The Bedford Introduction to Drama

SEVENTH EDITION

Lee A. Jacobus
University of Connecticut

BEDFORD / ST. MARTIN'S
Boston ◆ New York

For Bedford/St. Martin's

Senior Developmental Editor: Caroline Thompson
Production Supervisor: Samuel Jones
Senior Marketing Manager: Stacey Propps
Editorial Assistant: Regina Tavani
Project Management: Lifland et al., Bookmakers
Photo Research Manager: Martha Friedman
Permissions Manager: Kalina K. Ingham
Senior Art Director: Anna Palchik
Text Design: Claire Seng-Niemoeller
Cover Design: Donna Lee Dennison
Cover Photo: Dion Johnstone as Caliban in *The Tempest*, Stratford Shakespeare
    Festival 2010. Courtesy the Stratford Shakespeare Festival Archives. Photography
    by David Hou.
Composition: S4Carlisle Publishing Services
Printing and Binding: Quad/Graphics

President, Bedford/St. Martin's: Denise B. Wydra
Presidents, Macmillan Higher Education: Joan E. Feinberg and Tom Scotty
Editor in Chief: Karen S. Henry
Director of Marketing: Karen R. Soeltz
Production Director: Susan W. Brown
Associate Production Director: Elise S. Kaiser
Manager, Publishing Services: Andrea Cava

Library of Congress Control Number: 2012942238

Manufactured in the United States of America.

7   6   5   4   3   2
f   e   d   c   b   a

For information, write: Bedford/St. Martin's, 75 Arlington Street, Boston, MA 02116
(617-399-4000)

ISBN 978-1-4576-0632-8

Acknowledgments

Preface for Instructors

With an abundance of plays, commentaries, and useful editorial features, *The Bedford Introduction to Drama* has always provided a diverse overview of dramatic literature with enough breadth and flexibility to complement a variety of pedagogical approaches. In its seventh edition, it remains the most complete anthology available: a collection of fifty-four important plays that have shaped dramatic literature from the time of the early Greek dramatists to the present. The anthology includes several American multicultural plays, strong representation of female playwrights (with twelve plays by women), and an impressive selection of contemporary plays (with eight plays that have premiered since 2000). The book also offers a full array of background material about the plays and playwrights, encouraging students to think critically about all aspects of a play as a work of literature and performance.

Even when it appears most timeless, all drama, like all literature, is a product not only of language and style but also of its era, including a complex range of political, social, and ethnic influences. *The Bedford Introduction to Drama* offers a succinct but thorough history of Western drama, complemented by coverage of Asian drama. A general introduction gives an overview of the great ages of drama, the major genres and elements, and the cultural value of drama. Throughout the book, introductions to significant periods of drama, the playwrights, and the plays focus on the cultural contexts of the works and on their stage history. The timeline following the introduction to each dramatic period presents important developments in theater history in their appropriate cultural contexts.

Accompanying all the plays are thorough biographical and critical introductions; brief performance histories; commentaries by playwrights, directors, actors, reviewers, and critics; and photographs of landmark productions. These play-specific materials are complemented by four casebooks interspersed throughout the book. The casebooks present background materials—journal entries, letters, newspaper accounts, and essays—about specific plays or periods, enabling students to think critically about a play or group of plays through a focused study of important cultural and historical contexts.

A number of features emphasize plays in performance. Richly illustrated sections on staging and theater design in each historical introduction include detailed diagrams of period theaters, along with a discussion of the major technical innovations in staging. An illustrated section on "The Actor" in each historical introduction explores the development of acting styles, methods, and techniques in every major period of drama. A marginal quotation, often an appreciative comment by an actor, director, or other playwright, accompanies each biographical introduction, illuminating a particular playwright or work. More than 200 photographs and stage diagrams throughout the book help students visualize the plays in performance.

The Bedford Introduction to Drama is also a complete resource for the beginning student. In the general introduction, a discussion of the elements of drama defines important terms and concepts and demonstrates these concepts in action, drawing its examples from Lady Isabella Augusta Gregory's one-act play *The Rising of the Moon*. The anthology presents two major playwrights in particular depth—with three plays by William Shakespeare and two by Sophocles—offering students a unique opportunity to study and write about significant figures in the development of drama.

"Writing about Drama" at the end of the book offers students possible approaches for commenting on dramatic literature and points the way for developing ideas that can result in probing critical essays. From prewriting to outlining and drafting, the process of writing about drama is illustrated by reference to *The Rising of the Moon*, and a sample essay on the play provides one model of drama criticism for students. Especially useful for assignments involving attendance at theater productions, the section "Writing a Review" analyzes professional reviews and offers suggestions for students who are writing reviews.

The "Glossary of Dramatic Terms" clearly and concisely defines concepts and terms. When these terms are first introduced and defined in the text, they appear in boldface.

New to This Edition

New Plays

Fifteen plays are new to the seventh edition, spanning the major eras of drama, from Euripides' *The Bacchae*, to John Gay's *The Beggar's Opera*, to Samuel Beckett's *Endgame*, to Sarah Ruhl's *Eurydice*. The selection of new contemporary plays is informed by research into the most frequently produced plays of recent seasons, increasing the likelihood that students will have opportunities to see performances of the plays they read. Among the new contemporary prize-winners are John Patrick Shanley's *Doubt*, Yasmina Reza's *God of Carnage*, Tracy Letts's *August: Osage County*, and Lynn Nottage's *Ruined*. *Fefu and Her Friends* by María Irene Fornés, *Cloud Nine* by Caryl Churchill, and *Topdog/Underdog* by Suzan-Lori Parks strengthen the selection of works by female playwrights. Tennessee Williams's *Cat on a Hot Tin Roof*, a reviewer favorite from previous editions, returns in this edition, and Tom Stoppard's *Arcadia* and Conor McPherson's *The Seafarer* appear in the anthology for the first time.

New Casebook

The Bedford Introduction to Drama continues to offer the strongest coverage of Shakespeare in any introductory anthology. In addition to *Hamlet* and *A Midsummer Night's Dream*, the seventh edition now includes *The Tempest*, accompanied by a new Critical Casebook designed to help students understand Shakespeare's cultural influence and develop their own critical approach to the play. Excerpts from William Strachey's *True Repertory of the Wreck* and Montaigne's *Of the Cannibals* provide context, and writings by Samuel Taylor Coleridge, Robert Browning, E. K. Chambers, Aimé Césaire, Ania Loomba,

Maureen Connolly McFeely, Hofstra University; Donald McManus, Emory University; Richard Noggle, University of Kansas; Rachel Poulsen, Edgewood College; Korey Rothman, University of Maryland; Leah Roy, Wake Forest University; Gloria Olchowy Rozeboom, Grant MacEwan University; J. Richard Smith, Cornish College of the Arts; Tammy Veach, Eastern Illinois University; and Carol Westcamp, University of Arkansas at Fort Smith. Tammy Veach of Eastern Illinois University also assisted in updating and creating new resources for the companion Web site.

I am especially grateful to the people who worked behind the scenes at Bedford/St. Martin's to produce this book. I thank editorial assistant Regina Tavani for coordinating reviews, managing tasks large and small to prepare the manuscript for production, and overseeing the development of content for the Web site. Project manager Sally Lifland managed the production of this complex project with aplomb and kept the book on schedule. Art director Donna Dennison designed the stunning cover.

As always, I owe an immense debt of gratitude to the imaginative and intelligent guidance of Denise Wydra, president of Bedford/St. Martin's; Joan Feinberg, president of Macmillan Higher Education; and their predecessor, Charles Christensen. They have been friends of this book from the beginning and have helped give it special meaning. Karen Henry, my editor and muse for the first three editions of this book, is a passionate fan of theater and the values for which this book stands. Even now she remains close to this project. Mika De Roo, my editor for the fifth edition, was enthusiastic and helpful from the first. Maura Shea, my editor for the fourth edition, and again happily for the sixth edition, sets a standard that few can match. Her taste, judgment, and editorial eye helped make this book what it is. She is my vision of the ideal editor, both talented and skilled, and aiming unerringly to help make this the best book it can be. Carrie Thompson, editor for the current edition, was remarkable in her devotion to this project. She read all the plays we considered and made shrewd and splendid suggestions that I happily followed. Having an editor passionate about drama, as Carrie is, supporting a project as huge and challenging as this is, has made the entire experience a great pleasure. She raised the bar on this edition. Great editors like Carrie are a national treasure.

Lee A. Jacobus
University of Connecticut, Storrs

and Marjorie Garber offer a range of critical approaches and responses to the play.

New Design and Web Site

The seventh edition is designed to be not only visually striking but more readable and teachable than ever. The new design highlights the rich contextual features of the book, including historical introductions, timelines, casebooks, and commentaries, while increasing the readability of the plays. As in previous editions, plenty of space is devoted to performance photographs and illustrations. Photographs are integrated into the texts of the plays in the very scenes that they depict to help students visualize the performance.

New marginal notes throughout the book refer students to free and open resources on the book's fully updated and redesigned companion site, **bedfordstmartins.com/jacobus**. The site offers extensive materials to help students succeed in the course, including discussion questions and assignments for every play, links to additional resources on each of the playwrights and casebooks, in-depth drama tutorials, and annotated links to drama organizations, theaters, and other drama resources. The full text of Anna Cora Mowatt's *Fashion* is available for download on the site for the convenience of instructors who wish to assign a full-length American melodrama. An additional cultural casebook (from the fourth edition) focusing on the Abbey Theatre and the Irish Literary Renaissance is also available.

Instructor Resources and DVD/VHS Library

Resources for instructors include a selected bibliography for each major dramatic period and its playwrights, a list of suggested audiovisual resources, and additional assignment ideas. These resources can be downloaded from **bedfordstmartins.com/jacobus** or **bedfordstmartins.com/jacobus/catalog**.

A selection of DVDs and videotapes of plays included in the book is available for qualified adopters. Contact your Bedford/St. Martin's sales representative for more information.

Compact Edition

The Bedford Introduction to Drama, Seventh Edition, is also available in a compact edition containing twenty-eight plays, twenty-six commentaries, and two casebooks focusing on *The Tempest* and *Death of a Salesman*. The compact edition retains all of the longer book's editorial features for those instructors who want a smaller, less expensive anthology. For more information and a complete table of contents, visit **bedfordstmartins.com/jacobus/catalog**. To order the compact edition, use ISBN 978-1-4576-0633-5.

Acknowledgments

I am grateful to the following reviewers who offered suggestions and advice for the seventh edition: Debra E. Best, California State University, Dominguez Hills; Jamie Libby Boyle, University of South Carolina; Anne Brannen, Duquesne University; Patricia Lewis Browne, Nazareth College of Rochester; Mark Cosdon, Allegheny College; Keith Cushman, University of North Carolina at Greensboro; Laura Early, Bellarmine University; Joel G. Fink, Roosevelt University; Anita Hagerman, Webster University; Patrick J. Immel, Northwest Missouri State University; Desiree Libengood, Crown College;

Contents

Medieval Drama   196

Renaissance Drama   242

Medieval Drama   196

Renaissance Drama   242

Nineteenth-Century Drama Through the Turn of the Twentieth Century   667

Drama in the Early and Mid-Twentieth Century   890

Contemporary Drama   1282

Writing about Drama   1847

Introduction:
Thinking about Drama

The word *drama* comes from an early Greek word, *dran*, meaning "to do something." Drama implies doing something of considerable importance. In modern terms, a dramatic action is the plot or storyline of a play. The ingredients of any drama are the plot; the characters, represented on stage by actors; their actions, described by gestures and movement; thought—the ideas in the play—revealed in dialogue and behavior; spectacle, represented by scenery, music, costume, and lighting; and, finally, audiences who respond to the entire mixture.

When we are in the theater, we see the actors, hear the lines, are aware of the setting, and sense the theatrical community of which we are a part. Even when reading a play, we should imagine actors speaking lines and visualize a setting in which those lines are spoken. Drama is an experience in which we participate on many levels simultaneously. On one level, we may believe that what we see is really happening; on another level, we know it is only make-believe. On one level we may be amused, but on another level we realize that serious statements about human nature are being made. Drama both entertains and instructs.

What Is Drama? When Aristotle wrote about drama in the *Poetics,* a work providing one of the earliest and most influential theories of drama, he began by explaining drama as the imitation of an action (**mimesis**). Those analyzing his work have interpreted this statement in several ways. One interpretation is that drama imitates life. On the surface, this observation may seem simple, even obvious. But on reflection, we begin to find complex significance in his comment. The drama of the Greeks, for example, with its intense mythic structure, its formidable speeches, and its profound actions, often seems larger than life or other than life. Yet we recognize characters saying words that we ourselves are capable of saying, doing things that we ourselves might do. The great Greek tragedies are certainly lifelike and certainly offer literary mirrors in which we can examine human nature. And the same is true of Greek comedies.

The relationship between drama and life has always been subtle and complex. In some plays, such as Luigi Pirandello's *Six Characters in Search of an Author,* it is one of the central issues. We begin our reading or viewing of most plays knowing that the dramatic experience is not absolutely real in the sense that, for example, the actor playing Hamlet does not truly die or truly see a ghost or truly frighten his mother. The play imitates those imagined actions, but when done properly it is realistic enough to make us fear, if only for a moment, that they could be real.

We see significance in the actions Hamlet imitates; his actions help us live our own lives more deeply, more intensely, because they give us insight into the possibilities of life. In an important sense, we share the experience of a character such as Hamlet when, for example, he soliloquizes over the question of whether it is better to die than to live in a world filled with sin and crime. We are all restricted to living this life as ourselves; drama is one art form that helps us realize the potential of life, for both the good and the bad.

Drama and Ritual

Such imaginative participation is only a part of what we derive from drama. In its origins, drama seems to have evolved from ancient Egyptian and Greek rituals, ceremonies that were performed the same way again and again and were thought to have a propitious effect on the relationship between the people and their gods.

In ancient Egypt, some religious rituals evolved into repeated passion plays, such as those celebrating Isis and Osiris at the festivals of Heb-Seb at Sakkara some three thousand years ago. Greek drama was first performed during yearly religious celebrations dedicated to the god Dionysus. The early Greek playwrights, such as Sophocles in *Oedipus Rex* and *Antigone,* emphasized the interaction between the will of the gods and the will of human beings, often pitting the truths of men and women against the truths of the gods. The interpretation of the myths by the Greek playwrights over a two-hundred-year period helped the Greek people participate in the myths, understand them, and relate them to their daily lives.

In the thirteenth and fourteenth centuries, drama thrived in Japan, reaching a pinnacle in the Nō drama of Zeami Motokiyo and his father, Kan'ami. Japanese Nō drama combines music and movement in intricate patterns of ritualistic formality. Nō developed in a Buddhist environment and expressed the deep religious values associated with Buddhism. Although it began as a provincial form, the beauty of Nō—its deep meditative pauses and extraordinary dancelike movement—quickly made it the major style of drama in medieval Japan.

The rebirth of Western drama in the Middle Ages—after the fall of Rome and the loss of classical artistic traditions—took place first in monasteries, then later in and about the cathedrals of Europe. It evolved from medieval religious ceremonies that helped the faithful understand more about their own moral predicament. *Everyman,* a late play in the medieval theater (it was written about 1500), concerns itself with the central issue of reward and punishment for the immortal soul after this life.

Drama: The Illusion of Reality

From the beginning, drama has had the capacity to hold up an illusion of reality like the reflection in a mirror: we take the reality for granted while recognizing that it is nonetheless illusory. As we have seen, Aristotle described drama, or **dramatic illusion,** as an imitation of an action. But unlike the reflection in a mirror, the action of most drama is drawn not from our actual experience of life but from our potential or imagined experience. In the great Greek dramas, the illusion includes the narratives of ancient myths that were thought to offer profound illumination.

Different ages have had different approaches to representing reality onstage. Greek actors spoke in verse and wore masks. Except in the case of some comedies and **satyr plays,** the staging consisted of very little setting and no special costumes. Medieval drama was sometimes acted on pageant wagons and carts, but the special machinery developed to suggest hellfire and the presence of devils was said to be so realistic as to be frightening. Audiences of the Elizabethan age (named for Elizabeth I, who ruled England from 1558 to 1603) were accustomed to actors who spoke directly to the crowds at their feet near the apron of the stage. All Elizabethan plays were done in essentially contemporary clothing, often with no more scenery than a suggestion in the spoken descriptions of the players. The actors recited their lines in verse, except when the author had a particular reason to use prose—for example, to imply that the speaker was of low social station. Yet Elizabethans reported that their theater was much like life itself.

In Shakespeare's *A Midsummer Night's Dream,* fairies, enchantments, an ass's head on the shoulders of a man all are presented as illusions, and we accept them. They inform the audience—in Shakespeare's day and in modern times—not by showing us ourselves in a mirror but by demonstrating that even fantastic realities have significance for us.

Certainly *A Midsummer Night's Dream* gives us insight into the profound range of human emotions. We learn about the pains of rejection when we see Helena longing for Demetrius, who in turn longs for Hermia. We learn about jealousy and possessiveness when we see Oberon cast a spell on his wife, Titania, over a dispute concerning a changeling. And we learn, too, about the worldly ambitions of the "rude mechanicals" who themselves put on a play whose reality they fear might frighten their audience. They solve the problem by reminding their audience that it is only a play and that they need not fear that reality will spoil their pleasure.

In modern drama, the dramatic illusion of reality includes not just the shape of an action, the events, and the characters but also the details of everyday life. When the action changes locale, the setting changes as well. Some contemporary playwrights make an effort to re-create a reality close to the one we live in. Some modern plays, such as August Wilson's *Fences,* make a precise representation of reality a primary purpose, shaping the tone of the language to reflect the way modern people speak, re-creating contemporary reality in the setting, language, and other elements of the drama.

But describing a play as an illusion of reality in no way means that it represents the precise reality that we take for granted in our everyday experience. Rather, drama ranges widely and explores multiple realities, some of which may seem very close to our own and some of which may seem improbably removed from our everyday experience.

Seeing a Play Onstage

For an audience, drama is one of the most powerful artistic experiences. When we speak about participating in drama, we mean that as a member of the audience we become a part of the action that unfolds. This is a mysterious phenomenon.

When we see a play today, we are usually seated in a darkened theater looking at a lighted stage. In ages past, this contrast was not the norm. Greek plays took place outdoors during the morning and the afternoon; most Elizabethan plays were staged outdoors in the afternoon; in the Renaissance, some plays began to be staged indoors with ingenious systems of lighting that involved candles and reflectors. In the early nineteenth century, most theaters used gaslight onstage; electricity took over in the later part of the century, and its use has grown increasingly complex. In most large theaters today, computerized lighting boards have replaced Renaissance candles.

Sitting in the darkness has made the experience of seeing Greek and Elizabethan plays much different for us than it was for the original audiences. We do not worry about being seen by the "right people" or about studying the quality of the audience, as people did during the Restoration in the late seventeenth century. The darkness isolates us from all except those who sit adjacent to us. Yet we instantly respond when others in the audience laugh, when they gasp, when they shift restlessly. We recognize in those moments that we are part of a larger community drawn together by theater and that we are all involved in the dramatic experience.

Theaters and Their Effect

Different kinds of theaters make differing demands on actors and audiences. Despite its huge size, the open **arena** style theater of the early Greeks brought the audience into a special kind of intimacy with the actors. The players came very close to the first rows of seats, and the acoustics sometimes permitted even a whisper onstage to be audible in the far seats. The Greek theater also imparted a sense of formality to the occasion of drama. For one thing, its symmetry and circularity were accompanied by a relatively rigid seating plan. Public officials and nobility sat in special seats. Then each section of the theater was given over to specific families, and the less desirable edges of the seating area were devoted to travelers and strangers to the town. One knew one's place in the Greek theater. Its regularity gave the community a sense of order.

Medieval theater also gave its audiences a sense of community, both when it used playing areas called *mansions* inside and outside the churches and when it used wagons wheeled about in processions in the streets or outside the city walls. That the medieval theater repeated the same cycles of plays again and again for about two hundred years, to the delight of many European communities, tells us something about the stability of those communities. Their drama was integrated with their religion, and both helped them express their sense of belonging to the church and the community.

In some medieval performances, the actors came into the audience, breaking the sense of distance or the illusion of separation. It is difficult for us to know how much participation and involvement in the action the medieval audience felt. Modern audiences have responded very well to productions of medieval plays such as *The Second Shepherds' Pageant, Noah's Flood,* and *Everyman,* and we have every reason to think that medieval audiences enjoyed their dramas immensely. The guilds that performed them took pride in making their plays as exciting and involving as possible.

The Elizabethan playhouse was a wooden structure providing an enclosed space, approximately seventy-two feet in diameter, around a courtyard open to the sky. A covered stage thrust into the courtyard. As in the Greek theater, the audience was arranged somewhat by social station. Around the stage, which was about five feet off the ground, stood the groundlings, those who paid the least for their entrance. Then in covered galleries in the building itself sat patrons who paid extra for a seat. The effect of the enclosed structure was of a small, contained world. Actors were in the habit of speaking directly to members of the audience, and the audience rarely kept a polite silence. It was a busy, humming theater that generated intimacy and involvement between actors and audience.

The proscenium stage of the nineteenth and twentieth centuries distanced the audience from the play, providing a clear frame (the **proscenium**) behind which the performers acted out their scenes. This detachment was especially effective for plays that demanded a high degree of realism because the effect of the proscenium is to make the audience feel that it is witnessing the action as a silent observer, looking in as if through an imaginary fourth wall on a living room or other intimate space in which the action takes place. The proscenium arch gives the illusion that the actors are in a world of their own, unaware of the audience's presence.

In the twentieth century, some of the virtues of the Greek arena theater, or **theater in the round**, were rediscovered. In an effort to close the distance between audience and players, Antonin Artaud, the French actor and director, developed in the 1920s and 1930s a concept called the *theater of cruelty*. Using theater in the round, Artaud robbed the audience of the comfort of watching a distant stage and pressed his actors into the space of the viewers. His purpose was to force theatergoers to deal with the primary issues of the drama by stripping them of the security of darkness and anonymity. Theaters in the Soviet Union and Britain developed similar spaces in the 1930s and 1940s, and since the 1950s the Arena Theater in Washington, D.C., and the Circle in the Square in New York City have continued the tradition.

The thrust stage, a modern revision of Shakespeare's Globe Theatre stage, was designed in 1948 by Sir Tyrone Guthrie for the Assembly Hall in Edinburgh, Scotland. He further refined it in the Festival Theatre in Stratford, Ontario (1957), and in his famous Tyrone Guthrie Theater (1963) in Minneapolis. The audience sits on three sides of a stage that thrusts out from a flat area incorporating balconies, doors, and sometimes stairs. The thrust stage often intensifies the intimacy of the dramatic experience.

Twenty-first-century theater is eclectic. It uses thrust, arena, proscenium, and every other kind of stage already described. Some contemporary site-specific theater also converts nontheatrical space, such as warehouses or city streets, into space for performance.

Reading a Play

Reading a play is a different experience from seeing it enacted. For one thing, readers do not have the benefit of the interpretations made by a director, actors, and scene designers in presenting a performance. These interpretations are all critical judgments based on a director's ideas of how the play should be presented and on actors' insights into the meaning of the play.

A reading of a play produces an interpretation that remains in our heads and is not translated to the stage. The dramatic effect of the staging is lost to us unless we make a genuine effort to visualize it and to understand its contribution to the dramatic experience. For a fuller experience of the drama when reading plays, one should keep in mind the historical period and the conventions of staging that are appropriate to the period and that are specified by the playwright.

Some plays were prepared by their authors for reading as well as for staging, as evident in plays whose stage directions supply information that would be unavailable to an audience, such as the color of the characters' eyes, characters' secret motives, and other such details. Occasionally, stage directions, such as those of Bernard Shaw and Tennessee Williams, are written in a poetic prose that can be appreciated only by a reader.

It is not a certainty that seeing a play will produce an experience more "true" to the play's meaning than reading it. Every act of reading silently or speaking the lines aloud is an act of interpretation. No one can say which is the best interpretation. Each has its own merits, and the ideal is probably to read *and* see any play.

For links to theaters, drama organizations, and reviews, click on *Drama Links* at bedfordstmartins.com/jacobus.

The Great Ages of Drama

Certain historical periods have produced great plays and great playwrights, although why some periods generate more dramatic activity than others is still a matter of conjecture by scholars examining the social, historical, and religious conditions of the times. Each of the great ages of drama has affected the way plays have been written, acted, and staged in successive ages. In every age, drama borrows important elements from each earlier period.

Egyptian Drama

Although scholars disagree in their interpretations of archaeological evidence, it is quite likely that ancient Egyptian drama was highly developed. One of the key artifacts supporting this assertion is an incised stone stela (c. 1868 BCE) describing the roles that an official named Ikhernofret played in a celebration that included characters and dramatic action. The Abydos Passion Play, as some modern scholars call this event, was performed annually from approximately 2500 to 500 BCE. It is the story of Osiris (the equivalent of the Greek Dionysus), who was murdered in an act of trickery by his jealous brother Seth. Osiris was dismembered (as was Dionysus in Greek myth) and his parts scattered over the land. Isis, both wife and sister of Osiris, gathered most of the parts of Osiris in order to make possible his resurrection. The celebration seems to have been timed to reflect a pattern of agricultural renewal that the rebirth myth of Osiris satisfies. In his account of his role in the event, as recorded on the stela, Ikhernofret says,

> I did everything that His Person commanded, putting into effect my lord's command for his father, Osiris-Khentyamentiu, Lord of Abydos, great of power, who is in the Thinite nome. I acted as beloved son of Osiris-Khentyamentiu. I embellished his great barque of eternity; I made for it a shrine which displays the beauties of Khentyamentiu, in gold, silver, lapis-lazuli, bronze, sesnedjem-wood and cedar[?]. I fashioned the gods in his train. I made their shrines anew. I caused the temple priesthood to do their duties, I caused them to know the custom of every day, the festival of the Head-of-the-Year. I controlled work on the neshmet-barque; I fashioned the shrine and adorned the breast of the Lord of Abydos with lapis-lazuli and turquoise, electrum and every precious stone, as an adornment of the divine limbs. I changed the clothes of the god at his appearance, in the office of Master of Secrets and in my job as sem-priest. I was clean of arm in adoring the god, a sem clean of fingers.
>
> I organized the going forth of Wepwawet when he proceeded to avenge his father; I drove away the rebels from the neshmet-barque; I overthrew the enemies of Osiris; I celebrated the great going forth. I followed the god at his going, and

caused the ship to sail, Thoth steering the sailing. I equipped the barque with a chapel and affixed (Osiris's) beautiful adornments when he proceeded to the district of Peqer. I cleared the ways of the god to his tomb before Peqer. I avenged Wennefer that day of the great fight; I overthrew all his enemies upon the sandbanks of Nedyt; I caused him to proceed into the great barque. It raised up his beauties, I making glad the people/tomb owners of the Eastern Desert, creating joy amongst the people/tomb owners of the Western Desert; they saw the beauties of the neshmet-barque when it touched land at Abydos, when it brought Osiris-Khentyamentiu to his palace; I followed the god to his house, I carried out his purification and extended his seat and solved the problems of his residence [. . . and amongst] his entourage.[1]

Parts of the celebration were public in the outdoors, but parts were also played within the walls of the temple by priests. Little if anything is known about the mysteries they performed, but Herodotus (c. 484–c. 430 BCE), who claimed to have traveled in Egypt, reported seeing public participation in mock battles associated with the celebration.

Another festival, called the Heb-Seb, performed at the pyramid complex of Sakkara in the thirtieth year of a pharaoh's reign (and then every third year following), involved dance, music, and pageantry that closely resembled dramatic action. The purpose of the festival was to celebrate the longevity of the pharaoh and the resultant wellness of the land. The associated "Pyramid Texts" from Sakkara (c. 3000 BCE) also treat the resurrection of Osiris and may imply the existence of an early form of the celebration of Heb-Seb. All these festivals, supplemented by those from Busiris and Memphis in Egypt, suggest that although the Greeks believed they had invented drama, it is much more likely that the Egyptians had done so.

Greek Drama

The Greeks of the fifth century BCE are credited with the first masterful dramatic age, which lasted from the birth of Aeschylus (c. 525 BCE) to the death of Aristophanes (c. 385 BCE). Their theaters were supported by public funds, and the playwrights competed for prizes during the great festivals of Dionysus. Sometimes as many as ten to fifteen thousand people sat in the theaters and watched with a sense of delight and awe as the actors played out their tales.

Theater was extremely important to the Greeks as a way of interpreting their relationships with their gods and of reinforcing their sense of community. The fifth-century-BCE audience, mostly wealthy citizens, came early in the morning and spent the entire day in the theater. Drama for the Greeks was not mere escapism or entertainment, not a frill or a luxury. Connected as it was with religious festivals, it was a cultural necessity.

Sophocles' plays *Oedipus Rex* and *Antigone* are examples of the powerful tragedies that have transfixed audiences for centuries. Euripides, slightly younger than Sophocles, was also a prize-winning tragedian. His *Trojan Women*, *Alcestis*, *Medea*, *The Bacchae*, and *Elektra* [*Electra*] are still performed and still exert an influence on today's drama. The same is true of Aeschylus, who was slightly older than both and whose *Agamemnon*, *The Libation Bearers*, *The Eumenides* (known collectively as the *Oresteia*), and *Prometheus Bound* have all been among the most lasting of plays.

[1]From http://www.touregypt.net/passionplay.htm; also in Henry Breasted's *Ancient Records of Egypt*, part 2 (1906–07).

In addition to such great tragedians, the Greeks also produced the important comedians Aristophanes and Menander (late fourth century BCE), whose work has been plundered for plays as diverse as a Shakespeare comedy and a Broadway musical. Aristophanes' *Lysistrata,* in which the Athenian and Spartan women agree to withhold sex from their husbands until the men promise to stop making war, is a sometimes crude social comedy. Menander produced a more refined type of comedy that made the culture laugh at itself. Both styles of comedy are staples of popular entertainment even today. Menander's comedies were the basis of later social comedy in which society's ways of behavior are criticized. Such social comedy is exemplified in William Congreve's eighteenth-century *The Way of the World* and Molière's *Tartuffe.*

Roman Drama

The Romans became aware of Greek drama in the third century BCE and began to import Greek actors and playwrights. Because of many social and cultural differences between the societies, however, drama never took a central role in the life of the average Roman. Seneca, who is now viewed as Rome's most important tragedian, almost certainly wrote his plays to be read rather than to be seen onstage.

Roman comedy produced two great playwrights, Plautus and Terence, who helped develop the **stock** (or type) **character**, such as the skinflint or the prude. Plautus was the great Roman comedian in the tradition of Menander. Plautus's best-known plays are *The Braggart Warrior* and *The Twin Menaechmi;* during the Renaissance, when all European schoolchildren read Latin, his works were favorites.

Terence's work was praised during the Middle Ages and the Renaissance as being smoother, more elegant, and more polished and refined than Plautus's. In his own age, Terence was less admired by the general populace but more admired by connoisseurs of drama. His best-known plays—*The Woman of Andros, Phormio,* and *The Brothers*—are rarely performed today.

Drama took its place beside many other forms of entertainment in Roman culture—sports events, gladiator battles to the death, chariot races, the slaughter of wild beasts, and sacrifices of Christians and others to animals. The Roman public, when it did attend plays, enjoyed farces and relatively coarse humor. The audiences for Plautus and Terence, aristocratic in taste, may not have represented the cross-section of the community that was typical of Greek audiences.

Medieval Drama

After the fall of Rome and the spread of the Goths and Visigoths across southern Europe in the fifth century CE, Europe experienced a total breakdown of the strong central government Rome had provided. When Rome fell, Greek and Roman culture virtually disappeared. The great classical texts went largely unread until the end of the medieval period in the fourteenth and fifteenth centuries; however, expressions of culture, including art forms such as drama, did not entirely disappear. During the medieval period, the power and influence of the Church grew extensively, and it tried to fill the gap left by the demise of the Roman empire. The Church became a focus of both religious and secular activity for people all over Europe.

After almost five centuries of relative inactivity, European drama was reborn in religious ceremonies in monasteries. It moved inside churches, then out of doors by the twelfth century, perhaps because its own demands outgrew its circumstances. Drama had become more than an adjunct to the religious ceremonies that had spawned it.

One reason the medieval European communities regarded their drama so highly is that it expressed many of their concerns and values. The age was highly religious; in addition, the people who produced the plays were members of guilds whose personal pride was represented in their work. Their plays came to be called **mystery plays** because the trade that each guild represented was a special skill—a mystery to the average person. Of course, the pun on religious mystery was understood by most audiences.

Many of these plays told stories drawn from the Bible. The tales of Noah's Ark, Abraham and Isaac, and Samson and Delilah all had dramatic potential, and the mystery plays capitalized on that potential, as did plays on the life and crucifixion of Christ. Among mystery plays, *The Second Shepherds' Pageant* and *Abraham and Isaac* are still performed regularly.

Most mystery plays were gathered into groups of plays called **cycles,** dramatizing incidents from the Bible, among other sources. They were usually performed outdoors, at times on movable wagons that doubled as stages. Either the audience moved from wagon to wagon to see each play in a cycle or the wagons moved among the audience.

In the fifteenth and sixteenth centuries, a form of play developed that was not associated with cycles or with the guilds. These were the **morality plays,** and their purpose was to touch on larger contemporary issues that had a moral overtone. *Everyman,* the best known of the morality plays, was performed in many nations in various languages.

Renaissance Drama

The revival of learning in the Renaissance, beginning in Italy in the fourteenth century, had considerable effect on drama because classical Greek and Roman plays were discovered and studied. In the academies in Italy, some experiments in re-creating Greek and Roman plays introduced music into drama. New theaters, such as Teatro Olympico in Vicenza (1579), were built to produce these plays; they allow us to see how the Renaissance reconceived the classical stage. Some of these experiments developed into modern opera. The late medieval traditions of the Italian theater's **commedia dell'arte**, a stylized improvisational slapstick comedy performed by actors' guilds, began to move beyond Italy into other European nations. The commedia's stock characters, Harlequins and Pulcinellas, began to appear in many countries in Europe.

Elizabethan drama and Jacobean drama (named for King James I, who succeeded Elizabeth and reigned from 1603 to 1625) developed most fully during the fifty years from approximately 1590 to 1640. Audiences poured into the playhouses eager for plays about history and for the great tragedies of Christopher Marlowe, such as *Doctor Faustus,* and of Shakespeare, including *Macbeth, Hamlet, Othello, Julius Caesar,* and *King Lear.* But there were others as well: Middleton and Rowley's *The Changeling,* Cyril Tourneur's *Revenger's Tragedy,* John Webster's *The White Devil* and his sensational *The Duchess of Malfi.*

The great comedies of the age came mostly from the pen of William Shakespeare: *A Midsummer Night's Dream, The Comedy of Errors, As You Like It, Much Ado about Nothing, The Taming of the Shrew,* and *Twelfth Night.* Many of these plays derived from Italian originals, usually novellas or popular poems and sometimes comedies. But Shakespeare, of course, elevated and vastly improved everything he borrowed.

Ben Jonson, a playwright who was significantly influenced by the classical writers, was also well represented on the Elizabethan stage, with *Volpone,*

The Alchemist, Every Man in His Humour, Bartholomew Fair, and other durable comedies. Jonson is also important for his contributions to the **masque**, an aristocratic entertainment that featured music, dance, and fantastic costuming. His *Masque of Blackness* was performed in the royal court with the queen as a performer.

The Elizabethan stage sometimes grew bloody, with playwrights and audiences showing a passion for tragedies that, like *Hamlet,* centered on revenge and often ended with most of the characters meeting a premature death. Elizabethan plays also show considerable variety, with many plays detailing the history of English kings and, therefore, the history of England. It was a theater of powerful effect, and contemporary diaries indicate that the audiences delighted in it.

Throughout the Renaissance, women were not allowed on stage; men and boys played the female roles. Theaters in Shakespeare's day were built outside city limits in seamy neighborhoods near brothels and bear-baiting pits, where chained bears were set upon by large dogs for the crowd's amusement. Happily, the theaters' business was good; the plays were constructed of remarkable language that seems to have fascinated all social classes, since all flocked to the theater by the thousands.

Theaters also flourished in Spain in this period, producing Lope de Vega (1562–1635), who may have written as many as seventeen hundred plays. Vega's immediate successor, Pedro Calderón de la Barca (1600–1681), is sometimes considered to be more polished in style, but also more stiffly aristocratic in appeal. He wrote fewer plays than Vega, but still produced an amazing body of work. He is said to have written at least 111 dramas and seventy or eighty *auto sacramentales,* the Spanish equivalent of religious morality plays, designed for special religious ceremonies. Calderón is best known for *La vida es sueño (Life Is a Dream),* which is still performed today.

Late-Seventeenth- and Eighteenth-Century Drama

After the Puritan reign in England from 1642 (when the theaters were closed) to 1660, during which dramatic productions were almost nonexistent, the theater was suddenly revived. In 1660, Prince Charles, having been sent to France by his father during the English Civil War, was invited back to be king, thus beginning what was known in England as the Restoration. It was a gay, exciting period, in stark contrast to the gray Puritan era. During the Restoration, new indoor theaters modeled on those in France were built, and a new generation of actors and actresses (women took part in plays for the first time in England) came forth to participate in the dramatic revival.

Since the mid-seventeenth century, French writers, interpreting Aristotle's description of Greek drama, had leaned toward development of a classical theater, which was supposed to observe the "unities" of time, place, and action: a play had one plot and one setting and covered the action of one day. In 1637, Pierre Corneille wrote *Le Cid,* using relatively modern Spanish history as his theme and following certain classical techniques. Jean-Baptiste Racine was Corneille's successor, and his plays became even more classical by focusing on classical topics. His work includes *Andromache, Britannicus,* and, possibly his best play, *Phaedra.* Racine retired from the stage at the end of the seventeenth century, but he left a powerful legacy of classicism that reached well into the eighteenth century.

Molière, an actor and producer, was the best comedian of seventeenth-century France. *Tartuffe, The Misanthrope,* and several of his other plays are still produced regularly. Molière was classical in his way, borrowing ancient comedy's technique of using type, or stock, characters in his social satires.

Among the important English playwrights of the new generation were Aphra Behn, the first female professional writer, whose play *The Rover* was one of the most popular plays of the late seventeenth century, and William Congreve, whose best-known play, *The Way of the World,* is still often produced. The latter is a lively comedy that aimed to chasten as well as entertain Congreve's audiences.

The eighteenth century saw the tradition of social comedy continued in Richard Brinsley Sheridan's *School for Scandal* and Oliver Goldsmith's *She Stoops to Conquer.* The drama of this period focuses on social manners, and much of it is **satire**—that is, drama that offers mild criticism of society and holds society up to comic ridicule. But underlying that ridicule is the relatively noble motive of reforming society. We can see some of that motive at work in the plays of Molière and Goldsmith. We see it even more in John Gay's *The Beggar's Opera,* the most popular drama of the eighteenth century.

During much of the eighteenth century, theater in France centered on the court and was controlled by a small coterie of snobbish people. The situation in England was not quite the same, although the audiences were snobbish and socially conscious. They went to the theater to be seen, and they often went in claques—groups of like-minded patrons who applauded or booed together to express their views. Theater was important, but attendance at it was like a material possession, something to be displayed for others to admire.

A wide variety of drama was extant in Japan in the late sixteenth and early seventeenth centuries. Kabuki theater, the most remarkable form of popular Japanese drama and a lasting form still seen today in theaters around the world, evolved in this period. Kabuki is performed with music, and the resulting intensity would have surprised Western playwrights and audiences of that time. The emphasis shifted from the personality of the player to the situations and circumstances portrayed in the drama. Chikamatsu Monzaemon developed the form and was the most inventive of the Kabuki playwrights. His play *The Love Suicides at Sonezaki* was based on a genuine love suicide (*shinjū* in Japanese) and created a craze for love suicide plays that resulted in an edict in 1722 that banned them entirely. Some modern writers claim that the quality of his drama was not equaled in Japan for more than two hundred years.

Drama from the Nineteenth Century through the Turn of the Twentieth Century

English playwrights alone produced more than thirty thousand plays during the nineteenth century. Most of the plays were sentimental, melodramatic, and dominated by a few very powerful actors, stars who often overwhelmed the works written for them. The audiences were quite different from those of the seventeenth and eighteenth centuries. The upwardly mobile urban middle classes and the moneyed factory and mill owners who had benefited economically from the industrial revolution demanded a drama that would entertain them.

The audiences were generally not well educated, nor were they interested in plays that were intellectually demanding. Instead, they wanted escapist and sentimental entertainment that was easy to respond to and did not challenge their basic values. Revivals of old plays and adaptations of Shakespeare were also common in the age, with great stars like Edmund Kean, Sir Henry Irving, Edwin Forrest, Edwin Booth, and William Macready using the plays as platforms for overwhelming, and sometimes overbearing, performances. Thrillers were especially popular, as were historical plays and melodramatic plays featuring a helpless heroine.

As an antidote to such a diet, the new Realist movement in literature, exemplified by the achievements of French novelists Émile Zola and Gustave Flaubert, finally reached the stage in the 1870s and 1880s in plays by August Strindberg and Henrik Ibsen. Revolutionizing Western drama, these Scandinavians forced their audiences to confront more important issues and deeper psychological concerns than those facing earlier audiences.

Strindberg's *Miss Julie,* a psychological study, challenged social complacency based on class and social differences. Ibsen's *A Doll House* struck a blow for feminism, but it did not amuse all audiences. Some were horrified at the thought that Nora Helmer was to be taken as seriously as her husband. Such a view was heretical, but it was also thrilling for a newly awakened European conscience. Those intellectuals and writers who responded positively to Ibsen, including Bernard Shaw, acted as the new conscience and began a move that soon transformed drama. Feminism is also a theme, but perhaps less directly, of Ibsen's *Hedda Gabler,* the story of a woman whose frustration at being cast in an inferior role contributes to a destructive—and ultimately self-destructive—impulse. Both plays are acted in a physical setting that seems to be as ordinary as a nineteenth-century sitting room, with characters as small—and yet as large—as the people who watched them.

The Russian Anton Chekhov's plays *Three Sisters, Uncle Vanya,* and *The Cherry Orchard,* written at the turn of the twentieth century, are realistic as well, but they are also patient examinations of character, rather than primarily problem plays like Ibsen's *Ghosts* and *The Master Builder.* Chekhov was aware of social change in Russia, especially the changes that revealed a hitherto repressed class of peasants evolving into landowners and merchants. *The Cherry Orchard* is suffused with an overpowering sense of inevitability through which Chekhov depicts the conflict between the necessity for change and a nostalgia for the past. The comedies of Oscar Wilde, such as *Lady Windermere's Fan* and *The Importance of Being Earnest,* poke fun at the foibles of the upper classes. Amusing as these plays are, their satirical quality constitutes social criticism.

These plays introduced a modern realism of a kind that was rare in earlier drama. Melodrama of the nineteenth century was especially satisfying to mass audiences because the good characters were very good, the bad characters were very bad, and justice was meted out at the end. But it is difficult in Chekhov to be sure who the heroes and villains are. Nothing is as clear-cut in these plays as it is in popular melodramas. Instead, Chekhov's plays are as complicated as life itself. Such difficulties of distinction have become the norm of the most important of contemporary drama.

Drama in the Early and Mid-Twentieth Century

The drama of the early twentieth century nurtured the seeds of late-nineteenth-century realism into bloom, but sometimes this drama experimented with audience expectations. Eugene O'Neill's *Desire under the Elms* is a tragedy that features the ordinary citizen rather than the noble. This play focuses on New

England farmers as tragic characters. Arthur Miller's *Death of a Salesman* invokes a sense of dreadful inevitability within the world of the commercial salesman, the ordinary man. As in many other twentieth-century tragedies, the point is that the life of the ordinary man can be as tragic as that of Oedipus.

Luigi Pirandello experiments with reality in *Six Characters in Search of an Author,* a play that has a distinctly absurd quality, since it expects us to accept the notion that the characters on the stage are waiting for an author to put them into a play. Pirandello plays with our sense of illusion and of expectation and realism to such an extent that he forces us to reexamine our concepts of reality.

Bertolt Brecht's *Mother Courage,* an example of what the playwright called **epic drama**, explores war from a complex series of viewpoints. On the one hand, Courage is a powerful figure who has been seen as a model of endurance, but Brecht also wanted his audience to see that Courage brings on much of her own suffering by trying to profit from war. The sole act of self-sacrifice in the play comes at the end, when Kattrin beats her drum to warn villagers of the approach of a destroying army. Brecht produced the play early in World War II as a protest. Playwrights around the world responded to events such as World War I, the Communist revolution, and the Great Depression by writing plays that no longer permitted audiences to sit comfortably and securely in darkened theaters. Brecht and other playwrights instead came out to get their audiences, to make them feel and think, to make them realize their true condition.

Samuel Beckett's dramatic career began with *Waiting for Godot,* which audiences interpreted as an examination of humans' eternal vigilance for the revelation of God or of some transcendent meaning in their lives. In the play, Godot never comes, yet the characters do not give up hope. *Endgame*'s characters seem to be awaiting the end of the world: in the 1950s, the shadow of nuclear extinction cast by the cold war dominated most people's imagination.

Tennessee Williams relied on personal experience in writing *Cat on a Hot Tin Roof,* which portrays themes of homosexuality and marital sexual tension — themes that were not discussed in contemporary American theater except in veiled mythic terms, in the manner, for example, of O'Neill's *Desire under the Elms.*

Nigerian playwright Wole Soyinka, who won the Nobel Prize for literature in 1986, portrays the complex intersection of a person's past and the present in his play *The Strong Breed,* set in an African village reminiscent of the Greek *polis.* He experiments with Greek tragic forms in *The Bacchae of Euripides,* which is also set in Africa. Soyinka's insights into the nature of culture and drama provide us with a new way of reflecting on drama's power in our lives.

Modern dramatists from the turn of the twentieth century to the Korean War explored in many different directions and developed new approaches to themes of dramatic illusion as well as to questions concerning the relationship of an audience to the stage and the players.

Contemporary Drama

The twenty-first-century stage is vibrant. The great commercial theaters of England and the United States are sometimes hampered by high production costs, but regional theaters everywhere are producing fine drama. The National Theatre in London has made inexpensive seats available for most of its plays, and other theaters are doing the same. In Latin America, Germany, Japan,

China, France, and elsewhere, the theater is active and exciting. Poland's experiments in drama, led by Jerzy Grotowski's "Poor Theater," inspired experimentation that has spread throughout the world of drama. Russia, too, has produced a number of plays that have achieved worldwide currency.

The hallmark of many of these plays has been experimentalism. Caryl Churchill's *Top Girls* features characters who claim to be Pope Joan, Patient Griselda, and Lady Nijo, as well as being "themselves"—all this in the milieu of a feminist employment agency. Her newer play, *Far Away,* is a portrait of an apocalyptic world as viewed by a girl.

Sam Shepard, well known as an actor, was for many years among the most experimental playwrights living in New York's Greenwich Village. His *True West* begins as a relatively straightforward play about Austin and Lee, two brothers, but quickly reveals the drama that lies beneath the surface. Lee has arrived to steal his mother's television set but ends by stealing something of his brother's personality. *Buried Child* examines some frightening secrets in a dysfunctional family.

Suzan-Lori Parks has made a career of writing experimental plays, from the Brechtian *The Death of the Last Black Man in the Whole Entire World,* which structures itself in "panels" (brief, intense scenes that connect imaginatively), to *365 Days/365 Plays,* for which she wrote a play a day for a year. Tony Kushner employs similar techniques in *Angels in America.* Its brilliantly staged scenes are filled with emotional intensity, and the audience is carried on waves of imaginative speculation on America's history as well as on America's present. Moisés Kaufman and the members of the Tectonic Theater Project used highly inventive means to produce *The Laramie Project,* a play built around the murder of a young gay man, Matthew Shepherd, in Wyoming. It was a shocking crime both to the nation at large and to the local community in Laramie. The members of the project conducted many interviews with people in Laramie over a period of more than a year, and the resultant drama, largely developed from the interviews, revealed a range of surprising responses and surprising emotions. Experimentation is probably at the heart of the work of many playwrights, although it still does not please mainstream audiences to the same degree that traditional drama does.

Not all modern theater is experimental, however. August Wilson's *Fences* shows us the pain of life at the lower end of the economic ladder in a form that is recognizably realistic and plausible. The play is set in the 1950s and focuses on Troy Maxson, a black man, and his relationship with his son and his wife. Tenement life is one subject of the play, but the most important subject is the courage it takes to keep going after tasting defeat. The entire drama develops within the bounds of conventional nineteenth-century realism.

The most celebrated of contemporary playwrights seem to mix experimental and conventional dramatic techniques. Tom Stoppard, whose work is cerebral and witty, as in his pastiche of *Hamlet* called *Rosencrantz and Guildenstern Are Dead,* continues to delve into literature for much of his work. *The Invention of Love* treats the hopeless love of the Oxford classical scholar and poet A. E. Housman for a young athlete, Moses Jackson. The play begins with Housman crossing the river Styx into the underworld. Throughout, the older Housman watches himself as a young man and offers his sentiments. *Arcadia,* unlike some of Stoppard's early works, is a deeply emotional play about a thirteen-year-old girl, Lady Thomasina Coverly, gifted mathematically in an age in which such fields of study were reserved for men. The play takes place in one country house in Derbyshire, England, in both 1809 and 1989, contrasting several modes of thought and feeling—classical, romantic, and modern.

Paula Vogel's plays frequently interrupt the dramatic action with asides, but they are also imaginatively structured so that time feels fluid and the action moves in emotionally significant sweeps. *The Baltimore Waltz,* derived from Vogel's experience of watching her brother die of AIDS, brings humor to a tragic situation. Similarly, *How I Learned to Drive,* which sensitively treats the subject of sexual molestation in families, also has comic moments.

Recent Irish playwrights have provided us with a range of powerful plays that invoke horror, joy, and the supernatural. *Faith Healer, Translations, Dancing at Lughnasa,* and *Molly Sweeney* are only some of Brian Friel's celebrated plays. Friel has experimented with using both a single character and a full cast and has used many unusual techniques. For example, in *Translations,* English- and Irish-speaking characters are unable to communicate with one another, although in reality the actors all speak English for the audience. Conor McPherson's *Shining City* includes a bit of supernatural mystery typical of his work; *The Weir* incorporates a ghost story, and *The Seafarer* contains echoes of Irish myth and an appearance by the Devil. Martin McDonagh has had multiple plays running on Broadway and London's West End at the same time. *The Beauty Queen of Leenane, The Lonesome West, The Lieutenant of Inishmore,* and *The Pillowman* have all been nominated for Tony Awards.

Among other contemporary successes that have been produced internationally and in regional theaters are Sarah Ruhl's plays, which have stimulated audiences with their adventurous productions. *The Clean House* features a Brazilian housekeeper who searches for the perfect joke, which she eventually tells in Portuguese. *Eurydice* is a moving interpretation of the Greek myth of Orpheus and Eurydice, written as a hymn to Ruhl's father, who had died of cancer. *In the Next Room or the Vibrator Play*, a Tony Award nominee in 2010, examines late-nineteenth-century treatments of hysteria. Ruhl's satire is based on the assumption by some early psychologists that the vast majority of women's problems could be cured with the vibrator.

Other writers who have made an impact on contemporary theater include John Patrick Shanley, whose *Doubt* won the Pulitzer Prize for drama and the Tony Award for best play in 2005; Yasmina Reza, a French playwright whose plays *Art* and *God of Carnage* won Tony Awards in 1998 and 2009; Tracy Letts, whose *August: Osage County*, a portrait of a highly volatile family, won the Pulitzer Prize and the Tony Award for best play in 2008; and Lynn Nottage, who followed her plays *Poof!, Crumbs from the Table of Joy*, and *Intimate Apparel* with *Ruined*, a tale set in modern Africa that won the Pulitzer Prize in 2009. The theater of the twenty-first century continues with extraordinary energy to explore issues of social, historical, and psychological importance, using a wide range of techniques to which audiences respond positively.

Genres of Drama

Drama since the great age of the Greeks has taken several different forms. As we have seen, tragedies were one genre that pleased Greek audiences, and comedies pleased the Romans. In later ages, a blend of the comic and the tragic produced a hybrid genre: tragicomedy. In our time, unless a play is modeled on the Greek or Shakespearean tragedies, as is O'Neill's *Desire under the Elms,* it is usually considered tragicomic rather than tragic. Our age still enjoys the kind of comedy that people laugh at, although most plays that are strictly comedy are frothy, temporarily entertaining, and not lasting.

Tragedy

Tragedy demands a specific worldview. Aristotle, in his *Poetics,* points out that the tragic hero or heroine should be noble of birth, perhaps a king like Oedipus or a princess like Antigone. This has often been interpreted to mean that the tragic hero or heroine should be more magnanimous, more daring, and larger in spirit than the average person.

Modern tragedies have rediscovered tragic principles, and while O'Neill and Miller rely on Aristotle's precepts, they have shown that in a modern society shorn of the distinctions between noble and peasant, it is possible for audiences to see the greatness in all classes. This insight has given us a new way of orienting ourselves to the concept of fate; to **hamartia,** the wrong act that leads a person to a tragic end; and to the hero's or heroine's relationship to the social order.

Aristotle suggested that plot was the heart and soul of tragedy and that character came second. But most older tragedies take the name of the tragic hero or heroine as their title; this signifies the importance that dramatists invested in their tragic characters. Yet they also heeded Aristotle's stipulation that tragic action should have one plot rather than the double or triple plots that often characterize comedies. (Shakespeare was soundly criticized in the eighteenth century for breaking this rule in his tragedies.) And older tragedies paid attention to the concept of **peripeteia,** which specifies that the progress of the tragic characters sometimes leads them to a reversal: they get what they want, but what they want turns out to be destructive. Aristotle especially valued a plot in which the reversal takes place simultaneously with the recognition of the truth, or the shift from ignorance to awareness, as it does in Sophocles' *Oedipus Rex.*

Playwrights in the seventeenth and eighteenth centuries in France were especially interested in following classical precepts. They were certain that Greek tragedy and Roman comedy were the epitome of excellence in drama. They interpreted Aristotle's discussion of dramatic integrity as a set of rules governing dramatic form. These became known as drama's **three unities,** specifying one plot, a single action that takes place in one day, and a single setting. The neoclassical reinterpretation of the unities was probably much stricter than Aristotle intended.

Comedy

Two kinds of comedy developed among the ancient Greeks: **Old Comedy,** which resembles **farce** (light drama characterized by broad satirical comedy and an improbable plot) and often pokes fun at individuals with social and political power, and **New Comedy,** which is a more refined commentary on the condition of society.

Old Comedy survives in the masterful works of Aristophanes, such as *Lysistrata,* while New Comedy hearkens back to the lost plays of Menander and resurfaces in plays such as Molière's *Tartuffe.* Molière uses humor but mixes it with a serious level of social commentary. Modern **comedy of manners** studies and sometimes ridicules modern society, as in Oscar Wilde's *The Importance of Being Earnest.*

Comedy is not always funny. Chekhov thought *The Cherry Orchard* was a comedy, whereas his producer, the great Constantin Stanislavski, who trained actors to interpret Chekhov's lines and who acted in other Chekhov plays, thought it was a tragedy. The argument may have centered on the ultimate effect of the play on its audiences, but it may also have centered on the question of laughter. There are laughs in *The Cherry Orchard,* but they usually come at the expense of a character or a social group. This is true, as well, of Samuel Beckett's *Waiting for Godot* and *Krapp's Last Tape.* We may laugh, but we know that the play is at heart very serious.

Tragicomedy

Since the early seventeenth century, serious plays have been called **tragicomedies** when they do not adhere strictly to the structure of tragedy, which emphasizes the nobility of the hero or heroine, fate, the wrong action of the hero or heroine, and a resolution that includes death, exile, or a similar end. Many serious plays have these qualities, but they also have some of the qualities of comedy: a commentary on society, raucous behavior that draws laughs, and a relatively happy ending. Yet their darkness is such that we can hardly feel comfortable regarding them as comedies.

Plays such as Sam Shepard's *Buried Child* and Lorraine Hansberry's *A Raisin in the Sun* can be considered tragicomedy. Indeed, the modern temperament has especially relied on the mixture of comic and tragic elements for its most serious plays. Eugene O'Neill, Tennessee Williams, Harold Pinter, Caryl Churchill, Yasmina Reza, Sarah Ruhl, and Tracy Letts have all been masters of tragicomedy.

In contemporary drama, tragicomedy takes several forms. One is the play whose seriousness is relieved by comic moments; another is the play whose comic structure absorbs a tragic moment and continues to express affirmation. Yet another is the dark comedy whose sardonic humor leaves us wondering how we can laugh at something that is ultimately frightening. This is the case with some absurdist comedies, which insist that there is no meaning in events other than the meaning we invent for ourselves. Pinter's *The Homecoming* and Beckett's *Endgame* are such plays. They are funny yet sardonic, and when we laugh we do so uneasily.

Other genres of drama exist, although they are generally versions of tragedy, comedy, and tragicomedy. Improvisational theater, in which actors use no scripts and may switch roles at any moment, defies generic description. Musical comedies and operas are dramatic entertainments that have established their own genres related in some ways to the standard genres of drama.

Genre distinctions are useful primarily because they establish expectations in the minds of audiences with theatrical experience. Tragedies and comedies make different demands on an audience. According to Marsha Norman's explanation of the "rules" of drama, you have to know in a play just what is at stake. Understanding the principles that have developed over the centuries to create the genres of drama helps us know what is at stake.

Elements of Drama

All plays share some basic elements with which playwrights and producers work: plots, characters, settings, dialogue, movement, and themes. In addition, many modern plays pay close attention to lighting, costuming, music, and props. When we respond to a play, we observe the elements of drama in action together, and the total experience is rich, complex, and subtle. Occasionally, we respond primarily to an individual element—the theme or characterization, for instance—but that is rare. Our awareness of the elements of drama is most useful when we are thinking analytically about a play and the way it affects us.

For the sake of discussion, we will consider the way the basic elements of drama function in Lady Gregory's one-act play *The Rising of the Moon* (which follows this section). It has all the elements we expect from drama, and it is both a brief and a very successful play.

Plot

Plot is a term for the action of a drama. Plot implies that the **action** has a shape and form that will ultimately prove satisfying to the audience. Generally, a carefully plotted play begins with **exposition**, an explanation of what happened before the play began and of how the characters arrived at their present situation. The play continues, using **suspense** to build tension in the audience and in the characters and to develop further the pattern of **rising action**. The audience wonders what is going to happen, sees the characters set in motion, and then watches as certain questions implied by the drama are answered one by one. The action achieves its greatest tension as it moves to a point of **climax**, when a revelation is experienced, usually by the chief characters. Once the climax has been reached, the plot continues, sometimes very briefly, in a pattern of **falling action** as the drama reaches its conclusion and the characters understand their circumstances and themselves better than they did at the beginning of the play.

The function of plot is to give action a form that helps us understand elements of the drama in relation to one another. Plays can have several interrelated plots or only one. Lady Gregory's *The Rising of the Moon* has one very simple plot: a police sergeant is sent out with two policemen to make sure a political rebel does not escape from the area. The effect of the single plot is that the entire play focuses intensely on the interaction between the rebel, disguised as a ballad singer, and the sergeant. The sergeant meets the rebel, listens to him sing ballads, and then recognizes in him certain qualities they share. The audience wonders whether a reward of one hundred pounds will encourage the sergeant to arrest the ballad singer or, instead, the ballad singer's sense that his cause is just will persuade the sergeant to let him go. The climax of the action occurs when the sergeant's two policemen return and, as the ballad singer hides behind a barrel, ask whether the sergeant has seen any signs of the rebel. Not until that moment does the audience know for sure what the sergeant will do. When he gives his answer, the falling action begins.

Plots depend on **conflict** between characters, and in *The Rising of the Moon* the conflict is very deep. It is built into the characters themselves, but it is also part of the institution of law that the sergeant serves and the ongoing struggle for justice that the ballad singer serves. This conflict, still evident today, was a very significant national issue in Ireland when the play was first produced in Dublin in 1907.

Lady Gregory works subtly with the conflict between the sergeant and the ballad singer, showing that although they are on completely opposite sides of the law—and of the important political issues—they are more alike than they are different. The ballad singer begins to sing the "Granuaile," a revolutionary

For a tutorial on the elements of drama, click on *VirtualLit Drama Tutorials* at **bedfordstmartins.com/jacobus**.

song about England's unlawful dominance over Ireland through seven centuries; when he leaves out a line, the sergeant supplies it. In that action the sergeant reveals that even though he is paid by the English to keep law and order, his roots lie with the Irish people. By his knowledge of the revolutionary songs he reveals his sympathies.

Characterization

Lady Gregory has effectively joined **character** and conflict in *The Rising of the Moon:* as the conflict is revealed, the characters of the sergeant and the ballad singer are also revealed. At first the sergeant seems eager to get the reward, and he acts bossy with Policeman X and Policeman B. And when he first meets the ballad singer, he seems demanding and policemanlike. It is only when he begins to sense who the ballad singer really is that he changes and reveals a deep, sympathetic streak.

Lady Gregory, in a note to the play, said that in Ireland when the play was first produced, those who wanted Ireland to become part of England were incensed to see a policeman portrayed so as to show his sympathies with rebels. Those who wished Ireland to become a separate nation from England were equally shocked to see a policeman portrayed so sympathetically.

The sergeant and the ballad singer are both major characters in the play, but it is not clear that either is the villain or the hero. When the play begins, the sergeant seems to be the hero because he represents the law, and the ballad singer appears to be the villain because he has escaped from prison. But as the action develops, those characterizations change. What replaces them is an awareness of the complications that underlie the relationship between the law and the lawbreaker in some circumstances. This is part of the point of Lady Gregory's play.

Lady Gregory has given a very detailed portrait of both main characters, although in a one-act play she does not have enough space to be absolutely thorough in developing them. Yet we get an understanding of the personal ambitions of each character, and we understand both their relationship to Ireland and their particular allegiances as individuals. They speak with each other in enough detail to show that they understand each other, and when the ballad singer hides behind the barrel at the approach of the other two policemen, he indicates that he trusts the sergeant not to reveal him.

Policeman X and Policeman B are only sketched in. Yet their presence is important. It is with them that the sergeant reveals his official personality, and it is their presence at the end that represents the most important threat to the security of the ballad singer. We know, though, little or nothing about them personally. They are functionaries, a little like Rosencrantz and Guildenstern in *Hamlet,* but without the differentiating characterizations that Shakespeare was able to give minor players in his full-length play.

The plays collected in this book have some of the most remarkable characters ever created in literature. Tragedy usually demands complex characters, such as Oedipus, Antigone, Medea, Hamlet, and Willy Loman. We come to know them through their own words, through their interaction with other characters, through their expression of feelings, through their decisions, and through their presence onstage depicted in movement and gesture.

Tragicomedies offer individualized and complex characters, such as Madame Ranevskaya in *The Cherry Orchard,* Miss Julie in Strindberg's play by that name, and Nora Helmer in *A Doll House*. But just as effective in certain kinds of drama are characters drawn as types, such as Alceste, the misanthrope in Molière's play, and Everyman in medieval drama.

In many plays we see that the entire shape of the action derives from the characters, from their strengths and weaknesses. In such plays we do not feel that the action lies outside the characters and that they must live through an arbitrary sequence of events. Instead we believe that they create their own opportunities and problems.

Setting

The **setting** of a play includes many things. First, this term refers to the time and place in which the action occurs. Second, it refers to the scenery, the physical elements that appear onstage to vivify the author's stage directions. In Lady Gregory's play, we have a dock with barrels to suggest the locale, and darkness suggests night. These are important details that influence the emotional reaction of the audience.

Some plays make use of very elaborate settings; for example, August Wilson's *Fences* is produced with a detailed tenement backyard onstage. Others make use of simple settings, such as the empty stage of Pirandello's *Six Characters in Search of an Author*.

Lady Gregory's setting derives from her inspiration for the play. She visited the quays—places where boats dock and leave with goods—as a young girl and imagined how someone might escape from the nearby prison and make his getaway "under a load of kelp" in one of the ships. The quay represents the meeting of the land and water, and it represents the getaway, the possibility of freedom. The barrel is a symbol of trade, and the sergeant and the ballad singer sit on its top and trade the words of a revolutionary song with each other.

The title of the play refers to another element of the setting: the moonlight. The night protects the ballad singer, and it permits the sergeant to bend his sworn principles a bit. The rising of the moon, as a rebel song suggests, signifies a change in society, the time when "the small shall rise up and the big shall fall down." Lady Gregory uses these elements in the play in a very effective way, interrelating them so that their significance becomes increasingly apparent as the play progresses.

Dialogue

Plays depend for their unfolding on dialogue. The **dialogue** is the verbal exchanges between the characters. Since there is no description or commentary on the action, as there is in most novels, the dialogue must tell the whole story. Fine playwrights have developed ways of revealing character, advancing action, and introducing themes by a highly efficient use of dialogue.

Dialogue is spoken by one character to another, who then responds. But sometimes, as in Shakespeare's *Hamlet*, a character delivers a **soliloquy**, in which he or she speaks onstage to him- or herself. Ordinarily, such speeches take on importance because they are thought to be especially true. Characters, when they speak to each other, may well wish to deceive, but generally, when they speak to themselves, they have no reason to say anything but the truth.

In *The Rising of the Moon*, Lady Gregory has written an unusual form of dialogue that reveals a regional way of speaking. Lady Gregory was Anglo-Irish, but she lived in the west of Ireland and was familiar with the speech patterns that the characters in this play would have used. She has been recognized for her ability to re-create the speech of the rural Irish, and passages such as the following are meant to reveal the peculiarities of the rhythms and syntax of English as it was spoken in Ireland at the turn of the century:

> SERGEANT: Is he as bad as that?
> MAN: He is then.
> SERGEANT: Do you tell me so?

Lady Gregory makes a considerable effort to create dialogue that is rich in local color as well as in spirit. John Millington Synge, another Irish playwright, whose dialogue in *Riders to the Sea* is also an effort to re-create the sounds and rhythms of rural Irish speech, once said, "In a good play every speech should be as fully flavored as a nut or apple, and such speeches cannot be written by anyone who works among people who have shut their lips on poetry." Lady Gregory, who produced Synge's plays at the Abbey Theatre in Dublin, would certainly agree, as her dialogue in *The Rising of the Moon* amply shows.

Music

Lady Gregory introduces another dramatic element: music. In *The Rising of the Moon*, the music is integral to the plot because it allows the ballad singer, by omitting a line of a rebel song, gradually to expose the sergeant's sympathies with the rebel cause. The sergeant is at first mindful of his duty and insists that the balladeer stop, but eventually he is captivated by the music. As the ballad singer continues, he sings a song containing the title of the play, and the audience or reader realizes that the title exposes the play's rebel sympathies.

Incidental music is present in a great many of Shakespeare's plays. His songs are often cited for their particular excellence. Ophelia's song in act IV of *Hamlet* is deeply touching as a revelation of her mental disturbance. The song moves Laertes, who says, "Do you see this, O God?," and the audience, too, is moved. In the last act of *A Midsummer Night's Dream*, Shakespeare includes both music and dance to intensify the celebration of young lovers. The most frequently produced play of the eighteenth century, John Gay's *The Beggar's Opera*, used sixty-nine popular ballad tunes to punctuate the action. The *melo* in *melodrama* signals music, and nineteenth-century melodramas often began and ended with musical interludes.

Movement

We as readers or witnesses are energized by the movement of the characters in a play. As we read, stage directions inform us where the characters are, when they move, how they move, and perhaps even what the significance of their movement is. In modern plays, the author may give many directions for the action; in earlier plays, stage directions are few and often supplemented by those of a modern editor. In performance, the movements that you see may well have been invented by the director, although the text of a play often requires certain actions, as in the ghost scene and the final dueling scene in *Hamlet*. In some kinds of drama, such as musical comedy and Greek drama, part of the action may be danced.

Lady Gregory moves the ballad singer and the sergeant in telling ways. They move physically closer to each other as they become closer in their thinking. Their movement seems to pivot around the barrel, and in one of the most charming moments of the play, their eyes meet when the ballad singer sits on the barrel and comments on the way the sergeant is pacing back and forth. They then both sit on the barrel, facing in opposite directions, and share a pipe between them, almost as a peace offering.

Theme

The **theme** of a play is its message, its central concerns—in short, what the play is about. It is by no means a simple thing to decide what the theme of a play is, and many plays contain several themes rather than a single one. Often, the search for a theme tempts us to oversimplify, reducing a complex play to a relatively simple catchphrase.

Sophocles' *Antigone* focuses on the conflict between human law and the law of the gods when following both sets of laws seems to be impossible. Antigone wishes to honor the gods by burying her brother, but the law of Kreon decrees that he shall have no burial, since he is technically a traitor to the state. Similar themes are present in other Greek plays. *Hamlet* has many themes. On a very elementary level, the main theme of *Hamlet* is revenge. This is played out in the obligation of a son to avenge the murder of a father, even when the murderer is a kinsman. Another theme centers on corruption in the state of Denmark.

Lady Gregory's play has revolution as one theme. The rising of the moon is a sign for "the rising," or revolution, of the people against their English oppressors. The sergeant is an especially English emblem of oppression because the police were established by an Englishman, Robert Peele. At one point, the balladeer suggests the song "The Peeler and the Goat," but rejects it because in slang a "peeler" is a policeman.

Another important theme in *The Rising of the Moon* is that of unity among the Irish people. The sergeant seems to be at an opposite pole from the ballad singer when the play opens. He is posting signs announcing a reward that he could well use, since he is a family man. But as the play proceeds, the sergeant moves closer in thought to the Irish people, represented by the rebel, the ballad singer.

If concerned that readers and viewers will miss their thematic intentions, playwrights sometimes reveal these in one or two speeches. Usually, a careful reader or viewer has already divined the theme, and the speeches are intrusive. But Lady Gregory is able to introduce thematic material in certain moments of dialogue, as in this comment by the sergeant, revealing that the police are necessary to prevent a revolution:

> SERGEANT: Well, we have to do our duty in the force. Haven't we the whole country depending on us to keep law and order? It's those that are down would be up and those that are up would be down, if it wasn't for us.

For the most part, the thematic material in *The Rising of the Moon* is spread evenly throughout, as is the case in most good plays.

In every play, the elements of drama will work differently, sometimes giving us the feeling that character is dominant over theme, or plot over character, or setting over both. Ordinarily, critics believe that character, plot, and theme are the most important elements of drama, while setting, dialogue, music, and movement come next. But in the best of dramas each has its importance and each balances the others. The plays in this collection strive for that harmony and achieve it memorably.

Lady Gregory

Isabella Augusta Persse (1852–1932) was born in the west of Ireland. Her family was known as "ascendancy stock"—that is, they were educated, wealthy, and Protestant, living in a land that was largely uneducated, poverty-ridden, and Roman Catholic. A gulf existed between the rich ascendancy families, who lived in great houses with considerable style, partaking in lavish hunts and balls, and the impoverished Irish, who lived in one-room straw-roofed homes and worked the soil with primitive tools.

Lady Gregory took a strong interest in the Irish language, stimulated in part by a nurse who often spoke the language to her when she was a child. Her nurse was an important source of Irish folklore and a contact with the people who lived in the modest cottages around her family estate. It was extraordinary for any wealthy Protestant to pay attention to the language or the life of the poor laborers of the west of Ireland. Yet these are the people who figure most prominently in the plays that Lady Gregory wrote in later life.

Isabella Persse met Sir William Gregory when she was on a family trip to Nice and Rome. They were actually neighbors in Ireland but only slightly acquainted. He was also of Irish ascendancy stock and had been governor of Ceylon. They were married a year after they met, when she was twenty-eight and he was sixty-three. Their marriage was apparently quite successful, and in 1881 their son, Robert Gregory, was born. They used the family home, Coole Park, as a retreat for short periods, but most of their time was spent traveling and living in London, where Sir William was a trustee of the National Gallery of Art. W. B. Yeats, Bernard Shaw, and numerous other important literary figures spent time in Coole Park and its beautiful great house in the early part of the twentieth century.

Lady Gregory led a relatively conventional life until Sir William Gregory died in 1892. According to the laws of that time, the estate passed to her son, so she anticipated a life of relatively modest circumstances. In the process of finishing Sir William's memoirs, she found herself to be a gifted writer. She used some of her spare time to learn Irish well enough to talk with the old cottagers in the hills, where she went to gather folklore and old songs. Although W. B. Yeats and others had collected volumes of Irish stories and poems, they did not know Irish well enough to authenticate what they heard. Lady Gregory published her Kiltartan tales (she had dubbed her neighborhood Kiltartan) as a way of preserving the rapidly disappearing myths and stories that were still told around the hearth as a matter of course in rural Ireland.

She was already an accomplished writer when she met W. B. Yeats in 1894. Their meeting was of immense importance for the history of drama, since they decided to marshal their complementary talents and abilities to create an Irish theater. Their discussions included certain Irish neighbors, among them Edward Martyn, a Catholic whose early plays had been very successful. They also talked with Dr. Douglas Hyde, a mythographer and linguist and the first president of modern Ireland. Another neighbor who took part, the flamboyant George Moore, was a well-established novelist and playwright.

The group's first plays—Yeats's *The Countess Cathleen* and Martyn's *The Heather Field*—were performed on May 8 and 9, 1899, under the auspices of the newly formed Irish Literary Theatre in Dublin at the Ancient Concert

Rooms. Dedicated to producing plays by Irish playwrights on Irish themes, the Irish Literary Theatre became an immediate success. The greatest problem the founders faced was finding more plays. Lady Gregory tried her own hand and became, at age fifty, a playwright.

Her ear for people's speech was unusually good—good enough that she was able to give the great poet Yeats lessons in dialogue and to help him prepare his own plays for the stage. She collaborated with Yeats on *The Pot of Broth* in 1902, the year she wrote her first plays, *The Jackdaw* and *A Losing Game*. Her first produced play, *Twenty-Five,* was put on in 1903. By 1904, the group had rented the historic Abbey Theatre. Some of her plays were quite popular and were successful even in later revivals: *Spreading the News* (1904); *Kincora* and *The White Cockade* (1905); and *Hyacinth Halvey, The Doctor in Spite of Himself, The Gaol Gate,* and *The Canavans* (all 1906). The next year, there were troubles at the Abbey over John Millington Synge's *Playboy of the Western World*. The middle-class audience resented the portrait of Irish peasants as people who would celebrate a self-confessed father-killer, even though he had not actually done the "gallous deed." Lady Gregory faced down rioting audience members who were protesting what she was convinced was excellent drama.

In 1918, her son, a World War I pilot, was shot down over Italy. The years that followed were to some extent years of struggle. Lady Gregory managed the Abbey Theatre, directed its affairs, and developed new playwrights, among them Sean O'Casey. During the Irish Civil War (1920–1922), she was physically threatened, and eventually her family home, Roxborough, was burned. In 1926, after discovering that she had cancer, she made arrangements to sell Coole Park to the government with the agreement that she could remain there for life. She died in 1932, the writer of a large number of satisfying plays and the prime mover in developing one of the twentieth century's most important literary theaters.

The Rising of the Moon

One of Lady Gregory's shortest but most popular plays, *The Rising of the Moon* is openly political in its themes. Lady Gregory had been writing plays only a short time, and she was directing the Abbey Theatre Company when it produced this play in 1907. Her interest in Irish politics developed, she said, when she was going through the papers of a distant relative of her husband. That man had been in the Castle, the offices of the English authorities given the task of ruling Ireland from Dublin. She said that the underhanded dealings revealed in those papers persuaded her that Ireland would need to be a nation apart from England if justice were ever to be done.

In 1907, the question of union with England or separation and nationhood was on everyone's lips. Ireland was calm, and people in Dublin were relatively prosperous and by no means readying for a fight or a revolution. Yet there had been a tradition of risings against the English dating back to the Elizabethan age and earlier. In 1907, the average Irish person believed that revolution was a thing of the past; actually, it was less than ten years in the future. Certain organizations, notably the widespread Gaelic League and the less-known Sinn Féin (We Ourselves), had been developing to promote Irish lore, language, and culture. English was the dominant language in Ireland, since it was the language of commerce, but its use tended to obliterate the Irish culture. Lady Gregory's work with the Abbey Theatre, which was making one of the age's most important contributions to Irish culture, thus coincided with growing interest throughout Ireland in rediscovering its literary past.

The title *The Rising of the Moon* comes from a popular old rebel song that pointed to the rising of the moon as the signal for the rising of peoples against oppression. The main characters of the play represent the two opposing forces in Ireland: freedom and independence, personified by the ballad singer ("a Ragged Man"), and law and order, represented by the sergeant. The ballad singer is aligned with those who want to change the social structure of Ireland so that the people now on the bottom will be on top. The sergeant's job is to preserve the status quo and avoid such a turning of the tables.

In an important way, the sergeant and the ballad singer represent the two alternatives that face the modern Irish—now as in the past. One alternative is to accept the power of the English and be in their pay, like the sergeant; such a person would be well fed and capable of supporting a family. The other alternative is to follow the revolutionary path of the ballad singer and risk prison, scorn, and impoverishment. The ballad singer is a ragged man because he has been totally reduced in circumstances by his political choices.

For Lady Gregory, this play was a serious political statement. She and W. B. Yeats—both aristocratic Protestant Irish—were sympathetic to Irish revolutionary causes. They each wrote plays that struck a revolutionary note during this period. Neither truly expected a revolution; when the Easter Uprising of 1916 was put down with considerable loss of life, Yeats lamented that his plays may have sent some young men to their deaths.

The success of *The Rising of the Moon* lies in Lady Gregory's exceptional ear for dialogue. She captures the way people speak, and she also manages to draw the characters of the sergeant and the ballad singer so as to gain our sympathies for both. In a remarkably economic fashion, she dramatizes the problem of politics in Ireland, characterizing the two polarities and revealing some of the complexities that face anyone who tries to understand them.

For discussion questions and assignments on *The Rising of the Moon,* visit bedfordstmartins.com/jacobus.

LADY GREGORY (1852–1932)

The Rising of the Moon   1907

Persons

SERGEANT
POLICEMAN X
POLICEMAN B
A RAGGED MAN

Scene: *Side of a quay in a seaport town. Some posts and chains. A large barrel. Enter three policemen. Moonlight.*

(Sergeant, who is older than the others, crosses the stage to right and looks down steps. The others put down a pastepot and unroll a bundle of placards.)

POLICEMAN B: I think this would be a good place to put up a notice. (*He points to barrel.*)

POLICEMAN X: Better ask him. (*Calls to Sergeant.*) Will this be a good place for a placard?

(*No answer.*)

POLICEMAN B: Will we put up a notice here on the barrel?

(*No answer.*)

SERGEANT: There's a flight of steps here that leads to the water. This is a place that should be minded well. If he got down here, his friends might have a boat to meet him; they might send it in here from outside.

POLICEMAN B: Would the barrel be a good place to put a notice up?

SERGEANT: It might; you can put it there.

(*They paste the notice up.*)

SERGEANT (*reading it*): Dark hair—dark eyes, smooth face, height five feet five—there's not much to take hold of in that—It's a pity I had no chance of seeing him before he broke out of jail. They say he's a wonder, that it's he makes all the plans for the whole organization. There isn't another man in Ireland would have broken jail the way he did. He must have some friends among the jailers.

POLICEMAN B: A hundred pounds is little enough for the Government to offer for him. You may be sure any man in the force that takes him will get promotion.

SERGEANT: I'll mind this place myself. I wouldn't wonder at all if he came this way. He might come slipping along there (*points to side of quay*), and his friends might be waiting for him there (*points down steps*), and once he got away it's little chance we'd have of finding him; it's maybe under a load of kelp he'd be in a fishing boat, and not one to help a married man that wants it to the reward.

POLICEMAN X: And if we get him itself, nothing but abuse on our heads for it from the people, and maybe from our own relations.

SERGEANT: Well, we have to do our duty in the force. Haven't we the whole country depending on us to keep law and order? It's those that are down would be up and those that are up would be down, if it wasn't for us. Well, hurry on, you have plenty of other places to placard yet, and come back here then to me. You can take the lantern. Don't be too long now. It's very lonesome here with nothing but the moon.

POLICEMAN B: It's a pity we can't stop with you. The Government should have brought more police into the town, with *him* in jail, and at assize° time too. Well, good luck to your watch.

(*They go out.*)

SERGEANT (*walks up and down once or twice and looks at placard*): A hundred pounds and promotion sure. There must be a great deal of spending in a hundred pounds. It's a pity some honest man not to be better of that.

(*A Ragged Man appears at left and tries to slip past. Sergeant suddenly turns.*)

SERGEANT: Where are you going?

assize: Judicial inquest.

MAN: I'm a poor ballad-singer, your honor. I thought to sell some of these (*holds out bundle of ballads*) to the sailors.

(*He goes on.*)

SERGEANT: Stop! Didn't I tell you to stop? You can't go on there.

MAN: Oh, very well. It's a hard thing to be poor. All the world's against the poor!

SERGEANT: Who are you?

MAN: You'd be as wise as myself if I told you, but I don't mind. I'm one Jimmy Walsh, a ballad-singer.

SERGEANT: Jimmy Walsh? I don't know that name.

MAN: Ah, sure, they know it well enough in Ennis. Were you ever in Ennis, sergeant?

SERGEANT: What brought you here?

MAN: Sure, it's to the assizes I came, thinking I might make a few shillings here or there. It's in the one train with the judges I came.

SERGEANT: Well, if you came so far, you may as well go farther, for you'll walk out of this.

MAN: I will, I will; I'll just go on where I was going.

(*Goes toward steps.*)

SERGEANT: Come back from those steps; no one has leave to pass down them tonight.

MAN: I'll just sit on the top of the steps till I see will some sailor buy a ballad off me that would give me my supper. They do be late going back to the ship. It's often I saw them in Cork carried down the quay in a handcart.

SERGEANT: Move on, I tell you. I won't have anyone lingering about the quay tonight.

MAN: Well, I'll go. It's the poor have the hard life! Maybe yourself might like one, sergeant. Here's a good sheet now. (*Turns one over.*) "Content and a pipe"—that's not much. "The Peeler and the goat"—you wouldn't like that. "Johnny Hart"—that's a lovely song.

SERGEANT: Move on.

MAN: Ah, wait till you hear it. (*Sings.*)

There was a rich farmer's daughter lived near the town of Ross;
She courted a Highland soldier, his name was Johnny Hart;
Says the mother to her daughter, "I'll go distracted mad
If you marry that Highland soldier dressed up in Highland plaid."

SERGEANT: Stop that noise.

(*Man wraps up his ballads and shuffles toward the steps.*)

SERGEANT: Where are you going?

MAN: Sure you told me to be going, and I am going.

SERGEANT: Don't be a fool. I didn't tell you to go that way; I told you to go back to the town.

MAN: Back to the town, is it?

SERGEANT (*taking him by the shoulder and shoving him before him*): Here, I'll show you the way. Be off with you. What are you stopping for?

MAN (*who has been keeping his eye on the notice, points to it*): I think I know what you're waiting for, sergeant.

SERGEANT: What's that to you?

MAN: And I know well the man you're waiting for—I know him well—I'll be going.

(*He shuffles on.*)

SERGEANT: You know him? Come back here. What sort is he?

MAN: Come back is it, sergeant? Do you want to have me killed?

SERGEANT: Why do you say that?

MAN: Never mind. I'm going. I wouldn't be in your shoes if the reward was ten times as much. (*Goes on off stage to left.*) Not if it was ten times as much.

SERGEANT (*rushing after him*): Come back here, come back. (*Drags him back.*) What sort is he? Where did you see him?

MAN: I saw him in my own place, in the County Clare. I tell you you wouldn't like to be looking at him. You'd be afraid to be in the one place with him. There isn't a weapon he doesn't know the use of, and as to strength, his muscles are as hard as that board (*slaps barrel*).

SERGEANT: Is he as bad as that?

MAN: He is then.

SERGEANT: Do you tell me so?

MAN: There was a poor man in our place, a sergeant from Ballyvaughan.—It was with a lump of stone he did it.

SERGEANT: I never heard of that.

MAN: And you wouldn't, sergeant. It's not everything that happens gets into the papers. And there was a policeman in plain clothes, too. . . . It is in Limerick he was. . . . It was after the time of the attack on the police barrack at Kilmallock. . . . Moonlight . . . just like this . . . waterside. . . . Nothing was known for certain.

SERGEANT: Do you say so? It's a terrible county to belong to.

MAN: That's so, indeed! You might be standing there, looking out that way, thinking you saw him coming up this side of the quay (*points*), and he might be coming up this other side (*points*), and he'd be on you before you knew where you were.

SERGEANT: It's a whole troop of police they ought to put here to stop a man like that.

MAN: But if you'd like me to stop with you, I could be looking down this side. I could be sitting up here on this barrel.

SERGEANT: And you know him well, too?

MAN: I'd know him a mile off, sergeant.

SERGEANT: But you wouldn't want to share the reward?

MAN: Is it a poor man like me, that has to be going the roads and singing in fairs, to have the name on him that he took a reward? But you don't want me. I'll be safer in the town.

SERGEANT: Well, you can stop.

MAN (*getting up on barrel*): All right, sergeant. I wonder, now, you're not tired out, sergeant, walking up and down the way you are.

SERGEANT: If I'm tired I'm used to it.

MAN: You might have hard work before you tonight yet. Take it easy while you can. There's plenty of room up here on the barrel, and you see farther when you're higher up.

SERGEANT: Maybe so. (*Gets up beside him on barrel, facing right. They sit back to back, looking different ways.*) You made me feel a bit queer with the way you talked.

MAN: Give me a match, sergeant (*he gives it and man lights pipe*); take a draw yourself? It'll quiet you. Wait now till I give you a light, but you needn't turn round. Don't take your eye off the quay for the life of you.

SERGEANT: Never fear, I won't. (*Lights pipe. They both smoke.*) Indeed it's a hard thing to be in the force, out at night and no thanks for it, for all the danger we're in. And it's little we get but abuse from the people, and no choice but to obey our orders, and never asked when a man is sent into danger, if you are a married man with a family.

MAN (*sings*): As through the hills I walked to view the hills and shamrock plain,
I stood awhile where nature smiles to view the rocks and streams,
On a matron fair I fixed my eyes beneath a fertile vale,
And she sang her song it was on the wrong of poor old Granuaile.

SERGEANT: Stop that; that's no song to be singing in these times.

MAN: Ah, sergeant, I was only singing to keep my heart up. It sinks when I think of him. To think of us two sitting here, and he creeping up the quay, maybe, to get to us.

SERGEANT: Are you keeping a good lookout?

MAN: I am; and for no reward too. Amn't I the foolish man? But when I saw a man in trouble, I never could help trying to get him out of it. What's that? Did something hit me?

(*Rubs his heart.*)

SERGEANT (*patting him on the shoulder*): You will get your reward in heaven.

MAN: I know that, I know that, sergeant, but life is precious.

SERGEANT: Well, you can sing if it gives you more courage.

MAN (*sings*): Her head was bare, her hands and feet with iron bands were bound,
Her pensive strain and plaintive wail mingles with the evening gale,
And the song she sang with mournful air, I am old Granuaile.
Her lips so sweet that monarchs kissed . . .

SERGEANT: That's not it. . . . "Her gown she wore was stained with gore." . . . That's it—you missed that.

MAN: You're right, sergeant, so it is; I missed it. (*Repeats line.*) But to think of a man like you knowing a song like that.

SERGEANT: There's many a thing a man might know and might not have any wish for.

MAN: Now, I daresay, sergeant, in your youth, you used to be sitting up on a wall, the way you are sitting up on this barrel now, and the other lads beside you, and you singing "Granuaile"? . . .

SERGEANT: I did then.

MAN: And the "Shan Van Vocht"? . . .

SERGEANT: I did then.

MAN: And the "Green on the Cape"?

SERGEANT: That was one of them.

MAN: And maybe the man you are watching for tonight used to be sitting on the wall, when he was young, and singing those same songs. . . . It's a queer world. . . .

SERGEANT: Whisht! . . . I think I see something coming. . . . It's only a dog.

MAN: And isn't it a queer world? . . . Maybe it's one of the boys you used to be singing with that time you will be arresting today or tomorrow, and sending into the dock. . . .

SERGEANT: That's true indeed.

MAN: And maybe one night, after you had been singing, if the other boys had told you some plan they had, some plan to free the country, you might have joined with them . . . and maybe it is you might be in trouble now.

SERGEANT: Well, who knows but I might? I had a great spirit in those days.

MAN: It's a queer world, sergeant, and it's little any mother knows when she sees her child creeping on the floor what might happen to it before it has gone through its life, or who will be who in the end.

SERGEANT: That's a queer thought now, and a true thought. Wait now till I think it out. . . . If it wasn't for the sense I have, and for my wife and family, and for me joining the force the time I did, it might be myself now would be after breaking jail and hiding in the dark, and it might be him that's hiding in the dark and that got out of jail would be sitting up here where I am on this barrel. . . . And it might be myself would be creeping up trying to make my escape from himself, and it might be himself would be keeping the law, and myself would be breaking it, and myself would be trying to put a bullet in his head, or to take up a lump of stone the way you said he did . . . no, that myself did. . . . Oh! (*Gasps. After a pause.*) What's that? (*Grasps man's arm.*)

MAN (*jumps off barrel and listens, looking out over water*): It's nothing, sergeant.

SERGEANT: I thought it might be a boat. I had a notion there might be friends of his coming about the quays with a boat.

MAN: Sergeant, I am thinking it was with the people you were, and not with the law you were, when you were a young man.

SERGEANT: Well, if I was foolish then, that time's gone.

MAN: Maybe, sergeant, it comes into your head sometimes, in spite of your belt and your tunic, that it might have been as well for you to have followed Granuaile.

SERGEANT: It's no business of yours what I think.

MAN: Maybe, sergeant, you'll be on the side of the country yet.

SERGEANT (*gets off barrel*): Don't talk to me like that. I have my duties and I know them. (*Looks round.*) That was a boat; I hear the oars.

(*Goes to the steps and looks down.*)

MAN (*sings*): O, then, tell me, Shawn O'Farrell,
   Where the gathering is to be.
In the old spot by the river
   Right well known to you and me!

SERGEANT: Stop that! Stop that, I tell you!

MAN (*sings louder*): One word more, for signal token,
   Whistle up the marching tune,
With your pike upon your shoulder,
   At the Rising of the Moon.

SERGEANT: If you don't stop that, I'll arrest you.

(*A whistle from below answers, repeating the air.*)

SERGEANT: That's a signal. (*Stands between him and steps.*) You must not pass this way. . . . Step farther back. . . . Who are you? You are no ballad-singer.

MAN: You needn't ask who I am; that placard will tell you. (*Points to placard.*)

SERGEANT: You are the man I am looking for.

MAN (*takes off hat and wig. Sergeant seizes them*): I am. There's a hundred pounds on my head. There is a friend of mine below in a boat. He knows a safe place to bring me to.

SERGEANT (*looking still at hat and wig*): It's a pity! It's a pity. You deceived me. You deceived me well.

MAN: I am a friend of Granuaile. There is a hundred pounds on my head.

SERGEANT: It's a pity, it's a pity!

MAN: Will you let me pass, or must I make you let me?

SERGEANT: I am in the force. I will not let you pass.

MAN: I thought to do it with my tongue. (*Puts hand in breast.*) What is that?

VOICE OF POLICEMAN X (*outside*): Here, this is where we left him.

SERGEANT: It's my comrades coming.

MAN: You won't betray me . . . the friend of Granuaile. (*Slips behind barrel.*)

VOICE OF POLICEMAN B: That was the last of the placards.

POLICEMAN X (*as they come in*): If he makes his escape it won't be unknown he'll make it.

(*Sergeant puts hat and wig behind his back.*)

POLICEMAN B: Did anyone come this way?

SERGEANT (*after a pause*): No one.

POLICEMAN B: No one at all?

SERGEANT: No one at all.

POLICEMAN B: We had no orders to go back to the station; we can stop along with you.

SERGEANT: I don't want you. There is nothing for you to do here.

POLICEMAN B: You bade us to come back here and keep watch with you.

SERGEANT: I'd sooner be alone. Would any man come this way and you making all that talk? It is better the place to be quiet.

POLICEMAN B: Well, we'll leave you the lantern anyhow.

(*Hands it to him.*)

SERGEANT: I don't want it. Bring it with you.

POLICEMAN B: You might want it. There are clouds coming up and you have the darkness of the night before you yet. I'll leave it over here on the barrel. (*Goes to barrel.*)

SERGEANT: Bring it with you, I tell you. No more talk.

POLICEMAN B: Well, I thought it might be a comfort to you. I often think when I have it in my hand and can be flashing it about into every dark corner (*doing so*) that it's the same as being beside the fire at home, and the bits of bogwood blazing up now and again.

(*Flashes it about, now on the barrel, now on Sergeant.*)

SERGEANT (*furious*): Be off the two of you, yourselves and your lantern!

(*They go out. Man comes from behind barrel. He and Sergeant stand looking at one another.*)

SERGEANT: What are you waiting for?

MAN: For my hat, of course, and my wig. You wouldn't wish me to get my death of cold?

(*Sergeant gives them.*)

MAN (*going toward steps*): Well, good night, comrade, and thank you. You did me a good turn tonight, and I'm obliged to you. Maybe I'll be able to do as much for you when the small rise up and the big fall down . . . when we all change places at the Rising (*waves his hand and disappears*) of the Moon.

SERGEANT (*turning his back to audience and reading placard*): A hundred pounds reward! A hundred pounds! (*Turns toward audience.*) I wonder, now, am I as great a fool as I think I am?

Greek Drama

Because our historical knowledge of Greek drama is limited to what we can glean from the available contemporary commentaries and from partial archaeological remains—in the form of ruined theaters—we do not know when Greek theater began or what its original impulses were. Our best information points to 534 BCE as the beginning of the formal competitions among playwrights for coveted prizes that continued to be awarded for several centuries. Thespis, credited as the first tragedy writer, seems to have changed the nature of the form by stepping out of the chorus and taking a solo part. But the origin of *tragedy,* the Greek word for which translates to "goat-song" or "song for the sacrificial goat," is obscure. One theory is that tragedy may have developed from the rites of rural cults that sacrificed a she-goat at some Dionysian festivals or from masked animal dances at certain cult celebrations.

One source that may well have influenced the Greeks was the Egyptian civilization of the first millennium BCE. Egyptian culture was fully formed, brilliant, and complex, with numerous religious festivals and a pantheon of gods who resembled, and possibly inspired, those of the Greeks. Although it is not certain that Egypt produced a fully formed dramatic literature, certain major festivals and ceremonies that were performed annually, such as the Abydos Passion Play outlining the death and resurrection of Osiris, seem to have counterparts in Greek rituals and drama. The Abydos Passion Play tells the story of the betrayal and murder of Osiris by his jealous brother Seth, the scattering of his remains, and the efforts of Isis to reclaim and reassemble them to permit his rebirth.

The closest Greek counterpart to Osiris was **Dionysus**, who inspired orgiastic celebrations that found their way into early Greek drama. Dionysus was an agricultural deity, the Greek god of wine and the symbol of life-giving power. In several myths, he, like Osiris, was ritually killed and dismembered and his parts scattered through the land. These myths paralleled the agricultural cycle of death and disintegration during the winter, followed by cultivation and rebirth in the spring, and reinforced the Greeks' understanding of the meaning of birth, life, and death.

The Development of Greek Drama

Drama developed in ancient Greece in close connection with the Dionysia, religious celebrations dedicated to Dionysus. Four Dionysiac celebrations were held each winter in Athens, beginning at the grape harvest and culminating during the first wine tastings: the Rural Dionysia in December, the Lenaia in January, the Anthesteria in February, and the City Dionysia in March. Except for the Anthesteria, the festivals featured drama contests among playwrights, and some of the works performed in those competitions have endured through the centuries. Theories that connect the origins of drama with religion hypothesize that one function of the religious festivals within which the drama competitions took place was the ritual attempt to guarantee fertility and the growth of the crops, on which the society depended.

The **City Dionysia**, the most lavish of the festivals, lasted from five to seven days. It was open to non-Athenians and therefore offered Athenians the opportunity to show off their wealth, their glorious history, and their heroes, who were often honored in parades the day before the plays began. There is some question about what was presented on each day. Two days were probably taken up with dithyrambic contests among the ten tribes of Athens. Generally each tribe presented two choruses—one of men and one of boys—each singing a narrative lyric called a **dithyramb**. Three days were devoted to contests among tragedians, most of whom worked for half the year on three tragedies and a **satyr play**, an erotic piece of comic relief that ended the day's performance. A tragedian's three plays sometimes had related themes or myths, but often they did not. The tragedians wrote the plays; trained and rehearsed the actors; composed music; and created the setting, dances, costumes, and masks. Judges chosen by lottery awarded prizes. First prize went to the tragedian whose four plays were most powerful and most beautifully conceived.

After 486 BCE, when the first comedy competition was held, five and later three comedies were also presented during the festival. The performances were paid for by wealthy Athenians as part of their civic duty. The great Greek plays thus were not commercial enterprises but an important part of civic and religious festivals.

The Greeks and Their Gods

The great achievement of Greek religion was the humanizing of their gods. Apollo, Zeus, Aphrodite, Athena, and Bacchus had recognizable emotions and pleasures. The Greeks built temples to their gods and made offerings at appropriate times to avoid catastrophe and bad luck. But the Greeks had no official religious text, no system of religious belief that they all followed, and few ethical teachings derived from religion. The impression we have today is that Greeks' efforts to define and know the gods were shaped by great artists such as Phidias, who sculpted Zeus at Olympia; Homer, who portrayed the gods in *The Iliad* and *The Odyssey*; and the great Greek playwrights, who sometimes revealed the actions of the gods. Our present knowledge of Greek gods resides in the literary and artistic remains of Greek culture.

Fortunately for us, most Greek drama was associated with important celebrations designed to honor Greek gods. We would not, however, call this drama religious in nature—as we characterize the medieval drama designated to celebrate Christian holidays. What we learn from Greek drama is that the gods can favor individual humans for reasons of their own. And likewise, the gods can choose to punish individual humans. To some extent Greek drama is designed to explain the divine approach to favor and disfavor.

The Greek Stage

At the center of the Greek theater was the **orchestra**, where the chorus sang and danced (*orches* is derived from the Greek for "dancing place"). The audience, sometimes numbering fifteen thousand, sat in rising rows on three sides of the orchestra. The steep sides of a hill formed a natural amphitheater for Greek audiences. Eventually, on the rim of the orchestra, an oblong building called the **skene**, or scene house, developed as a space for the actors and a background for the action. The term **proskenion** was sometimes used to refer to a raised stage added in later times in front of the *skene* where the actors performed. The theater in Epidaurus (Figure 1) was a model for the Greek theater plan (Figure 2).

Greek theaters were widely dispersed from Greece to present-day Turkey, to Sicily, and even to southern France. Wherever the Greeks developed new colonies and city-states, they built theaters. In many of the surviving theaters the acoustics are so fine that a human voice onstage can be heard from any seat in the theater.

Perhaps the most spectacular theatrical device used by the Greek playwrights, the **mekane** ("machine"), was implemented onstage by means of elaborate booms or derricks. Actors were lowered onto the stage to enact the roles of Olympian gods intervening in the affairs of humans. Some commentators, such as Aristotle (384–322 BCE), believed that the *mekane* should be used only if the intercession of deities was in keeping with the character of the play. The last of the great Greek tragedians, Euripides (c. 485–c. 406 BCE), used the device in almost half of his tragedies. In *Medea*, Euripides uses the *mekane* to lift Medea to the roof of the *skene* and into her dragon chariot as a means of resolving the play's conflict. At the end of the play, Medea is beyond

Figure 1. The theater in Epidaurus, Greece, looking east. The best preserved (and now restored) Greek theater, it remains in use today. Built in the fourth century BCE by Polykleitos the Younger and approximately 124 feet in diameter, it seats twelve thousand people and has excellent acoustics.

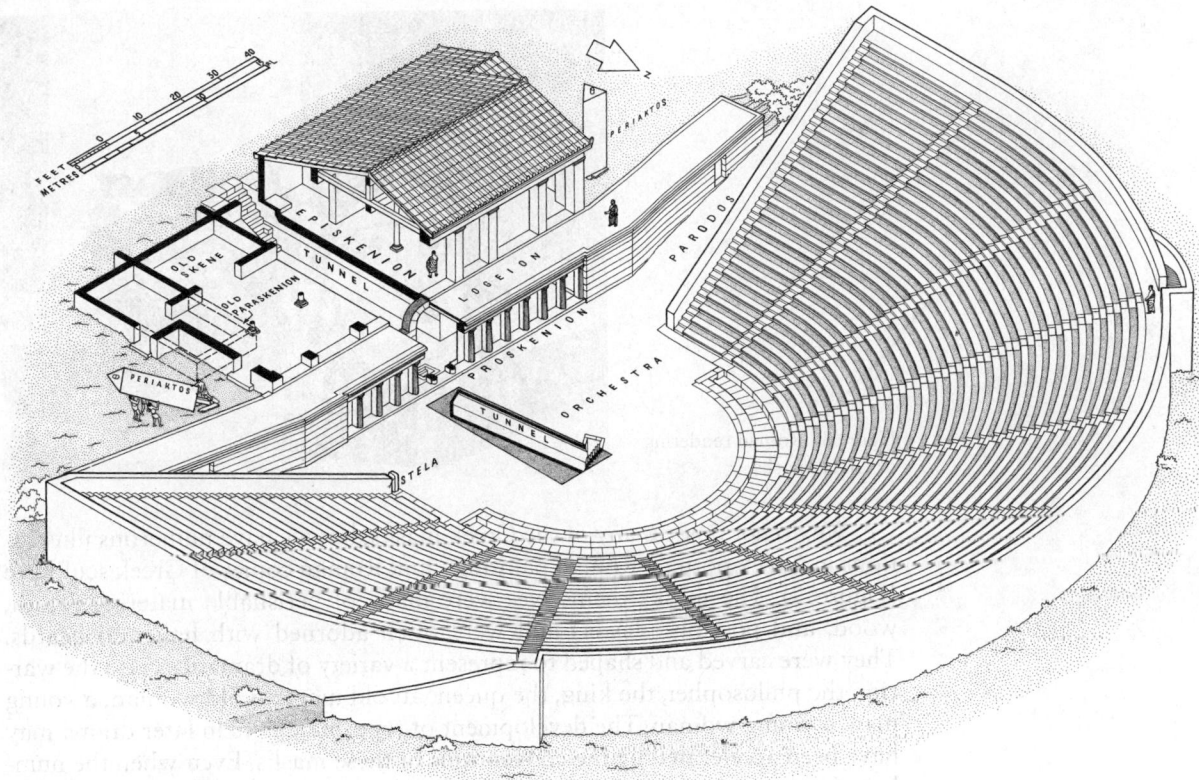

Figure 2. The Hellenistic theater in Eretria, Greece.

her persecutors' reach and is headed for safety in another country. Modern dramatists use a metaphorical version of this device called *deus ex machina* (literally, "the god from the machine") when they rescue characters at the last moment by improbable accidents or strokes of luck. Usually, these are unsatisfying means of solving dramatic problems.

The Greek Actor

According to legend, Thespis (sixth century BCE) was the first actor—the first person to step from the chorus to act in dialogue with it—thus creating the **agon,** or dramatic confrontation. He won the first prize for tragedy in 534 BCE. As the only actor, he took several parts, wearing **masks** to distinguish the different characters. One actor was the norm in tragedies until Aeschylus (c. 525–456 BCE), the first important Greek tragedian whose work survives, introduced a second actor and then Sophocles (c. 496–c. 406 BCE) added a third. Later, comedy used four actors. The chorus and all the actors were male.

Like the actors, the members of the chorus wore masks. At first the masks were simple, but they became more ornate, often decorated with details that established the gender, age, or station of each character. Despite the excellent acoustics in the largest of theaters, the actor had to project his voice for some distance, and certain masks were designed to amplify the voice to reach the most distant rows.

Figure 3. Roman rendering of Greek masks.

We do not possess any of the Greek masks, but we have numerous illustrations in Greek pottery, Roman paintings, and Roman copies of Greek sculpture (Figure 3). The masks themselves were made of perishable materials (cloth, wood, and possibly plaster) and were often adorned with hair and beards. They were carved and shaped to represent a variety of dramatic types: the warrior, the philosopher, the king, the queen, an old man, an old woman, a young man, a young woman. The development of type characters in later drama may have been accelerated by the conventions of these masks. Even when the number of actors was increased to four, masks were used to permit them to assume many roles and create a high level of dramatic complexity.

The demands on Greek actors were considerable. They were expected to be in good physical condition so as to dance with grace. Their voices had to be full and expressive, as well as flexible enough to represent different characters. The audience members sitting close to the actors were often taken by the sincerity or expressiveness of the eyes seen within the mask. Often the authors themselves, such as Thespis and Aeschylus, were among the most prominent actors of their time and were celebrated for their dramatic abilities.

Genres of Greek Drama

Greek drama developed three distinct genres: tragedy, satyr plays, and comedy. The most fully developed and valued genre is tragedy: the story, usually based on Greek myth, of the downfall of a noble figure. The satyr play followed a trilogy of tragedies. A chorus of satyrs, each half man and half goat or beast, enacted scenes from Greek myth in a sometimes crude and farcical fashion. Until the development of comedy, satyr plays provided the emotional relief needed after watching three tragedies. Comedy developed in two subgenres. Old Comedy, associated with Aristophanes, was often coarse and ribald, satirizing the foibles of important politicians and sometimes even important playwrights. New Comedy, associated with Menander, was more refined and avoided criticizing individuals while expressing a broad social criticism.

Tragedy

Greek tragedy focused on a person of noble birth who often had risen to a great height and then fell precipitately. Tragedies showed humans at the mercy of **moira**, their fate, which they only partly understood. One objective of

Greek drama was to have the audience experience a **catharsis**, which Aristotle describes as a purging or purifying of the emotions of pity and fear. According to the Greeks, these are emotions that a person associates with the fall of someone in a high social station, such as a king or queen. A central character, or **protagonist**, of noble birth was therefore an essential element for the playwright striving to evoke catharsis in an audience. Twentieth-century experiments with tragic figures who are ordinary people, such as Arthur Miller's *Death of a Salesman,* as masterful as they are, would not have made sense to the Greeks. For the Greeks, tragedy could befall only the great.

The modern critic Kenneth Burke identified a pattern for Greek tragedies. The tragic figure—for whom the play is usually named—experiences three stages of development: purpose, passion, and perception. The play begins with a purpose, such as finding the source of the plague in *Oedipus Rex.* Then, as the path becomes tangled and events unfold, the tragic figure begins an extensive process of soul-searching and suffers an inner agony—the passion. The perception of the truth involves a fate that the tragic figure would rather not face. It might be death or, as in *Oedipus Rex,* exile. It always involves separation from the human community. For the Greeks, that was the greatest punishment.

According to Aristotle, the tragic hero's perception of the truth is the most intense moment in the drama. He calls it **anagnorisis**, or recognition. Aristotle believed that when this recognition came at the same moment that the tragic figure's fortunes reversed—the **peripeteia**—the tragedy was most fulfilling for the audience. This is the case in *Oedipus Rex.* Aristotle's comments in his *Poetics* on the structure and effect of *Oedipus Rex* remain the most significant critical observations made by a contemporary on Greek theater. (See the excerpt from the *Poetics* that begins on page 95.)

The earliest tragedies seem to have developed from the emotional, intense dithyrambs sung by Athenian choruses. The **chorus** in most tragedies numbered twelve or fifteen men, who usually represented the citizenry in the drama. They dressed simply, and their song was sometimes sung in unison, sometimes delivered by the chorus leader. Originally, there were no actors separate from the chorus.

Eventually the structure of the plays became elaborated into a series of alternations between the characters' dialogue and the choral odes, with each speaking part developing the action or responding to it. Often crucial information furthering the action came from the mouth of a messenger, as in *Oedipus Rex.* The tragedies were structured in three parts: the **prologue** established the conflict; the episodes, or agons, developed the dramatic relationships between characters; and the **exodos** concluded the action. Between these sections the chorus performed different songs: **parodos** while moving onto the stage and **stasima** while standing still. In some plays, the chorus sang choral **odes** called the **strophe** as it moved from right to left. It sang the **antistrophe** while moving back to the right. The actors' episodes consisted of dialogue with each other and with the chorus. The scholar Bernhard Zimmerman has plotted the structure of *Oedipus Rex* in this fashion:

Prologue: Dialogue with Oedipus, the Priests, and Kreon establishing that the plague afflicting Thebes will cease when Laios's murderer is found.
Parodos: The opening hymn of the Chorus appealing to the gods.
First Episode: Oedipus seeks the murderer; Teiresias says it is Oedipus.
First Stasimon: The Chorus supports Oedipus, disbelieving Teiresias.

Second Episode: Oedipus accuses Kreon of being in league with Teiresias and the real murderer. Iokaste pleads for Kreon and tells the oracle of Oedipus's birth and of the death of Laios at the fork of a road. Oedipus sends for the eyewitness of the murder.

Second Stasimon: The Chorus, in a song, grows agitated for Oedipus.

Third Episode: The messenger from Oedipus's "hometown" tells him that his adoptive father has died and is not his real father. Iokaste guesses the truth and Oedipus becomes deeply worried.

Third Stasimon: The Chorus delivers a reassuring, hopeful song.

Fourth Episode: Oedipus, the Shepherd, and the Messenger confront the facts and Oedipus experiences the turning point of the play: he realizes he is the murderer he seeks.

Fourth Stasimon: The Chorus sings of the illusion of human happiness.

Exodos: Iokaste kills herself; Oedipus puts out his eyes; the Chorus and Kreon try to decide the best future action.

As this brief structural outline of *Oedipus Rex* demonstrates, the chorus assumed an important part in the tragedies. In Aeschylus's *Agamemnon*, it represents the elders of the community. In Sophocles' *Oedipus Rex*, it is a group of concerned citizens who give Oedipus advice and make demands on him. In *Antigone*, the chorus consists of men loyal to the state. In Euripides' *Medea*, the chorus is a group of the important women of Corinth.

Satyr Plays

The drama competitions held regularly from 534 BCE consisted usually of the work of three playwrights who each produced three tragedies and one satyr play, a form of comic relief. In a satyr play, the chorus dressed as satyrs, cavorting with a **phallus**, a mock penis, and engaging in riotous, almost slapstick antics. The characters were not psychologically developed, as they were in tragedy; the situations were not socially instructive, as they were in comedy. Rough-hewn and lighthearted, the satyr plays may have been a necessary antidote to the intensity of the tragedies.

Only one satyr play survives, perhaps an indication that the form was not as highly valued as tragedy. In Euripides' *Cyclops,* based on Odysseus's confrontation with the one-eyed giant who dined on a number of his men, Odysseus outwits the giant with the aid of a well-filled wineskin. The powers of Bacchus (Dionysus) are often alluded to, and drunkenness is a prime ingredient. The play is witty, entertaining, and brief. It might well have been the perfect way to end an otherwise serious drama festival.

Comedy

No coherent Greek theories on comedy have come down to us. (Aristotle is said to have written a lost treatise on comedy.) In the *Poetics,* Aristotle points out that comedy shows people from a lower social order than the nobility, who are the main figures in tragedy.

The two greatest Greek comic writers were Aristophanes (c. 448–c. 385 BCE), whose *Lysistrata* appears in this collection, and Menander (c. 342–c. 291 BCE). The first was a master of **Old Comedy** (which lasted from c. 486 to c. 400 BCE), in which individuals—sometimes well known to the audience—could be attacked personally. The humor was often ribald, coarse, and brassy, but according to

Aristotle, it was not vicious. Physical devices onstage, such as the erect phalluses beneath the men's garments in *Lysistrata,* accompanied ribald lines, and Athenian audiences were mightily entertained. Comedy appears to have provided release, but for entirely different emotions from those evoked by tragedy.

The Old Comedy of Aristophanes concentrated on buffoonery and farce. Although we know little about it, a form known as **Middle Comedy** seems to have flourished from approximately 400 to 320 BCE. Our evidence is from statuettes of players that indicate a more realistic portrayal of character and thus a less broad and grotesque form of comedy than in some of the plays of Aristophanes. The **New Comedy** of Menander and others whose work is now lost provided a less ribald humor that centered on the shortcomings of the middle classes. Although Menander enjoyed a great reputation in his own time and was highly regarded by Roman playwrights much later, very little of his work has survived. He is said to have written just over one hundred plays, but only one, *The Grouch,* survives intact. Twenty-three of his plays existed in a manuscript in Constantinople in the sixteenth century, but nothing of that volume seems to have survived. We know a number of titles, such as *The Lady from Andros, The Flatterer,* and *The Suspicious Man.* And we know that the Romans pilfered liberally from his plays. Beyond that we know little.

Menander's New Comedy concentrated on social manners. Instead of attacking individuals, as Aristophanes frequently did, Menander was more likely to attack a vice, such as vanity, or to portray the foibles of a social class. He aimed at his own middle class and established the pattern of parents or guardians struggling, usually over the issue of marriage, against the wishes of their children. The children ordinarily foil their parents' wishes, frequently with the help of an acerbic slave who provides the comedy with most of its humor. This pattern has proved so durable that it is used virtually every day in modern situation comedies on television.

Both Old and New Comedy have influenced theater from the time of the Greeks to the present. The nineteenth-century comedy of Oscar Wilde (in this collection) is an example of New Comedy, and the Marx Brothers' and Three Stooges' movies are examples of Old Comedy.

The Great Age of Greek Drama

The fifth century BCE was not only the great creative age of Athenian theater but also the age of Athenian power in Greek politics. By the beginning of the century, Greece dominated trade in the Mediterranean and therefore in many of the major civilized urban centers of the world. The most important threat to Greek power came from the Persians, living to the east. After the Persians attacked in 490 BCE, Greek city-states such as Athens formed the Delian League to defend themselves, pouring their funds into the treasury at Delos. When the Persians threatened again in 483 BCE, Themistocles (525?–460? BCE), Athenian soldier and statesman, realized he could not win a battle on land. By skillful political moves he managed to create a powerful navy. When the Persians attacked Athens in 480 BCE, Themistocles left a small rear guard to defend the Acropolis, the city's religious fortress. The Persians took the fortress, burned everything, and were lured by a clever ruse to Salamis, where they thought that a puny Athenian navy was making a getaway. Once the Persians set sail for Salamis, Themistocles turned on them and unleashed a powerful fighting force that defeated the Persians once and for all.

In the years immediately following, Athens overstated its role in the Persian defeat and assumed an air of imperial importance. It appropriated the gold in the Delian League treasury, using it to rebuild the Acropolis beginning in 448 BCE. The great Greek general and leader Pericles (495?–429? BCE) chose his friend Phidias to supervise the construction of the Parthenon and the other main buildings that are on the Acropolis even today. The threat of Athenian domination seems to have triggered the Peloponnesian Wars (431–406 BCE), which pitted the Spartan alliance against the Athenian alliance. Athens eventually lost the war and its democratic government.

The events of these years—dominated by interminable wars, threats of a return to tyranny, and cultural instability—are coterminous with the great flourishing of Greek art, drama, and philosophy. The geniuses of Greek drama cluster in the period dating from the birth of Aeschylus (c. 525 BCE) to the death of the philosopher Socrates (399 BCE). Aeschylus wrote *The Persians* (472 BCE); *Seven against Thebes* (467 BCE); and the *Oresteia* (458 BCE), a trilogy centering on Orestes and consisting of *Agamemnon, The Libation Bearers,* and *The Eumenides. The Suppliants* and *Prometheus Bound* are of uncertain dates.

Aeschylus's introduction of a second actor made it possible to intensify the dramatic value of each *agon,* the confrontation between **antagonists.** He is also notable for giving minor characters, such as the watchman who opens *Agamemnon,* both dimension and depth. Aeschylus's *Oresteia,* the only surviving trilogy, tells of the death of Agamemnon and the efforts of his son Orestes to avenge that death.

Sophocles (c. 496–c. 406 BCE) and Euripides (c. 485–406 BCE) learned from Aeschylus and from each other, because they were all sometimes rivals. In addition to *Oedipus Rex* (c. 429 BCE), Sophocles is known today for *Ajax* (c. 442 BCE), *Philoctetes* (c. 409 BCE), *Oedipus at Colonus* (406 BCE), and *Electra* (date uncertain).

Euripides, the last of the great tragedians, may have written as many as ninety-two plays. Of the eighteen that survive, the best known are *Alcestis* (438 BCE), *Medea* (431 BCE), *Electra* (c. 417 BCE), *The Trojan Women* (415 BCE), and *The Bacchae* (produced in 405 BCE). He is especially noteworthy for his portrayal of women and for his experimental approach to theater.

These three tragedians, along with Aristophanes, provide us with insight into the Greek dramatic imagination. They also reveal something of our common humanity, since their achievement—lost though it was for many centuries—shapes our current dramatic practice. The Greeks gave us not only the beginnings of drama but also the basis of drama. We build on it today whenever a play is written and whenever we witness a play.

Date	Theater	Political	Social/Cultural
1000–800 BCE			Classic paganism is in full bloom in Greece.
			Temple of Hera, oldest surviving temple in Olympia, Greece, is built.
			9th century: Age of the Homeric epic; *The Iliad, The Odyssey*
800–700		First Messenian War: Sparta gains power in Greece.	Choral music and dramatic music develop.
			Hesiod, poet whose *Works and Days* classified the five ages of mankind: Golden (peaceful), Silver (less happy), Bronze (art and warfare), Heroic (Trojan War), and Iron (the present)
			776: First Olympian Festival (predecessor of the modern Olympic games). Only one event is featured: a footrace of approximately 200 meters.
700–600		First written laws of Athens are recorded by Draco.	Sappho of Lesbos, Greek poet
			Archilochus, Greek lyricist and author of fables
			Construction of the Acropolis begins in Athens.
600–500	**534:** First contest for best tragedy is held in Athens as part of the annual City Dionysia, a major religious festival. The winning playwright (and actor) is Thespis.	**594:** Solon's law allows for the Council of Four Hundred and various reforms pertaining to land ownership and civil liberties.	The influence of the oracle at Delphi and its priestess is at its height.
	c. 501: Satyr plays are added to the City Dionysia play competition. Each playwright now has to present a trilogy of tragedies and a satyr play.	**c. 525–459:** Themistocles, Athenian statesman and naval commander, builds a Greek navy and fortifications.	The theater of Delphi is built.
		525–405: Persians conquer Egypt.	**c. 582–507:** Pythagoras, philosopher, mathematician, and musical theorist
			Public libraries in Athens
			c. 563–483: Siddhartha, founder of Buddhism, begins his religious journey in 534.
			c. 520–438: Pindar, Greek musician and poet
500–400	**487–486:** Comedy is introduced as a dramatic form in the City Dionysia.	**500–449:** Persian Wars	**c. 460–370:** Hippocrates, Greek physician who did much to separate medicine from superstition
	c. 471: Aeschylus introduces the second actor in the performance of tragedy at the City Dionysia.	**494:** King Darius of Persia annexes all of Greece.	**485–424:** Herodotus, Greek historian, writes the history of the Persian Wars.
		490: Athenians defeat the Persians in the Battle of Marathon.	

Date	Theater	Political	Social/Cultural
500–400 BCE (continued)	**c. 468:** Sophocles is credited with introducing the third actor in the performance of tragedy at the City Dionysia. **458:** First performance of Aeschylus's trilogy the *Oresteia* at the City Dionysia **458:** *Skene,* or scene house, is introduced in Greek theater. **c. 441:** First performance of Sophocles' *Antigone* at the City Dionysia **c. 430–425:** First Performance of Sophocles' *Oedipus Rex* at the City Dionysia **411:** First performance of Aristophanes' *Lysistrata*	**480:** At the Battle of Thermopylae, the Spartans defeat the Persians. **479:** Xerxes, son of Darius, returns to Persia; the Persian Wars end. **462–429:** Periclean Athens **431:** The Peloponnesian War begins; Athens is defeated in 404. Thucydides records the events in his history *The Peloponnesian War*.	**460–370:** Democritus, Greek philosopher who believed that all living things are composed of atoms **438:** The Parthenon is completed.
400–300	**400–c. 320:** Era of Middle Comedy, which concentrates on more accurately portraying daily life rather than the more fantastic plots of Old Comedy (Aristophanes) **336–300:** Era of New Comedy. Menander and others move further away from Aristophanes; stock characters are common. **335–323:** Aristotle writes *Poetics*.	**395:** The Corinthian War begins. Athens joins with Corinth, Thebes, and Argos to attack Sparta. Athens emerges from the ten-year war as a partially restored power. **332:** Alexander the Great conquers Egypt. **321:** Alexander the Great dies of a fever at age thirty-three. His successors divide the empire into Macedon, Egypt, and the Seleucid empire.	**399:** Socrates is tried and executed for corrupting the youth of Athens. **373:** Plato writes *Republic*. **340–271:** Epicurus, Greek philosopher who believed in pleasure, spontaneity, and freedom of will **320–30:** Hellenistic period of Greek art **307:** The museum and library of Alexandria are begun under Ptolemy Soter.
300–100	**277:** Artists of Dionysus, a performing artists' guild, is formed.		**275–195:** Eratosthenes, Greek scientist, suggests that the earth moves around the sun and makes close estimates of the earth's circumference.
100 BCE–300 CE		**100 BCE–1 CE:** Alexandria is the Mediterranean center of culture and commerce.	
300–400 CE			**346–359:** The Roman emperor Theodosius forbids the celebration of Olympic games in Greece.

Aeschylus

Very little is known for certain about the life of Aeschylus (c. 525–456 BCE), despite a first attempt at a biographical sketch in 300 BCE. What is known is that he was born in Eleusis near Athens at a time when Athens was beginning to be an important power in Greece and the cradle of Western art and thought. When Aeschylus was born, Athens was under the control of tyrants, a control that ended between 510 and 508 BCE; when he died, Athens was a democracy and one of the strongest states in the Greek confederation. The great threat to Athens's security came from the Persians, powerful Eastern warriors whose aim was the destruction of Greek economic power. Of the three great playwrights who lived in these times, Aeschylus is the only one who actually went to war against the Persians.

Records reveal that in 490 BCE Aeschylus fought at the battle of Marathon, in which his brother was killed. The Persians were defeated at Marathon, and their king, Darius, died shortly thereafter. For ten years, the Athenians enjoyed an uneasy peace, but in 480 BCE the Persians returned under King Xerxes with a powerful fleet and army. Aeschylus fought at Salamis and probably also at a later victory in Plataea.

Aeschylus seems to have been writing tragedies for fifteen years before his first victory in the drama competitions. He began competing between 499 and 496 BCE; he won his first victory in 484 BCE. Aeschylus went on to win a total of thirteen competitions with thirteen tetralogies: groups of three tragedies and a satyr play. He may have written as many as ninety plays; the titles of eighty-three have come down to us, with seven plays and many fragments surviving. *Agamemnon* is the first play in the *Oresteia*, the only surviving trilogy of Greek tragedies that we know were produced together. Sophocles' Oedipus plays, by contrast, were composed over a long period of time and were never performed as a trilogy until recent times.

Many efforts have been made to connect Aeschylus's plays to his life and times, but on the whole such efforts have been unprofitable. Clearly, though, he wrote some plays that spoke to the times, such as *The Persians* (472 BCE), undoubtedly inspired by Athenian success in the Persian Wars. *The Persians* won first prize, and its expenses were paid by Athens's ruler Pericles, who, after the battle of Salamis, rebuilt the Acropolis with the Parthenon and the other important buildings, such as the Erectheum, that still stand there. Aeschylus also wrote plays associated with specific places, such as *The Women of Aetna*, produced in Sicily near Mount Aetna.

Aeschylus is credited with a rough and powerful style expressed in a language that sometimes forced him to make up new words. The power of his language is always remarked on by those who read his plays in the original Greek, and his translators have often been poets in their own right. By contrast, the younger Sophocles uses a language that is smoother, more lyrical, and more graceful. Some critics have asserted that the younger playwrights profited from Aeschylus's development of tragic style.

Aeschylus died at age sixty-eight in Gela, Sicily, where he spent time at the request of a friendly tyrant, Hieron. The story surrounding Aeschylus's death

For links to resources about Aeschylus, click on *AuthorLinks* at **bedfordstmartins.com/jacobus.**

has been told many times and is probably only legend. It is said that an eagle grasping a tortoise flew high into the air and accidentally dropped the tortoise on Aeschylus's head, killing him. His death came at the height of the development of Greek tragedy.

Agamemnon

Agamemnon is the first play in the *Oresteia,* the only extant trilogy of Greek tragedies. The trilogy was performed in 458 BCE, winning first prize in the drama competition. It is named for Orestes, son of Agamemnon, even though Orestes does not appear until the second play, *The Libation Bearers,* and does not become the center of the action until the third play, *The Eumenides.* As many commentators have observed, the three plays are in essence three acts of one larger play.

Underlying the action of the three plays is a memory of the horror that has befallen the House of Atreus, the family to which Agamemnon and Orestes belong. Centuries before Aeschylus, Homer had told part of the story, which was a myth of significant proportions by the time Aeschylus dramatized it. Pelops, son of Tantalus, had two sons: Atreus and Thyestes. The legend has several forms, but in essence Atreus and Thyestes have a falling out over the throne of their father. In addition, Atreus suspects that Thyestes has slept with his wife. With Atreus in control of the kingdom, Thyestes is invited to return for a reconciliation, but Atreus plans a fearful revenge. Pretending to prepare a feast of slaughtered animals, Atreus serves Thyestes his own two children chopped into a stew. Once he has eaten, Thyestes is shown the heads, hands, and feet of his children and vomits. He then flees into exile with his remaining infant son, Aegisthus.

Atreus's sons were Menelaus (who led the Greeks to Troy to regain his errant wife, Helen) and Agamemnon (who returned victorious from Troy). Agamemnon's children were Iphigenia, Electra (who figures in *The Libation Bearers*), and Orestes. The *Oresteia* works out the gods' age-old curse on the house of Atreus.

Agamemnon reveals several forceful characters. Clytemnestra, the wife of Agamemnon, presents herself as a faithful, long-suffering wife waiting patiently for her husband to return from war. However, the Chorus, composed of older men, knows that she has taken a lover, Aegisthus. Clytemnestra faces up to the rumors of her infidelity when Agamemnon returns, daring anyone to contradict her. Secretly, though, she plans (with the help of Aegisthus) to kill Agamemnon. Her discovery that her husband is returning with a female slave, the prophetess Cassandra, as his concubine gives her further motivation.

To ensnare Agamemnon, Clytemnestra has woven an intricate web—the image of the spider is invoked in the play. She is warned of his return by the pillars of fire that are set from Troy to Greece as Agamemnon returns, so she is prepared. She produces a richly woven purple cloth—the equivalent of what we call a red carpet—on which she expects Agamemnon to walk into the palace. Knowing that to do so could offend the gods, he at first refuses. Ultimately he yields to her entreaties and enters the palace, leaving Cassandra outside to prophesy his death—and hers—to the unbelieving Chorus. Inside, Clytemnestra continues the pattern by winding a regal cloak about Agamemnon as he is in the bath, disabling him so that she is able to stab him mortally.

When Clytemnestra confesses to the murder of Agamemnon and Cassandra, she tells the Chorus that she is exacting revenge against Agamemnon for sacrificing their daughter Iphigenia in order to get a favorable wind to sail to Troy. Later, Aegisthus justifies his role in the killing as revenge against the crimes of Agamemnon's father, Atreus.

Throughout, *Agamemnon* emphasizes issues of gender. Often the Chorus comments on Clytemnestra's speaking with the authority of a man. The invocation of the god Apollo throughout the trilogy has been taken to imply an important cultural shift that Aeschylus recognizes. Is he referring to a distant past in which female deities were dominant, later having been replaced by masculine deities? Such speculation is impossible to verify (see Lois Spatz's commentary on page 64), but it is clear that the women in the *Oresteia* are powerful in their presence, assertive in their actions, and insistent in their demand for justice. *Agamemnon* ends with Clytemnestra facing down an angry and mistrustful Chorus and with Aegisthus claiming the throne and governing as a tyrant.

For discussion questions and assignments on *Agamemnon*, visit bedfordstmartins.com/jacobus.

Agamemnon in Performance

The first production of Aeschylus's trilogy in 458 BCE won first prize in the drama competition. Although tragedies were not usually revived, it seems that this trilogy was played again at Greek festivals a few years after Aeschylus's death in 456 BCE. Unfortunately, after the demise of the Greek festivals, Aeschylus was not performed again until the sixteenth century. Early in the twentieth century, the *Oresteia* was produced in Greek in the United States to a limited but enthusiastic audience. Harvard University produced *Agamemnon* in 1906, using all male actors, who spoke the lines in Greek. Max Reinhardt produced the trilogy in Berlin in 1915, but problems with the size of the theater and the nature of the stage resulted in an unsuccessful production. Beginning in 1977 in New York, Andrei Serban experimented with performing *Agamemnon* in a mixture of English and Greek because, as he said, "Greek sounds have the power to catch the real emotional experience of the text." Serban produced the play at the Vivian Beaumont Theater in Lincoln Center. The high-tech staging, with exposed metal mesh floors and walls, created powerful effects. The Royal Shakespeare Company in 1980 put together an eleven-hour sequence of plays of Aeschylus, Euripides, and Sophocles on the fall of Troy, calling it *The Greeks;* it was successful both in England and abroad. The National Theatre in London produced the *Oresteia* in 1981 to considerable acclaim. Interestingly, the reviews of that production describe *Agamemnon* as having been eclipsed in dramatic importance by *The Libation Bearers,* which "becomes the great dramatic moment of the trilogy." Combining Euripides' *Iphigenia in Aulis* with the trilogy, the French Théâtre du Soleil performed *Les Atrides* in Paris, Montreal, and New York in 1992. Ariane Mnouchkine directed and conceived the production (in French with simultaneous translation), using only five actors. Paul Nadler compared *Les Atrides* with bullfights, which "deal with killers and victims acting out their fates upon fields of honor." The Royal National Theatre performed a shortened version of the *Oresteia* in January 2000 in London. The text was translated by the noted English poet Ted Hughes. *Agamemnon* was performed in its entirety to good reviews. The highly lauded production of *Agamemnon* at the Getty Villa in Malibu, California, in 2008 was directed by Stephen Wadsworth and starred Delroy Lindo as Agamemnon and Tyne Daly as Clytemnestra. Within the last few years, a number of interesting loose adaptations of the play have been staged, such as Maria Kotzamani's *Agamemnon (The Ghost Sonata)* in a warehouse in Athens in 2000, which focused more on Agamemnon than on Clytemnestra, and Jeremy Menekseoglu's Chicago Dream Theater production in 2010, which concentrated on the relationship between Agamemnon and Cassandra.

AESCHYLUS (c. 525–456 BCE)

Agamemnon 458 BCE

TRANSLATED BY DAVID GRENE AND WENDY DONIGER O'FLAHERTY

Dramatis Personae

SENTRY
CHORUS, *old men of Argos left behind after the Argives went to Troy*
CLYTEMNESTRA, *queen of Argos in the absence of King Agamemnon at Troy*
HERALD *from the Greek army*
KING AGAMEMNON
CASSANDRA, *princess of Troy, daughter of King Priam*
AEGISTHUS

SENTRY: You gods, release me.
Crouched like a dog, I watch always, all year long,
on the tower of the sons of Atreus.
I have come to know the nightly gathering of the
    stars
and those radiant dynasts of the firmament that
5   lead them.
They bring winter and summer to men.
Now I watch for a flaming light,
the beacon fire, the tell-tale witness that Troy is
    captured.
Such are my orders, orders from a hopeful queen
10 who thinks with the mind of a man.
I have a bed here, soaked with dew, always shifting.
But no dreams. Fear is my visitor, not sleep.
I cannot close my eyes for fear.
Sometimes I whistle or hum;
15 the tunes are my drug against my sleepiness.
But then the sorrow comes.
This house is in bitter trouble.
Once it was well governed; not now.
Still, may the fire of good news light the darkness
20 to be the lucky release from our troubles.

The beacon! Day out of night!
The dances everywhere in Argos!
Thanks, good beacon!
My lady, Agamemnon's wife, get out of bed!
Cry aloud a blessing on this beacon,   25
since Troy is surely captured.
I will myself begin the dance, for I'll score to
    myself, too,
the winning dice that the beacon threw for my
    master.
Oh, that I could touch with this hand of mine
the hand that I love, my lord's.   30
As for the rest, I haven't a word;
a great ox stands on my tongue.
If the house itself had a voice to speak,
it would tell the clearest story.
I choose to speak to those who understand;   35
for the others, I am all forgetfulness.

CHORUS: This is the tenth year
since they launched from this land
the Greek fleet of a thousand ships
to help right wrongs done.   40
They launched it, King Menelaus,
great plaintiff against Priam,
and Agamemnon his brother;
twin the yoke joining them in honor and throne,
twin their shared grace of God.   45
From their hearts the great war cry;
they screamed like eagles,
that wheel and wheel high above their eyries,
driven by the oarage of their wings,
in lonely agony for the loss of their nestlings,   50
and all the watchful care they had spent guarding
    them.

But One yet higher up, some Apollo or Pan or
    Zeus,°
hears the shrill-voiced sorrow of these settlers in his
    kingdom
and sends on the evildoers
55   the Fury that brings punishment, however late.
So a Lord greater than the kings, Zeus god of
    guest-friends,
sends the sons of Atreus on Alexander;°
in this quarrel over a woman of many men,
he would lay upon Greeks and Trojans alike
60   many wrestlings where the limbs grow heavy
and the knee is pressed into the dust
and the spear is shattered in the first rites of
    engagement.
Yet it is now as it is.
Fulfillment moves toward what is fated.
And not with burnt offerings nor with pouring on
65   of wine
nor sacrifice to the gods below
will you assuage that stubborn anger.

But we, dishonored for the ancientness of our flesh,
were left behind then when the army went;
we remain, propping on staffs a strength like
70   a child's.
For the child's marrow, too, leaps within his breast
but is only the match of an old man's;
the god of war is not there either.
And the overold, the leafage already withering,
walks his three-footed way,° no stronger than
75   a child;
wanders, a dream in the daylight.

You, daughter of Tyndareus, Queen Clytemnestra,
What's the matter? What's the news? What have
    you heard?
What message do you trust, that you order sacrifices
80   at all the altars?
Of all the gods that hold our city,
of those above and those beneath the earth,
of those at the doorpost and those at the
    marketplace,
the altars blaze with offerings.
85   Here one torch sends its flames to the sky,
and another raises its light,
charmed by the soft, guileless urgings of pure
    streams of oil
drawn from the depth of the royal store.
Tell us what you can and what may be said
90   about all these things.
Cure this care that now broods darkly on our minds.

But then hope, shining out of the sacrifice,
turns away the insatiable thoughts that might
    otherwise
eat out the heart in sorrow.

It is mine to declare the omens of victory   95
given to princely men on the journey.
For by God's grace, old age, which grows with
    life, my life,
still breathes on my lips persuasion,
the strength of song.
I tell how the princes of the Achaeans,   100
twin-throned, single-hearted
lords of the youth of Greece,
were sent against the land of Troy
with spear in hand to exact vengeance.
The furious omen-birds° sent them,   105
one black eagle, one white-tail,
the kings of birds to the kings of the ships.
Near the palace they came on the spear-striking
    side,
perched where all could see them
as they fed on the womb's gravid load of leverets,°   110
mother and all, pulled down in the hare's last
    course.
✳ Cry sorrow, sorrow, but let the good prevail.

Yet the honest prophet of the army saw
the two sons of Atreus,
twin in military spirit,   115
and knew the princely leaders and hare-
    devourers—
knew that they were one and the same.
And so he declared in his prophecy,
"In time, this journey will capture Troy, Priam's°
    city;
and all the communal herds that graze before her
    towers   120
shall Fate give violently to plunder.
I only pray that no anger from the God will cast a
    cloud
upon this army forged from before to be
a great iron bit in the mouth of Troy.
For Queen Artemis° is full of pity out of jealousy   125
against those winged hounds of her father
who devour in sacrifice
the unhappy cowering mother with her brood
before they come to birth.
She hates the eagles' feast.   130
Cry sorrow, sorrow, but let the good prevail.

---

52. **Apollo or Pan or Zeus:** Greek gods with the power to
avenge crimes.   57. **Alexander:** Also known as Paris, Alexander
was the son of King Priam and Queen Hecuba of Troy. He
carried off Helen, the wife of Greek commander Menelaus
(Agamemnon's brother), and this action caused the Trojan
War.   75. **three-footed way:** Walking with a cane or staff.

105. **omen-birds:** Eagles, thought to be messengers of the gods.
110. **leverets:** Young hares.   119. **Priam:** King of Troy at the
time of the Trojan War.   125. **Artemis:** Greek goddess who was
the daughter of Zeus and sister of Apollo. Artemis was the protector of young animals. Angered at the slaughter of the leverets,
she caused contrary winds to prevent the Greeks from sailing
for Troy. Agamemnon was forced to sacrifice his daughter Iphigenia to appease Artemis and secure favorable winds.

Yes, she is kindly, that beautiful one,
to cubs, scarcely crawling, of savage lions,
and she finds her delight in all the breast-loving
    infants
135 of wild things of the field.
Yet she grants fulfillment of what the omens imply:
grant, Lady, favorable fulfillment, and void
    the other.
I call on Apollo the Healer
140 to keep her from setting against the Greeks
those contrary winds, winds that hold ships,
staying winds, winds that stop sailing altogether.
She might do this in eagerness for a different
    sacrifice,
one that is lawless and horrible,
a trueborn craftsman of quarrels,
145 that has no awe of a husband.
For full of terrors it lurks,
house keeping, crafty, long-memoried,
an anger that punishes child-slaughter."

Such were the prophecies of Calchas's° voice,
150 mingled with the good things,
and all predicted for our royal house
from omens on the way.
In harmony with these,
cry sorrow, sorrow, but let the good prevail.

155 ✻ Zeus, whoever he is,
if it is dear to him to be so called,
this is how I call him.
I have thrown all into the scale,
but cannot find his likeness—
160 there is only Zeus,
if I must cast my burden of vain care from the heart
in honest truth.

Not he that once was great,
swelling with daring, challenging all comers,
165 shall even be spoken of, for he is of the past.
And he that came after him
has had his three falls wrestling,
and is gone.
But whoever sings to Zeus
170 the victory song from a full heart,
he shall win all that his heart desires.

✻ Zeus it is that has made man's road;
he it is who has laid down the rule
that understanding comes through suffering.
175 Instead of sleep, there drips before the heart
the recollected sorrow of past pain.
It is against our wills that we become wise.
Forced indeed upon us is the grace of our gods
that sit on their solemn thrones.

So on that day, the old leader of the Greek ships, 180
faulting no prophet, caught his breath at his
    sudden calamity,
when the Greek host was burdened
with ships halted and empty holds,
as they held the coast over against Chalcis,°
at Aulis° where the tides roar to and fro. 185

The hurricane that came from Strymon,°
breeding deadly delays, starvation, lost anchorages,
driving crews to aimless wanderings,
sparing neither ships nor cables,
wore down the flower of the Argives, 190
doubling their time with enforced lingering.
So when the prophet's voice rang out,
proclaiming to the princes another cure for the
    bitter storm,
a cure yet heavier to bear,
he backed his prophecies with Artemis's name, 195
and the twin sons of Atreus beat the ground with
    their staves
and could not hold back their tears.
Then the old king spoke and said,
"Heavy indeed my fate if I disobey,
but heavy, too, if I must butcher my child, 200
the glory of my house, polluting a father's hands
with streams of a virgin's blood beside the altar.
Which of these two things is without evil?
How shall I become a deserter of my fleet and fail
    my allies?
There is sacred law on their side, that they
    passionately covet 205
a virgin's blood as sacrifice to quell the winds.
May it turn out well."

When he put on the harness of Necessity,
his spirit veered in a breath of change—
to impiety, to unholiness, to desecration, 210
and from it he drew audacity for his heart
to stop at nothing.
For indeed there is a wretched distraction
    of the wits,
a primal source of ruin,
that puts recklessness in man's mind 215
and counsels ugliness.
So he dared to become his daughter's sacrificer
to aid the war waged for a woman—
first rites of deliverance for the ships.
Her prayers, and her cries of "Father," and her
    maiden life 220
they set at nothing, those military umpires.
Her father ordered his servants to lift her
carefully over the altar

---

149. Calchas: A prophet who accompanied the Greek army
to Troy.

184. Chalcis: City in Asia Minor across the straits from
Aulis, where the Greeks were detained by contrary winds.
185. Aulis: City where the Greek fleet collected before sailing to
Troy.   **186. Strymon:** River in Asia Minor across from Aulis.

after the prayer, swooning, her clothes all round her,
225   like a young goat,
and with a gag on her beautiful lips
to restrain the cry that would curse his house.
Constrained to voicelessness by the violence of the
     bit,
she slipped to the ground her saffron robes,
and with darting, pitiful eyes struck each of her
230   sacrificers.
She stood out, like a figure in a picture, struggling
     to speak,
for often she had sung in her father's hospitable halls,
and with pure maiden voice lovingly honored
her beloved father's victory hymn,
235   with its triple libation to bring good luck.
What happened after that I neither saw nor tell.
But Calchas's divining art bore fruit;
the scales of justice have come down and brought,
with suffering, understanding.
240   You will learn the future when it happens.
Till then, let it be.
To do otherwise is to have sorrow before you need.
For it will come clear with the dawn's light.

(*Enter Clytemnestra.*)

But at the end of all this let there be good fortune.
245   Surely that is the wish of this (*turning to the queen*)
our sole and closest bulwark against trouble in
     Argos.
I have come, Queen Clytemnestra, to pay you my
     respects;
for it is right, in the absence of the prince,
to honor the wife of the man whose throne is empty.
250   I would be glad to know
if you are sure of good tidings or not.
Is it in the hope of happy news
that you are ordering sacrifice?
But I won't resent it if you must be silent.
255   CLYTEMNESTRA: As the proverb goes,
"May dawn be the dawn of good news
as she comes from her mother night"—
you shall learn of a joy greater than you hope.
For the Argives have captured Priam's city.
CHORUS: What? I cannot believe you; I cannot
260   understand.
CLYTEMNESTRA: Troy is the Greeks' city now. Are my
     words clear?
CHORUS: Joy steals over me, and calls out tears, too.
CLYTEMNESTRA: Your eyes proclaim you a subject true
     and loyal.
CHORUS: What makes you trust the news? Have you
     proof of it?
CLYTEMNESTRA: I have, of course—unless the gods
265   deceived me.
CHORUS: Dream visions? Do you believe in them?
CLYTEMNESTRA: No sleeping mind for me, no, nor its
     fancies.
CHORUS: Have flying rumors bloated you?
CLYTEMNESTRA: As if I were a child, you taunt me.

CHORUS: But when was it that the city was sacked?   270
CLYTEMNESTRA: In this last night that brought this
     dawn to birth.
CHORUS: What messenger can be as quick as that?
CLYTEMNESTRA: The god of fire, sending his brilliant
     glow from Mount Ida.
Beacon sent beacon here with courier fires,
Ida to the crag of Hermes in Lemnos;°   275
then from that island a third flame sent on
was welcomed by the heights of Athos that belong
     to Zeus;
and high, spanning the sea's back,
the strength of the escorting flame went joyously
     onward.
The pine fire sent its golden blaze, almost a sun,   280
to the watchtowers of Macistus.
He didn't hesitate nor carelessly succumb to sleep,
but passed his share of the message,
and from afar, over the streams of Euripus,
he gave to the sentries of Messapion   285
the sign that the beacon's light had traveled to him.
They in their turn lit up and sent the message farther,
firing a great heap of ancient gorse.
Still strong, the beacon's light never flagged,
but leapt over the plain of Asopus like a radiant
     moon,   290
to Mount Cithaeron, and there awakened
another relay of traveling fire.
The guard station did not refuse the far-escorted
     flame;
it kindled more than was ordered, and launched its
     light
over the Gorgon lake; and coming to   295
the goat-haunted mountain,
urged the watchman not to scant the ordinance of
     fire.
They lit a huge beard of flame that burnt
     ungrudgingly,
and sent it over the Saronic gulf, now become its
     mirror,
beyond the headland, till it struck the heights of
     Arachnus,   300
our neighboring sentry post here, and then again
struck right here on this roof of the sons of
     Atreus—
this fire that is the grandchild of that fire on
     Mount Ida.
Such were the courses of the torchbearers,
one from the other in relays,   305
and victor is he that ran first and last.
Such proof I have and such confirmation,
sent me out of Troy by my man.

273–275. Mount Ida . . . Lemnos: Mountain in Asia Minor
southeast of Troy from which the gods could view the battles. The place names that follow trace the course of beacon
fires set to bring the news of the Greek victory from Troy to
Greece.

CHORUS: My lady, to the gods once again
310   I shall give my prayer of thanks,
   but I would like you to tell me all this again,
   that I might hear the words and marvel at them
   from beginning to end.
CLYTEMNESTRA: Troy is captured; this is the day; the
     Greeks hold it.
315   Within that city there rings out
   a volume of cries that do not mingle.
   This is how I see it.
   Mix oil and vinegar in the same jar
   and you could not call them friends;
320   they will not be at one.
   So in Troy you might hear two sorts of crying:
   the conquered and the conquerors.
   The act is single, the meaning double.
   Here are these:
325   throwing themselves on the dead bodies
   of husbands and brothers,
   children on the bodies of their fathers,
   all sorrowing for the destiny of their dead,
   they cry from throats no longer free.
330   Then there are the others:
   roving all night after the fight
   sets them down hungry to breakfast
   on such foods as the city has;
   they all share, no rank or place assigned,
335   but as each has got the luck of the draw.
   They are already living in Troy's captured houses,
   free of the frost beneath the sky, free of the dews.
   They will sleep all night long without a guard,
   like happy men.
   If they revere the gods of that city in that captured
340   land,
   if they revere the gods' sacred places,
   they who are conquerors will not be reconquered.
   Only let no lust seize the army first,
   let no greed conquer them,
345   to make them ravish what they should not.
   They must still make the home voyage safely,
   travel the other leg of the double track.
   But even if the army came through offenseless
   in the sight of the gods,
350   the wrong done to the dead may yet awaken,
   seeking to contrive some sudden mischief.
   This is what you hear from me, a woman.
   But may the good prevail for all to see, past dispute.
   Of the many good things I might have,
355   this is what I would choose.
CHORUS: My lady, you talk wisely, like a sensible man.
   I have learned from you your convincing proofs,
   and now again I prepare to greet the gods.
   Surely we should thank them for what they have
     done for us.
360   O Zeus the king, and friendly night,
   that has endowed us with great glory,
   you that have cast upon the towers of Troy
   a close-fitting mesh so that no one young or old
   can overleap the great net of slavery,

the all-catching trap of ruin—   365
great Zeus of guest-friends I revere.
He has done all this. He has forever bent his bow
against Alexander, that no bolt should fail,
neither missing the mark nor scaling the stars.
They can say, "It is the stroke of Zeus";   370
the track of it is clear to see.
Zeus has acted as he has determined.
Someone has said,
"The gods do not deign to take heed of mortals
who trample underfoot the grace of holiness."   375
But he that said that had no piety in him.
The recklessness stands revealed
of those who breathe war beyond justice.
It is a recklessness that breeds consequences
when houses are overcrammed   380
beyond the measure of the best.
So I escape harm, let but a sufficiency be mine,
with abundance of good judgment.
For wealth gives no defense
for the man insolent with gorging,   385
who kicks the great altar of justice
to where none can see it.
Wretched persuasion,
intolerable child of forecounseling ruin,
drives him on violently.   390
And all cure is vain. It is not hidden, no—
the mischief shines, a lamp of evil light.
The black grain in Paris° shows through the test,
like base copper rubbed bare with use.
He has been like a child that chases a bird;   395
he has brought on this city an intolerable infection,
and no one of the gods will hear his prayer—
rather, pull down the unjust man
conversant with such things.
Such a one is Paris, who came   400
to the house of the sons of Atreus
and stained with shame the table of his host
by the theft of that host's wife.
She has left to her fellow citizens
the clanging of shields, the arming of sailors,
   ambushes.   405
To Ilium she has brought ruin instead of dowry.
Her daring defying all limits,
she darted quickly through the gates.
And many a groan there was
among those that spoke for the palace: 410
"Ah me, ah me, for the house, the house and the
   princes.
Ah me for the bed and the tracks of the love of
   men on it."
There one can see the silence—
dishonored, unreviling, inexorable—
of him that sits apart.   415
Through yearning for the one gone over the sea,
a ghost will seem to rule the house.

---

393. Paris: A prince of Troy, Paris abducted Helen of Greece, thus defying Zeus's law of hospitality.

The grace of beautiful statues is hateful to the man.
Their eyes are empty, and before them
420 all passionate love falls dead.
Fancies haunt him in dreams persuasively;
theirs is a grace without substance.
Unsubstantial it is, when one sees,
and dreaming reaches to the touch,
and the phantom is gone, quickly slipping through
      his hands,
425 as it follows the winged paths of sleep.
Such are the sorrows at home at the hearth;
but there are worse than these for all,
for those who joined the fleet and left the land of
      Greece.
430 In the house of every one of these
preeminent there is grief that reaches the heart.
They know whom they have sent forth, but
      instead of men
there come home urns and ashes to each house.
The war god is a money changer;
435 men's bodies are his money.
He holds the scales in the battle of the spear.
From Ilium he sends back to those who loved them
the scrapings of dust made heavy with their tears;
he loads the elegant urns with the dust that was
      once a man.
440 They mourn this man as they praise him—
how skilled he was in the fight—and another—
how gallantly he fell in his blood—
for another man's woman.
That is what they whisper and snarl;
445 and pain creeps about, full of ill will
toward the plaintiffs, the sons of Atreus.
But those others keep to their graves in all their
      beauty,
where they were, around the walls of Troy.
The enemy land that they have taken at last
450 has taken them, hidden them in itself.
The malicious speech of citizens is hard to bear;
it is the equal of a public curse.
And still I am troubled, lest I come to hear
something hidden in dark night.

455 For watchful are the gods' eyes
for those that kill by the thousands.
The black Furies reduce to dim nothingness
the man whose success has no justice in it,
wear him down, reversing his life's fortune.
460 And when he is among those we cannot see,
there is no help for him.
To be too well spoken of is heavy indeed.
For the thunderbolt is hurled from the eyes of Zeus.
May I not be a city-sacker, nor yet look upon my
      own life,
465 captured by others.
Swift is the rumor coursing through the city,
spurred by the fire of good tidings.
But whether it is true, who knows, or whether
somehow the gods deceive us.

Who is there so childish, so maimed of wit, 470
that the messages of fire should kindle his heart
only to sicken later when the news changes?
It is like the mettle of a woman's spirit
to praise the gracious gift before it is certainly there.
The limits of a woman's belief can be 475
as easily and quickly crossed
as cattle graze across a boundary.
But quickly, too, dies the report
a woman utters.
Soon we shall know about the lights from the
      beacons 480
and all the exchange of watch fires:
whether they are true or whether, like dreams,
a light of joy has stolen upon us and cheated our
      minds.
Here I see the herald coming from the shore,
shaded with twigs of olive. 485
The thirsty dust, twin sister of mud across the
      boundary,
is my witness; it witnesses to me that he has a *real*
      voice,
and so his testimony is not one of the smoky fire
of some wood on the hillside.
He will rather speak out and tell us to be glad, 490
or—God forbid it is the contrary message.
There *have* been good things that have shown
      through;
grant that this is their consummation.
Whoever prays anything else for this city,
I would he might reap the fruit of his mistaken
      thoughts. 495

(*Enter a herald.*)

HERALD: O my fathers' earth, Argos, Argos,
ten long years and I have come to you;
so many shipwrecked hopes, and one a winner.
I never dreamed that I would have for my share in
      death
a piece of dearest Argive land. 500
Now welcome earth, welcome the light of sun,
and Zeus supreme lord; and the Pythian King,°
no longer shooting his arrows against us;
you were harsh enough along Scamander's banks,
but now you are different, now you are savior and
      healer, 505
King Apollo. My greetings to all the gods in
      assembly.
My greeting to my patron god, Hermes, dear herald,
whom all heralds worship.
My greetings to the heroes that sent us out
and kindly welcome back what's left of us after
      the fight. 510
Hail, royal halls, roofs I have loved,
hail, holy seats and you divinities that face the
      sunlight.

502. **Pythian King:** The god Apollo.

Receive now with faces bright in joy—
if ever you did in days gone by—
515 now receive the king in glory after so long.
He comes and brings light after night's darkness,
a light to you and to all these—
King Agamemnon.
Give him true welcome; truly it belongs to him,
the king who dug down Troy with the spade of
520   God's justice,
made plowland of Troy;
and the seed has perished from all their country.
Their altars and the shrines of their gods are gone.
Such a yoking chain has he cast on Troy,
525 the king, Atreus's son, the old and happy man.
And now he comes here, most worthy of all
that now live and die.
Neither Paris nor the city that supports him
can boast that they have done more than they have
        paid for.
530 He was condemned for rape and theft—
lost what he carried off.
He has reaped for harvest
the utter ruin of his father's house.
And doubly have the sons of Priam paid for their
        offenses.
CHORUS: Herald of the Argive army, joy on your
535   homecoming!
HERALD: Joy, indeed. If the gods should end my life now,
        I'd not deny them.
CHORUS: Has the love of your lost homeland tortured
        you so?
HERALD: Yes; the tears you see are tears of joy.
CHORUS: That disease had its pleasure for you, all the
540   same.
HERALD: What disease? What should I understand by
        that?
CHORUS: Love's stroke. But you got love for the love
        you gave.
HERALD: You mean this land has missed the army as
        we missed you?
CHORUS: We were faint and weak and so have
        groaned for you.
HERALD: Why so uneasy? What horror was in your
545   mind?
CHORUS: I say nothing and am safe—a long, long
        silence.
HERALD: How could that be? Your king was away;
        did you fear others?
CHORUS: As you said just now, I would have
        welcomed death.
HERALD: It *has* been a success. Of course, in the
        length of time,
550 one must say some things have gone well, some ill.
Who except the gods lives the whole span of his life
without trouble?
Yes, if I were to speak of the hard work
and the bad quarters,
555 the narrow gangways and the hard beds,
there's plenty to complain about.

Then there were the troubles on land,
disgusting things, too.
Our beds were under the enemy's walls.
Rain from the sky and dew from the grass soaked us   560
and kept rotting our clothing
and bred lice in our hair.
I could talk about the winter, which killed the
        birds;
Mount Ida and its snow made that intolerable.
And then there was the heat,   565
when the sea fell on its noontide bed and slept.
Not a breath of wind, not a stir on the waves—
Oh, why should I still feel pain for all this?
It's over, isn't it, all the trouble?
It's over indeed, for them, too, the dead;   570
they'll never have to trouble about getting up again.
Why should I reckon up the numbers of those who
        are gone?
Why should the living grieve because
fortune turned against us?
I'm ready to say a long goodbye to all that's
        happened.   575
For us that are left of the Greek army,
the gain certainly wins out,
and the bad side of things doesn't weigh it down.
So, those of us who have sped over land and sea
can stand facing the sunlight and make our boast: 580
"There was a day when the Argive army took Troy.
They have nailed the spoils of it
on the homes of the gods throughout Greece
to be a glory forever and ever."
When they hear this, men must praise   585
the city and its generals.
We shall also honor the grace of God
who brought it to pass.
That's my whole speech.
CHORUS: What you say wins me over; I admit it.   590
To be ready to learn is what makes a young man
out of an old one.
But it is this house and Clytemnestra
that the news most concerns,
though I, too, am the richer for it.   595
CLYTEMNESTRA: I rejoiced long ago,
and raised the cry of joy over the news,
when first the fire came as my messenger in the night,
telling of Troy's capture and destruction.
That was when everyone found fault with me: 600
"Is it beacon fires that convince you
that Troy has now been sacked?
How like a woman's heart to be so lifted up."
In rumors such as these I appeared
to have gone astray in my wits.   605
But yet I made the sacrifices,
and following this "woman's fashion"
they all raised the chant, now here, now there,
throughout the city,
the songs of blessing at the gods' shrines,   610
and there they lulled to sleep
the sweet-smelling sacrificial fires.

Why *now* should I depend on you to tell me more?
I shall learn the whole story from my lord himself.
615 How shall I make best haste to receive him home,
my honored husband?
What sweeter day for a wife's eye to see
than when she opens the doors to her man
coming from the army,
620 when the gods have brought him safely back to her?
Tell my husband this:
bid him come as quick as he can,
the city's darling.
And when he comes may he find his wife
625 true as he left her,
the watchdog of his house,
devoted to him, enemy to his enemies,
the same always and ever.
I never broke the seal
630 in all those years.
I know of no pleasure with another man
nor any talk or evil gossip against me,
anymore than I know how to dip this blade
to temper it.
635 Such is my boast, so full of truth
that even a well-bred wife
need not blush to utter it.

                    (*Exit Clytemnestra*.)

CHORUS: She has spoken very suitably
for those who understand her.
640 But tell me, Herald,
what of Menelaus?
Was he among the returning army?
Is he safe among you?
And will he come back home again, our dear prince?
645 HERALD: I don't know how to put a fair face on lies:
my friends would only have good of it
for a short time anyway.
CHORUS: Why can't you tell news that is both good
and true?
When you separate them, you can't get away with it.
HERALD: Then—the man has vanished from the
650 Greek army,
he and his ship. *That* is not a lie.
CHORUS: Did you see him set forth from Ilium on his
own?
Or did some storm that struck you all together
snatch him away?
655 HERALD: You've hit it exactly;
in a few words you've covered a long, sad story.
CHORUS: What do the rest of his shipmates think?
Do they say he's alive or dead?
HERALD: No one knows how to tell the news clearly—
660 except the sun, there, that gives life to the world.
CHORUS: What do you mean? Was there a storm
that came upon the fleet by the gods' anger
and then ended?
HERALD: A day of good news—one should not
infect it
665 with the tongue of bad news.

The honor due to the two kinds of gods
is separate.
When a messenger with a gloomy face bears
cursed news
of an army's downfall,
there is one common injury which is public,   670
and then, besides, many a man is banned from his
home;
this is the double lash that the god of war loves,
a two-speared ruin, a bloody pair.
When, I say, a messenger is loaded with such
calamities,
he must sing his news as his hymn to the Furies.   675
But when the saving messenger of good news
comes to a city that rejoices in well-being
—how should I mingle good with bad
in telling you of this storm
which surely did proceed from the gods' anger   680
against the Greeks?
For fire and sea, those two oldest and deepest of
enemies,
swore a conspiracy and pledged their common
allegiance
to destroy the wretched Greek army.
In the night, waves lashed by the storm   685
arose to plague us.
For the Thracian winds battered ship on ship.
Butting one another savagely
in the hurricane and sheets of hail,
they sank from sight, as our evil shepherd   690
drove us here and there.
When the clear light of the day came back,
we saw the sea blooming,
and its flowers were dead Greeks and wrecks.
For ourselves and our boat, we went unharmed;   695
some god stole us through it or begged us off;
he must have steered us himself,
for no man touched the steering oar.
Luck chose to become our savior, and sat on our
ship,
so that we missed the driving waves when we were
at anchor,   700
nor were driven aground on the rugged land.
Afterward, when we had escaped our watery
hell,
in the white light of day, we hardly dared to trust
our luck;
and in our own thoughts we were constantly
shepherds of some new calamity,   705
seeing how the fleet had been pounded and ground
to pieces.
Now, if any of them still breathes,
they speak of us as lost; of course they do.
We have much the same idea about them.
Let it turn out well. For Menelaus,   710
in all likelihood you may expect him back.
For if the beams of the sun discover him living
and seeing,
through the workings of God—

715   for surely God will not yet blot out
       the whole family—
       there is some hope that he'll come home again.
       This is really the truth that you have heard.

                                                    (*Exit herald.*)

CHORUS: Who can have named her so,
            with such truth, utterly?
720   Could it be someone we cannot see,
       with foreknowledge of destiny,
       that used his tongue in harmony with fortune?
       She was called Helen,°
       the bride won by the spear, sought in strife.
725   Helen means death, and death indeed she was,
       death to ships and men and city
       as she sailed out of the delicate fabrics of her
            curtained room,
       fanned by the breeze of giant Zephyr;°
       and the man-swarm of shield-bearing hunters
730   came on the track of her,
       the vanished track of the oar blades
       which beached on the ever-green shores of Simoeis
       on the heels of their bloody quarrel.

       To Ilium it drove her,
735   the wrath that brings fulfillment,
       and again the word proved true, that equates
       marriage and mourning,
       for the wrath exacted vengeance at the last
       for the guest-table dishonored at the hearth shared
            by Zeus.
740   Wrath punished as victims those men,
       the new marriage kinsmen,
       who on that day must celebrate,
       sing out of full throats
       the hymn that honored the bride.
745   Perhaps that ancient city of Priam
       has learned another tune now,
       a tuneful dirge that calls him
       Paris the dismally bedded;
       the city has endured the ruin of its life,
750   the voice of countless lamentations,
       through the wretched bloodletting of its citizens.
       Once on a time there was a man
       who raised a lion cub in his home.
       It was a little thing, starved of milk,
755   still a suckling, still in the first rituals of its life,
       gentle, a friend of children,
       and a delight to the old.
       Many a time it lay in their arms,
       like a young baby;
760   its face was bright as it fawned on the hand
       at the dictates of its belly's needs.
       But time passed, and it showed
       what disposition it had from its breeding;

723. **Helen:** Daughter of Zeus and Leda, a mortal woman, Helen was the wife of the Greek commander Menelaus before she was abducted by Paris and brought to Troy.   728. **Zephyr:** God of the west wind.

       it requited the grace of those that brought it up
       by horrid slaughtering of their sheep,
765   an unbidden dinner guest.
       And the house was confused and befouled with blood;
       an evil it was that the servants couldn't fight,
       a very murderous mischief.
       God reared the lion in the house to become   770
       an additional priest of ruin.
       But on that first day—as I tell the story—
       she came to the city of Ilium
       a spirit of windless calm,
       the delicate glory of wealth,   775
       the soft arrow darting from her eyes,
       the flower of love that bites the heart.
       Then she changed direction, and brought
       a bitter ending to the marriage,
       hastening to the daughters of Priam   780
       to sit with them and live with them
       to their ruin.
       Zeus, the god of guests, brought her there,
       a Fury to make wives weep.
       There is an old saying among men, first spoken
            long ago,   785
       that a man's great prosperity, when perfected,
       gives birth and doesn't die childless,
       but from that good fortune in true descent
       there grows an ever-greedy misery.
       In this, my mind is different from others'.   790
       No, I say, it is the wicked deed
       that breeds more wickedness, and like to its own
            kind.
       For the house that is straight-dealing and just
       is fated always to have good children.
       The ancient deed of sacrilege always breeds a
            young one,   795
       full of disaster for man, now or then,
       when comes the dawn appointed for its birth.
       A spirit but a clansman—
       one cannot war against him nor fight him—
       he is a thing unholy,   800
       a daring, a black ruin to the halls,
       and very like his parents.
       For justice shines in houses grimed with smoke,
       and she honors the good man.
       And those gilded palaces where hands are dirty   805
       she leaves, averting her eyes;
       she goes to what is clean,
       for she doesn't honor power
       whose coinage is misstamped by the praise of the
            rich.
       And she guides everything to its due end.   810

(*Enter Agamemnon and Cassandra.*)

       My lord, conqueror of Troy, descendant of Atreus,
       how shall I greet you, how do you reverence,
       neither exceeding nor scanting due measure of
            praise?
       Many men, indeed, who transgress justice,
       honor appearance over reality.   815

Everyone is ready to cry over the unfortunate,
but the bite of that sorrow doesn't reach the heart.
So, too, there are those that seem to share joy,
yet the faces that they force have no laughter in
    them.
820　When one is a good judge of stock,
one doesn't miss the meaning of the man's eyes,
fawning in watery friendship
when they seem all loyalty.
In the days when you led the expedition from
    Greece,
825　for Helen's sake,
I saw you painted in ugly colors—
I will not hide that from you—
as one who had an unskillful hand
on the rudder of his wits
830　when you tried to win back through men's dying
a willing whore.
But now from the depth of my heart, in true
    friendship,
I say, May the work be kind to those who did it
    so well.
In time you shall know by enquiry
835　which of your citizens that stayed here at home
dealt justly, and which did wrong.

AGAMEMNON: First Argos and my country's gods,
I must address you; you and I are coauthors
of my home return and the justice
840　I exacted from Priam's city.
The causes were not spoken aloud,
but the gods heard them
and cast their votes with no opposing voices
into the bloody urn: for Ilium's destruction
845　and the deaths of men.
To the other urn nothing drew near
but the shadowy hope of a hand;
there was no filling that urn.
You can still see the smoke from the city's capture.
850　The hot blasts of ruin live there yet,
but there is ash, too, dying
as it sends into the air its breaths fattened on rich
    things.
For all of this we should pay our gods
much-remembering thanks.
855　We have taken vengeance for insolent robbery.
And for the sake of a woman a city has been
    leveled
by the biting beast of Argos, the colt,
the shield-bearing host,
that made its leap about the time of the setting
    Pleiades.
860　A ravening lion leaped over the wall
and licked its fill of royal blood.
So far my prelude stretches; that's for the gods.
What you've said of your feelings, I've heard and
    remember.
I say the same. You have me as your advocate.
865　In very few men is it native
to admire a successful friend without envying him.

For the poison of malice, settling on the heart,
doubles its weight in one who is stricken with envy.
He suffers under the load of his own troubles,
and groans to see the prosperity of the other man.　870
I know of what I speak; I very well understand
the glassy mirror of comradeship, that shadow of
    a shade,
which those prove to be who seemed my truest
    friends.
Only Odysseus,° who joined the fleet unwillingly,
once he was yoked was for me a ready trace horse.　875
Even as I speak of him, I do not know
if I speak of the dead or the living.
For other matters, we will set up public meetings
and take counsel in full assembly.
What is now well shall remain well; we shall see
    to it.　880
But where there is need for healing medicines,
we will try by surgery or cautery°
intelligently to avert the disease.
Now I will go in, into my halls, my hearth, my
    home,
and there I will first greet the gods　885
who sent me forth and brought me back again.
Victory has followed us;
let her be ours still, constantly!

(*Enter Clytemnestra.*)

CLYTEMNESTRA: You citizens, elders of Argos,
I will not be ashamed of speaking to you　890
of how I love my husband.
Modest inhibition is something
that dies away in human dealings.
I will tell of how wretched my life has been
while this man was in Troy—　895
at first hand I will tell it; it has been *my* life.
First, that a woman should sit in her house,
lonely without her male,
is something terrifying.
She hears so many hateful rumors;　900
here's one has come, and then another,
announcing a greater disaster still,
mouthing the ruin of the house.
If this man here had had as many wounds
as streams of rumor would have it,　905
he would have had more holes in him than a net.
If he had died, as his deaths multiplied in stories
    of him,
he must have had three bodies, like Geryon;
he would have boasted of taking a triple
shroud of earth to himself.　910
It was because of these hateful reports
that others, not I, have loosened many a cord
as it tightened round my neck.

874. **Odysseus:** Throughout the *Iliad*, Homer's story of the Trojan War, Odysseus is a brave soldier. He gives wise, even wily, advice to the Greeks.　882. **cautery:** The process of burning with a hot iron in order to heal.

And that is why your son
915   doesn't stand beside me as he should,
the proof of our trust, mine to you, yours to me,
our Orestes.
Do not wonder at this; a loyal ally keeps him safe,
Strophius the Phocian.°
920   He spoke to me of twin troubles:
your danger at Ilium, and then that here, too,
the anarchy of the people's voices
might overturn good counsel.
Indeed, it is inbred in men
925   to kick the man that's down.
That's the advice of Strophius, and there's no deceit
in it.
For my own part, the gushing springs of my grief
have dried up;
there's not a drop left.
930   My eyes are in pain from late watching,
weeping for the beacons that should tell of you,
but never called for firing.
In my dreams, I have started up,
roused by the light strokes of the gnat's flight;
935   I have seen so much more happen to you
than could be contained within the time
with which I shared my sleep.
But now I have come through all this;
my heart is free of sorrow;
940   and so I can describe this man of mine—
a watchdog of the house,
the saving forestay of the ship,
the rooted pillar of the towering roof,
the single child of a father,
the land seen by sailors when they had given over
945   hope,
the fairest day to see after the storm,
the springwater stream for the thirsty traveler.
It is sweet indeed to escape the harsh stroke of
necessity.
Such terms of address would, I think, belong to him.
950   But let no one be jealous.
Many, indeed, were the evils we endured before.
Now, dear heart,
step from the carriage, but do not place on earth,
my king,
this foot that trod Troy to destruction.
955   Servants, to whom I have commanded the task
of strewing his path to the house with tapestries—
let his way lie straight before him strewn with purple,
that justice may guide him to the home he never
hoped for.
Everything else earned by fate
960   an unsleeping mind, with the help of the gods,
will arrange justly.
AGAMEMNON: Daughter of Leda,° guardian of my house,

919. Strophius the Phocian: A family friend with whom Orestes stayed at the time of Agamemnon's murder. **962. Leda:** Mother of Clytemnestra by her husband, Tyndareus, and of Helen by Zeus, who approached Leda in the form of a swan.

your speech is a good fit for my absence:
both have stretched out long.
But to praise me in due fashion   965
is an honor that others should give.
Besides, do not make much of me in this woman's
fashion,
nor grovel and gape flatteringly, like some foreigner,
nor strew my path with garments that would make it
an object of ill will;   970
it is the gods one should honor with such things.
For one who is mortal, for me certainly,
to walk on subtly woven beauties like these
cannot be without fear.
I tell you, honor me as man, not god.   975
Footmats and embroideries—they sound differently,
they are different.
Not to be presumptuous
is the greatest gift the gods can give you.
It's only when a life has ended, and ended well,   980
that one dare say, "Well done."
I would be cheerful if my life
were like this in everything.
CLYTEMNESTRA: Then tell me this, and let it be your
own true judgment.
AGAMEMNON: Be sure, I will not falsify that judgment.   985
CLYTEMNESTRA: Was it through fear of the gods
that you made this vow?
AGAMEMNON: I said, if any man ever did, what I
knew would happen.
CLYTEMNESTRA: And what of Priam, if he had
conquered as you have?
AGAMEMNON: He would certainly have trodden on
the tapestry.   990
CLYTEMNESTRA: Don't be ashamed, then, of human
reproach.
AGAMEMNON: Yes, but the ill repute of the people's
voices
has a great power.
CLYTEMNESTRA: He that is not envied is also not
admired.
AGAMEMNON: A woman should not long so for a fight.   995
CLYTEMNESTRA: In those that win, yielding is graceful.
AGAMEMNON: Do you set such store on victory in
this dispute?
CLYTEMNESTRA: Let me have my way. You are the victor
if you yield readily.
AGAMEMNON: Well, if you will—here, someone
undo my sandals,   1000
that are like slaves for the treading of my foot.
And as I walk upon these lovely cloths,
I pray against the envious eye of the gods
lest from afar it strike me.
It's a great shame to spoil a house's wealth,   1005
these weavings so dear in price, with the dirt of
treading feet.
Enough of this.
Bring in this stranger here, and use her kindly.
The god looks from afar with approval
on the merciful conqueror.   1010

No one chooses to become a slave.
This woman is the very flower, picked out
from the spoils of war;
as a gift from the army to me, she followed me.
1015 Well, since I've been subdued to listen to you,
I will go into my house, treading on purple.
CLYTEMNESTRA: There is a sea—and who shall
        drain it dry?—
nourishing a spring, always new, an abundance of
        purple
to be bought with silver for the dyeing of garments.
1020 This house, my lord, has store enough of it,
thanks be to the gods.
This house does not know poverty.
I would have vowed the treading of many garments,
had I been so ordered by the shrines of the oracles,
1025 to win the safe return of your life.
When the root is there, the leaf comes to the
        house,
and stretches its shade against the dog star's heat.
And when you came to this house and hearth of
        yours,
it meant what heat means in the winter time.
1030 And when Zeus makes wine from the bitter grape,
it is still cool within the house,
when its perfected lord paces through the halls.
Zeus, Zeus, that brings all to <u>perfection</u>,
perfect my prayer.
1035 Bring to perfection all you have to do.
CHORUS: Why this fluttering, insistent terror
that keeps guard before my heart?
Is the song prophetic
that rises unhired and unbidden?
1040 My grounded mind has no confidence to dismiss it
like an obscure nightmare.
Time has grown old since the boats,
their hawsers all thrown out along the sands,
set out to Ilium.
1045 With my eyes I am my own witness
to their homecoming.
But nonetheless, my spirit within me
drones this tune of the Furies,
accompanied by no lyre,
1050 a song taught by none but itself.
It has none of the dear confidence of hope.
Not for nothing is the boding of my entrails,
the whirling of my heart, harmonized with
eddies of my mind that will surely bring fulfillment.
1055 But I pray that what I expect may fall away,
a lie, into unfulfillment.
There is no limit in health;
it is insatiable.
For disease is its next-door neighbor;
1060 there is but a single wall between them.
A man's destiny, facing straight ahead,
often crashes on the hidden reef.
Yet, if beforehand in prudent fear,
he casts overboard part of what he owns
1065 with the derrick of good measure,

his whole house does not sink utterly,
though overloaded to overflowing,
nor does the frame of the ship sink.
Many times the generous gifts of Zeus,
and those of the furrows yearly tilled,   1070
banish the disease of hunger.
But the black blood of a man,
when once it has fallen to the earth in his death,
who shall conjure it back again with any
        incantation?
Did not Zeus, for the safety of the world,   1075
stop the wizard who would raise the dead?
If there were no fates appointed by the gods
which checked other fates from having overmuch,
my heart would have outstripped my tongue
and poured this out.   1080
But now in the dark it mutters, in heart-anguish,
with never a hope of spinning out of my burning
        mind
what is right for this moment.
CLYTEMNESTRA: In with you too, now, Cassandra,
since Zeus (you cannot be angry with Zeus)   1085
has made you a sharer in the sacrifices in our
        house,
standing near the altar with many slaves that we
        own.
Get down from that carriage;
none of your high spirit of pride.
They say that Heracles, Alcmene's son,°   1090
was sold and forced to eat the bread of slavery.
If then the necessity of fate's scales
has forced this on you,
you should be very grateful for masters anciently
        rich.
Those who have reaped a harvest they never
        expected   1095
are always excessive in harshness toward their
        slaves.
From us you will have all the usual treatment.
CHORUS: She has finished; it is to you she spoke,
and what she says is clear enough.
You are taken, a quarry in fate's net;   1100
obey her, then—
though I will understand if you don't.
CLYTEMNESTRA: If she has anything besides her
        swallow twitterings,
a barbaric speech that no one knows,
I'll try to persuade her within her understanding.   1105
CHORUS: Follow her. What she says is the best there
        is for you;
leave the carriage; obey her.
CLYTEMNESTRA: I have no time to waste here with her
        outside the palace.
The sheep stand ready for slaughter   1110
in front of the hearth at the center of the house.

1090. **Heracles, Alcmene's son:** Heracles was a popular Greek
hero. According to legend, he was sold into slavery to Omphale,
Queen of Lydia.

(*To Cassandra.*)

> You, if you're going to do anything that I tell you,
> do it quickly.
> But if you disobey because you don't take in my
> words—

(*To Chorus.*)

1115
> Here, you!
> Don't speak to her any more; use your hands;
> that's all these foreigners understand.

CHORUS: I think the woman needs a good interpreter;
> she looks like a wild thing newly caught.

CLYTEMNESTRA: She's crazy; she hears only her
1120
> distraught mind.
> Of course she does, she that has left her newly
> captured city,
> come here not yet knowing how to wear the curb bit,
> till she's frothed out her spirit in blood.
> I won't throw any more words at her to be belittled.

(*Exit Clytemnestra.*)

1125
CHORUS: I pity her, and so I won't be angry.
> Come, you poor girl, desert your place in the
> carriage;
> yield to what must be; wear your yoke for the first
> time.

CASSANDRA: Oh! Oh! Oh! Oh, the land!
> Lord Apollo! Lord Apollo!

1130
CHORUS: Why do you raise such dismal cries to
> Apollo?
> He is no god for the singer of dirges.

CASSANDRA: Oh! Oh! Oh! Oh, the land!
> Lord Apollo! Lord Apollo!

1135
CHORUS: Again she calls with her ill omens
> upon the god who has no suitable place
> at scenes of mourning.

CASSANDRA: Lord Apollo! Lord Apollo! God of the
> streets,
> god of destruction! Now again, god of my
> destruction,
1140
> and so easily.

CHORUS: She seems to me about to prophesy her own
> misfortunes.
> The gift of prophecy still sticks
> even though the mind is now a slave's.

CASSANDRA: Lord Apollo! Lord Apollo!
1145
> God of my destruction! God of the streets!
> Through what streets have you led me now,
> to what house?

CHORUS: To that of the sons of Atreus. If you don't
> know that,
> that I can tell you. And you won't say it's a lie.

1150
CASSANDRA: Yes, to a house the gods hate;
> it has been witness of so many
> murders of kin, butcheries,
> bowl full of man's blood, ground soaked in shed
> blood.

CHORUS: The stranger has a nose as keen as a hound;
1155
> she's on the trail of a murder and will find it.

CASSANDRA: What convinces me are the witnesses—
> the children, the babies screaming of their cut
> throats,
> of their flesh roasted and eaten by their father.

CHORUS: We have heard of your fame as a prophet;
> but we need no foretellers here.   1160

CASSANDRA: Oh, what does she plan?
> What is the great new grief?
> It is a great evil against the house
> that she is planning.
> It is unbearable for its friends, uncurable.   1165
> Defense stands aloof and keeps away.

CHORUS: These last foretellings are quite beyond my
> understanding;
> the others I know—indeed the whole city cries
> them aloud.

CASSANDRA: Oh, you wretched woman,
> is this what you bring to consummation?   1170
> You have cleaned him in the bath
> till his skin shined,
> the husband to share your bed.
> And how shall I tell the consummation?
> It would be quick: the line of clutching hands,   1175
> stretching out, one hooked to another.

CHORUS: I don't understand that yet;
> you spoke riddles before,

Lilo Baur as Cassandra in the National Theatre's 2000 production of the *Oresteia*, translated by Ted Hughes and directed by Katie Mitchell.

but now what baffles me is the dimness
1180   of what comes from the gods in words.
CASSANDRA: Oh! Oh! Oh! What is this that appears?
         A net, a net of death. Can it be so?
         But the meshes are the bedfellow, the accomplice
            in murder.
         Let the pack that ravens insatiate against the family
1185   bay for a sacrifice that merits death by stoning.
CHORUS: What Fury is this you bid raise its cries
         against the house?
         I find no cleaning in your words.
         To my heart rush back the blood drops of
            yellowing stain,
         as when the eyes grow dim at the setting of a life's
1190   day,
         a man falling by the point of a spear.
         And destruction comes quick.
CASSANDRA: Look at that! Look at that!
         Keep away the bull from the cow!
1195   She will take him in the folds of the robe
         with the trick of the black horn.
         She strikes! He falls! He falls
         in the water of the bath.
         That is his end, I tell you,
         a treacherous murder in a cauldron.
1200 CHORUS: I will not boast of being a keen judge of
            prophecy,
         but this certainly looks like something evil.

Anyway, what good word ever came to mankind
from the prophets?
It is through evils that the wordy tricks of the
   prophets   1205
bring terrors for us to understand.
CASSANDRA: Oh, the ill boding of my own sad fate!
         For it is my own suffering, on top of his,
         that my tongue spills out.

(*To the god.*)

         Where is this you have brought me to in my
            sorrow?
         For nothing but to share his death; what else?   1210
CHORUS: You are someone god-possessed;
         the god carries you along.
         It is for yourself you cry out this tuneless tune.
         Like the brown nightingale,° that can never have   1215
            enough of song,
         as she cries "Itys! Itys!" for her life rich in sorrows,
         and her mind loves pity for herself.

1215–1222. Like the brown nightingale . . . cries of sorrow: The
Chorus alludes to the story of Philomela, who was raped by
her brother-in-law, Tereus. Although her tongue was cut out to
prevent her from telling anyone of the crime, Philomela sent her
sister a piece of embroidery that revealed all. The sisters took
their revenge on Tereus by tricking him into eating his son, Itys.
According to some accounts, the gods turned Philomela into a
nightingale.

A scene from the
American Repertory
Theater's 1994 production
of the *Oresteia*, directed
by François Rochaix.

CASSANDRA: Oh! The life of the shrill-voiced
      nightingale!
1220 The gods covered *her* with a feathered body;
      I tell you, they gave her a *sweet* life,
      and her cries are not cries of sorrow.
      But what remains for me
      is the splitting of the flesh with the two-edged
      spear.
1225 CHORUS: Where do they come from, these rushes
      of useless agony carried by the god?
      You make music that is a mixture,
      ugly cries of terror and high-pitched melodies.
      Where did you get the milestones of evil words
1230 that mark your prophetic journey?
      CASSANDRA: The marriage! The marriage of Paris,
      deadly to those who loved him.
      Scamander, river that my fathers drank of,
      in that time I was raised on your shores;
1235 but now around the banks of Cocytus and Acheron,°
      the rivers of death, I am likely to prophesy,
      and soon.
      CHORUS: What is this word you have spoken all too
      clearly?
      A newborn child could understand.
1240 The bite of murder has pierced me
      as you whimper at your painful fortune.
      It is a heartbreak to hear you.
      CASSANDRA: The agony, agony of the city utterly ruined.
      The sacrifices that my father made before the walls,
      the multiplied slaughter of cattle and woolly sheep.
1245 None of it helped; it was no cure.
      The city suffered as it was fated to suffer.
      And I shall soon be thrown on the ground
      in my own warm blood.
      CHORUS: What you say now follows what you said
      before.
      Some malevolent god who falls on you with
1250 fearful weight
      makes you a singer of these deadly mournful things.
      But as for the end—I am at a loss.
      CASSANDRA: Now my prophecy shall no longer peer
      from behind veils
      like a newly married bride.
1255 No, it will rush on, a wind brightly blowing
      into the sun's rising,
      to send disaster surging like a wave to meet the
      sunbeams,
      a disaster yet greater than this.
      I will not school you in riddles any longer.
1260 And do you be my witness that my nose is keen
      and my tracking by shortcuts
      on the path of crimes committed long ago.
      Never do they leave the house,
      that chorus that sings in ugly harmony.
1265 For their speech is of evil.

1235. Cocytus and Acheron: Rivers flowing together at the
entrance to the kingdom of death.

The revelers have drunk, to whet their courage
      more,
      man's blood, and so they abide in the house,
      and none shall expel them: they are the Furies,
      that attend on the murder of kin.
      The song they sing as they beleaguer the house   1270
      is the song of the primal destruction,
      when the mind is blinded.
      And each of the Furies has spat in disgust
      on the brother's bed that hates its violator.
      Hah! Am I an archer that missed,   1275
      or have I hit the mark?
      Or am I a false prophet
      that raps on doors and babbles?
      Be my witness, you, but first make your sworn oath
      that I know the story of the ancient sins   1280
      of this house.
      CHORUS: How would such an oath, even plighted in
      all honesty,
      serve as any kind of cure?
      True, I do wonder at you,
      that you, reared beyond the sea and speaking a
      strange tongue   1285
      should talk of these things as if you had been there.
      CASSANDRA: It was Apollo the prophet
      that charged me with the office of prophecy.
      CHORUS: He fell in love with you?
      Is that possible for a god?   1290
      CASSANDRA: Till now I was ashamed to speak of it.
      CHORUS: As long as things go well, one has one's
      delicacy.
      CASSANDRA: He was a wrestler, that breathed his
      grace into me.
      CHORUS: Did you come to the breeding of children,
      like other couples?   1295
      CASSANDRA: I promised the god and cheated him.
      CHORUS: Had you already got your gift of prophecy?
      CASSANDRA: Oh yes, I used to tell my countrymen
      all that would happen.
      CHORUS: How did you escape the god's anger?   1300
      CASSANDRA: Since my offense against him,
      no one believed a word of mine.
      CHORUS: Ah, but to us right now, you seem to
      prophesy truly.
      CASSANDRA: Oh, oh, my agony! There it is again!
      The fearful pain of true prophecy   1305
      that twists me, that drives me wild;
      and it is still only prelude.
      Look! Look! You see them! The young ones,
      sitting on the house like dream phantoms.
      They are the likenesses of those children dead and
      gone,   1310
      killed by those they loved;
      their hands are full of meat, their own flesh.
      You can see it clearly; they carry the pitiful load
      of their guts, and their father has tasted them.
      I tell you, there is punishment for this,   1315
      and someone is plotting it,
      a lion, but a coward, that wallows, a housekeeper

in the bed of the returning lord—
O mine, *my* lord—for I must bear the yoke of
    slavery.
1320 The captain of the ships, the sacker of Ilium,
he knows not what tongue is licking him,
the tongue of the hateful bitch, her ears pricked,
like a secret blind vengeance,
that will work out his evil fate.
1325 So far her daring reaches:
the woman will murder the man.
She is—what shall I call her and be right?
this monstrous, biting creature.
A snake with poison at both ends;
1330 some Scylla° living in the rocks, death to sailors;
some murderous, raging mother of hell;
some truceless god of war;
a war she has declared upon her loved ones!
So let her cry her war cry,
1335 whose daring knows no limit,
as at the moment when the battle turns.
Yet she seems to rejoice that he has come safe home.
It is all one to me, if you do not believe any of this;
what difference?
1340 It is to be and will come.
Soon you will stand here and say of me, in pity,
she was too true a prophet.
CHORUS: The feast of Thyestes, and the flesh of the
    children,
I understand and shudder; fear is on me
1345 as I hear the truth, and no mere likenesses.
But for the rest I heard from you,
I have fallen off the course and run wide.
CASSANDRA: I tell you, you will live to see
    Agamemnon's death.
CHORUS: Wretched girl, hold your tongue in piety.
1350 CASSANDRA: No, no holy god of healing presides over
    this story.
CHORUS: True, if what you say is so; but God forbid it
    should be.
CASSANDRA: You are all for God forbidding;
but their job is killing.
CHORUS: What man is he that furnishes this grief?
CASSANDRA: You have surely fallen astray of my
1355   prophecies.
CHORUS: Yes, for I do not understand how the plotter
will make his plan work.
CASSANDRA: Yet I know Greek rather too well.
CHORUS: So does the Delphic oracle;° but it's hard to
    understand,
1360 all the same.
CASSANDRA: Oh! It attacks me like fire!
Oh! Oh! O god! O Lycian Apollo!

1330. **Scylla:** A sea monster living in a cave opposite the whirlpool Charybdis. Ships could not escape the double threat.
1359. **Delphic oracle:** The chief oracle of ancient Greece, presided over by Apollo. The utterings of the oracle were ambiguous and had to be interpreted.

There she is, the lioness, two-footed bedfellow of the
    wolf,
in the absence of the true-bred lion.
She will kill me. Like one that brews a potion, 1365
She will put my reward, too, in the drink.
She cries her glee in triumph, as she whets the knife
for a man, to pay him in murder for bringing me
    here.

(*She starts tearing off her robe and garlands.*)

Why should I have these mockeries about me,
this staff, the prophet's garlands round my neck? 1370
Before I die myself, I shall at least destroy you.
Go; you shall be no more. Lie on the ground as
    you fall.
Thus I requite you.
Enrich some other girl with blinded madness,
some other girl than me. 1375
Look, Apollo himself undoes his prophetess
of her prophetic mantle; he has watched me
laughed to scorn even in this trumpery,
laughed at by friends turned foes,
with never a quiver in the scale—what hollowness! 1380
Ill-treated like a wandering beggar priest,
in misery half-starved to death, I still endured.
But now the prophet has unmade the prophet
and brought me here to meet my chance death.
No father's altar, but a chopping block, waits for me, 1385
to be warmed with my blood as I am butchered,
the preliminary victim. Yet, all the same, I shall
    not die
dishonored by the gods.
But another will come° to take vengeance for me;
he will kill the mother in whom he was seeded, 1390
and will avenge his father.
A wanderer outcast, grown alien to this land,
who will return from exile
to put a coping stone of ruin for those he loved,
for he has sworn a great oath by the gods 1395
that his father's corpse shall bring him home again.
Why do I go on this way, crying, full of self-pity?—
now that I have seen Troy's ruin, as I saw it,
now as Troy's conquerors come off in the god's
    judgment,
as I see them now. 1400
I will go and face it; I will face my death.
These gates before me here, I call you now by name:
the gates of death.
But I pray that the stroke that reaches me
may be a mortal stroke, 1405
that without struggle, as the blood runs freely,
in easy death I may close these eyes of mine.
CHORUS: You are a woman that has suffered much,
and have understood much; and you have said
    much.

1389. **another will come:** Reference to Orestes, who avenges his
father's murder in the second part of Aeschylus's trilogy.

1410 But if you truly know your fate,
why do you walk up to the altar steadfastly,
like an ox?
CASSANDRA: There is no escape, my friends; the time
is full.
CHORUS: Yet the latest moment has a special value.
CASSANDRA: This day has come; there is little I would
1415 gain by flight.
CHORUS: How courageous and steadfast!
CASSANDRA: No one who's happy hears these
compliments.
CHORUS: But death, if fame comes with it,
comes still with grace to those that must die anyway.
CASSANDRA: I weep for you, father, and for your
1420 noble children.

(*She recoils.*)

CHORUS: What is it? What is the fear that turns you
back?

(*Cassandra shudders.*)

CHORUS: What made you shudder?
Is it something in your mind that disgusts you?
CASSANDRA: The house! It reeks of murder, of
dripping blood!
1425 CHORUS: What? It's just the blood of sacrificed animals.
CASSANDRA: No, it is just like the smell of a grave.
CHORUS: It is no delicate Syrian incense in the house
that you speak of.
CASSANDRA: Still—I will go into the house,
to mourn with cries my own and Agamemnon's
1430 deaths.
I have enough of life.
My friends, I'm not scared
like a bird startled at a bush
in empty terror.
1435 When I die, you will be my witness to this,
when a woman dies to match my woman's death,
when a man falls to match that other man,
whose wife was his assassin.
This friendly office I lay on you, as I die now.
1440 CHORUS: Poor girl, I pity you for your death,
that the god predicted.
CASSANDRA: I have one more speech to make,
or shall I call it a dirge, just for myself.
As I face this last sunlight,
1445 I call on those who shall be my avengers
to make my enemies pay for *my* murder too,
only a dead slave, such an easy victory.
Men's fortunes, when they are good,
one might say of them, "They are like shadows
only."
1450 When they're bad, a wet sponge
with one stroke wipes it all out.
The first truth has my pity, far more than the second.
                                        (*Exit Cassandra.*)
CHORUS: To be successful is to be endlessly hungry
for more;
all men are so.

There is no one who banishes good fortune from
his house,   1455
so long as fingers point at it.
No man says, "Do not come here again, good
fortune."
Here is this king, to whom the blessed gods
granted
the sacking of Priam's city;
he came home with all the honors that the gods
gave him.   1460
But now, if he shall pay for the blood of the past
and dying render the price of others' deaths,
who that hears this and must die himself
dare boast that a man may be born
to live a whole life unharmed?   1465
AGAMEMNON (*from within*): I've been hit! I am hurt
to death.
CHORUS: Hush! Who is it that cries out, hurt to
death?
AGAMEMNON: I'm hit again!
CHORUS: It is the king crying out; I think all is over.
But let us plan safety for ourselves—if we can.   1470
1. My vote is to cry, Help! to the citizens
to come to the palace.
2. Yes, and at once, I think,
to catch them red-handed with dripping sword.
3. I think you're right; at least we should do
something.   1475
It certainly isn't the moment for hesitation.
4. But we can see. This is a kind of first act;
it looks like the beginning of a tyranny.
5. Yes, it does—because we're wasting time.
Their hands don't sleep, and they trample
underfoot   1480
the good reputation of delay.
6. I really do not know what would be best.
Those who do the deed of course find it easy to
plan.
7. Yes, I am with you. Anyhow,
one cannot by talking bring the dead to life again.   1485
8. Are we then, in order to stretch our own lives,
to yield to a government that shames our royal
house?
9. No, that is awful. Death is better than that.
Death is better than subjection to a tyranny.
10. Is the evidence of the cries good enough?   1490
Are we right to predict that the man is dead?
11. Yes, one must know before one gets angry.
Knowing the truth is very far from guessing.
12. I have the support of many voices among you:
that we should be told clearly how it is with
Agamemnon.   1495

(*Enter Clytemnestra.*)

CLYTEMNESTRA: Till now I have said much to meet
the occasion,
but now I will not be ashamed to say the opposite.
How could one, rendering hate to those who hated
but looked like loved ones,

1500 hedge the trap about with sides too high to be
leapt over?
This was my day of trial; I have thought of it
enough and long enough, a trial of an old quarrel
years and years old.
Now I stand here where I have struck him.
1505 He is dead, and the sequence ended.
This is how I managed—I will not disavow it—
that he should not escape, nor defend himself from
death.
I threw about him an encompassing net,
as it might be for fish, all-entangling,
1510 an evil wealth of cloak.
I struck him twice. He gave two groans,
and his body went limp;
as he lay there, I gave him a third,
in honor of the Zeus that keeps the dead
1515 securely in the underworld.
This was my grace and prayer for him.
So, as he lay there, he gasped out his spirit,
choking, poured out a sharp stream of his blood
and struck me with the dark bloody shower.
1520 I rejoiced as much as the new-sown earth
rejoices in the glad rain of Zeus,
when the buds strike in earth's womb.
So it is, you old men of Argos here;
be glad, if you can. I triumph in it.
1525 If it were right to pour libations
on a dead man's body, I would have done so to
him,
and more than justly done so.
Here's a bowl of horrors, cursed horrors,
that he filled within our house,
1530 and then he came and drank it off himself.
CHORUS: I wonder at your tongue, how boldly it wags,
that you should boast like this over a dead husband.
CLYTEMNESTRA: You try me out as if I were
a woman that cannot think.
1535 But my heart doesn't tremble,
and I speak to you who know;
whether you wish to praise or blame me is all one
to me.
Here is Agamemnon, my husband, now a corpse—
his death the work of this right hand of mine,
1540 an efficient craftsman.
That is how *that* is.
CHORUS: Woman, what evil thing have you eaten
that grows in the earth,
what draught have you tasted that comes from the
salt sea,
1545 that you have taken upon you so horrible a sacrifice
and the curse of the people's voice?
You have cast away, you have torn apart,
and you shall be cast and torn away from the city,
a monstrous object of hate to the citizens.
CLYTEMNESTRA: Now it's against me that you
1550 proclaim banishment,
that the hatred and curses of the citizens shall be
mine,

but in the old days you brought nothing against
that man,
who, with all the indifference of one whose
pastures are full
of teeming flocks, rich in wool,
had no care for the death of a lamb.   1555
He sacrificed his own daughter,
dearest pain of my womb,
to charm the contrariness of Thracian winds.
For this, should you not have banished him,
payment for his polluting wickedness?   1560
No, you are a careful hearer and harsh judge
only of *my* acts.
Threaten away! I tell you now, if once you
conquer me
in a fair fight, I'll be your subject;
but if God gives another outcome,   1565
you will get an education in discretion
and learn it thoroughly, though the knowledge
comes very late.
CHORUS: You think big thoughts, and you scream
proud defiance,
as though the bloody smear of your success   1570
had maddened your mind.
The smear of blood—I can see it in your eyes.
But still you must pay stroke for stroke,
with no friend to take your part.
CLYTEMNESTRA: You may now hear the solemn
swearing of my oath: 1575
By the justice due to my child, and now perfected,
by the Spirit of Destruction and the Fury,
in whose honor I cut this man's throat,
my hope treads not within the hall of Fear
so long as Aegisthus lights the hearth fire for me,   1580
my loyal friend, as he has always been,
shield for my daring—no small one.
There lies Agamemnon, this girl's seducer—
he was the darling of all the women of Troy—
and there she is, our prophet, prisoner of war,   1585
that shared his bed, a faithful whore
that spoke her auguries for him, and knew as well
the rubbing of the sailors' benches.
Both have suffered as they deserved.
He died as I said, and she has sung her swan song
in death,   1590
and lies with him, her lover.
But to me she has brought an additional side dish
to *my* pleasure in bed.
CHORUS: What day of doom may I look for soon,
one with not too much pain, not too long
bedridden,   1595
that shall bring me the sleep that has no ending,
now that my kindest of guardians has been
overcome,
suffering so much at a woman's hands.
By a woman his life has perished.
Curse on you, crazy Helen, that were the single
murderess   1600
of all those lives, those many lives,

lost under Troy's walls;
now you have made the fulfillment,
the fine flowering, of whatever it was,
1605 that quarrel within the house
built to bring a man to misery.
You have perfected it,
through bloodshed that cannot be washed out.

CLYTEMNESTRA: Do not pray for your end in death
1610 because of the burden of your grief in this,
nor turn your anger against Helen,
as the man-killer who destroyed
those many lives of the Greeks,
and brought into being an incurable pain.

CHORUS: Spirit that attacks the house of the sons of
1615 Atreus,
you master me to the breaking of my heart;
your power is wielded by two women of like soul.
And now you stand like an evil raven,
and croak over the dead a lawless hymn of victory.

1620 CLYTEMNESTRA: Now indeed you have made right
the judgment of your mouth,
as you name the thrice-glutted spirit of this race.
It is through him that the love of blood-licking
is nourished in the belly,
1625 and before the old wound has healed,
new pus comes.

CHORUS: Yes, the one you name is indeed great,
the spirit whose anger lies heavy on this house.
And the tale you have to tell is evil;
it has an endless appetite for the events of blind
1630 madness.
But surely these are through Zeus,
who is cause of all, who brings all to pass.
For what is there that is fulfilled for man,
except through Zeus?
1635 What is there of all this
that is not of God's accomplishment?
O my king, my king,
how shall I sorrow for you?
What shall I say from a heart that loves you?
1640 You lie there in that spider's web,
gasping out your life in an unholy death.
Oh, oh! Conquered by deadly treachery,
to fall to such an ignoble bed
by a wife's hand and a double-edged blade.

1645 CLYTEMNESTRA: You cry aloud on this as *my* work;
but do not call me Agamemnon's wife.
No, it is the old, bitter, Evil Genius
of Atreus, giver of the cruel feast,
that has likened himself to the wife of this dead man
1650 and has paid him off, sacrificing a full-grown victim
in fulfillment for those young children.

CHORUS: But who will bear you witness
that you are guiltless of the murder?
How, how so? It is true, there may be,
1655 on his father's side, the Evil Genius to help you.
And the black god of war presses on
through tides of kindred blood
to the place of his advance,

where he pays just requital
for the congealed fragments of the eaten children. 1660
O my king, my king,
how shall I sorrow for you?
What shall I say from a heart that loves you?
You lie there in that spider's web,
gasping out your life in an unholy death. 1665
Oh, oh! Conquered by deadly treachery,
to fall to such an ignoble bed
by a wife's hand and a double-edged blade.

CLYTEMNESTRA: Did *he* not also lay upon the house
a treacherous destruction? 1670
The victim, my daughter, raised from his loins,
Iphigeneia, whom I mourn for.
What he did is what he suffered for.
Let him not boast of anything in the house of death,
for he paid for what he had done 1675
with death by the mischief of the sword.

CHORUS: I am all bewildered about what road to take
as the house falls;
my wits are deserted by their skillful carefulness.
I fear the crash of the bloody torrent of rain 1680
that will shake the house to its foundation.
Now it is a shower no longer.
Fate is whetting its justice on other whetstones
for another deed of injury.
Earth, Earth, would you had received me 1685
before I lived to see him in his lowly couch
in a silver-sided bath.
Who shall bury him? Who shall keen him?
Will you dare to do this, to make lament for him,
you who killed him, your husband? 1690
Will you accomplish for his soul a grace no grace
as thanks for his great deeds?
Who shall stand at the grave and chant
a praise of the hero
with tears in the eye and truthful sorrow at heart? 1695

CLYTEMNESTRA: The care of that concerns you not at
all.
It is by our hand that he fell, that he died,
and we shall bury him
with no cries of mourning from this house.
But his daughter Iphigeneia, as is right, 1700
will welcome her father by the swift-flowing passage
over the River of Sorrows
and throw her arms around him and kiss him.

CHORUS: This is but the exchange of insult for insult;
it is hard to judge the issue of such a fight. 1705
The pirate plunders the pirate,
the killer pays for the killing.
Still there remains, as long as Zeus remains on his
throne,
the rule that he who has acted shall suffer
accordingly.
That is the divine law. 1710
Who shall expel from the house the brood of curses?
The whole race is welded to destruction.

CLYTEMNESTRA: In what you say now, the prophecy has
become truth.

For my part, I am willing to make a sworn
    compact
1715 with the evil spirit of this house
to be satisfied with things as they are, however bad,
on condition that he, in the days to come,
may go from our house and wear out some other
    breed
with murders of one another in the family.
1720 I will be utterly content with a small part of wealth,
if I can banish from these halls
the madness of mutual bloodletting.

(Enter Aegisthus.)

AEGISTHUS: O happy light, day of justified revenge!
    Now I will say that the gods
1725 in watchfulness so high above the earth
still bear an eye on the sorrows of mortals to
    avenge them.
Now I take pleasure to have seen this man
lying here in the robes that were
the nets of the Furies for him,
1730 paying for the plots his father's hand contrived.
For Atreus, ruler of this land, was this man's father,
and his brother Thyestes was my father.
Both were Pelops's sons; this is the plain story.
The two of them were in dispute about the throne,
1735 and Atreus banished my father from city and home.
The unlucky Thyestes later returned,
a suppliant at Atreus's hearth, and found safety
    there—
I mean for his own part, for he did not die
nor stained his fatherland with blood.
1740 But the vile Atreus, father of the dead man here,
with show of eagerness rather than love,
gave my father a banquet of welcome.
He pretended to celebrate a day of feasting
on flesh slaughtered for meat,
1745 in all hospitality,
but the meat he gave my father was his own
    children's.
The feet and the ends of the fingers he put apart
    and hid,
as the guests sat man by man at separate tables.
So Thyestes in ignorance ate the other parts,
a meal that brought a curse, as you see, on all the
1750   race.
Later, when he discovered what awful act he had
    committed,
he moaned aloud, recoiled, and vomited up the
    bloody mess.
"A doom intolerable will overtake," he said,
"the house of Pelops."
1755 He kicked the dinner over to back the oath,
crying, "So perish every one of all your breed."
That is why you can see this man fallen dead here,
and I am justly the one who stitched together his
    murder.
I was the third son, and while I was still in
    swaddling clothes

he drove me out along with my luckless father.   1760
But when I grew to manhood, justice brought me
    back.
And so I laid my hand on him, though not face to
    face;
mine was the whole contriving of the evil plot.
So glorious the result,
that now I would welcome death itself,   1765
having seen him in the traps of justice.
CHORUS: Aegisthus, I do not respect insolence
at the moment of calamity.
Do you say that with aforethought you killed
    Agamemnon,
that you alone planned this miserable murder?   1770
In that case, I do not think your life will escape
the justice of the public curse, the stoning.
That's what I think.
AEGISTHUS: Do you talk back to me, you who sit at
    the lower oar,
when we are in possession of the upper deck?   1775
You will find out, despite your age,
how uncomfortable such learning is for an old man,
when discretion is the lesson set.
Chains in old age and hunger's pangs
are the very sharpest healing prophets of the mind.   1780
Don't you see this when you see?
Kick not against the pricks, lest your own striking
    hurt you.
CHORUS: Woman, you who were his housekeeper
and at the same time sullied his bed,
did you plot his death when the victors were
    newly home   1785
and he had been their general?
AEGISTHUS: These words of yours are true progenitors
    of sorrows.
Yours is a tongue the opposite of Orpheus's:
he led all things his captive through the joy of his
    own voice,
but you with silly yappings arouse others to lead
    you captive.   1790
Once you are mastered, you'll be a tamer animal.
CHORUS: I suppose you'll be the sovereign of the
    Argives,
you, who when you plotted this man's murder
didn't dare to do the deed with your own hand.
AEGISTHUS: Well, no. The treachery was a woman's part,   1795
clearly so. I would be suspected as his old enemy.
But his wealth will give me a base to rule the
    citizens,
and the disobedient man I will yoke in heavy chains;
he will not be, I assure you, like a full-fed young
    trace horse.
No, unwelcome hunger and a dark cell   1800
will see him through into submission.
CHORUS: Why didn't you kill him yourself, with your
    cowardly soul?
No, your partner, the woman, did the killing,
to be the pollution of the land and of the gods of
    the land.

1805 But I tell you, Orestes still sees the light of day,
that he may come home, and with good luck on
his side
be conquerer and the death of both of you.
AEGISTHUS: Since you're resolved to act and talk like
this,
you'll soon know—
1810 here, my bodyguards, this is your work, right here.
CHORUS: Here, let each one of you be ready, hand on
sword hilt.
AEGISTHUS: I, too, hold the hilt of my sword.
I will face my death.
CHORUS: You talk of death; I welcome it. But I will
1815 try my chances.
CLYTEMNESTRA: No, dearest, no. Let us do no further
evils.
Those that there are, are many, a bloody harvest;
we have a good store of calamity.
No, no bloodletting.
1820 Good old men, off with you to your houses.
Yield to what must be, before you suffer.
What we did had to be done.
If this should be all of troubles, I would gladly
welcome it,

though struck with misfortune
by the heavy hoof of the evil spirit. 1825
That is a woman's word, if anyone should think it
worth heeding.
AEGISTHUS: No, but to have them letting their
tongues
blossom in insolence, to throw their empty threats
about—
"That they would try their chances"— 1830
You lack all brains, so to abuse your master.
CHORUS: It does not fit an Argive to fawn on a villain.
AEGISTHUS: I will get even with you in the days to
come.
CHORUS: Not if the Spirit brings Orestes home.
AEGISTHUS: I know the diet of exiles is rich in hope. 1835
CHORUS: Yes, do things, grow fat, pollute justice—
while you can.
AEGISTHUS: You know you will pay me for your
foolishness.
CHORUS: Boast, do; be bold—a cock beside your hen.
CLYTEMNESTRA: Do not pay heed to their vain
yappings. I
and you together will make all things well, 1840
for we are masters of this house.

COMMENTARY

LOIS SPATZ (b. 1940)

Oresteia: Trilogy Preserved 1982

In her examination of Aeschylus, Lois Spatz discusses how he conceived of the three plays of the *Oresteia* as a unified whole. She also provides some of the key background information that most of the original Greek audience would have known. Spatz connects the plays to events of the time in Athens so that we can better understand *Agamemnon* in the context of history and the other two plays to which it is linked.

The *Oresteia* won first prize at the Great Dionysia of 458 BCE, just two years before Aeschylus's death. The three tragedies, *Agamemnon, The Libation Bearers* (*Choephoroi*), and *The Eumenides,* were presented in a sequence which concluded with a lost satyr play, *Proteus,* about the wanderings of Agamemnon's brother, Menelaus. Modern readers often study *Agamemnon* alone, although it is extremely difficult to follow and does not resolve the dramatic questions it raises, but the ancient spectators would have considered the drama as a first act in a larger whole. The trilogy is composed so that the *Agamemnon* and *The Libation Bearers* define a conflict which can only be resolved by a third and different action. *Agamemnon,* taken alone, seems an obscure play, for the extreme complexity of image, diction, and action is a dramatic device which conveys the moral, emotional, and political confusion of the initial situation. In the second play, where the next generation of characters better understand their positions and motivations, the action is clearer. In *The Eumenides*, Aeschylus illuminates the issues underlying the action and resolves them.

Because one must study the parts together to appreciate the whole, the trilogy will be treated as a single play. Although Aeschylus begins his drama *in medias res*, as Agamemnon is about to return from Troy, the audience was familiar with the stories concerning the crimes of Agamemnon's father, Atreus. Therefore, it would have suspected with increasing dread some relationship between the events of the present generation and the horrors of the past, which the poet does not mention directly until the last third of the play, when the curse on the House of Atreus becomes a central theme of the trilogy. Atreus was head of the house and ruler of Argos when Thyestes, his brother, raped his wife and attempted to steal his property and power. First Atreus exiled his brother, but judging that penalty inadequate, he invited him home and cooked and served Thyestes' children to him at a feast celebrating the reunion. When Thyestes discovered he had eaten his own sons, he cursed Atreus, promising revenge, and left Argos with his one remaining son, Aegisthus.

The curse arising from this horrible act brought misfortune to the next generation. Atreus's sons, Agamemnon and Menelaus, had married sisters, Clytemnestra and Helen, respectively. Helen, the most beautiful woman in Greece, was seduced and stolen away from the hearth of the House of Atreus by their guest, Paris (Alexander), son of King Priam of Troy. Paris's adultery was a violation of the sacred relationship between guest and host protected by Zeus Xenios ("Guest-Friend"). Therefore, the Argives considered it a serious crime demanding revenge and launched the Trojan War, subject of the *Iliad* and epic cycle.

The Greek warriors who had sworn to support Menelaus met at Aulis under the leadership of Agamemnon, elder brother of the wronged husband and most powerful king in Greece. When rough seas prevented the fleet's passage to Troy, the priest Calchas informed Agamemnon that he must sacrifice his daughter, Iphigenia, to the goddess Artemis in order to calm the winds. Agamemnon, confident of the justice of the war and fearful of his restive troops, decided to slaughter Iphigenia so that the expedition could set sail.

Aeschylus begins his drama just as the Argives receive the news that Agamemnon has defeated Troy. The audience would know, however, from such sources as the *Odyssey*, the return stories of the cycle, and the *Oresteia* by the lyric poet Stesichorus, that, during these ten years of war, Clytemnestra had sent her son Orestes away and taken Aegisthus as a lover, and that the Greek soldiers in Troy had committed crimes which were punished on the return voyages. Aeschylus's gradual and sparing presentation of this background increases the mystery surrounding the events of the play itself.

Act I and Act II are both return and revenge stories. In *Agamemnon* several characters in sequence, the watchman, citizen/chorus, Queen Clytemnestra, and the herald, express hope and anxiety about the general's experiences in the Trojan War and his safe victorious return. Tension builds because the expectation of victory as the just punishment of Troy is constantly undercut by suggestions that the general and his men have themselves committed atrocities to ensure victory. In fact, the Greek fleet has already been punished, destroyed by a god-sent storm at sea. At the midpoint in the drama, Agamemnon enters in triumph with his war prize, Cassandra, and is welcomed with Eastern pomp by his queen, Clytemnestra, who entices him to enter the palace on a luxurious tapestry. This greeting initiates the revenge story. After Agamemnon's entrance into the palace, Cassandra, the Trojan priestess of Apollo, predicts his murder and hers and relates it to the bloody history of the House of Atreus. Then Clytemnestra murders Agamemnon and his mistress and justifies her deed to the citizens as divine retribution for his sacrifice of their daughter, Iphigenia. Aegisthus, Clytemnestra's lover, later explains that history more precisely, justifying his part in Agamemnon's death as revenge for his uncle Atreus's slaughter of his brothers. Thus, the cycle of revenge as punishment which demands further revenge is clearly established by the end of the play. It is equally clear that Clytemnestra's act of revenge cannot break the cycle. She and her lover plan to replace Agamemnon as rulers of Argos, but they respond with threats of violence to the chorus's protests against their tyranny. *Agamemnon* ends with the chorus cowed for the moment, but predicting that Orestes, Agamemnon's son, sent away by Clytemnestra, will someday return to avenge the death of his father and assume his rightful place as head of the family and ruler of the state.

Act II, *The Libation Bearers,* also exhibits the return and revenge patterns, in dramatizing the murder of Agamemnon's murderers. First Orestes returns, fulfilling the hopes of his sister, Electra, and the chorus of household slaves, captives from Troy loyal to their conqueror, Agamemnon. Orestes later learns that his return has also fulfilled the nightmares of his mother, Clytemnestra. He enters, not as a conquering hero like his father, to be warmly welcomed and then duped, but as an exile in disguise, announcing his own death in order to deceive his mother and her lover. He has been spurred on by Apollo's demand that he avenge his father's death or suffer dire punishments, but he also acts from private motives as son, disinherited heir, and legitimate ruler of Argos. After praying with his sister and the chorus at the tomb of Agamemnon to invoke the aid of the gods and the powerful dead, he tricks Clytemnestra, kills Aegisthus, and then confronts his mother again. She tries to dissuade him, but he leads her into the house for the slaughter. When Orestes afterwards proclaims the justice of the matricide to the satisfied chorus, he does not gloat, as his mother before him did, for he recognizes that his deed was a crime as well as a necessity. He confesses that his pollution is a danger to himself and his community and prepares to leave Argos to be purified of blood guilt by Apollo. As he announces his plans, however, madness overtakes him; he seems to see the very Furies (Erinyes) from Hell descending on him to avenge his matricide. The chorus is puzzled that this act has not ended the chain of reciprocal revenge in the House of Atreus but sends him forward to Apollo with prayers for success.

Act III, *The Eumenides,* introduces a new story pattern, "suppliant received"; a new setting, the shrines of the gods in Delphi and Athens; and new characters, the gods themselves—Apollo, the Furies, and Athena. The play begins at the shrine of Apollo in Delphi, where Orestes has arrived as a suppliant begging asylum from the Furies and release from blood guilt. Although Apollo has temporarily drugged the Furies into sleep, he cannot permanently protect Orestes from their vengeance. The god directs the matricide to the shrine of Athena in the Acropolis of Athens, where the goddess will release him from the curse. Once Orestes has fled, the ghost of Clytemnestra angrily arouses the sleeping Furies and sends them to track their prey. Orestes arrives in Athens and clings to the goddess's shrine, but the Furies enter soon after and threaten to destroy him. Athena returns just in time, and after questioning Orestes and the chorus of Furies, she decides the conflict is too important for her to resolve alone. Instead, she establishes a homicide court (modeled on the murder trials of the Court of the Areopagus) where citizen-judges (dicasts) will hear arguments for both sides and decide between them. The two present their cases, with Apollo supporting Orestes' plea. When the jury's vote is equally split, Orestes is set free by Athena's order. Before he returns home, he thanks Apollo, Athena, and the court, promising eternal peace between Argos and Athens and wishing the city prosperity and victory forever. The Furies, incensed by the verdict, call down curses on Athens, but Athena persuades them to become honored participants in the new procedure, ever punishing injustice, but showering blessings on the good as well. When they accept her offer, they exchange their loathsome black garments for the red robes of metics (foreign residents in Athens), a visible sign of their transformation from Furies to Eumenides ("Kindly Ones"). The trilogy ends with a torchlight procession, similar to the Panathenaic Festival, in which the citizens escort the goddesses to their new home, a hallowed cave at the foot of the Acropolis.

It is a long way from the polluted House of Atreus in Argos, whose bloody Furies roost like metics on the roof (*L.B.*, 1023), to the clear bright light of Athens, with its court system, public festivals, rites of Apollo, and the patronage of Zeus's daughter, Athena. Aeschylus has chosen a primitive myth about a blood-vendetta which extends for generations and includes cannibalism and child sacrifice. But he has dramatized the saga in a way which makes it relevant to his fifth-century audience. In none of the earlier versions of the story (i.e., *Odyssey, Cypria, Nostoi,* Stesichorus's *Oresteia*) was Orestes freed by a verdict of the Court of the Areopagus in Athens. Aeschylus originated this resolution so that he could trace the development of human justice—from the blood-vendetta carried out by the family with the support of the Furies who automatically avenge kindred bloodshed, through the purification rituals performed at the shrines of Apollo, to its culmination in the state court system, established by Athena with Zeus's blessing.[1] In dramatizing the progress of justice from vendetta to trial, he is also tracing the evolution of social institutions, from family and clan united by kindred blood, through cult united by ritual and a common patron, up to its perfection in the democratic polis, exemplified by Athens, where the families were ruled by law, the gods supported the new institutions, and the citizens united into a harmonious and effective whole.[2] No Athenian could sit unmoved while Athena voted like a citizen according to the procedures established in mythic time, but still in effect in 458 BCE. Nor could he watch without pride the imitation of his great Panathenaic Festival and the respectful acceptance of the dread Furies as metics in his own state. Thus would the contemporary Athenian recognize the ideals and glory of his city in the resolution of the myth.

[1]For a different opinion of Apollo's place, see George Derwent Thomson, *Aeschylus and Athens: A Study in the Social Origins of Drama,* 2nd ed. (London: Lawrence & Wishart, 1967), pp. 259–61, and R. P. Winnington-Ingram, "The Role of Apollo in the *Oresteia,*" *Classical Review* 47(1933): 97–104. On the relation of purification to the laws on homicide, see D. M. MacDowell, *Athenian Homicide Law in the Age of the Orators* (Manchester: University of Manchester Press, 1963), pp. 4–5,141–50.

[2]The family remained important, however, even in the legal prosecution for homicide, as MacDowell points out (*Athenian Homicide,* pp. 8–30). For a study of this evolution, see Richard Kuhns, *The House, the City, and the Judge: The Growth of Moral Awareness in the "Oresteia"* (Indianapolis: Bobbs-Merrill, 1962). George Thomson also traces the development from tribe to state and its influence on the form and ideas of drama, and on the *Oresteia* in particular (*Aeschylus,* pp. 229–78).

But if this resolution represents the culmination of human progress, at least two problems disturbed the polis in 458. The Court of the Areopagus (the aristocratic body of ex-archons which once functioned as supreme overseer of the laws of the land) had recently been a target of the democratic reform. In 462, Ephialtes and Pericles carried through the Assembly an act which removed the court's right to interfere with democratic legislation and reduced its jurisdiction to cases of premeditated murder. The aristocrats were incensed and Ephialtes himself was assassinated. Although Aeschylus's own position on this democratic reform cannot be determined with certainty, in *The Eumenides* the court's function as a tribunal for murder is given a divine validation. Ephialtes and Pericles had also favored challenging Spartan hegemony in Greece by allying with Argos, Sparta's main rival in the Peloponnese. In 461, the leader of the aristocrats, Cimon, was ostracized and the alliance with Argos approved. This change, which also produced fierce debate in the ensuing years, received attention from Aeschylus in the *Oresteia*. Orestes is clearly a political representative of Argos who allies himself with Athens, seemingly with Aeschylus's approval.[3]

It is not as important to label Aeschylus an aristocrat or radical as it is to recognize in the entire trilogy a paradigm for necessary compromise between disparate elements in the state.[4] If political vendettas are not controlled, there can be no civil order and consequently no peace and prosperity. Traditional groups like the Furies must be reconciled to the new system, treated with honor, and allowed to serve the state so that they can preserve for themselves and the community whichever of their principles remain valuable. Athena, establishing the Court of the Areopagus, defines its functions in words which echo the Furies' defense of their grim penalties:

> Here the reverence
> of citizens, their fear and kindred do-no-wrong
> shall hold by day and in the blessing of night alike
> all while the people do not muddy their own laws
> with foul infusions. But if bright water you stain
> with mud, you nevermore will find it fit to drink.
> No anarchy, no rule of a single master. Thus
> I advise my citizens to govern and to grace,
> and not to cast fear utterly from your city. What
> man who fears nothing at all is ever righteous? Such
> be your just terrors, and you may deserve and have
> salvation for your citadel, your land's defence
> such as is nowhere else found among men...
> (*The Eumenides*, 11. 690–702)[5]

Her admonitions provide not only an eternal definition of good government, but also a timely warning to a population recently embroiled in civil strife.

---

[3]The debate about Aeschylus's position on the reforms is summarized by Anthony J. Podlecki in *The Political Background of Aeschylean Tragedy* (Ann Arbor: U of Michigan P, 1966), pp. 81–92.

[4]A forceful spokesman for this view is E. R. Dodds, "Morals and Politics," from *The Ancient Concept of Progress and Other Essays* (Oxford UP, 1973), pp. 54–62.

[5]I have used the translation of Richmond Lattimore that appears in *The Complete Greek Tragedies: Aeschylus 1* (New York, n.d.).

Sophocles

Sophocles (c. 496–c. 406 BCE) won more prizes than any other tragedian in the Greek drama competitions, and he never came in lower than second place. His first victory was against the grand old master Aeschylus in 468 BCE. Sophocles' last plays, which he wrote in his eighties, were among his greatest. We have fragments of some ninety plays or poems and seven complete tragedies, and records suggest that his output numbered something over a hundred and twenty plays.

Sophocles lived in interesting times. He would have recalled the first defeat of the Persians in 490 BCE, when the news came via a messenger who had run twenty-six miles from Marathon to Athens. In his adolescence, Athens achieved its astonishing and decisive victory over the Persians at Salamis. His popularity as a tragedian and as a statesman coincided with the development of an imperial attitude in Athens. Athenian society honored the greatness of such men as Aeschylus, Sophocles, Euripides, the historian Herodotus, and all the politicians and artists that Pericles drew to Athens for its rebuilding. It was a golden age shadowed by war.

Sophocles was both sociable and religious, serving as the priest of several religious cults. He was also a man of action, popular enough to be elected as one of Athens's twelve generals; he participated with Pericles in the Samian War (440–439 BCE). His plays—especially *Antigone* (441 BCE), which preceded his election to generalship—often reflect deep political issues. One of his primary themes concerns the relation of the individual to the *polis,* the state itself. Since the Greeks valued the individual and at the same time regarded the *polis* as a sacred bulwark against a return to barbarism, conflicts between the individual and the *polis* were immensely painful.

When Sophocles began writing, he broke with an old tradition. From the time of Thespis (mid-sixth century BCE), each playwright had acted in his own plays. Aeschylus probably did so, but it is on record that Sophocles' voice was not strong enough to permit him to take a part in his plays. He played the lyre well enough to appear onstage, and he participated in a game of ball in one of his plays, but he did not appear as an actor. He also introduced innovations in the structure of his plays by changing the size of the chorus from twelve to fifteen and by adding painted scenery, more props, and a third actor to the two that Aeschylus and other tragedians had used. Sophocles wrote some of his plays with specific actors in mind, much as Shakespeare, Molière, and many other first-rank playwrights have done.

Sophocles was versed in the epics of Homer. Some of his plays derive from the *Iliad* or the *Odyssey,* although Sophocles always adapted the material of others to his own purposes. His nickname was the Attic Bee because he could read their work and always return with a useful idea of his own. The approach he took to the structure of the play, measuring the effect of the rising action of complication and then ensuring that the moment of recognition occurred at the same time the falling action began, was recognized as a supremely elegant skill. Nowhere is this illustrated more definitively than in *Oedipus Rex.*

Bust of Sophocles. The
Capitoline Museum,
Rome.

The plays of Aeschylus, powerful though they are, have a somewhat
simpler construction than do Sophocles' more intricately structured plays.
The structure of the plays of Euripides, Sophocles' successor, was never as
fully worked out; and when Aristotle discussed the nature of tragedy in his
Poetics, it was to Sophocles that he turned for a model, not to the other two
master playwrights of the genre.

Besides the Oedipus plays, Sophocles' other surviving plays are *Philoctetes,
Ajax, Trachiniae,* and *Electra.*

Oedipus Rex

Oedipus Rex is one of three plays by Sophocles that treat the fate of Oedipus
and his children. The plays were written over a period of thirty years: *Antigone*
(first produced in 441 BCE), *Oedipus Rex* (produced approximately fifteen
years later, between 430 and 427 BCE), and *Oedipus at Colonus* (produced
in 401 BCE, after Sophocles' death). When these plays are produced together
today, they are usually performed in the order in which the events took place

in Oedipus's and Antigone's lives—*Oedipus Rex, Oedipus at Colonus,* and *Antigone*—almost like the trilogies that Athenian audiences often viewed in the early years of the drama competitions. In fact, the plays were never a unified trilogy, and one of Sophocles' distinctions is that he did not present as trilogies plays that were thematically related, as poets before him had done.

The original narratives of the Oedipus plays were known to Sophocles' audience—with the possible exception of the story of Antigone—and one of the special pleasures for the audience watching the action of *Oedipus Rex* was that they knew the outcome. They watched for the steps, the choices, that led Oedipus to his fate.

Oedipus Rex is the story of a noble man who seeks knowledge that in the end destroys him. His greatness is measured in part by the fact that the gods have prophesied his fate: the gods take interest only in significant men. Before the action of the play begins, Oedipus has set out to discover whether he is truly the son of Polybos and Merope, the people who have reared him. He learns from the oracle of Apollo at Delphi, the most powerful interpreter of the voice and the will of the gods, that he will kill his father and marry his mother. His response is overwhelmingly human: he has seen his *moira,* his fate, and he cannot accept it. His reaction is to do everything he can, including leaving his homeland as quickly as possible, to avoid the possibility of killing Polybos and marrying Merope.

The Greek audience would have known that Oedipus was a descendant of Kadmos, founder of Thebes, who had sown the dragon teeth that produced the Spartoi (the sown men). Legend determined that the rulership of Thebes would be in dispute, with fraternal rivalry resembling that of the Spartoi, who fought and killed each other. This bloody legacy follows Oedipus, but it also reaches into all the plays of the trilogy. For example, in *Antigone* we learn that Antigone's brothers Polyneices and Eteocles killed each other in the shadow of the city walls. Thus, the fate Oedipus attempts to avoid actually dooms most of the characters in the three plays, including his true father, Laios, and his daughter Antigone.

Sophocles develops the drama in terms of **irony**—the disjunction between what seems to be true and what is true. Knowing the outcome of the action, the audience savors the ironic moments from the beginning of the play to the end. Oedipus flees his homeland to avoid fulfilling the prophecy, only to run headlong into the fate foretold by the oracle. He unwittingly returns to his original home, Thebes, and to his parents, murdering Laios, his true father, at a crossroads on the way and marrying Iokaste, his true mother, and becoming king of Thebes. The blind seer Teiresias warns Oedipus not to pursue the truth, but, in human fashion, Oedipus refuses to heed Teiresias's warnings. When the complete truth becomes clear to Oedipus, he physically blinds himself in horror and expiation. Like the blind Teiresias, Oedipus must now look inward for the truth, without the distractions of surface experiences.

The belief that the moral health of the ruler directly affected the security of the *polis* was widespread in Athenian Greece. Indeed, the Athenians regarded their state as fragile—like a human being whose health, physical and moral, could change suddenly. Because the Greeks were concerned for the well-being of their state, the *polis* often figures in the tragedies. The Sophoclean Oedipus plays are usually called "the Theban plays," a nomenclature that reminds us that the story of Oedipus can be read as the story of an individual or as the story of a state.

The underlying conflict in *Oedipus Rex* is political. The political relationship of human beings to the gods, the arbiters of their fate, is dramatized in Oedipus's relationship with the seer Teiresias. If he had his way, Oedipus might disregard Teiresias entirely. But Oedipus cannot command everything, even as ruler. His incomplete knowledge, despite his wisdom, is symptomatic of the limitations of every individual.

The contrast of Oedipus and Kreon, Iokaste's brother, is one of political style. Oedipus is a fully developed character who reveals himself as sympathetic but willful. He acts on his misunderstanding of the prophecy without reconsulting the oracle. He then marries Iokaste and blinds himself, again without reconsulting the oracle. Kreon, who is much less complicated, never acts without consulting the oracle and thoughtfully reflecting on the oracle's message. Oedipus sometimes behaves tyrannically, and he appears eager for power. Kreon takes power only when forced to do so.

The depth of Sophocles' character development was matched only by the work of his contemporary Euripides until the work of Shakespeare almost two thousand years later. Sophocles' drama is one of psychological development. His audiences saw Oedipus as a model for human greatness but also as a model for the human capacity to fall from a great height. The play is about the limits of human knowledge; it is also about the limits and frailty of human happiness.

For discussion questions and assignments on *Oedipus Rex*, visit **bedfordstmartins.com/jacobus**.

Oedipus Rex in Performance

Oedipus Rex has enjoyed great popularity since its first performance. The Greeks, who originally restricted their plays to one performance, eventually began to revive plays of the masters. *Oedipus* was one of the most popular. In modern times, performance has been almost constant since the seventeenth century. Great dramatists have produced their own adaptations—Corneille (1659), John Dryden (1679), Voltaire (1718), William Butler Yeats (1923), and Jean Cocteau (1931)—proving the durability of the themes and the adaptability of the play. The early American performances (beginning in 1881) were in Greek, but these soon gave way to productions in English. In his *New York Times* review of the October 2000 production in City Center, New York, Ben Brantley said, "Few productions have so hauntingly conveyed the brutal isolation of those who would be king as the National Theatre of Greece's exquisitely staged *Oedipus Rex*, directed by Vassilis Papavassileiou." This production was also presented at the Roman Colosseum, the first theatrical event in that space in 1,500 years. Currently, Greek companies perform the play regularly in the theater of Dionysus in Athens as well as in Epidaurus and elsewhere.

SOPHOCLES (C. 496–C. 406 BCE)

Oedipus Rex   C. 430 BCE

TRANSLATED BY DUDLEY FITTS AND ROBERT FITZGERALD

Characters

OEDIPUS, *King of Thebes, supposed son of Polybos and Merope, King and Queen of Corinth*
IOKASTE, *wife of Oedipus and widow of the late King Laios*
KREON, *brother of Iokaste, a prince of Thebes*
TEIRESIAS, *a blind seer who serves Apollo*
PRIEST
MESSENGER, *from Corinth*
SHEPHERD, *former servant of Laios*
SECOND MESSENGER, *from the palace*
CHORUS OF THEBAN ELDERS
CHORAGOS, *leader of the Chorus*
ANTIGONE *and* ISMENE, *young daughters of Oedipus and Iokaste. They appear in the Exodos but do not speak.*
SUPPLIANTS, GUARDS, SERVANTS

The Scene: *Before the palace of Oedipus, King of Thebes. A central door and two lateral doors open onto a platform which runs the length of the facade. On the platform, right and left, are altars; and three steps lead down into the orchestra, or chorus-ground. At the beginning of the action these steps are crowded by suppliants who have brought branches and chaplets of olive leaves and who sit in various attitudes of despair. Oedipus enters.*

PROLOGUE°

OEDIPUS: My children, generations of the living
   In the line of Kadmos,° nursed at his ancient hearth:
   Why have you strewn yourselves before these altars
   In supplication, with your boughs and garlands?
5 The breath of incense rises from the city
   With a sound of prayer and lamentation.
                  Children,
   I would not have you speak through messengers,
   And therefore I have come myself to hear you—
   I, Oedipus, who bear the famous name.
   (*To a Priest.*) You, there, since you are eldest in
10   the company,
   Speak for them all, tell me what preys upon you,
   Whether you come in dread, or crave some blessing:

Prologue: Portion of the play explaining the background and current action. **2. Kadmos:** Founder of Thebes.

Tell me, and never doubt that I will help you
   In every way I can; I should be heartless
   Were I not moved to find you suppliant here.   15
PRIEST: Great Oedipus, O powerful king of Thebes!
   You see how all the ages of our people
   Cling to your altar steps: here are boys
   Who can barely stand alone, and here are priests
   By weight of age, as I am a priest of God,   20
   And young men chosen from those yet unmarried;
   As for the others, all that multitude,
   They wait with olive chaplets in the squares,
   At the two shrines of Pallas,° and where Apollo°
   Speaks in the glowing embers.
                Your own eyes   25
   Must tell you: Thebes is tossed on a murdering sea
   And can not lift her head from the death surge.
   A rust consumes the buds and fruits of the earth;
   The herds are sick; children die unborn,
   And labor is vain. The god of plague and pyre   30
   Raids like detestable lightning through the city,
   And all the house of Kadmos is laid waste,
   All emptied, and all darkened: Death alone
   Battens upon the misery of Thebes.

You are not one of the immortal gods, we know;   35
   Yet we have come to you to make our prayer
   As to the man surest in mortal ways
   And wisest in the ways of God. You saved us
   From the Sphinx,° that flinty singer, and the tribute
   We paid to her so long; yet you were never   40
   Better informed than we, nor could we teach you:
   A god's touch, it seems, enabled you to help us.

Therefore, O mighty power, we turn to you:
   Find us our safety, find us a remedy,
   Whether by counsel of the gods or of men.   45
   A king of wisdom tested in the past
   Can act in a time of troubles, and act well.
   Noblest of men, restore
   Life to your city! Think how all men call you
   Liberator for your boldness long ago;   50
   Ah, when your years of kingship are remembered,

24. Pallas: Pallas Athene, daughter of Zeus and goddess of wisdom. **Apollo:** Son of Zeus and god of the sun, of light and truth. **39. Sphinx:** A winged monster with the body of a lion and the face of a woman, the Sphinx had tormented Thebes with her riddle, killing those who could not solve it. When Oedipus solved the riddle, the Sphinx killed herself.

Let them not say *We rose, but later fell*—
Keep the State from going down in the storm!
Once, years ago, with happy augury,
55   You brought us fortune; be the same again!
No man questions your power to rule the land:
But rule over men, not over a dead city!
Ships are only hulls, high walls are nothing,
When no life moves in the empty passageways.
60   OEDIPUS: Poor children! You may be sure I know
All that you longed for in your coming here.
I know that you are deathly sick; and yet,
Sick as you are, not one is as sick as I.
Each of you suffers in himself alone
65   His anguish, not another's; but my spirit
Groans for the city, for myself, for you.

I was not sleeping, you are not waking me.
No, I have been in tears for a long while
And in my restless thought walked many ways.
70   In all my search I found one remedy,
And I have adopted it: I have sent Kreon,
Son of Menoikeus, brother of the queen,
To Delphi,° Apollo's place of revelation,
To learn there, if he can,
75   What act or pledge of mine may save the city.
I have counted the days, and now, this very day,
I am troubled, for he has overstayed his time.
What is he doing? He has been gone too long.
Yet whenever he comes back, I should do ill
80   Not to take any action the god orders.
PRIEST: It is a timely promise. At this instant
They tell me Kreon is here.
OEDIPUS: O Lord Apollo!
May his news be fair as his face is radiant!
PRIEST: Good news, I gather! he is crowned with bay,
The chaplet is thick with berries.
85   OEDIPUS: We shall soon know;
He is near enough to hear us now.   (*Enter Kreon.*)
     O prince:
Brother: son of Menoikeus:
What answer do you bring us from the god?
KREON: A strong one. I can tell you, great afflictions
90   Will turn out well, if they are taken well.
OEDIPUS: What was the oracle? These vague words
Leave me still hanging between hope and fear.
KREON: Is it your pleasure to hear me with all these
Gathered around us? I am prepared to speak,
But should we not go in?
95   OEDIPUS: Speak to them all,
It is for them I suffer, more than for myself.
KREON: Then I will tell you what I heard at Delphi.
In plain words
The god commands us to expel from the land of
     Thebes
100 An old defilement we are sheltering.

73. Delphi: Site of the oracle, source of religious authority and
prophecy, under the protection of Apollo.

It is a deathly thing, beyond cure;
We must not let it feed upon us longer.
OEDIPUS: What defilement? How shall we rid
ourselves of it?
KREON: By exile or death, blood for blood. It was
Murder that brought the plague-wind on the city.   105
OEDIPUS: Murder of whom? Surely the god has
named him?
KREON: My Lord: Laios once ruled this land,
Before you came to govern us.
OEDIPUS: I know;
I learned of him from others; I never saw him.
KREON: He was murdered; and Apollo commands us
now   110
To take revenge upon whoever killed him.
OEDIPUS: Upon whom? Where are they? Where shall
we find a clue
To solve that crime, after so many years?
KREON: Here in this land, he said. Search reveals
Things that escape an inattentive man.   115
OEDIPUS: Tell me: Was Laios murdered in his house,
Or in the fields, or in some foreign country?
KREON: He said he planned to make a pilgrimage.
He did not come home again.
OEDIPUS: And was there no one,
No witness, no companion, to tell what happened?   120
KREON: They were all killed but one, and he got away
So frightened that he could remember one thing
only.
OEDIPUS: What was that one thing? One may be the
key
To everything, if we resolve to use it.
KREON: He said that a band of highwaymen attacked
them,   125
Outnumbered them, and overwhelmed the king.
OEDIPUS: Strange, that a highwayman should be so
daring—
Unless some faction here bribed him to do it.
KREON: We thought of that. But after Laios' death
New troubles arose and we had no avenger.   130
OEDIPUS: What troubles could prevent your hunting
down the killers?
KREON: The riddling Sphinx's song
Made us deaf to all mysteries but her own.
OEDIPUS: Then once more I must bring what is dark
to light.
It is most fitting that Apollo shows,   135
As you do, this compunction for the dead.
You shall see how I stand by you, as I should,
Avenging this country and the god as well,
And not as though it were for some distant friend,
But for my own sake, to be rid of evil.   140
Whoever killed King Laios might—who knows?—
Lay violent hands even on me—and soon.
I act for the murdered king in my own interest.

Come, then, my children: leave the altar steps,
Lift up your olive boughs!
                                    One of you go   145

And summon the people of Kadmos to gather here.
I will do all that I can; you may tell them that.
                                        (*Exit a Page.*)
So, with the help of God,
We shall be saved—or else indeed we are lost.

150 **PRIEST:** Let us rise, children. It was for this we came,
And now the king has promised it.
Phoibos° has sent us an oracle; may he descend
Himself to save us and drive out the plague.

(*Exeunt° Oedipus and Kreon into the palace by the central door. The Priest and the Suppliants disperse right and left. After a short pause the Chorus enters the orchestra.*)

PARODOS° • Strophe° 1

CHORUS: What is God singing in his profound
      Delphi of gold and shadow?
    What oracle for Thebes, the Sunwhipped city?
    Fear unjoints me, the roots of my heart tremble.
5   Now I remember, O Healer, your power, and
        wonder:
    Will you send doom like a sudden cloud, or
        weave it
    Like nightfall of the past?
    Speak to me, tell me, O
    Child of golden Hope, immortal Voice.

Antistrophe° 1

10 Let me pray to Athene, the immortal daughter of Zeus,
      And to Artemis° her sister
    Who keeps her famous throne in the market ring,
    And to Apollo, archer from distant heaven—
    O gods, descend! Like three streams leap against
15 The fires of our grief, the fires of darkness;
    Be swift to bring us rest!
    As in the old time from the brilliant house
    Of air you stepped to save us, come again!

Strophe 2

    Now our afflictions have no end,
20 Now all our stricken host lies down
    And no man fights off death with his mind;
    The noble plowland bears no grain,
    And groaning mothers can not bear—
    See, how our lives like birds take wing,
25 Like sparks that fly when a fire soars,
    To the shore of the god of evening.

---

152. **Phoibos:** Apollo. 153. [S.D.] ***Exeunt:*** Latin for "they go out." **Parados:** Song or ode chanted by the Chorus on their entry. **Strophe:** Song sung by the Chorus as they danced from stage right to stage left. **Antistrophe:** Song sung by the Chorus following the Strophe, as they danced back from stage left to stage right. **11. Artemis:** The huntress, daughter of Zeus, twin sister of Apollo.

Antistrophe 2

    The plague burns on, it is pitiless,
    Though pallid children laden with death
    Lie unwept in the stony ways,
    And old gray women by every path   30
    Flock to the strand about the altars
    There to strike their breasts and cry
    Worship of Phoibos in wailing prayers:
    Be kind, God's golden child!

Strophe 3

    There are no swords in this attack by fire,   35
    No shields, but we are ringed with cries.
    Send the besieger plunging from our homes
    Into the vast sea-room of the Atlantic
    Or into the waves that foam eastward of
        Thrace—
    For the day ravages what the night spares—   40
    Destroy our enemy, lord of the thunder!
    Let him be riven by lightning from heaven!

Antistrophe 3

    Phoibos Apollo, stretch the sun's bowstring,
    That golden cord, until it sing for us,
    Flashing arrows in heaven!
                          Artemis, Huntress,   45
    Race with flaring lights upon our mountains!
    O scarlet god,° O golden-banded brow,
    O Theban Bacchos in a storm of Maenads,°

(*Enter Oedipus, center.*)

    Whirl upon Death, that all the Undying hate!
    Come with blinding torches, come in joy!   50

SCENE 1

OEDIPUS: Is this your prayer? It may be answered.
        Come,
    Listen to me, act as the crisis demands,
    And you shall have relief from all these evils.

    Until now I was a stranger to this tale,
    As I had been a stranger to the crime.   5
    Could I track down the murderer without a
        clue?
    But now, friends,
    As one who became a citizen after the murder,

---

47. **scarlet god:** Bacchus, god of wine and revelry; also called Dionysus. 48. **Maenads:** Female worshipers of Bacchus (Dionysus).

Douglas Campbell as Oedipus
in a 1957 Tyrone Guthrie
production.

I make this proclamation to all Thebans:
If any man knows by whose hand Laios, son of
10   Labdakos,
Met his death, I direct that man to tell me everything,
No matter what he fears for having so long
    withheld it.
Let it stand as promised that no further trouble
Will come to him, but he may leave the land in
    safety.
Moreover: If anyone knows the murderer to be
15   foreign,
Let him not keep silent: he shall have his reward
    from me.
However, if he does conceal it; if any man
Fearing for his friend or for himself disobeys this
    edict,
Hear what I propose to do:

20   I solemnly forbid the people of this country,
Where power and throne are mine, ever to receive
    that man
Or speak to him, no matter who he is, or let him
Join in sacrifice, lustration,° or in prayer.
I decree that he be driven from every house,
25   Being, as he is, corruption itself to us: the Delphic
Voice of Apollo has pronounced this revelation.
Thus I associate myself with the oracle
And take the side of the murdered king.

As for the criminal, I pray to God—

Whether it be a lurking thief, or one of a number— 30
I pray that that man's life be consumed in evil and
    wretchedness.
And as for me, this curse applies no less
If it should turn out that the culprit is my guest here,
Sharing my hearth.
            You have heard the penalty.
I lay it on you now to attend to this 35
For my sake, for Apollo's, for the sick
Sterile city that heaven has abandoned.
Suppose the oracle had given you no command:
Should this defilement go uncleansed for ever?
You should have found the murderer: your king, 40
A noble king, had been destroyed!
                Now I,
Having the power that he held before me,
Having his bed, begetting children there
Upon his wife, as he would have, had he lived—
Their son would have been my children's brother, 45
If Laios had had luck in fatherhood!
(And now his bad fortune has struck him
    down)—
I say I take the son's part, just as though
I were his son, to press the fight for him
And see it won! I'll find the hand that brought 50
Death to Labdakos' and Polydoros' child,
Heir of Kadmos' and Agenor's line.°
And as for those who fail me,
May the gods deny them the fruit of the earth,
Fruit of the womb, and may they rot utterly! 55

23. **lustration:** Ceremonial purification.

51–52. **Labdakos, Polydoros, Kadmos, and Agenor:** Father, grandfather, great-grandfather, and great-great-grandfather of Laios.

Let them be wretched as we are wretched, and
    worse!

For you, for loyal Thebans, and for all
Who find my actions right, I pray the favor
Of justice, and of all the immortal gods.

60 CHORAGOS: Since I am under oath, my lord, I swear
    I did not do the murder; I can not name
    The murderer. Phoibos ordained the search;
    Why did he not say who the culprit was?

OEDIPUS: An honest question. But no man in the world
65   Can make the gods do more than the gods will.

CHORAGOS: There is an alternative, I think—

OEDIPUS: Tell me.
    Any or all, you must not fail to tell me.

CHORAGOS: A lord clairvoyant to the lord Apollo,
    As we all know, is the skilled Teiresias.
    One might learn much about this from him,
70   Oedipus.

OEDIPUS: I am not wasting time:
    Kreon spoke of this, and I have sent for him—
    Twice, in fact; it is strange that he is not here.

CHORAGOS: The other matter—that old report—
    seems useless.

75 OEDIPUS: What was that? I am interested in all reports.

CHORAGOS: The king was said to have been killed by
    highwaymen.

OEDIPUS: I know. But we have no witnesses to that.

CHORAGOS: If the killer can feel a particle of dread,
    Your curse will bring him out of hiding!

OEDIPUS: No.
80   The man who dared that act will fear no curse.

(Enter the blind seer Teiresias, led by a Page.)

CHORAGOS: But there is one man who may detect the
    criminal.
    This is Teiresias, this is the holy prophet
    In whom, alone of all men, truth was born.

OEDIPUS: Teiresias: seer: student of mysteries,
85   Of all that's taught and all that no man tells,
    Secrets of Heaven and secrets of the earth:
    Blind though you are, you know the city lies
    Sick with plague; and from this plague, my lord,
    We find that you alone can guard or save us.

90   Possibly you did not hear the messengers?
    Apollo, when we sent to him,
    Sent us back word that this great pestilence
    Would lift, but only if we established clearly
    The identity of those who murdered Laios.
    They must be killed or exiled.

95   Can you use
    Birdflight° or any art of divination
    To purify yourself, and Thebes, and me
    From this contagion? We are in your hands.
    There is no fairer duty
100   Than that of helping others in distress.

96. **Birdflight:** Prophets used the flight of birds to predict the future.

TEIRESIAS: How dreadful knowledge of the truth
    can be
    When there's no help in truth! I knew this well,
    But did not act on it; else I should not have come.

OEDIPUS: What is troubling you? Why are your eyes
    so cold?

TEIRESIAS: Let me go home. Bear your own fate, and   105
    I'll
    Bear mine. It is better so: trust what I say.

OEDIPUS: What you say is ungracious and unhelpful
    To your native country. Do not refuse to speak.

TEIRESIAS: When it comes to speech, your own is
    neither temperate   110
    Nor opportune. I wish to be more prudent.

OEDIPUS: In God's name, we all beg you—

TEIRESIAS: You are all ignorant.
    No; I will never tell you what I know.
    Now it is my misery; then, it would be yours.

OEDIPUS: What! You do know something, and will
    not tell us?   115
    You would betray us all and wreck the State?

TEIRESIAS: I do not intend to torture myself, or you.
    Why persist in asking? You will not persuade me.

OEDIPUS: What a wicked old man you are! You'd try
    a stone's
    Patience! Out with it! Have you no feeling at all?   120

TEIRESIAS: You call me unfeeling. If you could only
    see
    The nature of your own feelings . . .

OEDIPUS: Why,
    Who would not feel as I do? Who could endure
    Your arrogance toward the city?

TEIRESIAS: What does it matter?
    Whether I speak or not, it is bound to come.

OEDIPUS: Then, if "it" is bound to come, you are   125
    bound to tell me.

TEIRESIAS: No, I will not go on. Rage as you please.

OEDIPUS: Rage? Why not!
                              And I'll tell you what I think:
    You planned it, you had it done, you all but
    Killed him with your own hands: if you had eyes,   130
    I'd say the crime was yours, and yours alone.

TEIRESIAS: So? I charge you, then,
    Abide by the proclamation you have made:
    From this day forth
    Never speak again to these men or to me;   135
    You yourself are the pollution of this country.

OEDIPUS: You dare say that! Can you possibly think
    you have
    Some way of going free, after such insolence?

TEIRESIAS: I have gone free. It is the truth sustains me.

OEDIPUS: Who taught you shamelessness? It was not
    your craft.

TEIRESIAS: You did. You made me speak. I did not
    want to.   140

OEDIPUS: Speak what? Let me hear it again more
    clearly.

TEIRESIAS: Was it not clear before? Are you tempting me?

OEDIPUS: I did not understand it. Say it again.

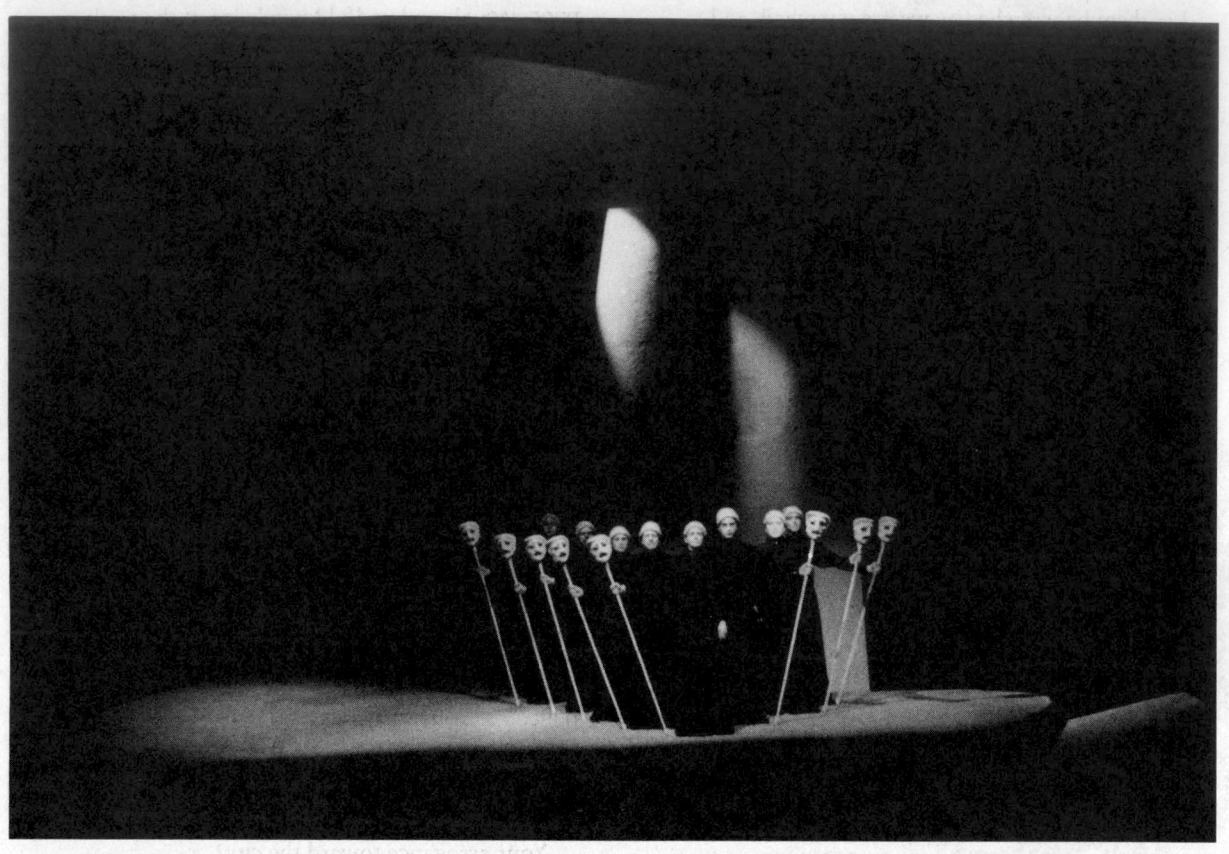

Franz Mertz's design for a 1952 production of *Oedipus Rex* directed by G. R. Sellner at Darmstadt Landestheater.

TEIRESIAS: I say that you are the murderer whom you
    seek.
OEDIPUS: Now twice you have spat out infamy.
145   You'll pay for it!
TEIRESIAS: Would you care for more? Do you wish to
    be really angry?
OEDIPUS: Say what you will. Whatever you say is
    worthless.
TEIRESIAS: I say you live in hideous shame with those
    Most dear to you. You can not see the evil.
150 OEDIPUS: Can you go on babbling like this for ever?
TEIRESIAS: I can, if there is power in truth.
OEDIPUS: There is:
155   But not for you, not for you,
    You sightless, witless, senseless, mad old man!
TEIRESIAS: You are the madman. There is no one here
    Who will not curse you soon, as you curse me.
OEDIPUS: You child of total night! I would not touch
    you;
    Neither would any man who sees the sun.
TEIRESIAS: True: it is not from you my fate will come.
    That lies within Apollo's competence,
    As it is his concern.

OEDIPUS: Tell me, who made   160
    These fine discoveries? Kreon? or someone else?
TEIRESIAS: Kreon is no threat. You weave your own
    doom.
OEDIPUS: Wealth, power, craft of statemanship!
    Kingly position, everywhere admired!
    What savage envy is stored up against these,   165
    If Kreon, whom I trusted, Kreon my friend,
    For this great office which the city once
    Put in my hands unsought—if for this power
    Kreon desires in secret to destroy me!

He has bought this decrepit fortune-teller, this   170
    Collector of dirty pennies, this prophet fraud—
    Why, he is no more clairvoyant than I am!
                                          Tell us:
    Has your mystic mummery ever approached the
        truth?
    When that hellcat the Sphinx was performing here,
    What help were you to these people?   175
    Her magic was not for the first man who came
        along:
    It demanded a real exorcist. Your birds—

What good were they? or the gods, for the matter
　　　of that?
　　But I came by,
180　Oedipus, the simple man, who knows nothing—
　　I thought it out for myself, no birds helped me!
　　And this is the man you think you can destroy,
　　That you may be close to Kreon when he's king!
　　Well, you and your friend Kreon, it seems to me,
185　Will suffer most. If you were not an old man,
　　You would have paid already for your plot.

CHORAGOS: We can not see that his words or yours
　　Have been spoken except in anger, Oedipus,
　　And of anger we have no need. How to accomplish
190　The god's will best: that is what most concerns us.

TEIRESIAS: You are a king. But where argument's
　　　concerned
　　I am your man, as much a king as you.
　　I am not your servant, but Apollo's.
　　I have no need of Kreon or Kreon's name.

195　Listen to me. You mock my blindness, do you?
　　But I say that you, with both your eyes, are blind:
　　You can not see the wretchedness of your life,
　　Nor in whose house you live, no, nor with whom.
　　Who are your father and mother? Can you tell me?
200　You do not even know the blind wrongs
　　That you have done them, on earth and in the
　　　world below.
　　But the double lash of your parents' curse will
　　　whip you
　　Out of this land some day, with only night
　　Upon your precious eyes.
205　Your cries then—where will they not be heard?
　　What fastness of Kithairon° will not echo them?
　　And that bridal-descant of yours—you'll know it
　　　then,
　　The song they sang when you came here to Thebes
　　And found your misguided berthing.
210　All this, and more, that you can not guess at now,
　　Will bring you to yourself among your children.

　　Be angry, then. Curse Kreon. Curse my words.
　　I tell you, no man that walks upon the earth
　　Shall be rooted out more horribly than you.

215　OEDIPUS: Am I to bear this from him?—Damnation
　　Take you! Out of this place! Out of my sight!

TEIRESIAS: I would not have come at all if you had
　　　not asked me.

OEDIPUS: Could I have told that you'd talk nonsense,
　　　that
　　You'd come here to make a fool of yourself, and
　　　of me?

TEIRESIAS: A fool? Your parents thought me sane
220　　enough.

206. **Kithairon:** The mountain where Oedipus was abandoned
as an infant.

OEDIPUS: My parents again!—Wait: who were my
　　parents?

TEIRESIAS: This day will give you a father, and break
　　your heart.

OEDIPUS: Your infantile riddles! Your damned
　　abracadabra!

TEIRESIAS: You were a great man once at solving
　　riddles.

OEDIPUS: Mock me with that if you like; you will
　　find it true.　　　　　　　　　　　　　　　　225

TEIRESIAS: It was true enough. It brought about your ruin.

OEDIPUS: But if it saved this town?

TEIRESIAS (*to the Page*): Boy, give me your hand.

OEDIPUS: Yes, boy; lead him away.
　　　　　　　　　　　　　　—While you are here
　　We can do nothing. Go; leave us in peace.　　230

TEIRESIAS: I will go when I have said what I have to say.
　　How can you hurt me? And I tell you again:
　　The man you have been looking for all this time,
　　The damned man, the murderer of Laios,
　　That man is in Thebes. To your mind he is
　　　foreign-born,　　　　　　　　　　　　　235
　　But it will soon be shown that he is a Theban,
　　A revelation that will fail to please.
　　　　　　　　　　　　　　　　A blind man,
　　Who has his eyes now; a penniless man, who is
　　　rich now;
　　And he will go tapping the strange earth with
　　　his staff.
　　To the children with whom he lives now he will be　240
　　Brother and father—the very same; to her
　　Who bore him, son and husband—the very same
　　Who came to his father's bed, wet with his father's
　　　blood.
　　Enough. Go think that over.
　　If later you find error in what I have said,　　245
　　You may say that I have no skill in prophecy.

(*Exit Teiresias, led by his Page.
Oedipus goes into the palace.*)

ODE° 1 • Strophe 1

CHORUS: The Delphic stone of prophecies
　　Remembers ancient regicide
　　And a still bloody hand.
　　That killer's hour of flight has come.
　　He must be stronger than riderless　　　　　5
　　Coursers of untiring wind,
　　For the son of Zeus° armed with his father's thunder
　　Leaps in lightning after him;
　　And the Furies° hold his track, the sad Furies.

Ode: Song sung by the Chorus. **7. son of Zeus:** Apollo.
9. Furies: Spirits called on to avenge crimes, especially against kin.

Antistrophe 1

10 Holy Parnassos'° peak of snow
    Flashes and blinds that secret man,
    That all shall hunt him down:
    Though he may roam the forest shade
    Like a bull gone wild from pasture
15 To rage through glooms of stone.
    Doom comes down on him; flight will not avail him;
    For the world's heart calls him desolate,
    And the immortal voices follow, for ever follow.

Strophe 2

    But now a wilder thing is heard
    From the old man skilled at hearing Fate in the
20   wing-beat of a bird.
    Bewildered as a blown bird, my soul hovers and
        can not find
    Foothold in this debate, or any reason or rest of mind.
    But no man ever brought—none can bring
    Proof of strife between Thebes' royal house,
25 Labdakos' line, and the son of Polybos;°
    And never until now has any man brought word
    Of Laios' dark death staining Oedipus the King.

Antistrophe 2

    Divine Zeus and Apollo hold
    Perfect intelligence alone of all tales ever told;
    And well though this diviner works, he works in
30   his own night;
    No man can judge that rough unknown or trust in
        second sight,
    For wisdom changes hands among the wise.
    Shall I believe my great lord criminal
    At a raging word that a blind old man let fall?
35 I saw him, when the carrion woman° faced him of old,
    Prove his heroic mind. These evil words are lies.

SCENE 2

KREON: Men of Thebes:
    I am told that heavy accusations
    Have been brought against me by King Oedipus.

    I am not the kind of man to bear this tamely.

5   If in these present difficulties
    He holds me accountable for any harm to him
    Through anything I have said or done—why, then,
    I do not value life in this dishonor.
    It is not as though this rumor touched upon
10 Some private indiscretion. The matter is grave.
    The fact is that I am being called disloyal
    To the State, to my fellow citizens, to my friends.

---

10. Parnassos: Mountain sacred to Apollo.   **25. Polybos:** King who adopted Oedipus.   **35. woman:** The Sphinx.

CHORAGOS: He may have spoken in anger, not from
    his mind.
KREON: But did you not hear him say I was the one
    Who seduced the old prophet into lying?   15
CHORAGOS: The thing was said; I do not know how
    seriously.
KREON: But you were watching him! Were his eyes
    steady?
    Did he look like a man in his right mind?
CHORAGOS: I do not know.
    I can not judge the behavior of great men.
    But here is the king himself.

(Enter Oedipus.)

OEDIPUS: So you dared come back.   20
    Why? How brazen of you to come to my house,
    You murderer!
                     Do you think I do not know
    That you plotted to kill me, plotted to steal my
        throne?
    Tell me, in God's name: am I coward, a fool,
    That you should dream you could accomplish   25
        this?
    A fool who could not see your slippery game?
    A coward, not to fight back when I saw it?
    You are the fool, Kreon, are you not? hoping
    Without support or friends to get a throne?
    Thrones may be won or bought: you could do
        neither.   30
KREON: Now listen to me. You have talked; let me
    talk, too.
    You can not judge unless you know the facts.
OEDIPUS: You speak well: there is one fact; but I find
    it hard
    To learn from the deadliest enemy I have.
KREON: That above all I must dispute with you.   35
OEDIPUS: That above all I will not hear you deny.
KREON: If you think there is anything good in being
    stubborn
    Against all reason, then I say you are wrong.
OEDIPUS: If you think a man can sin against his own
    kind
    And not be punished for it, I say you are mad.   40
KREON: I agree. But tell me: what have I done to
    you?
OEDIPUS: You advised me to send for that wizard,
    did you not?
KREON: I did. I should do it again.
OEDIPUS: Very well. Now tell me:
    How long has it been since Laios—
KREON: What of Laios?
OEDIPUS: Since he vanished in that onset by the road?   45
KREON: It was long ago, a long time.
OEDIPUS: And this prophet,
    Was he practicing here then?
KREON: He was; and with
    honor, as now.
OEDIPUS: Did he speak of me at that time?
KREON: He never did,
    At least, not when I was present.

Josef Svoboda's stage design for
M. Machacek's 1963 production of
Oedipus Rex in Prague.

OEDIPUS: But . . . the enquiry?
    I suppose you held one?
50 KREON: We did, but we learned nothing.
    OEDIPUS: Why did the prophet not speak against me then?
    KREON: I do not know; and I am the kind of man
      Who holds his tongue when he has no facts to go on.
    OEDIPUS: There's one fact that you know, and you
      could tell it.
55 KREON: What fact is that? If I know it, you shall have it.
    OEDIPUS: If he were not involved with you, he could
      not say
      That it was I who murdered Laios.
    KREON: If he says that, you are the one that knows it!—
      But now it is my turn to question you.
60 OEDIPUS: Put your questions. I am no murderer.
    KREON: First, then: You married my sister?
    OEDIPUS: I married your sister.
    KREON: And you rule the kingdom equally with her?
    OEDIPUS: Everything that she wants she has from me.

KREON: And I am the third, equal to both of you?
OEDIPUS: That is why I call you a bad friend.   65
KREON: No. Reason it out, as I have done.
  Think of this first: would any sane man prefer
  Power, with all a king's anxieties,
  To that same power and the grace of sleep?
  Certainly not I.   70
  I have never longed for the king's power—only his
    rights.
  Would any wise man differ from me in this?
  As matters stand, I have my way in everything
  With your consent, and no responsibilities.
  If I were king, I should be a slave to policy.   75
  How could I desire a scepter more
  Than what is now mine—untroubled influence?
  No, I have not gone mad; I need no honors,
  Except those with the perquisites I have now.
  I am welcome everywhere; every man salutes me,   80
  And those who want your favor seek my ear,

Since I know how to manage what they ask.
Should I exchange this ease for that anxiety?
Besides, no sober mind is treasonable.
85 I hate anarchy
And never would deal with any man who likes it.
Test what I have said. Go to the priestess
At Delphi, ask if I quoted her correctly.
And as for this other thing: if I am found
90 Guilty of treason with Teiresias,
Then sentence me to death. You have my word
It is a sentence I should cast my vote for—
But not without evidence!
                  You do wrong
When you take good men for bad, bad men for good.
95 A true friend thrown aside—why, life itself
Is not more precious!
                In time you will know this well:
For time, and time alone, will show the just man,
Though scoundrels are discovered in a day.
CHORAGOS: This is well said, and a prudent man
    would ponder it.
100 Judgments too quickly formed are dangerous.
OEDIPUS: But is he not quick in his duplicity?
And shall I not be quick to parry him?
Would you have me stand still, hold my peace, and let
This man win everything, through my inaction?
105 KREON: And you want—what is it, then? To banish me?
OEDIPUS: No, not exile. It is your death I want,
So that all the world may see what treason means.
KREON: You will persist, then? You will not believe me?
OEDIPUS: How can I believe you?
KREON: Then you are a fool.
OEDIPUS: To save myself?
110 KREON: In justice, think of me.
OEDIPUS: You are evil incarnate.
KREON: But suppose that you are wrong?
OEDIPUS: Still I must rule.
KREON: But not if you rule badly.
OEDIPUS: O city, city!
KREON: It is my city, too!
CHORAGOS: Now, my lords, be still. I see the queen,
115 Iokaste, coming from her palace chambers;
And it is time she came, for the sake of you both.
This dreadful quarrel can be resolved through her.

(*Enter Iokaste.*)

IOKASTE: Poor foolish men, what wicked din is this?
With Thebes sick to death, is it not shameful
120 That you should take some private quarrel up?
(*To Oedipus.*) Come into the house.
                —And you, Kreon, go now:
Let us have no more of this tumult over nothing.
KREON: Nothing? No, sister: what your husband
    plans for me
Is one of two great evils: exile or death.
OEDIPUS: He is right.
125   Why, woman I have caught him squarely
Plotting against my life.
KREON: No! Let me die
Accurst if ever I have wished you harm!

IOKASTE: Ah, believe it, Oedipus!
In the name of the gods, respect this oath of his
For my sake, for the sake of these people here! 130

Strophe 1

CHORAGOS: Open your mind to her, my lord. Be
    ruled by her, I beg you!
OEDIPUS: What would you have me do?
CHORAGOS: Respect Kreon's word. He has never
    spoken like a fool,
And now he has sworn an oath.
OEDIPUS: You know what you ask?
CHORAGOS: I do.
OEDIPUS: Speak on, then.
CHORAGOS: A friend so sworn should not be
    baited so, 135
In blind malice, and without final proof.
OEDIPUS: You are aware, I hope, that what you say
Means death for me, or exile at the least.

Strophe 2

CHORAGOS: No, I swear by Helios, first in heaven!
May I die friendless and accurst, 140
The worst of deaths, if ever I meant that!
It is the withering fields
    That hurt my sick heart:
Must we bear all these ills,
And now your bad blood as well? 145
OEDIPUS: Then let him go. And let me die, if I must,
Or be driven by him in shame from the land of
    Thebes.
It is your unhappiness, and not his talk,
That touches me.
             As for him—
Wherever he goes, hatred will follow him. 150
KREON: Ugly in yielding, as you were ugly in rage!
Natures like yours chiefly torment themselves.
OEDIPUS: Can you not go? Can you not leave me?
KREON: I can.
You do not know me; but the city knows me,
And in its eyes I am just, if not in yours. 155

             (*Exit Kreon.*)

Antistrophe 1

CHORAGOS: Lady Iokaste, did you not ask the King
    to go to his chambers?
IOKASTE: First tell me what has happened.
CHORAGOS: There was suspicion without evidence;
    yet it rankled
As even false charges will.
IOKASTE: On both sides?
CHORAGOS: On both.
IOKASTE: But what was said? 160

CHORAGOS: Oh let it rest, let it be done with!
    Have we not suffered enough?

OEDIPUS: You see to what your decency has brought
    you:
    You have made difficulties where my heart saw
    none.

Antistrophe 2

CHORAGOS: Oedipus, it is not once only I have told
165   you—
    You must know I should count myself unwise
    To the point of madness, should I now forsake
    you—
            You, under whose hand,
                In the storm of another time,
170   Our dear land sailed out free.
    But now stand fast at the helm!

IOKASTE: In God's name, Oedipus, inform your wife
    as well:
    Why are you so set in this hard anger?

OEDIPUS: I will tell you, for none of these men
    deserves
175   My confidence as you do. It is Kreon's work,
    His treachery, his plotting against me.

IOKASTE: Go on, if you can make this clear to me.

OEDIPUS: He charges me with the murder of Laios.

IOKASTE: Has he some knowledge? Or does he speak
    from hearsay?

OEDIPUS: He would not commit himself to such a
180   charge,
    But he has brought in that damnable soothsayer
    To tell his story.

IOKASTE: Set your mind at rest.
    If it is a question of soothsayers, I tell you
    That you will find no man whose craft gives
        knowledge
    Of the unknowable.
185   Here is my proof:
    An oracle was reported to Laios once
    (I will not say from Phoibos himself, but from
    His appointed ministers, at any rate)
    That his doom would be death at the hands of his
        own son—
190   His son, born of his flesh and of mine!

    Now, you remember the story: Laios was killed
    By marauding strangers where three highways
        meet;
    But his child had not been three days in this world
    Before the king had pierced the baby's ankles
195   And left him to die on a lonely mountainside.

    Thus, Apollo never caused that child
    To kill his father, and it was not Laios' fate
    To die at the hands of his son, as he had feared.
    This is what prophets and prophecies are worth!
    Have no dread of them.
200   It is God himself

Who can show us what he wills, in his own way.

OEDIPUS: How strange a shadowy memory crossed
    my mind,
    Just now while you were speaking; it chilled my
    heart.

IOKASTE: What do you mean? What memory do you
    speak of?

OEDIPUS: If I understand you, Laios was killed   205
    At a place where three roads meet.

IOKASTE: So it was said;
    We have no later story.

OEDIPUS: Where did it happen?

IOKASTE: Phokis, it is called: at a place where the
    Theban Way
    Divides into the roads toward Delphi and Daulia.

OEDIPUS: When?

IOKASTE: We had the news not long before you came 210
    And proved the right to your succession here.

OEDIPUS: Ah, what net has God been weaving for me?

IOKASTE: Oedipus! Why does this trouble you?

OEDIPUS: Do not ask me yet.
    First, tell me how Laios looked, and tell me
    How old he was.

IOKASTE: He was tall, his hair just touched 215
    With white; his form was not unlike your own.

OEDIPUS: I think that I myself may be accurst
    By my own ignorant edict.

IOKASTE: You speak strangely.
    It makes me tremble to look at you, my king.

OEDIPUS: I am not sure that the blind man can not see. 220
    But I should know better if you were to tell me—

IOKASTE: Anything—though I dread to hear you ask
    it.

OEDIPUS: Was the king lightly escorted, or did he ride
    With a large company, as a ruler should?

IOKASTE: There were five men with him in all: one
    was a herald;   225
    And a single chariot, which he was driving.

OEDIPUS: Alas, that makes it plain enough!
                                        But who—
    Who told you how it happened?

IOKASTE: A household servant,
    The only one to escape.

OEDIPUS: And is he still
    A servant of ours?

IOKASTE: No; for when he came back at last 230
    And found you enthroned in the place of the dead
        king,
    He came to me, touched my hand with his, and
        begged
    That I would send him away to the frontier district
    Where only the shepherds go—
    As far away from the city as I could send him.   235
    I granted his prayer; for although the man was a
        slave,
    He had earned more than this favor at my hands.

OEDIPUS: Can he be called back quickly?

IOKASTE: Easily.
    But why?

240 OEDIPUS: I have taken too much upon myself
   Without enquiry; therefore I wish to consult him.
IOKASTE: Then he shall come.
                              But am I not one also
   To whom you might confide these fears of yours?
OEDIPUS: That is your right; it will not be denied you,
245   Now least of all; for I have reached a pitch
   Of wild foreboding. Is there anyone
   To whom I should sooner speak?

   Polybos of Corinth is my father.
   My mother is a Dorian: Merope.
250 I grew up chief among the men of Corinth
   Until a strange thing happened—
   Not worth my passion, it may be, but strange.
   At a feast, a drunken man maundering in his cups
   Cries out that I am not my father's son!
255 I contained myself that night, though I felt anger
   And a sinking heart. The next day I visited
   My father and mother, and questioned them. They
       stormed,
   Calling it all the slanderous rant of a fool;
   And this relieved me. Yet the suspicion
260 Remained always aching in my mind;
   I knew there was talk; I could not rest;
   And finally, saying nothing to my parents,
   I went to the shrine at Delphi.

   The god dismissed my question without reply;
   He spoke of other things.
265   Some were clear,
   Full of wretchedness, dreadful, unbearable:
   As, that I should lie with my own mother, breed
   Children from whom all men would turn their
       eyes;
   And that I should be my father's murderer.

270 I heard all this, and fled. And from that day
   Corinth to me was only in the stars
   Descending in that quarter of the sky,
   As I wandered farther and farther on my way
   To a land where I should never see the evil
275 Sung by the oracle. And I came to this country
   Where, so you say, King Laios was killed.

   I will tell you all that happened there, my lady.
   There were three highways
   Coming together at a place I passed;
   And there a herald came towards me, and a
280   chariot
   Drawn by horses, with a man such as you describe
   Seated in it. The groom leading the horses
   Forced me off the road at his lord's command;
   But as this charioteer lurched over towards me
285 I struck him in my rage. The old man saw me
   And brought his double goad down upon my head
   As I came abreast.
                      He was paid back, and more!
   Swinging my club in this right hand I knocked him

Out of his car, and he rolled on the ground.
                              I killed him.

I killed them all.   290
Now if that stranger and Laios were—kin,
Where is a man more miserable than I?
More hated by the gods? Citizen and alien alike
Must never shelter me or speak to me—
I must be shunned by all.
                           And I myself   295
Pronounced this malediction upon myself!

Think of it: I have touched you with these hands,
These hands that killed your husband. What
    defilement!

Am I all evil, then? It must be so,
Since I must flee from Thebes, yet never again   300
See my own countrymen, my own country,
For fear of joining my mother in marriage
And killing Polybos, my father.
                                  Ah,
If I was created so, born to this fate,
Who could deny the savagery of God?   305
O holy majesty of heavenly powers!
May I never see that day! Never!
Rather let me vanish from the race of men
Than know the abomination destined me!
CHORAGOS: We too, my lord, have felt dismay at this.   310
   But there is hope: you have yet to hear the shepherd.
OEDIPUS: Indeed, I fear no other hope is left me.
IOKASTE: What do you hope from him when he
    comes?
OEDIPUS: This much:
   If his account of the murder tallies with yours,
   Then I am cleared.
IOKASTE: What was it that I said   315
   Of such importance?
OEDIPUS: Why, "marauders," you said.
   Killed the king, according to this man's story,
   If he maintains that still, if there were several,
   Clearly the guilt is not mine: I was alone.
   But if he says one man, singlehanded, did it,   320
   Then the evidence all points to me.
IOKASTE: You may be sure that he said there were
       several;
   And can he call back that story now? He can not.
   The whole city heard it as plainly as I.
   But suppose he alters some detail of it: 325
   He can not ever show that Laios' death
   Fulfilled the oracle: for Apollo said
   My child was doomed to kill him; and my child—
   Poor baby!—it was my child that died first.

   No. From now on, where oracles are concerned,   330
   I would not waste a second thought on any.
OEDIPUS: You may be right.
                              But come: let someone go
   For the shepherd at once. This matter must be settled.

IOKASTE: I will send for him.
335   I would not wish to cross you in anything,
         And surely not in this.—Let us go in.

                              (*Exeunt into the palace.*)

ODE 2 • Strophe 1

CHORUS: Let me be reverent in the ways of right,
         Lowly the paths I journey on;
         Let all my words and actions keep
         The laws of the pure universe
5   From highest Heaven handed down.
         For Heaven is their bright nurse,
         Those generations of the realms of light;
         Ah, never of mortal kind were they begot,
         Nor are they slaves of memory, lost in sleep:
10   Their Father is greater than Time, and ages not.

Antistrophe 1

         The tyrant is a child of Pride
         Who drinks from his great sickening cup
         Recklessness and vanity,
         Until from his high crest headlong
15   He plummets to the dust of hope.
         That strong man is not strong.
         But let no fair ambition be denied;
         May God protect the wrestler for the State
         In government, in comely policy,
20   Who will fear God, and on his ordinance wait.

Strophe 2

         Haughtiness and the high hand of disdain
         Tempt and outrage God's holy law;
         And any mortal who dares hold
         No immortal Power in awe
25   Will be caught up in a net of pain:
         The price for which his levity is sold.
         Let each man take due earnings, then,
         And keep his hands from holy things,
         And from blasphemy stand apart—
30   Else the crackling blast of heaven
         Blows on his head, and on his desperate heart.
         Though fools will honor impious men,
         In their cities no tragic poet sings.

Antistrophe 2

         Shall we lose faith in Delphi's obscurities,
35   We who have heard the world's core
         Discredited, and the sacred wood
         Of Zeus at Elis praised no more?

The deeds and the strange prophecies
Must make a pattern yet to be understood.
Zeus, if indeed you are lord of all,   40
Throned in light over night and day,
Mirror this in your endless mind:
Our masters call the oracle
Words on the wind, and the Delphic vision blind!
Their hearts no longer know Apollo,   45
And reverence for the gods has died away.

SCENE 3

(*Enter Iokaste.*)

IOKASTE: Princes of Thebes, it has occurred to me
         To visit the altars of the gods, bearing
         These branches as a suppliant, and this incense.
         Our king is not himself: his noble soul
         Is overwrought with fantasies of dread,   5
         Else he would consider
         The new prophecies in the light of the old.
         He will listen to any voice that speaks disaster,
         And my advice goes for nothing. (*She approaches
           the altar, right.*)
                        To you, then, Apollo,
         Lycean lord, since you are nearest, I turn in prayer   10
         Receive these offerings, and grant us deliverance
         From defilement. Our hearts are heavy with fear
         When we see our leader distracted, as helpless
           sailors
         Are terrified by the confusion of their helmsman.

(*Enter Messenger.*)

MESSENGER: Friends, no doubt you can direct me: 15
         Where shall I find the house of Oedipus,
         Or, better still, where is the king himself?
CHORAGOS: It is this very place, stranger; he is inside.
         This is his wife and mother of his children.
MESSENGER: I wish her happiness in a happy house,   20
         Blest in all the fulfillment of her marriage.
IOKASTE: I wish as much for you: your courtesy
         Deserves a like good fortune. But now, tell me:
         Why have you come? What have you to say to us?
MESSENGER: Good news, my lady, for your house and
           your husband.   25
IOKASTE: What news? Who sent you here?
MESSENGER: I am from Corinth.
         The news I bring ought to mean joy for you,
         Though it may be you will find some grief in it.
IOKASTE: What is it? How can it touch us in both
           ways?
MESSENGER: The word is that the people of the
           Isthmus   30
         Intend to call Oedipus to be their king.
IOKASTE: But old King Polybos—is he not reigning
           still?
MESSENGER: No. Death holds him in his sepulchre.
IOKASTE: What are you saying? Polybos is dead?

MESSENGER: If I am not telling the truth, may I die
35   myself.
IOKASTE (*to a Maidservant*): Go in, go quickly; tell
         this to your master.
     O riddlers of God's will, where are you now!
     This was the man whom Oedipus, long ago,
     Feared so, fled so, in dread of destroying him—
40   But it was another fate by which he died.

(*Enter Oedipus, center.*)

OEDIPUS: Dearest Iokaste, why have you sent for me?
IOKASTE: Listen to what this man says, and then
         tell me
     What has become of the solemn prophecies.
OEDIPUS: Who is this man? What is his news for me?
IOKASTE: He has come from Corinth to announce
45   your father's death!
OEDIPUS: Is it true, stranger? Tell me in your own
         words.
MESSENGER: I can not say it more clearly: the king is
         dead.
OEDIPUS: Was it by treason? Or by an attack of
         illness?
MESSENGER: A little thing brings old men to their
         rest.
OEDIPUS: It was sickness, then?
50   MESSENGER: Yes, and his many years.
OEDIPUS: Ah!
     Why should a man respect the Pythian hearth,° or
     Give heed to the birds that jangle above his head?
     They prophesied that I should kill Polybos,
55   Kill my own father; but he is dead and buried,
     And I am here—I never touched him, never,
     Unless he died of grief for my departure,
     And thus, in a sense, through me. No. Polybos
     Has packed the oracles off with him underground.
     They are empty words.
60   IOKASTE: Had I not told you so?
OEDIPUS: You had; it was my faint heart that
         betrayed me.
IOKASTE: From now on never think of those things
         again.
OEDIPUS: And yet—must I not fear my mother's bed?
IOKASTE: Why should anyone in this world be afraid
65   Since Fate rules us and nothing can be foreseen?
     A man should live only for the present day.

     Have no more fear of sleeping with your mother:
     How many men, in dreams, have lain with their
         mothers!
     No reasonable man is troubled by such things.
70   OEDIPUS: That is true, only—
     If only my mother were not still alive!
     But she is alive. I can not help my dread.
IOKASTE: Yet this news of your father's death is
         wonderful.
OEDIPUS: Wonderful. But I fear the living woman.

52. **Pythian hearth**: Delphi.

MESSENGER: Tell me, who is this woman that you
         fear?   75
OEDIPUS: It is Merope, man; the wife of King
         Polybos.
MESSENGER: Merope? Why should you be afraid of
         her?
OEDIPUS: An oracle of the gods, a dreadful saying.
MESSENGER: Can you tell me about it or are you
         sworn to silence?
OEDIPUS: I can tell you, and I will.   80
     Apollo said through his prophet that I was the
         man
     Who should marry his own mother, shed his
         father's blood
     With his own hands. And so, for all these years
     I have kept clear of Corinth, and no harm has
         come—
     Though it would have been sweet to see my
         parents again.   85
MESSENGER: And is this the fear that drove you out
         of Corinth?
OEDIPUS: Would you have me kill my father?
MESSENGER: As for that
     You must be reassured by the news I gave you.
OEDIPUS: If you could reassure me, I would reward
         you.
MESSENGER: I had that in mind, I will confess: I
         thought   90
     I could count on you when you returned to
         Corinth.
OEDIPUS: No: I will never go near my parents again.
MESSENGER: Ah, son, you still do not know what you
         are doing—
OEDIPUS: What do you mean? In the name of God
         tell me!
MESSENGER: —If these are your reasons for not going
         home.   95
OEDIPUS: I tell you, I fear the oracle may come true.
MESSENGER: And guilt may come upon you through
         your parents?
OEDIPUS: That is the dread that is always in my heart.
MESSENGER: Can you not see that all your fears
         are groundless?
OEDIPUS: Groundless? Am I not my parents' son?   100
MESSENGER: Polybos was not your father.
OEDIPUS: Not my father?
MESSENGER: No more your father than the man
         speaking to you.
OEDIPUS: But you are nothing to me!
MESSENGER: Neither was he.
OEDIPUS: Then why did he call me son?
MESSENGER: I will tell you:
     Long ago he had you from my hands, as a gift.   105
OEDIPUS: Then how could he love me so, if I was not
         his?
MESSENGER: He had no children, and his heart
         turned to you.
OEDIPUS: What of you? Did you buy me? Did you
         find me by chance?

MESSENGER: I came upon you in the woody vales of
          Kithairon.
OEDIPUS: And what were you doing there?
110   MESSENGER: Tending my flocks.
OEDIPUS: A wandering shepherd?
MESSENGER: But your savior, son, that day.
OEDIPUS: From what did you save me?
MESSENGER: Your ankles should tell you that.
OEDIPUS: Ah, stranger, why do you speak of that
          childhood pain?
MESSENGER: I pulled the skewer that pinned your feet
          together.
OEDIPUS: I have had the mark as long as I can
115   remember.
MESSENGER: That was why you were given the name°
          you bear.
OEDIPUS: God! Was it my father or my mother who
          did it?
          Tell me!
MESSENGER: I do not know. The man who gave you
          to me
          Can tell you better than I.
120   OEDIPUS: It was not you that found me, but another?
MESSENGER: It was another shepherd gave you
          to me.
OEDIPUS: Who was he? Can you tell me who he was?
MESSENGER: I think he was said to be one of Laios'
          people.
OEDIPUS: You mean the Laios who was king here
          years ago?
MESSENGER: Yes; King Laios; and the man was one
125   of his herdsmen.
OEDIPUS: Is he still alive? Can I see him?
MESSENGER: These men here
          Know best about such things.
OEDIPUS: Does anyone here
          Know this shepherd that he is talking about?
          Have you seen him in the fields, or in the town?
          If you have, tell me. It is time things were made
130   plain.
CHORAGOS: I think the man he means is that same
          shepherd
          You have already asked to see. Iokaste perhaps
          Could tell you something.
OEDIPUS: Do you know anything
          About him, Lady? Is he the man we have
          summoned?
          Is that the man this shepherd means?
135   IOKASTE: Why think of him?
          Forget this herdsman. Forget it all.
          This talk is a waste of time.
OEDIPUS: How can you say that,
          When the clues to my true birth are in my hands?
IOKASTE: For God's love, let us have no more
          questioning!
140   Is your life nothing to you?
          My own is pain enough for me to bear.

116. name: *Oedipus* literally means "swollen foot."

OEDIPUS: You need not worry. Suppose my mother a
          slave,
          And born of slaves: no baseness can touch you.
IOKASTE: Listen to me, I beg you: do not do this thing!
OEDIPUS: I will not listen; the truth must be made
          known.   145
IOKASTE: Everything that I say is for your own good!
OEDIPUS: My own good
          Snaps my patience, then; I want none of it.
IOKASTE: You are fatally wrong! May you never learn
          who you are!
OEDIPUS: Go, one of you, and bring the shepherd here.
          Let us leave this woman to brag of her royal name. 150
IOKASTE: Ah, miserable!
          That is the only word I have for you now.
          That is the only word I can ever have.

                              (*Exit into the palace.*)

CHORAGOS: Why has she left us, Oedipus? Why has
          she gone
          In such a passion of sorrow? I fear this silence: 155
          Something dreadful may come of it.
OEDIPUS: Let it come!
          However base my birth, I must know about it.
          The Queen, like a woman, is perhaps ashamed
          To think of my low origin. But I
          Am a child of Luck, I can not be dishonored.   160
          Luck is my mother; the passing months, my
          brothers,
          Have seen me rich and poor.
                              If this is so,
          How could I wish that I were someone else?
          How could I not be glad to know my birth?

ODE 3 • Strophe

CHORUS: If ever the coming time were known
          To my heart's pondering,
          Kithairon, now by Heaven I see the torches
          At the festival of the next full moon
          And see the dance, and hear the choir sing   5
          A grace to your gentle shade:
          Mountain where Oedipus was found,
          O mountain guard of a noble race!
          May the god° who heals us lend his aid,
          And let that glory come to pass   10
          For our king's cradling-ground.

Antistrophe

          Of the nymphs that flower beyond the years,
          Who bore you,° royal child,

9. god: Apollo.   **13. Who bore you:** The Chorus is asking if
Oedipus is the son of an immortal nymph and a god: Pan,
Apollo, Hermes, or Dionysus.

To Pan° of the hills or the timberline Apollo,
15   Cold in delight where the upland clears,
     Or Hermes° for whom Kyllene's° heights are piled?
     Or flushed as evening cloud,
     Great Dionysos,° roamer of mountains,
     He—was it he who found you there,
20   And caught you up in his own proud
     Arms from the sweet god-ravisher
     Who laughed by the Muses'° fountains?

SCENE 4

OEDIPUS: Sirs: though I do not know the man,
     I think I see him coming, this shepherd we want:
     He is old, like our friend here, and the men
     Bringing him seem to be servants of my house.
5   But you can tell, if you have ever seen him.

(*Enter Shepherd escorted by Servants.*)

CHORAGOS: I know him, he was Laios' man. You can
     trust him.
OEDIPUS: Tell me first, you from Corinth: is this the
     shepherd
     We were discussing?
MESSENGER: This is the very man.
OEDIPUS (*to Shepherd*): Come here. No, look at me.
     You must answer
10   Everything I ask.—You belonged to Laios?
SHEPHERD: Yes: born his slave, brought up in his
     house.
OEDIPUS: Tell me: what kind of work did you do for
     him?
SHEPHERD: I was a shepherd of his, most of my life.
OEDIPUS: Where mainly did you go for pasturage?
SHEPHERD: Sometimes Kithairon, sometimes the hills
15   near-by.
OEDIPUS: Do you remember ever seeing this man out
     there?
SHEPHERD: What would he be doing there? This
     man?
OEDIPUS: This man standing here. Have you ever
     seen him before?
SHEPHERD: No. At least, not to my recollection.
MESSENGER: And that is not strange, my lord. But I'll
20   refresh
     His memory: he must remember when we two
     Spent three whole seasons together, March to
     September,
     On Kithairon or thereabouts. He had two flocks;

14. **Pan:** God of nature, forests, flocks, and shepherds, depicted
as half man and half goat.   16. **Hermes:** Son of Zeus, messenger
of the gods.   **Kyllene:** Mountain reputed to be the birthplace
of Hermes; also the center of a cult to Hermes.   18. **Dionysos:**
Dionysus, god of wine around whom wild, orgiastic rituals developed; also called Bacchus.   22. **Muses:** Nine sister goddesses
who presided over poetry and music, art and sciences.

I had one. Each autumn I'd drive mine home
     And he would go back with his to Laios'
     sheepfold.—   25
     Is this not true, just as I have described it?
SHEPHERD: True, yes; but it was all so long ago.
MESSENGER: Well, then: do you remember, back in
     those days,
     That you gave me a baby boy to bring up as my
     own?
SHEPHERD: What if I did? What are you trying
     to say?
MESSENGER: King Oedipus was once that little child.   30
SHEPHERD: Damn you, hold your tongue!
OEDIPUS: No more of that!
     It is your tongue needs watching, not this man's.
SHEPHERD: My king, my master, what is it I have
     done wrong?
OEDIPUS: You have not answered his question about
     the boy.   35
SHEPHERD: He does not know . . . He is only making
     trouble . . .
OEDIPUS: Come, speak plainly, or it will go hard with
     you.
SHEPHERD: In God's name, do not torture an old
     man!
OEDIPUS: Come here, one of you; bind his arms
     behind him.
SHEPHERD: Unhappy king! What more do you wish
     to learn?   40
OEDIPUS: Did you give this man the child he speaks
     of?
SHEPHERD: I did.
     And I would to God I had died that very day.
OEDIPUS: You will die now unless you speak the
     truth.
SHEPHERD: Yet if I speak the truth, I am worse than
     dead.
OEDIPUS (*to Attendant*): He intends to draw it out,
     apparently—   45
SHEPHERD: No! I have told you already that I gave
     him the boy.
OEDIPUS: Where did you get him? From your house?
     From somewhere else?
SHEPHERD: Not from mine, no. A man gave him
     to me.
OEDIPUS: Is that man here? Whose house did he
     belong to?
SHEPHERD: For God's love, my king, do not ask me
     any more!   50
OEDIPUS: You are a dead man if I have to ask you
     again.
SHEPHERD: Then . . . Then the child was from the
     palace of Laios.
OEDIPUS: A slave child? or a child of his own line?
SHEPHERD: Ah, I am on the brink of dreadful speech!
OEDIPUS: And I of dreadful hearing. Yet I must hear.   55
SHEPHERD: If you must be told, then . . .
                         They said it was Laios' child;
     But it is your wife who can tell you about that.

The Shepherd (Oliver Cliff) tells Oedipus (Kenneth Welsh) the truth about his birth in the Guthrie Theater Company's 1973 production directed by Michael Langham.

OEDIPUS: My wife—Did she give it to you?
SHEPHERD: My lord, she did.
OEDIPUS: Do you know why?
SHEPHERD: I was told to get rid of it.
OEDIPUS: Oh heartless mother!
60 SHEPHERD: But in dread of prophecies . . .
OEDIPUS: Tell me.
SHEPHERD: It was said that the boy would kill his
        own father.
OEDIPUS: Then why did you give him over to this old
        man?
SHEPHERD: I pitied the baby, my king,
    And I thought that this man would take him far away
    To his own country.
65   He saved him—but for what a fate!
    For if you are what this man says you are,
    No man living is more wretched than Oedipus.
OEDIPUS: Ah God!
    It was true!
            All the prophecies!
                    —Now,
70 O Light, may I look on you for the last time!
    I, Oedipus,
    Oedipus, damned in his birth, in his marriage
        damned,
    Damned in the blood he shed with his own hand!

(*He rushes into the palace.*)

ODE 4 • Strophe 1

CHORUS: Alas for the seed of men.
    What measure shall I give these generations
    That breathe on the void and are void
    And exist and do not exist?
5   Who bears more weight of joy
    Than mass of sunlight shifting in images,
    Or who shall make his thought stay on
    That down time drifts away?
    Your splendor is all fallen.
10 O naked brow of wrath and tears,
    O change of Oedipus!
    I who saw your days call no man blest—
    Your great days like ghosts gone.

Antistrophe 1

    That mind was a strong bow.
15 Deep, how deep you drew it then, hard archer,
    At a dim fearful range,
    And brought dear glory down!
    You overcame the stranger°—
    The virgin with her hooking lion claws—
20 And though death sang, stood like a tower

---

18. stranger: The Sphinx.

To make pale Thebes take heart.
Fortress against our sorrow!
True king, giver of laws,
Majestic Oedipus!
No prince in Thebes had ever such renown,   25
No prince won such grace of power.

Strophe 2

And now of all men ever known
Most pitiful is this man's story:
His fortunes are most changed; his state
Fallen to a low slave's   30
Ground under bitter fate.
O Oedipus, most royal one!
The great door° that expelled you to the light
Gave at night—ah, gave night to your glory:
As to the father, to the fathering son.   35
All understood too late.
How could that queen whom Laios won,
The garden that he harrowed at his height,
Be silent when that act was done?

Antistrophe 2

But all eyes fail before time's eye,   40
All actions come to justice there.
Though never willed, though far down the deep
    past,
Your bed, your dread sirings,
Are brought to book at last.
Child by Laios doomed to die,   45
Then doomed to lose that fortunate little
    death,
Would God you never took breath in this air
That with my wailing lips I take to cry:
For I weep the world's outcast.
I was blind, and now I can tell why: 50
Asleep, for you had given ease of breath
To Thebes, while the false years went by.

EXODOS°

(*Enter, from the palace, Second Messenger.*)

SECOND MESSENGER: Elders of Thebes, most honored
    in this land,
    What horrors are yours to see and hear, what
        weight
    Of sorrow to be endured, if, true to your birth,
    You venerate the line of Labdakos!
    I think neither Istros nor Phasis, those great   5
        rivers,
    Could purify this place of all the evil

---

33. door: Iokaste's womb.   Exodos: Final scene.

It shelters now, or soon must bring to light—
Evil not done unconsciously, but willed.

The greatest griefs are those we cause ourselves.
CHORAGOS: Surely, friend, we have grief enough
10   already;
What new sorrow do you mean?
SECOND MESSENGER: The queen is dead.
CHORAGOS: O miserable queen! But at whose hand?
SECOND MESSENGER: Her own.
The full horror of what happened you can not
      know,
15 For you did not see it; but I, who did, will tell you
As clearly as I can how she met her death.

When she had left us,
In passionate silence, passing through the court,
She ran to her apartment in the house,
20 Her hair clutched by the fingers of both hands.
She closed the doors behind her; then, by that bed
Where long ago the fatal son was conceived—
That son who should bring about his father's
      death—
We heard her call upon Laios, dead so many
      years,
And heard her wail for the double fruit of her
      marriage,
25 A husband by her husband, children by her child.

Exactly how she died I do not know:
For Oedipus burst in moaning and would not
      let us
Keep vigil to the end: it was by him
As he stormed about the room that our eyes were
      caught.
From one to another of us he went, begging a
      sword,
30 Hunting the wife who was not his wife, the
      mother
Whose womb had carried his own children and
      himself.
I do not know: it was none of us aided him,
35 But surely one of the gods was in control!
For with a dreadful cry
He hurled his weight, as though wrenched out of
      himself,
At the twin doors: the bolts gave, and he rushed in.
And there we saw her hanging, her body swaying
From the cruel cord she had noosed about her
40   neck.
A great sob broke from him, heartbreaking to hear,
As he loosed the rope and lowered her to the
      ground.

I would blot out from my mind what happened
      next!
For the king ripped from her gown the golden
      brooches

That were her ornament, and raised them, and
      plunged them down
Straight into his own eyeballs, crying, "No more,   45
No more shall you look on the misery about me,
The horrors of my own doing! Too long you have
      known
The faces of those whom I should never have seen,
Too long been blind to those for whom I was
      searching!
From this hour, go in darkness!" And as he spoke, 50
He struck at his eyes—not once, but many times;
And the blood spattered his beard,
Bursting from his ruined sockets like red hail.

So from the unhappiness of two this evil has sprung,
A curse on the man and woman alike. The old   55
Happiness of the house of Labdakos
Was happiness enough: where is it today?
It is all wailing and ruin, disgrace, death—all
The misery of mankind that has a name—
And it is wholly and for ever theirs.   00
CHORAGOS: Is he in agony still? Is there no rest for
      him?
SECOND MESSENGER: He is calling for someone to
      open the doors wide
So that all the children of Kadmos may look upon
His father's murderer, his mother's—no,
I can not say it!
                  And then he will leave Thebes,   65
Self-exiled, in order that the curse
Which he himself pronounced may depart from
      the house.
He is weak, and there is none to lead him,
So terrible is his suffering.
                              But you will see:
Look, the doors are opening; in a moment   70
You will see a thing that would crush a heart of
      stone.

(*The central door is opened; Oedipus, blinded, is led in.*)

CHORAGOS: Dreadful indeed for men to see.
Never have my own eyes
Looked on a sight so full of fear.

Oedipus!   75
What madness came upon you, what demon
Leaped on your life with heavier
Punishment than a mortal man can bear?
No: I can not even
Look at you, poor ruined one.   80
And I would speak, question, ponder,
If I were able. No.
You make me shudder.
OEDIPUS: God. God.
Is there a sorrow greater?   85
Where shall I find harbor in this world?
My voice is hurled far on a dark wind.
What has God done to me?
CHORAGOS: Too terrible to think of, or to see.

A rehearsal for a production of *Oedipus Rex* at the Roman Colosseum in 2000.

Strophe 1

90   OEDIPUS: O cloud of night,
    Never to be turned away: night coming on,
    I can not tell how: night like a shroud!
    My fair winds brought me here.
                     O God. Again
    The pain of the spikes where I had sight,
95   The flooding pain
    Of memory, never to be gouged out.
  CHORAGOS: This is not strange.
    You suffer it all twice over, remorse in pain,
    Pain in remorse.

Antistrophe 1

100 OEDIPUS: Ah dear friend
    Are you faithful even yet, you alone?
    Are you still standing near me, will you stay here,
    Patient, to care for the blind?
                   The blind man!
    Yet even blind I know who it is attends me,
105   By the voice's tone—
    Though my new darkness hide the comforter.
  CHORAGOS: Oh fearful act!
    What god was it drove you to rake black
    Night across your eyes?

Strophe 2

OEDIPUS: Apollo. Apollo. Dear   110
    Children, the god was Apollo.
    He brought my sick, sick fate upon me.
    But the blinding hand was my own!
    How could I bear to see
    When all my sight was horror everywhere?   115
CHORAGOS: Everywhere; that is true.
OEDIPUS: And now what is left?
    Images? Love? A greeting even,
    Sweet to the senses? Is there anything?
    Ah, no, friends: lead me away.   120
    Lead me away from Thebes.
                 Lead the great wreck
    And hell of Oedipus, whom the gods hate.
CHORAGOS: Your misery, you are not blind to that.
    Would God you had never found it out!

Antistrophe 2

OEDIPUS: Death take the man who unbound   125
    My feet on that hillside
    And delivered me from death to life! What life?
    If only I had died,
    This weight of monstrous doom
    Could not have dragged me and my darlings down.   130

CHORAGOS: I would have wished the same.
OEDIPUS: Oh never to have come here
   With my father's blood upon me! Never
   To have been the man they call his mother's
      husband!
135   Oh accurst! Oh child of evil,
   To have entered that wretched bed—
                              the selfsame one!
   More primal than sin itself, this fell to me.
CHORAGOS: I do not know what words to offer you.
   You were better dead than alive and blind.
OEDIPUS: Do not counsel me any more. This
140   punishment
   That I have laid upon myself is just.
   If I had eyes,
   I do not know how I could bear the sight
   Of my father, when I came to the house of Death,
   Or my mother: for I have sinned against them
145   both
   So vilely that I could not make my peace
   By strangling my own life.
                        Or do you think my children,
   Born as they were born, would be sweet to my
      eyes?
   Ah never, never! Nor this town with its high walls,
   Nor the holy images of the gods.
150   For I,
   Thrice miserable!—Oedipus, noblest of all the
      line
   Of Kadmos, have condemned myself to enjoy
   These things no more, by my own malediction
   Expelling that man whom the gods declared
155   To be a defilement in the house of Laios.
   After exposing the rankness of my own guilt,
   How could I look men frankly in the eyes?
   No, I swear it,
   If I could have stifled my hearing at its source,
160   I would have done it and made all this body
   A tight cell of misery, blank to light and sound:
   So I should have been safe in my dark mind
   Beyond external evil.
                     Ah Kithairon!
   Why did you shelter me? When I was cast upon
      you,
165   Why did I not die? Then I should never
   Have shown the world my execrable birth.

   Ah Polybos! Corinth, city that I believed
   The ancient seat of my ancestors: how fair
   I seemed, your child! And all the while this evil
   Was cancerous within me!
170   For I am sick
   In my own being, sick in my origin.
   O three roads, dark ravine, woodland and way
   Where three roads met; you, drinking my father's
      blood,
   My own blood, spilled by my own hand: can you
      remember
175   The unspeakable things I did there, and the things

I went on from there to do?
                        O marriage, marriage!
   The act that engendered me, and again the act
   Performed by the son in the same bed—
                                       Ah, the net
   Of incest, mingling fathers, brothers, sons,
   With brides, wives, mothers: the last evil   180
   That can be known by men: no tongue can say
   How evil!
            No. For the love of God, conceal me
   Somewhere far from Thebes; or kill me; or hurl me
   Into the sea, away from men's eyes for ever.

   Come, lead me. You need not fear to touch me.   185
   Of all men, I alone can bear this guilt.

(*Enter Kreon.*)

CHORAGOS: Kreon is here now. As to what you ask,
   He may decide the course to take. He only
   Is left to protect the city in your place.
OEDIPUS: Alas, how can I speak to him? What right
      have I   190
   To beg his courtesy whom I have deeply wronged?
KREON: I have not come to mock you, Oedipus,
   Or to reproach you, either.
   (*To Attendants.*)   —You, standing there:
   If you have lost all respect for man's dignity,
   At least respect the flame of Lord Helios:°   195
   Do not allow this pollution to show itself
   Openly here, an affront to the earth
   And Heaven's rain and the light of day. No, take
      him
   Into the house as quickly as you can,
   For it is proper   200
   That only the close kindred see his grief.
OEDIPUS: I pray you in God's name, since your
      courtesy
   Ignores my dark expectation, visiting
   With mercy this man of all men most execrable:
   Give me what I ask—for your good, not for mine.   205
KREON: And what is it that you turn to me begging
      for?
OEDIPUS: Drive me out of this country as quickly as
      may be
   To a place where no human voice can ever greet
      me.
KREON: I should have done that before now—only,
   God's will had not been wholly revealed to me.   210
OEDIPUS: But his command is plain: the parricide
   Must be destroyed. I am that evil man.
KREON: That is the sense of it, yes; but as things are,
   We had best discover clearly what is to be done.
OEDIPUS: You would learn more about a man
      like me?   215
KREON: You are ready now to listen to the god.
OEDIPUS: I will listen. But it is to you
   That I must turn for help. I beg you, hear me.

195. **Lord Helios:** The sun god.

The woman is there—
220   Give her whatever funeral you think proper:
She is your sister.
                    —But let me go, Kreon!
Let me purge my father's Thebes of the pollution
Of my living here, and go out to the wild hills,
To Kithairon, that has won such fame with me,
225   The tomb my mother and father appointed for me,
And let me die there, as they willed I should.
And yet I know
Death will not ever come to me through sickness
Or in any natural way: I have been preserved
230   For some unthinkable fate. But let that be.

As for my sons, you need not care for them.
They are men, they will find some way to live.
But my poor daughters, who have shared my table,
Who never before have been parted from their
        father—
235   Take care of them, Kreon; do this for me.

And will you let me touch them with my hands
A last time, and let us weep together?
Be kind, my lord,
Great prince, be kind!
                    Could I but touch them,
240   They would be mine again, as when I had my eyes.

(*Enter Antigone and Ismene, attended.*)

Ah, God!
Is it my dearest children I hear weeping?
Has Kreon pitied me and sent my daughters?
KREON: Yes, Oedipus: I knew that they were dear
        to you
245   In the old days, and know you must love them still.
OEDIPUS: May God bless you for this—and be a
        friendlier
Guardian to you than he has been to me!

Children, where are you?
Come quickly to my hands: they are your
        brother's—
Hands that have brought your father's once clear
250   eyes
To this way of seeing—
                    Ah dearest ones,
I had neither sight nor knowledge then, your father
By the woman who was the source of his own life!
And I weep for you—having no strength to see
        you—,
255   I weep for you when I think of the bitterness
That men will visit upon you all your lives.
What homes, what festivals can you attend
Without being forced to depart again in tears?
And when you come to marriageable age,
260   Where is the man, my daughters, who would dare
Risk the bane that lies on all my children?
Is there any evil wanting? Your father killed
His father; sowed the womb of her who bore him;

Engendered you at the fount of his own existence!
That is what they will say of you.

                                    Then, whom   265
Can you ever marry? There are no bridegrooms
        for you,
And your lives must wither away in sterile dreaming.

O Kreon, son of Menoikeus!
You are the only father my daughters have,
Since we, their parents, are both of us gone for ever.   270
They are your own blood: you will not let them
Fall into beggary and loneliness;
You will keep them from the miseries that are mine!
Take pity on them; see, they are only children,
Friendless except for you. Promise me this,   275
Great prince, and give me your hand in token of it.

(*Kreon clasps his right hand.*)

Children:
I could say much, if you could understand me,
But as it is, I have only this prayer for you:
Live where you can, be as happy as you can—   280
Happier, please God, than God has made your
        father.
KREON: Enough. You have wept enough. Now go
        within.
OEDIPUS: I must, but it is hard.
KREON: Time eases all things.
OEDIPUS: You know my mind, then?
KREON: Say what you desire.
OEDIPUS: Send me from Thebes!
KREON: God grant that I may!   285
OEDIPUS: But since God hates me . . .
KREON: No, he will grant your wish.
OEDIPUS: You promise?
KREON: I can not speak beyond my knowledge.
OEDIPUS: Then lead me in.
KREON: Come now, and leave your children.   290
OEDIPUS: No! Do not take them from me!
KREON: Think no longer
That you are in command here, but rather think
How, when you were, you served your own
        destruction.

(*Exeunt into the house all but
the Chorus; the Choragos
chants directly to the audience.*)

CHORAGOS: Men of Thebes: look upon Oedipus.

This is the king who solved the famous riddle   295
And towered up, most powerful of men.
No mortal eyes but looked on him with envy,
Yet in the end ruin swept over him.

Let every man in mankind's frailty
Consider his last day; and let none   300
Presume on his good fortune until he find
Life, at his death, a memory without pain.

COMMENTARIES

Critical comment on the plays of Sophocles has been rich and various and has spanned the centuries. We are especially fortunate to have a commentary from the great age of Greek thought a century after Sophocles himself flourished. In *Oedipus Rex*, Sophocles gave the philosopher Aristotle a perfect drama on which to build a theory of tragedy, and Aristotle's observations have remained the most influential comments made on drama in the West. In some ways they have established the function, limits, and purposes of drama. In the twentieth century, for instance, when Bertolt Brecht tried to create a new theory of the drama, he specifically described his ideas as an alternative to Aristotelian notions.

Although not a critic, Sigmund Freud saw in the Oedipus myth as interpreted by Sophocles a basic psychological phenomenon experienced by all people in their infancy. This "Oedipus complex" is now well established in the history of psychology and in the popular imagination.

The extraordinary range of commentary on the Oedipus story is demonstrated nowhere more amazingly than in Claude Lévi-Strauss's structural reading of the myth, both in Sophocles' version and in other versions. Lévi-Strauss shows that a pattern emerges when certain actions in the play are placed side by side. If he is correct, his theory offers a way to interpret myths and to see why they were valued so highly by the Greeks in their drama.

ARISTOTLE (384–322 BCE)

Poetics: Comedy and Epic and Tragedy c. 334–323 BCE

TRANSLATED BY GERALD F. ELSE

Aristotle was Plato's most brilliant student and the heir to his teaching mantle. He remained with Plato for twenty years and then began his own school, called the Lyceum. His extant work consists mainly of his lectures, which were recorded by his students and carefully preserved. Called his treatises, they greatly influenced later thought and deal with almost every branch of philosophy, science, and the arts. His *Poetics* remains, more than two thousand years later, a document of immense importance for literary criticism. Although sometimes ambiguous, difficult, and unfinished, it provides insight into the theoretical basis of Greek tragedy and comedy, and it helps us see that the drama was significant enough in intellectual life to warrant an examination by the best Greek minds.

Comedy

Comedy is, as we said it was, an imitation of persons who are inferior; not, however, going all the way to full villainy, but imitating the ugly, of which the ludicrous is one part. The ludicrous, that is, is a failing or a piece of ugliness which causes no pain or destruction; thus, to go on farther, the comic mask° is something ugly and distorted but painless.

Now the stages of development of tragedy, and the men who were responsible for them, have not escaped notice but comedy did escape notice in the beginning because it was not taken seriously. (In fact it was late in its history that the presiding magistrate officially "granted a chorus" to the comic poets; until then they were volunteers.) Thus comedy already possessed certain defining characteristics when the first "comic poets," so-called, appear in the record. Who gave it masks, or prologues, or troupes of actors and all that sort of thing is not known. The composing of plots came originally from Sicily; of the Athenian poets, Crates° was the first to abandon the lampooning mode and compose arguments, that is, plots, of a general nature.

Epic and Tragedy

Well, then, epic poetry followed in the wake of tragedy up to the point of being a (1) good-sized (2) imitation (3) in verse (4) of people who are to be taken seriously; but in its having its verse unmixed with any other and being narrative in character, there they differ. Further, so far as its length is concerned, tragedy tries as hard as it can to exist during a single daylight period, or to vary but little, while the epic is not limited in its time and so differs in that respect. Yet originally they used to do this in tragedies just as much as they did in epic poems.

The constituent elements are partly identical and partly limited to tragedy. Hence anybody who knows about good and bad tragedy knows about epic also; for the elements that the epic possesses appertain to tragedy as well, but those of tragedy are not all found in the epic.

Tragedy and Its Six Constituent Elements

Our discussions of imitative poetry in hexameters,° and of comedy, will come later; at present let us deal with tragedy, recovering from what has been said so far the definition of its essential nature, as it was in development. Tragedy, then, is a process of imitating an action which has serious implications, is complete, and possesses magnitude; by means of language which has been made sensuously attractive, with each of its varieties found separately in the parts; enacted by the persons themselves and not presented through narrative; through a course of pity and fear completing the purification of tragic acts which have those emotional characteristics. By "language made sensuously attractive" I mean language that has rhythm and melody, and by "its varieties found separately" I mean the fact that certain parts of the play are carried on through spoken verses alone and others the other way around, through song.

---

the comic mask: Actors in Greek drama wore masks behind which they spoke their lines. The masks were made individually for each character.

Crates: Greek actor and playwright (fl. 470 BCE), credited by Aristotle with developing Greek comedy into a fully plotted, credible form. Aristophanes (c. 448–c. 385 BCE), another Greek comic playwright, says that Crates was the first to portray a drunkard onstage.

hexameters: The first known metrical form for classical verse. Each line had six metrical feet, some of which were prescribed in advance. It is the meter used for epic poetry and for poetry designed to teach a lesson. The form has sometimes been used in comparatively modern poetry but rarely with success except in French.

Now first of all, since they perform the imitation through action (by acting it), the adornment of their visual appearance will perforce constitute some part of the making of tragedy; and song-composition and verbal expression also, for those are the media in which they perform the imitation. By "verbal expression" I mean the actual composition of the verses, and by "song-composition" something whose meaning is entirely clear.

Next, since it is an imitation of an action and is enacted by certain people who are performing the action, and since those people must necessarily have certain traits both of character and thought (for it is thanks to these two factors that we speak of people's actions also as having a defined character, and it is in accordance with their actions that all either succeed or fail); and since the imitation of the action is the plot, for by "plot" I mean here the structuring of the events, and by the "characters" that in accordance with which we say that the persons who are acting have a defined moral character, and by "thought" all the passages in which they attempt to prove some thesis or set forth an opinion—it follows of necessity, then, that tragedy as a whole has just six constituent elements, in relation to the essence that makes it a distinct species; and they are plot, characters, verbal expression, thought, visual adornment, and song-composition. For the elements by which they imitate are two (i.e., verbal expression and song-composition), the manner in which they imitate is one (visual adornment), the things they imitate are three (plot, characters, thought), and there is nothing more beyond these. These then are the constituent forms they use.

The Relative Importance of the Six Elements

The greatest of these elements is the structuring of the incidents. For tragedy is an imitation not of men but of a life, an action, and they have moral quality in accordance with their characters but are happy or unhappy in accordance with their actions; hence they are not active in order to imitate their characters, but they include the characters along with the actions for the sake of the latter. Thus the structure of events, the plot, is the goal of tragedy, and the goal is the greatest thing of all.

Again: a tragedy cannot exist without a plot, but it can without characters: thus the tragedies of most of our modern poets are devoid of character, and in general many poets are like that; so also with the relationship between Zeuxis and Polygnotus,° among the painters: Polygnotus is a good portrayer of character, while Zeuxis's painting has no dimension of character at all.

Again: if one strings end to end speeches that are expressive of character and carefully worked in thought and expression, he still will not achieve the result which we said was the aim of tragedy; the job will be done much better by a tragedy that is more deficient in these other respects but has a plot, a structure of events. It is much the same case as with painting: the most beautiful pigments smeared on at random will not give as much pleasure as a black-and-white outline picture. Besides, the most powerful means tragedy has for swaying our feelings, namely the peripeties and recognitions,° are elements of plot.

Zeuxis and Polygnotus: Zeuxis (fl. 420–390 BCE) developed a method of painting in which the figures were rounded and apparently three-dimensional. Thus, he was an illusionistic painter, imitating life in a realistic style. Polygnotus (c. 470–440 BCE) was famous as a painter, and his works were on the Acropolis as well as at Delphi. His draftsmanship was especially praised.

peripeties and recognitions: The turning about of fortune and the recognition, on the part of the tragic hero, of the truth. This is, for Aristotle, a critical moment in the drama, especially if both events happen simultaneously, as they do in *Oedipus Rex*. It is quite possible for these moments to occur at separate times.

Again: an indicative sign is that those who are beginning a poetic career manage to hit the mark in verbal expression and character portrayal sooner than they do in plot construction; and the same is true of practically all the earliest poets.

So plot is the basic principle, the heart and soul, as it were, of tragedy, and the characters come second: [. . .] it is the imitation of an action and imitates the persons primarily for the sake of their action.

Third in rank is thought. This is the ability to state the issues and appropriate points pertaining to a given topic, an ability which springs from the arts of politics and rhetoric; in fact the earlier poets made their characters talk "politically" the present-day poets rhetorically. But "character" is that kind of utterance which clearly reveals the bent of a man's moral choice (hence there is no character in that class of utterances in which there is nothing at all that the speaker is choosing or rejecting), while "thought" is the passages in which they try to prove that something is so or not so, or state some general principle.

Fourth is the verbal expression of the speeches. I mean by this the same thing that was said earlier, that the "verbal expression" is the conveyance of thought through language: a statement which has the same meaning whether one says "verses" or "speeches."

The song-composition of the remaining parts is the greatest of the sensuous attractions, and the visual adornment of the dramatic persons can have a strong emotional effect but is the least artistic element, the least connected with the poetic art; in fact the force of tragedy can be felt even without benefit of public performance and actors, while for the production of the visual effect the property man's art is even more decisive than that of the poets.

General Principles of the Tragic Plot

With these distinctions out of the way, let us next discuss what the structuring of the events should be like, since this is both the basic and the most important element in the tragic art. We have established, then, that tragedy is an imitation of an action which is complete and whole and has some magnitude (for there is also such a thing as a whole that has no magnitude). "Whole" is that which has beginning, middle, and end. "Beginning" is that which does not necessarily follow on something else, but after it something else naturally is or happens; "end," the other way around, is that which naturally follows on something else, either necessarily or for the most part, but nothing else after it; and "middle" that which naturally follows on something else and something else on it. So, then, well constructed plots should neither begin nor end at any chance point but follow the guidelines just laid down.

Furthermore, since the beautiful, whether a living creature or anything that is composed of parts, should not only have these in a fixed order to one another but also possess a definite size which does not depend on chance—for beauty depends on size and order; hence neither can a very tiny creature turn out to be beautiful (since our perception of it grows blurred as it approaches the period of imperceptibility) nor an excessively huge one (for then it cannot all be perceived at once and so its unity and wholeness are lost), if for example there were a creature a thousand miles long—so, just as in the case of living creatures they must have some size, but one that can be taken in a single view, so with plots: they should have length, but such that they are easy to remember. As to a limit of the length, the one is determined by the tragic competitions and the ordinary span of attention. (If they had to compete with a hundred tragedies they would compete by the water clock, as they say used to be done [?].) But the limit fixed by the very nature of the case is: the longer the plot, up to the point of still being perspicuous as a whole, the finer it is so far as size is concerned; or to put it in general terms, the length in which, with things happening in unbroken sequence, a shift takes place either probably or necessarily from bad to good fortune or from good to bad—that is an acceptable norm of length.

But a plot is not unified, as some people think, simply because it has to do with a single person. A large, indeed an indefinite number of things can happen to a given individual, some of which go to constitute no unified event; and in the same way there can be many acts of a given individual from which no single action emerges. Hence it seems clear that those poets are wrong who have composed *Heracleïds, Theseïds,* and the like. They think that since Heracles was a single person it follows that the plot will be single too. But Homer, superior as he is in all other respects, appears to have grasped this point well also, thanks either to art or nature, for in composing an *Odyssey* he did not incorporate into it everything that happened to the hero, for example how he was wounded on Mt. Parnassus° or how he feigned madness at the muster, neither of which events, by happening, made it at all necessary or probable that the other should happen. Instead, he composed the *Odyssey*—and the *Iliad* similarly—around a unified action of the kind we have been talking about.

A poetic imitation, then, ought to be unified in the same way as a single imitation in any other mimetic field, by having a single object: since the plot is an imitation of an action, the latter ought to be both unified and complete, and the component events ought to be so firmly compacted that if any one of them is shifted to another place, or removed, the whole is loosened up and dislocated; for an element whose addition or subtraction makes no perceptible extra difference is not really a part of the whole.

From what has been said it is also clear that the poet's job is not to report what has happened but what is likely to happen: that is, what is capable of happening according to the rule of probability or necessity. Thus the difference between the historian and the poet is not in their utterances being in verse or prose (it would be quite possible for Herodotus's work to be translated into verse, and it would not be any the less a history with verse than it is without it); the difference lies in the fact that the historian speaks of what has happened, the poet of the kind of thing that *can* happen. Hence also poetry is a more philosophical and serious business than history; for poetry speaks more of universals, history of particulars. "Universal" in this case is what kind of person is likely to do or say certain kinds of things, according to probability or necessity; that is what poetry aims at, although it gives its persons particular names afterward; while the "particular" is what Alcibiades did or what happened to him.

In the field of comedy this point has been grasped: our comic poets construct their plots on the basis of general probabilities and then assign names to

Mt. Parnassus: A mountain in central Greece traditionally sacred to Apollo. In legend, Odysseus was wounded there, but the point Aristotle is making is that the writer of epics need not include every detail of his hero's life in a given work. Homer, in writing the *Odyssey,* was working with a hero, Odysseus, whose story had been legendary long before Homer began writing.

the persons quite arbitrarily, instead of dealing with individuals as the old iambic poets° did. But in tragedy they still cling to the historically given names. The reason is that what is possible is persuasive; so what has not happened we are not yet ready to believe is possible, while what has happened is, we feel, obviously possible: for it would not have happened if it were impossible. Nevertheless, it is a fact that even in our tragedies, in some cases only one or two of the names are traditional, the rest being invented, and in some others none at all. It is so, for example, in Agathon's *Antheus*—the names in it are as fictional as the events—and it gives no less pleasure because of that. Hence the poets ought not to cling at all costs to the traditional plots, around which our tragedies are constructed. And in fact it is absurd to go searching for this kind of authentication, since even the familiar names are familiar to only a few in the audience and yet give the same kind of pleasure to all.

So from these considerations it is evident that the poet should be a maker of his plots more than of his verses, insofar as he is a poet by virtue of his imitations and what he imitates is actions. Hence even if it happens that he puts something that has actually taken place into poetry, he is none the less a poet; for there is nothing to prevent some of the things that have happened from being the kind of things that can happen, and that is the sense in which he is their maker.

Simple and Complex Plots

Among simple plots and actions the episodic are the worst. By "episodic" plot I mean one in which there is no probability or necessity for the order in which the episodes follow one another. Such structures are composed by the bad poets because they are bad poets, but by the good poets because of the actors: in composing contest pieces for them, and stretching out the plot beyond its capacity, they are forced frequently to dislocate the sequence.

Furthermore, since the tragic imitation is not only of a complete action but also of events that are fearful and pathetic,° and these come about best when they come about contrary to one's expectation yet logically, one following from the other; that way they will be more productive of wonder than if they happen merely at random, by chance—because even among chance occurrences the ones people consider most marvelous are those that seem to have come about as if on purpose: for example the way the statue of Mitys at Argos killed the man who had been the cause of Mitys's death, by falling on him while he was attending the festival; it stands to reason, people think, that such things don't happen by chance—so plots of that sort cannot fail to be artistically superior.

Some plots are simple, others are complex; indeed the actions of which the plots are imitations already fall into these two categories. By "simple" action I mean one the development of which being continuous and unified in the manner stated above,

---

old iambic poets: Aristotle may be referring to Archilochus (fl. 650 BCE) and the iambic style he developed. The iamb is a metrical foot of two syllables, a short and a long syllable, and was the most popular metrical style before the time of Aristotle. "Dealing with individuals" implies using figures already known to the audience rather than figures whose names can be arbitrarily assigned because no one knows who they are.

fearful and pathetic: Aristotle said that tragedy should evoke two emotions: terror and pity. The terror results from our realizing that what is happening to the hero might just as easily happen to us; the pity results from our human sympathy with a fellow sufferer. Therefore, the fearful and pathetic represent significant emotions appropriate to our witnessing drama.

the reversal comes without peripety or recognition, and by "complex" action one in which the reversal is continuous but with recognition or peripety or both. And these developments must grow out of the very structure of the plot itself, in such a way that on the basis of what has happened previously this particular outcome follows either by necessity or in accordance with probability; for there is a great difference in whether these events happen because of those or merely after them.

"Peripety" is a shift of what is being undertaken to the opposite in the way previously stated, and that in accordance with probability or necessity as we have just been saying; as for example in the *Oedipus* the man who has come, thinking that he will reassure Oedipus, that is, relieve him of his fear with respect to his mother, by revealing who he once was, brings about the opposite; and in the *Lynceus,* as he (Lynceus) is being led away with every prospect of being executed, and Danaus pursuing him with every prospect of doing the executing, it comes about as a result of the other things that have happened in the play that *he* is executed and Lynceus is saved. And "recognition" is, as indeed the name indicates, a shift from ignorance to awareness, pointing in the direction either of close blood ties or of hostility, of people who have previously been in a clearly marked state of happiness or unhappiness.

The finest recognition is one that happens at the same time as a peripety, as is the case with the one in the *Oedipus.* Naturally, there are also other kinds of recognition: it is possible for one to take place in the prescribed manner in relation to inanimate objects and chance occurrences, and it is possible to recognize whether a person has acted or not acted. But the form that is most integrally a part of the plot, the action, is the one aforesaid; for that kind of recognition combined with peripety will excite either pity or fear (and these are the kinds of action of which tragedy is an imitation according to our definition), because both good and bad fortune will also be most likely to follow that kind of event. Since, further, the recognition is a recognition of persons, some are of one person by the other one only (when it is already known who the "other one" is), but sometimes it is necessary for both persons to go through a recognition, as for example Iphigenia is recognized by her brother° through the sending of the letter, but of him by Iphigenia another recognition is required.

These then are two elements of plot: peripety and recognition; third is the *pathos.* Of these, peripety and recognition have been discussed; a *pathos* is a destructive or painful act, such as deaths on stage, paroxysms of pain, woundings, and all that sort of thing.

SIGMUND FREUD (1856–1939)

The Oedipus Complex 1900–1930°

TRANSLATED BY JAMES STRACHEY

Sigmund Freud was the most celebrated psychiatrist of the twentieth century and the father of psychoanalytic theory. His research into the unconscious changed the way we think about the human mind, and his explorations into the symbolic

---

her brother: Orestes is Iphigenia's brother. Aristotle may be referring to a lost play.
1900–1930: *Interpretation of Dreams* was first published in 1900 and was updated regularly by Freud through eight editions. This passage is taken from the eighth edition, published in 1930.

meaning of dreams have been widely regarded as a breakthrough in connecting the meaning of world myth to personal life.

In his *Interpretation of Dreams* he turned to Sophocles' drama and developed his theories of the Oedipus complex and the Electra complex: the desire to kill one parent and marry the other may be rooted in the deepest natural psychological development of the individual. The following passage provides insight not only into a psychological state that, according to Freud, all humans may share but also into the way in which a man of Freud's temperament read and interpreted a great piece of literature. Like Sophocles himself, Freud believed that the myth underlying *Oedipus Rex* has a meaning and importance for all human beings.

In my experience, which is already extensive, the chief part in the mental lives of all children who later become psychoneurotics is played by their parents. Being in love with the one parent and hating the other are among the essential constituents of the stock of psychical impulses which is formed at that time and which is of such importance in determining the symptoms of the later neurosis. It is not my belief, however, that psychoneurotics differ sharply in this respect from other human beings who remain normal—that they are able, that is, to create something absolutely new and peculiar to themselves. It is far more probable—and this is confirmed by occasional observations on normal children—that they are only distinguished by exhibiting on a magnified scale feelings of love and hatred to their parents which occur less obviously and less intensely in the minds of most children.

This discovery is confirmed by a legend that has come down to us from classical antiquity: a legend whose profound and universal power to move can only be understood if the hypothesis I have put forward in regard to the psychology of children has an equally universal validity. What I have in mind is the legend of King Oedipus and Sophocles' drama which bears his name.

Oedipus, son of Laïus, King of Thebes, and of Jocasta, was exposed [to the elements and left to die] as an infant because an oracle had warned Laïus that the still unborn child would be his father's murderer. The child was rescued and grew up as a prince in an alien court, until, in doubts as to his origin, he too questioned the oracle and was warned to avoid his home since he was destined to murder his father and take his mother in marriage. On the road leading away from what he believed was his home, he met King Laïus and slew him in a sudden quarrel. He came next to Thebes and solved the riddle set him by the Sphinx who barred his way. Out of gratitude the Thebans made him their king and gave him Jocasta's hand in marriage. He reigned long in peace and honor, and she who, unknown to him, was his mother bore him two sons and two daughters. Then at last a plague broke out and the Thebans made inquiry once more of the oracle. It is at this point that Sophocles' tragedy opens. The messengers bring back the reply that the plague will cease when the murderer of Laïus has been driven from the land.

> But he, where is he? Where shall now be read
> The fading record of this ancient guilt?[1]

The action of the play consists in nothing other than the process of revealing, with cunning delays and ever-mounting excitement—a process that can be likened to the work of a psychoanalysis—that Oedipus himself is the murderer of Laïus, but further that he is the son of the murdered man and of Jocasta. Appalled at the

---

[1] Lewis Campbell's translation (1883), lines 108ff [Dudley Fitts and Robert Fitzgerald, *Sophocles: The Oedipus Cycle, an English Version* (Harcourt Brace & Company, 1949), Prologue, lines 112–13].

abomination which he has unwittingly perpetrated, Oedipus blinds himself and forsakes his home. The oracle has been fulfilled.

Oedipus Rex is what is known as a tragedy of destiny. Its tragic effect is said to lie in the contrast between the supreme will of the gods and the vain attempts of mankind to escape the evil that threatens them. The lesson which, it is said, the deeply moved spectator should learn from the tragedy is submission to the divine will and realization of his own impotence. Modern dramatists have accordingly tried to achieve a similar tragic effect by weaving the same contrast into a plot invented by themselves. But the spectators have looked on unmoved while a curse or an oracle was fulfilled in spite of all the efforts of some innocent man: later tragedies of destiny have failed in their effect.

If *Oedipus Rex* moves a modern audience no less than it did the contemporary Greek one, the explanation can only be that its effect does not lie in the contrast between destiny and human will, but is to be looked for in the particular nature of the material on which that contrast is exemplified. There must be something which makes a voice within us ready to recognize the compelling force of destiny in the *Oedipus,* while we can dismiss as merely arbitrary such dispositions as are laid down in [Grillparzer's] *Die Ahnfrau* or other modern tragedies of destiny. And a factor of this kind is in fact involved in the story of King Oedipus. His destiny moves us only because it might have been ours—because the oracle laid the same curse upon us before our birth as upon him. It is the fate of all of us, perhaps, to direct our first sexual impulse toward our mother and our first hatred and our first murderous wish against our father. Our dreams convince us that that is so. King Oedipus, who slew his father Laïus and married his mother Jocasta, merely shows us the fulfillment of our own childhood wishes. But, more fortunate than he, we have meanwhile succeeded, in so far as we have not become psychoneurotics, in detaching our sexual impulses from our mothers and in forgetting our jealousy of our fathers. Here is one in whom these primeval wishes of our childhood have been fulfilled, and we shrink back from him with the whole force of the repression by which those wishes have since that time been held down within us. While the poet, as he unravels the past, brings to light the guilt of Oedipus, he is at the same time compelling us to recognize our own inner minds, in which those same impulses, though suppressed, are still to be found. The contrast with which the closing Chorus leaves us confronted—

> . . . Fix on Oedipus your eyes,
> Who resolved the dark enigma, noblest champion and most wise.
> Like a star his envied fortune mounted beaming far and wide:
> Now he sinks in seas of anguish, whelmed beneath a raging tide . . .[2]

—strikes as a warning at ourselves and our pride, at us who since our childhood have grown so wise and so mighty in our own eyes. Like Oedipus, we live in ignorance of these wishes, repugnant to morality, which have been forced upon us by Nature, and after their revelation we may all of us well seek to close our eyes to the scenes of our childhood.[3]

---

[2]Lewis Campbell's translation, lines 1524ff [Fitts and Fitzgerald, antistrophe 2, lines 292–96].

[3][*Footnote added by Freud in 1914 edition.*] None of the findings of psychoanalytic research has provoked such embittered denials, such fierce opposition—or such amusing contortions—on the part of critics as this indication of the childhood impulses toward incest which persist in the unconscious. An attempt has even been made recently to make out, in the face of all experience, that the incest should only be taken as "symbolic."—Ferenczi (1912) has proposed an ingenious "overinterpretation" of the Oedipus myth, based on a passage in one of Schopenhauer's letters. [*Added 1919.*] Later studies have shown that the "Oedipus complex," which was touched upon for the first time in the above paragraphs in the *Interpretation of Dreams,* throws a light of undreamt-of importance on the history of the human race and the evolution of religion and morality.

There is an unmistakable indication in the text of Sophocles' tragedy itself that the legend of Oedipus sprang from some primeval dream material which had as its content the distressing disturbance of a child's relation to his parents owing to the first stirrings of sexuality. At a point when Oedipus, though he is not yet enlightened, has begun to feel troubled by his recollection of the oracle, Jocasta consoles him by referring to a dream which many people dream, though, as she thinks, it has no meaning:

> Many a man ere now in dreams hath lain
> With her who bare him. He hath least annoy
> Who with such omens troubleth not his mind.[4]

Today, just as then, many men dream of having sexual relations with their mothers, and speak of the fact with indignation and astonishment. It is clearly the key to the tragedy and the complement to the dream of the dreamer's father being dead. The story of Oedipus is the reaction of the imagination to these two typical dreams. And just as these dreams, when dreamt by adults, are accompanied by feelings of repulsion, so too the legend must include horror and self-punishment. Its further modification originates once again in a misconceived secondary revision of the material, which has sought to exploit it for theological purposes. . . . The attempt to harmonize divine omnipotence with human responsibility must naturally fail in connection with this subject matter just as with any other.

CLAUDE LÉVI-STRAUSS (1908–2009)

From The Structural Study of Myth   1955

Claude Lévi-Strauss was one of a handful of modern anthropologists whose interests span the range of thought, culture, and understanding. His work has been of immense influence on French intellectual life and, by extension, on the intellectual life of modern times. His works include *Triste Tropiques* (translated as *A World on the Wane*), about his own experiences as an anthropologist; *Structural Anthropology,* about the ways in which the study of anthropology implies a study of the structure of thought; and *Mythologies*, a four-volume summation of his thought. The excerpt that follows is structuralist in scope in that it attempts to understand the myth of Oedipus by examining the patterns of repetition in the original narrative. By setting up a grid, Lévi-Strauss begins to sort out the implications of the myth and to seek a meaning that is not necessarily apparent in the chronological order of the narrative. He examines the myth diachronically — across the lines of time — and thereby sees a new range of implications, which he treats as the structural implications of the myth. His reading is complex, suggesting that the Oedipus myth is a vegetation myth explaining the origins of mankind. Lévi-Strauss gives us a new way to interpret the significance of literary myths.

The time has come to give a concrete example of the method we propose. We will use the Oedipus myth which has the advantage of being well known to everybody and for which no preliminary explanation is therefore needed. By doing so,

---

[4]Lewis Campbell's translation, lines 982ff [Fitts and Fitzgerald, scene 3, lines 67–69].

I am well aware that the Oedipus myth has only reached us under late forms and through literary transfigurations concerned more with esthetic and moral preoccupations than with religious or ritual ones, whatever these may have been. But as will be shown later, this apparently unsatisfactory situation will strengthen our demonstration rather than weaken it.

The myth will be treated as would be an orchestra score perversely presented as a unilinear series and where our task is to reestablish the correct disposition. As if, for instance, we were confronted with a sequence of the type: 1,2,4,7,8,2,3,4,6, 8,1,4,5,7,8,1,2,5,7,3,4,5,6,8 . . . , the assignment being to put all the 1's together, all the 2's, the 3's, etc.; the result is a chart:

```
1   2     4      7   8
    2 3 4     6       8
1         4 5     7   8
1   2        5    7
        3 4 5
               6     8
```

We will attempt to perform the same kind of operation on the Oedipus myth, trying out several dispositions. [. . .] Let us suppose, for the sake of argument, that the best arrangement is the following (although it might certainly be improved by the help of a specialist in Greek mythology):

Kadmos seeks his sister Europa ravished by Zeus.		
	Kadmos kills the dragon.	
	The Spartoi kill each other.	
		Labdacos (Laios's father) = *lame* (?).
	Oedipus kills his father Laios.	Laios (Oedipus's father) = *left-sided* (?).
	Oedipus kills the Sphinx.	
Oedipus marries his mother Jocasta.		
	Eteocles kills his brother Polyneices.	Oedipus = *swollen-foot* (?).
Antigone buries her brother Polyneices despite prohibition.		

Thus, we find ourselves confronted with four vertical columns each of which includes several relations belonging to the same bundle. Were we to *tell* the myth, we would disregard the columns and read the rows from left to right and from top to bottom. But if we want to *understand* the myth, then we will have to disregard one half of the diachronic° dimension (top to bottom) and read from left to right, column after column, each one being considered as a unit.

All the relations belonging to the same column exhibit one common feature which it is our task to unravel. For instance, all the events grouped in the first column on the left have something to do with blood relations which are overemphasized, i.e., are subject to a more intimate treatment than they should be. Let us say, then, that the first column has as its common feature the *overrating of blood relations*. It is obvious that the second column expresses the same thing, but inverted: *underrating of blood relations*. The third column refers to monsters being slain. As to the fourth, a word of clarification is needed. The remarkable connotation of the surnames in Oedipus's father-line has often been noticed. However, linguists usually disregard it, since to them the only way to define the meaning of a term is to investigate all the contexts in which it appears, and personal names, precisely because they are used as such, are not accompanied by any context. With the method we propose to follow the objection disappears since the myth itself provides its own context. The meaningful fact is no longer to be looked for in the eventual sense of each name, but in the fact that all the names have a common feature: i.e., that they may eventually mean something and that all these hypothetical meanings (which may well remain hypothetical) exhibit a common feature, namely they refer to *difficulties to walk and to behave straight*.

What is then the relationship between the two columns on the right? Column three refers to monsters. The dragon is a chthonian° being which has to be killed in order that mankind be born from the earth; the Sphinx is a monster unwilling to permit men to live. The last unit reproduces the first one which has to do with the *autochthonous*° origin of mankind. Since the monsters are overcome by men, we may thus say that the common feature of the third column is *the denial of the autochthonous origin of man*.

This immediately helps us to understand the meaning of the fourth column. In mythology it is a universal character of men born from the earth that at the moment they emerge from the depth, they either cannot walk or do it clumsily. This is the case of the chthonian beings in the mythology of the Pueblo: Masauwu, who leads the emergence, and the chthonian Shumaikoli are lame ("bleeding-foot," "sore-foot"). The same happens to the Koskimo of the Kwakiutl after they have been swallowed by the chthonian monster, Tsiakish: when they returned to the surface of the earth "they limped forward or tripped sideways." Then the common feature of the fourth column is: *the persistence of the autochthonous origin of man*. It follows that column four is to column three as column one is to column two. The inability to connect two kinds of relationships is overcome (or rather replaced) by the positive statement that contradictory relationships are identical inasmuch as they are both self-contradictory in a similar way. Although this is still a provisional formulation of the structure of mythical thought, it is sufficient at this stage.

diachronic: Not ordered linearly in time but through time.
chthonian: From the underworld.
autochthonous: Native, aboriginal; in this case, born of the earth.

Turning back to the Oedipus myth, we may now see what it means. The myth has to do with the inability, for a culture which holds the belief that mankind is autochthonous [. . . ,] to find a satisfactory transition between this theory and the knowledge that human beings are actually born from the union of man and woman. Although the problem obviously cannot be solved, the Oedipus myth provides a kind of logical tool which, to phrase it coarsely, replaces the original problem: born from one or born from two? born from different or born from same? By a correlation of this type, the overrating of blood relations is to the underrating of blood relations as the attempt to escape autochthony is to the impossibility to succeed in it [that escape]. Although experience contradicts theory, social life verifies the cosmology by its similarity of structure. Hence cosmology is true.

Two remarks should be made at this stage.

In order to interpret the myth, we were able to leave aside a point which has until now worried the specialists, namely, that in the earlier (Homeric) versions of the Oedipus myth, some basic elements are lacking, such as Jocasta killing herself and Oedipus piercing his own eyes. These events do not alter the substance of the myth although they can easily be integrated, the first one as a new case of autodestruction (column three) while the second is another case of crippledness (column four). At the same time there is something significant in these additions since the shift from foot to head is to be correlated with the shift from: autochthonous origin negated to: self-destruction.

Thus, our method eliminates a problem which has been so far one of the main obstacles to the progress of mythological studies, namely, the quest for the *true* version, or the *earlier* one. On the contrary, we define the myth as consisting of all its versions; to put it otherwise: a myth remains the same as long as it is felt as such. A striking example is offered by the fact that our interpretation may take into account, and is certainly applicable to, the Freudian use of the Oedipus myth. Although the Freudian problem has ceased to be that of autochthony *versus* bisexual reproduction, it is still the problem of understanding how *one* can be born from *two*: how is it that we do not have only one procreator, but a mother plus a father? Therefore, not only Sophocles, but Freud himself, should be included among the recorded versions of the Oedipus myth on a par with earlier or seemingly more "authentic" versions.

Antigone

Antigone was Sophocles' thirty-second play, produced in March 441 BCE, when he was in his mid-fifties. It draws a powerful response from its audience partly because it portrays the conflict between two proud, willful people: Antigone, a daughter of Oedipus and Iokaste, and Kreon, Iokaste's brother and the king of Thebes. Its original success was due in part to its portrayal of the individual's struggle against a tyrannical king. After enjoying thirty years of peace with its archrival Sparta, Athens was moving slowly toward war; and the memory of previous tyrants—both good ones, like Peisistratus, and bad ones, like his son Hippias—remained in the minds of Sophocles' audience.

The main conflict in *Antigone* centers on a distinction between law and justice, the conflict between a human law and a higher law. Kreon, the uncle of

Antigone and Ismene, has made a decree: Polyneices, the brother of Antigone and Ismene, is guilty not only of killing his brother Eteocles but also of attacking the state and, like all traitors, will be denied a proper burial. When the action of the play begins, Antigone is determined to give her brother the burial that ancient tradition and her religious beliefs demand.

The opening dialogue with Ismene clarifies the important distinction between human law and the higher law on which Antigone says she must act. Ismene declares simply that she cannot go against the law of the citizens. Kreon has been willful in establishing the law, but it is nonetheless the law. Antigone, knowing full well the consequences of defying Kreon, nonetheless acts on her principles.

The complex conflict between Antigone and Kreon occurs on the level of citizen and ruler and is affected on the personal level by the relationship between Haimon, Kreon's son, and his intended bride, Antigone. The antagonism between Kreon and Haimon begins slowly, as Haimon appears to yield to the will of his father, but culminates in Haimon's ultimate rejection of his father by choosing to join Antigone in death.

When Teiresias reveals a prophecy of death and punishment and begs Kreon, for the sake of the suffering Thebes, to rescind his decree and give Polyneices a proper burial, Kreon willfully continues to heed his own declarations rather than oracular wisdom or the pleas of others.

By the time Kreon accepts Teiresias's prophecy, it is too late: he has lost his son, and his wife has killed herself. Power not only has corrupted Kreon but also has taken from him the people about whom he cared most. He emerges as an unyielding tyrant, guilty of making some of the same mistakes that haunted Oedipus.

It has never been easy to determine which of the two main characters is correct. The portrayal of Kreon as a tyrant content to take up the state as his private property tells us that he is not to be fully trusted. At the same time, Antigone knows that the social mores of Thebes require that a citizen obey the ruler. Antigone's great courage makes the audience feel sympathy and admiration for her. She is a martyr to her beliefs, an ancient Joan of Arc.

Antigone emerges as a heroine who presses forward in the full conviction that she is right. She must honor her dead brother at all costs. Even if she must break the law of the state, she must answer to what she regards as a higher law. As she says early in the play, she has "dared the crime of piety." Yet she has within her the complexity of all humans: she in one sense acts in the knowledge that she is right but in another dares Kreon to punish her. She challenges Kreon so boldly that her every move forces the proud Kreon to harden his position and set in motion the ultimate tragedy—the loss of all he holds dear. This is yet one more tragic irony in the Theban trilogy.

For a Drama in Depth tutorial on *Antigone*, click on *VirtualLit Drama Tutorials* at **bedfordstmartins.com/jacobus**.

Antigone in Performance

Since the eighteenth century, *Antigone* has been produced in Europe and the Western Hemisphere in more or less its original form and in various adaptations and rewritings. Jean Cocteau combined his version with music by Arthur Honegger in 1930. It was rewritten and produced by Walter Hasenclever in 1917 as a protest against the First World War and then in 1944 by Jean

Anouilh as a protest against Nazi occupation of Paris during World War II. The Royal Shakespeare Company produced *Antigone* along with all the other surviving Greek tragedies in 1980. Bertolt Brecht's production of *Antigone* in 1948 introduced a Gestapo officer and Nazi brutality. Athol Fugard's *The Island* (1973) features a remarkable production of *Antigone* as a play within a play, produced by convicts in a South African island jail as a Christmas entertainment for their jailers and specially invited white guests. Fugard found, as have so many other adapters and producers, that the political power of *Antigone* leaps out for virtually all contemporary audiences. Janusz Glowacki, a Polish playwright, produced *Antigone in New York* at the Arena Stage in Washington in March 1993. Inspired by both Sophocles and Beckett, it is set in Tompkins Square Park in New York. The action centers on a homeless Puerto Rican woman's efforts to bury a homeless man in the park. A highly regarded student production at Oxford in February 2004, directed by Zeynep Kayachin, was distinguished by the use of a new translation by a classics student, Lauren Curtiz. In recent years, student productions have, like the Oxford production, used video, projections, and contemporary music to advantage. In whatever format, the play demonstrates the durability of *Antigone*'s basic concept — that giving the deceased a decent burial is an essential attribute of humanity.

SOPHOCLES (c. 496–c. 406 BCE)

Antigone   441 BCE

TRANSLATED BY DUDLEY FITTS AND ROBERT FITZGERALD

Characters

ANTIGONE, } *daughters of Oedipus*
ISMENE,
EURYDICE, *wife of Kreon*
KREON, *King of Thebes*
HAIMON, *son of Kreon*
TEIRESIAS, *a blind seer*
A SENTRY
A MESSENGER
CHORUS

Scene: *Before the palace of Kreon, King of Thebes. A central double door, and two lateral doors. A platform extends the length of the facade, and from this platform three steps lead down into the orchestra, or chorus-ground.*

Time: *Dawn of the day after the repulse of the Argive army from the assault on Thebes.*

PROLOGUE°

(*Antigone and Ismene enter from the central door of the palace.*)

ANTIGONE: Ismene, dear sister,
    You would think that we had already suffered
      enough
    For the curse on Oedipus.°

Prologue: Portion of the play explaining the background and current action.   **3. curse on Oedipus:** Oedipus, king of Thebes and the father of Antigone and Ismene, was abandoned by his parents as an infant after the oracle foretold that he would one day kill his father and marry his mother. Rescued by a shepherd and raised by the king of Corinth, Oedipus returned years later to Thebes and unknowingly lived out the oracle's prophecy by killing Laios and marrying Iokaste. After his two sons, Eteocles and Polyneices, killed each other in combat, the throne went to Kreon, Iokaste's brother.

I cannot imagine any grief

5   That you and I have not gone through. And now—
Have they told you of the new decree of our King
Kreon?

ISMENE: I have heard nothing: I know

That two sisters lost two brothers, a double death

In a single hour; and I know that the Argive army

10   Fled in the night; but beyond this, nothing.

ANTIGONE: I thought so. And that is why I wanted
you

To come out here with me. There is something we
must do.

ISMENE: Why do you speak so strangely?

ANTIGONE: Listen, Ismene:

15   Kreon buried our brother Eteocles

With military honors, gave him a soldier's funeral,

And it was right that he should; but Polyneices,

Who fought as bravely and died as miserably,—

They say that Kreon has sworn

20   No one shall bury him, no one mourn for him,

But his body must lie in the fields, a sweet treasure

For carrion birds to find as they search for food.

That is what they say, and our good Kreon is
coming here

To announce it publicly; and the penalty—

Stoning to death in the public square!

25   There it is,

And now you can prove what you are:

A true sister, or a traitor to your family.

ISMENE: Antigone, you are mad! What could I
possibly do?

ANTIGONE: You must decide whether you will help
me or not.

30 ISMENE: I do not understand you. Help you in what?

ANTIGONE: Ismene, I am going to bury him. Will you
come?

ISMENE: Bury him! You have just said the new law
forbids it.

ANTIGONE: He is my brother. And he is your brother,
too.

ISMENE: But think of the danger! Think what Kreon
will do!

ANTIGONE: Kreon is not strong enough to stand in my

35   way.

ISMENE: Ah sister!

Oedipus died, everyone hating him

For what his own search brought to light, his eyes

Ripped out by his own hand; and Iocaste died,

His mother and wife at once: she twisted the

40   cords

That strangled her life; and our two brothers
died,

Each killed by the other's sword. And we are left:

But oh, Antigone,

Think how much more terrible than these

Our own death would be if we should go against

45   Kreon

And do what he has forbidden! We are only
women,

We cannot fight with men, Antigone!

The law is strong, we must give in to the law

In this thing, and in worse. I beg the Dead

To forgive me, but I am helpless: I must yield   50

To those in authority. And I think it is dangerous
business

To be always meddling.

ANTIGONE: If that is what you think,

I should not want you, even if you asked to
come.

You have made your choice, you can be what you
want to be.

But I will bury him; and if I must die,   55

I say that this crime is holy: I shall lie down

With him in death, and I shall be as dear

To him as he to me.

                It is the dead,

Not the living, who make the longest demands:

We die for ever . . .

             You may do as you like,   60

Since apparently the laws of the gods mean
nothing to you.

ISMENE: They mean a great deal to me; but I have no
strength

To break laws that were made for the public
good.

ANTIGONE: That must be your excuse, I suppose. But
as for me,

I will bury the brother I love.

ISMENE: Antigone,   65

I am so afraid for you!

ANTIGONE: You need not be:

You have yourself to consider, after all.

ISMENE: But no one must hear of this, you must tell
no one!

I will keep it a secret, I promise!

ANTIGONE: O tell it! Tell everyone!

Think how they'll hate you when it all comes out   70

If they learn that you knew about it all the time!

ISMENE: So fiery! You should be cold with fear.

ANTIGONE: Perhaps. But I am doing only what I
must.

ISMENE: But can you do it? I say that you cannot.

ANTIGONE: Very well: when my strength gives out,   75

I shall do no more.

ISMENE: Impossible things should not be tried at all.

ANTIGONE: Go away, Ismene:

I shall be hating you soon, and the dead will too,

For your words are hateful. Leave me my foolish
plan: 80

I am not afraid of the danger; if it means death,

It will not be the worst of deaths—death without
honor.

ISMENE: Go then, if you feel that you must.

You are unwise,

But a loyal friend indeed to those who love you.   85

(*Exit into the palace. Antigone goes off, left. Enter the
Chorus.*)

PARODOS° • Strophe° 1

CHORUS: Now the long blade of the sun, lying
　　Level east to west, touches with glory
　　Thebes of the Seven Gates. Open, unlidded
　　Eye of golden day! O marching light
5　　Across the eddy and rush of Dirce's stream,°
　　Striking the white shields of the enemy
　　Thrown headlong backward from the blaze of
　　　　morning!
CHORAGOS:° Polyneices their commander

Parodos: Song or ode chanted by the Chorus on its entry.
Strophe: Song sung by the Chorus as it danced from stage
right to stage left.　**5. Dirce's stream:** River near Thebes.
8. Choragos: Leader of the Chorus.

Roused them with windy phrases,
He the wild eagle screaming   10
Insults above our land,
His wings their shields of snow,
His crest their marshalled helms.

Antistrophe° 1

CHORUS: Against our seven gates in a yawning ring
　　The famished spears came onward in the night;   15
　　But before his jaws were sated with our blood,
　　Or pinefire took the garland of our towers,

Antistrophe: Song sung by the Chorus following the Strophe,
as they danced back from stage left to stage right.

Ismene tries to dissuade Antigone
(Martha Henry) in the Repertory
Theatre of Lincoln Center production
of *Antigone* at the Vivian Beaumont
Theater, directed by John Hirsch in
1971.

He was thrown back, and as he turned, great
   Thebes—
No tender victim for his noisy power—
20   Rose like a dragon behind him, shouting war.
CHORAGOS: For God hates utterly
   The bray of bragging tongues;
   And when he beheld their smiling,
   Their swagger of golden helms,
25   The frown of his thunder blasted
   Their first man from our walls.

Strophe 2

CHORUS: We heard his shout of triumph high in the air
   Turn to a scream; far out in a flaming arc
   He fell with his windy torch, and the earth struck him.
30   And others storming in fury no less than his
   Found shock of death in the dusty joy of battle.
CHORAGOS: Seven captains at seven gates
   Yielded their clanging arms to the god
   That bends the battle-line and breaks it.
35   These two only, brothers in blood,
   Face to face in matchless rage,
   Mirroring each the other's death
   Clashed in long combat.

Antistrophe 2

CHORUS: But now in the beautiful morning of victory
40   Let Thebes of the many chariots sing for joy!
   With hearts for dancing we'll take leave of war:
   Our temples shall be sweet with hymns of praise,
   And the long nights shall echo with our chorus.

SCENE 1

CHORAGOS: But now at last our new King is coming:
   Kreon of Thebes, Menoikeus' son.
   In this auspicious dawn of his reign
   What are the new complexities
5   That shifting Fate has woven for him?
   What is his counsel? Why has he summoned
   The old men to hear him?

(*Enter Kreon from the palace, center. He addresses the Chorus from the top step.*)

KREON: Gentlemen: I have the honor to inform you that
   our Ship of State, which recent storms have threat-
10   ened to destroy, has come safely to harbor at last,
   guided by the merciful wisdom of Heaven. I have
   summoned you here this morning because I know
   that I can depend upon you: your devotion to King
   Laios was absolute; you never hesitated in your
15   duty to our late ruler Oedipus; and when Oedipus
   died, your loyalty was transferred to his children.

Unfortunately, as you know, his two sons, the princes
Eteocles and Polyneices, have killed each other in
battle; and I, as the next in blood, have succeeded to
the full power of the throne.   20

I am aware, of course, that no Ruler can expect
complete loyalty from his subjects until he has been
tested in office. Nevertheless, I say to you at the very
outset that I have nothing but contempt for the kind
of Governor who is afraid, for whatever reason, to   25
follow the course that he knows is best for the State;
and as for the man who sets private friendship above
the public welfare,—I have no use for him, either. I
call God to witness that if I saw my country headed
for ruin, I should not be afraid to speak out plainly;   30
and I need hardly remind you that I would never
have any dealings with an enemy of the people. No
one values friendship more highly than I; but we
must remember that friends made at the risk of
wrecking our Ship are not real friends at all.   35

These are my principles, at any rate, and that is
why I have made the following decision concerning
the sons of Oedipus: Eteocles, who died as a man
should die, fighting for his country, is to be buried
with full military honors, with all the ceremony that   40
is usual when the greatest heroes die; but his brother
Polyneices, who broke his exile to come back with
fire and sword against his native city and the shrines
of his fathers' gods, whose one idea was to spill
the blood of his blood and sell his own people into   45
slavery—Polyneices, I say, is to have no burial:
no man is to touch him or say the least prayer for
him; he shall lie on the plain, unburied; and the birds
and the scavenging dogs can do with him whatever   50
they like.

This is my command, and you can see the wisdom
behind it. As long as I am King, no traitor is going to
be honored with the loyal man. But whoever shows
by word and deed that he is on the side of the
State,—he shall have my respect while he is living   55
and my reverence when he is dead.
CHORAGOS: If that is your will, Kreon son of
   Menoikeus,
You have the right to enforce it: we are yours.
KREON: That is my will. Take care that you do your
   part.
CHORAGOS: We are old men: let the younger ones
   carry it out.   60
KREON: I do not mean that: the sentries have been
   appointed.
CHORAGOS: Then what is it that you would have us
   do?
KREON: You will give no support to whoever breaks
   this law.
CHORAGOS: Only a crazy man is in love with death!
KREON: And death it is; yet money talks, and the wisest   65
   Have sometimes been known to count a few coins
   too many.

(*Enter Sentry from left.*)

Kreon (Philip Bosco), Antigone (Martha Henry), and Haimon (David Birney).

SENTRY: I'll not say that I'm out of breath from running,
 King, because every time I stopped to think about
70 what I have to tell you, I felt like going back. And all
 the time a voice kept saying, "You fool, don't you
 know you're walking straight into trouble?"; and then
 another voice: "Yes, but if you let somebody else get
 the news to Kreon first, it will be even worse than that
75 for you!" But good sense won out, at least I hope it
 was good sense, and here I am with a story that makes
 no sense at all; but I'll tell it anyhow, because, as they
 say, what's going to happen's going to happen and—
KREON: Come to the point. What have you to say?
80 SENTRY: I did not do it. I did not see who did it.
 You must not punish me for what someone else has done.
KREON: A comprehensive defense! More effective, perhaps,
 If I knew its purpose. Come: what is it?
SENTRY: A dreadful thing . . . I don't know how to
 put it—
KREON: Out with it!
85 SENTRY: Well, then;

The dead man—
          Polyneices—

(*Pause. The Sentry is overcome, fumbles for words.
Kreon waits impassively.*)

                              out there—
                                        someone,—
 New dust on the slimy flesh!

(*Pause. No sign from Kreon.*)

 Someone has given it burial that way, and
 Gone . . .

(*Long pause. Kreon finally speaks with deadly control.*)

KREON: And the man who dared do this?
SENTRY: I swear I
 Do not know! You must believe me!
                              Listen: 90
 The ground was dry, not a sign of digging, n
 Not a wheeltrack in the dust, no trace of an

It was when they relieved us this morning: and
  one of them,
The corporal, pointed to it.
         There it was,
The strangest—
95   Look:
The body, just mounded over with light dust: you
  see?
Not buried really, but as if they'd covered it
Just enough for the ghost's peace. And no sign
Of dogs or any wild animal that had been there.

100 And then what a scene there was! Every man of us
Accusing the other: we all proved the other man
  did it.
We all had proof that we could not have done it.
We were ready to take hot iron in our hands,
Walk through fire, swear by all the gods,
105 *It was not I!*
I do not know who it was, but it was not I!

(*Kreon's rage has been mounting steadily, but the Sentry
is too intent upon his story to notice it.*)

And then, when this came to nothing, someone
  said
A thing that silenced us and made us stare
Down at the ground: you had to be told the
  news,
110 And one of us had to do it! We threw the dice,
And the bad luck fell to me. So here I am,
No happier to be here than you are to have me:
Nobody likes the man who brings bad news.
CHORAGOS: I have been wondering, King: can it be
  that the gods have done this?
115 KREON (*furiously*): Stop!
Must you doddering wrecks
Go out of your heads entirely? "The gods"!
Intolerable!
The gods favor this corpse? Why? How had he
  served them?
120 Tried to loot their temples, burn their images,
Yes, and the whole State, and its laws with it!
Is it your senile opinion that the gods love to
  honor bad men?
A pious thought!—
       No, from the very beginning
There have been those who have whispered
  together,
125 Stiff-necked anarchists, putting their heads
  together,
Scheming against me in alleys. These are the men,
And they have bribed my own guard to do this
  thing.

(*Sententiously.*) Money!

There's nothing in the world so demoralizing as
  money.
130 Down go your cities,
Homes gone, men gone, honest hearts corrupted,
Crookedness of all kinds, and all for money!

(*To Sentry.*)   But you—
I swear by God and by the throne of God,
The man who has done this thing shall pay for it!
Find that man, bring him here to me, or your death   135
Will be the least of your problems: I'll string you
  up
Alive, and there will be certain ways to make you
Discover your employer before you die;
And the process may teach you a lesson you seem
  to have missed:
The dearest profit is sometimes all too dear: 140
That depends on the source. Do you understand
  me?
A fortune won is often misfortune.
SENTRY: King, may I speak?
KREON: Your very voice distresses me.
SENTRY: Are you sure that it is my voice, and not
  your conscience?
KREON: By God, he wants to analyze me now!   145
SENTRY: It is not what I say, but what has been done,
  that hurts you.
KREON: You talk too much.
SENTRY: Maybe; but I've done nothing.
KREON: Sold your soul for some silver: that's all
  you've done.
SENTRY: How dreadful it is when the right judge
  judges wrong!
KREON: Your figures of speech   150
May entertain you now; but unless you bring me
  the man,
You will get little profit from them in the end.

         (*Exit Kreon into the palace.*)

SENTRY: "Bring me the man"—!
I'd like nothing better than bringing him the man!
But bring him or not, you have seen the last of me
  here.   155
At any rate, I am safe!   (*Exit Sentry.*)

ODE° 1 • Strophe 1

CHORUS: Numberless are the world's wonders, but
  none
More wonderful than man; the stormgray sea
Yields to his prows, the huge crests bear him high;
Earth, holy and inexhaustible, is graven
With shining furrows where his plows have gone   5
Year after year, the timeless labor of stallions.

Antistrophe 1

The lightboned birds and beasts that cling to
  cover,
The lithe fish lighting their reaches of dim water,
All are taken, tamed in the net of his mind;
The lion on the hill, the wild horse windy-maned,   10

Ode: Song sung by the Chorus.

Resign to him; and his blunt yoke has broken
The sultry shoulders of the mountain bull.

Strophe 2

Words also, and thought as rapid as air,
He fashions to his good use; statecraft is his
15 And his the skill that deflects the arrows of snow,
The spears of winter rain: from every wind
He has made himself secure—from all but one:
In the late wind of death he cannot stand.

Antistrophe 2

O clear intelligence, force beyond all measure!
20 O fate of man, working both good and evil!
When the laws are kept, how proudly his city
  stands!
When the laws are broken, what of his city then?
Never may the anarchic man find rest at my
  hearth,
Never be it said that my thoughts are his
  thoughts.

SCENE 2

(*Reenter Sentry leading Antigone.*)

CHORAGOS: What does this mean? Surely this captive
  woman
  Is the Princess, Antigone. Why should she be
  taken?
SENTRY: Here is the one who did it! We caught her
  In the very act of burying him.—Where is
  Kreon?
CHORAGOS: Just coming from the house.

(*Enter Kreon, center.*)

5 KREON: What has happened?
  Why have you come back so soon?
SENTRY: (*expansively*):   O King,
  A man should never be too sure of anything:
  I would have sworn
  That you'd not see me here again: your anger
10 Frightened me so, and the things you threatened
    me with;
  But how could I tell then
  That I'd be able to solve the case so soon?
  No dice-throwing this time: I was only too glad to
    come!
  Here is this woman. She is the guilty one:
15 We found her trying to bury him.
  Take her, then; question her; judge her as you will.
  I am through with the whole thing now, and glad
    of it.
KREON: But this is Antigone! Why have you brought
  her here?
SENTRY: She was burying him, I tell you!

KREON: (*severely*):   Is this the truth? 20
SENTRY: I saw her with my own eyes. Can I say more?
KREON: The details: come, tell me quickly!
SENTRY: It was like this:
  After those terrible threats of yours, King,
  We went back and brushed the dust away from
    the body.
  The flesh was soft by now, and stinking,   25
  So we sat on a hill to windward and kept guard.
  No napping this time! We kept each other awake.
  But nothing happened until the white round sun
  Whirled in the center of the round sky over us:
  Then, suddenly,
  A storm of dust roared up from the earth, and the
    sky   30
  Went out, the plain vanished with all its trees
  In the stinging dark. We closed our eyes and
    endured it.
  The whirlwind lasted a long time, but it passed;
  And then we looked, and there was Antigone!   35
  I have seen
  A mother bird come back to a stripped nest, heard
  Her crying bitterly a broken note or two
  For the young ones stolen. Just so, when this girl
  Found the bare corpse, and all her love's work
    wasted,   40
  She wept, and cried on heaven to damn the hands
  That had done this thing.
                        And then she brought more dust
  And sprinkled wine three times for her brother's
    ghost.
  We ran and took her at once. She was not afraid,
  Not even when we charged her with what she had
    done.
  She denied nothing.   45
                        And this was a comfort to me,
  And some uneasiness: for it is a good thing
  To escape from death, but it is no great pleasure
  To bring death to a friend.
                        Yet I always say
  There is nothing so comfortable as your own safe
    skin!   50
KREON (*slowly, dangerously*): And you, Antigone,
  You with your head hanging,—do you confess
    this thing?
ANTIGONE: I do. I deny nothing.
KREON (*to Sentry*):   You may go.
                        (*Exit Sentry.*)
  (*To Antigone.*) Tell me, tell me briefly:
  Had you heard my proclamation touching this
    matter?   55
ANTIGONE: It was public. Could I help hearing it?
KREON: And yet you dared defy the law.
ANTIGONE: I dared.
  It was not God's proclamation. That final Justice
  That rules the world below makes no such laws.

  Your edict, King, was strong,
  But all your strength is weakness itself against

The immortal unrecorded laws of God.
They are not merely now: they were, and shall be,
Operative for ever, beyond man utterly.

65   I knew I must die, even without your decree:
I am only mortal. And if I must die
Now, before it is my time to die,
Surely this is no hardship: can anyone
Living, as I live, with evil all about me,
Think Death less than a friend? This death of mine
70   Is of no importance; but if I had left my brother
Lying in death unburied, I should have suffered.
Now I do not.
              You smile at me. Ah Kreon,
Think me a fool, if you like; but it may well be
That a fool convicts me of folly.
CHORAGOS: Like father, like daughter: both headstrong,
75   deaf to reason!
She has never learned to yield.
KREON: She has much to learn.
The inflexible heart breaks first, the toughest iron
Cracks first, and the wildest horses bend their necks
At the pull of the smallest curb.
                      Pride? In a slave?
80   This girl is guilty of a double insolence,
Breaking the given laws and boasting of it.
Who is the man here,
She or I, if this crime goes unpunished?
Sister's child, or more than sister's child,
85   Or closer yet in blood—she and her sister
Win bitter death for this!
(*To Servants.*)   Go, some of you,
Arrest Ismene. I accuse her equally.
Bring her: you will find her sniffling in the house
    there.

Her mind's a traitor: crimes kept in the dark
90   Cry for light, and the guardian brain shudders;
But how much worse than this
Is brazen boasting of barefaced anarchy!
ANTIGONE: Kreon, what more do you want than my
    death?
KREON: Nothing.
That gives me everything.
ANTIGONE: Then I beg you: kill me.
95   This talking is a great weariness: your words
Are distasteful to me, and I am sure that mine
Seem so to you. And yet they should not seem so:
I should have praise and honor for what I have
    done.
All these men here would praise me
100   Were their lips not frozen shut with fear of you.
(*Bitterly.*) Ah the good fortune of kings,
Licensed to say and do whatever they please!
KREON: You are alone here in that opinion.
ANTIGONE: No, they are with me. But they keep their
    tongues in leash.
105 KREON: Maybe. But you are guilty, and they are not.
ANTIGONE: There is no guilt in reverence for the dead.

KREON: But Eteocles—was he not your brother too?
ANTIGONE: My brother too.
KREON: And you insult his memory?
ANTIGONE (*softly*): The dead man would not say that
    I insult it.
KREON: He would: for you honor a traitor as much
    as him.   110
ANTIGONE: His own brother, traitor or not, and equal
    in blood.
KREON: He made war on his country. Eteocles
    defended it.
ANTIGONE: Nevertheless, there are honors due all the
    dead.
KREON: But not the same for the wicked as for the
    just.
ANTIGONE: Ah Kreon, Kreon,   115
    Which of us can say what the gods hold wicked?
KREON: An enemy is an enemy, even dead.
ANTIGONE: It is my nature to join in love, not hate.
KREON (*finally losing patience*): Go join them then; if
    you must have your love,
    Find it in hell!   120
CHORAGOS: But see, Ismene comes:

(*Enter Ismene, guarded.*)

    Those tears are sisterly, the cloud
    That shadows her eyes rains down gentle sorrow.
KREON: You too, Ismene,
    Snake in my ordered house, sucking my blood   125
    Stealthily—and all the time I never knew
    That these two sisters were aiming at my throne!
                                Ismene,
    Do you confess your share in this crime, or deny it?
    Answer me.
ISMENE: Yes, if she will let me say so. I am guilty.   130
ANTIGONE (*coldly*): No, Ismene. You have no right to
    say so.
    You would not help me, and I will not have you
    help me.
ISMENE: But now I know what you meant; and I am
    here
    To join you, to take my share of punishment.
ANTIGONE: The dead man and the gods who rule the
    dead   135
    Know whose act this was. Words are not friends.
ISMENE: Do you refuse me, Antigone? I want to die
    with you:
    I too have a duty that I must discharge to the dead.
ANTIGONE: You shall not lessen my death by sharing it.
ISMENE: What do I care for life when you are dead?   140
ANTIGONE: Ask Kreon. You're always hanging on his
    opinions.
ISMENE: You are laughing at me. Why, Antigone?
ANTIGONE: It's a joyless laughter, Ismene.
ISMENE: But can I do nothing?
ANTIGONE: Yes. Save yourself. I shall not envy you.
    There are those who will praise you; I shall have
    honor, too.   145
ISMENE: But we are equally guilty!

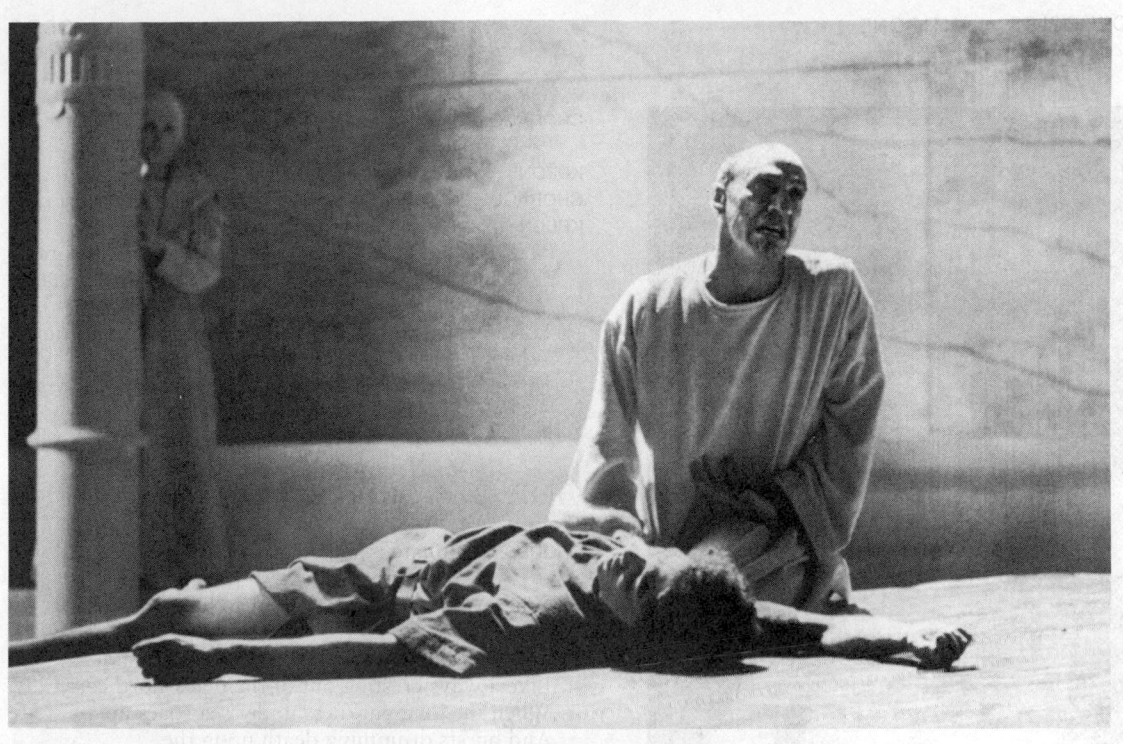

[TOP] Kreon (F. Murray Abraham) in a scene from the 1982 New York Shakespeare Festival production directed by Joseph Chaikin. [LEFT] Antigone (Lisa Banes) steadfastly admitting her guilt.

Randle Mell as Kreon and Alyssa Bresnahan as Antigone in the South Coast Repertory's 2004 production of *Antigone,* directed by Kate Whoriskey.

ANTIGONE: No more, Ismene.
    You are alive, but I belong to Death.
KREON (*to the Chorus*): Gentlemen, I beg you to
    observe these girls:
    One has just now lost her mind; the other,
150   It seems, has never had a mind at all.
ISMENE: Grief teaches the steadiest minds to waver,
    King.
KREON: Yours certainly did, when you assumed guilt
    with the guilty!
ISMENE: But how could I go on living without her?
KREON: You are.
    She is already dead.
ISMENE: But your own son's bride!
155 KREON: There are places enough for him to push his plow.
    I want no wicked women for my sons!
ISMENE: O dearest Haimon, how your father wrongs
    you!
KREON: I've had enough of your childish talk of
    marriage!

CHORAGOS: Do you really intend to steal this girl
    from your son?
KREON: No; Death will do that for me.
CHORAGOS: Then she must die?   160
KREON (*ironically*): You dazzle me.
               —But enough of this talk!
    (*To Guards.*) You, there, take them away and guard
    them well:
    For they are but women, and even brave men run
    When they see Death coming.
         (*Exeunt° Ismene, Antigone, and Guards.*)

ODE 2 • Strophe 1

CHORUS: Fortunate is the man who has never tasted
    God's vengeance!
Where once the anger of heaven has struck, that
    house is shaken
For ever: damnation rises behind each child
Like a wave cresting out of the black northeast,
When the long darkness under sea roars up   5
And bursts drumming death upon the
    windwhipped sand.

Antistrophe 1

I have seen this gathering sorrow from time long
    past
Loom upon Oedipus' children: generation from
    generation
Takes the compulsive rage of the enemy god.
So lately this last flower of Oedipus' line   10
Drank the sunlight! but now a passionate word
And a handful of dust have closed up all its beauty.

Strophe 2

What mortal arrogance
    Transcends the wrath of Zeus?
Sleep cannot lull him nor the effortless long months   15
Of the timeless gods: but he is young for ever,
And his house is the shining day of high Olympos.
    All that is and shall be,
    And all the past, is his.
No pride on earth is free of the curse of heaven.   20

Antistrophe 2

The straying dreams of men
    May bring them ghosts of joy:
But as they drowse, the waking embers burn them;   25
Or they walk with fixed eyes, as blind men walk.
But the ancient wisdom speaks for our own time:
    Fate works most for woe

164. [S.D.] *Exeunt*: Latin for "they go out."

With Folly's fairest show.
Man's little pleasure is the spring of sorrow.

SCENE 3

CHORAGOS: But here is Haimon, King, the last of all
    your sons.
    Is it grief for Antigone that brings him here,
    And bitterness at being robbed of his bride?

(*Enter Haimon.*)

KREON: We shall soon see, and no need of diviners.
                                                    —Son,
5   You have heard my final judgment on that girl:
    Have you come here hating me, or have you come
    With deference and with love, whatever I do?

HAIMON: I am your son, father. You are my guide.
    You make things clear for me, and I obey you.
    No marriage means more to me than your
10   continuing wisdom.

KREON: Good. That is the way to behave:
        subordinate
    Everything else, my son, to your father's will.
    This is what a man prays for, that he may get
    Sons attentive and dutiful in his house,
15   Each one hating his father's enemies,
    Honoring his father's friends. But if his sons
    Fail him, if they turn out unprofitably,
    What has he fathered but trouble for himself
    And amusement for the malicious?
                            So you are right
20   Not to lose your head over this woman.
    Your pleasure with her would soon grow cold,
        Haimon,
    And then you'd have a hellcat in bed and
        elsewhere.
    Let her find her husband in Hell!
    Of all the people in this city, only she
25   Has had contempt for my law and broken it.

    Do you want me to show myself weak before the
        people?
    Or to break my sworn word? No, and I will not.
    The woman dies.
    I suppose she'll plead "family ties." Well, let her.
30   If I permit my own family to rebel,
    How shall I earn the world's obedience?
    Show me the man who keeps his house in hand,
    He's fit for public authority.
                        I'll have no dealings
    With lawbreakers, critics of the government:
35   Whoever is chosen to govern should be obeyed—
    Must be obeyed, in all things, great and small,
    Just and unjust! O Haimon,
    The man who knows how to obey, and that man
        only,
    Knows how to give commands when the time
        comes.

You can depend on him, no matter how fast   40
The spears come: he's a good soldier, he'll stick it
    out.
Anarchy, anarchy! Show me a greater evil!
This is why cities tumble and the great houses rain
    down,
This is what scatters armies!
No, no: good lives are made so by discipline.   45
We keep the laws then, and the lawmakers,
And no woman shall seduce us. If we must lose,
Let's lose to a man, at least! Is a woman stronger
    than we?

CHORAGOS: Unless time has rusted my wits,
    What you say, King, is said with point and dignity.   50

HAIMON (*boyishly earnest*): Father:
    Reason is God's crowning gift to man, and you
        are right
    To warn me against losing mine. I cannot say—
    I hope that I shall never want to say!—that you
    Have reasoned badly. Yet there are other men   55
    Who can reason, too; and their opinions might be
        helpful.
    You are not in a position to know everything
    That people say or do, or what they feel:
    Your temper terrifies—everyone
    Will tell you only what you like to hear.   60
    But I, at any rate, can listen; and I have heard
        them
    Muttering and whispering in the dark about this
        girl.
    They say no woman has ever, so unreasonably,
    Died so shameful a death for a generous act:
    "She covered her brother's body. Is this indecent?   65
    She kept him from dogs and vultures. Is this a
        crime?
    Death?—She should have all the honor that we
        can give her!"

This is the way they talk out there in the city.
You must believe me:
Nothing is closer to me than your happiness.   70
What could be closer? Must not any son
Value his father's fortune as his father does his?
I beg you, do not be unchangeable:
Do not believe that you alone can be right.
The man who thinks that,   75
The man who maintains that only he has the power
To reason correctly, the gift to speak, the soul—
A man like that, when you know him, turns out
    empty.
It is not reason never to yield to reason!

In flood time you can see how some trees bend,   80
And because they bend, even their twigs are safe,
While stubborn trees are torn up, roots and all.
And the same thing happens in sailing:
Make your sheet fast, never slacken,—and over
    you go,
Head over heels and under: and there's your

Forget you are angry! Let yourself be moved!
I know I am young; but please let me say this:
The ideal condition
Would be, I admit, that men should be right by
     instinct;
90 But since we are all too likely to go astray,
The reasonable thing is to learn from those who
     can teach.
CHORAGOS: You will do well to listen to him, King,
If what he says is sensible. And you, Haimon,
Must listen to your father.—Both speak well.
KREON: You consider it right for a man of my years
95   and experience
To go to school to a boy?
HAIMON: It is not right
If I am wrong. But if I am young, and right,
What does my age matter?
KREON: You think it right to stand up for an anarchist?
100 HAIMON: Not at all. I pay no respect to criminals.
KREON: Then she is not a criminal?
HAIMON: The City would deny it, to a man.
KREON: And the City proposes to teach me how to rule?
HAIMON: Ah. Who is it that's talking like a boy now?
KREON: My voice is the one voice giving orders in
105   this City!
HAIMON: It is no City if it takes orders from one voice.
KREON: The State is the King!
HAIMON: Yes, if the State is a desert.

(Pause.)

KREON: This boy, it seems, has sold out to a woman.
HAIMON: If you are a woman: my concern is only for
           you.
KREON: So? Your "concern"! In a public brawl with
110   your father!
HAIMON: How about you, in a public brawl with
           justice?
KREON: With justice, when all that I do is within my
           rights?
HAIMON: You have no right to trample on God's right.
KREON (completely out of control): Fool, adolescent
           fool! Taken in by a woman!
115 HAIMON: You'll never see me taken in by anything vile.
KREON: Every word you say is for her!
HAIMON (quietly, darkly):   And for you.
And for me. And for the gods under the earth.
KREON: You'll never marry her while she lives.
HAIMON: Then she must die.—But her death will
           cause another.
120 KREON: Another?
Have you lost your senses? Is this an open threat?
HAIMON: There is no threat in speaking to emptiness.
KREON: I swear you'll regret this superior tone of
           yours!
You are the empty one!
HAIMON: If you were not my father,
125 I'd say you were perverse.
KREON: You girl-struck fool, don't play at words with
           me!

HAIMON: I am sorry. You prefer silence.
KREON: Now, by God—
I swear, by all the gods in heaven above us,
You'll watch it, I swear you shall!
(To the Servants.)   Bring her out!
Bring the woman out! Let her die before his eyes! 130
Here, this instant, with her bridegroom beside her!
HAIMON: Not here, no; she will not die here, King.
And you will never see my face again.
Go on raving as long as you've a friend to endure
     you.   (Exit Haimon.)
CHORAGOS: Gone, gone.   135
Kreon, a young man in a rage is dangerous!
KREON: Let him do, or dream to do, more than a
     man can.
He shall not save these girls from death.
CHORAGOS: These girls?
You have sentenced them both?
KREON: No, you are right.
I will not kill the one whose hands are clean.   140
CHORAGOS: But Antigone?
KREON (somberly):   I will carry her far away
Out there in the wilderness, and lock her
Living in a vault of stone. She shall have food,
As the custom is, to absolve the State of her
     death.
And there let her pray to the gods of hell: 145
They are her only gods:
Perhaps they will show her an escape from death,
Or she may learn,
                  though late,
That piety shown the dead is pity in vain.
                                  (Exit Kreon.)

ODE 3 • Strophe

CHORUS: Love, unconquerable
     Waster of rich men, keeper
     Of warm lights and all-night vigil
     In the soft face of a girl:
     Sea-wanderer, forest-visitor!   5
     Even the pure Immortals cannot escape you,
     And mortal man, in his one day's dusk,
     Trembles before your glory.

Antistrophe

     Surely you swerve upon ruin
     The just man's consenting heart,   10
     As here you have made bright anger
     Strike between father and son—
     And none has conquered but Love!
     A girl's glance working the will of heaven:
     Pleasure to her alone who mocks us,   15
     Merciless Aphrodite.°

16. Aphrodite: Goddess of love and beauty.

SCENE 4

CHORAGOS (*as Antigone enters guarded*): But I can
          no longer stand in awe of this,
     Nor, seeing what I see, keep back my tears.
     Here is Antigone, passing to that chamber
     Where all find sleep at last.

Strophe 1

5   ANTIGONE: Look upon me, friends, and pity me
          Turning back at the night's edge to say
          Good-by to the sun that shines for me no longer;
          Now sleepy Death
          Summons me down to Acheron,° that cold shore:
10   There is no bridesong there, nor any music.
     CHORUS: Yet not unpraised, not without a kind of
          honor,
          You walk at last into the underworld
          Untouched by sickness, broken by no sword.
          What woman has ever found your way to death?

Antistrophe 1

15   ANTIGONE: How often I have heard the story of
          Niobe,°
          Tantalos' wretched daughter, how the stone
          Clung fast about her, ivy-close: and they say
          The rain falls endlessly
          And sifting soft snow; her tears are never done.
20   I feel the loneliness of her death in mine.
     CHORUS: But she was born of heaven, and you
          Are woman, woman born. If her death is yours,
          A mortal woman's, is this not for you
          Glory in our world and in the world beyond?

Strophe 2

25   ANTIGONE: You laugh at me. Ah, friends, friends,
          Can you not wait until I am dead? O Thebes,
          O men many-charioted, in love with Fortune,
          Dear springs of Dirce, sacred Theban grove,
          Be witnesses for me, denied all pity,
30   Unjustly judged! and think a word of love
          For her whose path turns
          Under dark earth, where there are no more tears.
     CHORUS: You have passed beyond human daring and
          come at last
          Into a place of stone where Justice sits.
35   I cannot tell
          What shape of your father's guilt appears in this.

9. Acheron: River in Hades, domain of the dead.   15. Niobe:
When Niobe's many children (up to twenty in some accounts)
were slain in punishment for their mother's boastfulness, Niobe
was turned into a stone on Mount Sipylus. Her tears became
the mountain's streams.

Antistrophe 2

ANTIGONE: You have touched it at last: that bridal
          bed
     Unspeakable, horror of son and mother
          mingling:
     Their crime, infection of all our family!
     O Oedipus, father and brother!   40
     Your marriage strikes from the grave to murder
          mine.
     I have been a stranger here in my own land:
     All my life
     The blasphemy of my birth has followed me.
CHORUS: Reverence is a virtue, but strength   45
     Lives in established law: that must prevail.
     You have made your choice,
     Your death is the doing of your conscious
          hand.

Epode°

ANTIGONE: Then let me go, since all your words are
          bitter,
     And the very light of the sun is cold to me.   50
     Lead me to my vigil, where I must have
     Neither love nor lamentation; no song, but silence.

(*Kreon interrupts impatiently.*)

KREON: If dirges and planned lamentations could put
          off death,
     Men would be singing for ever.
     (*To the Servants.*)   Take her, go!
     You know your orders: take her to the vault   55
     And leave her alone there. And if she lives or dies,
     That's her affair, not ours: our hands are clean.
ANTIGONE: O tomb, vaulted bride-bed in eternal rock,
     Soon I shall be with my own again
     Where Persephone° welcomes the thin ghosts
          underground: 60
     And I shall see my father again, and you, mother,
     And dearest Polyneices—
                              dearest indeed
     To me, since it was my hand
     That washed him clean and poured the ritual wine:
     And my reward is death before my time!   65

     And yet, as men's hearts know, I have done no
          wrong,
     I have not sinned before God. Or if I have,
     I shall know the truth in death. But if the guilt
     Lies upon Kreon who judged me, then, I pray,
     May his punishment equal my own.
CHORAGOS: O passionate heart,   70
     Unyielding, tormented still by the same winds!

Epode: Song sung by the Chorus while standing still after singing the strophe and antistrophe.   60. Persephone: Abducted
by Pluto, god of the underworld, to be his queen.

KREON: Her guards shall have good cause to regret
    their delaying.
ANTIGONE: Ah! That voice is like the voice of death!
KREON: I can give you no reason to think you are
    mistaken.
75 ANTIGONE: Thebes, and you my fathers' gods,
    And rulers of Thebes, you see me now, the last
    Unhappy daughter of a line of kings,
    Your kings, led away to death. You will remember
    What things I suffer, and at what men's hands,
80   Because I would not transgress the laws of heaven.
             (*To the Guards, simply.*) Come: let us wait no
    longer.   (*Exit Antigone, left, guarded.*)

ODE 4 • Strophe 1

CHORUS: All Danae's beauty was locked away
    In a brazen cell where the sunlight could not come:
    A small room still as any grave, enclosed her.
    Yet she was a princess too,
5   And Zeus in a rain of gold poured love upon her.°
    O child, child,
    No power in wealth or war
    Or tough sea-blackened ships
    Can prevail against untiring Destiny!

Antistrophe 1

10 And Dryas's, son° also, that furious king,
    Bore the god's prisoning anger for his pride:
    Sealed up by Dionysos in deaf stone,
    His madness died among echoes.
    So at the last he learned what dreadful power
15   His tongue had mocked:
    For he had profaned the revels,
    And fired the wrath of the nine
    Implacable Sisters° that love the sound of the
    flute.

Strophe 2

And old men tell a half-remembered tale
20 Of horror° where a dark ledge splits the sea
    And a double surf beats on the gray shores:
    How a king's new woman, sick

1–5. **All Danae's beauty . . . poured love upon her:** Locked
away to prevent the fulfillment of a prophecy that she would
bear a son who would kill her father, Danae was nonetheless
impregnated by Zeus, who came to her in a shower of gold.
The prophecy was fulfilled by the son that came of their union.
10. Dryas's son: King Lycurgus of Thrace, whom Dionysus, god
of wine, caused to be stricken with madness. **18. Sisters:** The
Muses, nine sister goddesses who presided over poetry and music, arts and sciences. **19–20. half-remembered tale of horror:**
The second wife of King Phineas blinded the sons of his first
wife, Cleopatra, whom Phineas had imprisoned in a cave.

With hatred for the queen he had imprisoned,
Ripped out his two sons' eyes with her bloody
    hands
While grinning Ares° watched the shuttle plunge   25
Four times: four blind wounds crying for revenge,

Antistrophe 2

Crying, tears and blood mingled.—Piteously born,
Those sons whose mother was of heavenly birth!
Her father was the god of the North Wind
And she was cradled by gales,   30
She raced with young colts on the glittering hills
And walked untrammeled in the open light:
But in her marriage deathless Fate found means
To build a tomb like yours for all her joy.

SCENE 5

(*Enter blind Teiresias, led by a boy. The opening
speeches of Teiresias should be in singsong contrast to
the realistic lines of Kreon.*)

TEIRESIAS: This is the way the blind man comes,
    Princes, Princes,
    Lockstep, two heads lit by the eyes of one.
KREON: What new thing have you to tell us, old
    Teiresias?
TEIRESIAS: I have much to tell you: listen to the
    prophet, Kreon.
KREON: I am not aware that I have ever failed to
    listen.   5
TEIRESIAS: Then you have done wisely, King, and
    ruled well.
KREON: I admit my debt to you. But what have you
    to say?
TEIRESIAS: This, Kreon: you stand once more on the
    edge of fate.
KREON: What do you mean? Your words are a kind
    of dread.
TEIRESIAS: Listen, Kreon: 10
    I was sitting in my chair of augury, at the place
    Where the birds gather about me. They were all a-
    chatter,
    As is their habit, when suddenly I heard
    A strange note in their jangling, a scream, a
    Whirring fury; I knew that they were fighting,   15
    Tearing each other, dying
    In a whirlwind of wings clashing. And I was afraid.
    I began the rites of burnt-offering at the altar
    But Hephaistos° failed me: instead of bright flame,
    There was only the sputtering slime of the fat
    thigh-flesh
    Melting: the entrails dissolved in gray smoke,   20

---

25. Ares: God of war.   **19. Hephaistos:** God of fire.

The bare bone burst from the welter. And no
    blaze!

This was a sign from heaven. My boy described it,
Seeing for me as I see for others.
25 I tell you, Kreon, you yourself have brought
This new calamity upon us. Our hearths and altars
Are stained with the corruption of dogs and
    carrion birds
That glut themselves on the corpse of Oedipus's
    son.
The gods are deaf when we pray to them, their fire
30 Recoils from our offering, their birds of omen
Have no cry of comfort, for they are gorged
With the thick blood of the dead.
                              O my son,
These are no trifles! Think: all men make mistakes,
But a good man yields when he knows his course
    is wrong,
35 And repairs the evil. The only crime is pride.

Give in to the dead man, then: do not fight with a
    corpse—
What glory is it to kill a man who is dead?
Think, I beg you:
It is for your own good that I speak as I do.
40 You should be able to yield for your own good.
KREON: It seems that prophets have made me their
    especial province.
All my life long
I have been a kind of butt for the dull arrows
Of doddering fortune-tellers!
                          No, Teiresias:
45 If your birds—if the great eagles of God himself
Should carry him stinking bit by bit to heaven,
I would not yield. I am not afraid of pollution:
No man can defile the gods.
                      Do what you will,
Go into business, make money, speculate
50 In India gold or that synthetic gold from Sardis,
Get rich otherwise than by my consent to bury
    him.
Teiresias, it is a sorry thing when a wise man
Sells his wisdom, lets out his words for hire!
TEIRESIAS: Ah Kreon! Is there no man left in the
    world—
55 KREON: To do what?—Come, let's have the aphorism!
TEIRESIAS: No man who knows that wisdom
    outweighs any wealth?
KREON: As surely as bribes are baser than any
    baseness.
TEIRESIAS: You are sick, Kreon! You are deathly sick!
KREON: As you say: it is not my place to challenge a
    prophet.
60 TEIRESIAS: Yet you have said my prophecy is for sale.
KREON: The generation of prophets has always loved
    gold.
TEIRESIAS: The generation of kings has always loved
    brass.

KREON: You forget yourself! You are speaking to
    your King.
TEIRESIAS: I know it. You are a king because of me.
KREON: You have a certain skill; but you have sold
    out.   65
TEIRESIAS: King, you will drive me to words that—
KREON: Say them, say them!
    Only remember: I will not pay you for them.
TEIRESIAS: No, you will find them too costly.
KREON: No doubt. Speak:
    Whatever you say, you will not change my will.
TEIRESIAS: Then take this, and take it to heart!   70
The time is not far off when you shall pay back
Corpse for corpse, flesh of your own flesh.
You have thrust the child of this world into living
    night,
You have kept from the gods below the child that
    is theirs:
The one in a grave before her death, the other,   75
Dead, denied the grave. This is your crime:
And the Furies° and the dark gods of Hell
Are swift with terrible punishment for you.

Do you want to buy me now, Kreon?

                                  Not many days,
And your house will be full of men and women
    weeping,   80
And curses will be hurled at you from far
Cities grieving for sons unburied, left to rot
Before the walls of Thebes.

These are my arrows, Kreon: they are all for you.

(To Boy.) But come, child: lead me home.   85
Let him waste his fine anger upon younger men.
Maybe he will learn at last
To control a wiser tongue in a better head.

                              (Exit Teiresias.)

CHORAGOS: The old man has gone, King, but his words
    Remain to plague us. I am old, too,   90
    But I cannot remember that he was ever false.
KREON: That is true.... It troubles me.
    Oh it is hard to give in! but it is worse
    To risk everything for stubborn pride.
CHORAGOS: Kreon: take my advice.
KREON: What shall I do?   95
CHORAGOS: Go quickly: free Antigone from her vault
    And build a tomb for the body of Polyneices.
KREON: You would have me do this!
CHORAGOS: Kreon, yes!
    And it must be done at once: God moves
    Swiftly to cancel the folly of stubborn men.   100
KREON: It is hard to deny the heart! But I
    Will do it: I will not fight with destiny.

77. **Furies:** Spirits called on to avenge crimes, especially those
against kin.

CHORAGOS: You must go yourself, you cannot leave
　　it to others.
KREON: I will go.
　　　　—Bring axes, servants:
　　Come with me to the tomb. I buried her, I
105　Will set her free.
　　　　　　Oh quickly!
　　My mind misgives—
　　The laws of the gods are mighty, and a man must
　　　　serve them
　　To the last day of his life!　　　　(*Exit Kreon.*)

PAEAN° • Strophe 1

CHORAGOS: God of many names
CHORUS:　　　　　　　　O Iacchos
　　　　　　　　　　　　　　son
　　of Kadmeian Semele
　　　　　　　　O born of the Thunder!
　　Guardian of the West
　　　　　　　　　　Regent
　　of Eleusis' plain
　　　　　　　　O Prince of maenad Thebes
5　and the Dragon Field by rippling Ismenos:°

Antistrophe 1

CHORAGOS: God of many names
CHORUS:　　　　　　　　　　the flame of torches
　　flares on our hills
　　　　　　　　the nymphs of Iacchos
　　dance at the spring of Castalia:°
　　from the vine-close mountain
　　　　　　　　　　come ah come in ivy:
10　*Evohe evohe!*° sings through the streets of Thebes

Strophe 2

CHORAGOS: God of many names
CHORUS:　　　　　　　　　Iacchos of Thebes
　　heavenly Child
　　　　　　　　of Semele bride of the Thunderer!
　　The shadow of plague is upon us:
　　　　　　　　　　come

Paean: A song of praise or prayer. **1–5. God of many names . . .
rippling Ismenos:** A litany of names for Dionysus (Iacchos): he
was son of Zeus ("Thunder") and Semele; he was honored in
secret rites at Eleusis; and he was worshiped by the Maenads
of Thebes. Kadmos, Semele's father, sowed dragon's teeth in
a field beside the river Ismenos from which sprang warriors
who became the first Thebans.　**8. spring of Castalia:** A spring
on Mount Parnassus used by priestesses of Dionysus in rites of
purification.　**10. *Evohe evohe!*:** Cry of the Maenads to Dionysus.

with clement feet
　　　　　　oh come from Parnasos
down the long slopes
　　　　　　across the lamenting water　　15

Antistrophe 2

CHORAGOS: Io Fire! Chorister of the throbbing stars!
　　O purest among the voices of the night!
　　Thou son of God, blaze for us!
CHORUS: Come with choric rapture of circling
　　　Maenads
　　Who cry *Io Iacche!*°
　　　　　　God of many names!　　20

EXODOS°

(*Enter Messenger from left.*)

MESSENGER: Men of the line of Kadmos, you who
　　live
　　Near Amphion's citadel,°
　　　　　　　　　I cannot say
　　Of any condition of human life "This is fixed,
　　This is clearly good, or bad." Fate raises up,
　　And Fate casts down the happy and unhappy alike:　5
　　No man can foretell his Fate.
　　　　　　　　Take the case of Kreon:
　　Kreon was happy once, as I count happiness:
　　Victorious in battle, sole governor of the land,
　　Fortunate father of children nobly born.
　　And now it has all gone from him! Who can say　10
　　That a man is still alive when his life's joy fails?
　　He is a walking dead man. Grant him rich,
　　Let him live like a king in his great house:
　　If his pleasure is gone, I would not give
　　So much as the shadow of smoke for all he owns.　15
CHORAGOS: Your words hint at sorrow: what is your
　　news for us?
MESSENGER: They are dead. The living are guilty of
　　their death.
CHORAGOS: Who is guilty? Who is dead? Speak!
MESSENGER:　　　　　　　　　Haimon.
　　Haimon is dead; and the hand that killed him
　　Is his own hand.
CHORAGOS:　　　His father's? or his own?　　20
MESSENGER: His own, driven mad by the murder his
　　father had done.
CHORAGOS: Teiresias, Teiresias, how clearly you saw
　　it all!
MESSENGER: This is my news: you must draw what
　　conclusions you can from it.
CHORAGOS: But look: Eurydice, our Queen:

20. *Io Iacche!*: Ritual cry.　**Exodos:** Final scene.　**2. Amphion's
citadel:** A name for Thebes.

25   Has she overheard us?

(*Enter Eurydice from the palace, center.*)

EURYDICE: I have heard something, friends:
As I was unlocking the gate of Pallas'° shrine,
For I needed her help today, I heard a voice
Telling of some new sorrow. And I fainted
There at the temple with all my maidens
30   about me.
But speak again: whatever it is, I can bear it:
Grief and I are no strangers.
MESSENGER: Dearest Lady,
I will tell you plainly all that I have seen.
I shall not try to comfort you: what is the use,
35   Since comfort could lie only in what is not true?
The truth is always best.
                          I went with Kreon
To the outer plain where Polyneices was lying,
No friend to pity him, his body shredded by dogs.
We made our prayers in that place to Hecate
And Pluto,° that they would be merciful. And we
40   bathed
The corpse with holy water, and we brought
Fresh-broken branches to burn what was left of it,
And upon the urn we heaped up a towering
        barrow
Of the earth of his own land.
                          When we were done, we ran
To the vault where Antigone lay on her couch of
45   stone.
One of the servants had gone ahead,
And while he was yet far off he heard a voice
Grieving within the chamber, and he came back
And told Kreon. And as the King went closer,
50   The air was full of wailing, the words lost,
And he begged us to make all haste. "Am I a
        prophet?"
He said, weeping, "And must I walk this road,
The saddest of all that I have gone before?
My son's voice calls me on. Oh quickly, quickly!
55   Look through the crevice there, and tell me
If it is Haimon, or some deception of the gods!"

We obeyed; and in the cavern's farthest corner
We saw her lying:
She had made a noose of her fine linen veil
60   And hanged herself. Haimon lay beside her,
His arms about her waist, lamenting her,
His love lost under ground, crying out
That his father had stolen her away from him.

When Kreon saw him the tears rushed to his eyes
And he called to him: "What have you done,
65   child? speak to me.

27. **Pallas:** Pallas Athene, goddess of wisdom.   39–40. **Hecate
and Pluto:** Goddess of witchcraft and sorcery and King of
Hades, the underworld.

What are you thinking that makes your eyes so
        strange?
O my son, my son, I come to you on my knees!"
But Haimon spat in his face. He said not a word,
Staring—
            And suddenly drew his sword
And lunged. Kreon shrank back, the blade missed;
        and the boy,   70
Desperate against himself, drove it half its length
Into his own side, and fell. And as he died
He gathered Antigone close in his arms again,
Choking, his blood bright red on her white cheek.
And now he lies dead with the dead, and she is his   75
At last, his bride in the house of the dead.

                (*Exit Eurydice into the palace.*)

CHORAGOS: She has left us without a word. What
        can this mean?
MESSENGER: It troubles me, too; yet she knows what
        is best,
Her grief is too great for public lamentation,
And doubtless she has gone to her chamber to
        weep   80
For her dead son, leading her maidens in his dirge.

(*Pause.*)

CHORAGOS: It may be so: but I fear this deep silence.
MESSENGER: I will see what she is doing. I will go in.
                (*Exit Messenger into the palace.*)

(*Enter Kreon with attendants, bearing Haimon's body.*)

CHORAGOS: But here is the king himself: oh look at him,
        Bearing his own damnation in his arms.   85
KREON: Nothing you say can touch me any more.
My own blind heart has brought me
From darkness to final darkness. Here you see
The father murdering, the murdered son—
And all my civic wisdom!   90

Haimon my son, so young, so young to die,
I was the fool, not you; and you died for me.
CHORAGOS: That is the truth; but you were late in
        learning it.
KREON: This truth is hard to bear. Surely a god
Has crushed me beneath the hugest weight of
        heaven,   95
And driven me headlong a barbaric way
To trample out the thing I held most dear.

The pains that men will take to come to pain!

(*Enter Messenger from the palace.*)

MESSENGER: The burden you carry in your hands is
        heavy,
But it is not all: you will find more in your house.   100
KREON: What burden worse than this shall I find
        there?
MESSENGER: The Queen is dead.
KREON: O port of death, deaf world,

Is there no pity for me? And you, Angel of evil,
105 I was dead, and your words are death again.
Is it true, boy? Can it be true?
Is my wife dead? Has death bred death?
MESSENGER: You can see for yourself.

(*The doors are opened and the body of Eurydice is disclosed within.*)

KREON: Oh pity!
110 All true, all true, and more than I can bear!
O my wife, my son!
MESSENGER: She stood before the altar, and her heart
Welcomed the knife her own hand guided,
And a great cry burst from her lips for Megareus°
dead,
And for Haimon dead, her sons; and her last
115 breath
Was a curse for their father, the murderer of her sons.
And she fell, and the dark flowed in through her
closing eyes.
KREON: O God, I am sick with fear.
Are there no swords here? Has no one a blow for
me?
MESSENGER: Her curse is upon you for the deaths of
120 both.

114. Megareus: Son of Kreon and brother of Haimon, Megareus sacrificed himself in the unsuccessful attack upon Thebes, believing that his death was necessary to save Thebes.

KREON: It is right that it should be. I alone am guilty.
I know it, and I say it. Lead me in,
Quickly, friends.
I have neither life nor substance. Lead me in.
CHORAGOS: You are right, if there can be right in so
much wrong. 125
The briefest way is best in a world of sorrow.
KREON: Let it come,
Let death come quickly, and be kind to me.
I would not ever see the sun again.
CHORAGOS: All that will come when it will; but we,
meanwhile, 130
Have much to do. Leave the future to itself.
KREON: All my heart was in that prayer!
CHORAGOS: Then do not pray any more: the sky is deaf.
KREON: Lead me away. I have been rash and foolish.
I have killed my son and my wife. 135
I look for comfort; my comfort lies here dead.
Whatever my hands have touched has come to
nothing.
Fate has brought all my pride to a thought of dust.

(*As Kreon is being led into the house, the Choragos advances and speaks directly to the audience.*)

CHORAGOS: There is no happiness where there is no
wisdom;
No wisdom but in submission to the gods. 140
Big words are always punished,
And proud men in old age learn to be wise.

COMMENTARY

OLIVER TAPLIN (b. 1943)

Emotion and Meaning in Greek Tragedy 1983

Scholar Oliver Taplin focuses on one of Aristotle's concerns in his commentary on tragedy: the emotions aroused by drama. Tragedies were noted for their capacity to evoke pity and fear in the audience. Taplin helps us understand how an audience's emotional response can clarify our critical view of tragedy. He explores the argument that devalues an emotional response to tragedy, and then he considers the proposition that "tragedy is essentially the emotional experience of its audience."

It seems to me, then, that Gorgias° is right that tragedy is essentially the *emotional experience of its audience.* Whatever it tells us about the world is conveyed by means of these emotions. Plato agreed with Gorgias in this, but he disapproved of the process and regarded it as harmful. Aristotle agreed with him too, but, contrary to Plato, regarded it as beneficial and salutary. Plato's objection was that such emotions are not the province of the highest part of the soul, the intellectual part. This is the forefather of the error made by so many later critics who have not acknowledged the centrality of emotion in the communication of tragedy. They think that if tragedy is essentially an emotional experience, it must be *solely* that; and they think this because they assume that strong emotion is necessarily in opposition to thought, that the psychic activities are mutually exclusive. But is this right? Understanding, reason, learning, moral discrimination; these things are not, in my experience, incompatible with emotion (nor presumably in the experience of Gorgias and Aristotle): What is incompatible is cold insensibility. Whether or not emotion is inimical to such intellectual processes depends on the *circumstances in which it is aroused.*

The characteristic tragic emotions—pity, horror, fascination, indignation, and so forth—are felt in many other situations besides in the theater. Above all we suffer them in the face of the misfortunes of real life, of course. What distinguishes the experience of a great tragedy? For one thing, as already remarked, we feel for the fortunes of people who have no direct personal relation to us: While this does not decrease the intensity of the emotion, it affords us some distance and perspective. We can feel and at the same time observe from outside. But does this distinguish tragedy from other "contrived" emotional experiences (most of them tending to the anti-intellectual), for example an animal hunt, a football match, an encounter group, reading a thriller, or watching a horror movie? Well, the experience of tragedy is by no means a random series of sensations. Our emotional involvement has perspective and context at the same time, and not just in retrospect. Thus the events of the tragedy are in an ordered *sequence,* a sequence which gives shape and comprehensibility to what we feel. And, most important of all, the affairs of the characters which move us are given a moral setting which is argued and explored in the play. They act and suffer within situations of moral conflict, or social, intellectual, and theological conflict. The quality of the tragedy depends *both* on its power to arouse our emotions *and* on the setting of those emotions in a sequence of moral and intellectual complications which is set out and examined. Tragedy evokes our feelings for others, like much else; but it is distinguished by the order and significance it imparts to suffering. So if the audience is not moved, then the tragedy, however intellectual, is a total failure: If its passions are aroused, but in a thoughtless, amorphous way, then it is merely a bad tragedy, sensational, melodramatic.

Thus it is that our emotions in the theater, far from driving out thought and meaning, are indivisible from them: They are simultaneous and mutually dependent. The experience of tragedy can achieve this coherence in a way that the emotional experiences of real life generally cannot because they are too close, too cluttered with detail and partiality, to be seen in perspective. Tragedy makes us feel that we understand life in its tragic aspects. We have the sense that we can better sympathize with and cope with suffering, misfortune, and waste. It is this sense of understanding (not isolated pearls of wisdom) that is the "message" of a

---

Gorgias: Greek orator and rhetorician (c. 483–376 BCE).

tragedy, that the great playwright imparts. This is well put in T. S. Eliot's° essay "Shakespeare and the Stoicism of Seneca," where he argues that it is the quality of the emotional expression rather than the quality of the philosophy which makes literature great, which makes it "strong, true and informative . . . useful and beneficial in the sense in which poetry is useful and beneficial." "All great poetry," Eliot writes, "gives the illusion of a view of life . . . for every precise emotion tends towards intellectual formulation."

T. S. Eliot: Poet and critic (1888–1965).

Euripides

Euripides (c. 485–c. 406 BCE), last of the great Greek tragedians, did not enjoy the personal popularity accorded Aeschylus and Sophocles, possibly because his work criticized Athenian politics and society. Moreover, he was not highly regarded because he broke away from the formality of language and theme of his predecessors.

Euripides was raised in Salamis, the island from which the Greeks decisively defeated the Persians in 480 BCE. This victory heralded the Periclean Age (c. 462–404 BCE), when Athens enjoyed its greatest power. During that time, however, the Athenians spent almost three decades fighting the Peloponnesian Wars (431–404 BCE), which drained their energies and treasury. Eventually, they were forced to relinquish their dominance to Sparta. In such an environment, the officials and patriots of Athens were not happy with the work of someone who reminded them of their mistakes and questioned their values.

Euripides is especially noted for shifting the focus of dramatic events from the gods to humans. He valued individual human beings and the working of their wills. Influenced by the teaching of the Sophists, wandering professors who taught argument and philosophy, he agreed with Protagoras's principle "Man is the measure of all things." The ancients sometimes referred to Euripides as the philosopher of the stage.

Euripides continued Aeschylus's innovations in his use of the *skene*. Instead of representing the front of a palace, the *skene* in Euripides' plays sometimes represented a peasant's hut, a rural shrine, or some other common structure. He was interested in theatrical devices, especially machines that gave him the opportunity to achieve dramatic effects. He often used the *mekane*—a crane or derrick that lifted actors in or out of the play—to resolve his dramas when his characters found themselves in impossible situations. His choral odes, although beautiful, are sometimes considered detachable from the episodes of dramatic action. Moreover, his dialogue is more colloquial—closer to everyday speech—than is the dialogue found in other Greek tragedies. All these deviations from the dramatic norm emphasize the humanity in Euripides' plays and elevate human values over those of the gods.

One aspect of his dramatic critique of Greek culture was an unusual emphasis on women. Medea is the first thoroughly developed female character in Greek drama. She is treated as an independent woman, not just as Jason's wife or as someone's mother. She is herself. Athenians, intolerant of foreigners and women, considered both groups to be inferior to aristocratic Greek men. It is no wonder that of the twenty plays Euripides produced at the feasts of Dionysus, only five won prizes. Ten of Euripides' surviving plays place women at their center.

Eighteen months before his death, Euripides left Athens for the court of King Archelaus in Macedon. His departure may have signaled his dissatisfaction with the politics of Athens, or it may have been prompted by the indifference of Athens to his talents. This indifference did not persist, however;

Euripides' works were performed long after his death, and, ironically, his posthumous popularity dwarfed that of the other tragic playwrights.

Of Euripides' ninety-two plays, eighteen survive—more than twice as many as survive from any other Greek tragedian: *Alcestis* (438 BCE), *Medea* (431), *The Children of Heracles* (c. 430), *Hippolytus* (428), *Andromache* (426?), *Hecuba* (c. 424), *Cyclops* (c. 423), *The Suppliants* (c. 422), *Electra* (c. 417), *Heracles* (c. 417), *The Trojan Women* (415), *Helen* (412), *Iphegenia in Taurus* (c. 412), *The Phoenician Women* (c. 412–408), *Ion* (c. 411), *Orestes* (408), *The Bacchae* (405), and *Iphigenia in Aulis* (405). Another play, *Rhesus*, long attributed to Euripides, is now thought to have been written by an anonymous fourth-century-BCE playwright.

For links to resources about Euripides, click on *AuthorLinks* at bedfordstmartins.com/jacobus.

The Bacchae

Among the last of Euripides' plays, performed in the Theatre of Dionysus in Athens after his death (406 BCE), *The Bacchae* has been referred to as his finest work. It is also his most mysterious work, a play that has been interpreted in a dizzying variety of ways, particularly psychologically as a confrontation between intellect and passions. Dionysus (also called Bacchus) is the god of wine and pleasure. He is opposed in this play by a young man, King Pentheus, a moralistic upholder of the political establishment of Thebes.

Dionysus in his first speech establishes the conflict: he has returned to Thebes from an extensive tour of Asia, where he has spread his religious cult, to counter rumors that he is not the son of the god Zeus but the son of a mortal man. He has returned in the form of a man to reveal himself as a god. He has already enchanted the women of Thebes and sent them to the mountains, into an Eden-like environment in which they are in complete harmony with nature, wearing skins instead of cloth, touching and communing with a great many animals. In essence, they revel in their animal nature, which we are to understand as implying a potential for both innocence and profound violence.

Pentheus, perhaps because he is young, takes a hard-line position against Dionysus, in part because he believes that the women in the mountains are participating in some form of sexual orgy. During Euripides' life, certain religious cults were sometimes orgiastic in their expression. However, Dionysus tells us that the Bacchantes are completely chaste. The older men, the seer Teiresius and Cadmus, grandfather of Pentheus and Dionysus, both dressed in "Dionysiac costume," try to soften Pentheus's position, insisting that he is foolish to try to suppress the expression of the cult of Dionysus because the dionysian forces are part of our nature—the god is in us.

The violence ultimately unleashed on Pentheus is foreshadowed in his own speech complaining about "the women [who] wander off / to hidden nooks where they serve the lusts of men" (222–23), in which he refers to hunting down all the women and caging them, including his mother and Autonoe, the mother of Actaeon, who was torn to pieces in an earlier hunt by his own hounds. The tearing apart and eating of animals is natural in the animal world, but in Pentheus's world, the world of intellectual civilization, it is unnatural. Yet Pentheus himself threatens to capture Dionysus and "By god, I'll have his head cut off!" (241).

Ultimately, the conflict between a mortal and a god must end with the god wreaking havoc. As critics have observed, Pentheus is in the wrong in trying to prevent the worship of Dionysus, as well as in his condemnation of the Bacchantes' rites. Euripides seems to be saying that there is in all of us an animal nature that at proper times must have an outlet, or else the suppression of our animal spirits will result in destruction, much like the destruction of the palace in this play. Civilization, in other words, is built on a volcano.

In the final scenes, Pentheus, dressed as a woman to observe the rites of the priestesses, is discovered and hunted down. His mother, Agave, driven mad by Dionysus, imagines Pentheus as a lion, kills him, and carries his head on a stake, only to find to her horror that she has killed her own son. The violence of the god may be inexplicable, but we are to understand that it is the nature of the godhead. Our modern sense of what it means to worship a god is irrelevant to the Greek sense of worship—for the Greeks, to worship simply means to do as the god demands we do. As American classicist William Arrowsmith has said, Dionysus is necessity.

The story of Dionysus was noted in Homer's *Iliad* (6.130–140) three centuries before Euripides chose the material for his play. And Aeschylus had written a now-lost play treating the same mythic material, which he entitled *Pentheus,* in keeping with the Greek tradition of naming tragedies after the protagonist. But Euripides named his play after the women in the chorus, the Bacchantes. To enhance the status of the mass of women in the play was, for Euripides, an unusual decision. His other plays portray few morally superior women, something for which he was often criticized.

The Bacchae in Performance

The play may have been produced in Macedonia, the hill country where Euripides spent his last years in exile. But its first production took place in Athens under the guidance of his son in a trilogy of his last three plays—*The Bacchae, Iphigenia at Aulis,* and *Alcmaeon in Corinth* (a lost play)—in 406 BCE, the year of Euripides' death. Euripides was awarded one of his few first prizes for that production. After the great age of Greek drama, the opportunities for performance were few. In the late nineteenth century, *The Bacchae* was still considered a morally questionable play. But since then there have been many different adaptations and a great many productions throughout the world. The most controversial is probably Richard Schechner's *Dionysus in '69,* performed in a garage in New York, with relatively few lines from the play. This production involved the audience in an improvised "orgy" supposedly evoking the spirit of Bacchus. A film version of the production was made by Brian de Palma. In 1973, Wole Soyinka produced a London version that added a second chorus of slaves. Playwrights such as Ingmar Bergman, Charles Mee, and Caryl Churchill have produced radical interpretations of *The Bacchae*; operas and films have been made in English and other languages. Alan Cumming portrayed Dionysus in a 2007 Edinburgh production that later opened on the West End in London and in Lincoln Center in 2008. JoAnne Akalaitis's Public Theater production was done in the open air in Central Park in 2009. Francis Blessington's translation was used in the well-reviewed 2009 production in the Boston Center for the Arts. *The Bacchae* is many things to many directors.

EURIPIDES (C. 480 BCE–C. 406 BCE)

The Bacchae   405 BCE

TRANSLATED BY WILLIAM ARROWSMITH

Characters

DIONYSUS (*also called Bromius, Evius, and Bacchus*)
CHORUS OF ASIAN BACCHAE (*followers of Dionysus*)
TEIRESIAS
CADMUS
PENTHEUS
ATTENDANT
FIRST MESSENGER
SECOND MESSENGER
AGAVE
CORYPHAEUS (*chorus leader*)

Scene: *Before the royal palace at Thebes. On the left is the way to Cithaeron; on the right, to the city. In the center of the orchestra stands, still smoking, the vine-covered tomb of Semele, mother of Dionysus.*

Enter Dionysus. He is of soft, even effeminate, appearance. His face is beardless; he is dressed in a fawn-skin and carries a thyrsus (i.e., a stalk of fennel tipped with ivy leaves). On his head he wears a wreath of ivy, and his long blond curls ripple down over his shoulders. Throughout the play he wears a smiling mask.

DIONYSUS: I am Dionysus, the son of Zeus,
come back to Thebes, this land where I was born.
My mother was Cadmus' daughter, Semele by name,
midwived by fire, delivered by the lightning's
blast.

5   And here I stand, a god incognito,
disguised as man, beside the stream of Dirce
and the waters of Ismenus. There before the palace
I see my lightning-married mother's grave,
and there upon the ruins of her shattered house
10   the living fire of Zeus still smolders on
in deathless witness of Hera's violence and rage
against my mother. But Cadmus wins my praise:
he has made this tomb a shrine, sacred to my mother.
It was I who screened her grave with the green
of the clustering vine.

Far behind me lie
those golden-rivered lands, Lydia and Phrygia,
where my journeying began. Overland I went,
across the steppes of Persia where the sun strikes hotly
15   down, through Bactrian fastness and the grim waste
of Media. Thence to rich Arabia I came;
and so, along all Asia's swarming littoral
of towered cities where Greeks and foreign nations,
mingling, live, my progress made. There

I taught my dances to the feet of living men,
establishing my mysteries and rites
that I might be revealed on earth for what I am:
a god.
And thence to Thebes.

This city, first   20
in Hellas, now shrills and echoes to my women's cries,
their ecstasy of joy. Here in Thebes
I bound the fawn-skin to the women's flesh and armed
their hands with shafts of ivy. For I have come   25
to refute that slander spoken by my mother's sisters—
those who least had right to slander her.
They said that Dionysus was no son of Zeus,
but Semele had slept beside a man in love
and fathered off her shame on Zeus—a fraud, they
    sneered,   30
contrived by Cadmus to protect his daughter's name.
They said she lied, and Zeus in anger at that lie
blasted her with lightning.

Because of that offense
I have stung them with frenzy, hounded them from home
up to the mountains where they wander, crazed of mind,
and compelled to wear my orgies' livery.
Every woman in Thebes—but the women only—   35
I drove from home, mad. There they sit,
rich and poor alike, even the daughters of Cadmus,
beneath the silver firs on the roofless rocks.
Like it or not, this city must learn its lesson:
it lacks initiation in my mysteries;   40
that I shall vindicate my mother Semele
and stand revealed to mortal eyes as the god
she bore to Zeus.

Cadmus the king has abdicated,
leaving his throne and power to his grandson Pentheus;
who now revolts against divinity, in *me*;   45
thrusts *me* from his offerings; forgets *my* name
in his prayers. Therefore I shall *prove* to him
and every man in Thebes that I am god
indeed. And when my worship is established here,
and all is well, then I shall go my way
and be revealed to other men in other lands.   50
But if the men of Thebes attempt to force
my Bacchae from the mountainside by threat of arms,
I shall marshal my Maenads° and take the field.
To these ends I have laid my deity aside
and go disguised as man.

(He wheels and calls offstage.)

53. Maenads: Ecstatic women followers of Dionysus.

Alan Cumming as Dionysus in the
Lincoln Center Festival production
directed by John Tiffany, 2008.

55   On, my women,
women who worship me, women whom I led
out of Asia where Tmolus heaves its rampart
over Lydia!
          On, comrades of my progress here!
Come, and with your native Phrygian drum—
60   Rhea's drum and mine—pound at the palace doors
of Pentheus! Let the city of Thebes behold you,
while I return among Cithaeron's forest glens
where my Bacchae wait and join their whirling dances.

(*Exit Dionysus as the Chorus of Asian Bacchae comes
     dancing in from the right. They are dressed in
     fawn-skins, crowned with ivy, and carry thyrsi,
                    timbrels, and flutes.*)

CHORUS: Out of the land of Asia,
65   down from holy Tmolus,
speeding the service of god,
for Bromius° we come!

67. Bromius: Another name for Dionysus, meaning "roarer."

Hard are the labors of god;
hard, but his service is sweet.
Sweet to serve, sweet to cry:
                Bacchus!   Evohé!
—You on the streets!
                —You on the roads!
                          —Make way!
—Let every mouth be hushed. Let no ill-omened
     words   70
  profane your tongues.
                —Make way! Fall back!
                          —Hush.
—For now I raise the old, old hymn to Dionysus.
—Blessèd, blessèd are those who know the
     mysteries of god.
—Blessèd is he who hallows his life in the worship
     of god, he whom the spirit of god possesseth,
     who is one with those who belong to the holy
     body of god.   75
—Blessèd are the dancers and those who are purified,
     who dance on the hill in the holy dance of god.

—Blessèd are they who keep the rite of Cybele° the
    Mother.
—Blessèd are the thyrsus-bearers, those who wield
    in their hands the holy wand of god.
—Blessèd are those who wear the crown of the ivy
    of god.
—Blessèd, blessèd are they: Dionysus is their god!

—On, Bacchae, on, you Bacchae,
    bear your god in triumph home!
    Bear on the god, son of god,
    escort your Dionysus home!
    Bear him down from Phrygian hill,
    attend him through the streets of Hellas!

—So his mother bore him once
    in labor bitter; lightning-struck,
    forced by fire that flared from Zeus,
    consumed, she died, untimely torn,
    in childbed dead by blow of light!
    Of light the son was born!

—Zeus it was who saved his son;
    with speed outrunning mortal eye,
    bore him to a private place,
    bound the boy with clasps of gold;
    in his thigh as in a womb,
    concealed his son from Hera's eyes.

—And when the weaving Fates fulfilled the time,
    the bull-horned god was born of Zeus. In joy
    he crowned his son, set serpents on his head—
    wherefrom, in piety, descends to us
    the Maenad's writhing crown, her *chevelure*° of
    snakes.

—O Thebes, nurse of Semele,
    crown your hair with ivy!
    Grow green with bryony!
    Redden with berries! O city,
    with boughs of oak and fir,
    come dance the dance of god!
    Fringe your skins of dappled fawn
    with tufts of twisted wool!
    Handle with holy care
    the violent wand of god!
    And let the dance begin!
    He is Bromius who runs
    to the mountain!
            to the mountain!
    where the throng of women waits,
    driven from shuttle and loom,
    possessed by Dionysus!

—And I praise the holies of Crete,
    the caves of the dancing Curetes,
    there where Zeus was born,
    where helmed in triple tier

around the primal drum
the Corybantes° danced. They,
they were the first of all
whose whirling feet kept time
to the strict beat of the taut hide
and the squeal of the wailing flute.
Then from them to Rhea's hands
the holy drum was handed down;
but, stolen by the raving Satyrs,
fell at last to me and now
accompanies the dance
which every other year
celebrates your name:
    Dionysus!

—He is sweet upon the mountains. He drops to the
    earth from the running packs.
He wears the holy fawn-skin. He hunts the wild
    goat and kills it.
He delights in the raw flesh.
He runs to the mountains of Phrygia, to the
    mountains of Lydia he runs!
He is Bromius who leads us! *Evohé!*

—With milk the earth flows! It flows with wine!
    It runs with the nectar of bees!

—Like frankincense in its fragrance
is the blaze of the torch he bears.
Flames float out from his trailing wand
    as he runs, as he dances,
    kindling the stragglers,
    spurring with cries,
and his long curls stream to the wind!

—And he cries, as they cry, *Evohé!*—
    On, Bacchae!
    On, Bacchae!
Follow, glory of golden Tmolus,
    hymning god
    with a rumble of drums,
with a cry, *Evohé!* to the Evian god,
with a cry of Phrygian cries,
when the holy flute like honey plays
the sacred song of those who go
to the mountain!
            to the mountain!

—Then, in ecstasy, like a colt by its grazing mother,
    the Bacchante runs with flying feet, she leaps!

*(The Chorus remains grouped in two semicircles about
the orchestra as Teiresias makes his entrance. He is
incongruously dressed in the bacchant's fawn-skin
and is crowned with ivy. Old and blind,
he uses his thyrsus to tap his way.)*

TEIRESIAS: Ho there, who keeps the gates?
            Summon Cadmus—

80
85
90
95
100
105
110
115
120
125
130
135
140
145
150
155
160
165
170

---

78. Cybele: The mother goddess in ancient Phrygia, in what is
now Turkey.   **104.** *chevelure*: A head of hair.

125. Corybantes: Women followers of Cybele.

André De Shields as Teiresias in JoAnne Akalaitis's 2009 production in Central Park.

The Chorus dances, 2009.

Cadmus, Agenor's son, the stranger from Sidon
who built the towers of our Thebes.

                    Go, someone.
Say Teiresias wants him. He will know what errand
175 brings me, that agreement, age with age, we made
to deck our wands, to dress in skins of fawn
and crown our heads with ivy.

*(Enter Cadmus from the palace. Dressed in Dionysiac
costume and bent almost double with age, he is an
incongruous and pathetic figure.)*

CADMUS: My old friend,
I knew it must be you when I heard your summons.
For there's a wisdom in his voice that makes
the man of wisdom known.

                But here I am,
180 dressed in the costume of the god, prepared to go.
Insofar as we are able, Teiresias, we must
do honor to this god, for he was born
my daughter's son, who has been revealed to men,
the god, Dionysus.

             Where shall we go, where
shall we tread the dance, tossing our white heads
in the dances of god?

185   Expound to me, Teiresias.
For in such matters you are wise.

                Surely
I could dance night and day, untiringly
beating the earth with my thyrsus! And how sweet it is
to forget my old age.

TEIRESIAS: It is the same with me.
190 I too feel young, young enough to dance.

CADMUS: Good. Shall we take our chariots to the
    mountain?

TEIRESIAS: Walking would be better. It shows more honor
    to the god.

CADMUS: So be it. I shall lead, my old age
conducting yours.

TEIRESIAS: The god will guide us there
with no effort on our part.

195 CADMUS: Are we the only men
who will dance for Bacchus?

TEIRESIAS: They are all blind.
Only we can see.

CADMUS: But we delay too long.
Here, take my arm.

TEIRESIAS: Link my hand in yours.

CADMUS: I am a man, nothing more. I do not scoff at
heaven.

200 TEIRESIAS: We do not trifle with divinity.
No, we are the heirs of customs and traditions
hallowed by age and handed down to us
by our fathers. No quibbling logic can topple *them,*
whatever subtleties this clever age invents.
People may say: "Aren't you ashamed? At your age,
205 going dancing, wreathing your head with ivy?"
Well, I am *not* ashamed. Did the god declare
that just the young or just the old should dance?
No, he desires his honor from all mankind.

He wants no one excluded from his worship.

CADMUS: Because you cannot see, Teiresias, let me be 210
interpreter for you this once. Here comes
the man to whom I left my throne, Echion's son,
Pentheus, hastening toward the palace. He seems
excited and disturbed. Yes, listen to him.

*(Enter Pentheus from the right. He is a young man of
athletic build, dressed in traditional Greek dress; like
Dionysus, he is beardless. He enters excitedly, talking
to the attendants who accompany him.)*

PENTHEUS: I happened to be away, out of the city, 215
but reports reached me of some strange mischief here,
stories of our women leaving home to frisk
in mock ecstasies among the thickets on the
    mountain,
dancing in honor of the latest divinity,
a certain Dionysus, whoever he may be! 220
In their midst stand bowls brimming with wine.
And then, one by one, the women wander off
to hidden nooks where they serve the lusts of men.
Priestesses of Bacchus they claim they are,
but it's really Aphrodite they adore. 225
I have captured some of them; my jailers
have locked them away in the safety of our prison.
Those who run at large shall be hunted down
out of the mountains like the animals they are—
yes, my own mother Agave, and Ino
and Autonoë, the mother of Actaeon. 230
In no time at all I shall have them trapped
in iron nets and stop this obscene disorder.
    I am also told a foreigner has come to Thebes
from Lydia, one of those charlatan magicians,
with long yellow curls smelling of perfumes, 235
with flushed cheeks and the spells of Aphrodite
in his eyes. His days and nights he spends
with women and girls, dangling before them the joys
of initiation in his mysteries.
But let me bring him underneath that roof
and I'll stop his pounding with his wand and tossing 240
his head. By god, I'll have his head cut off!
And *this* is the man who claims that Dionysus
is a god and was sewn into the thigh of Zeus,
when, in point of fact, that same blast of lightning
consumed him and his mother both for her lie 245
that she had lain with Zeus in love. Whoever
this stranger is, aren't such impostures,
such unruliness, worthy of hanging?

*(For the first time he sees Teiresias and
Cadmus in their Dionysiac costumes.)*

                      What!
But this is incredible! Teiresias the seer
tricked out in a dappled fawn-skin!

                 And *you,*
you, my own grandfather, playing at the bacchant 250
with a wand!

          Sir, I shrink to see your old age
so foolish. Shake that ivy off, grandfather!

Now drop that wand. Drop it, I say.

(*He wheels on Teiresias.*)

Aha,

255　I see: this is *your* doing, Teiresias.
Yes, you want still another god revealed to men
so you can pocket the profits from burnt offerings
and bird-watching. By heaven, only your age
restrains me now from sending you to prison
with those Bacchic women for importing here to
　　Thebes
260　these filthy mysteries. When once you see
the glint of wine shining at the feasts of women,
then you may be sure the festival is rotten.

CORYPHAEUS: What blasphemy! Stranger, have you no
　　respect
for heaven? For Cadmus who sowed the dragon teeth?
265　Will the son of Echion disgrace his house?

TEIRESIAS: Give a wise man an honest brief to plead
and his eloquence is no remarkable achievement.
But you are glib; your phrases come rolling out
smoothly on the tongue, as though your words were
　　wise
instead of foolish. The man whose glibness flows
270　from his conceit of speech declares the thing he is:
a worthless and a stupid citizen.

　　　　　　　　　I tell you,
this god whom you ridicule shall someday have
enormous power and prestige throughout Hellas.
Mankind, young man, possesses two supreme
　　blessings.
275　First of these is the goddess Demeter, or Earth—
whichever name you choose to call her by.
It was she who gave to man his nourishment of grain.
But after her there came the son of Semele,
who matched her present by inventing liquid wine
as his gift to man. For filled with that good gift,
280　suffering mankind forgets its grief; from it
comes sleep; with it oblivion of the troubles
of the day. There is no other medicine
for misery. And when we pour libations
to the gods, we pour the god of wine himself
285　that through his intercession man may win
the favor of heaven.

　　　　　　　　You sneer, do you, at that story
that Dionysus was sewed into the thigh of Zeus?
Let me teach you what that really means. When Zeus
rescued from the thunderbolt his infant son,
he brought him to Olympus. Hera, however,
290　plotted at heart to hurl the child from heaven.
Like the god he is, Zeus countered her. Breaking off
a tiny fragment of that ether which surrounds the world,
he molded from it a dummy Dionysus.
This he *showed* to Hera, but with time men garbled
295　the word and said that Dionysus had been *sewed*
into the thigh of Zeus. This was their story,
whereas, in fact, Zeus *showed* the dummy to Hera
and gave it as a hostage for his son.

　　　　　　　　　　Moreover,

this is a god of prophecy. His worshippers,
like madmen, are endowed with mantic powers.
For when the god enters the body of a man　　300
he fills him with the breath of prophecy.

　　　　　　　　　　Besides,
he has usurped even the functions of warlike Ares.
Thus, at times, you see an army mustered under arms
stricken with panic before it lifts a spear.
This panic comes from Dionysus.

　　　　　　　　　Someday
you shall even see him bounding with his torches　　305
among the crags at Delphi, leaping the pastures
that stretch between the peaks, whirling and waving
his thyrsus: great throughout Hellas.

　　　　　　　　　Mark my words,
Pentheus. Do not be so certain that power　　310
is what matters in the life of man; do not mistake
for wisdom the fantasies of your sick mind.
Welcome the god to Thebes; crown your head;
pour him libations and join his revels.

Dionysus does not, I admit, *compel* a woman
to be chaste. Always and in every case　　315
it is her character and nature that keeps
a woman chaste. But even in the rites of Dionysus,
the chaste woman will not be corrupted.

　　　　　　　　　Think:
you are pleased when men stand outside your doors
and the city glorifies the name of Pentheus.　　320
And so the god: he too delights in glory.
But Cadmus and I, whom you ridicule, will crown
our heads with ivy and join the dances of the god—
an ancient foolish pair perhaps, but dance
we must. Nothing you have said would make me
change my mind or flout the will of heaven.　　325
You are mad, grievously mad, beyond the power
of any drugs to cure, for you are drugged
with madness.

CORYPHAEUS:　　　　Apollo would approve your words.
Wisely you honor Bromius: a great god.

CADMUS:　　　　　　　　　　　　My boy,
Teiresias advises well. Your home is here　　330
with us, with our customs and traditions, not
outside, alone. Your mind is distracted now,
and what you think is sheer delirium.
Even if this Dionysus is no god,
as you assert, persuade yourself that he is.
The fiction is a noble one, for Semele will seem　　335
to be the mother of a god, and this confers
no small distinction on our family.

　　　　　　　　　You saw
that dreadful death your cousin Actaeon died
when those man-eating hounds he had raised himself
savaged him and tore his body limb from limb
because he boasted that his prowess in the hunt
　　surpassed　　340
the skill of Artemis.

　　　　　　　Do not let his fate be yours.
Here, let me wreathe your head with leaves of ivy.
Then come with us and glorify the god.

PENTHEUS: Take your hands off me! Go worship your
     Bacchus,
   but do not wipe your madness off on me.
345 By god, I'll make him pay, the man who taught you
   this folly of yours.

                              (*He turns to his attendants.*)
                 Go, someone, this instant,
   to the place where this prophet prophesies.
   Pry it up with crowbars, heave it over,
   upside down; demolish everything you see.
350 Throw his fillets out to wind and weather.
   That will provoke him more than anything.
   As for the rest of you, go and scour the city
   for that effeminate stranger, the man who infects our
     women
   with this strange disease and pollutes our beds.
355 And when you take him, clap him in chains
   and march him here. He shall die as he deserves—
   by being stoned to death. He shall come to rue
   his merrymaking here in Thebes.

                              (*Exeunt attendants.*)

TEIRESIAS: Reckless fool,
   you do not know the consequences of your words.
   You talked madness before, but this is raving
   lunacy!
360   Cadmus, let us go and pray
   for this raving fool and for this city too,
   pray to the god that no awful vengeance strike
   from heaven.
             Take your staff and follow me.
   Support me with your hands, and I shall help you too
   lest we stumble and fall, a sight of shame,
   two old men together.
365   But go we must,
   acknowledging the service that we owe to god,
   Bacchus, the son of Zeus.
                   And yet take care
   lest someday your house repent of Pentheus
   in its sufferings. I speak not prophecy
   but fact. The words of fools finish in folly.

                              (*Exeunt Teiresias and Cadmus.
                              Pentheus retires into the palace.*)

CHORUS:
370 —Holiness, queen of heaven,
     Holiness on golden wing
     who hovers over earth,
     do you hear what Pentheus says?
     Do you hear his blasphemy
375 against the prince of the blessèd,
     the god of garlands and banquets,
     Bromius, Semele's son?
     These blessings he gave:
     laughter to the flute
380 and the loosing of cares
     when the shining wine is spilled
     at the feast of the gods,
385 and the wine-bowl casts its sleep
     on feasters crowned with ivy.

—A tongue without reins,
   defiance, unwisdom—
   their end is disaster.
   But the life of quiet good,
   the wisdom that accepts—   390
   these abide unshaken,
   preserving, sustaining
   the houses of men,
   Far in the air of heaven,
   the sons of heaven live.
   But they watch the lives of men.
   And what passes for wisdom is not;   395
   unwise are those who aspire,
   who outrange the limits of man.
   Briefly, we live. Briefly,
   then die. Wherefore, I say,
   he who hunts a glory, he who tracks
   some boundless, superhuman dream,
   may lose his harvest here and now
   and garner death. Such men are mad,   400
     their counsels evil.

—O let me come to Cyprus,
   island of Aphrodite,
   homes of the loves that cast
   their spells on the hearts of men!   405
   Or Paphos where the hundred-
   mouthed barbarian river
   brings ripeness without rain!
   To Pieria, haunt of the Muses,   410
   and the holy hill of Olympus!
   O Bromius, leader, god of joy,
   Bromius, take me there!
   There the lovely Graces go,
   and there Desire, and there
   the right is mine to worship   415
     as I please.

—The deity, the son of Zeus,
   in feast, in festival, delights.
   He loves the goddess Peace,
   generous of good,
   preserver of the young.
   To rich and poor he gives   420
   the simple gift of wine,
   the gladness of the grape.
   But him who scoffs he hates,
   and him who mocks his life,
   the happiness of those
   for whom the day is blessed   425
   but doubly blessed the night;
   whose simple wisdom shuns the thoughts
   of proud, uncommon men and all
   their god-encroaching dreams.
   But what the common people do,   430
   the things that simple men believe,
     I too believe and do.

(*As Pentheus reappears from the palace, enter from the
   left several attendants leading Dionysus captive.*)

ATTENDANT: Pentheus, here we are; not empty-handed either.
435   We captured the quarry you sent us out to catch.
But our prey here was tame: refused to run
or hide, held out his hands as willing as you please,
completely unafraid. His ruddy cheeks were flushed
as though with wine, and he stood there smiling,
440   making no objection when we roped his hands
and marched him here. It made me feel ashamed.
"Listen, stranger," I said, "I am not to blame.
We act under orders from Pentheus. He ordered
your arrest."
             As for those women you clapped in chains
445   and sent to the dungeon, they're gone, clean away,
went skipping off to the fields crying on their god
Bromius. The chains on their legs snapped apart
by themselves. Untouched by any human hand,
the doors swung wide, opening of their own accord.
450   Sir, this stranger who has come to Thebes is full
of many miracles. I know no more than that.
The rest is your affair.
PENTHEUS: Untie his hands.
We have him in our net. He may be quick,
but he cannot escape us now, I think.

(*While the servants untie Dionysus' hands, Pentheus
attentively scrutinizes his prisoner. Then the servants
step back, leaving Pentheus and Dionysus face to face.*)
               So,
you *are* attractive, stranger, at least to women—
which explains, I think, your presence here in Thebes.
Your curls are long. You do not wrestle, I take it.   455
And what fair skin you have—you must take care
   of it—
no daylight complexion; no, it comes from the night
when you hunt Aphrodite with your beauty.
                  Now then,
who are you and from where?
DIONYSUS: It is nothing   460
to boast of and easily told. You have heard, I suppose,
of Mount Tmolus and her flowers?
PENTHEUS: I know the place.
It rings the city of Sardis.
DIONYSUS: I come from there.
My country is Lydia.
PENTHEUS: Who is this god whose worship
you have imported into Hellas?

Pentheus (Cal MacAninch)
confronts the captured Dionysus
(Alan Cumming), 2008.

465 DIONYSUS: Dionysus, the son of Zeus.
    He initiated me.
    PENTHEUS: You have some local Zeus
    who spawns new gods?
    DIONYSUS: He is the same as yours—
    the Zeus who married Semele.
    PENTHEUS: How did you see him?
    In a dream or face to face?
    DIONYSUS: Face to face.
    He gave me his rites.
470 PENTHEUS: What form do they take,
    these mysteries of yours?
    DIONYSUS: It is forbidden
    to tell the uninitiate.
    PENTHEUS: Tell me the benefits
    that those who know your mysteries enjoy.
    DIONYSUS: I am forbidden to say. But they are worth
    knowing.
    PENTHEUS: Your answers are designed to make me curious.
475 DIONYSUS: No:
    our mysteries abhor an unbelieving man.
    PENTHEUS: You say you saw the god. What form did he
    assume?
    DIONYSUS: Whatever form he wished. The choice was
    his, not mine.
    PENTHEUS: You evade the question.
    DIONYSUS: Talk sense to a fool
    and he calls you foolish.
480 PENTHEUS: Have you introduced
    your rites in other cities too? Or is Thebes the
    first?
    DIONYSUS: Foreigners everywhere now dance for
    Dionysus.
    PENTHEUS: They are more ignorant than Greeks.
    DIONYSUS: In this matter
    they are not. Customs differ.
    PENTHEUS: Do you hold your rites
    during the day or night?
485 DIONYSUS: Mostly by night.
    The darkness is well suited to devotion.
    PENTHEUS: Better suited to lechery and seducing women.
    DIONYSUS: You can find debauchery by daylight too.
    PENTHEUS: You shall regret these clever answers.
    DIONYSUS: And you,
    your stupid blasphemies.
490 PENTHEUS: What a bold bacchant!
    You wrestle well—when it comes to words.
    DIONYSUS: Tell me,
    what punishment do you propose?
    PENTHEUS: First of all,
    I shall cut off your girlish curls.
    DIONYSUS: My hair is holy.
    My curls belong to god.

    (*Pentheus shears away the god's curls.*)

    PENTHEUS: Second, you will surrender
    your wand.
495 DIONYSUS: You take it. It belongs to Dionysus.

    (*Pentheus takes the thyrsus.*)

PENTHEUS: Last, I shall place you under guard and
    confine you in the palace.
DIONYSUS: The god himself will set me free
    whenever I wish.
PENTHEUS: You will be with your women in prison
    when you call on him for help.
DIONYSUS: He is here now
    and sees what I endure from you.
PENTHEUS: Where is he?   500
    I cannot see him.
DIONYSUS: With me. Your blasphemies
    have made you blind.
PENTHEUS: (*to attendants*)
                        Seize him. He is mocking me
    and Thebes.
DIONYSUS: I give you sober warning, fools:
    place no chains on *me*.
PENTHEUS: But *I* say: chain him.
    And I am the stronger here.
DIONYSUS: You do not know   505
    the limits of your strength. You do not know
    what you do. You do not know who you are.
PENTHEUS: I am Pentheus, the son of Echion and Agave.
DIONYSUS: Pentheus: you shall repent that name.
PENTHEUS: Off with him.
    Chain his hands; lock him in the stables by the palace.
    Since he desires the darkness, give him what he wants. 510
    Let him dance down there in the dark.

    (*As the attendants bind Dionysus' hands, the Chorus
    beats on its drums with increasing agitation as though
    to emphasize the sacrilege.*)
                          As for these women,
    your accomplices in making trouble here,
    I shall have them sold as slaves or put to work
    at my looms. That will silence their drums.

                          (*Exit Pentheus.*)

DIONYSUS: I go,   515
    though not to suffer, since that cannot be.
    But Dionysus whom you outrage by your acts,
    who you deny is god, will call you to account.
    When you set chains on me, you manacle the god.

    (*Exeunt attendants with Dionysus captive.*)

CHORUS:
—O Dirce, holy river,   520
child of Achelöus' water,
yours the springs that welcomed once
divinity, the son of Zeus!
For Zeus the father snatched his son
from deathless flame, crying: 525
Dithyrambus,° come!
Enter my male womb.
I name you Bacchus and to Thebes
proclaim you by that name.
But now, O blessèd Dirce,   530
you banish me when to your banks I come,
crowned with ivy, bringing revels.
O Dirce, why am I rejected?

526. **Dithyrambus:** A hymn sung to Dionysus.

535 By the clustered grapes I swear,
by Dionysus' wine,
someone you shall come to know
the name of *Bromius!*

—With fury, with fury, he rages,
540 Pentheus, son of Echion,
born of the breed of Earth,
spawned by the dragon, whelped by Earth!
Inhuman, a rabid beast,
a giant in wildness raging,
storming, defying the children of heaven.
545 He has threatened me with bonds
though my body is bound to god.
He cages my comrades with chains;
he has cast them in prison darkness.
550 O lord, son of Zeus, do you see?
O Dionysus, do you see
how in shackles we are held
unbreakably, in the bonds of oppressors?
Descend from Olympus, lord!
Come, whirl your wand of gold
555 and quell with death this beast of blood
whose violence abuses man and god outrageously.

—O lord, where do you wave your wand
among the running companies of god?
There on Nysa, mother of beasts?
There on the ridges of Corycia?
560 Or there among the forests of Olympus
where Orpheus fingered his lyre
and mustered with music the trees,
mustered the wilderness beasts?
565 O Pieria, you are blessed!
Evius honors you. He comes to dance,
bringing his Bacchae, fording the race
570 where Axios runs, bringing his Maenads
whirling over Lydias,
generous father of rivers
and famed for his lovely waters
575 that fatten a land of good horses.

(*Thunder and lightning. The earth trembles.
The Chorus is crazed with fear.*)

DIONYSUS: (*from within*)
Ho!
Hear me! Ho, Bacchae!
Ho, Bacchae! Hear my cry!
CHORUS: Who cries?
Who calls me with that cry
of Evius? Where are you, lord?
580 DIONYSUS: Ho! Again I cry—
the son of Zeus and Semele!
CHORUS: O lord, lord Bromius!
Bromius, come to us now!
DIONYSUS: *Let the earthquake come! Shatter the floor of*
585 *the world!*
CHORUS:
—Look there, how the palace of Pentheus totters.
—Look, the palace is collapsing!

—Dionysus is within. Adore him!
—We adore him!   590
—Look there!
—Above the pillars, how the great stones
gape and crack!
—Listen. Bromius cries his victory!
DIONYSUS: *Launch the blazing thunderbolt of god! O*
lightnings,
come! Consume with flame the palace of Pentheus!   595

(*A burst of lightning flares across the façade of the
palace and tongues of flame spurt up from the tomb of
Semele. Then a great crash of thunder.*)

CHORUS: Ah,
look how the fire leaps up
on the holy tomb of Semele,
the flame of Zeus of Thunders,
his lightnings, still alive,
blazing where they fell!
Down, Maenads,   600
fall to the ground in awe! He walks
among the ruins he has made!
He has brought the high house low!
He comes, our god, the son of Zeus!

(*The Chorus falls to the ground in oriental fashion,
bowing their heads in the direction of the palace. A
hush; then Dionysus appears, lightly picking his way
among the rubble. Calm and smiling still, he speaks to
the Chorus with a solicitude approaching banter.*)

DIONYSUS: What, women of Asia? Were you so overcome with fright
you fell to the ground? I think then you must have seen   605
how Bacchus jostled the palace of Pentheus. But come, rise.
Do not be afraid.
CORYPHAEUS: O greatest light of our holy revels,
how glad I am to see your face! Without you I was lost.
DIONYSUS: Did you despair when they led me away to
cast me down   610
in the darkness of Pentheus' prison?
CORYPHAEUS: What else could I do?
Where would I turn for help if something happened
to you?
But how did you escape that godless man?
DIONYSUS: With ease.
No effort was required.
CORYPHAEUS: But the manacles on your wrists?   615
DIONYSUS: There I, in turn, humiliated him, outrage for
outrage.
He seemed to think that he was chaining me but
never once
so much as touched my hands. He fed on his desires.
Inside the stable he intended as my jail, instead of me,
he found a bull and tried to rope its knees and hooves.
He was panting desperately, biting his lips with his teeth, 620
his whole body drenched with sweat, while I sat nearby,
quietly watching. But at that moment Bacchus came,
shook the palace and touched his mother's grave
with tongues
of fire. Imagining the palace was in flames,

Pentheus went rushing here and there, shouting to
625   his slaves
to bring him water. Every hand was put to work: in vain.
Then, afraid I might escape, he suddenly stopped short,
drew his sword and rushed to the palace. There, it
    seems,
630 Bromius had made a shape, a phantom which
    resembled me,
within the court. Bursting in, Pentheus thrust and
    stabbed
at that thing of gleaming air as though he thought
    it me.
And then, once again, the god humiliated him.
He razed the palace to the ground where it lies,
    shattered
in utter ruin—his reward for my imprisonment.
At that bitter sight, Pentheus dropped his sword,
635   exhausted
by the struggle. A man, a man, and nothing more,
yet he presumed to wage a war with god.
               For my part,
I left the palace quietly and made my way outside.
For Pentheus I care nothing.
                But judging from the sound
of tramping feet inside the court, I think our man
640 will soon be here. What, I wonder, will he have to say?
But let him bluster. I shall not be touched to rage.
Wise men know constraint: our passions are
    controlled.

(Enter Pentheus, stamping heavily,
from the ruined palace.)

PENTHEUS: But this is mortifying. That stranger, that man
I clapped in irons, has escaped.

(He catches sight of Dionysus.)

645   What! *You?*
Well, what do you have to say for yourself?
How did you escape? Answer me.
DIONYSUS: Your anger
walks too heavily. Tread lightly here.
PENTHEUS: *How did you escape?*
DIONYSUS: Don't you remember?
Someone, I said, would set me free.
650 PENTHEUS: Someone?
But who? Who is this mysterious someone?
DIONYSUS: [He who makes the grape grow its clusters
    for mankind.]
PENTHEUS: A splendid contribution, that.
DIONYSUS: You disparage the gift that is his chiefest glory.
PENTHEUS: [If I catch him here, he will not escape my
    anger.]
I shall order every gate in every tower
to be bolted tight.
DIONYSUS: And so? Could not a god
hurdle your city walls?
655 PENTHEUS: You are clever—very—
but not where it counts.
DIONYSUS: Where it counts the most,
there I *am* clever.

(Enter a messenger, a herdsman from Mount
Cithaeron.)

           But hear this messenger
who brings you news from the mountain of
    Cithaeron.
We shall remain where we are. Do not fear:
we will not run away.
MESSENGER: Pentheus, king of Thebes, 660
I come from Cithaeron where the gleaming flakes of
    snow
fall on and on forever—
PENTHEUS: Get to the point.
What is your message, man?
MESSENGER: Sir, I have seen
the holy Maenads, the women who ran barefoot 665
and crazy from the city, and I wanted to report
to you and Thebes what weird fantastic things,
what miracles and more than miracles,
these women do. But may I speak freely
in my own way and words, or make it short?
I fear the harsh impatience of your nature, sire, 670
too kingly and too quick to anger.
PENTHEUS: Speak freely.
You have my promise: I shall not punish you.
Displeasure with a man who speaks the truth is
    wrong.
However, the more terrible this tale of yours,
that much more terrible will be the punishment 675
I impose upon that man who taught our womenfolk
this strange new magic.
MESSENGER: About that hour
when the sun lets loose its light to warm the earth,
our grazing herds of cows had just begun to climb
the path along the mountain ridge. Suddenly
I saw three companies of dancing women, 680
one led by Autonoë, the second captained
by your mother Agave, while Ino led the third.
There they lay in the deep sleep of exhaustion,
some resting on boughs of fir, others sleeping
where they fell, here and there among the oak
    leaves— 685
but all modestly and soberly, not, as you think,
drunk with wine, nor wandering, led astray
by the music of the flute, to hunt their Aphrodite
through the woods.
              But your mother heard the lowing
of our horned herds, and springing to her feet, 690
gave a great cry to waken them from sleep.
And they too, rubbing the bloom of soft sleep
from their eyes, rose up lightly and straight—
a lovely sight to see: all as one,
the old women and the young and the unmarried
    girls.
First they let their hair fall loose, down 695
over their shoulders, and those whose straps had
    slipped
fastened their skins of fawn with writhing snakes
that licked their cheeks. Breasts swollen with milk,
new mothers who had left their babies behind at
    home

700 nestled gazelles and young wolves in their arms,
suckling them. Then they crowned their hair with
      leaves,
ivy and oak and flowering bryony. One woman
struck her thyrsus against a rock and a fountain
705 of cool water came bubbling up. Another drove
her fennel in the ground, and where it struck the earth,
at the touch of god, a spring of wine poured out.
Those who wanted milk scratched at the soil
710 with bare fingers and the white milk came welling up.
Pure honey spurted, streaming, from their wands.
If you had been there and seen these wonders for
      yourself,
you would have gone down on your knees and
      prayed
to the god you now deny.
                                                    We cowherds and shepherds
715 gathered in small groups, wondering and arguing
among ourselves at these fantastic things,
the awful miracles those women did.
But then a city fellow with the knack of words
rose to his feet and said: "All you who live
upon the pastures of the mountain, what do you say?
720 Shall we earn a little favor with King Pentheus
by hunting his mother Agave out of the revels?"
Falling in with his suggestion, we withdrew
and set ourselves in ambush, hidden by the leaves
among the undergrowth. Then at a signal
all the Bacchae whirled their wands for the revels
to begin. With one voice they cried aloud:
"O Iacchus! Son of Zeus!" "O Bromius!"
725   they cried
until the beasts and all the mountain seemed
wild with divinity. And when they ran,
everything ran with them.
                                        It happened, however,
that Agave ran near the ambush where I lay
730 concealed. Leaping up, I tried to seize her,
but she gave a cry: "Hounds who run with me,
men are hunting us down! Follow, follow me!
Use your wands for weapons."
                                              At this we fled
and barely missed being torn to pieces by
      the women.
735 Unarmed, they swooped down upon the herds of
cattle grazing there on the green of the meadow.
      And then
you could have seen a single woman with bare hands
tear a fat calf, still bellowing with fright,
in two, while others clawed the heifers to pieces.
There were ribs and cloven hooves scattered
740   everywhere,
and scraps smeared with blood hung from the fir
      trees.
And bulls, their raging fury gathered in their horns,
lowered their heads to charge, then fell, stumbling
745 to the earth, pulled down by hordes of women
and stripped of flesh and skin more quickly, sire,
than you could blink your royal eyes. Then,
carried up by their own speed, they flew like birds

across the spreading fields along Asopus' stream
where most of all the ground is good for harvesting.   750
Like invaders they swooped on Hysiae
and on Erythrae in the foothills of Cithaeron.
Everything in sight they pillaged and destroyed.
They snatched the children from their homes. And
      when
they piled their plunder on their backs, it stayed in   755
      place,
untied. Nothing, neither bronze nor iron,
fell to the dark earth. Flames flickered
in their curls and did not burn them. Then the
      villagers,
furious at what the women did, took to arms.
And *there*, sire, was something terrible to see.   760
For the men's spears were pointed and sharp, and yet
drew no blood, whereas the wands the women threw
inflicted wounds. And then the men *ran*,
routed by women! Some god, I say, was with them.
The Bacchae then returned where they had started,   765
by the springs the god had made, and washed their
      hands
while the snakes licked away the drops of blood
that dabbled their cheeks.
                                          Whoever this god may be,
sire, welcome him to Thebes. For he is great
in many other ways as well. It was he,   770
or so they say, who gave to mortal men
the gift of lovely wine by which our suffering
is stopped. And if there is no god of wine,
there is no love, no Aphrodite either,
nor other pleasure left to men.

                                            (*Exit messenger.*)

CORYPHAEUS: I tremble   775
to speak the words of freedom before the tyrant.
But let the truth be told: there is no god
greater than Dionysus.
PENTHEUS: Like a blazing fire
this Bacchic violence spreads. It comes too close.
We are disgraced, humiliated in the eyes
of Hellas. This is no time for hesitation.   780

                              (*He turns to an attendant.*)

You there. Go down quickly to the Electran gates
and order out all heavy-armored infantry;
call up the fastest troops among our cavalry,
the mobile squadrons and the archers. We march
against the Bacchae! Affairs are out of hand   785
when we tamely endure such conduct in our
      women.

                                          (*Exit attendant.*)

DIONYSUS: Pentheus, you do not hear, or else you
      disregard
my words of warning. You have done me wrong,
and yet, in spite of that, I warn you once
again: do not take arms against a god.
Stay quiet here. Bromius will not let you   790
drive his women from their revels on the mountain.

PENTHEUS: Don't you lecture me. You escaped from prison.
Or shall I punish you again?
DIONYSUS: If I were you,
I would offer him a sacrifice, not rage
795 and kick against necessity, a man defying
god.
PENTHEUS: I shall give your god the sacrifice
that he deserves. His victims will be his women.
I shall make a great slaughter in the woods of
Cithaeron.
DIONYSUS: You will all be routed, shamefully defeated,
when their wands of ivy turn back your shields
of bronze.
800 PENTHEUS: It is hopeless to wrestle with this man.
Nothing on earth will make him hold his tongue.
DIONYSUS: Friend,
you can still save the situation.
PENTHEUS: How?
By accepting orders from my own slaves?
DIONYSUS: No.
I undertake to lead the women back to Thebes.
Without bloodshed.
PENTHEUS: This is some trap.
805 DIONYSUS: A trap?
How so, if I save you by my own devices?
PENTHEUS: I know.
You and they have conspired to establish your rites
forever.
DIONYSUS: True, I have conspired—with god.
PENTHEUS: Bring my armor, someone. And you stop
810   talking.

(Pentheus strides toward the left, but when he is almost
offstage, Dionysus calls imperiously to him.)

DIONYSUS: Wait!
Would you like to see their revels on the mountain?
PENTHEUS: I would pay a great sum to see that sight.
DIONYSUS: Why are you so passionately curious?
PENTHEUS: Of course
I'd be sorry to see them drunk—
815 DIONYSUS: But for all your sorrow,
you'd like very much to see them?
PENTHEUS: Yes, very much.
I could crouch beneath the fir trees, out of sight.
DIONYSUS: But if you try to hide, they may track you
down.
PENTHEUS: Your point is well taken. I will go openly.
DIONYSUS: Shall I lead you there now? Are you ready
to go?
PENTHEUS: The sooner the better. The loss of even a
820   moment
would be disappointing now.
DIONYSUS: First, however,
you must dress yourself in women's clothes.
PENTHEUS: What?
You want me, a man, to wear a woman's dress. But
why?
DIONYSUS: If they knew you were a man, they would kill
you instantly.

PENTHEUS: True. You are an old hand at cunning, I see.
DIONYSUS: Dionysus taught me everything I know.   825
PENTHEUS: Your advice is to the point. What I fail to see
is what we do.
DIONYSUS: I shall go inside with you
and help you dress.
PENTHEUS: Dress? In a woman's dress,
you mean? I would die of shame.
DIONYSUS: Very well.
Then you no longer hanker to see the Maenads?
PENTHEUS: What is this costume I must wear?
DIONYSUS: On your head   830
I shall set a wig with long curls.
PENTHEUS: And then?
DIONYSUS: Next, robes to your feet and a net for your hair.
PENTHEUS: Yes? Go on.
DIONYSUS: Then a thyrsus for your hand
and a skin of dappled fawn.
PENTHEUS: I could not bear it.   835
I cannot bring myself to dress in women's clothes.
DIONYSUS: Then you must fight the Bacchae. That
means bloodshed.
PENTHEUS: Right. First we must go and reconnoiter.
DIONYSUS: Surely a wiser course than that of hunting
bad with worse.
PENTHEUS: But how can we pass through the city
without being seen?
DIONYSUS: We shall take deserted streets.   840
I will lead the way.
PENTHEUS: Any way you like,
provided those women of Bacchus don't jeer at me.
First, however, I shall ponder your advice,
whether to go or not.
DIONYSUS: Do as you please.
I am ready, whatever you decide.
PENTHEUS: Yes.
Either I shall march with my army to the mountain
or act on your advice.   845

(Exit Pentheus into the palace.)

DIONYSUS: Women, our prey now thrashes
in the net we threw. He shall see the Bacchae
and pay the price with death.
                    O Dionysus,
now action rests with you. And you are near.
Punish this man. But first distract his wits;   850
bewilder him with madness. For sane of mind
this man would never wear a woman's dress;
but obsess his soul and he will not refuse.
After those threats with which he was so fierce,
I want him made the laughingstock of Thebes,
paraded through the streets, a woman.
                              Now   855
I shall go and costume Pentheus in the clothes
which he must wear to Hades when he dies, butchered
by the hands of his mother. He shall come to know
Dionysus, son of Zeus, consummate god,   860
most terrible, and yet most gentle, to mankind.

(Exit Dionysus into the palace.)

CHORUS:
—When shall I dance once more
  with bare feet the all-night dances,
  tossing my head for joy
865   in the damp air, in the dew,
  as a running fawn might frisk
  for the green joy of the wide fields,
  free from fear of the hunt,
870   free from the circling beaters
  and the nets of woven mesh
  and the hunters hallooing on
  their yelping packs? And then, hard pressed,
  she sprints with the quickness of wind,
  bounding over the marsh, leaping
875   to frisk, leaping for joy,
  gay with the green of the leaves,
  to dance for joy in the forest,
  to dance where the darkness is deepest,
    where no man is.

—What is wisdom? What gift of the gods
  is held in honor like this:
  to hold your hand victorious
880   over the heads of those you hate?
  Honor is precious forever.

—Slow but unmistakable
  the might of the gods moves on.
  It punishes that man,
  infatuate of soul
885   and hardened in his pride,
  who disregards the gods.
  The gods are crafty:
  they lie in ambush
  a long step of time
890   to hunt the unholy.
  Beyond the old beliefs,
  no thought, no act shall go.
  Small, small is the cost
  to believe in this:
  whatever is god is strong;
  whatever long time has sanctioned,
  that is a law forever;
895   the law tradition makes
  is the law of nature.

—What is wisdom? What gift of the gods
  is held in honor like this:
  to hold your hand victorious
900   over the heads of those you hate?
  Honor is precious forever.

—Blessèd is he who escapes a storm at sea,
    who comes home to his harbor.
—Blessèd is he who emerges from under affliction.
—In various ways one man outraces another in the
905   race for wealth and power.
—Ten thousand men possess ten thousand hopes.
—A few bear fruit in happiness; the others go awry.

—But he who garners day by day the good of life,
  he is happiest. Blessèd is he.   910

*(Re-enter Dionysus from the palace. At the threshold
he turns and calls back to Pentheus.)*

DIONYSUS: Pentheus if you are still so curious to see
  forbidden sights, so bent on evil still,
  come out. Let us see you in your woman's dress,
  disguised in Maenad clothes so you may go and spy   915
  upon your mother and her company.

*(Enter Pentheus from the palace. He wears a long linen
dress which partially conceals his fawn-skin. He carries a
thyrsus in his hand; on his head he wears a wig with long
blond curls bound by a snood. He is dazed and completely
in the power of the god who has now possessed him.)*

              Why,
you look exactly like one of the daughters of Cadmus.
PENTHEUS: I seem to see two suns blazing in the
  heavens.
And now two Thebes, two cities, and each
with seven gates. And you—you are a bull   920
who walks before me there. Horns have sprouted
from your head. Have you always been a beast?
But now I see a bull.
DIONYSUS: It is the god you see.
Though hostile formerly, he now declares a truce
and goes with us. You see what you could not
when you were blind.
PENTHEUS: *(coyly primping)*
                Do I look like anyone?   925
Like Ino or my mother Agave?
DIONYSUS: So much alike
I almost might be seeing one of them. But look:
one of your curls has come loose from under the snood
where I tucked it.
PENTHEUS: It must have worked loose
when I was dancing for joy and shaking my head.   930
DIONYSUS: Then let me be your maid and tuck it back.
  Hold still.
PENTHEUS: Arrange it. I am in your hands completely.

(Dionysus tucks the curl back under the snood.)

DIONYSUS: And now your strap has slipped. Yes,   935
  and your robe hangs askew at the ankles.
PENTHEUS: *(bending backward to look)*
                    I think so.
At least on my right leg. But on the left the hem
lies straight.
DIONYSUS: You will think me the best of friends
when you see to your surprise how chaste the
  Bacchae are.   940
PENTHEUS: But to be a real Bacchante, should I hold
  the wand in my right hand? Or this way?
DIONYSUS: No.
In your right hand. And raise it as you raise
your right foot. I commend your change of heart.
PENTHEUS: Could I lift Cithaeron up, do you think?   945
  Shoulder the cliffs, Bacchae and all?

DIONYSUS: If you wanted.
Your mind was once unsound, but now you think
as sane men do.
PENTHEUS: Should we take crowbars with us?
950 Or should I put my shoulder to the cliffs
and heave them up?
DIONYSUS: What? And destroy the haunts
of the nymphs, the holy groves where Pan plays
his woodland pipe?
PENTHEUS: You are right. In any case,
women should not be mastered by brute strength.
I will hide myself beneath the firs instead.
955 DIONYSUS: You will find all the ambush you deserve,
creeping up to spy on the Maenads.
PENTHEUS: Think.
I can see them already, there among the bushes,
mating like birds, caught in the toils of love.
DIONYSUS: Exactly. This is your mission: you go to watch.
960 You may surprise them—or they may surprise you.
PENTHEUS: Then lead me through the very heart of
      Thebes,
since I, alone of all this city, dare to go.
DIONYSUS: You and you alone will suffer for your city.
A great ordeal awaits you. But you are worthy
965 of your fate. I shall lead you safely there;
someone else shall bring you back.
PENTHEUS: Yes, my mother.
DIONYSUS: An example to all men.
PENTHEUS: It is for that I go.
DIONYSUS: You will be carried home—
PENTHEUS: O luxury!
DIONYSUS: cradled in your mother's arms.
PENTHEUS: You will spoil me.
DIONYSUS: I *mean* to spoil you.
970 PENTHEUS: I go to my reward.
DIONYSUS: You are an extraordinary young man,
      and you go
to an extraordinary experience. You shall win
a glory towering to heaven and usurping
god's.

                              (*Exit Pentheus.*)

      Agave and you daughters of Cadmus,
reach out your hands! I bring this young man
975 to a great ordeal. The victor? Bromius.
Bromius—and I. The rest the event shall show.

                              (*Exit Dionysus.*)

CHORUS:
—Run to the mountain, fleet hounds of madness!
Run, run to the revels of Cadmus' daughters!
980 Sting them against the man in women's clothes,
the madman who spies on the Maenads, who peers
from behind the rocks, who spies from a vantage!
985 His mother shall see him first. She will cry
to the Maenads: "Who is this spy who has come
to the mountains to peer at the mountain-revels
of the women of Thebes? What bore him, Bacchae?
This man was born of no woman. Some lioness
990 give him birth, some one of the Libyan gorgons!"

—O Justice, principle of order, spirit of custom,
come! Be manifest; reveal yourself with a sword!
Stab through the throat that godless man,
the mocker who goes, flouting custom and
      outraging god!
O Justice, stab the evil earth-born spawn of Echion!   995

—Uncontrollable, the unbeliever goes,
in spitting rage, rebellious and amok,
madly assaulting the mysteries of god,
profaning the rites of the mother of god.
Against the unassailable he runs, with rage   1000
obsessed. Headlong he runs to death.
For death the gods exact, curbing by that bit
the mouths of men. They humble us with death
that we remember what we are who are not god,
but men. We run to death. Wherefore, I say;
accept, accept:
humility is wise; humility is blest.
But what the world calls wise I do not want.   1005
Elsewhere the chase. I hunt another game,
those great, those manifest, those certain goals,
achieving which, our mortal lives are blest.
Let these things be the quarry of my chase:
purity; humility; an unrebellious soul,
accepting all. Let me go the customary way,
the timeless, honored, beaten path of those who walk
with reverence and awe beneath the sons of heaven.   1010

—O Justice, principle of order, spirit of custom,
come! Be manifest; reveal yourself with a sword!
Stab through the throat that godless man,
the mocker who goes, flouting custom and outrag-
      ing god!
O Justice, destroy the evil earth-born sprawn of
      Echion!   1015

—O Dionysus, reveal yourself a bull! Be manifest,
a snake with darting heads, a lion breathing fire!
O Bacchus, come! Come with your smile!
Cast your noose about this man who hunts
your Bacchae! Bring him down, trampled   1020
underfoot by the murderous herd of your Maenads!

                    (*Enter a messenger from Cithaeron.*)

MESSENGER: How prosperous in Hellas these halls once
      were,
this house founded by Cadmus, the stranger from Sidon 1025
who sowed the dragon seed in the land of the snake!
I am a slave and nothing more, yet even so
I mourn the fortunes of this fallen house.
CORYPHAEUS: What is it?
Is there news of the Bacchae?
MESSENGER: This is my news:
Pentheus, the son of Echion, is dead.   1030
CORYPHAEUS: All hail to Bromius! Our god is a great god!
MESSENGER: What is this you say, women? You dare to
      rejoice
at these disasters which destroy this house?

CORYPHAEUS: I am no Greek. I hail my god
　　in my own way. No longer need I
1035　shrink with fear of prison.
MESSENGER: If you suppose this city is so short of men—
CORYPHAEUS: Dionysus, Dionysus, not Thebes,
　　has power over me.
MESSENGER: Your feelings might be forgiven, then. But this,
1040　this exultation in disaster—it is not right.
CORYPHAEUS: Tell us how the mocker died.
　　How was he killed?
MESSENGER: There were three of us in all: Pentheus and I,
　　attending my master, and that stranger who
　　　volunteered
　　his services as guide. Leaving behind us
　　the last outlying farms of Thebes, we forded
1045　the Asopus and struck into the barren scrubland
　　of Cithaeron.
　　　　　　　There in a grassy glen we halted,
　　unmoving, silent, without a word,
1050　so we might see but not be seen. From that vantage,
　　in a hollow cut from the sheer rock of the cliffs,
　　a place where water ran and the pines grew dense
　　with shade, we saw the Maenads sitting, their hands
　　busily moving at their happy tasks. Some
1055　wound the stalks of their tattered wands with tendrils
　　of fresh ivy; others, frisking like fillies
　　newly freed from the painted bridles, chanted
　　in Bacchic songs, responsively.
　　　　　　　But Pentheus—
　　unhappy man—could not quite see the companies
　　of women. "Stranger," he said, "from where I stand,
1060　I cannot see these counterfeited Maenads.
　　But if I climbed that towering fir that overhangs
　　the banks, then I could see their shameless orgies
　　better."
　　　　　And now the stranger worked a miracle.
　　Reaching for the highest branch of a great fir,
1065　he bent it down, down, down to the dark earth,
　　till it was curved the way a taut bow bends
　　or like a rim of wood when forced about the circle
　　of a wheel. Like that he forced that mountain fir
　　down to the ground. No mortal could have done it.
1070　Then he seated Pentheus at the highest tip
　　and with his hands let the trunk rise straightly up,
　　slowly and gently, lest it throw its rider.
　　And the tree rose, towering to heaven, with my master
　　huddled at the top. And now the Maenads saw him
　　more clearly than he saw them. But barely had they
1075　　seen,
　　when the stranger vanished and there came a great
　　　voice
　　out of heaven—Dionysus', it must have been—
　　crying: "Women, I bring you the man who has
　　　mocked
1080　at you and me and at our holy mysteries.
　　Take vengeance upon him." And as he spoke
　　a flash of awful fire bound earth and heaven.
　　The high air hushed, and along the forest glen
1085　the leaves hung still; you could hear no cry of beasts.

The Bacchae heard that voice but missed its words,
and leaping up, they stared, peering everywhere.
Again that voice. And now they knew his cry,
the clear command of god. And breaking loose
like startled doves, through grove and torrent, 　1090
over jagged rocks, they flew, their feet maddened
by the breath of god. And when they saw my master
perching in his tree, they climbed a great stone 　1095
that towered opposite his perch and showered him
with stones and javelins of fir, while the others
hurled their wands. And yet they missed their target,
poor Pentheus in his perch, barely out of reach 　1100
of their eager hands, treed, unable to escape.
Finally they splintered branches from the oaks
and with those bars of wood tried to lever up the tree
by prying at the roots. But every effort failed. 　1105
Then Agave cried out: "Maenads, make a circle
about the trunk and grip it with your hands.
Unless we take this climbing beast, he will reveal
the secrets of the god." With that, thousands of hands
tore the fir tree from the earth, and down, down 　1110
from his high perch fell Pentheus, tumbling
to the ground, sobbing and screaming as he fell,
for he knew his end was near. His own mother,
like a priestess with her victim, fell upon him
first. But snatching off his wig and snood 　1115
so she would recognize his face, he touched her
　cheeks,
screaming, "*No, no, Mother! I am Pentheus,
your own son, the child you bore to Echion!
Pity me, spare me, Mother! I have done a wrong,* 　1120
but do not kill your own son for my offense."
But she was foaming at the mouth, and her crazed
　eyes
rolling with frenzy. She was mad, stark mad,
possessed by Bacchus. Ignoring his cries of pity,
she seized his left arm at the wrist; then, planting 　1125
her foot upon his chest, she pulled, wrenching away
the arm at the shoulder—not by her own strength,
for the god had put inhuman power in her hands.
Ino, meanwhile, on the other side, was scratching off
his flesh. Then Autonoë and the whole horde 　1130
of Bacchae swarmed upon him. Shouts everywhere,
he screaming with what little breath was left,
they shrieking in triumph. One tore off an arm,
another a foot still warm in its shoe. His ribs
were clawed clean of flesh and every hand 　1135
was smeared with blood as they played ball with
　scraps
of Pentheus' body.
　　　　　　　The pitiful remains lie scattered,
one piece among the sharp rocks, others
lying lost among the leaves in the depths
of the forest. His mother, picking up his head, 　1140
impaled it on her wand. She seems to think it is
some mountain lion's head which she carries in
　triumph
through the thick of Cithaeron. Leaving her sisters
at the Maenad dances, she is coming here, gloating

1145　over her grisly prize. She calls upon Bacchus:
　　　he is her "fellow-huntsman," "comrade of the chase,
　　　crowned with victory." But all the victory
　　　she carries home is her own grief.
　　　　　　　　　　　　　　　　　Now,
　　　before Agave returns, let me leave
　　　this scene of sorrow. Humility,
1150　a sense of reverence before the sons of heaven—
　　　of all the prizes that a mortal man might win,
　　　these, I say, are wisest; these are best.

　　　　　　　　　　　　　　　(*Exit Messenger.*)

CHORUS:
　　　—We dance to the glory of Bacchus!
　　　We dance to the death of Pentheus,
1155　　the death of the spawn of the dragon!
　　　　He dressed in woman's dress;
　　　　he took the lovely thyrsus;
　　　　it waved him down to death,
　　　　led by a bull to Hades.
1160　　Hail, Bacchae! Hail, women of Thebes!
　　　Your victory is fair, fair the prize,
　　　　this famous prize of grief!
　　　Glorious the game! To fold your child
　　　in your arms, streaming with his blood!
CORYPHAEUS: But look: there comes Pentheus' mother,
1165　　Agave,
　　　running wild-eyed toward the palace.
　　　　　　　　　　　　　　　　—Welcome,
　　　welcome to the reveling band of the god of joy!

　　　(*Enter Agave with other Bacchantes. She is covered
　　　with blood and carries the head of Pentheus impaled
　　　　　　　　　　　　　　　　upon her thyrsus.*)

AGAVE: Bacchae of Asia—
CHORUS:　　　　　　　　Speak, speak.
AGAVE: We bring this branch to the palace,
1170　　this fresh-cut spray from the mountains.
　　　Happy was the hunting.
CHORUS:　　　　　　　　I see.
　　　I welcome our fellow-reveler of god.
AGAVE: The whelp of a wild mountain lion,
　　　and snared by me without a noose.
1175　Look, look at the prize I bring.
CHORUS: Where was he caught?
AGAVE:　　　　　　　　On Cithaeron—
CHORUS: On Cithaeron?
AGAVE:　　　　　　Our prize was killed.
CHORUS: Who killed him?
AGAVE:　　　　　　　I struck him first.
1180　The Maenads call me "Agave the blest."
CHORUS: And then?
AGAVE:　　　　Cadmus'—
CHORUS:　　　　　　　Cadmus'?
AGAVE:　　　　　　　　　　Daughters.
　　　After me, they reached the prey.
　　　After me. Happy was the hunting.
CHORUS: Happy indeed.
AGAVE:　　　　　　Then share my glory,
　　　share the feast.

CHORUS:　　　　Share, unhappy woman?
AGAVE: See, the whelp is young and tender.   1185
　　　Beneath the soft mane of its hair,
　　　the down is blooming on the cheeks.
CHORUS: With that mane he *looks* a beast.
AGAVE: Our god is wise. Cunningly, cleverly,   1190
　　　Bacchus the hunter lashed the Maenads
　　　against his prey.
CHORUS:　　　　　Our king is a hunter.
AGAVE: You praise me now?
CHORUS:　　　　　　　I praise you.
AGAVE: The men of Thebes—
CHORUS:　　　　　　　And Pentheus, your son?
AGAVE: Will praise his mother. She caught   1195
　　　a great quarry, this lion's cub.
CHORUS: Extraordinary catch.
AGAVE:　　　　　　　Extraordinary skill.
CHORUS: You are proud?
AGAVE:　　　　　Proud and happy.
　　　I have won the trophy of the chase,
　　　a great prize, manifest to all.
CORYPHAEUS: Then, poor woman, show the citizens of
　　　　Thebes   1200
　　　this great prize, this trophy you have won
　　　in the hunt.

　　　(*Agave proudly exhibits her thyrsus with the head
　　　　　　of Pentheus impaled upon the point.*)

AGAVE:　　　　　You citizens of this towered city,
　　　men of Thebes, behold the trophy of your women's
　　　hunting! *This* is the quarry of our chase, taken
　　　not with nets nor spears of bronze but by the white   1205
　　　and delicate hands of women. What are they worth,
　　　your boastings now and all that uselessness
　　　your armor is, since we, with our bare hands,
　　　captured this quarry and tore its bleeding body
　　　limb from limb?
　　　　　　　　—But where is my father Cadmus?   1210
　　　He should come. And my son. Where is Pentheus?
　　　Fetch him. I will have him set his ladder up
　　　against the wall and, there upon the beam,
　　　nail the head of this wild lion I have killed
　　　as a trophy of my hunt.

　　　(*Enter Cadmus, followed by attendants who bear upon
　　　　　　a bier the dismembered body of Pentheus.*)

CADMUS:　　　　　　Follow me, attendants.   1215
　　　Bear your dreadful burden in and set it down,
　　　there before the palace.

　　　　　　　　　(*The attendants set down the bier.*)

　　　　　　　　This was Pentheus
　　　whose body, after long and weary searchings
　　　I painfully assembled from Cithaeron's glens
　　　where it lay, scattered in shreds, dismembered
　　　throughout the forest, no two pieces   1220
　　　in a single place.
　　　　　　　Old Teiresias and I
　　　had returned to Thebes from the orgies on the mountain
　　　before I learned of this atrocious crime

1225 my daughters did. And so I hurried back
to the mountain to recover the body of this boy
murdered by the Maenads. There among the oaks
I found Aristaeus' wife, the mother of Actaeon,
Autonoë, and with her Ino, both
still stung with madness. But Agave, they said,
1230 was on her way to Thebes, still possessed.
And what they said was true, for there she is,
and not a happy sight.

AGAVE: Now, Father,
yours can be the proudest boast of living men.
For you are now the father of the bravest
      daughters
1235 in the world. All of your daughters are brave,
but I above the rest. I have left my shuttle
at the loom; I raised my sight to higher things—
to hunting animals with my bare hands.
                                              You see?
Here in my hands I hold the quarry of my chase,
1240 a trophy for our house. Take it, Father, take it.
Glory in my kill and invite your friends to share
the feast of triumph. For you are blest, Father,
by this great deed I have done.

CADMUS: This is a grief
so great it knows no size. I cannot look.
1245 *This* is the awful murder your hands have done.
This, this is the noble victim you have slaughtered
to the gods. And to share a feast like this
you now invite all Thebes and me?
                                              O gods,
how terribly I pity you and then myself.
Justly—too, too justly—has lord Bromius,
1250 this god of our own blood, destroyed us all,
every one.

AGAVE: How scowling and crabbed is old age
in men. I hope my son takes after his mother
and wins, as she has done, the laurels of the chase
when he goes hunting with the younger men of
      Thebes.
1255 But all my son can do is quarrel with god.
He should be scolded, Father, and you are the one
who should scold him. Yes, someone call him out
so he can see his mother's triumph.

CADMUS: Enough. No more.
When you realize the horror you have done,
1260 you shall suffer terribly. But if with luck
your present madness lasts until you die,
you will seem to have, not having, happiness.

AGAVE: Why do you reproach me? Is there something
      wrong?

CADMUS: First raise your eyes to the heavens.

1265 AGAVE: There.
But why?

CADMUS: Does it look the same as it did before?
Or has it changed?

AGAVE: It seems—somehow—clearer,
brighter than it was before.

CADMUS: Do you still feel
the same flurry inside you?

AGAVE: The same—flurry?

No, I feel—somehow—calmer. I feel as though—   1270
my mind were somehow—changing.

CADMUS: Can you still hear me?
Can you answer clearly?

AGAVE: No. I have forgotten
what we were saying, Father.

CADMUS: Who was your husband?

AGAVE: Echion—a man, they said, born of the dragon
      seed.

CADMUS: What was the name of the child you bore your
      husband?   1275

AGAVE: Pentheus.

CADMUS: And whose head do you hold in your hands?

AGAVE: (*averting her eyes*)
A lion's head—or so the hunters told me.

CADMUS: Look directly at it. Just a quick glance.

AGAVE: What is it? What am I holding in my hands?   1280

CADMUS: Look more closely still. Study it carefully.

AGAVE: *No!* O gods, I see the greatest grief there is.

CADMUS: Does it look like a lion now?

AGAVE: No, no. It is—
Pentheus' head—I hold—

CADMUS: And mourned by me   1285
before you ever knew.

AGAVE: But *who* killed him?
Why am *I* holding him?

CADMUS: O savage truth,
what a time to come!

AGAVE: For god's sake, speak.
My heart is beating with terror.

CADMUS: *You* killed him.
You and your sisters.

AGAVE: But where was he killed?   1290
Here at home? Where?

CADMUS: He was killed on Cithaeron,
there where the hounds tore Actaeon to pieces.

AGAVE: But why? Why had Pentheus gone to Cithaeron?

CADMUS: He went to your revels to mock the god.

AGAVE: But *we*—
what were we doing on the mountain?

CADMUS: You were mad.   1295
The whole city was possessed.

AGAVE: Now, now I see:
Dionysus has destroyed us all.

CADMUS: You outraged him.
You denied that he was truly god.

AGAVE: Father,
where is my poor boy's body now?

CADMUS: There it is.
I gathered the pieces with great difficulty.

AGAVE: Is his body entire? Has he been laid out well?   1300

CADMUS: [All but the head. The rest is mutilated
      horribly.]

AGAVE: But why should Pentheus suffer for
      my crime?

CADMUS: He, like you, blasphemed the god. And so
the god has brought us all to ruin at one blow,
you, your sisters, and this boy. All our house
the god has utterly destroyed and, with it,
me. For I have no sons left, no male heir;   1305

and I have lived only to see this boy,
this branch of your own body, most horribly
and foully killed.

(*He turns and addresses the corpse.*)

      —To you my house looked up.
Child, you were the stay of my house; you were
1310   my daughter's son. Of you this city stood in awe.
No one who once had seen your face dared
      outrage
the old man, or if he did, you punished him.
Now I must go, a banished and dishonored man—
I, Cadmus the great, who sowed the soldiery
1315   of Thebes and harvested a great harvest. My son,
dearest to me of all men—for even dead,
I count you still the man I love the most—
never again will your hand touch my chin;
no more, child, will you hug me and call me
1320   "Grandfather" and say, "Who is wronging you?
Does anyone trouble you or vex your heart,
      old man?
Tell me, Grandfather, and I will punish him."
No, now there is grief for me; the mourning
for you; pity for your mother; and for her sisters,
sorrow.
1325   If there is still any mortal man
who despises or defies the gods, let him look
on this boy's death and believe in the gods.
CORYPHAEUS: Cadmus, I pity you. Your daughter's son
has died as he deserved, and yet his death
bears hard on you.

[*At this point there is a break in the manuscript
of nearly fifty lines. The following speeches of Agave
and Coryphaeus and the first part of Dionysus'
speech have been conjecturally reconstructed from
fragments and later material which made use of the
Bacchae. Lines which can plausibly be assigned to
the lacuna are otherwise not indicated. My own inventions are designed, not to complete the speeches,
but to effect a transition between the fragments, and
are bracketed.*—TRANS.]

AGAVE: O Father, now you can see
how everything has changed. I am in anguish now,
tormented, who walked in triumph minutes past,
exulting in my kill. And that prize I carried home
with such pride was my own curse. Upon these hands
I bear the curse of my son's blood. How then
with these accursed hands may I touch his body?
How can I, accursed with such a curse, hold him
to my breast? O gods, what dirge can I sing
[that there might be] a dirge [for every]
broken limb?

. . . .

      Where is a shroud to cover up his corpse?
O my child, what hands will give you proper care
unless with my own hands I lift my curse?

(*She lifts up one of Pentheus' limbs and asks the help of
Cadmus in piecing the body together. She mourns each
piece separately before replacing it on the bier.*)

Come, Father. We must restore his head
to this unhappy boy. As best we can, we shall make
him whole again.
      —O dearest, dearest face!
Pretty boyish mouth! Now with this veil
I shroud your head, gathering with loving care
these mangled bloody limbs, this flesh I brought
to birth

. . . .

CORYPHAEUS: Let this scene teach those [who see these
     things:
Dionysus is the son] of Zeus.

(*Above the palace Dionysus appears in epiphany.*)

DIONYSUS: [I am Dionysus, the son of Zeus, returned to
     Thebes, revealed,
a god to men.] But the men [of Thebes] blasphemed me.
They slandered me; they said I came of mortal man,
and not content with speaking blasphemies,
[they dared to threaten my person with violence.]
These crimes this people whom I cherished well
did from malice to their benefactor. Therefore,
I now disclose the sufferings in store for them.
Like [enemies], they shall be driven from this city
to other lands; there, submitting to the yoke
of slavery, they shall wear out wretched lives,
captives of war, enduring much indignity.

(*He turns to the corpse of Pentheus.*)

This man has found the death which he deserved,
torn to pieces among the jagged rocks.
You are my witnesses: he came with outrage;
he attempted to chain my hands, abusing me
[and doing what he should least of all have done.]
And therefore he has rightly perished by the hands
of those who should the least of all have murdered
     him.
What he suffers, he suffers justly.
           Upon you,
Agave, and on your sisters I pronounce this doom:
you shall leave this city in expiation
of the murder you have done. You are unclean,
and it would be a sacrilege that murderers
should remain at peace beside the graves [of those
whom they have killed].

(*He turns to Cadmus.*)

. . . .

        Next I shall disclose the trials
which await this man. You, Cadmus, shall be changed   1330
to a serpent, and your wife, the child of Ares,
immortal Harmonia, shall undergo your doom,
a serpent too. With her, it is your fate
to go a journey in a car drawn on by oxen,
leading behind you a great barbarian host.
For thus decrees the oracle of Zeus.
With a host so huge its numbers cannot be counted,   1335
you shall ravage many cities; but when your army
plunders the shrine of Apollo, its homecoming
shall be perilous and hard. Yet in the end

the god Ares shall save Harmonia and you
and bring you both to live among the blest.
1340   So say I, born of no mortal father,
Dionysus, true son of Zeus. If then,
when you would not, you had muzzled your madness,
you should have an ally now in the son of Zeus.
CADMUS: We implore you, Dionysus. We have done
   wrong.
DIONYSUS: Too late. When there was time, you did not
1345   know me.
CADMUS: We have learned. But your sentence is too
   harsh.
DIONYSUS: I am a god. I was blasphemed by you.
CADMUS: Gods should be exempt from human passions.
DIONYSUS: Long ago my father Zeus ordained these
   things.
AGAVE: It is fated, Father. We must go.
1350 DIONYSUS: Why then delay?
For you must go.
CADMUS: Child, to what a dreadful end
have we all come, you and your wretched sisters
and my unhappy self. An old man, I must go
1355 to live a stranger among barbarian peoples, doomed
to lead against Hellas a motley foreign army.
Transformed to serpents, I and my wife,
Harmonia, the child of Ares, we must captain
spearsmen against the tombs and shrines of Hellas.
1360 Never shall my sufferings end; not even
over Acheron shall I have peace.
AGAVE: (*embracing Cadmus*)
                     O Father,
to be banished, to live without you!
CADMUS: Poor child,
1365 like a white swan warding its weak old father,
why do you clasp those white arms about my neck?

AGAVE: But banished! Where shall I go?
CADMUS: I do not know,
my child. Your father can no longer help you.
AGAVE: Farewell, my home! City, farewell.
O bridal bed, banished I go,   1370
in misery, I leave you now.
CADMUS: Go, poor child, seek shelter in Aristaeus' house.
AGAVE: I pity you, Father.
CADMUS: And I pity you, my child,
and I grieve for your poor sisters. I pity them.
AGAVE: Terribly has Dionysus brought   1375
disaster down upon this house.
DIONYSUS: I was terribly blasphemed,
my name dishonored in Thebes.
AGAVE: Farewell, Father.
CADMUS: Farewell to you, unhappy child.
Fare well. But you shall find your faring hard.   1380

(*Exit Cadmus.*)

AGAVE: Lead me, guides, where my sisters wait,
poor sisters of my exile. Let me go
where I shall never see Cithaeron more,   1385
where that accursed hill may not see me,
where I shall find no trace of thyrsus!
That I leave to other Bacchae.

(*Exit Agave with attendants.*)

CHORUS: The gods have many shapes.
The gods bring many things
to their accomplishment.
And what was most expected   1390
has not been accomplished.
But god has found his way
for what no man expected.
So ends the play.

COMMENTARY

ALBRECHT DIHLE (b. 1923)

The Bacchae 1994

In his book *A History of Greek Literature from Homer to the Hellenistic Period* (1994), Albrecht Dihle provides a masterful overview of the achievement of Greek drama in the fifth century BCE. Dihle was a professor at the University of Cologne and at the University of Heidelberg. He is now a full member of the Heidelberg Academy of Sciences and is regarded as one of Germany's leading classical scholars. His comments on *The Bacchae* center on the tradition of ecstatic cults in contemporary Greece.

[Euripides'] last play, the *Bacchae* [. . .] is arguably his most powerful play, and so different from all his others, particularly his late works, that it would probably not have been attributed to him at all if the posthumous date of performance (405 BC) and its authorship had not been reliably verified by external proof. (*Iphigenia in Aulis* was written even later but never completed, and has suffered so much through revisions that it is disregarded here.)

Even the technical details of the *Bacchae* are entirely unreminiscent of Euripidean style. The number of tetrameter scenes is small; the chorus is crucially involved in the action, there are no arias in the New Music style, and the prologue leads directly into the action. All this is more evocative of Aeschylean monumentality and directness. On his victorious advance through the world, Dionysus comes to Thebes, the native city of his mother. Everywhere he has instilled women with divine madness, luring them away from their children and looms and sweeping them off in droves into the virgin mountain forest to surrender themselves in blissful ecstasy to his divine presence. Pentheus, ruler of the city, seeks to put a stop to these events, but all his drastic measures fail in the face of the miraculous intervention of the god, who easily releases his adherents from prison. He also bewitches Pentheus, making him dress in maenad clothing and set off for the mountain forest himself to observe the Dionysiac rites of the women. There, however, the god exposes him to the fury of the frenzied women. His own mother, in the belief that she sees a lion before her, tears off his head, carrying it back to the city in triumph. Her awakening from this enchanted state is terrible. At a loss, all those involved acquiesce to the incomprehensible power of the new god.

This tragedy has been interpreted in the most contradictory ways. It has been seen as the last and most vehement protest by Euripides the 'educator' against the amorality of traditional religion. Two of the subsidiary roles in the play are invoked as an additional argument for this interpretation. Cadmus, the aged founder of the city, and the equally elderly seer Teiresias, seek with priestly, anxiety-ridden piety to come to terms with the appearance of the new god, making themselves utterly ridiculous by dressing up as maenads. They totally fail to grasp that this god is not even remotely interested in them.

Other exegetes, on the other hand, have seen the *Bacchae* as evidence of 'repentance' on the part of the old poet. They point chiefly to the unequivocally negative portrayal of Pentheus, who is presented as a ruthless and capricious tyrant who scents behind the Dionysiac cult merely clandestine promiscuity. It is to E. R. Dodds (1966) that scholarship owes an interpretation of the play in terms of religious history. He shows how Euripides depicted with extraordinary precision the typical manifestations of an ecstatic cult. Originally, the cult of Dionysus was an ecstatic religion that at certain times released its adherents from the constraints of their normal lives to disregard all the precepts of state and cult. Athens gradually domesticated this religion, incorporating it into its regular festival calendar, and sublimating its impulses into the magnificent creative achievements of tragedy, comedy and dithyramb. Nevertheless, the Greek world was seized again and again by epidemic waves of unfettered ecstatic piety. Most of these originated in Asia Minor, which was later to produce rather similar movements in the Montanism of the early Christian era and the dervishes of the Islamic era. Such cults also seem to have been indigenous, in a primeval, undomesticated form, to Macedon and Thrace in the northern Balkans, where the population was closely related to that of Anatolia. It was probably here that Euripides had an opportunity to observe them, spending the last two years of his life as a guest at Pella on the invitation of the King of Macedon. Here he may have come to know and understand the elemental power of Dionysiac ecstasy, of which the ancient myths and regulated cults of Classical Greece were mere pale reflections.

The story of Pentheus is a companion to others about the punished persecutors of the new god, such as that of the Thracian Lycurgus dealt with in a tetralogy by Aeschylus. In Euripides' version of the Pentheus tradition we thus find an ecstatic, orgiastic kind of piety that sweeps people to the very heights of proximity to the deity. After this glorious enthusiasm, however, they are left in a state of profound disenchantment that dissolves all the usual constraints of law and order, eclipsing the individual as a responsible person for a brief span. Euripides shows the impossibility of evaluating all this by means of the moral criteria used by the Greeks for centuries to derive ever purer and more sublime notions of the nature of the gods. The sheer power of Dionysus as revealed in the activities of his female adherents is not only mightier than that of the tyrant, but is contemptuous of attempts to organise it into the categories customarily used by people in their conduct towards one another and their gods.

At the end of a productive phase of tragedy writing, therefore, Euripides succeeded in illustrating the mysterious forces to which the Dionysiac cult, and hence tragedy itself, owed their origins. Whereas a major proportion of reflection on the content of myth found in Euripidean tragedies tended to demystify it and detach stage performance from its links with the cults and piety of the Attic *polis*,° the *Bacchae* made clear once again the roots of the dramatic art in a level of elemental human piety that defies categorisation by any civilisation. It was not by chance that a poet as erudite as Euripides entirely dispensed in the conception of this drama with poetic, musical and dramaturgical innovations of any kind.

polis: Citizens of the city-states.

Aristophanes

The best known of the Greek comic playwrights, Aristophanes (c. 448–c. 385 BCE) lived through some of the most difficult times in Athenian history. He watched Athenian democracy fade and decay as factionalism and war took their toll on the strength of the city-state. By the time he died, Athens was caught up in a fierce struggle between supporters of democracy and supporters of oligarchy, government by a small group of leaders.

Aristophanes' plays are democratic in that they appealed to sophisticated and unsophisticated theatergoers alike. Skilled at complex wordplay, he also enjoyed spirited and rowdy comedy. Since his plays were often sharply critical of Athenian policies, his ability to make people laugh was essential to conveying his message. He was a practitioner of what we now call Old Comedy, an irreverent form that ridiculed and insulted prominent people and important institutions. By Aristophanes' time, Old Comedy had become fiercely satirical, especially concerning political matters. Because Aristophanes held strong opinions, he found satire an ideal form for his talents.

Of his more than thirty known plays, only eleven survive. They come from three main periods in his life, beginning, according to legend, when he was a young man, in 427 BCE. *The Acharnians* (425 BCE), from his first period, focuses on the theme of peace. Dicaeopolis (whose name means "honest" or "good citizen") decides to make a separate peace after the Spartans have ravaged the Acharnian vineyards. The Acharnians vow revenge, but Dicaeopolis explains that peace must begin as an individual decision. Aristophanes saw war as a corporate venture; peacemaking was easier for an individual than for a group or a nation.

The Acharnians was followed by *The Peace* in 421 BCE, just before Sparta and Athens signed a treaty, and it seems clearly to have been written in support of the Athenian peace party, whose power had been growing from the time of *The Acharnians* and whose cause had been aided by that play.

His second period was also dominated by the problems of war. Athens's ill-fated expedition to Sicily in violation of the Treaty of Nicias lies thematically beneath the surface of *The Birds* (414 BCE), in which some citizens build Cloud-Cuckoo-Land to come between the world of humans and the world of the gods. *Lysistrata* (411 BCE) is also from this period; its frank antiwar theme is related to the Sicilian wars and to the ultimately devastating Peloponnesian Wars. These were wars fought by Greek city-states in the areas south of Athens, the Peloponnesus. The states had voluntarily contributed money to arm and support Athens against the Persians in 480 BCE — resulting in the Athenian victory at Salamis. The states later became angry when Pericles, the Athenian leader, demanded that they continue giving contributions, much of which he used to fund the rebuilding of the Acropolis and other civic projects in Athens.

The leaders of the other Greek city-states believed that Athens was becoming imperialistic and was overreaching. War broke out between the city-states in 431 BCE and lasted for nearly thirty years. These struggles and the difficulties of conducting a costly, long-distance war in Sicily combined eventually to exhaust the Athenian resources of men and funds. Soundly defeated in 405 BCE,

Athens surrendered to Sparta in 404. Aristophanes lived to see the Spartan ships at rest in the harbors of Athens's chief port, the Piraeus. And he saw, too, the destruction of the walls of the city, leaving it essentially defenseless.

Aristophanes' third and final period, from 393 BCE to his death, includes *The Ecclesiazusae* (c. 392 BCE) (translated as "The Women in Government"), in which women dress as men, find their way into parliament, and pass a new constitution. It is a highly topical play that points to the current situation in Athens and the people's general discontent and anxiety. The last part of *The Plutus,* written five years later, is an allegory about the god of wealth, who is eventually encouraged to make the just wealthy and the unjust poor.

Among the best known of Aristophanes' plays are several whose names refer to the disguises or costumes of the chorus, among them *The Knights, The Wasps,* and *The Frogs. The Frogs* (405 BCE) is especially interesting for its focus on literary issues. It features a contest in the underworld between Aeschylus, who had been dead more than fifty years, and Euripides, who had just died at a relatively young age. Aristophanes uses the contest to make many enlightening comments about Greek tragedy and the skills of the two authors.

Even in his last period Aristophanes was an innovative force in theater. His last surviving play virtually does away with the chorus as an important character in the action. His later plays resemble modern comedies partly because the chorus does not intrude on the action. His genius helped shape later developments in comedy.

For links to resources about Aristophanes, click on *AuthorLinks* at **bedfordstmartins.com/jacobus.**

Lysistrata

At the time *Lysistrata* was written (411 BCE), Athens had suffered a steady diet of war for more than twenty years. Political groups were actively trying to persuade Athenian leaders to discontinue the policies that had alienated Athens from the other city-states that were once its supporters in the Delian League, the group that had funded Athens's struggle against the Persian threat. Aristophanes opposed the imperialist attitudes that conflicted with the democratic spirit of only a generation earlier.

Lysistrata makes it clear that war was the central business of the nation at that time. No sooner is one campaign ended than another begins. The men encountered by the heroine Lysistrata (whose name means "disband the army") on the Acropolis—men who guard the national security and the national treasury—are old and decrepit. The young men are in the field. As Kalonike tells Lysistrata, her man has been away for five months. Such separations were common, and these women are fed up. Lysistrata has gathered the discontented women together to propose a scheme to bring peace and negotiate a treaty.

The scheme is preposterous, but, as is typical of Old Comedy, its very outrageousness is the source of its strength. In time, the idea begins to seem almost reasonable: Lysistrata asks the women to refuse to engage in sex with their husbands until the men stop making war. The women also seize the Acropolis and hold the treasury hostage. Without the national treasury, there can be no war. And because they are confident of getting the support of the larger community of women in other nations—who suffer as they do—they do not fear the consequences of their acts.

In amusing scenes generated by this situation, Aristophanes pokes fun at both sexes. We hear the gossipy conversation of the women, all of whom arrive late to Lysistrata's meeting. The men are dependent, helpless, and ineffectual, and they cannot resist the takeover. When the truth begins to settle in, the men solicit their wives' attention with enormous erections protruding beneath their gowns, one example of the exaggerated visual humor Aristophanes counted on. The double meanings in the conversations are also a great source of humor.

The wonderful scene 3 between Myrrhine and her husband Kinesias is predicated on the agony of the husband whose wife repeatedly promises sexual favors and then reneges, in order to build his sexual excitement to a fever pitch. It is no wonder that Lysistrata can eventually bring the men to sign any treaties she wants.

This heterosexual hilarity is balanced by a number of homosexual allusions. Kleisthenes, possibly a bisexual Athenian, stands ready to relieve some of the men's sexual discomfort, while Lysistrata admits that if the men do not capitulate, the women will have to satisfy their own needs. Such frankness is typical of Athenian comedy.

Women dominate the action of the play, although we must remember that male actors played women's roles. The women see the stupidity and waste of the war and devise a plan that will end it. Observing that they are the ones who suffer most from the effects of war, the women also note that they pay their taxes in babies. The suffering of women had been a major theme in the tragedies of Euripides, and everyone in Aristophanes' audience would have understood Lysistrata's motivation. The idea that a woman should keep her place is expressed by several characters. And since Athenian audiences would have agreed that women should not meddle in war or government, Aristophanes offered them a fantasy that challenged them on many levels.

Aristophanes praises Lysistrata's ingenuity and her perseverance. When the other women want to give up the plan because of their own sexual needs, she holds firm. She demands that they stand by their resolve. The picture of a strong, independent, intelligent, and capable woman obviously pleased the Athenians because they permitted this play to be performed more than once—an unusual practice. Lysistrata became a recognizable and admirable character in Athenian life.

The following translation of *Lysistrata* has several interesting features. It is composed of scenes, a division not made in the original Greek. Instead of having a chorus of elders, as in *Antigone*, Aristophanes uses two choruses—one of men and one of women—that are truly representative of the people: they are as divided and antagonistic as Sophocles' chorus is united and wise. The **koryphaios** (leader) of the men's chorus speaks alone, often in opposition to the koryphaios of the women's chorus.

The rhyming patterns of some of the songs are approximated in English, and the sense of dialect is maintained in the speech of Lampito, who represents a kind of country bumpkin. She is very muscular from the workouts that she and all other Spartans engaged in; Aristophanes reveals certain Athenian prejudices toward the Spartans in the scene where Lampito is taunted for her physique.

For discussion questions and assignments on *Lysistrata*, visit bedfordstmartins.com/jacobus.

Lysistrata in Performance

Lysistrata has enjoyed and still enjoys numerous productions, on both college and commercial stages. Because it is a bawdy play, it has sometimes run into trouble. In 1932, the New York police shut down a performance and sent out a warrant for the arrest of "Arthur" Aristophanes. In 1959, Dudley Fitts's translation (used here) was performed at the Phoenix Theatre in New York with "women . . . wearing simulated breasts, tipped with sequins, and the ruttish old men stripped down to union suits." Hunter College's 1968 production used rock music, hippie beads, and headbands. Less controversial productions include the first modern version, by Maurice Donnay in Paris (1892), in which Lysistrata takes a general as a lover. The Moscow Art Theater produced a highly acclaimed version in 1923 and brought it to the United States in 1925. That version, modified by Gilbert Seldes (published in book form with illustrations by Picasso), was produced throughout the 1930s. All-black versions of the play have been staged several times since 1938. Since 2001 this play has been produced in many countries, including France in 2006. It was performed in Boston, with Cherry Jones as Lysistrata, in 2002. Theodora Skipitares' well-reviewed version at La Mama in New York in February 2011 experimented with multimedia projections and life-size puppets that helped advance the comedic elements of the play. A surprising Broadway musical version, *Lysistrata Jones*, which opened in December 2011, portrays Lysistrata as a member of a women's basketball team that has not won a game in thirty years. Team members hope to break that streak by withholding sex from their boyfriends. Clearly the essence of Aristophanes' play appeals to modern audiences.

ARISTOPHANES (c. 448–c. 385 BCE)

Lysistrata   411 BCE

TRANSLATED BY DUDLEY FITTS

Persons Represented

LYSISTRATA, ⎫
KALONIKE, ⎬ *Athenian women*
MYRRHINE, ⎭
LAMPITO, *a Spartan woman*
CHORUS
COMMISSIONER
KINESIAS, *husband of Myrrhine*
SPARTAN HERALD
SPARTAN AMBASSADOR
A SENTRY

[BABY SON OF KENESIAS
STRATYLLIS
SPARTANS
ATHENIANS]

Scene: *Athens. First, a public square; later, beneath the walls of the Akropolis;° later, a courtyard within the Akropolis.*

Akropolis: Fortress of Athens, sacred to the goddess Athena.

PROLOGUE°

(*Athens; a public square; early morning; Lysistrata alone.*)

LYSISTRATA: If someone had invited them to a
    festival—
of Bacchos,° say; or to Pan's° shrine, or to
    Aphrodite's°
over at Kolias—, you couldn't get through the
    streets,
what with the drums and the dancing. But now,
not a woman in sight!
5   Except—oh, yes!

(*Enter Kalonike.*)

    Here's one of my neighbors, at last. Good
      morning, Kalonike.
KALONIKE: Good morning, Lysistrata.
                            Darling,
don't frown so! You'll ruin your face!
LYSISTRATA: Never mind my face.
Kalonike,
the way we women behave! Really, I don't blame
10   the men
for what they say about us.
KALONIKE: No; I imagine they're right.
LYSISTRATA: For example: I call a meeting
to think out a most important matter—and what
    happens?
The women all stay in bed!
15 KALONIKE: Oh, they'll be along.
It's hard to get away, you know: a husband, a cook,
a child . . . Home life can be *so* demanding!
LYSISTRATA: What I have in mind is even more
    demanding.
KALONIKE: Tell me: what is it?
LYSISTRATA: It's big.
KALONIKE: Goodness! *How* big?
LYSISTRATA: Big enough for all of us.
KALONIKE: But we're not all here!
LYSISTRATA: We would be, if *that's* what was up!
20   No, Kalonike,
this is something I've been turning over for nights,
long sleepless nights.
KALONIKE: It must be getting worn down, then,
if you've spent so much time on it.
LYSISTRATA: Worn down or not,
it comes to this: Only we women can save Greece!
KALONIKE: Only we women? Poor Greece!
25 LYSISTRATA: Just the same,

it's up to us. First, we must liquidate
the Peloponnesians—
KALONIKE: Fun, fun!
LYSISTRATA: —and then the Boiotians.°
KALONIKE: Oh! But not those heavenly eels!
LYSISTRATA: You needn't worry.
I'm not talking about eels.—But here's the point:
If we can get the women from those places—   30
all those Boiotians and Peloponnesians—
to join us women here, why, we can save all Greece!
KALONIKE: But dearest Lysistrata!
How can women do a thing so austere, so
political? We belong at home. Our only armor's   35
our perfumes, our saffron dresses and
our pretty little shoes!
LYSISTRATA: Exactly. Those
transparent dresses, the saffron, the perfume, those
    pretty shoes—
KALONIKE: Oh?
LYSISTRATA: Not a single man would lift
his spear—
KALONIKE: I'll send my dress to the dyer's tomorrow!
LYSISTRATA: —or grab a shield—
KALONIKE: The sweetest little negligee—   40
LYSISTRATA: —or haul out his sword.
KALONIKE: I know where
I can buy the dreamiest sandals!
LYSISTRATA: Well, so you see. Now, shouldn't
the women have come?
KALONIKE: Come? They should have *flown*!
LYSISTRATA: Athenians are always late.
                      But imagine!
There's no one here from the South Shore, or from
    Salamis.   45
KALONIKE: Things are hard over in Salamis, I swear.
They have to get going at dawn.
LYSISTRATA: And nobody from Acharnai.
I thought they'd be here hours ago.
KALONIKE: Well, you'll get
that awful Theagenes woman: she'll be
a sheet or so in the wind.
                      But look!   50
Someone at last! Can you see who they are?

(*Enter Myrrhine and other women.*)

LYSISTRATA: They're from Anagyros.
KALONIKE: They certainly are.
You'd know them anywhere, by the scent.
MYRRHINE: Sorry to be late, Lysistrata.
                      Oh come,
don't scowl so. Say something!
LYSISTRATA: My dear Myrrhine,   55
what is there to say? After all,
you've been pretty casual about the whole thing.

Prologue: Portion of the play explaining the background and
current action. **2. Bacchos:** Bacchus, god of wine and the
object of wild, orgiastic ritual and celebration; also called
Dionysus. **Pan:** God of nature, forests, flocks, and shepherds,
depicted as half man and half goat. Pan was considered playful
and lecherous. **Aphrodite:** Goddess of love.

27. Boiotians: Crude-mannered inhabitants of Boiotia, which
was noted for its seafood.

MYRRHINE: Couldn't find
my girdle in the dark, that's all.
                                    But what *is*
"the whole thing"?

KALONIKE: No, we've got to wait
60   for those Boiotians and Peloponnesians.

LYSISTRATA: That's more like it.—But, look!
Here's Lampito!

(Enter Lampito with women from Sparta.)

LYSISTRATA: Darling Lampito,
how pretty you are today! What a nice color!
Goodness, you look as though you could strangle a
65   bull!

LAMPITO: Ah think Ah could! It's the work-out
in the gym every day; and, of co'se that dance of ahs
where y' kick yo' own tail.

KALONIKE: What an adorable figure!

LAMPITO: Lawdy, when y' touch me lahk that,
Ah feel lahk a heifer at the altar!

70   LYSISTRATA: And this young lady?
Where is she from?

LAMPITO: Boiotia. Social-Register type.

LYSISTRATA: Ah. "Boiotia of the fertile plain."

KALONIKE: And if you look,
you'll find the fertile plain has just been mowed.

LYSISTRATA: And this lady?

LAMPITO: Hagh, wahd, handsome.
75   She comes from Korinth.

KALONIKE: High and wide's the word for it.

LAMPITO: Which one of you
called this heah meeting, and why?

LYSISTRATA: I did.

LAMPITO: Well, then, tell us:
What's up?

MYRRHINE: Yes, darling, what *is* on your mind, after
                                    all?

LYSISTRATA: I'll tell you.—But first, one little question.

MYRRHINE: Well?

LYSISTRATA: It's your husbands. Fathers of your
80   children. Doesn't it bother you
that they're always off with the Army? I'll stake my
        life,
not one of you has a man in the house this minute!

KALONIKE: Mine's been in Thrace the last five months,
        keeping an eye
on that General.

MYRRHINE: Mine's been in Pylos for seven.

LAMPITO: And mahn,
85   whenever he gets a *dis*charge, he goes raht back
with that li'l ole shield of his, and enlists again!

LYSISTRATA: And not the ghost of a lover to be found!
From the very day the war began—
                        those Milesians!
I could skin them alive!
                        —I've not seen so much, even,
90   as one of those leather consolation prizes.—
But there! What's important is: If I've found a way
to end the war, are you with me?

MYRRHINE: I should *say* so!
Even if I have to pawn my best dress and
drink up the proceeds.

KALONIKE: Me, too! Even if they split me
right up the middle, like a flounder.

LAMPITO: Ah'm shorely with you.   95
Ah'd crawl up Taygetos° on mah knees
if that'd bring peace.

LYSISTRATA: All right, then; here it is:
Women! Sisters!
If we really want our men to make peace,
we must be ready to give up—

MYRRHINE: Give up what?   100
Quick, tell us!

LYSISTRATA: But *will* you?

MYRRHINE: We will, even if it kills us.

LYSISTRATA: Then we must give up going to bed with
        our men.

(Long silence.)

Oh? So now you're sorry? Won't look at me?
Doubtful? Pale? All teary-eyed?
                            But come: be frank with me.
Will you do it, or not? Well? Will you do it?

MYRRHINE: I couldn't. No.   105
Let the war go on.

KALONIKE: Nor I. Let the war go on.

LYSISTRATA: You, you little flounder,
ready to be split up the middle?

KALONIKE: Lysistrata, no!
I'd walk through fire for you—you *know* I
        would!—but don't
ask us to give up *that!* Why, there's nothing like it!   110

LYSISTRATA: And you?

BOIOTIAN: No. I must say *I'd* rather walk
        through fire.

LYSISTRATA: What an utterly perverted sex we women
        are!
No wonder poets write tragedies about us.
There's only one thing we can think of.
                                    But you from Sparta:
if you stand by me, we may win yet! Will you?   115
It means so much!

LAMPITO: Ah sweah, it means *too* much!
By the Two Goddesses,° it does! Asking a girl
to sleep—Heaven knows how long!—in a great
        big bed
with nobody there but herself! But Ah'll stay with
        you!
Peace comes first!

LYSISTRATA: Spoken like a true Spartan!   120

---

96. **Taygetos:** A mountain range. 117. **Two Goddesses:** A
woman's oath referring to Demeter, the earth goddess, and her
daughter Persephone, who was associated with seasonal cycles
of fertility.

KALONIKE: But if—
                    oh dear!
                    —if we give up what you tell us to,
    will there *be* any peace?
LYSISTRATA: Why, mercy, of course there will!
    We'll just sit snug in our very thinnest gowns,
    perfumed and powdered from top to bottom, and
        those men
125   simply won't stand still! And when we say No,
    they'll go out of their minds! And there's your peace.
    You can take my word for it.
LAMPITO: Ah seem to remember
    that Colonel Menelaos threw his sword away
    when he saw Helen's breast° all bare.
KALONIKE: But, goodness me!
    What if they just get up and leave us?
130 LYSISTRATA: In that case
    we'll have to fall back on ourselves, I suppose.
    But they won't.
KALONIKE: I must say that's not much help. But
    what if they drag us into the bedroom?
LYSISTRATA: Hang on to the door.
KALONIKE: What if they slap us?
LYSISTRATA: If they do, you'd better give in.
135   But be sulky about it. Do I have to teach you how?
    You know there's no fun for men when they have
        to force you.
    There are millions of ways of getting them to see
        reason.
    Don't you worry: a man
    doesn't like it unless the girl cooperates.
140 KALONIKE: I suppose so. Oh, all right. We'll go along.
LAMPITO: Ah imagine us Spahtans can arrange a
        peace. But you
    Athenians! Why, you're just war-mongers!
LYSISTRATA: Leave that to me.
    I know how to make them listen.
LAMPITO: Ah don't see how.
    After all, they've got their boats; and there's lots
        of money
    piled up in the Akropolis.
145 LYSISTRATA: The Akropolis? Darling,
    we're taking over the Akropolis today!
    That's the older women's job. All the rest of us
    are going to the Citadel to sacrifice—you
        understand me?
    And once there, we're in for good!
LAMPITO: Whee! Up the rebels!
    Ah can see you're a good strat*ee*gist.
150 LYSISTRATA: Well, then, Lampito,
    what we have to do now is take a solemn oath.
LAMPITO: Say it. We'll sweah.
LYSISTRATA: This is it.
    —But where's our Inner Guard?
                    —Look. Guard: you see this shield?

Put it down here. Now bring me the victim's entrails.
KALONIKE: But the oath?
LYSISTRATA: You remember how in Aischylos'
                                Seven°   155
    they killed a sheep and swore on a shield? Well,
        then?
KALONIKE: But I don't see how you can swear for
    peace on a shield.
LYSISTRATA: What else do you suggest?
KALONIKE: Why not a white horse?
    We could swear by that.
LYSISTRATA: And where will you get a white horse?
KALONIKE: I never thought of that. *What* can we do?
LYSISTRATA: I have it!   160
    Let's set this big black wine-bowl on the ground
    and pour in a gallon or so of Thasian,° and swear
    not to add one drop of water.
LAMPITO: Ah lahk *that* oath!
LYSISTRATA: Bring the bowl and the wine-jug.
KALONIKE: Oh, what a simply *huge* one!
LYSISTRATA: Set it down. Girls, place your hands on
        the gift-offering.   165
    O Goddess of Persuasion! And thou, O Loving-cup:
    Look upon this our sacrifice, and
    be gracious!
KALONIKE: See the blood spill out. How red and pretty
    it is!
LAMPITO: And Ah must say it smells good.
MYRRHINE: Let me swear first!   170
KALONIKE: No, by Aphrodite, we'll match for it!
LYSISTRATA: Lampito: all of you women: come, touch
        the bowl,
    and repeat after me—remember, this is an oath—:
    I WILL HAVE NOTHING TO DO WITH MY
        HUSBAND OR MY LOVER
KALONIKE: *I will have nothing to do with my husband
    or my lover*   175
LYSISTRATA: THOUGH HE COME TO ME IN
    PITIABLE CONDITION
KALONIKE: *Though he come to me in pitiable condition*
    (Oh Lysistrata! This is killing me!)
LYSISTRATA: IN MY HOUSE I WILL BE
    UNTOUCHABLE
KALONIKE: *In my house I will be untouchable*   180
LYSISTRATA: IN MY THINNEST SAFFRON SILK
KALONIKE: *In my thinnest saffron silk*
LYSISTRATA: AND MAKE HIM LONG FOR ME.
KALONIKE: *And make him long for me.*
LYSISTRATA: I WILL NOT GIVE MYSELF   185
KALONIKE: *I will not give myself*
LYSISTRATA: AND IF HE CONSTRAINS ME
KALONIKE: *And if he constrains me*
LYSISTRATA: I WILL BE COLD AS ICE AND NEVER
    MOVE

127–128. **Colonel Menelaos . . . Helen's breast:** Helen, wife of
King Menelaos of Sparta, was abducted by Paris and taken to
Troy. The incident led to the Trojan War.

155. *Seven:* Aeschylus's *Seven against Thebes,* which deals with
the war between the sons of Oedipus for the throne of Thebes.
162. **Thasian:** Wine from Thasos.

190　KALONIKE: *I will be cold as ice and never move*
　　LYSISTRATA: I WILL NOT LIFT MY SLIPPERS
　　　　　TOWARD THE CEILING
　　KALONIKE: *I will not lift my slippers toward the ceiling*
　　LYSISTRATA: OR CROUCH ON ALL FOURS LIKE
　　　　　THE LIONESS IN THE CARVING
　　KALONIKE: *Or crouch on all fours like the lioness in
　　　　　the carving*
　　LYSISTRATA: AND IF I KEEP THIS OATH LET ME
195　　　　　DRINK FROM THIS BOWL
　　KALONIKE: *And if I keep this oath let me drink from
　　　　　this bowl*
　　LYSISTRATA: IF NOT, LET MY OWN BOWL BE
　　　　　FILLED WITH WATER.
　　KALONIKE: *If not, let my own bowl be filled with
　　　　　water.*
　　LYSISTRATA: You have all sworn?
　　MYRRHINE:　　　　　　　　We have.
　　LYSISTRATA:　　　　　　　　　　Then thus
　　　I sacrifice the victim.

(*Drinks largely.*)

200　KALONIKE:　　　　　Save some for us!
　　　Here's to you, darling, and to you, and to you!

(*Loud cries offstage.*)

　　LAMPITO: What's all *that* whoozy-goozy?
　　LYSISTRATA:　　　　　　Just what I told you.
　　　The older women have taken the Akropolis.
　　　Now you, Lampito,
　　　rush back to Sparta. We'll take care of things here.
205　　　Leave
　　　these girls here for hostages.
　　　　　　　　　　The rest of you,
　　　up to the Citadel: and mind you push in the bolts.
　　KALONIKE: But the men? Won't they be after us?
　　LYSISTRATA:　　　　　　Just you leave
　　　the men to me. There's not fire enough in the world,
210　　　or threats either, to make me open these doors
　　　except on my own terms.
　　KALONIKE:　　　　　I hope not, by Aphrodite!
　　　After all,
　　　we've got a reputation for bitchiness to live up to.

　　　　　　　　　　　　　(*Exeunt.°*)

PARODOS:°
CHORAL EPISODE

(*The hillside just under the Akropolis. Enter Chorus
of Old Men with burning torches and braziers; much
puffing and coughing.*)

213. [S.D.] *Exeunt:* Latin for "they go out."　**Parodos:** Song or
ode chanted by the Chorus on their entry.

KORYPHAIOS(man):° Forward march, Drakes, old friend:
　　never you mind
　　that damn big log banging hell down on your back.

Strophe° 1

CHORUS(men): There's this to be said for longevity:
　　You see things you thought that you'd never see.
　　　Look, Strymodoros, who would have thought it?　5
　　　We've caught it—
　　　　　　　　the New Femininity!
　　The wives of our bosom, our board, our bed—
　　Now, by the gods, they've gone ahead
　　And taken the Citadel (Heaven knows why!),
　　Profanèd the sacred statuar-y,　　　　　　　10
　　　　　　　　And barred the doors,
　　　　　　　　The subversive whores!
KORYPHAIOS(m): Shake a leg there, Philurgos, man: the
　　Akropolis or bust!
　　Put the kindling around here. We'll build one
　　　almighty big
　　bonfire for the whole bunch of bitches, every last one;　15
　　and the first we fry will be old Lykon's woman.

Antistrophe° 1

CHORUS(m): They're not going to give me the old
　　horse-laugh!
　　No, by Demeter, they won't pull this off!
　　　Think of Kleomenes: even he
　　　Didn't go free
　　　　　　　till he brought me his stuff.　　　20
　　A good man he was, all stinking and shaggy,
　　Bare as an eel except for the bag he
　　Covered his rear with. God, what a mess!
　　Never a bath in six years, I'd guess.
　　　　　　　　　Pure Sparta, man!　25
　　　　　　　　　He also ran.
KORYPHAIOS(m): That was a siege, friends! Seventeen
　　ranks strong
　　we slept at the Gate. And shall we not do as much
　　against these women, whom God and Euripides hate?
　　If we don't, I'll turn in my medals from Marathon.　30

Strophe 2

CHORUS(m): Onward and upward! A little push,
　　And we're there.

1. **Koryphaios:** Leader of the Chorus; also called Choragos.
There are two Choruses and two Koryphaioi, one male and
one female. **Strophe:** Song sung by the Chorus as it danced
from stage right to stage left.　**Antistrophe:** Song sung by the
Chorus following the Strophe, as it danced back from stage
left to stage right.

Ouch, my shoulders! I could wish
   For a pair
35 Of good strong oxen. Keep your eye
   On the fire there, it mustn't die.
        Akh! Akh!
The smoke would make a cadaver cough!

Antistrophe 2

Holy Herakles, a hot spark
40   Bit my eye!
Damn this hellfire, damn this work!
   So say I.
Onward and upward just the same.
(Laches, remember the Goddess: for shame!)
45   Akh! Akh!
The smoke would make a cadaver cough!

KORYPHAIOS(m): At last (and let us give suitable thanks
   to God
for his infinite mercies) I have managed to bring
my personal flame to the common goal. It
   breathes, it lives.
50 Now, gentlemen, let us consider. Shall we insert
the torch, say, into the brazier, and thus extract
a kindling brand? And shall we then, do you think,
push on to the gate like valiant sheep? On the whole
   yes.
But I would have you consider this, too: if they—
55 I refer to the women—should refuse to open,
what then? Do we set the doors afire
and smoke them out? At ease, men. Meditate.
Akh, the smoke! Woof! What we really need
is the loan of a general or two from the Samos
   Command.°
60 At least we've got this lumber off our backs.
That's something. And now let's look to our fire.
O Pot, brave Brazier, touch my torch with flame!
Victory, Goddess, I invoke thy name!
Strike down these paradigms of female pride
65 And we shall hang our trophies up inside.

(*Enter Chorus of Old Women on the walls of the
Akropolis, carrying jars of water.*)

KORYPHAIOS(woman): Smoke, girls, smoke! There's smoke
   all over the place!
Probably fire, too. Hurry, girls! Fire! Fire!

Strophe 1

CHORUS(women): Nikodike, run!
   Or Kalyke's done
70 To a turn, and poor Kritylla's
Smoked like a ham.
        Damn
These old men! Are we too late?

59. Samos Command: Headquarters of the Athenian military.

I nearly died down at the place
Where we fill our jars:
   Slaves pushing and jostling—
   Such a hustling   75
I never saw in all my days.

Antistrophe 1

But here's water at last.
Haste, sisters, haste!
Slosh it on them, slosh it down,
The silly old wrecks!   80
         Sex
Almighty! What they want's
A hot bath? Good. Send one down.
Athena of Athens town,
   Trito-born!° Helm of Gold!   85
   Cripple the old
Firemen! Help us help them drown!

(*The old men capture a woman, Stratyllis.*)

STRATYLLIS: Let me go! Let me go!
KORYPHAIOS(w):   You walking corpses,
   have you no shame?
KORYPHAIOS(m):   I wouldn't have believed it!
An army of women in the Akropolis!   90
KORYPHAIOS(w): So we scare you, do we? Grandpa,
   you've seen
only our pickets yet!
KORYPHAIOS(m):   Hey, Phaidrias!
Help me with the necks of these jabbering hens!
KORYPHAIOS(w): Down with your pots, girls! We'll need
   both hands
if these antiques attack us!
KORYPHAIOS(m):   Want your face kicked in?   95
KORYPHAIOS(w): Want your balls chewed off?
KORYPHAIOS(m):   Look out! I've got a stick!
KORYPHAIOS(w): You lay a half-inch of your stick on
   Stratyllis,
and you'll never stick again!
KORYPHAIOS(m): Fall apart!
KORYPHAIOS(w):   I'll spit up your guts!
KORYPHAIOS(m):   Euripides! Master!
How well you knew women!
KORYPHAIOS(w):   Listen to him, Rhodippe,   100
   up with the pots!
KORYPHAIOS(m):   Demolition of God,
   what good are your pots?
KORYPHAIOS(w):   You refugee from the tomb,
   what good is your fire?
KORYPHAIOS(m):   Good enough to make a pyre
   to barbecue you!
KORYPHAIOS(w):   We'll squizzle your kindling!
KORYPHAIOS(m): You think so?
KORYPHAIOS(w):   Yah! Just hang around a while!   105
KORYPHAIOS(m): Want a touch of my torch?

85. Trito-born: Athena, goddess of wisdom, was said to have
been born near Lake Tritonis in Libya.

KORYPHAIOS⁽ʷ⁾:   It needs a good soaping.
KORYPHAIOS⁽ᵐ⁾: How about you?
KORYPHAIOS⁽ʷ⁾:   Soap for a senile bridegroom!
KORYPHAIOS⁽ᵐ⁾: Senile? Hold your trap
KORYPHAIOS⁽ʷ⁾:   Just *you* try to hold it!
KORYPHAIOS⁽ᵐ⁾: The yammer of women!
KORYPHAIOS⁽ʷ⁾:   Oh is that so?
110   You're not in the jury room now, you know.
KORYPHAIOS⁽ᵐ⁾: Gentlemen, I beg you, burn off that
        woman's hair!
KORYPHAIOS⁽ʷ⁾: Let it come down!

(*They empty their pots on the men.*)

KORYPHAIOS⁽ᵐ⁾: What a way to drown!
KORYPHAIOS⁽ʷ⁾:   Hot, hey?
KORYPHAIOS⁽ᵐ⁾:   Say, enough!
KORYPHAIOS⁽ʷ⁾: Dandruff
115   needs watering. I'll make you
        nice and fresh.
KORYPHAIOS⁽ᵐ⁾: For God's sake, you,
        hold off!

SCENE 1

(*Enter a Commissioner accompanied by four
constables.*)

COMMISSIONER: These degenerate women! What a
        racket of little drums,
    what a yapping for Adonis° on every house-top!
    It's like the time in the Assembly when I was listening
    to a speech — out of order, as usual — by that fool
5   Demostratos,° all about troops for Sicily,°
    that kind of nonsense—
                        and there was his wife
    trotting around in circles howling
    Alas for Adonis! —
                    and Demostratos insisting
    we must draft every last Zakynthian that can walk—
10 and his wife up there on the roof,
    drunk as an owl, yowling
    Oh weep for Adonis! —
                        and that damned ox Demostratos
    mooing away through the rumpus. That's what we
        get
    for putting up with this wretched woman-business!
KORYPHAIOS⁽ᵐ⁾: Sir, you haven't heard the half of it.
15   They laughed at us!
    Insulted us! They took pitchers of water
    and nearly drowned us! We're still wringing out our
        clothes,
    for all the world like unhousebroken brats.

COMMISSIONER: Serves you right, by Poseidon!
    Whose fault is it if these women-folk of ours   20
    get out of hand? We coddle them,
    we teach them to be wasteful and loose. You'll see a
        husband
    go into a jeweler's. "Look," he'll say,
    "jeweler," he'll say, "you remember that gold choker
    you made for my wife? Well, she went to a dance
        last night   25
    and broke the clasp. Now, I've got to go to Salamis,
    and can't be bothered. Run over to my house tonight,
    will you, and see if you can put it together for her."
    Or another one
    goes to a cobbler — a good strong workman, too,   30
    with an awl that was never meant for child's play.
        "Here,"
    he'll tell him, "one of my wife's shoes is pinching
    her little toe. Could you come up about noon
    and stretch it out for her?"
                        Well, what do you expect?
    Look at me, for example, I'm a Public Officer,   35
    and it's one of my duties to pay off the sailors.
    And where's the money? Up there in the Akropolis!
    And those blasted women slam the door in my face!
    But what are we waiting for?
                        —Look here, constable,
    stop sniffing around for a tavern, and get us   40
    some crowbars. We'll force their gates! As a matter
        of fact,
    I'll do a little forcing myself.

(*Enter Lysistrata, above, with Myrrhine, Kalonike, and
the Boiotian.*)

LYSISTRATA: No need of forcing.
    Here I am, of my own accord. And all this talk
    about locked doors—! We don't need locked doors,
    but just the least bit of common sense.   45
COMMISSIONER: Is that so, ma'am!
                        —Where's my constable?
                        —Constable,
    arrest that woman, and tie her hands behind her.
LYSISTRATA: If he touches me, I swear by Artemis
    there'll be one scamp dropped from the public
        pay-roll tomorrow!
COMMISSIONER: Well, constable? You're not afraid, I
        suppose? Grab her,   50
    two of you, around the middle!
KALONIKE: No, by Pandrosos!°
    Lay a hand on her, and I'll jump on you so hard
    your guts will come out the back door!
COMMISSIONER: That's what *you* think!
    Where's the sergeant?—Here, you: tie up that
        trollop first,
    the one with the pretty talk!

---

2. **Adonis:** Fertility god, loved by Aphrodite. 5. **Demostratos:**
Athenian orator and politician. **Sicily:** Reference to the Sicilian Expedition (415–413 BCE) in which Athens was decisively
defeated.

51. **Pandrosos:** A woman's oath referring to one of the daughters of the founder of Athens.

55 MYRRHINE: By the Moon-Goddess,°
 just try! They'll have to scoop you up with a spoon!
COMMISSIONER: Another one!
                              Officer, seize that woman!
                                             I swear
 I'll put an end to this riot!
BOIOTIAN: By the Taurian,°
 one inch closer, you'll be one screaming bald-head!
COMMISSIONER: Lord, what a mess! And my
60   constables seem ineffective.
 But—women get the best of us? By God, no!
                                        —Skythians!°
 Close ranks and forward march!
LYSISTRATA: "Forward," indeed!
 By the Two Goddesses, what's the sense in *that*?
 They're up against four companies of women
 armed from top to bottom.
65 COMMISSIONER: Forward, my Skythians!
LYSISTRATA: Forward, yourselves, dear comrades!
 You grainlettucebeanseedmarket girls!
 You garlicandonionbreadbakery girls!
 Give it to 'em! Knock 'em down! Scratch 'em!
 Tell 'em what you think of 'em!

(*General melee, the Skythians yield.*)

70   —Ah, that's enough!
 Sound a retreat: good soldiers don't rob the dead.
COMMISSIONER: A nice day *this* has been for the police!
LYSISTRATA: Well, there you are.—Did you really
    think we women
 would be driven like slaves? Maybe now you'll admit
 that a woman knows something about spirit.
75 COMMISSIONER: Spirit enough,
 especially spirits in bottles! Dear Lord Apollo!
KORYPHAIOS⁽ᵐ⁾: Your Honor, there's no use talking to
    them. Words
 mean nothing whatever to wild animals like these.
 Think of the sousing they gave us! and the water
80 was not, I believe, of the purest.
KORYPHAIOS⁽ʷ⁾: You shouldn't have come after us.
    And if you try it again,
 you'll be one eye short!—Although, as a matter of
    fact,
 what I like best is just to stay at home and read,
 like a sweet little bride: never hurting a soul, no,
85 never going out. But if you *must* shake hornets' nests,
 look out for the hornets.

Strophe

CHORUS⁽ᵐ⁾: Of all the beasts that God hath wrought
 What monster's worse than woman?

Who shall encompass with his thought
    Their guile unending? No man.   90

They've seized the Heights, the Rock, the Shrine—
    But to what end? I wot not.
Sure there's some clue to their design!
    Have you the key? I thought not.
KORYPHAIOS⁽ᵐ⁾: We might question them, I suppose.
    But I warn you, sir,   95
 don't believe anything you hear! It would be un-
    Athenian
 not to get to the bottom of this plot.
COMMISSIONER: Very well.
 My first question is this: Why, so help you God,
 did you bar the gates of the Akropolis?
LYSISTRATA: Why?
 To keep the money, of course. No money, no war.   100
COMMISSIONER: You think that money's the cause of
    war?
LYSISTRATA: I do.
 Money brought about that Peisandros° business
 and all the other attacks on the State. Well and good!
 They'll not get another cent here!
COMMISSIONER: And what will you do? 105
LYSISTRATA: What a question! From now on, we intend
 to control the Treasury.
COMMISSIONER: Control the Treasury!
LYSISTRATA: Why not? Does that seem strange?
    After all,
 we control our household budgets.
COMMISSIONER: But that's different!
LYSISTRATA: "Different"? What do you mean?
COMMISSIONER: I mean simply this: 110
 it's the Treasury that pays for National Defense.
LYSISTRATA: Unnecessary. We propose to abolish war.
COMMISSIONER: Good God.—And National
    Security?
LYSISTRATA: Leave that to us.
COMMISSIONER: You?
LYSISTRATA: Us.
COMMISSIONER: We're done for, then!
LYSISTRATA: Never mind.   115
 We women will save you in spite of yourselves.
COMMISSIONER: What nonsense!
LYSISTRATA: If you like. But you must accept it, like it
    or not.
COMMISSIONER: Why, this is downright subversion!
LYSISTRATA: Maybe it is.
 But we're going to save you, Judge.
COMMISSIONER: I don't *want* to be saved.
LYSISTRATA: Tut. The death-wish. All the more reason.   120
COMMISSIONER: But the idea of women bothering
    themselves about peace and war!
LYSISTRATA: Will you listen to me?

---

55. **Moon-Goddess:** Artemis, goddess of the hunt and of fertility, daughter of Zeus.   58. **Taurian:** Reference to Artemis, who
was said to have been worshiped in a cult at Taurica Chersone-
sos.   61. **Skythians:** Athenian archers.

103. **Peisandros:** A politician who plotted against the Athenian
democracy.

COMMISSIONER: Yes. But be brief, or I'll—
LYSISTRATA: This is no time for stupid threats.
COMMISSIONER: By the gods,
I can't stand any more!
AN OLD WOMAN: Can't stand? Well, well.
125 COMMISSIONER: That's enough out of you, you old
buzzard!
Now, Lysistrata: tell me what you're thinking.
LYSISTRATA: Glad to.
                     Ever since this war began
We women have been watching you men, agreeing
with you,
keeping our thoughts to ourselves. That doesn't mean
we were happy: we weren't, for we saw how
130 things were going;
but we'd listen to you at dinner
arguing this way and that.
                                    —Oh you, and your big
Top Secrets!—
               And then we'd grin like little patriots
(though goodness knows we didn't feel like
grinning) and ask you:
"Dear, did the Armistice come up in Assembly
135 today?"
And you'd say, "None of your business! Pipe
down!" you'd say.
And so we would.
AN OLD WOMAN: *I* wouldn't have, by God!
COMMISSIONER: You'd have taken a beating, then!
                                            —Go on.
LYSISTRATA: Well, we'd be quiet. But then, you know,
all at once
140 you men would think up something worse than ever.
Even *I* could see it was fatal. And, "Darling,"
I'd say,
"have you gone completely mad?" And my husband
would look at me
and say, "Wife, you've got your weaving to attend
to.
Mind your tongue, if you don't want a slap.
145 'War's a man's affair!'"°
COMMISSIONER: Good words, and well pronounced.
LYSISTRATA: You're a fool if you think so.
                              It was hard enough
to put up with all this banquet-hall strategy.
But then we'd hear you out in the public square:
150 "Nobody left for the draft-quota here in Athens?"
you'd say; and, "No," someone else would say, "not
a man!"
And so we women decided to rescue Greece.
You might as well listen to us now: you'll have to,
later.
COMMISSIONER: *You* rescue Greece? Absurd.

LYSISTRATA: You're the absurd one.
COMMISSIONER: You expect me to take orders from a
woman?
            I'd die first!   155
LYSISTRATA: Heavens, if that's what's bothering you,
take my veil,
here, and wrap it around your poor head.
KALONIKE: Yes
and you can have my market-basket, too.
Go home, tighten your girdle, do the washing, mind
your beans! "War's   160
a woman's affair!"
KORYPHAIOS(w):   Ground pitchers! Close ranks!

Antistrophe

CHORUS(w): This is a dance that I know well,
My knees shall never yield.
Wobble and creak I may, but still
I'll keep the well-fought field.   165
Valor and grace march on before,
Love prods us from behind.
Our slogan is EXCELSIOR,
Our watchword SAVE MANKIND.
KORYPHAIOS(w): Women, remember your grandmothers!
Remember   170
that little old mother of yours, what a stinger she
was!
On, on, never slacken. There's a strong wind astern!
LYSISTRATA: O Eros of delight! O Aphrodite! Kyprian!°
If ever desire has drenched our breasts or dreamed
in our thighs, let it work so now on the men of
Hellas°   175
that they shall tail us through the land, slaves, slaves
to Woman, Breaker of Armies!
COMMISSIONER: And if we do?
LYSISTRATA: Well, for one thing, we shan't have to
watch you
going to market, a spear in one hand, and heaven
knows
what in the other.
KALONIKE: Nicely said, by Aphrodite!   180
LYSISTRATA: As things stand now, you're neither men
nor women.
Armor clanking with kitchen pans and pots—
You sound like a pack of Korybantes!°
COMMISSIONER: A man must do what a man must do.
LYSISTRATA: So I'm told.
But to see a General, complete with Gorgon-shield,   185
jingling along the dock to buy a couple of herrings!

---

145. **'War's a man's affair!':** Quoted from Homer's *Iliad*, VI, 492, Hector's farewell to his wife, Andromache.

173. **Kyprian:** Reference to Aphrodite's association with Cyprus (Kyprus), a place sacred to her and a center for her worship.
175. **Hellas:** Greece. 183. **Korybantes:** Priestesses of Cybele, a fertility goddess, who was celebrated in frenzied rituals accompanied by the beating of cymbals.

KALONIKE: *I* saw a Captain the other day—lovely
    fellow he was,
    nice curly hair—sitting on his horse; and—can
    you believe it?—
    he'd just bought some soup, and was pouring it
    into his helmet!
190 And there was a soldier from Thrace
    swishing his lance like something out of Euripides,
    and the poor fruit-store woman got so scared
    that she ran away and let him have his figs free!
COMMISSIONER: All this is beside the point.
                        Will you be so kind
    as to tell me how you mean to save Greece?
195 LYSISTRATA: Of course.
    Nothing could be simpler.
COMMISSIONER: I assure you, I'm all ears.
LYSISTRATA: Do you know anything about weaving?
    Say the yarn gets tangled: we thread it
    this way and that through the skein, up and down,
200 until it's free. And it's like that with war.
    We'll send our envoys
    up and down, this way and that, all over Greece,
    until it's finished.
COMMISSIONER: Yarn? Thread? Skein?
    Are you out of your mind? I tell you,
    war is a serious business.
205 LYSISTRATA: So serious
    that I'd like to go on talking about weaving.
COMMISSIONER: All right. Go ahead.
LYSISTRATA: The first thing we have to do
    is to wash our yarn, get the dirt out of it.
    You see? Isn't there too much dirt here in Athens?
    You must wash those men away.
210   Then our spoiled wool—
    that's like your job-hunters, out for a life
    of no work and big pay. Back to the basket,
    citizens or not, allies or not,
    or friendly immigrants.
                        And your colonies?
215 Hanks of wool lost in various places. Pull them
    together, weave them into one great whole,
    and our voters are clothed for ever.
COMMISSIONER: It would take a woman
    to reduce state questions to a matter of carding and
    weaving.
LYSISTRATA: You fool! Who were the mothers whose
    sons sailed off
    to fight for Athens in Sicily?
220 COMMISSIONER: Enough!
    I beg you, do not call back those memories.
LYSISTRATA: And then,
    instead of the love that every woman needs,
    we have only our single beds, where we can
    dream
    of our husbands off with the Army.
                        Bad enough for wives!
225 But what about our girls, getting older every day,
    and older, and no kisses?
COMMISSIONER: Men get older, too.

LYSISTRATA: Not in the same sense.
                        A soldier's discharged,
    and he may be bald and toothless, yet he'll find
    a pretty young thing to go to bed with.
                        But a woman!
    Her beauty is gone with the first gray hair.   230
    She can spend her time
    consulting the oracles and the fortune-tellers,
    but they'll never send her a husband.
COMMISSIONER: Still, if a man can rise to the
    occasion—
LYSISTRATA: Rise? Rise, yourself!   235
(Furiously.)
    Go invest in a coffin!
                You've money enough.
                        I'll bake you
    a cake for the Underworld.
                And here's your funeral wreath!
(She pours water upon him.)
MYRRHINE: And here's another!
(More water.)
KALONIKE: And here's
    my contribution!
(More water.)
LYSISTRATA: What are you waiting for?
    All aboard Styx Ferry!
                Charon's° calling for you!   240
    It's sailing-time: don't disrupt the schedule!
COMMISSIONER: The insolence of women! And
    to me!
    No, by God, I'll go back to town and show
    the rest of the Commission what might happen to
    them.   (*Exit Commissioner.*)
LYSISTRATA: Really, I suppose we should have laid
    out his corpse   245
    on the doorstep, in the usual way.
                        But never mind.
    We'll give him the rites of the dead tomorrow
    morning.

        (*Exit Lysistrata with Myrrhine and Kalonike.*)

PARABASIS:°
CHORAL EPISODE • Ode° 1

KORYPHAIOS[(m)]: Sons of Liberty, awake! The day of
    glory is at hand.

---

240. Charon: The god who ferried the souls of the newly dead
across the river Styx to Hades. **Parabasis:** Section of the
play in which the author presented his own views through the
Koryphaios directly to the audience. The parabasis in *Lysistrata*
is shorter than those in Aristophanes' other works and unusual in that the Koryphaios does not speak directly for the
author. **Ode:** Song sung by the Chorus.

CHORUS(m): I smell tyranny afoot, I smell it rising from
  the land.
  I scent a trace of Hippias,° I sniff upon the breeze
  A dismal Spartan hogo that suggests King
    Kleisthenes.°
5   Strip, strip for action, brothers!
    Our wives, aunts, sisters, mothers
  Have sold us out: the streets are full of godless
    female rages.
  Shall we stand by and let our women confiscate
    our wages?

[Epirrhema° 1]

KORYPHAIOS(m): Gentlemen, it's a disgrace to Athens, a
  disgrace
  to all that Athens stands for, if we allow these
10   grandmas
  to jabber about spears and shields and making
    friends
  with the Spartans. What's a Spartan? Give me a
    wild wolf
  any day. No. They want the Tyranny back, I
    suppose.
15 Are we going to take that? No. Let us look like
  the innocent serpent, but be the flower under it,
  as the poet sings. And just to begin with,
  I propose to poke a number of teeth
  down the gullet of that harridan over there.

Antode° 1

KORYPHAIOS(w): Oh, is that so? When you get home,
    your own mamma won't know you!
CHORUS(w): Who do you think we are, you senile
20   bravos? Well, I'll show you.
  I bore the sacred vessels in my eighth year,° and at ten
  I was pounding out the barley for Athena Goddess;°
    then
    They made me Little Bear
    At the Brauronian Fair;°
25 I'd held the Holy Basket° by the time I was of age,
  The Blessed Dry Figs had adorned my plump
    decolletage.

[Antepirrhema° 1]

3. **Hippias:** An Athenian tyrant.   4. **Kleisthenes:** A bisexual
Athenian.   **Epirrhema:** A part of the parabasis spoken by the
Koryphaios following an ode delivered by his or her half of the
Chorus.   **Antode:** Lyric song sung by half of the Chorus in response to the ode sung by the other half.   21. **eighth year:** Young
girls between the ages of seven and eleven served in the temple of
Athena in the Akropolis.   22. **pounding out the barley for Athena
Goddess:** At age ten a girl could be chosen to grind the sacred grain
of Athena.   24. **Brauronian Fair:** A ritual in the cult of Artemis,
who is associated with wild beasts, in which young girls dressed
up as bears and danced for the goddess.   25. **Holy Basket:** In one
ritual to Athena, young girls carried baskets of objects sacred to
the goddess.   **Antepirrhema:** The speech delivered by the second
Koryphaios after the second half of the Chorus had sung an ode.

KORYPHAIOS(w): A "disgrace to Athens," and I, just at
    the moment
  I'm giving Athens the best advice she ever had?
  Don't I pay taxes to the State? Yes, I pay them
  in baby boys. And what do you contribute,   30
  you impotent horrors? Nothing but waste: all
  our Treasury,° dating back to the Persian Wars,
  gone! rifled! And not a penny out of your pockets!
  Well, then? Can you cough up an answer to that?
  Look out for your own gullet, or you'll get a crack   35
  from this old brogan that'll make your teeth see
    stars!

Ode 2

CHORUS(m): Oh insolence!
  Am I unmanned?
  Incontinence!
  Shall my scarred hand   40
  Strike never a blow
  To curb this flow-
  ing female curse?

  Leipsydrion!°
  Shall I betray
  The laurels won   45
  On that great day?
  Come, shake a leg,
  Shed old age, beg
  The years reverse!   50

(Epirrhema 2)

KORYPHAIOS(m): Give them an inch, and we're done
    for! We'll have them
  launching boats next and planning naval
    strategy,
  sailing down on us like so many Artemisias.
  Or maybe they have ideas about the cavalry.
  That's fair enough, women are certainly good   55
  in the saddle. Just look at Mikon's paintings,
  all those Amazons wrestling with all those men!
  On the whole, a straitjacket's their best uniform.

Antode 2

CHORUS(w): Tangle with me,
  And you'll get cramps.   60
  Ferocity
  's no use now, Gramps!
  By the Two,
  I'll get through
  To you wrecks yet!   65

32. **Treasury:** Athenian politicians were raiding the funds
that were collected by Athens to finance a war against Persia.
44. **Leipsydrion:** A place where Athenian patriots had hero-
ically fought.

I'll scramble your eggs,
I'll burn your beans,
With my two legs.
You'll see such scenes
70   As never yet
Your two eyes met.
A curse? You bet!

                                        [Antepirrhema 2]

KORYPHAIOS(w): If Lampito stands by me, and that
      delicious Theban girl,
      Ismenia—what good are *you*? You and your
         seven
75   Resolutions! Resolutions? Rationing Boiotian eels
      and making our girls go without them at Hekate's°
         Feast!
      That was statesmanship! And we'll have to put up
         with it
      and all the rest of your decrepit legislation
      until some patriot—God give him strength!—
80   grabs you by the neck and kicks you off the Rock.

SCENE 2

(*Reenter Lysistrata and her lieutenants.*)

KORYPHAIOS(w) (*tragic tone*): Great Queen, fair
      Architect of our emprise,
   Why lookst thou on us with foreboding eyes?
LYSISTRATA: The behavior of these idiotic women!
   There's something about the female temperament
   that I can't bear!
5   KORYPHAIOS(w):   What in the world do you mean?
LYSISTRATA: Exactly what I say.
KORYPHAIOS(w): What dreadful thing has happened?
   Come, tell us: we're all your friends.
LYSISTRATA: It isn't easy
   to say it; yet, God knows, we can't hush it up.
KORYPHAIOS(w): Well, then? Out with it!
10   LYSISTRATA: To put it bluntly,
   we're dying to get laid.
KORYPHAIOS(w):   Almighty God!
LYSISTRATA: Why bring God into it?—No, it's just as
      I say.
   I can't manage them any longer: they've gone
      man-crazy,
   they're all trying to get out.
                              Why, look:
15   one of them was sneaking out the back door
   over there by Pan's cave; another
   was sliding down the walls with rope and tackle;
   another was climbing aboard a sparrow, ready to
      take off
   for the nearest brothel—I dragged *her* back by the
      hair!

---

76. **Hekate:** Patron of successful wars, object of a Boiotian cult
(later associated with sorcery).

They're all finding some reason to leave.
                              Look there!   20
   There goes another one.
                        —Just a minute, you!
   Where are you off to so fast?
FIRST WOMAN: I've got to get home.
   I've a lot of Milesian wool, and the worms are
      spoiling it.
LYSISTRATA: Oh bother you and your worms! Get back
      inside!
FIRST WOMAN: I'll be back right away, I swear I will.   25
   I just want to get it stretched out on my bed.
LYSISTRATA: You'll do no such thing. You'll stay
      right here.
FIRST WOMAN: And my wool?
   You want it ruined?
LYSISTRATA: Yes, for all I care.
SECOND WOMAN: Oh dear! My lovely new flax from
      Amorgos—
   I left it at home, all uncarded!
LYSISTRATA: Another one!   30
   And all she wants is someone to card her flax.
   Get back in there!
SECOND WOMAN: But I swear by the Moon-Goddess
   the minute I get it done, I'll be back!
LYSISTRATA: I say No.
   If you, why not all the other women as well?
THIRD WOMAN: O Lady Eileithyia!° Radiant goddess!
   Thou   35
   intercessor for women in childbirth! Stay, I pray thee,
   oh stay this parturition. Shall I pollute
   a sacred spot?°
LYSISTRATA: And what's the matter with *you*?
THIRD WOMAN: I'm having a baby—any minute now.
LYSISTRATA: But you weren't pregnant yesterday.
THIRD WOMAN: Well, I am today.   40
   Let me go home for a midwife, Lysistrata:
   there's not much time.
LYSISTRATA: I never heard such nonsense.
   What's that bulging under your cloak?
THIRD WOMAN: A little baby boy.
LYSISTRATA: It certainly isn't. But it's something hollow,
   like a basin or—Why, it's the helmet of Athena!   45
   And you said you were having a baby.
THIRD WOMAN: Well, I am! So there!
LYSISTRATA: Then why the helmet?
THIRD WOMAN: I was afraid that my pains
   might begin here in the Akropolis; and I wanted
   to drop my chick into it, just as the dear doves do.
LYSISTRATA: Lies! Evasions!—But at least one thing's
      clear: 50
   you can't leave the place before your purification.°

---

35. **Eileithyia:** Goddess of childbirth.   37–38. **pollute a sacred
spot:** Giving birth on the Akropolis was forbidden because it
was sacred ground.   51. **purification:** A ritual cleansing of a
woman after childbirth.

THIRD WOMAN: But I can't stay here in the Akropolis!
    Last night I dreamed
  of the Snake.
FIRST WOMAN: And those horrible owls, the noise they
    make!
  I can't get a bit of sleep; I'm just about dead.
LYSISTRATA: You useless girls, that's enough: Let's have
    no more lying.
55
  Of course you want your men. But don't you imagine
  that they want you just as much? I'll give you my
    word,
  their nights must be pretty hard.
                        Just stick it out!
  A little patience, that's all, and our battle's won.
60
  I have heard an Oracle. Should you like to hear it?
FIRST WOMAN: An Oracle? Yes, tell us!
LYSISTRATA: Here is what it says:
  WHEN SWALLOWS SHALL THE HOOPOE
    SHUN AND SPURN HIS HOT DESIRE,
  ZEUS WILL PERFECT WHAT THEY'VE BEGUN
65
    AND SET THE LOWER HIGHER.
FIRST WOMAN: Does that mean we'll be on top?
LYSISTRATA: BUT IF THE SWALLOWS SHALL FALL
    OUT
    AND TAKE THE HOOPOE'S BAIT,
  A CURSE MUST MARK THEIR HOUR OF
    DOUBT,
70
    INFAMY SEAL THEIR FATE.
THIRD WOMAN: I swear, *that* Oracle's all too clear.
FIRST WOMAN: Oh the dear gods!
LYSISTRATA: Let's not be downhearted, girls. Back to
    our places!
  The god has spoken. How can we possibly fail him?

      (*Exit Lysistrata with the dissident women.*)

CHORAL EPISODE • Strophe

CHORUS(m): I know a little story that I learned way
    back in school
  Goes like this:
  Once upon a time there was a young man—and no
    fool—
  Named Melanion; and his
5
  One aversion was marriage. He loathed the very
    thought.
  So he ran off to the hills, and in a special grot
  Raised a dog, and spent his days
  Hunting rabbits. And it says
  That he never never never did come home.
10
  It might be called a refuge *from* the womb.
  All right,
      all right,
          all right!
  We're as bright as young Melanion, and we hate
    the very sight
  Of you women!
A MAN: How about a kiss, old lady?

A WOMAN: Here's an onion for your eye!   15
A MAN: A kick in the guts, then?
A WOMAN: Try, old bristle-tail, just try!
A MAN: Yet they say Myronides
  On hands and knees
  Looked just as shaggy fore and aft as I!   20

Antistrophe

CHORUS(w): Well, *I* know a little story, and it's just as
    good as yours.
  Goes like this:
  Once there was a man named Timon—a rough
    diamond, of course,
  And that whiskery face of his
  Looked like murder in the shrubbery. By God, he
    was a son   25
  Of the Furies, let me tell you! And what did he do
    but run
  From the world and all its ways,
  Cursing mankind! And it says
  That his choicest execrations as of then
  Were leveled almost wholly at *old* men.   30
  All right,
      all right,
          all right!
  But there's one thing about Timon: he could
    always stand the sight
  of us women.
A WOMAN: How about a crack in the jaw, Pop?
A MAN: I can take it, Ma—no fear!   35
A WOMAN: How about a kick in the face?
A MAN: You'd reveal your old caboose?
A WOMAN: What I'd show,
  I'll have you know,
  Is an instrument you're too far gone to use.   40

SCENE 3

(*Reenter Lysistrata.*)

LYSISTRATA: Oh, quick, girls, quick! Come here!
A WOMAN: What is it?
LYSISTRATA: A man.
  A man simply bulging with love.
                   O Kyprian Queen,°
  O Paphian, O Kythereian! Hear us and aid us!
A WOMAN: Where is this enemy?
LYSISTRATA: Over there, by Demeter's shrine.
A WOMAN: Damned if he isn't. But who *is* he?
MYRRHINE: My husband.   5
  Kinesias.
LYSISTRATA: Oh then, get busy! Tease him! Undermine
    him!

2. **Kyprian Queen:** Aphrodite.

Cherry Jones as Lysistrata in the American Repertory Theater's 2002 production directed by Robert Brustein.

Geraldine James (far left) as Lysistrata in the Old Vic Theatre production in London, 1993.

The Théâtre La Licorne 2006 performance of *Lysistrata*, adapted by Claire Dancoisne.

Wreck him! Give him everything—kissing,
   tickling, nudging,
whatever you generally torture him with—: give
   him everything
except what we swore on the wine we would not
   give.
MYRRHINE: Trust me.
10 LYSISTRATA: I do. But I'll help you get him started.
   The rest of you women, stay back.

(*Enter Kinesias.*)

KINESIAS: Oh God! Oh my God!
   I'm stiff from lack of exercise. All I can do to stand
   up.
LYSISTRATA: Halt! Who are you, approaching our lines?
KINESIAS: Me? I.
LYSISTRATA: A man?
KINESIAS: You have eyes, haven't you?
15 LYSISTRATA: Go away.
KINESIAS: Who says so?

LYSISTRATA: Officer of the Day.
KINESIAS: Officer, I beg you,
   by all the gods at once, bring Myrrhine out.
LYSISTRATA: Myrrhine? And who, my good sir, are
   you?
KINESIAS: Kinesias. Last name's Pennison. Her husband.
LYSISTRATA: Oh, of course. I beg your pardon. We're
   glad to see you.   20
   We've heard so much about you. Dearest Myrrhine
   is always talking about Kinesias—never nibbles an
      egg
or an apple without saying
   "Here's to Kinesias!"
KINESIAS: Do you really mean it?
LYSISTRATA: I do.
   When we're discussing men, she always says   25
   "Well, after all, there's nobody like Kinesias!"
KINESIAS: Good God.—Well, then, please send her
   down here.
LYSISTRATA: And what do *I* get out of it?
KINESIAS: A standing promise.
LYSISTRATA: I'll take it up with her.
                        (*Exit Lysistrata.*)
KINESIAS: But be quick about it!
   Lord, what's life without a wife? Can't eat. Can't
   sleep.   30
   Every time I go home, the place is so empty, so
   insufferably sad. Love's killing me, Oh,
   hurry!

(*Enter Manes, a slave, with Kinesias's baby; the voice
of Myrrhine is heard offstage.*)

MYRRHINE: But of course I love him! Adore him—
                                But no,
   he hates love. No. I won't go down.

(*Enter Myrrhine, above.*)

KINESIAS: Myrrhine!
   Darlingest Myrrhinette! Come down quick!   35
MYRRHINE: Certainly not.
KINESIAS: Not? But why, Myrrhine?
MYRRHINE: Why? You don't need me.
KINESIAS: Need you? My God, *look* at me!
MYRRHINE: So long!

(*Turns to go.*)

KINESIAS: Myrrhine, Myrrhine, Myrrhine!
   If not for my sake, for our child!

(*Pinches Baby.*)

                   —All right, you: pipe up!
BABY: Mummie! Mummie! Mummie!
KINESIAS: You hear that? 40
   Pitiful, I call it. Six days now
   with never a bath; no food; enough to break your
   heart!
MYRRHINE: My darlingest child! What a father *you*
   acquired!
KINESIAS: At least come down for his sake.

MYRRHINE: I suppose I must.
45   Oh, this mother business!   (*Exit.*)
KINESIAS: How pretty she is! And younger!
        The harder she treats me, the more bothered I get.

(*Myrrhine enters, below.*)

MYRRHINE: Dearest child,
        you're as sweet as your father's horrid. Give me a kiss.
KINESIAS: Now don't you see how wrong it was to
        get involved
50   in this scheming League of women? It's bad
        for us both.
MYRRHINE: Keep your hands to yourself!
KINESIAS: But our house
        going to rack and ruin?
MYRRHINE: *I don't care.*
KINESIAS: And your knitting
        all torn to pieces by the chickens? Don't you care?
MYRRHINE: Not at all.
55   KINESIAS: And our debt to Aphrodite?
        Oh, *won't* you come back?
MYRRHINE: No.—At least, not until you men
        make a treaty and stop this war.
KINESIAS: Why, I suppose
        that might be arranged.
MYRRHINE: Oh? Well, I suppose
        I might come down then. But meanwhile,
        I've sworn not to.
60   KINESIAS: Don't worry.—Now let's have fun.
MYRRHINE: No! Stop it! I said no!
                              —Although, of course,
        I *do* love you.
KINESIAS: I know you do. Darling Myrrhine:
        come, shall we?
MYRRHINE: Are you out of your mind? In front of the
        child?
KINESIAS: Take him home, Manes.
                        (*Exit Manes with Baby.*)
                        There. He's gone.
                              Come on!
        There's nothing to stop us now.
65   MYRRHINE: You devil! But where?
KINESIAS: In Pan's cave. What could be snugger than that?
MYRRHINE: But my purification before I go back to
        the Citadel?
KINESIAS: Wash in the Klepsydra.°
MYRRHINE: And my oath?
KINESIAS: Leave the oath to me.
        After all, I'm the man.
MYRRHINE: Well . . . if you say so.
                        I'll go find a bed.
KINESIAS: Oh, bother a bed! The ground's good
70   enough for me.
MYRRHINE: No. You're a bad man, but you deserve
        something better than dirt.   (*Exit Myrrhine.*)
KINESIAS: What a love she is! And how thoughtful!

---

68. **Klepsydra:** A water clock beneath the walls of the Akropolis. Kinesias's suggestion borders on blasphemy.

(*Reenter Myrrhine.*)

MYRRHINE: Here's your bed.
        Now let me get my clothes off.
                              But, good horrors!
        We haven't a mattress.
KINESIAS: Oh, forget the mattress!
MYRRHINE: No.
        Just lying on blankets? Too sordid.
KINESIAS: Give me a kiss.   75
MYRRHINE: Just a second.   (*Exit Myrrhine.*)
KINESIAS: I swear, I'll explode!

(*Reenter Myrrhine.*)

MYRRHINE: Here's your mattress.
        I'll just take my dress off.
                        But look—
        where's our pillow?
KINESIAS: I don't *need* a pillow!
MYRRHINE: Well, *I* do.
                              (*Exit Myrrhine.*)
KINESIAS: I don't suppose even Herakles°
        would stand for this!

(*Reenter Myrrhine.*)

MYRRHINE: There we are. Ups-a-daisy!   80
KINESIAS: So we are. Well, come to bed.
MYRRHINE: But I wonder:
        is everything ready now?
KINESIAS: I can swear to that. Come, darling!
MYRRHINE: Just getting out of my girdle.
                              But remember, now,
        what you promised about the treaty.
KINESIAS: Yes, yes, yes!
MYRRHINE: But no coverlet!
KINESIAS: Damn it, I'll be your coverlet!   85
MYRRHINE: Be right back.   (*Exit Myrrhine.*)
KINESIAS: This girl and her coverlets
        will be the death of me.

(*Reenter Myrrhine.*)

MYRRHINE: Here we are. Up you go!
KINESIAS: Up? I've been up for ages.
MYRRHINE: Some perfume?
KINESIAS: No, by Apollo!
MYRRHINE: Yes, by Aphrodite!
        I don't care whether you want it or not.   90
                              (*Exit Myrrhine.*)
KINESIAS: For love's sake, hurry!

(*Reenter Myrrhine.*)

MYRRHINE: Here, in your hand. Rub it right in.
KINESIAS: Never cared for perfume.
        And this is particularly strong. Still, here goes.
MYRRHINE: What a nitwit I am! I brought you the
        Rhodian bottle.
KINESIAS: Forget it.
                                                      95

---

79. **Herakles:** Greek hero (Hercules) known for his Twelve Labors.

MYRRHINE: No trouble at all. You just wait here.
                                   (*Exit Myrrhine.*)
KINESIAS: God damn the man who invented perfume!

(*Reenter Myrrhine.*)

MYRRHINE: At last! The right bottle!
KINESIAS: I've got the tightest bottle of all,
     and it's right here waiting for you.
     Darling, forget everything else. Do come to bed.
MYRRHINE: Just let me get my shoes off.
100   —And, by the way,
     you'll vote for the treaty?
KINESIAS: I'll think about it.
                         (*Myrrhine runs away.*)
     There! That's done it! The damned woman,
     she gets me all bothered, she half kills me,
     and off she runs! What'll I do? Where
     can I get laid?
105   —And you, little prodding pal,
     who's going to take care of *you*? No, you and I
     had better get down to old Foxdog's Nursing Clinic.
CHORUS(m): Alas for the woes of man, alas
          Specifically for you.
110 She's brought you to a pretty pass:
          What are you going to do?
     Split, heart! Sag, flesh! Proud spirit, crack!
          Myrrhine's got you on your back.
KINESIAS: The agony, the protraction!
KORYPHAIOS(m):   Friend,
115   What woman's worth a damn?
     They bitch us all, world without end.
KINESIAS: Yet they're so damned sweet, man!
KORYPHAIOS(m): Calamitous, that's what I say.
     You should have learned that much today.
120 CHORUS(m): O blessed Zeus, roll womankind
          Up into one great ball;
     Blast them aloft on a high wind,
          And once there, let them fall.
     Down, down they'll come, the pretty dears,
125   And split themselves on our thick spears.
                              (*Exit Kinesias.*)

SCENE 4

(*Enter a Spartan Herald.*)

HERALD: Gentlemen, Ah beg you will be so kind
     as to direct me to the Central Committee.
     Ah have a communication.

(*Reenter Commissioner.*)

COMMISSIONER: Are you a man,
     or a fertility symbol?
HERALD: Ah refuse to answer that question!
5   Ah'm a certified herald from Spahta, and Ah've come
     to talk about an ahmistice.
COMMISSIONER: Then why
     that spear under your cloak?
HERALD: Ah have no speah!

COMMISSIONER: You don't walk naturally, with your tunic
     poked out so. You have a tum or, maybe,
     or a hernia?
HERALD: You lost yo' mahnd, man?
COMMISSIONER: Well,   10
     something's up, I can see that. And I don't like it.
HERALD: Colonel, Ah resent this.
COMMISSIONER: So I see. But what *is* it?
HERALD: A staff
     with a message from Spahta.
COMMISSIONER: Oh, I know about those staffs.
     Well, then, man, speak out: How are things in Sparta?
HERALD: Hahd, Colonel, hahd! We're at a standstill.   15
     Cain't seem to think of anything but women.
COMMISSIONER: How curious! Tell me, do you
          Spartans think
     that maybe Pan's to blame?
HERALD: Pan? No, Lampito and her little naked friends.
     They won't let a man come nigh them.   20
COMMISSIONER: How are you handling it?
HERALD: Losing our mahnds,
     if y' want to know, and walking around hunched over
     lahk men carrying candles in a gale.
     The women have swohn they'll have nothing to do
          with us
     until we get a treaty.
COMMISSIONER: Yes, I know.   25
     It's a general uprising, sir, in all parts of Greece.
     But as for the answer—
                    Sir: go back to Sparta
     and have them send us your Armistice Commission.
     I'll arrange things in Athens.
                    And I may say
     that my standing is good enough to make them listen.   30
HERALD: A man after mah own haht! Seh, Ah thank
     you.   (*Exit Herald.*)

CHORAL EPISODE • Strophe

CHORUS(m): Oh these women! Where will you find
     A slavering beast that's more unkind?
          Where's a hotter fire?
     Give me a panther, any day.
     He's not so merciless as they,   5
          And panthers don't conspire.

Antistrophe

CHORUS(w): We may be hard, you silly old ass,
     But who brought you to this stupid pass?
          You're the ones to blame.
     Fighting with us, your oldest friends,   10
     Simply to serve your selfish ends—
          Really, you have no shame!
KORYPHAIOS(m): No, I'm through with women for ever.
KORYPHAIOS(w):   If you say so.
     Still, you might put some clothes on. You look too
          absurd
     standing around naked. Come, get into this cloak.   15

KORYPHAIOS(m): Thank you; you're right. I merely took
  it off
because I was in such a temper.
KORYPHAIOS(w):   That's much better.
  Now you resemble a man again.
                         Why have you been so horrid?
  And look: there's some sort of insect in your eye.
  Shall I take it out?
20 KORYPHAIOS(m):   An insect, is it? So that's
  what's been bothering me. Lord, yes: take it out!
KORYPHAIOS(w): You might be more polite.
                              —But, heavens!
  What an enormous mosquito!
KORYPHAIOS(m):   You've saved my life.
  That mosquito was drilling an artesian well
  in my left eye.
25 KORYPHAIOS(w):   Let me wipe
  those tears away.—And now: one little kiss?
KORYPHAIOS(m): No, no kisses.
KORYPHAIOS(w): You're so difficult.
KORYPHAIOS(m): You impossible women! How you do
  get around us!
  The poet was right: Can't live with you, or without
30   you.
  But let's be friends.
  And to celebrate, you might join us in an Ode.

Strophe 1

CHORUS(m and w): Let it never be said
    That my tongue is malicious:
35   Both by word and by deed
  I would set an example that's noble and gracious.
    We've had sorrow and care
    Till we're sick of the tune.
    Is there anyone here
40   Who would like a small loan?
      My purse is crammed,
      As you'll soon find;
  And you needn't pay me back if the Peace gets signed.

Strophe 2

    I've invited to lunch
45   Some Karystian rips°—
    An esurient bunch,
  But I've ordered a menu to water their lips.
    I can still make soup
    And slaughter a pig.
50   You're all coming, I hope?
    But a bath first, I beg!
      Walk right up

45. **Karystian rips:** The Karystians were allies of Athens but
were scorned for their primitive ways and loose morals.

As though you owned the place,
And you'll get the front door slammed to in your
  face.

SCENE 5

(*Enter Spartan Ambassador, with entourage.*)

KORYPHAIOS(m): The Commission has arrived from
  Sparta.
            How oddly they're walking!
                Gentlemen, welcome to Athens!
  How is life in Lakonia?
AMBASSADOR: Need we discuss that?
  Simply use your eyes.
CHORUS(m):   The poor man's right:
            What a sight!
AMBASSADOR: Words fail me.   5
  But come, gentlemen, call in your Commissioners,
  and let's get down to a Peace.
CHORAGOS(m):   The state we're in! Can't bear
  a stitch below the waist. It's a kind of pelvic
  paralysis.
COMMISSIONER: Won't somebody call Lysistrata?—
                            Gentlemen,
  we're no better off than you.
AMBASSADOR: So I see.   10
A SPARTAN: Seh, do y'all feel a certain strain early in the
  morning?
AN ATHENIAN: I do, sir. It's worse than a strain.
  A few more days, and there's nothing for us but
      Kleisthenes,
  that broken blossom.
CHORAGOS(m):   But you'd better get dressed again.
  You know these people going around Athens with
      chisels   15
  looking for statues of Hermes.°
ATHENIAN: Sir, you are right.
SPARTAN: He certainly is! Ah'll put mah own clothes
  back on.

(*Enter Athenian Commissioners.*)

COMMISSIONER: Gentlemen from Sparta, welcome.
  This is a sorry business.
SPARTAN (*to one of his own group*): Colonel, we got
    dressed just in time. Ah sweah,
  if they'd seen us the way we were, there'd have been
    a new wah   20
  between the states.
COMMISSIONER: Shall we call the meeting to order?
                            Now, Lakonians,
  what's your proposal?
AMBASSADOR: We propose to consider peace.

16. **statues of Hermes:** The usual representation of Hermes
was with an erect phallus. Statues of Hermes were scattered
throughout Athens and were attacked by vandals just before
the Sicilian Expedition.

COMMISSIONER: Good. That's on our minds, too.
                                    —Summon Lysistrata.
    We'll never get anywhere without her.

25 AMBASSADOR: Lysistrata?
        Summon Lysis-*any*body! Only, summon!

KORYPHAIOS(m):   No need to summon:
    here she is, herself.

(*Enter Lysistrata.*)

COMMISSIONER: Lysistrata! Lion of women!
    This is your hour to be
    hard and yielding, outspoken and shy, austere and
30 gentle. You see here
    the best brains of Hellas (confused, I admit,
    by your devious charming) met as one man
    to turn the future over to you.

LYSISTRATA: That's fair enough,
    unless you men take it into your heads
35 to turn to each other instead of to us. But I'd know
    soon enough if you did.
                            —Where is Reconciliation?
    Go, some of you: bring her here.

                            (*Exeunt two women.*)
                            And now, women,
    lead the Spartan delegates to me: not roughly
    or insultingly, as our men handle them, but gently,
40 politely, as ladies should. Take them by the hand,
    or by anything else if they won't give you their hands.

(*The Spartans are escorted over.*)

    There.—The Athenians next, by any convenient
        handle.

(*The Athenians are escorted.*)

    Stand there, please.—Now, all of you, listen to me.

(*During the following speech the two women reenter,
carrying an enormous statue of a naked girl; this is
Reconciliation.*)

    I'm only a woman, I know; but I've a mind,
45 and, I think, not a bad one: I owe it to my father
    and to listening to the local politicians.
    So much for that.
                    Now, gentlemen,
    since I have you here, I intend to give you a scolding.
    We are all Greeks.
50 Must I remind you of Thermopylai,° of Olympia,
    of Delphoi? names deep in all our hearts?
    Are they not a common heritage?
                            Yet you men
    go raiding through the country from both sides,
    Greek killing Greek, storming down Greek cities—
55 and all the time the Barbarian across the sea
    is waiting for his chance!
                        —That's my first point.

50. **Thermopylai:** A narrow pass where, in 480 BCE, an army of three hundred Spartans held out for three days against a superior Persian force.

AN ATHENIAN: Lord! I can hardly contain myself.
LYSISTRATA: As for you Spartans:
    Was it so long ago that Perikleides°
    came here to beg our help? I can see him still,
    his gray face, his sombre gown. And what did he
        want?   60
    An army from Athens. All Messene
    was hot at your heels, and the sea-god splitting your
        land.
    Well, Kimon and his men,
    four thousand strong, marched out and saved all
        Sparta.
    And what thanks do we get? You come back to
        murder us.   65
AN ATHENIAN: They're aggressors, Lysistrata!
A SPARTAN: Ah admit it.
    When Ah look at those laigs, Ah sweah Ah'll
        aggress mahself!
LYSISTRATA: And you, Athenians: do you think you're
        blameless?
    Remember that bad time when we were helpless,
    and an army came from Sparta,   70
    and that was the end of the Thessalian menace,
    the end of Hippias and his allies.
                        And that was Sparta,
    and only Sparta; but for Sparta, we'd be
    cringing slaves today, not free Athenians.

(*From this point, the male responses are less to
Lysistrata than to the statue.*)

A SPARTAN: A well shaped speech.
AN ATHENIAN: Certainly it has its points.   75
LYSISTRATA: Why are we fighting each other? With all
        this history
    of favors given and taken, what stands in the way
    of making peace?
AMBASSADOR: Spahta is ready, ma'am,
    so long as we get that place back.
LYSISTRATA: What place, man?
AMBASSADOR: Ah refer to Pylos.
COMMISSIONER: Not a chance, by God!   80
LYSISTRATA: Give it to them, friend.
COMMISSIONER: But—what shall we have to bargain
        with?
LYSISTRATA: Demand something in exchange.
COMMISSIONER: Good idea.—Well, then:
    Cockeville first, and the Happy Hills, and the
    country between the Legs of Megara.
AMBASSADOR: Mah government objects.   85
LYSISTRATA: Overruled. Why fuss about a pair of legs?

(*General assent. The statue is removed.*)

AN ATHENIAN: I want to get out of these clothes and
        start my plowing.
A SPARTAN: Ah'll fertilize mahn first, by the Heavenly
        Twins!

58. **Perikleides:** Spartan ambassador to Athens who successfully urged Athenians to aid Sparta in quelling a rebellion.

LYSISTRATA: And so you shall,
90   once you've made peace. If you are serious,
go, both of you, and talk with your allies.
COMMISSIONER: Too much talk already. No, we'll
        stand together.
We've only one end in view. All that we want
is our women; and I speak for our allies.
AMBASSADOR: Mah government concurs.
95 AN ATHENIAN: So does Karystos.
LYSISTRATA: Good.—But before you come inside
to join your wives at supper, you must perform
the usual lustration. Then we'll open
our baskets for you, and all that we have is yours.
100   But you must promise upright good behavior
from this day on. Then each man home with his
        woman!
AN ATHENIAN: Let's get it over with.
A SPARTAN: Lead on. Ah follow.
AN ATHENIAN: Quick as a cat can wink!
                    (*Exeunt all but the Choruses.*)

Antistrophe 1

CHORUS(w): Embroideries and
105   Twinkling ornaments and
        Pretty dresses—I hand
Them all over to you, and with never a qualm.
        They'll be nice for your daughters
        On festival days
110   When the girls bring the Goddess
        The ritual prize.
        Come in, one and all:
        Take what you will.
I've nothing here so tightly corked that you can't
        make it spill.

Antistrophe 2

115   You may search my house
        But you'll not find
        The least thing of use,
Unless your two eyes are keener than mine.
        Your numberless brats
120   Are half starved? and your slaves?
        Courage, grandpa! I've lots
        Of grain left, and big loaves.
        I'll fill your guts,
        I'll go the whole hog;
But if you come too close to me, remember: 'ware
125   the dog!   (*Exeunt Choruses.*)

EXODOS°

(*A Drunken Citizen enters, approaches the gate, and is
halted by a sentry.*)

Exodos: Final scene.

CITIZEN: Open. The. Door.
SENTRY: Now, friend, just shove along!
    —So you want to sit down. If it weren't such an old
        joke,
    I'd tickle your tail with this torch. Just the sort of
        gag
    this audience appreciates.
CITIZEN: I. Stay. Right. Here.
SENTRY: Get away from there, or I'll scalp you!   5
    The gentlemen from Sparta
    are just coming back from dinner.

(*Exit Citizen; the general company reenters; the two
Choruses now represent Spartans and Athenians.*)

A SPARTAN: Ah must say,
    Ah never tasted better grub.
AN ATHENIAN: And those Lakonians!
    They're gentlemen, by the Lord! Just goes to show,
    a drink to the wise is sufficient.
COMMISSIONER: And why not?   10
    A sober man's an ass.
    Men of Athens, mark my words: the only efficient
    Ambassador's a drunk Ambassador. Is that clear?
    Look: we go to Sparta,
    and when we get there we're dead sober. The result?   15
    Everyone cackling at everyone else. They make
        speeches;
    and even if we understand, we get it all wrong
    when we file our reports in Athens. But today—!
    Everybody's happy. Couldn't tell the difference
    between *Drink to Me Only* and   20
    The Star-Spangled Athens.
                    What's a few lies,
    washed down in good strong drink?

(*Reenter the Drunken Citizen.*)

SENTRY: God almighty,
    he's back again!
CITIZEN: I. Resume. My. Place.
A SPARTAN (*to an Athenian*): Ah beg yo', seh,
    take yo' instrument in yo' hand and play for us.   25
    Ah'm told
    yo' understand the intricacies of the floot?
    Ah'd lahk to execute a song and dance
    in honor of Athens,
                    and, of cohse, of Spahta.
CITIZEN: Toot. On. Your. Flute.   30

(*The following song is a solo—an aria—accompanied
by the flute. The Chorus of Spartans begins a slow
dance.*)

A SPARTAN: O Memory,
    Let the Muse speak once more
    In my young voice. Sing glory.
    Sing Artemision's shore,
    Where Athens fluttered the Persians. *Alalai,*°   35

35. *Alalai:* War cry.

Sing glory, that great
Victory! Sing also
Our Leonidas and his men,
Those wild boars, sweat and blood
40   Down in a red drench. Then, then
The barbarians broke, though they had stood
Numberless as the sands before!

O Artemis,
Virgin Goddess, whose darts
45   Flash in our forests: approve
This pact of peace and join our hearts,
From this day on, in love.
Huntress, descend!

LYSISTRATA: All that will come in time.
                                  But now, Lakonians,
50   take home your wives. Athenians, take yours.
Each man be kind to his woman; and you, women
be equally kind. Never again, pray God,
shall we lose our way in such madness.

KORYPHAIOS(Athenian):   And now let's dance our joy.

(*From this point the dance becomes general.*)

CHORUS(Athenian): Dance, you Graces
                          Artemis, dance
Dance, Phoibos,° Lord of dancing
55   Dance,
In a scurry of Maenads,° Lord Dionysos
                          Dance, Zeus Thunderer
                 Dance, Lady Hera°
Queen of the sky
                 Dance, dance, all you gods

---

55. Phoibos: Apollo, god of the sun.   **56. Maenads:** Female
worshipers of Bacchus (Dionysus).   **57. Hera:** Wife of Zeus.

Dance witness everlasting of our pact
Evohi Evohe°   60
Dance for the dearest
                      the Bringer of Peace
Deathless Aphrodite!

COMMISSIONER: Now let us have another song from
    Sparta.

CHORUS(Spartan): From Taygetos, from Taygetos,
Lakonian Muse, come down.   65
Sing to the Lord Apollo
    Who rules Amyklai Town.

Sing Athena of the House of Brass!°
Sing Leda's Twins,° that chivalry
    Resplendent on the shore   70
Of our Eurotas; sing the girls
    That dance along before:
Sparkling in dust their gleaming feet,
    Their hair a Bacchant fire,
And Leda's daughter, thyrsos° raised,   75
    Leads their triumphant choir.

CHORUS(S and A): *Evohe!*
                      Evohai!
                           Evohe!
                                We pass
                      Dancing
                           dancing
                                to greet
Athena of the House of Brass.

---

60. *Evohi Evohe:* "Come forth! Come forth!" (an orgiastic cry
associated with rituals of Bacchus).   **68. *House of Brass:*** Temple to Athena on the Akropolis of Sparta.   **69. Leda's Twins:**
Leda, raped by Zeus, bore quadruplets, two daughters (one of
whom was Helen) and two sons.   **75. thyrsos:** A staff twined
with ivy and carried by Bacchus and his followers.

Roman Drama

Indigenous Sources

Roman drama depended heavily on Greek drama, whose myths it often reinterpreted. For centuries plays were performed much as they had been in Greece, although the Romans had less of a taste for tragedy than the Greeks; they preferred comedy. The Roman plays that have come down to us are mostly comic, and those that are tragic seem to have been intended to be read, not performed. Because Roman drama, rather than Greek drama, was known throughout Europe in the Medieval period and the Renaissance, it is of considerable importance. Even through the Elizabethan Age and up to the eighteenth century, Roman drama exerted a greater influence than Greek drama did on the development of modern drama.

Beginning with wood, then moving to stone, the Romans built excellent theaters throughout their realm. Many still exist.

Roman drama has several sources, not all of them well understood. The first and most literary is Greek drama, but among the more curious are the indigenous sources, which are especially difficult to trace. One such source might be the Etruscans, members of an old and obscure civilization in northern Italy that reached its height in the sixth century BCE and that the Romans eventually absorbed. The Etruscans had developed an improvised song and dance that was very entertaining. The town of Atella provided another indigenous comic tradition known as the **Atellan farce**, a very broad and sometimes coarse popular comedy. Such entertainments may have been acted in open spaces or at fairs, probably not on a stage at first.

The Atellan farce is especially interesting for developments in later Roman drama and world drama. The characters in these farces seem to have been **stock characters**, characters who are always recognizable and whose antics are predictable. The most common stock characters in the Atellan farce are Maccus, the clown; Bucco, the stupid, and probably fat, clown; Pappus, the foolish or stubborn old man; and the hunchbacked, wily slave Dossennus. At first these pieces of drama were improvised to a repeatable pattern, often involving a master who tries to get his slave to do his bidding but who somehow ends up being made to look the fool by the cunning slave. When the farces began to develop in Rome, they were written down and played onstage.

The concept of the stock character is associated with the masters of Roman comedy, Plautus and Terence, who often adapted Greek plays and made them their own. The braggart warrior (*miles gloriosus*), a stock character on the Roman stage, reappears in modern plays. The miser has been a mainstay in literature since Roman times and probably is best known today in the form of Scrooge in Dickens's *A Christmas Carol* and *The Miser* of Molière. The parasite was Roman in origin and can be seen today in numerous television situation comedies. Another Roman invention is the use of identical twins for comic effect. Because it permitted a wide range of comic misunderstandings, this device has been used by many playwrights, including Shakespeare in *The Comedy of Errors*. The Roman use of masks made the twins device much easier to employ than it would be in today's productions.

According to legend, in 240 BCE, a slave, Livius Andronicus, presented performances of his Latin translations of a Greek tragedy and a Greek comedy, giving the Romans their first real taste of Greek drama and literature. Livius soon earned his freedom, and his literary career became so firmly established that his translations from the Greek were those read in Rome for more than two hundred years. His translation of the *Odyssey* was the standard text through the time of Cicero (first century BCE).

Roman comedy derived primarily from the New Comedy of Menander, although it could, like Aristophanes' Old Comedy, sometimes be risqué. Comedies were the most well attended and the most performed of Roman dramas. That is not to say that the Romans produced no tragedies. They did, and the influence of Roman tragedy has been as long-lasting as that of Roman comedy. Still, the Roman people preferred to laugh rather than to feel the pity and terror of tragic emotion.

Just as the Greek plays developed in connection with festivals, the Roman plays became associated with games held several times a year. During the games, performances were offered on average every five to eleven days. The Megalesian Games took place in early April, in honor of the Great Mother, the goddess Cybele, whose temple stood on the Palatine Hill. In late April, the Floral Games were held in front of the temple of Flora on the Aventine Hill. The most important were the Roman Games in September and the Plebeian Games in November.

The Greek drama competitions had no counterpart among the Romans, for whom drama was not the primary entertainment during the festivals. Roman playwrights and actors were hired to put on performances to entertain and divert the impatient audiences, who could choose among a variety of spectacles, including gladiator fights, chariot races, and animal baiting. The producer had to please the audience or lose his chance to supply more entertainment.

Roman comedies were sometimes revisions or amalgamations of Greek plays. The themes and characters of Roman tragedies also derived from Greek originals. Figuring often in Roman tragedies was the Trojan War; its characters were reworked into new situations and their agonies reinterpreted.

For costumes the actors wore the Greek tunic (called a **chiton**) and a long white cloak or mantle called the **pallium**. Like the Greeks, the Romans wore a low slipper, called the **sock,** for comedy and shoes with an elevated sole, the **buskin,** for tragedy. For plays that had a totally Roman setting and narrative, the actors wore the Roman toga. Eventually, Roman actors used traditional Greek masks that immediately identified the characters for the audience. (The question of whether the earliest Roman actors wore masks has not been resolved.) The younger Roman characters wore black wigs, older characters wore white wigs, and characters representing slaves wore red wigs.

One of the most intriguing questions concerning Roman plays is the importance of music in the drama. In Greek plays the chorus took most of the responsibility for the music, but in Roman drama actors may have sung their lines, so the Roman plays may have resembled musical comedies. The dialogue in some comedies introduces an interlude of flute playing, indicating that there were times with no actor onstage, no spoken words, and no mimed action, but only a musician to entertain the audience.

The Roman Stage

In the third century BCE, the Romans began building wooden stages that could be taken down quickly and moved as necessary. Eventually, they built stone theaters that followed Greek plans but varied from the Greek model in a number of important respects. They were built on flat ground, rather than on hillsides as were the Greek theaters. The influence of the Romans' early wooden stage was reflected in the permanent buildings in several ways. The Roman stage was elevated, and since there was little or no chorus, the orchestra, in which the chorus moved from place to place, was no longer needed. The **scaena**, or background, against which the action took place, was often three stories tall and was proportionally longer than the Greek *skene* (as in Figure 4). This wide but shallow stage was exploited by the playwrights, who often set their plays on a street with various houses, temples, and other buildings along it.

Figure 4. Roman theater at Sabratha, Libya, with the *frons scaena* still in good shape. This photograph shows how the Romans modified the basic Greek design.

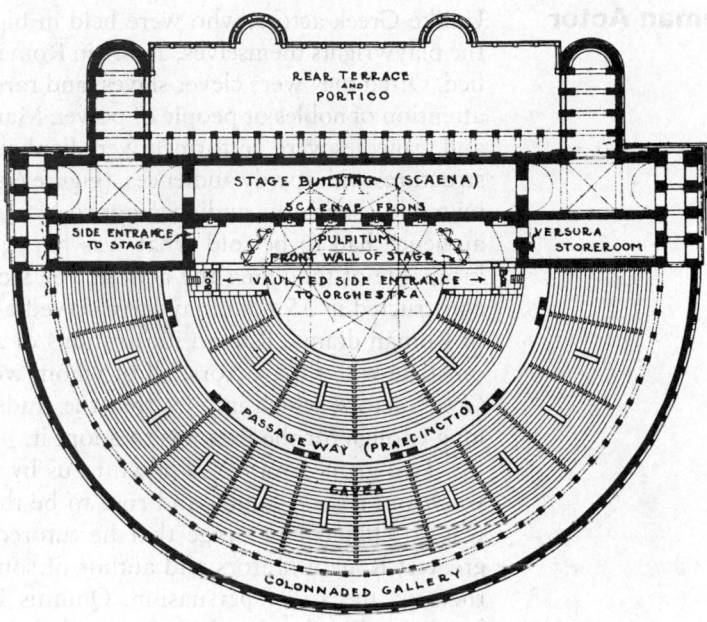

REAR TERRACE
AND
PORTICO

STAGE BUILDING (SCAENA)
SCAENAE FRONS
PULPITUM
FRONT WALL OF STAGE

SIDE ENTRANCE
TO STAGE

VERSURA
STOREROOM

← VAULTED SIDE ENTRANCE →
TO ORCHESTRA

PASSAGE WAY (PRAECINCTIO)

CAVEA

COLONNADED GALLERY

Figure 5. Theater of
Marcellus.

The space in front of the *scaena* was known as the **proscaena**, from which
the **proscenium arch**, which frames the stage and separates the actors from the
audience, developed much later in the Renaissance. The action took place on the
pulpitum, behind the *proscaena.* The potential for the proscenium arch is evident
in the plan of the Theater of Marcellus (Figure 5), where the sections to the left and
the right of the stage (*pulpitum*) already indicate a separation from the audience.

As in the plan of the Theater of Marcellus, the *frons scaena* (the front wall,
or façade) usually had three doors (some had only two), which were ordinarily
established to be doors of separate buildings, sometimes a temple and the
homes of chief characters. These doors were active "participants" in the drama;
it has been said that the most common line heard in a Roman play is a statement that the door is opening and someone is coming in. The standard Roman
play takes great care to justify the entrances and exits of its characters, which
may indicate that Roman audiences expected more realism in their comedies
than did their Greek counterparts.

The *frons scaena,* the front of the theater, not only was several stories
high but also was much more architecturally developed than the *skene* of the
Greek theater. The typical Roman architectural devices of multiple arches, columns, and pilasters decorated the *scaena,* giving it a stately appearance. Like
the Greek theater, the Roman theater used machinery that permitted actors to
be moved through the air and to make entrances from the heavens.

The greatest of the Roman dramatists, Plautus and Terence, would have had
their plays produced originally on early wooden stages or on Greek stages. The
characteristic Roman theater did not emerge until more than a hundred years
after their deaths, in the period of the empire. Seneca could have seen his plays
produced in the Roman theater, but they may not ever have been produced in
Roman times. His plays may have been closet dramas, designed only to be read.

The Roman Actor

Unlike Greek actors, who were held in high esteem even when they were not the playwrights themselves, actors in Roman times were thought to be undignified. Often they were clever slaves, and rarely were they thought worthy of the attention of nobles or people of power. Many of the theaters in which comedies and tragedies were performed were haphazardly built, uncomfortable wooden structures with rowdy audiences. (Figure 6 shows a scene from a comedy.) Some texts plead with the audience not to hiss after the play; others imply that the audience had to be told what was happening onstage, as though they were incapable of following the action. The stone theaters (the first of which was constructed in 55 BCE) may have served a better audience despite the waning of Roman drama. Roman illustrations of actors show that an altar was often on stage with three actors, all of whom wore masks similar to those worn by Greek actors, which implies that the tradition of masks had been carried on long enough for the Romans to adopt it.

Two great actors are known to us by name. Clodius Aesopus (fl. 55 BCE) was from a good family and rose to be the most noted actor for tragedy. He was so eloquent on stage that he tutored Cicero (106–43 BCE), one of the greatest Roman orators and author of some of the most significant books on rhetoric, the art of persuasion. Quintus Roscius Gallus (c. 126–c. 62 BCE), known as Roscius, was born a slave but, because of his extraordinary skills as a comic actor, rose to freedom and a high rank in Roman society. He too is said to have instructed Cicero, who wrote an oration called *Pro Roscio comoedo* (*For Roscius the Comedian*). The connection between Roman oration and the Roman actor is not accidental. The principles of oration, as laid down by Aristotle in his *Rhetoric* and later developed by Romans such as Quintilian and Cicero, were as useful to the actor as to the politician. Early treatises on acting stress the skills of the orator in the training of the actor.

Figure 6. A Roman bas-relief depicting actors performing a comic scene.

Date	Theater	Political	Social/Cultural
800–600 BCE			**753:** Rome is founded.
600–500			**6th century:** The Circus Maximus is constructed for chariot races and athletic contests. **527–509:** Roman Republic
500–400			**450:** Roman law is codified in the Twelve Tables.
400–300		**390:** Rome is rebuilt after a Gallic invasion.	
300–200	**3rd century:** Atellan farce, lively improvised scenarios based on domestic life, is imported from southern Italy to Rome. **240:** Ludi Romani, a festival in honor of Jupiter, incorporates comedy and tragedy for the first time. The festival, established by the elder Tarquin, Etruscan ruler of Rome, already included chariot races, boxing matches, and other popular entertainments. The plays performed at the festival in 240 are probably translations or imitations of Greek plays. **205–184:** Titus Maccius Plautus writes his plays, including *The Twin Menaechmi*.	**272:** Rome conquers central and southern Italy. **264–241:** First Punic War with Carthage **222:** Rome conquers northern Italy. **218–201:** Second Punic War	**c. 300:** Roman consul Appius Claudius Crassus builds the Appian Way, which stretches from Rome to Capua. **287:** Full equality between plebeians and patricians in Rome
200–100	**160:** Publius Terentius Afer (Terence) writes *The Brothers*. **c. 126–c. 62:** Roscius, a popular Roman actor	**195:** Cato the Elder becomes consul and initiates many reforms in urban development and government representation. **149–146:** The Third Punic War. Rome destroys Carthage and Corinth and conquers Greece. **133:** Tiberius Gracchus, Roman reformer, is murdered at the instigation of the Senate.	**186:** Wild animals are exhibited at the Circus Maximus. Contests between wild animals and humans begin shortly thereafter. **106–43:** Cicero, Roman orator **105:** Gladiatorial contests become part of state festivals.

Date	Theater	Political	Social/Cultural
100 BCE–1 CE	**1st century:** Theaters are built throughout the Roman empire.	**69 BCE:** Cleopatra is born. She reigns as queen of Egypt from 51 to 49 and from 48 to her death in 30.	**87–54:** Catullus, Roman poet
	90: Vitruvius writes *De Architectura*, a treatise on Roman architecture that discusses theatre architecture in Greece and Rome.	**60:** First Triumvirate (Pompey, Crassus, and Julius Caesar) rules Rome.	**70–19:** Virgil (P. Virgilius Maro), poet and author of the *Aeneid*
			47: The library of Ptolemy in Alexandria destroyed by fire; many valuable manuscripts and works of art are lost.
	55: The first permanent stone theater is built in Rome.	**47:** Herod is appointed King of Judea.	
	fl. 55: Clodius Aesopus, Roman tragedian actor	**45:** Julius Caesar is declared dictator by Roman Senate.	**46:** Julius Caesar stages the first *naumachia* (mock sea battle).
		44: On the Ides of March Caesar is assassinated.	**43 BCE–17 CE:** Ovid (Publius Ovidius Naso), poet and author of the *Metamorphoses*
		43–28: The Second Triumvirate (Antony, Lepidus, and Octavius) rules Rome.	
		27 BCE–476 CE: Roman empire	
		27: Gaius Octavius, Julius Caesar's grand-nephew, becomes the first emperor of the Roman empire, assuming the name Augustus.	**22:** Roman pantomime, a predecessor of modern ballet, is introduced by Pylades and Bathyllus.
	4 BCE–65 CE: Seneca. Dates for his plays, including *Medea,* are unknown. Seneca commits suicide after suffering a decline in power and influence.		**19:** Horace (65–8 BCE) writes *Ars Poetica.*
			4: Birth of Jesus
1–100		**14:** Augustus dies, and his stepson Tiberius becomes emperor.	**c. 30:** Crucifixion of Jesus
		37: Tiberius's grand-nephew Gaius Caesar (Caligula) is named emperor.	
		41: Caligula is assassinated by his own guards; his wife and young daughter are also murdered. Caligula's uncle Claudius is named emperor.	
		54: Claudius is allegedly poisoned by his wife, Julia Agrippina. Claudius's stepson Nero is named emperor.	**64:** Much of Rome is destroyed by fire. Nero blames the fire on Rome's increasing Christian population and initiates the first large-scale persecution of Christians in Rome.
		68: Nero commits suicide.	
		69: Vespasian is named emperor. He is succeeded by his son Titus.	**79:** Mount Vesuvius erupts, destroying Pompeii.
			80: The Colosseum is completed.

Date	Theater	Political	Social/Cultural
100–200		**117:** Hadrian becomes emperor.	
		120: Hadrian commissions the building of the Pantheon ("the place of all gods").	
		122–126: Hadrian's Wall is extended across Great Britain.	
	197–202: Tertullian writes *De Spectaculis*, denouncing the theater as anti-Christian.	**138:** Hadrian dies and is succeeded by Antonius Pius and then by Marcus Aurelius.	**c. 130–200:** Galen, Roman physicist and pioneer in anatomy and physiology
			164–180: A devastating plague sweeps the Roman empire.
200–300	**c. 300:** Records of earliest religious plays	Roman citizenship is given to every freeborn subject in the empire.	
		Under Roman rule, Carthage regains prominence as a center of culture and commerce.	
		220: Goths invade the Balkan Peninsula and Asia Minor.	
		257: Goths invade the Black Sea provinces.	
300–400		**313:** Edict of Milan. Emperor Constantine establishes toleration of Christianity.	
		331: Emperor Constantine moves the Roman capital from Rome to Constantinople.	**354–430:** St. Augustine, author of the influential *City of God* and *Confessions*
		360: Huns invade Europe.	**c. 360:** Scrolls begin to be replaced by books.
400–500		**401–403:** Visigoths invade Italy.	**c. 400:** In part because of the rise of Christianity, state festivals honoring pagan gods cease in Rome.
			404: Gladiatorial contests are abolished.
		410: Alaric, king of Visigoths, sacks Rome.	**c. 410:** Experiments with alchemy begin.
			523: Wild animal contests are abolished.

Roman Dramatists   The surviving Roman plays come from just three hands: Plautus (254–184 BCE), Terence (c. 190–159 BCE), and Seneca (4 BCE–65 CE). The comedies of Plautus are raucous, broad, and farcical; those of Terence are polished and carefully structured. Seneca wrote tragedies that were well known to Elizabethans such as Marlowe and Shakespeare, and it is clear that the Elizabethan Age found **Senecan tragedy** to be peculiarly suited to its own temperament.

Plautus

All surviving Roman comedy shows the influence of Greek originals. Plautus is among Rome's most famous playwrights and may have been a member of a troupe that performed Atellan comedy. His middle name is Maccius (a form of Maccus, the clown of the farces), possibly alluding to the role he had habitually played. Tradition has it that he was in the theater for a good while before he began writing comedies. His first plays date from 205 BCE, about thirty-five years after Livius introduced Greek drama to the Romans. No one knows how many plays he wrote, and many unauthenticated titles have been assigned to him. About twenty-one plays exist that are thought to be his, the most famous of which are *Amphitryon, The Pot of Gold, The Captives, Curculio, The Braggart Warrior, The Rope,* and *The Twin Menaechmi.*

The last play is probably the best known Roman comedy. It features Menaechmus from Syracuse, who goes to Epidamnus searching for his lost twin. There he meets people who mistake him for his brother: a cook; a prostitute; Sponge, a typical parasite; and even his brother's wife and father-in-law. The comedy exploits all the confusions inherent in mistaken identity.

The Twin Menaechmi

The Twin Menaechmi was the first ancient play to be translated into a modern language and put on the stage (1486 in Italy). It has been adapted by numerous modern playwrights, including Shakespeare in *The Comedy of Errors* and, more recently, Rodgers and Hart in *The Boys from Syracuse* (1938), a musical that ran on Broadway for 235 performances. *Boys* has been revived numerous times and is still a popular summer theater play. The following scene from the beginning of Act III of *The Twin Menaechmi* shows the parasite Sponge mistaking Menaechmus of Syracuse for Sponge's friend Menaechmus of Epidamnus. They have a great go-around over a dress in a typical mixup of the kind that originated with Roman comedies and has been popular in farces and comedies ever since.

PLAUTUS (254–184 BCE)

From The Twin Menaechmi   c. 205–184 BCE

TRANSLATED BY LIONEL CASSON

Act III

SPONGE: I'm over thirty now, and never have I ever in all those years pulled a more damned fool stunt than the one I pulled today: There was this town meeting, and *I* had to dive in and come up right in the middle of it. While I'm standing there with my mouth open, Menaechmus sneaks off on me. I'll bet he's gone to his girlfriend. Perfectly willing to leave me behind, too!

(*Paces up and down a few times, shaking his head bitterly. Then, in a rage.*) Damn, damn, damn the fellow who first figured out town meetings! All they do is keep a busy man away from his business. Why don't people pick a panel of men of leisure for this kind of thing? Hold a roll call at each meeting and whoever doesn't answer gets fined on the spot. There are plenty of persons around who need only one meal a day; they don't have business hours to keep because they don't go after dinner invitations or give them out. They're the ones to fuss with town meetings and town elections. If that's how things were run, I wouldn't have lost my lunch today. He sure wanted me along, didn't he? I'll go in, anyway. There's still hope of leftovers to soothe my soul. (*He is about to go up to the door when it suddenly swings open and Menaechmus of Syracuse appears, standing on the threshold with a garland, a little askew, on his head; he is holding the dress and listening to Lovey who is chattering at him from inside. Sponge quickly backs off into a corner.*) What's this I see? Menaechmus—and he's leaving, garland and all! The table's been cleared! I sure came in time—in time to walk him home. Well, I'll watch what his game is, and then I'll go and have a word with him.

MENAECHMUS OF SYRACUSE (*to Lovey inside*): Take it easy, will you! I'll have it back to you today in plenty of time, altered and trimmed to perfection. (*Slyly.*) Believe me, you'll say it's not your dress; you won't know it any more.

SPONGE (*to the audience*): He's bringing the dress to the dressmaker. The dining's done, the drinks are down—and Sponge spent the lunch hour outside. God damn it I'm not the man I think I am if I don't get even with him for this, but really even. You just watch. I'll give it to him, I will.

MENAECHMUS OF SYRACUSE (*closing the door and walking downstage; to the audience, jubilantly*): Good god, no one ever expected less—and got more blessings from heaven in one day than me. I dined, I wined, I wenched, and (*holding up the dress*) made off with this to which, from this moment on, she hereby forfeits all right, title, and interest.

SPONGE (*straining his ears, to the audience*): I can't make out what he's saying from back here. Is that full-belly talking about me and my right title and interest?

MENAECHMUS OF SYRACUSE (*to the audience*): She said I stole it from my wife and gave it to her. I saw she was mistaking me for someone else, so I promptly played it as if she and I were having a hot and heavy affair and began to yes her; I agreed right down the line to everything she said. Well, to make a long story short, I never had it so good for so little.

SPONGE (*clenching his fists, to the audience*): I'm going up to him. I'm itching to give him the works. (*Leaves his corner and strides belligerently toward Menaechmus.*)

MENAECHMUS OF SYRACUSE (*to the audience*): Someone coming up to me. Wonder who it is?

SPONGE (*roaring*): Well! You featherweight, you filth, you slime, you disgrace to the human race, you double-crossing good-for-nothing! What did I ever do to you that you had to ruin my life? You sure gave me the slip downtown a little while ago! You killed off the day all right—and held the funeral feast without me. Me who was coheir under the will! Where do you come off to do a thing like that!

MENAECHMUS OF SYRACUSE (*too pleased with life to lose his temper*): Mister, will you please tell me what business you and I have that gives you the right to use language like that to a stranger here, someone you never saw in your life? You hand me that talk and I'll hand you something you won't like.

SPONGE (*dancing with rage*): God damn it, you already have! I know god damned well you have!

MENAECHMUS OF SYRACUSE (*amused and curious*): What's your name, mister?

SPONGE (*as before*): Still making jokes, eh? As if you don't know my name!

MENAECHMUS OF SYRACUSE: So help me, so far as I know, I never heard of you or saw you till this minute. But I know one thing for sure: whoever you are, you'd better behave yourself and stop bothering me.

SPONGE (*taken aback for a minute*): Menaechmus! Wake up!

MENAECHMUS OF SYRACUSE (*genially*): Believe me, to the best of my knowledge, I am awake.

SPONGE: You don't know me?

MENAECHMUS OF SYRACUSE (*as before*): If I did, I wouldn't say I didn't.

SPONGE (*incredulously*): You don't know your own parasite?

MENAECHMUS OF SYRACUSE: Mister, it looks to me as if you've got bats in your belfry.

SPONGE (*shaken, but not convinced*): Tell me this: Didn't you steal that dress there from your wife today and give it to Lovey?

MENAECHMUS OF SYRACUSE: Good god, no! I don't have a wife, I never gave anything to any Lovey, and I never stole any dress. Are you in your right mind?

SPONGE (*aside, groaning*): A dead loss, the whole affair. (*To Menaechmus.*) But you came out of your house wearing the dress! I saw you myself!

MENAECHMUS OF SYRACUSE (*exploding*): Damn you! You think everybody's a pervert just because you are? I was wearing this dress? Is that what you're telling me?

SPONGE: I most certainly am.

MENAECHMUS OF SYRACUSE: Now you go straight to the one place fit for you! No — get yourself to the lunatic asylum; you're stark-raving mad.

SPONGE (*venomously*): God damn it, there's one thing nobody in the world is going to stop me from doing: I'm telling the whole story, exactly what happened, to your wife this minute. All these insults are going to boomerang back on your own head. Believe you me, you'll pay for eating that whole lunch yourself. (*Dashes into the house of Menaechmus of Epidamnus.*)

MENAECHMUS OF SYRACUSE (*throwing his arms wide, to the audience*): What's going on here? Must everyone I lay eyes on play games with me this way? Wait—I hear the door.

(*The door of Lovey's house opens, and one of her maids comes out holding a bracelet. She walks over to Menaechmus and, as he looks on blankly, hands it to him.*)

MAID: Menaechmus, Lovey says would you please do her a big favor and drop this at the jeweler's on your way? She wants you to give him an ounce of gold and have him make the whole bracelet over.

MENAECHMUS OF SYRACUSE (*with alacrity*): Tell her I'll not only take care of this but anything else she wants taken care of. Anything at all. (*He takes the piece and examines it absorbedly.*)

MAID (*watching him curiously, in surprise*): Don't you know what bracelet it is?

MENAECHMUS OF SYRACUSE: Frankly no—except that it's gold.

MAID: It's the one you told us you stole from your wife's jewel box when nobody was looking.

MENAECHMUS OF SYRACUSE (*forgetting himself, in high dudgeon*): I never did anything of the kind!

MAID: You mean you don't remember it? Well, if that's the case, you give it right back!

MENAECHMUS OF SYRACUSE (*after a few seconds of highly histrionic deep thought*): Wait a second. No, I *do* remember it. Of course—this is the one I gave her. Oh, and there's something else: Where are the armlets I gave her at the same time?

MAID (*puzzled*): You never gave her any armlets.

MENAECHMUS OF SYRACUSE (*quickly*): Right you are. This was all I gave her.

MAID: Shall I tell her you'll take care of it?

MENAECHMUS OF SYRACUSE: By all means, tell her. I'll take care of it, all right. I'll see she gets it back the same time she gets the dress back.

MAID (*going up to him and stroking his cheek*): Menaechmus dear, will you do me a favor too? Will you have some earrings made for me? Drop earrings, please; ten grams of gold in each. (*Meaningfully.*) It'll make me *so* glad to see you every time you come to the house.

MENAECHMUS OF SYRACUSE: Sure. (*With elaborate carelessness.*) Just give me the gold. I'll pay for the labor myself.

MAID: Please, you pay for the gold too. I'll make it up to you afterward.

MENAECHMUS OF SYRACUSE: No, you pay for the gold. I'll make it up to *you* afterward. Double.

MAID: I don't have the money.

MENAECHMUS OF SYRACUSE (*with a great air of magnanimity*): Well, any time you get it, you just let me have it.

MAID (*turning to go*): I'm going in now. Anything I can do for you?

MENAECHMUS OF SYRACUSE: Yes. Tell her I'll see to both things—(*sotto voce, to the audience*) that they get sold as quickly as possible for whatever they'll bring. (*As the maid starts walking toward the door.*) Has she gone in yet? (*Hearing a slam.*) Ah, she's in, the door's closed. (*Jubilantly.*) The lord loves me! I've had a helping hand from heaven! (*Suddenly looks about warily.*) But why hang around when I have the time and chance to get away from this (*jerking his thumb at Lovey's house*) pimping parlor here? Menaechmus! Get a move on, hit the road, forward march! I'll take off this garland and toss it to the left here (*doing so*). Then, if anyone tries to follow me, he'll think I went that way. Now I'll go and see if I can find my servant. I want to let him know all the blessings from heaven I've had.

(*He races off, stage right. The stage is now empty.*)

Terence

Terence is said to have been a North African slave brought to Rome, whose master realized he was unusually intelligent and gifted. After he was freed, Terence took his place in Roman literary life and produced a body of six plays, all of which still exist: *The Woman of Andros, The Self-Tormentor, The Eunuch, Phormio, The Mother-in-Law,* and *The Brothers.* Terence's plays are notable for carefully including a subplot or secondary action and for avoiding the technique of addressing the audience directly.

The Romans preferred Plautus's broad farcical humor to Terence's more carefully plotted, elegantly styled plays. Terence borrowed liberally from Greek sources, often more than one for each of his plays, to develop unusually complicated plots. A manager or producer worked with him on all his plays, and the musician who worked with him was a slave, Flaccus. Terence's productive life was relatively short. He died on a trip to Greece, apparently worrying over a piece of missing luggage said to have contained new plays.

Terence's situation was unusual: he had two wealthy Roman patrons who were interested in seeing the best Greek comedy brought to the Romans. Consequently, they paid for his productions and gave him more support than the average comic playwright could have expected. In sharp contrast with Plautus's work, which was repetitive in nature, Terence's plays exhibited considerable development of his dramatic skills from the beginning to the end of his work. Terence was more than a translator, but he wrote at a time when Romans were interested in emulating the Greeks, and his fidelity to Greek originals was one of his strongest recommendations.

The Brothers

The ending of *The Brothers,* generally recognized as Terence's masterpiece and certainly the most influential of his plays, has Demea planning a reversal on his brother, Micio. Micio is a good, easygoing bachelor who wishes others well. Demea has been a stern father to one of his sons, Ctesipho, and has tried to steer him in a direction other than the one Ctesipho wants to follow. Demea has entrusted the upbringing of his second son, Aeschinus, to his lenient brother, Micio. Both sons deceive both brothers and end up with the women they want rather than the women the brothers want for them. Meanwhile, Demea gives up and turns the tables on Micio, engineering his brother's marriage to Aeschinus's mother-in-law. In the process of all this, Demea decides to adopt the gentle, easygoing ways of his brother and to forsake his former stern behavior.

This play was adapted in the seventeenth century by Marston, Beaumont and Fletcher, and others. Molière relied on it for his *School for Wives.* At least five plays were adapted from it for the eighteenth-century English stage.

TERENCE (c. 190–159 BCE)

From The Brothers   160 BCE

TRANSLATED BY ROBERT GRAVES

From Act V

MICIO (*to Syrus, within*): My brother ordered it,° say ye! Where is he? . . . Hah, Brother, was it you who ordered this?

DEMEA: Yes, that I did! And in this and all things else I'm ready to do whatever may conduce to the uniting, serving, helping, and the joining together of both families.

My brother ordered it: Demea ordered the breaking down of a wall to allow the two families to communicate. In this way Demea imitates the good-naturedness of his brother, Micio, and traps him into marrying Aeschinus's mother-in-law.

AESCHINUS (*to Micio*): Pray, Sir, let it be so!

MICIO: Well, I've nothing to say against it.

DEMEA: Truth, 'tis no more than we are obliged to do. For first, she's your son's mother-in-law . . .

MICIO: What then?

DEMEA: A very virtuous and modest woman . . .

MICIO: So they say indeed.

DEMEA: Not weighed down by years . . .

MICIO: Not yet.

DEMEA: But past child-bearing: a lonesome woman whom nobody esteems . . .

MICIO (*aside*): What the Devil is he at?

DEMEA: . . . Therefore you ought to marry her; and you Aeschinus, should do what you can to bring this about.

MICIO: Who? I marry?

DEMEA: Yes, you.

MICIO: I, prithee?

DEMEA: Yes, you I say.

MICIO: Pho, you are fooling us, surely?

DEMEA (*to Aeschinus*): If thou hast any life in thee, persuade him to it.

AESCHINUS: Dear Father . . .

MICIO: (*interrupting*): Blockhead! Dost thou take in earnest what he says?

DEMEA: 'Tis in vain to refuse; it can't be avoided.

MICIO: Pho, you are in your dotage!

AESCHINUS: Good Sir, let me win this one favor.

MICIO (*angrily*): Art out of thy wits, let me alone!

DEMEA: Come, come! Hearken for once to what your son says.

MICIO: Haven't ye played the fool enough yet? Shall I at threescore and five marry an old woman who's ready to drop into the grave? This is your wise counsel, is it?

AESCHINUS: Pray, Sir, do; I've promised you shall.

MICIO: You promised, with a mischief! Promise for thyself, thou chit!

DEMEA: Fie, fie! What if he had begged a greater favor from you?

MICIO: As if there were any greater favor than this!

DEMEA: Pray grant his request.

AESCHINUS: Good Sir, be not so hard-hearted.

DEMEA: Pho, promise him for once!

MICIO: Will ye never leave baiting me?

AESCHINUS: Not till I've prevailed, Sir.

MICIO: Truth, this is downright forcing a man.

DEMEA: Come, Micio, be good-natured and consent.

MICIO: Though this be the most damned, foolish, ridiculous whim, and the most averse to my nature that could possibly be, yet since you are so extremely set upon it, I'll humor ye for once.

AESCHINUS: That is excellent, I'm obliged to ye beyond measure.

DEMEA (*aside*): Well, what's next? . . . What shall I say next? This is as I'd have it. . . . What's more to be done?

(*To Micio.*)

Ho! There's Hegio our poor kinsman, and nearest relation; in truth, we ought in conscience to do something for him.

MICIO: What, pray?

DEMEA: There's a small plot of land in the suburbs, which you farm out—pray let's give him that to live on.

MICIO: A small one, say ye?

DEMEA: Though it were a great one, you might yet give it to him. He has been as good as a father to Pamphila; he's a very honest man, our kinsman, and you couldn't bestow it better. Besides, Brother, there's a certain proverb (none of my own, I assure you) which you so well and wisely made use of: "That age has always this ill effect of making us more worldly, as well as wiser." We should do well to avoid this scandal. 'Tis a true proverb, Brother, and ought to be held in mind.

MICIO: What's all this? . . . Well, so let it be, if he has need of it.

AESCHINUS: Brave Father, I vow!

DEMEA: Now you are my true brother, both in body and soul.

MICIO: I'm glad of it.

DEMEA (*aside, laughing*): I've stabbed him with his own weapons, i'fack!

(*Enter Syrus, with a pick-axe upon his shoulders.*)

SYRUS (*to Demea*): The job is done as ye ordered, Sir.

DEMEA: Thou art an honest lad. . . . And upon my conscience I think Syrus deserves his freedom.

MICIO: He, his freedom? For what exploit?

DEMEA: O, for a thousand.

SYRUS: O dear Mr. Demea, you are a rare gentleman, edad you are! You know I've looked after the young gentlemen from their cradles. I taught them, advised them, and instructed them all I possibly could.

DEMEA: Nothing more evident! Nay, more than that, he catered for them, pimped for them, and in the morning took care of a debauchee for them. These are no ordinary accomplishments, I can assure ye.

SYRUS: Your worship's very merry.

DEMEA: Besides, he was prime mover in buying this music-girl. It was he who managed the whole intrigue, and 'tis no more than justice to reward him, as an encouragement to others! In short, Aeschinus desires the same thing.

MICIO (*to Aeschinus*): Do you desire it too?

AESCHINUS: Yes, if you please, Sir.

MICIO: Since 'tis so, come hither, Syrus! Thou art a free man.

(*Syrus kneels down, Micio lays his hand on his head, and after that gives him a cuff on the ear.*)

SYRUS (*rising up*): Generously done! A thousand thanks to ye all, and to you, Mr. Demea.

DEMEA: I'm well satisfied.

AESCHINUS: And I too.

SYRUS: I won't question it, Sir. But I wish heartily my joy were more complete, that my poor spouse Phrygia might be made as free as I am.

DEMEA: Truth, she's a mighty good woman.

SYRUS: And your grandson's first foster-mother, too.

DEMEA: Faith, in good earnest, if for that, she deserves her freedom before any woman in the world.

MICIO: What! For that simple service?

DEMEA: Yes, indeed! In fine, I'll pay for her freedom myself.

SYRUS: God's blessing light upon your worship, and grant all your wishes.

MICIO: Syrus, thou hast made a good day's work of it.

DEMEA: Besides, Brother, it would be a deed of charity to lend him a little money to set up in business that he may face the world without fear. I undertake that he'll soon repay it.

MICIO: Not a penny-piece!

AESCHINUS: He's a very honest fellow, Sir.

SYRUS: Upon my word, I'll repay you the loan. Do but trust me!

AESCHINUS: Pray do, Sir.

MICIO: I'll consider the matter with care.

DEMEA: He shall pay ye, I'll see to that.

SYRUS (*to Demea*): Egad, you're the best man alive.

AESCHINUS: And the pleasantest in the world.

MICIO: What's the meaning of this, Brother? How comes this sudden change of humor? Why this gallant squandering and profusion?

DEMEA: I'll tell ye, Brother. These sons of yours don't reckon you a sweet-natured and pleasant man because you live as you should and do what is just and reasonable, but because you fawn upon them, cocker them up, and give them what they'll spend. Now, son Aeschinus, if you are dissatisfied with my course of life, because I wouldn't indulge you in all things, right or wrong, then I'll not trouble my head with you any further. Be free to squander, buy mistresses, and do what you will! But if you wish me to advise ye, and set ye up, and help ye too in matters of which your youth can give ye but little understanding—matters of which you are over-fond, and don't well consider—see, here I'm ready to stand by you.

AESCHINUS: Dear Sir, we commit ourselves wholly to your charge; for you know what's fitting to be done far better than we . . . But what will ye do for my brother Ctesipho?

DEMEA: Why, let him take the music-girl; and so bid adieu to general wenching.

AESCHINUS: That's very reasonable. (*To the spectators.*) Gentlemen, your favor!

(Exeunt° all.)

[s.D.] *Exeunt:* Latin for "they go out."

Seneca

Senecan tragedies were based on either Greek or Roman themes and included murder, other bloodthirsty actions (many of which did not occur on stage but were described), horror of various kinds, ghosts, and long, bombastic speeches. Signs of Senecan influence can be seen in Elizabethan drama, with its taste for many of these devices; plays like *Hamlet* are notable for ending in a pool of blood, with most of the actors lying dead onstage. The theme of revenge was prized by Seneca and, later, by the Elizabethans.

Not a professional theater person, Seneca was wealthy and learned, a philosopher active in the government of Emperor Nero's Rome. His plays, most of which were adapted from Euripides, were probably written only to be read, as was common at the time, or perhaps recited, although there is no record of their having been performed. The Roman people thirsted for mime and farce but had much less taste for serious plays.

Ten plays attributed to Seneca exist, nine of which are surely his and one of which is only possibly his. His most famous are *Mad Hercules, The Phoenician Women, Medea, Phaedra, Agamemnon, Thyestes,* and *The Trojan Women.*

Thyestes

Thyestes, probably adapted from the *Oresteia* of Aeschylus, influenced a number of Elizabethan revenge tragedies, such as Shakespeare's *Hamlet.* The story is gruesome even by modern standards. Thyestes seduces his brother Atreus's wife, and Atreus banishes him. When Thyestes is summoned to Atreus's home, he is suspicious, but he goes, hoping to be able to see his children. The banquet Atreus holds for Thyestes seems to signal reconciliation between the brothers. But when it is over, Atreus brings in the heads of Thyestes' children, revealing that Thyestes has just eaten their bodies in the feast.

The second scene from act V—before Thyestes is told about the meal he has eaten—follows in its entirety. It shows Thyestes wrestling with himself in a passion of uncertainty. Thyestes' soliloquy is a psychological study of the effects of grief, care, uncertainty, and fear. Seneca's plays have many such soliloquies, and their revelations of complex emotional states deeply impressed the age of Shakespeare.

SENECA (4 BCE–65 CE)

From Thyestes

TRANSLATED BY ELLA ISABEL HARRIS

Act V • *Scene II*

(Thyestes sits alone at the banquet table, half overcome with wine; he tries to sing and be gay, but some premonition of evil weighs upon him.)

THYESTES *(to himself)*: By long grief dulled, put by thy cares, my heart,
  Let fear and sorrow fly and bitter need,
  Companion of thy timorous banishment,
  And shame, hard burden of afflicted souls.
  Whence thou has fallen profits more to know
  Than whither; great is he who with firm step
  Moves on the plain when fallen from the height;
  He who, oppressed by sorrows numberless
  And driven from his realm, with unbent neck
  Carries his burdens, not degenerate
  Or conquered, who stands firm beneath the weight
  Of all his burdens, he is great indeed.
  Now scatter all the clouds of bitter fate,
  Put by all signs of thy unhappy days,

In happy fortunes show a happy face,
Forget the old Thyestes. Ah, this vice
Still follows misery: never to trust
In happy days; though better fortunes come,
Those who have borne afflictions find it hard
To joy in better days. What holds me back,
Forbids me celebrate the festal tide?
What cause of grief, arising causelessly,
Bids me to weep? What art thou that forbids
That I should crown my head with festal wreath?
It does forbid, forbid! Upon my head
The roses languish, and my hair that drips
With ointment rises as with sudden fear,
My face is wet with showers of tears that fall
Unwillingly, and groans break off my song.
Grief loves accustomed tears, the wretched feel
That they must weep. I would be glad to make
Most bitter lamentation, and to wail,
And rend this robe with Tyrian purple dyed.
My mind gives warning of some coming grief,
Presages future ills. The storm that smites
When all the sea is calm weighs heavily
Upon the sailor. Fool! What grief, what storm,
Dost thou conceive? Believe thy brother now.
Be what it may, thou fearest now too late,
Or causelessly. I do not wish to be
Unhappy, but vague terror smites my breast.
No cause is evident and yet my eyes
O'erflow with sudden tears. What can it be,
Or grief, or fear? Or has great pleasure tears?

The surviving Roman plays offer enough variety to give us an idea of what the drama achieved. Like so much of Roman culture, Roman drama rested in the shadow of Greek accomplishments. The Romans were responsible for maintaining the Greek texts, allowing us to see a great deal of their work. Although it may be true that much of the Roman drama that was produced no longer exists, what survives shows variety and high quality.

Medieval Drama

The medieval period in Europe (476 CE–1500 CE) began with the collapse of Rome, a calamity of such magnitude that the years between then and the beginning of the Crusades in 1095 have been traditionally, if erroneously, called the Dark Ages. Historians used this term to refer to their lack of knowledge about a time in which no great central powers organized society or established patterns of behavior and standards in the arts.

Drama, or at least records of it, all but disappeared. The major Western institution to profit from the fall of the Roman empire was the Roman Catholic Church, which in the ninth and tenth centuries enjoyed considerable power and influence. Many bishops considered drama a godless activity, a distraction from the piety that the church demanded of its members. During the great age of cathedral building and the great ages of religious painting and religious music—from the seventh century to the thirteenth—drama was reborn in the Church.

The Role of the Church

The Church may well have intended nothing more than the simple dramatization of its message. Or the people may have craved drama, and the Church's response could have been an attempt to answer their needs. In either event, the Church could never have foreseen the outcome of adding a few moments of drama to the liturgy, the church services. **Liturgical drama** began in the tenth century with **tropes**, or embellishments, which were sung during parts of the Mass (the public celebration of the Eucharist). The earliest known example of a trope, called the *Quem Quaeritis* ("Whom seek ye?"), developed at the monastery at Limoges, c. 923–934 CE:

> ANGEL: Whom seek ye in the sepulchre, O ye Christians?
> THREE MARYS: Jesus of Nazareth, who was crucified, O ye Angels.
> ANGEL: He is not here; he is risen as he has foretold.
>   Go, announce that he is risen from the sepulchre.

Some scholars think that in its earliest form this trope was sung by four monks in a dialogue pattern, three monks representing the three Marys at Christ's tomb and the other representing the angel. Tropes like the *Quem*

Quaeritis evolved over the years to include a number of participants as the tropes spread from church to church throughout the Continent. These dramatic interpolations never became dramas separate from the Mass itself, although their success and popularity led to experiments with other dramatic sequences centering on moments in the Mass and in the life of Christ. The actors in these pieces did not think of themselves as specialists or professionals; they were simply monks who belonged to the church. The churchgoers obviously enjoyed the tropes, and more were created to amplify the liturgy.

In the tenth century, Hrosvitha entertained herself and her fellow nuns with imitations of the Roman dramatist Terence. Although her own subject matter was holy in nature, she admired Terence as an amusing comic writer with a polished style. She referred to herself as the "strong voice of Gandersheim," her community in Saxony, and said that she had "not hesitated to imitate in my writings a poet whose works are so widely read, my object being to glorify, within the limits of my poor talent, the laudable chastity of Christian virgins." Her plays are very short moral tales, often illustrating moments in the lives of Christian martyred women. As far as is known, these plays do not seem to have gone beyond the nuns' walls; therefore, they had little effect on the drama developing in the period.

Once dramatic scenes were added that took the action outside of the liturgy, it was not long before dramas were being staged outside the church. The Anglo-Norman drama *Adam,* dating from the twelfth century, has explicit stage directions establishing its setting outside the church. The play is to be staged on the west side of the church with a platform extending from the steps. The characters of Adam, Eve, God (called Figura), and the Devil and his assistants are given costumes and extensive dialogue. The dramatic detail in this play implies a considerable development of plot and action, which, despite its theological matter, is plainly too elaborate to be contained within the service of the Mass.

Once outside the church, drama flourished and soon became independent, although its themes continued to be religious and productions were connected with religious festivals. In 1264, Pope Urban IV added to the religious calendar a new, important feast: Corpus Christi, celebrated beginning on the first Thursday after Trinity Sunday, about two months after Easter. The purpose of the feast was to celebrate the doctrine declaring that the body of Christ was real and present in the Host (consecrated bread or wafer) taken by the faithful in the sacrament of the Eucharist (Communion).

At first, the feast of Corpus Christi was localized in Liège, Belgium. But by decree of Pope Clement V in 1311, it became one of the chief feasts of the church. Among other things, it featured a procession and pageant in which the Host was displayed publicly through the streets of a town. Because of the importance and excitement of this feast, entire communities took part in the celebration.

Miracle Plays

Miracle plays on the subject of miracles performed by saints developed late in the twelfth century both in England and on the Continent. Typically, these plays focused on the Virgin Mary and St. Nicholas, both of whom had strong followings (sometimes described as cults) during the medieval period. Mary is often portrayed as helping those in need or in danger—often at the last minute. Some of those she saved may have seemed to a pious audience to be unsavory sinners, but the point was that the saint saved all who truly wished to be saved.

Although they quickly became public entertainments removed from the church building and were popular as Corpus Christi entertainments throughout the fifteenth century, few miracle plays survive in English because King Henry VIII banned them during his reformation of the Church. As a result, they were not performed or preserved.

The craft guilds—professional organizations of workers involved in the same trade (carpenters, wool merchants, and so on)—soon began competing with each other in producing plays that could be performed during the feast of Corpus Christi. Most of their plays derived from Bible stories and the life of Christ. Religious guilds, such as the Confrèrie of the Passion, produced plays in Paris and elsewhere on the Continent. Because the Bible is silent on many details of Christ's life, some plays invented new material and illuminated dark areas, thereby satisfying the intense curiosity medieval Christians had about events the Bible omitted.

Mystery Plays

The Church did not ignore drama after it left the church buildings. Since plays had religious subject matter and could be used to teach the Bible and to model Christian behavior, they remained of considerable value to the Church.

First performed by the clergy, religious plays dramatized the mystery of Christ's Passion. Later, the Corpus Christi plays were produced by members of craft guilds, and they became known as **craft plays** or **mystery plays**. Beginning in the medieval period, the word *mystery* was used to describe a skill or trade known only to a few who apprenticed and mastered its special techniques; it also referred to religious mysteries.

By the fifteenth century, mystery plays and the feast of Corpus Christi were popular almost everywhere in Europe, and in England certain towns produced exceptionally elaborate cycles with unusually complex and ambitious plays. The **cycles** were groups of from twenty-four to forty-eight plays. Four cycles have been preserved: the Chester, York, Towneley (Wakefield), and N-Town cycles, named for their towns of origin. N-Town plays were a generic version of plays that any town could take and use as its own, although the plays were probably written near Lincoln.

The plays were performed annually, and the texts were carefully preserved. Some of the plays, such as *The Fall of Lucifer,* are very short. Others are longer and more complex and resemble modern plays: *Noah,* from the Wakefield Cycle, which has been produced regularly in recent history; *The Slaughter of Innocents;* and *The Second Shepherds' Pageant,* one of the most entertaining mystery plays.

The producers of the plays often had a sense of appropriateness in their choice of subjects. For example, the Water-Drawers guild sponsored *Noah's Flood;* the Butchers (because they sold "flesh"), *Temptation* and *The Woman Taken in Adultery;* and the Shipwrights, *The Building of the Ark.*

Among the best known mystery plays is the somewhat farcical *The Second Shepherds' Pageant,* which is both funny and serious. It tells of a crafty shepherd named Mak who steals a lamb from his fellow shepherds and takes it home. His wife, Gill, then places it in a cradle and pretends it is her baby. Eventually the shepherds—who suspect Mak from the first—smoke out the fraud and give Mak a blanket-tossing for their trouble. But after they do so, they see a star in the heavens and turn their attention to the birth of baby Jesus, the Lamb of God. They join the Magi and come to pay homage to the Christ Child.

The easy way in which the profane elements of everyday life coexisted with the sacred in medieval times has long interested scholars. The *Second Shepherds' Pageant* virtually breaks into two parts, the first dedicated to the wickedness of Mak and Gill and the horseplay of the shepherds. But once Mak has had his due, the play alters in tone and the sense of devotion to Christian teachings becomes uppermost. The fact that the mystery plays moved away from liturgical Latin to the vernacular (local) language made such a juxtaposition of sacred and profane much more possible.

The dominance of the guilds in producing mystery plays suggests that guilds were enjoying increasing political power and authority. The guilds grew stronger and more influential—probably at the expense of the Church. Some historians have seen this development as crucial to the growing secularization of the Middle Ages.

Morality Plays

Morality plays were never part of any cycle but developed independently as moral tales in the late fourteenth or early fifteenth century on the Continent and in England. They do not illustrate moments in the Bible, nor do they describe the life of Christ or the saints. Instead, they describe the lives of people facing the temptations of the world. The plays are careful to present a warning to the unwary that their souls are always in peril, that the devil is on constant watch, and that people must behave properly if they are to be saved.

One feature of morality plays is their reliance on **allegory**, a favorite medieval device. Allegory is the technique of giving abstract ideas or values a physical representation. In morality plays, abstractions such as goodness became characters in the drama. In modern times, we sometimes use allegory in art, as when we represent justice as a blindfolded woman. Allegorically, justice should act impartially because she does not "see" any distinctions, such as those of rank or privilege, that characterize people standing before a judge.

The use of allegory permitted medieval dramatists to personify abstract values such as sloth, greed, daintiness, vanity, strength, and hope by making them characters and placing them onstage in action. The dramatist specified symbols, clothing, and gestures appropriate to these abstract figures, thus helping the audience recognize the ideas the characters represented. The use of allegory was an extremely durable technique, already established in medieval painting, printed books, and books of emblems, in which, for example, sloth would be shown as a man reclining lazily on a bed or greed would be represented as overwhelmingly fat and vanity as a figure completely absorbed in a mirror.

The central problem in the morality play was the salvation of human beings: an individual's struggle to avoid sin and damnation and achieve salvation in the otherworld. As in *Everyman* (c. 1495), a late-medieval play that is the best known of the morality plays, the subjects were usually abstract battles between certain vices and specific virtues for the possession of the human soul, a theme repeated in the Elizabethan Age in Marlowe's *Doctor Faustus*.

In many ways, the morality play was a dramatized sermon designed to teach a moral lesson. Marked by high seriousness, it was nevertheless entertaining. Using allegory to represent abstract qualities allowed the didactic playwrights to draw clear-cut lines of moral force: Satan was always bad; angels were always good. The allegories were clear, direct, and apparent to all who witnessed the plays.

We do not have much knowledge of the origins of morality plays. Many of them are lost, but some of those that remain are occasionally performed: *The Pride of Life* (the earliest extant morality play), *The Castle of Perseverance, Wisdom, Mankind,* and *Everyman* are the best known. They enjoyed a remarkable popularity in the latter part of the medieval period, all the way up to the early Renaissance.

Japanese Drama

Although Chinese drama and Japanese drama neither influenced nor were influenced by Western drama in the medieval period, from roughly the late twelfth to the beginning of the seventeenth centuries they, like Western drama, were connected to temples, shrines, and religious ceremony. During this period, Japanese Nō drama developed as a highly refined, deliberate, and ritualized form involving ceremonial dance and music as well as a narrative. Centuries later, Nō drama had an influence on Western literature, particularly on writers such as Ezra Pound and playwrights such as W. B. Yeats and Samuel Beckett.

Nō drama developed from a popular form of drama called sarugaku Nō, invented by Kan'ami (1333–1384) in the fourteenth century. The rulers of Japan at that time, shoguns (generals) of the samurai warrior class, enjoyed theater and supported performances of highly sophisticated drama. They preferred sarugaku, or "monkey music"—a form that included gymnastic action, music, dance, and a story line. Kan'ami refined sarugaku into sarugaku Nō, a more deliberate and controlled form that elevated the actor and demanded more skill—the word *Nō* means "skill"—from performers. The refinement Kan'ami brought to the drama was associated with Zen Buddhism, the form of religion favored by the shogun of the period.

Nō drama, which relies on masks, ritual costume, dance, and music, is produced around the world even today. Nō emerged late in the fourteenth century out of Kan'ami's innovations, but it was his son, Zeami Motokiyo (1363–1443), who developed Nō into a serious form marked by the restraint and control associated with Zen Buddhism. The religious influences on Nō drama led to an emphasis on self-control, honorable behavior, and purity of action. Zeami produced a body of drama that can be seen today in the West as well as in the East. *Lady Han (Hanjo)* deals with a realistic situation in which a prostitute falls in love with a traveling captain. Before he leaves, they exchange fans on which a painting of the moon will identify them. Such romances were not uncommon, and the emotions portrayed in Nō drama are derived from living experience.

The Medieval Stage

Relatively little commentary survives about the conventions of medieval staging in Europe, and some of it is contradictory. We know that in the earliest years—after the tropes developed into full-blown religious scenes acted inside

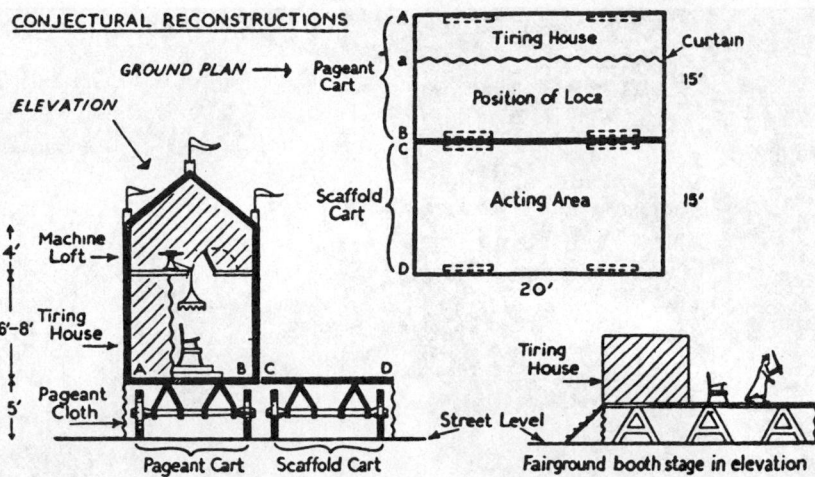

Figure 7. Pageant wagon.

the cathedrals—certain sections of the church were devoted to specific short plays. The later platforms outside the church became known as **mansions**; each mansion represented a building or physical place known to the audience. The audience moved from one mansion to another, seeing play after play, absorbing the dramatic representation of the events, characters, and locale associated with each mansion.

The tradition of moving from mansion to mansion carried over into the performances that took place on wagons with raised stages (Figure 7). Usually, the wagons remained stationary and the audience moved from one to another. During the guild cycles, the pageant carts would move; the performers would give their plays at several locales so that many people could see them (Figure 8).

According to medieval descriptions, drawings, and reconstructions, a **pageant cart** could also be simply a flat surface, drawn on wheels, that had a wagon next to it; these structures touched on their long side. In some cases, a figure could descend from an upper area as if from the clouds, or actors could descend from the pageant cart to the audience's level to enact a descent into an underworld. The stage was, then, a raised platform visible to the audience below.

A curtain concealed a space, usually inside or below the wagon, for changing costumes. The actors used costumes and props, sometimes very elaborate and expensive, in an effort to make the drama more impressive. Indeed, between the thirteenth and the sixteenth centuries, a number of theatrical effects were developed to please a large audience. For instance, in the morality and mystery plays, the devils were often portrayed as frightening, grotesque, and sometimes even comic figures. They became crowd pleasers. A sensational element was developed in some of the plays in the craft cycles, especially those about the lives of the saints and martyrs, in which there were plenty of chances to portray horrifying tortures.

The prop that seems to have pleased audiences the most was a complex machine known as the **mouth of hell** or "Hell mouth," usually a large fish-shaped orifice from which smoke and explosions, fueled by gunpowder, belched

Figure 8. A detail of Denis Van Alsloot's painting *Procession of the Ommeganck at Brussels in 1615* shows horse-drawn pageant wagons on the move, with several plays being performed simultaneously.

constantly. The devils took great delight in stuffing their victims into these maws. According to a contemporary account, one of the machines required seventeen men to operate.

The level of realism achieved by medieval plays was at times startling. In addition to visual realism, medieval plays involved a level of psychological participation on the part of both audience and actor. Sometimes the plays demanded that the actors suffer in accord with the characters they played. Some records attest to characters playing Christ on the cross having to be revived after their hearts stopped, and at least one Judas apparently was hanged just a little too long and had to be resuscitated.

The Medieval Actor

In the early days of liturgical drama, the actors in the tropes were monks, and those in the mystery plays were drawn from the guilds. At first all the actors were male, but records show that eventually women may have taken important roles.

The demands of more sophisticated plays encouraged the development of special skills required for the design and operation of complex stage machines and for the performance of the acrobatics that were expected of certain characters, such as devils. As actors developed facility in delivering lines and as writers found ways to incorporate more challenging elements in their plays, a professionalism no doubt arose, even if actors and writers had few opportunities to earn a living on the stage.

As medieval drama developed in England, France, and Germany, a few plays demanded a large number of actors—sometimes hundreds. The guilds that produced the plays could not always field enough actors from their own numbers and occasionally put out calls for auditions, usually conducted by a committee of the best available actors. Apparently it did not take long for guilds and other producing societies to recognize that some actors were skilled enough to demand recognition and consideration. By the sixteenth century, individual actors were noted for their skills as type characters and sometimes performed the same roles over a period of years. The costuming of actors, as illustrated in contemporary accounts, became extensive and demanding and clearly defined. The devils were attired in red with bizarre masks and performed characteristic wild movements. Military figures wore armor, and noble figures wore rich garments. Essentially, contemporary medieval dress was used in a manner that clarified the character type quickly for the convenience of the audience.

Most of the original early medieval plays were short, but in later years, up through the early sixteenth century, plays became longer. Some took as long as twenty-four hours to produce and involved a great many actors. The early mystery plays were often produced several times during a pageant. When the stage was moved to a new location and a new audience, the actors paraded behind the pageant cart. Because the plays were in the open, the most crucial element of the actor's skill-set was the voice. It was even more important for the medieval actor than for the Greek actor that the voice be commanding and powerful enough to project into the crowd.

By the second half of the sixteenth century, the early Renaissance, groups of wandering actors were producing highly demanding and sophisticated plays, and writers such as Shakespeare were able to join them and make a living. When these professionals secured their own theaters, they had no problems filling them with good drama, with actors, and with an audience.

Dramatic techniques developed in the medieval period were put to good use in the Renaissance theater. For example, the colorful and dramatic devil characters that stalked the mystery plays were transformed into sophisticated villains in Elizabethan drama. The devil Mephistopheles (Mephistophilis) behaves like a smooth Tudor lawyer in Marlowe's *Doctor Faustus;* Iago in *Othello* is suspected of having cloven hooves. Perhaps one important difference is that the Elizabethan devil-villains are truly frightening, since they are so recognizably human in their villainy.

Timeline | Medieval Drama

Date	Theater	Political	Social/Cultural
400–500		**476:** The fall of Rome and beginning of the Dark Ages **483–565:** Byzantine Emperor Justinian, author of the Code of Civil Laws	**480–524:** Boëthius, Roman scholar, philosopher, and theologian, is executed for treason.
500–600	**500–1000:** Traveling performers proliferate in Europe.		**570–632:** Muhammed, founder of Islam **590–594:** Devastating plague spreads through Europe and kills half the population.
600–700		**614:** Persians take Damascus and Jerusalem.	**636:** Anglo-Saxons are introduced to Christianity. **695:** Jews are persecuted in Spain.
700–800		**768–814:** Charlemagne reigns in France and is crowned Holy Roman Emperor on Christmas Day in 800 by Pope Leo III in Rome. **792:** Beginning of the Viking era in Britain	**c. 710:** Buddhist monasteries in Japan become centers of civilization. **787:** The Council of Nicaea officially rejects iconoclasm.
800–900	**9th century:** Beginnings of liturgical drama	**843:** Treaty of Verdun divides the Holy Roman Empire into German, French, and Italian kingdoms. **850:** Rurik, a Northman, becomes ruler of Kiev, an important Russian trading post. Trade begins with Constantinople, which remains a commercial and cultural center throughout the Dark Ages.	**c. 800–1000:** *Beowulf*, one of the first long poems written in English **855:** Earliest known attempts at polyphonic music **863:** Cyril and Methodius invent a Slavic alphabet called Cyrillic.
900–1000	**c. 900:** Farces make their first appearance since classical times. **925:** Earliest extant Easter trope **965–975:** Compilation of the *Regularis Concordia* (Monastic Agreement) by Ethelwood, bishop of Winchester, England. The *Regularis Concordia* contains the text of the earliest extant playlet in Europe, with directions for its performance. **970:** Plays of Hrosvitha, a German nun and the first known female playwright. The six plays are modeled on the comedies of Terence but deal with serious religious matters.	**c. 970–c. 1020:** Leif Ericson, possibly the first European to venture to North America	**c. 900:** The beginnings of the famous Arabian tales called *A Thousand and One Nights* **975:** Arabic arithmetical notation is brought to Europe by the Arabs. **980–1037:** Avicenna (Ibn Sina), Arab physician and philosopher **990:** Development of systemic musical notation

Date	Theater	Political	Social/Cultural
1000–1100		**1066:** The Normans conquer Britain. **1086:** Compilation of the *Domesday Book,* a survey of the British economy, population, and land ownership at that time **1096–1099:** First Crusade. Crusaders take Jerusalem from the Arabs.	**1054**: The Great Schism separates Eastern and Western Churches in Europe. **1079–1142:** Peter Abelard, French theologian and philosopher
1100–1200	**12th century:** Religious plays are first performed outside churches.	**1109–1113:** Anglo-French War **1147–1149:** Second Crusade. Crusaders lose Jerusalem to the Arabs. **1167–1227:** Genghis Khan, founder of Mongol empire **1189–1193:** Third Crusade. Crusaders fail to recapture Jerusalem.	**c. 1125:** Beginnings of French troubadour and trouvère music **1133–1855:** St. Bartholomew's Fair, London, England **1167:** Oxford University is founded.
1200–1300	**13th century:** Beginnings of zaju drama in China **1250:** *Easter Play of Muri,* beginnings of German drama **1276–1277:** French poet Adam de la Halle writes *The Play of the Greenwood,* the oldest extant medieval secular drama.	**1202–1204:** Fourth Crusade. Crusaders seize Constantinople. **1212:** Children's Crusade. Thousands of children are sent as crusaders to Jerusalem; most die or are sold as slaves. **1215:** King John of England signs the Magna Carta, guaranteeing habeas corpus, trial by jury, and restrictions on the power of the king. **1224–1227:** Anglo-French War **1228:** Sixth Crusade **1248:** Seventh Crusade	**c. 1202:** Court jesters appear at European courts. **1225:** Guillaume de Lorris writes *Roman de la Rose,* a story of courtly wooing. **1225–1274:** Thomas Aquinas, important Scholastic philosopher **1254–1324:** Marco Polo, Venetian traveler whose accounts of life in China became famous in the West **1264:** First celebration of the feast of Corpus Christi **c. 1282:** Florence emerges as the leading European city of commerce and finance.
1300–1400	**14th century**: Beginnings of Nō drama in Japan **c. 1385–1450:** *The Second Shepherds' Pageant,* part of the English Wakefield Cycle **1398–1548:** Confrèrie de la Passion at Paris performs religious plays.	**1337:** Hundred Years War begins.	**c. 1302:** Dante's *Divine Comedy* **1304–1374:** Petrarch, Italian poet **1347–1351:** The Black Death kills approximately 75 million people throughout Europe. **1360–1400:** *Piers Plowman* and *Sir Gawain and the Green Knight:* achievements of Middle English literature **1387:** Chaucer's *Canterbury Tales*

Date	Theater	Political	Social/Cultural
1400–1500	**c. 1425:** *The Castle of Perseverance,* English morality play **1429:** Plautus's plays are rediscovered in Italy. **c. 1470:** *Pierre Patheline,* most renowned of medieval French farces **1490:** *Corpus Christi* play of Eger, Bohemia **c. 1495:** *Everyman,* best known English morality play	**1429:** Joan of Arc's troops resist the British siege of Orléans, an important turning point in the Hundred Years War. **1431:** Joan of Arc is captured and burned as a heretic. **1453:** France wins the Hundred Years War and becomes an important continental power. England abandons the Continent to develop its naval forces. **1481:** Spanish Inquisition **1482–1485:** Reign of Richard III. Richard maintains a company of actors at court, which tours surrounding towns when not needed by His Majesty. **1485–1509:** Reign of Henry VII, first of the Tudor rulers. Like Richard III, Henry maintains a company of actors.	**1400–1455:** Fra Angelico, Italian painter **c. 1406–1469:** Fra Lippo Lippi, Italian painter best known for his frescoes **c. 1430:** Modern English develops from Middle English. **c. 1450:** Gutenberg invents movable type. **1485:** Sir Thomas Malory publishes *Le Morte Darthur,* one of the first books printed in England. **1492:** Columbus sets sail across the Atlantic.
1500–1600	**1527:** Henry VIII builds a House of Revels in which to stage court entertainments. **1548:** Production of plays is forbidden in Paris. **1558:** Elizabeth I forbids performance of all religious plays.	**1509–1547:** Reign of Henry VIII **1534:** Henry VIII breaks with the Roman Catholic Church. Drama is used as a political instrument to attack or defend opposing viewpoints. **1558–1603:** Reign of Elizabeth I	**1509:** Pope Clement V resides at Avignon, beginning the Babylonian Captivity, during which Rome is not the papal seat. **1545–1563:** The Council of Trent is convened by the Catholic Church to solidify its control over expressions of Church doctrine. Medieval religious plays are deemed provocative and controversial.

Hrosvitha

"I have been able to pick up some threads and scraps torn from the old mantle of philosophy, to weave them into the stuff of my own book."

–Hrosvitha

The German nun Hrosvitha (c. 935–1000) (also Hroswitha, Roswitha, Hrotsvit, and Hrotsuit) belonged to the Benedictine convent in Gandersheim, founded in 852. Her name translates to "strong voice," a term she uses to describe herself in her writing. Her voice is that of a learned woman, and today it can be heard as a feminist voice in a time and society that were unquestioningly patriarchal.

Hrosvitha is considered not only the earliest German female poet but the first female dramatist in Europe. A Saxon noblewoman, she entered the convent in approximately 959, living with nuns who were themselves of noble birth. The abbey was under the protection of Otto I (912–973), who united a powerful Germany and produced a long-lasting period of peace and development. Otto became the Holy Roman Emperor on February 13, 962. His rule, dubbed the Ottonian Renaissance, favored religion, learning, the arts, and music.

During this period, the abbey at Gandersheim was obligated not to the Church but to the king himself, and Otto eventually released it from his direct governance, permitting it to maintain a law court and to coin money. While such political issues may not have affected Hrosvitha, the fact that the period was one of learning and scholarship was of great importance. Hrosvitha was educated in the liberal arts, beginning with the quadrivium (geometry, arithmetic, music, and astronomy) and continuing with the trivium (grammar, rhetoric, and logic). Her studies were conducted in Latin, the language in which she wrote her plays. Her education was comparable to that of liberally educated men and of the nuns who lived with her.

Hrosvitha's work is deeply rooted in her religious beliefs. Her religious order meditated on the drama of the lives of Christian saints and especially on their often spectacular martyrdoms. The abbey gave its inhabitants a life of contemplation, removed from the world. But it is also clear that the nuns had the talent, education, and opportunities to write religious tracts and, in the case of Hrosvitha, religious drama. The question of whether Hrosvitha's plays were actually produced is not settled.

Hrosvitha wrote six plays and several other prose and poetic works. The plays reject the temptations of the world in the name of Christ. In *Gallicanus*, the title character is promised the hand of Constantia if he wins a specific battle, but Constantia, daughter of the Christian emperor Constantine, has taken a vow of chastity. Eventually, with the aid of saints, Gallicanus converts to Christianity and becomes a martyr. The conversion of an important Roman is the theme of *Callimachus,* and the conversion theme dominates *Paphnutius* and *Abraham. Sapientia* also emphasizes martyrdom. Sapientia's three daughters, whose names translate as Faith, Hope, and Charity, offer a threat to the stability of Emperor Hadrian's rule. They are tortured brutally but survive without pain until Hadrian beheads them. Eventually Sapientia joins her daughters in heavenly bliss, inspiring the local women who have witnessed the events.

For links to resources about Hrosvitha, click on *AuthorLinks* at **bedfordstmartins.com/jacobus.**

Dulcitius

Dulcitius is probably the second of Hrosvitha's plays. It was rediscovered in 1494 in an eleventh-century manuscript along with her other dramatic works. Its first printing was in 1501 in an edition with woodcuts by Albrecht Dürer, indicating its importance at the time. The play is plainly didactic and was designed to teach a lesson rather than merely to entertain. The lesson, as in all of Hrosvitha's plays, is a moral one, urging listeners or readers to live a life of purity and virtue in order to celebrate the greatness of God. In this sense, Hrosvitha wrote in the medieval literary tradition of Europe. Her plays are fascinating to the modern reader, however, because she purposely emulated the techniques of the Roman playwright Terence.

She chose Terence as her model because his texts were used in education and were therefore widely known in Europe. Moreover, they were amusing comedies written with such great style that they were models of elocution. Hrosvitha admits to imitating Terence, but her motives were subversive. She wished to use the eloquent style of Terence not to entertain her audience with secular amusement and charming courtesans but to honor the virtue of chaste virgins who praised God and Christian virtues.

Dulcitius, a jail governor, lusts after the three virgins Agape, Chionia, and Hirena (Love, Purity, and Peace). Hrosvitha emphasizes his power, but all his worldly power comes to nothing in the face of the virgins' beliefs. In this sense, Hrosvitha celebrates how the apparent weakness of females in her own society can confound the apparent strength of males. Despite his position and power, Dulcitius's lust cannot be satisfied.

The three virgins are problematic not only to Dulcitius but to Emperor Diocletian as well. When Agape tells Diocletian that it is dangerous to offend almighty God, Diocletian asks, "Dangerous to whom?" She responds, "To you and to the state you rule." Hrosvitha therefore establishes not only the power of the virgins but also that of the Christian religion. Astonishingly, this "new-fangled religion" threatens Rome itself, which is why Diocletian persecuted Christians so brutally during his reign.

The play's short lines, quick realistic dialogue, and carefully focused interaction are recognizably like Terence's. The present translation uses virgules (/) to indicate the end of lines as they were printed in the original Latin. The broad farcical humor of the "miraculous" scene in which Dulcitius embraces pots and pans in the kitchen, thinking they are the three virgins—a scene performed while the virgins watch through the crack in the door—is also in the tradition of Roman comedy.

Despite the three virgins' ultimate martyrdom, the play is a comedy. The soldiers and Dulcitius will end up in "Tartarus," while the virgins "will enter the heavenly bridal chamber of the Eternal King." For the devout canonness Hrosvitha, no ending could be happier.

For discussion questions and assignments on *Dulcitius*, visit bedfordstmartins.com/jacobus.

Dulcitius in Performance

In the opinion of most scholars, the plays of Hrosvitha were not produced but instead were read as **closet drama**. However, comic scenes such as the one in which Dulcitius blackens his face against the pots and pans have led some theater historians to speculate that the plays were performed by the nuns themselves in the abbey. In any event, *Dulcitius* would not have had a public audience and may not have influenced other medieval drama. It is, however, a remarkable moment in the history of drama. As Hrosvitha tells us, "I, the strong voice of Gandersheim, have not hesitated to imitate in my writings a poet whose works are so widely read, my object being to glorify, within the limits of my poor talent, the laudable chastity of Christian virgins in that self-same form of composition which has been used to describe the shameless acts of licentious women."

Dulcitius has recently sparked the interest of a number of small theaters. Theatre Unbound in Minneapolis, which concentrates on female playwrights, produced the play in 2005 in a grouping called *Girls Got Pluck*. The ADC Theatre of the University of Cambridge, England, produced a version of the play in 2008.

HROSVITHA (c. 935–1000)

Dulcitius c. 965

The Martyrdom of the Holy Virgins Agape, Chionia, and Hirena

TRANSLATED BY K. M. WILSON

[Characters

DIOCLETIAN
AGAPE   WIFE (OF DULCITIUS)
CHIONIA   SISSINUS
HIRENA   SOLDIERS
DULCITIUS   GUARDS]

The martyrdom of the holy virgins° Agape, Chionia, and Hirena, whom, in the silence of the night, Governor Dulcitius secretly visited, desiring to delight in their embrace. But as soon as he entered, / he became demented / and kissed and hugged the pots and pans, mistaking them for the girls until his face and his clothes were soiled with disgusting black dirt. Afterward Count Sissinus, acting on orders, / was given the girls so he might put them to tortures. / He, too, was deluded miraculously / but finally ordered that Agape and Chionia be burnt and Hirena be slain by an arrow.

DIOCLETIAN: The renown of your free and noble descent / and the brightness of your beauty demand / that you

The martyrdom of the holy virgins: The martyrdom of the three virgins occurred in 290 during Diocletian's persecution of the Christians in Thessalonica.

be married to one of the foremost men of my court. This will be done according to our command if you deny Christ° and comply by bringing offerings to our gods.°   5
AGAPE: Be free of care, / don't trouble yourself to prepare our wedding / because we cannot be compelled under any duress / to betray Christ's holy name, which we must confess, / nor to stain our virginity.   10
DIOCLETIAN: What madness possesses you? What rage drives you three? /
AGAPE: What signs of our madness do you see? /
DIOCLETIAN: An obvious and great display. /
AGAPE: In what way? /   15
DIOCLETIAN: Chiefly in that renouncing the practices of ancient religion / you follow the useless, new-fangled ways of the Christian superstition. /
AGAPE: Heedlessly you offend the majesty of the omnipotent God. That is dangerous . . .   20
DIOCLETIAN: Dangerous to whom?
AGAPE: To you and to the state you rule. /
DIOCLETIAN: She is mad; remove the fool! /

5. deny Christ: Deny the vow of virginity they made in the name of Christ. **6. our gods:** Gods acknowledged by the Roman empire.

CHIONIA: My sister is not mad; she rightly reprehended
25   your folly. /

DIOCLETIAN: She rages even more madly; remove her
from our sight and arraign the third girl. /

HIRENA: You will find the third, too, a rebel / and resisting
you forever. /

30   DIOCLETIAN: Hirena, although you are younger in birth, /
be greater in worth! /

HIRENA: Show me, I pray, how? /

DIOCLETIAN: Bow your neck to the gods, set an example
for your sisters, and be the cause for their freedom! /

35   HIRENA: Let those worship idols, Sire, / who wish to incur
God's ire. / But I won't defile my head, anointed with
royal unguent by debasing myself at the idols' feet. /

DIOCLETIAN: The worship of gods brings no dishonor /
but great honor. /

40   HIRENA: And what dishonor is more disgraceful, / what
disgrace is any more shameful / than when a slave is
venerated as a master? /

DIOCLETIAN: I don't ask you to worship slaves / but the
mighty gods of princes and greats. /

45   HIRENA: Is he not anyone's slave / who, for a price, is up
for sale? /

DIOCLETIAN: For her speech so brazen, / to the tortures
she must be taken. /

HIRENA: This is just what we hope for, this is what we
50   desire, / that for the love of Christ through tortures
we may expire. /

DIOCLETIAN: Let these insolent girls / who defy our decrees
and words / be put in chains and kept in the squalor
of prison until Governor Dulcitius can examine them. /

55   DULCITIUS: Bring forth, soldiers, the girls whom you
hold sequestered. /

SOLDIERS: Here they are whom you requested. /

DULCITIUS: Wonderful, indeed, how beautiful, how graceful, how admirable these little girls are! /

60   SOLDIERS: Yes, they are perfectly lovely. /

DULCITIUS: I am captivated by their beauty. /

SOLDIERS: That is understandable. /

DULCITIUS: To draw them to my heart, I am eager. /

SOLDIERS: Your success will be meager. /

65   DULCITIUS: Why? /

SOLDIERS: Because they are firm in faith. /

DULCITIUS: What if I sway them by flattery? /

SOLDIERS: They will despise it utterly. /

DULCITIUS: What if with tortures I frighten them? /

70   SOLDIERS: Little will it matter to them. /

DULCITIUS: Then what should be done, I wonder? /

SOLDIERS: Carefully you should ponder. /

DULCITIUS: Place them under guard in the inner room of
the pantry, where they keep the servants' pots. /

75   SOLDIERS: Why in that particular spot? /

DULCITIUS: So that I may visit them often at my leisure. /

SOLDIERS: At your pleasure. /

DULCITIUS: What do the captives do at this time of night? /

SOLDIERS: Hymns they recite. /

80   DULCITIUS: Let us go near. /

SOLDIERS: From afar we hear their tinkling little voices
clear. /

DULCITIUS: Stand guard before the door with your
lantern / but I will enter / and satisfy myself in their
longed-for embrace. /   85

SOLDIERS: Enter. We will guard this place. /

AGAPE: What is that noise outside the door? /

HIRENA: That wretched Dulcitius coming to the fore. /

CHIONIA: May God protect us! /

AGAPE: Amen. /   90

CHIONIA: What is the meaning of this clash of the pots
and the pans? /

HIRENA: I will check. / Come here, please, and look
through the crack! /

AGAPE: What is going on? /   95

HIRENA: Look, the fool, the madman base, / he thinks he
is enjoying our embrace. /

AGAPE: What is he doing? /

HIRENA: Into his lap he pulls the utensils, / he embraces
the pots and the pans, giving them tender kisses. /   100

CHIONIA: Ridiculous! /

HIRENA: His face, his hands, his clothes, are so soiled, so
filthy, that with all the soot that clings to him, he
looks like an Ethiopian. /

AGAPE: It is only right that he should appear in body the   105
way he is in his mind: possessed by the Devil. /

HIRENA: Wait! He prepares to leave. Let us watch how
he is greeted, / and how he is treated / by the soldiers
who wait for him. /

SOLDIERS: Who is coming out? / A demon without doubt. /   110
Or rather, the Devil himself is he; / let us flee! /

DULCITIUS: Soldiers, where are you taking yourselves in
flight? / Stay! Wait! Escort me home with your light! /

SOLDIERS: The voice is our master's tone / but the look
the Devil's own. / Let us not stay! / Let us run away;   115
the apparition will slay us! /

DULCITIUS: I will go to the palace and complain, / and
reveal to the whole court the insults I had to sustain. /

DULCITIUS: Guards, let me into the palace; / I must have
a private audience. /   120

GUARDS: Who is this vile and detestable monster covered in torn and despicable rags? Let us beat him, /
from the steps let us sweep him; / he must not be
allowed to enter. /

DULCITIUS: Alas, alas, what has happened? Am I not   125
dressed in splendid garments? Don't I look neat and
clean? / Yet anyone who looks at my mien / loathes
me as a foul monster. To my wife I shall return, / and
from her learn / what has happened. But there is my
spouse, / with disheveled hair she leaves the house, /   130
and the whole household follows her in tears. /

WIFE: Alas, alas, my Lord Dulcitius, what has happened
to you? / You are not sane; the Christians have made
a laughing stock out of you. /

DULCITIUS: Now I know at last. I owe this mockery to   135
their witchcraft. /

WIFE: What upsets me so, what makes me more sad is that you were ignorant of all that happened to you.

140 DULCITIUS: I command that those insolent girls be led forth, / and that they be publicly stripped of all their clothes, / so that they experience similar mockery in retaliation for ours.

SOLDIERS: We labor in vain; / we sweat without gain. /
145 Behold, their garments stick to their virginal bodies like skin, / and he who urged us to strip them snores in his seat, / and he cannot be awakened from his sleep. / Let us go to the Emperor and report what has happened.

DIOCLETIAN: It grieves me very much / to hear that Gover-
150 nor Dulcitius has been so greatly deluded, / so greatly insulted, / so utterly humiliated. / But these vile young women shall not boast with impunity of having made a mockery of our gods and those who worship them. I shall direct Count Sissinus to take due vengeance.

155 SISSINUS: Soldiers, where are those insolent girls who are to be tortured?

SOLDIERS: They are kept in prison.

SISSINUS: Leave Hirena there, / bring the others here. /

SOLDIERS: Why do you except the one?

160 SISSINUS: Sparing her youth. Perchance, she may be converted easier, if she is not intimidated by her sisters' presence. /

SOLDIERS: That makes sense. /

SOLDIERS: Here are the girls whose presence you
165 requested.

SISSINUS: Agape and Chionia, give heed, / and to my council accede! /

AGAPE: We will not give heed. /

SISSINUS: Bring offerings to the gods.

170 AGAPE: We bring offerings of praise forever / to the true Father eternal, / and to His Son co-eternal, / and also to the Holy Spirit.

SISSINUS: This is not what I bid, / but on pain of penalty prohibit. /

175 AGAPE: You cannot prohibit it; neither shall we ever sacrifice to demons.

SISSINUS: Cease this hardness of heart, and make your offerings. But if you persist, / then I shall insist / that you be killed according to the Emperor's orders.

180 CHIONIA: It is only proper that you should obey the orders of your Emperor, whose decrees we disdain, as you know. For if you wait and try to spare us, then you could be rightfully killed.

SISSINUS: Soldiers, do not delay, / take these blaspheming
185 girls away, / and throw them alive into the flames.

SOLDIERS: We shall instantly build the pyre you asked for, and we will cast these girls into the raging fire, and thus we'll put an end to these insults at last. /

AGAPE: O Lord, nothing is impossible for Thee; / even
190 the fire forgets its nature and obeys Thee; / but we are weary of delay; / therefore, dissolve the earthly bonds that hold our souls, we pray, / so that as our earthly bodies die, / our souls may sing your praise in Heaven.

SOLDIERS: Oh, marvel, oh stupendous miracle! Behold
195 their souls are no longer bound to their bodies, / yet no traces of injury can be found; / neither their hair, nor their clothes are burnt by the fire, / and their bodies are not at all harmed by the pyre. /

SISSINUS: Bring forth Hirena.

SOLDIERS: Here she is.   200

SISSINUS: Hirena, tremble at the deaths of your sisters and fear to perish according to their example.

HIRENA: I hope to follow their example and expire, / so with them in Heaven eternal joy I may acquire. /

SISSINUS: Give in, give in to my persuasion. /   205

HIRENA: I will never yield to evil persuasion. /

SISSINUS: If you don't yield, I shall not give you a quick and easy death, but multiply your sufferings.

HIRENA: The more cruelly I'll be tortured, / the more glo-
riously I'll be exalted. /   210

SISSINUS: You fear no tortures, no pain? / What you abhor, I shall ordain. /

HIRENA: Whatever punishment you design, / I will escape with help Divine. /

SISSINUS: To a brothel you will be consigned, / where   215
your body will be shamefully defiled. /

HIRENA: It is better that the body be dirtied with any stain than that the soul be polluted with idolatry.

SISSINUS: If you are so polluted in the company of harlots, you can no longer be counted among the vir-   220
ginal choir.

HIRENA: Lust deserves punishment, but forced compli-
ance the crown. With neither is one considered guilty, / unless the soul consents freely. /

SISSINUS: In vain have I spared her, in vain have I pitied   225
her youth.

SOLDIERS: We knew this before; / for on no possible score / can she be moved to adore our gods, nor can she be broken by terror.

SISSINUS: I shall spare her no longer. /   230

SOLDIERS: Rightly you ponder. /

SISSINUS: Seize her without mercy, / drag her with cruelty, / and take her in dishonor to the brothel. /

HIRENA: They will not do it. /

SISSINUS: Who can prohibit it? /   235

HIRENA: He whose foresight rules the world. /

SISSINUS: I shall see . . . /

HIRENA: Sooner than you wish, it will be. /

SISSINUS: Soldiers, be not afraid / of what this blasphem-
ing girl has said. /   240

SOLDIERS: We are not afraid, / but eagerly follow what you bade. /

SISSINUS: Who are those approaching? How similar they are to the men / to whom we gave Hirena just then. / They are the same. Why are you returning so   245
fast? / Why so out of breath, I ask? /

SOLDIERS: You are the one for whom we look. /

SISSINUS: Where is she whom you just took? /
SOLDIERS: On the peak of the mountain.
250 SISSINUS: Which one?
SOLDIERS: The one close by.
SISSINUS: Oh you idiots, dull and blind. / You have completely lost your mind! /
SOLDIERS: Why do you accuse us, / why do you abuse us, /
255 why do you threaten us with menacing voice and face?
SISSINUS: May the gods destroy you!
SOLDIERS: What have we committed? What harm have we done? How have we transgressed against your orders?
260 SISSINUS: Have I not given the orders that you should take that rebel against the gods to a brothel?
SOLDIERS: Yes, so you did command, / and we were eager to fulfill your demand, / but two strangers intercepted us / saying that you sent them to us / to lead
265 Hirena to the mountain's peak.
SISSINUS: That's new to me. /
SOLDIERS: We can see. /
SISSINUS: What were they like? /
SOLDIERS: Splendidly dressed and an awe-inspiring sight. /
270 SISSINUS: Did you follow? /
SOLDIERS: We did so. /
SISSINUS: What did they do? /
SOLDIERS: They placed themselves on Hirena's left and right, / and told us to be forthright / and not to hide
275 from you what happened.
SISSINUS: I see a sole recourse, / that I should mount my horse / and seek out those who so freely made sport with us.

SISSINUS: Hmm, I don't know what to do. I am bewildered by the witchcraft of these Christians. I keep going 280 around the mountain and keep finding this track / but I neither know how to proceed nor how to find my way back. /
SOLDIERS: We are all deluded by some intrigue; / we are afflicted with a great fatigue; / if you allow this insane person to stay alive, / then neither you nor we 285 shall survive. /
SISSINUS: Anyone among you, / I don't care which, string a bow, and shoot an arrow, and kill that witch! /
SOLDIERS: Rightly so. / 290
HIRENA: Wretched Sissinus, blush for shame, and proclaim your miserable defeat because without the help of weapons, you cannot overcome a tender little virgin as your foe. /
SISSINUS: Whatever the shame that may be mine, I will 295 bear it more easily now because I know for certain that you will die.
HIRENA: This is the greatest joy I can conceive, / but for you this is a cause to grieve, / because you shall be damned in Tartarus° for your cruelty, / while I shall 300 receive the martyr's palm and the crown of virginity; / thus I will enter the heavenly bridal chamber of the Eternal King, to whom are all honor and glory in all eternity. /

300. **Tartarus:** Hell.

COMMENTARY

SUE-ELLEN CASE (b. 1942)

Re-viewing Hrotsvit   1983

Sue-Ellen Case not only examines the plays of Hrosvitha but has actually produced them. She discusses the feminist issues in the plays and demonstrates the significance of the plays of Hrosvitha for a modern audience.

Hrotsvit's plays were not collected for circulation until the sixteenth century. They were not translated into modern Romance languages until the mid-nineteenth century and not into English until the twentieth century. The relative unavailability of her texts made production before the twentieth century improbable. Yet in the twentieth century, it is important to note that productions of her plays were often by women or in times in which women's issues were important to the theater world. A good example of the latter condition is the production history of Hrotsvit's work in London. The first major production of *Paphnutius* was directed by Edith Craig (daughter of Ellen Terry and sister of Gordon) in London in 1914. The production was by the Pioneer Players, a group founded and directed by Edith Craig, with Ellen Terry playing the role of the abbess in the convent in which Thais was confined. The translation was done by Christopher St. John, a *nom de plume* (indicative practice) for Christabel Marshall. Marshall had recently adapted the suffragette play *How the Vote Was Won* in 1909 and the play *The First Actress* in 1911—an indication that her interest in the text of Hrotsvit probably came from an interest in a woman playwright. Indeed, there was a movement in London theater at that time to be concerned with women's issues—particularly the vote. In 1908, actresses had formed a franchise league to support the suffrage movement, which produced plays about the vote and satires of male chauvinism.[1] The English women did not get the vote until 1928, and the decade of the 1920s was filled with the issue. Within this context, the 1920 production of *Callimachus* at the Art Theatre, the 1924 production of *Paphnutius* at the Maddermarket Theatre, the founding of the Roswitha club in 1926, the new translations by St. John, Waley and Tillyard during the decade, and the cessation of Hrotsvit productions after that decade can be easily understood.

My production of her works in 1982 came as a result of teaching a class on women and theater and becoming familiar with all of the new productions and critical studies evolving from the works of women playwrights and women's theater groups. The first problem in producing Hrotsvit is the obscurity of her name and play titles. The second is the short playing time of her texts. I decided to solve both problems by directing three plays in one evening and creating a title which might attract the Seattle women's community by identifying the plays according to the social roles of their three heroines: "The Virgin (*Dulcitius*), The Whore (*Paphnutius*), and The Desperate One" (*Callimachus*). My choice of production concept was determined by my goal of producing the first woman playwright. In order to emphasize her historical role, I decided to direct the play as a period piece. This introduces another set of difficulties, since the theater has no tradition of staging plays from the early Middle Ages and hence no concept of costumes, sets, or playing style. We took the costumes from mosaics and illuminations around the period and decided on flats, imitating the two-dimensional painting style of the time, with edifices found in Ottonian manuscript illuminations. The playing style was a combination of a classical sense of formal blocking and gestures, combined with intense, personal purpose. A projection screen rose from the back of a steeply raked stage and a processional ramp ran from the front of the stage through the center of the audience. This combination created the feeling of the space in a cathedral. The elevated ramp gave the Saints elevation and dominance. Between the plays, early medieval music was performed. All this allowed a style to emerge which was . . . an imitation of [both] classical formality and liturgical ceremony.

The context of Christianity and its trappings often created an audience response which was marked in its silent reverence. People seemed afraid to wiggle or whisper. At other times, this same sense turned into an active irreverence, manifested by laughter and something close to jeering. Contemporary staging of a Christian play is complicated to understand. Shakespeare productions have prepared an audience for the Elizabethan world of superstition, and Greek plays have prepared them for the world of pagan mythology, but the relative absence of medieval productions leaves the

[1]Michelene Wandor, *Understudies: Theatre and Sexual Politics* (London: Eyre Methuen, 1981), p. 10.

world of medieval Christianity to be understood by personal opinions about Christianity rather than the sense of it as a historical world view. Thus, for some feminists, the Christianity was seen as offensive and patriarchal. Particularly in these times of the Moral Majority, Hrotsvit's plays seemed to them to be written by an "Uncle Tom" trapped by male values. Many audience members laughed hysterically at the miracles, the voice of God, and the resurrections—seeing them not as stage conventions but as bygone beliefs. Christopher St. John records a similar reaction to the plays in their early London productions, citing a scene in *Callimachus* "Drusiana's prayer that she might die rather than yield to Callimachus was greeted with shouts of laughter." I think the only solution to this problem lies not in the staging concept of such scenes, but in establishing a familiarity with the playwright and her conventions through productions and an acquaintance with her texts in theater history and criticism classes.

For the actors, this problem translates into ways for them to individually understand the dilemma of their characters. The women identified instances of martyrdom and conviction which meant something to them. These ranged from pictures of concentration camp women, which some of the Jewish women brought to rehearsal, to stories of guerrillas in El Salvador or instances of rape victims who resisted. They did not focus so much on religious experiences as on sexual ones, political ones, or psychological approaches to their own fears and strengths. The men in the cast resisted identifying with the male aggression and cruelty portrayed by many of the characters. When asked to torment one of the young virgins in a flirtatious manner, they insisted they didn't know how. This identification came slowly, through memories of teasing girls in grade school, to early experiences of seduction and sexual aggression. For the men playing Saints, the problem was in giving focus to the women onstage and learning how to respond to the power of the women in a realistic fashion. This involved investigating their own fears of women's power.

For the actors, one of the most difficult aspects of Hrotsvit's work was her contiguous sense of form and her compressed, almost fragmentary sense of a scene. Characters have extremely short speeches of only one or two sentences, compressed into scenes of relatively scant dialogue and often no physical action. Fortunately, recent productions of plays by such authors as Beckett and Kroetz provided the actors with some experience in this style. The method which seemed most useful was to play the entire scene by improvising a long, literal development of its situation and then compress it moment by moment until it played in Hrotsvit's form. One fortunate consequence of this playing style is that the concentration and deliberation required by the actor made him or her oblivious to the sometimes raucous audience response.

Finally, the response of the critics illustrated an interesting aspect of viewing the plays. Almost all announcements and reviews of the plays included the words "rape" and "necrophilia" in their titles. One critic pointed out that these plays should make contemporary audiences feel less defensive about violence on TV, since it was already popular in the early Middle Ages. The titles are surprising, since neither the rapes nor the necrophilia ever occur. They are the intentions of the male characters but are foiled by heavenly intervention. The preoccupation by critics with these intentions might suggest that they were watching the male characters more than the females, even though it was not the focus of the text nor of the blocking. In fact, given the staging of resurrections and other such miracles, these dramatic intentions seemed minor parts of the staging. Yet they were the focus of critical reviews. This critical reception points out the necessity for a re-viewing of Hrotsvit from a feminist point of view and underlines the sense that her position and its implications in the world of theater [are] still long overdue.

The Second Shepherds' Pageant

The author of *The Second Shepherds' Pageant* (c. 1385–1450) has not been identified, but his style is distinct enough to permit scholars to refer to him simply as the Wakefield Master. His work is so clearly superior to that of the other writers of mystery pageants that some critics have dubbed him a medieval literary genius. Because he used a distinctive poetic meter and rhyming style, we know that he wrote several other plays in the Wakefield Cycle, including *Noah and the Ark, The First Shepherds' Play, Herod the Great,* and *The Buffeting.* None of the thirty-two plays in the Wakefield Cycle—nor any play in other English cycles—combines the wit, cleverness, farce, and seriousness of *The Second Shepherds' Pageant.*

The Wakefield Cycle is the group of plays performed by the guilds of Wakefield during the Corpus Christi holiday, which falls eight weeks after Easter, in either late May or early June. The performances began at sunrise and continued until late in the evening, usually outdoors in good weather. The plays in all the cycles begin with the creation and continue narrating important biblical moments, such as stories of Abraham, Herod, Julius Caesar, the shepherds at the nativity, the scourging of Christ, and even the hanging of Judas. Sometimes called the Towneley Cycle because the Towneley family owned the fifteenth-century manuscripts, the Wakefield Cycle represented a highly developed tradition that was of considerable economic significance to Wakefield. Large numbers of people came from surrounding towns to see the pageants and therefore represented important tourist traffic for local inns and businesses. The towns of York, Chester, and Coventry enjoyed the same benefits.

One of the important functions of the mystery plays was their presentation of significant and familiar biblical stories. Much of the medieval audience was illiterate or had limited access to books. Consequently, people learned or reviewed some basic Bible stories by watching these plays. The entertainment value of the plays was considered secondary, although it is plain from *The Second Shepherds' Pageant* that, by the late fifteenth century, audiences were familiar enough with the material that adding a bit of farce tended to energize the drama. It is clear that the Wakefield Master, who seems to have been a minor cleric, fully understood his rural and urban audiences' need for amusement as well as instruction.

In the Wakefield Cycle the same author wrote two Shepherd plays. As far as we can tell, the play presented here was the second of the two. They were the twelfth and thirteenth plays in the cycle of thirty-two. Some scholars have suggested that the first play is a first draft or early version and that *The Second Shepherds' Pageant* is an improved or more fully developed play. The evidence does not support such a view, however, because Mak and Gib, the two shepherds who are at the center of the comic action, are missing from the first play. In addition, some references in the second play to characters in the first play would be meaningless to an audience who had not seen the first play.

It is likely that the Wakefield Cycle was a processional cycle, in which the pageant carts carrying the guilds moved from location to location, each guild

For discussion questions and assignments on *The Second Shepherds' Pageant*, visit **bedfordstmartins.com/jacobus**.

performing the same play in each locale. Audience members in each location, if they stayed through the day, would have seen all the plays in succession. On the other hand, some evidence suggests that it may have been a stationary cycle, in which the plays were performed in succession, in a single courtyard or open space, to one audience.

If the cycle was processional, we have no idea which guild sponsored *The Second Shepherds' Pageant;* nothing has come down to us to indicate a choice. However, we do know that the town of York began heavily taxing the wool industries in the early fifteenth century, and consequently those industries moved to towns like Wakefield. It may well be that the development of those industries accounts for the plural number of shepherd plays.

The Second Shepherds' Pageant joins together two well-known stories. The more important is the story in Luke 2.15–20 of the birth of Jesus as witnessed by shepherds. The second narrative was also familiar from folklore: Mak's story of a shepherd who steals a lamb and tries to pass it off as his baby. The conjunction of these two stories offered the Wakefield Master a great deal of imaginative reinforcement for each narrative line. The metaphor of Jesus as a lamb dated from Roman times and arose in part because Jesus was offered as a sacrifice for the human race. Representing the lamb as an infant—and connecting that infant to the Christ child—thus helps intensify the concept of Christ's sacrifice. When the shepherds discover Mak's ruse—a process that not only takes some time but also involves a great deal of humor—they toss Mak in a blanket in what is essentially an act of good humor. In other words, they offer Mak the same kind of charity that Christians associate with the Christ child, and in return, they are invited to be in the presence of the Christ child.

The Second Shepherds' Pageant in Performance

In medieval times, the play was performed by amateurs, ostensibly members of the guild that produced the play. It would probably have been staged on a pageant wagon of the kind shown in Figure 7 (p. 201). Assuming that the Wakefield Cycle was extant in the early 1400s, it is remarkable to consider that one of the last known early performances of the play was in Tudor times in 1533. This means that the social issues described in the play, the hardships experienced by ordinary folk, and the complaints about taxation and rising prices were all relevant to a later generation.

Today, *The Second Shepherds' Pageant* is a favorite Christmas production at a number of universities. Mystery plays in general have grown in popularity. The Broomhill Opera of South Africa staged an abbreviated version of the traditional cycle in 2001 and 2002. Merging African drumming and choral music with the traditional plays resulted in an intense and highly successful production. The York Cycle was staged in the streets of York, England, in 1975, and a selection of nine of the plays was staged again in 1994. The Chester Cycle is staged in Chester every five years, with the most recent performance in 2008 and the next scheduled for 2013. Toronto produced the York Cycle in 1998; the Players of St. Peter put on selections from the mystery plays each December in St. Clement, Eastcheap, London.

Mystery plays such as *The Second Shepherds' Pageant* are still emotionally resonant for a large number of people, and today's performances attract sizable audiences.

THE WAKEFIELD MASTER

The Second Shepherds' Pageant   (c. 1385–1450)

EDITED BY A. C. CAWLEY

Characters

COLL, *the First Shepherd*
GIB, *the Second Shepherd*
DAW, *the Third Shepherd*
MAK, *the Sheep-stealer*
GILL, *Mak's Wife*
ANGEL
MARY, *with the Christ-child*

SCENE I

The open fields

1 SHEPHERD: Lord, what these weathers are cold! And
   I am ill happed.°
I am near-hand dold,° so long have I napped;
My legs they fold,° my fingers are chapped.
It is not as I would, for I am lapped°
5   In sorrow.
In storms and tempest,
Now in the east, now in the west,
Woe is him has never rest
Mid-day nor morrow!

10   But we sely husbands° that walk on the moor,
In faith, we are near-hands out of the door.°
No wonder, as it stands, if we be poor,
For the tilth° of our lands lies fallow as the
   floor,
As ye ken.
15   We are so hammed,°
Fortaxed and rammed,°
We are made hand-tamed
With these gentlery-men.°
Thus they reave us our rest, our Lady them
   wary!°

These men that are lord-fast,° they cause the plough
   tarry.   20
That, men say, is for the best; we find it contrary.
Thus are husbands oppressed, in point to miscarry
On live.°
Thus hold they us under,
Thus they bring us in blunder;°   25
It were great wonder
And ever° should we thrive.

For may he get a paint sleeve or a brooch,
   nowadays,°
Woe is him that him grieve, or once again-says!°
Dare no man him repreve, what mastery he
   mays;°   30
And yet may no man lieve° one word that he
   says—
No letter.
He can make purveyance°
With boast and bragance,°
And all is through maintenance°   35
Of men that are greater.

There shall come a swain as proud as a po;°
He must borrow my wain, my plough also;
Then I am full fain to grant ere he go.
Thus live we in pain, anger, and woe   40
By night and day.
He must have, if he langed,
If I should forgang it;°
I were better be hanged
Than once say him nay.   45

It does me good, as I walk thus by mine own,°
Of this world for to talk in manner of moan.°
To my sheep will I stalk and harken anon,
There abide on a balk,° or sit on a stone

1. **Lord ... ill happed:** How cold this weather is! And I am poorly clad. **2. near-hand dold:** Nearly numb. **3. fold:** Give way. **4. lapped:** Wrapped. **10. But we sely husbands:** But we poor husbandmen. **11. We are ... the door:** We are nearly homeless. **13. tilth:** Arable part. **15. hammed:** Crippled. **16. Fortaxed and rammed:** Overtaxed and crushed. **17–18. We are ... gentlery-men:** We are reduced to submission by these gentry. **19. Thus ... wary:** They rob us of our rest, our Lady curse them!

20. **lord-fast:** Bound to a lord. **22–23. in ... live:** In danger of coming to mortal harm. **25. Blunder:** Trouble. **27. ever:** If. **28. For ... nowadays:** If he is able to get an embroidered sleeve (i.e., a lord's livery). **29. again-says:** Gainsays. **30. Dare ... mays:** No man dare reprove him, no matter what force he uses. **31. lieve:** Believe. **33. He ... purveyance:** He can requisition (our belongings). **34. bragance:** Bragging. **35. maintenance:** Support. **37. po:** Peacock. **42–43. He must ... forgang it:** He must have what he wants, even if I have to go without it. **46. mine own:** Myself. **47. manner of moan:** Grumble. **49. balk:** A strip of rough grassland dividing two ploughed portions of a common field.

217

Mak becomes Joseph (Malcolm Storry) and Gill becomes Mary (Avril Carson), while the First Shepherd (Philip McGough) kneels before the manger in the 1978 Royal Shakespeare Company production, adapted by John Barton, titled *The Shepherds' Play,* and directed by David Tucker.

Philip McGough as the First Shepherd, Malcolm Storry as Mak, and Hilton McRae and David Bradley as the other two shepherds in the 1978 Royal Shakespeare Company production.

50   Full soon;
      For I trow, pardie,°
      True men if they be,
      We get more company
      Ere it be noon.

[*Enter Second Shepherd*]

55   2 SHEP.: Benste° and Dominus, what may this bemean?°
      Why fares this world thus? Oft have we not seen.°
      Lord, these weathers are spitous, and the winds
         full keen,°
      And the frosts so hideous they water mine een°—
      No lie.
60   Now in dry, now in wet,
      Now in snow, now in sleet,
      When my shoon freeze to my feet
      It is not all easy.

      But as far as I ken, or yet as I go,
65   We sely wedmen dree mickle woe:
      We have sorrow then and then; it falls oft so.°
      Silly Copple, our hen, both to and fro
      She cackles;
      But begin she to croak,
70   To groan or to cluck,
      Woe is him our cock,°
      For he is in the shackles.

      These men that are wed have not all their will;
      When they are full hard sted, they sigh full still.°
75   God wot they are led full hard and full ill;
      In bower nor in bed they say nought theretill.
      This tide
      My part have I fun,°
      I know my lesson:
80   Woe is him that is bun,°
      For he must abide.°

      But now late in our lives—a marvel to me,
      That I think my heart rives° such wonders to see;
      What that destiny drives it should so be°—
85   Some men will have two wives, and some men three
      In store;
      Some are woe° that have any.
      But so far can° I:
      Woe is him that has many,
90   For he feels sore.°

But, young men, of wooing, for God that you
   bought,°
Be well ware° of wedding, and think in your thought:
'Had I wist' is a thing that serveth of nought.°
Mickle still° mourning has wedding home brought,
And griefs,   95
With many a sharp° shower;
For thou mayst catch in an hour
That shall sow thee full sour°
As long as thou lives.

For, as ever read I epistle, I have one to my fere°   100
As sharp as thistle, as rough as a briar.
She is browed like a bristle, with a sour-loten cheer;°
Had she once wet her whistle, she could sing full clear
Her paternoster.
She is as great as a whale,   105
She has a gallon of gall;
By him that died for us all,
I would I had run to° I had lost her!
1 SHEP.: God look over the raw! Full deafly ye stand.°
2 SHEP.: Yea, the devil in thy maw, so tariand!   110
   Saw'st thou awre of Daw?
1 SHEP.:   Yea, on a lea-land
   Heard I him blow.° He comes here at hand,
   Not far.
   Stand still.
2 SHEP.:   Why?
1 SHEP.: For he comes, hope° I.   115
2 SHEP.: He will make° us both a lie,
   But if° we beware.

[*Enter Third Shepherd*]

3 SHEP.: Christ's cross me speed, and Saint Nicholas!
   Thereof had I need; it° is worse than it was.
   Whoso could take heed and let the world pass,   120
   It is ever in dread and brickle as glass,
   And slithes.
   This world fared never so,°
   With marvels mo° and mo—

51. **pardie:** By God.   55. **Benste:** Benedicite (bless us).   **bemean:** Mean.   56. **Oft have we not seen:** We have not often seen the like.   57. **keen:** Cruel.   58. **een:** Eyes.   64–66. **But . . . oft so:** But as far as I know or as my experience goes, we poor married men suffer much woe: we have sorrow time and again.   71. **Woe is him our cock:** Unhappy is our cock.   74. **When . . . full still:** When they are hard put to it, they sigh unceasingly.   76–78. **In bower . . . I fun:** They never answer back. Now I've found out what I have to do.   80. **bun:** Bound (in marriage).   81. **abide:** Remain so.   83. **rives:** Breaks.   84. **What that . . . so be:** Whatever destiny compels must come to pass.   87. **woe:** Miserable.   88. **can:** Know.   90. **sore:** Pain.

91. **But . . . bought:** But young men, as for wooing, by God who redeemed you.   92. **Well ware:** Very wary.   93. **'Had I wist' . . . nought:** 'If only I had known' is something that doesn't help you.   94. **Mickle still:** Constant.   96. **sharp:** Pang.   98. **That shall . . . full sour:** What shall grieve you most bitterly.   100. **I have one to my fere:** I have one for my mate.   102. **She is . . . sour-loten cheer:** She has bristly brows and a sour-looking face.   108. **to:** Till.   109. **God . . . ye stand:** God save the audience! You stand there as deaf as a post. (The First Shepherd has evidently been trying to attract the other's attention.)   110–112. **Yea, the devil . . . him blow:** The devil in your belly for tarrying so long! Have you Seen Daw anywhere? . . . Yea, in a fallow field I heard him blow (his horn).   115. **hope:** Think.   116. **make:** Tell.   117. **But if:** Unless.   119. **it:** Here, the world.   120–123. **Whoso could . . . never so:** Anyone who could look on and let the world go by (would see that) it is always fearful and as brittle as glass, and slides away (i.e., is transitory). But the world never behaved in this way before.   124. **mo:** More.

125   Now in weal, now in woe,
       And all thing writhes.°

       Was never since Noah's flood such floods seen,
       Winds and rains so rude, and storms so keen:
       Some stammered, some stood in doubt, as I ween.°
130   Now God turn all to good! I say as I mean,
       For ponder:°
       These floods so they drown,
       Both in fields and in town,
       And bear all down;
135   And that is a wonder.

       We that walk on the nights our cattle to keep,
       We see sudden sights when other men sleep.
       Yet methink my heart lights;° I see shrews° peep.
       Ye are two all-wights°—I will give my sheep
140   A turn.
       But full ill have I meant;
       As I walk on this bent,
       I may lightly repent,
       My toes if I spurn.°

145   Ah, sir, God you save, and master mine!
       A drink fain would I have, and somewhat to dine.
1 SHEP.: Christ's curse, my knave, thou art a lither
       hine!°
2 SHEP.: What, the boy list rave! Abide unto syne;
       We have made it.°
150   Ill thrift° on thy pate!
       Though the shrew came late,
       Yet is he in state°
       To dine—if he had it.

3 SHEP.: Such servants as I, that sweat and swinks,°
155   Eat our bread full dry, and that me forthinks.°
       We are oft wet and weary when master-men winks;°
       Yet come full lately° both dinners and drinks.
       But nately°
       Both our dame and our sire,
160   When we have run in the mire,
       They can nip at our hire,°
       And pay us full lately.
       But hear my truth, master: for the fare that ye make,
       I shall do thereafter—work as I take.
165   I shall do a little, sir, and among ever lake,°

       For yet lay my supper never on my stomach
       In fields.
       Whereto should I threap?°
       With my staff can I leap;
       And men say 'Light cheap   170
       Litherly foryields.'

1 SHEP.: Thou wert an ill lad to ride on wooing
       With a man that had but little of spending.°
2 SHEP.: Peace, boy, I bade. No more jangling,
       Or I shall make thee full rad, by the heaven's king! 175
       With thy gauds—
       Where are our sheep, boy?—we scorn.°
3 SHEP.: Sir, this same day at morn
       I them left in the corn,
       When they rang Lauds.°   180

       They have pasture good, they cannot go wrong.
1 SHEP.: That is right. By the rood,° these nights are
       long!
       Yet I would, ere we yode,° one gave us a song.
2 SHEP.: So I thought as I stood, to mirth us among.°
3 SHEP.: I grant.   185
1 SHEP.: Let me sing the tenory.°
2 SHEP.: And I the treble so high.
3 SHEP.: Then the mean falls to me.
       Let see how ye chant.   [*They sing.*

Then Mak enters with a cloak covering his tunic.

MAK: Now, Lord, for thy names seven, that made both
       moon and starns
       Well more than I can neven, thy will, Lord, of me 190
       tharns.
       I am all uneven; that moves oft my harns.°
       Now would God I were in heaven, for there weep
       no bairns
       So still.°
1 SHEP.: Who is that pipes so poor?°   195
MAK: Would God ye wist° how I foor!°
       Lo, a man that walks on the moor,
       And has not all his will.

2 SHEP.: Mak, where hast thou gone? Tell us tiding.°
3 SHEP.: Is he come? Then ilkone° take heed to
       his thing.   200

---

126. writhes: Changes. **129. ween:** Fear. **131. ponder:** Consider. **138. lights:** Grows light. **shrews:** Rogues. **139. all-wights:** Monsters. **139–144. I will give...I spurn:** I will turn my sheep away. But I have been ill disposed (to the shepherds); as I walk on this field, I may stub my toes in easy penance. **147. lither hine:** Lazy hind. **148–149. What, the boy...made it:** What, the boy is pleased to rave! Wait till later; we have finished it (i.e., our meal). **150. thrift:** Luck. **152. in state:** Ready. **154. swinks:** Toil. **155. forthinks:** Displeases. **156. winks:** Sleep. **157. lately:** Tardily. **158. nately:** Thoroughly. **161. They can nip at our hire:** They can stint our wages. **163–165. But hear...ever lake:** But hear my promise, master: in return for the food you provide, I shall do accordingly—work as I'm paid. I shall do but little, sir, and betweenwhiles play all the time.

168. threap: Haggle. **170–173. And men...spending:** 'A cheap bargain repays badly.' ... You'd be the wrong lad for anyone that's hard up to take a-wooing with him (cf. *Othello,* III, iii, 71). **174–177. Peace, boy,...we scorn:** Stop your wrangling, or I'll quickly make you, by the king of heaven! We scorn your pranks—where are our sheep, boy? **180. Lauds:** The first of the seven canonical offices, usually sung at daybreak. **182. rood:** Cross. **183. yode:** Went. **184. to mirth us among:** To gladden us meanwhile. **186. tenory:** Tenor. **190–192. Now, Lord,...my harns:** Now, Lord, by thy seven names, who made both moon and stars far more than I can name, thy will concerning me, Lord, is lacking. I am all at sixes and sevens; that often unsettles my brain. **194. still:** Incessantly. **195. Who is that pipes so poor:** Who is it that cries so piteously? **196. wist:** Knew. **foor:** Fared. **199. tiding:** News. **200. ilkone:** Everyone.

He takes Mak's cloak from him.

MAK: What! I be a yeoman, I tell you, of the king.
   The self and the same, sond° from a great lording,
   And sich.°
   Fie on you! Go hence
205   Out of my presence!
   I must have reverence.
   Why, who be ich?

1 SHEP.: Why make ye it so quaint?° Mak, ye do wrong.
2 SHEP.: But, Mak, list ye saint? I trow that ye long.°
3 SHEP.: I trow° the shrew can paint, the devil might him
210   hang!
MAK: I shall make complaint, and make you all to thwang°
   At a word,
   And tell even how ye doth.°
1 SHEP.: But, Mak, is that sooth?
215   Now take out that Southern tooth,°
   And set° in a turd!

2 SHEP.: Mak, the devil in your eye! A stroke would I
      lene° you.
3 SHEP.: Mak, know ye not me? By God, I could teen°
      you.
MAK: God look° you all three! Methought I had seen you.
   Ye are a fair company.
220 1 SHEP.:   Can ye now mean you?°
2 SHEP.: Shrew, peep!°
   Thus late as thou goes,
   What will men suppose?°
   And thou hast an ill noise°
225   Of° stealing of sheep.
MAK: And I am true as steel, all men wot;
   But a sickness I feel that holds me full hot:°
   My belly fares not well, it is out of estate.°
3 SHEP.: Seldom lies the devil dead by the gate.°
230 MAK: Therefore
   Full sore am I and ill;
   If I stand stone-still,
   I eat not a needle°
   This month and more.

235 1 SHEP.: How fares thy wife? By my hood, how fares she?
MAK: Lies waltering°—by the rood—by the fire, lo!
   And a house full of brood.° She drinks well, too;

Ill speed other good that she will do!°
But she
Eats as fast as she can,   240
And ilk° year that comes to man
She brings forth a lakan°—
And, some years, two

But were I now more gracious,° and richer by far,
I were eaten out of house and of harbour.°   245
Yet is she a foul dowse,° if ye come near;
There is none that trows nor knows a war°
Than ken I.
Now will ye see what I proffer?
To give all in my coffer   250
To-morn at next to offer
Her head-masspenny.°

2 SHEP.: I wot so forwaked° is none in this shire;
I would sleep if I taked less to my hire.°
3 SHEP.: I am cold and naked, and would have a fire.   255
1 SHEP.: I am weary, forraked,° and run in the mire—
Wake thou!
2 SHEP.: Nay, I will lie down by.°
For I must sleep, truly.
3 SHEP.: As good a man's son was I   260
As any of you.

But, Mak, come hither! Between° shalt thou lie
   down.
MAK: Then might I let you bedene of that ye would
      rown,
No dread.°   263–264
From my top to my toe,   [*He recites a night-spell.* 265
Manus tuas commendo,
Pontio Pilato.
Christ's cross me speed!

Now were time for a man that lacks what
   he would
To stalk privily then unto a fold,   270
And nimbly to work then, and be not too bold,
For he might abuy the bargain, if it were told
At the ending.°
Now were time for to reel;°
But he needs good counsel   275
That fain would fare well,

202. **sond:** Messenger. 203. **sich:** Such like. 208. **Why make ye it so quaint:** Why are you so uppish? 209. **But, Mak, . . . ye long:** But, Mak, do you want to play the saint? I believe you do. 210. **trow:** Believe. 211. **and make you all to thwang:** And have you all flogged. 213. **doth:** Do. 215. **Southern tooth:** Southern speech. (Mak has been trying to talk Southern English.) 216. **set:** Put. 217. **lene:** Give. 218. **teen:** Hurt. 219. **look:** Save. 220. **Can ye now mean you?:** Can you remember now? 221. **peep:** Pry about. 223. **suppose:** Suspect. 224. **ill noise:** Reputation. 225. **Of:** For. 227. **full hot:** Severely. 228. **estate:** Condition. 229. **Seldom . . . the gate:** Seldom lies the devil dead by the roadside (i.e., appearances may be deceptive). 232–233. **If . . . a needle:** May I be turned to stone if I have eaten a morsel. 236. **waltering:** Sprawling. 237. **brood:** children.

238. **Ill speed . . . will do:** There is no hope of her doing much else. 241. **ilk:** Every. 242. **lakan:** Baby. 244. **gracious:** Prosperous. 245. **harbour:** Home. 246. **dowse:** Wench. 247. **There is . . . a war:** There is none who believes (he knows) or (really) knows a worse one. 250–252. **To give . . . masspenny:** Tomorrow at the latest to give all in my coffer as an offering for her soul. 253. **forwaked:** Wearied with waking. 254. **if I taked . . . my hire:** Even if I should get less wages. 256. **forraked:** Worn out with walking. 258. **by:** Nearby. 262. **Between:** Between us. 263–264. **Then might . . . dread:** Then I might keep you from whispering what you want, no doubt. 272–273. **For he might . . . ending:** For he might pay dearly for it, if it came to a final reckoning. 274. **reel:** Move quickly.

And has but little spending.°

But about you a circle,° as round as a moon,
To I have done what I will, till that it be noon,
280 That ye lie stone-still to that I have done;
And I shall say theretill of good words a fone:°
'On height,°
Over your heads, my hand I lift.
Out go your eyes! Fordo your sight!'
285 But yet I must make better shift,
And it be right.

Lord, what they sleep hard!—that may ye all hear.°
Was I never a shepherd, but now will I lere.°
If the flock be scared, yet shall I nip near.°
290 How! draw hitherward! Now mends our cheer
From sorrow
A fat sheep, I dare say,
A good fleece, dare I lay.
Eft-quit° when I may,
295 But this will I borrow.

[*He goes home with the sheep.*

SCENE II

Mak's cottage

MAK: How, Gill, art thou in? Get us some light.
WIFE: Who makes such din this time of the night?
I am set for to spin; I hope not I might
Rise a penny to win, I shrew them on height!
300 So fares
A housewife that has been,
To be raised thus between,
Here may no note be seen
For such small chares.°

MAK: Good wife, open the heck!° See'st thou not what
305 I bring?
WIFE: I may thole thee draw the sneck.° Ah, come in, my
sweeting!
MAK: Yea, thou thar not reck of my long standing.°
WIFE: By the naked neck art thou like for to hang.

277. **spending:** Money. 278. **circle:** Magic circle. 281. **And
I . . . a fone:** And I shall also say a few good words. 282.
height: High. 284–287. **Out go . . . ye all hear:** 'Lose your
power of sight.' But yet I must make better efforts, if things
are to come right. Lord, how soundly they sleep! 288. **lere:**
Learn. 289. **yet shall I nip near:** Yet I shall grab (a sheep)
tightly. 290–292. **How! . . . dare say:** Now a fat sheep shall
comfort us. 294. **Eft-quit:** Repay. 298–304. **I am set . . .
chares:** I don't think I can earn a penny by getting up (from
my spinning), curse them! Any woman who has been a housewife knows what it means to be got up from her work continually. I have no work to show because of such small chores.
305. **heck:** Inner door. 306. **I may . . . the sneck:** I will let you
draw the latch. 307. **Yea, thou . . . standing:** You needn't mind
about my standing (outside) so long.

MAK: Do way!°
I am worthy my meat,°   310
For in a strait° can I get
More than they that swink° and sweat
All the long day.

Thus it fell to my lot, Gill; I had such grace.
WIFE: It were a foul blot° to be hanged for the case.   315
MAK: I have scaped, Jelott, oft as hard a glase.°
WIFE: 'But so long goes the pot to the water,' men says,
'At last
Comes it home broken.'
MAK: Well know I the token,°   320
But let it never be spoken!
But come and help fast.
I would he were flain; I list well eat.
This twelvemonth was I not so fain of one sheep-meat.°
WIFE: Come they ere he be slain, and hear the sheep
bleat—   325
MAK: Then might I be ta'en: that were a cold sweat!
Go spar°
The gate-door.°
WIFE: Yes, Mak,
For° and they come at thy back—
MAK: Then might I buy, for all the pack,   330
The devil of the war.°

WIFE: A good bourd° have I spied, since thou canst° none;
Here shall we him hide, till they be gone,
In my cradle. Abide! Let me alone,
And I shall lie beside in childbed and groan.   335
MAK: Thou red,°
And I shall say thou wast light°
Of a knave-child° this night.
WIFE: Now well is me day bright
That ever was I bred!   340
This is a good guise and a far cast;°
Yet a woman's advice helps at the last.
I wot never who spies; again go thou fast.°
MAK: But I come ere they rise, else° blows a cold blast!
I will go sleep.   345
Yet sleep all this meny;°
And I shall go stalk privily,
As it had never been I
That carried their sheep.

309. **Do way!:** Enough! 310. **meat:** Food. 311. **strait:**
Fix. 312. **swink:** Toil. 315. **blot:** Deed. 316. **glase:**
Blow. 320. **token:** Portent. 323–324. **I would . . . sheep-
meat:** I wish he were skinned; I am eager to eat. At no time
this year have I been so glad of a meal of mutton. 327. **spar:**
Fasten. 328. **gate-door:** Outer door. 329. **For:** If. 330–331.
Then might I . . . the war: Then I may get the devil of a bad time
from the whole pack of them. 332. **bourd:** Jest. **canst:** Knowest. 336. **red:** Get ready. 337. **wast light:** Delivered. 338.
knave-child: Boy. 339–341. **Now . . . a far cast:** I'm happy when
I think of the bright day I was born! This is a good method and a
cunning trick. 343. **again go thou fast:** Return again quickly (to
the others). 344. **else:** Unless. 346. **meny:** Company.

SCENE III

The open fields

350 1 SHEP.: *Resurrex a mortruus!* have hold my hand!
    Judas carnas dominus!° I may not well stand:
    My foot sleeps, by Jesus, and I walter fastand.°
    I thought that we laid us full near England.
  2 SHEP.: Ah, yea?°
355   Lord, what I have slept well!°
    As fresh as an eel,
    As light I me feel
    As leaf on a tree.
  3 SHEP.: Benste° be herein! So me quakes,
360   My heart is out of skin, what-so it makes.°
    Who makes all this din? So my brow blakes,°
    To the door will I win.° Hark, fellows, wakes!°
    We were four:
    See ye awre of Mak now?°
365 1 SHEP.: We were up ere thou.
  2 SHEP.: Man, I give God avow
    Yet yede he nawre.°
  3 SHEP.: Methought he was lapped in a wolf-skin.
  1 SHEP.: So are many happed now—namely within.°
  3 SHEP.: When we had long napped, methought with a
370   gin°
    A fat sheep he trapped; but he made no din.
  2 SHEP.: Be still!
    Thy dream makes thee wood;°
    It is but phantom, by the rood.
375 1 SHEP.: Now God turn all to good,
    If it be his will.
  2 SHEP.: Rise, Mak, for shame! Thou liest right
    long.
  MAK: Now Christ's holy name be us among!
    What is this? For Saint Jame,° I may not well
    gang!°
380   I trow I be the same. Ah, my neck has lain wrong
    Enough.°   [*They help him to get up.*
    Mickle thank! Since yester-even,
    Now by Saint Stephen,
    I was flayed with a sweven—
385   My heart out of slough.°

350–351. *Resurrex a mortruus*!...*Judas carnas dominus*!:
Bad Latin for "rise from the dead" and "Judas carnate Lord."
352. and I walter fastand: I'm tottering with hunger.
354. Ah, yea?: Oh, really?   355. Lord, what I have slept well:
How well I have slept!   359. Benste: Blessing.   359–360. So
me...makes: I tremble so much, my heart is in my mouth,
whatever the reason for it.   361. blakes: Darkens.   362. win:
Go.   wakes!: Wake up!   364. See ye awre of Mak now?: Have
you seen Mak anywhere?   366–367. Man,...he nawre: I vow
to God he's gone nowhere yet.   369. So are...within: Many
are covered like that nowadays—especially underneath.   370.
gin: Snare.   373. wood: Mad.   379. For Saint Jame: By Saint
James.   gang: Walk.   380–381. Ah, my neck...enough: My
neck has been lying very crookedly.   384–385. I was flayed...of
slough: I was terrified by a dream—I nearly jumped out of my skin.

I thought Gill began to croak and travail full sad,°
Well-nigh at the first cock, of a young lad
For to mend° our flock. Then be I never glad;
I have tow on my rock more than ever I had.°
Ah, my head!   390
A house full of young tharms,°
The devil knock out their harns!°
Woe is him has many bairns,
And thereto little bread.

I must go home, by your leave, to Gill, as I thought.°   395
I pray you look° my sleeve, that I steal nought;
I am loath you to grieve or from you take aught.
3 SHEP.: Go forth, ill might thou chieve!° Now would
    I we sought,
    This morn,
    That we had all our store.°   400
1 SHEP.: But I will go before.
    Let us meet.
2 SHEP.:   Where?
3 SHEP.: At the crooked thorn.

SCENE IV

Mak's cottage

MAK: Undo this door! Who is here? How long shall I
    stand?
WIFE: Who makes such a bere?° Now walk in the wenyand!°   405
MAK: Ah, Gill, what cheer? It is I, Mak, your husband.
WIFE: Then may we see here the devil in a band,°
    Sir Guile!
    Lo, he comes with a lote,°
    As he were holden° in the throat.   410
    I may not sit at my note°
    A hand-long° while.

MAK: Will ye hear what fare she makes to get her a
    glose?°
    And does naught but lakes,° and claws her toes.
WIFE: Why, who wanders, who wakes? Who comes, who   415
    goes?
    Who brews, who bakes? What makes me thus
    hoarse?
    And then
    It is ruth° to behold—
    Now in hot, now in cold,°

---

386. full sad: Hard.   388. mend: Increase.   389. I have tow...
ever I had: I have more tow on my distaff (i.e., more trouble
in store) than ever I had.   391. tharms: Bellies.   392. harns:
Brains.   395. thought: Intended.   396. look: Examine.   398.
chieve: Prosper.   398–400. Now...our store: Now I want us
this morning to see that we have all our stock.   405. bere: Din.
wenyand: waning moon (i.e., at an unlucky time).   407. band:
Noose.   409. lote: Noise.   410. holden: Held by.   411. note:
Work.   412. hand-long: Brief.   413. Will...glose: Will you
listen to the fuss she makes in the hope of excusing herself?
414. lakes: Play.   418. ruth: A pity.   419. Now in hot, now in
cold: At all times.

420 Full woeful is the household
That wants° a woman.

But what end hast thou made with the herds,° Mak?
MAK: The last word that they said when I turned my back.
They would look that they had their sheep, all the
pack.
I hope° they will not be well paid° when they their
425 sheep lack,
Pardie!
But how-so° the game goes,
To me they will suppose,°
And make a foul noise,
430 And cry out upon me.

But thou must do as thou hight.
WIFE: I accord me theretill;°
I shall swaddle him right in my cradle.
If it were a greater sleight, yet could I help till.°
I will lie down straight.° Come hap° me.
MAK: I will.
435 WIFE: Behind!
Come Coll and his marrow,°
They will nip us full narrow.°
MAK: But I may cry 'Out, harrow!'°
The sheep if they find.

440 WIFE: Harken ay when they call; they will come anon.
Come and make ready all, and sing by thine own;
Sing lullay° thou shall, for I must groan,
And cry out by the wall on Mary and John,
For sore.°
445 Sing lullay on fast,°
When thou hearest at the last;
And but I play a false cast,°
Trust me no more.

SCENE V

The crooked thorn

3 SHEP.: Ah, Coll, good morn! Why sleepest thou not?
1 SHEP.: Alas, that ever was I born! We have a foul
450   blot—
A fat wether have we lorn.°
3 SHEP.:   Marry, God's forbot!°
2 SHEP.: Who should do us that scorn?° That were a foul
spot.°

---

1 SHEP.: Some shrew.
I have sought with my dogs
All Horbury° shrogs,°   455
And, of fifteen hogs,
Found I but one ewe.°
3 SHEP.: Now trow me, if ye will—by Saint Thomas of
Kent,°
Either Mak or Gill was at that assent.°
1 SHEP.: Peace, man, be still! I saw when he went.   460
Thou slander'st him ill; thou ought to repent
Good speed.°
2 SHEP.: Now as ever might I thee,°
If I should even here die,
I would say it were he   465
That did that same deed.

3 SHEP.: Go we thither, I rede,° and run on our
feet.
Shall I never eat bread, the sooth to I wit.°
1 SHEP.: Nor drink in my head, with him till I meet.
2 SHEP.: I will rest in no stead° till that I him greet,   470
My brother.°
One I will hight:°
Till I see him in sight,
Shall I never sleep one night
There° I do another.   475

SCENE VI

Mak's cottage

3 SHEP.: Will ye hear how they hack? Our sire list
croon.°
1 SHEP.: Heard I never none crack° so clear out
of tone.°
Call on him.
2 SHEP.:   Mak, undo your door soon!°
MAK: Who is it that spake, as it were noon,
On loft?°   480
Who is that, I say?
3 SHEP.: Good fellows, were it° day.
MAK: As far as ye may,
Good,° speak soft,

---

421. **wants:** Lacks. 422. **herds:** Shepherds. 425. **hope:**
Think. **paid:** Pleased. 427. **how-so:** However. 428. **To me**
...suppose: They will suspect me. 431. **hight...theretill:**
Promised; I agree to that. 433. **sleight...till:** Trick; I could
still help with it. 434. **straight:** Straightaway. **hap:** Cover.
436. **marrow:** Mate. 437. **full narrow:** Hard. 438. **'Out,**
harrow!': A cry for help. 442. **lullay:** Lullaby. 444. **sore:**
Pain. 445. **fast:** Quickly. 447. **And but...cast:** And if I
don't play a false trick. 451. **lorn:** Lost. **God's forbot:** God
forbid. 452. **do us that scorn:** Insult us. **foul spot:** Disgrace.

455. **Horbury:** Near Wakefield. **shrogs:** Thickets. 456–457.
And of...one ewe: Among fifteen hogs (or young sheep) I
found only one ewe (i.e., the wether was missing). 458. **Saint**
Thomas of Kent: St. Thomas of Canterbury. 459. **Either...**
assent: Either Mak or Gill was a party to it. 462. **Good**
speed: Quickly. 463. **Now...I thee:** As I hope to prosper. 467. **rede:** Advise. 468. **the sooth to I wit:** Till I know
the truth. 470. **stead:** Place. 471. **My brother:** A friendly
form of address. 472. **One I will hight:** One thing I will promise. 475. **There:** Where. 476. **Will ye...list croon:** Do you
hear them trilling? Our gentleman is pleased to croon.
477. **crack:** Bawl. **tone:** Tune. 478. **soon:** Immediately.
479–480. **Who is it...on loft?:** Who is it that spoke aloud,
as though it were noon? 482. **were it:** If only it were.
484. **Good:** Good sirs.

485　Over a sick woman's head, that is at malease;
　　I had liefer be dead ere she had any disease.°
WIFE: Go to another stead! I may not well quease;°
　　Each foot that ye tread goes thorough my nose
　　So high.°
490　1 SHEP.: Tell us, Mak, if ye may,
　　How fare ye, I say?
MAK: But are ye in this town to-day?
　　Now how fare ye?

　　Ye have run in the mire, and are wet yet;
495　I shall make you a fire, if ye will sit.
　　A nurse would I hire. Think ye on yet?
　　Well quit is my hire—my dream, this is it°—
　　A season.
　　I have bairns, if ye knew,
500　Well more than enew;°
　　But we must drink as we brew,
　　And that is but reason.

　　I would ye dined ere ye yode.° Methink that ye sweat.
2 SHEP.: Nay, neither mends our mood drink nor meat.
505　MAK: Why, sir, ails you aught but good?°
3 SHEP.:　　　　　　　　　　　Yea, our sheep that we gete°
　　Are stolen as they yode. Our loss is great.
MAK: Sirs, drink!
　　Had I been there,
　　Some should have bought it full sore.°
510　1 SHEP.: Marry, some men trow that ye were,
　　And that us forthinks.°

2 SHEP.: Mak, some men trows° that it should be ye.
3 SHEP.: Either ye or your spouse, so say we.
MAK: Now if ye have suspouse° to Gill or to me,
515　Come and rip° our house, and then may ye see
　　Who had her.
　　If I any sheep fot,°
　　Either cow or stot°—
　　And Gill, my wife, rose not
520　Here since she laid her—

　　As I am true and leal,° to God here I pray
　　That this be the first meal that I shall eat this day.
1 SHEP.: Mak, as have I sele, advise thee, I say:
　　He learned timely to steal that could not say nay.°

WIFE: I swelt!°   525
　　Out, thieves, from my wones!°
　　Ye come to rob us for the nonce.°
MAK: Hear ye not how she groans?
　　Your hearts should melt.

WIFE: Out, thieves, from my bairn! Nigh him not there.°   530
MAK: Wist ye how she had farn,° your hearts would be sore.
　　Ye do wrong, I you warn, that thus come before
　　To a woman that has farn;° but I say no more.
WIFE: Ah, my middle!
　　I pray to God so mild,   535
　　If ever I you beguiled,
　　That I eat° this child
　　That lies in this cradle.
MAK: Peace, woman, for God's pain, and cry not so!
　　Thou spillest° thy brain, and makest me full woe.   540
2 SHEP.: I trow our sheep be slain. What find ye two?
3 SHEP.: All work we in vain; as well may we go.
　　But hatters!°
　　I can find no flesh,
　　Hard nor nesh,°   545
　　Salt nor fresh,
　　But two tome platters.°

　　Quick cattle but this, tame nor wild,
　　None, as have I bliss, as loud as he smelled.°
WIFE: No, so God me bless, and give me joy of my child! 550
1 SHEP.: We have marked amiss;° I hold us beguiled.
2 SHEP.: Sir, don.°
　　Sir—our Lady him save!—
　　Is your child a knave?°
MAK: Any lord might him have,   555
　　This child, to his son.

　　When he wakens he kips;° that joy is to see.
3 SHEP.: In good time to his hips, and in sely.°
　　But who were his gossips° so soon ready?
MAK: So fair fall their lips!
1 SHEP. [*Aside*]:　　　　　　Hark now, a lie!   560
MAK: So God them thank,°
　　Parkin, and Gibbon Waller, I say,
　　And gentle John Horne,° in good fay°—

485–486. Over...disease: Because of a sick woman who is in distress; I had rather die than she should suffer any discomfort. 487. quease: Breathe. 488–489. Each...high: Every step you tread goes through my nose so strongly (i.e., goes right through my head). 496–498. A nurse...it: I would like to hire a nurse. Do you still remember (my dream about a new addition to the family)? I've been paid my wages in full for a while—this is my dream come true. 500. enew: Enough. 503. yode: Went. 505. Why sir...good: Why, sir, is anything wrong with you? 506. gete: Tend. 509. full sore: Paid for. 511. forthinks: Displeases. 512. trows: Believe. 514. suspouse: Suspicion. 515. rip: Ransack. 517. fot: Fetched. 518. stot: Heifer. 521. leal: Honest. 523–524. Mak...say nay: Mak, as I hope for happiness, take thought I say: he learned early to steal who could not say no (to another's property).

525. swelt: Feel faint. 526. wones: House. 527. Ye come ...nonce: You come on purpose to rob us. 530. Nigh him not there: Do not go near him there. 531. Wist ye...farn: If you knew what she had been through. 533. To...farn: To a woman who has been in labor. 537. eat: May eat. 540. spillest: Injure. 543. hatters!: Confound it! 545. nesh: Soft. 547. But two tome platters: Only two empty platters. 548–549. Quick cattle...smelled: Live stock but this (i.e., the "baby" in the cradle), tame or wild, none (have I found), as I hope to be happy, that smelled as loud as he (i.e., the missing sheep). 551. marked amiss: Aimed wrongly (i.e., made a mistake). 552. don: Completely. 554. Knave: Boy. 557. kips: Snatches. 558. In good...sely: A good and happy future to him. 559. gossips: Godparents. 561. So God them thank: Good luck to them. 563. John Horne: The shepherd in *The First Shepherds' Play* who quarrels with Gyb about the pasturing of an imaginary flock of sheep. fay: Faith.

He made all the garray°—
565   With the great shank.°
2 SHEP.: Mak, friends will we be, for we are all one.°
MAK: We? Now I hold for me, for mends get I none.°
   Farewell all three!—all glad were ye gone.°
3 SHEP.: Fair words may there be, but love is there
   none
570   This year.   [*They leave the cottage.*
1 SHEP.: Gave ye the child anything?
2 SHEP.: I trow not one farthing.
3 SHEP.: Fast again will I fling;°
   Abide ye me there.   [*He returns to the cottage.*

575   Mak, take it to no grief,° if I come to thy bairn.
MAK: Nay, thou dost me great reprief, and foul hast
   thou farn.°
3 SHEP.: The child will it not grieve, that little day-
   starn.°
   Mak, with your leave, let me give your bairn
   But sixpence.
580 MAK: Nay, do way! He sleeps.
3 SHEP.: Methink he peeps.
MAK: When he wakens he weeps.
   I pray you go hence.

3 SHEP.: Give me leave him to kiss, and lift up the
   clout.°   [*He glimpses the sheep.*
585   What the devil is this? He has a long snout!
1 SHEP.: He is marked amiss. We wait ill about.
2 SHEP.: Ill-spun weft, iwis, ay comes foul out.°
   Aye, so!   [*He recognizes the sheep.*
   He is like to our sheep!
590 3 SHEP.: How, Gib, may I peep?
1 SHEP.: I trow kind will creep
   Where it may not go.

2 SHEP.: This was a quaint gaud and a far cast;°
   It was a high fraud.
3 SHEP.:   Yea , sirs, was't.
595   Let burn this bawd and bind her fast.
   A false scold hangs at the last;
   So shalt thou.
   Will ye see how they swaddle
   His four feet in the middle?
600   Saw I never in a cradle
   A horned lad ere now.

564. garray: Commotion. 565. shank: Long legs. 566. all
one: Agreed. 567. Now I . . . none: For my own part, I'm
holding back, for I get no amends. 568. all glad were ye
gone: (I should be) very glad if you were gone. (Probably an
aside.) 573. Fast . . . fling: I will dash back. 575. Mak . . .
grief: Don't take offense. 576. thou dost . . . farn: Nay, you
do me great shame, and you have behaved badly. 577. day-
starn: Star. 584. clout: Cloth. 586–587. He is . . . foul out:
He is misshapen. We do wrong to pry about. . . . Ill-spun
weft, indeed, always comes out badly (i.e., what is bred in the
bone will come out in the flesh). 591–593. kind . . . far cast:
Nature will creep where it cannot walk (i.e., assert itself in
one way or another). . . . This was a clever dodge and a cunning trick.

MAK: Peace, bid I. What, let be your fare!°
   I am he that him begat, and yond woman him bare.
1 SHEP.: What devil shall be hat,° Mak? Lo,
   God, Mak's heir!   605
2 SHEP.: Let be all that. Now God give him care,°
   I sagh.°
WIFE: A pretty child is he
   As sits on a woman's knee;
   A dillydown,° pardie,
   To gar° a man laugh.   610

3 SHEP.: I know him by the ear-mark; that is a good
   token.
MAK: I tell you, sirs, hark! his nose was broken.
   Since told me a clerk that he was forspoken.°
1 SHEP.: This is a false work; I would fain be wroken.°
   Get weapon!   615
WIFE: He was taken with° an elf,
   I saw it myself;
   When the clock struck twelve,
   Was he forshapen.°
2 SHEP.: Ye two are well feft sam in a stead.°   620
1 SHEP.: Since they maintain their theft, let do them
   to dead.°
MAK: If I trespass eft,° gird° off my head.
   With you will I be left.
3 SHEP.:   Sirs, do my rede:°
   For this trespass
   We will neither ban ne flite,°   625
   Fight nor chide,
   But have done as tite,°
   And cast him in canvas.

[*They toss Mak in a blanket.*

SCENE VII

The open fields

1 SHEP.: Lord, what I am sore, in point for to burst!
   In faith, I may no more; therefore will I rest.   630
2 SHEP.: As a sheep of seven score he weighed in my fist.
   For to sleep aywhere methink that I list.°
3 SHEP.: Now I pray you
   Lie down on this green.
1 SHEP.: On these thieves yet I mean.°   635
3 SHEP.: Whereto should ye teen?°
   Do as I say you.

602. fare: Uproar. 604. hat: Be called. 606. care: Sorrow. sagh: Saw (the sheep myself). 609. dillydown: Darling. 610. gar: Make. 613. forspoken: Bewitched. 614.
wroken: Avenged. 616. with: By. 619. forshapen: Transformed. 620. Ye two . . . stead: You two are well endowed
together in one place (i.e., are as clever a pair of rascals as ever
lived under one roof). 621. dead: Death. 622. eft: Again.
gird: Strike. 623. With you . . . my rede: I throw myself on
your mercy. . . . Take my advice. 625. neither ban ne flite:
Neither curse nor quarrel. 627. as tite: At once. 632. For to
sleep . . . I list: I think I would be glad to sleep anywhere. 635.
mean: Think. 636. teen: Vex yourself.

An Angel sings 'Gloria in excelsis,' and then says:

ANGEL: Rise, herdmen hend,° for now is he born
   That shall take from the fiend that Adam had lorn;
640 That warlock° to shend,° this night is he born.
   God is made your friend now at this morn,
   He behests.°
   At Bedlem° go see
   There lies that free°
645 In a crib full poorly,
   Betwixt two beasts.

1 SHEP.: This was a quaint steven° that ever yet I heard.
   It is a marvel to neven,° thus to be scared.
2 SHEP.: Of God's son of heaven he spoke upward.°
650 All the wood on a leven methought that he gard
   Appear.°
3 SHEP.: He spake of a bairn
   In Bedlem, I you warn.
1 SHEP.: That betokens yond starn;
655 Let us seek him there.

2 SHEP.: Say, what was his song? Heard ye not how he
     cracked° it,
   Three breves to a long?
3 SHEP.:   Yea, marry, he hacked° it:
   Was no crochet wrong, nor no thing that lacked it.°
1 SHEP.: For to sing us among, right as he knacked° it,
660 I can.
2 SHEP.: Let see how ye croon.
   Can ye bark at the moon?
3 SHEP.: Hold your tongues! Have done!
1 SHEP.: Hark after, then.   [*Sings.*

665 2 SHEP.: To Bedlem he bade that we should gang;°
   I am full adrad° that we tarry too long.
3 SHEP.: Be merry and not sad—of mirth is our song!
   Everlasting glad to meed may we fang
   Without noise.°
670 1 SHEP.: Hie we thither forthy,°
   If° we be wet and weary,
   To that child and that lady;
   We have it not to lose.°

2 SHEP.: We find by the prophecy—let be your din!—
675 Of David and Isay,° and more than I min°—
   They prophesied by clergy°—that in a virgin
   Should he light° and lie, to sloken° our sin,
   And slake° it,

Our kind,° from woe;
For Isay said so: 680
Ecce virgo
Concipiet a child that is naked.°

3 SHEP.: Full glad may we be, and abide that day
   That lovely to see, that all mights may.
   Lord, well were me for once and for ay,°   685
   Might I kneel on my knee, some word for to say
   To that child.
   But the angel said
   In a crib was he laid;
   He was poorly arrayed,   690
   Both meek and mild.

1 SHEP.: Patriarchs that have been, and prophets
     beforn,°
   They desired to have seen this child that is born.
   They are gone full clean; that have they lorn.°
   We shall see him, I ween, ere it be morn,   695
   To token.°
   When I see him and feel,
   Then wot I full well
   It is true as steel
   That prophets have spoken: 700

   To so poor as we are that he would appear
   First find, and declare by his messenger.°
2 SHEP.: Go we now, let us fare; the place is us near.

3 SHEP.: I am ready and yare;° go we in fere°
   To that bright °   705
   Lord, if thy will be—
   We are lewd° all three—
   Thou grant us some kins glee
   To comfort thy wight.°

SCENE VIII

The stable in Bethlehem

1 SHEP.: Hail, comely and clean;° hail, young child!   710
   Hail, maker, as I mean, of° a maiden so mild!
   Thou hast waried,° I ween, the warlock so wild:
   The false guiler of teen, now goes he beguiled.°
   Lo, he merries,°

638. hend: Gentle. **640. warlock:** The devil. **shend:** Destroy.
642. behests: Promises. **643. Bedlem:** Bethlehem. **644.
There lies that free:** Where lies that noble one. **647. quaint
steven:** Elegant voice. **648. neven:** Tell of. **649. upward:**
On high. **650–651. All . . . appear:** I thought he made the
whole wood appear as if lit up by lightning. **656. cracked:**
Sang. **658. hacked:** Trilled. **659. Was . . . it:** No crochet
was wrong, and there was nothing it lacked. **660. knacked:**
Sang. **665. gang:** Go. **666. adrad:** Afraid. **668–669. Everlasting . . . noise:** We can get everlasting joy as our reward
without any fuss. **670. forthy:** Therefore. **671. If:** Even if.
673. We . . . lose: We must not forget it. **675. Isay:** Isaiah.
min: Remember. **676. clergy:** Learning. **677. light:** Alight.
sloken: Quench. **678. slake:** Relieve.

679. kind: Race. **681–682.** *Ecce virgo concipiet:* Behold, a
virgin shall conceive. **684–685. That lovely . . . for ay:** To
see that lovely one who is almighty. Lord, I would be happy
for once and all. **692. beforn:** In the past. **694. that have
they lorn:** That chance have they lost. **696. To token:** As
a sign. **702. First . . . messenger:** Find (us) first of all, and
make known (his birth) through his messenger. **704. yare:**
Eager. **in fere:** Together. **705. bright:** Bright one. **707.
lewd:** Simple. **708–709. Thou grant . . . thy wight:** Grant us
some joyful way of comforting thy child. **710. clean:** Pure.
711. of: Born of. **712. waried:** Cursed. **713. The false guiler
of teen:** The false and malicious deceiver (i.e., the devil).
714. merries: Is merry.

715   Lo, he laughs, my sweeting!
      A well fare° meeting!
      I have holden my heting:°
      Have a bob° of cherries.

      2 SHEP.: Hail, sovereign saviour, for thou hast us
               sought!
720   Hail, freely food and flower,° that all thing has
         wrought!
      Hail, full of favour, that made all of nought!
      Hail! I kneel and I cower. A bird have I brought
      To my bairn.
      Hail, little tiny mop!°
725   Of our creed thou art crop;
      I would drink on thy cop,°
      Little day-starn.

      3 SHEP.: Hail, darling dear, full of Godhead!
      I pray thee be near when that I have need.
730   Hail, sweet is thy cheer! My heart would bleed
      To see thee sit here in so poor weed,°
      With no pennies.
      Hail! Put forth thy dall!°
      I bring thee but a ball:

Have and play thee withal,   735
And go to the tennis.

MARY: The Father of heaven, God omnipotent,
      That set all on seven,° his Son has he sent.
      My name could he neven, and light ere he went.
      I conceived him full even through might, as he
         meant;°   740
      And now is he born.
      He keep you from woe! —
      I shall pray him so.
      Tell forth as ye go,
      And min° on this morn.   745

1 SHEP.: Farewell, lady, so fair to behold,
         With thy child on thy knee.
2 SHEP.:   But he lies full cold.
      Lord, well is me! Now we go, thou behold.
3 SHEP.: Forsooth, already it seems to be told
         Full oft.   750
1 SHEP.: What grace we have fun!
2 SHEP.: Come forth; now are we won!°
3 SHEP.: To sing are we bun:°
      Let take on loft.°

716. **well fare:** Very fine.   717. **I have . . . heting:** I have kept my promise.   718. **bob:** Bunch.   720. **food and flower:** Noble child.   724. **mop:** Moppet.   725–726. **Of . . . thy cop:** You are the head of our faith; I would drink in your cup (i.e., the cup of the Eucharist).   731. **weed:** Clothing.   733. **dall:** Hand.

738. **That set all on seven:** That made all the world in seven days.   739–740. **My name . . . he meant:** He named my name and alighted in me before He went. I conceived him indeed through God's might, as His purpose was.   745. **min:** Remembered.   752. **won:** Redeemed.   753. **bun:** Bound.   754. **Let take on loft:** Let us begin loudly.

Everyman

The late medieval play *Everyman* may have origins in northern Europe. A Flemish play, *Elckerlijk* ("Everyman"), dates from c. 1495, and the question of whether the English *Everyman* was translated from the Flemish play or whether the latter is a translation of the English *Everyman* has not been settled. Both plays may have had a common origin in an unknown play. The English *Everyman* was produced frequently in the fifteenth and early sixteenth centuries. Its drama was largely theological, its purpose to reform the audience. One indication that entertainment was not the primary goal of this morality play is its lack of the comic moments found in other plays, such as *The Second Shepherds' Pageant*.

The author of the play may have been a priest. This long-standing assumption is based on the fact that the play has much theological content and offers a moral message of the kind one might expect to hear from the pulpit. The theme of the play is fundamental: the inevitability of death. And for that reason, in part, the play continues to have a universal appeal. Modern productions may not give the audience a suitable medieval chill, but the message of the play is still relevant for everyone.

The medieval reliance on allegory is apparent in the naming of the characters in *Everyman*: Death, Kindred, Cousin, Goods, Knowledge, Strength, Beauty, and Everyman himself. Each character does not just stand for a specific quality; he or she *is* that quality. The allegorical way of thinking derived from the medieval faith that everything in the world had a moral meaning. Morality plays depended on this belief and always articulated setting, characters, and circumstances in terms of their moral value. This approach was in keeping with the medieval belief that the soul was always in jeopardy and that life was a test of one's moral condition. When Everyman meets a character, the most important information about his or her moral value is communicated instantly in the character's name, as well as through costumes and props. The character Good Deeds is simply good deeds: there is no need for psychological development because the medieval audience had a full understanding of what good deeds meant and how Good Deeds as a character would behave.

The structure of *Everyman* resembles a journey. Everyman undertakes to see who among all his acquaintances will accompany him on his most important trip: to the grave and the judgment of God Almighty. Seeing life as a journey—or as part of a journey—was especially natural for the medieval mind, which had as models the popular and costly religious pilgrimages to holy shrines and to the Holy Land itself. If life on earth is only part of the journey of the soul, then the morality play helps to put it in clear perspective. This life is not, the play tells us, the most important part of the soul's existence.

At its core, *Everyman* has a profound commercial metaphor: Everyman is called to square accounts with God. The metaphor of accounting appears early in the play, when Everyman talks about his accounts and reckonings as if they appeared in a book that should go with him to heaven. His life will be examined; if he is found wanting, he will go into the fires of hell. If he has lived profitably from a moral viewpoint, he will enjoy life everlasting. The language of the play is heavily loaded with accounting metaphors that identify it as the product of a society quite unlike that of the Greeks or the Romans. Such metaphors suggest that *Everyman* directs its message to middle-class merchants for whom accounting was a significant concept.

Like many sermons, *Everyman* imparts a lesson that its auditors were expected to heed. Hence the key points of the play are repeated at the end by the Doctor. For modern audiences, didactic plays are sometimes tedious. For the medieval mind, they represented a delightful way of learning important messages.

For discussion questions and assignments on *Everyman*, visit **bedfordstmartins.com/jacobus.**

Everyman in Performance

Very little is known about early productions of *Everyman*. It was produced in Holland and England for seventy-five years beginning in the mid-fifteenth century. The play disappeared from the stage for centuries, finally resurfacing in 1901 in a production under the auspices of the Elizabethan Stage

Society in London, directed by William Poel. Poel designed the costumes and set, directed, and at first played the part of Death; when he got older, he played the part of God. Poel produced *Everyman* many times over the next fifteen years.

The 1901 production was followed by a 1902 revival in New York starring Edith Wynne Matthison and produced by Ben Greet, marking the play's first American performance. Greet continued producing *Everyman* for the next thirty-five years in both England and America.

After seeing Poel's production, Max Reinhardt, the legendary German director, decided to produce *Everyman* in Germany. The Austrian poet and playwright Hugo von Hofmannsthal wrote a new German adaptation, *Jedermann,* for Reinhardt. The adaptation features Everyman as a wealthy burgher, and central to the play is an ornate banquet scene in which Death appears. Hofmannsthal's German adaptation marked a shift in emphasis from the simpler and more personal English *Everyman* to the spectacular *Jedermann* that concentrates on a wealthy man's lustful life and his attempts to get into heaven. *Jedermann* was first produced in Berlin on December 1, 1911. In 1913, Reinhardt produced the play in Salzburg, Austria, at the Salzburg Cathedral square, and except for the years of World War II, Reinhardt's version of *Jedermann* has been performed regularly at the annual Salzburg Festival. The critic Brooks Atkinson found Reinhardt's production "nothing short of miraculous." In a review of Reinhardt's 1927 production, the critic Gilbert Gabriel found *Jedermann* "crammed with splendors for the eye, largesse of bells and uplifting voices for the ear." A reviewer at the 1936 Salzburg Festival production of *Jedermann* wrote that the play "has everything but simplicity."

The popularity of the Reinhardt productions of *Jedermann* paved the way for numerous productions of *Everyman* over the years. In 1936, during the Great Depression in the United States, the WPA (Works Progress Administration) held special Sunday church performances of *Everyman.* Other notable productions include a 1941 *Everyman* in New York, performed by refugee actors from Europe, and a 1955 tour with college casts in New England and California. In 1922, a new English adaptation of the German *Jedermann* by Sir John Martin-Harvey was presented at Stratford-on-Avon. This production toured to London and New York in 1923. In 1936, Sir John's adaptation was performed at the Hollywood Bowl in California with Peggy Wood and Lionel Braham. Long popular with college and community groups, the play continues to be performed around the world.

ANONYMOUS

Everyman c. 1495

EDITED BY A. C. CAWLEY

Characters

GOD	KNOWLEDGE
MESSENGER	CONFESSION
DEATH	BEAUTY
EVERYMAN	STRENGTH
FELLOWSHIP	DISCRETION
KINDRED	FIVE WITS
COUSIN	ANGEL
GOODS	DOCTOR
GOOD DEEDS	

*Here beginneth a treatise how the high Father of
Heaven sendeth Death to summon every creature to
come and give account of their lives in this world, and
is in manner of a moral play.*

MESSENGER: I pray you all give your audience,
    And hear this matter with reverence,
    By figure° a moral play:
    The *Summoning of Everyman* called it is,
5   That of our lives and ending shows
    How transitory we be all day.°
    This matter is wondrous precious,
    But the intent of it is more gracious,
    And sweet to bear away.
10   The story saith: Man, in the beginning
    Look well, and take good heed to the ending,
    Be you never so gay!
    Ye think sin in the beginning full sweet,
    Which in the end causeth the soul to weep,
15   When the body lieth in clay.
    Here shall you see how Fellowship and Jollity,
    Both Strength, Pleasure, and Beauty,
    Will fade from thee as flower in May;
    For ye shall hear how our Heaven King
20   Calleth Everyman to a general reckoning:
    Give audience, and hear what he doth say.

        (Exit.)

(God speaketh.)

GOD: I perceive, here in my majesty,
    How that all creatures be to me unkind,°
    Living without dread in worldly prosperity:
25   Of ghostly sight° the people be so blind,
    Drowned in sin, they know me not for their God;

3. **By figure:** In form.   6. **all day:** Always.   23. **unkind:** Ungrateful.   25. **ghostly sight:** Spiritual vision.

In worldly riches is all their mind,
They fear not my righteousness, the sharp rod.
My law that I showed, when I for them died,
They forget clean, and shedding of my blood red;   30
I hanged between two, it cannot be denied;
To get them life I suffered to be dead;
I healed their feet, with thorns hurt was my head.
I could do no more than I did, truly;
And now I see the people do clean forsake me: 35
They use the seven deadly sins damnable,
As pride, covetise, wrath, and lechery
Now in the world be made commendable;
And thus they leave of angels the heavenly company.
Every man liveth so after his own pleasure,   40
And yet of their life they be nothing sure:
I see the more that I them forbear
The worse they be from year to year.
All that liveth appaireth° fast;
Therefore I will, in all the haste,   45
Have a reckoning of every man's person;
For, and° I leave the people thus alone
In their life and wicked tempests,
Verily they will become much worse than beasts;
For now one would by envy another up eat;   50
Charity they do all clean forget.
I hoped well that every man
In my glory should make his mansion,
And thereto I had them all elect;
But now I see, like traitors deject,°   55
They thank me not for the pleasure that
    I to them meant,
Nor yet for their being that I them have lent.
I proffered the people great multitude of mercy,
And few there be that asketh it heartily.
They be so cumbered with worldly riches   60
That needs on them I must do justice,
On every man living without fear.
Where art thou, Death, thou mighty messenger?

(Enter Death.)

DEATH: Almighty God, I am here at your will,
    Your commandment to fulfill.   65
GOD: Go thou to Everyman,
    And show him, in my name,
    A pilgrimage he must on him take,
    Which he in no wise may escape;

44. **appaireth:** Degenerates.   47. **and:** If.   55. **deject:** Abject.

70 And that he bring with him a sure reckoning
   Without delay or any tarrying.

                                   (*God withdraws.*)

DEATH: Lord, I will in the world go run overall,
   And cruelly outsearch both great and small;
   Every man will I beset that liveth beastly
75 Out of God's laws, and dreadeth not folly.
   He that loveth riches I will strike with my dart,
   His sight to blind, and from heaven to depart°—
   Except that alms be his good friend—
   In hell for to dwell, world without end.
80 Lo, yonder I see Everyman walking.
   Full little he thinketh on my coming;
   His mind is on fleshly lusts and his treasure,
   And great pain it shall cause him to endure
   Before the Lord, Heaven King.

(*Enter Everyman.*)

85 Everyman, stand still! Whither art thou going
   Thus gaily? Hast thou thy Maker forget?
EVERYMAN: Why askest thou?
   Wouldest thou wit?°
DEATH: Yea, sir; I will show you:
90 In great haste I am sent to thee
   From God out of his majesty.
EVERYMAN: What, sent to me?
DEATH: Yea, certainly.
   Though thou have forget him here,
95 He thinketh on thee in the heavenly sphere,
   As, ere we depart, thou shalt know.
EVERYMAN: What desireth God of me?
DEATH: That shall I show thee:
   A reckoning he will needs have
100 Without any longer respite.
EVERYMAN: To give a reckoning longer leisure I crave;
   This blind matter troubleth my wit.
DEATH: On thee thou must take a long journey;
   Therefore thy book of count° with thee thou bring,
105 For turn° again thou cannot by no way.
   And look thou be sure of thy reckoning,
   For before God thou shalt answer, and show
   Thy many bad deeds, and good but a few;
   How thou hast spent thy life, and in what wise,
110 Before the chief Lord of paradise.
   Have ado that we were in that way,°
   For, wit thou well, thou shalt make none attorney.°
EVERYMAN: Full unready I am such reckoning to give.
   I know thee not. What messenger art thou?
115 DEATH: I am Death, that no man dreadeth,°
   For every man I rest,° and no man spareth;
   For it is God's commandment
   That all to me should be obedient.
EVERYMAN: O Death, thou comest when I had thee least
   in mind!

In thy power it lieth me to save;   120
   Yet of my good° will I give thee, if thou will be kind:
   Yea, a thousand pound shalt thou have,
   And defer this matter till another day.
DEATH: Everyman, it may not be, by no way.
   I set not by gold, silver, nor riches,   125
   Ne by pope, emperor, king, duke, ne princes;
   For, and I would receive gifts great,
   All the world I might get;
   But my custom is clean contrary.
   I give thee no respite. Come hence, and not tarry.   130
EVERYMAN: Alas, shall I have no longer respite?
   I may say Death giveth no warning!
   To think on thee, it maketh my heart sick,
   For all unready is my book of reckoning.
   But twelve year and I might have abiding,°   135
   My counting-book I would make so clear
   That my reckoning I should not need to fear.
   Wherefore, Death, I pray thee, for God's mercy,
   Spare me till I be provided of remedy.
DEATH: Thee availeth not to cry, weep, and pray;   140
   But haste thee lightly that thou were gone that
      journey,°
   And prove thy friends if thou can;
   For, wit thou well, the tide abideth no man,
   And in the world each living creature
   For Adam's sin must die of nature.°   145
EVERYMAN: Death, if I should this pilgrimage take,
   And my reckoning surely make,
   Show me, for saint charity,°
   Should I not come again shortly?
DEATH: No, Everyman; and thou be once there,   150
   Thou mayst never more come here,
   Trust me verily.
EVERYMAN: O gracious God in the high seat celestial,
   Have mercy on me in this most need!
   Shall I have no company from this vale terrestrial 155
   Of mine acquaintance, that way me to lead?
DEATH: Yea, if any be so hardy
   That would go with thee and bear thee company.
   Hie thee that thou were gone to God's magnificence,
   Thy reckoning to give before his presence.   160
   What, weenest° thou thy life is given thee,
   And thy worldly goods also?
EVERYMAN: I had wend° so, verily.
DEATH: Nay, nay; it was but lent thee;
   For as soon as thou art go,   165
   Another a while shall have it, and then go therefro,
   Even as thou has done.
   Everyman, thou art mad! Thou hast thy wits five,
   And here on earth will not amend thy life;
   For suddenly I do come.   170

---

77. **depart:** Separate. 88. **wit:** Know. 104. **count:** Account.
105. **turn:** Return. 111. **Have ado . . . that way:** Let us see about making that journey. 112. **none attorney:** No one (your) advocate. 115. **no man dreadeth:** Fears no man.
116. **rest:** Arrest.

121. **good:** Goods. 135. **But twelve year . . . abiding:** If I could stay for just twelve more years. 141. **But haste thee . . . that journey:** But set off quickly on your journey. 145. **of nature:** In the course of nature. 148. **for saint charity:** In the name of holy charity. 161. **weenest:** Suppose. 163. **wend:** Supposed.

EVERYMAN: O wretched caitiff,° whither shall I flee,
That I might scape this endless sorrow?
Now, gentle Death, spare me till to-morrow,
That I may amend me
175 With good advisement.
DEATH: Nay, thereto I will not consent,
Nor no man will I respite;
But to the heart suddenly I shall smite
Without any advisement.
180 And now out of thy sight I will me hie;
See thou make thee ready shortly,
For thou mayst say this is the day
That no man living may scape away.

(*Exit Death.*)

EVERYMAN: Alas, I may well weep with
sighs deep!
185 Now have I no manner of company
To help me in my journey, and me to keep;
And also my writing is full unready,
How shall I do now for to excuse me?
I would to God I had never be get!°
190 To my soul a full great profit it had be;
For now I fear pains huge and great.
The time passeth. Lord, help, that all wrought!
For though I mourn it availeth nought.
The day passeth, and is almost ago;°
195 I wot not well what for to do.
To whom were I best my complaint to make?
What and I to Fellowship thereof spake,
And showed him of this sudden chance?
For in him is all mine affiance;°
200 We have in the world so many a day
Be good friends in sport and play.
I see him yonder, certainly.
I trust that he will bear me company;
Therefore to him will I speak to ease my sorrow.
205 Well met, good Fellowship, and good morrow!

(*Fellowship speaketh.*)

FELLOWSHIP: Everyman, good morrow, by this day!
Sir, why lookest thou so piteously?
If any thing be amiss, I pray thee me say,
That I may help to remedy.
210 EVERYMAN: Yea, good Fellowship, yea;
I am in great jeopardy.
FELLOWSHIP: My true friend, show to me your mind;
I will not forsake thee to my life's end,
In the way of good company.
215 EVERYMAN: That was well spoken, and lovingly.
FELLOWSHIP: Sir, I must needs know your heaviness;°
I have pity to see you in any distress.
If any have you wronged, ye shall revenged be,
Though I on the ground be slain for thee—
220 Though that I know before that I should die.
EVERYMAN: Verily, Fellowship, gramercy.°

FELLOWSHIP: Tush! by thy thanks I set not a straw.
Show me your grief, and say no more.
EVERYMAN: If I my heart should to you break,°
And then you to turn your mind from me,   225
And would not me comfort when ye hear me speak,
Then should I ten times sorrier be.
FELLOWSHIP: Sir, I say as I will do indeed.
EVERYMAN: Then be you a good friend at need:
I have found you true herebefore.   230
FELLOWSHIP: And so ye shall evermore;
For, in faith, and thou go to hell,
I will not forsake thee by the way.
EVERYMAN: Ye speak like a good friend; I believe
you well.
I shall deserve° it, and I may.   235
FELLOWSHIP: I speak of no deserving, by this day!
For he that will say, and nothing do,
Is not worthy with good company to go;
Therefore show me the grief of your mind,
As to your friend most loving and kind.   240
EVERYMAN: I shall show you how it is:
Commanded I am to go a journey,
A long way, hard and dangerous,
And give a strait count, without delay,
Before the high Judge, Adonai.°   245
Wherefore, I pray you, bear me company,
As ye have promised, in this journey.
FELLOWSHIP: That is matter indeed.° Promise is duty;
But, and I should take such a voyage on me,
I know it well, it should be to my pain;   250
Also it maketh me afeard, certain.
But let us take counsel here as well as we can,
For your words would fear a strong man.
EVERYMAN: Why, ye said if I had need
Ye would me never forsake, quick ne dead,   255
Though it were to hell, truly.
FELLOWSHIP: So I said, certainly,
But such pleasures be set aside, the sooth to say;
And also, if we took such a journey,
When should we come again?   260
EVERYMAN: Nay, never again, till the day of doom.
FELLOWSHIP: In faith, then will not I come there!
Who hath you these tidings brought?
EVERYMAN: Indeed, Death was with me here.
FELLOWSHIP: Now, by God that all hath bought,°   265
If Death were the messenger,
For no man that is living to-day
I will not go that loath journey—
Not for the father that begat me!
EVERYMAN: Ye promised otherwise, pardie.°   270
FELLOWSHIP: I wot well I said so, truly;
And yet if thou wilt eat, and drink, and make good
cheer,
Or haunt to women the lusty company,°

171. **caitiff:** Captive.   189. **be get:** Been born.   194. **ago:**
Gone.   199. **affiance:** Trust.   216. **heaviness:** Sorrow.   221.
gramercy: Thanks.

224. **break:** Open.   235. **deserve:** Repay.   245. **Adonai:**
Hebrew name for God.   248. **That is matter indeed:** That
is a good reason indeed (for asking me).   265. **bought:**
Redeemed.   270. **pardie:** By God.   273. **haunt to women the
lusty company:** Frequent the lively company of women.

I would not forsake you while the day is clear,°
275   Trust me verily.
EVERYMAN: Yea, thereto ye would be ready!
To go to mirth, solace, and play,
Your mind will sooner apply,
Than to bear me company in my long journey.
280   FELLOWSHIP: Now, in good faith, I will not that way.
But and thou will murder, or any man kill,
In that I will help thee with a good will.
EVERYMAN: O, that is a simple advice indeed.
Gentle fellow, help me in my necessity!
285   We have loved long, and now I need;
And now, gentle Fellowship, remember me.
FELLOWSHIP: Whether ye have loved me or no,
By Saint John, I will not with thee go.
EVERYMAN: Yet, I pray thee, take the labor, and do so
much for me
290   To bring me forward, for saint charity,
And comfort me till I come without the town.
FELLOWSHIP: Nay, and thou would give me a new gown,
I will not a foot with thee go;
But, and thou had tarried, I would not have left thee
so.
295   And as now God speed thee in thy journey,
For from thee I will depart as fast as I may.
EVERYMAN: Whither away, Fellowship? Will thou forsake
me?
FELLOWSHIP: Yea, by my fay!° To God I betake° thee.
EVERYMAN: Farewell, good Fellowship; for thee my heart
is sore.
300   Adieu for ever! I shall see thee no more.
FELLOWSHIP: In faith, Everyman, farewell now at the
ending;
For you I will remember that parting is mourning.

(*Exit Fellowship.*)

EVERYMAN: Alack! shall we thus depart° indeed—
Ah, Lady, help!—without any more comfort?
305   Lo, Fellowship forsaketh me in my most need.
For help in this world whither shall I resort?
Fellowship herebefore with me would merry make,
And now little sorrow for me doth he take.
It is said, "In prosperity men friends may find,
310   Which in adversity be full unkind."
Now whither for succor shall I flee,
Sith° that Fellowship hath forsaken me?
To my kinsmen I will, truly,
Praying them to help me in my necessity;
315   I believe that they will do so,
For kind will creep where it may not go.°
I will go say,° for yonder I see them.
Where be ye now, my friends and kinsmen?

(*Enter Kindred and Cousin.*)

KINDRED: Here be we now at your commandment.
Cousin, I pray you show us your intent   320
In any wise, and do not spare.
COUSIN: Yea, Everyman, and to us declare
If ye be disposed to go anywhither;
For, wit you well, we will live and die together.
KINDRED: In wealth and woe we will with you hold,   325
For over his kin a man may be bold.°
EVERYMAN: Gramercy, my friends and kinsmen kind.
Now shall I show you the grief of my mind:
I was commanded by a messenger,
That is a high king's chief officer;   330
He bade me go a pilgrimage, to my pain,
And I know well I shall never come again;
Also I must give a reckoning strait,
For I have a great enemy° that hath me in wait,°
Which intendeth me for to hinder.   335
KINDRED: What account is that which ye must render?
That would I know.
EVERYMAN: Of all my works I must show
How I have lived and my days spent;
Also of ill deeds that I have used   340
In my time, sith life was me lent;
And of all virtues that I have refused.
Therefore, I pray you, go thither with me
To help to make mine account, for saint charity.
COUSIN: What, to go thither? Is that the matter?   345
Nay, Everyman, I had liefer fast bread and water°
All this five year and more.
EVERYMAN: Alas, that ever I was bore!
For now shall I never be merry,
If that you forsake me.   350
KINDRED: Ah, sir, what ye be a merry man!
Take good heart to you, and make no moan.
But one thing I warn you, by Saint Anne—
As for me, ye shall go alone.
EVERYMAN: My Cousin, will you not with me go?   355
COUSIN: No, by our Lady! I have the cramp in my toe.
Trust not to me, for, so God me speed,
I will deceive you in your most need.
KINDRED: It availeth not us to tice.°
Ye shall have my maid with all my heart;   360
She loveth to go to feasts, there to be nice,°
And to dance, and abroad to start:
I will give her leave to help you in that journey,
If that you and she may agree.
EVERYMAN: Now show me the very effect° of your
mind: 365
Will you go with me, or abide behind?
KINDRED: Abide behind? Yea, that will I, and I may!
Therefore farewell till another day.

(*Exit Kindred.*)

---

274. **while the day is clear:** Until daybreak.   298. **fay:** Faith.
betake: Commend.   303. **depart:** Part.   312. **Sith:** Since.
316. **for kind will creep where it may not go:** For kinship will
creep where it cannot walk (i.e., blood is thicker than water).
317. **say:** Essay, try.

326. **For over his kin . . . may be bold:** For a man may be sure
of his kinsfolk.   334. **enemy:** Devil.   **hath me in wait:** Has me
under observation.   346. **liefer fast bread and water:** Rather
fast on bread and water.   359. **tice:** Entice.   361. **nice:** Wanton.
365. **effect:** Tenor.

EVERYMAN: How should I be merry or glad?
370   For fair promises men to me make,
    But when I have most need they me forsake.
    I am deceived; that maketh me sad.
COUSIN: Cousin Everyman, farewell now,
    For verily I will not go with you.
375   Also of mine own an unready reckoning
    I have to account; therefore I make tarrying.
    Now God keep thee, for now I go.

                        (Exit Cousin.)

EVERYMAN: Ah, Jesus, is all come hereto?
    Lo, fair words maketh fools fain;°
380   They promise, and nothing will do, certain.
    My kinsmen promised me faithfully
    For to abide with me steadfastly,
    And now fast away do they flee:
    Even so Fellowship promised me.
385   What friend were best me of to provide?°
    I lose my time here longer to abide.
    Yet in my mind a thing there is:
    All my life I have loved riches;
    If that my Good° now help me might,
390   He would make my heart full light.
    I will speak to him in this distress—
    Where art thou, my Goods and riches?

(Goods speaks from a corner.)

GOODS: Who calleth me? Everyman? What! hast thou
      haste?
    I lie here in corners, trussed and piled so high,
395   And in chests I am locked so fast,
    Also sacked in bags. Thou mayst see with thine eye
    I cannot stir; in packs low I lie.
    What would ye have? Lightly° me say.
EVERYMAN: Come hither, Good, in all the haste thou may,
400   For of counsel I must desire thee.
GOODS: Sir, and ye in the world have sorrow or adversity,
    That can I help you to remedy shortly.
EVERYMAN: It is another disease that grieveth me;
    In this world it is not, I tell thee so.
405   I am sent for, another way to go,
    To give a strait count general
    Before the highest Jupiter of all;
    And all my life I have had joy and pleasure in thee,
    Therefore, I pray thee, go with me;
410   For, peradventure, thou mayst before God Almighty
    My reckoning help to clean and purify;
    For it is said ever among
    That money maketh all right that is wrong.
GOODS: Nay, Everyman, I sing another song.
415   I follow no man in such voyages;
    For, and I went with thee,
    Thou shouldst fare much the worse for me;
    For because on me thou did set thy mind,
    Thy reckoning I have made blotted and blind,
420   That thine account thou cannot make truly;

And that hast thou for the love of me.
EVERYMAN: That would grieve me full sore,
    When I should come to that fearful answer.
    Up, let us go thither together.
GOODS: Nay, not so! I am too brittle, I may not endure;   425
    I will follow no man one foot, be ye sure.
EVERYMAN: Alas, I have thee loved, and had great pleasure
    All my life-days on good and treasure.
GOODS: That is to thy damnation, without leasing,°
    For my love is contrary to the love everlasting;   430
    But if thou had me loved moderately during,
    As to the poor to give part of me,
    Then shouldst thou not in this dolor be,
    Nor in this great sorrow and care.
EVERYMAN: Lo, now was I deceived ere I was ware,   435
    And all I may wite° misspending of time.
GOODS: What, weenest thou that I am thine?
EVERYMAN: I had wend so.
GOODS: Nay, Everyman, I say no.
    As for a while I was lent thee;   440
    A season thou hast had me in prosperity.
    My condition is man's soul to kill;
    If I save one, a thousand I do spill.°
    Weenest thou that I will follow thee?
    Nay, not from this world, verily.   445
EVERYMAN: I had wend otherwise.
GOODS: Therefore to thy soul Good is a thief;
    For when thou art dead, this is my guise—
    Another to deceive in this same wise
    As I have done thee, and all to his soul's reprief.°   450
EVERYMAN: O false Good, cursed may thou be,
    Thou traitor to God, that hast deceived me
    And caught me in thy snare!
GOODS: Marry, thou brought thyself in care,
    Whereof I am glad;   455
    I must needs laugh, I cannot be sad.
EVERYMAN: Ah, Good, thou hast had long my heartly
      love;
    I gave thee that which should be the Lord's
      above.
    But wilt thou not go with me indeed?
    I pray thee truth to say.   460
GOODS: No, so God me speed!
    Therefore farewell, and have good day.

                        (Exit Goods.)

EVERYMAN: O, to whom shall I make my moan
    For to go with me in that heavy journey?
    First Fellowship said he would with me gone;   465
    His words were very pleasant and gay,
    But afterward he left me alone.
    Then spake I to my kinsmen, all in despair,
    And also they gave me words fair;
    They lacked no fair speaking,   470
    But all forsook me in the ending.
    Then went I to my Goods, that I loved best,

---

379. fain: Glad. **385. me of to provide:** To provide myself with. **389. Good:** Goods. **398. Lightly:** Quickly.

429. without leasing: Without a lie (i.e., truly). **436. wite:** Blame. **443. spill:** Ruin. **450. reprief:** Shame.

In hope to have comfort, but there had I least;
For my Goods sharply did me tell
475 That he bringeth many into hell.
Then of myself I was ashamed,
And so I am worthy to be blamed;
Thus may I well myself hate.
Of whom shall I now counsel take?
480 I think that I shall never speed
Till that I go to my Good Deed.
But, alas, she is so weak
That she can neither go nor speak;
Yet will I venture on her now.
485 My Good Deeds, where be you?

(*Good Deeds speaks from the ground.*)

GOOD DEEDS: Here I lie, cold in the ground;
Thy sins hath me sore bound,
That I cannot stir.
EVERYMAN: O Good Deeds, I stand in fear!
490 I must you pray of counsel,
For help now should come right well.°
GOOD DEEDS: Everyman, I have understanding
That ye be summoned account to make
Before Messias, of Jerusalem King;
And you do by me,° that journey with you will I
495 take.
EVERYMAN: Therefore I come to you, my moan to make;
I pray you that ye will go with me.
GOOD DEEDS: I would full fain, but I cannot stand,
verily.
EVERYMAN: Why, is there anything on you fall?
500 GOOD DEEDS: Yea, sir, I may thank you of° all;
If ye had perfectly cheered me,
Your book of count full ready had be.
Look, the books of your works and deeds eke!°
Behold how they lie under the feet,
505 To your soul's heaviness.
EVERYMAN: Our Lord Jesus help me!
For one letter here I cannot see.
GOOD DEEDS: There is a blind reckoning in time of
distress.
EVERYMAN: Good Deeds, I pray you help me in this need,
510 Or else I am for ever damned indeed;
Therefore help me to make reckoning
Before the Redeemer of all thing,
That King is, and was, and ever shall.
GOOD DEEDS: Everyman, I am sorry of your fall,
515 And fain would I help you, and I were able.
EVERYMAN: Good Deeds, your counsel I pray you give
me.
GOOD DEEDS: That shall I do verily;
Though that on my feet I may not go,
I have a sister that shall with you also,
520 Called Knowledge, which shall with you abide,
To help you to make that dreadful reckoning.

(*Enter Knowledge.*)

KNOWLEDGE: Everyman, I will go with thee, and be thy
guide,
In thy most need to go by thy side.
EVERYMAN: In good condition I am now in every
thing,
And am wholly content with this good thing, 525
Thanked be God my creator.
GOOD DEEDS: And when she hath brought you there
Where thou shalt heal thee of thy smart,
Then go you with your reckoning and your Good
Deeds together,
For to make you joyful at heart 530
Before the blessed Trinity.
EVERYMAN: My Good Deeds, gramercy!
I am well content, certainly,
With your words sweet.
KNOWLEDGE: Now go we together lovingly 535
To Confession, that cleansing river.
EVERYMAN: For joy I weep; I would we were there!
But, I pray you, give me cognition
Where dwelleth that holy man, Confession.
KNOWLEDGE: In the house of salvation: 540
We shall find him in that place,
That shall us comfort, by God's grace.

(*Knowledge takes Everyman to Confession.*)

Lo, this is Confession. Kneel down and ask mercy,
For he is in good conceit° with God Almighty.
EVERYMAN: O glorious fountain, that all uncleanness
doth clarify, 545
Wash from me the spots of vice unclean,
That on me no sin may be seen.
I come with Knowledge for my redemption,
Redempt with heart° and full contrition;
For I am commanded a pilgrimage to take, 550
And great accounts before God to make.
Now I pray you, Shrift, mother of salvation,
Help my Good Deeds for my piteous exclamation.
CONFESSION: I know your sorrow well, Everyman.
Because with Knowledge ye come to me, 555
I will you comfort as well as I can,
And a precious jewel I will give thee,
Called penance, voider of adversity;
Therewith shall your body chastised be,
With abstinence and perseverance in God's service. 560
Here shall you receive that scourge of me,
Which is penance strong that ye must endure,
To remember thy Savior was scourged for thee
With sharp scourges, and suffered it patiently;
So must thou, ere thou scape that painful
pilgrimage. 565
Knowledge, keep him in this voyage,
And by that time Good Deeds will be with thee.
But in any wise be siker° of mercy,
For your time draweth fast; and° ye will saved be,

---

491. should come right well: Would be very welcome. **495. by me:** As I advise. **500. of:** For. **503. eke:** Also.

544. conceit: Esteem. **549. heart:** Heartfelt. **568. siker:** Sure. **569. and:** If.

570　　Ask God mercy, and he will grant truly.
　　　When with the scourge of penance man doth him
　　　　　bind,
　　　The oil of forgiveness then shall he find.
　　EVERYMAN: Thanked be God for his gracious work!
　　　For now I will my penance begin;
575　　This hath rejoiced and lighted my heart,
　　　Though the knots be painful and hard within.
　　KNOWLEDGE: Everyman, look your penance that ye
　　　　　fulfill,
　　　What pain that ever it to you be;
　　　And Knowledge shall give you counsel at will
580　　How your account ye shall make clearly.
　　EVERYMAN: O eternal God, O heavenly figure,
　　　O way of righteousness, O goodly vision,
　　　Which descended down in a virgin pure
　　　Because he would every man redeem,
585　　Which Adam forfeited by his disobedience:
　　　O blessed Godhead, elect and high divine,
　　　Forgive my grievous offense;
　　　Here I cry thee mercy in this presence.°
　　　O ghostly treasure, O ransomer and redeemer,
590　　Of all the world hope and conductor,
　　　Mirror of joy, and founder of mercy,
　　　Which enlumineth heaven and earth thereby,
　　　Hear my clamorous complaint, though it late be;
　　　Receive my prayers, of thy benignity;
595　　Though I be a sinner most abominable,
　　　Yet let my name be written in Moses' table.°
　　　O Mary, pray to the Maker of all thing,
　　　Me for to help at my ending;
　　　And save me from the power of my enemy,
600　　For Death assaileth me strongly.
　　　And, Lady, that I may by mean of thy prayer
　　　Of your Son's glory to be partner,
　　　By the means of his passion, I it crave;
　　　I beseech you help my soul to save.
605　　Knowledge, give me the scourge of penance;
　　　My flesh therewith shall give acquittance:°
　　　I will now begin, if God give me grace.
　　KNOWLEDGE: Everyman, God give you time and space!
　　　Thus I bequeath you in the hands of our Saviour;
610　　Now may you make your reckoning sure.
　　EVERYMAN: In the name of the Holy Trinity,
　　　My body sore punished shall be:
　　　Take this, body, for the sin of the flesh!

(*Scourges himself.*)

　　　Also° thou delightest to go gay and fresh,
615　　And in the way of damnation thou did me bring,
　　　Therefore suffer now strokes and punishing.

---

588. **in this presence:** In the presence of this company.
596. **Moses' table:** Medieval theologians regarded the two
tablets given to Moses on Mount Sinai as symbols of baptism
and penance. Thus Everyman is asking to be numbered among
those who have escaped damnation by doing penance for their
sins. 606. **acquittance:** Satisfaction (as part of the sacrament
of penance). 614. **Also:** As.

Now of penance I will wade the water clear,
To save me from purgatory, that sharp fire.

(*Good Deeds rises from the ground.*)

GOOD DEEDS: I thank God, now I can walk and go,
　And am delivered of my sickness and woe.　　　　　620
　Therefore with Everyman I will go, and not
　　　spare;
　His good works I will help him to declare.
KNOWLEDGE: Now, Everyman, be merry and glad!
　Your Good Deeds cometh now; ye may not
　　　be sad.
　Now is your Good Deeds whole and sound,　　　　625
　Going upright upon the ground.
EVERYMAN: My heart is light, and shall be evermore;
　Now will I smite° faster than I did before.
GOOD DEEDS: Everyman, pilgrim, my special friend,
　Blessed be thou without end;　　　　　　　　　　630
　For thee is preparate the eternal glory.
　Ye have me made whole and sound,
　Therefore I will bide by thee in every stound.°
EVERYMAN: Welcome, my Good Deeds; now I hear thy
　　　voice,
　I weep for very sweetness of love.　　　　　　　　635
KNOWLEDGE: Be no more sad, but ever rejoice;
　God seeth thy living in his throne above.
　Put on this garment to thy behoof,°
　Which is wet with your tears,
　Or else before God you may it miss,　　　　　　　640
　When ye to your journey's end come shall.
EVERYMAN: Gentle Knowledge, what do ye it call?
KNOWLEDGE: It is a garment of sorrow:
　From pain it will you borrow;°
　Contrition it is,　　　　　　　　　　　　　　　645
　That geteth forgiveness;
　It pleaseth God passing well.
GOOD DEEDS: Everyman, will you wear it for your
　　　heal?°
EVERYMAN: Now blessed be Jesu, Mary's Son,
　For now have I on true contrition.　　　　　　　650
　And let us go now without tarrying;
　Good Deeds, have we clear our reckoning?
GOOD DEEDS: Yea, indeed, I have it here.
EVERYMAN: Then I trust we need not fear;
　Now, friends, let us not part in twain.　　　　　655
KNOWLEDGE: Nay, Everyman, that will we not,
　　　certain.
GOOD DEEDS: Yet must thou lead with thee
　Three persons of great might.
EVERYMAN: Who should they be?
GOOD DEEDS: Discretion and Strength they hight,°　660
　And thy Beauty may not abide behind.
KNOWLEDGE: Also ye must call to mind
　Your Five Wits as for your counsellors.

---

628. **smite:** Strike. 633. **stound:** Trial. 638. **behoof:** Advantage. 644. **borrow:** Release. 648. **heal:** Salvation. 660.
hight: Are called.

GOOD DEEDS: You must have them ready at all hours.
665   EVERYMAN: How shall I get them hither?
KNOWLEDGE: You must call them all together,
     And they will hear you incontinent.°
EVERYMAN: My friends, come hither and be present,
     Discretion, Strength, my Five Wits, and Beauty.

(*Enter Beauty, Strength, Discretion, and Five Wits.*)

670   BEAUTY: Here at your will we be all ready.
     What will ye that we should do?
GOOD DEEDS: That ye would with Everyman go,
     And help him in his pilgrimage.
     Advise you, will ye with him or not in that voyage?
675   STRENGTH: We will bring him all thither,
     To his help and comfort, ye may believe me.
DISCRETION: So will we go with him all together.
EVERYMAN: Almighty God, lofed° may thou be!
     I give thee laud that I have hither brought
     Strength, Discretion, Beauty, and Five Wits. Lack I
680   nought.
     And my Good Deeds, with Knowledge clear,
     All be in my company at my will here;
     I desire no more to my business.
STRENGTH: And I, Strength, will by you stand in
          distress,
685   Though thou would in battle fight on the ground.
FIVE WITS: And though it were through the world
          round,
     We will not depart for sweet ne sour.
BEAUTY: No more will I unto death's hour,
     Whatsoever thereof befall.
690   DISCRETION: Everyman, advise you first of all;
     Go with a good advisement and deliberation.
     We all give you virtuous monition°
     That all shall be well.
EVERYMAN: My friends, harken what I will tell:
695   I pray God reward you in his heavenly sphere.
     Now harken, all that be here,
     For I will make my testament
     Here before you all present:
     In alms half my good I will give with my hands twain
700   In the way of charity, with good intent,
     And the other half still shall remain
     In queth,° to be returned there it ought to be.°
     This I do in despite of the fiend of hell,
     To go quit out of his peril°
705   Ever after and this day.
KNOWLEDGE: Everyman, harken what I say:
     Go to priesthood, I you advise,
     And receive of him in any wise°
     The holy sacrament and ointment together.
710   Then shortly see ye turn again hither;
     We will all abide you here.

667. **incontinent:** Immediately. 678. **lofed:** Praised.
692. **monition:** Forewarning. 702. **queth:** Bequest. **returned**
there it ought to be: This line probably refers to restitution—
that is, the restoration to its proper owner of unlawfully
acquired property. 704. **quit out of his peril:** Free out of his
power. 708. **in any wise:** Without fail.

FIVE WITS: Yea, Everyman, hie you that ye ready were.
     There is no emperor, king, duke, ne baron,
     That of God hath commission
     As hath the least priest in the world being;   715
     For of the blessed sacraments pure and benign
     He beareth the keys, and thereof hath the cure°
     For man's redemption—it is ever sure—
     Which God for our soul's medicine
     Gave us out of his heart with great pine.°   720
     Here in this transitory life, for thee and me,
     The blessed sacraments seven there be:
     Baptism, confirmation, with priesthood good,
     And the sacrament of God's precious flesh and
          blood,
     Marriage, the holy extreme unction, and penance;   725
     These seven be good to have in remembrance,
     Gracious sacraments of high divinity.
EVERYMAN: Fain would I receive that holy body,
     And meekly to my ghostly father I will go.
FIVE WITS: Everyman, that is the best that ye can do.   730
     God will you to salvation bring,
     For priesthood exceedeth all other thing:
     To us Holy Scripture they do teach,
     And converteth man from sin heaven to reach;
     God hath to them more power given   735
     Than to any angel that is in heaven.
     With five words° he may consecrate,
     God's body in flesh and blood to make,
     And handleth his Maker between his hands.
     The priest bindeth and unbindeth all bands,   740
     Both in earth and in heaven.
     Thou ministers all the sacraments seven;
     Though we kissed thy feet, thou were worthy;
     Thou art surgeon that cureth sin deadly:
     No remedy we find under God   745
     But all only priesthood.°
     Everyman, God gave priests that dignity,
     And setteth them in his stead among us to be;
     Thus be they above angels in degree.

(*Everyman goes to the priest to receive the last sacra-*
ments.)

KNOWLEDGE: If priests be good, it is so, surely.   750
     But when Jesus hanged on the cross with
          great smart,
     There he gave out of his blessed heart
     The same sacrament in great torment:
     He sold them not to us, that Lord omnipotent.
     Therefore Saint Peter the apostle doth say   755
     That Jesu's curse hath all they
     Which God their Savior do buy or sell,
     Or they for any money do take or tell.°

717. **cure:** Charge. 720. **pine:** Suffering. 737. **five words:**
Hoc est enim Corpus meum ("For this is my body," the words
of the consecration of the body of Christ at Mass). 746.
But all only priesthood: Except only from the priesthood. 755–758. **Therefore Saint Peter . . . do take or tell:**
Reference to the sin of simony, the selling of church offices or
benefits. **tell:** Count out (i.e., sell).

Sinful priests giveth the sinners example bad;
Their children sitteth by other men's fires, I have
760 heard;
And some haunteth women's company
With unclean life, as lusts of lechery:
These be with sin made blind.
FIVE WITS: I trust to God no such may we find;
765 Therefore let us priesthood honor,
And follow their doctrine for our souls' succor.
We be their sheep, and they shepherds be
By whom we all be kept in surety.
Peace, for yonder I see Everyman come,
770 Which hath made true satisfaction.
GOOD DEEDS: Methink it is he indeed.

(*Reenter Everyman.*)

EVERYMAN: Now Jesu be your alder speed!°
I have received the sacrament for my redemption,
And then mine extreme unction:
775 Blessed be all they that counselled me to take it!
And now, friends, let us go without longer
respite;
I thank God that ye have tarried so long.
Now set each of you on this rood° your hand,
And shortly follow me:
780 I go before there I would be; God be our guide!
STRENGTH: Everyman, we will not from you go
Till ye have done this voyage long.
DISCRETION: I, Discretion, will bide by you also.
KNOWLEDGE: And though this pilgrimage be never so
strong,°
785 I will never part you fro.
STRENGTH: Everyman, I will be as sure by thee
As ever I did by Judas Maccabee.°

(*Everyman comes to his grave.*)

EVERYMAN: Alas, I am so faint I may not stand;
My limbs under me doth fold.
790 Friends, let us not turn again to this land,
Not for all the world's gold;
For into this cave must I creep
And turn to earth, and there to sleep.
BEAUTY: What, into this grave? Alas!
EVERYMAN: Yea, there shall ye consume, more
795 and less.
BEAUTY: And what, should I smother here?
EVERYMAN: Yea, by my faith, and never more appear.
In this world live no more we shall,
But in heaven before the highest Lord of all.
800 BEAUTY: I cross out all this;° adieu, by Saint John!

Scene from the Guthrie Theater production of *Everyman*,
directed by Robert Benedetti.

I take my cap in my lap,° and am gone.
EVERYMAN: What, Beauty, whither will ye?
BEAUTY: Peace, I am deaf; I look not behind me,
Not and thou wouldest give me all the gold in thy
chest.

(*Exit Beauty.*)

---

772. **your alder speed:** The helper of you all.   778. **rood:**
Cross.   784. **strong:** Grievous.   787. **Judas Maccabee:** Judas
Maccabeus, who overcame Syrian domination and won religious freedom for the Jews in 165 BCE, believed that his strength
came not from worldly might but from heaven (1 Maccabees
3:19).   800. **I cross out all this:** I cancel all this (i.e., my promise to stay with you).

801. **I take my cap in my lap:** Doff my cap (so low that it comes)
into my lap.

805 EVERYMAN: Alas, whereto may I trust?
Beauty goeth fast away from me;
She promised with me to live and die.
STRENGTH: Everyman, I will thee also forsake and
deny;
Thy game liketh° me not at all.
810 EVERYMAN: Why, then, ye will forsake me all?
Sweet Strength, tarry a little space.
STRENGTH: Nay, sir, by the rood of grace!
I will hie me from thee fast,
Though thou weep till thy heart to-brast.°
815 EVERYMAN: Ye would ever bide by me, ye said.
STRENGTH: Yea, I have you far enough conveyed.
Ye be old enough, I understand,
Your pilgrimage to take on hand;
I repent me that I hither came.
820 EVERYMAN: Strength, you to displease I am to blame;
Yet promise is debt, this ye well wot.
STRENGTH: In faith, I care not.
Thou art but a fool to complain;
You spend your speech and waste your brain.
825 Go thrust thee into the ground!   (*Exit Strength.*)
EVERYMAN: I had wend surer I should you have
found.
He that trusteth in his Strength
She him deceiveth at the length.
Both Strength and Beauty forsaketh me;
830 Yet they promised me fair and lovingly.
DISCRETION: Everyman, I will after Strength be
gone;
As for me, I will leave you alone.
EVERYMAN: Why, Discretion, will ye forsake me?
DISCRETION: Yea, in faith, I will go from thee,
835 For when Strength goeth before
I follow after evermore.
EVERYMAN: Yet, I pray thee, for the love of the Trinity,
Look in my grave once piteously.
DISCRETION: Nay, so nigh will I not come;
840 Farewell, every one!   (*Exit Discretion.*)
EVERYMAN: O, all thing faileth, save God alone—
Beauty, Strength, and Discretion;
For when Death bloweth his blast,
They all run from me full fast.
845 FIVE WITS: Everyman, my leave now of thee I take;
I will follow the other, for here I thee forsake.
EVERYMAN: Alas, then may I wail and weep,
For I took you for my best friend.
FIVE WITS: I will no longer thee keep;
850 Now farewell, and there an end.   (*Exit Five Wits.*)
EVERYMAN: O Jesu, help! All hath forsaken me.
GOOD DEEDS: Nay, Everyman; I will bide with thee.
I will not forsake thee indeed;
Thou shalt find me a good friend at need.
EVERYMAN: Gramercy, Good Deeds! Now may I true
855 friends see.
They have forsaken me, every one;

I loved them better than my Good Deeds alone.
Knowledge, will ye forsake me also?
KNOWLEDGE: Yea, Everyman, when ye to Death shall go;
But not yet, for no manner of danger.   860
EVERYMAN: Gramercy, Knowledge, with all my heart.
KNOWLEDGE: Nay, yet I will not from hence depart
Till I see where ye shall become.
EVERYMAN: Methink, alas, that I must be gone
To make my reckoning and my debts pay,   865
For I see my time is nigh spent away.
Take example, all ye that this do hear or see,
How they that I loved best do forsake me,
Except my Good Deeds that bideth truly.
GOOD DEEDS: All earthly things is but vanity: 870
Beauty, Strength, and Discretion do man forsake,
Foolish friends, and kinsmen, that fair spake—
All fleeth save Good Deeds, and that am I.
EVERYMAN: Have mercy on me, God most mighty;
And stand by me, thou mother and maid, holy
Mary.   875
GOOD DEEDS: Fear not; I will speak for thee.
EVERYMAN: Here I cry God mercy.
GOOD DEEDS: Short our end, and minish our pain;
Let us go and never come again.
EVERYMAN: Into thy hands, Lord, my soul I
commend;   880
Receive it, Lord, that it be not lost.
As thou me boughtest, so me defend,
And save me from the fiend's boast,
That I may appear with that blessed host
That shall be saved at the day of doom.   885
In manus tuas, of mights most
For ever, *commendo spiritum meum.*°

(*He sinks into his grave.*)

KNOWLEDGE: Now hath he suffered that we all shall
endure;
The Good Deeds shall make all sure.
Now hath he made ending;   890
Methinketh that I hear angels sing,
And make great joy and melody
Where Everyman's soul received shall be.
ANGEL: Come, excellent elect spouse, to Jesu!
Hereabove thou shalt go   895
Because of thy singular virtue.
Now the soul is taken the body fro,
Thy reckoning is crystal-clear.
Now shalt thou into the heavenly sphere,
Unto the which all ye shall come   900
That liveth well before the day of doom.

(*Enter Doctor.*)

DOCTOR: This moral men may have in mind.
Ye hearers, take it of worth, old and young,
And forsake Pride, for he deceiveth you in the end;

---

809. **liketh:** Pleases.   814. **brast:** Break.

886–887. *In manus tuas . . . commendo spiritum meum:* Into
your hands, most mighty One for ever, I commend my spirit.

And remember Beauty, Five Wits, Strength, and
905   Discretion,
They all at the last do every man forsake,
Save his Good Deeds there doth he take.
But beware, for and they be small
Before God, he hath no help at all;
910   None excuse may be there for every man.
Alas, how shall he do then?
For after death amends may no man make,
For then mercy and pity doth him forsake.
If his reckoning be not clear when he doth come,

God will say: "*Ite, maledicti, in ignem eternum.*"°   915
And he that hath his account whole and sound,
High in heaven he shall be crowned;
Unto which place God bring us all thither,
That we may live body and soul together.
Thereto help the Trinity!   920
Amen, say ye, for saint charity.

Thus endeth this moral play of Everyman.

915: "*Ite maledicti, in ignem eternum*": Depart, ye cursed,
into everlasting fire.

Renaissance Drama

The period following the Middle Ages in Europe, from about the fourteenth to the seventeenth centuries, is known as the *Renaissance,* a term meaning "rebirth." In this period, a shift away from medieval values and culture was motivated by a revival of classical learning; advances in physics, astronomy, and the biological sciences; exploration of the "New World" of the Americas; and political and economic developments. This shift was not abrupt, however; it was gradual, like a thaw. It began in the south, in Italy, late in the fourteenth century and moved northward through the activities of scholars, travelers, performers, and writers, until it reached England sometime late in the fifteenth century.

The Renaissance built on medieval culture and at the same time developed a secular understanding of the individual in society that eventually transformed this culture, long dominated by the Roman Catholic Church in many spheres—artistic, intellectual, political, as well as spiritual. The transformation was influenced by the work of great writers, scholars, philosophers, and scientists such as Desiderius Erasmus (1466?–1536), Niccolò Machiavelli (1469–1527), Nicolaus Copernicus (1473–1543), Francis Bacon (1561–1626), and Galileo Galilei (1564–1642). In addition, the rise in power of the guilds and the increase in wealth of the successful Italian trading states, which produced large and influential families in cities such as Florence, Venice, Milan, and Genoa, contributed to the erosion of the Church's dominance.

Italian scholars, following classical models, began in the last decades of the fourteenth century to center their studies on human achievements. Such studies, known as the humanities, became the chief concern of the most innovative thinkers of the day. Their interests were well served by the rediscovery of ancient Greek philosophical and scientific texts. Although ancient texts had been preserved in monasteries for centuries, knowledge of them was restricted. A new demand for classical texts, fed by the humanists' focus on ancient models as the source of wisdom and by their return to a liberal arts curriculum established by the Greeks, led to the wide dissemination of the works of Plato, Aristotle, Cicero, and important Greek dramatists during the Renaissance. The achievement of the ancients was an inspiration to Renaissance writers and reaffirmed their conviction that a study of the humanities was the key to transforming the old medieval attitudes into a new, dynamic worldview.

The Italian Theater

Most medieval Italian theater depended on portable stages, but it was clear in the last decades of the fourteenth century that to present the newly rediscovered Roman or Greek plays, something more closely resembling the original Greek theater would be necessary. Fortunately, *The Ten Books of Architecture* (written c. 16–13 BCE) of the great Roman architect Vitruvius was rediscovered in a manuscript in the monastery of St. Gall in Switzerland. It included detailed plans for the Greek-inspired Roman theater.

Using Vitruvius's designs, the Italians began building stages that consisted of raised platforms with a **frons scaena**, the flat front wall used in the Roman theater. The earliest Italian woodcuts show the stages to be relatively simple, with pillars supporting a roof or cover. Curtains stretched between the pillars permitted the actors to enter and exit. Usually, three "doors," with a name over each, indicated the houses of specific characters.

The study of Roman architecture eventually produced, in 1584, one of the wonders of the Renaissance, the Olympic Theatre (Teatro Olimpico) in Vicenza, designed by the great Renaissance architect Andrea Palladio (1508–1580), whose interpretation of Roman architecture was so compelling that it influenced architecture all over the world (Figure 9). The Olympic Theatre, which has been preserved and is still used for performances, has an orchestra, a semicircular seating area, and a multistory frons scaena. It also has several vistas of streets constructed in three-dimensional forced perspective running backward from the frons scaena.

The Olympic Theatre was built with an essentially conservative design that worked well for Roman plays but not for Renaissance plays. It did not inspire new theater designs. In newer theaters, Italian plays had begun to use scenery and painted backdrops that could be changed to suggest a change in location of the action. Carefully painted backdrops were also effective in increasing illusion: one backdrop could immediately locate an action on a city street, and another could help shift the audience imaginatively to a woodland scene. These innovations proved difficult to implement in the Olympic Theatre.

The theory of vanishing-point perspective, developed by the architect Filippo Brunelleschi (1377–1446) and published by Leon Battista Alberti in *On Painting* in 1435, helped revolutionize the design of flat theatrical backdrops. Earlier Renaissance painters had had no way to establish a firm sense of perspective on a flat surface, so all three-dimensional objects appeared flat; all space in a landscape or cityscape seemed shortened and unreal. The use of a single vanishing point—in which lines were lightly drawn from the edges of the canvas (or theatrical backdrop) so that they met in a single point in the center—made it possible to show buildings, trees, and figures in their proper proportion to one another (Figure 10). For the first time, Renaissance painters could achieve lifelike illusions on a flat surface. It was possible to use three-dimensional scenery in the Olympic Theatre—as well as some others—at this time, and the illusion of reality was thus intensified.

The designer Sebastiano Serlio (1475–1554) used the vanishing-point technique, intensified by receding lines of tiles in the floor and on the painted backdrop. Serlio established all-purpose settings for comedy, tragedy, and satire. The rigidity of the backdrops for comedy and tragedy—both used a piazza, a small town square, ringed by stone buildings—restricted their use. But the setting for satire was rustic: trees, bushes, a couple of cottages. Until the nineteenth century, European theaters were equipped with sets of backdrops and wingpieces derived from Serlio's designs.

Figure 9. Designed by Andrea Palladio, the Teatro Olimpico (begun 1579) in Vicenza, Italy, was the first indoor theater of the Renaissance. The scaena's openings produced an illusion of depth.

The most important and long-lasting development of Italian theater design in the mid-sixteenth century was the **proscenium arch**, a "frame" that surrounds the stage, permitting the audience to look in on the scene, whether in a room or in a town square. The arch lent a finished touch to the theater, separating the action from the audience and distancing the actors. The proscenium arch is common in theaters today.

Commedia dell'Arte

Renaissance Italy had two traditions of theater. *Commedia erudita* was learned, almost scholarly, in its interests in Roman staging and Roman plays. **Commedia dell'arte** was less reverent, more slapstick, and generally more popular. It is difficult, however, to say which had more influence on literature over the years. Each made its contribution.

In terms of acting and storytelling, the influence of the commedia dell'arte is almost unparalleled. The term means "comedy performed by professionals." The actors usually had grown up in performing families that made their living touring the countryside, performing at fairs and on feast days. From the early Renaissance through the eighteenth century, the commedia dell'arte entertained all of Europe and influenced comic theater in every nation.

The essence of commedia dell'arte was improvised scripts. A general narrative outline served as a basis, but the speeches were improvised to a degree (with some reliance on set elements and on experience with performing the same role many times). The principal characters were types who soon became familiar all over Europe: Pantalone, the often magisterial but miserly old man, and Arlecchino (Harlequin), the cunning clown. Pulcinella, the Punch of Punch and Judy, and Columbina, the innocent *zanni* (servant characters), began as clowns. They joined a host of other **stock characters** such as pedantic lawyers, a braggart captain, and a serving maid. Certain versions of general characters—such as Arlecchino, who began as a simple *zanno*—became famous and were copied in many countries. When Volpone calls Mosca a "zany" near the end of Ben Jonson's *Volpone*, he reminds his audience that his characters are indebted to the *zanni* in commedia dell'arte. Knowing who the characters were even before the play began was a convenience that Renaissance audiences enjoyed.

Figure 10. Perspective setting designed by Baldassare Peruzzi (1481–1536).

The youthful lovers in the commedia did not require masks, but the old men, the *zanni,* and other characters all had masks that identified them and made them look, to modern eyes, rather grotesque. These masks survive today in the carnival, in Venice, where the commedia began. Stock characters thrive in popular comedies everywhere. Molière and, much later, Bernard Shaw depended on them. One of comedy's greatest sources of energy lies in the delight that audiences have always taken in stock characters. Today hardly a situation comedy on television could survive without them.

The staging of commedia dell'arte was simple. The performances often took place in open air, but sometimes indoors in a more formal theatrical setting. Sometimes performers dispensed with the stage altogether and worked in marketplaces. Their scenarios were farcical crowd pleasers filled with buffoonery. They were based on the **burla** and the **lazzo**. The *burla* was the general plot for any given performance. *Lazzi* were comic routines something like Abbott and Costello's "Who's on First?" skit. Abbott and Costello developed their routine for burlesque, a form of comedy popular in the first half of the twentieth century centering on broad gags, routines, and running jokes. *Lazzi* were carefully planned to seem to be spontaneous interruptions of the action.

Elizabethan Drama

The reign of Queen Elizabeth I (1558–1603) is known as the Elizabethan Age in England — a period of discovery and prosperity as well as a period of great achievement in the arts, especially drama. Sir Francis Drake and Sir Walter Raleigh ventured across the Atlantic Ocean to the "New World," and England secured its economic future by defeating the invasion attempt of the Spanish Armada in 1588. England had become Protestant in the 1530s — one reason Catholic Spain believed it needed to subdue the nation.

Elizabethan England, especially after the defeat of the Armada, produced one of the great ages of drama, rivaling the great age of Greece. During this period, playwrights such as Thomas Kyd (1558–1594), Christopher Marlowe (1564–1593), William Shakespeare (1564–1616), Ben Jonson (1572–1637), John Marston (1576–1634), John Fletcher (1579–1625), John Webster (1580?–1625?), Thomas Middleton (1580?–1627), and John Ford (1586?–c. 1639) drew crowds by the thousands.

That the Elizabethans enjoyed plays with a moral basis is plain from the fact that so much of the great drama of the late sixteenth century and early seventeenth century is moral in character. Still, early Elizabethan plays were less obviously moralistic than the then-popular morality plays. They did not aim specifically to teach a moral lesson, although there are many lessons to be learned from Shakespeare and his contemporaries.

During Shakespeare's youth, wandering players put on a number of plays from **repertory**, their stock of perhaps a dozen current plays they could perform. How many players there were and what their source of plays was we do not know. Much of what we know comes directly from *Hamlet* and the appearance of the players who perform Hamlet's "Mouse-trap." What we learn there tells us that dramatic styles had developed in the English countryside and that theater was thriving.

The Elizabethan Theater

The design of the Elizabethan theater is a matter of some speculation. Many of the plays popular before the theaters were built were performed in a square inn yard, with a balcony above. Audience members looked out their windows or stood in the yard. One location of the earliest English drama is the Inns of Court, essentially a college for law students in London, where students staged plays. The audience there would have been learned, bright, and imaginative. Indeed, the first English tragedy, *Gorboduc,* by Thomas Sackville and Thomas Norton, was played indoors at the Inner Temple, one of the Inns of Court, in 1562, before Marlowe and Shakespeare were born.

The early theaters were often octagonal or circular, like the bear pits in which bears, tied to stakes, were baited by dogs for the amusement of the audience. The stage was raised about five feet from the ground, with levels of seating in several galleries. Approximately half the area over the stage was roofed and contained machinery to lower actors from the "heavens"; it was painted blue with stars to simulate the sky. Some stages were approximately twenty-five by forty feet. Doors or curtained openings at the back of the stage served for entrances and exits, and at the back of the stage was a special room for costume changes. The stage may have contained a section that was normally curtained but that opened to reveal an interior, such as a bedroom. The existence of this feature is, however, in considerable dispute.

Although professional players' groups had long been licensed to perform in France and Italy, until the 1570s professional actors—those who had no other trade—did not enjoy favor in England. Such people could be arrested for vagrancy. The law, however, changed, and actors with royal patronage were permitted to perform. The history of theater changed, too. In 1576, James Burbage (d. 1597) built the first building made specially for plays in England, called simply The Theatre.

Soon there were other theaters: the Swan, the Globe (Figure 11), the Rose, the Fortune, the Hope. The Globe was large enough to accommodate two to three thousand people. Because these theaters were open-air, they could not be used in winter, but all were extraordinarily successful. Shakespeare, who was part owner of the Globe and, later, of the second indoor Blackfriars Theatre, received money from admission fees and from his role as chief playwright. He became rich enough to retire in splendid style to Stratford, his hometown. Few other Elizabethan actors and playwrights had as much of a financial stake in their work as did Shakespeare.

The Elizabethan Actor

In the early 1500s, professional companies roamed the countryside with, usually, four actors and a boy who could play the female roles. They may have been accompanied by musicians. They found work where they could, and sometimes they stirred up controversy and were prevented from performing. Numerous laws enacted to restrict them were rarely enforced. Queen Elizabeth issued a license for a professional company to James Burbage in 1576, the year he built the first theater in England. Burbage's son, Richard Burbage (1567–1619), who was born in Stratford-on-Avon (like Shakespeare, his partner in the theater), became one of the most distinguished actors of the age. He played all the important tragic roles in Shakespeare's plays. By the time the Globe Theatre was built in 1599, their company, The Chamberlain's Men, included some of the

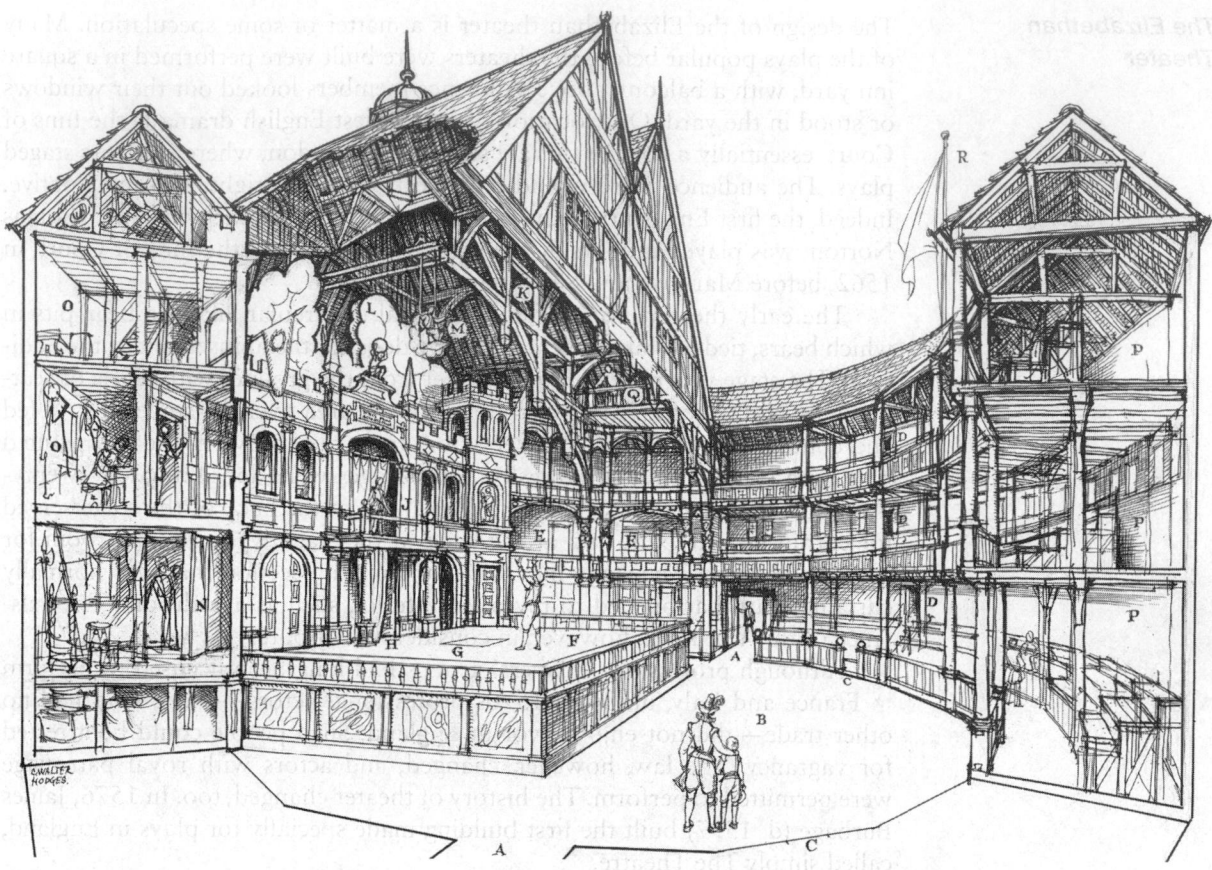

Figure 11. A conjectural reconstruction of the (second) Globe Theatre, 1614–1644.

AA	Main entrances to auditorium	L	Backing painted with clouds. A shutter is here shown open to allow a god's throne to travel forward. (c.f. "Cymbeline," Act V sc. IV)
B	Yard for standing spectators		
CC	Entrances to lowest gallery		
DD	Entrances to staircase leading to upper galleries	M	The throne about to descend to the stage
EE	"Gentlemen's Rooms"	N	Backstage area (or "Tiring-house")
F	The stage	O	Wardrobe and dressing-rooms
G	The stage trap (leading from the "Hell" beneath the stage)	P	Spectator galleries
		Q	"Fly" gallery in the Heavens
H	Curtained space for "discovery" scenes	R	Playhouse flag (reached from top landing of staircase, and raised to denote performance days)
J	Upper stage		
K	The "Heavens." (This area was probably covered with a stretched canopy that was painted to represent the sky.)		

most acclaimed actors of the day. One of them, Will Kempe (fl. 1600), was the most noted comic actor of the age (Figure 12). He was both a gifted clown and a brilliant dancer. However, as popular as he was with the audience, he left the company suddenly for reasons still unknown and acted elsewhere. His great roles—the Fool in *King Lear*, the first grave digger in *Hamlet,* and Dogberry in *Much Ado About Nothing*—were filled by another actor, Robert Armin (1568–1615), whose reputation grew as large as Kempe's.

Figure 12. William Kempe, a principal comic actor in Shakespeare's earlier plays, is shown dancing next to a musician.

The popularity of actors such as Burbage, Kempe, and Armin indicates how powerful and far-reaching the stage was in Elizabethan England. Despite their successes, actors were still regarded as somewhat disreputable, and stories were told of actors disguised as royalty stopping in a tavern for a drink and fooling the populace, who grew surly at such tricks.

The contemporary styles of acting were probably developed by wandering players throughout the early and mid-sixteenth century—and perhaps even earlier. In *Hamlet*, Shakespeare introduces a group of roaming players and offers us a sample of their high-style formal dialogue, which contrasts sharply with Shakespeare's dialogue. Hamlet critiques and instructs the players, whose style is overdone. In the open-air theaters, this style of acting seems to have evolved into a declamatory mode, in which the actor stands and makes his voice heard throughout the large and sometimes noisy audience. The style Hamlet critiques is probably one that he saw on stages in London. Many of the Elizabethan actors played to the audience as much as they related to each other, a trait that seems to have developed in response to the structure of the stage, with the audience on three sides and with some notables actually sitting on the stage itself. In contrast to many theaters, the Globe Theatre reportedly permitted actors to speak more naturally to one another and thus to render a more realistic performance.

The Elizabethan Audience

The entrance fee to the theaters was a penny, probably the equivalent of five to ten dollars in today's money. For another penny one could take a seat, probably on a bench, in one of the upper galleries. In some theaters, more private spaces were available as well. A great many playgoers were satisfied to stand around the stage and were thus nicknamed "groundlings." Hamlet calls them the "understanding gentlemen of the ground." The more academic playwrights, Marlowe and Jonson, used the term to mean those who would not perfectly understand the significance of the plays.

Shakespeare and other Elizabethan playwrights expected a widely diverse audience—from coarse to extraordinarily polished. Shakespeare had the gift, as did Marlowe and even Jonson in his comedies, to appeal to them all. Shakespeare's plays were given in public playhouses open to everyone. They were also given in university theaters, as in the case of *Macbeth;* in indoor private theaters; and in royal command performances. Shakespeare's universality reveals itself in his appeal to many different kinds of people.

Female Characters on the English Stage

Because the theater was considered morally questionable, women were not allowed to act on English stages. Boys and young men played the parts of young female characters. No Elizabethan commentator makes any complaint about having to put up with a boy playing the part of Juliet or any of Shakespeare's other love interests, such as Desdemona in *Othello,* Ophelia in *Hamlet,* or even Queen Cleopatra. Older women, such as the Nurse in *Romeo and Juliet,* were played by some of the gifted male character actors of the company.

The Masque

The Elizabethan **masque** was a special entertainment for royalty. It was a celebration that included a rudimentary plot, a great deal of singing and dancing, and magnificent costumes and lighting. Masques were usually performed only once, often to celebrate a royal marriage. Masque audiences participated in the dances and were usually delighted by complex machinery that lifted or lowered characters from the skies. The masque was devised in Italy in the 1570s by Count Giovanni Bardi, founder of the Florentine Camerata, a Renaissance group of theatergoers sponsored by Lorenzo de' Medici.

The geniuses of the masque are generally considered to have been Ben Jonson and Inigo Jones. Jones was the architect whose Banqueting Hall at Whitehall in London, which still stands, provided the setting for most of the great masques of the seventeenth century. Jonson and Jones worked together from 1605 to 1631 to produce a remarkable body of masques that today resemble the bones of a dinosaur: what we read on the page suggests in only the vaguest way what the presentation must have been like when the masques were mounted.

Because of the expenses of costuming and staging, most masques were too costly to be produced more than once. The royal treasury was often burdened in Queen Elizabeth's time, and more so after King James took the throne in 1603. Masque costumes were impressive, the scenery astounding, and the effects amazing. In all of this, the words—which are, after all, at the center of Shakespeare's plays as well as other plays of the period—were of least account. As a result of the emphasis on the machinery and designs—the work of Inigo Jones—Jonson abandoned their partnership in a huff, complaining that he could not compete with the scene painters and carpenters.

The value placed on spectacle in the masques tells us something about the taste of the aristocrats, who enjoyed sumptuous foods, clothes, and amusements. Eventually, audiences of the public theaters hungered for spectacle, too. Their appetite was satisfied by masques inserted in the plays of Marston, Webster, and Shakespeare, whose masque in *The Tempest* is a delightful short tribute to the genre. An added device for achieving spectacular effects onstage was huge storm machines installed in the Globe. Some say that one reason Shakespeare wrote *The Tempest* was to take advantage of the new equipment.

Foreign visitors described London theaters as gorgeous places of entertainment far surpassing their own. The quest for more intense spectacle eventually led to disaster in one theater. The Globe actually burned down in 1613 because a cannon in the roof above the stage misfired and brought the house down in real flames.

The royal demand for masques was unaffected by the tragedy of the Globe fire. As Francis Bacon said in his essay "On Masques" (1625), "These things are but toys to come amongst such serious observations. But yet, since princes will have such things, it is better they should be graced with elegancy than daubed with cost. Dancing to song is a thing of great state and pleasure."

Spanish Drama

The Spanish independently developed a corral, or open theatrical space, resembling the Elizabethan inn yard, in which they produced plays. This development may have been an accident of architecture—because of the widespread need for inns and for places to store horses—that permitted the symmetry of growth of the English Elizabethan and the Spanish Golden Age theaters.

The most important playwright of the Spanish theater was Lope de Vega (1562–1635), who is said to have written twelve hundred plays (seven hundred fifty survive). Many of them are relatively brief, and some resemble the scenarios for the commedia dell'arte. A good number, though, are full-length and impressive works, such as *The Sheep Well*, *The King*, *The Greatest Alcalde*, and *The Gardener's Dog*. Pedro Calderón de la Barca (1600–1681) became, on Lope de Vega's death, the reigning Spanish playwright. His *Life Is a Dream* is performed regularly throughout the world. Calderón became a priest in 1651 and wrote religious plays that occasionally got him into trouble with the Inquisition, an agency of the Catholic Church that searched out and punished heresy. He was especially imaginative in his use of stage machinery and especially gifted in producing philosophical and poetic dialogue.

Renaissance Drama

Date	Theater	Political	Social/Cultural
1300–1400	**1377–1446:** Filippo Brunelleschi, an Italian architect, develops vanishing-point perspective, which allows theatrical scenery to be drawn in realistic proportions.		**1348–1353:** Boccaccio's *Decameron* becomes a model for Italian prose. **c. 1386–1466:** Donatello, Italian painter and major innovator in Renaissance sculpture
1400–1500	**1414:** Rediscovery of Vitruvius's *De Architectura* (16–13 BCE). After its publication in 1486, the treatise significantly influences the development of staging practices. **1495:** The Dutch morality play *Elckerlijk* by Peter Dorland van Diest, possibly the prototype for the English *Everyman*	**1494:** The Parliament of Drogheda marks the subservience of Ireland to England.	**1450:** Florence under the Medici family becomes the center of the Renaissance and humanism. **1452–1519:** Leonardo da Vinci, brilliant inventor, architect, musician, and artist **1469–1527:** Niccolò Machiavelli, who writes the political treatise *The Prince* in 1513 and the comedy *Mandragola* between 1513 and 1520 **1473–1543:** Nicolaus Copernicus, founder of modern astronomy **1496:** Henry VII commissions Venetian navigator John Cabot (1450–1498) to discover a new trade route to Asia. **1497:** Cabot reaches the east coast of North America. **1497:** Vasco da Gama (c. 1469–1524) rounds the Cape of Good Hope.
1500–1600	**1508:** Vernacular drama begins in Italy with Ludovico Ariosto's *The Casket*. **1508:** The Hôtel de Bourgogne, a permanent theater building, opens in Paris. **1512:** The word *masque* is first used to denote a poetic drama. **1550–1650:** Golden Age of Spanish drama. The two principal playwrights are Lope de Vega (1562–1635) and Pedro Calderón de la Barca (1600–1681).	**1503:** James IV of Scotland marries Margaret Tudor, daughter of Henry VII. **1517:** Martin Luther protests the sale of indulgences by posting his 95 theses on a church door in Wittenberg, Germany, thus launching the Protestant Reformation in Germany. **1534:** Henry VIII (reigned 1509–1547) breaks with the Roman Catholic Church. **1535:** Henry VIII's Act of Supremacy names him head of the Church of England. Sir Thomas More is executed after refusing to comply with the Act.	**1507:** Pope Julius II announces the sale of indulgences to finance the rebuilding of St. Peter's Basilica in Rome. **1509–1564:** John Calvin, Swiss reformer **c. 1509:** A massive slave trade begins in the New World. **1512:** Copernicus's *Commentariolus* states that the earth and other planets turn around the sun. **1514–1564:** Andreas Vesalius, Dutch physician, founder of modern anatomy **1516–1547:** Henry Howard, Earl of Surrey, English poet **1519:** Hernando Cortés enters Tenochtitlán, capital of Mexico; is received by Montezuma, the Aztec ruler; and assumes control of Mexico in 1521. **1522:** Luther translates the New Testament into German. (He translates the Old Testament in 1534.) **1547–1616:** Miguel de Cervantes, author of the novel *Don Quixote* and many plays

Date	Theater	Political	Social/Cultural
1500–1600 (continued)	**1558–1594:** Playwright Thomas Kyd, author of *The Spanish Tragedy* (c. 1587)	**1547:** Ivan IV (the Terrible) becomes czar of Russia. Moscow is destroyed by fire in the same year.	**c. 1552–1599:** Edmund Spenser, English poet, author of *Faerie Queene*
	1562: The First English tragedy, *Gorboduc,* is performed at the Inns of Court.	**1553–1558:** Reign of Mary I of England. The country returns temporarily to Catholicism.	**1554–1586:** Sir Philip Sidney, poet and soldier, author of *An Apology for Poetry*
	1564–1593: Christopher Marlowe, author of *Doctor Faustus* (c. 1588), *Tamburlaine* (1587), and *Edward the Second* (c. 1592)	**1558–1603:** Reign of Elizabeth I in England. Protestantism becomes the religion of the realm. England emerges as a world power.	**1561–1626:** Francis Bacon, English philosopher and statesman
	1564–1616: William Shakespeare		**1564–1642:** Galileo Galilei, Italian astronomer
	c. 1568: Formation of the Italian commedia dell'arte company I Gelosi	**1570:** Japan opens the port of Nagasaki to trade with the West.	**1571–1630:** Johannes Kepler, German astronomer. His laws accurately describe the revolutions of the planets around the sun.
	1572–1637: Playwright Ben Jonson, author of *Volpone* (1605) and *Bartholomew Fair* (1614)	**1572:** At the Saint Bartholomew's Day Massacre in France, thousands of Protestants are killed.	**1572–1631:** John Donne, English metaphysical poet
	1574: The Earl of Leicester's Men, the first important acting troupe in London, is licensed.		
	1575: *Gammer Gurton's Needle,* early English farce, author unknown		
	1576: James Burbage builds The Theatre for the public performance of plays. Blackfriars, London's first private theater, is also built.		
	1577: John Northbrooke publishes *A Treatise against Dicing, Dancing, Plays, and Interludes,* one of several tracts attacking the growing professional theater.		**1577:** *Chronicles of England, Scotland and Ireland* is published by Raphael Holinshed and provides Shakespeare with information for his historical plays.
	1580–1627: Playwright Thomas Middleton, author of *The Changeling* (with William Rowley, 1622) *and A Chaste Maid in Cheapside* (1630)		**1580:** Sir Francis Drake is the first Englishman to circumnavigate the globe.
	1584: Completion of the Teatro Olimpico in Vicenza, Italy, designed by architect Andrea Palladio (1508–1580)	**1587:** The Catholic Mary Stuart, queen of Scotland, is executed in England.	**1583:** Sir Philip Sidney's *Defence of Poesy* argues for literature's importance in teaching morality and virtue.
	1586?–c. 1639: Playwright John Ford, author of *'Tis Pity She's a Whore* (1633)	**1587–1649:** John Winthrop, first governor of the Massachusetts Bay Colony	
		1588: The English fleet defeats the Spanish Armada.	
		1589: Henry IV, first of the Bourbon line, becomes king of France.	

Date	Theater	Political	Social/Cultural
1500–1600 (continued)	**1593:** London theaters are closed because of a plague, opening again in 1594.	**1589:** Russian czar Boris Godunov separates Moscow's church from that in Constantinople.	
	1595–1596: Shakespeare's comedy *A Midsummer Night's Dream*	**1595:** The Dutch begin to colonize the East Indies.	
		1598: The Edict of Nantes grants French Huguenots freedom of worship. (It is revoked in 1685.)	**1596–1650:** René Descartes, French philosopher, mathematician, and scientist
	1599: The Globe Theatre is built in London.		
1600–1700	**1600–1601:** Shakespeare's *Hamlet*	**1603:** Death of Elizabeth I. James VI of Scotland, son of Mary Stuart, becomes James I of England.	**1600:** Dutch opticians invent the telescope.
			1602: The Dutch East India Company is established to trade with the Far East.
	1611–1612: Shakespeare's *The Tempest*	**1605:** The Gunpowder Plot, an attempt to blow up the English Parliament and James I, is uncovered.	**1606–1669:** Rembrandt van Rijn, greatest master of the Dutch school of painting
	1613: Fire destroys the Globe Theatre.	**1618–1648:** The Thirty Years War is initiated by a Protestant revolt in Bohemia against the authority of the Holy Roman emperor.	**1607:** Jamestown, Virginia, the first permanent settlement across the Atlantic, is founded.
			1608–1674: John Milton, English poet, author of *Paradise Lost*
		1625: Death of James I. His son becomes Charles I of England.	**1611:** The King James Bible is published.
		1630: John Winthrop founds Boston.	**1619:** The first slaves from Africa arrive in Virginia.
	1633: The Oberammergau Passion play is first performed in Germany.	**1642:** Civil war begins in England.	**1620:** The Pilgrims land at Plymouth Rock, Massachusetts.
		1643: Louis XIV becomes king of France at age four.	**1626:** Peter Minuit purchases Manhattan Island from native Indian chiefs.
		1649: Charles I is beheaded in England, beginning the Commonwealth and Protectorate.	
	1642: The English Parliament closes the theaters.	**1648:** The Treaty of Westphalia ends the Thirty Years War.	**1632–1704:** John Locke, English philosopher, founder of empiricism

Christopher Marlowe

"Had in him those brave translunary things / That the first poets had"

–Michael Drayton

Christopher Marlowe (1564–1593) was born two months before William Shakespeare and in somewhat similar social circumstances. Marlowe's father was a shoemaker, Shakespeare's a glovemaker. But unlike Shakespeare, Marlowe won a scholarship to Cambridge, where he remained six years and began his career as a playwright. His first play, *Tamburlaine*, was finished before he left the university. When it was performed in London, it had the benefit of Edward Alleyn, the finest actor of his time, playing the title role.

The son-in-law of Philip Henslowe, who owned the Rose, the Fortune, and the Hope theaters in London, Alleyn was a rhetorical actor with a commanding voice and gestures. His style was perfect for declaiming what Ben Jonson called Marlowe's "Mighty line": his **iambic pentameter blank verse**, which moves in stately rhythms and dominated the Elizabethan stage. Marlowe's blank verse—especially in the emotional moments of Faustus's career, as in his invocation of the devils in act I, scene iii—resonates and rolls from the tongue in mighty billows. It has a virtually incantatory effect on the listener, and in a London theater of the time, as spoken by Edward Alleyn, it must have been mesmerizing.

Marlowe also had considerable success as a poet and as a translator of the classics. His version of Ovid's *Amores* is very lively, and his long poem *Hero and Leander* is a dynamic contribution to the poetry of Renaissance humanism. It shows his affection for the classics in a form that Shakespeare also employed: the longer narrative poem.

Marlowe's university scholarship was intended for those studying for the ministry, but instead of entering the ministry, he went up to London in 1587. Some of his friends revealed that his beliefs were close to those of atheism, a charge that in his time could have resulted in death. Fortunately, when he applied for his master's degree and was on the verge of having it denied, Queen Elizabeth intervened on his behalf. Her involvement has made subsequent generations think that he must have been a spy on her behalf during at least some of the time he was in Catholic sections of France.

Partly as a result of his connection with Elizabeth, Marlowe has often been portrayed as a romantic swashbuckler in the heart of complex intrigues. He was also well known to most of the literary people of London: Shakespeare, Sir Walter Raleigh, Francis Bacon, Thomas Kyd, and Thomas Harriot (an astronomer and writer) were all close associates. They and Marlowe were also acquainted with the remarkable magician Dr. John Dee. As members of a group dubbed the School of Night, they met privately to discuss ideas of the occult, alchemy, and skeptic philosophy—subjects that could not easily be talked about in the open.

For links to resources about Marlowe, click on *AuthorLinks* at **bedfordstmartins.com/jacobus**.

Marlowe's first play was *Tamburlaine* (1587; in two parts), followed by *The Jew of Malta* (1589) and *Edward the Second* (1592). They are all powerful plays that feature a great tragic character. *The Massacre at Paris* (1593) is based on the St. Bartholomew Day's Massacre in 1572, when some thirty thousand Huguenots—French Protestants—were killed by Catholics in Paris.

Marlowe's knowledge of the details of the events seems to have been considerable, although the play itself is not as powerful as his earlier tragedies. *Dido, Queen of Carthage* (1593; with Thomas Nashe) is a typical collaboration of the period. None of these plays, good as they are, come to the level of *Doctor Faustus,* which stands as one of the greatest plays of the Elizabethan Age.

Apparently quick to anger, Marlowe was involved in one murder before he himself was murdered over a bar bill at the inn of the Widow Bull in Deptford. He was drinking with an acquaintance, Ingram Frizer, who worked for the great Walsingham family, a patron of Marlowe's. During an argument Marlowe grabbed Frizer from behind, but Frizer broke free and stabbed Marlowe, who died instantly. At the time of Marlowe's death, Shakespeare was just beginning his career as a playwright.

Doctor Faustus

Doctor Faustus was probably written between 1588 and 1593, shortly before Marlowe died. There is a record of its being readied for the press in 1601, but if that version was printed, no copies survive. The first printed version, now called the A-text, is from 1604; an amplified version, called the B-text, came out in 1616. Neither had been supervised by Marlowe, and to make things more complicated, records indicate that Philip Henslowe paid two writers a substantial sum to add to the original text. What the additions were—or what the original text was—we probably will never know.

Current scholarship leads us to believe that the 1616 text, printed here, is actually closer to the original acting version than the 1604 text was. The breaking of the text into five acts and their scenes is a modern convention, as is the supplying of most of the stage directions. The five-act pattern common in classical plays is natural to Elizabethan plays as well.

The influence of the medieval stage is readily apparent in *Doctor Faustus.* The emphasis on the devils, the seven deadly sins, and the terrifying vision of hell in act V is reminiscent of the devils of the mystery plays and their reliance on frightening hell's mouth props. The allusion to medieval theater's tradition of the mansion in Mephistophilis's speech in act V also echoes the basic message of the morality plays:

> Ay, Faustus, now thou hast no hope of heaven;
> Therefore despair. Think only upon hell,
> For that must be thy mansion, there to dwell.

Doctor Faustus differs from the morality plays in one very important way, though. We are never led to think that Faustus would have lived a better or more interesting life if he had restrained his ambition. Faustus is a hero, especially of the romantic sort that strove to achieve great things and challenge the gods. The Elizabethans admired Faustus much more than they condemned him, no matter what moral tags Marlowe might have put in the play to satisfy society's official view of itself.

Among the sources of the play are a medieval folklore tradition connected with the wizard who sold his soul to the devil for greater powers and a German

For discussion questions and assignments on *Doctor Faustus,* visit **bedfordstmartins.com/jacobus.**

book called *Historia von D. Johan Fausten,* published in 1587. Marlowe may have seen the book or, more likely, an English translation of 1592 called *The History of the Damnable Life, and Deserved Death of Doctor John Faustus.* In any event, the Faust legend goes back to the early medieval period and could have reached Marlowe in any number of ways.

But *Doctor Faustus* has a modern twist that takes it out of the medieval mold. The Renaissance was a period of expansion, especially the expansion of knowledge. Astronomy was symbolic of the new age: telescopes were beginning to give Europeans a sense of the vastness and complexity of the universe. When Faustus asks information of Mephistophilis, he begins with questions about the planets and the universe, knowledge of which had long been thought to be somehow secret. Mastering that knowledge was symbolic of mastering the knowledge of the innermost workings of science.

Faustus's quest for knowledge became for some people a Renaissance theme. The magicians referred to in the text, such as Roger Bacon and Cornelius Agrippa, were actual people. Their work was read throughout Europe, and the kinds of magic actions that Faustus aspires to were thought possible. The Elizabethans definitely believed in the presence of spirits, of ghosts, of intervention through witches of the otherworld. *Doctor Faustus* fed the contemporary interest in the occult. Faustus quests for forbidden knowledge; he must sell his soul to the devil to acquire it. His lust for knowledge—he says at the outset that he has dominated all the world of learning available to him—is without bounds.

Doctor Faustus is one of the earliest English tragedies. Its hero is in many ways larger than life, and though not a member of the nobility, he is at ease with royalty and clearly superior in intellectual abilities. The richness of the psychological portrayal of Faustus—as well as of Wagner and Mephistophilis—elevates the play above the best earlier efforts of English and European dramatists. Faustus's University of Wittenberg produced the most important Protestant of the sixteenth century, Martin Luther. His daring—comparable in some ways to Faustus's overreaching—led to the Reformation, one of the most cataclysmic changes in European thought in the Renaissance. Hamlet is also a student at Wittenberg, a fact that gives us insight into the Elizabethan imagination. Wittenberg to the Elizabethans meant fierce intellectual energy and daring.

Like many of Shakespeare's tragedies, *Doctor Faustus* has interludes of comic relief, with the horse coursers who are bilked by Faustus and with other clowns and mechanicals who wonder openly about the terrifying skills of the magician. This linking of magic and comic has annoyed some critics who have agreed with Aristotle that such a mixture is problematic and tends to diffuse the effect of the drama. Actually, in performance the comic scenes are in no way a dilution of effect. They tend to buoy the energy of the play and help us focus anew on the insatiable Faustus.

Many in Marlowe's audience would have seen in Doctor Faustus an allusion to the magus John Dee, who cast the horoscope of Queen Elizabeth. Marlowe knew Dee, on whom the description of Faustus is based. Known throughout Europe for his almost supernormal intellectual capacity, Dee was learned in many sciences. His introduction to the first English edition of Euclid's *Geometry* made him not only respected in Europe but eventually known throughout the New World. Dee's version of Euclid was used at Harvard University until the late eighteenth century. Because Dee was a wizard, his house at Mortlake was attacked and burned to the ground by frightened peasants while he was abroad. With his house went one of the most impressive personal libraries in Europe.

Faustus was willing to seek forbidden knowledge—in the way Adam and Eve did—at all costs, in full awareness that he risked the loss of his soul. And while Marlowe condemns Faustus to hell and does not save him at the end, we have the feeling—as did Elizabethans—that there is something grand and heroic about Faustus's risk taking. He fails, yes, but he does so in a way that makes mediocre citizens who would never have had his imagination or daring seem pallid and weak. We find ourselves involved in Faustus's struggle.

Doctor Faustus in Performance

Marlowe may not have seen *Doctor Faustus* performed. There are no performance records until 1594, when Philip Henslowe and the Royal Admiral's Men produced the play. Productions were frequent until 1598, and Henslowe's records indicate that the play was extremely popular. The great actor Edward Alleyn portrayed Faustus. Along with several reissuings of printed versions of the play, productions seem to have continued into the early part of the seventeenth century, when a number of writers were hired at different times to add lines to the original text. After the Restoration in 1660 and the reopening of the theaters, *Doctor Faustus* was again played frequently, with Thomas Betterton in the title role. In the eighteenth century, the play was sometimes staged as a farce and in some cases reduced to a puppet show. In the nineteenth century, however, audiences were given the chance to see the play as a serious tragedy, with Sir Henry Irving, one of the greatest of the nineteenth-century actors, performing in London at the Lyceum Theatre in 1885.

Twentieth-century performances included a number of amateur productions, including one during wartime by the great director Peter Brook in 1942. Orson Welles performed the title role in a 1937 Works Progress Administration (WPA) production in New York; reviews were mixed. Welles, himself a magician, emphasized the magical elements, so trapdoors and special effects provided great moments of entertainment. The Phoenix Theatre's 1964 production in New York continued that tradition, with fireworks accompanying the entrance of the "hot whore." That production emphasized the blackness of the play, with dark sets and glittering dark costumes. At the end of the play, Faustus was faced with the yawning pit of hellfire. Productions of the play were also popular in Germany in the first half of the twentieth century. In his novel *Doctor Faustus,* Thomas Mann saw in the play a metaphor for Germany's having sold its soul to Hitler.

CHRISTOPHER MARLOWE (1564–1593)

The Tragical History of the Life and Death of Doctor Faustus   c. 1593

EDITED BY IRVING RIBNER

The Players

THE CHORUS
DOCTOR FAUSTUS
WAGNER, *his student and servant*
VALDES
CORNELIUS
THREE SCHOLARS
AN OLD MAN

POPE ADRIAN
RAYMOND, *King of Hungary*
BRUNO, *the rival Pope*
TWO CARDINALS
THE ARCHBISHOP OF RHEIMS
CHARLES V, *Emperor of Germany*

MARTINO
FREDERICK } *Gentlemen of the Emperor's court*
BENVOLIO

BEELZEBUB
DUKE OF SAXONY
DUKE OF ANHOLT
DUCHESS OF ANHOLT
ROBIN, *the clown, a hostler*
DICK
A VINTNER
A HORSE-COURSER
A CARTER
HOSTESS

GOOD ANGEL
BAD ANGEL
LUCIFER
MEPHISTOPHILIS
PRIDE
COVETOUSNESS
ENVY
WRATH } *The Seven Deadly Sins*
GLUTTONY
SLOTH
LECHERY
ALEXANDER, THE GREAT
HIS PARAMOUR
DARIUS, *King of Persia*
HELEN OF TROY
TWO CUPIDS
DEVILS, BISHOPS, MONKS, FRIARS, SOLDIERS

Note: Material in brackets has been added by the editor.

The Scene: *Wittenberg, Rome, the Emperor's court at Innsbruck, court of the Duke of Anholt, and the neighboring countryside.*

PROLOGUE

(*Enter Chorus.*)

CHORUS: Not marching in the fields of Trasimene
    Where Mars° did mate° the warlike Carthagens,°
    Nor sporting in the dalliance of love
    In courts of kings where state° is overturned,
    Nor in the pomp of proud audacious deeds   5
    Intends our muse to vaunt his heavenly verse.
    Only this, gentles: we must now perform
    The form of Faustus' fortunes, good or bad.
    And now to patient judgments we appeal,
    And speak for Faustus in his infancy.   10
    Now is he born, of parents base of stock,
    In Germany, within a town called Rhode.
    At riper years to Wittenberg he went,
    Whereas his kinsmen chiefly brought him up.
    So much he profits in divinity,   15
    The fruitful plot of scholarism graced,°
    That shortly he was graced with doctor's name,
    Excelling all whose sweet delight disputes°
    In th'heavenly matters of theology,
    Till swoll'n with cunning of a self-conceit,   20
    His waxen wings did mount above his reach,
    And melting,° heavens conspired his overthrow;
    For, falling to a devilish exercise
    And glutted now with learning's golden gifts,
    He surfeits upon cursèd necromancy.   25
    Nothing so sweet as magic is to him,
    Which he prefers before his chiefest bliss;
    And this the man that in his study sits.

Prologue. 1–2. Trasimene . . . Carthagens: Perhaps an allusion to a lost play about the Carthaginian Hannibal, who achieved one of his greatest victories at Lake Trasimene in 217 BCE. **2. Mars:** Roman god of war. **mate:** Rival, meet in battle. **4. state:** Government. **16. fruitful plot . . . graced:** Adorned the university. **18. whose sweet delight disputes:** Who takes pleasure in disputing. **21–22. waxen wings . . . melting:** Metaphor referring to Icarus's attempt to fly with waxen wings, which melted when he ignored his father's warning and flew too near the sun.

259

ACT I • Scene 1

(*Faustus in his study.*)

FAUSTUS: Settle thy studies, Faustus, and begin
    To sound the depth of that thou wilt profess,
    Having commenced,° be a divine in show;
    Yet level° at the end of every art,
5   And live and die in Aristotle's works.
    Sweet Analytics, 'tis thou hast ravished me!
    Bene' disserere est finis logices.°
    Is to dispute well logic's chiefest end?
    Affords this art no greater miracle?
10   Then read no more; thou hast attained that end.
    A greater subject fitteth Faustus' wit!
    Bid *On cay mae on*° farewell, Galen° come.
    Seeing *ubi desinit philosophus ibi incipit medicus,*°
    Be a physician, Faustus; heap up gold,
15   And be eternized for some wondrous cure.
    Summum bonum medicinae sanitas.°
    The end of physic is our body's health.
    Why, Faustus, hast thou not attained that end?
    Is not thy common talk sound aphorisms?
20   Are not thy bills° hung up as monuments,
    Whereby whole cities have escaped the plague,
    And divers desperate maladies been cured?
    Yet art thou still but Faustus and a man.
    Couldst thou make men to live eternally,
25   Or, being dead, raise them to life again,
    Then this profession were to be esteemed.
    Physic, farewell! Where is Justinian?°
    Si una eademque res legatus duobus,   [*He reads.*]
    Alter rem, alter valorem rei, etc.°
30   A petty case of paltry legacies!
    Exhaereditare filium nan potest pater nisi —
                          [*He reads.*]
    Such is the subject of the Institute
    And universal body of the law.
    This study fits a mercenary drudge
35   Who aims at nothing but external trash,
    Too servile and illiberal for me.

When all is done, divinity is best.
Jeromè's Bible,° Faustus, view it well:
Stipendium peccati mors est.° Ha! *Stipendium, etc.*
                          [*He reads.*]
The reward of sin is death. That's hard.   40
Si pecasse negamus, fallimur   [*He reads.*]
Et nulla est in nobis veritas.°
If we say that we have no sin,
We deceive ourselves, and there's no truth in us.
Why then belike we must sin,   45
And so consequently die.
Ay, we must die an everlasting death.
What doctrine call you this? *Che serà, serà:*
What will be, shall be! Divinity, adieu!
These metaphysics of magicians,   50
And necromantic books are heavenly.
Lines, circles, signs, letters, and characters—
Ay, these are those that Faustus most desires.
O, what a world of profit and delight,
Of power, of honor, of omnipotence   55
Is promised to the studious artisan!
All things that move between the quiet poles
Shall be at my command. Emperors and kings
Are but obeyed in their several provinces,
Nor can they raise the wind or rend the clouds,   60
But his dominion that exceeds in this
Stretcheth as far as doth the mind of man.
A sound magician is a demi-god.
Here try thy brains to get a deity!
Wagner!

(*Enter Wagner.*)

    Commend me to my dearest friends,   65
The German Valdes and Cornelius;
Request them earnestly to visit me.
WAGNER: I will sir.
                               (*Exit.*)
FAUSTUS: Their conference will be a greater help to me
    Than all my labors, plod I ne'er so fast.   70

(*Enter the Good Angel and the Evil Angel.*)

GOOD ANGEL: O, Faustus, lay that damnèd book aside,
    And gaze not on it, lest it tempt thy soul
    And heap God's heavy wrath upon thy head.
    Read, read the Scriptures. That is blasphemy.
BAD ANGEL: Go forward, Faustus, in that famous art   75
    Wherein all nature's treasury is contained.
    Be thou on earth as Jove is in the sky,
    Lord and commander of these elements.
                      (*Exeunt*° *Angels.*)
FAUSTUS: How am I glutted with conceit° of this!
    Shall I make spirits fetch me what I please,   80

I, i. **3. commenced:** Taken a degree. **4. level:** Aim. **7. *Bene'**
disserere est finis logices: The end of logic is to dispute well. A
tenet of the anti-Aristotelian system introduced at Cambridge
when Marlowe was a student there. **12. *On cay mae on:*** From
Aristotle, being or not being. **Galen:** Greek physician regarded
throughout the Middle Ages as a medical authority. **13. *ubi***
desinit philosophus ibi incipit medicus: Where the philosopher
stops, the doctor begins. **16. *Summum . . . sanitas:*** Health is
the highest good of the practice of medicine. **20. bills:** Medical prescriptions. **27. Justinian:** Roman emperor of Constantinople (527–565), responsible for assembling the Roman
law and renowned throughout the Middle Ages as a jurist.
28–29. *Si . . . rei, etc.:* If the same object is willed to two
persons, let one have the thing itself and the other its value,
etc. This is an incorrect version of one of Justinian's rules.
31. *Exhaereditare . . . nisi—:* The father cannot disinherit the
son except—; another of Justinian's rules roughly paraphrased.

38. Jeromè's Bible: St. Jerome's Vulgate (Latin) translation of the Bible. **39. *Stipendium . . . est:*** Translated in line
40 (Rom. 6:23). **41–42. *Si . . . veritas:*** Translated in lines
43–44 (1 John 1:8). **78. [s.d.] *Exeunt:*** Latin for "they go out."
79. conceit: The conception of attaining.

Resolve me of° all ambiguities,
Perform what desperate enterprise I will?
I'll have them fly to India for gold,
Ransack the ocean for orient pearl,
85   And search all corners of the new-found world
For pleasant fruits and princely delicates.
I'll have them read me strange philosophy
And tell the secrets of all foreign kings;
I'll have them wall all Germany with brass
90   And make swift Rhine circle fair Wittenberg.°
I'll have them fill the public schools with silk
Wherewith the students shall be bravely clad.
I'll levy soldiers with the coin they bring
And chase the Prince of Parma from our land
95   And reign sole king of all the provinces.°
Yea, stranger engines for the brunt of war
Than was the fiery keel at Antwerp's bridge°
I'll make my servile spirits to invent.
Come, German Valdes and Cornelius,
                                                    [*He calls within.*]
100   And make me blessed with your sage conference!

(*Enter Valdes and Cornelius.*)

Valdes, sweet Valdes, and Cornelius,
Know that your words have won me at the last
To practice magic and concealed arts;
Yet not your words only, but mine own fantasy
105   That will receive no object, for my head
But ruminates on necromantic skill.
Philosophy is odious and obscure;
Both law and physic are for petty wits;
Divinity is basest of the three,
110   Unpleasant, harsh, contemptible and vile.
'Tis, magic, magic, that hath ravished me.
Then, gentle friends, aid me in this attempt,
And I, that have with subtle syllogisms
Gravelled° the pastors of the German church,
115   And made the flowering pride of Wittenberg
Swarm to my problems° as th'infernal spirits
On sweet Musaeus° when he came to hell,
Will be as cunning as Agrippa was,
Whose shadows° made all Europe honor him.
120   VALDES: Faustus, these books, thy wit, and our experience
Shall make all nations to canonize us.
As Indian Moors° obey their Spanish lords,

So shall the spirits of every element
Be always serviceable to us three.
Like lions shall they guard us when we please,   125
Like Almain rutters° with their horsemen's staves
Or Lapland giants trotting by our sides,
Sometimes like women or unwedded maids,
Shadowing° more beauty in their airy brows
Than in the white breasts of the queen of love.   130
From Venice shall they drag huge argosies,
And from America the golden fleece
That yearly stuffs old Philip's treasury,
If learnèd Faustus will be resolute.
FAUSTUS: Valdes, as resolute am I in this   135
As thou to live; therefore object it not.
CORNELIUS: The miracles that magic will perform
Will make thee vow to study nothing else.
He that is grounded in astrology,
Enriched with tongues,° well seen in minerals,   140
Hath all the principles magic doth require.
Then doubt not, Faustus, but to be renowned
And more frequented for this mystery
Than heretofore the Delphian oracle.°
The spirits tell me they can dry the sea   145
And fetch the treasure of all foreign wracks,
Yea, all the wealth that our forefathers hid
Within the massy entrails of the earth.
Then tell me, Faustus, what shall we three want?
FAUSTUS: Nothing, Cornelius. O, this cheers my soul!   150
Come, show me some demonstrations magical,
That I may conjure in some lusty grove
And have these joys in full possession.
VALDES: Then haste thee to some solitary grove,
And bear wise Bacon's and Abanus' works,°   155
The Hebrew Psalter, and New Testament;
And whatsoever else is requisite
We will inform thee ere our conference cease.
CORNELIUS: Valdes, first let him know the words of art,
And then, all other ceremonies learned,   160
Faustus may try his cunning by himself.
VALDES: First I'll instruct thee in the rudiments,
And then wilt thou be perfecter than I.
FAUSTUS: Then come and dine with me, and after meat
We'll canvass every quiddity° thereof,   165
For ere I sleep I'll try what I can do.
This night I'll conjure, though I die therefore.
                                                    (*Exeunt.*)

---

81. **Resolve me of:** Explain to me.   90. **Rhine...Wittenberg:** Wittenberg is actually on the Elbe River, not the Rhine.   95. **provinces:** The Netherlands.   97. **fiery...bridge:** In April 1584, the Dutch used a fireship to destroy a bridge built across a river by the Prince of Parma in an attempt to blockade Antwerp.   114. **Gravelled:** Puzzled and amazed.   116. **problems:** Public disputations.   117. **Musaeus:** A semimythical Greek poet. Following Virgil, Marlowe has him visit hell like the mythical Orpheus.   118–119. **Agrippa...shadows:** Cornelius Agrippa (1486?–1535), a German physician and student of the occult, was said to have power to raise spirits (shadows) from the dead.   122. **Indian Moors:** American Indians.

126. **Almain rutters:** German cavalry.   129. **Shadowing:** Harboring, sheltering.   140. **Enriched with tongues:** Fluent in Latin, the language used for communicating with spirits.   144. **Delphian oracle:** The high priest of Apollo at Delphi who had power to foretell the future. (An oracle is the response of a god to a question asked by one who worships the god. The Delphic Oracle was the chief oracle of Greece, presided over by Apollo.)   155. **Bacon's...works:** Roger Bacon (1214?–1294) and Pietro D'Abano (1250–1316) were famous in the Middle Ages for their feats of magic.   165. **quiddity:** Essential element (a term from scholastic logic).

Scene II

(*Enter two Scholars.*)

FIRST SCHOLAR: I wonder what's become of Faustus, that
was wont to make our schools ring with *sic probo.*°

(*Enter Wagner.*)

SECOND SCHOLAR: That shall we presently know; here
comes his boy.

5 FIRST SCHOLAR: How now sirrah! Where's thy master?

WAGNER: God in heaven knows.

SECOND SCHOLAR: Why, dost not thou know then?

WAGNER: Yes, I know, but that follows not.

FIRST SCHOLAR: Go to, sirrah! Leave your jesting and tell

10 us where he is.

WAGNER: That follows not by force of argument, which
you, being licentiates,° should stand upon; therefore
acknowledge your error and be attentive.

SECOND SCHOLAR: Then you will not tell us?

15 WAGNER: You are deceived, for I will tell you. Yet if you
were not dunces, you would never ask me such a
question. For is he not *corpus naturale,* and is not
that *mobile?*° Then wherefore should you ask such a
question? But that I am by nature phlegmatic, slow

20 to wrath, and prone to lechery—to love, I would
say—it were not for you to come within forty foot
of the place of execution, although I do not doubt
but to see you both hanged the next sessions. Thus
having triumphed over you, I will set my counte-

25 nance like a precisian° and begin to speak thus:
Truly, my dear brethren, my master is within at dinner with Valdes and Cornelius, as this wine, if it
could speak, would inform your worships. And so,
the Lord bless you, preserve you, and keep you, my

30 dear brethren.

(*Exit.*)

FIRST SCHOLAR: O Faustus, then I fear that which I
have long suspected.
That thou art fall'n into that damnèd art
For which they two are infamous through the
world.

SECOND SCHOLAR: Were he a stranger, not allied
to me,

35 The danger of his soul would make me mourn.
But come, let us go and inform the rector.°
It may be his grave counsel may reclaim him.

FIRST SCHOLAR: I fear me nothing will reclaim
him now.

SECOND SCHOLAR: Yet let us see what we
can do.

(*Exeunt.*)

I, ii. 2. *sic probo:* Thus I prove (used in scholastic argument).
12. licentiates: Holders of university degrees. 17–18. *corpus
naturale . . . mobile:* The subject matter of physics, in scholastic terms, was *corpus naturale seu mobile* (natural body in
motion). 25. precisian: Puritan. 36. rector: Head of the
university.

Scene III

(*Thunder. Enter [above] Lucifer and four Devils. Enter
Faustus to conjure.*)

FAUSTUS: Now that the gloomy shadow of the night,
Longing to view Orion's drizzling look,
Leaps from th'Antarctic° world unto the sky
And dims the welkin° with her pitchy breath,
Faustus begin thine incantations,   5
And try if devils will obey thy hest,
Seeing thou hast prayed and sacrificed to them.
Within this circle is Jehovah's name,
Forward and backward anagrammatized,
Th'abbreviated names of holy saints,   10
Figures of every adjunct to the heavens,
And characters of signs and erring° stars,
By which the spirits are enforced to rise.
Then fear not, Faustus, to be resolute,
And try the utmost magic can perform.   15

(*Thunder.*)

*Sint mihi Dei Acherontis propitii! Valeat numen
triplex Jehovae. Ignei, aerii, aquatani spiritus, salvete!
Orientis princeps, Beelzebub, inferni ardentis monar-
cha, et Demogorgon, propitiamus vos, ut appareat et
surgat Mephistophilis. Quid tu moraris? Per Jehovam*   20
*Gehennam, et consecratam aquam quam nunc spargo,
signumque crucis quod nunc facto, et per vota nostra,
ipse nunc surgat nobis dicatus Mephistophilis.*°

(*Enter [Mephistophilis,] a Devil.*)

I charge thee to return and change thy shape;
Thou art too ugly to attend on me.   25
Go, and return an old Franciscan friar;
That holy shape becomes a devil best.

(*Exit Devil.*)

I see there's virtue in my heavenly words.
Who would not be proficient in this art?
How pliant is this Mephistophilis,   30
Full of obedience and humility.
Such is the force of magic and my spells.
Now Faustus, thou art conjurer laureate,
That canst command great Mephistophilis.
Quin redis Mephistophilis fratris imagine.°   35

(*Enter Mephistophilis [dressed like a Franciscan friar].*)

MEPHISTOPHILIS: Now Faustus, what wouldst thou
have me do?

I, iii. 4. welkin: Sky. 12. erring: wandering. 16–23. *Sint . . .
Mephistophilis:* May the gods of Acheron be propitious to me.
Let the triple name of Jehova (the trinity) be gone. Hail spirits
of fire, air, and water. Prince of the East, Beelzebub, monarch
of burning hell, and Demogorgon, we petition you that
Mephistophilis may appear and rise. Why do you linger? By
Jehova, Gehenna, and the holy water which I now sprinkle and
the sign of the cross which I now make and by our vows, let
Mephistophilis himself now rise to serve us. 35. *Quin . . .
imagine:* Return, Mephistophilis, in the shape of a friar.

FAUSTUS: I charge thee wait upon me whilst I live,
To do whatever Faustus shall command,
Be it to make the moon drop from her sphere
40   Or the ocean to overwhelm the world.
MEPHISTOPHILIS: I am a servant to great Lucifer
And may not follow thee without his leave.
No more than he commands must we perform.
FAUSTUS: Did not he charge thee to appear to me?
45 MEPHISTOPHILIS: No, I came hither of mine own accord.
FAUSTUS: Did not my conjuring speeches raise thee?
Speak.
MEPHISTOPHILIS: That was the cause, but yet *per
accidens,*°
For when we hear one rack the name of God,
Abjure the Scriptures and his Savior Christ,
50   We fly in hope to get his glorious soul;
Nor will we come unless he use such means
Whereby he is in danger to be damned.
Therefore the shortest cut for conjuring
Is stoutly to abjure the Trinity
55   And pray devoutly to the prince of hell.
FAUSTUS: So Faustus hath
Already done, and holds this principle:
There is no chief but only Beelzebub,
To whom Faustus doth dedicate himself.
60   This word "damnation" terrifies not me,
For I confound hell in Elysium.
My ghost° be with the old philosophers!
But leaving these vain trifles of men's souls,
Tell me what is that Lucifer thy lord?
MEPHISTOPHILIS: Arch-regent and commander of all
65   spirits.
FAUSTUS: Was not that Lucifer an angel once?
MEPHISTOPHILIS: Yes Faustus, and most dearly loved
of God.
FAUSTUS: How comes it then that he is prince of devils?
MEPHISTOPHILIS: O, by aspiring pride and insolence,
70   For which God threw him from the face of heaven.
FAUSTUS: And what are you that live with Lucifer?
MEPHISTOPHILIS: Unhappy spirits that fell with
Lucifer,
Conspired against our God with Lucifer,
And are for ever damned with Lucifer.
FAUSTUS: Where are you damned?
75 MEPHISTOPHILIS: In hell.
FAUSTUS: How comes it then that thou art out of hell?
MEPHISTOPHILIS: Why this is hell, nor am I out of it.
Think'st thou that I who saw the face of God
And tasted the eternal joys of heaven
80   Am not tormented with ten thousand hells
In being deprived of everlasting bliss?
O Faustus, leave these frivolous demands
Which strike a terror to my fainting soul.
FAUSTUS: What, is great Mephistophilis so passionate
85   For being deprivèd of the joys of heaven?

Learn thou of Faustus' manly fortitude,
And scorn those joys thou never shalt possess.
Go bear these tidings to great Lucifer:
Seeing Faustus hath incurred eternal death
By desperate thoughts against Jove's deity,   90
Say he surrenders up to him his soul,
So he will spare him four and twenty years,
Letting him live in all voluptuousness,
Having thee ever to attend on me,
To give me whatsoever I shall ask,   95
To tell me whatsoever I demand,
To slay mine enemies, and aid my friends,
And always be obedient to my will.
Go, and return to mighty Lucifer,
And meet me in my study at midnight,   100
And then resolve me of thy master's mind.
MEPHISTOPHILIS: I will, Faustus.
                                          (*Exit.*)
FAUSTUS: Had I as many souls as there be stars,
I'd give them all for Mephistophilis.
By him I'll be great emperor of the world,   105
And make a bridge thorough the moving air,
To pass the ocean with a band of men.
I'll join the hills that bind° the Afric shore,
And make that country continent to Spain,
And both contributory to my crown.   110
The Emperor shall not live but by my leave,
Nor any potentate of Germany.
Now that I have obtained what I desire,
I'll live in speculation of this art
Till Mephistophilis return again.   115

                                          (*Exit.*)

Scene IV

(*Enter Wagner and [Robin,] the Clown.*)

WAGNER: Come hither, sirrah boy.
ROBIN: Boy! O disgrace to my person. Zounds, boy
in your face! You have seen many boys with such
pickedevants,° I am sure.
WAGNER: Sirrah, hast thou no comings in?°   5
ROBIN: Yes, and goings out too, you may see, sir.
WAGNER: Alas, poor slave! See how poverty jests in his
nakedness. I know the villain's out of service, and so
hungry that I know he would give his soul to the devil
for a shoulder of mutton, though it were blood-raw. 10
ROBIN: Not so neither. I had need to have it well roasted,
and good sauce to it, if I pay so dear, I can tell you.
WAGNER: Sirrah, wilt thou be my man and wait on me,
and I will make thee go like *Qui mihi discipulus?*°

47. **cause . . . *per accidens:*** The terms are from scholastic logic.
62. **ghost:** Spirit.

108. **bind:** Enclose.   I, IV. 4. **pickedevants:** Pointed beards.
5. **comings in:** Earnings.   16. ***Qui mihi discipulus?:*** Who is my
disciple? (the opening words of a Latin poem by William Lyly,
well known to Elizabethan schoolboys).

15 ROBIN: What, in verse?

WAGNER: No slave; in beaten° silk and staves-acre.°

ROBIN: Staves-acre? That's good to kill vermin. Then, belike, if I serve you I shall be lousy.

20 WAGNER: Why, so thou shalt be, whether thou dost it or no; for, sirrah, if thou dost not presently bind thyself to me for seven years, I'll turn all the lice about thee into familiars° and make them tear thee in pieces.

ROBIN: Nay sir, you may save yourself a labor, for they are as familiar with me as if they paid for their meat 25 and drink, I can tell you.

WAGNER: Well, sirrah, leave your jesting and take these guilders.

ROBIN: Yes, marry sir, and I thank you too.

WAGNER: So, now thou art to be at an hour's warning, 30 whensoever and wheresoever the devil shall fetch thee.

ROBIN: Here, take your guilders again. I'll none of 'em.

WAGNER: Not I. Thou art pressed.° Prepare thyself, for I will presently raise up two devils to carry thee away. 35 Banio! Belcher!

ROBIN: Belcher? And Belcher come here, I'll belch him. I am not afraid of a devil.

(*Enter two Devils.*)

WAGNER: How now, sir? Will you serve me now?

ROBIN: Ay, good Wagner; take away the devil then.

40 WAGNER: Spirits away! Now, sirrah, follow me.

[*Exeunt Devils.*]

ROBIN: I will sir. But hark you, master, will you teach me this conjuring occupation?

WAGNER: Ay, sirrah. I'll teach thee to turn thyself to a dog, or a cat, or a mouse, or a rat, or any thing.

45 ROBIN: A dog, or a cat, or a mouse, or a rat! O brave Wagner!

WAGNER: Villain, call me Master Wagner, and see that you walk attentively, and let your right eye be always diametrally° fixed upon my left heel, that thou may'st 50 *quasi vestigial nostras insistere.°*

ROBIN: Well, sir, I warrant you.

(*Exeunt.*)

ACT II • Scene I

(*Enter Faustus in his Study.*)

FAUSTUS: Now Faustus must thou needs be damned, And canst thou not be saved. What boots° it then to think on God or heaven? Away with such vain fancies, and despair; 5 Despair in God, and trust in Beelzebub. Now go not backward; Faustus, be resolute.

16. **beaten:** Embroidered with metal. **staves-acre:** A plant used for killing vermin. 22. **familiars:** Attendant evil spirits. 33. **pressed:** Enlisted into service in exchange for money. 49. **diametrally:** In a straight line. 50. *quasi . . . insistere:* As if to walk in our tracks. **II, i. 3. boots:** Avails.

Why waver'st thou? O, something soundeth in mine ear: "Abjure this magic; turn to God again." Ay, and Faustus will turn to God again! To God? He loves thee not. 10 The God thou serv'st is thine own appetite, Wherein is fixed the love of Beelzebub. To him I'll build an altar and a church, And offer lukewarm blood of new-born babes.

(*Enter the two Angels.*)

BAD ANGEL: Go forward, Faustus, in that famous art. 15

GOOD ANGEL: Sweet Faustus, leave that execrable art.

FAUSTUS: Contrition, prayer, repentance—what of these?

GOOD ANGEL: O, they are means to bring thee unto heaven.

BAD ANGEL: Rather illusions, fruits of lunacy, That make men foolish that do use them most. 20

GOOD ANGEL: Sweet Faustus, think of heaven and heavenly things.

BAD ANGEL: No Faustus, think of honor and wealth.

(*Exeunt Angels.*)

FAUSTUS: Wealth? Why, the signory of Emden° shall be mine. When Mephistophilis shall stand by me, What power can hurt me? Faustus thou art safe. 25 Cast no more doubts. Mephistophilis, come And bring glad tidings from great Lucifer. Is't not midnight? Come, Mephistophilis. *Veni,° veni, Mephistophile.*

(*Enter Mephistophilis.*)

Now tell me what saith Lucifer, thy lord? 30

MEPHISTOPHILIS: That I shall wait on Faustus whilst he lives, So he will buy my service with his soul.

FAUSTUS: Already Faustus hath hazarded that for thee.

MEPHISTOPHILIS: But now thou must bequeath it solemnly And write a deed of gift with thine own blood, 35 For that security craves great Lucifer. If thou deny it, I must back to hell.

FAUSTUS: Stay, Mephistophilis! Tell me what good Will my soul do thy lord.

MEPHISTOPHILIS: Enlarge his kingdom.

FAUSTUS: Is that the reason why he tempts us thus? 40

MEPHISTOPHILIS: *Solamen miseris socios habuisse doloris.°*

FAUSTUS: Why, have you any pain that torture others?

MEPHISTOPHILIS: As great as have the human souls of men. But tell me, Faustus, shall I have thy soul?

23. **Emden:** The chief city of East Friesland near the mouth of the river Ems, which had considerable trade relations with Elizabethan England. 29. *Veni:* Come. 41. *Solamen . . . doloris:* It is a consolation in misery to have a fellow sufferer.

45 And I will be thy slave and wait on thee
    And give thee more than thou hast wit to ask.
    FAUSTUS: Ay, Mephistophilis, I'll give it him.
    MEPHISTOPHILIS: Then Faustus, stab thy arm
        courageously,
    And bind thy soul that at some certain day
50 Great Lucifer may claim it as his own,
    And then be thou as great as Lucifer.
    FAUSTUS: [stabbing his arm] Lo, Mephistophilis, for
        love of thee,
    I cut mine arm, and with my proper° blood
    Assure my soul to be great Lucifer's,
55 Chief lord and regent of perpetual night.
    View here this blood that trickles from mine arm,
    And let it be propitious for my wish.
    MEPHISTOPHILIS: But Faustus,
        Write it in manner of a deed of gift.
60 FAUSTUS: Ay, so I do. [He writes.] But Mephistophilis,
    My blood congeals, and I can write no more.
    MEPHISTOPHILIS: I'll fetch thee fire to dissolve it straight.
                                                    (Exit.)
    FAUSTUS: What might the staying of my blood portend?
    Is it unwilling I should write this bill?
65 Why streams it not that I may write afresh?
    "Faustus gives to thee his soul." Ah, there it stayed.
    Why shouldst thou not? Is not thy soul thine own?
    Then write again: "Faustus gives to thee his soul."

    (Enter Mephistophilis with the chafer of fire.)

    Mephistophilis: See Faustus, here is fire. Set it on.°
70 FAUSTUS: So. Now the blood begins to clear again.
    Now will I make an end immediately.

                                                [He writes.]

    MEPHISTOPHILIS: [Aside.] What will not I do to obtain
        his soul?
    FAUSTUS: Consummatum est;° this bill is ended,
    And Faustus hath bequeathed his soul to Lucifer.
75 But what is this inscription on mine arm?
    Homo fuge!° Whither should I fly?
    If unto God, he'll throw me down to hell.
    My senses are deceived; here's nothing writ.
    O yes, I see it plain. Even here is writ
80 Homo fuge! Yet shall not Faustus fly.
    MEPHISTOPHILIS: [Aside.] I'll fetch him somewhat to
        delight his mind.

                                                    (Exit.)

    (Enter Devils, giving crowns and rich apparel to Faustus.
    They dance and then depart. Enter Mephistophilis.)

    FAUSTUS: What means this show? Speak Mephistophilis.
    MEPHISTOPHILIS: Nothing, Faustus, but to delight thy
        mind
    And let thee see what magic can perform.

FAUSTUS: But may I raise such spirits when I please?   85
MEPHISTOPHILIS: Ay Faustus, and do greater things
    than these.
FAUSTUS: Then, Mephistophilis, receive this scroll,
    A deed of gift of body and of soul,
    But yet conditionally that thou perform
    All covenants and articles between us both.   90
MEPHISTOPHILIS: Faustus, I swear by hell and Lucifer
    To effect all promises between us made.
FAUSTUS: Then hear me read it Mephistophilis.
    On these conditions following:
    First, that Faustus may be a spirit in form and sub-   95
    stance;
    Secondly, that Mephistophilis shall be his servant and
    be at his command;
    Thirdly, that Mephistophilis shall do for him and
    bring him whatsoever;   100
    Fourthly, that he shall be in his chamber or house
    invisible;
    Lastly, that he shall appear to the said John Faustus
    at all times, in what form or shape soever he please:
    I, John Faustus, of Wittenberg, doctor, by these   105
    presents, do give both body and soul to Lucifer,
    Prince of the East, and his minister, Mephistophilis;
    and furthermore grant unto them that four and
    twenty years being expired, the articles above written
    inviolate, full power to fetch or carry the said John   110
    Faustus, body and soul, flesh, blood, or goods, into
    their habitation wheresoever.

                                    By me, John Faustus.

MEPHISTOPHILIS: Speak Faustus. Do you deliver this as
    your deed?
FAUSTUS: Ay, take it, and the devil give thee good of it.   115
MEPHISTOPHILIS: So now, Faustus, ask me what thou wilt.
FAUSTUS: First will I question with thee about hell.
    Tell me, where is the place that men call hell?
MEPHISTOPHILIS: Under the heavens.
FAUSTUS: Ay, so are all things else. But whereabouts?   120
MEPHISTOPHILIS: Within the bowels of these elements,
    Where we are tortured and remain for ever.
    Hell hath no limits, nor is circumscribed
    In one self place, but where we are is hell,
    And where hell is, there must we ever be.   125
    And, to be short, when all the world dissolves
    And every creature shall be purified,
    All places shall be hell that is not heaven.
FAUSTUS: I think hell's a fable.
MEPHISTOPHILIS: Ay, think so still, till experience change
    thy mind.   130
FAUSTUS: Why, dost thou think that Faustus shall be
    damned?
MEPHISTOPHILIS: Ay, of necessity, for here's the scroll
    In which thou hast given thy soul to Lucifer.
FAUSTUS: Ay, and body too. But what of that?
    Think'st thou that Faustus is so fond° to imagine   135

---

53. **proper:** Own.   69. **Set it on:** Set the dish of blood on the
fire.   73. ***Consummatum est:*** It is completed (the words of
Jesus at his Crucifixion; John 19:30).   76. ***Homo fuge:*** Fly, man.

135. **fond:** Foolish.

That after this life there is any pain?
No, these are trifles and mere old wives' tales.
MEPHISTOPHILIS: But I am an instance to prove the
contrary,
For I tell thee I am damned and now in hell.
140 FAUSTUS: Nay, and this be hell, I'll willingly be damned.
What? Sleeping, eating, walking and disputing?
But, leaving off this, let me have a wife,
The fairest maid in Germany,
For I am wanton and lascivious,
145 And cannot live without a wife.
MEPHISTOPHILIS: I prithee, Faustus, talk not of a wife.
FAUSTUS: Nay, sweet Mephistophilis, fetch me one, for I
will have one.
MEPHISTOPHILIS: Well, Faustus, thou shalt have a wife.
Sit there till I come.   [*Exit.*]
(*Enter* [*Mephistophilis*] *with a Devil dressed like a
woman, with fireworks.*)
150 FAUSTUS: What sight is this?
MEPHISTOPHILIS: Now Faustus, how dost thou like thy
wife?
FAUSTUS: Here's a hot whore indeed! No, I'll no wife.
MEPHISTOPHILIS: Marriage is but a ceremonial toy,
And if thou lovest me, think no more of it.
155 I'll cull thee out the fairest courtesans
And bring them every morning to thy bed.
She whom thine eye shall like, thy heart shall have,
Were she as chaste as was Penelope,°
As wise as Saba,° or as beautiful
160 As was bright Lucifer before his fall.
Hold; take this book; peruse it thoroughly.
The iterating of these lines brings gold;
The framing of this circle on the ground
Brings thunder, whirlwinds, storm and lightning.
165 Pronounce this thrice devoutly to thyself,
And men in harness° shall appear to thee,
Ready to execute what thou command'st.
FAUSTUS: Thanks, Mephistophilis, for this sweet book.
This will I keep as chary as my life.

(*Exeunt.*)

Scene II

(*Enter Faustus in his study and Mephistophilis.*)

FAUSTUS: When I behold the heavens, then I repent
And curse thee, wicked Mephistophilis,
Because thou hast deprived me of those joys.
MEPHISTOPHILIS: 'Twas thine own seeking, Faustus;
thank thyself.
5 But think'st thou heaven is such a glorious thing?

I tell thee, Faustus, 'tis not half so fair
As thou, or any man that breathes on earth.
FAUSTUS: How prov'st thou that?
MEPHISTOPHILIS: 'Twas made for man; then he's more
excellent.
FAUSTUS: If heaven was made for man, 'twas made for
me.   10
I will renounce this magic and repent.
(*Enter the two Angels.*)
GOOD ANGEL: Faustus repent; yet God will pity thee.
BAD ANGEL: Thou art a spirit;° God cannot pity thee.
FAUSTUS: Who buzzeth in mine ears I am a spirit?
Be I a devil, yet God may pity me;   15
Yea, God will pity me if I repent.
BAD ANGEL: Ay, but Faustus never shall repent.
                                          (*Exeunt angels.*)
FAUSTUS: My heart is hardened; I cannot repent.
Scarce can I name salvation, faith, or heaven,
But fearful echoes thunder in mine ears: 20
"Faustus, thou art damned!" Then swords and
knives,
Poison, guns, halters, and envenomed steel
Are laid before me to dispatch myself;
And long ere this I should have done the deed,
Had not sweet pleasure conquered deep despair.   25
Have not I made blind Homer sing to me
Of Alexander's love and Oenone's death?°
And hath not he, that built the walls of Thebes
With ravishing sound of his melodious harp,°
Made music with my Mephistophilis?   30
Why should I die then, or basely despair?
I am resolved; Faustus shall not repent.
Come, Mephistophilis, let us dispute again
And reason of divine astrology.
Speak; are there many spheres above the moon?   35
Are all celestial bodies but one globe,
As is the substance of this centric earth?
MEPHISTOPHILIS: As are the elements, such are the
heavens,
Even from the moon unto the empyreal orb,
Mutually folded in each others' spheres,   40
And jointly move upon one axle-tree.
Whose terminè° is termed the world's wide pole;
Nor are the names of Saturn, Mars, or Jupiter
Feigned, but are erring stars.°
FAUSTUS: But have they all
One motion, both *situ et tempore?*°   45

---

158. **Penelope:** The faithful wife of Ulysses in Homer's
Odyssey. 159. **Saba:** The Queen of Sheba. 166. **harness:**
Armor.

II, ii. 13. spirit: Devil. **27. Alexander's . . . death:** Paris (also
called Alexander) loved the nymph Oenone when he lived as
a shepherd on Mt. Ida. Oenone died of a broken heart when
he left her. **28–29. he . . . harp:** Amphion, son of Zeus and
Antiope, caused stones to move and the walls of Thebes to be
built simply by playing on the lyre given to him by Hermes.
42. terminè: Limit. **44. erring stars:** Planets. **45. *situ et tempore:*** In position (direction of movement) and in the time they
take to revolve about the earth.

MEPHISTOPHILIS: All move from east to west in four and twenty hours upon the poles of the world, but differ in their motions upon the poles of the zodiac.

FAUSTUS: These slender questions Wagner can decide.
50   Hath Mephistophilis no greater skill?
Who knows not the double motion of the planets?
That the first is finished in a natural day?
The second thus? Saturn in thirty years?
Jupiter in twelve; Mars in four; the sun, Venus and
55   Mercury in a year, the moon in twenty eight days.
These are freshmen's suppositions. But tell me hath every sphere a dominion or *intelligentia?*°

MEPHISTOPHILIS: Ay.

FAUSTUS: How many heavens or spheres are there?

60   MEPHISTOPHILIS: Nine—the seven planets, the firmament, and the empyreal heaven.

FAUSTUS: But is there not *coelum igneum, et crystallinum?*°

MEPHISTOPHILIS: No, Faustus, they be but fables.

65   FAUSTUS: Resolve me then in this one question: why are not conjunctions, oppositions, aspects, eclipses° all at one time, but in some years we have more, in some less?

MEPHISTOPHILIS: *Per inaequalem motum respectu totius.*°

70   FAUSTUS: Well, I am answered. Now tell me who made the world.

MEPHISTOPHILIS: I will not.

FAUSTUS: Sweet Mephistophilis, tell me.

MEPHISTOPHILIS: Move me not, Faustus.

75   FAUSTUS: Villain, have not I bound thee to tell me any thing?

MEPHISTOPHILIS: Ay, that is not against our kingdom. This is. Thou art damned. Think thou of hell.

FAUSTUS: Think, Faustus, upon God that made the world.

80   MEPHISTOPHILIS: Remember this.

(*Exit.*)

FAUSTUS: Ay, go accursèd spirit to ugly hell.
'Tis thou hast damned distressèd Faustus' soul.
Is't not too late?

(*Enter the two Angels.*)

BAD ANGEL: Too late.

85   GOOD ANGEL: Never too late, if Faustus will repent.

BAD ANGEL: If thou repent, devils will tear thee in pieces.

GOOD ANGEL: Repent, and they shall never raze thy skin.

(*Exeunt Angels.*)

FAUSTUS: O Christ, my Savior, my Savior,
Help to save distressèd Faustus' soul.

(*Enter Lucifer, Beelzebub, and Mephistophilis.*)

90   LUCIFER: Christ cannot save thy soul, for he is just.
There's none but I have interest in the same.

FAUSTUS: O, what art thou that look'st so terribly?

LUCIFER: I am Lucifer,
And this is my companion prince in hell.

95   FAUSTUS: O, Faustus, they are come to fetch thy soul.

BEELZEBUB: We are come to tell thee thou dost injure us.

LUCIFER: Thou call'st on Christ, contrary to thy promise.

BEELZEBUB: Thou shouldst not think on God.

LUCIFER: Think on the devil.

100   BEELZEBUB: And his dam too.

FAUSTUS: Nor will I henceforth. Pardon me in this,
And Faustus vows never to look to heaven,
Never to name God, or to pray to him,
To burn his Scriptures, slay his ministers,
105   And make my spirits pull his churches down.

LUCIFER: So shalt thou show thyself an obedient servant,
And we will highly gratify thee for it.

BEELZEBUB: Faustus, we are come from hell in person to show thee some pastime. Sit down, and thou shalt behold the Seven Deadly Sins appear to thee in their 110 own proper shapes and likeness.

FAUSTUS: That sight will be as pleasant to me as Paradise was to Adam the first day of his creation.

LUCIFER: Talk not of Paradise or creation, but mark the show. Go, Mephistophilis, fetch them in. 115

[*Exit Mephistophilis.*]

(*Enter the Seven Deadly Sins, [with Mephistophilis, led by a Piper].*)

BEELZEBUB: Now Faustus, question them of their names and dispositions.

FAUSTUS: That shall I soon. What art thou, the first?

PRIDE: I am Pride. I disdain to have any parents. I am like to Ovid's flea:° I can creep into every corner of a 120 wench. Sometimes, like a periwig, I sit upon her brow. Next, like a necklace, I hang about her neck. Then, like a fan of feathers, I kiss her lips, and then, turning myself to a wrought smock, do what I list. But fie, what a smell is here! I'll not speak another 125 word unless the ground be perfumed and covered with cloth of Arras.°

FAUSTUS: Thou art a proud knave indeed. What art thou, the second?

COVETOUSNESS: I am Covetousness, begotten of an old 130 churl in a leather bag, and might I now obtain my wish, this house, you and all, should turn to gold, that I might lock you safe into my chest. O my sweet gold!

---

57. **dominion or** *intelligentia:* Governing angel.   62–63. *coelum . . . crystallinum:* The fiery heaven and crystalline sphere of Ptolemaic astronomy.   66. **conjunctions:** Seeming proximities of heavenly bodies.   **oppositions:** Divergences of heavenly bodies.   **aspects:** Any other relations of such bodies to one another.   **eclipses:** The blottings out of one heavenly body by another.   69. *Per . . . totius:* By their unequal movements in respect to the whole (i.e., the different speeds of the various planets within the total cosmos).

120. **Ovid's flea:** The medieval poem *Carmine de Pulice* (Poem of the Flea) was generally attributed to Ovid.   127. **cloth of Arras:** Flemish cloth used generally for tapestries.

Arthur Darvill (left) as Mephistophilis and Paul Hilton as Faustus in the Shakespeare's Globe 2011 production directed by Matthew Dunster.

135 FAUSTUS: And what art thou, the third?
ENVY: I am Envy, begotten of a chimney-sweeper and an oyster-wife. I cannot read and therefore wish all books burned. I am lean with seeing others eat. O, that there would come a famine over all the world,
140 that all might die, and I live alone; then thou shouldst see how fat I'd be. But must thou sit and I stand? Come down, with a vengeance.
FAUSTUS: Out envious wretch! But what are thou, the fourth?

Paul Hilton as Faustus, 2011.

WRATH: I am Wrath. I had neither father nor mother. I 145
leaped out of a lion's mouth when I was scarce an hour old, and ever since have run up and down the world with this case of rapiers, wounding myself when I could get none to fight withal. I was born in hell, and look to it, for some of you shall be my father. 150
FAUSTUS: And what are you, the fifth?
GLUTTONY: I am Gluttony. My parents are all dead, and the devil a penny they have left me but a small pension, and that buys me thirty meals a day and ten

155 bevers°—a small trifle to suffice nature. I come of a
royal pedigree. My father was a gammon of bacon,
and my mother was a hogshead of claret wine. My
godfathers were these: Peter Pickled-herring and
Martin Martlemas-beef.° But my godmother, O, she
160 was a jolly gentlewoman, and well beloved in every
good town and city; her name was Mistress Margery
March-beer.° Now Faustus, thou hast heard all my
progeny; wilt thou bid me to a supper.

FAUSTUS: Not I. Thou wilt eat up all my victuals.

165 GLUTTONY: Then the devil choke thee.

FAUSTUS: Choke thyself, glutton. What art thou, the
sixth?

SLOTH: Heigh ho! I am Sloth. I was begotten on a sunny
bank, where I have lain ever since, and you have done
170 me great injury to bring me from thence. Let me be
carried thither again by Gluttony and Lechery. Heigh
ho! I'll not speak a word more for a king's ransom.

FAUSTUS: And what are you Mistress Minx, the seventh
and last?

175 LECHERY: Who, I, sir? I am one that loves an inch of raw
mutton° better than an ell of fried stockfish,° and the
first letter of my name begins with lechery.

LUCIFER: Away to hell! Away! On piper!
(Exeunt the seven Sins [and the Piper].)

FAUSTUS: O, how this sight doth delight my soul!

180 LUCIFER: But Faustus, in hell is all manner of delight.

FAUSTUS: O, might I see hell and return again safe, how
happy were I then!

LUCIFER: Faustus, thou shalt. At midnight I will send
for thee. Meanwhile peruse this book and view it
185 thoroughly, and thou shalt turn thyself into what
shape thou wilt.

FAUSTUS: Thanks, mighty Lucifer.
This will I keep as chary as my life.

LUCIFER: Now Faustus, farewell.

190 FAUSTUS: Farewell, great Lucifer. Come, Mephistophilis.
(Exeunt, several ways.)

Scene III

(Enter the Clown, [Robin, holding a book].)

ROBIN: What, Dick, look to the horses there till I come
again. I have gotten one of Doctor Faustus' conjuring
books, and now we'll have such knavery as't passes.

(Enter Dick.)

DICK: What, Robin, you must come away and walk the
5   horses.

ROBIN: I walk the horses? I scorn't, 'faith. I have other
matters in hand. Let the horses walk themselves and
they will. [*He reads.*] *A per se a; t, h, e, the; o per se
o; deny orgon, gorgon.* Keep further from me, O thou
illiterate and unlearned hostler.   10

DICK: 'Snails,° what hast thou got there? A book? Why,
thou canst not tell ne'er a word on't.

ROBIN: That thou shalt see presently. Keep out of the
circle, I say, lest I send you into the hostry with a
vengeance.   15

DICK: That's like, 'faith. You had best leave your foolery,
for an my master come, he'll conjure you, 'faith.

ROBIN: My master conjure me? I'll tell thee what: an my
master come here, I'll clap as fair a pair of horns°
on's head as e'er thou sawest in thy life.   20

DICK: Thou needst not do that, for my mistress hath
done it.

ROBIN: Ay, there be of us here that have waded as deep
into matters as other men, if they were disposed to
talk.   25

DICK: A plague take you! I thought you did not sneak up
and down after her for nothing. But I prithee, tell me
in good sadness,° Robin, is that a conjuring book?

ROBIN: Do but speak what thou'lt have me to do, and
I'll do't. If thou'lt dance naked, put off thy clothes   30
and I'll conjure thee about presently. Or if thou'lt go
but to the tavern with me, I'll give thee white wine,
red wine, claret wine, sack, muscadine, malmesey
and whippincrust.° Hold belly, hold, and we'll not
pay one penny for it.   35

DICK: O brave! Prithee let's to it presently, for I am as
dry as a dog.

ROBIN: Come then, let's away.
(Exeunt.)

ACT III • Prologue

(Enter the Chorus.)

CHORUS: Learnèd Faustus,
To find the secrets of astronomy
Graven in the book of Jove's high firmament,
Did mount him up to scale Olympus' top,
Where, sitting in a chariot burning bright   5
Drawn by the strength of yokèd dragons' necks,
He views the clouds, the planets, and the stars,
The tropics, zones, and quarters of the sky,
From the bright circle of the hornèd moon
Even to the height of *Primum Mobile.*°   10

---

155. **bevers:** Light snacks taken between regular meals.
159. **Martlemas-beef:** Salted meat hung for the winter on
Martinmas, November 11.   162. **March-beer:** A fine ale made in
the springtime and aged for two years before being drunk.   175–
176. **raw mutton:** Common slang for "whore."   176. **stockfish:**
Dried codfish.

II, iii. 11. **'Snails:** By God's nails.   **19. horns:** The common sign
of a cuckold.   **28. sadness:** Seriousness.   **34. whippincrust:**
Possibly a corruption of *hippocras*, a highly spiced and sugared wine.   **III, Prologue. 10.** *Primum Mobile:* In Ptolemaic
astronomy, the outermost sphere of creation, which moves the
other nine spheres.

And whirling round with this circumference,
Within the concave compass of the pole,
From east to west his dragons swiftly glide
And in eight days did bring him home again.
15 Not long he stayed within his quiet house
To rest his bones after his weary toil,
But new exploits do hale him out again,
And mounted then upon a dragon's back,
That with his wings did part the subtle air,
20 He now is gone to prove cosmography,°
That measures coasts and kingdoms of the earth,
And, as I guess, will first arrive at Rome
To see the Pope and manner of his court
And take some part of holy Peter's feast,
25 The which this day is highly solemnized.

(*Exit.*)

Scene I

(*Enter Faustus and Mephistophilis.*)

FAUSTUS: Having now, my good Mephistophilis,
Passed with delight the stately town of Trier,
Environed round with airy mountain tops,
With walls of flint, and deep entrenchèd lakes,°
5 Not to be won by any conquering prince;
From Paris next, coasting the realm of France,
We saw the river Main fall into Rhine,
Whose banks are set with groves of fruitful vines;
Then up to Naples, rich Campania,
10 Whose buildings fair and gorgeous to the eye,
The streets straight forth and paved with finest brick,
Quarters the town in four equivalents.
There saw we learnèd Maro's° golden tomb,
The way he cut, an English mile in length,
15 Through a rock of stone in one night's space.°
From thence to Venice, Padua, and the rest,
In midst of which a sumptuous temple stands,
That threats the stars with her aspiring top,
Whose frame is paved with sundry colored stones,
20 And roofed aloft with curious work in gold.°
Thus hitherto hath Faustus spent his time.
But tell me now, what resting-place is this?
Hast thou, as erst I did command,
Conducted me within the walls of Rome?
MEPHISTOPHILIS: I have, my Faustus, and for proof thereof
25 This is the goodly palace of the Pope;

And 'cause we are no common guests,
I choose his privy chamber for our use.
FAUSTUS: I hope his holiness will bid us welcome.
MEPHISTOPHILIS: All's one, for we'll be bold with his venison.
30 But now, my Faustus, that thou may'st perceive
What Rome contains for to delight thine eyes,
Know that this city stands upon seven hills
That underprop the groundwork of the same.
Just through the midst runs flowing Tiber's stream, 35
With winding banks that cut it in two parts,
Over the which four stately bridges lean,
That make safe passage to each part of Rome.
Upon the bridge called Ponte Angelo
Erected is a castle passing strong, 40
Where thou shalt see such store of ordinance
As that the double cannons, forged of brass,
Do match the number of the days contained
Within the compass of one complete year;
Beside the gates and high pyramidès 45
That Julius Caesar brought from Africa.°
FAUSTUS: Now, by the kingdoms of infernal rule,
Of Styx, of Acheron, and the fiery lake
Of ever-burning Phlegethon, I swear
That I do long to see the monuments 50
And situation of bright-splendent Rome.
Come, therefore, let's away.
MEPHISTOPHILIS: Nay, stay my Faustus. I know you'd see the Pope
And take some part of holy Peter's feast,
The which, in state and high solemnity, 55
This day is held through Rome and Italy
In honor of the Pope's triumphant victory.
FAUSTUS: Sweet Mephistophilis, thou pleasest me.
Whilst I am here on earth, let me be cloyed
With all things that delight the heart of man. 60
My four and twenty years of liberty
I'll spend in pleasure and in dalliance,
That Faustus' name, whilst this bright frame doth stand,
May be admirèd through the furthest land.
MEPHISTOPHILIS: 'Tis well said, Faustus. Come then, stand by me 65
And thou shalt see them come immediately.
FAUSTUS: Nay, stay, my gentle Mephistophilis,
And grant me my request, and then I go.
Thou know'st within the compass of eight days
We viewed the face of heaven, of earth, and hell. 70
So high our dragons soared into the air,
That looking down, the earth appeared to me
No bigger than my hand in quantity.
There did we view the kingdoms of the world,
And what might please mine eye I there beheld. 75

20. **prove cosmography:** Explore the universe. **III, i. 4. entrenchèd lakes:** Castle moats. **13. Maro:** Virgil. **14–15. way . . . space:** A tunnel between the bays of Naples and Baiae, through Mt. Posilipo, was said to have been cut by Virgil (regarded as a magician in the Middle Ages) by supernatural art. **17–20. In midst . . . gold:** St. Mark's cathedral in Venice.

45–46. **gates . . . Africa:** Before the gates of St. Peter's there still stands the obelisk that was brought to Rome from Heliopolis by the Emperor Caligula in the first century CE.

Then in this show let me an actor be,
That this proud Pope may Faustus' cunning see.
MEPHISTOPHILIS: Let it be so, my Faustus. But, first stay
And view their triumphs° as they pass this way,
80 And then devise what best contents thy mind
By cunning in thine art to cross the Pope
Or dash the pride of this solemnity,
To make his monks and abbots stand like apes
And point like antics at his triple crown,
85 To beat the beads about the friars' pates
Or clap huge horns upon the cardinals' heads,
Or any villainy thou canst devise,
And I'll perform it, Faustus. Hark, they come.
This day shall make thee be admired in Rome.

(*Enter the Cardinals and Bishops, some bearing crosiers, some the pillars; Monks and Friars singing their procession. Then the Pope, and Raymond, King of Hungary, with Bruno, led in chains.*)

POPE: Cast down our footstool.
90 RAYMOND: Saxon Bruno, stoop,
Whilst on thy back his holiness ascends
Saint Peter's chair and state pontifical.
BRUNO: Proud Lucifer, that state belongs to me,
But thus I fall to Peter, not to thee.
95 POPE: To me and Peter shalt thou groveling lie
And crouch before the papal dignity.
Sound trumpets then, for thus Saint Peter's heir
From Bruno's back ascends Saint Peter's chair.

(*A flourish while he ascends.*)

Thus, as the gods creep on with feet of wool
100 Long ere with iron hands they punish men,
So shall our sleeping vengeance now arise
And smite with death thy hated enterprise.
Lord Cardinals of France and Padua,
Go forthwith to our holy consistory,
105 And read amongst the Statutes Decretal°
What, by the holy council held at Trent,°
The sacred synod hath decreed for him
That doth assume the papal government
Without election and a true consent.
110 Away, and bring us word with speed.
FIRST CARDINAL: We go my Lord.

                                    (*Exeunt Cardinals.*)

POPE: Lord Raymond.   [*They talk apart.*]
FAUSTUS: Go, haste thee, gentle Mephistophilis,
Follow the cardinals to the consistory,
115 And as they turn their superstitious books,
Strike them with sloth and drowsy idleness,
And make them sleep so sound that in their shapes

Thyself and I may parley with this Pope,
This proud confronter of the Emperor,
And in despite of all his holiness   120
Restore this Bruno to his liberty
And bear him to the states of Germany.
MEPHISTOPHILIS: Faustus, I go.
FAUSTUS: Dispatch it soon.
The Pope shall curse that Faustus came to Rome.   125
                        (*Exeunt Faustus and Mephistophilis.*)
BRUNO: Pope Adrian,° let me have some right of law.
I was elected by the Emperor.
POPE: We will depose the Emperor for that deed
And curse the people that submit to him.
Both he and thou shalt stand excommunicate   130
And interdict from church's privilege
And all society of holy men.
He grows too proud in his authority,
Lifting his lofty head above the clouds,
And like a steeple overpeers the church.   135
But we'll pull down his haughty insolence,
And as Pope Alexander, our progenitor,
Trod on the neck of German Frederick,°
Adding this golden sentence to our praise,
"That Peter's heirs should tread on emperors   140
And walk upon the dreadful adder's back,
Treading the lion and the dragon down
And fearless spurn the killing basilisk,"°
So will we quell that haughty schismatic,
And by authority apostolical   145
Depose him from his regal government.
BRUNO: Pope Julius swore to princely Sigismond,°
For him and the succeeding popes of Rome,
To hold the emperors their lawful lords.
POPE: Pope Julius did abuse the church's rites,   150
And therefore none of his decrees can stand.
Is not all power on earth bestowed on us?
And therefore, though we would, we cannot err.
Behold this silver belt, whereto is fixed
Seven golden keys fast sealed with seven seals   155
In token of our sevenfold power from heaven,
To bind or loose, lock fast, condemn or judge,
Resign, or seal, or whatso pleaseth us.

---

79. **triumphs:** Spectacular displays.   105. **Statutes Decretal:** Papal decrees concerning religious doctrine or ecclesiastical law.   106. **council . . . Trent:** The Council of Trent, held by the Church from 1545 to 1563.

126. **Pope Adrian:** Marlowe perhaps means Pope Hadrian IV (1154–1159), who tried to assert his authority over Frederick Barbarossa, the Holy Roman Emperor. What historicity there may be in these scenes at the papal court is badly confused. 137–138. **Pope Alexander . . . Frederick:** Pope Alexander III (1159–1181), successor to Hadrian IV, continued the struggle against Barbarossa, forcing him to acknowledge the papal supremacy at Canossa.   143. **basilisk:** A mythical monster with power to kill by its looks.   147. **Pope Julius . . . Sigismond:** None of the three popes named Julius was contemporary with the Emperor Sigismund (1368–1437). Sigismund did, however, in 1414 summon the Council of Constance, which sought to end the Great Schism (1378–1417), during which the papacy in Rome was challenged by a line of popes in Avignon.

Then he and thou and all the world shall stoop,
160 Or be assurèd of our dreadful curse
To light as heavy as the pains of hell.

(*Enter Faustus and Mephistophilis, like the Cardinals.*)

MEPHISTOPHILIS: Now tell me, Faustus, are we not fitted
well?
FAUSTUS: Yes, Mephistophilis, and two such
cardinals
Ne'er served a holy pope as we shall do.
165 But whilst they sleep within the consistory,
Let us salute his reverend fatherhood.
RAYMOND: Behold, my lord, the cardinals are
returned.
POPE: Welcome, grave fathers. Answer presently:
What have our holy council there decreed
170 Concerning Bruno and the Emperor,
In quittance of their late conspiracy
Against our state and papal dignity?
FAUSTUS: Most sacred patron of the church of Rome,
By full consent of all the synod
175 Of priests and prelates it is thus decreed:
That Bruno and the German Emperor
Be held as Lollards° and bold schismatics
And proud disturbers of the church's peace.
And if that Bruno by his own assent,
180 Without enforcement of the German peers,
Did seek to wear the triple diadem
And by your death to climb Saint Peter's chair,
The Statutes Decretal have thus decreed:
He shall be straight condemned of heresy
185 And on a pile of fagots burned to death.
POPE: It is enough. Here, take him to your charge,
And bear him straight to Ponte Angelo,
And in the strongest tower enclose him fast.
Tomorrow, sitting in our consistory
190 With all our college of grave cardinals,
We will determine of his life or death.
Here, take his triple crown along with you,
And leave it in the church's treasury.
Make haste again, my good lord cardinals,
195 And take our blessing apostolical.
MEPHISTOPHILIS: So, so. Was never devil thus blessed
before.
FAUSTUS: Away, sweet Mephistophilis, be gone.
The cardinals will be plagued for this anon.

(*Exeunt Faustus and Mephistophilis
[with Bruno].*)

POPE: Go presently and bring a banquet forth,
200 That we may solemnize Saint Peter's feast,
And with Lord Raymond, King of Hungary,
Drink to our late and happy victory. (*Exeunt.*)

177. Lollards: Followers of John Wyclif (1320?–1384), the English reformer.

Scene II

(*A sennet [is sounded] while the banquet is brought in; and then enter Faustus and Mephistophilis in their own shapes.*)

MEPHISTOPHILIS: Now, Faustus, come, prepare thyself
for mirth.
The sleepy cardinals are hard at hand
To censure Bruno, that is posted hence,
And on a proud-paced steed, as swift as thought,
Flies o'er the Alps to fruitful Germany, 5
There to salute the woeful Emperor.
FAUSTUS: The Pope will curse them for their sloth today,
That slept both Bruno and his crown away.
But now, that Faustus may delight his mind
And by their folly make some merriment, 10
Sweet Mephistophilis, so charm me here
That I may walk invisible to all
And do whate'er I please unseen of any.
MEPHISTOPHILIS: Faustus, thou shalt. Then kneel down
presently:
Whilst on thy head I lay my hand 15
And charm thee with this magic wand.
First wear this girdle; then appear
Invisible to all are here.
The planets seven, the gloomy air,
Hell and the Furies'° forkèd hair, 20
Pluto's blue fire, and Hecate's tree,°
With magic spells so compass thee
That no eye may thy body see.
So Faustus. Now, for all their holiness,
Do what thou wilt, thou shalt not be discerned. 25
FAUSTUS: Thanks, Mephistophilis. Now friars take heed
Lest Faustus make your shaven crowns to bleed.
MEPHISTOPHILIS: Faustus, no more. See where the
cardinals come.

(*Enter Pope and all the Lords. Enter the Cardinals with a book.*)

POPE: Welcome, lord cardinals. Come, sit down.
Lord Raymond, take your seat. Friars attend, 30
And see that all things be in readiness,
As best beseems this solemn festival.
FIRST CARDINAL: First, may it please your sacred holiness
To view the sentence of the reverend synod
Concerning Bruno and the Emperor? 35
POPE: What needs this question? Did I not tell you
Tomorrow we would sit i' th' consistory
And there determine of his punishment?
You brought us word even now; it was decreed
That Bruno and the cursèd Emperor 40
Were by the holy council both condemned
For loathèd Lollards and base schismatics.
Then wherefore would you have me view that book?

III, ii. 20. Furies: Spirits called on to avenge crimes, especially crimes against kin. **21. Hecate's tree:** Hecate is the goddess of witchcraft.

FIRST CARDINAL: Your grace mistakes. You gave us no
    such charge.
45 RAYMOND: Deny it not. We all are witnesses
    That Bruno here was late delivered you,
    With his rich triple crown to be reserved
    And put into the church's treasury.
  BOTH CARDINALS: By holy Paul, we saw them not.
50 POPE: By Peter, you shall die
    Unless you bring them forth immediately.
    Hale them to prison. Lade their limbs with gyves.°
    False prelates, for this hateful treachery
    Cursed be your souls to hellish misery.

            [*Exeunt the two Cardinals with Attendants.*]

55 FAUSTUS: So, they are safe. Now, Faustus, to the feast.
    The Pope had never such a frolic guest.
  POPE: Lord Archbishop of Rheims, sit down with us.
  ARCHBISHOP: I thank your holiness.
  FAUSTUS: Fall to. The devil choke you an you spare.°
60 POPE: Who's that spoke? Friars look about.
  FRIAR: Here's nobody, if it like your holiness.
  POPE: Lord Raymond, pray fall to. I am beholding
    To the Bishop of Milan for this so rare a present.
  FAUSTUS: I thank you, sir.   [*He snatches the dish.*]
65 POPE: How now? Who snatched the meat from me?
    Villains, why speak you not?
    My good Lord Archbishop, here's a most dainty dish
    Was sent me from a cardinal in France.
  FAUSTUS: I'll have that too.   [*He snatches the dish.*]
70 POPE: What Lollards do attend our holiness,
    That we receive such great indignity?
    Fetch me some wine.
  FAUSTUS: Ay, pray do, for Faustus is a-dry.
  POPE: Lord Raymond, I drink unto your grace.
75 FAUSTUS: I pledge your grace.   [*He snatches the cup.*]
  POPE: My wine gone too? Ye lubbers, look about
    And find the man that doth this villainy,
    Or by our sanctitude, you all shall die.
    I pray, my lords, have patience at this
80   Troublesome banquet.
  ARCHBISHOP: Please it your holiness, I think it be some
    ghost crept out of purgatory, and now is come unto
    your holiness for his pardon.
  POPE: It may be so.
85   Go then, command our priests to sing a dirge
    To lay the fury of this same troublesome ghost.
                [*Exit an attendant.*]
    Once again, my lord, fall to.
            (*The Pope crosseth himself.*)
  FAUSTUS: How now?
    Must every bit be spicèd with a cross?
90   Nay then, take that.   [*He strikes the Pope.*]

POPE: O I am slain. Help me, my lords.
    O come and help to bear my body hence.
    Damned be this soul for ever for this deed.

          (*Exeunt the Pope and his train.*)

MEPHISTOPHILIS: Now, Faustus, what will you do now?
    For I can tell you you'll be cursed with bell, book,   95
    and candle.°
FAUSTUS: Bell, book, and candle; candle, book, and bell,
    Forward and backward, to curse Faustus to hell.

(*Enter the Friars with bell, book, and candle for the
dirge.*)

FIRST FRIAR: Come, brethren, let's about our business
    with good devotion.   [*They chant.*] 100
    *Cursed be he that stole his holiness' meat from
    the table.*
       Maledicat Dominus!°
    *Cursed be he that struck his holiness a blow on
    the face.*
       Maledicat Dominus!
    *Cursed be he that struck Friar Sandelo a blow on
    the pate.*   105
       Maledicat Dominus!
    Cursed be he that disturbeth our holy dirge.
       Maledicat Dominus!
    Cursed be he that took away his holiness's wine.
       Maledicat Dominus! Et omnes sancti.°   110
    Amen.

([*Faustus and Mephistophilis*] *beat the Friars, fling
fireworks among them, and exeunt.*)

Scene III

(*Enter* [*Robin,*] *the clown, and Dick, with a cup.*)

DICK: Sirrah Robin, we were best look that your devil
    can answer the stealing of this same cup, for the vint-
    ner's boy follows us at the hard heels.
ROBIN: 'Tis no matter. Let him come. An he follow us,
    I'll so conjure him as he was never conjured in his   5
    life, I warrant him. Let me see the cup.

(*Enter Vintner.*)

DICK: Here 'tis. Yonder he comes. Now, Robin, now or
    never show thy cunning.
VINTNER: O, are you here? I am glad I have found you.
    You are a couple of fine companions. Pray, where's   10
    the cup you stole from the tavern?

---

52. **Lade . . . gyves:** Shackle their limbs.   **59. an you spare:** If
you hold back.

95–96. **bell, book, and candle:** Used traditionally in the rite of
excommunication.   102. *Maledicat Dominus:* May the Lord
curse him.   110. *Et omnes sancti:* And all the saints.

ROBIN: How, how? We steal a cup? Take heed what you
say. We look not like cup stealers, I can tell you.
VINTNER: Never deny's, for I know you have it, and I'll
15   search you.
ROBIN: Search me? Ay, and spare not. Hold the cup, Dick.
[*Aside to Dick.*] Come, come, search me, search me.

[*The Vintner searches Robin.*]

VINTNER: [*to Dick*] Come on, sirrah, let me search you now.
DICK: Ay, ay, do, do. Hold the cup, Robin. [*Aside to
20   Robin.*] I fear not your searching. We scorn to steal
your cups, I can tell you.

[*The Vintner searches Dick.*]

VINTNER: Never outface me for the matter, for sure the
cup is between you two.
ROBIN: Nay, there you lie. 'Tis beyond us both.
25   VINTNER: A plague take you! I thought 'twas your knavery to take it away. Come, give it me again.
ROBIN: Ay, much. When? Can you tell? Dick, make me
a circle, and stand close at my back, and stir not for
thy life. Vintner, you shall have your cup anon. Say
30   nothing, Dick, *O per se, O Demogorgon, Belcher and
Mephistophilis.*

(*Enter Mephistophilis.* [*Exit the Vintner, in fright.*])

MEPHISTOPHILIS: Monarch of hell, under whose black
survey
Great potentates do kneel with awful fear,
Upon whose altars thousand souls do lie,
35   How am I vexèd by these villains' charms!
From Constantinople have they brought me now,
Only for pleasure of these damnèd slaves.
ROBIN: By Lady, sir, you have had a shrewd journey of it.
Will it please you to take a shoulder of mutton to
40   supper and a tester° in your purse, and go back
again?
DICK: Ay, I pray you heartily, sir, for we called you but in
jest, I promise you.
MEPHISTOPHILIS: To purge the rashness of this cursed deed,
45   First be thou turnèd to this ugly shape,
For apish deeds transformèd to an ape.
ROBIN: O brave, an ape! I pray sir, let me have the carrying of him about to show some tricks.
MEPHISTOPHILIS: And so thou shalt. Be thou transformed
50   to a dog, and carry him upon thy back. Away, be
gone!
ROBIN: A dog? That's excellent. Let the maids look well
to their porridge pots, for I'll into the kitchen presently. Come, Dick, come.

(*Exeunt* [*Robin and Dick,*] *the two clowns.*)

MEPHISTOPHILIS: Now with the flames of everburning
55   fire,
I'll wing myself and forthwith fly amain
Unto my Faustus, to the great Turk's court.

(*Exit.*)

III, iii. 40. tester: Sixpence.

ACT IV • Prologue

(*Enter Chorus.*)

CHORUS: When Faustus had with pleasure ta'en the view
Of rarest things and royal courts of kings,
He stayed his course and so returnèd home;
Where such as bare his absence but with grief—
I mean his friends and nearest companions—   5
Did gratulate his safety with kind words,
And in their conference of what befell,
Touching his journey through the world and air,
They put forth questions of astrology,
Which Faustus answered with such learnèd skill   10
As they admired and wondered at his wit.
Now is his fame spread forth in every land.
Amongst the rest, the Emperor is one—
Carolus the fifth°—at whose palace now
Faustus is feasted 'mongst his noblemen.   15
What there he did in trial of his art
I leave untold, your eyes shall see performed.

(*Exit.*)

Scene I

(*Enter Martino and Frederick, at several doors.*)

MARTINO: What ho, officers, gentlemen,
Hie to the presences° to attend the Emperor.
Good Frederick, see the rooms be voided straight;
His majesty is coming to the hall.
Go back, and see the state° in readiness.   5
FREDERICK: But where is Bruno, our elected Pope,
That on a fury's back came post from Rome?
Will not his grace consort the Emperor?
MARTINO: O yes, and with him comes the German
conjurer,
The learnèd Faustus, fame of Wittenberg,   10
The wonder of the world for magic art;
And he intends to show great Carolus
The race of all his stout progenitors,
And bring in presence of his majesty
The royal shapes and warlike semblances   15
Of Alexander° and his beauteous paramour.
FREDERICK: Where is Benvolio?
MARTINO: Fast asleep, I warrant you.
He took his rouse with stoups° of Rhenish wine
So kindly yesternight to Bruno's health   20
That all this day the sluggard keeps his bed.
FREDERICK: See, see, his window's ope. We'll call to him.
MARTINO: What ho, Benvolio!

IV, Prologue. 14. Carolus the fifth: Charles V, King of Spain
(as Charles I) from 1516 to 1556 and Holy Roman Emperor
from 1519 to 1556.   IV, i. 2. presences: Emperor's chamber.
5. state: Throne.   16. Alexander: Alexander the Great.   19.
took . . . stoups: Had a drinking bout with brimming goblets.

(*Enter Benvolio above at a window, in his nightcap, buttoning.*)

BENVOLIO: What a devil ail you two?

25 MARTINO: Speak softly, sir, lest the devil hear you,
For Faustus at the court is late arrived,
And at his heels a thousand furies wait
To accomplish whatsoever the doctor please.

BENVOLIO: What of this?

MARTINO: Come, leave thy chamber first, and thou
30   shalt see
This conjurer perform such rare exploits
Before the Pope° and royal Emperor
As never yet was seen in Germany.

BENVOLIO: Has not the Pope enough of conjuring yet?
35   He was upon the devil's back late enough,
And if he be so far in love with him,
I would he would post with him to Rome again.

FREDERICK: Speak, wilt thou come and see this sport?

BENVOLIO: Not I.

MARTINO: Wilt thou stand in thy window and see it
40   then?

BENVOLIO: Ay, and I fall not asleep i' th' meantime.

MARTINO: The Emperor is at hand, who comes to see
What wonders by black spells may compassed be.

BENVOLIO: Well, go you attend the Emperor. I am con-
45   tent for this once to thrust my head out at a window,
for they say if a man be drunk overnight the devil
cannot hurt him in the morning. If that be true, I have
a charm in my head shall control him as well as the
conjurer, I warrant you.

(*Exit [Frederick, with Martino. Benvolio remains at the window above].*)

Scene II

(*A sennet [is sounded. Enter] Charles, the German Emperor Bruno, [the Duke of] Saxony, Faustus, Mephistophilis, Frederick, Martino, and Attendants.*)

EMPEROR: Wonder of men, renowned magician,
Thrice-learnèd Faustus, welcome to our court.
This deed of thine, in setting Bruno free
From his and our professèd enemy,
5   Shall add more excellence unto thine art
Than if by powerful necromantic spells
Thou couldst command the world's obedience.
Forever be beloved of Carolus,
And if this Bruno thou hast late redeemed°
10   In peace possess the triple diadem
And sit in Peter's chair despite of chance,
Thou shalt be famous through all Italy
And honored of the German Emperor.

FAUSTUS: These gracious words, most royal Carolus,
15   Shall make poor Faustus to his utmost power
Both love and serve the German Emperor

32. the Pope: Bruno.   IV, ii. 9. redeemed: Rescued.

And lay his life at holy Bruno's feet.
For proof whereof, if so your grace be pleased,
The doctor stands prepared by power of art
To cast his magic charms that shall pierce through   20
The ebon gates of ever-burning hell,
And hale the stubborn Furies from their caves
To compass whatsoe'er your grace commands.

BENVOLIO: [*above*] Blood, he speaks terribly, but for all
that, I do not greatly believe him. He looks as like a   25
conjurer as the Pope° to a costermonger.°

EMPEROR: Then, Faustus, as thou late did'st promise us,
We would behold that famous conqueror,
Great Alexander, and his paramour
In their true shapes and state majestical,   30
That we may wonder at their excellence.

FAUSTUS: Your majesty shall see them presently.
Mephistophilis, away,
And with a solemn noise of trumpets' sound
Present before this royal Emperor,   35
Great Alexander and his beauteous paramour.

MEPHISTOPHILIS: Faustus, I will.

[*Exit.*]

BENVOLIO: Well, master doctor, an your devils come not
away quickly, you shall have me asleep presently.
Zounds, I could eat myself for anger to think I have   40
been such an ass all this while, to stand gaping after
the devil's governor and can see nothing.

FAUSTUS: I'll make you feel something anon, if my art
fail me not
My lord, I must forewarn your majesty
That when my spirits present the royal shapes   45
Of Alexander and his paramour,
Your grace demand no questions of the king,
But in dumb silence let them come and go.

EMPEROR: Be it as Faustus please; we are content.

BENVOLIO: Ay, ay, and I am content too. And thou bring   50
Alexander and his paramour before the Emperor, I'll
be Actaeon and turn myself to a stag.

FAUSTUS: And I'll play Diana and send you the horns
presently.

(*[A] sennet [is sounded]. Enter at one [door] the Emperor Alexander, at the other Darius.° They meet [in combat]. Darius is thrown down; Alexander kills him, takes off his crown, and, offering to go out, his paramour meets him. He embraceth her and sets Darius' crown upon her head; and coming back, both salute the Emperor, who, leaving his state, offers to embrace them, which Faustus seeing, suddenly stays him. Then trumpets cease and music sounds.*)

My gracious lord, you do forget yourself.
These are but shadows, not substantial.   55

EMPEROR: O pardon me. My thoughts are so ravishèd

26. the Pope: Bruno.   Costermonger: Fruit vendor (a term of contempt).   53. [S.D.] *Darius:* King Darius III of Persia (336–330 BCE), defeated at Granicus in 334 BCE by the Greeks under Alexander the Great.

With sight of this renownèd emperor,
That in mine arms I would have compassed him.
But, Faustus, since I may not speak to them,
60 To satisfy my longing thoughts at full,
Let me this tell thee: I have heard it said
That this fair lady, whilst she lived on earth,
Had on her neck a little wart or mole;
How may I prove that saying to be true?
65 FAUSTUS: Your majesty may boldly go and see.
EMPEROR: Faustus, I see it plain,
And in this sight thou better pleasest me
Than if I gained another monarchy.
FAUSTUS: Away! Be gone!

(*Exit show.*)

70   See, see, my gracious lord, what strange beast is yon,
That thrusts his head out at window?
EMPEROR: O wondrous sight! See, Duke of Saxony,
Two spreading horns most strangely fastenèd
Upon the head of young Benvolio.
75 SAXONY: What? Is he asleep or dead?
FAUSTUS: He sleeps, my lord, but dreams not of his
horns.
EMPEROR: This sport is excellent. We'll call and wake
him.
What ho, Benvolio!
BENVOLIO: A plague upon you! Let me sleep a while.
80 EMPEROR: I blame thee not to sleep much, having such a
head of thine own.
SAXONY: Look up, Benvolio; 'tis the Emperor calls.
BENVOLIO: The Emperor? Where? O zounds, my head!
EMPEROR: Nay, and thy horns hold, 'tis no matter for thy
85 head, for that's armed sufficiently.
FAUSTUS: Why, how now, sir knight! What, hanged by
the horns? This is most horrible. Fie, fie, pull in your
head for shame. Let not all the world wonder at you.
BENVOLIO: Zounds, doctor, is this your villainy?
90 FAUSTUS: O say not so, sir. The doctor has no skill,
No art, no cunning, to present these lords
Or bring before this royal Emperor
The mighty monarch, warlike Alexander.
If Faustus do it, you are straight resolved
95 In bold Actaeon's shape to turn a stag.
And therefore, my lord, so please your majesty,
I'll raise a kennel of hounds shall hunt him so
As all his footmanship shall scarce prevail
To keep his carcass from their bloody fangs
100 Ho, Belimote, Argiron, Asterote!
BENVOLIO: Hold, hold! Zounds, he'll raise up a kennel of
devils, I think, anon. Good, my lord, entreat for me.
'Sblood, I am never able to endure these torments.
EMPEROR: Then, good master doctor,
105 Let me entreat you to remove his horns.
He has done penance now sufficiently.
FAUSTUS: My gracious lord, not so much for injury done
to me, as to delight your majesty with some mirth,
hath Faustus justly requited this injurious° knight;

which being all I desire, I am content to remove his   110
horns. Mephistophilis, transform him.

[*Mephistophilis removes the horns.*]

And hereafter, sir, look you speak well of scholars.
BENVOLIO: [*aside.*] Speak well of ye? 'Sblood, and scholars be such cuckold makers to clap horns of honest
men's heads o' this order, I'll ne'er trust smooth faces   115
and small ruffs° more. But an I be not revenged for
this, would I might be turned to a gaping oyster and
drink nothing but salt water.

[*Exit Benvolio above.*]

EMPEROR: Come, Faustus. While the Emperor lives,
In recompense of this thy high desert,   120
Thou shalt command the state of Germany
And live beloved of mighty Carolus.

(*Exeunt.*)

Scene III

(*Enter Benvolio, Martino, Frederick, and Soldiers.*)

MARTINO: Nay, sweet Benvolio, let us sway thy thoughts
From this attempt against the conjurer.
BENVOLIO: Away! You love me not to urge me thus.
Shall I let slip so great an injury,
When every servile groom jests at my wrongs   5
And in their rustic gambols proudly say,
"Benvolio's head was graced with horns today"?
O, may these eyelids never close again
Till with my sword I have that conjurer slain.
If you will aid me in this enterprise,   10
Then draw your weapons and be resolute.
If not, depart. Here will Benvolio die,
But Faustus' death shall quit° my infamy.
FREDERICK: Nay, we will stay with thee, betide what may,
And kill that doctor if he come this way.   15
BENVOLIO: Then, gentle Frederick, hie thee to the grove,
And place our servants and our followers
Close in an ambush there behind the trees.
By this, I know, the conjurer is near.
I saw him kneel and kiss the Emperor's hand   20
And take his leave, laden with rich rewards.
Then, soldiers, boldly fight. If Faustus die,
Take you the wealth; leave us the victory.
FREDERICK: Come, soldiers. Follow me unto the grove.
Who kills him shall have gold and endless love.   25

(*Exit Frederick with the Soldiers.*)

BENVOLIO: My head is lighter than it was by th'horns,
But yet my heart's more ponderous than my head
And pants until I see that conjurer dead.
MARTINO: Where shall we place ourselves, Benvolio?
BENVOLIO: Here will we stay to bide the first assault.   30
O, were that damnèd hell-hound but in place,
Thou soon shouldst see me quit my foul disgrace.
(*Enter Frederick.*)

---

109. injurious: Insulting.

116. small ruffs: Academic gowns.   **IV, iii. 13. quit:** Pay for.

Orson Welles as Faustus in the 1937 Broadway production of
The Tragical History of Dr. Faustus, which Welles also directed.

FREDERICK: Close, close, the conjurer is at hand
    And all alone comes walking in his gown.
35   Be ready then, and strike the peasant down.
BENVOLIO: Mine be that honor then. Now, sword, strike
    home.
    For horns he gave I'll have his head anon.

(*Enter Faustus with the false head.*)

MARTINO: See, see, he comes.
BENVOLIO: No words! This blow ends all.
    Hell take his soul; his body thus must fall.
                       [*He stabs Faustus.*]
40 FAUSTUS: [*falling*] Oh!
FREDERICK: Groan you, master doctor?
BENVOLIO: Break may his heart with groans! Dear
    Frederick, see,
    Thus will I end his griefs immediately.
MARTINO: Strike with a willing hand. His head is off.

[*Benvolio strikes off Faustus' false head.*]

45 BENVOLIO: The devil's dead. The Furies now may laugh.
FREDERICK: Was this that stern aspèct, that awful frown,
    Made the grim monarch of infernal spirits
    Tremble and quake at his commanding charms?
MARTINO: Was this that damnèd head whose heart
    conspired
50   Benvolio's shame before the Emperor?

BENVOLIO: Ay, that's the head, and here the body lies,
    Justly rewarded for his villainies.
FREDERICK: Come, let's devise how we may add more
    shame
    To the black scandal of his hated name.
BENVOLIO: First, on his head, in quittance of my wrongs, 55
    I'll nail huge forkèd horns and let them hang
    Within the window where he yoked° me first,
    That all the world may see my just revenge.
MARTINO: What use shall we put his beard to?
BENVOLIO: We'll sell it to a chimney-sweeper. It will 60
    wear out ten birchen brooms, I warrant you.
FREDERICK: What shall eyes do?
BENVOLIO: We'll put out his eyes, and they shall serve for
    buttons to his lips to keep his tongue from catching
    cold. 65
MARTINO: An excellent policy! And now, sirs, having
    divided him, what shall the body do?

[*Faustus rises.*]

BENVOLIO: Zounds, the devil's alive again.
FREDERICK: Give him his head, for God's sake.
FAUSTUS: Nay, keep it. Faustus will have heads and hands, 70
    Ay, all your hearts, to recompense this deed.
    Knew you not, traitors, I was limited
    For four-and-twenty years to breathe on earth?
    And had you cut my body with your swords,
    Or hewed this flesh and bones as small as sand, 75
    Yet in a minute had my spirit returned,
    And I had breathed a man made free from harm.
    But wherefore do I dally my revenge?
    Asteroth, Belimoth, Mephistophilis!

(*Enter Mephistophilis and other Devils.*)

    Go, horse these traitors on your fiery backs, 80
    And mount aloft with them as high as heaven;
    Thence pitch them headlong to the lowest hell.
    Yet stay. The world shall see their misery,
    And hell shall after plague their treachery.
    Go, Belimoth, and take this caitiff° hence 85
    And hurl him in some lake of mud and dirt.
    Take thou this other; drag him through the woods
    Amongst the pricking thorns and sharpest briars,
    Whilst with my gentle Mephistophilis
    This traitor flies unto some steepy rock 90
    That, rolling down, may break the villain's bones
    As he intended to dismember me.
    Fly hence. Dispatch my charge immediately.
FREDERICK: Pity us, gentle Faustus. Save our lives.
FAUSTUS: Away!
FREDERICK: He must needs go that the devil drives. 95

                  (*Exeunt Spirits with the Knights.*)

(*Enter the ambushed Soldiers.*)

FIRST SOLDIER: Come, sirs, prepare yourselves in
    readiness.
    Make haste to help these noble gentlemen;
    I heard them parley with the conjurer.

57. **yoked:** Placed the horns on.   85. **caitiff:** Despicable wretch.

SECOND SOLDIER: See where he comes. Dispatch and kill
the slave.
100 FAUSTUS: What's here? An ambush to betray my life?
Then, Faustus, try thy skill. Base peasants, stand,
For lo, these trees remove at my command
And stand as bulwarks 'twixt yourselves and me,
To shield me from your hated treachery.
105 Yet to encounter this your weak attempt,
Behold an army comes incontinent.°

(*Faustus strikes the door, and enter a Devil playing on
a drum, after him another bearing an ensign, and divers
with weapons, Mephistophilis with fireworks. They set
upon the Soldiers and drive them out. [Exit Faustus.]*)

Scene IV

(*Enter at several doors Benvolio, Frederick, and Martino, their heads and faces bloody and besmeared with
mud and dirt, all having horns on their heads.*)

MARTINO: What ho, Benvolio!
BENVOLIO: Here! What, Frederick, ho!
FREDERICK: O help me, gentle friend. Where is Martino?
MARTINO: Dear Frederick, here,
5   Half smothered in a lake of mud and dirt,
Through which the Furies dragged me by the heels.
FREDERICK: Martino, see! Benvolio's horns again.
MARTINO: O misery! How now, Benvolio!
BENVOLIO: Defend me, heaven. Shall I be haunted° still?
10 MARTINO: Nay, fear not man; we have not power to kill.
BENVOLIO: My friends transformèd thus! O hellish spite!
Your heads are all set with horns.
FREDERICK: You hit it right.
It is your own you mean. Feel on your head.
BENVOLIO: Zounds, horns again!
15 MARTINO: Nay, chafe not man. We all are sped.°
BENVOLIO: What devil attends this damned magician,
That, spite of spite, our wrongs are doublèd?
FREDERICK: What may we do, that we may hide our
shames?
BENVOLIO: If we should follow him to work revenge,
20 He'd join long asses' ears to these huge horns,
And make us laughing-stocks to all the world.
MARTINO: What shall we then do, dear Benvolio?
BENVOLIO: I have a castle joining near these woods,
And thither we'll repair and live obscure
25 Till time shall alter these our brutish shapes.
Sith black disgrace hath thus eclipsed our fame,
We'll rather die with grief than live with shame.

(*Exeunt omnes.°*)

Scene V°

(*Enter Faustus and Mephistophilis.*)

FAUSTUS: Now, Mephistophilis, the restless course
That time doth run with calm and silent foot,
Shortening my days and thread of vital life,
Calls for the payment of my latest years.
Therefore, sweet Mephistophilis, let us   5
Make haste to Wittenberg.
MEPHISTOPHILIS: What, will you go on horseback, or on
foot?
FAUSTUS: Nay, till I am past this fair and pleasant green,
I'll walk on foot.

[*Exit Mephistophilis.*]

(*Enter a Horse-Courser.°*)

HORSE-COURSER: I have been all this day seeking one   10
Master Fustian.° Mass, see where he is. God save
you, master doctor.
FAUSTUS: What, horse-courser! You are well met.
HORSE-COURSER: I beseech your worship, accept of these
forty dollars.   15
FAUSTUS: Friend, thou canst not buy so good a horse for
so small a price. I have no great need to sell him, but
if thou likest him for ten dollars more, take him, because I see thou hast a good mind to him.
HORSE-COURSER: I beseech you, sir, accept of this. I am   20
a very poor man and have lost very much of late by
horse-flesh, and this bargain will set me up again.
FAUSTUS: Well, I will not stand with thee.° Give me the
money.

[*The Horse-Courser gives Faustus money.*]

Now, sirrah, I must tell you that you may ride him   25
o'er hedge and ditch, and spare him not. But, do you
hear? In any case, ride him not into the water.
HORSE-COURSER: How sir? Not into the water? Why, will
he not drink of all waters?°
FAUSTUS: Yes, he will drink of all waters, but ride him   30
not into the water—o'er hedge and ditch, or where
thou wilt, but not into the water. Go, bid the hostler
deliver him unto you, and remember what I say.
HORSE-COURSER: I warrant you, sir. O joyful day!
Now am I a man made forever.   35

(*Exit.*)

FAUSTUS: What art thou, Faustus, but a man condemned
to die?
Thy fatal time draws to a final end.
Despair doth drive distrust into my thoughts.
Confound these passions with a quiet sleep.

IV, v. The first eleven lines of this scene do not appear in
all versions of the play, but they provide a transition to the
Horse-Courser episode and remind readers of Faustus's impending tragedy. **9.** [S.D.] *Horse-Courser:* One who deals
in horses. **11. Fustian:** The perversion of Faustus's name is a
deliberate attempt at humor. **23. stand with thee:** Bargain.
29. drink . . . waters: Be ready for anything (a common proverb
of the time).

106. incontinent: At once. IV, iv. 9. haunted: (1) Bewitched;
(2) hunted, pursued (since he is a stag). 15. sped: Provided
(with horns). 27. [S.D.] *Exeunt omnes:* Latin for "All go out."

40   Tush! Christ did call the thief upon the cross;
       Then rest thee, Faustus, quiet in conceit.°

(*He sits to sleep [in his chair].*)

(*Enter the Horse-Courser, wet.*)

HORSE-COURSER: O what a cozening doctor was this? I
       riding my horse into the water, thinking some hidden
       mystery° had been in the horse, I had nothing under
45   me but a little straw and had much ado to escape
       drowning. Well, I'll go rouse him and make him give
       me my forty dollars again. Ho, sirrah doctor, you
       cozening scab!° Master doctor, awake and rise, and
       give me my money again, for your horse is turned to
50   a bottle° of hay. Master doctor!

(*He [tries to wake Faustus, and in doing so] pulls off
his leg.*)

       Alas, I am undone! What shall I do? I have pulled
       off his leg.

[*Faustus awakes.*]

FAUSTUS: O, help, help! The villain hath murdered me.
HORSE-COURSER: Murder or not murder, now he has but
55   one leg, I'll outrun him and cast this leg into some
       ditch or other.
FAUSTUS: Stop him, stop him, stop him! Ha, ha, ha,
       Faustus hath his leg again, and the horse-courser a
       bundle of hay for his forty dollars.

(*Enter Wagner.*)

60   How now, Wagner, what news with thee?
WAGNER: If it please you, the Duke of Anholt doth ear-
       nestly entreat your company and hath sent some of his
       men to attend you with provision fit for your journey.
FAUSTUS: The Duke of Anholt's an honorable gentleman,
65   and one to whom I must be no niggard of my cun-
       ning. Come away.

                                        (*Exeunt.*)

Scene VI

(*Enter [Robin, the] Clown, Dick, [the] Horse-Courser,
and a Carter.°*)

CARTER: Come, my masters, I'll bring you to the best beer
       in Europe. What ho, hostess! Where be these whores?

(*Enter Hostess.*)

HOSTESS: How now, what lack you? What, my old
       guests, welcome.
5   ROBIN: Sirrah, Dick, dost thou know why I stand so
       mute?
DICK: No, Robin; why is't?
ROBIN: I am eighteen pence on the score.° But say noth-
       ing, see if she have forgotten me.
10 HOSTESS: Who's this that stands so solemnly by himself?
       What, my old guest?

---

41. **conceit:** Thoughts.   44. **mystery:** Quality.   48. **cozening
scab:** Deceitful, contemptible rascal.   50. **bottle:** Bundle.   **IV,
vi.** [S.D.] *Carter:* A person who drives a cart.   8. **on the score:**
In debt.

ROBIN: O hostess, how do you? I hope my score stands
       still.°
HOSTESS: Ay, there's no doubt of that, for methinks you
       make no haste to wipe it out.   15
DICK: Why, hostess, I say, fetch us some beer.
HOSTESS: You shall presently. Look up into th'hall there,
       ho!

                                          (*Exit.*)

DICK: Come, sirs, what shall we do now till mine hostess
       come?   20
CARTER: Marry, sir, I'll tell you the bravest tale how a
       conjurer served me. You know Doctor Fauster?
HORSE-COURSER: Ay, a plague take him. Here's some
       on's have cause to know him. Did he conjure thee
       too?   25
CARTER: I'll tell you how he served me. As I was going to
       Wittenberg t'other day with a load of hay, he met me
       and asked me what he should give me for as much
       hay as he could eat. Now, sir, I thinking that a little
       would serve his turn, bade him take as much as he   30
       would for three farthings. So he presently gave me
       my money and fell to eating; and as I am a cursen°
       man, he never left eating till he had eat up all my
       load of hay.
ALL: O monstrous! Eat a whole load of hay!   35
ROBIN: Yes, yes, that may be, for I have heard of one that
       has eat a load of logs.
HORSE-COURSER: Now, sirs, you shall hear how villain-
       ously he served me. I went to him yesterday to buy a
       horse of him, and he would by no means sell him   40
       under forty dollars. So, sir, because I knew him to be
       such a horse as would run over hedge and ditch and
       never tire, I gave him my money. So when I had my
       horse, Doctor Fauster bade me ride him night and
       day and spare him no time; but, quoth he, in any   45
       case ride him not into the water. Now sir, I thinking
       the horse had had some rare quality that he would
       not have me know of, what did I but rid him into
       a great river, and when I came just in the midst, my
       horse vanished away, and I sat straddling upon a   50
       bottle of hay.
ALL: O brave doctor!
HORSE-COURSER: But you shall hear how bravely I
       served him for it. I went me home to his house, and
       there I found him asleep. I kept a hallooing and   55
       whooping in his ears, but all could not wake him. I
       seeing that took him by the leg and never rested pull-
       ing till I had pulled me his leg quite off, and now 'tis
       at home in mine hostry.
ROBIN: And has the doctor but one leg then? That's excel-   60
       lent, for one of his devils turned me into the likeness
       of an ape's face.
CARTER: Some more drink, hostess.
ROBIN: Hark you, we'll into another room and drink a
       while, and then we'll go seek out the doctor.   65
                                          (*Exeunt.*)

12–13. **stands still:** Does not go higher.   32. **cursen:** Christened.

Scene VII

(*Enter the Duke of Anholt, his Duchess, Faustus, and Mephistophilis, [Servants and Attendants].*)

DUKE: Thanks, master doctor, for these pleasant sights. Nor know I how sufficiently to recompense your great deserts° in erecting that enchanted castle in the air, the sight whereof so delighted me, as nothing in the world could please me more.

FAUSTUS: I do think myself, my good lord, highly recompensed in that it pleaseth your grace to think but well of that which Faustus hath performed. But, gracious lady, it may be that you have taken no pleasure in those sights. Therefore, I pray you, tell me what is the thing you most desire to have; be it in the world, it shall be yours. I have heard that great-bellied women do long for things are rare and dainty.

DUCHESS: True, master doctor, and since I find you so kind, I will make known unto you what my heart desires to have. And were it now summer, as it is January, a dead time of the winter, I would request no better meat than a dish of ripe grapes.

FAUSTUS: This is but a small matter. Go, Mephistophilis, away!

(*Exit Mephistophilis.*)

Madam I will do more than this for your content.

(*Enter Mephistophilis again with the grapes.*)

Here; now taste ye these. They should be good, for they come from a far country, I can tell you.

DUKE: This makes me wonder more than all the rest, that at this time of year, when every tree is barren of his fruit, from whence you had these ripe grapes.

FAUSTUS: Please it, your grace, the year is divided into two circles over the whole world, so that when it is winter with us, in the contrary circle it is likewise summer with them, as in India, Saba,° and such countries that lie far east, where they have fruit twice a year. From whence, by means of a swift spirit that I have, I had these grapes brought, as you see.

DUCHESS: And trust me, they are the sweetest grapes that e'er I tasted.

(*The Clowns [Robin, Dick, the Carter, and the Horse-Courser] bounce at the gate within.*)

DUKE: What rude disturbers have we at the gate?
Go, pacify their fury. Set it ope,
And then demand of them what they would have.

[*Exit a Servant.*]

(*They knock again and call out to talk with Faustus.*)

[*Enter Servant to them.*]

SERVANT: Why, how now, masters, what a coil° is there? What is the reason you disturb the duke?

DICK: We have no reason for it; therefore a fig for him.

SERVANT: What, saucy varlets,° dare you be so bold?

HORSE-COURSER: I hope, sir, we have wit enough to be more bold than welcome.

SERVANT: It appears so. Pray be bold elsewhere, And trouble not the duke.

DUKE: What would they have?

SERVANT: They all cry out to speak with Doctor Faustus.

CARTER: Ay, and we will speak with him.

DUKE: Will you, sir? Commit the rascals.

DICK: Commit with us! He were as good commit with his father as commit with us.

FAUSTUS: I do beseech your grace, let them come in; They are good subject for a merriment.

DUKE: Do as thou wilt, Faustus. I give thee leave.

FAUSTUS: I thank your grace.

(*Enter Robin, Dick, Carter, and Horse-Courser.*)

Why, how now, my good friends?
'Faith you are too outrageous,° but come near;
I have procured your pardons. Welcome all!

ROBIN: Nay, sir, we will be welcome for our money, and we will pay for what we take. What ho! Give's half a dozen of beer here, and be hanged.

FAUSTUS: Nay, hark you; can you tell me where you are?

CARTER: Ay, marry can I: we are under heaven.

SERVANT: Ay, but sir sauce-box, know you in what place?

HORSE-COURSER: Ay, ay, the house is good enough to drink in. Zounds, fill us some beer, or we'll break all the barrels in the house and dash out all your brains with your bottles.

FAUSTUS: Be not so furious. Come, you shall have beer. My lord, beseech you give me leave a while: I'll gage my credit, 'twill content your grace.

DUKE: With all my heart, kind doctor. Please thyself; Our servants and our court's at thy command.

FAUSTUS: I humbly thank your grace. Then fetch some beer.

HORSE-COURSER: Ay, marry, there spake a doctor indeed, and 'faith,
I'll drink a health to thy wooden leg for that word.

FAUSTUS: My wooden leg? What dost thou mean by that?

CARTER: Ha, ha, ha! Dost hear him, Dick? He has forgot his leg.

HORSE-COURSER: Ay, ay, he does not stand much° upon that.

FAUSTUS: No, faith; not much upon a wooden leg.

CARTER: Good lord, that flesh and blood should be so frail with your worship! Do not you remember a horse-courser you sold a horse to?

FAUSTUS: Yes, I remember I sold one a horse.

CARTER: And do you remember you bid he should not ride into the water?

FAUSTUS: Yes, I do very well remember that.

CARTER: And do you remember nothing of your leg?

FAUSTUS: No, in good sooth.

CARTER: Then, I pray, remember your courtesy.°

FAUSTUS: I thank you, sir.

IV, vii. 3. **deserts:** Good deeds.   30. **Saba:** Sheba.   39. **coil:** Disturbance.   42. **varlets:** Knaves, rascals.

56. **outrageous:** Violent.   78. **stand much:** Make much of (with a quibble).   89. **courtesy:** Curtsy; or, leg.

CARTER: 'Tis not so much worth. I pray you, tell me one thing.

FAUSTUS: What's that?

95 CARTER: Be both your legs bedfellows every night together?

FAUSTUS: Wouldst thou make a Colossus° of me, that thou askest me such questions?

CARTER: No, truly, sir. I would make nothing of you, but I would fain know that.

(Enter Hostess with drink.)

100 FAUSTUS: Then, I assure thee, certainly they are.

CARTER: I thank you; I am fully satisfied.

FAUSTUS: But wherefore dost thou ask?

CARTER: For nothing, sir. But methinks you should have a wooden bedfellow of one of 'em.

105 HORSE-COURSER: Why, do you hear, sir; did not I pull off one of your legs when you were asleep?

FAUSTUS: But I have it again, now I am awake. Look you here, sir.

ALL: O horrible! Had the doctor three legs?

110 CARTER: Do you remember, sir, how you cozened me and ate up my load of—

[Faustus charms him dumb.]

DICK: Do you remember how you made me wear an ape's—

[Faustus charms him dumb.]

HORSE-COURSER: You whoreson conjuring scab, do you remember how you cozened me with a ho—

[Faustus charms him dumb.]

115 ROBIN: Ha' you forgotten me? You think to carry it away° with your *hey-pass* and *re-pass*; do you remember the dog's fa—

[Faustus charms him dumb.]   *(Exeunt Clowns.)*

HOSTESS: Who pays for the ale? Hear you, master doctor, now you have sent away my guests, I pray who shall

120 pay me for my a—

[Faustus charms her dumb.]   *(Exit Hostess.)*

DUCHESS: My lord,
We are much beholding to this learnèd man.

DUKE: So are we, madam, which we will recompense
With all the love and kindness that we may.

125 His artful sport drives all sad thoughts away.

(Exeunt.)

ACT V • Scene I

(Thunder and lightning. Enter Devils with covered dishes. Mephistophilis leads them into Faustus' study. Then enter Wagner.)

WAGNER: I think my master means to die shortly.
He has made his will and given me his wealth,
His house, his goods, and store of golden plate,

Besides two thousand ducats ready coined.
I wonder what he means. If death were nigh,   5
He would not frolic thus. He's now at supper
With the scholars, where there's such belly-cheer
As Wagner in his life ne'er saw the like.
And see where they come; belike the feast is done.

(Exit.)

(Enter Faustus, Mephistophilis, and two or three Scholars.)

FIRST SCHOLAR: Master Doctor Faustus, since our con-   10
ference about fair ladies, which was the beautifulest
in all the world, we have determined with ourselves
that Helen of Greece was the admirablest lady that
ever lived. Therefore, master doctor, if you will do us
so much favor as to let us see that peerless dame of   15
Greece, whom all the world admires for majesty, we
should think ourselves much beholding unto you.

FAUSTUS: Gentlemen,
For that I know your friendship is unfeigned,
And Faustus' custom is not to deny   20
The just requests of those that wish him well,
You shall behold that peerless dame of Greece,
No otherwise for pomp and majesty
Than when Sir Paris crossed the seas with her
And brought the spoils to rich Dardania.°   25
Be silent then, for danger is in words.

(Music sounds. Mephistophilis brings in Helen; she passeth over the stage.)

SECOND SCHOLAR: Was this fair Helen, whose admirèd worth
Made Greece with ten years' war afflict poor Troy?
Too simple is my wit to tell her praise,
Whom all the world admires for majesty.   30

THIRD SCHOLAR: No marvel though the angry Greeks pursued
With ten years' war the rape of such a queen,
Whose heavenly beauty passeth all compare.

FIRST SCHOLAR: Since we have seen the pride of nature's works
And only paragon of excellence,   35
We'll take our leaves and for this blessèd sight
Happy and blest be Faustus evermore.

FAUSTUS: Gentlemen, farewell; the same wish I to you.

(Exeunt Scholars.)

(Enter an Old Man.)

OLD MAN: O gentle Faustus, leave this damnèd art,
This magic that will charm thy soul to hell   40
And quite bereave thee of salvation.
Though thou hast now offended like a man,
Do not persevere in it like a devil.
Yet, yet, thou hast an amiable° soul,
If sin by custom grow not into nature.   45
Then, Faustus, will repentance come too late;

96. Colossus: A giant statue said to have stood with its legs astride at the entrance to the ancient harbor of Rhodes. **115–116. carry it away:** Come off best.

V, i. 22–25. peerless dame . . . Dardania: The Greek Helen (the "peerless dame"), wife of Menelaus, was carried off to Troy (Dardania) by Paris, sparking the Trojan War. **44. amiable:** Worthy of divine love or grace.

Then thou art banished from the sight of heaven.
No mortal can express the pains of hell.
It may be this my exhortation
50 Seems harsh and all unpleasant; let it not,
For, gentle son, I speak it not in wrath
Or envy of° thee, but in tender love
And pity of thy future misery.
And so have hope that this my kind rebuke,
55 Checking° thy body, may amend thy soul.
FAUSTUS: Where art thou, Faustus? Wretch, what hast
thou done?
Damned art thou, Faustus, damned; despair and die!
Hell claims his right, and with a roaring voice
Says, "Faustus, come; thine hour is almost come";
60 And Faustus now will come to do thee right.

(*Mephistophilis gives him a dagger.*)

OLD MAN: O stay, good Faustus, stay thy desperate steps.
I see an angel hovers o'er thy head,
And with a vial full of precious grace
Offers to pour the same into thy soul.
65 Then call for mercy and avoid despair.
FAUSTUS: Ah, my sweet friend, I feel thy words
To comfort my distressèd soul.
Leave me a while to ponder on my sins.
OLD MAN: Faustus, I leave thee, but with grief of heart,
70 Fearing the enemy of thy hapless soul.

(*Exit.*)

FAUSTUS: Accursèd Faustus, where is mercy now?
I do repent, and yet I do despair.
Hell strives with grace for conquest in my breast.
What shall I do to shun the snares of death?
75 MEPHISTOPHILIS: Thou traitor, Faustus, I arrest thy soul
For disobedience to my sovereign lord.
Revolt, or I'll in piecemeal tear thy flesh.
FAUSTUS: I do repent I e'er offended him.
Sweet Mephistophilis, entreat thy lord
80 To pardon my unjust presumption,
And with my blood again I will confirm
The former vow I made to Lucifer.
MEPHISTOPHILIS: Do it then, Faustus, with unfeignèd°
heart,
Lest greater dangers do attend thy drift.°

[*Faustus stabs his arm and writes on a paper with his
blood.*]

85 FAUSTUS: Torment, sweet friend, that base and agèd man
That durst dissuade me from thy Lucifer,
With greatest torment that our hell affords.
MEPHISTOPHILIS: His faith is great; I cannot touch his
soul,
But what I may afflict his body with
90 I will attempt, which is but little worth.
FAUSTUS: One thing, good servant, let me crave of thee
To glut the longing of my heart's desire—
That I may have unto my paramour

52. **envy of:** Ill will toward.   55. **Checking:** Admonishing.
83. **unfeignèd:** Honest.   84. **drift:** Purpose.

That heavenly Helen which I saw of late,
Whose sweet embracings may extinguish clear   95
Those thoughts that do dissuade me from my vow,
And keep mine oath I made to Lucifer.
MEPHISTOPHILIS: This, or what else my Faustus shall desire,
Shall be performed in twinkling of an eye.

(*Enter Helen again, passing over [the stage] between
two Cupids.*)

FAUSTUS: Was this the face that launched a thousand
ships   100
And burnt the topless towers of Ilium?
Sweet Helen, make me immortal with a kiss.

[*She kisses him.*]

Her lips suck forth my soul. See where it flies!
Come, Helen, come, give me my soul again.
Here will I dwell, for heaven is in these lips,   105
And all is dross that is not Helena.

[*Enter the Old Man.*]

I will be Paris, and for love of thee
Instead of Troy shall Wittenberg be sacked;
And I will combat with weak Menelaus°
And wear thy colors on my plumèd crest.   110
Yea, I will wound Achilles° in the heel
And then return to Helen for a kiss.
O, thou art fairer than the evening's air,
Clad in the beauty of a thousand stars.
Brighter art thou than flaming Jupiter°   115
When he appeared to hapless Semele,°
More lovely than the monarch of the sky
In wanton Arethusa's azured arms,°
And none but thou shalt be my paramour.

(*Exeunt [all but the Old Man].*)

OLD MAN: Accursèd Faustus, miserable man,   120
That from thy soul exclud'st the grace of heaven
And fliest the throne of his tribunal seat!

(*Enter the Devils.*)

Satan begins to sift me with his pride.
As in this furnace God shall try my faith,
My faith, vile hell, shall triumph over thee.   125
Ambitious fiends, see how the heavens smiles
At your repulse and laughs your state° to scorn.
Hence hell, for hence I fly unto my God.

(*Exeunt.*)

Scene II

(*Thunder. Enter [above] Lucifer, Beelzebub, and
Mephistophilis.*)

109. **Menelaus:** The husband of Helen of Troy.   111. **Achilles:**
The Greek hero of the Trojan War, wounded in the heel by
Paris.   115. **Jupiter:** Zeus.   116. **Semele:** The daughter of
Cadmus and Harmonia who bore Zeus the child Dionysus.
117–118. **monarch . . . arms:** Arethusa was a nymph, one of the
Nereids, who governed a fountain on the isle of Ortygia near
Syracuse.   127. **state:** Royal power.

LUCIFER: Thus from infernal Dis° do we ascend
  To view the subjects of our monarchy,
  Those souls which sin seals the black sons of hell,
  'Mong which as chief, Faustus, we come to thee,
5 Bringing with us lasting damnation
  To wait upon thy soul. The time is come
  Which makes it forfeit.
MEPHISTOPHILIS: And this gloomy night,
  Here in this room will wretched Faustus be.
BEELZEBUB: And here we'll stay
10 To mark him how he doth demean himself.
MEPHISTOPHILIS: How should he, but in desperate lunacy?
  Fond worldling, now his heart-blood dries with grief;
  His conscience kills it, and his laboring brain
  Begets a world of idle fantasies
15 To over-reach the devil. But all in vain;
  His store of pleasures must be sauced° with pain.
  He and his servant, Wagner, are at hand.
  Both come from drawing Faustus' latest will.
  See where they come.

(*Enter Faustus and Wagner.*)

20 FAUSTUS: Say, Wagner, thou has perused my will;
  How dost thou like it?
WAGNER: Sir, so wondrous well
  As in all humble duty I do yield
  My life and lasting service for your love.

(*Enter the Scholars.*)

FAUSTUS: Gramercies,° Wagner. Welcome, gentlemen.
                                [*Exit Wagner.*]
25 FIRST SCHOLAR: Now, worthy Faustus, methinks your
  looks are changed.
FAUSTUS: Ah, gentlemen!
SECOND SCHOLAR: What ails Faustus?
FAUSTUS: Ah, my sweet chamber-fellow, had I lived with
30 thee, then had I lived still, but now must die eternally.
  Look, sirs; comes he not? Comes he not?
FIRST SCHOLAR: O my dear Faustus, what imports this
  fear?
SECOND SCHOLAR: Is all our pleasure turned to
35 melancholy?
THIRD SCHOLAR: He is not well with being over-solitary.
SECOND SCHOLAR: If it be so, we'll have physicians, and
  Faustus shall be cured.
THIRD SCHOLAR: 'Tis but a surfeit sir; fear nothing.
40 FAUSTUS: A surfeit of deadly sin that hath damned both
  body and soul.
SECOND SCHOLAR: Yet Faustus, look up to heaven, and
  remember mercy is infinite.
FAUSTUS: But Faustus' offence can ne'er be pardoned.
45 The serpent that tempted Eve may be saved, but not
  Faustus. Ah gentlemen, hear me with patience and
  tremble not at my speeches. Though my heart pants
  and quivers to remember that I have been a student
  here these thirty years, O, would I had never seen
50 Wittenberg, never read book. And what wonders I

V, ii. 1. **Dis:** Hades, or hell.   16. **sauced:** Paid for.   24. **Gramercies:**
Thanks.

have done, all Germany can witness—yea, all the
world—for which Faustus hath lost both Germany
and the world, yea heaven itself, heaven the seat of
God, the throne of the blessed, the kingdom of joy,
and must remain in hell for ever. Hell, ah hell for   55
ever! Sweet friends, what shall become of Faustus,
being in hell for ever?
SECOND SCHOLAR: Yet Faustus, call on God.
FAUSTUS: On God, whom Faustus hath abjured? On
  God, whom Faustus hath blasphemed? Ah, my God,   60
  I would weep, but the devil draws in my tears. Gush
  forth blood instead of tears, yea life and soul. O, he
  stays my tongue! I would lift up my hands, but see,
  they hold 'em; they hold 'em.
ALL: Who, Faustus?   65
FAUSTUS: Why, Lucifer and Mephistophilis. Ah, gentlemen, I gave them my soul for my cunning.
ALL: God forbid!
FAUSTUS: God forbade it indeed, but Faustus hath done
  it. For the vain pleasure of four and twenty years   70
  hath Faustus lost eternal joy and felicity. I writ them
  a bill with mine own blood. The date is expired. This
  is the time, and he will fetch me.
FIRST SCHOLAR: Why did not Faustus tell us of this before, that divines might have prayed for thee?   75
FAUSTUS: Oft have I thought to have done so, but the
  devil threatened to tear me in pieces if I named God,
  to fetch me, body and soul, if I once gave ear to divinity. And now 'tis too late. Gentlemen away, lest you
  perish with me.   80
SECOND SCHOLAR: O, what may we do to save Faustus?
FAUSTUS: Talk not of me, but save yourselves and depart.
THIRD SCHOLAR: God will strengthen me; I will stay with
  Faustus.
FIRST SCHOLAR: Tempt not God, sweet friend, but let us   85
  into the next room and there pray for him.
FAUSTUS: Ay, pray for me, pray for me; and what noise
  soever you hear, come not unto me, for nothing can
  rescue me.
SECOND SCHOLAR: Pray thou, and we will pray that God   90
  may have mercy upon thee.
FAUSTUS: Gentlemen, farewell. If I live till morning, I'll
  visit you; if not, Faustus is gone to hell.
ALL: Faustus, farewell.

                              (*Exeunt Scholars.*)

MEPHISTOPHILIS: [*above*] Ay, Faustus, now thou hast no
  hope of heaven;   95
  Therefore despair. Think only upon hell,
  For that must be thy mansion, there to dwell.
FAUSTUS: O thou bewitching fiend, 'twas thy temptation
  Hath robbed me of eternal happiness.
MEPHISTOPHILIS: I do confess it, Faustus, and rejoice.   100
  'Twas I, that when thou wert i' the way to heaven,
  Damned up thy passage. When thou took'st the book
  To view the Scriptures, then I turned the leaves
  And led thine eye.
  What, weep'st thou? 'Tis too late. Despair! Farewell!   105
  Fools that will laugh on earth must weep in hell.

                              (*Exit.*)

(*Enter the Good Angel and the Bad Angel at several doors.*)

GOOD ANGEL: Ah, Faustus, if thou hadst given ear to me,
Innumerable joys had followed thee;
But thou didst love the world.

BAD ANGEL: Gave ear to me,
110 And now must taste hell's pains perpetually.

GOOD ANGEL: O what will all thy riches, pleasures, pomps
Avail thee now?

BAD ANGEL: Nothing but vex thee more,
To want in hell, that had on earth such store.

(*Music while the throne descends.*)

GOOD ANGEL: O, thou hast lost celestial happiness,
115 Pleasures unspeakable, bliss without end.
Hadst thou affected sweet divinity,
Hell or the devil had had no power on thee.
Hadst thou kept on that way, Faustus, behold
In what resplendent glory thou hadst sat
120 In yonder throne, like those bright shining saints,
And triumphed over hell. That hast thou lost,
And now, poor soul, must thy good angel leave thee.

[*The throne ascends.*]

The jaws of hell are open to receive thee.

                                                        (*Exit.*)

(*Hell is discovered.*)

BAD ANGEL: Now, Faustus, let thine eyes with horror stare
125 Into that vast perpetual torture-house.
There are the Furies tossing damnèd souls
On burning forks; their bodies boil in lead.
There are live quarters broiling on the coals,
That ne'er can die. This ever-burning chair
130 Is for o'er-tortured souls to rest them in.
These that are fed with sops of flaming fire
Were gluttons and loved only delicates
And laughed to see the poor starve at their gates.
But yet all these are nothing; thou shalt see
135 Ten thousand tortures that more horrid be.

FAUSTUS: O, I have seen enough to torture me.

BAD ANGEL: Nay, thou must feel them, taste the smart of all.
He that loves pleasure must for pleasure fall.
And so I leave thee, Faustus, till anon;
140 Then wilt thou tumble in confusion.

([*Hell disappears.*] *The clock strikes eleven.*)

FAUSTUS: Ah Faustus,
Now hast thou but one bare hour to live,
And then thou must be damned perpetually.
Stand still, you ever-moving spheres of heaven,
145 That time may cease and midnight never come.
Fair nature's eye, rise, rise again, and make
Perpetual day; or let this hour be but
A year, a month, a week, a natural day,

That Faustus may repent and save his soul.
O lente, lente currite noctis equi!°   150
The stars move still; time runs; the clock will strike;
The devil will come, and Faustus must be damned.
O, I'll leap up to my God! Who pulls me down?
See, see, where Christ's blood streams in the firmament!
One drop would save my soul, half a drop! Ah, my Christ!   155
Rend not my heart for naming of my Christ!
Yet will I call on him. O, spare me, Lucifer!
Where is it now? 'Tis gone. And see where God
Stretcheth out his arm and bends his ireful brows.
Mountains and hills, come, come, and fall on me,   160
And hide me from the heavy wrath of God.
No, no!
Then will I headlong run into the earth.
Earth, gape! O no, it will not harbor me!
You stars that reigned at my nativity,   165
Whose influence hath allotted death and hell,
Now draw up Faustus like a foggy mist
Into the entrails of yon laboring cloud,
That when you vomit forth into the air,
My limbs may issue from your smoky mouths,   170
So that my soul may but ascend to heaven.

(*The watch strikes.*)

Ah, half the hour is past; 'twill all be past anon.
O God,
If thou wilt not have mercy on my soul,
Yet for Christ's sake, whose blood hath ransomed me,   175
Impose some end to my incessant pain.
Let Faustus live in hell a thousand years,
A hundred thousand, and at last be saved.
O, no end is limited to damnèd souls.
Why wert thou not a creature wanting soul?   180
Or why is this immortal that thou hast?
Ah, Pythagoras' *metempsychosis,*° were that true,
This soul should fly from me and I be changed
Into some brutish beast. All beasts are happy,
For, when they die   185
Their souls are soon dissolved in elements,
But mine must live still to be plagued in hell.
Cursed be the parents that engendered me!
No, Faustus, curse thyself, curse Lucifer
That hath deprived thee of the joys of heaven.   190

(*The clock strikes twelve.*)

O, it strikes, it strikes! Now, body, turn to air,
Or Lucifer will bear thee quick° to hell.
O soul, be changed to little water-drops,
And fall into the ocean, ne'er be found!

(*Thunder, and enter the Devils.*)

My God, my God, look not so fierce on me!   195

150. *O . . . equi:* O slowly, slowly, run you horses of night (adapted from Ovid's *Amores*).   182. *metempsychosis:* Belief in the transmigration of souls, associated with the Greek philosopher Pythagoras of Samos.   192. **quick:** Alive.

Adders and serpents, let me breathe a while!
Ugly hell, gape not! Come not, Lucifer!
I'll burn my books! Ah, Mephistophilis!
                    (*Exeunt [Faustus and Devils].*)

Scene III

(*Enter the Scholars.*)

FIRST SCHOLAR: Come, gentlemen, let us go visit
    Faustus,
  For such a dreadful night was never seen
  Since first the world's creation did begin.
  Such fearful shrieks and cries were never heard.
5   Pray heaven the doctor have escaped the danger.
SECOND SCHOLAR: O help us, heaven! See, here are
    Faustus' limbs,
  All torn asunder by the hand of death.
THIRD SCHOLAR: The devils whom Faustus served have
    torn him thus;
  For 'twixt the hours of twelve and one, methought
10 I heard him shriek and call aloud for help,
  At which self time the house seemed all on fire
  With dreadful horror of these damnèd fiends.
SECOND SCHOLAR: Well, gentlemen, though Faustus' end
    be such
  As every Christian heart laments to think on,

Yet for he was a scholar, once admired   15
For wondrous knowledge in our German schools,
We'll give his mangled limbs due burial;
And all the students clothed in mourning black,
Shall wait upon° his heavy° funeral.
                    (*Exeunt.*)

EPILOGUE

(*Enter Chorus.*)

CHORUS: Cut is the branch that might have grown full
    straight,
  And burnèd is Apollo's laurel bough
  That sometime grew within this learnèd man.
  Faustus is gone. Regard his hellish fall,
  Whose fiendful fortune may exhort the wise   5
  Only to wonder at unlawful things,
  Whose deepness doth entice such forward wits
  To practice more than heavenly power permits.
                    (*Exit.*)

    Terminat hora diem; terminat auctor opus.°

V, iii. 19. **wait upon:** Be present at. **heavy:** Sorrowful.
Epilogue. 9. *Terminat . . . opus:* The hour ends the day; the author ends his work.

William Shakespeare

Despite the fact that Shakespeare wrote some thirty-seven plays, owned part of his theatrical company, acted in plays, and retired a relatively wealthy man in the city of his birth, there is much we do not know about him. His father was a glovemaker with pretensions to being a gentleman; Shakespeare himself had his coat of arms placed on his home, New Place, purchased in part because it was one of the grandest buildings in Stratford. Church records indicate that he was born in April 1564 and died in April 1616, after having been retired from the stage for two or three years. We know that he married Anne Hathaway in 1582, when he was eighteen and she twenty-six; that he had a daughter Susanna and twins, Judith and Hamnet; and that Hamnet, his only son, died at age eleven. Shakespeare has no direct descendants today.

We know very little about his education. We assume that he went to the local grammar school, since as the son of a burgess he was eligible to attend at no cost. If he did so, he would have received a very strong education based on

This engraving of William Shakespeare by Martin Droeshout appeared in the First Folio Edition, a collection of his plays published in 1623, seven years after his death, by two of his fellow actors.

rhetoric, logic, and classical literature. He would have been exposed to the comedies of Plautus, the tragedies of Seneca, and the poetry of Virgil, Ovid, and a host of other, lesser writers.

A rumor has persisted that he spent some time as a Latin teacher. No evidence exists to suggest that Shakespeare went to a university, although his general learning and knowledge are so extraordinary and broad that generations of scholars have speculated that he may have also gone to the Inns of Court to study law. This cannot be proved, though; thus, some people claim that another person, with considerable university education, must have written his plays. However, no one in the Elizabethan theater had an education of the sort often proposed for Shakespeare. Marlowe and Ben Jonson were the most learned of Elizabethan playwrights, but their work is quite different in character and feeling from that of Shakespeare.

One recent theory about Shakespeare's early years suggests that before going to London to work in theater, he belonged to a wandering company of actors much like those who appear in *Hamlet*. It is an ingenious theory and has much to recommend it, including the fact that it would explain how Shakespeare could take the spotlight so quickly as to arouse the anger of more experienced London writers.

Shakespeare did not begin his career writing for the stage but, in the more conventional approach for the age, as a poet. He sought the support of an aristocratic patron, the earl of Southampton. Like many wealthy and polished young courtiers, Southampton felt it a pleasant ornament to sponsor a poet whose works would be dedicated to him. Shakespeare wrote sonnets apparently with Southampton in mind, and, hoping for preferment, the long narrative poems *Venus and Adonis, The Rape of Lucrece,* and *The Phoenix and the Turtle.* However, Southampton eventually decided to become the patron of another poet, John Florio, an Italian who had translated Michel de Montaigne's *Essays.*

Shakespeare's response was to turn to the stage. His first plays were a considerable success: *King Henry VI* in three parts—three full-length plays. Satisfying London's taste for plays that told the history of England's tangled political past, Shakespeare won considerable renown with a lengthy series of plays ranging from *Richard II* through the two parts of *King Henry IV* to *Henry V.* Audiences were delighted; competing playwrights envied his triumphs. Francis Meres's famous book of the period, *Palladis Tamia: Wit's Treasury,* cites Shakespeare as a modern Plautus and Seneca, the best in both comedy and tragedy. Meres says that by 1598 Shakespeare was known for a dozen plays. That his success was firm by this time is demonstrated by his having purchased his large house, New Place, in Stratford in 1597. He could not have done this without financial security.

In the next few years, Shakespeare made a number of interesting purchases of property in Stratford; he also made deals with his own theater company to secure the rights to perform in London. These arrangements produced legal records that give us some of the clearest information we have concerning Shakespeare's activities during this period. His company was called the Lord Chamberlain's Men while Queen Elizabeth was alive but was renamed the King's Men by King James in the spring of 1603, less than two months after Elizabeth died. As the King's Men, Shakespeare's company had considerable

"He was not of an age, but for all time."

–Ben Jonson

For links to resources about Shakespeare, click on *AuthorLinks* at bedfordstmartins.com/jacobus.

power and success. Its audience sometimes included King James, as for the first performance of *Macbeth*.

Shakespeare was successful as a writer of histories, comedies, and tragedies. He also wrote in another genre, known as romance. These plays share elements with both comedies and tragedies, and they often depend on supernatural or improbable elements. *Cymbeline*, *The Winter's Tale*, and *The Tempest* are the best known of Shakespeare's romances. They are late works and have a fascinating complexity.

When Shakespeare died on April 23, 1616, he was buried as a gentleman in the church in which he had been baptized in Stratford-upon-Avon. His will left most of his money and possessions to his two daughters, Judith and Susanna.

A Midsummer Night's Dream

A Midsummer Night's Dream (1595–1596) is an early comedy and one of Shakespeare's most beloved works. It is also one of his most imaginative plays, introducing us to the world of fairies and the realm of dreams. Romantic painters, such as Fuseli, have long found in this play a rich store of images that stretch far beyond the limits of the real world of everyday experience.

For Shakespeare the fun of the play is in showing how the world of the fairies intersects with the world of real people, and we can interpret the play as a hint of what would happen if the world of dreams were to cross the world of real experience. The fact that these worlds are more alike than they are different gives Shakespeare the comic basis on which to work. He also finds some new and amusing ways to interpret the device of mistaken identities.

The play is set in Athens, with Duke Theseus about to wed Hippolyta, the queen of the Amazons. Helena and Hermia are young women in love with Demetrius and Lysander, respectively. Demetrius, however, wants to marry Hermia and has the blessing of Hermia's father. Hermia's refusal to follow her father's wishes drives her into the woods, where she is followed by both young men and by Helena, who does not want to lose Demetrius.

The four young people find themselves in the world of the fairies, although the humans cannot see the fairies. Puck, an impish sprite, is ordered by Oberon, king of the fairies, to put the juice of a certain flower in Demetrius's eyes so that he will fall in love with Helena. When Puck puts it in Lysander's eyes instead, the plot backfires: Lysander is suddenly in love with Helena, and Hermia is confounded. Oberon has Puck place the same juice in the eyes of Titania, the queen of the fairies, causing her to fall in love with the first creature she sees when she awakes.

For discussion questions and assignments on *A Midsummer Night's Dream*, visit bedfordstmartins.com/jacobus.

That creature is Bottom, the "rude mechanical" (ignorant artisan) whose head has been transformed into an ass's head. Such a trick opens up possibilities for wonderful comic elements. The richness of the illusions that operate onstage continually draws us to the question of how we ever can know the truth of our own experiences, especially when some of them are dreams whose imaginative power can be overwhelming.

Shakespeare plays here with some of the Aristotelian conventions of drama, especially Aristotle's view that drama imitates life. One of the great comic devices in *A Midsummer Night's Dream* is the play within a play that Bottom, Quince, Snug, Flute, and Starveling are to put on before Theseus and Hippolyta. It tells the story of Pyramus and Thisby, lovers who lose each other because they misinterpret signs. It is "Merry and tragical! Tedious and brief!" But it is also a wonderful parody of what playwrights—including Shakespeare—often do when operating in the Aristotelian mode. The aim of the play is realism, yet the players are naive and inexperienced in drama; they do their best to remind the audience that it is only a play.

With its comic ineptness, the rude mechanicals' play needs no disclaimers of this sort, and the immediate audience—Theseus, Hippolyta, Demetrius, Helena, Lysander, and Hermia—is amused by the ardor of the players. The audience in the theater is also mightily amused at the antics of the mechanicals, which on the surface are simply funny and a wonderful pastiche of artless playacting.

Beneath the surface, something more serious is going on. Shakespeare is commenting on the entire function of drama in our lives. He continually reminds us in this play that we are watching an illusion, even an illusion within an illusion, but he also convinces us that illusions teach us a great deal about reality. The real-world setting of *A Midsummer Night's Dream*—Athens—is quite improbable. The mechanicals all have obviously English names and are out of place in an Athenian pastoral setting. The play on the level of Athens is pure fantasy, with even more fantastic goings-on at the level of the fairy world. But fantasy nourishes us. It helps us interpret our own experiences by permitting us to distance ourselves from them and reflect on how they affect others, one of the deepest functions of drama.

As in most comedies, everything turns out exceptionally well. A multiple marriage, one of the delightful conventions of many comedies, ends the drama, and virtually everyone receives what she or he wanted. We are left with a sense of satisfaction because we, too, get our wish about how things should turn out. Puck, one of the greatest of Shakespeare's characters, turns out to be sympathetic and human in his feelings about people. And Bottom, a clown whose origins are certainly Greek and Roman, endears himself to us with his generosity and caring toward others. Shakespeare promotes a remarkably warm view of humanity in this play, leaving us with a sense of delight and a glow that is rare even in comedy.

A Midsummer Night's Dream in Performance

A Midsummer Night's Dream has attracted many great directors in modern times, although in the late seventeenth and eighteenth centuries the play was adapted essentially as a vehicle for presenting the world of the fairies. It even became an opera in 1692. Ludwig Tieck engaged Mendelssohn to write incidental music for the play in Berlin in 1843; their production was for many years the most influential post-Shakespearean adaptation. Beerbohm Tree's 1900 production in London's Savoy Theatre included real rabbits and many other highly realistic details; eventually it played to more than 220,000 patrons. After numerous adaptations, it was produced by Granville Barker in London from 1912 to 1914 in its original text, and in New York in 1915.

The Old Vic's 1954 production was so lavish that it was staged at the Metropolitan Opera House in New York. Peter Brook played down the fairies and explored the play as a study of love. His 1970 production is well remembered for having placed Oberon and Puck on trapezes set against a stark white background. He also used some costumes and other elements of commedia dell'arte to spark the comedy. The American Repertory Theater's 1986 Boston production (see photos on pp. 298–299) reflects the approach to staging that the Royal Shakespeare Company has taken in recent years. The themes of love and transformation inspire the players in a way that shows off the brilliance of the play.

A Midsummer's Night Dream has been filmed several times. In 1935, James Cagney and Mickey Rooney starred in a version that has some charm. In 1968, the Royal Shakespeare Company with Diana Rigg produced a somewhat less interesting film. The most recent version, with Kevin Kline, Michelle Pfeiffer, and Stanley Tucci, received generally good reviews in 1999.

WILLIAM SHAKESPEARE (1564–1616)

A Midsummer Night's Dream   c. 1596

[Dramatis Personae

THESEUS, *Duke of Athens*
EGEUS, *father to Hermia*
LYSANDER, ⎱ *in love with Hermia*
DEMETRIUS, ⎰
PHILOSTRATE, *Master of the Revels to Theseus*

QUINCE, *a carpenter*
SNUG, *a joiner*
BOTTOM, *a weaver*
FLUTE, *a bellows-mender*
SNOUT, *a tinker*
STARVELING, *a tailor*

HIPPOLYTA, *Queen of the Amazons, betrothed to Theseus*
HERMIA, *daughter to Egeus, in love with Lysander*

HELENA, *in love with Demetrius*
OBERON, *King of the Fairies*
TITANIA, *Queen of the Fairies*
PUCK, *or Robin Goodfellow*
PEASEBLOSSOM,
COBWEB,
MOTH, ⎬ *fairies*
MUSTARDSEED,
Other FAIRIES *attending their king and queen*
ATTENDANTS *on Theseus and Hippolyta*

Scene: *Athens, and a wood near it.*]

{ACT I • Scene I}°

(*Enter Theseus, Hippolyta, [Philostrate,] with others.*)

THESEUS: Now, fair Hippolyta, our nuptial hour
Draws on apace. Four happy days bring in
Another moon; but, O, methinks, how slow
This old moon wanes! She lingers° my desires

I, i. Location: The palace of Theseus.   **4. lingers:** Lengthens, protects.

Note: The text of *A Midsummer Night's Dream* has come down to us in different versions—such as the first quarto, the second quarto, and the First Folio. The text used here is largely drawn from the first quarto. Passages enclosed in square brackets are taken from one of the other versions.

5   Like to a step-dame° or a dowager°
    Long withering out a young man's revenue.
HIPPOLYTA: Four days will quickly steep themselves in
        night,
    Four nights will quickly dream away the time;
    And then the moon, like to a silver bow
10 New-bent in heaven, shall behold the night
    Of our solemnities.
THESEUS: Go, Philostrate,
    Stir up the Athenian youth to merriments,
    Awake the pert and nimble spirit of mirth,
    Turn melancholy forth to funerals;
15 The pale companion° is not for our pomp.°
                            [*Exit Philostrate.*]
    Hippolyta, I woo'd thee with my sword,°
    And won thy love doing thee injuries;
    But I will wed thee in another key,
    With pomp, with triumph,° and with reveling.

(*Enter Egeus and his daughter Hermia, and Lysander,
and Demetrius.*)

20 **EGEUS:** Happy be Theseus, our renowned Duke!
    THESEUS: Thanks, good Egeus. What's the news with
        thee?
    EGEUS: Full of vexation come I, with complaint
        Against my child, my daughter Hermia.
        Stand forth, Demetrius. My noble lord,
25   This man hath my consent to marry her.
        Stand forth, Lysander. And, my gracious Duke,
        This man hath bewitch'd the bosom of my child.
        Thou, thou, Lysander, thou hast given her rhymes
        And interchang'd love tokens with my child.
30   Thou hast by moonlight at her window sung
        With feigning voice verses of feigning° love,
        And stol'n the impression of her fantasy,°
        With bracelets of thy hair, rings, gauds,° conceits,°
        Knacks,° trifles, nosegays, sweetmeats—
            messengers
35   Of strong prevailment in unhardened youth.
        With cunning hast thou filch'd my daughter's heart,
        Turn'd her obedience, which is due to me,
        To stubborn harshness. And, my gracious Duke,
        Be it so she will not here before your Grace
40   Consent to marry with Demetrius,
        I beg the ancient privilege of Athens:
        As she is mine, I may dispose of her,

    Which shall be either to this gentleman
    Or to her death, according to our law
    Immediately° provided in that case.   45
THESEUS: What say you, Hermia? Be advis'd, fair maid.
    To you your father should be as a god—
    One that compos'd your beauties, yea, and one
    To whom you are but as a form in wax
    By him imprinted and within his power   50
    To leave° the figure or disfigure° it.
    Demetrius is a worthy gentleman.
HERMIA: So is Lysander.
THESEUS: In himself he is;
    But in this kind,° wanting° your father's voice,°
    The other must be held the worthier.   55
HERMIA: I would my father look'd but with my eyes.
THESEUS: Rather your eyes must with his judgment look.
HERMIA: I do entreat your Grace to pardon me.
    I know not by what power I am made bold,
    Nor how it may concern° my modesty,   60
    In such a presence here to plead my thoughts;
    But I beseech your Grace that I may know
    The worst that may befall me in this case,
    If I refuse to wed Demetrius.
THESEUS: Either to die the death, or to abjure   65
    Forever the society of men.
    Therefore, fair Hermia, question your desires,
    Know of your youth, examine well your blood,°
    Whether, if you yield not to your father's choice,
    You can endure the livery° of a nun,   70
    For aye° to be in shady cloister mew'd,°
    To live a barren sister all your life,
    Chanting faint hymns to the cold fruitless moon.
    Thrice blessed they that master so their blood
    To undergo such maiden pilgrimage,   75
    But earthlier happy° is the rose distill'd,
    Than that which withering on the virgin thorn
    Grows, lives, and dies in single blessedness.
HERMIA: So will I grow, so live, so die, my lord,
    Ere I will yield my virgin patent° up   80
    Unto his lordship, whose unwished yoke
    My soul consents not to give sovereignty.
THESEUS: Take time to pause; and, by the next new
        moon—
    The sealing-day betwixt my love and me
    For everlasting bond of fellowship—   85
    Upon that day either prepare to die
    For disobedience to your father's will,
    Or° else to wed Demetrius, as he would,
    Or on Diana's altar° to protest°
    For aye austerity and single life.   90

---

5. step-dame: Stepmother. **dowager:** Widow with a jointure or dower (an estate or title from her deceased husband).
15. companion: Fellow. **pomp:** Ceremonial magnificence.
16. with my sword: In a military engagement against the
Amazons, when Hippolyta was taken captive. **19. triumph:**
Public festivity. **31. feigning:** (1) Counterfeiting; (2) faining,
desirous. **32. And...fantasy:** And made her fall in love with
you (imprinting your image on her imagination) by stealthy and
dishonest means. **33. gauds:** Playthings. **conceits:** Fanciful
trifles. **34. Knacks:** Knickknacks.

45. Immediately: Expressly. **51. leave:** Leave unaltered.
disfigure: Obliterate. **54. kind:** Respect. **wanting:** Lacking. **voice:** Approval. **60. concern:** Befit. **68. blood:** Passions. **70. livery:** Habit. **71. aye:** Ever. **mew'd:** Shut in
(said of a hawk, poultry, etc.). **76. earthlier happy:** Happier
as respects this world. **80. patent:** Privilege. **88. Or:** Either.
89. Diana's altar: Diana was a virgin goddess. **protest:** Vow.

DEMETRIUS: Relent, sweet Hermia, and, Lysander, yield
  Thy crazed° title to my certain right.
LYSANDER: You have her father's love, Demetrius;
  Let me have Hermia's. Do you marry him.
95 **EGEUS:** Scornful Lysander! True, he hath my love,
  And what is mine my love shall render him.
  And she is mine, and all my right of her
  I do estate unto° Demetrius.
  LYSANDER: I am, my lord, as well deriv'd° as he,
100 As well possess'd;° my love is more than his;
  My fortunes every way as fairly° rank'd,
  If not with vantage,° as Demetrius';
  And, which is more than all these boasts can be,
  I am belov'd of beauteous Hermia.
105 Why should not I then prosecute my right?
  Demetrius, I'll avouch it to his head,°
  Made love to Nedar's daughter, Helena,
  And won her soul; and she, sweet lady, dotes,
  Devoutly dotes, dotes in idolatry,
110 Upon this spotted° and inconstant man.
  THESEUS: I must confess that I have heard so much,
  And with Demetrius thought to have spoke thereof;
  But, being over-full of self-affairs,
  My mind did lose it. But, Demetrius, come,
115 And come, Egeus, you shall go with me;
  I have some private schooling for you both.
  For you, fair Hermia, look you arm° yourself
  To fit your fancies° to your father's will;
  Or else the law of Athens yields you up—
120 Which by no means we may extenuate°—
  To death, or to a vow of single life.
  Come, my Hippolyta. What cheer, my love?
  Demetrius and Egeus, go° along.
  I must employ you in some business
125 Against° our nuptial, and confer with you
  Of something nearly that° concerns yourselves.
  EGEUS: With duty and desire we follow you.

    (Exeunt° [all but Lysander and Hermia].)

LYSANDER: How now, my love, why is your cheek so pale?
  How chance the roses there do fade so fast?
130 **HERMIA:** Belike° for want of rain, which I could well
  Beteem° them from the tempest of my eyes.
  LYSANDER: Ay me! For aught that I could ever read,
  Could ever hear by tale or history,
  The course of true love never did run smooth;
135 But either it was different in blood°—

HERMIA: O cross,° too high to be enthrall'd to low!
LYSANDER: Or else misgraffed° in respect of years—
HERMIA: O spite, too old to be engag'd to young!
LYSANDER: Or else it stood upon the choice of
  friends°—
HERMIA: O hell, to choose love by another's eyes! 140
LYSANDER: Or, if there were a sympathy in choice,
  War, death, or sickness did lay siege to it,
  Making it momentany° as a sound,
  Swift as a shadow, short as any dream,
  Brief as the lightning in the collied° night, 145
  That, in a spleen,° unfolds° both heaven and earth,
  And ere a man hath power to say "Behold!"
  The jaws of darkness do devour it up.
  So quick° bright things come to confusion.°
HERMIA: If then true lovers have been ever cross'd,° 150
  It stands as an edict in destiny.
  Then let us teach our trial patience,°
  Because it is a customary cross,
  As due to love as thoughts and dreams and sighs,
  Wishes and tears, poor fancy's° followers. 155
LYSANDER: A good persuasion. Therefore, hear me,
  Hermia.
  I have a widow aunt, a dowager
  Of great revenue, and she hath no child.
  From Athens is her house remote seven leagues;
  And she respects° me as her only son. 160
  There, gentle Hermia, may I marry thee,
  And to that place the sharp Athenian law
  Cannot pursue us. If thou lovest me, then,
  Steal forth thy father's house tomorrow night;
  And in the wood, a league without the town, 165
  Where I did meet thee once with Helena
  To do observance to a morn of May,°
  There will I stay for thee.
HERMIA: My good Lysander!
  I swear to thee, by Cupid's strongest bow,
  By his best arrow with the golden head,° 170
  By the simplicity° of Venus' doves,°
  By that which knitteth souls and prospers loves,
  And by that fire which burn'd the Carthage queen,
  When the false Troyan° under sail was seen,

---

136. **cross:** Vexation. 137. **misgraffed:** Ill grafted, badly matched.
139. **friends:** Relatives. 143. **momentany:** Lasting but a moment.
145. **collied:** Blackened (as with coal dust), darkened. 146. **in a
spleen:** In a swift impulse; in a violent flash. **unfolds:** Discloses.
149. **quick:** Quickly; or, perhaps, living, alive. **confusion:** Ruin.
150. **ever cross'd:** Always thwarted. 152. **teach . . . patience:**
Teach ourselves patience in this trial. 155. **fancy's:** Amorous
passion's. 160. **respects:** Regards. 167. **do . . . May:** Perform
the ceremonies of May Day. 170. **best arrow . . . golden head:**
Cupid's best gold-pointed arrows were supposed to induce love,
his blunt leaden arrows aversion. 171. **simplicity:** Innocence.
doves: Those that drew Venus's chariot. 173–174. **by that
fire . . . false Troyan:** Dido, Queen of Carthage, immolated herself on a funeral pyre after having been deserted by the Trojan
hero Aeneas.

---

92. **crazed:** Cracked, unsound. 98. **estate unto:** Settle or
bestow upon. 99. **deriv'd:** Descended (i.e., "as well born").
100. **possess'd:** Endowed with wealth. 101. **fairly:** Handsomely.
102. **vantage:** Superiority. 106. **head:** Face. 110. **spotted:**
Morally stained. 117. **look you arm:** Take care you prepare.
118. **fancies:** Likings, thoughts of love. 120. **extenuate:** Mitigate. 123. **go:** Come. 125. **Against:** In preparation for.
126. **nearly that:** That closely. 127. [S.D.] *Exeunt:* Latin for
"they go out." 130. **Belike:** Very likely. 131. **Beteem:** Grant,
afford. 135. **blood:** Hereditary station.

175 By all the vows that ever men have broke,
In number more than ever women spoke,
In that same place thou hast appointed me
Tomorrow truly will I meet with thee.
LYSANDER: Keep promise, love. Look, here comes
Helena.

(*Enter Helena.*)

180 HERMIA: God speed fair° Helena, whither away?
HELENA: Call you me fair? That fair again unsay.
Demetrius loves your fair.° O happy fair!°
Your eyes are lodestars,° and your tongue's sweet air°
More tuneable° than lark to shepherd's ear
185 When wheat is green, when hawthorn buds appear.
Sickness is catching. O, were favor° so,
Yours would I catch, fair Hermia, ere I go;
My ear should catch your voice, my eye your eye,
My tongue should catch your tongue's sweet melody.
190 Were the world mine, Demetrius being bated,°
The rest I'd give to be to you translated.°
O, teach me how you look, and with what art
You sway the motion° of Demetrius' heart.
HERMIA: I frown upon him, yet he loves me still.
HELENA: O that your frowns would teach my smiles
195 such skill!
HERMIA: I give him curses, yet he gives me love.
HELENA: O that my prayers could such affection°
move!°
HERMIA: The more I hate, the more he follows me.
HELENA: The more I love, the more he hateth me.
200 HERMIA: His folly, Helena, is no fault of mine.
HELENA: None, but your beauty. Would that fault were
mine!
HERMIA: Take comfort. He no more shall see my face.
Lysander and myself will fly this place.
Before the time I did Lysander see,
205 Seem'd Athens as a paradise to me.
O, then, what graces in my love do dwell,
That he hath turn'd a heaven unto a hell!
LYSANDER: Helen, to you our minds we will unfold.
Tomorrow night, when Phoebe° doth behold
210 Her silver visage in the wat'ry glass,°
Decking with liquid pearl the bladed grass,
A time that lovers' flights doth still° conceal,
Through Athens' gates have we devis'd to steal.
HERMIA: And in the wood, where often you and I
215 Upon faint° primrose beds were wont to lie,
Emptying our bosoms of their counsel° sweet,

There my Lysander and myself shall meet;
And thence from Athens turn away our eyes,
To seek new friends and stranger companies.
Farewell, sweet playfellow. Pray thou for us,   220
And good luck grant thee thy Demetrius!
Keep word, Lysander. We must starve our sight
From lovers' food till morrow deep midnight.
LYSANDER: I will, my Hermia.   (*Exit Hermia.*)
Helena, adieu.
As you on him, Demetrius dote on you!   225

(*Exit Lysander.*)

HELENA: How happy some o'er other some can be!°
Through Athens I am thought as fair as she.
But what of that? Demetrius thinks not so;
He will not know what all but he do know.
And as he errs, doting on Hermia's eyes,   230
So I, admiring of° his qualities.
Things base and vile, holding no quantity,°
Love can transpose to form and dignity.
Love looks not with the eyes, but with the mind,
And therefore is wing'd Cupid painted blind.   235
Nor hath Love's mind of any judgment taste;°
Wings, and no eyes, figure° unheedy haste.
And therefore is Love said to be a child,
Because in choice he is so oft beguil'd.
As waggish boys in game° themselves forswear,   240
So the boy Love is perjur'd everywhere.
For ere Demetrius look'd on Hermia's eyne,°
He hail'd down oaths that he was only mine;
And when this hail some heat from Hermia felt,
So he dissolv'd, and show'rs of oaths did melt.   245
I will go tell him of fair Hermia's flight.
Then to the wood will he tomorrow night
Pursue her; and for this intelligence°
If I have thanks, it is a dear° expense.°
But herein mean I to enrich my pain,   250
To have his sight thither and back again.   (*Exit.*)

{Scene II}°

(*Enter Quince the Carpenter, and Snug the Joiner, and
Bottom the Weaver, and Flute the Bellows-Mender, and
Snout the Tinker, and Starveling the Tailor.*)

QUINCE: Is all our company here?
BOTTOM: You were best to call them generally,° man by
man, according to the scrip.°

---

180. **fair:** Fair-complexioned (generally regarded by the Elizabethans as more beautiful than dark-complexioned). 182. **your fair:** Your beauty (even though Hermia is dark-complexioned). **happy fair:** Lucky fair one. 183. **lodestars:** Guiding stars. **air:** Music. 184. **tuneable:** Tuneful, melodious. 186. **favor:** Appearance, looks. 190. **bated:** Excepted. 191. **translated:** Transformed. 193. **motion:** Impulse. 197. **affection:** Passion. **move:** Arouse. 209. **Phoebe:** Diana, the moon. 210. **glass:** Mirror. 212. **still:** Always. 215. **faint:** Pale. 216. **counsel:** Secret thought.

226. **o'er ... can be:** Can be in comparison to some others. 231. **admiring of:** Wondering at. 232. **holding no quantity:** Unsubstantial, unshapely. 236. **Nor ... taste:** Nor has Love, which dwells in the fancy or imagination, any *taste* or least bit of judgment or reason. 237. **figure:** Are a symbol of. 240. **game:** Sport, jest. 242. **eyne:** Eyes (old form of plural). 248. **intelligence:** Information. 249. **dear:** Costly. **a dear expense:** A trouble worth taking. **I, ii. Location:** Athens. Quince's house (?). 2. **generally:** Bottom's blunder for *individually*. 3. **scrip:** Script, written list.

QUINCE: Here is the scroll of every man's name which
5   is thought fit, through all Athens, to play in our
  interlude before the Duke and the Duchess on his
  wedding-day at night.
BOTTOM: First, good Peter Quince, say what the play
  treats on, then read the names of the actors, and so
10   grow to° a point.
QUINCE: Marry,° our play is "The most lamentable comedy and most cruel death of Pyramus and Thisby."
BOTTOM: A very good piece of work, I assure you, and a
  merry. Now, good Peter Quince, call forth your
15   actors by the scroll. Masters, spread yourselves.
QUINCE: Answer as I call you. Nick Bottom, the weaver.
BOTTOM: Ready. Name what part I am for, and proceed.
QUINCE: You, Nick Bottom, are set down for Pyramus.
BOTTOM: What is Pyramus? A lover, or a tyrant?
20 QUINCE: A lover, that kills himself most gallant for love.
BOTTOM: That will ask some tears in the true performing
  of it. If I do it, let the audience look to their eyes. I
  will move storms; I will condole° in some measure.
  To the rest—yet my chief humor° is for a tyrant. I
25   could play Ercles° rarely, or a part to tear a cat° in, to
  make all split.°
  "The raging rocks
  And shivering shocks
  Shall break the locks
30   Of prison gates;
  And Phibbus' car°
  Shall shine from far
  And make and mar
    The foolish Fates."
35 This was lofty! Now name the rest of the players.
  This is Ercles' vein, a tyrant's vein. A lover is more
  condoling.
QUINCE: Francis Flute, the bellows-mender.
FLUTE: Here, Peter Quince.
40 QUINCE: Flute, you must take Thisby on you.
FLUTE: What is Thisby? A wand'ring knight?
QUINCE: It is the lady that Pyramus must love.
FLUTE: Nay, faith, let not me play a woman. I have a
  beard coming.
45 QUINCE: That's all one.° You shall play it in a mask, and
  you may speak as small° as you will.
BOTTOM: An° I may hide my face, let me play Thisby
  too. I'll speak in a monstrous little voice, "Thisne,
  Thisne!" "Ah Pyramus, my lover dear! Thy Thisby
50   dear, and lady dear!"
QUINCE: No, no; you must play Pyramus; and, Flute,
  you Thisby.
BOTTOM: Well, proceed.

QUINCE: Robin Starveling, the tailor.
STARVELING: Here, Peter Quince.
55 QUINCE: Robin Starveling, you must play Thisby's
  mother. Tom Snout, the tinker.
SNOUT: Here, Peter Quince.
QUINCE: You, Pyramus' father; myself, Thisby's father;
  Snug, the joiner, you, the lion's part; and I hope here
60   is a play fitted.
SNUG: Have you the lion's part written? Pray you, if it
  be, give it me, for I am slow of study.
QUINCE: You may do it extempore, for it is nothing but
  roaring.
65 BOTTOM: Let me play the lion too. I will roar that I will
  do any man's heart good to hear me. I will roar that I
  will make the Duke say, "Let him roar again, let him
  roar again."
QUINCE: An you should do it too terribly, you would
70   fright the Duchess and the ladies, that they would
  shriek; and that were enough to hang us all.
ALL: That would hang us, every mother's son.
BOTTOM: I grant you, friends, if you should fright the
  ladies out of their wits, they would have no more dis-
75   cretion but to hang us; but I will aggravate° my voice
  so that I will roar you° as gently as any sucking dove;
  I will roar you an 'twere any nightingale.
QUINCE: You can play no part but Pyramus; for Pyramus
  is a sweet-fac'd man, a proper° man as one shall see
80   in a summer's day, a most lovely gentleman-like man.
  Therefore you must needs play Pyramus.
BOTTOM: Well, I will undertake it. What beard were I best
  to play it in?
QUINCE: Why, what you will.
85 BOTTOM: I will discharge° it in either your° straw-color
  beard, your orange-tawny beard, your purple-in-
  grain° beard, or your French-crown-color° beard,
  your perfect yellow.
QUINCE: Some of your French crowns° have no hair at
90   all, and then you will play barefac'd. But, masters,
  here are your parts. [He distributes parts.] And I am
  to entreat you, request you, and desire you, to con°
  them by tomorrow night; and meet me in the palace
  wood, a mile without the town, by moonlight. There
95   will we rehearse; for if we meet in the city, we shall
  be dogg'd with company, and our devices° known. In
  the meantime I will draw a bill° of properties, such as
  our play wants. I pray you, fail me not.
BOTTOM: We will meet, and there we may rehearse most
100   obscenely° and courageously. Take pains, be perfect;°
  adieu.

---

10. grow to: Come to.   **11. Marry:** A mild oath, originally the name of the Virgin Mary.   **23. condole:** Lament, arouse pity. **24. humor:** Inclination, whim.   **25. Ercles:** Hercules (the tradition of ranting came from Seneca's *Hercules Furens*).   **tear a cat:** Rant.   **26. make all split:** Cause a stir, bring the house down.   **31. Phibbus' car:** Phoebus's, the sun-god's, chariot. **45. That's all one:** It makes no difference.   **46. small:** High-pitched.   **47. An:** If.

76. aggravate: Bottom's blunder for *diminish*.   **77. roar you:** Roar for you.   **80. proper:** Handsome.   **86. discharge:** Perform.   **your:** I.e., you know the kind I mean.   **87–88. purple-in-grain:** Dyed a very deep red (from *grain*, the name applied to the dried insect used to make the dye).   **88. French-crown-color:** Color of a French crown, a gold coin.   **90. crowns:** Heads bald from syphilis, the "French disease."   **93. con:** Learn by heart.   **97. devices:** Plans.   **98. bill:** List.   **101. obscenely:** An unintentionally funny blunder, whatever Bottom meant to say. **perfect:** Letter-perfect in memorizing your parts.

QUINCE: At the Duke's oak we meet.
BOTTOM: Enough. Hold, or cut bow-strings.°

(*Exeunt.*)

{ACT II • Scene I}°

(*Enter a Fairy at one door, and Robin Goodfellow [Puck] at another.*)

PUCK: How now, spirit! Whither wander you?
FAIRY: Over hill, over dale,
   Thorough° bush, thorough brier,
   Over park, over pale,°
5   Thorough flood, thorough fire,
   I do wander every where,
   Swifter than the moon's sphere;
   And I serve the Fairy Queen,
   To dew her orbs° upon the green.
10   The cowslips tall her pensioners° be.
   In their gold coats spots you see;
   Those be rubies, fairy favors,°
   In those freckles live their savors.°
   I must go seek some dewdrops here
15   And hang a pearl in every cowslip's ear.
   Farewell, thou lob° of spirits; I'll be gone.
   Our Queen and all her elves come here anon.°
PUCK: The King doth keep his revels here tonight.
   Take heed the Queen come not within his sight.
20   For Oberon is passing fell° and wrath,°
   Because that she as her attendant hath
   A lovely boy, stolen from an Indian king;
   She never had so sweet a changeling.°
   And jealous Oberon would have the child
25   Knight of his train, to trace° the forests wild.
   But she perforce° withholds the loved boy,
   Crowns him with flowers and makes him all her joy.
   And now they never meet in grove or green,
   By fountain° clear, or spangled starlight sheen,
30   But they do square,° that all their elves for fear
   Creep into acorn-cups and hide them there.
FAIRY: Either I mistake your shape and making quite,
   Or else you are that shrewd° and knavish sprite°
   Call'd Robin Goodfellow. Are not you he
35   That frights the maidens of the villagery,
   Skim milk, and sometimes labor in the quern,°
   And bootless° make the breathless huswife churn,

And sometime make the drink to bear no barm,°
Mislead night-wanderers, laughing at their harm?
Those that Hobgoblin call you and sweet Puck, 40
You do their work, and they shall have good luck.
Are you not he?
PUCK: Thou speakest aright;
I am that merry wanderer of the night.
I jest to Oberon and make him smile
When I a fat and bean-fed horse beguile, 45
Neighing in likeness of a filly foal;
And sometime lurk I in a gossip's° bowl,
In very likeness of a roasted crab,°
And when she drinks, against her lips I bob
And on her withered dewlap° pour the ale. 50
The wisest aunt,° telling the saddest° tale,
Sometime for three-foot stool mistaketh me;
Then slip I from her bum, down topples she,
And "tailor"° cries, and falls into a cough;
And then the whole quire° hold their hips and 55
   laugh,
And waxen° in their mirth and neeze° and swear
A merrier hour was never wasted there.
But, room, fairy! Here comes Oberon.
FAIRY: And here my mistress. Would that he were
   gone!

(*Enter [Oberon] the King of Fairies at one door, with his train; and [Titania] the Queen at another, with hers.*)

OBERON: Ill met by moonlight, proud Titania. 60
TITANIA: What, jealous Oberon? Fairies, skip hence.
   I have forsworn his bed and company.
OBERON: Tarry, rash wanton.° Am not I thy lord?
TITANIA: Then I must be thy lady; but I know
   When thou hast stolen away from fairy land, 65
   And in the shape of Corin° sat all day,
   Playing on pipes of corn° and versing love
   To amorous Phillida.° Why art thou here,
   Come from the farthest steep° of India,
   But that, forsooth, the bouncing Amazon, 70
   Your buskin'd° mistress and your warrior love,
   To Theseus must be wedded, and you come
   To give their bed joy and prosperity.
OBERON: How canst thou thus for shame, Titania,
   Glance at my credit with Hippolyta,° 75
   Knowing I know thy love to Theseus?
   Didst not thou lead him through the glimmering
   night

---

104. Hold ... bow-strings: An archer's expression not definitely explained, but probably meaning here "keep your promises, or give up the play." **II, i. Location:** A wood near Athens. **3. Thorough:** Through. **4. pale:** Enclosure. **9. orbs:** Circles (i.e., fairy rings). **10. pensioners:** Retainers, members of the royal bodyguard. **12. favors:** Love tokens. **13. savors:** Sweet smells. **16. lob:** Country bumpkin. **17. anon:** At once. **20. passing fell:** Exceedingly angry. **wrath:** Wrathful. **23. changeling:** Child exchanged for another by the fairies. **25. trace:** Range through. **26. perforce:** Forcibly. **29. fountain:** Spring. **30. square:** Quarrel. **33. shrewd:** Mischievous. **sprite:** Spirit. **36. quern:** Handmill. **37. bootless:** In vain.

38. barm: Yeast, head on the ale. **47. gossip's:** Old woman's. **48. crab:** Crab apple. **50. dewlap:** Loose skin on neck. **51. aunt:** Old woman. **saddest:** Most serious. **54. tailor:** Possibly because she ends up sitting cross-legged on the floor, looking like a tailor. **55. quire:** Company. **56. waxen:** Increase. **neeze:** Sneeze. **63. wanton:** Headstrong creature. **66, 68. Corin, Phillida:** Conventional names of pastoral lovers. **67. corn:** Here, oat stalks. **69. steep:** Mountain range. **71. buskin'd:** Wearing half-boots called buskins. **75. Glance ... Hippolyta:** Make insinuations about my favored relationship with Hippolyta.

From Perigenia,° whom he ravished?
And make him with fair Aegles° break his faith,
80 With Ariadne° and Antiopa?°
TITANIA: These are the forgeries of jealousy;
And never, since the middle summer's spring,°
Met we on hill, in dale, forest, or mead,
By paved° fountain or by rushy° brook,
85 Or in° the beached margent° of the sea,
To dance our ringlets° to the whistling wind,
But with thy brawls thou hast disturb'd our sport.
Therefore the winds, piping to us in vain,
As in revenge, have suck'd up from the sea
90 Contagious° fogs; which falling in the land
Hath every pelting° river made so proud
That they have overborne their continents.°
The ox hath therefore stretch'd his yoke in vain,
The ploughman lost his sweat, and the green corn°
95 Hath rotted ere his youth attain'd a beard;
The fold° stands empty in the drowned field,
And crows are fatted with the murrion° flock;
The nine men's morris° is fill'd up with mud,
And the quaint mazes° in the wanton° green
100 For lack of tread are undistinguishable.
The human mortals want° their winter° here;
No night is now with hymn or carol bless'd.
Therefore° the moon, the governess of floods,
Pale in her anger, washes all the air,
105 That rheumatic diseases° do abound.
And thorough this distemperature° we see
The seasons alter: hoary-headed frosts
Fall in the fresh lap of the crimson rose,
And on old Hiems'° thin and icy crown
110 An odorous chaplet of sweet summer buds
Is, as in mockery, set. The spring, the summer,

The childing° autumn, angry winter, change
Their wonted liveries,° and the mazed° world,
By their increase,° now knows not which is which.
And this same progeny of evils comes 115
From our debate,° from our dissension;
We are their parents and original.°
OBERON: Do you amend it then; it lies in you.
Why should Titania cross her Oberon?
I do but beg a little changeling boy, 120
To be my henchman.°
TITANIA: Set your heart at rest.
The fairy land buys not the child of me.
His mother was a vot'ress° of my order,
And, in the spiced Indian air, by night,
Full often hath she gossip'd by my side, 125
And sat with me on Neptune's yellow sands,
Marking th' embarked traders° on the flood,°
When we have laugh'd to see the sails conceive
And grow big-bellied with the wanton° wind;
Which she, with pretty and with swimming gait, 130
Following—her womb then rich with my young
squire—
Would imitate, and sail upon the land
To fetch me trifles, and return again,
As from a voyage, rich with merchandise.
But she, being mortal, of that boy did die; 135
And for her sake do I rear up her boy,
And for her sake I will not part with him.
OBERON: How long within this wood intend you stay?
TITANIA: Perchance till after Theseus' wedding-day.
If you will patiently dance in our round° 140
And see our moonlight revels, go with us;
If not, shun me, and I will spare° your haunts.
OBERON: Give me that boy, and I will go with thee.
TITANIA: Not for thy fairy kingdom. Fairies, away!
We shall chide downright, if I longer stay. 145

(*Exeunt [Titania with her train].*)

OBERON: Well, go thy way. Thou shalt not from° this
grove
Till I torment thee for this injury.
My gentle Puck, come hither. Thou rememb'rest
Since° once I sat upon a promontory,
And heard a mermaid on a dolphin's back 150
Uttering such dulcet and harmonious breath°
That the rude sea grew civil at her song
And certain stars shot madly from their spheres,
To hear the sea-maid's music.
PUCK: I remember.
OBERON: That very time I saw, but thou couldst not, 155

78. **Perigenia:** Perigouna, one of Theseus's conquests. (This and the following women are named in Thomas North's translation of Plutarch's *Life of Theseus*.) 79. **Aegles:** Aegle, for whom Theseus deserted Ariadne according to some accounts. 80. **Ariadne:** The daughter of Minos, King of Crete, who helped Theseus escape the labyrinth after killing the Minotaur; later she was abandoned by Theseus. **Antiopa:** Queen of the Amazons and wife of Theseus; elsewhere identified with Hippolyta, but here thought of as a separate woman. 82. **middle summer's spring:** Beginning of midsummer. 84. **paved:** With pebbled bottom. **rushy:** Bordered with rushes. 85. **in:** On. **margent:** Edge, border. 86. **ringlets:** Dances in a ring (see *orbs* in line 9). 90. **Contagious:** Noxious. 91. **pelting:** Paltry; or, striking, moving forcefully. 92. **continents:** Banks that contain them. 94. **corn:** Grain of any kind. 96. **fold:** Pen for sheep or cattle. 97. **murrion:** Having died of the murrain, plague. 98. **nine men's morris:** Portion of the village green marked out in a square for a game played with nine pebbles or pegs. 99. **quaint mazes:** Intricate paths marked out on the village green to be followed rapidly on foot as a kind of contest. **wanton:** Luxuriant. 101. **want:** Lack. **winter:** Regular winter season; or, proper observances of winter, such as the *hymn or carol* in the next line (?). 103. **Therefore:** I.e., as a result of our quarrel. 105. **rheumatic diseases:** Colds, flu, and other respiratory infections. 106. **distemperature:** Disturbance in nature. 109. **Hiems:** The winter god.

112. **childing:** Fruitful, pregnant. 113. **wonted liveries:** Usual apparel. **mazed:** Bewildered. 114. **their increase:** Their yield, what they produce. 116. **debate:** Quarrel. 117. **original:** Origin. 121. **henchman:** Attendant, page. 123. **vot'ress:** Female votary; devotee, worshiper. 127. **traders:** Trading vessels. **flood:** Flood tide. 129. **wanton:** Sportive. 140. **round:** Circular dance. 142. **spare:** Shun. 146. **from:** Go from. 149. **Since:** When. 151. **breath:** Voice, song.

Flying between the cold moon and the earth,
Cupid all° arm'd. A certain aim he took
At a fair vestal° throned by the west,
And loos'd his love-shaft smartly from his bow,
160 As° it should pierce a hundred thousand hearts;
But I might° see young Cupid's fiery shaft
Quench'd in the chaste beams of the wat'ry moon,
And the imperial vot'ress passed on,
In maiden meditation, fancy-free.°
165 Yet mark'd I where the bolt of Cupid fell:
It fell upon a little western flower,
Before milk-white, now purple with love's wound,
And maidens call it love-in-idleness.°
Fetch me that flow'r; the herb I showed thee once.
170 The juice of it on sleeping eyelids laid
Will make or man or° woman madly dote
Upon the next live creature that it sees.
Fetch me this herb, and be thou here again
Ere the leviathan° can swim a league.
175 PUCK: I'll put a girdle round about the earth
In forty° minutes.   [*Exit.*]
OBERON: Having once this juice,
I'll watch Titania when she is asleep,
And drop the liquor of it in her eyes.
The next thing then she waking looks upon,
180 Be it on lion, bear, or wolf, or bull,
On meddling monkey, or on busy ape,
She shall pursue it with the soul of love.
And ere I take this charm from off her sight,
As I can take it with another herb,
185 I'll make her render up her page to me.
But who comes here? I am invisible,
And I will overhear their conference.

(*Enter Demetrius, Helena following him.*)

DEMETRIUS: I love thee not, therefore pursue me not.
Where is Lysander and fair Hermia?
190 The one I'll slay, the other slayeth me.
Thou told'st me they were stol'n unto this wood;
And here am I, and wode° within this wood,
Because I cannot meet my Hermia.
Hence, get thee gone, and follow me no more.
195 HELENA: You draw me, you hard-hearted adamant;°
But yet you draw not iron, for my heart
Is true as steel. Leave° you your power to draw,
And I shall have no power to follow you.

DEMETRIUS: Do I entice you? Do I speak you fair?°
Or, rather, do I not in plainest truth   200
Tell you I do not nor I cannot love you?
HELENA: And even for that do I love you the more.
I am your spaniel; and, Demetrius,
The more you beat me, I will fawn on you.
Use me but as your spaniel, spurn me, strike me,   205
Neglect me, lose me; only give me leave,
Unworthy as I am, to follow you.
What worser place can I beg in your love—
And yet a place of high respect with me—
Than to be used as you use your dog?   210
DEMETRIUS: Tempt not too much the hatred of my
    spirit,
For I am sick when I do look on thee.
HELENA: And I am sick when I look not on you.
DEMETRIUS: You do impeach° your modesty too much
To leave the city and commit yourself   215
Into the hands of one that loves you not,
To trust the opportunity of night
And the ill counsel of a desert° place
With the rich worth of your virginity.
HELENA: Your virtue° is my privilege.° For that°   220
It is not night when I do see your face,
Therefore I think I am not in the night;
Nor doth this wood lack worlds of company,
For you in my respect° are all the world.
Then how can it be said I am alone,   225
When all the world is here to look on me?
DEMETRIUS: I'll run from thee and hide me in the
    brakes,°
And leave thee to the mercy of wild beasts.
HELENA: The wildest hath not such a heart as you.
Run when you will, the story shall be chang'd: 230
Apollo flies and Daphne holds the chase,°
The dove pursues the griffin,° the mild hind°
Makes speed to catch the tiger—bootless° speed,
When cowardice pursues and valor flies.
DEMETRIUS: I will not stay° thy questions.° Let me go! 235
Or if thou follow me, do not believe
But I shall do thee mischief in the wood.
HELENA: Ay, in the temple, in the town, the field,
You do me mischief. Fie, Demetrius!
Your wrongs do set a scandal on my sex.   240
We cannot fight for love, as men may do;
We should be woo'd and were not made to woo.
                              [*Exit Demetrius.*]

---

157. all: Fully. **158. vestal:** Vestal virgin (contains a complimentary allusion to Queen Elizabeth as a votaress of Diana and probably refers to an actual entertainment in her honor at Elvetham in 1591). **160. As:** As if. **161. might:** Could. **164. fancy-free:** Free of love's spell. **168. love-in-idleness:** Pansy, heartsease. **171. or...or:** Either...or. **174. leviathan:** Sea monster, whale. **176. forty:** Used indefinitely. **192. wode:** Mad (pronounced "wood" and often spelled so). **195. adamant:** Lodestone, magnet (with pun on *hard-hearted,* since adamant was also thought to be the hardest of all stones and was confused with the diamond). **197. Leave:** Give up.

199. fair: Courteously. **214. impeach:** Call into question. **218. desert:** Deserted. **220. virtue:** Goodness or power to attract. **privilege:** Safeguard, warrant. **For that:** Because. **224. in my respect:** As far as I am concerned. **227. brakes:** Thickets. **231. Apollo...chase:** In the ancient myth, Daphne fled from Apollo and was saved from rape by being transformed into a laurel tree; here it is the female who *holds the chase,* or pursues, instead of the male. **232. griffin:** A fabulous monster with the head of an eagle and the body of a lion. **hind:** Female deer. **233. bootless:** Fruitless. **235. stay:** Wait for. **questions:** Talk or argument.

[ABOVE] Oberon instructing Puck in the power of the "little western flower" in the American Repertory Theater's 1986 production. [BELOW] Kevin Kline as Bottom and Michelle Pfeiffer as Titania in a touching moment from the 1999 film *William Shakespeare's A Midsummer Night's Dream,* directed by Michael Hoffman.

[LEFT] Oberon with Titania upon his shoulder. [RIGHT] The rude mechanicals: Moonshine with Lion.

I'll follow thee and make a heaven of hell,
To die upon° the hand I love so well.   [*Exit.*]
OBERON: Fare thee well, nymph. Ere he do leave this
245   grove,
Thou shalt fly him and he shall seek thy love.

(*Enter Puck.*)

Hast thou the flower there? Welcome, wanderer.
PUCK: Ay, there it is.   [*Offers the flower.*]
OBERON: I pray thee, give it me.
I know a bank where the wild thyme blows,°
250   Where oxlips° and the nodding violet grows,
Quite over-canopied with luscious woodbine,°
With sweet musk-roses° and with eglantine.°
There sleeps Titania sometime of the night
Lull'd in these flowers with dances and delight;

And there the snake throws° her enamel'd skin,   255
Weed° wide enough to wrap a fairy in.
And with the juice of this I'll streak° her eyes,
And make her full of hateful fantasies.
Take thou some of it, and seek through this grove.
                    [*Gives some love-juice.*]
A sweet Athenian lady is in love   260
With a disdainful youth. Anoint his eyes,
But do it when the next thing he espies
May be the lady. Thou shalt know the man
By the Athenian garments he hath on.
Effect it with some care, that he may prove   265
More fond on° her than she upon her love;
And look thou meet me ere the first cock crow.
PUCK: Fear not, my lord, your servant shall do so.
                    (*Exeunt.*)

244. upon: By. **249. blows:** Blooms. **250. oxlips:** Flowers
resembling cow-slip and primrose. **251. woodbine:** Honeysuckle. **252. musk-roses:** A kind of large, sweet-scented rose.
eglantine: Sweetbriar, another kind of rose.

255. throws: Sloughs off, sheds. **256. Weed:** Garment.
257. streak: Anoint, touch gently. **266. fond on:** Doting on.

{Scene II}°

(*Enter Titania, Queen of Fairies, with her train.*)

TITANIA: Come, now a roundel° and a fairy song;
  Then, for the third part of a minute, hence—
  Some to kill cankers° in the musk-rose buds,
  Some war with rere-mice° for their leathern wings,
5 To make my small elves coats, and some keep back
  The clamorous owl, that nightly hoots and wonders
  At our quaint° spirits. Sing me now asleep.
  Then to your offices and let me rest.

(*Fairies sing.*)

FIRST FAIRY: You spotted snakes with double° tongue,
10   Thorny hedgehogs, be not seen;
  Newts° and blindworms, do no wrong,
    Come not near our fairy queen.
    [*Chorus.*] Philomel,° with melody
    Sing in our sweet lullaby;
15 Lulla, lulla, lullaby, lulla, lulla, lullaby.
    Never harm,
    Nor spell nor charm,
  Come our lovely lady nigh.
  So, good night, with lullaby.
20 FIRST FAIRY: Weaving spiders, come not here;
    Hence, you long-legg'd spinners, hence!
  Beetles black, approach not near;
    Worm nor snail, do no offense.
    [*Chorus.*] Philomel, with melody, etc.
25 SECOND FAIRY: Hence, away! Now all is well.
  One aloof stand sentinel.

                    [*Exeunt Fairies. Titania sleeps.*]

(*Enter Oberon [and squeezes the flower on Titania's eyelids].*)

OBERON: What thou seest when thou dost wake,
  Do it for thy true-love take;
  Love and languish for his sake.
30 Be it ounce,° or cat, or bear,
  Pard,° or boar with bristled hair,
  In thy eye that shall appear
  When thou wak'st, it is thy dear
  Wake when some vile thing is near.   [*Exit.*]

(*Enter Lysander and Hermia.*)

35 LYSANDER: Fair love, you faint with wand'ring in the
      wood;
  And to speak troth,° I have forgot our way.
  We'll rest us, Hermia, if you think it good,

And tarry for the comfort of the day.
HERMIA: Be 't so, Lysander. Find you out a bed,
  For I upon this bank will rest my head.   40
LYSANDER: One turf shall serve as pillow for us both,
  One heart, one bed, two bosoms, and one troth.°
HERMIA: Nay, good Lysander; for my sake, my dear,
  Lie further off yet, do not lie so near.
LYSANDER: O, take the sense, sweet, of my
      innocence!°   45
  Love takes the meaning in love's conference.°
  I mean, that my heart unto yours is knit
  So that but one heart we can make of it;
  Two bosoms interchained with an oath—
  So then two bosoms and a single troth.   50
  Then by your side no bed-room me deny,
  For lying so, Hermia, I do not lie.°
HERMIA: Lysander riddles very prettily.
  Now much beshrew° my manners and my pride
  If Hermia meant to say Lysander lied.   55
  But, gentle friend, for love and courtesy
  Lie further off, in human° modesty;
  Such separation as may well be said
  Becomes a virtuous bachelor and a maid,
  So far be distant; and, good night, sweet friend. 60
  Thy love ne'er alter till thy sweet life end!
LYSANDER: Amen, amen, to that fair prayer, say I,
  And then end life when I end loyalty!
  Here is my bed. Sleep give thee all his rest!
HERMIA: With half that wish the wisher's eyes be
      press'd!°   65
    [*They sleep, separated by a short distance.*]

(*Enter Puck.*)

PUCK: Through the forest have I gone,
  But Athenian found I none
  On whose eyes I might approve°
  This flower's force in stirring love.
  Night and silence.—Who is here?   70
  Weeds of Athens he doth wear.
  This is he, my master said,
  Despised the Athenian maid;
  And here the maiden, sleeping sound,
  On the dank and dirty ground.   75
  Pretty soul! She durst not lie
  Near this lack-love, this kill-courtesy.
  Churl, upon thy eyes I throw
  All the power this charm doth owe.°
                    [*Applies the love-juice.*]
  When thou wak'st, let love forbid   80
  Sleep his seat on thy eyelid.

II, ii. **Location:** The wood.   1. **roundel:** Dance in a ring.
3. **cankers:** Cankerworms.   4. **rere-mice:** Bats.   7. **quaint:**
Dainty.   9. **double:** Forked.   11. **Newts:** water lizards (considered poisonous, as were blindworms—small snakes with
tiny eyes—and spiders).   13. **Philomel:** The nightingale.
(Philomela, daughter of King Pandion, was transformed into
a nightingale, according to Ovid's *Metamorphoses,* after she
had been raped by her sister Procne's husband, Tereus.)
30. **ounce:** Lynx.   31. **Pard:** Leopard.   36. **troth:** Truth.

42. **troth:** Faith, troth-plight.   45. **take . . . innocence:** Interpret my intention as innocent.   46. **Love . . . conference:** When
lovers confer, love teaches each lover to interpret the other's
meaning lovingly.   52. **lie:** Tell a falsehood (with a riddling
pun on *lie,* recline).   54. **beshrew:** Curse (but mildly meant).
57. **human:** Courteous.   65. **With . . . press'd:** May we share
your wish, so that your eyes too are *press'd,* closed, in sleep.
68. **approve:** Test.   79. **owe:** Own.

So awake when I am gone,
For I must now to Oberon.   (*Exit*.)

(*Enter Demetrius and Helena, running*.)

HELENA: Stay, though thou kill me, sweet Demetrius.
DEMETRIUS: I charge thee, hence, and do not haunt
85   me thus.
HELENA: O, wilt thou darkling° leave me? Do not so.
DEMETRIUS: Stay, on thy peril!° I alone will go.
                                                [*Exit*.]
HELENA: O, I am out of breath in this fond° chase!
The more my prayer, the lesser is my grace.°
90   Happy is Hermia, wheresoe'er she lies,°
For she hath blessed and attractive eyes.
How came her eyes so bright? Not with salt tears;
If so, my eyes are oft'ner wash'd than hers.
No, no, I am as ugly as a bear;
95   For beasts that meet me run away for fear.
Therefore no marvel though Demetrius
Do, as a monster, fly my presence thus.
What wicked and dissembling glass of mine
Made me compare with Hermia's sphery eyne?°
100 But who is here? Lysander, on the ground?
Dead, or asleep? I see no blood, no wound.
Lysander, if you live, good sir, awake.
LYSANDER [*awaking*]: And run through fire I will for
    thy sweet sake.
Transparent° Helena! Nature shows art,
105 That through thy bosom makes me see thy heart.
Where is Demetrius? O, how fit a word
Is that vile name to perish on my sword!
HELENA: Do not say so, Lysander, say not so.
What though he love your Hermia? Lord, what
    though?
110 Yet Hermia still loves you. Then be content.
LYSANDER: Content with Hermia? No! I do repent
The tedious minutes I with her have spent.
Not Hermia but Helena I love.
Who will not change a raven for a dove?
115 The will of man is by his reason sway'd,
And reason says you are the worthier maid.
Things growing are not ripe until their season;
So I, being young, till now ripe not° to reason.
And touching° now the point° of human skill,°
120 Reason becomes the marshal to my will
And leads me to your eyes, where I o'erlook°
Love's stories written in love's richest book.
HELENA: Wherefore was I to this keen mockery born?
When at your hands did I deserve this scorn?
125 Is 't not enough, is 't not enough, young man,
That I did never, no, nor never can,

Deserve a sweet look from Demetrius' eye,
But you must flout my insufficiency?
Good troth,° you do me wrong, good sooth,° you do,
In such disdainful manner me to woo.   130
But fare you well. Perforce I must confess
I thought you lord of° more true gentleness.
O, that a lady, of° one man refus'd,
Should of another therefore be abus'd!°   (*Exit*.)
LYSANDER: She sees not Hermia. Hermia, sleep thou
    there,   135
And never mayst thou come Lysander near!
For as a surfeit of the sweetest things
The deepest loathing to the stomach brings,
Or as the heresies that men do leave
Are hated most of those they did deceive,   140
So thou, my surfeit and my heresy,
Of all be hated, but the most of me!
And, all my powers, address your love and might
To honor Helen and to be her knight!   (*Exit*.)
HERMIA [*awaking*]: Help me, Lysander, help me! Do
    thy best   145
To pluck this crawling serpent from my breast!
Ay me, for pity! What a dream was here!
Lysander, look how I do quake with fear.
Methought a serpent eat° my heart away,
And you sat smiling at his cruel prey.°   150
Lysander! What, remov'd? Lysander! Lord!
What, out of hearing? Gone? No sound, no word?
Alack, where are you? Speak, an if you hear,
Speak, of all loves!° I swoon almost with fear.
No? Then I well perceive you are not nigh.   155
Either death, or you I'll find immediately.
                    (*Exit*. [*Manet*° *Titania lying asleep*.])

{ACT III • Scene I}°

(*Enter the Clowns* [*Quince, Snug, Bottom, Flute, Snout, and Starveling*].)

BOTTOM: Are we all met?
QUINCE: Pat, pat; and here's a marvailes° convenient
    place for our rehearsal. This green plot shall be our
    stage, this hawthorn brake° our tiring-house,° and
    we will do it in action as we will do it before the   5
    Duke.
BOTTOM: Peter Quince?
QUINCE: What sayest thou, bully° Bottom?
BOTTOM: There are things in this comedy of Pyramus and
    Thisby that will never please. First, Pyramus must 10
    draw a sword to kill himself, which the ladies cannot
    abide. How answer you that?

---

86. **darkling:** In the dark.   87. **on thy peril:** On pain of danger to you if you don't obey me and stay.   88. **fond:** Doting.   89. **my grace:** The favor I obtain.   90. **lies:** Dwells.   99. **sphery eyne:** Eyes as bright as stars in their spheres.   104. **Transparent:** (1) Radiant; (2) able to be seen through.   118. **ripe not:** (Am) not ripened.   119. **touching:** Reaching. **point:** Summit. **skill:** Judgment.   121. **o'erlook:** Read.

129. **Good troth, good sooth:** Indeed, truly.   132. **lord of:** Possessor of. **gentleness:** Courtesy.   133. **of:** By.   134. **abus'd:** Ill treated.   149. **eat:** Ate (pronounced "et").   150. **prey:** Act of preying.   154. **of all loves:** For all love's sake.   156. [S.D.] *Manet:* Latin for "she remains."   **III, i. Location:** Scene continues.   2. **marvailes:** Marvelous.   4. **brake:** Thicket. **tiring-house:** Attiring area, hence backstage.   8. **bully:** Worthy, jolly, fine fellow.

SNOUT: By 'r lakin,° a parlous° fear.

STARVELING: I believe we must leave the killing out,
15   when all is done.°

BOTTOM: Not a whit. I have a device to make all well.
Write me° a prologue; and let the prologue seem to
say, we will do no harm with our swords and that
Pyramus is not kill'd indeed; and, for the more better
20   assurance, tell them that I Pyramus am not Pyramus,
but Bottom the weaver. This will put them out of
fear.

QUINCE: Well, we will have such a prologue, and it shall
be written in eight and six.°

25 **BOTTOM:** No, make it two more; let it be written in eight
and eight.

SNOUT: Will not the ladies be afeard of the lion?

STARVELING: I fear it, I promise you.

BOTTOM: Masters, you ought to consider with your-
30   selves, to bring in—God shield us!—a lion among
ladies,° is a most dreadful thing. For there is not a
more fearful° wild-fowl than your lion living; and we
ought to look to 't.

SNOUT: Therefore another prologue must tell he is not
35   a lion.

BOTTOM: Nay, you must name his name, and half his
face must be seen through the lion's neck, and he
himself must speak through, saying thus, or to the
same defect:° "Ladies"—or "Fair ladies—I would
40   wish you"—or "I would request you"—or "I
would entreat you"—not to fear, not to tremble;
my life for yours.° If you think I come hither as a
lion, it were pity of my life.° No, I am no such thing,
I am a man as other men are." And there indeed let
45   him name his name, and tell them plainly he is Snug
the joiner.

QUINCE: Well, it shall be so. But there is two hard
things: that is, to bring the moonlight into a chamber; for, you know, Pyramus and Thisby meet by
50   moonlight.

SNOUT: Doth the moon shine that night we play our
play?

BOTTOM: A calendar, a calendar! Look in the almanac
Find out moonshine, find out moonshine.

[*They consult an almanac.*]

QUINCE: Yes, it doth shine that night.

55 **BOTTOM:** Why then may you leave a casement of the
great chamber window, where we play, open, and the
moon may shine in at the casement.

QUINCE: Ay; or else one must come in with a bush of
thorns° and a lantern, and say he comes to disfigure,°
or to present,° the person of Moonshine. Then there   60
is another thing: we must have a wall in the great
chamber; for Pyramus and Thisby, says the story, did
talk through the chink of a wall.

SNOUT: You can never bring in a wall. What say you,
Bottom?   65

BOTTOM: Some man or other must present Wall. And let
him have some plaster, or some loam, or some rough-
cast° about him, to signify wall; and let him hold his
fingers thus, and through that cranny shall Pyramus
and Thisby whisper.   70

QUINCE: If that may be, then all is well. Come, sit
down, every mother's son, and rehearse your parts.
Pyramus, you begin. When you have spoken your
speech, enter into that brake, and so every one
according to his cue.   75

(*Enter Robin [Puck].*)

PUCK: What hempen° home-spuns have we swagg'ring
here,
So near the cradle of the Fairy Queen?
What, a play toward?° I'll be an auditor;°
An actor too perhaps, if I see cause.

QUINCE: Speak, Pyramus. Thisby, stand forth.   80

BOTTOM: "Thisby, the flowers of odious savors
sweet,"—

QUINCE: Odors, odors.

BOTTOM: "Odors savors sweet;
So hath thy breath, my dearest Thisby dear.
But hark, a voice! Stay thou but here awhile,   85
And by and by I will to thee appear."   (*Exit.*)

PUCK: A stranger Pyramus than e'er played here.°

[*Exit.*]

FLUTE: Must I speak now?

QUINCE: Ay, marry, must you; for you must understand
he goes but to see a noise that he heard, and is to   90
come again.

FLUTE: "Most radiant Pyramus, most lily-white of hue,
Of color like the red rose on triumphant brier,
Most brisky juvenal° and eke° most lovely Jew,°
As true as truest horse that yet would never tire.   95
I'll meet thee, Pyramus, at Ninny's tomb."

QUINCE: "Ninus°' tomb," man. Why, you must not speak
that yet. That you answer to Pyramus. You speak all

---

13. By 'r lakin: By our ladykin, the Virgin Mary. **parlous:**
Perilous. **15. when all is done:** When all is said and done.
17. Write me: Write at my suggestion. **24. eight and six:** Alternate lines of eight and six syllables, a common ballad measure.
30–31. lion among ladies: A contemporary pamphlet tells how
at the christening in 1594 of Prince Henry, eldest son of King
James VI of Scotland, later James I of England, a "blackmoor"
instead of a lion drew the triumphal chariot, since the lion's
presence might have "brought some fear to the nearest."
32. fearful: Fear-inspiring. **39. defect:** Bottom's blunder for
effect. **42. my life for yours:** I pledge my life to make your
lives safe. **43. it were . . . life:** My life would be endangered.

58–59. bush of thorns: Bundle of thornbush faggots (part of the
accoutrements of the man in the moon, according to the popular notions of the time, along with his lantern and his dog).
59. disfigure: Quince's blunder for *prefigure.* **60. present:**
Represent. **67–68. rough-cast:** A mixture of lime and gravel
used to plaster the outside of buildings. **76. hempen:** Made of
hemp, a rough fiber. **78. toward:** About to take place. **auditor:** One who listens (i.e., part of the audience). **87. here:** In
this theater (?). **94. brisky juvenal:** Brisk youth. **eke:** Also.
Jew: Probably an absurd repetition of the first syllable of *juvenal.* **97. Ninus:** Mythical founder of Nineveh (whose wife,
Semiramis, was supposed to have built the walls of Babylon
where the story of Pyramus and Thisby takes place).

100 your part at once, cues and all. Pyramus enter. Your
cue is past; it is, "never tire."

FLUTE: O—"As true as truest horse, that yet would
never tire."

[*Enter Puck, and Bottom as Pyramus with the ass head.*]°

BOTTOM: "If I were fair,° Thisby, I were° only thine."

QUINCE: O monstrous! O strange! We are haunted.
Pray, masters! Fly, masters! Help!

[*Exeunt Quince, Snug, Flute, Snout, and Starveling.*]

105 PUCK: I'll follow you, I'll lead you about a round,°
Through bog, through bush, through brake, through
brier.
Sometime a horse I'll be, sometime a hound,
A hog, a headless bear, sometime a fire,°
And neigh, and bark, and grunt, and roar, and burn,
110 Like horse, hound, hog, bear, fire, at every turn.
(*Exit.*)

BOTTOM: Why do they run away? This is a knavery of
them to make me afeard.

(*Enter Snout.*)

SNOUT: O Bottom, thou art chang'd! What do I see on
thee?

115 BOTTOM: What do you see? You see an ass-head of your
own, do you?   [*Exit Snout.*]

(*Enter Quince.*)

QUINCE: Bless thee, Bottom, bless thee! Thou art translated.°   (*Exit.*)

BOTTOM: I see their knavery. This is to make an ass of
120 me, to fright me, if they could. But I will not stir from
this place, do what they can. I will walk up and down
here, and I will sing, that they shall hear I am not
afraid.   [*Sings.*]
The woosel cock° so black of hue,
125   With orange-tawny bill,
The throstle° with his note so true,
    The wren with little quill°—

TITANIA [*awaking*]: What angel wakes me from my
flow'ry bed?

BOTTOM [*sings*]: The finch, the sparrow, and the lark,
130   The plain-song° cuckoo grey,
Whose note full many a man doth mark,
    And dares not answer nay°—
For, indeed, who would set his wit to so foolish a
bird? Who would give a bird the lie,° though he cry
135 "cuckoo" never so?°

101. [S.D.] *with the ass head*: This stage direction, taken from
the Folio, presumably refers to a standard stage property.
102. **fair**: Handsome. **were**: Would be. 105. **about a round**:
Roundabout. 108. **fire**: Will-o'-the-wisp. 117–118. **translated**: Transformed. 124. **woosel cock**: Male ousel or ouzel,
blackbird. 126. **throstle**: Song thrush. 127. **quill**: Literally,
a reed pipe; hence, the bird's piping song. 130. **plain-song**:
Singing a melody without variations. 132. **dares . . . nay**:
Cannot deny that he is a cuckold. 134. **give . . . lie**: Call the
bird a liar. 135. **never so**: Ever so much.

TITANIA: I pray thee, gentle mortal, sing again.
Mine ear is much enamored of thy note;
So is mine eye enthralled to thy shape;
And thy fair virtue's force° perforce doth move me
On the first view to say, to swear, I love thee.   140

BOTTOM: Methinks, mistress, you should have little reason for that. And yet, to say the truth, reason and
love keep little company together nowadays. The
more the pity that some honest neighbors will not
make them friends. Nay, I can gleek° upon occasion.   145

TITANIA: Thou art as wise as thou art beautiful.

BOTTOM: Not so, neither. But if I had wit enough to get
out of this wood, I have enough to serve mine own
turn.°

TITANIA: Out of this wood do not desire to go.   150
Thou shalt remain here, whether thou wilt or no.
I am a spirit of no common rate.°
The summer still° doth tend upon my state;°
And I do love thee. Therefore, go with me.
I'll give thee fairies to attend on thee,   155
And they shall fetch thee jewels from the deep,
And sing while thou on pressed flowers dost sleep.
And I will purge thy mortal grossness so
That thou shalt like an airy spirit go.
Peaseblossom, Cobweb, Moth,° and
    Mustardseed!   160

(*Enter four Fairies [Peaseblossom, Cobweb, Moth, and
Mustardseed].*)

PEASEBLOSSOM: Ready.

COBWEB: And I.

MOTH: And I

MUSTARDSEED: And I.

ALL: Where shall we go?

TITANIA: Be kind and courteous to this gentleman.
Hop in his walks and gambol in his eyes;
Feed him with apricocks and dewberries,   165
With purple grapes, green figs, and mulberries;
The honey-bags steal from the humble-bees,
And for night-tapers crop their waxen thighs
And light them at the fiery glow-worm's eyes,
To have my love to bed and to arise;   170
And pluck the wings from painted butterflies
To fan the moonbeams from his sleeping eyes.
Nod to him, elves, and do him courtesies.

PEASEBLOSSOM: Hail, mortal!

COBWEB: Hail!   175

MOTH: Hail!

MUSTARDSEED: Hail!

BOTTOM: I cry your worship's mercy, heartily. I beseech
your worship's name.

139. **thy . . . force**: The power of your beauty. 145. **gleek**:
Scoff, jest. 148–149. **serve . . . turn**: Answer my purpose.
152. **rate**: Rank, value. 153. **still**: Ever always. **doth . . .
state**: Waits upon me as part of my royal retinue. 160. **Moth**:
Mote, speck. (The two words *moth* and *mote* were pronounced
alike.)

180 COBWEB: Cobweb.

BOTTOM: I shall desire you of more acquaintance, good
Master Cobweb. If I cut my finger, I shall make bold
with you.° Your name, honest gentleman?

PEASEBLOSSOM: Peaseblossom.

185 BOTTOM: I pray you, commend me to Mistress Squash,°
your mother, and to Master Peascod,° your father.
Good Master Peaseblossom, I shall desire you of more
acquaintance too. Your name, I beseech you, sir?

MUSTARDSEED: Mustardseed.

190 BOTTOM: Good Master Mustardseed, I know your
patience° well. That same cowardly, giant-like ox-
beef hath devour'd many a gentleman of your house.
I promise you your kindred hath made my eyes
water ere now. I desire you of more acquaintance,
195 good Master Mustardseed.

TITANIA: Come wait upon him; lead him to my bower.
The moon methinks looks with a wat'ry eye;
And when she weeps,° weeps every little flower,
Lamenting some enforced° chastity.
200 Tie up my lover's tongue, bring him silently.

(*Exeunt.*)

{Scene II}°

(*Enter [Oberon,] King of Fairies.*)

OBERON: I wonder if Titania be awak'd;
Then, what it was that next came in her eye,
Which she must dote on in extremity.

([*Enter*] *Robin Goodfellow [Puck].*)

Here comes my messenger. How now, mad spirit?
5 What night-rule° now about this haunted° grove?

PUCK: My mistress with a monster is in love.
Near to her close° and consecrated bower,
While she was in her dull° and sleeping hour,
A crew of patches,° rude mechanicals,°
10 That work for bread upon Athenian stalls,
Were met together to rehearse a play
Intended for great Theseus' nuptial day.
The shallowest thick-skin of that barren sort,°
Who Pyramus presented,° in their sport
15 Forsook his scene° and ent'red in a brake.
When I did him at this advantage take,
An ass's nole° I fixed on his head.

Anon his Thisby must be answered,
And forth my mimic° comes. When they him spy,
As wild geese that the creeping fowler eye, 20
Or russet-pated choughs,° many in sort,°
Rising and cawing at the gun's report,
Sever° themselves and madly sweep the sky,
So, at his sight, away his fellows fly;
And, at our stamp, here o'er and o'er one falls; 25
He murder cries and help from Athens calls.
Their sense thus weak, lost with their fears thus
strong,
Made senseless things begin to do them wrong,
For briers and thorns at their apparel snatch;
Some, sleeves—some, hats; from yielders all things
catch. 30
I led them on in this distracted fear
And left sweet Pyramus translated there,
When in that moment, so it came to pass,
Titania wak'd and straightway lov'd an ass.

OBERON: This falls out better than I could devise. 35
But hast thou yet latch'd° the Athenian's eyes
With the love-juice, as I did bid thee do?

PUCK: I took him sleeping—that is finish'd too—
And the Athenian woman by his side,
That, when he wak'd, of force° she must be ey'd. 40

(*Enter Demetrius and Hermia.*)

OBERON: Stand close. This is the same Athenian.

PUCK: This is the woman, but not this the man.
[*They stand aside.*]

DEMETRIUS: O, why rebuke you him that loves you so?
Lay breath so bitter on your bitter foe.

HERMIA: Now I but chide; but I should use thee worse, 45
For thou, I fear, hast given me cause to curse.
If thou hast slain Lysander in his sleep,
Being o'er shoes in blood, plunge in the deep,
And kill me too.
The sun was not so true unto the day 50
As he to me. Would he have stolen away
From sleeping Hermia? I'll believe as soon
This whole° earth may be bor'd and that the moon
May through the center creep and so displease
Her brother's° noontide with th' Antipodes.° 55
It cannot be but thou has murd'red him;
So should a murderer look, so dead,° so grim.

DEMETRIUS: So should the murdered look, and so
should I,
Pierc'd through the heart with your stern cruelty.
Yet you, the murderer, look as bright, as clear, 60
As yonder Venus in her glimmering sphere.

HERMIA: What's this to my Lysander? Where is he?
Ah, good Demetrius, wilt thou give him me?

182–183. If . . . you: Cobwebs were used to stanch bleeding.
185. Squash: Unripe pea pod. 186. Peascod: Ripe pea pod.
190–191. your patience: What you have endured. 198. she
weeps: I.e., she causes dew. 199. enforced: Forced, violated;
or, possibly, constrained (since Titania at this moment is
hardly concerned about chastity). III, ii. Location: The wood.
5. night-rule: Diversion for the night. haunted: Much frequented. 7. close: Secret, private. 8. dull: Drowsy. 9. patches:
Clowns, fools. rude mechanicals: Ignorant artisans. 13. barren
sort: Stupid company or crew. 14. presented: Acted. 15. scene:
Playing area. 17. nole: Noddle, head.

19. mimic: Burlesque actor. 21. russet-pated choughs: Gray-
headed jackdaws. in sort: In a flock. 23. Sever: Scatter.
36. latch'd: Moistened, anointed. 40. of force: Perforce.
53. whole: Solid. 55. Her brother's: I.e., the sun's. th' Antipodes: The people on the opposite side of the earth. 57. dead:
Deadly; or, deathly pale.

DEMETRIUS: I had rather give his carcass to my hounds.

HERMIA: Out dog! Out cur! Thou driv'st me past the

65   bounds

Of maiden's patience. Hast thou slain him, then?

Henceforth be never numb'red among men!

O, once tell true, tell true, even for my sake!

Durst thou have look'd upon him being awake,

70   And hast thou kill'd him sleeping? O brave touch!°

Could not a worm,° an adder, do so much?

An adder did it, for with doubler tongue

Than thine, thou serpent, never adder stung.

DEMETRIUS: You spend your passion° on a mispris'd

       mood.°

75   I am not guilty of Lysander's blood,

Nor is he dead, for aught that I can tell.

HERMIA: I pray thee, tell me then that he is well.

DEMETRIUS: An if I could, what should I get

       therefore?

HERMIA: A privilege never to see me more.

80   And from thy hated presence part I so.

See me no more, whether he be dead or no.

                            (Exit.)

DEMETRIUS: There is no following her in this fierce

       vein.

Here therefore for a while I will remain.

So sorrow's heaviness doth heavier° grow

85   For debt that bankrupt° sleep doth sorrow owe;

Which now in some slight measure it will pay,

If for his tender here I make some stay.°

                 (Lie down [and sleep].)

OBERON: What hast thou done? Thou hast mistaken

       quite

And laid the love-juice on some true-love's sight.

90   Of thy misprision° must perforce ensue

Some true love turn'd and not a false turn'd true.

PUCK: Then fate o'er-rules, that, one man holding

       troth,°

A million fail, confounding oath on oath.°

OBERON: About the wood go swifter than the wind,

95   And Helena of Athens look thou find.

All fancy-sick° she is and pale of cheer°

With sighs of love, that cost the fresh blood° dear.

By some illusion see thou bring her here.

I'll charm his eyes against she do appear.°

PUCK: I go, I go; look how I go   100

Swifter than arrow from the Tartar's bow.°

                         [Exit.]

OBERON: Flower of this purple dye,

Hit with Cupid's archery.

Sink in angle of his eye.

      [Applies love-juice to Demetrius' eyes.]

When his love he doth espy,   105

Let her shine as gloriously

As the Venus of the sky.

When thou wak'st, if she be by,

Beg of her for remedy.

(Enter Puck.)

PUCK: Captain of our fairy band,   110

Helena is here at hand,

And the youth, mistook by me,

Pleading for a lover's fee.°

Shall we their fond pageant° see?

Lord, what fools these mortals be!   115

OBERON: Stand aside. The noise they make

Will cause Demetrius to awake.

PUCK: Then will two at once woo one;

That must needs be sport alone;°

And those things do best please me   120

That befall prepost'rously.°

                  [They stand aside.]

(Enter Lysander and Helena.)

LYSANDER: Why should you think that I should woo in

       scorn?

Scorn and derision never come in tears.

Look when° I vow, I weep; and vows so born,

In their nativity all truth appears.°   125

How can these things in me seem scorn to you,

Bearing the badge° of faith, to prove them true?

HELENA: You do advance° your cunning more and

       more.

When truth kills truth,° O devilish-holy fray!

These vows are Hermia's. Will you give her o'er?   130

Weigh oath with oath, and you will nothing weigh.

Your vows to her and me, put in two scales

Will even weigh, and both as light as tales.°

LYSANDER: I had no judgment when to her I swore.

HELENA: Nor none, in my mind, now you give her o'er.   135

LYSANDER: Demetrius loves her, and he loves not you.

DEMETRIUS [*awaking*]: O Helen, goddess, nymph,

       perfect, divine!

To what, my love, shall I compare thine eyne?

---

70. **brave touch:** Noble exploit (said ironically). 71. **worm:** Serpent. 74. **passion:** Violent feelings. **mispris'd mood:** Anger based on misconception. 84. **heavier:** (1) Harder to bear; (2) drowsier. 85. **bankrupt:** Demetrius is saying that his sleepiness adds to the weariness caused by sorrow. 86–87. **Which . . . stay:** To a small extent I will be able to "pay back" and hence find some relief from sorrow, if I pause here a while (*make some stay*) while sleep *tenders*, or offers itself, by way of paying the debt owed to sorrow. 90. **misprision:** Mistake. 92. **troth:** Faith. 93. **confounding . . . oath:** Invalidating one oath with another. 96. **fancy-sick:** Lovesick. **cheer:** Face. 97. **sighs . . . blood:** An allusion to the physiological theory that each sigh costs the heart a drop of blood. 99. **against . . . appear:** In anticipation of her coming.

101. **Tartar's bow:** Tartars were famed for their skill with the bow 113. **fee:** Privilege, reward. 114. **fond pageant:** Foolish exhibition. 119. **alone:** Unequaled. 121. **prepost'rously:** Out of the natural order. 124. **Look when:** Whenever. 124–125. **vows . . . appears:** Vows made by one who is weeping give evidence thereby of their sincerity. 127. **badge:** Identifying device such as that worn on servants' livery. 128. **advance:** Carry forward, display. 129. **truth kills truth:** One of Lysander's vows must invalidate the other. 133. **tales:** Lies.

Crystal is muddy. O, how ripe in show°
140 Thy lips, those kissing cherries, tempting grow!
That pure congealed white, high Taurus'° snow,
Fann'd with the eastern wind, turns to a crow°
When thou hold'st up thy hand. O, let me kiss
This princess of pure white, this seal° of bliss!

145 HELENA: O spite! O hell! I see you all are bent
To set against me for your merriment.
If you were civil and knew courtesy,
You would not do me thus much injury.
Can you not hate me, as I know you do,
150 But you must join in souls to mock me too?
If you were men, as men you are in show,
You would not use a gentle lady so—
To vow, and swear, and superpraise° my parts,°
When I am sure you hate me with your hearts.
155 You both are rivals, and love Hermia;
And now both rivals, to mock Helena.
A trim° exploit, a manly enterprise,
To conjure tears up in a poor maid's eyes
With your derision! None of noble sort
160 Would so offend a virgin and extort°
A poor soul's patience, all to make you sport.

LYSANDER: You are unkind, Demetrius. Be not so;
For you love Hermia; this you know I know.
And here, with all good will, with all my heart,
165 In Hermia's love I yield you up my part;
And yours of Helena to me bequeath,
Whom I do love and will do till my death.

HELENA: Never did mockers waste more idle breath.

DEMETRIUS: Lysander, keep thy Hermia; I will none.°
170 If e'er I lov'd her, all that love is gone.
My heart to her but as guest-wise sojourn'd,
And now to Helen is it home return'd.
There to remain.

LYSANDER: Helen, it is not so.

DEMETRIUS: Disparage not the faith thou dost not know,
175 Lest, to thy peril, thou aby° it dear.
Look where thy love comes; yonder is thy dear.

(Enter Hermia.)

HERMIA: Dark night, that from the eye his° function
takes,
The ear more quick of apprehension makes;
Wherein it doth impair the seeing sense,
180 It pays the hearing double recompense.
Thou art not by mine eye, Lysander, found;
Mine ear, I thank it, brought me to thy sound.
But why unkindly didst thou leave me so?

LYSANDER: Why should he stay, whom love doth press
to go?

HERMIA: What love could press Lysander from my
side? 185

LYSANDER: Lysander's love, that would not let him
bide,
Fair Helena, who more engilds the night
Than all yon fiery oes° and eyes of light.
Why seek'st thou me? Could not this make thee
know,
The hate I bear thee made me leave thee so? 190

HERMIA: You speak not as you think. It cannot be.

HELENA: Lo, she is one of this confederacy!
Now I perceive they have conjoin'd all three
To fashion this false sport, in spite of me.°
Injurious Hermia, most ungrateful maid! 195
Have you conspir'd, have you with these contriv'd°
To bait° me with this foul derision?
Is all the counsel° that we two have shar'd,
The sisters' vows, the hours that we have spent,
When we have chid the hasty-footed time 200
For parting us—O, is all forgot?
All school-days friendship, childhood innocence?
We, Hermia, like two artificial° gods,
Have with our needles created both one flower,
Both on one sampler, sitting on one cushion, 205
Both warbling of one song, both in one key,
As if our hands, our sides, voices, and minds
Had been incorporate. So we grew together,
Like to a double cherry, seeming parted,
But yet an union in partition; 210
Two lovely° berries molded on one stem;
So, with two seeming bodies, but one heart;
Two of the first, like coats in heraldry,
Due but to one and crowned with one crest.°
And will you rent° our ancient love asunder, 215
To join with men in scorning your poor friend?
It is not friendly, 'tis not maidenly.
Our sex, as well as I, may chide you for it,
Though I alone do feel the injury.

HERMIA: I am amazed at your passionate words. 220
I scorn you not. It seems that you scorn me.

HELENA: Have you not set Lysander, as in scorn,
To follow me and praise my eyes and face?
And made your other love, Demetrius,
Who even but now did spurn me with his foot, 225
To call me goddess, nymph, divine and rare,
Precious, celestial? Wherefore speaks he this
To her he hates? And wherefore doth Lysander
Deny your love, so rich within his soul,
And tender° me, forsooth, affection, 230
But by your setting on, by your consent?

---

139. **show:** Appearance. 141. **Taurus:** A lofty mountain range in Asia Minor. 142. **turns to a crow:** Seems black by contrast. 144. **seal:** Pledge. 153. **superpraise:** Overpraise. **parts:** Qualities. 157. **trim:** Pretty, fine (said ironically). 160. **extort:** Twist, torture. 169. **will none:** Wish none of her. 175. **aby:** Pay for. 177. **his:** Its.

188. **oes:** Circles, orbs, stars. 194. **in spite of me:** To vex me. 196. **contriv'd:** Plotted. 197. **bait:** Torment, as one sets on dogs to bait a bear. 198. **counsel:** Confidential talk. 203. **artificial:** Skilled in art or creation. 211. **lovely:** Loving. 213–214. **Two . . . crest:** We have two separate bodies, just as a coat of arms in heraldry can be represented twice on a shield but surmounted by a single crest. 215. **rent:** Rend. 230. **tender:** Offer.

What though I be not so in grace° as you,
So hung upon with love, so fortunate,
But miserable most, to love unlov'd?
235   This you should pity rather than despise.
HERMIA: I understand not what you mean by this.
HELENA: Ay, do! Persever, counterfeit sad° looks,
  Make mouths° upon° me when I turn my back,
  Wink each at other, hold the sweet jest up.
240   This sport, well carried,° shall be chronicled.
  If you have any pity, grace, or manners,
  You would not make me such an argument.°
  But fare ye well. 'Tis partly my own fault,
  Which death, or absence, soon shall remedy.
245 **LYSANDER:** Stay, gentle Helena; hear my excuse,
  My love, my life, my soul, fair Helena!
HELENA: O excellent!
HERMIA: Sweet, do not scorn her so.
DEMETRIUS: If she cannot entreat,° I can compel.
LYSANDER: Thou canst compel no more than she
    entreat.
  Thy threats have no more strength than her weak
250   prayers.
  Helen, I love thee, by my life, I do!
  I swear by that which I will lose for thee,
  To prove him false that says I love thee not.
DEMETRIUS: I say I love thee more than he can do.
255 **LYSANDER:** If thou say so, withdraw, and prove it too.
DEMETRIUS: Quick, come!
HERMIA: Lysander, whereto tends all this?
LYSANDER: Away, you Ethiope!°
    [He tries to break away from Hermia.]
DEMETRIUS: No, no; he'll
  Seem to break loose; take on as you would follow,
  But yet come not. You are a tame man, go!
LYSANDER: Hang off,° thou cat, thou burr! Vile thing,
260   let loose,
  Or I will shake thee from me like a serpent!
HERMIA: Why are you grown so rude? What change is
    this,
  Sweet love?
LYSANDER: Thy love? Out, tawny Tartar, out!
  Out, loathed med'cine!° O hated potion, hence!
HERMIA: Do you not jest?
265 **HELENA:**   Yes, sooth,° and so do you.
LYSANDER: Demetrius, I will keep my word with thee.
DEMETRIUS: I would I had your bond, for I perceive
  A weak bond° holds you. I'll not trust your word.
LYSANDER: What, should I hurt her, strike her, kill her
    dead?
270   Although I hate her, I'll not harm her so.

HERMIA: What, can you do me greater harm than hate?
  Hate me? Wherefore? O me, what news,° my love?
  Am not I Hermia? Are not you Lysander?
  I am as fair now as I was erewhile.°
  Since night you lov'd me; yet since night you left me. 275
  Why, then you left me—O, the gods forbid!—
  In earnest, shall I say?
LYSANDER: Ay, by my life!
  And never did desire to see thee more.
  Therefore be out of hope, of question, of doubt;
  Be certain, nothing truer. 'Tis no jest 280
  That I do hate thee and love Helena.
HERMIA: O me! You juggler! You cankerblossom!°
  You thief of love! What, have you come by night
  And stol'n my love's heart from him?
HELENA: Fine, i' faith!
  Have you no modesty, no maiden shame, 285
  No touch of bashfulness? What, will you tear
  Impatient answers from my gentle tongue?
  Fie, fie! You counterfeit, you puppet,° you!
HERMIA: Puppet? Why so? Ay, that way goes the game.
  Now I perceive that she hath made compare 290
  Between our statures; she hath urg'd her height,
  And with her personage, her tall personage,
  Her height, forsooth, she hath prevail'd with him.
  And are you grown so high in his esteem,
  Because I am so dwarfish and so low? 295
  How low am I, thou painted maypole? Speak!
  How low am I? I am not yet so low
  But that my nails can reach unto thine eyes.
    [She flails at Helena but is restrained.]
HELENA: I pray you, though you mock me, gentlemen,
  Let her not hurt me. I was never curst;° 300
  I have no gift at all in shrewishness;
  I am a right° maid for my cowardice.
  Let her not strike me. You perhaps may think,
  Because she is something° lower than myself,
  That I can match her.
HERMIA: Lower! Hark, again! 305
HELENA: Good Hermia, do not be so bitter with me.
  I evermore did love you, Hermia,
  Did ever keep your counsels, never wrong'd you;
  Save that, in love unto Demetrius,
  I told him of your stealth° unto this wood. 310
  He followed you; for love I followed him.
  But he hath chid me hence and threat'ned me
  To strike me, spurn me, nay, to kill me too.
  And now, so° you will let me quiet go,
  To Athens will I bear my folly back 315
  And follow you no further. Let me go.
  You see how simple and how fond° I am.
HERMIA: Why, get you gone. Who is 't that hinders you?

---

232. grace: Favor. **237. sad:** Grave, serious. **238. mouths:**
Maws, faces, grimaces. **upon:** At. **240. carried:** Managed.
242. argument: Subject for a jest. **248. entreat:** Succeed by
entreaty. **257. Ethiope:** Referring to Hermia's relatively dark
hair and complexion; see also *tawny Tartar* six lines later.
260. Hang off: Let go. **264. med'cine:** Poison. **265. sooth:**
Truly. **268. weak bond:** Hermia's arm (with a pun on *bond*,
oath, in the previous line).

272. what news: What is the matter. **274. erewhile:** Just now.
282. cankerblossom: Worm that destroys the flower bud (?).
288. puppet: (1) Counterfeit; (2) dwarfish woman (in reference to Hermia's smaller stature). **300. curst:** Shrewish.
302. right: True. **304. something:** Somewhat. **310. stealth:**
Stealing away. **314. so:** If only. **317. fond:** Foolish.

HELENA: A foolish heart, that I leave here behind.

HERMIA: What, with Lysander?

320 HELENA: With Demetrius.

LYSANDER: Be not afraid; she shall not harm thee,
    Helena.

DEMETRIUS: No, sir, she shall not, though you take
    her part.

HELENA: O, when she is angry, she is keen and
    shrewd!°

She was a vixen when she went to school;

325 And though she be but little, she is fierce.

HERMIA: "Little" again! Nothing but "low" and
    "little"!

Why will you suffer her to flout me thus?

Let me come to her.

LYSANDER: Get you gone, you dwarf!

You minimus,° of hind'ring knot-grass° made!

You bead, you acorn!

330 DEMETRIUS: You are too officious

In her behalf that scorns your services.

Let her alone. Speak not of Helena;

Take not her part. For, if thou dost intend°

Never so little show of love to her,

Thou shalt aby° it.

LYSANDER: Now she holds me not;   335

Now follow, if thou dar'st, to try whose right,

Of thine or mine, is most in Helena.   [*Exit.*]

DEMETRIUS: Follow? Nay, I'll go with thee, cheek by
    jowl.°

[*Exit, following Lysander.*]

HERMIA: You, mistress, all this coil° is 'long of° you.

Nay, go not back.°

HELENA: I will not trust you, I,   340

Nor longer stay in your curst company.

Your hands than mine are quicker for a fray;

My legs are longer, though, to run away.   [*Exit.*]

---

323. shrewd: Shrewish.   **329. minimus:** Diminutive creature. **knot-grass:** A weed, an infusion of which was thought to stunt the growth.

333. intend: Give sign of.   **335. aby:** Pay for.   **338. cheek by jowl:** Side by side.   **339. coil:** Turmoil, dissension.   **'long of:** On account of.   **340. go not back:** Don't retreat. (Hermia is again proposing a fight.)

F. Murray Abraham (left) as Bottom, playing Pyramus in 1987.

Elizabeth McGovern as Helena in the 1987 New York Shakespeare festival production of *A Midsummer Night's Dream*, directed by A. J. Antoon.

HERMIA: I am amaz'd, and know not what to say.

(Exit.)

345   **OBERON:** This is thy negligence. Still thou mistak'st,
    Or else committ'st thy knaveries willfully.
  PUCK: Believe me, king of shadows, I mistook.
    Did not you tell me I should know the man
    By the Athenian garments he had on?
350   And so far blameless proves my enterprise
    That I have 'nointed an Athenian's eyes;
    And so far am I glad it so did sort°
    As this their jangling I esteem a sport.
  OBERON: Thou see'st these lovers seek a place to fight.
355   Hie therefore, Robin, overcast the night;
    The starry welkin° cover thou anon
    With drooping fog as black as Acheron,°
    And lead these testy rivals so astray
    As° one come not within another's way.
360   Like to Lysander sometime frame thy tongue,
    Then stir Demetrius up with bitter wrong;°
    And sometime rail thou like Demetrius.
    And from each other look thou lead them thus,

Till o'er their brows death-counterfeiting sleep
With leaden legs and batty° wings doth creep.   365
Then crush this herb° into Lysander's eye,

[Gives herb.]

Whose liquor hath this virtuous° property,
To take from thence all error with his° might
And make his eyeballs roll with wonted° sight.
When they next wake, all this derision°   370
Shall seem a dream and fruitless vision,
And back to Athens shall the lovers wend
With league whose date° till death shall never end.
Whiles I in this affair do thee employ,
I'll to my queen and beg her Indian boy;   375
And then I will her charmed eye release
From monster's view, and all things shall be peace.
PUCK: My fairy lord, this must be done with haste,
    For night's swift dragons° cut the clouds full fast,
    And yonder shines Aurora's harbinger,°   380

---

352. sort: Turn out.   **356. welkin:** Sky.   **357. Acheron:** River of Hades (here representing Hades itself).   **359. As:** That.   **361. wrong:** Insults.

365. batty: Batlike.   **366. this herb:** The antidote (mentioned in II, i, 184) to love-in-idleness.   **367. virtuous:** Efficacious.   **368. his:** Its.   **369. wonted:** Accustomed.   **370. derision:** Laughable business.   **373. date:** Term of existence.   **379. dragons:** Supposed to be yoked to the car of the goddess of night.   **380. Aurora's harbinger:** The morning star, precursor of dawn.

At whose approach, ghosts, wand'ring here and
    there,
Troop home to churchyards. Damned spirits all,
That in crossways and floods have burial,°
Already to their wormy beds are gone.
385   For fear lest day should look their shames upon,
They willfully themselves exile from light
And must for aye° consort with black-brow'd night.
OBERON: But we are spirits of another sort.
   I with the Morning's love° have oft made sport,
390   And, like a forester,° the groves may tread
Even till the eastern gate, all fiery-red,
Opening on Neptune with fair blessed beams,
Turns into yellow gold his salt green streams.
But, notwithstanding, haste; make no delay.
395   We may effect this business yet ere day.   [Exit.]
PUCK: Up and down, up and down,
   I will lead them up and down.
I am fear'd in field and town.
Goblin, lead them up and down.
400   Here comes one.

(Enter Lysander.)

LYSANDER: Where art thou, proud Demetrius? Speak
   thou now.
PUCK [mimicking Demetrius]: Here, villain, drawn°
   and ready. Where art thou?
LYSANDER: I will be with thee straight.°
PUCK: Follow me, then,
   To plainer° ground.
        [Lysander wanders about, following the voice.]°

(Enter Demetrius.)

DEMETRIUS: Lysander! Speak again!
405   Thou runaway, thou coward, art thou fled?
Speak! In some bush? Where dost thou hide thy
   head?
PUCK: [mimicking Lysander]: Thou coward, art thou
   bragging to the stars,
Telling the bushes that thou look'st for wars,
And wilt not come? Come, recreant;° come, thou
   child,
410   I'll whip thee with a rod. He is defil'd
That draws a sword on thee.
DEMETRIUS: Yea, art thou there?
PUCK: Follow my voice. We'll try° no manhood here.
                        (Exeunt.)

383. crossways . . . burial: Those who had committed suicide
were buried at crossways, with a stake driven through them;
those drowned (i.e., buried in floods or great waters) were
condemned to wander disconsolate for want of burial rites.
387. for aye: Forever.   389. Morning's love: Cephalus, a beautiful youth beloved by Aurora; or, perhaps, the goddess of
the dawn herself.   390. forester: Keeper of a royal forest.
402. drawn: With drawn sword.   403. straight: Immediately.
404. plainer: Smoother.   404. [s.d.] Lysander wanders about:
It is not clearly necessary that Lysander exit at this point;
neither exit nor reentrance is indicated in the early texts.
409. recreant: Cowardly wretch.   412. try: Test.

[Lysander returns.]

LYSANDER: He goes before me and still dares me on.
   When I come where he calls, then he is gone.
The villain is much lighter-heel'd than I.   415
I followed fast, but faster he did fly,
That fallen am I in dark uneven way,
And here will rest me. [Lies down.] Come, thou
   gentle day!
For if but once thou show me thy gray light,
I'll find Demetrius and revenge this spite.   [Sleeps.]   420

([Enter] Robin [Puck] and Demetrius.)

PUCK: Ho, ho, ho! Coward, why com'st thou not?
DEMETRIUS: Abide me, if thou dar'st; for well I wot°
   Thou runn'st before me, shifting every place,
And dar'st not stand nor look me in the face.
Where art thou now?
PUCK: Come hither. I am here.   425
DEMETRIUS: Nay, then, thou mock'st me. Thou shalt
   buy° this dear,°
If ever I thy face by daylight see.
Now, go thy way. Faintness constraineth me
To measure out my length on this cold bed.
By day's approach look to be visited.   430
                   [Lies down and sleeps.]

(Enter Helena.)

HELENA: O weary night, O long and tedious night,
   Abate° thy hours! Shine, comforts, from the east,
That I may back to Athens by daylight,
From these that my poor company detest;
And sleep, that sometimes shuts up sorrow's eye,   435
Steal me awhile from mine own company.
              [Lies down and] sleep[s].
PUCK: Yet but three? Come one more;
   Two of both kinds makes up four.
Here she comes, curst and sad.
Cupid is a knavish lad,   440
Thus to make poor females mad.

[Enter Hermia.]

HERMIA: Never so weary, never so in woe,
   Bedabbled with the dew and torn with briers,
I can no further crawl, no further go;
My legs can keep no pace with my desires.   445
Here will I rest me till the break of day.
Heavens shield Lysander, if they mean a fray!
             [Lies down and sleeps.]
PUCK: On the ground
   Sleep sound.
   I'll apply   450
   To your eye,
Gentle lover, remedy.
        [Squeezing the juice on Lysander's eyes.]
   When thou wak'st,
   Thou tak'st

422. wot: Know.   426. buy: Pay for. dear: Dearly.   432. Abate:
Lessen, shorten.

460 True delight
In the sight
Of thy former lady's eye;
And the country proverb known,
That every man should take his own,
465 In your waking shall be shown:
Jack shall have Jill;
Nought shall go ill;
The man shall have his mare again, and all shall
be well.   [*Exit. Manent the four lovers.*]

{ACT IV • Scene I}°

(*Enter [Titania,] Queen of Fairies, and [Bottom] the Clown, and Fairies; and [Oberon,] the King, behind them.*)

TITANIA: Come, sit thee down upon this flow'ry bed,
While I thy amiable° cheeks do coy,°
And stick musk-roses in thy sleek smooth head,
And kiss thy fair large ears, my gentle joy.
[*They recline.*]
5 BOTTOM: Where's Peaseblossom?
PEASEBLOSSOM: Ready.
BOTTOM: Scratch my head, Peaseblossom. Where's
Mounsieur Cobweb?
COBWEB: Ready.
10 BOTTOM: Mounsieur Cobweb, good mounsieur, get you
your weapons in your hand, and kill me a red-hipp'd
humble-bee on the top of a thistle; and, good moun-
sieur, bring me the honey-bag. Do not fret yourself
too much in the action, mounsieur; and, good moun-
15 sieur, have a care the honey-bag break not; I would
be loath to have you overflown with a honey-bag,
signior. Where's Mounsieur Mustardseed?
MUSTARDSEED: Ready.
BOTTOM: Give me your neaf,° Mounsieur Mustardseed.
20 Pray you, leave your curtsy,° good mounsieur.
MUSTARDSEED: What's your will?
BOTTOM: Nothing, good mounsieur, but to help
Cavalery° Cobweb° to scratch. I must to the barber's,
mounsieur; for methinks I am marvailes hairy about
25 the face; and I am such a tender ass, if my hair do but
tickle me, I must scratch.
TITANIA: What, wilt thou hear some music, my sweet
love?
BOTTOM: I have a reasonable good ear in music. Let's
30 have the tongs and the bones.°
[*Music: tongs, rural music.*]°
TITANIA: Or say, sweet love, what thou desirest to eat.

BOTTOM: Truly, a peck of provender. I could munch your
good dry oats. Methinks I have a great desire to a
bottle° of hay. Good hay, sweet hay, hath no fellow.°
TITANIA: I have a venturous fairy that shall seek   35
The squirrel's hoard, and fetch thee new nuts.
BOTTOM: I had rather have a handful or two of dried
peas. But, I pray you, let none of your people stir me.
I have an exposition° of sleep come upon me.
TITANIA: Sleep thou, and I will wind thee in my arms.   40
Fairies, be gone, and be all ways° away.
[*Exeunt fairies.*]
So doth the woodbine the sweet honeysuckle
Gently entwist; the female ivy so
Enrings the barky fingers of the elm.
Oh, how I love thee! How I dote on thee!   45
[*They sleep.*]

(*Enter Robin Goodfellow [Puck].*)

OBERON [*advancing*]: Welcome, good Robin. See'st thou
this sweet sight?
Her dotage now I do begin to pity.
For, meeting her of late behind the wood,
Seeking sweet favors° for this hateful fool,
I did upbraid her and fall out with her.   50
For she his hairy temples then had rounded
With coronet of fresh and fragrant flowers;
And that same dew, which sometime° on the buds
Was wont to swell like round and orient pearls,°
Stood now within the pretty flouriets'° eyes   55
Like tears that did their own disgrace bewail.
When I had at my pleasure taunted her,
And she in mild terms begg'd my patience,
I then did ask of her her changeling child;
Which straight she gave me, and her fairy sent   60
To bear him to my bower in fairy land.
And, now I have the boy, I will undo
This hateful imperfection of her eyes.
And, gentle Puck, take this transformed scalp
From off the head of this Athenian swain,   65
That, he awaking when the other° do,
May all to Athens back again repair,
And think no more of this night's accidents
But as the fierce vexation of a dream.
But first I will release the Fairy Queen.   70
[*Squeezes juice in her eyes.*]
Be as thou wast wont to be;
See as thou wast wont to see.
Dian's bud° o'er Cupid's flower

IV, i. Location: Scene continues. The four lovers are still asleep onstage. **2. amiable:** Lovely. **coy:** Caress. **19. neaf:** Fist. **20. leave your curtsy:** Put on your hat. **23. Cavalery:** Cavalien (form of address for a gentleman). **23. Cobweb:** Seemingly an error, since Cobweb has been sent to bring honey, whereas Peaseblossom has been asked to scratch. **30. tongs ... bones:** Instruments for rustic music. (The tongs were played like a triangle, whereas the bones were held between the fingers and used as clappers.) [S.D.] *Music ... music:* This stage direction is added from the Folio.

34. bottle: Bundle. **fellow:** Equal. **39. exposition:** Bottom's word for *disposition.* **41. all ways:** In all directions. **49. favors:** I.e., gifts of flowers. **53. sometime:** Formerly. **54. orient pearls:** The most beautiful of all pearls, those coming from the Orient. **55. flouriets':** Flowerets'. **66. other:** Others. **73. Dian's bud:** Perhaps the flower of the *agnus castus,* or chaste-tree, supposed to preserve chastity; or perhaps referring simply to Oberon's herb by which he can undo the effects of "Cupid's flower," the love-in-idleness of II, i, 165–168.

Hath such force and blessed power.

75   Now, my Titania, wake you, my sweet queen.

TITANIA [*waking*]: My Oberon! What visions have I
      seen!
   Methought I was enamor'd of an ass.

OBERON: There lies your love.

TITANIA: How came these things to pass?
   O, how mine eyes do loathe his visage now!

80   OBERON: Silence awhile. Robin, take off this head.
   Titania, music call, and strike more dead
   Than common sleep of all these five° the sense.

TITANIA: Music, ho! Music, such as charmeth sleep!

                                              [*Music.*]

PUCK [*removing the ass's head*]: Now, when thou
   wak'st, with thine own fool's eyes peep.

OBERON: Sound, music! Come, my queen, take hands
85   with me,
   And rock the ground whereon these sleepers be.

                                              [*Dance.*]

   Now thou and I are new in amity,
   And will tomorrow midnight solemnly°
   Dance in Duke Theseus' house triumphantly
90   And bless it to all fair prosperity.
   There shall the pairs of faithful lovers be
   Wedded, with Theseus, all in jollity.

PUCK: Fairy King, attend, and mark:
   I do hear the morning lark.

95   OBERON: Then, my queen, in silence sad,°
   Trip we after night's shade.
   We the globe can compass soon,
   Swifter than the wand'ring moon.

TITANIA: Come, my lord, and in our flight
100   Tell me how it came this night
   That I sleeping here was found
   With these mortals on the ground.   (*Exeunt.*)
                                      (*Wind horn [within].*)

(*Enter Theseus and all his train; [Hippolyta, Egeus].*)

THESEUS: Go, one of you, find out the forester,
   For now our observation° is perform'd;
105   And since we have the vaward° of the day,
   My love shall hear the music of my hounds.
   Uncouple in the western valley; let them go.
   Dispatch, I say, and find the forester.

                                      [*Exit an Attendant.*]

   We will, fair queen, up to the mountain's top
110   And mark the musical confusion
   Of hounds and echo in conjunction.

HIPPOLYTA: I was with Hercules and Cadmus° once,
   When in a wood of Crete they bay'd° the bear
   With hounds of Sparta.° Never did I hear

Such gallant chiding; for, besides the groves,   115
   The skies, the fountains, every region near
   Seem'd all one mutual cry. I never heard
   So musical a discord, such sweet thunder.

THESEUS: My hounds are bred out of the Spartan kind,
   So flew'd,° so sanded;° and their heads are hung   120
   With ears that sweep away the morning dew;
   Crook-knee'd, and dewlapp'd° like Thessalian bulls;
   Slow in pursuit, but match'd in mouth like bells,
   Each under each.° A cry° more tuneable°
   Was never holla'd to, nor cheer'd with horn,   125
   In Crete, in Sparta, nor in Thessaly.
   Judge when you hear. [*Sees the sleepers.*] But, soft!
      What nymphs are these?

EGEUS: My lord, this' my daughter here asleep;
   And this, Lysander; this Demetrius is;
   This Helena, old Nedar's Helena.   130
   I wonder of their being here together.

THESEUS: No doubt they rose up early to observe
   The rite of May, and, hearing our intent,
   Came here in grace of our solemnity.°
   But speak, Egeus. Is not this the day   135
   That Hermia should give answer of her choice?

EGEUS: It is, my lord.

THESEUS: Go, bid the huntsmen wake them with their
      horns.

                                      [*Exit an Attendant.*]

(*Shout within. Wind horns. They all start up.*)

   Good morrow, friends. Saint Valentine° is past.
   Begin these wood-birds but to couple now?   140

LYSANDER: Pardon, my lord.   [*They kneel.*]

THESEUS: I pray you all, stand up.
   I know you two are rival enemies;
   How comes this gentle concord in the world,
   That hatred is so far from jealousy
   To sleep by hate and fear no enmity?   145

LYSANDER: My lord, I shall reply amazedly,
   Half sleep, half waking; but as yet, I swear,
   I cannot truly say how I came here.
   But, as I think—for truly would I speak,
   And now I do bethink me, so it is—   150
   I came with Hermia hither. Our intent
   Was to be gone from Athens, where° we might,
   Without° the peril of the Athenian law—

EGEUS: Enough, enough, my lord; you have enough.
   I beg the law, the law, upon his head.   155
   They would have stol'n away; they would, Demetrius,

---

82. **these five**: I.e., the four lovers and Bottom.   88. **solemnly**:
Ceremoniously.   95. **sad**: Sober.   104. **observation**: Observance to a morn of May (I, i, 167).   105. **vaward**: Vanguard
(i.e., earliest part).   112. **Cadmus**: Mythical founder of Thebes. (This story about him is unknown.)   113. **bay'd**: Brought
to bay.   114. **hounds of Sparta**: Breed famous in antiquity for
their hunting skill.

120. **So flew'd**: Similarly having large hanging chaps or fleshy
covering of the jaw.   **sanded**: Of sandy color.   122. **dewlapp'd**:
Having pendulous folds of skin under the neck.   123–124.
match'd . . . under each: Harmoniously matched in their
various cries like a set of bells, from treble down to bass.
124. **cry**: Pack of hounds.   **tuneable**: Well tuned, melodious.   134. **solemnity**: Observance of these same rites of
May.   139. **Saint Valentine**: Birds were supposed to choose
their mates on St. Valentine's Day.   152. **where**: Wherever; or,
to where.   153. **Without**: Outside of, beyond.

Thereby to have defeated you and me,
You of your wife and me of my consent,
Of my consent that she should be your wife.

DEMETRIUS: My lord, fair Helen told me of their
160   stealth,
Of this their purpose hither to this wood,
And I in fury hither followed them,
Fair Helena in fancy following me.
But, my good lord, I wot not by what power—
165 But by some power it is—my love to Hermia,
Melted as the snow, seems to me now
As the remembrance of an idle gaud.°
Which in my childhood I did dote upon;
And all the faith, the virtue of my heart,
170 The object and the pleasure of mine eye,
Is only Helena. To her, my lord,
Was I betroth'd ere I saw Hermia,
But like a sickness did I loathe this food;
But, as in health, come to my natural taste,
175 Now I do wish it, love it, long for it,
And will for evermore be true to it.

THESEUS: Fair lovers, you are fortunately met.
Of this discourse we more will hear anon.
Egeus, I will overbear your will;
180 For in the temple, by and by, with us
These couples shall eternally be knit.
And, for° the morning now is something° worn,
Our purpos'd hunting shall be set aside.
Away with us to Athens. Three and three,
185 We'll hold a feast in great solemnity.
Come, Hippolyta.

        [*Exeunt Theseus, Hippolyta, Egeus, and train.*]

DEMETRIUS: These things seem small and
      undistinguishable,
Like far-off mountains turned into clouds.

HERMIA: Methinks I see these things with parted° eye,
When every thing seems double.

190 HELENA: So methinks;
And I have found Demetrius like a jewel,
Mine own, and not mine own.°

DEMETRIUS: Are you sure
That we are awake? It seems to me
That yet we sleep, we dream. Do not you think
195 The Duke was here, and bid us follow him?

HERMIA: Yea, and my father.

HELENA: And Hippolyta.

LYSANDER: And he did bid us follow to the temple.

DEMETRIUS: Why, then, we are awake. Let's follow him,
And by the way let us recount our dreams.

                      [*Exeunt.*]

BOTTOM [*awaking*]: When my cue comes, call me, and I 200
will answer. My next is, "Most fair Pyramus."
Heigh-ho! Peter Quince! Flute, the bellows-mender!
Snout, the tinker! Starveling! God's my life, stol'n
hence, and left me asleep! I have had a most rare
vision. I have had a dream, past the wit of man to say 205
what dream it was. Man is but an ass, if he go about°
to expound this dream. Methought I was—there is
no man can tell what. Methought I was—and me
thought I had—but man is but a patch'd° fool, if he
will offer° to say what me-thought I had. The eye of 210
man hath not heard, the ear of man hath not seen,
man's hand is not able to taste, his tongue to conceive, nor his heart to report, what my dream was. I
will get Peter Quince to write a ballad of this dream.
It shall be call'd "Bottom's Dream," because it hath 215
no bottom; and I will sing it in the latter end of a
play, before the Duke. Peradventure, to make it the
more gracious, I shall sing it at her° death.   [*Exit.*]

{Scene II}°

(*Enter Quince, Flute, [Snout, and Starveling].*)

QUINCE: Have you sent to Bottom's house? Is he come
home yet?

STARVELING: He cannot be heard of. Out of doubt he is
transported.°

FLUTE: If he come not, then the play is marr'd. It goes 5
not forward, doth it?

QUINCE: It is not possible. You have not a man in all
Athens able to discharge° Pyramus but he.

FLUTE: No, he hath simply the best wit of any handicraft
man in Athens. 10

QUINCE: Yea, and the best person too; and he is a very
paramour for a sweet voice.

FLUTE: You must say "paragon." A paramour is, God
bless us, a thing of naught.

(*Enter Snug the Joiner.*)

SNUG: Masters, the Duke is coming from the temple, 15
and there is two or three lords and ladies more married. If our sport had gone forward, we had all been
made men.

FLUTE: O sweet bully Bottom! Thus hath he lost sixpence a day° during his life; he could not have scap'd 20
sixpence a day. An the Duke had not given him sixpence a day for playing Pyramus, I'll be hang'd. He
would have deserv'd it. Sixpence a day in Pyramus,
or nothing.

(*Enter Bottom.*)

---

167. **idle gaud:** Worthless trinket. 182. **for:** Since. **something:** Somewhat. 189. **parted:** Improperly focused. 191–
192. **like...not mine own:** Like a jewel that one finds by
chance and therefore possesses but cannot certainly consider
one's own property.

206. **go about:** Attempt. 209. **patch'd:** Wearing motley (i.e.,
a dress of various colors). 210. **offer:** Venture. 218. **her:**
Thisby's (?). **IV, ii. Location:** Athens, Quince's house (?).
4. **transported:** Carried off by fairies; or, possibly, transformed.
8. **discharge:** Perform. 19–20. **sixpence a day:** As a royal
pension.

Stage model of the set for Max Reinhardt's 1913 production of *A Midsummer Night's Dream* at the Deutsches Theater in Berlin. The design called for an entire forest to be built on a stage that revolved as the action shifted.

25   **BOTTOM:** Where are these lads? Where are these hearts?°

  QUINCE: Bottom! O most courageous day! O most
    happy hour!

  BOTTOM: Masters, I am to discourse wonders.° But ask
    me not what; for if I tell you, I am no true Athenian. I
30   will tell you everything, right as it fell out.

  QUINCE: Let us hear, sweet Bottom.

  BOTTOM: Not a word of° me. All that I will tell you is,
    that the Duke hath din'd. Get your apparel together,
    good strings° to your beards, new ribands° to your
35   pumps, meet presently° at the palace, every man look
    o'er his part; for the short and the long is, our play
    is preferr'd.° In any case, let Thisby have clean linen;
    and let not him that plays the lion pare his nails, for
    they shall hang out for the lion's claws. And, most
40   dear actors, eat no onions nor garlic, for we are to
    utter sweet breath; and I do not doubt but to hear
    them say, it is a sweet comedy. No more words.
    Away! go, away!   [*Exeunt.*]

25. hearts: Good fellows. **28. am . . . wonders:** Have wonders
to relate. **32. of:** Out of. **34. strings:** To attach the beards.
ribands: Ribbons. **35. presently:** Immediately. **37. preferr'd:**
Selected for consideration.

{ACT V • Scene I}°

(*Enter Theseus, Hippolyta, and Philostrate,* [*Lords, and
Attendants*].)

HIPPOLYTA: 'Tis strange, my Theseus, that° these lovers
    speak of.

THESEUS: More strange than true. I never may° believe
    These antic° fables, nor these fairy toys.°
    Lovers and madmen have such seething brains
    Such shaping fantasies,° that apprehend   5
    More than cool reason ever comprehends.
    The lunatic, the lover, and the poet
    Are of imagination all compact.°
    One sees more devils than vast hell can hold;
    That is the madman. The lover, all as frantic,   10
    Sees Helen's° beauty in a brow of Egypt.°
    The poet's eye, in a fine frenzy rolling,

V, i. Location: Athens. The palace of Theseus. **1. that:** That
which. **2. may:** Can. **3. antic:** Strange, grotesque (with
additional punning sense of *antique,* ancient). **fairy toys:**
Trifling stories about fairies. **5. fantasies:** Imaginations.
8. compact: Formed, composed. **11. Helen's:** Of Helen of
Troy, pattern of beauty. **brow of Egypt:** Face of a gypsy.

Doth glance from heaven to earth, from earth to
   heaven;
And as imagination bodies forth
15 The forms of things unknown, the poet's pen
Turns them to shapes and gives to airy nothing
A local habitation and a name.
Such tricks hath strong imagination
That, if it would but apprehend some joy,
20 It comprehends some bringer° of that joy;
Or in the night, imagining some fear,°
How easy is a bush suppos'd a bear!
HIPPOLYTA: But all the story of the night told over,
And all their minds transfigur'd so together,
25 More witnesseth than fancy's images°
And grows to something of great constancy;°
But, howsoever,° strange and admirable.°

(*Enter lovers: Lysander, Demetrius, Hermia, and
Helena.*)

THESEUS: Here come the lovers, full of joy and mirth.
  Joy, gentle friends! Joy and fresh days of love
  Accompany your hearts!
30 LYSANDER: More than to us
  Wait in your royal walks, your board, your bed!
THESEUS: Come now, what masques, what dances shall
   we have,
To wear away this long age of three hours
Between our after-supper and bed-time?
35 Where is our usual manager of mirth?
What revels are in hand? Is there no play,
To ease the anguish of a torturing hour?
Call Philostrate.
PHILOSTRATE: Here, mighty Theseus.
THESEUS: Say, what abridgement° have you for this
   evening?
40 What masque? What music? How shall we beguile
The lazy time, if not with some delight?
PHILOSTRATE: There is a brief° how many sports are
   ripe.
Make choice of which your Highness will see first.
                          [*Giving a paper.*]
THESEUS [*reads*]: "The battle with the Centaurs,° to be
   sung
45 By an Athenian eunuch to the harp."
We'll none of that. That have I told my love,
In glory of my kinsman° Hercules.

[*Reads.*] "The riot of the tipsy Bacchanals,
Tearing the Thracian singer in their rage."°
That is an old device; and it was play'd   50
When I from Thebes came last a conqueror.
[*Reads.*] "The thrice three Muses mourning for the
   death
Of Learning, late deceas'd in beggary."°
That is some satire, keen and critical,
Not sorting with° a nuptial ceremony.   55
[*Reads.*] "A tedious brief scene of young Pyramus
And his love Thisby; very tragical mirth."
Merry and tragical? Tedious and brief?
That is, hot ice and wondrous strange° snow.
How shall we find the concord of this discord?   60
PHILOSTRATE: A play there is, my lord, some ten words
   long,
Which is as brief as I have known a play;
But by ten words, my lord, it is too long,
Which makes it tedious. For in all the play
There is not one word apt, one player fitted.   65
And tragical, my noble lord, it is,
For Pyramus therein doth kill himself.
Which, when I saw rehears'd, I must confess,
Made mine eyes water, but more merry tears
The passion of loud laughter never shed.   70
THESEUS: What are they that do play it?
PHILOSTRATE: Hard-handed men that work in Athens
   here,
Which never labor'd in their minds till now,
And now have toil'd° their unbreathed° memories
With this same play, against° your nuptial.   75
THESEUS: And we will hear it.
PHILOSTRATE: No, my noble lord,
It is not for you. I have heard it over,
And it is nothing, nothing in the world;
Unless you can find sport in their intents,
Extremely stretch'd° and conn'd° with cruel pain,   80
To do you service.
THESEUS: I will hear that play;
For never anything can be amiss'
When simpleness and duty tender it.
Go, bring them in; and take your places, ladies.

      [*Philostrate goes to summon the players.*]

HIPPOLYTA: I love not to see wretchedness o'ercharg'd°   85
And duty in his service° perishing.
THESEUS: Why, gentle sweet, you shall see no such thing.

---

20. **bringer:** Source. 21. **fear:** Object of fear. 25. **More...
images:** Testifies to something more substantial than mere imaginings. 26. **constancy:** Certainty. 27. **howsoever:** In any case.
admirable: A source of wonder. 39. **abridgement:** Pastime (to
abridge or shorten the evening). 42. **brief:** Short written statement, list. 44. **"battle...Centaurs":** Probably refers to the
battle of the Centaurs and the Lapithae, when the Centaurs
attempted to carry off Hippodamia, bride of Theseus's friend
Pirothous. 47. **kinsman:** Plutarch's *Life of Theseus* states that
Hercules and Theseus were near-kinsmen. Theseus is referring
to a version of the battle of the Centaurs in which Hercules was
said to be present.

48–49. **"The riot ... rage":** This was the story of the death of
Orpheus, as told in *Metamorphoses*. 52–53. **"The thrice ...
beggary":** Possibly an allusion to Spenser's *Teares of the Muses*
(1591), though "satires" deploring the neglect of learning
and the creative arts were commonplace. 55. **sorting with:**
Befitting. 59. **strange:** Seemingly an error for some adjective
that would contrast with *snow*, just as *hot* contrasts with *ice*.
74. **toil'd:** Taxed. **unbreathed:** Unexercised. 75. **against:** In
preparation for. 80. **stretch'd:** Strained. **conn'd:** Memorized.
85. **wretchedness o'ercharg'd:** Incompetence overburdened. 86.
his service: Its attempt to serve.

HIPPOLYTA: He says they can do nothing in this kind.°
THESEUS: The kinder we, to give them thanks for
    nothing.
90 Our sport shall be to take what they mistake;
    And what poor duty cannot do, noble respect
    Takes it in might, not merit.°
    Where I have come, great clerks° have purposed
    To greet me with premeditated welcomes;
95 Where I have seen them shiver and look pale,
    Make periods in the midst of sentences,
    Throttle their practic'd accent° in their fears,
    And in conclusion dumbly have broke off,
    Not paying me a welcome. Trust me, sweet,
100 Out of this silence yet I pick'd a welcome;
    And in the modesty of fearful duty
    I read as much as from the rattling tongue
    Of saucy and audacious eloquence.
    Love, therefore, and tongue-tied simplicity
105 In least° speak most, to my capacity.°

[*Philostrate returns.*]

PHILOSTRATE: So please your Grace, the Prologue° is
    address'd.°
THESEUS: Let him approach.   [*Flourish of trumpets.*]

(*Enter the Prologue* [*Quince*].)

PROLOGUE: If we offend, it is with our good will.
    That you should think, we come not to offend,
110 But with good will. To show our simple skill,
    That is the true beginning of our end.
    Consider, then, we come but in despite.
    We do not come, as minding° to content you,
    Our true intent is. All for your delight
115 We are not here. That you should here repent you,
    The actors are at hand; and, by their show,
    You shall know all that you are like to know.
THESEUS: This fellow doth not stand upon points.°
LYSANDER: He hath rid his prologue like a rough° colt;
120 he knows not the stop.° A good moral, my lord: it is
    not enough to speak, but to speak true.
HIPPOLYTA: Indeed he hath play'd on his prologue like
    a child on a recorder;° a sound, but not in govern-
    ment.°
125 THESEUS: His speech was like a tangled chain, nothing°
    impair'd, but all disorder'd. Who is next?

---

88. **kind:** Kind of thing. 92. **Takes ... merit:** Values it for
the effort made rather than for the excellence achieved. 93.
clerks: Learned men. 97. **practic'd accent:** Rehearsed speech;
or, usual way of speaking. 105. **least:** Saying least. **to my
capacity:** In my judgment and understanding. 106. **Prologue:**
Speaker of the prologue. **address'd:** Ready. 113. **minding:**
Intending. 118. **stand upon points:** (1) Heed niceties or small
points; (2) pay attention to punctuation in his reading. (The
humor of Quince's speech is in the blunders of its punctuation.) 119. **rough:** Unbroken. 120. **stop:** (1) The stopping of
a colt by reining it in; (2) punctuation mark. 123. **recorder:**
A wind instrument like a flute. 123–124. **government:** Control. 125. **nothing:** Not at all.

(*Enter Pyramus and Thisby, and Wall, and
Moonshine, and Lion.*)

PROLOGUE: Gentles, perchance you wonder at this
    show;
    But wonder on, till truth make all things plain.
    This man is Pyramus, if you would know;
    This beauteous lady Thisby is certain.   130
    This man, with lime and rough-cast, doth present
    Wall, that vile Wall which did these lovers sunder;
    And through Wall's chink, poor souls, they are
        content
    To whisper. At the which let no man wonder.
    This man, with lantern, dog, and bush of thorn,   135
    Presenteth Moonshine; for, if you will know,
    By moonshine did these lovers think no scorn°
    To meet at Ninus' tomb, there, there to woo.
    This grisly beast, which Lion hight° by name,
    The trusty Thisby, coming first by night,   140
    Did scare away, or rather did affright;
    And, as she fled, her mantle she did fall,°
    Which Lion vile with bloody mouth did stain.
    Anon comes Pyramus, sweet youth and tall,°
    And finds his trusty Thisby's mantle slain;   145
    Whereat, with blade, with bloody blameful blade,
    He bravely broach'd° his boiling bloody breast.
    And Thisby, tarrying in mulberry shade,
    His dagger drew, and died. For all the rest,
    Let Lion, Moonshine, Wall, and lovers twain   150
    At large° discourse, while here they do remain.

            (*Exeunt Lion, Thisby, and Moonshine.*)

THESEUS: I wonder if the lion be to speak.
DEMETRIUS: No wonder, my lord. One lion may, when
    many asses do.
WALL: In this same interlude it doth befall   155
    That I, one Snout by name, present a wall;
    And such a wall, as I would have you think,
    That had in it a crannied hole or chink,
    Through which the lovers, Pyramus and Thisby,
    Did whisper often very secretly.   160
    This loam, this rough-cast, and this stone doth show
    That I am that same wall; the truth is so.
    And this the cranny is, right and sinister,°
    Through which the fearful lovers are to whisper.
THESEUS: Would you desire lime and hair to speak better?   165
DEMETRIUS: It is the wittiest partition° that ever I heard
    discourse, my lord.

[*Pyramus comes forward.*]

THESEUS: Pyramus draws near the wall. Silence!

---

137. **think no scorn:** Think it no disgraceful matter. 139. **hight:**
Is called. 142. **fall:** Let fall. 144. **tall:** Courageous. 147.
broach'd: Stabbed. 151. **At large:** In full, at length. 163. **right
and sinister:** The right side of it and the left (*sinister*); or, running from right to left, horizontally. 166. **partition:** (1) Wall;
(2) section of a learned treatise or oration.

PYRAMUS: O grim-look'd° night! O night with hue so
    black!
170   O night, which ever art when day is not!
    O night, O night! Alack, alack, alack,
    I fear my Thisby's promise is forgot.
    And thou, O wall, O sweet, O lovely wall,
    That stand'st between her father's ground and mine,
175   Thou wall, O wall, O sweet and lovely wall,
    Show me thy chink, to blink through with mine eyne!

               [*Wall holds up his fingers.*]

    Thanks, courteous wall. Jove shield thee well for this!
    But what see I? No Thisby do I see.
    O wicked wall, through whom I see no bliss!
180   Curs'd be thy stones for thus deceiving me!
THESEUS: The wall, methinks, being sensible,° should
    curse again.
PYRAMUS: No, in truth, sir, he should not. "Deceiving
    me" is Thisby's cue: she is to enter now, and I am to
185   spy her through the wall. You shall see, it will fall pat
    as I told you. Yonder she comes.

(*Enter Thisby.*)

THISBY: O wall, full often hast thou heard my moans,
    For parting my fair Pyramus and me.
    My cherry lips have often kiss'd thy stones,
190   Thy stones with lime and hair knit up in thee.
PYRAMUS: I see a voice. Now will I to the chink,
    To spy an° I can hear my Thisby's face.
    Thisby!
THISBY: My love! Thou art my love, I think.
195 PYRAMUS: Think what thou wilt, I am thy lover's grace;°
    And, like Limander° am I trusty still.
THISBY: And I like Helen,° till the Fates me kill.
PYRAMUS: Not Shafalus° to Procrus° was so true.
THISBY: As Shafalus to Procrus, I to you.
200 PYRAMUS: O, kiss me through the hole of this vile wall!
THISBY: I kiss the wall's hole, not your lips at all.
PYRAMUS: Wilt thou at Ninny's tomb meet me
    straightway?
THISBY: 'Tide° life, 'tide death, I come without delay.

             [*Exeunt Pyramus and Thisby.*]

WALL: Thus have I, Wall, my part discharged so;
205   And, being done, thus Wall away doth go.   [*Exit.*]
THESEUS: Now is the mural down between the two
    neighbors.
DEMETRIUS: No remedy, my lord, when walls are so will-
    ful to hear° without warning.°
210 HIPPOLYTA: This is the silliest stuff that ever I heard.

THESEUS: The best in this kind° are but shadows;° and
    the worst are no worse, if imagination amend them.
HIPPOLYTA: It must be your imagination then, and not
    theirs.
THESEUS: If we imagine no worse of them than they of 215
    themselves, they may pass for excellent men. Here
    come two noble beasts in, a man and a lion.

(*Enter Lion and Moonshine.*)

LION: You, ladies, you, whose gentle hearts do fear
    The smallest monstrous mouse that creeps on floor,
    May now perchance both quake and tremble here,   220
    When lion rough in wildest rage doth roar.
    Then know that I, as Snug the joiner, am
    A lion fell,° nor else no lion's dam;
    For, if I should as lion come in strife
    Into this place, 'twere pity on my life.   225
THESEUS: A very gentle beast, and of a good conscience.
DEMETRIUS: The very best at a beast, my lord, that e'er
    I saw.
LYSANDER: This lion is a very fox for his valor.°
THESEUS: True; and a goose for his discretion.°   230
DEMETRIUS: Not so, my lord; for his valor cannot carry
    his discretion; and the fox carries the goose.
THESEUS: His discretion, I am sure, cannot carry his
    valor, for the goose carries not the fox. It is well.
    Leave it to his discretion, and let us listen to the 235
    moon.
MOON: This lanthorn° doth the horned moon present—
DEMETRIUS: He should have worn the horns on his head.°
THESEUS: He is no crescent, and his horns are invisible
    within the circumference.   240
MOON: This lanthorn doth the horned moon present;
    Myself the man i' th' moon do seem to be.
THESEUS: This is the greatest error of all the rest. The
    man should be put into the lanthorn. How is it else
    the man i' th' moon?   245
DEMETRIUS: He dares not come there for the° candle; for,
    you see, it is already in snuff.°
HIPPOLYTA: I am aweary of this moon. Would he would
    change!
THESEUS: It appears, by his small light of discretion, that 250
    he is in the wane; but yet, in courtesy, in all reason,
    we must stay the time.
LYSANDER: Proceed, Moon.

169. **grim-look'd:** Grim-looking. **181. sensible:** Capable
of feeling. **192. an:** If. **195. lover's grace:** Gracious lover.
196. Limander: Blunder for *Leander.* **197. Helen:** Blunder
for *Hero.* **198. Shafalus, Procrus:** Blunders for *Cephalus*
and *Procris,* also famous lovers. **203. 'Tide:** Betide, come.
209. to hear: As to hear. **without warning:** Without warning
the parents.

211. **in this kind:** Of this sort. **shadows:** Likenesses, repre-
sentations. **223. lion fell:** Fierce lion (with a play on the idea
of *lion skin*). **229. is . . . valor:** His valor consists of crafti-
ness and discretion. **230. goose . . . discretion:** As discreet as
a goose (that is, more foolish than discreet). **237. lanthorn:**
This original spelling may suggest a play on the *horn* of which
lanterns were made and also on a cuckold's horns, but the
spelling *lanthorn* is not used consistently for comic effect in
this play or elsewhere. In V, i, 135, for example, the word is *lantern* in the original. **238. on his head:** As a sign of cuckoldry.
246. for the: Because of the. **247. in snuff:** (1) Offended;
(2) in need of snuffing.

MOON: All that I have to say is to tell you that the lanthorn is the moon, I, the man in the moon, this thorn-
bush my thorn-bush, and this dog my dog.
DEMETRIUS: Why, all these should be in the lanthorn; for
all these are in the moon. But silence! Here comes
Thisby.

(*Enter Thisby.*)

THISBY: This is old Ninny's tomb. Where is my love?
LION [*roaring*]: Oh— [*Thisby runs off.*]
DEMETRIUS: Well roar'd, Lion.
THESEUS: Well run, Thisby.
HIPPOLYTA: Well shone, Moon. Truly, the moon shines
with a good grace.

[*The Lion shakes Thisby's mantle, and exit.*]

THESEUS: Well mous'd,° Lion.
DEMETRIUS: And then came Pyramus.
LYSANDER: And so the lion vanish'd.

(*Enter Pyramus.*)

PYRAMUS: Sweet Moon, I thank thee for thy sunny
beams;
I thank thee, Moon, for shining now so bright;
For, by thy gracious, golden, glittering gleams,
I trust to take of truest Thisby sight.
But stay, O spite!
But mark, poor knight,
What dreadful dole° is here!
Eyes, do you see?
How can it be?
O dainty duck! O dear!
Thy mantle good,
What, stain'd with blood!
Approach, ye Furies fell!°
O Fates, come, come,
Cut thread and thrum;°
Quail,° crush, conclude, and quell!°
THESEUS: This passion, and the death of a dear friend,
would go near to make a man look sad.°
HIPPOLYTA: Beshrew my heart, but I pity the man.
PYRAMUS: O wherefore, Nature, didst thou lions frame?
Since lion vile hath here deflow'r'd my dear,
Which is—no, no—which was the fairest dame
That liv'd, that lov'd, that lik'd, that look'd with
cheer.°
Come, tears, confound,
Out, sword, and wound
The pap of Pyramus;
Ay, that left pap,
Where heart doth hop. [*Stabs himself.*]
Thus die I, thus, thus, thus.

Now am I dead,
Now am I fled;
My soul is in the sky.
Tongue, lose thy light;
Moon, take thy flight. [*Exit Moonshine.*]
Now die, die, die, die, die. [*Dies.*]
DEMETRIUS: No die, but an ace,° for him; for he is but
one.°
LYSANDER: Less than an ace, man; for he is dead, he is
nothing.
THESEUS: With the help of a surgeon he might yet re
cover, and yet prove an ass.°
HIPPOLYTA: How chance Moonshine is gone before
Thisby comes back and finds her lover?
THESEUS: She will find him by starlight. Here she comes;
and her passion ends the play.

[*Enter Thisby.*]

HIPPOLYTA: Methinks she should not use a long one for
such a Pyramus. I hope she will be brief.
DEMETRIUS: A mote will turn the balance, which
Pyramus, which° Thisby, is the better: he for a man
God warr'nt us; she for a woman, God bless us.
LYSANDER: She hath spied him already with those sweet
eyes.
DEMETRIUS: And thus she means,° videlicet:°
THISBY: Asleep, my love?
What, dead, my dove?
O Pyramus, arise!
Speak, speak. Quite dumb?
Dead, dead? A tomb
Must cover thy sweet eyes.
These lily lips,
This cherry nose,
These yellow cowslip cheeks,
Are gone, are gone!
Lovers, make moan.
His eyes were green as leeks.
O Sisters Three,°
Come, come to me,
With hands as pale as milk;
Lay them in gore,
Since you have shore°
With shears his thread of silk.
Tongue, not a word.
Come, trusty sword,
Come, blade, my breast imbrue!° [*Stabs herself.*]
And farewell, friends.
Thus Thisby ends.
Adieu, adieu, adieu. [*Dies.*]

---

266. **mous'd:** Shaken. 275. **dole:** Grievous event. 281. **fell:**
Fierce. 283. **thread and thrum:** The warp in weaving and the
loose end of the warp. 284. **Quail:** Overpower. **quell:** Kill,
destroy. 285–286. **This . . . sad:** If one had other reason to
grieve, one might be sad, but not from this absurd portrayal of
passion. 291. **cheer:** Countenance.

304. **ace:** The side of the die featuring the single pip, or
spot. (The pun is on *die* as a singular of *dice;* Bottom's
performance is not worth a whole *die* but rather one single
face of it, one small portion.) 305. **one:** (1) An individual
person; (2) unique. 309. **ass:** With a pun on *ace.* 316–
317. **which . . . which:** Whether . . . or. 321. **means:** Moans,
laments. **videlicet:** To wit. 334. **Sisters Three:** The Fates.
338. **shore:** Shorn. 342. **imbrue:** Stain with blood.

THESEUS: Moonshine and Lion are left to bury the dead.

DEMETRIUS: Ay, and Wall too.

BOTTOM [*starting up*]: No, I assure you; the wall is
down that parted their fathers. Will it please you to
350 see the epilogue, or to hear a Bergomask dance° between two of our company?

THESEUS: No epilogue, I pray you; for your play needs
no excuse. Never excuse; for when the players are all
dead, there need none to be blam'd. Marry, if he that
355 writ it had play'd Pyramus and hang'd himself in
Thisby's garter, it would have been a fine tragedy;
and so it is, truly, and very notably discharg'd. But,
come, your Bergomask. Let your epilogue alone.

[A dance.]

The iron tongue of midnight hath told° twelve.
360 Lovers, to bed; 'tis almost fairy time.
I fear we shall outsleep the coming morn
As much as we this night have overwatch'd.°
This palpable-gross° play hath well beguil'd
The heavy° gait of night. Sweet friends, to bed.
365 A fortnight hold we this solemnity,
In nightly revels and new jollity.   (*Exeunt.*)

(*Enter Puck*)

PUCK: Now the hungry lion roars,
      And the wolf behowls the moon;
Whilst the heavy ploughman snores,
370   All with weary task fordone.°
Now the wasted brands° do glow,
      Whilst the screech-owl, screeching loud,
Puts the wretch that lies in woe
      In remembrance of a shroud.
375 Now it is the time of night
      That the graves, all gaping wide,
Every one lets forth his sprite,°
      In the churchway paths to glide.
And we fairies, that do run
380   By the triple Hecate's° team
From the presence of the sun,
      Following darkness like a dream,
Now are frolic.° Not a mouse
Shall disturb this hallowed house.
385 I am sent with broom before,
To sweep the dust behind° the door.

(*Enter* [*Oberon and Titania,*] *King and Queen of
Fairies, with all their train.*)

OBERON: Through the house give glimmering light,
      By the dead and drowsy fire;
Every elf and fairy sprite
390   Hop as light as bird from brier;
And this ditty, after me,
Sing, and dance it trippingly.

TITANIA: First, rehearse your song by rote,
To each word a warbling note.
395 Hand in hand, with fairy grace,
Will we sing, and bless this place.

[Song and dance.]

OBERON: Now, until the break of day,
Through this house each fairy stray.
To the best bride-bed will we,
400 Which by us shall blessed be;
And the issue there create°
Ever shall be fortunate.
So shall all the couples three
Ever true in loving be;
405 And the blots of Nature's hand
Shall not in their issue stand;
Never mole, hare lip, nor scar,
Nor mark prodigious,° such as are
Despised in nativity,
410 Shall upon their children be.
With this field-dew consecrate,°
Every fairy take his gait,°
And each several° chamber bless,
Through this palace, with sweet peace;
415 And the owner of it blest
Ever shall in safety rest.
Trip away; make no stay;
Meet me all by break of day.

(Exeunt [Oberon, Titania, and train].)

PUCK: If we shadows have offended,
420 Think but this, and all is mended,
That you have but slumb'red here°
While these visions did appear.
And this weak and idle theme,
No more yielding but° a dream,
425 Gentles, do not reprehend.
If you pardon, we will mend.
And, as I am an honest Puck,
If we have unearned luck
Now to scape the serpent's tongue,°
430 We will make amends ere long;
Else the Puck a liar call.
So, good night unto you all.
Give me your hands,° if we be friends,
And Robin shall restore amends.   [*Exit.*]

---

350. **Bergomask dance:** A rustic dance named for Bergamo,
a province in the state of Venice. 359. **told:** Counted, struck
(tolled). 362. **overwatch'd:** Stayed up too late. 363. **palpable-
gross:** Obviously crude. 364. **heavy:** Drowsy, dull. 370.
fordone: Exhausted. 371. **wasted brands:** Burned-out logs.
377. **Every . . . sprite:** Every grave lets forth its ghost. 380. **triple
Hecate's:** Hecate ruled in three capacities: as Luna or Cynthia in heaven, as Diana on earth, and as Proserpina in hell.
383. **frolic:** Merry. 386. **behind:** From behind. (Robin Goodfellow was a household spirit who helped good housemaids and
punished lazy ones.)

401. **create:** Created. 408. **prodigious:** Monstrous, un-
natural. 411. **consecrate:** Consecrated. 412. **take his gait:**
Go his way. 413. **several:** Separate. 421. **That . . . here:**
That it is a "midsummer night's dream." 424. **No . . . but:**
Yielding no more than. 429. **serpent's tongue:** Hissing.
433. **Give . . . hands:** Applaud.

COMMENTARIES

Some of the finest critical commentary ever written has been devoted to the works of Shakespeare. From the seventeenth century to the present, critics have taken a considerable interest in the nuances of his work.

In the following commentaries on *A Midsummer Night's Dream*, we find contrasting responses. In a specifically feminist observation, critic Linda Bamber shows how assumptions regarding power in a male-female relationship affect our interpretation of the play.

Peter Brook, one of the most notable contemporary directors of Shakespeare and the producer of a landmark production of *A Midsummer Night's Dream* (1970), gives us a director's view of the play. He centers the discussion on love, which in many forms is at the heart of the play. See his review of the production on page 322.

Contemporary reviews of Shakespeare's plays take a very different approach to the plays than do critical studies. The reviewers are concerned first with the actors and their interpretation of the drama. They then assess the director's insights and sense of pacing. In addition to focusing on the actors' and director's roles, critics aim to communicate a sense of the dynamics of the production as a whole. Peter Brook's production of *A Midsummer Night's Dream*, for example, was perhaps most startling for its all-white set and backdrop and for the marvelous scenes staged with principal actors lolling on simple white swings. Critics can give us insight into the staging of a work and the ways in which the staging imparts meaning to the drama.

LINDA BAMBER (b. 1945)

On *A Midsummer Night's Dream* 1982

The question of masculine and feminine is central to *A Midsummer Night's Dream*. Much of the action is precipitated by a power struggle between Titania and Oberon, and the young Athenians who rush off to the woods are there because a father has decided to oppose the will of his daughter regarding her marriage. Linda Bamber is a feminist critic interested in examining the centers of power in the play, particularly with an eye for what we accept as the natural order of relationships. She shows that the action of the comedy is essentially tied into questions of gender, which begin to become questions of genre.

The best example [in Shakespeare] of the relationship between male dominance and the status quo comes in *A Midsummer Night's Dream*, which begins with a rebellion of the feminine against the power of masculine authority. Hermia refuses the man both Aegeus and Theseus order her to marry; her refusal sends us off into the forest, beyond the power of the father and the masculine state. Once in the forest, of course, we find the social situation metaphorically repeated in this world of imagination and nature. The fairy king, Oberon, rules the forest. His rule, too, is troubled by the rebellion of the feminine. Titania has refused to give him her page, the child of a human friend who died in childbirth. But by the end of the story Titania is conquered, the child relinquished, and order restored. Even here the comic upheavals, whether we see them as May games or bad dreams, are associated with an uprising of women. David P. Young has pointed out how firmly this play connects order with masculine dominance and the disruption of order with the rebellion of the feminine:

> It is appropriate that Theseus, as representative of daylight and right reason, should have subdued his bride-to-be to the rule of his masculine will. That is the natural order of things. It is equally appropriate that Oberon, as king of darkness and fantasy, should have lost control of his wife, and that the corresponding natural disorder described by Titania should ensue.[1]

The natural order, the status quo, is for men to rule women. When they fail to do so, we have the exceptional situation, the festive, disruptive, disorderly moment of comedy.

A Midsummer Night's Dream is actually an anomaly among the festive comedies. It is unusual for the forces of the green world to be directed, as they are here, by a masculine figure. Because the green world here is a partial reproduction of the social world, the feminine is reduced to a kind of first cause of the action while a masculine power directs it. In the other festive comedies the feminine Other presides. She does not *command* the forces of the alternative world, as Oberon does, but since she acts in harmony with these forces her will and desire often prevail.

Where are we to bestow our sympathies? On the forces that make for the disruption of the status quo and therefore for the plot? Or on the force that asserts itself against the disruption and reestablishes a workable social order? Of course we cannot choose. We can only say that in comedy we owe our holiday to such forces as the tendency of the feminine to rebel, whereas to the successful reassertion of masculine power we owe our everyday order. Shakespearean comedy endorses both sides. Holiday is, of course, the subject and the analogue of each play; but the plays always end in a return to everyday life. The optimistic reading of Shakespearean comedy says that everyday life is clarified and enriched by our holiday from it; according to the pessimistic reading the temporary subversion of the social order has revealed how much that order excludes, how high a price we pay for it. But whether our return to everyday life is a comfortable one or not, the return itself is the inevitable conclusion to the journey out.

Does this make the comedies sexist? Is the association of women with the disruption of the social order an unconscious and insulting projection? It seems to begin as such; but as the form of Shakespearean comedy develops, the Otherness of the feminine develops into as powerful a force in the drama as the social authority of the masculine Self. For the feminine in Shakespearean comedy begins as a shrew but develops into a comic heroine. The shrew's rebellion directly challenges masculine authority, whereas the comic heroine merely presides over areas of experience to which masculine authority is irrelevant. But the shrew is essentially powerless against the social system, whereas the comic heroine is in alliance with forces that can never be finally overcome. The shrew is defeated by the superior strength, physical and social, of a man, or by women who support the status quo. She provokes a battle of the sexes, and the outcome of this battle, from Shakespeare's point of

---

[1]David P. Young, *Something of Great Constancy* (New Haven, CT: Yale UP, 1966), 183.

view, is inevitable. The comic heroine, on the other hand, does not fight the system but merely surfaces, again and again, when and where the social system is temporarily subverted. The comic heroine does not actively resist the social and political hegemony° of the men, but as an irresistible version of the Other she successfully competes for our favor with the (masculine) representatives of the social Self. The development of the feminine from the shrew to the comic heroine indicates a certain consciousness on the author's part of sexual politics; and it indicates a desire, at least, to create conditions of sexual equality within the drama even while reflecting the unequal conditions of men and women in the society at large.

PETER BROOK (b. 1925)

The Play Is the Message ...   1987

When a distinguished director becomes a critic, we have the opportunity to understand a play from the point of view of one who has to make the play work in front of an audience. Brook's production of *A Midsummer Night's Dream* was a sensation in England and the United States in 1970. It featured absolutely white lighting, white sets, and actors in swings. Brook's analysis of the play led him to see love as its constant concern, "constantly repeated." He concluded that to present the play, the players must embody the concept of love. They must bring to the play their own realization of the play's themes — even to the point of seeing theater anew, like the mechanicals "who are touching an extraordinary world with the tips of their fingers, a world which transcends their daily experience and which fills them with wonder" — the effect of the love they bring to their task.

People have often asked me: "What is the theme of *A Midsummer Night's Dream?*" There is only one answer to that question, the same as one would give regarding a cup. The quality of a cup is its cupness. I say this by way of introduction, to show that if I lay so much stress on the dangers involved in trying to define the themes of the *Dream* it is because too many productions, too many attempts at visual interpretation are based on preconceived ideas, as if these had to be illustrated in some way. In my opinion we should first of all try to rediscover the play as a living thing; then we shall be able to analyze our discoveries. Once I have finished working on the play, I can begin to produce my theories. It was fortunate that I did not attempt to do so earlier because the play would not have yielded up its secrets.

At the center of the *Dream,* constantly repeated, we find the word "love." Everything comes back to this, even the structure of the play, even its music. The quality the play demands from its performers is to build up an atmosphere of love during the performance itself, so that this abstract idea — for the word "love" is in itself a complete abstraction — may become palpable. The play presents us with forms of love which become less and less blurred as it goes on. "Love" soon begins to resound like a musical scale, and little by little we are introduced to its various modes and tones.

hegemony: Overriding authority.

Love is, of course, a theme which touches all men. No one, not even the most hardened, the coldest, or the most despairing, is insensitive to it, even if he does not know what love is. Either his practical experience confirms its existence or he suffers from its absence, which is another way of recognizing that it exists. At every moment the play touches something which concerns everyone.

As this is theater, there must be conflicts, so this play about love is also a play about the opposite of love, love and its opposite force. We are brought to realize that love, liberty, and imagination are closely connected. Right at the beginning of the play, for example, the father in a long speech tries to obstruct his daughter's love and we are surprised that such a character, apparently a secondary role, should have so long a speech—until we discover the real importance of his words. What he says not only reflects a generation gap (a father opposing his daughter's love because he had intended her for someone else), it also explains the reasons for his feeling of suspicion toward the young man whom his daughter loves. He describes him as an individual prone to fantasy, led by his imagination—an unpardonable weakness in the father's eyes.

From this starting point we see, as in any of Shakespeare's plays, a confrontation. Here it is between love and its opposing qualities, between fantasy and solid common sense—caught in an endless series of mirrors. As usual, Shakespeare confuses the issue. If we asked someone's opinion on the father's point of view, he might say, for example, that "The father is in the wrong because he is against freedom of the imagination," a very widespread attitude today.

In this way, for most present-day audiences, the girl's father comes over as the classical father figure who misunderstands young people and their flights of fancy. But later on, we discover surprisingly that he is right, because the imaginative world in which this lover lives causes him to behave in a quite disgusting way toward the very same daughter: as soon as a drop of liquid falls into his eyes, acting as a drug which liberates natural tendencies, he not only jilts her but his love is transformed into violent hate. He uses words which might well be borrowed from *Measure for Measure*, denouncing the girl with the kind of vehemence that, in the Middle Ages, led people to burn one another at the stake. Yet at the end of the play we are once more in agreement with the Duke, who rejects the father in the name of love. The young man has now been transformed.

So we observe this game of love in a psychological and metaphysical context; we hear Titania's assertion that the opposition between herself and Oberon is fundamental, primordial. But Oberon's acts deny this, for he perceives that within their opposition a reconciliation is possible.

The play covers an extraordinarily broad range of universal forces and feelings in a mythical world, which suddenly changes, in the last part, into high society. We find ourselves back in the very real palace. And the same Shakespeare who, a few pages earlier, offered us a scene of pure fantasy between Titania and Oberon, where it would be absurd to ask prosaic questions like "Where does Oberon live?" or "When describing a queen like Titania did Shakespeare wish to express political ideas?," now takes us into a precise social environment. We are present at the meeting point of two worlds, that of the workmen and the court, the world of wealth and elegance, and alleged sensitivity, the world of people who have had the leisure to cultivate fine sentiments and are now shown as insensitive and even disgusting in their superior attitude toward the poor.

At the beginning of the court scene we see our former heroes, who have spent the entire play involved in the theme of love, and would no doubt be quite capable of giving academic lectures on the subject, suddenly finding themselves plunged into a context which has apparently nothing to do with love (with their own love, since all their problems have been solved). Now they are in the context of a relationship with each other and with another social class, and they are at a loss. They do not realize that here too scorn eliminates love.

We see how well Shakespeare has situated everything. Athens in the *Dream* resembles our Athens in the sixties: the workmen, as they state in the first scene, are very much afraid of the authorities; if they commit the slightest error they will be hanged, and there is nothing comical about that. Indeed, they risk hanging as soon as they shed their anonymity. At the same time they are irresistibly attracted by the carrot of "sixpence a day" which will enable them to escape poverty. Yet their real motive is neither glory nor adventure nor money (that is made very clear and should guide the actors who perform this scene). Those simple men who have only ever worked with their hands apply to the use of the imagination exactly the same quality of love which traditionally underlies the relationship between a craftsman and his tools. That is what gives these scenes both their strength and their comic quality. These craftsmen make efforts which are grotesque in one sense because they push awkwardness to its limit, but at another level they set themselves to their task with such love that the meaning of their clumsy efforts changes before our eyes.

The spectators can easily decide to adopt the same attitude as the courtiers: to find all this quite simply ridiculous and laugh with the complacency of people who quite confidently mock the efforts of others. Yet the audience is invited to take a step back: to feel it cannot quite identify with the court, with people who are too grand and too unkind. Little by little, we come to see that the craftsmen, who behave with little understanding but who approach their new job with love, are discovering theater—an imaginary world for them, toward which they instinctively feel great respect. In fact, the "mechanicals" scene is often misinterpreted because the actors forget to look at theater through innocent eyes, they take a professional actor's views of good or bad acting, and in so doing they diminish the mystery and the sense of magic felt by these amateurs, who are touching an extraordinary world with the tips of their fingers, a world which transcends their daily experience and which fills them with wonder.

We see this quite clearly in the part of the boy who plays the girl, Thisby. At first sight this tough lad is irresistibly absurd, but by degrees, through his love for what he is doing, we discover what more is involved. In our production, the actor playing the part is a professional plumber, who took to acting only a short while ago. He well understands what is involved, what it means to feel this nameless and shapeless kind of love. This boy, himself new to theater, acts the part of someone who is new to theater. Through his conviction and his identification we discover that these awkward craftsmen, without knowing it, are teaching us a lesson—or it might be preferable to say that a lesson is being taught us through them. These craftsmen are able to make the connection between love for their trade and for a completely different task, whereas the courtiers are not capable of linking the love about which they talk so well with their simple role as spectators.

Nonetheless, little by little the courtiers become involved, even touched by the play within the play, and if we follow very closely what is there in the text, we see that for a moment the situation is completely transformed. One of the central images of the play is a wall, which, at a given moment, vanishes. Its disappearance, to which Bottom draws our attention, is caused by an act of love. Shakespeare is showing us how love can pervade a situation and act as a transforming force.

The *Dream* touches lightly on the fundamental question of the transformations which may occur if certain things are better understood. It requires us to reflect on the nature of love. All the landscapes of love are thrown into relief, and we are given a particular social context through which the other situations can be measured. Through the subtlety of its language the play removes all kinds of barriers. It is therefore not a play which provokes resistance or creates disturbance in the usual sense. Rival politicians could sit side by side at a performance of *A Midsummer Night's Dream* and each leave with the impression that the play fits his point of view perfectly. But if they give it a fine, sensitive attention they cannot fail to perceive a world just like their own, more and more riddled with contradictions and, like their own, waiting for that mysterious force, love, without which harmony will never return.

Hamlet

Hamlet (1600–1601), Shakespeare's boldest, most profound play, is a landmark in the poet's work. It coincides with the new century and the uncertainties of the last years of the old regime, which ended with the death of Queen Elizabeth in 1603. Until the very moment of her death, the succession was in doubt, but at her death she indicated that her cousin James of Scotland would take the throne. The new age was in many ways more complicated, more ambiguous, and more democratic than the old. It was also more dangerous because it was more uncertain.

Hamlet returns to a Denmark and a court that he hardly recognizes, to a mother newly wed to his uncle and in many ways not the woman he remembers, and, finally, to a ghostly father who will not rest until the crimes against him have been avenged. Like Marlowe's *Faustus*, Hamlet had been a scholar at the University of Wittenberg, where he presumably had studied theology and therefore acquired a special knowledge of the world of the spirits. Perhaps he had studied medicine and law as well. He gives evidence of knowing literature and having a taste for theater, and he is a ready hand with weapons when necessary.

Hamlet is also a melancholic. To the Elizabethan, *melancholic* did not mean depressed, although Hamlet dresses in black and still mourns for his father, even against the wishes of his uncle. The melancholic, rather, was introspective, thoughtful, perhaps world-weary, and possibly a touch sardonic. Above all things, he was an intellectual, a person of wide-ranging knowledge and intelligence, a reliable commentator with a probing mind.

Hamlet's broad intelligence and the penetrating introspection revealed in his soliloquies, such as his famous "To be, or not to be" meditation on suicide, make him a character with more psychological dimension, more "soul," than many people we know in life. In this sense the play is thoroughly modern; it satisfies our modern need to know the interior lives of characters who engage us onstage. Hamlet's range of feeling, his range of felt and expressed emotion, is impressive to any audience.

For a Drama in Depth tutorial on *Hamlet,* click on *VirtualLit Drama Tutorials* at **bedfordstmartins.com/jacobus.**

Hamlet is a revenge tragedy, a type of play that was especially appealing to the Elizabethans. Thomas Kyd's *The Spanish Tragedy* and John Marston's *Antonio's Revenge* are two examples of successful Elizabethan revenge tragedies. Shakespeare had written an earlier play that could be termed a revenge tragedy, *Titus Andronicus,* in 1594. Below are some characteristic elements of the revenge tragedy.

The revenge of a relative's murder or rape

The revenge of a father by a son, or vice versa

The appearance of a ghost

The hesitancy or delay of the hero

Tricks or devices to achieve revenge

The use of real or pretended insanity

Suicide

Political intrigue in a court

An able, scheming villain who is a ruler above the law

Philosophical soliloquies

Sensational use of horror (murder and gore onstage)

All these elements are present in *Hamlet.* But the play has other important qualities as well. The minor characters are developed in unexpected ways. Ophelia, the innocent, loving woman, becomes a touching figure in her own right. Unable to understand the nature of evil in the Danish court and driven to insanity by Hamlet's rejection of her and by her father's murder, she permits herself to sink to a watery death in a stream. Audiences are moved by her songs, her insane ramblings, and her devotion to her father as well as to Hamlet.

Characters such as Gertrude, Hamlet's mother, reveal a richness of psychology that sometimes startles us. Polonius, Ophelia's father, is virtually a stock character—the old, foolish philosopher—but he takes on special significance when he urges Ophelia to spy for him and when he ultimately dies at the hand of Hamlet. As Hamlet says, it was an unnecessary death for a "wretched, rash, intruding fool." But Polonius's son, Laertes, loved his father, and when Laertes returns grief-stricken, he does not hesitate a moment to get his revenge.

Hamlet's hesitancy is linked with his reputation as a melancholic. Because he thinks things through so deeply, he does not act instantly, as does Laertes. Even when the ghost reveals himself as his father and tells him that he has been murdered and must be avenged, Hamlet fears that the apparition might be a dangerous fakery of the devil to lure him to murder.

But Hamlet shows that he can act swiftly—indeed, rashly. His killing of Polonius is a rash act. He thinks the man behind the tapestry in his mother's bedroom is his uncle, since no other man but her husband has any right to be there. When Hamlet is sent to England with Rosencrantz and Guildenstern, he quickly senses a plot, undoes it, leaps aboard a pirate ship, and negotiates his way home with alacrity. This is not the behavior of a man who cannot act. In the graveyard scene, he acts just as impulsively as Laertes would when he leaps into Ophelia's grave.

Hamlet's talents exhibited in his welcoming of the players in act II show him to be an experienced theatergoer, one with some skills onstage. He is also an expert writer; his additions to *The Murder of Gonzago* convert that imaginary play into a "mousetrap" baited to catch the murderer of his father. In early Renaissance paintings, the mousetrap is a symbol for Jesus Christ, who catches the devil. The allusion would not have been lost on the Elizabethan audience, who would have seen Hamlet's psychological approach as quite reasonable.

Emotions are of great importance to Hamlet. He feels deeply and he watches others to see what their feelings are. He knows that their demeanor may not reveal them as they are, so he must be a careful student of behavior. As he tells his mother, "I know not 'seems.'" What seems is only what is apparent; his procedure is always to penetrate the surfaces of things to know their reality, which is why he uses drama as an instrument to penetrate psychological surfaces.

Hamlet in Performance

Richard Burbage played Hamlet in its original production, which was probably in 1601 but may have been in 1600. He continued playing the part for the rest of his life. *Hamlet* was staged on an English ship off the coast of Africa in 1607. The first American production was in 1759. When one thinks of productions of the play, one thinks of the great actors who played the role. Their names read like a *Who's Who* of acting: David Garrick (1717–1779), Edmund Kean (1789–1833), William Charles Macready (1793–1873), and Sir Henry Irving (1838–1905) were all identified with the role.

In the twentieth century, the two towering Hamlets were John Gielgud and Laurence Olivier, who both acted for the Old Vic Theatre. To interpret the part, Olivier studied psychoanalyst Ernest Jones's essay on Hamlet's Oedipus complex. Jones was a disciple of Freud, who discussed Hamlet in his *Interpretation of Dreams*. Paul Scofield, in Peter Brook's 1955 production, found the part so challenging that he said playing it "feels like trespassing." Since the mid-1950s, Christopher Plummer, Derek Jacobi, and Jonathan Pryce have played the part to acclaim, both on stage and in films. Richard Burton played Hamlet in New York in 1964. Michael Pennington's version for the Royal Shakespeare Company's 1980 production (see photos on p. 358) was well received by both critics and audiences. Pennington believed that the part tested not only one's skill but also one's character. He said, "When things go well you could do three performances a day and still be the last to leave the party, and at other times the part shakes you like a rat."

The number of major productions in the 1980s alone was astonishing: Christopher Walken for the American Shakespeare Festival in Stratford, Connecticut (1982); Roger Rees for the Royal Shakespeare Company in Stratford, England (1984); Kevin Kline for the New York Shakespeare Festival (1986); Ingmar Bergman's acclaimed production in Swedish in Sweden and New York (1988); Daniel Day-Lewis for the National Theatre in London (1989); and Austin Pendleton for the Riverside Shakespeare Company in New York (1989).

Franco Zeffirelli cast Mel Gibson in his 1990 film, which presents a credible Hamlet capable of deep emotional outburst. The setting of the film is lavish, and the interaction between Hamlet and Gertrude has a special psychological valence. *Hamlet* had a banner year in 1995, when Liam Neeson played the

Danish prince in London and New York to considerable acclaim. That production was marked by a careful deemphasis of the great soliloquies. Ralph Fiennes, in the wake of a film success in *Schindler's List*, played Hamlet in Edwardian clothes on Broadway, using madness as "a way of acting out." Keanu Reeves, another film actor, performed the part at the Royal Manitoba Theatre Centre in Winnipeg, Canada. One critic said of Reeves's performance, "His hairstyle changed with his moods." Robert Wilson, known for massive semioperatic productions, played entirely alone, in a production called *Hamlet: A Monologue* that premiered in Houston. In this production, Hamlet, on his deathbed, relives his story in flashbacks; he provides critical speeches of other characters himself. Among his efforts at Shakespeare, Kenneth Branagh took on the title role in a lavish production of *Hamlet* in 1996.

Hamlet has been the dream role not only of great actors but of great actresses as well. Sarah Bernhardt played Hamlet in the late nineteenth century, and Eva Le Gallienne, Siobhan McKenna, and Judith Anderson took on the part in the twentieth century. *Hamlet* has also given rise to numerous spinoffs, the best of which is Tom Stoppard's *Rosencrantz and Guildenstern Are Dead* (1967). Heiner Müller's *Hamlet-machine* (1977) is a respected avantgarde version of the play. Lee Blessing's *Fortinbras* (1991) is an innovative retelling of the play from the point of view of a minor character—except that this character becomes the king. Blessing's success suggests that *Hamlet* is rich enough and inspiring enough to generate numerous further redactions and interpretations. Michael Almereyda's 2000 film version of *Hamlet* starred Ethan Hawke as Hamlet, Sam Shepard as the Ghost, Kyle MacLachlan as Claudius, and Bill Murray as Polonius. It is one of many filmed versions of the play. Today productions of *Hamlet* are being staged in most countries on every continent, from the Globe Theatre in London to the coast of Zealand in Denmark. There is no end in sight for creative interpretations of this great play.

WILLIAM SHAKESPEARE (1564–1616)

Hamlet, Prince of Denmark   c. 1600

[Dramatis Personae

CLAUDIUS, *King of Denmark*
HAMLET, *son to the late King Hamlet, and nephew to the present King*
POLONIUS, *Lord Chamberlain*
HORATIO, *friend to Hamlet*
LAERTES, *son to Polonius*

VOLTIMAND,
CORNELIUS,
ROSENCRANTZ, } *courtiers*
GUILDENSTERN,
OSRIC,
GENTLEMAN,
PRIEST, OR DOCTOR OF DIVINITY

MARCELLUS, } *officers*
BERNARDO,
FRANCISCO, *a solider*
REYNALDO, *servant to Polonius*
PLAYERS
TWO CLOWNS, *grave-diggers*
FORTINBRAS, *Prince of Norway*
CAPTAIN
ENGLISH AMBASSADORS

GERTRUDE, *Queen of Denmark, mother to Hamlet*
OPHELIA, *daughter to Polonius*

LORDS, LADIES, OFFICERS, SOLDIERS, SAILORS, MESSENGERS,
    AND OTHER ATTENDANTS
GHOST *of Hamlet's father*

Scene: Denmark.]

{ACT I • Scene I}°

(*Enter Bernardo and Francisco, two sentinels,* [*meeting*].)

BERNARDO: Who's there?
FRANCISCO: Nay, answer me.° Stand and unfold yourself.
BERNARDO: Long live the King!
FRANCISCO: Bernardo?
5 BERNARDO: He.
FRANCISCO: You come most carefully upon your hour.
BERNARDO: 'Tis now struck twelve. Get thee to bed,
    Francisco.
FRANCISCO: For this relief much thanks. 'Tis bitter cold,
    And I am sick at heart.
BERNARDO: Have you had quiet guard?
10 FRANCISCO: Not a mouse stirring.
BERNARDO: Well, good night.
    If you do meet Horatio and Marcellus,
    The rivals° of my watch, bid them make haste.

(*Enter Horatio and Marcellus.*)

FRANCISCO: I think I hear them. Stand, ho! Who is there?
HORATIO: Friends to this ground.
15 MARCELLUS: And liegemen to the Dane.°
FRANCISCO: Give you° good night.
MARCELLUS: O, farewell, honest soldier.
    Who hath relieved you?
FRANCISCO: Bernardo hath my place.
    Give you good night.   (*Exit Francisco.*)

Note: The text of *Hamlet* has come down to us in different
versions—such as the first quarto, the second quarto, and the
First Folio. The text used here is largely drawn from the second
quarto. Passages enclosed in square brackets are taken from
one of the other versions, in most cases the First Folio.
I, i. Location: Elsinore castle. A guard platform.   **2. me:** Francisco
emphasizes that *he* is the sentry currently on watch.   **13. rivals:**
Partners.   **15. liegemen to the Dane:** Men sworn to serve the
Danish king.   **16. Give you:** God give you.

MARCELLUS: Holla, Bernardo!
BERNARDO: Say,
    What, is Horatio there?
HORATIO: A piece of him.
BERNARDO: Welcome, Horatio. Welcome, good
    Marcellus.   20
HORATIO: What, has this thing appear'd again tonight?
BERNARDO: I have seen nothing.
MARCELLUS: Horatio says 'tis but our fantasy,
    And will not let belief take hold of him
    Touching this dreaded sight, twice seen of us.   25
    Therefore I have entreated him along
    With us to watch the minutes of this night,
    That if again this apparition come
    He may approve° our eyes and speak to it.
HORATIO: Tush, tush, 'twill not appear.
BERNARDO: Sit down awhile,   30
    And let us once again assail your ears,
    That are so fortified against our story,
    What we have two nights seen.
HORATIO: Well, sit we down,
    And let us hear Bernardo speak of this.
BERNARDO: Last night of all,   35
    When yond same star that's westward from the pole°
    Had made his° course t' illume that part of heaven
    Where now it burns, Marcellus and myself,
    The bell then beating one—

(*Enter Ghost.*)

MARCELLUS: Peace, break thee off! Look where it
    comes again!   40
BERNARDO: In the same figure, like the King that's dead.
MARCELLUS: Thou art a scholar.° Speak to it, Horatio.
BERNARDO: Looks 'a° not like the King? Mark it, Horatio.
HORATIO: Most like. It harrows me with fear and
    wonder.
BERNARDO: It would be spoke to.
MARCELLUS: Speak to it,° Horatio.   45
HORATIO: What art thou that usurp'st this time of
    night,
    Together with that fair and warlike form
    In which the majesty of buried Denmark°
    Did sometimes° march? By heaven I charge thee
    speak!
MARCELLUS: It is offended.
BERNARDO: See, it stalks away.   50
HORATIO: Stay! Speak, speak. I charge thee, speak.
                           (*Exit Ghost.*)
MARCELLUS: 'Tis gone, and will not answer.
BERNARDO: How now, Horatio? You tremble and
    look pale.
    Is not this something more than fantasy?
    What think you on 't?   55

29. approve: Corroborate.   **36. pole:** Polestar.   **37. his:** Its.
42. scholar: One learned in Latin and able to address spirits.
43. 'a: He.   **45. It . . . it:** A ghost could not speak until spoken to.   **48. buried Denmark:** The buried king of Denmark.
49. sometimes: Formerly.

HORATIO: Before my God, I might not this believe
　　Without the sensible° and true avouch
　　Of mine own eyes.
MARCELLUS:　　　　　　Is it not like the King?
HORATIO: As thou art to thyself.
60　　Such was the very armor he had on
　　When he the ambitious Norway° combated.
　　So frown'd he once when, in an angry parle,°
　　He smote the sledded° Polacks° on the ice.
　　'Tis strange.
MARCELLUS: Thus twice before, and jump° at this
65　　　　dead hour,
　　With martial stalk hath he gone by our watch.
HORATIO: In what particular thought to work I know
　　　　not,
　　But, in the gross and scope° of mine opinion,
　　This bodes some strange eruption to our state.
MARCELLUS: Good now,° sit down, and tell me, he
70　　　　that knows,
　　Why this same strict and most observant watch
　　So nightly toils° the subject° of the land,
　　And why such daily cast° of brazen cannon,
　　And foreign mart° for implements of war,
75　　Why such impress° of shipwrights, whose sore task
　　Does not divide the Sunday from the week.
　　What might be toward,° that this sweaty haste
　　Doth make the night joint-laborer with the day?
　　Who is 't that can inform me?
HORATIO:　　　　　　　　That can I,
80　　At least, the whisper goes so. Our last king,
　　Whose image even but now appear'd to us,
　　Was, as you know, by Fortinbras of Norway,
　　Thereto prick'd on° by a most emulate° pride,
　　Dar'd to the combat; in which our valiant
　　　　Hamlet—
　　For so this side of our known world esteem'd
85　　　　him—
　　Did slay this Fortinbras; who, by a seal'd compact,
　　Well ratified by law and heraldry,
　　Did forfeit, with his life, all those his lands
　　Which he stood seiz'd° of, to the conqueror;
90　　Against the° which a moi'ty competent°
　　Was gaged° by our king, which had return'd
　　To the inheritance of Fortinbras
　　Had he been vanquisher, as, by the same comart°
　　And carriage° of the article design'd,

His fell to Hamlet. Now, sir, young Fortinbras,　　95
　　Of unimproved° mettle hot and full,
　　Hath in the skirts° of Norway here and there
　　Shark'd up° a list of lawless resolutes°
　　For food and diet° to some enterprise
　　That hath a stomach° in 't, which is no other—　　100
　　As it doth well appear unto our state—
　　But to recover of us, by strong hand
　　And terms compulsatory, those foresaid lands
　　So by his father lost. And this, I take it,
　　Is the main motive of our preparations,　　105
　　The source of this our watch, and the chief head°
　　Of this post-haste and romage° in the land.
BERNARDO: I think it be no other but e'en so.
　　Well may it sort° that this portentous figure
　　Comes armed through our watch so like the King　　110
　　That was and is the question of these wars.
HORATIO: A mote° it is to trouble the mind's eye.
　　In the most high and palmy° state of Rome,
　　A little ere the mightiest Julius fell,
　　The graves stood tenantless and the sheeted° dead　　115
　　Did squeak and gibber in the Roman streets;
　　As° stars with trains of fire and dews of blood,
　　Disasters° in the sun; and the moist star°
　　Upon whose influence Neptune's° empire stands°
　　Was sick almost to doomsday° with eclipse.　　120
　　And even the like precurse° of fear'd events,
　　As harbingers° preceding still° the fates
　　And prologue to the omen° coming on,
　　Have heaven and earth together demonstrated
　　Unto our climatures° and countrymen.　　125

(Enter Ghost.)

　　But soft, behold! Lo where it comes again!
　　I'll cross° it, though it blast me. Stay, illusion!
　　If thou hast any sound, or use of voice,
　　Speak to me!　　　　　　(*It spreads his arms.*)
　　If there be any good thing to be done　　130
　　That may to thee do ease and grace to me,
　　Speak to me!
　　If thou art privy to thy country's fate,
　　Which, happily,° foreknowing may avoid,

---

57. sensible: Confirmed by the senses.　**61. Norway:** King of Norway.　**62. parle:** Parley.　**63. sledded:** Traveling on sleds. **Polacks:** Poles.　**65. jump:** Exactly.　**68. gross and scope:** General view.　**70. Good now:** An expression denoting entreaty or expostulation.　**72. toils:** Causes to toil. **subject:** Subjects.　**73. cast:** Casting.　**74. mart:** Buying and selling.　**75. impress:** Impressment, conscription.　**77. toward:** In preparation.　**83. prick'd on:** Incited. **emulate:** Ambitious.　**89. seiz'd:** Possessed.　**90. Against the:** In return for. **moi'ty competent:** Sufficient portion.　**91. gaged:** Engaged, pledged.　**93. comart:** Joint bargain (?).　**94. carriage:** Import, bearing.

96. unimproved: Not turned to account (?) or untested (?). **97. skirts:** Outlying regions, outskirts.　**98. Shark'd up:** Got together in haphazard fashion. **resolutes:** Desperadoes. **99. food and diet:** No pay but their keep.　**100. stomach:** Relish of danger.　**106. head:** Source.　**107. romage:** Bustle, commotion.　**109. sort:** Suit.　**112. mote:** Speck of dust. **113. palmy:** Flourishing.　**115. sheeted:** Shrouded.　**117. As:** This abrupt transition suggests that matter has possibly been omitted between lines 116 and 117.　**118. Disasters:** Unfavorable signs of aspects. **moist star:** Moon, governing tides. **119. Neptune:** God of the sea. **stands:** Depends.　**120. sick . . . doomsday:** See Matt. 24:29 and Rev. 6:12.　**121. precurse:** Heralding, foreshadowing.　**122. harbingers:** Forerunners. **still:** Continually.　**123. omen:** Calamitous event.　**125. climatures:** Regions.　**127. cross:** Meet, face directly.　**134. happily:** Haply, perchance.

135 O, speak!
Or if thou hast uphoarded in thy life
Extorted treasure in the womb of earth,
For which, they say, you spirits oft walk in death,
                                        (*The cock crows.*)
Speak of it. Stay, and speak! Stop it, Marcellus.
140 MARCELLUS: Shall I strike at it with my partisan?°
HORATIO: Do, if it will not stand.   [*They strike at it.*]
BERNARDO: 'Tis here!
HORATIO: 'Tis here!
MARCELLUS: 'Tis gone.   [*Exit Ghost.*]
We do it wrong, being so majestical,
To offer it the show of violence;
145 For it is, as the air, invulnerable,
And our vain blows malicious mockery.
BERNARDO: It was about to speak when the cock
        crew.
HORATIO: And then it started like a guilty thing
Upon a fearful summons. I have heard,
150 The cock, that is the trumpet to the morn,
Doth with his lofty and shrill-sounding throat
Awake the god of day, and, at his warning,
Whether in sea or fire, in earth or air,
Th' extravagant and erring° spirit hies
155 To his confine; and of the truth herein
This present object made probation.°
MARCELLUS: It faded on the crowing of the cock.
Some say that ever 'gainst° that season comes
Wherein our Savior's birth is celebrated,
160 The bird of dawning singeth all night long,
And then, they say, no spirit dare stir abroad;
The nights are wholesome, then no planets strike,°
No fairy takes,° nor witch hath power to charm,
So hallowed and so gracious° is that time.
165 HORATIO: So have I heard and do in part believe it.
But, look, the morn, in russet mantle clad,
Walks o'er the dew of yon high eastward hill.
Break we our watch up, and by my advice
Let us impart what we have seen tonight
170 Unto young Hamlet; for, upon my life,
This spirit, dumb to us, will speak to him.
Do you consent we shall acquaint him with it,
As needful in our loves, fitting our duty?
MARCELLUS: Let's do 't, I pray, and I this morning know
175 Where we shall find him most conveniently.
                                        (*Exeunt.*)°

{Scene II}°

(*Flourish. Enter Claudius, King of Denmark, Gertrude
the Queen, Councilors, Polonius and his son Laertes,
Hamlet, cum aliis*° [*including Voltimand and Cornelius*].)

140. **partisan:** Long-handled spear.   154. **extravagant and
erring:** Wandering. (The words have similar meanings.)
156. **probation:** Proof.   158. **'gainst:** Just before.   162. **strike:**
Exert evil influence.   163. **takes:** Bewitches.   164. **gracious:**
Full of goodness.   175. [S.D.] *Exeunt:* Latin for "they go out."
I, ii. **Location:** The castle.   [S.D.] *cum aliis:* With others.

KING: Though yet of Hamlet our dear brother's death
The memory be green, and that it us befitted
To bear our hearts in grief and our whole kingdom
To be contracted in one brow of woe,
Yet so far hath discretion fought with nature   5
That we with wisest sorrow think on him,
Together with remembrance of ourselves.
Therefore our sometime sister, now our queen,
Th' imperial jointress° to this warlike state,
Have we, as 'twere with a defeated joy—   10
With an auspicious and a dropping eye,
With mirth in funeral and with dirge in marriage,
In equal scale weighing delight and dole—
Taken to wife. Nor have we herein barr'd
Your better wisdoms, which have freely gone   15
With this affair along. For all, our thanks.
Now follows that you know° young Fortinbras,
Holding a weak supposal° of our worth,
Or thinking by our late dear brother's death
Our state to be disjoint and out of frame,   20
Colleagued with° this dream of his advantage,°
He hath not fail'd to pester us with message
Importing° the surrender of those lands
Lost by his father, with all bands° of law,
To our most valiant brother. So much for him.   25
Now for ourself and for this time of meeting.
Thus much the business is: we have here writ
To Norway, uncle of young Fortinbras—
Who, impotent and bed-rid, scarcely hears
Of this his nephew's purpose—to suppress   30
His° further gait° herein, in that the levies,
The lists, and full proportions are all made
Out of his subject;° and we here dispatch
You, good Cornelius, and you, Voltimand,
For bearers of this greeting to old Norway,   35
Giving to you no further personal power
To business with the King, more than the scope
Of these delated° articles allow.   [*Gives a paper.*]
Farewell, and let your haste commend your duty.
CORNELIUS, VOLTIMAND: In that, and all things, will
        we show our duty.   40
KING: We doubt it nothing. Heartily farewell.

                [*Exit Voltimand and Cornelius.*]

And now, Laertes, what's the news with you?
You told us of some suit; what is 't, Laertes?
You cannot speak of reason to the Dane°
And lose your voice.° What wouldst thou beg,
        Laertes,   45

9. **jointress:** Woman possessed of a joint tenancy of an estate.
17. **know:** Be informed (that).   18. **weak supposal:** Low estimate.   21. **Colleagued with:** Joined to, allied with.   **dream . . .
advantage:** Illusory hope of success.   23. **Importing:** Pertaining to.   24. **bands:** Contracts.   31. **His:** Fortinbras's.   **gait:**
Proceeding.   31–33. **in that . . . subject:** Since the levying
of troops and supplies is drawn entirely from the King of
Norway's own subjects.   38. **delated:** Detailed (variant of
dilated).   44. **the Dane:** The Danish king.   45. **lose your voice:**
Waste your speech.

That shall not be my offer, not thy asking?
The head is not more native° to the heart,
The hand more instrumental° to the mouth,
Than is the throne of Denmark to thy father.
What wouldst thou have, Laertes?

50 LAERTES: My dread lord,
Your leave and favor to return to France,
From whence though willingly I came to Denmark
To show my duty in your coronation,
Yet now I must confess, that duty done,
55 My thoughts and wishes bend again toward France
And bow them to your gracious leave and pardon.°

KING: Have you your father's leave? What says
    Polonius?

POLONIUS: H'ath, my lord, wrung from me my slow
    leave
By laborsome petition, and at last
60 Upon his will I seal'd my hard° consent.
I do beseech you, give him leave to go.

KING: Take thy fair hour, Laertes. Time be thine,
And thy best graces spend it at thy will!
But now, my cousin° Hamlet, and my son—

65 HAMLET: A little more than kin, and less than kind.°

KING: How is it that the clouds still hang on you?

HAMLET: Not so, my lord. I am too much in the sun.°

QUEEN: Good Hamlet, cast thy nighted color off,
And let thine eye look like a friend on Denmark.
70 Do not forever with thy veiled° lids
Seek for thy noble father in the dust.
Thou know'st 'tis common,° all that lives must die,
Passing through nature to eternity.

HAMLET: Ay, madam, it is common.

QUEEN: If it be,
75 Why seems it so particular with thee?

HAMLET: Seems, madam! Nay, it is. I know not "seems."
'Tis not alone my inky cloak, good mother,
Nor customary suits of solemn black,
Nor windy suspiration of forc'd breath,
80 No, nor the fruitful° river in the eye,
Nor the dejected havior of the visage,
Together with all forms, moods, shapes of grief,
That can denote me truly. These indeed seem,
For they are actions that a man might play.
85 But I have that within which passes show;
These but the trappings and the suits of woe.

KING: 'Tis sweet and commendable in your nature,
    Hamlet,
To give these mourning duties to your father.

But you must know your father lost a father,
That father lost, lost his, and the survivor bound   90
In filial obligation for some term
To do obsequious° sorrow. But to persever°
In obstinate condolement° is a course
Of impious stubbornness. 'Tis unmanly grief.
It shows a will most incorrect to heaven,   95
A heart unfortified, a mind impatient,
An understanding simple and unschool'd.
For what we know must be and is as common
As any the most vulgar thing to sense,°
Why should we in our peevish opposition   100
Take it to heart? Fie, 'tis a fault to heaven,
A fault against the dead, a fault to nature,
To reason most absurd, whose common theme
Is death of fathers, and who still hath cried,
From the first corse° till he that died today,   105
"This must be so." We pray you, throw to earth
This unprevailing° woe, and think of us
As of a father; for let the world take note,
You are the most immediate° to our throne,
And with no less nobility of love   110
Than that which dearest father bears his son
Do I impart toward you. For your intent
In going back to school in Wittenberg,°
It is most retrograde° to our desire,
And we beseech you, bend you° to remain   115
Here in the cheer and comfort of our eye,
Our chiefest courtier, cousin, and our son.

QUEEN: Let not thy mother lose her prayers, Hamlet.
I pray thee stay with us, go not to Wittenberg.

HAMLET: I shall in all my best obey you, madam.   120

KING: Why, 'tis a loving and a fair reply.
Be as ourself in Denmark. Madam, come.
This gentle and unforc'd accord of Hamlet
Sits smiling to my heart, in grace whereof
No jocund° health that Denmark drinks today   125
But the great cannon to the clouds shall tell,
And the King's rouse° the heaven shall bruit again,°
Respeaking earthly thunder.° Come away.

(Flourish. Exeunt all but Hamlet.)

HAMLET: O, that this too too sullied° flesh would melt,
Thaw, and resolve itself into a dew!   130
Or that the Everlasting had not fix'd
His canon° 'gainst self-slaughter! O God, God,
How weary, stale, flat, and unprofitable

---

47. **native:** Closely connected, related. 48. **instrumental:** Serviceable. 56. **leave and pardon:** Permission to depart. 60. **hard:** Reluctant. 64. **cousin:** Any kin not of the immediate family. 65. **A little . . . kind:** Closer than an ordinary nephew (since I am stepson), and yet more separated in natural feeling (with pun on *kind*, meaning affectionate and natural, lawful). This line is often read as an aside, but it need not be. 67. **sun:** The sunshine of the King's royal favor (with pun on *son*). 70. **veiled:** Downcast. 72. **common:** Of universal occurrence. (But Hamlet plays on the sense of vulgar in line 74.) 80. **fruitful:** Abundant.

92. **obsequious:** Suited to obsequies or funerals. **persever:** Persevere. 93. **condolement:** Sorrowing. 99. **As . . . sense:** As the most ordinary experience. 105. **corse:** Corpse. 107. **unprevailing:** Unavailing. 109. **most immediate:** Next in succession. 113. **Wittenberg:** Famous German university founded in 1502. 114. **retrograde:** Contrary. 115. **bend you:** Incline yourself. 125. **jocund:** Merry. 127. **rouse:** Draft of liquor. **bruit again:** Loudly echo. 128. **thunder:** Of trumpet and kettledrum sounded when the King drinks; see I, iv, 8–12. 129. **sullied:** Defiled. (The early quartos read *sallied,* the Folio *solid.*) 132. **canon:** Law.

Seem to me all the uses of this world!
135 Fie on 't, ah, fie! 'Tis an unweeded garden
That grows to seed. Things rank and gross in
    nature
Possess it merely.° That it should come to this!
But two months dead—nay, not so much, not two.
So excellent a king, that was to° this
140 Hyperion° to a satyr; so loving to my mother
That he might not beteem° the winds of heaven
Visit her face too roughly. Heaven and earth,
Must I remember? Why, she would hang on him
As if increase of appetite had grown
145 By what it fed on, and yet, within a month—
Let me not think on 't. Frailty, thy name is
    woman!—
A little month, or ere those shoes were old
With which she followed my poor father's body,
Like Niobe,° all tears, why she, even she—
150 O God, a beast, that wants discourse of reason,°
Would have mourn'd longer—married with my
    uncle,
My father's brother, but no more like my father
Than I to Hercules. Within a month,
Ere yet the salt of most unrighteous tears
155 Had left the flushing in her galled° eyes,
She married. O, most wicked speed, to post
With such dexterity to incestuous° sheets!
It is not nor it cannot come to good.
But break, my heart, for I must hold my tongue.

(*Enter Horatio, Marcellus, and Bernardo.*)

HORATIO: Hail to your lordship!
160 HAMLET: I am glad to see you well.
    Horatio!—or I do forget myself.
HORATIO: The same, my lord, and your poor servant
    ever.
HAMLET: Sir, my good friend; I'll change° that name
    with you.
    And what make° you from Wittenberg, Horatio?
165 Marcellus?
MARCELLUS: My good lord.
HAMLET: I am very glad to see you. [*To Bernardo.*]
    Good even, sir.—
    But what, in faith, make you from Wittenberg?
HORATIO: A truant disposition, good my lord.
170 HAMLET: I would not hear your enemy say so,
    Nor shall you do my ear that violence

To make it truster of your own report
Against yourself. I know you are no truant.
But what is your affair in Elsinore?
We'll teach you to drink deep ere you depart.   175
HORATIO: My lord, I came to see your father's
    funeral.
HAMLET: I prithee do not mock me, fellow student;
    I think it was to see my mother's wedding.
HORATIO: Indeed, my lord, it followed hard° upon.
HAMLET: Thrift, thrift, Horatio! The funeral bak'd
    meats   180
Did coldly furnish forth the marriage tables.
Would I had met my dearest° foe in heaven
Or° ever I had seen that day, Horatio!
My father!—Methinks I see my father.
HORATIO: Where, my lord?
HAMLET: In my mind's eye, Horatio.   185
HORATIO: I saw him once. 'A° was a goodly king.
HAMLET: 'A was a man, take him for all in all,
    I shall not look upon his like again.
HORATIO: My lord, I think I saw him yesternight.
HAMLET: Saw? Who?   190
HORATIO: My lord, the King your father.
HAMLET: The King my father?
HORATIO: Season your admiration° for a while
    With an attent° ear, till I may deliver,
    Upon the witness of these gentlemen,
    This marvel to you.
HAMLET: For God's love, let me hear!   195
HORATIO: Two nights together had these gentlemen,
    Marcellus and Bernardo, on their watch,
    In the dead waste and middle of the night,
    Been thus encount'red. A figure like your father,
    Armed at point° exactly, cap-a-pe,°   200
    Appears before them, and with solemn march
    Goes slow and stately by them. Thrice he walk'd
    By their oppress'd and fear-surprised eyes
    Within his truncheon's° length, whilst they, distill'd
    Almost to jelly with the act° of fear,   205
    Stand dumb and speak not to him. This to me
    In dreadful secrecy impart they did,
    And I with them the third night kept the watch,
    Where, as they had delivered, both in time,
    Form of the thing, each word made true and good,   210
    The apparition comes. I knew your father;
    These hands are not more like.
HAMLET: But where was this?
MARCELLUS: My lord, upon the platform where we
    watch.
HAMLET: Did you not speak to it?
HORATIO: My lord, I did,
    But answer made it none. Yet once methought   215
    It lifted up it° head and did address

---

137. **merely:** Completely.   139. **to:** In comparison to.   140.
Hyperion: Titan sun-god, father of Helios.   141. **beteem:** Allow.   149. **Niobe:** Tantalus's daughter, Queen of Thebes, who
boasted that she had more sons and daughters than Leto; for
this, Apollo and Artemis, children of Leto, slew her fourteen
children. She was turned by Zeus into a stone that continually dropped tears.   150. **wants . . . reason:** Lacks the faculty
of reason.   155. **galled:** Irritated, inflamed.   157. **incestuous:**
In Shakespeare's day, a marriage like that of Claudius, to his
deceased brother's wife, was considered incestuous.   163.
change: Exchange (i.e., the name of friend).   164. **make:** Do.

179. **hard:** Close.   182. **dearest:** Direst.   183. **Or:** Ere, before.
186. **'A:** He.   192. **Season your admiration:** Restrain your
astonishment.   193. **attent:** Attentive.   200. **at point:** Completely.   **cap-a-pe:** From head to foot.   204. **truncheon:** Officer's staff.   205. **act:** Action, operation.   216. **it:** Its.

Itself to motion, like as it would speak;
But even then the morning cock crew loud,
And at the sound it shrunk in haste away,
And vanish'd from our sight.

220 HAMLET: 'Tis very strange.
HORATIO: As I do live, my honor'd lord, 'tis true,
And we did think it writ down in our duty
To let you know of it.
HAMLET: Indeed, indeed, sirs. But this troubles me.
Hold you the watch tonight?

225 ALL: We do, my lord.
HAMLET: Arm'd, say you?
ALL: Arm'd, my lord.
HAMLET: From top to toe?
ALL: My lord, from head to foot.
HAMLET: Then saw you not his face?

230 HORATIO: O, yes, my lord. He wore his beaver° up.
HAMLET: What, looked he frowningly?
HORATIO: A countenance more
In sorrow than in anger.
HAMLET: Pale or red?
HORATIO: Nay, very pale.
HAMLET: And fix'd his eyes upon you?
HORATIO: Most constantly.
HAMLET: I would I had been there.

235 HORATIO: It would have much amaz'd you.
HAMLET: Very like, very like. Stay'd it long?
HORATIO: While one with moderate haste might tell°
a hundred.
MARCELLUS, BERNARDO: Longer, longer.
HORATIO: Not when I saw 't.
HAMLET: His beard was grizzl'd,—no?

240 HORATIO: It was, as I have seen it in his life,
A sable silver'd.°
HAMLET: I will watch tonight.
Perchance 'twill walk again.
HORATIO: I warr'nt it will.
HAMLET: If it assume my noble father's person,
I'll speak to it, though hell itself should gape

245 And bid me hold my peace. I pray you all,
If you have hitherto conceal'd this sight,
Let it be tenable° in your silence still,
And whatsomever else shall hap tonight,
Give it an understanding, but no tongue.

250 I will requite your loves. So, fare you well.
Upon the platform, 'twixt eleven and twelve,
I'll visit you.
ALL: Our duty to your honor.
HAMLET: Your loves, as mine to you. Farewell.
                    (*Exeunt* [*all but Hamlet*].)
My father's spirit in arms! All is not well.
I doubt° some foul play. Would the night were
255   come!

---

230. **beaver:** Visor on the helmet.   237. **tell:** Count.   241. **sable silver'd:** Black mixed with white.   247. **tenable:** Held tightly.   255. **doubt:** Suspect.

Till then sit still, my soul. Foul deeds will rise,
Though all the earth o'erwhelm them, to men's eyes.
                     (*Exit.*)

{Scene III}°

(*Enter Laertes and Ophelia, his sister.*)

LAERTES: My necessaries are embark'd. Farewell.
And, sister, as the winds give benefit
And convoy is assistant,° do not sleep
But let me hear from you.
OPHELIA: Do you doubt that?
LAERTES: For Hamlet, and the trifling of his favor,   5
Hold it a fashion and a toy in blood,°
A violet in the youth of primy° nature,
Forward,° not permanent, sweet, not lasting,
The perfume and suppliance° of a minute—
No more.
OPHELIA: No more but so?
LAERTES: Think it no more.   10
For nature crescent° does not grow alone
In thews° and bulk, but, as this temple° waxes,
The inward service of the mind and soul
Grows wide withal.° Perhaps he loves you now,
And now no soil° nor cautel° doth besmirch   15
The virtue of his will;° but you must fear,
His greatness weigh'd,° his will is not his own.
[For he himself is subject to his birth.]
He may not, as unvalued persons do,
Carve° for himself; for on his choice depends   20
The safety and health of this whole state,
And therefore must his choice be circumscrib'd
Unto the voice and yielding° of that body
Whereof he is the head. Then if he says he loves
    you,
It fits your wisdom so far to believe it   25
As he in his particular act and place
May give his saying deed,° which is no further
Than the main voice of Denmark goes withal.
Then weigh what loss your honor may sustain
If with too credent° ear you list° his songs,   30
Or lose your heart, or your chaste treasure open
To his unmaster'd importunity.
Fear it, Ophelia, fear it, my dear sister,
And keep you in the rear of your affection,
Out of the shot° and danger of desire.   35

I, iii. Location: Polonius's chambers.   **3. convoy is assistant:** Means of conveyance are available.   **6. toy in blood:** Passing amorous fancy.   **7. primy:** In its prime, springtime.   **8. Forward:** Precocious.   **9. suppliance:** Supply, filler.   **11. crescent:** Growing, waxing.   **12. thews:** Bodily strength. **temple:** Body.   **14. Grows wide withal:** Grows along with it.   **15. soil:** Blemish. **cautel:** Deceit.   **16. will:** Desire.   **17. greatness weigh'd:** High position considered.   **20. Carve:** Choose pleasure.   **23. voice and yielding:** Assent, approval.   **27. deed:** Effect.   **30. credent:** Credulous. **list:** Listen to.   **35. shot:** Range.

The chariest° maid is prodigal enough
If she unmask her beauty to the moon.
Virtue itself scapes not calumnious strokes.
The canker galls° the infants of the spring
40 Too oft before their buttons° be disclos'd,°
And in the morn and liquid dew° of youth
Contagious blastments° are most imminent.
Be wary then; best safety lies in fear.
Youth to itself rebels, though none else near.

45 OPHELIA: I shall the effect of this good lesson keep
As watchman to my heart. But, good my brother,
Do not, as some ungracious pastors do,
Show me the steep and thorny way to heaven,
Whiles, like a puff'd° and reckless libertine,
50 Himself the primrose path of dalliance treads,
And recks° not his own rede.°

(*Enter Polonius.*)

LAERTES: O, fear me not.
I stay too long. But here my father comes.
A double blessing is a double° grace;
Occasion° smiles upon a second leave.

POLONIUS: Yet here, Laertes? Aboard, aboard, for
55   shame!
The wind sits in the shoulder of your sail,
And you are stay'd for. There—my blessing with
    thee!
And these few precepts in thy memory
Look thou character.° Give thy thoughts no tongue
60 Nor any unproportion'd thought his° act.
Be thou familiar,° but by no means vulgar.°
Those friends thou hast, and their adoption tried,°
Grapple them to thy soul with hoops of steel,
But do not dull thy palm with entertainment
65 Of each new-hatch'd, unfledg'd courage.° Beware
Of entrance to a quarrel, but, being in,
Bear't that° th' opposed may beware of thee.
Give every man thy ear, but few thy voice;
Take each man's censure,° but reserve thy judgment.
70 Costly thy habit as thy purse can buy,
But not express'd in fancy; rich, not gaudy,
For the apparel oft proclaims the man,
And they in France of the best rank and station
Are of a most select and generous chief° in that.
75 Neither a borrower nor a lender be,
For loan oft loses both itself and friend,
And borrowing dulleth edge of husbandry.°

This above all: to thine own self be true,
And it must follow, as the night the day,
Thou canst not then be false to any man.   80
Farewell. My blessing season° this in thee!

LAERTES: Most humbly do I take my leave, my lord.

POLONIUS: The time invests° you. Go, your servants
    tend.°

LAERTES: Farewell, Ophelia, and remember well
What I have said to you.   85

OPHELIA: 'Tis in my memory lock'd,
And you yourself shall keep the key of it.

LAERTES: Farewell.   (*Exit Laertes.*)

POLONIUS: What is 't, Ophelia, he hath said to you?

OPHELIA: So please you, something touching the Lord
    Hamlet.   90

POLONIUS: Marry,° well bethought.
'Tis told me he hath very oft of late
Given private time to you, and you yourself
Have of your audience been most free and
    bounteous.
If it be so—as so 'tis put on° me,   95
And that in way of caution I must tell you
You do not understand yourself so clearly
As it behooves my daughter and your honor.
What is between you? Give me up the truth.

OPHELIA: He hath, my lord, of late made many
    tenders°
Of his affection to me.   100

POLONIUS: Affection? Pooh! You speak like a green
    girl,
Unsifted° in such perilous circumstance.
Do you believe his tenders, as you call them?

OPHELIA: I do not know, my lord, what I should think. 105

POLONIUS: Marry, I will teach you. Think yourself a
    baby
That you have ta'en these tenders° for true pay,
Which are not sterling.° Tender° yourself more
    dearly,
Or—not to crack the wind° of the poor phrase,
Running it thus—you'll tender me a fool.°   110

OPHELIA: My lord, he hath importun'd me with love
In honorable fashion.

POLONIUS: Ay, fashion° you may call it. Go to, go to.

OPHELIA: And hath given countenance° to his speech,
    my lord,
With almost all the holy vows of heaven.   115

---

36. chariest: Most scrupulously modest. **39. canker galls:** Cankerworm destroys. **40. buttons:** Buds. **disclos'd:** Opened. **41. liquid dew:** Time when dew is fresh. **42. blastments:** Blights. **49. puff'd:** Bloated. **51. recks:** Heeds. **rede:** Counsel. **53. double:** I.e., Laertes has already bidden his father good bye. **54. Occasion:** Opportunity. **59. character:** Inscribe. **60. his:** Its. **61. familiar:** Sociable. **vulgar:** Common. **62. tried:** Tested. **65. courage:** Young man of spirit. **67. Bear't that:** Manage it so that. **69. censure:** Opinion, judgment. **74. generous chief:** Noble eminence (?). **77. husbandry:** Thrift.

81. season: Mature. **83. invests:** Besieges. **tend:** Attend, wait. **91. Marry:** By the Virgin Mary (a mild oath). **95. put on:** Impressed on, told to. **100. tenders:** Offers. **103. Unsifted:** Untried. **107. tenders:** With added meaning here of "promise to pay." **108. sterling:** Legal currency. **Tender:** Hold. **109. crack the wind:** Run it until it is broken, winded. **110. tender me a fool:** (1) Show yourself to me as a fool; (2) show me up as a fool; (3) present me with a grandchild (*fool* was a term of endearment for a child). **113. fashion:** Mere form, pretense. **114. countenance:** Credit, support.

POLONIUS: Ay, springes° to catch woodcocks.° I do know,
  When the blood burns, how prodigal the soul
  Lends the tongue vows. These blazes, daughter,
  Giving more light than heat, extinct in both
120 Even in their promise, as it is a-making,
  You must not take for fire. From this time
  Be something scanter of your maiden presence.
  Set your entreatments° at a higher rate
  Than a command to parle.° For Lord Hamlet,
125 Believe so much in him° that he is young,
  And with a larger tether may he walk
  Than may be given you. In few,° Ophelia,
  Do not believe his vows, for they are brokers,°
  Not of that dye° which their investments° show,
130 But mere implorators° of unholy suits,
  Breathing° like sanctified and pious bawds,
  The better to beguile. This is for all:
  I would not, in plain terms, from this time forth
  Have you so slander° any moment leisure
135 As to give words or talk with the Lord Hamlet.
  Look to 't, I charge you. Come your ways.
OPHELIA: I shall obey, my lord.   (*Exeunt.*)

{Scene IV}°

(*Enter Hamlet, Horatio, and Marcellus.*)

HAMLET: The air bites shrewdly; it is very cold.
HORATIO: It is a nipping and an eager air.
HAMLET: What hour now?
HORATIO: I think it lacks of twelve.
MARCELLUS: No, it is struck.
HORATIO: Indeed? I heard it not.
5 It then draws near the season
  Wherein the spirit held his wont to walk.

    (*A flourish of trumpets, and two pieces° go off
    [within].*)

What does this mean, my lord?
HAMLET: The King doth wake° tonight and takes his rouse,°
  Keeps wassail,° and the swagg'ring up-spring° reels;

116. springes: Snares. woodcocks: Birds easily caught; here used to connote gullibility. 123. entreatments: Negotiations for surrender (a military term). 124. parle: Discuss terms with the enemy. (Polonius urges his daughter, in the metaphor of military language, not to meet with Hamlet and consider giving in to him merely because he requests an interview.) 125. so . . . him: This much concerning him. 127. In few: Briefly. 128. brokers: Go-betweens, procurers. 129. dye: Color or sort. investments: Clothes (i.e., they are not what they seem). 130. mere implorators: Out-and-out solicitors. 131. Breathing: Speaking. 134. slander: Bring disgrace or reproach upon. I, iv. Location: The guard platform. 6. [s.d.] pieces: I.e., of ordnance, cannon. 8. wake: Stay awake and hold revel. rouse: Carouse, drinking bout. 9. wassail: Carousal. up-spring: Wild German dance.

And as he drains his draughts of Rhenish° down,   10
  The kettle-drum and trumpet thus bray out
  The triumph of his pledge.°
HORATIO: Is it a custom?
HAMLET: Ay, marry, is 't,
  But to my mind, though I am native here
  And to the manner° born, it is a custom   15
  More honor'd in the breach than the observance.°
  This heavy-headed revel east and west°
  Makes us traduc'd and tax'd of° other nations.
  They clepe° us drunkards, and with swinish phrase°
  Soil our addition;° and indeed it takes   20
  From our achievements, though perform'd at height,°
  The pith and marrow of our attribute.
  So, oft it chances in particular men,
  That for some vicious mole of nature° in them,
  As in their birth—wherein they are not guilty,   25
  Since nature cannot choose his° origin—
  By the o'ergrowth of some complexion,°
  Oft breaking down the pales° and forts of reason,
  Or by some habit that too much o'er-leavens°
  The form of plausive° manners, that these men,   30
  Carrying, I say, the stamp of one defect,
  Being nature's livery,° or fortune's star,°
  Their virtues else, be they as pure as grace,
  As infinite as man may undergo,
  Shall in the general censure take corruption   35
  From that particular fault. The dram of eale°
  Doth all the noble substance of a doubt°
  To his own scandal.°

(*Enter Ghost.*)

HORATIO: Look, my lord, it comes!
HAMLET: Angels and ministers of grace defend us!
  Be thou a spirit of health° or goblin damn'd,   40
  Bring with thee airs from heaven or blasts from hell,
  Be thy intents wicked or charitable,
  Thou com'st in such a questionable° shape

10. Rhenish: Rhine wine. 12. triumph . . . pledge: His feat in draining the wine in a single draft. 15. manner: Custom (of drinking). 16. More . . . observance: Better neglected than followed. 17. east and west: I.e., everywhere. 18. tax'd of: Censured by. 19. clepe: Call. with swinish phrase: By calling us swine. 20. addition: Reputation. 21. at height: Outstandingly. 24. mole of nature: Natural blemish in one's constitution. 26. his: Its. 27. complexion: Humor (i.e., one of the four humors or fluids thought to determine temperament). 28. pales: Palings, fences (as of a fortification). 29. o'er-leavens: Induces a change throughout (as yeast works in dough). 30. plausive: Pleasing. 32. nature's livery: Endowment from nature. fortune's star: Mark placed by fortune. 36. dram of eale: Small amount of evil (?). 37. of a doubt: A famous crux, sometimes emended to *of about or often dout* (i.e., often erase or do out) or to *antidote* (counteract). 38. To . . . scandal: To the disgrace of the whole enterprise. 40. of health: Of spiritual good. 43. questionable: Inviting question or conversation.

That I will speak to thee. I'll call thee Hamlet,
45 King, father, royal Dane. O, answer me!
Let me not burst in ignorance, but tell
Why thy canoniz'd° bones, hearsed° in death,
Have burst their cerements;° why the sepulcher
Wherein we saw thee quietly interr'd
50 Hath op'd his ponderous and marble jaws
To cast thee up again. What may this mean,
That thou, dead corse, again in complete steel
Revisits thus the glimpses of the moon,°
Making night hideous, and we fools of nature°
55 So horridly to shake our disposition
With thoughts beyond the reaches of our souls?
Say, why is this? Wherefore? What should we do?
                                   ([Ghost] beckons [Hamlet].)
HORATIO: It beckons you to go away with it,
As if it some impartment° did desire
60 To you alone.
MARCELLUS: Look with what courteous action
It waves you to a more removed ground.
But do not go with it.
HORATIO: No, by no means.
HAMLET: It will not speak. Then I will follow it.
HORATIO: Do not, my lord.
65 HAMLET: Why, what should be the fear?
I do not set my life at a pin's fee,°
And for my soul, what can it do to that,
Being a thing immortal as itself?
It waves me forth again. I'll follow it.
HORATIO: What if it tempt you toward the flood, my
70 Lord
Or to the dreadful summit of the cliff
That beetles o'er° his° base into the sea,
And there assume some other horrible form
Which might deprive your sovereignty of reason,°
75 And draw you into madness? Think of it.
The very place puts toys of desperation,°
Without more motive, into every brain
That looks so many fathoms to the sea
And hears it roar beneath.
HAMLET: It waves me still.
80 Go on, I'll follow thee.
MARCELLUS: You shall not go, my lord.
                                   [They try to stop him.]
HAMLET: Hold off your hands!
HORATIO: Be rul'd, you shall not go.
HAMLET: My fate cries out,
And makes each petty artery° in this body
As hardy as the Nemean lion's° nerve.°

Still am I call'd. Unhand me, gentlemen.   85
By heaven, I'll make a ghost of him that lets° me!
I say, away! Go on. I'll follow thee.
                                   (Exeunt Ghost and Hamlet.)
HORATIO: He waxes desperate with imagination.
MARCELLUS: Let's follow. 'Tis not fit thus to obey him.
HORATIO: Have after. To what issue° will this come?   90
MARCELLUS: Something is rotten in the state of Denmark.
HORATIO: Heaven will direct it.°
MARCELLUS: Nay, let's follow him. *(Exeunt.)*

{Scene V}°

(Enter Ghost and Hamlet.)

HAMLET: Whither wilt thou lead me? Speak. I'll go
     no further.
GHOST: Mark me.
HAMLET: I will.
GHOST: My hour is almost come,
When I to sulph'rous and tormenting flames
Must render up myself.
HAMLET: Alas, poor ghost!
GHOST: Pity me not, but lend thy serious hearing   5
To what I shall unfold.
HAMLET: Speak. I am bound to hear.
GHOST: So art thou to revenge, when thou shalt hear.
HAMLET: What?
GHOST: I am thy father's spirit,   10
Doom'd for a certain term to walk the night,
And for the day confin'd to fast° in fires,
Till the foul crimes° done in my days of nature
Are burnt and purg'd away. But that° I am forbid
To tell the secrets of my prison-house,   15
I could a tale unfold whose lightest word
Would harrow up thy soul, freeze thy young blood,
Make thy two eyes, like stars, start from their
     spheres,°
Thy knotted and combined locks° to part,
And each particular hair to stand an end,°   20
Like quills upon the fearful porpentine.°
But this eternal blazon° must not be
To ears of flesh and blood. List, list, O, list!
If thou didst ever thy dear father love—
HAMLET: O God!   25
GHOST: Revenge his foul and most unnatural murder.
HAMLET: Murder?

---

47. canoniz'd: Buried according to the canons of the church.
hearsed: Coffined.   **48. cerements:** Grave-clothes. **53. glimpses of
the moon:** Earth by night.   **54. fools of nature:** Mere men, limited
to natural knowledge. **59. impartment:** Communication.   **66.
fee:** Value. **72. beetles o'er:** Overhangs threateningly.   **his:** Its.
74. deprive . . . reason: Take away the rule of reason over your
mind. **76. toys of desperation:** Fancies of desperate acts (i.e., suicide).   **83. artery:** Sinew.   **84. Nemean lion:** One of the monsters
slain by Hercules in his twelve labors.   **nerve:** Sinew.

86. lets: Hinders.   **90. issue:** Outcome.   **92. it:** The outcome.
I, v. Location: The battlements of the castle.   **12. fast:** Do
penance.   **13. crimes:** Sins.   **14. But that:** Were it not that.
18. spheres: Eye sockets, here compared to the orbits or transparent revolving spheres in which, according to Ptolemaic astronomy, the heavenly bodies were fixed.   **19. knotted . . . locks:**
Hair neatly arranged and confined.   **20. an end:** On end.
21. fearful porpentine: Frightened porcupine.   **22. eternal
blazon:** Revelation of the secrets of eternity.

GHOST: Murder most foul, as in the best it is,
    But this most foul, strange, and unnatural.
HAMLET: Haste me to know 't, that I, with wings as
30   swift
    As meditation or the thoughts of love,
    May sweep to my revenge.
GHOST: I find thee apt;
    And duller shouldst thou be than the fat weed
    That roots itself in ease on Lethe° wharf,°
35   Wouldst thou not stir in this. Now, Hamlet, hear.
    'Tis given out that, sleeping in my orchard,
    A serpent stung me. So the whole ear of Denmark
    Is by a forged process° of my death
    Rankly abus'd.° But know, thou noble youth,
40   The serpent that did sting thy father's life
    Now wears his crown.
HAMLET: O my prophetic soul!
    My uncle!
GHOST: Ay, that incestuous, that adulterate° beast,
    With witchcraft of his wits, with traitorous gifts—
45   O wicked wit and gifts, that have the power
    So to seduce!—won to his shameful lust
    The will of my most seeming-virtuous queen.
    O Hamlet, what a falling-off was there!
    From me, whose love was of that dignity
50   That it went hand in hand even with the vow
    I made to her in marriage, and to decline
    Upon a wretch whose natural gifts were poor
    To those of mine!
    But virtue, as it never will be moved,
55   Though lewdness court it in a shape of heaven,°
    So lust, though to a radiant angel link'd,
    Will sate itself in a celestial bed,
    And prey on garbage.
    But, soft, methinks I scent the morning air.
60   Brief let me be. Sleeping within my orchard,
    My custom always of the afternoon,
    Upon my secure° hour thy uncle stole,
    With juice of cursed hebona° in a vial,
    And in the porches of my ears did pour
65   The leprous° distillment, whose effect
    Holds such an enmity with blood of man
    That swift as quicksilver it courses through
    The natural gates and alleys of the body,
    And with a sudden vigor it doth posset°
70   And curd, like eager° droppings into milk,
    The thin and wholesome blood. So did it mine,
    And a most instant tetter° bark'd° about,

Most lazar-like,° with vile and loathsome crust,
    All my smooth body.
    Thus was I, sleeping, by a brother's hand   75
    Of life, of crown, of queen, at once dispatch'd,°
    Cut off even in the blossoms of my sin,
    Unhous'led,° disappointed,° unanel'd,°
    No reck'ning made, but sent to my account
    With all my imperfections on my head.   80
    O, horrible! O, horrible, most horrible!
    If thou hast nature° in thee, bear it not.
    Let not the royal bed of Denmark be
    A couch for luxury° and damned incest.
    But, howsomever thou pursues this act,   85
    Taint not thy mind, nor let thy soul contrive
    Against thy mother aught. Leave her to heaven
    And to those thorns that in her bosom lodge,
    To prick and sting her. Fare thee well at once.
    The glow-worm shows the matin° to be near,   90
    And 'gins to pale his uneffectual fire.°
    Adieu, adieu, adieu! Remember me.   [*Exit.*]
HAMLET: O all you host of heaven! O earth! What
    else?
    And shall I couple° hell? O fie! Hold, hold, my
    heart,
    And you, my sinews, grow not instant old,   95
    But bear me stiffly up. Remember thee!
    Ay, thou poor ghost, whiles memory holds a seat
    In this distracted globe.° Remember thee!
    Yea, from the table° of my memory
    I'll wipe away all trivial fond° records,   100
    All saws° of books, all forms,° all pressures° past
    That youth and observation copied there,
    And thy commandment all alone shall live
    Within the book and volume of my brain,
    Unmix'd with baser matter. Yes, by heaven!   105
    O most pernicious woman!
    O villain, villain, smiling, damned villain!
    My tables—meet it is I set it down,
    That one may smile, and smile, and be a villain.
    At least I am sure it may be so in Denmark.   110
                    [*Writing.*]
    So, uncle, there you are. Now to my word;
    It is "Adieu, adieu! Remember me."
    I have sworn 't.

(*Enter Horatio and Marcellus.*)

HORATIO: My lord, my lord!
MARCELLUS: Lord Hamlet!
HORATIO: Heavens secure him!

---

34. Lethe: The river of forgetfulness in Hades. **wharf:** Bank. **38. forged process:** Falsified account. **39. abus'd:** Deceived. **43. adulterate:** Adulterous. **55. shape of heaven:** Heavenly form. **62. secure:** Confident, unsuspicious. **63. hebona:** Poison. (The word seems to be a form of *ebony*, though it is thought perhaps to be related to *henbane*, a poison, or to *ebenus*, yew.) **65. leprous:** Causing leprosy-like disfigurement. **69. posset:** Coagulate, curdle. **70. eager:** Sour, acid. **72. tetter:** Eruption of scabs. **bark'd:** Covered with a rough covering, like bark on a tree.

73. lazar-like: Leper-like. **76. dispatch'd:** Suddenly deprived. **78. Unhous'led:** Without having received the sacrament (of Holy Communion). **disappointed:** Unready (spiritually) for the last journey. **unanel'd:** Without having received extreme unction. **82. nature:** The promptings of a son. **84. luxury:** Lechery. **90. matin:** Morning. **91. uneffectual fire:** Cold light. **94. couple:** Add. **98. globe:** Head. **99. table:** Writing tablet. **100. fond:** Foolish. **101. saws:** Wise sayings. **forms:** Images. **pressures:** Impressions stamped.

115 HAMLET: So be it!
    MARCELLUS: Illo, ho, ho, my lord!
    HAMLET: Hillo, ho, ho,° boy! Come, bird, come.
    MARCELLUS: How is 't, my noble lord?
    HORATIO: What news, my lord?
    HAMLET: O, wonderful!
    HORATIO: Good my lord, tell it.
120 HAMLET: No, you will reveal it.
    HORATIO: Not I, my lord, by heaven.
    MARCELLUS: Nor I, my lord.
    HAMLET: How say you, then, would heart of man
          once think it?
       But you'll be secret?
    HORATIO, MARCELLUS: Ay, by heaven, my lord.
    HAMLET: There's never a villain dwelling in all
          Denmark
125   But he's an arrant° knave.
    HORATIO: There needs no ghost, my lord, come from
          the grave
       To tell us this.
    HAMLET: Why, right, you are in the right.
       And so, without more circumstance° at all,
       I hold it fit that we shake hands and part,
130   You, as your business and desire shall point you—
       For every man hath business and desire,
       Such as it is—and for my own poor part,
       Look you, I'll go pray.
    HORATIO: These are but wild and whirling words, my
          lord.
135 HAMLET: I am sorry they offend you, heartily;
       Yes, faith, heartily.
    HORATIO: There's no offense, my lord.
    HAMLET: Yes, by Saint Patrick,° but there is, Horatio,
       And much offense too. Touching this vision here,
       It is an honest° ghost, that let me tell you.
140   For your desire to know what is between us,
       O'ermaster 't as you may. And now, good friends
       As you are friends, scholars, and soldiers,
       Give me one poor request.
    HORATIO: What is 't, my lord? We will.
    HAMLET: Never make known what you have seen
145   tonight.
    HORATIO, MARCELLUS: My lord, we will not.
    HAMLET: Nay, but swear 't.
    HORATIO: In faith,
       My lord, not I.
    MARCELLUS: Nor I, my lord, in faith.
    HAMLET: Upon my sword.°   [Holds out his sword.]
    MARCELLUS: We have sworn, my lord, already.
    HAMLET: Indeed, upon my sword, indeed.
                            (Ghost cries under the stage.)

GHOST: Swear.   150
HAMLET: Ha, ha, boy, say'st thou so? Art thou there,
       truepenny?°
    Come on, you hear this fellow in the cellarage.
    Consent to swear.
HORATIO: Propose the oath, my lord.
HAMLET: Never to speak of this that you have seen,
    Swear by my sword.   155
GHOST [beneath]: Swear.
HAMLET: Hic et ubique?° Then we'll shift our ground.
                            [He moves to another spot.]
    Come hither, gentlemen,
    And lay your hands again upon my sword.
    Swear by my sword   160
    Never to speak of this that you have heard.
GHOST [beneath]: Swear by his sword.
HAMLET: Well said, old mole! Canst work i' th' earth
       so fast?
    A worthy pioner!° Once more remove, good friends.
                            [Moves again.]
HORATIO: O day and night, but this is wondrous
       strange!   165
HAMLET: And therefore as a stranger give it welcome.
    There are more things in heaven and earth, Horatio,
    Than are dreamt of in your philosophy.°
    But come;
    Here, as before, never, so help you mercy,   170
    How strange or odd soe'er I bear myself—
    As I perchance hereafter shall think meet
    To put an antic° disposition on—
    That you, at such times seeing me, never shall,
    With arms encumb'red° thus, or this headshake,   175
    Or by pronouncing of some doubtful phrase,
    As "Well, well, we know," or "We could, an if°
       we would,"
    Or "If we list° to speak," or "There be, an if they
       might,"
    Or such ambiguous giving out,° to note°
    That you know aught of me—this do swear,   180
    So grace and mercy at your most need help you.
GHOST [beneath]: Swear.   [They swear.]
HAMLET: Rest, rest, perturbed spirit! So, gentlemen,
    With all my love I do commend me to you;
    And what so poor a man as Hamlet is   185
    May do, t' express his love and friending to you,
    God willing, shall not lack. Let us go in together,
    And still° your fingers on your lips, I pray.
    The time is out of joint. O cursed spite,
    That ever I was born to set it right!   190
                            [They wait for him to leave first.]
    Nay, come, let's go together.   (Exeunt.)

---

117. **Hillo, ho, ho:** A falconer's call to a hawk in air. Hamlet is playing upon Marcellus's *Illo* (i.e., *halloo*). 125. **arrant:** Thoroughgoing. 128. **circumstance:** Ceremony. 137. **Saint Patrick:** The keeper of purgatory and patron saint of all blunders and confusion. 139. **honest:** I.e., a real ghost and not an evil spirit. 148. **sword:** The hilt in the form of a cross.

151. **truepenny:** Honest old fellow. 157. **Hic et ubique:** Here and everywhere (Latin). 164. **pioner:** Pioneer, digger, miner. 168. **your philosophy:** This subject called "natural philosophy" or "science" that people talk about. 173. **antic:** Fantastic. 175. **encumb'red:** Folded or entwined. 177. **an if:** If. 178. **list:** Were inclined. 179. **giving out:** Profession of knowledge. **note:** Give a sign, indicate. 188. **still:** Always.

{ACT II • Scene I}°

(*Enter old Polonius, with his man [Reynaldo].*)

POLONIUS: Give him this money and these notes,
    Reynaldo.
REYNALDO: I will, my lord.
POLONIUS: You shall do marvel's° wisely, good
    Reynaldo,
    Before you visit him, to make inquire
    Of his behavior.
5 REYNALDO: My lord, I did intend it.
POLONIUS: Marry, well said, very well said. Look you,
    sir,
    Inquire me first what Danskers° are in Paris,
    And how, and who, what means,° and where they
        keep,°
    What company, at what expense; and finding
10   By this encompassment° and drift° of question
    That they do know my son, come you more nearer
    Than your particular demands will touch it.°
    Take° you, as 'twere, some distant knowledge
        of him,
    As thus, "I know his father and his friends,
15   And in part him." Do you mark this, Reynaldo?
REYNALDO: Ay, very well, my lord.
POLONIUS: "And in part him, but," you may say, "not
    well.
    But, if 't be he I mean, he's very wild,
    Addicted so and so," and there put on° him
20   What forgeries° you please—marry, none so rank
    As may dishonor him, take heed of that,
    But, sir, such wanton,° wild, and usual slips
    As are companions noted and most known
    To youth and liberty.
REYNALDO: As gaming, my lord.
25 POLONIUS: Ay, or drinking, fencing, swearing,
    Quarreling, drabbing°—you may go so far.
REYNALDO: My lord, that would dishonor him.
POLONIUS: Faith, no, as you may season° it in the
    charge.
    You must not put another scandal on him
30   That he is open to incontinency;°
    That's not my meaning. But breathe his faults so
        quaintly°
    That they may seem the taints of liberty,°
    The flash and outbreak of a fiery mind,

    A savageness in unreclaimed° blood,
    Of general assault.°
REYNALDO: But, my good lord—   35
POLONIUS: Wherefore should you do this?
REYNALDO: Ay, my lord,
    I would know that.
POLONIUS: Marry, sir, here's my drift,
    And, I believe, it is a fetch of wit.°
    You laying these slight sullies on my son,
    As 'twere a thing a little soil'd i' th' working,°   40
    Mark you,
    Your party in converse,° him you would
        sound,°
    Having ever° seen in the prenominate crimes°
    The youth you breathe° of guilty, be assur'd
    He closes with you in this consequence:°   45
    "Good sir," or so, or "friend," or "gentleman,"
    According to the phrase or the addition°
    Of man and country.
REYNALDO: Very good, my lord.
POLONIUS: And then, sir, does 'a this—'a does—
    what was I about to say?
    By the mass, I was about to say something.   50
    Where did I leave?
REYNALDO: At "closes in the consequence."
POLONIUS: At "closes in the consequence," ay, marry.
    He closes thus: "I know the gentleman;
    I saw him yesterday, or th' other day,
    Or then, or then, with such, or such, and, as you say,   55
    There was 'a gaming, there o'ertook in 's rouse,°
    There falling out° at tennis," or perchance,
    "I saw him enter such a house of sale,"
    Videlicet,° a brothel, or so forth. See you now,
    Your bait of falsehood takes this carp° of truth;   60
    And thus do we of wisdom and of reach,°
    With windlasses° and with assays of bias,°
    By indirections find directions° out.
    So by my former lecture and advice
    Shall you my son. You have me, have you not?   65
REYNALDO: My lord, I have.
POLONIUS: God buy ye; fare ye well.
REYNALDO: Good my lord.
POLONIUS: Observe his inclination in yourself.°

---

34. **unreclaimed:** Untamed.   35. **general assault:** Tendency that assails all unrestrained youth.   38. **fetch of wit:** Clever trick.   40. **soil'd i' th' working:** Shopworn.   42. **converse:** Conversation.   **sound:** Sound out.   43. **Having ever:** If he has ever.   **prenominate crimes:** Before-mentioned offenses.   44. **breathe:** Speak.   45. **closes . . . consequence:** Follows your lead in some fashion as follows.   47. **addition:** Title.   56. **o'ertook in 's rouse:** Overcome by drink.   57. **falling out:** Quarreling.   59. **Videlicet:** Namely.   60. **carp:** A fish.   61. **reach:** Capacity, ability.   62. **windlasses:** Circuitous paths (literally, circuits made to head off the game in hunting).   **assays of bias:** Attempts through indirection (like the curving path of the bowling ball, which is biased or weighted to one side).   63. **directions:** The way things really are.   68. **in yourself:** In your own person (as well as by asking questions).

II, i. Location: Polonius's chambers.   **3. marvel's:** Marvelous(ly).   **7. Danskers:** Danes.   **8. what means:** What wealth (they have).   **keep:** Dwell.   **10. encompassment:** Roundabout talking.   **drift:** Gradual approach or course.   **11–12. come . . . it:** You will find out more this way than by asking pointed questions (particular demands).   **13. Take:** Assume, pretend.   **19. put on:** Impute to.   **20. forgeries:** Invented tales.   **22. wanton:** Sportive, unrestrained.   **26. drabbing:** Whoring.   **28. season:** Temper, soften.   **30. incontinency:** Habitual loose behavior.   **31. quaintly:** Delicately, ingeniously.   **32. taints of liberty:** Faults resulting from freedom.

REYNALDO: I shall, my lord.
POLONIUS: And let him ply° his music.
70 REYNALDO: Well, my lord.
POLONIUS: Farewell.   (*Exit Reynaldo.*)

(*Enter Ophelia.*)

                        How now, Ophelia, what's the matter?
OPHELIA: O, my lord, my lord, I have been so affrighted!
POLONIUS: With what, i' th' name of God?
OPHELIA: My lord, as I was sewing in my closet,°
75   Lord Hamlet, with his doublet° all unbrac'd,°
      No hat upon his head, his stockings fouled,
      Ungart'red, and down-gyved to his ankle,°
      Pale as his shirt, his knees knocking each other,
      And with a look so piteous in purport
80   As if he had been loosed out of hell
      To speak of horrors—he comes before me.
POLONIUS: Mad for thy love?
OPHELIA: My lord, I do not know,
      But truly I do fear it.
POLONIUS: What said he?
OPHELIA: He took me by the wrist and held me hard.
85   Then goes he to the length of all his arm,
      And, with his other hand thus o'er his brow
      He falls to such perusal of my face
      As 'a would draw it. Long stay'd he so.
      At last, a little shaking of mine arm
90   And thrice his head thus waving up and down,
      He rais'd a sigh so piteous and profound
      As it did seem to shatter all his bulk°
      And end his being. That done, he lets me go,
      And, with his head over his shoulder turn'd,
95   He seem'd to find his way without his eyes,
      For out o' doors he went without their helps,
      And, to the last, bended their light on me.
POLONIUS: Come, go with me. I will go seek the King.
      This is the very ecstasy° of love
100   Whose violent property° fordoes° itself
      And leads the will to desperate undertakings
      As oft as any passion under heaven
      That does afflict our natures. I am sorry.
      What, have you given him any hard words of late?
105 OPHELIA: No, my good lord, but, as you did command,
      I did repel his letters and denied
      His access to me.
POLONIUS: That hath made him mad.
      I am sorry that with better heed and judgment
      I had not quoted° him. I fear'd he did but trifle
      And meant to wrack thee; but, beshrew my
110   jealousy!°

By heaven, it is as proper to our age°
To cast beyond° ourselves in our opinions
As it is common for the younger sort
To lack discretion. Come, go we to the King.
This must be known, which, being kept close,°   115
   might move
More grief to hide than hate to utter love.°
Come.

                                        (*Exeunt.*)

{Scene II}°

(*Flourish. Enter King and Queen, Rosencrantz, and Guildenstern [with others].*)

KING: Welcome, dear Rosencrantz and Guildenstern.
   Moreover that° we much did long to see you,
   The need we have to use you did provoke
   Our hasty sending. Something have you heard
   Of Hamlet's transformation—so call it,   5
   Sith° nor th' exterior nor° the inward man
   Resembles that° it was. What it should be,
   More than his father's death, that thus hath put him
   So much from th' understanding of himself,
   I cannot dream of. I entreat you both   10
   That, being of so young days° brought up with him,
   And sith so neighbor'd to his youth and havior,
   That you vouchsafe your rest° here in our court
   Some little time, so by your companies
   To draw him on to pleasures, and to gather   15
   So much as from occasion you may glean,
   Whether aught to us unknown afflicts him thus,
   That, open'd,° lies within our remedy.
QUEEN: Good gentlemen, he hath much talk'd of you
   And sure I am two men there is not living   20
   To whom he more adheres. If it will please you
   To show us so much gentry° and good will
   As to expend your time with us awhile
   For the supply and profit° of our hope,
   Your visitation shall receive such thanks   25
   As fits a king's remembrance.
ROSENCRANTZ: Both your Majesties
   Might, by the sovereign power you have of us,
   Put your dread pleasures more into command
   Than to entreaty.

---

70. **let him ply:** See that he continues to study.   74. **closet:**
Private chamber.   75. **doublet:** Close-fitting jacket.   **unbrac'd:**
Unfastened.   77. **down-gyved to his ankle:** Fallen to the ankles
(like gyves or fetters).   92. **bulk:** Body.   99. **ecstasy:** Madness.
100. **property:** Nature.   **fordoes:** Destroys.   109. **quoted:** Observed.   110. **beshrew my jealousy:** A plague upon my suspicious nature.

111. **proper . . . age:** Characteristic of us (old) men.   112. **cast
beyond:** Overshoot, miscalculate.   115. **close:** Secret.   115–
116. **might . . . love:** Might cause more grief (to others) by hiding the knowledge of Hamlet's strange behavior to Ophelia than
hatred by telling it.   **II, ii. Location:** The castle.   2. **Moreover
that:** Besides the fact that.   6. **Sith:** Since.   **nor . . . nor:** Neither . . . nor.   7. **that:** What.   11. **of . . . days:** From such early
youth.   13. **vouchsafe your rest:** Please to stay.   18. **open'd:**
Revealed.   22. **gentry:** Courtesy.   24. **supply and profit:** Aid
and successful outcome.

GUILDENSTERN: But we both obey,
30 And here give up ourselves in the full bent°
To lay our service freely at your feet,
To be commanded.
KING: Thanks, Rosencrantz and gentle Guildenstern.
QUEEN: Thanks, Guildenstern and gentle Rosencrantz.
35 And I beseech you instantly to visit
My too much changed son. Go, some of you,
And bring these gentlemen where Hamlet is.
GUILDENSTERN: Heavens make our presence and our
practices
Pleasant and helpful to him!
QUEEN: Ay, amen!

(*Exeunt Rosencrantz
and Guildenstern* [*with
some Attendants*].)

(*Enter Polonius.*)

POLONIUS: Th' ambassadors from Norway, my good
40 lord,
Are joyfully return'd.
KING: Thou still° hast been the father of good news.
POLONIUS: Have I, my lord? I assure my good liege,
I hold my duty, as I hold my soul,
45 Both to my God and to my gracious king;
And I do think, or else this brain of mine
Hunts not the trail of policy so sure
As it hath us'd to do, that I have found
The very cause of Hamlet's lunacy.
50 KING: O, speak of that! That do I long to hear.
POLONIUS: Give first admittance to th' ambassadors.
My news shall be the fruit° to that great feast.
KING: Thyself do grace to them, and bring them in.

(*Exit Polonius.*)

He tells me, my dear Gertrude, he hath found
55 The head and source of all your son's distemper.
QUEEN: I doubt° it is no other but the main,°
His father's death, and our o'erhasty marriage.

(*Enter Ambassadors* [*Voltimand and Cornelius, with
Polonius*].)

KING: Well, we shall sift him.—Welcome, my good
friends!
Say, Voltimand, what from our brother Norway?
VOLTIMAND: Most fair return of greetings and
60 desires.
Upon our first,° he sent out to suppress
His nephew's levies, which to him appear'd
To be a preparation 'gainst the Polack,
But, better look'd into, he truly found
65 It was against your Highness. Whereat griev'd
That so his sickness, age, and impotence
Was falsely borne in hand,° sends out arrests

On Fortinbras, which he, in brief, obeys,
Receives rebuke from Norway, and in fine°
70 Makes vow before his uncle never more
To give th' assay° of arms against your Majesty.
Whereon old Norway, overcome with joy,
Gives him three score thousand crowns in annual
fee,
And his commission to employ those soldiers,
75 So levied as before, against the Polack,
With an entreaty, herein further shown,

[*Giving a paper.*]

That it might please you to give quiet pass
Through your dominions for this enterprise,
On such regards of safety and allowance°
80 As therein are set down.
KING: It likes° us well;
And at our more consider'd° time we'll read,
Answer, and think upon this business.
Meantime we thank you for your well-took labor.
Go to your rest; at night we'll feast together.
Most welcome home! (*Exeunt Ambassadors.*)
85 POLONIUS: This business is well ended.
My liege, and madam, to expostulate°
What majesty should be, what duty is,
Why day is day, night night, and time is time,
Were nothing but to waste night, day, and time.
90 Therefore, since brevity is the soul of wit,°
And tediousness the limbs and outward flourishes,
I will be brief. Your noble son is mad.
Mad call I it, for, to define true madness,
What is 't but to be nothing else but mad?
But let that go.
QUEEN: More matter, with less art.
95 POLONIUS: Madam, I swear I use no art at all.
That he is mad, 'tis true; 'tis true 'tis pity,
And pity 'tis 'tis true—a foolish figure,°
But farewell it, for I will use no art.
100 Mad let us grant him, then, and now remains
That we find out the cause of this effect,
Or rather say, the cause of this defect,
For this effect defective comes by cause.°
Thus it remains, and the remainder thus.
105 Perpend.°
I have a daughter—have while she is mine—
Who, in her duty and obedience, mark,
Hath given me this. Now gather, and surmise.
[*Reads the letter.*] "To the celestial and my soul's
idol,
110 the most beautified Ophelia"—
That's an ill phrase, a vile phrase; "beautified" is a
vile

---

30. **in . . . bent:** To the utmost degree of our capacity. 42. **still:** Always. 52. **fruit:** Dessert. 56. **doubt:** Fear, suspect. **main:** Chief point, principal concern. 61. **Upon our first:** At our first words on the business. 67. **borne in hand:** Deluded, taken advantage of.

69. **in fine:** In the end. 71. **assay:** Trial. 79. **On . . . allowance:** With such pledges of safety and provisos. 80. **likes:** Pleases. 81. **consider'd:** Suitable for deliberation. 86. **expostulate:** Expound. 90. **wit:** Sound sense or judgment. 98. **figure:** Figure of speech. 103. **For . . . cause:** I.e., for this defective behavior, this madness has a cause. 105. **Perpend:** Consider.

phrase. But you shall hear. Thus: [*Reads.*]
   "In her excellent white bosom, these, etc."
QUEEN: Came this from Hamlet to her?
POLONIUS: Good madam, stay awhile; I will be
115   faithful.

                                                     [*Reads.*]
   "Doubt° thou the stars are fire,
      Doubt that the sun doth move,
      Doubt truth to be a liar,
      But never doubt I love.
120   O dear Ophelia, I am ill at these numbers.° I have
   not art to reckon° my groans. But that I love thee
   best, O most best, believe it. Adieu.
             Thine evermore, most dear lady, whilst this
                   machine° is to him, Hamlet."
125   This in obedience hath my daughter shown me,
   And, more above,° hath his solicitings,
   As they fell out° by time, by means, and place,
   All given to mine ear.
KING: But how hath she
   Receiv'd his love?
POLONIUS: What do you think of me?
130   KING: As of a man faithful and honorable.
POLONIUS: I would fain prove so. But what might you
      think,
   When I had seen this hot love on the wing—
   As I perceiv'd it, I must tell you that,
   Before my daughter told me—what might you,
135   Or my dear Majesty your Queen here, think,
   If I had play'd the desk or table-book,°
   Or given my heart a winking,° mute and dumb,
   Or look'd upon this love with idle sight?°
   What might you think? No, I went round° to work,
   And my young mistress thus I did bespeak:°
   "Lord Hamlet is a prince, out of thy star;°
   This must not be." And then I prescripts gave her,
   That she should lock herself from his resort,
   Admit no messengers, receive no tokens.
145   Which done, she took the fruits of my advice;
   And he, repelled—a short tale to make—
   Fell into a sadness, then into a fast,
   Thence to a watch,° thence into a weakness,
   Thence to a lightness,° and, by this declension,°
150   Into the madness wherein now he raves,
   And all we mourn for.
KING: Do you think this?
QUEEN: It may be, very like.

POLONIUS: Hath there been such a time—I would fain
      know that—
   That I have positively said "'Tis so,"
   When it prov'd otherwise?
KING: Not that I know.   155
POLONIUS [*pointing to his head and shoulder*]: Take
      this from this, if this be otherwise.
   If circumstances lead me, I will find
   Where truth is hid, though it were hid indeed
   Within the center.°
KING: How may we try it further?
POLONIUS: You know, sometimes he walks four hours
      together   160
   Here in the lobby.
QUEEN: So he does indeed.
POLONIUS: At such a time I'll loose my daughter to him.
   Be you and I behind an arras° then.
   Mark the encounter. If he love her not
   And be not from his reason fall'n thereon,°   165
   Let me be no assistant for a state,
   But keep a farm and carters.
KING: We will try it.

(*Enter Hamlet* [*reading on a book*].)

QUEEN: But look where sadly the poor wretch comes
      reading.
POLONIUS: Away, I do beseech you both, away.
   I'll board° him presently.

      (*Exeunt King and Queen* [*with Attendants*].)

                   O, give me leave.   170
   How does my good Lord Hamlet?
HAMLET: Well, God-a-mercy.°
POLONIUS: Do you know me, my lord?
HAMLET: Excellent well. You are a fishmonger.°
POLONIUS: Not I, my lord.   175
HAMLET: Then I would you were so honest a man.
POLONIUS: Honest, my lord?
HAMLET: Ay, sir. To be honest, as this world goes, is
   to be one man pick'd out of ten thousand.
POLONIUS: That's very true, my lord.   180
HAMLET: For if the sun breed maggots in a dead dog, be-
   ing a good kissing carrion°—Have you a daughter?
POLONIUS: I have, my lord.
HAMLET: Let her not walk i' th' sun.° Conception° is a
   blessing, but as your daughter may conceive, friend, 185
   look to 't.

---

116. **Doubt:** Suspect, question.   120. **ill . . . numbers:** Unskilled
at writing verses.   121. **reckon:** (1) Count; (2) number met-
rically, scan.   124. **machine:** Body.   126. **more above:** Moreover.   127. **fell out:** Occurred.   136. **play'd . . . table-book:**
Remained shut up, concealing the information.   137. **winking:** Closing of the eyes.   138. **with idle sight:** Complacently
or uncomprehendingly.   139. **round:** Roundly, plainly.   140.
bespeak: Address.   141. **out of thy star:** Above your sphere,
position.   148. **watch:** State of sleeplessness.   149. **lightness:**
Light-headedness.   **declension:** Decline, deterioration.

159. **center:** Middle point of the earth (which is also the center of the Ptolemaic universe).   163. **arras:** Hanging, tapestry.
165. **thereon:** On that account.   170. **board:** Accost.
172. **God-a-mercy:** Thank you.   174. **fishmonger:** Fish merchant (with connotation of *bawd*, procurer [?]).   182. **good
kissing carrion:** A good piece of flesh for kissing or for the sun
to kiss.   184. **i' th' sun:** With additional implication of the
sunshine of princely favors.   **Conception:** (1) Understanding;
(2) pregnancy.

POLONIUS [*aside*]: How say you by that? Still harping on my daughter. Yet he knew me not at first; 'a said I was a fishmonger. 'A is far gone. And truly in my youth I suff'red much extremity for love, very near this. I'll speak to him again.—What do you read, my lord?

HAMLET: Words, words, words.

POLONIUS: What is the matter,° my lord?

HAMLET: Between who?

POLONIUS: I mean, the matter that you read, my lord.

HAMLET: Slanders, sir, for the satirical rogue says here that old men have gray beards, that their faces are wrinkled, their eyes purging° thick amber and plum-tree gum, and that they have a plentiful lack of wit, together with most weak hams. All which, sir, though I most powerfully and potently believe, yet I hold it not honesty° to have it thus set down, for you yourself, sir, shall grow old as I am, if like a crab you could go backward. *method in the madness*

POLONIUS [*aside*]: Though this be madness, yet there is method in 't.—Will you walk out of the air, my lord?

HAMLET: Into my grave.

190
195
200
205

194. **matter:** Substance (but Hamlet plays on the sense of basis for a dispute). 199. **purging:** Discharging. 203. **honesty:** Decency.

POLONIUS: Indeed, that's out of the air. [*Aside*.] How pregnant° sometimes his replies are! A happiness° that often madness hits on, which reason and sanity could not so prosperously° be deliver'd of. I will leave him, [and suddenly contrive the means of meeting between him] and my daughter.—My honorable lord, I will most humbly take my leave of you.

HAMLET: You cannot, sir, take from me any thing that I will more willingly part withal—except my life, except my life, except my life.

(*Enter Guildenstern and Rosencrantz.*)

POLONIUS: Fare you well, my lord.

HAMLET: These tedious old fools! *he doesn't actually like them*

POLONIUS: You go to seek the Lord Hamlet; there he is.

ROSENCRANTZ [*to Polonius*]: God save you, sir!

[*Exit Polonius.*]

GUILDENSTERN: My honor'd lord!

ROSENCRANTZ: My most dear lord!

HAMLET: My excellent good friends! How dost thou, Guildenstern? Ah, Rosencrantz! Good lads, how do you both?

210
215
220
225

210. **pregnant:** Full of meaning. **happiness:** Felicity of expression. 212. **prosperously:** Successfully. 220. **old fools:** I.e., old men like Polonius.

Hamlet returns to Denmark. Left to right, Voltimand (Jeremy Geidt), Gertrude (Christine Estabrook), Claudius (Mark Metcalf), Hamlet (Mark Rylance), and Laertes (Derek Smith) in the 1991 American Repertory Theater production of *Hamlet,* directed by Ron Daniels.

The dumb-show sequence with Candy Buckley as the Player Queen.

ROSENCRANTZ: As the indifferent° children of the earth.

GUILDENSTERN: Happy in that we are not over-happy.
230   On Fortune's cap we are not the very button.

HAMLET: Nor the soles of her shoe?

ROSENCRANTZ: Neither, my lord.

HAMLET: Then you live about her waist, or in the middle of her favors?

235   GUILDENSTERN: Faith, her privates° we.

HAMLET: In the secret parts of Fortune? O, most true; she is a strumpet.° What news?

ROSENCRANTZ: None, my lord, but the world's grown honest.

240   HAMLET: Then is doomsday near. But your news is not true. [Let me question more in particular. What have you, my good friends, deserv'd at the hands of Fortune that she sends you to prison hither?

GUILDENSTERN: Prison, my lord?

245   HAMLET: Denmark's a prison.

ROSENCRANTZ: Then is the world one.

HAMLET: A goodly one, in which there are many confines,° wards,° and dungeons, Denmark being one o' th' worst.

250   ROSENCRANTZ: We think not so, my lord.

HAMLET: Why then 'tis none to you, for there is nothing either good or bad but thinking makes it so. To me it is a prison.

ROSENCRANTZ: Why then, your ambition makes it one.
255   'Tis too narrow for your mind.

228. **indifferent:** Ordinary.   235. **privates:** Close acquaintances (with sexual pun on *private parts*).   237. **strumpet:** Prostitute (a common epithet for indiscriminate Fortune; see line 497, p. 348).   247–248. **confines:** Places of confinement.   248. **wards:** Cells.

HAMLET: O God, I could be bounded in a nutshell and count myself a king of infinite space, were it not that I have had dreams.

GUILDENSTERN: Which dreams indeed are ambition, for the very substance of the ambitious° is merely the   260 shadow of a dream.

HAMLET: A dream itself is but a shadow.

ROSENCRANTZ: Truly, and I hold ambition of so airy and light a quality that it is but a shadow's shadow.

HAMLET: Then are our beggars bodies,° and our mon-   265 archs and outstretch'd° heroes the beggars' shadows. Shall we to th' court? For, by my fay,° I cannot reason.

ROSENCRANTZ, GUILDENSTERN: We'll wait upon° you.

HAMLET: No such matter. I will not sort° you with the   270 rest of my servants, for, to speak to you like an honest man, I am most dreadfully attended.°] But, in the beaten way° of friendship, what make° you at Elsinore?

ROSENCRANTZ: To visit you, my lord, no other occasion.   275

HAMLET: Beggar that I am, I am even poor in thanks; but I thank you, and sure, dear friends, my thanks are too dear a halfpenny.° Were you not sent for? Is it your own inclining? Is it a free visitation? Come, come,

260. **the very . . . ambitious:** That seemingly very substantial thing which the ambitious pursue.   265. **bodies:** Solid substances rather than shadows (since beggars are not ambitious).   266. **outstretch'd:** (1) Far-reaching in their ambition; (2) elongated as shadows.   267. **fay:** Faith.   269. **wait upon:** Accompany, attend.   270. **sort:** Class, associate.   272. **dreadfully attended:** Waited upon in slovenly fashion.   273. **beaten way:** Familiar path.   **make:** Do.   278. **dear a halfpenny:** Expensive at the price of a halfpenny (i.e., of little worth).

280 　deal justly with me. Come, come; nay, speak.
　　GUILDENSTERN: What should we say, my lord?
　　HAMLET: Why, anything, but to th' purpose. You were
　　　sent for; and there is a kind of confession in your
　　　looks which your modesties have not craft enough
285 　to color. I know the good King and Queen have sent
　　　for you.
　　ROSENCRANTZ: To what end, my lord?
　　HAMLET: That you must teach me. But let me conjure°
　　　you, by the rights of our fellowship, by the conso-
290 　nancy of our youth,° by the obligation of our ever-
　　　preserv'd love, and by what more dear a better
　　　proposer° could charge° you withal, be even° and
　　　direct with me, whether you were sent for, or no?
　　ROSENCRANTZ [aside to Guildenstern]: What say you?
295 　HAMLET [aside]: Nay then, I have an eye of° you.—If
　　　you love me, hold not off.
　　GUILDENSTERN: My lord, we were sent for.
　　HAMLET: I will tell you why; so shall my anticipation
　　　prevent your discovery,° and your secrecy to the King
300 　and Queen molt no feather.° I have of late—but
　　　wherefore I know not—lost all my mirth, forgone
　　　all custom of exercises; and indeed it goes so heavily
　　　with my disposition that this goodly frame, the earth,
　　　seems to me a sterile promontory; this most excellent
305 　canopy, the air, look you, this brave° o'erhanging fir-
　　　mament, this majestical roof fretted° with golden fire,
　　　why, it appeareth nothing to me but a foul and pesti-
　　　lent congregation of vapors. What a piece of work is
　　　a man! How noble in reason, how infinite in faculties,
310 　in form and moving how express° and admirable, in
　　　action how like an angel, in apprehension how like
　　　a god! The beauty of the world, the paragon of ani-
　　　mals! And yet, to me, what is this quintessence° of
　　　dust? Man delights not me—no, nor woman neither,
315 　though by your smiling you seem to say so.
　　ROSENCRANTZ: My lord, there was no such stuff in my
　　　thoughts.
　　HAMLET: Why did you laugh then, when I said "man
　　　delights not me"?
320 　ROSENCRANTZ: To think, my lord, if you delight not in
　　　man, what lenten entertainment° the players shall
　　　receive from you. We coted° them on the way, and
　　　hither are they coming, to offer you service.
　　HAMLET: He that plays the king shall be welcome; his
325 　Majesty shall have tribute of me. The adventurous

knight shall use his foil and target,° the lover shall
not sigh gratis, the humorous man° shall end his part
in peace, [the clown shall make those laugh whose
lungs are tickle o' th' sere°], and the lady shall say her
mind freely, or the blank verse shall halt° for 't. What 330
players are they?
ROSENCRANTZ: Even those you were wont to take such
delight in, the tragedians of the city.
HAMLET: How chances it they travel? Their residence,°
both in reputation and profit, was better both ways. 335
ROSENCRANTZ: I think their inhibition° comes by the
means of the innovation.°
HAMLET: Do they hold the same estimation they did when
I was in the city? Are they so follow'd?
ROSENCRANTZ: No, indeed, are they not.° 340
[HAMLET: How comes it? Do they grow rusty?
ROSENCRANTZ: Nay, their endeavor keeps in the
wonted° pace. But there is, sir, an aery° of children,
little eyases,° that cry out on the top of question,°
and are most tyrannically° clapp'd for 't. These are 345
now the fashion, and so berattle° the common
stages°—so they call them—that many wearing
rapiers° are afraid of goose-quills° and dare scarce
come thither.
HAMLET: What, are they children? Who maintains 'em? 350
How are they escoted?° Will they pursue the quality°
no longer than they can sing?° Will they not say
afterwards, if they should grow themselves to com-
mon° players—as it is most like, if their means are
no better—their writers do them wrong, to make 355
them exclaim against their own succession?°
ROSENCRANTZ: Faith, there has been much to do° on
both sides, and the nation holds it no sin to tarre°
them to controversy. There was, for a while, no
money bid for argument° unless the poet and the 360
player went to cuffs in the question.°

326. **foil and target:** Sword and shield. 327. **humorous man:** Eccentric character, dominated by one trait, or "humor." 329. **tickle o' th' sere:** Easy on the trigger, ready to laugh easily. (*Sere* is part of a gunlock.) 330. **halt:** Limp. 334. **residence:** Remaining in one place (i.e., in the city). 336. **inhibition:** Formal prohibition (from acting plays in the city). 337. **innovation:** I.e., the new fashion in satirical plays performed by boy actors in the "private" theaters; or, possibly, a political uprising or the strict limitations set on the theater in London in 1600. 340. **No . . . not:** The following passage (lines 341–367), omitted from the early quartos, alludes to the so-called War of the Theatres, 1599–1602, the rivalry between the child companies and the adult actors. 343. **wonted:** Usual. **aery:** Nest. 344. **eyases:** Young hawks. **cry . . . question:** Speak shrilly, dominating the controversy (in decrying the public theaters). 345. **tyrannically:** Outrageous. 346. **berattle:** Berate. 346–347. **common stages:** Public theaters. 347–348. **many wearing rapiers:** Many men of fashion, who were afraid to patronize the common players for fear of being satirized by the poets who wrote for the children. 348. **goose-quills:** Pens of satirists. 351. **escoted:** Maintained. **quality:** (Acting) profession. 352. **no longer . . . sing:** Only until their voices change. 353–354. **common:** Regular, adult. 356. **succession:** Future careers. 357. **to do:** Ado. 358. **tarre:** Set on (as dogs). 360. **argument:** Plot for a play. 361. **went . . . question:** Came to blows in the play itself.

288. **conjure:** Adjure, entreat. 289–290. **consonancy of our youth:** The fact that we are of the same age. 291–292. **better proposer:** More skillful propounded. 292. **charge:** Urge. **even:** Straight, honest. 295. **of:** On. 299. **prevent your discovery:** Forestall your disclosure. 300. **molt no feather:** Not diminish in the least. 305. **brave:** Splendid. 306. **fretted:** Adorned (with fret-work, as in a vaulted ceiling). 310. **express:** Well-framed (?), exact (?). 313. **quintessence:** The fifth essence of ancient philosophy, beyond earth, water, air, and fire, supposed to be the substance of the heavenly bodies and to be latent in all things. 321. **lenten entertainment:** Meager reception (appropriate to Lent). 322. **coted:** Overtook and passed beyond.

HAMLET: Is 't possible?

GUILDENSTERN: O, there has been much throwing about of brains.

365   HAMLET: Do the boys carry it away?°

ROSENCRANTZ: Ay, that they do, my lord—Hercules and his load° too.]

HAMLET: It is not very strange, for my uncle is King of Denmark, and those that would make mouths° at him while my father liv'd, give twenty, forty, fifty, a
370   hundred ducats° apiece for his picture in little.° 'Sblood,° there is something in this more than natural, if philosophy could find it out.

(*A flourish [of trumpets within*].)

GUILDENSTERN: There are the players.

375   HAMLET: Gentlemen, you are welcome to Elsinore. Your hands, come then. Th' appurtenance of welcome is fashion and ceremony. Let me comply° with you in this garb,° lest my extent° to the players, which, I tell you, must show fairly outwards,° should more appear
380   like entertainment° than yours. You are welcome. But my uncle-father and aunt-mother are deceiv'd.

GUILDENSTERN: In what, my dear lord?

HAMLET: I am but mad north-north-west.° When the wind is southerly I know a hawk from a handsaw.°

(*Enter Polonius.*)   *I'm only cray-cray sometimes*

385   POLONIUS: Well be with you, gentlemen!

HAMLET: Hark you, Guildenstern, and you too; at each ear a hearer. That great baby you see there is not yet out of his swaddling-clouts.°

ROSENCRANTZ: Happily° he is the second time come to
390   them; for they say an old man is twice a child.

HAMLET: I will prophesy he comes to tell me of the players; mark it.—You say right, sir, o' Monday morning, 'twas then indeed.

POLONIUS: My lord, I have news to tell you.

395   HAMLET: My lord, I have news to tell you. When Roscius° was an actor in Rome—

POLONIUS: The actors are come hither, my lord.

HAMLET: Buzz,° buzz!   *stale news*

POLONIUS: Upon my honor—

400   HAMLET: Then came each actor on his ass—

POLONIUS: The best actors in the world, either for tragedy, comedy, history, pastoral, pastoral-comical, historical-pastoral, tragical-historical, tragical-comical-historical-pastoral, scene individable,° or poem unlimited.° Seneca° cannot be too heavy, nor   405 Plautus° too light. For the law of writ and the liberty,° these are the only men.

HAMLET: O Jephthah, judge of Israel,° what a treasure hadst thou!

POLONIUS: What a treasure had he, my lord?   410

HAMLET: Why,
   "One fair daughter, and no more,
   The which he loved passing° well."

POLONIUS [*aside*]: Still on my daughter.

HAMLET: Am I not i' th' right, old Jephthah?   415

POLONIUS: If you call me Jephthah, my lord, I have a daughter that I love passing well.

HAMLET: Nay, that follows not.

POLONIUS: What follows, then, my lord?

HAMLET: Why,   *there's a song*   420
   "As by lot, God wot,"°
   and then, you know,
   "It came to pass, as most like° it was."
The first row° of the pious chanson° will show you more, for look where my abridgement° comes.   425

(*Enter the Players.*)

You are welcome, masters; welcome, all. I am glad to see thee well. Welcome, good friends. O, old friend! Why, thy face is valanc'd° since I saw thee last. Com'st thou to beard° me in Denmark? What, my young lady° and mistress? By 'r lady, your   430 ladyship is nearer to heaven than when I saw you last, by the altitude of a chopine.° Pray God your voice, like a piece of uncurrent° gold, be not crack'd within the ring.° Masters, you are all welcome. We'll e'en to 't like French falconers, fly at anything   435 we see. We'll have a speech straight.° Come, give us a taste of your quality; come, a passionate speech.

---

365. **carry it away:** Win the day. 366–367. **Hercules . . . load:** Thought to be an allusion to the sign of the Globe Theatre, which was Hercules bearing the world on his shoulder. 369. **mouths:** Faces. 371. **ducats:** Gold coins. **in little:** In miniature. 372. **'Sblood:** By His (God's, Christ's) blood. 377. **comply:** Observe the formalities of courtesy. 378. **garb:** Manner. **my extent:** The extent of my showing courtesy. 379. **show fairly outwards:** Look cordial to outward appearances. 380. **entertainment:** A (warm) reception. 383. **north-north-west:** Only partly, at times. 384. **hawk, handsaw:** Mattock (or *hack*) and a carpenter's cutting tool, respectively; also birds, with a play on *hernshaw*, or heron. 388. **swaddling-clouts:** Cloths in which to wrap a newborn baby. 389. **Happily:** Haply, perhaps. 396. **Roscius:** A famous Roman actor who died in 62 BCE. 398. **Buzz:** An interjection used to denote stale news.

404. **scene individable:** A play observing the unity of place. 405. **poem unlimited:** A play disregarding the unities of time and place. **Seneca:** Writer of Latin tragedies. 406. **Plautus:** Writer of Latin comedy. **law . . . liberty:** Dramatic composition both according to rules and without rules (i.e., "classical" and "romantic" dramas). 408. **Jephthah . . . Israel:** Jephthah had to sacrifice his daughter; see Judges 11. Hamlet goes on to quote from a ballad on the theme. 413. **passing:** Surpassingly. 421. **wot:** Knows. 423. **like:** Likely, probable. 424. **row:** Stanza. **chanson:** Ballad, song. 425. **my abridgement:** Something that cuts short my conversation; also, a diversion. 428. **valanc'd:** Fringed (with a beard). 429. **beard:** Confront (with obvious pun). 430. **young lady:** Boy playing women's parts. 432. **chopine:** Thick-soled shoe of Italian fashion. 433. **uncurrent:** Not passable as lawful coinage. 433–434. **crack'd . . . ring:** Changed from adolescent to male voice, no longer suitable for women's roles. (Coins featured rings enclosing the sovereign's head; if the coin was cracked within this ring, it was unfit for currency.) 436. **straight:** At once.

FIRST PLAYER: What speech, my good lord?

HAMLET: I heard thee speak me a speech once, but it
was never acted, or, if it was, not above once, for the
play, I remember, pleas'd not the million; 'twas caviary to the general.° But it was—as I receiv'd it, and
others, whose judgments in such matters cried in
the top of° mine—an excellent play, well digested
in the scenes, set down with as much modesty as
cunning.° I remember one said there were no sallets°
in the lines to make the matter savory, nor no matter
in the phrase that might indict° the author of affectation, but call'd it an honest method, as wholesome as
sweet, and by very much more handsome than fine.°
One speech in 't I chiefly lov'd: 'twas Aeneas' tale to
Dido, and thereabout of it especially when he speaks
of Priam's slaughter.° If it live in your memory, begin
at this line: let me see, let me see—
"The rugged Pyrrhus,° like th' Hyrcanian beast"°—
'Tis not so. It begins with Pyrrhus:
"The rugged Pyrrhus, he whose sable° arms,
Black as his purpose, did the night resemble
When he lay couched in the ominous horse,°
Hath now this dread and black complexion
    smear'd
With heraldry more dismal.° Head to foot
Now is he total gules,° horridly trick'd°
With blood of fathers, mothers, daughters, sons,
Bak'd and impasted° with the parching streets,°
That lend a tyrannous and a damned light
To their lord's° murder. Roasted in wrath and fire,
And thus o'er-sized° with coagulate gore,
With eyes like carbuncles, the hellish Pyrrhus
Old grandsire Priam seeks."
So proceed you.

POLONIUS: 'Fore God, my lord, well spoken, with good
accent and good discretion.

FIRST PLAYER: "Anon he finds him
Striking too short at Greeks. His antique sword,
Rebellious to his arm, lies where it falls,
Repugnant° to command. Unequal match'd,

Pyrrhus at Priam drives, in rage strikes wide,
But with the whiff and wind of his fell° sword
Th' unnerved father falls. [Then senseless Ilium,°]
Seeming to feel this blow, with flaming top
Stoops to his° base, and with a hideous crash
Takes prisoner Pyrrhus' ear. For, lo! His sword,
Which was declining on the milky head
Of reverend Priam, seem'd i' th' air to stick.
So as a painted° tyrant Pyrrhus stood,
And, like a neutral to his will and matter,°
Did nothing.
But, as we often see, against° some storm,
A silence in the heavens, the rack° stand still,
The bold winds speechless, and the orb below
As hush as death, anon the dreadful thunder
Doth rend the region,° so, after Pyrrhus' pause,
Aroused vengeance sets him new a-work,
And never did the Cyclops'° hammers fall
On Mars's armor forg'd for proof eterne°
With less remorse than Pyrrhus' bleeding sword
Now falls on Priam.
Out, out, thou strumpet Fortune! All you gods,
In general synod,° take away her power!
Break all the spokes and fellies° from her wheel,
And bowl the round nave° down the hill of
    heaven,
As low as to the fiends!"

POLONIUS: This is too long.

HAMLET: It shall to the barber's with your beard.—
Prithee say on. He's for a jig° or a tale of bawdry, or
he sleeps. Say on, come to Hecuba.°

FIRST PLAYER: "But who, ah woe! had seen the
    mobled° queen"—

HAMLET: "The mobled queen?"

POLONIUS: That's good. "Mobled queen" is good.

FIRST PLAYER: "Run barefoot up and down, threat'ning
    the flames
With bisson rheum,° a clout° upon that head
Where late the diadem stood, and for a robe,
About her lank and all o'er-teemed° loins,
A blanket, in the alarm of fear caught up—
Who this had seen, with tongue in venom steep'd,
'Gainst Fortune's state° would treason have
    pronounc'd.°
But if the gods themselves did see her then

441–442. **caviary to the general:** Caviar in the multitude (i.e., a choice dish too elegant for coarse tastes). 443–444. **cried in the top of:** Spoke with greater authority than. 446. **cunning:** Skill. **sallets:** Salad (i.e., spicy improprieties). 448. **indict:** Convict. 450. **fine:** Elaborately ornamented, showy. 453. **Priam's slaughter:** The slaying of the ruler of Troy, when the Greeks finally took the city. 455. **Pyrrhus:** A Greek hero in the Trojan War, also known as Neoptolemus, son of Achilles. **Hyrcanian beast:** I.e., the tiger. (See Virgil, *Aeneid*, IV, 266; compare the whole speech with Marlowe's *Dido Queen of Carthage*, II, i, 214 ff.) 457. **sable:** Black (for reasons of camouflage during the episode of the Trojan horse). 459. **ominous horse:** Trojan horse, by which the Greeks gained access to Troy. 461. **dismal:** Ill-omened. 462. **gules:** Red (a heraldic term). **trick'd:** Adorned, decorated. 464. **impasted:** Crusted, like a thick paste. **with . . . streets:** By the parching heat of the streets (because of the fires everywhere). 466. **their lord's:** Priam's. 467. **o'er-sized:** Covered as with size or glue. 475. **Repugnant:** Disobedient, resistant.

477. **fell:** Cruel. 478. **senseless Ilium:** Insensate Troy. 480. **his:** Its. 484. **painted:** Painted in a picture. 485. **like . . . matter:** As though poised indecisively between his intention and its fulfillment. 487. **against:** Just before. 488. **rack:** Mass of clouds. 491. **region:** Sky. 493. **Cyclops:** Giant armor makers in the smithy of Vulcan. 494. **proof eterne:** Eternal resistance to assault. 498. **synod:** Assembly. 499. **fellies:** Pieces of wood forming the rim of a wheel. 500. **nave:** Hub. 504. **jig:** Comic song and dance often given at the end of a play. 505. **Hecuba:** Wife of Priam. 506. **mobled:** Muffled. 510. **bisson rheum:** Blinding tears. **clout:** Cloth. 512. **o'er-teemed:** Worn out with bearing children. 515. **state:** Rule, managing. **pronounc'd:** Proclaimed.

When she saw Pyrrhus make malicious sport
In mincing with his sword her husband's limbs,
The instant burst of clamor that she made,
520 Unless things mortal move them not at all,
Would have made milch° the burning eyes of
   heaven,
And passion in the gods."
POLONIUS: Look whe'er° he has not turn'd his color and
has tears in 's eyes. Prithee, no more.
525 HAMLET: 'Tis well; I'll have thee speak out the rest of
this soon. Good my lord, will you see the players
well bestow'd?° Do you hear, let them be well us'd,
for they are the abstract° and brief chronicles of the
time. After your death you were better have a bad
530 epitaph than their ill report while you live.
POLONIUS: My lord, I will use them according to their
desert. *I'll give them what they deserve*
HAMLET: God's bodkin,° man, much better! Use every
man after his desert, and who shall scape whipping?
535 Use them after your own honor and dignity. The less
they deserve, the more merit is in your bounty. Take
them in. *no one deserves, but give them off*
POLONIUS: Come, sirs.
HAMLET: Follow him, friends. We'll hear a play tomor-
540 row. [*As they start to leave, Hamlet detains the First
Player.*] Dost thou hear me, old friend? Can you play
the Murder of Gonzago?
FIRST PLAYER: Ay, my lord.
HAMLET: We'll ha 't tomorrow night. You could, for
545 need, study a speech of some dozen or sixteen lines,
which I would set down and insert in 't, could you
not?
FIRST PLAYER: Ay, my lord.
HAMLET: Very well. Follow that lord, and look you
550 mock him not.—My good friends, I'll leave you till
night. You are welcome to Elsinore.
               (*Exeunt Polonius and Players.*)
ROSENCRANTZ: Good my lord!
               (*Exeunt [Rosencrantz and Guildenstern].*)
HAMLET: Ay, so, God buy you.—Now I am alone.
O, what a rogue and peasant slave am I!
555 Is it not monstrous that this player here,
But in a fiction, in a dream of passion,
Could force his soul so to his own conceit°
That from her working all his visage wann'd,°
Tears in his eyes, distraction in his aspect,
560 A broken voice, and his whole function suiting
With forms to his conceit?° And all for nothing!
For Hecuba!
What's Hecuba to him, or he to Hecuba, *mourning further lost sons*

Second Soliloquy

521. **milch:** Milky moist with tears. 523. **whe'er:** Whether.
527. **bestow'd:** Lodged. 528. **abstract:** Summary account.
533. **God's bodkin:** By God's (Christ's) little body, *bodykin*
(not to be confused with *bodkin,* dagger). 557. **conceit:**
Conception. 558. **wann'd:** Grew pale. 560–561. **his whole ...
conceit:** His whole being responded with actions to suit his
thought.

---

if he the player
H. felt like he wanted
to have just entered
be a show

That he should weep for her? What would he do,
Had he the motive and the cue for passion   565
That I have? He would drown the stage with tears
And cleave the general ear with horrid speech,
Make mad the guilty and appall the free,°
Confound the ignorant, and amaze indeed
The very faculties of eyes and ears. Yet I,   570
A dull and muddy-mettled° rascal, peak,°
Like John-a-dreams,° unpregnant of° my cause,
And can say nothing—no, not for a king
Upon whose property° and most dear life
A damn'd defeat was made. Am I a coward?   575
Who calls me villain? Breaks my pate across?
Plucks off my beard, and blows it in my face?
Tweaks me by the nose? Gives me the lie° i' th'
   throat,
As deep as to the lungs? Who does me this?
Ha, 'swounds, I should take it; for it cannot be   580
But I am pigeon-liver'd,° and lack gall
To make oppression bitter, or ere this
I should have fatted all the region kites°
With this slave's offal. Bloody, bawdy villain!
Remorseless, treacherous, lecherous, kindless° villain!   585
[O, vengeance!]
Why, what an ass am I! This is most brave,
That I, the son of a dear father murder'd,
Prompted to my revenge by heaven and hell,
Must, like a whore, unpack my heart with words,   590
And fall a-cursing, like a very drab,°
A stallion!° Fie upon 't, foh! About,° my brains!
Hum, I have heard
That guilty creatures sitting at a play
Have by the very cunning of the scene   595
Been struck so to the soul that presently°
They have proclaim'd their malefactions;
For murder, though it have no tongue, will speak
With most miraculous organ. I'll have these
   Players
Play something like the murder of my father   600
Before mine uncle. I'll observe his looks;
I'll tent° him to the quick. If 'a do blench,°
I know my course. The spirit that I have seen
May be the devil, and the devil hath power
T' assume a pleasing shape; yea, and perhaps   605
Out of my weakness and my melancholy,
As he is very potent with such spirits,°

He'll use the play to see if C. killed his father

568. **free:** Innocent. 571. **muddy-mettled:** Dull-spirited.
peak: Mope, pine. 572. **John-a-dreams:** Sleepy dreaming
idler. **unpregnant of:** Not quickened by. 574. **property:** The
crown; perhaps also character, quality. 578. **Gives me the
lie:** Calls me a liar. 581. **pigeon-liver'd:** The pigeon or dove
was popularly supposed to be mild because it secreted no gall.
583. **region kites:** Kites (birds of prey) of the air, from the
vicinity. 585. **kindless:** Unnatural. 591. **drab:** Prostitute.
592. **stallion:** Prostitute (male or female). (Many editors follow
the Folio reading of *scullion.*) **About:** About it, to work.
596. **presently:** At once. 602. **tent:** Probe. **blench:** Quail,
flinch. 607. **spirits:** Humors (of melancholy).

Abuses° me to damn me. I'll have grounds
More relative° than this. The play's the thing
610 Wherein I'll catch the conscience of the King.

                                          (*Exit.*)

{ACT III • Scene I}°

(*Enter King, Queen, Polonius, Ophelia, Rosencrantz, Guildenstern, Lords.*)

KING: And can you, by no drift of conference,°
    Get from him why he puts on this confusion,
    Grating so harshly all his days of quiet
    With turbulent and dangerous lunacy?
5   ROSENCRANTZ: He does confess he feels himself
        distracted,
    But from what cause 'a will by no means speak.
GUILDENSTERN: Nor do we find him forward° to be
        sounded,°
    But with a crafty madness keeps aloof
    When we would bring him on to some confession
    Of his true state.
10 QUEEN: Did he receive you well?
ROSENCRANTZ: Most like a gentleman.
GUILDENSTERN: But with much forcing of his
        disposition.°
ROSENCRANTZ: Niggard of question,° but of our
        demands
    Most free in his reply.
QUEEN: Did you assay° him
15 To any pastime?
ROSENCRANTZ: Madam, it so fell out that certain players
    We o'er-raught° on the way. Of these we told him,
    And there did seem in him a kind of joy
    To hear of it. They are here about the court,
20 And, as I think, they have already order
    This night to play before him.
POLONIUS: 'Tis most true,
    And he beseech'd me to entreat your Majesties
    To hear and see the matter.
KING: With all my heart, and it doth much content me
25 To hear him so inclin'd.
    Good gentlemen, give him a further edge,°
    And drive his purpose into these delights.
ROSENCRANTZ: We shall, my lord.
              (*Exeunt Rosencrantz and Guildenstern.*)
KING: Sweet Gertrude, leave us too,
    For we have closely° sent for Hamlet hither,
30 That he, as 'twere by accident, may here

Affront° Ophelia.
    Her father and myself, [lawful espials,°]
    Will so bestow ourselves that seeing, unseen,
    We may of their encounter frankly judge,
    And gather by him, as he is behav'd,   35
    If 't be th' affliction of his love or no
    That thus he suffers for.
QUEEN: I shall obey you.
    And for your part, Ophelia, I do wish
    That your good beauties be the happy cause
    Of Hamlet's wildness. So shall I hope your virtues 40
    Will bring him to his wonted way again,
    To both your honors.
OPHELIA: Madam, I wish it may.
                                          [*Exit Queen.*]
POLONIUS: Ophelia, walk you here.—Gracious,° so
        please you,
    We will bestow ourselves. [*To Ophelia.*] Read on
        this book,   [*Gives her a book.*]
    That show of such an exercise° may color°   45
    Your loneliness. We are oft to blame in this—
    'Tis too much prov'd°—that with devotion's visage
    And pious action we do sugar o'er
    The devil himself.
KING [*aside*]: O, 'tis too true!   50
    How smart a lash that speech doth give my
        conscience!
    The harlot's cheek, beautied with plast'ring art,
    Is not more ugly to° the thing° that helps it
    Than is my deed to my most painted word.
    O heavy burden!   55
POLONIUS: I hear him coming. Let's withdraw, my lord.
                        [*King and Polonius withdraw.°*]

(*Enter Hamlet. [Ophelia pretends to read a book.]*)

HAMLET: To be, or not to be, that is the question:
    Whether 'tis nobler in the mind to suffer
    The slings and arrows of outrageous fortune,
    Or to take arms against a sea of troubles,   60
    And by opposing end them. To die, to sleep—
    No more—and by a sleep to say we end
    The heart-ache and the thousand natural shocks
    That flesh is heir to. 'Tis a consummation
    Devoutly to be wish'd. To die, to sleep;   65
    To sleep, perchance to dream. Ay, there's the rub,°
    For in that sleep of death what dreams may come
    When we have shuffled° off this mortal coil,°

---

608. Abuses: Deludes. **609. relative:** Closely related, pertinent. **III, i. Location:** The castle. **1. drift of conference:** Direction of conversation. **7. forward:** Willing. **sounded:** Tested deeply. **12. disposition:** Inclination. **13. question:** Conversation. **14. assay:** Try to win. **17. o'er-raught:** Overtook and passed. **26. edge:** Incitement. **29. closely:** Privately.

31. Affront: Confront, meet. **32. espials:** Spies. **43. Gracious:** Your Grace (i.e., the King). **45. exercise:** Act of devotion. (The book she reads is a book of devotions, or prayers.) **color:** Give a plausible appearance to. **47. too much prov'd:** Too often shown to be true, too often practiced. **53. to:** Compared to. **thing:** I.e., the cosmetic. **56. [s.d.] withdraw:** The King and Polonius may retire behind an arras. The stage directions specify that they "enter" again near the end of the scene. **66. rub:** Literally, an obstacle in the game of bowls. **68. shuffled:** Sloughed, cast. **coil:** Turmoil.

70   Must give us pause. There's the respect°
     That makes calamity of so long life.°
     For who would bear the whips and scorns of time,
     Th' oppressor's wrong, the proud man's
         contumely,°
     The pangs of despis'd° love, the law's delay,
     The insolence of office,° and the spurns
75   That patient merit of th' unworthy takes,
     When he himself might his quietus° make
     With a bare bodkin?° Who would fardels° bear,
     To grunt and sweat under a weary life,
     But that the dread of something after death,
80   The undiscover'd country from whose bourn°
     No traveler returns, puzzles the will,
     And makes us rather bear those ills we have
     Than fly to others that we know not of?
     Thus conscience does make cowards of us all
85   And thus the native hue° of resolution
     Is sicklied o'er with the pale cast° of thought,
     And enterprises of great pitch° and moment°
     With this regard° their currents° turn awry,
     And lose the name of action.—Soft you now,
90   The fair Ophelia. Nymph, in thy orisons°
     Be all my sins rememb'red.
     OPHELIA: Good my lord,
     How does your honor for this many a day?
     HAMLET: I humbly thank you; well, well, well.
     OPHELIA: My lord, I have remembrances of yours,
95   That I have longed long to re-deliver.
        I pray you, now receive them.   [Offers tokens.]
     HAMLET: No, not I, I never gave you aught.
     OPHELIA: My honor'd lord, you know right well
         you did,
        And with them words of so sweet breath compos'd
100   As made these things more rich. Their perfume lost,
        Take these again, for to the noble mind
        Rich gifts wax poor when givers prove unkind.
        There, my lord.   [Gives tokens.]
     HAMLET: Ha, ha! Are you honest?°
105 OPHELIA: My lord?
     HAMLET: Are you fair?°
     OPHELIA: What means your lordship?
     HAMLET: That if you be honest and fair, your honesty°
        should admit no discourse° to your beauty.
110 OPHELIA: Could beauty, my lord, have better commerce°
        than with honesty?

HAMLET: Ay, truly, for the power of beauty will sooner
   transform honesty from what it is to a bawd than the
   force of honesty can translate beauty into his likeness. This was sometime° a paradox,° but now the   115
   time° gives it proof. I did love you once.
OPHELIA: Indeed, my lord, you made me believe so.
HAMLET: You should not have believ'd me, for virtue
   cannot so inoculate° our old stock but we shall relish
   of it.° I lov'd you not.   120
OPHELIA: I was the more deceiv'd.
HAMLET: Get thee to a nunn'ry.° Why wouldst thou be a
   breeder of sinners? I am myself indifferent honest;°
   but yet I could accuse me of such things that it were
   better my mother had not borne me: I am very proud, 125
   revengeful, ambitious, with more offenses at my
   beck° than I have thoughts to put them in, imagination to give them shape, or time to act them in. What
   should such fellows as I do crawling between earth
   and heaven? We are arrant knaves, all; believe none   130
   of us. Go thy ways to a nunn'ry. Where's your father?
OPHELIA: At home, my lord.
HAMLET: Let the doors be shut upon him, that he may
   play the fool nowhere but in 's own house.
   Farewell.   135
OPHELIA: O, help him, you sweet heavens!
HAMLET: If thou dost marry, I'll give thee this plague for
   thy dowry: be thou as chaste as ice, as pure as snow,
   thou shalt not escape calumny. Get thee to a nunn'ry,
   farewell. Or, if thou wilt needs marry, marry a fool,   140
   for wise men know well enough what monsters°
   you° make of them. To a nunn'ry, go, and quickly
   too. Farewell.
OPHELIA: Heavenly powers, restore him!
HAMLET: I have heard of your paintings too, well   145
   enough. God hath given you one face, and you make
   yourselves another. You jig,° and amble, and you lisp,
   you nickname God's creatures, and make your wantonness your ignorance.° Go to, I'll no more on 't;
   it hath made me mad. I say, we will have no moe   150
   marriage. Those that are married already—all but
   one—shall live. The rest shall keep as they are. To a
   nunn'ry, go.   (Exit.)
OPHELIA: O, what a noble mind is here o'erthrown!
   The courtier's, soldier's, scholar's, eye, tongue, sword, 155
   Th' expectancy and rose of the fair state,°

---

69. **respect:** Consideration.   70. **of . . . life:** So long-lived.
72. **contumely:** Insolent abuse.   73. **despis'd:** Rejected.
74. **office:** Officialdom.   **spurns:** Insults.   76. **quietus:** Acquittance; here, death.   77. **bodkin:** Dagger.   **fardels:** Burdens.
80. **bourn:** Boundary.   85. **native hue:** Natural color, complexion.   86. **cast:** Shade of color.   87. **pitch:** Height (as of a
falcon's flight).   **moment:** Importance.   88. **regard:** Respect,
consideration.   **currents:** Courses.   90. **orisons:** Prayers.
104. **honest:** (1) Truthful; (2) chaste.   106. **fair:** (1) Beautiful; (2) just, honorable.   108. **your honesty:** Your chastity.
109. **discourse:** Familiar dealings.   110. **commerce:** Dealings.

115. **sometime:** Formerly.   **paradox:** A view opposite to commonly held opinion.   115–116. **the time:** The present age.
119. **inoculate:** Graft, be engrafted to.   119–120. **but . . . it:**
That we do not still have about us a taste of the old stock
(i.e., retain our sinfulness).   122. **nunn'ry:** (1) Convent;
(2) brothel.   123. **indifferent honest:** Reasonably virtuous.
127. **beck:** Command.   141. **monsters:** An allusion to the
horns of a cuckold.   142. **you:** You women.   147. **jig:** Dance
and sing affectedly and wantonly.   148–149. **make . . . ignorance:** Excuse your affection on the grounds of your ignorance.
156. **Th' expectancy . . . state:** The hope and ornament of the
kingdom made fair (by him).

Telling the actor how to do that [handwritten]   ACT III • SCENE II

The glass of fashion and the mold of form,°
Th' observ'd of all observers,° quite, quite down!
And I, of ladies most deject and wretched,
160 That suck'd the honey of his music vows,
Now see that noble and most sovereign reason, *O, is going to get crazy* [handwritten]
Like sweet bells jangled, out of time and harsh,
That unmatch'd form and feature of blown° youth
Blasted with ecstasy.° O, woe is me,
165 T' have seen what I have seen, see what I see!

(*Enter King and Polonius.*)

KING: Love? His affections do not that way tend; *H. isn't lovesick,* [handwritten]
Nor what he spake, though it lack'd form a little,
Was not like madness. There's something in his soul *so he'll be sent to England to collect money* [handwritten]
O'er which his melancholy sits on brood,
170 And I do doubt° the hatch and the disclose°
Will be some danger; which for to prevent,
I have in quick determination
Thus set it down: he shall with speed to England,
For the demand of° our neglected tribute.
175 Haply the seas and countries different
With variable° objects shall expel
This something-settled° matter in his heart,
Whereon his brains still beating puts him thus
From fashion of himself.° What think you on 't?
180 POLONIUS: It shall do well. But yet do I believe
The origin and commencement of his grief
Sprung from neglected love.—How now,
     Ophelia?
You need not tell us what Lord Hamlet said;
We heard it all.—My lord, do as you please,
185 But, if you hold it fit, after the play
Let his queen mother all alone entreat him
To show his grief. Let her be round° with him;
And I'll be plac'd, so please you, in the ear
Of all their conference. If she find him not,
190 To England send him, or confine him where
Your wisdom best shall think.
KING: It shall be so.
Madness in great ones must not unwatch'd go.
                                   (*Exeunt.*)

{Scene II}°

(*Enter Hamlet and three of the Players.*)

HAMLET: Speak the speech, I pray you, as I pronounc'd
it to you, trippingly on the tongue. But if you mouth

---

it, as many of our players° do, I had as lief the town-
crier spoke my lines. Nor do not saw the air too
much with your hand, thus, but use all gently; for in 5
the very torrent, tempest, and, as I may say, whirlwind of your passion, you must acquire and beget
a temperance that may give it smoothness. O, it offends me to the soul to hear a robustious° periwig-
pated° fellow tear a passion to tatters, to very rags, to 10
split the ears of the groundlings,° who for the most
part are capable of° nothing but inexplicable dumb-
shows and noise. I would have such a fellow whipp'd
for o'er-doing Termagant.° It out-herods Herod.°
Pray you, avoid it.   15
FIRST PLAYER: I warrant your honor.
HAMLET: Be not too tame neither, but let your own discretion be your tutor. Suit the action to the word, the
word to the action, with this special observance, that
you o'erstep not the modesty of nature. For anything 20
so o'erdone is from° the purpose of playing, whose
end, both at the first and now, was and is, to hold, as
't were, the mirror up to nature, to show virtue her
feature, scorn her own image, and the very age and
body of the time his° form and pressure.° Now this 25
overdone, or come tardy off,° though it makes the
unskillful laugh, cannot but make the judicious
grieve, the censure of which one° must in your allowance o'erweigh a whole theater of others. O, there
be players that I have seen play, and heard others 30
praise, and that highly, not to speak it profanely,
that, neither having th' accent of Christians nor the
gait of Christian, pagan, nor man, have so strutted
and bellow'd that I have thought some of nature's
journeymen° had made men and not made them 35
well, they imitated humanity so abominably.
FIRST PLAYER: I hope we have reform'd that indifferently°
with us, sir.
HAMLET: O, reform it altogether. And let those that play
your clowns speak no more than is set down for 40
them; for there be of them° that will themselves
laugh, to set on some quantity of barren° spectators
to laugh too, though in the mean time some necessary question of the play be then to be consider'd.

---

157. The glass . . . form: The mirror of fashion and the pattern
of courtly behavior. 158. observ'd . . . observers: The center
of attention and honor in the court. 163. blown: Bloom-
ing. 164. ecstasy: Madness. 170. doubt: Fear. disclose:
Disclosure. 174. For . . . of: To demand. 176. variable:
Various. 177. something-settled: Somewhat settled. 179.
From . . . himself: Out of his natural manner. 187. round:
Blunt. III, ii. Location: The castle.

3. our players: Indefinite use (i.e., players nowadays). 9. robus-
tious: Violent, boisterous. 9–10. periwig-pated: Wearing a wig.
11. groundlings: Spectators who paid least and stood in the
yard of the theater. 12. capable of: Susceptible of being influenced by. 14. Termagant: A god of the Saracens. (In the
St. Nicholas play, one of his worshipers, leaving him in charge
of goods, returns to find them stolen, whereupon he beats the
god or idol, which howls vociferously.) Herod: Herod of
Jewry. (In *The Slaughter of the Innocents* and other cycle plays,
the part was played with great noise and fury.) 21. from: Contrary to. 25. his: Its. pressure: Stamp, impressed character.
26. come tardy off: Inadequately done. 28. the censure . . .
one: The judgment of even one of whom. 35. journeymen:
Laborers not yet masters in their trade. 37. indifferently:
Tolerably. 41. of them: Some among them. 42. barren: I.e.,
of wit.

45 That's villainous, and shows a most pitiful ambition
 in the fool that uses it. Go, make you ready.

          [Exeunt Players.]

(Enter Polonius, Guildenstern, and Rosencrantz.)

 How now, my lord? Will the King hear this piece
 of work?
POLONIUS: And the Queen too, and that presently.°
50 HAMLET: Bid the players make haste.

         [Exit Polonius.]

 Will you two help to hasten them?
ROSENCRANTZ: Ay, my lord.   *(Exeunt they two.)*
HAMLET: What ho, Horatio!

(Enter Horatio.)

HORATIO: Here, sweet lord, at your service.
HAMLET: Horatio, thou art e'en as just a man
55 As e'er my conversation cop'd withal.°
HORATIO: O, my dear lord—
HAMLET: Nay, do not think I flatter;
 For what advancement may I hope from thee
 That no revenue hast but thy good spirits,
 To feed and clothe thee? Why should the poor be
  flatter'd?
60 No, let the candied° tongue lick absurd pomp,
 And crook the pregnant° hinges of the knee
 Where thrift° may follow fawning. Dost thou hear?
 Since my dear soul was mistress of her choice
 And could of men distinguish her election,
65 Sh' hath seal'd thee for herself, for thou hast been
 As one, in suff'ring all, that suffers nothing,
 A man that Fortune's buffets and rewards
 Hast ta'en with equal thanks; and blest are those
 Whose blood° and judgment are so well commeddled°
70 That they are not a pipe for Fortune's finger
 To sound what stop° she please. Give me that man
 That is not passion's slave, and I will wear him
 In my heart's core, ay, in my heart of heart,
 As I do thee.—Something too much of this.—
75 There is a play tonight before the King.
 One scene of it comes near the circumstance
 Which I have told thee of my father's death.
 I prithee, when thou seest that act afoot,
 Even with the very comment of thy soul°
80 Observe my uncle. If his occulted° guilt
 Do not itself unkennel in one speech,
 It is a damned° ghost that we have seen,
 And my imaginations are as foul
 As Vulcan's stithy.° Give him heedful note,

both will watch him and compare

 For I mine eyes will rivet to his face,   85
 And after we will both our judgments join
 In censure of his seeming.°
HORATIO: Well, my lord.
 If 'a steal aught the whilst this play is playing,
 And scape detecting, I will pay the theft.

*([Flourish.] Enter trumpets and kettledrums, King,
Queen, Polonius, Ophelia, [Rosencrantz, Guildenstern,
and other Lords, with Guards carrying torches].)*

HAMLET: They are coming to the play. I must be idle. Get 90
 you a place. *[The King, Queen, and courtiers sit.]*
KING: How fares our cousin Hamlet?
HAMLET: Excellent, i' faith, of the chameleon's dish:°
 I eat the air, promise-cramm'd. You cannot feed
 capons so.   95

*This so in ds [?]
the a gecoby [?]*

KING: I have nothing with° this answer, Hamlet. These
 words are not mine.°
HAMLET: No, nor mine now. *[To Polonius.]* My lord, you
 played once i' th' university, you say?
POLONIUS: That did I, my lord; and was accounted a 100
 good actor.
HAMLET: What did you enact?
POLONIUS: I did enact Julius Caesar. I was killed i' th'
 Capitol; Brutus kill'd me.
HAMLET: It was a brute part of him to kill so capital a 105
 calf there. Be the players ready?
ROSENCRANTZ: Ay, my lord; they stay upon your
 patience.
QUEEN: Come hither, my dear Hamlet, sit by me.
HAMLET: No, good mother, here's metal more attractive. 110
POLONIUS *[to the King]*: O, ho, do you mark that?
HAMLET: Lady, shall I lie in your lap?

        [Lying down at Ophelia's feet.]

OPHELIA: No, my lord.
[HAMLET: I mean, my head upon your lap?
OPHELIA: Ay, my lord.]   115
HAMLET: Do you think I meant country° matters?
OPHELIA: I think nothing, my lord.
HAMLET: That's a fair thought to lie between maids' legs.
OPHELIA: What is, my lord?
HAMLET: Nothing.   120
OPHELIA: You are merry, my lord.
HAMLET: Who, I?
OPHELIA: Ay, my lord.
HAMLET: O God, your only jig-maker.° What should a
 man do but be merry? For look you how cheerfully 125
 my mother looks, and my father died within 's° two
 hours.

---

49. presently: At once. **55. my . . . withal:** My contact with
people provided opportunity for encounter with. **60. candied:**
Sugared, flattering. **61. pregnant:** Compliant. **62. thrift:**
Profit. **69. blood:** Passion. **commeddled:** Commingled.
71. stop: Hole in a wind instrument for controlling the
sound. **79. very . . . soul:** Inward and sagacious criticism.
80. occulted: Hidden. **82. damned:** In league with Satan.
84. stithy: Smithy, place of stiths (anvils).

87. censure of his seeming: Judgment of his appearance or behavior. **93. chameleon's dish:** Chameleons were supposed to
feed on air. Hamlet deliberately misinterprets the King's *fares*
as *feeds*. By his phrase *eat the air* he also plays on the idea of
feeding himself with the promise of succession, of being the
heir. **96. have . . . with:** Make nothing of it. **97. are not mine:**
Do not respond to what I asked. **116. country:** With a bawdy
pun. **124. only jig-maker:** Very best composer of jigs (song
and dance). **126. within 's:** Within this.

OPHELIA: Nay, 'tis twice two months, my lord.

HAMLET: So long? Nay then, let the devil wear black for
130   I'll have a suit of sables.° O heavens! Die two months
ago, and not forgotten yet? Then there's hope a great
man's memory may outlive his life half a year. But,
by 'r lady, 'a must build churches, then, or else shall
'a suffer not thinking on,° with the hobby-horse,
135   whose epitaph is "For, O, for, O, the hobby-horse is
forgot."°

(*The trumpets sound. Dumb show follows.*)

(*Enter a King and a Queen [very lovingly]; the Queen
embracing him, and he her. [She kneels and makes show
of protestation unto him.] He takes her up, and declines
his head upon her neck. He lies him down upon a bank
of flowers. She, seeing him asleep, leaves him. Anon
comes in another man, takes off his crown, kisses it,
pours poison in the sleeper's ears, and leaves him. The
Queen returns; finds the King dead, makes passionate
action. The Poisoner, with some three or four, come in
again, seem to condole with her. The dead body is carried away. The Poisoner woos the Queen with gifts; she
seems harsh awhile but in the end accepts love.*)

                                                    [*Exeunt.*]

OPHELIA: What means this, my lord?

HAMLET: Marry, this' miching mallecho;° it means
mischief.

140   OPHELIA: Belike° this show imports the argument° of
the play.

(*Enter Prologue.*)

HAMLET: We shall know by this fellow. The players cannot keep counsel;° they'll tell all.

OPHELIA: Will 'a tell us what this show meant?

145   HAMLET: Ay, or any show that you will show him. Be not
you° asham'd to show, he'll not shame to tell you
what it means.

OPHELIA: You are naught, you are naught.° I'll mark the
play.

150   PROLOGUE: For us, and for our tragedy,
Here stooping° to your clemency,
We beg your hearing patiently.   [*Exit.*]

HAMLET: Is this a prologue, or the posy of a ring?°

OPHELIA: 'Tis brief, my lord.

155   HAMLET: As woman's love.

(*Enter [two Players as] King and Queen.*)

PLAYER KING: Full thirty times hath Phoebus' cart°
gone round
Neptune's salt wash° and Tellus'° orbed ground,
And thirty dozen moons with borrowed° sheen
About the world have times twelve thirties been,
Since love our hearts and Hymen° did our hands   160
Unite commutual° in most sacred bands.

PLAYER QUEEN: So many journeys may the sun and
moon
Make us again count o'er ere love be done!
But, woe is me, you are so sick of late,
So far from cheer and from your former state,   165
That I distrust you. Yet, though I distrust,°
Discomfort you, my lord, it nothing° must.
For women's fear and love hold quantity;°
In neither aught, or in extremity.
Now, what my love is, proof° hath made you know,   170
And as my love is siz'd, my fear is so.
Where love is great, the littlest doubts are fear;
Where little fears grow great, great love grows
there.

PLAYER KING: Faith, I must leave thee, love, and
shortly too;
My operant° powers their functions leave to do.°   175
And thou shalt live in this fair world behind,
Honor'd, belov'd; and haply one as kind
For husband shalt thou—

PLAYER QUEEN: O, confound the rest!
Such love must needs be treason in my breast.
In second husband let me be accurst!   180
None wed the second but who kill'd the first.

HAMLET: Wormwood, wormwood.

PLAYER QUEEN: The instances° that second marriage
move°
Are base respects of thrift,° but none of love.
A second time I kill my husband dead,   185
When second husband kisses me in bed.

PLAYER KING: I do believe you think what now you
speak,
But what we do determine oft we break.
Purpose is but the slave to memory,°
Of violent birth, but poor validity,°   190
Which now, like fruit unripe, sticks on the tree,
But fall unshaken when they mellow be.

---

130. **suit of sables:** Garments trimmed with the fur of the sable
and hence suited for a wealthy person, not a mourner (with
a pun on *sable*, black).   134. **suffer . . . on:** Undergo oblivion.   135–136. **"For . . . forgot":** Verse of a song occurring
also in *Love's Labor's Lost*, III, i, 30. The hobby-horse was
a character made up to resemble a horse, appearing in the
Morris dance and such May-game sports. This song laments
the disappearance of such customs under pressure from the
Puritans.   138. **this' miching mallecho:** This is sneaking mischief.   140. **Belike:** Probably.   **argument:** Plot.   143. **counsel:**
Secret.   145–146. **Be not you:** If you are not.   148. **naught:**
Indecent.   151. **stooping:** Bowing.   153. **posy . . . ring:** Brief
motto in verse inscribed in a ring.

156. **Phoebus' cart:** The sun god's chariot.   157. **salt wash:**
The sea. **Tellus:** Goddess of the earth, of the *orbed ground*.
158. **borrowed:** Reflected.   160. **Hymen:** God of matrimony.
161. **commutual:** Mutually.   166. **distrust:** Am anxious about.
167. **nothing:** Not at all.   168. **hold quantity:** Keep proportion with one another.   170. **proof:** Experience.   175.
operant: Active. **leave to do:** Cease to perform.   183.
instances: Motives. **move:** Motivate.   184. **base . . . thrift:** Ignoble considerations of material prosperity.   189. **Purpose . . .
memory:** Our good intentions are subject to forgetfulness.
190. **validity:** Strength, durability.

Most necessary 'tis that we forget
To pay ourselves what to ourselves is debt.°
195 What to ourselves in passion we propose,
The passion ending, doth the purpose lose.
The violence of either grief or joy
Their own enactures° with themselves destroy.
Where joy most revels, grief doth most lament;
200 Grief joys, joy grieves, on slender accident.
This world is not for aye,° nor 'tis not strange
That even our loves should with our fortunes
      change;
For 'tis a question left us yet to prove,
Whether love lead fortune, or else fortune love.
205 The great man down, you mark his favorite flies;
The poor advanc'd makes friends of enemies.
And hitherto doth love on fortune tend;
For who not needs° shall never lack a friend,
And who in want° a hollow friend doth try,°
210 Directly seasons him° his enemy.
But, orderly to end where I begun,
Our wills and fates do so contrary run
That our devices still° are overthrown;
Our thoughts are ours, their ends° none of our own.
215 So think thou wilt no second husband wed,
But die thy thoughts when thy first lord is dead.

PLAYER QUEEN: Nor earth to me give food, nor
      heaven light,
Sport and repose lock from me day and night,
To desperation turn my trust and hope,
220 An anchor's cheer° in prison be my scope!°
Each opposite° that blanks° the face of joy
Meet what I would have well and it destroy!
Both here and hence° pursue me lasting strife,
If, once a widow, ever I be wife!

225 HAMLET: If she should break it now!

PLAYER KING: 'Tis deeply sworn. Sweet, leave me here
      awhile;
My spirits grow dull, and fain I would beguile
The tedious day with sleep.   [*Sleeps.*]

PLAYER QUEEN: Sleep rock thy brain,
230   And never come mischance between us twain!

                                               [*Exit.*]

HAMLET: Madam, how like you this play?

QUEEN: The lady doth protest too much, methinks.

HAMLET: O, but she'll keep her word.

KING: Have you heard the argument?° Is there no
235   offense in 't?

[handwritten: Gertrude doesn't like the play]

193–194. **Most . . . debt:** It's inevitable that in time we forget
the obligations we have imposed on ourselves. 198. **enac-
tures:** Fulfillments. 201. **aye:** Ever. 208. **who not needs:**
He who is not in need (of wealth). 209. **who in want:** He
who is in need. **try:** Test (his generosity). 210. **seasons him:** Rip-
ens him into. 213. **devices still:** Intentions continually. 214.
ends: Results. 220. **anchor's cheer:** Anchorite's or hermit's
fare. **my scope:** The extent of my happiness. 222. **opposite:**
Adverse thing. **blanks:** Causes to blanch or grow pale. 223.
hence: In the life hereafter. 234. **argument:** Plot.

HAMLET: No, no, they do but jest, poison in jest; no
offense i' th' world.

KING: What do you call the play?

HAMLET: "The Mouse-trap." Marry, how? Tropically.°
240 This play is the image of a murder done in Vienna.
Gonzago is the Duke's name; his wife, Baptista. You
shall see anon. 'Tis a knavish piece of work, but what
of that? Your Majesty, and we that have free° souls, it
touches us not. Let the gall'd jade° winch,° our with-
245 ers° are unwrung.°

(*Enter Lucianus.*)

This is one Lucianus, nephew to the King.

OPHELIA: You are as good as a chorus,° my lord.

HAMLET: I could interpret between you and your love, if
I could see the puppets dallying.°

250 OPHELIA: You are keen, my lord, you are keen.

HAMLET: It would cost you a groaning to take off mine
edge.

OPHELIA: Still better, and worse.°

HAMLET: So° you mistake° your husbands. Begin, mur-
255 derer, leave thy damnable faces, and begin. Come,
the croaking raven doth bellow for revenge.

LUCIANUS: Thoughts black, hands apt, drugs fit, and time
agreeing,
Confederate season,° else no creature seeing,
260 Thou mixture rank, of midnight weeds collected,
With Hecate's ban° thrice blasted, thrice infected,
Thy natural magic and dire property
On wholesome life usurp immediately.
               [*Pours the poison into the sleeper's ears.*]

HAMLET: 'A poisons him i' th' garden for his estate. His
265 name's Gonzago. The story is extant, and written in
very choice Italian. You shall see anon how the murderer gets the love of Gonzago's wife.

               [*Claudius rises.*]

OPHELIA: The King rises.

[HAMLET: What, frighted with false fire?°]

QUEEN: How fares my lord?
270 POLONIUS: Give o'er the play.

239. **Tropically:** Figuratively. (The first quarto reading, *trapi-
cally,* suggests a pun on *trap* in *Mouse-trap.*) 243. **free:** Guiltless. 244. **gall'd jade:** Horse whose hide is rubbed by saddle
or harness. **winch:** Wince. 244–245. **withers:** The part between the horse's shoulder blades. 245. **unwrung:** Not rubbed
sore. 247. **chorus:** In many Elizabethan plays, the forthcoming action was explained by an actor known as the "chorus";
at a puppet show, the actor who spoke the dialogue was
known as an "interpreter," as indicated by the lines following.
249. **dallying:** With sexual suggestion, continued in *keen* (i.e.,
sexually aroused), *groaning* (i.e., moaning in pregnancy), and
edge (i.e., sexual desire or impetuosity). 253. **Still . . . worse:**
More keen-witted and less decorous. 254. **So:** Even thus (in
marriage). **mistake:** Mistake, take erringly, falseheartedly.
259. **Confederate season:** The time and occasion conspiring (to
assist the murderer). 261. **Hecate's ban:** The curse of Hecate,
the goddess of witchcraft. 269. **false fire:** The blank discharge
of a gun loaded with powder but not shot.

KING: Give me some light. Away!
POLONIUS: Lights, lights, lights!

(Exeunt all but Hamlet and Horatio.)

HAMLET: "Why, let the strucken deer go weep, The hart
275   ungalled° play.
        For some must watch,° while some must sleep;
            Thus runs the world away."°
        Would not this,° sir, and a forest of feathers°—if the
        rest of my fortunes turn Turk with° me—with two
280   Provincial roses° on my raz'd° shoes, get me a fellow-
        ship in a cry of players?°
HORATIO: Half a share.
HAMLET: A whole one, I.
        "For thou dost know, O Damon dear,
285   This realm dismantled° was
        Of Jove himself, and now reigns here
            A very, very—pajock."°
HORATIO: You might have rhym'd.
HAMLET: O good Horatio, I'll take the ghost's word for
290   a thousand pound. Didst perceive?
HORATIO: Very well, my lord.
HAMLET: Upon the talk of pois'ning?
HORATIO: I did very well note him.
HAMLET: Ah, ha! Come, some music! Come, the
295   recorders!°
        "For if the King like not the comedy,
        Why then, belike, he likes it not, perdy"°
        Come, some music!

(Enter Rosencrantz and Guildenstern.)

GUILDENSTERN: Good my lord, vouchsafe me a word
300   with you.
HAMLET: Sir, a whole history.
GUILDENSTERN: The King, sir—
HAMLET: Ay, sir, what of him?
GUILDENSTERN: Is in his retirement marvelous dis-
305   temp'red.
HAMLET: With drink, sir?
GUILDENSTERN: No, my lord, with choler.°
HAMLET: Your wisdom should show itself more richer to
        signify this to the doctor, for for me to put him to
310   his purgation would perhaps plunge him into more
        choler.

GUILDENSTERN: Good my lord, put your discourse into
        some frame° and start not so wildly from my affair.
HAMLET: I am tame, sir. Pronounce.
GUILDENSTERN: The Queen, your mother, in most great   315
        affliction of spirit, hath sent me to you.
HAMLET: You are welcome.
GUILDENSTERN: Nay, good my lord, this courtesy is not
        of the right breed. If it shall please you to make me
        a wholesome answer, I will do your mother's com-   320
        mandment; if not, your pardon° and my return shall
        be the end of my business.
HAMLET: Sir, I cannot.
ROSENCRANTZ: What, my lord?
HAMLET: Make you a wholesome answer; my wit's dis-   325
        eas'd. But, sir, such answer as I can make, you shall
        command, or rather, as you say, my mother. There-
        fore no more, but to the matter. My mother, you
        say—
ROSENCRANTZ: Then thus she says: your behavior hath   330
        struck her into amazement and admiration.°
HAMLET: O wonderful son, that can so stonish a mother!
        But is there no sequel at the heels of this mother's
        admiration? Impart.
ROSENCRANTZ: She desires to speak with you in her   335
        closet,° ere you go to bed.
HAMLET: We shall obey, were she ten times our mother.
        Have you any further trade with us?
ROSENCRANTZ: My lord, you once did love me.
HAMLET: And do still, by these pickers and stealers.°   340
ROSENCRANTZ: Good my lord, what is your cause of dis-
        temper? You do surely bar the door upon your own
        liberty, if you deny your griefs to your friend.
HAMLET: Sir, I lack advancement.
ROSENCRANTZ: How can that be, when you have the   345
        voice of the King himself for your succession in
        Denmark?
HAMLET: Ay, sir, but "While the grass grows"°—the
        proverb is something° musty.

(Enter the Players with recorders.)

        O, the recorders! Let me see one. [*He takes a recorder.*]   350
        To withdraw° with you: why do you go about to re-
        cover the wind° of me, as if you would drive me into
        a toil?°
GUILDENSTERN: O, my lord, if my duty be too bold, my
        love is too unmannerly.°   355
HAMLET: I do not well understand that. Will you play
        upon this pipe?

---

275. **ungalled:** Unafflicted. 276. **watch:** Remain awake.
274–277. **Why . . . away:** Probably from an old ballad, with
allusion to the popular belief that a wounded deer retires
to weep and die; cf. *As You Like It,* II, i, 66. 278. **this:** The
play. **feathers:** Allusion to the plumes that Elizabethan actors
were fond of wearing. 279. **turn Turk with:** Turn renegade
against, go back on. 280. **Provincial roses:** Rosettes of ribbon like the roses of a part of France. **raz'd:** With ornamental slashing. 280–281. **fellowship . . . players:** Partnership in
a theatrical company. 285. **dismantled:** Stripped, divested.
287. **pajock:** Peacock, a bird with a bad reputation (here substituted for the obvious rhyme-word *ass*). 295. **recorders:** Wind
instruments like the flute. 297. **perdy:** A corruption of the
French *par dieu,* by God. 307. **choler:** Anger. (But Hamlet takes
the word in its more basic humors sense of bilious disorder.)

313. **frame:** Order. 321. **pardon:** Permission to depart.
331. **admiration:** Wonder. 336. **closet:** Private chamber.
340. **pickers and stealers:** Hands (so called from the catechism, "to keep my hands from picking and stealing").
348. **While . . . grows:** The rest of the proverb is "the silly horse
starves"; Hamlet may not live long enough to succeed to the
kingdom. 349. **something:** Somewhat. 351. **withdraw:** Speak
privately. 352. **recover the wind:** Get the windward
side. 353. **toil:** Snare. 354–355. **if . . . unmannerly:** If I am
using an unmannerly boldness, it is my love that occasions it.

GUILDENSTERN: My lord, I cannot.

HAMLET: I pray you.

360 GUILDENSTERN: Believe me, I cannot.

HAMLET: I do beseech you.

GUILDENSTERN: I know no touch of it, my lord.

HAMLET: It is as easy as lying. Govern these ventages°
with your fingers and thumb, give it breath with your
365 mouth, and it will discourse most eloquent music.
Look you, these are the stops.

GUILDENSTERN: But these cannot I command to any
utt'rance of harmony; I have not the skill.

HAMLET: Why, look you now, how unworthy a thing
370 you make of me! You would play upon me, you
would seem to know my stops, you would pluck out
the heart of my mystery, you would sound me from
my lowest note to the top of my compass,° and there
is much music, excellent voice, in this little organ,°
375 yet cannot you make it speak. 'Sblood, do you think
I am easier to be play'd on than a pipe? Call me what
instrument you will, though you can fret° me, you
cannot play upon me.

"play me for a fool"

(*Enter Polonius.*)

God bless you, sir!

380 POLONIUS: My lord, the Queen would speak with you,
and presently.°

HAMLET: Do you see yonder cloud that's almost in shape
of a camel?

POLONIUS: By th' mass, and 'tis like a camel, indeed.

385 HAMLET: Methinks it is like a weasel.

POLONIUS: It is back'd like a weasel.

*Polonius would agree
any thing*

HAMLET: Or like a whale?

POLONIUS: Very like a whale.

HAMLET: Then I will come to my mother by and by.°

390 [*Aside.*] They fool me° to the top of my bent.°—I
will come by and by.

POLONIUS: I will say so.   [*Exit.*]

HAMLET: "By and by" is easily said. Leave me, friends.

[*Exeunt all but Hamlet.*]

'Tis now the very witching time° of night,
395 When churchyards yawn and hell itself breathes out
Contagion to this world. Now could I drink hot
blood,
And do such bitter business as the day
Would quake to look on. Soft, now to my mother.
O heart, lose not thy nature! Let not ever
400 The soul of Nero° enter this firm bosom.

Let me be cruel, not unnatural;
I will speak daggers to her, but use none.
My tongue and soul in this be hypocrites:
How in my words somever° she be shent,°
To give them seals° never, my soul, consent!   405

(*Exit.*)

{Scene III}°

(*Enter King, Rosencrantz, and Guildenstern.*)

*he's sending
R & G
w/ Hamlet
to England*

KING: I like him not, nor stands it safe with us
To let his madness range. Therefore prepare you.
I your commission will forthwith dispatch,°
And he to England shall along with you.
The terms° of our estate° may not endure   5
Hazard so near 's as doth hourly grow
Out of his brows.°

GUILDENSTERN: We will ourselves provide.
Most holy and religious fear it is
To keep those many many bodies safe
That live and feed upon your Majesty.   10

ROSENCRANTZ: The single and peculiar° life is bound
With all the strength and armor of the mind
To keep itself from noyance,° but much more
That spirit upon whose weal depends and rests
The lives of many. The cess° of majesty   15
Dies not alone, but like a gulf° doth draw
What's near it with it; or it is a messy wheel
Fix'd on the summit of the highest mount,
To whose huge spokes ten thousand lesser things
Are mortis'd and adjoin'd, which, when it falls,   20
Each small annexment, petty consequence,
Attends° the boist'rous ruin. Never alone
Did the King sigh, but with a general groan.

KING: Arm° you, I pray you, to this speedy voyage,
For we will fetters put about this fear,   25
Which now goes too free-footed.

ROSENCRANTZ: We will haste us.

(*Exeunt Gentlemen [Rosencrantz
and Guildenstern].*)

(*Enter Polonius.*)

POLONIUS: My lord, he's going to his mother's closet.
Behind the arras° I'll convey myself

↑ tapestry

---

404. How . . . somever: However much by my words. shent:
Rebuked. 405. give them seals: Confirm them with deeds.
III, iii. Location: The castle. 3. dispatch: Prepare, cause to be
drawn up. 5. terms: Condition, circumstances. our estate:
My royal position. 7. brows: Effronteries, threatening frowns
(?), brain (?). 11. single and peculiar: Individual and private.
13. noyance: Harm. 15. cess: Decease. 16. gulf: Whirlpool.
22. Attends: Participates in. 24. Arm: Prepare. 28. arras:
Screen of tapestry placed around the walls of household apartments. (On the Elizabethan stage, the arras was presumably over
a door or discovery space in the tiring-house façade.)

---

363. ventages: Stops of the recorder. 373. compass: Range (of
voice). 374. organ: Musical instrument. 377. fret: Irritate
(with a quibble, or pun, on *fret* meaning the piece of wood,
gut, or metal that regulates the fingering on an instrument). 381.
presently: At once. 389. by and by: Immediately. 390. fool
me: Make me play the fool. top of my bent: Limit of my ability or endurance (literally, the extent to which a bow may be
bent). 394. witching time: Time when spells are cast and evil is
abroad. 400. Nero: Murderer of his mother, Agrippina.

Is that supposed to be a skull?

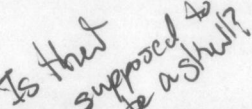

[TOP LEFT] Michael Pennington as Hamlet. [TOP MIDDLE] A scene from the Royal Shakespeare Company's 1980 production. [TOP RIGHT] The grave-digger holds up Yorick's skull as Hamlet and Horatio (Tom Wilkinson) look on. [BOTTOM LEFT] Hamlet, played by Kenneth Branagh, duels Laertes, played by Michael Maloney. Branagh directed this 1996 film. [BOTTOM RIGHT] Carol Royle as Ophelia with Hamlet in the nunnery scene.

To hear the process.° I'll warrant she'll tax him
      home,°
30   And, as you said, and wisely was it said,
     'Tis meet that some more audience than a mother,
     Since nature makes them partial, should o'erhear
     The speech, of vantage.° Fare you well, my liege.
     I'll call upon you ere you go to bed,
     And tell you what I know.
35   KING: Thanks, dear my lord.
                              (*Exit [Polonius].*)
     O, my offense is rank, it smells to heaven;
     It hath the primal eldest curse° upon 't,
     A brother's murder. Pray can I not,
     Though inclination be as sharp as will.°
40   My stronger guilt defeats my strong intent,
     And, like a man to double business bound,
     I stand in pause where I shall first begin,
     And both neglect. What if this cursed hand
     Were thicker than itself with brother's blood,
45   Is there not rain enough in the sweet heavens
     To wash it white as snow? Whereto serves mercy
     But to confront the visage of offense?°
     And what's in prayer but this twofold force,
     To be forestalled° ere we come to fall,
50   Or pardon'd being down? Then I'll look up;
     My fault is past. But, O, what form of prayer
     Can serve my turn? "Forgive me my foul
        murder"?
     That cannot be, since I am still possess'd
     Of those effects for which I did the murder,
55   My crown, mine own ambition, and my queen.
     May one be pardon'd and retain th' offense?
     In the corrupted currents° of this world
     Offense's gilded hand° may shove by justice,
     And oft 'tis seen the wicked prize° itself
60   Buys out the law. But 'tis not so above.
     There is no shuffling,° there the action lies°
     In his° true nature, and we ourselves compell'd,
     Even to the teeth and forehead° of our faults,
     To give in evidence. What then? What rests?°
65   Try what repentance can. What can it not?
     Yet what can it, when one cannot repent?
     O wretched state! O bosom black as death!
     O limed° soul, that, struggling to be free,

[handwritten: He doesn't just confessed]

Art more engag'd!° Help, angels! Make assay.°
Bow, stubborn knees, and heart with strings of steel,   70
Be soft as sinews of the new-born babe!
All may be well.
                              [*He kneels.*]

(*Enter Hamlet [with sword drawn].*)

HAMLET: Now might I do it pat,° now 'a is a-praying;
   And now I'll do 't. And so 'a goes to heaven;
   And so am I reveng'd. That would be scann'd:°   75
   A villain kills my father, and for that,
   I, his sole son, do this same villain send
   To heaven.
   Why, this is hire and salary, not revenge.
   'A took my father grossly,° full of bread,°   80
   With all his crimes broad blown,° as flush° as
      May;
   And how his audit° stands who knows save
      heaven?
   But in our circumstance and course° of thought,
   'Tis heavy with him. And am I then reveng'd,
   To take him in the purging of his soul,   85
   When he is fit and season'd for his passage?
   No!
   Up, sword, and know thou a more horrid hent.°
                              [*Puts up his sword.*]
   When he is drunk asleep, or in his rage,
   Or in th' incestuous pleasure of his bed,   90
   At game a-swearing, or about some act
   That has no relish of salvation in 't—
   Then trip him, that his heels may kick at heaven,
   And that his soul may be as damn'd and black
   As hell, whereto it goes. My mother stays.   95
   This physic° but prolongs thy sickly days.   (*Exit.*)
KING: My words fly up, my thoughts remain below.
   Words without thoughts never to heaven go.
                              (*Exit.*)

[handwritten: trying to confess]
[handwritten: He can't kill him while confessing he wouldn't go to hell then]

{Scene IV}°

(*Enter [Queen] Gertrude and Polonius.*)

POLONIUS: 'A will come straight. Look you lay° home
      to him.
   Tell him his pranks have been too broad° to bear
      with,

---

29. **process:** Proceedings.   **tax him home:** Reprove him severely.
33. **of vantage:** From an advantageous place.   37. **primal eldest curse:** The curse of Cain, the first murderer; he killed his brother Abel.   39. **Though . . . will:** Though my desire is as strong as my determination.   46–47. **Whereto . . . offense:** For what function does mercy serve other than to undo the effects of sin?   49. **forestalled:** Prevented (from sinning).   57. **currents:** Courses.   58. **gilded hand:** Hand offering gold as a bribe.   59. **wicked prize:** Prize won by wickedness.   61. **shuffling:** Escape by trickery.   **the action lies:** The accusation is made manifest, comes up for consideration (a legal metaphor).   62. **his:** Its.   63. **teeth and forehead:** Face to face, concealing nothing.   64. **rests:** Remains.   68. **limed:** Caught as with birdlime, a sticky substance used to ensnare birds.

69. **engag'd:** Embedded.   **assay:** Trial.   73. **pat:** Opportunely.
75. **would be scann'd:** Needs to be looked into.   80. **grossly:** Not spiritually prepared.   **full of bread:** Enjoying his worldly pleasures. (See Ezek. 16:49.)   81. **crimes broad blown:** Sins in full bloom.   **flush:** Lusty.   82. **audit:** Account.   83. **in . . . course:** As we see it in our mortal situation.   88. **know . . . hent:** Await to be grasped by me on a more horrid occasion.
96. **physic:** Purging (by prayer).   **III, iv. Location:** The queen's private chamber.   1. **lay:** Thrust (i.e., reprove him soundly).
2. **broad:** Unrestrained.

And that your Grace hath screen'd and stood between
Much heat° and him. I'll sconce° me even here.
5   Pray you, be round° [with him.
HAMLET (*within*): Mother, mother, mother!]
QUEEN: I'll warrant you, fear me not.
     Withdraw, I hear him coming.
                    [*Polonius hides behind the arras.*]

(*Enter Hamlet.*)

HAMLET: Now, mother, what's the matter?
10   QUEEN: Hamlet, thou hast thy father° much offended.
HAMLET: Mother, you have my father much offended.
QUEEN: Come, come, you answer with an idle° tongue.
HAMLET: Go, go, you question with a wicked tongue.
QUEEN: Why, how now, Hamlet?
HAMLET: What's the matter now?
QUEEN: Have you forgot me?
15   HAMLET: No, by the rood,° not so:
     You are the Queen, your husband's brother's wife
     And—would it were not so!—you are my mother.
QUEEN: Nay, then, I'll set those to you that can speak.
HAMLET: Come, come, and sit you down; you shall not budge.
20   You go not till I set you up a glass
     Where you may see the inmost part of you.
QUEEN: What wilt thou do? Thou wilt not murder me?
     Help, ho!
POLONIUS [*behind*]: What, ho! Help!
HAMLET [*drawing*]: How now? A rat? Dead, for a
25   ducat, dead!
                    [*Makes a pass through the arras.*]
POLONIUS [*behind*]: O, I am slain! [*Falls and dies.*]
QUEEN: O me, what hast thou done?
HAMLET: Nay, I know not. Is it the King?
QUEEN: O, what a rash and bloody deed is this!
HAMLET: A bloody deed—almost as bad, good mother,
30   As kill a king, and marry with his brother.
QUEEN: As kill a king!
HAMLET: Ay, lady, it was my word.
                    [*Parts the arras and discovers Polonius.*]
     Thou wretched, rash, intruding fool, farewell!
     I took thee for thy better. Take thy fortune.
     Thou find'st to be too busy is some danger.—
35   Leave wringing of your hands. Peace, sit you down,
     And let me wring your heart, for so I shall,
     If it be made of penetrable stuff,
     If damned custom° have not braz'd° it so
     That it be proof° and bulwark against sense.°

QUEEN: What have I done, that thou dar'st wag thy tongue   40
     In noise so rude against me?
HAMLET: Such an art
     That blurs the grace and blush of modesty,
     Calls virtue hypocrite, takes off the rose
     From the fair forehead of an innocent love
     And sets a blister° there, makes marriage-vows   45
     As false as dicers' oaths. O, such a deed
     As from the body of contraction° plucks
     The very soul, and sweet religion° makes
     A rhapsody° of words. Heaven's face does glow
     O'er this solidity and compound mass   50
     With heated visage, as against the doom,
     Is thought-sick at the act.°
QUEEN: Ay me, what act,
     That roars so loud and thunders in the index?°
HAMLET: Look here, upon this picture, and on this,
     The counterfeit presentment° of two brothers.   55
                    [*Shows her two likenesses.*]
     See, what a grace was seated on this brow:
     Hyperion's° curls, the front° of Jove himself,
     An eye like Mars, to threaten and command,
     A station° like the herald Mercury
     New-lighted on a heaven-kissing hill—   60
     A combination and a form indeed,
     Where every god did seem to set his seal,
     To give the world assurance of a man.
     This was your husband. Look you now, what follows:
     Here is your husband, like a mildew'd ear,°   65
     Blasting his wholesome brother. Have you eyes?
     Could you on this fair mountain leave to feed,
     And batten° on this moor?° Ha, have you eyes?
     You cannot call it love, for at your age
     The heyday° in the blood is tame, it's humble,   70
     And waits upon the judgment, and what judgment
     Would step from this to this? Sense,° sure, you have,
     Else could you not have motion, but sure that sense
     Is apoplex'd,° for madness would not err,

4. Much heat: The king's anger. **sconce:** Ensconce, hide. **5. round:** Blunt. **10. thy father:** Your stepfather, Claudius. **12. idle:** Foolish. **15. rood:** Cross. **38. damned custom:** Habitual wickedness. **braz'd:** Brazened, hardened. **39. proof:** Armor. **sense:** Feeling.

45. sets a blister: Brands as a harlot. **47. contraction:** The marriage contract. **48. religion:** Religious vows. **49. rhapsody:** Senseless string. **49–52. Heaven's . . . act:** Heaven's face flushes with anger to look down upon this solid world, this compound mass, with hot face as though the day of doom were near, and is thought-sick at the deed (i.e., Gertrude's marriage). **53. index:** Table of contents, prelude, or preface. **55. counterfeit presentment:** Portrayed representation. **57. Hyperion:** The sun-god. **front:** Brow. **59. station:** Manner of standing. **65. ear:** I.e., of grain. **68. batten:** Gorge. **moor:** Barren upland. **70. heyday:** State of excitement. **72. Sense:** Perception through the five senses (the functions of the middle or sensible soul). **74. apoplex'd:** Paralyzed. (Hamlet goes on to explain that without such a paralysis of will, mere madness would not so err, nor would the five senses so enthrall themselves to *ecstasy* or lunacy; even such deranged states of mind would be able to make the obvious choice between Hamlet Senior and Claudius.)

75 Nor sense to ecstasy was ne'er so thrall'd
    But it reserv'd some quantity of choice
    To serve in such a difference. What devil was 't
    That thus hath cozen'd° you at hoodman-blind?°
    Eyes without feeling, feeling without sight,
80 Ears without hands or eyes, smelling sans° all,
    Or but a sickly part of one true sense
    Could not so mope.°
    O shame, where is thy blush? Rebellious hell,
    If thou canst mutine° in a matron's bones,
85 To flaming youth let virtue be as wax,
    And melt in her own fire. Proclaim no shame
    When the compulsive ardor gives the charge,
    Since frost itself as actively doth burn,
    And reason panders will.°

90 QUEEN: O Hamlet, speak no more!
    Thou turn'st mine eyes into my very soul,
    And there I see such black and grained° spots
    As will not leave their tinct.°

    HAMLET: Nay, but to live
    In the rank sweat of an enseamed° bed,
95 Stew'd in corruption, honeying and making love
    Over the nasty sty—

    QUEEN: O, speak to me no more.
    These words, like daggers, enter in my ears.
    No more, sweet Hamlet!

    HAMLET: A murderer and a villain,
100 A slave that is not twentieth part the tithe°
    Of your precedent° lord, a vice° of kings,
    A cutpurse of the empire and the rule,
    That from a shelf the precious diadem stole,
    And put it in his pocket!

105 QUEEN: No more!

    (*Enter Ghost* [*in his nightgown*].)

    HAMLET: A king of shreds and patches°—
    Save me, and hover o'er me with your wings,
    You heavenly guards! What would your gracious
        figure?

    QUEEN: Alas, he's mad!

110 HAMLET: Do you not come your tardy son to chide,
    That, laps'd in time and passion,° lets go by
    Th' important° acting of your dread command?
    O, say!

---

78. **cozen'd:** Cheated. **hoodman-blind:** Blindman's bluff.
80. **sans:** Without. 82. **mope:** Be dazed, act aimlessly.
84. **mutine:** Mutiny. 86–89. **Proclaim . . . will:** Call it no shameful business when the compelling ardor of youth delivers the attack (i.e., commits lechery), since the frost of advanced age burns with as active a fire of lust and reason perverts itself by fomenting lust rather than restraining it. 92. **grained:** Dyed in grain, indelible. 93. **tinct:** Color. 94. **enseamed:** Laden with grease. 100. **tithe:** Tenth part. 101. **precedent:** Former (i.e., the elder Hamlet). **vice:** Buffoon (a reference to the vice of the morality plays). 106. **shreds and patches:** Motley, the traditional costume of the clown or fool. 111. **laps'd . . . passion:** Having allowed time to lapse and passion to cool. 112. **important:** Importunate, urgent.

GHOST: Do not forget. This visitation
    Is but to whet thy almost blunted purpose.   115
    But, look, amazement° on thy mother sits.
    O, step between her and her fighting soul!
    Conceit° in weakest bodies strongest works.
    Speak to her, Hamlet.

    HAMLET: How is it with you, lady?

    QUEEN: Alas, how is 't with you,   120
    That you do bend your eye on vacancy,
    And with th' incorporal° air do hold discourse?
    Forth at your eyes your spirits wildly peep,
    And, as the sleeping soldiers in th' alarm,
    Your bedded° hair, like life in excrements,°   125
    Start up and stand an° end. O gentle son,
    Upon the heat and flame of thy distemper
    Sprinkle cool patience. Whereon do you look?

    HAMLET: On him, on him! Look you how pale he
        glares!
    His form and cause conjoin'd,° preaching to stones,   130
    Would make them capable.°—Do not look
        upon me,
    Lest with this piteous action you convert
    My stern effects.° Then what I have to do
    Will want true color—tears perchance for blood.°

    QUEEN: To whom do you speak this?   135

    HAMLET: Do you see nothing there?

    QUEEN: Nothing at all, yet all that is I see.

    HAMLET: Nor did you nothing hear?

    QUEEN: No, nothing but ourselves.

    HAMLET: Why, look you there, look how it steals away! 140
    My father, in his habit° as he lived!
    Look, where he goes, even now, out at the portal!

                                    (*Exit Ghost.*)

    QUEEN: This is the very coinage of your brain.
    This bodiless creation ecstasy°
    Is very cunning in.   145

    HAMLET: Ecstasy?
    My pulse, as yours, doth temperately keep time,
    And makes as healthful music. It is not madness
    That I have utter'd. Bring me to the test,
    And I the matter will reword, which madness   150
    Would gambol° from. Mother, for love of grace,
    Lay not that flattering unction° to your soul
    That not your trespass but my madness speaks.
    It will but skin and film the ulcerous place,
    Whiles rank corruption, mining° all within,   155

---

116. **amazement:** Distraction. 118. **Conceit:** Imagination. 122. **incorporal:** Immaterial. 125. **bedded:** Laid in smooth layers. **excrements:** Outgrowths. 126. **an:** On. 130. **His . . . conjoin'd:** His appearance joined to his cause for speaking. 131. **capable:** Receptive. 132–133. **convert . . . effects:** Divert me from my stern duty. 134. **want . . . blood:** Lack plausibility so that (with a play on the normal sense of *color*) I shall shed tears instead of blood. 141. **habit:** Dress. 144. **ecstasy:** Madness. 151. **gambol:** Skip away. 152. **unction:** Ointment. 155. **mining:** Working under the surface.

Bill Murray as Polonius and
Julia Stiles as Ophelia in
Michael Almereyda's 2000 film
adaptation of *Hamlet,* which
also starred Ethan Hawke as
Hamlet, Sam Shepard as the
Ghost of Hamlet's father, and
Kyle MacLachlan as Claudius.

Infects unseen. Confess yourself to heaven,
Repent what's past, avoid what is to come,
And do not spread the compost° on the weeds
To make them ranker. Forgive me this my virtue;°
160 For in the fatness° of these pursy° times
Virtue itself of vice must pardon beg,
Yea, curb° and woo for leave° to do him good.
QUEEN: O Hamlet, thou hast cleft my heart in twain.
HAMLET: O, throw away the worser part of it,
165   And live the purer wit the other half.
Good night. But go not to my uncle's bed;
Assume a virtue, if you have it not.
That monster, custom, who all sense doth eat,°
Of habits devil,° is angel yet in this,
170   That to the use of actions fair and good
He likewise gives a frock or livery°
That aptly is put on. Refrain tonight,
And that shall lend a kind of easiness
To the next abstinence; the next more easy;
175   For use° almost can change the stamp of nature,
And either° . . . the devil, or throw him out
With wondrous potency. Once more, good night;
And when you are desirous to be bless'd,°

*he's really
bad at being
nice to his
mom.*

I'll blessing beg of you. For this same lord,
                    [*Pointing to Polonius.*]
I do repent; but heaven hath pleas'd it so   180
To punish me with this, and this with me,
That I must be their scourge and minister.°
I will bestow° him, and will answer well
The death I gave him. So, again, good night.
I must be cruel only to be kind.   185
Thus bad begins and worse remains behind.°
One word more, good lady.
QUEEN: What shall I do?
HAMLET: Not this, by no means, that I bid you do:
Let the bloat° king tempt you again to bed,
Pinch wanton on your cheek, call you his mouse, 190
And let him, for a pair of reechy° kisses,
Or paddling in your neck with his damn'd fingers,
Make yon to ravel all this matter out,
That I essentially am not in madness,
But mad in craft. 'Twere good° you let him know, 195
For who that's but a queen, fair, sober, wise,
Would from a paddock,° from a bat, a gib,°
Such dear concernings° hide? Who would do so?
No, in despite of sense and secrecy,
Unpeg the basket° on the house's top,   200

158. compost: Manure. **159. this my virtue:** My virtuous talk
in reproving you. **160. fatness:** Grossness. **pursy:** Short-
winded, corpulent. **162. curb:** Bow, bend the knee. **leave:**
Permission. **168. who . . . eat:** Who consumes all proper or
natural feeling. **169. Of habits devil:** Devil-like in prompting evil habits. **171. livery:** An outer appearance, a customary garb (and hence a predisposition easily assumed in time
of stress). **175. use:** Habit. **176. And either:** A defective line
usually emended by inserting the word *master* after *either,* following the fourth quarto and early editors. **178. be bless'd:**
Become blessed (i.e., repentant).

182. their scourge and minister: Agent of heavenly retribution.
(By *scourge,* Hamlet also suggests that he himself will eventually suffer punishment in the process of fulfilling heaven's
will.) **183. bestow:** Stow, dispose of. **186. behind:** To come.
189. bloat: Bloated. **191. reechy:** Dirty, filthy. **195. good:**
Said ironically; also the following eight lines. **197. paddock:**
Toad. **gib:** Tomcat. **198. dear concernings:** Important affairs. **200. Unpeg the basket:** Open the cage (i.e., let out the
secret).

Let the birds fly, and, like the famous ape,°
To try conclusions,° in the basket creep
And break your own neck down.
QUEEN: Be thou assur'd, if words be made of breath,
205 And breath of life, I have no life to breathe
What thou hast said to me.
HAMLET: I must to England; you know that?
QUEEN: Alack,
I had forgot. 'Tis so concluded on.
HAMLET: There's letters seal'd, and my two school-
fellows,
210 Whom I will trust as I will adders fang'd,
They bear the mandate; they must sweep my way,°
And marshal me to knavery. Let it work.
For 'tis the sport to have the enginer°
Hoist with° his own petar,° and 't shall go hard
215 But I will delve one yard below their mines,°
And blow them at the moon. O, 'tis most sweet,
When in one line two crafts° directly meet.
This man shall set me packing.°
I'll lug the guts into the neighbor room.
220 Mother, good night indeed. This counselor
Is now most still, most secret, and most grave,
Who was in life a foolish prating knave.
Come, sir, to draw toward an end° with you.
Good night, mother.

(*Exeunt* [*severally, Hamlet dragging in Polonius*].)

{ACT IV • Scene I}°

(*Enter King and Queen, with Rosencrantz and Guildenstern.*)

KING: There's matter in these sighs, these profound
heaves
You must translate; 'tis fit we understand them.
Where is your son?
QUEEN: Bestow this place on us a little while.

[*Exeunt Rosencrantz and Guildenstern.*]

5 Ah, mine own lord, what have I seen tonight!
KING: What, Gertrude? How does Hamlet?
QUEEN: Mad as the sea and wind when both contend
Which is the mightier. In his lawless fit,

Behind the arras hearing something stir,
Whips out his rapier, cries, "A rat, a rat!" 10
And, in this brainish apprehension,° kills
The unseen good old man.
KING: O heavy deed!
It had been so with us, had we been there.
His liberty is full of threats to all—
To you yourself, to us, to everyone. 15
Alas, how shall this bloody deed be answer'd?
It will be laid to us, whose providence°
Should have kept short,° restrain'd, and out of haunt°
This mad young man. But so much was our love
We would not understand what was most fit, 20
But, like the owner of a foul disease,
To keep it from divulging,° let it feed
Even on the pith of life. Where is he gone?
QUEEN: To draw apart the body he hath kill'd,
O'er whom his very madness, like some ore° 25
Among a mineral° of metals base,
Shows itself pure: 'a weeps for what is done.
KING: O Gertrude, come away!
The sun no sooner shall the mountains touch
But we will ship him hence, and this vile deed 30
We must, with all our majesty and skill,
Both countenance and excuse. Ho, Guildenstern!

(*Enter Rosencrantz and Guildenstern.*)

Friends both, go join you with some further aid.
Hamlet in madness hath Polonius slain,
And from his mother's closet hath he dragg'd him. 35
Go seek him out; speak fair, and bring the body
Into the chapel. I pray you, haste in this.

[*Exeunt Rosencrantz and Guildenstern.*]

Come, Gertrude, we'll call up our wisest friends
And let them know both what we mean to do
And what's untimely done........ 40
Whose whisper o'er the world's diameter,°
As level° as the cannon to his blank,°
Transports his pois'ned shot, may miss our name,
And hit the woundless° air. O, come away!
My soul is full of discord and dismay. (*Exeunt.*) 45

{Scene II}°

(*Enter Hamlet.*)

HAMLET: Safely stow'd.
[ROSENCRANTZ, GUILDENSTERN (*within*): Hamlet! Lord
Hamlet!]

201. **famous ape:** In a story now lost. 202. **conclusions:** Experiments (in which the ape apparently enters a cage from which birds have been released and then tries to fly out of the cage as they have done, falling to his death). 211. **sweep my way:** Go before me. 213. **enginer:** Constructor of military contrivances. 214. **Hoist with:** Blown up by. **petar:** Petard, an explosive used to blow in a door or make a breach. 215. **mines:** Tunnels used in warfare to undermine the enemy's emplacements; Hamlet will countermine by going under their mines. 217. **crafts:** Acts of guile, plots. 218. **set me packing:** Set me to making schemes and set me to lugging (him) and, also, send me off in a hurry. 223. **draw . . . end:** Finish up (with a pun on *draw,* pull). **IV, i. Location:** The castle.

11. **brainish apprehension:** Headstrong conception. 17. **providence:** Foresight. 18. **short:** On a short tether. **out of haunt:** Secluded. 22. **divulging:** Becoming evident. 25. **ore:** Vein of gold. 26. **mineral:** Mine. 40. **And . . . done:** A defective line; conjectures as to the missing words include *so, haply, slander* (Capell and others); *for, haply, slander* (Theobald and others). 41. **diameter:** Extent from side to side. 42. **As level:** With as direct aim. **blank:** White spot in the center of a target. 44. **woundless:** Invulnerable. **IV, ii. Location:** The castle.

HAMLET: But soft, what noise? Who calls on Hamlet?
    O, here they come.

5

(*Enter Rosencrantz and Guildenstern.*)

ROSENCRANTZ: What have you done, my lord, with the
    dead body?
HAMLET: Compounded it with dust, whereto 'tis kin.
ROSENCRANTZ: Tell us where 'tis, that we may take it
    thence
    And bear it to the chapel.
HAMLET: Do not believe it.   *[you're stupid → sponge]*
ROSENCRANTZ: Believe what?
HAMLET: That I can keep your counsel and not mine
    own. Besides, to be demanded of° a sponge, what
    replication° should be made by the son of a king?
ROSENCRANTZ: Take you me for a sponge, my lord?
HAMLET: Ay, sir, that soaks up the King's countenance,°
    his rewards, his authorities. But such officers do the
    King best service in the end. He keeps them, like an
    ape an apple, in the corner of his jaw, first mouth'd,
    to be last swallow'd. When he needs what you have
    glean'd, it is but squeezing you, and, sponge, you
    shall be dry again.
ROSENCRANTZ: I understand you not, my lord.
HAMLET: I am glad of it. A knavish speech sleeps in° a
    foolish ear.
ROSENCRANTZ: My lord, you must tell us where the body
    is, and go with us to the King.
HAMLET: The body is with the King, but the King is not
    with the body.° The King is a thing—
GUILDENSTERN: A thing, my lord?
HAMLET: Of nothing.° Bring me to him. [Hide fox, and
    all after.°]   (*Exeunt.*)

10

15

20

25

30

Hamlet is a great actor

{Scene III}°

(*Enter King, and two or three.*)

KING: I have sent to seek him, and to find the body.
    How dangerous is it that this man goes loose!
    Yet must not we put the strong law on him.   *He's loved by the people*
    He's lov'd of the distracted° multitude,
    Who like not in their judgment, but their eyes,
    And where 'tis so, th' offender's scourge° is weigh'd,°
    But never the offense. To bear° all smooth and even,
    This sudden sending him away must seem

5

---

13. **demanded of:** Questioned by.   14. **replication:** Reply.
16. **countenance:** Favor.   24. **sleeps in:** Has no meaning to.
28–29. **The . . . body:** Perhaps alludes to the legal commonplace of "the king's two bodies," which drew a distinction between the sacred office of kingship and the particular mortal
who possessed it at any given time.   31. **Of nothing:** Of no
account.   31–32. **Hide . . . after:** An old signal cry in the game
of hide-and-seek, suggesting that Hamlet now runs away from
them.   **IV, iii. Location:** The castle.   4. **distracted:** Fickle, unstable.   6. **scourge:** Punishment.   **weigh'd:** Taken into consideration.   7. **bear:** Manage.

Deliberate pause.° Diseases desperate grown
By desperate appliance are reliev'd,
Or not at all.

10

(*Enter Rosencrantz, [Guildenstern,] and all the rest.*)   *What happened*

    How now? What hath befall'n?
ROSENCRANTZ: Where the dead body is bestow'd, my
    lord,
    We cannot get from him.   *He won't tell them where the body is*
KING: But where is he?
ROSENCRANTZ: Without, my lord; guarded, to know your
    pleasure.
KING: Bring him before us.
ROSENCRANTZ: Ho! Bring in the lord.

15

(*They enter [with Hamlet].*)

KING: Now, Hamlet, where's Polonius?
HAMLET: At supper.
KING: At supper? Where?
HAMLET: Not where he eats, but where 'a is eaten. A   *he's done for worms*
    certain convocation of politic worms° are e'en at
    him. Your worm is your only emperor for diet.° We   20
    fat all creatures else to fat us, and we fat ourselves
    for maggots. Your fat king and your lean beggar is
    but variable service,° two dishes, but to one table—
    that's the end.   25
KING: Alas, alas!
HAMLET: A man may fish with the worm that hath eat°
    of a king, and eat of the fish that hath fed of that
    worm.
KING: What dost thou mean by this?   30
HAMLET: Nothing but to show you how a king may go a
    progress° through the guts of a beggar.
KING: Where is Polonius?
HAMLET: In heaven. Send thither to see. If your messen-
    ger find him not there, seek him i' th' other place   35
    yourself. But if indeed you find him not within this
    month, you shall nose him as you go up the stairs
    into the lobby.
KING [*to some Attendants*]: Go seek him there.
HAMLET: 'A will stay till you come.   40

                                [*Exit Attendants.*]

KING: Hamlet, this deed, for thine especial safety,—
    Which we do tender,° as we dearly° grieve
    For that which thou hast done—must send thee
        hence
    [With fiery quickness.] Therefore prepare thyself.
    The bark° is ready, and the wind at help,   45
    Th' associates tend,° and everything is bent°
    For England.   *get ready / you're going to England / for your own protection*

---

9. **Deliberate pause:** Carefully considered action.   20. **politic
worms:** Crafty worms (suited to a master spy like Polonius).
21. **diet:** Food, eating (with perhaps a punning reference to the
Diet of Worms, a famous convocation held in 1521).   24. **variable service:** Different courses of a single meal.   27. **eat:** Eaten
(pronounced "et").   32. **progress:** Royal journey of state.
42. **tender:** Regard, hold dear.   **dearly:** Intensely.   45. **bark:**
Sailing vessel.   46. **tend:** Wait.   **bent:** In readiness.

HAMLET: For England!

KING: Ay, Hamlet.

50 HAMLET: Good.

KING: So is it, if thou knew'st our purposes.

HAMLET: I see a cherub° that sees them. But, come, for
England! Farewell, dear mother.

KING: Thy loving father, Hamlet.

55 HAMLET: My mother. Father and mother is man and
wife, man and wife is one flesh, and so, my mother.
Come, for England! (*Exit.*)

KING: Follow him at foot;° tempt him with speed
aboard.

Delay it not; I'll have him hence tonight.

60 Away! For everything is seal'd and done
That else leans on° th' affair. Pray you, make haste.

[*Exeunt all but the King.*]

And, England,° if my love thou hold'st at aught—
As my great power thereof may give thee sense,
Since yet thy cicatrice° looks raw and red

65 After the Danish sword, and thy free awe°
Pays homage to us—thou mayst not coldly set°
Our sovereign process,° which imports at full,
By letters congruing° to that effect,
The present° death of Hamlet. Do it, England,

70 For like the hectic° in my blood he rages,
And thou must cure me. Till I know 'tis done,
Howe'er my haps,° my joys were ne'er begun.

(*Exit.*)

{Scene IV}°

(*Enter Fortinbras with his Army over the stage.*)

FORTINBRAS: Go, captain, from me greet the Danish
king.
Tell him that, by his license,° Fortinbras
Craves the conveyance° of a promis'd march
Over his kingdom. You know the rendezvous.

5 If that his Majesty would aught with us,
We shall express our duty in his eye;°
And let him know so.

CAPTAIN: I will do 't, my lord.

FORTINBRAS: Go softly° on. [*Exeunt all but the
Captain.*]

(*Enter Hamlet, Rosencrantz, [Guildenstern,] etc.*)

HAMLET: Good sir, whose powers° are these?

10 CAPTAIN: They are of Norway, sir.

HAMLET: How purposed, sir, I pray you?

CAPTAIN: Against some part of Poland.

HAMLET: Who commands them, sir?

CAPTAIN: The nephew to old Norway, Fortinbras.

HAMLET: Goes it against the main° of Poland, sir, 15
Or for some frontier?

CAPTAIN: Truly to speak, and with no addition,°
We go to gain a little patch of ground
That hath in it no profit but the name.
To pay° five ducats, five, I would not farm it;° 20
Nor will it yield to Norway or the Pole
A ranker° rate, should it be sold in fee.°

HAMLET: Why, then the Polack never will defend it.

CAPTAIN: Yes, it is already garrison'd.

HAMLET: Two thousand souls and twenty thousand
ducats 25
Will not debate the question of this straw.°
This is th' imposthume° of much wealth and
peace,
That inward breaks, and shows no cause without
Why the man dies. I humbly thank you, sir.

CAPTAIN: God buy you, sir. [*Exit.*]

ROSENCRANTZ: Will 't please you go, my lord? 30

HAMLET: I'll be with you straight. Go a little before.

[*Exit all except Hamlet.*]

How all occasions do inform against° me,
And spur my dull revenge! What is a man,
If his chief good and market of° his time
Be but to sleep and feed? A beast, no more. 35
Sure he that made us with such large discourse,°
Looking before and after, gave us not
That capability and god-like reason
To fust° in us unus'd. Now, whether it be
Bestial oblivion,° or some craven scruple 40
Of thinking too precisely on th' event°—
A thought which, quarter'd, hath but one part
wisdom
And ever three parts coward—I do not know
Why yet I live to say "This thing's to do,"
Sith° I have cause and will and strength and means 45
To do 't. Examples gross° as earth exhort me:
Witness this army of such mass and charge°
Led by a delicate and tender prince,
Whose spirit, with divine ambition puff'd
Makes mouths° at the invisible event, 50
Exposing what is mortal and unsure
To all that fortune, death, and danger dare,

---

52. **cherub:** Cherubim are angels of knowledge.   58. **at foot:**
Close behind, at heel.   61. **leans on:** Bears upon, is related to.
62. **England:** King of England.   64. **cicatrice:** Scar.   65. **free
awe:** Voluntary show of respect.   66. **set:** Esteem.   67. **process:** Command.   68. **congruing:** Agreeing.   69. **present:**
Immediate.   70. **hectic:** Persistent fever.   72. **haps:** Fortunes.
IV, iv. Location: The coast of Denmark.   2. **license:** Permission.   3. **conveyance:** Escort, convoy.   6. **eye:** Presence.
8. **softly:** Slowly.   9. **powers:** Forces.

15. **main:** Main part.   17. **addition:** Exaggeration.   20. **To
pay:** I.e., for a yearly rental of.   **farm it:** Take a lease of it.
22. **ranker:** Higher.   **in fee:** Fee simple, outright.   26. **debate . . .
straw:** Settle this trifling matter.   27. **imposthume:** Abscess.
32. **inform against:** Denounce, betray; take shape against.   34.
market of: Profit of compensation for.   36. **discourse:** Power
of reasoning.   39. **fust:** Grow moldy.   40. **oblivion:** Forgetfulness.   41. **event:** Outcome.   45. **Sith:** Since.   46. **gross:**
Obvious.   47. **charge:** Expense.   50. **Makes mouths:** Makes
scornful faces.

Even for an egg-shell. Rightly to be great
Is not to stir without great argument,
55   But greatly to find quarrel in a straw
When honor's at the stake. How stand I then,
That have a father kill'd, a mother stain'd,
Excitements of° my reason and my blood,
And let all sleep, while, to my shame, I see
60   The imminent death of twenty thousand men,
That, for a fantasy° and trick° of fame,
Go to their graves like beds, fight for a plot°
Whereon the numbers cannot try the cause,°
Which is not tomb enough and continent°
65   To hide the slain? O, from this time forth,
My thoughts be bloody, or be nothing worth!

                                                        (*Exit.*)

[handwritten: This is the emotional climax]

{Scene V}°

(*Enter Horatio, [Queen] Gertrude, and a Gentleman.*)

QUEEN: I will not speak with her.
GENTLEMAN: She is importunate, indeed distract.
   Her mood will needs be pitied.
QUEEN: What would she have?
GENTLEMAN: She speaks much of her father, says she
      hears
5   There's tricks° i' th' world, and hems, and beats
      her heart,°
   Spurns enviously at straws,° speaks things in doubt°
   That carry but half sense. Her speech is nothing,
   Yet the unshaped use° of it doth move
   The hearers to collection;° they yawn° at it,
10   And botch° the words up fit to their own thoughts,
   Which, as her winks and nods and gestures yield°
      them,
   Indeed would make one think there might be
      thought,°
   Though nothing sure, yet much unhappily.
HORATIO: 'Twere good she were spoken with, for she may
      strew
15   Dangerous conjectures in ill-breeding° minds.
QUEEN: Let her come in.   [*Exit Gentlemen.*]
   [*Aside.*] To my sick soul, as sin's true nature is,
   Each toy° seems prologue to some great amiss.°

So full of artless jealousy is guilt,
It spills itself in fearing to be spilt.°   20

[handwritten: She has a bad feeling about this]

(*Enter Ophelia [distracted].*)

OPHELIA: Where is the beauteous majesty of Denmark?
QUEEN: How now, Ophelia?
OPHELIA (*she sings*): "How should I your true love:
      know
   From another one?
   By his cockle hat° and staff,   25
      And his sandal shoon."°
QUEEN: Alas, sweet lady, what imports this song?
OPHELIA: Say you? Nay, pray you, mark.
   "He is dead and gone, lady,   (*Song.*)
      He is dead and gone;   30
   At his head a grass-green turf,
      At his heels a stone."
   O, ho!
QUEEN: Nay, but Ophelia—
OPHELIA: Pray you mark.   35
   [*Sings.*] "White his shroud as the mountain
      snow"—

(*Enter King.*)

QUEEN: Alas, look here, my lord.
OPHELIA: "Larded° all with flowers   (*Song.*)
   Which bewept to the ground did not go
      With true love showers."   40
KING: How do you, pretty lady?
OPHELIA: Well, God 'ild° you! They say the owl° was a
   baker's daughter. Lord, we know what we are, but
   know not what we may be. God be at your table!
KING: Conceit° upon her father.   45
OPHELIA: Pray let's have no words of this; but when they
   ask you what it means, say you this:
   "Tomorrow is Saint Valentine's° day.   (*Song.*)
      All in the morning betime,
   And I a maid at your window,   50
      To be your Valentine.
   Then up he rose, and donn'd his clo'es,
      And dupp'd° the chamber-door,
   Let in the maid, that out a maid
      Never departed more."   55
KING: Pretty Ophelia!
OPHELIA: Indeed, la, without an oath, I'll make an end
      on 't:
   [*Sings.*] "By Gis° and by Saint Charity,

---

58. Excitements of: Promptings by.   **61. fantasy:** Fanciful
caprice.   **trick:** Trifle.   **62. plot:** I.e., of ground.   **63. Whereon . . . cause:** On which there is insufficient room for the soldiers
needed to engage in a military contest.   **64. continent:** Receptacle, container.   **IV, v. Location:** The castle.   **5. tricks:** Deceptions.   **heart:** Breast.   **6. Spurns . . . straws:** Kicks spitefully,
takes offense at trifles.   **in doubt:** Obscurely.   **8. unshaped use:**
Distracted manner.   **9. collection:** Inference, a guess at some
sort of meaning.   **yawn:** Wonder, grasp.   **10. botch:** Patch.
11. yield: Deliver, bring forth (her words).   **12. thought:**
Conjectures.   **15. ill-breeding:** Prone to suspect the worst.
18. toy: Trifle.   **amiss:** Calamity.

19–20. So . . . spilt: Guilt is so full of suspicion that it
unskillfully betrays itself in fearing betrayal.   **25. cockle hat:**
Hat with cockleshell stuck in it as a sign that the wearer had
been a pilgrim to the shrine of St. James of Compostella in
Spain.   **26. shoon:** Shoes.   **38. Larded:** Decorated.   **42. God
'ild:** God yield or reward.   **owl:** Refers to a legend about a
baker's daughter who was turned into an owl for refusing
Jesus bread.   **45. Conceit:** Brooding.   **48. Valentine's:** This
song alludes to the belief that the first girl seen by a man on the
morning of this day was his valentine or true love.   **53. dupp'd:**
Opened.   **59. Gis:** Jesus.

Alack, and fie for shame!
60 Young men will do 't, if they come to 't;
By Cock,° they are to blame.
Quoth she, 'Before you tumbled me,
You promised me to wed.'"
He answers:
65 "'So would I ha' done, by yonder sun,
An thou hadst not come to my bed.'"
KING: How long hath she been thus?
OPHELIA: I hope all will be well. We must be patient, but
I cannot choose but weep, to think they would lay
70 him i' th' cold ground. My brother shall know of it;
and so I thank you for your good counsel. Come, my
coach! Good night, ladies; good night, sweet ladies;
good night, good night.

[*Exit.*]

KING: Follow her close; give her good watch, I pray
you.   [*Exit Horatio.*]
75 O, this is the poison of deep grief; it springs
All from her father's death—and now behold!
O Gertrude, Gertrude,
When sorrows come, they come not single spies,°
But in battalions. First, her father slain;
80 Next, your son gone, and he most violent author
Of his own just remove; the people muddied,°
Thick and unwholesome in their thoughts and
whispers,
For good Polonius' death; and we have done but
greenly,°
In hugger-mugger° to inter him; poor Ophelia
85 Divided from herself and her fair judgment,
Without the which we are pictures, or mere beasts;
Last, and as much containing as all these,
Her brother is in secret come from France,
Feeds on his wonder, keeps himself in clouds,°
90 And wants° not buzzers° to infect his ear
With pestilent speeches of his father's death,
Wherein necessity, of matter beggar'd,°
Will nothing stick our person to arraign
In ear and ear.° O my dear Gertrude, this,
95 Like to a murd'ring-piece,° in many places
Gives me superfluous death.   (*A noise within.*)
[QUEEN: Alack, what noise is this?]
KING: Attend!
Where are my Switzers?° Let them guard the door.

(*Enter a Messenger.*)

What is the matter?
100 MESSENGER: Save yourself, my lord!

The ocean, overpeering of his list,°
Eats not the flats° with more impiteous° haste
Than young Laertes, in a riotous head,°
O'erbears your officers. The rabble call him lord,
And, as° the world were now but to begin,   105
Antiquity forgot, custom not known,
The ratifiers and props° of every word,°
They cry, "Choose we! Laertes shall be king!"
Caps, hands, and tongues applaud it to the clouds,
"Laertes shall be king, Laertes king!"   110
(*A noise within.*)
QUEEN: How cheerfully on the false trail they cry!
O, this is counter,° you false Danish dogs!

(*Enter Laertes with others.*)

KING: The doors are broke.
LAERTES: Where is this King? Sirs, stand you all without.
ALL: No, let's come in.
LAERTES: I pray you, give me leave.   115
ALL: We will, we will.
[*They retire without the door.*]
LAERTES: I thank you. Keep the door. O thou vile king,
Give me my father!
QUEEN: Calmly, good Laertes.
[*She tries to hold him back.*]
LAERTES: That drop of blood that's calm proclaims
me bastard,
Cries cuckold to my father, brands the harlot   120
Even here, between the chaste unsmirched brow
Of my true mother.
KING: What is the cause, Laertes,
That thy rebellion looks so giant-like?
Let him go, Gertrude. Do not fear our° person.
There's such divinity doth hedge a king   125
That treason can but peep to what it would,°
Acts little of his will.° Tell me, Laertes,
Why thou art thus incens'd. Let him go, Gertrude.
Speak, man.
LAERTES: Where is my father?
KING: Dead.
QUEEN: But not by him.
KING: Let him demand his fill.   130
LAERTES: How came he dead? I'll not be juggled with.
To hell, allegiance! Vows, to the blackest devil!
Conscience and grace, to the profoundest pit!
I dare damnation. To this point I stand,
That both the worlds I give to negligence,°   135

---

62. Cock: A perversion of *God* in oaths.   **78. spies:** Scouts sent in advance of the main force.   **81. muddied:** Stirred up, confused.   **83. greenly:** Imprudently, foolishly.   **84. hugger-mugger:** Secret haste.   **89. in clouds:** I.e., of suspicion and rumor.   **90. wants:** Lacks.   **buzzers:** Gossipers, informers.   **92. of matter beggar'd:** Unprovided with facts.   **93–94. Will . . . and ear:** Will not hesitate to accuse my (royal) person in everybody's ears.   **95. murd'ring-piece:** Cannon loaded so as to scatter its shot.   **99. Switzers:** Swiss guards, mercenaries.

101. overpeering of his list: Overflowing its shore.   **102. flats:** Flatlands near shore.   **impiteous:** Pitiless.   **103. head:** Armed force.   **105. as:** As if.   **107. ratifiers and props:** Refer to *antiquity* and *custom*.   **word:** Promise.   **112. counter:** A hunting term meaning to follow the trail in a direction opposite to that which the game has taken.   **124. fear our:** Fear for my.   **126. can . . . would:** Can only glance, as from far off or through a barrier, at what it would intend.   **127. Acts . . . will:** (But) performs little of what it intends.   **135. both . . . negligence:** Both this world and the next are of no consequence to me.

I'll get revenge for my father!

Let come what comes, only I'll be reveng'd
Most throughly° for my father.

KING: Who shall stay you?

LAERTES: My will, not all the world's.°
And for my means, I'll husband them so well,
140   They shall go far with little.

KING: Good Laertes,
If you desire to know the certainty
Of your dear father, is 't writ in your revenge
That, swoopstake,° you will draw both friend and
    foe,
Winner and loser?

145   LAERTES: None but his enemies.

KING: Will you know them then?

LAERTES: To his good friends thus wide I'll ope my arms,
And, like the kind life-rend'ring pelican,°
Repast° them with my blood.

KING: Why, now you speak
Like a good child and a true gentleman.
150   That I am guiltless of your father's death,
And am most sensibly° in grief for it,
It shall as level° to your judgment 'pear
As day does to your eye.

                (*A noise within:*) "Let her come in."

LAERTES: How now? What noise is that?

(*Enter Ophelia.*)

155   O heat, dry up my brains! Tears seven times salt
Burn out the sense and virtue° of mine eye!
By heaven, thy madness shall be paid with weight°
Till our scale turn the beam.° O rose of May!
Dear maid, kind sister, sweet Ophelia!
160   O heavens, is 't possible a young maid's wits
Should be as mortal as an old man's life?
[Nature is fine in° love, and where 'tis fine,
It sends some precious instance° of itself
After the thing it loves.°]

I'll get revenge for your insanity for her. Laertes love and wants life

165   OPHELIA: "They bore him barefac'd on the bier;

                (*Song.*)

[Hey non nonny, nonny, hey nonny,]
And in his grave rain'd many a tear"—
Fare you well, my dove!

LAERTES: Hadst thou thy wits, and didst persuade°
        revenge,
170   It could not move thus.

OPHELIA: You must sing "A-down a-down,
And you call him a-down-a."

O, how the wheel° becomes it! It is the false steward°
that stole his master's daughter.

LAERTES: This nothing's more than matter.°   175

OPHELIA: There's rosemary,° that's for remembrance;
pray you, love, remember. And there is pansies,° that's
for thoughts.

LAERTES: A document° in madness, thoughts and remembrance fitted.   180

OPHELIA: There's fennel° for you, and columbines.°
There's rue° for you, and here's some for me; we may
call it herb of grace o' Sundays. You may wear your
rue with a difference.° There's a daisy.° I would give
you some violets,° but they wither'd all when my   185
father died. They say 'e made a good end—
[*Sings.*] "For bonny sweet Robin is all my joy."

LAERTES: Thought° and affliction, passion, hell itself,
She turns to favor° and to prettiness.

OPHELIA: "And will 'a not come again?   (*Song.*) 190
And will 'a not come again?
    No, no, he is dead,
    Go to thy death-bed,
He never will come again.

"His beard was as white as snow,   195
All flaxen was his poll.°
    He is gone, he is gone,
    And we cast away moan.
God 'a' mercy on his soul!

Bye Ophelia

And of all Christians' souls, I pray God. God buy you. 200
                                            [*Exit.*]

LAERTES: Do you see this, O God?

KING: Laertes, I must commune with your grief,
Or you deny me right. Go but apart,
Make choice of whom your wisest friends you will,
And they shall hear and judge 'twixt you and me.   205
If by direct or by collateral° hand
They find us touch'd,° we will our kingdom give,
Our crown, our life, and all that we call ours,
To you in satisfaction; but if not,
Be you content to lend your patience to us,   210
And we shall jointly labor with your soul
To give it due content.

---

137. **throughly:** Thoroughly. 138. **My will ... world's:** I'll stop (*stay*) when my will is accomplished, not for anyone else's. 143. **swoopstake:** Literally, taking all stakes on the gambling table at once (i.e., indiscriminately); *draw* is also a gambling term. 147. **pelican:** Refers to the belief that the female pelican fed its young with its own blood. 148. **Repast:** Feed. 151. **sensibly:** Feelingly. 152. **level:** Plain. 156. **virtue:** Faculty, power. 157. **paid with weight:** Repaid, avenged equally or more. 158. **beam:** Crossbar of a balance. 162. **fine in:** Refined by. 163. **instance:** Token. 164. **After ... loves:** Into the grave, along with Polonius. 169. **persuade:** Argue cogently for.

173. **wheel:** Spinning wheel as accompaniment to the song, or refrain. **false steward:** The story is unknown. 175. **This ... matter:** This seeming nonsense is more meaningful than sane utterance. 176. **rosemary:** Used as a symbol of remembrance both at weddings and at funerals. 177. **pansies:** Emblems of love and courtship; perhaps from French *pensées*, thoughts. 179. **document:** Instruction, lesson. 181. **fennel:** Emblem of flattery. **columbines:** Emblems of unchastity (?) or ingratitude (?). 182. **rue:** Emblem of repentance; when mingled with holy water, it was known as *herb of grace*. 184. **with a difference:** Suggests that Ophelia and the queen have different causes of sorrow and repentance; perhaps with a play on *rue* in the sense of ruth, or pity. **daisy:** Emblem of dissembling, faithlessness. 185. **violets:** Emblems of faithfulness. 188. **Thought:** Melancholy. 189. **favor:** Grace. 196. **poll:** Head. 206. **collateral:** Indirect. 207. **us touch'd:** Me implicated.

LAERTES: Let this be so.
His means of death, his obscure funeral—
No trophy,° sword, nor hatchment° o'er his bones,
215   No noble rite nor formal ostentation°—
Cry to be heard, as 'twere from heaven to earth,
That I must call 't in question.
KING: So you shall;
And where th' offense is, let the great ax fall.
I pray you go with me.   (*Exeunt.*)

may the guilty be punished w/ death

{Scene VI}°

(*Enter Horatio and others.*)

HORATIO: What are they that would speak with me?
GENTLEMAN: Seafaring men, sir. They say they have let-
ters for you.
HORATIO: Let them come in.   [*Exit Gentleman.*]
5   I do not know from what part of the world
I should be greeted, if not from lord Hamlet.

(*Enter Sailors.*)

FIRST SAILOR: God bless you sir.
HORATIO: Let him bless thee too.
FIRST SAILOR: 'A shall, sir, an 't please him. There's a letter
10   for you, sir—it came from th' ambassador that was
bound for England—if your name be Horatio, as I
am let to know it is.   [*Gives letter.*]
HORATIO [*reads*]: "Horatio, when thou shalt have
overlook'd this, give these fellows some means° to the
15   King; they have letters for him. Ere we were two days
old at sea, a pirate of very warlike appointment° gave
us chase. Finding ourselves too slow of sail, we put
on a compell'd valor, and in the grapple I boarded
them. On the instant they got clear of our ship, so I
20   alone became their prisoner. They have dealt with me
like thieves of mercy,° but they knew what they did:
I am to do a good turn for them. Let the King have
the letters I have sent, and repair thou to me with as
much speed as thou wouldest fly death. I have words
25   to speak in thine ear will make thee dumb; yet are
they much too light for the bore° of the matter. These
good fellows will bring thee where I am. Rosencrantz
and Guildenstern hold their course for England. Of
them I have much to tell thee. Farewell.
30   He that thou knowest thine, Hamlet."
Come, I will give you way for these your letters,
And do 't the speedier that you may direct me
To him from whom you brought them.   (*Exeunt.*)

{Scene VII}°

(*Enter King and Laertes.*)

KING: Now must your conscience my acquittance seal,°
And you must put me in your heart for friend,
Sith you have heard, and with a knowing ear,
That he which hath your noble father slain
Pursued my life.
LAERTES: It well appears. But tell me   5
Why you proceeded not against these feats°
So criminal and so capital° in nature,
As by your safety, greatness, wisdom, all things else,
You mainly° were stirr'd up.
KING: O, for two special reasons,
Which may to you, perhaps, seem much unsinew'd,°
But yet to me th' are strong. The Queen his mother
Lives almost by his looks, and for myself—
My virtue or my plague, be it either which—
She's so conjunctive° to my life and soul
That, as the star moves not but in his sphere,°   15
I could not but by her. The other motive,
Why to a public count° I might not go,
Is the great love the general gender° bear him,
Who, dipping all his faults in their affection,
Would, like the spring° that turneth wood to stone,
Convert his gyves° to graces, so that my arrows,   20
Too slightly timber'd° for so loud° a wind,
Would have reverted to my bow again
And not where I had aim'd them.
LAERTES: And so have I a noble father lost,   25
A sister driven into desp'rate terms,°
Whose worth, if praises may go back° again,
Stood challenger on mount° of all the age
For her perfections. But my revenge will come.
KING: Break not your sleeps for that. You must not
think   30
That we are made of stuff so flat and dull
That we can let our beard be shook with danger
And think it pastime. You shortly shall hear more.
I lov'd your father, and we love ourself;
And that, I hope, will teach you to imagine—   35

(*Enter a Messenger with letters.*)

[How now? What news?]
MESSENGER: [Letters, my lord, from Hamlet:]

I didn't tell any because his mother and the people love him

---

214. **trophy:** Memorial. **hatchment:** Tablet displaying the
armorial bearings of a deceased person. 215. **ostentation:**
Ceremony. **IV, vi. Location:** The castle. 14. **means:** Means
of access. 16. **appointment:** Equipage. 21. **thieves of mercy:**
Merciful thieves. 26. **bore:** Caliber (i.e., importance).

IV, vii. Location: The castle. 1. **my acquittance seal:** Confirm
or acknowledge my innocence. 6. **feats:** Acts. 7. **capital:**
Punishable by death. 9. **mainly:** Greatly. 10. **unsinew'd:**
Weak. 14. **conjunctive:** Closely united. 15. **sphere:** The hollow sphere in which, according to Ptolemaic astronomy, the
planets moved. 17. **count:** Account, reckoning. 18. **general
gender:** Common people. 20. **spring:** A spring with such a
concentration of lime that it coats a piece of wood with lime-
stone, in effect gilding it. 21. **gyves:** Fetters (which, gilded
by the people's praise, would look like badges of honor).
22. **slightly timber'd:** Light. **loud:** Strong. 26. **terms:** State,
condition. 27. **go back:** Recall Ophelia's former virtues.
28. **on mount:** On high.

These to your Majesty, this to the Queen.
                                        [*Gives letters.*]
KING: From Hamlet? Who brought them?
MESSENGER: Sailors, my lord, they say; I saw them not.
40   They were given me by Claudio. He receiv'd them
      Of him that brought them.
KING: Laertes, you shall hear them.
      Leave us.   [*Exit Messenger.*]
      [*Reads.*] "High and mighty, you shall know I am set
      naked° on your kingdom. Tomorrow shall I beg leave
45   to see your kingly eyes, when I shall, first asking your
      pardon° thereunto, recount the occasion of my sud-
      den and more strange return.   Hamlet."
      What should this mean? Are all the rest come back?
      Or is it some abuse,° and no such thing?
      LAERTES: Know you the hand?
50   KING: 'Tis Hamlet's character.° "Naked!"
      And in a postscript here, he says "alone."
      Can you devise° me?
      LAERTES: I am lost in it, my lord. But let him come.
      It warms the very sickness in my heart
55   That I shall live and tell him to his teeth,
      "Thus didst thou."
      KING: If it be so, Laertes—
      As how should it be so? How otherwise?°—
      Will you be ruled by me?
      LAERTES: Ay, my lord,
      So° you will not o'errule me to a peace.
60   KING: To thine own peace. If he be now returned,
      As checking at° his voyage, and that he means
      No more to undertake it, I will work him
      To an exploit, now ripe in my device,
      Under the which he shall not choose but fall;
65   And for his death no wind of blame shall breathe,
      But even his mother shall uncharge the practice°
      And call it accident.
      LAERTES: My lord, I will be rul'd,
      The rather if you could devise it so
      That I might be the organ.°
      KING: It falls right.
70   You have been talk'd of since your travel much,
      And that in Hamlet's hearing, for a quality
      Wherein, they say, you shine. Your sum of parts°
      Did not together pluck such envy from him
      As did that one, and that, in my regard,
75   Of the unworthiest siege.°
      LAERTES: What part is that, my lord?
      KING: A very riband in the cap of youth,
      Yet needful too, for youth no less becomes

The light and careless livery that it wears
Than settled age his sables° and his weeds,°   80
Importing health° and graveness. Two months since
Here was a gentleman of Normandy.
I have seen myself, and serv'd against, the French,
And they can well° on horseback, but this gallant
Had witchcraft in 't; he grew unto his seat,   85
And to such wondrous doing brought his horse
As had he been incorps'd and demi-natured°
With the brave beast. So far he topp'd° my thought
That I, in forgery° of shapes and tricks,
Come short of what he did.
LAERTES: A Norman was 't?   90
KING: A Norman.
LAERTES: Upon my life, Lamord.
KING: The very same.
LAERTES: I know him well. He is the brooch° indeed
And gem of all the nation.
KING: He made confession° of you,   95
And gave you such a masterly report
For art and exercise in your defense,
And for your rapier most especial,
That he cried out, 'twould be a sight indeed,
If one could match you. The scrimers° of their
      nation,   100
He swore, had neither motion, guard, nor eye,
If you oppos'd them. Sir, this report of his
Did Hamlet so envenom with his envy
That he could nothing do but wish and beg
Your sudden coming o'er to play° with you.   105
Now, out of this—
LAERTES: What out of this, my lord?
KING: Laertes, was your father dear to you?
Or are you like the painting of a sorrow,
A face without a heart?
LAERTES: Why ask you this?
KING: Not that I think you did not love your father, 110
But that I know love is begun by time,°
And that I see, in passages of proof,°
Time qualifies° the spark and fire of it.
There lives within the very flame of love
A kind of wick or snuff° that will abate it,   115
And nothing is at a like goodness still,°
For goodness, growing to a plurisy,°
Dies in his own too much.° That° we would do,
We should do when we would; for this "would"
      changes

80. **sables:** Rich robes furred with sable. **weeds:** Garments.
81. **Importing health:** Indicating prosperity. 84. **can well:**
Are skilled. 87. **incorps'd and demi-natur'd:** Of one body
and nearly of one nature (like the centaur). 88. **topp'd:** Surpassed. 89. **forgery:** Invention. 93. **brooch:** Ornament. 95.
confession: Admission of superiority. 100. **scrimers:** Fencers.
105. **play:** Fence. 111. **begun by time:** Subject to change.
112. **passages of proof:** Actual instances. 113. **qualifies:**
Weakens. 115. **snuff:** The charred part of a candlewick.
116. **nothing . . . still:** Nothing remains at a constant level of
perfection. 117. **plurisy:** Excess, plethora. 118. **in . . . much:**
Of its own excess. **That:** That which.

44. **naked:** Destitute, unarmed, without following. 46. **pardon:** Permission. 49. **abuse:** Deceit. 50. **character:** Handwriting. 52. **devise:** Explain to. 57. **As . . . otherwise:** How
can this (Hamlet's return) be true? Yet how otherwise than true
(since we have the evidence of his letter). 59. **So:** Provided
that. 61. **checking at:** Turning aside from (like a falcon leaving the quarry to fly at a chance bird). 66. **uncharge the practice:** Acquit the stratagem of being a plot. 69. **organ:** Agent,
instrument. 72. **Your . . . parts:** All your other virtues.
75. **unworthiest siege:** Least important rank.

120 And hath abatements° and delays as many
   As there are tongues, are hands, are accidents,°
   And then this "should" is like a spendthrift's sigh,°
   That hurts by easing.° But, to the quick o' th' ulcer;
   Hamlet comes back. What would you undertake
125 To show yourself your father's son in deed
   More than in words?

LAERTES: To cut his throat i' th' church!

KING: No place, indeed, should murder sanctuarize;°
   Revenge should have no bounds. But, good Laertes,
   Will you do this,° keep close within your chamber.
130 Hamlet return'd shall know you are come home.
   We'll put on those° shall praise your excellence
   And set a double varnish on the fame
   The Frenchman gave you, bring you in fine°
      together,
   And wager on your heads. He, being remiss,°
135 Most generous,° and free from all contriving,
   Will not peruse the foils, so that, with ease,
   Or with a little shuffling, you may choose
   A sword unbated,° and in a pass of practice°
   Requite him for your father.

LAERTES: I will do 't.
140 And for that purpose I'll anoint my sword.
   I bought an unction° of a mountebank°
   So mortal that, but dip a knife in it,
   Where it draws blood no cataplasm° so rare,
   Collected from all simples° that have virtue
145 Under the moon, can save the thing from death
   That is but scratch'd withal. I'll touch my point
   With this contagion, that, if I gall° him slightly,
   It may be death.

KING: Let's further think of this,
   Weigh what convenience both of time and means
150 May fit us to our shape.° If this should fail,
   And that our drift look through our bad
      performance,°
   'Twere better not assay'd. Therefore this project
   Should have a back or second, that might hold
   If this did blast in proof.° Soft, let me see.
155 We'll make a solemn wager on your cunnings—
   I ha 't!
   When in your motion you are hot and dry—
   As° make your bouts more violent to that end—
   And that he calls for drink, I'll have prepar'd him
   A chalice for the nonce,° whereon but sipping,   160
   If he by chance escape your venom'd stuck,°
   Our purpose may hold there. [*A cry within.*] But
      stay, what noise?

(*Enter Queen.*)

QUEEN: One woe doth tread upon another's heel,
   So fast they follow. Your sister's drowned, Laertes.

LAERTES: Drown'd! O, where?   165

QUEEN: There is a willow grows askant° the brook
   That shows his hoar° leaves in the glassy stream;
   Therewith fantastic garlands did she make
   Of crow-flowers, nettles, daisies, and long purples°
   That liberal° shepherds give a grosser name,   170
   But our cold° maids do dead men's fingers call them.
   There on the pendent boughs her crownet° weeds
   Clamb'ring to hang, an envious sliver° broke,
   When down her weedy° trophies and herself
   Fell in the weeping brook. Her clothes spread wide, 175
   And mermaid-like awhile they bore her up,
   Which time she chanted snatches of old lauds,°
   As one incapable° of her own distress,
   Or like a creature native and indued°
   Unto that element. But long it could not be   180
   Till that her garments, heavy with their drink,
   Pull'd the poor wretch from her melodious lay
   To muddy death.

LAERTES: Alas, then she is drown'd?

QUEEN: Drown'd, drown'd.

LAERTES: Too much of water hast thou, poor Ophelia,   185
   And therefore I forbid my tears. But yet
   It is our trick;° nature her custom holds,
   Let shame say what it will. [*He weeps.*] When
      these are gone,
   The woman will be out.° Adieu, my lord.
   I have a speech of fire, that fain would blaze,   190
   But that this folly drowns it.   (*Exit.*)

KING: Let's follow, Gertrude.
   How much I had to do to calm his rage!
   Now fear I this will give it start again;
   Therefore let's follow.   (*Exeunt.*)

---

120. **abatements:** Diminutions.   121. **accidents:** Occurrences, incidents.   122. **spendthrift's sigh:** An allusion to the belief that each sigh cost the heart a drop of blood.   123. **hurts by easing:** Costs the heart blood even while it affords emotional relief.   127. **sanctuarize:** Protect from punishment (alludes to the right of sanctuary with which certain religious places were invested).   129. **Will you do this:** If you wish to do this. 131. **put on those:** Instigate those who.   133. **in fine:** Finally. 134. **remiss:** Negligently unsuspicious.   135. **generous:** Noble-minded.   138. **unbated:** Not blunted, having no button.   **pass of practice:** Treacherous thrust.   141. **unction:** Ointment. **mountebank:** Quack doctor.   143. **cataplasm:** Plaster or poultice.   144. **simples:** Herbs.   147. **gall:** Graze, wound. 150. **shape:** Part that we propose to act.   151. **drift . . . performance:** I.e., our intention be disclosed by our bungling. 154. **blast in proof:** Burst in the test (like a cannon).

158. **As:** And you should.   160. **nonce:** Occasion.   161. **stuck:** Thrust (from *stoccado*, a fencing term).   166. **askant:** Aslant. 167. **hoar:** White or gray.   169. **long purples:** Early purple orchids.   170. **liberal:** Free-spoken.   171. **cold:** Chaste.   172. **crownet:** Made into a chaplet or coronet.   173. **envious sliver:** Malicious branch.   174. **weedy:** I.e., of plants.   177. **lauds:** Hymns.   178. **incapable:** Lacking capacity to apprehend.   179. **indued:** Adapted by nature.   187. **It is our trick:** Weeping is our natural way (when sad).   188–189. **When . . . out:** When my tears are all shed, the woman in me will be expended, satisfied.

[Handwritten margin note: "...Did Ophelia kill herself. Really. Drowning is one of the least pleasant ways to go and below a noble nobleman"]

{ACT V • Scene I}°

(*Enter two Clowns*° [*with spades, etc.*])

FIRST CLOWN: Is she to be buried in Christian burial when
she willfully seeks her own salvation?
SECOND CLOWN: I tell thee she is; therefore make her
grave straight.° The crowner° hath sat on her, and
5 finds it Christian burial.
FIRST CLOWN: How can that be, unless she drown'd herself in her own defense?
SECOND CLOWN: Why, 'tis found so.
FIRST CLOWN: It must be "se offendendo";° it cannot
10 be else. For here lies the point: if I drown myself
wittingly, it argues an act, and an act hath three
branches—it is to act, to do, and to perform. Argal,°
she drown'd herself wittingly.
SECOND CLOWN: Nay, but hear you, goodman delver—
15 **FIRST CLOWN:** Give me leave. Here lies the water; good.
Here stands the man; good. If the man go to this
water, and drown himself, it is, will he,° nill he, he
goes, mark you that. But if the water come to him
and drown him, he drowns not himself. Argal, he
20 that is not guilty of his own death shortens not his
own life.
SECOND CLOWN: But is this law?
FIRST CLOWN: Ay, marry, is 't—crowner's quest° law.
SECOND CLOWN: Will you ha' the truth on 't? If this had
25 not been a gentlewoman, she should have been buried out o' Christian burial.
FIRST CLOWN: Why, there thou say'st.° And the more
pity that great folk should have count'nance° in this
world to drown or hang themselves, more than their
30 even-Christen.° Come, my spade. There is no ancient
gentlemen but gard'ners, ditchers, and grave-makers.
They hold up Adam's profession.
SECOND CLOWN: Was he a gentleman?
FIRST CLOWN: 'A was the first that ever bore arms.
35 [**SECOND CLOWN:** Why, he had none.
FIRST CLOWN: What, art a heathen? How dost thou understand the Scripture? The Scripture says "Adam
digg'd." Could he dig without arms?] I'll put another
question to thee. If thou answerest me not to the pur-
40 pose, confess thyself°— *[Handwritten note: "the graves and the their occupants"]*
SECOND CLOWN: Go to.
FIRST CLOWN: What is he that builds stronger than either
the mason, the shipwright, or the carpenter?
SECOND CLOWN: The gallows-maker, for that frame
45 outlives a thousand tenants.

FIRST CLOWN: I like thy wit well, in good faith. The gallows does well, but how does it well? It does well to
those that do ill. Now thou dost ill to say the gallows
is built stronger than the church. Argal, the gallows
50 may do well to thee. To 't again, come.
SECOND CLOWN: "Who builds stronger than a mason, a
shipwright, or a carpenter?"
FIRST CLOWN: Ay, tell me that, and unyoke.°
SECOND CLOWN: Marry, now I can tell.
55 **FIRST CLOWN:** To 't.
SECOND CLOWN: Mass,° I cannot tell.

(*Enter Hamlet and Horatio* [*at a distance*].)

FIRST CLOWN: Cudgel thy brains no more about it, for
your dull ass will not mend his pace with beating;
and, when you are ask'd this question next, say "a
60 grave-maker." The houses he makes lasts till doomsday. Go, get thee in, and fetch me a stoup° of liquor.

[*Exit Second Clown. First Clown digs.*]
(*Song.*)

"In youth, when I did love, did love,°
   Methought it was very sweet,
To contract—O—the time for—a—my behove,°
   O, methought there—a—was nothing—a—
   meet."°
65
HAMLET: Has this fellow no feeling of his business, that
'a sings at grave-making? *[Handwritten note: "he sings while digging graves"]*
HORATIO: Custom hath made it in him a property of
easiness.°
HAMLET: 'Tis e'en so. The hand of little employment hath
70 the daintier sense.° *[Handwritten note: "nobles"]*
(*Song.*)
FIRST CLOWN: "But age, with his stealing steps,
   Hath claw'd me in his clutch,
And hath shipped me into the land,°
   As if I had never been such."
75
[*Throws up a skull.*]
HAMLET: That skull had a tongue in it, and could sing
once. How the knave jowls° it to the ground, as if
'twere Cain's jaw-bone, that did the first murder!
This might be the pate of a politician,° which this ass
80 now o'erreaches,° one that would circumvent God,
might it not? *[Handwritten note: "Now he's just tossing skulls around they were once alive"]*
HORATIO: It might, my lord.

53. **unyoke:** After this great effort they may unharness the team
of your wits.   56. **Mass:** By the Mass.   61. **stoup:** Two-quart
measure.   62. **In . . . love:** This and the two following stan-
zas, with nonsensical variations, are from a poem attributed
to Lord Vaux and printed in *Tottel's Miscellany* (1557). The
O and *a* (for "ah") seemingly are the grunts of the digger.
64. **To contract . . . behove:** To make a betrothal agreement for
my benefit (?).   65. **meet:** Suitable (i.e., more suitable).   68–69.
property of easiness: Something he can do easily and without thinking.   71. **daintier sense:** More delicate sense of feeling.   74. **into the land:** Toward my grave (?) (but note the lack
of rhyme in *steps, land*).   77. **jowls:** Dashes.   79. **politician:**
Schemer, plotter.   80. **o'erreaches:** Circumvents, gets the better
of (with a quibble on the literal sense).

V, i. Location: A churchyard. [S.D.] *Clowns:* Rustics.   **4. straight:**
Straightway, immediately.   **crowner:** Coroner.   **9. se offendendo:**
A comic mistake for *se defendendo*, term used in verdicts of jus-
tifiable homicide.   **12. Argal:** Corruption of *ergo*, therefore.   **17.**
will he: Will he not.   **23. quest:** Inquest.   **27. there thou say'st:**
That's right.   **28. count'nance:** Privilege.   **30. even-Christen:**
Fellow Christian.   **40. confess thyself:** The saying continues, "and
be hanged."

HAMLET: Or of a courtier, which could say "Good morrow, sweet lord! How dost thou, sweet lord?" This
85 might be my Lord Such-a-one, that prais'd my Lord
Such-a-one's horse when 'a meant to beg it, might it
not?

HORATIO: Ay, my lord.

HAMLET: Why, e'en so, and now my Lady Worm's
90 chapless,° and knock'd about the mazzard° with a
sexton's spade. Here's fine revolution,° an° we had
the trick to see 't. Did these bones cost no more the
breeding,° but to play at loggats° with them? Mine
ache to think on 't.

(Song.)

95 FIRST CLOWN: "A pick-axe, and a spade, a spade,
    For and° a shrouding sheet;
    O, a pit of clay for to be made
    For such a guest is meet."

                    [*Throws up another skull.*]

HAMLET: There's another. Why may not that be the
100 skull of a lawyer? Where be his quiddities° now, his
quillities,° his cases, his tenures,° and his tricks? Why
does he suffer this mad knave now to knock him
about the sconce° with a dirty shovel, and will not
tell him of his action of battery? Hum! This fellow
105 might be in 's time a great buyer of land, with his
statutes, his recognizances,° his fines, his double°
vouchers,° his recoveries.° [Is this the fine of his fines,
and the recovery of his recoveries,] to have his fine
pate full of fine dirt?° Will his vouchers vouch him
110 no more of his purchases, and double [ones too],
than the length and breadth of a pair of indentures?°
The very conveyances° of his lands will scarcely lie
in this box,° and must th' inheritor° himself have no
more, ha?

115 HORATIO: Not a jot more, my lord.

HAMLET: Is not parchment made of sheep-skins?

HORATIO: Ay, my lord, and of calf-skins too.

HAMLET: They are sheep and calves which seek out
assurance in that.° I will speak to this fellow.—
Whose grave's this, sirrah?°   120

FIRST CLOWN: Mine, sir.

    [*Sings.*] "O, a pit of clay for to be made
    [For such a guest is meet]."

HAMLET: I think it be thine, indeed, for thou liest in 't.

FIRST CLOWN: You lie out on 't, sir, and therefore 'tis not 125
yours. For my part, I do not lie in 't, yet it is mine.

HAMLET: Thou dost lie in 't, to be in 't and say it is thine.
'Tis for the dead, not for the quick;° therefore thou
liest.

FIRST CLOWN: 'Tis a quick lie, sir; 'twill away again 130
from me to you.

HAMLET: What man dost thou dig it for?

FIRST CLOWN: For no man, sir.

HAMLET: What woman, then?

FIRST CLOWN: For none, neither.   135

HAMLET: Who is to be buried in 't?

FIRST CLOWN: One that was a woman, sir, but, rest her
soul, she's dead.

HAMLET: How absolute° the knave is! We must speak
by the card,° or equivocation° will undo us. By the 140
Lord, Horatio, this three years I have taken note of it:
the age is grown so pick'd° that the toe of the peasant comes so near the heel of the courtier, he galls his
kibe.° How long hast thou been a grave-maker?

FIRST CLOWN: Of all the days i' th' year, I came to 't that 145
day that our last king Hamlet overcame Fortinbras.

HAMLET: How long is that since?

FIRST CLOWN: Cannot you tell that? Every fool can tell
that. It was that very day that young Hamlet was
born—he that is mad, and sent into England.   150

HAMLET: Ay, marry, why was he sent into England?

FIRST CLOWN: Why, because 'a was mad. 'A shall recover
his wits there, or, if 'a do not, 'tis no great matter
there.

HAMLET: Why?   155

FIRST CLOWN: 'Twill not be seen in him there. There the
men are as mad as he.

HAMLET: How came he mad?

FIRST CLOWN: Very strangely, they say.

HAMLET: How strangely?   160

FIRST CLOWN: Faith, e'en with losing his wits.

HAMLET: Upon what ground?

FIRST CLOWN: Why, here in Denmark. I have been sexton
here, man and boy, thirty years.

HAMLET: How long will a man lie i' th' earth ere he rot? 165

FIRST CLOWN: Faith, if 'a be not rotten before 'a die—
as we have many pocky° corses [now-a-days], that

90. chapless: Having no lower jaw. **mazzard:** Head (literally,
a drinking vessel). **91. revolution:** Change. **an:** If. **93. the
breeding:** In the breeding, raising. **loggats:** A game in which
pieces of hardwood are thrown to lie as near as possible to a
stake. **96. For and:** And moreover. **100. quiddities:** Subtleties, quibbles (from Latin *quid*, a thing). **101. quillities:** Verbal
niceties, subtle distinctions (variation of *quiddities*). **tenures:**
The holding of a piece of property or office; or, the conditions
or period of such holding. **103. sconce:** Head. **106. statutes,
recognizances:** Legal documents guaranteeing a debt by attaching land and property. **106–107. fines, recoveries:** Ways
of converting entailed estates into "fee simple" or freehold.
106. double: Signed by two signatories. **107. vouchers:** Guarantee of the legality of a title to real estate. **107–109. fine
of his fines . . . fine pate . . . fine dirt:** End of his legal maneuvers . . . elegant head . . . minutely sifted dirt. **111. pair of
indentures:** Legal document drawn up in duplicate on a single
sheet and then cut apart on a zigzag line so that each pair was
uniquely matched. (Hamlet may refer to two rows of teeth,
or dentures.) **112. conveyances:** Deeds. **113. this box:** The
skull. **inheritor:** Possessor, owner.

119. assurance in that: Safety in legal parchments. **120. sirrah:**
Term of address to inferiors. **128. quick:** Living. **139. absolute:** Positive, decided. **140. by the card:** By the mariner's card
on which the points of the compass were marked (i.e., with
precision). **equivocation:** Ambiguity in the use of terms.
142. pick'd: Refined, fastidious. **143–144. galls his kibe:**
Chafes the courtier's chilblain (a swelling or sore caused by
cold). **167. pocky:** Rotten, diseased (literally, with the pox, or
syphilis).

will scarce hold the laying in — 'a will last you some
eight year or nine year. A tanner will last you nine
170 year.

HAMLET: Why he more than another?

FIRST CLOWN: Why, sir, his hide is so tann'd with his
trade that 'a will keep out water a great while, and
your water is a sore decayer of your whoreson dead
175 body. [*Picks up a skull.*] Here's a skull now hath lain
you° i' th' earth three and twenty years.

HAMLET: Whose was it?

FIRST CLOWN: A whoreson mad fellow's it was. Whose do
you think it was?

180 HAMLET: Nay, I know not.

FIRST CLOWN: A pestilence on him for a mad rogue! 'A
pour'd a flagon of Rhenish° on my head once. This
same skull, sir, was Yorick's skull, the King's jester.

HAMLET: This?

185 FIRST CLOWN: E'en that.

HAMLET: [Let me see.] [*Takes the skull*] Alas, poor
Yorick! I knew him, Horatio, a fellow of infinite jest,
of most excellent fancy. He hath borne me on his
back a thousand times; and now, how abhorr'd in
190 my imagination it is! My gorge rises at it. Here hung
those lips that I have kiss'd I know not how oft.
Where be your gibes now? Your gambols, your
songs, your flashes of merriment that were wont to
set the table on a roar? Not one now, to mock your
195 own grinning? Quite chap-fall'n?° Now get you to
my lady's chamber, and tell her, let her paint an inch
thick, to this favor° she must come; make her laugh
at that. Prithee, Horatio, tell me one thing.

HORATIO: What's that, my lord?

200 HAMLET: Dost thou think Alexander look'd o' this fashion i' th' earth?

HORATIO: E'en so.

HAMLET: And smelt so? Pah! [*Puts down the skull.*]

HORATIO: E'en so, my lord.

205 HAMLET: To what base uses we may return, Horatio!
Why may not imagination trace the noble dust of
Alexander, till 'a find it stopping a bung-hole?

HORATIO: 'Twere to consider too curiously,° to consider so.

HAMLET: No, faith, not a jot, but to follow him thither
210 with modesty° enough, and likelihood to lead it.
[As thus]: Alexander died, Alexander was buried,
Alexander returneth to dust; the dust is earth; of
earth we make loam;° and why of that loam, whereto
he was converted, might they not stop a beer-barrel?
215 Imperious° Caesar, dead and turn'd to clay,
Might stop a hole to keep the wind away.
O, that that earth which kept the world in awe

Should patch a wall t' expel the winter's flaw!°
But soft, but soft awhile! Here comes the King.

(*Enter King, Queen, Laertes, and the Corse [of Ophelia,
in procession, with Priest, Lords etc.].*)

The Queen, the courtiers. Who is this they follow?   220
And with such maimed rites? This doth betoken
The corse they follow did with desp'rate hand
Fordo it° own life. 'Twas of some estate.°
Couch° we awhile, and mark.
                    [*He and Horatio conceal themselves.
                    Ophelia's body is taken to the grave.*]

LAERTES: What ceremony else?   225

HAMLET [*to Horatio*]: That is Laertes, a very noble
        youth. Mark.

LAERTES: What ceremony else?

PRIEST: Her obsequies have been as far enlarg'd
As we have warranty. Her death was doubtful,
And, but that great command o'ersways the order,   230
She should in ground unsanctified been lodg'd
Till the last trumpet. For° charitable prayers,
Shards,° flints, and pebbles should be thrown on her.
Yet here she is allow'd her virgin crants,°
Her maiden strewments,° and the bringing home   235
Of bell and burial.°

LAERTES: Must there no more be done?

PRIEST: No more be done.
We should profane the service of the dead
To sing a requiem and such rest to her
As to peace-parted souls.

LAERTES: Lay her i' th' earth,   240
And from her fair and unpolluted flesh
May violets° spring! I tell thee, churlish priest,
A minist'ring angel shall my sister be
When thou liest howling!

HAMLET [*to Horatio*]:   What, the fair Ophelia!

QUEEN [*scattering flowers*]: Sweets to the sweet!
        Farewell.   245
I hoped thou shouldst have been my Hamlet's wife.
I thought thy bride-bed to have deck'd, sweet maid,
And not have strew'd thy grave.

LAERTES: O, treble woe
Fall ten times treble on that cursed head
Whose wicked deed thy most ingenious sense°   250
Depriv'd thee of! Hold off the earth awhile,
Till I have caught her once more in mine arms.
        [*Leaps into the grave and embraces Ophelia.*]
Now pile your dust upon the quick and dead,
Till of this flat a mountain you have made

175–176. **lain you:** Lain.   182. **Rhenish:** Rhine wine.
195. **chap-fall'n:** (1) Lacking the lower jaw; (2) dejected.
197. **favor:** Aspect, appearance.   208. **curiously:** Minutely.
210. **modesty:** Moderation.   213. **loam:** Clay mixture for
brickmaking or other clay use.   215. **Imperious:** Imperial.

218. **flaw:** Gust of wind.   223. **Fordo it:** Destroy its.   **estate:**
Rank.   224. **Couch:** Hide, lurk.   232. **For:** In place of.
233. **Shards:** Broken bits of pottery.   234. **crants:** Garland.
235. **strewments:** Traditional strewing of flowers.   235–236.
bringing . . . burial: Laying to rest of the body in consecrated
ground, to the sound of the bell.   242. **violets:** See IV, v, 186
and note.   250. **ingenious sense:** Mind endowed with finest
qualities.

255 T 'o'ertop old Pelion,° or the skyish head
  Of blue Olympus.°
 HAMLET [*coming forward*]: What is he whose grief
  Bears such an emphasis, whose phrase of sorrow
  Conjures the wand'ring stars,° and makes them stand
260 Like wonder-wounded hearers? This is I,
  Hamlet the Dane.°
 LAERTES: The devil take thy soul!

           [*Grappling with him.*]

 HAMLET: Thou pray'st not well.
  I prithee, take thy fingers from my throat;
  For, though I am not splenitive° and rash,
265 Yet have I in me something dangerous,
  Which let thy wisdom fear. Hold off thy hand.
 KING: Pluck them asunder.
 QUEEN: Hamlet, Hamlet!
 ALL: Gentlemen!
 HORATIO: Good my lord, be quiet.

      [*Hamlet and Laertes are parted.*]

 HAMLET: Why, I will fight with him upon this theme
270 Until my eyelids will no longer wag.
 QUEEN: O my son, what theme?
 HAMLET: I lov'd Ophelia. Forty thousand brothers
  Could not with all their quantity of love
  Make up my sum. What wilt thou do for her?
275 KING: O, he is mad, Laertes.
 QUEEN: For love of God, forbear him.
 HAMLET: 'Swounds,° show me what thou' do.
  Woo 't° weep? Woo 't fight? Woo 't fast? Woo 't
   tear thyself?
  Woo 't drink up eisel?° Eat a crocodile?
280 I'll do 't. Dost thou come here to whine?
  To outface me with leaping in her grave?
  Be buried quick° with her, and so will I.
  And, if thou prate of mountains, let them throw
  Millions of acres on us, till our ground,
285 Singeing his pate° against the burning zone,°
  Make Ossa° like a wart! Nay, an thou 'lt mouth,°
  I'll rant as well as thou.
 QUEEN: This is mere° madness,
  And thus a while the fit will work on him;
  Anon, as patient as the female dove
290 When that her golden couplets° are disclos'd,°
  His silence will sit drooping.
 HAMLET: Hear you, sir.
  What is the reason that you use me thus?

  I lov'd you ever. But it is no matter.
  Let Hercules himself do what he may,
  The cat will mew, and dog will have his day.° 295
 KING: I pray thee, good Horatio, wait upon him.

     (*Exit Hamlet and Horatio.*)

 [*To Laertes.*] Strengthen your patience in° our last
   night's speech;
  We'll put the matter to the present push.°
  Good Gertrude, set some watch over your son.—
  This grave shall have a living° monument. 300
  An hour of quiet shortly shall we see;
  Till then, in patience our proceeding be. (*Exeunt.*)

{Scene II}°

(*Enter Hamlet and Horatio.*)

 HAMLET: So much for this, sir; now shall you see the
   other.°
  You do remember all the circumstance?
 HORATIO: Remember it, my lord!
 HAMLET: Sir, in my heart there was a kind of
   fighting
  That would not let me sleep. Methought I lay 5
  Worse than the mutines° in the bilboes.° Rashly,°
  And prais'd be rashness for it—let us know,°
  Our indiscretion sometime serves us well
  When our deep plots do pall,° and that should
   learn° us
  There's a divinity that shapes our ends, 10
  Rough-hew° them how we will—
 HORATIO: That is most certain.
 HAMLET: Up from my cabin,
  My sea-gown scarf'd about me, in the dark
  Grop'd I to find out them, had my desire,
  Finger'd° their packet, and in fine° withdrew 15
  To mine own room again, making so bold,
  My fears forgetting manners, to unseal
  Their grand commission; where I found, Horatio—
  Ah, royal knavery!—an exact command,
  Larded° with many several sorts of reasons 20
  Importing° Denmark's health and England's too,
  With, ho, such bugs° and goblins in my life,°
  That, on the supervise,° no leisure bated,°

255, 256. **Pelion, Olympus:** Mountains in the north of Thessaly; see also the reference to Ossa at line 286. **259. wand'ring stars:** Planets. **261. the Dane:** This title normally signifies the king; see I, i, 15 and note. **264. splenitive:** Quick-tempered. **277. 'Swounds:** By His (Christ's) wounds. **278. Woo 't:** Wilt thou. **279. eisel:** Vinegar. **282. quick:** Alive. **285. his pate:** Its head (i.e., top). **burning zone:** Sun's orbit. **286. Ossa:** Another mountain in Thessaly. (In their war against the Olympian gods, the giants attempted to heap Ossa, Pelion, and Olympus on one another to scale heaven.) **mouth:** Rant. **287. mere:** Utter. **290. golden couplets:** Two baby pigeons, covered with yellow down. **disclos'd:** Hatched.

294–295. Let . . . day: Despite any blustering attempts at interference, every person will sooner or later do what he must do. **297. in:** By recalling. **298. present push:** Immediate test. **300. living:** Lasting; also refers (for Laertes' benefit) to the plot against Hamlet. **V, ii. Location:** The castle. **1. see the other:** Hear the other news. **6. mutines:** Mutineers. **bilboes:** Shackles. **Rashly:** On impulse (this adverb goes with lines 12ff.). **7. know:** Acknowledge. **9. pall:** Fail. **learn:** Teach. **11. Rough-hew:** Shape roughly. **15. Finger'd:** Pilfered, pinched. **in fine:** Finally, in conclusion. **20. Larded:** Enriched. **21. Importing:** Relating to. **22. bugs:** Bugbears, hobgoblins. **in my life:** To be feared if I were allowed to live. **23. supervise:** Reading. **leisure bated:** Delay allowed.

No, not to stay the grinding of the axe,
My head should be struck off.

25 HORATIO: Is 't possible?

HAMLET: Here's the commission; read it at more
   leisure.   [*Gives document.*]
But wilt thou hear now how I did proceed?

HORATIO: I beseech you.

HAMLET: Being thus benetted round with villainies,
30   Or I could make a prologue to my brains,
They had begun the play.° I sat me down,
Devis'd a new commission, wrote it fair.°
I once did hold it, as our statists° do,
A baseness° to write fair, and labor'd much
35 How to forget that learning, but, sir, now
It did me yeoman's° service. Wilt thou know
Th' effect° of what I wrote?

HORATIO: Ay, good my lord.

HAMLET: An earnest conjuration from the King,
As England was his faithful tributary,
40 As love between them like the palm might flourish,
As peace should still her wheaten garland° wear
And stand a comma° 'tween their amities,
And many such-like as's° of great charge,°
That, on the view and knowing of these contents,
45 Without debasement further, more or less,
He should those bearers put to sudden death,
Not shriving time° allow'd.

HORATIO: How was this seal'd?

HAMLET: Why, even in that was heaven ordinant.°
I had my father's signet° in my purse,
50 Which was the model of that Danish seal;
Folded the writ up in the form of th' other,
Subscrib'd° it, gave 't th' impression,° plac'd it safely,
The changeling° never known. Now, the next day
Was our sea-fight, and what to this was sequent
55 Thou knowest already.

HORATIO: So Guildenstern and Rosencrantz go to 't.

HAMLET: [Why, man, they did make love to this
   employment.]
They are not near my conscience. Their defeat
Does by their own insinuation° grow.
60 'Tis dangerous when the baser nature comes
Between the pass° and fell° incensed points
Of mighty opposites.

HORATIO: Why, what a king is this!

HAMLET: Does it not, think thee, stand° me now
  upon—
He that hath killed my king and whor'd my mother,
65 Popp'd in between th' election° and my hopes,
Thrown out his angle° for my proper° life,
And with such coz'nage°—is 't not perfect
  conscience
[To quit° him with this arm? And is 't not to be
  damn'd
To let this canker° of our nature come
70 In further evil?

HORATIO: It must be shortly known to him from
  England
What is the issue of the business there.

HAMLET: It will be short. The interim is mine,
And a man's life 's no more than to say "One."°
75 But I am very sorry, good Horatio,
That to Laertes I forgot myself,
For by the image of my cause I see
The portraiture of his. I'll court his favors.
But, sure, the bravery° of his grief did put me
Into a tow'ring passion.

HORATIO: Peace, who comes here?]   80

(*Enter a Courtier* [*Osric*].)

OSRIC: Your lordship is right welcome back to Denmark.

HAMLET: I humbly thank you, sir. [*To Horatio.*] Dost
know this water-fly?

HORATIO: No, my good lord.

HAMLET: Thy state is the more gracious, for 'tis a vice to   85
know him. He hath much land, and fertile. Let a
beast be lord of beasts, and his crib shall stand at the
King's mess.° 'Tis a chough,° but, as I say, spacious in
the possession of dirt.

OSRIC: Sweet lord, if your lordship were at leisure, I   90
should impart a thing to you from his Majesty.

HAMLET: I will receive it, sir, with all diligence of spirit.
Put your bonnet to his right use; 'tis for the head.

OSRIC: I thank your lordship, it is very hot.

HAMLET: No, believe me, 'tis very cold; the wind is   95
northerly.

OSRIC: It is indifferent° cold, my lord, indeed.

HAMLET: But yet methinks it is very sultry and hot for
my complexion.°

OSRIC: Exceedingly, my lord; it is very sultry, as   100
'twere—I cannot tell how. My lord, his Majesty bade
me signify to you that 'a has laid a great wager on
your head. Sir, this is the matter—

30–31. Or . . . play: Before I could consciously turn my brain to
the matter, it had started working on a plan. (*Or* means "ere.")
32. fair: In a clear hand.   **33. statists:** Statesmen.   **34. baseness:**
Lower-class trait.   **36. yeoman's:** Substantial, workmanlike.
37. effect: Purport.   **41. wheaten garland:** Symbolic of fruitful
agriculture, of peace.   **42. comma:** Indicating continuity, link.
43. as's: (1) The "whereases" of formal document; (2) asses.
charge: (1) Import; (2) burden.   **47. shriving time:** Time for
confession and absolution.   **48. ordinant:** Directing.   **49. sig-
net:** Small seal.   **52. Subscrib'd:** Signed.   **impression:** With a
wax seal.   **53. changeling:** The substituted letter (literally, a
fairy child substituted for a human one).   **59. insinuation:** Interference.   **61. pass:** Thrust.   **fell:** Fierce.

63. stand: Become incumbent.   **65. election:** The Danish
monarch was "elected" by a small number of high-
ranking electors.   **66. angle:** Fishing line.   **proper:** Very.
67. coz'nage: Trickery.   **68. quit:** Repay.   **69. canker:** Ulcer.
74. a man's . . . "One": To take a man's life requires no more
than to count to one as one duels.   **79. bravery:** Bravado.
86–88. Let . . . mess: If a man, no matter how beastlike, is as
rich in possessions as Osric, he may eat at the king's table.
88. chough: Chattering jackdaw.   **97. indifferent:** Somewhat.
99. complexion: Temperament.

HAMLET: I beseech you, remember—

[*Hamlet moves him to put on his hat.*]

105 OSRIC: Nay, good my lord; for my ease,° in good faith. Sir, here is newly come to court Laertes—believe me, an absolute gentleman, full of most excellent differences,° of very soft society° and great showing.° Indeed, to speak feelingly° of him, he is the card° or
110 calendar° of gentry,° for you shall find in him the continent of what part° a gentleman would see.

HAMLET: Sir, his definement° suffers no perdition° in you, though, I know, to divide him inventorially° would dozy° th' arithmetic of memory, and yet
115 but yaw° neither° in respect of° his quick sail. But, in the verity of extolment,° I take him to be a soul of great article,° and his infusion° of such dearth and rareness,° as, to make true diction° of him, his semblable° is his mirror, and who else would trace° him,
120 his umbrage,° nothing more.

OSRIC: Your lordship speaks most infallibly of him.

HAMLET: The concernancy,° sir? Why do we wrap the gentleman in our more rawer breath?°

OSRIC: Sir?

125 HORATIO: Is 't not possible to understand in another tongue?° You will do 't,° sir, really.

HAMLET: What imports the nomination° of this gentleman?

OSRIC: Of Laertes?

130 HORATIO [*to Hamlet*]: His purse is empty already; all 's golden words are spent.

HAMLET: Of him, sir.

OSRIC: I know you are not ignorant—

HAMLET: I would you did, sir; yet, in faith, if you did, it
135 would not much approve° me. Well, sir?

OSRIC: You are not ignorant of what excellence Laertes is—

HAMLET: I dare not confess that, lest I should compare° with him in excellence; but to know a man well were to know himself.°   140

OSRIC: I mean, sir, for his weapon; but in the imputation laid on him by them,° in his meed° he's unfellow'd.°

HAMLET: What's his weapon?

OSRIC: Rapier and dagger.

HAMLET: That's two of his weapons—but well.   145

OSRIC: The King, sir, hath wager'd with him six Barbary horses, against the which he has impawn'd,° as I take it, six French rapiers and poniards, with their assigns,° as girdle, hangers,° and so. Three of the carriages,° in faith, are very dear to fancy,° very responsive° to the hilts, most delicate° carriages, and of very liberal conceit.°   150

HAMLET: What call you the carriages?

HORATIO [*to Hamlet*]: I knew you must be edified by the margent° ere you had done.   155

OSRIC: The carriages, sir, are the hangers.

HAMLET: The phrase would be more germane to the matter if we could carry a cannon by our sides; I would it might be hangers till then. But, on: six Barb'ry horses against six French swords, their assigns, and
160 three liberal-conceited carriages; that's the French bet against the Danish. Why is this impawn'd, as you call it?

OSRIC: The King, sir, hath laid,° sir, that in a dozen passes° between yourself and him, he shall not   165
exceed you three hits. He hath laid on twelve for nine, and it would come to immediate trial, if your lordship would vouchsafe the answer.

HAMLET: How if I answer no?

OSRIC: I mean, my lord, the opposition of your person   170
in trial.

HAMLET: Sir, I will walk here in the hall. If it please his Majesty, it is the breathing time° of day with me. Let the foils be brought, the gentleman willing, and the King hold his purpose, I will win for him an I can; if   175
not, I will gain nothing but my shame and the odd hits.

---

105. **for my ease:** A conventional reply declining the invitation to put his hat back on. 107–108. **differences:** Special qualities. **soft society:** Agreeable manners. 108. **great showing:** Distinguished appearance. 109. **feelingly:** With just perception. **card:** Chart, map. 110. **calendar:** Guide. **gentry:** Good breeding. 110–111. **the continent ... part:** One who contains in him all the qualities (a *continent* is that which contains). 112. **definement:** Definition. (Hamlet proceeds to mock Osric by using his lofty diction back at him.) **perdition:** Loss, diminution. 113. **divide him inventorially:** Enumerate his graces. 114. **dozy:** Dizzy. 115. **yaw:** To move unsteadily (said of a ship). **neither:** For all that. **in respect of:** In comparison with. 116. **in ... extolment:** In true praise (of him). 117. **article:** Moment or importance. **infusion:** Essence, character imparted by nature. 117–118. **dearth and rareness:** Rarity. 118. **make true diction:** Speak truly. 119. **semblable:** Only true likeness. **who ... trace:** Any person who would wish to follow. 120. **umbrage:** Shadow. 122. **concernancy:** Import, relevance. 123. **breath:** Speech. 125–126. **to understand ... tongue:** For Osric to understand when someone else speaks in his manner. (Horatio twits Osric for not being able to understand the kind of flowery speech he himself uses when Hamlet speaks in such a vein.) 126. **You will do 't:** You can if you try. 127. **nomination:** Naming. 135. **approve:** Commend.

138. **compare:** Seem to compete. 139–140. **but ... himself:** For, to recognize excellence in another man, one must know oneself. 141–142. **imputation ... them:** Reputation given him by others. 142. **meed:** Merit. **unfellow'd:** Unmatched. 147. **impawn'd:** Staked, wagered. 149. **assigns:** Appurtenances. **hangers:** Straps on the sword belt (*girdle*) from which the sword hung. 149–150. **carriages:** An affected way of saying *hangers;* literally, gun-carriages. 150. **dear to fancy:** Fancifully designed, tasteful. 150–151. **responsive:** Corresponding closely, matching. 151. **delicate:** I.e., in workmanship. 152. **liberal conceit:** Elaborate design. 155. **margent:** Margin of a book, place for explanatory notes. 164. **laid:** Wagered. 165. **passes:** Bouts. (The odds of the betting are hard to explain. Possibly the king bets that Hamlet will win at least five out of twelve, at which point Laertes raises the odds against himself by betting he will win nine.) 173. **breathing time:** Exercise period.

OSRIC: Shall I deliver you so?

HAMLET: To this effect, sir—after what flourish your
180   nature will.

OSRIC: I commend my duty to your lordship.

HAMLET: Yours, yours. [*Exit Osric.*] He does well to
    commend it himself; there are no tongues else for 's
    turn.

185 HORATIO: This lapwing° runs away with the shell on his
    head.

HAMLET: 'A did comply, sir, with his dug,° before 'a
    suck'd it. Thus has he—and many more of the same
    breed that I know the drossy° age dotes on—only
190   got the tune° of the time and, out of an habit of
    encounter,° a kind of yesty° collection,° which car-
    ries them through and through the most fann'd and
    winnow'd° opinions; and do but blow them to their
    trial, the bubbles are out.°

(*Enter a Lord.*)

195 LORD: My lord, his Majesty commended him to you by
    young Osric, who brings back to him that you attend
    him in the hall. He sends to know if your pleasure
    hold to play with Laertes, or that you will take longer
    time.

200 HAMLET: I am constant to my purposes; they follow the
    King's pleasure. If his fitness speaks,° mine is ready;
    now or whensoever, provided I be so able as now.

LORD: The King and Queen and all are coming down.

HAMLET: In happy time.°

205 LORD: The Queen desires you to use some gentle enter-
    tainment° to Laertes before you fall to play.

HAMLET: She well instructs me.   [*Exit Lord.*]

HORATIO: You will lose, my lord.

HAMLET: I do not think so. Since he went into France, I
210   have been in continual practice; I shall win at the
    odds. But thou wouldst not think how ill all's here
    about my heart; but it is no matter.

HORATIO: Nay, good my lord—

HAMLET: It is but foolery, but it is such a kind of gain-
215   giving,° as would perhaps trouble a woman.

HORATIO: If your mind dislike anything, obey it. I will
    forestall their repair hither, and say you are not fit.

HAMLET: Not a whit, we defy augury. There is special
    providence in the fall of a sparrow. If it be now, 'tis
220   not to come; if it be not to come, it will be now, if it

---

be not now, yet it will come. The readiness is all.
Since no man of aught he leaves knows what is 't to
leave betimes,° let be.

(*A table prepar'd. [Enter] trumpets, drums, and Officers
with cushions; King, Queen, [Osric,] and all the State;
foils, daggers, [and wine borne in;] and Laertes.*)

KING: Come, Hamlet, come, and take this hand from me.
    [*The King puts Laertes' hand into Hamlet's.*]

HAMLET: Give me your pardon, sir. I have done you
    wrong,   225
    But pardon 't, as you are a gentleman.
    This presence° knows,
    And you must needs have heard, how I am punish'd
    With a sore distraction. What I have done
    That might your nature, honor, and exception°   230
    Roughly awake, I here proclaim was madness.
    Was 't Hamlet wrong'd Laertes? Never Hamlet.
    If Hamlet from himself be ta'en away,
    And when he's not himself does wrong Laertes,
    Then Hamlet does it not, Hamlet denies it.   235
    Who does it, then? His madness. If 't be so,
    Hamlet is of the faction that is wrong'd;
    His madness is poor Hamlet's enemy.
    [Sir, in this audience,]
    Let my disclaiming from a purpos'd evil
    Free me so far in your most generous thoughts   240
    That I have shot my arrow o'er the house
    And hurt my brother.

LAERTES: I am satisfied in nature,°
    Whose motive in this case should stir me most
    To my revenge. But in my terms of honor   245
    I stand aloof, and will no reconcilement
    Till by some elder masters of known honor
    I have a voice° and precedent of peace
    To keep my name ungor'd. But till that time,
    I do receive your offer'd love like love,   250
    And will not wrong it.

HAMLET: I embrace it freely,
    And will this brothers' wager frankly play.
    Give us the foils. Come on.

LAERTES: Come, one for me.

HAMLET: I'll be your foil,° Laertes. In mine ignorance
    Your skill shall, like a star i' th' darkest night,   255
    Stick fiery off° indeed.

LAERTES: You mock me, sir.

HAMLET: No, by this hand.

KING: Give them the foils, young Osric. Cousin Hamlet,
    You know the wager?

HAMLET: Very well, my lord.
    Your Grace has laid the odds o' th' weaker side.   260

---

185. lapwing: A bird that draws intruders away from its
nest and was thought to run about when newly hatched
with its head in the shell; a seeming reference to Osric's hat.
187. comply . . . dug: Observe ceremonious formality toward
his mother's teat. **189. drossy:** Frivolous. **190. tune:** Temper, mood, manner of speech. **190–191. habit of encounter:**
Demeanor of social intercourse. **191. yesty:** Yeasty, frothy.
collection: I.e., of current phrases. **192–193. fann'd and
winnow'd:** Select and refined. **193–194. blow . . . out:** Put them
to the test, and their ignorance is exposed. **201. If . . . speaks:**
If his readiness answers to the time. **204. In happy time:** A
phrase of courtesy indicating acceptance. **205–206. entertainment:** Greeting. **214–215. gain-giving:** Misgiving.

222–223. what . . . betimes: What is the best time to leave it.
227. presence: Royal assembly. **230. exception:** Disapproval.
243. in nature: As to my personal feelings. **248. voice:**
Authoritative pronouncement. **254. foil:** Thin metal background which sets a jewel off (with pun on the blunted rapier
for fencing). **256. Stick fiery off:** Stand out brilliantly.

KING: I do not fear it; I have seen you both.
But since he is better'd,° we have therefore odds.
LAERTES: This is too heavy, let me see another.
[*Exchanges his foil for another.*]
HAMLET: This likes me well. These foils have all a length?
[*They prepare to play.*]

265 OSRIC: Ay, my good lord.
KING: Set me the stoups of wine upon that table.
If Hamlet give the first or second hit,
Or quit° in answer of the third exchange,
Let all the battlements their ordnance fire.

270 The King shall drink to Hamlet's better breath,
And in the cup an union° shall he throw,
Richer than that which four successive kings
In Denmark's crown have worn. Give me the cups,
And let the kettle° to the trumpet speak,

275 The trumpet to the cannoneer without,
The cannons to the heavens, the heaven to earth,
"Now the King drinks to Hamlet." Come, begin.
(*Trumpets the while.*)
And you, the judges, bear a wary eye.
HAMLET: Come on sir.

280 LAERTES: Come, my lord. [*They play. Hamlet scores a hit.*]
HAMLET: One.
LAERTES: No.
HAMLET: Judgment.
OSRIC: A hit, a very palpable hit.
(*Drum, trumpets, and shot. Flourish. A piece goes off.*)
LAERTES: Well, again.

285 KING: Stay, give me drink. Hamlet, this pearl is thine.
[*He throws a pearl in Hamlet's cup and drinks.*]
Here's to thy health. Give him the cup.
HAMLET: I'll play this bout first, set it by awhile.
Come. [*They play.*] Another hit; what say you?
LAERTES: A touch, a touch. I do confess 't.
KING: Our son shall win.

290 QUEEN: He's fat,° and scant of breath.
Here, Hamlet, take my napkin,° rub thy brows.
The Queen carouses° to thy fortune, Hamlet.
HAMLET: Good madam!
KING: Gertrude, do not drink.

295 QUEEN: I will, my lord; I pray you pardon me.
[*Drinks.*]
KING [*aside*]: It is the pois'ned cup. It is too late.
HAMLET: I dare not drink yet, madam; by and by.
QUEEN: Come, let me wipe thy face.
LAERTES [*to King*]: My lord, I'll hit him now.
KING: I do not think 't.
LAERTES [*aside*]: And yet it is almost against my

300 conscience.

HAMLET: Come, for the third Laertes. You do but dally.
I pray you, pass with your best violence;
I am afeard you make a wanton of me.°
LAERTES: Say you so? Come on. [*They play.*]
OSRIC: Nothing, neither way.
LAERTES: Have at you now! 305
[*Laertes wounds Hamlet; then, in scuffling, they change rapiers,° and Hamlet wounds Laertes.*]
KING: Part them! They are incens'd.
HAMLET: Nay, come, again. [*The Queen falls.*]
OSRIC: Look to the Queen there, ho!
HORATIO: They bleed on both sides. How is it, my lord?
OSRIC: How is 't, Laertes?
LAERTES: Why, as a woodcock° to mine own springe, Osric; 310
I am justly kill'd with mine own treachery.
HAMLET: How does the Queen?
KING: She swoons to see them bleed.
QUEEN: No, no, the drink, the drink—O my dear Hamlet—
The drink, the drink! I am pois'ned. [*Dies.*]
HAMLET: O villainy! Ho, let the door be lock'd! 315
Treachery! Seek it out. [*Laertes falls.*]
LAERTES: It is here, Hamlet. Hamlet, thou art slain.
No med'cine in the world can do thee good;
In thee there is not half an hour's life.
The treacherous instrument is in thy hand, 320
Unbated° and envenom'd. The foul practice
Hath turn'd itself on me. Lo, here I lie,
Never to rise again. Thy mother's pois'ned.
I can no more. The King, the King's to blame.
HAMLET: The point envenom'd too? Then, venom, to
thy work. [*Stabs the King.*] 325
ALL: Treason! Treason!
KING: O, yet defend me, friends; I am but hurt.
HAMLET: Here, thou incestuous, murd'rous, damned Dane,
[*He forces the King to drink the poisoned cup.*]
Drink off this potion. Is thy union° here?
Follow my mother. [*King dies.*]
LAERTES: He is justly serv'd. 330
It is a poison temper'd° by himself.
Exchange forgiveness with me, noble Hamlet.
Mine and my father's death come not upon thee,
Nor thine on me! [*Dies.*]

262. **is better'd:** Has improved; is the odds-on favorite.
268. **quit:** Repay (with a hit). 271. **union:** Pearl (so called, according to Pliny's *Natural History*, IX, because pearls are *unique,* never identical). 274. **kettle:** Kettledrum. 290. **fat:** Not physically fit, out of training. 291. **napkin:** Handkerchief. 292. **carouses:** Drinks a toast.

303. **make . . . me:** Treat me like a spoiled child, holding back to give me an advantage. 306. [S.D.] ***in scuffling, they change rapiers:*** This stage direction occurs in the Folio. According to a widespread stage tradition, Hamlet receives a scratch, realizes that Laertes' sword is unbated, and accordingly forces an exchange. 310. **woodcock:** A bird, a type of stupidity or decoy. **springe:** Trap, snare. 321. **Unbated:** Not blunted with a button. 329. **union:** Pearl (see line 271; with grim puns on the word's other meanings: marriage, shared death [?]). 331. **temper'd:** Mixed.

335 HAMLET: Heaven make thee free of it! I follow thee.
    I am dead, Horatio. Wretched Queen, adieu!
    You that look pale and tremble at this chance,
    That are but mutes° or audience to this act,
    Had I but time—as this fell° sergeant,° Death,
340 Is strict in his arrest—O, I could tell you—
    But let it be. Horatio, I am dead;
    Thou livest. Report me and my cause aright
    To the unsatisfied.
HORATIO: Never believe it.
    I am more an antique Roman° than a Dane.
    Here's yet some liquor left.

        [*He attempts to drink from the poisoned cup.*
              Hamlet prevents him.]

345 HAMLET: As th' art a man,
    Give me the cup! Let go! By heaven, I'll ha 't.
    O God, Horatio, what a wounded name,
    Things standing thus unknown, shall I leave
      behind me!
    If thou didst ever hold me in thy heart,
350 Absent thee from felicity awhile,
    And in this harsh world draw thy breath in pain
    To tell my story.
        (*A march afar off* [*and a volley within*].)
        What warlike noise is this?
OSRIC: Young Fortinbras, with conquest come from
    Poland,
    To the ambassadors of England gives
    This warlike volley.
355 HAMLET: O, I die, Horatio!
    The potent poison quite o'ercrows° my spirit.
    I cannot live to hear the news from England,
    But I do prophesy th' election lights
    On Fortinbras. He has my dying voice.°
360 So tell him, with th' occurrents° more and less
    Which have solicited°—the rest is silence.   [*Dies.*]
HORATIO: Now cracks a noble heart. Good night,
    sweet prince;
    And flights of angels sing thee to thy rest!
                  [*March within.*]
    Why does the drum come hither?

(*Enter Fortinbras, with the* [*English*] *Ambassadors*
[*with drum, colors, and attendants*].)

FORTINBRAS: Where is this sight?
365 HORATIO: What is it you would see?
    If aught of woe or wonder, cease your search.
FORTINBRAS: This quarry° cries on havoc.° O proud
    Death.
    What feast is toward° in thine eternal cell,

    That thou so many princes at a shot
    So bloodily hast struck?
FIRST AMBASSADOR: The sight is dismal;   370
    And our affairs from England come too late.
    The ears are senseless that should give us hearing,
    To tell him his commandment is fulfill'd,
    That Rosencrantz and Guildenstern are dead.
    Where should we have our thanks?
HORATIO: Not from his° mouth,   375
    Had it th' ability of life to thank you.
    He never gave commandment for their death.
    But since, so jump° upon this bloody question,°
    You from the Polack wars, and you from England,
    Are here arriv'd, give order that these bodies   380
    High on a stage° be placed to the view,
    And let me speak to th' yet unknowing world
    How these things came about. So shall you hear
    Of carnal, bloody, and unnatural acts,
    Of accidental judgments,° casual° slaughters,   385
    Of deaths put on° by cunning and forc'd cause,
    And, in this upshot, purposes mistook
    Fall'n on th' inventors' heads. All this can I
    Truly deliver.
FORTINBRAS: Let us haste to hear it,
    And call the noblest to the audience.   390
    For me, with sorrow I embrace my fortune.
    I have some rights of memory° in this kingdom,
    Which now to claim my vantage° doth invite me.
HORATIO: Of that I shall have also cause to speak,
    And from his mouth whose voice will draw on
      more.°   395
    But let this same be presently° perform'd,
    Even while men's minds are wild, lest more
      mischance
    On° plots and errors happen.
FORTINBRAS: Let four captains
    Bear Hamlet, like a soldier, to the stage,
    For he was likely, had he been put on,°   400
    To have prov'd most royal; and, for his passage,°
    The soldiers' music and the rite of war
    Speak loudly for him.
    Take up the bodies. Such a sight as this
    Becomes the field,° but here shows much amiss.   405
    Go, bid the soldiers shoot.
        (*Exeunt* [*marching, bearing off the dead bodies;*
               a peal of ordnance is shot off].)

---

338. **mutes:** Silent observers. **339. fell:** Cruel. **sergeant:** Sheriff's officer. **344. Roman:** It was the Roman custom to follow masters in death. **356. o'ercrows:** Triumphs over. **359. voice:** Vote. **360. occurrents:** Events, incidents. **361. solicited:** Moved, urged. **367. quarry:** Heap of dead. **cries on havoc:** Proclaims a general slaughter. **368. toward:** In preparation.

375. **his:** Claudius's. **378. jump:** Precisely. **question:** Dispute. **381. stage:** Platform. **385. judgments:** Retributions. **casual:** Occurring by chance. **386. put on:** Instigated. **392. of memory:** Traditional, remembered. **393. vantage:** Presence at this opportune moment. **395. voice...more:** Vote will influence still others. **396. presently:** Immediately. **398. On:** On the basis of. **400. put on:** Invested in royal office and so put to the test. **401. passage:** Death. **405. field:** I.e., of battle.

COMMENTARIES

The great Shakespearean Andrew Cecil Bradley was professor of poetry at Oxford when he wrote one of the most highly regarded of all critical texts on Shakespeare: *Shakespearean Tragedy* (1904). He limited himself to discussing four plays: *Hamlet, Othello, King Lear,* and *Macbeth*. His insights into all these plays are still useful guides for any reader. In the commentary below, he considers Hamlet's role as the "melancholy Dane."

T. S. Eliot, one of the twentieth century's most important poets and an equally important literary critic, was a great student of Elizabethan and Jacobean drama. His discussion centers on the difficulties he sees with *Hamlet*.

A. C. BRADLEY (1851–1935)

Hamlet's Melancholy 1904

Bradley offers us an analysis of Hamlet's character, with an emphasis on what Shakespeare may have meant by describing him as melancholy. The term today implies little more than sadness, but in the sixteenth and seventeenth centuries it pointed to something quite different. The term suggested that Hamlet was philosophical and capable of inward analysis — it meant that he was, in a modern sense, a deep person. Bradley reviews the ways in which Hamlet seems to fulfill the seventeenth-century concept of Melancholy.

Let us first ask ourselves what we can gather from the play, immediately or by inference, concerning Hamlet as he was just before his father's death. And I begin by observing that the text does not bear out the idea that he was one-sidedly reflective and indisposed to action. Nobody who knew him seems to have noticed this weakness. Nobody regards him as a mere scholar who has "never formed a resolution or executed a deed." In a court which certainly would not much admire such a person he is the observed of all observers. Though he has been disappointed of the throne everyone shows him respect; and he is the favorite of the people, who are not given to worship philosophers. Fortinbras, a sufficiently practical man, considered that he was likely, had he been put on, to have proved most royally. He has Hamlet borne by four captains "like a soldier" to his grave; and Ophelia says that Hamlet *was* a soldier. If he was fond of acting, an aesthetic pursuit, he was equally fond of fencing, an athletic one: he practiced it assiduously even in his worst days.[1] So far as we can conjecture from what we see of him in those bad days, he must normally have been charmingly frank, courteous and kindly to everyone, of whatever rank, whom he liked or respected, but by no means timid or deferential to others; indeed, one would gather that he was rather the reverse, and also that he was apt to be decided and even imperious if thwarted or interfered with. He must always have

---

[1] He says so to Horatio, whom he has no motive for deceiving [V, ii, 209–210]. His contrary statement [II, ii, 301–302] is made to Rosencrantz and Guildenstern.

been fearless—in the play he appears insensible to fear of any ordinary kind. And, finally, he must have been quick and impetuous in action; for it is downright impossible that the man we see rushing after the Ghost, killing Polonius, dealing with the King's commission on the ship, boarding the pirate, leaping into the grave, executing his final vengeance, could *ever* have been shrinking or slow in an emergency. Imagine Coleridge doing any of these things!

If we consider all this, how can we accept the notion that Hamlet's was a weak and one-sided character? "Oh, but he spent ten or twelve years at a University!" Well, even if he did, it is possible to do that without becoming the victim of excessive thought. But the statement that he did rests upon a most insecure foundation.

Where then are we to look for the seeds of danger?

(1) Trying to reconstruct from the Hamlet of the play, one would not judge that his temperament was melancholy in the present sense of the word; there seems nothing to show that; but one would judge that by temperament he was inclined to nervous instability, to rapid and perhaps extreme changes of feeling and mood, and that he was disposed to be, for the time, absorbed in the feeling or mood that possessed him, whether it were joyous or depressed. This temperament the Elizabethans would have called melancholic; and Hamlet seems to be an example of it, as Lear is of a temperament mixedly choleric and sanguine. And the doctrine of temperaments was so familiar in Shakespeare's time—as Burton, and earlier prose writers, and many of the dramatists show—that Shakespeare may quite well have given this temperament to Hamlet consciously and deliberately. Of melancholy in its developed form, a habit, not a mere temperament, he often speaks. He more than once laughs at the passing and half-fictitious melancholy of youth and love; in Don John in *Much Ado* he has sketched the sour and surly melancholy of discontent; in Jaques a whimsical self-pleasing melancholy; in Antonio in the *Merchant of Venice* a quiet but deep melancholy, for which neither the victim nor his friends can assign any cause.[2] He gives to Hamlet a temperament which would not develop into melancholy unless under some exceptional strain, but which still involved a danger. In the play we see the danger realized, and find a melancholy quite unlike any that Shakespeare had as yet depicted, because the temperament of Hamlet is quite different.

(2) Next, we cannot be mistaken in attributing to the Hamlet of earlier days an exquisite sensibility, to which we may give the name "moral," if that word is taken in the wide meaning it ought to bear. This, though it suffers cruelly in later days, as we saw in criticizing the sentimental view of Hamlet, never deserts him; it makes all his cynicism, grossness and hardness appear to us morbidities, and has an inexpressibly attractive and pathetic effect. He had the soul of the youthful poet as Shelley and Tennyson have described it, an unbounded delight and faith in everything good and beautiful. We know this from himself. The world for him was *herrlich wie am ersten Tag°*—"this goodly frame the earth, this most excellent canopy the air, this brave o'erhanging firmament, this majestical roof fretted with golden fire." And not nature only: "What a piece of work is a man! how noble in reason! how infinite in faculty! in form and moving how express and admirable! in action how like an angel! in apprehension how like a god!" This is no commonplace to Hamlet; it is the language of a heart thrilled with wonder and swelling into ecstasy.

---

[2] The critics have labored to find a cause, but it seems to me Shakespeare simply meant to portray a pathological condition; and a very touching picture he draws. Antonio's sadness, which he describes in the opening lines of the play, would never drive him to suicide, but it makes him indifferent to the issue of the trial, as all his speeches in the trial scene show.

herrlich . . . Tag: As wonderful as the first day.

Doubtless it was with the same eager enthusiasm he turned to those around him. Where else in Shakespeare is there anything like Hamlet's adoration of his father? The words melt into music whenever he speaks of him. And, if there are no signs of any such feeling toward his mother, though many signs of love, it is characteristic that he evidently never entertained a suspicion of anything unworthy in her—characteristic, and significant of his tendency to see only what is good unless he is forced to see the reverse. For we find this tendency elsewhere, and find it going so far that we must call it a disposition to idealize, to see something better than what is there, or at least to ignore deficiencies. He says to Laertes, "I loved you ever," and he describes Laertes as a "very noble youth," which he was far from being. In his first greeting of Rosencrantz and Guildenstern, where his old self revives, we trace the same affectionateness and readiness to take men at their best. His love for Ophelia, too, which seems strange to some, is surely the most natural thing in the world. He saw her innocence, simplicity and sweetness, and it was like him to ask no more; and it is noticeable that Horatio, though entirely worthy of his friendship, is, like Ophelia, intellectually not remarkable. To the very end, however clouded, this generous disposition, this "free and open nature," this unsuspiciousness survive. They cost him his life; for the King knew them, and was sure that he was too "generous and free from all contriving" to "peruse the foils." To the very end, his soul, however sick and tortured it may be, answers instantaneously when good and evil are presented to it, loving the one and hating the other. He is called a skeptic who has no firm belief in anything, but he is never skeptical about *them*.

And the negative side of his idealism, the aversion to evil, is perhaps even more developed in the hero of the tragedy than in the Hamlet of earlier days. It is intensely characteristic. Nothing, I believe, is to be found elsewhere in Shakespeare (unless in the rage of the disillusioned idealist Timon) of quite the same kind as Hamlet's disgust at his uncle's drunkenness, his loathing of his mother's sensuality, his astonishment and horror at her shallowness, his contempt for everything pretentious or false, his indifference to everything merely external. This last characteristic appears in his choice of the friend of his heart, and in a certain impatience of distinctions of rank or wealth. When Horatio calls his father "a goodly king," he answers, surely with an emphasis on "man,"

> He was a man, take him for all in all,
> I shall not look upon his like again.

He will not listen to talk of Horatio being his "servant." When the others speak of their "duty" to him, he answers, "Your love, as mine to you." He speaks to the actor precisely as he does to an honest courtier. He is not in the least a revolutionary, but still, in effect, a king and a beggar are all one to him. He cares for nothing but human worth, and his pitilessness toward Polonius and Osric and his "schoolfellows" is not wholly due to morbidity, but belongs in part to his original character.

Now, in Hamlet's moral sensibility there undoubtedly lay a danger. Any great shock that life might inflict on it would be felt with extreme intensity. Such a shock might even produce tragic results. And, in fact, *Hamlet* deserves the title "tragedy of moral idealism" quite as much as the title "tragedy of reflection."

(3) With this temperament and this sensibility we find, lastly, in the Hamlet of earlier days, as of later, intellectual genius. It is chiefly this that makes him so different from all those about him, good and bad alike, and hardly less different from

most of Shakespeare's other heroes. And this, though on the whole the most important trait in his nature, is also so obvious and so famous that I need not dwell on it at length. But against one prevalent misconception I must say a word of warning. Hamlet's intellectual power is not a specific gift, like a genius for music or mathematics or philosophy. It shows itself, fitfully, in the affairs of life as unusual quickness of perception, great agility in shifting the mental attitude, a striking rapidity and fertility in resource; so that, when his natural belief in others does not make him unwary, Hamlet easily sees through them and masters them, and no one can be much less like the typical helpless dreamer. It shows itself in conversation chiefly in the form of wit or humor; and, alike in conversation and in soliloquy, it shows itself in the form of imagination quite as much as in that of thought in the stricter sense. Further, where it takes the latter shape, as it very often does, it is not philosophic in the technical meaning of the word. There is really nothing in the play to show that Hamlet ever was "a student of philosophies," unless it be the famous lines which, comically enough, exhibit this supposed victim of philosophy as its critic:

> There are more things in heaven and earth, Horatio,
> Than are dreamt of in your philosophy.[3]

His philosophy, if the word is to be used, was, like Shakespeare's own, the immediate product of the wondering and meditating mind; and such thoughts as that celebrated one, "There is nothing either good or bad but thinking makes it so," surely needed no special training to produce them. Or does Portia's remark, "Nothing is good without respect," *i.e.,* out of relation, prove that she had studied metaphysics?

Still Hamlet had speculative genius without being a philosopher, just as he had imaginative genius without being a poet. Doubtless in happier days he was a close and constant observer of men and manners, noting his results in those tables which he afterwards snatched from his breast to make in wild irony his last note of all, that one may smile and smile and be a villain. Again and again we remark that passion for generalization which so occupied him, for instance, in reflections suggested by the King's drunkenness that he quite forgot what it was he was waiting to meet upon the battlements. Doubtless, too, he was always considering things, as Horatio thought, too curiously. There was a necessity in his soul driving him to penetrate below the surface and to question what others took for granted. That fixed habitual look which the world wears for most men did not exist for him. He was forever unmaking his world and rebuilding it in thought, dissolving what to others were solid facts, and discovering what to others were old truths. There were no old truths for Hamlet. It is for Horatio a thing of course that there's a divinity that shapes our ends, but for Hamlet it is a discovery hardly won. And throughout this kingdom of the mind, where he felt that man, who in action is only like an angel, is in apprehension like a god, he moved (we must imagine) more than content, so that even in his dark days he declares he could be bounded in a nutshell and yet count himself a king of infinite space, were it not that he had bad dreams.

If now we ask whether any special danger lurked *here,* how shall we answer? We must answer, it seems to me, "Some danger, no doubt, but, granted the ordinary chances of life, not much." For, in the first place, that idea which so many critics quietly take for granted—the idea that the gift and the habit of meditative and speculative thought tend to produce irresolution in the affairs of life—would be

---

[3] Of course "your" does not mean Horatio's philosophy in particular. "Your" is used as the Gravedigger uses it when he says that "your water is a sore decayer of your ... dead body."

Hamlet's reluctance to kill Claudius is what really sells H. as a great mind, because he has to think about everything so thoroughly.

found by no means easy to verify. Can you verify it, for example, in the lives of the philosophers, or again in the lives of men whom you have personally known to be addicted to such speculation? I cannot. Of course, individual peculiarities being set apart, absorption in *any* intellectual interest, together with withdrawal from affairs, may make a man slow and unskillful in affairs; and doubtless, individual peculiarities being again set apart, a mere student is likely to be more at a loss in a sudden and great practical emergency than a soldier or a lawyer. But in all this there is no difference between a physicist, a historian, and a philosopher; and again, slowness, want of skill, and even helplessness are something totally different from the peculiar kind of irresolution that Hamlet shows. The notion that speculative thinking specially tends to produce *this* is really a mere illusion.

In the second place, even if this notion were true, it has appeared that Hamlet did *not* live the life of a mere student, much less of a mere dreamer, and that his nature was by no means simply or even one-sidedly intellectual, but was healthily active. Hence, granted the ordinary chances of life, there would seem to be no great danger in his intellectual tendency and his habit of speculation; and I would go further and say that there was nothing in them, taken alone, to unfit him even for the extraordinary call that was made upon him. In fact, if the message of the Ghost had come to him within a week of his father's death, I see no reason to doubt that he would have acted on it as decisively as Othello himself, though probably after a longer and more anxious deliberation. And therefore the Schlegel-Coleridge view (apart from its descriptive value) seems to me fatally untrue, for it implies that Hamlet's procrastination was the normal response of an overspeculative nature confronted with a difficult practical problem.

On the other hand, under conditions of a peculiar kind, Hamlet's reflectiveness certainly might prove dangerous to him, and his genius might even (to exaggerate a little) become his doom. Suppose that violent shock to his moral being of which I spoke; and suppose that under this shock, any possible action being denied to him, he began to sink into melancholy; then, no doubt, his imaginative and generalizing habit of mind might extend the effects of this shock through his whole being and mental world. And if, the state of melancholy being thus deepened and fixed, a sudden demand for difficult and decisive action in a matter connected with the melancholy arose, this state might well have for one of its symptoms an endless and futile mental dissection of the required deed. And, finally, the futility of this process, and the shame of his delay, would further weaken him and enslave him to his melancholy still more. Thus the speculative habit would be *one* indirect cause of the morbid state which hindered action; and it would also reappear in a degenerate form as one of the *symptoms* of this morbid state.

Now this is what actually happens in the play. Turn to the first words Hamlet utters when he is alone; turn, that is to say, to the place where the author is likely to indicate his meaning most plainly. What do you hear?

> O, that this too too solid flesh would melt,
> Thaw and resolve itself into a dew!
> Or that the Everlasting had not fix'd
> His canon 'gainst self-slaughter! O God! God!
> How weary, stale, flat and unprofitable,
> Seem to me all the uses of this world!
> Fie on't! ah fie! 'tis an unweeded garden,
> That grows to seed; things rank and gross in nature
> Possess it merely.

Here are a sickness of life, and even a longing for death, so intense that nothing stands between Hamlet and suicide except religious awe. And what has caused them? The rest of the soliloquy so thrusts the answer upon us that it might seem impossible to miss it. It was not his father's death; that doubtless brought deep grief, but mere grief for someone loved and lost does not make a noble spirit loathe the world as a place full only of things rank and gross. It was not the vague suspicion that we know Hamlet felt. Still less was it the loss of the crown; for though the subserviency of the electors might well disgust him, there is not a reference to the subject in the soliloquy, nor any sign elsewhere that it greatly occupied his mind. It was the moral shock of the sudden ghastly disclosure of his mother's true nature, falling on him when his heart was aching with love, and his body doubtless was weakened by sorrow. And it is essential, however disagreeable, to realize the nature of this shock. It matters little here whether Hamlet's age was twenty or thirty: in either case his mother was a matron of mature years. All his life he had believed in her, we may be sure, as such a son would. He had seen her not merely devoted to his father, but hanging on him like a newly wedded bride, hanging on him

> As if increase of appetite had grown
> By what it fed on.

He had seen her following his body "like Niobe, all tears." And then within a month—"O God! a beast would have mourned longer"—she married again, and married Hamlet's uncle, a man utterly contemptible and loathsome in his eyes; married him in what to Hamlet was incestuous wedlock;[4] married him not for any reason of state, nor even out of old family affection, but in such a way that her son was forced to see in her action not only an astounding shallowness of feeling but an eruption of coarse sensuality, "rank and gross,"[5] speeding posthaste to its horrible delight. Is it possible to conceive an experience more desolating to a man such as we have seen Hamlet to be; and is its result anything but perfectly natural? It brings bewildered horror, then loathing, then despair of human nature. His whole mind is poisoned. He can never see Ophelia in the same light again: she is a woman, and his mother is a woman: if she mentions the word "brief" to him, the answer drops from his lips like venom, "as woman's love." The last words of the soliloquy, which is *wholly* concerned with this subject, are,

> But break, my heart, for I must hold my tongue!

He can do nothing. He must lock in his heart, not any suspicion of his uncle that moves obscurely there, but that horror and loathing; and if his heart ever found relief, it was when those feelings, mingled with the love that never died out in him,

---

[4] This aspect of the matter leaves *us* comparatively unaffected, but Shakespeare evidently means it to be of importance. The Ghost speaks of it twice, and Hamlet thrice (once in his last furious words to the King). If, as we must suppose, the marriage was universally admitted to be incestuous, the corrupt acquiescence of the court and the electors to the crown would naturally have a strong effect on Hamlet's mind

[5] It is most significant that the metaphor of this soliloquy reappears in Hamlet's adjuration to his mother [III, iv, 158–159]:

> Repent what's past; avoid what is to come;
> And do not spread the compost on the weeds
> To make them ranker.

poured themselves forth in a flood as he stood in his mother's chamber beside his father's marriage bed.[6]

If we still wonder, and ask why the effect of this shock should be so tremendous, let us observe that *now* the conditions have arisen under which Hamlet's highest endowments, his moral sensibility and his genius, become his enemies. A nature morally blunter would have felt even so dreadful a revelation less keenly. A slower and more limited and positive mind might not have extended so widely through its world the disgust and disbelief that have entered it. But Hamlet has the imagination which, for evil as well as good, feels and sees all things in one. Thought is the element of his life, and his thought is infected. He cannot prevent himself from probing and lacerating the wound in his soul. One idea, full of peril, holds him fast, and he cries out in agony at it, but is impotent to free himself ("Must I remember?" "Let me not think on't"). And when, with the fading of his passion, the vividness of this idea abates, it does so only to leave behind a boundless weariness and a sick longing for death.

And this is the time which his fate chooses. In this hour of uttermost weakness, this sinking of his whole being toward annihilation, there comes on him, bursting the bounds of the natural world with a shock of astonishment and terror, the revelation of his mother's adultery and his father's murder, and, with this, the demand on him, in the name of everything dearest and most sacred, to arise and act. And for a moment, though his brain reels and totters, his soul leaps up in passion to answer this demand. But it comes too late. It does but strike home the last rivet in the melancholy which holds him bound.

> The time is out of joint! O cursed spite
> That ever I was born to set it right,—

so he mutters within an hour of the moment when he vowed to give his life to the duty of revenge; and the rest of the story exhibits his vain efforts to fulfill this duty, his unconscious self-excuses and unavailing self-reproaches, and the tragic results of his delay.

"Melancholy," I said, not dejection, nor yet insanity. That Hamlet was not far from insanity is very probable. His adoption of the pretense of madness may well have been due in part to fear of the reality; to an instinct of self-preservation, a forefeeling that the pretense would enable him to give some utterance to the load that pressed on his heart and brain, and a fear that he would be unable altogether to repress such utterance. And if the pathologist calls his state melancholia, and even proceeds to determine its species, I see nothing to object to in that; I am grateful to him for emphasizing the fact that Hamlet's melancholy was no mere common depression of spirits; and I have no doubt that many readers of the play would understand it better if they read an account of melancholia in a work on mental diseases. If we like to use the word "disease" loosely, Hamlet's condition may truly be called diseased. No exertion of will could have dispelled it. Even if he had been able at once to do the bidding of the Ghost he would doubtless have still remained for some time under the cloud. It would be absurdly unjust to call *Hamlet* a study of melancholy, but it contains such a study.

---

[6] If the reader will now look at the only speech of Hamlet's that precedes the soliloquy, and is more than one line in length–the speech beginning "Seems, madam! nay, it *is*"–he will understand what, surely, when first we come to it, sounds very strange and almost boastful. It is not, in effect, about Hamlet himself at all; it is about his mother (I do not mean that it is intentionally and consciously so; and still less that she understood it so).

But this melancholy is something very different from insanity, in anything like the usual meaning of that word. No doubt it might develop into insanity. The longing for death might become an irresistible impulse to self-destruction; the disorder of feeling and will might extend to sense and intellect; delusions might arise; and the man might become, as we say, incapable and irresponsible. But Hamlet's melancholy is some way from this condition. It is a totally different thing from the madness which he feigns; and he never, when alone or in company with Horatio alone, exhibits the signs of that madness. Nor is the dramatic use of this melancholy, again, open to the objections which would justly be made to the portrayal of an insanity which brought the hero to a tragic end. The man who suffers as Hamlet suffers—and thousands go about their business suffering thus in greater or less degree—is considered irresponsible neither by other people nor by himself: he is only too keenly conscious of his responsibility. He is therefore, so far, quite capable of being a tragic agent, which an insane person, at any rate according to Shakespeare's practice, is not. And, finally, Hamlet's state is not one which a healthy mind is unable sufficiently to imagine. It is probably not further from average experience, nor more difficult to realize, than the great tragic passions of Othello, Antony or Macbeth.

Let me try to show now, briefly, how much this melancholy accounts for.

It accounts for the main fact, Hamlet's inaction. For the *immediate* cause of that is simply that his habitual feeling is one of disgust at life and everything in it, himself included—a disgust which varies in intensity, rising at times into a longing for death, sinking often into weary apathy, but is never dispelled for more than brief intervals. Such a state of feeling is inevitably adverse to *any* kind of decided action; the body is inert, the mind indifferent or worse; its response is, "it does not matter," "it is not worth while," "it is no good." And the action required of Hamlet is very exceptional. It is violent, dangerous, difficult to accomplish perfectly, on one side repulsive to a man of honor and sensitive feeling, on another side involved in a certain mystery (here come in thus, in their subordinate place, various causes of inaction assigned by various theories). These obstacles would not suffice to prevent Hamlet from acting, if his state were normal; and against them there operate, even in his morbid state, healthy and positive feelings, love of his father, loathing of his uncle, desire of revenge, desire to do duty. But the retarding motives acquire an unnatural strength because they have an ally in something far stronger than themselves, the melancholic disgust and apathy; while the healthy motives, emerging with difficulty from the central mass of diseased feeling, rapidly sink back into it and "lose the name of action." We *see* them doing so; and sometimes the process is quite simple, no analytical reflection on the deed intervening between the outburst of passion and the relapse into melancholy.[7] But this melancholy is perfectly consistent also with that incessant dissection of the task assigned, of which the Schlegel-Coleridge theory makes so much. For those endless questions (as we may imagine them), "Was I deceived by the Ghost? How am I to do the deed? When? Where? What will be the consequence of attempting it— success, my death, utter misunderstanding, mere mischief to the State? Can it be right to do it, or noble to kill a defenseless man? What is the good of doing it in such a world as this?"—all this, and whatever else passed in a sickening round through Hamlet's mind, was not the healthy and right deliberation of a man with such a task, but otiose thinking hardly deserving the name of thought, an unconscious weaving of

---

[7] *E.g.* in the transition, referred to above, from desire for vengeance into the wish never to have been born; in the soliloquy, "O what a rogue"; in the scene at Ophelia's grave. The Schlegel-Coleridge theory does not account for the psychological movement in those passages.

[handwritten marginalia: He is very proud of his mind and his abilities. Perhaps Horatio is at play.]

[handwritten marginalia: what?]

pretexts for inaction, aimless tossings on a sick bed, symptoms of melancholy which only increased it by deepening self-contempt.

Again, (*a*) this state accounts for Hamlet's energy as well as for his lassitude, those quick decided actions of his being the outcome of a nature normally far from passive, now suddenly stimulated, and producing healthy impulses which work themselves out before they have time to subside. (*b*) It accounts for the evidently keen satisfaction which some of these actions give to him. He arranges the play scene with lively interest, and exults in its success, not really because it brings him nearer to his goal, but partly because it has hurt his enemy and partly because it has demonstrated his own skill [III, ii, 274–298]. He looks forward almost with glee to countermining the King's designs in sending him away [III, iv, 215], and looks back with obvious satisfaction, even with pride, to the address and vigor he displayed on the voyage [V, ii, 4–55]. These were not *the* action on which his morbid self-feeling had centered; he feels in them his old force, and escapes in them from his disgust. (*c*) It accounts for the pleasure with which he meets old acquaintances, like his "school-fellows" or the actors. The former observed (and we can observe) in him a "kind of joy" at first, though it is followed by "much forcing of his disposition" as he attempts to keep this joy and his courtesy alive in spite of the misery which so soon returns upon him and the suspicion he is forced to feel. (*d*) It accounts no less for the painful features of his character as seen in the play, his almost savage irritability on the one hand, and on the other his self-absorption, his callousness, his insensibility to the fates of those whom he despises, and to the feelings even of those whom he loves. These are frequent symptoms of such melancholy, and (*e*) they sometimes alternate, as they do in Hamlet, with bursts of transitory, almost hysterical, and quite fruitless emotion. It is to these last (of which a part of the soliloquy, "O what a rogue," gives a good example) that Hamlet alludes when, to the Ghost, he speaks of himself as "lapsed in *passion*," and it is doubtless partly his conscious weakness in regard to them that inspires his praise of Horatio as a man who is not "passion's slave."[8]

Finally, Hamlet's melancholy accounts for two things which seem to be explained by nothing else. The first of these is his apathy or "lethargy." We are bound to consider the evidence which the text supplies of this, though it is usual to ignore it. When Hamlet mentions, as one possible cause of his inaction, his "thinking too precisely on the event," he mentions another, "bestial oblivion"; and the thing against which he inveighs in the greater part of that soliloquy (IV, iv) is not the excess or the misuse of reason (which for him here and always is godlike), but this *bestial* oblivion or "*dullness*," this "letting all *sleep*," this allowing of heaven-sent reason to "fust unused":

> What is a man,
> If his chief good and market of his time
> Be but to *sleep* and feed? a *beast,* no more.[9]

---

[8]Hamlet's violence at Ophelia's grave, though probably intentionally exaggerated, is another example of this want of self-control. The Queen's description of him [V, i, 287–291],

> This is mere madness;
> And thus awhile the fit will work on him;
> Anon, as patient as the female dove,
> When that her golden couplets are disclosed,
> His silence will sit drooping,

may be true to life, though it is evidently prompted by anxiety to excuse his violence on the ground of his insanity.

[9]Throughout, I italicize to show the connection of ideas.

So, in the soliloquy in II, ii he accuses himself of being "a *dull* and muddy-mettled rascal," who "peaks [mopes] like John-a-dreams, unpregnant of his cause," dully indifferent to his cause. So, when the Ghost appears to him the second time, he accuses himself of being tardy and lapsed in *time*; and the Ghost speaks of his purpose being almost *blunted,* and bids him not to *forget* (cf. "oblivion"). And so, what is emphasized in those undramatic but significant speeches of the player king and of Claudius is the mere dying away of purpose or of love. Surely what all this points to is not a condition of excessive but useless mental activity (indeed there is, in reality, curiously little about that in the text), but rather one of dull, apathetic, brooding gloom, in which Hamlet, so far from analyzing his duty, is not thinking of it at all, but for the time literally *forgets* it. It seems to me we are driven to think of Hamlet *chiefly* thus during the long time which elapsed between the appearance of the Ghost and the events presented in the Second Act. The Ghost, in fact, had more reason than we suppose at first for leaving with Hamlet as his parting injunction the command, "Remember me," and for greeting him, on reappearing, with the command, "Do not forget." These little things in Shakespeare are not accidents.

T. S. ELIOT (1888–1965)

Hamlet and His Problems   1934

Not only a leading poet of the twentieth-century modernist period, T. S. Eliot also produced extremely interesting criticism of Elizabethan literature. His several collections of essays defined important critical terms that later readers have used to gain insight into great writers. One of those terms is developed here: the objective correlative, which Eliot believes is missing in *Hamlet*. His argument is provocative and revealing.

Few critics have ever admitted that *Hamlet* the play is the primary problem, and Hamlet the character only secondary. And Hamlet the character has had an especial temptation for that most dangerous type of critic: the critic with a mind which is naturally of the creative order, but which through some weakness in creative power exercises itself in criticism instead. These minds often find in Hamlet a vicarious existence for their own artistic realization. Such a mind had Goethe, who made of Hamlet a Werther; and such had Coleridge, who made of Hamlet a Coleridge; and probably neither of these men in writing about Hamlet remembered that his first business was to study a work of art. The kind of criticism that Goethe and Coleridge produced, in writing of Hamlet, is the most misleading kind possible. For they both possessed unquestionable critical insight, and both make their critical aberrations the more plausible by the substitution—of their own Hamlet for Shakespeare's—which their creative gift effects. We should be thankful that Walter Pater° did not fix his attention on this play.

Two writers of our time, Mr. J. M. Robertson and Professor Stoll of the University of Minnesota, have issued small books which can be praised for moving in the

---

Walter Pater: English writer and critic (1839–1894). His writings were often overelaborate.

other direction. Mr. Stoll performs a service in recalling to our attention the labors of the critics of the seventeenth and eighteenth centuries, observing that

> they knew less about psychology than more recent Hamlet critics, but they were nearer in spirit to Shakespeare's art; and as they insisted on the importance of the effect of the whole rather than on the importance of the leading character, they were nearer, in their old-fashioned way, to the secret of dramatic art in general.

Qua work of art, the work of art cannot be interpreted; there is nothing to interpret; we can only criticize it according to standards, in comparison to other works of art; and for "interpretation" the chief task is the presentation of relevant historical facts which the reader is not assumed to know. Mr. Robertson points out, very pertinently, how critics have failed in their "interpretation" of *Hamlet* by ignoring what ought to be very obvious: that *Hamlet* is a stratification, that it represents the efforts of a series of men, each making what he could out of the work of his predecessors. The *Hamlet* of Shakespeare will appear to us very differently if, instead of treating the whole action of the play as due to Shakespeare's design, we perceive his *Hamlet* to be superposed upon much cruder material which persists even in the final form.

We know that there was an older play by Thomas Kyd, that extraordinary dramatic (if not poetic) genius who was in all probability the author of two plays so dissimilar as the *Spanish Tragedy* and *Arden of Feversham;* and what this play was like we can guess from three clues: from the *Spanish Tragedy* itself, from the tale of Belleforest upon which Kyd's *Hamlet* must have been based, and from a version acted in Germany in Shakespeare's lifetime which bears strong evidence of having been adapted from the earlier, not from the later, play. From these three sources it is clear that in the earlier play the motive was a revenge motive simply; that the action or delay is caused, as in the *Spanish Tragedy,* solely by the difficulty of assassinating a monarch surrounded by guards; and that the "madness" of Hamlet was feigned in order to escape suspicion, and successfully. In the final play of Shakespeare, on the other hand, there is a motive which is more important than that of revenge, and which explicitly "blunts" the latter; the delay in revenge is unexplained on grounds of necessity or expediency; and the effect of the "madness" is not to lull but to arouse the king's suspicion. The alteration is not complete enough, however, to be convincing. Furthermore, there are verbal parallels so close to the *Spanish Tragedy* as to leave no doubt that in places Shakespeare was merely *revising* the text of Kyd. And finally there are unexplained scenes — the Polonius-Laertes and the Polonius-Reynaldo scenes — for which there is little excuse; these scenes are not in the verse style of Kyd, and not beyond doubt in the style of Shakespeare. These Mr. Robertson believes to be scenes in the original play of Kyd reworked by a third hand, perhaps Chapman,° before Shakespeare touched the play. And he concludes, with very strong show of reason, that the original play of Kyd was, like certain other revenge plays, in two parts of five acts. The upshot of Mr. Robertson's examination is, we believe, irrefragable: that Shakespeare's *Hamlet,* so far as it is Shakespeare's, is a play dealing with the effect of a mother's guilt upon her son, and that Shakespeare was unable to impose this motive successfully upon the "intractable" material of the old play.

Of the intractability there can be no doubt. So far from being Shakespeare's masterpiece, the play is most certainly an artistic failure. In several ways the play is puzzling, and disquieting as is none of the others. Of all the plays it is the longest and is possibly the one on which Shakespeare spent most pains; and yet he has left

Chapman: George Chapman (1559?–1634), Elizabethan poet and playwright.

in it superfluous and inconsistent scenes which even hasty revision should have noticed. The versification is variable. Lines like

> Look, the morn, in russet mantle clad,
> Walks o'er the dew of yon high eastern hill,

are of the Shakespeare of *Romeo and Juliet*. The lines in act V, scene ii,

> Sir, in my heart there was a kind of fighting
> That would not let me sleep . . .
> Up from my cabin,
> My sea-gown scarf'd about me, in the dark
> Grop'd I to find out them: had my desire;
> Finger'd their packet;

are of his quite mature. Both workmanship and thought are in an unstable position. We are surely justified in attributing the play, with that other profoundly interesting play of "intractable" material and astonishing versification, *Measure for Measure,* to a period of crisis, after which follow the tragic successes which culminate in *Coriolanus. Coriolanus* may be not as "interesting" as *Hamlet,* but it is, with *Antony and Cleopatra,* Shakespeare's most assured artistic success. And probably more people have thought *Hamlet* a work of art because they found it interesting than have found it interesting because it is a work of art. It is the *Mona Lisa* of literature.

The grounds of *Hamlet*'s failure are not immediately obvious. Mr. Robertson is undoubtedly correct in concluding that the essential emotion of the play is the feeling of a son toward a guilty mother:

> [Hamlet's] tone is that of one who has suffered tortures on the score of his mother's degradation. . . . The guilt of a mother is an almost intolerable motive for drama, but it had to be maintained and emphasized to supply a psychological solution, or rather a hint of one.

This, however, is by no means the whole story. It is not merely the "guilt of a mother" that cannot be handled as Shakespeare handled the suspicion of Othello, the infatuation of Antony, or the pride of Coriolanus. The subject might conceivably have expanded into a tragedy like these, intelligible, self-complete, in the sunlight. *Hamlet,* like the sonnets, is full of some stuff that the writer could not drag to light, contemplate, or manipulate into art. And when we search for this feeling, we find it, as in the sonnets, very difficult to localize. You cannot point to it in the speeches; indeed, if you examine the two famous soliloquies, you see the versification of Shakespeare but a content which might be claimed by another, perhaps by the author of the *Revenge of Bussy d'Ambois,*° act V, scene i. We find Shakespeare's Hamlet not in the action, not in any quotations that we might select, so much as in an unmistakable tone which is unmistakably not in the earlier play.

The only way of expressing emotion in the form of art is by finding an "objective correlative"; in other words, a set of objects, a situation, a chain of events which shall be the formula of that *particular* emotion; such that when the external facts, which must terminate in sensory experience, are given, the emotion is immediately evoked. If you examine any of Shakespeare's more successful tragedies, you will find this exact equivalence; you will find that the state of mind of Lady Macbeth walking in her sleep has been communicated to you by a skillful accumulation of imagined sensory impressions; the words of Macbeth on hearing of his wife's death strike us as if, given the sequence of events, these words were

---

Revenge of Bussy d'Ambois: Tragedy (1610–1611) by George Chapman, dealing with the reluctance of Clement d'Ambois to avenge his brother's death.

Eliot says it's / mind it limits him / what limits him / if only he were a poet

automatically released by the last event in the series. The artistic "inevitability" lies in this complete adequacy of the external to the emotion; and this is precisely what is deficient in *Hamlet*. Hamlet (the man) is dominated by an emotion which is inexpressible, because it is in *excess* of the facts as they appear. And the supposed identity of Hamlet with his author is genuine to this point: that Hamlet's bafflement at the absence of objective equivalent to his feelings is a prolongation of the bafflement of his creator in the face of his artistic problem. Hamlet is up against the difficulty that his disgust is occasioned by his mother, but that his mother is not an adequate equivalent for it; his disgust envelops and exceeds her. It is thus a feeling which he cannot understand; he cannot objectify it, and it therefore remains to poison life and obstruct action. None of the possible actions can satisfy it; and nothing that Shakespeare can do with the plot can express Hamlet for him. And it must be noticed that the very nature of the *données* of the problem precludes objective equivalence. To have heightened the criminality of Gertrude would have been to provide the formula for a totally different emotion in Hamlet; it is just *because* her character is so negative and insignificant that she arouses in Hamlet the feeling which she is incapable of representing.

The "madness" of Hamlet lay to Shakespeare's hand; in the earlier play a simple ruse, and to the end, we may presume, understood as a ruse by the audience. For Shakespeare it is less than madness and more than feigned. The levity of Hamlet, his repetition of phrase, his puns, are not part of a deliberate plan of dissimulation, but a form of emotional relief. In the character Hamlet it is the buffoonery of an emotion which can find no outlet in action; in the dramatist it is the buffoonery of an emotion which he cannot express in art. The intense feeling, ecstatic or terrible, without an object or exceeding its object, is something which every person of sensibility has known; it is doubtless a subject of study for pathologists. It often occurs in adolescence: the ordinary person puts these feelings to sleep, or trims down his feelings to fit the business world; the artist keeps them alive by his ability to intensify the world to his emotions. The Hamlet of Laforgue° is an adolescent; the Hamlet of Shakespeare is not, he has not that explanation and excuse. We must simply admit that here Shakespeare tackled a problem which proved too much for him. Why he attempted it at all is an insoluble puzzle; under compulsion of what experience he attempted to express the inexpressibly horrible, we cannot ever know. We need a great many facts in his biography; and we should like to know whether, and when, and after or at the same time as what personal experience, he read Montaigne's *Apologie de Raimond Sebond*. We should have, finally, to know something which is by hypothesis unknowable, for we assume it to be an experience which, in the manner indicated, exceeded the facts. We should have to understand things which Shakespeare did not understand himself.

The Tempest

One of Shakespeare's most thought-provoking plays, *The Tempest* links Renaissance Italy, Elizabethan England, and the discoveries of the New World. Shakespeare had an interest in the Virginia Company, an investment group that sent a flotilla of ships to Virginia in 1609. Its flagship, carrying the governor-to-be of Virginia, Sir Thomas Gates, was lost in a July storm and washed up

---

Laforgue: Jules Laforgue (1860–1887), French poet who was an important influence on Eliot.

on Bermuda, then reputed to be the Isle of Devils. Admiral Sir George Somers built new boats and, with Gates and the rest of the crew, continued the journey, arriving in Jamestown in May 1610. All this news was reported in England as Shakespeare was preparing to write a new play for the Globe Theatre. With the "still-vexed Bermudas" of *The Tempest* (not to mention its opening storm), drama now touched on current events in the Elizabethan world of politics and adventure.

There is also a connection between Prospero, the philosopher-magician of *The Tempest*, and the most celebrated Elizabethan magician of the time, John Dee (1527–1608). This learned mathematician was also an astrologer, whom Queen Elizabeth consulted when she wanted to have her horoscope cast. His fame as a necromancer—one who called the spirits to do his bidding—took him as far as Poland to perform magic. While he was there in 1583, an English mob, certain Dee was a dangerous wizard, destroyed his library, furnishings, and laboratories. He was known by reputation to the audiences of the original productions of *The Tempest*, in November 1611 and again in 1612–1613.

King James I, who was almost surely at its first performances, took a special interest in magic. The play was performed at courtly festivities celebrating the marriage of James's daughter Elizabeth. The marriage of Miranda and Ferdinand paralleled this real-life marriage. Moreover, the masque that the spirits perform for Miranda and Ferdinand (act IV, scene i) served as a special wedding celebration, since masques were dedicated to Hymen, the god of marriage.

Apart from relying on current events, *The Tempest* is notable in that it is one of the few plays for which Shakespeare did not use an earlier source from fiction, drama, or history. The plot—the good duke and his daughter being cast adrift by his evil brother and then ending on an island that the duke controls through his magic—seems entirely original. Early critics saw the play as a moral excursion in which the power of good, after great trial, eventually overcomes evil. However, Shakespeare leaves a loose end at the conclusion of the play. While most of those who colluded to remove Prospero from his dukedom are contrite and ashamed—and express honest regret at their earlier actions—Prospero's brother Antonio remains unrepentant at the end. Prospero, whose magic controls everyone on the island, forsakes magic when he declares that he will return to Milan. Thus he leaves himself potentially defenseless against a possible repetition of his brother's crimes. This detail emphasizes the island as a magical place, while reminding us of the existence of evil in the world of Renaissance politics.

The political aspect of the play hints at governmental negligence. Antonio is hungry for power, but Prospero is neglectful of it. Some critics have suggested that Niccoló Machiavelli (1469–1527) may have provided some thematic underpinning for the play in his political treatise *The Prince*, which insists that a prince (or duke) should hold on to power by any means possible. While spending his time cultivating magic, Prospero neglects his political duties, leaving the way open to his usurping brother.

The Tempest in Performance

[handwritten marginal note:] Why wasn't the Tempest a hit?

Curiously, *The Tempest* does not seem to have made a stir when it was first performed in 1611. Unlike *Titus Andronicus, Henry V, Romeo and Juliet, Hamlet,* and thirteen other plays, *The Tempest* was not printed in a convenient small quarto-size book in Shakespeare's lifetime. The quarto (so called because the pages were one quarter the size of the full-size paper fed into printing presses of the time) was a cheap but not always accurate text. Quartos were produced

Was the closing of theater a contributing factor of S.'s death?

when printers thought the popularity of a play would sell the book. Only in 1623, after Shakespeare's death, was *The Tempest* printed in the First Folio (whose pages were created with a single fold of the full-size paper) by members of his theater company.

In 1642, the Puritans, part of a movement that had been becoming increasingly powerful in London, gained control of the city, at the beginning of what was to be a civil war. The Puritans believed that entertainment was sinful, and in September of that year they ordered all theaters closed. The theaters remained closed for the next eighteen years. After the theaters were closed, *The Tempest* seems not to have been acted in private, although no records survive. After England's restoration of the crown in 1660, the play was revived in the form of a broad adaptation by John Dryden (1631–1700) and William D'Avenant (1606–1668). Their play *The Enchanted Island* (1667) was produced during the Restoration, when women could take roles on stage. Soon after, in 1674, Thomas Shadwell (1642–1692) turned Dryden and D'Avenant's version into an opera, which became one of the most often produced adaptations of *The Tempest.* The original play was not produced successfully in London until 1838. Since then, it has been adapted and revised countless times as an opera and broadly adapted by novelists and poets.

Modern productions of the play are often based on their interpretations of Prospero's role. Late-nineteenth-century actors were not as drawn to the role of Prospero. When Beerbohm Tree, an important Shakespearean actor, produced *The Tempest* in the early 1900s, he took the part of Caliban. He enjoyed the ambiguity of that role, which he played sympathetically.

John Gielgud was the most durable Prospero of the twentieth century, playing the role numerous times, from 1930 at the Old Vic to 1991 in Peter Greenaway's film *Prospero's Books,* an adaptation that used mime and opera. In 1957, Gielgud played Prospero in Peter Brook's first production, which emphasized the theme of revenge. After his second production (1963), Brook said that *The Tempest* "includes all the themes from [Shakespeare's] earlier work—kingship, inheritance, treachery, conscience, identity, love, music, God; he draws them together as if to find the key to it all, but there is no such key. There is no grand order and Prospero returns to Milan not bathed in tranquility, but a wreck."

Peter Hall's 1974 production at London's National Theatre presented Gielgud in makeup that made him resemble John Dee, the Elizabethan magus. The emphasis on magic was clear and powerful. As Prospero, Patrick Stewart began what was supposed to be a limited run in a 1995 production directed by George Wolfe but went on to become a Broadway hit. Stewart was known to the public from the television sci-fi series *Star Trek: The Next Generation,* but his training with the Royal Shakespeare Company was evident in his powerful Prospero. This production also brought out a post-colonial issue—the tension between Ariel and Caliban as two members of oppressed tribes.

Sam Mendes cast Stephen Dillane as Prospero in the Bridge Project's brilliant production at the Brooklyn Academy of Music in February 2010. Julie Taymor's 2010 film *The Tempest* emphasized the colonialist reading of the play but surprised audiences by casting Helen Mirren as Prospera. Ralph Fiennes played Prospero onstage at the Haymarket in London in 2011, in a more traditional reading of the play. This spate of very different interpretations demonstrates the enduring mystery of *The Tempest,* which seems to grow in our imagination rather than diminish.

WILLIAM SHAKESPEARE (1564–1616)

The Tempest 1611

Names of the Actors

ALONSO, *King of Naples*
SEBASTIAN, *his brother*
PROSPERO, *the right Duke of Milan*
ANTONIO, *his brother, the usurping Duke of Milan*
FERDINAND, *son to the King of Naples*
GONZALO, *an honest old councillor*
ADRIAN,
FRANCISCO, } *lords*
CALIBAN, *a savage and deformed slave*
TRINCULO, *a jester*
STEPHANO, *a drunken butler*
MASTER, *of a ship*
BOATSWAIN
MARINERS

MIRANDA, *daughter to Prospero*

ARIEL, *an airy Spirit*
IRIS,
CERES,
JUNO, } *[presented by] Spirits*
NYMPHS,
REAPERS,

[*Other Spirits attending Prospero*]

Scene: *An uninhabited island*

ACT I • Scene I°

(*A tempestuous noise of thunder and lightning heard.
Enter a Shipmaster and a Boatswain.*)

MASTER: Boatswain!
BOATSWAIN: Here, Master. What cheer?
MASTER: Good,° speak to the mariners. Fall to 't
yarely,° or we run ourselves aground. Bestir,
5 bestir!   (*Exit.*)

(*Enter Mariners.*)

BOATSWAIN: Heigh, my hearts! Cheerly,° cheerly, my
hearts! Yare, yare! Take in the topsail. Tend° to the

I, i. **Location:** On board ship, off the island's coast.
3. **Good:** I.e., it's good you've come; or, my good fellow.
4. **yarely:** Nimbly.   6. **Cheerly:** Cheerily.   7. **Tend:** Attend.

Master's whistle.—Blow° till thou burst thy wind, if
room enough!°

(*Enter Alonso, Sebastian, Antonio, Ferdinand, Gonzalo,
and others.*)

ALONSO: Good Boatswain, have care. Where's the   10
Master? Play the men.°
BOATSWAIN: I pray now, keep° below.
ANTONIO: Where is the Master, Boatswain?
BOATSWAIN: Do you not hear him? You mar our labor.
Keep° your cabins! You do assist the storm.   15
GONZALO: Nay, good,° be patient.
BOATSWAIN: When the sea is. Hence!° What cares
these roarers° for the name of king? To cabin! Silence!
Trouble us not.
GONZALO: Good, yet remember whom thou hast   20
aboard.
BOATSWAIN: None that I more love than myself. You are
a councillor; if you can command these elements
to silence and work the peace of the present,° we
will not hand° a rope more. Use your authority. If   25
you cannot, give thanks you have lived so long
and make yourself ready in your cabin for the mis-
chance° of the hour, if it so hap.°—Cheerly, good
hearts!—Out of our way, I say.   (*Exit.*)
GONZALO: I have great comfort from this fellow.   30
Methinks he hath no drowning mark upon him;
his complexion is perfect gallows.° Stand fast,
good Fate, to his hanging! Make the rope of his
destiny our cable, for our own doth little advantage.° If he be not born to be hanged, our case is   35
miserable.°   (*Exeunt.*)°

8. **Blow:** Addressed to the wind.   8–9. **if room enough:**
As long as we have sea room enough.   11. **Play the men:**
Act like men (?), ply, urge the men to exert themselves (?).
12. **keep:** Stay.   15. **Keep:** Remain in.   16. **good:** Good fellow.
17. **Hence:** Get away.   18. **roarers:** Waves or winds or both;
spoken of as though they were "bullies" or "blusterers."
24. **work . . . present:** Bring calm to our present circumstances.   25. **hand:** Handle.   28. **mischance:** Misfortune.
hap: Happen.   32. **complexion . . . gallows:** Appearance shows
he was born to be hanged (and therefore, according to the
proverb, in no danger of drowning).   34–35. **our . . . advantage:** I.e., our own cable is of little benefit.   35–36. **case is miserable:** Circumstances are desperate.   36. [S.D.] *Exeunt:* Latin
for "they go out."

(*Enter Boatswain.*)

BOATSWAIN: Down with the topmast! Yare! Lower, lower!
Bring her to try wi' the main course.° (*A cry within.*)
A plague upon this howling! They are louder than
the weather or our office.°

(*Enter Sebastian, Antonio, and Gonzalo.*)

Yet again? What do you here? Shall we give o'er° and
drown? Have you a mind to sink?

SEBASTIAN: A pox o' your throat, you bawling, blas-
phemous, incharitable dog!

BOATSWAIN: Work you, then.

ANTONIO: Hang, cur! Hang, you whoreson, insolent
noisemaker! We are less afraid to be drowned than
thou art.

GONZALO: I'll warrant him for drowning,° though the
ship were no stronger than a nutshell and as leaky as
an unstanched° wench.

BOATSWAIN: Lay her ahold,° ahold! Set her two courses.°
Off to sea again! Lay her off!

(*Enter Mariners, wet.*)

MARINERS: All lost! To prayers, to prayers! All lost!
[*Exeunt Mariners.*]

BOATSWAIN: What, must our mouths be cold?°

GONZALO: The King and Prince at prayers! Let's
assist them,
For our case is as theirs.

SEBASTIAN: I am out of patience.

ANTONIO: We are merely° cheated of our lives by
drunkards.
This wide-chapped° rascal! Would thou mightst lie
drowning
The washing of ten tides!°

GONZALO: He'll be hanged yet,
Though every drop of water swear against it
And gape at wid'st° to glut° him.
(*A confused noise within.*)   "Mercy on us!"—
"We split,° we split!"—"Farewell my wife and
children!"—
"Farewell, brother!"—"We split, we split, we split!"

[*Exit Boatswain.*]

ANTONIO: Let's all sink wi' the King.

SEBASTIAN: Let's take leave of him.

(*Exit [with Antonio].*)

GONZALO: Now would I give a thousand furlongs of sea
for an acre of barren ground: long heath,° brown
furze,° anything. The wills above be done! But I
would fain° die a dry death.   (*Exit.*)

wishes his death to be dry

Scene II°

(*Enter Prospero [in his magic cloak] and Miranda.*)

MIRANDA: If by your art,° my dearest father, you
have
Put the wild waters in this roar,° allay° them.
The sky, it seems, would pour down stinking
pitch,°
But that the sea, mounting to th' welkin's
cheek,°
Dashes the fire out. O, I have suffered
With those that I saw suffer! A brave° vessel,
Who had, no doubt, some noble creature in her,
Dashed all to pieces. O, the cry did knock
Against my very heart! Poor souls, they perished.
Had I been any god of power, I would
Have sunk the sea within the earth or ere°
It should the good ship so have swallowed and
The freighting° souls within her.

PROSPER: Be collected.°
No more amazement.° Tell your piteous° heart
There's no harm done.

MIRANDA: O, woe the day!

PROSPERO: No harm.
I have done nothing but° in care of thee,
Of thee, my dear one, thee, my daughter, who
Art ignorant of what thou art, naught knowing
Of whence I am, nor that I am more better°
Than Prospero, master of a full° poor cell,

The King & Prince are on board.

---

38. **Bring . . . course:** Sail her close to the wind by means of the mainsail.   40. **our office:** I.e., the noise we make at our work.   41. **give o'er:** Give up.   49. **warrant him for drowning:** Guarantee that he will never be drowned.   51. **unstanched:** Insatiable, loose, unrestrained.   52. **ahold:** Ahull, close to the wind.   **courses:** Sails (i.e., foresail as well as mainsail), set in an attempt to get the ship back out into open water.   55. **must . . . cold:** I.e., must we drown in the cold sea; or, let us heat up our mouths with liquor.   58. **merely:** Utterly.   59. **wide-chapped:** With mouth wide open.   59–60. **lie . . . tides:** Pirates were hanged on the shore and left until three tides had come in.   62. **at wid'st:** Wide.   **glut:** Swallow.   63. **split:** Break apart.

68. **heath:** Heather.   69. **furze:** Gorse, a weed growing on wasteland.   70. **fain:** Rather.   **I, ii. Location:** The island. Prospero's cell is visible, and on the Elizabethan stage it presumably remains so throughout the play, although in some scenes the convention of flexible distance allows us to imagine characters in other parts of the island.   1. **art:** Magic   2. **roar:** Uproar.   **allay:** Pacify.   3. **pitch:** A thick, viscous substance produced by boiling down tar or turpentine   4. **welkin's cheek:** Sky's face.   6. **brave:** Gallant, splendid.   11. **or ere:** Before.   13. **freighting:** Forming the cargo.   **collected:** Calm, composed.   14. **amazement:** Consternation.   **piteous:** Pitying.   16. **but:** Except.   19. **more better:** Of higher rank.   20. **full:** Very.

40

45

50

55

60

65

70

5

10

15

20

Akiya Henry as Miranda and Joseph Mydell as Prospero at
the Regent's Park Open Air Theatre in London, 2009.

And thy no greater father.
MIRANDA: More to know
Did never meddle° with my thoughts.
PROSPERO: 'Tis time
I should inform thee farther. Lend thy hand
And pluck my magic garment from me. So,
            [*Laying down his magic cloak and staff.*]
Lie there, my art.—Wipe thou thine eyes. Have
25 comfort.
The direful spectacle of the wreck,° which touched
The very virtue° of compassion in thee,
I have with such provision° in mine art
So safely ordered that there is no soul—
30 No, not so much perdition° as an hair
Betid° to any creature in the vessel

22. **meddle:** Mingle. 26. **wreck:** Shipwreck. 27. **virtue:**
Essence. 28. **provision:** Foresight. 30. **perdition:** Loss.
31. **Betid:** Happened.

Which° thou heardst cry, which thou sawst sink.
     Sit down,
For thou must now know farther.
MIRANDA [*sitting*]:   You have often
Begun to tell me what I am, but stopped
And left me to a bootless inquisition,°   35
Concluding, "Stay, not yet."
PROSPERO: The hour's now come;
The very minute bids thee ope° thine ear.
Obey, and be attentive. Canst thou remember
A time before we came unto this cell?
I do not think thou canst, for then thou wast
     not   40
Out° three years old.
MIRANDA: Certainly, sir, I can.
PROSPERO: By what? By any other house or person?
Of anything the image, tell me, that
Hath kept with thy remembrance.
MIRANDA: 'Tis far off,
And rather like a dream than an assurance   45
That my remembrance warrants.° Had I not
Four or five women once that tended° me?
PROSPERO: Thou hadst, and more, Miranda. But
     how is it
That this lives in thy mind? What seest thou else
In the dark backward and abysm of time?°   50
If thou rememberest aught° ere thou cam'st here,
How thou cam'st here thou mayst.
MIRANDA: But that I do not.
PROSPERO: Twelve year since, Miranda, twelve year
     since,
Thy father was the Duke of Milan and
A prince of power.
MIRANDA: Sir, are not you my father?   55
PROSPERO: Thy mother was a piece° of virtue, and
She said thou wast my daughter; and thy father
Was Duke of Milan, and his only heir
And princess no worse issued.°
MIRANDA: O the heavens!
What foul play had we, that we came from
     thence?   60
Or Blessed was 't we did?
PROSPERO: Both, both, my girl.
By foul play, as thou sayst, were we heaved
     thence,
But blessedly holp° hither.
MIRANDA: O, my heart bleeds
To think o' the teen that I have turned you to,°
Which is from° my remembrance! Please you,
     farther.   65

32. **Which:** Whom. 35. **bootless inquisition:** Profitless inquiry. 37. **ope:** Open. 41. **Out:** Fully. 45–46. **assurance . . .
warrants:** Certainty that my memory guarantees. 47. **tended:**
Attended, waited upon. 50. **backward . . . time:** Abyss of
the past. 51. **aught:** Anything. 56. **piece:** Masterpiece,
exemplar. 59. **no worse issued:** No less nobly born, descended.
63. **holp:** Helped. 64. **teen . . . to:** Trouble I've caused you to
remember or put you to. 65. **from:** Out of.

[handwritten: he was on the ship]

PROSPERO: My brother and thy uncle, called
        Antonio—
    I pray thee, mark me, that a brother should
    Be so perfidious!—he whom next° thyself
    Of all the world I loved, and to him put
70 The manage° of my state, as at that time
    Through all the seigniories° it was the first,
    And Prospero the prime° duke, being so reputed
    In dignity, and for the liberal arts
    Without a parallel; those being all my study,
75 The government I cast upon my brother
    And to my state grew stranger,° being
        transported°
    And rapt in secret studies. Thy false uncle—
    Dost thou attend me?
MIRANDA: Sir, most heedfully.
PROSPERO: Being once perfected° how to grant suits,
80 How to deny them, who t' advance and who
    To trash° for overtopping,° new created
    The creatures° that were mine, I say, or changed
        'em
    Or else new formed 'em;° having both the key°
    Of officer and office, set all hearts i' the state
85 To what tune pleased his ear, that° now he was
    The ivy which had hid my princely trunk
    And sucked my verdure° out on 't.° Thou
        attend'st not.
MIRANDA: O, good sir, I do.
PROSPERO: I pray thee, mark me.
    I, thus neglecting worldly ends, all dedicated
90 To closeness° and the bettering of my mind
    With that which, but by being so retired,
    O'erprized all popular rate,° in my false brother
    Awaked an evil nature; and my trust,
    Like a good parent,° did beget of° him
95 A falsehood in its contrary as great
    As my trust was, which had indeed no limit,
    A confidence sans° bound. He being thus lorded°
    Not only with what my revenue yielded
    But what my power might else° exact, like one

[handwritten marginal notes: the Pros began to love the uncle / P's trust was too much and / should b Duke himself / t thought he himself]

    Who, having into° truth by telling of it,   100
    Made such a sinner of his memory
    To° credit his own lie,° he did believe
    He was indeed the Duke, out o'° the substitution
    And executing th' outward face of royalty°
    With all prerogative. Hence his ambition
        growing—   105
    Dost thou hear?
MIRANDA: Your tale, sir, would cure deafness.
PROSPERO: To have no screen between this part he
        played
    And him he played it for,° he needs° will be
    Absolute Milan.° Me, poor man, my library
    Was dukedom large enough. Of temporal
        royalties°   110
    He thinks me now incapable; confederates°—
    So dry° he was for sway°—wi' the King of
        Naples
    To give him° annual tribute, do him homage,
    Subject his coronet to his° crown, and bend°
    The dukedom yet° unbowed—alas, poor Milan!— 115
    To most ignoble stooping.
MIRANDA: O the heavens!
PROSPERO: Mark his condition° and th' event,° then
        tell me
    If this might be a brother.
MIRANDA: I should sin
    To think but° nobly of my grandmother.
    Good wombs have borne bad sons.
PROSPERO: Now the condition, 120
    This King of Naples, being an enemy
    To me inveterate, hearkens° my brother's suit,
    Which was that he, in lieu o' the premises°
    Of homage and I know not how much tribute,
    Should presently extirpate° me and mine   125
    Out of the dukedom and confer fair Milan,
    With all the honors, on my brother. Whereon
    A treacherous army levied, one midnight
    Fated to th' purpose did Antonio open
    The gates of Milan, and, i' the dead of darkness, 130
    The ministers for the purpose° hurried thence°

[handwritten marginal note: Milan is under Naples control]

---

68. **next:** Next to. 70. **manage:** Management, administration. 71. **seigniories:** City-states of northern Italy. 72. **prime:** Of highest rank. 76. **to...stranger:** Withdrew from my responsibilities as duke. **transported:** Carried away. 79. **perfected:** Grown skillful. 81. **trash:** Check a hound by tying a cord or weight to its neck. **overtopping:** Running too far ahead of the pack; surmounting, exceeding one's authority. 82. **creatures:** Dependents. 82–83. **or changed...formed 'em:** Either changed their loyalties and duties or else created new ones. 83. **key:** (1) Key for unlocking; (2) tool for tuning stringed instruments. 85. **that:** So that. 87. **verdure:** Vitality. **on 't:** Of it. 90. **closeness:** Retirement, seclusion. 91–92. **but...rate:** Simply because it was done in such seclusion, had a value not appreciated by popular opinion. 94. **good parent:** Alludes to the proverb that good parents often bear bad children; see also line 120. **of:** In. 97. **sans:** Without. **lorded:** Raised to lordship, with power and wealth. 99. **else:** Otherwise, additionally.

100–102. **Who...lie:** Who, by repeatedly telling the lie (that he was indeed Duke of Milan), made his memory such a confirmed sinner against truth that he began to believe his own lie. **into:** Unto, against. **To:** So as to. 103. **out o':** As a result of. 104. **And...royalty:** And (as a result of) his carrying out all the ceremonial functions of royalty. 107–108. **To have...it for:** To have no separation or barrier between his role and himself. (Antonio wanted to act in his own person, not as substitute.) 108. **needs:** Necessarily. 109. **Absolute Milan:** Unconditional duke of Milan. 110. **temporal royalties:** Practical prerogatives and responsibilities of a sovereign. 111. **confederates:** Conspires, allies himself. 112. **dry:** Thirsty. **sway:** Power. 113. **him:** The King of Naples. 114. **his...his:** Antonio's... the King of Naples's. **bend:** Make bow down. 115. **yet:** Hitherto. 117. **condition:** Pact. **event:** Outcome. 119. **but:** Other than. 122. **hearkens:** Listens to. 123. **in...premises:** In return for the stipulation. 125. **presently extirpate:** At once remove. 131. **ministers...purpose:** Agents employed to do this. **thence:** From there.

Me and thy crying self.
MIRANDA: Alack, for pity!
I, not remembering how I cried out then,
Will cry it o'er again. It is a hint°
That wrings° mine eyes to 't.
135 PROSPERO: Hear a little further,
And then I'll bring thee to the present business
Which now's upon 's, without the which this
        story
Were most impertinent.°
MIRANDA: Wherefore° did they not
That hour destroy us?
PROSPERO: Well demanded,° wench.°
My tale provokes that question. Dear, they durst
140   not,
So dear the love my people bore me, nor set
A mark so bloody° on the business, but
With colors fairer° painted their foul ends.
In few,° they hurried us aboard a bark,°
Bore us some leagues to sea, where they
145   prepared
A rotten carcass of a butt,° not rigged,
Nor tackle,° sail, nor mast; the very rats
Instinctively have quit° it. There they hoist us
To cry to th' sea that roared to us, to sigh
150 To th' winds whose pity, sighing back again,
Did us but loving wrong.°
MIRANDA: Alack, what trouble
Was I then to you!
PROSPERO: O, a cherubin°
Thou wast that did preserve me. Thou didst
        smile,
Infusèd with a fortitude from heaven,
155 When I have decked° the sea with drops full salt,
Under my burden groaned, which° raised in me
An undergoing stomach,° to bear up
Against what should ensue.
MIRANDA: How came we ashore?
160 PROSPERO: By Providence divine.
Some food we had, and some fresh water, that
A noble Neapolitan, Gonzalo,
Out of his charity, who being then appointed
Master of this design, did give us, with
165 Rich garments, linens, stuffs,° and necessaries,

Which since have steaded much.° So, of his
        gentleness,
Knowing I loved my books, he furnished me
From mine own library with volumes that
I prize above my dukedom.
MIRANDA: Would° I might
But ever° see that man!
PROSPERO: Now I arise.   170
        [*He puts on his magic cloak.*]
Sit still and hear the last of our sea sorrow.°
Here in this island we arrived; and here
Have I, thy schoolmaster, made thee more profit°
Than other princess'° can, that have more time
For vainer° hours and tutors not so careful.   175
MIRANDA: Heavens thank you for 't! And now, I
        pray you, sir—
For still 'tis beating in my mind—your reason
For raising this sea storm?
PROSPERO: Know thus far forth:
By accident most strange, bountiful Fortune,
Now my dear lady, hath mine enemies   180
Brought to this shore; and by my prescience
I find my zenith° doth depend upon
A most auspicious star, whose influence°
If now I court not, but omit,° my fortunes
Will ever after droop. Here cease more
        questions.   185
Thou art inclined to sleep. 'Tis a good dullness,°
And give it way.° I know thou canst not choose.
        [*Miranda sleeps.*]
Come away,° servant, come! I am ready now.
Approach, my Ariel, come.

(*Enter Ariel.*)

ARIEL: All hail, great master, grave sir, hail! I come   190
        To answer thy best pleasure; be 't to fly,
        To swim, to dive into the fire, to ride
        On the curled clouds, to thy strong bidding task°
        Ariel and all his quality.°
PROSPERO: Hast thou, spirit,
Performed to point° the tempest that I bade thee?   195
ARIEL: To every article.
        I boarded the King's ship. Now on the beak,°
        Now in the waist,° the deck,° in every cabin,
        I flamed amazement.° Sometimes I'd divide

They tried to make their deaths look like an accident so they put them on a rotting boat.

---

134. hint: Occasion.   **135. wrings:** (1) Constraints; (2) wrings tears from.   **138. impertinent:** Irrelevant.   **Wherefore:** Why.
139. demanded: Asked.   **wench:** Here, term of endearment.
141–142. set . . . bloody: Make obvious their murderous intent (from the practice of marking with the blood of the prey those who have participated in a successful hunt).   **143. fairer:** Apparently more attractive.   **144. few:** Few words.   **bark:** Ship.   **146. butt:** Cask, tub.   **147. Nor tackle:** Neither rigging (i.e., the pulleys and ropes designed for hoisting sails).
148. quit: Abandoned.   **151. loving wrong:** I.e., the winds pitied Prospero and Miranda though of necessity they blew them from shore.   **152. cherubin:** Angel.   **155. decked:** Covered (with salt tears), adorned.   **156. which:** I.e., the smile.
157. undergoing stomach: Courage to go on.   **165. stuffs:** Supplies.

166. steaded much: Been of much use.   **169. Would:** I wish.
170. But ever: Someday.   **171. sea sorrow:** Sorrowful adventure at sea.   **173. more profit:** Profit more.   **174. princess':** Princesses. (Or the word may be *princes*, referring to royal children both male and female.)   **175. vainer:** More foolishly spent.
182. zenith: Height of fortune (astrological term).   **183. influence:** Astrological power.   **184. omit:** Ignore.   **186. dullness:** Drowsiness.   **187. give it way:** Let it happen (i.e., don't fight it).
188. Come away: Come.   **193. task:** Make demands upon.
194. quality: (1) Fellow spirits; (2) abilities.   **195. to point:** To the smallest detail.   **197. beak:** Prow.   **198. waist:** Midships.   **deck:** Poop deck at the stern.   **199. flamed amazement:** Struck terror in the guise of fire (i.e., Saint Elmo's fire).

Julian Bleach as Ariel and
Patrick Stewart as Prospero
in the Royal Shakespeare
Company's 2006 production
directed by Gregory Doran.

200   And burn in many places; on the topmast,
      The yards, and the bowsprit would I flame distinctly,°
      Then meet and join. Jove's lightning, the precursors
      O' the dreadful thunderclaps, more momentary
      And sight-outrunning° were not. The fire and cracks
205   Of sulfurous roaring the most mighty Neptune°
      Seem to besiege and make his bold waves tremble,
      Yea, his dread trident shake.
PROSPERO: My brave spirit!
      Who was so firm, so constant, that this coil°
      Would not infect his reason?
ARIEL: Not a soul
210   But felt a fever of the mad° and played
      Some tricks of desperation. All but mariners
      Plunged in the foaming brine and quit the vessel,
      Then all afire with me. The King's son,
         Ferdinand,
      With hair up-staring°—then like reeds, not hair—
215   Was the first man that leapt; cried, "Hell is empty,
      And all the devils are here!"
PROSPERO: Why, that's my spirit!
      But was not this nigh shore?
ARIEL: Close by, my master.
PROSPERO: But are they, Ariel, safe?
ARIEL: Not a hair perished.
      On their sustaining garments° not a blemish,
220   But fresher than before; and, as thou bad'st° me,

      In troops° I have dispersed them 'bout the isle.
      The King's son have I landed by himself,
      Whom I left cooling of° the air with sighs
      In an odd angle° of the isle, and sitting,
      His arms in this sad knot.°   [*He folds his arms.*]
PROSPERO: Of the King's ship,   225
      The mariners, say how thou hast disposed,
      And all the rest o' the fleet.
ARIEL: Safely in harbor
      Is the King's ship; in the deep nook,° where once
      Thou calledst me up at midnight to fetch dew
      From the still-vexed Bermudas,° there she's hid;   230
      The mariners all under hatches stowed,
      Who, with a charm joined to their suffered labor,°
      I have left asleep. And for the rest o' the fleet,
      Which I dispersed, they all have met again
      And are upon the Mediterranean float°   235
      Bound sadly home for Naples,
      Supposing that they saw the King's ship wrecked
      And his great person perish.
PROSPERO: Ariel, thy charge
      Exactly is performed. But there's more work.
      What is the time o' the day?
ARIEL: Past the mid season.°   240
PROSPERO: At least two glasses.° The time twixt six
      and now

201. **distinctly:** In different places.   204. **sight-outrunning:**
Swifter than sight.   205. **Neptune:** Roman god of the sea.
208. **coil:** Tumult.   210. **of the mad:** I.e., such as madmen
feel.   214. **up-staring:** Standing on end.   219. **sustaining garments:** Garments that buoyed them up in the sea.   220. **bad'st:**
Ordered.

221. **troops:** Groups.   223. **cooling of:** Cooling.   224. **angle:**
Corner.   225. **sad knot:** Folded arms are indicative of mel-
ancholy.   228. **nook:** Bay.   230. **still-vexed Bermudas:**
Ever-stormy Bermudas. (Perhaps refers to the then-recent
Bermuda shipwreck; see pages 394–395. The Folio text reads
Bermoothes.)   232. **with . . . labor:** By means of a spell
added to all the labor they have undergone.   235. **float:** Sea.
240. **mid season:** Noon.   241. **glasses:** Hourglasses.

Must by us both be spent most preciously.
ARIEL: Is there more toil? Since thou dost give me pains,°
Let me remember° thee what thou hast promised,
Which is not yet performed me.
245 PROSPERO: How now? Moody?
What is 't thou canst demand?
ARIEL: My liberty.
PROSPERO: Before the time be out? No more!
ARIEL: I prithee,
Remember I have done thee worthy service,
Told thee no lies, made thee no mistakings, served
250 Without or grudge or rumblings. Thou did promise
To bate° me a full year.
PROSPERO: Dost thou forget
From what a torment I did free thee?
ARIEL: No.
PROSPERO: Thou dost, and think'st it much to tread
the ooze
Of the salt deep,
255 To run upon the sharp wind of the north,
To do me° business in the veins° o' the earth
When it is baked° with frost.
ARIEL: I do not, sir.
PROSPERO: Thou liest, malignant thing! Hast thou forgot
The foul witch Sycorax, who with age and envy°
260 Was grown into a hoop?° Hast thou forgot her?
ARIEL: No, sir.
PROSPERO: Thou hast. Where was she born? Speak.
Tell me.
ARIEL: Sir, in Algiers.
PROSPERO: O, was she so? I must
Once in a month recount what thou hast been
Which thou forgett'st. This damned witch
Sycorax,
265
For mischiefs manifold and sorceries terrible
To enter human hearing, from Algiers,
Thou know'st, was banished. For one thing she
did°
They would not take her life. Is not this true?
270 ARIEL: Ay, sir.
PROSPERO: This blue-eyed° hag was hither brought
with child°
And here was left by the sailors. Thou, my slave,
As thou report'st thyself, was then her servant;
And, for° thou wast a spirit too delicate
275 To act her earthy and abhorred commands,
Refusing her grand hests,° she did confine thee,
By help of her more potent ministers

And in her most unmitigable rage,
Into a cloven pine, within which rift
Imprisoned thou didst painfully remain   280
A dozen years; within which space she died
And left thee there, where thou didst vent thy
groans
As fast as mill wheels strike.° Then was this
island—
Save° for the son that she did litter° here,
A freckled whelp,° hag-born°—not honored
with   285
A human shape.
ARIEL: Yes, Caliban her son.
PROSPERO: Dull thing, I say so:° he, that Caliban
Whom now I keep in service. Thou best know'st
What torment I did find thee in. Thy groans
Did make wolves howl, and penetrate the breasts   290
Of ever-angry bears. It was a torment
To lay upon the damned, which Sycorax
Could not again undo. It was mine art,
When I arrived and heard thee, that made gape°
The pine and let thee out.
ARIEL: I thank thee, master.   295
PROSPERO: If thou more murmur'st, I will rend an
oak
And peg thee in his° knotty entrails till
Thou hast howled away twelve winters.
ARIEL: Pardon, master.
I will be correspondent° to command
And do my spriting° gently.°   300
PROSPERO: Do so, and after two days
I will discharge thee.
ARIEL: That's my noble master!
What shall I do? Say what? What shall I do?
PROSPERO: Go make thyself like a nymph o' the sea.
Be subject
To no sight but thine and mine, invisible   305
To every eyeball else. Go take this shape
And hither come in 't. Go, hence with diligence!
                              (*Exit* [*Ariel*].)
Awake, dear heart, awake! Thou hast slept well.
Awake!
MIRANDA: The strangeness of your story put
Heaviness° in me.
PROSPERO: Shake it off. Come on,   310
We'll visit Caliban, my slave, who never
Yields us kind answer.
MIRANDA: 'Tis a villain, sir,
I do not love to look on.

---

243. **pains:** Labors.   244. **remember:** Remind.   251. **bate:**
Remit, deduct.   256. **do me:** Do for me.   **veins:** Veins of minerals; or, underground streams thought to be analogous to the
veins of the human body.   257. **baked:** Hardened.   259. **envy:**
Malice.   260. **grown into a hoop:** I.e., so bent over with
age as to resemble a hoop.   268. **one . . . did:** Perhaps a reference to her pregnancy, for which her life would be spared.
271. **blue-eyed:** With dark circles under the eyes or with
blue eyelids, implying pregnancy.   **with child:** Pregnant.
274. **for:** Because.   276. **hests:** Commands.

283. **as mill wheels strike:** As the blades of a mill wheel strike the
water.   284. **Save:** Except.   **litter:** Give birth to.   285. **whelp:**
Offspring (used of animals).   **hag-born:** Born of a female
demon.   287. **Dull . . . so:** I.e., exactly, that's what I said, you
dullard.   294. **gape:** Open wide.   297. **his:** Its.   299. **correspondent:** Responsive, submissive.   300. **spriting:** Duties as
a spirit.   **gently:** Willingly, ungrudgingly.   310. **Heaviness:**
Drowsiness.

PROSPERO: But, as 'tis,
We cannot miss° him. He does make our fire,
315   Fetch in our wood, and serves in offices°
That profit us.—What ho! Slave! Caliban!
Thou earth, thou! Speak.
CALIBAN (*within*):   There's wood enough within.
PROSPERO: Come forth, I say! There's other business
      for thee.
      Come, thou tortoise! When?°

(*Enter Ariel like a water nymph.*)

320   Fine apparition! My quaint° Ariel,
Hark in thine ear.   [*He whispers.*]
ARIEL: My lord, it shall be done.   (*Exit.*)
PROSPERO: Thou poisonous slave, got° by the devil
      himself
Upon thy wicked dam,° come forth!

(*Enter Caliban.*)

CALIBAN: As wicked° dew as e'er my mother
      brushed
325   With raven's feather from unwholesome fen°
Drop on you both! A southwest° blow on ye
And blister you all o'er!
PROSPERO: For this, be sure, tonight thou shalt have
      cramps,
Side-stitches that shall pen thy breath up.
      Urchins°
330   Shall forth at vast° of night that they may work
All exercise on thee. Thou shalt be pinched
As thick as honeycomb,° each pinch more stinging
Than bees that made 'em.°
CALIBAN: I must eat my dinner.
This island's mine, by Sycorax my mother,
Which thou tak'st from me. When thou cam'st
335   first,
Thou strok'st me and made much of me, wouldst
      give me
Water with berries in 't, and teach me how
To name the bigger light, and how the less,°
That burn by day and night. And then I loved
      thee
340   And showed thee all the qualities o' th' isle,
The fresh springs, brine pits, barren place and
      fertile.

Cursed be I that did so! All the charms°
Of Sycorax, toads, beetles, bats, light on you!
For I am all the subjects that you have,
Which first was mine own king; and here you
      sty° me   345
In this hard rock, whiles you do keep from me
The rest o' th' island.
PROSPERO: Thou most lying slave,
Whom stripes° may move, not kindness! I have
      used thee,
Filth as thou art, with humane° care, and lodged
      thee
In mine own cell, till thou didst seek to violate   350
The honor of my child.
CALIBAN: Oho, Oho! Would 't had been done!
Thou didst prevent me; I had peopled else°
This isle with Calibans.
MIRANDA: Abhorrèd slave,°
Which any print° of goodness wilt not take,   355
Being capable of all ill! I pitied thee,
Took pains to make thee speak, taught thee each
      hour
One thing or other. When thou didst not, savage
Know thine own meaning, but wouldst gabble like
A thing most brutish, I endowed thy purposes°   360
With words that made them known. But thy
      vile race,°
Though thou didst learn, had that in 't which
      good natures
Could not abide to be with; therefore wast thou
Deservedly confined into this rock,
Who hadst deserved more than a prison.   365
CALIBAN: You taught me language, and my profit on 't
Is I know how to curse. The red plague° rid° you
For learning° me your language!
PROSPERO: Hagseed,° hence!
Fetch us in fuel, and be quick, thou'rt best,°
To answer other business.° Shrugg'st thou,
      malice?   370
If thou neglect'st or dost unwillingly
What I command, I'll rack thee with old°
      cramps,
Fill all thy bones with aches,° make thee roar
That beasts shall tremble at thy din.
CALIBAN: No, pray thee.
[*Aside.*] I must obey. His art is of such power   375

---

314. miss: Do without. **315. offices:** Functions, duties.
319. When: An exclamation of impatience. **320. quaint:**
Ingenious. **322. got:** Begotten, sired. **323. dam:** Mother
(used of animals). **324. wicked:** Mischievous, harmful.
325. fen: Marsh, bog. **326. southwest:** I.e., wind thought to
bring disease. **329. Urchins:** Hedgehogs; here, suggesting goblins in the guise of hedgehogs. **330. vast:** Lengthy, desolate
time. (Malignant spirits were thought to be restricted to the
hours of darkness.) **332. As thick as honeycomb:** I.e., all over,
with as many pinches as a honeycomb has cells. **333. 'em:** I.e.,
the honeycomb. **338. the bigger . . . less:** I.e., the sun and the
moon. (See Genesis 1:16: "God then made two great lights: the
greater light to rule the day, and the less light to rule the night.")

342. charms: Spells. **345. sty:** Confine as in a sty. **348.
stripes:** Lashes. **349. humane:** Not distinguished as a word
from *human*. **353. peopled else:** Otherwise populated.
354–365. Abhorrèd . . . prison: These lines are sometimes assigned by editors to Prospero. **355. print:** Imprint, impression. **360. purposes:** Meanings, desires. **361. race:** Natural
disposition; species, nature. **367. red plague:** Plague characterized by red sores and evacuation of blood. **rid:** Destroy.
368. learning: Teaching. **Hagseed:** Offspring of a female demon. **369. thou'rt best:** You'd be well advised. **370. answer
other business:** Perform other tasks. **372. old:** Such as old
people suffer; or, plenty of. **373. aches:** Pronounced "aitches."

[ABOVE] Helen Mirren as Prospera, Felicity Jones as Miranda, and Djimon Hounsou as Caliban in Julie Taymor's 2010 film.
[BELOW] Stephen Dillane as Prospero and Juliet Rylance as Miranda in a production directed by Sam Mendes at the Old Vic in London, 2010.

Is P. supposed to look crazed?

It would control my dam's god, Setebos,°
And make a vassal of him.

PROSPERO: So, slave, hence!

(*Exit Caliban.*)

(*Enter Ferdinand; and Ariel, invisible,° playing
and singing. [Ferdinand does not see Prospero and
Miranda.]*)

(*Ariel's Song.*)

ARIEL: Come unto these yellow sands,
     And then take hands;
380   Curtsied when you have,° and kissed
          The wild waves whist,°
     Foot it featly° here and there,
          And, sweet sprites,° bear
     The burden.° Hark, hark!
385   (*Burden, dispersedly° [within].*) Bow-wow.
     The watchdogs bark.
               [*Burden, dispersedly within*]. Bow-wow.
     Hark, hark! I hear
     The strain of strutting chanticleer
390   Cry Cock-a-diddle-dow.

FERDINAND: Where should this music be? I' th' air or th'
          earth?
     It sounds no more and sure it waits upon°
     Some god o' th' island. Sitting on a bank,°
     Weeping again the King my father's wreck,
395   This music crept by me upon the waters,
     Allaying both their fury and my passion°
     With its sweet air. Thence° I have followed it,
     Or it hath drawn me rather. But 'tis gone.
     No, it begins again.

(*Ariel's Song.*)

400   ARIEL: Full fathom five thy father lies.
          Of his bones are coral made.
     Those are pearls that were his eyes.
          Nothing of him that doth fade
     But doth suffer a sea change
405   Into something rich and strange.
     Sea nymphs hourly ring his knell.°
               (*Burden [within].*) Ding dong.
     Hark, now I hear them, ding dong bell.

FERDINAND: The ditty does remember° my drowned
          father.
410   This is no mortal business, nor no sound
     That the earth owes.° I hear it now above me.

PROSPERO [*to Miranda*]: The fringed curtains of
          thine eye advance°
     And say what thou seest yond.

MIRANDA: What is 't? A spirit?
     Lord, how it looks about! Believe me, sir,
     It carries a brave° form. But 'tis a spirit.   415

PROSPERO: No, wench, it eats and sleeps and hath
          such senses
     As we have, such. This gallant which thou seest
     Was in the wreck; and, but° he's something stained°
     With grief, that's beauty's canker,° thou mightst
          call him
     A goodly person. He hath lost his fellows   420
     And strays about to find 'em.

MIRANDA: I might call him
     A thing divine, for nothing natural
     I ever saw so noble.

PROSPERO [*aside*]:   It goes on,° I see,
     As my soul prompts it.—Spirit, fine spirit, I'll
          free thee
     Within two days for this.

FERDINAND [*seeing Miranda*]: Most sure, the goddess   425
     On whom these airs° attend!—Vouchsafe° my
          prayer
     May know° if you remain° upon this island,
     And that you will some good instruction give
     How I may bear me° here. My prime° request,
     Which I do last pronounce, is—O you
          wonder!°—   430
     If you be maid or no?°

MIRANDA: No wonder, sir,
     But certainly a maid.

FERDINAND: My language? Heavens!
     I am the best° of them that speak this speech,
     Were I but where 'tis spoken.

PROSPERO [*coming forward*]:   How? The best?
     What wert thou if the King of Naples heard thee?   435

FERDINAND: A single° thing, as I am now, that wonders
     To hear thee speak of Naples.° He does hear me,°
     And that he does I weep.° Myself am Naples,
     Who with mine eyes, never since at ebb,° beheld
     The King my father wrecked.

MIRANDA: Alack, for mercy!   440

FERDINAND: Yes, faith, and all his lords, the Duke of
          Milan

---

376. **Setebos:** A god of the Patagonians, named in Robert Eden's *History of Travel* (1577).   377. [s.d.] *Ariel, invisible:* Ariel wears a garment that by convention indicates he is invisible to the other characters.   380. **Curtsied . . . have:** When you have curtsied.   380–381. **kissed . . . whist:** Kissed the waves into silence; or, kissed while the waves are being hushed.   382. **Foot it featly:** Dance nimbly.   383. **sprites:** Spirits.   384. **burden:** Refrain, undersong.   385. [s.d.] *dispersedly*: From all directions, not in unison.   392. **waits upon:** Serves, attends.   393. **bank:** Sandbank.   396. **passion:** Grief.   397. **Thence:** From the bank on which he sat.   406. **knell:** Announcement of a death by the tolling of a bell.   409. **remember:** Commemorate.   411. **owes:** Owns.

412. **advance:** Raise.   415. **brave:** Excellent.   418. **but:** Except that. **something stained:** Somewhat disfigured.   419. **canker:** Cankerworm (feeding on buds and leaves).   423. **It goes on:** I.e., my plan works.   426. **airs:** Songs. **Vouchsafe:** Grant.   427. **May know:** I.e., that I may know. **remain:** Dwell.   429. **bear me:** Conduct myself. **prime:** Chief.   430. **wonder:** Miranda's name means "to be wondered at."   431. **maid or no:** I.e., a human maiden as opposed to a goddess or married woman.   433. **best:** I.e., in birth.   436. **single:** (1) Solitary, being at once King of Naples and myself; (2) feeble.   437. **Naples:** The King of Naples. **He does hear me:** I.e., the King of Naples does hear my words, for I am King of Naples.   438. **And . . . weep:** I.e., and I weep at this reminder that my father is seemingly dead, leaving me heir.   439. **at ebb:** I.e., dry, not weeping.

And his brave son° being twain.

PROSPERO [*aside*]:   The Duke of Milan
And his more braver° daughter could control°
   thee,
If now 'twere fit to do 't. At the first sight
445 They have changed eyes.°—Delicate Ariel,
I'll set thee free for this. [*To Ferdinand*.] A word,
   good sir.
I fear you have done yourself some wrong.° A word!

MIRANDA [*aside*]: Why speaks my father so
   ungently? This
Is the third man that e'er I saw, the first
450 That e'er I sighed for. Pity move my father
To be inclined my way!

FERDINAND: O, if a virgin,
And your affection not gone forth, I'll make you
The Queen of Naples.

PROSPERO: Soft, sir! One word more.
[*aside*.] They are both in either's° powers; but this
   swift business
455 I must uneasy° make, lest too light winning
Make the prize light.° [*To Ferdinand*.] One word
   more: I charge thee
That thou attend° me. Thou dost here usurp
The name thou ow'st° not, and hast put thyself
Upon this island as a spy, to win it
From me, the lord on 't.°

460 FERDINAND: No, as I am a man.

MIRANDA: There's nothing ill can dwell in such a
   temple.
If the ill spirit have so fair a house,
Good things will strive to dwell with 't.°

PROSPERO: Follow me.—
Speak not you for him, he's a traitor.—Come,
465 I'll manacle thy neck and feet together.
Seawater shalt thou drink; thy food shall be
The fresh-brook mussels, withered roots, and husks
Wherein the acorn cradled. Follow.

FERDINAND: No!
I will resist such entertainment° till
Mine enemy has more power.
     (*He draws and is charmed° from moving.*)

470 MIRANDA: O dear father,
Make not too rash° a trial of him, for
He's gentle,° and not fearful.°

PROSPERO: What, I say,

My foot° my tutor?—Put thy sword up, traitor,
Who mak'st a show but dar'st not strike, thy
   conscience
Is so possessed with guilt. Come from thy ward,° 475
For I can here disarm thee with this stick
And make thy weapon drop.
     [*He brandishes his staff.*]

MIRANDA [*trying to hinder him*]: Beseech you, father!

PROSPERO: Hence! Hang not on my garments.

MIRANDA: Sir, have pity!
I'll be his surety.°

PROSPERO: Silence! One word more
Shall make me chide thee, if not hate thee.
   What, 480
An advocate for an impostor? Hush!
Thou think'st there is no more such shapes as he,
Having seen but him and Caliban. Foolish wench,
To° the most of men this is a Caliban,
And they to him are angels.

MIRANDA: My affections 485
Are then most humble; I have no ambition
To see a goodlier man.

PROSPERO [*to Ferdinand*]: Come on, obey.
Thy nerves° are in their infancy again
And have no vigor in them.

FERDINAND: So they are.
My spirits,° as in a dream, are all bound up. 490
My father's loss, the weakness which I feel,
The wreck of all my friends, nor this man's threats
To whom I am subdued, are but light° to me
Might I but through my prison once a day
Behold this maid. All corners else° o' th' earth 495
Let liberty make use of; space enough
Have I in such a prison.

PROSPERO [*aside*]: It works. [*To Ferdinand*.] Come
on.—Thou hast done well, fine Ariel! [*To
Ferdinand*.] Follow me.
[*To Ariel*.] Hark what thou else shalt do me.°

MIRANDA [*to Ferdinand*]:   Be of comfort.
My father's of a better nature, sir, 500
Than he appears by speech. This is unwonted°
Which now came from him.

PROSPERO [*to Ariel*]:   Thou shalt be as free
As mountain winds; but then° exactly do
All points of my command.

ARIEL: To th' syllable.

PROSPERO [*to Ferdinand*]: Come, follow. [*To
Miranda*.] Speak not for him. 505
     (*Exeunt.*)

---

442. son: The only reference in the play to a son of Antonio. 443. more braver: More splendid. control: Refute. 445. changed eyes: Exchanged amorous glances. 447. done . . . wrong: I.e., spoken falsely. 454. both in either's: Each in the other's. 455. uneasy: Difficult. 455–456. light . . . light: Easy . . . cheap. 457. attend: Follow, obey. 458. ow'st: Ownest. 460. on 't: Of it. 463. strive . . . with 't: I.e., expel the evil and occupy the *temple*, the body. 469. entertainment: Treatment. 470. [s.d.] charmed: Magically prevented. 471. rash: Harsh. 472. gentle: Well born. fearful: Frightening, dangerous; or, perhaps, cowardly.

473. foot: Subordinate. (Miranda, the foot, presumes to instruct Prospero, the head.) 475. ward: Defensive posture (in fencing). 479. surety: Guarantee. 484. To: Compared to. 488. nerves: Sinews. 490. spirits: Vital powers. 493. light: Unimportant. 495. corners else: Other corners, regions. 499. me: For me. 501. unwonted: Unusual. 503. then: Until then, or if that is to be so.

ACT II • Scene I°

(*Enter Alonso, Sebastian, Antonio, Gonzalo, Adrian, Francisco, and others.*)

GONZALO [*to Alonso*]: Beseech you, sir, be merry. You have cause,
So have we all, of joy, for our escape
Is much beyond° our loss. Our hint of° woe
Is common; every day some sailor's wife,
The masters of some merchant, and the merchant°

5 Have just° our theme of woe. But for the miracle,
I mean our preservation, few in millions
Can speak like us. Then wisely, good sir, weigh
Our sorrow with° our comfort.

ALONSO: Prithee, peace.

10 SEBASTIAN [*to Antonio*]: He receives comfort like cold porridge.°

ANTONIO [*to Sebastian*]: The visitor° will not give him o'er° so.

SEBASTIAN: Look, he's winding up the watch of his
15 wit; by and by it will strike.

GONZALO: [*to Alonso*]: Sir—

SEBASTIAN: [*to Antonio*]: One. Tell.°

GONZALO: When every grief is entertained
That's offered, comes to th' entertainer°—

20 SEBASTIAN: A dollar.°

GONZALO: Dolor comes to him, indeed. You have spoken
truer than you purposed.

SEBASTIAN: You have taken it wiselier than I meant
you should.

25 GONZALO [*to Alonso*]: Therefore, my lord—

ANTONIO: Fie, what a spendthrift is he of his tongue!

ALONSO [*To Gonzalo*]: I prithee, spare.°

GONZALO: Well, I have done. But yet—

SEBASTIAN: He will be talking.

30 ANTONIO: Which, of he or Adrian, for a good wager, first
begins to crow?°

SEBASTIAN: The old cock.°

ANTONIO: The cockerel.°

SEBASTIAN: Done. The wager?

ANTONIO: A laughter.° 35

SEBASTIAN: A match!°

ADRIAN: Though this island seem to be desert°—

ANTONIO: Ha, ha, ha!

SEBASTIAN: So, you're paid.°

ADRIAN: Uninhabitable and almost inaccessible— 40

SEBASTIAN: Yet—

ADRIAN: Yet—

ANTONIO: He could not miss 't.°

ADRIAN: It must needs be° of subtle, tender, and
delicate temperance.° 45

ANTONIO: Temperance° was a delicate° wench.

SEBASTIAN: Ay, and a subtle,° as he most learnedly
delivered.°

ADRIAN: The air breathes upon us here most sweetly.

SEBASTIAN: As if it had lungs, and rotten ones. 50

ANTONIO: Or as 'twere perfumed by a fen.

GONZALO: Here is everything advantageous to life.

ANTONIO: True, save° means to live.

SEBASTIAN: Of that there's none, or little.

GONZALO: How lush and lusty° the grass looks! How 55
green!

ANTONIO: The ground indeed is tawny.°

SEBASTIAN: With an eye° of green in 't.

ANTONIO: He misses not much.

SEBASTIAN: No. He doth but° mistake the truth totally. 60

GONZALO: But the rarity of it is—which is indeed almost
beyond credit—

SEBASTIAN: As many vouched° rarities are.

GONZALO: That our garments, being, as they were,
drenched in the sea, hold notwithstanding their 65
freshness and glosses, being rather new-dyed than
stained with salt water.

ANTONIO: If but one of his pockets° could speak, would
it not say he lies?

II, i. Location: Another part of the island. **3. much beyond:** More remarkable than. **hint of:** Occasion for. **5. masters . . . the merchant:** Officers of some merchant vessel and the merchant himself, the owner (or else the ship itself). **6. just:** Exactly. **9. with:** Against. **11. porridge:** With a pun on *peace* (line 9) and *peas* or *pease*, a common ingredient of porridge. **12. visitor:** One taking nourishment and comfort to the sick (i.e., Gonzalo). **12–13. give him o'er:** Abandon him. **17. Tell:** Keep count. **18–19. When . . . entertainer:** When every sorrow that presents itself is accepted without resistance, there comes to the recipient. **20. dollar:** Widely circulated coin, the German thaler and the Spanish piece of eight. (Sebastian puns on *entertainer* in the sense of innkeeper; to Gonzalo, *dollar* suggests *dolor*, grief.) **27. spare:** Forbear, cease. **30–31. Which . . . crow:** Which of the two, Gonzalo or Adrian, do you bet will speak (crow) first? **32. old cock:** I.e., Gonzalo. **33. cockerel:** I.e., Adrian.

35. laughter: (1) Burst of laughter; (2) sitting of eggs. (When Adrian, the *cockerel*, begins to speak two lines later, Sebastian loses the bet. The Folio speech prefixes in lines 38–39 are here reversed so that Antonio enjoys his laugh as the prize for winning, as in the proverb "He who laughs last laughs best" or "He laughs that wins." The Folio assignment can work in the theater, however, if Sebastian pays for losing with a sardonic laugh of concession.) **36. A match:** A bargain; agreed. **37. desert:** Uninhabited. **39. you're paid:** I.e., you've had your laugh. **43. miss 't:** (1) Avoid saying "Yet"; (2) miss the island. **44. must needs be:** Has to be. **45. Temperance:** Mildness of climate. **46. Temperance:** A girl's name. **delicate:** Here it means "given to pleasure, voluptuous"; in line 44, "pleasant." (Antonio is evidently suggesting that *tender, and delicate temperance* sounds like a Puritan phrase, which Antonio then mocks by applying the words to a woman rather than an island. He began this bawdy comparison with a double entendre on *inaccessible*, line 40.) **47. subtle:** Here it means "tricky, sexually crafty"; in line 44, "delicate." **48. delivered:** Uttered. (Sebastian joins Antonio in baiting the Puritans with his use of the pious cant phrase *learnedly delivered*.) **53. save:** Except. **55. lusty:** Healthy. **57. tawny:** Dull brown, yellowish. **58. eye:** Tinge or spot (perhaps with reference to Gonzalo's eye or judgment). **60. but:** Merely. **63. vouched:** Certified. **68. pockets:** I.e., because they are muddy.

70 SEBASTIAN: Ay, or very falsely pocket up° his report.°
    GONZALO: Methinks our garments are now as fresh as when we put them on first in Afric, at the marriage of the King's fair daughter Claribel to the King of Tunis.
75 SEBASTIAN: 'Twas a sweet marriage, and we prosper well in our return.
    ADRIAN: Tunis was never graced before with such a paragon to° their queen.
    GONZALO: Not since widow Dido's° time.
80 ANTONIO: Widow! A pox o' that! How came that "widow" in? Widow Dido!
    SEBASTIAN: What if he had said "widower Aeneas" too? Good Lord, how you take° it!
    ADRIAN: "Widow Dido" said you? You make me
85 study of° that. She was of Carthage, not of Tunis.
    GONZALO: This Tunis, sir, was Carthage.
    ADRIAN: Carthage?
    GONZALO: I assure you, Carthage.
    ANTONIO: His word is more than the miraculous
90 harp.°
    SEBASTIAN: He hath raised the wall, and houses too.
    ANTONIO: What impossible matter will he make easy next?
95 SEBASTIAN: I think he will carry this island home in his pocket and give it his son for an apple.
    ANTONIO: And, sowing the kernels° of it in the sea, bring forth more islands.
    GONZALO: Ay.°
    ANTONIO: Why, in good time.°
100 GONZALO [to Alonso]: Sir, we were talking° that our garments seem now as fresh as when we were at Tunis at the marriage of your daughter, who is now queen.
    ANTONIO: And the rarest° that e'er came there.
    SEBASTIAN: Bate,° I beseech you, widow Dido.
105 ANTONIO: O, widow Dido? Ay, widow Dido.
    GONZALO: Is not, sir, my doublet° as fresh as the first day I wore it? I mean, in a sort.°
    ANTONIO: That "sort"° was well fished for.

    GONZALO: When I wore it at your daughter's marriage.
110 ALONSO: You cram these words into mine ears against The stomach° of my sense.° Would I had never Married° my daughter there! For, coming thence, My son is lost and, in my rate,° she too, Who is so far from Italy removed
115 I ne'er again shall see her. O thou mine heir Of Naples and of Milan, what strange fish Hath made his meal° on thee?
    FRANCISCO: Sir, he may live. I saw him beat the surges° under him
120 And ride upon their backs. He trod the water, Whose enmity he flung aside, and breasted The surge most swoll'n that met him. His bold head 'Bove the contentious waves he kept, and oared Himself with his good arms in lusty° stroke To th' shore, that o'er his wave-worn basis bowed,°
125 As° stooping to relieve him. I not° doubt He came alive to land.°
    ALONSO: No, no, he's gone.
    SEBASTIAN [to Alonso]: Sir, you may thank yourself for this great loss, That° would not bless our Europe with your daughter, But rather° loose° her to an African,
130 Where she at least is banished from your eye,° Who hath cause to wet the grief on 't.°
    ALONSO: Prithee, peace.
    SEBASTIAN: You were kneeled to and importuned° otherwise By all of us, and the fair soul herself Weighed between loathness and obedience at Which end o' the beam should bow.° We have
135 lost your son, I fear, forever. Milan and Naples have More widows in them of this business' making° Than we bring men to comfort them. The fault's your own.
140 ALONSO: So is the dear'st° o' the loss.
    GONZALO: My lord Sebastian, The truth you speak doth lack some gentleness And time° to speak it in. You rub the sore

---

70. pocket up: I.e., conceal, suppress; often used in the sense of "receive unprotestingly, fail to respond to a challenge." **his report:** Sebastian's jest is that the evidence of Gonzalo's soggy and sea-stained pockets would confute Gonzalo's speech and his reputation for truth telling. **78. to:** For. **79. widow Dido:** Queen of Carthage, deserted by Aeneas. (She was in fact a widow when Aeneas, a widower, met her, but Antonio may be amused at Gonzalo's prudish use of the term *widow* to describe a woman deserted by her lover.) **83. take:** Understand, respond to, interpret. **85. study of:** Think about. **89–90. miraculous harp:** Alludes to Amphion's harp, with which he raised the walls of Thebes; Gonzalo has exceeded that deed by creating a modern Carthage—walls *and houses*—mistakenly on the site of Tunis. **96. kernels:** Seeds. **98. Ay:** Gonzalo may be reasserting his point about Carthage, or he may be responding ironically to Antonio, who in turn answers sarcastically. **99. in good time:** An expression of ironical acquiescence or amazement (i.e., "Sure, right away"). **100. talking:** Saying. **103. rarest:** Most remarkable, beautiful. **104. Bate:** Abate, except, leave out. (Sebastian may be saying either "Don't forget Dido" or "Let's have no more talk of Dido.") **106. doublet:** Close-fitting jacket. **107. in a sort:** In a way. **108. "sort":** Antonio plays on the idea of drawing lots.

110–111. against . . . sense: I.e., against my will. **stomach:** Appetite. **112. Married:** Given in marriage. **113. rate:** Estimation, opinion. **117. made his meal:** Fed himself. **118. surges:** Waves. **123. lusty:** Vigorous. **124. that . . . bowed:** I.e., that projected out over the base of the cliff that had been eroded by the surf, thus seeming to bend down toward the sea. **125. As:** As if. **I not:** I do not. **126. came . . . land:** Reached land alive. **128. That:** You who. **129. rather:** Would rather. **loose:** (1) Release, let loose; (2) lose. **130. is banished from your eye:** Is not constantly before your eye to serve as a reproachful reminder of what you have done. **131. Who . . . on 't:** I.e., your eye which has good reason to weep because of this; or, Claribel, who has good reason to weep for it. **132. importuned:** Urged, implored. **133–135. the fair . . . bow:** I.e., Claribel herself was poised uncertainly between unwillingness to marry and obedience to her father as to which end of the scale should sink, which should prevail. **137. of . . . making:** On account of this marriage. **140. dear'st:** Heaviest, most costly. **143. time:** Appropriate time.

When you should bring the plaster.°
SEBASTIAN: Very well.
145 ANTONIO: And most chirurgeonly.°
GONZALO [*to Alonso*]:
     It is foul weather in us all, good sir,
     When you are cloudy.
SEBASTIAN [*to Antonio*]: Fowl° weather?
ANTONIO [*to Sebastian*]:   Very foul.
GONZALO: Had I plantation° of this isle, my lord—
ANTONIO [*to Sebastian*]:
     He'd sow 't with nettle seed.
150 SEBASTIAN: Or docks, or mallows.°
GONZALO: And were the king on 't, what would I do?
SEBASTIAN: Scape° being drunk for want° of wine.
GONZALO: I' the commonwealth I would by contraries°
     Execute all things; for no kind of traffic°
155 Would I admit; no name of magistrate;
     Letters° should not be known; riches, poverty,
     And use of service,° none; contract, succession,°
     Bourn,° bound of land,° tilth,° vineyard, none;
     No use of metal, corn,° or wine, or oil;
160 No occupation; all men idle, all,
     And women too, but innocent and pure;
     No sovereignty—
SEBASTIAN: Yet he would be king on 't.
ANTONIO: The latter end of his commonwealth forgets
     the beginning.
165 GONZALO: All things in common nature should produce
     Without sweat or endeavor. Treason, felony,
     Sword, pike,° knife, gun, or need of any engine°
     Would I not have; but nature should bring forth,
     Of its own kind, all foison,° all abundance,
170 To feed my innocent people.
SEBASTIAN: No marrying 'mong his subjects?
ANTONIO: None, man, all idle—whores and knaves.
GONZALO: I would with such perfection govern, sir,
     T' excel the Golden Age.°
SEBASTIAN: Save° His Majesty!
ANTONIO: Long live Gonzalo!
175 GONZALO: And—do you mark me, sir?
ALONSO: Prithee, no more. Thou dost talk nothing to me.
GONZALO: I do well believe Your Highness, and did it
     to minister occasion° to these gentlemen, who are of

such sensible° and nimble lungs that they always use°
     to laugh at nothing.   180
ANTONIO: 'Twas you we laughed at.
GONZALO: Who in this kind of merry fooling am nothing
     to you; so you may continue, and laugh at nothing
     still.
ANTONIO: What a blow was there given!   185
SEBASTIAN: An° it had not fallen flat-long.°
GONZALO: You are gentlemen of brave mettle:° you
     would lift the moon out of her sphere° if she would
     continue in it five weeks without changing.

(*Enter Ariel [invisible] playing solemn music.*)

SEBASTIAN: We would so, and then go a-batfowling.°   190
ANTONIO: Nay, good my lord, be not angry.
GONZALO: No, I warrant you, I will not adventure my
     discretion so weakly.° Will you laugh me asleep? For
     I am very heavy.°
ANTONIO: Go sleep, and hear us.°   195

          [*All sleep except Alonso, Sebastian, and
                                          Antonio.*]

ALONSO: What, all so soon asleep? I wish mine eyes
     Would, with themselves, shut up my thoughts.° I find
     They are inclined to do so.
SEBASTIAN: Please you, sir,
     Do not omit° the heavy° offer of it.
     It seldom visits sorrow; when it doth,   200
     It is a comforter.
ANTONIO: We two, my lord,
     Will guard your person while you take your rest,
     And watch your safety.
ALONSO: Thank you. Wondrous heavy.
          [*Alonso sleeps. Exit Ariel.*]
SEBASTIAN: What a strange drowsiness possesses them!
ANTONIO: It is the quality o' the climate.
SEBASTIAN: Why   205
     Doth it not then our eyelids sink? I find not
     Myself disposed to sleep.
ANTONIO: Nor I. My spirits are nimble.
     They fell together all, as by consent,°
     They dropped, as by a thunderstroke. What might,
     Worthy Sebastian, O, what might—? No more.   210

---

144. plaster: A medical application. **145. chirurgeonly:** Like a skilled surgeon. (Antonio mocks Gonzalo's medical analogy of a *plaster* applied curatively to a wound.) **148. Fowl:** With a pun on *foul*, returning to the imagery of lines 30–35. **149. plantation:** Colonization (with subsequent wordplay on the literal meaning). **150. docks, mallows:** Weeds used as antidotes for nettle stings. **152. Scape:** Escape. **want:** Lack. (Sebastian jokes sarcastically that this hypothetical ruler would be saved from dissipation only by the barrenness of the island.) **153. by contraries:** By what is directly opposite to usual custom. **154. traffic:** Trade. **156. Letters:** Learning. **157. use of service:** Custom of employing servants. **succession:** Holding of property by right of inheritance. **158. Bourn:** Boundaries. **bound of land:** Landmarks. **tilth:** Tillage of soil. **159. corn:** Grain. **167. pike:** Lance. **engine:** Instrument of warfare. **169. foison:** Plenty. **174. the Golden Age:** The age, according to Hesiod, when Cronus, or Saturn, ruled the world; an age of innocence and abundance. **Save:** God save. **178. minister occasion:** Furnish opportunity.

179. sensible: Sensitive. **use:** Are accustomed. **186. An:** If. **flat-long:** With the flat of the sword—i.e., ineffectually. (Compare "fallen flat.") **187. mettle:** Temperament, courage. (The sense of *metal*, indistinguishable as a form from *mettle*, continues the metaphor of the sword.) **188. sphere:** Orbit (literally one of the concentric zones occupied by planets in the Ptolemaic astronomy). **190. a-batfowling:** Hunting birds at night with lantern and *bat* or stick; also, gulling a simpleton. (Gonzalo is the simpleton, or fowl, and Sebastian will use the moon as his lantern.) **192–193. adventure . . . weakly:** Risk my reputation for discretion for so trivial a cause (by getting angry at these sarcastic fellows). **194. heavy:** Sleepy. **195. Go . . . us:** Let our laughing send you to sleep; or, go to sleep and hear us laugh at you. **197. Would . . . thoughts:** Would shut off my melancholy brooding when they close themselves in sleep. **199. omit:** Neglect. **heavy:** Drowsy. **208. consent:** Common agreement.

[handwritten margin note: They may be asleep but you and be king are deep]

And yet methinks I see it in thy face,
What thou shouldst be. Th' occasion° speaks thee,° and
My strong imagination sees a crown
Dropping upon thy head.
SEBASTIAN: What, art thou waking?
ANTONIO: Do you not hear me speak?
215 SEBASTIAN: I do, and surely
It is a sleepy language, and thou speak'st
Out of thy sleep. What is it thou didst say?
This is a strange repose, to be asleep
With eyes wide open—standing, speaking, moving—
And yet so fast asleep.
220 ANTONIO: Noble Sebastian,
Thou lett'st thy fortune sleep—die, rather; wink'st°
Whiles thou art waking.
SEBASTIAN: Thou dost snore distinctly;°
There's meaning in thy snores.
ANTONIO: I am more serious than my custom. You
225 Must be so too, if heed° me; which to do
Trebles thee o'er.°
SEBASTIAN: Well, I am standing water.°
ANTONIO: I'll teach you how to flow.
SEBASTIAN: Do so. To ebb°
Hereditary sloth° instructs me.
ANTONIO: O,
If you but knew how you the purpose cherish
230 Whiles thus you mock it!° How, in stripping it,
You more invest° it! Ebbing men, indeed,
Most often do so near the bottom° run
By their own fear or sloth.
SEBASTIAN: Prithee, say on.
The setting° of thine eye and cheek proclaim
235 A matter° from thee, and a birth indeed
Which throes° thee much to yield.°
ANTONIO: Thus, sir:
Although this lord° of weak remembrance,° this
Who shall be of as little memory
When he is earthed,° hath here almost persuaded—

[handwritten margin note: I want to make you king, you aren't lazy]

For he's a spirit of persuasion, only   240
Professes to persuade°—the King his son's alive,
'Tis as impossible that he's undrowned
As he that sleeps here swims.
SEBASTIAN: I have no hope
That he's undrowned.
ANTONIO: O, out of that "no hope"
What great hope have you! No hope that way° is   245
Another way so high a hope that even
Ambition cannot pierce a wink° beyond,
But doubt discovery there.° Will you grant with
  me
That Ferdinand is drowned?
SEBASTIAN: He's gone.
ANTONIO: Then tell me,
Who's the next heir of Naples?
SEBASTIAN: Claribel.   250
ANTONIO: She that is Queen of Tunis, she that dwells
Ten leagues beyond man's life;° she that from Naples
Can have no note,° unless the sun were post°—
The man i' the moon's too slow—till newborn chins
Be rough and razorable,° she that from° whom   255
We all were sea-swallowed, though some cast°
  again,
And by that destiny to perform an act
Whereof what's past is prologue, what to come
In yours and my discharge.°
SEBASTIAN: What stuff is this? How say you?   260
'Tis true my brother's daughter's Queen of Tunis,
So is she heir of Naples, twixt which regions
There is some space.
ANTONIO: A space whose every cubit°
Seems to cry out, "How shall that Claribel
Measure us° back to Naples? Keep° in Tunis,   265
And let Sebastian wake."° Say this were death
That now hath seized them, why, they were no
  worse
Than now they are. There be° that can rule Naples
As well as he that sleeps, lords that can prate°
As amply and unnecessarily   270
As this Gonzalo. I myself could make
A chough of as deep chat.° O, that you bore
The mind that I do! What a sleep were this
For your advancement! Do you understand me?

[handwritten margin note: c. can't be queen, if you were king you'll be king]

---

212. **occasion:** Opportunity of the moment. **speaks thee:** I.e., calls upon you, proclaims you usurper of Alonso's crown. 221. **wink'st:** (You) shut your eyes. 222. **distinctly:** Articulately. 225. **if heed:** If you heed. 226. **Trebles thee o'er:** Makes you three times as great and rich. **standing water:** Water that neither ebbs nor flows, at a standstill. 227. **ebb:** Recede, decline. 228. **Hereditary sloth:** Natural laziness and the position of younger brother, one who cannot inherit. 229–230. **If . . . mock it:** I.e., if you only knew how much you really enhance the value of ambition even while your words mock your purpose. 230–231. **How . . . invest it:** I.e., how the more you speak flippantly of ambition, the more you in effect affirm it. **invest:** Clothe. (Antonio's paradox is that by skeptically stripping away illusions Sebastian can see the essence of a situation and the opportunity it presents or by disclaiming and deriding his purpose Sebastian shows how he values it.) 232. **the bottom:** I.e., on which unadventurous men may go aground and miss the tide of fortune. 234. **setting:** Set expression (of earnestness). 235. **matter:** Matter of importance. 236. **throes:** Causes pain, as in giving birth. **yield:** Give forth, speak about. 237. **this lord:** I.e., Gonzalo. **remembrance:** (1) Power of remembering; (2) being remembered after his death. 239. **earthed:** Buried.

240–241. **only . . . persuade:** I.e., whose whole function (as a privy councilor) is to persuade. 245. **that way:** I.e., in regard to Ferdinand's being saved. 247–248. **Ambition . . . there:** Ambition itself cannot see any further than that hope (of the crown), but is unsure of itself in seeing even so far, is dazzled by daring to think so high. 247. **wink:** Glimpse. 252. **Ten . . . life:** I.e., it would take more than a lifetime to get there. 253. **note:** News, intimation. **post:** Messenger. 255. **razorable:** Ready for shaving. **from:** On our voyage from. 256. **cast:** Were disgorged (with a pun on *casting* of parts for a play). 259. **discharge:** Performance. 263. **cubit:** Ancient measure of length, about twenty inches. 265. **Measure us:** I.e., traverse the cubits, find her way. **Keep:** Stay (addressed to Claribel). 266. **wake:** I.e., to his good fortune. 268. **There be:** There are those. 269. **prate:** Speak foolishly. 271–272. **I . . . chat:** I could teach a jackdaw to talk as wisely or be such a garrulous talker myself.

SEBASTIAN: Methinks I do.

275 ANTONIO: And how does your content°
Tender° your own good fortune?

SEBASTIAN: I remember
You did supplant your brother Prospero.

ANTONIO: True.
And look how well my garments sit upon me,
Much feater° than before. My brother's servants
280 Were then my fellows. Now they are my men.

SEBASTIAN: But, for your conscience?

ANTONIO: Ay, sir, where lies that? If 'twere a kibe,°
'Twould put me to° my slipper; but I feel not
This deity in my bosom. Twenty consciences
285 That stand twixt me and Milan,° candied° be they
And melt ere they molest!° Here lies your brother,
No better than the earth he lies upon,
If he were that which now he's like—that's dead,
Whom I, with this obedient steel, three inches of it,
290 Can lay to bed forever; whiles you, doing thus,°
To the perpetual wink° for aye° might put
This ancient morsel, this Sir Prudence, who
Should not° upbraid our course. For all the rest,
They'll take suggestion° as a cat laps milk;
295 They'll tell the clock° to any business that
We say befits the hour.

SEBASTIAN: Thy case, dear friend,
Shall be my precedent. As thou gott'st Milan,
I'll come by Naples. Draw thy sword. One stroke
Shall free thee from the tribute° which thou payest,
And I the king shall love thee.

300 ANTONIO: Draw together;
And when I rear my hand, do you the like
To fall it° on Gonzalo.   [They draw.]

SEBASTIAN: O, but one word.
                    [They talk apart.]

(Enter Ariel [invisible], with music and song.)

ARIEL: My master through his art foresees the danger
That you, his friend, are in, and sends me forth—
305 For else his project dies—to keep them living.
                    (Sings in Gonzalo's ear.)
While you here do snoring lie,
Open-eyed conspiracy
    His time° doth take.
If of life you keep a care,
310 Shake off slumber, and beware.
    Awake, awake!

ANTONIO: Then let us both be sudden.°

GONZALO [waking]: Now, good angels preserve the King!
                    [The others wake.]

ALONSO: Why, how now, ho, awake? Why are you
    drawn?
Wherefore this ghastly looking?

GONZALO: What's the matter? 315

SEBASTIAN: Whiles we stood here securing° your
    repose,
Even now, we heard a hollow burst of bellowing
Like bulls, or rather lions. Did 't not wake you?
It struck mine ear most terribly.

ALONSO: I heard nothing.

ANTONIO: O, 'twas a din to fright a monster's ear, 320
To make an earthquake! Sure it was the roar
Of a whole herd of lions.

ALONSO: Heard you this, Gonzalo?

GONZALO: Upon mine honor, sir, I heard a humming,
And that a strange one too, which did awake me.
I shaked you, sir, and cried.° As mine eyes opened, 325
I saw their weapons drawn. There was a noise,
That's verily.° 'Tis best we stand upon our guard,
Or that we quit this place. Let's draw our weapons.

ALONSO: Lead off this ground, and let's make further
    search 330
For my poor son.

GONZALO: Heavens keep him from these beasts!
For he is, sure, i' th' island.

ALONSO: Lead away.

ARIEL [aside]: Prospero my lord shall know what I
    have done.
So, King, go safely on to seek thy son.
                    (Exeunt [separately].)

Scene II°

(Enter Caliban with a burden of wood. A noise of
thunder heard.)

CALIBAN: All the infections that the sun sucks up
From bogs, fens, flats,° on Prosper fall, and make him
By inchmeal° a disease! His spirits hear me,
And yet I needs must° curse. But they'll nor° pinch,
Fright me with urchin shows,° pitch me i' the mire, 5
Nor lead me, like a firebrand,° in the dark
Out of my way, unless he bid 'em. But
For every trifle are they set upon me,
Sometimes like apes, that mow° and chatter at me

---

275. **content:** Desire, inclination. 276. **Tender:** Regard, look after. 279. **feater:** More becomingly, fittingly. 282. **kibe:** Chilblain; here, a sore on the heel. 283. **put me to:** Oblige me to wear. 285. **Milan:** The dukedom of Milan. **candied:** Frozen, congealed in crystalline form. **be they:** May they be. 286. **molest:** Interfere. 290. **thus:** The actor makes a stabbing gesture. 291. **wink:** Sleep, closing of eyes. **aye:** Ever. 293. **Should not:** Would not then be able to. 294. **take suggestion:** Respond to prompting. 295. **tell the clock:** I.e., agree, answer appropriately, chime. 299. **tribute:** See I, ii, 113–124. 302. **fall it:** Let it fall. 308. **time:** Opportunity.

312. **sudden:** Quick. 316. **securing:** Standing guard over. 326. **cried:** Called out. 328. **verily:** True. **II, ii. Location:** Another part of the island. 2. **flats:** Swamps. 3. **By inchmeal:** Inch by inch. 4. **needs must:** Have to. **nor:** neither. 5. **urchin shows:** Elvish apparitions shaped like hedgehogs. 6. **like a firebrand:** In the guise of a will-o'-the-wisp. 9. **mow:** Make faces.

[Handwritten annotations:] Curse P, I hope he gets sick

[Handwritten annotations:] Is this man or fish? It's a native. I'll hide under his cloak.

10   And after bite me; then like hedgehogs, which
Lie tumbling in my barefoot way and mount
Their pricks at my footfall. Sometimes am I
All wound with° adders, who with cloven
      tongues
Do hiss me into madness.

(Enter Trinculo.)

Lo, now, lo!

[Handwritten:] I'll hide from the spirit

15   Here comes a spirit of his, and to torment me
For bringing wood in slowly. I'll fall flat.
Perchance he will not mind° me. [*He lies down.*]

TRINCULO: Here's neither bush nor shrub to bear off°
any weather at all. And another storm brewing; I
20   hear it sing i' the wind. Yond same black cloud
yond huge one, looks like a foul bombard° that
would shed his° liquor. If it should thunder as it
did before, I know not where to hide my head.
Yond same cloud cannot choose but fall by pailfuls.
25   [*Seeing Caliban.*] What have we here, a man or a
fish? Dead or alive? A fish, he smells like a fish; a
very ancient and fishlike smell; a kind of not-of-
the-newest Poor John.° A strange fish! Were I in
England now, as once I was, and had but this fish
30   painted,° not a holiday fool there but would give
a piece of silver. There would this monster make
a man.° Any strange beast there makes a man.
When they will not give a doit° to relieve a lame
beggar, they will lay out ten to see a dead Indian.
35   Legged like a man, and his fins like arms! Warm,
o' my troth!° I do now let loose my opinion, hold
it° no longer: this is no fish, but an islander, that
hath lately suffered° by a thunderbolt. [*Thunder.*]
Alas, the storm is come again! My best way is to
40   creep under his gaberdine.° There is no other shelter
hereabout. Misery acquaints a man with strange
bedfellows. I will here shroud° till the dregs° of the
storm be past.

[*He creeps under Caliban's garment.*]

(Enter Stephano, singing, [a bottle in his hand].)

STEPHANO: "I shall no more to sea, to sea,
45   Here shall I die ashore—"
This is a very scurvy tune to sing at a man's funeral.

Well, here's my comfort. *(Drinks.)*
(Sings.)
"The master, the swabber,° the boatswain, and I,
      The gunner and his mate,
Loved Mall, Meg, and Marian, and Margery,   *[Handwritten:]* w/ them   50
      But none of us cared for Kate.
      For she had a tongue with a tang,°
      Would cry to a sailor, 'Go hang!'
She loved not the savor of tar nor of pitch,
Yet a tailor might scratch her where'er she did itch.°   55
      Then to sea, boys, and let her go hang!"

This is a scurvy tune too. But here's my comfort.
(Drinks.)

[Handwritten:] He speaks their language. If I tone her help...

CALIBAN: Do not torment me!° O!
STEPHANO: What's the matter?° Have we devils here?
Do you put tricks upon 's° with savages and men   60
of Ind,° ha? I have not scaped drowning to be
afeard now of your four legs. For it hath been said,
"As proper° a man as ever went on four legs° cannot make him give ground"; and it shall be said so
again while Stephano breathes at° nostrils.   65
CALIBAN: This spirit torments me! O!
STEPHANO: This is some monster of the isle with four
legs, who hath got, as I take it, an ague.° Where
the devil should he learn° our language? I will give
him some relief, if it be but for that.° If I can re-   70
cover° him and keep him tame and get to Naples
with him, he's a present for any emperor that ever
trod on neat's leather.°
CALIBAN: Do not torment me, prithee. I'll bring my
wood home faster.   75
STEPHANO: He's in his fit now and does not talk after
the wisest.° He shall taste of my bottle. If he have
never drunk wine afore,° it will go near to° remove
his fit. If I can recover° him and keep him tame, I
will not take too much° for him. He shall pay for   80
him that hath° him,° and that soundly.

---

13. **wound with:** Entwined by.   17. **mind:** Notice.   18. **bear
off:** Keep off.   21. **foul bombard:** Dirty leather jug.   22. **his:**
Its.   28. **Poor John:** Salted fish, type of poor fare.   30. **painted:**
I.e., painted on a sign set up outside a booth or tent at a fair.
31–32. **make a man:** (1) Make one's fortune; (2) be indistinguishable
from an Englishman.   33. **doit:** Small coin.   36. **o' my troth:** By
my faith.   36–37. **hold it:** Hold it in.   38. **suffered:** I.e., died.
40. **gaberdine:** Cloak, loose upper garment.   42. **shroud:** Take
shelter.   **dregs:** Last remains (as in a *bombard* or jug, line 21).

48. **swabber:** Crew member whose job is to wash the decks.
52. **tang:** Sting.   55. **tailor...itch:** A dig at tailors for their
supposed effeminacy and a bawdy suggestion of satisfying a
sexual craving.   58. **Do...me:** Caliban assumes that one
of Prospero's spirits has come to punish him.   59. **What's
the matter:** What's going on here?   60. **put tricks upon 's:**
Trick us with conjuring shows.   61. **Ind:** India.   63. **proper:**
Handsome.   **four legs:** The conventional phrase would
supply *two legs*.   65. **at':** At the.   68. **ague:** Fever. (Probably both Caliban and Trinculo are quaking; see lines 58
and 83.)   69. **should he learn:** Could he have learned.
70. **for that:** I.e., for knowing our language.   71. **recover:**
Restore.   73. **neat's leather:** Cowhide.   76–77. **after the
wisest:** In the wisest fashion.   78. **afore:** Before.   **go near
to:** Nearly.   79–80. **I will...much:** I.e., no sum can be too
much.   80–81. **He shall...hath him:** I.e., anyone who wants
him will have to pay dearly for him.   81. **hath:** Possesses,
receives.

CALIBAN: Thou does me yet but little hurt; thou wilt anon,° I know it by thy trembling. Now Prosper works upon thee.

85 STEPHANO: Come on your ways. Open your mouth. Here is that which will give language to you, cat. Open your mouth.° This will shake your shaking, I can tell you, and that soundly. [*Giving Caliban a drink.*] You cannot tell who's your friend. Open
90 your chaps° again.

TRINCULO: I should know that voice. It should be— but he is drowned, and these are devils. O, defend me!

STEPHANO: Four legs and two voices—a most deli-
95 cate° monster! His forward voice now is to speak well of his friend, his backward voice° is to utter foul speeches and to detract. If all the wine in my bottle will recover him,° I will help° his ague. Come. [*Giving a drink.*] Amen! I will pour some in
100 thy other mouth.

TRINCULO: Stephano!

STEPHANO: Doth thy other mouth call me?° Mercy, mercy! This is a devil, and no monster. I will leave him. I have no long spoon.°

105 TRINCULO: Stephano! If thou beest Stephano, touch me and speak to me, for I am Trinculo—be not afeard—thy good friend Trinculo.

STEPHANO: If thou beest Trinculo, come forth. I'll pull thee by the lesser legs. If any be Trinculo's legs,
110 these are they. [*Pulling him out.*] Thou art very Trinculo indeed! How cam'st thou to be the siege° of this mooncalf?° Can he vent° Trinculos?

TRINCULO: I took him to be killed with a thunder-stroke. But art thou not drowned, Stephano? I
115 hope now thou art not drowned. Is the storm over-blown?° I hid me under the dead mooncalf's gaber-dine for fear of the storm. And art thou living, Stephano? O Stephano, two Neapolitans scaped!

[*He capers with Stephano.*]

STEPHANO: Prithee, do not turn me about. My stomach
120 is not constant.°

CALIBAN: These be fine things, an if° they be not spirits.
That's a brave° god, and bears° celestial liquor.
I will kneel to him.

STEPHANO: How didst thou scape? How cam'st thou hither? Swear by this bottle how thou cam'st 125 hither. I escaped upon a butt of sack° which the sailors heaved o'erboard—by this bottle,° which I made of the bark of a tree with mine own hands since° I was cast ashore.

CALIBAN [*kneeling*]: I'll swear upon that bottle to be 130 thy true subject, for the liquor is not earthly.

STEPHANO: Here. Swear then how thou escapedst.

TRINCULO: Swum ashore, man, like a duck. I can swim like a duck, I'll be sworn.

STEPHANO: Here, kiss the book.° Though thou canst 135 swim like a duck, thou art made like a goose.

[*Giving him a drink.*]

TRINCULO: O Stephano, hast any more of this?

STEPHANO: The whole butt, man. My cellar is in a rock by the seaside, where my wine is hid.—How now, mooncalf? How does thine ague? 140

CALIBAN: Hast thou not dropped from heaven?

STEPHANO: Out o' the moon, I do assure thee. I was the man i' the moon when time was.°

CALIBAN: I have seen thee in her, and I do adore thee. My mistress showed me thee, and thy dog, and thy bush.° 145

STEPHANO: Come, swear to that. Kiss the book. I will furnish it anon with new contents. Swear.

[*Giving him a drink.*]

TRINCULO: By this good light,° this is a very shallow monster! I afeard of him? A very weak monster! The man i' the moon? A most poor credulous 150 monster! Well drawn,° monster, in good sooth!°

CALIBAN [*to Stephano*]: I'll show thee every fertile inch o'th'island,
And I will kiss thy foot. I prithee, be my god.

TRINCULO: By this light, a most perfidious and drunken monster! When 's god's asleep, he'll rob 155 his bottle.°

---

83. **anon:** Presently.   86–87. **cat...mouth:** Allusion to the proverb "Good liquor will make a cat speak."   90. **chaps:** Jaws.   94–95. **delicate:** Ingenious.   96. **backward voice:** Trinculo and Caliban are facing in opposite directions. Stephano supposes the monster to have a rear end that can emit *foul speeches* or foul-smelling wind at the monster's *other mouth*, line 100.   97–98. **If...him:** Even if it takes all the wine in my bottle to cure him.   98. **help:** Cure.   102. **call me:** I.e., call me by name, know supernaturally who I am.   104. **long spoon:** Allusion to the proverb "He that sups with the devil has need of a long spoon."   111. **siege:** Excrement.   112. **mooncalf:** Monstrous or misshapen creature (whose deformity is caused by the malignant influence of the moon). **vent:** Excrete, defecate.   115–116. **overblown:** Blown over.   120. **not constant:** Unsteady.

121. **an if:** If.   122. **brave:** Fine, magnificent. **bears:** He carries.   126. **butt of sack:** Barrel of Canary wine.   127. **by this bottle:** I.e., I swear by this bottle.   128. **since:** After.   135. **book:** I.e., bottle (but with ironic reference to the practice of kissing the Bible in swearing an oath; see *I'll be sworn* in line 134).   143. **when time was:** Once upon a time.   145. **dog...bush:** The man in the moon was popularly imagined to have with him a dog and a bush of thorn.   148. **By...light:** By God's light, by this good light from heaven.   151. **Well drawn:** Well pulled (on the bottle). **in good sooth:** Truly, indeed.   155–156. **When...bottle:** I.e., Caliban wouldn't even stop at robbing his god of his bottle if he could catch him asleep.

They think they're the only ones who survived

CALIBAN: I'll kiss thy foot. I'll swear myself thy
     subject.
STEPHANO: Come on then. Down, and swear.
                                        [*Caliban kneels.*]
160 TRINCULO: I shall laugh myself to death at this puppy-
     headed monster. A most scurvy monster! I could
     find in my heart to beat him—
STEPHANO: Come, kiss.
TRINCULO: But that the poor monster's in drink.° An
165   abominable monster!
CALIBAN: I'll show thee the best springs. I'll pluck
     thee berries.
     I'll fish for thee and get thee wood enough.
     A plague upon the tyrant that I serve!
     I'll bear him no more sticks, but follow thee,
170   Thou wondrous man.
TRINCULO: A most ridiculous monster, to make a
     wonder of a poor drunkard!
CALIBAN: I prithee, let me bring thee where crabs°
     grow;
     And I with my long nails will dig thee pignuts,°
175 Show thee a jay's nest, and instruct thee how
     To snare the nimble marmoset.° I'll bring thee
     To clustering filberts, and sometimes I'll get thee
     Young scamels° from the rock. Wilt thou go with
     me?
STEPHANO: I prithee now, lead the way without any
180   more talking.— Trinculo, the King and all our
     company else° being drowned, we will inherit°
     here.—Here, bear my bottle.—Fellow Trinculo,
     we'll fill him by and by again.
CALIBAN (*sings drunkenly*): Farewell, master, farewell,
185   farewell!
TRINCULO: A howling monster; a drunken monster!
CALIBAN: No more dams I'll make for fish,
     Nor fetch in firing°
     At requiring,
190 Nor scrape trenchering,° nor wash dish.
          'Ban, 'Ban, Ca-Caliban
          Has a new master. Get a new man!°
     Freedom, high-day!° High-day, freedom!
     Freedom, high-day, freedom!
195 STEPHANO: O brave monster! Lead the way.
                                        (*Exeunt.*)

C. is now ↑ 3 S's servant.

164. **in drink:** Drunk.   173. **crabs:** Crab apples; or, perhaps,
crabs.   174. **pignuts:** Earthnuts, edible tuberous roots.   176.
marmoset: Small monkey.   178. **scamels:** Possibly *seamews,*
mentioned in William Strachey's report on the shipwreck he
endured (see p. 434); possibly shellfish; or, perhaps, from *squa-
melle,* furnished with little scales. Contemporary French and
Italian travel accounts report that the natives of Patagonia in
South America ate small fish described as *fort scameux* and
squame.   181. **else:** In addition, besides ourselves.   **inherit:**
Take possession.   188. **firing:** Firewood.   190. **trenchering:**
Trenchers, wooden plates.   192. **Get a new man:** Addressed to
Prospero.   193. **high-day:** Holiday.

ACT III • Scene I°

They're willing to work, though he's off. W. it does really work for him.

(*Enter Ferdinand, bearing a log.*)

FERDINAND: There be some sports° are painful,° and their labor
     Delight in them sets off.° Some kinds of
     baseness°
     Are nobly undergone,° and most poor° matters
     Point to rich ends. This my mean° task
     Would be as heavy to me as odious, but°   5
     The mistress which I serve quickens° what's
     dead
     And makes my labors pleasures. O, she is
     Ten times more gentle than her father's crabbèd,
     And he's composed of harshness. I must
     remove
     Some thousands of these logs and pile them up,   10
     Upon a sore injunction.° My sweet mistress
     Weeps when she sees me work and says such
     baseness
     Had never like executor.° I forget;°
     But these sweet thoughts do even refresh my
     labors,
     Most busy lest when I do it.°

(*Enter Miranda; and Prospero [at a distance, unseen].*)

rest, please
studying 2-3 more hours

MIRANDA: Alas now, pray you,   15
     Work not so hard. I would the lightning had
     Burnt up those logs that you are enjoined° to
     pile!
     Pray, set it down and rest you. When this° burns,
     'Twill weep° for having wearied you. My father
     Is hard at study. Pray now, rest yourself.   20
     He's safe for these° three hours.
FERDINAND: O most dear mistress,
     The sun will set before I shall discharge°
     What I must strive to do.
MIRANDA: If you'll sit down,
     I'll bear your logs the while. Pray, give me that.
     I'll carry it to the pile.

III, i. **Location:** Before Prospero's cell.   1. **sports:** Pastimes,
activities.   **painful:** Laborious.   1–2. **and their . . . sets off:**
I.e., but the pleasure we get from those pastimes compensates
for the effort.   2. **baseness:** Menial activity.   3. **undergone:**
Undertaken.   **most poor:** Poorest.   4. **mean:** Lowly.   5. **but:**
Were it not that.   6. **quickens:** Gives life to.   11. **sore injunction:** Severe command.   13. **Had . . . executor:** I.e., was
never before undertaken by one of my noble rank.   **I forget:**
I.e., I forget that I'm supposed to be working; or, I forget my
happiness, oppressed by my labor.   15. **Most . . . it:** I.e., least
troubled by my labor, and most active in my thoughts, when
I think of her (?). (The line may be in need of emendation.)
17. **enjoined:** Commanded.   18. **this:** I.e., the log.   19. **weep:**
I.e., exude resin.   21. **these:** I.e., the next.   22. **discharge:**
Complete.

25 FERDINAND: No, precious creature,
    I had rather crack my sinews, break my back,
    Than you should such dishonor undergo
    While I sit lazy by.
    MIRANDA: It would become me
    As well as it does you; and I should do it
30 With much more ease, for my good will is to it,
    And yours it is against.
    PROSPERO [aside]:   Poor worm, thou art
        infected!
    This visitation° shows it.
    MIRANDA: You look wearily.
    FERDINAND: No, noble mistress, 'tis fresh morning
        with me
    When you are by° at night. I do beseech you—
35 Chiefly that I might set it in my prayers—
    What is your name?
    MIRANDA: Miranda.—O my father,
    I have broke your hest° to say so.
    FERDINAND: Admired Miranda!°
    Indeed the top of admiration, worth
    What's dearest° to the world! Full many a lady
40 I have eyed with best regard,° and many a time
    The harmony of their tongues hath into
        bondage
    Brought my too diligent° ear. For several° virtues
    Have I liked several women, never any
    With so full soul but some defect in her
45 Did quarrel with the noblest grace she owed°
    And put it to the foil.° But you, O you,
    So perfect and so peerless, are created
    Of° every creature's best!
    MIRANDA: I do not know
    One of my sex; no woman's face remember,
50 Save, from my glass, mine own. Nor have I seen
    More that I may call men than you, good friend,
    And my dear father. How features are abroad°
    I am skilless° of; but, by my modesty,°
    The jewel in my dower, I would nor wish
55 Any companion in the world but you;
    Nor can imagination form a shape,
    Besides yourself, to like of.° But I prattle
    Something° too wildly, and my father's precepts
    I therein do forget.
    FERDINAND: I am in my condition°

    A prince, Miranda; I do think, a king—   60
    I would, not so!—and would° no more endure
    This wooden slavery° than to suffer
    The flesh-fly° blow° my mouth. Hear my soul
        speak:
    The very instant that I saw you did
    My heart fly to your service; there resides   65
    To make me slave to it, and for your sake
    Am I this patient log-man.
    MIRANDA: Do you love me?
    FERDINAND: O heaven, O earth, bear witness to this
        sound,
    And crown what I profess with kind event°
    If I speak true! If hollowly,° invert°   70
    What best is boded° me to mischief!° I
    Beyond all limit of what° else i' the world
    Do love, prize, honor you.
    MIRANDA [weeping]:   I am a fool
    I weep at what I am glad of.
    PROSPERO [aside]:   Fair encounter
    Of two most rare affections! Heavens rain grace 75
    On that which breeds between 'em!
    FERDINAND: Wherefore weep you?
    MIRANDA: At mine unworthiness, that dare not
        offer
    What I desire to give, and much less take
    What I shall die° to want.° But this is trifling,
    And all the more it seeks to hide itself   80
    The bigger bulk it shows. Hence, bashful
        cunning,°
    And prompt me, plain and holy innocence!
    I am your wife, if you will marry me;
    If not, I'll die your maid.° To be your fellow°
    You may deny me, but I'll be your servant   85
    Whether you will° or no.
    FERDINAND: My mistress,° dearest,
    And I thus humble ever.
    MIRANDA: My husband, then?
    FERDINAND: Ay, with a heart as willing°
    As bondage e'er of freedom. Here's my hand.   90
    MIRANDA [clasping his hand]: And mine, with my
        heart in 't. And now farewell
    Till half an hour hence.
    FERDINAND: A thousand thousand!°
        (Exeunt [Ferdinand and Miranda, separately].)

32. visitation: (1) Visit of the sick; (2) visitation of the plague (i.e., infection of love). 34. by: Nearby. 37. hest: Command. Admired Miranda: Her name means "to be admired or wondered at." 39. dearest: Most treasured. 40. best regard: Thoughtful and approving attention. 42. diligent: Attentive. several: Various (also in line 43). 45. owed: Owned. 46. put . . . foil: (1) Overthrew it (as in wrestling); (2) served as a foil, or contrast, to set it off. 48. Of: Out of. 52. How . . . abroad: What people look like in other places. 53. skilless: Ignorant. modesty: Virginity. 57. like of: Be pleased with, be fond of. 58. Something: Somewhat. 59. condition: Rank.

61. would: Wish (it were). 62. wooden slavery: Being compelled to carry wood. 63. flesh-fly: Insect that deposits its eggs in dead flesh. blow: Befoul with fly eggs. 69. kind event: Favorable outcome. 70. hollowly: Insincerely, falsely. invert: Turn. 71. boded: Destined for. mischief: Evil. 72. what: Whatever. 79. die: Probably with an unconscious sexual meaning that underlies all of lines 77–81. want: Lack. 81. bashful cunning: Coyness. 84. maid: Handmaiden, servant. fellow: Mate, equal. 86. will: Desire it. My mistress: I.e., the woman I adore and serve (not an illicit sexual partner). 89. willing: Desirous. 92. A thousand thousand: I.e., a thousand thousand farewells.

PROSPERO: So glad of this as they I cannot be,
95   Who are surprised with all;° but my rejoicing
     At nothing can be more. I'll to my book,
     For yet ere suppertime must I perform
     Much business appertaining.°   (*Exit.*)

Scene II°

(*Enter Caliban, Stephano, and Trinculo.*)

STEPHANO: Tell not me. When the butt is out,° we will
     drink water, not a drop before. Therefore bear up
     and board 'em.° Servant monster, drink to me.
TRINCULO: Servant monster? The folly of° this island!
5   They say there's but five upon this isle. We are
     three of them; if th' other two be brained° like us,
     the state totters.
STEPHANO: Drink, servant monster, when I bid thee.
     Thy eyes are almost set° in thy head.
                                          [*Giving a drink.*]
10 TRINCULO: Where should they be set° else? He were a
     brave° monster indeed if they were set in his tail.
STEPHANO: My man-monster hath drowned his
     tongue in sack. For my part, the sea can-
     not drown me. I swam, ere I could recover° the
15   shore, five and thirty leagues° off and on.° By this
     light,° thou shalt be my lieutenant, monster, or my
     standard.°
TRINCULO: Your lieutenant, if you list.° He's no standard.°
STEPHANO: We'll not run,° Monsieur Monster.
20 TRINCULO: Nor go° neither, but you'll lie° like dogs
     and yet say nothing neither.
STEPHANO: Mooncalf, speak once in thy life, if thou
     beest a good mooncalf.
CALIBAN: How does thy honor? Let me lick thy
     shoe.
25   I'll not serve him. He is not valiant.

TRINCULO: Thou liest, most ignorant monster, I am in
     case to jostle a constable.° Why, thou debauched
     fish, thou, was there ever man a coward that hath
     drunk so much sack° as I today? Wilt thou tell a
     monstrous lie, being but half a fish and half a   30
     monster?
CALIBAN: Lo, how he mocks me! Wilt thou let him,
     my lord?
TRINCULO: "Lord," quoth he? That a monster should
     be such a natural!°
CALIBAN: Lo, lo, again! Bite him to death, I prithee.   35
STEPHANO: Trinculo, keep a good tongue in your
     head. If you prove a mutineer—the next tree!°
     The poor monster's my subject, and he shall not
     suffer indignity.
CALIBAN: I thank my noble lord. Wilt thou be
     pleased   40
     To hearken once again to the suit I made to
     thee?
STEPHANO: Marry,° will I. Kneel and repeat it. I will
     stand, and so shall Trinculo. [*Caliban kneels.*]

(*Enter Ariel, invisible.°*)

CALIBAN: As I told thee before, I am subject to a
     tyrant,
     A sorcerer, that by his cunning hath   45
     Cheated me of the island.
ARIEL [*mimicking Trinculo*]: Thou liest.
CALIBAN: Thou liest, thou jesting monkey, thou!
     I would my valiant master would destroy thee.
     I do not lie.
STEPHANO: Trinculo, if you trouble him any more in 's 50
     tale, by this hand, I will supplant° some of your
     teeth.
TRINCULO: Why, I said nothing.
STEPHANO: Mum, then, and no more.—Proceed.
CALIBAN: I say by sorcery he got this isle;   55
     From me he got it. If thy greatness will
     Revenge it on him—for I know thou dar'st,
     But this thing° dare not—
STEPHANO: That's most certain.
CALIBAN: Thou shalt be lord of it, and I'll serve thee. 60
STEPHANO: How now shall this be compassed?°
     Canst thou bring me to the party?
CALIBAN: Yea, yea, my lord. I'll yield him thee
     asleep,
     Where thou mayst knock a nail into his head.

---

95. with all: By everything that has happened; or, *withal,* with it.   **98. appertaining:** Related to this.   **III, ii. Location:** Another part of the island.   **1. out:** Empty.   **2–3. bear . . . 'em:** Stephano uses the terminology of maneuvering at sea and boarding a vessel under attack as a way of urging an assault on the liquor supply.   **4. folly of:** I.e., stupidity found on.   **6. be brained:** Are endowed with intelligence.   **9. set:** Fixed in a drunken state; or, sunk, like the sun.   **10. set:** Placed.   **11. brave:** Fine, splendid.   **14. recover:** Gain, reach.   **15. leagues:** Units of distance each equaling about three miles.   **off and on:** Intermittently.   **By this light:** An oath by the light of the sun.   **16. standard:** Standard-bearer, ensign (as distinguished from *lieutenant,* lines 15–17).   **17. list:** Prefer.   **17–18. no standard:** I.e., not able to stand up.   **19. run:** (1) Retreat; (2) urinate (taking Trinculo's *standard,* line 17, in the old sense of "conduit").   **20. go:** Walk.   **lie:** (1) Tell lies; (2) lie prostrate; (3) excrete.

26–27. in case . . . constable: I.e., in fit condition, made valiant by drink, to taunt or challenge the police.   **29. sack:** Spanish white wine.   **34. natural:** (1) Idiot; (2) natural as opposed to unnatural, monsterlike.   **37. the next tree:** I.e., you'll hang.   **42. Marry:** I.e., indeed. (Originally an oath: by the Virgin Mary.)   **43. [s.d.]** *invisible:* I.e., wearing a garment to connote invisibility, as at I, ii, 377.   **51. supplant:** Uproot, displace.   **58. this thing:** I.e., Trinculo.   **61. compassed:** Achieved.

65 ARIEL: Thou liest; thou canst not.
CALIBAN: What a pied ninny's° this! Thou scurvy
  patch!°—
I do beseech thy greatness, give him blows
And take his bottle from him. When that's gone
He shall drink naught but brine, for I'll not show
  him
70 Where the quick freshes° are.
STEPHANO: Trinculo, run into no further danger. Interrupt the monster one word further° and, by this
  hand, I'll turn my mercy out o' doors° and make a
  stockfish° of thee.
75 TRINCULO: Why, what did I? I did nothing. I'll go farther off.°
STEPHANO: Didst thou not say he lied?
ARIEL: Thou liest.
STEPHANO: Do I so? Take thou that. [*He beats
80 Trinculo.*] As you like this, give me the lie° another
  time.
TRINCULO: I did not give the lie. Out o' your wits and
  hearing too? A pox o' your bottle! This can sack
  and drinking do. A murrain° on your monster, and
85 the devil take your fingers!
CALIBAN: Ha, ha, ha!
STEPHANO: Now, forward with your tale. [*To Trinculo.*]
  Prithee, stand further off.
CALIBAN: Beat him enough. After a little time
  I'll beat him too.
90 STEPHANO: Stand farther.—Come, proceed.
CALIBAN: Why, as I told thee, tis a custom with him
I' th' afternoon to sleep. There thou mayst brain
  him,
Having first seized his books; or with a log
Batter his skull, or paunch° him with a stake,
95 Or cut his weasand° with thy knife. Remember
First to possess his books, for without them
He's but a sot,° as I am, nor hath not
One spirit to command. They all do hate him
As rootedly as I. Burn but his books.
100 He has brave utensils°—for so he calls them—
Which, when he has a house, he'll deck withal.°
And that most deeply to consider is
The beauty of his daughter. He himself
Calls her a nonpareil. I never saw a woman
105 But only Sycorax my dam and she;
But she as far surpasseth Sycorax

As great'st does least.
STEPHANO: Is it so brave° a lass?
CALIBAN: Ay, lord. She will become° thy bed, I
  warrant,
And bring thee forth brave brood.
110 STEPHANO: Monster, I will kill this man. His daughter
  and I will be king and queen—save Our
  Graces!—and Trinculo and thyself shall be
  viceroys. Dost thou like the plot, Trinculo?
TRINCULO: Excellent.
115 STEPHANO: Give me thy hand. I am sorry I beat thee;
  but, while thou liv'st, keep a good tongue in thy
  head.
CALIBAN: Within this half hour will he be asleep. Wilt
  thou destroy him then?
120 STEPHANO: Ay, on mine honor.
ARIEL [*aside*]: This will I tell my master.
CALIBAN: Thou mak'st me merry; I am full of
  pleasure.
Let us be jocund.° Will you troll the catch°
You taught me but whilere?°
125 STEPHANO: At thy request, monster, I will do reason,
  any reason.° Come on, Trinculo, let us sing.
                                        (*Sings.*)
"Flout° 'em and scout° 'em
And scout 'em and flout 'em!
  Thought is free."
130 CALIBAN: That's not the tune.
            (*Ariel plays the tune on a tabor° and pipe.*)
STEPHANO: What is this same?
TRINCULO: This is the tune of our catch, played by the
  picture of Nobody.°
135 STEPHANO: If thou beest a man, show thyself in thy
  likeness. If thou beest a devil, take 't as thou list.°
TRINCULO: O, forgive me my sins!
STEPHANO: He that dies pays all debts. I defy thee.
  Mercy upon us!
140 CALIBAN: Art thou afeard?
STEPHANO: No, monster, not I.
CALIBAN: Be not afeard. The isle is full of noises,
  Sounds, and sweet airs, that give delight and hurt
    not.
Sometimes a thousand twangling instruments
Will hum about mine ears, and sometimes voices
145 That, if I then had waked after long sleep,

---

66. **pied ninny:** Fool in motley.   **patch:** Fool.   70. **quick freshes:** Running springs.   72. **one word further:** I.e., one more time.   73. **turn . . . doors:** I.e., forget about being merciful.   74. **stockfish:** Dried cod beaten before cooking.   76. **off:** Away.   80. **give me the lie:** Call me a liar to my face.   84. **murrain:** Plague (literally, a cattle disease).   94. **paunch:** Stab in the belly.   95. **weasand:** Windpipe.   97. **sot:** Fool.   100. **brave utensils:** Fine furnishings.   101. **deck withal:** Furnish it with.

108. **brave:** Splendid, attractive.   109. **become:** Suit.   124. **jocund:** Jovial, merry.   **troll the catch:** Sing the round.   125. **but whilere:** Only a short time ago.   126–127. **reason, any reason:** Anything reasonable.   128. **Flout:** Scoff at.   **scout:** Deride.   131. [s.d.] **tabor:** Small drum.   134. **picture of Nobody:** Refers to a familiar figure with head, arms, and legs but no trunk.   136. **take 't . . . list:** I.e., take my defiance as you please, as best you can.

Will make me sleep again; and then, in dreaming,
The clouds methought would open and show
    riches
Ready to drop upon me, that when I waked
150 I cried to dream° again.
STEPHANO: This will prove a brave kingdom to me,
    where I shall have my music for nothing.
CALIBAN: When Prospero is destroyed.
STEPHANO: That shall be by and by.° I remember the
155 story.
TRINCULO: The sound is going away. Let's follow it, and
    after do our work.
STEPHANO: Lead, monster; we'll follow. I would I could
    see this laborer! He lays it on.°
160 **TRINCULO:** Wilt come? I'll follow Stephano.
                (*Exeunt [following Ariel's music].*)

Scene III°

(*Enter Alonso, Sebastian, Antonio, Gonzalo, Adrian, Francisco, etc.*)

GONZALO: By 'r lakin,° I can go no further, sir.
    My old bones aches. Here's a maze trod indeed
    Through forthrights and meanders!° By your
        patience,
    I needs must° rest me.
ALONSO: Old lord, I cannot blame thee,
5   Who am myself attached° with weariness,
    To the dulling of my spirits.° Sit down and rest.
    Even here I will put off my hope, and keep it
    No longer for° my flatterer. He is drowned
    Whom thus we stray to find, and the sea mocks
10 Our frustrate° search on land. Well, let him go.
                [*Alonso and Gonzalo sit.*]
ANTONIO [*aside to Sebastian*]: I am right° glad that
    he's so out of hope.°
    Do not, for° one repulse, forgo the purpose
    That you resolved t' effect.
SEBASTIAN [*to Antonio*]:   The next advantage
    Will we take throughly.°
ANTONIO [*to Sebastian*]:   Let it be tonight,
15 For, now° they are oppressed with travel,° they

Will not, nor cannot, use° such vigilance
As when they are fresh.
SEBASTIAN [*to Antonio*]:   I say tonight. No more.
                (*Solemn and strange music; and
                Prospero on the top,° invisible.*)
ALONSO: What harmony is this? My good friends,
    hark!
GONZALO: Marvelous sweet music!

(*Enter several strange shapes, bringing in a banquet, and dance about it with gentle actions of salutations; and, inviting the King, etc., to eat, they depart.*)

ALONSO: Give us kind keepers,° heavens! What were
    these?   20
SEBASTIAN: A living° drollery.° Now I will believe
    That there are unicorns; that in Arabia
    There is one tree, the phoenix'° throne, one
        phoenix
    At this hour reigning there.
ANTONIO: I'll believe both;
    And what does else want credit,° come to me   25
    And I'll be sworn 'tis true. Travelers ne'er did lie,
    Though fools at home condemn 'em.
GONZALO: If in Naples
    I should report this now, would they believe me
    If I should say I saw such islanders?
    For, certes,° these are people of the island,   30
    Who though they are of monstrous shape, yet
        note,
    Their manners are more gentle, kind, than of
    Our human generation you shall find
    Many, nay, almost any.
PROSPERO [*aside*]:   Honest lord,
    Thou hast said well, for some of you there
        present   35
    Are worse than devils.
ALONSO: I cannot too much muse°
    Such shapes, such gesture, and such sound,
        expressing—
    Although they want° the use of tongue—a kind
    Of excellent dumb discourse.
PROSPERO [*aside*]:   Praise in departing.°

---

150. **to dream:** Desirous of dreaming.   154. **by and by:** Very soon.   159. **lays it on:** I.e., plays the drum skillfully and energetically.   **III, iii. Location:** Another part of the island. 1. **By 'r lakin:** By our Ladykin, by our Lady.   3. **forthrights and meanders:** Paths straight and crooked.   4. **needs must:** Have to.   5. **attached:** Seized.   6. **To . . . spirits:** To the point of being dull-spirited.   8. **for:** As.   10. **frustrate:** Frustrated.   11. **right:** Very.   **out of hope:** Despairing, discouraged.   12. **for:** Because of.   14. **throughly:** Thoroughly.   15. **now:** Now that.   **travel:** Spelled *trauaile* in the Folio and carrying the sense of labor as well as traveling.

16. **use:** Apply.   17. [S.D.] **on the top:** At some high point of the tiring-house or the theater, on a third level above the gallery.   20. **kind keepers:** Guardian angels.   21. **living:** With live actors.   **drollery:** Comic entertainment, caricature, puppet show.   23. **phoenix:** Mythical bird consumed to ashes every five to six hundred years, only to be renewed into another cycle.   25. **want credit:** Lack credence.   30. **certes:** Certainly.   36. **muse:** Wonder at.   38. **want:** Lack.   39. **Praise in departing:** I.e., save your praise until the end of the performance (proverbial).

FRANCISCO: They vanished strangely.

40 SEBASTIAN: No matter, since
    They have left their viands° behind, for we have
        stomachs.°
    Will 't please you taste of what is here?

ALONSO: Not I.

GONZALO: Faith, sir, you need not fear. When we
        were boys,
    Who would believe that there were
        mountaineers°
45 Dewlapped° like bulls, whose throats had
        hanging et 'em
    Wallets° of flesh? Or that there were such men
    Whose heads stood in their breasts?° Which
        now we find

Each putter-out of five for one° will bring us
Good warrant° of.

ALONSO: I will stand to° and feed,
50 Although my last°—no matter, since I feel
    The best° is past. Brother, my lord the Duke,
    Stand to, and do as we.

                        [*They approach the table.*]

(*Thunder and lightning. Enter Ariel, like a harpy,° claps
his wings upon the table, and with a quaint device° the
banquet vanishes.°*)

---

41. **viands:** Provisions. **stomachs:** Appetites. **44. mountain-eers:** Mountain dwellers. **45. Dewlapped:** Having a *dewlap,* or fold of skin hanging from the neck, like cattle. **46. Wallets:** Pendent folds of skin, wattles. **47. in their breasts:** I.e., like the Anthropophagi described in *Othello,* I, iii, 146.

48. **putter-out . . . one:** One who invests money or gambles on the risks of travel on the condition that, if he returns safely, he is to receive five times the amount deposited; hence, any trav-eler. **49. Good warrant:** Assurance. **stand to:** Fall to; take the risk. **50. Although my last:** Even if this were to be my last meal. **51. best:** Best part of life. **52.** [S.D.] *harpy:* A fabulous monster with a woman's face and breasts and a vulture's body, supposed to be a minister of divine vengeance. *quaint device:* Ingenious stage contrivance. *the banquet vanishes:* I.e., the food vanishes; the table remains until line 82.

Christian Camargo as Ariel, directed by Sam Mendes, 2010.

ARIEL: You are three men of sin, whom Destiny—
    That hath to° instrument this lower world
55 And what is in 't—the never-surfeited sea
    Hath caused to belch up you, and on this island
    Where man doth not inhabit, you 'mongst men
    Being most unfit to live. I have made you mad;
    And even with suchlike valor° men hang and
      drown
    Their proper° selves.

                  [Alonso, Sebastian, and
                  Antonio draw their swords.]
60   You fools! I and my fellows
    Are ministers of Fate. The elements
    Of whom° your swords are tempered° may as
      well
    Wound the loud winds, or with bemocked-at°
      stabs
    Kill the still-closing° waters, as diminish
    One dowl° that's in my plume. My fellow
65   ministers
    Are like° invulnerable. If° you could hurt,
    Your swords are now too massy° for your
      strengths
    And will not be uplifted. But remember—
    For that's my business to you—that you three
70 From Milan did supplant good Prospero;
    Exposed unto the sea, which hath requit° it,
    Him and his innocent child; for which foul deed
    The powers, delaying, not forgetting, have
    Incensed the seas and shores, yea, all the creatures,
75 Against your peace. Thee of thy son, Alonso,
    They have bereft; and do pronounce by me
    Lingering perdition,° worse than any death
    Can be at once, shall step by step attend
    You and your ways; whose° wraths to guard you
      from—
80 Which here, in this most desolate isle, else° falls
    Upon your heads—is nothing° but heart's
      sorrow
    And a clear° life ensuing.

(He vanishes in thunder; then, to soft music, enter the shapes again, and dance, with mocks and mows,° and carrying out the table.)

PROSPERO: Bravely° the figure of this harpy hast
    thou

Performed, my Ariel; a grace it had devouring.°
    Of my instruction hast thou nothing bated°   85
    In what thou hadst to say. So,° with good life°
    And observation strange,° my meaner° ministers
    Their several kinds° have done. My high charms
      work,
    And these mine enemies are all knit up
    In their distractions. They now are in my power; 90
    And in these fits I leave them, while I visit
    Young Ferdinand, whom they suppose is drowned,
    And his and mine loved darling.   *[Exit above.]*
GONZALO: I' the name of something holy, sir, why°
      stand you
    In this strange stare?
ALONSO: O, it° is monstrous, monstrous! 95
    Methought the billows° spoke and told me of it;
    The winds did sing it to me, and the thunder,
    That deep and dreadful organ pipe, pronounced
    The name of Prosper; it did bass my trespass.°
    Therfor° my son i' th' ooze is bedded; and   100
    I'll seek him deeper than e'er plummet° sounded,°
    And with him there lie mudded.   *(Exit.)*
SEBASTIAN: But one fiend at a time,
    I'll fight their legions o'er.°
ANTONIO: I'll be thy second.

    (Exeunt [Sebastian and Antonio].)

GONZALO: All three of them are desperate.° Their 105
      great guilt,
    Like poison given to work a great time after,
    Now 'gins to bite the spirits.° I do beseech you
    That are of suppler joints, follow them swiftly
    And hinder them from what this ecstasy°
    May now provoke them to.
ADRIAN.   Follow, I pray you. 110
                (Exeunt omnes.°)

---

84. **a grace . . . devouring:** I.e., you gracefully caused the banquet to disappear as if you had consumed it (with puns on *grace* meaning "gracefulness" and "a blessing on the meal" and on *devouring* meaning "a literal eating" and "an all-consuming or ravishing grace"). 85. **bated:** Abated, omitted. 86. **So:** In the same fashion. **good life:** Faithful reproduction. 87. **observation strange:** Exceptional attention to detail. **meaner:** I.e., subordinate to Ariel. 88. **several kinds:** Individual parts. 94. **why:** Gonzalo was not addressed in Ariel's speech to the *three men of sin* (line 53) and is not, as they are, in a maddened state; see lines 105–107. 95. **it:** I.e., my sin (also in line 96). 96. **billows:** Waves. 99. **bass my trespass:** Proclaim my trespass like a bass note in music. 100. **Therfor:** In consequence of this. 101. **plummet:** A lead weight attached to a line for testing depth. **sounded:** Probed, tested the depth of. 104. **o'er:** One after another. 105. **desperate:** Despairing and reckless. 107. **bite the spirits:** Sap their vital powers through anguish. 109. **ecstasy:** Mad frenzy. 110. [S.D.] **omnes:** Latin for "all."

---

54. **to:** I.e., as its. 59. **suchlike valor:** I.e., the reckless valor derived from madness. 60. **proper:** Own. 62. **whom:** Which. **tempered:** Composed and hardened. 63. **bemocked-at:** Scorned. 64. **still-closing:** Always closing again when parted. 65. **dowl:** Soft, fine feather. 66. **like:** Likewise, similarly. **If:** Even if. 67. **massy:** Heavy. 71. **requit:** Requited, avenged. 77. **perdition:** Ruin, destruction. 79. **whose:** Refers to the heavenly powers. 80. **else:** Otherwise. 81. **is nothing:** There is no way. 82. **clear:** Unspotted, innocent. [S.D.] *mocks and mows:* Mocking gestures and grimaces. 83. **Bravely:** Finely, dashingly.

ACT IV • Scene I°

(Enter Prospero, Ferdinand, and Miranda.)

PROSPERO: If I have too austerely° punished you,
Your compensation makes amends, for I
Have given you here a third° of mine own life,
Or that for which I live; who once again
5 I tender to thy hand. All thy vexations°
Were but my trials of thy love, and thou
Hast strangely° stood the test. Here, afore Heaven,
I ratify this my rich gift. O Ferdinand,
Do not smile at me that I boast her off,°
10 For thou shalt find she will outstrip all praise
And make it halt° behind her.

FERDINAND: I do believe it
Against an oracle.°

PROSPERO: Then, as my gift and thine own
acquisition
Worthily purchased, take my daughter. But
15 If thou dost break her virgin-knot before
All sanctimonious° ceremonies may
With full and holy rite be ministered,
No sweet aspersion° shall the heavens let fall
To make this contract grow; but barren hate
20 Sour-eyed disdain, and discord shall bestrew
The union of your bed with weeds° so loathly
That you shall hate it both. Therefore take heed,
As Hymen's lamps shall light you.°

FERDINAND: As I hope
For quiet days, fair issue,° and long life,
25 With such love as 'tis now, the murkiest den,
The most opportune place, the strong'st
suggestion°
Our worser genius° can,° shall never melt
Mine honor into lust, to° take away
The edge° of that day's celebration
When I shall think or° Phoebus' steeds are
30 foundered°
Or Night kept chained below.

PROSPERO: Fairly spoke.
Sit then and talk with her. She is thine own.
[Ferdinand and Miranda sit and talk together.]
What,° Ariel! My industrious servant, Ariel!

(Enter Ariel.)

ARIEL: What would my potent master? Here I am.

PROSPERO: Thou and thy meaner fellows° your last
service   35
Did worthily perform, and I must use you
In such another trick.° Go bring the rabble,°
O'er whom I give thee power, here to this place.
Incite them to quick motion, for I must
Bestow upon the eyes of this young couple   40
Some vanity° of mine art. It is my promise,
And they expect it from me.

ARIEL: Presently?°

PROSPERO: Ay, with a twink.°

ARIEL: Before you can say "Come" and "Go,"
And breathe twice, and cry "So, so,"
Each one, tripping on his toe,   45
Will be here with mop and mow.°
Do you love me, master? No?

PROSPERO: Dearly, my delicate Ariel. Do not
approach
Till thou dost hear me call.

ARIEL: Well, I conceive.°   50
(Exit.)

PROSPERO: Look thou be true;° do not give dalliance
Too much the rein. The strongest oaths are straw
To the fire i' the blood. Be more abstemious,
Or else good night° your vow!

FERDINAND: I warrant° you, sir,
The white cold virgin snow upon my heart°   55
Abates the ardor of my liver.°

PROSPERO: Well.
Now come, my Ariel! Bring a corollary,°
Rather than want° a spirit. Appear, and
pertly!°—
No tongue!° All eyes! Be silent.   *(Soft music.)*

(Enter Iris.°)

IRIS: Ceres,° most bounteous lady, thy rich leas°   60

IV, i. **Location:** Before Prospero's cell. **1. austerely:** Severely.
3. a third: I.e., Miranda, into whose education Prospero
has put a third of his life (?) or who represents a large part
of what he cares about, along with his dukedom and his
learned study (?). **5. vexations:** Torments. **7. strangely:**
Extraordinarily. **9. boast her off:** I.e., praise her so; or, perhaps, an error for *boast of her*; the Folio reads *boast her of*.
11. halt: Limp. **12. Against an oracle:** I.e., even if an oracle should declare otherwise. **16. sanctimonious:** Sacred.
18. aspersion: Dew, shower. **21. weeds:** In place of the flowers customarily strewn on the marriage bed. **23. As . . . you:**
I.e., as you long for happiness and concord in your marriage.
(Hymen was the Greek and Roman god of marriage; his
symbolic torches, the wedding torches, were supposed to
burn brightly for a happy marriage, smokily for a troubled
one.) **24. issue:** Offspring. **26. suggestion:** Temptation.
27. worser genius: Evil genius; or, evil attendant spirit. **can:**
Is capable of. **28. to:** So as to. **29. edge:** Keen enjoyment,
sexual ardor. **30. or:** Either. **foundered:** Broken down, made
lame. (Ferdinand will wait impatiently for the bridal night.)

---

33. What: Now then. **35. meaner fellows:** Subordinates.
37. trick: Device. **rabble:** Band (i.e., the *meaner fellows* of line
35). **41. vanity:** (1) Illusion; (2) trifle; (3) desire for admiration, conceit. **42. Presently:** Immediately. **43. with a twink:**
In the twinkling of an eye, in an instant. **47. mop and mow:**
Gestures and grimaces. **50. conceive:** Understand. **51. true:**
True to your promise. **54. good night:** I.e., say good bye to.
warrant: Guarantee. **55. The white . . . heart:** I.e., the ideal of
chastity and consciousness of Miranda's chaste innocence en-
shrined in my heart. **56. liver:** As the presumed seat of the
passions. **57. corollary:** Surplus, extra supply. **58. want:**
Lack. **pertly:** Briskly. **59. No tongue:** All the beholders are
to be silent (lest the spirits vanish). [s.D.] ***Iris:*** Goddess of the
rainbow and Juno's messenger. **60. Ceres:** Goddess of the gen-
erative power of nature. **leas:** Meadows.

(handwritten: op Ceres, get but out of here...)

Of wheat, rye, barley, vetches,° oats, and peas;
Thy turfy mountains, where live nibbling sheep,
And flat meads° thatched with stover,° them to
   keep;
Thy banks with pionèd and twillèd° brims,
65 Which spongy° April at thy hest betrims
To make cold nymphs chaste crowns; and thy
   broom groves,°
Whose shadow the dismissèd bachelor° loves
Being lass-lorn; thy poll-clipped° vineyard;
And thy sea marge,° sterile and rocky hard,
Where thou thyself dost air: the queen o' the
70   sky,°
Whose watery arch° and messenger am I,
Bids thee leave these, and with her sovereign
   grace,
      (Juno descends° [slowly in her car].)
Here on this grass plot, in this very place,
To come and sport. Her peacocks° fly amain.°
75 Approach, rich Ceres, her to entertain.°

(Enter Ceres.)

CERES: Hail, many-colored messenger, that ne'er
Dost disobey the wife of Jupiter,
Who with thy saffron° wings upon my flowers
Diffusest honeydrops, refreshing showers,
80 And with each end of thy blue bow° dost crown
My bosky° acres and my unshrubbed down,°
Rich scarf to my proud earth. Why hath thy
   queen
Summoned me hither to this short-grassed green?

IRIS: A contract of true love to celebrate,
85 And some donation freely to estate°
On the blest lovers.

CERES: Tell me, heavenly bow,
If Venus or her son,° as° thou dost know,
Do now attend the Queen? Since they did plot
The means that dusky° Dis my daughter got,°
90 Her° and her blind boy's scandaled° company
I have forsworn.

IRIS: Of her society°

(handwritten: cupid and venus tried to make M.f. do the thing but they failed)

Be not afraid. I met her deity°
Cutting the clouds towards Paphos,° and her son
Dove-drawn° with her. Here thought they to have done°
Some wanton charm° upon this man and maid,   95
Whose vows are that no bed-right shall be paid
Till Hymen's torch be lighted, but in vain.
Mars's hot minion° is returned° again;
Her waspish-headed° son has broke his arrows,
Swears he will shoot no more, but play with
   sparrows°   100
And be a boy right out.°

(handwritten: Kts bless the couple)

[Juno alights.]

CERES: Highest Queen of state,°
Great Juno, comes; I know her by her gait.°

JUNO: How does my bounteous sister? Go with me
To bless this twain, that they may prosperous be
And honored in their issue.°   *(They sing.)* 105

JUNO: Honor, riches, marriage blessing,
Long continuance, and increasing,
Hourly joys be still° upon you!
Juno sings her blessings on you,

CERES: Earth's increase, foison plenty,°   110
Barns and garners° never empty,
Vines with clustering bunches growing,
Plants with goodly burden bowing;

Spring come to you at the farthest
In the very end of harvest!°   115
Scarcity and want shall shun you;
Ceres' blessing so is on you.

(handwritten: I want to be here forever)

FERDINAND: This is a most majestic vision, and
Harmonious charmingly.° May I be bold
To think these spirits?

PROSPERO: Spirits, which by mine art 120
I have from their confines called to enact
My present fancies.

FERDINAND: Let me live here ever!
So rare a wondered° father and a wife
Makes this place Paradise.

    (Juno and Ceres whisper, and send Iris on
                        employment.)

PROSPERO: Sweet now, silence!
Juno and Ceres whisper seriously;   125
There's something else to do. Hush and be mute.

---

61. **vetches:** Plants for forage, fodder. 63. **meads:** Meadows. **stover:** Winter fodder for cattle. 64. **pionèd and twillèd:** Undercut by the swift current and protected by roots and branches that tangle to form a barricade. 65. **spongy:** Wet. 66. **broom groves:** Clumps of broom, gorse, yellow-flowered shrub. 67. **dismissèd bachelor:** Rejected male lover. 68. **poll-clipped:** Pruned, looped at the top; or, *pole-clipped*, hedged in with poles. 69. **sea marge:** Shore. 70. **queen o' the sky:** I.e., Juno. 71. **watery arch:** Rainbow. 72. [s.d.] *Juno descends:* I.e., starts her descent from the "heavens" above the stage (?). 74. **peacocks:** Birds sacred to Juno and used to pull her chariot. **amain:** With full speed. 75. **entertain:** Receive. 78. **saffron:** Yellow. 80. **bow:** I.e., rainbow. 81. **bosky:** Wooded. **down:** Upland. 85. **estate:** Bestow. 87. **son:** I.e., Cupid. **as:** As far as. 89. **dusky:** Dark. **Dis...got:** Pluto, or Dis, god of the infernal regions, carried off Persephone, daughter of Ceres, to be his bride in Hades. 90. **Her:** I.e., Venus's. **scandaled:** Scandalous. 91. **society:** Company.

92. **her deity:** I.e., Her highness. 93. **Paphos:** Place on the island of Cyprus sacred to Venus. 94. **Dove-drawn:** Venus's chariot was drawn by doves. **done:** Placed. 95. **wanton charm:** Lustful spell. 98. **Mars's hot minion:** I.e., Venus, the beloved of Mars. **returned:** I.e., returned to Paphos. 99. **waspish-headed:** Fiery, hotheaded, peevish. 100. **sparrows:** Supposed lustful and sacred to Venus. 101. **right out:** Outright. **Highest...state:** Most majestic Queen. 102. **gait:** I.e., majestic bearing. 105. **issue:** Offspring. 108. **still:** Always. 110. **foison plenty:** Plentiful harvest. 111. **garners:** Granaries. 115. **In...harvest:** I.e., with no winter in between. 119. **charmingly:** Enchantingly. 123. **wondered:** Wonder-performing, wondrous.

Or else our spell is marred.
IRIS: You nymphs, called naiads,° of the windring°
    brooks,
  With your sedged° crowns and ever-harmless°
    looks,
  Leave your crisp° channels, and on this green
130   land
  Answer your summons; Juno does command.
  Come, temperate° nymphs, and help to celebrate
  A contract of true love. Be not too late.

(*Enter certain nymphs.*)

  You sunburnt sicklemen,° of August weary,°
135 Come hither from the furrow° and be merry.
  Make holiday; your rye-straw hats put on,
  And these fresh nymphs encounter° every one
  In country footing.°

(*Enter certain reapers, properly° habited. They join
with the nymphs in a graceful dance, toward the end
whereof Prospero starts suddenly, and speaks; after
which, to a strange, hollow, and confused noise, they
heavily° vanish.*)

PROSPERO [*aside*]: I had forgot that foul conspiracy
140 Of the beast Caliban and his confederates
  Against my life. The minute of their plot
  Is almost come. [*To the Spirits.*] Well done!
    Avoid;° no more!
FERDINAND [*to Miranda*]: This is strange. Your
    father's in some passion
  That works° him strongly.
MIRANDA: Never till this day
145 Saw I him touched with anger so distempered.
PROSPERO: You do look, my son, in a moved sort,°
  As if you were dismayed. Be cheerful, sir.
  Our revels° now are ended. These our actors,
  As I foretold you, were all spirits and
150 Are melted into air, into thin air;
  And, like the baseless° fabric of this vision,
  The cloud-capped towers, the gorgeous palaces,
  The solemn temples, the great globe° itself,
  Yea, all which it inherit,° shall dissolve,
155 And, like this insubstantial pageant faded,
  Leave not a rack° behind. We are such stuff
  As dreams are made on,° and our little life
  Is rounded° with a sleep. Sir, I am vexed.

Bear with my weakness. My old brain is
  troubled.
Be not disturbed with my infirmity.   160
If you be pleased, retire° into my cell
And there repose. A turn or two I'll walk
To still my beating° mind.
FERDINAND, MIRANDA: We wish your peace.
    (*Exeunt [Ferdinand and Miranda].*)
PROSPERO: Come with a thought!° I thank thee,
  Ariel. Come.

(*Enter Ariel.*)

ARIEL: Thy thoughts I cleave° to. What's thy pleasure?
PROSPERO: Spirit,   165
  We must prepare to meet with Caliban.
ARIEL: Ay, my commander. When I presented° Ceres,
  I thought to have told thee of it, but I feared
  Lest I might anger thee.
PROSPERO: Say again, where didst thou leave these
  varlets?   170
ARIEL: I told you, sir, they were red-hot with
  drinking,
  So full of valor that they smote the air
  For breathing in their faces, beat the ground
  For kissing of their feet, yet always bending°
  Towards their project. Then I beat my tabor,   175
  At which, like unbacked° colts, they pricked their
    ears,
  Advanced° their eyelids, lifted up their noses
  As° they smelt music. So I charmed their ears
  That calflike they my lowing° followed through
  Toothed briers, sharp furzes, pricking gorse,° and
    thorns,   180
  Which entered their frail shins. At last I left them
  I' the filthy-mantled° pool beyond your cell,
  There dancing up to the chins, that the foul lake
  O'erstunk° their feet.
PROSPERO: This was well done, my bird.
  Thy shape invisible retain thou still.   185
  The trumpery° in my house, go bring it hither,
  For stale° to catch these thieves.
ARIEL: I go. I go.   (*Exit.*)
PROSPERO: A devil, a born devil, on whose nature
  Nurture can never stick; on whom my pains,
  Humanely taken, all, all lost, quite lost!   190
  And as with age his body uglier grows,

---

128. **naiads:** Nymphs of springs, rivers, or lakes. **windring:** Wandering, winding (?). 129. **sedged:** Made of reeds. **ever-harmless:** Ever-innocent. 130. **crisp:** Curled, rippled. 132. **temperate:** Chaste. 134. **sicklemen:** Harvesters, field workers who cut down grain and grass. **weary:** I.e., weary of the hard work of the harvest. 135. **furrow:** I.e., plowed fields. 137. **encounter:** Join. 138. **country footing:** Country dancing. [s.d.] *properly:* Suitably. *heavily:* Slowly, dejectedly. 142. **Avoid:** Depart, withdraw. 144. **works:** Affects, agitates. 146. **moved sort:** Troubled state, condition. 148. **revels:** Entertainment, pageant. 151. **baseless:** Without substance. 153. **great globe:** With a glance at the Globe Theatre. 154. **which it inherit:** Who subsequently occupy it. 156. **rack:** Wisp of cloud. 157. **on:** Of. 158. **rounded:** Surrounded; or, crowned, rounded off.

161. **retire:** Withdraw, go. 163. **beating:** Agitated. 164. **with a thought:** I.e., on the instant or summoned by my thought, no sooner thought of than here. 165. **cleave:** Cling, adhere. 167. **presented:** Acted the part of; or, introduced. 174. **bending:** Aiming. 176. **unbacked:** Unbroken, unridden. 177. **Advanced:** Lifted up. 178. **As:** As if. 179. **lowing:** Mooing. 180. **furzes ... gorse:** Prickly shrubs. 182. **filthy-mantled:** Covered with a slimy coating. 184. **O'erstunk:** Smelled worse than; or, caused to stink terribly. 186. **trumpery:** Cheap goods, the *glistering apparel* mentioned in the following stage direction. 187. **stale:** (1) Decoy; (2) out-of-fashion garments (with possible further suggestions of *fit for a stale*, or prostitute; *stale*, meaning "horse piss," line 199; and *steal*, pronounced like *stale*).

So his mind cankers.° I will plague them all,
Even to roaring.

(*Enter Ariel, loaden with glistering apparel, etc.*)

Come, hang them on this line.°

([*Ariel hangs up the showy finery; Prospero and Ariel remain,° invisible.*] *Enter Caliban, Stephano, and Trinculo, all wet.*)

CALIBAN: Pray you, tread softly, that the blind mole
may
195   Not hear a footfall. We now are near his cell.
STEPHANO: Monster, your fairy, which you say is a
harmless fairy, has done little better than played the
jack° with us.
TRINCULO: Monster, I do smell all horse piss, at which
200   my nose is in great indignation.
STEPHANO: So is mine. Do you hear, monster? If I
should take a displeasure against you, look you—
TRINCULO: Thou wert but a lost monster.
CALIBAN: Good my lord, give me thy favor still.
205   Be patient, for the prize I'll bring thee to
Shall hoodwink° this mischance.° Therefore
speak softly.
All's hushed as midnight yet.
TRINCULO: Ay, but to lose our bottles in the pool—
STEPHANO: There is not only disgrace and dishonor in
210   that, monster, but an infinite loss.
TRINCULO: That's more to me than my wetting. Yet this is
your harmless fairy, monster!
STEPHANO: I will fetch off my bottle, though I be o'er my
ears° for my labor.
215   CALIBAN: Prithee, my king, be quiet. Seest thou here,
This is the mouth o' the cell. No noise, and
enter.
Do that good mischief which may make this
island
Thine own forever, and I thy Caliban
For aye thy footlicker.
220   STEPHANO: Give me thy hand. I do begin to have bloody
thoughts.
TRINCULO [*seeing the finery*]: O King Stephano! O
peer!° O worthy Stephano! Look what a wardrobe
here is for thee!
225   CALIBAN: Let it alone, thou fool, it is but trash.
TRINCULO: Oho, monster! We know what belongs to
a frippery.° O King Stephano! [*He takes a gown.*]
STEPHANO: Put off° that gown, Trinculo. By this hand,
I'll have that gown.
230   TRINCULO: Thy Grace shall have it.

---

192. cankers: Festers, grows malignant.   **193. line:** Lime tree or linden.   [S.D.] *Prospero and Ariel remain:* The staging is uncertain. They may instead exit here and return with the spirits at line 256.   **198. jack:** (1) Knave; (2) will-o'-the wisp.   **206. hoodwink:** Cover up, make you not see (a hawking term).   **mischance:** Mishap, misfortune.   **213–214. o'er ears:** I.e., totally submerged and perhaps drowned.   **222–223. King . . . peer:** Alludes to the old ballad beginning "King Stephen was a worthy peer."   **227. frippery:** Place where cast-off clothes are sold.   **228. Put off:** Put down; or, take off.

CALIBAN: The dropsy° drown this fool! What do you
mean
To dote thus on such luggage?° Let 't alone
And do the murder first. If he awake,
From toe to crown° he'll fill our skins with
pinches,
Make us strange stuff.
STEPHANO: Be you quiet, monster.—Mistress line,° is   235
not this my jerkin? [*He takes it down.*] Now is the
jerkin under the line.° Now, jerkin, you are like° to
lose your hair and prove a bald° jerkin.
TRINCULO: Do, do!° We steal by line and level,° an 't   240
like° Your Grace.
STEPHANO: I thank thee for that jest. Here's a garment
for 't. [*He gives a garment.*] Wit shall not go unre-
warded while I am king of this country. "Steal by
line and level" is an excellent pass of pate.° There's   245
another garment for 't.
TRINCULO: Monster, come, put some lime° upon your
fingers, and away with the rest.
CALIBAN: I will have none on 't. We shall lose our
time,
And all be turned to barnacles,° or to apes   250
With foreheads villainous° low.
STEPHANO: Monster, lay to° your fingers. Help to bear
this° away where my hogshead° of wine is, or I'll
turn you out of my kingdom. Go to,° carry this.
TRINCULO: And this.   255
STEPHANO: Ay, and this.
[*They load Caliban with more and more garments.*]

(*A noise of hunters heard. Enter divers spirits, in shape of dogs and hounds, hunting them about, Prospero and Ariel setting them on.*)

PROSPERO: Hey, Mountain, hey!
ARIEL: Silver! There it goes, Silver!

---

231. dropsy: Disease characterized by the accumulation of fluid in the connective tissue of the body.   **232. luggage:** Cumbersome trash.   **234. crown:** Head.   **236. Mistress line:** Addressed to the linden or lime tree upon which, at line 193, Ariel hung the *glistering apparel*.   **237. jerkin:** Jacket made of leather.   **238. under the line:** Under the lime tree (with punning sense of being south of the equinoctial line or equator; sailors on long voyages to the southern regions were popularly supposed to lose their hair from scurvy or other diseases. Stephano also quibbles handily on losing hair through syphilis, and in *Mistress* and *jerkin*).   **like:** Likely.   **239. bald:** (1) Hairless, napless; (2) meager.   **240. Do, do:** I.e., bravo. (Said in response to the jesting or the taking of the jerkin or both.)   **by line and level:** I.e., by means of plumb line and carpenter's level, methodically (with pun on *line*, or lime tree, line 238, and *steal*, pronounced like *stale*, or prostitute, continuing Stephano's bawdy quibble).   **240–241. an 't like:** If it please.   **245. pass of pate:** Sally of wit. (The metaphor is from fencing.)   **247. lime:** Birdlime, sticky substance (to give Caliban sticky fingers).   **250. barnacles:** Barnacle geese, formerly supposed to be hatched from seashells attached to trees and to fall thence into the water; here evidently used, like *apes*, as types of simpletons.   **251. villainous:** Miserably.   **252. lay to:** Start using.   **253. this:** I.e., the *glistering apparel*.   **hogshead:** Large cask.   **254. Go to:** An expression of exhortation or remonstrance.

Ralph Fiennes as Prospero in a production directed by Trevor Nunn at the Theatre Royal Haymarket, 2011.

PROSPERO: Fury, Fury! There, Tyrant, there! Hark! Hark!

[*Caliban, Stephano, and Trinculo are driven out.*]

    Go, charge my goblins that they grind their
260   joints
    With dry° convulsions,° shorten up their sinews
    With agèd° cramps, and more pinch-spotted
        make them
    Than pard° or cat o' mountain.°
ARIEL: Hark, they roar!
PROSPERO: Let them be hunted soundly.° At this hour
265   Lies at my mercy all mine enemies.
    Shortly shall all my labors end, and thou
    Shalt have the air at freedom. For a little°
    Follow, and do me service.   (*Exeunt.*)

ACT V • Scene I°

(*Enter Prospero in his magic robes, [with his staff,] and Ariel.*)

PROSPERO: Now does my project gather to a head.
    My charms crack° not, my spirits obey, and Time

---

261. **dry:** Associated with age, arthritic (?). **convulsions:** Cramps.   262. **agèd:** Characteristic of old age.   263. **pard:** Panther or leopard.   **cat o' mountain:** Wildcat.   264. **soundly:** Thoroughly.   267. **little:** Little while longer.   V, i. **Location:** Before Prospero's cell.   2. **crack:** Collapse, fail. (The metaphor is probably alchemical, as in *project* and *gather to a head*, line 1.)

426

Goes upright with his carriage.° How's the day?
ARIEL: On° the sixth hour, at which time, my lord,
    You said our work should cease.
PROSPERO: I did say so,   5
    When first I raised the tempest. Say, my spirit,
    How fares the King and 's followers?
ARIEL: Confined together
    In the same fashion as you gave in charge,
    Just as you left them; all prisoners, sir,
    In the line grove° which weather-fends° your cell.
    They cannot budge till your release.° The King,
    His brother, and yours abide all three distracted,°
    And the remainder mourning over them,
    Brim full of sorrow and dismay; but chiefly
    Him that you termed, sir, the good old lord,
        Gonzalo.   15
    His tears runs down his beard like winter's drops
    From eaves of reeds.° Your charm so strongly
        works 'em
    That if you now beheld them your affections°
    Would become tender.
PROSPERO: Dost thou think so, spirit?
ARIEL: Mine would, sir, were I human.
PROSPERO: And mine shall.   20
    Hast thou, which art but air, a touch° a feeling
    Of their afflictions, and shall not myself,
    One of their kind, that relish all as sharply
    Passion as they,° be kindlier° moved than thou
        art?
    Though with their high wrongs I am struck to
        the quick,
    Yet with my nobler reason 'gainst my fury   25
    Do I take part. The rarer° action is
    In virtue than in vengeance. They being penitent,
    The sole drift of my purpose doth extend
    Not a frown further. Go release them, Ariel.   30
    My charms I'll break, their senses I'll restore,
    And they shall be themselves.
ARIEL: I'll fetch them, sir.
                                        (*Exit.*)
    [*Prospero traces a charmed circle with his staff.*]

PROSPERO: Ye elves of hills, brooks, standing lakes,
        and groves,°
    And ye that on the sands with printless foot
    Do chase the ebbing Neptune, and do fly him   35

---

3. **his carriage:** Its burden. (Time is no longer heavily burdened and so can go upright, standing straight and unimpeded.)   4. **On:** Approaching.   10. **line grove:** Grove of lime trees.   **weather-fends:** Protects from the weather.   11. **your release:** You release them.   12. **distracted:** Out of their wits.   17. **eaves of reeds:** Thatched roofs.   18. **affections:** Feelings.   21. **touch:** Sense, feeling.   23–24. **that...they:** I.e., I who am just as sensitive to suffering as they.   24. **kindlier:** (1) More sympathetically; (2) more naturally humanly.   27. **rarer:** Nobler.   33–50. **Ye...art:** This famous passage is an embellished paraphrase of Golding's translation of Ovid's *Metamorphoses*, 7, 197–219.

When he comes back; you demi-puppets° that
By moonshine do the green sour ringlets° make,
Whereof the ewe not bites; and you whose pastime
Is to make midnight mushrooms,° that rejoice
40   To hear the solemn curfew,° by whose aid,
Weak masters though ye be, I have bedimmed
The noontide sun, called forth the mutinous winds,
And twixt the green sea and the azured vault°
Set roaring war; to the dread rattling thunder
45   Have I given fire,° and rifted,° Jove's stout oak
With his own bolt;° the strong-based promontory
Have I made shake, and by the spurs° plucked up
The pine and cedar; graves at my command
Have waked their sleepers, oped, and let 'em forth
50   By my so potent art. But this rough° magic
I here abjure, and when I have required°
Some heavenly music—which even now I do—
To work mine end upon their senses that°
This airy charm° is for, I'll break my staff,
55   Bury it certain fathoms in the earth,
And deeper than did ever plummet sound
I'll drown my book.   (Solemn music.)

(*Here enters Ariel before; then Alonso, with a frantic gesture, attended by Gonzalo; Sebastian and Antonio in like manner, attended by Adrian and Francisco. They all enter the circle which Prospero had made, and there stand charmed; which Prospero observing, speaks.*)

[*To Alonso.*] A solemn air,° and° the best comforter
To an unsettled fancy,° cure thy brains,
Now useless, boiled within thy skull! [*To
60   Sebastian and Antonio.*] There stand,
For you are spell-stopped.—
Holy Gonzalo, honorable man,
Mine eyes, e'en sociable° to the show° of thine,
Fall° fellowly drops. [*Aside.*] The charm dissolves apace,
65   And as the morning steals upon the night,
Melting the darkness, so their rising senses
Begin to chase the ignorant fumes° that mantle°

Their clearer° reason.—O good Gonzalo,
My true preserver, and a loyal sir
To him thou follow'st! I will pay thy graces°   70
Home° both in word and deed.—Most cruelly
Didst thou, Alonso, use me and my daughter.
Thy brother was a furtherer° in the act.—
Thou art pinched° for 't now, Sebastian. [*To
   Antonio.*] Flesh and blood,
You, brother mine, that entertained ambition,   75
Expelled remorse° and nature,° whom,° with
   Sebastian,
Whose inward pinches therefore are most strong,
Would here have killed your king, I do forgive
   thee,
Unnatural though thou art.—Their
   understanding
Begins to swell, and the approaching tide   80
Will shortly fill the reasonable shore°
That now lies foul and muddy. Not one of them
That yet looks on me, or would know me.—
   Ariel,
Fetch me the hat and rapier in my cell.

[*Ariel goes to the cell and returns immediately.*]

I will disease° me and myself present   85
As I was sometime Milan.° Quickly, spirit!
Thou shalt ere long be free.

                (*Ariel sings and helps to attire him.*)

ARIEL: Where the bee sucks, there suck I.
   In a cowslip's bell I lie;
   There I couch° when owls do cry.   90
   On the bat's back I do fly
   After° summer merrily.
   Merrily, merrily shall I live now
   Under the blossom that hangs on the bough.
PROSPERO: Why, that's my dainty Ariel! I shall miss
      thee,   95
But yet thou shalt have freedom. So, so, so.°
To the King's ship, invisible as thou art!
There shalt thou find the mariners asleep
Under the hatches. The Master and the Boatswain
Being awake, enforce them to this place,   100
And presently,° I prithee.
ARIEL: I drink the air before me and return
   Or ere° your pulse twice beat.   (*Exit.*)
GONZALO: All torment, trouble, wonder, and
      amazement

---

36. **demi-puppets:** Puppets of half size (i.e., elves and fairies).   37. **green sour ringlets:** Fairy rings, circles in grass (actually produced by mushrooms).   39. **midnight mushrooms:** Mushrooms appearing overnight.   40. **curfew:** Evening bell, usually rung at nine o'clock, ushering in the time when spirits are abroad.   43. **the azured vault:** I.e., the sky.   44–45. **to . . . fire:** I have discharged the dread rattling thunderbolt.   45. **rifted:** Riven, split.   46. **bolt:** Lightning bolt.   47. **spurs:** Roots.   50. **rough:** Violent.   51. **required:** Requested.   53. **their senses that:** The senses of those whom.   54. **airy charm:** I.e., music.   58. **air:** Song. **and:** I.e., which is.   59. **fancy:** Imagination.   63. **sociable:** Sympathetic. **show:** Appearance.   64. **Fall:** Let fall.   67. **ignorant fumes:** Fumes that render them incapable of comprehension. **mantle:** Envelop.

68. **clearer:** Growing clearer.   70. **pay thy graces:** Reward your favors.   71. **Home:** Fully.   73. **furtherer:** Accomplice.   74. **pinched:** Punished, afflicted.   76. **remorse:** Pity. **nature:** Natural feeling. **whom:** I.e., who.   81. **reasonable shore:** Shores of reason—i.e., minds. (Their reason returns like the incoming tide.)   85. **disease:** Disrobe.   86. **As . . . Milan:** In my former appearance as Duke of Milan.   90. **couch:** Lie.   92. **After:** I.e., pursuing.   96. **So, so, so:** Expresses approval of Ariel's help as valet.   101. **presently:** Immediately.   103. **Or ere:** Before.

105 Inhabits here. Some heavenly power guide us
    Out of this fearful° country!
PROSPERO: Behold, sir King,
    The wrongèd Duke of Milan, Prospero.
    For more assurance that a living prince
    Does now speak to thee, I embrace thy body;
110 And to thee and thy company I bid
    A hearty welcome.   [Embracing him.]
ALONSO: Whe'er thou be'st he or no,
    Or some enchanted trifle° to abuse° me,
    As late° I have been, I not know. Thy pulse
    Beats as of flesh and blood; and, since I saw
        thee,
115 Th' affliction of my mind amends, with which
    I fear a madness held me. This must crave°—
    An if this be at all°—a most strange story.°
    Thy dukedom I resign,° and do entreat
    Thou pardon me my wrongs.° But how should
        Prospero
    Be living, and be here?

120 PROSPERO [to Gonzalo]: First, noble friend,
    Let me embrace thine age,° whose honor cannot
    Be measured or confined.   [Embracing him.]
GONZALO: Whether this be
    Or be not, I'll not swear.
PROSPERO: You do yet taste
    Some subtleties° o' th' isle, that will not let you
125 Believe things certain. Welcome, my friends all!
    [Aside to Sebastian and Antonio.] But you, my
        brace° of lords, were I so minded,
    I here could pluck His Highness' frown upon
        you
    And justify you° traitors. At this time
    I will tell no tales.
SEBASTIAN: The devil speaks in him.
PROSPERO: No.
    [To Antonio.] For you, most wicked sir, whom to
130   call brother
    Would even infect my mouth, I do forgive
    Thy rankest fault—all of them; and require
    My dukedom of thee, which perforce° I know
    Thou must restore.
ALONSO: If thou be'st Prospero,
135 Give us particulars of thy preservation,
    How thou hast met us here, whom° three hours
        Since

Were wrecked upon this shore; where I have
    lost—
How sharp the point of this remembrance is!—
My dear son Ferdinand.
PROSPERO: I am woe° for 't, sir.
ALONSO: Irreparable is the loss, and Patience   140
    Says it is past her cure.
PROSPERO: I rather think
    You have not sought her help, of whose soft
        grace°
    For the like loss I have her sovereign° aid
    And rest myself content.
ALONSO: You the like loss?
PROSPERO: As great to me as late,° and supportable 145
    To make the dear loss, have I° means much
        weaker
    Than you may call to comfort you; for I
    Have lost my daughter.
ALONSO: A daughter?
    O heavens, that they were living both in Naples, 150
    The king and queen there! That° they were, I
        wish
    Myself were mudded° in that oozy bed
    Where my son lies. When did you lose your
        daughter?
PROSPERO: In this last tempest. I perceive these lords
    At this encounter do so much admire°   155
    That they devour their reason° and scarce think
    Their eyes do offices of truth, their words
    Are natural breath.° But, howsoever you have
    Been jostled from your senses, know for certain
    That I am Prospero and that very duke   160
    Which was thrust forth of° Milan, who most
        strangely
    Upon this shore, where you were wrecked, was
        landed
    To be the lord on 't. No more yet of this,
    For 'tis a chronicle of day by day,°
    Not a relation for a breakfast nor   165
    Befitting this first meeting. Welcome, sir.
    This cell's my court. Here have I few attendants,
    And subjects none abroad.° Pray you, look in.
    My dukedom since you have given me again,
    I will requite° you with as good a thing,   170
    At least bring forth a wonder to content ye
    As much as me my dukedom.

---

106. **fearful:** Frightening. 112. **trifle:** Trick of magic. **abuse:** Deceive. 113. **late:** Lately. 116. **crave:** Require. 117. **An ... all:** If this is actually happening. **story:** I.e., explanation. 118. **Thy ... resign:** Alonso made an arrangement with Antonio at the time of Prospero's banishment for Milan to pay tribute to Naples; see I, ii, 113–127. 119. **wrongs:** Wrongdoings. 121. **thine age:** Your venerable self. 124. **subtleties:** Illusions, magical powers. 126. **brace:** Pair. 128. **justify you:** Prove you to be. 133. **perforce:** Necessarily. 136. **whom:** I.e., who.

139. **woe:** Sorry. 142. **of ... grace:** By whose mercy. 143. **sovereign:** Efficacious. 145. **late:** Recent. 145–146. **supportable ... have I:** To make the deeply felt loss bearable, I have. 151. **That:** So that. 152. **mudded:** Buried in the mud. 155. **admire:** Wonder. 156. **devour their reason:** I.e., are dumbfounded. 156–158. **scarce ... breath:** Scarcely believe that their eyes inform them accurately what they see or that their words are naturally spoken. 161. **of:** From. 164. **of day by day:** Requiring days to tell. 168. **abroad:** Away from here, anywhere else. 170. **requite:** Repay.

(*Here Prospero discovers° Ferdinand and Miranda playing at chess.*)

MIRANDA: Sweet lord, you play me false.

FERDINAND: No, my dearest love,

175   I would not for the world.

MIRANDA: Yes, for a score of kingdoms you should wrangle,
      And I would call it fair play.°

ALONSO: If this prove
      A vision° of the island, one dear son
      Shall I twice lose.

SEBASTIAN: A most high miracle!

FERDINAND [*approaching his father*]:

180   Though the seas threaten, they are merciful;
      I have cursed them without cause.   [*He kneels.*]

ALONSO: Now all the blessings
      Of a glad father compass° thee about!
      Arise, and say how thou cam'st here.

                            [*Ferdinand rises.*]

MIRANDA: O, wonder!
      How many goodly creatures are there here!
      How beauteous mankind is! O, brave° new

185   world,
      That has such people in 't!

PROSPERO: 'Tis new to thee.

ALONSO: What is this maid with whom thou wast
      at play?
      Your eld'st° acquaintance cannot be three hours.
      Is she the goddess that hath severed us
      And brought us thus together?

190   FERDINAND: Sir, she is mortal;
      But by immortal Providence she's mine.
      I chose her when I could not ask my father
      For his advice, nor thought I had one. She
      Is daughter to this famous Duke of Milan,

195   Of whom so often I have heard renown
      But never saw before, of whom I have
      Received a second life; and second father
      This lady makes him to me.

ALONSO: I am hers.
      But O, how oddly will it sound that I
      Must ask my child forgiveness!

200   PROSPERO: There, sir, stop.
      Let us not burden our remembrances with

A heaviness° that's gone.

GONZALO: I have inly° wept,
      Or should have spoke ere this. Look down, you
      gods,
      And on this couple drop a blessèd crown!
      For it is you that have chalked forth the way°   205
      Which brought us hither.

ALONSO: I say amen, Gonzalo!

GONZALO: Was Milan° thrust from Milan that his
      issue
      Should become kings of Naples? O, rejoice
      Beyond a common joy, and set it down
      With gold on lasting pillars: In one voyage   210
      Did Claribel her husband find at Tunis,
      And Ferdinand, her brother, found a wife
      Where he himself was lost; Prospero his dukedom
      In a poor isle; and all of us ourselves
      When no man was his own.°   215

ALONSO [*to Ferdinand and Miranda*]: Give me your
      hands.
      Let grief and sorrow still° embrace his° heart
      That° doth not wish you joy!

GONZALO: Be it so! Amen!

(*Enter Ariel, with the Master and Boatswain amazedly following.*)

      O, look, sir, look, sir! Here is more of us.
      I prophesied, if a gallows were on land,
      This fellow could not drown.—Now, blasphemy,°   220
      That swear'st grace o'erboard,° not an oath° on
      shore?
      Hast thou no mouth by land? What is the news?

BOATSWAIN: The best news is that we have safely found
      Our King and company; the next, our ship—   225
      Which, but three glasses° since, we gave out° split—
      Is tight and yare° and bravely° rigged as when
      We first put out to sea.

ARIEL [*aside to Prospero*]: Sir, all this service
      Have I done since I went.

PROSPERO [*aside to Ariel*]:   My tricksy° spirit!

ALONSO: These are not natural events; they
      strengthen°   230
      From strange to stranger. Say, how came you
      hither?

BOATSWAIN: If I did think, sir, I were well awake,
      I'd strive to tell you. We were dead of sleep,°

---

172. [S.D.] *discovers:* I.e., by opening a curtain, presumably rear stage.   176–177. **Yes . . . play:** I.e., yes, even if we were playing for twenty kingdoms, something less than the whole world, you would still contend mightily against me and play me false, and I would let you do it as though it were fair play; or, if you were to play not just for stakes but literally for kingdoms, my accusation of false play would be out of order in that your "wrangling" would be proper.   178. **vision:** Illusion.   182. **compass:** Encompass, embrace.   185. **brave:** Splendid, gorgeously appareled, handsome.   188. **eld'st:** Longest.

202. **heaviness:** Sadness.   **inly:** Inwardly.   205. **chalked . . . way:** Marked as with a piece of chalk the pathway.   207. **Was Milan:** Was the Duke of Milan.   214–215. **all . . . own:** All of us have found ourselves and our sanity when we all had lost our senses.   217. **still:** Always.   **his:** That person's.   218. **That:** Who.   221. **blasphemy:** I.e., blasphemer.   222. **That . . . o'erboard:** I.e., you who banish heavenly grace from the ship by your blasphemies.   **not an oath:** Aren't you going to swear an oath.   226. **glasses:** I.e., hours.   **gave out:** Reported, professed to be.   227. **yare:** Ready.   **bravely:** Splendidly.   229. **tricksy:** Ingenious, sportive.   230. **strengthen:** Increase.   233. **dead of sleep:** Deep in sleep.

And—how we know not—all clapped under
    hatches,
Where but even now, with strange and several°
235   noises
Of roaring, shrieking, howling, jingling chains,
And more diversity of sounds, all horrible,
We were awaked; straightway at liberty;
Where we, in all her trim, freshly beheld
240 Our royal, good, and gallant ship, our Master
Cap'ring to eye° her. On a trice,° so please you,
Even in a dream, were we divided from them°
And were brought moping° hither.
ARIEL [aside to Prospero]:   Was 't well done?
PROSPERO [aside to Ariel]: Bravely, my diligence.
    Thou shalt be free.
245 ALONSO: This is as strange a maze as e'er men trod,
And there is in this business more than nature
Was ever conduct° of. Some oracle
Must rectify our knowledge.
PROSPERO: Sir, my liege,
Do not infest° your mind with beating on°
250   The strangeness of this business. At picked°
    leisure,
Which shall be shortly, single° I'll resolve° you,
Which to you shall seem probable,° of every
These° happened accidents,° till when, be
    cheerful
And think of each thing well.° [Aside to Ariel.]
    Come hither, spirit.
255 Set Caliban and his companions free.
Untie the spell. [Exit Ariel.] How fares my
    gracious sir?
There are yet missing of your company
Some few odd° lads that you remember not.

(Enter Ariel, driving in Caliban, Stephano, and Trinculo
in their stolen apparel.)

STEPHANO: Every man shift° for all the rest,° and let
260   no man take care for himself; for all is but fortune.
Coraggio,° bully monster,° coraggio!
TRINCULO: If these be true spies° which I wear in my
    head, here's a goodly sight.
CALIBAN: O Setebos, these be brave° spirits indeed!
265   How fine° my master is! I am afraid
He will chastise me.

SEBASTIAN: Ha, ha!
What things are these, my lord Antonio?
Will money buy 'em?
ANTONIO: Very like. One of them
Is a plain fish, and no doubt marketable.   270
PROSPERO: Mark but the badges° of these men, my
    lords,
Then say if they be true.° This misshapen knave,
His mother was a witch, and one so strong
That could control the moon, make flows and ebbs,
And deal in her command without her power.°   275
These three have robbed me, and this
    demidevil—
For he's a bastard° one—had plotted with them
To take my life. Two of these fellows you
Must know and own.° This thing of darkness I
Acknowledge mine.
CALIBAN: I shall be pinched to death.   280
ALONSO: Is not this Stephano, my drunken butler?
SEBASTIAN: He is drunk now. Where had he wine?
ALONSO: And Trinculo is reeling ripe.° Where
    should they
Find this grand liquor that hath gilded° 'em?
[To Trinculo.] How cam'st thou in this pickle?°   285
TRINCULO: I have been in such a pickle since I saw
    you last that, I fear me, will never out of my bones.
    I shall not fear flyblowing.°
SEBASTIAN: Why, how now, Stephano?
STEPHANO: O, touch me not! I am not Stephano, but   290
    a cramp.
PROSPERO: You'd be king o' the isle, sirrah?°
STEPHANO: I should have been a sore° one, then.
ALONSO [pointing to Caliban]: This is a strange thing
    as e'er I looked on.   295
PROSPERO: He is as disproportioned in his manners
As in his shape.—Go, sirrah, to my cell.
Take with you your companions. As you look
To have my pardon, trim° it handsomely.
CALIBAN: Ay, that I will; and I'll be wise hereafter   300
And seek for grace. What a thrice-double ass
Was I to take this drunkard for a god
And worship this dull fool!
PROSPERO: Go to. Away!
ALONSO: Hence, and bestow your luggage where
    you found it.

235. several: Different, diverse. 241. Cap'ring to eye: Dancing
for joy to see. On a trice: In an instant. 242. them: I.e., the
other crew members. 243. moping: In a daze. 247. conduct:
Guide, leader. 249. infest: Harass, disturb. beating on: Worrying about. 250. picked: Chosen, convenient. 251. single:
I.e., by my own human powers. resolve: Satisfy, explain to.
252. probable: Explicable, plausible. 252–253. of every
These: About every one of these. 253. accidents: Occurrences. 254. well: Favorably. 258. odd: Unaccounted for.
259. shift: Provide. for all the rest: Stephano drunkenly
gets wrong the saying "Every man for himself." 261. Coraggio: Courage. bully monster: Gallant monster (ironical).
262. true spies: Accurate observers (i.e., sharp eyes).
264. brave: Handsome. 265. fine: Splendidly attired.

271. badges: Emblems of cloth or silver worn on the arms of retainers. (Prospero refers here to the stolen clothes as emblems of
their villainy.) 272. true: Honest. 275. deal . . . power: Wield
the moon's power, either without her authority or beyond her
influence. 277. bastard: Counterfeit. 279. own: Recognize,
admit as belonging to you. 283. reeling ripe: Stumblingly
drunk. 284. gilded: (1) Flushed, made drunk; (2) covered with
gilt (suggesting the horse urine in IV, i, 181–194, 199–200).
285. pickle: (1) Fix, predicament; (2) pickling brine (in this
case, horse urine). 288. flyblowing: I.e., being fouled by fly
eggs (from which he is saved by being pickled). 292. sirrah:
Standard form of address to an inferior, here expressing reprimand. 293. sore: (1) Tyrannical; (2) sorry, inept; (3) wracked
by pain. 299. trim: Prepare, decorate.

305 **SEBASTIAN:** Or stole it rather.
        [*Exeunt Caliban, Stephano, and Trinculo.*]
    PROSPERO: Sir, I invite Your Highness and your train
        To my poor cell, where you shall take your rest
        For this one night; which, part of it, I'll waste°
        With such discourse as, I not doubt, shall make
        it
310   Go quick away: the story of my life,
        And the particular accidents° gone by
        Since I came to this isle. And in the morn
        I'll bring you to your ship, and so to Naples,
        Where I have hope to see the nuptial
315   Of these our dear-belovèd solemnized;
        And thence retire me° to my Milan, where
        Every third thought shall be my grave.
    ALONSO: I long
        To hear the story of your life, which must
        Take° the ear strangely.
    PROSPERO: I'll deliver° all;
320   And promise you calm seas, auspicious gales,
        And sail so expeditious that shall catch
        Your royal fleet far off. [*Aside to Ariel.*] My
            Ariel, chick,
        That is thy charge. Then to the elements
        Be free, and fare thou well! — Please you, draw
            near.°

                    (*Exeunt omnes.*)

308. **waste:** Spend.   311. **accidents:** Occurrences.   316. **retire
me:** Return.   319. **Take:** Take effect upon, enchant.   **deliver:**
Declare, relate.   324. **draw near:** I.e., enter my cell.

EPILOGUE

(*Spoken by Prospero.*)

Now my charms are all o'erthrown,
And what strength I have 's mine own,
Which is most faint. Now, 'tis true,
I must be here confined by you
Or sent to Naples. Let me not,   5
Since I have my dukedom got
And pardoned the deceiver, dwell
In this bare island by your spell,
But release me from my bands°
With the help of your good hands.°   10
Gentle breath° of yours my sails
Must fill, or else my project fails,
Which was to please. Now I want°
Spirits to enforce,° art to enchant,
And my ending is despair   15
Unless I be relieved by prayer,°
Which pierces so that it assaults°
Mercy itself, and frees° all faults.
As you from crimes° would pardoned be,
Let your indulgence° set me free.   (*Exit.*)   20

Epilogue. 9. bands: Bonds.   **10. hands:** I.e., applause (the
noise of which would break the spell of silence).   **11. Gentle
breath:** Favorable breeze (produced by hands clapping or
favorable comment).   **13. want:** Lack.   **14. enforce:** Control.
16. prayer: I.e., Prospero's petition to the audience.   **17. as-
saults:** Rightfully gains the attention of.   **18. frees:** Obtains
forgiveness for.   **19. crimes:** Sins.   **20. indulgence:** (1) Humor-
ing, lenient approval; (2) remission of punishment for sin.

Shakespeare's *The Tempest*

Modern-day Shakespeareans find that *The Tempest*'s richness of characterization, impressive theatricality, and complex range of themes definitely support multiple critical perspectives. Early Shakespeare critics would have been
surprised by current interpretations of *The Tempest* that posit colonialism as
one of the primary themes of the play. Inspired as the play was by the colonizing efforts of the Virginia Company, such a reading is plausible. In these
interpretations, Prospero is not seen primarily as a benevolent father or as a
magnanimous and forgiving ruler who restores his uninvited guests to their
previously "wrecked" ship. Instead, taking Caliban's island from him, putting
Caliban into slavery, and demanding his obeisance cast Prospero as a representative of the Europeans who usurped the land of Native Americans and
enslaved them.

In part because it is one of Shakespeare's shortest plays and in part because it contains a masterful masque, the wedding celebration for Ferdinand
and Miranda, *The Tempest* has been thought of as an elaborate masque in its
own right. All the action takes place in one location on one day, observing
the Aristotelian unities. And because of Prospero's final speech, renouncing his
magic, it has long been thought to be one of the only plays in which Shakespeare
was being self-referential. Most early critics focused on the connection
between Prospero's magic and Shakespeare's magic on stage. Shortly after writing this play, Shakespeare retired and left London to go home to Stratford, a
move paralleling Prospero's return to Milan. Prospero claimed that "graves at
my command / Have waked their sleepers," but as the modern critic Stephen
Greenblatt says, "It is not Prospero, but Shakespeare who has commanded old
Hamlet to burst from the grave."[1] In this sense, the play is not about occult
magic, the kind that Sycorax is said to have derived from the devil, but about
the dramatic magic that is characteristic of all theaters, in which illusion becomes reality while remaining illusion.

It was conventional for playwrights in Shakespeare's day to derive dramatic material from Italian, French, or other literary sources. Shakespeare's

[1]Stephen Greenblatt, *Will in the World* (New York: W. W. Norton, 2004), p. 376.

early plays about the kings of England relied on histories such as *Holinshed's Chronicles* to provide a structure for the poetry. Scholars have tracked down the original sources for all of Shakespeare's plays except *The Tempest,* which seems to be the only one that did not derive its inspiration from another text, although there are slight echoes of Michel de Montaigne's essay "Of the Cannibals," as well as a few borrowings in one of Prospero's speeches from Ovid's *Metamorphoses.* But scholars early on pointed to reports of a shipwreck that took place in 1610 on the island of Bermuda, which seems to be referenced when Ariel refers to "the still-vexed Bermudas" (I, ii, 230). William Strachey (1572–1621) was a passenger on the wrecked *Sea Venture* and wrote back to England to provide a record of the experience. His was not the only news of the wreck, but scholars have assumed that Shakespeare, who had a financial interest in the Virginia Company, which owned the *Sea Venture*, would have had access to Strachey's report, even though it was suppressed by the company, which did not want to spread bad news. However influential Strachey's report might have been, Shakespeare set his island in the Mediterranean, not in the New World.

Critics such as Samuel Taylor Coleridge and E. K. Chambers focused their comments on the characters in the play, noting, for example, that Ariel may represent the elements of air and fire, while Caliban may represent the elements of earth and water. The four elements were important matters for the early and late Renaissance mind, and accommodating them in a drama was always suggestive of a balance of forces in the universe.

For Robert Browning, Caliban was essentially a monster, part human and part supernatural as a spawn of Sycorax. His poem is a "reading" of Caliban through Caliban's efforts to conceive the nature of God. Browning's Caliban imagines Setebos to be much like himself, willful and capricious, vicious when it suits him, and yet much more powerful. This poem is an experiment in imagining a natural religion as a result of savage reflection. While it may be a critical comment on *The Tempest,* it is also a critical comment on some of the theological questions being raised in Victorian England and continental Europe during the period of great colonial expansion, when the religious beliefs of many non-Europeans were first examined.

Since the 1950s, the general force of critical commentary on the play has centered on issues of colonialism. Ariel seeks his freedom, which Prospero grants only after the tasks he puts him to are complete. Caliban, however, is considered subhuman, and his freedom occurs only with Prospero's abandonment of the island. Aimé Césaire rewrote the play to accommodate his colonialist interpretation of Caliban. Ania Loomba examines Caliban and Sycorax through the lens of colonialism, while Marjorie Garber gives us a contemporary view of the play that honors the complexities introduced by our modern attitudes toward it. Clearly the play can sustain a wide variety of interpretations and is rich enough to accommodate them all.

WILLIAM STRACHEY (1572–1621)

From True Repertory of the Wreck 1610

Strachey was a literary man in the sense that he associated with some of the best writers of the day, especially Ben Jonson, John Donne, John Marston, and George Chapman, all members of the unofficial "club" that met at the Mermaid Tavern. Shakespeare was also associated with that group. Strachey was traveling to Virginia in search of a fortune when the *Sea Venture* ran aground in Bermuda in 1609. Several reports of the event were published in 1610; Strachey's was circulated privately in July 1610. Shakespeare had various connections to the Virginia Company; because the plot of his play reflects events recounted by Strachey and his language is similar to Strachey's, it seems certain that Shakespeare knew of Strachey's report and used it as a source for *The Tempest*.

A most dreadful tempest, the manifold deaths whereof are here to the life described—Their wrack on Bermuda, and the description of those islands.
[...]

We had followed this course so long as now we were within seven or eight days at the most, by Captain Newport's reckoning, of making Cape Henry upon the coast of Virginia, when on Saint James his day, July 24, being Monday, preparing for no less all the black night before—the clouds gathering thick upon us, and the winds singing and whistling most unusually, which made us to cast off our pinnace, towing the same until then astern—a dreadful storm and hideous began to blow from out the northeast, which swelling and roaring, as it were, by fits, some hours with more violence than others, at length did beat all light from heaven, which like an hell of darkness turned black upon us, so much the more fuller of horror, as in such cases horror and fear use to overrun the troubled and overmastered senses of all, which, taken up with amazement, the ears-lay so sensible to the terrible cries and murmurs of the winds and distraction of our company, as who was most armed and best prepared was not a little shaken. For surely (noble lady) as death comes not so sudden nor apparent, so he comes not so elvish and painful to men, especially even then in health and perfect habitudes of body, as at sea; who comes at no time so welcome but our frailty (so weak is the hold of hope in miserable demonstrations of danger) it makes guilty of many contrary changes and conflicts. For indeed death is accompanied at no time nor place with circumstances every way so uncapable of particularities of goodness and inward comforts as at sea. For it is most true there arises commonly no such unmerciful tempest, compound of so many contrary and diverse nations, but that it works upon the whole frame of the body, and most loathsomely affects all the powers thereof. And the manner of the sickness it lays upon the body, being so unsufferable, gives not the mind any free and quiet time to use her judgment and empire. Which made the poet say,

> Hostium uxores puerique caecos
> sentiant motus orientis Haedi &
> aequoris nigri fremitum & trementes
> verbere ripas°

For four and twenty hours the storm in a restless tumult had blown so exceedingly as we could not apprehend in our imaginations any possibility of greater violence. Yet did we still find it not only more terrible but more constant, fury added to fury, and one storm urging a second more outrageous than the former, whether it so wrought upon our fears or indeed met with new forces.

Sometimes strikes in our ship amongst women and passengers not used to such hurly and discomforts made us look one upon the other with troubled hearts and panting bosoms, our clamors drown'd in the winds, and the winds in thunder. Prayers might well be in the heart and lips, but drowned in the outcries of the officers, nothing heard that could give comfort, nothing seen that might encourage hope. It is impossible for me, had I the voice of Stentor, and expression of as many tongues as his throat of voices, to express the outcries and miseries, not languishing but wasting his spirits and art, constant to his own principles, but not prevailing.

Our sails, wound up, lay without their use. And if at any time we bore but a hullock, or half forecourse,° to guide her before the sea, six and sometimes eight men were not enough to hold the whipstaff in the steerage and the tiller below in the gunner room, by which may be imagined the strength of the storm in which the sea swelled above the clouds and gave battle unto heaven.

It could not be said to rain. The waters like whole rivers did flood in the air. And this I did still observe that whereas upon the land when a storm has poured itself forth once in drifts of rain, the wind, as beaten down and vanquished therewith, not long after endures. Here the glut of water, as if throttling the wind erewhile, was no sooner a little emptied and qualified but instantly the winds, as having gotten their mouths now free and at liberty, spake more loud, and grew more tumultuous and malignant. What shall I say?—Winds and seas were as mad as fury and rage could make them. For my own part, I had been in some storms before, as well upon the coast of Barbary and Algier in the Levant, and once more distressful in the Adriatic Gulf, in a bottom of Candy,° so as I may well say, *Ego quid sit ater Adriae novi sinus & quid albus peccet Iapex*.° Yet all that I had ever suffered gathered together might not hold comparison with this. There was not a moment in which the sudden splitting or instant oversetting of the ship was not expected.

Hostium . . . ripas: May our enemies' wives and children feel the blind motions of rising (Haedus) and the roaring of the black sea and the shore quaking with the blow. From Horace, *Europa Ode*.
   forecourse: Storm sail.
   Candy: Boat in Cyprus.
   Ego . . . Iapex: I know what the black gulf of the Adriatic is like and the mischief of the white west-nor'wester.

Howbeit this was not all. It pleased God to bring a greater affliction yet upon us, for in the beginning of the storm we had received likewise a mighty leak, and the ship in every joint almost having spewed out her oakum before we were aware (a casualty more desperate than any other that a voyage by sea draws with it) was grown five foot suddenly deep with water above her ballast, and we almost drowned within while we sat looking when to perish from above. This imparting no less terror than danger ran through the whole ship with much fright and amazement, startled and turned the blood, and took down the braves of the most hardy mariner of them all, insomuch as he that before happily felt not the sorrow of others now began to sorrow for himself when he saw such a pond of water so suddenly broken in, and which he knew could not without present avoiding but instantly sink him, so as joining only for his own sake, not yet worth the saving in the public safety.

There might be seen master, master's mate, boatswain, quartermaster, coopers, carpenters, and who not with candles in their hands, creeping along the ribs viewing the sides, searching every corner, and listening in every place, if they could hear the water run. Many a weeping leak was this way found and hastily stop'd, and at length one in the gunner room made up with I know not how many pieces of beef. But all was to no purpose: The leak (if it were but one) which drunk in our greatest seas and took in our destruction fastest could not then be found, nor ever was, by any labor, counsel, or search. The waters still increasing, and the pumps going, which at length choked with bringing up whole and continual biscuit—and indeed all we had, ten thousand weight it was conceived as most likely that the leak might be sprung in the bread room, whereupon the carpenter went down and rip'd up all the room, but could not find it so.

[. . .]

We found it to be the dangerous and dreaded island, or rather islands, of the Bermuda, whereof let me give Your Ladyship a brief description before I proceed to my narration; and that the rather, because they be so terrible to all that ever touched on them, and such tempests, thunders, and other fearful objects are seen and heard about them that they be called commonly "the Devil's Islands," and are feared and avoided of all sea travelers alive above any other place in the world. Yet it pleased our merciful God to make even this hideous and hated place both the place of our safety and means of our deliverance.

And hereby also I hope to deliver the world from a foul and general error: it being counted of most that they can be no habitation for men, but rather given over to devils and wicked spirits; whereas indeed we find them now by experience to be as habitable and commodious as most countries of the same climate and situation, insomuch as if the entrance into them were as easy as the place itself is contenting, it had long ere this been inhabited as well as other islands. Thus shall we make it appear that truth is the daughter of time, and that men ought not to deny everything which is not subject to their own sense.

[. . .]

This being thus laid,° and by such a one who had gotten an opinion, as I before rememb'red, of religion (when it was declared by those two accusers), not knowing what further ground it had or accomplices, it pleased the governor to let this his factious offense to have a public affront and contestation by these two witnesses

---

This being thus laid: The reference is to Stephen Hopkins, who began a movement to undermine the governor's authority, the beginnings of a mutiny.

before the whole company, who at the tolling of a bell assembled before a *corps du guard,* where the prisoner was brought forth in manacles, and both accused and suffered to make at large to every particular his answer, which was only full of sorrow and tears, pleading simplicity and denial. But he being only found at this time both the captain and the follower of this mutiny, and generally held worthy to satisfy the punishment of his offense with the sacrifice of his life, our governor passed the sentence of a martial court upon him, such as belongs to mutiny and rebellion. But so penitent he was, and made so much moan, alleging the ruin of his wife and children in this his trespass, as it wrought in the hearts of all the better sort of the company, who therefore with humble entreaties and earnest supplications went unto our governor, whom they besought, as likewise did Captain Newport and myself, and never left him until we had got his pardon.

In these dangers and devilish disquiets, while the Almighty God wrought for us and sent us, miraculously delivered from the calamities of the sea, all blessings upon the shore to content and bind us to gratefulness, thus enraged amongst ourselves to the destruction each of other, into what a mischief and misery had we been given up had we not had a governor with his authority to have suppressed the same? Yet was there a worse practice, faction, and conjuration afoot, deadly and bloody, in which the life of our governor with many others were threat'ned, and could not but miscarry in his fall. But such is ever the will of God, who in the execution of His judgments breaks the firebrands upon the head of him who first kindles them!

There were who conceived that our governor indeed neither dared nor had authority to put in execution or pass the act of justice upon anyone, how treacherous or impious soever, their own opinions so much deceiving them for the unlawfulness of any act which they would execute, daring to justify among themselves that if they should be apprehended before the performance, they should happily suffer as martyrs. They persevered therefore not only to draw unto them such a number and associates as they could work into the abandoning of our governor and to the inhabiting of this island, they had now purposed (also) to have made a surprise of the storehouse, and to have forced from thence what was therein either of meal, cloth, cables, arms, sails, oars, or what else it pleased God that we had recovered from the wrack, and was to serve our general necessity and use, either for the relief of us while we stayed here, or for the carrying of us from this place again, when our pinnace should have been furnished.

But as all giddy and lawless attempts have always something of imperfection, and that as well by the property of the action, which holds of disobedience and rebellion (both full of fear), as through the ignorance of the devisers themselves; so in this, besides those defects, there were some of the association who, not strong enough fortified in their own conceits, broke from the plot itself and before the time was ripe for the execution thereof discovered the whole order and every agent and actor thereof; who nevertheless were not suddenly apprehended by reason the confederates were divided and separated in place, some with us, and the chief with Sir George Summers in his island and indeed all his whole company, but good watch passed upon them, every man from thenceforth commanded to wear his weapon, without which before we freely walked from quarter to quarter and conversed among ourselves, and every man advised to stand upon his guard, his own life not being in safety while his next neighbor was not to be trusted.

The sentinels and nightwarders doubled, the passages of both the quarters were carefully observed, by which means nothing was further attempted until a gentleman amongst them, one Henry Paine, the thirteenth of March full of mischief and every hour preparing something or other, stealing swords, adzes, axes, hatchets, saws, augers, planes, mallets, etc. to make good his own bad end his watch night coming about, and being called by the captain of the same to be upon the guard, did not only give his said commander evil language but struck at him, doubled his blows, and when he was not suffered to close with him, went off the guard, scoffing at the double diligence and attendance of the watch appointed by the governor for much purpose, as he said. Upon which the watch telling him if the governor should understand of this his insolence, it might turn him to much blame, and happily be as much as his life were worth, the said Paine replied with a settled and bitter violence, and in such unreverent terms as I should offend the modest ear too much to express it in his own phrase, but the contents were how that the governor had no authority of that quality to justify upon anyone, how mean soever in the colony, an action of that nature, and therefore let the governor (said he) kiss, etc. Which words being with the omitted additions brought the next day unto every common and public discourse, at length they were delivered over to the governor, who examining well the fact the transgression so much the more exemplary and odious as being in a dangerous time, in a confederate, and the success of the same wish'dly listened after with a doubtful conceit what might be the issue of so notorious a boldness and impudency, calling the said Paine before him and the whole company, where, being soon convinced both by the witness of the commander, and many which were upon the watch with him, our governor, who had now the eyes of the whole colony fixed upon him, condemned him to be instantly hanged; and the ladder being ready, after he had made many confessions, he earnestly desired, being a gentleman, that he might be shot to death; and towards the evening he had his desire, the sun and his life setting together.

MICHEL EYQUEM DE MONTAIGNE (1533–1592)

From Of the Cannibals   1580

Montaigne became famous for his essays, which he and his younger contemporary Francis Bacon elevated to the state of literature. Montaigne was enormously influential in Shakespeare's time, especially after John Florio (1553–1625) translated his work in 1603. In this essay, Montaigne discusses the American Indians and their ways of living, as reported by numerous travelers of the age. The passage refers to the occasional habit of eating the flesh of defeated warriors and details some cultural habits of the "savages" of the New World.

They war against the nations that lie beyond their mountains, to which they go naked, having no other weapons than bows or wooden swords, sharp at one end as our broaches are. It is an admirable thing to see the constant resolution of their combats, which never end but by effusion of blood and murder; for they know not what fear or routs are. Every victor brings home the head of the enemy he hath slain as a trophy of his victory and fasteneth the same at the entrance of his dwelling place. After they have long time used and treated their prisoners well and with all commodities they can devise, he that is the master of them, summoning a great assembly of his acquaintance, tieth a cord to one of the prisoner's arms, by the end whereof he holds him fast, with some distance from him for fear he might offend him, and giveth the other arm, bound in like manner, to the dearest friend he hath, and both in the presence of all the assembly kill him with swords. Which done, they roast and then eat him in common and send some slices of him to such of their friends as are absent. It is not, as some imagine, to nourish themselves with it (as anciently the Scythians wont to do), but to represent an extreme and inexpiable revenge.

Which we prove thus: Some of them perceiving the Portugals, who had confederated themselves with their adversaries, to use another kind of death when they took them prisoners—which was to bury them up to the middle, and against the upper part of the body to shoot arrows, and then being almost dead, to hang them up—they supposed that these people of the other world (as they who had sowed the knowledge of many vices amongst their neighbors and were much more cunning in all kinds of evils and mischief than they) undertook not this manner of revenge without cause, and that consequently it was more smartful and cruel than theirs, and thereupon began to leave their old fashion to follow this.

I am not sorry we note the barbarous horror of such an action, but grieved that, prying so narrowly into their faults, we are so blinded in ours. I think there is more barbarism in eating men alive than to feed upon them being dead; to mangle by tortures and torments a body full of lively sense, to roast him in pieces, to make dogs and swine to gnaw and tear him in mammocks° (as we have not only read but seen very lately, yea and [in] our own memory, not amongst ancient enemies but our neighbors and fellow-citizens; and, which is worse, under pretense of piety and religion), than to roast and eat him after he is dead.

Chrysippus and Zeno, archpillars of the Stoic sect, have supposed that it was no hurt at all, in time of need and to what end soever, to make use of our carrion bodies and to feed upon them, as did our forefathers who, being besieged by Caesar in the city of Alexia, resolved to sustain the famine of the siege with the bodies of old men, women, and other persons unserviceable and unfit to fight.

> Gascons (as fame reports)
> Lived with meats of such sorts.
> Juven. *Sat.* XV.93.

And physicians fear not, in all kinds of compositions availful to our health, to make use of it, be it for outward or inward applications. But there was never any opinion found so unnatural and immodest that would excuse treason, treachery, disloyalty, tyranny, cruelty, and suchlike, which are our ordinary faults.

We may then well call them barbarous in regard of reason's rules, but not in respect of us that exceed them in all kind of barbarism. Their wars are noble and generous and have as much excuse and beauty as this human infirmity may admit; they aim at nought so much, and have no other foundation amongst them, but the mere jealousy of virtue. They contend not for the gaining of new lands; for to this day they yet enjoy that natural uberty° and fruitfulness which without laboring toil doth in such plenteous abundance furnish them with all necessary things that they need not enlarge their limits. They are yet in that happy estate as they desire no more than what their natural necessities direct them. Whatsoever is beyond it is to them superfluous. Those that are much about one age do generally inter-call one another

mammocks: Shreds.
uberty: Abundance.

brethren, and such as are younger they call children, and the aged are esteemed as fathers to all the rest. These leave this full possession of goods in common and without division to their heirs, without other claim or title but that which nature doth plainly impart unto all creatures, even as she brings them into the world. If their neighbors chance to come over the mountains to assail or invade them, and that they get the victory over them, the victors' conquest is glory and the advantage to be and remain superior in valor and virtue; else have they nothing to do with the goods and spoils of the vanquished, and so return into their country, where they neither want any necessary thing nor lack this great portion, to know how to enjoy their condition happily, and are contented with what nature affordeth them. So do these when their turn cometh. They require no other ransom of their prisoners but an acknowledgment and confession that they are vanquished. And in a whole age a man shall not find one that doth not rather embrace death than either by word or countenance remissly to yield one jot of an invincible courage. There is none seen that would not rather be slain and devoured than sue for life or show any fear. They use their prisoners with all liberty, that they may so much the more hold their lives dear and precious, and commonly entertain them with threats of future death, with the torments they shall endure, with the preparations intended for that purpose, with mangling and slicing of their members, and with the feast that shall be kept at their charge. All which is done to wrest some remiss and exact some faint-yielding speech of submission from them, or to possess them with a desire to escape or run away; that so they may have the advantage to have daunted and made them afraid and to have forced their constancy. For certainly true victory consisteth in that only point.

SAMUEL TAYLOR COLERIDGE (1772–1834)

From The Lectures of 1811–1812, Lecture IX 1812

Coleridge was one of the great Romantic poets, author of *The Rime of the Ancient Mariner, Kubla Khan,* and, with William Wordsworth, the volume *Lyrical Ballads.* In addition to being a major poet, Coleridge was a gifted critic and one of the most profound of Shakespeare interpreters. His lectures, delivered in London between 1810 and 1820, are credited with energizing nineteenth-century interest in Shakespeare, especially *Hamlet.* His comments here about Ariel emphasize that spirit's bondage to Prospero, and those about Miranda emphasize her wonder. Coleridge focuses on a quotation much ridiculed by Alexander Pope (1688–1744) in his critical poem *Peri Bathos, or The Art of Sinking in Poetry.*

But to return to *The Tempest,* and to the wondrous creation of Ariel. If a doubt could ever be entertained whether Shakespeare was a great poet, acting upon laws arising out of his own nature and not without law, as has sometimes been idly asserted, that doubt must be removed by the character of Ariel. The very first words uttered by this being introduce the spirit, not as an angel, above man; not a gnome, or a fiend, below man; but while the poet gives him the faculties and the advantages of reason, he divests him of all mortal character, not positively, it is true, but negatively. In air he lives, from air he derives his being, in air he acts; and all his colors and properties seem to have been obtained from the rainbow and the skies. There is nothing about Ariel that cannot be conceived to exist either at sunrise or at sunset: hence all that belongs to Ariel belongs to the delight the mind is capable of receiving from the most lovely external appearances. His answers to Prospero are directly to the question and nothing beyond; or where he expatiates, which is not unfrequently, it is to himself and upon his own delights, or upon the unnatural situation in which he is placed, though under a kindly power and to good ends.

Shakespeare has properly made Ariel's very first speech characteristic of him. After he has described the manner in which he had raised the storm and produced its harmless consequences, we find that Ariel is discontented—that he has been freed, it is true, from a cruel confinement, but still that he is bound to obey Prospero and to execute any commands imposed upon him. We feel that such a state of bondage is almost unnatural to him, yet we see that it is delightful for him to be so employed. It is as if we were to command one of the winds in a different direction to that which nature dictates, or one of the waves, now rising and now sinking, to recede before it bursts upon the shore: such is the feeling we experience, when we learn that a being like Ariel is commanded to fulfill any mortal behest.

When, however, Shakespeare contrasts the treatment of Ariel by Prospero with that of Sycorax, we are sensible that the liberated spirit ought to be grateful, and Ariel does feel and acknowledge the obligation; he immediately assumes the airy being, with a mind so elastically correspondent that when once a feeling has passed from it, not a trace is left behind.

Is there anything in nature from which Shakespeare caught the idea of this delicate and delightful being, with such childlike simplicity, yet with such preternatural powers? He is neither born of heaven, nor of earth; but, as it were, between both, like a May blossom kept suspended in air by the fanning breeze, which prevents it from falling to the ground, and only finally, and by compulsion, touching earth. This reluctance of the sylph to be under the command even of Prospero is kept up through the whole play, and in the exercise of his admirable judgment Shakespeare has availed himself of it in order to give Ariel an interest in the event, looking forward to that moment when he was to gain his last and only reward—simple and eternal liberty.

Another instance of admirable judgment and excellent preparation is to be found in the creature contrasted with Ariel—Caliban, who is described in such a manner by Prospero as to lead us to expect the appearance of a foul, unnatural monster. He is not seen at once: his voice is heard; this is the preparation; he was too offensive to be seen first in all his deformity, and in nature we do not receive so much disgust from sound as from sight. After we have heard Caliban's voice he does not enter until Ariel has entered like a water nymph. All the strength of contrast is thus acquired without any of the shock of abruptness, or of that unpleasant sensation, which we experience when the object presented is in any way hateful to our vision.

The character of Caliban is wonderfully conceived: he is a sort of creature of the earth, as Ariel is a sort of creature of the air. He partakes of the qualities of the brute, but is distinguished from brutes in two ways: by having mere understanding without moral reason; and by not possessing the instincts which pertain to absolute animals. Still, Caliban is in some respects a noble being: the poet has raised him far above contempt: he is a man in the sense of the imagination: all the images he uses are drawn from nature and are highly poetical; they fit in with the images of Ariel. Caliban gives us images from the earth, Ariel images from the air. Caliban talks of the difficulty of finding fresh water, of the situation of morasses, and of other circumstances which even brute instinct, without reason, could comprehend. No mean figure is employed, no mean passion displayed, beyond animal passion and repugnance to command.

The manner in which the lovers are introduced is equally wonderful, and it is the last point I shall now mention in reference to this, almost miraculous, drama. The same judgment is observable in every scene, still preparing, still inviting, and still gratifying, like a finished piece of music. I have omitted to notice one thing, and you must give me leave to advert to it before I proceed: I mean the conspiracy against the life of Alonzo. I want to show you how well the poet prepares the feelings of the reader for this plot, which was to execute the most detestable of all crimes, and which, in another play, Shakespeare has called "the murder of sleep."

Antonio and Sebastian at first had no such intention: it was suggested by the magical sleep cast on Alonzo and Gonzalo; but they are previously introduced scoffing and scorning at what was said by others, without regard to age or situation—without any sense of admiration for the excellent truths they heard delivered, but giving themselves up entirely to the malignant and unsocial feeling which induced them to listen to everything that was said, not for the sake of profiting by the learning and experience of others, but of hearing something that might gratify vanity and self-love, by making them believe that the person speaking was inferior to themselves.

This, let me remark, is one of the grand characteristics of a villain; and it would not be so much a presentiment as an anticipation of hell for men to suppose that all mankind were as wicked as themselves, or might be so, if they were not too great fools. Pope, you are perhaps aware, objected to this conspiracy; but in my mind, if it could be omitted, the play would lose a charm which nothing could supply.

Many, indeed innumerable, beautiful passages might be quoted from this play, independently of the astonishing scheme of its construction. Everybody will call to mind the grandeur of the language of Prospero in that divine speech, where he takes leave of his magic art; and were I to indulge myself by repetitions of the kind, I should descend from the character of a lecturer to that of a mere reciter. Before I terminate, I may particularly recall one short passage which has fallen under the very severe, but inconsiderate, censure of Pope and Arbuthnot, who pronounce it a piece of the grossest bombast. Prospero thus addresses his daughter, directing her attention to Ferdinand:

The fringed curtains of thine eye advance,
And say what thou seest yond.

Taking these words as a periphrase of—"Look what is coming yonder," it certainly may to some appear to border on the ridiculous and to fall under the rule I formerly laid down—that whatever, without injury, can be translated into a foreign language in simple terms, ought to be in simple terms in the original language; but it is to be borne in mind that different modes of expression frequently arise from difference of situation and education: a blackguard would use very different words, to express the same thing, to those a gentleman would employ, yet both would be natural and proper; difference of feeling gives rise to difference of language: a gentleman speaks in polished terms, with due regard to his own rank and position, while a blackguard, a person little better than half a brute, speaks like half a brute, showing no respect for himself nor for others.

But I am content to try the lines I have just quoted by the introduction to them; and then, I think, you will admit, that nothing could be more fit and appropriate than such language. How does Prospero introduce them? He has just told Miranda a wonderful story, which deeply affected her and filled her with surprise and astonishment, and for his own purposes he afterwards lulls her to sleep. When she awakes, Shakespeare has made her wholly inattentive to the present, but wrapped up in the past. An actress who understands the character of Miranda would have her eyes cast down and her eyelids almost covering them, while she was, as it were, living in her dream. At this moment Prospero sees Ferdinand and wishes to point him out to his daughter, not only with great, but with scenic solemnity, he standing before her and before the spectator in the dignified character of a great magician. Something was to appear to Miranda on the sudden, and as unexpectedly as if the hero of a drama were to be on the stage at the instant when the curtain is elevated. It is under such circumstances that Prospero says, in a tone calculated at once to arouse his daughter's attention,

> The fringed curtains of thine eye advance,
> And say what thou seest yond.

Turning from the sight of Ferdinand to his thoughtful daughter, his attention was first struck by the downcast appearance of her eyes and eyelids; and, in my humble opinion, the solemnity of the phraseology assigned to Prospero is completely in character, recollecting his preternatural capacity, in which the most familiar objects in nature present themselves in a mysterious point of view. It is much easier to find fault with a writer by reference to former notions and experience than to sit down and read him, recollecting his purpose, connecting one feeling with another, and judging of his words and phrases in proportion as they convey the sentiments of the persons represented. Of Miranda we may say that she possesses in herself all the ideal beauties that could be imagined by the greatest poet of any age or country; but it is not my purpose now so much to point out the high poetic powers of Shakespeare as to illustrate his exquisite judgment, and it is solely with this design that I have noticed a passage with which, it seems to me, some critics, and those among the best, have been unreasonably dissatisfied. If Shakespeare be the wonder of the ignorant, he is, and ought to be, much more the wonder of the learned: not only from profundity of thought, but from his astonishing and intuitive knowledge of what man must be at all times and under all circumstances, he is rather to be looked upon as a prophet than as a poet. Yet, with all these unbounded powers, with all this might and majesty of genius, he makes us feel as if he were unconscious of himself and of his high destiny, disguising the half god in the simplicity of a child.

ROBERT BROWNING (1812–1889)

Caliban upon Setebos; or, Natural Theology in the Island   1864

Robert Browning was the most important English poet of his time. One of his specialties was the dramatic monologue, a poem spoken by the protagonist directly to the audience. A dramatic monologue is much like one of Hamlet's soliloquies except that the reader is alone "listening" to the monologue rather than seeing it spoken on stage. Browning, affected by public discussions of Darwin's theory (which had been published in 1859), treats Caliban as a primitive "missing link" who tries to conceive the nature of Setebos, his god. In his search for understanding of theology, Caliban speaks of himself in the third person, then in the first person singular and plural. He imagines Setebos is much like him: whimsical, cruel when necessary, and essentially arbitrary.

'Thou thoughtest that I was altogether such a one as thyself.'

(David, Psalms 50:21)

['Will sprawl, now that the heat of day is best,
Flat on his belly in the pit's much mire,
With elbows wide, fists clenched to prop his chin.
And, while he kicks both feet in the cool slush,
And feels about his spine small eft-things course,
Run in and out each arm, and make him laugh:
And while above his head a pompion-plant,
Coating the cave-top as a brow its eye,
Creeps down to touch and tickle hair and beard,
10 And now a flower drops with a bee inside,
And now a fruit to snap at, catch and crunch,—
He looks out o'er yon sea which sunbeams cross
And recross till they weave a spider-web
(Meshes of fire, some great fish breaks at times)
And talks to his own self, howe'er he please,
Touching that other, whom his dam called God.
Because to talk about Him, vexes—ha,
Could He but know! and time to vex is now,
When talk is safer than in winter-time.
20 Moreover Prosper and Miranda sleep
In confidence he drudges at their task,
And it is good to cheat the pair, and gibe,
Letting the rank tongue blossom into speech.]

Setebos, Setebos, and Setebos!
'Thinketh, He dwelleth i' the cold o' the moon.

'Thinketh He made it, with the sun to match,
But not the stars; the stars came otherwise;
Only made clouds, winds, meteors, such as that:
Also this isle, what lives and grows thereon,
30 And snaky sea which rounds and ends the same.

'Thinketh, it came of being ill at ease:
He hated that He cannot change His cold,
Nor cure its ache. 'Hath spied an icy fish
That longed to 'scape the rock-stream where she lived,
And thaw herself within the lukewarm brine
O' the lazy sea her stream thrusts far amid,
A crystal spike 'twixt two warm walls of wave;
Only, she ever sickened, found repulse
At the other kind of water, not her life
40 (Green-dense and dim-delicious, bred o' the sun)
Flounced back from bliss she was not born to breathe,
And in her old bounds buried her despair,
Hating and loving warmth alike: so He.

'Thinketh, He made thereat the sun, this isle,
Trees and the fowls here, beast and creeping thing.
Yon otter, sleek-wet, black, lithe as a leech;
Yon auk, one fire-eye in a ball of foam,
That floats and feeds; a certain badger brown
He hath watched hunt with that slant white-wedge eye

By moonlight; and the pie with the long tongue   50
That pricks deep into oakwarts for a worm,
And says a plain word when she finds her prize,
But will not eat the ants; the ants themselves
That build a wall of seeds and settled stalks
About their hole—He made all these and more,
Made all we see, and us, in spite: how else?
He could not, Himself, make a second self
To be His mate; as well have made Himself:
He would not make what he mislikes or slights,
An eyesore to Him, or not worth His pains: 60
But did, in envy, listlessness or sport,
Make what Himself would fain, in a manner, be—
Weaker in most points, stronger in a few,
Worthy, and yet mere playthings all the while,
Things He admires and mocks too,—that is it.

Because, so brave, so better though they be,
It nothing skills if He begin to plague.
Look now, I melt a gourd-fruit into mash,
Add honeycomb and pods, I have perceived,
Which bite like finches when they bill and kiss,—   70
Then, when froth rises bladdery, drink up all,
Quick, quick, till maggots scamper through my brain;
Last, throw me on my back i' the seeded thyme,
And wanton, wishing I were born a bird.
Put case, unable to be what I wish,
I yet could make a live bird out of clay:
Would not I take clay, pinch my Caliban
Able to fly?—for, there, see, he hath wings,
And great comb like the hoopoe's to admire,
And there, a sting to do his foes offence,   80
There, and I will that he begin to live,
Fly to yon rock-top, nip me off the horns
Of grigs high up that make the merry din,
Saucy through their veined wings, and mind me not.
In which feat, if his leg snapped, brittle clay,
And he lay stupid-like,—why, I should laugh;
And if he, spying me, should fall to weep,
Beseech me to be good, repair his wrong,
Bid his poor leg smart less or grow again,—
Well, as the chance were, this might take or else   90
Not take my fancy: I might hear his cry,
And give the mankin three sound legs for one,
Or pluck the other off, leave him like an egg,
And lessoned he was mine and merely clay.
Were this no pleasure, lying in the thyme,
Drinking the mash, with brain become alive,
Making and marring clay at will? So He.

'Thinketh, such shows nor right nor wrong in Him,
Nor kind, nor cruel: He is strong and Lord.
'Am strong myself compared to yonder crabs   100
That march now from the mountain to the sea,
'Let twenty pass, and stone the twenty-first,
Loving not, hating not, just choosing so.
'Say, the first straggler that boasts purple spots
Shall join the file, one pincer twisted off;
'Say, this bruised fellow shall receive a worm,
And two worms he whose nippers end in red;
As it likes me each time, I do: so He.

Well then, 'supposeth He is good i' the main,
110   Placable if His mind and ways were guessed,
But rougher than His handiwork, be sure!
Oh, He hath made things worthier than Himself,
And envieth that, so helped, such things do more
Than He who made them! What consoles but this?
That they, unless through Him, do naught at all,
And must submit: what other use in things?
'Hath cut a pipe of pithless elder-joint
That, blown through, gives exact the scream o' the jay
When from her wing you twitch the feathers blue:
120   Sound this, and little birds that hate the jay
Flock within stone's throw, glad their foe is hurt:
Put case such pipe could prattle and boast forsooth
'I catch the birds, I am the crafty thing,
I make the cry my maker cannot make
With his great round mouth; he must blow through mine!'
Would not I smash it with my foot? So He.

But wherefore rough, why cold and ill at ease?
Aha, that is a question! Ask, for that,
What knows,—the something over Setebos
130   That made Him, or He, may be, found and fought,
Worsted, drove off and did to nothing, perchance.
There may be something quiet o'er His head,
Out of His reach, that feels nor joy nor grief,
Since both derive from weakness in some way.
I joy because the quails come; would not joy
Could I bring quails here when I have a mind:
This Quiet, all it hath a mind to, doth.
'Esteemeth stars the outposts of its couch,
But never spends much thought nor care that way.
140   It may look up, work up,—the worse for those
It works on! 'Careth but for Setebos
The many-handed as a cuttle-fish,
Who, making Himself feared through what He does,
Looks up, first, and perceives he cannot soar
To what is quiet and hath happy life;
Next looks down here, and out of very spite
Makes this a bauble-world to ape yon real,
These good things to match those as hips do grapes.
'Tis solace making baubles, ay, and sport.
150   Himself peeped late, eyed Prosper at his books
Careless and lofty, lord now of the isle:
Vexed, 'stitched a book of broad leaves, arrow-shaped,
Wrote thereon, he knows what, prodigious words;
Has peeled a wand and called it by a name;
Weareth at whiles for an enchanter's robe
The eyed skin of a supple oncelot;
And hath an ounce sleeker than youngling mole,
A four-legged serpent he makes cower and couch,
Now snarl, now hold its breath and mind his eye,
160   And saith she is Miranda and my wife:
'Keeps for his Ariel a tall pouch-bill crane
He bids go wade for fish and straight disgorge;
Also a sea-beast, lumpish, which he snared,
Blinded the eyes of, and brought somewhat tame,
And split its toe-webs, and now pens the drudge
In a hole o' the rock and calls him Caliban;
A bitter heart that bides its time and bites.

'Plays thus at being Prosper in a way,
Taketh his mirth with make-believes: so He.

His dam held that the Quiet made all things   170
Which Setebos vexed only: 'holds not so.
Who made them weak, meant weakness He might vex.
Had He meant other, while His hand was in,
Why not make horny eyes no thorn could prick,
Or plate my scalp with bone against the snow,
Or overscale my flesh 'neath joint and joint,
Like an orc's armour? Ay,—so spoil His sport!
He is the One now: only He doth all.

'Saith, He may like, perchance, what profits Him.
Ay, himself loves what does him good; but why?   180
'Gets good no otherwise. This blinded beast
Loves whoso places flesh-meat on his nose,
But, had he eyes, would want no help, but hate
Or love, just as it liked him: He hath eyes.
Also it pleaseth Setebos to work,
Use all His hands, and exercise much craft,
By no means for the love of what is worked.
'Tasteth, himself, no finer good i' the world
When all goes right, in this safe summer-time,
And he wants little, hungers, aches not much,   190
Than trying what to do with wit and strength.
'Falls to make something: 'piled yon pile of turfs,
And squared and stuck mere squares of soft white chalk,
And, with a fish-tooth, scratched a moon on each,
And set up endwise certain spikes of tree,
And crowned the whole with a sloth's skull a-top,
Found dead i' the woods, too hard for one to kill.
No use at all i' the work, for work's sole sake;
'Shall some day knock it down again: so He.

'Saith He is terrible: watch His feats in proof!   200
One hurricane will spoil six good months' hope.
He hath a spite against me, that I know,
Just as He favours Prosper, who knows why?
So it is, all the same, as well I find.
'Wove wattles half the winter, fenced them firm
With stone and stake to stop she-tortoises
Crawling to lay their eggs here: well, one wave,
Feeling the foot of Him upon its neck,
Gaped as a snake does, lolled out its large tongue,
And licked the whole labour flat: so much for spite.   210
'Saw a ball flame down late (yonder it lies)
Where, half an hour before, I slept i' the shade:
Often they scatter sparkles: there is force!
'Dug up a newt He may have envied once
And turned to stone, shut up inside a stone.
Please Him and hinder this?—What Prosper does?
Aha, if He would tell me how! Not He!
There is the sport: discover how or die!
All need not die, for of the things o' the isle
Some flee afar, some dive, some run up trees;   220
Those at His mercy,—why, they please Him most
When . . . when . . . well, never try the same way twice!
Repeat what act has pleased, He may grow wroth.
You must not know His ways, and play Him off,

Sure of the issue. 'Doth the like himself:
'Spareth a squirrel that it nothing fears
But steals the nut from underneath my thumb,
And when I threat, bites stoutly in defence:
'Spareth an urchin that contrariwise,
230 Curls up into a ball, pretending death
For fright at my approach: the two ways please.
But what would move my choler more than this,
That either creature counted on its life
Tomorrow and next day and all days to come,
Saying, forsooth, in the inmost of its heart,
'Because he did so yesterday with me,
And otherwise with such another brute,
So must he do henceforth and always.'—Ay?
Would teach the reasoning couple what 'must' means!
240 'Doth as he likes, or wherefore Lord? So He.

'Conceiveth all things will continue thus,
And we shall have to live in fear of Him
So long as He lives, keeps His strength: no change,
If He have done His best, make no new world
To please Him more, so leave off watching this, –
If He surprise not even the Quiet's self
Some strange day,—or, suppose, grow into it
As grubs grow butterflies: else, here are we,
And there is He, and nowhere help at all.
250 'Believeth with the life, the pain shall stop.
His dam held different, that after death
He both plagued enemies and feasted friends:
Idly! He doth His worst in this our life,
Giving just respite lest we die through pain,
Saving last pain for worst,—with which, an end.
Meanwhile, the best way to escape His ire
Is, not to seem too happy. 'Sees, himself,
Yonder two flies, with purple films and pink,
Bask on the pompion-bell above: kills both.
260 'Sees two black painful beetles roll their ball
On head and tail as if to save their lives:
Moves them the stick away they strive to clear.

Even so, 'would have Him misconceive, suppose
This Caliban strives hard and ails no less,
And always, above all else, envies Him;
Wherefore he mainly dances on dark nights,
Moans in the sun, gets under holes to laugh,
And never speaks his mind save housed as now:
Outside, 'groans, curses. If He caught me here,
270 O'erheard this speech, and asked 'What chuckles at?'
'Would, to appease Him, cut a finger off,
Or of my three kid yearlings burn the best,
Or let the toothsome apples rot on tree,
Or push my tame beast for the ore to taste:
While myself lit a fire, and made a song
And sung it, '*What I hate, be consecrate*
To celebrate Thee and Thy state, no mate
For Thee; what see for envy in poor me?'
Hoping the while, since evils sometimes mend,
280 Warts rub away and sores are cured with slime,
That some strange day, will either the Quiet catch
And conquer Setebos, or likelier He

Decrepit may doze, doze, as good as die.

[What, what? A curtain o'er the world at once!
Crickets stop hissing; not a bird—or, yes,
There scuds His raven that has told Him all!
It was fool's play, this prattling! Ha! The wind
Shoulders the pillared dust, death's house o' the move,
And fast invading fires begin! White blaze—
A tree's head snaps—and there, there, there, there, there,   290
His thunder follows! Fool to gibe at Him!
Lo! 'Lieth flat and loveth Setebos!
'Maketh his teeth meet through his upper lip,
Will let those quails fly, will not eat this month
One little mess of whelks, so he may 'scape!]

E. K. CHAMBERS (1866–1954)

The Tempest   1925

E. K. Chambers is considered one of the most important scholars of Medieval
and Renaissance drama. His several volumes on Shakespeare are still important
enough to influence twenty-first-century writers on Shakespeare's work. His brief
essay on *The Tempest* is drawn from *Shakespeare: A Survey*, in which he devotes
a chapter to each play. His critical analysis in the following essay aims at forming
a link between Shakespeare the dramatist and Prospero the magician. He sees
Shakespeare bidding playwriting a farewell just as Prospero bids magic farewell.
Ariel may be the spirit of poetry, but Caliban is an "earthy" creature, similar to those
for whom the missionaries labored tirelessly.

The Tempest, among Shakespeare's later plays, is a counterpart to the *Midsummer
Night's Dream* of his lyric youth. Here, too, is a dream, or, if you will, a fairy tale, in
which the protagonists are not men and women but imagined beings, taken partly
from folk-belief and partly from literature, to be the symbols of forces dimly perceived
by the poet as ruling that life, which is itself, after all, in another degree, but such stuff
as dreams are made on. And, like *A Midsummer Night's Dream*, the play must interest the spectator less through a strictly dramatic appeal to his emotions, than by the
strange romantic charm of its setting and its sensuous realization of the delicate and
the grotesque in the mysterious personages whom it brings before him. It is, in fact, to
be classed as dramatic *spectacle* rather than as drama proper, and the elaboration with
which it has been put upon the stage by modern managers may be regarded as not, in
this case, wholly out of keeping with the intention of the dramatist.

Apart, indeed, from its Ariel and its Caliban, and tried by the too rigid conception of drama which is blind to everything except just the interplay of human characters in action, *The Tempest* certainly fails to answer satisfactorily to the test. The
practical omnipotence which Prospero derives from his magic arts takes all vitality
from the plots which he unravels and from the conflict between hero and villains
which they represent. And, unless you are sentimentalist inveterate, your emotions
will not be more than faintly stirred by the blameless loves at first sight of Ferdinand
and Miranda, or by the quite superfluous obstacles, hollow as the property logs that
Ferdinand must carry, which are put in their way by the heavy father. The inexperienced but peerless maiden, advancing the fringed curtains of her eyes upon the "brave

new world that hath such people in it," only to have them dazzled by the first male being that crossed her path; the gallant but patient lover, of whom she very truly says, "Nothing natural I ever saw so noble"; they have much to answer for, it is to be feared, in the later development of rose-pink drawing-room fiction. Perhaps it would be a little hard to bear them a grudge for this. But even if they are not responsible for their great-great-grandchildren, do they not themselves share something of the colourless insipidity of their great-great-grandfather and grandmother, Daphnis and Chloe? And if you accept Miranda as a "nonpareil" and "the top of admiration" is it not rather because Shakespeare himself, through the mouths of Prospero and Ferdinand, tells you that that is what she is, than because of anything that she says or does as she stands before you? The device is an effective one in the hands of the novelist; but it is less available for the dramatist, who cannot, after all, escape from sooner or later producing his puppets, and making them speak and act for themselves upon his stage. Incidentally, it is a little curious to observe how the type of Shakespeare's women varies at different periods of his career. Miranda, Imogen, Perdita; set them against Rosalind, Beatrice, Helena. Is one to suppose that Shakespeare, like many more recent dramatists, found himself obliged to write "round" the personality of the "leading lady," who starred it for the time being in his company? Or is he merely following the wavering of the modish taste in heroines, a taste set perhaps, as some think, during the period of his final plays, by the sentimental tragicomedies of Beaumont and Fletcher?°

But if *The Tempest* is not exactly a slice cut straight from the red heart of humanity, still less can it be reasonably interpreted as a deliberate and consistent allegory. To prove, for example, in detail that it is not a formal exposition of the Baconian philosophy would carry me into regions of controversy which I do not propose, now or at any other time, to tread. The dream-formula is the true one. The play is no more than a dream, and as such dispensed from any obligation to logical completeness or continuity; an iridescent bubble, shot across by divers threads of symbolism and suggestion, independent of one other, but all reflecting tendencies of thought and feeling which were dominant in the mind of the poet at the time of its composition. Some of these tendencies may perhaps be indicated without breaking down the filmy texture of fancy by too heavy a burden of external comment.

That the general drift and structure of the play are peculiarly characteristic of Shakespeare's later mood of serene optimism, and that the invincible Prospero, biding his time to charm good out of ill and to make the odds all even, is in particular a kind of concrete embodiment of Providence, have become commonplaces of criticism. I need not labour them, or dwell upon the contrast between the spiritual temper which finds such expression and that which gave birth to the Titanic tragedies of *Macbeth* and *King Lear.* It is one which makes its first appearance in *Pericles,* and dominates *Cymbeline* and *The Winter's Tale*, as well as *The Tempest.* Further, one may readily agree with those who think that the play was written with an eye to the conditions of a court entertainment, rather than to those of the public stage. It is, in fact, a glorified mask. The ship of the first scene represents the "pageant" of carpenter's work, commonly introduced into such devices, and the dances, songs, and disguises of Ariel and his company are balanced, as in an anti-mask, by the clumsy revels of Stephano and his reeling-ripe fellows. The character of the formal mask introduced into the Fourth Act suggests a wedding, and at a Jacobean wedding the plain-spokenness of Prospero's sermon to the lovers would perhaps be neither intolerable nor uncalled for. The parallel to *A Midsummer Night's Dream*, probably performed at a

---

Beaumont and Fletcher: Francis Beaumont (1584–1616) and John Fletcher (1579–1625) were a popular team of playwrights who, along with their works, were known to Shakespeare.

court wedding in 1594 or 1595, and ending with an epithalamium,° is in this point exact. *The Tempest* is known to have been presented before the Princess Elizabeth, afterwards the unfortunate "Queen of Hearts," and Frederick the Elector Palatine, during the festivities accompanying their marriage on the 14th of February, 1613. It has even been supposed that it was originally written for this occasion. But the evidence for an earlier performance in 1611, which has now outlived suspicion, would make this theory untenable, even did Miranda not still more suggest a portrait of Elizabeth as she came into her new-washed world from the seclusion of Combe Abbey in 1611, than a portrait of Elizabeth after two years of court life in 1613. It is possible, however, although not, I think, more than possible, that the play may have been revised in the latter year, and the hymeneal mask, which is not particularly appropriate to its place in the action, inserted as a compliment to the bridal pair. However this may be, the hunt after topical allusions in Shakespeare's plays is surely not pursued with the discretion and saving sense of humour which it demands, when the escape of Ferdinand from drowning is interpreted as a reference to the untimely end of Henry, Prince of Wales, who died, not by drowning, but from typhoid fever, shortly before his sister's marriage. Ferdinand cannot stand both for Henry and for Frederick; nor is it the obvious way of condoling with a father on the death of a son, to point out that somebody else's son did not die. Even less willingly can one be induced to find in the triumphant magic of Prospero a delicate flattery of those political intrigues of James the First which had culminated in the alliance with the Elector. Shakespeare was willing enough, no doubt, to address a passing compliment to the king in *Macbeth.* He had more than once done as much for Gloriana° in earlier plays. But the dignified and patient Prospero is no more likely than Hamlet himself to be intended as a full-length portrait of the meanest and least picturesque of all the Stuarts. And so far, indeed, as there is any personal reference in Prospero at all, is it not clearly to one far greater than James the First, namely William Shakespeare himself? I find it impossible to doubt that in the famous address to the "elves of hills, brooks, standing lakes, and groves," in which Prospero recites how by their aid he has—

Bedimmed
The noontide sun, called forth the mutinous winds,
And 'twixt the green sea and the azured vault
Set roaring war,

and finally abjures his rough magic, breaks his staff, and drowns his book, Shakespeare is really making his own farewell to the stage and to the arts by which he has exercised a dominion even more elemental than that of the enchanter. This speech gives a key to one at least of the ideas which find expression in the play. Thus Ariel, who from another point of view is the agent and minister of an inscrutable Providence, becomes from this a symbol of the spirit of poetry found pegged in the cloven pine of the pre-Shakespearean drama, brought into the service of the creative imagination, and employed for his term in the fashioning of illusions to delight the eyes and move the hearts of men. And so it is hinted that at the end of the play the insubstantial pageant of the great Shakespearean drama shall fade for ever. Ariel shall have his freedom, and Prospero shall betake himself to the dukedom of Milan—which is Stratford.

Whether I am right in this or not, the scanty evidence available would seem to show that the year 1611, in which *The Tempest* was probably written, was also that in which Shakespeare bade good-bye to London and took up his abode for the rest of his life at New Place. He was then still a comparatively young man, and had been

epithalamium: A poem written to celebrate a marriage.
Gloriana: Queen Elizabeth I.

a dramatist for not more than a round score of years. The significance of so early a retirement has perhaps hardly been sufficiently appreciated. No doubt Shakespeare had made money and could afford, like Alleyn,° to enjoy his repose and the responsibilities of a landed proprietor. But his willingness to leave London and his triumphs and to bury himself at the age of forty-eight in the smug obscurity of a petty provincial town certainly suggests that his quality of actor and playwright had lost whatever attraction it may ever have possessed for him. The hints of dissatisfaction with the life of the mime, at a much earlier date, in the *Sonnets*, will not be forgotten. Plays and poems are full of these tantalizing glimpses of the man William Shakespeare behind them, and any attempt at interpretation lands one on the perilous ways of conjectural biography. It is, certainly, a merely conjectural reconstruction of the inadequate data when I suggest that Shakespeare as a lad was "dedicated to closeness and the bettering of his mind" and felt little desire for the career of a farmer and more or less prosperous burgess, which was that laid open to him by the traditions of his family. He cared not to be Duke of Milan. Literary ambitions, aided perhaps by some event capable at least of symbolical representation in a drama as an intrigue against him, drove him to London. But the actual conditions attending the calling of an actor and dramatist spelt disillusion. Shakespeare was more of a *bourgeois* than he had dreamed. The mayor's son, conscious of his father's coat-armour, rebelled against the disrepute attaching to an occupation whose members were only distinguished by a legal fiction from rogues and vagrants. The prospect of retirement was present to his mind from an early period. He saved money, invested it in Stratford, bought a house there, and, as soon as his affairs permitted, he gladly broke his pen, and returned to his rejected dukedom, to enjoy the dignities of New Place, to dig his garden, collect his tithes, sit through sermons, and entertain the preacher to sack and supper.

May one venture to think that something better and more spiritual than this merely respectable instinct helped to account for his flight? Is it possible that, in 1611, Shakespeare heard Warwickshire calling with a voice that would not be denied? London was a growing city in the early seventeenth century, and a note of revolt from urban life, hardly heard since the day of the poets of imperial Rome, was beginning to steal back into literature. Jonson translated his—

Beatus ille, qui procul negotiis,°

although Jonson, if any one, had Fleet Street in his veins; and doubtless many a poet flung himself across a table in the Half-Moon to write an ode about the shepherd's life and its sweet content. But the sentiment was a real one all the same, and there are signs in Shakespeare's latest plays that he shared it. In *The Winter's Tale* it reveals itself in the hints of conventional pastoral, always the townsman's dream of country life. In *The Tempest* it inspires the speculations of Gonzalo, borrowed from Montaigne though these may be, on the golden age and the pleasant liberties of its primitive civilization; and also surely the sweet out-of-doors air of the play, blown through and through with breaths from those voyages of discovery which brought so much romance and such a widening horizon into Elizabethan life.

And so we come to the enigmatic figure of Caliban, about which, it must be admitted, the ingenuity of the commentators has not been idle. I have rejected the temptation to suggest that, just as Ariel symbolizes the spirit of poetry brought by Shakespeare into the service of the creative imagination, so Caliban signifies the spirit of prose, born of Sycorax who is controversial theology, and imperfectly subdued by Shakespeare to the same service. There are some who follow

---

Alleyn: Edward Alleyn (1566–1626) was one of the best known actors of his age.
Beatus . . . negotiis: Happy those who are away from the business (from Horace, *Odes*).

Renan° in taking Caliban for a type of Demos, and regard his desire to "nor scrape trenchering nor wash dish" as eminently characteristic of political ideals which aim at nothing higher than the escape from reasonable labour. Of any political intention on Shakespeare's part in *The Tempest* I am profoundly sceptical; nor do I feel sure that, in the great political cleavage which was beginning to show itself in his day, he would have been so certainly a foe to Demos as is often assumed. Those who believe in his supposed aristocratic and divine-right sympathies, largely on the basis of the Jack Cade scenes in *Henry the Sixth* which he probably did not design, may be invited to compare the demeanour of the boatswain in the storm with that of the crowd of courtiers whose howling proved louder than the weather or his office. Shakespeare, at least, was the dupe neither of a theory nor of a title. "What cares these roarers for the name of king?"

Browning based on Caliban a semi-ironical disquisition on the genesis of natural religions and their anthropomorphism. Others have seen in him an anticipation of Darwinian theories as to the development of man. It is not necessary to attribute to Shakespeare prophetic gifts in the region of biology; but he does seem to be endeavouring to adumbrate in Caliban such a general conception of primitive humanity as the expanding knowledge of his day had opened out to him. Caliban is an earthy creature. He has the morals and the maliciousness of a troglodyte,° and must be taught the first elements of human knowledge—

> How
> To name the bigger light, and how the less,
> That burn by day and night—

and even the first principles of articulate speech. He will take no print of goodness, and can only be controlled and made serviceable by terror. On the other hand—and here we come back to the cravings after the life according to nature which the play in more than one point suggests—he is akin to earth in another sense. He knows all "the qualities of the isle," where the "quick freshes" are, and where the brine pits; and, in the fervour of his adoration for Stephano, vows—

> I'll show thee the best springs. I'll pluck thee berries.
> I'll fish for thee and get thee wood enough;

and again—

> I prithee, let me bring thee where crabs grow.
> And I with my long nails will dig thee pig-nuts;
> Show thee a jay's nest and instruct thee how
> To snare the nimble marmoset; I'll bring thee
> To clustering filberts and sometimes I'll get thee
> Young scamels from the rock.

And is it upon Caliban or upon the missionaries of European civilization that the irony falls, in his complaint against Prospero—

> You taught me language, and my profit on it
> Is, I know how to curse. The red plague rid you
> For teaching me your language!

or in the Rabelaisian scenes where the monster abases himself in the cult of the *dive bouteille*° and confesses of the drunken lackey who holds it—

> That's a brave god, and bears celestial liquor?

Renan: Ernest Renan (1823–1892) was famous for his *Life of Jesus* (1863), but he also wrote *Caliban* (1878). Demos refers to the common people—in Renan's case, perhaps the peasants.
troglodyte: Literally, a cave dweller, an extremely primitive human.
the cult of the *dive bouteille:* the cult of the "divine bottle" (i.e., the pursuit of drunkenness).

AIMÉ CÉSAIRE (1913–2008)

From A Tempest 1969

TRANSLATED BY RICHARD MILLER

Aimé Césaire was a poet, writer, and politician. He was born in Martinique but educated in Paris at the Sorbonne. In his student days, he associated with other black writers and intellectuals and took part in the development of negritude, a movement championing black thought and black politics. He spent much of his life as a teacher in Martinique. He also wrote important books and several plays condemning colonialism, including *A Season in the Congo* (1966), which he intended as part of a trilogy that ended with his play *A Tempest*. The excerpt below is from the ending of the play, in which Prospero and Caliban are left on the island together, with Prospero aged and Caliban free.

TRINCULO: Raise sail! But that's what we do all the time, Sire, Stephano and I . . . at least, we raise our glasses, from dawn till dusk till dawn. . . . The hard part is putting them down, landing, as you might say.

PROSPERO: Scoundrels! If only life could bring you to the safe harbors of Temperance and Sobriety!

ALONSO: (*indicating Caliban*) That is the strangest creature I've ever seen!

PROSPERO: And the most devilish too!

GONZALO: What's that? Devilish! You've reprimanded him, preached at him, you've ordered and made him obey and you say he is still indomitable!

PROSPERO: Honest Gonzalo, it is as I have said.

GONZALO: Well—and forgive me, Counsellor, if I give counsel—on the basis of my long experience the only thing left is exorcism. "Begone, unclean spirit, in the name of the Father, of the Son and of the Holy Ghost." That's all there is to it!

Caliban bursts out laughing.

GONZALO: You were absolutely right! And more so that you thought . . . He's not just a rebel, he's a real tough customer! (*To Caliban*) So much the worse for you, my friend. I have tried to save you. I give up. I leave you to the secular arm!

PROSPERO: Come here, Caliban. Have you got anything to say in your own defence? Take advantage of my good humor. I'm in a forgiving mood today.

CALIBAN: I'm not interested in defending myself. My only regret is that I've failed.

PROSPERO: What were you hoping for?

CALIBAN: To get back my island and regain my freedom.

PROSPERO: And what would you do all alone here on this island, haunted by the devil, tempest tossed?

CALIBAN: First of all, I'd get rid of you! I'd spit you out, all your works and pomps! Your "white" magic!

PROSPERO: That's a fairly negative program. . . .

CALIBAN: You don't understand it . . . I say I'm going to spit you out, and that's very positive . . .

PROSPERO: Well, the world is really upside down . . . We've seen everything now: Caliban as a dialectician! However, in spite of everything I'm fond of you, Caliban. Come, let's make peace. We've lived together for ten years and worked side by side! Ten years count for something, after all! We've ended up by becoming compatriots!

CALIBAN: You know very well that I'm not interested in peace. I'm interested in being free! Free, you hear?

PROSPERO: It's odd . . . no matter what you do, you won't succeed in making me believe that I'm a tyrant!

CALIBAN: Understand what I say, Prospero:

For years I bowed my head
for years I took it, all of it—

your insults, your ingratitude . . .
and worst of all, more degrading than all the rest,
your condescension.
But now, it's over!
Over, do you hear?
Of course, at the moment
You're still stronger than I am.
But I don't give a damn for your power
or for your dogs or your police or your inventions!
And do you know why?
It's because I know I'll get you.
I'll impale you! And on a stake that you've sharpened yourself!
You'll have impaled yourself!
Prospero, you're a great magician:
you're an old hand at deception.
And you lied to me so much,
about the world, about myself,
that you ended up by imposing on me
an image of myself:
underdeveloped, in your words, undercompetent
that's how you made me see myself!
And I hate that image . . . and it's false!
But now I know you, you old cancer,
And I also know myself!
And I know that one day
my bare fist, just that,
will be enough to crush your world!
The old world is crumbling down!

Isn't it true? Just look!
It even bores you to death.
And by the way . . . you have a chance to get it over with:
You can pick up and leave.
You can go back to Europe.
But the hell you will!
I'm sure you won't leave.
You make me laugh with your "mission"!
Your "vocation"!
Your vocation is to hassle me.
And that's why you'll stay,
just like those guys who founded the colonies
and who now can't live anywhere else.
You're just an old addict, that's what you are!

PROSPERO: Poor Caliban! You know that you're headed towards your own ruin. You're
    sliding towards suicide! You know I will be the stronger, and stronger all the time.
    I pity you!
CALIBAN: And I hate you!
PROSPERO: Beware! My generosity has its limits.
CALIBAN: (*shouting*)

Shango marches with strength
along his path, the sky!
Shango is a fire-bearer,
his steps shake the heavens
and the earth
Shango, Shango, ho!

PROSPERO: I have uprooted the oak and raised the sea,
    I have caused the mountain to tremble and have bared my chest to adversity.
    With Jove I have traded thunderbolt for thunderbolt.

Better yet—from a brutish monster I have made man!
But ah! To have failed to find the path to man's heart . . .
if that be where man is.
(*to Caliban*)
Well, I hate you as well!
For it is you who have made me
doubt myself for the first time.
(*to the Nobles*)
. . . My friends, come near. We must say farewell. . . . I shall not be going with you.
My fate is here: I shall not run from it.
ANTONIO: What, Sire?
PROSPERO: Hear me well.
I am not in any ordinary sense a master,
as this savage thinks,
but rather the conductor of a boundless score:
this isle,
summoning voices, I alone,
and mingling them at my pleasure,
arranging out of confusion
one intelligible line.
Without me, who would be able to draw music from all that?
This isle is mute without me.
My duty, thus, is here,
and here I shall stay.
GONZALO: Oh day full rich in miracles!
PROSPERO: Do not be distressed. Antonio, be you the lieutenant of my goods and
make use of them as procurator until that time when Ferdinand and Miranda
may take effective possession of them, joining them with the Kingdom of Naples. Nothing of that which has been set for them must be postponed: Let their
marriage be celebrated at Naples with all royal splendor. Honest Gonzalo, I
place my trust in your word. You shall stand as father to our princess at this
ceremony.
GONZALO: Count on me, Sire.
PROSPERO: Gentlemen, farewell.

They exit.

And now, Caliban, it's you and me!
What I have to tell you will be brief:
Ten times, a hundred times, I've tried to save you,
above all from yourself.
But you have always answered me with wrath
and venom,
like the opossum that pulls itself up by its own tail
the better to bite the hand that tears it from the darkness.
Well, my boy, I shall set aside my indulgent nature
and henceforth I will answer your violence
with violence!

*Time passes, symbolized by the curtain's being lowered halfway and reraised. In
semi-darkness Prospero appears, aged and weary. His gestures are jerky and automatic, his speech weak, toneless, trite.*

PROSPERO: Odd, but for some time now we seem to be overrun with opossums. They're
everywhere. Peccarys, wild boar, all this unclean nature! But mainly opossums.
Those eyes! The vile grins they have! It's as though the jungle was laying siege to the
cave. . . . But I shall stand firm. . . . I shall not let my work perish! (*Shouting*) I shall
protect civilization! (*He fires in all directions.*) They're done for! Now, this way I'll
be able to have some peace and quiet for a while. But it's cold. Odd how the climate's
changed. Cold on this island . . . Have to think about making a fire . . . Well, Caliban,

old fellow, it's just us two now, here on the island . . . only you and me. You and me. You-me . . . me-you! What in the hell is he up to? (*Shouting*) Caliban!

In the distance, above the sound of the surf and the chirping of birds, we hear snatches of Caliban's song:

FREEDOM HI-DAY, FREEDOM HI-DAY!

ANIA LOOMBA

Caliban and Sycorax   1989

Ania Loomba is professor of English and Comparative Literature at the University of Pennsylvania. Educated at the University of New Delhi and the University of Sussex, she specializes in drama, feminism, colonialism, and post-colonialism. Among her works are *Shakespeare, Race and Colonialism* (2002) and *Postcolonial Studies and Beyond* (2005). Her focus in this excerpt from *Gender, Race, Renaissance Drama* (1989) is on colonial preconceptions of Caliban and the position of Sycorax as the only strong female character referenced in the play.

The Black Rapist[1]

One of the reasons for the play's declining pertinence to contemporary third world politics has been identified as

> the difficulty of wresting from it any role for female defiance or leadership in a period when protest is coming increasingly from that quarter. Given that Caliban is without a female counterpart in his oppression and rebellion, and given the largely autobiographical cast of African and Caribbean appropriations of the play, it follows that all the writers who quarried from *The Tempest* an expression of their lot should have been men. (Nixon, p. 577)

It is true that the play poses a problem for a feminist, and especially a nonwestern feminist appropriation, if by "appropriation" we mean an amplification of the anti-colonial voices within the text. But such a difficulty does not arise simply from the lack of a strong female presence, black or white, in the play, but also from the play's representation of black male sexuality.

Caliban contests Prospero's account of his arrival on the island but not the accusation of attempted rape of Miranda. Identifying the political effects of Prospero's accusation, Paul Brown comments that "the issue here is not whether Caliban is actually a rapist or not, since Caliban accepts the charge." On the contrary, I suggest that this acceptance is important for assessing both colonial and anti-colonial readings of the play. An article written in 1892, which later became what Griffiths calls "a standard defence of Caliban" speaks of the rape as "an offence, an unpardonable offence, but *one that he was fated to commit*" (p. 166; emphasis added) and goes on to see Caliban as unfortunate, oppressed, but "like all these lower peoples, easily misled." This implies that sexual violence is part of the

---

[1] I am indebted to work on *The Tempest* by Barker and Hulme, Paul Brown and Rob Nixon, all of which has made this chapter possible.

black man's inferior nature, a view that amalgamates racist common-sense notions about black sexuality and animalism, and sexist assumptions about rape as an inevitable expression of frustrated male desire.

These notions were complexly employed in the influential *Psychologie de la colonisation* (1948) by Octave Mannoni, who seriously reassessed the play in order to propound a controversial view of the psychology of the colonised subject. Mannoni advocated the notion of the "Caliban complex" which he analyzed as the desire for dependency on the part of the native. Caliban (and the Madagascans, whose uprising of 1947–48 provided the impetus for the work) revolts not against slavery but because he is abandoned by Prospero. Analyzing Caliban's speech in Act 2, Mannoni came to the conclusion that "Caliban does not complain of being exploited: he complains of being betrayed." As other Caribbean and African intellectuals pointed out, Mannoni posited Caliban as an eager partner in his own colonization (Nixon, pp. 562–65).

Sycorax

Mannoni, significantly, edited out these opening lines of Caliban's version of Prospero's arrival on the island:

> This island's mine, by Sycorax my mother,
> Which thou tak'st from me.
>
> [I, ii, 334–35]

These lines had elicited the first recorded anti-imperialist response to the play in 1904, which found that in them "the whole case of the aboriginal against aggressive civilisation [was] dramatised before us" (Nixon, pp. 561–62). They were also focused by subsequent Caribbean and African appropriations, but although some of these indicated the matrilinear nature of many pre-colonial societies, gender was hardly ever seized upon by anti-colonial intellectuals as a significant dimension of racial oppression.

Sycorax is more than the justification for Caliban's territorial rights to the island—she operates as a powerful contrast to Miranda. Both Prospero and Caliban testify to her power; the former draws upon the language of misogyny as well as racism to construct her as a "foul witch" [I, ii, 259] the latter invokes her strength to express his hatred of his master [I, ii, 324–26, 342–43]. Prospero's descriptions of Sycorax emphasize both her non-European origins—she's "from Argier"—and her fertility—"This blue-ey'd hag was hither brought with child" [I, ii, 263, 271]. She is also "so strong / That could control the moon, make flows and ebbs, / And deal in her command without her power" [V, i, 272–74]. Hence she stands in complete contrast to the white, virginal and obedient Miranda. Between them they split the patriarchal stereotype of woman as the white devil—virgin and whore, goddess (Miranda is mistaken for one by Ferdinand) and witch.

But Sycorax is also Prospero's "other"; his repeated comparisons between their different magics and their respective reigns of the island are used by him to claim a superior morality, a greater strength and a greater humanity, and hence legitimize his takeover of the island and its inhabitants; but they also betray an anxiety that Sycorax's power has not been fully exorcised, for Caliban still invokes it for his own rebellion: "All the charms / Of Sycorax, toads, beetles, bats, light on you!" [I, ii, 342–43]. As George Lamming pointed out in *The Pleasures of Exile,* while

Miranda is like many an African slave child in never having known her mother, "the actual Caliban of *The Tempest* has the advantage . . . of having known the meaning and power of his mother Sycorax" (p. 111).

Prospero's takeover is both *racial* plunder and a transfer to *patriarchy*. The connections between witches and transgressive women, between witch-trials with the process of capital accumulation, and between the economic, ideological and sexual subordination of native women by colonial rule, have already been discussed [in *Gender, Race, Renaissance Drama,* chapters 1 and 3]. The restructuring of the colonized economy not only involved the export of raw material to factories in England, but also a redefinition of men and women's work, which economically dislocated women, and calcified patriarchal tendencies in the native culture. . . . In Burma, for example, British colonialists acknowledged that Burmese women had property and sexual rights unheard of in England. Accordingly, Fielding Hall, Political Officer in the British Colonial Administration in Burma, suggested that in order to "civilise" the Burmese people:

1. The men must be taught to kill and to fight for the British colonialists.
2. Women must surrender their liberty in the interests of men. (Mies, quoted by Rughani, p. 19)

Colonized women were also subjected to untold sexual harassment, rape, enforced marriage and degradation, both under direct slavery and otherwise. Sycorax's illegitimate pregnancy contrasts with Miranda's chastity and virginity, reminding us that the construction of the promiscuity of non-European women served to legitimize their sexual abuse and to demarcate them from white women.

Therefore Prospero as colonialist consolidates power which is specifically white and male, and constructs Sycorax as a black, wayward and wicked witch in order to legitimize it. If Caliban's version of past events prompts us to question Prospero's story, then this interrogation should include the re-telling of Sycorax's story. The distinctions drawn by generations of critics between his "white magic" and Sycorax's "black magic" only corroborate Prospero's narrative. African appropriations emphasized the brutality of Prospero's "reason" and its historical suppression of black culture, but they did not bring out the gender-value of these terms; they read the story of colonized and colonizing men but not of colonized and colonizing women, which is also told by Miranda's lonely presence on the island.

Brown, Paul, "'This thing of darkness I acknowledge mine': *The Tempest* and the discourse of colonialism," in Dollimore and Sinfield, eds., 1985, pp. 48–71.

Dollimore, Jonathan, and Sinfield, Alan, eds., *Political Shakespeare: New Essays in Cultural Materialism* (Manchester University Press, 1985).

Griffiths, Trevor R., "'This island's mine': Caliban and colonialism," *Yearbook of English Studies* 13 (1983), pp. 159–80.

Lamming, George, *The Pleasures of Exile* (London and New York, Allison and Busby, 1984).

Mies, Maria, *Patriarchy and Accumulation on a World Scale: Women in the International Division of Labour* (London and New Jersey, Zed Books, 1986).

Nixon, Rob, "Caribbean and African appropriations of *The Tempest*," *Critical Inquiry* 13 (Spring 1987), pp. 557–77.

Rughani, Pratap, "Kipling, India and Imperialism" (unpublished paper).

MARJORIE GARBER (b. 1944)

The Tempest and Colonialism   2004

Marjorie Garber is the William R. Kenan, Jr., Professor of English and Chair of the Committee on Dramatic Arts at Harvard University. *Shakespeare After All* (2004), from which the passage below is taken, was selected as one of the five best nonfiction books of the year by *Newsweek*. Garber examines *The Tempest* in detail in an effort to clarify the themes of colonialism that have attracted recent criticism while also examining the geography of the island, whose complexities complicate any absolute connection with the New World—or any world except that of the imagination.

Shakespeare's powerful late romance *The Tempest* has been addressed by modern critics from two important perspectives: as a fable of art and creation, and as a colonialist allegory. These readings very much depend on one's conception of European man's place in the universe, and on whether a figure like Prospero stands for all mankind or for one side of a conflict.

The first interpretation, following upon the ideas of Renaissance humanism and the place of the artist/playwright/magician, offers a story of mankind at the center of the universe, of "man" as creator and authority. Such a reading is, by its nature, at once aesthetic, philosophical, and skeptical. Prospero is man-the-artist, or man-the-scholar: Ariel and Caliban represent his ethereal and material selves—the one airy, imaginative, and swift; the second earthy, gross, and appetitive. Prospero has often been seen as a figure for the artist as creator—as Shakespeare's stand-in, so to speak, or Shakespeare's self-conception, an artist figure unifying the world around him by his "so potent art." By his magic, his *good* magic, or what has been described as *white* (or benevolent) magic, he subdues anarchic figures around him, like Caliban and his mother, Sycorax, the previous ruler of the island, who is also a magician (often thought of as a practitioner of *black,* or malevolent, magic). Prospero's magic books enable him as well to thwart the incipient revolts of both high and low conspirators, and to exact a species of revenge against those who usurped his dukedom and set him adrift on the sea—for *The Tempest* is one of Shakespeare's most compelling "revenge tragedies," turned, at the last moment, toward forgiveness.

But there is something troubling about this idealized picture of a Renaissance man accommodated with arts and crafts, dominance and power, in a little world, a little island, that he takes and makes his own. Many critical observers, especially in the later twentieth century, have seen Prospero as a colonizer of alien territory *not* his own, a European master who comes to an island in the New World, displaces its native ruler, enslaves its indigenous population (in this case emblematized by Caliban), and makes its rightful inhabitants work for him and his family as servants, fetching wood and water, while he and his daughter enjoy all the amenities of the temperate climate and the fertile land. The tensions between the aesthetic and the political lie at the heart of the play.

First staged in 1611, with King James present in the audience, *The Tempest* was subsequently performed as part of the marriage celebration for his daughter, the Princess Elizabeth, whom the King was about to "lose" to her husband, Frederick, the Elector Palatine—just as Prospero "loses" his daughter, Miranda, as he tells Alonso, King of Naples, "in this last tempest," to Ferdinand, the King's son. So the political and social context, the timeliness, of the play may have been evident from the beginning.

Although it takes the form of an extended scene of instruction between Prospero and Miranda, father and daughter, the play is fundamentally built on the continuous contrast between Prospero's two servants, Ariel and Caliban, mind and body, imagination and desire or lust. If Ariel is imagination personified, surely Caliban is something like libido (sexual desire) or id (basic human drives). If one thing is clear on Prospero's island, it is that, for all his anarchic and disruptive qualities, Caliban is *necessary*—like the body itself. "We cannot miss him," says Prospero (meaning, "We cannot do without him"). "He does make our fire, / Fetch in our wood, and serves in offices / That profit us" [I, ii, 314–16]. Later in the play, after Caliban foils the conspiracy against his life, Prospero will say ruefully of him, "This thing of darkness I / Acknowledge mine" [V, i, 278–79]. What Prospero acknowledges in this phrase is not only responsibility (Caliban is my slave), but also identity (Caliban, the "thing of darkness," is part of me).

In one way we might say that *The Tempest* is macrocosmic: Caliban is a spirit of earth and water, Ariel a spirit of fire and air, and together they are elements harnessed by Prospero, here a kind of magician and wonder-worker closely allied to Renaissance science. Together these figures give us a picture of the world. In another way we could say that *The Tempest* is microcosmic, its structural design a mirror of the human psyche: Caliban, who is necessary and burdensome, the libido, the id, a "thing of darkness" who must be acknowledged; Ariel the spirit of imagination incarnate, who cannot be possessed forever, and therefore must be allowed to depart in freedom. And in yet a third way the play's design illustrates the basic doctrines of Renaissance humanist philosophy. Mankind is a creature a little lower than the angels, caught between the bestial and the celestial, a creature of infinite possibilities. In all of these patterns Prospero stands between the poles marked out by Ariel and Caliban.

The second kind of interpretation, the colonial or postcolonial narrative, follows upon early modern voyages of exploration and discovery, "first contact," and the encounters with, and exploitation of, indigenous peoples in the New World. In this interpretive context *The Tempest* is not idealizing, aesthetic, and "timeless," but rather topical, contextual, "political," and in dialogue with the times. Yet manifestly this dichotomy will break down, both in literary analysis and in performance. It is perfectly possible for a play about a mage, artist, and father to be, at the same time, a play about a colonial governor, since Prospero himself is, or was, the Duke of Milan. His neglect of his ducal responsibilities ("rapt in secret studies," he allowed his brother to scheme against him) led first to his usurpation and exile, then to his establishment of an alternative government on the island, displacing and enslaving the native inhabitant Caliban, whose mother, Sycorax, had ruled there before Prospero's arrival and who, as Caliban says, "first was mine own king" [I, ii, 345].

Caliban's name is a variant of "cannibal" (deriving from "Carib," a fierce nation of the West Indies), and Shakespeare's play owes much to Montaigne's essay "Of Cannibals" (1580), which draws trenchant and unflattering comparisons between the supposedly civilized Europeans and the native islanders. "There is nothing savage or barbarous about those peoples, but that every man calls barbarous anything he is not accustomed to," Montaigne writes. Despite the nakedness and unfamiliar ways of these tribes, contemporary European societies "surpass them in every kind of barbarism," like treachery, disloyalty, tyranny, and cruelty, which "are everyday vices in us." As for cannibalism itself, there is "more barbarity in lacerating by rack and torture a body still fully able to feel things, in roasting him little by little . . . than in roasting and eating him after his death."

Colonialist readings have gained force in the last fifty years by analogy with the historical events of postcolonialism, whether in South Asia, Africa, or the Caribbean, but they are also entirely pertinent to Shakespeare's own time. During the years when *The Tempest* was written and first performed, Europe, and England in particular, was in the heyday of the period of colonial exploration. Sir Walter Ralegh is one important and charismatic figure who went from the Elizabethan court to the New World, and in his account, *The Discovery of the Large, Rich, and Beautiful Empire of Guiana* (1596), he describes encounters with native populations of just this kind. Captain John Smith set out with the Virginia colonists in 1606, and his *General History of Virginia, New England, and the Summer Isles* (1624) is another key source for this period, documenting the encounter of Englishmen (for which we may read Prospero's Italians/Europeans) with a native culture and climate in the New World.

There are moments in the play that clearly evoke the local historical context: as, for example, when Trinculo, the drunken jester, stumbling over the recumbent form of Caliban, imagines a fast way to make money, by exhibiting him back in the Old World for a fee:

> Were I in England now, as once I was, and had but this fish painted, not a holiday-fool there but would give a piece of silver. There would this monster make a man. Any strange beast there makes a man. When they will not give a doit to relieve a lame beggar, they will lay out ten to see a dead Indian.
>
> The Tempest [II, ii, 26–31]

"Were I in England" is Shakespeare's typical sly wit—an in-joke for the English audience, like the scene in which the gravedigger in *Hamlet* remarks that no one in England would detect Hamlet's infirmity: "There the men are as mad as he" [V, i, 142–43].

Many of the twentieth-century rewritings of *The Tempest* are inspired by New World concerns, and even are written from the point of view of the oppressed. The Uruguayan philosopher and critic José Enrique Rodó wrote his *Ariel* in 1900, calling upon Latin America to retain cultural values unsullied by the materialism of the United States; in 1913 he published *El Mirador de Próspero* (Prospero's Balcony). Martinican playwright Aimé Césaire published the first version of his *Une Tempête*, a radical adaptation of Shakespeare's play, in 1968, and the Cuban revolutionary intellectual Roberto Fernández Retamar wrote his *Calibán* in 1971. The story of *The Tempest* has intersected, repeatedly and always interestingly, with other "political" and colonial moments, through and beyond the postcolonial period of the mid-twentieth century. In many revisionist readings, Caliban becomes a more central and sympathetic figure. In some productions, dating as early as the turn of the last century, he is a loner and a misunderstood "hero," dispossessed of his birthright by the invading Europeans. From W. H. Auden's poem *The Sea and the Mirror* (1944) to Césaire's *Une Tempête*, an adaptation explicitly made "for a Black theater," to films as diverse as *Forbidden Planet* (1956) and *Prospero's Books* (1991), *The Tempest* has retained its power and fascination.

But is Prospero's enchanted island in the Old World or the New World? The play's indebtedness to many New World texts is evident in its descriptions: the storm in the "still-vexed Bermudas"; the native inhabitants, often associated by critics with American Indians; the echoes of Jamestown and the early Virginia tracts, as well as of Montaigne's influential account of New World natives. In literal geographical terms, however, the island must be located in the Mediterranean Sea, not far from the coast of Africa. The King and court party are returning from the wedding of Claribel to an African in Tunis, and Sycorax hails from Algiers ("Argier"). Scholars have also begun to remind us that an even closer island, one actually within the "British isles," was famed for the wildness of its inhabitants, linking Ireland as yet another colonial space evoked by the play's suggestively rich and elusive landscape. That *all* of these associations seem germane is now virtually taken for granted.

What is most magical about the isle, however, is that in being many places at once, geographically, culturally, and mythographically hybrid, it eludes location and becomes a space for poetry, and for dream. It is not found on any map. Prospero's enchanted island, while drawn from real explorations and published accounts, is ultimately a country of the mind. And this is made clear by the very structure of the play, which starts out in medias res,° in clamor, in shipwreck, and in darkness.

As *The Tempest* begins, the audience finds itself in the middle of a storm at sea. All around is confusion: "A tempestuous noise of thunder and lightning heard." Voices cry out, seemingly from nowhere, in disconnected fragments that recall other Shakespearean storms, and other romances.

BOATSWAIN: Keep your cabins; you do assist the storm.
GONZALO: Nay, good, be patient.

[I, i, 12–14]

These lines might have come from the shipwreck scene in *Pericles*, where the nurse Lychorida urges the King in very similar words: "Patience, good sir, do not assist the storm."

"What care these roarers for the name of king?" cries the Boatswain in despair. This is an echo of the storm in *The Winter's Tale*, in which the nobleman Antigonus was torn to pieces by the bear. Those waves, too, "roared," with no regard for such cultural niceties as rank and status. This present tempest, the tempest in the play that bears that name, is thus somehow the quintessential storm, the "perfect" storm, distilled of all the Shakespearean tempests we have weathered before, from *Othello* and *King Lear* to the romances. Indeed, this scene is often played in total darkness, emphasizing the confusion and disorder.

in medias res: In the middle of things.

Pedro Calderón de la Barca

Calderón (1600–1681) is one of Spain's greatest poets and dramatists of the Golden Age—the early and mid-seventeenth century. This was a time when Lope de Vega (1562–1635) dominated the stage and fashioned the form of the popular drama as a three-act structure, with the opening act establishing the issues and characters, the second act developing the conflict, and the third act resolving the problems raised by the drama. Lope established the form of the *comedia* (tragicomic social drama) in his *The New Art of Play Writing* (1609), and Calderón followed Lope's structure.

The Golden Age also produced Spain's greatest painters—El Greco (1541–1614), Murillo (1617–1682), and Velásquez (1599–1660). The abundance and significance of art during the Golden Age resulted in part from the fact that, during most of this period, King Philip IV brought artists to court and provided them with studios. Velásquez painted many portraits of King Philip, who visited his studio daily. Likewise, the theater was nurtured by the court throughout this period. Lope was the first court playwright; when he died in 1635, Calderón took his place.

Calderón came from a well-to-do family ruled by a difficult and tyrannical father. He went first to the University of Alcalá and then to the university at Salamanca, where he studied law and probably theology. He changed his original plan to become a priest and began writing plays in 1623. Apparently the king—or perhaps the powerful prime minister, Olivares—became aware of Calderón's work and brought him into the court circle, giving him the opportunity to produce a variety of plays. Despite the fact that Spain's power and wealth were eroding rapidly, Philip's court maintained an extensive program of lavish entertainment. Some historians have seen this behavior as an escapist refusal to believe that most of the immense wealth in gold and silver brought back twice yearly from the Americas was already pledged to wars, insurrections, and entertainment. Not long after Calderón died, the nation was virtually bankrupt.

The opportunities afforded him at court made it possible for Calderón to produce elaborate entertainments, especially after Olivares built a new court suitable for more brilliant productions in 1634. The old court, the Alcázar, was dark, small, and depressing. The new court was large, elegant, and expressive. It demanded a steady stream of entertainments.

The popular stage was often an open-air theater similar to the Elizabethan theater of Shakespeare's time. Scenery was minimal, costumes rarely more than suggestions, and lighting natural. Plays were put on in the afternoon, at 3 o'clock in the summer and at 2 o'clock in the winter. But at court, lighting was provided by candles and oil lamps, scenic backgrounds were possible, and costuming was imaginative.

In Calderón's remarkable output as a playwright, he may have produced as many as a hundred one-act religious plays for the feast of Corpus Christi. These *auto sacramentales* are allegorical plays, usually about saints' lives and similar to medieval miracle plays. Some of these plays were widely admired, such as *The Constant Prince* (1629), about the martyrdom of Portuguese prince Ferdinand; *The Wonder-Working Magician* (1637), about a Faust character; and *The Two Lovers of Heaven* (1640). Nearly eighty of these plays survive.

Calderón wrote many secular dramas as well as *zarzuelas*, a form that combined music, dance, and drama and that developed into his operas, in which the dialogue is set to music. Among his most important secular plays are *The Surgeon of His Honor* (1635), *Life Is a Dream* (1635), *The Mayor of Zalamea* (1640), and *Daughter of the Air* (1653). Each of these plays is powerful, but *Life Is a Dream* has become the most enduring and the most often produced of his plays. He wrote it in his favorite baroque style—*Gongorism,* named for an earlier baroque poet, Luis de Góngora y Argote (1561–1627), whose style is marked by references to mythology, stylistic excesses, and complexity of language and thought. In translation many of these stylistic effects are lost, although *Life Is a Dream* is marked by complexity of thought even in English.

In 1651, Calderón took religious orders and retired from the popular stage, but he continued to write for the court. He eventually became an honorary chaplain to Philip and spent much of his time at court in Madrid even while officially assigned to Toledo.

Life Is a Dream

For discussion questions and assignments on *Life Is a Dream*, visit **bedfordstmartins.com/jacobus.**

The central action of *Life Is a Dream* is the conversion, or "rebirth," of Prince Sigismund. The action of the subplot is the recovery of Rossaura's honor after her seduction by the foreign duke Aistulf. These two strands of action intertwine when Rossaura helps Sigismund begin to understand the true nature of the world, and he helps her regain her honor once he is recognized by the people of Poland as the true heir of his father.

Life Is a Dream, often called Spain's *Hamlet,* is one of Calderón's philosophical plays. It centers on self-discovery and the untrustworthiness of illusion. Like Hamlet, Sigismund spends part of the second act of the play trying to decide the truth of his experiences: Were they real, or were they a dream? Is life real or a dream? The concept of life as a dream comes from Eastern thought and was commonly discussed in the seventeenth century. Skepticism—the reluctance to believe in the knowledge gathered by the senses—was widespread in this age. Both Shakespeare and Calderón were influenced by the revival of classical skepticism, and both examined experience in an effort to discover truth.

When the play opens, Sigismund is imprisoned and baffled at his lack of freedom. He does not know that his horoscope predicted at his birth that he would grow up to be a tyrant who would conquer his father, King Vasily. As a result, Vasily placed him in a prison with Clothold as his guard and tutor. But the aging Vasily, concerned with the succession of his throne, has second thoughts and suspects that the horoscope might be wrong. He releases Sigismund to observe his behavior: if he seems tyrannical, he will be reimprisoned and told that his moments of freedom were a dream; if he is prudent, he will inherit the crown.

Rossaura arrives searching for Aistulf, the man who wronged her. She is disguised as a man and is present when Vasily experiments with freeing Sigismund. Sigismund behaves tyrannically, doing what he wants when he wants with no thought for anyone else. He is in a sense a "natural" man because he had not been socialized in a normal family or in normal surroundings. But before he is returned to prison, he falls in love with Rossaura, and his love for her begins the process of his conversion.

Once returned to prison, Sigismund believes his experience of freedom was a dream until he reflects on Rossaura. His memory of her begins to convince him that he truly experienced freedom after all. Ultimately, the people resist the imposition of a foreign king, Aistulf, Duke of Muscovy, and storm the prison to free Sigismund. He is a changed man who realizes that he must temper his desires and consider other people's feelings. At the head of an army, he defeats his father, Vasily. When his father bows before him, he in turn bows before his father, thus demonstrating his allegiance and his conversion from a wrathful tyrant. Rossaura is a central part of Sigismund's metamorphosis. She may be an allegorical representation of feminine (and therefore civilizing) beauty or humanity. Sigismund pledges to help her recover her honor. Prince Aistulf is revealed as a seducer, and Sigismund is a wiser and more compassionate person.

Life Is a Dream in Performance

Like *Hamlet*, Calderón's *Life Is a Dream* has been produced often since its first appearance in 1635. Ironically, modern productions in Spain are infrequent because the Spanish are reluctant to tamper with the original verse, which is difficult and unusual. Federico García Lorca produced it in Spain in 1932, respecting the conventions of classic Spanish theater. The Teatro Español produced a full version in 1982. Productions in other parts of the world have, since the first English version in London in 1899, been frequent and interesting. Among the several modern New York versions was the 1981 production directed by María Irene Fornés. Anne Bogart did a highly praised "pictorially 'Spanish'" production in Cambridge, Massachusetts, in 1989 using Edwin Honig's translation. José Rivera's somewhat vaudevillean adaptation appeared in Hartford in 1998 and in New York in 2000, titled *Sueño*.

Another modern production was that by the Royal Lyceum Theatre Company of Scotland at the Brooklyn Academy of Music in 1999. This was a high-energy, powerful drama that concentrated on the pain and bewilderment of Sigismund, who appeared much of the time bearing a large chain, symbolic of his imprisonment. The stage was simple: a twenty-five-foot circle of broken stones over which hung a huge picture-frame mirror tilted to show only part of the action and to mirror the reality of the stage action in an unreal way throughout. The director, Calixto Bieito, from Barcelona, compressed the action into one two-hour act, relying for clarity on some long speeches of exposition and explanation. He also included two Spanish musicians singing Flamenco songs and beating Flamenco rhythms in the background—a haunting accompaniment.

In February 2007, the South Coast Repertory Theatre of Costa Mesa, California, produced *Life Is a Dream* in another new translation and adaptation by the Pulitzer Prize–winning playwright Nilo Cruz. Cruz, author of *Anna in the Tropics,* has said that this is his favorite play in part because of its lyrical language and the questions it poses about the nature of humanity. The Donmar Warehouse in London produced an adaptation of *Life Is a Dream* in two acts by Helen Edmundson in 2009, and the Santa Fe Opera produced Pulitzer Prize–winning composer Lewis Spratlan's operatic version in its 2010 season. Both of these productions received strong reviews.

The following translation by Michael Kidd is in prose rather than poetry. It achieves great accuracy by avoiding the linguistic difficulties imposed by the restrictions of English poetic forms.

PEDRO CALDERÓN DE LA BARCA (1600–1681)

Life Is a Dream 1635

TRANSLATED BY MICHAEL KIDD

Characters:

ROSSAURA, *a lady*
SIGISMUND, *a prince*
CLOTHOLD, *an old man*
STELLA, *a princess*
SOLDIERS

BUGLE, *a foolish lackey*
VASILY, *the king*
AISTULF, *a prince* [*and duke*]
GUARDS
MUSICIANS

[SERVANTS AND COURT ATTENDANTS]

ACT 1 • Scene 1

([*Deserted mountainside at twilight, near the entrance to a tower.*] *Enter Rossaura at the top of a mountain, disguised as a man dressed for the road. She makes her way down the mountain as she begins to speak, [addressing the horse from which she has been thrown*].)

ROSSAURA: Hippogriff,° monstrous hippogriff, peer of the wind! You're a lightning bolt with no flame, a bird with no colour, a fish with no scales, a brute with no base instinct. Where do you speed off to: bucking, lurching, and bolting before the obscure labyrinth of those barren crags? Stay, then, on this mountaintop, a Phaethon° to the brutes; while I, a woman with no direction but that offered by the laws of fate, will descend in blindness and desperation the twisted face of this lofty cliff, whose scowling brow withers in the sun. Poorly, Poland, do you greet the foreigner, for you write his entrance to your sands in blood, and hardly is he come when he comes into hardship. I'm at the mercy of my luck, but where did an unlucky wretch ever turn for mercy?

(*Enter Bugle, a foolish lackey.*)

BUGLE: Make that two unlucky wretches, and don't forget me back at camp when you start lodging complaints. For if it was two of us who left our fatherland to seek adventures, and two of us who, amid misfortune and madness, arrived at this spot, and two of us who came rolling down the mountain, can't I rightly

Note: Bracketed items are editorial interpolations.
hippogriff: Mythological beast that is part horse, part eagle, and part lion.   Phaethon: Son of Helios, who lets him drive the chariot of the sun for one day.

complain if you make me party to the sorrow and leave me out of the settlement?

ROSSAURA: I didn't want to involve you in my complaints, Bugle, and take away your right to consolation through the expression of your own distress; for there is such pleasure to be gained from complaining, a philosopher once said, that one should go in search of misfortunes just to be able to complain about them.

BUGLE: That philosopher was a scruffy drunk who deserves a thousand slaps in the face! I'd like to see how he enjoys lamenting then. But really, my lady, what are we to do now: on foot, alone, and lost at such an hour on a deserted mountainside, with the sun heading fast for the horizon?

ROSSAURA: Who ever heard of such strange happenings? Yet unless my vision suffers from the deceptions of fantasy, I think I see some kind of building in the flickering twilight.

BUGLE: Either my desire is deceiving me, or I see the same thing.

ROSSAURA: Lying crudely among the barren crags, it's a palace so minute that even the sunlight barely reaches it. Its crude architecture is such that it could pass for a boulder that rolled off the mountaintop and settled at the foot of all these rocks and crags that strive toward the sun's warmth.

BUGLE: Let's draw closer and not lose time in speculation, my lady, for it's preferable to be received with generosity by whoever lives inside.

ROSSAURA: The door — or better yet, the gloomy mouth — is open, and from its depths the night, conceived inside, issues forth.

(*They hear the sound of chains [from inside the tower].*)

BUGLE: What's that sound, heavens!

ROSSAURA: I'm paralyzed, a mass of frozen fire.

BUGLE: I hear the sound of chains; I'll be damned if it's not the ghost of a galley slave. My fear says it all.

(*Sigismund's voice is heard from inside the tower.*)

SIGISMUND: Oh, what a miserable, unlucky wretch am I!

ROSSAURA: What's that sad voice I hear! I'm struggling with new sufferings and torments!

BUGLE: And I with new fears.

ROSSAURA: Bugle!

BUGLE: My lady!

ROSSAURA: We must flee the severities of this haunted tower!

BUGLE: I don't even have the stomach to flee, should I be forced to.

ROSSAURA: Is there not a faint light in that decrepit glow, that pale star, which, in faltering swoons, flickering warmth, and trembling radiance, makes the dark room more shadowy with its feeble glow? Yes, for in its flicker I can make out, though from afar, a dark prison that serves as grave to a living corpse. And to my even greater astonishment, clothed in the skins of a beast lies a man bound in chains and accompanied only by the light. Since we can't flee, let's listen to his misfortunes from here and see what he says.

(*A curtain is drawn back to reveal Sigismund with a candle, bound in chains and dressed in animal skins.*)

SIGISMUND: Oh, what a miserable, unlucky wretch am I! I seek to understand, heavens, given the way you treat me, what crime I committed against you with my birth; although if I was born, I already understand my crime. Your sentence and its harshness have due cause, for birth itself is man's greatest offence. But I would just like to know, to ease my distress — leaving aside, heavens, the offence of birth — what else I did to merit further punishment. Weren't others born? And if so, what privileges were they granted that I've never enjoyed? Birds are born, and with the regalia that decorates them in finest beauty, hardly do they attain the stature of a feathered flower or a winged bouquet when they cut swiftly through the ethereal chambers, overcoming devotion to the nest that they leave behind in tranquillity. Yet I, with more soul, have less liberty? Brutes are born, with their coats of dappled beauty, and hardly do they reflect the constellations above, thanks to divine artistry, when they become reckless and cruel, and human necessity, teaching them cruelty, makes them monsters in its labyrinth. Yet I, with gentler instinct, have less liberty? Fish are born, unbreathing miscarriages of algae and slime, and hardly do these scaly ships see themselves upon the waves when they begin to lurch in all directions, measuring the ocean's vastness with the full capacity of their frigid core. Yet I, with greater will, have less liberty? Streams are born, snakes winding through the flowers, and hardly do these silvery serpents begin to twist among the flowers when they celebrate with music the mercy of the heavens that grant them majestic flight through the open field. Yet I, with more life, have less liberty? Suffering like this turns me into a volcano, an Etna, and I should like to rip pieces of my heart from my breast. What law, what sentence, what cause is capable of denying men the sweet privilege, the fundamental charter that God grants to crystalline waters, to fish, to brutes, and to birds?

ROSSAURA: His words have filled me with fear and pity.

SIGISMUND: Who's been listening to me? Is it Clothold?

BUGLE: (*Aside.*) Say yes.

ROSSAURA: It's only a poor wretch — Oh, miserable me! — who in these frigid caverns has overheard your melancholy words.

(*Sigismund grabs her.*)

SIGISMUND: Then you shall die by my hand, so you won't know that I know that you know my frailties. Simply because you've overheard me, I'm going to rip you to shreds in my mighty arms.

BUGLE: I'm deaf and haven't heard a word you've said.

ROSSAURA: If you're human by birth, my kneeling at your feet will be sufficient cause for you to spare me.

SIGISMUND: Your voice has filled me with sympathy; your appearance, with awe; and your deference, with confusion. Who are you? For although I know so little of the world here, for this tower is both my cradle and my grave; and although since birth, if mine can be called a birth, I know only this crude wasteland where I live miserably like a living skeleton or a breathing cadaver; and although I've never seen or spoken to anyone but the man who frequents this place and understands my misfortunes, from whom I know something of Heaven and earth: and although here — to give you more cause for astonishment, that you may call me a human monster — amid bewilderment and chimeras, I am a man among beasts and a beast among men; and although, amid such grim misfortunes, I have studied the art of government through the example of brutes and the counsel of birds, and have measured the orbits of the gentle heavenly bodies; you alone — you — have eased the agony of my anger, the bewilderment of my eyes, the amazement of my ears. Each glimpse of you increases my amazement, and the more I look at you the more I desire to look. My eyes must suffer from the dropsy,° since when drinking means death, they drink more, and thus, seeing that sight kills me, I'm dying to see. But let me see you and die, for now that I've succumbed I can't imagine, if seeing you brings me death, what not seeing you would bring. It would be beyond death; death of that sort — I've pondered its severity — would be savage ire, rage, and intense grief, for to give life to an unfortunate wretch is tantamount to giving death to a happy soul.

ROSSAURA: I'm so astonished by looking at you and so amazed by listening to you that I don't know what to say to you or what to ask you. I will say only that Heaven has led me here today in order to console me, if he who is unfortunate can gain consolation from seeing another even more so. The story is told of a wise man who one day reached such a point of poverty and misery that his only nourishment came from eating the grasses he picked. Can there be anyone else, he would say to himself, poorer and sadder than I? And when he turned his head he found the answer, for there was another wise man gathering the blades that he'd discarded. I lived in this world

dropsy: Disorder in which retention of liquid causes swelling.

John Ortiz as Sigismund hangs over Rossaura (Michi Barall) and Bugle (Jan Leslie Harding), who contemplate the significance of his imprisonment. From José Rivera's 1998 Hartford Stage Company production of *Sueño*. This scene is visually reminiscent of Leonardo da Vinci's drawing of the "measure of man" as well as emblems of the crucifixion.

resentful of fortune, and just when I was asking myself, Can there be anyone else with more miserable
luck? you responded mercifully, for in applying the
moral of my story, I find that you would have taken
up my sufferings and treated them as joys. And if by
chance my sufferings might give you some relief, listen to them carefully, and feel free to take any that
are left over. I am . . .

CLOTHOLD: (*Offstage.*) Tower guards! Through sleep
or cowardice, you've given passage to two people
who've broken through, the prison perimeter.

ROSSAURA: (*Aside.*) What new confusion is this!

SIGISMUND: That's Clothold, my jailer; my misfortunes
haven't ended yet.

CLOTHOLD: (*Offstage.*) Come quickly and, with vigilance, seize them or kill them before they can defend
themselves! (*In unison with the Guards, offstage.*)
Treason!

BUGLE: Tower guards who let us in here: since we have a
choice, I think seizing us would be easier.

(*Enter Clothold with a gun, accompanied by Soldiers,
all with their faces covered.*)

CLOTHOLD: Keep your faces covered, all of you; it's an
important precaution that will keep anyone from
recognizing us while we're here.

BUGLE: What's this, a damn costume party?

CLOTHOLD: O you, whose ignorance of this forbidden site
has led you past its enclosed perimeter against the
decree of the king, who has prohibited anyone from
daring to behold the monstrosity that lies amidst
these boulders; surrender your arms and your lives,
or this pistol, a metallic viper, will spit forth a piercing venom of two bullets, deafening the air with its
shots.

SIGISMUND: Before, O tyrannical master, you can offend
or injure them, my life will become the spoils of these
miserable fetters. For despite their restraint, by God,
I will tear myself to shreds with own my hands and
teeth, here among these very crags, before I consent
to the misfortune of these strangers and bewail their
abuse.

CLOTHOLD: If you know that your misfortunes, Sigismund,
are so great that even before your birth you were
condemned to die by the dictates of the stars; if you
know that these prison walls were built to serve as
brake and rein to your arrogant fury, what are you
boasting about? Guards, close the door to that narrow cell and lock him away inside.

[TOP] Sigismund (John Ortiz) in prison holding his symbolic
chains while Rossaura looks on in José Rivera's production
of *Sueño* at the Hartford Stage. [BOTTOM] George Anton as
Sigismund in Calixto Bieito's Royal Lyceum Theatre production of *Life Is a Dream* at the Brooklyn Academy of Music,
October 1999. The chains he carries symbolize his imprisonment and his torment.

(*They lock him in the tower, and he speaks from within.*)

SIGISMUND: Oh, heavens, how rightly you act in stripping me of my liberty, for otherwise I would fight you like a giant who, to shatter the crystal sphere of the sun, piles mountains of jasper atop foundations of stone.

CLOTHOLD: Perhaps, precisely so that you won't do so, you suffer so many hardships today.

ROSSAURA: I see how his pride so offended you, and I would be a fool if I didn't beg you humbly for my life, which lies in your power. Let yourself be moved by my submission, for it would be unduly severe if neither pride nor humility found favour with you.

BUGLE: And if you're unmoved by Humility and Pride, two characters that have moved and stirred a thousand allegorical plays, I shall, neither humbly nor proudly but somewhere in between, ask you for your help and shelter.

CLOTHOLD: [*To the Soldiers.*] Attention!

SOLDIERS: Sir!

CLOTHOLD: Strip them both of their arms and blindfold them, so they won't see how or from where they're leaving.

ROSSAURA: [*Touching her sword, still in its sheath.*] Here's my sword, which can be surrendered only to you because, after all, you're the commander, and it is incapable of surrendering to anyone of lesser rank.

BUGLE: Mine is such that it can be given to the lowest of the low. [*To one of the Soldiers.*] Here, you take it.

ROSSAURA: And if I am to die, I wish to leave you, as proof of my loyalty, an item whose value was determined by he who once wore it. I ask you to keep it safe because, although I don't know what secret it holds, I do know that this golden sword conceals great mysteries, for I have come to Poland to avenge a dishonour with nothing else to vouch for me. [*She unsheathes the sword and hands it to Clothold, who cannot contain his astonishment.*]

CLOTHOLD: (*Aside.*) Good heavens! What's the meaning of this? My sufferings and confusions, my anxieties and sorrows, are now compounded.

[*To Rossaura.*] Who gave it to you?

ROSSAURA: A woman.

CLOTHOLD: What was her name?

ROSSAURA: I'm obliged not to reveal that.

CLOTHOLD: How do you suspect or know that it holds some secret?

ROSSAURA: She who gave it to me said: "Leave for Poland and, through ingenuity, deliberation, or artifice, let the noble and powerful see you with this sword, for I know that one of them will offer you favour and shelter." She wouldn't say whom she meant in case he might be dead.

CLOTHOLD: (*Aside.*) Heaven help me! What am I hearing! Is this an illusion or reality? This is the sword I left with the lovely Viola, signalling that anyone who came back wearing it would find me as loving as a son and as faithful as a father. So what am I to do now—Oh, miserable me!—amid such confusion, when he who brings the sword seeking favour can find only death, insofar as he comes before me doomed by the king's edict? What terrible confusion! What sad fate! What inconstant luck! This is my son; his appearance confirms what I know in my heart, which, longing to see him, calls to my breast, beats its wings within, and, unable to break the lock, does as he who, confined indoors, leans out of the window upon hearing a noise in the street. And thus, not knowing what's happening, my heart hears the noise and rushes to look out through my eyes—the windows to my soul—through which it escapes in the form of tears. What am I to do? Heaven help me! What am I to do? To take him to the king is to take him—Oh, what tragedy!—to his death, and I can't hide him from the king without violating the laws of fealty. On the one hand I am swayed by self-interest, on the other by loyalty to the king. But how can there really be any doubt? Doesn't loyalty to the king come before all else? So loyalty it shall be, and away with self-interest. Besides, I recall now that he said he's come to Poland to avenge a dishonour, and everyone knows that a dishonoured man is contemptible, so he can't be my son. He's not my son and doesn't share my noble blood. But then again, if the affront was inescapable—for honour is of such fragile substance that it can be shattered with a single deed or blemished with a whisper—what more could a nobleman do in his defence, what more than to go looking for his remedy at all cost? He *is* my son, he *does* share my blood, for his courage is great! And thus, in the face of so much doubt, my best option is go to the king, inform him that he's my son, and acknowledge that he must die. Perhaps the very depth of my loyalty will move his heart; and if I manage to preserve my son's life, then I'll help him avenge his dishonour; but if the king remains steadfast in his severity and sentences him to death, then he shall die without knowing that I'm his father.

[*To Rossaura and Bugle.*] Come with me, foreigners. Fear not, no, that you lack company in your misfortunes; for amid such doubt, where life hangs in the balance, I don't know whose misfortunes are greater. [*Exit all.*]

Scene 2

([*Palace of King Vasily of Poland.*] *Enter, on one side, Aistulf in the company of Soldiers, and on the other, Stella with her Ladies-in-waiting. Music plays in the background.*)

AISTULF: Upon seeing the brilliant flashes that were comets, the drums and the trumpets along with the birds and the streams do well in mixing their diverse greetings; for, with equal music and awesome wonder before your celestial image, the birds are feathered bugles and the instruments, metallic birds. And thus you are greeted, my lady, as Queen by the salvos, as Aurora° by the birds, as Pallas° by the trumpets, and as Flora° by the flowers. Because, in mocking the day that the night now banishes, you are Aurora in happiness, Flora in peace, Pallas in war, and Queen in my soul.

STELLA: If words are to be judged by actions, you do not fare well in pronouncing courtly compliments that are so easily contradicted by all that clamorous brass [*pointing to the Soldiers*], which has already met my bold resistance; for the flattery I'm hearing from you, as I see it, does not agree with the severe show of force that I'm observing. And take note that it's a base action, worthy only of the deception and treachery of beasts, to flatter with the mouth and kill with the mind.

AISTULF: You're very poorly informed, Stella, in questioning the sincerity of my compliments, so I beseech you: hear my cause before you judge my intentions. When Eustorgius the Third, King of Poland, passed away, he left Vasily as his heir, along with two daughters, from whom you and I were born. I won't tire you with details that have no place here. Clorilyn, your mother and my superior, who now rests under a canopy of stars in a sweeter realm, was the eldest, and you're her daughter. Next came my mother and your aunt, the gallant Grethissunda, may God keep her a thousand years. She married the Duke of Muscovy and gave birth to me. Now here's the issue, my lady: Vasily, who's already succumbing to the inevitable contempt of time, and who was always more inclined to academic pursuits than to women, is widowed and childless, and you and I both aspire to this country's throne. You contend that you're the daughter of the elder sister; I, that I was born a man and that, even though my mother was the younger sister, I should receive preference. We have both informed our uncle of our intentions; he responded that he wished to resolve our dispute, and we settled on this place and this day. With this intention I left my land in Muscovy; with the same intention I have arrived here, unprepared to go to war, only to find you waging it against me. Oh, would that Love, a wise god, move the people, always a sound astrologer, to grant us a sound judgment today and end this meeting by making you Queen—Queen of my will. Thus you would be, to your greater honour, crowned by our uncle, rewarded by your valour, and recognized as sovereign by my love.

STELLA: To such courtly generosity my heart responds no less in turn, for I, simply to make this imperial monarchy yours, would be happy to claim it as mine; yet, though my love is not convinced that you are

insincere, in all you say I fear you are contradicted by that locket hanging about your breast.

AISTULF: I'll resolve your doubts about that . . . but not now, for all those clamorous instruments indicate that the king and his court are approaching.

(*Flourish. Enter King Vasily—an old man—and his Attendants.*)

STELLA: Wise Thales,°
AISTULF: Learned Euclid,°
STELLA: who governs today
AISTULF: who lives today
STELLA: by the constellations
AISTULF: by the stars
STELLA: and charts
AISTULF: and glosses and measures
STELLA: their courses,
AISTULF: their tracks,
STELLA: allow me, with humble bonds,
AISTULF: allow me, with tender embraces,
STELLA: to be the ivy upon your trunk.
AISTULF: to surrender myself at your feet.
VASILY: Dear niece and nephew, let me embrace you. And insofar as you both come here, true to my loving ways, with your own show of affection, trust that I will leave neither of you with cause for complaint, and you shall both be treated fairly. And now, confessing weariness from the heavy burden of my years, I solicit only your silence, for the subject matter itself will solicit your amazement. You know well—and please listen carefully, my beloved niece and nephew, illustrious court of Poland, vassals, relatives, and friends—you know well that my knowledge has earned me the nickname of Learned in world opinion; thus, in defiance of time and oblivion, paintings worthy of Timanthes° and sculptures worthy of Lysippus° proclaim me the great Vasily around the globe. You know also that the knowledge I most cultivate and admire lies in subtle mathematics, in whose name I rob time and exempt fame of the jurisdiction and task of making new revelations with the passing of each day. For when in my charts I witness happenings of the coming centuries, I earn the thanks owed to time for revealing what I have told. Those snowy spheres, those glass canopies illuminated by the sun's rays and encircled by the moon's beams, those diamond orbs, those crystalline globes adorned by the stars and crisscrossed by the Zodiac, have received the greatest attention of my years; they are the books in which, on diamond-studded paper bound in sapphire, with diverse characters etched in gold lines, Heaven records our deeds, whether adverse or auspicious. These books I read with such swiftness

---

Aurora: The goddess of dawn. **Pallas:** The goddess Athena, who appears with lance and shield. **Flora:** The goddess of flowers.

Thales: Greek astronomer (c. 624–546 BCE) considered the first Western philosopher. **Euclid:** Greek mathematician and geometer (fl. 300 BCE). **Timanthes:** Greek painter (c. 400 BCE). **Lysippus:** Greek sculptor (c. 300 BCE).

that I follow in spirit their rapid movements across the sky's corridors and pathways. If only Heaven had taken my life as the first casualty of its ire, if only I had foreseen my tragedy in its writings before my ingenuity began to gloss the margins and index the pages. Even success is a double-edged sword for the unlucky, and he who is pricked by knowledge ends up destroying himself. I say this to you myself, although my actions will speak more eloquently, and once again I ask that silence accompany your amazement. By Clorilyn, my wife, I had an unlucky son, upon whose birth the heavens ran out of omens before he had been freed into the beautiful light from the living grave of the womb, for thus are birth and death akin. Time and again his mother, seized by the images and hallucinations of dreams, watched as a monster in human form brazenly broke through her entrails and, drenched in her blood, killed her, a once-in-a-century human viper. The day of the birth arrived, and, in fulfilment of the omens—for the irreverent are often proved true—he was born under such a horoscope that the sun, reddened by its blood, was viciously entering into a duel with the moon; and with Earth as spectator, the two divine torches fought not in hand to hand combat but with the volleys of their brilliant rays. It was the greatest, most horrendous eclipse the sun has ever suffered since it shed tears of blood over Christ's death; and the globe, bathed in raging fires, presumed itself to be in the grips of the apocalypse. The heavens darkened, buildings trembled, the clouds rained stones, and the rivers ran with blood. Under this miserable, under this fatal planet or sign Sigismund was born, indicating his nature with the death of his mother, a savage act of which he said: "I am man, for already I've begun poorly to repay my benefactors." Resorting to my studies, I saw in them and in everything that Sigismund would be the wildest of men, the cruellest of princes, and the most perverse of monarchs, bringing polarization and division to the kingdom, like a school of treachery or an academy of vice; and that, driven by his fury and wavering between bewilderment and transgression, he would trample me beneath his heels, and I, vanquished and prostrate before his feet, would—what anxiety it causes me to say the words!—offer the grey hair of my beard as a doormat to his boots. Who doesn't take peril seriously, especially when it is revealed through the research on which his self-interest depends? Thus, lending credence to the soothsaying fates that had foretold the peril in their fatal prophecies, I determined to lock up the beast that had been born, to see if a wise man might master the stars. It was announced that the prince was stillborn, and I, ever cautious, had a tower built among the crags and bluffs of those mountains, where the light of day scarcely makes its way, so heavily do the crude obelisks guard the entrance. The severe penalties and laws that, by public proclamation, prohibited anyone from entering the mountain's forbidden zone were made necessary by the reasons I have told you. There lives Sigismund, in misery, destitution, and confinement, where only Clothold has spoken to him, dealt with him, and seen him. The only witness to his miseries, Clothold has taught him natural law and instructed him in the Catholic faith. Three conclusions may be drawn from all this. First, that I hold you in such esteem, Poland, that I wish to spare you the oppression and rule of a tyrannical king, because any ruler who put his fatherland and empire in such danger couldn't be considered benevolent. Second is the consideration that to deprive my heir of the right he was given by human and divine sanction is not an act of Christian charity, for no law allows me, in trying to keep someone else from becoming tyrannical and barbaric, to become so myself; yet if my son is a tyrant, in order to prevent him from committing crimes, I must commit them myself. Third and last, I realize how erroneous it was to place easy credence in predictions of the future; for although the prince's inclination may place ruinous obstacles in his path, he might very well avoid them, because even the most contemptuous fate, the most monstrous inclination, or the most perverse planet can only influence the will, not force it. And so, after hesitating and reflecting over my options, I've come up with a solution that is sure to leave you dumbstruck. Tomorrow I shall place Sigismund – for this is his name – without his knowing that he is my son and your king, under my canopy, upon my throne, and in place of me, where he will govern and command you and where you will all swear docile obedience to him. In this way I shall accomplish three things, with which I can now respond to the three conclusions I pointed out earlier. First, that if he turns out to be prudent, rational, and kind, in complete contradiction of the fate that predicted so many things of him, you will all enjoy the reign of your rightful prince, who has grown up a courtier to the mountain and a neighbour to its beasts. Second, that if he turns out to be defiant, brazen, barbaric, and cruel and runs with free rein through the field of his vices, I shall have loyally fulfilled my obligation; and then, in ousting him, I shall behave as a successful king, for returning him to prison would not be cruelty but rather punishment. Third, that if he turns out to be the prince I just described, out of my love for you, my subjects, I shall give you a king and queen more worthy of my crown and sceptre: for my niece and nephew, uniting their two claims to the throne and reconciled to each other through the sanctity of marriage, will have what they have earned. This I command of you as a king; this I ask of you as a father; this I beg of you as a sage; this I say to you as an elder; and if kings are the humble slaves of their republics as Seneca the Spaniard said, this I beseech of you as a slave.

AISTULF: If it's up to me to respond, as he who presumably has the greatest interest here in the matter, I'll speak for everyone in saying let Sigismund come forward, for his being your son is reason enough.

ALL: Give us our prince, for we want him as our king!

VASILY: Vassals, I appreciate and value your goodwill. Accompany my niece and nephew, Atlases° of my old age, to their quarters, and tomorrow you will see him.

ALL: Long live the great King Vasily!

(Exit all. Before the king can leave, Clothold enters with Rossaura and Bugle and detains him.)

CLOTHOLD: May I speak with you?

VASILY: Oh, Clothold! You are most welcome.

CLOTHOLD: Although bowing before your presence is always welcoming, this time, my lord, a gloomy and contemptuous fate has forced a break in the norms of protocol and custom.

VASILY: What's the matter?

CLOTHOLD: A grave misfortune, my lord, has befallen me, when it could have been a source of greatest joy.

VASILY: Explain.

CLOTHOLD: [*Pointing to Rossaura.*] This handsome young man, either daring or unknowing, entered the tower, my lord, where he saw the prince. And he's . . .

VASILY: Don't fret, Clothold. If this had happened another day, I confess I would have been alarmed. But I just spoke the tower's secret, so it doesn't matter that he knows it because I've revealed it. Come and see me later, because I have many things to report to you and much to ask of you; for you are to be, take note, the instrument of the greatest event the world has ever seen. And to those prisoners, so that you won't conclude I'm punishing your oversight, I grant pardon.

(Exit.)

CLOTHOLD: May you live a thousand centuries, great lord! (*Aside.*) Heaven has improved my luck. I won't tell anyone that he's my son now, since I can get by without doing so. [*To Rossaura and Bugle.*] Errant strangers, you are free to go.

ROSSAURA: I shall *adorn* your feet a thousand times with my kisses.

BUGLE: I'll just *adore* them from afar, for what's a letter or two between friends?

ROSSAURA: You have given me, sire, my life; and since I live in your debt, I shall be your eternal slave.

CLOTHOLD: What I've given you isn't life, for a well-born man has no life as long as he's dishonoured; and given that you've come here to avenge a dishonour, as you yourself have told me, I can't have given you life because you bring none with you; for a life lived in disrepute is no life. (*Aside.*) In this way I'll spur him on.

Atlas: Greek Titan who supported the earth on his back.

ROSSAURA: I confess that I remain without life despite receiving it from you; but through vengeance I shall leave my honour so unblemished that my life, in overcoming danger, may be recognized as your gift.

CLOTHOLD: Take back this burnished blade you brought with you, for I know that, when dyed in the blood of your enemy, it will be sufficient to avenge your dishonour; because any blade that was once mine—I mean "mine" in this instant, this brief period that I've held it in my power—is capable of avenging you.

ROSSAURA: In your name I arm myself with it a second time, and upon it I swear myself to revenge, even if my enemy were more powerful.

CLOTHOLD: Is he? By a lot?

ROSSAURA: So much so that I shall not tell you: not because I wouldn't entrust greater matters to your prudence but rather so that the advantage I behold in your devotion won't backfire on me.

CLOTHOLD: On the contrary, in telling me you would keep me on your side, for you would keep me from aiding your enemy. (*Aside.*) Oh, if only I could know who it is!

ROSSAURA: So that you won't think I underestimate your trust, know that my enemy is none other than Aistulf, Duke of Muscovy.

CLOTHOLD: (*Aside.*) This is more than I can bear, much worse than I'd imagined!

[*To Rossaura.*] Let's clarify matters. If you were born a Muscovite, your natural lord cannot have dishonoured you; return to your fatherland, then, and cast aside the burning impetuousness that propels you.

ROSSAURA: I'm certain that, even though he's my prince, he has dishonoured me.

CLOTHOLD: Impossible, even if he had dared to slap you in the face. (*Aside.*) Heavens!

ROSSAURA: My dishonour was greater.

CLOTHOLD: State it then, for you can't say anything more than I can imagine.

ROSSAURA: I would do so, but such is the respect with which I look upon you, the affection with which I worship you, the esteem in which I hold you, that I dare not tell you that my external trappings are a riddle, for their owner is not what appearances suggest. You decide: if I am not what I appear to be, and Aistulf has come here to marry Stella, can he not dishonour me? I have said enough.

(Exit Rossaura and Bugle.)

CLOTHOLD: Listen! Wait! Stop! What confusing labyrinth is this, where reason has lost its thread? My honour is besmirched, the enemy is powerful, I'm his vassal, and she's a woman: show me the way out, heavens! Although I'm not sure there is a way out when, in such a confusing abyss, Heaven is full of omens and earth is full of aberrations.

ACT 2 • Scene 1

(*[The palace.] Enter Vasily and Clothold.*)

CLOTHOLD: Everything has been carried out as you ordered.

VASILY: Tell me, Clothold, how it happened.

CLOTHOLD: In this way, my lord. With the soothing concoction you had compounded from a mixture of medicinal herbs, whose tyrannical properties and secret powers so dissipate, rob, and disorient human reasoning that they can turn a man into a living corpse, and whose potent qualities divest anyone under their influence of his senses and faculties . . . There's no need to prove that this is possible, for so many times, my lord, experience shows us, and it's true, that medicine is full of natural secrets, and there's no animal, plant, or stone that doesn't have a determined property; and if our human malice has experimented with a thousand poisons in search of their lethal qualities, is it surprising that, with a little less potency, a poison that kills could be made to induce sleep? Leaving aside doubts about whether this is possible, for it's been demonstrated through argument and evidence, I'll continue my story: with the concoction compounded of opium, belladonna, and henbane,° I descended to Sigismund's narrow prison. I talked with him a bit about the moral lessons he has been taught by the silence of the mountains and heavens, under whose divine instruction he has learned rhetoric from the birds and the beasts. To better elevate his spirit to the task you have in store for him, I proposed for discussion the swiftness of a majestic eagle that, as it scorned the sphere of the wind, was transformed, in the lofty regions of fire, into a feathery flare or a runaway comet. I praised its imperious flight, saying: "You are, after all, sovereign among birds, and thus it is natural that you consider yourself superior to all the rest." He needed no further prompting, for whenever the topic of sovereign power is discussed, he reasons with ambition and pride because his blood, of course, incites, moves, and animates him to great things, and he said: "To think that in the restive realm of birds there is one who commands obedience from all! In this matter my misfortunes console me, since, if I'm subservient to another, it's only by force, because I would never submit of my own free will to another man." Seeing him enraged by this idea, which tells the story of his grief, I invited him to drink from the potion, and hardly had the elixir passed from the glass to his breast when he surrendered his powers to sleep and a chill ran through his veins and organs such that, if I hadn't known it was a simulated death, I would have feared for his life. At this moment the people to whom you have entrusted the success of this endeavour are arriving and, placing him in a coach, are taking him to your quarters, which have been prepared with the majesty and grandeur worthy of his person. They will lay him upon your bed where, when the stupor wears off, they will attend to him as they do to you, my lord, for you have ordered it thus. And if having obeyed you has earned me any favour, I ask only — and forgive me my impropriety — that you tell me your intention in bringing Sigismund to the palace in this way.

VASILY: Clothold, your doubt is well founded, and I wish to satisfy it for you alone. The influence of my son Sigismund's star, as you know, threatens a thousand misfortunes and tragedies. I wish to study whether the stars — which are incapable of lying, especially when they've already given us, in the prince's cruel character, so many examples of their correctness — at least soften or temper their judgment and, won over through courage and prudence, retract their prediction; for man has mastery over the stars. I wish to study this matter by bringing the prince to a place where he'll discover he's my son and have his talent put to the test. If he overcomes his inclinations through magnanimity, he shall become king; but if he shows his cruel and tyrannical nature, I will return him to his chains. Now you'll ask why, for the purposes of the experiment, it was necessary to bring him asleep in this way. And I wish to answer all your doubts. If he were to discover today that he's my son and tomorrow found himself reduced again to his chains and misery, given his character he would no doubt fall into the sin of despair, because with the knowledge of who he is, what consolation would he have? And thus I have tried to leave myself an escape from that jeopardy by telling him that everything he saw was a dream. In this way two things may be examined. First: his character, for when he awakens, his actions will show us what he imagines and thinks. Second: a way to console him if he finds himself obeyed now and later reawakens in his cell, for he will conclude that he was dreaming, and he will be correct in that assumption because in this world, Clothold, everyone who lives dreams.

CLOTHOLD: I wouldn't be lacking in reasons to prove your error, but it's too late now for, from the look of things, the prince has awoken and is drawing near.

VASILY: I'm going to step out. You're his mentor; go to him and, with the truth, confront the many confusions that must be assailing his thoughts.

CLOTHOLD: So you give me permission to tell him the truth?

VASILY: Yes, for it may be that when he finds out, the danger will be more easily overcome because it's been understood.

(*Exit Vasily; enter Bugle.*)

BUGLE: (*Aside.*) At the expense of a good beating from a blond, halberd°-brandishing sentry whose beard matched the colour of his livery, I've pushed my way

---

henbane: A plant whose leaves, when combined with opium, can produce hysteria.

halberd: Lancelike weapon with an axe-head and sharp spike.

in to see all that's happening; because the best way to get an eyeful without bribing the usher is to focus elsewhere, for if you're shameless enough, there's more to see in the stands than on the stage.

CLOTHOLD: (*Aside.*) That's Bugle, servant to she who— Good heavens!—she who, dealing in misfortune, has relayed my offence to Poland.

[*To Bugle.*] Bugle, what's the news?

BUGLE: The news, my lord, is that the great generosity you show in your willingness to help Rossaura avenge her dishonour has encouraged her to resume dressing in her own clothing.

CLOTHOLD: A good decision, so that she not be judged indecent.

BUGLE: The news is that, changing her name and wisely calling herself your niece, she has enhanced her stature to such a degree that the remarkable Princess Stella has employed her as her lady-in-waiting.

CLOTHOLD: It is fitting that my name be used to defend her honour once and for all.

BUGLE: The news is that she's eagerly awaiting the moment in which you will act on behalf of her honour.

CLOTHOLD: That's a safe bet, for good things come to those who wait.

BUGLE: The news is that she is being pampered and attended to like a queen, thanks to calling herself your niece. And the news is that I, living beside her, am dying of hunger, for no one thinks about me, forgetting that my name is Bugle, and that if such a Bugle sounds off, it can inform the king, Aistulf, and Stella of everything that's happening; because bugles and servants are two things that don't get on very well with secrecy. And if silence ever abandons me, I may become the subject of that familiar tune, *A bugle that heralds the sun / Plays second to none.*

CLOTHOLD: Your complaint is well founded, and I shall attend to it; in the meantime, you may work for me.

BUGLE: Well here comes Sigismund.

(*Enter Musicians in song and Servants who are busily dressing Sigismund. The prince enters in astonishment.*)

SIGISMUND: Heaven help me, what am I seeing! Heaven help me, what am I watching! My doubt surpasses my dread. I, in a sumptuous palace? I, dressed in fine fabrics and brocades? I, surrounded by such elegant and refined servants? I, waking from sleep in such an exquisite bed? I, amid so many people intent on dressing me? To say I'm dreaming is deception; I know quite well that I'm awake. Am I not Sigismund? Heavens, reveal the truth to me. Tell me: what could have befallen my imagination as I slept, that I should find myself here? But whatever it was, why waste time wondering about it? Better to enjoy being served and let come what may.

SERVANT 2: He's so melancholy!

SERVANT 1: Well who wouldn't be, after going through this?

BUGLE: Me.

SERVANT 2: Go speak to him now.

SERVANT 1: [*To Sigismund.*] Shall I have them sing again?

SIGISMUND: No, I don't want any more singing.

SERVANT 2: You seem so shocked, I thought you might enjoy some entertainment.

SIGISMUND: I can't comfort my sorrows with their voices; military marches are the only music I enjoy listening to.

CLOTHOLD: Your Highness, my lord, allow me to kiss your hand; for my honour will be the first to offer you obedience.

SIGISMUND: (*Aside.*) This is Clothold, so how is it that he who mistreats me in prison now treats me with such respect? What's happening to me?

CLOTHOLD: In the immense confusion of your new surroundings, your thought and reason must be plagued by thousands of doubts. But I want to free you from all of them if—if that's possible—because you need to know, my lord, that you are the Crown Prince of Poland. If you have lived secluded and hidden from sight, it was due to the inclemency of fate, which sanctions a thousand tragedies for this realm once the kingly laurel leaf adorns your noble brow. Yet in the hope that, with caution, you might overcome the stars, for a virtuous man can do so, you've been brought to the palace from the tower in which you lived while your spirit was in the power of sleep. Your father, the king my lord, will come to see you shortly, and from him, Sigismund, you'll learn the rest.

SIGISMUND: Why you vile, contemptible traitor! What more need I learn, now that I know my true identity, in order to proclaim my pride and power from this point forward? How could you betray your fatherland by hiding me away, for you have denied me, against reason and law, my entitlement?

CLOTHOLD: Oh, miserable me!

SIGISMUND: You were a traitor to the law, a sycophant to the king, and a cruel jailor to me; and thus the king, the law, and I, amid such monstrous misfortune, condemn you to die by my hands.

SERVANT 2: My lord . . .

SIGISMUND: Let no one try to stop me, for it would be a useless endeavour and, by God, if you get in my way, I'll throw you out that window.

SERVANT 1: Flee, Clothold.

CLOTHOLD: (*Aside.*) Poor Sigismund, what excessive pride you demonstrate, unaware that it's all a dream! (*He flees.*)

SERVANT 2: Beware that . . .

SIGISMUND: Out of my way.

SERVANT 2: . . . he was obeying his king.

SIGISMUND: When the law isn't just, the king needn't be obeyed; and at any rate, I was his prince.

SERVANT 2: It wasn't for him to decide whether it was just or not.

SIGISMUND: You're asking for it, it would seem, with all that yapping.

BUGLE: What the prince says is very right, and what you did was very wrong.

SERVANT 1: Who gave you permission to speak?

BUGLE: I took it upon myself.

SIGISMUND: Who are you, pray tell?

BUGLE: A busybody, a job in which I reign supreme, because I'm the nosiest person on the face of the earth.

SIGISMUND: You're the only one in this princely world I find gratifying.

BUGLE: My lord, I'm a great gratifier of all worldly princes.

(*Enter Aistulf* [*hat in hand*].)

AISTULF: Infinitely lucky is this day, O prince, in which you proclaim yourself Poland's sun and fill its horizons with the brightness and bliss of your divine radiance, for you appear like the sun from beneath the mountains! Rise, then, and may the shining laurel leaf, so slow in crowning your brow, be as slow in withering. [*He dons his hat.*]

SIGISMUND: God keep you.

AISTULF: I'll forgive your meagre greeting only because you don't recognize me. I am Aistulf, Duke of Muscovy, and your cousin; we must treat each other as equals.

SIGISMUND: I said "God keep you." What more do you want? But since you don't find my greetings suitable to your high birth, next time I'll say "God damn you!"

SERVANT 2: (*To Aistulf.*) Consider, your highness, that he was raised in the mountains and treats everyone accordingly. (*To Sigismund.*) Aistulf, my lord, prefers to be addressed as . . .

SIGISMUND: I found it irritating the way he spoke to me so gravely, and the first thing he did was don his hat.

SERVANT 2: He's titled.

SIGISMUND: I'm more entitled!

SERVANT 2: All the same, it's fitting that there be greater decorum between the two of you than with others.

SIGISMUND: Who asked for your opinion anyway?

(*Enter Stella.*)

STELLA: Your highness, my lord, I welcome you warmly to the royal family, which gratefully receives you and desires your presence, and where, despite past deceptions, we wish you an august and celebrated reign and a life measured in centuries rather than years.

SIGISMUND: Tell me now, who is this imperial beauty? Who is this human goddess at whose divine feet Heaven surrenders its radiance? Who is this beautiful woman?

BUGLE: She is, my lord, your cousin Stella.

SIGISMUND: Stella . . . Stellar? More like Solar! [*To Stella.*] Although it were well to wish me well on the wealth that I inherit, I deserve more well-wishing just for having seen you today; and thus, I appreciate your well-wishing for finding myself before such unmerited wealth. Stella—whose waking is enough to please the brightest star—what is left for the sun to do if you rise with the day? Allow me to kiss your hand, from whose snowy chalice the gentle breeze drinks in radiance.

STELLA: Be a little more gentlemanly in the presence of the court.

AISTULF: (*Aside.*) If he takes her hand, I'm finished!

SERVANT 2: (*Aside.*) Aistulf's dismay is palpable; I must put a stop to this. (*To Sigismund.*) Beware, my lord, that it's not right to be so forward, and Aistulf is . . .

SIGISMUND: Didn't I tell you to stay out of my way?

SERVANT 2: I'm only saying what's right.

SIGISMUND: Everything you say annoys me. Nothing is right that contradicts my delight.

SERVANT 2: But my lord, I remember hearing you say that it's well to obey and serve what's right.

SIGISMUND: You also heard me say that I'd throw anyone who annoyed me off that balcony.

SERVANT 2: Men of my standing can't be treated that way.

SIGISMUND: Oh no? So help me God, I'll test that theory!

(*He grabs the Servant and rushes offstage, followed by the others. He returns shortly* [*with the others, minus the Servant*].)

AISTULF: I can't believe what I've just seen!

STELLA: Help, everyone! (*Exit.*)

SIGISMUND: Did you see how he dropped from the balcony to the sea below? By God, the test succeeded!

AISTULF: You should keep your rash impulses in greater check; for what separates men from beasts also separates a mountainside from a palace.

SIGISMUND: If you persist in acting so gravely and speaking with such presumption, next time you might not have a head to wear that hat on.

(*Exit Aistulf; enter Vasily.*)

VASILY: What's going on here?

SIGISMUND: Nothing. I threw a man who annoyed me off that balcony.

BUGLE: [*To Sigismund.*] Be aware that you're speaking to the king.

VASILY: Your first day here has already cost a life?

SIGISMUND: He told me it couldn't be done, and I won the bet.

VASILY: It's very distressing that, when I come to see you as prince, expecting to find you mindful, triumphing over fate and the stars, I find you acting with such severity that your first deed in power is a grave murder. How can I offer you love with open arms now, when I know your prideful embrace is trained in bringing death? Who ever looked without fear upon a naked dagger fresh from the kill? Who ever looked without emotion upon the bloody spot in which a man was murdered? Even the strongest among us responds to his instinct. And thus, seeing in your arms the instrument of this murder and recognizing the bloody spot where it happened, I withdraw from your arms; and, although I had planned to encircle your neck with loving embraces, I shall turn away empty-handed, for I fear the intent of your arms.

SIGISMUND: I can survive without your embraces as I have until now, for when a father is capable of using such severity against me and ungratefully casts me off, raises me like a beast, treats me like a monster, and solicits my death, it matters little that he withhold his embraces, for he has already denied me my humanity.

VASILY: By God and Heaven above, I wish I had never brought you into existence so as not to hear your voice and see your defiance now.

SIGISMUND: If you'd never brought me into existence, I'd have no complaint with you; but since you did, I do, because you then took it from me; for though to give is the noblest and most unique of all actions, to give only to take away later is the most despicable.

VASILY: What thanks I get for turning you from a poor and humble prisoner into the prince of Poland!

SIGISMUND: Well what's there to thank you for in that? You've been a tyrant to my free will. Old and decrepit, you're already at death's door, so what can you give me? Anything more than what's rightfully mine? You're my father and my king; thus all this splendour is mine by the rights of natural law. Thus, whatever rank I now enjoy I owe you nothing for, and I could even denounce you for the time you've kept me without liberty, life, and honour; so it is you who should thank me for not exacting from you what you owe.

VASILY: You are barbaric and reckless; the heavens have kept their word, and thus I appeal to the heavens now. So full of pride and presumption you are! And though you may now know your lineage and understand the deception in which you have lived, and though you find yourself in a place where you consider yourself superior to everyone else, take my advice seriously: act with humility and gentleness, for you might be dreaming even though you think you're awake. (*Exit.*)

SIGISMUND: Might be dreaming even though I think I'm awake? Impossible, for I feel and perceive the continuity between my past and present. And though you may be having second thoughts, there's no going back now; I know who I am, and you cannot, no matter how much you wail and moan, take away my birthright to this crown. And if you saw me before, weighed down by my chains, that was when I was unaware of my identity. But I know who I am now, and I know that I'm a composite of man and beast.

(*Enter Rossaura, dressed as a lady-in-waiting.*)

ROSSAURA: (*Aside.*) Now that I'm in the service of Stella, I'm in constant fear of running into Aistulf, for Clothold doesn't want him to know who I am or to see me because he says it's important for my honour. And I trust Clothold's intentions because I owe him a debt of gratitude for the refuge he has given my life and honour here in the palace.

BUGLE: What has pleased you most of all the wondrous things you've seen today?

SIGISMUND: Nothing has shocked me, for I was prepared for everything. Yet, if I had to name something truly amazing in the world, it would be the beauty of woman. I once read in my books that what cost God the greatest amount of effort was man, for he is a world writ small. Be that as it may, woman causes me more unease, for she is Heaven writ small and is as superior to man in beauty as Heaven is to earth, especially the one I'm looking at now.

ROSSAURA: (*Aside.*) The prince is here; I shall withdraw.

SIGISMUND: Hey, woman, stop! Don't couple sunset and sunrise with your speedy retreat; for in coupling sunrise and sunset, warmth and cold shadow, you will no doubt syncopate° the day.
(*Aside.*) But what's this I'm seeing?

ROSSAURA: (*Aside.*) I can't believe my own eyes.

SIGISMUND: (*Aside.*) I've seen this beauty before.

ROSSAURA: (*Aside.*) I've seen this splendour, this grandeur reduced to the confines of a narrow cell.

SIGISMUND: (*Aside.*) My life has returned.
[*To Rossaura.*] Woman—for this term is the best compliment a man can pay—who are you, that without recognizing you I recall your affection, and my spirit grasps for you so strongly that I'm convinced I've seen you before? Who are you, beautiful woman?

ROSSAURA: (*Aside.*) I must keep my identity a secret.
[*To Sigismund.*] Just a lowly lady-in-waiting to Princess Stella.

SIGISMUND: You misspeak; you are the sun on whose flame that Stellar beauty lives, for she takes her resplendence from your rays. I have seen, in the scented realm, the deity of the rose rule over the ordinary flowers, empress through her greater beauty; I have seen, in the mines of the learned academy of precious stones, the diamond crowned emperor because of his greater brilliance; I have seen, in the beautiful palaces of the restless constellations, the morning star, first in rank, rule as king; I have seen, in the perfect spheres of heaven, the sun call the planets to court, presiding over them as a great oracle of light. So how is it that flowers, stones, constellations, and planets defer to the most beautiful among them, yet you serve one of lesser beauty while you, ever more beautiful and lovely, are the sun, the morning star, the diamond, and the rose?

(*Enter Clothold, unseen.*)

CLOTHOLD: (*Aside.*) I must restrain Sigismund, for I'm the one, after all, who raised him. But what's this I'm seeing now?

ROSSAURA: I cherish your kindness, but silence will be my most eloquent response; when reason falters, my lord, the most articulate are those who keep quiet.
[*She turns to exit.*]

SIGISMUND: Do not leave; wait. How can you wish to leave my senses in the dark like that?

ROSSAURA: I request your Highness's permission.

SIGISMUND: To go so abruptly is not a request; it's a demand.

syncopate: To shorten (shorten the day).

ROSSAURA: Well, if you don't grant me permission, I'll have no other choice.

SIGISMUND: You're going to force me from politeness to boorishness, because resistance is a cruel venom to my patience.

ROSSAURA: Well even if that venom, full of fury, severity, and wrath, were to overcome your patience, it wouldn't dare attack my honour, nor could it.

SIGISMUND: You'll make me lose the inhibitions your beauty inspires in me, just to see if I can, for I'm strongly inclined to overcome the impossible. Today I threw a man off that balcony who said it couldn't be done; and thus, have no doubt that I'll throw your honour out the window, just to see if I can.

CLOTHOLD: (*Aside.*) His rashness knows no bounds. What am I to do, heavens, before such mad desire when I find my honour at risk a second time?

ROSSAURA: Not in vain were the warnings that this unlucky realm would suffer, at the hands of your tyranny, terrible upheavals of crime, treason, wrath, and death. Yet what is to be expected of a man who is human in name only: reckless, inhuman, cruel, prideful, barbaric, and tyrannical, a man born among beasts?

SIGISMUND: Precisely so you wouldn't hurl that insult at me, I was polite with you, thinking I could win you over with such measures. But if this is what you call barbaric, then I might as well live up to your insults. [*To Bugle.*] You there, leave us alone, close the door, and make sure no one comes in.

(*Exit Bugle.*)

ROSSAURA: (*Aside.*) I'm finished!
    [*To Sigismund.*] Beware . . .

SIGISMUND: I'm a tyrant, remember? So your attempts to restrain me are in vain.

CLOTHOLD: (*Aside.*) Oh, what an awful predicament! I must stop him, even if he kills me.
    [*To Sigismund.*] My lord, listen to reason.

SIGISMUND: This is the second time you've provoked my ire, you decrepit old madman. Do you take my anger and severity lightly? How did you get in here?

CLOTHOLD: Summoned by the cries of her voice, I'm here to tell you to be more pleasant if you desire to rule and that you needn't resort to cruelty to assert yourself over others, because this may be a dream.

SIGISMUND: You provoke my rage by lecturing me about reality. I'll kill you and test whether this is a dream or reality.

(*As he goes to unsheathe his sword, Clothold detains him and kneels before him.*)

CLOTHOLD: I'm hoping this gesture will spare my life.

SIGISMUND: Take your brazen hand off my blade.

CLOTHOLD: Until someone arrives who can restrain your severity and quick temper. I shall not let you go.

ROSSAURA: Good heavens!

SIGISMUND: Let go I say, you decrepit madman, you barbaric fiend, or . . . (*They fight.*) . . . I'll kill you with my bare hands.

ROSSAURA: Come quickly, everyone, he's killing Clothold!
    (*Exit.*)

(*As Aistulf enters, Clothold falls at his feet, and the duke steps between the two antagonists.*)

AISTULF: What's all this about, gentle prince? You would tarnish your valiant blade with an old man's blood? Return your illustrious sword to its sheath.

SIGISMUND: As soon as I've drenched it in his contemptible blood.

AISTULF: His life has sought refuge at my feet; I must give some purpose to my arrival.

SIGISMUND: Let death be your purpose; that way I can also avenge your earlier insolence.

AISTULF: I act in self-defence, not lese-majesty.

(*They unsheathe their swords. Enter Vasily and Stella.*)

CLOTHOLD: Don't hurt him, my lord.

VASILY: What's this? Swords drawn in the palace?

STELLA: (*Aside.*) It's Aistulf! Oh miserable me, what cruel torment!

VASILY: What's going on?

AISTULF: Nothing, my lord, now that you're here.

(*They sheathe their swords.*)

SIGISMUND: A great deal, my lord, despite your arrival. I tried to kill that old man.

VASILY: You would show no respect for his grey hair?

CLOTHOLD: Don't fret, my lord; my grey hair is unimportant.

SIGISMUND: It is in vain to hope that I show respect for grey hair; why, I might even see yours [*gesturing at Vasily*] at my feet one day, because I still haven't had my revenge for the unjust manner in which you raised me. (*Exit.*)

VASILY: Well before you reach that point, you'll return to sleep in a place where you'll believe that all that has happened to you, since it was of this world, was a dream.

(*Exit Vasily and Clothold. Stella and Aistulf remain onstage.*)

AISTULF: How seldom fate errs in predicting misfortune, for it is as accurate in foretelling evil as it is inaccurate in foretelling good. What an excellent astrologer it would be if it made only cruel predictions, for there's no doubt that they would always come true! This theory, Stella, is confirmed in the case of both Sigismund and myself, for in each of us there was a different prediction. In Sigismund's case, it foresaw severity, excessive pride, misfortune, and death, and it was right in each instance because it's all happening. But in my case—where, upon seeing, my lady, your exquisite brilliance, of which the sun is but a shadow and Heaven a meagre imitation, it predicted good fortune, trophies, acclaim, and wealth—it spoke incorrectly but also correctly, for it can only be correct when it promises kindness and delivers contempt.

STELLA: I'm sure that your compliments are heartfelt; yet I suspect they're intended for another lady, whose portrait you were wearing in the locket around your neck when you first came to see me, Aistulf. That being the case, she alone deserves your flattery; go to her to claim your reward, for insincere compliments and misrepresentations are no more valid in love's court than they are in the king's.

(*Enter Rossaura, hidden.*)

ROSSAURA: (*Aside.*) Thank God my cruel misfortunes are finally coming to an end, for anyone who suffers through this is prepared for anything!

AISTULF: I'll banish the locket's picture from my breast to make way for your beautiful image. Where Stella is present, shadows have no place . . .
(*Aside.*) . . . nor do Stellar glimmers in the presence of the sun.
[*To Stella.*] I'll go and get the locket.
(*Aside.*) Forgive me, lovely Rossaura, for this offence, but men and women are no more faithful than this when they're apart. (*Exit.*)

ROSSAURA: (*Aside.*) I was so worried he'd see me that I didn't catch anything they said.

STELLA: Astraea?

ROSSAURA: My lady?

STELLA: I'm glad it's you, because you're the only one I can trust with a secret.

ROSSAURA: You're too kind, my lady, to one who serves you.

STELLA: In the short time I've known you, Astraea, you've earned the keys to my conscience; for this reason, and because of who you are, I'm going to trust you with a secret that I'm not even comfortable with myself.

ROSSAURA: I am your slave.

STELLA: Well, to make a long story short, my first cousin Aistulf — *first* in more ways than one, if you know what I mean — is to marry me, if in fact fortune decides to remedy so much adversity with a single act of joy. I was distressed that the first day I saw him he was wearing the portrait of another lady around his neck. I spoke to him about it politely; he's a gallant and sincere lover, so he went to get the locket and is going to bring it here. But I feel awkward accepting it from him directly. Stay here, and when he comes, tell him to hand it over to you. I'll say no more; you're discreet and beautiful — surely you know what it means to be in love. (*Exit.*)

ROSSAURA: If only I didn't! Heaven help me! What woman is careful and prudent enough to figure a way out of such a dilemma? Can there be anyone else in the world that the merciless stars assail with more misfortune and besiege with more sorrow? What shall I do amid such confusion, where it seems impossible to find a solution that comforts me or a comfort that consoles me? Since the first misfortune, every event or blunder has turned into another, for they succeed one another like heirs. In imitation of the phoenix, they breed one another, living on what kills them; and their urn is always alive with their ashes. Misfortunes are cowardly, a philosopher once said, because they never seem to walk alone; but I say they're courageous, since they always push forward and never look back. Whoever is escorted by misfortunes can aim for the stars, for he never need fear that they will abandon him. I can say so because so many have occurred in my life that I've never found myself without them, and they never give up until they find me, wounded by fortune or in the arms of death. Oh, miserable me! What shall I do in these circumstances? If I reveal my identity, Clothold, to whose protection and honour I owe my life, might be offended, for he has asked me to keep quiet while I await his remedy to my dishonour. But if I don't reveal my identity, how can I keep up the charade if Aistulf recognizes me? For even if I attempt to disguise myself with my voice, my speech, and my eyes, my soul will expose them as liars. What shall I do? But why reflect on what to do, when it's evident that, no matter how I prepare, reflect, and think, when the moment arrives, my grief will do as it sees fit? For no one is master of his sorrow. And since my soul dares not determine a course of action, let my grief culminate today and let my sorrow reach its extreme, but let me be freed of doubting and guessing once and for all. But until then, give me strength, heavens, give me strength!

(*Enter Aistulf with the locket.*)

AISTULF: Here's the locket, my lady . . . but . . . Oh, God!

ROSSAURA: What's the matter, my lord? What's got you so shocked?

AISTULF: Hearing your voice, Rossaura, and seeing you here.

ROSSAURA: Rossaura? You are mistaken, my lord, if you take me for another lady; for I am Astraea, and my humble station is not worthy of the joy caused by your confused affection.

AISTULF: Enough with the deception, Rossaura, for the soul never lies; and though mine may look upon you as Astraea, it loves you as Rossaura.

ROSSAURA: I don't understand, my lord, so I don't know how to respond. All I can say is that Stella — who is at least as Stellar as Venus — has ordered me to wait here for you and to ask you, on her behalf, to hand over that locket and to take it to her myself. It is a most reasonable request. Stella wishes it thus, for even the tiniest things, if they work to my disadvantage, are Stellar in design.

AISTULF: Try as you might, Rossaura, you're a most unconvincing liar! Tell your eyes to harmonize their music to your voice; for such a cacophonous instrument must stutter and falter in attempting to adjust and calibrate the falsehoods of the speaker to the truth of his sentiments.

ROSSAURA: I repeat that I'm here only for the locket.

AISTULF: Well, since you insist on carrying on with this charade, I'll reply in kind. You may tell the princess, Astraea, that I hold her in such esteem that, when she asks me for a portrait. I consider it in poor taste to send it to her; rather, that she may treasure and revere it, I'll send her the original. And you may take it to her, for you carry it in yourself—when you're not beside yourself.

ROSSAURA: When a determined, proud, and courageous man agrees to undertake a mission, if he returns without reaching the goal—even if he acquires something more valuable in the process—he faces ridicule and humiliation. I'm here for a portrait, and even if I take back an original of greater worth, I'll be ridiculed. Give me the locket, my lord, for I shall not return without it.

AISTULF: Well how do you expect to take it if I don't give it to you?

ROSSAURA: Like this! [*She grabs for the locket.*] Give it to me, you ingrate!

AISTULF: Your efforts are in vain.

ROSSAURA: By God, it's not for another woman's hands!

AISTULF: You're ferocious today.

ROSSAURA: And you're a two-timing scoundrel!

AISTULF: That's enough, my Rossaura.

ROSSAURA: I'm not your Rossaura, you swine!

([*They continue struggling.*] *Enter Stella.*)

STELLA: Astraea, Aistulf, what's going on here?

AISTULF: (*Aside.*) Oh no, it's Stella!

ROSSAURA: (*Aside.*) May love grant me the ingenuity to get my locket back.
(*To Stella.*) If you wish to know what's going on, my lady, I'll tell you.

AISTULF: (*Aside* [*to Rossaura*].) What do you think you're doing?

ROSSAURA: You ordered me to wait here for Aistulf and to ask him for a locket on your behalf. I was left alone, and as related topics associate freely in the mind, your talk of lockers reminded me that I was carrying one of my own in my sleeve. I decided to look at it, for people always entertain themselves with nonsense when they're alone. I accidentally dropped it on the floor, and Aistulf, who'd just arrived to give you the other lady's locket, picked it up; and not only is he unwilling to hand over the one you'd asked him for, but he also wants to take mine. And since he wouldn't give it back even though I begged and beseeched him, I grew angry and impatient and tried to take it back by force. That one he holds in his hand now is mine: you'll know as soon as you see the resemblance it bears to me.

STELLA: Give me the locket, Aistulf. (*She takes it from him.*)

AISTULF: My lady!

STELLA: A faithful copy of the original.

ROSSAURA: So you agree it's mine?

STELLA: Could there be any doubt?

ROSSAURA: Now tell him to give you the other one.

STELLA: Take your locket and go.

ROSSAURA: (*Aside.*) At least I got my locket back. The rest is their problem. (*Exit.*)

STELLA: Now give me the locket I asked you for; for though I shall never look at you or speak to you again, I don't want it to remain in your power— no—if only because I so foolishly asked you for it.

AISTULF: (*Aside.*) How can I get myself out of this one? [*To Stella.*] Although I should like, beautiful Stella, to serve and obey you, I can't give you the locket you request because . . .

STELLA: You're a swine and a boorish suitor! Keep it, for I wouldn't want to be reminded, in accepting it, that I ever asked you for anything! (*Exit.*)

AISTULF: Wait . . . listen . . . look . . . I . . . ! Goddamn you, Rossaura! Where, how, and why did you turn up in Poland today? You're going to destroy yourself and me with you! (*Exit.*)

Scene 2

([*The tower.*] *Sigismund, bound in chains and dressed in animal skins as at the beginning of the play, is revealed asleep on the floor. Enter Clothold, Bugle, and two Servants.*)

CLOTHOLD: (*To the Servants.*) Leave him here, and his excessive pride will end today where it began.

SERVANT: I've secured the chain as before.

BUGLE: Better not to wake up, Sigismund; you'll only find yourself destroyed, your fate reversed, your false grandeur reduced to a shadow of life and a glow of death.

CLOTHOLD: Anyone who speaks so glibly should have a nice place in which to debate himself at length. [*To the Servants.*] Seize this man and lock him away in that room.

BUGLE: Why me?

CLOTHOLD: Because a bugle with so many secrets must be kept locked away in a harsh prison, where it can't sound off.

BUGLE: Have I, by chance, tried to kill my father? No. Am I the one who threw little Icarus off the balcony? Is my death or rebirth the issue? Does my dreaming or sleeping matter? What's your purpose in locking me up?

CLOTHOLD: You're Bugle.

BUGLE: Well I'll call myself Horn from now on, and I'll keep quiet, as befits those with horns.

(*They take him away. Enter King Vasily, his face hidden behind a cloak.*)

VASILY: Clothold?

CLOTHOLD: My lord! Why does Your Majesty come in disguise?

VASILY: A foolish curiosity to see what happens with Sigismund—Oh, miserable me!—has brought me here in this fashion.

CLOTHOLD: Behold him there, reduced to his miserable state.

VASILY: Oh. unfortunate prince, born at such a sad moment! [*To Clothold.*] Go wake him now, for the lotus he drank should be wearing off.

CLOTHOLD: He is restless, my lord, and talking in his sleep.

VASILY: What could he be dreaming now? Let's listen.

SIGISMUND: (*In his sleep.*) Faithful is the prince who punishes tyrants. Clothold shall die by my hands! My father shall kiss my feet!

CLOTHOLD: He threatens me with death.

VASILY: And me with severity and disrespect.

CLOTHOLD: He means to take my life.

VASILY: He schemes to subjugate me at his feet.

SIGISMUND: (*In his sleep.*) On the broad public square that is the great stage of the world, my unequalled valour shall be the star. For my vengeance to take shape, all must watch Prince Sigismund triumph over his father. (*He awakens.*) But—Oh, miserable me!—where am I?

VASILY: (*Aside to Clothold.*) He mustn't see me. You know what to do. I'll listen from over there. (*He withdraws from the prince's view.*)

SIGISMUND: Is this really me? Am I the one I see reduced to this state, a chained captive? Are you not my grave, tower? Yes. Good god, what a torrent of dreams!

CLOTHOLD: (*Aside.*) It's up to me to pull off the deception. [*To Sigismund.*] Is it finally time to wake up?

SIGISMUND: Yes, it's finally time to wake up.

CLOTHOLD: Must you spend all day sleeping? You haven't woken up since I left to follow the flight of that majestic eagle while you stayed put?

SIGISMUND: No, nor am I awake now, for as I see it, Clothold, I'm still sleeping. My reasoning is sound because, if what seemed so palpable and true to me was only a dream, then what I'm seeing now mustn't be trusted. And it's no surprise that, if I can see in my sleep, exhaustion should lead me to dream while awake.

CLOTHOLD: Tell me what you dreamed.

SIGISMUND: Even assuming it was a dream, I won't say what I dreamed, Clothold, but rather what I saw, yes. I awoke to find myself—What cruel flattery!—upon a bed that could have been, with a bit of detail and colour, a bed of flowers woven by Spring, where a thousand noblemen, bowing at my feet, called me their prince and adorned me in fine clothes and precious stones. You turned the numbness of my senses into happiness by announcing the good news; for, although this is my lot here, there I was Prince of Poland.

CLOTHOLD: You must have given me a handsome reward.

SIGISMUND: Not really. With a valiant and mighty spirit, I twice tried to kill you for your treason.

CLOTHOLD: Such severity toward me?

SIGISMUND: I was lord over all, and I wanted revenge on everyone. My only love was for a woman, and I believe it was real because, while everything else has vanished, it alone has remained with me.

(*Exit the King.*)

CLOTHOLD: (*Aside.*) The king has left, filled with pity at the princes's remarks.
[*To Sigismund.*] Because we had spoken about that eagle, when you slept you dreamt of empire. But in your dreams it would be fitting, Sigismund, to show more respect to he who raised you with such care; for even in dreams doing what's right mustn't be overlooked.

(*Exit.*)

SIGISMUND: This is true. So we must repress this savage character, this fury, this ambition, in case we dream again. And we no doubt shall, for we live in such a singular world that living is no more than dreaming; and experience teaches me that the man who lives dreams what he is until waking. The king dreams he's king, and he lives under this deception commanding, planning, and governing; and his acclaim, which he receives on loan, he scribbles on the wind, where death turns it to ash. What grave misfortune! To think that anyone should try to govern knowing that he will awaken in the sleep of death! The rich man dreams of his riches, which bring him more worries; the poor man dreams he suffers in misery and poverty; the man who improves his lot dreams; the man who toils and solicits dreams; the man who insults and offends dreams. And in this world, in short, everyone dreams what he is though no one realizes it. I dream that I'm here, weighed down by these chains, and I dreamt that I found myself in another, more flattering state. What is life? A frenzy. What is life? An illusion, a shadow, a fiction; and the greatest good is fleeting, for all life is a dream, and even dreams are but dreams.

ACT 3 • Scene 1

([*The tower.*] *Enter Bugle.*)

BUGLE: In a haunted tower, because of what I know, I'm being held captive. What will they do to me for my ignorance if they axe me for my knowledge? To think that a fellow should be sentenced to a life of starving to death! I feel sorry for myself! Everyone will say, "I can believe it," and I'm sure they can, for in my opinion this silence doesn't befit the name Bugle, and I can't keep my mouth shut. My company here, if I can bring myself to say it, are spiders and mice: what lovely goldfinches! My dreams last night filled my poor head with shawms,° trumpets, and tomfoolery; and with processions, crucifixes, and penitents marching up and down and fainting at the sight of one another's blood. Yet I, to tell the truth, am fainting from hunger, for this prison's favourite

---

shawms: Musical instruments similar to oboes.

philosopher is Empty-Plato and its only creed is the Frail-Mary. If silence be considered saintly, then Saint Secret is my man, for I fast in his honour and never feast! But the punishment I suffer is well deserved, for I'm a servant who kept his mouth shut, which is the greatest sacrilege.

(*A sound of drums and people is heard, and a voice speaks from offstage.*)

SOLDIER 1: This is the tower he's in. Knock down the door; everybody in!

BUGLE: By God! They must be looking for me, for they say I'm in here! What can they want with me?

(*Enter as many Soldiers as possible.*)

SOLDIER 1: Inside, inside.

SOLDIER 2: [*Pointing to Bugle.*] Here he is.

BUGLE: No he isn't.

SOLDIERS: My lord . . .

BUGLE: [*Aside.*] Are these guys drunk or what?

SOLDIER 2: You are our prince; we don't want and won't accept anyone but our rightful lord, not a foreign prince, Give us all your feet, that we may bow before them.

SOLDIERS: Long live our great prince!

BUGLE: (*Aside.*) By God, it's for real! Can it be a custom of this kingdom to take a new prisoner each day, make him prince, and then return him to the lower? Apparently, for I've seen it happen twice now. I'll have to play my role.

SOLDIERS: Give us the soles of your feet. [*They kneel to kiss his feet.*]

BUGLE: I can't because I need them for myself, and I wouldn't do you much good as a desolated prince.

SOLDIER 2: We all told your father himself that we recognize only you as our prince, not the Muscovite.

BUGLE: You talked back to my father? You're a bunch of lowlifes!

SOLDIER 1: It was the loyalty of our hearts speaking.

BUGLE: If it was loyalty, then I forgive you.

SOLDIER 2: Come forth and restore your rule. Long live Sigismund!

ALL: Long live Sigismund!

BUGLE: (*Aside.*) Why do they call me Sigismund? It must be the name they reserve for all their bogus princes.

(*Enter Sigismund.*)

SIGISMUND: Who calls Sigismund's name?

BUGLE: (*Aside.*) Is my time as prince already up?

SOLDIER 2: Which of you is Sigismund?

SIGISMUND: I am.

SOLDIER 2: [*To Bugle.*] You impudent fool! How dare you call yourself Sigismund?

BUGLE: Me, call myself Sigismund? I deny that charge. You're the ones who Sigismunded me, so you're the impudent fools.

SOLDIER 1: Great Prince Sigismund—your appearance confirms your identity, though our faith has already affirmed you as our lord—your father, the great King

Vasily, fearful lest the stars fulfil a prediction that says he will end up at your feet, vanquished by your might, is attempting to deny you your rightful authority and give it to Aistulf, Duke of Muscovy. For this purpose he convened his court, and the masses, learning of the events and realizing that they have a natural-born prince, refuse to be ruled by a foreigner. And thus, nobly overlooking the inclemency of fate, they've come looking for you where you're held prisoner so that, aided by their weapons, you may break out of this tower and recover your imperial crown and sceptre, stripping them from a tyrant. Come forth, then, for on that barren mount a numerous army of outlaws and peasants salutes you. Freedom awaits you; listen to its chant.

VOICES: [*Offstage.*] Long live Sigismund! Long live the prince!

SIGISMUND: (*Aside.*) What's happening, heavens? Do you wish me to dream again of greatness that will be undone by time? Am I to glimpse again the shadowy outlines of majesty and pomp that will be swept away by the wind? Must I come to grips with the truth again, that human power is born of jeopardy and lives in uncertainty? It shall not be; it shall not be. Here I am, again a prisoner of my fortune. And since I know that this life is all a dream, be gone shadows, you who today give body and voice to my deadened senses, when truth holds that you have neither body nor voice. For I don't want counterfeit majesty and pomp, no. Fanciful illusions that unravel at the slightest touch of the breeze—just like the budding almond tree whose flowers, without warning or counsel, bloom early and expire at the first cold wind, withering and tarnishing the beauty, brightness, and colour of their rosy buds—I see you, I recognize you, and I know you play the same game with everyone who falls asleep. I won't be fooled this time, for I've learned the truth and know that life is a dream.

SOLDIER 2: If you think we're deceiving you, turn your gaze toward that defiant mountainside and you'll see the people who wait there to obey your command.

SIGISMUND: I've seen this before as clearly and distinctly as I'm seeing it now, and it was a dream.

SOLDIER 1: Great things, my lord, are always foreshadowed, which explains how you could have dreamt this moment.

SIGISMUND: You speak convincingly: it was a foreshadowing.

(*Aside.*) And in case that be true, since life is so short, let's dream, my soul, let's dream again. But we must do so with vigilance and with the awareness that we may awaken from this delight at the best moment; if we keep that in mind, the truth will sting less, for to be prepared for harm is to avoid it. And with the caveat that, even if this is not a dream, all power is on loan and must be returned to its owner, let us stop at nothing.

[*To the Soldiers.*] Vassals, I appreciate your loyalty. You may count on my boldness and skill to liberate you from slavery to a foreigner. Sound the call to arms, and shortly you will see my immense valour in action. I aim to take arms against my father and prove the stars true; soon I shall have him at my feet. (*Aside.*) Yet, in case I should wake up before then, wouldn't it be better to avoid making promises that I can't keep?

ALL: [*Offstage.*] Long live Sigismund! Long live the prince!

(*Enter Clothold.*)

CLOTHOLD: What's all this commotion, heavens?

SIGISMUND: Clothold.

CLOTHOLD: My lord . . .
   (*Aside.*) My life will be the test of his cruelty.

BUGLE: (*Aside.*) I'll bet he throws him off the mountain. (*Exit.*)

CLOTHOLD: I come before your royal feet, certain of my death. [*He kneels before the prince.*]

SIGISMUND: On your feet, father, on your feet; you will be the compass and guide to whom I entrust my accomplishments, for I know I owe my upbringing to your great loyalty. Let me embrace you.

CLOTHOLD: What are you saying?

SIGISMUND: That I'm dreaming, and that I wish to do what's right; for good works mustn't be overlooked, even in dreams.

CLOTHOLD: Well, my lord, if doing what's right is now your motto, then you won't be offended if I appeal to it today. You would wage war against your father; I cannot counsel you or come to your aid against my king. I am at your mercy; kill me.

SIGISMUND: Swine! Traitor! Ingrate!
   (*Aside.*) But heavens! It behoves me to exercise restraint, for I still don't know if I'm awake.
   [*To Clothold.*] Clothold, I envy and appreciate your valour. Go and serve the king, and we'll meet again on the battlefield. [*To his Soldiers.*] Sound the call to arms.

CLOTHOLD: [*Rising.*] I kiss your feet a thousand times. (*Exit.*)

SIGISMUND: Off we go, fortune, to claim my throne. Don't wake me if I'm sleeping, and don't lull me to sleep if it's real. Yet, whether it's reality or a dream, doing what's right is what matters. If it's reality, then for the sake of reality; if it's a dream, then for the purpose of winning friends for when we awake. (*Exit all amid the call to arms.*)

Scene 2

([*The palace.*] *Enter Vasily and Aistulf.*)

VASILY: Who, Aistulf, is wise enough to curb the fury of a runaway horse? Who can detain the current of a defiant river in its downhill rush to the sea? Who is valiant enough to stop a boulder that has broken free of the mountaintop? Well that's all easy in comparison to halting a defiant and reckless mob. The proof is in the clashing cries of Poland's rival parties, which penetrate the innermost mountains with thunderous echoes of "Long live Aistulf!" or "Long live Sigismund!" The coronation site, fallen prey to wayward aspirations and hidden loyalties, has become a gloomy theatre where importunate fortune stages her tragedies.

AISTULF: We must suspend the celebration and postpone the applause and flattering delights that your fortunate hand promised me; for if Poland, which I hope to rule, today refuses obedience to me, it is to make me earn it first. Give me a horse, and let him who boasts with thunder descend like lightning, full of arrogance. (*Exit.*)

VASILY: The inevitable has little remedy, and the foreseen carries considerable risk; if it's meant to be, there's no defence against it, for he who most tries to avoid it most precipitates its arrival. What harsh logic! What awful circumstances! What tremendous horror! He who believes he's running from danger ends up running into it. In trying to avoid it, I have ruined myself. I, and I alone, have destroyed my fatherland.

(*Enter Stella.*)

STELLA: If you do not act, your majesty, to put a stop to the chaos that has broken out and, spreading from one side to the next, polarizes streets and squares, you will soon find your kingdom swimming in waves of scarlet, dyed in the crimson of its own blood; sadly, misfortune and tragedy are already widespread. Such is the ruin of your empire, such the might of harsh and bloody inclemency that it amazes the eyes and alarms the ears. The sun is startled and the wind falters; the rocks form tombstones and the flowers cluster on gravesites; every building is a mausoleum and every soldier, a living skeleton.

(*Enter Clothold.*)

CLOTHOLD: Thank God I've made it here alive!

VASILY: Clothold, what can you tell us of Sigismund?

CLOTHOLD: A monstrous mob, reckless and blind, has broken into the tower and liberated the prince from its depths. Finding his power seconded a second time, he became valiant, proclaiming fiercely that he will prove the stars right.

VASILY: Give me a horse, for I wish valiantly to defeat my ungrateful son in person. In defence of my crown, may steel triumph where knowledge has failed. (*Exit.*)

STELLA: And I, flanking the sun, shall act as Bellona.° I hope to write my name next to yours [*Gesturing toward Vasily as he exits*], for on obedient wings I shall fly in competition with the deity of Pallas. (*Exit amid the call to arms.*)

(*Enter Rossaura, who detains Clothold.*)

ROSSAURA: I realize that we're in the midst of war; but even if your valour is bursting in your breast, hear me

---

Bellona: Roman goddess of war.

out. You know that I arrived in Poland poor, humble, and unfortunate, and that, aided by your valour, I found mercy in your person, You ordered me—Oh, heavens!—to live in disguise in the palace and to attempt, concealing my jealousy, to keep away from Aistulf. But he saw me in the end, and so recklessly does he trample my honour that he speaks to Stella in front of me every night in the garden. I've stolen the key, with which I can provide the means for you to enter the garden and put an end to my troubles. There, with bluster, daring, and might, you can restore my honour since you are already resolved to avenge me with his death.

CLOTHOLD: It's true that from the moment I first saw you, Rossaura, I was moved to do for you—as your sobs bore witness—whatever my life allowed. The first thing I did was to get you to change that outfit you were wearing so that, if Aistulf were to see you, he'd see you in your own clothes and not take for indecency the mad temerity that besmirches honour. I've since been trying to determine how to recover your lost honour even if it meant—so much does your honour preoccupy me—killing Aistulf. What wayward madness! Although, given that he's not my king, I am neither cowed nor awed by him. I was planning to kill him when Sigismund tried to kill me, and then he arrived and, overlooking the danger to himself, demonstrated a degree of altruism in my defence that went past courage to temerity. So tell me, how am I now to kill the person who saved my life, when my soul is full of gratitude? And thus, torn between the effect of his action and my obligation to you. having given you life and received it from him, I don't know which party to go to or to help; for to you I'm bound on account of giving, and to him I'm bound on account of receiving. And thus, in the matter at hand, nothing satisfies my loving nature because my active and passive sides are in conflict.

ROSSAURA: I needn't remind you that, in men of distinction, receiving is as base an action as giving is noble. Accepting this principle, you have no reason to be grateful to him given that, if he gave you life and you gave me life, it's obvious that he forced your noble nature to commit a base act while I facilitated its generosity. Therefore you should consider yourself offended by him and indebted to me, for you have given to me what you have received from him. And thus you should attend to my honour, which is at great risk, for it gives me precedence in the conflict between giving and receiving.

CLOTHOLD: Although nobility lives from giving, gratitude for noble actions corresponds to those who receive. And as I have not held back in giving, I have become known as generous in addition to noble. Let me be known also as grateful, for I can be grateful and generous simultaneously, for giving and receiving are equally honourable.

ROSSAURA: You gave me life and, in doing so, said yourself that a life lived in dishonour is no life. Therefore I have received nothing from you, for your hand has dispensed death, not life. And if you must be generous before being grateful—as you yourself have said—I expect you to give me my life, which you have yet to do; and, since giving is more ennobling, be generous first, and you will be grateful later.

CLOTHOLD: Your reasoning has convinced me, and I shall be generous first. I shall, Rossaura, give you my inheritance, with which you may retire to a convent. The solution I am suggesting is well considered, since in fleeing from a crime you will take refuge in a sanctuary. For when a divided kingdom is burdened with misfortunes, I don't wish to multiply them, for I was born noble. With this remedy I can be loyal to my country, generous to you, and grateful to Aistulf. It behoves you to accept this remedy, which we'll keep between the two of us, for I wouldn't do anything more even if—By God!—I were your father.

ROSSAURA: If you were my father, I would accept this insult; but as you're not, I won't.

CLOTHOLD: Well, then what is it you plan to do?

ROSSAURA: Kill the duke.

CLOTHOLD: Can a lady who never knew her father have such courage?

ROSSAURA: Yes.

CLOTHOLD: Who drives you?

ROSSAURA: My reputation.

CLOTHOLD: Beware that Aistulf is about to become . . .

ROSSAURA: He tramples over all my honour.

CLOTHOLD: . . . your king and Stella's husband.

ROSSAURA: By God, it shall not happen!

CLOTHOLD: This is madness.

ROSSAURA: I know.

CLOTHOLD: You must overcome it.

ROSSAURA: I cannot.

CLOTHOLD: You'll lose . . .

ROSSAURA: I know.

CLOTHOLD: . . . life and honour.

ROSSAURA: I know.

CLOTHOLD: What do you want?

ROSSAURA: My death.

CLOTHOLD: Beware, that's sacrilege.

ROSSAURA: It's honour.

CLOTHOLD: It's folly.

ROSSAURA: It's valour.

CLOTHOLD: It's frenzy.

ROSSAURA: It's rage, it's wrath.

CLOTHOLD: So there's no compromising with your obsession?

ROSSAURA: No.

CLOTHOLD: Who will assist you?

ROSSAURA: I'll assist myself.

CLOTHOLD: There's no solution?

ROSSAURA: There's no solution.

CLOTHOLD: Think well; there must be another way.

ROSSAURA: Only another form of self-destruction. (*Exit.*)

CLOTHOLD: Well, since you're bent on destroying yourself, wait for me, my daughter, and we'll go down together. (*Exit.*)

Scene 3

([*A wilderness area, somewhere between the palace and the tower.*] *Amid the call to arms, Soldiers, Bugle, and Sigismund march out, the latter dressed in animal skins.*)

SIGISMUND: If Rome at the height of her youthful vigour could see me today, how thrilled she would be at the rare chance to have her mighty armies led by a beast whose insolent bravado strikes at the firmament itself! But let's come down to earth, my spirit, lest we shatter this tenuous glory, for I'll only be disappointed, upon waking, at having achieved so much only to lose it; for the lesser the glory, the less its loss will be felt.

(*A bugle sounds offstage.*)

BUGLE: We are approached by a swift horse—forgive me, for it demands careful description—upon whom a careful map is drawn in which its body is earth, fire is the soul trapped in its chest, its spittle is the sea, and the air is its breath; the motley figure inspires chaos, for its soul, spittle, body, and breath form a monstrosity of fire, earth, sea, and wind. Upon its coarse coat of dapple grey sits a gallant woman who digs in the spurs and bids it fly rather than gallop toward your presence.

SIGISMUND: I'm blinded by her aura.

BUGLE: (*Aside.*) By God, it's Rossaura! (*Exit.*)

SIGISMUND: Heaven has restored her to my presence.

(*Enter Rossaura with a splendid cloak, a sword, and a dagger.*)

ROSSAURA: Generous Sigismund, whose heroic majesty emerges into the light of its deeds from the darkness of its shadows: may your rise in the world, shining sun of Poland, imitate the greatest of heavenly bodies, which, in the arms of dawn, recovers its shining throne before flowers and roses and, stepping out newly crowned, spreads its light and casts its rays over oceans and mountains, bathing high peaks and adorning frothy waves. Take pity on this unlucky woman who today throws herself at your feet; being both unfortunate and a woman, she has two reasons to expect charity from a man who prides himself on his valour, either of which is enough, both of which are more than enough. Three times now you have beheld me with awe, three times without knowing who I am, for on each occasion you've seen me in different attire and character. The first time was in your cruel prison, where you took me for a man and your life played flattery to my misfortunes. The second time—when your majestic splendour was but a dream, a ghost, a shadow—you beheld me as a woman. The third time is today, where I, a monstrous hybrid, am adorned in the fine clothes of a woman and the arms of a man. And so that pity may move you to come to my aid, listen to the tragic story of my life. I was born at court in Muscovy to a noble mother who, to judge from her misfortunes, must have been very beautiful. She caught the eye of a treacherous scoundrel, whose name can't cross my lips because it is unknown to them, although his character informs my own; and thus, as the product of his desire, I regret now not being born pagan so that I could madly convince myself that he was one of those gods who, transformed into a shower of gold, a swan, or a bull, are lamented by Danae, Leda, and Europa.° While I thought that by citing dastardly tales I would merely lengthen my speech, I see now that I have foreshadowed how my mother, swept away in the game of love, was more beautiful than any other woman and as unlucky as all of them. She was so completely duped by that foolish old ruse of a secret wedding vow that she relives it even today; and her betrayer was such an Aeneas° to her honour that he even left her a sword. Its blade will remain sheathed for now, but I shall reveal it before my story is over. From this poorly tied knot, which neither binds nor imprisons, from this marriage, from this crime—for it's all the same thing—I was born, so similar to my mother that I was her living portrait, her double, if not in loveliness then in luck and circumstances. And so it goes without saying that my stormy fate drove me to shipwreck. The most I can tell you about myself is the name of the lord who steals the prizes of my honour, the spoils of my reputation: Aistulf. Oh, miserable me! At the mention of his name my heart fills with anger and choler, a natural reaction to an allusion to the enemy. Aistulf was the ungrateful lord who, forgetful of love's delight—for in a past love, even memories are forgotten—came to Poland, lured by conquest, to marry Stella, his sunrise and my sunset. Who would guess that lovers brought together by stellar design would now be separated by Stella's design? Humiliated and mocked, I was left feeling sad, demented, dead; I was left with myself, and I raged with the confusion of hell and the chaos of Babel. And refusing to talk about it, because some suffering and anguish is better left to feelings than to words, I spoke my sufferings in silence until one day, when I was alone with my mother Viola—Oh, heavens!—she broke them free of their prison, and they all poured out together, tripping over one another in their haste. I was not ashamed to relate them, for when a person confesses his faults to someone he knows has similar faults, it seems as though he feels free and uninhibited in doing so, for there are times when a bad example does some good. In any case, my mother listened dutifully to my laments and tried to console me with her own. How easily a guilty judge forgives! And having learned from her own experience—whereby, having entrusted the remedy of her dishonour to idle liberty and lenient time, she now had no way to remedy my own misfortunes—she considered it best that I go after him and oblige him, with overpowering arguments, to pay the debt of my honour; and to make it easier, fortune suggested dressing me in the clothes of

Danae, Leda, and Europa: Three women seduced by Zeus in the forms of a shower of gold, a swan, and a white bull, respectively. **Aeneas:** Hero of Virgil's *Aeneid*; he abandoned queen Dido.

a man. She took down an old sword, this one you see me wearing—now's the time to unsheathe its blade as I promised—for my mother, trusting in its design, said to me: "Make your way to Poland, Rossaura, and do your best to have the nobles there see you wearing this sword, for in one of them your fortune may find a merciful welcome and your anguish, consolation." Thus I arrived in Poland. Let's pass quickly over details that are unimportant or already known: that a bucking beast brought me to your cave, where you were astonished to see me; that Clothold took pity on me, asked the king to spare my life, and the king granted his request; that Clothold, informed of my identity, persuaded me to wear my normal clothes and enter the service of Stella, where I ingeniously thwarted Aistulf's courtship and prevented Stella from becoming his wife; and that there, in the palace, you were again baffled at the sight of me, this time dressed as a woman, my past and present appearances confused in your mind. Let's turn our attention to how Clothold, convinced that Aistulf should marry the lovely Stella and rule jointly with her, advised me, in an affront to my honour, to end my crusade. But now that, O valiant Sigismund, your turn at vengeance has arrived, for Heaven has allowed you to break free of the confines of that crude prison, where your temperament was a savage to sorrow and a rock to suffering; now that you are taking up arms against your fatherland and against your father, I am here to offer my help, combining the rich garments of Diana° and the armament of Pallas, dressed in cloth as well as steel, for I am suited to both. Let's move quickly, then, brave chief, for we both have an interest in preventing and annulling this arranged marriage: I, to stop the man who would be my husband from marrying another; you, to nullify the threat posed by the strength and power that their countries, once united, would represent. As a woman, I come to move you to the cause of my honour; as a man, I come to encourage you to recover your crown. As a woman, I come to request your sympathy by throwing myself at your feet; as a man, I come to serve you by aiding your soldiers. As a woman, I come to request your support in my dishonour and anguish; as a man, I come to support you with my sword and my character. And finally, consider that if you see me now as a woman and try to seduce me, I will become a man and slay you in legitimate defence of my honour; for to recover it I must act as a lovesick woman in complaining and as a man in accruing fame.

SIGISMUND: (*Aside.*) Heavens, if I'm really dreaming, then restrain my memory, for it's impossible for a dream to have so many twists and turns. God help me! Who could escape them all or avoid thinking about any of them? Who ever heard of such enigmatic torments? If that splendour in which I found myself was a dream, how is it that this woman can now describe it to me in such vivid detail? So it was real, not a dream. But if it was real, then it's no less confusing, for why does my

Diana: Roman goddess of hunting.

life call it a dream? Are delights so akin to dreams that the real ones are taken for lies and the fake ones for genuine? Is there so little difference between one and the other that it's debatable whether what's seen and enjoyed is real or made up? Is the copy so close to the original that the mind doubts which is which? If so, and all grandiosity and power, all majesty and splendour will eventually fade into shadow, then we must take advantage of this moment while we can, for it affords us delights that are found only in dreams. Rossaura is in my power; my soul longs for her loveliness. Let's enjoy, then, the moment and allow love to violate the understanding of bravery and trust with which she kneels before me. This is a dream, and that being the case, let's dream of delights now, for they will become sorrows later. And yet I can use the same argument to convince myself differently. If it's a dream, a show, who would risk losing divine glory for the sake of human ego? What past pleasure is not a dream? Who has never thought, in looking back on his most heroic escapades, "I'm sure this was all a dream"? If this is my epiphany, if I know pleasure is a lovely flame that will be reduced to ash by the first breeze that blows, then we must hearken to the eternal, or fame everlasting, where joy never sleeps and grandeur never rests. Rossaura is without honour, and it is more fitting for a prince to give honour than to take it away. By God, I must recover her honour before my own crown! We must overcome the temptation of this moment.
[*To a Soldier.*] Sound the call to arms, for today I shall begin battle before dark shadows bury the sun's golden rays in waves of greenish black!

ROSSAURA: My lord, are you going to turn away just like that? My problems and anguish don't merit a single word from you in reply? How can you ignore me so completely? You won't even show me your face?

SIGISMUND: Rossaura, honour demands, in order to be merciful, that I be cruel to you now. My voice is silent so that my honour may respond; I don't speak to you because I want my actions to speak for me; I don't look at you because it's essential, when you're so helpless, that he who is to look after your honour not look upon your beauty.

(*Exit Sigismund and Soldiers.*)

ROSSAURA: What enigmatic talk is this, heavens? After so much sorrow, must I still put up with equivocal replies!

(*Enter Bugle.*)

BUGLE: My lady, do you have a minute?

ROSSAURA: Oh, Bugle! Where have you been?

BUGLE: Locked away in a tower wondering when death might appear in the cards for me, for they could have zapped me at any moment.

ROSSAURA: Why?

BUGLE: Because I know the secret of your identity. You see, Clothold (*Offstage, the drums of war are heard.*) . . . but what's all that racket?

ROSSAURA: What could it be?

BUGLE: An armed squadron is spilling out of the besieged palace in hopes of resisting and defeating the one commanded by the fierce Sigismund.

ROSSAURA: Well how can I stand here like a coward when so much cruelty is being unleashed in defiance of order and law? I must rush to his side and astonish the world. (*Exit.*)

SOLDIERS: (*Offstage, one group.*) Long live our invincible king!

(*Offstage, another group.*) Long live our freedom!

BUGLE: I say, long live freedom *and* the king! Let them live with my blessing, for as long as they look out for me, I have no problem with anything. And now, amid such confusion, I shall be as pitiless as Nero° as he watched Rome burn. Though if I have to take pity on something, it might as well be me. If I hide, I can watch the whole party from here among the crags. It's a safe place where death won't find me, so to hell with death! (*He [makes an obscene gesture, directed at Death, and] hides.*)

(*The sound of war intensifies. Enter the king, Clothold, and Aistulf, in retreat.*)

VASILY: Has there ever been an unluckier king? Has there ever been a more persecuted father?

CLOTHOLD: Your army, now defeated, retreats in disorder.

AISTULF: The traitors have become victors.

VASILY: In battles such as this, loyalty belongs to the winners and treachery to the defeated. We must flee, Clothold, from the cruel and inhuman severity of a tyrannical son.

(*A shot is heard offstage, and Bugle falls wounded from his hiding place.*)

BUGLE: Heaven help me!

AISTULF: Who is this unlucky soldier fallen at our feet, drenched in blood?

BUGLE: Just an unfortunate man who, in trying to run from death, ran right into her, for there's no hiding place she can't find. Which goes to show that he who most tries to flee her reach is the one who will fall within her reach. So return, return to the bloody fighting immediately, for you're safer amid arms and open fire than on the most remote mountaintop, and there's no sure way past destiny's power and fate's inclemency. And thus, although you aim to free yourselves from death by fleeing, consider that, if it's God's will that you die, then you shall die. (*He falls dead offstage.*)

VASILY: Consider that, if it's God's will that you die, then you shall die. How easily, O heavens, we are brought from error and ignorance to greater understanding by this corpse that speaks through the mouth of an open wound, which, like a bloody tongue, teaches us that all of man's attempts to cheat fate are in vain! And thus I, in attempting to save my fatherland from sedition and death, have in the end turned it over to the very people from whom I was attempting to save it.

CLOTHOLD: Although fate, my lord, sees all and is capable of finding its target among the darkest crags, it's

Nero: 15–68 CE; one of Rome's most sadistic and violent emperors.

not a Christian sentiment to say that there's no way around its wrath. There is, for the prudent man can triumph over fate; and now, unless you desire more suffering and tragedy, you must find a place where you can protect yourself.

AISTULF: My lord, Clothold speaks with the wisdom of old age, and I with the valour of youth. Over there in the thicket is a horse, swift miscarriage of the wind; use it to flee, and I shall guard your back.

VASILY: If it's God's will that I die or if death awaits me here, today I shall seek her out and await her face to face.

(*The call to arms is sounded, and Sigismund enters accompanied by his Soldiers.*)

SIGISMUND: Among the crags and thickets of the mountain hides the king. Seek him out; let no shrub on the summit go unexamined, trunk by trunk and branch by branch!

CLOTHOLD: [*To the king.*] Flee, my lord!

VASILY: To what end?

AISTULF: What do you intend to do?

VASILY: Step aside, Aistulf.

CLOTHOLD: What do you intend to do?

VASILY: Something that must be done, Clothold. [*To Sigismund.*] If I'm the one you're looking for, you have me at your mercy, my prince. Use my grey hairs as a mat for your feet; trample my neck and tread upon my crown; humiliate me and drag my good name through the mud; take your vengeance on my honour, and treat me as your captive. After so many attempts to circumvent it, let fate claim its reward; let the stars keep their word.

SIGISMUND: Illustrious Court of Poland, witness to so many amazing events, listen carefully, for your prince wishes to address you. What is determined by Heaven and written by God's finger on the azure tablet—of which the numerous blue leaves adorned in gold letters are the signs and annotations—never lies or deceives; the lies and deceptions come from the one who, wishing to manipulate the information, undertakes to decipher it. My father, who is present among us, in order to avoid the wrath of my character, turned me into a brute, a human beast; thus, whereas my gallant nobility, genteel lineage, and generous nature should have made me congenial and humble, my living conditions and upbringing were sufficient to cultivate a ferocious disposition. What a way to cheat fate! If any man were told, "One day you will be killed by an inhuman beast," would it be a good solution for him to wake one up while it was sleeping? If he were told, "That sword you're wearing will one day be the death of you," to take it out and point it at his chest would prove a futile remedy. If he were told, "Your grave will lie beneath walls of water and bear tombstones of silvery waves," he would be foolish to set sail just when the defiant sea was whipping up frothy mountains of glass. My father has ended up just like the one who, threatened by a beast, woke it up; like the one who, fearful of the sword, unsheathed it; and like the one who stirred up the waves of a tempest. But even if—and listen well—my wrath were a dormant beast, my fury a temperate sword, and my severity a calm sea, fortune could not be overcome through injustice and vengeance, for such measures only make matters worse. And thus, whoever wishes to overcome his fortune must do so through prudence and temperance. He who foresees a danger can't remove himself from its path; yes, he can take a few humble measures to guard against it, but not until the moment is upon him, for there's no way of forestalling its arrival. Of this there's no better proof than this extraordinary spectacle, this bizarre event, horrible and monstrous to behold. Just look and you'll see, despite all efforts to the contrary, a father vanquished at my foot, a monarch grovelling in defeat. This was Heaven's judgment; no matter how he tried to prevent it, he was unable. And I—inferior to him in years, valour, and knowledge—shall succeed where he failed. Rise, my lord, and give me your hand; now that the stars have shown you the error in your attempts to overcome them, my neck humbly awaits your vengeance, I am at your mercy.

VASILY: My son, you are prince, for such a noble action remoulds you from my flesh; the laurel and the palm are yours. You have triumphed; your deeds shall be your crown.

ALL: Long live Sigismund! Long live Sigismund!

[*Enter Rossaura.*]

SIGISMUND: [*Observing Rossaura.*] My valour promises great victories, and today the greatest of all will be my victory over myself. Aistulf, promise your hand to Rossaura immediately, for you know that you're a debtor to her honour, and I intend to make you pay.

AISTULF: Although it's true I owe her something, bear in mind that she doesn't know who her father is; and it would be a low and infamous deed for someone like me to marry a woman who . . .

CLOTHOLD: Do not go on; hold your tongue and listen. Rossaura is just as noble as you, Aistulf, and I will argue her case with my sword if I have to. She is my daughter, and that's all you need to know.

AISTULF: What are you saying?

CLOTHOLD: Until I saw her promised in noble marriage and her honour avenged, I didn't want to reveal her identity. It's a very long story, but the point is that she's my daughter.

AISTULF: Well, that being the case, I'll honour my word.

SIGISMUND: And now, so Stella won't feel left out, given that she's lost a prince of such merit and reputation, by my own hand I shall wed her to a man who is, in distinction and good fortune, if not greater than Aistulf, at least his equal. Give me your hand, my lady.

STELLA: I'm honoured to be worthy of such joy.

SIGISMUND: To Clothold, who served my father loyally, I offer my warm embrace together with any favours that he might ask of me.

SOLDIER 1: If that's how you reward someone who never served you, what do I get for inciting the uprising in the kingdom and for freeing you from the tower in which you were imprisoned?

SIGISMUND: The tower. And so that you'll never emerge until you die, you'll be under the constant watch of the guards, for traitors are of no use once their treachery has passed.

VASILY: Your ingenuity amazes us all.

AISTULF: What a change of character!

ROSSAURA: What discretion, what prudence!

SIGISMUND: Hence comes your amazement, your shock, given that my teacher was a dream? I still fear, deep down inside, that I'll wake up and find myself locked away again in my dark prison. And if that doesn't happen, it's enough to dream it so, for that's how I came to realize that all human happiness is, in the end, as ephemeral as a dream. So I'd like to take advantage of this happy moment while I can . . . [*To the audience.*] . . . and ask you to overlook our flaws, for forgiveness comes naturally to noble souls.

COMMENTARY

ED MORALES (b. 1955)

Review of José Rivera's Production of *Sueño* 1998

In this extensive discussion of José Rivera's adaptation of *Life Is a Dream*, Morales examines the reasoning behind Rivera's reworking of Calderón's language and Rivera's emphasis on the philosophical issues that lie beneath the surface of the play. Morales also gives us some insight into the challenges faced by a modern producer of a seventeenth-century drama, especially in light of the ways in which both the theater and its audiences have changed.

Sueño, José Rivera's adaptation of Calderón de la Barca's classic *La Vida es Sueño* (*Life Is a Dream*), starts out impressively enough. When John Ortiz's hirsute, muscular, and scantily clad body appears onstage suspended in midair by long red ropes, Hartford Stage Company audiences can't help but hold their collective breath and expect a wild theatrical ride. Ortiz plays Segismundo, the son of a Spanish monarch held in a dungeon because of his original sin — killing his mother in childbirth — but about to be freed from his misery to have a go at his birthright as a ruler. The sharp contrast between his captivity and deliverance causes Segismundo to blur the line between reality and dreams and allows Calderón to explore the big philosophical questions (What is existence? *Is* life a dream, and if so, who is dreaming *us*? God?) that have made *La Vida es Sueño* so enduring. However, it's hard not to wonder what kind of resonance these issues can have for a twentieth-century audience, when a good chunk of reality is virtual or simulated.

At first glance, *Sueño's* theatrical strategy seems to be a variation on what might be called the New York Shakespeare Festival style of reinventing the classics. The characters engage in a contemporary sassiness; they draw out some of the contemporaneous subtext from seventeenth-century situations; and traditionally cross-dressed roles are augmented by nontraditionally cross-dressed ones. But on closer inspection, Rivera's *Sueño* proves to be a true adaptation, not a recontextualization; there are no TV sets or gang paraphernalia in this production. The costumes are faithful to their origins in Spain. Indeed, it's not the surface aspects of the production that offer a contemporary spin on Calderón's metaphysical musings: it is the *language* that has been changed, shifting from the baroque Spanish verse of the 1600s to the contemporary rhythms of America at the end of the twentieth century.

From Segismundo's opening soliloquies, where he proclaims himself "a storm of chemical responses pretending to have a soul," Rivera has reclaimed Calderón's florid use of metaphor and made it his own, spiced with science, sarcasm, and sweetness. "I wanted to find the language Calderón would have used if he was a forty-two-year-old playwright living in California," the theater and television writer says on the phone from his home in Los Angeles. That blending of the contemporary and the antiquated can have some surprising results. For instance, when Segismundo says he is "God's wild virus," you can feel all the implications of imagined or real modern-day plagues while simultaneously acknowledging their roots in an empire engaged in conquering a New World.

Rivera was not only faced with the task of reinventing Calderón's language, but also the challenge of making the play, which is long on plot and short on characterization, "actable." By doing case studies of people who had experienced long-term isolation, Rivera was able to create a realistic psychological profile for Segismundo and enliven his character with appropriate behavior, particularly in the early scenes between him and Rosaura (Michi Barall), a young noblewoman bent on revenge. Long monologues were replaced with short, snappy, almost sit-com-esque interactions, a possible by-product of the time Rivera has done in Hollywood. (The writer professes to have given up television work, particularly since the demise of *Eerie, Indiana*, a series he created that some claim was too smart to remain on the air.)

In this way, the wordplay between Lord Astolfo (Damian Young) and Princess Estrella (Alene Dawson) — two scheming nobles who have their eyes on the throne — is one of the highlights of the production. "Flowers are dishrags compared to you," carps Astolfo in his parodic wooing of a noblewoman in line to succeed the reigning monarch. "Helen? A slutbox.... Aphrodite? Maggot poop." Young and Jan Leslie Harding, in her drag interpretation of Rosaura's clownish manservant Clarin (the character is traditionally played by a male), provide comic relief from the dark antics Segismundo engages in when he's given a chance to prove he might be worthy of nobility.

By showcasing these underlying comedic moments, *Sueño* moves away from the tragically cerebral aura that traditionally surrounds Calderón's work. Nevertheless, the play's dramatic impact is reinvigorated by Rivera's commitment to updating its contextual underpinnings. In the post-Freud era, there are echoes of the Oedipus complex in Segismundo's attacks on his father Basilio's kingship. Perhaps more important, their relationship strongly resembles the one between Prospero and Caliban in *The Tempest*. Segismundo is portrayed as a vulgar, uneducated beast, an id looking to inflict severe psychological, as well as physical, pain. Basilio, on the other hand, seems to be uncertain about his moral imperative: he is vaguely aware of his own complicity in the brutal conquest of the New World. Even as he obsesses over a lunar eclipse (the evil omen that marks the birth of his son), another spherical object, the Aztec calendar, lurks center stage for much of the play.

For Rivera, this zigzagging between the old and the new in some ways mirrors the ambivalence of the Hispanic phenomenon and may explain Latino interest in the Hartford Stage production. (The fact that the theater coordinated a major community relations drive didn't hurt either.) According to Rivera, while Hispanics may not feel directly connected to Spain, they still relate to intrinsic elements of the culture. "There's this code of honor that we all seem to be struggling with," muses Rivera. "Being Latino in the U.S. is like being caught in the middle between tradition and nontradition. But we have come to feel comfortable with contradiction."

While Rivera's rewrite may make Calderón's work more accessible and contemporary, *Sueño* has even more profound implications. Instead of saying, "If the Fates decree that now's your time to die / There's nothing you can do," Clarin declares, "If God wants your ass, he's going to get your ass." While the change works as humor, these lines are also helping Rivera establish the idea that the presence of mortal life is no longer just an extension of the proof of the existence of God. "In the original, Segismundo gets attached to the idea that if everything is a dream, the dreamer must be God," says Rivera. "What my version is trying to say is that the idea of God is unreliable."

In transferring Calderón's psyche into his own, Rivera is making a statement about American reality and the way it represents the difference between Old World and New World thinking. The romantic pairings that climax the original— Astolfo-Rosaura and Segismundo-Estrella—are reversed. Rosaura turns her back on nobility and urges Segismundo to join her in a quest for free will and the overturning of the rigid class structures of Europe. It's a moment that brings out an idea buried in Calderón's text, that a New World is about to begin. In José Rivera's own sly and spiritual way, *Sueño* carries the enormous implication that we're on the verge of that kind of history happening all over again.

Late-Seventeenth- and Eighteenth-Century Drama

Theater in England continued to thrive after Shakespeare's death, thanks to the efforts of a host of successful playwrights, including John Webster (1580?–1638?), Francis Beaumont (c. 1584–1616) and his collaborator John Fletcher (1579–1625), Philip Massinger (1583–1640), Thomas Middleton (1580–1627), John Ford (1586–c. 1655) and James Shirley (1596–1666). All of these playwrights were busy working independently or in collaboration. Fletcher, chosen successor to Shakespeare at the Globe, furnished the theater with as many as four plays a year. But in 1642, long-standing religious and political conflicts between King Charles I and Parliament finally erupted into civil war, with the Parliament, under the influence of Puritanism, eventually winning.

The Puritans were religious extremists with narrow, specific values. They were essentially an emerging merchant class of well-to-do citizens who viewed the aristocracy as wastrels. Theater for them was associated with both the aristocracy and the low life. Theatergoing was synonymous with wasting time; the theaters were often a focus for immoral activity, and the neighborhoods around the theaters were as unsavory as any in England. Under the Puritan government, all theaters in England were closed for almost twenty years. When the new king, Charles II, was crowned in 1660, those that had not been converted to other uses had become completely outmoded.

As a young prince, Charles, with his mother and brother, had been sent to the Continent in the early stages of the civil war. When his father, Charles I, was beheaded, the future king and his family were in France, where they were in a position to see the remarkable achievements of French comedy and French classical tragedy. Charles II developed a taste for theater that accompanied him back to England. And when he returned in triumph to usher in the exciting and swashbuckling period known as the Restoration, he permitted favorites to build new theaters.

Theater on the Continent: Neoclassicism

Interaction among the leading European countries — England, Spain, and France — was sporadic at best in the seventeenth century because of intermittent wars among the nations, yet the development of theater in all three countries took similar turns throughout the early 1600s.

By the 1630s, the French were aware of Spanish achievements in the theater; Pierre Corneille (1606–1684), who emerged as France's leading playwright of the time, adapted a Spanish story by de Castro that became one of his most important plays, *Le Cid*.

By the time Charles II took up residence in France in the 1640s, the French had developed a suave, polished, and intellectually demanding approach to drama. Corneille and the neoclassicists were part of a large movement in European culture and the arts that tried to codify and emulate the achievement of the ancients. Qualities such as harmony, symmetry, balance in everything structural, and clear moral themes were most sought after. Because **neoclassicism** valued thought over feeling, the thematic material in neoclassical drama was very important. That material was sometimes political, reflecting the values of Augustan Rome — 27 BCE to 17 CE — when Caesar Augustus lived and when it was appropriate to think in terms of subordinating the self to the interests of the state. Neoclassical dramatists focused on honor, moral integrity, self-sacrifice, and heroic political subjects.

French Tragedy

One school of critics held playwrights strictly to the Aristotelian concepts of the unities of time, place, character, and action. These "rules critics" demanded a perfect observance of the unities — that is, they wanted a play to have one plot, a single action that takes place in one day, and a single setting. In most cases the plays that satisfied them are now often thought of as static, cold, limited, and dull. Their perfection is seen today as rigid and emotionally icy.

Corneille's work did not please such critics, and they turned to a much younger competitor, Jean Racine (1639–1699), who brought the tradition of French tragedy to its fullest. Most of Racine's plays are on classical subjects, beginning in 1667 with *Andromache*, continuing with *Britannicus* (1669), *Iphigenia* (1674), and *Mithridate* (1673), and ending in 1677 with his most famous and possibly best play, *Phaedra*.

Phaedra is a deeply passionate, moral play centering on the love of Phaedra for her stepson, Hippolytus. Venus is responsible for her incestuous love — which is the playwright's way of saying that Phaedra is impelled by the gods or by destiny, almost against her will.

The French stage, unlike the English, never substituted boys for female roles, and so plays such as *Phaedra* were opportunities for brilliant actresses. Phaedra, in particular, dominates the stage — she is a commanding and infinitely complex figure. It is no wonder that this play was a favorite of Sarah Bernhardt (1844–1923), one of France's greatest actresses.

French Comedy: Molière

At the same time that Racine commanded the tragic stage, Jean Baptiste Poquelin (1622–1673), known as Molière, began his dominance of the comic stage. He was aware of Racine's achievements and applauded them strongly. His career started with a small theater company that spent most of its time touring the countryside beyond Paris. When the company settled in Paris, its plays were influenced by some of the stock characters and situations of the commedia dell'arte, but they also began to reflect Molière's own genius for composition.

Seeing a performance by Molière's company in 1658, King Louis XIV found it so much to his liking that he installed the company in a theater and demanded to see more of its work. From that time on, Molière wrote, produced, and acted in one comedy after another, most of which have become part of the permanent repertoire of the French stage. Plays such as *The Misanthrope* (1666), *The Miser* (1669), *The Bourgeois Gentleman* (1670), *The Imaginary Invalid* (1673), and his satire on the theme of religious hypocrisy, *Tartuffe* (1669), are also staged all over the world.

Theater in England: The Restoration

The English Restoration began in 1660 with the return of King Charles II to England after nearly two decades in France. The new age craved glitter, excitement, sensuality, and dramatic dazzle. Audiences wanted upbeat comedies that poked fun at stuffed shirts and old-fashioned institutions. Charles was influenced by the French theaters, which were often constructed on a pattern of the French tennis court — a long, narrow, rectangular space that served well for French performances.

The Great Fire of 1666, which destroyed most of London, occasioned extensive reconstruction that, in the 1670s, included the building of new theaters. They too were long and narrow, but, unlike most Elizabethan theaters, they were enclosed and depended on artificial lighting. Restoration theaters operated year-round, and the prices of seats depended on their location. The first-level boxes against the walls were the most expensive seats; the middle-priced seats — actually backless benches — filled the pit before the proscenium-arched stage (Figure 13); and the lowest-priced seats were in the upper ranges of the galleries.

The structure of the new theater permitted realistic scene design, with a receding space that accommodated painted backdrops. Actors could enter and leave by side doors directly on stage or could retreat to the **flies** through the scenic stage. The proscenium was not framed as in later theaters but, rather, permitted actors to move close to those sitting in the pit. The space allotted to the actors in the Drury Lane Theatre was considerable, facilitating rousing fight scenes and crowd scenes. The **apron** also produced an intimacy between actor and audience that encouraged a more natural presentation. The drama-starved audiences favored a new style of comedy—one that was socially observant—and a new style of tragedy—one that may be called heroic, as in the plays of John Dryden (1631–1700), whose *All for Love* was a "rewrite" of Shakespeare's *Antony and Cleopatra*. New plays for the Restoration often consisted of rewritings of great Elizabethan plays (including a version of *King Lear* with a happy ending) or reworkings of plots of French, Italian, and Spanish plays. The age required high fashion, superficial brilliance, and sensual entertainment in the style of a sometimes lewd court and more open society.

Not everyone applauded these developments, however. The clergyman and critic Jeremy Collier, in *A Short View of the Immorality and Profaneness of the English Stage* (1698), attacked the contemporary theater for its immorality, its satiric portrayal of ministers of the church, and its casual references to the Bible. He condemned not only the theater of his age but also the plays of Shakespeare and the great Elizabethan dramatists, whose work was quite different in tone from the contemporary drama. The effect he had on theater

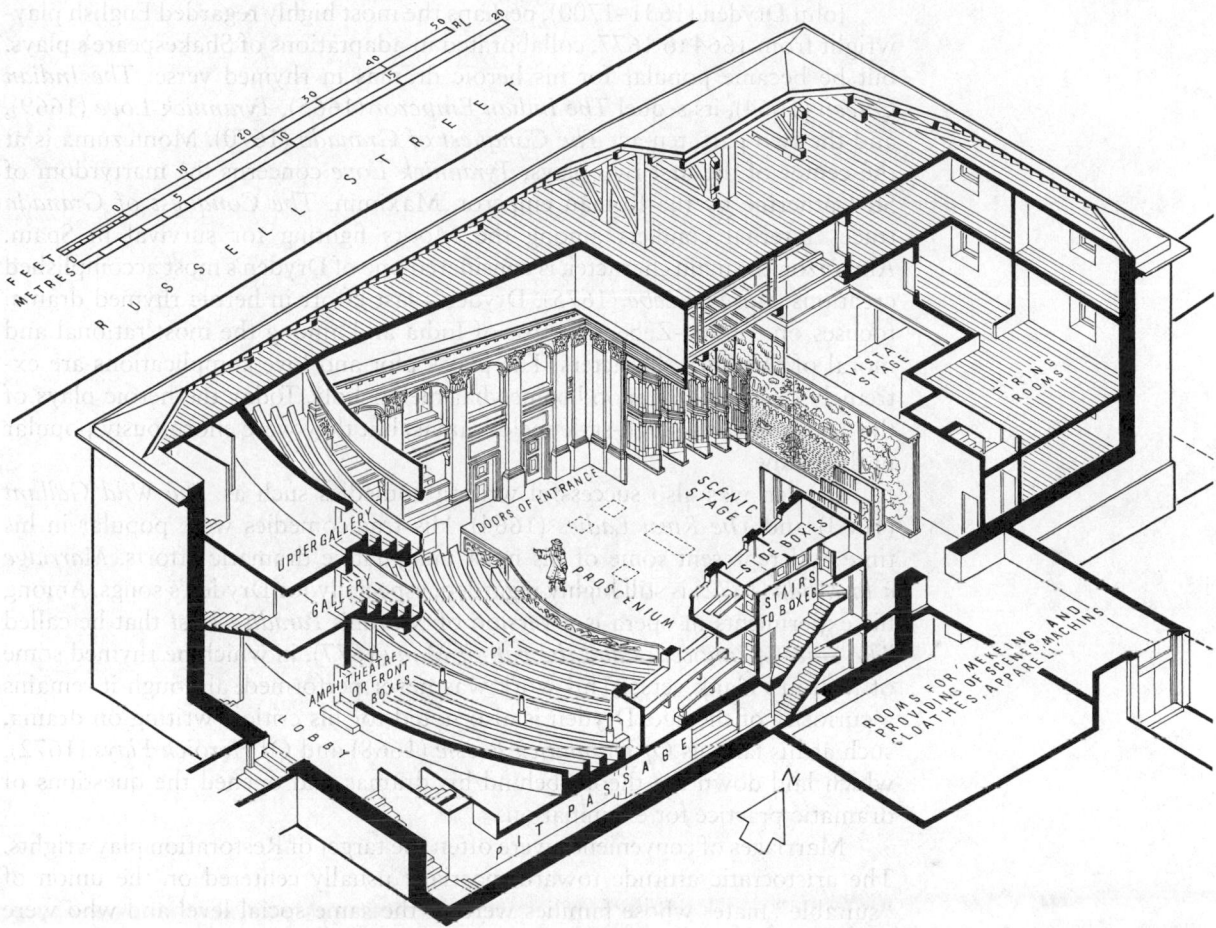

Figure 13. Theatre Royal, Drury Lane, 1676, designed by Sir Christopher Wren.

was extensive, in part because, during his reign a decade earlier, James II had taken up the cry to reform the theater. Major playwrights were fined for their productions, which certainly had a dampening effect on later productions by important actors and companies.

Among England's notable playwrights from 1660 through the eighteenth century were Aphra Behn (1640–1689), the first professional female playwright on the English stage and author of *The Rover*, one of the most frequently performed plays of the period; William Wycherley (1640–1716), whose best works are thought to be *The Plain Dealer*, indebted to Molière, and *The Country Wife*; William Congreve (1670–1729), whose *The Way of the World* is justly famous; and Richard Brinsley Sheridan (1751–1816), whose *School for Scandal* is still bright, lively, and engaging for modern audiences. Other important playwrights whose work is still performed are George Farquhar (1678–1707), especially known for *The Beaux Stratagem* (1707); John Gay (1685–1732), whose *Beggar's Opera* has been revived repeatedly since its first performance in 1728; and Oliver Goldsmith (1730–1774), author of *She Stoops to Conquer* (1773).

John Dryden (1631–1700), perhaps the most highly regarded English playwright from 1664 to 1677, collaborated in adaptations of Shakespeare's plays, but he became popular for his heroic dramas in rhymed verse: *The Indian Queen* (1664), its sequel *The Indian Emperor* (1665), *Tyrannick Love* (1669), and the two-part, ten-act *The Conquest of Granada* (1670). Montezuma is at the center of the first two plays; *Tyrannick Love* concerns the martyrdom of St. Catherine by the Roman emperor, Maximin. *The Conquest of Granada* traces internal conflicts among the Moors fighting for survival in Spain. Almanzor, the main character, is considered one of Dryden's most accomplished creations. *Aureng-Zebe* (1675), Dryden's last effort in heroic rhymed drama, focuses on Aureng-Zebe, emperor of India and among the most rational and moral of Dryden's characters. The play's plot and love complications are extremely dense and its mood somewhat melancholy. Today the heroic plays of the 1660s resemble high-style melodramas, but they were enormously popular in their time.

Dryden was also successful writing comedies such as *The Wild Gallant* (1663) and *The Rival Ladies* (1664). His tragicomedies were popular in his time and represent some of his most imaginative dramatic efforts. *Marriage à-la-Mode* (1672) is still highly regarded, especially for Dryden's songs. Among his experiments in opera is a version of Milton's *Paradise Lost* that he called *The State of Innocence and the Fall of Man* (1677), in which he rhymed some of Milton's blank verse. This work was never performed, although it remains a curiosity of the age. Dryden is also noted for his critical writing on drama, such as his famous *Of Dramatick Poesie* (1668) and *Of Heroick Plays* (1672), which laid down the theory behind his dramas and opened the questions of dramatic practice for examination.

Marriages of convenience were often the target of Restoration playwrights. The aristocratic attitude toward marriage usually centered on the union of "suitable" mates whose families were of the same social level and who were financially attractive to each other. Consequently, impoverished gentlemen of good name would sometimes seek out wealthy women, and vice versa. Marriages were based sometimes on love but more often on financial or social convenience. As a result, conflicts in choosing marriage partners often involved elaborate dealings between parents and children. Once married, husbands and wives played complex games of adultery and betrayal, negotiating terms of financial settlements while engaging in witty repartee and riposte, as in William Congreve's immortal *The Way of the World*. It is not until the end of the eighteenth century that the sentimental comedy appeared, introducing recognizable emotional responses that appear normal to present-day audiences. Aristocratic attitudes toward marriage are evident in drama as late as the end of the nineteenth century, as in Oscar Wilde's *The Importance of Being Earnest*.

The English playwrights produced a wide range of comedy, to fulfill their audiences' desire for bright, gay, and witty entertainment. The comedies of the period came to be known in the twentieth century as **comedies of manners** because they revealed the foibles of the society that watched them. Society enjoyed laughing at itself. Although some of the English dramas of the eighteenth century developed a moralistic tone and were heavily classical, the earlier **restoration comedies** focused less on reforming the society than on capitalizing on its faults.

Eighteenth-Century Drama

Eighteenth-century Europe absorbed much of the spirit of France and the French neoclassicists. England, like other European countries, began to see the effects of neoclassicism in the arts and literature. Emulation of classical art and classical values was common throughout Europe, and critics established standards of excellence in the arts to guarantee quality.

The most famous name in eighteenth-century English drama is David Garrick (1717–1779), the legendary actor and manager of the Drury Lane Theatre. The theaters, including his own, often reworked French drama and earlier English and Italian drama, but they began to develop a new **sentimental comedy** to balance the neoclassical heroic tragedies of the period. It was comedy that played on, manipulated, and exploited the emotions of the audience to arouse sympathy for the characters in the play.

Sentimental comedy flourished after 1720, but Colley Cibber (1671–1757) is sometimes credited with originating this form with his *Love's Last Shift* (1696). The play centers on Loveless, who wanders from his marriage only to find that his wife has disguised herself as a prostitute to win him back. As in all sentimental comedies, what the audience most wants is what it gets: a certain amount of tears, an equal amount of laughter, and a happy ending. As an actor, Cibber was especially well known for his portrayal of fops, his way of poking satiric fun at his own society and its pretensions.

Sir Richard Steele (1672–1729) wrote one of the best known sentimental comedies, *The Conscious Lovers* (1722). Steele's coauthor on *The Spectator*, Joseph Addison (1672–1719), also distinguished himself with his contribution to the heroic tragedy of the age, the long neoclassical *Cato* (1713). It was considered to be the finest example of the moral heroic style. Today it is not a playable drama because the action is too slow, the speeches too long, and the theme too obscure, although it is a perfect model of what the age preferred in heroic tragedy. George Lillo (1693–1739) in *The London Merchant* (1731) produced a bourgeois tragedy in which the main character was from the middle class. It was one of the most frequently produced plays of its time.

The audiences at the time enjoyed bright, amusing comedies that often criticized wayward youth, overprotective parents, dishonest financial dealings, and social expectations. Their taste in tragedies veered toward a moralizing heroism that extolled the values of the community and self-sacrifice on the part of the hero.

The Seventeenth- and Eighteenth-Century Actor

Although the tradition of acting in England had been interrupted for almost twenty years before the Restoration, some important actors, such as Thomas Betterton (1635–1710), were able to continue many of the features of Shakespeare's staging. Betterton was especially noted for his performances as Hamlet, a part that was popular throughout the eighteenth century. In this period in England, actors received praise if they had fine figures and strong and mellow voices, and used facial expressions to reveal emotion at the proper dramatic moment. Commentary on acting stressed naturalness of expression as a prerequisite for excellence. However, the age's concept of what was natural was much different from ours; the acting of the age would seem grossly exaggerated to us.

In France, women had been on stage for some time, and during the Restoration, actresses appeared on the English stage and proved enormously

Figure 14. Nell Gwynne, the best known actress of her age, in a portrait by Sir Peter Lely (c. 1675).

popular. Actresses were often the most important draw in English theaters in the seventeenth century. Nell Gwynne (1650–1687), one of the most famous actresses of the age (Figure 14), was also mistress to Charles II. She was discovered by her actor husband while selling flowers near a theater at age 15. Her lightheartedness and sometimes risqué manner were part of her stage appeal. The great diarist Samuel Pepys saw her in a comedy and vowed that "so great a performance of a comical part was never, I believe, in the world before." She was so remarkable that John Dryden, poet laureate, wrote comic parts specifically for her.

Actors in this period employed numerous stage tricks, sometimes called **claptraps,** designed to elicit applause because they were conventional theatrical exaggerations. (Hamlet's startled reaction when he first sees his father's ghost is a good example.) Actors often "milked" a scene for applause by using various ingenious means of showing horror and alarm. Even the "pregnant" pause was used by Betterton and others to draw the audience in. Conventions such as broad gestures with the upstage hand and sudden kneeling on the downstage knee were widely employed for dramatic effect, along with impetuous turns to the audience, especially from the apron. Some of the older actors were also skilled at the rant—raising the voice, grotesquely twisting the body, and grimacing while driving home a point. These were tricks that actors such as David Garrick (1717–1779) often railed against in an effort to promote a more subdued style of acting. Although eighteenth-century commentators note that he sometimes used mild forms of the very tricks he disliked, Garrick's purpose was to exhibit a natural style on stage, and he was widely complimented for having done so.

Garrick's greatest role was Richard III, and he was praised for his ability to reveal a variety of emotions in his face, especially in the tent scene on Bosworth field (Figure 15). He practiced moving from joy to horror to surprise to alarm to grief to guilt—and even more emotions, one after another—all in a convincing manner. Garrick and other eighteenth-century actors had the advantage of modern theaters such as the Drury Lane (which he managed), in which the apron was close to the pit. The intimate, enclosed space made it possible for actors to be heard easily and to be seen well enough for their facial expressions to convey reactions that in ages past necessitated broad gesturing. The evolution of the theater's design made it possible for Garrick to achieve the effects for which he was so widely praised. Garrick occasionally went so far as to burlesque the overly theatrical style of some of his competitors, although sometimes only a portion of the audience got the joke.

Many good actors with fine reputations appeared on the stage of the period: James Quin (1693–1766), said to be the finest Falstaff of his age; Charles Macklin (1699–1797), a playwright also known for his sensitive portrayal

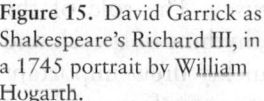

Figure 15. David Garrick as Shakespeare's Richard III, in a 1745 portrait by William Hogarth.

of Shylock and his virtual invention of the stage Irishman; Sarah Siddons (1755–1831) and her brother John Philip Kemble (1757–1823), praised for their smooth and careful acting style. Siddons and Kemble sometimes acted together to great acclaim, and their style evolved over time into a melodramatic exaggeration that was to become dominant in the early nineteenth century.

Drama in Japan

During the period of the Tokugawa shogunate (1603–1868), Japan attempted to seal itself off from the Western world. Although the Portuguese had a trading facility in Nagasaki, their influence was limited in range and scope. The great playwrights and actors of the Tokugawa period in Edo (Tokyo), Kyoto, and Osaka were generally unaware of traditions of Western drama, and in some cases they had never read or seen a foreign play.

Although Japan was essentially a military dictatorship at the time, the period was peaceful and prosperous, with a rising merchant middle class that demanded entertainment that represented their own values and interests. The shogun, or leader, was a warrior, and the warrior class—the samurai—had much to say about the forms of entertainment available. They were interested in theater partly because with peacetime came leisure time and the opportunity for indulgence. The pleasure district, or "floating world," of Kyoto permitted prostitution and various theatrical and circus-like entertainments for men. It was in this atmosphere that traditions of kabuki theater and puppet theater flourished.

Kabuki began from a dance performed in 1603 by a female entertainer named Okuni, whose popularity was such that she developed numerous imitators, especially prostitutes who danced kabuki in order to attract customers. The dance was enlarged with sketches from contemporary life accompanied by a popular three-stringed instrument called a *shamisen*. The role of the *shamisen* musician in kabuki plays was to establish the rhythms of speech and help stimulate the motions of the audience. Kabuki quickly drew important actors who used elaborate makeup and brilliant costumes to perform multiact plays over an entire day.

After women were banned from the stage in 1629, men performed all the parts in kabuki plays. Audiences found kabuki exciting because it was designed to stimulate the masses. This popular entertainment form narrated stories of contemporary life and sometimes captured the audience's dissatisfaction with the inequities they perceived in their own society. Kabuki also produced numerous highly gifted actors, many from the samurai class, who became a draw in their own right.

Partly because the actors became difficult and demanding, some of the important playwrights of the time, including Chikamatsu Monzaemon (1653–1725), turned to the *jōruri*, or puppet plays. Unlike actors, puppets made no demands on authors and never stole the show. They were also versatile enough to create remarkably subtle expressions of emotion, thought, and action. Some plays were produced in both kabuki and *jōruri* forms, but because incredible special effects were possible with puppets—effects that could not be achieved with actors—*jōruri* theater flourished in the early eighteenth century.

Chikamatsu, the greatest of Japanese playwrights, was born into a samurai family that had little influence in society. He drifted into kabuki theater and now enjoys the reputation of being Japan's first professional playwright. His early plays were for particularly important kabuki actors. He specialized in history plays, which were popular because they educated people not only about their own history but also about faraway places. His domestic plays, especially his tragedies, which are primarily puppet plays, are more frequently produced today, partly because their subjects—middle-class suffering and emotional longing—seem more modern to us. *The Love Suicides at Sonezaki*, one of a series of love suicide plays, was so influential as to help cause the entire genre to be banned.

During this period, kabuki acting and stagecraft developed quickly, with highly stylized masks, extraordinary costumes, and complex sets. Eventually, complex stage machinery—trap doors and revolving stages—made the drama all the more interesting. The puppet stage depended on a chanter who recited the lines of all the characters and sometimes the narrator. Eventually, puppets operated by a single person gave way to more complex, three-person puppets requiring unusual coordination and skill and producing subtle expressions and effects. Today both forms of theater still exist in Japan and are performed throughout the world.

Date	Theater	Political	Social/Cultural
1600–1700	**1603:** Okuni creates the first kabuki dance.	**1603:** Beginning of the Tokugawa shogunate in Edo, Japan, a long period of peace	**1606–1669:** Rembrandt van Rijn, Dutch painter
	1606–1684: French playwright Pierre Corneille, author of *Le Cid* (1636)	**1605:** Gun Powder Plot in London; execution of Guy Fawkes	**1608–1674:** John Milton, English author
	1622–1673: Molière (born Jean Baptiste Poquelin), French dramatist and actor, author of *The Misanthrope* (1666), *Tartuffe* (1669), and *The Learned Ladies* (1672)		**1610:** Galileo's first observations through a telescope
			1620: Voyage of the *Mayflower*
			1628: William Harvey describes the circulation of blood.
	c. 1634–1691: Sir George Etherege, author of *Love in a Tub* and *The Man of Mode* (1676)		**1631–1700:** John Dryden, English author and playwright
			1633: John Donne's *Poems*, the complete collection of his poetry, is published.
	1635–1710: Thomas Betterton, perhaps the Restoration's most important actor		**1637:** René Descartes's *Discourse on Method*, an exploration of mathematics and laws
	1639–1699: Jean Racine, French playwright, author of *Phaedra* (1677)		**1638:** Anne Hutchinson is expelled from the Massachusetts Bay Colony and founds Rhode Island.
	1640–1689: Aphra Behn, first professional female playwright in the English theater, author of *The Rover* (1677)	**1642:** Beginning of the English Civil War	
		1643: Louis XIV becomes king of France at age four.	**1645:** Gian Lorenzo Bernini begins his *Ecstasy of St. Theresa.*
	1650–1687: Nell Gwynne, English actress and mistress of Charles II	**1649:** Charles I is beheaded by order of Parliament.	
		1655: Oliver Cromwell prohibits Anglican church services and divides England into eleven districts governed by major-generals.	**1650:** Anne Bradstreet publishes *The Tenth Muse*, the first collection of poetry from the New World.
	1656: First use of Italianate scenery in England in a production of *The Siege of Rhodes,* designed by John Webb		
	1658: Molière's troupe, the Illustre Théâtre, is invited to perform at the court of Louis XIV. The company is subsequently given permission to remain in Paris, as the Troupe de Monsieur, and allowed to use the Petit Bourbon for public performances.	**1658:** Cromwell dissolves Parliament and then dies in September.	
	1660: Theatrical activity resumes in London (after being halted in 1642) when Charles II issues patents to Thomas Killigrew and William Davenant. Women are permitted on the English stage for the first time.	**1660:** Restoration of the English monarchy and end of the Commonwealth; Charles II, son of the executed Charles I, is crowned.	**1660:** Samuel Pepys begins his diary. **1660:** Dutch Boers settle on the Cape of Good Hope. **1661–1731:** Daniel Defoe, English author

Date	Theater	Political	Social/Cultural
1600–1700 (continued)	**1664:** Japanese playwright Fukui Yagozaemon writes *The Outcast's Revenge,* the first full-length kabuki play.	**1664:** The British annex New Amsterdam and rename it New York.	**1664–1666:** Isaac Newton (1642–1727), English mathematician and physicist, discovers the law of universal gravitation and begins to develop calculus.
	1670–1729: William Congreve, author of *Love for Love* (1695) and *The Way of the World* (1700)	**1682:** Louis XIV moves the French court to Versailles.	**1665:** Plague devastates London.
	1680: The Comédie-Française, the first national theater, opens in Paris.	**1682–1725:** Peter the Great reigns as czar of Russia and calls for political and cultural reforms.	**1666:** Great Fire of London
		1685: Louis XIV revokes the Edict of Nantes, and persecution of the Huguenots (French Protestants) ensues.	**1685–1750:** J. S. Bach, German composer
	1695–1715: Proliferation of female playwrights in England. Thirty-seven new plays by women are produced on the London stage during this period by playwrights such as Mary Pix (1666–1706), Susanna Centlivre (c. 1670–1723), Mary Delarivière Manley (c. 1672–1724), and Catharine Trotter (1679–1749).	**1688:** William of Orange invades England with the encouragement of prominent Protestants, who fear James II's Catholicism. James flees to France. William III and Mary II (daughter of James II) are crowned in 1689.	**1687:** Isaac Newton publishes *Mathematical Principles*.
			1688–1704: Alexander Pope, English poet
	1698: Jeremy Collier's *A Short View of the Immorality and Profaneness of the English Stage*, the most effective of several attacks on the theater published at the turn of the century	**1690:** An Irish uprising in favor of James II is suppressed by William III at the Battle of the Boyne.	**1692:** Salem witchcraft trials
			1694–1778: François Marie Arouet de Voltaire, French author often described as the embodiment of the Enlightenment
		1697: The last remains of Mayan civilization are destroyed by the Spanish.	
1700–1800	**1703:** Chikamatsu creates the genre of love suicide plays with *The Love Suicides at Sonezaki.*	**1703:** Peter the Great lays the foundation for St. Petersburg.	**1703–1758:** Jonathan Edwards, American theologian
	1707–1793: Carlo Goldoni, Italian playwright, author of *The Servant of Two Masters* (1743)	**1707:** The Act of Union unites Scotland and England, which become Great Britain.	**1709–1784:** Samuel Johnson, English literary critic, scholar, poet, and lexicographer
	1717–1779: David Garrick, greatest English actor of the eighteenth century and owner and manager of the Drury Lane Theatre in London	**1714:** The House of Hanover begins its rule of Great Britain with the accession of George I.	
		1715: Louis XIV, France's Sun King, dies.	**1720:** First serialization of novels in newspapers
	1720–1806: Carlo Gozzi, Italian playwright, author of *King Stag* (1762) and *Turandot* (1762)		**1724–1804:** Emmanuel Kant, German metaphysics philosopher

Date	Theater	Political	Social/Cultural
1700–1800 (continued)	**1728:** John Gay (1685–1732) writes *The Beggar's Opera,* arguably the most popular English play of the eighteenth century.		**1726:** Jonathan Swift writes *Gulliver's Travels.*
	1730–1774: Oliver Goldsmith, author of *The Vicar of Wakefield*, *The Deserted Village*, and *She Stoops to Conquer*		**1732:** Covent Garden opera house opens in London.
	1729–1781: Gotthold Ephraim Lessing, Germany's first important playwright, author of *Minna von Barnhelm* (1767) and *Emilia Galotti* (1772)		**1732–1809:** Franz Josef Haydn, prolific Austrian composer
	1737: The Licensing Act in England prohibits the performance of any play not previously licensed by the Lord Chamberlain. A number of such laws regulating theatrical activity are enacted throughout the eighteenth century.	**1740:** Frederick the Great introduces freedom of press and worship in Prussia.	**1742:** Cotton factories are established in Birmingham and Northampton, England.
	1749–1832: Johann Wolfgang von Goethe, German writer whose early works include the play *Götz von Berlichingen* (1773) and the novel *The Sorrows of Young Werther* (1774)	**1756:** Frederick begins the Seven Years War, pitting Prussia and Great Britain against Russia, Austria, and France.	**1746–1828:** Francisco de Goya, Spanish painter and political cartoonist
			1751: Denis Diderot, French writer and philosopher, publishes the first volume of his *Encyclopédie*.
	1751–1816: Richard Brinsley Sheridan, playwright and statesman, author of *The School for Scandal* (1777)	**1762:** Catherine the Great (b. 1729) becomes empress of Russia after overthrowing her husband, Peter III; she reigns until her death in 1796.	**1756–1791:** Wolfgang Amadeus Mozart, Austrian composer
	1762: English actor-manager David Garrick prohibits audience members from sitting on the stage.	**1763:** The Treaty of Paris ends the Seven Years War. Prussia emerges as an important European power. France loses many colonial possessions.	**1757–1827:** William Blake, Romantic poet and artist, author of *Songs of Innocence* and *Songs of Experience*
			1759–1797: Mary Wollstonecraft, English writer and early feminist, author of *Vindication of the Rights of Woman* (1792)
		1765: British Parliament passes the Stamp Act. Nine colonies in the New World draw up a declaration of rights and liberties.	**1762:** The Sorbonne library opens in Paris.
	c. 1769: Spectators are banned from sitting on the stage in Paris.	**1766:** Catherine the Great grants freedom of worship in Russia.	
		1776: U.S. Declaration of Independence	**1791:** James Boswell publishes his *Life of Johnson*.

Molière

Molière (1622–1673, born Jean Baptiste Poquelin) came from a family attached to the glittering court of Louis XIV, the Sun King. His father had purchased an appointment to the king, and as a result the family was familiar with the exciting court life of Paris, although not on intimate terms with the courtiers who surrounded the king. Molière's father was a furnisher and upholsterer to the king; the family, while well-to-do and possessing some power, was still apart from royalty and the privileged aristocracy.

Molière's education was exceptional. He went to Jesuit schools and spent more than five years at Collège de Clermont, which he left in 1641, having studied both the humanities and philosophy. His knowledge of philosophy was unusually deep, and his background in the classics was exceptionally strong. He also took a law degree in 1641, at Orléans, but never practiced. His father's dream was that Molière should inherit his father's appointment as furnisher to the king, thereby guaranteeing himself a comfortable future.

That, however, was not to be. Instead of following the law, Molière decided at the last minute to abandon his secure future, change his name so as not to scandalize his family, and take up a career in the theater. He began by joining a company of actors run by the Béjart family. They established a theater based in Paris called the Illustre Théâtre. It was run by Madeleine Béjart, with whom Molière had a professional and personal relationship until she died in 1672.

The famed commedia dell'arte actor Tiberio Fiorillo, known as Scaramouche, was a close friend of Molière and perhaps was responsible for Molière's choice of a career in theater. Scaramouche may have been part of the Illustre Théâtre, or he may have acted in it on occasion. Unfortunately, the Illustre Théâtre lasted only a year. It was one of several Parisian theatrical groups, and none of them prospered.

The company went bankrupt in 1644, and Molière had to be bailed out of debtors' prison. Forced to leave Paris for about thirteen years, he played in the provinces and remote towns. What was left of the Béjart group merged with another company on tour, and Molière became director of that company. During this time he suffered most of the indignities typical of the traveling life, including poverty.

Eventually Molière began writing plays, but only after he had worked extensively as an actor. In October 1658, Louis XIV saw Molière's troupe acting in one of his comedies at the Louvre. The royal court was so impressed with what it saw that the king gave Molière the use of a theater. Molière's work remained immensely popular and controversial. He acted in and produced his own plays and wrote a succession of major works that are still favorites.

Because other companies envied Molière's success and favor with the king, a number of "scandals" arose around his plays. The first play to invite controversy was *The School for Wives* (1662), in which Arnolphe reacts in horror to the infidelities he sees in the wives all around him. He decides that his wife-to-be must be raised far from the world, where she will be ignorant of the wayward lives of the Parisians. A man who intends to seduce her tells Arnolphe (not knowing who he is) how he will get her out of Arnolphe's grasp. The play is highly comic, but groups of theatergoers protested that it was immoral and scandalous. In response Molière wrote *Criticism of the School for Wives* (1663), in which the debate over the play is enacted.

Though not his most comic play, *The Misanthrope* (1666), is one of his most often produced and most thought-provoking. Molière himself acted the part of Alceste, and his wife acted opposite him as Célimène; most of the players realized that the play was making fun of the couple's own marriage. It was not so serious a portrayal as to dampen the spirits of the audience, because Molière introduced enough humor to keep it light. Yet the play had enough substance to keep audiences focused on the opposing sentiments of the couple. Alceste hates society and refuses to be polite and tell people nice things when he feels they deserve rebuke. Célimène loves society and especially loves the way she can dominate it and be its center, enjoying the attention of many suitors.

The Misanthrope examines the character of each person on stage and, by extension, the character of those in the audience—a privileged, refined stratum of society. One reason the play did not satisfy its earliest audiences may be that the lovers adhere to their opposite views of the world and, as a result, do not marry in the end. A conventional comedy would have found a means to join them, but this is not a conventional comedy.

Among Molière's other successes are *The Miser* (1668), *The Bourgeois Gentleman* (1670), and his final play, *The Imaginary Invalid* (1673). Molière had a bad cough for most of the last decade of his life, which onstage he often made to seem the cough of the character he was playing. But Molière was genuinely ill; he died playing the title role in *The Imaginary Invalid*.

Tartuffe

Molière first produced *Tartuffe, or The Hypocrite* in three acts at Versailles at a royal fête in 1664. Although the king recognized the value of the play and liked to have it read at court as a private entertainment, he immediately banned it from public production. While the king was away from court, Molière rewrote the play as *Panulphe, or the Hypocrite,* but that also was deemed too irreverent to be produced publicly.

Because Molière's satirical comedies were already thought to be problematic for French society, the clergy, who wielded considerable power with the king, kept careful watch on Molière's productions. The Society of the Holy Sacrament thought that it was being satirized in *Tartuffe* and protested the play as immoral and an attack on the Church. The Bishop of Autun also believed, perhaps correctly, that he was being satirized in the character of Tartuffe. Molière was denounced as a "demon," and a writ of excommunication was ordered against all who performed in or went to see the play.

In 1669, after the Society of the Holy Sacrament had been dissolved and after the king had managed to assuage the clergy, a permit was issued for the production of the present version of the play in five acts. Its immediate success established it as a permanent repertory piece, and it has been performed regularly ever since. Its satire on religious hypocrisy is timeless and meaningful in virtually all societies.

Tartuffe is a beggar who somehow cons Orgon, a wealthy man with a large estate, into taking him into his home. Tartuffe tricks Orgon by convincing him that he is a man of God who cares nothing for the material goods of the world and whose only duty is to God. Orgon's mother, Madame Pernelle, is thoroughly convinced that Tartuffe is virtuous and that the family must listen to and respect him. Orgon's son Damis sees Tartuffe for a fraud but is silenced and disowned by his father, who will not listen to reason. He has made up his mind and cannot be swayed by argument.

Molière immediately introduces the comic convention of the father forcing his daughter to marry against her will when Orgon announces that Mariane must give up her love for Valère and marry Tartuffe. She is an obedient daughter and seems to comply, though reluctantly. In one of the most amusing scenes in drama (act 2, scene 3), Mariane's maid Dorine cleverly persuades her to disobey her father and marry Valère. The interchange between Mariane and Valère in scene 4 reveals the high spirits of both lovers, who demonstrate their stubbornness and whose irritation with each other is smoothed over by the clever maid, a staple of drama since the Greeks.

Tartuffe, who does not appear until act 3, proposes adultery to Orgon's wife, Elmire, who plays along with him to undo Orgon's plans to marry off Mariane. It is a wonderfully comic scene (act 3, scene 3) marked by memorable lines, such as Tartuffe's "I offer you, my dear Elmire, / Love without scandal, pleasure without fear." Later he adds, "It's scandal, madame, which makes it an offense / And it's no sin to sin in confidence" (act 4, scene 5). Elmire finally plots to expose Tartuffe to her husband by having Orgon hide while Tartuffe tries to seduce her. But the plan almost backfires because Orgon madly signed over his estate to Tartuffe and upbraided his family for abusing a pious man.

The level of satire in the play is broad enough to bring laughter to virtually all audiences, and the portrait of a supposedly pious, religious, and zealous person who is fundamentally a hypocrite and fraud is so brilliantly established that Tartuffe has become the stereotype of the hypocrite. The many such frauds exposed in the press in our own era make it clear that little has changed since Molière's time.

Richard Wilbur's translation, in rhymed couplets, respects the original French, which is also in rhymed couplets. The French verse is twelve-syllable rhymed couplets, called Alexandrines. Rhyming is much easier to do in French than in English, but Wilbur produces some marvelous rhymes, such as Tartuffe's seductive lines "Madam, forget such fears, and be my pupil, / And I shall teach you how to conquer scruple" (act 4, scene 5, 99–100). The artificiality of rhyme mirrors the artificiality of some of the characters and of their society — probably even more effectively in modern English than it did in seventeenth-century France, when it was unusual for plays to be written in prose.

Molière observes the unities in *Tartuffe* by having the action take place in one day, in one setting, with no subplots. The result is that intensity builds relentlessly until the unusual resolution of the action, which comes at the very last minute. As in most comedies, the lovers are permitted to marry, the villain is revealed and chastised, and the family is restored to its rightful position. But in the process, society is exposed as gullible, naive, and easily manipulated. In this sense, the play is a moral play, rather than the dangerous immoral work that the clergy condemned.

Tartuffe in Performance

Molière played the part of Orgon at the first public performance in February 1669, at the Palais Royale in Paris. The Théâtre-Français, which still produces the play regularly, featured Nicholas Auge as Tartuffe in 1776. His first entrance in act 3 was notable for his bringing out a gigantic handkerchief to hide Dorine's bosom, while delivering the line "Hide that breast" with a lustful leer and obvious lecherous looks — a convention later followed and developed by that company throughout the nineteenth century. One of the strangest productions was that of the Athénée theater in Paris in 1950, with Louis Jouvet as a truly pious Tartuffe struggling with himself over the temptation of Elmire! Jouvet's Tartuffe was not a slovenly, fat, lecherous figure with a dangling crucifix, as conventional Tartuffes were. Audiences for that production were annoyed at what they saw as a misreading of the text, and reviews indicate that there were very few laughs. However, the production ran for 139 performances. A similar interpretation in Paris in 1964 with Michel Auclair, a dashing leading man of the era, emphasized a possible unconscious homosexual connection between Tartuffe and Orgon as an explanation for Orgon's strange behavior. The stage was decorated with huge black-and-white religious paintings that depicted a naked Christ, thus introducing the images of flesh even before the play began. In 1965, the Repertory Theatre of Lincoln Center produced the Richard Wilbur translation with Michael O'Sullivan as Tartuffe; the production ran for five months, alternating with an Arthur Miller play. Tyrone Guthrie's 1967 production at the Old Vic starred John Gielgud as Orgon but was criticized for its weak, rural clown Tartuffe. However, it was praised for avoiding modern psychological interpretations and sticking with the text in such a way that the *deus ex machina* of the king's messenger at the end was more intelligible as a force that restores proper order to a disordered world. Freyda Thomas adapted the play at Circle in the Square in New York in 1996 as *Tartuffe: Born Again*. This production portrayed Tartuffe as a modern televangelist, a comparison that begged to be made in the 1990s. In 2002, London's National Theatre produced a rollicking *Tartuffe* with Martin Clunes, a TV sitcom star of considerable girth, playing the role broadly for laughs in a translation that sometimes verged on the scatological. The Yale Repertory Theatre productions took the same approach, first in 1984 and most recently in 2007. Austin Pendleton performed Tartuffe at Yale, and his comic interpretation will be long remembered. The popularity of *Tartuffe* continues, with 2011 productions at Brigham Young University, Dordt College, the Workshop Theatre and Pearl Theatre in New York, the Los Angeles Stage, the Theatricum Botanicum, and the English Touring Theatre, in an adaptation by Roger McGough. Hypocrisy seems to be a lively dramatic subject in any age.

For discussion questions and assignments on *Tartuffe,* visit bedfordstmartins.com/jacobus.

MOLIÈRE (1622–1673)

Tartuffe   1669

TRANSLATED BY RICHARD WILBUR

Characters

MME PERNELLE, *Orgon's mother*
ORGON, *Elmire's husband*
ELMIRE, *Orgon's wife*
DAMIS, *Orgon's son, Elmire's stepson*
MARIANE, *Orgon's daughter, Elmire's stepdaughter, in
    love with Valère*
VALÈRE, *in love with Mariane*
CLÉANTE, *Orgon's brother-in-law*
TARTUFFE, *a hypocrite*
DORINE, *Mariane's lady's-maid*
M. LOYAL, *a bailiff*
A POLICE OFFICER
FLIPOTE, *Mme Pernelle's maid*

The scene throughout: Orgon's house in Paris.

ACT I • Scene 1

[*Madame Pernelle and Flipote, her maid, Elmire,
Mariane, Dorine, Damis, Cléante.*]

MADAME PERNELLE: Come, come, Flipote; it's time I
    left this place.
ELMIRE: I can't keep up, you walk at such a pace.
MADAME PERNELLE: Don't trouble, child; no need to
    show me out.
    It's not your manners I'm concerned about.
5 ELMIRE: We merely pay you the respect we owe.
    But, Mother, why this hurry? Must you go?
MADAME PERNELLE: I must. This house appalls me.
        No one in it
    Will pay attention for a single minute.
    Children, I take my leave much vexed in spirit.
10 I offer good advice, but you won't hear it.
    You all break in and chatter on and on.
    It's like a madhouse with the keeper gone.
DORINE: If . . .
MADAME PERNELLE: Girl, you talk too much,
        and I'm afraid
    You're far too saucy for a lady's-maid.
15 You push in everywhere and have your say.
DAMIS: But . . .
MADAME PERNELLE: You, boy, grow more
        foolish every day.
    To think my grandson should be such a dunce!
    I've said a hundred times, if I've said it once,
    That if you keep the course on which you've
        started,

You'll leave your worthy father broken-hearted.   20
MARIANE: I think . . .
MADAME PERNELLE: And you, his sister,
        seem so pure,
    So shy, so innocent, and so demure.
    But you know what they say about still waters.
    I pity parents with secretive daughters.
ELMIRE: Now, Mother . . .
MADAME PERNELLE: And as for you,
        child, let me add   25
    That your behavior is extremely bad,
    And a poor example for these children, too.
    Their dear, dead mother did far better than you.
    You're much too free with money, and I'm distressed
    To see you so elaborately dressed.   30
    When it's one's husband that one aims to please,
    One has no need of costly fripperies.
CLÉANTE: Oh, Madam, really . . .
MADAME PERNELLE: You are her brother, Sir,
    And I respect and love you; yet if I were
    My son, this lady's good and pious spouse,   35
    I wouldn't make you welcome in my house.
    You're full of worldly counsels which, I fear,
    Aren't suitable for decent folk to hear.
    I've spoken bluntly, Sir; but it behooves us
    Not to mince words when righteous fervor moves us.   40
DAMIS: Your man Tartuffe is full of holy speeches . . .
MADAME PERNELLE: And practices precisely what he
    preaches.
    He's a fine man, and should be listened to.
    I will not hear him mocked by fools like you.
DAMIS: Good God! Do you expect me to submit   45
    To the tyranny of that carping hypocrite?
    Must we forgo all joys and satisfactions
    Because that bigot censures all our actions?
DORINE: To hear him talk—and he talks all the time—
    There's nothing one can do that's not a crime.   50
    He rails at everything, your dear Tartuffe.
MADAME PERNELLE: Whatever he reproves deserves
    reproof.
    He's out to save your souls, and all of you
    Must love him, as my son would have you do.
DAMIS: Ah no, Grandmother, I could never take   55
    To such a rascal, even for my father's sake.
    That's how I feel, and I shall not dissemble.
    His every action makes me seethe and tremble
    With helpless anger, and I have no doubt
    That he and I will shortly have it out.   60
DORINE: Surely it is a shame and a disgrace
    To see this man usurp the master's place—

To see this beggar who, when first he came,
Had not a shoe or shoestring to his name
65   So far forget himself that he behaves
As if the house were his, and we his slaves.
MADAME PERNELLE: Well, mark my words, your souls
      would fare far better
If you obeyed his precepts to the letter.
DORINE: You see him as a saint. I'm far less awed;
70   In fact, I see right through him. He's a fraud.
MADAME PERNELLE: Nonsense!
DORINE: His man Laurent's the same, or
      worse;
I'd not trust either with a penny purse.
MADAME PERNELLE: I can't say what his servant's
      morals may be;
His own great goodness I can guarantee.
75   You all regard him with distaste and fear
Because he tells you what you're loath to hear,
Condemns your sins, points out your moral flaws,
And humbly strives to further Heaven's cause.
DORINE: If sin is all that bothers him, why is it
80   He's so upset when folk drop in to visit?
Is Heaven so outraged by a social call
That he must prophesy against us all?
I'll tell you what I think: if you ask me,
He's jealous of my mistress' company.
MADAME PERNELLE: Rubbish! (*To Elmire.*) He's not
85   alone, child, in complaining
Of all your promiscuous entertaining.
Why, the whole neighborhood's upset, I know,
By all these carriages that come and go,
With crowds of guests parading in and out
90   And noisy servants loitering about.
In all of this, I'm sure there's nothing vicious;
But why give people cause to be suspicious?
CLÉANTE: They need no cause; they'll talk in any case.
Madam, this world would be a joyless place
95   If, fearing what malicious tongues might say,
We locked our doors and turned our friends away.
And even if one did so dreary a thing,
D'you think those tongues would cease their
      chattering?
One can't fight slander; it's a losing battle;
100   Let us instead ignore their tittle-tattle.
Let's strive to live by conscience' clear decrees,
And let the gossips gossip as they please.
DORINE: If there is talk against us, I know the source:
It's Daphne and her little husband, of course.
105   Those who have greatest cause for guilt and shame
Are quickest to besmirch a neighbor's name.
When there's a chance for libel, they never miss it;
When something can be made to seem illicit
They're off at once to spread the joyous news,
110   Adding to fact what fantasies they choose.
By talking up their neighbor's indiscretions
They seek to camouflage their own transgressions,
Hoping that others' innocent affairs
Will lend a hue of innocence to theirs,
115   Or that their own black guilt will come to seem

Part of a general shady color-scheme.
MADAME PERNELLE: All that is quite irrelevant.
      I doubt
That anyone's more virtuous and devout
Than dear Orante; and I'm informed that she
Condemns your mode of life most vehemently.   120
DORINE: Oh, yes, she's strict, devout, and has no
      taint
Of worldliness; in short, she seems a saint.
But it was time which taught her that disguise;
She's thus because she can't be otherwise.
So long as her attractions could enthrall,   125
She flounced and flirted and enjoyed it all,
But now that they're no longer what they were
She quits a world which fast is quitting her,
And wears a veil of virtue to conceal
Her bankrupt beauty and her lost appeal.   130
That's what becomes of old coquettes today;
Distressed when all their lovers fall away,
They see no recourse but to play the prude,
And so confer a style on solitude.
Thereafter, they're severe with everyone,   135
Condemning all our actions, pardoning none,
And claiming to be pure, austere, and zealous
When, if the truth were known, they're merely
      jealous,
And cannot bear to see another know
The pleasures time has forced them to forgo.   140
MADAME PERNELLE (*initially to Elmire*): That sort of
      talk is what you like to hear;
Therefore you'd have us all keep still, my dear,
While Madam rattles on the livelong day.
Nevertheless, I mean to have my say.
I tell you that you're blest to have Tartuffe   145
Dwelling, as my son's guest, beneath this roof;
That Heaven has sent him to forestall its wrath
By leading you, once more, to the true path;
That all he reprehends is reprehensible,
And that you'd better heed him, and be sensible.   150
These visits, balls, and parties in which you revel
Are nothing but inventions of the Devil.
One never hears a word that's edifying:
Nothing but chaff and foolishness and lying,
As well as vicious gossip in which one's neighbor   155
Is cut to bits with epee, foil, and saber.
People of sense are driven half-insane
At such affairs, where noise and folly reign
And reputations perish thick and fast.
As a wise preacher said on Sunday last,   160
Parties are Towers of Babylon, because
The guests all babble on with never a pause;
And then he told a story which, I think . . .
      (*To Cléante.*)
I heard that laugh, Sir, and I saw that wink!
Go find your silly friends and laugh some more!   165
Enough; I'm going; don't show me to the door.
I leave this household much dismayed and vexed;
I cannot say when I shall see you next.
      (*Slapping Flipote.*)

Wake up, don't stand there gaping into space!
170 I'll slap some sense into that stupid face.
Move, move, you slut.

Scene 2   [*Cléante, Dorine.*]

CLÉANTE: I think I'll stay behind;
I want no further pieces of her mind.
How that old lady . . .
DORINE: Oh, what wouldn't she say
If she could hear you speak of her that way!
5   She'd thank you for the *lady*, but I'm sure
She'd find the *old* a little premature.
CLÉANTE: My, what a scene she made, and what a din!
And how this man Tartuffe has taken her in!
DORINE: Yes, but her son is even worse deceived;
10   His folly must be seen to be believed.
In the late troubles, he played an able part
And served his king with wise and loyal heart,
But he's quite lost his senses since he fell
Beneath Tartuffe's infatuating spell.
15   He calls him brother, and loves him as his life,
Preferring him to mother, child, or wife.
In him and him alone will he confide;
He's made him his confessor and his guide;
He pets and pampers him with love more tender
20   Than any pretty mistress could engender,
Gives him the place of honor when they dine,
Delights to see him gorging like a swine,
Stuffs him with dainties till his guts distend,
And when he belches, cries "God bless you, friend!"
25   In short, he's mad; he worships him; he dotes;
His deeds he marvels at, his words he quotes,
Thinking each act a miracle, each word
Oracular as those that Moses heard.
Tartuffe, much pleased to find so easy a victim,
30   Has in a hundred ways beguiled and tricked him,
Milked him of money, and with his permission
Established here a sort of Inquisition.
Even Laurent, his lackey, dares to give
Us arrogant advice on how to live;
35   He sermonizes us in thundering tones
And confiscates our ribbons and colognes.
Last week he tore a kerchief into pieces
Because he found it pressed in a *Life of Jesus*:
He said it was a sin to juxtapose
40   Unholy vanities and holy prose.

Scene 3   [*Elmire, Mariane, Damis, Cléante, Dorine.*]

ELMIRE (*to Cléante*): You did well not to follow; she stood in the door
And said *verbatim* all she'd said before.
I saw my husband coming. I think I'd best
Go upstairs now, and take a little rest.

CLÉANTE: I'll wait and greet him here; then I must go.   5
I've really only time to say hello.
DAMIS: Sound him about my sister's wedding, please,
I think Tartuffe's against it, and that he's
Been urging Father to withdraw his blessing,
As you well know, I'd find that most distressing.   10
Unless my sister and Valère can marry,
My hopes to wed *his* sister will miscarry,
And I'm determined . . .
DORINE: He's coming.

Scene 4   [*Orgon, Cléante, Dorine.*]

ORGON: Ah, Brother,
good-day.
CLÉANTE: Well, welcome back. I'm sorry I can't stay.
How was the country? Blooming, I trust, and
green?
ORGON: Excuse me, Brother; just one moment.
(*To Dorine.*)
Dorine . . .
(*To Cleante.*)
To put my mind at rest, I always learn   5
The household news the moment I return.
(*To Dorine.*)
Has all been well, these two days I've been gone?
How are the family? What's been going on?
DORINE: Your wife, two days ago, had a bad fever,   10
And a fierce headache which refused to leave her.
ORGON: Ah. And Tartuffe?
DORINE: Tartuffe? Why, he's round
and red,
Bursting with health, and excellently fed.
ORGON: Poor fellow!
DORINE: That night, the mistress was
unable
To take a single bite at the dinner-table.   15
Her headache-pains, she said, were simply hellish.
ORGON: Ah. And Tartuffe?
DORINE: He ate his meal with relish,
And zealously devoured in her presence
A leg of mutton and a brace of pheasants.
ORGON: Poor fellow!
DORINE: Well, the pains continued strong,   20
And so she tossed and tossed the whole night long,
Now icy-cold, now burning like a flame.
We sat beside her bed till morning came.
ORGON: Ah. And Tartuffe?
DORINE: Why, having eaten, he rose
And sought his room, already in a doze,   25
Got into his warm bed, and snored away
In perfect peace until the break of day.
ORGON: Poor fellow!
DORINE: After much ado, we talked her
Into dispatching someone for the doctor.
He bled her, and the fever quickly fell.   30

ORGON: Ah. And Tartuffe?
DORINE: He bore it very well.
   To keep his cheerfulness at any cost,
   And make up for the blood *Madame* had lost,
   He drank, at lunch, four beakers full of port.
ORGON: Poor fellow!
35 DORINE: Both are doing well, in short.
   I'll go and tell *Madame* that you've expressed
   Keen sympathy and anxious interest.

Scene 5   [*Orgon, Cléante.*]

CLÉANTE: That girl was laughing in your face, and
      though
   I've no wish to offend you, even so
   I'm bound to say that she had some excuse.
   How can you possibly be such a goose?
5 Are you so dazed by this man's hocus-pocus
   That all the world, save him, is out of focus?
   You've given him clothing, shelter, food, and care;
   Why must you also . . .
ORGON: Brother, stop right there.
   You do not know the man of whom you speak.
CLÉANTE: I grant you that. But my judgment's not so
10   weak
   That I can't tell, by his effect on others . . .
ORGON: Ah, when you meet him, you two will be
      like brothers!
   There's been no loftier soul since time began.
   He is a man who . . . a man who . . . an excellent man.
15 To keep his precepts is to be reborn,
   And view this dunghill of a world with scorn.
   Yes, thanks to him I'm a changed man indeed.
   Under his tutelage my soul's been freed
   From earthly loves, and every human tie:
20 My mother, children, brother, and wife could die,
   And I'd not feel a single moment's pain.
CLÉANTE: That's a fine sentiment, Brother; most humane.
ORGON: Oh, had you seen Tartuffe as I first knew him,
   Your heart, like mine, would have surrendered to
      him.
25 He used to come into our church each day
   And humbly kneel nearby, and start to pray.
   He'd draw the eyes of everybody there
   By the deep fervor of his heartfelt prayer;
   He'd sigh and weep, and sometimes with a sound
30 Of rapture he would bend and kiss the ground;
   And when I rose to go, he'd run before
   To offer me holy-water at the door.
   His serving-man, no less devout than he,
   Informed me of his master's poverty;
35 I gave him gifts, but in his humbleness
   He'd beg me every time to give him less.
   "Oh, that's too much," he'd cry, "too much by
      twice!
   I don't deserve it. The half, Sir, would suffice."

And when I wouldn't take it back, he'd share
   Half of it with the poor, right then and there.   40
   At length, Heaven prompted me to take him in
   To dwell with us, and free our souls from sin.
   He guides our lives, and to protect my honor
   Stays by my wife, and keeps an eye upon her;
   He tells me whom she sees, and all she does,   45
   And seems more jealous than I ever was!
   And how austere he is! Why, he can detect
   A mortal sin where you would least suspect;
   In smallest trifles, he's extremely strict.
   Last week, his conscience was severely pricked   50
   Because, while praying, he had caught a flea
   And killed it, so he felt, too wrathfully.
CLÉANTE: Good God, man! Have you lost your
      common sense—
   Or is this all some joke at my expense?
   How can you stand there and in all sobriety . . .   55
ORGON: Brother, your language savors of impiety.
   Too much free-thinking's made your faith unsteady,
   And as I've warned you many times already,
   'Twill get you into trouble before you're through.
CLÉANTE: So I've been told before by dupes like you: 60
   Being blind, you'd have all others blind as well;
   The clear-eyed man you call an infidel,
   And he who sees through humbug and pretense
   Is charged, by you, with want of reverence.
   Spare me your warnings, Brother; I have no fear   65
   Of speaking out, for you and Heaven to hear,
   Against affected zeal and pious knavery.
   There's true and false in piety, as in bravery,
   And just as those whose courage shines the most
   In battle, are the least inclined to boast,   70
   So those whose hearts are truly pure and lowly
   Don't make a flashy show of being holy.
   There's a vast difference, so it seems to me,
   Between true piety and hypocrisy:
   How do you fail to see it, may I ask?   75
   Is not a face quite different from a mask?
   Cannot sincerity and cunning art,
   Reality and semblance, be told apart?
   Are scarecrows just like men, and do you hold
   That a false coin is just as good as gold?   80
   Ah, Brother, man's a strangely fashioned creature
   Who seldom is content to follow Nature,
   But recklessly pursues his inclination
   Beyond the narrow bounds of moderation,
   And often, by transgressing Reason's laws,   85
   Perverts a lofty aim or noble cause.
   A passing observation, but it applies.
ORGON: I see, dear Brother, that you're profoundly wise;
   You harbor all the insight of the age.
   You are our one clear mind, our only sage,   90
   The era's oracle, its Cato° too,
   And all mankind are fools compared to you.

91. Cato: Roman statesman (234–149 BCE) noted for his virtue
and wisdom.

CLÉANTE: Brother, I don't pretend to be a sage,
    Nor have I all the wisdom of the age.
95   There's just one insight I would dare to claim;
    I know that true and false are not the same;
    And just as there is nothing I more revere
    Than a soul whose faith is steadfast and sincere,
    Nothing that I more cherish and admire
100   Than honest zeal and true religious fire,
    So there is nothing that I find more base
    Than specious piety's dishonest face—
    Than these bold mountebanks, these histrios
    Whose impious mummeries and hollow shows
105   Exploit our love of Heaven, and make a jest
    Of all that men think holiest and best;
    These calculating souls who offer prayers
    Not to their Maker, but as public wares,
    And seek to buy respect and reputation
110   With lifted eyes and sighs of exaltation;
    These charlatans, I say, whose pilgrim souls
    Proceed, by way of Heaven, toward earthly goals,
    Who weep and pray and swindle and extort,
    Who preach the monkish life, but haunt the court,
115   Who make their zeal the partner of their vice—
    Such men are vengeful, sly, and cold as ice,
    And when there is an enemy to defame
    They cloak their spite in fair religion's name,
    Their private spleen and malice being made
120   To seem a high and virtuous crusade,
    Until, to mankind's reverent applause,
    They crucify their foe in Heaven's cause.
    Such knaves are all too common; yet, for the wise,
    True piety isn't hard to recognize,
125   And, happily, these present times provide us
    With bright examples to instruct and guide us.
    Consider Ariston and Périandre;
    Look at Oronte, Alcidamas, Clitandre;
    Their virtue is acknowledged; who could
      doubt it?
130   But you won't hear them beat the drum about it.
    They're never ostentatious, never vain,
    And their religion's moderate and humane;
    It's not their way to criticize and chide:
    They think censoriousness a mark of pride,
135   And therefore, letting others preach and rave,
    They show, by deeds, how Christians should
      behave.
    They think no evil of their fellow man,
    But judge of him as kindly as they can.
    They don't intrigue and wangle and conspire;
140   To lead a good life is their one desire;
    The sinner wakes no rancorous hate in them;
    It is the sin alone which they condemn;
    Nor do they try to show a fiercer zeal
    For Heaven's cause than Heaven itself could feel.
145   These men I honor, these men I advocate
    As models for us all to emulate.
    Your man is not their sort at all, I fear:
    And, while your praise of him is quite sincere,

    I think that you've been dreadfully deluded.
ORGON: Now then, dear Brother, is your speech
    concluded?   150
CLÉANTE: Why, yes.
ORGON: Your servant, Sir.

[*He turns to go.*]

CLÉANTE: No, Brother; wait.
    There's one more matter. You agreed of late
    That young Valère might have your daughter's
      hand.
ORGON: I did.
CLÉANTE: And set the date, I understand.
ORGON: Quite so.
CLÉANTE: You've now postponed it; is that
      true?   155
ORGON: No doubt.
CLÉANTE: The match no longer pleases you?
ORGON: Who knows?
CLÉANTE: D'you mean to go back on
    your word?
ORGON: I won't say that.
CLÉANTE: Has anything occurred
    Which might entitle you to break your pledge?
ORGON: Perhaps.
CLÉANTE: Why must you hem, and haw, and
      hedge?   160
    The boy asked me to sound you in this affair . . .
ORGON: It's been a pleasure.
CLÉANTE: But what shall I tell
    Valère?
ORGON: Whatever you like.
CLÉANTE: But what have you
    decided?
    What are your plans?
ORGON: I plan, Sir, to be guided
    by Heaven's will.
CLÉANTE: Come, Brother, don't talk rot.   165
    You've given Valère your word; will you keep it,
    or not?
ORGON : Good day.
CLÉANTE: This looks like poor Valère's
    undoing;
    I'll go and warn him that there's trouble brewing.

ACT II • Scene 1   [*Orgon, Mariane.*]

ORGON: Mariane.
MARIANE: Yes, Father?
ORGON: A word with you; come here.
MARIANE: What are you looking for?
ORGON (*peering into a small closet*):
                                Eavesdroppers, dear.
    I'm making sure we shan't be overheard.
    Someone in there could catch our every word.
    Ah, good, we're safe. Now, Mariane, my child,   5

You're a sweet girl who's tractable and mild,
Whom I hold dear, and think most highly of.
MARIANE: I'm deeply grateful, Father, for your love.
ORGON: That's well said, Daughter; and you can
    repay me
10 If, in all things, you'll cheerfully obey me.
MARIANE: To please you, Sir, is what delights me best.
ORGON: Good, good. Now, what d'you think of
    Tartuffe, our guest?
MARIANE: I, Sir?
ORGON: Yes. Weigh your answer; think it through.
MARIANE: Oh, dear. I'll say whatever you wish me to.
ORGON: That's wisely said, my Daughter. Say of him,
15   then,
That he's the very worthiest of men,
And that you're fond of him, and would rejoice
In being his wife, if that should be my choice.
    Well?
MARIANE: What?
ORGON: What's that?
MARIANE: I . . .
ORGON: Well?
MARIANE: Forgive me,
    pray.
ORGON: Did you not hear me?
MARIANE: Of *whom,* Sir, must I
20   say
That I am fond of him, and would rejoice
In being his wife, if that should be your choice?
ORGON: Why, of Tartuffe.
MARIANE: But, Father, that's false, you
    know.
Why would you have me say what isn't so?
25 ORGON: Because I am resolved it shall be true.
That it's my wish should be enough for you.
MARIANE: You can't mean, Father . . .
ORGON: Yes, Tartuffe
    shall be
Allied by marriage to this family,
And he's to be your husband, is that clear?
30 It's a father's privilege . . .

Scene 2   [*Dorine, Orgon, Mariane.*]

ORGON (*to Dorine*):   What are you doing in
    here?
Is curiosity so fierce a passion
With you, that you must eavesdrop in this
    fashion?
DORINE: There's lately been a rumor going about—
Based on some hunch or chance remark, no
5   doubt—
That you mean Mariane to wed Tartuffe.
I've laughed it off, of course, as just a spoof.
ORGON: You find it so incredible?
DORINE: Yes, I do.
I won't accept that story, even from you.

ORGON: Well, you'll believe it when the thing is
    done.   10
DORINE: Yes, yes, of course. Go on and have your
    fun.
ORGON: I've never been more serious in my life.
DORINE: Ha!
ORGON: Daughter, I mean it; you're to be his wife.
DORINE: No, don't believe your father; it's all a hoax.
ORGON: See here, young woman . . .
DORINE: Come, Sir, no
    more jokes;   15
You can't fool us.
ORGON: How dare you talk that way?
DORINE: All right, then: we believe you, sad to say.
But how a man like you, who looks so wise
And wears a moustache of such splendid size,
Can be so foolish as to . . .
ORGON: Silence, please!   20
My girl, you take too many liberties.
I'm master here, as you must not forget.
DORINE: Do let's discuss this calmly; don't be upset.
You can't be serious, Sir, about this plan.
What should that bigot want with Mariane?   25
Praying and fasting ought to keep him busy.
And then, in terms of wealth and rank, what
    is he?
Why should a man of property like you
Pick out a beggar son-in-law?
ORGON: That will do.
Speak of his poverty with reverence.   30
His is a pure and saintly indigence
Which far transcends all worldly pride and pelf.
He lost his fortune, as he says himself,
Because he cared for Heaven alone, and so
Was careless of his interests here below.   35
I mean to get him out of his present straits
And help him to recover his estates—
Which, in his part of the world, have no small
    fame.
Poor though he is, he's a gentleman just the same.
DORINE: Yes, so he tells us; and, Sir, it seems to me   40
Such pride goes very ill with piety.
A man whose spirit spurns this dungy earth
Ought not to brag of lands and noble birth;
Such worldly arrogance will hardly square
With meek devotion and the life of prayer.   45
. . . But this approach, I see, has drawn a blank;
Let's speak, then, of his person, not his rank.
Doesn't it seem to you a trifle grim
To give a girl like her to a man like him?
When two are so ill-suited, can't you see   50
What the sad consequence is bound to be?
A young girl's virtue is imperilled, Sir,
When such a marriage is imposed on her;
For if one's bridegroom isn't to one's taste,
It's hardly an inducement to be chaste,   55
And many a man with horns upon his brow
Has made his wife the thing that she is now.
It's hard to be a faithful wife, in short,

To certain husbands of a certain sort,
60 And he who gives his daughter to a man she hates
Must answer for her sins at Heaven's gates.
Think, Sir, before you play so risky a role.
ORGON: This servant-girl presumes to save my soul!
DORINE: You would do well to ponder what I've said.
65 ORGON: Daughter, we'll disregard this dunderhead.
Just trust your father's judgment. Oh, I'm aware
That I once promised you to young Valère;
But now I hear he gambles, which greatly
    shocks me;
What's more, I've doubts about his orthodoxy.
70 His visits to church, I note, are very few.
DORINE: Would you have him go at the same hours
    as you,
And kneel nearby, to be sure of being seen?
ORGON: I can dispense with such remarks, Dorine.
    (*To Mariane.*)
Tartuffe, however, is sure of Heaven's blessing,
75 And that's the only treasure worth possessing.
This match will bring you joys beyond all
    measure;
Your cup will overflow with every pleasure;
You two will interchange your faithful loves
Like two sweet cherubs, or two turtle-doves.
80 No harsh word shall be heard, no frown be seen,
And he shall make you happy as a queen.
DORINE: And she'll make him a cuckold, just wait
    and see.
ORGON: What language!
DORINE: Oh, he's a man of destiny;
He's *made* for horns, and what the stars demand
85 Your daughter's virtue surely can't withstand.
ORGON: Don't interrupt me further. Why can't you
    learn
That certain things are none of your concern?
DORINE: It's for your own sake that I interfere.

[*She repeatedly interrupts Orgon just as he is turning to speak to his daughter.*]

ORGON: Most kind of you. Now, hold your tongue,
    d'you hear?
DORINE: If I didn't love you . . .
ORGON: Spare me your
90   affection.
DORINE: I'll love you, Sir, in spite of your objection.
ORGON: Blast!
DORINE: I can't bear, Sir, for your honor's sake,
To let you make this ludicrous mistake.
ORGON: You mean to go on talking?
DORINE: If I didn't protest
95 This sinful marriage, my conscience couldn't rest.
ORGON: If you don't hold your tongue, you little
    shrew . . .
DORINE: What, lost your temper? A pious man like
    you?
ORGON: Yes! Yes! You talk and talk. I'm maddened
    by it.
Once and for all, I tell you to be quiet.

DORINE: Well, I'll be quiet. But I'll be thinking hard. 100
ORGON: Think all you like, but you had better guard
That saucy tongue of yours, or I'll . . .
    (*Turning back to Mariane.*)
                           Now, child,
I've weighed this matter fully.
DORINE (*aside*):   It drives me wild
that I can't speak.

[*Orgon turns his head, and she is silent.*]

ORGON: Tartuffe is no young dandy,
But, still, his person . . .
DORINE (*aside*):   Is as sweet as candy. 105
ORGON: Is such that, even if you shouldn't care
For his other merits . . .

[*He turns and stands facing Dorine, arms crossed.*]

DORINE (*aside*):   They'll make a lovely pair.
If I were she, no man would marry me
Against my inclination, and go scot-free.
He'd learn, before the wedding-day was over, 110
How readily a wife can find a lover.
ORGON (to *Dorine*): It seems you treat my orders as
    a joke.
DORINE: Why, what's the matter? 'Twas not to you I
    spoke.
ORGON: What *were* you doing?
DORINE: Talking to myself,
    that's all.
ORGON: Ah! (*Aside.*) One more bit of impudence and
    gall, 115
And I shall give her a good slap in the face.

(*He puts himself in position to slap her; Dorine, whenever he glances at her, stands immobile and silent.*)

Daughter, you shall accept, and with good grace,
The husband I've selected . . . Your wedding-day . . .
    (*To Dorine.*).
Why don't you talk to yourself?
DORINE: I've nothing to say.
ORGON: Come, just one word.
DORINE: No thank you, Sir, I
    pass. 120
ORGON: Come, speak; I'm waiting.
DORINE: I'd not be such an ass.
ORGON (*turning to Mariane*): In short, dear
    Daughter, I mean to be obeyed,
And you must bow to the sound choice I've made.
DORINE (*moving away*): I'd not wed such a monster,
    even in jest.

[*Orgon attempts to slap her, but misses.*]

ORGON: Daughter, that maid of yours is a thorough
    pest; 125
She makes me sinfully annoyed and nettled.
I can't speak further; my nerves are too
    unsettled.
She's so upset me by her insolent talk,
I'll calm myself by going for a walk.

Scene 3   [*Dorine, Mariane.*]

DORINE (*returning*): Well, have you lost your tongue, girl? Must I play
    Your part, and say the lines you ought to say?
    Faced with a fate so hideous and absurd,
    Can you not utter one dissenting word?
MARIANE: What good would it do? A father's power is great.
5
DORINE: Resist him now, or it will be too late.
MARIANE: But . . .
DORINE: Tell him one cannot love at a father's whim,
    That you shall marry for yourself, not him;
    That once it's you who are to be the bride,
10
    It's you, not he, who must be satisfied;
    And that if his Tartuffe is so sublime,
    He's free to marry him at any time.
MARIANE: I've bowed so long to Father's strict control,
    I couldn't oppose him now, to save my soul.
DORINE: Come, come, Mariane. Do listen to reason, won't you?
15
    Valère has asked your hand. Do you love him, or don't you?
MARIANE: Oh, how unjust of you! What can you mean
    By asking such a question, dear Dorine?
    You know the depth of my affection for him;
20
    I've told you a hundred times how I adore him.
DORINE: I don't believe in everything I hear;
    Who knows if your professions were sincere?
MARIANE: They were, Dorine, and you do me wrong to doubt it;
    Heaven knows that I've been all too frank about it.
DORINE: You love him, then?
MARIANE: Oh, more than I can express.
25
DORINE: And he, I take it, cares for you no less?
MARIANE: I think so.
DORINE: And you both, with equal fire,
    Burn to be married?
MARIANE: That is our one desire.
DORINE: What of Tartuffe, then? What of your father's plan?
MARIANE: I'll kill myself, if I'm forced to wed that man.
30
DORINE: I hadn't thought of that recourse. How splendid!
    Just die, and all your troubles will be ended!
    A fine solution. Oh, it maddens me
    To hear you talk in that self-pitying key.
MARIANE: Dorine, how harsh you are! It's most unfair.
35
    You have no sympathy for my despair.
DORINE: I've none at all for people who talk drivel
    And, faced with difficulties, whine and snivel.
MARIANE: No doubt I'm timid, but it would be wrong . . .

DORINE: True love requires a heart that's firm and strong.
40
MARIANE: I'm strong in my affection for Valère,
    But coping with my father is his affair.
DORINE: But if your father's brain has grown so cracked
    Over his dear Tartuffe that he can retract
    His blessing, though your wedding-day was named,
45
    It's surely not Valère who's to be blamed.
MARIANE: If I defied my father, as you suggest,
    Would it not seem unmaidenly, at best?
    Shall I defend my love at the expense
    Of brazenness and disobedience?
50
    Shall I parade my heart's desires, and flaunt . . .
DORINE: No, I ask nothing of you. Clearly you want
    To be Madame Tartuffe, and I feel bound
    Not to oppose a wish so very sound.
    What right have I to criticize the match?
55
    Indeed, my dear, the man's a brilliant catch.
    Monsieur Tartuffe! Now, there's a man of weight!
    Yes, yes, Monsieur Tartuffe, I'm bound to state,
    Is quite a person; that's not to be denied;
    'Twill be no little thing to be his bride.
60
    The world already rings with his renown;
    He's a great noble—in his native town;
    His ears are red, he has a pink complexion,
    And all in all, he'll suit you to perfection.
MARIANE: Dear God!
DORINE: Oh, how triumphant you will feel
65
    At having caught a husband so ideal!
MARIANE: Oh, do stop teasing, and use your cleverness
    To get me out of this appalling mess.
    Advise me, and I'll do whatever you say.
DORINE: Ah no, a dutiful daughter must obey
70
    Her father, even if he weds her to an ape.
    You've a bright future; why struggle to escape?
    Tartuffe will take you back where his family lives,
    To a small town aswarm with relatives—
    Uncles and cousins whom you'll be charmed to meet.
75
    You'll be received at once by the elite,
    Calling upon the bailiff's wife, no less—
    Even, perhaps, upon the mayoress,
    Who'll sit you down in the *best* kitchen chair.
    Then, once a year, you'll dance at the village fair
80
    To the drone of bagpipes—two of them, in fact—
    And see a puppet-show, or an animal act.
    Your husband . . .
MARIANE: Oh, you turn my blood to ice!
    Stop torturing me, and give me your advice.
DORINE (*threatening to go*): Your servant, Madam.
MARIANE: Dorine, I beg of you . . .
85
DORINE: No, you deserve it; this marriage must go through.
MARIANE: Dorine!
DORINE: No.

MARIANE: Not Tartuffe! You know I think him . . .

DORINE: Tartuffe's your cup of tea, and you shall
      drink him.

MARIANE: I've always told you everything, and
      relied . . .

90   DORINE: No. You deserve to be tartutified.

MARIANE: Well, since you mock me and refuse to care,
      I'll henceforth seek my solace in despair:
      Despair shall be my counsellor and friend,
      And help me bring my sorrows to an end.

                               [*She starts to leave.*]

DORINE: There now, come back; my anger has
95   subsided.
      You do deserve some pity, I've decided.

MARIANE: Dorine, if Father makes me undergo
      This dreadful martyrdom, I'll die, I know.

DORINE: Don't fret; it won't be difficult to discover
      Some plan of action . . . But here's Valère, your
100   lover.

Scene 4   [*Valère, Mariane, Dorine.*]

VALÈRE: Madam. I've just received some wondrous news
      Regarding which I'd like to hear your views.

MARIANE: What news?

VALÈRE: You're marrying Tartuffe.

MARIANE: I find
      That Father does have such a match in mind.

VALÈRE: Your father, Madam . . .

MARIANE: . . . has just this
5   minute said
      That it's Tartuffe he wishes me to wed.

VALÈRE: Can he be serious?

MARIANE: Oh, indeed he can;
      He's clearly set his heart upon the plan.

VALÈRE: And what position do you propose to take,
      Madam?

MARIANE: Why—I don't know.

10   VALÈRE: For heaven's sake—
      You don't know?

MARIANE: No.

VALÈRE: Well, well!

MARIANE: Advise me, do.

VALÈRE: Marry the man. That's my advice to you.

MARIANE: That's your advice?

VALÈRE: Yes.

MARIANE: Truly?

VALÈRE: Oh, absolutely.
      You couldn't choose more wisely, more astutely.

MARIANE: Thanks for this counsel; I'll follow it, of
15   course.

VALÈRE: Do, do; I'm sure 'twill cost you no remorse.

MARIANE: To give it didn't cause your heart to break.

VALÈRE: I gave it, Madam, only for your sake.

MARIANE: And it's for your sake that I take it, Sir.

DORINE (*withdrawing to the rear of the stage*): Let's
20   see which fool will prove the stubborner.

VALÈRE: So! I am nothing to you, and it was flat
      Deception when you . . .

MARIANE: Please, enough of that.
      You've told me plainly that I should agree
      To wed the man my father's chosen for me,
      And since you've deigned to counsel me so wisely,   25
      I promise, Sir, to do as you advise me.

VALÈRE: Ah, no, 'twas not by me that you were
      swayed.
      No, your decision was already made;
      Though now, to save appearances, you protest
      That you're betraying me at my behest.   30

MARIANE: Just as you say.

VALÈRE: Quite so. And I now see
      That you were never truly in love with me.

MARIANE: Alas, you're free to think so if you choose.

VALÈRE: I choose to think so, and here's a bit of news:
      You've spurned my hand, but I know where to
      turn   35
      For kinder treatment, as you shall quickly learn.

MARIANE: I'm sure you do. Your noble qualities
      Inspire affection . . .

VALÈRE: Forget my qualities, please.
      They don't inspire you overmuch, I find.
      But there's another lady I have in mind   40
      Whose sweet and generous nature will not scorn
      To compensate me for the loss I've borne.

MARIANE: I'm no great loss, and I'm sure that you'll
      transfer
      Your heart quite painlessly from me to her.

VALÈRE: I'll do my best to take it in my stride.   45
      The pain I feel at being cast aside
      Time and forgetfulness may put an end to.
      Or if I can't forget, I shall pretend to.
      No self respecting person is expected
      To go on loving once he's been rejected.   50

MARIANE: Now, that's a fine, high-minded sentiment.

VALÈRE: One to which any sane man would assent.
      Would you prefer it if I pined away
      In hopeless passion till my dying day?
      Am I to yield you to a rival's arms   55
      And not console myself with other charms?

MARIANE: Go then: console yourself; don't hesitate.
      I wish you to; indeed, I cannot wait.

VALÈRE: You wish me to?

MARIANE: Yes.

VALÈRE: That's the final straw.
      Madam, farewell. Your wish shall be my law.   60

[*He starts to leave, and then returns: this repeatedly.*]

MARIANE: Splendid.

VALÈRE (*coming back again*):
                This breach, remember, is of your
      making;
      It's you who've driven me to the step I'm taking.

MARIANE: Of course.

VALÈRE (*coming back again*):
                Remember, too, that I am merely
      Following your example.

MARIANE: I see that clearly.

65 VALÈRE: Enough. I'll go and do your bidding, then.

MARIANE: Good.

VALÈRE (*coming back again*):
      You shall never see my face again.

MARIANE: Excellent.

VALÈRE (*walking to the door, then turning about*):
      Yes?

MARIANE: What?

VALÈRE: What's that? What did
  you say?

MARIANE: Nothing. You're dreaming.

VALÈRE: Ah. Well, I'm on
  my way.
  Farewell, *Madame.*
    [*He moves slowly away.*]

MARIANE: Farewell.

DORINE (*to Mariane*):   If you ask me,
70 Both of you are as mad as mad can be.
  Do stop this nonsense, now. I've only let you
  Squabble so long to see where it would get you.
  Whoa there, Monsieur Valère!

[*She goes and seizes Valère by the arm; he makes a great show of resistance.*]

VALÈRE: What's this, Dorine?

DORINE: Come here.

VALÈRE: No, no, my heart's too full of
  spleen.
75 Don't hold me back; her wish must be obeyed.

DORINE: Stop!

VALÈRE: It's too late now; my decision's made.

DORINE: Oh, pooh!

MARIANE (*aside*): He hates the sight of me, that's
  plain.
  I'll go, and so deliver him from pain.

DORINE (*leaving Valère, running after Mariane*): And
  now *you* run away! Come back.

MARIANE: No, no.
80 Nothing you say will keep me here. Let go!

VALÈRE (*aside*): She cannot bear my presence, I
  perceive.
  To spare her further torment, I shall leave.

DORINE (*leaving Mariane, running after Valère*):
  Again! You'll not escape, Sir; don't you try it.
  Come here, you two. Stop fussing, and be quiet.

[*She takes Valère by the hand, then Mariane, and draws them together.*]

VALÈRE (*to Dorine*): What do you want of me?

MARIANE (*to Dorine*):   What
85 is the point of this?

DORINE: We're going to have a little armistice.
      (*To Valère.*)
  Now, weren't you silly to get so overheated?

VALÈRE: Didn't you see how badly I was treated?

DORINE (*to Mariane*): Aren't you a simpleton, to have
  lost your head?

90 MARIANE: Didn't you hear the hateful things he said?

DORINE (*to Valère*): You're both great fools. Her sole
  desire, Valère,
  Is to be yours in marriage. To that I'll swear.
      (*To Mariane.*)
  He loves you only, and he wants no wife
  But you, Mariane. On that I'll stake my life.

MARIANE (*to Valère*): Then why you advised me so,
  I cannot see.   95

VALÈRE (*to Mariane*): On such a question, why ask
  advice of *me?*

DORINE: Oh, you're impossible. Give me your hands,
  you two.
      (*To Valère.*)
  Yours first.

VALÈRE (*giving Dorine his hand*):
      But why?

DORINE (*to Mariane*): And now a hand from you.

MARIANE (*also giving Dorine her hand*): What are
  you doing?

DORINE: There: a perfect fit.
  You suit each other better than you'll admit.   100

[*Valère and Mariane hold hands for some time without looking at each other.*]

VALÈRE (*turning toward Mariane*): Ah, come, don't be so
  haughty. Give a man
  A look of kindness, won't you Mariane?
      [*Mariane turns toward Valère and smiles.*]

DORINE: I tell you, lovers are completely mad!

VALÈRE (*to Mariane*): Now come, confess that you
  were very bad
  To hurt my feeling as you did just now.
  I have a just complaint, you must allow.   105

MARIANE: *You* must allow that you were most
  unpleasant . . .

DORINE: Let's table that discussion for the present;
  Your father has a plan which must be stopped.

MARIANE: Advise us, then; what means must we
  adopt?   110

DORINE: We'll use all manner of means, and all at
  once.
      (*To Mariane.*)
  Your father's addled; he's acting like a dunce.
  Therefore you'd better humor the old fossil.
  Pretend to yield to him, be sweet and docile,
  And then postpone, as often as necessary,   115
  The day on which you have agreed to marry.
  You'll thus gain time, and time will turn the trick.
  Sometimes, for instance, you'll be taken sick,
  And that will seem good reason for delay;
  Or some bad omen will make you change the day—   120
  You'll dream of muddy water, or you'll pass
  A dead man's hearse, or break a looking-glass.
  If all else fails, no man can marry you
  Unless you take his ring and say "I do."
  But now, let's separate. If they should find   125
  Us talking here, our plot might be divined.
      (*To Valère.*)

Go to your friends, and tell them what's occurred,
And have them urge her father to keep his word.
Meanwhile, we'll stir her brother into action,
130 And get Elmire, as well, to join our faction.
Good-bye.
VALÈRE (*to Mariane*):
            Though each of us will do his best,
It's your true heart on which my hopes shall rest.
MARIANE (*to Valère*): Regardless of what Father may
    decide,
None but Valère shall claim me as his bride.
VALÈRE: Oh, how those words content me! Come
135   what will . . .
DORINE: Oh, lovers, lovers! Their tongues are never
    still.
Be off, now.
VALÈRE (*turning to go, then turning back*):
                One last word . . .
DORINE: No time to chat:
You leave by this door; and *you* leave by that.

[*Dorine pushes them, by the shoulders, toward opposing doors.*]

ACT III • Scene 1   [*Damis, Dorine.*]

DAMIS: May lightning strike me even as I speak,
May all men call me cowardly and weak,
If any fear or scruple holds me back
From settling things, at once, with that great
    quack!
5 DORINE: Now, don't give way to violent emotion.
Your father's merely talked about this notion,
And words and deeds are far from being one.
Much that is talked about is left undone.
DAMIS: No, I must stop that scoundrel's
    machinations;
10 I'll go and tell him off; I'm out of patience.
DORINE: Do calm down and be practical. I had rather
My mistress dealt with him—and with your father.
She has some influence with Tartuffe, I've noted.
He hangs upon her words, seems most devoted,
15 And may, indeed, be smitten by her charm.
Pray Heaven it's true! 'Twould do our cause no
    harm.
She sent for him, just now, to sound him out
On this affair you're so incensed about;
She'll find out where he stands, and tell him, too,
20 What dreadful strife and trouble will ensue
If he lends countenance to your father's plan.
I couldn't get in to see him, but his man
Says that he's almost finished with his prayers.
Go, now. I'll catch him when he comes
    downstairs.
25 DAMIS: I want to hear this conference, and I will.
DORINE: No, they must be alone.
DAMIS: Oh, I'll keep still.

DORINE: Not you. I know your temper. You'd start a brawl,
And shout and stamp your foot and spoil it all.
Go on.
DAMIS: I won't; I have a perfect right . . .
DORINE: Lord, you're a nuisance! He's coming; get
    out of sight.   30

[*Damis conceals himself in a closet at the rear of the stage.*]

Scene 2   [*Tartuffe, Dorine.*]

TARTUFFE (*observing Dorine, and calling to his
    manservant offstage*): Hang up my hair-shirt,
    put my scourge in place,
And pray, Laurent, for Heaven's perpetual grace.
I'm going to the prison now, to share
My last few coins with the poor wretches there.
DORINE (*aside*): Dear God, what affectation! What a
    fake!   5
TARTUFFE: You wished to see me?
DORINE: Yes . . .
TARTUFFE (*taking a handkerchief from his pocket*):
                        For mercy's sake,
Please take this handkerchief, before you speak.
DORINE: What?
TARTUFFE: Cover that bosom, girl. The flesh is weak,
And unclean thoughts are difficult to control.

Debra Gillett as Dorine and Martin Clunes as Tartuffe in the "handkerchief" scene from London's National Theatre production in 2002.

10   Such sights as that can undermine the soul.
    DORINE: Your soul, it seems, has very poor defenses,
      And flesh makes quite an impact on your senses.
      It's strange that you're so easily excited;
      My own desires are not so soon ignited,
15   And if I saw you naked as a beast,
      Not all your hide would tempt me in the least.
    TARTUFFE: Girl, speak more modestly; unless you do,
      I shall be forced to take my leave of you.
    DORINE: Oh, no, it's I who must be on my way;
20   I've just one little message to convey.
      Madame is coming down, and begs you, Sir,
      To wait and have a word or two with her.
    TARTUFFE: Gladly.
    DORINE (*aside*):   *That* had a softening effect!
      I think my guess about him was correct.
    TARTUFFE: Will she be long?
25   DORINE: No: that's her step I hear.
      Ah, here she is, and I shall disappear.

Scene 3   [*Elmire, Tartuffe.*]

    TARTUFFE: May Heaven, whose infinite goodness we
      adore,
      Preserve your body and soul forevermore,
      And bless your days, and answer thus the plea
      Of one who is its humblest votary.
5   ELMIRE: I thank you for that pious wish. But please,
      Do take a chair and let's be more at ease.

[*They sit down.*]

    TARTUFFE: I trust that you are once more well and
      strong?
    ELMIRE: Oh, yes: the fever didn't last for long.
    TARTUFFE: My prayers are too unworthy. I am sure,
      To have gained from Heaven this most gracious
10   cure;
      But lately, Madam, my every supplication
      Has had for object your recuperation.
    ELMIRE: You shouldn't have troubled so. I don't
      deserve it.
    TARTUFFE: Your health is priceless, Madam, and to
      preserve it
15   I'd gladly give my own, in all sincerity.
    ELMIRE: Sir, you outdo us all in Christian charity.
      You've been most kind. I count myself your
      debtor.
    TARTUFFE: 'Twas nothing, Madam. I long to serve
      you better.
    ELMIRE: There's a private matter I'm anxious to
      discuss.
20   I'm glad there's no one here to hinder us.
    TARTUFFE: I too am glad; it floods my heart with bliss
      To find myself alone with you like this.
      For just this chance I've prayed with all my
      power —
      But prayed in vain, until this happy hour.

    ELMIRE: This won't take long, Sir, and I hope
      you'll be
25
      Entirely frank and unconstrained with me.
    TARTUFFE: Indeed, there's nothing I had rather do
      Than bare my inmost heart and soul to you.
      First, let me say that what remarks I've made
      About the constant visits you are paid
30
      Were prompted not by any mean emotion,
      But rather by a pure and deep devotion,
      A fervent zeal . . .
    ELMIRE: No need for explanation.
      Your sole concern, I'm sure, was my salvation.
    TARTUFFE (*taking Elmire's hand and pressing her
      fingertips*): Quite so; and such great fervor
      do I feel . . .
35
    ELMIRE: Ooh! Please! You're pinching!
    TARTUFFE: 'Twas from
      excess of zeal.
      I never meant to cause you pain, I swear.
      I'd rather . . .

[*He places his hand on Elmire's knee.*]

    ELMIRE: What can your hand be doing there?
    TARTUFFE: Feeling your gown; what soft, fine-woven
      stuff!
    ELMIRE: Please, I'm extremely ticklish. That's enough.   40

[*She draws her chair away; Tartuffe pulls his after her.*]

    TARTUFFE (*fondling the lace collar of her gown*): My,
      my, what lovely lacework on your dress!
      The workmanship's miraculous, no less.
      I've not seen anything to equal it.
    ELMIRE: Yes, quite. But let's talk business for a bit.
      They say my husband means to break his word   45
      And give his daughter to you, Sir. Had you heard?
    TARTUFFE: He did once mention it. But I confess
      I dream of quite a different happiness.
      It's elsewhere, Madam, that my eyes discern
      The promise of that bliss for which I yearn.   50
    ELMIRE: I see: you care for nothing here below.
    TARTUFFE: Ah, well—my heart's not made of stone,
      you know.
    ELMIRE: All your desires mount heavenward, I'm
      sure,
      In scorn of all that's earthly and impure.
    TARTUFFE: A love of heavenly beauty does not
      preclude   55
      A proper love for earthly pulchritude;
      Our senses are quite rightly captivated
      By perfect works our Maker has created.
      Some glory clings to all that Heaven has made;
      In you, all Heaven's marvels are displayed.   60
      On that fair face, such beauties have been
      lavished.
      The eyes are dazzled and the heart is ravished;
      How could I look on you, O flawless creature,
      And not adore the Author of all Nature,
      Feeling a love both passionate and pure   65
      For you, his triumph of self-portraiture?

At first, I trembled lest that love should be
A subtle snare that Hell had laid for me;
I vowed to flee the sight of you, eschewing
70 A rapture that might prove my soul's undoing;
But soon, fair being, I became aware
That my deep passion could be made to square
With rectitude, and with my bounden duty.
I thereupon surrendered to your beauty.
75 It is, I know, presumptuous on my part
To bring you this poor offering of my heart,
And it is not my merit, Heaven knows,
But your compassion on which my hopes repose.
You are my peace, my solace, my salvation;
80 On you depends my bliss—or desolation;
I bide your judgment and, as you think best,
I shall be either miserable or blest.
ELMIRE: Your declaration is most gallant, Sir,
But don't you think it's out of character?
85 You'd have done better to restrain your passion
And think before you spoke in such a fashion.
It ill becomes a pious man like you . . .
TARTUFFE: I may be pious, but I'm human too:
With your celestial charms before his eyes,
90 A man has not the power to be wise.
I know such words sound strangely, coming
       from me,
But I'm no angel, nor was meant to be,
And if you blame my passion, you must needs
Reproach as well the charms on which it feeds.
95 Your loveliness I had no sooner seen
Than you became my soul's unrivalled queen;
Before your seraph glance, divinely sweet,
My heart's defenses crumbled in defeat,
And nothing fasting, prayer, or tears might do
100 Could stay my spirit from adoring you.
My eyes, my sighs have told you in the past
What now my lips make bold to say at last,
And if, in your great goodness, you will deign
To look upon your slave, and ease his pain,—
105 If, in compassion for my soul's distress,
You'll stoop to comfort my unworthiness,
I'll raise to you, in thanks for that sweet manna,
An endless hymn, an infinite hosanna.
With me, of course, there need be no anxiety,
110 No fear of scandal or of notoriety.
These young court gallants, whom all the ladies
       fancy,
Are vain in speech, in action rash and chancy;
When they succeed in love, the world soon
       knows it;
No favor's granted them but they disclose it
115 And by the looseness of their tongues profane
The very altar where their hearts have lain.
Men of my sort, however, love discreetly,
And one may trust our reticence completely.
My keen concern for my good name insures
120 The absolute security of yours;
In short, I offer you, my dear Elmire,
Love without scandal, pleasure without fear.

ELMIRE: I've heard your well-turned speeches to
       the end,
And what you urge I clearly apprehend.
Aren't you afraid that I may take a notion   125
To tell my husband of your warm devotion,
And that, supposing he were duly told,
His feelings toward you might grow rather cold?
TARTUFFE: I know, dear lady, that your exceeding
       charity
Will lead your heart to pardon my temerity;   130
That you'll excuse my violent affection
As human weakness, human imperfection;
And that—O fairest!—you will bear in mind
That I'm but flesh and blood, and am not blind.
ELMIRE: Some women might do otherwise, perhaps,   135
But I shall be discreet about your lapse;
I'll tell my husband nothing of what's occurred
If, in return, you'll give your solemn word
To advocate as forcefully as you can
The marriage of Valère and Mariane,   140
Renouncing all desires to dispossess
Another of his rightful happiness,
And . . .

Scene 4   [*Damis, Elmire, Tartuffe.*]

DAMIS (*emerging from the closet where he has been
       hiding*): No! We'll not hush up this vile affair;
I heard it all inside that closet there,
Where Heaven, in order to confound the pride
Of this great rascal, prompted me to hide.
Ah, now I have my long-awaited chance   5
To punish his deceit and arrogance,
And give my father clear and shocking proof
Of the black character of his dear Tartuffe.
ELMIRE: Ah no, Damis; I'll be content if he
Will study to deserve my leniency.   10
I've promised silence—don't make me break my
       word;
To make a scandal would be too absurd.
Good wives laugh off such trifles, and forget them;
Why should they tell their husbands, and upset them?
DAMIS: You have your reasons for taking such a
       course,   15
And I have reasons, too, of equal force.
To spare him now would be insanely wrong.
I've swallowed my just wrath for far too long
And watched this insolent bigot bringing strife
And bitterness into our family life.   20
Too long he's meddled in my father's affairs,
Thwarting my marriage-hopes, and poor Valère's.
It's high time that my father was undeceived,
And now I've proof that can't be disbelieved—
Proof that was furnished me by Heaven above.   25
It's too good not to take advantage of.
This is my chance, and I deserve to lose it
If, for one moment, I hesitate to use it.

ELMIRE: Damis . . .
DAMIS: No, I must do what I think right.
30   Madam, my heart is bursting with delight,
     And, say whatever you will, I'll not consent
     To lose the sweet revenge on which I'm bent.
     I'll settle matters without more ado;
     And here, most opportunely, is my cue.

Scene 5   [*Orgon, Damis, Tartuffe, Elmire.*]

DAMIS: Father, I'm glad you've joined us. Let us
        advise you
     Of some fresh news which doubtless will surprise
        you.
     You've just now been repaid with interest
     For all your loving-kindness to our guest.
5   He's proved his warm and grateful feelings
        toward you;
     It's with a pair of horns he would reward you.
     Yes, I surprised him with your wife, and heard
     His whole adulterous offer, every word.
     She, with her all too gentle disposition,
10   Would not have told you of his proposition;
     But I shall not make terms with brazen lechery,
     And feel that not to tell you would be treachery.
ELMIRE: And I hold that one's husband's peace of
        mind
     Should not be spoilt by tattle of this kind.
15   One's honor doesn't require it: to be proficient
     In keeping men at bay is quite sufficient.
     These are my sentiments, and I wish, Damis,
     That you had heeded me and held your peace.

Scene 6   [*Orgon, Damis, Tartuffe.*]

ORGON: Can it be true, this dreadful thing I hear?
TARTUFFE: Yes, Brother, I'm a wicked man, I fear:
     A wretched sinner, all depraved and twisted,
     The greatest villain that has ever existed.
     My life's one heap of crimes, which grows each
5   minute;
     There's naught but foulness and corruption in it;
     And I perceive that Heaven, outraged by me,
     Has chosen this occasion to mortify me.
     Charge me with any deed you wish to name;
10   I'll not defend myself, but take the blame.
     Believe what you are told, and drive Tartuffe
     Like some base criminal from beneath your roof;
     Yes, drive me hence, and with a parting curse:
     I shan't protest, for I deserve far worse.
ORGON (*to Damis*): Ah, you deceitful boy, how dare
15   you try
     To stain his purity with so foul a lie?
DAMIS: What! Are you taken in by such a bluff?
     Did you not hear . . . ?
ORGON: Enough, you rogue, enough!

TARTUFFE: Ah, Brother, let him speak: you're being
        unjust.
     Believe his story; the boy deserves your trust.   20
     Why, after all, should you have faith in me?
     How can you know what I might do, or be?
     Is it on my good actions that you base
     Your favor? Do you trust my pious face?
     Ah, no, don't be deceived by hollow shows;   25
     I'm far, alas, from being what men suppose;
     Though the world takes me for a man of worth,
     I'm truly the most worthless man on earth.
        (*To Damis.*)
     Yes, my dear son, speak out now: call me the chief
     Of sinners, a wretch, a murderer, a thief;   30
     Load me with all the names men most abhor;
     I'll not complain; I've earned them all, and more;
     I'll kneel here while you pour them on my head
     As a just punishment for the life I've led.
ORGON (*to Taruffe*): This is too much, dear Brother.
        (*To Damis.*)
                          Have you no heart?   35
DAMIS: Are you so hoodwinked by this rascal's art . . . ?
ORGON: Be still, you monster.
        (*To Tartuffe.*)
                          Brother, I pray you, rise.
        (*To Damis.*)
     Villain!
DAMIS: But . . .
ORGON: Silence!
DAMIS: Can't you realize . . . ?
ORGON: Just one word more, and I'll tear you limb
        from limb.
TARTUFFE: In God's name, Brother, don't be harsh
        with him.
     I'd rather far be tortured at the stake   40
     Than see him bear one scratch for my poor
        sake.
ORGON (*to Damis*): Ingrate!
TARTUFFE: If I must beg you, on bended knee,
     To pardon him . . .
ORGON (*falling to his knees, addressing Tartuffe*):
                   Such goodness cannot be!
        (*To Damis.*)
     Now, *there's* true charity!
DAMIS: What, you . . . ?
ORGON: Villain, be still!   45
     I know your motives; I know you wish him ill:
     Yes, all of you—wife, children, servants, all—
     Conspire against him and desire his fall,
     Employing every shameful trick you can
     To alienate me from this saintly man.   50
     Ah, but the more you seek to drive him away,
     The more I'll do to keep him. Without delay,
     I'll spite this household and confound its pride
     By giving him my daughter as his bride.
DAMIS: You're going to force her to accept his hand?   55
ORGON: Yes, and this very night, d'you understand?
     I shall defy you all, and make it clear
     That I'm the one who gives the orders here.

Come, wretch, kneel down and clasp his blessed feet,
60 And ask his pardon for your black deceit.
DAMIS: I ask that swindler's pardon? Why, I'd
    rather . . .
ORGON: So! You insult him, and defy your father!
    A stick! A stick! (*To Tartuffe.*) No, no—release
    me, do.
    (*To Damis.*)
    Out of my house this minute! Be off with you,
65 And never dare set foot in it again.
DAMIS: Well, I shall go, but . . .
ORGON: Well, go quickly, then
    I disinherit you; an empty purse
    Is all you'll get from me—except my curse!

Scene 7   [*Orgon, Tartuffe.*]

ORGON: How he blasphemed your goodness! What
    a son!
TARTUFFE: Forgive him, Lord, as I've already done.
    (*To Orgon.*)
    You can't know how it hurts when someone
    tries
    To blacken me in my dear Brother's eyes.
ORGON: Ahh!
5 TARTUFFE: The mere thought of such ingratitude
    Plunges my soul into so dark a mood . . .
    Such horror grips my heart . . . I gasp for breath,
    And cannot speak, and feel myself near death.
ORGON:

[*He runs, in tears, to the door through which he has just
driven his son.*]

    You blackguard! Why did I spare you? Why did
    I not
10 Break you in little pieces on the spot?
    Compose yourself, and don't be hurt, dear friend.
TARTUFFE: These scenes, these dreadful quarrels, have
    got to end.
    I've much upset your household, and I perceive
    That the best thing will be for me to leave.
ORGON: What are you saying!
TARTUFFE: They're all against me
15 here;
    They'd have you think me false and insincere.
ORGON: Ah, what of that? Have I ceased believing
    in you?
TARTUFFE: Their adverse talk will certainly continue,
    And charges which you now repudiate
20 You may find credible at a later date.
ORGON: No, Brother, never.
TARTUFFE: Brother, a wife can sway
    Her husband's mind in many a subtle way.
ORGON: No, no.
TARTUFFE: To leave at once is the solution;
    Thus only can I end their persecution.
25 ORGON: No, no, I'll not allow it; you shall remain.

TARTUFFE: Ah, well; 'twill mean much martyrdom
    and pain,
    But if you wish it . . .
ORGON: Ah!
TARTUFFE: Enough; so be it.
    But one thing must be settled, as I see it.
    For your dear honor, and for our friendship's
    sake,
    There's one precaution I feel bound to take.   30
    I shall avoid your wife, and keep away . . .
ORGON: No, you shall not, whatever they may say.
    It pleases me to vex them, and for spite
    I'd have them see you with her day and night.
    What's more, I'm going to drive them to despair   35
    By making you my only son and heir;
    This very day, I'll give to you alone
    Clear deed and title to everything I own.
    A dear, good friend and son-in-law-to-be
    Is more than wife, or child, or kin to me.   40
    Will you accept my offer, dearest son?
TARTUFFE: In all things, let the will of Heaven be
    done.
ORGON: Poor fellow! Come, we'll go draw up
    the deed.
    Then let them burst with disappointed greed!

ACT IV • Scene 1   [*Cléante, Tartuffe.*]

CLÉANTE: Yes, all the town's discussing it, and truly,
    Their comments do not flatter you unduly.
    I'm glad we've met, Sir, and I'll give my view
    Of this sad matter in a word or two.
    As for who's guilty, that I shan't discuss;   5
    Let's say it was Damis who caused the fuss;
    Assuming, then, that you have been ill-used
    By young Damis, and groundlessly accused,
    Ought not a Christian to forgive, and ought
    He not to stifle every vengeful thought?   10
    Should you stand by and watch a father make
    His only son an exile for your sake?
    Again I tell you frankly, be advised:
    The whole town, high and low, is scandalized;
    This quarrel must be mended, and my advice is   15
    Not to push matters to a further crisis.
    No, sacrifice your wrath to God above,
    And help Damis regain his father's love.
TARTUFFE: Alas, for my part I should take great joy
    In doing so. I've nothing against the boy.   20
    I pardon all, I harbor no resentment;
    To serve him would afford me much contentment.
    But Heaven's interest will not have it so:
    If he comes back, then I shall have to go.
    After his conduct—so extreme, so vicious—   25
    Our further intercourse would look suspicious.
    God knows what people would think! Why, they'd
    describe
    My goodness to him as a sort of bribe;

They'd say that out of guilt I made pretense
30 Of loving-kindness and benevolence—
That, fearing my accuser's tongue, I strove
To buy his silence with a show of love.
CLÉANTE: Your reasoning is badly warped and
stretched,
And these excuses, Sir, are most far-fetched.
35 Why put yourself in charge of Heaven's cause?
Does Heaven need our help to enforce its laws?
Leave vengeance to the Lord, Sir; while we live,
Our duty's not to punish, but forgive;
And what the Lord commands, we should obey
40 Without regard to what the world may say.
What! Shall the fear of being misunderstood
Prevent our doing what is right and good?
No, no; let's simply do what Heaven ordains,
And let no other thoughts perplex our brains.
45 TARTUFFE: Again, Sir, let me say that I've forgiven
Damis, and thus obeyed the laws of Heaven;
But I am not commanded by the Bible
To live with one who smears my name with libel.
CLÉANTE: Were you commanded, Sir, to indulge the
whim
50 Of poor Orgon, and to encourage him
In suddenly transferring to your name
A large estate to which you have no claim?
TARTUFFE: 'Twould never occur to those who know
me best
To think I acted from self-interest.
55 The treasures of this world I quite despise;
Their specious glitter does not charm my eyes;
And if I have resigned myself to taking
The gift which my dear Brother insists on
making,
I do so only, as he well understands,
60 Lest so much wealth fall into wicked hands,
Lest those to whom it might descend in time
Turn it to purposes of sin and crime,
And not, as I shall do, make use of it
For Heaven's glory and mankind's benefit.
CLÉANTE: Forget these trumped-up fears. Your
65 argument
Is one the rightful heir might well resent;
It is a moral burden to inherit
Such wealth, but give Damis a chance to bear it.
And would it not be worse to be accused
70 Of swindling, than to see that wealth misused?
I'm shocked that you allowed Orgon to broach
This matter, and that you feel no self-reproach;
Does true religion teach that lawful heirs
May freely be deprived of what is theirs?
75 And if the Lord has told you in your heart
That you and young Damis must dwell apart,
Would it not be the decent thing to beat
A generous and honorable retreat,
Rather than let the son of the house be sent,
80 For your convenience, into banishment?
Sir, if you wish to prove the honesty
Of your intentions . . .

TARTUFFE: Sir, it is half-past three.
I've certain pious duties to attend to,
And hope my prompt departure won't offend you.
CLÉANTE (alone): Damn.   85

Scene 2   [Elmire, Mariane, Cléante, Dorine.]

DORINE: Stay, Sir, and help Mariane,
for Heaven's sake!
She's suffering so, I fear her heart will break.
Her father's plan to marry her off tonight
Has put the poor child in a desperate plight.
I hear him coming. Let's stand together, now,   5
And see if we can't change his mind, somehow,
About this match we all deplore and fear.

Scene 3   [Orgon, Elmire, Mariane, Cléante, Dorine.]

ORGON: Halt! Glad to find you all assembled here.
(To Mariane.)
This contract, child, contains your happiness,
And what it says I think your heart can guess.
MARIANE (falling to her knees): Sir, by that Heaven
which sees me here distressed,
And by whatever else can move your breast,   5
Do not employ a father's power, I pray you,
To crush my heart and force it to obey you,
Nor by your harsh commands oppress me so
That I'll begrudge the duty which I owe—
And do not so embitter and enslave me   10
That I shall hate the very life you gave me.
If my sweet hopes must perish, if you refuse
To give me to the one I've dared to choose,
Spare me at least—I beg you, I implore—
The pain of wedding one whom I abhor;   15
And do not, by a heartless use of force,
Drive me to contemplate some desperate course.
ORGON (feeling himself touched by her): Be firm, my
soul. No human weakness, now.
MARIANE: I don't resent your love for him. Allow
Your heart free rein, Sir; give him your property, 20
And if that's not enough, take mine from me;
He's welcome to my money; take it, do,
But don't, I pray, include my person too.
Spare me, I beg you; and let me end the tale
Of my sad days behind a convent veil.   25
ORGON: A convent! Hah! When crossed in their
amours,
All lovesick girls have the same thought as yours.
Get up! The more you loathe the man, and dread
him,
The more ennobling it will be to wed him.
Marry Tartuffe, and mortify your flesh!   30
Enough; don't start that whimpering afresh.
DORINE: But why . . . ?

ORGON: Be still, there. Speak when
    you're spoken to.
    Not one more bit of impudence out of you.
CLÉANTE: If I may offer a word of counsel here . . .
35 ORGON: Brother, in counseling you have no peer;
    All your advice is forceful; sound, and clever;
    I don't propose to follow it, however.
ELMIRE (*to Orgon*): I am amazed, and don't know
    what to say;
    Your blindness simply takes my breath away.
40   You are indeed bewitched, to take no warning
    From our account of what occurred this morning.
ORGON: Madam, I know a few plain facts, and one
    Is that you're partial to my rascal son;
    Hence, when he sought to make Tartuffe the
    victim
45   Of a base lie, you dared not contradict him.
    Ah, but you underplayed your part, my pet;
    You should have looked more angry, more upset.
ELMIRE: When men make overtures, must we reply
    With righteous anger and a battle-cry?
50   Must we turn back their amorous advances
    With sharp reproaches and with fiery glances?
    Myself, I find such offers merely amusing,
    And make no scenes and fusses in refusing;
    My taste is for good-natured rectitude,
55   And I dislike the savage sort of prude
    Who guards her virtue with her teeth and claws,
    And tears men's eyes out for the slightest cause:
    The Lord preserve me from such honor as that,
    Which bites and scratches like an alley-cat!
60   I've found that a polite and cool rebuff
    Discourages a lover quite enough.
ORGON: I know the facts, and I shall not be shaken.
ELMIRE: I marvel at your power to be mistaken.
    Would it, I wonder, carry weight with you
65   If I could *show* you that our tale was true?
ORGON: Show me?
ELMIRE: Yes.
ORGON: Rot.
ELMIRE: Come, what if I found a way
    To make you see the facts as plain as day?
ORGON: Nonsense.
ELMIRE: Do answer me; don't be absurd.
    I'm not now asking you to trust our word.
70   Suppose that from some hiding-place in here
    You learned the whole sad truth by eye and ear—
    What would you say of your good friend, after
    that?
ORGON: Why, I'd say . . . nothing, by Jehoshaphat!
    It can't be true.
ELMIRE: You've been too long deceived,
75   And I'm quite tired of being disbelieved.
    Come now: let's put my statements to the test,
    And you shall see the truth made manifest.
ORGON: I'll take that challenge. Now do your
    uttermost.
    We'll see how you make good your empty boast.
ELMIRE (*to Dorine*): Send him to me.

DORINE: He's crafty; it
    may be hard   80
    To catch the cunning scoundrel off his guard.
ELMIRE: No, amorous men are gullible. Their conceit
    So blinds them that they're never hard to cheat.
    Have him come down (*To Cléante and Mariane.*)
    Please leave us, for a bit.

Scene 4   [*Elmire, Orgon.*]

ELMIRE: Pull up this table, and get under it.
ORGON: What?
ELMIRE: It's essential that you be well-hidden.
ORGON: Why there?
ELMIRE: Oh, Heavens! Just do as you are
    bidden.
    I have my plans; we'll soon see how they fare.
    Under the table, now; and once you're there,   5
    Take care that you are neither seen nor heard.
ORGON: Well, I'll indulge you, since I gave my word
    To see you through this infantile charade.
ELMIRE: Once it is over, you'll be glad we played.

(*To her husband, who is now under the table.*)

    I'm going to act quite strangely, now, and you   10
    Must not be shocked at anything I do.
    Whatever I may say, you must excuse
    As part of that deceit I'm forced to use.
    I shall employ sweet speeches in the task
    Of making that imposter drop his mask;   15
    I'll give encouragement to his bold desires,
    And furnish fuel to his amorous fires.
    Since it's for your sake, and for his destruction,
    That I shall seem to yield to his seduction,
    I'll gladly stop whenever you decide   20
    That all your doubts are fully satisfied.
    I'll count on you, as soon as you have seen
    What sort of man he is, to intervene,
    And not expose me to his odious lust
    One moment longer than you feel you must.   25
    Remember: you're to save me from my plight
    Whenever . . . He's coming! Hush! Keep out of
    sight!

Scene 5   [*Tartuffe, Elmire, Orgon.*]

TARTUFFE: You wish to have a word with me, I'm told.
ELMIRE: Yes. I've a little secret to unfold.
    Before I speak, however, it would be wise
    To close that door, and look about for spies.

[*Tartuffe goes to the door, closes it, and returns.*]

    The very last thing that must happen now   5
    Is a repetition of this morning's row.
    I've never been so badly caught off guard.
    Oh, how I feared for you! You saw how hard

Aaron Hendry as Tartuffe, Misha Bouvion as Elmire, and Ted Barton as Orgon at the Will Geer Theatricum Botanicum, 2011.

I tried to make that troublesome Damis
10   Control his dreadful temper, and hold his peace.
In my confusion, I didn't have the sense
Simply to contradict his evidence;
But as it happened, that was for the best,
And all has worked out in our interest.
15   This storm has only bettered your position;
My husband doesn't have the least suspicion,
And now, in mockery of those who do,
He bids me be continually with you.
And that is why, quite fearless of reproof,
20   I now can be alone with my Tartuffe,
And why my heart—perhaps too quick to yield—
Feels free to let its passion be revealed.
TARTUFFE: Madam, your words confuse me. Not long ago,
You spoke in quite a different style, you know.
25   ELMIRE: Ah, Sir, if that refusal made you smart,
It's little that you know of woman's heart,
Or what that heart is trying to convey
When it resists in such a feeble way!

Always, at first, our modesty prevents
The frank avowal of tender sentiments;   30
However high the passion which inflames us,
Still, to confess its power somehow shames us.
Thus we reluct, at first, yet in a tone
Which tells you that our heart is overthrown,
That what our lips deny, our pulse confesses,   35
And that, in time, all noes will turn to yesses.
I fear my words are all too frank and free,
And a poor proof of woman's modesty;
But since I'm started, tell me, if you will—
Would I have tried to make Damis be still,   40
Would I have listened, calm and unoffended,
Until your lengthy offer of love was ended,
And been so very mild in my reaction,
Had your sweet words not given me satisfaction?
And when I tried to force you to undo   45
The marriage-plans my husband has in view.
What did my urgent pleading signify
If not that I admired you, and that I
Deplored the thought that someone else might own

50　　Part of a heart I wished for mine alone?
　　TARTUFFE: Madam, no happiness is so complete
　　　　As when, from lips we love, come words so sweet;
　　　　Their nectar floods my every sense, and drains
　　　　In honeyed rivulets through all my veins.
55　　　　To please you is my joy, my only goal;
　　　　Your love is the restorer of my soul;
　　　　And yet I must beg leave, now, to confess
　　　　Some lingering doubts as to my happiness.
　　　　Might this not be a trick? Might not the catch
60　　　　Be that you wish me to break off the match
　　　　With Mariane, and so have feigned to love me?
　　　　I shan't quite trust your fond opinion of me
　　　　Until the feelings you've expressed so sweetly
　　　　Are demonstrated somewhat more concretely,
65　　　　And you have shown, by certain kind concessions,
　　　　That I may put my faith in your professions.
　　ELMIRE (She coughs, to warn her husband): Why be
　　　　in such a hurry? Must my heart
　　　　Exhaust its bounty at the very start?
　　　　To make that sweet admission cost me dear,
70　　　　But you'll not be content, it would appear,
　　　　Unless my store of favors is disbursed
　　　　To the last farthing, and at the very first.
　　TARTUFFE: The less we merit, the less we dare to hope,
　　　　And with our doubts, mere words can never cope.
75　　　　We trust no promised bliss till we receive it;
　　　　Not till a joy is ours can we believe it.
　　　　I, who so little merit your esteem,
　　　　Can't credit this fulfillment of my dream,
　　　　And shan't believe it, Madam, until I savor
80　　　　Some palpable assurance of your favor.
　　ELMIRE: My, how tyrannical your love can be,
　　　　And how it flusters and perplexes me!
　　　　How furiously you take one's heart in hand,
　　　　And make your every wish a fierce command!
85　　　　Come, must you hound and harry me to death?
　　　　Will you not give me time to catch my breath?
　　　　Can it be right to press me with such force,
　　　　Give me no quarter, show me no remorse,
　　　　And take advantage, by your stern insistence,
90　　　　Of the fond feelings which weaken my resistance?
　　TARTUFFE: Well, if you look with favor upon my love,
　　　　Why, then, begrudge me some clear proof thereof?
　　ELMIRE: But how can I consent without offense
　　　　To Heaven, toward which you feel such reverence?
　　TARTUFFE: If Heaven is all that holds you back, don't
95　　　　worry.
　　　　I can remove that hindrance in a hurry.
　　　　Nothing of that sort need obstruct our path.
　　ELMIRE: Must one not be afraid of Heaven's wrath?
　　TARTUFFE: Madam, forget such fears, and be my pupil,
100　　And I shall teach you how to conquer scruple.
　　　　Some joys, it's true, are wrong in Heaven's eyes;
　　　　Yet Heaven is not averse to compromise;
　　　　There is a science, lately formulated,
　　　　Whereby one's conscience may be liberated,
105　　And any wrongful act you care to mention
　　　　May be redeemed by purity of intention.
　　　　I'll teach you, Madam, the secrets of that science;

　　　　Meanwhile, just place on me your full reliance.
　　　　Assuage my keen desires, and feel no dread:
　　　　The sin, if any, shall be on my head.　　　　110

[Elmire coughs, this time more loudly.]
　　　　You've a bad cough.
　　ELMIRE:　　　　　　Yes, yes. It's bad indeed.
　　TARTUFFE (producing a little paper bag): A bit of
　　　　licorice may be what you need.
　　ELMIRE: No, I've a stubborn cold, it seems. I'm sure it
　　　　Will take much more than licorice to cure it.
　　TARTUFFE: How aggravating.
　　ELMIRE:　　　　　　Oh, more than I can say.　　115
　　TARTUFFE: If you're still troubled, think of things
　　　　this way:
　　　　No one shall know our joys, save us alone,
　　　　And there's no evil till the act is known;
　　　　It's scandal, Madam, which makes it an offense,
　　　　And it's no sin to sin in confidence.　　　　120
　　ELMIRE (having coughed once more): Well, clearly
　　　　I must do as you require,
　　　　And yield to your importunate desire.
　　　　It is apparent, now, that nothing less
　　　　Will satisfy you, and so I acquiesce.
　　　　To go so far is much against my will;　　　　125
　　　　I'm vexed that it should come to this; but still,
　　　　Since you are so determined on it, since you
　　　　Will not allow mere language to convince you,
　　　　And since you ask for concrete evidence, I
　　　　See nothing for it, now, but to comply.　　　　130
　　　　If this is sinful, if I'm wrong to do it,
　　　　So much the worse for him who drove me to it.
　　　　The fault can surely not be charged to me.
　　TARTUFFE: Madam, the fault is mine, if fault there be,
　　　　And . . .
　　ELMIRE:　　Open the door a little, and peek out;　　135
　　　　I wouldn't want my husband poking about.
　　TARTUFFE: Why worry about the man? Each day he grows
　　　　More gullible; one can lead him by the nose.
　　　　To find us here would fill him with delight,
　　　　And if he saw the worst, he'd doubt his sight.　　140
　　ELMIRE: Nevertheless, do step out for a minute
　　　　Into the hall, and see that no one's in it.

Scene 6　[Orgon, Elmire.]

ORGON (coming out from under the table): That man's a
　　　　perfect monster, I must admit!
　　　　I'm simply stunned. I can't get over it.
　　ELMIRE: What, coming out so soon? How premature!
　　　　Get back in hiding, and wait until you're sure.
　　　　Stay till the end, and be convinced completely;　　5
　　　　We mustn't stop till things are proved concretely.
　　ORGON: Hell never harbored anything so vicious!
　　ELMIRE: Tut, don't be hasty. Try to be judicious.
　　　　Wait, and be certain that there's no mistake.
　　　　No jumping to conclusions, for Heaven's sake!　　10

[She places Orgon behind her, as Tartuffe re-enters.]

Scene 7 [*Tartuffe, Elmire, Orgon.*]

TARTUFFE (*not seeing Orgon*): Madam, all things
     have worked out to perfection;
  I've given the neighboring rooms a full inspection;
  No one's about; and now I may at last . . .
ORGON (*intercepting him*): Hold on, my passionate
     fellow, not so fast!
5 I should advise a little more restraint.
  Well, so you thought you'd fool me, my dear saint!
  How soon you wearied of the saintly life—
  Wedding my daughter, and coveting my wife!
  I've long suspected you, and had a feeling
10 That soon I'd catch you at your double-dealing.
  Just now, you've given me evidence galore;
  It's quite enough; I have no wish for more.
ELMIRE (*to Tartuffe*): I'm sorry to have treated you so slyly,
  But circumstances forced me to be wily.
TARTUFFE: Brother, you can't think . . .
15 ORGON: No more talk from you;
  Just leave this household, without more ado.
TARTUFFE: What I intended . . .
  ORGON: That seems fairly clear.
  Spare me your falsehoods and get out of here.
TARTUFFE: No, I'm the master, and you're the one to go!
20 This house belongs to me, I'll have you know,
  And I shall show you that you can't hurt *me*
  By this contemptible conspiracy,
  That those who cross me know not what they do,
  And that I've means to expose and punish you,
25 Avenge offended Heaven, and make you grieve
  That ever you dared order me to leave.

Scene 8 [*Elmire, Orgon.*]

ELMIRE: What was the point of all that angry chatter?
ORGON: Dear God, I'm worried. This is no laughing
     matter.
ELMIRE: How so?
ORGON: I fear I understood his drift.
  I'm much disturbed about that deed of gift.
ELMIRE: You gave him . . . ?
ORGON: Yes, it's all been drawn
5   and signed.
  But one thing more is weighing on my mind.
ELMIRE: What's that?
ORGON: I'll tell you; but first let's see if there's
  A certain strong-box in his room upstairs.

ACT V • Scene 1 [*Orgon, Cléante.*]

CLÉANTE: Where are you going so fast?
ORGON: God knows!
CLÉANTE: Then wait;
  Let's have a conference, and deliberate
  On how this situation's to be met.
ORGON: That strong-box has me utterly upset;

This is the worst of many, many shocks.   5
CLÉANTE: Is there some fearful mystery in that box?
ORGON: My poor friend Argas brought that box to me
  With his own hands, in utmost secrecy;
  'Twas on the very morning of his flight.
  It's full of papers which, if they came to light, 10
  Would ruin him—or such is my impression.
CLÉANTE: Then why did you let it out of your possession?
ORGON: Those papers vexed my conscience, and it
     seemed best
  To ask the counsel of my pious guest.
  The cunning scoundrel got me to agree   15
  To leave the strong-box in his custody,
  So that, in case of an investigation,
  I could employ a slight equivocation
  And swear I didn't have it, and thereby,
  At no expense to conscience, tell a lie.   20
CLÉANTE: It looks to me as if you're out on a limb.
  Trusting him with that box, and offering him
  That deed of gift, were actions of a kind
  Which scarcely indicate a prudent mind.
  With two such weapons, he has the upper hand,   25
  And since you're vulnerable, as matters stand,
  You erred once more in bringing him to bay.
  You should have acted in some subtler way.
ORGON: Just think of it: behind that fervent face,
  A heart so wicked, and a soul so base!   30
  I took him in, a hungry beggar, and then . . .
  Enough, by God! I'm through with pious men:
  Henceforth I'll hate the whole false brotherhood,
  And persecute them worse than Satan could.
CLÉANTE: Ah, there you go—extravagant as ever!   35
  Why can you not be rational? You never
  Manage to take the middle course, it seems,
  But jump, instead, between absurd extremes.
  You've recognized your recent grave mistake
  In falling victim to a pious fake;   40
  Now, to correct that error, must you embrace
  An even greater error in its place,
  And judge our worthy neighbors as a whole
  By what you've learned of one corrupted soul?
  Come, just because one rascal made you swallow 45
  A show of zeal which turned out to be hollow,
  Shall you conclude that all men are deceivers,
  And that, today, there are no true believers?
  Let atheists make that foolish inference;
  Learn to distinguish virtue from pretense,   50
  Be cautious in bestowing admiration,
  And cultivate a sober moderation.
  Don't humor fraud, but also don't asperse
  True piety; the latter fault is worse,
  And it is best to err, if err one must,   55
  As you have done, upon the side of trust.

Scene 2 [*Damis, Orgon, Cléante.*]

DAMIS: Father, I hear that scoundrel's uttered threats
  Against you; that he pridefully forgets
  How, in his need, he was befriended by you,

And means to use your gifts to crucify you.
5 ORGON: It's true, my boy. I'm too distressed for tears.
DAMIS: Leave it to me, Sir; let me trim his ears.
Faced with such insolence, we must not waver.
I shall rejoice in doing you the favor
Of cutting short his life, and your distress.
10 CLÉANTE: What a display of young hotheadedness!
Do learn to moderate your fits of rage.
In this just kingdom, this enlightened age,
One does not settle things by violence.

Scene 3   [*Madame Pernelle, Mariane, Elmire, Dorine, Damis, Orgon, Cléante.*]

MADAME PERNELLE: I hear strange tales of very strange
events.
ORGON: Yes, strange events which these two eyes beheld.
The man's ingratitude is unparalleled.
I save a wretched pauper from starvation,
5 House him, and treat him like a blood relation,
Shower him every day with my largesse,
Give him my daughter, and all that I possess;

Angelika Thomas as Madame Pernelle and Peter Jordan as
Orgon in *Der Tartuffe* at the 2006 Salzburg Festival.

And meanwhile the unconscionable knave
Tries to induce my wife to misbehave;
And not content with such extreme rascality,   10
Now threatens me with my own liberality,
And aims, by taking base advantage of
The gifts I gave him out of Christian love,
To drive me from my house, a ruined man,
And make me end a pauper, as he began.   15
DORINE: Poor fellow!
MADAME PERNELLE: No, my son, I'll never bring
Myself to think him guilty of such a thing.
ORGON: How's that?
MADAME PERNELLE: The righteous always were
maligned.
ORGON: Speak clearly, Mother. Say what's on your
mind.
MADAME PERNELLE: I mean that I can smell a rat, my
dear.   20
You know how everybody hates him, here.
ORGON: That has no bearing on the case at all.
MADAME PERNELLE: I told you a hundred times, when you
were small,
That virtue in this world is hated ever;
Malicious men may die, but malice never.   25
ORGON: No doubt that's true, but how does it apply?
MADAME PERNELLE: They've turned you against him by
a clever lie.
ORGON: I've told you, I was there and saw it done.
MADAME PERNELLE: Ah, slanderers will stop at nothing,
Son.
ORGON: Mother, I'll lose my temper . . . For the last
time,   30
I tell you I was witness to the crime.
MADAME PERNELLE: The tongues of spite are busy night
and noon,
And to their venom no man is immune.
ORGON: You're talking nonsense. Can't you realize
I saw it; saw it; saw it with my eyes?   35
Saw, do you understand me? Must I shout it
Into your ears before you'll cease to doubt it?
MADAME PERNELLE: Appearances can deceive, my son.
Dear me,
We cannot always judge by what we see.
ORGON: Drat! Drat!
MADAME PERNELLE:
                    One often interprets things awry; 40
Good can seem evil to a suspicious eye.
ORGON: Was I to see his pawing at Elmire
As an act of charity?
MADAME PERNELLE: Till his guilt is clear,
A man deserves the benefit of the doubt.
You should have waited, to see how things turned
out.   45
ORGON: Great God in Heaven, what more proof did
I need?
Was I to sit there, watching, until he'd . . .
You drive me to the brink of impropriety.
MADAME PERNELLE: No, no, a man of such surpassing
piety
Could not do such a thing. You cannot shake me.   50

I don't believe it, and you shall not make me.
ORGON: You vex me so that, if you weren't my
    mother,
I'd say to you . . . some dreadful thing or other.
DORINE: It's your turn now, Sir, not to be listened to;
55   You'd not trust us, and now she won't trust you.
CLÉANTE: My friends, we're wasting time which
    should be spent
In facing up to our predicament.
I fear that scoundrel's threats weren't made
    in sport.
DAMIS: Do you think he'd have the nerve to go to
    court?
60 ELMIRE: I'm sure he won't: they'd find it all too crude
A case of swindling and ingratitude.
CLÉANTE: Don't be too sure. He won't be at a loss
To give his claims a high and righteous gloss;
And clever rogues with far less valid cause
65   Have trapped their victims in a web of laws.
I say again that to antagonize
A man so strongly armed was most unwise.
ORGON: I know it; but the man's appalling cheek
Outraged me so, I couldn't control my pique.
70 CLÉANTE: I wish to Heaven that we could devise
Some truce between you, or some compromise.
ELMIRE: If I had known what cards he held, I'd not
Have roused his anger by my little plot.
ORGON (*to Dorine, as M. Loyal enters*): What is that
    fellow looking for? Who is he?
75   Go talk to him—and tell him that I'm busy.

Scene 4 [*Monsieur Loyal, Madame Pernelle, Orgon, Damis, Mariane, Dorine, Elmire, Cléante.*]

MONSIEUR LOYAL: Good day, dear sister. Kindly let
    me see
Your master.
DORINE: He's involved with company,
And cannot be disturbed just now, I fear.
MONSIEUR LOYAL: I hate to intrude; but what has brought
    me here
5   Will not disturb your master, in any event.
Indeed, my news will make him most content.
DORINE: Your name?
MONSIEUR LOYAL: Just say that I bring greetings
    from
Monsieur Tartuffe, on whose behalf I've come.
DORINE (*to Orgon*): Sir, he's a very gracious man,
    and bears
10   A message from Tartuffe, which he declares,
Will make you most content.
CLÉANTE: Upon my word,
I think this man had best be seen, and heard.
ORGON: Perhaps he has some settlement to suggest.
How shall I treat him? What manner would be best?
15 CLÉANTE: Control your anger, and if he should mention
Some fair adjustment, give him your full attention.

MONSIEUR LOYAL: Good health to you, good Sir.
    May Heaven confound
Your enemies, and may your joys abound.
ORGON (*aside, to Cléante*): A gentle salutation: it
    confirms
My guess that he is here to offer terms.   20
MONSIEUR LOYAL: I've always held your family most
    dear;
I served your father, Sir, for many a year.
ORGON: Sir, I must ask your pardon; to my shame,
I cannot now recall your face or name.
MONSIEUR LOYAL: Loyal's my name; I come from
    Normandy,   25
And I'm a bailiff, in all modesty.
For forty years, praise God, it's been my boast
To serve with honor in that vital post,
And I am here, Sir, if you will permit
The liberty, to serve you with this writ . . .   30
ORGON: To—*what?*
MONSIEUR LOYAL: Now, please, Sir, let us have no
    friction:
It's nothing but an order of eviction.
You are to move your goods and family out
And make way for new occupants, without
Deferment or delay, and give the keys . . .   35
ORGON: I? Leave this house?
MONSIEUR LOYAL: Why yes, Sir, if you please.
This house, Sir, from the cellar to the roof,
Belongs now to the good Monsieur Tartuffe,
And he is lord and master of your estate
By virtue of a deed of present date,   40
Drawn in due form, with clearest legal phrasing . . .
DAMIS: Your insolence is utterly amazing!
MONSIEUR LOYAL: Young man, my business here is
    not with you,
But with your wise and temperate father, who,
Like every worthy citizen, stands in awe   45
Of justice, and would never obstruct the law.
ORGON: But . . .
MONSIEUR LOYAL:
        Not for a million, Sir, would you rebel
Against authority; I know that well.
You'll not make trouble, Sir, or interfere
With the execution of my duties here.   50
DAMIS: Someone may execute a smart tattoo
On that black jacket of yours, before you're through.
MONSIEUR LOYAL: Sir, bid your son be silent. I'd much
    regret
Having to mention such a nasty threat
Of violence, in writing my report.   55
DORINE (*aside*): This man Loyal's a most disloyal sort!
MONSIEUR LOYAL: I love all men of upright character,
And when I agreed to serve these papers, Sir,
It was your feelings that I had in mind.
I couldn't bear to see the case assigned   60
To someone else, who might esteem you less
And so subject you to unpleasantness.
ORGON: What's more unpleasant than telling a man
    to leave

His house and home?

MONSIEUR LOYAL: You'd like a short reprieve?
65   If you desire it, Sir, I shall not press you,
      But wait until tomorrow to dispossess you.
      Splendid. I'll come and spend the night here, then,
      Most quietly, with half a score of men.
      For form's sake, you might bring me, just before
70   You go to bed, the keys to the front door.
      My men, I promise, will be on their best
      Behavior, and will not disturb your rest.
      But bright and early, Sir, you must be quick
      And move out all your furniture, every stick:
75   The men I've chosen are both young and strong,
      And with their help it shouldn't take you long.
      In short, I'll make things pleasant and convenient,
      And since I'm being so extremely lenient,
      Please show me, Sir, a like consideration,
80   And give me your entire cooperation.
ORGON (aside): I may be all but bankrupt, but I vow
      I'd give a hundred louis, here and now,
      Just for the pleasure of landing one good clout
      Right on the end of that complacent snout.
CLÉANTE: Careful; don't make things worse.
85 DAMIS: My bootsole itches
      To give that beggar a good kick in the breeches.
DORINE: Monsieur Loyal, I'd love to hear the whack
      Of a stout stick across your fine broad back.
MONSIEUR LOYAL: Take care: a woman too may go
          to jail if
90   She uses threatening language to a bailiff.
CLÉANTE: Enough, enough, Sir. This must not go on.
      Give me that paper, please, and then begone.
MONSIEUR LOYAL: Well, *au revoir*. God give you all
          good cheer!
ORGON: May God confound you, and him who sent
          you here!

Scene 5   [*Orgon, Cléante, Mariane, Elmire, Madame Pernelle, Dorine, Damis.*]

ORGON: Now, Mother, was I right or not? This
          writ
      Should change your notion of Tartuffe a bit.
      Do you perceive his villainy at last?
MADAME PERNELLE: I'm thunderstruck. I'm utterly
          aghast.
5 DORINE: Oh, come, be fair. You mustn't take offense
      At this new proof of his benevolence.
      He's acting out of selfless love, I know.
      Material things enslave the soul, and so
      He kindly has arranged your liberation
10   From all that might endanger your salvation.
ORGON: Will you not ever hold your tongue, you
          dunce?
CLÉANTE: Come, you must take some action, and at
          once.
ELMIRE: Go tell the world of the low trick he's tried.

The deed of gift is surely nullified
By such behavior, and public rage will not   15
Permit the wretch to carry out his plot.

Scene 6   [*Valère, Orgon, Cléante, Elmire, Mariane, Madame Pernelle, Damis, Dorine.*]

VALÈRE: Sir, though I hate to bring you more bad
          news,
      Such is the danger that I cannot choose.
      A friend who is extremely close to me
      And knows my interest in your family
      Has, for my sake, presumed to violate   5
      The secrecy that's due to things of state,
      And sends me word that you are in a plight
      From which your one salvation lies in flight.
      That scoundrel who's imposed upon you so
      Denounced you to the King an hour ago   10
      And, as supporting evidence, displayed
      The strong-box of a certain renegade
      Whose secret papers, so he testified,
      You had disloyally agreed to hide.
      I don't know just what charges may be pressed,   15
      But there's a warrant out for your arrest;
      Tartuffe has been instructed, furthermore,
      To guide the arresting officer to your door.
CLÉANTE: He's clearly done this to facilitate
      His seizure of your house and your estate.   20
ORGON: That man, I must say, is a vicious beast!
VALÈRE: Quick, Sir; you mustn't tarry in the least.
      My carriage is outside, to take you hence;
      This thousand louis should cover all expense.
      Let's lose no time, or you shall be undone;   25
      The sole defense, in this case, is to run.
      I shall go with you all the way, and place you
      In a safe refuge to which they'll never trace you.
ORGON: Alas, dear boy, I wish that I could show
          you
      My gratitude for everything I owe you.   30
      But now is not the time; I pray the Lord
      That I may live to give you your reward.
      Farewell, my dears; be careful . . .
CLÉANTE: Brother, hurry.
      We shall take care of things; you needn't worry.

Scene 7   [*The Officer, Tartuffe, Valère, Orgon, Elmire, Mariane, Madame Pernelle, Dorine, Cléante, Damis.*]

TARTUFFE: Gently, Sir, gently; stay right where you are.
      No need for haste; your lodging isn't far.
      You're off to prison, by order of the Prince.
ORGON: This is the crowning blow, you wretch; and since
      It means my total ruin and defeat,   5
      Your villainy is now at last complete.

John Beatty's set design (with ensemble cast) for the Roundabout Theatre Company's 2002–2003 production.

TARTUFFE: You needn't try to provoke me; it's no use.
    Those who serve Heaven must expect abuse.
CLÉANTE: You are indeed most patient, sweet, and blameless.
DORINE: How he exploits the name of Heaven! It's
10   shameless.
TARTUFFE: Your taunts and mockeries are all for naught;
    To do my duty is my only thought.
MARIANE: Your love of duty is most meritorious,
    And what you've done is little short of glorious.
15 TARTUFFE: All deeds are glorious, Madam, which obey
    The sovereign prince who sent me here today.
ORGON: I rescued you when you were destitute;
    Have you forgotten that, you thankless brute?
TARTUFFE: No, no, I well remember everything;
20   But my first duty is to serve my King.
    That obligation is so paramount
    That other claims, beside it, do not count;
    And for it I would sacrifice my wife,
    My family, my friend, or my own life.
ELMIRE: Hypocrite!
25 DORINE: All that we most revere, he uses
    To cloak his plots and camouflage his ruses.
CLÉANTE: If it is true that you are animated
    By pure and loyal zeal, as you have stated,
    Why was this zeal not roused until you'd sought
30   To make Orgon a cuckold, and been caught?
    Why weren't you moved to give your evidence
    Until your outraged host had driven you hence?

I shan't say that the gift of all his treasure
Ought to have damped your zeal in any measure;
But if he is a traitor, as you declare,   35
How could you condescend to be his heir?
TARTUFFE (*to the officer*): Sir, spare me all this clamor;
    it's growing shrill.
    Please carry out your orders, if you will.
OFFICER: Yes, I've delayed too long, Sir. Thank you kindly.
    You're just the proper person to remind me.   40
    Come, you are off to join the other boarders
    In the King's prison, according to his orders.
TARTUFFE: Who? I, Sir?
OFFICER: Yes.
TARTUFFE: To prison? This can't be true!
OFFICER: I owe an explanation, but not to you.
                  (*To Orgon.*)
    Sir, all is well; rest easy, and be grateful.   45
    We serve a Prince to whom all sham is hateful,
    A Prince who sees into our inmost hearts,
    And can't be fooled by any trickster's arts.
    His royal soul, though generous and human,
    Views all things with discernment and acumen;   50
    His sovereign reason is not lightly swayed,
    And all his judgments are discreetly weighed.
    He honors righteous men of every kind,
    And yet his zeal for virtue is not blind,
    Nor does his love of piety numb his wits   55
    And make him tolerant of hypocrites.
    'Twas hardly likely that this man could cozen

A King who's foiled such liars by the dozen.
With one keen glance, the King perceived the whole
60 Perverseness and corruption of his soul,
And thus high Heaven's justice was displayed:
Betraying you, the rogue stood self-betrayed.
The King soon recognized Tartuffe as one
Notorious by another name, who'd done
65 So many vicious crimes that one could fill
Ten volumes with them, and be writing still.
But to be brief: our sovereign was appalled
By this man's treachery toward you, which he called
The last, worst villainy of a vile career,
70 And bade me follow the impostor here
To see how gross his impudence could be,
And force him to restore your property.
Your private papers, by the King's command,
I hereby seize and give into your hand.
75 The King, by royal order, invalidates
The deed which gave this rascal your estates,
And pardons, furthermore, your grave offense
In harboring an exile's documents.
By these decrees, our Prince rewards you for
80 Your loyal deeds in the late civil war,
And shows how heartfelt is his satisfaction

In recompensing any worthy action,
How much he prizes merit, and how he makes
More of men's virtues than of their mistakes.
DORINE: Heaven be praised!
MADAME PERNELLE: I breathe again, at last. 85
ELMIRE: We're safe.
MARIANE: I can't believe the danger's past.
ORGON (to Tartuffe): Well, traitor, now you see . . .
CLÉANTE: Ah, Brother, please,
Let's not descend to such indignities.
Leave the poor wretch to his unhappy fate,
And don't say anything to aggravate 90
His present woes; but rather hope that he
Will soon embrace an honest piety,
And mend his ways, and by a true repentance
Move our just King to moderate his sentence.
Meanwhile, go kneel before your sovereign's throne 95
And thank him for the mercies he has shown.
ORGON: Well said: let's go at once and, gladly kneeling,
Express the gratitude which all are feeling.
Then, when that first great duty has been done,
We'll turn with pleasure to a second one, 100
And give Valère, whose love has proven so true,
The wedded happiness which is his due.

COMMENTARY

MEL GUSSOW (1933–2005)

Review of Tartuffe   1991

Mel Gussow, in his *New York Times* review of the Yale Repertory Theatre's 1991 production of *Tartuffe*, comments on the effects of the stage set, which was dominated by huge mahogany doors, and on the visual elements that help qualify the diminutive stature of Tartuffe as played by the irrepressible Austin Pendleton.

In Walton Jones's production of *Tartuffe* at the Yale Repertory Theatre, a row of large mahogany-like doors is positioned against a *trompe l'oeil* background. The doors are used for quick entrances, exits, and punchlines. They slide across the stage on tracks, swing open and slam on cue, and are filled with concealed crannies for depositing plot-advancing objects.

In using the jack-in-the-box set, the design of Kevin Rupnik, the director offers a well-carpentered, occasionally tricked-up approach to Molière, but with merit in its breathlessness. It is enlivened by several performances, especially by that of Austin Pendleton in the title role.

Mr. Pendleton takes to Tartuffe as a hypocrite to a hairshirt. Although his characterization is larger than life, he is undeniably short, and he uses his lowness to comic effect, even to playing one scene on his knees behind a portable pulpit that is the height of a go-cart. From his first entrance in an itch-provoking gown that almost reaches to his bare feet, he plays Tartuffe like a saint set for martyrdom. When he throws away his propriety and makes an advance on Orgon's wife (Frances Conroy), he does so with a sudden gale of energy. "I may be pious," he proclaims, "but I'm human too," and he raises his hand as if signaling the cavalry into action.

When he is caught in a flagrantly compromising position with the lady of the house, he looks at the almost cuckolded Orgon with the expression of an innocent child. "Brother, you can't think . . . ," says Tartuffe, and the actor takes a long, laughable pause before realizing that his game is up.

The key to Mr. Pendleton's success is that he is portraying a fanatic. This could be regarded as a Pendleton specialty—on stage and also on television, as witness his Mr. Entertainment, a helplessly stagestruck song-and-dance man, the amateur Sinatra of *St. Elsewhere*.

With Tartuffe loose in the household, the interfering maid Dorine (a pert performance by Fran Brill) mobilizes her allies, who include most of the other characters in the play, for an all-out siege on the villain. Subplot humor is provided by her attempt to wake up her employer, Orgon (Jerome Dempsey), a nearsighted fool who holds fast to his astigmatism. Mr. Dempsey is a master of the slow burn, as demonstrated in the scene in which he, aroused from his gullibility, tries to convince his still skeptical mother of Tartuffe's deceit. Patiently he describes the dastard, and she blithely dismisses the charge as slander. His carefully timed delivery of the line "Mother, I'll lose my temper" is done with apoplectic finesse.

Barring a certain amount of busyness—too much swirling through those doors—and a tentativeness at the conclusion, this is a mirthful *Tartuffe* that begins the Yale Repertory season. A final word is due Richard Wilbur's verse translation. In common with his other versions of Molière comedies, it is an eloquent example of the adapter's art.

Aphra Behn

> "All women together ought to let flowers fall upon the tomb of Aphra Behn . . . for it was she who earned them the right to speak their minds."
> – Virginia Woolf

Although not technically England's first female playwright or the first woman to earn a living by her pen, Aphra Behn (c. 1640–1689) was the first notably successful female playwright. She wrote twenty plays, several novels, among them *Oroonoko* (c. 1688), and *Poems on Several Occasions* (1684). She also published translations and edited volumes of poetry.

Behn grew up in an England governed by the Puritan Commonwealth. Throughout the 1650s, Oliver Cromwell was Protector, and the theaters were closed. The Puritans were, in Behn's eyes, dull, hypocritical, and repressive. Her allegiance was to the Stuarts, whose Charles I was beheaded by order of Parliament in 1649. His sons, Charles and James, were forced into exile on the Continent, along with many Stuart courtiers, such as the gallants who appear in *The Rover*. When Charles II was restored to the throne in 1660, the period known as the Restoration began. Behn was twenty years old.

Very little is known of her, and much of that is guesswork based on her writing. For example, *Oroonoko* is a novel set in Surinam, in South America, which was a British colony when she visited there with members of her family in 1663–1664. Before returning to London, she may have acted as a political informant under the name of Astrea. She married Mr. Behn, possibly a Dutch merchant in England, who died two years later. She seems to have been persuaded by the writer and theater manager Thomas Killigrew to become an English spy in Antwerp. She was residing there when the Great Fire of 1666 destroyed most of London. Her services were so little valued that she was not paid and ended up for a brief time in debtors' prison when she returned to England.

Once out of prison, she took advantage of her friendship with Thomas Betterton, who belonged to a theater company at Lincoln's Inn Fields. He played the lead in her first play, *The Forced Marriage* (1670), which ran successfully for six nights. The record for the first run of a play was thirteen nights. In 1670, Behn reached a mostly courtly audience, those politically aligned with Charles II or somehow involved in court politics.

Behn succeeded again with *The Amorous Prince* in 1671. Those first two plays were wholly original, but she quickly resorted to the Shakespearean device of adapting the work of others. Like Shakespeare, she made considerable changes and improved the material she borrowed. After the success of *The Rover* (1677), she was accused of plagiarism and answered the charge in the Postscript to the play. She did borrow some characters and details from Thomas Killigrew's *Thomaso; or, The Wanderer,* a closet drama, or play intended to be read, not staged (1654; published 1664); but, as she says in her Postscript, no one would have taken notice if her play had not been so successful—and written by a woman. Playwrights commonly adapted earlier material because they had to produce many plays in a short time to earn a meager living.

The theme of her first play, loveless and unhappy marriages arranged by families, recurs throughout Behn's work. All we know about her own marriage is that it was brief; she did not remarry despite having long-term relationships. But she concerned herself with the fate of women in her society. A young

For links to resources about Behn, click on *AuthorLinks* at **bedfordstmartins.com/jacobus.**

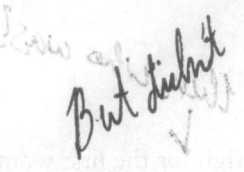

woman could not hope to marry if she was not a virgin. Once she was married, a woman's property became her husband's, and her legal identity was melded with his. Consequently, she was at her husband's mercy since she had no recourse in law against any of his excesses.

However, the alternative to marriage was considered worse. If a woman was seduced and people found out, she could expect to lose her status and forsake marriage. As a result, she would be forced to earn her own living, a harsh prospect since women were not given the same education as men and could not take part in any of the professions. One fate of many such women was to become prostitutes. In the meantime, men pursued their goal of seduction, as they do in *The Rover* and other Behn plays, with no thought given to the welfare of the women they seduced. Furthermore, they frequently threatened women with rape if the women were uncompliant. The theme of rape echoes through Behn's plays. By necessity Behn had to appeal to a predominantly male audience, but even so she expresses some of her deeper concerns for the welfare of her sex. She exposes the unfairness and pain of arranged marriages and portrays women as complex and intelligent. Her work seems to reflect the influence of Shakespeare's female characters, such as Helena and Hermia in *A Midsummer Night's Dream* and Beatrice in *Much Ado about Nothing*.

Behn's plays include *Abdelazer* (1676), *The Town Fop* (1676), *The Lucky Chance* (1686), and *The Emperor of the Moon* (1687). Her last play, *The Widow Ranter* (1689), produced posthumously, was a failure. But it is an interesting portrait of the settlement of the Virginias, and was likely informed by her own experience in the New World. The prefaces to Behn's plays treat important issues, such as the unequal education of women. She points out, however, that in playwriting the lack of education in Greek and Latin is no handicap. She reminds her readers that Shakespeare and Jonson did very well with limited education and that "gownmen" (scholars) talked incessantly and to little account. What was needed for the stage was experience and a good ear, and Aphra Behn had both.

The Rover; or, The Banished Cavaliers

The English rakes who swagger through this play are displaced Royalist cavaliers who lived perilously in exile during the Puritan interregnum of the 1650s as they awaited the restoration of Charles II to the throne. Their concerns in Naples are warlike and lusty. Their frequent dueling delighted the audiences of 1677 and caused *The Rover* to be one of Behn's best received plays. Beneath the brawling, however, is a more serious struggle between the sexes.

It is pre-Lenten carnival time in Naples, when all the people dress in masquerade. The players in *The Rover* disguise themselves — Hellena as a gypsy or a page, Belvile as Antonio, the others in costumes that make them unrecognizable — from the first act to the last. Such masquerading permits the young men and women to meet and talk without supervision. Among the characters, the most stable are Florinda and Belvile, who love each other from the beginning and who end up married despite the objections of Florinda's brother Pedro and their father, who has promised Florinda to Don Vincentio, a wealthy old man.

Behn's favorite theme of arranged or forced marriage thus surfaces quickly in this play, and much of the action involves its circumvention. A related theme also develops quickly: forcible rape. The Cavaliers, or rakes, treat women of lower social class as if they were whores. In this play, Florinda faces rape not once but twice. First Willmore, the Rover, treats her as "an errant harlot" and forces her to scream "rape" (3, 5). When Frederick and Belvile intervene, Willmore explains that he was drunk and not to blame. Florinda's second close call comes with Blunt. When she runs into his apartment to escape discovery on the street, Blunt decides to avenge his disgrace at the hands of Lucetta by raping Florinda—thus punishing the entire sex for his mishandling. This time Frederick, without knowing who Florinda is, decides both to help Blunt and to rape her as well. When she gives them a ring that reveals her to be an aristocrat, a woman of quality, Frederick says, "'twould anger us vilely to be trussed up for a rape upon a maid of quality, when we only believe we ruffle a harlot" (4, 5, 150–52).

These scenes are painful from our modern perspective and must have been even more so to women in Behn's audience. Part of her purpose, though, is to point out that men treated women differently according to class. Aristocrats such as these cavaliers were sometimes willfully brutal toward women in a lower class. Behn builds sympathy for Florinda and, by extension, for all women who are treated viciously by men. It is conceivable that some men in the audiences of Behn's day might not have been conscious of her purpose, since they may have approved of behavior such as Blunt's and Frederick's.

Like Florinda, the other female characters in *The Rover* face obstacles with wit and resourcefulness, but not all the women are successful. Behn's portrait of the courtesan Angellica is laced with irony. Against her will and better judgment, Angellica finds herself falling in love with Willmore. When she takes Willmore as a lover without demanding from him the usual thousand crowns, her handmaid Moretta watches in horror, realizing that her mistress is giving away something she would normally sell at a dear price. Angellica is smitten by Willmore—just as Hellena is smitten by the same rover—but once Willmore enjoys Angellica's pleasures, he dismisses her from his mind. Angellica the courtesan knows that this is the way men relate to women. But Angellica the woman, who gave Willmore her "virgin heart," is as deceived as any woman could be.

Hellena, promised to the church as a nun by her father, begins the play revealing her plans to avoid the convent at all costs. Her brother Pedro does not say so, but he seems to expect that when she is in the convent he will have access to the 300,000 crowns her uncle has bequeathed her. Pedro attempts to force Hellena to "marry" the church in the same way that he attempts to force Florinda to marry a man she does not love. Neither sister will have any of it.

The play centers more on the success of Florinda and Hellena than it does on Belvile or Willmore. Hellena, by virtue of her wit—which is equal to Willmore's—and her understanding of social realities, forces Willmore to submit to her will. He is all for making love, but she demands that Hymen, the god of marriage, be invoked before their lovemaking. When he tells her

were they popular because they were shocking?

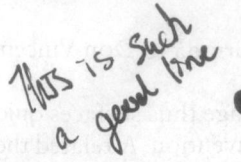

This is such a good line

that she should be content with love and not demand marriage, she replies, "What shall I get? A cradle full of noise and mischief, with a pack of repentance at my back?" (5, 514–16). She is more than his match. The play ends with Florinda, Hellena, and Valeria all winning the husbands of their choice on their own terms.

The Rover; or, The Banished Cavaliers in Performance

Charles II attended the March 24, 1677, production of *The Rover*, and successive royal performances were commanded before different monarchs in 1724 and 1729. Some seventy performances of the play took place between 1700 and 1725, and even more were recorded between 1726 and 1760. However, after 1790 the play was not produced for many decades.

Today's productions indicate a modern understanding of the play's feminist themes and its subtle wit-play between the sexes. The Folger Theatre Group in Washington, D.C., produced the work in 1982, playing it broadly for its humor. Critics praised the play for its vitality but complained that the production overdid the "business"—stage gestures, movement, and action—and the actors did not clearly deliver their lines. Christopher Reeve played Willmore in the Williamstown Theatre production in 1987, with Kate Burton as Florinda. The director, John Rubinstein, moved the setting from Naples to the West Indies. One of the most interesting, although not wholly satisfying, productions was in 1986 by the Royal Shakespeare Company. Jeremy Irons played Willmore and Imogen Stubbs played Hellena. The director, John Barton, adapted the text using the earlier source play *Thomaso; or, The Wanderer* by Thomas Killigrew. Critics of the Royal Shakespeare production were struck by the modernity of Behn's play. The King's County Shakespeare Company of Brooklyn, New York, produced the play to some acclaim in 2003. D.J.R. Bruckner, in the *New York Times,* said the play was "as fresh as tomorrow." The cast used period costume and period weaponry, which is not always done with this play. The version of the play produced by the Chance Theatre Company of Anaheim, California, in 2005 employed modern casual dress, casting the women as adolescent girls having a fantasy and using stuffed animals and Barbie and Ken dolls as weapons. These modern productions focus on the feminist issues in the text. London's Tabard Theatre produced a very lively carnivalesque version in 2007. The University of Pennsylvania and several other universities adapted the play to the modern stage in 2011.

For discussion questions and assignments on *The Rover,* visit **bedfordstmartins.com/jacobus.**

APHRA BEHN (c. 1640–1689)

The Rover; or, The Banished Cavaliers   1677

PROLOGUE

Wits, like physicians, never can agree,
When of a different society.
And Rabel's drops° were never more cried down
By all the learned doctors of the town,
5   Than a new play whose author is unknown.
Nor can those doctors with more malice sue
(And powerful purses) the dissenting few,
Than those, with an insulting pride, do rail
At all who are not of their own cabal.°
10   If a young poet hit your humor right,
You judge him then out of revenge and spite.
So amongst men there are ridiculous elves,
Who monkeys hate for being too like themselves.
So that the reason of the grand debate
15   Why wit so oft is damned when good plays take,
Is that you censure as you love, or hate.
    Thus like a learned conclave poets sit,
Catholic° judges both of sense and wit,
And damn or save as they themselves think fit.
20   Yet those who to others' faults are so severe,
Are not so perfect but themselves may err.
Some write correct, indeed, but then the whole
(Bating° their own dull stuff i'th' play) is stole:
As bees do suck from flowers their honeydew,
25   So they rob others striving to please you.
    Some write their characters genteel and fine,
But then they do so toil for every line,
That what to you does easy seem, and plain,
Is the hard issue of their laboring brain.
30   And some th' effects of all their pains, we see,
Is but to mimic good extempore.°
Others, by long converse about the town,
Have wit enough to write a lewd lampoon,
But their chief skill lies in a bawdy song.
35   In short, the only wit that's now in fashion,
Is but the gleanings of good conversation.
As for the author of this coming play,
I asked him what he thought fit I should say
In thanks for your good company today:
40   He called me fool, and said it was well known
You came not here for our sakes, but your own.

New plays are stuffed with wits, and with deboches,°
That crowd and sweat like cits° in May-Day°
    coaches.°

Written by a Person of Quality

The Actors' Names

[Men]
DON ANTONIO, *the Viceroy's son*
DON PEDRO, *a noble Spaniard, his friend*
BELVILE, *an English colonel in love with Florinda*
WILLMORE, *the Rover*
FREDERICK, *an English gentleman, and friend to Belvile
    and Blunt*
BLUNT, *an English country gentleman*
STEPHANO, *servant to Don Pedro*
PHILIPPO, *Lucetta's gallant*
SANCHO, *pimp to Lucetta*
BISKEY *and* SEBASTIAN, *two bravos° to Angellica*
OFFICER *and* SOLDIERS
[DIEGO,] *Page to Don Antonio*

[Women]
FLORINDA, *sister to Don Pedro*
HELLENA, *a gay young woman designed for a nun, and
    sister to Florinda*
VALERIA, *a kinswoman to Florinda*
ANGELLICA BIANCA, *a famous courtesan*
MORETTA, *her woman*
CALLIS, *governess to Florinda and Hellena*
LUCETTA, *a jilting wench*
SERVANTS, other MASQUERADERS, MEN and WOMEN

The Scene: *Naples, in Carnival time.*

ACT I • Scene I

(*A Chamber. Enter Florinda and Hellena.*)

FLORINDA: What an impertinent thing is a young girl
    bred in a nunnery! How full of questions! Prithee
    no more, Hellena; I have told thee more than thou
    understand'st already.

---

3. Rabel's drops: A patent medicine.   **9. cabal:** A small, secret political group.   **18. Catholic:** Having broad tastes or interests.   **23. Bating:** Leaving out.   **31. extempore:** A performance given without a script or rehearsal.

42. deboches: Orgies, debauches.   **43. cits:** Residents of cities.   **May-Day:** May 1, celebrated as a spring festival.   **coaches:** Carriages on parade during a May Day celebration.   [**The Actors' Names**] **bravos:** Villains, adventurers.

[handwritten margin note: Does the play low key whore rhyme?]

5   HELLENA: The more's my grief. I would fain know as
       much as you, which makes me so inquisitive; nor is't
       enough I know you're a lover, unless you tell me too
       who 'tis you sigh for.
     FLORINDA: When you're a lover I'll think you fit for a
10   secret of that nature.
     HELLENA: 'Tis true, I never was a lover yet, but I begin to
       have a shrewd guess what 'tis to be so, and fancy it
       very pretty to sigh, and sing, and blush, and wish,
       and dream and wish, and long and wish to see the
15   man, and when I do, look pale and tremble, just as
       you did when my brother brought home the fine
       English colonel to see you. What do you call him?
       Don Belvile?
     FLORINDA: Fie, Hellena. *[handwritten: who's the mmn? to Google.]*
20   HELLENA: That blush betrays you. I am sure 'tis so. Or is
       it Don Antonio the Viceroy's son? Or perhaps the
       rich old Don Vincentio, whom my father designs you
       for a husband? Why do you blush again?
     FLORINDA: With indignation; and how near soever my
25   father thinks I am to marrying that hated object, I
       shall let him see I understand better what's due to my
       beauty, birth, and fortune, and more to my soul, than
       to obey those unjust commands.
     HELLENA: Now hang me, if I don't love thee for that
30   dear disobedience. I love mischief strangely, as most
       of our sex do who are come to love nothing else.
       But tell me, dear Florinda, don't you love that fine
       Anglese?° For I vow, next to loving him myself, 'twill
       please me most that you do so, for he is so gay and
35   so handsome.
     FLORINDA: Hellena, a maid designed for a nun ought not
       to be so curious in a discourse of love.
     HELLENA: And dost thou think that ever I'll be a nun?
       Or at least till I'm so old I'm fit for nothing else?
40   Faith no, sister; and that which makes me long to
       know whether you love Belvile, is because I hope he
       has some mad companion or other that will spoil my
       devotion. Nay, I'm resolved to provide myself this
       Carnival, if there be e'er a handsome proper fellow of
45   my humor above ground,° though I ask first.
     FLORINDA: Prithee be not so wild.
     HELLENA: Now you have provided yourself of a man
       you take no care of poor me. Prithee tell me, what
       dost thou see about me that is unfit for love? Have I
50   not a world of youth? A humor gay? A beauty pass-
       able? A vigor desirable? Well shaped? Clean limbed?
       Sweet breathed? And sense enough to know how all
       these ought to be employed to the best advantage?
       Yes, I do and will; therefore lay aside your hopes of
55   my fortune by my being a devote,° and tell me how
       you came acquainted with this Belvile. For I perceive
       you knew him before he came to Naples.
     FLORINDA: Yes, I knew him at the siege of Pamplona; he

[handwritten vertical margin note: Why does she keep mentioning truly youth and fortune?]

was then a colonel of French horse,° who when the
town was ransacked, nobly treated my brother and   60
myself, preserving us from all insolences. And I must
own, besides great obligations, I have I know not
what that pleads kindly for him about my heart, and
will suffer no other to enter. But see, my brother.

(*Enter Don Pedro, Stephano with a masking habit,° and
Callis.*)

PEDRO: Good morrow, sister. Pray when saw you your   65
  lover Don Vincentio?
FLORINDA: I know not, sir. Callis, when was he here? For
  I consider it so little I know not when it was.
PEDRO: I have a command from my father here to tell
  you you ought not to despise him, a man of so vast a   70
  fortune, and such a passion for you.—Stephano, my
  things.

(*Puts on his masking habit.*)

FLORINDA: A passion for me? 'Tis more than e'er I saw,
  or he had a desire should be known. I hate Vincentio,
  sir, and I would not have a man so dear to me as my   75
  brother follow the ill customs of our country and
  make a slave of his sister. And, sir, my father's will
  I'm sure you may divert.
PEDRO: I know not how dear I am to you, but I wish only
  to be ranked in your esteem equal with the English   80
  colonel Belvile. Why do you frown and blush? Is
  there any guilt belongs to the name of that cavalier?
FLORINDA: I'll not deny I value Belvile. When I was exposed to such dangers as the licensed lust of common soldiers threatened when rage and conquest   85
  flew through the city, then Belvile, this criminal for
  my sake, threw himself into all dangers to save my
  honor. And will you not allow him my esteem?
PEDRO: Yes, pay him what you will in honor, but you
  must consider Don Vincentio's fortune, and the join-   90
  ture° he'll make you.
FLORINDA: Let him consider my youth, beauty, and fortune, which ought not to be thrown away on his age
  and jointure.
PEDRO: 'Tis true, he's not so young and fine a gentleman   95
  as that Belvile. But what jewels will that cavalier
  present you with? Those of his eyes and heart?
HELLENA: And are not those better than any Don
  Vincentio has brought from the Indies?
PEDRO: Why, how now! Has your nunnery breeding   100
  taught you to understand the value of hearts and eyes?
HELLENA: Better than to believe Vincentio's deserve value
  from any woman. He may perhaps increase her bags,
  but not her family.°

---

33. *Anglese:* The English colonel Belvile. 45. **above ground:**
In the real world (i.e., outside the convent). 55. **devote:** Nun.

59. **of French horse:** In the French cavalry. 64. [S.D.] *masking
habit:* Costume for the Carnival masquerades. 90–91. **jointure:** An estate given by a husband to a wife in lieu of her
dowry. 103–104. **increase her bags . . . family:** Give her material goods but not enhance her family's standing.

[handwritten: Marriage against your will is a problem theme already]

PEDRO: This is fine! Go! Up to your devotion! You are 105
not designed for the conversation of lovers.

HELLENA (*aside*): Nor saints yet a while, I hope.—Is't not
enough you make a nun of me, but you must cast my
sister away too, exposing her to a worse confinement
than a religious life? 110

PEDRO: The girl's mad! It is a confinement to be carried
into the country to an ancient villa belonging to the
family of the Vincentios these five hundred years, and
have no other prospect than that pleasing one of seeing all her own that meets her eyes: a fine air, large 115
fields, and gardens where she may walk and gather
flowers?

HELLENA: When, by moonlight? For I am sure she dares
not encounter with the heat of the sun; that were a
task only for Don Vincentio and his Indian breeding, 120
who loves it in the dog days.° And if these be her
daily divertissements,° what are those of the night?
To lie in a wide moth-eaten bed-chamber with furniture in fashion in the reign of King Sancho the First;°
the bed, that which his forefathers lived and died in. 125

PEDRO: Very well.

HELLENA: This apartment, new furbushed° and fitted
out for the young wife, he out of freedom makes his
dressing room; and being a frugal and a jealous coxcomb,° instead of a valet to uncase° his feeble carcass, 130
he desires you to do that office. Signs of favor, I'll assure you, and such as you must not hope for unless
your woman be out of the way.

PEDRO: Have you done yet?

HELLENA: That honor being past, the giant stretches 135
itself, yawns and sighs a belch or two loud as a musket, throws himself into bed, and expects you in his
foul sheets; and ere you can get yourself undressed,
calls you with a snore or two. And are not these fine
blessings to a young lady? 140

PEDRO: Have you done yet?

[handwritten: truth]

HELLENA: And this man you must kiss, nay you must kiss
none but him too, and nuzzle through his beard to
find his lips. And this you must submit to for threescore years, and all for a jointure. 145

PEDRO: For all your character of Don Vincentio, she is as
like to marry him as she was before.

HELLENA: Marry Don Vincentio! Hang me, such a wedlock would be worse than adultery with another man.
I had rather see her in the *Hostel de Dieu,*° to waste 150
her youth there in vows, and be a handmaid to lazars°
and cripples, than to lose it in such a marriage.

PEDRO: You have considered, sister, that Belvile has no
fortune to bring you to; is banished his country, despised at home, and pitied abroad. 155

HELLENA: What then? The Viceroy's son is better than
that old Sir Fifty. Don Vincentio! Don Indian! He thinks
he's trading to Gambo° still, and would barter himself—
that bell and bauble—for your youth and fortune.

PEDRO: Callis, take her hence and lock her up all this 160
Carnival, and at Lent she shall begin her everlasting
penance in a monastery.

HELLENA: I care not; I had rather be a nun than be
obliged to marry as you would have me if I were designed for't. 165

PEDRO: Do not fear the blessing of that choice. You shall
be a nun.

HELLENA (*aside*): Shall I so? You may chance to be mistaken in my way of devotion. A nun! Yes, I am like to
make a fine nun! I have an excellent humor for a 170
grate!° No, I'll have a saint of my own to pray to
shortly, if I like any that dares venture on me.

PEDRO: Callis, make it your business to watch this
wildcat.—As for you, Florinda, I've only tried you all
this while and urged my father's will; but mine is that 175
you would love Antonio: He is brave and young, and
all that can complete the happiness of a gallant maid.
This absence of my father will give us opportunity to
free you from Vincentio by marrying here, which you
must do tomorrow. 180

FLORINDA: Tomorrow!

PEDRO: Tomorrow, or 'twill be too late. 'Tis not my
friendship to Antonio which makes me urge this, but
love to thee and hatred to Vincentio; therefore resolve
upon tomorrow. 185

FLORINDA: Sir, I shall strive to do as shall become your
sister.

PEDRO: I'll both believe and trust you. Adieu.

(*Exeunt*° *Pedro and Stephano.*)

HELLENA: As becomes his sister! That is to be as resolved
your way as he is his. 190

(*Hellena goes to Callis.*)

FLORINDA: I ne'er till now perceived my ruin near.
I've no defense against Antonio's love,
For he has all the advantages of nature,
The moving arguments of youth and fortune.

HELLENA: But hark you, Callis, you will not be so cruel to 195
lock me up indeed, will you?

CALLIS: I must obey the commands I have. Besides, do
you consider what a life you are going to lead?

HELLENA: Yes, Callis, that of a nun; and till then I'll be indebted a world of prayers to you if you'll let me now 200
see what I never did, the divertissements of a Carnival.

CALLIS: What, go in masquerade? 'Twill be a fine farewell to the world, I take it. Pray what would you do
there?

HELLENA: That which all the world does, as I am told: 205

---

121. **dog days:** The hot days of summer.   122. **divertissements:**
Amusements.   124. **King Sancho the First:** King of Spain,
probably Sancho I of Castile (970–1035).   127. **new fur-
brushed:** Refurbished.   129–130. **coxcomb:** Conceited person,
fop.   130. **uncase:** Disrobe.   150. *Hostel de Dieu:* Hospital
operated by a group of nuns.   151. **lazars:** Lepers.

158. **Gambo:** British colony in West Africa.   171. **grate:** The
grille covering the windows in a convent (i.e., the convent).
188. [S.D.] *Exeunt:* Latin for "they go out."

Be as mad as the rest and take all innocent freedoms.
Sister, you'll go too, will you not? Come, prithee be
not sad. We'll outwit twenty brothers if you'll be
ruled by me. Come, put off this dull humor with your
210 clothes, and assume one as gay and as fantastic as
the dress my cousin Valeria and I have provided, and
let's ramble.

FLORINDA: Callis, will you give us leave to go?

CALLIS (aside): I have a youthful itch of going myself.—
215 Madam, if I thought your brother might not know it,
and I might wait on you; for by my troth I'll not trust
young girls alone.

FLORINDA: Thou seest my brother's gone already, and
thou shalt attend and watch us.

(Enter Stephano.)

220 STEPHANO: Madam, the habits are come, and your cousin
Valeria is dressed and stays for you.

FLORINDA (aside): 'Tis well. I'll write a note, and if I
chance to see Belvile and want an opportunity to
speak to him, that shall let him know what I've
225 resolved in favor of him.

HELLENA: Come, let's in and dress us.   *(Exeunt.)*

Scene II

*(A long street. Enter Belvile, melancholy; Blunt and
Frederick.)*

FREDERICK: Why, what the devil ails the colonel, in a
time when all the world is gay to look like mere Lent
thus? Hadst thou been long enough in Naples to
have been in love, I should have sworn some such
5 judgment had befallen thee.

BELVILE: No, I have made no new amours since I came
to Naples.

FREDERICK: You have left none behind you in Paris?

BELVILE: Neither.

10 FREDERICK: I cannot divine the cause then, unless the
old cause, the want of money.

BLUNT: And another old cause, the want of a wench.
Would not that revive you?

BELVILE: You are mistaken, Ned.

15 BLUNT: Nay, 'adsheartlikins,° then thou'rt past cure.

FREDERICK: I have found it out: Thou hast renewed thy
acquaintance with the lady that cost thee so many
sighs at the siege of Pamplona—pox on't, what d'ye
call her—her brother's a noble Spaniard, nephew to
20 the dead general. Florinda. Ay, Florinda. And will
nothing serve thy turn but that damned virtuous
woman, whom on my conscience thou lov'st in spite
too, because thou seest little or no possibility of gaining her.

25 BELVILE: Thou art mistaken; I have int'rest enough in
that lovely virgin's heart to make me proud and vain,

were it not abated by the severity of a brother, who,
perceiving my happiness—

FREDERICK: Has civilly forbid thee the house?

BELVILE: 'Tis so, to make way for a powerful rival, the 30
Viceroy's son, who has the advantage of me in being
a man of fortune, a Spaniard, and her brother's
friend; which gives him liberty to make his court,
whilst I have recourse only to letters and distant
looks from her window, which are as soft and kind as 35
those which heaven sends down on penitents.

BLUNT: Heyday! 'Adsheartlikins, simile! By this light the
man is quite spoiled. Fred, what the devil are we made
of that we cannot be thus concerned for a wench?
'Adsheartlikins, our Cupids are like the cooks of the 40
camp: They can roast or boil a woman, but they have
none of the fine tricks to set 'em off; no hogoes° to
make the sauce pleasant and the stomach sharp.

FREDERICK: I dare swear I have had a hundred as young,
kind, and handsome as this Florinda; and dogs eat 45
me if they were not as troublesome to me i'th' morning as they were welcome o'er night.

BLUNT: And yet I warrant he would not touch another
woman if he might have her for nothing.

BELVILE: That's thy joy, a cheap whore. 50

BLUNT: Why, 'adsheartlikins, I love a frank soul. When
did you ever hear of an honest woman that took a
man's money? I warrant 'em good ones. But gentlemen, you may be free; you have been kept so poor
with parliaments and protectors that the little stock 55
you have is not worth preserving. But I thank my
stars I had more grace than to forfeit my estate by
cavaliering.

BELVILE: Methinks only following the court should be
sufficient to entitle 'em to that. 60

BLUNT: 'Adsheartlikins, they know I follow it to do it
no good, unless they pick a hole in my coat for lending you money now and then, which is a greater
crime to my conscience, gentlemen, than to the commonwealth. 65

(Enter Willmore.)

WILLMORE: Ha! Dear Belvile! Noble colonel!

BELVILE: Willmore! Welcome ashore, my dear rover!
What happy wind blew us this good fortune?

WILLMORE: Let me salute my dear Fred, and then command me.—How is't, honest lad? 70

FREDERICK: Fair, sir, the old compliment, infinitely the
better to see my dear mad Willmore again. Prithee,
why earnest thou ashore? And where's the Prince?°

WILLMORE: He's well, and reigns still lord of the wat'ry
element. I must aboard again within a day or two, 75
and my business ashore was only to enjoy myself a
little this Carnival.

BELVILE: Pray know our new friend, sir; he's but bashful,
a raw traveler, but honest, stout, and one of us.

---

15. **'adsheartlikins:** Expostulation equivalent to "As God
loves us."

42. **hogoes:** Relishes.   73. **Prince:** Charles II, in exile on the
Continent during the reign of Cromwell.

(*Embraces Blunt.*)

80 WILLMORE: That you esteem him gives him an int'rest here.

BLUNT: Your servant, sir.

WILLMORE: But well, faith, I'm glad to meet you again in
85 a warm climate, where the kind sun has its godlike
power still over the wine and women. Love and
mirth are my business in Naples, and if I mistake not
the place, here's an excellent market for chapmen° of
my humor.

BELVILE: See, here be those kind merchants of love you
90 look for.

(*Enter several men in masking habits, some playing on
music, others dancing after; women dressed like courtesans, with papers pinned on their breasts, and baskets
of flowers in their hands.*)

BLUNT: 'Adsheartlikins, what have we here?

FREDERICK: Now the game begins.

WILLMORE: Fine pretty creatures! May a stranger have
leave to look and love? What's here? "Roses for every
95 month"? (*Reads the papers.*)

BLUNT: Roses for every month? What means that?

DELVILE: They are, or would have you think they're courtesans, who here in Naples are to be hired by the
month.

100 WILLMORE: Kind and obliging to inform us, pray where
do these roses grow? I would fain plant some of 'em
in a bed of mine.

WOMAN: Beware such roses, sir.

WILLMORE: A pox of fear: I'll be baked with thee
105 between a pair of sheets, and that's thy proper still;
so I might but strew such roses over me and under
me. Fair one, would you would give me leave to
gather at your bush this idle month; I would go near
to make somebody smell of it all the year after.

110 BELVILE: And thou hast need of such a remedy, for thou
stink'st of tar and ropes' ends like a dock or pesthouse.

(*The Woman puts herself into the hands of a man and
exeunt.*)

WILLMORE: Nay, nay, you shall not leave me so.

BELVILE: By all means use no violence here.

WILLMORE: Death! Just as I was going to be damnably
115 in love, to have her led off! I could pluck that rose out
of his hand, and even kiss the bed the bush grew in.

FREDERICK: No friend to love like a long voyage at sea.

BLUNT: Except a nunnery, Fred.

WILLMORE: Death! But will they not be kind? Quickly
120 be kind? Thou know'st I'm no tame sigher, but a
rampant lion of the forest.

(*Advances from the farther end of the scenes two men
dressed all over with horns° of several sorts, making
grimaces at one another, with papers pinned on their
backs.*)

BELVILE: Oh the fantastical rogues, how they're dressed!
'Tis a satire against the whole sex.

WILLMORE: Is this a fruit that grows in this warm country?

BELVILE: Yes, 'tis pretty to see these Italians start, swell, 125
and stab at the word cuckold, and yet stumble at
horns on every threshold.

WILLMORE: See what's on their back. (*Reads.*) "Flowers
of every night." Ah, rogue! And more sweet than
roses of every month! This is a gardener of Adam's 130
own breeding.

(*They dance.*)

BELVILE: What think you of these grave people? Is a wake
in Essex half so mad or extravagant?

WILLMORE: I like their sober grave way; 'tis a kind of
legal authorized fornication, where the men are not 135
chid° for't, nor the women despised, as amongst our
dull English. Even the monsieurs° want that part of
good manners.

BELVILE: But here in Italy, a monsieur is the humblest
best-bred gentleman: Duels are so baffled by bravos 140
that an age shows not one but between a Frenchman
and a hangman, who is as much too hard for him on
the Piazza as they are for a Dutchman on the New
Bridge. But see, another crew.

(*Enter Florinda, Hellena, and Valeria, dressed like
gypsies; Callis and Stephano, Lucetta, Philippo, and
Sancho in masquerade.*)

HELLENA: Sister, there's your Englishman, and with him 145
a handsome proper fellow. I'll to him, and instead of
telling him his fortune, try my own.

WILLMORE: Gypsies, on my life. Sure these will prattle if
a man cross their hands.° (*Goes to Hellena.*)—Dear,
pretty, and, I hope, young devil, will you tell an amo- 150
rous stranger what luck he's like to have?

HELLENA: Have a care how you venture with me, sir, lest
I pick your pocket, which will more vex your English
humor than an Italian fortune will please you.

WILLMORE: How the devil cam'st thou to know my coun- 155
try and humor?

HELLENA: The first I guess by a certain forward impudence, which does not displease me at this time; and
the loss of your money will vex you because I hope
you have but very little to lose. 160

WILLMORE: Egad, child, thou'rt i'th' right; it is so little I
dare not offer it thee for a kindness. But cannot you
divine what other things of more value I have about
me that I would more willingly part with?

HELLENA: Indeed no, that's the business of a witch, and 165
I am but a gypsy yet. Yet without looking in your
hand, I have a parlous° guess 'tis some foolish heart
you mean, an inconstant English heart, as little worth
stealing as your purse.

---

87. **chapmen:** Merchants, in this case merchants of love.
121. [s.d.] *horns:* Emblem of the cuckold, a man whose wife is
unfaithful.

136. **chid:** Chided, reproached. 137. **monsieurs:** Frenchmen.
149. **cross their hands:** Cross their hands with silver; pay them
to tell his fortune. 167. **parlous:** Dangerously cunning, clever
(from *perilous*).

[handwritten: Hellena wants to be a nun]

170 WILLMORE: Nay, then thou dost deal with the devil, that's certain. Thou hast guessed as right as if thou hadst been one of that number it has languished for. I find you'll be better acquainted with it, nor can you take it in a better time; for I am come from sea, child, and

175 Venus not being propitious to me in her own element,° I have a world of love in store. Would you would be good-natured and take some on't° off my hands.

HELLENA: Why, I could be inclined that way, but for a foolish vow I am going to make to die a maid.

180 WILLMORE: Then thou art damned without redemption, and as I am a good Christian, I ought in charity to divert so wicked a design. Therefore prithee, dear creature, let me know quickly when and where I shall begin to set a helping hand to so good a work.

185 HELLENA: If you should prevail with my tender heart, as I begin to fear you will, for you have horrible loving eyes, there will be difficulty in't that you'll hardly undergo for my sake.

WILLMORE: Faith, child, I have been bred in dangers, and

190 wear a sword that has been employed in a worse cause than for a handsome kind woman. Name the danger; let it be anything but a long siege, and I'll undertake it.

HELLENA: Can you storm?

195 WILLMORE: Oh, most furiously.

HELLENA: What think you of a nunnery wall? For he that wins me must gain that first.

WILLMORE: A nun! Oh, now I love thee for't! There's no sinner like a young saint. Nay, now there's no deny-

200 ing me; the old law had no curse to a woman like dying a maid: Witness Jeptha's daughter.°

HELLENA: A very good text this, if well handled; and I perceive, Father Captain, you would impose no severe penance on her who were inclined to console

205 herself before she took orders.°

WILLMORE: If she be young and handsome.

HELLENA: Ay, there's it. But if she be not—

WILLMORE: By this hand, child, I have an implicit faith, and dare venture on thee with all faults. Besides, 'tis

210 more meritorious to leave the world when thou hast tasted and proved the pleasure on't. Then 'twill be a virtue in thee, which now will be pure ignorance.

HELLENA: I perceive, good Father Captain, you design only to make me fit for heaven. But if, on the con-

215 trary, you should quite divert me from it, and bring me back to the world again, I should have a new man to seek, I find. And what a grief that will be; for when I begin, I fancy I shall love like anything; I never tried yet.

---

175. Venus . . . element: Venus, the goddess of love, was supposedly born from the foam of the sea. 177. on't: Of it. 201. Jeptha's daughter: To fulfill a vow, Jeptha sacrificed his only child, a virgin daughter, whom he allowed to go off to the mountains for two months to "bewail" her virginity before he killed her. "And it became a custom in Israel that the daughters of Israel went year by year to lament the daughter of Jeptha . . . four days in the year" (Judges 11:39–40). 205. took orders: Entered the convent.

WILLMORE: Egad, and that's kind! Prithee, dear crea- 220 ture, give me credit for a heart, for faith, I'm a very honest fellow. Oh, I long to come first to the banquet of love! And such a swinging appetite I bring. Oh, I'm impatient. Thy lodging, sweetheart, thy lodging, or I'm a dead man! 225

HELLENA: Why must we be either guilty of fornication or murder if we converse with you men? And is there no difference between leave to love me, and leave to lie with me? *[handwritten: Why must you have sex to love!]*

WILLMORE: Faith, child, they were made to go together. 230

LUCETTA (*pointing to Blunt*): Are you sure this is the man?

SANCHO: When did I mistake your game?

LUCETTA: This is a stranger, I know by his gazing; if he be brisk he'll venture to follow me, and then, if I 235 understand my trade, he's mine. He's English, too, and they say that's a sort of good-natured loving people, and have generally so kind an opinion of themselves that a woman with any wit may flatter 'em into any sort of fool she pleases. 240

(*She often passes by Blunt and gazes on him; he struts and cocks, and walks and gazes on her.*)

BLUNT: 'Tis so, she is taken; I have beauties which my false glass° at home did not discover.

FLORINDA (*aside*): This woman watches me so, I shall get no opportunity to discover myself to him, and so miss the intent of my coming.—[*To Belvile.*] But as I 245 was saying, sir, by this line you should be a lover. (*Looking in his hand.*)

BELVILE: I thought how right you guessed: All men are in love, or pretend to be so. Come, let me go; I'm weary of this fooling. (*Walks away.*)

FLORINDA: I will not, sir, till you have confessed whether 250 the passion that you have vowed Florinda be true or false.

(*She holds him; he strives to get from her.*)

BELVILE: Florinda! (*Turns quick toward her.*)

FLORINDA: Softly.

BELVILE: Thou hast nam'd one will fix me here forever. 255

FLORINDA: She'll be disappointed then, who expects you this night at the garden gate. And if you fail not, as— (*Looks on Callis, who observes 'em.*) Let me see the other hand—you will go near to do, she vows to die or make you happy. 260

BELVILE: What canst thou mean?

FLORINDA: That which I say. Farewell.

(*Offers to go.*)

BELVILE: O charming sibyl,° stay; complete that joy which as it is will turn into distraction! Where must I be? At the garden gate? I know it. At night, you say? 265 I'll sooner forfeit heaven than disobey.

(*Enter Don Pedro and other maskers, and pass over the stage.*)

---

242. false glass: Lying mirror. 263. sibyl: A female prophet; fortune-teller.

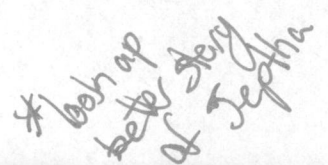

[handwritten: # look up better story of Jeptha]

CALLIS: Madam, your brother's here.

FLORINDA: Take this to instruct you farther.

(Gives him a letter, and goes off.)

FREDERICK: Have a care, sir, what you promise; this may
270   be a trap laid by her brother to ruin you.

BELVILE: Do not disturb my happiness with doubts.

(Opens the letter.)

WILLMORE: My dear pretty creature, a thousand blessings
on thee! Still in this habit, you say? And after dinner
at this place?

275   HELLENA: Yes, if you will swear to keep your heart and
not bestow it between this and that.

WILLMORE: By all the little gods of love, I swear; I'll leave
it with you, and if you run away with it, those deities
of justice will revenge me.

(Exeunt all the women [except Lucetta].)

280   FREDERICK: Do you know the hand?

BELVILE: 'Tis Florinda's.
All blessings fall upon the virtuous maid.

FREDERICK: Nay, no idolatry; a sober sacrifice I'll allow
you.

286   BELVILE: Oh friends, the welcom'st news! The softest
letter! Nay, you shall all see it. And could you now
be serious, I might be made the happiest man the sun
shines on!

WILLMORE: The reason of this mighty joy?

290   BELVILE: See how kindly she invites me to deliver her
from the threatened violence of her brother. Will you
not assist me?

WILLMORE: I know not what thou mean'st, but I'll make
one at any mischief where a woman's concerned. But
295   she'll be grateful to us for the favor, will she not?

BELVILE: How mean you?

WILLMORE: How should I mean? Thou know'st there's
but one way for a woman to oblige me.

BELVILE: Do not profane; the maid is nicely virtuous.

300   WILLMORE: Who, pox, then she's fit for nothing but a
husband. Let her e'en go, colonel.

FREDERICK: Peace, she's the colonel's mistress, sir.

WILLMORE: Let her be the devil; if she be thy mistress, I'll
serve her. Name the way.

305   BELVILE: Read here this postscript. *(Gives him a letter.)*

WILLMORE *(reads):* "At ten at night, at the garden gate,
of which, if I cannot get the key, I will contrive a
way over the wall. Come attended with a friend or
two."—Kind heart, if we three cannot weave a string
310   to let her down a garden wall, 'twere pity but the
hangman wove one for us all.

FREDERICK: Let her alone for that; your woman's wit,
your fair kind woman, will outtrick a broker or a
Jew, and contrive like a Jesuit° in chains. But see,
315   Ned Blunt is stolen out after the lure of a damsel.

(Exeunt Blunt and Lucetta.)

BELVILE: So, he'll scarce find his way home again unless
we get him cried by the bellman in the market place.
And 'twould sound prettily: "A lost English boy of
thirty."

FREDERICK: I hope 'tis some common crafty sinner, one   320
that will fit him. It may be she'll sell him for Peru:°
The rogue's sturdy, and would work well in a mine.
At least I hope she'll dress him for our mirth, cheat
him of all, then have him well-favoredly banged, and
turned out at midnight.   325

WILLMORE: Prithee what humor is he of, that you wish
him so well?

BELVILE: Why, of an English elder brother's humor: educated in a nursery, with a maid to tend him till fifteen,
and lies with his grandmother till he's of age; one that 330
knows no pleasure beyond riding to the next fair, or
going up to London with his right worshipful father
in parliament time, wearing gay clothes, or making
honorable love to his lady mother's laundry maid;
gets drunk at a hunting match, and ten to one then   335
gives some proofs of his prowess. A pox upon him,
he's our banker, and has all our cash about him; and
if he fail, we are all broke.

FREDERICK: Oh, let him alone for that matter; he's of a
damned stingy quality that will secure our stock. I   340
know not in what danger it were indeed if the jilt
should pretend she's in love with him, for 'tis a kind
believing coxcomb; otherwise, if he part with more
than a piece of eight,° geld° him—for which offer
he may chance to be beaten if she be a whore of the   345
first rank.

BELVILE: Nay, the rogue will not be easily beaten; he's
stout enough. Perhaps if they talk beyond his capacity he may chance to exercise his courage upon some
of them, else I'm sure they'll find it as difficult to beat 350
as to please him.

WILLMORE: 'Tis a lucky devil to light upon so kind a
wench!

FREDERICK: Thou hadst a great deal of talk with thy
little gypsy; couldst thou do no good upon her? For   355
mine was hardhearted.

WILLMORE: Hang her, she was some damned honest person of quality, I'm sure, she was so very free and
witty. If her face be but answerable to her wit and
humor, I would be bound to constancy this month to   360
gain her. In the meantime, have you made no kind
acquaintance since you came to town? You do not
use to be honest° so long, gentlemen.

FREDERICK: Faith, love has kept us honest: We have
been all fir'd with a beauty newly come to town, the 365
famous Paduana° Angellica Bianca.

WILLMORE: What, the mistress of the dead Spanish
general?

---

314. Jew . . . Jesuit: Anti-Semitic and anti-Catholic attitudes of
the time portrayed Jews and Jesuits as cunning and not worthy
of trust.

321. sell him for Peru: Sell him as a slave. 344. piece of eight:
Spanish money. geld: Castrate. 363. honest: Sexually inac-
tive. 366. Paduana: Angellica was born in Padua, Italy.

370 BELVILE: Yes, she's now the only ador'd beauty of all
the youth in Naples, who put on all their charms to
appear lovely in her sight: Their coaches, liveries,
and themselves all gay as on a monarch's birthday
to attract the eyes of this fair charmer, while she
375 has the pleasure to behold all languish for her that
see her.

FREDERICK: 'Tis pretty to see with how much love the
men regard her, and how much envy the women.

WILLMORE: What gallant has she?

BELVILE: None; she's exposed to sale, and four days in the
380 week she's yours, for so much a month.

WILLMORE: The very thought of it quenches all manner of
fire in me. Yet prithee, let's see her.

BELVILE: Let's first to dinner, and after that we'll pass the
day as you please. But at night ye must all be at my
385 devotion.

WILLMORE: I will not fail you.   [*Exeunt.*]

ACT II • Scene I

(*The long street. Enter Belvile and Frederick in masking habits, and Willmore in his own clothes, with a
vizard° in his hand.*)

WILLMORE: But why thus disguised and muzzled?

BELVILE: Because whatever extravagances we commit in
these faces, our own may not be obliged to answer
'em.

5 WILLMORE: I should have changed my eternal buff,°
too; but no matter, my little gypsy would not have
found me out then. For if she should change hers, it is
impossible I should know her unless I should hear her
prattle. A pox on't, I cannot get her out of my head.
10 Pray heaven, if ever I do see her again, she prove
damnably ugly, that I may fortify myself against her
tongue.

BELVILE: Have a care of love, for o' my conscience she
was not of a quality to give thee any hopes.

15 WILLMORE: Pox on 'em, why do they draw a man in
then? She has played with my heart so, that 'twill
never lie still till I have met with some kind wench
that will play the game out with me. Oh, for my arms
full of soft, white, kind woman—such as I fancy
20 Angellica.

BELVILE: This is her house, if you were but in stock to get
admittance. They have not dined yet; I perceive the
picture is not out.°

(*Enter Blunt.*)

WILLMORE: I long to see the shadow of the fair substance;
25 a man may gaze on that for nothing.

BLUNT: Colonel, thy hand. And thine, Fred. I have been
an ass, a deluded fool, a very coxcomb from my birth
till this hour, and heartily repent my little faith.

BELVILE: What the devil's the matter with thee, Ned?

BLUNT: Oh, such a mistress, Fred! Such a girl!   30

WILLMORE: Ha! Where?

FREDERICK: Ay, where?

BLUNT: So fond, so amorous, so toying, and so fine! And
all for sheer love, ye rogue! Oh, how she looked and
kissed! And soothed my heart from my bosom! I can-   35
not think I was awake, and yet methinks I see and
feel her charms still. Fred, try if she have not left the
taste of her balmy kisses upon my lips. (*Kisses him.*)

BELVILE: Ha! Ha! Ha!

WILLMORE: Death, man, where is she?   40

BLUNT: What a dog was I to stay in dull England so long!
How have I laughed at the colonel when he sighed
for love! But now the little archer° has revenged
him! And by this one dart I can guess at all his joys,
which then I took for fancies, mere dreams and   45
fables. Well, I'm resolved to sell all in Essex and plant
here forever.

BELVILE: What a blessing 'tis, thou hast a mistress thou
dar'st boast of; for I know thy humor is rather to
have a proclaimed clap than a secret amour.   50

WILLMORE: Dost know her name?

BLUNT: Her name? No, 'adsheartlikins. What care I for
names? She's fair, young, brisk and kind, even to rav-
ishment! And what a pox care I for knowing her by
any other title?   55

WILLMORE: Didst give her anything?

BLUNT: Give her? Ha! Ha! Ha! Why, she's a person of
quality. That's a good one! Give her? 'Adsheartlikins,
dost think such creatures are to be bought? Or are
we provided for such a purchase? Give her, quoth ye? 60
Why, she presented me with this bracelet for the toy
of a diamond I used to wear. No, gentlemen, Ned
Blunt is not everybody. She expects me again tonight.

WILLMORE: Egad, that's well; we'll all go.

BLUNT: Not a soul! No, gentlemen, you are wits; I am a   65
dull country rogue, I.

FREDERICK: Well, sir, for all your person of quality, I shall
be very glad to understand your purse be secure; 'tis
our whole estate at present, which we are loath to
hazard in one bottom.° Come sir, unlade.   70

BLUNT: Take the necessary trifle useless now to me, that
am beloved by such a gentlewoman. 'Adsheartlikins,
money! Here, take mine too.

FREDERICK: No, keep that to be cozened,° that we may
laugh.   75

WILLMORE: Cozened? Death! Would I could meet with
one that would cozen me of all the love I could spare
tonight.

FREDERICK: Pox, 'tis some common whore, upon my life.

[S.D.] **vizard:** Face mask.   **5. buff:** Military coat made of buff
(leather).   **23. picture is not out:** Hanging her picture outside the house is a sign that she is open for business. (See lines
111–112 later in the scene.)

43. little archer: Cupid.   **70. hazard in one bottom:** Keep in
one place, as in the hold (bottom) of a ship.   **74. cozened:**
Cheated.

So they can't have Angelica?

80 BLUNT: A whore? Yes, with such clothes, such jewels, such a house, such furniture, and so attended! A whore!

BELVILE: Why yes, sir, they are whores, though they'll neither entertain you with drinking, swearing, or
85 bawdry; are whores in all those gay clothes and right° jewels; are whores with those great houses richly furnished with velvet beds, store of plate,° handsome attendance, and fine coaches; are whores, and errant° ones.

90 WILLMORE: Pox on't, where do these fine whores live?

BELVILE: Where no rogues in office, ycleped° constables, dare give 'em laws, nor the wine-inspired bullies of the town break their windows; yet they are whores though this Essex calf° believe 'em persons of quality

95 BLUNT: 'Adsheartlikins, y'are all fools. There are things about this Essex calf that shall take with the ladies, beyond all your wit and parts. This shape and size, gentlemen, are not to be despised; my waist, too, tolerably long, with other inviting signs that shall be
100 nameless.

WILLMORE: Egad, I believe he may have met with some person of quality that may be kind to him.

BELVILE: Dost thou perceive any such tempting things about him that should make a fine woman, and of
105 quality, pick him out from all mankind to throw away her youth and beauty upon; nay, and her dear heart, too? No, no, Angellica has raised the price too high.

WILLMORE: May she languish for mankind till she die,
110 and be damned for that one sin alone.

(*Enter two Bravos and hang up a great picture of Angellica's against the balcony, and two little ones at each side of the door.*)

BELVILE: See there the fair sign to the inn where a man may lodge that's fool enough to give her price.

(*Willmore gazes on the picture.*)

BLUNT: 'Adsheartlikins, gentlemen, what's this?

BELVILE: A famous courtesan, that's to be sold.

115 BLUNT: How? To be sold? Nay, then I have nothing to say to her. Sold? What impudence is practiced in this country; with what order and decency whoring's established here by virtue of the Inquisition!° Come, let's be gone; I'm sure we're no chapmen for this
120 commodity.

FREDERICK: Thou art none, I'm sure, unless thou couldst have her in thy bed at a price of a coach in the street.

WILLMORE: How wondrous fair she is! A thousand crowns a month? By heaven, as many kingdoms were

too little! A plague of this poverty, of which I ne'er 125 complain but when it hinders my approach to beauty which virtue ne'er could purchase.

(*Turns from the picture.*)

BLUNT: What's this? (*Reads.*) "A thousand crowns a month"! 'Adsheartlikins, here's a sum! Sure 'tis a mistake.—[*To one of the Bravos.*] Hark you, friend, 130 does she take or give so much by the month?

FREDERICK: A thousand crowns! Why, 'tis a portion for the Infanta!°

BLUNT: Hark ye, friends, won't she trust?°

BRAVO: This is a trade, sir, that cannot live by credit. 135

(*Enter Don Pedro in masquerade, followed by Stephano.*)

BELVILE: See, here's more company; let's walk off a while.

(*Exeunt English,° Pedro reads.*)

PEDRO: Fetch me a thousand crowns; I never wished to buy this beauty at an easier rate. (*Passes off.*)

(*Enter Angellica and Moretta in the balcony, and draw a silk curtain.*) *I wonder if they'll be selling her—*

ANGELLICA: Prithee, what said those fellows to thee?

BRAVO: Madam, the first were admirers of beauty only, 140 but no purchasers; they were merry with your price and picture, laughed at the sum, and so passed off.

ANGELLICA: No matter, I'm not displeased with their rallying; their wonder feeds my vanity, and he that wishes but to buy gives me more pride than he that 145 gives my price can make my pleasure.

BRAVO: Madam, the last I knew through all his disguises to be Don Pedro, nephew to the general, and who was with him in Pamplona.

ANGELLICA: Don Pedro? My old gallant's nephew? 150 When his uncle died he left him a vast sum of money; it is he who was so in love with me at Padua, and who used to make the general so jealous.

MORETTA: Is this he that used to prance before our window, and take such care to show himself an amorous 155 ass? If I am not mistaken, he is the likeliest man to give your price.

ANGELLICA: The man is brave and generous, but of a humor so uneasy and inconstant that the victory over his heart is as soon lost as won; a slave that can add 160 little to the triumph of the conqueror. But inconstancy's the sin of all mankind, therefore I'm resolved that nothing but gold shall charm my heart.

MORETTA: I'm glad on't; 'tis only interest that women of our profession ought to consider, though I wonder 165 what has kept you from that general disease of our sex so long; I mean, that of being in love.

ANGELLICA: A kind but sullen star under which I had the happiness to be born. Yet I have had no time for love; the bravest and noblest of mankind have purchased 170

---

86. right: Real. **87. plate:** Silverware. **89. errant:** Unmitigated. **91. ycleped:** Past participle of *clepe:* called. **94. Essex calf:** Derogatory term meaning "fool," referring to Essex, England, Blunt's home. **118. Inquisition:** The Spanish Inquisition (1478–1834) forced prostitutes out of Spain and into neighboring countries.

132–133. portion for the Infanta: Dowry for the Spanish princess. **134. trust:** Extend credit for payment. **136. [S.D.] English:** All the English characters.

The King's County
Shakespeare Company's
2003 production of *The
Rover* with Tessa Martin
and Jon Fordham.

my favors at so dear a rate, as if no coin but gold were
current with our trade. But here's Don Pedro again;
fetch me my lute, for 'tis for him or Don Antonio
the Viceroy's son that I have spread my nets.

*(Enter at one door Don Pedro, Stephano; Don Antonio
and Diego [his page] at the other door, with people following him in masquerade, antically attired, some with
music. They both go up to the picture.)*

175   ANTONIO: A thousand crowns! Had not the painter flat-
       tered her, I should not think it dear.
       PEDRO: Flattered her? By heaven, he cannot. I have seen
       the original, nor is there one charm here more than
       adorns her face and eyes; all this soft and sweet, with
180   a certain languishing air that no artist can represent.
       ANTONIO: What I heard of her beauty before had fired
       my soul, but this confirmation of it has blown it to
       a flame.
       PEDRO: Ha!
185   PAGE: Sir, I have known you throw away a thousand
       crowns on a worse face, and though y'are near your
       marriage, you may venture a little love here; Florinda
       will not miss it.
       PEDRO (*aside*): Ha! Florinda! Sure 'tis Antonio.
190   ANTONIO: Florinda! Name not those distant joys; there's
       not one thought of her will check my passion here.
       PEDRO (*aside*): Florinda scorned! (*A noise of a lute
       above.*) And all my hopes defeated of the possession

of Angellica! (*Antonio gazes up.*) Her injuries, by
heaven, he shall not boast of!   195

(Song to a lute above.)

Song

[I]
*When Damon first began to love
He languished in a soft desire,
And knew not how the gods to move,
To lessen or increase his fire.
For Caelia in her charming eyes*   200
Wore all love's sweets, and all his cruelties.

II
*But as beneath a shade he lay,
Weaving of flowers for Caelia's hair,
She chanced to lead her flock that way,
And saw the am'rous shepherd there.*   205
*She gazed around upon the place,
And saw the grove, resembling night,
To all the joys of love invite,
Whilst guilty smiles and blushes dressed her face.
At this the bashful youth all transport grew,*   210
*And with kind force he taught the virgin how
To yield what all his sighs could never do.*

*(Angellica throws open the curtains and bows to Antonio,
who pulls off his vizard and bows and blows up kisses.
Pedro, unseen, looks in's face. [The curtains close.])*

why is Ang. so valuable? Just bc she's pretty.

ANTONIO: By heaven, she's charming fair!

PEDRO (*aside*): 'Tis he, the false Antonio!

ANTONIO (*to the Bravo*): Friend, where must I pay my
215   off'ring of love?
    My thousand crowns I mean.

PEDRO: That off'ring I have designed to make,
    And yours will come too late.

ANTONIO: Prithee begone; I shall grow angry else,
220   And then thou art not safe.

PEDRO: My anger may be fatal, sir, as yours,
    And he that enters here may prove this truth.

ANTONIO: I know not who thou art, but I am sure thou'rt
    worth my killing, for aiming at Angellica.

                                   (*They draw and fight.*)

(*Enter Willmore and Blunt, who draw and part 'em.*)

225 BLUNT: Adsheartlikins, here's fine doings.

WILLMORE: Tilting for the wench, I'm sure. Nay, gad, if
    that would win her I have as good a sword as the best
    of ye. Put up, put up, and take another time and
    place, for this is designed for lovers only.

                                   (*They all put up.*)

PEDRO: We are prevented; dare you meet me tomorrow
230   on the Molo?°
    For I've a title to a better quarrel,
    That of Florinda, in whose credulous heart
    Thou'st made an int'rest, and destroyed my hopes.

ANTONIO: Dare!
235   I'll meet thee there as early as the day.

PEDRO: We will come thus disguised, that whosoever
    chance to get the better, he may escape unknown.

ANTONIO: It shall be so.

                         (*Exeunt Pedro and Stephano.*)

—Who should this rival be? Unless the English
240   colonel, of whom I've often heard Don Pedro speak.
    It must be he, and time he were removed who lays a
    claim to all my happiness.

(*Willmore, having gazed all this while on the picture[s],
pulls down a little one.*)

WILLMORE: This posture's loose and negligent;
    The sight on't would beget a warm desire
245   In souls whom impotence and age had chilled.
    This must along with me.

BRAVO: What means this rudeness, sir? Restore the
    picture.

ANTONIO: Ha! Rudeness committed to the fair Angellica!—
250   Restore the picture, sir.

WILLMORE: Indeed I will not, sir.

ANTONIO: By heaven, but you shall.

WILLMORE: Nay, do not show your sword; if you do, by
    this dear beauty, I will show mine too.

255 ANTONIO: What right can you pretend to't?

WILLMORE: That of possession, which I will maintain.

230. Molo: Wharf.

You, perhaps, have a thousand crowns to give for
    the original.

ANTONIO: No matter, sir, you shall restore the picture.

(*[The curtains open.] Angellica and Moretta above.*)

ANGELLICA: Oh, Moretta, what's the matter?   260

ANTONIO: Or leave your life behind.

WILLMORE: Death! You lie; I will do neither.

(*They fight. The Spaniards join with Antonio, Blunt
laying on like mad.*)

ANGELLICA: Hold, I command you, if for me you fight.

(*They leave off and bow.*)

WILLMORE (*aside*): How heavenly fair she is! Ah, plague
    of her price! *She must be gorgeous*   265

ANGELLICA: You sir, in buff, you that appear a soldier,
    that first began this insolence—

WILLMORE: 'Tis true, I did so, if you call it insolence for
    a man to preserve himself. I saw your charming pic-
    ture and was wounded; quite through my soul each   270
    pointed beauty ran; and wanting a thousand crowns
    to procure my remedy, I laid this little picture to my
    bosom, which, if you cannot allow me, I'll resign.

ANGELLICA: No, you may keep the trifle.

ANTONIO: You shall first ask me leave, and this.   275

(*Fight again as before.*)

(*Enter Belvile and Frederick, who join with the English.*)

ANGELLICA: Hold! Will you ruin me?—Biskey! Sebastian!
    Part 'em!

(*The Spaniards are beaten off.*)

MORETTA: Oh, madam, we're undone. A pox upon that
    rude fellow; he's set on to ruin us. We shall never see
    good days again till all these fighting poor rogues are   280
    sent to the galleys.

(*Enter Belvile, Blunt, Frederick, and Willmore with's
shirt bloody.*)

BLUNT: Adsheartlikins, beat me at this sport and I'll
    ne'er wear sword more.

BELVILE (*to Willmore*): The devil's in thee for a mad fel-
    low; thou art always one at an unlucky adventure.   285
    Come, let's be gone whilst we're safe, and remember
    these are Spaniards, a sort of people that know how
    to revenge an affront.

FREDERICK: You bleed! I hope you are not wounded.

WILLMORE: Not much. A plague on your dons; if they   290
    fight no better they'll ne'er recover Flanders.° What
    the devil was't to them that I took down the picture?

BLUNT: Took it! Adsheartlikins, we'll have the great one
    too; 'tis ours by conquest. Prithee help me up and I'll
    pull it down.   295

291. ne'er recover Flanders: In 1659, the Spanish gave Flanders,
which had been part of the Spanish Netherlands, to France as
settlement to end a war.

ANGELLICA [to Willmore]: Stay, sir, and ere you affront me farther let me know how you durst commit this outrage. To you I speak, sir, for you appear a gentleman.

WILLMORE: To me, madam? — Gentlemen, your servant.

(Belvile stays him.°)

300 BELVILE: Is the devil in thee? Dost know the danger of ent'ring the house of an incensed courtesan?

WILLMORE: I thank you for your care, but there are other matters in hand, there are, though we have no great temptation. Death! Let me go!

305 FREDERICK: Yes, to your lodging if you will, but not in here. Damn these gay harlots; by this hand I'll have as sound and handsome a whore for a patacoon.° Death, man, she'll murder thee!

WILLMORE: Oh, fear me not. Shall I not venture where a
310 beauty calls? A lovely charming beauty! For fear of danger? When, by heaven, there's none so great as to long for her whilst I want money to purchase her.

FREDERICK: Therefore 'tis loss of time unless you had the thousand crowns to pay.

315 WILLMORE: It may be she may give a favor; at least I shall have the pleasure of saluting her when I enter and when I depart.

BELVILE: Pox, she'll as soon lie with thee as kiss thee, and sooner stab than do either. You shall not go.

320 ANGELLICA: Fear not, sir, all I have to wound with is my eyes.

BLUNT: Let him go. Adsheartlikins, I believe the gentlewoman means well.

BELVILE: Well, take thy fortune; we'll expect you in the
325 next street. Farewell, fool, farewell.

WILLMORE: Bye, colonel.   (Goes in.)

FREDERICK: The rogue's stark mad for a wench.

                                                               (Exeunt.)

Scene II

(A fine chamber. Enter Willmore, Angellica, and Moretta.)

ANGELLICA: Insolent sir, how durst you pull down my picture?

WILLMORE: Rather, how durst you set it up to tempt poor am'rous mortals with so much excellence,
5 which I find you have but too well consulted by the unmerciful price you set upon't. Is all this heaven of beauty shown to move despair in those that cannot buy? And can you think th'effects of that despair should be less extravagant than I have shown?

10 ANGELLICA: I sent for you to ask my pardon, sir, not to aggravate your crime. I thought I should have seen you at my feet imploring it.

WILLMORE: You are deceived. I came to rail at you, and rail such truths too, as shall let you see the vanity of
15 that pride which taught you how to set such price on sin.

For such it is whilst that which is love's due
Is meanly bartered for.

ANGELLICA: Ha! Ha! Ha! Alas, good captain, what pity
20 'tis your edifying doctrine will do no good upon me. Moretta, fetch the gentleman a glass,° and let him survey himself to see what charms he has. — (Aside, in a soft tone.) And guess my business.

MORETTA: He knows himself of old: I believe those breeches and he have been acquainted ever since he
25 was beaten at Worcester.°

ANGELLICA: Nay, do not abuse the poor creature.

MORETTA: Good weather-beaten corporal, will you march off? We have no need of your doctrine, though you have of our charity. But at present we have no
30 scraps; we can afford no kindness for God's sake. In fine, sirrah, the price is too high i'th' mouth° for you, therefore troop, I say.

WILLMORE: Here, good forewoman of the shop, serve me and I'll be gone.
35

MORETTA: Keep it to pay your laundress; your linen stinks of the gun room. For here's no selling by retail.

WILLMORE: Thou hast sold plenty of thy stale ware at a cheap rate.

MORETTA: Ay, the more silly kind heart I, but this is an
40 age wherein beauty is at higher rates. In fine, you know the price of this.

WILLMORE: I grant you 'tis here set down, a thousand crowns a month. Pray, how much may come to my share for a pistole?° Bawd, take your black lead° and
45 sum it up, that I may have a pistole's worth of this vain gay thing, and I'll trouble you no more.

MORETTA: Pox on him, he'll fret me to death! Abominable fellow, I tell thee we only sell by the whole piece.
50

WILLMORE: 'Tis very hard, the whole cargo or nothing. Faith, madam, my stock will not reach it; I cannot be your chapman. Yet I have countrymen in town, merchants of love like me; I'll see if they'll put in for a share. We cannot lose much by it, and what we have
55 no use for, we'll sell upon the Friday's mart at "Who gives more?" — I am studying, madam, how to purchase you, though at present I am unprovided of money.

ANGELLICA (aside): Sure this from any other man would
60 anger me; nor shall he know the conquest he has made. — Poor angry man, how I despise this railing.

WILLMORE: Yes, I am poor. But I'm a gentleman,
And one that scorns this baseness which you practice.
Poor as I am I would not sell myself,
65
No, not to gain your charming high-prized person.
Though I admire you strangely for your beauty,
Yet I contemn your mind.
And yet I would at any rate enjoy you;

---

299. [s.d.] stays him: Keeps him from leaving.   307. patacoon: Portuguese or Spanish coin of small denomination.

21. glass: Mirror.   26. Worcester: Charles II was routed by Cromwell at Worcester in 1651 and was forced into exile on the Continent.   32. high i'th' mouth: High.   44–45. how much . . . pistole: How much will my pistole (a Spanish coin) buy?   45. black lead: Pencil.

[handwritten at top: you're beautiful but worthless if you can't see my beauty inside]

70   At your own rate; but cannot. See here
      The only sum I can command on earth:
      I know not where to eat when this is gone.
      Yet such a slave I am to love and beauty
      This last reserve I'll sacrifice to enjoy you.
75   Nay, do not frown, I know you're to be bought,
      And would be bought by me. By me,
      For a meaning trifling sum, if I could pay it down.
      Which happy knowledge I will still repeat,
      And lay it to my heart: It has a virtue in't,
80   And soon will cure those wounds your eyes have made.
      And yet, there's something so divinely powerful
            there—
      Nay, I will gaze, to let you see my strength.

(*Holds her, looks on her, and pauses and sighs.*)

      By heav'n, bright creature, I would not for the world
      Thy fame were half so fair as is thy face.

(*Turns her away from him.*)

ANGELLICA (*aside*): His words go through me to the
85   very soul.— *[handwritten: She likes him for sure]*
      If you have nothing else to say to me—
WILLMORE: Yes, you shall hear how infamous you are—
      For which I do not hate thee—
      But that secures my heart, and all the flames it feels
90   Are but so many lusts:
      I know it by their sudden bold intrusion.
      The fire's impatient and betrays; 'tis false.
      For had it been the purer flame of love,
      I should have pined and languished at your feet,
95   Ere found the impudence to have discovered it.
      I now dare stand your scorn and your denial.
MORETTA: Sure she's bewitched, that she can stand thus
      tamely and hear his saucy railing.—Sirrah, will you
      be gone?
100 ANGELLICA (*to Moretta*): How dare you take this lib-
      erty! Withdraw!—Pray tell me, sir, are not you guilty
      of the same mercenary crime? When a lady is pro-
      posed to you for a wife, you never ask how fair,
      discreet, or virtuous she is, but what's her fortune;
105 which, if but small, you cry "She will not do my busi-
      ness," and basely leave her, though she languish for
      you. Say, is not this as poor? *[handwritten: a you're only after his money]*
WILLMORE: It is a barbarous custom, which I will scorn *[handwritten: her]*
      to defend in our sex, and do despise in yours.
ANGELLICA: Thou'rt a brave fellow! Put up thy gold,
110   and know,
      That were thy fortune as large as is thy soul,
      Thou shouldst not buy my love
      Couldst thou forget those mean effects of vanity
      Which set me out to sale,
115 And as a lover prize my yielding joys.
      Canst thou believe they'll be entirely thine,
      Without considering they were mercenary?
WILLMORE: I cannot tell, I must bethink me first.
      (*Aside.*) Ha! Death, I'm going to believe her.
120 ANGELLICA: Prithee confirm that faith, or if thou canst not,
      Flatter me a little: 'Twill please me from thy mouth.

Jeremy Irons, as Willmore, and Sinéad Cusack, as Angellica, in the Royal Shakespeare Company's 1986 production directed by John Barton.

WILLMORE (*aside*): Curse on thy charming tongue!
      Dost thou return
      My feigned contempt with so much subtlety?—
      Thou'st found the easiest way into my heart,
      Though I yet know that all thou say'st is false.   125

(*Turning from her in rage.*)

ANGELLICA: By all that's good, 'tis real;
      I never loved before, though oft a mistress.
      Shall my first vows be slighted?
WILLMORE (*aside*): What can she mean?
ANGELLICA (*in an angry tone*): I find you cannot credit me.   130
WILLMORE: I know you take me for an errant ass,
      An ass that may be soothed into belief,
      And then be used at pleasure;
      But, madam, I have been so often cheated
      By perjured, soft, deluding hypocrites,   135
      That I've no faith left for the cozening sex,
      Especially for women of your trade.
ANGELLICA: The low esteem you have of me perhaps
      May bring my heart again:
      For I have pride that yet surmounts my love.   140

(*She turns with pride; he holds her.*)

WILLMORE: Throw off this pride, this enemy to bliss,
      And show the power of love: 'Tis with those arms
      I can be only vanquished, made a slave.

ANGELLICA: Is all my mighty expectation vanished?
145　No, I will not hear thee talk; thou hast a charm
In every word that draws my heart away,
And all the thousand trophies I designed
Thou hast undone. Why art thou soft?
Thy looks are bravely rough, and meant for war.
150　Couldst thou not storm on still?
I then perhaps had been as free as thou.
WILLMORE (aside): Death, how she throws her fire
about my soul!—
Take heed, fair creature, how you raise my hopes,
Which once assumed pretends to all dominion:
155　There's not a joy thou hast in store
I shall not then command.
For which I'll pay you back my soul, my life!
Come, let's begin th'account this happy minute!
ANGELLICA: And will you pay me then the price I ask?
WILLMORE: Oh, why dost thou draw me from an
160　awful worship,
By showing thou art no divinity.
Conceal the fiend, and show me all the angel!
Keep me but ignorant, and I'll be devout
And pay my vows forever at this shrine.

(Kneels and kisses her hand.)

165　ANGELLICA: The pay I mean is but thy love for mine.
Can you give that?
WILLMORE: Entirely. Come, let's withdraw where I'll renew my vows, and breathe 'em with such ardor thou
shalt not doubt my zeal.
170　ANGELLICA: Thou hast a power too strong to be resisted.

(Exeunt Willmore and Angellica.)

MORETTA: Now my curse go with you! Is all our project
fallen to this? To love the only enemy to our trade?
Nay, to love such a shameroon;° a very beggar; nay, a
pirate beggar, whose business is to rifle and be gone;
175　a no-purchase, no-pay tatterdemalion,° and English
picaroon;° a rogue that fights for daily drink, and
takes a pride in being loyally lousy? Oh, I could curse
now, if I durst. This is the fate of most whores.
Trophies, which from believing fops we win,
180　*Are spoils to those who cozen us again.*　[Exit.]

ACT III • Scene I

(A street. Enter Florinda, Valeria, Hellena, in antic°
different dresses from what they were in before; Callis
attending.)

FLORINDA: I wonder what should make my brother in so
ill a humor? I hope he has not found out our ramble
this morning.

173. **shameroon:** Shameful person. 175. **tatterdemalion:** Ragamuffin. 176. **picaroon:** Wandering rogue. [S.D.] *antic:* Absurd, ludicrous, strange.

HELLENA: No, if he had, we should have heard on't at
both ears, and have been mewed up° this afternoon,　5
which I would not for the world should have happened. Hey ho, I'm as sad as a lover's lute.
VALERIA: Well, methinks we have learnt this trade of
gypsies as readily as if we had been bred upon the
road to Loretto;° and yet I did so fumble when I told　10
the stranger his fortune that I was afraid I should
have told my own and yours by mistake. But methinks Hellena has been very serious ever since.
FLORINDA: I would give my garters she were in love,
to be revenged upon her for abusing me. How is't,　15
Hellena?
HELLENA: Ah, would I had never seen my mad monsieur.
And yet, for all your laughing, I am not in love. And
yet this small acquaintance, o' my conscience, will
never out of my head.　20
VALERIA: Ha! Ha! Ha! I laugh to think how thou art fitted with a lover, a fellow that I warrant loves every
new face he sees.
HELLENA: Hum, he has not kept his word with me here,
and may be taken up. That thought is not very pleas-　25
ant to me. What the deuce should this be now that I
feel?
VALERIA: What is't like?
HELLENA: Nay, the Lord knows, but if I should be
hanged I cannot choose but be angry and afraid　30
when I think that mad fellow should be in love with
anybody but me. What to think of myself I know not:
Would I could meet with some true damned gypsy,
that I might know my fortune.
VALERIA: Know it! Why there's nothing so easy: Thou　35
wilt love this wand'ring inconstant till thou find'st
thyself hanged about his neck, and then be as mad to
get free again.
FLORINDA: Yes, Valeria, we shall see her bestride his baggage horse and follow him to the campaign.　40
HELLENA: So, so, now you are provided for there's no
care taken of poor me. But since you have set my
heart a-wishing, I am resolved to know for what, I
will not die of the pip,° so I will not.
FLORINDA: Art thou mad to talk so? Who will like thee　45
well enough to have thee, that hears what a mad
wench thou art?
HELLENA: Like me? I don't intend every he that likes me
shall have me, but he that I like. I should have stayed
in the nunnery still if I had liked my lady abbess as　50
well as she liked me. No, I came thence not, as my
wise brother imagines, to take an eternal farewell of
the world, but to love and to be beloved; and I will be
beloved, or I'll get one of your men, so I will.
VALERIA: Am I put into° the number of lovers?　55

5. **mewed up:** Shut in, imprisoned.　10. **Loretto:** Loretto is an Italian town on the Adriatic coast, a destination for pilgrims visiting the cottage of the Virgin Mary.　44. **pip:** A disease of poultry and birds, applied vaguely, usually humorously, to various ailments in humans.　55. **Am I put into:** Do you include me among?

HELLENA: You? Why, coz, I know thou'rt too good-natured to leave us in any design; thou wouldst venture a cast° though thou comest off a loser, especially with such a gamester. I observed your man, and your willing ear incline that way; and if you are not a lover, 'tis an art soon learnt—that I find.   (*Sighs.*)

FLORINDA: I wonder how you learnt to love so easily. I had a thousand charms to meet my eyes and ears ere I could yield, and 'twas the knowledge of Belvile's merit, not the surprising person, took my soul. Thou art too rash, to give a heart at first sight.

HELLENA: Hang your considering lover! I never thought beyond the fancy that 'twas a very pretty, idle, silly kind of pleasure to pass one's time with: to write little soft nonsensical billets,° and with great difficulty and danger receive answers in which I shall have my beauty praised, my wit admired, though little or none, and have the vanity and power to know I am desirable. Then I have the more inclination that way because I am to be a nun, and so shall not be suspected to have any such earthly thoughts about me; but when I walk thus—and sigh thus—they'll think my mind's upon my monastery, and cry, "How happy 'tis she's so resolved." But not a word of man.

FLORINDA: What a mad creature's this!

HELLENA: I'll warrant, if my brother hears either of you sigh, he cries gravely, "I fear you have the indiscretion to be in love, but take heed of the honor of our house, and your own unspotted fame"; and so he conjures on till he has laid the soft winged god in your hearts, or broke the bird's nest.° But see, here comes your lover, but where's my inconstant? Let's step aside, and we may learn something.

(*Go aside.*)

(*Enter Belvile, Frederick, and Blunt.*)

BELVILE: What means this! The picture's taken in.

BLUNT: It may be the wench is good-natured, and will be kind gratis.° Your friend's a proper handsome fellow.

BELVILE: I rather think she has cut his throat and is fled; I am mad he should throw himself into dangers. Pox on't, I shall want him, too, at night. Let's knock and ask for him.

HELLENA: My heart goes a-pit, a-pat, for fear 'tis my man they talk of.

(*Knock; Moretta above.*)

MORETTA: What would you have?

BELVILE: Tell the stranger that entered here about two hours ago that his friends stay here for him.

MORETTA: A curse upon him for Moretta: Would he were at the devil! But he's coming to you.

(*Enter Willmore.*)

HELLENA: Ay, ay 'tis he. Oh, how this vexes me!

BELVILE: And how and how, dear lad, has fortune smiled? Are we to break her windows, or raise up altars to her, hah?

WILLMORE: Does not my fortune sit triumphant on my brow? Dost not see the little wanton god there all gay and smiling? Have I not an air about my face and eyes that distinguish me from the crowd of common lovers? By heaven, Cupid's quiver has not half so many darts as her eyes! Oh, such a *bona roba*!° To sleep in her arms is lying *in fresco*,° all perfumed air about me.

HELLENA (*aside*): Here's fine encouragement for me to fool on!

WILLMORE: Hark'ee, where didst thou purchase that rich Canary° we drank today? Tell me, that I may adore the spigot and sacrifice to the butt.° The juice was divine; into which I must dip my rosary, and then bless all things that I would have bold or fortunate.

BELVILE: Well, sir, let's go take a bottle and hear the story of your success.

FREDERICK: Would not French wine do better?

WILLMORE: Damn the hungry balderdash!° Cheerful sack° has a generous virtue in't inspiring a successful confidence, gives eloquence to the tongue and vigor to the soul, and has in a few hours completed all my hopes and wishes! There's nothing left to raise a new desire in me. Come, let's be gay and wanton. And, gentlemen, study; study what you want, for here are friends that will supply gentlemen. [*Jingles gold.*] Hark what a charming sound they make! 'Tis he and she gold whilst here, and shall beget new pleasures every moment.

BLUNT: But hark'ee, sir, you are not married, are you?

WILLMORE: All the honey of matrimony but none of the sting, friend.

BLUNT: 'Adsheartlikins, thou'rt a fortunate rogue!

WILLMORE: I am so, sir: let these inform you! Ha, how sweetly they chime! Pox of poverty: It makes a man a slave, makes wit and honor sneak. My soul grew lean and rusty for want of credit.

BLUNT: 'Adsheartlikins, this I like well; it looks like my lucky bargain! Oh, how I long for the approach of my squire, that is to conduct me to her house again. Why, here's two provided for!

FREDERICK: By this light, y'are happy men.

BLUNT: Fortune is pleased to smile on us, gentlemen, to smile on us.

(*Enter Sancho and pulls down Blunt by the sleeve; they go aside.*)

SANCHO: Sir, my lady expects you. She has removed all that might oppose your will and pleasure, and is impatient till you come.

57–58. **venture a cast:** Throw the dice.   70. **billets:** Brief letters, notes.   85–86. **laid . . . bird's nest:** Ruined your chances.   91. **gratis:** Free of charge.

112. *bona roba*: A courtesan.   113. *in fresco*: In the fresh air out of doors.   118. **Canary:** A light sweet wine from the Canary Islands.   119. **butt:** Large wine cask.   125. **hungry balderdash:** Cheap mixture of liquor.   126. **sack:** Dry white Spanish wine.

BLUNT: Sir, I'll attend you.—Oh the happiest rogue! I'll
take no leave, lest they either dog me or stay me.

(*Exit with Sancho.*)

BELVILE: But then the little gypsy is forgot?

WILLMORE: A mischief on thee for putting her into my
thoughts! I had quite forgot her else, and this night's
debauch had drunk her quite down.

HELLENA: Had it so, good captain!

(*Claps him on the back.*)

WILLMORE (*aside*): Ha! I hope she did not hear me!

HELLENA: What, afraid of such a champion?

WILLMORE: Oh, you're a fine lady of your word, are you
not? To make a man languish a whole day—

HELLENA: In tedious search of me.

WILLMORE: Egad, child, thou'rt in the right. Hadst thou
seen what a melancholy dog I have been ever since
I was a lover, how I have walked the streets like a
Capuchin,° with my hands in my sleeves—faith,
sweetheart, thou wouldst pity me.

HELLENA (*aside*): Now if I should be hanged I can't be
angry with him, he dissembles so heartily.—Alas,
good captain, what pains you have taken; now were
I ungrateful not to reward so true a servant.

WILLMORE: Poor soul, that's kindly said; I see thou
barest a conscience. Come then, for a beginning show
me thy dear face.

HELLENA: I'm afraid, my small acquaintance, you have
been staying that swinging stomach you boasted of
this morning. I then remember my little collation°
would have gone down with you without the sauce
of a handsome face. Is your stomach so queasy now?

WILLMORE: Faith, long fasting, child, spoils a man's
appetite. Yet if thou durst treat, I could so lay about
me still—

HELLENA: And would you fall to before a priest says
grace?

WILLMORE: O' fie, fie, what an old out-of-fashioned
thing hast thou named? Thou couldst not dash me
more out of countenance shouldst thou show me an
ugly face.

(*Whilst he is seemingly courting Hellena, enter Angellica,
Moretta, Biskey, and Sebastian, all in masquerade.
Angellica sees Willmore and stares.*)

ANGELLICA: Heavens, 'tis he! And passionately fond to
see another woman!

MORETTA: What could you less expect from such a
swaggerer?

ANGELLICA: Expect? As much as I paid him: a heart entire,
Which I had pride enough to think when'er I gave,
It would have raised the man above the vulgar,
Made him all soul, and that all soft and constant.

HELLENA: You see, captain, how willing I am to be
friends with you, till time and ill luck make us lovers;
and ask you the question first rather than put your

169. **Capuchin:** Franciscan monk.   180. **collation:** Snack.

modesty to the blush by asking me. For alas, I know
you captains are such strict men, and such severe
observers of your vows to chastity, that 'twill be hard
to prevail with your tender conscience to marry a
young willing maid.

WILLMORE: Do not abuse me, for fear I should take thee
at thy word and marry thee indeed, which I'm sure
will be revenge sufficient.

HELLENA: O' my conscience, that will be our destiny,
because we are both of one humor: I am as inconstant as you, for I have considered, captain, that a
handsome woman has a great deal to do whilst her
face is good. For then is our harvest-time to gather
friends, and should I in these days of my youth catch
a fit of foolish constancy, I were undone: 'tis loitering
by daylight in our great journey. Therefore, I declare
I'll allow but one year for love, one year for indifference, and one year for hate; and then go hang yourself, for I profess myself the gay, the kind, and the
inconstant. The devil's in't if this won't please you!

WILLMORE: Oh, most damnably. I have a heart with a
hole quite through it too; no prison mine, to keep a
mistress in.

ANGELLICA (*aside*): Perjured man! How I believe thee
now!

HELLENA: Well, I see our business as well as humors are
alike: yours to cozen as many maids as will trust you,
and I as many men as have faith. See if I have not as
desperate a lying look as you can have for the heart
of you. (*Pulls off her vizard; he starts.*) How do you
like it, captain?

WILLMORE: Like it! By heaven, I never saw so much
beauty! Oh, the charms of those sprightly black eyes!
That strangely fair face, full of smiles and dimples!
Those soft round melting cherry lips and small even
white teeth! Not to be expressed, but silently adored!
[*She replaces her mask.*] Oh, one look more, and strike
me dumb, or I shall repeat nothing else till I'm mad.

(*He seems to court her to pull off her vizard; she refuses.*)

ANGELLICA: I can endure no more. Nor is it fit to interrupt him, for if I do, my jealousy has so destroyed my
reason I shall undo him. Therefore I'll retire, and you,
Sebastian (*to one of her Bravos*), follow that woman
and learn who 'tis; while you (*to the other Bravo*) tell
the fugitive I would speak to him instantly.   (*Exit.*)

(*This while Florinda is talking to Belvile, who stands
sullenly; Frederick courting Valeria.*)

VALERIA [*to Belvile*]: Prithee, dear stranger, be not so
sullen, for though you have lost your love you see
my friend frankly offers you hers to play with in the
meantime.

BELVILE: Faith, madam, I am sorry I can't play at her
game.

FREDERICK [*to Valeria*]: Pray leave your intercession and
mind your own affair. They'll better agree apart: He's
a modest sigher in company, but alone no woman
'scapes him.

FLORINDA (*aside*): Sure he does but rally. Yet, if it should be true? I'll tempt him farther.—Believe me, noble stranger, I'm no common mistress. And for a little
260 proof on't, wear this jewel.° Nay, take it, sir, 'tis right, and bills of exchange may sometimes miscarry.

BELVILE: Madam, why am I chose out of all mankind to be the object of your bounty?

VALERIA: There's another civil question asked.

265 FREDERICK (*aside*): Pox of's modesty; it spoils his own markets and hinders mine.

FLORINDA: Sir, from my window I have often seen you, and women of my quality have so few opportunities for love that we ought to lose none.

270 FREDERICK [*to Valeria*]: Ay, this is something! Here's a woman! When shall I be blest with so much kindness from your fair mouth?—(*Aside to Belvile.*) Take the jewel, fool!

BELVILE: You tempt me strangely, madam, every way—

275 FLORINDA (*aside*): So, if I find him false, my whole repose is gone.

BELVILE: And but for a vow I've made to a very fair lady, this goodness had subdued me.

FREDERICK [*aside to Belvile*]: Pox on't, be kind, in pity to
280 me be kind. For I am to thrive here but as you treat her friend.

HELLENA: Tell me what you did in yonder house, and I'll unmask.

WILLMORE: Yonder house? Oh, I went to a—to—why,
285 there's a friend of mine lives there.

HELLENA: What, a she or a he friend?

WILLMORE: A man, upon honor, a man. A she friend? No, no, madam, you have done my business, I thank you.

290 HELLENA: And was't your man friend that had more darts in's eyes than Cupid carries in's whole budget of arrows?

WILLMORE: So—

HELLENA: "Ah, such a *bona roba*! To be in her arms is
295 lying *in fresco*, all perfumed air about me." Was this your man friend too?

WILLMORE: So—

HELLENA: That gave you the he and the she gold, that begets young pleasures?

300 WILLMORE: Well, well, madam, then you can see there are ladies in the world that will not be cruel. There are, madam, there are.

HELLENA: And there be men, too, as fine, wild, inconstant fellows as yourself. There be, captain, there be, if you
305 go to that now. Therefore, I'm resolved—

WILLMORE: Oh!

HELLENA: To see your face no more—

WILLMORE: Oh!

HELLENA: Till tomorrow.

310 WILLMORE: Egad, you frighted me.

HELLENA: Nor then neither, unless you'll swear never to see that lady more.

260. jewel: A locket with her picture in it.

WILLMORE: See her! Why, never to think of womankind again.

HELLENA: Kneel and swear.   315

(*Kneels, she gives him her hand.*)

WILLMORE: I do, never to think, to see, to love, nor lie, with any but thyself.

HELLENA: Kiss the book.

WILLMORE: Oh, most religiously.   (*Kisses her hand.*)

HELLENA: Now what a wicked creature am I, to damn a   320
proper fellow.

CALLIS (*to Florinda*): Madam, I'll stay no longer: 'tis e'en dark.

FLORINDA [*to Belvile*]: However, sir, I'll leave this with you, that when I'm gone you may repent the oppor-   325
tunity you have lost by your modesty.

(*Gives him the jewel, which is her picture, and exit. He gazes after her.*)

WILLMORE [*to Hellena*]: 'Twill be an age till tomorrow, and till then I will most impatiently expect you. Adieu, my dear pretty angel.

(*Exeunt all the women.*)

BELVILE: Ha! Florinda's picture! 'Twas she herself. What   330
a dull dog was I! I would have given the world for one minute's discourse with her.

FREDERICK: This comes of your modesty. Ah, pox o' your vow; 'twas ten to one but we had lost the jewel by't.

BELVILE: Willmore, the blessed'st opportunity lost!   335
Florinda, friends, Florinda!

WILLMORE: Ah, rogue! Such black eyes! Such a face! Such a mouth! Such teeth! And so much wit!

BELVILE: All, all, and a thousand charms besides.

WILLMORE: Why, dost thou know her?   340

BELVILE: Know her! Ay, ay, and a pox take me with all my heart for being so modest.

WILLMORE: But hark'ee, friend of mine, are you my rival? And have I been only beating the bush all this while?

BELVILE: I understand thee not. I'm mad! See here—   345

(*Shows the picture.*)

WILLMORE: Ha! Whose picture's this? 'Tis a fine wench!

FREDERICK: The colonel's mistress, sir.

WILLMORE: Oh, oh, here. (*Gives the picture back.*) I thought't had been another prize. Come, come, a bottle will set thee right again.   350

BELVILE: I am content to try, and by that time 'twill be late enough for our design.

WILLMORE: Agreed.
Love does all day the soul's great empire keep,
But wine at night lulls the soft god asleep.   355

(*Exeunt.*)

Scene II

(*Lucetta's house. Enter Blunt and Lucetta with a light.*)

LUCETTA: Now we are safe and free: no fears of the com-ing home of my old jealous husband, which made me a little thoughtful when you came in first. But now love is all the business of my soul.

5   BLUNT: I am transported!—(*Aside.*) Pox on't, that I had but some fine things to say to her, such as lovers use. I was a fool not to learn of Fred a little by heart before I came. Something I must say. 'Adsheartlikins, sweet soul, I am not used to compliment, but I'm an honest
10   gentleman, and thy humble servant.

LUCETTA: I have nothing to pay for so great a favor, but such a love as cannot but be great, since at first sight of that sweet face and shape it made me your absolute captive.

15   BLUNT (*aside*): Kind heart, how prettily she talks! Egad, I'll show her husband a Spanish trick: Send him out of the world and marry her; she's damnably in love with me, and will ne'er mind settlements,° and so there's that saved.

20   LUCETTA: Well, sir, I'll go and undress me, and be with you instantly.

BLUNT: Make haste then, for 'adsheartlikins, dear soul, thou canst not guess at the pain of a longing lover when his joys are drawn within the compass of a few
25   minutes.

LUCETTA: You speak my sense, and I'll make haste to prove it.   (*Exit.*)

BLUNT: 'Tis a rare girl, and this one night's enjoyment with her will be worth all the days I ever passed in
30   Essex. Would she would go with me into England, though to say truth, there's plenty of whores already. Put a pox on 'em, they are such mercenary prodigal whores that they want such a one as this, that's free and generous, to give 'em good examples. Why, what
35   a house she has, how rich and fine!

(*Enter Sancho.*)

SANCHO: Sir, my lady has sent me to conduct you to her chamber.

BLUNT: Sir, I shall be proud to follow.—(*Aside.*) Here's one of her servants too; 'adsheartlikins, by this garb
40   and gravity he might be a justice of peace in Essex, and is but a pimp here.

(*Exeunt.*)

Scene III

(*The scene changes to a chamber with an alcove bed in't, a table, etc.; Lucetta in bed. Enter Sancho and Blunt, who takes the candle of Sancho at the door.*)

SANCHO: Sir, my commission reaches no farther.

BLUNT: Sir, I'll excuse your compliment.

[*Exit Sancho.*]
—What, in bed, my sweet mistress?

LUCETTA: You see, I still outdo you in kindness.

5   BLUNT: And thou shalt see what haste I'll make to quit scores. Oh, the luckiest rogue!

18. **will ne'er mind settlements:** Won't require the gifts of property usually settled on a wife after marriage.

(*He undresses himself.*)

LUCETTA: Should you be false or cruel now—

BLUNT: False! 'Adsheartlikins, what dost thou take me for, a Jew? An insensible heathen? A pox of thy old jealous husband: An° he were dead, egad, sweet soul,
10   it should be none of my fault if I did not marry thee.

LUCETTA: It never should be mine.

BLUNT: Good soul! I'm the fortunatest dog!

LUCETTA: Are you not undressed yet?

BLUNT: As much as my impatience will permit.   15

(*Goes toward the bed in his shirt, drawers, etc.*)

LUCETTA: Hold, sir, put out the light; it may betray us else.

BLUNT: Anything; I need no other light but that of thine eyes.—(*Aside.*) 'Adsheartlikins, there I think I had it.

(*Puts out the candle; the bed descends; he gropes about to find it.*)

Why, why, where am I got? What, not yet? Where are   20
you, sweetest?—Ah, the rogue's silent now. A pretty love-trick this; how she'll laugh at me anon!—You need not, my dear rogue, you need not! I'm all on fire already; come, come, now call me, in pity.—Sure I'm enchanted! I have been round the chamber, and can   25
find neither woman nor bed. I locked the door; I'm sure she cannot go that way, or if she could, the bed could not.—Enough, enough, my pretty wanton; do not carry the jest too far! (*Lights on a trap, and is let down.*)—Ha! Betrayed! Dogs! Rogues! Pimps! Help!   30
Help!

(*Enter Lucetta, Philippo, and Sancho with a light.*)

PHILIPPO: Ha! Ha! Ha! He's dispatched finely.

LUCETTA: Now, sir, had I been coy, we had missed of this booty.

PHILIPPO: Nay, when I saw 'twas a substantial fool, I   35
was mollified. But when you dote upon a serenading coxcomb, upon a face, fine clothes, and a lute, it makes me rage.

LUCETTA: You know I was never guilty of that folly, my dear Philippo, but with yourself. But come, let's see   40
what we have got by this.

PHILIPPO: A rich coat; sword and hat; these breeches, too, are well lined! See here, a gold watch! A purse—Ha! Gold! At least two hundred pistoles! A bunch of diamond rings, and one with the family arms! A gold   45
box, with a medal of his king, and his lady mother's picture! These were sacred relics, believe me. See, the waistband of his breeches have a mine of gold—old queen Bess's!° We have a quarrel to her ever since eighty-eight,° and may therefore justify the theft: The   50
Inquisition might have committed it.

LUCETTA: See, a bracelet of bowed gold! These his sisters tied about his arm at parting. But well, for all this, I

10. **An:** If.   **48–49. old queen Bess's:** Queen Elizabeth I (reigned 1558–1603).   **50. eighty-eight:** The year the Spanish Armada was defeated by the English (1588).

55 fear his being a stranger may make a noise and hinder our trade with them hereafter.

PHILIPPO: That's our security: He is not only a stranger to us, but to the country too. The common shore° into which he is descended, thou know'st, conducts

60 him into another street, which this light will hinder him from ever finding again. He knows neither your name, nor that of the street where your house is; nay, nor the way to his own lodgings.

LUCETTA: And art thou not an unmerciful rogue, not to afford him one night for all this? I should not have

65 been such a Jew.

PHILIPPO: Blame me not, Lucetta, to keep as much of thee as I can to myself. Come, that thought makes me wanton; let's to bed.—Sancho, lock up these.

> *This is the fleece which fools do bear,*
70 > *Designed for witty men to shear.*   (*Exeunt.*)

Scene IV

(*The scene changes, and discovers Blunt creeping out of a common shore; his face, etc., all dirty.*)

BLUNT (*climbing up*): Oh, Lord, I am got out at last, and, which is a miracle, without a clue. And now to damning and cursing! But if that would ease me, where shall I begin? With my fortune, myself, or the

5 quean° that cozened me? What a dog was I to believe in woman! Oh, coxcomb! Ignorant conceited coxcomb! To fancy she could be enamored with my person! At first sight enamored! Oh, I'm a cursed puppy! 'Tis plain, fool was writ upon my forehead! She per-

10 ceived it; saw the Essex calf there. For what allurements could there be in this countenance, which I can endure because I'm acquainted with it. Oh dull, silly dog, to be thus soothed into a cozening! Had I been drunk, I might fondly have credited the young quean;

15 but as I was in my right wits to be thus cheated, confirms it: I am a dull believing English country fop. But my comrades! Death and the devil, there's the worst of all! Then a ballad will be sung tomorrow on the Prado,° to a lousy tune of the enchanted squire and

20 the annihilated damsel. But Fred—that rogue and the colonel will abuse me beyond all Christian patience. Had she left me my clothes, I have a bill of exchange at home would have saved my credit. But now all hope is taken from me. Well, I'll home, if I

25 can find the way, with this consolation: that I am not the first kind believing coxcomb; but there are, gallants, many such good natures amongst ye.

> *And though you've better arts to hide your follies,*
> *'Adsheartlikins, y'are all as errant cullies.°*

(*Exit.*)

57. **common shore**: Sewer. 5. **quean**: Harlot, tramp. 18–19. **ballad . . . Prado**: A song satirizing him will be sung on the Prado, a fashionable promenade in Madrid, for common amusement. 29. *cullies*: A cully is one easily fooled—a simpleton.

Scene V

(*Scene: the garden in the night. Enter Florinda in an undress,° with a key and a little box.*)

FLORINDA: Well, thus far I'm in my way to happiness. I have got myself free from Callis; my brother too, I find by yonder light, is got into his cabinet,° and thinks not of me; I have by good fortune got the key of the garden back door. I'll open it to prevent

5 Belvile's knocking: A little noise will now alarm my brother. Now am I as fearful as a young thief. (*Unlocks the door.*) Hark! What noise is that? Oh, 'twas the wind that played amongst the boughs. Belvile stays long, methinks; it's time. Stay, for fear of

10 a surprise, I'll hide these jewels in yonder jasmine.

(*She goes to lay down the box.*)

(*Enter Willmore, drunk.*)

WILLMORE: What the devil is become of these fellows Belvile and Frederick? They promised to stay at the next corner for me, but who the devil knows the cor-

15 ner of a full moon? Now, whereabouts am I? Ha, what have we here? A garden! A very convenient place to sleep in. Ha! What has God sent us here? A female! By this light, a woman! I'm a dog if it be not a very wench!

20 FLORINDA: He's come! Ha! Who's there?

WILLIMORE: Sweet soul, let me salute thy shoestring.

FLORINDA [*aside*]: 'Tis not my Belvile. Good heavens, I know him not!—Who are you, and from whence come you?

25 WILLMORE: Prithee, prithee, child, not so many hard questions! Let it suffice I am here, child. Come, come kiss me.

FLORINDA: Good gods! What luck is mine?

WILLMORE: Only good luck, child, parlous° good luck.

30 Come hither.—'Tis a delicate shining wench. By this hand, she's perfumed, and smells like any nosegay.—Prithee, dear soul, let's not play the fool and lose time—precious time. For as Gad shall save me, I'm as honest a fellow as breathes, though I'm a little

35 disguised° at present. Come, I say. Why, thou mayst be free with me: I'll be very secret. I'll not boast who 'twas obliged me, not I; for hang me if I know thy name.

FLORINDA: Heavens! What a filthy beast is this!

40 WILLMORE: I am so, and thou ought'st the sooner to lie with me for that reason. For look you, child, there will be no sin in't, because 'twas neither designed nor premeditated: 'Tis pure accident on both sides. That's a certain thing now. Indeed, should I make love to

45 you, and you vow fidelity, and swear and lie till you believed and yielded—that were to make it willful fornication, the crying sin of the nation. Thou art,

[S.D.] *undress*: Undergarment. 3. **cabinet**: Private room. 29. **parlous**: Excessively, with pun on *perilous*. 35. **disguised**: I.e., by liquor.

therefore, as thou art a good Christian, obliged in conscience to deny me nothing. Now, come be kind
50   without any more idle prating.
FLORINDA: Oh, I am ruined! Wicked man, unhand me!
WILLMORE: Wicked? Egad, child, a judge, were he young and vigorous, and saw those eyes of thine, would know 'twas they gave the first blow, the first
55   provocation. Come, prithee let's lose no time, I say. This is a fine convenient place.
FLORINDA: Sir, let me go, I conjure° you, or I'll call out.
WILLMORE: Ay, ay, you were best to call witness to see how finely you treat me. Do!
60 FLORINDA: I'll cry murder, rape, or anything, if you do not instantly let me go!
WILLMORE: A rape? Come, come, you lie, you baggage, you lie. What! I'll warrant you would fain have the world believe now that you are not so forward as I.
65   No, not you. Why at this time of night was your cobweb door set open, dear spider, but to catch flies? Ha! Come, or I shall be damnably angry. Why, what a coil° is here!
FLORINDA: Sir, can you think—
70 WILLMORE: That you would do't for nothing? Oh, oh, I find what you would be at. Look here, here's a pistole for you. Here's a work indeed! Here, take it, I say!
FLORINDA: For heaven's sake, sir, as you're a gentle-man—
75 WILLMORE: So now, now, she would be wheedling me for more! What, you will not take it then? You are resolved you will not? Come, come, take it or I'll put it up again, for look ye, I never give more. Why, how now, mistress, are you so high i'th' mouth a pistole
80   won't down with you? Ha! Why, what a work's here! In good time! Come, no struggling to be gone. But an y'are good at a dumb wrestle, I'm for ye. Look ye, I'm for ye.   (*She struggles with him.*)

(*Enter Belvile and Frederick.*)

BELVILE: The door is open. A pox of this mad fellow!
85   I'm angry that we've lost him; I durst have sworn he had followed us.
FREDERICK: But you were so hasty, colonel, to be gone.
FLORINDA: Help! Help! Murder! Help! Oh, I am ruined!
BELVILE: Ha! Sure that's Florinda's voice! (*Comes up to*
90   *them.*) A man!—Villain, let go that lady!

(*A noise; Willmore turns and draws; Frederick interposes.*)

FLORINDA: Belvile! Heavens! My brother too is coming, and 'twill be impossible to escape. Belvile, I con-jure you to walk under my chamber window, from whence I'll give you some instructions what to do.
95   This rude man has undone us.   (*Exit.*)
WILLMORE: Belvile!

(*Enter Pedro, Stephano, and other servants, with lights.*)

PEDRO: I'm betrayed! Run, Stephano, and see if Florinda be safe.

    (*Exit Stephano.*)

(*They fight, and Pedro's party beats 'em out.*)

—So, whoe'er they be, all is not well. I'll to Florinda's chamber.   (*Going out, meets Stephano.*)   100
STEPHANO: You need not, sir: The poor lady's fast asleep, and thinks no harm. I would not awake her, sir, for fear of frighting her with your danger.
PEDRO: I'm glad she's there.—Rascals, how came the garden door open?   105
STEPHANO: That question comes too late, sir. Some of my fellow servants masquerading, I'll warrant.
PEDRO: Masquerading! A lewd custom to debauch our youth! There's something more in this than I imagine.

    (*Exeunt.*)

Scene VI

(*Scene changes to the street. Enter Belvile in rage, Frederick holding him, Willmore melancholy.*)

WILLMORE: Why, how the devil should I know Florinda?
BELVILE: Ah, plague of your ignorance! If it had not been Florinda, must you be a beast? A brute? A senseless swine?
WILLMORE: Well, sir, you see I am endued° with pa-   5
tience: I can bear. Though egad, y'are very free with me, methinks. I was in good hopes the quarrel would have been on my side, for so uncivilly interrupting me.
BELVILE: Peace, brute, whilst thou'rt safe. Oh, I'm dis-   10
tracted!
WILLMORE: Nay, nay, I'm an unlucky dog, that's certain.
BELVILE: Ah, curse upon the star that ruled my birth, or whatsoever other influence that makes me still so wretched.   15
WILLMORE: Thou break'st my heart with these com-plaints. There is no star in fault, no influence but sack, the cursed sack I drunk.
FREDERICK: Why, how the devil came you so drunk?
WILLMORE: Why, how the devil came you so sober?   20
BELVILE: A curse upon his thin skull, he was always be-forehand that way.
FREDERICK: Prithee, dear colonel, forgive him; he's sorry for his fault.
BELVILE: He's always so after he has done a mischief. A   25
plague on all such brutes!
WILLMORE: By this light, I took her for an errant harlot.
BELVILE: Damn your debauched opinion! Tell me, sot, hadst thou so much sense and light about thee to dis-tinguish her woman, and couldst not see something   30
about her face and person to strike an awful rever-ence into thy soul?

---

57. **conjure:** Entreat, implore.   68. **coil:** Noisy disturbance.

5. **endued:** Endowed.

WILLMORE: Faith no, I considered her as mere a woman
as I could wish.

35 BELVILE: 'Sdeath, I have no patience. Draw, or I'll kill
you!

WILLMORE: Let that alone till tomorrow, and if I set not
all right again, use your pleasure.

BELVILE: Tomorrow! Damn it,

40   The spiteful light will lead me to no happiness.
Tomorrow is Antonio's, and perhaps
Guides him to my undoing. Oh, that I could meet
This rival, this powerful fortunate!

WILLMORE: What then?

45 BELVILE: Let thy own reason, or my rage, instruct thee.

WILLMORE: I shall be finely informed then, no doubt.
Hear me, colonel, hear me; show me the man and I'll
do his business.

BELVILE: I know him no more than thou, or if I did I

50   should not need thy aid.

WILLMORE: This you say is Angellica's house; I promised
the kind baggage to lie with her tonight.

(*Offers to go in.*)

(*Enter Antonio and his Page. Antonio knocks on the
hilt of's sword.*)

ANTONIO: You paid the thousand crowns I directed?

PAGE: To the lady's old woman, sir, I did.

55 WILLMORE: Who the devil have we here?

BELVILE: I'll now plant myself under Florinda's window,
and if I find no comfort there, I'll die.

(*Exeunt Belvile and Frederick.*)

(*Enter Moretta.*)

MORETTA: Page?

PAGE: Here's my lord.

60 WILLMORE: How is this? A picaroon going to board my
frigate? —Here's one chase gun for you!

(*Drawing his sword, justles Antonio, who turns and
draws. They fight; Antonio falls.*)

MORETTA: Oh, bless us! We're all undone!

(*Runs in and shuts the door.*)

PAGE: Help! Murder!

(*Belvile returns at the noise of fighting.*)

BELVILE: Ha! The mad rogue's engaged in some unlucky

65   adventure again.

(*Enter two or three Masqueraders.*)

MASQUERADER: Ha! A man killed!

WILLMORE: How, a man killed? Then I'll go home to
sleep.

(*Puts up and reels out. Exeunt Masqueraders another
way.*)

BELVILE: Who should it be? Pray heaven the rogue is safe,

70   for all my quarrel to him.

(*As Belvile is groping about, enter an Officer and six
Soldiers.*)

SOLDIER: Who's there?

OFFICER: So, here's one dispatched. Secure the murderer.

BELVILE: Do not mistake my charity for murder! I came
to his assistance!   (*Soldiers sieze on Belvile.*)   75

OFFICER: That shall be tried, sir. St. Jago! Swords drawn
in the Carnival time!   (*Goes to Antonio.*)

ANTONIO: Thy hand, prithee.

OFFICER: Ha! Don Antonio! Look well to the villain
there. —How is it, sir?   80

ANTONIO: I'm hurt.

BELVILE: Has my humanity made me a criminal?

OFFICER: Away with him!

BELVILE: What a curst chance is this!

(*Exeunt soldiers with Belvile.*)

ANTONIO [*aside*]: This is the man that has set upon me   85
twice. —(*To the officer.*) Carry him to my apartment
till you have further orders from me.

(*Exit Antonio, led.*)

ACT IV • Scene I

(*A fine room. Discovers Belvile as by dark alone.*)

BELVILE: When shall I be weary of railing on fortune,
who is resolved never to turn with smiles upon me?
Two such defeats in one night none but the devil and
that mad rogue could have contrived to have plagued
me with. I am here a prisoner. But where, heaven   5
knows. And if there be murder done, I can soon
decide the fate of a stranger in a nation without
mercy. Yet this is nothing to the torture my soul
bows with when I think of losing my fair, my dear
Florinda. Hark, my door opens. A light! A man, and   10
seems of quality. Armed, too! Now shall I die like a
dog, without defense.

(*Enter Antonio in a nightgown, with a light; his arm in
a scarf, and a sword under his arm. He sets the candle
on the table.*)

ANTONIO: Sir, I come to know what injuries I have done
you, that could provoke you to so mean an action
as to attack me basely without allowing time for my   15
defense?

BELVILE: Sir, for a man in my circumstances to plead
innocence would look like fear. But view me well,
and you will find no marks of coward on me, nor
anything that betrays that brutality you accuse me   20
with.

ANTONIO: In vain, sir, you impose upon my sense. You
are not only he who drew on me last night, but yesterday before the same house, that of Angellica. Yet
there is something in your face and mien° that makes   25
me wish I were mistaken.

25. **mien:** Demeanor, appearance.

BELVILE: I own I fought today in the defense of a friend of mine with whom you, if you're the same, and your party were first engaged. Perhaps you think this
30 crime enough to kill me; but if you do, I cannot fear you'll do it basely.

ANTONIO: No sir, I'll make you fit for a defense with this.

(Gives him the sword.)

BELVILE: This gallantry surprises me, nor know I how to
35 use this present, sir, against a man so brave.

ANTONIO: You shall not need. For know, I come to snatch you from a danger that is decreed against you: perhaps your life, or long imprisonment. And 'twas with so much courage you offended, I cannot see you
40 punished.

BELVILE: How shall I pay this generosity?

ANTONIO: It had been safer to have killed another than have attempted me. To show your danger, sir, I'll let you know my quality: And 'tis the Viceroy's son
45 whom you have wounded.

BELVILE: The Viceroy's son!—*(Aside.)* Death and confusion! Was this plague reserved to complete all the rest? Obliged by° him, the man of all the world I would destroy!

50 ANTONIO: You seem disordered, sir.

BELVILE: Yes, trust me, I am, and 'tis with pain that man receives such bounties who wants the power to pay 'em back again.

ANTONIO: To gallant spirits 'tis indeed uneasy, but you
55 may quickly overpay me, sir.

BELVILE *(aside)*: Then I am well. Kind heaven, but set us even, that I may fight with him and keep my honor safe.—Oh, I'm impatient, sir, to be discounting the mighty debt I owe you. Command me quickly.

60 ANTONIO: I have a quarrel with a rival, sir, about the maid we love.

BELVILE *(aside)*: Death, 'tis Florinda he means! That thought destroys my reason, and I shall kill him.

ANTONIO: My rival, sir, is one has all the virtues man can
65 boast of—

BELVILE *(aside)*: Death, who should this be?

ANTONIO: He challenged me to meet him on the Molo as soon as day appeared, but last night's quarrel has made my arm unfit to guide a sword.

70 BELVILE: I apprehend you, sir. You'd have me kill the man that lays a claim to the maid you speak of. I'll do't. I'll fly to do't!

ANTONIO: Sir, do you know her?

BELVILE: No, sir, but 'tis enough she is admired by you.

75 ANTONIO: Sir, I shall rob you of the glory on't, for you must fight under my name and dress.

BELVILE: That opinion must be strangely obliging that makes you think I can personate the brave Antonio, whom I can but strive to imitate.

80 ANTONIO: You say too much to my advantage. Come, sir, the day appears that calls you forth. Within, sir, is the habit.°

(Exit Antonio.)

48. Obliged by: Favored by. **82. habit:** Antonio's clothing.

BELVILE: Fantastic fortune, thou deceitful light,
That cheats the wearied traveler by night,
Though on a precipice each step you tread, 85
I am resolved to follow where you lead. *(Exit.)*

Scene II

(The Molo. Enter Florinda and Callis in masks, with Stephano.)

FLORINDA *(aside)*: I'm dying with my fears: Belvile's not coming as I expected under my window makes me believe that all those fears are true.—Canst thou not tell with whom my brother fights?

STEPHANO: No, madam, they were both in masquerade. 5
I was by when they challenged one another, and they had decided the quarrel then, but were prevented by some cavaliers; which made 'em put it off till now. But I am sure 'tis about you they fight.

FLORINDA *(aside)*: Nay, then, 'tis with Belvile, for what other 10
lover have I that dares fight for me except Antonio, and he is too much in favor with my brother. If it be he, for whom shall I direct my prayers to heaven?

STEPHANO: Madam, I must leave you, for if my master see me, I shall be hanged for being your conductor. I 15
escaped narrowly for the excuse I made for you last night i'th' garden.

FLORINDA: I'll reward thee for't. Prithee, no more.

(Exit Stephano.)

(Enter Don Pedro in his masking habit.)

PEDRO: Antonio's late today; the place will fill, and we may be prevented. *(Walks about.)* 20

FLORINDA *(aside)*: Antonio? Sure I heard amiss.

PEDRO: But who will not excuse a happy lover
When soft fair arms confine the yielding neck,
And the kind whisper languishingly breathes
"Must you be gone so soon?" 25
Sure I had dwelt forever on her bosom—
But stay, he's here.

(Enter Belvile dressed in Antonio's clothes.)

FLORINDA *[aside]*: 'Tis not Belvile; half my fears are vanished.

PEDRO: Antonio! 30

BELVILE *(aside)*: This must be he.—You're early, sir; I do not use to be outdone this way.

PEDRO: The wretched, sir, are watchful, and 'tis enough you've the advantage of me in Angellica.

BELVILE *(aside)*: Angellica! Or° I've mistook my man, or 35
else Antonio! Can he forget his interest in Florinda and fight for common prize?

PEDRO: Come, sir, you know our terms.

BELVILE *(aside)*: By heaven, not I.—No talking; I am ready, sir. 40

(Offers to fight; Florinda runs in.)

35. Or: Either.

FLORINDA (*to Belvile*): Oh, hold! Whoever you be, I do conjure you hold! If you strike here, I die!

PEDRO: Florinda!

BELVILE: Florinda imploring for my rival!

45 PEDRO: Away; this kindness is unseasonable.

(*Puts her by; they fight; she runs in just as Belvile disarms Pedro.*)

FLORINDA: Who are you, sir, that dares deny my prayers?

BELVILE: Thy prayers destroy him; if thou wouldst preserve him, do that thou'rt unacquainted with, and curse him.

(*She holds him.*)

50 FLORINDA: By all you hold most dear, by her you love, I do conjure you, touch him not.

BELVILE: By her I love?
See, I obey, and at your feet resign
The useless trophy of my victory.

(*Lays his sword at her feet.*)

55 PEDRO: Antonio, you've done enough to prove you love Florinda.

BELVILE: Love Florinda! Does heaven love adoration, prayer, or penitence? Love her? Here, sir, your sword again.

(*Snatches up the sword and gives it to him.*)

60 Upon this truth I'll fight my life away.

PEDRO: No, you've redeemed my sister, and my friendship.

(*He gives him Florinda, and pulls off his vizard to show his face, and puts it on again.*)

BELVILE: Don Pedro!

PEDRO: Can you resign your claims to other women, and 65 give your heart entirely to Florinda?

BELVILE: Entire, as dying saints' confessions are!
I can delay my happiness no longer:
This minute let me make Florinda mine.

PEDRO: This minute let it be. No time so proper: This 70 night my father will arrive from Rome, and possibly may hinder what we purpose.

FLORINDA: O, heavens! This minute?

(*Enter Masqueraders and pass over.*)

BELVILE: Oh, do not ruin me!

PEDRO: The place begins to fill, and that we may not 75 be observed, do you walk off to St. Peter's church, where I will meet you and conclude your happiness.

BELVILE: I'll meet you there.—(*Aside.*) If there be no more saints' churches in Naples.

FLORINDA: Oh, stay, sir, and recall your hasty doom! 80 Alas, I have not yet prepared my heart To entertain so strange a guest.

PEDRO: Away; this silly modesty is assumed too late.

BELVILE: Heaven, madam, what do you do?

FLORINDA: Do? Despise the man that lays a tyrant's claim
85 To what he ought to conquer by submission.

BELVILE: You do not know me. Move a little this way.
(*Draws her aside.*)

FLORINDA: Yes, you may force me even to the altar,
But not the holy man that offers there
Shall force me to be thine.

(*Pedro talks to Callis this while.*)

BELVILE: Oh, do not lose so blest an opportunity!   90

(*Pulls off his vizard.*)

See, 'tis your Belvile, not Antonio,
Whom your mistaken scorn and anger ruins.

FLORINDA: Belvile!
Where was my soul it could not meet thy voice,
And take this knowledge in.   95

(*As they are talking, enter Willmore, finely dressed, and Frederick.*)

WILLMORE: No intelligence? No news of Belvile yet? Well, I am the most unlucky rascal in nature. Ha! Am I deceived, or is it he? Look, Fred! 'Tis he, my dear Belvile!

(*Runs and embraces him; Belvile's vizard falls out on's hand.*)

BELVILE: Hell and confusion seize thee!   100

PEDRO: Ha! Belvile! I beg your pardon, sir.

(*Takes Florinda from him.*)

BELVILE: Nay, touch her not. She's mine by conquest, sir; I won her by my sword.

WILLMORE: Didst thou so? And egad, child, we'll keep her by the sword.   105

(*Draws on Pedro; Belvile goes between.*)

BELVILE: Stand off!
Thou'rt so profanely lewd, so curst by heaven,
All quarrels thou espousest must be fatal.

WILLMORE: Nay, an you be so hot, my valor's coy,
And shall be courted when you want it next.   110
(*Puts up his sword.*)

BELVILE (*to Pedro*): You know I ought to claim a victor's right,
But you're the brother to divine Florinda,
To whom I'm such a slave. To purchase her
I durst not hurt the man she holds so dear.

PEDRO: 'Twas by Antonio's, not by Belvile's sword   115
This question should have been decided, sir.
I must confess much to your bravery's due,
Both now and when I met you last in arms;
But I am nicely punctual in my word,
As men of honor ought, and beg your pardon: 120
For this mistake another time shall clear.

(*Aside to Florinda as they are going out.*)

—This was some plot between you and Belvile,
But I'll prevent you.

[*Exeunt Pedro and Florinda.*]

(*Belvile looks after her and begins to walk up and down in rage.*)

WILLMORE: Do not be modest now and lose the woman. But if we shall fetch her back so—

BELVILE: Do not speak to me!

WILLMORE: Not speak to you? Egad, I'll speak to you, and will be answered, too.

BELVILE: Will you, sir?

WILLMORE: I know I've done some mischief, but I'm so dull a puppy that I'm the son of a whore if I know how or where. Prithee inform my understanding.

BELVILE: Leave me, I say, and leave me instantly!

WILLMORE: I will not leave you in this humor, nor till I know my crime.

BELVILE: Death, I'll tell you, sir—

(*Draws and runs at Willmore; he runs out, Belvile after hint; Frederick interposes.*)

(*Enter Angellica, Moretta, and Sebastian.*)

ANGELLICA: Ha! Sebastian, is that not Willmore?
Haste! haste and bring him back.

[*Exit Sebastian.*]

FREDERICK [*aside*]: The colonel's mad: I never saw him thus before. I'll after 'em lest he do some mischief, for I am sure Willmore will not draw on him.   (*Exit.*)

ANGELLICA: I am all rage! My first desires defeated!
For one for aught he knows that has no
Other merit than her quality.
Her being Don Pedro's sister. He loves her!
I know 'tis so. Dull, dull, insensible,
He will not see me now, though oft invited,
And broke his word last night. False perjured man!
He that but yesterday fought for my favors,
And would have made his life a sacrifice
To've gained one night with me,
Must now be hired and courted to my arms.

MORETTA: I told you what would come on't, but Moretta's an old doting fool. Why did you give him five hundred crowns, but to set himself out for other lovers? You should have kept him poor if you had meant to have had any good from him.

ANGELLICA: Oh, name not such mean trifles! Had I given
Him all my youth has earned from sin,
I had not lost a thought nor sigh upon't.
But I have given him my eternal rest,
My whole repose, my future joys, my heart!
My virgin heart, Moretta! Oh, 'tis gone!

MORETTA: Curse on him, here he comes. How fine she has made him, too.

(*Enter Willmore and Sebastian; Angellica turns and walks away.*)

WILLMORE: How now, turned shadow?
Fly when I pursue, and follow when I fly? (*Sings.*)
Stay, gentle shadow of my dove,
And tell me ere I go,

Whether the substance may not prove
A fleeting thing like you.

(*As she turns she looks on him.*)

There's a soft kind look remaining yet.

ANGELLICA: Well, sir, you may be gay: All happiness, all joys pursue you still. Fortune's your slave, and gives you every hour choice of new hearts and beauties, till you are cloyed° with the repeated bliss which others vainly languish for. But know, false man, that I shall be revenged.

(*Turns away in rage.*)

WILLMORE: So, gad, there are of those faint-hearted lovers, whom such a sharp lesson next their hearts would make as impotent as fourscore.° Pox o' this whining; my business is to laugh and love. A pox on't, I hate your sullen lover: A man shall lose as much time to put you in humor now as would serve to gain a new woman.

ANGELLICA: I scorn to cool that fire I cannot raise,
Or do the drudgery of your virtuous mistress.

WILLMORE: A virtuous mistress? Death, what a thing thou hast found out for me! Why, what the devil should I do with a virtuous woman, a sort of ill-natured creature that takes a pride to torment a lover. Virtue is but an infirmity in woman, a disease that renders even the handsome ungrateful; whilst the ill-favored, for want of solicitations and address, only fancy themselves so. I have lain with a woman of quality who has all the while been railing at whores.

ANGELLICA: I will not answer for your mistress's virtue,
Though she be young enough to know no guilt;
And I could wish you would persuade my heart
'Twas the two hundred thousand crowns you
courted.

WILLMORE: Two hundred thousand crowns! What story's this? What trick? What woman, ha?

ANGELLICA: How strange you make it. Have you forgot the creature you entertained on the Piazzo last night?

WILLMORE (*aside*): Ha! My gypsy worth two hundred thousand crowns! Oh, how I long to be with her! Pox, I knew she was of quality.

ANGELLICA: False man! I see my ruin in thy face.
How many vows you breathed upon my bosom
Never to be unjust. Have you forgot so soon?

WILLMORE: Faith, no; I was just coming to repeat 'em. But here's a humor indeed would make a man a saint.—(*Aside.*) Would she would be angry enough to leave me, and command me not to wait on her.

(*Enter Hellena dressed in man's clothes.*)

HELLENA: This must be Angellica: I know it by her mumping° matron here. Ay, ay, 'tis she. My mad captain's with her, too, for all his swearing. How this

---

176. cloyed: Full to bursting.   **181. as fourscore:** As an eighty-year-old.   **217. mumping:** Moping.

unconstant humor makes me love him!—Pray, good
grave gentlewoman, is not this Angellica?

MORETTA: My too young sir, it is.—[*Aside.*] I hope 'tis
one from Don Antonio.   (*Goes to Angellica.*)

HELLENA (*aside*): Well, something I'll do to vex him for
this.

ANGELLICA: I will not speak with him. Am I in humor to
receive a lover?

WILLMORE: Not speak with him? Why, I'll be gone, and
wait your idler minutes. Can I show less obedience to
the thing I love so fondly?

(*Offers to go.*)

ANGELLICA: A fine excuse this! Stay—

WILLMORE: And hinder your advantage? Should I repay
your bounties so ungratefully?

ANGELLICA [*to Hellena*]: Come hither, boy.—
[*To Willmore.*] That I may let you see

How much above the advantages you name
I prize one minute's joy with you.

WILLMORE (*impatient to be gone*): Oh, you destroy me
with this endearment.—[*Aside.*] Death, how shall
I get away?—Madam, 'twill not be fit I should be
seen with you. Besides, it will not be convenient. And
I've a friend—that's dangerously sick.

ANGELLICA: I see you're impatient. Yet you shall stay.

WILLMORE (*aside*): And miss my assignation with my
gypsy.

(*Walks about impatiently; Moretta brings Hellena, who
addresses herself to Angellica.*)

HELLENA: Madam,
You'll hardly pardon my intrusion
When you shall know my business,
And I'm too young to tell my tale with art;
But there must be a wondrous store of goodness
Where so much beauty dwells.

ANGELLICA: A pretty advocate, whoever sent thee.
Prithee proceed.

(*To Willmore, who is stealing off.*)
—Nay, sir, you shall not go.

WILLMORE (*aside*): Then I shall lose my dear gypsy forever. Pox on't, she stays me out of spite.

HELLENA: I am related to a lady, madam,
Young, rich, and nobly born, but has the fate
To be in love with a young English gentleman.
Strangely she loves him, at first sight she loved him,
But did adore him when she heard him speak;
For he, she said, had charms in every word
That failed not to surprise, to wound and conquer.

WILLMORE (*aside*): Ha! Egad, I hope this concerns me.

ANGELLICA (*aside*): 'Tis my false man he means. Would
he were gone:
This praise will raise his pride, and ruin me.
(*To Willmore.*)—Well,
Since you are so impatient to be gone,
I will release you, sir.

WILLMORE (*aside*): Nay, then I'm sure 'twas me he
spoke of: This cannot be the effects of kindness in

her.—No, Madam, I've considered better on't, and
will not give you cause of jealousy.

ANGELLICA: But sir, I've business that—

WILLMORE: This shall not do; I know 'tis but to try me.

ANGELLICA: Well, to your story, boy.—(*Aside.*) Though
'twill undo me.

HELLENA: With this addition to his other beauties,
He won her unresisting tender heart.
He vowed, and sighed, and swore he loved her dearly;
And she believed the cunning flatterer,
And thought herself the happiest maid alive.
Today was the appointed time by both
To consummate their bliss:
The virgin, altar, and the priest were dressed;
And whilst she languished for th'expected
bridegroom,
She heard he paid his broken vows to you.

WILLMORE (*aside*): So, this is some dear rogue that's in
love with me, and this way lets me know it. Or, if
it be not me, he means someone whose place I may
supply.

ANGELLICA: Now I perceive
The cause of thy impatience to be gone,
And all the business of this glorious dress.

WILLMORE: Damn the young prater; I know not what he
means.

HELLENA: Madam,
In your fair eyes I read too much concern
To tell my further business.

ANGELLICA: Prithee, sweet youth, talk on: Thou mayst
perhaps
Raise here a storm that may undo my passion,
And then I'll grant thee anything.

HELLENA: Madam, 'tis to entreat you (oh
unreasonable)
You would not see this stranger.
For if you do, she vows you are undone;
Though nature never made a man so excellent,
And sure he 'ad been a god, but for inconstancy.

WILLMORE (*aside*): Ah, rogue, how finely he's instructed!
'Tis plain, some woman that has seen me *en passant.*°

ANGELLICA: Oh, I shall burst with jealousy! Do you know
the man you speak of?

HELLENA: Yes, madam, he used to be in buff and scarlet.

ANGELLICA (*to Willmore*): Thou false as hell, what canst
thou say to this?

WILLMORE: By heaven—

ANGELLICA: Hold, do not damn thyself—

HELLENA: Nor hope to be believed.

(*He walks about; they follow.*)

ANGELLICA: Oh perjured man!
Is't thus you pay my generous passion back?

HELLENA: Why would you, sir, abuse my lady's faith?

ANGELLICA: And use me so unhumanely.

HELLENA: A maid so young, so innocent—

---

306. *en passant:* In passing.

320 WILLMORE: Ah, young devil!

ANGELLICA: Dost thou not know thy life is in my
power?

HELLENA: Or think my lady cannot be revenged?

WILLMORE (*aside*): So, so, the storm comes finely on.

325 ANGELLICA: Now thou art silent: Guilt has struck thee
dumb.
Oh, hadst thou still been so, I'd lived in safety.

(*She turns away and weeps.*)

WILLMORE (*aside to Hellena*): Sweetheart, the lady's
name and house—quickly! I'm impatient to be with
her.

(*Looks toward Angellica to watch her turning, and as
she comes towards them he meets her.*)

330 HELLENA (*aside*): So, now is he for another woman.

WILLMORE: The impudent'st young thing in nature:
I cannot persuade him out of his error, madam.

ANGELLICA: I know he's in the right; yet thou'st a
tongue
That would persuade him to deny his faith.

(*In rage walks away.*)

335 WILLMORE (*said softly to Hellena*): Her name, her
name, dear boy!

HELLENA: Have you forgot it, sir?

WILLMORE (*aside*): Oh, I perceive he's not to know I am
a stranger to his lady.—Yes, yes, I do know, but I

340 have forgot the—(*Angellica turns.*)—By heaven,
such early confidence I never saw.

ANGELLICA: Did I not charge you with this mistress,
sir?
Which you denied, though I beheld your perjury.
This little generosity of thine has rendered back my
heart.   (*Walks away.*)

345 WILLMORE (*to Hellena*): So, you have made sweet work
here, my little mischief. Look your lady be kind
and good-natured now, or I shall have but a cursed
bargain on't. (*Angellica turns toward them.*)—The
rogue's bred up to mischief; art thou so great a fool

350 to credit him?

ANGELLICA: Yes, I do, and you in vain impose upon me.
Come hither, boy. Is not this he you spake of?

HELLENA: I think it is. I cannot swear, but I vow he has
just such another lying lover's look.

(*Hellena looks in his face; he gazes on her.*)

355 WILLMORE (*aside*): Ha! Do I not know that face? By
heaven, my little gypsy! What a dull dog was I: Had I
but looked that way I'd known her. Are all my hopes
of a new woman banished?—Egad, if I do not fit
thee for this, hang me.—[*To Angellica.*] Madam, I

360 have found out the plot.

HELLENA [*aside*]: Oh lord, what does he say? Am I discovered now?

WILLMORE: Do you see this young spark here?

HELLENA [*aside*]: He'll tell her who I am.

365 WILLMORE: Who do you think this is?

HELLENA [*aside*]: Ay, ay, he does know me.—Nay, dear
captain, I am undone if you discover me.

WILLMORE: Nay, nay, no cogging;° she shall know what a
precious mistress I have.

HELLENA: Will you be such a devil?   370

WILLMORE: Nay, nay, I'll teach you to spoil sport you will
not make.—This small ambassador comes not from
a person of quality, as you imagine and he says, but
from a very errant gypsy: the talking'st, prating'st,
canting'st little animal thou ever saw'st.   375

ANGELLICA: What news you tell me, that's the thing I
mean.

HELLENA (*aside*): Would I were well off the place! If ever
I go a-captain-hunting again—

WILLMORE: Mean that thing? That gypsy thing? Thou   380
mayst as well be jealous of thy monkey or parrot as
of her. A German motion° were worth a dozen of her,
and a dream were a better enjoyment—a creature of
a constitution fitter for heaven than man.

HELLENA (*aside*): Though I'm sure he lies, yet this vexes 385
me.

ANGELLICA: You are mistaken: she's a Spanish woman
made up of no such dull materials.

WILLMORE: Materials? Egad, an she be made of any
that will either dispense or admit of love, I'll be   390
bound to continence.

HELLENA (*aside to him*): Unreasonable man, do you
think so?

WILLMORE: You may return, my little brazen head, and
tell your lady, that till she be handsome enough to be 395
beloved, or I dull enough to be religious, there will be
small hopes of me.

ANGELLICA: Did you not promise, then, to marry her?

WILLMORE: Not I, by heaven.

ANGELLICA: You cannot undeceive my fears and tor-   400
ments, till you have vowed you will not marry her.

HELLENA (*aside*): If he swears that, he'll be revenged on
me indeed for all my rogueries.

ANGELLICA: I know what arguments you'll bring against
me: fortune and honor.   405

WILLMORE: Honor! I tell you, I hate it in your sex; and
those that fancy themselves possessed of that fop-
pery are the most impertinently troublesome of all
womankind, and will transgress nine commandments to keep one. And to satisfy your jealousy, I   410
swear—

HELLENA (*aside to him*): Oh, no swearing, dear captain.

WILLMORE: If it were possible I should ever be inclined
to marry, it should be some kind young sinner: one
that has generosity enough to give a favor hand-   415
somely to one that can ask it discreetly, one that has
wit enough to manage an intrigue of love. Oh, how
civil such a wench is to a man that does her the honor
to marry her.

ANGELLICA: By heaven, there's no faith in anything he   420
says.

(*Enter Sebastian.*)

368. **cogging:** Fawning, coaxing.   382. **motion:** Puppet show.

SEBASTIAN: Madam, Don Antonio—

ANGELLICA: Come hither.

425 HELLENA [aside]: Ha! Antonio! He may be coming hither, and he'll certainly discover me. I'll therefore retire without a ceremony.   (Exit Hellena.)

ANGELLICA: I'll see him. Get my coach ready.

SEBASTIAN: It waits you, madam.

430 WILLMORE [aside]: This is lucky.—What, madam, now I may be gone and leave you to the enjoyment of my rival?

ANGELLICA: Dull man, that canst not see how ill, how poor,
      That false dissimulation looks. Be gone,
      And never let me see thy cozening face again,
435   Lest I relapse and kill thee.

WILLMORE: Yes, you can spare me now. Farewell, till you're in better humor.—[Aside.] I'm glad of this release. Now for my gypsy:
      For though to worse we change, yet still we find
440   New joys, new charms, in a new miss that's kind.
                              (Exit Willmore.)

ANGELLICA: He's gone, and in this ague° of my soul
      The shivering fit returns.
      Oh, with what willing haste he took his leave,
      As if the longed-for minute were arrived
445   Of some blest assignation.
      In vain I have consulted all my charms,
      In vain this beauty prized, in vain believed
      My eyes could kindle any lasting fires;
      I had forgot my name, my infamy,
450   And the reproach that honor lays on those
      That dare pretend a sober passion here.
      Nice reputation, though it leave behind
      More virtues than inhabit where that dwells,
      Yet that once gone, those virtues shine no more.
455   Then since I am not fit to be beloved,
      I am resolved to think on a revenge
      On him that soothed° me thus to my undoing.
                              (Exeunt.)

Scene III

(A street. Enter Florinda and Valeria in habits different from what they have been seen in.)

FLORINDA: We're happily escaped, and yet I tremble still.

VALERIA: A lover, and fear? Why, I am but half an one, and yet I have courage for any attempt. Would Hellena were here: I would fain have had her as deep in 5 this mischief as we; she'll fare but ill else, I doubt.

FLORINDA: She pretended a visit to the Augustine nuns; but I believe some other design carried her out; pray heaven we light on her. Prithee, what didst do with Callis?

441. **ague:** Fever, accompanied by shivering. 457. **soothed:** Advised.

VALERIA: When I saw no reason would do good on her, I 10 followed her into the wardrobe, and as she was looking for something in a great chest, I toppled her in by the heels, snatched the key of the apartment where you were confined, locked her in, and left her bawling for help. 15

FLORINDA: 'Tis well you resolve to follow my fortunes, for thou darest never appear at home again after such an action.

VALERIA: That's according as the young stranger and I shall agree. But to our business. I delivered your note 20 to Belvile when I got out under pretense of going to mass. I found him at his lodging, and believe me it came seasonably, for never was man in so desperate a condition. I told him of your resolution of making your escape today if your brother would be absent 25 long enough to permit you; if not, to die rather than be Antonio's.

FLORINDA: Thou should'st have told him I was confined to my chamber upon my brother's suspicion that the business on the Molo was a plot laid between him 30 and I.

VALERIA: I said all this, and told him your brother was now gone to his devotion; and he resolves to visit every church till he find him, and not only undeceive him in that, but caress him so as shall delay his return 35 home.

FLORINDA: Oh heavens! He's here, and Belvile with him, too.

(They put on their vizards.)

(Enter Don Pedro, Belvile, Willmore; Belvile and Don Pedro seeming in serious discourse.)

VALERIA: Walk boldly by them, and I'll come at a distance, lest he suspect us. 40

(She walks by them and looks back on them.)

WILLMORE: Ha! A woman, and of excellent mien!

PEDRO: She throws a kind look back on you.

WILLMORE: Death, 'tis a likely wench and that kind look shall not be cast away. I'll follow her.

BELVILE: Prithee do not. 45

WILLMORE: Do not? By heavens, to the antipodies,° with such an invitation.

                    (She goes out, and Willmore follows her.)

BELVILE: 'Tis a mad fellow for a wench.

(Enter Frederick.)

FREDERICK: Oh, colonel, such news!

BELVILE: Prithee what? 50

FREDERICK: News that will make you laugh in spite of fortune.

BELVILE: What, Blunt has had some damned trick put upon him? Cheated, banged, or clapped?°

46. **antipodies:** Antipodes; parts of the earth diametrically opposite. 54. **clapped:** Given gonorrhea.

55 FREDERICK: Cheated, sir, rarely cheated of all but his shirt and drawers; the unconscionable whore too turned him out before consummation, so that, traversing the streets at midnight, the watch found him in this *fresco* and conducted him home. By heaven, 60 'tis such a sight, and yet I durst as well been hanged as laughed at him or pity him: He beats all that do but ask him a question, and is in such an humor.

PEDRO: Who is't has met with this ill usage, sir?

BELVILE: A friend of ours whom you must see for mirth's 65 sake.—(*Aside.*) I'll employ him to give Florinda time for an escape.

PEDRO: What is he?

BELVILE: A young countryman of ours, one that has been educated at so plentiful a rate he yet ne'er knew 70 the want of money; and 'twill be a great jest to see how simply he'll look without it. For my part, I'll lend him none: And the rogue know not how to put on a borrowing face and ask first, I'll let him see how good 'tis to play our parts whilst I play his. Prithee, 75 Fred, do you go home and keep him in that posture till we come. (*Exeunt.*)

(*Enter Florinda from the farther end of the scene, looking behind her.*)

FLORINDA: I am followed still. Ha! My brother too advancing this way! Good heavens defend me from being seen by him! (*She goes off.*)

(*Enter Willmore, and after him Valeria, at a little distance.*)

80 WILLMORE: Ah, there she sails! She looks back as she were willing to be boarded; I'll warrant her prize.°

(*He goes out, Valeria following.*)

(*Enter Hellena, just as he goes out, with a page.*)

HELLENA: Ha, is not that my captain that has a woman in chase? 'Tis not Angellica.—Boy, follow those people at a distance, and bring me an account where 85 they go in. (*Exit Page.*) —I'll find his haunts, and plague him everywhere. Ha! My brother!

(*Belvile, Willmore, Pedro cross the stage; Hellena runs off.*)

Scene IV

(*Scene changes to another street. Enter Florinda.*)

FLORINDA: What shall I do? My brother now pursues me. Will no kind power protect me from his tyranny? Ha! Here's a door open; I'll venture in, since nothing can be worse than to fall into his hands. My life and 5 honor are at stake, and my necessity has no choice. (*She goes in.*)

81. **warrant her prize:** Consider her worthy of pursuing.

(*Enter Valeria, Hellena's Page peeping after Florinda.*)

PAGE: Here she went in; I shall remember this house. (*Exit Boy.*)

VALERIA: This is Belvile's lodging, she's gone in as readily as if she knew it. Ha! Here's that mad fellow again; I dare not venture in. I'll watch my opportunity. (*Goes aside.*)

(*Enter Willmore, gazing about him.*)

WILLMORE: I have lost her hereabouts. Pox on't, she 10 must not 'scape me so. (*Goes out.*)

Scene V

(*Scene changes to Blunt's chamber, discovers him sitting on a couch in his shirt and drawers, reading.*)

BLUNT: So, now my mind's a little at peace, since I have resolved revenge. A pox on this tailor, though, for not bringing home the clothes I bespoke. And a pox of all poor cavaliers: A man can never keep a spare suit for 'em, and I shall have these rogues come in and find me 5 naked, and then I'm undone. But I'm resolved to arm myself: The rascals shall not insult over me too much. (*Puts on an old rusty sword and buff belt.*) Now, how like a morris dancer° I am equipped! A fine ladylike whore to cheat me thus without affording me a kindness for my money! A pox light on her, I shall never be 10 reconciled to the sex more; she has made me as faithless as a physician, as uncharitable as a churchman, and as ill-natured as a poet. Oh, how I'll use all womankind hereafter! What would I give to have one of 15 'em within my reach now! Any mortal thing in petticoats, kind fortune, send me, and I'll forgive thy last night's malice.—Here's a cursed book, too—a warning to all young travelers—that can instruct me how to prevent such mischiefs now 'tis too late. Well, 'tis a 20 rare convenient thing to read a little now and then, as well as hawk and hunt.

(*Sits down again and reads.*)

(*Enter to him Florinda.*)

FLORINDA: This house is haunted, sure: 'Tis well furnished, and no living thing inhabits it. Ha! A man! Heavens, how he's attired! Sure 'tis some rope 25 dancer, or fencing master. I tremble now for fear, and yet I must venture now to speak to him.—Sir, if I may not interrupt your meditations—

(*He starts up and gazes.*)

BLUNT: Ha, what's here? Are my wishes granted? And is not that a she creature? 'Adsheartlikins, 'tis.—What 30 wretched thing art thou, ha?

FLORINDA: Charitable sir, you've told yourself already

9. **morris dancer:** The morris dance is a lively dance performed by men wearing costumes and bells.

what I am: a very wretched maid, forced by a strange
unlucky accident to seek a safety here, and must be
35   ruined if you do not grant it.

BLUNT: Ruined! Is there any ruin so inevitable as that
which now threatens thee? Dost thou know, miserable woman, into what den of mischiefs thou art
40   fallen; what abyss of confusion, ha? Dost not see
something in my looks that frights thy guilty soul,
and makes thee wish to change that shape of woman
for any humble animal, or devil? For those were safer
for thee, and less mischievous.

FLORINDA: Alas, what mean you, sir? I must confess,
45   your looks have something in 'em makes me fear, but
I beseech you, as you seem a gentleman, pity a harmless virgin that takes your house for sanctuary.

BLUNT: Talk on, talk on; and weep, too, till my faith
so return. Do, flatter me out of my senses again. A
50   harmless virgin with a pox; as much one as t'other,
'adsheartlikins. Why, what the devil, can I not be safe
in my house for you, not in my chamber? Nay, not
even being naked too cannot secure me? This is an
impudence greater than has invaded me yet. Come,
55   no resistance.   (*Pulls her rudely.*)

FLORINDA: Dare you be so cruel?

BLUNT: Cruel? 'Adsheartlikins, as a galley slave, or a
Spanish whore. Cruel? Yes, I will kiss and beat thee
all over, kiss and see thee all over; thou shalt lie with
60   me too, not that I care for the enjoyment, but to let
thee see I have ta'en deliberated malice to thee, and
will be revenged on one whore for the sins of another.
I will smile and deceive thee; flatter thee, and beat
thee; embrace thee and rob thee, as she did me; fawn
65   on thee, and strip thee stark naked; then hang thee
out at my window by the heels, with a paper of
scurvy verses fastened to thy breast in praise of damnable women. Come, come, along.

FLORINDA: Alas, sir, must I be sacrificed for the crimes
70   of the most infamous of my sex? I never understood
the sins you name.

BLUNT: Do, persuade the fool you love him, or that, one
of you can be just or honest; tell me I was not an easy
coxcomb, or any strange impossible tale: It will be
75   believed sooner than thy false showers or protestations. A generation of damned hypocrites! To flatter
my very clothes from my back! Dissembling witches!
Are these the returns you make an honest gentleman
that trusts, believes, and loves you? But if I be not
80   even with you—Come along, or I shall—(*Pulls her
again.*)

(*Enter Frederick.*)

FREDERICK: Ha, what's here to do?

BLUNT: 'Adsheartlikins, Fred, I am glad thou art come, to
be a witness of my dire revenge.

FREDERICK: What's this, a person of quality too, who is
85   upon the ramble° to supply the defects of some grave
impotent husband?

85. **upon the ramble:** Rambling, wandering.

BLUNT: No, this has another pretense: Some very unfortunate accident brought her hither, to save a life pursued by I know not who or why, and forced to take
sanctuary here at fool's haven. 'Adsheartlikins, to me   90
of all mankind for protection? Is the ass to be cajoled
again, think ye? No, young one, no prayers or tears
shall mitigate my rage; therefore prepare for both
my pleasures of enjoyment and revenge. For I am resolved to make up my loss here on thy body: I'll take   95
it out in kindness and in beating.

FREDERICK: Now, mistress of mine, what do you think
of this?

FLORINDA: I think he will not, dares not be so barbarous.

FREDERICK: Have a care, Blunt, she fetched a deep sigh;   100
she is enamored with thy shirt and drawers. She'll
strip thee even of that; there are of her calling such
unconscionable baggages and such dexterous thieves,
they'll flea° a man and he shall ne'er miss his skin till
he feels the cold. There was a countryman of ours   105
robbed of a row of teeth whilst he was a-sleeping,
which the jilt made him buy again when he waked.
You see, lady, how little reason we have to trust you.

BLUNT: 'Adsheartlikins, why this is most abominable!

FLORINDA: Some such devils there may be, but by all   110
that's holy, I am none such. I entered here to save a
life in danger.

BLUNT: For no goodness, I'll warrant her.

FREDERICK: Faith, damsel, you had e'en confessed the
plain truth, for we are fellows not to be caught twice   115
in the same trap. Look on that wreck: a tight vessel
when he set out of haven, well trimmed and laden.
And see how a female picaroon of this island of
rogues has shattered him, and canst thou hope for
any mercy?   120

BLUNT: No, no, gentlewoman, come along; 'adsheartlikins, we must be better acquainted.—We'll both lie
with her, and then let me alone to bang her.

FREDERICK: I'm ready to serve you in matters of revenge
that has a double pleasure in't.   125

BLUNT: Well said.—You hear, little one, how you are
condemned by public vote to the bed within; there's
no resisting your destiny, sweetheart.

(*Pulls her.*)

FLORINDA: Stay, sir. I have seen you with Belvile, an
English cavalier. For his sake, use me kindly. You   130
know him, sir.

BLUNT: Belvile? Why yes, sweeting, we do know Belvile,
and wish he were with us now. He's a cormorant at
whore and bacon:° He'd have a limb or two of thee,
my virgin pullet. But 'tis no matter; we'll leave him   135
the bones to pick.

FLORINDA: Sir, if you have any esteem for that Belvile, I
conjure you to treat me with more gentleness; he'll
thank you for the justice.

FREDERICK: Hark'ee, Blunt, I doubt we are mistaken in   140
this matter.

104. **flea:** Strip off the skin (flay).   **133–134. cormorant . . .
bacon:** Glutton for sex.

FLORINDA: Sir, if you find me not worth Belvile's care, use me as you please. And that you may think I merit better treatment than you threaten, pray take this
145 present.

(*Gives him a ring; he looks on it.*)

BLUNT: Hum, a diamond! Why, 'tis a wonderful virtue now that lies in this ring, a mollifying virtue. 'Adsheartlikins, there's more persuasive rhetoric in't than all her sex can utter.

150 FREDERICK: I begin to suspect something, and 'twould anger us vilely to be trussed up for a rape upon a maid of quality, when we only believe we ruffle a harlot.

BLUNT: Thou art a credulous fellow, but 'adsheartlikins, I have no faith yet. Why, my saint prattled as par-
155 lously as this does; she gave me a bracelet, too, a devil on her! But I sent my man to sell it today for necessaries, and it proved as counterfeit as her vows of love.

FREDERICK: However, let it reprieve her till we see
160 Belvile.

BLUNT: That's hard, yet I will grant it.

(*Enter a Servant.*)

SERVANT: Oh, sir, the colonel is just come in with his new friend and a Spaniard of quality, and talks of having you to dinner with 'em.

165 BLUNT: 'Adsheartlikins, I'm undone! I would not see 'em for the world. Hark'ee, Fred, lock up the wench in your chamber.

FREDERICK: Fear nothing, madam: Whate'er he threatens, you are safe whilst in my hands.

(*Exeunt Frederick and Florinda.*)

170 BLUNT: And sirrah, upon your life, say I am not at home, or that I'm asleep, or—or—anything. Away; I'll prevent their coming this way.

(*Locks the door, and exeunt.*)

ACT V

(*Blunt's chamber. After a great knocking as at his chamber door, enter Blunt softly crossing the stage, in his shirt and drawers as before.*)

[VOICES] (*call within*): Ned! Ned Blunt! Ned Blunt!

BLUNT: The rogues are up in arms. 'Adsheartlikins, this villainous Frederick has betrayed me: They have heard of my blessed fortune.

5 [VOICES] (*and knocking within*): Ned Blunt! Ned! Ned!

BELVILE [*within*]: Why, he's dead, sir, without dispute dead; he has not been seen today. Let's break open the door. Here, boy—

BLUNT: Ha, break open the door? 'Adsheartlikins, that
10 mad fellow will be as good as his word.

BELVILE [*within*]: Boy, bring something to force the door.

(*A great noise within, at the door again.*)

BLUNT: So, now must I speak in my own defense, I'll try what rhetoric will do.—Hold, hold! What do you mean, gentlemen, what do you mean?

BELVILE (*within*): Oh, rogue, art alive? Prithee open the
15 door and convince us.

BLUNT: Yes, I am alive, gentlemen, but at present a little busy.

BELVILE (*within*): How, Blunt grown a man of business? Come, come, open and let's see this miracle.
20

BLUNT: No, no, no, no, gentlemen, 'tis no great business. But—I am—at—my devotion. 'Adsheartlikins, will you not allow a man time to pray?

BELVILE (*within*): Turned religious? A greater wonder than the first! Therefore open quickly, or we shall
25 unhinge, we shall.

BLUNT [*aside*]: This won't do.—Why hark'ee, colonel, to tell you the truth, I am about a necessary affair of life: I have a wench with me. You apprehend me?— The devil's in't if they be so uncivil as to disturb me
30 now.

WILLMORE [*within*]: How, a wench? Nay then, we must enter and partake. No resistance. Unless it be your lady of quality, and then we'll keep our distance.

BLUNT: So, the business is out.
35

WILLMORE [*within*]: Come, come, lend's more hands to the door. Now heave, all together. (*Breaks open the door.*) So, well done, my boys.

(*Enter Belvile [and his Page], Willmore, Frederick, and Pedro. Blunt looks simply, they all laugh at him; he lays his hand on his sword, and comes up to Willmore.*)

BLUNT: Hark'ee, sir, laugh out your laugh quickly, d'ye hear, and be gone. I shall spoil your sport else, 'ads-
40 heartlikins, sir. I shall. The jest has been carried on too long.—(*Aside.*) A plague upon my tailor!

WILLMORE: 'Sdeath, how the whore has dressed him! Faith, sir, I'm sorry.

BLUNT: Are you so, sir? Keep't to yourself then, sir, I
45 advise you, d'ye hear, for I can as little endure your pity as his mirth.

(*Lays his hand on's sword.*)

BELVILE: Indeed, Willmore, thou wert a little too rough with Ned Blunt's mistress. Call a person of quality whore, and one so young, so handsome, and so elo-
50 quent? Ha, ha, he.

BLUNT: Hark'ee, sir, you know me, and know I can be angry. Have a care, for 'adsheartlikins, I can fight, too, I can, sir. Do you mark me? No more.

BELVILE: Why so peevish, good Ned? Some disappoint-
55 ments, I'll warrant. What, did the jealous count, her husband, return just in the nick?

BLUNT: Or the devil, sir. (*They laugh.*) D'ye laugh? Look ye settle me a good sober countenance, and that quickly, too, or you shall know Ned Blunt is not—
60

BELVILE: Not everybody, we know that.

BLUNT: Not an ass to be laughed at, sir.

WILLMORE: Unconscionable sinner! To bring a lover so near his happiness—a vigorous passionate lover—

65 and then not only cheat him of his movables, but his very desires, too.

BELVILE: Ah, sir, a mistress is a trifle with Blunt; he'll have a dozen the next time he looks abroad. His eyes have charms not to be resisted; there needs no more 70 than to expose that taking person to the view of the fair, and he leads 'em all in triumph.

PEDRO: Sir, though I'm a stranger to you, I am ashamed at the rudeness of my nation; and could you learn who did it, would assist you to make an example of 75 'em.

BLUNT: Why ay, there's one speaks sense now, and handsomely. And let me tell you, gentlemen, I should not have showed myself like a jack pudding° thus to have made you mirth, but that I have revenge within my 80 power. For know, I have got into my possession a female, who had better have fallen under any curse than the ruin I design her. 'Adsheartlikins, she assaulted me here in my own lodgings, and had doubtless committed a rape upon me, had not this sword 85 defended me.

FREDERICK: I know not that, but o' my conscience thou had ravished her, had she not redeemed herself with a ring. Let's see't, Blunt.

(Blunt shows the ring.)

BELVILE [*aside*]: Ha! The ring I gave Florinda when we 90 exchanged our vows!—Hark'ee, Blunt—

(Goes to whisper to him.)

WILLMORE: No whispering, good colonel, there's a woman in the case. No whispering.

BELVILE [*aside to Blunt*]: Hark'ee, fool, be advised, and conceal both the ring and the story for your reputa-95 tion's sake. Do not let people know what despised cullies we English are; to be cheated and abused by one whore, and another rather bribe thee than be kind to thee, is an infamy to our nation.

WILLMORE: Come, come, where's the wench? We'll see 100 her; let her be what she will, we'll see her.

PEDRO: Ay, ay, let us see her. I can soon discover whether she be of quality, or for your diversion.

BLUNT: She's in Fred's custody.

WILLMORE: Come, come, the key—

(To Frederick, who gives him the key; they are going.)

105 BELVILE [*aside*]: Death, what shall I do?—Stay, gentlemen.—[*Aside.*] Yet if I hinder 'em, I shall discover all.—Hold, let's go one at once.° Give me the key.

WILLMORE: Nay, hold there, colonel, I'll go first.

FREDERICK: Nay, no dispute, Ned and I have the propri-110 ety of her.

WILLMORE: Damn propriety! Then we'll draw cuts. *(Belvile goes to whisper [to] Willmore.)* Nay, no corruption, good colonel. Come, the longest sword carries her.

78. **jack pudding:** Clown.   107. **one at once:** One after the other.

(They all draw, forgetting Don Pedro, being a Spaniard, had the longest.)

BLUNT: I yield up my interest to you, gentlemen, and 115 that will be revenge sufficient.

WILLMORE *(to Pedro)*: The wench is yours.—[*Aside.*] Pox of his Toledo,° I had forgot that.

FREDERICK: Come, sir, I'll conduct you to the lady.

(Exeunt Frederick and Pedro.)

BELVILE *(aside)*: To hinder him will certainly discover 120 her.—Dost know, dull beast, what mischief thou hast done?

(Willmore walking up and down, out of humor.)

WILLMORE: Ay, ay, to trust our fortune to lots! A devil on't, 'twas madness, that's the truth on't.

BELVILE: Oh, intolerable sot— 125

(Enter Florinda running, masked, Pedro after her; Willmore gazing round her.)

FLORINDA *(aside)*: Good heaven defend me from discovery!

PEDRO: 'Tis but in vain to fly me; you're fallen to my lot.

BELVILE [*aside*]: Sure she's undiscovered yet, but now I fear there is no way to bring her off. 130

WILLMORE [*aside*]: Why, what a pox, is not this my woman, the same I followed but now?

(Pedro talking to Florinda, who walks up and down.)

PEDRO: As if I did not know ye, and your business here.

FLORINDA *(aside)*: Good heaven, I fear he does indeed!

PEDRO: Come, pray be kind; I know you meant to be so 135 when you entered here, for these are proper gentlemen.

WILLMORE: But sir, perhaps the lady will not be imposed upon: She'll choose her man.

PEDRO: I am better bred than not to leave her choice 140 free.

(Enter Valeria, and is surprised at sight of Don Pedro.)

VALERIA *(aside)*: Don Pedro here! There's no avoiding him.

FLORINDA *(aside)*: Valeria! Then I'm undone.

VALERIA *(to Pedro, running to him)*: Oh, I have found 145 you, sir! The strangest accident—if I had breath—to tell it.

PEDRO: Speak! Is Florinda safe? Hellena well?

VALERIA: Ay, ay, sir. Florinda is safe.—[*Aside.*] From any fears of you. 150

PEDRO: Why, where's Florinda? Speak!

VALERIA: Ay, where indeed, sir; I wish I could inform you. But to hold you no longer in doubt—

FLORINDA *(aside)*: Oh, what will she say?

VALERIA: She's fled away in the habit—of one of her 155 pages, sir. But Callis thinks you may retrieve her yet,

118. **Toledo:** His sword, which won the draw, was made in Toledo, Spain.

if you make haste away. She'll tell you, sir, the rest.—
(*Aside.*) If you can find her out.

160 PEDRO: Dishonorable girl, she has undone my aim.—
[*To Belvile.*] Sir, you see my necessity of leaving you,
and I hope you'll pardon it. My sister, I know, will
make her flight to you, and if she do, I shall expect
she should be rendered back.

BELVILE: I shall consult my love and honor, sir.

(*Exit Pedro.*)

165 FLORINDA (*to Valeria*): My dear preserver, let me embrace thee.

WILLMORE: What the devil's all this?

BLUNT: Mystery, by this light.

VALERIA: Come, come, make haste and get yourselves
170 married quickly, for your brother will return again.

BELVILE: I'm so surprised with fears and joys, so amazed
to find you here in safety, I can scarce persuade my
heart into a faith of what I see.

WILLMORE: Hark'ee, colonel, is this that mistress who has
175 cost you so many sighs, and me so many quarrels
with you?

BELVILE: It is.—[*To Florinda.*] Pray give him the honor
of your hand.

WILLMORE: Thus it must be received, then. (*Kneels and*
180 *kisses her hand.*) And with it give your pardon, too.

FLORINDA: The friend to Belvile may command me
anything.

WILLMORE (*aside*): Death, would I might; 'tis a surprising
beauty.

185 BELVILE: Boy, run and fetch a father instantly.

(*Exit Boy.*)

FREDERICK: So, now do I stand like a dog, and have not
a syllable to plead my own cause with. By this hand,
madam, I was never thoroughly confounded before,
nor shall I ever more dare look up with confidence,
190 till you are pleased to pardon me.

FLORINDA: Sir, I'll be reconciled to you on one condition:
that you'll follow the example of your friend in marrying a maid that does not hate you, and whose fortune, I believe, will not be unwelcome to you.

195 FREDERICK: Madam, had I no inclinations that way, I
should obey your kind commands.

BELVILE: Who, Fred marry? He has so few inclinations
for womankind that had he been possessed of paradise he might have continued there to this day, if no
200 crime but love could have disinherited him.

FREDERICK: Oh, I do not use to boast of my intrigues.

BELVILE: Boast! Why, thou cost nothing but boast. And I
dare swear, wert thou as innocent from the sin of the
grape as thou art from the apple, thou might'st yet
205 claim that right in Eden which our first parents lost
by too much loving.

FREDERICK: I wish this lady would think me so modest
a man.

VALERIA: She would be sorry then, and not like you half
210 so well. And I should be loath to break my word with
you, which was, that if your friend and mine agreed,
it should be a match between you and I.

(*She gives him her hand.*)

FREDERICK: Bear witness, colonel, 'tis a bargain.

(*Kisses her hand.*)

BLUNT (*to Florinda*): I have a pardon to beg, too; but
215 'adsheartlikins, I am so out of countenance that I'm a
dog if I can say anything to purpose.

FLORINDA: Sir, I heartily forgive you all.

BLUNT: That's nobly said, sweet lady.—Belvile, prithee
present her her ring again, for I find I have not cour-
220 age to approach her myself.

(*Gives him the ring; he gives it to Florinda.*)

(*Enter Boy.*)

BOY: Sir, I have brought the father that you sent for.

[*Exit Boy.*]

BELVILE: 'Tis well. And now, my dear Florinda, let's fly to
complete that mighty joy we have so long wished and
sighed for.—Come, Fred, you'll follow?

FREDERICK: Your example, sir, 'twas ever my ambition 225
in war, and must be so in love.

WILLMORE: And must not I see this juggling° knot tied?

BELVILE: No, thou shalt do us better service and be our
guard, lest Don Pedro's sudden return interrupt the
ceremony. 230

WILLMORE: Content; I'll secure this pass.

(*Exeunt Belvile, Florinda, Frederick, and Valeria.*)

(*Enter Boy.*)

BOY (*to Willmore*): Sir, there's a lady without would
speak to you.

WILLMORE: Conduct her in; I dare not quit my post.

BOY [*to Blunt*]: And sir, your tailor waits you in your 235
chamber.

BLUNT: Some comfort yet: I shall not dance naked at the
wedding.

(*Exeunt Blunt and Boy.*)

(*Enter again the Boy, conducting in Angellica in a*
masking habit and a vizard. Willmore runs to her.)

WILLMORE [*aside*]: This can be none but my pretty
gypsy.—Oh, I see you can follow as well as fly. 240
Come, confess thyself the most malicious devil in
nature; you think you have done my business with
Angellica—

ANGELLICA: Stand off, base villain!

(*She draws a pistol and holds it to his breast.*)

WILLMORE: Ha, 'tis not she! Who art thou, and what's 245
thy business?

ANGELLICA: One thou hast injured, and who comes to
kill thee for't.

WILLMORE: What the devil canst thou mean?

ANGELLICA: By all my hopes to kill thee— 250

(*Holds still the pistol to his breast; he going back, she*
following still.)

WILLMORE: Prithee, on what acquaintance? For I know
thee not.

---

227. **juggling:** Based on trickery or deception.

ANGELLICA: Behold this face so lost to thy
    remembrance,   (*Pulls off her vizard.*)
    And then call all thy sins about thy soul
255   And let 'em die with thee.
WILLMORE: Angellica!
ANGELLICA: Yes, traitor! Does not thy guilty blood run
    shivering through thy veins? Hast thou no horror at
    this sight, that tells thee thou hast not long to boast
260   thy shameful conquest?
WILLMORE: Faith, no, child. My blood keeps its old
    ebbs and flows still, and that usual heat too, that
    could oblige thee with a kindness, had I but opportu-
    nity.
265 ANGELLICA: Devil! Dost wanton with my pain? Have at
    thy heart!
WILLMORE: Hold, dear virago!° Hold thy hand a little;
    I am not now at leisure to be killed. Hold and hear
    me.—(*Aside.*) Death, I think she's in earnest.
270 ANGELLICA (*aside, turning from him*): Oh, if I take not
    heed, my coward heart will leave me to his mercy.—
    What have you, sir, to say?—But should I hear thee,
    thoud'st talk away all that is brave about me, and I
    have vowed thy death by all that's sacred.

(*Follows him with the pistol to his breast.*)

275 WILLMORE: Why then, there's an end of a proper hand-
    some fellow, that might 'a lived to have done good
    service yet. That's all I can say to't.
ANGELLICA (*pausingly*): Yet—I would give thee time
    for—penitence.
280 WILLMORE: Faith, child, I thank God I have ever took
    care to lead a good, sober, hopeful life, and am of a
    religion that teaches me to believe I shall depart in
    peace.
ANGELLICA: So will the devil! Tell me,
285   How many poor believing fools thou hast undone?
    How many hearts thou hast betrayed to ruin?
    Yet these are little mischiefs to the ills
    Thou'st taught mine to commit: Thou'st taught it
    love.
WILLMORE: Egad, 'twas shrewdly hurt the while.
290 ANGELLICA: Love, that has robbed it of its unconcern,
    Of all that pride that taught me how to value it.
    And in its room
    A mean submissive passion was conveyed,
    That made me humbly bow, which I ne'er did
295   To anything but heaven.
    Thou, perjured man, didst this; and with thy
        oaths,
    Which on thy knees thou didst devoutly make,
    Softened my yielding heart, and then I was a slave.
    Yet still had been content to've worn my chains,
300   Worn 'em with vanity and joy forever,
    Hadst thou not broke those vows that put them on.
    'Twas then I was undone.

(*All this while follows him with the pistol to his breast.*)

267. virago: A woman of great stature, strength, and courage.

WILLMORE: Broke my vows? Why, where hast thou lived?
    Amongst the gods? For I never heard of mortal man
    that has not broke a thousand vows.   305
ANGELLICA: Oh, impudence!
WILLMORE: Angellica, that beauty has been too long
    tempting, not to have made a thousand lovers lan-
    guish; who, in the amorous fever, no doubt have
    sworn like me. Did they all die in that faith, still ador-   310
    ing? I do not think they did.
ANGELLICA: No, faithless man; had I repaid their vows,
    as I did thine, I would have killed the ingrateful that
    had abandoned me.
WILLMORE: This old general has quite spoiled thee: 315
    Nothing makes a woman so vain as being flattered.
    Your old lover ever supplies the defects of age with
    intolerable dotage, vast charge, and that which you
    call constancy; and attributing all this to your own
    merits, you domineer, and throw your favors in's   320
    teeth, upbraiding him still with the defects of age,
    and cuckold him as often as he deceives your expec-
    tations. But the gay, young, brisk lover, that brings his
    equal fires, and can give you dart for dart, you'll find
    will be as nice as you sometimes.   325
ANGELLICA: All this thou'st made me know, for which I
    hate thee.
    Had I remained in innocent security,
    I should have thought all men were born my slaves,
    And worn my power like lightning in my eyes,
    To have destroyed at pleasure when offended.   330
    But when love held the mirror, the undeceiving
        glass
    Reflected all the weakness of my soul, and made me
        know
    My richest treasure being lost, my honor,
    All the remaining spoil could not be worth
    The conqueror's care or value.   335
    Oh, how I fell, like a long-worshiped idol,
    Discovering all the cheat.
    Would not the incense and rich sacrifice
    Which blind devotion offered at my altars
    Have fallen to thee?   340
    Why wouldst thou then destroy my fancied power?
WILLMORE: By heaven, thou'rt brave, and I admire thee
        strangely.
    I wish I were that dull, that constant thing
    Which thou wouldst have, and nature never meant
        me.
    I must, like cheerful birds, sing in all groves,   345
    And perch on every bough,
    Billing the next kind she that flies to meet me;
    Yet, after all, could build my nest with thee,
    Thither repairing when I'd loved my round,
    And still reserve a tributary flame.   350
    To gain your credit, I'll pay you back your charity,
    And be obliged for nothing but for love.

(*Offers her a purse of gold.*)

ANGELLICA: Oh, that thou wert in earnest!
    So mean a thought of me

355   Would turn my rage to scorn, and I should pity
          thee,
      And give thee leave to live;
      Which for the public safety of our sex,
      And my own private injuries, I dare not do.
      Prepare——   (*Follows still, as before.*)
360   I will no more be tempted with replies.

WILLMORE: Sure——

ANGELLICA: Another word will damn thee! I've heard
      thee talk too long.

(*She follows him with the pistol ready to shoot; he
retires, still amazed. Enter Don Antonio, his arm in a
scarf, and lays hold on the pistol.*)

ANTONIO: Ha! Angellica!

365 ANGELLICA: Antonio! What devil brought thee hither?

ANTONIO: Love and curiosity, seeing your coach at door.
      Let me disarm you of this unbecoming instrument of
      death. (*Takes away the pistol.*) Amongst the number
      of your slaves was there not one worthy the honor to
370   have fought your quarrel?——[*To Willmore.*] Who are
      you, sir, that are so very wretched to merit death
      from her?

WILLMORE: One, sir, that could have made a better end
      of an amorous quarrel without you, than with you.

375 ANTONIO: Sure 'tis some rival. Ha! The very man took
      down her picture yesterday; the very same that set on
      me last night! Blessed opportunity——

(*Offers to shoot him.*)

ANGELLICA: Hold, you're mistaken, sir.

ANTONIO: By heaven, the very same!——Sir, what preten-
380   sions have you to this lady?

WILLMORE: Sir, I do not use to be examined, and am ill at
      all disputes but this——

(*Draws; Antonio offers to shoot.*)

ANGELLICA (*to Willmore*): Oh, hold! You see he's armed
      with certain death.
      ——And you, Antonio, I command you hold,
385   By all the passion you've so lately vowed me.

(*Enter Don Pedro, sees Antonio, and stays.*)

PEDRO (*aside*): Ha! Antonio! And Angellica!

ANTONIO: When I refuse obedience to your will,
      May you destroy me with your mortal hate.
      By all that's holy, I adore you so,
390   That even my rival, who has charms enough
      To make him fall a victim to my jealousy,
      Shall live; nay, and have leave to love on still.

PEDRO (*aside*): What's this I hear?

ANGELLICA (*pointing to Willmore*): Ah thus, 'twas thus he
      talked, and I believed.
395   Antonio, yesterday
      I'd not have sold my interest in his heart
      For all the sword has won and lost in battle.
      ——But now, to show my utmost of contempt,
      I give thee life; which, if thou wouldst preserve,
400   Live where my eyes may never see thee more.

Live to undo someone whose soul may prove
So bravely constant to revenge my love.

(*Goes out. Antonio follows, but Pedro pulls him back.*)

PEDRO: Antonio, stay.

ANTONIO: Don Pedro!

PEDRO: What coward fear was that prevented thee from   405
      meeting me this morning on the Molo?

ANTONIO: Meet thee?

PEDRO: Yes, me; I was the man that dared thee to't.

ANTONIO: Hast thou so often seen me fight in war, to
      find no better cause to excuse my absence? I sent my   410
      sword and one to do thee right, finding myself unca-
      pable to use a sword.

PEDRO: But 'twas Florinda's quarrel that we fought, and
      you, to show how little you esteemed her, sent me
      your rival, giving him your interest. But I have found   415
      the cause of this affront, and when I meet you fit for
      the dispute, I'll tell you my resentment.

ANTONIO: I shall be ready, sir, ere long, to do you rea-
      son.   (*Exit Antonio.*)

PEDRO: If I could find Florinda, now whilst my anger's   420
      high, I think I should be kind, and give her to Belvile
      in revenge.

WILLMORE: Faith, sir, I know not what you would do, but
      I believe the priest within has been so kind.

PEDRO: How? My sister married?   425

WILLMORE: I hope by this time he is, and bedded too, or
      he has not my longings about him.

PEDRO: Dares he do this? Does he not fear my power?

WILLMORE: Faith, not at all; if you will go in and thank
      him for the favor he has done your sister, so; if not, sir, 430
      my power's greater in this house than yours: I have
      a damned surly crew here that will keep you till the
      next tide, and then clap you on board for prize. My
      ship lies but a league off the Molo, and we shall show
      your donship a damned Tramontana° rover's trick.   435

(*Enter Belvile.*)

BELVILE: This rogue's in some new mischief. Ha! Pedro
      returned!

PEDRO: Colonel Belvile, I hear you have married my
      sister.

BELVILE: You have heard truth then, sir.   440

PEDRO: Have I so? Then, sir, I wish you joy.

BELVILE: How?

PEDRO: By this embrace I do, and I am glad on't.

BELVILE: Are you in earnest?

PEDRO: By our long friendship and my obligations to   445
      thee, I am; the sudden change I'll give you reasons for
      anon. Come, lead me to my sister, that she may know
      I now approve her choice.

(*Exit Belvile with Pedro.*)

(*Willmore goes to follow them. Enter Hellena, as before
in boy's clothes, and pulls him back.*)

_____

435. **Tramontana:** Region of Italy north of the Alps.

WILLMORE: Ha! My gypsy! Now a thousand blessings
on thee for this kindness. Egad, child, I was e'en in
despair of ever seeing thee again; my friends are all
provided for within, each man his kind woman.

HELLENA: Ha! I thought they had served me some such
trick!

WILLMORE: And I was e'en resolved to go aboard, and
condemn myself to my lone cabin, and the thoughts
of thee.

HELLENA: And could you have left me behind? Would
you have been so ill natured?

WILLMORE: Why, 'twould have broke my heart, child.
But since we are met again, I defy foul weather to
part us.

HELLENA: And would you be a faithful friend now, if a
maid should trust you?

WILLMORE: For a friend I cannot promise: Thou art of a
form so excellent, a face and humor too good for
cold dull friendship. I am parlously afraid of being in
love, child; and you have not forgotten how severely
you have used me?

HELLENA: That's all one; such usage you must still look
for: to find out all your haunts, to rail at you to all
that love you, till I have made you love only me in
your own defense, because nobody else will love you.

WILLMORE: But hast thou no better quality to recommend
thyself by?

HELLENA: Faith, none, captain. Why, 'twill be the greater
charity to take me for thy mistress. I am a lone child,
a kind of orphan lover, and why I should die a maid,
and in a captain's hands too, I do not understand.

WILLMORE: Egad, I was never clawed away with broad-
sides from any female before. Thou hast one virtue I
adore—good nature. I hate a coy demure mistress,
she's as troublesome as a colt, I'll break none. No,
give me a mad mistress when mewed, and in flying,
one I dare trust upon the wing, that whilst she's kind
will come to the lure.°

HELLENA: Nay, as kind as you will, good captain, whilst
it lasts. But let's lose no time.

WILLMORE: My time's as precious to me as thine can be.
Therefore, dear creature, since we are so well agreed,
let's retire to my chamber; and if ever thou wert
treated with such savory love! Come, my bed's prepared for such a guest all clean and sweet as thy fair
self. I love to steal a dish and a bottle with a friend,
and hate long graces. Come, let's retire and fall to.

HELLENA: 'Tis but getting my consent, and the business is
soon done. Let but old gaffer Hymen° and his priest
say amen to's, and I dare lay my mother's daughter
by as proper a fellow as your father's son, without
fear or blushing.

WILLMORE: Hold, hold, no bug words,° child. Priest and
Hymen? Prithee add a hangman to 'em to make

up the consort. No, no, we'll have no vows but love,
child, nor witness but the lover: The kind deity en-
joins naught but love and enjoy. Hymen and priest
wait still upon portion and jointure; love and beauty
have their own ceremonies. Marriage is as certain a
bane to love as lending money is to friendship. I'll
neither ask nor give a vow, though I could be content
to turn gypsy and become a left-handed bridegroom
to have the pleasure of working that great miracle of
making a maid a mother, if you durst venture. 'Tis
upse gypsy° that, and if I miss I'll lose my labor.

HELLENA: And if you do not lose, what shall I get? A
cradle full of noise and mischief, with a pack of
repentance at my back? Can you teach me to weave
incle° to pass my time with? 'Tis upse gypsy that, too.

WILLMORE: I can teach thee to weave a true love's knot
better.

HELLENA: So can my dog.

WILLMORE: Well, I see we are both upon our guards, and
I see there's no way to conquer good nature but by
yielding. Here, give me thy hand: One kiss, and I am
thine.

HELLENA: One kiss! How like my page he speaks! I am
resolved you shall have none, for asking such a sneaking sum. He that will be satisfied with one kiss will
never die of that longing. Good friend single-kiss, is
all your talking come to this? A kiss, a caudle!° Farewell, captain single-kiss.

(Going out; he stays her.)

WILLMORE: Nay, if we part so, let me die like a bird upon
a bough, at the sheriff's charge. By heaven, both
the Indies shall not buy thee from me. I adore thy
humor and will marry thee, and we are so of one
humor it must be a bargain. Give me thy hand.
(Kisses her hand.) And now let the blind ones, love
and fortune, do their worst.

HELLENA: Why, god-a-mercy, captain!

WILLMORE: But hark'ee: the bargain is now made, but is
it not fit we should know each other's names, that
when we have reason to curse one another hereafter,
and people ask me who 'tis I give to the devil, I may
at least be able to tell what family you came of?

HELLENA: Good reason, captain, and where I have
cause, as I doubt not but I shall have plentiful, that I
may know at whom to throw my—blessings, I
beseech ye your name.

WILLMORE: I am called Robert the Constant.

HELLENA: A very fine name! Pray was it your faulkner°
or butler that christened you? Do they not use to
whistle when they call you?

WILLMORE: I hope you have a better, that a man may
name without crossing himself—you are so merry
with mine.

484–486. flying . . . lure: I.e., one who will be faithful as long
as that doesn't interfere with her wishes.   **497. Hymen:** God of
marriage.   **501. bug words:** Words that inspire fear.

513. upse gypsy: Gypsy fashion.   **517. incle:** Linen yarn or
tape.   **529. caudle:** A warm drink made of gruel and wine or
ale, sweetened and spiced, given to the sick.   **549. faulkner:**
Falconer, trainer of hawks.

555 HELLENA: I am called Hellena the Inconstant.

(*Enter Pedro, Belvile, Florinda, Frederick, Valeria.*)

PEDRO: Ha! Hellena!

FLORINDA: Hellena!

HELLENA: The very same. Ha! My brother! Now, captain,
show your love and courage; stand to your arms and
560 defend me bravely, or I am lost forever.

PEDRO: What's this I hear? False girl, how came you
hither, and what's your business? Speak!

(*Goes roughly to her.*)

WILLMORE: Hold off, sir; you have leave to parley° only.

(*Puts himself between.*)

HELLENA: I had e'en as good tell it, as you guess it. Faith,
565 brother, my business is the same with all living creatures of my age: to love and be beloved—and here's
the man.

PEDRO: Perfidious maid, hast thou deceived me too;
deceived thyself and heaven?

570 HELLENA: 'Tis time enough to make my peace with that;
Be you but kind, let me alone with heaven.

PEDRO: Belvile, I did not expect this false play from you.
Was't not enough you'd gain Florinda, which I pardoned, but your lewd friends too must be enriched
575 with the spoils of a noble family?

BELVILE: Faith, sir, I am as much surprised at this as you
can be. Yet, sir, my friends are gentlemen, and ought
to be esteemed for their misfortunes, since they have
the glory to suffer with the best of men and kings.
580 'Tis true, he's a rover of fortune, yet a prince aboard
his little wooden world.

PEDRO: What's this to the maintenance of a woman of
her birth and quality?

WILLMORE: Faith, sir, I can boast of nothing but a sword
585 which does me right where'er I come, and has
defended a worse cause than a woman's, and since
I loved her before I either knew her birth or name, I
must pursue my resolution and marry her.

PEDRO: And is all your holy intent of becoming a nun
590 debauched into a desire of man?

HELLENA: Why, I have considered the matter, brother, and
find the three hundred thousand crowns my uncle
left me, and you cannot keep from me, will be better laid out in love than in religion, and turn to as
595 good an account. Let most voices carry it: for heaven
or the captain?

ALL CRY: A captain! A captain!

HELLENA: Look ye, sir, 'tis a clear case.

PEDRO: Oh, I am mad!—(*Aside.*) If I refuse, my life's in
600 danger.—Come, there's one motive induces me. Take
her; I shall now be free from fears of her honor.
Guard it you now, if you can; I have been a slave to't
long enough. (*Gives her to him.*)

563. parley: Speak or discuss.

WILLMORE: Faith, sir, I am of a nation that are of opinion
a woman's honor is not worth guarding when she 605
has a mind to part with it.

HELLENA: Well said, captain.

PEDRO (*to Valeria*): This was your plot, mistress, but
I hope you have married one that will revenge my
quarrel to you. 610

VALERIA: There's no altering destiny, sir.

PEDRO: Sooner than a woman's will; therefore I forgive
you all, and wish you may get my father's pardon as
easily, which I fear.

(*Enter Blunt dressed in a Spanish habit, looking very
ridiculous; his Man adjusting his band.*)

MAN: 'Tis very well, sir. 615

BLUNT: Well, sir! 'Adsheartlikins, I tell you 'tis damnable
ill, sir. A Spanish habit! Good Lord! Could the devil
and my tailor devise no other punishment for me but
the mode of a nation I abominate?

BELVILE: What's the matter, Ned? 620

BLUNT: Pray view me round, and judge.

(*Turns round.*)

BELVILE: I must confess thou art a kind of an odd figure.

BLUNT: In a Spanish habit with a vengeance! I had rather
be in the Inquisition for Judaism° than in this doublet
and breeches; a pillory were an easy collar to this, 625
three handfuls high; and these shoes, too, are worse
than the stocks, with the sole an inch shorter than my
foot. In fine, gentlemen, methinks I look like a bag of
bays° stuffed full of fool's flesh.

BELVILE: Methinks 'tis well, and makes thee look e'en 630
cavalier. Come, sir, settle your face and salute our
friends. Lady—

BLUNT (*to Hellena*): Ha! Sayst thou so, my little rover?
Lady, if you be one, give me leave to kiss your hand,
and tell you, 'adsheartlikins, for all I look so, I am 635
your humble servant. A pox of my Spanish habit!
(*Music is heard to play.*)

WILLMORE: Hark! What's this?

(*Enter Boy.*)

BOY: Sir, as the custom is, the gay people in masquerade,
who make every man's house their own, are coming
up. 640

(*Enter several men and women in masking habits, with
music; they put themselves in order and dance.*)

BLUNT: 'Adsheartlikins, would 'twere lawful to pull off
their false faces, that I might see if my doxy° were
not amongst 'em.

BELVILE (*to the maskers*): Ladies and gentlemen, since
you are come so *a propos,*° you must take a small 645
collation with us.

624. **Inquisition for Judaism:** The Spanish Inquisition, which
persecuted heretics, Jews, and Muslims. **628–629. bag of
bays:** Spices wrapped in cloth and used for flavoring in cooking. **642. doxy:** Mistress, prostitute. **645.** *a propos:* In a
timely fashion; appropriately.

WILLMORE (*to Hellena*): Whilst we'll to the good man
  within, who stays to give us a cast of his office.° Have
  you no trembling at the near approach?
650 HELLENA: No more than you have in an engagement or
  a tempest.
WILLMORE: Egad, thou'rt a brave girl, and I admire thy
  love and courage.
      Lead on; no other dangers they can dread,
655   *Who venture in the storms o'th' marriage bed.*
                                        (*Exeunt.*)

EPILOGUE

The banished cavaliers! A roving blade!
A popish carnival! A masquerade!
The devil's in't if this will please the nation
In these our blessed times of reformation,
5   When conventickling° is so much in fashion.
And yet—
That mutinous tribe less factions do beget,
Than your continual differing in wit.
Your judgment's, as your passion's, a disease:
10 Nor muse nor miss your appetite can please;
You're grown as nice as queasy consciences,
Whose each convulsion, when the spirit moves,
Damns everything that maggot° disapproves.
    With canting° rule you would the stage refine,
15 And to dull method all our sense confine.
With th'insolence of commonwealths you rule,
Where each gay fop and politic grave fool
On monarch wit impose, without control.
As for the last, who seldom sees a play,
20 Unless it be the old Blackfriars° way;
Shaking his empty noddle o'er bamboo,°
He cries, "Good faith, these plays will never do!
Ah, sir, in my young days, what lofty wit,
What high-strained scenes of fighting there were writ.
25 These are slight airy toys. But tell me, pray,
What has the House of Commons done today?"
Then shows his politics, to let you see
Of state affairs he'll judge as notably
As he can do of wit and poetry.
30 The younger sparks, who hither do resort,
Cry,
"Pox o' your genteel things! Give us more sport'!

Damn me, I'm sure 'twill never please the court."
    Such fops are never pleased, unless the play
Be stuffed with fools as brisk and dull as they.   35
Such might the half-crown spare, and in a glass
At home behold a more accomplished ass.
Where they may set their cravats, wigs, and faces,
And practice all their buffoonry grimaces:
See how this huff becomes, this damny,° stare,   40
Which they at home may act because they dare,
But must with prudent caution do elsewhere.
Oh that our Nokes, or Tony Lee,° could show
A fop but half so much to th' life as you.

POSTSCRIPT

This play had been sooner in print, but for a report
about the town (made by some either very malicious
or very ignorant) that 'twas *Thomaso°* altered; which
made the booksellers fear some trouble from the proprietor of that admirable play, which indeed has wit   5
enough to stock a poet, and is not to be pieced or
mended by any but the excellent author himself. That
I have stolen some hints from it, may be a proof that
I valued it more than to pretend to alter it, had I the
dexterity of some poets, who are not more expert in   10
stealing than in the art of concealing, and who even
that way outdo the Spartan boys.° I might have appropriated all to myself; but I, vainly proud of my
judgment, hang out the sign of Angellica (the only
stolen object) to give notice where a great part of the   15
wit dwelt; though if the *Play of the Novella°* were
as well worth remembering as *Thomaso*, they might
(bating° the name) have as well said I took it from
thence. I will only say the plot and business (not to
boast on't) is my own; as for the words and charac-   20
ters, I leave the reader to judge and compare 'em with
Thomaso, to whom I recommend the great entertainment of reading it. Though had this succeeded ill, I
should have had no need of imploring that justice
from the critics, who are naturally so kind to any that   25
pretend to usurp their dominion, especially of our
sex: They would doubtless have given me the whole
honor on't. Therefore I will only say in English what
the famous Vergil does in Latin: I make verses, and
others have the fame.   30

---

648. stays . . . office: The priest waits to perform his office (i.e.,
to marry them).   5. conventickling: A pun—a conventicle was
a secret meeting of religious dissenters (those who were not
members of the Church of England).   13. maggot: Conscience.
14. canting: Hypocritical.   20. Blackfriars: The Blackfriars
Theatre (1576–1655), considered old-fashioned in Behn's time.
21. o'er bamboo: Over a cane, implying old age.

40. damny: Damn me.   43. Nokes . . . Lee: The best low comedians of the day. James Nokes performed in Thomas Betterton's
company.   3. Thomaso: Thomas Killigrew's *Thomaso; or, The
Wanderer* (1654; published 1664).   12. Spartan boys: Those
who hid in the Trojan horse.   16. *Play of the Novella*: *The
Novella* (1632) by Richard Brome, from which Behn borrowed
several ideas.   18. bating: Excepting.

ELAINE HOBBY (b. 1956)

Courtship and Marriage
in *The Rover* 1989

Elaine Hobby closely examines *The Rover* to help us understand the conventions of romantic love in Aphra Behn's work. Her essay is especially enlightening on the questions of marriage and rape and on the differences in the viewpoints of men and women characters in the play. Hobby notes the complexities implied in the characterization of Angellica, the courtesan.

Commonly, Behn's plays feature at least two pairs of young lovers, whose attitudes to love and marriage serve as contrasting strategies in courtship. A common pattern is that of the "constant couple," who remain true to one another, and finally marry, despite parental opposition and, usually, confusions over one another's true identity and conduct. These lovers are not, however, idyllically well matched or perfectly happy. In *The Rover*, Florinda and Belvile are just such a constant couple. From the beginning they are in love with one another, and resolved to accept no other partner. Except for her stubbornness on this one issue, Florinda is all quiet obedience, failing to argue her case against an arranged marriage. Her passivity is no ideal. Twice in the course of the play she narrowly escapes being raped by the friends of her beloved, and on each occasion is only saved because her obvious high social class causes her attackers to hesitate, fearing retribution from her relatives. The second of these incidents is a nightmare scene where, seeking refuge in Blunt's house, she is regarded by him as the perfect target for his revenge against all women (and Lucetta in particular) for making fun of him. When Frederick, the play's great upholder of patriarchal morality, arrives, the two men agree to rape her.

> BLUNT: We'll both lie with her, and then let me alone to bang her.
> FREDERICK: I'm ready to serve you in matters of revenge that has a double
>   pleasure in't.

(IV, v, 123–26)

In a world where men can choose to rape a woman, any woman, for spite, there is no safety for the romantic heroine. In Behn's plays, as in her novels, rape or the threat of it is shown to be an almost routine masculine strategy to bully and manipulate women. In *The Amorous Prince*, Frederick threatens to rape Laura at knifepoint to humble her for scorning him, and in the same play Silvio threatens to rape his "sister" Cleonte. Sir Timothy Tawdrey in *The Town-Fopp*, when threatening to rape Phillis, tells her that old patriarchal lie: that all women want to be forcibly taken. Phillis's fate is the most terrible of all. Having no economic choices (like Philadelphia in Behn's novel *The Unfortunate Happy Lady*), she has no option but to marry her would-be rapist.

Setting out with a theme of courtship and marriage, Behn writes about rape and prostitution, constructing scenarios that show how closely connected these fates are for women. Where Florinda's reliance on "true love" for her salvation twice brings her to the brink of being raped, the courtesan Angellica Bianca in the same play is betrayed by her final inability to escape from the tempting lies of romance. Early in the play, she makes a cool assessment of women's position, explaining that she had opted to sell her body for the solid return of financial reward, rather than trusting to illusory male fidelity: "Nothing but gold shall charm my heart" (II, i, 163). She knows, too, that marriage for money is a no less mercenary affair than prostitution. Disaster arrives, however, because she has seriously misjudged the power structure of her society. She arrives in town hoping to captivate either the viceroy's son Don Antonio, or Don Pedro, the nephew of her deceased "protector." Had she been married to her old lover, Don Pedro would have been her kin, and had some social duty to support her. As it is, she is left to live on her wits and her transitory physical charms. When Willmore, the "rover" of the title, finally rejects her in favor of the wealthy virgin Hellena, she is forced to recognize that her chosen independence was illusory. In a world where men make the rules, her only salable item is her virginity. Having sold that in the wrong market, she is damned.

When Angellica falls hopelessly for the feckless Willmore, she wants to believe that love and romance can be dissociated from social and economic structures, that "true love" in her world can be above financial considerations. She calls on him to see things her way and, blinded by this desire, does not recognize that he is using her for his pleasure.

> ANGELLICA: Thou'rt a brave fellow! Put up thy gold, and know,
> That were thy fortune large as is thy soul,
> Thou shouldst not buy my love
> Couldst thou forget these mean effects of vanity
> Which set me out to sale,
> And as a lover prize my yielding joys.
> Canst thou believe they'll be entirely thine,
> Without considering they were mercenary?   (II, ii, 110–17)

In the course of the play, Willmore's repeated answer to this is a resounding "No." Having worshiped her beauty, tasted the pleasures of her body, and spent her money to attract a wealthier woman, he leaves her for a better catch.

Angellica is a troubling and uncomfortable figure in the play, disrupting the wit and airiness of scenes between Hellena and Willmore and undercutting the conventional "happy ending" of true lovers united. Realizing she has been betrayed by Willmore despite giving him "My virgin heart . . . Oh! 'tis gone!" (IV, ii, 163) she plots her revenge "for the public safety of our sex" (V, 357). Trapping him at gunpoint she decides, however, to let him live: he is not worth the trouble of an execution: "But now, to show my utmost of contempt, / I give thee life" (V, 398–99). Through Willmore, she has learned that male protestations of devotion, and all their courtly love rhetoric, are for them just a game. There is no true power, no safety, for women.[. . .]

In many of Behn's plays, men's obsessions with their courtship conventions prevent them from understanding the women they address. Romance is a male invention, and women are jeopardized and often betrayed if they believe such declarations of undying passion. The task for the witty heroine who is at the center of many of Behn's plays, as Hellena is in *The Rover*, is to discover as much as possible about her man's true intentions, beneath his courtly facade. Willmore refers to both Angellica and to Hellena as his "angel" in high-flown rhetoric, but where

Angellica is briefly fooled by this worship, Hellena is quite clear-sighted about the limit of his commitment. As far as possible, she takes control of her situation, disguising herself and playing parts, testing out and then capturing the man she has chosen. Disguised, she watches him court and promise fidelity to Angellica, and in a bitter but witty scene mocks him, throwing back at him the overblown promises she has heard him make (III, 1). She has no interest in traditional courtship rituals, thinking them "a very pretty, idle, silly kind of pleasure to pass one's time with" (III, 1, 67–68), but she is not deceived by Willmore's forthright arguments in favor of unfettered sensuality. She knows already what Angellica shows the audience: Marriage is a necessity for women, otherwise, as she challenges Willmore, "What shall I get? A cradle full of noise and mischief, with a pack of repentance at my back?" (V, 514–16).

She gets her man, but it is a tawdry victory and the audience knows it, with Angellica there to remind them. Willmore has shown himself to be insensitive, capricious, and dangerous to women, and there is no reason to imagine that he will be faithful to Hellena for longer than the month that he originally resolves to sacrifice to gain her. In *The Second Part of the Rover*, where Willmore again chooses between two women (and this time chooses the prostitute), it is revealed in passing that Hellena had died at sea within three months of the marriage.

The world of courtship and marriage depicted by Behn in these plays is a bleak one. Bright, witty women like Hellena use daring and imagination in a desperate attempt to evade the arranged marriages or confinements to nunneries destined them by their families. They race against time, trying their best to negotiate when all power lies in others' hands. None of the dashing young blades they choose and test out are admirable characters, but they seem preferable to a fool like Haunce van Ezel (in *The Dutch Lover*) or an odious tyrant like Octavio (in *The Feign'd Curtizans*). Woven in with the wit and humor, music and spectacle, are hard, sober women's truths about the debauchery of the Restoration court and its acolytes. Armed with wit and driven by necessity, like her heroines, Aphra Behn succeeded in dramatizing in marketable form the dilemmas that faced her and her sisters.

Chikamatsu Monzaemon

Generally regarded as the most significant Japanese playwright, Chikamatsu Monzaemon (1653–1725) was born in the province of Echizen into a minor samurai family. His family name was Sugimori, but he changed it when he began writing plays. In his lifetime—during the celebrated Tokugawa shogunate (1603–1868)—hundreds of thousands of samurai did not serve the shogun or a *daimyo*, or master. Chikamatsu was among those called *rōnin*, samurai who lived without a master and who were therefore without a clear direction. Trained as warriors and supported by the farmer class in Japan during the extended peace of the period, the samurai had little to do. Some of them left the samurai class and, like Chikamatsu, changed their names and went into theater or into some form of business.

The class structure of Japan at this time consisted essentially of peasant farmers, the samurai, the nobility, and merchants. (Some commentators add a class of artisans.) During the late seventeenth and eighteenth centuries, the merchants grew into a wealthy class and often held power over the nobility through debts and other obligations. Chikamatsu was especially interesting because, although he experienced life as part of the samurai class, he also appears to have been connected with a Buddhist monastery as a youth. He may have taken his pseudonym from the Chikamatsu temple at which he stayed for some time. At age nineteen, he became a page in a noble family and experienced palace life. Some sources suggest that he was employed by nobleman Ogimachi Kimmochi (1653–1733), who wrote puppet plays; others suggest he worked for Lord Ichijo Eikan, a connoisseur of puppet plays. Regardless, it was probably this experience that impelled Chikamatsu to give up his position and become Japan's first professional playwright. In essence, Chikamatsu had personal experience in three of the four primary classes in Japanese culture.

Unfortunately, we do not know a great deal about Chikamatsu. We do not know which was his first play, nor do we know how many plays he wrote. Estimates run from 130 to 140 plays, the majority of which are *jōruri*, or puppet plays, and the rest kabuki plays using live actors.

Kabuki, whose linguistic root implies subversive behavior, began with a dance in the "floating world," or pleasure quarter of Kyoto. This was an area licensed for the entertainment of samurai and nobles and permitting prostitution and many forms of entertainment for men, including theater. If we think of Nō drama as refined and religious at heart, we can think of kabuki as profane and appealing to the masses. Its beginning was in 1603 in the dances of a woman named Okuni. Scholar James Brandon, an expert on classical Japanese theater, says of kabuki, "it was the rock entertainment of the seventeenth century. Okuni performed the first Japanese plays of contemporary urban life: numerous painted screens and scrolls show her outrageously garbed as a handsome young warrior, exotic Christian rosary draped on her bosom, conducting an assignation with a prostitute."[1] Eventually, prostitutes took up the practice

For links to resources about Chikamatsu, click on *AuthorLinks* at **bedfordstmartins.com/jacobus**.

---

[1]James Brandon, *The Cambridge Guide to Asian Theatre* (Cambridge: Cambridge University Press, 1993), p. 147.

of kabuki in narrative plays that were sometimes based on current events and that used live actors aiming at an essentially realistic theatre. The authorities eventually cracked down and in 1629 banned female actors, giving rise to the highly specialized *onnagata*, male actors who represented women on stage.

Chikamatsu was most renowned for his puppet plays, but early in his career he also wrote for the kabuki theater. At that time puppet plays were known as *jōruri*, but the more common term now is *bunraku*. Both forms of theater, kabuki and bunraku, are performed in Japan and elsewhere today. Chikamatsu's earliest plays for the puppet theater were probably written in 1683. The puppet theater relied on chanters—virtuoso speakers with highly trained voices—to deliver the lines of the characters. One of the greatest chanters of this period, Takemoto Gidayū (1651–1714), is known to have produced a number of Chikamatsu's earliest plays, among them *Kagekiyo Victorious* (1686).

Chikamatsu's early kabuki plays seem to have been inspired by especially popular actors, among them the brilliant Sakata Tōjūrō (1647–1709). One problem with kabuki actors in the late seventeenth century was that many grew arrogant and difficult. A cult of personality as strong as anything connected with contemporary film stars grew up around the kabuki actors, resulting in a drama that focused not on the play itself but on the presence of the actor.

The puppet theater had the advantage of eliminating this complication. In addition, during the early part of the eighteenth century, the drama that was possible with puppets was similar to what is possible today with computer-generated imagery (CGI) in animated and live-action films. Impossible situations could be enacted with puppets: caesarian operations, quick transformations, dismemberments, and more. When Chikamatsu was writing *jōruri* plays, each puppet was operated by a single person, usually dressed in black (as they are today) so as to permit the puppets to seem to be acting on their own. Each puppet head was painted in a way that signaled to the audience whether it was a good or a villainous figure. Chikamatsu went beyond these limitations, however, and created characters of some moral ambiguity and considerable complexity.

His works are usually divided into history plays and domestic plays, often domestic tragedies. The most successful of his history plays is *The Battles of Coxinga* (1715), set in China. Because Japan was essentially sealed off from foreigners and no Japanese were allowed to travel at this time, the foreign setting added to its appeal. Chikamatsu also invented the successful genre called *shinjū-mono*, or love-suicide play. *The Love Suicides at Sonezaki* (1703) was the first of a series of love-suicide plays written by Chikamatsu as well as other playwrights of the time. It was based on an actual event that had constituted a minor scandal only weeks before he produced his play. He refined the genre in several more plays, including *The Love Suicides at the Women's Temple* (1708) and the unusually modern and complex *The Love Suicides at Amijima* (c. 1720).

The genre was so popular that it became a societal threat. In response to these plays, a great many people committed their own love-suicides, and consequently the authorities banned all such plays in 1722. (Curiously, a similar cult of suicide developed in Europe after the publication of Goethe's *The Sorrows of Young Werther* [1774].)

After 1705, Chikamatsu moved to Osaka, where he was the resident playwright for Gidayū's puppet theater until his death in 1725. His work matured, and his subtle and complex use of language, especially rhyme patterns and puns, established him as one of Japan's greatest writers. He is noted for a technique known as the "pivot-word"—a word that has a double meaning, functioning one way in the beginning of a line and another way in the rest of the line. His skill as a poet makes reading his plays almost as rewarding as seeing them enacted.

The Love Suicides at Sonezaki

For discussion questions and assignments on *The Love Suicides at Sonezaki*, visit **bedfordstmartins.com/jacobus**.

Sonezaki shinjū is the first *shinjū-mono*, or love-suicide play. Chikamatsu wrote some dozen such plays himself, and other playwrights contributed their own. Taken from a current event, the story is direct and moving. Tokubei falls in love with Ohatsu, a young prostitute whose freedom he cannot afford to buy. In desperation, Tokubei sees only one way out of their dilemma: suicide.

In this play, Chikamatsu explores a number of interesting issues. It was not uncommon for a visitor to the floating world to fall in love with a courtesan. Japanese society maintained a clear double standard: men were permitted to enjoy the favors of prostitutes in the licensed areas, whereas their wives were threatened with execution if they committed adultery. In some plays a brother and father approved the killing of an unfaithful woman by her husband. Wives who maintained silence in face of such activity were praised. Those who complained or grew jealous were often divorced, and once divorced they were ruined. Prostitutes were unmarried entertainers whose job was to attract the attention of men and to please them. They were owned by the establishments they served and could be purchased for a high price.

One of the first things one notices about *The Love Suicides at Sonezaki* is that the characters are essentially part of what we would think of today as the middle class. The play is a representational drama, a domestic tragedy, that attempts to present characters speaking as they would if they were encountered in actual society. Tokubei works for a company that sells soy sauce. The villain Kuheiji is a powerful oil merchant. One of Ohatsu's customers is a "country bumpkin." Chikamatsu reveals ordinary people experiencing powerful emotions. It would take another 150 years for such serious middle-class drama to appear on European stages.

The play is also interesting because it respects the Aristotelian unities even though Chikamatsu could have known nothing of Aristotle or of any foreign play. The action takes place in a twenty-four-hour period, the characters develop clearly and consistently, and there is no subplot. As a result, the play seems modern to the Western reader.

The popularity of this and other love-suicide plays, which led to a ban on the genre in 1722, continued in the public imagination for a few years after the ban was enacted, but then the form faded into obscurity. After Chikamatsu's death, the puppet theater developed much more technically advanced production values. The development of three-person puppets, which required considerable coordination among the puppeteers, permitted more surprising effects and more subtle and amazing movements. Chikamatsu's plays were sometimes rewritten to take advantage of these and other developments, such as a revolving stage (about a century before a similar development in Europe). Therefore, most of the current texts of the plays have the marks of a modern rewriting. In the text given here, however, Chikamatsu's 1703 version, except for a brief introductory passage, appears as it was originally played.

Because the chanter controls the dialogue in the puppet play, he also acts as a narrator commenting on and advancing the action. The narrator chants some of the most beautiful poetry in the third scene. A passage known as the *michi-yuki*, or "lovers' journey," offers Chikamatsu the opportunity to raise the level of diction and explore the emotions implied in the action of lovers journeying toward their death. It begins,

> Farewell to this world, and to the night farewell.
> We who walk the road to death, to what should we be likened?
> To the frost by the road that leads to the graveyard,
> Vanishing with each step we take ahead:
> How sad is this dream of a dream!

The inclusion of religion, Amida Buddhism, in this and other plays that have at their root erotic content is not unusual. Most of the better kabuki plays treated religion as important. Ohatsu and Tokubei end *The Love Suicides at Sonezaki* with a sense of religious assurance that may seem odd to Western audiences. At the heart of this play and other love-suicide dramas is the conflict of two important values of Japanese society: *giri*, the obligations one has to family and society, and *ninjō*, the personal human feelings to which one responds. Like yin and yang, these elements must be balanced. If one worries only about obligation to others and ignores emotion, one can miss important life experiences. If one is dominated only by personal emotion and desire, society will suffer. In this play Tokubei is torn between his obligation to his master and his feelings for Ohatsu. In addition, he is humiliated by the clever Kuheiji and loses his honor. Ohatsu realizes the situation Tokubei is in and proposes a way out for them both. The narrator, obviously moved by the lovers' situation, sees them as moving toward paradise.

One of the details that makes this play seem so modern, especially in relation to European plays of the eighteenth century, is its emphasis on money. Tokubei seems naïve in lending his money even to a good friend, considering what is at stake. But it is the forfeit of the money through Kuheiji's cleverness that drives Tokubei to the play's ultimate resolution. One way or another, Tokubei seems doomed because of the considerable sum of money he has received from his master.

The Love Suicides at Sonezaki in Performance

A key element of all *jōruri* puppet plays is the musician, who plays a three-string instrument called the *shamisen*. Performers on this instrument were successful entertainers before they collaborated with chanters and puppets, and even today the musician has a prominent role in both kabuki and bunraku (puppet) productions. The chanter stands or sits to the side of the stage, and the handlers of the puppets are usually in a lowered section of the stage so that they remain inconspicuous. In modern performances, the handlers are often dressed in absolute black, including face masks, and from a slight distance they are almost unnoticeable. The puppets are elaborate and capable of expressing considerable emotion, especially in conjunction with the shamisen musician.

The stage itself has grown wider since Chikamatsu's age, but it still relies on painted scenery and realistic representation of the various locations of the drama. Like a number of other important puppet plays, *The Love Suicides at Sonezaki* has also been performed as a kabuki play with living actors, usually wearing masks and elaborate costumes. Contemporary productions of puppet plays, those of both Chikamatsu and other playwrights, take advantage of the scale of large Western theaters, a development that was adopted largely after World War II. These plays are remarkably effective in those spaces.

CHIKAMATSU MONZAEMON   (1653–1725)

The Love Suicides at Sonezaki   1703

TRANSLATED BY DONALD KEENE

Cast of Characters

TOKUBEI, *aged 25, employee of a dealer in soy sauce*
KUHEIJI, *an oil merchant*
HOST *of Temma House*
CHŌZŌ, *an apprentice*
CUSTOMER *of Ohatsu*
TOWNSMEN
OHATSU, *aged 19, a courtesan*
HOSTESS
COURTESANS
SERVANTS

Scene One: *The grounds of the Ikudama Shrine in Osaka. Time: May 21, 1703.*

NARRATOR:
This graceful young man has served many springs
With the firm of Hirano in Uchihon Street;
He hides the passion that burns in his breast
Lest word escape and the scandal spread.
He drinks peach wine, a cup at a time,
And combs with care his elegant locks.
"Toku" he is called, and famed for his taste,
But now, his talents buried underground,
He works as a clerk, his sleeves stained with oil,

A slave to his sweet remembrances of love.
Today he makes the rounds of his clients
With a lad who carries a cask of soy:
They have reached the shrine of Ikudama.

A woman's voice calls from a bench inside a refreshment stand.

OHATSU: Tokubei—that's you, isn't it?

NARRATOR: She claps her hands, and Tokubei nods in recognition.

TOKUBEI: Chōzō, I'll be following later. Make the rounds of the temples in Tera Street and the uptown mansions, and then return to the shop. Tell them that I'll be back soon. Don't forget to call on the dyer's in Azuchi Street and collect the money he owes us. And stay away from Dōtombori.

NARRATOR: He watches as long as the boy remains in sight, then lifts the bamboo blinds.

TOKUBEI: Ohatsu—what's the matter?

NARRATOR: He starts to remove his bamboo hat.

OHATSU: Please keep your hat on just now. I have a customer from the country today who's making a pilgrimage to all thirty-three temples of Kwannon. He's been boasting that he intends to spend the whole day drinking. At the moment he's gone off to hear the impersonators' show, but if he returns and finds us together, there might be trouble. All the chair-bearers know you. It's best you keep your face covered.

But to come back to us. Lately you haven't written me a word. I've been terribly worried but, not knowing what the situation might be in your shop, I couldn't very well write you. I must have called a hundred times at the Tamba House, but they hadn't any news of you either. Somebody—yes, it was Taichi, the blind musician—asked his friends, and they said you'd gone back to the country. I couldn't believe it was true. You've really been too cruel. Didn't you even want to ask about me? Perhaps you hoped things would end that way, but I've been sick with worry. If you think I'm lying, feel this swelling!

NARRATOR: She takes his hand and presses it to her breast, weeping reproachful and entreating tears, exactly as if they were husband and wife. Man though he is, he also weeps.

TOKUBEI: You're right, entirely right, but what good would it have done to tell you and make you suffer? I've been going through such misery that I couldn't be more distracted if Bon, New Year, the Ten Nights, and every other feast in the calendar came all at once. My mind's been in a turmoil, and my finances in chaos. To tell the truth, I went up to Kyoto to raise some money, among other things. It's a miracle I'm still alive. If they make my story into a three-act play, I'm sure the audiences will weep.

NARRATOR: Words fail and he can only sigh.

OHATSU: And is this the comic relief of your tragedy? Why couldn't you have trusted me with your worries when you tell me even trivial little things? You must've had some reason for hiding. Why don't you take me into your confidence?

NARRATOR: She leans over his knee. Bitter tears soak her handkerchief.

TOKUBEI: Please don't cry or be angry with me. I wasn't hiding anything, but it wouldn't have helped to involve you. At any rate, my troubles have largely been settled, and I can tell you the whole story now.

My master has always treated me with particular kindness because I'm his nephew. For my part, I've served him with absolute honesty. There's never been a penny's discrepancy in the accounts. It's true that recently I used his name when I bought on credit a bolt of Kaga silk to make into a summer kimono, but that's the one and only time, and if I have to raise the money on the spot, I can always sell back the kimono without taking a loss. My master has been so impressed by my honesty that he proposed I marry his wife's niece with a dowry of two *kamme*,° and promised to set me up in business. That happened last year, but how could I shift my affections when I have you? I didn't give his suggestion a second thought, but in the meantime my mother—she's really my stepmother—conferred with my master, keeping it a secret from me. She went back

kamme: A considerable sum of money.

to the country with the two *kamme* in her clutches. Fool that I am, I never dreamt what had happened.

The trouble began last month when they tried to force me to marry. I got angry and said, "Master, you surprise me. You know how unwilling I am to get married, and yet you've inveigled my old mother into giving her consent. You've gone too far, master. I can't understand the mistress's attitude either. If I took as my wife this young lady whom I've always treated with the utmost deference and accepted her dowry in the bargain, I'd spend my whole life dancing attendance on my wife. How could I ever assert myself? I've refused once, and even if my father were to return from his grave, the answer would still be no."

The master was furious that I should have answered so bluntly. His voice shook with rage. "I know your real reasons. You're involved with Ohatsu, or whatever her name is, from the Temma House in Dōjima. That's why you seem so averse to my wife's niece. Very well—after what's been said, I'm no longer willing to give you the girl, and since there's to be no wedding, return the money. Settle without fail by the twenty-second of the month and clear your business accounts. I'll chase you from Osaka and never let you set foot here again!"

I too have my pride as a man. "Right you are!" I answered, and rushed off to my village. But my so-called mother wouldn't let the money from her grip, not if this world turned into the next. I went to Kyoto, hoping to borrow the money from the wholesale soy sauce dealers in the Fifth Ward. I've always been on good terms with them. But, as ill luck would have it, they had no money to spare. I retraced my steps to the country, and this time, with the intercession of the whole village, I managed to extract the money from my mother. I intended to return the dowry immediately and settle things for once and for all. But if I can't remain in Osaka, how shall I be able to meet you?

My bones may be crushed to powder, my flesh be torn away, and I may sink, an empty shell, in the slime of Shijimi River. Let that happen if it must, but if I am parted from you, what shall I do?

NARRATOR: He weeps, suffocated by his grief. Ohatsu, holding back the welling tears of sympathy, strengthens and comforts him.

OHATSU: How you've suffered! And when I think that it's been because of me, I feel happy, sad, and most grateful all at once. But please, show more courage. Pull yourself together. Your uncle may have forbidden you to set foot in Osaka again, but you haven't committed robbery or arson. I'll think of some way to keep you here. And if a time should come when we can no longer meet, did our promises of love hold only for this world? Others before us have chosen reunion through death. To die is simple enough—none will hinder and none be hindered on the journey to the Mountain of Death and the River of Three Ways.

NARRATOR: Ohatsu falters among these words of encouragement, choked by tears. She resumes.

OHATSU: The twenty-second is tomorrow. Return the money early, since you must return it anyway. Try to get in your master's good graces again.

TOKUBEI: I want to, and I'm impatient to return the money, but on the thirteenth of the month Kuheiji the oil merchant—I think you know him—begged me desperately for the money. He said he needed it only for one day, and promised to return it by the morning of the eighteenth. I decided to lend him the money since I didn't need it until the twenty-second, and it was for a friend close as a brother. He didn't get in touch with me on the eighteenth or nineteenth. Yesterday he was out and I couldn't see him. I intended to call on him this morning, but I've spent it making the rounds of my customers in order to wind up my business by tomorrow. I'll go to him this evening and settle everything. He's a man of honor and he knows my predicament. I'm sure nothing will go wrong. Don't worry. Oh—look there, Ohatsu!

NARRATOR:

"Hatsuse is far away,
Far too is Naniwa-dera:
So many temples are renowned
For the sound of their bells,
Voices of the Eternal Law.
If, on an evening in spring,
You visit a mountain temple
You will see..."

At the head of a band of revelers

TOKUBEI: Kuheiji! That's a poor performance! You've no business running off on excursions when you haven't cleared up your debt with me. Today we'll settle our account.

NARRATOR: He grasps Kuheiji's arm and restrains him. Kuheiji's expression is dubious.

KUHEIJI: What are you talking about, Tokubei? These people with me are all residents of the ward. We've had a meeting in Ueshio Street to raise funds for a pilgrimage to Ise. We've drunk a little saké, but we're on our way home now. What do you mean by grabbing my arm? Don't be rowdy!

NARRATOR: He removes his wicker hat and glares at Tokubei.

TOKUBEI: I'm not being rowdy. All I ask is that you return the two *kamme* of silver I lent you on the thirteenth, which you were supposed to repay on the eighteenth.

NARRATOR: Before he can finish speaking, Kuheiji bursts out laughing.

KUHEIJI: Are you out of your mind, Tokubei? I can't remember having borrowed a penny from you in all the years I've known you. Don't make any accusations which you'll regret.

NARRATOR: He shakes himself free. His companions also remove their hats. Tokubei pales with astonishment.

TOKUBEI: Don't say that, Kuheiji! You came to me in tears, saying that you couldn't survive your monthly bills, and I thought that this was the kind of emergency for which we'd been friends all these years. I lent you the money as an act of generosity, though I needed it desperately myself. I told you that I didn't even require a receipt, but you insisted on putting your seal to one, for form's sake. You made me write out a promissory note and you sealed it. Don't try to deny it, Kuheiji!

NARRATOR: Tokubei rebukes him heatedly.

KUHEIJI: What's that? I'd like to see the seal.

TOKUBEI: Do you think I'm afraid to show you?

NARRATOR: He produces the paper from his wallet.

TOKUBEI: If these gentlemen are from the ward, I am sure that they will recognize your seal. Will you still dispute it?

NARRATOR: When he unfolds the paper and displays it, Kuheiji claps his hands in recollection.

KUHEIJI: Yes, it's my seal all right. Oh, Tokubei, I never thought you'd do such a thing, not even if you were starving and forced to eat dirt. On the tenth of the month I lost a wallet containing the seal. I advertised for it everywhere, but without success, so as of the sixteenth of this month, as I've informed these gentlemen, I've changed my seal. Could I have affixed the seal I lost on the tenth to a document on the thirteenth? No—what happened was that you found my wallet, wrote the promissory note, and affixed my seal. Now you're trying to extort money from me—that makes you a worse criminal than a forger. You'd do better, Tokubei, to commit out-and-out robbery. You deserve to have your head cut off, but for old times' sake, I'll forgive you. Let's see if you can make any money out of this!

NARRATOR: He throws the note in Tokubei's face and glares at him fiercely in an extraordinary display of feigned innocence. Tokubei, furious, cries aloud.

TOKUBEI: You've been damned clever. You've put one over on me. I'm dishonored. What am I to do? Must I let you take my money brazenly from me? You've planned everything so cleverly that even if I go to court, I'm sure to lose. I'll take back my money with my fists! See here! I'm Tokubei of the Hirano-ya, a man of honor. Do you follow me? I'm not a man to trick a friend out of his money the way you have. Come on!

NARRATOR: He falls on Kuheiji.

KUHEIJI: You impudent little apprentice! I'll knock the insolence out of you!

NARRATOR: He seizes the front of Tokubei's kimono and they grapple, trading blows and shoves. Ohatsu rushes barefoot to them.

OHATSU (*to townsmen*): Please everybody, stop the fight! He's a friend of mine. Where are the chair-bearers? Why don't they do something? Tokubei's being beaten!

NARRATOR: She writhes in anguish, but is helpless. Her customer, country bumpkin that he is, bundles her forcibly into a palanquin.

CUSTOMER: It won't do for you to get hurt.

OHATSU: Please wait just a moment! Oh, I'm so un-happy!

NARRATOR: The palanquin is rushed off, leaving only the echoes of her weeping voice.

Tokubei is alone; Kuheiji has five companions. Men rush out from the nearby booths and drive them all with sticks to the lotus pond. Who tramples Tokubei? Who beats him? There is no way to tell. His hair is disheveled, his sash undone. He stumbles and falls to this side and that.

TOKUBEI: Kuheiji, you swine! Do you think I'll let you escape alive?

NARRATOR: He staggers about searching for Kuheiji, but he has fled and vanished. Tokubei falls heavily in his tracks and, weeping bitterly, he cries aloud.

TOKUBEI (*to bystanders*): I feel humiliated and ashamed that you've seen me this way. There was not a false word in my accusation. I've always treated Kuheiji like a brother, and when he begged me for the money, saying he'd never forget it as long as he lived, I lent it to him, sure that he'd do the same for me, though the money was precious as life, and I knew that without it tomorrow, the twenty-first, I'd have to kill myself. He made me write the note in my own hand, then put his seal to it. But it was a seal which he had already reported as lost, and now he's turned the accusations against me! It's mortifying, infuriating—to be kicked and beaten this way, dishonored and forced to my knees. It would've been better if I had died while smashing and biting him!

NARRATOR: He strikes the ground and gnashes his teeth, clenches his fists and moans, a sight to stir compassion.

TOKUBEI: There's no point in my talking this way. Before three days have passed I, Tokubei, will make amends by showing all Osaka the purity at the bottom of my heart.

NARRATOR: The meaning of these words is later known.

TOKUBEI: I'm sorry to have bothered you all. Please forgive me.

NARRATOR: He speaks his apologies, picks up his battered hat and puts it on. His face, downcast in the sinking rays of the sun, is clouded by tears that engulf him. Dejectedly he leaves, a sight too pitiful to behold.

Scene Two: *Inside the Temma House. Time: Evening of the same day.*

NARRATOR:
The breezes of love are all-pervasive
By Shijimi River, where love-drowned guests
Like empty shells, bereft of their senses,
Wander the dark ways of love
Lit each night by burning lanterns,
Fireflies that glow in the four seasons,
Stars that shine on rainy nights.

By Plum Bridge, blossoms show even in summer.
Rustics on a visit, city connoisseurs,
All journey the varied roads of love,
Where adepts wander and novices play:
What a lively place this New Quarter is!

But alas for Ohatsu of the Temma House—even after she returns the day's events still weigh on her. She cannot swallow her saké, she feels on edge. As she sits weeping, some courtesans from the neighboring houses and other friends come for a little chat.

FIRST COURTESAN: Have you heard, Ohatsu? They say that Toku was given a thrashing for something bad he did. Is it true?

SECOND COURTESAN: No, my customer told me that Toku was trampled to death.

NARRATOR: They say he was lettered for fraud or trussed for counterfeiting a seal. Not one decent thing have they to report: every expression of sympathy makes their visit the more painful.

OHATSU: No, please, not another word. The more I hear, the worse my breast pains me. I'm sure I'll be the first to die. I wish I were dead already.

NARRATOR: She can only weep. But amidst her tears she happens to look outside and catches a glimpse of Tokubei, a pathetic figure wearing a wicker hat, even at night. Her heart leaps, and she wants to run to him, but in the sitting room are the master and his wife, and by the entrance stands the cook, while in the kitchen a maid is hovering: with so many sharp eyes watching, she cannot do as she pleases.

OHATSU: I feel terribly depressed. I think I'll step outside for a moment.

NARRATOR: She slips out softly.

OHATSU: What happened? I've heard rumors of every sort about you. They've driven me out of my mind with worry.

NARRATOR: She thrusts her face under the brim of his wicker hat and weeps in secret, soundless, painful tears. He too is lost in tears.

TOKUBEI: I've been made the victim of a clever plot, as no doubt you've heard, and the more I struggle, the worse off I am. Everything has turned against me now. I can't survive this night. I've made up my mind to it.

NARRATOR: As he whispers, voices are heard from within.

VOICES: Come inside, Ohatsu. There's enough gossip about you as it is.

OHATSU: There—did you hear? We can't go on talking. Do as I show you.

NARRATOR: She hides him under the train of her mantle. He crawls behind her to the garden door, where he slips beneath the porch at the step. Ohatsu sits by the entrance and, pulling the tobacco tray to her, lights her pipe. She assumes an air of unconcern.

At this moment Kuheiji and a couple of his loud-mouthed friends burst in, accompanied by a blind musician.

KUHEIJI: Hello, girls. You're looking lonesome. Would you like me for a customer? Hello there, host. I haven't seen you in ages.

NARRATOR: He strides arrogantly into the room.

HOST: Bring a tobacco tray and some saké cups.

NARRATOR: He makes the customary fuss over the guests.

KUHEIJI: No, don't bother about saké. We were drinking before we came. I have something to tell you. Tokubei, the number one customer of your Ohatsu, found a seal I'd lost and tried to cheat me out of two *kamme* in silver with a forged note. The facts were too much for him, and he finally met with some unpleasantness from which he was lucky to escape alive. His reputation has been ruined. Be on your guard if he comes here again. Everybody will tell you that I speak the truth, so even if Tokubei tells you the exact opposite, don't believe him for a moment. You'd do best not to let him in at all. Sooner or later he's bound to end up on the gallows.

NARRATOR: He pours out his words convincingly. Tokubei, underneath the porch, gnashes his teeth and trembles with rage. Ohatsu, afraid that he may reveal himself, calms him with her foot, calms him gently. The host is loath to answer yes or no, for Tokubei's a customer of long standing.

HOST: Well, then, how about some soup?

NARRATOR: Covering his confusion, he leaves the room. Ohatsu, weeping bitterly, exclaims.

OHATSU: You needn't try your clever words on me. Tokubei and I have been intimate for years. We've told each other our inmost secrets. He hasn't a particle of deceit in him, the poor boy. His generosity has been his undoing. He's been tricked, but he hasn't the evidence to prove it. After what has happened Tokubei has no choice but to kill himself. I wish I knew whether or not he was resolved to die.

NARRATOR: She pretends to be talking to herself, but with her foot she questions him. He nods, and taking her ankle, passes it across his throat, to let her know that he is bent on suicide.

OHATSU: I knew it. I knew it. No matter how long one lives, it comes to the same thing. Only death can wipe out the disgrace.

NARRATOR: Kuheiji is startled by her words.

KUHEIJI: What is Ohatsu talking about? Why should Tokubei kill himself? Well, if he kills himself, I'll take good care of you after he is gone! I think you've fallen for me too!

OHATSU: That's most generous of you, I'm sure. But would you object if, by way of thanks for your kindness, I killed you? Could I go on living even a moment if separated from Toku? Kuheiji, you dirty thief! Anyone hearing your silly lies can only suspect you. I'm sure that Toku intends to die with me, as I with him.

NARRATOR: She taps with her foot, and Tokubei, weeping, takes it in his hands and reverently touches it to his forehead. He embraces her knees and sheds tears

of love. She too can hardly conceal her emotions. Though no word is spoken, answering each other heart to heart, they silently weep. That no one knows makes it sadder still.

Kuheiji feels uncomfortable.

KUHEIJI: The wind's against us today. Let's get out of here. The whores in this place are certainly peculiar—they seem to have an aversion for customers like ourselves with plenty of money to spend. Let's stop at the Asa House and have a drink there. We'll rattle around a couple of gold pieces, then go home to bed. Oh—my wallet is so heavy I can hardly walk.

NARRATOR: Spewing forth all manner of abuse, they noisily depart. The host and his wife call to the servants.

HOST: It's time to put out the lights for the night. Lay out beds for the guests who are staying on. Ohatsu, you sleep upstairs. Get to bed early.

OHATSU (*to herself*): Master, mistress, I shall probably never see you again. Farewell. Farewell to all the servants too.

NARRATOR: Thus inwardly taking leave, she goes to her bedchamber. Later they will learn that this was a parting for life; how pitiful the foolish hearts of men who do not realize the truth in time!

HOST: See that the fire is out under the kettle. Don't let the mice get at the relishes.

NARRATOR: They shut the place and bar the gate. Hardly have their heads touched their pillows than all are snoring merrily. So short is the night that before they've had a chance to dream, two o'clock in the morning has come. Ohatsu is dressed for death, a black cloak dark as the ways of love thrown over her kimono of spotless white. She tiptoes to the staircase and looks down. Tokubei shows his face from under the porch. He beckons, nods, points, communicating his intent without a word. Below the stairs a servant girl is sleeping. A hanging lantern brightly shines. Ohatsu in desperation attaches her fan to a palm-leaf broom, and from the second step of the staircase attempts in vain to extinguish the flame. At last, by stretching every inch, she puts it out, only to tumble suddenly down the stairs. The lamp is out, and in the darkness the servant girl turns in her sleep. Trembling, the lovers grope for each other—a fearful moment. The host awakens in his room to the back.

HOST: What was that noise just now? Servants! The night lamp has gone out. Get up and light it!

NARRATOR: The servant girl, aroused, sleepily rubs her eyes and gets up from bed stark naked.

SERVANT: I can't find the flint box.

NARRATOR: She wanders about the room searching, and Ohatsu, faint with terror, dodges this way and that to avoid her. At last she catches Tokubei's hand, and softly they creep to the entranceway. They unfasten the latch, but the hinges creak, and frightened by the noise, they hesitate. Just then the maid begins to strike the flints; they time their actions to the rasping

sound, and with each rasp open the door farther until, huddled together and their sleeves twisted round
them, they pass through the door one after the other,
feeling as though they tread on a tiger's tail. They
exchange glances and cry out for joy, happy that
they are to die—a painful, heart-rending sight. The
life left them now is as brief as sparks that fly from
blocks of flint.

Scene Three: *The journey from Dōjima to the Sonezaki
Shrine.*

NARRATOR:
Farewell to this world, and to the night farewell.
We who walk the road to death, to what should we
    be likened?
To the frost by the road that leads to the graveyard,
Vanishing with each step we take ahead:
How sad is this dream of a dream!

TOKUBEI:
Ah, did you count the bell? Of the seven strokes
That mark the dawn, six have sounded.
The remaining one will be the last echo
We shall hear in this life.

OHATSU:
It will echo the bliss of nirvana.

NARRATOR:
Farewell, and not to the bell alone—
They look a last time on the grass, the trees, the sky.
The clouds, the river go by unmindful of them;
The Dipper's bright reflection shines in the water.

TOKUBEI:
Let's pretend that Umeda Bridge
Is the bridge the magpies built
Across the Milky Way, and make a vow
To be husband and wife stars for eternity.

OHATSU:
I promise. I'll be your wife forever.

NARRATOR:
They cling together—the river waters
Will surely swell with the tears they shed.
Across the river, in a teahouse upstairs,
Some revelers, still not gone to bed,
Are loudly talking under blazing lamps—
No doubt gossiping about the good or bad
Of this year's crop of lovers' suicides;
Their hearts sink to hear these voices.

TOKUBEI:
How strange! but yesterday, even today,
We spoke as if such things did not concern us.
Tomorrow we shall figure in their gossip.
If the world will sing about us, let it sing.

NARRATOR:
This is the song that now they hear.
    "I'm sure you'll never have me for your wife,
    I know my love means nothing to you..."
Yes, for all our love, for all our grieving,
Our lives, our lots, have not been as we wished.
Never, until this very day, have we known
A single night of heart's relaxation—

Instead, the tortures of an ill-starred love.
    "What is this bond between us?
I cannot forget you.
But you would shake me off and go—
I'll never let you!
Kill me with your hands, then go.
I'll never release you!"
So she said in tears.

OHATSU:
Of all the many songs, that one, tonight!

TOKUBEI:
Who is it singing? We who listen

BOTH:
Suffer the ordeal of those before us.

NARRATOR:
They cling to each other, weeping bitterly.
Any other night would not matter
If tonight were only a little longer,
But the heartless summer night, as is its wont,
Breaks as cockcrows hasten their last hour.

TOKUBEI:
It will be worse if we wait for dawn.
Let us die in the wood of Tenjin.

NARRATOR:
He leads her by the hand.
At Umeda Embankment, the night ravens.

TOKUBEI:
Tomorrow our bodies may be their meal.

OHATSU:
It's strange, this is your unlucky year
Of twenty-five, and mine of nineteen.
It's surely proof how deep are our ties
That we who love each other are cursed alike.
All the prayers I have made for this world
To the gods and to the Buddha, I here and now
Direct to the future: in the world to come
May we be reborn on the same lotus!

NARRATOR:
One hundred eight the beads her fingers tell
On her rosary;° tears increase the sum.
No end to her grief, but the road has an end:
Their minds are numbed, the sky is dark, the wind
    still,
They have reached the thick wood of Sonezaki.
    Shall it be here, shall it be there? When they brush
    the grass, the falling dew vanishes even quicker
    than their lives, in this uncertain world a
    lightning flash—or was it something else?

OHATSU: I'm afraid. What was that now?

TOKUBEI: That was a human spirit. I thought we alone
    would die tonight, but someone else has preceded
    us. Whoever it may be, we'll have a companion on
    the journey to the Mountain of Death. *Namu Amida
    Butsu. Namu Amida Butsu.*°

---

rosary: A Buddhist rosary. ***Namu Amida Butsu:*** Calling the
name of the Amida Buddha, an incarnation of Siddhartha
Gautama, with sincerity should grant the individual eternal life
in The Pure Land—hence Pure Land Buddhism.

NARRATOR: She weeps helplessly.

OHATSU: To think that others are dying tonight too! How heartbreaking!

NARRATOR: Man though he is, his tears fall freely.

TOKUBEI: Those two spirits flying together—do you suppose they belong to anyone else? They must be yours and mine!

OHATSU: Those two spirits? Then, are we dead already?

TOKUBEI: Normally, if we saw a spirit, we'd knot our clothes and murmur prayers to keep our souls with us, but now we hurry towards our end, hoping instead our two souls will find the same dwelling. Do not mistake the way, do not lose me!

NARRATOR: They embrace, flesh to flesh, then fall to the ground and weep—how pitiful they are! Their strings of tears unite like entwining branches, or the pine and palm that grow from a single trunk, a symbol of eternal love. Here the dew of their unhappy lives will at last settle.

TOKUBEI: Let this be the spot.

NARRATOR: He unfastens the sash of his cloak. Ohatsu removes her tear-stained outer robe, and throws it on the palm tree; the frond might now serve as a broom to sweep away the sad world's dust. Ohatsu takes a razor from her sleeve.

OHATSU: I had this razor prepared in case we were overtaken on the way and separated. I was determined not to forfeit our name as lovers. How happy I am that we are to die together as we hoped!

TOKUBEI: How wonderful of you to have thought of that! I am so confident in our love that I have no fears even about death. And yet it would be unfortunate if because of the pain we are to suffer people said that we looked ugly in death. Let us secure our bodies to this twin-trunked tree and die immaculately! We will become an unparalleled example of a lovers' suicide.

OHATSU: Yes, let us do that.

NARRATOR: Alas! She little thought she thus would use her light blue undersash! She draws it taut, and with her razor slashes it through.

OHATSU: The sash is cut, but you and I will never be torn apart.

NARRATOR: She sits, and he binds her twice, thrice to the tree, firmly so that she will not stir.

TOKUBEI: Is it tight?

OHATSU: Very tight.

NARRATOR: She looks at her husband, and he at her—they burst into tears.

BOTH: This is the end of our unhappy lives!

TOKUBEI: No I mustn't give way to grief.

NARRATOR: He lifts his head and joins his hands in prayer.

TOKUBEI: My parents died when I was a boy, and I grew up thanks to the efforts of my uncle, who was my master. It disgraces me to die without repaying his kindness. Instead I shall cause him trouble which will last even after my death. Please forgive my sins.

Soon I shall see my parents in the other world. Father, Mother, welcome me there!

NARRATOR: He weeps. Ohatsu also joins her hands.

OHATSU: I envy you. You say you will meet your parents in the world of the dead. My father and mother are in this world and in good health. I wonder when I shall see them again. I heard from them this spring, but I haven't seen them since the beginning of last autumn. Tomorrow, when word reaches the village of our suicides, how unhappy they will be! Now I must bid farewell for this life to my parents, my brothers and sisters. If at least my thoughts can reach you, please appear before me, if only in dreams. Dear Mother, beloved Father!

NARRATOR: She sobs and wails aloud. Her husband also cries out and sheds incessant tears in all too understandable emotion.

OHATSU: We could talk forever, but it serves no purpose. Kill me, kill me quickly!

NARRATOR: She hastens the moment of death.

TOKUBEI: I'm ready.

NARRATOR: He swiftly draws his dagger.

TOKUBEI: The moment has come. *Namu Amida. Namu Amida.*

NARRATOR: But when he tries to bring the blade against the skin of the woman he's loved, and held and slept with so many months and years, his eyes cloud over, his hand shakes. He tries to steady his weakening resolve, but still he trembles, and when he thrusts, the point misses. Twice or thrice the flashing blade deflects this way and that until a cry tells it has struck her throat.

TOKUBEI: *Namu Amida. Namu Amida. Namu Amida Butsu.*

NARRATOR: He twists the blade deeper and deeper, but the strength has left his arm. When he sees her weaken, he stretches forth his hands. The last agonies of death are indescribable.

TOKUBEI: Must I lag behind you? Let's draw our last breaths together.

NARRATOR: He thrusts and twists the razor in his throat, until it seems the handle or the blade must snap. His eyes grow dim, and his last painful breath is drawn away at its appointed hour. No one is there to tell the tale, but the wind that blows through Sonezaki Wood transmits it, and high and low alike gather to pray for these lovers who beyond a doubt will in the future attain Buddhahood. They have become models of true love.

COMMENTARY

DONALD H. SHIVELY (1921–2005)

The Development
of Theater Buildings   1978

Donald Shively discusses the development of the kabuki theater from 1600, beginning with the theater of Nō drama, through its use of revolving stages in 1830. The experience of the audience was radically altered by the changes in theater design, especially the hanamichi, a runway that took the actor into the audience while still maintaining his distance from both the main action and the onlookers.

The earliest kabuki performances [...] were staged in rudimentary enclosures which could be hastily constructed if subscription *nō* stages were not already available in the amusement quarters at the edge of the cities. From about 1617 Kyoto began issuing licenses to operate theaters. As was true of houses of prostitution, the theaters were increasingly restricted to certain quarters of the city. In Kyoto they were clustered in the area of Shijō, just east of the river, and although as many as seven licenses were issued by 1669, it is not clear how many were in operation at one time.[1] This concentration parallels the establishment of the large prostitution quarters at Shimabara, several miles to the southwest, in 1641. The Shijō theater area and riverbank was a large amusement center in which kabuki was one of many dozens of diversions. There were smaller playhouses, puppet theaters, and a number of wayside entertainers who recited tales from military epics, the *Taiheiki* and *Heike monogatari*. There were fortune-tellers, dentists, *sumō* wrestlers, jugglers, and tightrope walkers. There were sideshows exhibiting such freaks as the female giant and the armless woman archer. There were exotic animals—tigers, bears, porcupines, eagles and peacocks, performing monkeys, and dancing dogs. Teahouses, restaurants, and refreshment stands lined the streets. Paintings of the period show these establishments crowded together, thronged with people of every description.[2]

Edo performances of women's kabuki and youths' kabuki took place as early as 1617 in the Yoshiwara and the nearby amusement area of Nakabashi. The first theater

[1]Dōmoto Kansei (Yatarō), *Kamigata engeki shi* (Tokyo: Shun'yōdō, 1934), p. 41; Takano Tatsuyuki, *Nihon engeki shi* (Tokyo: Tōkyō-dō, 1948), II:265–269. Dōmoto believes that seven theaters were licensed as early as 1624, but Takano's opinion that this did not happen until 1669–1670 seems more probable.

[2]There are many illustrations of the scene at the Shijō riverbank, including performances of *onna kabuki*, *wakashu kabuki*, and a variety of sideshows in screen paintings of the second quarter of the seventeenth century, as in Kondō Ichitarō, *Japanese Genre Painting: The Lively Art of Renaissance Japan*, trans. R. A. Miller (Tokyo: Charles E. Tuttle Co., 1961), plates 4, 66–71, pp. 22 and 24; also Kikuchi Sadao et al., eds., *Kinsei fūzoku zukan* (Tokyo: Mainichi Shimbunsha, 1974), II:109; and Kyoto Kokuritsu Hakubutsukan, comp., *Rakuchū rakugai zu* (Tokyo: Kadokawa Shoten, 1966), unnumbered plates at back.

to be licensed was the Saruwaka-za in Nakabashi in 1624, later renamed Nakamura-za, which continued to operate at a succession of locations until 1893. It serves as a particularly remarkable example of the exercise of an hereditary license to operate a theater. This and later kabuki theaters were ordered to move from time to time and finally, after the Meireki fire of 1657 forced the Yoshiwara far outside the city, were restricted to Sakai-chō and Kobiki-chō and shortly limited to four in number. The Tokugawa government continued to follow a policy of treating the prostitution and theater quarters as parallel concerns. When the theater quarters burned in 1841, nearly two centuries later, they were ordered to move to Saruwaka-chō in Asakusa, close by the Yoshiwara. In Osaka too, where the issuing of regular licenses to theaters followed the Edo precedent, they were restricted from the 1660s to Dōtombori and Horie.

With the issuing of licenses permitting the construction of permanent theaters, the buildings became gradually more substantial. The mat fence was replaced by solid board walls, and a row of boxes (*sajiki*) was built along the two sides of the parquet (*doma*) for spectators who required more comfort and privacy. Later boxes were added at the rear of the parquet. City officials, seeking to keep kabuki a simple form of entertainment, forbade the construction of roofs over the parquet. But resourceful theater owners devised a method of stretching mats across the parquet to serve as makeshift shelters which provided shade from the sun and protection against light showers. Over a period of two centuries the theater buildings became gradually more elaborate and comfortable as the authorities made concessions, alternating between a resigned attitude and a stricter policy of sumptuary regulation.

Set back slightly from the street so as not to obstruct traffic, the theater façade was dominated by a tower on which ornamental spears were mounted to indicate possession of an official license. This spear (or drum) tower was draped with a cloth bunting featuring the large design of the theater's crest. The Nakamura-za first used the wheeling crane (*maizuru*) design. The Ichimura-za chose a rounded crane within an octagon.[3] Most theaters placed large billboards on the tower, the center board announcing in bold characters the name of the proprietor, those on either side the names of leading actors. Lower billboards, typically four in number if the offering was a four-act play, gave the title of each act. From the 1720s a tableau from each act was painted above the title.

Before these signs stood low platforms where barkers waved their fans to attract the attention of passersby and entice them into the theater. In addition to the cruder techniques of whistling and calling to onlookers, they would attempt to draw a crowd by staging impersonations of the leading actors, imitating their voices as they recited tantalizing lines from the play, and parodying their characteristic poses and gestures. Contemporary paintings record the remarkably exuberant commitment of these *kido geisha* (entrance performers) to their task.[4]

The early theaters had only one entrance, located in the center of the building under the drum tower. It was a small opening with a high threshold which the customer

[3]The use of the crane became taboo in 1690 because the word for crane (*tsuru*) was used by the shōgun Tsunayoshi in his daughter's name, Tsuruhime. Thereafter the Nakamura-za used a gingko leaf design, and the Ichimura-za changed its crest to an orange-tree design. Suda Atsuo, *Nihon gekijō shi no kenkyū* (Tokyo: Sagami Shobō, 1957), p. 330.

[4]The six-fold screen (Tokyo National Museum) of the Nakamura-za with its new gingko-leaf crest and stage, attributed to Hishikawa Moronobu (d. 1694), appears in Kondō, plate 76 (identified inexplicably as the Morita-za); Gunji Masakatsu, *Kabuki* (New York: Kodansha America, 1969), plate 416; and Suwa Haruo, *Kabuki kaika* (Tokyo: Kadokawa Shoten, 1970), plate 58.

had to step over while ducking under a low overhead. Aptly called the mouse-entrance (*nezumi kido*), it was a holdover from the enclosures used for subscription *nō* and was presumably designed to make it difficult for anyone to slip in quickly without paying. As the theaters grew larger in the eighteenth century, an entrance was provided on each side of the drum tower for admission to the parquet. The stoop entrance was abandoned and a short curtain (*noren*) hung across the top of the doorway, as is customary in Japanese shops. Tickets were purchased outside and other fees paid within for the rental of a reed mat (*hanjō*) and a length of smoldering cord to light one's pipe. On each side of the front of the building an entrance was added for guests going to boxes in order to avoid jostling by the plebs. Inside, stairs led to the upper level of boxes.

The price of tickets ranged widely between the cheapest and the best seats. In 1714, boxes in Edo theaters commanded 1200 *mon*, single spaces 200 *mon*. Parquet tickets averaged 64 *mon*. When space was available, single-act tickets were sold for 12 *mon*. Rental of a mat was 6 *mon* additional.[5] These prices increased rather steadily through much of the Tokugawa period, probably following the general inflationary trend, but exacerbated at certain times by the escalating salaries of the star actors. Attending a major theater was not cheap. The cost of a box seat in 1828 was 1 *ryō* 2 *bu,* the equivalent of 3 bales (*hyō*) of rice or a servant's salary for three or four months. When a performance was popular, the price of tickets rose abruptly.[6]

While the Nakamura-za in Edo provides a detailed illustration of the physical design of a theater, it should be noted that no two were identical. Theaters were, moreover, periodically rebuilt, for fires frequently ravaged Edo. In the 1690s the outer dimensions of the Nakamura-za were 71.5 feet by 97.5 feet, or 6,971 square feet.[7] At its largest in 1809, it measured 80 feet by 138.5 feet, or 11,080 square feet.[8] The structure remained a fraction of the size of the present Kabuki-za in Tokyo, which has 39,000 square feet of space on the ground floor, seating 1,078 people, approximately the same number as the Tokugawa structure. But the modern building has five floors with 120,000 square feet of floor space and accommodates an additional 1,522 people on the mezzanine and balconies.[9] The Nakamura-za of 1720 had a row of boxes along the two sides and across the back. Although only one tier was allowed at that time, by 1724 a second tier of boxes had been added. It was repeatedly forbidden to hang bamboo blinds across the front of the boxes and to install screens or other partitions which would provide privacy for the occupants. However, a number of paintings from this period show such items in use, partially concealing from the gaze of the populace ladies-in-waiting of the shogun's or daimyo's households, members of the Buddhist clergy, and rich merchants.[10]

The parquet (*doma*) of the Nakamura-za, 52 feet wide and 82.4 feet deep in 1720, had a capacity of 800 persons. Later, the front half with its better seats was divided

[5]Takano, II:242–243.

[6]Gunji Masakatsu, *Kabuki to Yoshiwara* (Tokyo: Awaji Shobo, 1956), pp. 62–63; Gunji (1969), pp. 51–52. Only the large theaters of the three cities are discussed in this chapter, but there were also small, low-priced theaters known as *miyachi shibai* located on temple grounds, which were permitted to give performances for one hundred days during the year. Gunji (1956), pp. 38–42.

[7]Suda, p. 328.

[8]Zushi Yoshihiko, *Nihon no gekijō kaiko* (Tokyo: Sagami Shobō, 1947), p. 61. The largest Kyoto theaters seem to have been somewhat larger, at least in 1689 when one measured 106 by 196 feet, over 20,000 square feet. Suda, p. 330.

[9]Yoshida Teruji, ed., *Kabuki-za* (Tokyo: Kabuki-za Shuppanbu, 1951), p. 324.

[10]Zushi, p. 60; Suda, pp. 331–333; Takano, II:341. Three-tiered boxes are mentioned in 1701, but this perhaps means two tiers raised above the floor, allowing space underneath. Suda, p. 331.

into partitions (*masu*) not quite five feet square which narrowly accommodated seven or eight people.[11] Rear parquet space was unreserved. The last back seats, called the *ōmukō* (greatly beyond) were so far from the stage that they were also known as the "deaf gallery." Thus, including boxes and the cheapest parquet seats, the theater held about 1,200.[12] Operating policy was to crowd in as many as possible. According to a book of 1703, "The people came in pushing and jostling, and eight persons sat knee over knee on a mat. It is very pleasant to see them pressed together like human *sushi*."[13]

By the early eighteenth century, wooden roofs occasionally sheltered part of the pit, although not officially sanctioned until 1724. Thereafter tile roofs were recommended to decrease the danger of fire from flying embers. Even after the theaters added roofs, artificial lighting remained proscribed because of the danger to the wooden structure from the open flame of oil lamps and candles. Performances, expected to end about 5 P.M., depended on natural light from windows with translucent paper-covered *shōji* installed on both sides of the theater behind or above the upper row of boxes.[14]

Dressing rooms, located directly behind the stage, were built in two stories by the 1670s. Before the end of the century the Morita-za in Edo added a third level.[15] This section of the building was built high to take as little ground space as necessary from the stage and parquet. A passageway leading to the dressing room section was constructed behind the boxes. Though intended for use by actors to gain access to the end of the runway (*hanamichi*), it was soon traveled by actors summoned to boxes or patrons visiting dressing rooms.[16] The usual arrangement called for baths and quarters for musicians, writers, and *wakashu* on the first floor, *onnagata* on the second, and players of men's roles on the third. A large rehearsal area also occupied the third level. Leading players had individual dressing rooms, although partitions had not received official sanction.[17]

The early kabuki stage basically recreated the square *nō* stage with pillars in the four corners supporting a thatched roof. The main platform had two narrow appendages, one of the right used by the chorus in the *nō*, the other at the rear for the musicians. Off the left of the stage a "bridge" (*hashigakari*) for entrances and exits extended back at an oblique angle with a railing on each side and a long roof. These features of the *nō* stage were gradually modified in the kabuki theater, although it is surprising how long they persisted. The stage itself was only 19 feet square at the outset. Rather than alter its design, more space was gained by greatly widening the bridge and eliminating its handrails. It then emerged as a secondary performing area, a rectangle set back slightly from the main stage. A platform was appended to the front of the stage (*tsuke-butai*) which jutted into the audience. Though these changes were not completed until the first decades of the eighteenth century, some stages had already become quite large. That of the Nakamura-za measured 32.5 feet by 37.7 feet in 1724. Not until 1796, however, was the roof over the main stage eliminated.[18]

[11] From 1772, wooden partitions replaced ropes to divide the *masu*, and later the size of the *masu* was reduced until finally there was space for only four people. Suda, 339.

[12] Takano, II:343; Iizuka Tomoichirō, *Kabuki gairon* (Tokyo: Hakubunkan, 1928), p. 469; Gunji (1969),p. 50.

[13] *"(Kyō-Ōsaka) Yakusha hyōban iro jamisen,"* in *Kabuki hyōbanki shūsei* (Tokyo: Iwanami Shoten, 1973), III:327a; Takano, II:343.

[14] Suda, p. 333.

[15] Suda, p. 327.

[16] Suda, pp. 327, 329.

[17] Suda, pp. 335, 345.

[18] Suda, p. 337. The present Kabuki-za stage is 77 feet by 95 feet.

One of the most distinctive inventions of the kabuki theater is the *hanamichi*, a five-foot-wide runway which extends from the left side of the stage to the rear of the audience. It is used for more dramatic entrances and exits and as an occasional pivot of activity. Its origins are unclear. The more obvious assumption, that it began as a second *hashigakari* directed through the audience, appears to be incorrect. Perhaps as early as the 1650s a small platform was attached to the stage slightly left of center where members of the audience placed gifts (*hana*) of money or goods for their favorite actors. These were called *hana* because the gift was attached to a flower (*hana*) branch. Such a platform appears in a drawing of the Nakamura-za in 1687.[19] By 1724, at least, the *hanamichi* was a runway 52 feet long, set at an oblique angle, probably ending toward the rear end of the row of boxes on the left side of the hall. Although the word *hanamichi* may originally have meant "a path for gifts," by the 1720s and perhaps several decades earlier, it was used primarily as an extension of the stage. Woodblock prints of the next decade show actors standing or seated upon it. Occasionally a small platform called the *nanori-dai* was added about the midway point where an actor could stand almost dead center of the parquet to announce the name and pedigree (*nanori*) of the character he was portraying. After 1780 another, narrower runway was sometimes erected on the right side of the hall. Perhaps as a result, the main *hanamichi* was set at right angles to the stage, parallel to its narrower companion.[20]

[19] Suda, p. 329. There is some evidence that it was used as part of the stage by 1668. Iizuka, p. 421; Takano, II:361–363.

[20] Suda, pp. 337–341.

Perspective view of Kyogen play stage by artist Okumura Masanobu.

Artist Utagawa Toyokuni III's woodblock print of an eighteenth-century stage, with the galleries at the edges of the stage and the two balconies, the arhat dais and the yoshino.

Most of the physical features of the theater discussed on the preceding pages are illustrated in a woodblock print by Okumura Masanobu (1686–1764) of the Ichimura-za in Edo in 1744. The *nō* stage with its roof and front pillars, the appended *hashigakari* stage right and *tsuke-butai* stage front, and the *hanamichi* are clearly evident. There is a raised walk (*ayumi*) across the hall for easier access by customers and vendors to the front part of the pit. A tea and a food vendor pass through the audience. The stage curtain is drawn to stage right. Boxes of the first tier were known as quail boxes (*uzura sajiki*) because their wooden bars made them resemble crates for keeping quail. The second tier of boxes retained eaves from the days, a few decades earlier, when there was no roof over the pit. Sliding doors of translucent paper let in daylight above the boxes.[21]

In such a theater the play moved easily into the audience. The tiers of boxes at the front of the hall were alongside the stage. Later in the eighteenth century a low balcony intruded behind the left corner of the stage (stage right). Known as the *rakandai* (arhat dais), its tightly lined-up spectators hovered over the stage like the five hundred arhats of a Buddhist painting. A seventeen-syllable satirical poem (*senryū*) observes: "The five hundred went home, having seen the actors' backs."

[21] The pillar at stage left bears the name of the play, *Nanakusa wakayagi Soga*, followed by the name of the theater, Ichimura-za. The other pillar gives the name of the scene, "Yaoya Oshichi kyōdai biraki." On the beam joining the pillars we see that the Ichimura-za has reclaimed its crane crest. On stage beside her shop counter stands the vegetable dealer (*yaoya*) Oshichi, played by Segawa Kikujirō in this performance of the first month of 1744. Kichizō, played by Onoe Kikugorō, approaches on the *hanamichi*. A stage attendant waves his fan to quiet the audience. This print is an example of the Western-style perspective picture (*ukie*, "floating picture") which came into vogue about 1736. Yoshida Teruji, *Kabuki-e no kenkyū* (Tokyo: Ryokuen Shobō, 1936, 1963), pp. 98–101. The print is in the collection of the Atami Bijutsu-kan.

A second balcony inevitably grew above this. It was called *tsūten* (passing through to heaven), or Yoshino (a mountain district noted for cherry blossoms), as its perspective barely penetrated the artificial cherry blossoms suspended from the ceiling of the hall. A woodblock print of the last decades of the Tokugawa period shows the plebs, crammed in these galleries at the edge of the stage, watching gleefully, mouths agape, as the actors perform, almost within reach.[22] When the play was a great success, the management, not impervious to the potential boon, seated customers on the stage itself. This practice is recorded by the satirical poems: "A big hit—the action is performed in a six-foot square," and "Spectators and actors are lined up together—a big hit."[23] With an audience thus gathered on three sides of the performers and cheap balcony seating available over one corner of the stage, no concept of a platform-framing proscenium arch emerged.

[22] Detail of a print of a theater interior by Utagawa Toyokuni III (1786–1864), in the collection of the Waseda Daigaku Engeki Hakubutsukan (The Tsubouchi Memorial Theatre Museum, Waseda University). The entire print is reproduced in Gunji (1969), plate 448.

[23] Gunji (1956), pp. 59–60.

William Congreve

Although born in England, William Congreve (1670–1729) was educated in Ireland, first at Kilkenny School and then at Trinity College, Dublin. Jonathan Swift, whose poetry praised Congreve, was also at Kilkenny and Trinity during part of this time. They were lifelong friends and central figures in literary London. Later, Congreve read law at the Middle Temple in London and was able to make good use of his legal training in several of his plays.

Congreve's literary career began with a novel, *Incognita* (1691), which he wrote in his teens. John Dryden praised the novel and, later, Congreve's plays. After Congreve's first play was produced, the poet Thomas Southerne named Congreve the likely inheritor of Dryden's crown as poet laureate.

His first play, *The Old Bachelor* (1693), was an immediate success, establishing him as an important playwright. Later in 1693, he produced his second play, *The Double Dealer*, which had a mixed reception. Dryden, in a letter, said, "The women thinke he has exposed their Bitchery too much and the Gentlemen are offended with him; for the discovery of their follyes: & the way of their Intrigues, under the notion of Friendship to their Ladyes Husbands." Maskwell, the double dealer, is a classic manipulator who advances his own interests while damaging those of other characters. Congreve defended the play as a moral fable, but it was not until Queen Mary requested a command performance that the play was restored in the eyes of the public. *Love for Love* (1695) was for many years Congreve's most popular and best liked play. It is the story of the worthy Valentine, who is about to lose an inheritance to a younger brother. In the end Valentine's intelligence wins out, and by pretending madness he secures his beloved, the wealthy heiress Angelica, as well as his own estate. Thomas Betterton, the acclaimed Restoration actor, played Valentine in the first performances; his theater company at Lincoln's Inn Fields produced all of Congreve's work. John Gielgud played Valentine in London, opening on April 8, 1943, to considerable acclaim and continuing for 471 performances through World War II. Laurence Olivier and Lynn Redgrave played in the 1965 revival, also a success. Congreve's one tragedy, *The Mourning Bride* (1697), was very successful, although it was not revived in the twentieth century.

Congreve's career as a playwright lasted only seven years. He left the stage after the production of *The Way of the World* (1700), ostensibly because of its cool reception. Although not technically a failure, the play was not received with the enthusiasm Congreve thought it deserved. He had already been stung by Jeremy Collier's criticism of Restoration playwrights in *A Short View of the Immorality and Profaneness of the English Stage* (1698). Congreve was also annoyed by the rise of the new sentimental middle-class drama. During the rest of his life, he wrote occasional poetry, such as *A Pindarique Ode on the Victorious Progress of Her Majesties Arms* (1706), and libretti for several operas: *The Judgment of Paris* (1701), *A Hymn to Harmony* (1703), and *The Tears of Amarylis* (1703). He spent much of his later years as a retiring gentleman in the company of the duchess of Marlborough, with whom he probably had a child, Lady Mary Godolphin, who inherited his estate.

Congreve was buried in the Poets' Corner of Westminster Abbey, near Aphra Behn, who was buried at the entrance to the cloisters. Critics in his time and in succeeding generations have regarded his plays as among the purest examples of the English comic style of the late seventeenth century. *The Way of the World* has been especially singled out for praise because even though it is witty, brisk, and amusing, it is pungent and serious at the core, with characters whose intelligence and essential worth help animate a drama that vies with those of Molière.

The Way of the World

The Way of the World, Congreve's fifth and last play, has been his most enduring and—taking the long view—his most successful. It is an intellectual romp, with plot twists, disguises, and numerous complications. The names of the characters—Fainall, Mirabell, Wilfull, Witwoud, Waitwell, and Petulant—indicate Congreve's use of **stock** or **type characters**, characters immediately recognizable for their stereotypical behavior and traits. However, he always moves beneath the surface of types and reveals a satisfying complexity. Type characters have been used to advantage in all ages of comic drama, but especially in the English Restoration.

Congreve's genius shows up in his witty use of **repartee,** or quick replies. He is a master of the one-liner and the **riposte,** a sharp return in speech. Wit was a rapier in the late seventeenth century, to be used for the amusement of those intelligent enough to follow the exchanges. Early on, Witwoud says, "A wit should no more be sincere than a woman constant; one argues a decay of parts, as t'other of beauty." Mirabell tells Mrs. Fainall, "You should have just so much disgust for your husband as may be sufficient to make you relish your lover." Such a witty comment on early-eighteenth-century marriage, once we get to know Fainall and his essential viciousness, takes on a serious cast.

The plot of *The Way of the World* centers on marriage, adultery, and family fortunes. Man-about-town Mirabell wishes to marry Mrs. Millamant, who has inherited six thousand pounds and will receive another six thousand pounds if she marries in accord with the wishes of her aunt, Lady Wishfort (an older woman "full of the vigor of fifty-five"). Lady Wishfort, however, feels betrayed by Mirabell, who pretended to love her to get close to Millamant. Lady Wishfort wants Millamant to marry Sir Wilfull Witwoud, and Mirabell's efforts to make Lady Wishfort relent in this wish are carried forth on a wave of deception, disguise, and comic mixups. Mirabell and Millamant resemble traditional Shakespearean lovers such as Petruchio and Katharine in *The Taming of the Shrew* and Benedick and Beatrice in *Much Ado about Nothing*. They also resemble Aphra Behn's Willmore and Hellena and Molière's Alceste and Célimène. Millamant is every bit a match for Mirabell, and as a result, their comic scenes are intense and engaging even as they reveal the limits of Congreve's society.

The "contract" scene in act 4, in which Millamant and Mirabell discuss their intentions to marry, is both funny and very serious. Their use of

For discussion questions and assignments on *The Way of the World*, visit bedfordstmartins.com/jacobus.

legal language in what is ostensibly a romantic situation is pointedly ironic. Millamant is no starry-eyed bride. She knows that once she is married, all her possessions will belong to her husband; she will be like his chattel, to do with as he pleases. Having had the advantage of studying the marriages around her, she covenants in this scene for her independence.

The villain in the play is Fainall. While having an affair with Mrs. Marwood, he discovers that she is seriously attracted to Mirabell. No longer interested in Mrs. Marwood, he cannot turn away from her because she can expose him to his wife as an adulterer. Fainall's wife is Lady Wishfort's daughter, once married to a Mr. Languish, who has died. Before becoming involved with Fainall, Mrs. Fainall was Mirabell's mistress, but when she feared she was pregnant, Mirabell arranged the hasty marriage to Fainall, knowing that Fainall needed the widow's money and that Mrs. Fainall needed the respectability of marriage. It turned out that Mrs. Fainall was not pregnant, and now she regrets her marriage. In act 2, when she asks Mirabell why she married, he responds, "Why do we daily commit disagreeable and dangerous actions? To save that idol, reputation." Of her husband, Fainall, he says, "When you are weary of him, you know your remedy." (The epigraph at the beginning of the play warns us that adultery is the subject of the drama.) These circumstances demonstrate that Fainall, for all his villainy, is also being used by the Wishfort family.

Mirabell, like Fainall, is a manipulator but is not a villain at heart. He respects Millamant and manages ultimately to find a way to undo Fainall's schemes to control Millamant's fortune. The play does not end with everyone happy, but with Mirabell and Millamant possessing the advantage and looking forward to marriage and children. Eventually, all deceptions are revealed, the proper lovers are joined, and the complications are smoothed out. Because of its careful examination of the relationship between the sexes and of the impediments a sophisticated society can throw between them, *The Way of the World* is virtually a timeless comedy.

The Way of the World in Performance

After the play's initial poor reception, Alexander Pope praised *The Way of the World* as having "so much bullion in it as would serve to lace fifty modern comedies." It was revived relatively soon after 1701 in London, and according to theater historian Emmet Avery, it played 285 times in the eighteenth century. It was one of the first plays at the new Covent Garden Theatre on December 7, 1732, and is said to be among the most produced English comedies ever since. It is manifestly a vehicle for female stars. The great actress Dame Peggy Ashcroft, along with Dame Edith Evans, starred in the London production of 1942. The play has been produced steadily in the United States since the 1920s. The Tyrone Guthrie Theater in Minneapolis produced it in 1965 to rave notices; Jessica Tandy as Lady Wishfort essentially stole the show. Britain's Actors' Company brought it to the Brooklyn Academy of Music in 1974, with the characters wearing cutaway formal clothes, top hats, and tails instead of eighteenth-century garb. The production used telephones and other modern conveniences to demonstrate that the play is not a museum piece. Robin Phillips's 1976 Stratford, Ontario, production was described as "nothing short of brilliant." Maggie Smith played Millamant several times in the 1980s, joining Jessica Tandy in her role as Lady Wishfort. Smith's performance in the January 1985 London production underscored the fact that the role is ideal for a great comic actress. She made the play her own. A good number of recent productions, since Ray Vitra's for the Pearl Theatre in New York's East Village in 2000, have been well reviewed, despite concerns regarding the text's intelligibility for unprepared audiences.

WILLIAM CONGREVE (1670–1729)

The Way of the World   1700

Audire est operae pretium, procedere recte
Qui moechis non vultis.   — HORACE, *Satires*°

—Metuat doti deprensa.°

PROLOGUE

(*Spoken by Mr. Fainall.*)

Of those few fools who with ill stars are curst,
Sure scribbling fools, call'd poets, fare the worst;
For they're a sort of fools which Fortune makes,
And after she has made 'em fools, forsakes.
With Nature's oafs 'tis quite a different case,   5
For Fortune favors all her idiot-race;
In her° own nest the cuckoo-eggs we find,
O'er which she broods to hatch the
    changeling-kind.°
No portion for her own she has to spare,
So much she dotes on her adopted care.   10
  Poets are bubbles,° by the town drawn in,
Suffer'd at first some trifling stakes to win;
But what unequal hazards do they run!
Each time they write, they venture all they've won;

The squire that's buttered° still, is sure to be
    undone.   15
This author, heretofore, has found your favor,
But pleads no merit from his past behavior.
To build on that might prove a vain presumption,
Should grants to poets made admit resumption;
And in Parnassus° he must lose his seat,   20
If that be found a forfeited estate.
  He owns, with toil he wrought the following
    scenes,
But, if they're naught, ne'er spare him for his pains;
Damn him the more; have no commiseration
For dullness on mature deliberation.   25
He swears he'll not resent one hiss'd-off scene,
Nor, like those peevish wits, his play maintain,
Who, to assert their sense, your taste arraign.
Some plot we think he has, and some new thought;
Some humor too, no farce; but that's a fault.   30
Satire, he thinks, you ought not to expect;
For so reform'd a town who dares correct?
To please, this time, has been his sole pretense;
He'll not instruct, lest it should give offense.
Should he by chance a knave or fool expose,   35
That hurts none here, sure here are none of those.
In short, our play shall (with your leave to show it)
Give you one instance of a passive poet,
Who to your judgments yields all resignation;
So save or damn, after your own discretion.   40

[Epigraphs] Audire . . . vultis: Horace, *Satires* 1.2.37–38: "Ye that do not wish well to the proceedings of adulterers, it is worth your while to hear how they are hampered on all sides" (trans. Christopher Smart).   **Metuat doti deprensa:** Ibid., line 131. The context of the lines in which the epigraph appears is "Nor am I apprehensive, while I am in her company, . . . lest the maid . . . should be in apprehension for her limbs, *the detected wife for her portion* [dowry], I for myself" (trans. Smart). **7. her:** Fortune's.   **8. O'er which . . . changeling-kind:** The cuckoo lays its eggs in the nests of other birds to which they are left to be hatched. The implication is that Fortune is favorable to fools.   **11. bubbles:** Dupes.

15. buttered: Abundantly flattered.   **20. Parnassus:** The Greek mountain sacred to Apollo and the Muses.

Dramatis Personae

Men

FAINALL, *in love with Mrs. Marwood*
MIRABELL, *in love with Mrs. Millamant*
WITWOUD, } *followers of Mrs. Millamant*
PETULANT, }
SIR WILFULL WITWOUD, *half brother to Witwoud, and nephew to Lady Wishfort*
WAITWELL, *servant to Mirabell*

Women

LADY WISHFORT, *enemy to Mirabell, for having falsely pretended love to her*
MRS. MILLAMANT, *a fine lady, niece to Lady Wishfort, and loves Mirabell*
MRS. MARWOOD, *friend to Mr. Fainall, and likes Mirabell*
MRS. FAINALL, *daughter to Lady Wishfort, and wife to Fainall, formerly friend to Mirabell*
FOIBLE, *woman to Lady Wishfort*
MINCING, *woman to Mrs. Millamant*
BETTY, *waiting-maid at a chocolate-house*
PEG, *maid to Lady Wishfort*
DANCERS, FOOTMEN, *and* ATTENDANTS

Scene: London. The time equal to that of the presentation.

ACT I

(A Chocolate-House. Mirabell and Fainall, rising from cards; Betty waiting.)

MIRABELL: You are a fortunate man, Mr. Fainall.
FAINALL: Have we done?
MIRABELL: What you please. I'll play on to entertain you.
5 FAINALL: No, I'll give you your revenge another time, when you are not so indifferent; you are thinking of something else now, and play too negligently. The coldness of a losing gamester lessens the pleasure of the winner. I'd no more play with a man that slighted
10 his ill fortune than I'd make love to a woman who undervalued the loss of her reputation.
MIRABELL: You have a taste extremely delicate and are for refining on your pleasures.
FAINALL: Prithee, why so reserved? Something has put
15 you out of humor.
MIRABELL: Not at all. I happen to be grave today, and you are gay; that's all.
FAINALL: Confess, Millamant and you quarreled last night, after I left you; my fair cousin has some
20 humors° that would tempt the patience of a Stoic.°

---

20. **humors:** Moods.   **Stoic:** One who subscribes to the Stoic school of philosophy, which teaches freedom from passion and indifference to pleasure and pain.

What, some coxcomb° came in, and was well received by her, while you were by.
MIRABELL: Witwoud and Petulant, and what was worse, her aunt, your wife's mother, my evil genius; or to sum up all in her own name, my old Lady Wishfort 25
came in.
FAINALL: Oh, there it is then! She has a lasting passion for you, and with reason. What, then my wife was there?
MIRABELL: Yes, and Mrs. Marwood, and three or four 30
more, whom I never saw before. Seeing me, they all put on their grave faces, whispered one another; then complained aloud of the vapors,° and after fell into a profound silence.
FAINALL: They had a mind to be rid of you. 35
MIRABELL: For which reason I resolved not to stir. At last the good old lady broke through her painful taciturnity with an invective against long visits. I would not have understood her, but Millamant joining in the argument, I rose, and, with a constrained smile, told 40
her, I thought nothing was so easy as to know when a visit began to be troublesome. She reddened, and I withdrew, without expecting° her reply.
FAINALL: You were to blame to resent what she spoke only in compliance with her aunt. 45
MIRABELL: She is more mistress of herself than to be under the necessity of such a resignation.
FAINALL: What? though half her fortune depends upon her marrying with my lady's approbation?
MIRABELL: I was then in such a humor that I should have 50
been better pleased if she had been less discreet.
FAINALL: Now I remember, I wonder not they were weary of you. Last night was one of their cabal nights; they have 'em three times a week, and meet by turns at one another's apartments, where they come together 55
like the coroner's inquest, to sit upon the murdered reputations of the week. You and I are excluded; and it was once proposed that all the male sex should be excepted. But somebody moved that, to avoid scandal, there might be one man of the community; upon 60
which motion Witwoud and Petulant were enrolled members.°
MIRABELL: And who may have been the foundress of this sect? My Lady Wishfort, I warrant, who publishes her detestation of mankind, and full of the vigor of 65
fifty-five, declares for a friend° and ratafia,° and let posterity shift for itself, she'll breed no more.
FAINALL: The discovery of your sham addresses to her, to conceal your love to her niece, has provoked this separation; had you dissembled better, things might 70
have continued in the state of nature.
MIRABELL: I did as much as man could, with any reasonable conscience; I proceeded to the very last act

---

21. **coxcomb:** Conceited person, fop.   33. **vapors:** Boredom.
43. **expecting:** Awaiting.   61–62. **Witwoud ... members:** The implication is that Witwoud and Petulant are but half-men.
66. **friend:** Lover. When applied to a lady, the word carries the meaning of "mistress."   **ratafia:** Fruit-flavored liqueur.

of flattery with her, and was guilty of a song in her
75 commendation. Nay, I got a friend to put her into a
lampoon, and compliment her with the imputation
of an affair with a young fellow, which I carried so
far that I told her the malicious town took notice that
she was grown fat of a sudden; and when she lay in
80 of a dropsy,° persuaded her she was reported to be in
labor. The devil's in't, if an old woman is to be flattered further, unless a man should endeavor downright personally to debauch° her; and that my virtue
forbade me. But for the discovery of this amour I am
85 indebted to your friend, or your wife's friend, Mrs.
Marwood.

FAINALL: What should provoke her to be your enemy,
unless she has made you advances which you have
slighted? Women do not easily forgive omissions of
90 that nature.

MIRABELL: She was always civil to me till of late. I confess
I am not one of those coxcombs who are apt to interpret a woman's good manners to her prejudice, and
think that she who does not refuse 'em everything
95 can refuse 'em nothing.

FAINALL: You are a gallant man, Mirabell; and though
you may have cruelty enough not to satisfy a lady's
longing, you have too much generosity not to be tender of her honor. Yet you speak with an indifference
100 which seems to be affected, and confesses you are
conscious of a negligence.

MIRABELL: You pursue the argument with a distrust that
seems to be unaffected, and confesses you are conscious of a concern for which the lady is more in-
105 debted to you than is your wife.

FAINALL: Fie, fie, friend! If you grow censorious, I must
leave you. I'll look upon the gamesters in the next
room.

MIRABELL: Who are they?

110 FAINALL: Petulant and Witwoud. (*To Betty.*) Bring me
some chocolate. (*Exit.*)

MIRABELL: Betty, what says your clock?

BETTY: Turned of the last canonical hour,° sir.
(*Exit.*)

MIRABELL: How pertinently the jade° answers me! (*Look-
115 ing on his watch.*) Ha? almost one o'clock! O, y'are
come!

(*Enter a Footman.*)

Well, is the grand affair over? You have been something tedious.

FOOTMAN: Sir, there's such coupling at Pancras° that they

stand behind one another, as 'twere in a country 120
dance. Ours was the last couple to lead up, and no
hopes appearing of dispatch, besides the parson
growing hoarse, we were afraid his lungs would have
failed before it came to our turn, so we drove round to
Duke's place,° and there they were riveted in a trice.° 125

MIRABELL: So, so, you are sure they are married.

FOOTMAN: Married and bedded, sir; I am witness.

MIRABELL: Have you the certificate?

FOOTMAN: Here it is, sir.

MIRABELL: Has the tailor brought Waitwell's clothes 130
home, and the new liveries?

FOOTMAN: Yes, sir.

MIRABELL: That's well. Do you go home again, d'ye
hear, and adjourn the consummation till further
order; bid Waitwell shake his ears, and Dame Partlet° 135
rustle up her feathers, and meet me at one o'clock
by Rosamond's Pond,° that I may see her before she
returns to her lady; and as you tender your ears, be
secret.

(*Exit Footman.*)

(*Reenter Fainall and Betty.*)

FAINALL: Joy of your success, Mirabell; you look 140
pleased.

MIRABELL: Aye, I have been engaged in a matter of some
sort of mirth, which is not yet ripe for discovery. I am
glad this is not a cabal night. I wonder, Fainall, that
you who are married, and of consequence should be 145
discreet, will suffer your wife to be of such a party.

FAINALL: Faith, I am not jealous. Besides, most who are
engaged are women and relations; and for the men,
they are of a kind too contemptible to give scandal.

MIRABELL: I am of another opinion. The greater the cox- 150
comb, always the more the scandal; for a woman
who is not a fool can have but one reason for associ-
ating with a man who is one.

FAINALL: Are you jealous as often as you see Witwoud
entertained by Millamant? 155

MIRABELL: Of her understanding I am, if not of her
person.

FAINALL: You do her wrong; for, to give her her due, she
has wit.

MIRABELL: She has beauty enough to make any man 160
think so, and complaisance enough not to contradict
him who shall tell her so.

FAINALL: For a passionate lover, methinks you are a
man somewhat too discerning in the failings of your
mistress. 165

MIRABELL: And for a discerning man, somewhat too
passionate a lover; for I like her with all her faults,
nay, like her for her faults. Her follies are so natural,

---

80. **dropsy:** An excessive accumulation of fluid in the body.
83. **debauch:** Seduce. 113. **canonical hour:** It was only during
the canonical hours (eight in the morning to twelve noon) that
marriages could be legally performed. 114. **jade:** Derogatory
term for a woman. 119. **Pancras:** St. Pancras Church, where
marriages were performed without license and outside the
canonical hours.

125. **Duke's place:** St. James's Church, Aldgate. **riveted in a
trice:** Married quickly. 135. **Dame Partlet:** Refers to Foible,
who has just been married to Waitwell. "Partlet" derives
from Pertelote, the hen in Chaucer's "Nun's Priest's Tale."
137. **Rosamond's Pond:** A lake in St. James's Park.

or so artful, that they become her, and those affectations which in another woman would be odious,
serve but to make her more agreeable. I'll tell thee,
Fainall, she once used me with that insolence, that
in revenge I took her to pieces, sifted° her, and separated her failings, I studied 'em, and got 'em by rote.°
The catalogue was so large that I was not without
hopes one day or other to hate her heartily: To which
end I so used° myself to think of 'em that at length,
contrary to my design and expectation, they gave me
every hour less and less disturbance, till in a few days
it became habitual to me to remember 'em without
being displeased. They are now grown as familiar to
me as my own frailties; and in all probability, in a
little time longer I shall like 'em as well.

FAINALL: Marry her, marry her! Be half as well acquainted
with her charms as you are with her defects, and my
life on't, you are your own man again.

MIRABELL: Say you so?

FAINALL: Aye, aye, I have experience; I have a wife, and
so forth.

(*Enter a Messenger.*)

MESSENGER: Is one Squire Witwoud here?

BETTY: Yes; what's your business?

MESSENGER: I have a letter for him, from his brother Sir
Wilfull, which I am charged to deliver into his own
hands.

BETTY: He's in the next room, friend; that way.
                                              (*Exit Messenger.*)

MIRABELL: What, is the chief of that noble family in town,
Sir Wilfull Witwoud?

FAINALL: He is expected today. Do you know him?

MIRABELL: I have seen him. He promises to be an
extraordinary° person; I think you have the honor to
be related to him.

FAINALL: Yes, he is half brother to this Witwoud by a former wife, who was sister to my Lady Wishfort, my
wife's mother. If you marry Millamant, you must call
cousins too.

MIRABELL: I had rather be his relation than his
acquaintance.

FAINALL: He comes to town in order to equip himself for
travel.

MIRABELL: For travel! Why the man that I mean is above
forty.°

FAINALL: No matter for that; 'tis for the honor of England
that all Europe should know we have blockheads of
all ages.

MIRABELL: I wonder there is not an act of parliament to
save the credit of the nation, and prohibit the exportation of fools.

FAINALL: By no means; 'tis better as 'tis. 'Tis better to

trade with a little loss than to be quite eaten up with
being overstocked.

MIRABELL: Pray, are the follies of this knight-errant and
those of the squire his brother anything related?

FAINALL: Not at all; Witwoud grows by the knight, like
a medlar grafted on a crab.° One will melt in your
mouth, and t'other set your teeth on edge; one is all
pulp, and the other all core.

MIRABELL: So one will be rotten before he be ripe, and
the other will be rotten without ever being ripe at all.

FAINALL: Sir Wilfull is an odd mixture of bashfulness and
obstinacy. But when he's drunk, he's as loving as the
monster in *The Tempest*,° and much after the same
manner. To give t'other his due, he has something of
good nature and does not always want wit.

MIRABELL: Not always; but as often as his memory fails
him, and his commonplace° of comparisons. He is
a fool with a good memory and some few scraps of
other folks' wit. He is one whose conversation can
never be approved, yet it is now and then to be endured. He has indeed one good quality, he is not
exceptious;° for he so passionately affects the reputation of understanding raillery° that he will construe
an affront into a jest and call downright rudeness
and ill language, satire and fire.

FAINALL: If you have a mind to finish his picture, you
have an opportunity to do it at full length. Behold
the original!

(*Enter Witwoud.*)

WITWOUD: Afford me your compassion, my dears! Pity
me, Fainall! Mirabell, pity me!

MIRABELL: I do from my soul.

FAINALL: Why, what's the matter?

WITWOUD: No letters for me, Betty?

BETTY: Did not a messenger bring you one but now, sir?

WITWOUD: Aye, but no other?

BETTY: No, sir.

WITWOUD: That's hard, that's very hard. A messenger, a
mule, a beast of burden! He has brought me a letter
from the fool my brother, as heavy as a panegyric°
in a funeral sermon, or a copy of commendatory
verses from one poet to another. And what's worse,
'tis as sure a forerunner of the author as an epistle
dedicatory.

MIRABELL: A fool, and your brother, Witwoud!

WITWOUD: Aye, aye, my half brother. My half brother he
is, no nearer upon honor.

MIRABELL: Then 'tis possible he may be but half a fool.

---

173. **sifted:** Examined closely.   174. **got 'em by rote:** Memorized them.   177. **used:** Accustomed.   200. **extraordinary:**
Somewhat eccentric.   211. **above forty:** It was customary for
a gentleman of quality to make a "grand tour" of continental
capitals in his early twenties.

224. **medlar grafted on a crab:** The medlar is like a crab apple
and is edible only when it begins to decay. The crab apple is
always sour.   231. **the monster in *The Tempest*:** Caliban (or
possibly Sycorax) in the adaptation of Shakespeare's play by
John Dryden and Sir William Davenant (1667).   235. **commonplace:** Commonplace book; scrapbook.   240. **exceptious:**
Inclined to take exceptions.   241. **raillery:** Good-humored
ridicule; banter.   257. **panegyric:** Eulogy, especially involving
elaborate praise.

WITWOUD: Good, good, Mirabell, *le drôle!*° Good, good; hang him, don't let's talk of him. Fainall, how does your lady? Gad, I say anything in the world to get this fellow out of my head. I beg pardon that I should ask a man of pleasure and the town a question at once so foreign and domestic.° But I talk like an old maid at a marriage, I don't know what I say; but she's the best woman in the world.°

FAINALL: 'Tis well you don't know what you say, or else your commendation would go near to make me either vain or jealous.

WITWOUD: No man in town lives well with a wife but Fainall. Your judgment, Mirabell?

MIRABELL: You had better step and ask his wife, if you would he credibly informed.

WITWOUD: Mirabell.

MIRABELL: Aye.

WITWOUD: My dear, I ask ten thousand pardons; gad, I have forgot what I was going to say to you!

MIRABELL: I thank you heartily, heartily.

WITWOUD: No, but prithee excuse me; my memory is such a memory.

MIRABELL: Have a care of such apologies, Witwoud; for I never knew a fool but he affected to complain, either of the spleen° or his memory.

FAINALL: What have you done with Petulant?

WITWOUD: He's reckoning his money — my money it was. I have no luck today.

FAINALL: You may allow him to win you at play, for you are sure to be too hard for him at repartee;° since you monopolize the wit that is between you, the fortune must be his, of course.

MIRABELL: I don't find that Petulant confesses the superiority of wit to be your talent, Witwoud.

WITWOUD: Come, come, you are malicious now, and would breed debates. Petulant's my friend, and a very honest fellow, and a very pretty fellow, and has a smattering — faith and troth,° a pretty deal of an odd sort of a small wit; nay, I'll do him justice. I'm his friend, I won't wrong him. And if he had any judgment in the world, he would not be altogether contemptible. Come, come, don't detract from the merits of my friend.

FAINALL: You don't take your friend to be over-nicely bred?

WITWOUD: No, no, hang him, the rogue has no manners at all, that I must own. No more breeding than a bum-baily,° that I grant you. 'Tis pity, faith; the fellow has fire and life.

MIRABELL: What, courage?

WITWOUD: Hum, faith I don't know as to that; I can't say as to that. Yes, faith, in a controversy he'll contradict anybody.

MIRABELL: Though 'twere a man whom he feared, or a woman whom he loved.

WITWOUD: Well, well, he does not always think before he speaks; we have all our failings. You are too hard upon him, you are, faith. Let me excuse him. I can defend most of his faults, except one or two. One he has, that's the truth on't; if he were my brother, I could not acquit him. That indeed I could wish were otherwise.

MIRABELL: Aye, marry, what's that, Witwoud?

WITWOUD: Oh, pardon me! Expose the infirmities of my friend? No, my dear, excuse me there.

FAINALL: What, I warrant he's unsincere, or 'tis some such trifle.

WITWOUD: No, no, what if he be? 'Tis no matter for that; his wit will excuse that. A wit should no more be sincere than a woman constant; one argues a decay of parts,° as t'other of beauty.

MIRABELL: Maybe you think him too positive?

WITWOUD: No, no, his being positive is an incentive to argument, and keeps up conversation.

FAINALL: Too illiterate?

WITWOUD: That! that's his happiness; his want of learning gives him the more opportunities to show his natural parts.

MIRABELL: He wants words?

WITWOUD: Aye, but I like him for that now; for his want of words gives me the pleasure very often to explain his meaning.

FAINALL: He's impudent?

WITWOUD: No, that's not it.

MIRABELL: Vain?

WITWOUD: No.

MIRABELL: What! he speaks unseasonable truths sometimes, because he has not wit enough to invent an evasion?

WITWOUD: Truths! ha! ha! ha! No, no; since you will have it, I mean he never speaks truth at all, that's all. He will lie like a chambermaid, or a woman of quality's porter. Now that is a fault.

(*Enter a Coachman.*)

COACHMAN: Is Master Petulant here, mistress?

BETTY: Yes.

COACHMAN: Three gentlewomen in a coach would speak with him.

FAINALL: O brave Petulant! Three!

BETTY: I'll tell him.

COACHMAN: You must bring two dishes of chocolate and a glass of cinnamon-water.°

(*Exeunt*° *Betty and Coachman.*)

---

266. *le drôle:* The wag.   271. **foreign and domestic:** Since he knows (by gossip) that the Fainall marriage is not working out very well, Witwoud plays on the words *foreign and domestic.* 273. **best woman in the world:** I.e., Mrs. Fainall. Witwoud realizes that he has blundered into a rather delicate situation. 290. **spleen:** Ill humor; peevishness.   295. **repartee:** Adroitness and cleverness in making replies in conversation.   303. **troth:** Loyalty, faithfulness.   313. **bum-baily:** An under-bailiff, a minor court officer.

335. **parts:** Personal endowments.   365. **cinnamon-water:** A cordial of spirits, cinnamon, and hot water, prescribed to aid digestion.   [S.D.] *Exeunt:* Latin for "they go out."

WITWOUD: That should be for two fasting strumpets,° and a bawd troubled with wind.° Now you may know what the three are.

MIRABELL: You are very free with your friend's acquaintance.

WITWOUD: Aye, aye, friendship without freedom is as dull as love without enjoyment, or wine without toasting. But to tell you a secret, these are trulls° whom he allows coach-hire, and something more, by the week, to call on him once a day at public places.

MIRABELL: How!

WITWOUD: You shall see how he won't go to 'em, because there's no more company here to take notice of him. Why, this is nothing to what he used to do; before he found out this way, I have known him call for himself.

FAINALL: Call for himself? What dost thou mean?

WITWOUD: Mean! Why, he would slip you out° of this chocolate-house, just when you had been talking to him; as soon as your back was turned, whip, he was gone! Then trip to his lodging, clap on a hood and scarf, and a mask, slap into a hackney-coach, and drive hither to the door again in a trice, where he would send in for himself; that I mean, call for himself, wait for himself. Nay, and what's more, not finding himself, sometimes leave a letter for himself.

MIRABELL: I confess this is something extraordinary. I believe he waits for himself now, he is so long a-coming. Oh! I ask his pardon.

(*Enter Petulant and Betty.*)

BETTY: Sir, the coach stays.

PETULANT: Well, well, I come. 'Sbud,° a man had as good be a professed midwife as a professed whoremaster, at this rate! To be knocked up and raised at all hours, and in all places! Pox on 'em, I won't come! D'ye hear, tell 'em I won't come. Let 'em snivel and cry their hearts out.

FAINALL: You are very cruel, Petulant.

PETULANT: All's one, let it pass. I have a humor to be cruel.

MIRABELL: I hope they are not persons of condition° that you use at this rate.

PETULANT: Condition! Condition's a dried fig, if I am not in humor! By this hand, if they were your—a—a—your what-d'ye-call-'ems themselves, they must wait or rub off,° if I want appetite.°

MIRABELL: What-d'ye-call-'ems! What are they, Witwoud?

WITWOUD: Empresses, my dear; by your what-d'ye-call-'ems he means sultana queens.

PETULANT: Aye, Roxolanas.°

MIRABELL: Cry you mercy!

FAINALL: Witwoud says they are—

PETULANT: What does he say th'are?

WITWOUD: I? Fine ladies, I say.

PETULANT: Pass on, Witwoud. Harkee, by this light his relations: two co-heiresses his cousins, and an old aunt, who loves caterwauling° better than a conventicle.°

WITWOUD: Ha! ha! ha! I had a mind to see how the rogue would come off. Ha! ha! ha! Gad, I can't be angry with him, if he had said they were my mother and my sisters.

MIRABELL: No!

WITWOUD: No; the rogue's wit and readiness of invention charm me. Dear Petulant!

BETTY: They are gone, sir, in great anger.

PETULANT: Enough, let 'em trundle. Anger helps complexion, saves paint.°

FAINALL: This continence is all dissembled; this is in order to have something to brag of the next time he makes court to Millamant, and swear he has abandoned the whole sex for her sake.

MIRABELL: Have you not left off your impudent pretensions there yet? I shall cut your throat some time or other, Petulant, about that business.

PETULANT: Aye, aye, let that pass. There are other throats to be cut.

MIRABELL: Meaning mine, sir?

PETULANT: Not I. I mean nobody; I know nothing. But there are uncles and nephews in the world, and they may be rivals. What then? All's one for that.

MIRABELL: How! harkee Petulant, come hither. Explain, or I shall call your interpreter.°

PETULANT: Explain! I know nothing. Why, you have an uncle, have you not, lately come to town, and lodges by my Lady Wishfort's?

MIRABELL: True.

PETULANT: Why, that's enough. You and he are not friends; and if he should marry and have a child, you may be disinherited, ha?

MIRABELL: Where hast thou stumbled upon all this truth?

PETULANT: All's one for that; why, then say I know something.

MIRABELL: Come, thou art an honest fellow, Petulant, and shalt make love to my mistress, thou sha't,° faith. What hast thou heard of my uncle?

PETULANT: I? Nothing I. If throats are to be cut, let swords clash! Snug's the word;° I shrug and am silent.

MIRABELL: Oh, raillery, raillery! Come, I know thou art in the women's secrets. What, you're a cabalist; I

366. **strumpets:** Prostitutes. 367. **wind:** Air in the stomach or bowels. 373. **trulls:** Women of easy virtue. 382. **slip you out:** Slip out. 395. **'Sbud:** "God's blood," a mild oath. 404. **condition:** Social distinction. 409. **rub off:** Go away. **want appetite:** Lack desire for them. 414. **Roxolanas:** Roxolana is the name of the Turkish sultana in Davenant's *The Siege of Rhodes* (1656), one of the first "heroic plays."

420. **caterwauling:** Noisy quarreling. 421. **conventicle:** A meetinghouse of nonconformist religious sects, especially Presbyterians. 431. **paint:** Makeup. 446. **interpreter:** Possibly a second, as in a duel. 459. **sha't:** Slangy contraction for "shalt." 462. **Snug's the word:** In modern slang, "Mum's the word."

know you stayed at Millamant's last night, after I
went. Was there any mention made of my uncle or
me? Tell me. If thou hadst but good nature equal to
thy wit, Petulant, Tony Witwoud, who is now thy
470 competitor in fame, would show as dim by thee as
a dead whiting's° eye by a pearl of orient;° he would
no more be seen by thee than Mercury is by the sun.°
Come, I'm sure thou wo't° tell me.

PETULANT: If I do, will you grant me common sense then
475 for the future?

MIRABELL: Faith, I'll do what I can for thee, and I'll pray
that Heaven may grant it thee in the meantime.

PETULANT: Well, harkee.

(Mirabell and Petulant talk apart.)

FAINALL: Petulant and you both will find Mirabell as
480 warm a rival as a lover.

WITWOUD: Pshaw! pshaw! That she laughs at Petulant is
plain. And for my part, but that it is almost a fashion
to admire her, I should—Harkee, to tell you a secret,
but let it go no further; between friends, I shall never
485 break my heart for her.

FAINALL: How?

WITWOUD: She's handsome; but she's a sort of an uncertain woman.

FAINALL: I thought you had died for her.

490 WITWOUD: Umh—no—

FAINALL: She has wit.

WITWOUD: 'Tis what she will hardly allow anybody else.
Now, demme,° I should hate that, if she were as
handsome as Cleopatra. Mirabell is not so sure of
495 her as he thinks for.

FAINALL: Why do you think so?

WITWOUD: We stayed pretty late there last night, and
heard something of an uncle to Mirabell, who is
lately come to town, and is between him and the
500 best part of his estate. Mirabell and he are at some
distance, as my Lady Wishfort has been told; and
you know she hates Mirabell worse than a Quaker
hates a parrot,° or than a fishmonger hates a hard
frost.° Whether this uncle has seen Mrs. Millamant
505 or not, I cannot say; but there were items of such a
treaty being in embryo, and if it should come to life,
poor Mirabell would be in some sort unfortunately
fobbed,° i'faith.

FAINALL: 'Tis impossible Millamant should hearken to
510 it.

WITWOUD: Faith, my dear, I can't tell; she's a woman, and
a kind of a humorist.°

MIRABELL: And this° is the sum of what you could collect
last night?

PETULANT: The quintessence. Maybe Witwoud knows 515
more; he stayed longer. Besides, they never mind him;
they say anything before him.

MIRABELL: I thought you had been the greatest favorite.

PETULANT: Aye, *tête à tête*,° but not in public, because I
make remarks. 520

MIRABELL: You do?

PETULANT: Aye, aye, pox, I'm malicious, man! Now he's
soft, you know; they are not in awe of him. The fellow's
well bred; he's what you call a what-d'ye-call-'em,
a fine gentleman; but he's silly withal. 525

MIRABELL: I thank you. I know as much as my curiosity
requires. Fainall, are you for the Mall?°

FAINALL: Aye, I'll take a turn before dinner.

WITWOUD: Aye, we'll walk in the Park; the ladies talked
of being there. 530

MIRABELL: I thought you were obliged to watch for your
brother Sir Wilfull's arrival.

WITWOUD: No, no, he comes to his aunt's, my Lady
Wishfort. Pox on him! I shall be troubled with him
too; what shall I do with the fool? 535

PETULANT: Beg him for his estate, that I may beg you
afterwards; and so have but one trouble with you
both.

WITWOUD: O rare Petulant! Thou art as quick as fire in a
frosty morning; thou shalt to the Mall with us, and 540
we'll be very severe.

PETULANT: Enough, I'm in a humor to be severe.

MIRABELL: Are you? Pray then walk by yourselves: Let
us not be accessory to your putting the ladies out
of countenance with your senseless ribaldry,° which 545
you roar out aloud as often as they pass by you; and
when you have made a handsome woman blush, then
you think you have been severe.

PETULANT: What, what? Then let 'em either show their
innocence by not understanding what they hear, or 550
else show their discretion by not hearing what they
would not be thought to understand.

MIRABELL: But hast not thou then sense enough to know
that thou oughtest to be most ashamed thyself, when
thou hast put another out of countenance? 555

PETULANT: Not I, by this hand! I always take blushing
either for a sign of guilt or ill breeding.

MIRABELL: I confess you ought to think so. You are in the
right, that you may plead the error of your judgment
in defense of your practice. 560

　　Where modesty's ill manners, 'tis but fit
　　That impudence and malice pass for wit.

(Exeunt.)

---

471. **whiting:** A kind of codfish. **pearl of orient:** Said to be
particularly brilliant. 472. **than Mercury is by the sun:** The
planet nearest the sun and of very low magnitude. 473. **wo't:**
Wilt. 493. **demme:** Contraction of *damn me.* 502–503.
Quaker . . . parrot: Parrots are proverbially known to
swear. 503–504. **fishmonger . . . frost:** Fishmongers peddled
fish and consequently hated very cold weather. 508. **fobbed:**
Cheated. 512. **humorist:** A moody or capricious person,
hence unreliable.

513. **And this:** During the dialogue of Fainall and Witwoud,
Mirabell and Petulant have been talking "apart." They now reenter the general dialogue. 519. *tête à tête:* Literally, "head
to head." One on one, in private. 527. **Mall:** A fashionable
walk in St. James's Park. 545. **ribaldry:** Coarse behavior or
language.

Scene from an updated version of *The Way of the World,* directed by Sharon Ott in 1992 at the Huntington Theatre in Boston.

ACT II

(St. James's Park. Enter Mrs. Fainall and Mrs. Marwood.)

MRS. FAINALL: Aye, aye, dear Marwood, if we will be happy, we must find the means in ourselves, and among ourselves. Men are ever in extremes, either doting or averse. While they are lovers, if they have
5   fire and sense, their jealousies are insupportable. And when they cease to love (we ought to think at least) they loathe; they look upon us with horror and distaste; they meet us like the ghosts of what we were, and as from such, fly from us.
10 **MRS. MARWOOD:** True, 'tis an unhappy circumstance of life that love should ever die before us; and that the man so often should outlive the lover. But say what you will, 'tis better to be left than never to have been loved. To pass our youth in dull indifference, to
15   refuse the sweets of life because they once must leave us, is as preposterous as to wish to have been born old, because we one day must be old. For my part, my youth may wear and waste, but it shall never rust in my possession.

MRS. FAINALL: Then it seems you dissemble an aversion   20 to mankind, only in compliance to my mother's humor?

MRS. MARWOOD: Certainly. To be free,° I have no taste of those insipid dry discourses with which our sex of force must entertain themselves, apart from men. We   25 may affect endearments to each other, profess eternal friendships, and seem to dote like lovers; but 'tis not in our natures long to persevere. Love will resume his empire in our breasts; and every heart, or soon or late, receive and readmit him as its lawful tyrant.   30

MRS. FAINALL: Bless me, how have I been deceived! Why, you profess a libertine!°

---

23. free: Frank.   **32. profess a libertine:** Speak as one who leads a loose, unconventional life.

MRS. MARWOOD: You see my friendship by my freedom. Come, be as sincere, acknowledge that your senti-
35   ments agree with mine.
MRS. FAINALL: Never!
MRS. MARWOOD: You hate mankind?
MRS. FAINALL: Heartily, inveterately.
MRS. MARWOOD: Your husband?
40   MRS. FAINALL: Most transcendently; aye, though I say it, meritoriously.
MRS. MARWOOD: Give me your hand upon it.
MRS. FAINALL: There.
MRS. MARWOOD: I join with you; what I have said has
45   been to try you.
MRS. FAINALL: Is it possible? Dost thou hate those vipers, men?
MRS. MARWOOD: I have done hating 'em; and am now come to despise 'em; the next thing I have to do, is
50   eternally to forget 'em.
MRS. FAINALL: There spoke the spirit of an Amazon, Penthesilea!°
MRS. MARWOOD: And yet I am thinking sometimes to carry my aversion further.
55   MRS. FAINALL: How?
MRS. MARWOOD: Faith, by marrying; if I could but find one that loved me very well and would be thoroughly sensible of ill usage, I think I should do myself the violence of undergoing the ceremony.
60   MRS. FAINALL: You would not make him a cuckold?
MRS. MARWOOD: No, but I'd make him believe I did, and that's as bad.
MRS. FAINALL: Why had not you as good do it?
MRS. MARWOOD: Oh, if he should ever discover it, he
65   would then know the worst, and be out of his pain; but I would have him ever to continue upon the rack of fear and jealousy.
MRS. FAINALL: Ingenious mischief! Would thou wert mar-
ried to Mirabell.
70   MRS. MARWOOD: Would I were!
MRS. FAINALL: You change color.
MRS. MARWOOD: Because I hate him.
MRS. FAINALL: So do I; but I can hear him named. But what reason have you to hate him in particular?
75   MRS. MARWOOD: I never loved him; he is, and always was, insufferably proud.
MRS. FAINALL: By the reason you give for your aversion, one would think it dissembled; for you have laid a fault to his charge of which his enemies must acquit
80   him.
MRS. MARWOOD: Oh, then it seems you are one of his fa-
vorable enemies. Methinks you look a little pale, and now you flush again.
MRS. FAINALL: Do I? I think I am a little sick o' the
85   sudden.
MRS. MARWOOD: What ails you?

MRS. FAINALL: My husband. Don't you see him? He turned short upon me unawares, and has almost overcome me.

(*Enter Fainall and Mirabell.*)

MRS. MARWOOD: Ha! ha! ha! He comes opportunely for   90
you.
MRS. FAINALL: For you, for he has brought Mirabell with him.
FAINALL: My dear!
MRS. FAINALL: My soul!   95
FAINALL: You don't look well today, child.
MRS. FAINALL: D'ye think so?
MIRABELL: He is the only man that does, madam.
MRS. FAINALL: The only man that would tell me so at least; and the only man from whom I could hear it   100
without mortification.
FAINALL: O my dear, I am satisfied of your tenderness; I know you cannot resent anything from me, especially what is in effect of my concern.
MRS. FAINALL: Mr. Mirabell, my mother interrupted you   105
in a pleasant relation last night; I would fain hear it out.
MIRABELL: The persons concerned in that affair have yet a tolerable reputation. I am afraid Mr. Fainall will be censorious.   110
MRS. FAINALL: He has a humor more prevailing than his curiosity and will willingly dispense with the hearing of one scandalous story, to avoid giving an occasion to make another by being seen to walk with his wife. This way, Mr. Mirabell, and I dare promise you will   115
oblige us both.

(*Exeunt Mrs. Fainall and Mirabell.*)

FAINALL: Excellent creature! Well, sure if I should live to be rid of my wife, I should be a miserable man.
MRS. MARWOOD: Aye!
FAINALL: For having only that one hope, the accomplish-   120
ment of it, of consequence, must put an end to all my hopes; and what a wretch is he who must survive his hopes! Nothing remains when that day comes, but to sit down and weep like Alexander,° when he wanted other worlds to conquer.   125
MRS. MARWOOD: Will you not follow 'em?
FAINALL: Faith, I think not.
MRS. MARWOOD: Pray let us; I have a reason.
FAINALL: You are not jealous?
MRS. MARWOOD: Of whom?   130
FAINALL: Of Mirabell.
MRS. MARWOOD: If I am, is it inconsistent with my love to you that I am tender of your honor?
FAINALL: You would intimate, then, as if there were a fellow-feeling between my wife and him.   135
MRS. MARWOOD: I think she does not hate him to that degree she would be thought.

---

52. **Penthesilea:** Queen of the Amazons, the mythical race of women warriors. After befriending Priam following the death of Hector, she was killed by Achilles, who fell in love with her as she lay dying.

124. **Alexander:** Alexander the Great (356–323 BCE), the powerful ruler and conqueror.

FAINALL: But he, I fear, is too insensible.

MRS. MARWOOD: It may be you are deceived.

140 FAINALL: It may be so. I do now begin to apprehend it.

MRS. MARWOOD: What?

FAINALL: That I have been deceived, madam, and you are false.

MRS. MARWOOD: That I am false! What mean you?

145 FAINALL: To let you know I see through all your little arts. Come, you both love him; and both have equally dissembled your aversion. Your mutual jealousies of one another have made you clash till you have both struck fire. I have seen the warm confes-
150 sion reddening on your cheeks and sparkling from your eyes.

MRS. MARWOOD: You do me wrong.

FAINALL: I do not. 'Twas for my ease to oversee° and willfully neglect the gross advances made him by my
155 wife; that by permitting her to be engaged, I might continue unsuspected in my pleasures, and take you oftener to my arms in full security. But could you think, because the nodding husband would not awake, that e'er the watchful lover slept?

160 MRS. MARWOOD: And wherewithal can you reproach me?

FAINALL: With infidelity, with loving another, with love of Mirabell.

MRS. MARWOOD: 'Tis false! I challenge you to show an
165 instance that can confirm your groundless accusation. I hate him.

FAINALL: And wherefore do you hate him? He is insensible, and your resentment follows his neglect. An instance? The injuries you have done him are a proof,
170 your interposing in his love. What cause had you to make discoveries of his pretended passion? to undeceive the credulous aunt, and be the officious obstacle of his match with Millamant?

MRS. MARWOOD: My obligations to my lady urged me; I
175 had professed a friendship to her, and could not see her easy nature so abused by that dissembler.

FAINALL: What, was it conscience then? Professed a friendship! Oh, the pious friendships of the female sex!

180 MRS. MARWOOD: More tender, more sincere, and more enduring, than all the vain and empty vows of men, whether professing love to us, or mutual faith to one another.

FAINALL: Ha! ha! ha! You are my wife's friend too.

185 MRS. MARWOOD: Shame and ingratitude! Do you reproach me? You, you upbraid me? Have I been false to her, through strict fidelity to you, and sacrificed my friendship to keep my love inviolate? And have you the baseness to charge me with the guilt, unmindful
190 of the merit? To you it should be meritorious, that I have been vicious, and do you reflect that guilt upon me, which should lie buried in your bosom?

FAINALL: You misinterpret my reproof. I meant but to remind you of the slight account you once could make

153. **oversee:** Overlook.

of strictest ties, when set in competition with your 195 love to me.

MRS. MARWOOD: 'Tis false; you urged it with deliberate malice! 'Twas spoke in scorn, and I never will forgive it.

FAINALL: Your guilt, not your resentment, begets your 200 rage. If yet you loved, you could forgive a jealousy; but you are stung to find that you are discovered.

MRS. MARWOOD: It shall be all discovered. You too shall be discovered, be sure you shall. I can but be exposed. If I do it myself, I shall prevent° your baseness. 205

FAINALL: Why, what will you do?

MRS. MARWOOD: Disclose it to your wife; own what has passed between us.

FAINALL: Frenzy!

MRS. MARWOOD: By all my wrongs I'll do't! I'll publish 210 to the world the injuries you have done me, both in my fame and fortune! With both I trusted you, you bankrupt in honor, as indigent of wealth.

FAINALL: Your fame I have preserved. Your fortune has been bestowed as the prodigality of your love would 215 have it, in pleasures which we both have shared. Yet, had not you been false, I had ere this repaid it. 'Tis true, had you permitted Mirabell with Millamant to have stolen their marriage, my lady had been incensed beyond all means of reconcilement, Millamant 220 had forfeited the moiety° of her fortune, which then would have descended to my wife. And wherefore did I marry, but to make lawful prize of a rich widow's wealth, and squander it on love and you?

MRS. MARWOOD: Deceit and frivolous pretense! 225

FAINALL: Death, am I not married! What's pretense? Am I not imprisoned, fettered? Have I not a wife? nay a wife that was a widow, a young widow, a handsome widow; and would be again a widow, but that I have a heart of proof,° and something of a constitution to 230 bustle through the ways of wedlock and this world! Will you yet be reconciled to truth and me?

MRS. MARWOOD: Impossible. Truth and you are inconsistent. I hate you, and shall for ever.

FAINALL: For loving you? 235

MRS. MARWOOD: I loathe the name of love after such usage; and next to the guilt with which you would asperse me, I scorn you most. Farewell!

FAINALL: Nay, we must not part thus.

MRS. MARWOOD: Let me go. 240

FAINALL: Come, I'm sorry.

MRS. MARWOOD: I care not, let me go, break my hands, do! I'd leave 'em to get loose.

FAINALL: I would not hurt you for the world. Have I no other hold to keep you here? 245

MRS. MARWOOD: Well, I have deserved it all.

FAINALL: You know I love you.

MRS. MARWOOD: Poor dissembling! Oh, that—well, It is not yet—

205. **prevent:** Anticipate.   221. **moiety:** Half.   230. **heart of proof:** A heart that is proof against such wishes.

250 FAINALL: What? what is it not? what is it not yet? It is not yet too late—

MRS. MARWOOD: No, it is not yet too late; I have that comfort.

FAINALL: It is, to love another.

255 MRS. MARWOOD: But not to loathe, detest, abhor mankind, myself, and the whole treacherous world.

FAINALL: Nay, this is extravagance. Come, I ask your pardon. No tears. I was to blame; I could not love you and be easy in my doubts. Pray, forbear. I be-
260 lieve you. I'm convinced I've done you wrong; and any way, every way will make amends. I'll hate my wife yet more, damn her! I'll part with her, rob her of all she's worth, and we'll retire somewhere, anywhere, to another world. I'll marry thee; be pacified.
265 'Sdeath,° they come; hide your face, your tears. You have a mask;° wear it a moment. This way, this way. Be persuaded.

(*Exeunt.*)

(*Reenter Mirabell and Mrs. Fainall.*)

MRS. FAINALL: They are here yet.

MIRABELL: They are turning into the other walk.

270 MRS. FAINALL: While I only hated my husband, I could bear to see him; but since I have despised him, he's too offensive.

MIRABELL: Oh, you should hate with prudence.

MRS. FAINALL: Yes, for I have loved with indiscretion.

275 MIRABELL: You should have just so much disgust for your husband as may be sufficient to make you relish your lover.

MRS. FAINALL: You have been the cause that I have loved without bounds, and would you set limits to that
280 aversion of which you have been the occasion? Why did you make me marry this man?

MIRABELL: Why do we daily commit disagreeable and dangerous actions? To save that idol, reputation. If the familiarities of our loves had produced that con-
285 sequence of which you were apprehensive, where could you have fixed a father's name with credit, but on a husband?° I knew Fainall to be a man lavish of his morals, an interested and professing° friend, a false and a designing lover; yet one whose wit and
290 outward fair behavior have gained a reputation with the town enough to make that woman stand excused who has suffered herself to be won by his addresses. A better man ought not to have been sacrificed to the occasion; a worse had not answered to the purpose.
295 When you are weary of him, you know your remedy.

265. 'Sdeath: "God's death," an oath.   266. mask: Ladies' masks were fashionable and reputable except when worn at the theater, where they were construed as the mark of a loose woman.   283–287. If the familiarities . . . husband: Mirabell refers to his affair with Mrs. Fainall, after the death of her first husband, Mr. Languish, and prior to her marriage to Fainall. She feared that she was pregnant by Mirabell, and as a result Mirabell urged her to marry Fainall.   288. professing: Self-interested and dissembling.

MRS. FAINALL: I ought to stand in some degree of credit with you, Mirabell.

MIRABELL: In justice to you, I have made you privy to my whole design, and put it in your power to ruin or advance my fortune.
300

MRS. FAINALL: Whom have you instructed to represent your pretended uncle?

MIRABELL: Waitwell, my servant.

MRS. FAINALL: He is an humble servant° to Foible, my mother's woman, and may win her to your interest.
305

MIRABELL: Care is taken for that. She is won and worn by this time. They were married this morning.

MRS. FAINALL: Who?

MIRABELL: Waitwell and Foible. I would not tempt my servant to betray me by trusting him too far. If
310 your mother, in hopes to ruin me, should consent to marry my pretended uncle, he might, like Mosca in *The Fox,*° stand upon terms;° so I made him sure beforehand.

MRS. FAINALL: So if my poor mother is caught in a con-
315 tract, you will discover the imposture betimes, and release her by producing a certificate of her gallant's former marriage?

MIRABELL: Yes, upon condition that she consent to my marriage with her niece, and surrender the moiety of
320 her fortune in her possession.°

MRS. FAINALL: She talked last night of endeavoring at a match between Millamant and your uncle.

MIRABELL: That was by Foible's direction, and my instruction, that she might seem to carry it more privately.°
325

MRS. FAINALL: Well, I have an opinion of your success for I believe my lady will do anything to get a husband; and when she has this, which you have provided for her, I suppose she will submit to anything to get rid of him.
330

MIRABELL: Yes, I think the good lady would marry anything that resembled a man, though 'twere no more than what a butler could pinch out of a napkin.°

MRS. FAINALL: Female frailty! We must all come to it, if we live to be old and feel the craving of a false
335 appetite when the true is decayed.

MIRABELL: An old woman's appetite is depraved like that of a girl. 'Tis the green sickness° of a second

304. servant: Suitor.   312–313. Mosca . . . Fox: Mosca, the crafty servant in Ben Jonson's play *Volpone; or, The Fox* (1606).   313. stand upon terms: Insist on the proper terms of a binding contract, as Mosca does in the denouement of the Jonson play.   319–321. condition that she . . . possession: Lady Wishfort has control of half of Mrs. Millamant's (her niece's) fortune, which Millamant will acquire on her marriage, provided Lady Wishfort approves of the match; should Millamant marry without her aunt's approval, she forfeits the half of her fortune in trust.   325. she might . . . privately: I.e., to allay any suspicions Lady Wishfort might have about the validity of Mirabell's "uncle."   333. pinch out of a napkin: It was fashionable to pinch table napkins into curious and fancy shapes.   338. green sickness: An anemia prevalent in adolescent girls, marked by a sallow yellow-green complexion.

340 childhood; and, like the faint offer of a latter spring, serves but to usher in the fall, and withers in an affected bloom.

MRS. FAINALL: Here's your mistress.

(*Enter Mrs. Millamant, Witwoud, and Mincing.*)

MIRABELL: Here she comes, i'faith, full sail, with her fan
345 spread and streamers out, and a shoal of fools for tenders.° Ha, no, I cry her mercy!

MRS. FAINALL: I see but one poor empty sculler,° and he tows her woman after him.

MIRABELL (*to Mrs. Millamant*): You seem to be unat-
350 tended, madam. You used to have the *beau monde*° throng after you, and a flock of gay, fine perukes° hovering round you.

WITWOUD: Like moths about a candle. I had like to have lost my comparison for want of breath.

355 MRS. MILLAMANT: Oh, I have denied myself airs today. I have walked as fast through the crowd–

WITWOUD: As a favorite just disgraced, and with as few followers.

MRS. MILLAMANT: Dear Mr. Witwoud, truce with your si-
360 militudes;° for I'm as sick of 'em—

WITWOUD: As a physician of a good air. I cannot help it, madam, though 'tis against myself.

MRS. MILLAMANT: Yet again! Mincing, stand between me and his wit.

365 WITWOUD: Do, Mrs. Mincing, like a screen before a great fire. I confess I do blaze today; I am too bright.

MRS. FAINALL: But, dear Millamant, why were you so long?

MRS. MILLAMANT: Long! Lord, have I not made violent
370 haste? I have asked every living thing I met for you; I have inquired after you, as after a new fashion.

WITWOUD: Madam, truce with your similitudes. No, you met her husband, and did not ask him for her.

MIRABELL: By your leave, Witwoud, that were like in-
375 quiring after an old fashion, to ask a husband for his wife.

WITWOUD: Hum, a hit! a hit! a palpable hit!° I confess it.

MRS. FAINALL: You were dressed before I came abroad.

MRS. MILLAMANT: Aye, that's true. Oh, but then I had—
Mincing, what had I? Why was I so long?

380 MINCING: O mem,° your laship° stayed to peruse a pecket° of letters.

MRS. MILLAMANT: Oh, aye, letters; I had letters. I am persecuted with letters. I hate letters. Nobody knows how to write letters, and yet one has 'em, one does
385 not know why. They serve one to pin up one's hair.

WITWOUD: Is that the way? Pray, madam, do you pin up your hair with all your letters? I find I must keep copies.

MRS. MILLAMANT: Only with those in verse, Mr. Witwoud.
390 I never pin up my hair with prose, I think I tried once, Mincing.

MINCING: O mem, I shall never forget it.

MRS. MILLAMANT: Aye, poor Mincing tiffed° and tiffed all the morning.

395 MINCING: Till I had the cremp in my fingers, I'll vow, mem. And all to no purpose. But when your laship pins it up with poetry, it sits so pleasant the next day as anything, and is so pure and so crips.°

WITWOUD: Indeed, so crips?

400 MINCING: You're such a critic, Mr. Witwoud.

MRS. MILLAMANT: Mirabell, did you take exceptions last night? Oh, aye, and went away. Now I think on't, I'm angry. No, now I think on't, I'm pleased; for I believe I gave you some pain.

405 MIRABELL: Does that please you?

MRS. MILLAMANT: Infinitely; I love to give pain.

MIRABELL: You would affect a cruelty which is not in your nature; your true vanity is in the power of pleasing.

410 MRS. MILLAMANT: Oh, I ask your pardon for that. One's cruelty is one's power; and when one parts with one's cruelty, one parts with one's power; and when one has parted with that, I fancy one's old and ugly.

MIRABELL: Aye, aye, suffer your cruelty to ruin the ob-
415 ject of your power, to destroy your lover, and then how vain, how lost a thing you'll be! Nay, 'tis true: You are no longer handsome when you've lost your lover; your beauty dies upon the instant. For beauty is the lover's gift; 'tis he bestows your charms, your
420 glass is all a cheat. The ugly and the old, whom the looking-glass mortifies, yet after commendation° can be flattered by it, and discover beauties in it; for that reflects our praises, rather than your face.

MRS. MILLAMANT: Oh, the vanity of these men! Fainall,
425 d'ye hear him? If they did not commend us, we were not handsome! Now, you must know they could not commend one, if one was not handsome. Beauty the lover's gift! Lord, what is a lover, that it can give? Why, one makes lovers as fast as one pleases, and
430 they live as long as one pleases, and they die as soon as one pleases; and then, if one pleases, one makes more.

WITWOUD: Very pretty. Why, you make no more of making of lovers, madam, than of making so many card
435 matches.°

MRS. MILLAMANT: One no more owes one's beauty to a lover than one's wit to an echo. They can but reflect what we look and say; vain empty things if we are silent or unseen, and want a being.

---

345. tenders: Small boats that attend larger ships. **346. sculler:** A man operating a rowboat (i.e., Witwoud). **349. *beau monde*:** People of fashion. **350. perukes:** Suitors, referring to the wigs worn by gentlemen of the period. **359. similitudes:** Witwoud is a tireless (and tiresome) maker of comparisons, or similes. See "his commonplace [book] of comparisons" in act 1. **376. a palpable hit:** See Osric in *Hamlet*, V, ii: "A hit, a very palpable hit." **380. mem:** Madam. **laship:** Ladyship. **381. pecket:** Packet.

393. tiffed: Arranged. **398. crips:** Crisp. **421. commendation:** Praise. **434–435. card matches:** Matches made from pieces of heavy paper tipped with sulfur.

440 MIRABELL: Yet to those two vain empty things you owe two° the greatest pleasures of your life.

MRS. MILLAMANT: How so?

MIRABELL: To your lover you owe the pleasure of hearing yourselves praised; and to an echo the pleasure of 445 hearing yourselves talk.

WITWOUD: But I know a lady that loves talking so incessantly, she won't give an echo fair play; she has that everlasting rotation of tongue, that an echo must wait till she dies, before it can catch her last words.

450 MRS. MILLAMANT: Oh, fiction! Fainall, let us leave these men.

MIRABELL (*aside to Mrs. Fainall*): Draw off Witwoud.

MRS. FAINALL: Immediately. I have a word or two for Mr. Witwoud.

(*Exeunt Witwoud and Mrs. Fainall.*)

455 MIRABELL: I would beg a little private audience too. You had the tyranny to deny me last night, though you knew I came to impart a secret to you that concerned my love.

MRS. MILLAMANT: You saw I was engaged.

460 MIRABELL: Unkind! You had the leisure to entertain a herd of fools; things who visit you from their excessive idleness, bestowing on your easiness that time which is the encumbrance of their lives. How can you find delight in such society? It is impossible they 465 should admire you; they are not capable. Or if they were, it should be to you as a mortification, for sure to please a fool is some degree of folly.

MRS. MILLAMANT: I please myself. Besides, sometimes to converse with fools is for my health.

470 MIRABELL: Your health! Is there a worse disease than the conversation of fools?

MRS. MILLAMANT: Yes, the vapors; fools are physic° for it, next to assafetida.°

MIRABELL: You are not in a course of fools?°

475 MRS. MILLAMANT: Mirabell, if you persist in this offensive freedom, you'll displease me. I think I must resolve, after all, not to have you; we shan't agree.

MIRABELL: Not in our physic, it may be.

MRS. MILLAMANT: And yet our distemper,° in all likeli-480 hood, will be the same; for we shall be sick of one another. I shan't endure to be reprimanded nor instructed; 'tis so dull to act always by advice, and so tedious to be told of one's faults—I can't bear it. Well, I won't have you, Mirabell, I'm resolved—I 485 think—you may go. Ha! ha! ha! What would you give that you could help loving me?

MIRABELL: I would give something that you did not know I could not help it.

MRS. MILLAMANT: Come, don't look grave then. Well, 490 what do you say to me?

MIRABELL: I say that a man may as soon make a friend by his wit, or a fortune by his honesty, as win a woman with plain dealing° and sincerity.

MRS. MILLAMANT: Sententious Mirabell! Prithee, don't look with that violent and inflexible wise face, like 495 Solomon at the dividing of the child° in an old tapestry hanging.

MIRABELL: You are merry, madam, but I would persuade you for a moment to be serious.

MRS. MILLAMANT: What, with that face? No, if you 500 keep your countenance, 'tis impossible I should hold mine. Well, after all, there is something very moving in a lovesick face. Ha! ha! ha! Well, I won't laugh; don't be peevish. Heigho! now I'll be melancholy, as melancholy as a watchlight.° Well, Mirabell, if ever 505 you will win me, woo me now. Nay, if you are so tedious, fare you well; I see they are walking away.

MIRABELL: Can you not find in the variety of your disposition one moment—

MRS. MILLAMANT: To hear you tell me Foible's married, 510 and your plot like to speed? No.

MIRABELL: But how you came to know it—

MRS. MILLAMANT: Without the help of the devil, you can't imagine; unless she should tell me herself, Which of the two it may have been, I will leave you 515 to consider; and when you have done thinking of that, think of me.

(*Exeunt Mrs. Millamant with Mincing.*)

MIRABELL: I have something more—Gone! Think of you! To think of a whirlwind, though 'twere in a whirlwind, were a case of more steady contempla-520 tion; a very tranquility of mind and mansion. A fellow that lives in a windmill has not a more whimsical dwelling than the heart of a man that is lodged in a woman. There is no point of the compass to which they cannot turn, and by which they are not turned; 525 and by one as well as another; for motion, not method, is their occupation. To know this, and yet continue to be in love, is to be made wise from the dictates of reason, and yet persevere to play the fool by the force of instinct. Oh, here come my pair of 530 turtles!° What, billing so sweetly? Is not Valentine's Day over with you yet?

(*Enter Waitwell and Foible.*)

Sirrah, Waitwell, why, sure you think you were married for your own recreation, and not for my conveniency.

441. **two:** Two of. 472. **physic:** Medicine. 473. **assafetida:** A gum resin prescribed by doctors as an antidote to "the vapors." 474. **course of fools:** Series of treatments. 479. **distemper:** Illness.

493. **plain dealing:** Honesty, frankness. 496. **Solomon … child:** The Old Testament Solomon, king of Israel, was known for his wisdom. When confronted with two women both claiming to be the mother of a newborn baby, Solomon said he would divide the baby in two and give one half to each woman. When one of the women told the king not to slay the baby but to let it live and give it whole to the other woman, Solomon declared the first woman the baby's true mother (I Kings 3:16–28). 505. **watchlight:** A small night candle. 530–531. **pair of turtles:** Turtle doves; lovers.

535 WAITWELL: Your pardon, sir. With submission, we have
indeed been solacing° in lawful delights; but still with
an eye to business, sir. I have instructed her as well
as I could. If she can take your directions as readily
as my instructions, sir, your affairs are in a prosper-
540 ous way.
MIRABELL: Give you joy, Mrs. Foible.
FOIBLE: O las, sir, I'm so ashamed! I'm afraid my lady has
been in a thousand inquietudes for me. But I protest,
sir, I made as much haste as I could.
545 WAITWELL: That she did indeed, sir. It was my fault that
she did not make more.
MIRABELL: That I believe.
FOIBLE: But I told my lady as you instructed me, sir that
I had a prospect of seeing Sir Rowland, your uncle;
550 and that I would put her ladyship's picture in my
pocket to show him, which I'll be sure to say has
made him so enamored of her beauty, that he burns
with impatience to lie at her ladyship's feet and worship the original.
555 MIRABELL: Excellent Foible! Matrimony has made you
eloquent in love.
WAITWELL: I think she has profited, sir. I think so.
FOIBLE: You have seen Madam Millamant, sir?
MIRABELL: Yes.
560 FOIBLE: I told her, sir, because I did not know that you
might find an opportunity; she had so much company last night.
MIRABELL: Your diligence will merit more. In the
meantime—   (*Gives money.*)
565 FOIBLE: O dear sir, your humble servant!
WAITWELL: Spouse.
MIRABELL: Stand off, sir, not a penny! Go on and prosper,
Foible; the lease shall be made good and the farm
stocked, if we succeed.°
570 FOIBLE: I don't question your generosity, sir; and you
need not doubt of success. If you have no more commands, sir, I'll be gone, I'm sure my lady is at her toilet and can't dress till I come. Oh, dear, I'm sure that
(*looking out*) was Mrs. Marwood that went by in a
575 mask; if she has seen me with you, I'm sure she'll tell
my lady. I'll make haste home and prevent her. Your
servant, sir. B'w'y,° Waitwell.   (*Exit.*)
WAITWELL: Sir Rowland, if you please. The jade's so pert
upon her preferment° she forgets herself.
580 MIRABELL: Come, sir, will you endeavor to forget yourself, and transform into Sir Rowland?
WAITWELL: Why, sir, it will be impossible I should remember myself. Married, knighted, and attended° all
in one day! 'Tis enough to make any forget himself.
585 The difficulty will be how to recover my acquaintance and familiarity with my former self, and fall
from my transformation to a reformation into

536. **solacing:** Taking pleasure. 568–569. **the lease . . . succeed:** I.e., If our little plot succeeds, I'll be even more generous. 577. **B'w'y:** A slurred form of "God be with you."
579. **preferment:** Her advancement in the world; her new status
as a wife. 583. **attended:** Waited upon.

Waitwell. Nay, I shan't be quite the same Waitwell
neither; for, now I remember me, I'm married and
can't be my own man again.   590
Aye, there's my grief; that's the sad change of life,
To lose my title, and yet keep my wife.

(*Exeunt.*)

ACT III

(*A room in Lady Wishfort's house. Lady Wishfort at
her toilet, Peg waiting.*)

LADY WISHFORT: Merciful! no news of Foible yet?
PEG: No, madam.
LADY WISHFORT: I have no more patience. If I have not
fretted myself till I am pale again, there's no veracity
in me! Fetch me the red; the red, do you hear, sweet-   5
heart? An arrant ash-color, as I'm a person! Look you
how this wench stirs! Why dost thou not fetch me a
little red? Didst thou not hear me, mopus?°
PEG: The red ratafia° does your ladyship mean, or the
cherry-brandy?   10
LADY WISHFORT: Ratafia, fool! No, fool! Not the ratafia,
fool. Grant me patience! I mean the Spanish paper,°
idiot; complexion, darling. Paint, paint, paint; dost
thou understand that, changeling,° dangling thy
hands like bobbins° before thee? Why dost thou not   15
stir, puppet? thou wooden thing upon wires!
PEG: Lord, madam, your ladyship is so impatient! I
cannot come at the paint, madam; Mrs. Foible has
locked it up and carried the key with her.
LADY WISHFORT: A pox take you both! Fetch me the   20
cherry-brandy then. (*Exit Peg.*) I'm as pale and as
faint, I look like Mrs. Qualmsick, the curate's wife,
that's always breeding. Wench, come, come, wench,
what art thou doing? sipping? tasting? Save thee,
dost thou not know the bottle?   25

(*Reenter Peg with a bottle and china cup.*)

PEG: Madam, I was looking for a cup.
LADY WISHFORT: A cup, save thee! and what a cup hast
thou brought! Does thou take me for a fairy, to
drink out of an acorn? Why didst thou not bring thy
thimble? Hast thou ne'er a brass thimble clinking in   30
thy pocket with a bit of nutmeg? I warrant thee.
Come, fill, fill! So; again. (*One knocks.*) See who
that is. Set down the bottle first. Here, here under the
table. What, wouldst thou go with the bottle in thy
hand, like a tapster?° As I'm a person, this wench has 35
lived in an inn upon the road, before she came to me,
like Maritornes the Asturian in *Don Quixote*!° No
Foible yet?

8. **mopus:** Idiot; dull-witted girl. 9. **ratafia:** Fruit-flavored
brandy. 12. **Spanish paper:** Cosmetic rouge. 14. **changeling:**
Simpleton. 15. **bobbins:** Spools of yarn. 35. **tapster:** A person
who taps beer in a tavern. 37. **Maritornes . . . *Don Quixote*:** In
Cervantes's *Don Quixote* (part 1, chapter 16), Maritornes is an
Austrian chambermaid with whom the Don fancies himself in love.

PEG: No, madam; Mrs. Marwood.

40 LADY WISHFORT: Oh, Marwood; let her come in. Come in, good Marwood.

(*Enter Mrs. Marwood.*)

MRS. MARWOOD: I'm surprised to find your ladyship in *déshabillé*° at this time of day.

LADY WISHFORT: Foible's a lost thing; has been abroad
45 since morning, and never heard of since.

MRS. MARWOOD: I saw her but now, as I came masked through the park, in conference with Mirabell.

LADY WISHFORT: With Mirabell! You call my blood into my face, with mentioning that traitor. She durst not
50 have the confidence! I sent her to negotiate an affair in which, if I'm detected, I'm undone. If that wheedling villain has wrought upon Foible to detect me, I'm ruined. O my dear friend, I'm a wretch of wretches if I'm detected.

55 MRS. MARWOOD: O madam, you cannot suspect Mrs. Foible's integrity.

LADY WISHFORT: Oh, he carries poison in his tongue that would corrupt integrity itself! If she has given him an opportunity, she has as good as put her
60 integrity into his hands. Ah, dear Marwood, what's integrity to an opportunity? Hark! I hear her! Go, you thing, and send her in. (*Exit Peg.*) Dear friend, retire into my closet,° that I may examine her with more freedom. You'll pardon me, dear friend; I can
65 make bold with you. There are books over the chimney, Quarles° and Prynne,° and the *Short View of the Stage,*° with Bunyan's works,° to entertain you.
(*Exit Mrs. Marwood.*)

(*Enter Foible.*)

O Foible, where hast thou been? What hast thou been doing?

70 FOIBLE: Madam, I have seen the party.

LADY WISHFORT: But what hast thou done?

FOIBLE: Nay, 'tis your ladyship has done, and are to do; I have only promised. But a man so enamored, so transported! Well, if worshiping of pictures be a sin,
75 poor Sir Rowland, I say.

LADY WISHFORT: The miniature has been counted like. But hast thou not betrayed me, Foible? Hast thou not detected me to that faithless Mirabell? What hadst

thou to do with him in the Park? Answer me, has he got nothing out of thee?

80

FOIBLE (*aside*): So the devil has been beforehand with me. What shall I say? (*Aloud.*) Alas, madam, could I help it, if I met that confident thing? Was I in fault? If you had heard how he used me, and all upon your ladyship's account, I'm sure you would not suspect
85 my fidelity. Nay, if that had been the worst, I could have borne; but he had a fling at your ladyship too. And then I could not hold; but i'faith I gave him his own.

LADY WISHFORT: Me? what did the filthy fellow say?
90

FOIBLE: O madam! 'tis a shame to say what he said, with his taunts and his fleers, tossing up his nose. "Humh!" says he. "What, you are a-hatching some plot," says he, "you are so early abroad, or catering," says he. "Ferreting for some disbanded° officer,
95 I warrant. Half-pay is but thin subsistence," says he. "Well, what pension does your lady propose? Let me see," says he. "What, she must come down pretty deep now, she's superannuated,"° says he, "and—"

LADY WISHFORT: Ods° my life, I'll have him, I'll have
100 him murdered! I'll have him poisoned! Where does he eat? I'll marry a drawer° to have him poisoned in his wine! I'll send for Robin° from Locket's° immediately.

FOIBLE: Poison him? Poisoning's too good fur him.
105 Starve him, madam, starve him; marry Sir Rowland, and get him disinherited. Oh, you would bless yourself to hear what he said!

LADY WISHFORT: A villain! "superannuated"!

FOIBLE: "Humh," says he. "I hear you are laying
110 designs against me too," says he, "and Mrs. Millamant is to marry my uncle" (he does not suspect a word of your ladyship); "but," says he, "I'll fit you for that." "I warrant you," says he. "I'll hamper you for that," says he. "You and your old frippery° too,"
115 says he. "I'll handle you—"

LADY WISHFORT: Audacious villain! "handle" me; would he durst! "Frippery! old frippery!" Was there ever such a foul-mouthed fellow? I'll be married tomorrow; I'll be contracted tonight.
120

FOIBLE: The sooner the better, madam.

LADY WISHFORT: Will Sir Rowland be here, sayest thou? When, Foible?

FOIBLE: Incontinently,° madam. No new sheriff's wife expects the return of her husband after knighthood
125 with that impatience in which Sir Rowland burns for the dear hour of kissing your ladyship's hands after dinner.

---

43. *déshabillé*: Casual attire.   63. closet: Private sitting room.
66. Quarles: Francis Quarles, devotional poet, author of *Emblems, Divine and Moral* (1635).   Prynne: William Prynne, Puritan author of *Histrio-Mastix* (1633), an attack on the immorality of the stage.   66–67. *Short View of the Stage*: By Jeremy Collier, an attack on "the Immorality and Profaneness of the English Stage" (1698), directly aimed at the earlier plays of Congreve. Dryden answered the censures of Collier in his Preface to the *Fables* (1700).   67. Bunyan's works: John Bunyan, the great Puritan writer and preacher. A one-volume edition of the *Works of That Eminent Servant of Christ, Mr. John Bunyan* had appeared in 1692.

---

95. disbanded: Discharged.   99. superannuated: Old and infirm.   100. Ods: God's.   102. drawer: One who draws wine or ale; a waiter.   103. Robin: Common name for a waiter. Locket's: A fashionable restaurant in Charing Cross.   115. old frippery: Old clothes, as applied to Lady Wishfort, "old clotheshorse."   124. Incontinently: Immediately, and with the added suggestion of passionate impatience.

LADY WISHFORT: "Frippery! superannuated! frippery!"
130 I'll frippery the villain; I'll reduce him to frippery and
rags! A tatterdemalion!° I hope to see him hung with
tatters, like a Long Lane penthouse° or a gibbet thief.
A slander-mouthed railer! I warrant the spendthrift
prodigal's in debt as much as the million lottery,° or
135 the whole court upon a birthday.° I'll spoil his credit
with his tailor. Yes, he shall have my niece with her
fortune, he shall!
FOIBLE: He! I hope to see him lodge in Ludgate° first,
and angle into Blackfriars° for brass farthings with
140 an old mitten.°
LADY WISHFORT: Aye, dear Foible; thank thee for that,
dear Foible. He has put me out of all patience. I shall
never recompose my features to receive Sir Rowland
with any economy of face.° This wretch has fretted
145 me that I am absolutely decayed. Look, Foible.
FOIBLE: Your ladyship has frowned a little too rashly,
indeed, madam. There are some cracks discernible in
the white varnish.
LADY WISHFORT: Let me see the glass. "Cracks," sayest
150 thou? Why I am arrantly fleaed;° I look like an old
peeled wall. Thou must repair me, Foible, before Sir
Rowland comes, or I shall never keep up to my
picture.°
FOIBLE: I warrant you, madam, a little art once made
155 your picture like you; and now a little of the same art
must make you like your picture. Your picture must
sit for you, madam.
LADY WISHFORT: But art thou sure Sir Rowland will not
fail to come? Or will 'a not fail when he does come?
160 Will he be importunate, Foible, and push? For if he
should not be importunate, I shall never break decorums. I shall die with confusion, if I am forced to
advance. Oh no, I can never advance! I shall swoon if
he should expect advances. No, I hope Sir Rowland
165 is better bred than to put a lady to the necessity of
breaking her forms. I won't be too coy neither. I
won't give him despair; but a little disdain is not
amiss, a little scorn is alluring.
FOIBLE: A little scorn becomes your ladyship.

---

131. tatterdemalion: Ragamuffin.   **132. Long Lane penthouse:**
A shed with a sloping roof in Long Lane, a district famous
for its shops of old and secondhand clothes.   **134. million
lottery:** A wild scheme to raise a million pounds by the sale
of lottery tickets.   **135. the whole ... birthday:** Since custom demanded gifts on such an occasion, a royal birthday
was an expensive event.   **138. Ludgate:** The debtors' prison.
139. angle into Blackfriars: Ludgate Prison abutted on the pre-
cinct of Blackfriars, the area of London between Ludgate Hill
and the river.   **140. old mitten:** It was the practice of Ludgate
prisoners to beg money from passersby, probably by lowering
an old mitten on a string from a high window.   **144. economy
of face:** The sense is that Lady Wishfort has been so distressed
by Foible's account of Mirabell's words that her makeup has
been ruined, and the cosmetics necessary to make her face presentable to Sir Rowland will be very expensive.   **150. fleaed:**
Flayed; skinned.   **152–153. keep ... picture:** I.e., look as lovely
as I do in my picture.

LADY WISHFORT: Yes, but tenderness becomes me best,   170
a sort of dyingness. You see that picture has a sort of
a — ha, Foible? a swimmingness in the eyes. Yes, I'll
look so. My niece affects it; but she wants features. Is
Sir Rowland handsome? Let my toilet be removed.
I'll dress above. I'll receive Sir Rowland here. Is he   175
handsome? Don't answer me. I won't know; I'll be
surprised, I'll be taken by surprise.
FOIBLE: By storm, madam. Sir Rowland's a brisk man.
LADY WISHFORT: Is he! Oh, then he'll importune, if he's
a brisk man. I shall save decorums if Sir Rowland   180
importunes. I have a mortal terror at the apprehension of offending against decorums. Oh, I'm glad he's
a brisk man. Let my things be removed, good Foible.
(*Exit.*)

(*Enter Mrs. Fainall.*)

MRS. FAINALL: O Foible, I have been in a fright, lest I
should come too late! That devil Marwood saw you   185
in the Park with Mirabell, and I'm afraid will discover it to my lady.
FOIBLE: Discover what, madam?
MRS. FAINALL: Nay, nay, put not on that strange face. I
am privy to the whole design, and know that Wait-   190
well, to whom thou wert this morning married, is to
personate Mirabell's uncle, and as such, winning my
lady, to involve her in those difficulties from which
Mirabell only must release her, by his making his
conditions to have my cousin and her fortune left to   195
her own disposal.
FOIBLE: O dear madam, I beg your pardon. It was not
my confidence in your ladyship that was deficient;
but I thought the former good correspondence
between your ladyship and Mr. Mirabell might have   200
hindered his communicating this secret.
MRS. FAINALL: Dear Foible, forget that.
FOIBLE: O dear madam, Mr. Mirabell is such a sweet,
winning gentleman, but your ladyship is the pattern
of generosity. Sweet lady, to be so good! Mr. Mirabell   205
cannot choose but be grateful. I find your ladyship
has his heart still. Now, madam, I can safely tell your
ladyship our success. Mrs. Marwood had told my
lady, but I warrant I managed myself. I turned it all
for the better. I told my lady that Mr. Mirabell railed   210
at her. I laid horrid things to his charge, I'll vow; and
my lady is so incensed that she'll be contracted to Sir
Rowland tonight, she says. I warrant I worked her
up, that he may have her for asking for, as they say of
a Welsh maidenhead.   215
MRS. FAINALL: O rare Foible!
FOIBLE: I beg your ladyship to acquaint Mr. Mirabell of
his success. I would be seen as little as possible to
speak to him; besides, I believe Madam Marwood
watches me. She has a month's mind;° but I know   220
Mr. Mirabell can't abide her. (*Calls.*) John! Remove
my lady's toilet. Madam, your servant. My lady is so
impatient, I fear she'll come for me if I stay.

---

220. month's mind: A longing, desire.

MRS. FAINALL: I'll go with you up the back stairs, lest I
should meet her.   (*Exeunt.*)

(*Reenter Mrs. Marwood alone.*)

MRS. MARWOOD: Indeed, Mrs. Engine,° is it thus with
you? Are you become a go-between of this importance? Yes, I shall watch you. Why, this wench is the
passe-partout, a very master-key to everybody's
strong-box. My friend Fainall,° have you carried it so
swimmingly? I thought there was something in it; but
it seems it's over with you.° Your loathing is not from
a want of appetite then, but from a surfeit. Else you
could never be so cool to fall from a principal to be
an assistant; to procure for him! "A pattern of generosity," that I confess. Well, Mr. Fainall, you have
met with your match. O man, man! woman, woman!
the devil's an ass; if I were a painter, I would draw
him like an idiot, a driveller with a bib and bells.
Man should have his head and horns,° and woman
the rest of him. Poor simple fiend! "Madam Marwood
has a month's mind, but he can't abide her." 'Twere
better for him you had not been his confessor
in that affair, without° you could have kept his counsel closer. I shall not prove another "pattern of generosity." He has not obliged me to that with those
excesses of himself; and now I'll have none of him.
Here comes the good lady, panting ripe; with a heart
full of hope, and a head full of care, like any chemist
upon the day of projection.°

(*Reenter Lady Wishfort.*)

LADY WISHFORT: O dear Marwood, what shall I say for
this rude forgetfulness? But my dear friend is all
goodness.
MRS. MARWOOD: No apologies, dear madam. I have
been very well entertained.
LADY WISHFORT: As I'm a person, I am in a very chaos
to think I should so forget myself, but I have such an
olio of affairs,° really I know not what to do. (*Calls.*)
Foible! I expect my nephew, Sir Wilfull, every moment too. (*Calls.*) Why, Foible! He means to travel
for improvement.
MRS. MARWOOD: Methinks Sir Wilfull should rather
think of marrying than travelling at his years. I hear
he is turned of forty.

LADY WISHFORT: Oh, he's in less danger of being spoiled
by his travels. I am against my nephew's marrying too
young. It will be time enough when he comes back
and has acquired discretion to choose for himself.
MRS. MARWOOD: Methinks Mrs. Millamant and he
would make a very fit match. He may travel afterwards. 'Tis a thing very usual with young gentlemen.
LADY WISHFORT: I promise you I have thought on't; and
since 'tis your judgment, I'll think on't again. I assure
you I will; I value your judgment extremely. On my
word, I'll propose it.

(*Reenter Foible.*)

Come, come, Foible, I had forgot my nephew will be
here before dinner. I must make haste.
FOIBLE: Mr. Witwoud and Mr. Petulant are come to dine
with your ladyship.
LADY WISHFORT: Oh, dear, I can't appear till I am
dressed. Dear Marwood, shall I be free with you
again, and beg you to entertain 'em? I'll make all
imaginable haste. Dear friend, excuse me.

(*Exeunt Lady Wishfort and Foible.*)

(*Enter Mrs. Millamant and Mincing.*)

MRS. MILLAMANT: Sure never anything was so unbred
as that odious man! Marwood, your servant.
MRS. MARWOOD: You have a color; what's the matter?
MRS. MILLAMANT: That horrid fellow, Petulant, has
provoked me into a flame. I have broke my fan.
Mincing, lend me yours; is not all the powder out of
my hair?
MRS. MARWOOD: No. What has he done?
MRS. MILLAMANT: Nay, he has done nothing; he has
only talked. Nay, he has said nothing neither; but he
has contradicted everything that has been said. For
my part, I thought Witwoud and he would have
quarreled.
MINCING: I vow, mem, I thought once they would have
fit.°
MRS. MILLAMANT: Well, 'tis a lamentable thing, I swear,
that one has not the liberty of choosing one's acquaintance as one does one's clothes.
MRS. MARWOOD: If we had that liberty, we should be as
weary of one set of acquaintance, though never so
good, as we are of one suit, though never so fine. A
fool and a doily stuff° would now and then find days
of grace, and be worn for variety.
MRS. MILLAMANT: I could consent to wear 'em, if they
would wear alike; but fools never wear out, they are
such *drap-de-Berry*° things! without one could give
'em to one's chambermaid after a day or two.
MRS. MARWOOD: 'Twere better so indeed. Or what
think you of the playhouse? A fine, gay, glossy fool

---

226. **Mrs. Engine:** I.e., Foible, the agent of the plot, which
Mrs. Marwood has discovered by eavesdropping on the
discourse between Foible and Mrs. Fainall.   230. **Fainall:**
Mrs. Fainall.   232. **it seems ... you:** Among other things,
Mrs. Marwood has learned of Mrs. Fainall's affair with
Mirabell before her marriage to Fainall.   240. **horns:** The
traditional sign of the cuckold, a man whose wife is unfaithful.   244. **without:** Unless.   249–250. **like any chemist ...
projection:** The comparison refers to the attempts of the alche-
mists to transmute base metals into gold. The "day of projection" is the last day of the experiment, when success or failure
will be known.   257–258. **such an olio of affairs:** I.e., such a
number of things on my mind.

298. **fit:** Fought.   305. **doily stuff:** A coarse woolen material.
309. *drap-de-Berry:* Woolen cloth, probably coarse but sturdy,
from the French province of Berry.

should be given there, like a new masking habit, after the masquerade is over, and we have done with the
315 disguise. For a fool's visit is always a disguise, and never admitted by a woman of wit, but to blind° her affair with a lover of sense. If you would but appear barefaced now, and own Mirabell, you might as easily put off Petulant and Witwoud as your hood and
320 scarf. And indeed 'tis time, for the town has found it; the secret is grown too big for the pretense. 'Tis like Mrs. Primly's great belly, she may lace it down before, but it burnishes° on her hips. Indeed, Millamant, you can no more conceal it than my Lady
325 Strammel can her face, that goodly face, which, in defiance of her Rhenish-wine tea,° will not be comprehended in a mask.°

MRS. MILLAMANT: I'll take my death, Marwood, you are more censorious than a decayed beauty, or a dis-
330 carded toast. Mincing, tell the men they may come up. My aunt is not dressing here; their folly is less provoking than your malice. (*Exit Mincing.*) "The town has found it!" What has it found? That Mirabell loves me is no more a secret than it is a secret that
335 you discovered it to my aunt, or than the reason why you discovered it is a secret.

MRS. MARWOOD: You are nettled.°

MRS. MILLAMANT: You're mistaken. Ridiculous!

MRS. MARWOOD: Indeed, my dear, you'll tear another
340 fan, if you don't mitigate those violent airs.

MRS. MILLAMANT: O silly! ha! ha! ha! I could laugh immoderately. Poor Mirabell! His constancy to me has quite destroyed his complaisance for all the world beside. I swear, I never enjoined it him to be so coy. If
345 I had the vanity to think he would obey me, I would command him to show more gallantry. 'Tis hardly well-bred to be so particular° on one hand, and so insensible on the other. But I despair to prevail, and so let him follow his own way, ha! ha! ha! Pardon
350 me, dear creature, I must laugh, ha! ha! ha! though I grant you 'tis a little barbarous, ha! ha! ha!

MRS. MARWOOD: What pity 'tis, so much fine raillery, and delivered with so significant gesture, should be so unhappily directed to miscarry!
355 MRS. MILLAMANT: Ha? Dear creature, I ask your pardon. I swear I did not mind you.°

MRS. MARWOOD: Mr. Mirabell and you both may think it a thing impossible, when I shall tell him by telling you—
360 MRS. MILLAMANT: Oh, dear, what? For it is the same thing if I hear it, ha! ha! ha!

MRS. MARWOOD: That I detest him, hate him, madam.

---

316. **blind:** Camouflage.   323. **burnishes:** Is all the more evident.
326. **Rhenish-wine tea:** Rhenish white wine was supposed to reduce corpulence.   326–327. **will not...mask:** The sense is that the lady's face was so fat that no mask would fit it.
337. **nettled:** Annoyed.   347. **particular:** Attentive to one lady (i.e., Millamant).   356. **I did not mind you:** I did not have you in mind.

MRS. MILLAMANT: O madam, why so do I. And yet the creature loves me, ha! ha! ha! How can one forbear laughing to think of it! I am a sibyl° if I am not 365 amazed to think what he can see in me. I'll take my death, I think you are handsomer and, within a year or two as young; if you could but stay for me, I should overtake you, but that cannot be. Well, that thought makes me melancholic. Now, I'll be sad. 370

MRS. MARWOOD: Your merry note may be changed sooner than you think.

MRS. MILLAMANT: D'ye say so? Then I'm resolved I'll have a song to keep up my spirits.

(*Reenter Mincing.*)

MINCING: The gentlemen stay but to comb,° madam, 375 and will wait on you.

MRS. MILLAMANT: Desire Mrs.—, that is in the next room, to sing the song I would have learnt yesterday. You shall hear it, madam, not that there's any great matter in it, but 'tis agreeable to my humor. 380

(*Song.*)

[*Set by Mr. John Eccles.*°]

I
Love's but the frailty of the mind,
    When 'tis not with ambition join'd;
A sickly flame, which, if not fed, expires,
And feeding, wastes in self-consuming fires.

II
'Tis not to wound a wanton boy   385
    Or am'rous youth, that gives the joy;
But 'tis the glory to have pierc'd a swain,
For whom inferior beauties sigh'd in vain.

III
Then I alone the conquest prize,
    When I insult a rival's eyes;   390
If there's delight in love, 'tis when I see
That heart, which others bleed for, bleed for me.

(*Enter Petulant and Witwoud.*)

MRS. MILLAMANT: Is your animosity composed, gentlemen?

WITWOUD: Raillery, raillery, madam; we have no ani-   395
mosity. We hit off a little wit now and then, but no animosity. The falling-out of wits is like the falling-out of lovers; we agree in the main, like treble and bass. Ha, Petulant?

PETULANT: Aye, in the main, but when I have a humor to   400
contradict.

WITWOUD: Aye, when he has a humor to contradict, then I contradict too. What, I know my cue. Then we contradict one another like two battledores; for contradictions beget one another like Jews.   405

---

365. **sibyl:** A female prophet or seer.   375. **comb:** I.e., comb their wigs.   380. [S.D.] **John Eccles:** English composer (1668–1735), who set these verses to music.

PETULANT: If he says black's black, if I have a humor to say 'tis blue, let that pass; all's one for that. If I have a humor to prove it, it must be granted.

WITWOUD: Not positively must, but it may, it may.

410 PETULANT: Yes, it positively must, upon proof positive.

WITWOUD: Aye, upon proof positive it must; but upon proof presumptive it only may. That's a logical distinction now, madam.

MRS. MARWOOD: I perceive your debates are of importance and very learnedly handled.

415 PETULANT: Importance is one thing, and learning's another; but a debate's a debate, that I assert.

WITWOUD: Petulant's an enemy to learning; he relies altogether on his parts.

420 PETULANT: No, I'm no enemy to learning; it hurts not me.

MRS. MARWOOD: That's a sign indeed it's no enemy to you.

PETULANT: No, no, it's no enemy to anybody but them that have it.

425 MRS. MILLAMANT: Well, an illiterate man's my aversion; I wonder at the impudence of any illiterate man to offer to make love.

WITWOUD: That I confess I wonder at too.

MRS. MILLAMANT: Ah! to marry an ignorant that can
430 hardly read or write!

PETULANT: Why should a man be any further from being married, though he can't read, than he is from being hanged? The ordinary's° paid for setting the psalm, and the parish priest for reading the ceremony. And
435 for the rest which is to follow in both cases, a man may do it without book; so all's one for that.

MRS. MILLAMANT: D'ye hear the creature? Lord, here's company; I'll be gone.

(*Exeunt Mrs. Millamant and Mincing.*)

(*Enter Sir Wilfull Witwoud in a riding dress, and a Footman to Lady Wishfort.*)

WITWOUD: In the name of Bartlemew and his fair,° what
440 have we here?

MRS. MARWOOD: 'Tis your brother, I fancy. Don't you know him?

WITWOUD: Not I. Yes, I think it is he. I've almost forgot him; I have not seen him since the Revolution.°

445 FOOTMAN (*to Sir Wilfull*): Sir, my lady's dressing. Here's company; if you please to walk in, in the meantime.

SIR WILFULL: Dressing! What, it's but morning here, I warrant, with you in London; we should count it towards afternoon in our parts, down in Shropshire.
450 Why then, belike my aunt han't dined yet, ha, friend?

FOOTMAN: Your aunt, sir?

433. **ordinary's:** The ordinary was the chaplain of a prison, who prepared criminals for death. 439. **Bartlemew and his fair:** Bartholomew Fair was held in August of each year at Smithfield. Since it was specially renowned for its sale of country cloths, Witwoud may here be referring to the inappropriateness of his brother's riding habit in a London drawing room. 444. **Revolution:** The bloodless Revolution of 1688, which marked the defeat of James II and the accession to the throne of William and Mary.

SIR WILFULL: My aunt, sir! Yes, my aunt, sir, and your lady, sir; your lady is my aunt, sir. Why, what, dost thou not know me, friend? Why, then send somebody hither that does. How long hast thou lived with
455 thy lady, fellow, ha?

FOOTMAN: A week, sir; longer than anybody else in the house, except my lady's woman.

SIR WILFULL: Why then, belike thou dost not know thy lady, if thou seest her, ha, friend?
460

FOOTMAN: Why truly, sir, I cannot safely swear to her face in a morning, before she is dressed. 'Tis like I may give a shrewd guess at her by this time.

SIR WILFULL: Well, prithee try what thou canst do; if thou canst not guess, inquire her out, dost hear, fel-
465 low? And tell her, her nephew, Sir Wilfull Witwoud, is in the house.

FOOTMAN: I shall, sir.

SIR WILFULL: Hold ye, hear me, friend; a word with you in your ear. Prithee who are these gallants?
470

FOOTMAN: Really, sir, I can't tell; here come so many here, 'tis hard to know 'em all.   (*Exit.*)

SIR WILFULL: Oons,° this fellow knows less than a starling;° I don't think 'a knows his own name.

MRS. MARWOOD: Mr. Witwoud, your brother is not
475 behind-hand in forgetfulness; I fancy he has forgot you too.

WITWOUD: I hope so. The devil take him that remembers first, I say.

SIR WILFULL: Save you, gentlemen and lady!
480

MRS. MARWOOD: For shame, Mr. Witwoud; why won't you speak to him? And you, sir.

WITWOUD: Petulant, speak.

PETULANT: And you, sir.

SIR WILFULL: No offense, I hope.
485
(*Salutes Mrs. Marwood.*)

MRS. MARWOOD: No sure, sir.

WITWOUD: This is a vile dog; I see that already. No offense! Ha! ha! ha! to him; to him, Petulant, smoke° him.

PETULANT: It seems as if you had come a journey, sir;
490 hem, hem.   (*Surveying him round.*)

SIR WILFULL: Very likely, sir, that it may seem so.

PETULANT: No offense, I hope, sir.

WITWOUD: Smoke the boots, the boots; Petulant, the boots, ha! ha! ha!
495

SIR WILFULL: Maybe not, sir; thereafter as 'tis meant,° sir.

PETULANT: Sir, I presume upon the information of your boots.

SIR WILFULL: Why, 'tis like you may, sir. If you are not
500 satisfied with the information of my boots, sir, if you will step to the stable, you may inquire further of my horse, sir.

PETULANT: Your horse, sir! Your horse is an ass, sir!

473. **Oons:** God's wounds, an oath. 473–474. **starling:** Proverbially a stupid bird. 488. **smoke:** "To affront a stranger at his coming in" (Summers, *Dictionary of the Canting Crew*). 496. **as 'tis meant:** According to the way it is meant.

505   SIR WILFULL: Do you speak by way of offense, sir?

     MRS. MARWOOD: The gentleman's merry, that's all, sir. (*Aside.*) 'Slife,° we shall have a quarrel betwixt an horse and an ass, before they find one another out.

510   (*Aloud.*) You must not take anything amiss from your friends, sir. You are among your friends here, though it may be you don't know it. If I am not mistaken, you are Sir Wilfull Witwoud.

     SIR WILFULL: Right, lady; I am Sir Wilfull Witwoud, so I write myself; no offense to anybody, I hope; and

515   nephew to the Lady Wishfort of this mansion.

     MRS. MARWOOD: Don't you know this gentleman, sir?

     SIR WILFULL: Hum! What, sure 'tis not—yea by'r Lady, but 'tis. 'Sheart° I know not whether 'tis or no. Yea, but 'tis, by the Wrekin.° Brother Antony! What, Tony,

520   i'faith! What, dost thou not know me? By'r Lady, nor I thee, thou art so becravated° and so beperiwigged.° 'Sheart, why dost not speak? Art thou o'erjoyed?

     WITWOUD: Odso, brother, is it you? Your servant, brother.

525   SIR WILFULL: Your servant! Why, yours, sir. Your servant again, 'sheart, and your friend and servant to that, and a—(*puff*) and a flapdragon for your service,° sir! and a hare's foot, and a hare's scut° for your service, sir, an you be so cold and so courtly!

530   WITWOUD: No offense, I hope, brother.

     SIR WILFULL: 'Sheart, sir, but there is, and much offense! A pox, is this your Inns o' Court° breeding, not to know your friends and your relations, your elders and your betters?

535   WITWOUD: Why, brother Wilfull of Salop,° you may be as short as a Shrewsbury° cake, if you please. But I tell you 'tis not modish to know relations in town. You think you're in the country, where great lubberly° brothers slabber° and kiss one another when

540   they meet, like a call of serjeants.° 'Tis not the fashion here, 'tis not indeed, dear brother.

     SIR WILFULL: The fashion's a fool; and you're a fop, dear brother. 'Sheart, I've suspected this. By'r Lady, I conjectured you were a fop, since you began to

545   change the style of your letters, and write in a scrap of paper, gilt round the edges, no broader than a *subpoena.*° I might expect this when you left off, "Honored brother," and "hoping you are in good health," and so forth, to begin with a "Rat me,° knight, I'm so

sick of a last night's debauch," ods heart, and then 550 tell a familiar tale of a cock and a bull,° and a whore and a bottle, and so conclude. You could write news before you were out of your time,° when you lived with honest Pumple Nose, the attorney of Furnival's Inn,° you could entreat to be remembered then to 555 your friends round the Wrekin. We could have gazettes, then, and *Dawks's Letter,*° and the *Weekly Bill,*° till of late days.

     PETULANT: 'Slife, Witwoud, were you ever an attorney's clerk? of the family of the Furnivals? Ha! ha! ha! 560

     WITWOUD: Aye, aye, but that was but for a while, not long, not long. Pshaw! I was not in my own power then; an orphan, and this fellow was my guardian. Aye, aye, I was glad to consent to that man to come to London. He had the disposal of me then. If I had 565 not agreed to that, I might have been bound prentice to a felt maker in Shrewsbury; this fellow would have bound me to a maker of felts.

     SIR WILFULL: 'Sheart, and better than to be bound to a maker of fops, where, I suppose, you have served 570 your time; and now you may set up for yourself.

     MRS. MARWOOD: You intend to travel, sir, as I'm informed.

     SIR WILFULL: Belike I may, madam. I may chance to sail upon the salt seas, if my mind hold. 575

     PETULANT: And the wind serve.

     SIR WILFULL: Serve or not serve, I shan't ask license of you, sir; nor the weathercock your companion. I direct my discourse to the lady, sir. 'Tis like my aunt may have told you, madam. Yes, I have settled my 580 concerns, I may say now, and am minded to see foreign parts. If an how that the peace° holds, whereby, that is, taxes abate.

     MRS. MARWOOD: I thought you had designed for France at all adventures.° 585

     SIR WILFULL: I can't tell that; 'tis like I may, and 'tis like I may not. I am somewhat dainty in making a resolution, because when I make it, I keep it. I don't stand shill I, shall I,° then; if I say't, I'll do't. But I have thoughts to tarry a small matter in town, to learn 590 somewhat of your lingo first, before I cross the seas. I'd gladly have a spice of your French, as they say, whereby to hold discourse in foreign countries.

     MRS. MARWOOD: Here's an academy in town for that use. 595

     SIR WILFULL: There is? 'Tis like there may.

---

507. **'Slife:** God's life.   518. **'Sheart:** God's heart.   519. **Wrekin:** A hill in his native Shropshire.   521. **becravated:** Wearing a cravat, or tie.   **beperiwigged:** Wearing a wig.   527–528. **flapdragon . . . service:** Derived from the game of catching raisins out of burning brandy and meaning "a fig for your service."   528. **scut:** Tail.   532. **Inns o' Court:** The center of the legal world of London, used for the city itself. Sir Wilfull, the country squire, simply asks if Witwoud's rudeness is a mark of city manners.   535. **Salop:** Another name for Shropshire.   536. **Shrewsbury:** The capital of Shropshire.   538–539. **lubberly:** Loutish.   539. **slabber:** Slobber.   540. **serjeants:** When sergeants-at-law are admitted to the bar.   546–547. *subpoena:* A legal summons.   549. **"Rat me":** Contraction of the oath "May God rot me."

551. **tale . . . bull:** A wildly exaggerated tale.   553. **out of your time:** I.e., before he had finished his legal apprenticeship.   554–555. **Furnival's Inn:** One of the Inns of Court (Chancery) attached to Lincoln's Inn.   557. *Dawks's Letter:* A newsletter with a wide circulation in the provinces.   557–558. *Weekly Bill:* It reported all deaths in and around London.   582. **peace:** The Treaty of Ryswick (1697), which temporarily terminated the war between France on the one hand and England and her Continental allies on the other.   585. **at all adventures:** In any case.   589. **shill I, shall I:** Shilly-shally. Sir Wilfull is saying that he is not an indecisive man.

MRS. MARWOOD: No doubt you will return very much improved.

WITWOUD: Yes, refined, like a Dutch skipper from a whale-fishing.

(Reenter Lady Wishfort with Fainall.)

LADY WISHFORT: Nephew, you are welcome.

SIR WILFULL: Aunt, your servant.

FAINALL: Sir Wilfull, your most faithful servant.

SIR WILFULL: Cousin Fainall, give me your hand.

LADY WISHFORT: Cousin Witwoud, your servant; Mr. Petulant, your servant. Nephew, you are welcome again. Will you drink anything after your journey, nephew, before you eat? Dinner's almost ready.

SIR WILFULL: I'm very well, I thank you, aunt; however, I thank you for your courteous offer. 'Sheart I was afraid you would have been in the fashion too, and have remembered to have forgot your relations. Here's your cousin Tony; belike I mayn't call him brother for fear of offense.

LADY WISHFORT: O, he's a rallier,° nephew. My cousin's a wit; and your great wits always rally their best friends to choose.° When you have been abroad, nephew, you'll understand raillery better.

(Fainall and Mrs. Marwood talk apart.)

SIR WILFULL: Why then, let him hold his tongue in the meantime, and rail when that day comes.

(Reenter Mincing.)

MINCING: Mem, I come to acquaint your laship that dinner is impatient.

SIR WILFULL: Impatient? Why then, belike it won't stay till I pull off my boots. Sweetheart, can you help me to a pair of slippers? My man's with the horses, I warrant.

LADY WISHFORT: Fie, fie, nephew, you would not pull off your boots here. Go down into the hall; dinner shall stay for you. My nephew's a little unbred; you'll pardon him, madam. Gentlemen, will you walk? Marwood?

MRS. MARWOOD: I'll follow you, madam, before Sir Wilfull is ready.

(Exeunt all but Mrs. Marwood and Fainall.)

FAINALL: Why then, Foible's a bawd, an arrant, rank, match-making bawd. And I, it seems, am a husband, a rank husband; and my wife a very arrant, rank wife, all in the way of the world. 'Sdeath, to be a cuckold by anticipation, a cuckold in embryo!° Sure I was born with budding antlers, like a young satyr, or

a citizen's child.° 'Sdeath! to be outwitted, to be out-jilted, outmatrimonied! If I had kept my speed like a stag, 'twere somewhat; but to crawl after, with my horns, like a snail, and be out-stripped by my wife, 'tis scurvy wedlock.

MRS. MARWOOD: Then shake it off. You have often wished for an opportunity to part; and now you have it. But first prevent their plot; the half of Millamant's fortune is too considerable to be parted with, to a foe, to Mirabell.

FAINALL: Damn him! that had been mine, had you not made that fond° discovery. That had been forfeited, had they been married. My wife had added luster to my horns by that increase of fortune, I could have worn 'em tipped with gold, though my forehead had been furnished like a deputy lieutenant's hall.°

MRS. MARWOOD: They may prove a cap of mainte-nance° to you still, if you can away with° your wife. And she's no worse than when you had her. I dare swear she had given up her game before she was married.

FAINALL: Hum! that may be.

MRS. MARWOOD: You married her to keep you; and if you can contrive to have her keep you better than you expected, why should you not keep her longer than you intended?

FAINALL: The means, the means.

MRS. MARWOOD: Discover to my lady your wife's con-duct; threaten to part with her. My lady loves her, and will come to any composition° to save her repu-tation. Take the opportunity of breaking it, just upon the discovery of this imposture. My lady will be en-raged beyond bounds, and sacrifice niece and fortune and all, at that conjuncture. And let me alone to keep her warm; if she should flag in her part, I will not fail to prompt her.

FAINALL: Faith, this has an appearance.°

MRS. MARWOOD: I'm sorry I hinted to my lady to endeavor a match between Millamant and Sir Wilfull; that may be an obstacle.

FAINALL: Oh, for that matter leave me to manage him; I'll disable him for that. He will drink like a Dane;° after dinner, I'll set his hand in.°

---

615. **rallier:** A railer; one who delights in raillery, gentle mock-ery.   617. **to choose:** As they like.   637–638. **to be ... embryo:** In their "talk apart," Mrs. Marwood has told Mr. Fainall what she has learned of his wife's affair with Mirabell before her marriage to Fainall.

640. **citizen's child:** I.e., a cuckold's child. Many a child of an honest citizen was fathered by a gentleman of the town. 651. **fond:** Foolish.   654–655. **forehead ... hall:** I.e., though he had been cuckolded as many times as there are antlers of stags and deer decorating the country mansion of a deputy lieuten-ant.   656–657. **cap of maintenance:** A term in heraldry. The coat of arms of a royal bastard sometimes included a cap with two points behind, like the horns of a cuckold. Mrs. Marwood puns on the word *maintenance* since she is insinuating that, armed with this new information concerning his wife, Fainall may be in a better position to blackmail Lady Wishfort to the amount of Millamant's fortune that she controls.   657. **away with:** Continue to tolerate.   669. **come to any composition:** Agree to anything.   676. **an appearance:** Possibilities. 681. **drink like a Dane:** The Danes were known as heavy drinkers.   682. **I'll set ... in:** I.e., I'll involve him in the plot.

MRS. MARWOOD: Well, how do you stand affected towards your lady?

FAINALL: Why, faith, I'm thinking of it. Let me see. I am married already, so that's over. My wife has played the jade with me; well, that's over too. I never loved her, or if I had, why, that would have been over too by this time. Jealous of her I cannot be, for I am certain; so there's an end of jealousy. Weary of her I am, and shall be. No, there's no end of that; no, no, that were too much to hope. Thus far concerning my repose; now for my reputation. As to my own, I married not for it, so that's out of the question. And as to my part in my wife's, why, she had parted with hers before; so bringing none to me, she can take none from me. 'Tis against all rule of play that I should lose to one who has not wherewithal to stake.

MRS. MARWOOD: Besides, you forget marriage is honorable.

FAINALL: Hum! Faith, and that's well thought on. Marriage is honorable, as you say; and if so, wherefore should cuckoldom be a discredit, being derived from so honorable a root?

MRS. MARWOOD: Nay, I know not; if the root he honorable, why not the branches?°

FAINALL: So, so; why, this point's clear. Well, how do we proceed?

MRS. MARWOOD: I will contrive a letter which shall be delivered to my lady at the time when that rascal who is to act Sir Rowland is with her. It shall come as from an unknown hand, for the less I appear to know of the truth, the better I can play the incendiary. Besides, I would not have Foible provoked if I could help it, because you know she knows some passages.° Nay, I expect all will come out; but let the mine be sprung first, and then I care not if I am discovered.

FAINALL: If the worst come to the worst, I'll turn my wife to grass,° I have already a deed of settlement of the best part of her estate, which I wheedled out of her; and that you shall partake at least.

MRS. MARWOOD: I hope you are convinced that I hate Mirabell now; you'll be no more jealous?

FAINALL: Jealous! No, by this kiss. Let husbands be jealous; but let the lover still believe. Or if he doubt, let it be only to endear his pleasure, and prepare the joy that follows, when he proves his mistress true. But let husbands' doubts convert to endless jealousy; or if they have belief, let it corrupt to superstition and blind credulity. I am single, and will herd no more with 'em. True, I wear the badge, but I'll disown the order. And since I take my leave of 'em, I care not if I leave 'em a common motto to their common crest.

    All husbands must or pain or shame endure
    The wise too jealous are, fools too secure.

                             (*Exeunt.*)

ACT IV

([*Scene continues.*] *Enter Lady Wishfort and Foible.*)

LADY WISHFORT: Is Sir Rowland coming, sayest thou, Foible? and are things in order?

FOIBLE: Yes, madam, I have put wax-lights in the sconces, and placed the footmen in a row in the hall, in their best liveries, with the coachman and postillion to fill up the equipage.

LADY WISHFORT: Have you pulvilled° the coachman and postillion, that they may not stink of the stable when Sir Rowland comes by?

FOIBLE: Yes, madam.

LADY WISHFORT: And are the dancers and the music ready, that he may be entertained in all points with correspondence to his passion?

FOIBLE: All is ready, madam.

LADY WISHFORT: And—well, and how do I look, Foible?

FOIBLE: Most killing well, madam.

LADY WISHFORT: Well, and how shall I receive him? In what figure shall I give his heart the first impression? There is a great deal in the first impression. Shall I sit? No, I won't sit, I'll walk; aye, I'll walk from the door upon his entrance; and then turn full upon him. No, that will be too sudden. I'll lie, aye, I'll lie down. I'll receive him in my little dressing-room; there's a couch. Yes, yes, I'll give the first impression on a couch. I won't lie neither, but loll and lean upon one elbow; with one foot a little dangling off, jogging in a thoughtful way. Yes, and then as soon as he appears, start, aye, start and be surprised, and rise to meet him in a pretty disorder. Yes, oh, nothing is more alluring than a levee° from a couch, in some confusion; it shows the foot to advantage, and furnishes with blushes and recomposing airs beyond comparison. Hark! there's a coach.

FOIBLE: 'Tis he, madam.

LADY WISHFORT: Oh dear, has my nephew made his addresses to Millamant? I ordered him.

FOIBLE: Sir Wilfull is set in to drinking, madam, in the parlor.

LADY WISHFORT: Ods my life, I'll send him to her. Call her down, Foible; bring her hither. I'll send him as I go. When they are together, then come to me, Foible, that I may not be too long alone with Sir Rowland.

                             (*Exit.*)

---

707. branches: I.e., the cuckold's horns. **716–717. she knows some passages:** I.e., Foible knows of Mrs. Marwood's affair with Mr. Fainall and may divulge it. Indeed, she does, in the denouement of act 5. **720–721. turn . . . grass:** Turn her out, as he would an animal to graze.

7. pulvilled: Scented with a sweet-smelling powder. **31. levee:** Rising.

(*Enter Mrs. Millamant and Mrs. Fainall.*)

FOIBLE: Madam, I stayed here to tell your ladyship that
Mr. Mirabell has waited this half hour for an opportunity to talk with you, though my lady's orders
were to leave you and Sir Wilfull together. Shall I tell
Mr. Mirabell that you are at leisure?

MRS. MILLAMANT: No, what would the dear man have?
I am thoughtful, and would amuse myself; bid him
come another time.

    "There never yet was woman made,
      Nor shall, but to be curs'd."°
                 (*Repeating and walking about.*)
    That's hard!

MRS. FAINALL: You are very fond of Sir John Suckling today, Millamant, and the poets.

MRS. MILLAMANT: He? Aye, and filthy verses; so I am.

FOIBLE: Sir Wilfull is coming, madam. Shall I send
Mr. Mirabell away?

MRS. MILLAMANT: Aye, if you please, Foible, send him
away, or send him hither; just as you will, dear
Foible. I think I'll see him; shall I? Aye, let the wretch
come.

                     (*Exit Foible.*)
    "Thyrsis, a youth of the inspired train."°
                 (*Repeating.*)

Dear Fainall, entertain Sir Wilfull. Thou hast philosophy to undergo° a fool; thou art married and hast
patience. I would confer with my own thoughts.

MRS. FAINALL: I am obliged to you, that you would
make me your proxy in this affair; but I have business of my own.

(*Enter Sir Wilfull.*)

O Sir Wilfull, you are come at the critical instant.
There's your mistress up to the ears in love and contemplation; pursue your point, now or never.

SIR WILFULL: Yes; my aunt will have it so. I would
gladly have been encouraged with a bottle or two,
because I'm somewhat wary at first, before I am
acquainted. (*This while Millamant walks about
repeating to herself.*) But I hope, after a time, I shall
break my mind; that is, upon further acquaintance.
So for the present, cousin, I'll take my leave. If so be
you'll be so kind to make my excuse, I'll return to
my company.

MRS. FAINALL: Oh, fie, Sir Wilfull! What, you must not
be daunted.

SIR WILFULL: Daunted! No, that's not it. It is not so much
for that; for if so be that I set on't, I'll do't. But only
for the present; 'tis sufficient till further acquaintance, that's all. Your servant.

MRS. FAINALL: Nay, I'll swear you shall never lose so
favorable an opportunity, if I can help it. I'll leave
you together and lock the door.   (*Exit.*)

SIR WILFULL: Nay, nay, cousin. I have forgot my gloves.
What d'ye do? 'Sheart, 'a has locked the door indeed,
I think. Nay, Cousin Fainall, open the door! Pshaw,
what a vixen trick is this? Nay, now 'a has seen me
too. Cousin, I made bold to pass through as it were. I
think this door's enchanted!

MRS. MILLAMANT (*repeating*):
    "I prithee spare me, gentle boy,
      Press me no more for that slight toy—"°

SIR WILFULL: Anan?° Cousin, your servant.

MRS. MILLAMANT (*repeating*):
    "That foolish trifle of a heart—"
    Sir Wilfull!

SIR WILFULL: Yes. Your servant. No offense, I hope,
cousin.

MRS. MILLAMANT (*repeating*):
    "I swear it will not do its part,
    Though thou dost shine, employ'st thy pow'r
      and art."
    Natural, easy Suckling!

SIR WILFULL: Anan? Suckling? No such suckling neither, cousin, nor stripling! I thank Heaven, I'm no
minor.

MRS. MILLAMANT: Ah, rustic! ruder than Gothic.°

SIR WILFULL: Well, well, I shall understand your lingo one
of these days, cousin; in the meanwhile I must answer
in plain English.

MRS. MILLAMANT: Have you any business with me, Sir
Wilfull?

SIR WILFULL: Not at present, cousin. Yes, I made bold
to see, to come and know if that how you were disposed to fetch a walk this evening; if so be that I
might not be troublesome, I would have fought° a
walk with you.

MRS. MILLAMANT: A walk! What then?

SIR WILFULL: Nay, nothing. Only for the walk's sake,
that's all.

MRS. MILLAMANT: I nauseate walking; 'tis a country
diversion. I loathe the country and everything that
relates to it.

SIR WILFULL: Indeed! hah! Look ye, look ye, you do?
Nay, 'tis like you may. Here are choice of pastimes
here in town, as plays and the like; that must be confessed indeed.

MRS. MILLAMANT: Ah, *l'étourdi*!° I hate the town too.

SIR WILFULL: Dear heart, that's much. Hah! that you
should hate 'em both! Hah! 'tis like you may; there
are some can't relish the town, and others can't away

52–53. "There never . . . curs'd": The opening lines of a poem
by Sir John Suckling (1609–1642).   64. "Thyrsis . . . train":
The first line of *The Story Phoebus and Daphne, Applied,* a
poem by Edmund Waller (1606–1687), a poet much admired
by Dryden and renowned for the "sweetness" of his verse.
66. **undergo:** Put up with.

98–99. "I prithee . . . toy": The first two lines of a "Song" by
Suckling. The three lines quoted by Millamant in her next two
speeches complete the first stanza of the poem.   100. **Anan:**
I beg your pardon.   111. **Gothic:** The Restoration and early
eighteenth century considered the civilization of the Goths and
"Gothic" art rude and barbarous.   120. **fought:** A provincial
form of *fetched.*   132. *l'étourdi:* The silly fellow.

with the country. 'Tis like you may be one of those, cousin.

MRS. MILLAMANT: Ha! ha! ha! Yes, 'tis like I may. You have nothing further to say to me?

140 SIR WILFULL: Not at present, cousin. 'Tis like when I have an opportunity to he more private, I may break my mind in some measure. I conjecture you partly guess—however, that's as time shall try; but spare to speak and spare to speed,° as they say.

145 MRS. MILLAMANT: If it is of no great importance, Sir Wilfull, you will oblige me to leave me; I have just now a little business—

SIR WILFULL: Enough, enough, cousin, yes, yes, all a case;° when you're disposed, when you're disposed.
150 Now's as well as another time; and another time as well as now. All's one for that. Yes, yes, if your concerns call you, there's no haste; it will keep cold, as they say. Cousin, your servant. I think this door's locked.

155 MRS. MILLAMANT: You may go this way, sir.

SIR WILFULL: Your servant; then with your leave I'll return to my company.

MRS. MILLAMANT: Aye, aye; ha! ha! ha!
"Like Phoebus sung the no less am'rous boy."°

(*Enter Mirabell.*)

160 MIRABELL: "Like Daphne, she, as lovely and as coy."° Do you lock yourself up from me, to make my search more curious?° Or is this pretty artifice contrived, to signify that here the chase must end and my pursuit be crowned, for you can fly no further?

165 MRS. MILLAMANT: Vanity! No. I'll fly and be followed to the last moment. Though I am upon the very verge of matrimony, I expect you should solicit me as much as if I were wavering at the grate of a monastery, with one foot over the threshold. I'll be solicited to the
170 very last, nay, and afterwards.

MIRABELL: What, after the last?

MRS. MILLAMANT: Oh, I should think I was poor and had nothing to bestow, if I were reduced to an inglorious ease and freed from the agreeable fatigues of
175 solicitation.

MIRABELL: But do not you know that when favors are conferred upon instant and tedious solicitation, that they diminish in their value, and that both the giver loses the grace, and the receiver lessens his pleasure?

180 MRS. MILLAMANT: It may be in things of common application; but never sure in love. Oh, I hate a lover that can dare to think he draws a moment's air independent on the bounty of his mistress. There is not so impudent a thing in nature as the saucy look of an

assured man, confident of success. The pedantic arro-   185
gance of a very husband has not so pragmatical° an air. Ah! I'll never marry, unless I am first made sure of my will and pleasure.

MIRABELL: Would you have 'em both before marriage? Or will you be contented with the first now, and stay   190
for the other till after grace?

MRS. MILLAMANT: Ah! don't be impertinent. My dear liberty, shall I leave thee? My faithful solitude, my darling contemplation, must I bid you then adieu? Ay-h adieu, my morning thoughts, agreeable wak-   195
ings, indolent slumbers, all ye *douceurs,*° ye *sommeils du matin,*° adieu. I can't do't, 'tis more than impossible. Positively, Mirabell, I'll lie abed in a morning as long as I please.

MIRABELL: Then I'll get up in a morning as early as I   200
please.

MRS. MILLAMANT: Ah! idle creature, get up when you will. And d'ye hear, I won't be called names after I'm married; positively I won't be called names.

MIRABELL: Names!   205

MRS. MILLAMANT: Aye, as wife, spouse, my dear, joy, jewel, love, sweetheart, and the rest of that nauseous cant, in which men and their wives are so fulsomely familiar; I shall never bear that. Good Mirabell, don't let us be familiar or fond, nor kiss before folks,   210
like my Lady Fadler and Sir Francis; nor go to Hyde Park together the first Sunday in a new chariot, to provoke eyes and whispers, and then never be seen there together again, as if we were proud of one another the first week, and ashamed of one another   215
ever after. Let us never visit together, nor go to a play together. But let us be very strange and well-bred; let us be as strange as if we had been married a great while, and as well bred as if we were not married at all.   220

MIRABELL: Have you any more conditions to offer? Hitherto your demands are pretty reasonable.

MRS. MILLAMANT: Trifles! As liberty to pay and receive visits to and from whom I please; to write and receive letters, without interrogatories° or wry faces on your   225
part; to wear what I please, and choose conversation with regard only to my own taste; to have no obligation upon me to converse with wits that I don't like, because they are your acquaintance, or to be intimate with fools, because they may be your relations. Come   230
to dinner when I please; dine in my dressing-room when I'm out of humor, without giving a reason. To have my closet inviolate; to be sole empress of my tea-table, which you must never presume to approach without first asking leave. And lastly, wher-   235
ever I am, you shall always knock at the door before you come in. These articles subscribed, if I continue to

---

143–144. **spare to speak . . . speed:** Proverb meaning "If you hold your tongue, you won't get along in the world." 148–149. **all a case:** Idiomatic for "It's all the same." 159. **"Like Phoebus . . . boy":** The third line of Waller's *Story of Phoebus and Daphne, Applied.* 160. **"Like Daphne . . . coy":** The fourth line of Waller's poem. Mirabell completes the couplet begun by Millamant. 162. **curious:** Difficult.

186. **pragmatical:** Officious. 196. *douceurs:* Sweet pleasures. 196–197. *sommeils du matin:* Morning sleep. 225. **interrogatories:** Prying questions.

endure you a little longer, I may by degrees dwindle into a wife.

240 MIRABELL: Your bill of fare is something advanced in this latter account. Well, have I liberty to offer conditions, that when you are dwindled into a wife, I may not be beyond measure enlarged into a husband?

MRS. MILLAMANT: You have free leave. Propose your
245 utmost; speak and spare not.

MIRABELL: I thank you. *Imprimis*° then, I covenant° that your acquaintance be general; that you admit no sworn confidante, or intimate of your own sex; no she-friend to screen her affairs under your counte-
250 nance, and tempt you to make trial of a mutual secrecy. No decoy-duck to wheedle° you a fop, scrambling° to the play in a mask; then bring you home in a pretended fright, when you think you shall be found out, and rail at me for missing the play, and
255 disappointing the frolic which you had to pick me up and prove my constancy.

MRS. MILLAMANT: Detestable *imprimis!* I go to the play in a mask!

MIRABELL: *Item,*° I article that you continue to like your
260 own face, as long as I shall; and while it passes current with me, that you endeavor not to new-coin it. To which end, together with all vizards for the day, I prohibit all masks for the night, made of oiled skins and I know not what: hog's bones, hare's gall, pig
265 water, and the marrow of a roasted cat.° In short, I forbid all commerce with the gentle-woman in What-d'ye-call-it Court. *Item*, I shut my doors against all bawds with baskets, and pennyworths of muslin, china, fans, atlases,° etc. *Item*, when you shall be
270 breeding—

MRS. MILLAMANT: Ah! name it not.

MIRABELL: Which may be presumed, with a blessing on our endeavors—

MRS. MILLAMANT: Odious endeavors!

275 MIRABELL: I denounce against all strait-lacing, squeezing for a shape, till you mold my boy's head like a sugar-loaf, and instead of a man child, make me father to a crooked billet.° Lastly, to the dominion of the tea-table I submit, but with *proviso* that you
280 exceed not in your province, but restrain yourself to native and simple tea-table drinks, as tea, chocolate, and coffee, as likewise to genuine and authorized tea-table talk, such as mending of fashions, spoiling reputations, railing at absent friends, and so forth;
285 but that on no account you encroach upon the men's prerogative, and presume to drink healths, or toast fellows; for prevention of which, I banish all foreign forces, all auxiliaries to the tea-table, as orange brandy, all aniseed, cinnamon, citron, and Barbados
290 waters, together with ratafia and the most noble

spirit of clary.° But for cowslip wine, poppy water, and all dormitives,° those I allow. These *provisos* admitted, in other things I may prove a tractable and complying husband.

MRS. MILLAMANT: O horrid *provisos*! filthy strongwa- 295 ters! I toast fellows, odious men! I hate your odious *provisos*.

MIRABELL: Then we're agreed. Shall I kiss your hand upon the contract? And here comes one to be a witness to the sealing of the deed. 300

(Reenter Mrs. Fainall.)

MRS. MILLAMANT: Fainall, what shall I do? Shall I have him? I think I must have him.

MRS. FAINALL: Aye, aye, take him, take him; what should you do?

MRS. MILLAMANT: Well then—I'll take my death I'm in 305 a horrid fright. Fainall, I shall never say it. Well—I think—I'll endure you.

MRS. FAINALL: Fie! fie! have him, have him, and tell him so in plain terms; for I am sure you have a mind to him.

MRS. MILLAMANT: Are you? I think I have; and the horrid 310 man looks as if he thought so too. Well, you ridiculous thing you, I'll have you; I won't be kissed, nor I won't be thanked. Here, kiss my hand though. So, hold your tongue now; don't say a word.

MRS. FAINALL: Mirabell, there's a necessity for your obe- 315 dience; you have neither time to talk nor stay. My mother is coming; and in my conscience, if she should see you, would fall into fits and maybe not recover, time enough to return to Sir Rowland, who, as Foible tells me, is in a fair way to succeed. Therefore spare 320 your ecstacies for another occasion, and slip down the back stairs, where Foible waits to consult you.

MRS. MILLAMANT: Aye, go, go. In the meantime I suppose you have said something to please me.

MIRABELL: I am all obedience. *(Exit.)* 325

MRS. FAINALL: Yonder Sir Wilfull's drunk, and so noisy that my mother has been forced to leave Sir Rowland to appease him; but he answers her only with singing and drinking. What they may have done by this time I know not; but Petulant and he were upon quarrel- 330 ing as I came by.

MRS. MILLAMANT: Well, if Mirabell should not make a good husband, I am a lost thing; for I find I love him violently.

MRS. FAINALL: So it seems; for you mind not what's said 335 to you. If you doubt him, you had best take up with Sir Wilfull.

MRS. MILLAMANT: How can you name that superannuated lubber? Foh!

(Enter Witwoud, from drinking.)

MRS. FAINALL: So, is the fray made up, that you have left 340 'em?

---

246. *Imprimis:* First. **covenant:** Decree. **251. wheedle:** Procure. **252. scrambling:** Going without suitable dignity. **259. *Item:*** In addition. **264–265. hog's bones ... cat:** All were ingredients in cosmetics. **269. atlases:** A kind of satin. **278. billet:** Stick.

288–291. orange brandy ... clary: All these "auxiliaries" were cordials made of brandy and variously flavored. **292. dormitives:** Sedatives.

WITWOUD: Left 'em? I could stay no longer. I have laughed like ten christenings; I am tipsy with laughing. If I had stayed any longer I should have burst; I
345 must have been let out and pieced in the sides like an unsized camlet.° Yes, yes, the fray is composed; my lady came in like a *noli prosequi*° and stopped the proceedings.

MRS. MILLAMANT: What was the dispute?

350 WITWOUD: That's the jest; there was no dispute. They could neither of 'em speak for rage, and so fell asputtering at one another like two roasting apples.

(*Enter Petulant, drunk.*)

Now, Petulant? All's over, all's well? Gad, my head begins to whim° it about. Why dost thou not speak?
355 Thou art both as drunk and as mute as a fish.

PETULANT: Look you, Mrs. Millamant, if you can love me, dear nymph, say it, and that's the conclusion. Pass on, or pass off; that's all.

WITWOUD: Thou hast uttered volumes, folios, in less
360 than *decimo sexto*,° my dear Lacedemonian.° Sirrah, Petulant, thou art an epitomizer of words.°

PETULANT: Witwoud, you are an annihilator of sense.

WITWOUD: Thou art a retailer of phrases and dost deal in remnants of remnants, like a maker of pincush-
365 ions; thou art in truth (metaphorically speaking) a speaker of shorthand.

PETULANT: Thou art (without a figure) just one half of an ass, and Baldwin° yonder, thy half brother, is the rest. A Gemini° of asses split would make just four of you.

370 WITWOUD: Thou dost bite, my dear mustard seed; kiss me for that.

PETULANT: Stand off! I'll kiss no more males. I have kissed your twin yonder in a humor of reconciliation, till he (*hiccup*) rises upon my stomach like a radish.

375 MRS. MILLAMANT: Eh! filthy creature! What was the quarrel?

PETULANT: There was no quarrel; there might have been a quarrel.

WITWOUD: If there had been words enow between 'em to
380 have expressed provocation, they had gone together by the ears like a pair of castanets.

PETULANT: You were the quarrel.

MRS. MILLAMANT: Me!

PETULANT: If I have a humor to quarrel, I can make less
385 matters conclude premises. If you are not handsome, what then, if I have a humor to prove it? If I shall

have my reward, say so; if not, fight for your face the next time yourself. I'll go sleep.

WITWOUD: Do, wrap thyself up like a wood louse, and dream revenge; and hear me, if thou canst learn to 390
write by tomorrow morning, pen me a challenge. I'll carry it for thee.

PETULANT: Carry your mistress's monkey a spider! Go flea dogs, and read romances! I'll go to bed to my maid.   (*Exit.*) 395

MRS. FAINALL: He's horridly drunk. How came you all in this pickle?

WITWOUD: A plot! a plot! to get rid of the knight. Your husband's advice; but he sneaked off.

(*Reenter Sir Wilfull drunk, and Lady Wishfort.*)

LADY WISHFORT: Out upon't, out upon't! At years of 400
discretion, and comport yourself at this rantipole° rate!

SIR WILFULL: No offense, aunt.

LADY WISHFORT: Offense? As I'm a person, I'm ashamed of you. Fogh! how you stink of wine! D'ye 405
think my niece will ever endure such a borachio!° you're an absolute borachio.

SIR WILFULL: Borachio!

LADY WISHFORT: At a time when you should commence an amour, and put your best foot foremost— 410

SIR WILFULL: 'Sheart, an you grutch° me your liquor, make a hill. Give me more drink, and take my purse.

(*Sings.*) "Prithee fill me the glass
    Till it laugh in my face,
With ale that is potent and mellow; 415
    He that whines for a lass
    Is an ignorant ass,
For a bumper has not its fellow."

But if you would have me marry my cousin, say the word, and I'll do't. Wilfull will do't; that's the word. 420
Wilfull will do't; that's my crest. My motto I have forgot.

LADY WISHFORT: My nephew's a little overtaken,° cousin, but 'tis with drinking your health. O' my word you are obliged to him. 425

SIR WILFULL: *In vino veritas*,° aunt. If I drunk your health today, cousin, I am a borachio. But if you have a mind to be married, say the word, and send for the piper; Wilfull will do't. If not, dust it away, and let's have t'other round. Tony! Ods-heart, where's Tony? 430
Tony's an honest fellow; but he spits after a bumper, and that's a fault.

---

346. **unsized camlet:** I.e., like a piece of unstiffened satin.
347. *noli prosequi:* A legal term meaning that the plaintiff does not wish to continue the prosecution. 354. **whim:** Spin.
360. *decimo sexto:* A very tiny book. **Lacedemonian:** Spartan. (The Spartans were known to be very laconic people—that is, terse in their speech.) 361. **thou art . . . words:** I.e., You say much in few words. 368. **Baldwin:** The name of the ass in the medieval tale *Reynard the Fox*. 369. **Gemini:** Matched pair of twins. The constellation Gemini derives its name from the twin stars Castor and Pollux.

401. **rantipole:** Wild. 406. **borachio:** Spanish for "wine bag," a drunkard. Shakespeare has a character named Borachio in *Much Ado about Nothing*. 411. **grutch:** Grudge. 423. **overtaken:** Overcome by drink. 426. *In vino veritas:* In wine (there is) truth.

(*Sings.*) "We'll drink, and we'll never ha' done,
    boys,
    Put the glass then around with the sun, boys;
435 Let Apollo's example invite us;
    For he's drunk every night,
    And that makes him so bright,
That he's able next morning to light us."

The sun's a good pimple,° an honest soaker, he has a
440 cellar at your Antipodes.° If I travel, aunt, I touch at
your Antipodes; your Antipodes are a good, rascally sort of topsy-turvy fellows. If I had a bumper,
I'd stand upon my head and drink a health to 'em.
A match or no match, cousin, with the hard name.
445 Aunt, Wilfull will do't. If she has her maidenhead,
let her look to't, if she has not, let her keep her own
counsel in the meantime, and cry out at the nine
months' end.

MRS. MILLAMANT: Your pardon, madam, I can stay no
450 longer. Sir Wilfull grows very powerful. Egh! how he
smells! I shall be overcome if I stay. Come, cousin.

(*Exeunt Mrs. Millamant and Mrs. Fainall.*)

LADY WISHFORT: Smells! he would poison a tallow-
chandler° and his family! Beastly creature, I know
not what to do with him. Travel, quotha! aye, travel,
455 travel, get thee gone, get thee but far enough, to the
Saracens, or the Tartars, or the Turks, for thou art not
fit to live in a Christian commonwealth, thou beastly
pagan!

SIR WILFULL: Turks, no; no Turks, aunt; your Turks are
460 infidels, and believe not in the grape. Your Maho-
metan, your Mussulman, is a dry stinkard.° No offense, aunt. My map says that your Turk is not so
honest a man as your Christian. I cannot find by the
map that your mufti° is orthodox; whereby it is a
465 plain case that orthodox is a hard word, aunt, and
(*hiccup*) Greek for claret.

(*Sings.*) "To drink is a Christian diversion,
Unknown to the Turk or the Persian
    Let Mahometan fools
    Live by heathenish rules,
470 And be damn'd over teacups and coffee!
    But let British lads sing,
    Crown a health to the king,
And a fig for your sultan and sophy!"°

475 Ah, Tony!

(*Enter Foible, and whispers [to] Lady Wishfort.*)

LADY WISHFORT (*aside to Foible*): Sir Rowland impatient? Good lack! what shall I do with this beastly
tumbril?° (*Aloud.*) Go lie down and sleep, you sot!
or, as I'm a person, I'll have you bastinadoed° with
broomsticks. Call up the wenches with broomsticks. 480

(*Exit Foible.*)

SIR WILFULL: Ahey! Wenches, where are the wenches?
LADY WISHFORT: Dear Cousin Witwoud, get him away,
and you will bind me to you inviolably. I have an
affair of moment that invades me with some precipi-
tation. You will oblige me to all futurity. 485
WITWOUD: Come, knight. Pox on him, I don't know what
to say to him. Will you go to a cock match?
SIR WILFULL: With a wench, Tony? Is she a shakebag,°
Sirrah? Let me bite your cheek° for that.
WITWOUD: Horrible! he has a breath like a bagpipe! 490
Aye, aye, come, will you march, my Salopian?°
SIR WILFULL: Lead on, little Tony, I'll follow thee, my
Anthony, my Tantony. Sirrah, thou shalt be my
Tantony, and I'll be thy pig.°
    "And a fig for your sultan and sophy." 495

(*Exit singing with Witwoud.*)

LADY WISHFORT: This will never do. It will never make a
match; at least before he has been abroad.

(*Enter Waitwell, disguised as Sir Rowland.*)

Dear Sir Rowland, I am confounded with confusion
at the retrospection of my own rudeness! I have more
pardons to ask than the Pope distributes in the Year 500
of Jubilee.° But I hope, where there is likely to be so
near an alliance, we may unbend the severity of decorum, and dispense with a little ceremony.
WAITWELL: My impatience, madam, is the effect of my
transport; and till I have the possession of your 505
adorable person, I am tantalized on the rack, and do
but hang, madam, on the tenter° of expectation.
LADY WISHFORT: You have excess of gallantry, Sir
Rowland, and press things to a conclusion with a
most prevailing vehemence. But a day or two for 510
decency of marriage—
WAITWELL: For decency of funeral, madam! The delay
will break my heart; or, if that should fail, I shall
be poisoned. My nephew will get an inkling of my
designs, and poison me—and I would willingly 515
starve him before I die; I would gladly go out of the
world with that satisfaction. That would be some

---

439. **pimple:** Drinking companion. 440. **Antipodes:** The opposite end of the world or its inhabitants. 452–453. **tallow-
chandler:** Candle maker. 461. **dry stinkard:** A miserable
nondrinker. Mohammedans drink neither wine nor spirits.
464. **mufti:** An expert in Mohammedan religious law.
474. **sophy:** A former title of the Persian shah.

478. **tumbril:** Dump-cart. 479. **bastinadoed:** Beaten.
488. **shakebag:** A term in cock fighting for a very game or
sporting cock. 489. **bite your cheek:** I.e., give you a big kiss.
491. **Salopian:** Shropshireman. 494. **pig:** In art and legend, the pig is associated with St. Anthony the Great.
500–501. **Year of Jubilee:** The year (approximately every
twenty-fifth) in which the pope grants general remission from
the consequences of sin. 507. **tenter:** A tenterhook.

comfort to me, if I could but live so long as to be revenged on that unnatural viper.

520 LADY WISHFORT: Is he so unnatural, say you? Truly I would contribute much both to the saving of your life, and the accomplishment of your revenge. Not that I respect myself, though he has been a perfidious wretch to me.

525 WAITWELL: Perfidious to you!

LADY WISHFORT: O Sir Rowland, the hours that he has died away at my feet, the tears that he has shed, the oaths that he has sworn, the palpitations that he has felt, the trances and the tremblings, the ardors and 530 the ecstasies, the kneelings and the risings, the heart-heavings and the hand-gripings, the pangs and the pathetic regards of his protesting eyes! Oh, no memory can register!

WAITWELL: What, my rival! Is the rebel my rival? 'A 535 dies.

LADY WISHFORT: No, don't kill him at once, Sir Rowland; starve him gradually, inch by inch.

WAITWELL: I'll do't. In three weeks he shall be barefoot; in a month out at knees with begging an alms. He 540 shall starve upward and upward, till he has nothing living but his head, and then go out in a stink like a candle's end upon a save-all.°

LADY WISHFORT: Well, Sir Rowland, you have the way. You are no novice in the labyrinth of love; you have 545 the clue. But as I am a person, Sir Rowland, you must not attribute my yielding to any sinister appetite, or indigestion of widowhood: nor impute my complacency to any lethargy of continence. I hope you do not think me prone to any iteration° of nuptials—

550 WAITWELL: Far be it from me—

LADY WISHFORT: If you do, I protest I must recede, or think that I have made a prostitution of decorums; but in the vehemence of compassion, and to save the life of a person of so much importance—

555 WAITWELL: I esteem it so.

LADY WISHFORT: Or else you wrong my condescension.

WAITWELL: I do not, I do not!

LADY WISHFORT: Indeed you do.

WAITWELL: I do not, fair shrine of virtue!

560 LADY WISHFORT: If you think the least scruple of carnality° was an ingredient—

WAITWELL: Dear madam, no. You are all camphire° and frankincense, all chastity and odor.

LADY WISHFORT: Or that—

(*Reenter Foible.*)

565 FOIBLE: Madam, the dancers are ready; and there's one with a letter, who must deliver it into your own hands.

LADY WISHFORT: Sir Rowland, will you give me leave? Think favorably, judge candidly, and conclude you have found a person who would suffer racks in honor's cause, dear Sir Rowland, and will wait on 570 you incessantly.° (*Exit.*)

WAITWELL: Fie, fie! What a slavery have I undergone! Spouse, hast thou any cordial? I want spirits.

FOIBLE: What a washy° rogue art thou, to pant thus for a quarter of an hour's lying and swearing to a fine 575 lady!

WAITWELL: Oh, she is the antidote to desire! Spouse, thou wilt fare the worse for't. I shall have no appetite to "iteration of nuptials" this eight-and-forty hours. By this hand I'd rather be a chair-man° in the dog 580 days° than act Sir Rowland till this time tomorrow!

(*Reenter Lady Wishfort, with a letter.*)

LADY WISHFORT: Call in the dancers. Sir Rowland, we'll sit, if you please, and see the entertainment. (*Dance.*) Now, with your permission, Sir Rowland, I will peruse my letter. I would open it in your presence, 585 because I would not make you uneasy. If it should make you uneasy, I would burn it—speak if it does— but you may see, the superscription is like a woman's hand.

FOIBLE (*aside to Waitwell*): By Heaven! Mrs. Marwood's; 590 I know it. My heart aches. Get it from her.

WAITWELL: A woman's hand? No, madam, that's no woman's hand; I see that already. That's somebody whose throat must be cut.

LADY WISHFORT: Nay, Sir Rowland, since you give me a 595 proof of your passion by your jealousy, I promise you I'll make a return, by a frank communication. You shall see it; we'll open it together. Look you here. (*Reads.*) "Madam, though unknown to you." Look you there; 'tis from nobody that I know. "I have that 600 honor for your character, that I think myself obliged to let you know you are abused. He who pretends to be Sir Rowland is a cheat and a rascal." Oh, heavens! what's this?

FOIBLE (*aside*): Unfortunate! all's ruined!   605

WAITWELL: How, how, let me see, let me see! (*Reading.*) "A rascal, and disguised and suborned° for that imposture." O villainy! O villainy! "by the contrivance of—"

LADY WISHFORT: I shall faint, I shall die, oh!   610

FOIBLE (*aside to Waitwell*): Say 'tis your nephew's hand. Quickly, his plot, swear, swear it!

WAITWELL: Here's a villain! Madam, don't you perceive it? don't you see it?

LADY WISHFORT: Too well, too well! I have seen too 615 much.

---

542. **save-all:** A device in a candlestick to ensure that the candle will be completely burned.   549. **iteration:** Repetition. The sense seems to be that Lady Wishfort hopes Sir Rowland will not suspect her of a willingness to marry just any man. 560–561. **carnality:** Sensuality, lust.   562. **camphire:** Camphor was believed to reduce sexual desire.

571. **incessantly:** Immediately.   574. **washy:** Weak.   580. **chairman:** A sedan-chair carrier.   580–581. **dog days:** The sultriest days of the summer, a period of about six weeks beginning in early July.   607. **suborned:** Bribed.

Robert Hack, Carol Schultz, and Mikel Sarah Lambert in the Pearl Theatre Company's 2000 performance of *The Way of the World,* directed by Ray Vitra.

WAITWELL: I told you at first I knew the hand. A woman's hand? The rascal writes a sort of a large hand, your Roman hand. I saw there was a throat to be cut presently. If he were my son, as he is my 620 nephew, I'd pistol him!

FOIBLE: Oh, treachery! But are you sure, Sir Rowland, it is his writing?

WAITWELL: Sure? Am I here? Do I live? Do I love this pearl of India? I have twenty letters in my pocket 625 from him in the same character.°

LADY WISHFORT: How!

FOIBLE: Oh, what luck it is, Sir Rowland, that you were present at this juncture! This was the business that brought Mr. Mirabell disguised to Madam Millamant 630 this afternoon. I thought something was contriving, when he stole by me and would have hid his face.

LADY WISHFORT: How, how! I heard the villain was in the house indeed; and now I remember, my niece

626. **character:** Handwriting.

went away abruptly, when Sir Wilfull was to have 635 made his addresses.

FOIBLE: Then, then, madam, Mr. Mirabell waited for her in her chamber, but I would not tell your ladyship to discompose° you when you were to receive Sir Rowland. 640

WAITWELL: Enough, his date is short.

FOIBLE: No, good Sir Rowland, don't incur the law.

WAITWELL: Law? I care not for law. I can but die, and 'tis in a good cause. My lady shall be satisfied of my truth and innocence, though it cost me my life. 645

LADY WISHFORT: No, dear Sir Rowland, don't fight; if you should be killed, I must never show my face; or hanged! Oh, consider my reputation, Sir Rowland! No, you shan't fight. I'll go in and examine my niece; I'll make her confess. I conjure you, Sir Rowland, by 650 all your love, not to fight.

WAITWELL: I am charmed, madam; I obey. But some proof you must let me give you; I'll go for a black box, which contains the writings of my whole estate, and deliver that into your hands. 655

LADY WISHFORT: Aye, dear Sir Rowland, that will be some comfort; bring the black box.

WAITWELL: And may I presume to bring a contract to be signed this night? May I hope so far?

LADY WISHFORT: Bring what you will; but come alive, 660 pray come alive. Oh, this is a happy discovery!

WAITWELL: Dead or alive I'll come, and married we will be in spite of treachery; aye, and get an heir that shall defeat the last remaining glimpse of hope in my abandoned nephew. Come, my buxom widow. 665

    Ere long you shall substantial proof receive,
    That I'm an arrant knight—°

FOIBLE (*aside*):   Or arrant° knave.
                        (*Exeunt.*)

ACT V

([*Scene continues.*] *Enter Lady Wishfort and Foible.*)

LADY WISHFORT: Out of my house, out of my house, thou viper! thou serpent, that I have fostered! thou bosom traitress, that I raised from nothing! Begone! begone! begone! go! go! That I took from washing of old gauze and weaving of dead hair, with a bleak blue 5 nose, over a chafing-dish of starved embers, and dining behind a traverse rag,° in a shop no bigger than a birdcage! Go, go! starve again, do, do!

FOIBLE: Dear madam, I'll beg your pardon on my knees.

LADY WISHFORT: Away! out! out! Go set up for yourself 10 again! Do, drive a trade, do, with your three-penny-worth of small ware flaunting upon a pack-thread under a brandy-seller's bulk,° or against a dead wall

639. **discompose:** Distress, upset.   **667. arrant knight:** I.e., a true knight-errant. **arrant:** Downright. **7. traverse rag:** A curtain or hanging that serves as a screen. **13. bulk:** A booth where brandy is sold.

Douglas Campbell's set design and ensemble cast, including Zoe Caldwell and Jessica Tandy, in the Minnesota Theater Company's 1965 performance of *The Way of the World* at the Tyrone Guthrie Theater.

by a ballad-monger! Go, hang out an old frisoneer-
gorget,° with a yard of yellow colberteen° again. Do;
an old gnawed mask, two rows of pins, and a child's
fiddle; a glass necklace with the beads broken, and a
quilted nightcap with one ear. Go, go, drive a trade!
These were your commodities, you treacherous trull!
this was the merchandise you dealt in, when I took
you into my house, placed you next myself, and made
you governance of my whole family! You have forgot
this, have you, now you have feathered your nest?

FOIBLE: No, no, dear madam. Do but hear me; have but
a moment's patience. I'll confess all. Mr. Mirabell seduced me; I am not the first that he has wheedled
with his dissembling tongue. Your ladyship's own
wisdom has been deluded by him, then how should
I, a poor ignorant, defend myself? O madam, if you
knew but what he promised me, and how he assured
me your ladyship should come to no damage! Or else
the wealth of the Indies should not have bribed me to
conspire against so good, so sweet, so kind a lady as
you have been to me.

LADY WISHFORT: No damage? What, to betray me, to
marry me to a cast-servingman?° To make me a
receptacle, a hospital for a decayed pimp? "No damage"? O thou frontless° impudence, more than a big-
bellied actress!

FOIBLE: Pray do but hear me, madam; he could not
marry your ladyship, madam. No indeed; his marriage was to have been void in law, for he was married to me first, to secure your ladyship. He could not
have bedded your ladyship; for if he had consum-
mated with your ladyship, he must have run the risk
of the law and been put upon his clergy.° Yes indeed,
I inquired of the law in that case before I would
meddle or make.°

LADY WISHFORT: What, then I have been your property,
have I? I have been convenient to you, it seems!
While you were catering for Mirabell, I have been
broker° for you? What, have you made a passive
bawd of me? This exceeds all precedent; I am brought
to fine uses, to become a botcher° of second-hand

14–15. frisoneer-gorget: A kind of wimple, or head covering, made of coarse woolen cloth.   15. colberteen: A French lace of inferior quality.   36. cast-servingman: A discharged servant.

38. frontless: Shameless.   46. put upon his clergy: Forced to plead benefit of clergy. Clergy (and, later, people who could read or write) could claim exemption from punishment imposed by a secular court.   48. meddle or make: A colloquialism for "get mixed up in this business."   52. broker: Marriage broker.   54. botcher: A maker or mender.

marriages between Abigails° and Andrews!° I'll couple you! Yes, I'll baste you together, you and your Philander!° I'll Duke's-Place you, as I'm a person! Your turtle is in custody already; you shall coo in the same cage, if there be constable or warrant in the parish.   (*Exit.*)

FOIBLE: Oh, that ever I was born! Oh, that I was ever married! A bride! aye, I shall be a Bridewell-bride.° Oh!

(*Enter Mrs. Fainall.*)

MRS. FAINALL: Poor Foible, what's the matter?

FOIBLE: O madam, my lady's gone for a constable. I shall be had to a justice, and put to Bridewell to beat hemp. Poor Waitwell's gone to prison already.

MRS. FAINALL: Have a good heart, Foible; Mirabell's gone to give security for him. This is all Marwood's and my husband's doing.

FOIBLE: Yes, yes, I know it, madam; she was in my lady's closet, and overheard all that you said to me before dinner. She sent the letter to my lady; and that missing effect, Mr. Fainall laid this plot to arrest Waitwell, when he pretended to go for the papers; and in the meantime Mrs. Marwood declared all to my lady.

MRS. FAINALL: Was there no mention made of me in the letter? My mother does not suspect my being in the confederacy? I fancy Marwood has not told her, though she has told my husband.

FOIBLE: Yes, madam; but my lady did not see that part. We stifled the letter before she read so far. Has that mischievous devil told Mr. Fainall of your ladyship then?

MRS. FAINALL: Aye, all's out, my affair with Mirabell, everything discovered. This is the last day of our living together; that's my comfort.

FOIBLE: Indeed, madam, and so 'tis a comfort if you knew all. He has been even with your ladyship; which I could have told you long enough since, but I love to keep peace and quietness by my good will. I had rather bring friends together than set 'em at distance. But Mrs. Marwood and he are nearer related than ever their parents thought for.

MRS. FAINALL: Sayest thou so, Foible? Canst thou prove this?

FOIBLE: I can take my oath of it, madam; so can Mrs. Mincing. We have had many a fair word from Madam Marwood, to conceal something that passed in our chamber one evening when you were at Hyde Park and we were thought to have gone awalking; but we went up unawares, though we were sworn to secrecy too. Madam Marwood took a book and swore us upon it, but it was but a book of poems. So long as it was not a Bible oath, we may break it with a safe conscience.

MRS. FAINALL: This discovery is the most opportune thing I could wish. Now, Mincing?

(*Enter Mincing.*)

MINCING: My lady° would speak with Mrs. Foible, mem. Mr. Mirabell is with her; he has set your spouse at liberty, Mrs. Foible, and would have you hide yourself in my lady's closet till my old lady's anger is abated. Oh, my old lady is in a perilous passion at something Mr. Fainall has said, he swears, and my old lady cries. There's a fearful hurricane, I vow. He says, mem, how that he'll have my lady's fortune made over to him, or he'll be divorced.

MRS. FAINALL: Does your lady or Mirabell know that?

MINCING: Yes, mem, they have sent me to see if Sir Wilfull be sober and to bring him to them. My lady is resolved to have him, I think, rather than lose such a vast sum as six thousand pound. Oh, come, Mrs. Foible, I hear my old lady.

MRS. FAINALL: Foible, you must tell Mincing that she must prepare to vouch° when I call her.

FOIBLE: Yes, yes, madam.

MINCING: O yes, mem, I'll vouch anything for your ladyship's service, be what it will.

(*Exeunt Mincing and Foible.*)

(*Reenter Lady Wishfort, with, Mrs. Marwood.*)

LADY WISHFORT: O my dear friend, how can I enumerate the benefits that I have received from your goodness? To you I owe the timely discovery of the false vows of Mirabell, to you I owe the detection of the impostor, Sir Rowland. And now you are become an intercessor with my son-in-law, to save the honor of my house, and compound for the frailties of my daughter. Well, friend, you are enough to reconcile me to the bad world, or else I would retire to deserts and solitudes, and feed harmless sheep by groves and purling streams. Dear Marwood, let us leave the world, and retire by ourselves and be shepherdesses.

MRS. MARWOOD: Let us first dispatch the affair in hand, madam. We shall have leisure to think of retirement afterwards. Here is one who is concerned in the treaty.

LADY WISHFORT: O daughter, daughter, is it possible thou shouldst be my child, bone of my bone, and flesh of my flesh, and, as I may say, another me, and yet transgress the most minute particle of severe virtue? Is it possible you should lean aside to iniquity, who have been cast in the direct mold of virtue? I have not only been a mold but a pattern for you, and a model for you, after you were brought into the world.

MRS. FAINALL: I don't understand your ladyship.

LADY WISHFORT: Not understand? Why, have you not been naught?° Have you not been sophisticated?° Not understand? Here I am ruined to compound° for

---

55. **Abigails:** A maidservant in Beaumont and Fletcher's play *The Scornful Lady.* **Andrews:** A manservant in Fletcher and Massinger's *The Elder Brother.* 57. **Philander:** The lover in Beaumont and Fletcher's *The Laws of Candy.* 62. **Bridewell-bride:** Bridewell was a house of correction.

109. **My lady:** I.e., Millamant. 125. **vouch:** Testify. 155. **naught:** Naughty, wicked. **sophisticated:** Corrupted, debauched. 156. **compound:** Compensate. Lady Wishfort refers to Mr. Fainall's blackmailing tactics.

your caprices and your cuckoldoms. I must pawn my plate and my jewels, and ruin my niece, and all little enough.

160 MRS. FAINALL: I am wronged and abused, and so are you. 'Tis a false accusation, as false as hell, as false as your friend there, aye, or your friend's friend, my false husband.

MRS. MARWOOD: My friend, Mrs. Fainall? Your husband
165 my friend? What do you mean?

MRS. FAINALL: I know what I mean, madam, and so do you; and so shall the world at a time convenient.

MRS. MARWOOD: I am sorry to see you so passionate, madam. More temper° would look more like inno-
170 cence. But I have done. I am sorry my zeal to serve your ladyship and family should admit of misconstruction, or make me liable to affronts. You will pardon me, madam, if I meddle no more with an affair in which I am not personally concerned.

175 LADY WISHFORT: O dear friend, I am so ashamed that you should meet with such returns! (*To Mrs. Fainall.*) You ought to ask pardon on your knees, ungrateful creature; she deserves more from you than all your life can accomplish. (*To Mrs. Marwood.*) Oh, don't
180 leave me destitute in this perplexity! No, stick to me, my good genius.

MRS. FAINALL: I tell you, madam, you're abused. Stick to you? Aye, like a leech, to suck your best blood; she'll drop off when she's full. Madam, you shan't
185 pawn a bodkin,° nor part with a brass counter,° in composition for me. I defy 'em all. Let 'em prove their aspersions; I know my own innocence, and dare stand a trial.   (*Exit.*)

LADY WISHFORT: Why, if she should be innocent, if she
190 should be wronged after all, ha? I don't know what to think; and, I promise you, her education has been unexceptionable.° I may say it; for I chiefly made it my own care to initiate her very infancy in the rudiments of virtue, and to impress upon her tender years
195 a young odium° and aversion to the very sight of men. Aye, friend, she would ha' shrieked if she had but seen a man, till she was in her teens. As I'm a person 'tis true. She was never suffered to play with a male child, though but in coats; nay, her very babies°
200 were of the feminine gender. Oh, she never looked a man in the face but her own father, or the chaplain, and him we made a shift° to put upon her for a woman, by the help of his long garments and his sleek face, till she was going in her fifteen.°

205 MRS. MARWOOD: 'Twas much she should be deceived so long.

LADY WISHFORT: I warrant you, or she would never have borne to have been catechized by him; and have heard his long lectures against singing and dancing,
210 and such debaucheries, and going to filthy plays and profane music meetings, where the lewd trebles squeak nothing but bawdy, and the basses roar blasphemy. Oh, she would have swooned at the sight or name of an obscene playbook! And can I think, after
215 all this, that my daughter can be naught? What, a whore? and thought it excommunication to set her foot within the door of a playhouse! O dear friend, I can't believe it, no, no! As she says, let him prove it, let him prove it.

220 MRS. MARWOOD: Prove it, madam? What, and have your name prostituted in a public court? yours and your daughter's reputation worried at the bar by a pack of bawling lawyers? To be ushered in with an *Oyez*° of scandal, and have your case opened by an old
225 fumbling lecher in a quoif° like a man-midwife; to bring your daughter's infamy to light; to be a theme for legal punsters and quibblers by the statute, and become a jest against a rule of court, where there is no precedent for a jest in any record, not even in
230 Doomsday Book;° to discompose the gravity of the bench, and provoke naughty interrogatories in more naughty law Latin, while the good judge, tickled with the proceeding, simpers under a gray beard, and fidges° off and on his cushion as if he had swallowed
235 cantharides,° or sat upon cow-itch!°

LADY WISHFORT: Oh, 'tis very hard!

MRS. MARWOOD: And then to have my young revelers of the Temple° take notes, like prentices at a conventicle;° and after, talk it over again in Commons,° or
240 before drawers in an eating-house.

LADY WISHFORT: Worse and worse!

MRS. MARWOOD: Nay, this is nothing; if it would end here, 'twere well. But it must, after this, be consigned by the shorthand writers to the public press, and
245 from thence be transferred to the hands, nay into the throats and lungs of hawkers,° with voices more licentious than the loud flounder-man's.° And this you must hear till you are stunned; nay, you must hear nothing else for some days.

250 LADY WISHFORT: Oh, 'tis insupportable! No, no, dear friend; make it up, make it up; aye, aye, I'll compound. I'll give up all, myself and my all, my niece and her all, anything, everything for composition.

MRS. MARWOOD: Nay, madam, I advise nothing; I only
255 lay before you, as a friend, the inconveniencies which perhaps you have overseen. Here comes Mr. Fainall; if he will be satisfied to huddle up all in silence, I shall

---

169. **temper:** Temperateness.   185. **bodkin:** Needle or hairpin. **brass counter:** A farthing (a quarter of a penny).   192. **unexceptionable:** Exemplary.   195. **odium:** Dislike.   199. **babies:** Dolls.   202. **made a shift:** Devised a plan.   204. **in her fifteen:** Into her fifteenth year.

223. *Oyez:* The court crier's call for silence.   225. **quoif:** Coif, the lawyer's white cap.   230. **Doomsday Book:** A record of a survey of the lands of England made by order of William the Conqueror.   234. **fidges:** Fidgets.   235. **cantharides:** A powder made from dried beetles and used medicinally as a skin irritant.   **cow-itch:** Cowage, a plant that causes intense itching. 238. **Temple:** The courts of law.   238–239. **prentices at a conventicle:** It was customary for a Puritan master to require his apprentice to take notes on the Sunday sermon in the meetinghouse (conventicle).   239. **Commons:** The dining hall. 246. **hawkers:** Peddlers.   247. **flounder-man:** An actual flounder seller, well known to the Londoners of the day and noted for his "loud, but not unmusical" voice.

be glad. You must think I would rather congratulate
than condole with you.

(Enter Fainall.)

260 LADY WISHFORT: Aye, aye, I do not doubt it, dear
Marwood; no, no, I do not doubt it.
FAINALL: Well, madam, I have suffered myself to be
overcome by the importunity of this lady, your
friend, and am content you shall enjoy your own
265 proper estate during life, on condition you oblige
yourself never to marry, under such penalty as I think
convenient.
LADY WISHFORT: Never to marry?
FAINALL: No more Sir Rowlands; the next imposture may
270 not be so timely detected.
MRS. MARWOOD: That condition, I dare answer, my lady
will consent to, without difficulty; she has already
but too much experienced the perfidiousness of men.
Besides, madam, when we retire to our pastoral soli-
275 tude, we shall bid adieu to all other thoughts.
LADY WISHFORT: Aye, that's true; but in case of necessity, as of health, or some such emergency—
FAINALL: Oh, if you are prescribed marriage, you shall be
considered; I will only reserve to myself the power
280 to choose for you. If your physic be wholesome, it
matters not who is your apothecary. Next, my wife
shall settle on me the remainder of her fortune, not
made over already; and for her maintenance depend
entirely on my discretion.
285 LADY WISHFORT: This is most inhumanly savage,
exceeding the barbarity of a Muscovite° husband.
FAINALL: I learned it from his Czarish majesty's retinue,°
in a winter evening's conference over brandy and
pepper, amongst other secrets of matrimony and
290 policy, as they are at present practiced in the northern hemisphere. But this must be agreed unto, and
that positively. Lastly, I will be endowed, in right of
my wife, with that six thousand pound, which is the
moiety of Mrs. Millamant's fortune in your posses-
295 sion; and which she has forfeited (as will appear by
the last will and testament of your deceased husband,
Sir Jonathan Wishfort) by her disobedience in contracting herself against your consent or knowledge,
and by refusing the offered match with Sir Wilfull
300 Witwoud, which you, like a careful aunt, had provided for her.
LADY WISHFORT: My nephew was *non compos,*° and
could not make his addresses.
FAINALL: I come to make demands. I'll hear no objections.
305 LADY WISHFORT: You will grant me time to consider?
FAINALL: Yes, while the instrument° is drawing, to which
you must set your hand till more sufficient deeds can
be perfected; which I will take care shall be done
with all possible speed. In the meanwhile I will go for

the said instrument, and till my return you may bal- 310
ance this matter in your own discretion.

(Exit.)

LADY WISHFORT: This insolence is beyond all precedent,
all parallel; must I be subject to this merciless villain?
MRS. MARWOOD: 'Tis severe indeed, madam, that you
should smart for your daughter's wantonness. 315
LADY WISHFORT: 'Twas against my consent that she
married this barbarian, but she would have him,
though her year° was not out. Ah! her first husband,
my son Languish, would not have carried it thus.
Well, that was my choice, this is hers; she is matched 320
now with a witness.° I shall be mad! Dear friend, is
there no comfort for me? Must I live to be confiscated at this rebel-rate?° Here come two more of my
Egyptian plagues° too.

(Enter Mrs. Millamant and Sir Wilfull Witwoud.)

SIR WILFULL: Aunt, your servant. 325
LADY WISHFORT: Out, caterpillar, call not me aunt! I know
thee not!
SIR WILFULL: I confess I have been a little in disguise,° as
they say. 'Sheart! and I'm sorry for't. What would
you have? I hope I committed no offense, aunt, and 330
if I did, I am willing to make satisfaction; and what
can a man say fairer? If I have broke anything, I'll
pay for't, an it cost a pound. And so let that content for what's past, and make no more words. For
what's to come, to pleasure you I'm willing to marry 335
my cousin. So pray let's all be friends; she and I are
agreed upon the matter before a witness.
LADY WISHFORT: How's this, dear niece? Have I any comfort? Can this be true?
MRS. MILLAMANT: I am content to be a sacrifice to your 340
repose, madam; and to convince you that I had no
hand in the plot, as you were misinformed, I have
laid my commands on Mirabell to come in person,
and be a witness that I give my hand to this flower
of knighthood; and for the contract that passed be- 345
tween Mirabell and me, I have obliged him to make
a resignation of it in your ladyship's presence. He is
without, and waits your leave for admittance.
LADY WISHFORT: Well, I'll swear I am something revived
at this testimony of your obedience; but I cannot 350
admit that traitor. I fear I cannot fortify myself to
support his appearance. He is as terrible to me as a
Gorgon;° if I see him, I fear I shall turn to stone, pet-
rify incessantly.

---

286. Muscovite: Russian.   **287. Czarish majesty's retinue:**
Referring to Peter the Great's visit to England in 1697.
302. *non compos:* I.e., *non compos mentis,* not in his right
mind.   **306. instrument:** Formal agreement.

318. her year: Period of mourning for her first husband.
321. with a witness: Colloquialism meaning "with a vengeance."   **322–323. Must I live . . . rebel-rate:** The sense is
"Must I live to see my property and fortune confiscated in this
piratical fashion?"   **324. Egyptian plagues:** Referring to the
plagues of Egypt recorded in Exodus 7ff.   **328. disguise:** Drunk.
353. Gorgon: Any one of the three sisters in Greek legend
(Medusa was one) whose hair was wreathed with snakes and
whose glance turned the beholder to stone.

355 **MRS. MILLAMANT:** If you disoblige him, he may resent your refusal, and insist upon the contract still. Then 'tis the last time he will be offensive to you.

LADY WISHFORT: Are you sure it will be the last time? If I were sure of that! Shall I never see him again?

360 **MRS. MILLAMANT:** Sir Wilfull, you and he are to travel together, are you not?

SIR WILFULL: 'Sheart, the gentleman's a civil gentleman, aunt; let him come in. Why, we are sworn brothers and fellow travelers. We are to be Pylades and Orestes,° 365 he and I. He is to be my interpreter in foreign parts. He has been overseas once already; and with *proviso* that I marry my cousin, will cross 'em once again, only to bear me company. 'Sheart, I'll call him in. An I set on't once, he shall come in; and see who'll 370 hinder him.

(*Goes to the door and hems.*)

MRS. MARWOOD: This is precious fooling, if it would pass; but I'll know the bottom of it.

LADY WISHFORT: O dear Marwood, you are not going?

MRS. MARWOOD: Not far, madam; I'll return immedi- 375 ately. (*Exit.*)

(*Reenter Sir Wilfull with Mirabell.*)

SIR WILFULL: Look up, man, I'll stand by you; 'sbud and she do frown, she can't kill you, besides, harkee, she dare not frown desperately, because her face is none of her own. 'Sheart, an she should, her forehead 380 would wrinkle like the coat of a cream cheese; but mum for that, fellow traveler.

MIRABELL: If a deep sense of the many injuries I have offered to so good a lady, with a sincere remorse and a hearty contrition, can but obtain the least glance of 385 compassion, I am too happy. Ah, madam, there was a time! But let it be forgotten. I confess I have deservedly forfeited the high place I once held, of sighing at your feet. Nay, kill me not, by turning from me in disdain. I come not to plead for favor; nay, not for 390 pardon. I am a suppliant only for pity. I am going where I shall never behold you more.

SIR WILFULL: How, fellow traveler! You shall go by yourself then.

MIRABELL: Let me be pitied first, and afterwards forgot- 395 ten. I ask no more.

SIR WILFULL: By'r lady, a very reasonable request, and will cost you nothing, aunt. Come, come, forgive and forget, aunt; why, you must, an you are a Christian.

MIRABELL: Consider, madam, in reality you could not 400 receive much prejudice; it was an innocent device, though I confess it had a face of guiltiness. It was at most an artifice which love contrived, and errors which love produces have ever been accounted venial. At least think it is punishment enough that I 405 have lost what in my heart I hold most dear, that to your cruel indignation I have offered up this beauty, and with her my peace and quiet; nay, all my hopes of future comfort.

SIR WILFULL: An he does not move me, would I may never be o' the quorum!° An it were not as good a 410 deed as to drink, to give her to him again, I would I might never take shipping! Aunt, if you don't forgive quickly, I shall melt, I can tell you that. My contract went no farther than a little mouth-glue, and that's hardly dry; one doleful sigh more from my fellow 415 traveler, and 'tis dissolved.

LADY WISHFORT: Well, nephew, upon your account—ah, he has a false insinuating tongue! Well, sir, I will stifle my just resentment at my nephew's request. I will endeavor what I can to forget, but on *proviso* that 420 you resign the contract with my niece immediately.

MIRABELL: It is in writing, and with papers of concern; but I have sent my servant for it, and will deliver it to you, with all acknowledgments for your transcendent goodness. 425

LADY WISHFORT (*aside*): Oh, he has witchcraft in his eyes and tongue! When I did not see him, I could have bribed a villain to his assassination; but his appearance rakes the embers which have so long lain smothered in my breast. 430

(*Reenter Fainall and Mrs. Marwood.*)

FAINALL: Your date of deliberation, madam, is expired. Here is the instrument; are you prepared to sign?

LADY WISHFORT: If I were prepared, I am not empowered. My niece exerts a lawful claim, having matched herself by my direction to Sir Wilfull. 435

FAINALL: That sham is too gross to pass on me, though 'tis imposed on you, madam.

MRS. MILLAMANT: Sir, I have given my consent.

MIRABELL: And, sir, I have resigned my pretensions.

SIR WILFULL: And, sir, I assert my right; and will main- 440 tain it in defiance of you, sir, and of your instrument. 'Sheart, an you talk of an instrument, sir, I have an old fox° by my thigh shall hack your instrument of ram vellum° to shreds, sir! It shall not be sufficient for a *mittimus*° or a tailor's measure.° Therefore withdraw 445 your instrument, sir, or, by'r lady, I shall draw mine.

LADY WISHFORT: Hold, nephew, hold!

MRS. MILLAMANT: Good Sir Wilfull, respite° your valor.

FAINALL: Indeed? Are you provided of your guard, with your single beefeater° there? But I'm prepared for 450 you, and insist upon my first proposal. You shall submit your own estate to my management and absolutely make over my wife's to my sole use, as pursuant to the purpose and tenor of this other covenant.

---

364. Pylades and Orestes: In Greek legend, Pylades was the loyal and trusted friend of Orestes, son of Agamemnon and brother of Elektra.

410. quorum: An indispensable member of the legal bench. **443. fox:** Sword. **443–444. ram vellum:** Parchment (made from sheepskin). **445. *mittimus:*** Legal term for a warrant of commitment to prison. **tailor's measure:** Tailors' measurements were recorded on parchment. **448. respite:** Control. **450. beefeater:** A guard of the Tower of London.

455 (*To Mrs. Millamant.*) I suppose, madam, your consent is not requisite in this case; nor, Mr. Mirabell, your resignation; nor, Sir Wilfull, your right. You may draw your fox if you please, sir, and make a Bear Garden° flourish somewhere else; for here it will not
460 avail.—This, my Lady Wishfort, must be subscribed, or your darling daughter's turned adrift, like a leaky hulk, to sink or swim, as she and the current of this lewd town can agree.

LADY WISHFORT: Is there no means, no remedy to stop
465 my ruin? Ungrateful wretch! dost thou not owe thy being, thy subsistence, to my daughter's fortune?

FAINALL: I'll answer you when I have the rest of it in my possession.

MIRABELL (*to Lady Wishfort*): But that you would not ac-
470 cept of a remedy from my hands—I own I have not deserved you should owe any obligation to me; or else perhaps I could advise—

LADY WISHFORT: Oh, what? what? to save me and my child from ruin, from want, I'll forgive all that's past;
475 nay, I'll consent to anything to come, to be delivered from this tyranny.

MIRABELL: Aye, madam, but that is too late; my reward is intercepted. You have disposed of her who only could have made me a compensation for all my ser-
480 vices. But be it as it may, I am resolved I'll serve you; you shall not be wronged in this savage manner.

LADY WISHFORT: How! Dear Mr. Mirabell, can you be so generous at last? But it is not possible. Harkee, I'll break my nephew's match; you shall have my niece
485 yet, and all her fortune, if you can but save me from this imminent danger.

MIRABELL: Will you? I take you at your word. I ask no more. I must have leave for two criminals to appear.

LADY WISHFORT: Aye, aye; anybody, anybody!
490 MIRABELL: Foible is one, and a penitent.

(*Reenter Mrs. Fainall, Foible, and Mincing.*)

MRS. MARWOOD (*to Fainall*): O my shame! (*Mirabell and Lady Wishfort go to Mrs. Fainall and Foible.*) These corrupt things are brought hither to expose me.

FAINALL: If it must all come out, why let 'em know it; 'tis
495 but the way of the world. That shall not urge me to relinquish or abate one tittle of my terms; no, I will insist the more.

FOIBLE: Yes indeed, madam; I'll take my Bible oath of it.

MINCING: And so will I, mem.
500 LADY WISHFORT: O Marwood. Marwood, art thou false? my friend deceive me? Hast thou been a wicked accomplice with that profligate man?

MRS. MARWOOD: Have you so much ingratitude and injustice, to give credit against your friend to the asper-
505 sions of two such mercenary trulls?

MINCING: "Mercenary," mem? I scorn your words. 'Tis true we found you and Mr. Fainall in the blue

garret; by the same token, you swore us to secrecy upon Messalina's poems.° "Mercenary?" No, if we would have been mercenary, we should have held our 510 tongues; you would have bribed us sufficiently.

FAINALL: Go, you are an insignificant thing! Well, what are you the better for this? Is this Mr. Mirabell's expedient? I'll be put off no longer. You thing, that was a wife, shall smart for this! I will not leave thee 515 wherewithal to hide thy shame; your body shall be naked as your reputation.

MRS. FAINALL: I despise you, and defy your malice! You have aspersed me wrongfully. I have proved your falsehood. Go, you and your treacherous—I will not 520 name it, but starve together, perish!

FAINALL: Not while you are worth a groat,° indeed, my dear. Madam, I'll be fooled no longer.

LADY WISHFORT: Ah, Mr. Mirabell, this is small comfort, the detection of this affair. 525

MIRABELL: Oh, in good time. Your leave for the other offender and penitent to appear, madam.

(*Enter Waitwell, with a box of writings.*)

LADY WISHFORT: O Sir Rowland? Well, rascal?

WAITWELL: What your ladyship pleases. I have brought the black box at last, madam. 530

MIRABELL: Give it me. Madam, you remember your promise.

LADY WISHFORT: Aye, dear sir.

MIRABELL: Where are the gentlemen?

WAITWELL: At hand, sir, rubbing their eyes; just risen 535 from sleep.

FAINALL: 'Sdeath, what's this to me? I'll not wait your private concerns.

(*Enter Petulant and Witwoud.*)

PETULANT: How now? What's the matter? Whose hand's out?° 540

WITWOUD: Heyday! what, are you all got together, like players at the end of the last act?

MIRABELL: You may remember, gentlemen, I once requested your hands as witnesses to a certain parchment. 545

WITWOUD: Aye, I do; my hand I remember. Petulant set his mark.

MIRABELL: You wrong him, his name is fairly written, as shall appear. You do not remember, gentlemen, anything of what that parchment contained? 550

(*Undoing the box.*)

WITWOUD: No.

PETULANT: Not I. I writ. I read nothing.

458–459. **Bear Garden:** Bear baiting was a popular amusement in the London of the day, and the gardens in which it took place were notorious for brawls and rowdy behavior.

509. **Messalina's poems:** Mincing means a volume of *miscellaneous* poems. Her mistake presents an amusing irony, since Messalina, the wife of the Roman Emperor Claudius, was notorious for her avarice, treachery, and dissoluteness.   522. **groat:** An old silver coin worth about fourpence.   539–540. **Whose hand's out:** What is the trouble?

MIRABELL: Very well; now you shall know. Madam, your promise.

555 LADY WISHFORT: Aye, aye, sir, upon my honor.

MIRABELL: Mr. Fainall, it is now time that you should know that your lady, while she was at her own disposal, and before you had by your insinuations wheedled her out of a pretended settlement of the

560 greatest part of her fortune—

FAINALL: Sir! pretended!

MIRABELL: Yes, sir. I say that this lady, while a widow, having it seems received some cautions respecting your inconstancy and tyranny of temper, which

565 from her own partial opinion and fondness of you she could never have suspected—she did, I say, by the wholesome advice of friends and of sages learned in the laws of this land, deliver this same as her act and deed to me in trust, and to the uses within men-

570 tioned. You may read if you please (*holding out the parchment*), though perhaps what is written on the back may serve your occasions.

FAINALL: Very likely, sir. What's here? Damnation! (*Reads.*) "A deed of conveyance of the whole estate

575 real of Arabella Languish, widow, in trust to Edward Mirabell." Confusion?

MIRABELL: Even so, sir; 'tis the way of the world, sir, of the widows of the world. I suppose this deed may bear an elder° date than what you have obtained

580 from your lady?

FAINALL: Perfidious fiend! Then thus I'll be revenged.

(*Offers to run at Mrs. Fainall.*)

SIR WILFULL: Hold, sir! Now you may make your Bear Garden flourish somewhere else, sir.

FAINALL: Mirabell, you shall hear of this, sir; be sure you

585 shall. (*To Sir Wilfull.*) Let me pass, oaf!

(*Exit.*)

MRS. FAINALL (*to Mrs. Marwood*): Madam, you seem to stifle your resentment; you had better give it vent.

MRS. MARWOOD: Yes, it shall have vent, and to your confusion; or I'll perish in the attempt.   (*Exit.*)

590 LADY WISHFORT: O daughter, daughter, 'tis plain thou hast inherited thy mother's prudence.

MRS. FAINALL: Thank Mr. Mirabell, a cautious friend, to whose advice all is owing.

LADY WISHFORT: Well, Mr. Mirabell, you have kept your

595 promise, and I must perform mine. First, I pardon, for your sake, Sir Rowland there, and Foible. The next thing is to break the matter to my nephew, and how to do that—

MIRABELL: For that, madam, give yourself no trouble; let

600 me have your consent. Sir Wilfull is my friend; he has had compassion upon lovers, and generously engaged a volunteer° in this action, for our service, and now designs to prosecute his travels.

SIR WILFULL: 'Sheart, aunt, I have no mind to marry. My cousin's a fine lady, and the gentleman loves her, 605
and she loves him, and they deserve one another; my resolution is to see foreign parts. I have set on't, and when I'm set on't, I must do't. And if these two gentlemen would travel too, I think they may be spared.

PETULANT: For my part, I say little; I think things are best 610
off or on.°

WITWOUD: Egad, I understand nothing of the matter; I'm in a maze yet, like a dog in a dancing school.

LADY WISHFORT: Well, sir, take her, and with her all the joy I can give you.   615

MRS. MILLAMANT: Why does not the man take me? Would you have me give myself to you over again?

MIRABELL: Aye, and over and over again; (*kisses her hand*) for I would have you as often as possibly I can. Well, Heaven grant I love you not too well; that's all 620
my fear.

SIR WILFULL: 'Sheart, you'll have time enough to toy° after you're married; or if you will toy now, let us have a dance in the meantime, that we who are not lovers may have some other employment besides 625
looking on.

MIRABELL: With all my heart, dear Sir Wilfull. What shall we do for music?

FOIBLE: Oh, sir, some that were provided for Sir Rowland's entertainment are yet within call.   630

(*A dance.*)

LADY WISHFORT: As I am a person, I can hold out no longer. I have wasted my spirits so today already that I am ready to sink under the fatigue; and I cannot but have some fears upon me yet that my son Fainall will pursue same desperate course.   635

MIRABELL: Madam, disquiet not yourself on that account; to my knowledge his circumstances are such, he must of force° comply. For my part, I will contribute all that in me lies to a reunion; in the meantime, madam (*to Mrs. Fainall*), let me before 640
these witnesses restore to you this deed of trust; it may be a means, well-managed, to make you live easily, together.

From hence let those be warn'd, who mean to
   wed,
Lest mutual falsehood stain the bridal bed;   645
For each deceiver to his cost may find
That marriage frauds too oft are paid in kind.

(*Exeunt omnes.*)°

EPILOGUE

(*Spoken by Mrs. Millamant.*)

After our Epilogue this crowd dismisses,
I'm thinking how this play'll be pull'd to pieces.
But pray consider, ere you doom its fall,

---

579. **elder:** Earlier.   602. **a volunteer:** As a volunteer.

611. **off or on:** One way or the other.   622. **toy:** Play.   638. **of force:** Of necessity.   647. [S.D.] *omnes:* Latin for "all."

How hard a thing 'twould be to please you all.
5 There are some critics so with spleen diseas'd,
They scarcely come inclining to be pleas'd;
And sure he must have more than mortal skill,
Who pleases any one against his will.
Then, all bad poets we are sure are foes,
And how their number's swell'd the town well
10   knows;
In shoals I've mark'd 'em judging in the pit;
Though they're on no pretense for judgment fit,
But that they have been damn'd for want of wit.
Since when they, by their own offenses taught,
15 Set up for spies on plays, and finding fault.
Others there are whose malice we'd prevent;
Such who watch plays with scurrilous intent
To mark out who by characters are meant.
And though no perfect likeness they can trace,
20 Yet each pretends to know the copy'd face.
These with false glosses° feed their own ill nature,

21. **glosses:** Marginal notes.

And turn to libel what was meant a satire.°
May such malicious fops this fortune find,
To think themselves alone the fools design'd;
If any are so arrogantly vain,   25
To think they singly can support a scene,
And furnish fool enough to entertain.
For well the learn'd and the judicious know
That satire scorns to stoop so meanly low
As any one abstracted° fop to show.   30
For, as when painters form a matchless face
They from each fair one catch some diff'rent grace;
And shining features in one portrait blend,
To which no single beauty must pretend;
So poets oft do in one piece expose   35
Whole *belles assemblées*° of coquettes and beaux.

21–22. **nature . . . satire:** According to seventeenth-century pronunciation, *nature* and *satire* were good rhymes. **30. abstracted:** Particular. **36. *belles assemblées*:** Fine gatherings.

COMMENTARY

ARNOLD ARONSON (b. 1948)

Comedy, Manners, and Brickbats   1991

Arnold Aronson centers his comments on the 1991 production of *The Way of the World* at the Public Theater in New York. He reviews Jeremy Collier's attack on the theaters of the time and then comments on the current production. His discussion is less a review than an effort to position the comedy in relation to historical events and early-eighteenth-century attitudes toward sex and marriage.

Currently at the Public Theater and opening Tuesday is an elitist play that has been attacked roundly by conservative moralists, led by a demagogic clergyman. But it will not be shut down by incensed watchdog groups, since the play is nearly 300 years old: William Congreve's classic *The Way of the World*, in a revival directed by David Greenspan.

First presented in 1700, the work is generally considered the artistic culmination of the Restoration comedy of manners. The exquisite language, rapier-sharp repartee, and labyrinthine plot make the play somewhat daunting for modern audiences and actors. Yet the antipathy faced by Congreve and his colleagues in the late seventeenth century was not unlike that [encountered by] many theater artists today.

Jeremy Collier, a parson who campaigned against the stage with a vengeance, attacked Restoration playwrights in his famous 1698 diatribe, *A Short View of the Immorality and Profaneness of the English Stage*. He criticized them for "smuttiness of expression" and "swearing" and condemned a theater that "degrades human nature, sinks reason into appetite, and breaks down the distinction between man and beast." He was joined by the monarchs William and Mary and by members of Parliament who sought to restrict public behavior in the theater.

How could the situation have reached this state less than 100 years after Shakespeare? Whereas Elizabethan London had supported some half-dozen theaters catering to thousands of spectators, Restoration London never filled more than two theaters attended by an audience numbering in the hundreds, most of whom were associated with the court.

The transition began in 1642 when the Puritan rebellion led by Oliver Cromwell overthrew the monarchy. All the theaters were closed, and most of the courtiers escaped to Paris, where they remained until 1660, when Charles II took the throne. The returning nobility brought back a taste for French theater, especially its novel practice—for the English—of employing actresses. Under Charles II and James II the theater nearly became the private domain of the court. Thus the fops, pompous gallants, wits, and hypocrites who populate the plays (and bear the names of their characteristics—such as, in this play, Witwoud and Lady Wishfort, pronounced "Wish-for-it") are typically seen as both vicious caricatures and realistic portraits of the audience.

The plots usually revolve around sexual intrigue, and infidelity seems taken for granted — it is *The Way of the World*. Easily lost in this play is the fact that the seemingly admirable Mirabell (André Braugher) had an affair with Lady Wishfort's (Ruth Maleczech) daughter (Mary Shultz), and when he thought she might be pregnant, foisted her on his friend Fainall (René Rivera), who marries her, though he is having an affair with Mrs. Marwood (Caris Corfman).

The accusations of immorality focused, not surprisingly, on sexual content and disregarded the fact that such plays were satirical. The playwrights tried to defend themselves, through pamphlets and jibes in their texts. But the attackers achieved their end. The theaters began to censor themselves, the small audiences declined further, and Congreve ceased writing. A decade later, plays were emphasizing moral virtues, and comedies, like those by George Farquhar, stressed sentiment and natural goodness, while the settings changed to the countryside, where city slickers received their comeuppance.

What critics at the time failed to realize was that Restoration comedies are not about sex. A kiss is rare and seems almost vulgar when it occurs. The plays are about human passions sublimated into a brilliant display of language. It is excess and lack of control that [are] evil in Congreve's world. Rationality, order, and command over passions and language are rewarded. This may not be the same as morality, but it *is* civility.

John Gay

Although he was born in the countryside, John Gay (1685–1732) began his career in London as an apprentice to a silk merchant. With the standard grammar school education of the time, he was able to begin writing pastoral poetry, and he abandoned his apprenticeship to search for a patron who would support him by appointing him secretary or assistant. Aaron Hill, a childhood friend and a wealthy young man with a taste for the theater, introduced him to literary circles and may have helped him publish his first poems. The Duchess of Monmouth supported him for a short time as well. In *Rural Sports* (1713), a successful comic view of hunting and fishing in the country, he detailed the difficulties in finding and satisfying patrons—in particular, the fact that some of those who made promises never kept them.

Both Jonathan Swift (1667–1745) and Alexander Pope (1688–1744) took notice of Gay's early work and included him in their Scriblerus Club, a group that included Samuel Johnson (1709–1784), William Congreve (1670–1729), and John Arbuthnot (1667–1735). Jonathan Swift had enough influence to help Gay find an appointment at the court of the first Georgian king. Gay's dedication of *Rural Sports* to Pope began a long friendship with Pope, the reigning poet and satirist of his age, who gave Gay the gift of support and approval throughout his life. Pope encouraged Gay to write a volume of pastoral poems called *The Shepherd's Week* (1714), which ridiculed the work of a contemporary poet whom Pope abhorred. A number of Gay's early works failed to achieve the success he craved. *Trivia, or the Art of Walking the Streets of London* (1716) is said to be one of the best poems about daily life in London, but his play *Three Hours of Marriage* (1717) failed.

Gay made a good deal of money when he published *Poems on Several Occasions* (1720), because he published his book by subscription—signing up buyers in advance. With more than a thousand pounds at his disposal, he decided to invest in the South Sea Company, which sold stock in a scheme designed to make its shareholders rich with returns from a monopoly on trading with South American colonies, supplying goods, materials, expertise, and slaves. The scheme involved the English government, including members of the prime minister's cabinet. The stock went up wildly but then fell catastrophically, and Gay lost most of his money. The de facto prime minister, Robert Walpole (1676–1745), protected his own inner circle from criminal charges while many people lost their life savings in the collapse of the company's stock.

Despite the fact that he was provided a living in the palace at Whitehall, Gay lashed out at the court, particularly Robert Walpole and his circle, in his most famous work, *The Beggar's Opera* (1728), a ballad opera with sixty-nine tunes drawn from the popular songs of the day. Italian opera was all the rage at the time, but *The Beggar's Opera* was so successful that even George Frideric Handel abandoned opera and turned to oratorios. Gay's audience was quick to realize that *The Beggar's Opera* was a satire that likened Walpole to a dishonest ringleader of a gang of thieves. Gay soon paid a price for his satire: his sequel, *Polly*, never reached the stage because Walpole led the move to prohibit its performance.

Ironically, banning *Polly* made it all the more desirable to Gay's readers, and in 1729 it was published by subscription, earning Gay more than a thousand pounds. The Duchess of Queensbury, an enthusiastic supporter of Gay, was dismissed from court for soliciting subscriptions from courtiers, many of whom were also enthusiastic about the condemned play. The Duchess remained a friend for life, and her husband, the Duke of Queensbury, Gay's patron, provided him with quarters in which to live.

Gay's book of *Fables* (1727), a signal success, has been issued in 350 editions and translated into most European languages. Handel's opera *Acis and Galatea,* for which Gay had written the libretto in 1719, was performed in London in 1732, the year of Gay's death at age 47. Many of Gay's works were performed and published after his death, but his dramatic reputation rests on *The Beggar's Opera.* He is buried in the Poets' Corner of Westminster Abbey.

The Beggar's Opera

The Beggar's Opera is considered the most successful dramatic production of eighteenth-century London, having held the stage for an unheard of sixty-two performances and having been revived frequently. John Gay capitalized on the contemporary passion for sentimental Italian operas by introducing short songs set to ballad airs that almost everyone in the audience already knew; thus, although most of the lines are spoken, the play is known as a ballad opera. As the player says at the end of the play, "an opera must end happily," and by an act of fiat on the part of the Beggar, it does. But for its original audience, the core of the play was satirical, not sentimental. Macheath is based on a legendary criminal of the times, Jonathan Wild (1683–1725), who ran a gang of thieves preying on the recently wealthy class of Londoners by pretending to have "found" their lost wares and returning them for a "garnish," a bit of bribery.

For discussion questions and assignments on *The Beggar's Opera,* visit bedfordstmartins.com/jacobus.

As the play opens, the Beggar, who narrates the play, sets the stage. The Peachums discover that their daughter Polly has secretly married the most celebrated London thief, Macheath. The Peachums are a criminal couple themselves—the husband is both a thief-catcher and a receiver of stolen goods. At first, they are angry at Polly because her decision will cost them money, but eventually Peachum sets out to arrest Macheath and hang him so that Polly will get Macheath's criminal fortune.

Macheath goes to the local tavern filled with criminals and whores and is shocked to find that Jenny Diver and Suky Tawdry, hired by Peachum, have turned him over to the authorities. He is sent to a prison run by Lockit, whose daughter Lucy is angry at Macheath for not keeping his promise to marry her. Eventually Lucy takes her father's keys and lets Macheath escape. Polly, broken-hearted, finds Lucy and tries to come to some kind of agreement about their relationship with Macheath, but Lucy tries to poison Polly. Macheath is captured again, and both Lucy and Polly demand that their fathers save him. Meanwhile Macheath is surrounded by women who claim he has made them pregnant, and he realizes that he will indeed be hanged. But the Beggar intervenes.

When the play was performed in 1728, it was widely seen as a satire on Robert Walpole, the first prime minister of England. Technically, there was no such office during the reign of George I, but by 1725 Walpole's power was such that George II installed him in 10 Downing Street, today still the home of the prime minister. Walpole's power was considerable; he rewarded his friends and made life difficult for his enemies. When the colossal financial scheme called the South Sea Bubble went bad, he got his money out in time and did not punish the perpetrators of the scheme. He also tolerated the well-known misdeeds of the master criminal Jonathan Wild, the subject of numerous local ballads. Moreover, Walpole was highly suspicious of writers who were in a position to criticize the government. The first quarter of the eighteenth century was politically unstable because the Hanoverian succession of Georgian kings to the throne was not absolutely clear, and support for the ousted Stuarts kept the government on edge.

Walpole had many enemies, and a number of them were the most powerful writers of the era: Henry Fielding (1707–1754), whose novel *Jonathan Wild* was a satire on Walpole, and Alexander Pope, whose *Rape of the Lock* satirized Walpole's class. Jonathan Swift satirized the government in *Gulliver's Travels*. Both Pope and Swift encouraged Gay in his writing of *The Beggar's Opera*.

Because Walpole's government operated at his will and practiced the garnishment (bribery) typical of Lockit in Newgate Prison, Gay pointedly represents the operations of the thieves, whores, and prison officials as a parody of the behavior of Walpole's "gang." The Beggar says at the end of the play, "you may observe such a similitude of manners in high and low life, that it is difficult to determine whether…the fine gentlemen imitate the gentlemen of the road, or the gentlemen of the road the fine gentlemen."

The popularity of the play, along with other satirical treatments of his government, led Walpole to push through a Theatrical Licensing Act, which put an end to dramatic political satires in England. But Gay's play was revived often after Walpole's death, and today it has probably been best served by Bertolt Brecht and Kurt Weill's adaptation as *The Threepenny Opera* (1928), originally written in German and also a satirical piece.

For a modern audience, *The Beggar's Opera* has lost its satirical references, but it still has a powerful appeal in its portrayals of Polly and Lucy, each of whom imagines herself the wife of Macheath, himself a dashing criminal character whose amorality and professions of faithfulness and honor amuse audiences in all ages. Macheath is a ladies man, as is revealed in act 2, scene 4, as well as in act 3, scene 15, but most of his ladies are unsavory and eager to turn him in and collect the reward.

The formula of sentimental comedy, the lover's pursuit and ultimate marriage, is fulfilled in the play, but in a hitherto unheard of manner. Both Polly and Lucy are outright in their pursuit of Macheath, and both recognize that he is unfaithful despite his protestations of absolute faithfulness: "Suspect my honour, my courage, suspect anything but my love. May my pistols miss fire, and my mare slip her shoulder while I am pursued, if I ever forsake thee!" (act 1, scene 13). He, meanwhile, tells us he cannot live without women: "I must have women. There is nothing unbends the mind like them" (act 2, scene 4).

And the comic convention of parents as characters blocking their daughters' desires is retained, but Peachum and his wife do not want Polly to marry at all, much less marry for love, just as Lockit is appalled at Lucy's love for Macheath. These parents want their daughters to marry for money and then lose their husbands to the gallows so that they become wealthy widows. These ironies are modern in their sensibility and help keep *The Beggar's Opera* entertaining for current audiences.

The Beggar's Opera in Performance

John Rich put on *The Beggar's Opera* in 1728, and the saying went around London that the play "made Rich gay and Gay rich." The success was immense and immediate. Lavinia Fenton (1708–1760) was made famous as Polly and played the role often, leaving the stage only to become a duchess. While the play had been staged frequently, one of its greatest successes was in 1920 when it played at the Lyric Theatre in Hammersmith, England, for an astounding 1463 performances, the greatest run for a musical play up to that time. Productions, particularly adaptations, in London, in Australia, and on the continent have continued to the present day. In 1928, on its two hundredth anniversary, Bertolt Brecht and Kurt Weill adapted the play as *The Threepenny Opera,* probably its most successful adaptation. Benjamin Britten, Wole Soyinka, and Václav Havel are among the distinguished and successful artists who have also adapted the play. The South African Broomhill Opera Company staged a vibrant version with many African musical and dramatic touches in Australia, England, and the United States from 2003 through 2005. In 2009, the Vanishing Point Theatre in Glasgow, Scotland, with the Royal Lyceum Theatre of Edinburgh, Scotland, and the Belgrade Theatre in Coventry, England, produced a highly charged reimagining of *The Beggar's Opera* using rock music, projections, and multimedia. Lucy Bailey directed the original version of the play in 2011 at The Open Air Theatre in Regent's Park, London.

JOHN GAY (1685–1732)

The Beggar's Opera 1728

Dramatis Personæ

Men:

PEACHUM
LOCKIT
MACHEATH
FILCH
JEMMY TWITCHER
CROOK-FINGERED JACK
WAT DREARY
ROBIN OF BAGSHOT } *Macheath's Gang*
NIMMING NED
HARRY PADINGTON
MATT OF THE MINT
BEN BUDGE
BEGGAR
PLAYER
CONSTABLES, DRAWER, TURNKEY, *etc.*

Women:

MRS. PEACHUM
POLLY PEACHUM
LUCY LOCKIT
DIANA TRAPES
MRS. COAXER
DOLLY TRULL
MRS. VIXEN
BETTY DOXY } *Women of the Town*
JENNY DIVER
MRS. SLAMMEKIN
SUKY TAWDRY
MOLLY BRAZEN

INTRODUCTION   *Beggar, Player*

BEGGAR: If poverty be a title to poetry, I am sure no-body can dispute mine. I own myself of the company of beggars; and I make one at their weekly festivals at St Giles's.° I have a small yearly salary for my catches,° and am welcome to a dinner there whenever I please, which is more than most poets can say.

PLAYER: As we live by the Muses, 'tis but gratitude in us to encourage poetical merit wherever we find it. The Muses, contrary to all other ladies, pay no distinction to dress, and never partially mistake the pertness of

St. Giles: One of the worst slums in London, near what is now the West End.   catches: Rounds, songs like "Row, Row Your Boat."

embroidery for wit, nor the modesty of want for dulness. Be the author who he will, we push his play as far as it will go. So (though you are in want) I wish you success heartily.

BEGGAR: This piece I own was originally writ for the celebrating the marriage of James Chanter and Moll Lay, two most excellent ballad-singers. I have introduced the similes that are in all your celebrated operas: the swallow, the moth, the bee, the ship, the flower, etc. Besides, I have a prison scene, which the ladies always reckon charmingly pathetic. As to the parts, I have observed such a nice impartiality to our two ladies, that it is impossible for either of them to take offence. I hope I may be forgiven, that I have not made my opera throughout unnatural, like those in vogue; for I have no recitative; excepting this, as I have consented to have neither prologue nor epilogue, it must be allowed an opera in all its forms. The piece indeed hath been heretofore frequently represented by ourselves in our great room at St. Giles's, so that I cannot too often acknowledge your charity in bringing it now on the stage.

PLAYER: But I see 'tis time for us to withdraw; the actors are preparing to begin.—Play away the overture.

(Exeunt)

ACT I • Scene I

Scene: *Peachum's house*

Peachum sitting at a table with a large book of accounts before him

Air I: *An old woman clothed in grey*

Through all the employments of life,
    Each neighbour abuses his brother;
Whore and rogue they call husband and wife:
    All professions be-rogue one another.
The priest calls the lawyer a cheat,
    The lawyer be-knaves the divine;
And the statesman, because he's so great,
    Thinks his trade as honest as mine.

PEACHUM: A lawyer is an honest employment; so is mine. Like me, too, he acts in a double capacity, both against rogues and for 'em; for 'tis but fitting that we should protect and encourage cheats, since we live by 'em.

The Beggar's Opera in an engraving by William Hogarth.

Scene II   *Peachum, Filch*

FILCH: Sir, Black Moll hath sent word her trial comes on in the afternoon, and she hopes you will order matters so as to bring her off.

PEACHUM: Why, she may plead her belly° at worst; to my knowledge she hath taken care of that security. But as the wench is very active and industrious, you may satisfy her that I'll soften the evidence.

FILCH: Tom Gagg, Sir, is found guilty.

PEACHUM: A lazy dog! When I took him the time before, I told him what he would come to if he did not mend his hand. This is death without reprieve. I may venture to book him.

(writes)

"For Tom Gagg, forty pounds." Let Betty Sly know that I'll save her from transportation,° for I can get more by her staying in England.

FILCH: Betty hath brought more goods into our lock to-year, than any five the gang; and in truth, 'tis a pity to lose so good a customer.

PEACHUM: If none of the gang take her off, she may, in the common course of business, live a twelve-month longer. I love to let women scape. A good sportsman always lets the hen partridges fly, because the breed of the game depends upon them. Besides, here the law allows us no reward; there is nothing to be got by the death of women—except our wives.

FILCH: Without dispute, she is a fine woman! 'Twas to her I was obliged for my education, and (to say a bold word) she hath trained up more young fellows to the business than the gaming table.

plead her belly: Pregnant women were spared the harshest punishment.

transportation: Being sent as a criminal to one of the colonies or the West Indies.

PEACHUM: Truly, Filch, thy observation is right. We and the surgeons are more beholden to women than all the professions besides.

Air II: *The bonny grey-eyed morn*

FILCH: 'Tis woman that seduces all mankind,
　　　　By her we first were taught the wheedling arts:
　　Her very eyes can cheat; when most she's kind,
　　　　She tricks us of our money with our hearts.
　　For her, like wolves by night we roam for prey,
　　　　And practise ev'ry fraud to bribe her charms;
　　For suits of love, like law, are won by pay,
　　　　And beauty must be fee'd into our arms.

PEACHUM: But make haste to Newgate,° boy, and let my friends know what I intend; for I love to make them easy one way or other.

FILCH: When a gentleman is long kept in suspense, penitence may break his spirit ever after. Besides, certainty gives a man a good air upon his trial, and makes him risk another without fear or scruple. But I'll away, for 'tis a pleasure to be the messenger of comfort to friends in affliction.

Scene III   *Peachum*

PEACHUM: But 'tis now high time to look about me for a decent execution against next sessions. I hate a lazy rogue, by whom one can get nothing till he is hanged. (*reading*) "A register of the gang. Crook-fingered Jack." A year and a half in the service. Let me see how much the stock owes to his industry; one, two, three, four, five gold watches, and seven silver ones. A mighty clean-handed fellow! Sixteen snuff-boxes, five of them of true gold. Six dozen of handkerchiefs, four silver-hilted swords, half a dozen of shirts, three tie-periwigs, and a piece of broadcloth. Considering these are only the fruits of his leisure hours, I don't know a prettier fellow, for no man alive hath a more engaging presence of mind upon the road. "Wat Dreary, alias Brown Will," an irregular dog, who hath an underhand way of disposing of his goods. I'll try him only for a session or two longer upon his good behaviour. "Harry Padington," a poor petty-larceny rascal, without the least genius; that fellow, though he were to live these six months, will never come to the gallows with any credit. "Slippery Sam"; he goes off the next sessions, for the villain hath the impudence to have views of following his trade as a tailor, which he calls an honest employment. "Matt of the Mint," listed not above a month ago, a promising sturdy fellow, and diligent in his way; somewhat too bold and hasty, and may raise good contributions on the public, if he does not cut himself short by murder. "Tom Tipple," a guzzling soaking sot, who is always too drunk to stand himself, or to make others

Newgate: Notorious prison in central London.

stand. A cart is absolutely necessary for him. "Robin of Bagshot, alias Gorgon, alias Bluff Bob, alias Carbuncle, alias Bob Booty—"

Scene IV   *Peachum, Mrs. Peachum*

MRS. PEACHUM: What of Bob Booty, husband? I hope nothing bad hath betided him. You know, my dear, he's a favourite customer of mine. 'Twas he made me a present of this ring.

PEACHUM: I have set his name down in the black-list, that's all, my dear; he spends his life among women, and as soon as his money is gone, one or other of the ladies will hang him for the reward, and there's forty pound lost to us forever.

MRS. PEACHUM: You know, my dear, I never meddle in matters of death; I always leave those affairs to you. Women indeed are bitter bad judges in these cases, for they are so partial to the brave, that they think every man handsome who is going to the camp or the gallows.

Air III: *Cold and raw*

　　If any wench Venus's girdle° wear,
　　　　Though she be never so ugly;
　　Lilies and roses will quickly appear,
　　　　And her face look wond'rous smugly.
　　Beneath the left ear so fit but a cord,
　　　　(A rope so charming a zone is!)
　　The youth in his cart hath the air of a lord,
　　　　And we cry, "There dies an Adonis!"

But really, husband, you should not be too hard-hearted, for you never had a finer, braver set of men than at present. We have not had a murder among them all, these seven months. And truly, my dear, that is a great blessing.

PEACHUM: What a dickens is the woman always a-wimpering about murder for? No gentleman is ever looked upon the worse for killing a man in his own defence; and if business cannot be carried on without it, what would you have a gentleman do?

MRS. PEACHUM: If I am in the wrong, my dear, you must excuse me, for nobody can help the frailty of an over-scrupulous conscience.

PEACHUM: Murder is as fashionable a crime as a man can be guilty of. How many fine gentlemen have we in Newgate every year, purely upon that article! If they have wherewithal to persuade the jury to bring it in manslaughter, what are they the worse for it? So, my dear, have done upon this subject. Was Captain Macheath here this morning, for the banknotes he left with you last week?

MRS. PEACHUM: Yes, my dear; and though the bank had stopped payment, he was so cheerful and so agreeable!

Venus' girdle: A magic belt that, when worn, made Venus, goddess of love, irresistible.

Sure there is not a finer gentleman upon the road than the captain! If he comes from Bagshot at any reasonable hour he hath promised to make one this evening with Polly and me, and Bob Booty, at a party of quadrille.° Pray, my dear, is the captain rich?

PEACHUM: The captain keeps too good company ever to grow rich. Marybone and the chocolate-houses are his undoing. The man that proposes to get money by play should have the education of a fine gentleman, and be trained up to it from his youth.

MRS. PEACHUM: Really, I am sorry upon Polly's account the captain hath not more discretion. What business hath he to keep company with lords and gentlemen? He should leave them to prey upon one another.

PEACHUM: "Upon Polly's account!" What a plague does the woman mean?—"Upon Polly's account!"

MRS. PEACHUM: Captain Macheath is very fond of the girl.

PEACHUM: And what then?

MRS. PEACHUM: If I have any skill in the ways of women, I am sure Polly thinks him a very pretty man.

PEACHUM: And what then? You would not be so mad to have the wench marry him! Gamesters and highwaymen are generally very good to their whores, but they are very devils to their wives.

MRS. PEACHUM: But if Polly should be in love, how should we help her, or how can she help herself? Poor girl, I am in the utmost concern about her.

Air IV: *Why is your faithful slave disdain'd?*

> If love the virgin's heart invade,
> How, like a moth, the simple maid
>   Still plays about the flame!
> If soon she be not made a wife,
> Her honour's sing'd, and then for life
>   She's—what I dare not name.

PEACHUM: Look ye, wife. A handsome wench in our way of business is as profitable as at the bar of a Temple coffeehouse, who looks upon it as her livelihood to grant every liberty but one. You see I would indulge the girl as far as prudently we can. In anything but marriage! After that, my dear, how shall we be safe? Are we not then in her husband's power? For a husband hath the absolute power over all a wife's secrets but her own. If the girl had the discretion of a court lady, who can have a dozen young fellows at her ear without complying with one, I should not matter it; but Polly is tinder, and a spark will at once set her on a flame. Married! If the wench does not know her own profit, sure she knows her own pleasure better than to make herself a property! My daughter to me should be, like a court lady to a minister of state, a key to the whole gang. Married! If the affair is not already done, I'll terrify her from it, by the example of our neighbours.

---

quadrille: A card game involving gambling, usually played in Marybone, the gambling district.

MRS. PEACHUM: Mayhap, my dear, you may injure the girl. She loves to imitate the fine ladies, and she may only allow the captain liberties in the view of interest.

PEACHUM: But 'tis your duty, my dear, to warn the girl against her ruin, and to instruct her how to make the most of her beauty. I'll go to her this moment, and sift her. In the meantime, wife, rip out the coronets and marks of these dozen of cambric handkerchiefs, for I can dispose of them this afternoon to a chap in the City.

Scene V   *Mrs. Peachum*

MRS. PEACHUM: Never was a man more out of the way in an argument than my husband! Why must our Polly, forsooth, differ from her sex, and love only her husband? And why must Polly's marriage, contrary to all observation, make her the less followed by other men? All men are thieves in love, and like a woman the better for being another's property.

Air V: *Of all the simple things we do*

> A maid is like the golden ore,
>   Which hath guineas intrinsical in't
> Whose worth is never known, before
>   It is tried and impress'd in the mint.
> A wife's like a guinea in gold,
>   Stamp'd with the name of her spouse;
> Now here, now there; is bought, or is sold;
>   And is current in every house.

Scene VI   *Mrs. Peachum, Filch*

MRS. PEACHUM: Come hither, Filch—(*aside*) I am as fond of this child as though my mind misgave me he were my own. He hath as fine a hand at picking a pocket as a woman, and is as nimble-fingered as a juggler.—If an unlucky session does not cut the rope of thy life, I pronounce, boy, thou wilt be a great man in history. Where was your post last night, my boy?

FILCH: I plied at the opera, Madam; and considering 'twas neither dark nor rainy, so that there was no great hurry in getting chairs and coaches, made a tolerable hand on't. These seven handkerchiefs, Madam.

MRS. PEACHUM: Coloured ones, I see. They are of sure sale from our warehouse at Redriff among the seamen.

FILCH: And this snuff-box.

MRS. PEACHUM: Set in gold! A pretty encouragement this to a young beginner.

FILCH: I had a fair tug at a charming gold watch. Pox take the tailors for making the fobs so deep and narrow! It stuck by the way, and I was forced to make my escape under a coach. Really, Madam, I fear I shall be cut off in the flower of my youth, so that every now and then (since I was pumped) I have thoughts of taking up and going to sea.

MRS. PEACHUM: You should go to Hockley in the Hole° and to Marybone, child, to learn valour. These are the schools that have bred so many brave men. I thought, boy, by this time thou hadst lost fear as well as shame. Poor lad! how little does he know as yet of the Old Bailey!° For the first fact I'll insure thee from being hanged; and going to sea, Filch, will come time enough upon a sentence of transportation. But now, since you have nothing better to do, even go to your book, and learn your catechism; for really a man makes but an ill figure in the ordinary's paper, who cannot give a satisfactory answer to his questions. But, hark you, my lad. Don't tell me a lie; for you know I hate a liar. Do you know of anything that hath passed between Captain Macheath and our Polly?

FILCH: I beg you, Madam, don't ask me; for I must either tell a lie to you or to Miss Polly; for I promised her I would not tell.

MRS. PEACHUM: But when the honour of our family is concerned—

FILCH: I shall lead a sad life with Miss Polly, if ever she come to know that I told you. Besides, I would not willingly forfeit my own honour by betraying anybody.

MRS. PEACHUM: Yonder comes my husband and Polly. Come, Filch, you shall go with me into my own room, and tell me the whole story. I'll give thee a most delicious glass of a cordial that I keep for my own drinking.

Scene VII   *Peachum, Polly*

POLLY: I know as well as any of the fine ladies how to make the most of myself and of my man too. A woman knows how to be mercenary, though she hath never been in a court or at an assembly. We have it in our natures, Papa. If I allow Captain Macheath some trifling liberties, I have this watch and other visible marks of his favour to show for it. A girl who cannot grant some things, and refuse what is most material, will make but a poor hand of her beauty, and soon be thrown upon the common.

Air VI: *What shall I do to show how much I love her?*

Virgins are like the fair flower in its lustre,
   Which in the garden enamels the ground;
Near it the bees in play flutter and cluster,
   And gaudy butterflies frolic around.
But, when once pluck'd, 'tis no longer alluring,
   To Covent Garden 'tis sent (as yet sweet),
There fades, and shrinks, and grows past all
      enduring,
   Rots, stinks, and dies, and is trod under feet.

PEACHUM: You know, Polly, I am not against your toying and trifling with a customer in the way of business, or to get out a secret, or so. But if I find out that you

Hockley in the Hole: Neighborhood in central London where bear-baiting and other forms of animal cruelty were popular entertainment.   **Old Bailey:** The Court in which trials are held.

have played the fool and are married, you jade you, I'll cut your throat, hussy. Now you know my mind.

Scene VIII   *Peachum, Polly, Mrs. Peachum*

Air VII: *Oh London is a fine town*

MRS. PEACHUM: (*in a very great passion*)
   Our Polly is a sad slut! nor heeds what we have taught
      her.
   I wonder any man alive will ever rear a daughter!
   For she must have both hoods and gowns, and hoops
      to swell her pride,
   With scarfs and stays, and gloves and lace; and she
      will have men beside;
   And when she's dress'd with care and cost, all-
      tempting, fine and gay,
   As men should serve a cowcumber,° she flings herself
      away.
      Our Polly is a sad slut, etc.

You baggage! you hussy! you inconsiderate jade! had you been hanged, it would not have vexed me, for that might have been your misfortune; but to do such a mad thing by choice! The wench is married, husband.

PEACHUM: Married! The captain is a bold man, and will risk anything for money; to be sure he believes her a fortune. Do you think your mother and I should have lived comfortably so long together, if ever we had been married? Baggage!

MRS. PEACHUM: I knew she was always a proud slut; and now the wench hath played the fool and married, because forsooth she would do like the gentry. Can you support the expense of a husband, hussy, in gaming, drinking and whoring? have you money enough to carry on the daily quarrels of man and wife about who shall squander most? There are not many husbands and wives who can bear the charges of plaguing one another in a handsome way. If you must be married, could you introduce nobody into our family but a highwayman? Why, thou foolish jade, thou wilt be as ill used, and as much neglected, as if thou hadst married a lord!

PEACHUM: Let not your anger, my dear, break through the rules of decency, for the captain looks upon himself in the military capacity, as a gentleman by his profession. Besides what he hath already, I know he is in a fair way of getting, or of dying; and both these ways, let me tell you, are most excellent chances for a wife.—Tell me, hussy, are you ruined or no?

MRS. PEACHUM: With Polly's fortune, she might very well have gone off to a person of distinction. Yes, that you might, you pouting slut!

PEACHUM: What, is the wench dumb? Speak, or I'll make you plead by squeezing out an answer from you. Are you really bound wife to him, or are you only upon liking?   (*pinches her*)

cowcumber: Cucumber, believed at the time to be fit only for cows to eat.

POLLY: (*screaming*) Oh!

MRS. PEACHUM: How the mother is to be pitied who hath handsome daughters! Locks, bolts, bars, and lectures of morality are nothing to them: they break through them all. They have as much pleasure in cheating a father and mother as in cheating at cards.

PEACHUM: Why, Polly, I shall soon know if you are married, by Macheath's keeping from our house.

Air VIII: *Grim king of the ghosts*

POLLY: Can love be controll'd by advice?
    Will Cupid our mothers obey?
Though my heart were as frozen as ice,
    At his flame 'twould have melted away.
When he kiss'd me so closely he press'd,
    'Twas so sweet that I must have comply'd:
So I thought it both safest and best
    To marry, for fear you should chide.

MRS. PEACHUM: Then all the hopes of our family are gone for ever and ever!

PEACHUM: And Macheath may hang his father and mother-in-law, in hope to get into their daughter's fortune.

POLLY: I did not marry him (as 'tis the fashion) coolly and deliberately for honour or money. But, I love him.

MRS. PEACHUM: Love him! worse and worse! I thought the girl had been better bred. O husband, husband! her folly makes me mad! my head swims! I'm distracted! I can't support myself—oh!   (*faints*)

PEACHUM: See, wench, to what a condition you have reduced your poor mother! a glass of cordial, this instant. How the poor woman takes it to heart! (*Polly goes out and returns with it.*) Ah, hussy, now this is the only comfort your mother has left!

POLLY: Give her another glass, Sir; my mama drinks double the quantity whenever she is out of order.—This, you see, fetches her.

MRS. PEACHUM: The girl shows such a readiness, and so much concern, that I could almost find in my heart to forgive her.

Air IX: *O Jenny, O Jenny, where hast thou been?*

    O Polly, you might have toy'd and kiss'd.
    By keeping men off, you keep them on.
POLLY: But he so teas'd me,
      And he so pleas'd me,
    What I did, you must have done.

MRS. PEACHUM: Not with a highwayman.—You sorry slut!

PEACHUM: A word with you, wife. 'Tis no new thing for a wench to take man without consent of parents. You know 'tis the frailty of woman, my dear.

MRS. PEACHUM: Yes, indeed, the sex is frail. But the first time a woman is frail, she should be somewhat nice, methinks, for then or never is the time to make her fortune. After that, she hath nothing to do but to guard herself from being found out, and she may do what she pleases.

PEACHUM: Make yourself a little easy; I have a thought shall soon set all matters again to rights. Why so melancholy, Polly? since what is done cannot be undone, we must all endeavour to make the best of it.

MRS. PEACHUM: Well, Polly; as far as one woman can forgive another, I forgive thee.—Your father is too fond of you, hussy.

POLLY: Then all my sorrows are at an end.

MRS. PEACHUM: A mighty likely speech, in troth, for a wench who is just married!

Air X: *Thomas, I cannot*

POLLY: I, like a ship in storms, was toss'd;
    Yet afraid to put in to land;
    For seiz'd in the port the vessel's lost,
    Whose treasure is contraband.
      The waves are laid,
      My duty's paid.
    Oh joy beyond expression!
      Thus, safe ashore,
      I ask no more,
    My all is in my possession.

PEACHUM: I hear customers in t'other room. Go, talk with 'em, Polly; but come to us again, as soon as they are gone.—But, hark ye, child, if 'tis the gentleman who was here yesterday about the repeating watch, say, you believe we can't get intelligence of it till tomorrow. For I lent it to Suky Straddle, to make a figure with it to-night at a tavern in Drury Lane. If t'other gentleman calls for the silver-hilted sword, you know Beetle-browed Jemmy hath it on, and he doth not come from Tunbridge till Tuesday night, so that it cannot be had till then.

Scene IX   *Peachum, Mrs. Peachum*

PEACHUM: Dear wife, be a little pacified. Don't let your passion run away with your senses. Polly, I grant you, hath done a rash thing.

MRS. PEACHUM: If she had had only an intrigue with the fellow, why the very best families have excused and huddled up a frailty of that sort. 'Tis marriage, husband, that makes it a blemish.

PEACHUM: But money, wife, is the true fuller's earth° for reputations: there is not a spot or a stain but what it can take out. A rich rogue now-a-days is fit company for any gentleman; and the world, my dear, hath not such a contempt for roguery as you imagine. I tell you, wife, I can make this match turn to our advantage.

MRS. PEACHUM: I am very sensible, husband, that Captain Macheath is worth money, but I am in doubt whether he hath not two or three wives already, and then if he should die in a session or two, Polly's dower would come into dispute.

PEACHUM: That, indeed, is a point which ought to be considered.

fuller's earth: Earth used to clean fabrics.

Air XI: *A soldier and a sailor*

> A fox may steal your hens, Sir,
> A whore your health and pence, Sir,
> Your daughter rob your chest, Sir,
> Your wife may steal your rest, Sir,
>   A thief your goods and plate.
> But this is all but picking;
> With rest, pence, chest, and chicken,
> It ever was decreed, Sir,
> If lawyer's hand is fee'd, Sir,
>   He steals your whole estate.

The lawyers are bitter enemies to those in our way. They don't care that anybody should get a clandestine livelihood but themselves.

Scene X   *Mrs. Peachum, Peachum, Polly*

POLLY: 'Twas only Nimming Ned. He brought in a damask window-curtain, a hoop-petticoat, a pair of silver candlesticks, a periwig, and one silk stocking, from the fire that happened last night.

PEACHUM: There is not a fellow that is cleverer in his way, and saves more goods out of the fire than Ned. But now, Polly, to your affair; for matters must not be left as they are. You are married then, it seems?

POLLY: Yes, Sir.

PEACHUM: And how do you propose to live, child?

POLLY: Like other women, Sir, upon the industry of my husband.

MRS. PEACHUM: What, is the wench turned fool? A highwayman's wife, like a soldier's, hath as little of his pay as of his company.

PEACHUM: And had not you the common views of a gentlewoman in your marriage, Polly?

POLLY: I don't know what you mean, Sir.

PEACHUM: Of a jointure,° and of being a widow.

POLLY: But I love him, Sir: how then could I have thoughts of parting with him?

PEACHUM: Parting with him! Why, that is the whole scheme and intention of all marriage articles. The comfortable estate of widowhood is the only hope that keeps up a wife's spirits. Where is the woman who would scruple to be a wife, if she had it in her power to be a widow whenever she pleased? If you have any views of this sort, Polly, I shall think the match not so very unreasonable.

POLLY: How I dread to hear your advice! Yet I must beg you to explain yourself.

PEACHUM: Secure what he hath got, have him peached the next sessions, and then at once you are made a rich widow.

POLLY: What, murder the man I love! The blood runs cold at my heart with the very thought of it.

jointure: Arrangement by which husband and wife hold their property jointly.

PEACHUM: Fie, Polly! What hath murder to do in the affair? Since the thing sooner or later must happen, I dare say the captain himself would like that we should get the reward for his death sooner than a stranger. Why, Polly, the captain knows that as 'tis his employment to rob, so 'tis ours to take robbers; every man in his business. So that there is no malice in the case.

MRS. PEACHUM: Ay, husband, now you have nicked the matter. To have him peached is the only thing could ever make me forgive her.

Air XII: *Now ponder well, ye parents dear*

POLLY: Oh, ponder well! be not severe;
>   So save a wretched wife!
>   For on the rope that hangs my dear
>   Depends poor Polly's life.

MRS. PEACHUM: But your duty to your parents, hussy, obliges you to hang him. What would many a wife give for such an opportunity!

POLLY: What is a jointure, what is widowhood to me? I know my heart. I cannot survive him.

Air XIII: *Le printemps rappelle aux armes*

> The turtle thus with plaintive crying,
>   Her lover dying,
> The turtle thus with plaintive crying,
>   Laments her dove.
> Down she drops, quite spent with sighing,
> Pair'd in death, as pair'd in love.

Thus, Sir, it will happen to your poor Polly.

MRS. PEACHUM: What, is the fool in love in earnest then? I hate thee for being particular. Why, wench, thou art a shame to thy very sex.

POLLY: But hear, me Mother.—If you ever loved—

MRS. PEACHUM: Those cursed play-books she reads have been her ruin. One word more, hussy, and I shall knock your brains out, if you have any.

PEACHUM: Keep out of the way, Polly, for fear of mischief, and consider of what is proposed to you.

MRS. PEACHUM: Away, hussy. Hang your husband, and be dutiful.

Scene XI   *Mrs. Peachum, Peachum*

(Polly listening)

MRS. PEACHUM: The thing, husband, must and shall be done. For the sake of intelligence we must take other measures, and have him peached the next session without her consent. If she will not know her duty, we know ours.

PEACHUM: But really, my dear, it grieves one's heart to take off a great man. When I consider his personal bravery, his fine stratagem, how much we have already got by him, and how much more we may get, methinks I can't find in my heart to have a hand in his death. I wish you could have made Polly undertake it.

MRS. PEACHUM: But in a case of necessity—our own lives are in danger.

PEACHUM: Then, indeed, we must comply with the customs of the world, and make gratitude give way to interest. He shall be taken off.

MRS. PEACHUM: I'll undertake to manage Polly.

PEACHUM: And I'll prepare matters for the Old Bailey.

Scene XII   *Polly*

POLLY: Now I'm a wretch, indeed.—Methinks I see him already in the cart, sweeter and more lovely than the nosegay in his hand!—I hear the crowd extolling his resolution and intrepidity!—What volleys of sighs are sent from the windows of Holborn, that so comely a youth should be brought to disgrace!—I see him at the tree! The whole circle are in tears!—even butchers weep!—Jack Ketch° himself hesitates to perform his duty, and would be glad to lose his fee by a reprieve. What then will become of Polly? As yet I may inform him of their design, and aid him in his escape.—It shall be so.—But then he flies, absents himself, and I bar myself from his dear, dear conversation! That too will distract me. If he keep out of the way, my papa and mama may in time relent, and we may be happy. If he stays, he is hanged, and then he is lost forever! He intended to lie concealed in my room, till the dusk of the evening. If they are abroad, I'll this instant let him out, lest some accident should prevent him.

(*Exit, and returns*)

Scene XIII   *Polly, Macheath*

Air XIV: *Pretty Parrot, say*

MACHEATH: Pretty Polly, say,
          When I was away,
      Did your fancy never stray
          To some newer lover?

POLLY: Without disguise,
          Heaving sighs,
          Doting eyes,
      My constant heart discover.
          Fondly let me loll!

MACHEATH: O pretty, pretty Poll.

POLLY: And are *you* as fond as ever, my dear?

MACHEATH: Suspect my honour, my courage, suspect anything but my love. May my pistols miss fire, and my mare slip her shoulder while I am pursued, if I ever forsake thee!

Jack Ketch: A notorious executioner (d. 1686) who frequently botched the job of beheading prisoners, resulting in horrifying spectacles.

POLLY: Nay, my dear, I have no reason to doubt you, for I find in the romance you lent me, none of the great heroes were ever false in love.

Air XV: *Pray, fair one, be kind*

MACHEATH: My heart was so free,
          It rov'd like the bee,
      Till Polly my passion requited;
      I sipp'd each flower,
      I chang'd ev'ry hour,
      But here ev'ry flower is united.

POLLY: Were you sentenced to transportation, sure, my dear you could not leave me behind you—could you?

MACHEATH: Is there any power, any force that could tear me from thee? You might sooner tear a pension out of the hands of a courtier, a fee from a lawyer, a pretty woman from a looking glass, or any woman from quadrille. But to tear me from thee is impossible!

Air XVI: *Over the hills and far away*

      Were I laid on Greenland's coast,
          And in my arms embrac'd my lass:
      Warm amidst eternal frost,
          Too soon the half year's night would pass.

POLLY: Were I sold on Indian soil,
          Soon as the burning day was clos'd,
      I could mock the sultry toil,
          When on my charmer's breast repos'd.

MACHEATH: And I would love you all the day,

POLLY: Every night would kiss and play,

MACHEATH: If with me you'd fondly stray

POLLY: Over the hills and far away.

POLLY: Yes, I would go with thee. But oh!—how shall I speak it? I must be torn from thee. We must part.

MACHEATH: How! Part!

POLLY: We must, we must. My papa and mama are set against thy life. They now, even now are in search after thee. They are preparing evidence against thee. Thy life depends upon a moment.

Air XVII: *Gin thou wert mine own thing*

      Oh, what pain it is to part!
          Can I leave thee, can I leave thee?
      Oh, what pain it is to part!
          Can thy Polly ever leave thee?
      But lest death my love should thwart,
      And bring thee to the fatal cart,
      Thus I tear thee from my bleeding heart!
          Fly hence, and let me leave thee.

One kiss and then—one kiss—begone—farewell.

MACHEATH: My hand, my heart, my dear, is so riveted to thine, that I cannot unloose my hold.

POLLY: But my papa may intercept thee, and then I should lose the very glimmering of hope. A few weeks, perhaps, may reconcile us all. Shall thy Polly hear from thee?

MACHEATH: Must I then go?

POLLY: And will not absence change your love?

MACHEATH: If you doubt it, let me stay—and be hanged.

POLLY: Oh, how I fear! how I tremble!—Go—but when safety will give you leave, you will be sure to see me again; for till then Polly is wretched.

Air XVIII: *O, the broom*

(Parting, and looking back at each other with fondness; he at one door, she at the other)

MACHEATH: The miser thus a shilling sees,
                      Which he's oblig'd to pay,
                  With sighs resigns it by degrees,
                      And fears 'tis gone for aye.

POLLY: The boy, thus, when his sparrow's flown,
                      The bird in silence eyes;
                  But soon as out of sight 'tis gone,
                      Whines, whimpers, sobs and cries.

ACT II • Scene I

Scene: *A tavern near Newgate*

Jemmy Twitcher, Crook-Fingered Jack, Wat Dreary, Robin of Bagshot, Nimming Ned, Harry Padington, Matt of the Mint, Ben Budge, and the rest of the gang, at the table, with wine, brandy and tobacco

BEN: But pr'ythee, Matt, what is become of thy brother Tom? I have not seen him since my return from transportation.

MATT: Poor brother Tom had an accident this time twelve-month, and so clever a made fellow he was, that I could not save him from those flaying rascals the surgeons; and now, poor man, he is among the otamys° at Surgeons' Hall.

BEN: So it seems, his time was come.

JEMMY: But the present time is ours, and nobody alive hath more. Why are the laws levelled at us? Are we more dishonest than the rest of mankind? What we win, gentlemen, is our own by the law of arms and the right of conquest.

JACK: Where shall we find such another set of practical philosophers, who to a man are above the fear of death?

WAT: Sound men, and true!

ROBIN: Of tried courage, and indefatigable industry!

NED: Who is there here that would not die for his friend?

HARRY: Who is there here that would betray him for his interest?

MATT: Show me a gang of courtiers that can say as much.

BEN: We are for a just partition of the world, for every man hath a right to enjoy life.

MATT: We retrench the superfluities of mankind. The world is avaricious, and I hate avarice. A covetous

otamys: Anatomy specimens at Surgeons' Hall.

fellow, like a jackdaw, steals what he was never made to enjoy, for the sake of hiding it. These are the robbers of mankind, for money was made for the free-hearted and generous, and where is the injury of taking from another what he hath not the heart to make use of?

JEMMY: Our several stations for the day are fix'd. Good luck attend us all. Fill the glasses.

Air XIX: *Fill ev'ry glass*

MATT: Fill ev'ry glass, for wine inspires us,
                  And fires us,
              With courage, love and joy.
              Women and wine should life employ.
              Is there aught else on earth desirous?

CHORUS: Fill ev'ry glass, etc.

Scene II   *To them enter Macheath*

MACHEATH: Gentlemen, well met. My heart hath been with you this hour; but an unexpected affair hath detained me. No ceremony, I beg you.

MATT: We were just breaking up to go upon duty. Am I to have the honour of taking the air with you, Sir, this evening upon the heath? I drink a dram now and then with the stage-coachmen in the way of friend-ship and intelligence, and I know that about this time there will be passengers upon the western road who are worth speaking with.

MACHEATH: I was to have been of that party—but—

MATT: But what, Sir?

MACHEATH: Is there any man who suspects my courage?

MATT: We have all been witnesses of it.

MACHEATH: My honour and truth to the gang?

MATT: I'll be answerable for it.

MACHEATH: In the division of our booty, have I ever shown the least marks of avarice or injustice?

MATT: By these questions something seems to have ruffled you. Are any of us suspected?

MACHEATH: I have a fixed confidence, gentlemen, in you all, as men of honour, and as such I value and respect you. Peachum is a man that is useful to us.

MATT: Is he about to play us any foul play? I'll shoot him through the head.

MACHEATH: I beg you, gentlemen, act with conduct and discretion. A pistol is your last resort.

MATT: He knows nothing of this meeting.

MACHEATH: Business cannot go on without him. He is a man who knows the world, and is a necessary agent to us. We have had a slight difference, and till it is accommodated I shall be obliged to keep out of his way. Any private dispute of mine shall be of no ill consequence to my friends. You must continue to act under his direction, for the moment we break loose from him, our gang is ruin'd.

MATT: As a bawd to a whore, I grant you, he is to us of great convenience.

MACHEATH: Make him believe I have quitted the gang, which I can never do but with life. At our private quarters I will continue to meet you. A week or so will probably reconcile us.

MATT: Your instructions shall be observed. 'Tis now high time for us to repair to our several duties; so till the evening at our quarters in Moorfields we bid you farewell.

MACHEATH: I shall wish myself with you. Success attend you.

(*sits down melancholy at the table*)

Air XX: *March in Rinaldo, with drums and trumpets*

MATT: Let us take the road.
 Hark! I hear the sound of coaches!
 The hour of attack approaches,
To your arms, brave boys, and load.
 See the ball I hold!
Let the chymists toil like asses,
Our fire their fire surpasses,
And turns all our lead to gold.

(*The gang, ranged in the front of the stage, load their pistols, and stick them under their girdles; then go off singing the first part in chorus.*)

Scene III   *Macheath, Drawer*

MACHEATH: What a fool is a fond wench! Polly is most confoundedly bit. I love the sex. And a man who loves money might as well be contented with one guinea, as I with one woman. The town perhaps hath been as much obliged to me, for recruiting it with free-hearted ladies, as to any recruiting officer in the army. If it were not for us and the other gentlemen of the sword, Drury Lane would be uninhabited.

Air XXI: *Would you have a young virgin*

If the heart of a man is depress'd with cares,
The mist is dispell'd when a woman appears;
 Like the notes of a fiddle, she sweetly, sweetly
Raises the spirits, and charms our ears.
 Roses and lilies her cheeks disclose,
 But her ripe lips are more sweet than those.
   Press her,
   Caress her
   With blisses,
   Her kisses
Dissolve us in pleasure, and soft repose.

I must have women. There is nothing unbends the mind like them. Money is not so strong a cordial for the time.—Drawer! (*Enter Drawer*) Is the porter gone for all the ladies, according to my directions?

DRAWER: I expect him back every minute. But you know, Sir, you sent him as far as Hockley in the Hole for three of the ladies, for one in Vinegar Yard, and for the rest of them somewhere about Lewkner's Lane. Sure some of them are below, for I hear the bar bell. As they come I will show them up.—Coming! coming!

Scene IV   *Macheath, Mrs. Coaxer, Dolly Trull, Mrs. Vixen, Betty Doxy, Jenny Diver, Mrs. Slammekin, Suky Tawdry, and Molly Brazen*

MACHEATH: Dear Mrs. Coaxer, you are welcome. You look charmingly today. I hope you don't want the repairs of quality, and lay on paint.—Dolly Trull! kiss me, you slut; are you as amorous as ever, hussy? You are always so taken up with stealing hearts, that you don't allow yourself time to steal anything else.—Ah Dolly, thou wilt ever be a coquette. Mrs. Vixen, I'm yours; I always loved a woman of wit and spirit; they make charming mistresses, but plaguy wives.—Betty Doxy! Come hither, hussy. Do you drink as hard as ever? You had better stick to good wholesome beer; for in troth, Betty, strong waters will in time ruin your constitution. You should leave those to your betters.—What! and my pretty Jenny Diver too! As prim and demure as ever! There is not any prude, though ever so high bred, hath a more sanctified look, with a more mischievous heart. Ah! thou art a dear artful hypocrite.—Mrs. Slammekin! as careless and genteel as ever! all you fine ladies, who know you own beauty, affect an undress.—But see, here's Suky Tawdry come to contradict what I was saying. Everything she gets one way, she lays out upon her back. Why, Suky, you must keep at least a dozen tally-men.—Molly Brazen! (*She kisses him.*) That's well done. I love a free-hearted wench. Thou hast a most agreeable assurance, girl, and art as willing as a turtle.—But hark! I hear music. The harper is at the door. "If music be the food of love, play on." Ere you seat yourselves, ladies, what think you of a dance?—Come in. (*Enter Harper*) Play the French tune, that Mrs. Slammekin was so fond of.

(*a dance* à la ronde *in the French manner; near the end of it this song and chorus*)

Air XXII: *Cotillon*

Youth's the season made for joys,
 Love is then our duty;
She alone who that employs,
 Well deserves her beauty.
  Let's be gay,
  While we may,
Beauty's a flower, despis'd in decay.
 Youth's the season, etc.

Let us drink and sport to-day,
 Ours is not to-morrow.
Love with youth flies swift away,
 Age is nought but sorrow.
  Dance and sing,
  Time's on the wing,
Life never knows the return of spring.

CHORUS: Let us drink, etc.

MACHEATH: Now, pray ladies, take your places.—Here, fellow. (*pays the Harper*) Bid the drawer bring us more wine. (*Exit Harper*) If any of the ladies choose gin, I hope they will be so free to call for it.

JENNY: You look as if you meant me. Wine is strong enough for me. Indeed, Sir, I never drink strong waters, but when I have the colic.

MACHEATH: Just the excuse of the fine ladies! Why, a lady of quality is never without the colic.—I hope, Mrs. Coaxer, you have had good success of late in your visits among the mercers.

COAXER: We have so many interlopers! Yet, with industry, one may still have a little picking. I carried a silver-flowered lutestring and a piece of black padesoy° to Mr. Peachum's lock but last week.

VIXEN: There's Molly Brazen hath the ogle of a rattle-snake. She riveted a linen-draper's eye so fast upon her, that he was nicked of three pieces of cambric before he could look off.

BRAZEN: O dear Madam! But sure nothing can come up to your handling of laces! And then you have such a sweet deluding tongue! To cheat a man is nothing; but the woman must have fine parts indeed who cheats a woman!

VIXEN: Lace, Madam, lies in a small compass, and is of easy conveyance. But you are apt, Madam, to think too well of your friends.

COAXER: If any woman hath more art than another, to be sure, 'tis Jenny Diver. Though her fellow be never so agreeable, she can pick his pocket as coolly as if money were her only pleasure. Now that is a command of the passions uncommon in a woman!

JENNY: I never go to the tavern with a man, but in the view of business. I have other hours, and other sort of men for my pleasure. But had I your address, Madam—

MACHEATH: Have done with your compliments, ladies; and drink about.—You are not so fond of me, Jenny, as you use to be.

JENNY: 'Tis not convenient, Sir, to show my fondness among so many rivals. 'Tis your own choice, and not the warmth of my inclination that will determine you.

Air XXIII: *All in a misty morning*

Before the barn-door crowing,
  The cock by hens attended,
His eyes around him throwing,
  Stands for a while suspended.
Then one he singles from the crew,
  And cheers the happy hen;
With how do you do, and how do you do,
  And how do you do again.

MACHEATH: Ah Jenny! thou art a dear slut.

TRULL: Pray, Madam, were you ever in keeping?

TAWDRY: I hope, Madam, I han't been so long upon the town, but I have met with some good fortune as well as my neighbours.

padesoy: Peau de soie, a type of silk fabric.

TRULL: Pardon me, Madam, I meant no harm by the question; 'twas only in the way of conversation.

TAWDRY: Indeed, Madam, if I had not been a fool, I might have lived very handsomely with my last friend. But upon his missing five guineas, he turned me off. Now I never suspected he had counted them.

SLAMMEKIN: Who do you look upon, Madam, as your best sort of keepers?

TRULL: That, Madam, is thereafter as they be.

SLAMMEKIN: I, Madam, was once kept by a Jew; and bating their religion, to women they are a good sort of people.

TAWDRY: Now for my part, I own I like an old fellow: for we always make them pay for what they can't do.

VIXEN: A spruce prentice, let me tell you, ladies, is no ill thing: they bleed freely. I have sent at least two or three dozen of them in my time to the plantations.

JENNY: But to be sure, Sir, with so much good fortune as you have had upon the road, you must be grown immensely rich.

MACHEATH: The road, indeed, hath done me justice, but the gaming-table hath been my ruin.

Air XXIV: *When once I lay with another man's wife*

JENNY: The gamesters and lawyers are jugglers alike,
    If they meddle, your all is in danger.
  Like gypsies, if once they can finger a souse,°
    Your pockets they pick, and they pilfer your
      house,
    And give your estate to a stranger.

A man of courage should never put anything to the risk but his life. (*She takes up his pistol*) These are the tools of a man of honour. Cards and dice are only fit for cowardly cheats, who prey upon their friends.
          (*Tawdry takes up the other*)

TAWDRY: This, Sir, is fitter for your hand. Besides your loss of money, 'tis a loss to the ladies. Gaming takes you off from women. How fond could I be of you! but before company, 'tis ill-bred.

MACHEATH: Wanton hussies!

JENNY: I must and will have a kiss to give my wine a zest.

(*They take him about the neck, and make signs to Peachum and Constables, who rush in upon him*)

Scene V   *To them, Peachum and Constables*

PEACHUM: I seize you, Sir, as my prisoner.

MACHEATH: Was this well done, Jenny?—Women are decoy ducks; who can trust them! Beasts, jades, jilts, harpies, furies, whores!

PEACHUM: Your case, Mr. Macheath, is not particular. The greatest heroes have been ruined by women. But, to do them justice, I must own they are a pretty sort of creatures, if we could trust them. You must now,

souse: A very small coin.

Sir, take your leave of the ladies, and if they have a mind to make you a visit, they will be sure to find you at home. The gentleman, ladies, lodges in Newgate. Constables, wait upon the captain to his lodgings.

Air XXV: *When first I laid siege to my Chloris*

MACHEATH: At the tree I shall suffer with pleasure,
   At the tree I shall suffer with pleasure.
    Let me go where I will,
    In all kinds of ill,
   I shall find no such furies as these are.

PEACHUM: Ladies, I'll take care the reckoning shall be discharged.

> (*Exit Macheath, guarded, with Peachum and Constables*)

Scene VI   *The Women remain*

VIXEN: Look ye, Mrs. Jenny, though Mr. Peachum may have made a private bargain with you and Suky Tawdry for betraying the captain, as we were all assisting, we ought all to share alike.

COAXER: I think Mr. Peachum, after so long an acquaintance, might have trusted me as well as Jenny Diver.

SLAMMEKIN: I am sure at least three men of his hanging, and in a year's time too (if he did me justice) should be set down to my account.

TRULL: Mrs. Slammekin, that is not fair. For you know one of them was taken in bed with me.

JENNY: As far as a bowl of punch or a treat, I believe Mrs. Suky will join with me. As for anything else, ladies, you cannot in conscience expect it.

SLAMMEKIN: Dear Madam—

TRULL: I would not for the world—

SLAMMEKIN: 'Tis impossible for me—

TRULL: As I hope to be saved, Madam—

SLAMMEKIN: Nay, then I must stay here all night.

TRULL: Since you command me.

> (*Exeunt with great ceremony*)

Scene VII

Scene: *Newgate*

Lockit, Turnkeys, Macheath, Constables

LOCKIT: Noble Captain, you are welcome. You have not been a lodger of mine this year and half. You know the custom, Sir. Garnish,° Captain, garnish. Hand me down those fetters there.

MACHEATH: Those, Mr. Lockit, seem to be the heaviest of the whole set. With your leave, I should like the further pair better.

Garnish: Money paid as a bribe.

LOCKIT: Look ye, Captain, we know what is fittest for our prisoners. When a gentleman uses me with civility, I always do the best I can to please him.—Hand them down, I say.—We have them of all prices, from one guinea to ten, and 'tis fitting every gentleman should please himself.

MACHEATH: I understand you, Sir. (*gives money*) The fees here are so many, and so exorbitant, that few fortunes can bear the expense of getting off handsomely, or of dying like a gentleman.

LOCKIT: Those, I see, will fit the captain better.—Take down the further pair.—Do but examine them, Sir—never was better work. How genteelly they are made! They will fit as easy as a glove, and the nicest man in England might not be ashamed to wear them. (*He puts on the chains*) If I had the best gentleman in the land in my custody I could not equip him more handsomely. And so, Sir—I now leave you to your private meditations.

Scene VIII   *Macheath*

Air XXVI: *Courtiers, courtiers, think it no harm*

Man may escape from rope and gun;
  Nay, some have out-liv'd the doctor's pill;
Who takes a woman must be undone,
  That basilisk is sure to kill.
The fly that sips treacle is lost in the sweets,
  So he that tastes woman, woman, woman,
He that tastes woman, ruin meets.

To what a woeful plight have I brought myself! Here must I (all day long, till I am hanged) be confined to hear the reproaches of a wench who lays her ruin at my door. I am in the custody of her father, and to be sure, if he knows of the matter I shall have a fine time on't betwixt this and my execution. But I promised the wench marriage. What signifies a promise to a woman? Does not man in marriage itself promise a hundred things that he never means to perform? Do all we can, women will believe us; for they look upon a promise as an excuse for following their own inclinations.—But here comes Lucy, and I cannot get from her. Would I were deaf!

LUCY: You base man, you—how can you look me in the face after what hath passed between us? See here, perfidious wretch, how I am forced to bear about the load of infamy you have laid upon me. O Macheath! thou hast robbed me of my quiet—to see thee tortured would give me pleasure.

Air XXVII: *A lovely lass to a friar came*

Thus when a good huswife sees a rat
  In her trap in the morning taken,
With pleasure her heart goes pit-a-pat
  In revenge for her loss of bacon.

Tom Randle as Macheath
in the Royal Opera's production in London, 2009.

Then she throws him
        To the dog or cat,
    To be worried, crushed and shaken.

MACHEATH: Have you no bowels, no tenderness, my dear
    Lucy, to see a husband in these circumstances?
LUCY: A husband!
MACHEATH: In every respect but the form, and that, my
    dear, may be said over us at any time. Friends should
    not insist upon ceremonies. From a man of honour,
    his word is as good as his bond.
LUCY: 'Tis the pleasure of all you fine men to insult the
    women you have ruined.

Air XXVIII: *'Twas when the sea was roaring*

    How cruel are the traitors,
        Who lie and swear in jest,
    To cheat unguarded creatures
        Of virtue, fame, and rest!
    Whoever steals a shilling
        Through shame the guilt conceals;
    In love the perjured villain
        With boasts the theft reveals.

MACHEATH: The very first opportunity, my dear (have but
    patience) you shall be my wife in whatever manner
    you please.
LUCY: Insinuating monster! And so you think I know
    nothing of the affair of Miss Polly Peachum.—I
    could tear thy eyes out!
MACHEATH: Sure, Lucy, you can't be such a fool as to be
    jealous of Polly!
LUCY: Are you not married to her, you brute, you?

MACHEATH: Married! Very good. The wench gives it out
    only to vex thee, and to ruin me in thy good opinion.
    'Tis true I go to the house; I chat with the girl, I kiss
    her, I say a thousand things to her (as all gentlemen
    do) that mean nothing, to divert myself; and now the
    silly jade hath set it about that I am married to her,
    to let me know what she would be at. Indeed, my
    dear Lucy, these violent passions may be of ill conse-
    quence to a woman in your condition.
LUCY: Come, come, Captain, for all your assurance, you
    know that Miss Polly hath put it out of your power
    to do me the justice you promised me.
MACHEATH: A jealous woman believes everything her
    passion suggests. To convince you of my sincerity, if
    we can find the ordinary,° I shall have no scruples of
    making you my wife; and I know the consequence of
    having two at a time.
LUCY: That you are only to be hanged, and so get rid of
    them both.
MACHEATH: I am ready, my dear Lucy, to give you
    satisfaction—if you think there is any in marriage.
    What can a man of honour say more?
LUCY: So then it seems, you are not married to Miss Polly.
MACHEATH: You know, Lucy, the girl is prodigiously con-
    ceited. No man can say a civil thing to her, but (like
    other fine ladies) her vanity makes her think he's her
    own for ever and ever.

Air XXIX: *The sun had loos'd his weary teams*

    The first time at the looking-glass
        The mother sets her daughter,

ordinary: The chaplain at Newgate. He can marry them.

The image strikes the smiling lass
    With self-love ever after.
Each time she looks, she, fonder grown,
    Thinks ev'ry charm grows stronger.
But alas, vain maid, all eyes but your own
    Can see you are not younger.

When women consider their own beauties, they are all alike unreasonable in their demands; for they expect their lovers should like them as long as they like themselves.

LUCY: Yonder is my father—perhaps this way we may light upon the ordinary, who shall try if you will be as good as your word. For I long to be made an honest woman.

Scene X   *Peachum, Lockit with an account-book*

LOCKIT: In this last affair, brother Peachum, we are agreed. You have consented to go halves in Macheath.

PEACHUM: We shall never fall out about an execution. But as to that article, pray how stands our last year's account?

LOCKIT: If you will run your eye over it, you'll find 'tis fair and clearly stated.

PEACHUM: This long arrear of the government is very hard upon us! Can it be expected that we should hang our acquaintance for nothing, when our betters will hardly save theirs without being paid for it? Unless the people in employment pay better, I promise them for the future, I shall let other rogues live besides their own.

LOCKIT: Perhaps, brother, they are afraid these matters may be carried too far. We are treated too by them with contempt, as if our profession were not reputable.

PEACHUM: In one respect, indeed, our employment may be reckoned dishonest, because, like great statesmen, we encourage those who betray their friends.

LOCKIT: Such language, brother, anywhere else might turn to your prejudice. Learn to be more guarded, I beg you.

Air XXX: *How happy are we*

When you censure the age,
    Be cautious and sage,
Lest the courtiers offended should be:
    If you mention vice or bribe,
    'Tis so pat to all the tribe;
Each cries—"That was levell'd at me."

PEACHUM: Here's poor Ned Clincher's name, I see. Sure, brother Lockit, there was a little unfair proceeding in Ned's case; for he told me in the condemned hold, that for value received, you had promised him a session or two longer without molestation.

LOCKIT: Mr. Peachum, this is the first time my honour was ever called in question.

PEACHUM: Business is at an end—if once we act dishonourably.

LOCKIT: Who accuses me?

PEACHUM: You are warm, brother.

LOCKIT: He that attacks my honour, attacks my livelihood. And this usage, Sir, is not to be borne.

PEACHUM: Since you provoke me to speak, I must tell you too, that Mrs. Coaxer charges you with defrauding her of her information-money, for the apprehending of Curl-pated Hugh. Indeed, indeed, brother, we must punctually pay our spies, or we shall have no information.

LOCKIT: Is this language to me, Sirrah—who have saved you from the gallows, Sirrah?   *(collaring each other)*

PEACHUM: If I am hanged, it shall be for ridding the world of an arrant rascal.

LOCKIT: This hand shall do the office of the halter you deserve, and throttle you—you dog!

PEACHUM: Brother, brother—we are both in the wrong—we shall be both losers in the dispute—for you know we have it in our power to hang each other. You should not be so passionate.

LOCKIT: Nor you so provoking.

PEACHUM: 'Tis our mutual interest; 'tis for the interest of the world we should agree. If I said anything, brother, to the prejudice of your character, I ask pardon.

LOCKIT: Brother Peachum—I can forgive as well as resent. Give me your hand. Suspicion does not become a friend.

PEACHUM: I only meant to give you occasion to justify yourself. But I must now step home, for I expect the gentleman about this snuff-box, that Filch nimmed two nights ago in the park. I appointed him at this hour.

Scene XI   *Lockit, Lucy*

LOCKIT: Whence come you, hussy?

LUCY: My tears might answer that question.

LOCKIT: You have then been whimpering and fondling, like a spaniel, over the fellow that hath abused you.

LUCY: One can't help love; one can't cure it. 'Tis not in my power to obey you, and hate him.

LOCKIT: Learn to bear your husband's death like a reasonable woman. 'Tis not the fashion, now-a-days, so much as to affect sorrow upon these occasions. No woman would ever marry, if she had not the chance of mortality for a release. Act like a woman of spirit, hussy, and thank your father for what he is doing.

Air XXXI: *Of a noble race was Shenkin*

LUCY: Is then his fate decreed, Sir?
    Such a man can I think of quitting?
When first we met, so moves me yet,
    Oh, see how my heart is splitting!

LOCKIT: Look ye, Lucy—there is no saving him. So, I think, you must even do like other widows—buy yourself weeds, and be cheerful.

Air XXXII

You'll think, ere many days ensue,
    This sentence not severe;
I hang your husband, child, 'tis true,
    But with him hang your care.
        Twang dang dillo dee.

Like a good wife, go moan over your dying husband. That, child, is your duty. Consider, girl, you can't have the man and the money too—so make yourself as easy as you can by getting all you can from him.

Scene XII   *Lucy, Macheath*

LUCY: Though the ordinary was out of the way to-day, I hope, my dear, you will, upon the first opportunity, quiet my scruples. Oh, Sir!—my father's hard heart is not to be softened, and I am in the utmost despair.

MACHEATH: But if I could raise a small sum—Would not twenty guineas, think you, move him? Of all the arguments in the way of business, the perquisite is the most prevailing. Your father's perquisites for the escape of prisoners must amount to a considerable sum in the year. Money well timed and properly applied will do anything.

Air XXXIII: *London ladies*

If you at an office solicit your due,
    And would not have matters neglected;
You must quicken the clerk with the perquisite too,
    To do what his duty directed.
Or would you the frowns of a lady prevent,
    She too has this palpable failing,
The perquisite softens her into consent;
    That reason with all is prevailing.

LUCY: What love or money can do shall be done: for all my comfort depends upon your safety.

Scene XIII   *Lucy, Macheath, Polly*

POLLY:. Where is my dear husband?—Was a rope ever intended for this neck! Oh, let me throw my arms about it, and throttle thee with love! Why dost thou turn away from me? 'Tis thy Polly—'tis thy wife.

MACHEATH: Was ever such an unfortunate rascal as I am!

LUCY: Was there ever such another villain!

POLLY: O Macheath! was it for this we parted? Taken! imprisoned! tried! hanged!—cruel reflection! I'll stay with thee till death—no force shall tear thy dear wife from thee now. What means my love? Not one kind word! not one kind look! think what thy Polly suffers to see thee in this condition.

Randle with Leah-Marian Jones as Polly Peachum and Sarah Fox as Lucy Lockit.

Air XXXIV: *All in the Downs*

Thus when the swallow, seeking prey,
    Within the sash is closely pent,
His consort, with bemoaning lay,
    Without sits pining for th' event.
Her chatt'ring lovers all around her skim;
She heeds them not (poor bird!)—her soul's with him.

MACHEATH: (*aside*) I must disown her.—The wench is distracted.

LUCY: Am I then bilked of my virtue? Can I have no reparation? Sure, men were born to lie, and women to believe them! O villain! villain!

POLLY: Am I not thy wife? Thy neglect of me, thy aversion to me, too severely proves it. Look on me. Tell me, am I not thy wife?

LUCY: Perfidious wretch!

POLLY: Barbarous husband!

LUCY: Hadst thou been hanged five months ago, I had been happy.

POLLY: And I too. If you had been kind to me till death, it would not have vexed me—and that's no very unreasonable request (though from a wife) to a man who hath not above seven or eight days to live.

LUCY: Art thou then married to another? Hast thou two wives, monster?

MACHEATH: If women's tongues can cease for an answer—hear me.

LUCY: I won't. Flesh and blood can't bear my usage.

POLLY: Shall I not claim my own? Justice bids me speak.

Air XXXV: *Have you heard of a frolicsome ditty?*

MACHEATH: How happy could I be with either,
    Were t'other dear charmer away!
    But while you thus tease me together,
    To neither a word will I say;
    But tol de rol, etc.

POLLY: Sure, my dear, there ought to be some preference shown to a wife! At least she may claim the appearance of it. He must be distracted with his misfortunes, or he could not use me thus!

LUCY: O villain, villain! thou hast deceived me—I could even inform against thee with pleasure. Not a prude wishes more heartily to have facts against her intimate acquaintance, than I now wish to have facts against thee. I would have her satisfaction, and they should all out.

Air XXXVI: *Irish trot*

POLLY: I'm bubbled.

LUCY: —I'm bubbled.°

POLLY: Oh, how I am troubled!

LUCY: Bamboozled, and bit!

POLLY: —My distresses are doubled.

---

bubbled: Cheated.

LUCY: When you come to the tree, should the hangman refuse,
    These fingers, with pleasure, could fasten the noose.

POLLY: I'm bubbled, etc.

MACHEATH: Be pacified, my dear Lucy—this is all a fetch of Polly's to make me desperate with you in case I get off. If I am hanged, she would fain have the credit of being thought my widow.—Really, Polly, this is no time for a dispute of this sort; for whenever you are talking of marriage, I am thinking of hanging.

POLLY: And hast thou the heart to persist in disowning me?

MACHEATH: And hast thou the heart to persist in persuading me that I am married? Why, Polly, dost thou seek to aggravate my misfortunes?

LUCY: Really, Miss Peachum, you but expose yourself. Besides, 'tis barbarous in you to worry a gentleman in his circumstances.

Air XXXVII

POLLY: Cease your funning;
         Force or cunning
    Never shall my heart trapan.°
         All these sallies
         Are but malice
    To seduce my constant man.
         'Tis most certain,
         By their flirting,
    Women oft have envy shown;
         Pleas'd, to ruin
         Others' wooing;
    Never happy in their own!

Decency, Madam, methinks, might teach you to behave yourself with some reserve with the husband, while his wife is present.

MACHEATH: But, seriously, Polly, this is carrying the joke a little too far.

LUCY: If you are determined, Madam, to raise a disturbance in the prison, I shall be obliged to send for the turnkey to show you the door. I am sorry, Madam, you force me to be so ill-bred.

POLLY: Give me leave to tell you, Madam, these forward airs don't become you in the least, Madam. And my duty, Madam, obliges me to stay with my husband, Madam.

Air XXXVIII: *Good-morrow, gossip Joan*

LUCY: Why, how now, Madam Flirt?
    If you thus must chatter;
    And are for flinging dirt,
        Let's try who best can spatter;
            Madam Flirt!

---

trapan: Ensnare.

POLLY: Why, how now, saucy jade;
    Sure, the wench is tipsy!
    (*to him*) How can you see me made
    The scoff of such a gypsy?
    (*to her*) Saucy jade!

Scene XIV   *Lucy, Macheath, Polly, Peachum*

PEACHUM: Where's my wench? Ah, hussy! hussy! Come you home, you slut; and when your fellow is hanged, hang yourself, to make your family some amends.

POLLY: Dear, dear father, do not tear me from him—I must speak; I have more to say to him.—Oh! twist thy fetters about me, that he may not haul me from thee!

PEACHUM: Sure all women are alike! If ever they commit the folly, they are sure to commit another by exposing themselves.—Away—not a word more—you are my prisoner now, hussy.

AIR XXXIX: *Irish howl*

POLLY: No power on earth can e'er divide
    The knot that sacred love hath tied.
    When parents draw against our mind,
    The true-love's knot they faster bind.
      Ho ho ra in ambora,—*etc.*
      (*holding Macheath, Peachum pulling her*)

Scene XV   *Lucy, Macheath*

MACHEATH: I am naturally compassionate, wife, so that I could not use the wench as she deserved; which made you at first suspect there was something in what she said.

LUCY: Indeed, my dear, I was strangely puzzled.

MACHEATH: If that had been the case, her father would never have brought me into this circumstance. No, Lucy, I had rather die than be false to thee.

LUCY: How happy am I if you say this from your heart! For I love thee so, that I could sooner bear to see thee hanged than in the arms of another.

MACHEATH: But couldst thou bear to see me hanged?

LUCY: O Macheath, I can never live to see that day.

MACHEATH: You see, Lucy, in the account of love you are in my debt, and you must now be convinced that I rather choose to die than be another's. Make me, if possible, love thee more, and let me owe my life to thee. If you refuse to assist me, Peachum and your father will immediately put me beyond all means of escape.

LUCY: My father, I know, hath been drinking hard with the prisoners, and I fancy he is now taking his nap in his own room. If I can procure the keys, shall I go off with thee, my dear?

MACHEATH: If we are together, 'twill be impossible to lie concealed. As soon as the search begins to be a little cool, I will send to thee. Till then my heart is thy prisoner.

LUCY: Come then, my dear husband—owe thy life to me—and though you love me not, be grateful. But that Polly runs in my head strangely.

MACHEATH: A moment of time may make us unhappy forever.

Air XL: *The lass of Patie's mill*

LUCY: I like the fox shall grieve,
    Whose mate hath left her side,
  Whom hounds, from morn to eve,
    Chase o'er the country wide.
  Where can my lover hide?
    Where cheat the wary pack?
  If love be not his guide,
    He never will come back!

ACT III • Scene I

Scene: *Newgate   Lockit, Lucy*

LOCKIT: To be sure, wench, you must have been aiding and abetting to help him to this escape.

LUCY: Sir, here hath been Peachum and his daughter Polly, and to be sure they know the ways of Newgate as well as if they had been born and bred in the place all their lives. Why must all your suspicion light upon me?

LOCKIT: Lucy, Lucy, I will have none of these shuffling answers.

LUCY: Well then—if I know anything of him I wish I may be burnt!

LOCKIT: Keep your temper, Lucy, or I shall pronounce you guilty.

LUCY: Keep yours, Sir. I do wish I may be burnt. I do!— and what can I say more to convince you?

LOCKIT: Did he tip handsomely? How much did he come down with? Come, hussy, don't cheat your father, and I shall not be angry with you. Perhaps you have made a better bargain with him than I could have done. How much, my good girl?

LUCY: You know, Sir, I am fond of him, and would have given money to have kept him with me.

LOCKIT: Ah, Lucy! thy education might have put thee more upon thy guard; for a girl in the bar of an alehouse is always besieged.

LUCY: Dear Sir, mention not my education—for 'twas to that I owe my ruin.

Air XLI: *If love's a sweet passion*

When young at the bar you first taught me to
    score,
And bid me be free of my lips, and no more;
I was kiss'd by the parson, the squire, and the sot.
When the guest was departed, the kiss was
    forgot.

But his kiss was so sweet, and so closely he
   press'd,
That I langush'd and pin'd till I granted the rest.

If you can forgive me, Sir, I will make a fair confession, for to be sure, he hath been a most barbarous
villain to me.

LOCKIT: And so you have let him escape, hussy—have
you?

LUCY: When a woman loves, a kind look, a tender word
can persuade her to anything—and I could ask no
other bribe.

LOCKIT: Thou wilt always be a vulgar slut, Lucy. If you
would not be looked upon as a fool, you should never
do anything but upon the foot of interest. Those that
act otherwise are their own bubbles.

LUCY: But love, Sir, is a misfortune that may happen to
the most discreet woman, and in love we are all fools
alike. Notwithstanding all he swore, I am now fully
convinced that Polly Peachum is actually his wife.
Did I let him escape (fool that I was!) to go to her?
Polly will wheedle herself into his money, and then
Peachum will hang him, and cheat us both.

LOCKIT: So I am to be ruined, because, forsooth, you
must be in love!—a very pretty excuse!

LUCY: I could murder that impudent happy strumpet: I
gave him his life, and that creature enjoys the sweets
of it. Ungrateful Macheath!

Air XLII: *South-Sea ballad*

My love is all madness and folly,
      Alone I lie,
      Toss, tumble, and cry,
What a happy creature is Polly!
      Was e'er such a wretch as I!
With rage I redden like scarlet,
That my dear inconstant varlet,
      Stark blind to my charms,
      Is lost in the arms
Of that jilt, that inveigling harlot!
      Stark blind to my charms,
      Is lost in the arms
Of that jilt, that inveigling harlot!
      This, this my resentment alarms.

LOCKIT: And so, after all this mischief, I must stay here
to be entertained with your caterwauling, Mistress
Puss! Out of my sight, wanton strumpet! you shall
fast and mortify yourself into reason, with now and
then a little handsome discipline to bring you to your
senses. Go!

Scene II   *Lockit*

LOCKIT: Peachum then intends to outwit me in this affair; but I'll be even with him. The dog is leaky in

his liquor, so I'll ply him that way, get the secret
from him, and turn this affair to my own advantage.
Lions, wolves, and vultures don't live together in
herds, droves or flocks. Of all animals of prey, man
is the only sociable one. Every one of us preys upon
his neighbour, and yet we herd together. Peachum is
my companion, my friend. According to the custom
of the world, indeed, he may quote thousands of
precedents for cheating me—and shall not I make
use of the privilege of friendship to make him a
return?

Air XLIII: *Packington's pound*

Thus gamesters united in friendship are found,
Though they know that their industry all is a
         cheat;
They flock to their prey at the dice-box's sound,
And join to promote one another's deceit.
      But if by mishap
      They fail of a chap,
To keep in their hands, they each other entrap.
Like pikes, lank with hunger, who miss of their ends,
They bite their companions, and prey on their
         friends.

Now, Peachum, you and I, like honest tradesmen,
are to have a fair trial which of us two can over-
reach the other. Lucy! (*Enter Lucy.*) Are there any of
Peachum's people now in the house?

LUCY: Filch, Sir, is drinking a quartern of strong waters in
the next room with Black Moll.

LOCKIT: Bid him come to me.   (*Exit Lucy*)

Scene III   *Lockit, Filch*

LOCKIT: Why, boy, thou lookest as if thou wert half
starved; like a shotten herring.

FILCH: One had need have the constitution of a horse to
go thorough the business. Since the favourite child-
getter was disabled by a mishap, I have picked up
a little money by helping the ladies to a pregnancy
against their being called down to sentence. But if
a man cannot get an honest livelihood any easier
way, I am sure 'tis what I can't undertake for another
session.

LOCKIT: Truly, if that great man should tip off, 'twould
be an irreparable loss. The vigour and prowess of a
knight errant never saved half the ladies in distress
that he hath done. But, boy, canst thou tell me where
thy master is to be found?

FILCH: At his lock, Sir, at the Crooked Billet.

LOCKIT: Very well. I have nothing more with you. (*Exit
Filch*) I'll go to him there, for I have many important
affairs to settle with him; and in the way of those

transactions I'll artfully get into his secret. So that Macheath shall not remain a day longer out of my clutches. (*Exit*)

Scene IV

Scene: *A Gaming-House*

Macheath in a fine tarnished coat, Ben Budge, Matt of the Mint

MACHEATH: I am sorry, gentlemen, the road was so barren of money. When my friends are in difficulties, I am always glad that my fortune can be serviceable to them. (*gives them money*) You see, gentlemen, I am not a mere court friend, who professes everything and will do nothing.

Air XLIV: *Lillibullero*

The modes of the court so common are grown
   That a true friend can hardly be met;
Friendship for interest is but a loan,
   Which they let out for what they can get.
      'Tis true, you find
      Some friends so kind,
Who will give you good counsel themselves to
      defend.
      In sorrowful ditty,
      They promise, they pity,
But shift you, for money, from friend to friend.

But we, gentlemen, have still honour enough to break through the corruptions of the world. And while I can serve you, you may command me.

BEN: It grieves my heart that so generous a man should be involved in such difficulties as oblige him to live with such ill company, and herd with gamesters.

MATT: See the partiality of mankind! One man may steal a horse, better than another look over a hedge. Of all mechanics, of all servile handicraftsmen, a gamester is the vilest. But yet, as many of the quality are of the profession, he is admitted amongst the politest company. I wonder we are not more respected.

MACHEATH: There will be deep play to-night at Marybone and consequently money may be picked up upon the road. Meet me there, and I'll give you the hint who is worth setting.

MATT: The fellow with a brown coat with a narrow gold binding, I am told, is never without money.

MACHEATH: What do you mean, Matt? Sure you will not think of meddling with him! He's a good honest kind of a fellow, and one of us.

BEN: To be sure, Sir, we will put ourselves under your direction.

MACHEATH: Have an eye upon the money-lenders. A rouleau° or two would prove a pretty sort of an expedition. I hate extortion.

rouleau: A roll of coins used in gambling.

MATT: Those rouleaus are very pretty things. I hate your bank bills—there is such a hazard in putting them off.

MACHEATH: There is a certain man of distinction who in his time hath nicked me out of a great deal of the ready. He is in my cash, Ben; I'll point him out to you this evening, and you shall draw upon him for the debt.—The company are met; I hear the dice-box in the other room. So, gentlemen, your servant! You'll meet me at Marybone. (*Exeunt*)

Scene V

Scene: *Peachum's lock*

A table with wine, brandy, pipes and tobacco
Peachum, Lockit

LOCKIT: The coronation account, brother Peachum, is of so intricate a nature that I believe it will never be settled.

PEACHUM: It consists, indeed, of a great variety of articles. It was worth to our people, in fees, of different kinds, above ten instalments. This is part of the account, brother, that lies open before us.

LOCKIT: A lady's tail of rich brocade—that, I see, is disposed of.

PEACHUM: To Mrs. Diana Trapes, the tally-woman, and she will make a good hand on't in shoes and slippers, to trick out young ladies, upon their going into keeping.

LOCKIT: But I don't see any article of the jewels.

PEACHUM: Those are so well known that they must be sent abroad. You'll find them entered under the article of exportation. As for the snuff-boxes, watches, swords, etc., I thought it best to enter them under their several heads.

LOCKIT: Seven and twenty women's pockets complete, with the several things therein contained; all sealed, numbered, and entered.

PEACHUM: But, brother, it is impossible for us now to enter upon this affair. We should have the whole day before us. Besides, the account of the last half-year's plate is in a book by itself, which lies at the other office.

LOCKIT: Bring us then more liquor. To-day shall be for pleasure—to-morrow for business.—Ah brother, those daughters of ours are two slippery hussies. Keep a watchful eye upon Polly, and Macheath in a day or two shall be our own again.

Air XLV: *Down in the North Country*

What gudgeons° are we men!
   Ev'ry woman's easy prey.
Though we have felt the hook, again
   We bite and they betray.

gudgeons: Small fish easily caught.

The bird that hath been trapp'd,
    When he hears his calling mate,
To her he flies, again he's clapp'd
    Within the wiry grate.

PEACHUM: But what signifies catching the bird, if your daughter Lucy will set open the door of the cage?

LOCKIT: If men were answerable for the follies and frailties of their wives and daughters, no friends could keep a good correspondence together for two days. This is unkind of you, brother; for among good friends, what they say or do goes for nothing.

(*Enter a Servant*)

SERVANT: Sir, here's Mrs. Diana Trapes wants to speak with you.

PEACHUM: Shall we admit her, brother Lockit?

LOCKIT: By all means—she's a good customer, and a fine-spoken woman, and a woman who drinks and talks so freely will enliven the conversation.

PEACHUM: Desire her to walk in.   (*Exit Servant*)

Scene VI   *Peachum, Lockit, Mrs. Trapes*

PEACHUM: Dear Mrs. Dye, your servant!—one may know by your kiss that your gin is excellent.

TRAPES: I was always very curious in my liquors.

LOCKIT: There is no perfumed breath like it. I have been long acquainted with the flavour of those lips—han't I, Mrs. Dye?

TRAPES: Fill it up. I take as large draughts of liquor as I did of love. I hate a flincher in either.

Air XLVI: *A shepherd kept sheep*

In the days of my youth I could bill like a dove, fa, la, la, etc.
Like a sparrow at all times was ready for love, fa, la, la, etc.
The life of all mortals in kissing should pass
Lip to lip while we're young—then the lip to the glass, fa, la, etc.

But now, Mr. Peachum, to our business. If you have blacks of any kind, brought in of late: manteaus—velvet scarfs—petticoats—let it be what it will—I am your chap—for all my ladies are very fond of mourning.

PEACHUM: Why, look ye, Mrs. Dye—you deal so hard with us, that we can afford to give the gentlemen, who venture their lives for the goods, little or nothing.

TRAPES: The hard times oblige me to go very near in my dealing. To be sure, of late years I have been a great sufferer by the parliament. Three thousand pounds would hardly make me amends. The act for destroying the Mint° was a severe cut upon our business.

Mint: Area in south London where, until 1722, debtors could stay without being prosecuted.

'Till then, if a customer stepped out of the way—we knew where to have her. No doubt you know Mrs. Coaxer—there's a wench now (till to-day) with a good suit of clothes of mine upon her back, and I could never set eyes upon her for three months together.—Since the act too against imprisonment for small sums, my loss there too hath been very considerable; and it must be so, when a lady can borrow a handsome petticoat, or a clean gown, and I not have the least hank upon her! And, o' my conscience, now-a-days most ladies take a delight in cheating, when they can do it with safety.

PEACHUM: Madam, you had a handsome gold watch of us t'other day for seven guineas. Considering we must have our profit—to a gentleman upon the road, a gold watch will be scarce worth the taking.

TRAPES: Consider, Mr. Peachum, that watch was remarkable and not of very safe sale. If you have any black velvet scarfs—they are a handsome winter wear, and take with most gentlemen who deal with my customers. 'Tis I that put the ladies upon a good foot. 'Tis not youth or beauty that fixes their price. The gentlemen always pay according to their dress, from half a crown to two guineas; and yet those hussies make nothing of bilking of me. Then, too, allowing for accidents—I have eleven fine customers now down under the surgeon's hands; what with fees and other expenses, there are great goings-out, and no comings-in, and not a farthing to pay for at least a month's clothing. We run great risks—great risks indeed.

PEACHUM: As I remember, you said something just now of Mrs. Coaxer.

TRAPES: Yes, Sir. To be sure, I stripped her of a suit of my own clothes about two hours ago, and have left her as she should be, in her shift, with a lover of hers, at my house. She called him upstairs, and he was going to Marybone in a hackney coach. And I hope, for her own sake and mine, she will persuade the captain to redeem her, for the captain is very generous to the ladies.

LOCKIT: What captain?

TRAPES: He thought I did not know him. An intimate acquaintance of yours, Mr. Peachum—only Captain Macheath—as fine as a lord.

PEACHUM: To-morrow, dear Mrs. Dye, you shall set your own price upon any of the goods you like. We have at least half a dozen velvet scarfs, and all at your service. Will you give me leave to make you a present of this suit of nightclothes for your own wearing? But are you sure it is Captain Macheath?

TRAPES: Though he thinks I have forgot him; nobody knows him better. I have taken a great deal of the captain's money in my time at second hand, for he always loved to have his ladies well dressed.

PEACHUM: Mr. Lockit and I have a little business with the captain—you understand me—and we will satisfy you for Mrs. Coaxer's debt.

LOCKIT: Depend upon it—we will deal like men of honour.

TRAPES: I don't enquire after your affairs—so whatever happens, I wash my hands on't. It hath always been my maxim, that one friend should assist another. But if you please, I'll take one of the scarfs home with me: 'tis always good to have something in hand.   (*Exeunt*)

Scene VII

Scene: *Newgate*

Lucy

LUCY: Jealousy, rage, love and fear are at once tearing me to pieces. How I am weatherbeaten and shattered with distresses!

Air XLVII: *One evening, having lost my way*

I'm like a skiff on the ocean toss'd,
    Now high, now low, with each billow borne,
With her rudder broke, and her anchor lost,
    Deserted and all forlorn.
While thus I lie rolling and tossing all night,
That Polly lies sporting on seas of delight!
    Revenge, revenge, revenge,
Shall appease my restless sprite.

I have the ratsbane ready. I run no risk, for I can lay her death upon the gin, and so many die of that naturally that I shall never be called in question. But say I were to be hanged—I never could be hanged for anything that would give me greater comfort than the poisoning that slut.

(*Enter Filch*)

FILCH: Madam, here's our Miss Polly come to wait upon you.
LUCY: Show her in.   (*Exit Filch*)

Scene VIII   *Lucy, Polly*

LUCY: Dear Madam, your servant. I hope you will pardon my passion, when I was so happy to see you last. I was so overrun with the spleen, that I was perfectly out of myself. And really, when one hath the spleen everything is to be excused by a friend.

Air XLVIII: *Now Roger, I'll tell thee, because thou'rt my son*

    When a wife's in her pout,
      (As she's sometimes, no doubt),
The good husband, as meek as a lamb,
      Her vapours to still,
      First grants her her will,
And the quieting draught is a dram.
Poor man! And the quieting draught is a dram.

—I wish all our quarrels might have so comfortable a reconciliation.
POLLY: I have no excuse for my own behaviour, Madam, but my misfortunes. And really, Madam, I suffer too upon your account.
LUCY: But, Miss Polly—in the way of friendship, will you give me leave to propose a glass of cordial to you?
POLLY: Strong waters are apt to give me the headache—I hope, Madam, you will excuse me.
LUCY: Not the greatest lady in the land could have better in her closet, for her own private drinking. You seem mighty low in spirits, my dear.
POLLY: I am sorry, Madam, my health will not allow me to accept of your offer. I should not have left you in the rude manner I did when we met last, Madam, had not my papa hauled me away so unexpectedly. I was indeed somewhat provoked, and perhaps might use some expressions that were disrespectful. But really, Madam, the captain treated me with so much contempt and cruelty that I deserved your pity, rather than your resentment.
LUCY: But since his escape no doubt all matters are made up again. Ah Polly! Polly! 'tis I am the unhappy wife, and he loves you as if you were only his mistress.
POLLY: Sure, Madam, you cannot think me so happy as to be the object of your jealousy. A man is always afraid of a woman who loves him too well—so that I must expect to be neglected and avoided.
LUCY: Then our cases, my dear Polly, are exactly alike. Both of us, indeed, have been too fond.

Air XLIX: *Oh, Bessy Bell*

POLLY: A curse attends that woman's love,
      Who always would be pleasing.
LUCY: The pertness of the billing dove,
      Like tickling, is but teasing.
POLLY: What then in love can woman do?
LUCY: If we grow fond they shun us.
POLLY: And when we fly them, they pursue.
LUCY: But leave us when they've won us.

LUCY: Love is so very whimsical in both sexes, that it is impossible to be lasting. But my heart is particular, and contradicts my own observation.
POLLY: But really, Mistress Lucy, by his last behaviour, I think I ought to envy you. When I was forced from him, he did not show the least tenderness. But perhaps he hath a heart not capable of it.

Air L: *Would fate to me Belinda give*

Among the men, coquets we find,
Who court by turns all womankind;
And we grant all their hearts desir'd,
When they are flatter'd and admir'd.

The coquets of both sexes are self-lovers, and that is a love no other whatever can dispossess. I fear, my dear Lucy, our husband is one of those.

LUCY: Away with these melancholy reflections; indeed, my dear Polly, we are both of us a cup too low. Let me prevail upon you to accept of my offer.

Air LI: *Come, sweet lass*

> Come, sweet lass,
> Let's banish sorrow
> Till to-morrow;
> Come, sweet lass,
> Let's take a chirping glass.
>   Wine can clear
>   The vapours of despair;
>   And make us light as air;
>   Then drink, and banish care.

I can't bear, child, to see you in such low spirits. And I must persuade you to what I know will do you good. (*aside*) I shall now soon be even with the hypocritical strumpet.   (*Exit Lucy*)

Scene IX   *Polly*

POLLY: All this wheedling of Lucy cannot be for nothing. At this time, too, when I know she hates me! The dissembling of a woman is always the forerunner of mischief. By pouring strong waters down my throat, she thinks to pump some secrets out of me. I'll be upon my guard, and won't taste a drop of her liquor, I'm resolved.

Scene X   *Lucy, with strong waters   Polly*

LUCY: Come, Miss Polly.

POLLY: Indeed, child, you have given yourself trouble to no purpose. You must, my dear, excuse me.

LUCY: Really, Miss Polly, you are so squeamishly affected about taking a cup of strong waters as a lady before company. I vow, Polly, I shall take it monstrously ill if you refuse me. Brandy and men (though women love them never so well) are always taken by us with some reluctance—unless 'tis in private.

POLLY: I protest, Madam, it goes against me.—What do I see! Macheath again in custody! Now every glimmering of happiness is lost. (*drops the glass of liquor on the ground*)

LUCY (*aside*): Since things are thus, I'm glad the wench hath escaped: for by this event 'tis plain she was not happy enough to deserve to be poisoned.

Scene XI   *Lockit, Macheath, Peachum, Lucy, Polly*

LOCKIT: Set your heart to rest, Captain. You have neither the chance of love or money for another escape, for you are ordered to be called down upon your trial immediately.

PEACHUM: Away, hussies! This is not a time for a man to be hampered with his wives. You see, the gentleman is in chains already.

LUCY: O husband, husband, my heart longed to see thee; but to see thee thus distracts me!

POLLY: Will not my dear husband look upon his Polly? Why hadst thou not flown to me for protection? with me thou hadst been safe.

Air LII: *The last time I went o'er the moor*

POLLY: Hither, dear husband, turn your eyes.

LUCY: Bestow one glance to cheer me.

POLLY: Think, with that look, thy Polly dies.

LUCY: Oh, shun me not—but hear me.

POLLY: 'Tis Polly sues.

LUCY: —'Tis Lucy speaks.

POLLY: Is thus true love requited?

LUCY: My heart is bursting.

POLLY: —Mine too breaks.

LUCY: Must I

POLLY: —Must I be slighted?

MACHEATH: What would you have me say, ladies? You see, this affair will soon be at an end, without my disobliging either of you.

PEACHUM: But the settling this point, Captain, might prevent a law-suit between your two widows.

Air LIII: *Tom Tinker's my true love*

MACHEATH: Which way shall I turn me? how can I decide?
>   Wives, the day of our death, are as fond as a bride.
>   One wife is too much for most husbands to hear,
>   But two at a time there's no mortal can bear.
>   This way, and that way, and which way I will,
>   What would comfort the one, t'other wife would take ill.

POLLY: But if his own misfortunes have made him insensible to mine, a father sure will be more compassionate.—Dear, dear Sir, sink the material evidence, and bring him off at his trial—Polly upon her knees begs it of you.

Air LIV: *I am a poor shepherd undone*

> When my hero in court appears,
>   And stands arraign'd for his life;
> Then think of poor Polly's tears;
>   For ah! poor Polly's his wife.
> Like the sailor he holds up his hand,
>   Distress'd on the dashing wave.
> To die a dry death at land,
>   Is as bad as a wat'ry grave.
>   And alas, poor Polly!
>   Alack, and well-a-day!
>   Before I was in love,
>   Oh! every month was May.

LUCY: If Peachum's heart is hardened, sure you, Sir, will have more compassion on a daughter. I know the evidence is in your power. How then can you be a tyrant to me? (*kneeling*)

Air LV: *Ianthe the lovely*

When he holds up his hand arraign'd for his life,
Oh think of your daughter, and think I'm his wife!
What are cannons, or bombs, or clashing of swords?
For death is more certain by witnesses' words.
Then nail up their lips; that dread thunder allay;
And each month of my life will hereafter be May.

LOCKIT: Macheath's time is come, Lucy. We know our own affairs, therefore let us have no more whimpering or whining.

Air LVI: *A cobbler there was*

Ourselves, like the great, to secure a retreat,
  When matters require it, must give up our gang.
    And good reason why,
    Or, instead of the fry,
    Ev'n Peachum and I,
Like poor petty rascals, might hang, hang;
Like poor petty rascals might hang.

PEACHUM: Set your heart at rest, Polly. Your husband is to die to-day. Therefore, if you are not already provided, 'tis high time to look about for another. There's comfort for you, you slut.

LOCKIT: We are ready, Sir, to conduct you to the Old Bailey.

Air LVII: *Bonny Dundee*

MACHEATH: The charge is prepar'd; the lawyers are met,
  The judges all rang'd (a terrible show!)
I go, undismay'd—for death is a debt,
  A debt on demand. So, take what I owe.
Then farewell, my love—dear charmers, adieu!
  Contented I die—'tis the better for you.
    Here ends all dispute the rest of our lives,
    For this way at once I please all my wives.

Now, gentlemen, I am ready to attend you.

Scene XII   *Lucy, Polly, Filch*

POLLY: Follow them, Filch, to the court. And when the trial is over, bring me a particular account of his behaviour, and of everything that happened. You'll find me here with Miss Lucy. (*Exit Filch*)
But why is all this music?

LUCY: The prisoners whose trials are put off till next session are diverting themselves.

POLLY: Sure there is nothing so charming as music! I'm fond of it to distraction! But alas! now, all mirth seems an insult upon my affliction.—Let us retire, my dear Lucy, and indulge our sorrows. The noisy crew, you see, are coming upon us. (*Exeunt*)
(*a dance of prisoners in chains, etc.*)

Scene XIII

Scene: *The condemned hold*

Macheath, in a melancholy posture

Air LVIII: *Happy groves*

O cruel, cruel, cruel case!
Must I suffer this disgrace?

Air LIX: *Of all the girls that are so smart*

Of all the friends in time of grief,
  When threat'ning death looks grimmer,
Not one so sure can bring relief,
  As this best friend, a brimmer.   (*drinks*)

Air LX: *Britons, strike home*

Since I must swing—I scorn, I scorn to wince or whine.   (*rises*)

Air LXI: *Chevy Chase*

But now again my spirits sink;
I'll raise them high with wine.
       (*drinks a glass of wine*)

Air LXII: *To old Sir Simon the King*

But valour the stronger grows,
The stronger liquor we're drinking.
And how can we feel our woes,
When we've lost the trouble of thinking?   (*drinks*)

Air LXIII: *Joy to great Cæsar*

If thus—A man can die
Much bolder with brandy.
     (*pours out a bumper of brandy*)

Air LXIV: *There was an old woman*

So I drink off this bumper.—And now I can stand the test.
And my comrades shall see that I die as brave as the best.   (*drinks*)

Air LXV: *Did you ever hear of a gallant sailor*

But can I leave my pretty hussies,
Without one tear, or tender sigh?

Air LXVI: *Why are mine eyes still flowing*

> Their eyes, their lips, their busses,
> Recall my love.—Ah, must I die!

Air LXVII: *Greensleeves*

> Since laws were made for ev'ry degree,
> To curb vice in others, as well as me,
> I wonder we han't better company,
>   Upon Tyburn tree!
> But gold from law can take out the sting;
> And if rich men like us were to swing,
> 'Twould thin the land, such numbers to string
>   Upon Tyburn tree!

(*Enter Jailor*)

JAILOR: Some friends of yours, Captain, desire to be admitted. I leave you together.   (*Exit*)

Scene XIV   *Macheath, Ben Budge, Matt of the Mint*

MACHEATH: For my having broke prison, you see, gentlemen, I am ordered immediate execution. The sheriff's officers, I believe, are now at the door. That Jemmy Twitcher should peach me, I own surprised me! 'Tis a plain proof that the world is all alike, and that even our gang can no more trust one another than other people. Therefore, I beg you, gentlemen, look well to yourselves, for in all probability you may live some months longer.

MATT: We are heartily sorry, Captain, for your misfortune. But 'tis what we must all come to.

MACHEATH: Peachum and Lockit, you know, are infamous scoundrels. Their lives are as much in your power, as yours are in theirs. Remember your dying friend!—'tis my last request. Bring those villains to the gallows before you, and I am satisfied.

MATT: We'll do't.

(*Enter Jailor*)

JAILOR: Miss Polly and Miss Lucy intreat a word with you.

MACHEATH: Gentlemen, adieu.

Scene XV   *Lucy, Macheath, Polly*

MACHEATH: My dear Lucy—my dear Polly—whatsoever hath passed between us is now at an end. If you are fond of marrying again, the best advice I can give you is to ship yourselves off for the West Indies, where you'll have a fair chance of getting a husband apiece; or by good luck, two or three, as you like best.

POLLY: How can I support this sight!

LUCY: There is nothing moves one so much as a great man in distress.

Air LXVIII: *All you that must take a leap*

LUCY:	Would I might be hanged!
POLLY:	—And I would so too!
LUCY:	To be hanged with you
POLLY:	—My dear, with you.

MACHEATH: Oh, leave me to thought! I fear! I doubt! I tremble! I droop!—See, my courage is out.
                    (*turns up the empty bottle*)

POLLY: No token of love?

MACHEATH: —See, my courage is out.
                    (*turns up the empty pot*)

LUCY: No token of love?

POLLY: —Adieu!

LUCY: —Farewell!

MACHEATH: But hark! I hear the toll of the bell!

CHORUS: Tol de rol lol, etc.

(*Re-enter Jailor*)

JAILOR: Four women more, Captain, with a child apiece! See, here they come.

(*Enter Women and Children*)

MACHEATH: What—four wives more! This is too much.—Here—tell the sheriff's officers I am ready.
                    (*Exit Macheath guarded*)

Scene XVI   *To them enter Player and Beggar*

PLAYER: But, honest friend, I hope you don't intend that Macheath shall be really executed.

BEGGAR: Most certainly, Sir. To make the piece perfect, I was for doing strict poetical justice. Macheath is to be hanged; and for the other personages of the drama, the audience must have supposed they were all either hanged or transported.

PLAYER: Why then, friend, this is a downright deep tragedy. The catastrophe is manifestly wrong, for an opera must end happily.

BEGGAR: Your objection, Sir, is very just and is easily removed. For you must allow that in this kind of drama 'tis no matter how absurdly things are brought about.—So—you rabble there—run and cry a reprieve!—let the prisoner be brought back to his wives in triumph.

PLAYER: All this we must do, to comply with the taste of the town.

BEGGAR: Through the whole piece you may observe such a similitude of manners in high and low life, that it is difficult to determine whether (in the fashionable vices) the fine gentlemen imitate the gentlemen of the road, or the gentlemen of the road the fine gentlemen. Had the play remained as I at first intended, it would have carried a most excellent moral. 'Twould have shown that the lower sort of people have their vices in a degree as well as the rich; and that they are punished for them.

Scene XVII   *To them Macheath, with rabble, etc.*

MACHEATH: So, it seems, I am not left to my choice, but must have a wife at last.—Look ye, my dears; we will have no controversy now. Let us give this day to mirth, and I am sure she who thinks herself my wife will testify her joy by a dance.

ALL: Come, a dance—a dance.

MACHEATH: Ladies, I hope you will give me leave to present a partner to each of you. And (if I may without offence) for this time, I take Polly for mine. (*to Polly*) And for life, you slut—for we were really married.—As for the rest—But at present keep your own secret.   (*a dance*)

Air LXIX: *Lumps of pudding*

Thus I stand like the Turk, with his doxies around;
From all sides their glances his passion confound:
For black, brown, and fair, his inconstancy burns,
And the different beauties subdue him by turns:
Each calls forth her charms, to provoke his desires:
Though willing to all, with but one he retires.
But think of this maxim, and put off your sorrow,
The wretch of to-day may be happy to-morrow.

CHORUS: But think of this maxim, etc.

Nineteenth-Century Drama through the Turn of the Twentieth Century

The French Revolution of 1789 and the subsequent wars of the early nineteenth century established that century as a period of dynamic and dramatic change in Europe and the Americas. Not only was a democratizing wave surging throughout the western world, but dramatic literature was becoming increasingly serious. The Romantics treated the common people with great sympathy, finding in them sincerity and naturalness, in contrast to the shallow and sometimes cruel behavior of the aristocrats who dominated the social and political landscapes of the eighteenth century. Although Romantic plays were being written and produced in France, England, and Germany even after the end of the Napoleonic Wars in 1814, they have not proved as durable as the Romantic poetry and novels of the time. Later nineteenth-century drama introduced audiences to realism with the work of Henrik Ibsen and August Strindberg, in addition to the well-made melodramas of Dion Boucicault and René Pixérécourt, which were popular in France, Ireland, England, and the United States. The revolutionary movements that continued through the "Springtime of the People"—the revolutions of 1848 in France, Germany, Switzerland, Austria, Brazil, and other nations—pointed to profound social and economic change and the emergence of a considerable new middle class.

The Nineteenth-Century Theater

Technically, theaters changed more during the period between 1800 and 1900 than in any comparable earlier period. The introduction of gas jets early in the century had a major effect. Now, light could be dimmed or raised as needed; the house could be gradually and entirely darkened. With gaslight onstage, selective lighting contributed to the emotional effect of plays and allowed actors to move deeper into the stage instead of playing important scenes on the apron. With the advent of elaborate scenery, as in the Drottningholm Theatre in Sweden, lighting devices were often placed behind the proscenium pillars and scenery so that actors were more visible when they stood within the proscenium. The changes did not take place overnight, but as new theaters were built in the early nineteenth century (and as older theaters were refurbished), the apron shrank and the front doors leading to it disappeared. That change

Figure 16. Elaborately decorated proscenium arch. Auditorium, Chicago, 1889. (Chicago History Museum, HB-31105C, photograph by Hedrich Blessing.)

reinforced the nineteenth-century practice of treating the proscenium opening as the imaginary "fourth wall" of a room. The elaborate framing of Chicago's Auditorium (1889, Figure 16) allowed for complex lighting systems and made the proscenium a "window" into the dramatic action.

Numerous other technical innovations were introduced into the new theaters, such as London's Drury Lane Theatre, which was rebuilt in 1812. Highly sophisticated machinery lifted actors from below the stage, and flies, or fly galleries, above the stage permitted scene changes and other dramatic alterations and effects. At Theatre Royal, Drury Lane (Figure 17), the remodeling changed the shape of the apron and made space for an orchestra. The actors moving forward onto the apron were not able to reach the audience, which necessitated a change in the style of acting. Histrionic gestures were still visible, but intimate expressions of disdain or hatred were not as likely to elicit a response in the audience. Music, especially in the first half of the century, was usually part of the theater experience. In the United States, various kinds of

Figure 17. Theatre Royal, Drury Lane, 1812.

entertainment might share a bill with a play, and the entire experience might last five hours or more. At times it was thought impossible to succeed with a play if there were not dances or music between the acts.

Drury Lane drew a considerable audience from among the middle classes, and the entertainment was lively and often sentimental. However, the great plays of Shakespeare were still being produced—though usually in modified form and often with happy endings, even in the tragedies. France and England naturally influenced each other throughout the century, especially in stage design. The English stage designs in turn influenced North American designs.

The Nineteenth-Century Actor

Throughout the first half of the century in the United States, English actors essentially set the standard for acting. Edmund Kean and William Charles Macready were influenced by David Garrick, whose approach aimed at a "natural" style, although by our standards Kean and Macready still employed an enlarged and overdone mode of acting. Relative to earlier ages, however, it was

Figure 18. Edwin Forrest as Macbeth.

Figure 19. William Charles Macready as Macbeth.

a realistic and emotionally true method of acting that toned down the ranting, as well as the use of broad rhetorical gestures designed to dazzle the audience. English audiences were experienced enough to no longer need the exaggerated style that had appealed to some earlier theatergoers.

American actors, such as Edwin Forrest, Ira Aldrige, and Charlotte Cushman, continued a tradition of broad rhetorical acting, with some of the gestures and exaggerations that in earlier times thrilled English audiences. The English actors believed that the American audiences were less sophisticated and thus much more susceptible to the high drama of an actor such as Forrest.

One of the strangest events in the history of theater occurred on May 10, 1849, when the styles of two actors, the American Edwin Forrest (1806–1872) and the Englishman William Charles Macready (1793–1873)—both playing the role of Macbeth—were the subject of a serious riot! Forrest's American style featured exaggerated gestures and dramatic vocal expostulations—as in Figure 18, which shows his upstage hand gesturing profoundly and his cape rustling in a powerful wind. Macready, by contrast, was typically described as intellectual, cool, and refined in his gestures (Figure 19 shows him as Macbeth in the costume of an older-generation Scots lord). Writing in his diary six years before the riot, when he and Forrest were friends, Macready said of American acting, "From what I can learn the audiences of the United States have been accustomed to exaggeration in all its forms, and have applauded what has been most extravagant; it is not, therefore, surprising that they should bestow such little applause on me, not having their accustomed cues." Of Forrest, whom he had seen as Lear, he said,

> I had a very high opinion of his powers of mind when I saw him exactly seventeen years ago; I said then, if he would cultivate those powers and really study, where, as in England, his taste could be formed, he would make one of the very first actors of this or any day. But I thought he would not do so, as his countrymen were, by their extravagant applause, possessing him with the idea and with the fact, as far as remuneration was concerned, that it was unnecessary. I reluctantly, as far as my feelings towards him are interested, record my opinion that my prophetic soul foresaw the consequence. He has great physical power. But I could discern no imagination, no original thought, no poetry at all in his acting.

The Astor Place Riot took place because Macready's restrained style was thought to be effete and foppish in comparison with Forrest's. The unruly mobs of New York, egged on by several instigators who preferred Forrest over Macready, threw paving stones, rocks, and vegetables in the audience of the Opera House and became so threatening that no one could hear the performance. The police were called in to restore order. When they failed, the National Guard was called up to control the throng of 20,000. Like the police, the Guard faltered for a time, but it eventually gathered itself and fired point blank into the mob after a warning salvo over their heads. The death toll was approximately 20, but upwards of 100 were wounded. This was not the first theater riot, but it was the most famous and the most disastrous. Although Macready never returned, he left his mark on American theater, which began to evolve a more relaxed and realistic style of acting. The generations of actors in melodrama that followed were not always as restrained as Macready, but they were usually not as enthusiastic as Forrest.

Macready is credited with having insisted on several important changes in the production of Shakespeare's plays. He restored them to their original texts—not without criticism—and he insisted on doing considerable research to guarantee the authenticity of costuming and other historical details. In addition, he changed the way actors approached a play. Previously they had memorized their lines in isolation and come to the theater as they pleased, with no special thought to the overall nature of the drama at hand. Macready insisted that the actors respect the spirit of the play and unify their styles so they would be acting in concert. This approach was, ultimately, the beginning of the modern style of acting that dominated the later half of the century.

Romantic Drama

Early-nineteenth-century English Romantic poets produced a variety of plays espousing a new philosophy of the individual, a philosophy of democracy, and a cry for personal liberation, but unfortunately their plays failed to capture the popular stage. William Wordsworth's *The Borderers* (1796–1797), concerning political struggles on the border between England and Scotland, was a failure, perhaps because of its static, declamatory nature, evident in a production at Yale University. Even a play with an inherently dramatic subject—*The Fall of Robespierre* (1794) by Robert Southey and Samuel Taylor Coleridge, concerning the violent excesses of the French Revolution of 1789—could not stir popular audiences. John Keats wrote *Otho the Great* (1819) about a tenth-century dispute between brothers and a father and son. He hoped that the great actor and producer Edmund Kean would want to produce the play, but Kean declined. Percy Bysshe Shelley wrote *The Cenci* (1819) when he was in Italy, hoping it would be produced on the English stage, but it was banned by the censors. The style of Shelley's play has been compared with that of John Webster's *The Dutchess of Malfi* (1613); its themes include violent death and insanity. George Gordon, Lord Byron, wrote several plays that had admirers but were not successful. *Manfred* (1817) is a **closet drama**—a play meant to be read, not produced. It presents a powerful portrait of a brooding intellect comparable, in some ways, to Hamlet. Allardyce Nicoll, the British drama historian and critic, has said of this and other Romantic plays that "audiences and readers familiar with *Lear* and *Macbeth* and *Othello* could not be expected to feel a thrill of wonder and delight in the contemplation of works so closely akin to these in general aim and yet so far removed from them in freshness of imaginative power."

French and German Romantic dramatists were more successful than their English counterparts. Johann Wolfgang von Goethe (1749–1832), one of Germany's most important playwrights, produced a number of successful plays in the late eighteenth century. Then came his masterpiece, *Faust* (1808, 1832), in two parts, with a scope and grandeur of concept that challenged the theaters of his day. The play opens in heaven, with Mephistopheles presenting his plan for tempting Faust; Faust signs over his soul to Mephistopheles in return for one moment of perfect joy. Faust was willing to risk all in his efforts to live life to its fullest, and despite his sins he was admired as a hero. Faust's self-analytic individualism, marked by a love of excess and a capacity for deep feeling and frightening intensity, has fascinated the German mind ever since Goethe rediscovered him. His development of Faust as a psychologically complex character contrasts with Christopher Marlowe's version in *Doctor Faustus*.

Another important force in German theater was Johann Cristoph Friedrich von Schiller (1759–1805), whose early play *The Robbers* (1781) was written when he was twenty-two. This still-popular (and still-produced) play reminds English audiences of the legend of Robin Hood, since its hero, Karl von Moor, is a robber admirable for his generosity and seriousness. His adversary is his evil brother, who dominates the castle, the emblem of local repressive political power. Schiller was a highly successful playwright throughout the late eighteenth century. In the early nineteenth century, he produced several popular historical plays, such as *Maria Stuart* (1800) on Scotland's Queen Mary, the ill-fated cousin of Queen Elizabeth I. *The Maid of Orleans* (1801) told the story of Joan of Arc, the French heroine who led her army to victory, only to be burned at the stake to satisfy political and religious exigencies. Both plays evoke deep sympathy for their heroines, and both have been noted for their sentimentality. Schiller's last play, *William Tell* (1804), like *The Robbers,* tells the story of a heroic individual's fight against the oppressive forces of an evil baron. Schiller made the story of William Tell universal, and his theatrical successes were soon known throughout Europe and the Americas.

In France, the Romantic tragedy held sway for some time in the 1830s. Victor Hugo (1802–1885) had a great success in *Hernani* (1830), although critics and writers who insisted on classical rules were so disturbed by its innovation that they caused disruptions in the theater. They attended only to jeer the pardon of Hernani, an outlaw, by Don Carlos, king of Spain. At the end, Hernani and Donna Sol, his loved one, drink a poison so as to die together because they cannot live together. Alexandre Dumas (1802–1879), soon to be famous as a novelist, produced a number of successful, influential plays, among them *Henry III and His Court* (1829) and *The Tower of Nesle* (1832).

Melodrama

Melodrama developed in Germany and France in the mid- and late eighteenth century. The *melo* in *melodrama* means "song"; incidental music was a hallmark of melodrama. In England, certain regulations separated Covent Garden, Drury Lane, and the Haymarket—the three "major" theaters with exclusive licenses to produce spoken drama—from the "minor" theaters, which had to produce musical plays such as burlettas, which resembled our comic operettas. Eventually, the minor theaters began to produce plays with spoken dialogue and accompanying music, heralding a new, popular style. Melodrama proved to be one of the most durable innovations of the late eighteenth century.

August Friedrich Ferdinand von Kotzebue (1761–1819) and Guilbert de Pixérécourt (1773–1844), who coined the term *melodrama*, began developing the melodramatic play in Germany and France, respectively. Many of these dramas used background music that altered according to the mood of the scene, a tradition that continues today in films and on television. Nineteenth-century melodramas featured familiar crises: the virtuous maiden fallen into the hands of an unscrupulous landlord; the father who, lamenting over a portrait of his dead wife, discovers that he is speaking to his—until then—lost daughter. Nineteenth-century melodramas had well-defined heroes, heroines, and villains. The plots were filled with surprises and unlikely twists designed to amaze and delight the audience. Most of the plays were explicitly sentimental, depending on a strong emotional appeal with clear-cut and relatively decisive endings.

Though not popular later on, the plays of Kotzebue and Pixérécourt pleased their contemporary audiences and helped establish melodrama as a dominant style for the first six decades of the nineteenth century. Kotzebue published thirty-six plays (twenty-two were produced) and enjoyed immense popularity in England and the United States. Translated into several languages, his works influenced later popular playwrights, who admired his ability to invent and resolve complex plot situations. The ending of *La-Peyrouse* (1798) provides a taste of the mode. The hero, cast ashore on a desert island, falls in love with the "savage" Malvina. When he rejoins his wife, Adelaide, he is presented with the problem of what to do with Malvina. Here is the women's solution:

MALVINA (*turning affectionately, yet with trembling, to Adelaide*): I have prayed for thee, and for myself—let us be sisters!

ADELAIDE: Sisters! (*She remains some moments lost in thought.*) Sisters! Sweet girl, you have awakened a consoling idea in my bosom! Yes, we will be sisters, and this man shall be our brother! Share him we cannot, nor can either possess him singly. (*With enthusiasm.*) We, the sisters, will inhabit one hut, he shall dwell in another. We will educate our children, he shall assist us both—by day we will make but one family, at night we will separate—how say you? will you consent? . . . (*Extending her arms to La-Peyrouse.*) A sisterly embrace!

In France, Pixérécourt produced a similar and highly successful drama that pleased his audiences. Not everyone was pleased, however. Goethe resigned his office in the Weimar Court Theatre when Pixérécourt's *The Dog of Montargis* was produced in 1816 because he did not want to be associated with any play that had a dog as its hero.

Not all these plays have been forgotten. Alexandre Dumas's *La Dame aux camélias* (*Camille*) was a theatrical hit in 1852 and has remained popular ever since, inspiring the Verdi opera *La Traviata* (1853) and revivals and adaptations up to the present, including the British playwright Pam Gems's feminist version (1987), starring Kathleen Turner. Based on a woman Dumas knew in Paris, it is the story of a wealthy young man who falls in love with a courtesan, Marguerite Gauthier. Like Angellica in *The Rover*, she has manipulated men throughout her life, but now she is truly in love with Armand. The young man's father opposes the match, but even he is moved by the majesty of their love. Eventually, the father faces Marguerite and convinces her that if she really loves his son, she will let him go since their union can bring nothing but harm to Armand. She then feigns contempt for Armand and dismisses him, brokenhearted. Later, after they have been separated and she has fallen deathly ill, Armand learns the truth and rushes to her. On her deathbed, Armand professes his love as she dies in his arms.

In the United States, George Aiken produced another long-lasting and influential drama, *Uncle Tom's Cabin* (1852), based on Harriet Beecher Stowe's novel. Stowe, a prominent northern abolitionist, poured all her anger at slavery into her novel. Aiken's stage version played for three hundred nights in its first production and across the nation more than a quarter of a million times. Some of its characters—Uncle Tom, Little Eva, Sambo, Topsy, and Simon Legree—live on in the popular imagination, but despite the contemporary interest in Stowe and in this play, it reflects its era through features like the paternalistic subtitle: *Life among the Lowly*.

The Well-Made Play

Early in the nineteenth century, a Frenchman with an unusual theatrical gift for pleasing popular audiences began a career that spanned fifty successful years. Eugène Scribe (1791–1861) may have produced as many as four or five hundred plays. He employed collaborators and mined novels and stories for his plots, producing tragedies, comedies, opera libretti, and one-act vaudeville pieces. He quickly determined that plot held the attention of the audience and that rambling character studies were of lesser interest. Consequently, he developed a formula for dramatic action and made sure that all his works fit into it. The result was the creation of a "factory" for making plays. Among the elements of Scribe's formula were the following:

1. A careful exposition telling the audience what the situation is, usually including one or more secrets to be revealed later.
2. Surprises, such as letters to be opened at a critical moment and identities to be revealed later.
3. Suspense that builds steadily throughout the play, usually sustained by cliff-hanging situations and characters who miss each other by way of carefully timed entrances and exits. At critical moments, characters lose important papers or misplace identifying jewelry, for instance.
4. A **climax** late in the play when the secrets are revealed and the hero confronts his antagonists and succeeds.
5. A **denouement**, the resolution of the drama, when all the loose ends are drawn together and explanations are made that render all the action plausible.

It should be evident from this description that the **well-made play** still thrives, not only on the stage but also in films and on television. Scribe's emphasis on plot was sensational for his time, and his success was unrivaled; however, none of his plays has survived in contemporary performance. Only one, *Adrienne Lecouvreur* (1849), the story of a famous actress poisoned by a rival, is mentioned by critics as interesting because of its depth of characterization. Scribe was superficial and brilliant—a winning combination in theater at the time. He had numerous imitators and prepared the way for later developments in theater.

The Rise of Realism

Technical changes in theaters during the latter part of the nineteenth century continued at a rapid pace. When limelight was added to gas, the result was bright, intense lighting onstage; in the last decades of the century, electric light heralded a new era in lighting design. Good lighting generally demanded detailed and authentic scenery; the dreamy light produced by gas often hid imperfections that were now impossible to disguise. The new Madison Square Theater (1879) in New York City was built with elevators that allowed its stage, complete with detailed and realistic scenery as well as actors, to be raised into position. European theaters had developed similar capabilities.

In the 1840s, accurate period costumes began to be the norm for historical plays. In the Elizabethan theater, contemporary clothing had been worn onstage, but by the mid-nineteenth century costume designers were researching historical periods and producing costumes that aimed at historical accuracy.

In addition to offering lifelike scenery, lighting, and costumes, the theaters of the latter part of the century also featured plays whose circumstances and language were recognizable, contemporary, and believable. Even the sentimental melodramas seemed more realistic than productions of *King Lear* or *Macbeth*, plays that were still popular. The work of Scribe, including his historical plays, used a relatively prosaic everyday language. The situations may not seem absolutely lifelike to our eyes, but in their day they prepared the way for realism.

Changes in philosophy also contributed to the development of a realistic drama. Émile Zola (1840–1902) preached a doctrine of **naturalism**, demanding that drama avoid the artificiality of convoluted plot and urging a drama of natural, lifelike action. He intended his work to help change social conditions in France. His naturalistic novel *Nana* (1880) focused on a courtesan whose life came to a terrifying end. The play *Thérèse Raquin* (1873), based on Zola's novel of the same name, told the story of a woman and her lover who murder her husband and then commit suicide out of a sense of mutual guilt. There are no twists, surprises, or even much suspense in the play. Zola's subjects seem to have been uniformly grim, and naturalism became associated with the darker side of life.

Realism, which avoided mechanical "clockwork" plots with their artificially contrived conclusions, began to be evident in drama in the later years of the eighteenth century (some scholars claim to see evidence of it even earlier, in the work of Thomas Middleton [1580–1627]) and became progressively more common as the end of the nineteenth century approached. In the realistic plays of Henrik Ibsen (1828–1906) and August Strindberg (1849–1912), the details of the setting, the costuming, and the circumstances of the action were so fully realized as to convince audiences that they were listening in on life itself. (See Figure 20 for an example of a realistic stage setting.)

Figure 20. Realistic setting in a 1941 production of Anton Chekhov's *The Cherry Orchard*.

In Britain, Oscar Wilde (1854–1900), Irish poet, novelist, and playwright, offered an alternative to both melodrama and realistic drama near the end of the century. Wilde had spent much of his literary life promoting the philosophy of art for art's sake. He asserted that the pleasure of poetry was in its sounds, images, and thoughts; poetry and drama did not serve religious, political, social, or even personal goals. For Wilde, art served itself. He was such a brilliant conversationalist that the Irish poet-playwright W. B. Yeats declared him the only person he ever heard who spoke complete, rounded sentences that sounded as if he had written and polished them the night before. His witticisms were often barbed and vicious but always incisive and perceptive. He became famous for his bright, witty comedies. *The Importance of Being Earnest* (1895), sometimes wrongly accused of being about nothing, is the most often performed of Wilde's comedies. It is an unsentimental, witty, and sometimes brittle comedy dissecting English upper-class attitudes that most of his audience would have taken for granted.

Wilde competed with numerous comic playwrights in England and abroad, such as the enormously successful Arthur Wing Pinero (1855–1934) and W. S. Gilbert (1836-1911) in England and Georges Feydeau (1862–1921) in France. None, though, could manage the unusual combination of wit and seriousness that marks Wilde's achievements. Another important competitor was Irish playwright Bernard Shaw (1856–1950), whose plays were also comic and serious, such as *Arms and the Man* (1894), *You Never Can Tell* (1898), and *Pygmalion* (1913). But Shaw is probably best known for his plays of ideas—plays in which an underlying idea or principle drives the action—such as *Mrs. Warren's Profession* (1898), *Man and Superman* (1903), and *Major Barbara* (1905).

After a disappointing beginning as a playwright, Anton Chekhov (1860–1904) worked with the Moscow Art Theatre under the directorship of Konstantin Stanislavski (1865–1938), one of the most influential figures in modern Western drama. Stanislavski emphasized "inner realism," helping the actor become the character even in situations off stage by developing improvisational experiences to let the actor explore the character in situations other than those within the play. The Stanislavski Method helped the actor *become* the part, rather than just play the part. Chekhov and Stanislavski worked together to produce Chekhov's plays at a time when Chekhov believed himself a failure as a dramatist.

The first production of Chekhov's *The Seagull* (1896), his sixth major staged play, was a failure. Stanislavski persuaded Chekhov to give it to his company to produce, resulting in an important triumph. Chekhov then reworked an earlier play into *Uncle Vanya* (1899) for Stanislavski, and it, too, was a hit. *Three Sisters* (1901) was not successful in its first performances, but it later became known as one of Chekhov's finest works. His last play, *The Cherry Orchard* (1904), was put on by Stanislavski's company and has become one of the most important works of twentieth-century drama. Chekhov died of a heart attack soon after the play's first production. Today Chekhov's legacy continues, and all his major plays are staged throughout the world. Thus, one of the most important nineteenth-century writers led the way to new developments in twentieth-century drama that are still evident today on the stage, as well as in films and on television.

Timeline   Nineteenth-Century Drama

Date	Theater	Political	Social/Cultural
1700–1800	**1759–1805:** Friedrich von Schiller, German playwright, author of *The Robbers* (1781) and *Maria Stuart* (1800)		**1770–1827:** Ludwig van Beethoven, German composer
	1761–1819: August Friedrich Ferdinand von Kotzebue, German playwright and one of the early developers of melodrama	**1775:** The American War of Independence begins at Concord, Massachusetts.	**1775–1817:** Jane Austen, English novelist
	1767–1787: *Sturm und Drang* period in German drama featuring the work of Goethe, Schiller, and others who rebelled against eighteenth-century rationalism	**1776:** The Declaration of Independence is signed. **1783:** Peace of Versailles: Britain recognizes the independence of the United States.	
	1773: The Swedish National Theatre is established in Stockholm.	**1789:** French revolutionaries storm the Bastille as the French revolution sweeps over French society.	**1792–1822:** Percy Bysshe Shelley, English Romantic poet
	1773–1844: Guilbert de Pixérécourt, French playwright generally credited with originating the melodrama	**1793:** Louis XVI and his queen, Marie Antoinette, are guillotined. The Reign of Terror, a purge instituted by the revolutionary government of France, claims 35,000 lives in one year.	**1793:** Eli Whitney (1765–1825) invents the cotton gin. **1795:** British forces occupy the Cape of Good Hope. **1795–1821:** John Keats, English Romantic poet
	1791–1861: Eugène Scribe, French playwright, developer of the well-made play, author of *Adrienne Lecouvreur* (1849)	**1799:** Napoleon Bonaparte overthrows the Directory of France, the moderate government that replaced the Reign of Terror.	**1798:** *Lyrical Ballads* is published by Wordsworth and Coleridge. **1799–1837:** Alexander Pushkin, Russian poet
	1793–1873: William Charles Macready, English actor		
1800–1900	**1806–1872:** Edwin Forrest, America's first great native-born actor	**1803:** The Louisiana Purchase doubles the area of the United States.	**1802–1885:** Victor Hugo, French novelist
		1804: Napoleon I (1769–1821) declares himself emperor of France.	**1803–1882:** Ralph Waldo Emerson, American Transcendental philosopher, clergyman, and author
	1808 and 1832: German writer Johann Wolfgang von Goethe (1749–1832) produces his masterpiece, *Faust* (in two parts).	**1805:** Admiral Horatio Nelson's victory over Napoleon at Trafalgar establishes the supremacy of British naval forces.	**1805:** Gas lighting is introduced in Great Britain.
	1809–1852: Nikolai Gogol, Russian playwright, author of *The Inspector General* (1836)		**1809–1852:** Louis Braille, French inventor of reading system for the blind
	1812: Theatre Royal, Drury Lane, is rebuilt.	**1811–1820:** The Regency period: George, Prince of Wales, acts as regent for George III, who was declared insane.	
	1813–1837: Georg Büchner, German playwright, author of *Danton's Death* (1835) and *Woyzeck* (1836)	**1812:** The United States declares war on Britain.	**1812–1870:** Charles Dickens, English novelist
	1813–1883: Richard Wagner, German composer, among whose works is the four-part *Der Ring des Nibelungen* (1853–1874)	**1814:** Treaty of Ghent ends the War of 1812; Britain is defeated.	

Date	Theater	Political	Social/Cultural
1800–1900 (continued)	**1816:** Chestnut Street Theater in Philadelphia is the first theater to illuminate its stage with gas lighting.	**1815:** Napoleon is decisively defeated at the Battle of Waterloo.	**1816–1855:** Charlotte Brontë, English novelist
	1820–1890: Dion Boucicault, Irish American actor and writer of popular melodramas, among them *The Octoroon* (1859) and *The Colleen Bawn* (1860)	**1818:** Shaka ascends the Zulu throne in Southern Africa and initiates a period of military reform; he is assassinated in 1828.	**1817–1862:** Henry David Thoreau, American Transcendental writer and naturalist
		1820: Accession of George IV	**1820–1906:** Susan B. Anthony, American leader of the women's suffrage movement
	1828–1906: Henrik Ibsen, Norwegian playwright, whose best known works include *A Doll House* (1879) and *Hedda Gabler* (1890)	**1820:** The Missouri Compromise admits Maine as a free state and Missouri as a slave state.	**1821–1881:** Fyodor Dostoevsky, Russian novelist
			1828–1910: Leo Tolstoy, Russian novelist and philosopher
	1830: *Hernani,* by the French novelist and playwright Victor Hugo (1802–1885), traditionally marks the beginning of French romanticism.	**1821:** Mexico declares its independence.	**1830–1886:** Emily Dickinson, American poet
		1823: The Monroe Doctrine closes the American continent to European colonization.	**1831:** William Lloyd Garrison (1805–1879), American abolitionist, founds the *Liberator*.
	1837: William Charles Macready (1793–1873), an English actor, is the first to use the limelight (or Drummond light), a prototype of the spotlight.	**1837:** Queen Victoria begins her sixty-four-year reign in Great Britain.	**1833–1897:** Johannes Brahms, German composer
			1839: Louis Daguerre (1789–1851) invents the daguerreotype, an early type of photograph.
	1840–1902: Émile Zola, French writer and promoter of naturalism in literature, among whose works is the novel (also a play) *Thérèse Raquin* (1873)	**1839:** The First Opium War between Britain and China begins. The war ends in 1842 with the Treaty of Nanjing, which turns over Hong Kong to Britain and opens several Chinese ports to western trade.	**1840–1893:** Peter Ilyich Tchaikovsky, Russian composer
			1843–1916: Henry James, American realist novelist
			1844: The telegraph is used for the first time.
			1845: Frederick Douglass (c. 1817–1895), African American abolitionist, publishes *Narrative of the Life of Frederick Douglass*.
			1845–1849: The great potato famine in Ireland kills nearly a million Irish; 1,600,000 immigrate to the United States.
	1849: The Astor Place Riot in New York is a result of the rivalry between the actors William Charles Macready and Edwin Forrest; twenty-two people are killed.	**1846–1848:** Mexican War over the United States' annexation of Texas. The Treaty of Guadalupe Hidalgo (1848) cedes Texas to the United States.	**1848:** The First U.S. Women's Rights Convention is held in Seneca Falls, New York.
			1848: California gold rush
	1849–1923: Sarah Bernhardt, French performer, perhaps the greatest actress of the nineteenth century		**1848:** Karl Marx, German political philosopher, writes *The Communist Manifesto* with Friedrich Engels.
			1850: Tennyson succeeds Wordsworth as poet laureate of Great Britain.
	1849–1912: August Strindberg, Swedish playwright, among whose works are *Miss Julie* (1888) and *A Dream Play* (1902)		**1851:** Herman Melville (1819–1891) publishes *Moby Dick*.
		1852: Napoleon III declares himself emperor of France and rules until 1871.	**1852:** Harriet Beecher Stowe (1811–1896) publishes *Uncle Tom's Cabin*.

Timeline Nineteenth-Century Drama (continued)

Date	Theater	Political	Social/Cultural
1800–1900 (continued)	**1854–1900:** Oscar Wilde, Irish writer, whose plays include *A Woman of No Importance* (1893) and *The Importance of Being Earnest* (1895)	**1857:** Czar Alexander II begins emancipation of serfs in Russia.	**1854–1856:** Scottish explorer David Livingstone crosses Africa.
	1856–1950: Bernard Shaw, Irish playwright, among whose works are *Mrs. Warren's Profession* (1898), *Major Barbara* (1905), and *Pygmalion* (1913)	**1860:** Abraham Lincoln is elected president. South Carolina secedes from the Union.	**1859:** Charles Darwin (1809–1882) publishes *On the Origin of Species by Natural Selection.*
	1860–1904: Anton Chekhov, Russian writer, author of *The Seagull* (1896) and *The Cherry Orchard* (1903)	**1861:** Italy is unified under Victor Emmanuel II. **1861–1865:** The Civil War is fought in the United States.	**1860s:** Louis Pasteur (1822–1895), French chemist, develops pasteurization.
	1870–1900: Golden Age of Peking (Beijing) Opera	**1862:** Otto von Bismarck is appointed prime minister of Prussia.	**1865–1939:** William Butler Yeats, Irish poet and playwright
	1871–1896: Gilbert and Sullivan write their comic operas, among them *H.M.S. Pinafore* (1878) and *The Pirates of Penzance* (1879).	**1865:** Abraham Lincoln is assassinated by the actor John Wilkes Booth at Ford's Theatre in Washington, D.C. **1869:** The Suez Canal opens.	**1869:** The first transcontinental railroad in the United States is completed.
	1876: Opening of Richard Wagner's Festival Theatre in Bayreuth, Germany	**1870–1871:** Franco-Prussian War	**1869–1959:** Frank Lloyd Wright, preeminent American architect
	1881: The Savoy Theatre is the first theater in London to be completely illuminated by electric light.	**1871:** The German Empire is founded under Kaiser Wilhelm I.	**1876:** Alexander Graham Bell (1847–1922) invents the telephone.
	1887: Théâtre Libre is founded in Paris by André Antoine to pursue naturalism in subject matter and staging.	**1876:** At the Battle of the Little Bighorn, the Sioux defeat General George Custer's troops.	**1877:** Thomas Edison (1847–1931) invents the phonograph.
	1890–1930: Vaudeville becomes one of the most popular forms of entertainment in the United States.	**1885:** The Congo becomes a personal possession of King Leopold II of Belgium.	**1879:** Thomas Edison invents the lightbulb.
	1896: The first revolving stage is installed by Karl Lautenschlager at the Residenz Theater in Munich.	**1890:** The Battle of Wounded Knee ends the American Indians' wars of resistance; two hundred Indians are killed by the U.S. Army.	
	1898: The Moscow Art Theatre is founded under the direction of Konstantin Stanislavski and Vladimir Nemirovich-Danchenko.	**1898:** The Spanish-American War. Cuban patriots demand independence and receive the military support of the United States. The 1898 Treaty of Paris gives Puerto Rico, Guam, the Philippines, and Cuba to the United States.	**1898–1976:** Paul Robeson, African American singer, actor, and civil rights activist
		1899–1902: The Boer War (South African War) ends British supremacy in South Africa.	

Henrik Ibsen

Using the new style of realism, Henrik Ibsen (1828–1906) slowly and despite many setbacks became the most influential modern dramatist. Subjects that had been ignored on the stage became the center of his work. But his rise to fame was anything but direct. His family was extremely poor, and as a youth he worked in a drugstore in Grimstad, a seaport town in Norway. At seventeen he had an illegitimate child with a servant girl. At twenty-one he wrote his first play, in verse. In 1850, at the age of twenty-two, he left Grimstad for Oslo (then called Christiana) to become a student, but within a year he joined the new National Theatre, where he stayed for six years, writing and directing.

In the 1850s, Ibsen wrote numerous plays that did not bring him recognition: *St. John's Eve* (1853), *Lady Inger of Østraat* (1855), *Olaf Liljekrans* (1857), and *The Vikings at Helgeland* (1857). In the early 1860s, with a wife and daughter to support, he went through a period of serious self-doubt and despair, which was not improved when his first play in five years, *Love's*

Henrik Ibsen at age sixty-eight, seventeen years after the first production of *A Doll House*. He was the most influential playwright in Europe when this photograph was taken in 1896.

Comedy (1862), was turned down for performance. Eventually he got a job with the Christiana Theatre and had a rare success with *The Pretenders* (1864), a historical play about thirteenth-century warriors vying for the vacant throne of Norway.

Ibsen's breakthrough came with the publication in 1866 of the verse play *Brand,* which was written to be read, not performed. (It was first produced in 1885.) It is the portrait of a clergyman who takes the strictures of religion so seriously that he rejects the New Testament doctrine of love and accepts the Old Testament doctrine of the will of God. He destroys himself in the process and ends the play on a mountaintop in the Ice Church, facing an avalanche about to kill him. Out of the clouds comes the answer to his question of whether love or will achieves salvation: "He is the God of Love." *Brand* made Ibsen famous. He followed it with another successful closet drama, *Peer Gynt* (1867), about a character, quite unlike Brand, who avoids the rigors of morality and ends up uncertain whether he has been saved or condemned.

Despite these successes, Ibsen still struggled for recognition. It was not until 1877 that he had his first success in a play that experimented with the new realistic style of drama: *The Pillars of Society,* which probed behind the hypocrisies of Karsten Bernick, a merchant who prospers by all manner of double-dealing and betrayal of his relatives. Eventually, he admits his crimes and, instead of being punished, is welcomed back into society and is more successful than ever. This play gave Ibsen a reputation in Germany, where it was frequently performed, and prepared him for his great successes. *A Doll House* (1879), which he wrote in Italy, came two years later. It was more fully realistic in style than *The Pillars of Society* and, though immensely successful in Scandinavia, did not become widely known elsewhere for another ten years.

Ibsen's next play, *Ghosts* (1881), was denounced violently because it dared to treat a subject that had been taboo on the stage: syphilis. *Ghosts* introduced a respectable family, the Alvings, who harbor the secret that their late father contracted the disease and passed it on to Oswald, his son. In addition, the theme of incest is suggested in the presence of Alving's illegitimate daughter, Regina, who falls in love with Oswald. This kind of material was so foreign to the late-nineteenth-century stage that Ibsen was vilified and isolated by the literary community in Norway. He chose exile for a time in Rome, Amalfi, and Munich.

Ibsen's last years were filled with activity. He wrote some of his best known plays in rapid succession: *An Enemy of the People* (1882), *The Wild Duck* (1884), *Hedda Gabler* (1890), *The Master Builder* (1892), and *John Gabriel Borkman* (1896). In 1891, he returned to live in Norway, where he died fifteen years later.

The most influential European dramatist in the late nineteenth century, Ibsen inspired emerging writers in the United States, Ireland, and many other nations. But his full influence was not felt until the early decades of the twentieth century, when other writers were able to spread the revolutionary doctrine that was implied in realism as practiced by Ibsen and Strindberg. Being direct, honest, and unsparing in treating character and theme became the normal mode of serious drama after Ibsen.

For links to resources about Ibsen, click on *AuthorLinks* at **bedfordstmartins.com/jacobus.**

A Doll House

Once Henrik Ibsen found his voice as a realist playwright, he began to develop plays centering on social problems and the problems of the individual struggling against the demands of society. In *A Doll House* (1879), he focused on the repression of women—a subject that deeply offended conservatives and was very much on the minds of progressive and liberal Scandinavians. It was therefore a rather daring theme. The play opens with the dutiful, eager wife Nora Helmer twittering like a lark and pattering about like a squirrel, pleasing her husband, Torvald. Helmer is obsessed with propriety. As far as he is concerned, Nora is only a woman, an empty-headed ornament in a house designed to keep his life functioning smoothly.

Nora is portrayed as a macaroon-eating, sweet-toothed creature looking for ways to please her husband. When she reveals that she borrowed the money that took them to Italy for a year to save her husband's life, she shows us that she is made of much stronger stuff than anyone has given her credit for. Yet the manner in which she borrowed the money is technically criminal because she had to forge her father's signature, and she now finds herself at the mercy of the lender, Nils Krogstad.

From a modern perspective, Nora's action seems daring and imaginative rather than merely illegal and surreptitious. Torvald Helmer's moralistic position is to us essentially stifling. He condemns people for their crimes without considering their circumstances or motives. He is moralistic rather than moral.

For this 1906 production of Ibsen's *The Wild Duck,* the director, André Antoine, had the set constructed of Norwegian pine to achieve a high degree of realism.

Edvard Munch's 1906 stage design for Max Reinhardt's production of Ibsen's *Ghosts* at the Kammerspiele in Berlin. Although *Ghosts* (1881) was written in Ibsen's realistic style, Munch's expressionistic lines and shadows seem to reflect the tendency in Ibsen's late plays to move beyond realism to a more dreamlike structure.

The atmosphere of the Helmer household is oppressive. Everything is set up to amuse Torvald, and he lacks any awareness that other people might be his equals. Early in the play, Ibsen establishes Nora's longings: she explains that to pay back her loan she had to take in copying work, and, rather than resenting her labor, she observes that it made her feel wonderful, the way a man must feel. Ibsen said that his intention in the play was not primarily to promote the emancipation of women; it was to establish, as Ibsen's biographer Michael Meyer says, "that the primary duty of anyone was to find out who he or she really was and to become that person."

However, the play from the first was seen as addressing the problems of women, especially married women who were treated as their husbands' property. When the play was first performed, the slam of the door at Nora's leaving was much louder than it is today. It was shocking to late-nineteenth-century society, which took Torvald Helmer's attitudes for granted. The first audiences probably were split in their opinions about Nora's actions. As Meyer reminds us, "No play had ever before contributed so momentously to the social debate, or been so widely and furiously discussed among people who were not normally interested in theatrical or even artistic matters." Although the critics in Copenhagen (where the play was first produced) and London were very negative, the audiences were filled with curiosity and flocked to the theaters to see the play.

What the audiences saw was that once Nora is awakened, the kind of life Torvald imagines for her is death to Nora. Torvald cannot see how his self-absorbed concern and fear for his own social standing reveal his limitations and selfishness. Nora sees immediately the limits of his concern, and her only choice is to leave him so that she can grow morally and spiritually.

What she does and where she goes have been a matter of speculation since the play was first performed. Ibsen refused to encourage any specific conjecture. It is enough that she has the courage to leave. But the ending of the play bothered audiences as well as critics, and it was performed in Germany in 1880 with a revised ending that Ibsen himself wrote to forestall anyone else's doing so. Hedwig Niemann-Raabe, the first German actress to play the part, insisted that she would personally never leave her children and therefore would not do the play as written. In the revised version, instead of leaving, Nora is led to the door of her children's room and falls weeping as the curtain goes down. This so-called happy-ending version was played for a while in England and elsewhere. No one was satisfied with this ending, and eventually the play reverted to its original form.

Through the proscenium arch of the theater in Ibsen's day audiences were permitted to eavesdrop on themselves, since Ibsen clearly was analyzing their own mores. In a way the audience was looking at a dollhouse, but instead of containing miniature furniture and miniature people, it contained replicas of those watching. That very sense of intimacy, made possible by the late-nineteenth-century theater, heightened the intensity of the play.

A Doll House in Performance

A Doll House was first produced in the Royal Theatre, Copenhagen, in December 1879. Despite its immediate popular success in Scandinavia and Germany, two years passed before the play appeared elsewhere and ten years before it appeared in England and the United States in a complete and accurate text. An adaptation (also with the happy ending) titled *The Child Wife* was produced in Milwaukee in 1882. The first professional London production of the play in 1889 found favor with the public, but it was attacked in the press for being "unnatural, immoral and, in its concluding scene, essentially undramatic." Among other things, Ibsen was condemned for not providing a vibrant plot.

Among the play's memorable performances was Ethel Barrymore's version in New York in 1905. Barrymore was praised for a brilliant interpretation of "the child wife." Ruth Gordon played the part to acclaim in 1937, as did Claire Bloom in 1971 on the stage and in 1973 in film. Jane Fonda played the role in Joseph Losey's film version of 1973. The Norwegian actress Liv Ullmann performed the role in Lincoln Center in 1975 and was praised as "the most enchanting," the "most honest" Nora that the critic Walter Kerr had seen. Other critics were less kind, but it was a successful run. One of the most riveting of modern productions was Anthony Page's revival of *A Doll House*, starring Janet McTeer. This production began in London in 1997 and transferred to New York for a Broadway run the same year. Ben Brantley of the *New York Times* said of it, "Nothing can prepare you for the initial shock of Ms. McTeer's performance, which transforms the passive Nora Helmer, Ibsen's child-like plaything of a wife, into an electric, even aggressive presence" revealing "previously hidden nuances in Ibsen's landmark work." This production was faithful to the production values of Ibsen's original, using an essentially Victorian-era setting with period costumes. McTeer's energy transformed the play and gave Nora a new dimension that made the audience believe that she would do better than merely survive when she left her home. Lee Breuer's

For discussion questions and assignments on *A Doll House,* visit **bedfordstmartins.com/jacobus.**

2005 production of *Mabou Mines Dollhouse* set the stage as a dollhouse and used actresses who were six feet tall and actors who were five feet tall and shorter. The effect on the audience was to emphasize the power relationships between men and women. Controversy followed the Mabou Mines troupe tour, but it also awakened audiences to some of the underlying forces of the play. The play is performed regularly in college and regional theaters in the United States and elsewhere.

HENRIK IBSEN (1828–1906)

A Doll House 1879

TRANSLATED BY ROLF FJELDE

The Characters

TORVALD HELMER, *a lawyer*
NORA, *his wife*
DR. RANK
MRS. LINDE
NILS KROGSTAD, *a bank clerk*
THE HELMERS' THREE SMALL CHILDREN
ANNE-MARIE, *their nurse*
HELENE, *a maid*
A DELIVERY BOY

The action takes place in Helmer's residence.

ACT I

(*A comfortable room, tastefully but not expensively furnished. A door to the right in the back wall leads to the entryway; another to the left leads to Helmer's study. Between these doors, a piano. Midway in the left-hand wall a door, and further back a window. Near the window a round table with an armchair and a small sofa. In the right-hand wall, toward the rear, a door, and nearer the foreground a porcelain stove with two armchairs and a rocking chair beside it. Between the stove and the side door, a small table. Engravings*

Note: As Fjelde explains in his foreword to the translation, he does not use the possessive "A Doll's House" because "the house is not Nora's, as the possessive implies." Fjelde believes that Ibsen includes Torvald with Nora in the original title, "for the two of them at the play's opening are still posing like the little marzipan bride and groom atop the wedding cake."

on the walls. An étagère° with china figures and other small art objects; a small bookcase with richly bound books; the floor carpeted; a fire burning in the stove. It is a winter day.)

(*A bell rings in the entryway; shortly after we hear the door being unlocked. Nora comes into the room, humming happily to herself; she is wearing street clothes and carries an armload of packages, which she puts down on the table to the right. She has left the hall door open, and through it a Delivery Boy is seen holding a Christmas tree and a basket, which he gives to the Maid who let them in.*)

NORA: Hide the tree well, Helene. The children mustn't get a glimpse of it till this evening, after it's trimmed. (*To the Delivery Boy, taking out her purse.*) How much?

DELIVERY BOY: Fifty, ma'am.

NORA: There's a crown. No, keep the change. (*The Boy thanks her and leaves. Nora shuts the door. She laughs softly to herself while taking off her street things. Drawing a bag of macaroons from her pocket, she eats a couple, then steals over and listens at her husband's study door.*) Yes, he's home. (*Hums again as she moves to the table right.*)

HELMER (*from the study*): Is that my little lark twittering out there?

NORA (*busy opening some packages*): Yes, it is.

HELMER: Is that my squirrel rummaging around?

NORA: Yes!

HELMER: When did my squirrel get in?

NORA: Just now. (*Putting the macaroon bag in her pocket and wiping her mouth.*) Do come in, Torvald, and see what I've bought.

[S.D.] **étagère:** Cabinet with shelves.

HELMER: Can't be disturbed. (*After a moment he opens the door and peers in, pen in hand.*) Bought, you say? All that there? Has the little spendthrift been out throwing money around again?

NORA: Oh, but Torvald, this year we really should let ourselves go a bit. It's the first Christmas we haven't had to economize.

HELMER: But you know we can't go squandering.

NORA: Oh yes, Torvald, we can squander a little now. Can't we? Just a tiny, wee bit. Now that you've got a big salary and are going to make piles and piles of money.

HELMER: Yes—starting New Year's. But then it's a full three months till the raise comes through.

NORA: Pooh! We can borrow that long.

HELMER: Nora! (*Goes over and playfully takes her by the ear.*) Are your scatterbrains off again? What if today I borrowed a thousand crowns, and you squandered them over Christmas week, and then on New Year's Eve a roof tile fell on my head, and I lay there—

NORA (*putting her hand on his mouth*): Oh! Don't say such things!

HELMER: Yes, but what if it happened—then what?

NORA: If anything so awful happened, then it just wouldn't matter if I had debts or not.

HELMER: Well, but the people I'd borrowed from?

NORA: Them? Who cares about them! They're strangers.

HELMER: Nora, Nora, how like a woman! No, but seriously, Nora, you know what I think about that. No debts! Never borrow! Something of freedom's lost—and something of beauty, too—from a home that's founded on borrowing and debt. We've made a brave stand up to now, the two of us; and we'll go right on like that the little while we have to.

NORA (*going toward the stove*): Yes, whatever you say, Torvald.

HELMER (*following her*): Now, now, the little lark's wings mustn't droop. Come on, don't be a sulky squirrel. (*Taking out his wallet.*) Nora, guess what I have here.

NORA (*turning quickly*): Money!

HELMER: There, see. (*Hands her some notes.*) Good grief, I know how costs go up in a house at Christmastime.

NORA: Ten—twenty—thirty—forty. Oh, thank you, Torvald; I can manage no end on this.

HELMER: You really will have to.

NORA: Oh yes, I promise I will! But come here so I can show you everything I bought. And so cheap! Look, new clothes for Ivar here—and a sword. Here a horse and a trumpet for Bob. And a doll and a doll's bed here for Emmy; they're nothing much, but she'll tear them to bits in no time anyway. And here I have dress material and handkerchiefs for the maids. Old Anne-Marie really deserves something more.

HELMER: And what's in that package there?

NORA (*with a cry*): Torvald, no! You can't see that till tonight!

HELMER: I see. But tell me now, you little prodigal, what have you thought of for yourself?

NORA: For myself? Oh, I don't want anything at all.

HELMER: Of course you do. Tell me just what—within reason—you'd most like to have.

NORA: I honestly don't know. Oh, listen, Torvald—

HELMER: Well?

NORA (*fumbling at his coat buttons, without looking at him*): If you want to give me something, then maybe you could—you could—

HELMER: Come on, out with it.

NORA (*hurriedly*): You could give me money, Torvald. No more than you think you can spare; then one of these days I'll buy something with it.

HELMER: But Nora—

NORA: Oh, please, Torvald darling, do that! I beg you, please. Then I could hang the bills in pretty gilt paper on the Christmas tree. Wouldn't that be fun?

HELMER: What are those little birds called that always fly through their fortunes?

NORA: Oh yes, spendthrifts; I know all that. But let's do as I say, Torvald; then I'll have time to decide what I really need most. That's very sensible, isn't it?

HELMER (*smiling*): Yes, very—that is, if you actually hung onto the money I give you, and you actually used it to buy yourself something. But it goes for the house and for all sorts of foolish things, and then I only have to lay out some more.

NORA: Oh, but Torvald—

HELMER: Don't deny it, my dear little Nora. (*Putting his arm around her waist.*) Spendthrifts are sweet, but they use up a frightful amount of money. It's incredible what it costs a man to feed such birds.

NORA: Oh, how can you say that! Really, I save everything I can.

HELMER (*laughing*): Yes, that's the truth. Everything you can. But that's nothing at all.

NORA (*humming, with a smile of quiet satisfaction*): Hm, if you only knew what expenses we larks and squirrels have, Torvald.

HELMER: You're an odd little one. Exactly the way your father was. You're never at a loss for scaring up money; but the moment you have it, it runs right out through your fingers; you never know what you've done with it. Well, one takes you as you are. It's deep in your blood. Yes, these things are hereditary, Nora.

NORA: Ah, I could wish I'd inherited many of Papa's qualities.

HELMER: And I couldn't wish you anything but just what you are, my sweet little lark. But wait; it seems to me you have a very—what should I call it?—a very suspicious look today—

NORA: I do?

HELMER: You certainly do. Look me straight in the eye.

NORA (*looking at him*): Well?

HELMER (*shaking an admonitory finger*): Surely my sweet tooth hasn't been running riot in town today, has she?

NORA: No. Why do you imagine that?

HELMER: My sweet tooth really didn't make a little detour through the confectioner's?

NORA: No, I assure you, Torvald—

HELMER: Hasn't nibbled some pastry?

NORA: No, not at all.

HELMER: Not even munched a macaroon or two?

NORA: No, Torvald, I assure you, really—

HELMER: There, there now. Of course I'm only joking.

NORA (*going to the table, right*): You know I could never
think of going against you.

HELMER: No, I understand that; and you *have* given me
your word. (*Going over to her.*) Well, you keep your
little Christmas secrets to yourself, Nora darling. I
expect they'll come to light this evening, when the
tree is lit.

NORA: Did you remember to ask Dr. Rank?

HELMER: No. But there's no need for that, it's assumed
he'll be dining with us. All the same, I'll ask him when
he stops by here this morning. I've ordered some fine
wine. Nora, you can't imagine how I'm looking forward to this evening.

NORA: So am I. And what fun for the children, Torvald!

HELMER: Ah, it's so gratifying to know that one's gotten
a safe, secure job, and with a comfortable salary. It's
a great satisfaction, isn't it?

NORA: Oh, it's wonderful!

HELMER: Remember last Christmas? Three whole weeks
before, you shut yourself in every evening till long after midnight, making flowers for the Christmas tree,
and all the other decorations to surprise us. Ugh, that
was the dullest time I've ever lived through.

NORA: It wasn't at all dull for me.

HELMER (*smiling*): But the outcome *was* pretty sorry,
Nora.

NORA: Oh, don't tease me with that again. How could
I help it that the cat came in and tore everything to
shreds.

HELMER: No, poor thing, you certainly couldn't. You
wanted so much to please us all, and that's what
counts. But it's just as well that the hard times are
past.

NORA: Yes, it's really wonderful.

HELMER: Now I don't have to sit here alone, boring myself, and you don't have to tire your precious eyes
and your fair little delicate hands—

NORA (*clapping her hands*): No, is it really true, Torvald,
I don't have to? Oh, how wonderfully lovely to
hear! (*Taking his arm.*) Now I'll tell you just how
I've thought we should plan things. Right after
Christmas—(*The doorbell rings.*) Oh, the bell.
(*Straightening the room up a bit.*) Somebody would
have to come. What a bore!

HELMER: I'm not at home to visitors, don't forget.

MAID (*from the hall doorway*): Ma'am, a lady to see
you—

NORA: All right, let her come in.

MAID (*to Helmer*): And the doctor's just come too.

HELMER: Did he go right to my study?

MAID: Yes, he did.

(*Helmer goes into his room. The Maid shows in
Mrs. Linde, dressed in traveling clothes, and shuts the
door after her.*)

MRS. LINDE (*in a dispirited and somewhat hesitant voice*):
Hello, Nora.

NORA (*uncertain*): Hello—

MRS. LINDE: You don't recognize me.

NORA: No, I don't know—but wait, I think—
(*Exclaiming.*) What! Kristine! Is it really you?

MRS. LINDE: Yes, it's me.

NORA: Kristine! To think I didn't recognize you. But then,
how could I? (*More quietly.*) How you've changed,
Kristine!

MRS. LINDE: Yes, no doubt I have. In nine—ten long
years.

NORA: Is it so long since we met? Yes, it's all of that. Oh,
these last eight years have been a happy time, believe
me. And so now you've come in to town, too. Made
the long trip in the winter. That took courage.

MRS. LINDE: I just got here by ship this morning.

NORA: To enjoy yourself over Christmas, of course.
Oh, how lovely! Yes, enjoy ourselves, we'll do
that. But take your coat off. You're not still cold?
(*Helping her.*) There now, let's get cozy here by the
stove. No, the easy chair there! I'll take the rocker
here. (*Seizing her hands.*) Yes, now you have your
old look again; it was only in that first moment.
You're a bit more pale, Kristine—and maybe a bit
thinner.

MRS. LINDE: And much, much older, Nora.

NORA: Yes, perhaps a bit older; a tiny, tiny bit; not much
at all. (*Stopping short; suddenly serious.*) Oh, but
thoughtless me, to sit here, chattering away. Sweet,
good Kristine, can you forgive me?

MRS. LINDE: What do you mean, Nora?

NORA (*softly*): Poor Kristine, you've become a widow.

MRS. LINDE: Yes, three years ago.

NORA: Oh, I knew it, of course; I read it in the papers.
Oh, Kristine, you must believe me; I often thought of
writing you then, but I kept postponing it, and something always interfered.

MRS. LINDE: Nora dear, I understand completely.

NORA: No, it was awful of me, Kristine. You poor thing,
how much you must have gone through. And he left
you nothing?

MRS. LINDE: No.

NORA: And no children?

MRS. LINDE: No.

NORA: Nothing at all, then?

MRS. LINDE: Not even a sense of loss to feed on.

NORA (*looking incredulously at her*): But Kristine, how
could that be?

MRS. LINDE (*smiling wearily and smoothing her hair*):
Oh, sometimes it happens, Nora.

NORA: So completely alone. How terribly hard that must
be for you. I have three lovely children. You can't see
them now; they're out with the maid. But now you
must tell me everything—

MRS. LINDE: No, no, no, tell me about yourself.

NORA: No, you begin. Today I don't want to be selfish. I want to think only of you today. But there is something I must tell you. Did you hear of the wonderful luck we had recently?

MRS. LINDE: No, what's that?

NORA: My husband's been made manager in the bank, just think!

MRS. LINDE: Your husband? How marvelous!

NORA: Isn't it? Being a lawyer is such an uncertain living, you know, especially if one won't touch any cases that aren't clean and decent. And of course Torvald would never do that, and I'm with him completely there. Oh, we're simply delighted, believe me! He'll join the bank right after New Year's and start getting a huge salary and lots of commissions. From now on we can live quite differently—just as we want. Oh, Kristine, I feel so light and happy! Won't it be lovely to have stacks of money and not a care in the world?

MRS. LINDE: Well, anyway, it would be lovely to have enough for necessities.

NORA: No, not just for necessities, but stacks and stacks of money!

MRS. LINDE (*smiling*): Nora, Nora, aren't you sensible yet? Back in school you were such a free spender.

NORA (*with a quiet laugh*): Yes, that's what Torvald still says. (*Shaking her finger.*) But "Nora, Nora" isn't as silly as you all think. Really, we've been in no position for me to go squandering. We've had to work, both of us.

MRS. LINDE: You too?

NORA: Yes, at odd jobs—needlework, crocheting, embroidery, and such—(*casually*) and other things too. You remember that Torvald left the department when we were married? There was no chance of promotion in his office, and of course he needed to earn more money. But that first year he drove himself terribly. He took on all kinds of extra work that kept him going morning and night. It wore him down, and then he fell deathly ill. The doctors said it was essential for him to travel south.

MRS. LINDE: Yes, didn't you spend a whole year in Italy?

NORA: That's right. It wasn't easy to get away, you know. Ivar had just been born. But of course we had to go. Oh, that was a beautiful trip, and it saved Torvald's life. But it cost a frightful sum, Kristine.

MRS. LINDE: I can well imagine.

NORA: Four thousand, eight hundred crowns it cost. That's really a lot of money.

MRS. LINDE: But it's lucky you had it when you needed it.

NORA: Well, as it was, we got it from Papa.

MRS. LINDE: I see. It was just about the time your father died.

NORA: Yes, just about then. And, you know, I couldn't make that trip out to nurse him. I had to stay here, expecting Ivar any moment, and with my poor sick Torvald to care for. Dearest Papa, I never saw him

again, Kristine. Oh, that was the worst time I've known in all my marriage.

MRS. LINDE: I know how you loved him. And then you went off to Italy?

NORA: Yes. We had the means now, and the doctors urged us. So we left a month after.

MRS. LINDE: And your husband came back completely cured?

NORA: Sound as a drum!

MRS. LINDE: But—the doctor?

NORA: Who?

MRS. LINDE: I thought the maid said he was a doctor, the man who came in with me.

NORA: Yes, that was Dr. Rank—but he's not making a sick call. He's our closest friend, and he stops by at least once a day. No, Torvald hasn't had a sick moment since, and the children are fit and strong, and I am, too. (*Jumping up and clapping her hands.*) Oh, dear God, Kristine, what a lovely thing to live and be happy! But how disgusting of me—I'm talking of nothing but my own affairs. (*Sits on a stool close by Kristine, arms resting across her knees.*) Oh, don't be angry with me! Tell me, is it really true that you weren't in love with your husband? Why did you marry him, then?

MRS. LINDE: My mother was still alive, but bedridden and helpless—and I had my two younger brothers to look after. In all conscience, I didn't think I could turn him down.

NORA: No, you were right there. But was he rich at the time?

MRS. LINDE: He was very well off, I'd say. But the business was shaky, Nora. When he died, it all fell apart, and nothing was left.

NORA: And then—?

MRS. LINDE: Yes, so I had to scrape up a living with a little shop and a little teaching and whatever else I could find. The last three years have been like one endless workday without a rest for me. Now, it's over, Nora. My poor mother doesn't need me, for she's passed on. Nor the boys, either; they're working now and can take care of themselves.

NORA: How free you must feel—

MRS. LINDE: No—only unspeakably empty. Nothing to live for now. (*Standing up anxiously.*) That's why I couldn't take it any longer out in that desolate hole. Maybe here it'll be easier to find something to do and keep my mind occupied. If I could only be lucky enough to get a steady job, some office work—

NORA: Oh, but Kristine, that's so dreadfully tiring, and you already look so tired. It would be much better for you if you could go off to a bathing resort.

MRS. LINDE (*going toward the window*): I have no father to give me travel money, Nora.

NORA (*rising*): Oh, don't be angry with me.

MRS. LINDE (*going to her*): Nora dear, don't you be angry with me. The worst of my kind of situation is all the bitterness that's stored away. No one to work for, and yet you're always having to snap up your opportunities. You have to live; and so you grow self-ish. When you told me the happy change in your lot, do you know I was delighted less for your sakes than for mine?

NORA: How so? Oh, I see. You think maybe Torvald could do something for you.

MRS. LINDE: Yes, that's what I thought.

NORA: And he will, Kristine! Just leave it to me; I'll bring it up so delicately—find something attractive to humor him with. Oh, I'm so eager to help you.

MRS. LINDE: How very kind of you, Nora, to be so concerned over me—doubly kind, considering you really know so little of life's burdens yourself.

NORA: I—? I know so little—?

MRS. LINDE (*smiling*): Well, my heavens—a little needle-work and such—Nora, you're just a child.

NORA (*tossing her head and pacing the floor*): You don't have to act so superior.

MRS. LINDE: Oh?

NORA: You're just like the others. You all think I'm incapable of anything serious—

MRS. LINDE: Come now—

NORA: That I've never had to face the raw world.

MRS. LINDE: Nora dear, you've just been telling me all your troubles.

NORA: Hm! Trivial! (*Quietly.*) I haven't told you the big thing.

MRS. LINDE: Big thing? What do you mean?

NORA: You look down on me so, Kristine, but you shouldn't. You're proud that you worked so long and hard for your mother.

MRS. LINDE: I don't look down on a soul. But it is true: I'm proud—and happy, too—to think it was given to me to make my mother's last days almost free of care.

NORA: And you're also proud thinking of what you've done for your brothers.

MRS. LINDE: I feel I've a right to be.

NORA: I agree. But listen to this, Kristine—I've also got something to be proud and happy for.

MRS. LINDE: I don't doubt it. But whatever do you mean?

NORA: Not so loud. What if Torvald heard! He mustn't, not for anything in the world. Nobody must know, Kristine. No one but you.

MRS. LINDE: But what is it, then?

NORA: Come here. (*Drawing her down beside her on the sofa.*) It's true—I've also got something to be proud and happy for. I'm the one who saved Torvald's life.

MRS. LINDE: Saved—? Saved how?

NORA: I told you about the trip to Italy. Torvald never would have lived if he hadn't gone south—

MRS. LINDE: Of course; your father gave you the means—

NORA (*smiling*): That's what Torvald and all the rest think, but—

MRS. LINDE: But—?

NORA: Papa didn't give us a pin. I was the one who raised the money.

MRS. LINDE: You? That whole amount?

NORA: Four thousand, eight hundred crowns. What do you say to that?

MRS. LINDE: But Nora, how was it possible? Did you win the lottery?

NORA (*disdainfully*): The lottery? Pooh! No art to that.

MRS. LINDE: But where did you get it from then?

NORA (*humming, with a mysterious smile*): Hmm, tra-la-la-la.

MRS. LINDE: Because you couldn't have borrowed it.

NORA: No? Why not?

MRS. LINDE: A wife can't borrow without her husband's consent.

NORA (*tossing her head*): Oh, but a wife with a little business sense, a wife who knows how to manage—

MRS. LINDE: Nora, I simply don't understand—

NORA: You don't have to. Whoever said I *borrowed* the money? I could have gotten it other ways. (*Throwing herself back on the sofa.*) I could have gotten it from some admirer or other. After all, a girl with my ravishing appeal—

MRS. LINDE: You lunatic.

NORA: I'll bet you're eaten up with curiosity, Kristine.

MRS. LINDE: Now listen here, Nora—you haven't done something indiscreet?

NORA (*sitting up again*): Is it indiscreet to save your husband's life?

MRS. LINDE: I think it's indiscreet that without his knowledge you—

NORA: But that's the point: He mustn't know! My Lord, can't you understand? He mustn't ever know the close call he had. It was to *me* the doctors came to say his life was in danger—that nothing could save him but a stay in the south. Didn't I try strategy then! I began talking about how lovely it would be for me to travel abroad like other young wives; I begged and I cried; I told him please to remember my condition, to be kind and indulge me; and then I dropped a hint that he could easily take out a loan. But at that, Kristine, he nearly exploded. He said I was frivolous, and it was his duty as man of the house not to indulge me in whims and fancies—as I think he called them. Aha, I thought, now you'll just have to be saved—and that's when I saw my chance.

MRS. LINDE: And your father never told Torvald the money wasn't from him?

NORA: No, never. Papa died right about then. I'd considered bringing him into my secret and begging him never to tell. But he was too sick at the time—and then, sadly, it didn't matter.

MRS. LINDE: And you've never confided in your husband since?

NORA: For heaven's sake, no! Are you serious? He's so strict on that subject. Besides—Torvald, with all his masculine pride—how painfully humiliating for him if he ever found out he was in debt to me. That would just ruin our relationship. Our beautiful, happy home would never be the same.

MRS. LINDE: Won't you ever tell him?

NORA (*thoughtfully, half smiling*): Yes—maybe sometime years from now, when I'm no longer so attractive. Don't laugh! I only mean when Torvald loves me less than now, when he stops enjoying my dancing and dressing up and reciting for him. Then it might be wise to have something in reserve—(*Breaking off.*) How ridiculous! That'll never happen—Well, Kristine, what do you think of my big secret? I'm capable of something too, hm? You can imagine, of course, how this thing hangs over me. It really hasn't been easy meeting the payments on time. In the business world there's what they call quarterly interest and what they call amortization, and these are always so terribly hard to manage. I've had to skimp a little here and there, wherever I could, you know. I could hardly spare anything from my house allowance, because Torvald has to live well. I couldn't let the children go poorly dressed; whatever I got for them, I felt I had to use up completely—the darlings!

MRS. LINDE: Poor Nora, so it had to come out of your own budget, then?

NORA: Yes, of course. But I was the one most responsible, too. Every time Torvald gave me money for new clothes and such, I never used more than half; always bought the simplest, cheapest outfits. It was a godsend that everything looks so well on me that Torvald never noticed. But it did weigh me down at times, Kristine. It *is* such a joy to wear fine things. You understand.

MRS. LINDE: Oh, of course.

NORA: And then I found other ways of making money. Last winter I was lucky enough to get a lot of copying to do. I locked myself in and sat writing every evening till late in the night. Ah, I was tired so often, dead tired. But still it was wonderful fun, sitting and working like that, earning money. It was almost like being a man.

MRS. LINDE: But how much have you paid off this way so far?

NORA: That's hard to say, exactly. These accounts, you know, aren't easy to figure. I only know that I've paid out all I could scrape together. Time and again I haven't known where to turn. (*Smiling.*) Then I'd sit here dreaming of a rich old gentleman who had fallen in love with me—

MRS. LINDE: What! Who is he?

NORA: Oh, really! And that he'd died, and when his will was opened, there in big letters it said, "All my fortune shall be paid over in cash, immediately, to that enchanting Mrs. Nora Helmer."

MRS. LINDE: But Nora dear—who *was* this gentleman?

NORA: Good grief, can't you understand? The old man never existed; that was only something I'd dream up time and again whenever I was at my wits' end for money. But it makes no difference now; the old fossil can go where he pleases for all I care; I don't need him or his will—because now I'm free. (*Jumping up.*) Oh, how lovely to think of that, Kristine! Carefree! To know you're carefree, utterly carefree; to be

able to romp and play with the children, and to keep up a beautiful, charming home—everything just the way Torvald likes it! And think, spring is coming, with big blue skies. Maybe we can travel a little then. Maybe I'll see the ocean again. Oh yes, it *is* so marvelous to live and be happy!

(*The front doorbell rings.*)

MRS. LINDE (*rising*): There's the bell. It's probably best that I go.

NORA: No, stay. No one's expected. It must be for Torvald.

MAID (*from the hall doorway*): Excuse me, ma'am—there's a gentleman here to see Mr. Helmer, but I didn't know—since the doctor's with him—

NORA: Who is the gentleman?

KROGSTAD (*from the doorway*): It's me, Mrs. Helmer.

(*Mrs. Linde starts and turns away toward the window.*)

NORA (*stepping toward him, tense, her voice a whisper*): You? What is it? Why do you want to speak to my husband?

KROGSTAD: Bank business—after a fashion. I have a small job in the investment bank, and I hear now your husband is going to be our chief—

NORA: In other words, it's—

KROGSTAD: Just dry business, Mrs. Helmer. Nothing but that.

NORA: Yes, then please be good enough to step into the study. (*She nods indifferently as she sees him out by the hall door, then returns and begins stirring up the stove.*)

MRS. LINDE: Nora—who was that man?

NORA: That was a Mr. Krogstad—a lawyer.

MRS. LINDE: Then it really was him.

NORA: Do you know that person?

MRS. LINDE: I did once—many years ago. For a time he was a law clerk in our town.

NORA: Yes, he's been that.

MRS. LINDE: How he's changed.

NORA: I understand he had a very unhappy marriage.

MRS. LINDE: He's a widower now.

NORA: With a number of children. There now, it's burning. (*She closes the stove door and moves the rocker a bit to one side.*)

MRS. LINDE: They say he has a hand in all kinds of business.

NORA: Oh? That may be true; I wouldn't know. But let's not think about business. It's so dull.

(*Dr. Rank enters from Helmer's study.*)

RANK (*still in the doorway*): No, no, really—I don't want to intrude, I'd just as soon talk a little while with your wife. (*Shuts the door, then notices Mrs. Linde.*) Oh, beg pardon. I'm intruding here too.

NORA: No, not at all. (*Introducing him.*) Dr. Rank, Mrs. Linde.

RANK: Well now, that's a name much heard in this house. I believe I passed the lady on the stairs as I came.

MRS. LINDE: Yes, I take the stairs very slowly. They're rather hard on me.

RANK: Uh-hm, some touch of internal weakness?

MRS. LINDE: More overexertion, I'd say.

RANK: Nothing else? Then you're probably here in town to rest up in a round of parties?

MRS. LINDE: I'm here to look for work.

RANK: Is that the best cure for overexertion?

MRS. LINDE: One has to live, Doctor.

RANK: Yes, there's a common prejudice to that effect.

NORA: Oh, come on, Dr. Rank—you really do want to live yourself.

RANK: Yes, I really do. Wretched as I am, I'll gladly prolong my torment indefinitely. All my patients feel like that. And it's quite the same, too, with the morally sick. Right at this moment there's one of those moral invalids in there with Helmer—

MRS. LINDE (*softly*): Ah!

NORA: Who do you mean?

RANK: Oh, it's a lawyer, Krogstad, a type you wouldn't know. His character is rotten to the root—but even he began chattering all-importantly about how he had to live.

NORA: Oh? What did he want to talk to Torvald about?

RANK: I really don't know. I only heard something about the bank.

NORA: I didn't know that Krog—that this man Krogstad had anything to do with the bank.

RANK: Yes, he's gotten some kind of berth down there. (*To Mrs. Linde.*) I don't know if you also have, in your neck of the woods, a type of person who scuttles about breathlessly, sniffing out hints of moral corruption, and then maneuvers his victim into some sort of key position where he can keep an eye on him. It's the healthy these days that are out in the cold.

MRS. LINDE: All the same, it's the sick who most need to be taken in.

RANK (*with a shrug*): Yes, there we have it. That's the concept that's turning society into a sanatorium.

(*Nora, lost in her thoughts, breaks out into quiet laughter and claps her hands.*)

RANK: Why do you laugh at that? Do you have any real idea of what society is?

NORA: What do I care about dreary old society? I was laughing at something quite different—something terribly funny. Tell me, Doctor—is everyone who works in the bank dependent now on Torvald?

RANK: Is that what you find so terribly funny?

NORA (*smiling and humming*): Never mind, never mind! (*Pacing the floor.*) Yes, that's really immensely amusing: that we—that Torvald has so much power now over all those people. (*Taking the bag out of her pocket.*) Dr. Rank, a little macaroon on that?

RANK: See here, macaroons! I thought they were contraband here.

NORA: Yes, but these are some that Kristine gave me.

MRS. LINDE: What? I—?

NORA: Now, now, don't be afraid. You couldn't possibly know that Torvald had forbidden them. You see, he's worried they'll ruin my teeth. But hmp! Just this once! Isn't that so, Dr. Rank? Help yourself! (*Puts a macaroon in his mouth.*) And you too, Kristine. And I'll also have one, only a little one—or two, at the most. (*Walking about again.*) Now I'm really tremendously happy. Now there's just one last thing in the world that I have an enormous desire to do.

RANK: Well! And what's that?

NORA: It's something I have such a consuming desire to say so Torvald could hear.

RANK: And why can't you say it?

NORA: I don't dare. It's quite shocking.

MRS. LINDE: Shocking?

RANK: Well, then it isn't advisable. But in front of us you certainly can. What do you have such a desire to say so Torvald could hear?

NORA: I have such a huge desire to say—to hell and be damned!

RANK: Are you crazy?

MRS. LINDE: My goodness, Nora!

RANK: Go on, say it. Here he is.

NORA (*hiding the macaroon bag*): Shh, shh, shh!

(*Helmer comes in from his study, hat in hand, overcoat over his arm.*)

NORA (*going toward him*): Well, Torvald dear, are you through with him?

HELMER: Yes, he just left.

NORA: Let me introduce you—this is Kristine, who's arrived here in town.

HELMER: Kristine—? I'm sorry, but I don't know—

NORA: Mrs. Linde, Torvald dear. Mrs. Kristine Linde.

HELMER: Of course. A childhood friend of my wife's, no doubt?

MRS. LINDE: Yes, we knew each other in those days.

NORA: And just think, she made the long trip down here in order to talk with you.

HELMER: What's this?

MRS. LINDE: Well, not exactly—

NORA: You see, Kristine is remarkably clever in office work, and so she's terribly eager to come under a capable man's supervision and add more to what she already knows—

HELMER: Very wise, Mrs. Linde.

NORA: And then when she heard that you'd become a bank manager—the story was wired out to the papers—then she came in as fast as she could and—Really, Torvald, for my sake you can do a little something for Kristine, can't you?

HELMER: Yes, it's not at all impossible. Mrs. Linde, I suppose you're a widow?

MRS. LINDE: Yes.

HELMER: Any experience in office work?

MRS. LINDE: Yes, a good deal.

HELMER: Well, it's quite likely that I can make an opening for you—

NORA (*clapping her hands*): You see, you see!

HELMER: You've come at a lucky moment, Mrs. Linde.

MRS. LINDE: Oh, how can I thank you?

HELMER: Not necessary. (*Putting his overcoat on.*) But today you'll have to excuse me—

RANK: Wait, I'll go with you. (*He fetches his coat from the hall and warms it at the stove.*)

NORA: Don't stay out long, dear.

HELMER: An hour; no more.

NORA: Are you going too, Kristine?

MRS. LINDE (*putting on her winter garments*): Yes, I have to see about a room now.

HELMER: Then perhaps we can all walk together.

NORA (*helping her*): What a shame we're so cramped here, but it's quite impossible for us to—

MRS. LINDE: Oh, don't even think of it! Good-bye, Nora dear, and thanks for everything.

NORA: Good-bye for now. Of course you'll be back this evening. And you too, Dr. Rank. What? If you're well enough? Oh, you've got to be! Wrap up tight now.

(*In a ripple of small talk the company moves out into the hall; children's voices are heard outside on the steps.*)

NORA: There they are! There they are! (*She runs to open the door. The children come in with their nurse, Anne-Marie.*) Come in, come in! (*Bends down and kisses them.*) Oh, you darlings—! Look at them, Kristine. Aren't they lovely!

RANK: No loitering in the draft here.

HELMER: Come, Mrs. Linde—this place is unbearable now for anyone but mothers.

(*Dr. Rank, Helmer, and Mrs. Linde go down the stairs. Anne-Marie goes into the living room with the children. Nora follows, after closing the hall door.*)

NORA: How fresh and strong you look. Oh, such red cheeks you have! Like apples and roses. (*The children interrupt her throughout the following.*) And it was so much fun? That's wonderful. Really? You pulled both Emmy and Bob on the sled? Imagine, all together! Yes, you're a clever boy, Ivar. Oh, let me hold her a bit, Anne-Marie. My sweet little doll baby! (*Takes the smallest from the nurse and dances with her.*) Yes, yes, Mama will dance with Bob as well. What? Did you throw snowballs? Oh, if I'd only been there! No, don't bother, Anne-Marie—I'll undress them myself. Oh yes, let me. It's such fun. Go in and rest; you look half frozen. There's hot coffee waiting for you on the stove. (*The nurse goes into the room to the left. Nora takes the children's winter things off, throwing them about, while the children talk to her all at once.*) Is that so? A big dog chased you? But it didn't bite? No, dogs never bite little, lovely doll babies. Don't peek in the packages, Ivar! What is it? Yes, wouldn't you like to know. No, no, it's an ugly something. Well? Shall we play? What shall we play? Hide-and-seek? Yes, let's play hide-and-seek. Bob must hide first. I must? Yes, let me hide first. (*Laughing and shouting, she and the children play in and out of the living room and*

the adjoining room to the right. At last Nora hides under the table. The children come storming in, search, but cannot find her, then hear her muffled laughter, dash over to the table, lift the cloth up and find her. Wild shouting. She creeps forward as if to scare them. More shouts. Meanwhile, a knock at the hall door; no one has noticed it. Now the door half opens, and Krogstad appears. He waits a moment; the game goes on.*)

KROGSTAD: Beg pardon, Mrs. Helmer—

NORA (*with a strangled cry, turning and scrambling to her knees*): Oh! What do you want?

KROGSTAD: Excuse me. The outer door was ajar; it must be someone forgot to shut it—

NORA (*rising*): My husband isn't home, Mr. Krogstad.

KROGSTAD: I know that.

NORA: Yes—then what do you want here?

KROGSTAD: A word with you.

NORA: With—? (*To the children, quietly.*) Go in to Anne-Marie. What? No, the strange man won't hurt Mama. When he's gone, we'll play some more. (*She leads the children into the room to the left and shuts the door after them. Then, tense and nervous:*) You want to speak to me?

KROGSTAD: Yes, I want to.

NORA: Today? But it's not yet the first of the month—

KROGSTAD: No, it's Christmas Eve. It's going to be up to you how merry a Christmas you have.

NORA: What is it you want? Today I absolutely can't—

KROGSTAD: We won't talk about that till later. This is something else. You do have a moment to spare, I suppose?

NORA: Oh yes, of course—I do, except—

KROGSTAD: Good. I was sitting over at Olsen's Restaurant when I saw your husband go down the street—

NORA: Yes?

KROGSTAD: With a lady.

NORA: Yes. So?

KROGSTAD: If you'll pardon my asking: Wasn't that lady a Mrs. Linde?

NORA: Yes.

KROGSTAD: Just now come into town?

NORA: Yes, today.

KROGSTAD: She's a good friend of yours?

NORA: Yes, she is. But I don't see—

KROGSTAD: I also knew her once.

NORA: I'm aware of that.

KROGSTAD: Oh? You know all about it. I thought so. Well, then let me ask you short and sweet: Is Mrs. Linde getting a job in the bank?

NORA: What makes you think you can cross-examine me, Mr. Krogstad—you, one of my husband's employees? But since you ask, you might as well know—yes, Mrs. Linde's going to be taken on at the bank. And I'm the one who spoke for her, Mr. Krogstad. Now you know.

KROGSTAD: So I guessed right.

NORA (*pacing up and down*): Oh, one does have a tiny bit of influence, I should hope. Just because I am a woman, don't think it means that—When one has a subordinate position, Mr. Krogstad, one really ought to be careful about pushing somebody who—hm—

KROGSTAD: Who has influence?

NORA: That's right.

KROGSTAD (*in a different tone*): Mrs. Helmer, would you be good enough to use your influence on my behalf?

NORA: What? What do you mean?

KROGSTAD: Would you please make sure that I keep my subordinate position in the bank?

NORA: What does that mean? Who's thinking of taking away your position?

KROGSTAD: Oh, don't play the innocent with me. I'm quite aware that your friend would hardly relish the chance of running into me again; and I'm also aware now whom I can thank for being turned out.

NORA: But I promise you—

KROGSTAD: Yes, yes, yes, to the point: There's still time, and I'm advising you to use your influence to prevent it.

NORA: But Mr. Krogstad, I have absolutely no influence.

KROGSTAD: You haven't? I thought you were just saying—

NORA: You shouldn't take me so literally. I! How can you believe that I have any such influence over my husband?

KROGSTAD: Oh, I've known your husband from our student days. I don't think the great bank manager's more steadfast than any other married man.

NORA: You speak insolently about my husband, and I'll show you the door.

KROGSTAD: The lady has spirit.

NORA: I'm not afraid of you any longer. After New Year's, I'll soon be done with the whole business.

KROGSTAD (*restraining himself*): Now listen to me, Mrs. Helmer. If necessary, I'll fight for my little job in the bank as if it were life itself.

NORA: Yes, so it seems.

KROGSTAD: It's not just a matter of income; that's the least of it. It's something else—All right, out with it! Look, this is the thing. You know, just like all the others, of course, that once, a good many years ago, I did something rather rash.

NORA: I've heard rumors to that effect.

KROGSTAD: The case never got into court; but all the same, every door was closed in my face from then on. So I took up those various activities you know about. I had to grab hold somewhere; and I dare say I haven't been among the worst. But now I want to drop all that. My boys are growing up. For their sakes, I'll have to win back as much respect as possible here in town. That job in the bank was like the first rung in my ladder. And now your husband wants to kick me right back down in the mud again.

NORA: But for heaven's sake, Mr. Krogstad, it's simply not in my power to help you.

KROGSTAD: That's because you haven't the will to—but I have the means to make you.

NORA: You certainly won't tell my husband that I owe you money?

KROGSTAD: Hm—what if I told him that?

NORA: That would be shameful of you. (*Nearly in tears.*) This secret—my joy and my pride—that he should learn it in such a crude and disgusting way—learn it from you. You'd expose me to the most horrible unpleasantness—

KROGSTAD: Only unpleasantness?

NORA (*vehemently*): But go on and try. It'll turn out the worse for you, because then my husband will really see what a crook you are, and then you'll never be able to hold your job.

KROGSTAD: I asked if it was just domestic unpleasantness you were afraid of?

NORA: If my husband finds out, then of course he'll pay what I owe at once, and then we'd be through with you for good.

KROGSTAD (*a step closer*): Listen, Mrs. Helmer—you've either got a very bad memory, or else no head at all for business. I'd better put you a little more in touch with the facts.

NORA: What do you mean?

KROGSTAD: When your husband was sick, you came to me for a loan of four thousand, eight hundred crowns.

NORA: Where else could I go?

KROGSTAD: I promised to get you that sum—

NORA: And you got it.

KROGSTAD: I promised to get you that sum, on certain conditions. You were so involved in your husband's illness, and so eager to finance your trip, that I guess you didn't think out all the details. It might just be a good idea to remind you. I promised you the money on the strength of a note I drew up.

NORA: Yes, and that I signed.

KROGSTAD: Right. But at the bottom I added some lines for your father to guarantee the loan. He was supposed to sign down there.

NORA: Supposed to? He did sign.

KROGSTAD: I left the date blank. In other words, your father would have dated his signature himself. Do you remember that?

NORA: Yes, I think—

KROGSTAD: Then I gave you the note for you to mail to your father. Isn't that so?

NORA: Yes.

KROGSTAD: And naturally you sent it at once—because only some five, six days later you brought me the note, properly signed. And with that, the money was yours.

NORA: Well, then; I've made my payments regularly, haven't I?

KROGSTAD: More or less. But—getting back to the point—those were hard times for you then, Mrs. Helmer.

NORA: Yes, they were.

KROGSTAD: Your father was very ill, I believe.

NORA: He was near the end.

KROGSTAD: He died soon after?

NORA: Yes.

KROGSTAD: Tell me, Mrs. Helmer, do you happen to recall the date of your father's death? The day of the month, I mean.

NORA: Papa died the twenty-ninth of September.

KROGSTAD: That's quite correct; I've already looked into that. And now we come to a curious thing—(*taking out a paper*) which I simply cannot comprehend.

NORA: Curious thing? I don't know—

KROGSTAD: This is the curious thing: that your father co-signed the note for your loan three days after his death.

NORA: How—? I don't understand.

KROGSTAD: Your father died the twenty-ninth of September. But look. Here your father dated his signature October second. Isn't that curious, Mrs. Helmer? (*Nora is silent.*) Can you explain it to me? (*Nora remains silent.*) It's also remarkable that the words "October second" and the year aren't written in your father's hand, but rather in one that I think I know. Well, it's easy to understand. Your father forgot perhaps to date his signature, and then someone or other added it, a bit sloppily, before anyone knew of his death. There's nothing wrong in that. It all comes down to the signature. And there's no question about *that*, Mrs. Helmer. It really *was* your father who signed his own name here, wasn't it?

NORA (*after a short silence, throwing her head back and looking squarely at him*): No, it wasn't. *I* signed Papa's name.

KROGSTAD: Wait, now—are you fully aware that this is a dangerous confession?

NORA: Why? You'll soon get your money.

KROGSTAD: Let me ask you a question—why didn't you send the paper to your father?

NORA: That was impossible. Papa was so sick. If I'd asked him for his signature, I also would have had to tell him what the money was for. But I couldn't tell him, sick as he was, that my husband's life was in danger. That was just impossible.

KROGSTAD: Then it would have been better if you'd given up the trip abroad.

NORA: I couldn't possibly. The trip was to save my husband's life. I couldn't give that up.

KROGSTAD: But didn't you ever consider that this was a fraud against me?

NORA: I couldn't let myself be bothered by that. You weren't any concern of mine. I couldn't stand you, with all those cold complications you made, even though you knew how badly off my husband was.

KROGSTAD: Mrs. Helmer, obviously you haven't the vaguest idea of what you've involved yourself in. But I can tell you this: It was nothing more and nothing worse that I once did—and it wrecked my whole reputation.

NORA: You? Do you expect me to believe that you ever acted bravely to save your wife's life?

KROGSTAD: Laws don't inquire into motives.

NORA: Then they must be very poor laws.

KROGSTAD: Poor or not—if I introduce this paper in court, you'll be judged according to law.

NORA: This I refuse to believe. A daughter hasn't a right to protect her dying father from anxiety and care? A wife hasn't a right to save her husband's life? I don't

Krogstad (Robert Gerringer) explains the seriousness of her actions to Nora.

know much about laws, but I'm sure that somewhere in the books these things are allowed. And you don't know anything about it—you who practice the law? You must be an awful lawyer, Mr. Krogstad.

KROGSTAD: Could be. But business—the kind of business we two are mixed up in—don't you think I know about that? All right. Do what you want now. But I'm telling you *this:* If I get shoved down a second time, you're going to keep me company. (*He bows and goes out through the hall.*)

NORA (*pensive for a moment, then tossing her head*): Oh, really! Trying to frighten me! I'm not so silly as all that. (*Begins gathering up the children's clothes, but soon stops.*) But—? No, but that's impossible! I did it out of love.

THE CHILDREN (*in the doorway, left*): Mama, that strange man's gone out the door.

NORA: Yes, yes, I know it. But don't tell anyone about the strange man. Do you hear? Not even Papa!

THE CHILDREN: No, Mama. But now will you play again?

NORA: No, not now.

Nora (Claire Bloom) is troubled as Helmer (Donald Madden) kisses her in Patrick Garland's 1971 production.

THE CHILDREN: Oh, but Mama, you promised.

NORA: Yes, but I can't now. Go inside; I have too much to do. Go in, go in, my sweet darlings. (*She herds them gently back in the room and shuts the door after them. Settling on the sofa, she takes up a piece of embroidery and makes some stitches, but soon stops abruptly.*) No! (*Throws the work aside, rises, goes to the hall door and calls out.*) Helene! Let me have the tree in here. (*Goes to the table, left, opens the table drawer, and stops again.*) No, but that's utterly impossible!

MAID (*with the Christmas tree*): Where should I put it, ma'am?

NORA: There. The middle of the floor.

MAID: Should I bring anything else?

NORA: No, thanks. I have what I need.

(*The Maid, who has set the tree down, goes out.*)

NORA (*absorbed in trimming the tree*): Candles here— and flowers here. That terrible creature! Talk, talk, talk! There's nothing to it at all. The tree's going to

be lovely. I'll do anything to please you Torvald. I'll sing for you, dance for you—

(*Helmer comes in from the hall, with a sheaf of papers under his arm.*)

NORA: Oh! You're back so soon?

HELMER: Yes. Has anyone been here?

NORA: Here? No.

HELMER: That's odd. I saw Krogstad leaving the front door.

NORA: So? Oh yes, that's true. Krogstad was here a moment.

HELMER: Nora, I can see by your face that he's been here, begging you to put in a good word for him.

NORA: Yes.

HELMER: And it was supposed to seem like your own idea? You were to hide it from me that he'd been here. He asked you that, too, didn't he?

NORA: Yes, Torvald, but—

HELMER: Nora, Nora, and you could fall for that? Talk with that sort of person and promise him anything? And then in the bargain, tell me an untruth.

NORA: An untruth—?

HELMER: Didn't you say that no one had been here? (*Wagging his finger.*) My little songbird must never do that again. A songbird needs a clean beak to warble with. No false notes. (*Putting his arm about her waist.*) That's the way it should be, isn't it? Yes, I'm sure of it. (*Releasing her.*) And so, enough of that. (*Sitting by the stove.*) Ah, how snug and cozy it is here. (*Leafing among his papers.*)

NORA (*busy with the tree, after a short pause*): Torvald!

HELMER: Yes.

NORA: I'm so much looking forward to the Stenborgs' costume party, day after tomorrow.

HELMER: And I can't wait to see what you'll surprise me with.

NORA: Oh, that stupid business!

HELMER: What?

NORA: I can't find anything that's right. Everything seems so ridiculous, so inane.

HELMER: So my little Nora's come to *that* recognition?

NORA (*going behind his chair, her arms resting on its back*): Are you very busy, Torvald?

HELMER: Oh—

NORA: What papers are those?

HELMER: Bank matters.

NORA: Already?

HELMER: I've gotten full authority from the retiring management to make all necessary changes in personnel and procedure. I'll need Christmas week for that. I want to have everything in order by New Year's.

NORA: So that was the reason this poor Krogstad—

HELMER: Hm.

NORA (*still leaning on the chair and slowly stroking the nape of his neck*): If you weren't so very busy, I would have asked you an enormous favor, Torvald.

HELMER: Let's hear. What is it?

NORA: You know, there isn't anyone who has your good taste—and I want so much to look well at the costume party. Torvald, couldn't you take over and decide what I should be and plan my costume?

HELMER: Ah, is my stubborn little creature calling for a lifeguard?

NORA: Yes, Torvald, I can't get anywhere without your help.

HELMER: All right—I'll think it over. We'll hit on something.

NORA: Oh, how sweet of you. (*Goes to the tree again. Pause.*) Aren't the red flowers pretty—? But tell me, was it really such a crime that this Krogstad committed?

HELMER: Forgery. Do you have any idea what that means?

NORA: Couldn't he have done it out of need?

HELMER: Yes, or thoughtlessness, like so many others. I'm not so heartless that I'd condemn a man categorically for just one mistake.

NORA: No, of course not, Torvald!

HELMER: Plenty of men have redeemed themselves by openly confessing their crimes and taking their punishment.

NORA: Punishment—?

HELMER: But now Krogstad didn't go that way. He got himself out by sharp practices, and that's the real cause of his moral breakdown.

NORA: Do you really think that would—?

HELMER: Just imagine how a man with that sort of guilt in him has to lie and cheat and deceive on all sides, has to wear a mask even with the nearest and dearest he has, even with his own wife and children. And with the children, Nora—that's where it's most horrible.

NORA: Why?

HELMER: Because that kind of atmosphere of lies infects the whole life of a home. Every breath the children take in is filled with the germs of something degenerate.

NORA (*coming closer behind him*): Are you sure of that?

HELMER: Oh, I've seen it often enough as a lawyer. Almost everyone who goes bad early in life has a mother who's a chronic liar.

NORA: Why just—the mother?

HELMER: It's usually the mother's influence that's dominant, but the father's works in the same way, of course. Every lawyer is quite familiar with it. And still this Krogstad's been going home year in, year out, poisoning his own children with lies and pretense; that's why I call him morally lost. (*Reaching his hands out toward her.*) So my sweet little Nora must promise me never to plead his cause. Your hand on it. Come, come, what's this? Give me your hand. There, now. All settled. I can tell you it'd be impossible for me to work alongside of him. I literally feel physically revolted when I'm anywhere near such a person.

NORA (*withdraws her hand and goes to the other side of the Christmas tree*): How hot it is here! And I've got so much to do.

The *Mabou Mines Dollhouse*, a 2005 interpretation of Ibsen's play by Lee Breuer and the Mabou Mines troupe, paired female actors at least six feet tall with male actors five feet tall or shorter.

HELMER (*getting up and gathering his papers*): Yes, and I have to think about getting some of these read through before dinner. I'll think about your costume, too. And something to hang on the tree in gilt paper, I may even see about that. (*Putting his hand on her head.*) Oh you, my darling little songbird. (*He goes into his study and closes the door after him.*)

NORA (*softly, after a silence*): Oh, really! It isn't so. It's impossible. It must be impossible.

ANNE-MARIE (*in the doorway left*): The children are begging so hard to come in to Mama.

NORA: No, no, no, don't let them in to me! You stay with them, Anne-Marie.

ANNE-MARIE: Of course, ma'am. (*Closes the door.*)

NORA (*pale with terror*): Hurt my children—! Poison my home? (*A moment's pause; then she tosses her head.*) That's not true. Never. Never in all the world.

ACT II

(*Same room. Beside the piano the Christmas tree now stands stripped of ornament, burned-down candle stubs on its ragged branches. Nora's street clothes lie on the sofa. Nora, alone in the room, moves restlessly about; at last she stops at the sofa and picks up her coat.*)

NORA (*dropping the coat again*): Someone's coming! (*Goes toward the door, listens.*) No—there's no one. Of course—nobody's coming today, Christmas Day—or tomorrow, either. But maybe—(*Opens the door and looks out.*) No, nothing in the mailbox. Quite empty. (*Coming forward.*) What nonsense! He won't do anything serious. Nothing terrible could happen. It's impossible. Why, I have three small children.

(*Anne-Marie, with a large carton, comes in from the room to the left.*)

ANNE-MARIE: Well, at last I found the box with the masquerade clothes.

NORA: Thanks. Put it on the table.

ANNE-MARIE (*does so*): But they're all pretty much of a mess.

NORA: Ahh! I'd love to rip them in a million pieces!

ANNE-MARIE: Oh, mercy, they can be fixed right up. Just a little patience.

NORA: Yes, I'll go get Mrs. Linde to help me.

ANNE-MARIE: Out again now? In this nasty weather? Miss Nora will catch cold—get sick.

NORA: Oh, worse things could happen—How are the children?

ANNE-MARIE: The poor mites are playing with their Christmas presents, but—

NORA: Do they ask for me much?

ANNE-MARIE: They're so used to having Mama around, you know.

NORA: Yes, but Anne-Marie, I *can't* be together with them as much as I was.

ANNE-MARIE: Well, small children get used to anything.

NORA: You think so? Do you think they'd forget their mother if she was gone for good?

ANNE-MARIE: Oh, mercy—gone for good!

NORA: Wait, tell me. Anne-Marie—I've wondered so often—how could you ever have the heart to give your child over to strangers?

ANNE-MARIE: But I had to, you know, to become little Nora's nurse.

NORA: Yes, but how could you *do* it?

ANNE-MARIE: When I could get such a good place? A girl who's poor and who's gotten in trouble is glad enough for that. Because that slippery fish, he didn't do a thing for me, you know.

NORA: But your daughter's surely forgotten you.

ANNE-MARIE: Oh, she certainly has not. She's written to me, both when she was confirmed and when she was married.

NORA (*clasping her about the neck*): You old Anne-Marie, you were a good mother for me when I was little.

ANNE-MARIE: Poor little Nora, with no other mother but me.

NORA: And if the babies didn't have one, then I know that you'd—What silly talk! (*Opening the carton.*) Go in to them. Now I'll have to—Tomorrow you can see how lovely I'll look.

ANNE-MARIE: Oh, there won't be anyone at the party as lovely as Miss Nora. (*She goes off into the room, left.*)

NORA (*begins unpacking the box, but soon throws it aside*): Oh, if I dared to go out. If only nobody would come. If only nothing would happen here while I'm out. What craziness—nobody's coming. Just don't think. This muff—needs a brushing. Beautiful gloves, beautiful gloves. Let it go. Let it go! One, two, three, four, five, six—(*With a cry.*) Oh, there

they are! (*Poises to move toward the door, but remains irresolutely standing. Mrs. Linde enters from the hall, where she has removed her street clothes.*)

NORA: Oh, it's you, Kristine. There's no one else out there? How good that you've come.

MRS. LINDE: I hear you were up asking for me.

NORA: Yes, I just stopped by. There's something you really can help me with. Let's get settled on the sofa. Look, there's going to be a costume party tomorrow evening at the Stenborgs' right above, us, and now Torvald wants me to go as a Neapolitan peasant girl and dance the tarantella that I learned in Capri.

MRS. LINDE: Really, are you giving a whole performance?

NORA: Torvald says yes, I should. See, here's the dress. Torvald had it made for me down there; but now it's all so tattered that I just don't know—

MRS. LINDE: Oh, we'll fix that up in no time. It's nothing more than the trimmings—they're a bit loose here and there. Needle and thread? Good, now we have what we need.

NORA: Oh, how sweet of you!

MRS. LINDE (*sewing*): So you'll be in disguise tomorrow, Nora. You know what? I'll stop by then for a moment and have a look at you all dressed up. But listen, I've absolutely forgotten to thank you for that pleasant evening yesterday.

NORA (*getting up and walking about*): I don't think it was as pleasant as usual yesterday. You should have come to town a bit sooner, Kristine—Yes, Torvald really knows how to give a home elegance and charm.

MRS. LINDE: And you do, too, if you ask me. You're not your father's daughter for nothing. But tell me, is Dr. Rank always so down in the mouth as yesterday?

NORA: No, that was quite an exception. But he goes around critically ill all the time—tuberculosis of the spine, poor man. You know, his father was a disgusting thing who kept mistresses and so on—and that's why the son's been sickly from birth.

MRS. LINDE (*lets her sewing fall to her lap*): But my dearest Nora, how do you know about such things?

NORA (*walking more jauntily*): Hmp! When you've had three children, then you've had a few visits from—from women who know something of medicine, and they tell you this and that.

MRS. LINDE (*resumes sewing; a short pause*): Does Dr. Rank come here every day?

NORA: Every blessed day. He's Torvald's best friend from childhood, and *my* good friend, too. Dr. Rank almost belongs to this house.

MRS. LINDE: But tell me—is he quite sincere? I mean, doesn't he rather enjoy flattering people?

NORA: Just the opposite. Why do you think that?

MRS. LINDE: When you introduced us yesterday, he was proclaiming that he'd often heard my name in this house; but later I noticed that your husband hadn't the slightest idea who I really was. So how could Dr. Rank—?

NORA: But it's all true, Kristine. You see, Torvald loves me beyond words, and, as he puts it, he'd like to keep me all to himself. For a long time he'd almost be jealous if I even mentioned any of my old friends back home. So of course I dropped that. But with Dr. Rank I talk a lot about such things because he likes hearing about them.

MRS. LINDE: Now listen, Nora; in many ways you're still like a child. I'm a good deal older than you, with a little more experience. I'll tell you something: You ought to put an end to all this with Dr. Rank.

NORA: What should I put an end to?

MRS. LINDE: Both parts of it, I think. Yesterday you said something about a rich admirer who'd provide you with money—

NORA: Yes, one who doesn't exist—worse luck. So?

MRS. LINDE: Is Dr. Rank well off?

NORA: Yes, he is.

MRS. LINDE: With no dependents?

NORA: No, no one. But—

MRS. LINDE: And he's over here every day?

NORA: Yes, I told you that.

MRS. LINDE: How can a man of such refinement be so grasping?

NORA: I don't follow you at all.

MRS. LINDE: Now don't try to hide it, Nora. You think I can't guess who loaned you the forty-eight hundred crowns?

NORA: Are you out of your mind? How could you think such a thing! A friend of ours, who comes here every single day. What an intolerable situation that would have been!

MRS. LINDE: Then it really wasn't him.

NORA: No, absolutely not. It never even crossed my mind for a moment—And he had nothing to lend in those days; his inheritance came later.

MRS. LINDE: Well, I think that was a stroke of luck for you, Nora dear.

NORA: No, it never would have occurred to me to ask Dr. Rank—Still, I'm quite sure that if I had asked him—

MRS. LINDE: Which you won't, of course.

NORA: No, of course not. I can't see that I'd ever need to. But I'm quite positive that if I talked to Dr. Rank—

MRS. LINDE: Behind your husband's back?

NORA: I've got to clear up this other thing; *that's* also behind his back. I've *got* to clear it all up.

MRS. LINDE: Yes, I was saying that yesterday, but—

NORA (*pacing up and down*): A man handles these problems so much better than a woman—

MRS. LINDE: One's husband does, yes.

NORA: Nonsense. (*Stopping.*) When you pay everything you owe, then you get your note back, right?

MRS. LINDE: Yes, naturally.

NORA: And can rip it into a million pieces and burn it up—that filthy scrap of paper!

MRS. LINDE (*looking hard at her, laying her sewing aside, and rising slowly*): Nora, you're hiding something from me.

NORA: You can see it in my face?

MRS. LINDE: Something's happened to you since yesterday morning. Nora, what is it?

NORA (*hurrying toward her*): Kristine! (*Listening.*) Shh! Torvald's home. Look, go in with the children a while. Torvald can't bear all this snipping and stitching. Let Anne-Marie help you.

MRS. LINDE (*gathering up some of the things*): All right, but I'm not leaving here until we've talked this out. (*She disappears into the room, left, as Torvald enters from the hall.*)

NORA: Oh, how I've been waiting for you, Torvald dear.

HELMER: Was that the dressmaker?

NORA: No, that was Kristine. She's helping me fix up my costume. You know, it's going to be quite attractive.

HELMER: Yes, wasn't that a bright idea I had?

NORA: Brilliant! But then wasn't I good as well to give in to you?

HELMER: Good—because you give in to your husband's judgment? All right, you little goose, I know you didn't mean it like that. But I won't disturb you. You'll want to have a fitting, I suppose.

NORA: And you'll be working?

HELMER: Yes. (*Indicating a bundle of papers.*) See. I've been down to the bank. (*Starts toward his study.*)

NORA: Torvald.

HELMER (*stops*): Yes.

NORA: If your little squirrel begged you, with all her heart and soul, for something—?

HELMER: What's that?

NORA: Then would you do it?

HELMER: First, naturally, I'd have to know what it was.

NORA: Your squirrel would scamper about and do tricks, if you'd only be sweet and give in.

HELMER: Out with it.

NORA: Your lark would be singing high and low in every room—

HELMER: Come on, she does that anyway.

NORA: I'd be a wood nymph and dance for you in the moonlight.

HELMER: Nora—don't tell me it's that same business from this morning?

NORA (*coming closer*): Yes, Torvald, I beg you, please!

HELMER: And you actually have the nerve to drag that up again?

NORA: Yes, yes, you've got to give in to me; you *have* to let Krogstad keep his job in the bank.

HELMER: My dear Nora, I've slated his job for Mrs. Linde.

NORA: That's awfully kind of you. But you could just fire another clerk instead of Krogstad.

HELMER: This is the most incredible stubbornness! Because you go and give an impulsive promise to speak up for him, I'm expected to—

NORA: That's not the reason, Torvald. It's for your own sake. That man does writing for the worst papers; you said it yourself. He could do you any amount of harm. I'm scared to death of him—

HELMER: Ah, I understand. It's the old memories haunting you.

NORA: What do you mean by that?

HELMER: Of course, you're thinking about your father.

NORA: Yes, all right. Just remember how those nasty gossips wrote in the papers about Papa and slandered him so cruelly. I think they'd have had him dismissed if the department hadn't sent you up to investigate, and if you hadn't been so kind and open-minded toward him.

HELMER: My dear Nora, there's a notable difference between your father and me. Your father's official career was hardly above reproach. But mine is; and I hope it'll stay that way as long as I hold my position.

NORA: Oh, who can ever tell what vicious minds can invent? We could be so snug and happy now in our quiet, carefree home—you and I and the children, Torvald! That's why I'm pleading with you so—

HELMER: And just by pleading for him you make it impossible for me to keep him on. It's already known at the bank that I'm firing Krogstad. What if it's rumored around now that the new bank manager was vetoed by his wife—

NORA: Yes, what then—?

HELMER: Oh yes—as long as our little bundle of stubbornness gets her way—! I should go and make myself ridiculous in front of the whole office—give people the idea I can be swayed by all kinds of outside pressure. Oh, you can bet I'd feel the effects of that soon enough! Besides—there's something that rules Krogstad right out at the bank as long as I'm the manager.

NORA: What's that?

HELMER: His moral failings I could maybe overlook if I had to—

NORA: Yes, Torvald, why not?

HELMER: And I hear he's quite efficient on the job. But he was a crony of mine back in my teens—one of those rash friendships that crop up again and again to embarrass you later in life. Well, I might as well say it straight out: We're on a first-name basis. And that tactless fool makes no effort at all to hide it in front of others. Quite the contrary—he thinks that entitles him to take a familiar air around me, and so every other second he comes booming out with his, "Yes, Torvald!" and "Sure thing, Torvald!" I tell you, it's been excruciating for me. He's out to make my place in the bank unbearable.

NORA: Torvald, you can't be serious about all this.

HELMER: Oh no? Why not?

NORA: Because these are such petty considerations.

HELMER: What are you saying? Petty? You think I'm petty!

NORA: No, just the opposite, Torvald dear. That's exactly why—

HELMER: Never mind. You call my motives petty; then I might as well be just that. Petty! All right! We'll put a stop to this for good. (*Goes to the hall door and calls.*) Helene!

NORA: What do you want?

HELMER (*searching among his papers*): A decision. (*The Maid comes in.*) Look here; take this letter; go out with it at once. Get hold of a messenger and have him deliver it. Quick now. It's already addressed. Wait, here's some money.

MAID: Yes, sir. (*She leaves with the letter.*)

HELMER (*straightening his papers*): There, now, little Miss Willful.

NORA (*breathlessly*): Torvald, what was that letter?

HELMER: Krogstad's notice.

NORA: Call it back, Torvald! There's still time. Oh, Torvald, call it back! Do it for my sake—for your sake, for the children's sake! Do you hear, Torvald; do it! You don't know how this can harm us.

HELMER: Too late.

NORA: Yes, too late.

HELMER: Nora, dear, I can forgive you this panic, even though basically you're insulting me. Yes, you are! Or isn't it an insult to think that *I* should be afraid of a courtroom hack's revenge? But I forgive you anyway, because this shows so beautifully how much you love me. (*Takes her in his arms.*) This is the way it should be, my darling Nora. Whatever comes, you'll see: When it really counts, I have strength and courage enough as a man to take on the whole weight myself.

NORA (*terrified*): What do you mean by that?

HELMER: The whole weight, I said.

NORA (*resolutely*): No, never in all the world.

HELMER: Good. So we'll share it, Nora, as man and wife. That's as it should be. (*Fondling her.*) Are you happy now? There, there, there—not these frightened dove's eyes. It's nothing at all but empty fantasies—Now you should run through your tarantella and practice your tambourine. I'll go to the inner office, and shut both doors, so I won't hear a thing; you can make all the noise you like. (*Turning in the doorway.*) And when Rank comes, just tell him where he can find me. (*He nods to her and goes with his papers into the study, closing the door.*)

NORA (*standing as though rooted, dazed with fright, in a whisper*): He really could do it. He will do it. He'll do it in spite of everything. No, not that, never, never! Anything but that! Escape! A way out—(*The doorbell rings.*) Dr. Rank! Anything but that! Anything, whatever it is! (*Her hands pass over her face, smoothing it; she pulls herself together, goes over and opens the hall door. Dr. Rank stands outside, hanging his fur coat up. During the following scene, it begins getting dark.*)

NORA: Hello, Dr. Rank. I recognized your ring. But you mustn't go in to Torvald yet; I believe he's working.

RANK: And you?

NORA: For you, I always have an hour to spare—you know that. (*He has entered, and she shuts the door after him.*)

RANK: Many thanks. I'll make use of these hours while I can.

NORA: What do you mean by that? While you can?

RANK: Does that disturb you?

NORA: Well, it's such an odd phrase. Is anything going to happen?

RANK: What's going to happen is what I've been expecting so long—but I honestly didn't think it would come so soon.

NORA (gripping his arm): What is it you've found out? Dr. Rank, you have to tell me!

RANK (sitting by the stove): It's all over with me. There's nothing to be done about it.

NORA (breathing easier): Is it you—then—?

RANK: Who else? There's no point in lying to one's self. I'm the most miserable of all my patients, Mrs. Helmer. These past few days I've been auditing my internal accounts. Bankrupt! Within a month I'll probably be laid out and rotting in the churchyard.

NORA: Oh, what a horrible thing to say.

RANK: The thing itself is horrible. But the worst of it is all the other horror before it's over. There's only one final examination left; when I'm finished with that, I'll know about when my disintegration will begin. There's something I want to say. Helmer with his sensitivity has such a sharp distaste for anything ugly. I don't want him near my sickroom.

NORA: Oh, but Dr. Rank—

RANK: I won't have him in there. Under no condition. I'll lock my door to him—As soon as I'm completely sure of the worst, I'll send you my calling card marked with a black cross, and you'll know then the wreck has started to come apart.

NORA: No, today you're completely unreasonable. And I wanted you so much to be in a really good humor.

RANK: With death up my sleeve? And then to suffer this way for somebody else's sins. Is there any justice in that? And in every single family, in some way or another, this inevitable retribution of nature goes on—

NORA (her hands pressed over her ears): Oh, stuff! Cheer up! Please—be gay!

RANK: Yes, I'd just as soon laugh at it all. My poor, innocent spine, serving time for my father's gay army days.

NORA (by the table, left): He was so infatuated with asparagus tips and pâté de foie gras, wasn't that it?

HANK: Yes—and with truffles.

NORA: Truffles, yes. And then with oysters, I suppose?

RANK: Yes, tons of oysters, naturally.

NORA: And then the port and champagne to go with it. It's so sad that all these delectable things have to strike at our bones.

RANK: Especially when they strike at the unhappy bones that never shared in the fun.

NORA: Ah, that's the saddest of all.

RANK (looks searchingly at her): Hm.

NORA (after a moment): Why did you smile?

RANK: No, it was you who laughed.

NORA: No, it was you who smiled, Dr. Rank!

RANK (getting up): You're even a bigger tease than I'd thought.

NORA: I'm full of wild ideas today.

RANK: That's obvious.

NORA (putting both hands on his shoulders): Dear, dear Dr. Rank, you'll never die for Torvald and me.

RANK: Oh, that loss you'll easily get over. Those who go away are soon forgotten.

NORA (looks fearfully at him): You believe that?

RANK: One makes new connections, and then—

NORA: Who makes new connections?

RANK: Both you and Torvald will when I'm gone. I'd say you're well under way already. What was that Mrs. Linde doing here last evening?

NORA: Oh, come—you can't be jealous of poor Kristine?

RANK: Oh yes, I am. She'll be my successor here in the house. When I'm down under, that woman will probably—

NORA: Shh! Not so loud. She's right in there.

RANK: Today as well. So you see.

NORA: Only to sew on my dress. Good gracious, how unreasonable you are. (Sitting on the sofa.) Be nice now, Dr. Rank. Tomorrow you'll see how beautifully I'll dance; and you can imagine then that I'm dancing only for you—yes, and of course for Torvald, too—that's understood. (Takes various items out of the carton.) Dr. Rank, sit over here and I'll show you something.

RANK (sitting): What's that?

NORA: Look here. Look.

RANK: Silk stockings.

NORA: Flesh-colored. Aren't they lovely? Now it's so dark here, but tomorrow—No, no, no, just look at the feet. Oh well, you might as well look at the rest.

RANK: Hm—

NORA: Why do you look so critical? Don't you believe they'll fit?

RANK: I've never had any chance to form an opinion on that.

NORA (glancing at him a moment): Shame on you. (Hits him lightly on the ear with the stockings.) That's for you. (Puts them away again.)

RANK: And what other splendors am I going to see now?

NORA: Not the least bit more, because you've been naughty. (She hums a little and rummages among her things.)

RANK (after a short silence): When I sit here together with you like this, completely easy and open, then I don't know—I simply can't imagine—whatever would have become of me if I'd never come into this house.

NORA (smiling): Yes, I really think you feel completely at ease with us.

RANK (more quietly, staring straight ahead): And then to have to go away from it all—

NORA: Nonsense, you're not going away.

RANK (his voice unchanged):—and not even be able to leave some poor show of gratitude behind, scarcely a fleeting regret—no more than a vacant place that anyone can fill.

NORA: And if I asked you now for—No—

RANK: For what?

NORA: For a great proof of your friendship—

RANK: Yes, yes?

NORA: No, I mean—for an exceptionally big favor—

RANK: Would you really, for once, make me so happy?

NORA: Oh, you haven't the vaguest idea what it is.

RANK: All right, then tell me.

NORA: No, but I can't, Dr. Rank—it's all out of reason. It's advice and help, too—and a favor—

RANK: So much the better. I can't fathom what you're hinting at. Just speak out. Don't you trust me?

NORA: Of course. More than anyone else. You're my best and truest friend, I'm sure. That's why I want to talk to you. All right, then, Dr. Rank. There's something you can help me prevent. You know how deeply, how inexpressibly dearly Torvald loves me; he'd never hesitate a second to give up his life for me.

RANK (leaning close to her): Nora—do you think he's the only one—

NORA (with a slight start): Who—?

RANK: Who'd gladly give up his life for you.

NORA (heavily): I see.

RANK: I swore to myself you should know this before I'm gone. I'll never find a better chance. Yes, Nora, now you know. And also you know now that you can trust me beyond anyone else.

NORA (rising, natural and calm): Let me by.

RANK (making room for her, but still sitting): Nora—

NORA (in the hall doorway): Helene, bring the lamp in. (Goes over to the stove.) Ah, dear Dr. Rank, that was really mean of you.

RANK (getting up): That I've loved you just as deeply as somebody else? Was that mean?

NORA: No, but that you came out and told me. That was quite unnecessary—

RANK: What do you mean? Have you known—?

(The Maid comes in with the lamp, sets it on the table, and goes out again.)

RANK: Nora—Mrs. Helmer—I'm asking you: Have you known about it?

NORA: Oh, how can I tell what I know or don't know? Really, I don't know what to say—Why did you have to be so clumsy, Dr. Rank! Everything was so good.

RANK: Well, in any case, you now have the knowledge that my body and soul are at your command. So won't you speak out?

NORA (looking at him): After that?

RANK: Please, just let me know what it is.

NORA: You can't know anything now.

RANK: I have to. You mustn't punish me like this. Give me the chance to do whatever is humanly possible for you.

NORA: Now there's nothing you can do for me. Besides, actually, I don't need any help. You'll see—it's only my fantasies. That's what it is. Of course! (Sits in the rocker, looks at him, and smiles.) What a nice one you are, Dr. Rank. Aren't you a little bit ashamed, now that the lamp is here?

RANK: No, not exactly. But perhaps I'd better go—for good?

NORA: No, you certainly can't do that. You must come here just as you always have. You know Torvald can't do without you.

RANK: Yes, but you?

NORA: You know how much I enjoy it when you're here.

RANK: That's precisely what threw me off. You're a mystery to me. So many times I've felt you'd almost rather be with me than with Helmer.

NORA: Yes—you see, there are some people that one loves most and other people that one would almost prefer being with.

RANK: Yes, there's something to that.

NORA: When I was back home, of course I loved Papa most. But I always thought it was so much fun when I could sneak down to the maids' quarters, because they never tried to improve me, and it was always so amusing, the way they talked to each other.

RANK: Aha, so it's their place that I've filled.

NORA (jumping up and going to him): Oh, dear, sweet Dr. Rank, that's not what I meant at all. But you can understand that with Torvald it's just the same as with Papa—

(The Maid enters from the hall.)

MAID: Ma'am—please! (She whispers to Nora and hands her a calling card.)

NORA (glancing at the card): Ah! (Slips it into her pocket.)

RANK: Anything wrong?

NORA: No, no, not at all. It's only some—it's my new dress—

RANK: Really? But—there's your dress.

NORA: Oh, that. But this is another one—I ordered it—Torvald mustn't know—

RANK: Ah, now we have the big secret.

NORA: That's right. Just go in with him—he's back in the inner study. Keep him there as long as—

RANK: Don't worry. He won't get away. (Goes into the study.)

NORA (to the Maid): And he's standing waiting in the kitchen?

MAID: Yes, he came up by the back stairs.

NORA: But didn't you tell him somebody was here?

MAID: Yes, but that didn't do any good.

NORA: He won't leave?

MAID: No, he won't go till he's talked with you, ma'am.

NORA: Let him come in, then—but quietly. Helene, don't breathe a word about this. It's a surprise for my husband.

MAID: Yes, yes, I understand—(Goes out.)

NORA: This horror—it's going to happen. No, no, no, it can't happen, it mustn't. (She goes and bolts Helmer's door. The Maid opens the hall door for Krogstad and shuts it behind him. He is dressed for travel in a fur coat, boots, and a fur cap.)

NORA (going toward him): Talk softly. My husband's home.

KROGSTAD: Well, good for him.

NORA: What do you want?

KROGSTAD: Some information.

NORA: Hurry up, then. What is it?

KROGSTAD: You know, of course, that I got my notice.

NORA: I couldn't prevent it, Mr. Krogstad. I fought for you to the bitter end, but nothing worked.

KROGSTAD: Does your husband's love for you run so thin? He knows everything I can expose you to, and all the same he dares to—

NORA: How can you imagine he knows anything about this?

KROGSTAD: Ah, no—I can't imagine it either, now. It's not at all like my fine Torvald Helmer to have so much guts—

NORA: Mr. Krogstad, I demand respect for my husband!

KROGSTAD: Why, of course—all due respect. But since the lady's keeping it so carefully hidden, may I presume to ask if you're also a bit better informed than yesterday about what you've actually done?

NORA: More than you ever could teach me.

KROGSTAD: Yes, I *am* such an awful lawyer.

NORA: What is it you want from me?

KROGSTAD: Just a glimpse of how you are, Mrs. Helmer. I've been thinking about you all day long. A cashier, a night-court scribbler, a—well, a type like me also has a little of what they call a heart, you know.

NORA: Then show it. Think of my children.

KROGSTAD: Did you or your husband ever think of mine? But never mind. I simply wanted to tell you that you don't need to take this thing too seriously. For the present, I'm not proceeding with any action.

NORA: Oh no, really! Well—I knew that.

KROGSTAD: Everything can be settled in a friendly spirit. It doesn't have to get around town at all; it can stay just among us three.

NORA: My husband must never know anything of this.

KROGSTAD: How can you manage that? Perhaps you can pay me the balance?

NORA: No, not right now.

KROGSTAD: Or you know some way of raising the money in a day or two?

NORA: No way that I'm willing to use.

KROGSTAD: Well, it wouldn't have done you any good, anyway. If you stood in front of me with a fistful of bills, you still couldn't buy your signature back.

NORA: Then tell me what you're going to do with it.

KROGSTAD: I'll just hold onto it—keep it on file. There's no outsider who'll even get wind of it. So if you've been thinking of taking some desperate step—

NORA: I have.

KROGSTAD: Been thinking of running away from home—

NORA: I have!

KROGSTAD: Or even of something worse—

NORA: How could you guess that?

KROGSTAD: You can drop those thoughts.

NORA: How could you guess I was thinking of *that*?

KROGSTAD: Most of us think about *that* at first. I thought about it too, but I discovered I hadn't the courage—

NORA (lifelessly): I don't either.

KROGSTAD (relieved): That's true, you haven't the courage? You too?

NORA: I don't have it—I don't have it.

KROGSTAD: It would be terribly stupid, anyway. After that first storm at home blows out, why, then—I have here in my pocket a letter for your husband—

NORA: Telling everything?

KROGSTAD: As charitably as possible.

NORA (quickly): He mustn't ever get that letter. Tear it up. I'll find some way to get money.

KROGSTAD: Beg pardon, Mrs. Helmer, but I think I just told you—

NORA: Oh, I don't mean the money I owe you. Let me know how much you want from my husband, and I'll manage it.

KROGSTAD: I don't want any money from your husband.

NORA: What do you want, then?

KROGSTAD: I'll tell you what. I want to recoup, Mrs. Helmer; I want to get on in the world—and there's where your husband can help me. For a year and a half I've kept myself clean of anything disreputable—all that time struggling with the worst conditions; but I was satisfied, working my way up step by step. Now I've been written right off, and I'm just not in the mood to come crawling back. I tell you, I want to move on. I want to get back in the bank—in a better position. Your husband can set up a job for me—

NORA: He'll never do that!

KROGSTAD: He'll do it. I know him. He won't dare breathe a word of protest. And once I'm in there together with him, you just wait and see! Inside of a year, I'll be the manager's right-hand man. It'll be Nils Krogstad, not Torvald Helmer, who runs the bank.

NORA: You'll never see the day!

KROGSTAD: Maybe you think you can—

NORA: I have the courage now—for *that*.

KROGSTAD: Oh, you don't scare me. A smart, spoiled lady like you—

NORA: You'll see; you'll see!

KROGSTAD: Under the ice, maybe? Down in the freezing, coal-black water? There, till you float up in the spring, ugly, unrecognizable, with your hair falling out—

NORA: You don't frighten me.

KROGSTAD: Nor do you frighten me. One doesn't do these things, Mrs. Helmer. Besides what good would it be? I'd still have him safe in my pocket.

NORA: Afterwards? When I'm no longer—?

KROGSTAD: Are you forgetting that *I'll* be in control then over your final reputation? (Nora stands speechless, staring at him.) Good; now I've warned you. Don't do anything stupid. When Helmer's read my letter, I'll be waiting for his reply. And bear in mind that it's your husband himself who's forced me back to my old ways. I'll never forgive him for that. Good-bye, Mrs. Helmer. (He goes out through the hall.)

NORA (*goes to the hall door, opens it a crack, and listens*): He's gone. Didn't leave the letter. Oh no, no, that's impossible too! (*Opening the door more and more.*) What's that? He's standing outside—not going downstairs. He's thinking it over? Maybe he'll—? (*A letter falls in the mailbox; then Krogstad's footsteps are heard, dying away down a flight of stairs. Nora gives a muffled cry and runs over toward the sofa table. A short pause.*) In the mailbox. (*Slips warily over to the hall door.*) It's lying there. Torvald, Torvald—now we're lost!

MRS. LINDE (*entering with the costume from the room, left*): There now, I can't see anything else to mend. Perhaps you'd like to try—

NORA (*in a hoarse whisper*): Kristine, come here.

MRS. LINDE (*tossing the dress on the sofa*): What's wrong? You look upset.

NORA: Come here. See that letter? There! Look—through the glass in the mailbox.

MRS. LINDE: Yes, yes, I see it.

NORA: That letter's from Krogstad—

MRS. LINDE: Nora—it's Krogstad who loaned you the money!

NORA: Yes, and now Torvald will find out everything.

MRS. LINDE: Believe me, Nora, it's best for both of you.

NORA: There's more you don't know. I forged a name.

MRS. LINDE: But for heaven's sake—?

NORA: I only want to tell you that, Kristine, so that you can be my witness.

MRS. LINDE: Witness? Why should I—?

NORA: If I should go out of my mind—it could easily happen—

MRS. LINDE: Nora!

NORA: Or anything else occurred—so I couldn't be present here—

MRS. LINDE: Nora, Nora, you aren't yourself at all!

NORA: And someone should try to take on the whole weight, all of the guilt, you follow me—

MRS. LINDE: Yes, of course, but why do you think—?

NORA: Then you're the witness that it isn't true, Kristine. I'm very much myself; my mind right now is perfectly clear; and I'm telling you: Nobody else has known about this; I alone did everything. Remember that.

MRS. LINDE: I will. But I don't understand all this.

NORA: Oh, how could you ever understand it? It's the miracle now that's going to take place.

MRS. LINDE: The miracle?

NORA: Yes, the miracle. But it's so awful, Kristine. It mustn't take place, not for anything in the world.

MRS. LINDE: I'm going right over and talk with Krogstad.

NORA: Don't go near him; he'll do you some terrible harm!

MRS. LINDE: There was a time once when he'd gladly have done anything for me.

NORA: He?

MRS. LINDE: Where does he live?

NORA: Oh, how do I know? Yes. (*Searches in her pocket.*) Here's his card. But the letter, the letter—!

HELMER (*from the study, knocking on the door*): Nora!

NORA (*with a cry of fear*): Oh! What is it? What do you want?

HELMER: Now, now, don't be so frightened. We're not coming in. You locked the door—are you trying on the dress?

NORA: Yes, I'm trying it. I'll look just beautiful, Torvald.

MRS. LINDE (*who has read the card*): He's living right around the corner.

NORA: Yes, but what's the use? We're lost. The letter's in the box.

MRS. LINDE: And your husband has the key?

NORA: Yes, always.

MRS. LINDE: Krogstad can ask for his letter back unread; he can find some excuse—

NORA: But it's just this time that Torvald usually—

MRS. LINDE: Stall him. Keep him in there. I'll be back as quick as I can. (*She hurries out through the hall entrance.*)

NORA (*goes to Helmer's door, opens it, and peers in*): Torvald!

HELMER (*from the inner study*): Well—does one dare set foot in one's own living room at last? Come on, Rank, now we'll get a look—(*In the doorway.*) But what's this?

NORA: What, Torvald dear?

HELMER: Rank had me expecting some grand masquerade.

RANK (*in the doorway*): That was my impression, but I must have been wrong.

NORA: No one can admire me in my splendor—not till tomorrow.

HELMER: But Nora dear, you look so exhausted. Have you practiced too hard?

NORA: No, I haven't practiced at all yet.

HELMER: You know, it's necessary—

NORA: Oh, it's absolutely necessary, Torvald. But I can't get anywhere without your help. I've forgotten the whole thing completely.

HELMER: Ah, we'll soon take care of that.

NORA: Yes, take care of me, Torvald, please! Promise me that? Oh, I'm so nervous. That big party—You must give up everything this evening for me. No business—don't even touch your pen. Yes? Dear Torvald, promise?

HELMER: It's a promise. Tonight I'm totally at your service—you little helpless thing. Hm—but first there's one thing I want to—(*Goes toward the hall door.*)

NORA: What are you looking for?

HELMER: Just to see if there's any mail.

NORA: No, no, don't do that, Torvald!

HELMER: Now what?

NORA: Torvald, please. There isn't any.

HELMER: Let me look, though. (*Starts out. Nora, at the piano, strikes the first notes of the tarantella. Helmer, at the door, stops.*) Aha!

Cheryl Campbell as Nora in the 1981–1982 Royal Shakespeare Company production of *A Doll House*.

NORA: I can't dance tomorrow if I don't practice with you.

HELMER (*going over to her*): Nora dear, are you really so frightened?

NORA: Yes, so terribly frightened. Let me practice right now; there's still time before dinner. Oh, sit down and play for me, Torvald. Direct me. Teach me, the way you always have.

HELMER: Gladly, if it's what you want. (*Sits at the piano.*)

NORA (*snatches the tambourine up from the box, then a long, varicolored shawl, which she throws around herself, whereupon she springs forward and cries out*): Play for me now! Now I'll dance!

(*Helmer plays and Nora dances. Rank stands behind Helmer at the piano and looks on.*)

HELMER (*as he plays*): Slower. Slow down.

NORA: Can't change it.

HELMER: Not so violent, Nora!

NORA: Has to be just like this.

HELMER (*stopping*): No, no, that won't do at all.

NORA (*laughing and swinging her tambourine*): Isn't that what I told you?

RANK: Let me play for her.

HELMER (*getting up*): Yes, go on. I can teach her more easily then.

(*Rank sits at the piano and plays, Nora dances more and more wildly. Helmer has stationed himself by the stove and repeatedly gives her directions; she seems not to hear them; her hair loosens and falls over her shoulders; she does not notice, but goes on dancing. Mrs. Linde enters.*)

MRS. LINDE (*standing dumbfounded at the door*): Ah—!

NORA (*still dancing*): See what fun, Kristine!

HELMER: But Nora darling, you dance as if your life were at stake.

NORA: And it is.

HELMER: Rank, stop! This is pure madness. Stop it, I say!

(*Rank breaks off playing, and Nora halts abruptly.*)

HELMER (*going over to her*): I never would have believed it. You've forgotten everything I taught you.

NORA (*throwing away the tambourine*): You see for yourself.

HELMER: Well, there's certainly room for instruction here.

NORA: Yes, you see how important it is. You've got to teach me to the very last minute. Promise me that, Torvald?

HELMER: You can bet on it.

NORA: You mustn't, either today or tomorrow, think about anything else but me; you mustn't open any letters—or the mailbox—

HELMER: Ah, it's still the fear of that man—

NORA: Oh yes, yes, that too.

HELMER: Nora, it's written all over you—there's already a letter from him out there.

NORA: I don't know. I guess so. But you mustn't read such things now; there mustn't be anything ugly between us before it's all over.

RANK (*quietly to Helmer*): You shouldn't deny her.

HELMER (*putting his arm around her*): The child can have her way. But tomorrow night, after you've danced—

NORA: Then you'll be free.

MAID (*in the doorway, right*): Ma'am, dinner is served.

NORA: We'll be wanting champagne, Helene.

MAID: Very good, ma'am. (*Goes out.*)

HELMER: So—a regular banquet, hm?

NORA: Yes, a banquet—champagne till daybreak! (*Calling out.*) And some macaroons, Helene. Heaps of them—just this once.

HELMER (*taking her hands*): Now, now, now—no hysterics. Be my own little lark again.

NORA: Oh, I will soon enough. But go on in—and you, Dr. Rank. Kristine, help me put up my hair.

RANK (*whispering, as they go*): There's nothing wrong—really wrong, is there?

HELMER: Oh, of course not. It's nothing more than this childish anxiety I was telling you about. (*They go out, right.*)

NORA: Well?

MRS. LINDE: Left town.

NORA: I could see by your face.

MRS. LINDE: He'll be home tomorrow evening. I wrote him a note.

NORA: You shouldn't have. Don't try to stop anything now. After all, it's a wonderful joy, this waiting here for the miracle.

MRS. LINDE: What is it you're waiting for?

NORA: Oh, you can't understand that. Go in to them; I'll be along in a moment.

(*Mrs. Linde goes into the dining room. Nora stands a short while as if composing herself; then she looks at her watch.*)

NORA: Five. Seven hours to midnight. Twenty-four hours to the midnight after, and then the tarantella's done. Seven and twenty-four? <u>Thirty-one hours to live.</u>

HELMER (*in the doorway, right*): What's become of the little lark?

NORA (*going toward him with open arms*): Here's your lark!

ACT III

(*Same scene. The table, with chairs around it, has been moved to the center of the room. A lamp on the table is lit. The hall door stands open. Dance music drifts down from the floor above. Mrs. Linde sits at the table, absently paging through a book, trying to read, but apparently unable to focus her thoughts. Once or twice she pauses, tensely listening for a sound at the outer entrance.*)

MRS. LINDE (*glancing at her watch*): Not yet—and there's hardly any time left. If only he's not—(*Listening again.*) Ah, there it is. (*She goes out in the hall and cautiously opens the outer door. Quiet footsteps are heard on the stairs. She whispers.*) Come in. Nobody's here.

KROGSTAD (*in the doorway*): I found a note from you at home. What's back of all this?

MRS. LINDE: I just *had* to talk to you.

KROGSTAD: Oh? And it just *had* to be here in this house?

MRS. LINDE: At my place it was impossible; my room hasn't a private entrance. Come in, we're all alone. The maid's asleep, and the Helmers are at the dance upstairs.

KROGSTAD (*entering the room*): Well, well, the Helmers are dancing tonight? Really?

MRS. LINDE: Yes, why not?

KROGSTAD: How true—why not?

Why does this need to be private?

MRS. LINDE: All right, Krogstad, let's talk.

KROGSTAD: Do we two have anything more to talk about?

MRS. LINDE: We have a great deal to talk about.

KROGSTAD: I wouldn't have thought so.

MRS. LINDE: No, because you've never understood me, really.

KROGSTAD: Was there anything more to understand—except what's all too common in life? A calculating woman throws over a man the moment a better catch comes by.

MRS. LINDE: You think I'm so thoroughly calculating? You think I broke it off lightly?   *They were engaged*

KROGSTAD: Didn't you?

MRS. LINDE: Nils—is that what you really thought?

KROGSTAD: If you cared, then why did you write me the way you did?

MRS. LINDE: What else could I do? If I had to break off with you, then it was my job as well to root out everything you felt for me.

KROGSTAD (*wringing his hands*): So that was it. And this—all this, simply for money!

MRS. LINDE: Don't forget I had a helpless mother and two small brothers. We couldn't wait for you, Nils; you had such a long road ahead of you then.

KROGSTAD: That may be; but you still hadn't the right to abandon me for somebody else's sake.

MRS. LINDE: Yes—I don't know. So many, many times I've asked myself if I did have that right.

KROGSTAD (*more softly*): When I lost you, it was as if all the solid ground dissolved from under my feet. Look at me; I'm a half-drowned man now, hanging onto a wreck.

MRS. LINDE: Help may be near.

KROGSTAD: It was near—but then you came and blocked it off.

MRS. LINDE: Without my knowing it, Nils. Today for the first time I learned that it's you I'm replacing at the bank.

KROGSTAD: All right—I believe you. But now that you know, will you step aside?

MRS. LINDE: No, because that wouldn't benefit you in the slightest.

KROGSTAD: Not "benefit" me, hm! I'd step aside anyway.

MRS. LINDE: I've learned to be realistic. Life and hard, bitter necessity have taught me that.

KROGSTAD: And life's taught me never to trust fine phrases.

MRS. LINDE: Then life's taught you a very sound thing. But you do have to trust in actions, don't you?

KROGSTAD: What does that mean?

MRS. LINDE: You said you were hanging on like a half-drowned man to a wreck.

KROGSTAD: I've good reason to say that.

MRS. LINDE: I'm also like a half-drowned woman on a wreck. No one to suffer with; no one to care for.

KROGSTAD: You made your choice.

MRS. LINDE: There wasn't any choice then.

KROGSTAD: So—what of it?

[Handwritten at top: Does she really feel this way or is it Nora's behalf she's working on?]

MRS. LINDE: Nils, if only we two shipwrecked people could reach across to each other.

KROGSTAD: What are you saying?

MRS. LINDE: Two on one wreck are at least better off than each on his own.

KROGSTAD: Kristine!

MRS. LINDE: Why do you think I came into town?

KROGSTAD: Did you really have some thought of me?

MRS. LINDE: I have to work to go on living. All my born days, as long as I can remember, I've worked, and it's been my best and my only joy. But now I'm completely alone in the world; it frightens me to be so empty and lost. To work for yourself—there's no joy in that. Nils, give me something—someone to work for. *[Handwritten margin: She really does love him]*

KROGSTAD: I don't believe all this. It's just some hysterical feminine urge to go out and make a noble sacrifice.

MRS. LINDE: Have you ever found me to be hysterical?

KROGSTAD: Can you honestly mean this? Tell me—do you know everything about my past?

MRS. LINDE: Yes.

KROGSTAD: And you know what they think I'm worth around here.

MRS. LINDE: From what you were saying before, it would seem that with me you could have been another person.

KROGSTAD: I'm positive of that.

MRS. LINDE: Couldn't it happen still?

KROGSTAD: Kristine—you're saying this in all seriousness? Yes, you are! I can see it in you. And do you really have the courage, then—?

MRS. LINDE: I need to have someone to care for, and your children need a mother. We both need each other. Nils, I have faith that you're good at heart—I'll risk everything together with you.

KROGSTAD (*gripping her hands*): Kristine, thank you, thank you—Now I know I can win back a place in their eyes. Yes—but I forgot—

MRS. LINDE (*listening*): Shh! The tarantella. Go now! Go on!

KROGSTAD: Why? What is it?

MRS. LINDE: Hear the dance up there? When that's over, they'll be coming down.

KROGSTAD: Oh, then I'll go. But—it's all pointless. Of course, you don't know the move I made against the Helmers.

MRS. LINDE: Yes, Nils, I know.

KROGSTAD: And all the same, you have the courage to—?

MRS. LINDE: I know how far despair can drive a man like you.

KROGSTAD: Oh, if I only could take it all back.

MRS. LINDE: You easily could—your letter's still lying in the mailbox.

KROGSTAD: Are you sure of that?

MRS. LINDE: Positive. But—

KROGSTAD (*looks at her searchingly*): Is that the meaning of it, then? You'll save your friend at any price. Tell me straight out. Is that it? *[Handwritten: My thought exactly.]*

MRS. LINDE: Nils—anyone who's sold herself for somebody else once isn't going to do it again.

KROGSTAD: I'll demand my letter back.

MRS. LINDE: No, no.

KROGSTAD: Yes, of course. I'll stay here till Helmer comes down; I'll tell him to give me my letter again—that it only involves my dismissal—that he shouldn't read it—

MRS. LINDE: No, Nils, don't call the letter back.

KROGSTAD: But wasn't that exactly why you wrote me to come here?

MRS. LINDE: Yes, in that first panic. But it's been a whole day and night since then, and in that time I've seen such incredible things in this house. Helmer's got to learn everything; this dreadful secret has to be aired; those two have to come to a full understanding; all these lies and evasions can't go on.

KROGSTAD: Well, then, if you want to chance it. But at least there's one thing I can do, and do right away—

MRS. LINDE (*listening*): Go now, go, quick! The dance is over. We're not safe another second.

KROGSTAD: I'll wait for you downstairs.

MRS. LINDE: Yes, please do; take me home.

KROGSTAD: I can't believe it; I've never been so happy. (*He leaves by way of the outer door; the door between the room and the hall stays open.*)

MRS. LINDE (*straightening up a bit and getting together her street clothes*): How different now! How different! Someone to work for, to live for—a home to build. Well, it is worth the try! Oh, if they'd only come! (*Listening.*) Ah, there they are. Bundle up. (*She picks up her hat and coat. Nora's and Helmer's voices can be heard outside; a key turns in the lock, and Helmer brings Nora into the hall almost by force. She is wearing the Italian costume with a large black shawl about her; he has on evening dress, with a black domino open over it.*)

NORA (*struggling in the doorway*): No, no, no, not inside! I'm going up again. I don't want to leave so soon.

HELMER: But Nora dear—

NORA: Oh, I beg you, please, Torvald. From the bottom of my heart, *please*—only an hour more!

HELMER: Not a single minute, Nora darling. You know our agreement. Come on, in we go; you'll catch cold out here. (*In spite of her resistance, he gently draws her into the room.*)

MRS. LINDE: Good evening.

NORA: Kristine!

HELMER: Why, Mrs. Linde—are you here so late?

MRS. LINDE: Yes, I'm sorry, but I did want to see Nora in costume.

NORA: Have you been sitting here, waiting for me?

MRS. LINDE: Yes. I didn't come early enough; you were all upstairs; and then I thought I really couldn't leave without seeing you.

HELMER (*removing Nora's shawl*): Yes, take a good look. She's worth looking at, I can tell you that, Mrs. Linde. Isn't she lovely?

MRS. LINDE: Yes, I should say—

HELMER: A dream of loveliness, isn't she? That's what everyone thought at the party, too. But she's horribly

[Handwritten at bottom: He's a child showing off his toy...]

stubborn—this sweet little thing. What's to be done with her? Can you imagine, I almost had to use force to pry her away.

NORA: Oh, Torvald, you're going to regret you didn't indulge me, even for just a half hour more.

HELMER: There, you see. She danced her tarantella and got a tumultuous hand—which was well earned, although the performance may have been a bit too naturalistic—I mean it rather overstepped the proprieties of art. But never mind—what's important is, she made a success, an overwhelming success. You think I could let her stay on after that and spoil the effect? Oh no; I took my lovely little Capri girl—my capricious little Capri girl, I should say—took her under my arm; one quick tour of the ballroom, a curtsy to every side, and then—as they say in novels—the beautiful vision disappeared. An exit should always be effective, Mrs. Linde, but that's what I can't get Nora to grasp. Phew, It's hot in here. (*Flings the domino on a chair and opens the door to his room.*) Why's it dark in here? Oh yes, of course. Excuse me. (*He goes in and lights a couple of candles.*)

NORA (*in a sharp, breathless whisper*): So?

MRS. LINDE (*quietly*): I talked with him.

NORA: And—?

MRS. LINDE: Nora—you must tell your husband everything.

NORA (*dully*): I knew it.

MRS. LINDE: You've got nothing to fear from Krogstad, but you have to speak out.

NORA: I won't tell.

MRS. LINDE: Then the letter will.

NORA: Thanks, Kristine. I know now what's to be done. Shh!

HELMER (*reentering*): Well, then, Mrs. Linde—have you admired her?

MRS. LINDE: Yes, and now I'll say good night.

HELMER: Oh, come, so soon? Is this yours, this knitting?

MRS. LINDE: Yes, thanks. I nearly forgot it.

HELMER: Do you knit, then?

MRS. LINDE: Oh yes.

HELMER: You know what? You should embroider instead.

MRS. LINDE: Really? Why?

HELMER: Yes, because it's a lot prettier. See here, one holds the embroidery so, in the left hand, and then one guides the needle with the right—so—in an easy, sweeping curve—right?

MRS. LINDE: Yes, I guess that's—

HELMER: But, on the other hand, knitting—it can never be anything but ugly. Look, see here, the arms tucked in, the knitting needles going up and down—there's something Chinese about it. Ah, that was really a glorious champagne they served.

MRS. LINDE: Yes, good night, Nora, and don't be stubborn anymore.

HELMER: Well put, Mrs. Linde!

MRS. LINDE: Good night, Mr. Helmer.

HELMER (*accompanying her to the door*): Good night, good night. I hope you get home all right. I'd be very happy to—but you don't have far to go. Good night, good night. (*She leaves. He shuts the door after her and returns.*) There, now, at last we got her out the door. She's a deadly bore, that creature.

NORA: Aren't you pretty tired, Torvald?

HELMER: No, not a bit.

NORA: You're not sleepy?

HELMER: Not at all. On the contrary, I'm feeling quite exhilarated. But you? Yes, you really look tired and sleepy.

NORA: Yes, I'm very tired. Soon now I'll sleep.

HELMER: See! You see! I was right all along that we shouldn't stay longer.

NORA: Whatever you do is always right.

HELMER (*kissing her brow*): Now my little lark talks sense. Say, did you notice what a time Rank was having tonight?

NORA: Oh, was he? I didn't get to speak with him.

HELMER: I scarcely did either, but it's a long time since I've seen him in such high spirits. (*Gazes at her a moment, then comes nearer her.*) Hm—it's marvelous, though, to be back home again—to be completely alone with you. Oh, you bewitchingly lovely young woman!

NORA: Torvald, don't look at me like that!

HELMER: Can't I look at my richest treasure? At all that beauty that's mine, mine alone—completely and utterly.

NORA (*moving around to the other side of the table*): You mustn't talk to me that way tonight.

HELMER (*following her*): The tarantella is still in your blood. I can see—and it makes you even more enticing. Listen. The guests are beginning to go. (*Dropping his voice.*) Nora—it'll soon be quiet through this whole house.

NORA: Yes, I hope so.

HELMER: You do, don't you, my love? Do you realize—when I'm out at a party like this with you—do you know why I talk to you so little, and keep such a distance away; just send you a stolen look now and then—you know why I do it? It's because I'm imagining then that you're my secret darling, my secret young bride-to-be, and that no one suspects there's anything between us.

NORA: Yes, yes; oh, yes, I know you're always thinking of me.

HELMER: And then when we leave and I place the shawl over those fine young rounded shoulders—over that wonderful curving neck—then I pretend that you're my young bride, that we're just coming from the wedding, that for the first time I'm bringing you into my house—that for the first time I'm alone with you—completely alone with you, your trembling young beauty! All this evening I've longed for nothing but you. When I saw you turn and sway in the tarantella—my blood was pounding till I couldn't stand it—that's why I brought you down here so early—

[handwritten at top: Maybe not so manipulative, otherwise she'd use sex to distract him from work.]

NORA: Go away, Torvald! Leave me alone. I don't want all this.

HELMER: What do you mean? Nora, you're teasing me. You will, won't you? Aren't I your husband—?

(*A knock at the outside door.*)

NORA (*startled*): What's that?

HELMER (*going toward the hall*): Who is it?

RANK (*outside*): It's me. May I come in a moment?

HELMER (*with quiet irritation*): Oh, what does he want now? (*Aloud.*) Hold on. (*Goes and opens the door.*) Oh, how nice that you didn't just pass us by!

RANK: I thought I heard your voice, and then I wanted so badly to have a look in. (*Lightly glancing about.*) Ah, me, these old familiar haunts. You have it snug and cozy in here, you two.

HELMER: You seemed to be having it pretty cozy upstairs, too. *[handwritten: "Get out of here"]*

RANK: Absolutely. Why shouldn't I? Why not take in everything in life? As much as you can, anyway, and as long as you can. The wine was superb—

HELMER: The champagne especially. *[handwritten: he's drunk]*

RANK: You noticed that too? It's amazing how much I could guzzle down.

NORA: Torvald also drank a lot of champagne this evening.

RANK: Oh?

NORA: Yes, and that always makes him so entertaining.

RANK: Well, why shouldn't one have a pleasant evening after a well-spent day?

HELMER: Well spent? I'm afraid I can't claim that.

RANK (*slapping him on the back*): But I can, you see!

NORA: Dr. Rank, you must have done some scientific research today.

RANK: Quite so.

HELMER: Come now—little Nora talking about scientific research! *[handwritten: Rude & demeaning]*

NORA: And can I congratulate you on the results?

RANK: Indeed you may.

NORA: Then they were good?

RANK: The best possible for both doctor and patient—certainty.

NORA (*quickly and searchingly*): Certainty?

RANK: Complete certainty. So don't I owe myself a gay evening afterwards?

NORA: Yes, you're right, Dr. Rank.

HELMER: I'm with you—just so long as you don't have to suffer for it in the morning.

RANK: Well, one never gets something for nothing in life.

NORA: Dr. Rank—are you very fond of masquerade parties?

RANK: Yes, if there's a good array of odd disguises—

NORA: Tell me, what should we two go as at the next masquerade?

HELMER: You little featherhead—already thinking of the next! *[handwritten: this is a new one]*

RANK: We two? I'll tell you what: You must go as Charmed Life—

HELMER: Yes, but find a costume for that!

RANK: Your wife can appear just as she looks every day.

HELMER: That was nicely put. But don't you know what you're going to be?

RANK: Yes, Helmer, I've made up my mind.

HELMER: Well?

RANK: At the next masquerade I'm going to be invisible. *[handwritten: a ghost?]*

HELMER: That's a funny idea.

RANK: They say there's a hat—black, huge—have you never heard of the hat that makes you invisible? You put it on, and then no one on earth can see you.

HELMER (*suppressing a smile*): Ah, of course.

RANK: But I'm quite forgetting what I came for. Helmer, give me a cigar, one of the dark Havanas.

HELMER: With the greatest pleasure. (*Holds out his case.*)

RANK: Thanks. (*Takes one and cuts off the tip.*)

NORA (*striking a match*): Let me give you a light.

RANK: Thank you. (*She holds the match for him; he lights the cigar.*) And now good-bye.

HELMER: Good-bye, good-bye, old friend.

NORA: Sleep well, Doctor.

RANK: Thanks for that wish.

NORA: Wish me the same.

RANK: You? All right, if you like—Sleep well. And thanks for the light. (*He nods to them both and leaves.*)

HELMER (*his voice subdued*): He's been drinking heavily.

NORA (*absently*): Could be. (*Helmer takes his keys from his pocket and goes out in the hall.*) Torvald—what are you after?

HELMER: Got to empty the mailbox; it's nearly full. There won't be room for the morning papers.

NORA: Are you working tonight?

HELMER: You know I'm not. Why—what's this? Someone's been at the lock.

NORA: At the lock—?

HELMER: Yes, I'm positive. What do you suppose—? I can't imagine one of the maids—? Here's a broken hairpin. Nora, it's yours—

NORA (*quickly*): Then it must be the children—

HELMER: You'd better break them of that. Hm, hm—well, opened it after all. (*Takes the contents out and calls into the kitchen.*) Helene! Helene, would you put out the lamp in the hall. (*He returns to the room, shutting the hall door, then displays the handful of mail.*) Look how it's piled up. (*Sorting through them.*) Now what's this?

NORA (*at the window*): The letter! Oh, Torvald, no!

HELMER: Two calling cards—from Rank. *[handwritten: He won't read the letter, it'll be already over Rank]*

NORA: From Dr. Rank?

HELMER (*examining them*): "Dr. Rank, Consulting Physician." They were on top. He must have dropped them in as he left.

NORA: Is there anything on them?

HELMER: There's a black cross over the name. See? That's a gruesome notion. He could almost be announcing his own death.

NORA: That's just what he's doing.

[handwritten at bottom: He's going to kill himself. That's where he'll be invisible.]

HELMER: What! You've heard something? Something he's told you?

NORA: Yes. That when those cards came, he'd be taking his leave of us. He'll shut himself in now and die.

HELMER: Ah, my poor friend! Of course I knew he wouldn't be here much longer. But so soon—And then to hide himself away like a wounded animal.

NORA: If it has to happen, then it's best it happens in silence—don't you think so, Torvald?

HELMER (*pacing up and down*): He's grown right into our lives. I simply can't imagine him gone. He with his suffering and loneliness—like a dark cloud setting off our sunlit happiness. Well, maybe it's best this way. For him, at least. (*Standing still.*) And maybe for us too, Nora. Now we're thrown back on each other, completely. (*Embracing her.*) Oh you, my darling wife, how can I hold you close enough? You know what, Nora—time and again I've wished you were in some terrible danger, just so I could stake my life and soul and everything, for your sake.

NORA (*tearing herself away, her voice firm and decisive*): Now you must read your mail, Torvald.

HELMER: No, no, not tonight. I want to stay with you, dearest.

NORA: With a dying friend on your mind?

HELMER: You're right. We've both had a shock. There's ugliness between us—these thoughts of death and corruption. We'll have to get free of them first. Until then—we'll stay apart.

NORA (*clinging about his neck*): Torvald—good night! Good night!

HELMER (*kissing her on the cheek*): Good night, little songbird. Sleep well, Nora. I'll be reading my mail now. (*He takes the letters into his room and shuts the door after him.*)

NORA (*with bewildered glances, groping about, seizing Helmer's domino, throwing it around her, and speaking in short, hoarse, broken whispers*): Never see him again. Never, never. (*Putting her shawl over her head.*) Never see the children either—them, too. Never, never. Oh, the freezing black water! The depths—down—Oh, I wish it were over—He has it now; he's reading it—now. Oh no, no, not yet. Torvald, good-bye, you and the children—(*She starts for the hall; as she does, Helmer throws open his door and stands with an open letter in his hand.*)

HELMER: Nora!

NORA (*screams*): Oh—!

HELMER: What is this? You know what's in this letter?

NORA: Yes, I know. Let me go! Let me out!

HELMER (*holding her back*): Where are you going?

NORA (*struggling to break loose*): You can't save me, Torvald!

HELMER (*slumping back*): True! Then it's true what he writes? How horrible! No, no, it's impossible—it can't be true.

NORA: It *is* true. I've loved you more than all this world.

HELMER: Ah, none of your slippery tricks.

NORA (*taking one step toward him*): Torvald—!

HELMER: What *is* this you've blundered into!

NORA: Just let me loose. You're not going to suffer for my sake. You're not going to take on my guilt.

HELMER: No more playacting. (*Locks the hall door.*) You stay right here and give me a reckoning. You understand what you've done? Answer! You understand?

NORA (*looking squarely at him, her face hardening*): Yes. I'm beginning to understand everything now.

HELMER (*striding about*): Oh, what an awful awakening! In all these eight years—she who was my pride and joy—a hypocrite, a liar—worse, worse—a criminal! How infinitely disgusting it all is! The shame! (*Nora says nothing and goes on looking straight at him. He stops in front of her.*) I should have suspected something of the kind. I should have known. All your father's flimsy values—Be still! All your father's flimsy values have come out in you. No religion, no morals, no sense of duty—Oh, how I'm punished for letting him off! I did it for your sake, and you repay me like this.

NORA: Yes, like this.

HELMER: Now you've wrecked all my happiness—ruined my whole future. Oh, it's awful to think of. I'm in a cheap little grafter's hands; he can do anything he wants with me, ask for anything, play with me like a puppet—and I can't breathe a word. I'll be swept down miserably into the depths on account of a featherbrained woman.

NORA: When I'm gone from this world, you'll be free.

HELMER: Oh, quit posing. Your father had a mess of those speeches too. What good would that ever do me if you were gone from this world, as you say? Not the slightest. He can still make the whole thing known; and if he does, I could be falsely suspected as your accomplice. They might even think that I was behind it—that I put you up to it. And all that I can thank you for—you that I've coddled the whole of our marriage. Can you see now what you've done to me?

NORA (*icily calm*): Yes.

HELMER: It's so incredible, I just can't grasp it. But we'll have to patch up whatever we can. Take off the shawl. I said, take it off! I've got to appease him somehow or other. The thing has to be hushed up at any cost. And as for you and me, it's got to seem like everything between us is just as it was—to the outside world, that is. You'll go right on living in this house, of course. But you can't be allowed to bring up the children; I don't dare trust you with them—Oh, to have to say this to someone I've loved so much! Well, that's done with. From now on happiness doesn't matter; all that matters is saving the bits and pieces, the appearance—(*The doorbell rings. Helmer starts.*) What's that? And so late. Maybe the worst—? You think he'd—? Hide, Nora! Say you're sick. (*Nora remains standing motionless. Helmer goes and opens the door.*)

MAID (*half dressed, in the hall*): A letter for Mrs. Helmer.

HELMER: I'll take it. (*Snatches the letter and shuts the door.*) Yes, it's from him. You don't get it; I'm reading it myself.

NORA: Then read it.

HELMER (*by the lamp*): I hardly dare. We may be ruined, you and I. But—I've got to know. (*Rips open the letter, skims through a few lines, glances at an enclosure, then cries out joyfully.*) Nora! (*Nora looks inquiringly at him.*) Nora! Wait—better check it again—Yes, yes, it's true. I'm saved. Nora, I'm saved!

NORA: And I?

HELMER: You too, of course. We're both saved, both of us. Look. He's sent back your note. He says he's sorry and ashamed—that a happy development in his life—oh, who cares what he says! Nora, we're saved! No one can hurt you. Oh, Nora, Nora—but first, this ugliness all has to go. Let me see—(*Takes a look at the note.*) No, I don't want to see it; I want the whole thing to fade like a dream. (*Tears the note and both letters to pieces, throws them into the stove and watches them burn.*) There—now there's nothing left—He wrote that since Christmas Eve you—Oh, they must have been three terrible days for you, Nora.

NORA: I fought a hard fight.

HELMER: And suffered pain and saw no escape but—No, we're not going to dwell on anything unpleasant. We'll just be grateful and keep on repeating: It's over now, it's over! You hear me, Nora? You don't seem to realize—it's over. What's it mean—that frozen look? Oh, poor little Nora, I understand. You can't believe I've forgiven you. But I have, Nora; I swear I have. I know that what you did, you did out of love for me.

NORA: That's true.

HELMER: You loved me the way a wife ought to love her husband. It's simply the means that you couldn't judge. But you think I love you any the less for not knowing how to handle your affairs? No, no—just lean on me; I'll guide you and teach you. I wouldn't be a man if this feminine helplessness didn't make you twice as attractive to me. You mustn't mind those sharp words I said—that was all in the first confusion of thinking my world had collapsed. I've forgiven you, Nora; I swear I've forgiven you.

NORA: My thanks for your forgiveness. (*She goes out through the door, right.*)

HELMER: No, wait—(*Peers in.*) What are you doing in there?

NORA (*inside*): Getting out of my costume.

HELMER (*by the open door*): Yes, do that. Try to calm yourself and collect your thoughts again, my frightened little songbird. You can rest easy now; I've got wide wings to shelter you with. (*Walking about close by the door.*) How snug and nice our home is, Nora. You're safe here; I'll keep you like a hunted dove I've rescued out of a hawk's claws. I'll bring peace to your poor, shuddering heart. Gradually it'll happen, Nora; you'll see. Tomorrow all this will look different to you; then everything will be as it was. I won't have to go on repeating I forgive you; you'll feel it for yourself. How can you imagine I'd ever conceivably want to disown you—or even blame you in any way? Ah, you don't know a man's heart, Nora. For a man there's something indescribably sweet and satisfying in knowing he's forgiven his wife—and forgiven her out of a full and open heart. It's as if she belongs to him in two ways now: In a sense he's given her fresh into the world again, and she's become his wife and his child as well. From now on that's what you'll be to me—you little, bewildered, helpless thing. Don't be afraid of anything, Nora; just open your heart to me, and I'll be conscience and will to you both—(*Nora enters in her regular clothes.*) What's this? Not in bed? You've changed your dress?

NORA: Yes, Torvald, I've changed my dress.

HELMER: But why now, so late?

NORA: Tonight I'm not sleeping.

HELMER: But Nora dear—

NORA (*looking at her watch*): It's still not so very late. Sit down, Torvald; we have a lot to talk over. (*She sits at one side of the table.*)

HELMER: Nora—what is this? That hard expression—

NORA: Sit down. This'll take some time. I have a lot to say.

HELMER (*sitting at the table directly opposite her*): You worry me, Nora. And I don't understand you.

NORA: No, that's exactly it. You don't understand me. And I've never understood you either—until tonight. No, don't interrupt. You can just listen to what I say. We're closing out accounts, Torvald.

HELMER: How do you mean that?

NORA (*after a short pause*): Doesn't anything strike you about our sitting here like this?

HELMER: What's that?

NORA: We've been married now eight years. Doesn't it occur to you that this is the first time we two, you and I, man and wife, have ever talked seriously together?

HELMER: What do you mean—seriously?

NORA: In eight whole years—longer even—right from our first acquaintance, we've never exchanged a serious word on any serious thing.

HELMER: You mean I should constantly go and involve you in problems you couldn't possibly help me with?

NORA: I'm not talking of problems. I'm saying that we've never sat down seriously together and tried to get to the bottom of anything.

HELMER: But dearest, what good would that ever do you?

NORA: That's the point right there: You've never understood me. I've been wronged greatly, Torvald—first by Papa, and then by you.

HELMER: What! By us—the two people who've loved you more than anyone else?

NORA (*shaking her head*): You never loved me. You've thought it fun to be in love with me, that's all.

HELMER: Nora, what a thing to say!

NORA: Yes, it's true now, Torvald. When I lived at home with Papa, he told me all his opinions, so I had the same ones too; or if they were different I hid them, since he wouldn't have cared for that. He used to call me his doll-child, and he played with me the way I played with my dolls. Then I came into your house—

Nora and Torvald (Stephen Moore).

HELMER: How can you speak of our marriage like that?

NORA (*unperturbed*): I mean, then I went from Papa's hands into yours. You arranged everything to your own taste, and so I got the same taste as you—or I pretended to; I can't remember. I guess a little of both, first one, then the other. Now when I look back, it seems as if I'd lived here like a beggar—just from hand to mouth. I've lived by doing tricks for you, Torvald. But that's the way you wanted it. It's a great sin what you and Papa did to me. You're to blame that nothing's become of me.

HELMER: Nora, how unfair and ungrateful you are! Haven't you been happy here?

NORA: No, never. I thought so—but I never have.

HELMER: Not—not happy!

NORA: No, only lighthearted. And you've always been so kind to me. But our home's been nothing but a play-pen. I've been your doll-wife here, just as at home I was Papa's doll-child. And in turn the children have been my dolls. I thought it was fun when you played with me, just as they thought it fun when I played with them. That's been our marriage, Torvald.

HELMER: There's some truth in what you're saying—under all the raving exaggeration. But it'll all be different after this. Playtime's over; now for the schooling.

NORA: Whose schooling—mine or the children's?

HELMER: Both yours and the children's, dearest.

NORA: Oh, Torvald, you're not the man to teach me to be a good wife to you.

HELMER: And you can say that?

NORA: And I—how am I equipped to bring up children?

HELMER: Nora!

NORA: Didn't you say a moment ago that that was no job to trust me with?

HELMER: In a flare of temper! Why fasten on that?

NORA: Yes, but you were so very right. I'm not up to the job. There's another job I have to do first. I have to try to educate myself. You can't help me with that. I've got to do it alone. And that's why I'm leaving you now.

HELMER (*jumping up*): What's that?

NORA: I have to stand completely alone, if I'm ever going to discover myself and the world out there. So I can't go on living with you.

HELMER: Nora, Nora!

NORA: I want to leave right away. Kristine should put me up for the night—

HELMER: You're insane! You've no right! I forbid you!

NORA: From here on, there's no use forbidding me anything. I'll take with me whatever is mine. I don't want a thing from you, either now or later.

HELMER: What kind of madness is this!

NORA: Tomorrow I'm going home—I mean, home where I came from. It'll be easier up there to find something to do. *She's killing herself*

HELMER: Oh, you blind, incompetent child!

NORA: I must learn to be competent, Torvald.

HELMER: Abandon your home, your husband, your children! And you're not even thinking what people will say) ...*priorities man*

NORA: I can't be concerned about that. I only know how essential this is.

HELMER: Oh, it's outrageous. So you'll run out like this on your most sacred vows.

NORA: What do you think are my most sacred vows?

HELMER: And I have to tell you that! Aren't they your duties to your husband and children?

NORA: I have other duties equally sacred.

HELMER: That isn't true. What duties are they?

NORA: Duties to myself. *Women's RIGHTS!*

HELMER: Before all else, you're a wife and a mother.

NORA: I don't believe in that anymore. I believe that before all else, I'm a human being, no less than you—or anyway, I ought to try to become one. I know the majority thinks you're right, Torvald, and plenty of books agree with you, too. But I can't go on believing what the majority says, or what's written in books. I have to think over these things myself and try to understand them. *yes*

HELMER: Why can't you understand your place in your own home? On a point like that, isn't there one everlasting guide you can turn to? Where's your religion?

NORA: Oh, Torvald, I'm really not sure what religion is.

HELMER: What—?

NORA: I only know what the minister said when I was confirmed. He told me religion was this thing and that. When I get clear and away by myself, I'll go into that problem too. I'll see if what the minister said was right, or, in any case, if it's right for me.

HELMER: A young woman your age shouldn't talk like that. If religion can't move you, I can try to rouse your conscience. You do have some moral feeling? Or, tell me—has that gone too?

NORA: It's not easy to answer that, Torvald. I simply don't know. I'm all confused about these things. I just know I see them so differently from you. I find out for one thing, that the law's not at all what I'd thought—but I can't get it through my head that the law is fair. A woman hasn't a right to protect her dying father or save her husband's life! I can't believe that.

HELMER: You talk like a child. You don't know anything of the world you live in.

NORA: No, I don't. But now I'll begin to learn for myself. I'll try to discover who's right, the world or I. *Mistake*

HELMER: Nora, you're sick; you've got a fever. I almost think you're out of your head.

NORA: I've never felt more clearheaded and sure in my life.

Janet McTeer as Nora Helmer in Anthony Page's production of *A Doll House* at the Belasco Theater on Broadway, 1997. McTeer's interpretation of the role electrified audiences, who, according to Ben Brantley, found "previously hidden nuances in Ibsen's landmark work."

HELMER: And—clearheaded and sure—you're leaving your husband and children?

NORA: Yes.

HELMER: Then there's only one possible reason.

NORA: What?

HELMER: You no longer love me.

NORA: No. That's exactly it.

HELMER: Nora! You can't be serious!

NORA: Oh, this is so hard, Torvald—you've been so kind to me always. But I can't help it. I don't love you anymore.

HELMER (*struggling for composure*): Are you also clearheaded and sure about that?

NORA: Yes, completely. That's why I can't go on staying here.

HELMER: Can you tell me what I did to lose your love?

NORA: Yes, I can tell you. It was this evening when the miraculous thing didn't come—then I knew you weren't the man I'd imagined.

HELMER: Be more explicit; I don't follow you.

NORA: I've waited now so patiently eight long years—for, my Lord, I know miracles don't come every day. Then this crisis broke over me, and such a certainty filled me: *Now* the miraculous event would occur. While Krogstad's letter was lying out there, I never for an instant dreamed that you could give in to his terms. I was so utterly sure you'd say to him: Go on, tell your tale to the whole wide world. And when he'd done that—

HELMER: Yes, what then? When I'd delivered my own wife into shame and disgrace—!

NORA: When he'd done that, I was so utterly sure that you'd step forward, take the blame on yourself and say: I am the guilty one.

HELMER: Nora—!

NORA: You're thinking I'd never accept such a sacrifice from you? No, of course not. But what good would my protests be against you? That was the miracle I was waiting for, in terror and hope. And to stave that off, I would have taken my life.

HELMER: I'd gladly work for you day and night, Nora—and take on pain and deprivation. But there's no one who gives up honor for love.

NORA: Millions of women have done just that.

HELMER: Oh, you think and talk like a silly child.

NORA: Perhaps. But you neither think nor talk like the man I could join myself to. When your big fright was over—and it wasn't from any threat against me, only for what might damage you—when all the danger was past, for you it was just as if nothing had happened. I was exactly the same, your little lark, your doll, that you'd have to handle with double care now that I'd turned out so brittle and frail. (*Gets up.*) Torvald—in that instant it dawned on me that for eight years I've been living here with a stranger, and that I'd even conceived three children—oh, I can't stand the thought of it! I could tear myself to bits.

HELMER (*heavily*): I see. There's a gulf that's opened between us—that's clear. Oh, but Nora, can't we bridge it somehow?

NORA: The way I am now, I'm no wife for you.

HELMER: I have the strength to make myself over.

NORA: Maybe—if your doll gets taken away.

HELMER: But to part! To part from you! No, Nora, no—I can't imagine it.

NORA (*going out, right*): All the more reason why it has to be. (*She reenters with her coat and a small overnight bag, which she puts on a chair by the table.*)

HELMER: Nora, Nora, not now! Wait till tomorrow.

NORA: I can't spend the night in a strange man's room.

HELMER: But couldn't we live here like brother and sister—

NORA: You know very well how long that would last. (*Throws her shawl about her.*) Good-bye, Torvald. I won't look in on the children. I know they're in better hands than mine. The way I am now, I'm no use to them.

HELMER: But someday, Nora—someday—?

NORA: How can I tell? I haven't the least idea what'll become of me.

HELMER: But you're my wife, now and wherever you go.

NORA: Listen, Torvald—I've heard that when a wife deserts her husband's house just as I'm doing, then the law frees him from all responsibility. In any case, I'm freeing you from being responsible. Don't feel yourself bound, any more than I will. There has to be absolute freedom for us both. Here, take your ring back. Give me mine.

HELMER: That too?

NORA: That too.

HELMER: There it is.

NORA: Good. Well, now it's all over. I'm putting the keys here. The maids know all about keeping up the house—better than I do. Tomorrow, after I've left town, Kristine will stop by to pack up everything that's mine from home. I'd like those things shipped up to me.

HELMER: Over! All over! Nora, won't you ever think about me?

NORA: I'm sure I'll think of you often, and about the children and the house here.

HELMER: May I write you?

NORA: No—never. You're not to do that.

HELMER: Oh, but let me send you—

NORA: Nothing. Nothing.

HELMER: Or help you if you need it.

NORA: No. I accept nothing from strangers.

HELMER: Nora—can I never be more than a stranger to you?

NORA (*picking up the overnight bag*): Ah, Torvald—it would take the greatest miracle of all—

HELMER: Tell me the greatest miracle!

NORA: You and I both would have to transform ourselves to the point that—Oh, Torvald, I've stopped believing in miracles.

HELMER: But I'll believe. Tell me! Transform ourselves to the point that—?

NORA: That our living together could be a true marriage. (*She goes out down the hall.*)

HELMER (*sinks down on a chair by the door, face buried in his hands*): Nora! Nora! (*Looking about and rising.*) Empty. She's gone. (*A sudden hope leaps in him.*) The greatest miracle—?

(*From below, the sound of a door slamming shut.*)

COMMENTARIES

Ibsen wrote about his own work, both in his letters to producers and actors and in his notes describing the development of his plays. Such notes reveal his concern, his insights as he wrote the plays, and his motives. Sometimes what he says about the plays does not completely square with modern interpretations. On the other hand, he explains in his notes that the circumstances of women in modern society were much on his mind when he was working on *A Doll House*.

Ibsen's "Notes for the Modern Tragedy" is remarkable for suggesting a separate sensibility (spiritual law) for men and for women. His observations about the society in which women live—and in which Nora is confounded—sound as if they could have been written a century later than they were. Muriel C. Bradbrook's discussion of *A Doll House* focuses on the moral bankruptcy of Nora's situation, which is to say the situation of all wives of the period.

HENRIK IBSEN (1828–1906)

Notes for the Modern Tragedy   1878

TRANSLATED BY A. G. CHATER

Ibsen's first notes for *A Doll House* were jotted down on October 19, 1878. They show that his thinking on the relations between men and women was quite sophisticated and that the material for the play had been gestating for some time. His comments indicate that the essentially male society he knew was one of his central concerns in the play. *Why wasn't the women's rights movement sooner if this was so common then?*

There are two kinds of spiritual law, two kinds of conscience, one in man and another, altogether different, in woman. They do not understand each other; but in practical life the woman is judged by man's law, as though she were not a woman but a man.

The wife in the play ends by having no idea of what is right or wrong; natural feeling on the one hand and belief in authority on the other have altogether bewildered her.

A woman cannot be herself in the society of the present day, which is an exclusively masculine society, with laws framed by men and with a judicial system that judges feminine conduct from a masculine point of view.

Where does all the love go then?

She has committed forgery, and she is proud of it; for she did it out of love for her husband, to save his life. But this husband with his commonplace principles of honor is on the side of the law and looks at the question from the masculine point of view.

Spiritual conflicts. Oppressed and bewildered by the belief in authority, she loses faith in her moral right and ability to bring up her children. Bitterness. A mother in modern society, like certain insects who go away and die when she has

715

done her duty in the propagation of the race. Love of life, of home, of husband and children and family. Now and then a womanly shaking off of her thoughts. Sudden return of anxiety and terror. She must bear it all alone. The catastrophe approaches, inexorably, inevitably. Despair, conflict, and destruction.

(Krogstad has acted dishonorably and thereby become well-to-do; now his prosperity does not help him, he cannot recover his honor.)

MURIEL C. BRADBROOK (1909–1993)

A Doll's House: Ibsen the Moralist   1948

In her important study of Ibsen, *Ibsen: The Norwegian*, Muriel C. Bradbrook discusses all the important plays, but she reserves a special place for *A Doll House*. In her analysis she suggests that Nora slowly discovers the fundamental bankruptcy of her marriage. Bradbrook calls it "eight years' prostitution." She also shows the true extent of Torvald's possessiveness and immaturity. As Bradbrook says, the true moment of recognition — in the Greek tragic sense — occurs when Nora sees both herself and Torvald in their true nature. Bradbrook also helps us see the full implication of Nora's leaving her home. She can never hope again for the comforts she has enjoyed as Torvald's wife.

Poor Nora, living by playing her tricks like a little pet animal, sensing how to manage Torvald by those pettinesses in his character she does not know she knows of, is too vulnerably sympathetic to find her life-work in reading John Stuart Mill. At the end she still does not understand the strange world in which she has done wrong by forging a signature. She does understand that she has lived by what Virginia Woolf called "the slow waterlogged sinking of her will into his." And this picture is built up for her and for us by the power of structural implication, a form of writing particularly suited to drama, where the latent possibilities of a long stretch of past time can be thrown into relief by a crisis. In *A Doll's House,* the past is not only lighted up by the present, as a transparency might be lit up with a lamp; the past is changed by the present so that it becomes a different thing. Nora's marriage becomes eight years' prostitution, as she gradually learns the true nature of her relations with Torvald and the true nature of Torvald's feelings for her.

In act I, no less than six different episodes bring out the war that is secretly waged between his masculine dictatorship and her feminine wiles:

Her wheedling him for money with a simple transference: "Let us do as *you* suggest. . . ."

Her promise to Christine: "Just leave it to me: I will broach the matter very cleverly." She is evidently habituated to and aware of her own technique.

Her description of how she tried to coax Torvald into taking the holiday and how she was saving up the story of the bond "for when I am no longer as good-looking as I am now." She knows the precarious nature of her hold.

Her method of asking work for Christine by putting Christine also into a (completely bogus) position of worshiping subservience to Torvald.

Her boast to Krogstad about her influence. Whilst this may be a justifiable triumph over her tormentor, it is an unconscious betrayal of Torvald (witness his fury in act II at the idea of being thought uxorious).

After this faceted exposition, the treatment grows much broader. Nora admits Torvald's jealousy: Yet she flirts with Rank, aware but not acknowledging the grounds of her control. The pressure of implication remains constant throughout: It is comparable with the effect of a dialect, coloring all that is said. To take a few lines at random from the dialogue of Nora and Rank in act II:

> NORA (*putting her hand on his shoulder*): Dear, dear Dr. Rank! Death mustn't take you away from Torvald and me. [Nora is getting demonstrative as she senses Rank's responsiveness, and her hopes of obtaining a loan from him rise. Hence her warmth of feeling, purely seductive.]
>
> RANK: It is a loss you will easily recover from. Those who are gone away are soon forgotten. [Poor Rank is reminded by that "Torvald and me" how little he really counts to Nora.]
>
> NORA (*anxiously*): Do you believe that? [Rank has awakened her thoughts of what may happen if *she* has to go away.]

Her methods grow more desperate—the open appeal to Torvald to keep Krogstad and the frantic expedient of the tarantella. In the last act her fate is upon her; yet in spite of all her terror and Torvald's tipsy amorousness, she still believes in his chivalry and devotion. This extraordinary self-deception is perhaps the subtlest and most telling implication of all. Practice had left her theory unshaken: So when the crash comes, she cries, "I have been living with a strange man," yet it was but the kind of man her actions had always implied him to be. Her vanity had completely prevented her from recognizing what she was doing, even though she had become such an expert at doing it.

Torvald is more gradually revealed. In the first act he appears indulgent, perhaps a trifle inclined to nag about the macaroons and to preach, but virtually a more efficient David Copperfield curbing a rather better-trained Dora. In the second act, his resentment and his pleasure alike uncover the deeper bases of his dominance. His anger at the prospect of being thought under his wife's influence and his fury at the imputation of narrow-mindedness show that it is really based on his own cowardice, the need for something weaker to bully: This is confirmed when he gloats over Nora's panic as evidence of her love for him, and over her agitation in the tarantella ("you little helpless thing!"). His love of order and his fastidiousness, when joined to such qualities, betray a set personality; and the last act shows that he has neither control nor sympathy on the physical level. But he is no fool, and his integrity is not all cowardice. Doubtless, debt or forgery really was abhorrent to him.

The climax of the play comes when Nora sees Torvald and sees herself: It is an *anagnorisis*, a recognition. Her life is cored like an apple. For she has had no life apart from this. Behind the irrelevant program for self-education there stands a woman, pitifully inexperienced, numbed by emotional shock, but with a newfound will to face what has happened, to accept her bankruptcy, as, in a very different way, Peer Gynt had at last accepted his.

"Yes, I am beginning to understand. . . ." she says. "What you did," observes the now magnanimous Torvald, "you did out of love for me." "That is true," says Nora: And she calls him to a "settling of accounts," not in any spirit of hostility but in an attempt to organize vacancy. "I have made nothing of my life. . . . I must stand quite alone . . . it is necessary to me . . ." That is really the program. *Ainsi tout leur a craqué dans les mains.*°

The spare and laminated speech gains its effect by inference and riddle. But these are the characteristic virtues of Norse. Irony is its natural weapon. Ibsen was working with the grain of the language. It was no accident that it fell to a Norwegian to take that most finely tooled art, the drama, and bring it to a point and precision so nice that literally not a phrase is without its direct contribution to the structure. The unrelenting cohesion of *A Doll's House* is perhaps, like that of the *Oedipus the King,* too hard on the playgoer; he is allowed no relief. Nora cannot coo to her baby without saying: "My sweet little *baby doll!*" or play with her children without choosing, significantly, *Hide and Seek.* Ibsen will not allow the smallest action to escape from the psychopathology of everyday life. However, a play cannot be acted so that every moment is tense with significance, and, in practice, an actor, for the sake of light and shade, will probably slur some of Ibsen's points, deliberately or unconsciously. The tension between the characters is such that the slightest movement of one sets all the others quivering. But this is partly because they are seen with such detachment, like a clear-cut intaglio. The play is, above all, articulated.

That is not to say that it is the mere dissection of a problem. Perhaps Rank and Mrs. Linde would have been more subtly wrought into the action at a later date; but the tight control kept over Nora and Torvald does not mean that they can be exhausted by analysis or staled by custom. They are so far in advance of the characters of *Pillars of Society* that they are capable of the surprising yet inevitable development that marks the character conceived "in the round," the character that is, in Ibsen's phrase, fully "seen."

Consider, for example, Torvald's soliloquy whilst Nora is taking off her masquerade dress. It recalls at one moment Dickens's most unctuous hypocrites—"Here I will protect you like a hunted dove that I have saved from the claws of the hawk!"—at another Meredith's Willoughby Patterne°—"Only be frank and open with me and I will be both will and conscience to you"—yet from broadest caricature to sharpest analysis, it remains the self-glorified strut of the one character, the bank clerk in his pride, cousin to Peer Gynt, that typical Norwegian, and to Hjalmer Ekdal, the toiling breadwinner of the studio.

Whilst the Ibsenites might have conceded that Torvald is Art, they would probably have contended that Nora is Truth. Nora, however, is much more than a Revolting Wife. She is not a sour misanthropist or a fighting suffragette, but a lovely young woman who knows that she still holds her husband firmly infatuated after eight years of marriage. . . .

In leaving her husband Nora is seeking a fuller life as a human being. She is emancipating herself. Yet the seeking itself is also a renunciation, a kind of death—"I must stand alone." No less than Falk, or the hero of *On the Vidda,* she gives up something that has been her whole life. She is as broken as Torvald in the end: But she is a strong character and he is a weak one. In the "happy ending" which Ibsen reluctantly allowed to be used, it was the sight of the children that

---

Ainsi . . . mains: Thus everything has shattered in their hands.
Willoughby Patterne: The protagonist in George Meredith's novel *The Egoist* (1879), an arrogant aristocrat who lacks awareness of the needs and desires of the women in his life.

persuaded her to stay, and unless it is remembered that leaving Torvald means leaving the children, the full measure of Nora's decision cannot be taken. An actress gets her chance to make this point in the reply to Torvald's plea that Nora should stay for the children's sake.

It should be remembered, too, that the seriousness of the step she takes is lost on the present generation. She was putting herself outside society, inviting insult, destitution, and loneliness. She went out into a very dark night.

August Strindberg

The Swedish playwright August Strindberg (1849–1912) wrote fifty-eight plays, more than a dozen novels, and more than a hundred short stories, all collected now in fifty-five volumes. During the time he was producing this astonishing body of work, he was the victim of persistent paranoia, suffered the destruction of three marriages, and lived through a major nervous breakdown.

He was a man of enormous complexity whose work has traditionally been broken into two periods. The first consists of the work he wrote up to 1894, which includes *The Father* (1877), *Miss Julie* (1888), *The Creditors* (1889), and other naturalistic plays. The second consists of work he wrote after 1897, including *To Damascus* (1898–1901), *There Are Crimes and Crimes* (1899), *Easter* and *The Dance of Death* (both 1901), *A Dream Play* (1902), and *Ghost Sonata* (1907); these are largely expressionist plays. **Expressionism** disregarded the strict demands of naturalism to present a "slice of life" without artistic shaping of plot and resolution. Instead, expressionist drama used materials that resembled dreams—or nightmares—and focused on symbolic actions and a subjective interpretation of the world. Strindberg's later drama is often symbolic, taut, and psychological. His novel *Inferno* (1897) not only marks the transition between his early and late work but also gives this period of his life its name. Strindberg's *Inferno* period was a time of madness and paranoic behavior that virtually redirected his life for more than three years. During this time he was convinced that the secrets of life were wrapped in the occult, and his energies went into alchemical experiments and studies of cabalistic lore.

The first period of his dramatic career began with *Master Olof* (1872), a historical drama that he chose to write in prose, which he felt was a more natural medium than verse, the convention for such plays at the time. The play was turned down by the Royal Dramatic Theatre, and he rewrote it in verse in 1876. It was rejected for a second time but was finally produced the following year. At that time, Strindberg recorded, "In 1877 Antoine opened his Théâtre Libre in Paris, and *Thérèse Raquin*, although nothing but an adapted novel, became the dominant model. It was the powerful theme and the concentrated form that showed innovation, although the unity of time was not yet observed, and curtain falls were retained. It was then I wrote my dramas: *Lady Julie, The Father,* and *Creditors*." *Thérèse Raquin,* Émile Zola's naturalistic play, inspired Strindberg to move further toward his own interpretation of naturalism, which is perhaps most evident in *Miss Julie.* Strindberg was more subjective in his approach to naturalism, less scientific and deterministic, than Zola. Whereas Zola's approach might be described as photographic realism, Strindberg's was more selective and impressionistic but no less honest and true. He saw his characters operating out of "a whole series of deeply buried motives." They were not necessarily the product of their biology or their social circumstances, as the naturalists of Zola's stripe sometimes implied. Yet Strindberg saw clearly that class distinctions helped determine the behavior of many people. He seemed to accept the view that people were not created by their class but rather belonged to their class because of the kind of people they were. Strindberg probed deeply into the psychology of his characters, whose emotional lives, rather than outward social qualities, determined their actions.

Strindberg is often described as a woman-hater, a misogynist. For periods of his life he does seem to have been misogynistic, but he was nonetheless extremely contradictory in both behavior and belief. There is no simple way to talk about Strindberg's attitude toward women. On the one hand, he is conventional in his thinking that women belong in the home. On the other hand, he married a highly successful actress, Siri von Essen. As he said in a letter in 1895, "Woman is to me the earth and all its glory, the bond that binds, and of all the evil the worst evil I have seen is the female sex." A decade later, in *A Blue Book*, he wrote, "When I approach a woman as a lover, I look up to her, I see something of the mother in her, and this I respect. I assume a subordinate position, become childish and puerile and actually am subordinate, like most men. . . . I put her on a pedestal." In his views of women, as in many things, including his attitude toward dramatic techniques and style, Strindberg is a mass of contradictions and complexities of the sort sometimes associated with genius.

Miss Julie

For discussion questions and assignments on *Miss Julie*, visit **bedfordstmartins.com/jacobus.**

Miss Julie, the daughter of a count, and Jean, the count's valet, come from strikingly different social backgrounds. In ordinary circumstances, they might not be on friendly terms, much less become lovers, as they do. But the count is away, and Miss Julie and Jean are drawn into a sexual liaison marked by a struggle for dominance and control. Miss Julie's fiancé has been disposed of before the play begins because he refused to debase himself slavishly to her will. She is a free spirit, but her breeding is suspect because her mother, like her, took a lover and defied the count. Miss Julie's mother rebelled against her husband and punished him by burning their house down after the insurance expired. As further punishment and abasement, she humiliated the count by arranging to have her lover lend him the money to rebuild the house. Thus, Miss Julie's heritage is one of independence, rebellion, and unorthodoxy.

Under her mother's tutelage, Miss Julie was raised to manipulate men, but she cannot accept them totally. She also seems to feel contempt for herself as a woman mixed in with her contempt for men. In his preface to the play, Strindberg says that Julie is a modern "man-hating half-woman" who sells herself for honors of various kinds. (See the commentary on p. 738.)

The play has a mysterious quality. It takes place on Midsummer Eve, when lovers reveal themselves to one another and when almost anything can happen. In primitive fertility rites it was a time associated with sexual awakening. The cook, Kristine, mentions that it is the feast of St. John and alludes to his beheading for spurning Salome's advances. Jean (French for John) in one tense moment of the play beheads Julie's pet bird as a sign of the violence pent up in him. This incident foreshadows Miss Julie's death.

The fairy-tale quality that creeps into the play — as in *A Midsummer Night's Dream,* set on the same day — may seem out of place in a realistic drama, but it is profoundly compelling. It is also typical of Strindberg, who often uses symbolism to suggest a dream quality and deepen the significance of the action. (Dreams are a part of life that modern playwrights have taken great pains to explore.)

The count himself, Julie's father, never appears in the play, but his presence is always felt, ominous and intense, again much as in a fairy tale. Jean tells Miss Julie that he would willingly kill himself if the count were to order it. Kristine, like a witch, demands retribution because she was spurned by Jean, who was once her lover. Near the end of the play she prevents Julie and Jean from running away from the count by impounding the horses in the stable, thus taking revenge on both of them.

Although Julie may be seen as the princess, Jean has very little claim to being Prince Charming of the play, especially since he has little strength of character. He feels superior to his station as a valet, and Strindberg in his preface refers to him as a nobleman. However, like Kristine, he is coarse beneath his outwardly polished appearance. His highest ambition is to be the proprietor of a first-class hotel, a prospect he wants to share with Julie.

One of the most striking passages in the play is the story Jean tells Julie almost reluctantly. He tries to explain to her what it feels like to be "down below," where she has never been. When he was a boy, he thought of the apple trees in her father's garden as part of the "Garden of Eden, guarded by angry angels." He entered this enchanted place with his mother to weed onions and wandered into the outhouse — a building like a Turkish pavilion whose function he could not guess. While he was exploring it, he heard someone coming and had to exit beneath the outhouse and hide himself under a pile of weeds and "wet dirt that stank." From his hiding place he saw Julie in a pink dress and white stockings. He rushed to the millpond and jumped in to wash the filth off himself. Ironically, only a few moments after he tells her this story, he calls her a whore, and she, in response, says, "Oh, God in heaven, end my wretched life! Take me away from the filth I'm sinking into! Save me! Save me!"

Miss Julie falls under the power of her lover and cannot redirect her life; she sinks deeper and deeper into "filth." She has few choices at the end of the play, and the conclusion to *Miss Julie* is swift. The contrast between Julie's willfulness and Jean's caution makes their situation especially desperate. When Julie leaves at the end of the play to seal her fate, we sense the terrible weight of their society's values. Those values are symbolized by the return of the count and the expectations he had of Julie's behavior while he was gone.

Miss Julie in Performance

The first planned professional production of *Miss Julie* was canceled at the last minute by censors in Copenhagen on March 1, 1889. Although the play was performed privately on March 14, 1889, in Copenhagen University's Students' Union, it was not performed professionally in Stockholm until 1906. Some important early productions of the play were in Paris in André Antoine's distinguished Théâtre Libre in 1893 and in Berlin in Max Reinhardt's Kleines Theater in 1904. Reinhardt produced seventeen of Strindberg's plays and was one of his great champions. In 1907, Strindberg produced the play in his own Intimate Theatre in Stockholm, where it ran intermittently for 134 showings. He even arranged a special performance for Bernard Shaw. The first London production was in 1912, but since the 1930s the play has been revived many times, with many distinguished actors in all three major roles.

Among the notable modern productions is the Old Vic's 1966 version directed by Michael Elliott, with Maggie Smith and Albert Finney starring.

The Baxter Theatre of Johannesburg, South Africa, produced the play in 1985 with the black actor John Kani as Jean and the white Afrikaner actress Sandra Prinsloo as Julie. Some white audiences considered that casting outrageous. The sensational Ingmar Bergman production at the Brooklyn Academy of Music in 1991 stretched the play to two hours and made it more of a domestic tragedy—as John Simon said, "more like us, more believable, and, therefore, more terrifying."

Dramatist Frank McGuinness's translation of *Miss Julie* was produced at the Theatre Royal in London in 2000, with Christopher Eccleston and Aisling O'Sullivan in a carefully built period kitchen with period costumes. The sexual dynamic of the play was central to a production designed to attract a younger audience. In New York in 2005, the Rattlestick Playwrights Theatre produced a well-reviewed version, adapted by Craig Lucas, that emphasized the physicality of the protagonists and went so far as to show their lovemaking silhouetted behind a scrim during a scene change.

Filmed at least five times, *Miss Julie* has been televised as well. It is one of the most frequently produced modern plays.

AUGUST STRINDBERG (1849–1912)

Miss Julie   1888

TRANSLATED BY HARRY G. CARLSON

Characters

MISS JULIE, *25 years old*
JEAN, *her father's valet, 30 years old*
KRISTINE, *her father's cook, 35 years old*

(*The action takes place in the Count's kitchen on midsummer eve.*)

Setting: (*A large kitchen, the ceiling and side walls of which are hidden by draperies. The rear wall runs diagonally from down left to up right. On the wall down left are two shelves with copper, iron, and pewter utensils; the shelves are lined with scalloped paper. Visible to the right is most of a set of large, arched glass doors, through which can be seen a fountain with a statue of Cupid, lilac bushes in bloom, and the tops of some Lombardy poplars. At down left is the corner of a large tiled stove; a portion of its hood is showing. At right, one end of the servants' white pine dining table juts out; several chairs stand around it. The stove is decorated with birch branches; juniper twigs are strewn on the floor. On the end of the table stands a large*

Japanese spice jar, filled with lilac blossoms. An ice box, a sink, and a washstand. Above the door is an old-fashioned bell on a spring; to the left of the door, the mouthpiece of a speaking tube is visible.)

(*Kristine is frying something on the stove. She is wearing a light-colored cotton dress and an apron. Jean enters. He is wearing livery and carries a pair of high riding boots with spurs, which he puts down on the floor where they can be seen by the audience.*)

JEAN: Miss Julie's crazy again tonight; absolutely crazy!
KRISTINE: So you finally came back?
JEAN: I took the Count to the station and when I returned past the barn I stopped in for a dance. Who do I see but Miss Julie leading off the dance with the gamekeeper! But as soon as she saw me she rushed over to ask me for the next waltz. And she's been waltzing ever since—I've never seen anything like it. She's crazy!
KRISTINE: She always has been, but never as bad as the last two weeks since her engagement was broken off.
JEAN: Yes, I wonder what the real story was there. He was a gentleman, even if he wasn't rich. Ah! These

people have such romantic ideas. (*Sits at the end of the table.*) Still, it's strange, isn't it? I mean that she'd rather stay home with the servants on midsummer eve instead of going with her father to visit relatives?

KRISTINE: She's probably embarrassed after that row with her fiancé.

JEAN: Probably! He gave a good account of himself, though. Do you know how it happened, Kristine? I saw it, you know, though I didn't let on I had.

KRISTINE: No! You saw it?

JEAN: Yes, I did.————That evening they were out near the stable, and she was "training" him—as she called it. Do you know what she did? She made him jump over her riding crop, the way you'd teach a dog to jump. He jumped twice and she hit him each time. But the third time he grabbed the crop out of her hand, hit her with it across the cheek, and broke it in pieces. Then he left.

KRISTINE: So, that's what happened! I can't believe it!

JEAN: Yes, that's the way it went!————What have you got for me that's tasty, Kristine?

KRISTINE (*serving him from the pan*): Oh, it's only a piece of kidney I cut from the veal roast.

JEAN (*smelling the food*): Beautiful! That's my favorite *délice.*° (*Feeling the plate.*) But you could have warmed the plate!

KRISTINE: You're fussier than the Count himself, once you start! (*She pulls his hair affectionately.*)

JEAN (*angry*): Stop it, leave my hair alone! You know I'm touchy about that.

KRISTINE: Now, now, it's only love, you know that. (*Jean eats. Kristine opens a bottle of beer.*)

JEAN: Beer? On midsummer eve? No thank you! I can do better than that. (*Opens a drawer in the table and takes out a bottle of red wine with yellow sealing wax.*) See that? Yellow seal! Give me a glass! A wine glass! I'm drinking this *pur.*°

KRISTINE (*returns to the stove and puts on a small saucepan*): God help the woman who gets you for a husband! What a fussbudget.

JEAN: Nonsense! You'd be damned lucky to get a man like me. It certainly hasn't done you any harm to have people call me your sweetheart. (*Tastes the wine.*) Good! Very good! Just needs a little warming. (*Warms the glass between his hands.*) We bought this in Dijon. Four francs a liter, not counting the cost of the bottle, or the customs duty.————What are you cooking now? It stinks like hell!

KRISTINE: Oh, some slop Miss Julie wants to give Diana.

JEAN: Watch your language, Kristine. But why should you have to cook for that damn mutt on midsummer eve? Is she sick?

KRISTINE: Yes, she's sick! She sneaked out with the gatekeeper's dog—and now there's hell to pay. Miss Julie won't have it!

JEAN: Miss Julie has too much pride about some things and not enough about others, just like her mother was. The Countess was most at home in the kitchen and the cowsheds, but a *one*-horse carriage wasn't elegant enough for her. The cuffs of her blouse were dirty, but she had to have her coat of arms on her cufflinks.————And Miss Julie won't take proper care of herself either. If you ask me, she just isn't refined. Just now, when she was dancing in the barn, she pulled the gamekeeper away from Anna and made him dance with her. *We* wouldn't behave like that, but that's what happens when aristocrats pretend they're common people—they get *common!*———— But she is quite a woman! Magnificent! What shoulders, and what—et cetera!

KRISTINE: Oh, don't overdo it! I've heard what Clara says, and she dresses her.

JEAN: Ha, Clara! You're all jealous of each other! I've been out riding with her. . . . And the way she dances!

KRISTINE: Listen, Jean! You're going to dance with me, when I'm finished here, aren't you?

JEAN: Of course I will.

KRISTINE: Promise?

JEAN: Promise? When I say I'll do something, I do it! By the way, the kidney was very good. (*Corks the bottle.*)

JULIE (*in the doorway to someone outside*): I'll be right back! You go ahead for now! (*Jean sneaks the bottle back into the table drawer and gets up respectfully. Miss Julie enters and crosses to Kristine by the stove.*) Well? Is it ready? (*Kristine indicates that Jean is present.*)

JEAN (*gallantly*): Are you ladies up to something secret?

JULIE (*flicking her handkerchief in his face*): None of your business!

JEAN: Hmm! I like the smell of violets!

JULIE (*coquettishly*): Shame on you! So you know about perfumes, too? You certainly know how to dance. Ah, ah! No peeking! Go away.

JEAN (*boldly but respectfully*): Are you brewing up a magic potion for midsummer eve? Something to prophesy by under a lucky star, so you'll catch a glimpse of your future husband!

JULIE (*caustically*): You'd need sharp eyes to see him! (*To Kristine.*) Pour out half a bottle and cork it well.————Come and dance a schottische° with me, Jean . . .

JEAN (*hesitating*): I don't want to be impolite to anyone, and I've already promised this dance to Kristine . . .

JULIE: Oh, she can have another one—can't you, Kristine? Won't you lend me Jean?

KRISTINE: It's not up to me, ma'am. (*To Jean.*) If the mistress is so generous, it wouldn't do for you to say no. Go on, Jean, and thank her for the honor.

JEAN: To be honest, and no offense intended, I wonder whether it's wise for you to dance twice running with the same partner, especially since these people are quick to jump to conclusions . . .

JULIE (*flaring up*): What's that? What sort of conclusions? What do you mean?

---

délice: Delight.   *pur:* Pure; the first drink from the bottle.

schottische: A Scottish round dance resembling a polka.

JEAN (*submissively*): If you don't understand, ma'am, I must speak more plainly. It doesn't look good to play favorites with your servants. . . .

JULIE: Play favorites! What an idea! I'm astonished! As mistress of the house, I honor your dance with my presence. And when I dance, I want to dance with someone who can lead, so I won't look ridiculous.

JEAN: As you order, ma'am! I'm at your service!

JULIE (*gently*): Don't take it as an order! On a night like this we're all just ordinary people having fun, so we'll forget about rank. Now, take my arm!————Don't worry, Kristine! I won't steal your sweetheart! (*Jean offers his arm and leads Miss Julie out.*)

Mime

(*The following should be played as if the actress playing Kristine were really alone. When she has to, she turns her back to the audience. She does not look toward them, nor does she hurry as if she were afraid they would grow impatient. Schottische music played on a fiddle sounds in the distance. Kristine hums along with the music. She clears the table, washes the dishes, dries them, and puts them away. She takes off her apron. From a table drawer she removes a small mirror and leans it against the bowl of lilacs on the table. She lights a candle, heats a hairpin over the flame, and uses it to set a curl on her forehead. She crosses to the door and listens, then returns to the table. She finds the handkerchief Miss Julie left behind, picks it up, and smells it. Then, preoccupied, she spreads it out, stretches it, smoothes out the wrinkles, and folds it into quarters, and so forth.*)

JEAN (*enters alone*): God, she really *is* crazy! What a way to dance! Everybody's laughing at her behind her back. What do you make of it, Kristine?

KRISTINE: Ah! It's that time of the month for her, and she always gets peculiar like that. Are you going to dance with me now?

JEAN: You're not mad at me, are you, for leaving . . . ?

KRISTINE: Of course not!————Why should I be, for a little thing like that? Besides, I know my place . . .

JEAN (*puts his arm around her waist*): You're a sensible girl, Kristine, and you'd make a good wife . . .

JULIE (*entering; uncomfortably surprised; with forced good humor*): What a charming escort—running away from his partner.

JEAN: On the contrary, Miss Julie. Don't you see how I rushed back to the partner I abandoned!

JULIE (*changing her tone*): You know, you're a superb dancer!————But why are you wearing livery on a holiday? Take it off at once!

JEAN: Then I must ask you to go outside for a moment. You see, my black coat is hanging over here . . . (*Gestures and crosses right.*)

JULIE: Are you embarrassed about changing your coat in front of me? Well, go in your room then. Either that or stay and I'll turn my back.

JEAN: With your permission, ma'am! (*He crosses right. His arm is visible as he changes his jacket.*)

JULIE (*to Kristine*): Tell me, Kristine—you two are so close—. Is Jean your fiancé?

KRISTINE: Fiancé? Yes, if you wish. We can call him that.

JULIE: What do you mean?

KRISTINE: You had a fiancé yourself, didn't you? So . . .

JULIE: Well, we were properly engaged . . .

KRISTINE: But nothing came of it, did it? (*Jean returns dressed in a frock coat and bowler hat.*)

JULIE: *Très gentil, monsieur Jean! Très gentil!*

JEAN: *Vous voulez plaisanter, madame!*

JULIE: *Et vous voulez parler français!*° Where did you learn that?

JEAN: In Switzerland, when I was wine steward in one of the biggest hotels in Lucerne!

JULIE: You look like a real gentleman in that coat! *Charmant!*° (*Sits at the table.*)

JEAN: Oh, you're flattering me!

JULIE (*offended*): Flattering you?

JEAN: My natural modesty forbids me to believe that you would really compliment someone like me, and so I took the liberty of assuming that you were exaggerating, which polite people call flattering.

JULIE: Where did you learn to talk like that? You must have been to the theater often.

JEAN: Of course. And I've done a lot of traveling.

JULIE: But you come from here, don't you?

JEAN: My father was a farmhand on the district attorney's estate nearby. I used to see you when you were little, but you never noticed me.

JULIE: No! Really?

JEAN: Sure. I remember one time especially . . . but I can't talk about that.

JULIE: Oh, come now! Why not? Just this once!

JEAN: No, I really couldn't, not now. Some other time, perhaps.

JULIE: Why some other time? What's so dangerous about now?

JEAN: It's not dangerous, but there are obstacles.——Her, for example. (*Indicating Kristine, who has fallen asleep in a chair by the stove.*)

JULIE: What a pleasant wife she'll make! She probably snores, too.

JEAN: No, she doesn't, but she talks in her sleep.

JULIE (*cynically*): How do *you* know?

JEAN (*audaciously*): I've heard her! (*Pause, during which they stare at each other.*)

JULIE: Why don't you sit down?

JEAN: I couldn't do that in your presence.

JULIE: But if I order you to?

JEAN: Then I'd obey.

JULIE: Sit down, then.————No, wait. Can you get me something to drink first?

JEAN: I don't know what we have in the ice box. I think there's only beer.

Très gentil . . . français!: Very pleasing, Mr. Jean! Very pleasing. You would trifle with me, madam! And you want to speak French! *Charmant!:* Charming!

JULIE: Why do you say "only"? My tastes are so simple I prefer beer to wine. (*Jean takes a bottle of beer from the ice box and opens it. He looks for a glass and a plate in the cupboard and serves her.*)

JEAN: Here you are, ma'am.

JULIE: Thank you. Won't you have something yourself?

JEAN: I'm not partial to beer, but if it's an order . . .

JULIE: An order?———Surely a gentleman can keep his lady company.

JEAN: You're right, of course. (*Opens a bottle and gets a glass.*)

JULIE: Now, drink to my health! (*He hesitates.*) What? A man of the world—and shy?

JEAN (*in mock romantic fashion, he kneels and raises his glass*): Skål to my mistress!

JULIE: Bravo!———Now kiss my shoe, to finish it properly. (*Jean hesitates, then boldly seizes her foot and kisses it lightly.*) Perfect! You should have been an actor.

JEAN (*rising*): That's enough now, Miss Julie! Someone might come in and see us.

JULIE: What of it?

JEAN: People talk, that's what! If you knew how their tongues were wagging just now at the dance, you'd . . .

JULIE: What were they saying? Tell me!———Sit down!

JEAN (*sits*): I don't want to hurt you, but they were saying things———suggestive things, that, that . . . well, you can figure it out for yourself! You're not a child. If a woman is seen drinking alone with a man—let alone a servant—at night—then . . .

JULIE: Then what? Besides, we're not alone. Kristine is here.

JEAN: Asleep!

JULIE: Then I'll wake her up. (*Rising.*) Kristine! Are you asleep? (*Kristine mumbles in her sleep.*)

JULIE: Kristine!———She certainly can sleep!

KRISTINE (*in her sleep*): The Count's boots are brushed—put the coffee on—right away, right away—uh, huh—oh!

JULIE (*grabbing Kristine's nose*): Will you wake up!

JEAN (*severely*): Leave her alone—let her sleep!

JULIE (*sharply*): What?

JEAN: Someone who's been standing over a stove all day has a right to be tired by now. Sleep should be respected . . .

JULIE (*changing her tone*): What a considerate thought—it does you credit—thank you! (*Offering her hand.*) Come outside and pick some lilacs for me! (*During the following, Kristine awakens and shambles sleepily off right to bed.*)

JEAN: Go with you?

JULIE: With me!

JEAN: We couldn't do that! Absolutely not!

JULIE: I don't understand. Surely you don't imagine . . .

JEAN: No, I don't, but the others might.

JULIE: What? That I've fallen in love with a servant?

JEAN: I'm not a conceited man, but such things happen—and for these people, nothing is sacred.

JULIE: I do believe you're an aristocrat!

JEAN: Yes, I am.

JULIE: And I'm stepping down . . .

JEAN: Don't step down, Miss Julie, take my advice. No one'll believe you stepped down voluntarily. People will always say you fell.

JULIE: I have a higher opinion of people than you. Come and see!———Come! (*She stares at him broodingly.*)

JEAN: You're very strange, do you know that?

JULIE: Perhaps! But so are you!———For that matter, everything is strange. Life, people, everything. Like floating scum, drifting on and on across the water, until it sinks down and down! That reminds me of a dream I have now and then. I've climbed up on top of a pillar. I sit there and see no way of getting down. I get dizzy when I look down, and I must get down, but I don't have the courage to jump. I can't hold on firmly, and I long to be able to fall, but I don't fall. And yet I'll have no peace until I get down, no rest unless I get down, down on the ground! And if I did get down to the ground, I'd want to be under the earth . . . Have you ever felt anything like that?

JEAN: No. I dream that I'm lying under a high tree in a dark forest. I want to get up, up on top, and look out over the bright landscape, where the sun is shining, and plunder the bird's nest up there, where the golden eggs lie. And I climb and climb, but the trunk's so thick and smooth, and it's so far to the first branch. But I know if I just reached that first branch, I'd go right to the top, like up a ladder. I haven't reached it yet, but I will, even if it's only in a dream!

JULIE: Here I am chattering with you about dreams. Come, let's go out! Just into the park! (*She offers him her arm, and they start to leave.*)

JEAN: We'll have to sleep on nine midsummer flowers, Miss Julie, to make our dreams come true! (*They turn at the door. Jean puts his hand to his eye.*)

JULIE: Did you get something in your eye?

JEAN: It's nothing—just a speck—it'll be gone in a minute.

JULIE: My sleeve must have brushed against you. Sit down and let me help you. (*She takes him by the arm and seats him. She tilts his head back and with the tip of a handkerchief tries to remove the speck.*) Sit still, absolutely still! (*She slaps his hand.*) Didn't you hear me?———Why, you're trembling; the big, strong man is trembling! (*Feels his biceps.*) What muscles you have!

JEAN (*warning*): Miss Julie!

JULIE: Yes, *monsieur* Jean.

JEAN: *Attention! Je ne suis qu'un homme!*°

JULIE: Will you sit still!———There! Now it's gone! Kiss my hand and thank me.

JEAN (*rising*): Miss Julie, listen to me!———Kristine has gone to bed!———Will you listen to me!

Attention! Je ne suis qu'un homme!: Watch out! I am only a man!

JULIE: Kiss my hand first!

JEAN: Listen to me!

JULIE: Kiss my hand first!

JEAN: All right, but you've only yourself to blame!

JULIE: For what?

JEAN: For what? Are you still a child at twenty-five? Don't you know that it's dangerous to play with fire?

JULIE: Not for me. I'm insured.

JEAN (*boldly*): No, you're not! But even if you were, there's combustible material close by.

JULIE: Meaning you?

JEAN: Yes! Not because it's me, but because I'm young———

JULIE: And handsome—what incredible conceit! A Don Juan perhaps! Or a Joseph!° Yes, that's it, I do believe you're a Joseph!

JEAN: Do you?

JULIE: I'm almost afraid so. (*Jean boldly tries to put his arm around her waist and kiss her. She slaps his face.*) How dare you?

JEAN: Are you serious or joking?

JULIE: Serious.

JEAN: Then so was what just happened. You play games too seriously, and that's dangerous. Well, I'm tired of games. You'll excuse me if I get back to work. I haven't done the Count's boots yet and it's long past midnight.

JULIE: Put the boots down!

JEAN: No! It's the work I have to do. I never agreed to be your playmate, and never will. It's beneath me.

JULIE: You're proud.

JEAN: In certain ways, but not in others.

JULIE: Have you ever been in love?

JEAN: We don't use that word, but I've been fond of many girls, and once I was sick because I couldn't have the one I wanted. That's right, sick, like those princes in the Arabian Nights—who couldn't eat or drink because of love.

JULIE: Who was she? (*Jean is silent.*) Who was she?

JEAN: You can't force me to tell you that.

JULIE: But if I ask you as an equal, as a—friend! Who was she?

JEAN: You!

JULIE (*sits*): How amusing . . .

JEAN: Yes, if you like! It was ridiculous!———You see, that was the story I didn't want to tell you earlier. Maybe I will now. Do you know how the world looks from down below?———Of course you don't. Neither do hawks and falcons, whose backs we can't see because they're usually soaring up there above us. I grew up in a shack with seven brothers and sisters and a pig, in the middle of a wasteland, where there wasn't a single tree. But from our window I could see the tops of apple trees above the wall of your father's garden. That was the Garden of Eden, guarded by

angry angels with flaming swords. All the same, the other boys and I managed to find our way to the Tree of Life.———Now you think I'm contemptible, I suppose.

JULIE: Oh, all boys steal apples.

JEAN: You say that, but you think I'm contemptible anyway. Oh well! One day I went into the Garden of Eden with my mother, to weed the onion beds. Near the vegetable garden was a small Turkish pavilion in the shadow of jasmine bushes and over-grown with honeysuckle. I had no idea what it was used for, but I'd never seen such a beautiful building. People went in and came out again, and one day the door was left open. I sneaked close and saw walls covered with pictures of kings and emperors, and red curtains with fringes at the windows—now you know the place I mean. I———(*Breaks off a sprig of lilac and holds it in front of Miss Julie's nose.*)———I'd never been inside the manor house, never seen anything except the church—but this was more beautiful. From then on, no matter where my thoughts wandered, they returned—there. And gradually I got a longing to experience, just once, the full pleasure of—*enfin,*° I sneaked in, saw, and marveled! But then I heard someone coming! There was only one exit for ladies and gentlemen, but for me there was another, and I had no choice but to take it! (*Miss Julie, who has taken the lilac sprig, lets it fall on the table.*) Afterwards, I started running. I crashed through a raspberry bush, flew over a strawberry patch, and came up onto the rose terrace. There I caught sight of a pink dress and a pair of white stockings—it was you. I crawled under a pile of weeds, and I mean under—under thistles that pricked me and wet dirt that stank. And I looked at you as you walked among the roses, and I thought: If it's true that a thief can enter heaven and be with the angels, then why can't a farm-hand's son here on God's earth enter the manor house garden and play with the Count's daughter?

JULIE (*romantically*): Do you think all poor children would have thought the way you did?

JEAN (*at first hesitant, then with conviction*): If all poor—yes—of course. Of course!

JULIE: It must be terrible to be poor!

JEAN (*with exaggerated suffering*): Oh, Miss Julie! Oh!———A dog can lie on the Countess's sofa, a horse can have his nose patted by a young lady's hand, but a servant———(*Changing his tone.*)———oh, I know—now and then you find one with enough stuff in him to get ahead in the world, but how often?———Anyhow, do you know what I did then?———I jumped in the millstream with my clothes on, was pulled out, and got a beating. But the following Sunday, when my father and all the others went to my grandmother's, I arranged to stay home. I scrubbed myself with soap and water, put on my best clothes, and went to church so that I could see you!

Don Juan . . . Joseph: Don Juan in Spanish legend is a seducer of women; in Genesis, Joseph resists the advances of Potiphar's wife.

enfin: Finally.

I saw you and returned home, determined to die. But I wanted to die beautifully and pleasantly, without pain. And then I remembered that it was dangerous to sleep under an elder bush. We had a big one, and it was in full flower. I plundered its treasures and bedded down under them in the oat bin. Have you ever noticed how smooth oats are?—and soft to the touch, like human skin . . . ! Well, I shut the lid and closed my eyes. I fell asleep and woke up feeling very sick. But I didn't die, as you can see. What was I after?————I don't know. There was no hope of winning you, of course.———— You were a symbol of the hopelessness of ever rising out of the class in which I was born.

JULIE: You're a charming storyteller. Did you ever go to school?

JEAN: A bit, but I've read lots of novels and been to the theater often. And then I've listened to people like you talk—that's where I learned most.

JULIE: Do you listen to what we say?

JEAN: Naturally! And I've heard plenty, too, driving the carriage or rowing the boat. Once I heard you and a friend . . .

JULIE: Oh?————What did you hear?

JEAN: I'd better not say. But I was surprised a little. I couldn't imagine where you learned such words. Maybe at bottom there isn't such a great difference between people as we think.

JULIE: Shame on you! We don't act like you when we're engaged.

JEAN (*staring at her*): Is that true?————You don't have to play innocent with me, Miss . . .

JULIE: The man I gave my love to was a swine.

JEAN: That's what you all say—afterwards.

JULIE: All?

JEAN: I think so. I know I've heard that phrase before, on similar occasions.

JULIE: What occasions?

JEAN: Like the one I'm talking about. The last time . . .

JULIE (*rising*): Quiet! I don't want to hear any more!

JEAN: That's interesting—that's what *she* said, too. Well, if you'll excuse me, I'm going to bed.

JULIE (*gently*): To bed? On midsummer eve?

JEAN: Yes! Dancing with the rabble out there doesn't amuse me much.

JULIE: Get the key to the boat and row me out on the lake. I want to see the sun come up.

JEAN: Is that wise?

JULIE: Are you worried about your reputation?

JEAN: Why not? Why should I risk looking ridiculous and getting fired without a reference, just when I'm trying to establish myself. Besides, I think I owe something to Kristine.

JULIE: So, now it's Kristine . . .

JEAN: Yes, but you, too.————Take my advice, go up and go to bed!

JULIE: Am I to obey you?

JEAN: Just this once—for your own good! Please! It's very late. Drowsiness makes people giddy and liable

to lose their heads! Go to bed! Besides—unless I'm mistaken—I hear the others coming to look for me. And if they find us together, you'll be lost!

(*The Chorus approaches, singing.*)

The swineherd found his true love
a pretty girl so fair,
The swineherd found his true love
but let the girl beware.

For then he saw the princess
the princess on the golden hill,
but then saw the princess,
so much fairer still.

So the swineherd and the princess
they danced the whole night through,
and he forgot his first love,
to her he was untrue.

And when the long night ended,
and in the light of day, of day,
the dancing too was ended,
and the princess could not stay.

Then the swineherd lost his true love,
and the princess grieves him still,
and never more she'll wander
from atop the golden hill.

JULIE: I know all these people and I love them, just as they love me. Let them come in and you'll see.

JEAN: No, Miss Julie, they don't love you. They take your food, but they spit on it! Believe me! Listen to them, listen to what they're singing!————No. don't listen to them!

JULIE (*listening*): What are they singing?

JEAN: It's a dirty song! About you and me!

JULIE: Disgusting! Oh! How deceitful!————

JEAN: The rabble is always cowardly! And in a battle like this, you don't fight; you can only run away!

JULIE: Run away? But where? We can't go out—or into Kristine's room.

JEAN: True. But there's my room. Necessity knows no rules. Besides, you can trust me. I'm your friend and I respect you.

JULIE: But suppose—suppose they look for you in there?

JEAN: I'll bolt the door, and if anyone tries to break in, I'll shoot!————Come! (*On his knees.*) Come!

JULIE (*urgently*): Promise me . . . ?

JEAN: I swear! (*Miss Julie runs off right. Jean hastens after her.*)

Ballet

(*Led by a fiddler, the servants and farm people enter, dressed festively, with flowers in their hats. On the table they place a small barrel of beer and a keg of schnapps, both garlanded. Glasses are brought out, and the drinking starts. A dance circle is formed and "The Swineherd and the Princess" is sung. When the dance is finished, everyone leaves, singing.)*

(Miss Julie enters alone. She notices the mess in the kitchen, wrings her hands, then takes out her powder puff and powders her nose.)

JEAN *(enters, agitated)*: There, you see? And you heard them. We can't possibly stay here now, you know that.

JULIE: Yes, I know. But what can we do?

JEAN: Leave, travel, far away from here.

JULIE: Travel? Yes, but where?

JEAN: To Switzerland, to the Italian lakes. Have you ever been there?

JULIE: No. Is it beautiful?

JEAN: Oh, an eternal summer—oranges growing everywhere, laurel trees, always green . . .

JULIE: But what'll we do there?

JEAN: I'll open a hotel—with first-class service for first-class people.

JULIE: Hotel?

JEAN: That's the life, you know. Always new faces, new languages. No time to worry or be nervous. No hunting for something to do—there's always work to be done: bells ringing night and day, train whistles blowing, carriages coming and going, and all the while gold rolling into the till! That's the life!

JULIE: Yes, it sounds wonderful. But what'll I do?

JEAN: You'll be mistress of the house: the jewel in our crown! With your looks . . . and your manner—oh—success is guaranteed! It'll be wonderful! You'll sit in your office like a queen and push an electric button to set your slaves in motion. The guests will file past your throne and timidly lay their treasures before you.————You have no idea how people tremble when they get their bill.————I'll salt the hills° and you'll sweeten them with your prettiest smile.————Let's get away from here——*(Takes a timetable out of his pocket.)*————Right away, on the next train!————We'll be in Malmö six-thirty tomorrow morning, Hamburg at eight-forty; from Frankfort to Basel will take a day, then on to Como by way of the St. Gotthard Tunnel, in, let's see, three days. Three days!

JULIE: That's all very well! But Jean—you must give me courage!————Tell me you love me! Put your arms around me!

JEAN *(hesitating)*: I want to—but I don't dare. Not in this house, not again. I love you—never doubt that—you don't doubt it, do you, Miss Julie?

JULIE *(shy; very feminine)*: "Miss!"————Call me Julie! There are no barriers between us anymore. Call me Julie!

JEAN *(tormented)*: I can't! There'll always be barriers between us as long as we stay in this house. There's the past and there's the Count. I've never met anyone I had such respect for.————When I see his

---

salt the bills: Inflate or pad the bills.

---

gloves lying on a chair, I feel small.————When I hear that bell up there ring, I jump like a skittish horse.————And when I look at his boots standing there so stiff and proud, I feel like bowing! *(Kicking the boots.)* Superstitions and prejudices we learned as children—but they can easily be forgotten. If I can just get to another country, a republic, people will bow and scrape when they see my livery—*they'll* bow and scrape, you hear, not me! I wasn't *born* to cringe. I've got stuff in me, I've got character, and if I can only grab onto that first branch, you watch me climb! I'm a servant today, but next year I'll own my own hotel. In ten years I'll have enough to retire. Then I'll go to Rumania and be decorated. I could—mind you I said *could*—end up a count!

JULIE: Wonderful, wonderful!

JEAN: Ah, in Rumania you just buy your title, and so you'll be a countess after all. My countess!

JULIE: But I don't care about that—that's what I'm putting behind me! Show me you love me, otherwise—otherwise, what am I?

JEAN: I'll show you a thousand times—afterwards! Not here! And whatever you do, no emotional outbursts, or we'll both be lost! We must think this through coolly, like sensible people. *(He takes out a cigar, snips the end, and lights it.)* You sit there, and I'll sit here. We'll talk as if nothing happened.

JULIE *(desperately)*: Oh, my God! Have you no feelings?

JEAN: Me? No one has more feelings than I do, but I know how to control them.

JULIE: A little while ago you could kiss my shoe—and now!

JEAN *(harshly)*: Yes, but that was before. Now we have other things to think about.

JULIE: Don't speak harshly to me!

JEAN: I'm not—just sensibly! We've already done one foolish thing, let's not have any more. The Count could return any minute, and by then we've got to decide what to do with our lives. What do you think of my plans for the future? Do you approve?

JULIE: They sound reasonable enough. I have only one question: For such a big undertaking you need capital—do you have it?

JEAN *(chewing on the cigar)*: Me? Certainly! I have my professional expertise, my wide experience, and my knowledge of languages. That's capital enough, I should think!

JULIE: But all that won't even buy a train ticket.

JEAN: That's true. That's why I'm looking for a partner to advance me the money.

JULIE: Where will you find one quickly enough?

JEAN: That's up to you, if you want to come with me.

JULIE: But I can't; I have no money of my own. *(Pause.)*

JEAN: Then it's all off . . .

JULIE: And . . .

JEAN: Things stay as they are.

JULIE: Do you think I'm going to stay in this house as your lover? With all the servants pointing their fingers at me? Do you imagine I can face my father after

Marin Hinkle as Julie and Reg Rogers as Jean in the Rattlestick Playwrights Theatre 2005 production of *Miss Julie,* directed by Craig Lucas.

this? No! Take me away from here, away from shame and dishonor————Oh, what have I done! My God, my God! (*She cries.*)

JEAN: Now, don't start that old song!————What have you done? The same as many others before you.

JULIE (*screaming convulsively*): And now you think I'm contemptible!————I'm falling, I'm falling!

JEAN: Fall down to my level and I'll lift you up again.

JULIE: What terrible power drew me to you? The attraction of the weak to the strong? The falling to the rising? Or was it love? Was this love? Do you know what love is?

JEAN: Me? What do you take me for? You don't think this was my first time, do you?

JULIE: The things you say, the thoughts you think!

JEAN: That's the way I was taught, and that's the way I am! Now don't get excited and don't play the grand lady, because we're in the same boat now!———— Come on, Julie, I'll pour you a glass of something special! (*He opens a drawer in the table, takes out a wine bottle, and fills two glasses already used.*)

JULIE: Where did you get that wine?

JEAN: From the cellar.

JULIE: My father's burgundy!

JEAN: That'll do for his son-in-law, won't it?

JULIE: And I drink beer! Beer!

JEAN: That only shows I have better taste.

JULIE: Thief!

JEAN: Planning to tell?

JULIE: Oh, oh! Accomplice of a common thief! Was I drunk? Have I been walking in a dream the whole evening? Midsummer eve! A time of innocent fun!

JEAN: Innocent, eh?

JULIE (*pacing back and forth*): Is there anyone on earth more miserable than I am at this moment?

JEAN: Why should you be? After such a conquest? Think of Kristine in there. Don't you think she has feelings, too?

JULIE: I thought so awhile ago, but not any more. No, a servant is a servant . . .

JEAN: And a whore is a whore!

JULIE (*on her knees, her hands clasped*): Oh, God in heaven, end my wretched life! Take me away from the filth I'm sinking into! Save me! Save me!

JEAN: I can't deny I feel sorry for you. When I lay in that onion bed and saw you in the rose garden, well . . . I'll be frank . . . I had the same dirty thoughts all boys have.

Helen Mirren as Miss Julie in a 1971 production of Strindberg's play.

JULIE: And you wanted to die for me!

JEAN: In the oat bin? That was just talk.

JULIE: A lie, in other words!

JEAN (*beginning to feel sleepy*): More or less! I got the idea from a newspaper story about a chimney sweep who curled up in a firewood bin full of lilacs because he got a summons for not supporting his illegitimate child . . .

JULIE: So, that's what you're like . . .

JEAN: I had to think of something. And that's the kind of story women always go for.

JULIE: Swine!

JEAN: *Merde!*

JULIE: And now you've seen the hawk's back . . .

JEAN: Not exactly its *back* . . .

JULIE: And I was to be the first branch . . .

JEAN: But the branch was rotten . . .

JULIE: I was to be the sign on the hotel . . .

JEAN: And I the hotel . . .

JULIE: Sit at your desk, entice your customers, pad their bills . . .

JEAN: That I'd do myself . . .

JULIE: How can anyone be so thoroughly filthy?

JEAN: Better clean up then!

JULIE: You lackey, you menial, stand up, when I speak to you!

JEAN: Menial's strumpet, lackey's whore, shut up and get out of here! Who are you to lecture me on coarseness? None of my kind is ever as coarse as you were tonight. Do you think one of your maids would throw herself at a man the way you did? Have you ever seen any girl of my class offer herself like that? I've only seen it among animals and street-walkers.

JULIE (*crushed*): You're right. Hit me, trample on me. I don't deserve any better. I'm worthless. But help me! If you see any way out of this, help me, Jean, please!

JEAN (*more gently*): I'd be lying if I didn't admit to a sense of triumph in all this, but do you think that a person like me would have dared even to look at someone like you if you hadn't invited it? I'm still amazed . . .

JULIE: And proud . . .

JEAN: Why not? Though I must say it was too easy to be really exciting.

JULIE: Go on, hit me, hit me harder!

JEAN (*rising*): No! Forgive me for what I've said! I don't hit a man when he's down, let alone a woman. I can't deny though, that I'm pleased to find out that what looked so dazzling to us from below was only tinsel, that the hawk's back was only gray, after all, that the lovely complexion was only powder, that those polished fingernails had black edges, and that a dirty handkerchief is still dirty, even if it smells of perfume . . . ! On the other hand, it hurts me to find out that what I was striving for wasn't finer, more substantial. It hurts me to see you sunk so low that you're inferior to your own cook. It hurts like watching flowers beaten down by autumn rains and turned into mud.

JULIE: You talk as if you were already above me.

JEAN: I am. You see, I could make you a countess, but you could never make me a count.

JULIE: But I'm the child of a count—something you could never be!

JEAN: That's true. But I could be the father of counts—if . . .

JULIE: But you're a thief. I'm not.

JEAN: There are worse things than being a thief! Besides, when I'm working in a house, I consider myself sort of a member of the family, like one of the children. And you don't call it stealing when a child snatches a berry off a full bush. (*His passion is aroused again.*) Miss Julie, you're a glorious woman, much too good for someone like me! You were drinking and you lost your head. Now you want to cover up your mistake by telling yourself that you love me! You don't. Maybe there was a physical attraction—but then your love is no better than mine.————I could never be satisfied to be no more than an animal to you, and I could never arouse real love in you.

JULIE: Are you sure of that?

JEAN: You're suggesting it's possible————Oh, I could fall in love with you, no doubt about it. You're beautiful, you're refined————(*approaching and taking her hand*)————cultured, lovable when you want to be, and once you start a fire in a man, it never goes out. (*Putting his arm around her waist.*) You're like hot, spicy wine, and one kiss from you . . . (*He tries to lead her out, but she slowly frees herself.*)

JULIE: Let me go!?————You'll never win me like that.

JEAN: *How* then?————Not like that? Not with caresses and pretty speeches. Not with plans about the future or rescue from disgrace! *How* then?

JULIE: How? How? I don't know!————I have no idea!————I detest you as I detest rats, but I can't escape from you.

JEAN: Escape with me!

JULIE (*pulling herself together*): Escape? Yes, we must escape!————But I'm so tired. Give me a glass of wine? (*Jean pours the wine. She looks at her watch.*) But we must talk first. We still have a little time. (*She drains the glass, then holds it out for more.*)

JEAN: Don't drink so fast. It'll go to your head.

JULIE: What does it matter?

JEAN: What does it matter? It's vulgar to get drunk! What did you want to tell me?

JULIE: We must escape! But first we must talk, I mean I must talk. You've done all the talking up to now. You told about your life, now I want to tell about mine, so we'll know all about each other before we go off together.

JEAN: Just a minute! Forgive me! If you don't want to regret it afterwards, you'd better think twice before revealing any secrets about yourself.

JULIE: Aren't you my friend?

JEAN: Yes, sometimes! But don't rely on me.

JULIE: You're only saying that.———— Besides, everyone already knows my secrets.————You see, my mother was a commoner—very humble background. She was brought up believing in social equality, women's rights, and all that. The idea of marriage repelled her. So, when my father proposed, she replied that she would never become his wife, but he could be her lover. He insisted that he didn't want the woman he loved to be less respected than he. But his passion ruled him, and when she explained that the world's respect meant nothing to her, he accepted her conditions.

But now his friends avoided him and his life was restricted to taking care of the estate, which couldn't satisfy him. I came into the world—against my mother's wishes, as far as I can understand. She wanted to bring me up as a child of nature, and, what's more, to learn everything a boy had to learn, so that I might be an example of how a woman can be as good as a man. I had to wear boy's clothes and learn to take care of horses, but I was never allowed in the cowshed. I had to groom and harness the horses and go hunting—and even had to watch them slaughter animals—that was disgusting! On the estate men were put on women's jobs and women on men's jobs—with the result that the property became run down and we became the laughingstock of the district. Finally, my father must have awakened from his trance because he rebelled and changed everything his way. My parents were then married quietly. Mother became ill—I don't know what illness it was—but she often had convulsions, hid in the attic and in the garden, and sometimes stayed out all night. Then came the great fire, which you've heard about. The house, the stables, and the cowshed all burned down, under very curious circumstances, suggesting arson, because the accident happened the day after the insurance had expired. The quarterly premium my father sent in was delayed because of a messenger's carelessness and didn't arrive in time. (*She fills her glass and drinks.*)

JEAN: Don't drink any more!

JULIE: Oh, what does it matter.————We were left penniless and had to sleep in the carriages. My father had no idea where to find money to rebuild the house because he had so slighted his old friends that they had forgotten him. Then my mother suggested that he borrow from a childhood friend of hers, a brick manufacturer who lived nearby. Father got the loan without having to pay interest, which surprised him. And that's how the estate was rebuilt.————(*Drinks again.*) Do you know who started the fire?

JEAN: The Countess, your mother.

JULIE: Do you know who the brick manufacturer was?

JEAN: Your mother's lover?

JULIE: Do you know whose money it was?

JEAN: Wait a moment—no, I don't.

JULIE: It was my mother's.

JEAN: You mean the Count's, unless they didn't sign an agreement when they were married.

JULIE: They didn't.————My mother had a small inheritance which she didn't want under my father's control, so she entrusted it to her—friend.

JEAN: Who stole it!

JULIE: Exactly! He kept it.————All this my father found out, but he couldn't bring it to court, couldn't repay his wife's lover, couldn't prove it was his wife's money! It was my mother's revenge for being forced into marriage against her will. It nearly drove him to suicide—there was a rumor that he tried with a pistol, but failed. So, he managed to live through it and my mother had to suffer for what she'd done. You can imagine that those were a terrible five years for me. I loved my father, but I sided with my mother because I didn't know the circumstances. I learned from her to hate men—you've heard how she hated the whole male sex—and I swore to her I'd never be a slave to any man.

JEAN: But you got engaged to that lawyer.

JULIE: In order to make him my slave.

JEAN: And he wasn't willing?

JULIE: He was willing, all right, but I wouldn't let him. I got tired of him.

JEAN: I saw it—out near the stable.

JULIE: What did you see?

JEAN: I saw—how he broke off the engagement.

JULIE: That's a lie! I was the one who broke it off. Has he said that he did? That swine . . .

JEAN: He was no swine, I'm sure. So, you hate men, Miss Julie?

JULIE: Yes!———Most of the time! But sometimes—when the weakness comes, when passion burns! Oh, God, will the fire never die out?

JEAN: Do you hate me, too?

JULIE: Immeasurably! I'd like to have you put to death, like an animal . . .

JEAN: I see—the penalty for bestiality—the woman gets two years at hard labor and the animal is put to death. Right?

JULIE: Exactly!

JEAN: But there's no prosecutor here—and no animal. So, what'll we do?

JULIE: Go away!

JEAN: To torment each other to death?

JULIE: No! To be happy for—two days, a week, as long as we can be happy, and then—die . . .

JEAN: Die? That's stupid! It's better to open a hotel!

JULIE: (*without listening*):———on the shore of Lake Como, where the sun always shines, where the laurels are green at Christmas and the oranges glow.

JEAN: Lake Como is a rainy hole, and I never saw any oranges outside the stores. But tourists are attracted there because there are plenty of villas to be rented out to lovers, and that's a profitable business.———Do you know why? Because they sign a lease for six months—and then leave after three weeks!

JULIE: (*naively*): Why after three weeks?

JEAN: They quarrel, of course! But they still have to pay the rent in full! And so you rent the villas out again. And that's the way it goes, time after time. There's never a shortage of love—even if it doesn't last long!

JULIE: You don't want to die with me?

JEAN: I don't want to die at all! For one thing, I like living, and for another, I think suicide is a crime against the Providence which gave us life.

JULIE: You believe in God? *You?*

JEAN: Of course I do. And I go to church every other Sunday.———To be honest, I'm tired of all this, and I'm going to bed.

JULIE: Are you? And do you think I can let it go at that? A man owes something to the woman he's shamed.

JEAN: (*taking out his purse and throwing a silver coin on the table*): Here! I don't like owing anything to anybody.

JULIE: (*pretending not to notice the insult*): Do you know what the law states . . .

JEAN: Unfortunately the law doesn't state any punishment for the woman who seduces a man!

JULIE: (*as before*): Do you see any way out but to leave, get married, and then separate?

JEAN: Suppose I refuse such a *mésalliance?*[°]

JULIE: *Mésalliance* . . .

JEAN: Yes, for me! You see, I come from better stock than you. There's no arsonist in my family.

JULIE: How do you know?

JEAN: You can't prove otherwise. We don't keep charts on our ancestors—there's just the police records! But I've read about your family. Do you know who the founder was? He was a miller who let the king sleep with his wife one night during the Danish War. I don't have any noble ancestors like that. I don't have any noble ancestors at all, but I could become one myself.

JULIE: This is what I get for opening my heart to someone unworthy, for giving my family's honor . . .

JEAN: Dishonor!———Well, I told you so: When people drink, they talk, and talk is dangerous!

JULIE: Oh, how I regret it!———How I regret it!———If you at least loved me.

JEAN: For the last time———what do you want? Shall I cry; shall I jump over your riding crop? Shall I kiss you and lure you off to Lake Como for three weeks, and then God knows what. . . ? What shall I do? What do you want? This is getting painfully embarrassing! But that's what happens when you stick your nose in women's business. Miss Julie! I see that you're unhappy. I know you're suffering, but I can't understand you. We don't have such romantic ideas; there's not this kind of hate between us. Love is a game we play when we get time off from work, but we don't have all day and night, like you. I think you're sick, really sick. Your mother was crazy, and her ideas have poisoned your life.

JULIE: Be kind to me. At least now you're talking like a human being.

JEAN: Be human yourself, then. You spit on me, and you won't let me wipe myself off———

JULIE: Help me! Help me! Just tell me what to do, where to go!

JEAN: In God's name, if I only knew myself!

JULIE: I've been crazy, out of my mind, but isn't there any way out?

JEAN: Stay here and keep calm! No one knows anything!

JULIE: Impossible! The others know and Kristine knows.

JEAN: No they don't, and they'd never believe a thing like that!

JULIE (*hesitantly*): But—it could happen again!

JEAN: That's true!

JULIE: And then?

JEAN (*frightened*): Then?———Why didn't I think about that? Yes, there is only one thing to do—get away from here! Right away! I can't come with you,

---

mésalliance: Misalliance or mismatch, especially regarding relative social status.

then we'd be finished, so you'll have to go alone —away—anywhere!

JULIE: Alone?———Where?———I can't do that!

JEAN: You must! And before the Count gets back! If you stay, you know what'll happen. Once you make a mistake like this, you want to continue because the damage has already been done.... Then you get bolder and bolder—until finally you're caught! So leave! Later you can write to the Count and confess everything—except that it was me! He'll never guess who it was, and he's not going to be eager to find out, anyway.

JULIE: I'll go if you come with me.

JEAN: Are you out of your head? Miss Julie runs away with her servant! In two days it would be in the newspapers, and that's something your father would never live through.

JULIE: I can't go and I can't stay! Help me! I'm so tired, so terribly tired.———Order me! Set me in motion— I can't think or act on my own . . .

JEAN: What miserable creatures you people are! You strut around with your noses in the air as if you were the lords of creation! All right, I'll order you. Go upstairs and get dressed! Get some money for the trip, and then come back down!

JULIE (in a half-whisper): Come up with me!

JEAN: To your room?———Now you're crazy again! (Hesitates for a moment.) No! Go, at once! (Takes her hand to lead her out.)

JULIE (as she leaves): Speak kindly to me, Jean!

JEAN: An order always sounds unkind—now you know how it feels. (Jean, alone, sighs with relief. He sits at the table, takes out a notebook and pencil, and begins adding up figures, counting aloud as he works. He continues in dumb show until Kristine enters, dressed for church. She is carrying a white tie and shirt front.)

KRISTINE: Lord Jesus, what a mess! What have you been up to?

JEAN: Oh, Miss Julie dragged everybody in here. You mean you didn't hear anything? You must have been sleeping soundly.

KRISTINE: Like a log.

JEAN: And dressed for church already?

KRISTINE: Of course! You remember you promised to come with me to communion today!

JEAN: Oh, yes, that's right.———And you brought my things. Come on, then! (He sits down. Kristine starts to put on his shirt front and tie. Pause. Jean begins sleepily.) What's the gospel text for today?

KRISTINE: On St. John's Day?—the beheading of John the Baptist, I should think!

JEAN: Ah, that'll be a long one, for sure.———Hey, you're choking me!———Oh, I'm sleepy, so sleepy!

KRISTINE: Yes, what have you been doing, up all night? Your face is absolutely green.

JEAN: I've been sitting here gabbing with Miss Julie.

KRISTINE: She has no idea what's proper, that one! (Pause.)

JEAN: You know, Kristine . . .

KRISTINE: What?

JEAN: It's really strange when you think about it. ———Her!

KRISTINE: What's so strange?

JEAN: Everything! (Pause.)

KRISTINE (looking at the half-empty glasses standing on the table): Have you been drinking together, too?

JEAN: Yes.

KRISTINE: Shame on you!———Look me in the eye!

JEAN: Well?

KRISTINE: Is it possible? Is it possible?

JEAN (thinking it over for a moment): Yes, it is.

KRISTINE: Ugh! I never would have believed it! No, shame on you, shame!

JEAN: You're not jealous of her, are you?

KRISTINE: No, not of her! If it had been Clara or Sofie I'd have scratched your eyes out!———I don't know why, but that's the way I feel.———Oh, it's disgusting!

JEAN: Are you angry at her, then?

KRISTINE: No, at you! That was an awful thing to do, awful! Poor girl!———No, I don't care who knows it—I won't stay in a house where we can't respect the people we work for.

JEAN: Why should we respect them?

KRISTINE: You're so clever, you tell me! Do you want to wait on people who can't behave decently? Do you? You disgrace yourself that way, if you ask me.

JEAN: But it's a comfort to know they aren't any better than us.

KRISTINE: Not for me. If they're no better, what do we have to strive for to better ourselves.———And think of the Count! Think of him! As if he hasn't had enough misery in his life! Lord Jesus! No, I won't stay in this house any longer!———And it had to be with someone like you! If it had been that lawyer, if it had been a real gentleman . . .

JEAN: What do you mean?

KRISTINE: Oh, you're all right for what you are, but there are men and gentlemen, after all!———No, this business with Miss Julie I can never forget. She was so proud, so arrogant with men, you wouldn't have believed she could just go and give herself—and to someone like you! And she was going to have poor Diana shot for running after the gatekeepers' mutt!———Yes, I'm giving my notice, I mean it—I won't stay here any longer. On the twenty-fourth of October, I leave!

JEAN: And then?

KRISTINE: Well, since the subject has come up, it's about time you looked around for something since we're going to get married, in any case.

JEAN: Where am I going to look? I couldn't find a job like this if I was married.

KRISTINE: No, that's true. But you can find work as a porter or as a caretaker in some government office. The state doesn't pay much, I know, but it's secure, and there's a pension for the wife and children . . .

JEAN (grimacing): That's all very well, but it's a bit early for me to think about dying for a wife and children. My ambitions are a little higher than that.

KRISTINE: Your ambitions, yes! Well, you have obligations, too! Think about them!

JEAN: Don't start nagging me about obligations. I know what I have to do! (*Listening for something outside.*) Besides, this is something we have plenty of time to think over. Go and get ready for church.

KRISTINE: Who's that walking around up there?

JEAN: I don't know, unless it's Clara.

KRISTINE (*going*): You don't suppose it's the Count, who came home without us hearing him?

JEAN (*frightened*): The Count? No, I don't think so. He'd have rung.

KRISTINE (*going*): Well, God help us! I've never seen anything like this before. (*The sun has risen and shines through the treetops in the park. The light shifts gradually until it slants in through the windows. Jean goes to the door and signals. Miss Julie enters, dressed in travel clothes and carrying a small bird cage, covered with a cloth, which she places on a chair.*)

JULIE: I'm ready now.

JEAN: Shh! Kristine is awake.

JULIE (*very nervous during the following*): Does she suspect something?

JEAN: She doesn't know anything. But my God, you look awful!

JULIE: Why? How do I look?

JEAN: You're pale as a ghost and—excuse me, but your face is dirty.

JULIE: Let me wash up then.————(*She goes to the basin and washes her hands and face.*) Give me a towel!———— Oh————the sun's coming up.

JEAN: Then the goblins will disappear.

JULIE: Yes, there must have been goblins out last night!————Jean, listen, come with me! I have some money now.

JEAN (*hesitantly*): Enough?

JULIE: Enough to start with. Come with me! I just can't travel alone on a day like this—midsummer day on a stuffy train—jammed in among crowds of people staring at me. Eternal delays at every station, while I'd wish I had wings. No, I can't, I can't! And then there'll be memories, memories of midsummer days when I was little. The church—decorated with birch leaves and lilacs; dinner at the big table with relatives and friends, the afternoons in the park, dancing, music, flowers, and games. Oh, no matter how far we travel, the memories will follow in the baggage car, with remorse and guilt!

JEAN: I'll go with you—but right away, before it's too late. Right this minute!

JULIE: Get dressed, then! (*Picking up the bird cage.*)

JEAN: But no baggage! It would give us away!

JULIE: No, nothing! Only what we can have in the compartment with us.

JEAN (*has taken his hat*): What've you got there? What is it?

JULIE: It's only my greenfinch. I couldn't leave her behind.

JEAN: What? Bring a bird cage with us? You're out of your head! Put it down!

JULIE: It's the only thing I'm taking from my home—the only living being that loves me, since Diana was unfaithful. Don't be cruel! Let me take her!

JEAN: Put the cage down, I said!————And don't talk so loudly—Kristine will hear us!

JULIE: No, I won't leave her in the hands of strangers! I'd rather you killed her.

JEAN: Bring the thing here, then, I'll cut its head off!

JULIE: Oh! But don't hurt her! Don't . . . no, I can't.

JEAN: Bring it here! I can!

JULIE (*taking the bird out of the cage and kissing it*): Oh, my little Serena, must you die and leave your mistress?

JEAN: Please don't make a scene! Your whole future is at stake! Hurry up! (*He snatches the bird from her, carries it over to the chopping block, and picks up a meat cleaver. Miss Julie turns away.*) You should have learned how to slaughter chickens instead of how to fire pistols. (*He chops off the bird's head.*) Then you wouldn't feel faint at the sight of blood.

JULIE (*screaming*): Kill me, too! Kill me! You, who can slaughter an innocent animal without blinking an eye! Oh, how I hate, how I detest you! There's blood between us now! I curse the moment I set eyes on you! I curse the moment I was conceived in my mother's womb!

JEAN: What good does cursing do? Let's go!

JULIE (*approaching the chopping block, as if drawn against her will*): No, I don't want to go yet. I can't . . . until I see . . . Shh! I hear a carriage————(*She listens, but her eyes never leave the cleaver and the chopping block.*) Do you think I can't stand the sight of blood? You think I'm so weak . . . Oh—I'd like to see your blood and your brains on a chopping block!————I'd like to see your whole sex swimming in a sea of blood, like my little bird . . . I think I could drink from your skull! I'd like to bathe my feet in your open chest and eat your heart roasted whole! ————You think I'm weak. You think I love you because my womb craved your seed. You think I want to carry your spawn under my heart and nourish it with my blood—bear your child and take your name! By the way, what is your family name? I've never heard it. ————Do you have one? I was to be Mrs. Bootblack—or Madame Pigsty.————You dog, who wears my collar, you lackey, who bears my coat of arms on your buttons—do I have to share you with my cook, compete with my own servant? Oh! Oh! Oh!————You think I'm a coward who wants to run away! No, now I'm staying—and let the storm break! My father will come home . . . to find his desk broken open . . . and his money gone! Then he'll ring—that bell . . . twice for his valet—and then he'll send for the police . . . and then I'll tell everything! Everything! Oh, what a relief it'll be to have it all end—if only it will end!————And then he'll have a stroke and die . . . That'll be the end of all of us—and there'll be peace . . . quiet . . . eternal rest!————And then our coat of arms will be broken against his coffin—the family title extinct—but the valet's line will go on in an orphanage . . . win laurels in the gutter, and end in jail!

JEAN: There's the blue blood talking! Very good, Miss Julie! Just don't let that miller out of the closet! (*Kristine enters, dressed for church, with a psalm-book in her hand.*)

JULIE (*rushing to Kristine and falling into her arms, as if seeking protection*): Help me, Kristine! Help me against this man!

KRISTINE (*unmoved and cold*): What a fine way to behave on a Sunday morning! (*Sees the chopping block.*) And look at this mess!————What does all this mean? Why all this screaming and carrying on?

JULIE: Kristine! You're a woman and my friend! Beware of this swine!

JEAN (*uncomfortable*): While you ladies discuss this, I'll go in and shave. (*Slips off right.*)

JULIE: You must listen to me so you'll understand!

KRISTINE: No, I could never understand such disgusting behavior! Where are you off to in your traveling clothes?————And he had his hat on.————Well?————Well?————

JULIE: Listen to me, Kristine! Listen, and I'll tell you everything————

KRISTINE: I don't want to hear it . . .

JULIE: But you must listen to me . . .

KRISTINE: What about? If it's about this silliness with Jean, I'm not interested, because it's none of my business. But if you're thinking of tricking him into running out, we'll soon put a stop to that!

JULIE (*extremely nervous*): Try to be calm now, Kristine, and listen to me! I can't stay here, and neither can Jean—so we must go away . . .

KRISTINE: Hm, hm!

JULIE (*brightening*): You see, I just had an idea————What if all three of us go—abroad—to Switzerland and start a hotel together?————I have money, you see—and Jean and I could run it—and I thought you, you could take care of the kitchen . . . Wouldn't that be wonderful?————Say yes! And come with us, and then everything will be settled!————Oh, do say yes! (*Embracing Kristine and patting her warmly.*)

KRISTINE (*coolly, thoughtfully*): Hm, hm!

JULIE (*presto tempo*):° You've never traveled, Kristine.————You must get out and see the world. You can't imagine how much fun it is to travel by train—always new faces—new countries.————And when we get to Hamburg, we'll stop off at the zoo—you'll like that.————and then we'll go to the theater and the opera—and when we get to Munich, dear, there we have museums, with Rubens and Raphael, the great painters, as you know.————You've heard of Munich, where King Ludwig lived—the king who went mad.————And then we'll see his castles—they're still there and they're like castles in fairy tales.————And from there it isn't far to Switzerland—and the Alps.————Imagine—the Alps have snow on them even in the middle of summer!————And oranges grow there and laurel trees that

presto tempo: At a rapid pace.

are green all year round————(*Jean can be seen in the wings right, sharpening his razor on a strop which he holds with his teeth and his left hand. He listens to the conversation with satisfaction, nodding now and then in approval. Miss Julie continues tempo prestissimo.*)° And then we'll start a hotel—and I'll be at the desk, while Jean greets the guests . . . does the shopping . . . writes letters.————You have no idea what a life it'll be—the train whistles blowing and the carriages arriving and the bells ringing in the rooms and down in the restaurant.————And I'll make out the bills—and I know how to salt them! . . . You'll never believe how timid travelers are when they have to pay their bills!————And you—you'll be in charge of the kitchen.————Naturally, you won't have to stand over the stove yourself.————And since you're going to be seen by people, you'll have to wear beautiful clothes.————And you, with your looks—no, I'm not flattering you—one fine day you'll grab yourself a husband!————You'll see!—A rich Englishman—they're so easy to————(*Slowing down.*)————catch—and then we'll get rich—and build ourselves a villa on Lake Como.————It's true it rains there a little now and then, but————(*Dully.*)————the sun has to shine sometimes—although it looks dark—and then . . . of course we could always come back home again————(*Pause.*)————here—or somewhere else————

KRISTINE: Listen, Miss Julie, do you believe all this?

JULIE (*crushed*): Do I believe it?

KRISTINE: Yes!

JULIE (*wearily*): I don't know. I don't believe in anything anymore. (*She sinks down on the bench and cradles her head in her arms on the table.*) Nothing! Nothing at all!

KRISTINE (*turning right to where Jean is standing*): So, you thought you'd run out!

JEAN (*embarrassed; puts the razor on the table*): Run out? That's no way to put it. You hear Miss Julie's plan, and even if she is tired after being up all night, it's still a practical plan.

KRISTINE: Now you listen to me! Did you think I'd work as a cook for that . . .

JEAN (*sharply*): You watch what you say in front of your mistress! Do you understand?

KRISTINE: Mistress!

JEAN: Yes!

KRISTINE: Listen to him! Listen to him!

JEAN: Yes, you listen! It'd do you good to listen more and talk less! Miss Julie is your mistress. If you despise her, you have to despise yourself for the same reason!

KRISTINE: I've always had enough self-respect————

JEAN:————to be able to despise other people!

KRISTINE:————to stop me from doing anything that's beneath me. You can't say that the Count's cook has been up to something with the groom or the swineherd! Can you?

JEAN: No, you were lucky enough to get hold of a gentleman!

tempo prestissimo: At a very rapid pace.

KRISTINE: Yes, a gentleman who sells the Count's oats from the stable.

JEAN: You should talk—taking a commission from the grocer and bribes from the butcher.

KRISTINE: What?

JEAN: And you say you can't respect your employers any longer. You, you, you!

KRISTINE: Are you coming to church with me, now? You could use a good sermon after your fine deed!

JEAN: No, I'm not going to church today. You'll have to go alone and confess what you've been up to.

KRISTINE: Yes, I'll do that, and I'll bring back enough forgiveness for you, too. The Savior suffered and died on the Cross for all our sins, and if we go to Him with faith and a penitent heart, He takes all our sins on Himself.

JEAN: Even grocery sins?

JULIE: And do you believe that, Kristine?

KRISTINE: It's my living faith, as sure as I stand here. It's the faith I learned as a child, Miss Julie, and kept ever since. "Where sin abounded, grace did much more abound!"

JULIE: Oh, if I only had your faith. If only . . .

KRISTINE: Well, you see, we can't have it without God's special grace, and that isn't given to everyone———

JULIE: Who is it given to then?

KRISTINE: That's the great secret of the workings of grace, Miss Julie, and God is no respecter of persons, for the last shall be the first . . .

JULIE: Then He does respect the last.

KRISTINE (continuing): . . . and it is easier for a camel to go through the eye of a needle, than for a rich man to enter the Kingdom of God. That's how it is, Miss Julie! Anyhow, I'm going now—alone, and on the way I'm going to tell the groom not to let any horses out, in case anyone wants to leave before the Count gets back!———Goodbye! (Leaves.)

JEAN: What a witch! ———And all this because of a greenfinch!———

JULIE (dully): Never mind the greenfinch!———Can you see any way out of this? Any end to it?

JEAN (thinking): No!

JULIE: What would you do in my place?

JEAN: In your place? Let's see—as a person of position, as a woman who had—fallen. I don't know—wait, now I know.

JULIE (taking the razor and making a gesture): You mean like this?

JEAN: Yes! But—understand—I wouldn't do it! That's the difference between us!

JULIE: Because you're a man and I'm a woman? What sort of difference is that?

JEAN: The usual difference—between a man and a woman.

JULIE (with the razor in her hand): I want to, but I can't!———My father couldn't either, the time he should have done it.

JEAN: No, he shouldn't have! He had to revenge himself first.

JULIE: And now my mother is revenged again, through me.

JEAN: Didn't you ever love your father, Miss Julie?

JULIE: Oh yes, deeply, but I've hated him, too. I must have done so without realizing it! It was he who brought me up to despise my own sex, making me half woman, half man. Whose fault is what's happened? My father's, my mother's, my own? My own? I don't have anything that's my own. I don't have a single thought that I didn't get from my father, not an emotion that I didn't get from my mother, and this last idea—that all people are equal—I got that from my fiancé.———That's why I called him a swine! How can it be my fault? Shall I let Jesus take on the blame, the way Kristine does?———No, I'm too proud to do that and too sensible—thanks to my father's teachings.———And as for someone rich not going to heaven, that's a lie. But Kristine won't get in—how will she explain the money she has in the savings bank? Whose fault is it?———What does it matter whose fault it is? I'm still the one who has to bear the blame, face the consequences . . .

JEAN: Yes, but . . . (The bell rings sharply twice. Miss Julie jumps up. Jean changes his coat.) The Count is back! Do you suppose Kristine—(He goes to the speaking tube, taps the lid, and listens.)

JULIE: He's been to his desk!

JEAN: It's Jean, sir! (Listening; the audience cannot hear the Count's voice.) Yes, sir! (Listening.) Yes, sir! Right away! (Listening.) At once, sir! (Listening.) I see, in half an hour!

JULIE (desperately frightened): What did he say? Dear Lord, what did he say?

JEAN: He wants his boots and his coffee in half an hour.

JULIE: So, in half an hour! Oh, I'm so tired. I'm not able to do anything. I can't repent, can't run away, can't stay, can't live—can't die! Help me now! Order me, and I'll obey like a dog! Do me this last service, save my honor, save his name! You know what I should do, but don't have the will to . . . You will it, you order me to do it!

JEAN: I don't know why———but now I can't either———I don't understand.———It's as if this coat made it impossible for me to order you to do anything.———And now, since the Count spoke to me—I—I can't really explain it—but—ah, it's the damn lackey in me!———I think if the Count came down here now—and ordered me to cut my throat, I'd do it on the spot.

JULIE: Then pretend you're he, and I'm you!——— You gave such a good performance before when you knelt at my feet.———You were a real nobleman.———Or—have you ever seen a hypnotist in the theater? (Jean nods.) He says to his subject: "Take the broom," and he takes it. He says: "Sweep," and he sweeps———

JEAN: But the subject has to be asleep.

JULIE (ecstatically): I'm already asleep.———The whole room is like smoke around me . . . and you look like an iron stove . . . shaped like a man in black, with a tall hat—and your eyes glow like coals when the fire is dying—and your face is a white patch, like ashes———(The sunlight has reached the *floor and now shines on Jean.*) ————— it's so warm and good————— (*She rubs her hands as if warming them before a fire.*) ————— and bright—and so peaceful!

JEAN (*taking the razor and putting it in her hand*): Here's the broom! Go now while it's bright—out to the barn—and . . . (*Whispers in her ear.*)

JULIE (*awake*): Thank you. I'm going now to rest! But just tell me—that those who are first can also receive the gift of grace. Say it, even if you don't believe it.

JEAN: The first? No, I can't————— But wait—Miss Julie—now I know! You're no longer among the first—you're now among—the last!

JULIE: That's true.—————I'm among the very last. I'm the last one of all! Oh!—————But now I can't go!—————Tell me once more to go!

JEAN: No, now I can't either! I can't!

JULIE: And the first shall be the last!

JEAN: Don't think, don't think! You're taking all my strength from me, making me a coward.————— What was that? I thought the bell moved!—————No! Shall we stuff paper in it?—————To be so afraid of a bell!—————But it isn't just a bell.—————There's someone behind it—a hand sets it in motion—and something else sets the hand in motion.—————Maybe if you cover your ears—cover your ears! But then it rings even louder! rings until someone answers.—————And then it's too late! And then the police come—and—then—————(*The bell rings twice loudly. Jean flinches, then straightens up.*) It's horrible! But there's no other way!—————Go! (*Miss Julie walks firmly out through the door.*)

COMMENTARY

AUGUST STRINDBERG (1849–1912)

From the Preface to Miss Julie 1888

TRANSLATED BY HARRY G. CARLSON

Strindberg's preface sets out his intentions in writing *Miss Julie*, a play concerned with the problem of "social climbing or falling, of higher or lower, better or worse, man or woman." He discusses the struggle for dominance between Miss Julie and Jean, and he characterizes Miss Julie as a woman forced to "wreak vengeance" on herself.

Miss Julie is a modern character. Not that the man-hating half-woman has not existed in all ages but because now that she has been discovered, she has come out in the open to make herself heard. The half-woman is a type who pushes her way ahead, selling herself nowadays for power, decorations, honors, and diplomas, as formerly she used to do for money. The type implies a retrogressive step in evolution, an inferior species who cannot endure. Unfortunately, they are able to pass on their wretchedness; degenerate men seem unconsciously to choose their mates from among them. And so they breed, producing an indeterminate sex for whom life is a torture. Fortunately, the offspring go under either because they are out of harmony with reality or because their repressed instincts break out uncontrollably or because their hopes of achieving equality with men are crushed. The type is tragic, revealing the drama of a desperate struggle against Nature, tragic as the romantic heritage now being dissipated by naturalism, which has a contrary aim: happiness, and happiness belongs only to the strong and skillful species.

But Miss Julie is also: a relic of the old warrior nobility now giving way to a new nobility of nerve and intellect, a victim of her own flawed constitution, a victim of the discord caused in a family by a mother's "crime," a victim of the delusions and conditions of her age—and together these are the equivalent of the concept of Destiny, or Universal Law, of antiquity. Guilt has been abolished by the naturalist, along with God, but the consequences of an action—punishment, imprisonment or the fear of it—that he cannot erase, for the simple reason that they remain, whether he pronounces acquittal or not. Those who have been injured are not as kind and understanding as an unscathed outsider can afford to be. Even if her father felt constrained not to seek revenge, his daughter would wreak vengeance upon herself, as she does here, out of an innate or acquired sense of honor, which the upper classes inherit—from where? From barbarism, from the ancient Aryan home of the race, from medieval chivalry. It is a beautiful thing, but nowadays a hindrance to the survival of the race. It is the nobleman's harikari, which compels him to slit open his own stomach when someone insults him and which survives in a modified form in the duel, that privilege of the nobility. That is why Jean, the servant, lives, while Miss Julie cannot live without honor. The slave's advantage over the nobleman is that he lacks this fatal preoccupation with honor. But in all of us Aryans there is something of the nobleman, or a Don Quixote. And so we sympathize with the suicide, whose act means a loss of honor. We are noblemen enough to be pained when we see the mighty fallen and as superfluous as a corpse, yes, even if the fallen should rise again and make amends through an honorable act. The servant Jean is a race-founder, someone in whom the process of differentiation can be detected. Born the son of a tenant farmer, he has educated himself in the things a gentleman should know. He has been quick to learn, has finely developed senses (smell, taste, sight) and a feeling for what is beautiful. He is already moving up in the world and is not embarrassed about using other people's help. He is alienated from his fellow servants, despising them as parts of a past he has already put behind him. He fears and flees them because they know his secrets, pry into his intentions, envy his rise, and look forward eagerly to his fall. Hence his dual, indecisive nature, vacillating between sympathy for people in high social positions and hatred for those who currently occupy those positions. He is an aristocrat, as he himself says, has learned the secrets of good society, is polished on the surface but coarse beneath, wears a frock coat tastefully but without any guarantee that his body is clean.

He has respect for Miss Julie, but is afraid of Kristine because she knows his dangerous secrets. He is sufficiently callous not to let the night's events disturb his plans for the future. With both a slave's brutality and a master's lack of squeamishness, he can see blood without fainting and shake off misfortune easily. Consequently, he comes through the struggle unscathed and will probably end up an innkeeper. And even if *he* does not become a Rumanian count, his son will become a university student and possibly a county police commissioner. . . .

Apart from the fact that Jean is rising in the world, he is superior to Miss Julie because he is a man. Sexually, he is an aristocrat because of his masculine strength, his more keenly developed senses, and his capacity for taking the initiative. His sense of inferiority is mostly due to the social circumstances in which be happens to be living, and he can probably shed it along with his valet's jacket.

His slave mentality expresses itself in the fearful respect he has for the Count (the boots) and his religious superstition; but he respects the Count mainly as the occupant of the kind of high position to which he himself aspires; and the respect remains even after he has conquered the daughter of the house and seen how empty the lovely shell was.

I do not believe that love in any "higher" sense can exist between two people of such different natures, and so I have Miss Julie's love as something she fabricates in order to protect and excuse herself; and I have Jean suppose himself capable of loving her under other social circumstances. I think it is the same with love as with the hyacinth, which must take root in darkness *before* it can produce a sturdy flower. Here a flower shoots up, blooms, and goes to seed all at once, and that is why it dies so quickly.

American Melodrama

The rise in popularity of melodrama in the United States in the nineteenth century—in contrast to the dominance of heroic drama, tragedy, and social satire in the previous century in England and Europe—has been attributed to the less sophisticated audiences in American cities. After the Revolutionary War and the War of 1812, the nation had freed itself from England's social domination and established its own mores, demanding an entertainment that was more intelligible, less subtle, and more immediate. The American audiences for melodramas included a more socially mixed population than the eighteenth-century English upper middle class. American audiences also enjoyed certain plays by Shakespeare and a few other important playwrights, but the overwhelming demand was for sentimental comedies and crime dramas that involved suspense, surprise, and excitement.

Melodrama is sometimes considered a less significant form of drama than the standard repertory of tragedies and comedies because it relies on stereotypes, simplified moral situations, conventional pieties that are never examined critically, and the inevitable happy ending that resolves all of the essentially artificial complications. The resolutions are often achieved by unexpected and unlikely means, such as a revealing birthmark that qualifies the lowly hero as the lost child of a noble family, who is then able to marry the Lady whom he has just saved from death. Many of the situations are unrealistic, and the complexities that might be the sole subject of a more serious drama are usually omitted altogether. Modern musicals have generally followed this formula with considerable success.

Although their plots were unrealistic, sentimental plays relied on spectacle that was realistic in appearance and effect. For example, complex water effects were common from the middle of the nineteenth century on, and machines that permitted horses to race on stage provided thrills and excitement. Trap doors, revolving stages, and scenery lowered from the flies all helped to intensify the spectacle of the melodrama. These innovations were enhanced by the replacement of gas lights with electric lights in the late 1880s. Bright or controllable light made it possible—and necessary—to achieve a high level of realism in the scenery and settings. The *mise en scene*, or design elements, such as furnishings, costumes, interior details, and outdoor scenes, all had to be realistic because they were so much more visible! This period was remarkable for major improvements in scene painting and scene construction, which was the primary draw for much of the audience. Actors, more visible in bright lights and capable of powerful dramatic effects in contrasting low lights, seized their advantage, especially in suspenseful scenes implying great danger and in tragic scenes that verged on the operatic. All of these new developments in lighting, set, and costume design paralleled and complemented the rise of melodrama in the United States.

Writing plays was not a lucrative profession in the United States in the nineteenth century, but acting in them often was, which is why many playwrights acted in the plays that made them famous. Born in France, Anna Cora Mowatt began her stage career in the United States after her husband died. Despite the fact that she had no training, she was an immediate success as an actor. Her play *Fashion* (1845) satirizes the ambitious attempts of American socialites to emulate the latest European styles.

The most successful American play of the nineteenth century was *Uncle Tom's Cabin* (1852), a melodrama by George L. Aiken. The play was derived from Harriet Beecher Stowe's novel, which had been published only six months before. Stowe came from a very religious family that condemned the stage outright, so there was never any question of her adapting the novel as a play. Aiken never received permission to write the play, and he earned very little money for his efforts, even though at least 500,000 people attended the play over its lifetime on the stage. The play depended on stereotypes, simplified situations, considerable sentimentality, and unlikely events. It also relied on spectacular effects that shocked and surprised the eager audiences. The play faithfully conveyed Stowe's disapproval of slavery and emerged as successful antislavery propaganda that, according to Abraham Lincoln, contributed to the start of the Civil War.

The Civil War (1861–1865) interrupted the development of theater in many parts of the nation, but it also became a major theme of later plays and melodramas. Bronson Howard's Civil War drama *Shenandoah* (1888) was enormously successful, even though it avoided discussion of the reasons for the war or the nature of the war itself. William Gillette's *Secret Service* (1895) and his earlier Civil War drama *Held by the Enemy* (1886) were successful in large part because he played the primary roles. He was already a matinee idol when he began a lifelong engagement playing the title role in *Sherlock Holmes* (1899), which ran well into the twentieth century and made him a wealthy man.

A prime ingredient of many melodramas of the period was the sensational crime that had to be solved before the play ended. Dion Boucicault, an Irish transplant in America, was the master of the sentimental melodrama and among the most productive playwrights of the age. His pre–Civil War drama *The Octoroon, or Life in Louisiana* (1859) also treated the question of slavery and was set on a southern plantation. Boucicault's play was very popular, in part because it treated the theme in such a way that southerners thought it approved of the southern way of life, whereas northerners thought it fueled the abolitionist cause of ending slavery. With the primary focus on solving a murder by ingenious technical means, the question of slavery was played down.

Today, when we read or see the sentimental melodramas of the nineteenth century, we may react to exaggerated dialogue and conventional platitudes much the way Hamlet reacts to the old style of acting when he instructs the players in *Hamlet*. The language may be easy to mock because it seems so completely artificial, but it is important to understand that the audiences of this period believed such dialogue was artistic. To them, the more high-flown, artificial, and stagy, the better. Instead of parodying it, these audiences imitated it. Thus, we must recognize that the drama that dominated the American theater scene in this century reflects the tastes of the audiences that demanded and rewarded it.

Anna Cora Mowatt

Anna Cora Mowatt (1819–1870) was eight years old when she left France for the United States with her American parents. Her father was an exporter and raised her in a comfortable upper-middle-class family. She was interested in the theater and acting from a very young age, appearing in a play when she was only five. When she was fifteen, Mowatt eloped with a wealthy lawyer, James Mowatt. They lived on Long island, where she was part of a social circle similar to the one portrayed in her play. She began writing fiction in the 1830s, but in 1840 her husband lost a great deal of money and became ill. Her writing, including the six-act play *Gulzara, or the Persian Star* (1840), took on greater importance and was a means of supporting the entire family, including her three young adopted children. Her task was made more difficult by her suffering from tuberculosis, which made brief periods of convalescence necessary.

During one of her periods of convalescence, Mowatt wrote the five-act comedy *Fashion*. The play was first performed in 1845 and enjoyed remarkable popular and critical success at the Park Theater in New York and at the Walnut Street Theater in Philadelphia a few days later, establishing her as a major force in dramatic literature. Although she did not act in the first performances, Mowatt played the part of Gertrude later in the year. She continued to act, appearing in Bulwer-Lytton's *The Lady of Lyons* at the Park Theater in June 1845, and was an immediate success. Her husband died in 1851, and her own health became so problematic that she had to retire in 1854. She remarried, but her new husband was a southerner and she eventually split with him over the question of slavery. She moved to Paris, to Florence, and then to England, where she lived until her death in 1870.

Fashion

In *Fashion*, Mowatt satirizes the American pretensions to European styles and the American worship of European aristocracy. This play is in many ways a farce, although its underlying message is clear. The excerpt here includes the complete act 5, wherein all the intrigues and deceptions are clarified and the problems of the play are resolved. In earlier acts, we are introduced to the important characters:

For the full text of *Fashion*, visit **bedfordstmartins.com/jacobus**.

ADAM TRUEMAN, a wealthy 72-year-old farmer from the frontier, rugged and, as his
    name suggests, a man who is a true American and plainspoken
COUNT JOLIMAITRE, a fraud acting as a Count
MRS. TIFFANY, a spendthrift duped by the Count

MR. TIFFANY, a businessman who forges documents in order to maintain his wife's lavish lifestyle

SNOBSON, Tiffany's clerk, who knows about the forgeries and blackmails Tiffany by demanding to be permitted to marry Tiffany's daughter

SERAPHINA, Tiffany's daughter, who falls for the Count

GERTRUDE, a governess who was raised in Geneva

CAPTAIN HOWARD, an officer in the U.S. Army who loves Gertrude

All of these characters are essentially stereotypes: the rustic American back-woodsman, the elegant con man, the vain and easily fooled wife, the bland and helpless husband, the villainous servant-clerk, the empty-headed girl, the misunderstood and undervalued heroine, and the dashing but empty military man.

According to Mowatt, Trueman is the one character who was drawn from life, having been modeled on a farmer whom she knew. He has all the lines that seem to establish the moral tone of the play and the desirable moral position of those in society. He delivers speeches such as "Fashion! And pray what is *fashion*, madam? An agreement between certain persons to live without using their souls! To substitute etiquette for virtue — decorum for purity — manners for morals! To affect a shame for the works of their Creator! And expend all their rapture upon the works of their tailors and dressmakers" (act 4). He plays the critical role in resolving the action in act 5.

In act 4, Gertrude concocts a scheme for exposing the fraudulent Count, but her plan backfires and act 5 begins with people believing she has com-promised herself with the Count. She had attempted to set up a tryst between Millinette, the French ladies' maid, and the Count, but she was discovered before she could bring the two of them together. As act 5 begins, she is under suspicion and tries, by being honest, to clear her name. A large part of the play's appeal in 1845 was its moral, which confirmed the value of American straightforwardness and warned against sacrificing a family's financial security for the sake of fashion.

ANNA CORA MOWATT (1819–1870)

From Fashion　　1845

Act V • *Scene 1*

Mrs. Tiffany's Drawing Room—same Scene as Act First. Gertrude seated at a table, with her head leaning on her hand; in the other hand she holds a pen. A sheet of paper and an ink-stand before her.

GERTRUDE: How shall I write to them? What shall I say? Prevaricate I cannot—(*Rises and comes forward.*) and yet if I write the truth—simple souls! how can they comprehend the motives for my conduct? Nay—the truly pure see no imaginary evil in others! It is only vice, that reflecting its own image, suspects, even the innocent. I have no time to lose—I must prepare them for my return. (*Resumes her seat and writes.*) What a true pleasure there is in daring to be frank! (*After writing a few lines more, pauses.*) Not so frank either,—there is one name that I cannot mention. Ah! that he should suspect—should despise me. (*Writes.*)

(*Enter Trueman.*)

TRUEMAN: There she is! If this girl's soul had only been as fair as her face,—yet she dared to speak the truth,—I'll not forget that! A woman who refuses to tell a lie has one spark of heaven in her still. (*Approaches her.*) Gertrude, (*Gertrude starts and looks up.*) what are you writing there? Plotting more mischief, eh, girl?

GERTRUDE: I was writing a few lines to some friends in Geneva.

TRUEMAN: The Wilsons, eh?

GERTRUDE (*surprised, rising*): Are you acquainted with them, Sir?

TRUEMAN: I shouldn't wonder if I was. I suppose you have taken good care not to mention the dark room—that foreign puppy in the closet—the pleasant surprise—and all that sort of thing, eh?

GERTRUDE: I have no reason for concealment, Sir! for I have done nothing of which I am ashamed!

TRUEMAN: Then I can't say much for your modesty.

GERTRUDE: I should not wish you to say more than I deserve.

TRUEMAN: There's a bold minx! (*Aside.*)

GERTRUDE: Since my affairs seem to have excited your interest—I will not say *curiosity*, perhaps you even feel a desire to inspect my correspondence? There, (*Handing the letter.*) I pride myself upon my good nature,—you may like to take advantage of it?

TRUEMAN: With what an air she carries it off! (*Aside.*) Take advantage of it? So I will. (*Reads.*) What's this? "French chambermaid—Count—impostor—infatuation—Seraphina—Millinette—disguised myself—expose him." Thunder and lightning! I see it all! Come and kiss me, girl! (*Gertrude evinces surprise.*) No, no—I forgot—it won't do to come to that yet! She's a rare girl! I'm out of my senses with joy! I don't know what to do with myself! Tol, de rol, de rol, de ra. (*Capers and sings.*)

GERTRUDE: What a remarkable old man! (*Aside.*) Then you do me justice, Mr. Trueman?

TRUEMAN: I say I don't! Justice? You're above all dependence upon justice! Hurrah! I've found one true woman at last? *True*? (*Pauses thoughtfully.*) Humph! I didn't think of that flaw! Plotting and manoeuvering—not much truth in that? An honest girl should be above stratagems!

GERTRUDE: But my *motive*, Sir, was good.

TRUEMAN: That's not enough—your *actions* must be *good* as well as your *motives*! Why could you not tell the silly girl that man was an imposter?

GERTRUDE: I did inform her of my suspicions—she ridiculed them; the plan I chose was an imprudent one, but I could not devise—

TRUEMAN: I hate devising! Give me a woman with the *firmness* to be *frank*! But no matter—I had no right to look for an angel out of Paradise; and I am as happy—as happy as a Lord! that is, ten times happier than any Lord ever was! Tol, de rol, de rol! Oh! you—you—I'll thrash every fellow that says a word against you!

GERTRUDE: You will have plenty of employment then, Sir, for I do not know of one just now who would speak in my favor!

TRUEMAN: Not *one*, eh? Why, where's your dear Mr. Twinkle? I know all about it—can't say that I admire your choice of a husband! But there's no accounting for a girl's taste.

GERTRUDE: Mr. Twinkle! Indeed you are quite mistaken!

TRUEMAN: No—really? Then you're not taken with him, eh?

GERTRUDE: Not even with his rhymes.

TRUEMAN: Hang that old mother meddle-much! What a fool she has made of me. And so you're quite free, and I may choose a husband for you myself? Heart-whole, eh?

GERTRUDE: I—I—I trust there is nothing *unsound* about my heart.

TRUEMAN: There it is again. Don't prevaricate, girl! I tell you an *evasion* is a *lie in contemplation*, and I hate lying! Out with the truth! Is your heart *free* or not?

GERTRUDE: Nay, Sir, since you *demand* an answer, permit *me* to demand by what right you ask the question?

(*Enter Howard.*)

Colonel Howard here!

TRUEMAN: I'm out again! What's the Colonel to her? (*Retires up.*)

HOWARD (*crosses to her*): I have come, Gertrude, to bid you farewell. To-morrow I resign my commission and leave this city, perhaps for ever. You, Gertrude, it is you who have exiled me! After last evening—

TRUEMAN (*coming forward to Howard*): What the plague have you got to say about last evening?

HOWARD: Mr. Trueman!

TRUEMAN: What have you got to say about last evening? and what have you to say to that little girl at all? It's Tiffany's precious daughter you're in love with.

HOWARD: Miss Tiffany? Never! I never had the slightest pretension—

TRUEMAN: That lying old woman! But I'm glad of it! Oh! Ah! Um! (*Looking significantly at Gertrude and then at Howard.*) I see how it is. So you don't choose to marry Seraphina, eh? Well now, whom do you choose to marry? (*Glancing at Gertrude.*)

HOWARD: I shall not marry at all!

TRUEMAN: You won't? (*Looking at them both again.*) Why you don't mean to say that you don't like—(*Points with his thumb to Gertrude.*)

GERTRUDE: Mr. Trueman, I may have been wrong to boast of my good nature, but do not presume too far upon it.

HOWARD: You like frankness, Mr. Trueman, therefore I will speak plainly. I have long cherished a dream from which I was last night rudely awakened.

TRUEMAN: And that's what you call speaking plainly? Well, I differ with you! But I can guess what you mean. Last night you suspected Gertrude there of—(*angrily*) of what no man shall ever suspect her again while I'm above ground! You did her injustice,—it was a mistake! There, now that matter's settled. Go, and ask her to forgive you,—she's woman enough to do it! Go, go!

HOWARD: Mr. Trueman, you have forgotten to whom you dictate.

TRUEMAN: Then you won't do it? you won't ask her pardon?

HOWARD: Most undoubtedly I will not—not at any man's bidding. I must first know—

TRUEMAN: You won't do it? Then if I don't give you a lesson in politeness—

HOWARD: It will be because you find me your *tutor* in the same science. I am not a man to brook an insult, Mr. Trueman! but we'll not quarrel in presence of the lady.

TRUEMAN: Won't we? I don't know that—

GERTRUDE: Pray, Mr. Trueman—Colonel Howard, pray desist, Mr. Trueman, for my sake! (*Taking hold of his arm to hold him back.*) Colonel Howard, if you will read this letter it will explain everything. (*Hands letter to Howard, who reads.*)

TRUEMAN: He don't deserve an explanation! Didn't I tell him that it was a mistake? Refuse to beg your pardon! I'll teach him, I'll teach him!

HOWARD (*after reading*): Gertrude, how have I wronged you!

TRUEMAN: Oh, you'll beg her pardon now? (*Between them.*)

HOWARD: Hers, Sir, and yours! Gertrude, I fear—

TRUEMAN: You needn't,—she'll forgive you. You don't know these women as well as I do,—they're always ready to pardon; it's their nature, and they can't help it. Come along, I left Antony and his wife in the dining room; we'll go and find them. I've a story of my own to tell! As for you, Colonel, you may follow. Come along. Come along!

(*Leads out Gertrude, followed by Howard.*)

(*Enter Mr. and Mrs. Tiffany, Mr. Tiffany with a bundle of bills in his hand.*)

MRS. TIFFANY: I beg you won't mention the subject again, Mr. Tiffany. Nothing is more plebeian than a discussion upon economy—nothing more *ungenteel* than looking over and fretting over one's bills!

TIFFANY: Then I suppose, my dear, it is quite as ungenteel to *pay* one's bills?

MRS. TIFFANY: Certainly! I hear the *ee-light* never condescend to do anything of the kind. The honor of their invaluable patronage is sufficient for the persons they employ!

TIFFANY: *Patronage* then is a newly invented food upon which the working classes fatten? What convenient appetites poor people must have! Now listen to what I am going to say. As soon as my daughter marries Mr. Snobson—

(*Enter Prudence, a three-cornered note in her hand.*)

PRUDENCE: Oh, dear! oh, dear! what shall we do! Such a misfortune! Such a disaster! Oh, dear! oh, dear!

MRS. TIFFANY: Prudence, you are the most tiresome creature! What *is* the matter?

PRUDENCE (*passing up and down the stage*): Such a disgrace to the whole family! But I always expected it. Oh, dear! oh, dear!

MRS. TIFFANY (*following her up and down the stage*): What are you talking about, Prudence? Will you tell me what has happened?

PRUDENCE (*still pacing, Mrs. Tiffany following*): Oh! I can't, I can't! You'll feel so dreadfully! How could she do such a thing! But I expected nothing else! I never did, I never did!

MRS. TIFFANY (*still following*): Good gracious! what do you mean, Prudence? Tell me, will you tell me? I shall get into such a passion! What *is* the matter?

PRUDENCE (*still pacing*): Oh, Betsy, Betsy! That your daughter should have come to that! Dear me, dear me!

TIFFANY: Seraphina? Did you say Seraphina? What has happened to her? what has she done?

(*Following Prudence up and down the stage on the opposite side from Mrs. Tiffany.*)

MRS. TIFFANY (*still following*): What *has* she done? what *has* she done?

PRUDENCE: Oh! something dreadful—dreadful—shocking!

TIFFANY (*still following*): Speak quickly and plainly—you torture me by this delay, Prudence, be calm, and speak! What is it?

PRUDENCE (*stopping*): Zeke just told me—he carried her travelling trunk himself—she gave him a whole dollar! Oh, my!

TIFFANY: Her trunk? where? where?

PRUDENCE: Round the corner!

MRS. TIFFANY: What did she want with her trunk? You are the most vexatious creature, Prudence! There is no bearing your ridiculous conduct!

PRUDENCE: Oh, you will have worse to bear—worse! Seraphina's gone!

TIFFANY: Gone! where?

PRUDENCE: Off!—eloped—eloped with the Count! Dear me, dear me! I always told you she would!

TIFFANY: Then I am ruined!

(*Stands with his face buried in his hands.*)

MRS. TIFFANY: Oh, what a ridiculous girl! And she might have had such a splendid wedding! What could have possessed her?

TIFFANY: The devil himself possessed her, for she has ruined me past all redemption! Gone, Prudence, did you say gone? Are you *sure* they are gone?

PRUDENCE: Didn't I tell you so! Just look at this note—one might know by the very fold of it—

TIFFANY (*snatching the note*): Let me see it! (*Opens the note and reads.*) "My dear Ma,—When you receive this I shall be a *countess*! Isn't it a sweet title? The Count and I were forced to be married privately, for reasons which I will explain in my next. You must pacify Pa, and put him in a good humour before I come back, though now I'm to be a countess I suppose I shouldn't care!" Undutiful huzzy! "We are going to make a little excursion and will be back in a week.

"Your dutiful daughter—Seraphina." A man's curse is sure to spring up at his own hearth,—here is mine! The sole curb upon that villain gone, I am wholly in his power! Oh! the first downward step from honor—he who takes it cannot pause in his mad descent and is sure to be hurried on to ruin!

MRS. TIFFANY: Why, Mr. Tiffany, how you do take on! And I dare say to elope was the most fashionable way after all!

(*Enter Trueman, leading Gertrude, and followed by Howard.*)

TRUEMAN: Where are all the folks? Here, Antony, you are the man I want. We've been hunting for you all over the house. Why—what's the matter? There's a face for a thriving city merchant! Ah! Antony, you never wore such a hang-dog look as that when you trotted about the country with your pack upon your back! Your shoulders are no broader now—but they've a heavier load to carry—that's plain!

MRS. TIFFANY: Mr. Trueman, such allusions are highly improper! What would my daughter, *the Countess*, say!

GERTRUDE: The Countess? Oh! Madam!

MRS. TIFFANY: Yes, the Countess! My daughter Seraphina, the Countess *dee* Jolimaitre! What have you to say to that? No wonder you are surprised after your *recherché, abimé°* conduct! I have told you already, Miss Gertrude, that you were not a proper person to enjoy the inestimable advantages of my patronage. You are dismissed—do you understand? Discharged!

recherché, abimé: Farfetched, awful.

TRUEMAN: Have you done? Very well, it's my turn now. Antony, perhaps what I have to say don't concern you as much as some others—but I want you to listen to me. You remember, Antony, (*his tone becomes serious*), a blue-eyed, smiling girl—

TIFFANY: Your daughter, Sir? I remember her well.

TRUEMAN: None ever saw her to forget her! Give me your hand, man. There—that will do! Now let me go on. I never coveted wealth—yet twenty years ago I found myself the richest farmer in Catteraugus. This cursed money made my girl an object of speculation. Every idle fellow that wanted to feather his nest was sure to come courting Ruth. There was one—my heart misgave me the instant I laid eyes upon him—for he was a city chap, and not over fond of the truth. But Ruth—ah! she was too pure herself to look for guile! His fine words and his fair looks—the old story—she was taken with him—I said, "no"—but the girl liked her own way better than her old father's—girls always do! and one morning—the rascal robbed me—not of my money, he would have been welcome to that—but of the only treasure I cherished—my daughter!

TIFFANY: But you forgave her!

TRUEMAN: I did! I knew she would never forgive herself—that was punishment enough! The scoundrel thought he was marrying my gold with my daughter—he was mistaken! I took care that they should never want; but that was all. She loved him—what will not woman love? The villain broke her heart—mine was tougher, or it wouldn't have stood what it did. A year after they were married, he forsook her! She came back to her old home—her old father! It couldn't last long—she pined—and pined—and—then—she died! Don't think me an old fool—though I am one—for grieving won't bring her back. (*Bursts into tears.*)

TIFFANY: It was a heavy loss!

TRUEMAN: So heavy, that I should not have cared how soon I followed her, but for the child she left! As I pressed that child in my arms, I swore that my unlucky wealth should never curse it, as it had cursed its mother! It was all I had to love—but I sent it away—and the neighbors thought it was dead. The girl was brought up tenderly but humbly by my wife's relatives in Geneva. I had her taught true independence—she had hands—capacities—and should use them! Money should never buy her a husband! for I resolved not to claim her until she had made her choice, and found the man who was willing to take her for herself alone. She turned out a rare girl! and it's time her old grandfather claimed her. Here he is to do it! And there stands Ruth's child! Old Adam's heiress! Gertrude, Gertrude!—my child! (*Gertrude rushes into his arms.*)

PRUDENCE (*after a pause*): Do tell; I want to know! But I knew it! I always said Gertrude would turn out somebody, after all!

MRS. TIFFANY: Dear me! Gertrude an heiress! My dear Gertrude, I always thought you a very charming girl—quite YOU-NICK—an heiress! I must give her a ball! I'll introduce her into society myself—of course an heiress must make a sensation! (*Aside.*)

HOWARD: I am too bewildered even to wish her joy. Ah! there will be plenty to do that now—but the gulf between us is wider than ever. (*Aside.*)

TRUEMAN: Step forward, young man, and let us know what you are muttering about. I said I would never claim her until she had found the man who loved her for herself. I *have* claimed her—yet I never break my word—I think I *have* found that man! and here he is. (*Strikes Howard on the shoulder.*) Gertrude's yours! There—never say a word, man—don't bore me with your thanks—you can cancel all obligations by making that child happy! There—take her!—Well, girl, and what do you say?

GERTRUDE: That I rejoice too much at having found a parent for my first act to be one of disobedience! (*Gives her hand to Howard.*)

TRUEMAN: How very dutiful! and how disinterested!

(*Tiffany retires up—and paces the stage, exhibiting great agitation.*)

PRUDENCE (*to Trueman*): All the *single folks* are getting married!

TRUEMAN: No they are not. You and I are single folks, and we're not likely to get married.

MRS. TIFFANY: My dear Mr. Trueman—my sweet Gertrude, when my daughter, the Countess, returns, she will be delighted to hear of this *deenooment*! I assure you that the Countess will be quite charmed!

GERTRUDE: The Countess? Pray, Madam, where *is* Seraphina?

MRS. TIFFANY: The Countess *dee* Jolimaitre, my dear, is at this moment on her way to—to Washington! Where after visiting all the fashionable curiosities of the day—including the President—she will return to grace her native city!

GERTRUDE: I hope you are only jesting, Madam? Seraphina is not married?

MRS. TIFFANY: Excuse me, my dear, my daughter had this morning the honor of being united to the Count *dee* Jolimaitre!

GERTRUDE: Madam! He is an imposter!

MRS. TIFFANY: Good gracious! Gertrude, how can you talk in that disrespectful way of a man of rank? An heiress, my dear, should have better manners! The Count—

(*Enter Millinette, crying.*)

MILLINETTE: Oh! Madame! I will tell everything—oh! dat monstre! He break my heart!

MRS. TIFFANY: Millinette, what is the matter?

MILLINETTE: Oh! he promise to marry me—I love him much—and now Zeke say he run away vid Mademoiselle Seraphina!

MRS. TIFFANY: What insolence! The girl is mad! Count Jolimaitre marry my *femmy de chamber*!°

MILLINETTE: Oh! Madame, he is not one Count, not at all! Dat is only de title he go by in dis country. De foreigners always take de large title ven dey do come here. His name *à Paris* vas Gustave Treadmill. But he not one Frenchman at all, but he do live one long time *à Paris*. First he live vid Monsieur Vermicelle—dere he vas de head cook! Den he live vid Monsieur Tire-nez, de barber! After dat he live wid Monsieur le Comte Frippon-fin—and dere he vas le Comte's valet! Dere, now I tell everyting I feel one great deal better!

MRS. TIFFANY: Oh! good gracious! I shall faint! Not a Count! What will everybody say? It's no such thing! I say he *is* a Count! One can see the foreign *jenny says quoi*° in his face! Don't you think I can tell a Count when I see one? I say he *is* a Count!

(*Enter Snobson, his hat on—his hands thrust in his pocket—evidently a little intoxicated.*)

SNOBSON: I won't stand it! I say I won't.

TIFFANY (*rushing up to him*): Mr. Snobson, for heaven's sake—(*Aside.*)

---

femmy de chamber: *Femme de chambre*, chambermaid.
jenny says quoi: *Je ne sais quoi*—literally, "I don't know what"; a certain something.

SNOBSON: Keep off! I'm a hard customer to get the better of! You'll see if I don't come out strong!

TRUEMAN (*quietly knocking off Snobson's hat with his stick*): Where are your manners, man?

SNOBSON: My business ain't with you, Catteraugus; you've waked up the wrong passenger!—Now the way I'll put it into Tiff will be a caution. I'll make him wince! That extra mint julep has put the true pluck in me. Now for it! (*Aside.*) Mr. Tiffany, Sir—you need n't think to come over me, Sir—you'll have to get up a little earlier in the morning before you do *that*, Sir! I'd like to know, Sir, how you came to assist your daughter in running away with that foreign loafer? It was a downright swindle, Sir. After the conversation I and you had on that subject she wasn't your property, Sir.

TRUEMAN: What, Antony, is that the way your city clerk bullies his boss?

SNOBSON: You're drunk, Catteraugus—don't expose your-self—you're drunk! Taken a little too much toddy, my old boy! Be quiet! I'll look after you, and they won't find it out. If you want to be busy, you may take care of my *hat*—I feel so deuced weak in the chest, I don't think I *could* pick it up myself.—Now to put the screws to Tiff. (*Aside.*) Mr. Tiffany, Sir—you have broken your word, as no virtuous individual—no honorable member—of—the—com—mu—ni—ty—

TIFFANY: Have some pity, Mr. Snobson, I beseech you! I had nothing to do with my daughter's elopement! I will agree to anything you desire—your salary shall be doubled—trebled—(*Aside to him.*)

SNOBSON (*aloud*): No you don't. No bribery and corruption.

TIFFANY: I implore you to be silent. You shall become partner of the concern, if you please—only do not speak. You are not yourself at this moment. (*Aside to him.*)

SNOBSON: Ain't I, though? I feel *twice* myself. I feel like two Snobsons rolled into one, and I'm chock full of the spunk of a dozen! Now Mr. Tiffany, Sir—

TIFFANY: I shall go distracted! Mr. Snobson, if you have one spark of manly feeling—(*Aside to him.*)

TRUEMAN: Antony, why do you stand disputing with that drunken jackass? Where's your nigger? Let him kick the critter out, and be of use for once in his life.

SNOBSON: Better be quiet, Catteraugus. This ain't your hash, so keep your spoon out of the dish. Don't expose yourself, old boy.

TRUEMAN: Turn him out, Antony!

SNOBSON: He daren't do it! Ain't I up to him? Ain't he in my power? Can't I knock him into a cocked hat with a word? And now he's got my steam up—I *will* do it!

TIFFANY (*beseechingly*): Mr. Snobson—my friend—

SNOBSON: It's no go—steam's up—and I don't stand at anything!

TRUEMAN: You won't *stand* here long unless you mend your manners—you're not the first man I've *upset* because he didn't know his place.

SNOBSON: I know where Tiff's place is, and that's in the *States' Prison*! It's bespoke already. He would have it! He wouldn't take pattern of me, and behave like a gentleman! He's a *forger*, Sir! (*Tiffany throws himself into a chair in an attitude of despair; the others stand transfixed with astonishment.*) He's been forging Dick Anderson's endorsements of his notes these ten months. He's got a couple in the bank that will send him to the wall anyhow—if he can't make a raise. I took them there myself! Now you know what he's worth. I said I'd expose him, and I have done it!

MRS. TIFFANY: Get out of the house! You ugly, little, drunken brute, get out! It's not true. Mr. Trueman, put him out; you have got a stick—put him out!

(*Enter Seraphina, in her bonnet and shawl—a parasol in her hand.*)

SERAPHINA: I hope Zeke hasn't delivered my note.

(*Stops in surprise at seeing the persons assembled.*)

MRS. TIFFANY: Oh, here is the Countess! (*Advances to embrace her.*)

TIFFANY (*starting from his seat, and seizing Seraphina violently by the arm*): Are—you—married?

SERAPHINA: Goodness, Pa, how you frighten me! No, I'm not married, *quite.*

TIFFANY: Thank heaven.

MRS. TIFFANY (*drawing Seraphina aside*): What's the matter? Why did you come back?

SERAPHINA: The clergyman wasn't at home—I came back for my jewels—the Count said nobility couldn't get on without them.

TIFFANY: I may be saved yet! Seraphina, my child, you will not see me disgraced—ruined! I have been a kind father to you—at least I have tried to be one—although your mother's extravagance made a *madman* of me! The Count is an imposter—you seemed to like him—(*pointing to Snobson*). Heaven forgive me! (*Aside.*) Marry *him* and save *me.* You, Mr. Trueman, you will be my friend in this hour of extreme need—you will advance the sum which I require—I pledge myself to return it. My wife—my child—who will support them were I—the thought makes me frantic! You will aid me? You had a child yourself.

TRUEMAN: But I did not *sell* her—it was her own doings. Shame on you, Antony! Put a price on your own flesh and blood! Shame on such foul traffic!

TIFFANY: Save me—I conjure you—for my father's sake.

TRUEMAN: For your *father's son's* sake I will *not* aid you in becoming a greater villain than you are!

GERTRUDE: Mr. Trueman—Father, I should say—save him—do not embitter our happiness by permitting this calamity to fall upon another—

TRUEMAN: Enough—I did not need your voice, child. I am going to settle this matter my own way.

(*Goes up to Snobson—who has seated himself and fallen asleep—tilts him out of the chair.*)

SNOBSON (*waking up*): Eh? Where's the fire? Oh! it's you, Catteraugus.

TRUEMAN: If I comprehend aright, you have been for some time aware of your principal's forgeries?

(*As he says this, he beckons to Howard, who advances as witness.*)

SNOBSON: You've hit the nail, Catteraugus! Old chap saw that I was up to him six months ago; left off throwing dust into my eyes—

TRUEMAN: Oh, he did!

SNOBSON: Made no bones of forging Anderson's name at my elbow.

TRUEMAN: Forged at your elbow? You saw him do it?

SNOBSON: I did.

TRUEMAN: Repeatedly.

SNOBSON: Re—pea—ted—ly.

TRUEMAN: Then you, Rattlesnake, if he goes to the States' Prison, you'll take up your quarters there too. You are an accomplice, an *accessory*!

(*Trueman walks away and seats himself, Howard rejoins Gertrude. Snobson stands for some time bewildered.*)

SNOBSON: The deuce, so I am! I never thought of that! I must make myself scarce. I'll be off! Tif, I say, Tif! (*Going up to him and speaking confidentially*) that drunken old rip has got us in his power. Let's give him the slip and be off. They want men of genius at the West,—we're sure to get on! You—you can set up for a writing master, and teach copying *signatures*; and I—I'll give lectures on *temperance*! You won't come, eh? Then I'm off without you. Good bye, Catteraugus! Which is the way to California? (*Steals off.*)

TRUEMAN: There's one debt your city owes me. And now let us see what other nuisances we can abate. Antony, I'm not given to preaching, therefore I shall not say much about what you have done. Your face speaks for itself,—the crime has brought its punishment along with it.

TIFFANY: Indeed it has, Sir! In *one year* I have lived a *century* of misery.

TRUEMAN: I believe you, and upon one condition I will assist you—

TIFFANY: My friend—my first, ever kind friend,—only name it!

TRUEMAN: You must sell your house and all these gew gaws, and bundle your wife and daughter off to the country. There let them learn economy, true independence, and home virtues, instead of foreign follies. As for yourself, continue your business—but let moderation, in future, be your counsellor, and let *honesty* be your confidential clerk.

TIFFANY: Mr. Trueman, you have made existence once more precious to me! My wife and daughter shall quit the city to-morrow, and—

PRUDENCE: It's all coming right! It's all coming right! We'll go to the county of Catteraugus. (*Walking up to Trueman.*)

TRUEMAN: No, you won't—I make that a stipulation, Antony; keep clear of Catteraugus. None of your fashionable examples there!

(*Jolimaitre appears in the Conservatory and peeps into the room unperceived.*)

COUNT: What can detain Seraphina? We ought to be off!

MILLINETTE (*turns round, perceives him, runs and forces him into the room.*): Here he is! Ah, Gustave, mon cher Gustave! I have you now and we never part no more. Don't frown, Gustave, don't frown—

TRUEMAN: Come forward, Mr. Count! and for the edification of fashionable society confess that you're an imposter.

COUNT: An imposter? Why, you abominable old—

TRUEMAN: Oh, your feminine friend has told us all about it, the cook—the valet—barber and all that sort of thing. Come, confess, and something may be done for you.

COUNT: Well, then, I do confess I am no count; but really, ladies and gentlemen, I may recommend myself as the most capital cook.

MRS. TIFFANY: Oh, Seraphina!

SERAPHINA: Oh, Ma! (*They embrace and retire up.*)

TRUEMAN: Promise me to call upon the whole circle of your fashionable acquaintances with your own advertisements and in your cook's attire, and I will set you up in business to-morrow. Better turn stomachs than turn heads!

MILLINETTE: But you will marry me?

COUNT: Give us your hand, Millinette! Sir, command me for the most delicate *paté*—the daintiest *croquette à la royale*—the most transcendent *omelette soufflée* that ever issued from a French pastry-cook's oven. I hope you will pardon my conduct, but I heard that in America, where you pay homage to titles while you profess to scorn them—where *Fashion* makes the basest coin current—where you have no kings, no princes, no *nobility*—

TRUEMAN: Stop there! I object to your use of that word. When justice is found only among lawyers—health among physicians—and patriotism among politicians, *then* may you say that there is no *nobility* where there are no titles! But we *have* kings, princes, and nobles in abundance—of *Nature's stamp*, if not of *Fashion's*,—we have honest men, warm hearted and brave, and we have women—gentle, fair, and true, to whom no *title* could add *nobility*.

Epilogue

PRUDENCE: I told you so! And now you hear and see.
    I told you *Fashion* would the fashion be!

TRUEMAN: Then both its point and moral I distrust.

COUNT: Sir, is that liberal?

HOWARD: Or is it just?

TRUEMAN: The guilty have escaped!

TIFFANY: Is, therefore, sin made charming? Ah! there's punishment within!
    Guilt ever carries his own scourge along.

GERTRUDE: Virtue her own reward!

TRUEMAN: You're right, I'm wrong.

MRS. TIFFANY: How we have been deceived!

PRUDENCE: I told you so.

SERAPHINA: To lose at once a title and a beau!

COUNT: A count no more, I'm no more of *account*.

TRUEMAN: But to a nobler title you may mount,
    And be in time—who knows?—an honest man!

COUNT: Eh, Millinette?

MILLINETTE: Oh, *oui*—I know you can!

GERTRUDE (*to audience*): But ere we close the scene, a word with you,—
    We charge you answer,—Is this picture true?
    Some little mercy to our efforts show,
    Then let the world your honest verdict know.
    Here let it see portrayed its ruling passion,
    And learn to prize at its just value—*Fashion*.

George L. Aiken

Harriet Beecher Stowe's novel *Uncle Tom's Cabin* was published only six months before George Aiken's play was first produced in 1852. At least one friend of Stowe's asked for her permission to stage the novel and was refused because Stowe, the daughter of a famous minister and the wife of a theologian, was convinced that the stage was unholy and led Christians to bad behavior. But she did not have the means to protect her novel from Aiken's adaptation, which in its first production ran for three hundred performances and was an instant success. Historians estimate that the play was seen by at least half a million people from 1852 to the early years of the twentieth century.

Very little is known about George Aiken. He had written some dime novels before he wrote this play, and so far as we know, he wrote no other plays. However, we do know that, like most playwrights of the period, he received very little for his script: $40 and a gold watch. He made his money acting in the drama. He played two roles in different productions: George Shelby, the white master who wants to buy back Uncle Tom in Act 6 (included here), and George Harris, the black slave who fights for and ultimately gains his freedom in Canada in the acts that precede this one.

There were several different dramatic versions of Stowe's novel in the nineteenth century, but Aiken's became the standard and was used as the basis of subsequent films in the early twentieth century because it was the only version that was published in book form. Stowe, who had never before been to a theater, eventually was spirited into a Washington theater by a friend, who arranged for Stowe to arrive in the manager's box through a private entrance and covered her so that she would not be recognized. The friend later reported that Stowe was moved to joy and tears, along with the rest of the audience.

Uncle Tom's Cabin

The play was originally written as two plays, which is one reason this version has six acts. The final scene, a wordless tableau, was added in 1853 to prevent people from leaving the theater abruptly, and on a down note, after Tom's death. The play also has two primary plots. The first, which opens the play, is the story of the slave George Harris. Harris complains about his master to his wife, Eliza, whose Christian beliefs console her with the thought that she must obey her master and suffer slavery. George is not content with resignation and speaks almost blasphemously about what he perceives as an uncaring God. He is perceptive and articulate as well:

> My master! And who made him my master? That's what I think of! What right has he to me? I'm as much of a man as he is! What right has he to make a dray-horse of me? — to take me from things I can do better than he can, and put me to work that any horse can do? He tries to do it; he says he'll bring me down and humble me, and he puts me to just the hardest, meanest and dirtiest work, on purpose.

George is a highly sympathetic character. Aided by a frontierman called Phineas Fletcher, who kills the slave hunter Loker, George and Eliza and their child cross over the half-frozen Ohio River to the North and eventually into Canada to begin a new life.

As in the novel, the portraits of blacks are uniformly sympathetic, and the portraits of whites are uniformly unsympathetic. The white characters are either violent and cruel, like Simon Legree, or well-meaning and weak, like George Shelby. Stowe's primary purpose was propagandistic—to protest and portray slavery as inhuman and cruel—and Aiken's play follows her lead entirely. The use of stereotypes advances the purposes of the novel and play.

The second plot is the story of Uncle Tom, the "good slave." He accepts his lot in life as he thinks a Christian should. Even here in act 6 he offers to

A scene from a 1901 stage production of *Uncle Tom's Cabin*, showing Eliza and George's flight through ice and snow to eventual freedom in Canada.

sacrifice himself for his oppressor if need be, because it is the Christian thing to do. Such behavior pleased the primarily white audiences of the nineteenth century, especially in the decade before the Civil War, when the question of slavery was hotly debated in the North. However, black commentators were not eager to accept the portrayal of any such obedient slave as being either desirable or realistic.

Because of financial setbacks that befall his master, Mr. Shelby, Uncle Tom is "sold down the river" into a frightening environment. But while on the riverboat he meets Eva, a little white girl whose sense of Christian charity matches Tom's, and the two of them form a special bond. When Eva falls off the boat, Tom saves her life, and Eva's father, St. Clare, buys Tom from the slave trader. Tom and Eva become friends who understand each other, but Eva dies of an illness. She is seen in a vision that helps people change their lives, and St. Clare promises to free Tom. However, St. Clare is killed in a fight, and ultimately Tom is bought by the evil Simon Legree, who embodies the stereotype of the cruel and inhuman slave driver. His brutality to the humane and sympathetic Uncle Tom makes Tom into a martyr in act 6.

GEORGE L. AIKEN (1830–1876)

From Uncle Tom's Cabin, or Life Among the Lowly   1852

Act VI • *Scene 1*

Dark landscape. An old, roofless shed.

(Tom is discovered in shed, lying on some old cotton bagging. Cassy kneels by his side, holding a cup to his lips.)

CASSY: Drink all ye want. I knew how it would be. It isn't the first time I've been out in the night, carrying water to such as you.

TOM (*returning cup*): Thank you, missis.

CASSY: Don't call me missis. I'm a miserable slave like yourself—a lower one than you can ever be! It's no use, my poor fellow, this you've been trying to do. You were a brave fellow. You had the right on your side; but it's all in vain for you to struggle. You are in the Devil's hands: he is the strongest, and you must give up.

TOM: Oh! how can I give up?

CASSY: You see *you* don't know anything about it; I do. Here you are, on a lone plantation, ten miles from any other, in the swamps; not a white person here who could testify, if you were burned alive. There's no law here that can do you, or any of us, the least good; and this man! there's no earthly thing that he is not bad enough to do. I could make one's hair rise, and their teeth chatter, if I should only tell what I've seen and been knowing to here; and it's no use resisting! Did I *want* to live with him? Wasn't I a woman delicately bred? and he!—Father in Heaven! what was he and is he? And yet I've lived with him these five years, and cursed every moment of my life, night and day.

TOM: Oh, heaven! have you quite forgot us poor critters?

CASSY: And what are these miserable low dogs you work with, that you should suffer on their account? Every one of them would turn against you the first time they get a chance. They are all of them as low and cruel to each other as they can be; there's no use in your suffering to keep from hurting them!

TOM: What made 'em cruel? If I give out, I shall get used to it and grow, little by little, just like 'em. No, no, missis, I've lost everything, wife, and children, and home, and a kind master, and he would have set me free if he'd only lived a day longer—I've lost everything in *this* world, and now I can't lose heaven, too; no, I can't get to be wicked besides all.

CASSY: But it can't be that He will lay sin to our account; he won't charge it to us when we are forced to it; he'll charge it to them that drove us to it. Can I do anything more for you? Shall I give you some more water?

TOM: Oh missis! I wish you'd go to Him who can give you living waters!

CASSY: Go to Him! Where is He? Who is He?

TOM: Our Heavenly Father!

CASSY: I used to see the picture of Him, over the altar, when I was a girl; but *he isn't here!* there's nothing here but sin, and long, long despair! There, there, don't talk any more, my poor fellow. Try to sleep, if you can. I must hasten back, lest my absence be noted. Think of me when I am gone, Uncle Tom, and pray, pray for me. (*Exit Cassy. Tom sinks back to sleep.*)

Scene 2

Street in New Orleans.

(*Enter George Shelby.*)

GEORGE: At length my mission of mercy is nearly finished; I have reached my journey's end. I have now but to find the house of Mr. St. Clare, re-purchase old Uncle Tom, and convey him back to his wife and children, in old Kentucky. Some one approaches; he may, perhaps, be able to give me the information I require. I will accost him.

(*Enter Marks.*)

Pray, sir, can you tell me where Mr. St. Clare dwells?

MARKS: Where I don't think you'll be in a hurry to seek him.

GEORGE: And where is that?

MARKS: In the grave!

GEORGE: Stay, sir! you may be able to give me some information concerning Mr. St. Clare.

MARKS: I beg pardon, sir, I am a lawyer; I can't afford to *give* anything.

GEORGE: But you would have no objections to selling it?

MARKS: Not the slightest.

GEORGE: What do you value it at?

MARKS: Well, say five dollars, that's reasonable.

GEORGE: There they are. (*Gives money.*) Now answer me to the best of your ability. Has the death of St. Clare caused his slaves to be sold?

MARKS: It has.

GEORGE: How were they sold?

MARKS: At auction—they went dirt cheap.

GEORGE: How were they bought—all in one lot?

MARKS: No, they went to different bidders.

GEORGE: Was you present at the sale?

MARKS: I was.

GEORGE: Do you remember seeing a negro among them called Tom.

MARKS: What, Uncle Tom?

GEORGE: The same—who bought him?

MARKS: A Mr. Legree.

GEORGE: Where is his plantation?

MARKS: Up in Louisiana, on the Red River; but a man never could find it unless he had been there before.

GEORGE: Who could I get to direct me there?

MARKS: Well, stranger, I don't know of any one just at present, 'cept myself, could find it for you; it's such an out-of-the-way sort of hole; and if you are a mind to come down handsomely, why, I'll do it.

GEORGE: The reward shall be ample.

MARKS: Enough said, stranger; let's take the steamboat at once. (*Exeunt.*)

Scene 3

A rough chamber.

(*Enter Legree. Sits.*)

LEGREE: Plague on that Sambo, to kick up this yer row between me and the new hands.

(*Cassy steals on, and stands behind him.*)

The fellow won't be fit to work for a week now, right in the press of the season.

CASSY: Yes, just like you.

LEGREE: Hah! you she-devil! you've come back, have you? (*Rises.*)

CASSY: Yes, I have; come to have my own way, too.

LEGREE: You lie, you jade! I'll be up to my word. Either behave yourself, or stay down in the quarters and fare and work with the rest.

CASSY: I'd rather, ten thousand times, live in the dirtiest hole in the quarters, than be under your hoof!

LEGREE: But you are under my hoof, for all that, that's one comfort; so sit down here and listen to reason. (*Grasps her wrist.*)

CASSY: Simon Legree, take care! (*Legree lets go his hold.*) You're afraid of me, Simon, and you've reason to be; for I've got the Devil in me!

LEGREE: I believe to my soul you have. After all, Cassy, why can't you be friends with me, as you used to?

CASSY (*bitterly*): Used to!

LEGREE: I wish, Cassy, you'd behave yourself decently.

CASSY: You talk about behaving decently! and what have you been doing? You haven't even sense enough to keep from spoiling one of your best hands, right in the most pressing season, just for your devilish temper.

LEGREE: I was a fool, it's a fact, to let any such brangle come up; but when Tom set up his will he had to be broke in.

CASSY: You'll never break *him* in.

LEGREE: Won't I? I'd like to know if I won't! He'll be the first nigger that ever come it round me! I'll break every bone in his body but he shall give up.

(*Enter Sambo, with a paper in his hand; he stands bowing.*)

LEGREE: What's that, you dog?

SAMBO: It's a witch thing, mas'r.

LEGREE: A what?

SAMBO: Something that niggers gits from witches. Keep 'em from feeling when they's flogged. He had it tied round his neck with a black string.

(*Legree takes the paper and opens it. A silver dollar drops on the stage, and a long curl of light hair twines around his finger.*)

LEGREE: Damnation. (*Stamping and writhing, as if the hair burned him.*) Where did this come from? Take it off! burn it up! burn it up! (*Throws the curl away.*) What did you bring it to me for?

SAMBO (*trembling*): I beg pardon, mas'r; I thought you would like to see 'um.

LEGREE: Don't you bring me any more of your devilish things. (*Shakes his fist at Sambo who runs off. Legree kicks the dollar after him.*) Blast it! where did he get that? If it didn't look just like—whoo! I thought I'd forgot that. Curse me if I think there's any such thing as forgetting anything, any how.

CASSY: What is the matter with you, Legree? What is there in a simple curl of fair hair to appal a man like you—you who are familiar with every form of cruelty.

LEGREE: Cassy, to-night the past has been recalled to me—the past that I have so long and vainly striven to forget.

CASSY: Hast aught on this earth power to move a soul like thine?

LEGREE: Yes, for hard and reprobate as I now seem, there has been a time when I have been rocked on the bosom of a mother, cradled with prayers and pious hymns, my now seared brow bedewed with the waters of holy baptism.

CASSIE (*aside*): What sweet memories of childhood can thus soften down that heart of iron?

LEGREE: In early childhood a fair-haired woman has led me, at the sound of Sabbath bells, to worship and to pray. Born of a hard-tempered sire, on whom that gentle woman had wasted a world of unvalued love, I followed in the steps of my father. Boisterous, unruly and tyrannical, I despised all her counsel, and would have none of her reproof, and, at an early age, broke from her to seek my fortunes on the sea. I never came home but once after that; and then my mother, with the yearning of a heart that must love something, and had nothing else to love, clung to me, and sought with passionate prayers and entreaties to win me from a life of sin.

CASSY: That was your day of grace, Legree; then good angels called you, and mercy held you by the hand.

LEGREE: My heart inly relented; there was a conflict, but sin got the victory, and I set all the force of my rough nature against the conviction of my conscience. I drank and swore, was wilder and more brutal than ever. And one night, when my mother, in the last agony of her despair, knelt at my feet, I spurned her from me, threw her senseless on the floor, and with brutal curses fled to my ship.

CASSY: Then the fiend took thee for his own.

LEGREE: The next I heard of my mother was one night while I was carousing among drunken companions. A letter was put in my hands. I opened and a lock of long, curling hair fell from it, and twined about my fingers, even as that lock twined but now. The letter told me that my mother was dead, and that dying she blest and forgave me! (*Buries his face in his hands.*)

CASSY: Why did you not even then renounce your evil ways?

LEGREE: There is a dread, unhallowed necromancy of evil, that turns things sweetest and holiest to phantoms of horror and affright. That pale, loving mother,—her dying prayers, her forgiving love,—wrought in my demoniac heart of sin only as a damning sentence, bringing with it a fearful looking for of judgment and fiery indignation.

CASSY: And yet you would not strive to avert the doom that threatened you.

LEGREE: I burned the lock of hair and I burned the letter; and when I saw them hissing and crackling in the flame, inly shuddered as I thought of everlasting fires! I tried to drink and revel, and swear away the memory; but often in the deep night, whose solemn stillness arraigns the soul in forced communion with itself, I have seen that pale mother rising by my bed-side, and felt the soft twining of that hair around my fingers, 'till the cold sweat would roll down my face, and I would spring from my bed in horror—horror! (*Falls in chair. After a pause.*) What the devil ails me? Large drops of sweat stand on my forehead, and my heart beats heavy and thick with fear. I thought I saw something white rising and glimmering in the gloom before me, and it seemed to bear my mother's face!

I know one thing; I'll let that fellow Tom alone, after this. What did I want with his cussed paper? I believe I am bewitched sure enough! I've been shivering and sweating ever since! Where did he get that hair? It couldn't have been that! I *burn'd* that up, I know I did! It would be a joke if hair could rise from the dead! I'll have Sambo and Quimbo up here to sing and dance one of their dances, and keep off these horrid notions. Here, Sambo! Quimbo! (*Exit.*)

CASSY: Yes, Legree, that golden tress was charmed; each hair had in it a spell of terror and remorse for thee, and was used by a mightier power to bind thy cruel hands from inflicting uttermost evil on the helpless! (*Exit.*)

Scene 4

Street.

(*Enter Marks, meeting Cute, who enters, dressed in an old faded uniform.*)

MARKS: By the land, stranger, but it strikes me that I've seen you somewhere before.

CUTE: By chowder! do you know now, that's just what I was going to say?

MARKS: Isn't your name Cute?

CUTE: You're right, I calculate. Yours is Marks, I reckon.

MARKS: Just so.

CUTE: Well, I swow, I'm glad to see you. (*They shake hands.*) How's your wholesome?

MARKS: Hearty as ever. Well, who would have thought of ever seeing you again. Why, I thought you was in Vermont?

CUTE: Well, so I was. You see I went there after that rich relation of mine—but the speculation didn't turn out well.

MARKS: How so?

CUTE: Why, you see, she took a shine to an old fellow—Deacon Abraham Perry—and married him.

MARKS: Oh, that rather put your nose out of joint in that quarter.

CUTE: Busted me right up, I tell you. The deacon did the handsome thing though; he said if I would leave the neighbourhood and go out South again, he'd stand the damage. I calculate I didn't give him much time to change his mind, and so, you see, here I am again.

MARKS: What are you doing in that soldier rig?

CUTE: Oh, this is my sign.

MARKS: Your sign?

CUTE: Yes; you see, I'm engaged just at present in an all-fired good speculation; I'm a Fillibusterow.

MARKS: A what?

CUTE: A Fillibusterow! Don't you know what that is? It's Spanish for Cuban Volunteer; and means a chap that goes the whole porker for glory and all that ere sort of thing.

MARKS: Oh! you've joined the order of the Lone Star!

CUTE: You've hit it. You see I bought this uniform at a second-hand clothing store; I puts it on and goes to a benevolent individual and I says to him,—appealing to his feelings,—I'm one of the fellows that went to Cuba and got massacred by the bloody Spaniards. I'm in a destitute condition—give me a trifle to pay my passage back, so I can whop the tyrannical cusses and avenge my brave fellow soger what got slewed there.

MARKS: How pathetic!

CUTE: I tell you it works up the feelings of benevolent individuals dreadfully. It draws tears from their eyes and money from their pockets. By chowder! one old chap gave me a hundred dollars to help on the cause.

MARKS: I admire a genius like yours.

CUTE: But I say, what are you up to?

MARKS: I am the travelling companion of a young gentleman by the name of Shelby, who is going to the plantation of a Mr. Legree, on the Red River, to buy an old darky who used to belong to his father.

CUTE: Legree—Legree? Well, now, I calculate I've heard that ere name afore.

MARKS: Do you remember that man who drew a bowie knife on you in New Orleans?

CUTE: By chowder! I remember the circumstance just as well as if it was yesterday; but I can't say that I recollect much about the man, for you see I was in something of a hurry about that time and didn't stop to take a good look at him.

MARKS: Well, that man was this same Mr. Legree.

CUTE: Do you know, now, I should like to pay that critter off?

MARKS: Then I'll give you an opportunity.

CUTE: Chowder! how will you do that?

MARKS: Do you remember the gentleman that interfered between you and Legree?

CUTE: Yes—well?

MARKS: He received the blow that was intended for you, and died from the effects of it. So, you see, Legree is a murderer, and we are the only witnesses of the deed. His life is in our hands.

CUTE: Let's have him right up and make him dance on nothing to the tune of Yankee Doodle!

MARKS: Stop a bit. Don't you see a chance for a profitable speculation?

CUTE: A speculation! Fire away, don't be bashful; I'm the man for a speculation.

MARKS: I have made a deposition to the Governor of the State of all the particulars of that affair at Orleans.

CUTE: What did you do that for?

MARKS: To get a warrant for his arrest.

CUTE: Oh! and have you got it?

MARKS: Yes, here it is. (*Takes out paper.*)

CUTE: Well, now, I don't see how you are going to make anything by that bit of paper?

MARKS: But I do. I shall say to Legree, I have got a warrant against you for murder; my friend, Mr. Cute, and myself are the only witnesses who can appear against you. Give us a thousand dollars, and we will tear up the warrant and be silent.

CUTE: Then Mr. Legree forks over a thousand dollars, and your friend Cute pockets five hundred of it. Is that the calculation?

MARKS: If you will join me in the undertaking.

CUTE: I'll do it, by chowder!

MARKS: Your hand to bind the bargain.

CUTE: I'll stick by you thro' thick and thin.

MARKS: Enough said.

CUTE: Then shake. (*They shake hands.*)

MARKS: But I say, Cute, he may be contrary and show fight.

CUTE: Never mind, we've got the law on our side, and we're bound to stir him up. If he don't come down handsomely, we'll present him with a neck-tie made of hemp!

MARKS: I declare you're getting spunky.

CUTE: Well, I reckon I am. Let's go and have something to drink. Tell you what, Marks, if we don't get *him*, we'll have his hide, by chowder! (*Exeunt, arm in arm.*)

Scene 5

Rough chamber.

(*Enter Legree, followed by Sambo.*)

LEGREE: Go and send Cassy to me.

SAMBO: Yes, mas'r. (*Exit.*)

LEGREE: Curse the woman! she's got a temper worse than the devil! I shall do her an injury one of these days if she isn't careful.

(*Re-enter Sambo, frightened.*)

What's the matter with you, you black scoundrel?

SAMBO: S'help me, mas'r, she isn't dere.

LEGREE: I suppose she's about the house somewhere?

SAMBO: No, she isn't, mas'r; I's been all over de house and I can't find nothing of her nor Emmeline.

LEGREE: Bolted, by the Lord! Call out the dogs! saddle my horse! Stop! are you sure they really have gone?

SAMBO: Yes, mas'r; I's been in every room 'cept the haunted garret, and dey wouldn't go dere.

LEGREE: I have it! Now, Sambo, you jest go and walk that Tom up here, right away! (*Exit Sambo.*) The old cuss is at the bottom of this yer whole matter; and I'll have it out of his infernal black hide, or I'll know the reason why! I *hate* him—I *hate* him! And isn't he *mine?* Can't I do what I like with him? Who's to hinder, I wonder?

(*Tom is dragged on by Sambo and Quimbo.*)

LEGREE (*grimly confronting Tom*): Well, Tom, do you know I've made up my mind to *kill* you?

TOM: It's very likely, Mas'r.

LEGREE: *I—have—done—just—that—thing*, Tom, unless you tell me what do you know about these yer gals? (*Tom is silent.*) D'ye hear? Speak!

TOM: I hain't got anything to tell, mas'r.

LEGREE: Do you dare to tell me, you old black rascal, you don't know? Speak! Do you know anything?

TOM: I know, mas'r; but I can't tell anything. I *can die!*

LEGREE: Hark ye, Tom! ye think, 'cause I have let you off before, I don't mean what I say; but, this time, I have made *up my mind*, and counted the cost. You've always stood it out agin me; now, I'll *conquer ye or kill ye!* one or t'other. I'll count every drop of blood there is in you, and take 'em one by one, 'till ye give up!

TOM: Mas'r, if you was sick, or in trouble, or dying, and I could save, I'd *give* you my heart's blood; and, if taking every drop of blood in this poor old body would save your precious soul, I'd give 'em freely. Do the worst you can, my troubles will be over soon; but if you don't repent, yours won't never end.

(*Legree strikes Tom down with the butt of his whip.*)

LEGREE: How do you like that?

SAMBO: He's most gone, mas'r!

TOM (*rises feebly on his hands*): There ain't no more you can do! I forgive you with all my soul. (*Sinks back, and is carried off by Sambo and Quimbo.*)

LEGREE: I believe he's done for finally. Well, his mouth is shut up at last—that's one comfort.

(*Enter George Shelby, Marks and Cute.*)

Strangers! Well, what do you want?

GEORGE: I understand that you bought in New Orleans a negro named Tom?

LEGREE: Yes, I did buy such a fellow, and a devil of a bargain I had of it, too! I believe he's trying to die, but I don't know as he'll make it out.

GEORGE: Where is he? Let me see him!

SAMBO: Dere he is! (*Points to Tom.*)

LEGREE: How dare you speak? (*Drives Sambo and Quimbo off. George exits.*)

CUTE: Now's the time to nab him.

MARKS: How are you, Mr. Legree?

LEGREE: What the devil brought you here?

MARKS: This little bit of paper. I arrest you for the murder of Mr. St. Clare. What do you say to that?

LEGREE: This is my answer! (*Makes a blow at Marks, who dodges, and Cute receives the blow. He cries out and runs off. Marks fires at Legree, and follows Cute.*) I am hit!—the game's up! (*Falls dead. Quimbo and Sambo return and carry him off laughing.*)

(*George Shelby enters, supporting Tom. Music. They advance and Tom falls, centre.*)

GEORGE: Oh! dear Uncle Tom! do wake—do speak once more! look up! Here's Master George—your own little Master George. Don't you know me?

TOM (*opening his eyes and speaking in a feeble tone*): Mas'r George! Bless de Lord! it's all I wanted! They hav'n't forgot me! It warms my soul; it does my old heart good! Now I shall die content!

GEORGE: You sha'n't die! you mustn't die, nor think of it. I have come to buy you, and take you home.

TOM: Oh, Mas'r George, you're too late. The Lord has bought me, and is going to take me home.

GEORGE: Oh! don't die. It will kill me—it will break my heart to think what you have suffered, poor, poor fellow!

TOM. Don't call me poor fellow. I *have* been poor fellow; but that's all past and gone now. I'm right in the door, going into glory! Oh, Mas'r George! *Heaven has come!* I've got the victory! the Lord has given it to me! Glory be to His name! (*Dies.*)

(*Solemn music. George covers Uncle Tom with his cloak, and kneels over him. Clouds work on and conceal them, and then work off.*)

Scene 7

(*Gorgeous clouds, tinted with sunlight. Eva, robed in white, is discovered on the back of a milk-white dove, with expanded wings, as if just soaring upward. Her hands are extended in benediction over St. Clare and Uncle Tom, who are kneeling and gazing up to her. Impressive music. Slow curtain.*)

Bronson Howard

Bronson Howard (1842–1908) has the distinction of being the first professional American playwright and the first to make a handsome living writing plays. He was followed by many more playwrights, but he demonstrated that there was money to be made not just by acting on stage but also by providing the texts for actors. He originally studied to attend Yale University, but an eye problem kept him home in Detroit, where he worked on the *Free Press*. He began producing plays very early in his career, in 1864, with *Fantine*, a dramatization of a segment of *Les Miserables;* its success was limited but encouraging. He left Detroit for the *Tribune* and the *Post* in New York, where, after the Civil War, he wrote *Saratoga* (1870), a farce produced by another important American playwright and producer, Augustin Daly. His play ran for 101 nights, guaranteeing him a living in the theater.

Among his eighteen plays, *The Banker's Daughter* (1878) and *The Henrietta* (1887) are significant because they both emphasize issues in American business, which Howard believed was one of the most important themes in American drama. None of these plays offered a significant analysis of American culture. Howard excelled in mild satire of the kind that helps audiences laugh at themselves without feeling the need to change their behavior. Howard's gift was that he understood what his late-nineteenth-century audiences really wanted and gave it to them. He was the essence of the popular playwright.

Howard's success was based in part on reflecting to his audience an image of itself. Audiences of the day found the language of even the most elevated and high-brow speeches stirring, and it moved them emotionally in ways that such language simply does not today. We need to remember, when we read his work, that the nineteenth-century audience believed that Howard offered a reliable portrait of human behavior. That is why Howard was so powerful a figure in American melodrama.

Howard's stagecraft was marked in some measure by the increasing availability around the country of theaters that emphasized the proscenium arch at the expense of the apron in front of it. The overacting of those who depended on asides to the audience (as in both *Fashion* and *Uncle Tom's Cabin* and, indeed, most melodramas before the Civil War) was rendered nearly impossible by Howard's practice of keeping the action within the proscenium. This approach also established a sense of realism and of detachment from the audience. The asides in *Shenandoah* are few and brief, although soliloquy sometimes does the same work that asides had done in earlier plays. One of Howard's means of building emotional intensity, as in *Shenandoah*, was to write each act as a single scene. This was in stark contrast to such melodramas as *Uncle Tom's Cabin* and Dion Boucicault's *The Octoroon*, in which all the acts are punctuated with numerous scenes and scene changes.

Howard's fortunes improved profoundly when he teamed with Charles Frohman, the American impresario and theater producer, whose skills helped Howard make *Shenandoah* one of the most successful nineteenth-century American dramas. Howard is said to have earned at least $100,000 from this play alone. He went on to establish, in 1891, what is now known as The Dramatists Guild as a means of helping dramatists earn royalties from their work. What he understood better than most playwrights before him was the business of the theater. Howard's posthumously published *Autobiography of a Play* (1914) recounts his experiences as a dramatist.

Shenandoah

The memory of the Civil War was still painful for many people in 1888, but dramas were beginning to use the war as their subject. Most plays, like Howard's *Shenandoah*, skirted many important issues, such as slavery and the motives for the secession of the states. Although *Shenandoah* begins in act 1 with the main characters anticipating the opening salvo of southern forces preparing to shell Fort Sumter, in Charlestown, South Carolina, their concerns are more immediately focused on the romances of Kerchival West, a northerner in love with a southern girl, Gertrude Ellingham, and Robert Ellingham, a southerner married to Kerchival's sister Madeline West. Once the cannonade is heard at the end of act 1, Kerchival and Robert, best of friends, face the possibility that they will meet on the field of battle. Both join their respective armies as colonels, and Kerchival and Gertrude are separated until act 3, when Kerchival is wounded and Gertrude helps nurse him.

Act 3, included here, focuses more on the war itself than does the rest of the play. Soldiers appear on stage; prisoners of war and the wounded appear; the sounds of cannons and of muskets punctuate the act as Kerchival tries to overcome his wound, rejoin his command, and attack the enemy. He is held back by General Haverill, who mistakenly thinks his wife has been unfaithful to him with Kerchival. Ultimately, Kerchival is arrested, Haverill moves out, and the Union soldiers are temporarily routed by Confederate General Early. The threat of infidelity during their three-year separation hangs over Kerchival and Gertrude as well, but by the end of act 3 it is clear that Gertrude has remained true to her love for Kerchival. The act ends with a reversal. The Union troops, harried by Kerchival, are turned back to the battle by the arrival of Union General Sheridan, who rides on stage on Gertrude's horse, Jack. Even Gertrude, the southerner, cheers him on. The drama of act 3 is responsible for much of the success of the play. It offers all the spectacle that an audience in search of thrilling inspiration could want.

Act 4, the last act of the drama, ties everything together. Mrs. Haverill is no longer under suspicion, and both pairs of lovers (Kerchival and Gertrude, Ellingham and Madeline) are reunited. The older married couple, the Haverills, are also together. Howard's purpose in using these romantic models may have been to symbolize the separation and reunion of the states themselves, in a nation now whole again when the play ends.

JENNY: "OH, IF A LACE HANDKERCHIEF CAN BE OF ANY USE TO YOU, CAPTAIN, DURING THE HARDSHIPS OF A CAMPAIGN-YOU-YOU MAY KEEP THAT ONE!"

An 1898 poster advertisement for Bronson Howard's *Shenandoah*.

BRONSON HOWARD (1842–1908)

From Shenandoah 1888

Act III

(*The scene is the same as in Act II. It is now bright daylight, with sunshine flecking the foreground and bathing the distant valley and mountains. As the curtain rises Jenny Buckthorn is sitting on the low stone post, in the center of the stage, looking toward the left. She imitates a Trumpet Signal on her closed fists.*)

JENNY: What a magnificent line! Guides posts! Every man and every horse is eager for the next command. There comes the flag! (*As the scene progresses, trumpet signals are heard without and she follows their various meanings in her speech.*) To the standard! The regiment is going to the front. Oh! I do wish I could go with it. I always do, the moment I hear the trumpets. Boots and Saddles! Mount! I wish I was in command of the regiment. It was born in me. Fours right! There they go! Look at those horses' ears! Forward. (*A military band is heard without, playing "The Battle Cry of Freedom." Jenny takes the attitude of holding a bridle and trotting.*) Bappity—plap—plap—plap, etc. (*She imitates the motions of a soldier on horseback, stepping down to the rock at side of post; thence to the ground and about the stage, with the various curvellings of a spirited horse. A chorus of soldiers is heard without, with the band. The music becomes more and more distant. Jenny gradually stops as the music is dying away, and stands, listening. As it dies entirely away, she suddenly starts to an enthusiastic attitude.)* Ah! If I were only a man! The enemy! On Third Battalion, left, front, into line, march! Draw sabres! Charge! *(Imitates a trumpet signal. As she finishes, she rises to her full height, with both arms raised, and trembling with enthusiasm.)* Ah! *(She suddenly drops her arms and changes to an attitude and expression of disappointment—pouting.)* And the first time Old Margery took me to Father, in her arms, she had to tell him I was a girl. Father was as much disgusted as I was. But he'd never admit it; he says I'm as good a soldier as any of 'em—just as I am.

(Enter Barket, on the veranda, his arm in a sling.)

BARKET: Miss Jenny!

JENNY: Barket! The regiment has marched away to the front, and we girls are left here, with just you and a corporal's guard to look after us.

BARKET: I've been watching the byes mesilf. *(Coming down.)* If a little military sugarplum like you, Miss Jenny, objects to not goin' wid 'em, what do you think of an ould piece of hard tack like me? I can't join the regiment till I've taken you and Miss Madeline back to Winchester, by your father's orders. But it is n't the first time I've escorted you, Miss Jenny. Many a time, when you was a baby, on the Plains, I commanded a special guard to accompany ye's from one fort to anither, and we gave the command in a whisper, so as not to wake ye's up.

JENNY: I told you to tell Father that I'd let him know when Madeline and I were ready to go.

BARKET: I tould him that I'd as soon move a train of army mules.

JENNY: I suppose we must start for home again to-day?

BARKET: Yes, Miss Jenny, in charge of an ould Sargeant wid his arm in a sling and a couple of convalescent throopers. This department of the United States Army will move to the rear in half an hour.

JENNY: Madeline and I only came yesterday morning.

BARKET: Whin your father got ye's a pass to the front, we all thought the fightin' in the Shenandoey Valley was over. It looks now as if it was just beginning. This is no place for women, now. Miss Gertrude Ellingham ought to go wid us, but she won't.

JENNY: Barket! Captain Heartsease left the regiment yesterday, and he has n't rejoined it; he is n't with them, now, at the head of his company. Where is he?

BARKET: I can't say where he is, Miss Jenny. *(Aside.)* Lyin' unburied in the woods, where he was shot, I'm afraid.

JENNY: When Captain Heartsease does rejoin the regiment, Barket, please say to him for me, that—that I—I may have some orders for him, when we next meet. *(Exit, on veranda.)*

BARKET: Whin they nixt mate. They tell us there is no such thing as marriage in Hiven. If Miss Jenny and Captain Heartsease mate there, they'll invint somethin' that's mighty like it. While I was lyin' wounded in General Buckthorn's house at Washington, last summer, and ould Margery was taking care of me, Margery tould me, confidentially, that they was in love wid aitch ither; and I think she was about right. I've often seen Captain Heartsease take a sly look at a little lace handkerchief, just before we wint into battle. *(Looking off the stage.)* Here's General Buckthorn himself. He and I must make it as aisy as we can for Miss Jenny's poor heart.

(*Enter General Buckthorn.*)

BUCKTHORN: Sergeant Barket! You have n't started with those girls yet?

BARKET: They're to go in half an hour, sir.

BUCKTHORN: Be sure they do go. Is General Haverill here?

BARKET: Yes, sur; in the house with some of his staff, and the Surgeon.

BUCKTHORN: Ah! The Surgeon. How is Colonel West, this morning, after the wound he received last night?

BARKET: He says, himself, that he's as well as iver he was; but the Colonel and Surgeon don't agray on that subject. The dochter says he must n't lave his room for a month. The knife wint dape; and there's something wrong inside of him. But the Colonel bein' on the outside himsilf, can't see it. He's as cross as a bear, baycause they would n't let him go to the front this morning, at the head of his regiment. I happened to raymark that the Chaplain was prayin' for his raycovery. The Colonel said he'd courtmartial him if he did n't stop that—quick; there's more important things for the Chaplain to pray for in his official capacity. Just at that moment the trumpets sounded, "Boots and Saddles." I had to dodge one of his boots, and the Surgeon had a narrow escape from the ither one. It was lucky for us both his saddle was n't in the room.

BUCKTHORN: That looks encouraging. I think Kerchival will get on.

BARKET: Might I say a word to you, sur, about Miss Jenny?

BUCKTHORN: Certainly, Barket. You and old Margery and myself have been a sort of triangular mother, so to speak, to the little girl since her own poor mother left her to our care, when she was only a baby, in the old fort on the Plains. (*He unconsciously rests his arm over Barket's shoulder, familiarly, and then suddenly draws up.*) Ahem! (*Gruffly.*) What is it? Proceed.

BARKET: Her mother's bosom would have been the softest place for her poor little head to rest upon, now, sur.

BUCKTHORN (*touching his eyes*): Well!

BARKET: Ould Margery tould me in Washington that Miss Jenny and Captain Heartsease were in love wid aitch ither.

BUCKTHORN (*starting*): In love!

BARKET: I approved of the match.

BUCKTHORN: What the devil!

(*Barket salutes quickly and starts up stage and out. Buckthorn moves up after him, and stops at the post. Barket stops in the road.*)

BARKET: So did ould Margery.

BUCKTHORN (*angrily*): March! (*Barket salutes suddenly and marches off.*) Heartsease! That young jackanapes! A mere fop; he'll never make a soldier. My girl in love with—bah! I don't believe it; she's too good a soldier, herself.

(*Enter Haverill, on the veranda.*)

Ah, Haverill!

HAVERILL: General Buckthorn! Have you heard anything of General Sheridan since I sent that dispatch to him last evening?

BUCKTHORN: He received it at midnight and sent back word that he considers it a ruse of the enemy. General Wright agrees with him. The reconnoissance yesterday showed no hostile force, on our right, and Crook reports that Early is retreating up the valley. But General Sheridan may, perhaps, give up his journey to Washington, and he has ordered some changes in our line, to be executed this afternoon at four o'clock. I rode over to give you your instructions in person. You may order General McCuen to go into camp on the right of Meadow Brook, with the second division.

(*Haverill is writing in his note-book.*)
(*Enter Jenny, on the veranda.*)

JENNY: Oh, Father! I'm so glad you've come. I've got something to say to you.

(*Running down and jumping into his arms, kissing him. He turns with her, and sets her down, squarely on her feet and straight before him.*)

BUCKTHORN: And I've got something to say to you—about Captain Heartsease.

JENNY: Oh! That's just what I wanted to talk about.

BUCKTHORN: Fall in! Front face! (*She jumps into military position, turning toward him.*) What's this I hear from Sergeant Barket? He says you've been falling in love.

JENNY: I have (*Saluting.*)

BUCKTHORN: Young woman! Listen to my orders. Fall out! (*Turns sharply and marches to Haverill.*) Order the Third Brigade of Cavalry, under Colonel Lowell, to occupy the left of the pike.

JENNY: Father! (*Running to him and seizing the tail of his coat.*) Father, dear!

BUCKTHORN: Close in Colonel Powell on the extreme left—(*slapping his coat-tails out of Jenny's hands, without looking around*)—and hold Custer on the second line, at Old Forge Road. That is all at present. (*Turning to Jenny.*) Goodbye, my darling! (*Kisses her.*) Remember your orders! You little pet! (*Chuckling, as he taps her chin; draws up suddenly and turns to Haverill.*) General! I bid you good-day.

HAVERILL: Good-day, General Buckthorn.

(*They salute with great dignity. Buckthorn starts up stage; Jenny springs after him, seizing his coat-tails.*)

JENNY: But I want to talk with you, Father; I can't fall out. I—I—have n't finished yet.

(*Clinging to his coat, as Buckthorn marches out rapidly, in the road, holding back with all her might.*)

HAVERILL: It may have been a ruse of the enemy, but I hope that General Sheridan has turned back from Washington. (*Looking at his note-book.*) We are to make changes in our line at four o'clock this afternoon. (*Returning the book to his pocket, he stands in thought.*) The Surgeon tells me that Kerchival West will get on well enough if he remains quiet; otherwise not. He shall not die by the hand of a common assassin; he has no right to die like that. My wife gave my own picture of herself to him—not to my son—and she looked so like an angel when she took it from my hand! They were both false to me, and they have been true to each other. I will save his life for myself.

(*Enter Gertrude, on the veranda.*)

GERTRUDE: General Haverill! (*Anxiously, coming down.*) Colonel West persists in disobeying the injunctions of the Surgeon. He is preparing to join his regiment at the front. Give him your orders to remain here. Compel him to be prudent!

HAVERILL (*quickly*): The honor of death at the front is not in reserve for him.

GERTRUDE: Eh? What did you say, General?

HAVERILL: Gertrude! I wish to speak to you, as your father's old friend; and I was once your guardian. Your father was my senior officer in the Mexican War. Without his care I should have been left dead in a foreign land. He, himself, afterwards fell fighting for the old flag.

GERTRUDE: The old flag. (*Aside.*) My father died for it, and he—(*looking toward the left*)—is suffering for it—the old flag!

HAVERILL: I can now return the kindness your father did to me, by protecting his daughter from something that may be worse than death.

GERTRUDE: What do you mean?

HAVERILL: Last night I saw you kneeling at the side of Kerchival West; you spoke to him with all the tender passion of a Southern woman. You said you loved him. But you spoke into ears that could not hear you. Has he ever heard those words from your lips? Have you ever confessed your love to him before?

GERTRUDE: Never. Why do you ask?

HAVERILL: Do not repeat those words. Keep your heart to yourself, my girl.

GERTRUDE: General! Why do you say this to me? And at such a moment—when his life—

HAVERILL: His life! (*Turning sharply.*) It belongs to me!

GERTRUDE: Oh!

KERCHIVAL: Sergeant! (*Without. He steps into the road, looking back. Haverill comes down.*) See that my horse is ready at once. General! (*Saluting.*) Are there any orders for my regiment beyond those given to Major Wilson, in my absence, this morning? I am about to ride on after the troops and reassume my command.

HAVERILL (*quietly*): It is my wish, Colonel, that you remain here under the care of the Surgeon.

KERCHIVAL: My wound is a mere trifle. This may be a critical moment in the campaign, and I cannot rest here. I must be with my own men.

HAVERILL (*quietly*): I beg to repeat the wish I have already expressed.

(*Kerchival walks to him, and speaks apart, almost under his breath, but very earnest in tone.*)

KERCHIVAL: I have had no opportunity, yet, to explain certain matters, as you requested me to do yesterday; but whatever there may be between us, you are now interfering with my duty and my privilege as a soldier; and it is my right to be at the head of my regiment.

HAVERILL (*quietly*): It is my positive order that you do not reassume your command.

KERCHIVAL: General Haverill, I protest against this—

HAVERILL (*quietly*): You are under arrest, sir.

KERCHIVAL: Arrest!

GERTRUDE: Ah!

(*Kerchival unclasps his belt and offers his sword to Haverill.*)

HAVERILL (*quietly*): Keep your sword; I have no desire to humiliate you; but hold yourself subject to further orders from me.

KERCHIVAL: My regiment at the front!—and I under arrest! (*Exit.*)

HAVERILL: Gertrude! If your heart refuses to be silent—if you feel that you must confess your love to that man—first tell him what I have said to you, and refer him to me for an explanation. (*Exit.*)

GERTRUDE: What can he mean? He would save me from something worse than death, he said. "His life—It belongs to me!" What can he mean? Kerchival told me that he loved me—it seems many years since that morning in Charleston—and when we met again, yesterday, he said that he had never ceased to love me. I will not believe that he has told me a falsehood. I have given him my love, my whole soul and my faith. (*Drawing up to her full height.*) My perfect faith!

(*Jenny runs in, to the road, and up the slope. She looks down the hill, then toward the left and enters.*)

JENNY: A flag of truce, Gertrude. And a party of Confederate soldiers, with an escort, coming up the hill. They are carrying someone; he is wounded.

(*Enter, up the slope, a Lieutenant of Infantry with an escort of Union Soldiers, their arms at right shoulder, and a party of Confederate Soldiers bearing a rustic stretcher. Lieutenant Frank Bedloe lies on the stretcher. Major Hardwick, a Confederate Surgeon, walks at his side. Madeline appears at the veranda, watching them. Gertrude stands with her back to the audience. The Lieutenant gives orders in a low tone, and the front escort moves toward the right, in the road. The Confederate bearers and the Surgeon pass through the gate. The rear escort moves on in the road, under the Lieutenant's orders. The bearers halt in the front of the stage; on a sign from the Surgeon, they leave the stretcher on the ground, stepping back.*)

MAJOR HARDWICK: Is General Haverill here?

GERTRUDE: Yes; what can we do, sir?

MADELINE: The General is just about mounting with his staff, to ride away. Shall I go for him, sir?

MAJOR HARDWICK: Say to him, please, that Colonel Robert Ellingham, of the Tenth Virginia, sends his respects and sympathy. He instructed me to bring this young officer to this point, in exchange for himself, as agreed upon between them last evening.

(*Exit Madeline.*)

JENNY: Is he unconscious or sleeping, sir?

MAJOR HARDWICK: Hovering between life and death. I thought he would bear the removal better. He is waking. Here, my lad! (*Placing his canteen to the lips of Frank, who moves, reviving.*) We have reached the end of our journey.

FRANK: My father!

MAJOR HARDWICK: He is thinking of his home.

(*Frank rises on one arm, assisted by the Surgeon.*)

FRANK: I have obeyed General Haverill's orders, and I have a report to make.

GERTRUDE: We have already sent for him. (*Stepping to him.*) He will be here in a moment.

FRANK (*looking into her face, brightly*): Is not this—Miss—Gertrude Ellingham?

GERTRUDE: You know me? You have seen me before?

FRANK: Long ago! Long ago! You know the wife of General Haverill?

GERTRUDE: I have no dearer friend in the world.

FRANK: She will give a message for me to the dearest friend I have in the world. My little wife! I must not waste even the moment we are waiting. Doctor! My note-book! (*Trying to get it from his coat. The Surgeon takes it out. A torn and blood stained lace handkerchief also falls out. Gertrude kneels at his side.)* Ah! I—I—have a message from another—*(holding up the handkerchief)*—from Captain Heartsease. *(Jenny makes a quick start toward him.)* He lay at my side in the hospital, when they brought me away; he had only strength enough to put this in my hand, and he spoke a woman's name; but I—I—forget what it is. The red spots upon it are the only message he sent.

(Gertrude takes the handkerchief and looks back at Jenny, extending her hand. Jenny moves to her, takes the handkerchief and turns back, looking down on it. She drops her face into her hands and goes out sobbing, on the veranda.)
(Enter Madeline on the veranda.)

MADELINE: General Haverill is coming. I was just in time. He was already on his horse.

FRANK: Ah! He is coming. *(Then suddenly.)* Write! Write! *(Gertrude writes in the note-book as he dictates.)* "To—my wife—Edith:—Tell our little son, when he is old enough to know—how his father died; not how he lived. And tell her who filled my own mother's place so lovingly—she is your mother, too—that my father's portrait of her, which she gave to me in Charleston, helped me to be a better man!" And—Oh! I must not forget this—"It was taken away from me while I was a prisoner in Richmond, and it is in the possession of Captain Edward Thornton, of the Confederate Secret Service. But her face is still beside your own in my heart. My best—warmest, last—love—to you, darling." I will sign it.

(Gertrude holds the book, and he signs it, then sinks back very quietly, supported by the Surgeon. Gertrude rises and walks away.)

MADELINE: General Haverill is here.

(The Surgeon lays the fold of the blanket over Frank's face and rises.)

GERTRUDE: Doctor!

MAJOR HARDWICK: He is dead.

(Madeline, on the veranda, turns and looks away. The Lieutenant orders the guard, "Present Arms.")

(Enter Haverill, on the veranda. He salutes the guard as he passes. The Lieutenant orders, "Carry Arms." Haverill comes down.)

HAVERILL: I am too late?

MAJOR HARDWICK: I'm sorry, General. His one eager thought as we came was to reach here in time to see you.

(Haverill moves to the bier, looks down at it, then folds back the blanket from the face. He starts slightly as he first sees it.)

HAVERILL: Brave boy! I hoped once to have a son like you. I shall be in your father's place to-day, at your grave. *(He replaces the blanket and steps back.)* We will carry him to his comrades in the front. He shall have a soldier's burial, in sight of the mountain-top beneath which he sacrificed his young life; that shall be his monument.

MAJOR HARDWICK: Pardon me, General. We Virginians are your enemies, but you cannot honor this young soldier more than we do. Will you allow my men the privilege of carrying him to his grave?

(Haverill inclines his head. The Surgeon motions to the Confederate Soldiers, who step to the bier and raise it gently.)

HAVERILL: Lieutenant!

(*The Lieutenant orders the guard "Left Face." The Confederate bearers move through the gate, preceded by Lieutenant Hardwick. Haverill draws his sword, reverses it, and moves up behind the bier with bowed head. The Lieutenant orders "Forward March," and the cortège disappears. While the girls are still watching it, the heavy sound of distant artillery is heard, with booming reverberations among the hills and in the valley.*)

MADELINE: What is that sound, Gertrude?

GERTRUDE: Listen!

(*Another and more prolonged distant sound, with long reverberations.*)

MADELINE: Again! Gertrude!

(*Gertrude raises her hand to command silence; listens. Distant cannon again.*)

GERTRUDE: It is the opening of a battle.

MADELINE: Ah! (*Running down stage. The sounds are heard again, prolonged.*)

GERTRUDE: How often have I heard that sound! (*Coming down.*) This is war, Madeline! You are face to face with it now.

MADELINE: And Robert is there! He may be in the thickest of the danger—at this very moment.

GERTRUDE: Yes. Let our prayers go up for him; mine do, with all a sister's heart.

(*Kerchival enters on veranda, without coat or vest, his sash about his waist, looking back as he comes in.*)

    Kerchival!

KERCHIVAL: Go on! Go on! Keep the battle to yourselves. I'm out of it. (*The distant cannon and reverberations are rising in volume.*)

MADELINE: I pray for Robert Ellingham—and for the *cause* in which he risks his life! (*Kerchival looks at her, suddenly; also Gertrude.*) Heaven forgive me if I am wrong, but I am praying for the enemies of my country. His people are my people, his enemies are my enemies. Heaven defend him and his, in this awful hour.

KERCHIVAL: Madeline! My sister!

MADELINE: Oh, Kerchival! (*Turning and dropping her face on his breast.*) I cannot help it—I cannot help it!

KERCHIVAL: My poor girl! Every woman's heart, the world over, belongs not to any country or any flag, but to her husband—and her lover. Pray for the man you love, sister—it would be treason not to. (*Passes her before him to the left of the stage. Looks across to Gertrude.*) Am I right? (*Gertrude drops her head. Madeline moves up veranda and out.*) Is what I have said to Madeline true?

GERTRUDE: Yes! (*Looks up.*) Kerchival!

KERCHIVAL: Gertrude! (*Hurries across to her, clasps her in his arms. He suddenly staggers and brings his hand to his breast.*)

GERTRUDE: Your wound!

(*Supporting him as he reels and sinks into seat.*)

KERCHIVAL: Wound! I have no wound! You do love me! (*Seizing her hand.*)

GERTRUDE: Let me call the Surgeon, Kerchival.

KERCHIVAL: You can be of more service to me than he can. (*Detaining her. Very heavy sounds of the battle; she starts, listening.*) Never mind that! It's only a battle. You love me!

GERTRUDE: Be quiet, Kerchival, dear. I do love you. I told you so, when you lay bleeding here, last night. But you could not hear me. (*At his side, resting her arm about him, stroking his head.*) I said that same thing to—to—another, more than three years ago. It is in that letter that General Buckthorn gave you. (*Kerchival starts.*) No—no—you must be very quiet, or I will not say another word. If you obey me, I will repeat that part of the letter, every word; I know it by heart, for I read it a dozen times. The letter is from Mrs. Haverill.

KERCHIVAL (*quietly*): Go on.

GERTRUDE: "I have kept your secret, my darling, but I was sorely tempted to betray the confidence you reposed in me at Charleston. If Kerchival West—(*she retires backward from him as she proceeds*)—had heard you say, as I did, when your face was hidden in my bosom, that night, that you loved him with your whole heart—"

KERCHIVAL: Ah!

(*Starting to his feet. He sinks back. She springs to support him.*)

GERTRUDE: I will go for help.

KERCHIVAL: Do not leave me at such a moment as this. You have brought me a new life. (*Bringing her to her knees before him and looking down at her.*) Heaven is just opening before me. (*His hands drop suddenly and his head falls back.*)

GERTRUDE: Ah! Kerchival? You are dying!

(*Musketry. A sudden sharp burst of musketry, mingled with the roar of artillery nearby. Kerchival starts, seizing Gertrude's arm and holding her away, still on her knees. He looks eagerly toward the left.*)

KERCHIVAL: The enemy is close upon us!

(*Barket runs in, up the slope.*)

BARKET: Colonel Wist! The devils have sprung out of the ground. They're pouring over our lift flank like Noah's own flood. The Union Army has started back for Winchester, on its way to the North Pole; our own regiment, Colonel, is coming over the hill in full retrate.

KERCHIVAL: My own regiment! (*Starting up.*) Get my horse, Barket. (*Turns.*) Gertrude, my life! (*Embraces Gertrude.*)

BARKET: Your horse is it? I'm wid ye! There's a row at Finnegan's ball, and we're in it. (*Springs to the road, and runs out.*)

KERCHIVAL (*turns away; stops*): I am under arrest.

(*The retreat begins. Fugitives begin to straggle across the stage from the left.*)

GERTRUDE: You must not go, Kerchival; it will kill you.

KERCHIVAL: Arrest be damned! (*Starts up toward the center, raising his arms above his head with clenched fist, and rising to full height.*) Stand out of my way, you cowards!

(*They cower away from him as he rushes out among them. The stream of fugitives passing across the stage swells in volume. Gertrude runs through them and up to the elevation, turning.*)

GERTRUDE: Men! Are you soldiers? Turn back! There is a leader for you! Turn back! Fight for your flag—and mine!—the flag my father died for! Turn back! (*She looks out toward the left and then turns toward the front.*) He has been marked for death already, and I—I can only pray. (*Dropping to her knees.*)

(*The stream of fugitives continues, now over the elevation also. Rough and torn uniforms, bandaged arms and legs; some limping and supported by others, some dragging their muskets after them, others without muskets, others using them as crutches. There is a variety of uniforms, both cavalry and infantry; flags are dragged on the ground, the rattle of near musketry and roar of cannon continue; two or three wounded fugitives drop down beside the hedge. Benson staggers in and drops upon a rock near the post. Artillerists, rough, torn and wounded, drag and force a field-piece across. Corporal Dunn, wounded, staggers to the top of elevation. There is a lull in the sounds of the battle. Distant cheers are heard without.*)

DUNN: Listen, fellows! Stop! Listen! Sheridan! General Sheridan is coming! (*Cheers from those on stage. Gertrude rises quickly. The wounded soldiers rise, looking over the hedge. All on stage stop, looking eagerly toward the left. The cheers without come nearer, with shouts of "Sheridan! Sheridan!"*) The horse is down; he is worn out.

GERTRUDE: No! He is up again! He is on my Jack! Now, for your life, Jack, and for me! You've never failed me yet. (*The cheers without now swell to full volume and are taken up by those on the stage. The horse sweeps by with General Sheridan.*) Jack! Jack!! Jack!!!

(*Waving her arms as he passes. She throws up her arms and falls backward, caught by Dunn. The stream of men is reversed and surges across the stage to the left, in the road and on the elevation, with shouts, and throwing up of hats. The field piece is forced up the slope with a few bold, rough movements; the artillerists are loading it, and the stream of returning fugitives is still surging by in the road as the curtain falls.*)

DION BOUCICAULT (1820–1890)

Notes on Acting

Boucicault was an Irish playwright and a gifted actor who became the darling of the English stage with plays such as *London Assurance* (1841), *The Vampire* (1852), *The Octoroon, or Life in Louisiana* (1859), *The Colleen Bawn* (1860), *The Shaughraun* (1874), and many others. His *Rip Van Winkle* (1866) made Joseph Jefferson, an American actor, a star. Jefferson played the part for most of the rest of his life. All of Boucicault's popular plays were melodramas, and his skill in writing for the popular stage was such that he has sometimes been regarded as the century's leading melodramatist. He lived for some time in the United States and died in New York. His comments on acting give us insight into the expectations for performance in the nineteenth century.

I must now go to a subject of a rather delicate nature, and that is really the first part of my subject—the voice. You know there are certain voices on the stage—you are perfectly aware of this—that the actor does not use off the stage; that are exclusively confined to tragedy. It is not the actor's ordinary voice. The idea is that the tragedian never has to use his own voice. Why? What is the reason? Before this century the great French tragedians before Talma and the great English tragedians before Kean used their treble voice—the teapot style. They did it as if they played on the flute. Then came the period when the tragedian played his part on the double bass. . . . There was no reason for it. Now we perform that part in the present age in what is called the medium voice. The reason is this. It is the transcendental drama tragedy. When I call it transcendental I mean unreal, poetic, to distinguish it from the realistic or the drama of ordinary life. The transcendental drama assumes that the dialogues are uttered by beings larger than life, who express ideas that no human being could pour out. The actor has accustomed himself to feel that he is in a different region; and, therefore, he feels if he uses his ordinary voice it might jar on the transcendental effect. I have fought out this very question with the great tragedians in France; and it seemed as if the tragedians were afraid of destroying the delicate illusion of the audience, who are sent about four hundred years back, as if they were living with people whom they had never seen and had no knowledge of. The consequence is those characters are too big for any ordinary human being, and the actor tries to make his manner and his voice correspond.

• • •

To the young beginner I would say, when you go upon the stage do not be full of yourself, but be full of your part. That is mistaking vanity for genius, and is the fault of many more than perhaps you are aware of. If actors' and actresses' minds be employed upon themselves, and not on the character they wish and aspire to perform, they never really get out of themselves. Many think they are studying their character when they are only studying themselves. They get their costume, they put it on, see how it fits, they cut and contrive it, but all that is not studying their character, but their costume. Actors and actresses frequently come to me and say, "Have you any part that will fit me?" They never dream of saying, "Have you any part that I can fit? that I can expand myself or contract myself into; that I can put myself inside of; that I, as a Protean, can shape myself into, even alter my voice and everything that nature has given to me, and be what you have contrived? I do not want you to contrive like a tailor to fit me." That is what is constantly happening. . . .

It was not so forty years ago. They had their faults many of them, but they did not constitute costume and make-up as the study of character, which it is not. I will tell you what did happen forty years ago. I was producing a comedy in which Mr. Farren, the father of the gentleman who so ably bears the same name (old Farren), played a leading part. He did not ask what he was going to wear, but he came to me, and said, "Who did you draw this party from; had you any type?" I said, "Yes, I had," and mentioned the names of two old fogies, who, at that time, were well known in London society. One he knew, the other he did not. He went and studied Sir Harcourt Courtley, and he studied by the speediest method, for the study was absolutely and literally out of the mouth of the man himself. That will give you an idea how they studied character. . . .

That is the way to study character, to get at the bottom of human nature, and I am happy to say that, amongst some young actors who have come out within the last ten or fifteen years, I have seen a natural instinct for the study of character and for the drawing of character most admirably, and much more faithfully than they drew it twenty or thirty years ago. There is a study of character that we may call good and true that has been accomplished within the last fifteen or sixteen years.

Now, I will say something by way of anecdote to show how utterly unnecessary it is for you to bother your minds so much about your dress. I was producing

The Shaughraun in New York. I generally had enough to employ my time. I get the actors and actresses to study their characters, and generally leave myself to the last. But the last morning before the play was produced I saw my dresser hobbling about, but afraid to come to the stage. At last he said, "Have you thought of your costume?" I said I had not done any such thing. It was about three o'clock in the afternoon, and I had to play about seven o'clock in the evening. I went upstairs, and said, "Have you got a red coat?" "Yes; we have got a uniform red hunting coat." "Oh, that is of no use!" "We have got one that was used in *She Stoops to Conquer*." That was brought, but it had broad lapels, and looked to belong to about one hundred and fifty years ago. "Oh!" said the man, "there is an old coat that was worn by Mr. Beckett as Goldfinch." When he came to that it reached all down to my feet, and was too long in the sleeves. So I cut them off with a big pair of shears, and by the shears and the scissors I got some sort of a fit. Then I got an old hunting cap, a pair of breeches, and sent for some old boots that cost about 2s 6d, and did not fit me, and that is how I came on the stage. The editor of one of the newspapers said, "Where on earth did you get that extraordinary costume from?"

Believe me, I mention these circumstances simply to show that the study of character should be from the inside; not from the outside! Great painters, I am told, used to draw a human figure in the nude form, and, when they were proposing to finish their pictures, to paint the costumes; then the costumes came right. That is exactly how an actor ought to study his art. He ought to paint his character in the nude form and put the costume on the last thing.

Now, let me give this particular advice to all persons going on the stage. Many of you are already on the stage, but others may be going on. Having arrived at that conclusion as to what your line is going to be, always try to select those kinds of characters and the line that is most suited and more nearly conforms to your own natural gifts. Nature knows best. If you happen to have a short, sharp face, a hard voice, an angular figure, you are suited for the intellectual characters of the drama, such as Hamlet and so forth. If you are of a soft, passionate nature—if you have a soft voice and that sort of sensuous disposition which seems to lubricate your entire form, your limbs, so that your movements are gentle and softer than others, then this character is fitted for a Romeo or an Othello. You will find, if you look back at the records of actors, there are few great actors that have shone in the two different lines, the intellectual and the sensual drama. Kemble could do Hamlet, but he could not do Othello. Kean could do Othello, but he could not do Hamlet. The one was passionate and sensual, the other was an intellectual, a noble, grand actor.

Now, after you have made this preliminary study you will recollect that in every great character, there are three characters really. We are all free men, in one sense, speaking, of course, of our inner life; but we have three characters. First there is the man by himself—as he is to himself—as he is to God. That is one man, the inner man, as he is when alone; the unclothed man. Then there is the native man, the domestic man, as he is to his family. Still there is a certain amount of disguise. He is not as he is to other men. Then there is the man as he stands before the world at large; as he is outside in society. Those are the three characters. They are all in the one man, and the dramatist does not know his business unless he puts them into one character. Look at Hamlet in his soliloquies, he is passionate, he is violent, he is intemperate in himself, he knows his faults and lashes his own weakness. But he has no sooner done that when Horatio comes on the stage with a few friends. Horatio is the mild, soft, gentle companion; with his arm round his neck, Hamlet forgets the other man; he gets a little on, but he is the same man to Horatio as he is to his mother, when he gets her in the closet. But when he encounters the world at large, he is the Prince! the condescending man! You have seen Hamlet played, and if you watched closely, you have seen those three phases of his character have been given on this stage! So it is in nearly all characters—comic or otherwise. You will find that the three characters always combine in the man. . . .

Now, ladies and gentlemen, I have kept you a long time. All I say now is that I have to give you most heartily and conscientiously, as an old man, an old dramatist, and an old actor, this advice. Whatever is done by an actor let it be done with circumspection, without anxiety or hurry, remembering that vehemence is not passion, that the public will feel and appreciate when the actor is not full of himself, but when he is full of character, with that deliberation without slowness, that calmness of resolution without coldness, that self-possession without over-weening confidence, which should combine in the actor so as to give grace to comic and importance to tragic presence. The audience are impressed with the unaffected character of one who moves forward with a fixed purpose, full of momentous designs. He expresses a passion with which they will sympathize, and radiates a command which they will obey. . . .

Oscar Wilde

Oscar Fingal O'Flahertie Wills Wilde (1854–1900) was born to a famous eye surgeon who maintained a home in Dublin's most exclusive neighborhood. Wilde's mother, known by her literary name, Speranza, was noted for collecting Irish folk stories in the western hills in the late 1870s. Her work was important to later literature, but it was especially important for its timing, since most of the storytellers in Ireland were gone by the turn of the century.

Wilde was a brilliant classics scholar at Trinity College, Dublin, where his tutor was the legendary Mahaffy, who later traveled with him in France. After Trinity, he went to Magdalen College, Oxford, where he earned a distinguished degree. Among his influences in Oxford was Slade Professor of Art John Ruskin, with whom Wilde had long walks and talks. Ruskin had published important books on northern Gothic art and on Italian art, especially the art of Venice. Art was one of Wilde's primary passions, especially the decorative arts. He agreed with Walter Pater, a contemporary art critic, that art must best serve the needs of art. He believed, for example, that poetry did not serve religious, political, social, or biographical goals. Its ends were aesthetic and its pleasures were in its sounds, images, and thoughts.

Partly because of his brilliance and partly because he was one of the age's greatest conversationalists, Wilde was soon in the company of the famous and amusing people of his generation. Some of his conversational gift is apparent in his plays.

By his own admission, his life was marked by an overindulgence in sensuality: "What paradox was to me in the sphere of thought, perversity became to me in the sphere of passion." He married Constance Lloyd in 1884, and the couple soon had two sons. But by 1891 Wilde had already had several homosexual liaisons, one of which was to bring him to ruin. His relationship with the much younger Lord Alfred Douglas ended with Douglas's father, the marquis of Queensberry, publicly denouncing Wilde as a sodomite. Wilde sued for libel but lost. As a result, in 1895 he was tried for sodomy, convicted, and sentenced to two years' hard labor. Wilde's actions have been seen as self-destructive, but they are also consistent with his efforts to force society to examine its own hypocrisy. Unfortunately, his efforts in court and prison ruined him, and he died in exile in Paris three years after his release.

His best known novel, *The Picture of Dorian Gray* (1891; expanded 1894), is the story of a young man whose sensual life eats away at him and eventually destroys him. The novel's failure when it was first published led Wilde to try writing for the stage, where he was a signal success. Remarkably, all his plays were written in the period between 1891 and his imprisonment in 1895. Most of his plays—*Salomé* (1891), *Lady Windermere's Fan* (1892), *A Woman of No Importance* (1893), *An Ideal Husband* (1895), and *The Importance of Being Earnest* (1895)—rank as witty, insightful, and sharp commentaries on the upper-class British society Wilde knew best. They owe a great deal to eighteenth-century comedies, such as William Congreve's *The Way of the World*. But they also owe a great deal to British and European farces and comedies of Wilde's own time, many of which he seems to have studied closely. Unlike those plays—many of which have never been published and no longer exist—Wilde's are still funny and still seem pertinent even though the class he criticized has long vanished.

The Importance of Being Earnest was a remarkable success when it opened at the St. James Theatre on Valentine's Day 1895, but it closed in two months after fewer than one hundred performances when the scandal of Wilde's conviction became public. Wilde's reputation as playwright was made and broken in a matter of a few years, and it was not restored until after his death.

The Importance of Being Earnest

For discussion questions and assignments on *The Importance of Being Earnest*, visit **bedfordstmartins.com/jacobus**.

The Importance of Being Earnest was originally written in four acts, but because the producer requested that it be cut, Wilde reworked it into three acts, agreeing that the excisions made the play stronger. Its subtitle, *A Trivial Comedy for Serious People*, has prompted commentators to think of the play as farcical fluff, a play about little or nothing that is nonetheless profoundly amusing. The *New York Times* commented after the play's first U.S. opening, "The thing is as slight in structure and as devoid of purpose as a paper balloon, but it is extraordinarily funny." Recent critics have challenged this view on the grounds that the play's subject matter centers on the questions of identity and reality. One current view is that its surfaces are slight but beneath the surface is a commentary on a society that judges things only by appearance.

The primary characters are Algernon Moncrieff and Jack Worthing, young gentlemen of marriageable age. Among the women are Algernon's cousin Gwendolen Fairfax, who adores the name Ernest and is in love with Jack; Lady Bracknell, her mother; and Cecily Cardew, Jack's ward. Bunbury, referred to by Algernon, seems to be a character, but is instead an invention. He is a convenience for Algernon, a country friend whose illnesses Algernon uses to avoid social events he dislikes, such as Lady Bracknell's dinners. Jack, who lives in the country, has created a similar figure to help him escape to town—an imaginary brother Ernest. In town, Jack pretends to be Ernest, and all his town acquaintances, including Algernon and Gwendolen, know Jack by that name.

The similarities with Restoration comedies are striking. The question of marriage is central in the play, and attitudes toward marriage in Wilde's social class are among the targets of his satire. When Lady Bracknell probes into Jack Worthing's background, she discovers distressing news about his family "line": Jack is a foundling who had been left in a handbag in Victoria Station. His family "line" is the Brighton Line! Gwendolen could also have stepped from a Restoration comedy. She is determined to have Jack Worthing, and when he seems sluggish about proposing she prompts him, offering a critique of his proposal by telling him he seems inexperienced at it.

The play owes perhaps even more to the farces of the 1880s and 1890s and a great deal to the well-made plays of Eugène Scribe and his successors. Critics often compare Wilde to Alexandre Dumas, the author of *La Dame aux camélias* (*Camille*), because both writers fashion their plays with a considerable degree of artificiality, planting information in the first act that would prove the solution to problems in the last act. Dumas also plays with questions of identity, disguise, and revelation at the last minute in much the way Wilde does here when he reveals the identity of Ernest.

In melodramas and well-made plays, the revelation at the end was not that the potential husband had the right name so much as that he had the right background: he was an aristocrat and not the commoner he seemed to be. Wilde has fun with this convention and many others. In an instant, he ridicules the trick of revealing the hero to be "marriageable" because of his birth by emphasizing the triviality of a name. Yet names are of great importance (as Shakespeare tells us in *Romeo and Juliet*), and the earnestness implied in Ernest is one ingredient that helps Jack Worthing succeed.

Critic Kerry Powell has demonstrated that almost every device in *The Importance of Being Earnest* was drawn from a contemporary farce or comedy. The device of the child lost in a piece of luggage was used in *The Lost Child* (1863), and *The Foundling* (1894) actually took place in Brighton. The name Bunbury and the concept of "Bunburying" come from *The Godpapa* (1891). Even the device of baptism was used in *Crimes and Christening* (1891). Wilde was adept at taking the theater conventions his audience was most familiar with and using them to his own ends—to entertain his audience, but at the same time to help him put an extra edge on his satire.

The Importance of Being Earnest in Performance

After the first production closed down in 1895, the play was revived in London in 1898 and 1902. An even more successful production in 1909 saw 324 performances. The benchmark for a truly successful play in those days seems to have been one hundred performances, and Wilde would have felt vindicated by the 1909 production, had he lived to see it. *The Importance of Being Earnest* has been produced so often in Great Britain and the United States that only a few productions can be taken into account here. The first New York production was in 1902. John Gielgud and Edith Evans played in the 1939 London production and then again in 1942. In 1947, Gielgud played in New York with Clifton Webb and Estelle Winwood. The reviews were especially strong, calling the play "as insolently monocled in manner and as killingly high-toned in language as mischievous tomfoolery can make it."

The play inspired at least five musicals between 1927 and 1984. The 1979 production at Stratford, Ontario, was called "a perfect play in a perfect production." A production by the Berlin Play Actors in 1987 used all men and relied on insights drawn from transvestite performers, but it was badly received. University productions of the play are fairly common, although, like the Yale Repertory production in 1986, they are not always able to pull off the comic demands of the play's exacting language. The original four-act version of the play, discovered in 1977 in the New York Public Library, was produced in Ohio in the John Carroll University's Marinello Theater in 1985. It was more a curiosity than a triumph. The 1993 production at the Aldwych in London received great praise for its dazzling sets that "matched Wilde's word pictures with bold stage pictures." Maggie Smith played Lady Bracknell. Sir Peter Hall toured his Theatre Royal Bath company successfully in 2006 with a strikingly energetic Lynn Redgrave as Lady Bracknell. The 2006 production at the Brooklyn Academy of Music was well received, although the Harvey Theatre's stage was faulted for not wholly accommodating the proscenium frame necessary for the drama.

The play is a witty tour de force of language. Its surfaces gleam, and the best productions play it straight. A spate of contemporary films has made Wilde's work available to a wide audience.

OSCAR WILDE (1854–1900)

The Importance of Being Earnest 1895

A Trival Comedy for Serious People

The Persons of the Play

JOHN WORTHING, J.P., *of the Manor House, Woolton, Hertfordshire*
ALGERNON MONCRIEFF, *his friend*
REV. CANON CHASUBLE, D.D., *rector of Woolton*
MERRIMAN, *butler to Mr. Worthing*
LANE, *Mr. Moncrieff's manservant*
LADY BRACKNELL
HON. GWENDOLEN FAIRFAX, *her daughter*
CECILY CARDEW, *John Worthing's ward*
MISS PRISM, *her governess*

The Scenes of the Play

Act I: *Algernon Moncrieff's Flat in Half Moon Street, W.*
Act II: *The Garden at the Manor House, Woolton*
Act III: *Morning Room at the Manor House, Woolton*

ACT I

(*Scene: Morning room in Algernon's flat in Half Moon Street. The room is luxuriously and artistically furnished. The sound of a piano is heard in the adjoining room. Lane is arranging afternoon tea on the table, and after the music has ceased, Algernon enters.*)

ALGERNON: Did you hear what I was playing, Lane?
LANE: I didn't think it polite to listen, sir.
ALGERNON: I'm sorry for that, for your sake. I don't play accurately—anyone can play accurately—but I play with wonderful expression. As far as the piano is concerned, sentiment is my forte. I keep science for Life.
LANE: Yes, sir.
ALGERNON: And, speaking of the science of Life, have you got the cucumber sandwiches cut for Lady Bracknell?
LANE: Yes, sir. (*Hands them on a salver.*)
ALGERNON (*inspects them, takes two, and sits down on the sofa*): Oh!—by the way, Lane, I see from your book that on Thursday night, when Lord Shoreham and Mr. Worthing were dining with me, eight bottles of champagne are entered as having been consumed.

LANE: Yes, sir; eight bottles and a pint.
ALGERNON: Why is it that at a bachelor's establishment the servants invariably drink the champagne? I ask merely for information.
LANE: I attribute it to the superior quality of the wine, sir. I have often observed that in married households the champagne is rarely of a first-rate brand.
ALGERNON: Good heavens! Is marriage so demoralizing as that?
LANE: I believe it *is* a very pleasant state, sir. I have had very little experience of it myself up to the present. I have only been married once. That was in consequence of a misunderstanding between myself and a young person.
ALGERNON (*languidly*): I don't know that I am much interested in your family life, Lane.
LANE: No, sir; it is not a very interesting subject. I never think of it myself.
ALGERNON: Very natural, I am sure. That will do, Lane, thank you.
LANE: Thank you, sir. (*Lane goes out.*)
ALGERNON: Lane's views on marriage seem somewhat lax. Really, if the lower orders don't set us a good example, what on earth is the use of them? They seem, as a class, to have absolutely no sense of moral responsibility.

(*Enter Lane.*)

LANE: Mr. Ernest Worthing.

(*Enter Jack. Lane goes out.*)

ALGERNON: How are you, my dear Ernest? What brings you up to town?
JACK: Oh, pleasure, pleasure! What else should bring one anywhere? Eating as usual, I see, Algy!
ALGERNON (*Stiffly*): I believe it is customary in good society to take some slight refreshment at five o'clock. Where have you been since last Thursday?
JACK (*sitting down on the sofa*): In the country.
ALGERNON: What on earth do you do there?
JACK (*pulling off his gloves*): When one is in town one amuses oneself. When one is in the country one amuses other people. It is excessively boring.
ALGERNON: And who are the people you amuse?
JACK (*airily*): Oh, neighbors, neighbors.

ALGERNON: Got nice neighbors in your part of Shropshire?

JACK: Perfectly horrid! Never speak to one of them.

ALGERNON: How immensely you must amuse them! (*Goes over and takes sandwich.*) By the way, Shropshire is your county, is it not?

JACK: Eh? Shropshire? Yes, of course. Hallo! Why all these cups? Why cucumber sandwiches? Why such reckless extravagance in one so young? Who is coming to tea?

ALGERNON: Oh! merely Aunt Augusta and Gwendolen.

JACK: How perfectly delightful!

ALGERNON: Yes, that is all very well; but I am afraid Aunt Augusta won't quite approve of your being here.

JACK: May I ask why?

ALGERNON: My dear fellow, the way you flirt with Gwendolen is perfectly disgraceful. It is almost as bad as the way Gwendolen flirts with you.

JACK: I am in love with Gwendolen. I have come up to town expressly to propose to her.

ALGERNON: I thought you had come up for pleasure? — I call that business.

JACK: How utterly unromantic you are!

ALGERNON: I really don't see anything romantic in proposing. It is very romantic to be in love. But there is nothing romantic about a definite proposal. Why, one may be accepted. One usually is, I believe. Then the excitement is all over. The very essence of romance is uncertainty. If ever I get married, I'll certainly try to forget the fact.

JACK: I have no doubt about that, dear Algy. The Divorce Court was specially invented for people whose memories are so curiously constituted.

ALGERNON: Oh! there is no use speculating on that subject. Divorces are made in heaven — (*Jack puts out his hand to take a sandwich. Algernon at once interferes.*) Please don't touch the cucumber sandwiches. They are ordered specially for Aunt Augusta. (*Takes one and eats it.*)

JACK: Well, you have been eating them all the time.

ALGERNON: That is quite a different matter. She is my aunt. (*Takes plate from below.*) Have some bread and butter. The bread and butter is for Gwendolen. Gwendolen is devoted to bread and butter.

JACK (*advancing to table and helping himself*): And very good bread and butter it is too.

ALGERNON: Well, my dear fellow, you need not eat as if you were going to eat it all. You behave as if you were married to her already. You are not married to her already, and I don't think you ever will be.

JACK: Why on earth do you say that?

ALGERNON: Well, in the first place, girls never marry the men they flirt with. Girls don't think it right.

JACK: Oh, that is nonsense!

ALGERNON: It isn't. It is a great truth. It accounts for the extraordinary number of bachelors that one sees all over the place. In the second place, I don't give my consent.

JACK: Your consent!

ALGERNON: My dear fellow, Gwendolen is my first cousin. And before I allow you to marry her, you will have to clear up the whole question of Cecily.

(*Rings bell.*)

JACK: Cecily! What on earth do you mean? What do you mean, Algy, by Cecily? I don't know anyone of the name of Cecily.

(*Enter Lane.*)

ALGERNON: Bring me that cigarette case Mr. Worthing left in the smoking room the last time he dined here.

LANE: Yes, sir.   (*Lane goes out.*)

JACK: Do you mean to say you have had my cigarette case all this time? I wish to goodness you had let me know. I have been writing frantic letters to Scotland Yard about it. I was very nearly offering a large reward.

ALGERNON: Well, I wish you would offer one. I happen to be more than usually hard up.

JACK: There is no good offering a large reward now that the thing is found.

(*Enter Lane with the cigarette case on a salver. Algernon takes it at once. Lane goes out.*)

ALGERNON: I think that is rather mean of you, Ernest, I must say. (*Opens case and examines it.*) However, it makes no matter, for, now that I look at the inscription inside, I find that the thing isn't yours after all.

JACK: Of course it's mine. (*Moving to him.*) You have seen me with it a hundred times, and you have no right whatsoever to read what is written inside. It is a very ungentlemanly thing to read a private cigarette case.

ALGERNON: Oh! it is absurd to have a hard-and-fast rule about what one should read and what one shouldn't. More than half of modern culture depends on what one shouldn't read.

JACK: I am quite aware of the fact, and I don't propose to discuss modern culture. It isn't the sort of thing one should talk of in private. I simply want my cigarette case back.

ALGERNON: Yes; but this isn't your cigarette case. This cigarette case is a present from someone of the name of Cecily, and you said you didn't know anyone of that name.

JACK: Well, if you want to know, Cecily happens to be my aunt.

ALGERNON: Your aunt!

JACK: Yes. Charming old lady she is, too. Lives at Tunbridge Wells. Just give it back to me, Algy.

ALGERNON (*retreating to back of sofa*): But why does she call herself little Cecily if she is your aunt and lives at Tunbridge Wells? (*Reading.*) "From little Cecily with her fondest love."

JACK (*moving to sofa and kneeling upon it*): My dear fellow, what on earth is there in that? Some aunts are tall, some aunts are not tall. That is a matter that surely an aunt may be allowed to decide for herself. You seem to think that every aunt should be exactly like your aunt! That is absurd! For heaven's sake give me back my cigarette case.

(*Follows Algernon round the room.*)

ALGERNON: Yes. But why does your aunt call you her uncle? "From little Cecily, with her fondest love to her dear Uncle Jack." There is no objection, I admit, to an aunt being a small aunt, but why an aunt, no matter what her size may be, should call her own nephew her uncle, I can't quite make out. Besides, your name isn't Jack at all; it is Ernest.

JACK: It isn't Ernest; it's Jack.

ALGERNON: You have always told me it was Ernest. I have introduced you to everyone as Ernest. You answer to the name of Ernest. You look as if your name was Ernest. You are the most earnest looking person I ever saw in my life. It is perfectly absurd your saying that your name isn't Ernest. It's on your cards. Here is one of them (*taking it from case*) "Mr. Ernest Worthing, B.4, The Albany." I'll keep this as a proof that your name is Ernest if ever you attempt to deny it to me, or to Gwendolen, or to anyone else.

(*Puts the card in his pocket.*)

JACK: Well, my name is Ernest in town and Jack in the country, and the cigarette case was given to me in the country.

ALGERNON: Yes, but that does not account for the fact that your small Aunt Cecily, who lives at Tunbridge Wells, calls you her dear uncle. Come, old boy, you had much better have the thing out at once.

JACK: My dear Algy, you talk exactly as if you were a dentist. It is very vulgar to talk like a dentist when one isn't a dentist. It produces a false impression.

ALGERNON: Well, that is exactly what dentists always do. Now, go on! Tell me the whole thing. I may mention that I have always suspected you of being a confirmed and secret Bunburyist; and I am quite sure of it now.

JACK: Bunburyist? What on earth do you mean by a Bunburyist?

ALGERNON: I'll reveal to you the meaning of that incomparable expression as soon as you are kind enough to inform me why you are Ernest in town and Jack in the country.

JACK: Well, produce my cigarette case first.

ALGERNON: Here it is. (*Hands cigarette case.*) Now produce your explanation, and pray make it improbable.

(*Sits on sofa.*)

JACK: My dear fellow, there is nothing improbable about my explanation at all. In fact it's perfectly ordinary. Old Mr. Thomas Cardew, who adopted me when I was a little boy, made me in his will guardian to his granddaughter, Miss Cecily Cardew. Cecily, who addresses me as her uncle from motives of respect that you could not possibly appreciate, lives at my place in the country under the charge of her admirable governess, Miss Prism.

ALGERNON: Where is that place in the country, by the way?

JACK: That is nothing to you, dear boy. You are not going to be invited—I may tell you candidly that the place is not in Shropshire.

ALGERNON: I suspected that, my dear fellow! I have Bunburyed all over Shropshire on two separate occasions. Now, go on. Why are you Ernest in town and Jack in the country?

JACK: My dear Algy, I don't know whether you will be able to understand my real motives. You are hardly serious enough. When one is placed in the position of guardian, one has to adopt a very high moral tone on all subjects. It's one's duty to do so. And as a high moral tone can hardly be said to conduce very much to either one's health or one's happiness, in order to get up to town I have always pretended to have a younger brother of the name of Ernest, who lives in the Albany, and gets into the most dreadful scrapes. That, my dear Algy, is the whole truth pure and simple.

ALGERNON: The truth is rarely pure and never simple. Modern life would be very tedious if it were either and modern literature a complete impossibility!

JACK: That wouldn't be at all a bad thing.

ALGERNON: Literary criticism is not your forte, my dear fellow. Don't try it. You should leave that to people who haven't been at a university. They do it so well in the daily papers. What you really are is a Bunburyist. I was quite right in saying you were a Bunburyist. You are one of the most advanced Bunburyists I know.

JACK: What on earth do you mean?

ALGERNON: You have invented a very useful younger brother called Ernest, in order that you may be able to come up to town as often as you like. I have invented an invaluable permanent invalid called Bunbury, in order that I may be able to go down into the country whenever I choose. Bunbury is perfectly invaluable. If it wasn't for Bunbury's extraordinary bad health, for instance, I wouldn't be able to dine with you at Willis's tonight, for I have been really engaged to Aunt Augusta for more than a week.

JACK: I haven't asked you to dine with me anywhere tonight.

ALGERNON: I know. You are absurdly careless about sending out invitations. It is very foolish of you. Nothing annoys people so much as not receiving invitations.

JACK: You had much better dine with your Aunt Augusta.

ALGERNON: I haven't the smallest intention of doing anything of the kind. To begin with, I dined there on Monday, and once a week is quite enough to dine with one's own relations. In the second place, whenever I do dine there I am always treated as a member of the family, and sent down with° either no woman at all, or two. In the third place, I know perfectly well whom she will place me next to, tonight. She will place me next Mary Farquhar, who always flirts with her own husband across the dinner table. That is not very pleasant. Indeed, it is not even decent—and that sort of thing is enormously on the increase. The

---

sent down with: Assigned a woman to escort into the dining room for dinner.

amount of women in London who flirt with their own husbands is perfectly scandalous. It looks so bad. It is simply washing one's clean linen in public. Besides, now that I know you to be a confirmed Bunburyist I naturally want to talk to you about Bunburying. I want to tell you the rules.

JACK: I'm not a Bunburyist at all. If Gwendolen accepts me, I am going to kill my brother, indeed I think I'll kill him in any case. Cecily is a little too much interested in him. It is rather a bore. So I am going to get rid of Ernest. And I strongly advise you to do the same with Mr.—with your invalid friend who has the absurd name.

ALGERNON: Nothing will induce me to part with Bunbury, and if you ever get married, which seems to me extremely problematic, you will be very glad to know Bunbury. A man who marries without knowing Bunbury has a very tedious time of it.

JACK: That is nonsense. If I marry a charming girl like Gwendolen, and she is the only girl I ever saw in my life that I would marry, I certainly won't want to know Bunbury.

ALGERNON: Then your wife will. You don't seem to realize, that in married life three is company and two is none.

JACK (*sententiously*): That, my dear young friend, is the theory that the corrupt French drama has been propounding for the last fifty years.

ALGERNON: Yes; and that the happy English home has proved in half the time.

JACK: For heaven's sake, don't try to be cynical. It's perfectly easy to be cynical.

ALGERNON: My dear fellow, it isn't easy to be anything nowadays. There's such a lot of beastly competition about. (*The sound of an electric bell is heard.*) Ah! that must be Aunt Augusta. Only relatives, or creditors, ever ring in that Wagnerian° manner. Now, if I get her out of the way for ten minutes, so that you can have an opportunity for proposing to Gwendolen, may I dine with you tonight at Willis's?

JACK: I suppose so, if you want to.

ALGERNON: Yes, but you must be serious about it. I hate people who are not serious about meals. It is so shallow of them.

(*Enter Lane.*)

LANE: Lady Bracknell and Miss Fairfax.

(*Algernon goes forward to meet them. Enter Lady Bracknell and Gwendolen.*)

LADY BRACKNELL: Good afternoon, dear Algernon, I hope you are behaving very well.

ALGERNON: I'm feeling very well, Aunt Augusta.

LADY BRACKNELL: That's not quite the same thing. In fact the two things rarely go together.

(*Sees Jack and bows to him with icy coldness.*)

Wagnerian: Referring to the operas of Richard Wagner (1813–1883), whose music was popularly thought to be loud.

ALGERNON (*to Gwendolen*): Dear me, you are smart!

GWENDOLEN: I am always smart! Aren't I, Mr. Worthing?

JACK: You're quite perfect, Miss Fairfax.

GWENDOLEN: Oh! I hope I am not that. It would leave no room for developments, and I intend to develop in many directions.

(*Gwendolen and Jack sit down together in the corner.*)

LADY BRACKNELL: I'm sorry if we are a little late Algernon, but I was obliged to call on dear Lady Harbury. I hadn't been there since her poor husband's death. I never saw a woman so altered; she looks quite twenty years younger. And now I'll have a cup of tea, and one of those nice cucumber sandwiches you promised me.

ALGERNON: Certainly, Aunt Augusta.

(*Goes over to tea table.*)

LADY BRACKNELL: Won't you come and sit here, Gwendolen?

GWENDOLEN: Thanks, Mama, I'm quite comfortable where I am.

ALGERNON (*picking up empty plate in horror*): Good heavens! Lane! Why are there no cucumber sandwiches? I ordered them specially.

LANE (*gravely*): There were no cucumbers in the market this morning, sir. I went down twice.

ALGERNON: No cucumbers?

LANE: No, sir. Not even for ready money.

ALGERNON: That will do, Lane, thank you.

LANE: Thank you, sir. (*Goes out.*)

ALGERNON: I am greatly distressed, Aunt Augusta, about there being no cucumbers, not even for ready money.

LADY BRACKNELL: It really makes no matter, Algernon. I had some crumpets with Lady Harbury, who seems to me to be living entirely for pleasure now.

ALGERNON: I hear her hair has turned quite gold from grief.

LADY BRACKNELL: It certainly has changed its color. From what cause I, of course, cannot say. (*Algernon crosses and hands tea.*) Thank you. I've quite a treat for you tonight, Algernon. I am going to send you down with Mary Farquhar. She is such a nice woman, and so attentive to her husband. It's delightful to watch them.

ALGERNON: I am afraid, Aunt Augusta, I shall have to give up the pleasure of dining with you tonight after all.

LADY BRACKNELL (*frowning*): I hope not, Algernon. It would put my table completely out. Your uncle would have to dine upstairs. Fortunately he is accustomed to that.

ALGERNON: It is a great bore, and, I need hardly say, a terrible disappointment to me, but the fact is I have just had a telegram to say that my poor friend Bunbury is very ill again. (*Exchanges glances with Jack.*) They seem to think I should be with him.

LADY BRACKNELL: It is very strange. This Mr. Bunbury seems to suffer from curiously bad health.

ALGERNON: Yes; poor Bunbury is a dreadful invalid.

LADY BRACKNELL: Well, I must say, Algernon, that I think it is high time that Mr. Bunbury made up his mind whether he was going to live or to die. This shilly-shallying with the question is absurd. Nor do I in any way approve of the modern sympathy with invalids. I consider it morbid. Illness of any kind is hardly a thing to be encouraged in others. Health is the primary duty of life. I am always telling that to your poor uncle, but he never seems to take much notice—as far as any improvement in his ailments goes. I should be much obliged if you would ask Mr. Bunbury, from me, to be kind enough not to have a relapse on Saturday, for I rely on you to arrange my music for me. It is my last reception, and one wants something that will encourage conversation, particularly at the end of the season when everyone has practically said whatever they had to say, which, in most cases, was probably not much.

ALGERNON: I'll speak to Bunbury, Aunt Augusta, if he is still conscious, and I think I can promise you he'll be all right by Saturday. Of course the music is a great difficulty. You see, if one plays good music, people don't listen, and if one plays bad music people don't talk. But I'll run over the program I've drawn out, if you will kindly come into the next room for a moment.

LADY BRACKNELL: Thank you, Algernon. It is very thoughtful of you. (*Rising, and following Algernon.*) I'm sure the program will be delightful, after a few expurgations. French songs I cannot possibly allow. People always seem to think that they are improper, and either look shocked, which is vulgar, or laugh, which is worse. But German sounds a thoroughly respectable language, and indeed, I believe is so. Gwendolen, you will accompany me.

GWENDOLEN: Certainly, Mama.

(*Lady Bracknell and Algernon go into the music room. Gwendolen remains behind.*)

JACK: Charming day it has been, Miss Fairfax.

GWENDOLEN: Pray don't talk to me about the weather Mr. Worthing. Whenever people talk to me about the weather, I always feel quite certain that they mean something else. And that makes me so nervous.

JACK: I do mean something else.

GWENDOLEN: I thought so. In fact, I am never wrong.

JACK: And I would like to be allowed to take advantage of Lady Bracknell's temporary absence—

GWENDOLEN: I would certainly advise you to do so. Mama has a way of coming back suddenly into a room that I have often had to speak to her about.

JACK (*nervously*): Miss Fairfax, ever since I met you I have admired you more than any girl—I have ever met since—I met you.

GWENDOLEN: Yes, I am quite aware of the fact. And I often wish that in public, at any rate, you had been more demonstrative. For me you have always had an irresistible fascination. Even before I met you I was far from indifferent to you. (*Jack looks at her in amazement.*) We live, as I hope you know Mr. Worthing, in an age of ideals. The fact is constantly

mentioned in the more expensive monthly magazines, and has reached the provincial pulpits I am told: And my ideal has always been to love someone of the name of Ernest. There is something in that name that inspires absolute confidence. The moment Algernon first mentioned to me that he had a friend called Ernest, I knew I was destined to love you.

JACK: You really love me, Gwendolen?

GWENDOLEN: Passionately!

JACK: Darling! You don't know how happy you've made me.

GWENDOLEN: My own Ernest!

JACK: But you don't mean to say that you couldn't love me if my name wasn't Ernest?

GWENDOLEN: But your name is Ernest.

JACK: Yes, I know it is. But supposing it was something else? Do you mean to say you couldn't love me then?

GWENDOLEN (*glibly*): Ah! that is clearly a metaphysical speculation, and like most metaphysical speculations has very little reference at all to the actual facts of real life, as we know them.

JACK: Personally, darling, to speak quite candidly, I don't much care about the name of Ernest—I don't think the name suits me at all.

GWENDOLEN: It suits you perfectly. It is a divine name. It has a music of its own. It produces vibrations.

JACK: Well, really, Gwendolen, I must say that I think there are lots of other much nicer names. I think Jack, for instance, a charming name.

GWENDOLEN: Jack?—No, there is very little music in the name Jack, if any at all, indeed. It does not thrill. It produces absolutely no vibrations—I have known several Jacks, and they all, without exception, were more than usually plain. Besides, Jack is a notorious domesticity for John! And I pity any woman who is married to a man called John. She would probably never be allowed to know the entrancing pleasure of a single moment's solitude. The only really safe name is Ernest.

JACK: Gwendolen, I must get christened at once—I mean we must get married at once. There is no time to be lost.

GWENDOLEN: Married, Mr. Worthing?

JACK (*astounded*): Well—surely. You know that I love you, and you led me to believe, Miss Fairfax that you were not absolutely indifferent to me.

GWENDOLEN: I adore you. But you haven't proposed to me yet. Nothing has been said at all about marriage. The subject has not even been touched on.

JACK: Well—may I propose to you now?

GWENDOLEN: I think it would be an admirable opportunity. And to spare you any possible disappointment, Mr. Worthing, I think it only fair to tell you quite frankly beforehand that I am fully determined to accept you.

JACK: Gwendolen!

GWENDOLEN: Yes, Mr. Worthing, what have you got to say to me?

JACK: You know what I have got to say to you.

GWENDOLEN: Yes, but you don't say it.

JACK: Gwendolen, will you marry me?

(*Goes on his knees.*)

GWENDOLEN: Of course I will, darling. How long you have been about it! I am afraid you have had very little experience in how to propose.

JACK: My own one, I have never loved anyone in the world but you.

GWENDOLEN: Yes, but men often propose for practice. I know my brother Gerald does. All my girlfriends tell me so. What wonderfully blue eyes you have, Ernest! They are quite, quite blue. I hope you will always look at me just like that, especially when there are other people present.

(*Enter Lady Bracknell.*)

LADY BRACKNELL: Mr. Worthing! Rise, sir, from this semi-recumbent posture. It is most indecorous.

GWENDOLEN: Mama! (*He tries to rise; she restrains him.*) I must beg you to retire. This is no place for you. Besides, Mr. Worthing has not quite finished yet.

LADY BRACKNELL: Finished what, may I ask?

GWENDOLEN: I am engaged to Mr. Worthing, Mama.

(*They rise together.*)

LADY BRACKNELL: Pardon me, you are not engaged to anyone. When you do become engaged to someone, I, or your father, should his health permit him, will inform you of the fact. An engagement should come on a young girl as a surprise, pleasant or unpleasant, as the case may be. It is hardly a matter that she could be allowed to arrange for herself—And now I have a few questions to put to you, Mr. Worthing. While I am making these inquiries, you, Gwendolen, will wait for me below in the carriage.

GWENDOLEN (*reproachfully*): Mama!

LADY BRACKNELL: In the carriage, Gwendolen! (*Gwendolen goes to the door. She and Jack blow kisses to each other behind Lady Bracknell's back. Lady Bracknell looks vaguely about as if she could not understand what the noise was. Finally turns round.*) Gwendolen, the carriage!

GWENDOLEN: Yes, Mama.

(*Goes out, looking back at Jack.*)

LADY BRACKNELL (*sitting down*): You can take a seat, Mr. Worthing.

(*Looks in her pocket for notebook and pencil.*)

JACK: Thank you, Lady Bracknell, I prefer standing.

LADY BRACKNELL (*pencil and notebook in hand*): I feel bound to tell you that you are not down on my list of eligible young men, although I have the same list as the dear Duchess of Bolton has. We work together, in fact. However, I am quite ready to enter your name, should your answers be what a really affectionate mother requires. Do you smoke?

JACK: Well, yes, I must admit I smoke.

LADY BRACKNELL: I am glad to hear it. A man should always have an occupation of some kind. There are far too many idle men in London as it is. How old are you?

JACK: Twenty-nine.

LADY BRACKNELL: A very good age to be married at. I have always been of opinion that a man who desires to get married should know either everything or nothing. Which do you know?

JACK (*after some hesitation*): I know nothing, Lady Bracknell.

LADY BRACKNELL: I am pleased to hear it. I do not approve of anything that tampers with natural ignorance. Ignorance is like a delicate exotic fruit; touch it and the bloom is gone. The whole theory of modern education is radically unsound. Fortunately in England, at any rate, education produces no effect whatsoever. If it did, it would prove a serious danger to the upper classes, and probably lead to acts of violence in Grosvenor Square. What is your income?

JACK: Between seven and eight thousand a year.

LADY BRACKNELL (*makes a note in her book*): In land, or in investments?

JACK: In investments, chiefly.

LADY BRACKNELL: That is satisfactory. What between the duties expected of one during one's lifetime, and the duties exacted from one after one's death, land has ceased to be either a profit or a pleasure. It gives one position, and prevents one from keeping it up. That's all that can be said about land.

JACK: I have a country house with some land, of course, attached to it, about fifteen hundred acres, I believe; but I don't depend on that for my real income. In fact, as far as I can make out, the poachers are the only people who make anything out of it.

LADY BRACKNELL: A country house! How many bedrooms? Well, that point can be cleared up afterwards. You have a town house, I hope? A girl with a simple, unspoiled nature, like Gwendolen, could hardly be expected to reside in the country.

JACK: Well, I own a house in Belgrave Square, but it is let by the year to Lady Bloxham. Of course, I can get it back whenever I like, at six months' notice.

LADY BRACKNELL: Lady Bloxham? I don't know her.

JACK: Oh, she goes about very little. She is a lady considerably advanced in years.

LADY BRACKNELL: Ah, nowadays that is no guarantee of respectability of character. What number in Belgrave Square?

JACK: 149.

LADY BRACKNELL (*shaking her head*): The unfashionable side. I thought there was something. However; that could easily be altered.

JACK: Do you mean the fashion, or the side?

LADY BRACKNELL (*sternly*): Both, if necessary, I presume. What are your politics?

JACK: Well, I am afraid I really have none. I am a Liberal Unionist.

LADY BRACKNELL: Oh, they count as Tories. They dine with us. Or come in the evening, at any rate. Now to minor matters. Are your parents living?

JACK: I have lost both my parents.

LADY BRACKNELL: Both? To lose one parent may be regarded as a misfortune—to lose *both* seems like carelessness. Who was your father? He was evidently a man of some wealth. Was he born in what the Radical papers call the purple of commerce, or did he rise from the ranks of the aristocracy?

JACK: I am afraid I really don't know. The fact is, Lady Bracknell, I said I had lost my parents. It would be nearer the truth to say that my parents seem to have lost me—I don't actually know who I am by birth. I was—well, I was found.

LADY BRACKNELL: Found!

JACK: The late Mr. Thomas Cardew, an old gentleman of a very charitable and kindly disposition, found me, and gave me the name of Worthing, because he happened to have a first-class ticket for Worthing in his pocket at the time. Worthing is a place in Sussex. It is a seaside resort.

LADY BRACKNELL: Where did the charitable gentleman who had a first-class ticket for this seaside resort find you?

JACK (*gravely*): In a handbag.

LADY BRACKNELL: A handbag?

JACK (*very seriously*): Yes, Lady Bracknell. I was in a handbag—a somewhat large, black leather handbag, with handles to it—an ordinary handbag in fact.

LADY BRACKNELL: In what locality did this Mr. James, or Thomas, Cardew come across this ordinary handbag?

JACK: In the cloakroom at Victoria Station. It was given to him in mistake for his own.

LADY BRACKNELL: The cloakroom at Victoria Station?

JACK: Yes. The Brighton line.

LADY BRACKNELL: The line is immaterial. Mr. Worthing, I confess I feel somewhat bewildered by what you have just told me. To be born, or at any rate bred, in a handbag, whether it had handles or not, seems to me to display a contempt for the ordinary decencies of family life that reminds one of the worst excesses of the French Revolution. And I presume you know what that unfortunate movement led to? As for the particular locality in which the handbag was found, a cloakroom at a railway station might serve to conceal a social indiscretion—has probably, indeed, been used for that purpose before now—but it could hardly be regarded as an assured basis for a recognized position in good society.

JACK: May I ask you then what you would advise me to do? I need hardly say I would do anything in the world to ensure Gwendolen's happiness.

LADY BRACKNELL: I would strongly advise you, Mr. Worthing, to try and acquire some relations as soon as possible, and to make a definite effort to produce at any rate one parent of either sex, before the season is quite over.

JACK: Well, I don't see how I could possibly manage to do that. I can produce the handbag at any moment. It is in my dressing room at home. I really think that should satisfy you, Lady Bracknell.

LADY BRACKNELL: Me, sir! What has it to do with me? You can hardly imagine that I and Lord Bracknell would dream of allowing our only daughter—a girl brought up with the utmost care—to marry into a cloakroom, and form an alliance with a parcel? Good morning, Mr. Worthing!

(*Lady Bracknell sweeps out in majestic indignation.*)

JACK: Good morning! (*Algernon, from the other room, strikes up the Wedding March. Jack looks perfectly furious, and goes to the door.*) For goodness' sake don't play that ghastly tune, Algy! How idiotic you are!

(*The music stops, and Algernon enters cheerily.*)

ALGERNON: Didn't it go off all right, old boy? You don't mean to say Gwendolen refused you? I know it is a way she has. She is always refusing people. I think it is most ill-natured of her.

JACK: Oh, Gwendolen is as right as a trivet. As far as she is concerned, we are engaged. Her mother is perfectly unbearable. Never met such a Gorgon°—I don't really know what a Gorgon is like, but I am quite sure that Lady Bracknell is one. In any case, she is a monster, without being a myth, which is rather unfair. I beg your pardon, Algy, I suppose I shouldn't talk about your own aunt in that way before you.

ALGERNON: My dear boy, I love hearing my relations abused. It is the only thing that makes me put up with them at all. Relations are simply a tedious pack of people, who haven't got the remotest knowledge of how to live, nor the smallest instinct about when to die.

JACK: Oh, that is nonsense!

ALGERNON: It isn't!

JACK: Well, I won't argue about the matter. You always want to argue about things.

ALGERNON: That is exactly what things were originally made for.

JACK: Upon my word, if I thought that, I'd shoot myself—(*A pause.*) You don't think there is any chance of Gwendolen becoming like her mother in about a hundred and fifty years, do you Algy?

ALGERNON: All women become like their mothers. That is their tragedy. No man does. That's his.

JACK: Is that clever?

ALGERNON: It is perfectly phrased! and quite as true as any observation in civilized life should be.

JACK: I am sick to death of cleverness. Everybody is clever nowadays. You can't go anywhere without meeting clever people. The thing has become an absolute public nuisance. I wish to goodness we had a few fools left.

Gorgon: In Greek myth, one of three very ugly sisters who had, among other characteristics, serpents for hair.

ALGERNON: We have.

JACK: I should extremely like to meet them. What do they talk about?

ALGERNON: The fools? Oh! about the clever people, of course.

JACK: What fools!

ALGERNON: By the way, did you tell Gwendolen the truth about your being Ernest in town, and Jack in the country?

JACK (*in a very patronizing manner*): My dear fellow, the truth isn't quite the sort of thing one tells to a nice sweet refined girl. What extraordinary ideas you have about the way to behave to a woman!

ALGERNON: The only way to behave to a woman is to make love to her if she is pretty, and to someone else if she is plain.

JACK: Oh, that is nonsense.

ALGERNON: What about your brother? What about the profligate Ernest?

JACK: Oh, before the end of the week I shall have got rid of him. I'll say he died in Paris of apoplexy. Lots of people die of apoplexy, quite suddenly, don't they?

ALGERNON: Yes, but it's hereditary, my dear fellow. It's a sort of thing that runs in families. You had much better say a severe chill.

JACK: You are sure a severe chill isn't hereditary, or anything of that kind?

ALGERNON: Of course it isn't!

JACK: Very well, then. My poor brother Ernest is carried off suddenly in Paris, by a severe chill. That gets rid of him.

ALGERNON: But I thought you said that—Miss Cardew was a little too much interested in your poor brother Ernest? Won't she feel his loss a good deal?

JACK: Oh, that is all right. Cecily is not a silly romantic girl, I am glad to say. She has got a capital appetite, goes on long walks, and pays no attention at all to her lessons.

ALGERNON: I would rather like to see Cecily.

JACK: I will take very good care you never do. She is excessively pretty, and she is only just eighteen.

ALGERNON: Have you told Gwendolen yet that you have an excessively pretty ward who is only just eighteen?

JACK: Oh! one doesn't blurt these things out to people. Cecily and Gwendolen are perfectly certain to be extremely great friends. I'll bet you anything you like that half an hour after they have met, they will be calling each other sister.

ALGERNON: Women only do that when they have called each other a lot of other things first. Now, my dear boy, if we want to get a good table at Willis's, we really must go and dress. Do you know it is nearly seven?

JACK (*irritably*): Oh! it always is nearly seven.

ALGERNON: Well, I'm hungry.

JACK: I never knew you when you weren't—

ALGERNON: What shall we do after dinner? Go to a theater?

JACK: Oh, no! I loathe listening.

ALGERNON: Well, let us go to the Club?

JACK: Oh, no! I hate talking.

ALGERNON: Well, we might trot round to the Empire° at ten?

JACK: Oh, no! I can't bear looking at things. It is so silly.

ALGERNON: Well, what shall we do?

JACK: Nothing!

ALGERNON: It is awfully hard work doing nothing. However, I don't mind hard work where there is no definite object of any kind.

(*Enter Lane.*)

LANE: Miss Fairfax.

(*Enter Gwendolen. Lane goes out.*)

ALGERNON: Gwendolen, upon my word!

GWENDOLEN: Algy, kindly turn your back. I have something very particular to say to Mr. Worthing.

ALGERNON: Really, Gwendolen, I don't think I can allow this at all.

GWENDOLEN: Algy, you always adopt a strictly immoral attitude towards life. You are not quite old enough to do that.

(*Algernon retires to the fireplace.*)

JACK: My own darling!

GWENDOLEN: Ernest, we may never be married. From the expression on Mama's face I fear we never shall. Few parents nowadays pay any regard to what their children say to them. The old-fashioned respect for the young is fast dying out. Whatever influence I ever had over Mama, I lost at the age of three. But although she may prevent us from becoming man and wife, and I may marry someone else, and marry often, nothing that she can possibly do can alter my eternal devotion to you.

JACK: Dear Gwendolen!

GWENDOLEN: The story of your romantic origin, as related to me by Mama, with unpleasing comments, has naturally stirred the deeper fibers of my nature. Your Christian name has an irresistible fascination. The simplicity of your character makes you exquisitely incomprehensible to me. Your town address at the Albany I have. What is your address in the country?

JACK: The Manor House, Woolton, Hertfordshire.

(*Algernon, who has been carefully listening, smiles to himself, and writes the address on his shirt cuff. Then picks up the Railway Guide.*)

GWENDOLEN: There is a good postal service, I suppose? It may be necessary to do something desperate. That of course will require serious consideration. I will communicate with you daily.

JACK: My own one!

Empire: Empire Theatre, a London music hall that was also a rendezvous for prostitutes.

Scene from the Huntington Theatre Company's 1994 production of *The Importance of Being Earnest.*

GWENDOLEN: How long do you remain in town?

JACK: Till Monday.

GWENDOLEN: Good! Algy, you may turn round now.

ALGERNON: Thanks, I've turned round already.

GWENDOLEN: You may also ring the bell.

JACK: You will let me see you to your carriage, my own darling?

GWENDOLEN: Certainly.

JACK (*to Lane, who now enters*): I will see Miss Fairfax out.

LANE: Yes, sir.   (*Jack and Gwendolen go off.*)

(*Lane presents several letters on a salver to Algernon. It is to be surmised that they are bills, as Algernon, after looking at the envelopes, tears them up.*)

ALGERNON: A glass of sherry, Lane.

LANE: Yes, sir.

ALGERNON: Tomorrow, Lane, I'm going Bunburying.

LANE: Yes, sir.

ALGERNON: I shall probably not be back till Monday. You can put up my dress clothes, my smoking jacket, and all the Bunbury suits—

LANE: Yes, sir.   (*Handing sherry.*)

ALGERNON: I hope tomorrow will be a fine day, Lane.

LANE: It never is, sir.

ALGERNON: Lane, you're a perfect pessimist.

LANE: I do my best to give satisfaction, sir.

(*Enter Jack. Lane goes off.*)

JACK: There's a sensible, intellectual girl! the only girl I ever cared for in my life. (*Algernon is laughing immoderately.*) What on earth are you so amused at?

ALGERNON: Oh, I'm a little anxious about poor Bunbury, that is all.

JACK: If you don't take care, your friend Bunbury will get you into a serious scrape some day.

ALGERNON: I love scrapes. They are the only things that are never serious.

JACK: Oh, that's nonsense, Algy. You never talk anything but nonsense.

ALGERNON: Nobody ever does.

(*Jack looks indignantly at him, and leaves the room. Algernon lights a cigarette, reads his shirt cuff, and smiles.*)

ACT II

(*Scene: Garden at the Manor House. A flight of gray stone steps leads up to the house. The garden, an old-fashioned one, full of roses. Time of year, July. Basket chairs, and a table covered with books, are set under a large yew tree. Miss Prism discovered seated at the table. Cecily is at the back watering flowers.*)

MISS PRISM (*calling*): Cecily, Cecily! Surely such a utilitarian occupation as the watering of flowers is rather Moulton's duty than yours? Especially at a moment when intellectual pleasures await you. Your German grammar is on the table. Pray open it at page fifteen. We will repeat yesterday's lesson.

CECILY (*coming over very slowly*): But I don't like German. It isn't at all a becoming language. I know perfectly well that I look quite plain after my German lesson.

MISS PRISM: Child, you know how anxious your guardian is that you should improve yourself in every way. He laid particular stress on your German, as he was leaving for town yesterday. Indeed, he always lays stress on your German when he is leaving for town.

CECILY: Dear Uncle Jack is so very serious! Sometimes he is so serious that I think he cannot be quite well.

MISS PRISM (*drawing herself up*): Your guardian enjoys the best of health, and his gravity of demeanor is especially to be commended in one so comparatively young as he is. I know no one who has a higher sense of duty and responsibility.

CECILY: I suppose that is why he often looks a little bored when we three are together.

MISS PRISM: Cecily! I am surprised at you. Mr. Worthing has many troubles in his life. Idle merriment and triviality would be out of place in his conversation. You must remember his constant anxiety about that unfortunate young man his brother.

CECILY: I wish Uncle Jack would allow that unfortunate young man, his brother, to come down here sometimes. We might have a good influence over him, Miss Prism. I am sure you certainly would. You know German, and geology, and things of that kind influence a man very much.

(*Cecily begins to write in her diary.*)

MISS PRISM (*shaking her head*): I do not think that even I could produce any effect on a character that according to his own brother's admission is irretrievably weak and vacillating. Indeed I am not sure that I would desire to reclaim him. I am not in favor of this modern mania for turning bad people into good people at a moment's notice. As a man sows so let him reap. You must put away your diary, Cecily. I really don't see why you should keep a diary at all.

CECILY: I keep a diary in order to enter the wonderful secrets of my life. If I didn't write them down I should probably forget all about them.

MISS PRISM: Memory, my dear Cecily, is the diary that we all carry about with us.

CECILY: Yes, but it usually chronicles the things that have never happened, and couldn't possibly have happened. I believe that Memory is responsible for nearly all the three-volume novels that Mudie sends us.

MISS PRISM: Do not speak slightingly of the three-volume novel, Cecily. I wrote one myself in earlier days.

CECILY: Did you really, Miss Prism? How wonderfully clever you are! I hope it did not end happily? I don't like novels that end happily. They depress me so much.

MISS PRISM: The good ended happily, and the bad unhappily. That is what Fiction means.

CECILY: I suppose so. But it seems very unfair. And was your novel ever published?

MISS PRISM: Alas! no. The manuscript unfortunately was abandoned. I use the word in the sense of lost or mislaid. To your work, child, these speculations are profitless.

CECILY (*smiling*): But I see dear Dr. Chasuble coming up through the garden.

MISS PRISM (*rising and advancing*): Dr. Chasuble! This is indeed a pleasure.

(*Enter Canon Chasuble.*)

CHASUBLE: And how are we this morning? Miss Prism, you are, I trust, well?

CECILY: Miss Prism has just been complaining of a slight headache. I think it would do her so much good to have a short stroll with you in the park, Dr. Chasuble.

MISS PRISM: Cecily, I have not mentioned anything about a headache.

CECILY: No, dear Miss Prism, I know that, but I felt instinctively that you had a headache. Indeed I was thinking about that, and not about my German lesson, when the Rector came in.

CHASUBLE: I hope, Cecily, you are not inattentive.

CECILY: Oh, I am afraid I am.

CHASUBLE: That is strange. Were I fortunate enough to be Miss Prism's pupil, I would hang upon her lips. (*Miss Prism glares.*) I spoke metaphorically.—My metaphor was drawn from bees. Ahem! Mr. Worthing, I suppose, has not returned from town yet?

MISS PRISM: We do not expect him till Monday afternoon.

CHASUBLE: Ah yes, he usually likes to spend his Sunday in London. He is not one of those whose sole aim is enjoyment, as, by all accounts, that unfortunate young man his brother seems to be. But I must not disturb Egeria° and her pupil any longer.

MISS PRISM: Egeria? My name is Lætitia, Doctor.

CHASUBLE (*bowing*): A classical allusion merely, drawn from the Pagan authors. I shall see you both no doubt at Evensong?

MISS PRISM: I think, dear Doctor, I will have a stroll with you. I find I have a headache after all, and a walk might do it good.

CHASUBLE: With pleasure, Miss Prism, with pleasure. We might go as far as the schools and back.

MISS PRISM: That would be delightful. Cecily, you will read your Political Economy in my absence. The chapter on the Fall of the Rupee° you may omit. It is somewhat too sensational. Even these metallic problems have their melodramatic side.

(*Goes down the garden with Dr. Chasuble.*)

CECILY (*picks up books and throws them back on table*): Horrid Political Economy! Horrid Geography! Horrid, horrid German!

(*Enter Merriman with a card on a salver.*)

MERRIMAN: Mr. Ernest Worthing has just driven over from the station. He has brought his luggage with him.

Egeria: Roman goddess of water.   Fall of the Rupee: Reference to the Indian rupee, whose steady deflation between 1873 and 1893 caused the Indian government finally to close the mints.

CECILY (*takes the card and reads it*): "Mr. Ernest Worthing, B.4, The Albany, W." Uncle Jack's brother! Did you tell him Mr. Worthing was in town?

MERRIMAN: Yes, Miss. He seemed very much disappointed. I mentioned that you and Miss Prism were in the garden. He said he was anxious to speak to you privately for a moment.

CECILY: Ask Mr. Ernest Worthing to come here. I suppose you had better talk to the housekeeper about a room for him.

MERRIMAN: Yes, Miss. (*Merriman goes off.*)

CECILY: I have never met any really wicked person before. I feel rather frightened. I am so afraid he will look just like everyone else.

(*Enter Algernon, very gay and debonair.*)

He does!

ALGERNON (*raising his hat*): You are my little cousin Cecily, I'm sure.

CECILY: You are under some strange mistake. I am not little. In fact, I believe I am more than usually tall for my age. (*Algernon is rather taken aback.*) But I am your cousin Cecily. You, I see from your card, are Uncle Jack's brother, my cousin Ernest, my wicked cousin Ernest.

ALGERNON: Oh! I am not really wicked at all, Cousin Cecily. You mustn't think that I am wicked.

CECILY: If you are not, then you have certainly been deceiving us all in a very inexcusable manner. I hope you have not been leading a double life, pretending to be wicked and being really good all the time. That would be hypocrisy.

ALGERNON (*looks at her in amazement*): Oh! Of course I have been rather reckless.

CECILY: I am glad to hear it.

ALGERNON: In fact, now you mention the subject, I have been very bad in my own small way.

CECILY: I don't think you should be so proud of that, though I am sure it must have been very pleasant.

ALGERNON: It is much pleasanter being here with you.

CECILY: I can't understand how you are here at all. Uncle Jack won't be back till Monday afternoon.

ALGERNON: That is a great disappointment. I am obliged to go up by the first train on Monday morning. I have a business appointment that I am anxious—to miss.

CECILY: Couldn't you miss it anywhere but in London?

ALGERNON: No: the appointment is in London.

CECILY: Well, I know, of course, how important it is not to keep a business engagement, if one wants to retain any sense of the beauty of life, but still I think you had better wait till Uncle Jack arrives. I know he wants to speak to you about your emigrating.

ALGERNON: About my what?

CECILY: Your emigrating. He has gone up to buy your outfit.

ALGERNON: I certainly wouldn't let Jack buy my outfit. He has no taste in neckties at all.

CECILY: I don't think you will require neckties. Uncle Jack is sending you to Australia.

ALGERNON: Australia! I'd sooner die.

CECILY: Well, he said at dinner on Wednesday night, that you would have to choose between this world, the next world, and Australia.

ALGERNON: Oh, well! The accounts I have received of Australia and the next world are not particularly encouraging. This world is good enough for me, Cousin Cecily.

CECILY: Yes, but are you good enough for it?

ALGERNON: I'm afraid I'm not that. That is why I want you to reform me. You might make that your mission, if you don't mind, Cousin Cecily.

CECILY: I'm afraid I've no time, this afternoon.

ALGERNON: Well, would you mind my reforming myself this afternoon?

CECILY: It is rather quixotic° of you. But I think you should try.

ALGERNON: I will. I feel better already.

CECILY: You are looking a little worse.

ALGERNON: That is because I am hungry.

CECILY: How thoughtless of me. I should have remembered that when one is going to lead an entirely new life, one requires regular and wholesome meals. Won't you come in?

ALGERNON: Thank you. Might I have a buttonhole° first? I never have any appetite unless I have a buttonhole first.

CECILY: A Maréchal Niel?°

ALGERNON: No, I'd sooner have a pink rose.

CECILY: Why? (*Cuts a flower.*)

ALGERNON: Because you are like a pink rose, Cousin Cecily.

CECILY: I don't think it can be right for you to talk to me like that. Miss Prism never says such things to me.

ALGERNON: Then Miss Prism is a shortsighted old lady. (*Cecily puts the rose in his buttonhole.*) You are the prettiest girl I ever saw.

CECILY: Miss Prism says that all good looks are a snare.

ALGERNON: They are a snare that every sensible man would like to be caught in.

CECILY: Oh! I don't think I would care to catch a sensible man. I shouldn't know what to talk to him about.

(*They pass into the house. Miss Prism and Dr. Chasuble return.*)

MISS PRISM: You are too much alone, dear Dr. Chasuble. You should get married. A misanthrope I can understand—a womanthrope, never!

CHASUBLE (*with a scholar's shudder*): Believe me, I do not deserve so neologistic a phrase. The precept as well as the practice of the Primitive Church was distinctly against matrimony.

---

quixotic: Foolishly impractical, from the idealistic hero of Cervantes' *Don Quixote*. **buttonhole:** Boutonniere. **Maréchal Niel:** A yellow rose.

MISS PRISM (*sententiously*): That is obviously the reason why the Primitive Church has not lasted up to the present day. And you do not seem to realize, dear Doctor, that by persistently remaining single, a man converts himself into a permanent public temptation. Men should be more careful; this very celibacy leads weaker vessels astray.

CHASUBLE: But is a man not equally attractive when married?

MISS PRISM: No married man is ever attractive except to his wife.

CHASUBLE: And often, I've been told, not even to her.

MISS PRISM: That depends on the intellectual sympathies of the woman. Maturity can always be depended on. Ripeness can be trusted. Young women are green. (*Dr. Chasuble starts.*) I spoke horticulturally. My metaphor was drawn from fruits. But where is Cecily?

CHASUBLE: Perhaps she followed us to the schools.

(*Enter Jack slowly from the back of the garden. He is dressed in the deepest mourning, with crepe hatband and black gloves.*)

MISS PRISM: Mr. Worthing!

CHASUBLE: Mr. Worthing?

MISS PRISM: This is indeed a surprise. We did not look for you till Monday afternoon.

JACK (*shakes Miss Prism's hand in a tragic manner*): I have returned sooner than I expected. Dr. Chasuble, I hope you are well?

CHASUBLE: Dear Mr. Worthing, I trust this garb of woe does not betoken some terrible calamity?

JACK: My brother.

MISS PRISM: More shameful debts and extravagance?

CHASUBLE: Still leading his life of pleasure?

JACK (*shaking his head*): Dead!

CHASUBLE: Your brother Ernest dead?

JACK: Quite dead.

MISS PRISM: What a lesson for him! I trust he will profit by it.

CHASUBLE: Mr. Worthing, I offer you my sincere condolence. You have at least the consolation of knowing that you were always the most generous and forgiving of brothers.

JACK: Poor Ernest! He had many faults, but it is a sad, sad blow.

CHASUBLE: Very sad indeed. Were you with him at the end?

JACK: No. He died abroad, in Paris, in fact. I had a telegram last night from the manager of the Grand Hotel.

CHASUBLE: Was the cause of death mentioned?

JACK: A severe chill, it seems.

MISS PRISM: As a man sows, so shall he reap.

CHASUBLE (*raising his hand*): Charity, dear Miss Prism, charity! None of us are perfect. I myself am peculiarly susceptible to drafts. Will the interment take place here?

JACK: No. He seemed to have expressed a desire to be buried in Paris.

CHASUBLE: In Paris! (*Shakes his head.*) I fear that hardly points to any very serious state of mind at the last. You would no doubt wish me to make some slight allusion to this tragic domestic affliction next Sunday. (*Jack presses his hand convulsively.*) My sermon on the meaning of the manna in the wilderness can be adapted to almost any occasion, joyful, or, as in the present case, distressing. (*All sigh.*) I have preached it at harvest celebrations, christenings, confirmations, on days of humiliation and festal days. The last time I delivered it was in the Cathedral, as a charity sermon on behalf of the Society for the Prevention of Discontent among the Upper Orders. The Bishop, who was present, was much struck by some of the analogies I drew.

JACK: Ah! that reminds me, you mentioned christenings I think, Dr. Chasuble? I suppose you know how to christen all right? (*Dr. Chasuble looks astounded.*) I mean, of course, you are continually christening, aren't you?

MISS PRISM: It is, I regret to say, one of the Rector's most constant duties in this parish. I have often spoken to the poorer classes on the subject. But they don't seem to know what thrift is.

CHASUBLE: But is there any particular infant in whom you are interested, Mr. Worthing? Your brother was, I believe, unmarried, was he not?

JACK: Oh yes.

MISS PRISM (*bitterly*): People who live entirely for pleasure usually are.

JACK: But it is not for any child, dear Doctor. I am very fond of children. No! the fact is, I would like to be christened myself, this afternoon, if you have nothing better to do.

CHASUBLE: But surely, Mr. Worthing, you have been christened already?

JACK: I don't remember anything about it.

CHASUBLE: But have you any grave doubts on the subject?

JACK: I certainly intend to have. Of course I don't know if the thing would bother you in any way, or if you think I am a little too old now.

CHASUBLE: Not at all. The sprinkling, and, indeed, the immersion of adults is a perfectly canonical practice.

JACK: Immersion!

CHASUBLE: You need have no apprehensions. Sprinkling is all that is necessary, or indeed I think advisable. Our weather is so changeable. At what hour would you wish the ceremony performed?

JACK: Oh, I might trot round about five if that would suit you.

CHASUBLE: Perfectly, perfectly! In fact I have two similar ceremonies to perform at that time. A case of twins that occurred recently in one of the outlying cottages on your own estate. Poor Jenkins the carter, a most hardworking man.

JACK: Oh! I don't see much fun in being christened along with other babies. It would be childish. Would half-past five do?

CHASUBLE: Admirably! Admirably! (*Takes out watch.*) And now, dear Mr. Worthing, I will not intrude any longer into a house of sorrow. I would merely beg you not to be too much bowed down by grief. What seem to us bitter trials are often blessings in disguise.

MISS PRISM: This seems to me a blessing of an extremely obvious kind.

(*Enter Cecily from the house.*)

CECILY: Uncle Jack! Oh, I am pleased to see you back. But what horrid clothes you have got on! Do go and change them.

MISS PRISM: Cecily!

CHASUBLE: My child! my child!

(*Cecily goes towards Jack; he kisses her brow in a melancholy manner.*)

CECILY: What is the matter, Uncle Jack? Do look happy! You look as if you had toothache, and I have got such a surprise for you. Who do you think is in the dining room? Your brother!

JACK: Who?

CECILY: Your brother Ernest. He arrived about half an hour ago.

JACK: What nonsense! I haven't got a brother.

CECILY: Oh, don't say that. However badly he may have behaved to you in the past he is still your brother. You couldn't be so heartless as to disown him. I'll tell him to come out. And you will shake hands with him, won't you, Uncle Jack?

(*Runs back into the house.*)

CHASUBLE: These are very joyful tidings.

MISS PRISM: After we had all been resigned to his loss, his sudden return seems to me peculiarly distressing.

JACK: My brother is in the dining room? I don't know what it all means. I think it is perfectly absurd.

(*Enter Algernon and Cecily hand in hand. They come slowly up to Jack.*)

JACK: Good heavens!   (*Motions Algernon away.*)

ALGERNON: Brother John, I have come down from town to tell you that I am very sorry for all the trouble I have given you, and that I intend to lead a better life in the future.

(*Jack glares at him and does not take his hand.*)

CECILY: Uncle Jack, you are not going to refuse your own brother's hand?

JACK: Nothing will induce me to take his hand. I think his coming down here disgraceful. He knows perfectly well why.

CECILY: Uncle Jack, do be nice. There is some good in everyone. Ernest has just been telling me about his poor invalid friend Mr. Bunbury whom he goes to visit so often. And surely there must be much good in one who is kind to an invalid, and leaves the pleasures of London to sit by a bed of pain.

JACK: Oh! he has been talking about Bunbury has he?

CECILY: Yes, he has told me all about poor Mr. Bunbury, and his terrible state of health.

JACK: Bunbury! Well, I won't have him talk to you about Bunbury or about anything else. It is enough to drive one perfectly frantic.

ALGERNON: Of course I admit that the faults were all on my side. But I must say that I think that Brother John's coldness to me is peculiarly painful. I expected a more enthusiastic welcome, especially considering it is the first time I have come here.

CECILY: Uncle Jack, if you don't shake hands with Ernest I will never forgive you.

JACK: Never forgive me?

CECILY: Never, never, never!

JACK: Well, this is the last time I shall ever do it.

(*Shakes hands with Algernon and glares.*)

CHASUBLE: It's pleasant, is it not, to see so perfect a reconciliation? I think we might leave the two brothers together.

MISS PRISM: Cecily, you will come with us.

CECILY: Certainly, Miss Prism. My little task of reconciliation is over.

CHASUBLE: You have done a beautiful action today, dear child.

MISS PRISM: We must not be premature in our judgments.

CECILY: I feel very happy.   (*They all go off.*)

JACK: You young scoundrel, Algy, you must get out of this place as soon as possible. I don't allow any Bunburying here.

(*Enter Merriman.*)

MERRIMAN: I have put Mr. Ernest's things in the room next to yours, sir. I suppose that is all right?

JACK: What?

MERRIMAN: Mr. Ernest's luggage, sir. I have unpacked it and put it in the room next to your own.

JACK: His luggage?

MERRIMAN: Yes, sir. Three portmanteaus, a dressing case, two hatboxes, and a large luncheon basket.

ALGERNON: I am afraid 1 can't stay more than a week this time.

JACK: Merriman, order the dog cart at once. Mr. Ernest has been suddenly called back to town.

MERRIMAN: Yes, sir.   (*Goes back into the house.*)

ALGERNON: What a fearful liar you are, Jack. I have not been called back to town at all.

JACK: Yes, you have.

ALGERNON: I haven't heard anyone call me.

JACK: Your duty as a gentleman calls you back.

ALGERNON: My duty as a gentleman has never interfered with my pleasures in the smallest degree.

JACK: I can quite understand that.

ALGERNON: Well, Cecily is a darling.

JACK: You are not to talk of Miss Cardew like that. I don't like it.

ALGERNON: Well, I don't like your clothes. You look perfectly ridiculous in them. Why on earth don't you go up and change? It is perfectly childish to be in deep mourning for a man who is actually staying for a whole week in your house as a guest. I call it grotesque.

JACK: You are certainly not staying with me for a whole week as a guest or anything else. You have got to leave—by the four-five train.

ALGERNON: I certainly won't leave you so long as you are in mourning. It would be most unfriendly. If I were in mourning you would stay with me, I suppose. I should think it very unkind if you didn't.

JACK: Well, will you go if I change my clothes?

ALGERNON: Yes, if you are not too long. I never saw anybody take so long to dress, and with such little result.

JACK: Well, at any rate, that is better than being always overdressed as you are.

ALGERNON: If I am occasionally a little overdressed, I make up for it by being always immensely overeducated.

JACK: Your vanity is ridiculous, your conduct an outrage, and your presence in my garden utterly absurd. However, you have got to catch the four-five, and I hope you will have a pleasant journey back to town. This Bunburying, as you call it, has not been a great success for you.

(*Goes into the house.*)

ALGERNON: I think it has been a great success. I'm in love with Cecily, and that is everything.

(*Enter Cecily at the back of the garden. She picks up the can and begins to water the flowers.*)

But I must see her before I go, and make arrangements for another Bunbury. Ah, there she is.

CECILY: Oh, I merely came back to water the roses. I thought you were with Uncle Jack.

ALGERNON: He's gone to order the dog cart for me.

CECILY: Oh, is he going to take you for a nice drive?

ALGERNON: He's going to send me away.

CECILY: Then have we got to part?

ALGERNON: I am afraid so. It's a very painful parting.

CECILY: It is always painful to part from people whom one has known for a very brief space of time. The absence of old friends one can endure with equanimity. But even a momentary separation from anyone to whom one has just been introduced is almost unbearable.

ALGERNON: Thank you.

(*Enter Merriman.*)

MERRIMAN: The dog cart is at the door, sir.

(*Algernon looks appealingly at Cecily.*)

CECILY: It can wait, Merriman—for—five minutes.

MERRIMAN: Yes, miss.   (*Exit Merriman.*)

ALGERNON: I hope, Cecily, I shall not offend you if I state quite frankly and openly that you seem to me to be in every way the visible personification of absolute perfection.

CECILY: I think your frankness does you great credit, Ernest. If you will allow me I will copy your remarks into my diary.

(*Goes over to table and begins writing in diary.*)

ALGERNON: Do you really keep a diary? I'd give anything to look at it. May I?

CECILY: Oh no. (*Puts her hand over it.*) You see, it is simply a very young girl's record of her own thoughts and impressions, and consequently meant for publication. When it appears in volume form I hope you will order a copy. But pray, Ernest, don't stop. I delight in taking down from dictation. I have reached "absolute perfection." You can go on. I am quite ready for more.

ALGERNON (*somewhat taken aback*): Ahem! Ahem!

CECILY: Oh, don't cough, Ernest. When one is dictating one should speak fluently and not cough. Besides, I don't know how to spell a cough.

(*Writes as Algernon speaks.*)

ALGERNON (*speaking very rapidly*): Cecily, ever since I first looked upon your wonderful and incomparable beauty, I have dared to love you wildly, passionately, devotedly, hopelessly.

CECILY: I don't think that you should tell me that you love me wildly, passionately, devotedly, hopelessly. Hopelessly doesn't seem to make much sense, does it?

ALGERNON: Cecily!

(*Enter Merriman.*)

MERRIMAN: The dog cart is waiting, sir.

ALGERNON: Tell it to come round next week, at the same hour.

MERRIMAN (*looks at Cecily, who makes no sign*): Yes, sir.
(*Merriman retires.*)

CECILY: Uncle Jack would be very much annoyed if he knew you were staying on till next week, at the same hour.

ALGERNON: Oh, I don't care about Jack. I don't care for anybody in the whole world but you. I love you, Cecily. You will marry me, won't you?

CECILY: You silly boy! Of course. Why, we have been engaged for the last three months.

ALGERNON: For the last three months?

CECILY: Yes, it will be exactly three months on Thursday.

ALGERNON: But how did we become engaged?

CECILY: Well, ever since dear Uncle Jack first confessed to us that he had a younger brother who was very wicked and bad, you of course have formed the chief topic of conversation between myself and Miss Prism. And of course a man who is much talked about is always very attractive. One feels there must be something in him after all. I daresay it was foolish of me, but I fell in love with you, Ernest.

ALGERNON: Darling! And when was the engagement actually settled?

CECILY: On the 14th of February last. Worn out by your entire ignorance of my existence, I determined to end the matter one way or the other, and after a long struggle with myself I accepted you under this dear old tree here. The next day I bought this little ring in your name, and this is the little bangle with the true lovers' knot I promised you always to wear.

ALGERNON: Did I give you this? It's very pretty, isn't it?

CECILY: Yes, you've wonderfully good taste, Ernest. It's the excuse I've always given for your leading such a bad life. And this is the box in which I keep all your dear letters.

(*Kneels at table, opens box, and produces letters tied up with blue ribbon.*)

ALGERNON: My letters! But my own sweet Cecily, I have never written you any letters.

CECILY: You need hardly remind me of that, Ernest. I remember only too well that I was forced to write your letters for you. I wrote always three times a week, and sometimes oftener.

ALGERNON: Oh, do let me read them, Cecily!

CECILY: Oh, I couldn't possibly. They would make you far too conceited. (*Replaces box.*) The three you wrote me after I had broken off the engagement are so beautiful, and so badly spelled, that even now I can hardly read them without crying a little.

ALGERNON: But was our engagement ever broken off?

CECILY: Of course it was. On the 22nd of last March. You can see the entry if you like. (*Shows diary.*) "Today I broke off my engagement with Ernest. I feel it is better to do so. The weather still continues charming."

ALGERNON: But why on earth did you break it off? What had I done? I had done nothing at all. Cecily, I am very much hurt indeed to hear you broke it off. Particularly when the weather was so charming.

CECILY: It would hardly have been a really serious engagement if it hadn't been broken off at least once. But I forgave you before the week was out.

ALGERNON (*crossing to her, and kneeling*): What a perfect angel you are, Cecily.

CECILY: You dear romantic boy. (*He kisses her; she puts her fingers through his hair.*) I hope your hair curls naturally, does it?

ALGERNON: Yes, darling, with a little help from others.

CECILY: I am so glad.

ALGERNON: You'll never break off our engagement again, Cecily?

CECILY: I don't think I could break it off now that I have actually met you. Besides, of course, there is the question of your name.

ALGERNON (*nervously*): Yes, of course.

CECILY: You must not laugh at me, darling, but it had always been a girlish dream of mine to love someone whose name was Ernest. (*Algernon rises, Cecily also.*) There is something in that name that seems to inspire absolute confidence. I pity any poor married woman whose husband is not called Ernest.

ALGERNON: But, my dear child, do you mean to say you could not love me if I had some other name?

CECILY: But what name?

ALGERNON: Oh, any name you like—Algernon—for instance—

CECILY: But I don't like the name of Algernon.

ALGERNON: Well, my own dear, sweet, loving little darling, I really can't see why you should object to the name of Algernon. It is not at all a bad name. In fact, it is rather an aristocratic name. Half of the chaps who get into the Bankruptcy Court are called Algernon. But seriously, Cecily—(*moving to her*)—if my name was Algy, couldn't you love me?

CECILY (*rising*): I might respect you, Ernest, I might admire your character, but I fear that I should not be able to give you my undivided attention.

ALGERNON: Ahem! Cecily! (*Picking up hat.*) Your Rector here is, I suppose, thoroughly experienced in the practice of all the rites and ceremonials of the Church?

CECILY: Oh yes. Dr. Chasuble is a most learned man. He has never written a single book, so you can imagine how much he knows.

ALGERNON: I must see him at once on a most important christening—I mean on most important business.

CECILY: Oh!

ALGERNON: I shan't be away more than half an hour.

CECILY: Considering that we have been engaged since February the 14th, and that I only met you today for the first time, I think it is rather hard that you should leave me for so long a period as half an hour. Couldn't you make it twenty minutes?

ALGERNON: I'll be back in no time.

(*Kisses her and rushes down the garden.*)

CECILY: What an impetuous boy he is! I like his hair so much. I must enter his proposal in my diary.

(*Enter Merriman.*)

MERRIMAN: A Miss Fairfax has just called to see Mr. Worthing. On very important business Miss Fairfax states.

CECILY: Isn't Mr. Worthing in his library?

MERRIMAN: Mr. Worthing went over in the direction of the Rectory some time ago.

CECILY: Pray ask the lady to come out here; Mr. Worthing is sure to be back soon. And you can bring tea.

MERRIMAN: Yes, miss. (*Goes out.*)

CECILY: Miss Fairfax! I suppose one of the many good elderly women who are associated with Uncle Jack in some of his philanthropic work in London. I don't quite like women who are interested in philanthropic work. I think it is so forward of them.

(*Enter Merriman.*)

MERRIMAN: Miss Fairfax.

(*Enter Gwendolen. Exit Merriman.*)

CECILY (*advancing to meet her*): Pray let me introduce myself to you. My name is Cecily Cardew.

GWENDOLEN: Cecily Cardew? (*Moving to her and shaking hands.*) What a very sweet name! Something tells me that we are going to be great friends. I like you already more than I can say. My first impressions of people are never wrong.

CECILY: How nice of you to like me so much after we have known each other such a comparatively short time. Pray sit down.

GWENDOLEN (*still standing up*): I may call you Cecily, may I not?

CECILY: With pleasure!

GWENDOLEN: And you will always call me Gwendolen, won't you?

CECILY: If you wish.

GWENDOLEN: Then that is all quite settled, is it not?

CECILY: I hope so.

(*A pause. They both sit down together.*)

GWENDOLEN: Perhaps this might be a favorable opportunity for my mentioning who I am. My father is Lord Bracknell. You have never heard of Papa, I suppose?

CECILY: I don't think so.

GWENDOLEN: Outside the family circle, Papa, I am glad to say, is entirely unknown. I think that is quite as it should be. The home seems to me to be the proper sphere for the man. And certainly once a man begins to neglect his domestic duties he becomes painfully effeminate, does he not? And I don't like that. It makes men so very attractive. Cecily, Mama, whose views on education are remarkably strict, has brought me up to be extremely shortsighted; it is part of her system, so do you mind my looking at you through my glasses?

CECILY: Oh! not at all, Gwendolen. I am very fond of being looked at.

GWENDOLEN (*after examining Cecily carefully through a lorgnette*): You are here on a short visit I suppose?

CECILY: Oh no! I live here.

GWENDOLEN (*severely*): Really? Your mother, no doubt, or some female relative of advanced years, resides here also?

CECILY: Oh no! I have no mother, nor, in fact, any relations.

GWENDOLEN: Indeed?

CECILY: My dear guardian, with the assistance of Miss Prism, has the arduous task of looking after me.

GWENDOLEN: Your guardian?

CECILY: Yes, I am Mr. Worthing's ward.

GWENDOLEN: Oh! It is strange he never mentioned to me that he had a ward. How secretive of him! He grows more interesting hourly. I am not sure, however, that the news inspires me with feelings of unmixed delight. (*Rising and going to her.*) I am very fond of you, Cecily; I have liked you ever since I met you! But I am bound to state that now that I know that you are Mr. Worthing's ward, I cannot help expressing a wish you were—well just a little older than you seem to be—and not quite so very alluring in appearance. In fact, if I may speak candidly—

CECILY: Pray do! I think that whenever one has anything unpleasant to say, one should always be quite candid.

GWENDOLEN: Well, to speak with perfect candor, Cecily, I wish that you were fully forty-two, and more than usually plain for your age. Ernest has a strong upright nature. He is the very soul of truth and honor. Disloyalty would be as impossible to him as deception. But even men of the noblest possible moral character are extremely susceptible to the influence of the physical charms of others. Modern, no less than Ancient History, supplies us with many most painful examples of what I refer to. If it were not so, indeed, History would be quite unreadable.

CECILY: I beg your pardon, Gwendolen, did you say Ernest?

GWENDOLEN: Yes.

CECILY: Oh, but it is not Mr. Ernest Worthing who is my guardian. It is his brother—his elder brother.

GWENDOLEN (*sitting down again*): Ernest never mentioned to me that he had a brother.

CECILY: I am sorry to say they have not been on good terms for a long time.

GWENDOLEN: Ah! that accounts for it. And now that I think of it I have never heard any man mention his brother. The subject seems distasteful to most men. Cecily, you have lifted a load from my mind. I was growing almost anxious. It would have been terrible if any cloud had come across a friendship like ours, would it not? Of course you are quite, quite sure that it is not Mr. Ernest Worthing who is your guardian?

CECILY: Quite sure. (*A pause.*) In fact, I am going to be his.

GWENDOLEN (*inquiringly*): I beg your pardon?

CECILY (*rather shy and confidingly*): Dearest Gwendolen, there is no reason why I should make a secret of it to you. Our little county newspaper is sure to chronicle the fact next week. Mr. Ernest Worthing and I are engaged to be married.

GWENDOLEN (*quite politely, rising*): My darling Cecily, I think there must be some slight error. Mr. Ernest Worthing is engaged to me. The announcement will appear in the *Morning Post* on Saturday at the latest.

CECILY (*very politely, rising*): I am afraid you must be under some misconception. Ernest proposed to me exactly ten minutes ago. (*Shows diary.*)

GWENDOLEN (*examines diary through her lorgnette carefully*): It is certainly very curious, for he asked me to be his wife yesterday afternoon at 5:30. If you would care to verify the incident, pray do so. (*Produces diary of her own.*) I never travel without my diary. One should always have something sensational to read in the train. I am so sorry, dear Cecily, if it is any disappointment to you, but I am afraid *I* have the prior claim.

CECILY: It would distress me more than I can tell you, dear Gwendolen, if it caused you any mental or physical anguish, but I feel bound to point out that since Ernest proposed to you he clearly has changed his mind.

GWENDOLEN (*meditatively*): If the poor fellow has been entrapped into any foolish promise I shall consider it my duty to rescue him at once, and with a firm hand.

CECILY (*thoughtfully and sadly*): Whatever unfortunate entanglement my dear boy may have got into, I will never reproach him with it after we are married.

GWENDOLEN: Do you allude to me, Miss Cardew, as an entanglement? You are presumptuous. On an occasion of this kind it becomes more than a moral duty to speak one's mind. It becomes a pleasure.

CECILY: Do you suggest, Miss Fairfax, that I entrapped Ernest into an engagement? How dare you? This is no time for wearing the shallow mask of manners. When I see a spade I call it a spade.

GWENDOLEN (*satirically*): I am glad to say that I have never seen a spade. It is obvious that our social spheres have been widely different.

(*Enter Merriman, followed by the Footman. He carries a salver, tablecloth, and plate stand. Cecily is about to retort. The presence of the servants exercises a restraining influence, under which both girls chafe.*)

MERRIMAN: Shall I lay tea here as usual, miss?

CECILY (*sternly, in a calm voice*): Yes, as usual.

(*Merriman begins to clear table and lay cloth. A long pause. Cecily and Gwendolen glare at each other.*)

GWENDOLEN: Are there many interesting walks in the vicinity, Miss Cardew?

CECILY: Oh! Yes! a great many. From the top of one of the hills quite close one can see five counties.

GWENDOLEN: Five counties! I don't think I should like that. I hate crowds.

CECILY (*sweetly*): I suppose that is why you live in town?

(*Gwendolen bites her lip, and beats her foot nervously with her parasol.*)

GWENDOLEN (*looking round*): Quite a well-kept garden this is, Miss Cardew.

CECILY: So glad you like it, Miss Fairfax.

GWENDOLEN: I had no idea there were any flowers in the country.

CECILY: Oh, flowers are as common here, Miss Fairfax, as people are in London.

GWENDOLEN: Personally I cannot understand how anybody manages to exist in the country, if anybody who is anybody does. The country always bores me to death.

CECILY: Ah! This is what the newspapers call agricultural depression, is it not? I believe the aristocracy are suffering very much from it just at present. It is almost an epidemic amongst them, I have been told. May I offer you some tea, Miss Fairfax?

GWENDOLEN (*with elaborate politeness*): Thank you. (*Aside.*) Detestable girl! But I require tea!

CECILY (*sweetly*): Sugar?

GWENDOLEN (*superciliously*): No, thank you. Sugar is not fashionable anymore.

(*Cecily looks angrily at her, takes up the tongs, and puts four lumps of sugar into the cup.*)

CECILY (*severely*): Cake or bread and butter?

GWENDOLEN (*in a bored manner*): Bread and butter, please. Cake is rarely seen at the best houses nowadays.

CECILY (*cuts a very large slice of cake, and puts it on the tray*): Hand that to Miss Fairfax.

(*Merriman does so, and goes out with Footman. Gwendolen drinks the tea and makes a grimace. Puts down cup at once, reaches out her hand to the bread and butter, looks at it, and finds it is cake. Rises in indignation.*)

GWENDOLEN: You have filled my tea with lumps of sugar, and though I asked most distinctly for bread and butter, you have given me cake. I am known for the gentleness of my disposition, and the extraordinary sweetness of my nature, but I warn you, Miss Cardew, you may go too far.

CECILY (*rising*): To save my poor, innocent, trusting boy from the machinations of any other girl there are no lengths to which I would not go.

GWENDOLEN: From the moment I saw you I distrusted you. I felt that you were false and deceitful. I am never deceived in such matters. My first impressions of people are invariably right.

CECILY: It seems to me, Miss Fairfax, that I am trespassing on your valuable time. No doubt you have many other calls of a similar character to make in the neighborhood.

(*Enter Jack.*)

GWENDOLEN (*catching sight of him*): Ernest! My own Ernest!

JACK: Gwendolen! Darling!   (*Offers to kiss her.*)

GWENDOLEN (*drawing back*): A moment! May I ask if you are engaged to be married to this young lady? (*Points to Cecily.*)

JACK (*laughing*): To dear little Cecily! Of course not! What could have put such an idea into your pretty little head?

GWENDOLEN: Thank you. You may!

(*Offers her cheek.*)

CECILY (*very sweetly*): I knew there must be some misunderstanding, Miss Fairfax. The gentleman whose arm is at present round your waist is my dear guardian, Mr. John Worthing.

GWENDOLEN: I beg your pardon?

CECILY: This is Uncle Jack.

GWENDOLEN (*receding*): Jack! Oh!

(*Enter Algernon.*)

CECILY: Here is Ernest.

ALGERNON (*goes straight over to Cecily without noticing anyone else*): My own love!

(*Offers to kiss her.*)

CECILY (*drawing back*): A moment, Ernest! May I ask you—are you engaged to be married to this young lady?

ALGERNON (*looking round*): To what young lady? Good heavens! Gwendolen!

CECILY: Yes! to good heavens, Gwendolen, I mean to Gwendolen.

ALGERNON (*laughing*): Of course not! What could have put such an idea into your pretty little head?

CECILY: Thank you. (*Presenting her cheek to be kissed.*) You may. (*Algernon kisses her.*)

GWENDOLEN: I felt there was some slight error, Miss Cardew. The gentleman who is now embracing you is my cousin, Mr. Algernon Moncrieff.

CECILY (*breaking away from Algernon*): Algernon Moncrieff! Oh!

(*The two girls move towards each other and put their arms round each other's waists as if for protection.*)

CECILY: Are you called Algernon?

ALGERNON: I cannot deny it.

CECILY: Oh!

GWENDOLEN: Is your name really John?

JACK (*standing rather proudly*): I could deny it if I liked. I could deny anything if I liked. But my name certainly is John. It has been John for years.

CECILY (*to Gwendolen*): A gross deception has been practiced on both of us.

GWENDOLEN: My poor wounded Cecily!

CECILY: My sweet wronged Gwendolen!

GWENDOLEN (*slowly and seriously*): You will call me sister, will you not?

(*They embrace. Jack and Algernon groan and walk up and down.*)

CECILY (*rather brightly*): There is just one question I would like to be allowed to ask my guardian.

GWENDOLEN: An admirable idea! Mr. Worthing, there is just one question I would like to be permitted to put to you. Where is your brother Ernest? We are both engaged to be married to your brother Ernest, so it is a matter of some importance to us to know where your brother Ernest is at present.

JACK (*slowly and hesitatingly*): Gwendolen—Cecily—it is very painful for me to be forced to speak the truth. It is the first time in my life that I have ever been reduced to such a painful position, and I am really quite inexperienced in doing anything of the kind. However I will tell you quite frankly that I have no brother Ernest. I have no brother at all. I never had a brother in my life, and I certainly have not the smallest intention of ever having one in the future.

CECILY (*surprised*): No brother at all?

JACK (*cheerily*): None!

GWENDOLEN (*severely*): Had you never a brother of any kind?

JACK (*pleasantly*): Never. Not even of any kind.

GWENDOLEN: I am afraid it is quite clear, Cecily, that neither of us is engaged to be married to anyone.

CECILY: It is not a very pleasant position for a young girl suddenly to find herself in. Is it?

GWENDOLEN: Let us go into the house. They will hardly venture to come after us there.

CECILY: No, men are so cowardly, aren't they?

(*They retire into the house with scornful looks.*)

JACK: This ghastly state of things is what you call Bunburying, I suppose?

ALGERNON: Yes, and a perfectly wonderful Bunbury it is. The most wonderful Bunbury I have ever had in my life.

JACK: Well, you've no right whatsoever to Bunbury here.

ALGERNON: That is absurd. One has a right to Bunbury anywhere one chooses. Every serious Bunburyist knows that.

JACK: Serious Bunburyist! Good heavens!

ALGERNON: Well, one must be serious about something, if one wants to have any amusement in life. I happen to be serious about Bunburying. What on earth you are serious about I haven't got the remotest idea. About everything, I should fancy. You have such an absolutely trivial nature.

JACK: Well, the only small satisfaction I have in the whole of this wretched business is that your friend Bunbury is quite exploded. You won't be able to run down to the country quite so often as you used to do, dear Algy. And a very good thing too.

ALGERNON: Your brother is a little off color, isn't he, dear Jack? You won't be able to disappear to London quite so frequently as your wicked custom was. And not a bad thing either.

JACK: As for your conduct towards Miss Cardew, I must say that your taking in a sweet, simple, innocent girl like that is quite inexcusable. To say nothing of the fact that she is my ward.

ALGERNON: I can see no possible defense at all for your deceiving a brilliant, clever, thoroughly experienced young lady like Miss Fairfax. To say nothing of the fact that she is my cousin.

JACK: I wanted to be engaged to Gwendolen, that is all. I love her.

ALGERNON: Well, I simply wanted to be engaged to Cecily. I adore her.

JACK: There is certainly no chance of your marrying Miss Cardew.

ALGERNON: I don't think there is much likelihood, Jack, of you and Miss Fairfax being united.

JACK: Well, that is no business of yours.

ALGERNON: If it was my business, I wouldn't talk about it. (*Begins to eat muffins.*) It is very vulgar to talk about one's business. Only people like stockbrokers do that, and then merely at dinner parties.

JACK: How you can sit there, calmly eating muffins when we are in this horrible trouble. I can't make out. You seem to me to be perfectly heartless.

ALGERNON: Well, I can't eat muffins in an agitated manner. The butter would probably get on my cuffs. One should always eat muffins quite calmly. It is the only way to eat them.

JACK: I say it's perfectly heartless your eating muffins at all, under the circumstances.

ALGERNON: When I am in trouble, eating is the only thing that consoles me. Indeed, when I am in really great trouble, as anyone who knows me intimately will tell you, I refuse everything except food and drink. At the present moment I am eating muffins because I am unhappy. Besides, I am particularly fond of muffins. (*Rising.*)

JACK (*rising*): Well, that is no reason why you should eat them all in that greedy way.

(*Takes muffins from Algernon.*)

ALGERNON (*offering tea cake*): I wish you would have tea cake instead. I don't like tea cake.

JACK: Good heavens! I suppose a man may eat his own muffins in his own garden.

ALGERNON: But you have just said it was perfectly heartless to eat muffins.

JACK: I said it was perfectly heartless of you, under the circumstances. That is a very different thing.

ALGERNON: That may be, but the muffins are the same. (*He seizes the muffin dish from Jack.*)

JACK: Algy, I wish to goodness you would go.

ALGERNON: You can't possibly ask me to go without having some dinner. It's absurd. I never go without my dinner. No one ever does, except vegetarians and people like that. Besides I have just made arrangements, with Dr. Chasuble to be christened at a quarter to six under the name of Ernest.

JACK: My dear fellow, the sooner you give up that nonsense the better. I made arrangements this morning with Dr. Chasuble to be christened myself at 5:30, and I naturally will take the name of Ernest. Gwendolen would wish it. We can't both be christened Ernest. It's absurd. Besides, I have a perfect right to be christened if I like. There is no evidence at all that I ever have been christened by anybody. I should think it extremely probable I never was, and so does Dr. Chasuble. It is entirely different in your case. You have been christened already.

ALGERNON: Yes, but I have not been christened for years.

JACK: Yes, but you have been christened. That is the important thing.

ALGERNON: Quite so. So I know my constitution can stand it. If you are not quite sure about your ever having been christened, I must say I think it rather dangerous your venturing on it now. It might make you very unwell. You can hardly have forgotten that someone very closely connected with you was very nearly carried off this week in Paris by a severe chill.

JACK: Yes, but you said yourself that a severe chill was not hereditary.

ALGERNON: It usen't to be, I know—but I daresay it is now. Science is always making wonderful improvements in things.

JACK (*picking up the muffin dish*): Oh, that is nonsense; you are always talking nonsense.

ALGERNON: Jack, you are at the muffins again! I wish you wouldn't. There are only two left. (*Takes them.*) I told you I was particularly fond of muffins.

JACK: But I hate tea cake.

ALGERNON: Why on earth then do you allow tea cake to be served up for your guests? What ideas you have of hospitality!

JACK: Algernon! I have already told you to go. I don't want you here. Why don't you go!

ALGERNON: I haven't quite finished my tea yet! and there is still one muffin left.

(*Jack groans, and sinks into a chair. Algernon still continues eating.*)

ACT III

(*Scene: Morning room at the Manor House. Gwendolen and Cecily are at the window, looking out into the garden.*)

GWENDOLEN: The fact that they did not follow us at once into the house, as anyone else would have done, seems to me to show that they have some sense of shame left.

CECILY: They have been eating muffins. That looks like repentance.

GWENDOLEN (*after a pause*): They don't seem to notice us at all. Couldn't you cough?

CECILY: But I haven't got a cough.

GWENDOLEN: They're looking at us. What effrontery!

CECILY: They're approaching. That's very forward of them.

GWENDOLEN: Let us preserve a dignified silence.

CECILY: Certainly. It's the only thing to do now.

(*Enter Jack followed by Algernon. They whistle some dreadful popular air from a British opera.*)

GWENDOLEN: This dignified silence seems to produce an unpleasant effect.

CECILY: A most distasteful one.

GWENDOLEN: But we will not be the first to speak.

CECILY: Certainly not.

GWENDOLEN: Mr. Worthing, I have something very particular to ask you. Much depends on your reply.

CECILY: Gwendolen, your common sense is invaluable. Mr. Moncrieff, kindly answer me the following question. Why did you pretend to be my guardian's brother?

ALGERNON: In order that I might have an opportunity of meeting you.

CECILY (*to Gwendolen*): That certainly seems a satisfactory explanation, does it not?

GWENDOLEN: Yes, dear, if you can believe him.

CECILY: I don't. But that does not affect the wonderful beauty of his answer.

GWENDOLEN: True. In matters of grave importance, style, not sincerity is the vital thing. Mr. Worthing, what explanation can you offer to me for pretending to have a brother? Was it in order that you might have an opportunity of coming up to town to see me as often as possible?

JACK: Can you doubt it, Miss Fairfax?

GWENDOLEN: I have the gravest doubts upon the subject. But I intend to crush them. This is not the moment for German skepticism. (*Moving to Cecily.*) Their explanations appear to be quite satisfactory, especially Mr. Worthing's. That seems to me to have the stamp of truth upon it.

CECILY: I am more than content with what Mr. Moncrieff said. His voice alone inspires one with absolute credulity.

GWENDOLEN: Then you think we should forgive them?

CECILY: Yes. I mean no.

GWENDOLEN: True! I had forgotten. There are principles at stake that one cannot surrender. Which of us should tell them? The task is not a pleasant one.

CECILY: Could we not both speak at the same time?

GWENDOLEN: An excellent idea! I nearly always speak at the same time as other people. Will you take the time from me?

CECILY: Certainly.

(*Gwendolen beats time with uplifted finger.*)

GWENDOLEN AND CECILY (*speaking together*): Your Christian names are still an insuperable barrier. That is all!

JACK AND ALGERNON (*speaking together*): Our Christian names! Is that all? But we are going to be christened this afternoon.

GWENDOLEN (*to Jack*): For my sake you are prepared to do this terrible thing?

JACK: I am!

CECILY (*to Algernon*): To please me you are ready to face this fearful ordeal?

ALGERNON: I am!

GWENDOLEN: How absurd to talk of the equality of the sexes! Where questions of self-sacrifice are concerned, men are infinitely beyond us.

JACK: We are! (*Clasps hands with Algernon.*)

CECILY: They have moments of physical courage of which we women know absolutely nothing.

GWENDOLEN (*to Jack*): Darling!

ALGERNON (*to Cecily*): Darling!

(*They fall into each other's arms.*)

(*Enter Merriman. When he enters he coughs loudly, seeing the situation.*)

MERRIMAN: Ahem! Ahem! Lady Bracknell!

JACK: Good heavens!

(*Enter Lady Bracknell. The couples separate, in alarm. Exit Merriman.*)

LADY BRACKNELL: Gwendolen! What does this mean?

GWENDOLEN: Merely that I am engaged to be married to Mr. Worthing, Mama.

LADY BRACKNELL: Come here. Sit down. Sit down immediately. Hesitation of any kind is a sign of mental decay in the young, of physical weakness in the old. (*Turns to Jack.*) Apprised, sir, of my daughter's sudden flight by her trusty maid, whose confidence I purchased by means of a small coin, I followed her at once by a luggage train. Her unhappy father is, I am glad to say, under the impression that she is attending a more than usually lengthy lecture by the University Extension Scheme on the influence of a permanent income on thought. I do not propose to undeceive him. Indeed I have never undeceived him on any question. I would consider it wrong. But of course, you will clearly understand that all communication between yourself and my daughter must cease immediately from this moment. On this point, as indeed on all points, I am firm.

JACK: I am engaged to be married to Gwendolen, Lady Bracknell!

LADY BRACKNELL: You are nothing of the kind, sir. And now, as regards Algernon!—Algernon!

ALGERNON: Yes, Aunt Augusta.

LADY BRACKNELL: May I ask if it is in this house that your invalid friend Mr. Bunbury resides?

ALGERNON (*stammering*): Oh! No! Bunbury doesn't live here. Bunbury is somewhere else at present. In fact, Bunbury is dead.

LADY BRACKNELL: Dead! When did Mr. Bunbury die? His death must have been extremely sudden.

ALGERNON (*airily*): Oh! I killed Bunbury this afternoon. I mean poor Bunbury died this afternoon.

LADY BRACKNELL: What did he die of?

ALGERNON: Bunbury? Oh, he was quite exploded.

LADY BRACKNELL: Exploded! Was he the victim of a revolutionary outrage? I was not aware that Mr. Bunbury was interested in social legislation. If so, he is well punished for his morbidity.

ALGERNON: My dear Aunt Augusta, I mean he was found out! The doctors found out that Bunbury could not live, that is what I mean—so Bunbury died.

LADY BRACKNELL: He seems to have had great confidence in the opinion of his physicians. I am glad, however, that he made up his mind at the last to some definite course of action, and acted under proper medical advice. And now that we have finally got rid of this Mr. Bunbury, may I ask, Mr. Worthing, who is that young person whose hand my nephew Algernon is now holding in what seems to me a peculiarly unnecessary manner?

JACK: That lady is Miss Cecily Cardew, my ward.

(*Lady Bracknell bows coldly to Cecily.*)

ALGERNON: I am engaged to be married to Cecily, Aunt Augusta.

Eric Stoltz and Schuyler Grant propose a toast in the Irish Repertory Theatre's 1996 production of *The Importance of Being Earnest*.

LADY BRACKNELL: I beg your pardon?

CECILY: Mr. Moncrieff and I are engaged to be married, Lady Bracknell.

LADY BRACKNELL (*with a shiver, crossing to the sofa and sitting down*): I do not know whether there is anything peculiarly exciting in the air of this particular part of Hertfordshire, but the number of engagements that go on seems to me considerably above the proper average that statistics have laid down for our guidance. I think some preliminary inquiry on my part would not be out of place. Mr. Worthing, is Miss Cardew at all connected with any of the larger railway stations in London? I merely desire information. Until yesterday I had no idea that there were any families or persons whose origin was a Terminus.

(*Jack looks perfectly furious, but restrains himself.*)

JACK (*in a clear, cold voice*): Miss Cardew is the granddaughter of the late Mr. Thomas Cardew of 149, Belgrave Square, S.W.; Gervase Park, Dorking, Surrey; and the Sporran, Fifeshire, N.B.

LADY BRACKNELL: That sounds not unsatisfactory. Three addresses always inspire confidence, even in tradesmen. But what proof have I of their authenticity?

JACK: I have carefully preserved the Court Guides of the period. They are open to your inspection, Lady Bracknell.

LADY BRACKNELL (*grimly*): I have known strange errors in that publication.

JACK: Miss Cardew's family solicitors are Messrs. Markby, Markby, and Markby.

LADY BRACKNELL: Markby, Markby, and Markby? A firm of the very highest position in their profession. Indeed I am told that one of the Mr. Markbys is occasionally to be seen at dinner parties. So far I am satisfied.

JACK (*very irritably*): How extremely kind of you, Lady Bracknell! I have also in my possession, you will be pleased to hear, certificates of Miss Cardew's birth, baptism, whooping cough, registration, vaccination, confirmation, and the measles; both the German and the English variety.

LADY BRACKNELL: Ah! A life crowded with incident I see; though perhaps somewhat too exciting for a young girl. I am not myself in favor of premature experiences. (*Rises, looks at her watch.*) Gwendolen! the time approaches for our departure. We have not a moment to lose. As a matter of form, Mr. Worthing, I had better ask you if Miss Cardew has any little fortune?

JACK: Oh! about a hundred and thirty thousand pounds in the Funds. That is all. Good-bye, Lady Bracknell. So pleased to have seen you.

LADY BRACKNELL (*sitting down again*): A moment, Mr. Worthing. A hundred and thirty thousand pounds! And in the Funds! Miss Cardew seems to me a most attractive young lady, now that I look at her. Few girls of the present day have any really solid qualities, any of the qualities that last, and improve with time. We live, I regret to say, in an age of surfaces. (*To Cecily.*) Come over here, dear. (*Cecily goes across.*) Pretty child! your dress is sadly simple, and your hair seems almost as Nature might have left it. But we can soon alter all that. A thoroughly experienced French maid produces a really marvelous result in a very brief space of time: I remember recommending one to young Lady Lancing, and after three months her own husband did not know her.

JACK (*aside*): And after six months nobody knew her.

LADY BRACKNELL (*glares at Jack for a few moments. Then bends, with a practiced smile, to Cecily*): Kindly turn round, sweet child. (*Cecily turns completely round.*) No, the side view is what I want. (*Cecily presents her profile.*) Yes, quite as I expected. There are distinct social possibilities in your profile. The two weak points in our age are its want of principle and its want of profile. The chin a little higher, dear. Style largely depends on the way the chin is worn. They are worn very high, just at present. Algernon!

ALGERNON: Yes, Aunt Augusta!

LADY BRACKNELL: There are distinct social possibilities in Miss Cardew's profile.

ALGERNON: Cecily is the sweetest, dearest, prettiest girl in the whole world. And I don't care twopence about social possibilities.

LADY BRACKNELL: Never speak disrespectfully of Society, Algernon. Only people who can't get into it do that. (*To Cecily.*) Dear child, of course you know that Algernon has nothing but his debts to depend upon. But I do not approve of mercenary marriages. When I married Lord Bracknell I had no fortune of any kind. But I never dreamed for a moment of allowing that to stand in my way. Well, I suppose I must give my consent.

ALGERNON: Thank you, Aunt Augusta.

LADY BRACKNELL: Cecily, you may kiss me!

CECILY (*kisses her*): Thank you, Lady Bracknell.

LADY BRACKNELL: You may also address me as Aunt Augusta for the future.

CECILY: Thank you, Aunt Augusta.

LADY BRACKNELL: The marriage, I think, had better take place quite soon.

ALGERNON: Thank you, Aunt Augusta.

CECILY: Thank you, Aunt Augusta.

LADY BRACKNELL: To speak frankly, I am not in favor of long engagements. They give people the opportunity of finding out each other's character before marriage, which I think is never advisable.

JACK: I beg your pardon for interrupting you, Lady Bracknell, but this engagement is quite out of the question. I am Miss Cardew's guardian, and she cannot marry without my consent until she comes of age. That consent I absolutely decline to give.

LADY BRACKNELL: Upon what grounds may I ask? Algernon is an extremely, I may almost say an ostentatiously, eligible young man. He has nothing, but he looks everything. What more can one desire?

JACK: It pains me very much to have to speak frankly to you, Lady Bracknell, about your nephew, but the fact is that I do not approve at all of his moral character. I suspect him of being untruthful.

(*Algernon and Cecily look at him in indignant amazement.*)

LADY BRACKNELL: Untruthful! My nephew Algernon? Impossible! He is an Oxonian.°

JACK: I fear there can be no possible doubt about the matter. This afternoon, during my temporary absence in London on an important question of romance, he obtained admission to my house by means of the false pretense of being my brother. Under an assumed name he drank, I've just been informed by my butler, an entire pint bottle of my Perrier-Jouêt, Brut, '89; a wine I was specially reserving for myself. Continuing his disgraceful deception, he succeeded in the course of the afternoon in alienating the affections of my only ward. He subsequently stayed to tea, and devoured every single muffin. And what makes his conduct all the more heartless is, that he was perfectly well aware from the first that I have no brother, that I never had a brother, and that I don't intend to have a brother, not even of any kind. I distinctly told him so myself yesterday afternoon.

LADY BRACKNELL: Ahem! Mr. Worthing, after careful consideration I have decided entirely to overlook my nephew's conduct to you.

JACK: That is very generous of you, Lady Bracknell. My own decision, however, is unalterable. I decline to give my consent.

LADY BRACKNELL (*to Cecily*): Come here, sweet child. (*Cecily goes over.*) How old are you, dear?

CECILY: Well, I am really only eighteen, but I always admit to twenty when I go to evening parties.

LADY BRACKNELL: You are perfectly right in making some slight alteration. Indeed, no woman should ever be quite accurate about her age. It looks so calculating—(*In a meditative manner.*) Eighteen but admitting to twenty at evening parties. Well, it will not be very long before you are of age and free from the restraints of tutelage. So I don't think your guardian's consent is, after all, a matter of any importance.

JACK: Pray excuse me, Lady Bracknell, for interrupting you again, but it is only fair to tell you that according to the terms of her grandfather's will Miss Cardew does not come legally of age till she is thirty-five.

Oxonian: Educated at Oxford University.

Lady Bracknell (Lynn Redgrave), with Algernon (Robert Petkoff) and Cecily (Charlotte Parry), in Sir Peter Hall's Theatre Royal Bath production, 2006.

LADY BRACKNELL: That does not seem to me to be a grave objection. Thirty-five is a very attractive age. London society is full of women of the very highest birth who have, of their own free choice, remained thirty-five for years. Lady Dumbleton is an instance in point. To my own knowledge she has been thirty-five ever since she arrived at the age of forty, which was many years ago now. I see no reason why our dear Cecily should not be even still more attractive at the age you mention than she is at present. There will be a large accumulation of property.

CECILY: Algy, could you wait for me till I was thirty-five?

ALGERNON: Of course I could, Cecily. You know I could.

CECILY: Yes, I felt it instinctively, but I couldn't wait all that time. I hate waiting even five minutes for anybody. It always makes me rather cross. I am not punctual myself, I know, but I do like punctuality in others, and waiting, even to be married, is quite out of the question.

ALGERNON: Then what is to be done, Cecily?

CECILY: I don't know, Mr. Moncrieff.

LADY BRACKNELL: My dear Mr. Worthing, as Miss Cardew states positively that she cannot wait till she is thirty-five—a remark which I am bound to say seems to me to show a somewhat impatient nature—I would beg of you to reconsider your decision.

JACK: But my dear Lady Bracknell, the matter is entirely in your own hands. The moment you consent to my marriage with Gwendolen, I will most gladly allow your nephew to form an alliance with my ward.

LADY BRACKNELL (*rising and drawing herself up*): You must be quite aware that what you propose is out of the question.

JACK: Then a passionate celibacy is all that any of us can look forward to.

LADY BRACKNELL: That is not the destiny I propose for Gwendolen. Algernon, of course, can choose for himself. (*Pulls out her watch.*) Come, dear; (*Gwendolen rises*) we have already missed five, if not six, trains. To miss any more might expose us to comment on the platform.

(*Enter Dr. Chasuble.*)

CHASUBLE: Everything is quite ready for the christenings.

LADY BRACKNELL: The christenings, sir! Is not that somewhat premature?

CHASUBLE (*looking rather puzzled, and pointing to Jack and Algernon*): Both these gentlemen have expressed a desire for immediate baptism.

LADY BRACKNELL: At their age? The idea is grotesque and irreligious! Algernon, I forbid you to be baptized. I will not hear of such excesses. Lord Bracknell would be highly displeased if he learned that that was the way in which you wasted your time and money.

CHASUBLE: Am I to understand then that there are to be no christenings at all this afternoon?

JACK: I don't think that, as things are now, it would be of much practical value to either of us, Dr. Chasuble.

CHASUBLE: I am grieved to hear such sentiments from you, Mr. Worthing. They savor of the heretical views of the Anabaptists,° views that I have completely refuted in four of my unpublished sermons. However, as your present mood seems to be one peculiarly secular, I will return to the church at once. Indeed, I

Anabaptists: A religious sect founded in the sixteenth century and advocating adult baptism and church membership for adults only.

have just been informed by the pew opener that for the last hour and a half Miss Prism has been waiting for me in the vestry.

LADY BRACKNELL (*starting*): Miss Prism! Did I hear you mention a Miss Prism?

CHASUBLE: Yes, Lady Bracknell. I am on my way to join her.

LADY BRACKNELL: Pray allow me to detain you for a moment. This matter may prove to be one of vital importance to Lord Bracknell and myself. Is this Miss Prism a female of repellent aspect, remotely connected with education?

CHASUBLE (*somewhat indignantly*): She is the most cultivated of ladies, and the very picture of respectability.

LADY BRACKNELL: It is obviously the same person. May I ask what position she holds in your household?

CHASUBLE (*severely*): I am a celibate, madam.

JACK (*interposing*): Miss Prism, Lady Bracknell, has been for the last three years Miss Cardew's esteemed governess and valued companion.

LADY BRACKNELL: In spite of what I hear of her, I must see her at once. Let her be sent for.

CHASUBLE (*looking off*): She approaches; she is nigh.

(*Enter Miss Prism hurriedly.*)

MISS PRISM: I was told you expected me in the vestry, dear Canon. I have been waiting for you there for an hour and three-quarters.

(*Catches sight of Lady Bracknell who has fixed her with a stony glare. Miss Prism grows pale and quails. She looks anxiously round as if desirous to escape.*)

LADY BRACKNELL (*in a severe, judicial voice*): Prism! (*Miss Prism bows her head in shame.*) Come here, Prism! (*Miss Prism approaches in a humble manner.*) Prism! Where is that baby? (*General consternation. The Canon starts back in horror. Algernon and Jack pretend to be anxious to shield Cecily and Gwendolen from hearing the details of a terrible public scandal.*) Twenty-eight years ago, Prism, you left Lord Bracknell's house, Number 104, Upper Grosvenor Street, in charge of a perambulator that contained a baby, of the male sex. You never returned. A few weeks later, through the elaborate investigations of the Metropolitan police, the perambulator was discovered at midnight, standing by itself in a remote corner of Bayswater. It contained the manuscript of a three-volume novel of more than usually revolting sentimentality. (*Miss Prism starts in involuntary indignation.*) But the baby was not there! (*Everyone looks at Miss Prism.*) Prism! Where is that baby?
(*A pause.*)

MISS PRISM: Lady Bracknell, I admit with shame that I do not know. I only wish I did. The plain facts of the case are these. On the morning of the day you mention, a day that is forever branded on my memory, I prepared as usual to take the baby out in its perambulator. I had also with me a somewhat old, but capacious handbag in which I had intended to place the manuscript of a work of fiction that I had written during my few unoccupied hours. In a moment of mental abstraction, for which I never can forgive myself, I deposited the manuscript in the bassinette, and placed the baby in the handbag.

JACK (*who has been listening attentively*): But where did you deposit the handbag?

MISS PRISM: Do not ask me, Mr. Worthing.

JACK: Miss Prism, this is a matter of no small importance to me. I insist on knowing where you deposited the handbag that contained that infant.

MISS PRISM: I left it in the cloakroom of one of the larger railway stations in London.

JACK: What railway station?

MISS PRISM (*quite crushed*): Victoria. The Brighton line.
(*Sinks into a chair.*)

JACK: I must retire to my room for a moment. Gwendolen, wait here for me.

GWENDOLEN: If you are not too long, I will wait here for you all my life.
(*Exit Jack in great excitement.*)

CHASUBLE: What do you think this means, Lady Bracknell?

LADY BRACKNELL: I dare not even suspect, Dr. Chasuble. I need hardly tell you that in families of high position strange coincidences are not supposed to occur. They are hardly considered the thing.

(*Noises heard overhead as if someone was throwing trunks about. Everyone looks up.*)

CECILY: Uncle Jack seems strangely agitated.

CHASUBLE: Your guardian has a very emotional nature.

LADY BRACKNELL: This noise is extremely unpleasant. It sounds as if he was having an argument. I dislike arguments of any kind. They are always vulgar, and often convincing.

CHASUBLE (*looking up*): It has stopped now.
(*The noise is redoubled.*)

LADY BRACKNELL: I wish he would arrive at some conclusion.

GWENDOLEN: This suspense is terrible. I hope it will last.

(*Enter Jack with a handbag of black leather in his hand.*)

JACK (*rushing over to Miss Prism*): Is this the handbag, Miss Prism? Examine it carefully before you speak. The happiness of more than one life depends on your answer.

MISS PRISM (*calmly*): It seems to be mine. Yes, here is the injury it received through the upsetting of a Gower Street omnibus in younger and happier days. Here is the stain on the lining caused by the explosion of a temperance beverage, an incident that occurred at Leamington. And here, on the lock, are my initials. I had forgotten that in an extravagant mood I had had them placed there. The bag is undoubtedly mine. I am delighted to have it so unexpectedly restored to me. It has been a great inconvenience being without it all these years.

JACK (*in a pathetic voice*): Miss Prism, more is restored to you than this handbag. I was the baby you placed in it.

MISS PRISM (*amazed*): You?

JACK (*embracing her*): Yes—mother!

MISS PRISM (*recoiling in indignant astonishment*): Mr. Worthing! I am unmarried!

JACK: Unmarried! I do not deny that is a serious blow. But after all, who has the right to cast a stone against one who has suffered? Cannot repentance wipe out an act of folly? Why should there be one law for men, and another for women? Mother, I forgive you. (*Tries to embrace her again.*)

MISS PRISM (*still more indignant*): Mr. Worthing, there is some error. (*Pointing to Lady Bracknell.*) There is the lady who can tell you who you really are.

JACK (*after a pause*): Lady Bracknell, I hate to seem inquisitive, but would you kindly inform me who I am?

LADY BRACKNELL: I am afraid that the news I have to give you will not altogether please you. You are the son of my poor sister, Mrs. Moncrieff, and consequently Algernon's elder brother.

JACK: Algy's elder brother! Then I have a brother after all. I knew I had a brother! I always said I had a brother! Cecily,—how could you have ever doubted that I had a brother. (*Seizes hold of Algernon.*) Dr. Chasuble, my unfortunate brother. Miss Prism, my unfortunate brother. Gwendolen, my unfortunate brother. Algy, you young scoundrel, you will have to treat me with more respect in the future. You have never behaved to me like a brother in all your life.

ALGERNON: Well, not till today, old boy, I admit. I did my best, however, though I was out of practice.

(*Shakes hands.*)

GWENDOLEN (*to Jack*): My own! But what own are you? What is your Christian name, now that you have become someone else?

JACK: Good heavens!—I had quite forgotten that point. Your decision on the subject of my name is irrevocable, I suppose?

GWENDOLEN: I never change, except in my affections.

CECILY: What a noble nature you have, Gwendolen!

JACK: Then the question had better be cleared up at once. Aunt Augusta, a moment. At the time when Miss Prism left me in the handbag, had I been christened already?

LADY BRACKNELL: Every luxury that money could buy, including christening, had been lavished upon you by your fond and doting parents.

JACK: Then I was christened! That is settled. Now, what name was I given? Let me know the worst.

LADY BRACKNELL: Being the eldest son you were naturally christened after your father.

JACK (*irritably*): Yes, but what was my father's Christian name?

LADY BRACKNELL (*meditatively*): I cannot at the present moment recall what the General's Christian name was. But I have no doubt he had one. He was eccentric, I admit. But only in later years. And that was the result of the Indian climate, and marriage, and indigestion, and other things of that kind.

JACK: Algy! Can't you recollect what our father's Christian name was?

ALGERNON: My dear boy, we were never even on speaking terms. He died before I was a year old.

JACK: His name would appear in the Army Lists of the period, I suppose, Aunt Augusta?

LADY BRACKNELL: The General was essentially a man of peace, except in his domestic life. But I have no doubt his name would appear in any military directory.

JACK: The Army Lists of the last forty years are here. These delightful records should have been my constant study. (*Rushes to bookcase and tears the books out.*) M. Generals—Mallam, Maxbohm, Magley, what ghastly names they have—Markby, Migsby, Mobbs, Moncrieff! Lieutenant 1840, Captain, Lieutenant-Colonel, Colonel, General 1869, Christian names, Ernest John. (*Puts book very quietly down and speaks quite calmly*.) I always told you, Gwendolen, my name was Ernest, didn't I? Well, it is Ernest after all. I mean it naturally is Ernest.

LADY BRACKNELL: Yes, I remember now that the General was called Ernest. I knew I had some particular reason for disliking the name.

GWENDOLEN: Ernest! My own Ernest! I felt from the first that you could have no other name!

JACK: Gwendolen, it is a terrible thing for a man to find out suddenly that all his life he has been speaking nothing but the truth. Can you forgive me?

GWENDOLEN: I can. For I feel that you are sure to change.

JACK: My own one!

CHASUBLE (*to Miss Prism*): Laetitia! (*Embraces her.*)

MISS PRISM (*enthusiastically*): Frederick! At last!

ALGERNON: Cecily! (*Embraces her.*) At last!

JACK: Gwendolen! (*Embraces her.*) At last!

LADY BRACKNELL: My nephew, you seem to be displaying signs of triviality.

JACK: On the contrary, Aunt Augusta, I've now realized for the first time in my life the vital Importance of Being Earnest.

COMMENTARY

JOSEPH DONOHUE (b. 1954)

Interview with Sir Peter Hall, Director of *The Importance of Being Earnest* 2006

The distinguished director is interviewed by professor Joseph Donohue concerning his reasons for directing Wilde's play for contemporary audiences. Hall explains why he believes the play is always timely and what he sees as its central issues. He also explores the gender issues buried in the play.

Q: Is there anything about the present time, the world situation, or our understanding of Oscar Wilde himself that makes mounting a production of *The Importance of Being Earnest* particularly appropriate now?

A: This is the second time I've done the play, and I believe it's an absolutely unique and original object. I don't think that you can write it off as a farce or a farcical comedy; I think it's as original as *Waiting for Godot*, and heaven knows what Wilde would've done if he had been spared, if we hadn't murdered him, because it is absolutely original. In that sense, it's a masterpiece, and in that sense, it's always timely. It's not easy to do, but I think the important thing about Wilde—I've done *Ideal Husband* several times, and *Earnest* twice—the important thing is to understand what his wit is about. It's not about standing on the stage and having like a tennis match of facetiousness of who can win. If you look at Wilde's plays carefully, the wit always covers over something which is very painful, or very extraordinary, something that can't be actually understood or said, for whatever reason. Wilde said, "Give a man a mask and he will tell you the truth," and Wilde's mask, for his characters, is always wit. It's like the English stiff upper lip of the nineteenth century. So you've got to look at *The Importance of Being Earnest* as a deeply serious play about the double life, about sexual desire, about the marriage market, and if you play it very seriously, it's excruciatingly funny. If you don't play it seriously, I think the comedy wears off.

But, why do it now? Well, I think it's always time to do it, in a sense. I don't think there's a deeply contemporary need to do it or anything. Masterpieces need revaluing for each generation.

Q: The original production of *The Importance of Being Earnest*, at George Alexander's St. James Theatre, in London in 1895, featured a three-act play text, cut down—probably mostly by Alexander himself—from the four-act play originally written by Wilde. Earlier, the author had written to Alexander offering him the play and telling him that the two men's parts of Jack and Algy were of equal prominence. In cutting the play to three acts Alexander seems to have made sure that his own part, Jack Worthing, outshone the part of Algy. That

807

choice was memorialized in the first edition of the play. What text do you plan to use for the production? The standard choice is the first edition text, based on Alexander's three-act play, but have you considered using at least some material from the original four-act text? If you chose to do that, would you try to restore more of a balance between the two roles of Jack and Algy, or do you like the greater centrality of Jack as the three-act text presents it? Do you have some other comments about the balancing of pairs of contrasting characters in the play—for example, Gwendolen and Cecily, Miss Prism and Canon Chasuble?

A: We're using the three-act text. When we did the play before, I looked into the fourth act very carefully and actually rehearsed some of it and did some of it, but not in performance. Whoever edited it to the three-act version, whether it was George Alexander or Wilde himself or a collaboration, I personally think they did well. There's something prolix and a little self-indulgent about the fourth act. Of course it's got some good things in it, but I don't think they finally help.

I don't understand the comment about an imbalance between the two roles. Algy is a superb part; he gets all the laughs. Ernest is the center of the play in the sense that Ernest is the man who has not yet come to terms with who he is, not come to terms with his own sexuality, among other things, and therefore needs to lead a double life. I think that's a wonderfully rich and extraordinary part. I don't think that Algy is a supporting role at all.

I think classically, from Plautus onward and certainly [in] Shakespeare, comedy is about couples. Couples who find out they're now mature enough to get married, or relate to each other in terms of love. I think the balancing of the characters is classic comedy.

Q: Is the play essentially a comedy, or essentially a farce? Or is it a mixed breed?

A: I never understand why people need to put some kind of label on things. It's like saying, "Are Shakespeare's late plays romances or comedies, or comedy/ romances, or what are they?" They're plays, and they're very original, and as I said, I think *The Importance of Being Earnest* is one of the most original plays in the English language. I certainly don't think it can be dismissed as a farce any more than I think that it can be just looked at as a serious play. It's the most extraordinary combination of critical comedy which illuminates what the people are about, and what their quest is, and what their pains are, and what their anguishes are. It's very serious, but it's excruciatingly funny. I don't know of any label for that; it's why I think Oscar Wilde is so original.

Q: Is the author in the play?

A: Well, the author's in the play. The author's in the play all the while. He's partly Algy always wanting to go off on some secret mission, for some nefarious, probably sexual, purpose. He's also Ernest trying to be a pillar of the community but actually leading a double life. Of course, *Ideal Husband* is another case in point. The first great play in the English language about bisexuality, if you actually look at it. And I don't think any writer leaves himself outside when he sits down to write his play. I think that looking at *The Importance of Being Earnest* as autobiography is altogether too crude. Certainly Wilde is there all the time.

Q: Lady Bracknell is a notorious blocking character—standing in the way, for over two acts, of Jack and Gwendolen's happiness. And yet hers is one of the most delicious roles in all of British comedy—or farce! How do these two aspects of the character factor into your direction of Lynn Redgrave in the role? Will there be some pressure for her to differentiate her approach to the role from such famous portrayers as Edith Evans or Judi Dench?

A: I was fortunate enough to do my other *Importance of Being Earnest* with Judi Dench, so perhaps I'm uniquely qualified to answer the question. I simply don't understand it, actually. I think what's wonderful about Lady Bracknell is that she's such a materialist, such a total exponent of the marriage market. She's out to sell her daughter to the highest bidder. She reveals that [she] had absolutely no money herself, but her marriage enabled her to become rich. She is, in many respects, a monster. But like other monsters, like Fagin, we like the enormity of their desires; we get a charge out of seeing someone behave quite so absolutely. . . . I don't think at all that Lady Bracknell wrecks the play, blocks the play, distorts the play. I think if she's played as a comic turn she wrecks the play; I've seen that happen. But if you understand what a rapacious lady she is, she really makes the serious heart of the play very evident. It's a curious thing, comedy—it has to be highly serious, and that's certainly true of Lady Bracknell.

Anton Chekhov

Anton Chekhov (1860–1904) spent most of his childhood in relative poverty. His family managed to set up household in Moscow after years spent in remote Taganrog, six hundred miles to the south. He studied medicine in Moscow and eventually received his degree. Although he practiced medicine most of his life, he said that if medicine was his wife, literature was his mistress. His earliest literary efforts were for the purpose of relieving his family's poverty; it was not long before he was earning more from writing than from medicine. By 1896 he had written more than three hundred short stories, most of them published in newspapers. Many of them are classics.

His first theatrical works, apart from his short farces, were not successful. *Ivanov* (1887–1889), rushed into production, was a failure, but the revised 1889 version, reflecting much of his personal life, was successful. *The Wood Demon* (1889), also a failure, helped Chekhov eventually produce his great plays: *The Seagull* (1896); *Uncle Vanya* (1897); *Three Sisters* (1901); and his last, *The Cherry Orchard* (1903). These plays essentially reshaped modern drama, creating a style that critic Richard Peace describes as a "subtle blend of naturalism and symbolism."

The Seagull attracted the attention of the Moscow Art Theatre. The play was not a success in its first production in 1896, but two years later it became one of the theater's triumphs. Konstantin Stanislavski, the great Russian director and actor, played Trigorin, the lead character, but Chekhov thought that he was overacting. They often had disagreements about the playwright's work, but the Moscow Art Theatre supported Chekhov fully.

The surfaces of Chekhov's plays are so lifelike that at times one feels his dramatic purposes are submerged, and to an extent that is true. Chekhov is the master of the **subtext**, a technique in which the dialogue on the surface seems innocuous or meandering, but deeper meanings are implied. Madame Ranevskaya's musings about her childhood in act 1 of *The Cherry Orchard* contrast with the purposeful dialogue of Lopakhin. Her long speeches in act 3 about the "millstone" she loves in Paris are also meandering, but they reveal an idealistic character doomed to suffer at the hands of a new generation of realists who have no time for her ramblings and sentimentalism.

Because subtexts are always present, to read Chekhov's work requires close attention. One must constantly probe, analyze, ask what is implied by what is being said. Chekhov resists "explaining" his plays by having key characters give key thematic speeches. Instead, the meaning builds slowly. Our grasp of what a situation or circumstance finally means will change as we read and as we gather more understanding of the subtleties veiled by surfaces.

Chekhov's style is remarkable for its clarity; on its surface, his writing is direct, simple, and effective. Even his short stories have a clear dramatic center, and the characters he chose to observe are exceptionally modern in that they are neither heroes nor villains. The dramatic concept of a larger-than-life Oedipus or of *Hamlet*'s devilish Claudius is nowhere to be seen in his work. Chekhov's characters are limited, recognizable, and in many ways completely ordinary.

Chekhov's genius was in showing such characters' ambitions, pain, and successes. He was quite aware of important social changes taking place in Russia; the old aristocratic classes, who once owned serfs, were being reduced to a genteel impoverishment, while the children of former slaves were beginning to succeed in business and real estate ventures. Since Chekhov's grandfather had been a serf who bought his freedom in 1841, it is likely that Chekhov was especially supportive of such social change; we see evidence of that in his best plays.

The Cherry Orchard

For discussion questions and assignments on *The Cherry Orchard*, visit **bedfordstmartins.com/jacobus**.

The Cherry Orchard (1903) premiered on Chekhov's birthday, January 17, in 1904. The Moscow Art Theatre performance was directed by Konstantin Stanislavski, an actor-director who pioneered a new method of realistic acting. (Stanislavski is still read and admired the world over. His techniques were modified in the United States and form the basis of **method acting**.) For the subtle effects that Chekhov wanted, however, he found Stanislavski too stagey, flamboyant, and melodramatic. They argued hotly over what should happen in his plays, and often Stanislavski prevailed.

One argument was over whether *The Cherry Orchard* was a tragedy. Chekhov steadfastly called it a comedy, but Stanislavski saw the ruin of Madame Ranevskaya and the destruction of the cherry orchard as tragic. Chekhov perhaps saw it the same way, but he also considered its potential as the impetus for a new, more realistic life for Madame Ranevskaya and her brother Gayev. Their impracticality was an important cause of their having lost their wealth and estate.

How audiences interpret Lopakhin depends on how they view the ambition of the new class of businessmen whose zeal, work, and cleverness earn them the estates that previously they could have hoped only to work on. Social change is fueled by money, which replaces an inherited aristocracy with ambitious moneymakers who earn the power to force changes on the old, less flexible aristocrats. In Russia, massive social change was eventually effected by revolution and the institution of communism. But *The Cherry Orchard* shows that change would have come to Russia in any event.

Perhaps Chekhov's peasant blood helped him see the play as more of a comedy than a tragedy, even though he portrays the characters with greater complexity than we might expect in comedy. Lopakhin is not a simple, unsympathetic character; Trofimov is not a simple dreamer. We need to look closely at what they do and why they do it. For example, when thinking about preserving the beauties of the cherry orchard, Trofimov reminds people that all of Russia is an orchard, that the world is filled with beautiful places. Such a view makes it difficult for him to feel nostalgia for aristocratic privilege.

Trofimov sounds a striking note about the practice of slavery in Russia. He tells Madame Ranevskaya and Gayev that they are living on credit, that they must repay debts to the Russian people. The cherry orchard is beautiful because each tree represents the soul of a serf. The class of beautiful people to which the impractical Madame Ranevskaya belongs owes its beauty and grace to the institution of slavery, and soon the note will be presented for payment. The sound of the breaking string in act 1, repeated at the end of the play, is Chekhov's way of symbolizing the losses and changes represented in the play.

Madame Ranevskaya, however, cannot change. Her habits of mind are fully formed before the play begins; nothing that Lopakhin can say will help change her. Even though she knows she is dangerously in debt, she gives a gold coin to a beggar. *Noblesse oblige*—the duty of the upper class to help the poor—is still part of her ethos, even if it also involves her own ruin.

A sense of tragedy is apparent in Madame Ranevskaya's feelings and her helplessness. She seems incapable of transforming herself, no matter how much she may wish to change. We see her as a victim of fate, a fate that is formed by her expectations and training. But the play also contains comic and nonsensical moments, as, for example, in the by-play of Varya, Yasha, and Yepikhodov over a game of billiards in act 3. In his letters Chekhov mentions that the play is happy and frivolous, "in places even a farce."

The Cherry Orchard in Performance

Since its first production in 1904, *The Cherry Orchard* has played to responsive audiences in Europe and abroad. It was produced in London in 1911, Berlin in 1919, and New York in 1923 (in Russian). Eva Le Gallienne produced it in New York in her English version in 1928. In 1968, she directed the play with Uta Hagen as Madame Ranevskaya. Tyrone Guthrie directed it at the Old Vic in 1933 and again in 1941. John Gielgud, Peggy Ashcroft, Judi Dench, and Dorothy Tutin performed in a powerful and well-reviewed version in London in 1961. When Joseph Papp produced an all-black *Cherry Orchard* in 1973, James Earl Jones was praised as a powerful Lopakhin.

Andrei Serban's 1977 production for Joseph Papp at Lincoln Center in New York was commended for its extraordinary stage effects. According to the reviewer at *Time* magazine,

> Serban's best images effectively magnify the play's conflict between the old order and the bright new world that is its doom: a frieze of peasants laboring beneath modern telegraph wires, a group of aristocrats watching the setting sun silhouette a factory on the horizon.

The American playwright Jean Claude van Italie revised the text for contemporary audiences. His version, produced at the John Drew Theater of Guild Hall in East Hampton in July 1985, was directed by Elinor Renfield. Amanda Plummer played Anya, and Joanna Merlin played Madame Ranevskaya. Peter Brook's 1987 New York production, with Brian Dennehy as a notable Lopakhin, had little scenery beyond a great number of Oriental rugs. It was played without intermissions at breakneck speed. *New York Times* critic Frank Rich said of it, "On this director's magic carpets, *The Cherry Orchard* flies." Other modern treatments of *The Cherry Orchard* include Michael Picardie's adaptation to South Africa and Brian Friel's adaptation to Ireland. In 1997, Galina Volchek staged a Russian-language version in the Martin Beck Theater on Broadway. Critic Peter Marks said the play was "communicated vividly." Theater critic David Finkle described the 2006 production by the Shakespeare Theatre of New Jersey as "the essence of Anton Chekhov." The set of this production, unlike most, included several trees in bloom so that the audience could actually see the orchard that was to be cut away for new housing. Zoë Wanamaker received glowing reviews for her portrayal of Madame Ranevskaya in London's National Theatre production of *The Cherry Orchard*, which was broadcast live in theaters around the world on June 30, 2011, making it the most widely viewed production of Chekhov's drama.

ANTON CHEKHOV (1860–1904)

The Cherry Orchard   1903

TRANSLATED BY ANN DUNNIGAN

Characters

RANEVSKAYA, LYUBOV ANDREYEVNA, *a landowner*
ANYA, *her daughter, seventeen years old*
VARYA, *her adopted daughter, twenty-four years old*
GAYEV, LEONID ANDREYEVICH, *Madame Ranevskaya's brother*
LOPAKHIN, YERMOLAI ALEKSEYEVICH, *a merchant*
TROFIMOV, PYOTR SERGEYEVICH *a student*
SEMYONOV-PISHCHIK, BORIS BORISOVICH, *a landowner*
CHARLOTTA IVANOVNA, *a governess*
YEPIKHODOV, SEMYON PANTELEYEVICH, *a clerk*
DUNYASHA, *a maid*
FIRS, *an old valet, eighty-seven years old*
YASHA, *a young footman*
A STRANGER
THE STATIONMASTER
A POST-OFFICE CLERK
GUESTS, SERVANTS

The action takes place on Madame Ranevskaya's estate.

ACT I

(*A room that is still called the nursery. One of the doors leads into Anya's room. Dawn; the sun will soon rise. It is May, the cherry trees are in bloom, but it is cold in the orchard; there is a morning frost. The windows in the room are closed. Enter Dunyasha with a candle, and Lopakhin with a book in his hand.*)

LOPAKHIN: The train is in, thank God. What time is it?

DUNYASHA: Nearly two. (*Blows out the candle.*) It's already light.

LOPAKHIN: How late is the train, anyway? A couple of hours at least. (*Yawns and stretches.*) I'm a fine one! What a fool I've made of myself! Came here on purpose to meet them at the station, and then overslept. . . . Fell asleep in the chair. It's annoying. . . . You might have waked me.

DUNYASHA: I thought you had gone. (*Listens.*) They're coming now, I think!

LOPAKHIN (*listens*): No . . . they've got to get the luggage and one thing and another. (*Pause.*) Lyubov Andreyevna has lived abroad for five years, I don't know what she's like now. . . . She's a fine person. Sweet-tempered, simple. I remember when I was a boy of fifteen, my late father—he had a shop in the village then—gave me a punch in the face and made my nose bleed. . . . We had come into the yard here for some reason or other, and he'd had a drop too much. Lyubov Andreyevna—I remember as if it were yesterday—still young, and so slender, led me to the washstand in this very room, the nursery. "Don't cry, little peasant," she said, "it will heal in time for your wedding. . . ." (*Pause.*) Little peasant . . . my father was a peasant, it's true, and here I am in a white waistcoat and tan shoes. Like a pig in a pastry shop. . . . I may be rich, I've made a lot of money, but if you think about it, analyze it, I'm a peasant through and through. (*Turning pages of the book.*) Here I've been reading this book, and I didn't understand a thing. Fell asleep over it. (*Pause.*)

DUNYASHA: The dogs didn't sleep all night: They can tell that their masters are coming.

LOPAKHIN: What's the matter with you, Dunyasha, you're so . . .

DUNYASHA: My hands are trembling. I'm going to faint.

Zoë Wanamaker played Madame Ranevskaya in London in 2011.

LOPAKHIN: You're much too delicate, Dunyasha. You dress like a lady, and do your hair like one, too. It's not right. You should know your place.

(*Enter Yepikhodov with a bouquet; he wears a jacket and highly polished boots that squeak loudly. He drops the flowers as he comes in.*)

YEPIKHODOV (*picking up the flowers*): Here, the gardener sent these. He says you're to put them in the dining room. (*Hands the bouquet to Dunyasha.*)

LOPAKHIN: And bring me some kvas.°

DUNYASHA: Yes, sir. (*Goes out.*)

YEPIKHODOV: There's a frost this morning—three degrees—and the cherry trees are in bloom. I cannot approve of our climate. (*Sighs.*) I cannot. Our climate is not exactly conducive. And now, Yermolai Alekseyevich, permit me to append: The day before yesterday I bought myself a pair of boots, which, I venture to assure you, squeak so that it's quite infeasible. What should I grease them with?

LOPAKHIN: Leave me alone. You make me tired.

YEPIKHODOV: Every day some misfortune happens to me. But I don't complain, I'm used to it, I even smile.

(*Dunyasha enters, serves Lopakhin the kvas.*)

YEPIKHODOV: I'm going. (*Stumbles over a chair and upsets it.*) There! (*As if in triumph.*) Now you see, excuse the expression . . . the sort of circumstance, incidentally. It's really quite remarkable! (*Goes out.*)

DUNYASHA: You know, Yermolai Alekseyich, I have to confess that Yepikhodov has proposed to me.

kvas: A Russian beer.

LOPAKHIN: Ah!

DUNYASHA: And I simply don't know. . . . He's a quiet man, but sometimes, when he starts talking, you can't understand a thing he says. It's nice, and full of feeling, only it doesn't make sense. I sort of like him. He's madly in love with me. But he's an unlucky fellow: Every day something happens to him. They tease him about it around here; they call him Two-and-twenty Troubles.

LOPAKHIN (*listening*): I think I hear them coming . . .

DUNYASHA: They're coming! What's the matter with me? I'm cold all over.

LOPAKHIN: They're really coming. Let's go and meet them. Will she recognize me? It's five years since we've seen each other.

DUNYASHA (*agitated*): I'll faint this very minute . . . oh, I'm going to faint!

(*Two carriages are heard driving up to the house. Lopakhin and Dunyasha go out quickly. The stage is empty. There is a hubbub in the adjoining rooms. Firs hurriedly crosses the stage leaning on a stick. He has been to meet Lyubov Andreyevna and wears old fashioned livery and a high hat. He mutters something to himself, not a word of which can be understood. The noise offstage grows louder and louder. A voice: "Let's go through here. . . ." Enter Lyubov Andreyevna, Anya, Charlotta Ivanovna with a little dog on a chain, all in traveling dress; Varya wearing a coat and kerchief; Gayev, Semyonov-Pishchik, Lopakhin, Dunyasha with a bundle and parasol; servants with luggage—all walk through the room.*)

ANYA: Let's go this way. Do you remember, Mama, what room this is?

LYUBOV ANDREYEVNA (*joyfully, through tears*): The nursery!

VARYA: How cold it is! My hands are numb. (*To Lyubov Andreyevna.*) Your rooms, both the white one and the violet one, are just as you left them, Mama.

LYUBOV ANDREYEVNA: The nursery ... my dear, lovely nursery.... I used to sleep here when I was little.... (*Weeps.*) And now, like a child, I ... (*Kisses her brother, Varya, then her brother again.*) Varya hasn't changed; she still looks like a nun. And I recognized Dunyasha.... (*Kisses Dunyasha.*)

GAYEV: The train was two hours late. How's that? What kind of management is that?

CHARLOTTA (*to Pishchik*): My dog even eats nuts.

PISHCHIK (*amazed*): Think of that now!

(*They all go out except Anya and Dunyasha.*)

DUNYASHA: We've been waiting and waiting for you.... (*Takes off Anya's coat and hat.*)

ANYA: I didn't sleep for four nights on the road ... now I feel cold.

DUNYASHA: It was Lent when you went away, there was snow and frost then, but now? My darling! (*Laughs and kisses her.*) I've waited so long for you, my joy, my precious ... I must tell you at once, I can't wait another minute....

ANYA (*listlessly*): What now?

DUNYASHA: The clerk, Yepikhodov, proposed to me just after Easter.

ANYA: You always talk about the same thing.... (*Straightening her hair.*) I've lost all my hairpins.... (*She is so exhausted she can hardly stand.*)

DUNYASHA: I really don't know what to think. He loves me—he loves me so!

ANYA (*looking through the door into her room, tenderly*): My room, my windows ... it's just as though I'd never been away. I am home! Tomorrow morning I'll get up and run into the orchard.... Oh, if could only sleep! I didn' sleep during the entire journey, I was so tormented by anxiety.

DUNYASHA: Pyotr Sergeich arrived the day before yesterday.

ANYA (*joyfully*): Petya!

DUNYASHA: He's asleep in the bathhouse, he's staying there. "I'm afraid of being in the way," he said. (*Looks at her pocket watch.*) I ought to wake him up, but Varvara Mikhailovna told me not to. "Don't you wake him," she said.

(*Enter Varya with a bunch of keys at her waist.*)

VARYA: Dunyasha, coffee, quickly ... Mama's asking for coffee.

DUNYASHA: This very minute. (*Goes out.*)

VARYA: Thank God, you've come! You're home again. (*Caressing her.*) My little darling has come back! My pretty one is here!

ANYA: I've been through so much.

VARYA: I can imagine!

ANYA: I left in Holy Week, it was cold then. Charlotta never stopped talking and doing her conjuring tricks the entire journey. Why did you saddle me with Charlotta?

VARYA: You couldn't have traveled alone, darling. At seventeen!

ANYA: When we arrived in Paris, it was cold, snowing. My French is awful.... Mama was living on the fifth floor, and when I got there, she had all sorts of Frenchmen and ladies with her, and an old priest with a little book, and it was full of smoke, dismal. Suddenly I felt sorry for Mama, so sorry. I took her head in my arms and held her close and couldn't let her go. Afterward she kept hugging me and crying....

VARYA (*through her tears*): Don't talk about it, don't talk about it....

ANYA: She had already sold her villa near Mentone, and she had nothing left, nothing. And I hadn't so much as a kopeck left, we barely managed to get there. But Mama doesn't understand! When we had dinner in a station restaurant, she always ordered the most expensive dishes and tipped each of the waiters a ruble. Charlotta is the same. And Yasha also ordered a dinner, it was simply awful. You know, Yasha is Mama's footman; we brought him with us.

VARYA: I saw the rogue.

ANYA: Well, how are things? Have you paid the interest?

VARYA: How could we?

ANYA: Oh, my God, my God!

VARYA: In August the estate will be put up for sale.

ANYA: My God!

(*Lopakhin peeps in at the door and moos like a cow.*)

LOPAKHIN: Moo-o-o! (*Disappears.*)

VARYA (*through her tears*): What I couldn't do to him! (*Shakes her fist.*)

ANYA (*embracing Varya, softly*): Varya, has he proposed to you? (*Varya shakes her head.*) But he loves you.... Why don't you come to an understanding, what are you waiting for?

VARYA: I don't think anything will come of it. He's too busy, he has no time for me ... he doesn't even notice me. I've washed my hands of him, it makes me miserable to see him.... Everyone talks of our wedding, they all congratulate me, and actually there's nothing to it—it's all like a dream.... (*In a different tone.*) You have a brooch like a bee.

ANYA (*sadly*): Mama bought it. (*Goes into her own room; speaks gaily, like a child.*) In Paris I went up in a balloon!

VARYA: My darling is home! My pretty one has come back!

(*Dunyasha has come in with the coffeepot and prepares coffee.*)

VARYA (*stands at the door of Anya's room*): You know, darling, all day long I'm busy looking after the house, but I keep dreaming. If we could marry you to a rich man I'd be at peace. I could go into a hermitage, then to Kiev, to Moscow, and from one holy place to another. . . . I'd go on and on. What a blessing!

ANYA: The birds are singing in the orchard. What time is it?

VARYA: It must be after two. Time you were asleep, darling. (*Goes into Anya's room.*) What a blessing!

(*Yasha enters with a lap robe and a traveling bag.*)

YASHA (*crosses the stage mincingly*): May one go through here?

DUNYASHA: A person would hardly recognize you, Yasha. Your stay abroad has done wonders for you.

YASHA: Hm. . . . And who are you?

DUNYASHA: When you left here I was only that high— (*indicating with her hand*). I'm Dunyasha, Fyodor Kozoyedov's daughter. You don't remember?

YASHA: Hm. . . . A little cucumber! (*Looks around, then embraces her; she cries out and drops a saucer. He quickly goes out.*)

VARYA (*in a tone of annoyance, from the doorway*): What's going on here?

DUNYASHA (*tearfully*): I broke a saucer.

VARYA: That's good luck.

ANYA: We ought to prepare Mama: Petya is here. . . .

VARYA: I gave orders not to wake him.

ANYA (*pensively*): Six years ago Father died, and a month later brother Grisha drowned in the river . . . a pretty little seven-year-old boy. Mama couldn't bear it and went away . . . went without looking back. . . . (*Shudders.*) How I understand her, if she only knew! (*Pause.*) And Petya Trofimov was Grisha's tutor, he may remind her. . . .

(*Enter Firs wearing a jacket and a white waistcoat.*)

FIRS (*goes to the coffeepot, anxiously*): The mistress will have her coffee here. (*Puts on white gloves.*) Is the coffee ready? (*To Dunyasha, sternly.*) You! Where's the cream?

DUNYASHA: Oh, my goodness! (*Quickly goes out.*)

FIRS (*fussing over the coffeepot*): Ah, what an addlepate! (*Mutters to himself.*) They've come back from Paris. . . . The master used to go to Paris . . . by carriage. . . . (*Laughs.*)

VARYA: What is it, Firs?

FIRS: If you please? (*Joyfully.*) My mistress has come home! At last! Now I can die. . . . (*Weeps with joy.*)

(*Enter Lyubov Andreyevna, Gayev, and Semyonov-Pishchik, the last wearing a sleeveless peasant coat of fine cloth and full trousers. Gayev, as he comes in, goes through the motions of playing billiards.*)

LYUBOV ANDREYEVNA: How does it go? Let's see if I can remember . . . cue ball into the corner! Double the rail to center table.

GAYEV: Cut shot into the corner! There was a time, sister, when you and I used to sleep here in this very room, and now I'm fifty-one, strange as it may seem. . . .

LOPAKHIN: Yes, time passes.

GAYEV: How's that?

LOPAKHIN: Time, I say, passes.

GAYEV: It smells of patchouli here.

ANYA: I'm going to bed. Good night, Mama. (*Kisses her mother.*)

LYUBOV ANDREYEVNA: My precious child. (*Kisses her hands.*) Are you glad to be home? I still feel dazed.

ANYA: Good night, Uncle.

GAYEV (*kisses her face and hands*): God bless you. How like your mother you are! (*To his sister.*) At her age you were exactly like her, Lyuba.

(*Anya shakes hands with Lopakhin and Pishchik and goes out, closing the door after her.*)

LYUBOV ANDREYEVNA: She's exhausted.

PISHCHIK: Must have been a long journey.

VARYA: Well, gentlemen? It's after two, high time you were going.

LYUBOV ANDREYEVNA (*laughs*): You haven't changed, Varya. (*Draws Varya to her and kisses her.*) I'll just drink my coffee and then we'll all go. (*Firs places a cushion under her feet.*) Thank you, my dear. I've got used to coffee. I drink it day and night. Thanks, dear old man. (*Kisses him.*)

VARYA: I'd better see if all the luggage has been brought in.

LYUBOV ANDREYEVNA: Is this really me sitting here? (*Laughs.*) I feel like jumping about and waving my arms. (*Buries her face in her hands.*) What if it's only a dream! God knows I love my country, love it dearly. I couldn't look out the train window, I was crying so! (*Through tears.*) But I must drink my coffee. Thank you, Firs, thank you, my dear old friend. I'm so glad you're still alive.

FIRS: The day before yesterday.

GAYEV: He's hard of hearing.

LOPAKHIN: I must go now, I'm leaving for Kharkov about five o'clock. It's so annoying! I wanted to have a good look at you, and have a talk. You're as splendid as ever.

PISHCHIK (*breathing heavily*): Even more beautiful. . . . Dressed like a Parisienne. . . . There goes my wagon, all four wheels!

LOPAKHIN: Your brother here, Leonid Andreich, says I'm a boor, a moneygrubber, but I don't mind. Let him talk. All I want is that you should trust me as you used to, and that your wonderful, touching eyes should look at me as they did then. Merciful God! My father was one of your father's serfs, and your grandfather's, but you yourself did so much for me once, that I've forgotten all that and love you as if you were my own kin—more than my kin.

LYUBOV ANDREYEVNA: I can't sit still, I simply cannot. (*Jumps up and walks about the room in great excitement.*) I cannot bear this joy. . . . Laugh at me, I'm silly. . . . My dear little bookcase . . . (*kisses bookcase*) my little table . . .

GAYEV: Nurse died while you were away.

LYUBOV ANDREYEVNA (*sits down and drinks coffee*): Yes, God rest her soul. They wrote me.

GAYEV: And Anastasy is dead. Petrushka Kosoi left me and is now with the police inspector in town. (*Takes a box of hard candies from his pocket and begins to suck one.*)

PISHCHIK: My daughter, Dashenka . . . sends her regards . . .

LOPAKHIN: I wish I could tell you something very pleasant and cheering. (*Glances at his watch.*) I must go directly, there's no time to talk, but . . . well, I'll say it in a couple of words. As you know, the cherry orchard is to be sold to pay your debts. The auction is set for August twenty-second, but you need not worry, my dear; you can sleep in peace, there is a way out. This is my plan. Now, please listen! Your estate is only twenty versts° from town, the railway runs close by, and if the cherry orchard and the land along the river were cut up into lots and leased for summer cottages, you'd have, at the very least, an income of twenty-five thousand a year.

GAYEV: Excuse me, what nonsense!

LYUBOV ANDREYEVNA: I don't quite understand you, Yermolai Alekseich.

LOPAKHIN: You will get, at the very least, twenty-five rubles a year for a two-and-a-half-acre lot, and if you advertise now, I guarantee you won't have a single plot of ground left by autumn, everything will be snapped up. In short, I congratulate you, you are saved. The site is splendid, the river is deep. Only, of course, the ground must be cleared . . . you must tear down all the old outbuildings, for instance, and this house, which is worthless, cut down the old cherry orchard.

LYUBOV ANDREYEVNA: Cut it down? Forgive me, my dear, but you don't know what you are talking about. If there is one thing in the whole province that is interesting, not to say remarkable, it's our cherry orchard.

LOPAKHIN: The only remarkable thing about this orchard is that it is very big. There's a crop of cherries every other year, and then you can't get rid of them, nobody buys them.

GAYEV: This orchard is even mentioned in the *Encyclopedia.*

LOPAKHIN (*glancing at his watch*): If we don't think of something and come to a decision, on the twenty-second of August the cherry orchard, and the entire estate, will be sold at auction. Make up your minds! There is no other way out, I swear to you. None whatsoever.

FIRS: In the old days, forty or fifty years ago, the cherries were dried, soaked, marinated, and made into jam, and they used to—

GAYEV: Be quiet, Firs.

FIRS: And they used to send cartloads of dried cherries to Moscow and Kharkov. And that brought in money! The dried cherries were soft and juicy in those days, sweet, fragrant. . . . They had a method then . . .

LYUBOV ANDREYEVNA: And what has become of that method now?

FIRS: Forgotten. Nobody remembers. . . .

---

versts: A verst is approximately equal to a kilometer, a little more than half a mile.

PISHCHIK: How was it in Paris? What's it like there? Did you eat frogs?

LYUBOV ANDREYEVNA: I ate crocodiles.

PISHCHIK: Think of that now!

LOPAKHIN: There used to be only the gentry and the peasants living in the country, but now these summer people have appeared. All the towns, even the smallest ones, are surrounded by summer cottages. And it is safe to say that in another twenty years these people will multiply enormously. Now the summer resident only drinks tea on his porch, but it may well be that he'll take to cultivating his acre and then your cherry orchard will be a happy, rich, luxuriant—

GAYEV (*indignantly*): What nonsense!

(*Enter Varya and Yasha.*)

VARYA: There are two telegrams for you, Mama. (*Picks out a key and with a jingling sound opens an old-fashioned bookcase.*) Here they are.

LYUBOV ANDREYEVNA: From Paris. (*Tears up the telegrams without reading them.*) That's all over. . . .

GAYEV: Do you know, Lyuba, how old this bookcase is? A week ago I pulled out the bottom drawer, and what do I see? Some figures burnt into it. The bookcase was made exactly a hundred years ago. What do you think of that? Eh? We could have celebrated its jubilee. It's an inanimate object, but nevertheless, for all that, it's a bookcase.

PISHCHIK: A hundred years . . . think of that now!

GAYEV: Yes . . . that is something. . . . (*Feeling the bookcase.*) Dear, honored bookcase. I salute thy existence, which for over one hundred years has served the glorious ideals of goodness and justice; thy silent appeal to fruitful endeavor, unflagging in the course of a hundred years, tearfully sustaining through generations of our family, courage and faith in a better future, and fostering in us ideals of goodness and social consciousness. . . .

(*A pause.*)

LOPAKHIN: Yes . . .

LYUBOV ANDREYEVNA: You are the same as ever, Lyonya.

GAYEV (*somewhat embarrassed*): Carom into the corner, cut shot to center table.

LOPAKHIN (*looks at his watch*): Well, time for me to go.

YASHA (*hands medicine to Lyubov Andreyevna*): Perhaps you will take your pills now.

PISHCHIK: Don't take medicaments, dearest lady, they do neither harm nor good. Let me have them, honored lady. (*Takes the pillbox, shakes the pills into his hand, blows on them, puts them into his mouth and washes them down with kvas.*) There!

LYUBOV ANDREYEVNA (*alarmed*): Why, you must be mad!

PISHCHIK: I've taken all the pills.

LOPAKHIN: What a glutton!

(*Everyone laughs.*)

FIRS: The gentleman stayed with us during Holy Week . . . ate half a bucket of pickles. . . . (*Mumbles.*)

LYUBOV ANDREYEVNA: What is he saying?

VARYA: He's been muttering like that for three years now. We've grown used to it.

YASHA: He's in his dotage.

(*Charlotta Ivanovna, very thin, tightly laced, in a white dress with a lorgnette at her belt, crosses the stage.*)

LOPAKHIN: Forgive me, Charlotta Ivanovna, I haven't had a chance to say how do you do to you. (*Tries to kiss her hand.*)

CHARLOTTA (*pulls her hand away*): If I permit you to kiss my hand you'll be wanting to kiss my elbow next, then my shoulder.

LOPAKHIN: I have no luck today. (*Everyone laughs.*) Charlotta Ivanovna, show us a trick!

LYUBOV ANDREYEVNA: Charlotta, show us a trick!

CHARLOTTA: No. I want to sleep. (*Goes out.*)

LOPAKHIN: In three weeks we'll meet again. (*Kisses Lyubov Andreyevna's hand.*) Good-bye till then. Time to go. (*To Gayev.*) Good-bye. (*Kisses Pishchik.*) Good bye. (*Shakes hands with Varya, then with Firs and Yasha.*) I don't feel like going. (*To Lyubov Andreyevna.*) If you make up your mind about the summer cottages and come to a decision, let me know; I'll get you a loan of fifty thousand or so. Think it over seriously.

VARYA (*angrily*): Oh, why don't you go!

LOPAKHIN: I'm going, I'm going. (*Goes out.*)

GAYEV: Boor. Oh, pardon. Varya's going to marry him, he's Varya's young man.

VARYA: Uncle dear, you talk too much.

LYUBOV ANDREYEVNA: Well, Varya, I shall be very glad. He's a good man.

PISHCHIK: A man, I must truly say . . . most worthy. . . . And my Dashenka . . . says, too, that . . . says all sorts of things. (*Snores but wakes up at once.*) In any case, honored lady, oblige me . . . a loan of two hundred and forty rubles . . . tomorrow the interest on my mortgage is due. . . .

VARYA (*in alarm*): We have nothing, nothing at all!

LYUBOV ANDREYEVNA: I really haven't any money.

PISHCHIK: It'll turn up. (*Laughs.*) I never lose hope. Just when I thought everything was lost, that I was done for, lo and behold—the railway line ran through my land . . . and they paid me for it. And before you know it, something else will turn up, if not today—tomorrow. . . . Dashenka will win two hundred thousand . . . she's got a lottery ticket.

LYUBOV ANDREYEVNA: The coffee is finished, we can go to bed.

FIRS (*brushing Gayev's clothes, admonishingly*): You've put on the wrong trousers again. What am I to do with you?

VARYA (*softly*): Anya's asleep. (*Quietly opens the window.*) The sun has risen, it's no longer cold. Look, Mama dear, what wonderful trees! Oh, Lord, the air! The starlings are singing!

GAYEV (*opens another window*): The orchard is all white. You haven't forgotten, Lyuba? That long avenue there that runs straight—straight as a stretched-out strap;

it gleams on moonlight nights. Remember? You've not forgotten?

LYUBOV ANDREYEVNA (*looking out the window at the orchard*): Oh, my childhood, my innocence! I used to sleep in this nursery, I looked out from here into the orchard, happiness awoke with me each morning, it was just as it is now, nothing has changed. (*Laughing with joy.*) All, all white! Oh, my orchard! After the dark, rainy autumn and the cold winter, you are young again, full of happiness, the heavenly angels have not forsaken you. . . . If I could cast off this heavy stone weighing on my breast and shoulders, if I could forget my past!

GAYEV: Yes, and the orchard will be sold for our debts, strange as it may seem. . . .

LYUBOV ANDREYEVNA: Look, our dead mother walks in the orchard . . . in a white dress! (*Laughs with joy.*) It is she!

GAYEV: Where?

VARYA: God be with you, Mama dear.

LYUBOV ANDREYEVNA: There's no one there, I just imagined it. To the right, as you turn to the summerhouse, a slender white sapling is bent over . . . it looks like a woman.

(*Enter Trofimov wearing a shabby student's uniform and spectacles.*)

LYUBOV ANDREYEVNA: What a wonderful orchard! The white masses of blossoms, the blue sky—

TROFIMOV: Lyubov Andreyevna! (*She looks around at him.*) I only want to pay my respects, then I'll go at once. (*Kisses her hand ardently.*) I was told to wait until morning, but I hadn't the patience.

(*Lyubov Andreyevna looks at him, puzzled.*)

VARYA (*through tears*): This is Petya Trofimov.

TROFIMOV: Petya Trofimov, I was Grisha's tutor. . . . Can I have changed so much?

(*Lyubov Andreyevna embraces him, quietly weeping.*)

GAYEV (*embarrassed*): There, there, Lyuba.

VARYA (*crying*): Didn't I tell you, Petya, to wait till tomorrow?

LYUBOV ANDREYEVNA: My Grisha . . . my little boy . . . Grisha . . . my son. . . .

VARYA: What can we do, Mama dear? It's God's will.

TROFIMOV (*gently, through tears*): Don't, don't. . . .

LYUBOV ANDREYEVNA (*quietly weeping*): My little boy dead, drowned. . . . Why? Why, my friend? (*In a lower voice.*) Anya is sleeping in there, and I'm talking loudly . . . making all this noise. . . . But Petya, why do you look so bad? Why have you grown so old?

TROFIMOV: A peasant woman in the train called me a mangy gentleman.

LYUBOV ANDREYEVNA: You were just a boy then, a charming little student, and now your hair is thin—and spectacles! Is it possible you are still a student? (*Goes toward the door.*)

TROFIMOV: I shall probably be an eternal student.

LYUBOV ANDREYEVNA: (*kisses her brother, then Varya*): Now, go to bed. . . . You've grown older too, Leonid.

PISHCHIK (*follows her*): Well, seems to be time to sleep. . . . Oh, my gout! I'm staying the night. Lyubov Andreyevna, my soul, tomorrow morning . . . two hundred and forty rubles. . . .

GAYEV: He keeps at it.

PISHCHIK: Two hundred and forty rubles . . . to pay the interest on my mortgage.

LYUBOV ANDREYEVNA: I have no money, my friend.

PISHCHIK: My dear, I'll pay it back. . . . It's a trifling sum.

LYUBOV ANDREYEVNA: Well, all right, Leonid will give it to you. . . . Give it to him, Leonid.

GAYEV: Me give it to him! . . . Hold out your pocket!

LYUBOV ANDREYEVNA: It can't be helped, give it to him. . . . He needs it. . . . He'll pay it back. *no he won't*

(*Lyubov Andreyevna, Trofimov, Pishchik, and Firs go out. Gayev, Varya, and Yasha remain.*)

GAYEV: My sister hasn't yet lost her habit of squandering money. (*To Yasha.*) Go away, my good fellow, you smell of the henhouse.

YASHA (*with a smirk*): And you, Leonid Andreyevich, are just the same as ever.

GAYEV: How's that? (*To Varya.*) What did he say?

VARYA: Your mother has come from the village; she's been sitting in the servants' room since yesterday, waiting to see you. . . .

YASHA: Let her wait, for God's sake!

VARYA: Aren't you ashamed?

YASHA: A lot I need her! She could have come tomorrow. (*Goes out.*)

VARYA: Mama's the same as ever, she hasn't changed a bit. She'd give away everything, if she could.

GAYEV: Yes. . . . (*A pause.*) If a great many remedies are suggested for a disease, it means that the disease is incurable. I keep thinking, racking my brains, I have many remedies, a great many, and that means in effect, that I have none. It would be good to receive a legacy from someone, good to marry our Anya to a very rich man, good to go to Yaroslav and try our luck with our aunt, the Countess. She is very, very rich, you know.

Anya's going to get married off & prest

VARYA (*crying*): If only God would help us!

GAYEV: Stop bawling. Auntie's very rich, but she doesn't like us. In the first place, sister married a lawyer, not a nobleman . . . (*Anya appears in the doorway.*) She married beneath her, and it cannot be said that she has conducted herself very virtuously. She is good, kind, charming, and I love her dearly, but no matter how much you allow for extenuating circumstances, you must admit she leads a sinful life. You feel it in her slightest movement.

VARYA (*in a whisper*): Anya is standing in the doorway.

GAYEV: What? (*Pause.*) Funny, something got into my right eye . . . I can't see very well. And Thursday, when I was in the district court . . .

(*Anya enters.*)

VARYA: Why aren't you asleep, Anya?

ANYA: I can't get to sleep. I just can't.

GAYEV: My little one! (*Kisses Anya's face and hands.*) My child. . . . (*Through tears.*) You are not my niece, you are my angel, you are everything to me. Believe me, believe . . .

ANYA: I believe you, Uncle. Everyone loves you and respects you, but, Uncle dear, you must keep quiet, just keep quiet. What were you saying just now about my mother, about your own sister? What made you say that?

GAYEV: Yes, yes. . . . (*Covers his face with her hand.*) Really, it's awful! My God! God help me! And today I made a speech to the bookcase . . . so stupid! And it was only when I had finished that I realized it was stupid.

VARYA: It's true, Uncle dear, you ought to keep quiet. Just don't talk, that's all.

ANYA: If you could keep from talking, it would make things easier for you, too.

GAYEV: I'll be quiet. (*Kisses Anya's and Varya's hands.*) I'll be quiet. Only this is about business. On Thursday I was in the district court, well, a group of us gathered together and began talking about one thing and another, this and that, and it seems it might be possible to arrange a loan on a promissory note to pay the interest at the bank.

VARYA: If only God would help us!

GAYEV: On Tuesday I'll go and talk it over again. (*To Varya.*) Stop bawling. (*To Anya.*) Your mama will talk to Lopakhin; he, of course, will not refuse her. . . . And as soon as you've rested, you will go to Yaroslav to the Countess, your great-aunt. In that way we shall be working from three directions—and our business is in the hat. We'll pay the interest, I'm certain of it. . . . (*Puts a candy in his mouth.*) On my honor, I'll swear by anything you like, the estate shall not be sold. (*Excitedly.*) By my happiness, I swear it! Here's my hand on it, call me a worthless, dishonorable man if I let it come to auction! I swear by my whole being!

ANYA (*a calm mood returns to her, she is happy*): How good you are, Uncle, how clever! (*Embraces him.*) Now I am at peace! I'm at peace! I'm happy!

(*Enter Firs.*)

FIRS (*reproachfully*): Leonid Andreich, have you no fear of God? When are you going to bed?

GAYEV: Presently, presently. Go away, Firs, I'll . . . all right, I'll undress myself. Well, children, bye-bye. . . . Details tomorrow, and now go to sleep. (*Kisses Anya and Varya.*) I am a man of the eighties. . . . They don't think much of that period today, nevertheless, I can say that in the course of my life I have suffered not a little for my convictions. It is not for nothing that the peasant loves me. You have to know the peasant! You have to know from what—

ANYA: There you go again, Uncle!

VARYA: Uncle dear, do be quiet.

FIRS (*angrily*): Leonid Andreich!

GAYEV: I'm coming, I'm coming. . . . Go to bed. A clean double rail shot to center table. . . . (*Goes out; Firs hobbles after him.*)

ANYA: I'm at peace now. I would rather not go to Yaroslav, I don't like my great-aunt, but still, I'm at peace, thanks to Uncle. (*She sits down.*)

VARYA: We must get some sleep. I'm going now. Oh, something unpleasant happened while you were away. In the old servants' quarters, as you know, there are only the old people: Yefimushka, Polya, Yevstignei, and, of course, Karp. They began letting in all sorts of rogues to spend the night—I didn't say anything. But then I heard they'd been spreading a rumor that I'd given an order for them to be fed nothing but dried peas. Out of stinginess, you see.... It was all Yevstignei's doing.... Very well, I think, if that's how it is, you just wait. I send for Yevstignei ... (*yawning*) he comes.... "How is it, Yevstignei," I say, "that you could be such a fool...." (*Looks at Anya.*) She's fallen asleep. (*Takes her by the arm.*) Come to your little bed.... Come along. (*Leading her.*) My little darling fell asleep. Come.... (*They go.*)

(*In the distance, beyond the orchard, a shepherd is playing on a reed pipe. Trofimov crosses the stage and, seeing Varya and Anya, stops.*)

VARYA: Sh! She's asleep ... asleep.... Come along, darling.

ANYA (*softly, half-asleep*): I'm so tired.... Those bells ... Uncle ... dear ... Mama and Uncle ...

VARYA: Come, darling, come along. (*They go into Anya's room.*)

TROFIMOV (*deeply moved*): My sunshine! My spring!

ACT II

(*A meadow. An old, lopsided, long-abandoned little chapel; near it a well, large stones that apparently were once tombstones, and an old bench. A road to the Gayev manor house can be seen. On one side, where the cherry orchard begins, tall poplars loom. In the distance a row of telegraph poles, and far, far away, on the horizon, the faint outline of a large town, which is visible only in very fine, clear weather. The sun will soon set. Charlotta, Yasha, and Dunyasha are sitting on the bench; Yepikhodov stands near playing something sad on the guitar. They are all lost in thought. Charlotta wears an old forage cap; she has taken a gun from her shoulder and is adjusting the buckle on the sling.*)

CHARLOTTA (*reflectively*): I haven't got a real passport, I don't know how old I am, but it always seems to me that I'm quite young. When I was a little girl, my father and mother used to travel from one fair to another giving performances—very good ones. And I did the *salto mortale*° and all sorts of tricks. Then when papa and Mama died, a German lady took me to live with her and began teaching me. Good. I grew up and became a governess. But where I come from and who I am—I do not know.... Who my parents were—perhaps they weren't even married—I don't know.

salto mortale: Somersault.

(*Takes a cucumber out of her pocket and eats it.*) I don't know anything. (*Pause.*) One wants so much to talk, but there isn't anyone to talk to ... I have no one.

YEPIKHODOV (*plays the guitar and sings*): "What care I for the clamorous world, what's friend or foe to me?" ... How pleasant it is to play a mandolin!

DUNYASHA: That's a guitar, not a mandolin. (*Looks at herself in a hand mirror and powders her face.*)

YEPIKHODOV: To a madman, in love, it is a mandolin.... (*Sings.*) "Would that the heart were warmed by the flame of requited love ...."

(*Yasha joins in.*)

CHARLOTTA: How horribly these people sing! ... Pfui! Like jackals!

DUNYASHA (*to Yasha*): Really, how fortunate to have been abroad!

YASHA: Yes, to be sure. I cannot but agree with you there. (*Yawns, then lights a cigar.*)

YEPIKHODOV: It stands to reason. Abroad everything has long since been fully constituted.

YASHA: Obviously.

YEPIKHODOV: I am a cultivated man, I read all sorts of remarkable books, but I am in no way able to make out my own inclinations, what it is I really want, whether, strictly speaking, to live or to shoot myself; nevertheless, I always carry a revolver on me. Here it is. (*Shows revolver.*)

CHARLOTTA: Finished. Now I'm going. (*Slings the gun over her shoulder.*) You're a very clever man, Yepikhodov, and quite terrifying; women must be mad about you. Brrr! (*Starts to go.*) These clever people are all so stupid, there's no one for me to talk to.... Alone, always alone, I have no one ... and who I am, and why I am, nobody knows.... (*Goes out unhurriedly.*)

YEPIKHODOV: Strictly speaking, all else aside, I must state regarding myself, that fate treats me unmercifully, as a storm does a small ship. If, let us assume, I am mistaken, then why, to mention a single instance, do I wake up this morning, and there on my chest see a spider of terrifying magnitude? ... Like that. (*Indicates with both hands.*) And likewise, I take up some kvas to quench my thirst, and there see something in the highest degree unseemly, like a cockroach. (*Pause.*) Have you read Buckle?° (*Pause.*) If I may trouble you, Avdotya Fyodorovna, I should like to have a word or two with you.

DUNYASHA: Go ahead.

YEPIKHODOV: I prefer to speak with you alone.... (*Sighs.*)

DUNYASHA (*embarrassed*): Very well ... only first bring me my little cape ... you'll find it by the cupboard.... It's rather damp here....

YEPIKHODOV: Certainly, ma'ma ... I'll fetch it, ma'ma.... Now I know what to do with my revolver.... (*Takes the guitar and goes off playing it.*)

Buckle: Thomas Henry Buckle (1821–1862) was a radical historian who formulated a scientific basis for history emphasizing the interrelationship of climate, food production, population, and wealth.

Laila Robins, Edmond Genest, and Alison Weller in the Shakespeare Theatre of New Jersey's 2006 production of *The Cherry Orchard*, which included a set with trees in bloom.

YASHA: Two-and-twenty Troubles! Between ourselves, a stupid fellow. (*Yawns.*)

DUNYASHA: God forbid that he should shoot himself. (*Pause.*) I've grown so anxious, I'm always worried. I was only a little girl when I was taken into the master's house, and now I'm quite unused to the simple life, and my hands are white as can be, just like a lady's. I've become so delicate, so tender and lady-like, I'm afraid of everything. . . . Frightfully so. And, Yasha, if you deceive me, I just don't know what will become of my nerves.

YASHA (*kisses her*): You little cucumber! Of course, a girl should never forget herself. What I dislike above everything is when a girl doesn't conduct herself properly.

DUNYASHA: I'm passionately in love with you, you're educated, you can discuss anything. (*Pause.*)

YASHA (*yawns*): Yes. . . . As I see it, it's like this: If a girl loves somebody, that means she's immoral. (*Pause.*) Very pleasant smoking a cigar in the open air. . . . (*Listens.*) Someone's coming this way. . . . It's the masters. (*Dunyasha impulsively embraces him.*) You go home, as if you'd been to the river to bathe; take that path, otherwise they'll see you and suspect me of having a rendezvous with you. I can't endure that sort of thing.

DUNYASHA (*with a little cough*): My head is beginning to ache from your cigar. . . . (*Goes out.*)

(*Yasha remains, sitting near the chapel. Lyubov Andreyevna, Gayev, and Lopakhin enter.*)

LOPAKHIN: You must make up your mind once and for all—time won't stand still. The question, after all, is quite simple. Do you agree to lease the land for summer cottages or not? Answer in one word: Yes or no? Only one word!

LYUBOV ANDREYEVNA: Who is it that smokes those disgusting cigars out here? (*Sits down.*)

GAYEV: Now that the railway line is so near, it's made things convenient. (*Sits down.*) We went to town and had lunch . . . cue ball to center! I feel like going to the house first and playing a game.

LYUBOV ANDREYEVNA: Later.

LOPAKHIN: Just one word! (*Imploringly.*) Do give me an answer!

GAYEV (*yawning*): How's that?

LYUBOV ANDREYEVNA (*looks into her purse*): Yesterday I had a lot of money, and today there' hardly any left. My poor Varya tries to economize by feeding everyone milk soup, and in the kitchen the old people get nothing but dried peas, while I squander money

821

foolishly.... (*Drops the purse, scattering gold coins.*) There they go.... (*Vexed.*)

YASHA: Allow me, I'll pick them up in an instant. (*Picks up the money.*)

LYUBOV ANDREYEVNA: Please do, Yasha. And why did I go to town for lunch? ... That miserable restaurant of yours with its music, and tablecloths smelling of soap.... Why drink so much, Lyonya? Why eat so much? Why talk so much? Today in the restaurant again you talked too much, and it was all so pointless. About the seventies, about the decadents. And to whom? Talking to waiters about the decadents!

LOPAKHIN: Yes.

GAYEV (*waving his hand*): I'm incorrigible, that's evident.... (*Irritably to Yasha.*) Why do you keep twirling about in front of me?

YASHA (*laughs*): I can't help laughing when I hear your voice.

GAYEV (*to his sister*): Either he or I—

LYUBOV ANDREYEVNA: Go away, Yasha, run along.

YASHA (*hands Lyubov Andreyevna her purse*): I'm going, right away. (*Hardly able to contain his laughter.*) This very instant.... (*Goes out.*)

LOPAKHIN: That rich man, Deriganov, is prepared to buy the estate. They say he's coming to the auction himself.

[ABOVE] The spare set in Ron Daniels's 1993 production of *The Cherry Orchard* at the American Repertory Theatre highlights the characters' emotional isolation.
[RIGHT] Claire Bloom as Madame Ranevskaya.

LYUBOV ANDREYEVNA: Where did you hear that?

LOPAKHIN: That's what they're saying in town.

LYUBOV ANDREYEVNA: Our aunt in Yaroslav promised to send us something, but when and how much, no one knows.

LOPAKHIN: How much do you think she'll send? A hundred thousand? Two hundred?

LYUBOV ANDREYEVNA: Oh . . . ten or fifteen thousand, and we'll be thankful for that.

LOPAKHIN: Forgive me, but I have never seen such frivolous, such queer, unbusinesslike people as you, my friends. You are told in plain language that your estate is to be sold, and it's as though you don't understand it.

LYUBOV ANDREYEVNA: But what are we to do? Tell us what to do.

LOPAKHIN: I tell you every day. Every day I say the same thing. Both the cherry orchard and the land must be leased for summer cottages, and it must be done now, as quickly as possible—the auction is close at hand. Try to understand! Once you definitely decide on the cottages, you can raise as much money as you like, and then you are saved.

LYUBOV ANDREYEVNA: Cottages, summer people—forgive me, but it's so vulgar.

GAYEV: I agree with you, absolutely.

LOPAKHIN: I'll either burst into tears, start shouting, or fall into a faint! I can't stand it! You've worn me out! (*To Gayev.*) You're an old woman!

GAYEV: How's that?

LOPAKHIN: An old woman! (*Starts to go.*)

LYUBOV ANDREYEVNA (*alarmed*): No, don't go, stay, my dear. I beg you. Perhaps we'll think of something!

LOPAKHIN: What is there to think of?

LYUBOV ANDREYEVNA: Don't go away, please. With you here it's more cheerful somehow. . . . (*Pause.*) I keep expecting something to happen, like the house caving in on us.

GAYEV (*in deep thought*): Double rail shot into the corner. . . . Cross table to the center. . . .

LYUBOV ANDREYEVNA: We have sinned so much. . . .

LOPAKHIN: What sins could you have—

GAYEV (*puts a candy into his mouth*): They say I've eaten up my entire fortune in candies. . . . (*Laughs.*)

LYUBOV ANDREYEVNA: Oh, my sins. . . . I've always squandered money recklessly, like a madwoman, and I married a man who did nothing but amass debts. My husband died from champagne—he drank terribly—then, to my sorrow, I fell in love with another man, lived with him, and just at that time—that was my first punishment, a blow on the head—my little boy was drowned . . . here in the river. And I went abroad, went away for good, never to return, never to see this river. . . . I closed my eyes and ran, beside myself, and *he* after me. . . . callously, without pity. I bought a villa near Mentone, becuase he fell ill there, and for three years I had no rest, day or night. The sick man wore me out, my soul dried up. Then last year, when the villa was sold to pay my debts, I went to Paris, and there he stripped me of everything, and left me for another woman; I tried to poison myself. . . . So stupid, so shameful. . . . And suddenly I felt a longing for Russia, for my own country, for my little girl. . . . (*Wipes away her tears.*) Lord, Lord, be merciful, forgive my sins! Don't punish me anymore! (*Takes a telegram out of her pocket.*) This came today from Paris. . . . He asks my forgiveness, begs me to return. . . . (*Tears up telegram.*) Do I hear music? (*Listens.*)

GAYEV: That's our famous Jewish band. You remember, four violins, a flute, and double bass.

LYUBOV ANDREYEVNA: It's still in existence? We ought to send for them sometime and give a party.

LOPAKHIN (*listens*): I don't hear anything. . . . (*Sings softly.*) "The Germans, for pay, will turn Russians into Frenchmen, they say." (*Laughs.*) What a play I saw yesterday at the theater—very funny!

LYUBOV ANDREYEVNA: There was probably nothing funny about it. Instead of going to see plays you ought to look at yourselves a little more often. How drab your lives are, how full of futile talk!

LOPAKHIN: That's true. I must say, this life of ours is stupid. . . . (*Pause.*) My father was a peasant, an idiot; he understood nothing, taught me nothing; all he did was beat me when he was drunk, and always with a stick. As a matter of fact, I'm as big a blockhead and idiot as he was. I never learned anything, my handwriting's disgusting, I write like a pig—I'm ashamed to have people see it.

LYUBOV ANDREYEVNA: You ought to get married, my friend.

LOPAKHIN: Yes . . . that's true.

LYUBOV ANDREYEVNA: To our Varya. She's a nice girl.

LOPAKHIN: Yes.

LYUBOV ANDREYEVNA: She's a girl who comes from simple people, works all day long, but the main thing is she loves you. Besides, you've liked her for a long time now.

LOPAKHIN: Well? I've nothing against it . . . She's a good girl. (*Pause.*)

GAYEV: I've been offered a place in the bank. Six thousand a year. . . . Have you heard?

LYUBOV ANDREYEVNA: How could you! You stay where you are. . . .

(*Firs enters carrying an overcoat.*)

FIRS (*to Gayev*): If you please, sir, put this on, it's damp.

GAYEV (*puts on the overcoat*): You're a pest, old man.

FIRS: Never mind. . . . You went off this morning without telling me. (*Looks him over.*)

LYUBOV ANDREYEVNA: How you have aged, Firs!

FIRS: What do you wish, madam?

LOPAKHIN: She says you've grown very old!

FIRS: I've lived a long time. They were arranging a marriage for me before your papa was born. . . . (*Laughs.*) I was already head footman when the emancipation came. At that time I wouldn't consent to my freedom, I stayed with the masters. . . . (*Pause.*) I remember, everyone was happy, but what they were happy about, they themselves didn't know.

LOPAKHIN: It was better in the old days. At least they flogged them.

FIRS (*not hearing*): Of course. The peasants kept to the masters, the masters kept to the peasants; but now they have all gone their own ways, you can't tell about anything.

GAYEV: Be quiet, Firs. Tomorrow I must go to town. I've been promised an introduction to a certain general who might let us have a loan.

LOPAKHIN: Nothing will come of it. And you can rest assured, you won't even pay the interest.

LYUBOV ANDREYEVNA: He's raving. There is no such general.

(*Enter Trofimov, Anya, and Varya.*)

GAYEV: Here come our young people.

ANYA: There's Mama.

LYUBOV ANDREYEVNA (*tenderly*): Come, come along, my darlings. (*Embraces Anya and Varya.*) If you only knew how I love you both! Sit here beside me—there, like that.

(*They all sit down.*)

LOPAKHIN: Our eternal student is always with the young ladies.

TROFIMOV: That's none of your business.

LOPAKHIN: He'll soon be fifty, but he's still a student.

TROFIMOV: Drop your stupid jokes.

LOPAKHIN: What are you so angry about, you queer fellow?

TROFIMOV: Just leave me alone.

LOPAKHIN (*laughs*): Let me ask you something: What do you make of me?

TROFIMOV: My idea of you, Yermolai Alekseich, is this: You're a rich man, you will soon be a millionaire. Just as the beast of prey, which devours everything that crosses its path, is necessary in the metabolic process, so are you necessary.

(*Everyone laughs.*)

VARYA: Petya, you'd better tell us something about the planets.

LYUBOV ANDREYEVNA: No, let's go on with yesterday's conversation.

TROFIMOV: What was it about?

GAYEV: About the proud man.

TROFIMOV: We talked a long time yesterday, but we didn't get anywhere. In the proud man, in your sense of the word, there's something mystical. And you may be right from your point of view, but if you look at it simply, without being abstruse, why even talk about pride? Is there any sense in it if, physiologically, man is poorly constructed, if, in the vast majority of cases, he is coarse, ignorant, and profoundly unhappy? We should stop admiring ourselves. We should just work, and that's all.

GAYEV: You die, anyway.

TROFIMOV: Who knows? And what does it mean—to die? It may be that man has a hundred senses, and at his death only the five that are known to us perish, and the other ninety-five go on living.

LYUBOV ANDREYEVNA: How clever you are, Petya!

LOPAKHIN (*ironically*): Terribly clever!

TROFIMOV: Mankind goes forward, perfecting its powers. Everything that is now unattainable will some day be comprehensible and within our grasp, only we must work, and help with all our might those who are seeking the truth. So far, among us here in Russia, only a very few work. The great majority of the intelligentsia that I know seek nothing, do nothing, and as yet are incapable of work. They call themselves the intelligentsia, yet they belittle their servants, treat the peasants like animals, are wretched students, never read anything serious, and do absolutely nothing; they only talk about science and know very little about art. They all look serious, have grim expressions, speak of weighty matters, and philosophize; and meanwhile anyone can see that the workers eat abominably, sleep without pillows, thirty of forty to a room, and everywhere there are bedbugs, stench, dampness, and immorality.... It's obvious that all our fine talk is merely to delude ourselves and others. Show me the day nurseries they are always talking about—and where are the reading rooms? They only write about them in novels, but in reality they don't exist. There is nothing but filth, vulgarity, asiaticism.°... I'm afraid of those very serious countenances, I don't like them, I'm afraid of serious conversations. We'd do better to remain silent.

LOPAKHIN: You know, I get up before five in the morning, and I work from morning to night; now, I'm always handling money, my own and other people's, and I see what people around me are like. You have only to start doing something to find out how few honest, decent people there are. Sometimes, when I can't sleep, I think: "Lord, Thou gavest us vast forests, boundless fields, broad horizons, and living in their midst we ourselves ought truly to be giants...."

LYUBOV ANDREYEVNA: Now you want giants! They're good only in fairy tales, otherwise they're frightening.

(*Yepikhodov crosses at the rear of the stage, playing the guitar.*)

LYUBOV ANDREYEVNA (*pensively*): There goes Yepikhodov...

ANYA (*pensively*): There goes Yepikhodov...

GAYEV: The sun has set, ladies and gentlemen.

TROFIMOV: Yes.

GAYEV (*in a low voice, as though reciting*): Oh, Nature, wondrous Nature, you shine with eternal radiance, beautiful and indifferent; you, whom we call mother, unite within yourself both life and death, giving life and taking it away....

---

asiaticism: Trofimov, expressing a common prejudice of the time, refers to Asian apathy.

VARYA (*beseechingly*): Uncle dear!

ANYA: Uncle, you're doing it again!

TROFIMOV: You'd better cue ball into the center.

GAYEV: I'll be silent, silent.

(*All sit lost in thought. The silence is broken only by the subdued muttering of Firs. Suddenly a distant sound is heard, as if from the sky, like the sound of a snapped string mournfully dying away.*)

LYUBOV ANDREYEVNA: What was that?

LOPAKHIN: I don't know. Somewhere far off in a mine shaft a bucket's broken loose. But somewhere very far away.

GAYEV: It might be a bird of some sort . . . like a heron.

TROFIMOV: Or an owl . . .

LYUBOV ANDREYEVNA (*shudders*): It's unpleasant somehow. . . . (*Pause.*)

FIRS: The same thing happened before the troubles: An owl hooted and the samovar hissed continually.

GAYEV: Before what troubles?

FIRS: Before the emancipation.

LYUBOV ANDREYEVNA: Come along, my friends, let us go, evening is falling. (*To Anya.*) There are tears in your eyes—what is it, my little one?

(*Embraces her.*)

ANYA: It's all right, Mama. It's nothing.

TROFIMOV: Someone is coming.

(*A Stranger appears wearing a shabby white forage cap and an overcoat. He is slightly drunk.*)

STRANGER: Permit me to inquire, can I go straight through here to the station?

GAYEV: You can. Follow the road.

STRANGER: I am deeply grateful to you. (*Coughs.*) Splendid weather. . . . (*Reciting.*) "My brother, my suffering brother . . . come to the Volga, whose groans" . . . (*To Varya.*) Mademoiselle, will you oblige a hungry Russian with thirty kopecks?

(*Varya, frightened, cries out.*)

LOPAKHIN (*angrily*): There's a limit to everything.

LYUBOV ANDREYEVNA (*panic-stricken*): Here you are—take this. . . . (*Fumbles in her purse.*) I have no silver. . . . Never mind, here's a gold piece for you. . . .

STRANGER: I am deeply grateful to you. (*Goes off.*)

(*Laughter.*)

VARYA (*frightened*): I'm leaving . . . I'm leaving. . . . Oh, Mama, dear, there's nothing in the house for the servants to eat, and you give him a gold piece!

LYUBOV ANDREYEVNA: What's to be done with such a silly creature? When we get home I'll give you all I've got. Yermolai Alekseyevich, you'll lend me some more!

LOPAKHIN: At your service.

LYUBOV ANDREYEVNA: Come, my friends, it's time to go. Oh, Varya, we have definitely made a match for you. Congratulations!

VARYA (*through tears*): Mama, that's not something to joke about.

LOPAKHIN: "Aurelia, get thee to a nunnery . . ."°

GAYEV: Look, my hands are trembling: It's a long time since I've played a game of billiards.

LOPAKHIN: "Aurelia, O Nymph, in thy orisons, be all my sins remember'd!"

LYUBOV ANDREYEVNA: Let us go, my friends, it will soon be suppertime.

VARYA: He frightened me. My heart is simply pounding.

LOPAKHIN: Let me remind you, ladies and gentlemen: On the twenty-second of August the cherry orchard is to be sold. Think about that!—Think!

(*All go out except Trofimov and Anya.*)

ANYA (*laughs*): My thanks to the stranger for frightening Varya, now we are alone.

TROFIMOV: Varya is so afraid we might suddenly fall in love with each other that she hasn't left us alone for days. With her narrow mind she can't understand that we are above love. To avoid the petty and the illusory, which prevent our being free and happy—that is the aim and meaning of life. Forward! We are moving irresistibly toward the bright star that burns in the distance! Forward! Do not fall behind, friends!

ANYA (*clasping her hands*): How well you talk! (*Pause.*) It's marvelous here today!

TROFIMOV: Yes, the weather is wonderful.

ANYA: What have you done to me, Petya, that I no longer love the cherry orchard as I used to? I loved it so tenderly, it seemed to me there was no better place on earth than our orchard.

TROFIMOV: All Russia is our orchard. It is a great and beautiful land, and there are many wonderful places in it. (*Pause.*) Just think, Anya: Your grandfather, your great-grandfather, and all your ancestors were serf-owners, possessors of living souls. Don't you see that from every cherry tree, from every leaf and trunk, human beings are peering out at you? Don't you hear their voices? To possess living souls—that has corrupted all of you, those who lived before and you who are living now, so that your mother, you, your uncle, no longer perceive that you are living in debt, at someone else's expense, at the expense of those whom you wouldn't allow to cross your threshold. . . . We are at least two hundred years behind the times, we have as yet absolutely nothing, we have no definite attitude toward the past, we only philosophize, complain of boredom, or drink vodka. Yet it's quite clear that to begin to live we must first atone for the past, be done with it, and we can atone for it only by suffering, only by extraordinary, unceasing labor. Understand this, Anya.

ANYA: The house we live in hasn't really been ours for a long time, and I shall leave it, I give you my word.

"*Aurelia . . . nunnery*": From Hamlet's famous line rejecting Ophelia (Lopakhin's next line is also from Shakespeare's *Hamlet*).

TROFIMOV: If you have the keys of the household, throw them into the well and go. Be as free as the wind.

ANYA (*in ecstasy*): How well you put that!

TROFIMOV: Believe me, Anya, believe me! I am not yet thirty, I am young, still a student, but I have already been through so much! As soon as winter comes, I am hungry, sick, worried, poor as a beggar, and—where has not fate driven me! Where have I not been? And yet always, every minute of the day and night, my soul was filled with inexplicable premonitions. I have a premonition of happiness, Anya, I can see it . . .

ANYA: The moon is rising.

(*Yepikhodov is heard playing the same melancholy song on the guitar. The moon rises. Somewhere near the poplars Varya is looking for Anya and calling: "Anya, where are you?"*)

TROFIMOV: Yes, the moon is rising. (*Pause*). There it is—happiness . . . It's coming, nearer and nearer, I can hear its footsteps. And if we do not see it, if we do not recognize it, what does it matter? Others will see it.

VARYA'S VOICE: Anya! Where are you?

TROFIMOV: That Varya again! (*Angrily*.) It's revolting!

ANYA: Well? Let's go down to the river. It's lovely there.

TROFIMOV: Come on. (*They go.*)

VARYA'S VOICE: Anya! Anya!

ACT III

(*The drawing room, separated by an arch from the ballroom. The chandelier is lighted. The Jewish band that was mentioned in act II is heard playing in the hall. It is evening. In the ballroom they are dancing a grand rond. The voice of Semyonov-Pishchik: "Promenade à une paire!"° They all enter the drawing room: Pishchik and Charlotta Ivanovna are the first couple, Trofimov and Lyubov Andreyevna the second, Anya and the Post-Office Clerk the third, Varya and the Stationmaster the fourth, etc. Varya, quietly weeping, dries her tears as she dances. Dunyasha is in the last couple. As they cross the drawing room Pishchik calls: "Grand rond, balancez!" and "Les cavaliers à genoux et remerciez vos dames!"° Firs, wearing a dress coat, brings in a tray with seltzer water. Pishchik and Trofimov come into the drawing room.*)

PISHCHIK: I'm a full-blooded man, I've already had two strokes, and dancing's hard work for me, but as they say, "If you run with the pack, you can bark or not, but at least wag your tail." At that, I'm as strong as a horse. My late father—quite a joker he was, God rest his soul—used to say, talking about our origins, that the ancient line of Semyonov-Pishchik was descended from the very horse that Caligula had

"*Promenade à une paire!*": French for "Walk in pairs!" "*Grand rond . . . dames!*": Instructions in the dance: "Large circle!" and "Gentlemen, kneel down and thank your ladies!"

seated in the Senate.° . . . (*Sits down.*) But the trouble is—no money! A hungry dog believes in nothing but meat. . . . (*Snores but wakes up at once.*) It's the same with me—I can think of nothing but money. . . .

TROFIMOV: You know, there really is something equine about your figure.

PISHCHIK: Well, a horse is a fine animal. . . . You can sell a horse.

(*There is the sound of a billiard game in the next room. Varya appears in the archway.*)

TROFIMOV (*teasing her*): Madame Lopakhina! Madame Lopakhina!

VARYA (*angrily*): Mangy gentleman!

TROFIMOV: Yes, I am a mangy gentleman, and proud of it!

VARYA (*reflecting bitterly*): Here we've hired musicians, and what are we going to pay them with? (*Goes out.*)

TROFIMOV (*to Pishchik*): If the energy you have expended in the course of your life trying to find money to pay interest had gone into something else, ultimately, you might very well have turned the world upside down.

PISHCHIK: Nietzsche . . . the philosopher . . . the greatest, most renowned . . . a man of tremendous intellect . . . says in his works that it is possible to forge banknotes.

TROFIMOV: And have you read Nietzsche?

PISHCHIK: Well . . . Dashenka told me. I'm in such a state now that I'm just about ready for forging. . . . The day after tomorrow I have to pay three hundred and ten rubles . . . I've got a hundred and thirty. . . . (*Feels in his pocket, grows alarmed.*) The money is gone! I've lost the money! (*Tearfully.*) Where is my money? (*Joyfully.*) Here it is, inside the lining. . . . I'm all in a sweat. . . .

(*Lyubov Andreyevna and Charlotta Ivanovna come in.*)

LYUBOV ANDREYEVNA (*humming a Lezginka*):° Why does Leonid take so long? What is he doing in town? (*To Dunyasha.*) Dunyasha, offer the musicians some tea.

TROFIMOV: In all probability, the auction didn't take place.

LYUBOV ANDREYEVNA: It was the wrong time to have the musicians, the wrong time to give a dance. . . . Well, never mind. . . . (*Sits down and hums softly.*)

CHARLOTTA (*gives Pishchik a deck of cards*): Here's a deck of cards for you. Think of a card.

PISHCHIK: I've thought of one.

CHARLOTTA: Now shuffle the pack. Very good. And now, my dear Mr. Pishchik, hand it to me. *Eins, zwei, drei!*° Now look for it—it's in your side pocket.

PISHCHIK: (*takes the card out of his side pocket*): The eight of spades—absolutely right! (*Amazed.*) Think of that, now!

CHARLOTTA (*holding the deck of cards in the palm of her hand, to Trofimov*): Quickly, tell me, which card is on top?

Caligula . . . Senate: Caligula (CE 12–41), a cavalry soldier, was Roman emperor (CE 37–41). **Lezginka:** A lively Russian tune for a dance. ***Eins, zwei, drei!:*** "One, two, three!" (German).

TROFIMOV: What? Well, the queen of spades.

CHARLOTTA: Right! (*To Pishchik.*) Now which card is on top?

PISHCHIK: The ace of hearts.

CHARLOTTA: Right! (*Claps her hands and the deck of cards disappears.*) What lovely weather we're having today! (*A mysterious feminine voice, which seems to come from under the floor, answers her: "Oh, yes, splendid weather, madam."*) You are so nice, you're my ideal. . . . (*The voice: "And I'm very fond of you, too, madam."*)

STATIONMASTER (*applauding*): Bravo, Madame Ventriloquist!

PISHCHIK (*amazed*): Think of that, now! Most enchanting Charlotta Ivanovna . . . I am simply in love with you. . . .

CHARLOTTA: In love? (*Shrugs her shoulders.*) Is it possible that you can love? *Guter Mensch, aber schlechter Musikant.*°

TROFIMOV (*claps Pishchik on the shoulder*): You old horse, you!

CHARLOTTA: Attention, please! One more trick. (*Takes a lap robe from a chair.*) Here's a very fine lap robe; I should like to sell it. (*Shakes it out.*) Doesn't anyone want to buy it?

PISHCHIK (*amazed*): Think of that, now!

CHARLOTTA: *Eins, zwei, drei!* (*Quickly raises the lap robe, behind it stands Anya, who curtsies, runs to her mother, embraces her, and runs back into the ballroom amid the general enthusiasm.*)

LYUBOV ANDREYEVNA (*applauding*): Bravo, bravo!

CHARLOTTA: Once again! *Eins, zwei, drei.* (*Raises the lap robe; behind it stands Varya, who bows.*)

PISHCHIK (*amazed*): Think of that, now!

CHARLOTTA: The end! (*Throws the robe at Pishchik, makes a curtsy, and runs out of the room.*)

PISHCHIK (*hurries after her*): The minx! . . . What a woman! What a woman! (*Goes out.*)

LYUBOV ANDREYEVNA: And Leonid still not here. What he is doing in town so long, I do not understand! It must be all over by now. Either the estate is sold, or the auction didn't take place—but why keep us in suspense so long!

VARYA (*trying to comfort her*): Uncle has bought it, I am certain of that.

TROFIMOV (*mockingly*): Yes.

VARYA: Great-aunt sent him power of attorney to buy it in her name and transfer the debt. She's doing it for Anya's sake. And I am sure, with God's help, Uncle will buy it.

LYUBOV ANDREYEVNA: Our great-aunt in Yaroslav sent fifteen thousand to buy the estate in her name—she doesn't trust us—but that's not even enough to pay the interest. (*Covers her face with her hands.*) Today my fate will be decided, my fate . . .

TROFIMOV (*teasing Varya*): Madame Lopakhina!

Guter Mensch, aber schlechter Musikant: "Good man, but poor musician" (German).

VARYA (*angrily*): Eternal student! Twice already you've been expelled from the university.

LYUBOV ANDREYEVNA: Why are you so cross, Varya? If he teases you about Lopakhin, what of it? Go ahead and marry Lopakhin if you want to. He's a nice man, he's interesting. And if you don't want to, don't. Nobody's forcing you, my pet.

VARYA: To be frank, Mama dear, I regard this matter seriously. He is a good man, I like him.

LYUBOV ANDREYEVNA: Then marry him. I don't know what you're waiting for!

VARYA: Mama, I can't propose to him myself. For the last two years everyone's been talking to me about him; everyone talks, but he is either silent or he jokes. I understand. He's getting rich, he's absorbed in business, he has no time for me. If I had some money, no matter how little, if it were only a hundred rubles, I'd drop everything and go far away. I'd go into a nunnery.

TROFIMOV: A blessing!

VARYA (*to Trofimov*): A student ought to be intelligent! (*In a gentle tone, tearfully.*) How homely you have grown, Petya, how old! (*To Lyubov Andreyevna, no longer crying.*) It's just that I cannot live without work, Mama. I must be doing something every minute.

(*Yasha enters.*)

YASHA (*barely able to suppress his laughter*): Yepikhodov has broken a billiard cue! (*Goes out.*)

VARYA: But why is Yepikhodov here? Who gave him permission to play billiards? I don't understand these people. . . . (*Goes out.*)

LYUBOV ANDREYEVNA: Don't tease her, Petya. You can see she's unhappy enough without that.

TROFIMOV: She's much too zealous, always meddling in other people's affairs. All summer long she's given Anya and me no peace—afraid a romance might develop. What business is it of hers? Besides, I've given no occasion for it, I am far removed from such banality. We are above love!

LYUBOV ANDREYEVNA: And I suppose I am beneath love. (*In great agitation.*) Why isn't Leonid here? If only I knew whether the estate had been sold or not! The disaster seems to me so incredible that I don't even know what to think, I'm lost. . . . I could scream this very instant . . . I could do something foolish. Save me, Petya. Talk to me, say something. . . .

TROFIMOV: Whether or not the estate is sold today—does it really matter? That's all done with long ago; there's no turning back, the path is overgrown. Be calm, my dear. One must not deceive oneself; at least once in one's life one ought to look the truth straight in the eye.

LYUBOV ANDREYEVNA: What truth? You can see where there is truth and where there isn't, but I seem to have lost my sight, I see nothing. You boldly settle all the important problems, but tell me, my dear boy, isn't it because you are young and have not yet had to suffer for a single one of your problems? You boldly look ahead, but isn't it because you neither see nor expect anything dreadful, since life is still hidden from your young eyes? You're bolder, more honest, deeper than we are, but think about it, be just a little bit magnanimous, and spare me. You see, I was born here, my mother and father lived here, and my grandfather. I love this house, without the cherry orchard my life has no meaning for me, and if it must be sold, then sell me with the orchard.... (*Embraces Trofimov and kisses him on the forehead.*) And my son was drowned here.... (*Weeps.*) Have pity on me, you good, kind man.

TROFIMOV: You know I feel for you with all my heart.

LYUBOV ANDREYEVNA: But that should have been said differently, quite differently.... (*Takes out her handkerchief and a telegram falls to the floor.*) My heart is heavy today, you can't imagine. It's so noisy here, my soul quivers at every sound, I tremble all over, and yet I can't go to my room. When I am alone the silence frightens me. Don't condemn me, Petya...I love you as if you were my own. I would gladly let you marry Anya, I swear it, only you must study, my dear, you must get your degree. You do nothing, fate simply tosses you from place to place—it's so strange.... Isn't that true? Isn't it? And you must do something about your beard, to make it grow somehow.... (*Laughs.*) You're so funny!

TROFIMOV (*picks up the telegram*): I have no desire to be an Adonis.°

LYUBOV ANDREYEVNA: That's a telegram from Paris. I get them every day. One yesterday, one today. That wild man has fallen ill again, he's in trouble again.... He begs my forgiveness, implores me to come, and really, I ought to go to Paris to be near him. Your face is stern, Petya, but what can one do, my dear? What am I to do? He is ill, he's alone and unhappy, and who will look after him there, who will keep him from making mistakes, who will give him his medicine on time? And why hide it or keep silent, I love him, that's clear. I love him, love him.... It's a millstone round my neck, I'm sinking to the bottom with it, but I love that stone, I cannot live without. it. (*Presses Trofimov's hand.*) Don't think badly of me, Petya, and don't say anything to me, don't say anything....

TROFIMOV (*through tears*): For God's sake, forgive my frankness: You know that he robbed you!

LYUBOV ANDREYEVNA: No, no, no, you mustn't say such things! (*Covers her ears.*)

TROFIMOV: But he's a scoundrel! You're the only one who doesn't know it! He's a petty scoundrel, a nonentity—

LYUBOV ANDREYEVNA (*angry, but controlling herself*): You are twenty-six or twenty-seven years old, but you're still a schoolboy!

TROFIMOV: That may be!

LYUBOV ANDREYEVNA: You should be a man, at your age you ought to understand those who love. And you ought to be in love yourself. (*Angrily.*) Yes, yes!

Adonis: From Greek myth, a beautiful young man.

It's not purity with you, it's simply prudery, you're a ridiculous crank, a freak—

TROFIMOV (*horrified*): What is she saying!

LYUBOV ANDREYEVNA: I am above love! You're not above love, you're just an addlepate, as Firs would say. Not to have a mistress at your age!

TROFIMOV (*in horror*): This is awful! What is she saying!.... (*Goes quickly toward the ballroom.*) This is awful...I can't...I won't stay here.... (*Goes out, but immediately returns.*) All is over between us! (*Goes out to the hall.*)

LYUBOV ANDREYEVNA (*calls after him*): Petya, wait! You absurd creature, I was joking! Petya!

(*In the hall there is the sound of someone running quickly downstairs and suddenly falling with a crash. Anya and Varya scream, but a moment later laughter is heard.*)

LYUBOV ANDREYEVNA: What was that?

(*Anya runs in.*)

ANYA (*laughing*): Petya fell down the stairs! (*Runs out.*)

LYUBOV ANDREYEVNA: What a funny boy that Petya is!

(*The Stationmaster stands in the middle of the ballroom and recites A. Tolstoy's° "The Sinner." Everyone listens to him, but he has no sooner spoken a few lines than the sound of a waltz is heard from the hall and recitation is broken off. They all dance. Trofimov, Anya, Varya, and Lyubov Andreyevna come in from the hall.*)

LYUBOV ANDREYEVNA: Come, Petya...come, you pure soul...please, forgive me.... Let's dance.... (*They dance.*)

(*Anya and Varya dance. Firs comes in, puts his stick by the side door. Yasha also comes into the drawing room and watches the dancers.*)

YASHA: What is it, grandpa?

FIRS: I don't feel well. In the old days, we used to have generals, barons, admirals, dancing at our balls, but now we send for the post office clerk and the stationmaster, and even they are none too eager to come. Somehow I've grown weak. The late master, their grandfather, dosed everyone with sealing wax, no matter what ailed them. I've been taking sealing wax every day for twenty years or more, maybe that's what's kept me alive.

YASHA: You bore me, grandpa. (*Yawns.*) High time you croaked.

FIRS: Ah, you...addlepate! (*Mumbles.*)

(*Trofimov and Lyubov Andreyevna dance from the ballroom into the drawing room.*)

LYUBOV ANDREYEVNA: *Merci.* I'll sit down a while. (*Sits.*) I'm tired.

(*Anya comes in.*)

A. Tolstoy: Aleksey Konstantinovich Tolstoy (1817–1875), Russian novelist, dramatist, and poet.

ANYA (*excitedly*): There was a man in the kitchen just now saying that the cherry orchard was sold today.

LYUBOV ANDREYEVNA: Sold to whom?

ANYA: He didn't say. He's gone. (*Dances with Trofimov; they go into the ballroom.*)

YASHA: That was just some old man babbling. A stranger.

FIRS: Leonid Andreich is not back yet, still hasn't come. And he's wearing the light, between-seasons overcoat; like enough he'll catch cold. Ah, when they're young they're green.

LYUBOV ANDREYEVNA: This is killing me. Yasha, go and find out who it was sold to.

YASHA: But that old man left long ago. (*Laughs.*)

LYUBOV ANDREYEVNA (*slightly annoyed*): Well, what are you laughing at? What are you so happy about?

YASHA: That Yepikhodov is very funny! Hopeless! Two-and-twenty Troubles.

LYUBOV ANDREYEVNA: Firs, if the estate is sold, where will you go?

FIRS: Wherever you tell me to go, I'll go.

LYUBOV ANDREYEVNA: Why do you look like that? Aren't you well? You ought to go to bed.

FIRS: Yes.... (*With a smirk.*) Go to bed, and without me who will serve, who will see to things? I'm the only one in the whole house.

YASHA (*to Lyubov Andreyevna*): Lyubov Andreyevna! Permit me to make a request, be so kind. If you go back to Paris again, do me the favor of taking me with you. It is positively impossible for me to stay here. (*Looking around, then in a low voice.*) There's no need to say it, you can see for yourself, it's an uncivilized country, the people have no morals, and the boredom! The food they give us in the kitchen is unmentionable, and besides, there's this Firs who keeps walking about mumbling all sorts of inappropriate things. Take me with you, be so kind!

(*Enter Pishchik.*)

PISHCHIK: May I have the pleasure of a waltz with you, fairest lady? (*Lyubov Andreyevna goes with him.*) I really must borrow a hundred and eighty rubles from you, my charmer ... I really must.... (*Dancing.*) Just a hundred and eighty rubles.... (*They pass into the ballroom.*)

YASHA (*softly sings*): "Wilt thou know my soul's unrest ..."

(*In the ballroom a figure in a gray top hat and checked trousers is jumping about, waving its arms; there are shouts of "Bravo, Charlotta Ivanovna!"*)

DUNYASHA (*stopping to powder her face*): The young mistress told me to dance — there are lots of gentlemen and not enough ladies — but dancing makes me dizzy, and my heart begins to thump. Firs Nikolayevich, the post office clerk just said something to me that took my breath away.

(*The music grows more subdued.*)

FIRS: What did he say to you?

DUNYASHA: "You," he said, "are like a flower."

YASHA (*yawns*): What ignorance.... (*Goes out.*)

DUNYASHA: Like a flower.... I'm such a delicate girl, I just adore tender words.

FIRS: You'll get your head turned.

(*Enter Yepikhodov.*)

YEPIKHODOV: Avdotya Fyodorovna, you are not desirous of seeing me.... I might almost be some sort of insect. (*Sighs.*) Ah, life!

DUNYASHA: What is it you want?

YEPIKHODOV: Indubitably, you may be right. (*Sighs.*) But, of course, if one looks at it from a point of view, then, if I may so express myself, and you will forgive my frankness, you have completely reduced me to a state of mind. I know my fate, every day some misfortune befalls me, but I have long since grown accustomed to that; I look upon my fate with a smile. But you gave me your word, and although I—

DUNYASHA: Please, we'll talk about it later, but leave me in peace now. Just now I'm dreaming.... (*Plays with her fan.*)

YEPIKHODOV: Every day a misfortune, and yet, if I may so express myself, I merely smile, I even laugh.

(*Varya enters from the ballroom.*)

VARYA: Are you still here, Semyon? What a disrespectful man you are, really! (*To Dunyasha.*) Run along, Dunyasha. (*To Yepikhodov.*) First you play billiards and break a cue, then you wander about the drawing room as though you were a guest.

YEPIKHODOV: You cannot, if I may so express myself, penalize me.

VARYA: I am not penalizing you, I'm telling you. You do nothing but wander from one place to another, and you don't do your work. We keep a clerk, but for what, I don't know.

YEPIKHODOV (*offended*): Whether I work, or wander about, or eat, or play billiards, these are matters to be discussed only by persons of discernment, and my elders.

VARYA: You dare say that to me! (*Flaring up.*) You dare? You mean to say I have no discernment? Get out of here! This instant!

YEPIKHODOV (*intimidated*): I beg you to express yourself in a more delicate manner.

VARYA (*beside herself*): Get out, this very instant! Get out! (*He goes to the door, she follows him.*) Two-and-twenty Troubles! Don't let me set eyes on you again!

YEPIKHODOV (*goes out, his voice is heard behind the door*): I shall lodge a complaint against you!

VARYA: Oh, you're coming back? (*Seizes the stick left near the door by Firs.*) Come, come on.... Come, I'll show you.... Ah, so you're coming, are you? Then take that—(*Swings the stick just as Lopakhin enters.*)

LOPAKHIN: Thank you kindly.

VARYA (*angrily and mockingly*): I beg your pardon.

LOPAKHIN: Not at all. I humbly thank you for your charming reception.

VARYA: Don't mention it. (*Walks away, then looks back and gently asks.*) I didn't hurt you, did I?

LOPAKHIN: No, it's nothing. A huge bump coming up, that's all.

(*Voices in the ballroom: "Lopakhin has come! Yermolai Alekseich!" Pishchik enters.*)

PISHCHIK: As I live and breathe! (*Kisses Lopakhin.*) There is a whiff of cognac about you, dear soul. And we've been making merry here, too.

(*Enter Lyubov Andreyevna.*)

LYUBOV ANDREYEVNA: Is that you, Yermolai Alekseich? What kept you so long? Where's Leonid?

LOPAKHIN: Leonid Andreich arrived with me, he's coming . . .

LYUBOV ANDREYEVNA (*agitated*): Well, what happened? Did the sale take place? Tell me!

LOPAKHIN (*embarrassed, fearing to reveal his joy*): The auction was over by four o'clock. . . . We missed the train, had to wait till half past nine. (*Sighing heavily.*) Ugh! My head is swimming. . . .

(*Enter Gayev; he carries his purchases in one hand and wipes away his tears with the other.*)

LYUBOV ANDREYEVNA: Lyonya, what happened? Well, Lyonya? (*Impatiently, through tears.*) Be quick, for God's sake!

GAYEV (*not answering her, simply waves his hand. To Firs, weeping*): Here, take these. . . . There's anchovies, Kerch herrings. . . . I haven't eaten anything all day. . . . What I have been through! (*The click of billiard balls is heard through the open door to the billiard room, and Yasha's voice: "Seven and eighteen!" Gayev's expression changes, he is no longer weeping.*) I'm terribly tired. Firs, help me change. (*Goes through the ballroom to his own room, followed by Firs.*)

PISHCHIK: What happened at the auction? Come on, tell us!

LYUBOV ANDREYEVNA: Is the cherry orchard sold?

LOPAKHIN: It's sold.

LYUBOV ANDREYEVNA: Who bought it?

LOPAKHIN: I bought it. (*Pause.*)

(*Lyubov Andreyevna is overcome; she would fall to the floor if it were not for the chair and table near which she stands. Varya takes the keys from her belt and throws them on the floor in the middle of the drawing room and goes out.*)

LOPAKHIN: I bought it! Kindly wait a moment, ladies and gentlemen, my head is swimming. I can't talk. . . . (*Laughs.*) We arrived at the auction, Deriganov was already there. Leonid Andreich had only fifteen thousand, and straight off Deriganov bid thirty thousand over and above the mortgage. I saw how the land lay, so I got into the fight and bid forty. He bid forty-five. I bid fifty-five. In other words, he kept raising it by five thousand, and I by ten. Well, it finally came to an end. I bid ninety thousand above the mortgage, and it was knocked down to me. The cherry orchard is now mine! Mine! (*Laughs uproariously.*) Lord! God in heaven! The cherry orchard is mine! Tell me I'm drunk, out of my mind, that I imagine it. . . . (*Stamps his feet.*) Don't laugh at me! If my father and my grandfather could only rise from their graves and see all that has happened, how their Yermolai, their beaten, half-literate Yermolai, who used to run about barefoot in winter, how that same Yermolai has bought an estate, the most beautiful estate in the whole world! I bought the estate where my father and grandfather were slaves, where they weren't even allowed in the kitchen. I'm asleep, this is just some dream of mine, it only seems to be. . . . It's the fruit of your imagination, hidden in the darkness of uncertainty. . . . (*Picks up the keys, smiling tenderly.*) She threw down the keys, wants to show that she's not mistress here anymore. . . . (*Jingles the keys.*) Well, no matter. (*The orchestra is heard tuning up.*) Hey, musicians, play, I want to hear you! Come on, everybody, and see how Yermolai Lopakhin will lay the ax to the cherry orchard, how the trees will fall to the ground! We're going to build summer cottages and our grandsons and great-grandsons will see a new life here. . . . Music! Strike up!

(*The orchestra plays. Lyubov Andreyevna sinks into a chair and weeps bitterly.*)

LOPAKHIN (*reproachfully*): Why didn't you listen to me, why? My poor friend, there's no turning back now. (*With tears.*) Oh, if only all this could be over quickly, if somehow our discordant, unhappy life could be changed!

PISHCHIK (*takes him by the arm; speaks in an undertone*): She's crying. Let's go into the ballroom, let her be alone. . . . Come on. . . . (*Leads him into the ballroom.*)

LOPAKHIN: What's happened? Musicians, play so I can hear you! Let everything be as I want it! (*Ironically.*) Here comes the new master, owner of the cherry orchard! (*Accidentally bumps into a little table, almost upsetting the candelabrum.*) I can pay for everything! (*Goes out with Pishchik.*)

(*There is no one left in either the drawing room or the ballroom except Lyubov Andreyevna, who sits huddled up and weeping bitterly. The music plays softly. Anya and Trofimov enter hurriedly. Anya goes to her mother and kneels before her. Trofimov remains in the doorway of the ballroom.*)

ANYA: Mama! . . . Mama, you're crying! Dear, kind, good Mama, my beautiful one, I love you . . . I bless you. The cherry orchard is sold, it's gone, that's true, true, but don't cry, Mama, life is still before you, you still have your good, pure soul. . . . Come with me, come, darling, we'll go away from here! . . . We'll plant a new orchard, more luxuriant than this one.

You will see it and understand; and joy, quiet, deep joy, will sink into your soul, like the evening sun, and you will smile, Mama! Come, darling, let us go. . . .

ACT IV

(*The scene is the same as act I. There are neither curtains on the windows nor pictures on the walls, and only a little furniture piled up in one corner, as if for sale. There is a sense of emptiness. Near the outer door, at the rear of the stage, suitcases, traveling bags, etc., are piled up. Through the open door on the left the voices of Varya and Anya can be heard. Lopakhin stands waiting. Yasha is holding a tray with little glasses of champagne. In the hall, Yepikhodov is tying up a box. Offstage, at the rear, there is a hum of voices. It is the peasants who have come to say good-bye. Gayev's voice: "Thanks, brothers, thank you."*)

YASHA: The peasants have come to say good-bye. In my opinion, Yermolai Alekseich, peasants are good-natured, but they don't know much.

(*The hum subsides. Lyubov Andreyevna enters from the hall with Gayev. She is not crying, but she is pale, her face twitches, and she cannot speak.*)

GAYEV: You gave them your purse, Lyuba. That won't do! That won't do!

LYUBOV ANDREYEVNA: I couldn't help it! I couldn't help it! (*They both go out.*)

LOPAKHIN (*in the doorway, calls after them*): Please, do me the honor of having a little glass at parting. I didn't think of bringing champagne from town, and at the station I found only one bottle. Please! What's the matter, friends, don't you want any? (*Walks away from the door.*) If I'd known that, I wouldn't have bought it. Well, then I won't drink any either. (*Yasha carefully sets the tray down on a chair.*) At least you have a glass, Yasha.

YASHA: To those who are departing! Good luck! (*Drinks.*) This champagne is not the real stuff, I can assure you.

LOPAKHIN: Eight rubles a bottle. (*Pause.*) It's devilish cold in here.

YASHA: They didn't light the stoves today; it doesn't matter, since we're leaving. (*Laughs.*)

LOPAKHIN: Why are you laughing?

YASHA: Because I'm pleased.

LOPAKHIN: It's October, yet it's sunny and still outside, like summer. Good for building. (*Looks at his watch, then calls through the door.*) Bear in mind, ladies and gentlemen, only forty-six minutes till train time! That means leaving for the station in twenty minutes. Better hurry up!

(*Trofimov enters from outside wearing an overcoat.*)

TROFIMOV: Seems to me it's time to start. The carriages are at the door. What the devil has become of my rubbers? They're lost. (*Calls through the door.*) Anya, my rubbers are not here. I can't find them.

LOPAKHIN: I've got to go to Kharkov. I'm taking the same train you are. I'm going to spend the winter in Kharkov. I've been hanging around here with you, and I'm sick and tired of loafing. I can't live without work, I don't know what to do with my hands; they dangle in some strange way, as if they didn't belong to me.

TROFIMOV: We'll soon be gone, then you can take up your useful labors again.

LOPAKHIN: Here, have a little drink.

TROFIMOV: No, I don't want any.

LOPAKHIN: So you're off for Moscow?

TROFIMOV: Yes, I'll see them into town, and tomorrow I'll go to Moscow.

LOPAKHIN: Yes. . . . Well, I expect the professors haven't been giving any lectures: They're waiting for you to come!

TROFIMOV: That's none of your business.

LOPAKHIN: How many years is it you've been studying at the university?

TROFIMOV: Can't you think of something new? That's stale and flat. (*Looks for his rubbers.*) You know we'll probably never see each other again, so allow me to give you one piece of advice at parting: Don't wave your arms about! Get out of that habit—of arm-waving. And another thing, building cottages and counting on the summer residents in time becoming independent farmers—that's just another form of arm-waving. Well, when all's said and done, I'm fond of you anyway. You have fine, delicate fingers, like an artist; you have a fine delicate soul.

LOPAKHIN (*embraces him*): Good-bye, my dear fellow. Thank you for everything. Let me give you some money for the journey, if you need it.

TROFIMOV: What for? I don't need it.

LOPAKHIN: But you haven't any!

TROFIMOV: I have. Thank you. I got some money for a translation. Here it is in my pocket. (*Anxiously.*) But where are my rubbers?

VARYA (*from the next room*): Here, take the nasty things! (*Flings a pair of rubbers onto the stage.*)

TROFIMOV: What are you so cross about, Varya? Hm. . . . But these are not my rubbers.

LOPAKHIN: In the spring I sowed three thousand acres of poppies, and now I've made forty thousand rubles clear. And when my poppies were in bloom, what a picture it was! So, I'm telling you, I've made forty thousand, which means I'm offering you a loan because I can afford to. Why turn up your nose? I'm a peasant—I speak bluntly.

TROFIMOV: Your father was a peasant, mine was a pharmacist—which proves absolutely nothing. (*Lopakhin takes out his wallet.*) No, don't—even if you gave me two hundred thousand I wouldn't take it. I'm a free man. And everything that is valued so highly and held so dear by all of you, rich and poor alike, has not the slightest power over me—it's like a feather floating in the air. I can get along without you, I can pass you by, I'm strong and proud.

Mankind is advancing toward the highest truth, the highest happiness attainable on earth, and I am in the front ranks!

LOPAKHIN: Will you get there?

TROFIMOV: I'll get there. (*Pause.*) I'll either get there or I'll show others the way to get there.

(*The sound of axes chopping down trees is heard in the distance.*)

LOPAKHIN: Well, good-bye, my dear fellow. It's time to go. We turn up our noses at one another, but life goes on just the same. When I work for a long time without stopping, my mind is easier, and it seems to me that I, too, know why I exist. But how many there are in Russia, brother, who exist nobody knows why. Well, it doesn't matter, that's not what makes the wheels go round. They say Leonid Andreich has taken a position in the bank, six thousand a year. . . . Only, of course, he won't stick it out, he's too lazy. . . .

ANYA (*in the doorway*): Mama asks you not to start cutting down the cherry orchard until she's gone.

TROFIMOV: Yes, really, not to have had the tact. . . . (*Goes out through the hall.*)

LOPAKHIN: Right away, right away. . . . Ach, what people. . . . (*Follows Trofimov out.*)

ANYA: Has Firs been taken to the hospital?

YASHA: I told them this morning. They must have taken him.

ANYA (*to Yepikhodov, who is crossing the room*): Semyon Panteleich, please find out if Firs has been taken to the hospital.

YASHA (*offended*): I told Yegor this morning. Why ask a dozen times?

YEPIKHODOV: It is my conclusive opinion that the venerable Firs is beyond repair; it's time he was gathered to his fathers. And I can only envy him. (*Puts a suitcase down on a hatbox and crushes it.*) There you are! Of course! I knew it! (*Goes out.*)

YASHA (*mockingly*): Two-and-twenty Troubles!

VARYA (*through the door*): Has Firs been taken to the hospital?

ANYA: Yes, he has.

VARYA: Then why didn't they take the letter to the doctor?

ANYA: We must send it on after them. . . . (*Goes out.*)

VARYA (*from the adjoining room*): Where is Yasha? Tell him his mother has come to say good-bye to him.

YASHA (*waves his hand*): They really try my patience.

(*Dunyasha has been fussing with the luggage; now that Yasha is alone she goes up to him.*)

DUNYASHA: You might give me one little look, Yasha. You're going away . . . leaving me. . . . (*Cries and throws herself on his neck.*)

YASHA: What's there to cry about? (*Drinks champagne.*) In six days I'll be in Paris again. Tomorrow we'll take the express, off we go, and that's the last you'll see of us. I can hardly believe it. *Vive la France*! This place is not for me, I can't live here. . . . It can't be helped.

I've had enough of this ignorance—I'm fed up with it. (*Drinks champagne.*) What are you crying for? Behave yourself properly, then you won't cry.

DUNYASHA (*looks into a small mirror and powders her face*): Send me a letter from Paris. You know, I loved you, Yasha, how I loved you! I'm such a tender creature, Yasha!

YASHA: Here they come. (*Busies himself with the luggage, humming softly.*)

(*Enter Lyubov Andreyevna, Gayev, Charlotta Ivanovna.*)

GAYEV: We ought to be leaving. There's not much time now. (*Looks at Yasha.*) Who smells of herring?

LYUBOV ANDREYEVNA: In about ten minutes we should be getting into the carriages. (*Glances around the room.*) Good-bye, dear house, old grandfather. Winter will pass, spring will come, and you will no longer be here, they will tear you down. How much these walls have seen? (*Kisses her daughter warmly.*) My treasure, you are radiant, your eyes are sparkling like two diamonds. Are you glad? Very?

ANYA: Very! A new life is beginning, Mama!

GAYEV (*cheerfully*): Yes, indeed, everything is all right now. Before the cherry orchard was sold we were all worried and miserable, but afterward, when the question was finally settled once and for all, everybody calmed down and felt quite cheerful. . . . I'm in a bank now, a financier . . . cue ball into the center . . . and you, Lyuba, say what you like, you look better, no doubt about it.

LYUBOV ANDREYEVNA: Yes. My nerves are better, that's true. (*Her hat and coat are handed to her.*) I sleep well. Carry out my things, Yasha, it's time. (*To Anya.*) My little girl, we shall see each other soon. . . . I shall go to Paris and live there on the money your great-aunt sent to buy the estate—long live Auntie!—but that money won't last long.

ANYA: You'll come back soon, Mama, soon . . . won't you? I'll study hard and pass my high school examinations, and then I can work and help you. We'll read all sorts of books together, Mama. . . . Won't we? (*Kisses her mother's hand.*) We'll read in the autumn evenings, we'll read lots of books, and a new and wonderful world will open up before us. . . . (*Dreaming.*) Mama, come back. . . .

LYUBOV ANDREYEVNA: I'll come, my precious. (*Embraces her.*)

(*Enter Lopakhin, Charlotta Ivanovna is softly humming a song.*)

GAYEV: Happy Charlotta: She's singing!

CHARLOTTA (*picks up a bundle and holds it like a baby in swaddling clothes*): Bye, baby, bye. . . . (*A baby's crying is heard, "Wah! Wah!"*) Be quiet, my darling, my dear little boy. ("*Wah! Wah!*") I'm so sorry for you! (*Throws the bundle down.*) You will find me a position, won't you? I can't go on like this.

LOPAKHIN: We'll find something, Charlotta Ivanovna, don't worry.

GAYEV: Everyone is leaving us, Varya's going away . . . all of a sudden nobody needs us.

CHARLOTTA: I have nowhere to go in town. I must go away. (*Hums.*) It doesn't matter . . .

(*Enter Pishchik.*)

LOPAKHIN: Nature's wonder!

PISHCHIK (*panting*): Ugh! Let me catch my breath. . . . I'm exhausted. . . . My esteemed friends. . . . Give me some water. . . .

GAYEV: After money, I suppose? Excuse me, I'm fleeing from temptation. . . . (*Goes out.*)

PISHCHIK: It's a long time since I've been to see you . . . fairest lady. . . . (*To Lopakhin*) So you're here. . . . Glad to see you, you intellectual giant. . . . Here . . . take it . . . four hundred rubles . . . I still owe you eight hundred and forty . . .

LOPAKHIN (*shrugs his shoulders in bewilderment*): I must be dreaming. . . . Where did you get it?

PISHCHIK: Wait . . . I'm hot. . . . A most extraordinary event. Some Englishmen came to my place and discovered some kind of white clay on my land. (*To Lyubov Andreyevna*) And four hundred for you . . . fairest, most wonderful lady. . . . (*Hands her the money.*) The rest later. (*Takes a drink of water.*) Just now a young man in the train was saying that a certain . . . great philosopher recommends jumping off roofs. . . . "Jump!" he says, and therein lies the whole problem. (*In amazement.*) Think of that, now! . . . Water!

LOPAKHIN: Who were those Englishmen?

PISHCHIK: I leased them the tract of land with the clay on it for twenty-four years. . . . And now, excuse me, I have no time . . . I must be trotting along . . . I'm going to Znoikov's . . . to Kardamanov's . . . I owe everybody. (*Drinks.*) Keep well . . . I'll drop in on Thursday . . .

LYUBOV ANDREYEVNA: We're just moving into town, and tomorrow I go abroad . . .

PISHCHIK: What? (*Alarmed.*) Why into town? That's why I see the furniture . . . suitcases. . . . Well, never mind. . . . (*Through tears.*) Never mind. . . . Men of the greatest intellect, those Englishmen. . . . Never mind. . . . Be happy . . . God will help you. . . . Never mind. . . . Everything in this world comes to an end. . . . (*Kisses Lyubov Andreyevna's hand.*) And should the news reach you that my end has come, just remember this old horse, and say: "There once lived a certain Semyonov-Pishchik, God rest his soul." . . . Splendid weather. . . . Yes. . . . (*Goes out greatly disconcerted, but immediately returns and speaks from the doorway.*) Dashenka sends her regards. (*Goes out.*)

LYUBOV ANDREYEVNA: Now we can go. I am leaving with two things on my mind. First—that Firs is sick. (*Looks at her watch.*) We still have about five minutes. . . .

ANYA: Mama, Firs has already been taken to the hospital. Yasha sent him there this morning.

LYUBOV ANDREYEVNA: My second concern is Varya. She's used to getting up early and working, and now, with no work to do, she's like a fish out of water. She's grown pale and thin, and cries all the time, poor girl. . . . (*Pauses.*) You know very well, Yermolai Alekseich, that I dreamed of marrying her to you, and everything pointed to your getting married. (*Whispers to Anya, who nods to Charlotta, and they both go out.*) She loves you, you are fond of her, and I don't know—I don't know why it is you seem to avoid each other. I can't understand it!

LOPAKHIN: To tell you the truth, I don't understand it myself. The whole thing is strange, somehow. . . . If there's still time, I'm ready right now. . . . Let's finish it up—and *basta,*° but without you I feel I'll never be able to propose to her.

LYUBOV ANDREYEVNA: Splendid! After all, it only takes a minute. I'll call her in at once. . . .

LOPAKHIN: And we even have the champagne. (*Looks at the glasses.*) Empty! Somebody's already drunk it. (*Yasha coughs.*) That's what you call lapping it up.

LYUBOV ANDREYEVNA (*animatedly*): Splendid! We'll leave you. . . . Yasha, *allez!*° I'll call her. . . . (*At the door.*) Varya, leave everything and come here. Come! (*Goes out with Yasha.*)

LOPAKHIN (*looking at his watch*): Yes. . . . (*Pause.*)

(*Behind the door there is smothered laughter and whispering; finally Varya enters.*)

VARYA (*looking over the luggage for a long time*): Strange, I can't seem to find it . . .

LOPAKHIN: What are you looking for?

VARYA: I packed it myself, and I can't remember . . . (*Pause.*)

LOPAKHIN: Where are you going now, Varya Mikhailovna?

VARYA: I? To the Ragulins'. . . . I've agreed to go there to look after the house . . . as a sort of housekeeper.

LOPAKHIN: At Yashnevo? That would be about seventy versts from here. (*Pause.*) Well, life in this house has come to an end. . . .

VARYA (*examining the luggage*): Where can it be? . . . Perhaps I put it in the trunk. . . . Yes, life in this house has come to an end . . . there'll be no more . . .

LOPAKHIN: And I'm off for Kharkov . . . by the next train. I have a lot to do. I'm leaving Yepikhodov here . . . I've taken him on.

VARYA: Really!

LOPAKHIN: Last year at this time it was already snowing, if you remember, but now it's still and sunny. It's cold though. . . . About three degrees of frost.

VARYA: I haven't looked. (*Pause.*) And besides, our thermometer's broken. (*Pause.*)

(*A voice from the yard calls: "Yermolai Alekseich!"*)

LOPAKHIN (*as if he had been waiting for a long time for the call*): Coming! (*Goes out quickly.*)

---

basta: Italian for "enough." *allez!:* French for "go!"

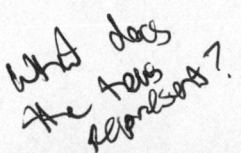

(*Varya sits on the floor, lays her head on a bundle of clothes, and quietly sobs. The door opens and Lyubov Andreyevna enters cautiously.*)

LYUBOV ANDREYEVNA: Well? (*Pause.*) We must be going.

VARYA (*no longer crying, dries her eyes*): Yes, it's time, Mama dear. I can get to the Ragulins' today, if only we don't miss the train.

LYUBOV ANDREYEVNA (*in the doorway*): Anya, put your things on!

(*Enter Anya, then Gayev and Charlotta Ivanovna. Gayev wears a warm overcoat with a hood. The servants and coachmen come in. Yepikhodov bustles about the luggage.*)

LYUBOV ANDREYEVNA: Now we can be on our way.

ANYA (*joyfully*): On our way!

GAYEV: My friends, my dear, cherished friends! Leaving this house forever, can I pass over in silence, can I refrain from giving utterance, as we say farewell, to those feelings that now fill my whole being—

ANYA (*imploringly*): Uncle!

VARYA: Uncle dear, don't!

GAYEV (*forlornly*): Double the rail off the white to center table . . . yellow into the side pocket. . . . I'll be quiet. . . .

(*Enter Trofimov, then Lopakhin.*)

TROFIMOV: Well, ladies and gentlemen, it's time to go!

LOPAKHIN: Yepikhodov, my coat!

LYUBOV ANDREYEVNA: I'll sit here just one more minute. It's as though I had never before seen what the walls of this house were like, what the ceilings were like, and now I look at them hungrily, with such tender love . . .

GAYEV: I remember when I was six years old, sitting on this windowsill on Whitsunday, watching my father going to church . . .

LYUBOV ANDREYEVNA: Have they taken all the things?

LOPAKHIN: Everything, I think. (*Puts on his overcoat.*) Yepikhodov, see that everything is in order.

YEPIKHODOV (*in a hoarse voice*): Rest assured, Yermolai Alekseich!

LOPAKHIN: What's the matter with your voice?

YEPIKHODOV: Just drank some water . . . must have swallowed something.

YASHA (*contemptuously*): What ignorance!

LYUBOV ANDREYEVNA: When we go—there won't be a soul left here. . . .

LOPAKHIN: Till spring.

VARYA (*pulls an umbrella out of a bundle as though she were going to hit someone; Lopakhin pretends to be frightened*): Why are you—I never thought of such a thing!

TROFIMOV: Ladies and gentlemen, let's get into the carriages—it's time now! The train will soon be in!

VARYA: Petya, there they are—your rubbers, by the suitcase. (*Tearfully.*) And what dirty old things they are!

TROFIMOV (*putting on his rubbers*): Let's go, ladies and gentlemen!

GAYEV (*extremely upset, afraid of bursting into tears*): The train . . . the station. . . . Cross table to the center, double the rail . . . on the white into the corner.

LYUBOV ANDREYEVNA: Let us go!

GAYEV: Are we all here? No one in there? (*Locks the side door on the left.*) There are some things stored in there, we must lock up. Let's go!

ANYA: Good-bye, house! Good-bye, old life!

TROFIMOV: Hail to the new life! (*Goes out with Anya.*)

(*Varya looks around the room and slowly goes out. Yasha and Charlotta with her dog go out.*)

LOPAKHIN: And so, till spring. Come along, my friends. . . . Till we meet! (*Goes out.*)

(*Lyubov Andreyevna and Gayev are left alone. As though they had been waiting for this, they fall onto each other's necks and break into quiet, restrained sobs, afraid of being heard.*)

GAYEV (*in despair*): My sister, my sister. . . .

LYUBOV ANDREYEVNA: Oh, my dear, sweet, lovely orchard! . . . My life, my youth, my happiness, good-bye! . . . Good-bye!

ANYA'S VOICE (*gaily calling*): Mama!

TROFIMOV'S VOICE (*gay and excited*): Aa-oo!

LYUBOV ANDREYEVNA: One last look at these walls, these windows. . . . Mother loved to walk about in this room. . . .

GAYEV: My sister, my sister!

ANYA'S VOICE: Mama!

TROFIMOV'S VOICE: Aa-oo!

LYUBOV ANDREYEVNA: We're coming! (*They go out.*)

(*The stage is empty. There is the sound of doors being locked, then of the carriages driving away. It grows quiet. In the stillness there is the dull thud of an ax on a tree, a forlorn, melancholy sound. Footsteps are heard. From the door on the right Firs appears. He is dressed as always in a jacket and white waistcoat, and wears slippers. He is ill.*)

FIRS (*goes to the door and tries the handle*): Locked. They have gone. . . . (*Sits down on the sofa.*) They've forgotten me. . . . Never mind. . . . I'll sit here awhile. . . . I expect Leonid Andreich hasn't put on his fur coat and has gone off in his overcoat. (*Sighs anxiously.*) And I didn't see to it. . . . When they're young, they're green! (*Mumbles something which cannot be understood.*) I'll lie down awhile. . . . There's no strength left in you, nothing's left, nothing. . . . Ach, you . . . addlepate! (*Lies motionless.*)

(*A distant sound is heard that seems to come from the sky, the sound of a snapped string mournfully dying away. A stillness falls, and nothing is heard but the thud of the ax on a tree far away in the orchard.*)

COMMENTARIES

ANTON CHEKHOV (1860–1904)

From Letters of Anton Chekov 1888–1903

TRANSLATED BY MICHAEL HENRY HEIM WITH SIMON KARLINSKY

Chekhov, like Ibsen, was an inveterate letter writer. In letters to family members and colleagues, he wrote quite frankly about his hopes, expectations, and difficulties regarding his work. Chekhov's letters concerning his purpose as an artist and his play *The Cherry Orchard* give us some insight into his anxieties and his hopes for his work. His awareness of the difficulties he faced in his writing helps us understand how his plays developed into complex and demanding works.

October 4, 1888

The people I fear are those who look for tendentiousness between the lines and are determined to see me as either liberal or conservative. I am neither liberal, nor conservative, nor gradualist, nor monk, nor indifferentist. I should like to be a free artist and nothing else. That is why I cultivate no particular predilection for policemen, butchers, scientists, writers, or the younger generation. I look upon tags and labels as prejudices. My holy of holies is the human body, health, intelligence, talent, inspiration, love and the most absolute freedom imaginable, freedom from violence and lies.

November 25, 1892

Keep in mind that the writers we call eternal or simply good, the writers who intoxicate us, have one highly important trait in common: They are moving towards something definite and beckon you to follow, and you feel with your entire being, not only with your mind, that they have a certain goal, like the ghost of Hamlet's father, which had a motive for coming and stirring Hamlet's imagination. Depending on their caliber, some have immediate goals—the abolition of serfdom, the liberation of one's country, politics, beauty, or simply vodka . . .—while the goals of others are more remote—God, life after death, the happiness of mankind, etc. The best of them are realistic and describe life as it is, but because each line is saturated with the consciousness of its goal, you feel life as it should be in addition to life as it is, and you are captivated by it. But what about us? Us! We describe life as it is and stop dead right there. We wouldn't lift a hoof if you lit into us with a whip. We have neither immediate nor remote goals, and there is an emptiness in our souls. We have no politics, we don't believe in revolution, there is no God, we're not afraid of ghosts, and I personally am not even afraid of death or blindness. If you want nothing, hope for nothing, and fear nothing, you cannot be an artist.

To K. S. Stanislavsky°
Yalta. Oct. 30, 1903

When I was writing Lopakhin, I thought of it as a part for you. If for any reason you don't care for it, take the part of Gayev. Lopakhin is a merchant, of course, but he is a very decent person in every sense. He must behave with perfect decorum, like an educated man, with no petty ways or tricks of any sort, and it seemed to me this part, the central one of the play, would come out brilliantly in your hands. . . . In choosing an actor for the part you must remember that Varya, a serious and religious girl, is in love with Lopakhin; she wouldn't be in love with a mere money-grubber. . . .

To Vl. I. Nemirovich-Danchenko°
Yalta. Nov. 2, 1903

. . . Pishchik is a Russian, an old man, worn out by the gout, age, and satiety; stout, dressed in a sleeveless undercoat (à la Simov [an actor in the Moscow Art Theatre]), boots without heels. Lopakhin—a white waistcoat, yellow shoes; when walking, swings his arms, a broad stride, thinks deeply while walking, walks as if on a straight line. Hair not short, and therefore often throws back his head; while in thought he passes his hand through his beard, combing it from the back forward, i. e., from the neck toward the mouth. Trofimov, I think, is clear. Varya—black dress, wide belt.

Three years I spent writing "The Cherry Orchard," and for three years I have been telling you that it is necessary to invite an actress for the role of Lyubov Andreyevna. And now you see you are trying to solve a puzzle that won't work out.

To K. S. Alekseyev (Stanislavsky)
Yalta, Nov. 5, 1903

The house in the play is two-storied, a large one. But in the third act does it not speak of a stairway leading down? Nevertheless, this third act worries me. . . . N. has it that the third act takes place in "some kind of hotel"; . . . evidently I made an error in the play. The action does not pass in "some kind of hotel," but in a *drawing room*. If I mention a hotel in the play, which I cannot now doubt, after Vl. Iv.'s [Nemirovich-Danchenko] letter, please telegraph me. We must correct it; we cannot issue it thus, with grave errors distorting its meaning.

The house must be large, solid; wooden (like Aksakov's, which, I think, S. T. Morozov has seen) or stone, it is all the same. It is very old and imposing; country residents do not take such houses; such houses are usually wrecked and the material employed for the construction of a country house. The furniture is ancient, stylish, solid; ruin and debt have not affected the surroundings.

When they buy such a house, they reason thus: it is cheaper and easier to build a new and smaller one than to repair this old one.

Your shepherd played well. That was most essential.

K. S. Stanislavsky: Konstantin Stanislavski (1863–1938), director with the Moscow Art Theatre, which produced most of Chekhov's plays.

Vl. I. Nemirovich-Danchenko: Vladimir Ivanovich Nemirovich-Danchenko (1858–1943), novelist and codirector of the Moscow Art Theatre.

PETER BROOK (b. 1925)

On Chekhov 1987

Peter Brook has established himself as one of the most distinguished directors of recent years. He was educated at Oxford University and has been a director of the Royal Shakespeare Company in England. In 1987, he directed *The Cherry Orchard* at the Brooklyn Academy of Music. Some of his thoughts as he prepared to direct the play are presented here, showing his awareness of Chekhov's "film sense" in a play that was written just as film was emerging as a popular form. He is also aware of Chekhov's personal vision of death and sees it expressed in the circumstances of the play.

Chekhov always looked for what's natural; he wanted performances and productions to be as limpid as life itself. Chekhov's writing is extremely concentrated, employing a minimum of words; in a way, it is similar to Pinter or Beckett. As with them, it is construction that counts, rhythm, the purely theatrical poetry that comes not from beautiful words but from the right word at the right moment. In the theater, someone can say "yes" in such a way that the "yes" is no longer ordinary—it can become a beautiful word, because it is the perfect expression of what cannot be expressed in any other way. With Chekhov, periods, commas, points of suspension are all of a fundamental importance, as fundamental as the "pauses" precisely indicated by Beckett. If one fails to observe them, one loses the rhythm and tensions of the play. In Chekhov's work, the punctuation represents a series of coded messages which record characters' relationships and emotions, the moments at which ideas come together or follow their own course. The punctuation enables us to grasp what the words conceal.

Chekhov is like a perfect filmmaker. Instead of cutting from one image to another—perhaps from one place to another—he switches from one emotion to another just before it gets too heavy. At the precise moment when the spectator risks becoming too involved in a character, an unexpected situation cuts across. Nothing is stable. Chekhov portrays individuals and a society in a state of perpetual change, he is the dramatist of life's movement, simultaneously smiling and serious, amusing and bitter—completely free from the "music," the Slav "nostalgia" that Paris nightclubs still preserve. He often stated that his plays were comedies—this was the central issue of his conflict with Stanislavsky.

But it's wrong to conclude that *The Cherry Orchard* should be performed as a vaudeville. Chekhov is an infinitely detailed observer of the human comedy. As a doctor, he knew the meaning of certain kinds of behavior, how to discern what was essential, to expose what he diagnosed. Although he shows tenderness and an attentive sympathy, he never sentimentalizes. One doesn't imagine a doctor shedding tears over the illnesses of his patients. He learns how to balance compassion with distance.

In Chekhov's work, death is omnipresent—he knew it well—but there is nothing negative or unsavory in its presence. The awareness of death is balanced with a desire to live. His characters possess a sense of the present moment, and the need to taste it fully. As in great tragedies, one finds a harmony between life and death.

Chekhov died young, having traveled, written, and loved enormously, having taken part in the events of his day, in great schemes of social reform. He died shortly after asking for some champagne, and his coffin was transported in a wagon bearing the inscription "Fresh Oysters." His awareness of death, and of the precious moments that could be lived, endows his work with a sense of the relative: in other words, a viewpoint from which the tragic is always a bit absurd.

In Chekhov's work, each character has its own existence: not one of them resembles another, particularly in *The Cherry Orchard,* which presents a microcosm of the political tendencies of the time. There are those who believe in social transformations, others attached to a disappearing past. None of them can achieve satisfaction or plenitude, and seen from outside, their existences might well appear empty, senseless. But they all burn with intense desires. They are not disillusioned, quite the contrary: In their own ways, they are all searching for a better quality of life, emotionally and socially. Their drama is that society—the outside world—blocks their energy. The complexity of their behavior is not indicated in the words, it emerges from the mosaic construction of an infinite number of details. What is essential is to see that these are not plays about lethargic people. They are hypervital people in a lethargic world, forced to dramatize the minutest happening out of a passionate desire to live. They have not given up.

Bernard Shaw

The Irish playwright Bernard Shaw[1] (1856–1950) was astonishing not only for the range of his writing but also for the length and vigor of his life. He was a public figure for most of his days, with an especially keen ability to catch public attention and to make his presence felt. His early work was devoted to criticism in newspapers and then to a series of fairly successful novels. He began writing plays in his late thirties; once he began, he realized that he had discovered his vocation, and he went on to write more than fifty. Some of them, such as *Arms and the Man* (1894), *Candida* (1897), *Mrs. Warren's Profession* (1898), *Man and Superman* (1901–1903), *Major Barbara* (1905), *Pygmalion* (1913), *Heartbreak House* (1919), and *St. Joan* (1923), are among the most often performed plays by any English-language writer of his time.

Shaw's gift of analysis and philosophical reflection created in his works a new kind of drama that has sometimes been named for him—Shavian. The term implies a deep interest in ideas rather than in character and a propensity for elaborate discourse between characters who represent different points of view. Shaw assumed that drama should amuse and entertain, but of much greater importance was his didactic motive. Drama should teach a lesson about something of great moral importance.

This is not to say that Shaw was unable to be entertaining. Some of his comedies, still played today, are bright and witty. *You Never Can Tell* (1898), a comedy about male-female relationships whose main character is a dentist, and *Pygmalion,* a comedy in which a man teaches a cockney girl how to speak with an upper-class accent with unexpected results, are both funny plays. *Pygmalion* was redone as a musical, *My Fair Lady*, and was Shaw's most financially successful play.

Still, Shaw was basically a philosophical writer. His plays can usually be seen as having a specific theme on which the characters continually discourse. Whether it was the relationship of England and Ireland, the state of the medical profession, genetics and propagation, or poverty, Shaw always focused on an issue, and he even commented that Shakespeare's shortcoming was that his plays have no message.

Shaw frequently wrote elaborate and lengthy prefaces to his published plays. In his prefaces, Shaw takes time to explain—and fully explore—the messages of his plays. He discusses the questions of genetic planning and the improvement of the race in his preface to *Man and Superman*; in the preface to *Candida,* he discusses the relationship of pity to love.

Shaw's lifelong socialism affected his work and his thinking, and he himself was a socialist politician for a short period. Consequently, it is not uncommon to see political concerns expressed and debated in his plays.

Shaw's political ideas were shaped by his interest in economics as a discipline. In 1884, he joined the Fabian Society, which had been established a year earlier as a group to study and promote socialism, and he remained active

[1]Shaw was born George Bernard Shaw and is sometimes referred to as GBS. He disliked the name George and preferred to be addressed as Bernard Shaw.

until 1911. Fabianism, unlike Marxism or communism, held that society need not be destroyed by revolution but could become an instrument of socialist reform. For this reason, Fabianism was known as evolutionary socialism. *Fabian Essays* (1889), which Shaw edited, was used by study groups that sprouted up throughout Great Britain to spread Fabian socialist ideas through politics, religion, and society. The result of this movement was the organization of a new political party, the Labour Party (1893), which still exists. The socialist government of Britain in the 1960s and 1970s was a direct outgrowth of Fabian theories.

As he studied economics, Shaw grew to believe that all social values were built on an economic base. He developed this idea in his Fabian essays and maintained it throughout his plays. He also maintained a presence as a critic of theater and accepted Ibsen as a major playwright at a time when most London critics found Ibsen's work unacceptable. Shaw's *Quintessence of Ibsenism* (1891; revised after Ibsen's death in 1913) is still a useful commentary on that playwright's work.

Mrs. Warren's Profession

For discussion questions and assignments on *Mrs. Warren's Profession*, visit bedfordstmartins.com/jacobus.

Shaw once described *Mrs. Warren's Profession* as being in "my most odious vein." But in a letter to actress Ellen Terry (May 28, 1897), Shaw wrote, "It's much my best play; but it makes my blood run cold: I can hardly bear the most appalling bits of it. Ah, when I wrote that, I had some nerve." The play was written in 1894 and inspired by Janet Achurch, the actress who played Nora in Ibsen's *A Doll House*. Achurch told Shaw the story of a play she was writing based on Guy de Maupassant's short story "Yvette." Shaw adopted the idea and hoped that when he finished his play, Achurch would play Vivie, the heroine. Shaw owed a great deal to other playwrights who had touched on similar themes—although none as directly as he had—but his story of a mother-daughter relationship in which the mother was a prostitute was original in that it proposed a "new woman" for the heroine, Vivie, and refused to permit Mrs. Warren to express shame for her professional decisions. This was a highly daring play for its time.

Indeed, the play had only two private performances in London in 1902 before it premiered in the United States in 1905. The play was banned or protested in several cities, especially after its first performances. By the time it was given its first public performances in London in 1926, Shaw had lost interest in the play and simply felt it was too late in production. The Comédie-Française considered it too amoral to produce as late as 1955, which demonstrates that Shaw hit a nerve that was still sensitive well beyond his own day.

The form of the play is essentially conventional for its time, although Shaw consciously employed techniques of Henrik Ibsen, whom he admired enough to have written the seminal study *The Quintessence of Ibsenism* (1891). He had learned from Ibsen how to address social issues directly and how to produce a female character whose ambiguities would intrigue an audience. Ibsen's emphasis on the "new woman"—the independent woman who could make her own decisions and her own way—is evident in *Mrs. Warren's Profession*.

The men in the play are generally dependent on the women. Mrs. Warren has a good business sense and has used the capital provided her by Sir George Crofts so well that Crofts need no longer worry about his own welfare. In one sense he is a kept man, living on the earnings of a woman. The Reverend Samuel Gardner has converted from a roué and former client of Mrs. Warren to an overly pious churchman worried about his reputation. His son, Frank, may or may not be a brother to Vivie, and although the play ends with Vivie declaring that she doesn't care whether he is her brother or not, the theme of incest seems underdeveloped. Yet Shaw believed it was an essential ingredient of the play. Frank plans not to work, is shiftless and indolent, and would be content to be supported by Vivie and her mother's money, just as Crofts is content to bask in the security provided by Mrs. Warren.

The underlying theme of economic opportunities for women drives this play. Many Victorians believed that prostitution, widespread in England, was one of the most serious social diseases of the time. But Shaw is keen enough in his analysis of English social life to realize that prostitutes were often forced into the profession because the alternatives were even worse. Mrs. Warren explains to Vivie in act 2 that she watched her two half-sisters follow the path of respectability: "One of them worked in a whitelead factory twelve hours a day for nine shillings a week until she died of lead poisoning. She only expected to get her hands a little paralyzed; but she died. The other was always held up to us as a model because she married a Government laborer in the Deptford victualling yard, and kept his room and the three children neat and tidy on eighteen shillings a week—until he took to drink."

The unrespectable sisters, Liz and Mrs. Warren, followed "the life" and ended up in control of their own situation. Liz, retired in a cathedral town, is emblematic of the height of respectability. Vivie is in a position to reject her mother's life, as well as Croft's offer of marriage and wealth and Frank's offer of marriage and love. But she is in this position because her mother provided her with a man's education at Cambridge. She describes herself as a "wrangler"—a term meaning an honors student in mathematics but also implying achievement in debate. This position was formerly available only to men (as Praed implies when he says nothing like that happened "in my day").

Vivie ends the play in the secure knowledge that she will succeed in the law profession and that the limited options available to her mother will never be her only options. Vivie, then, is heroic, and the play is comic in form.

Mr. Warren's Profession in Performance

Mrs. Warren's Profession was produced privately in London on January 5, 1902, at the New Lyric Club. On October 27, 1902, it was produced at the Hyperion Theater in New Haven, Connecticut, its first American production. H. Granville Barker, a distinguished actor and writer, played the part of Frank, and Fanny Brough was Mrs. Warren. It was performed again in New York in 1905 with the well-known actor Richard Mansfield, but the police commissioner closed the play for "offending public decency." A special court hearing in 1906 proclaimed the play "not pleasant" but did not declare it indecent.

After performances in Berlin (1907) and Glasgow (1913), the play's first public performance in England took place in Birmingham in 1925, when the

British censors finally cleared the play of charges of indecency. It ran in London at the Strand Theatre in 1926 for eighty-six performances.

John Loder and Estelle Winwood played Crofts and Mrs. Warren off-Broadway in 1950 for twenty-eight performances. Ruth Gordon and Lynn Redgrave played Mrs. Warren and Vivie in a 1976 New York Shakespeare Festival production in Lincoln Center that lasted for sixty-nine performances. Edward Herrmann played Frank, and Milo O'Shea played Reverend Gardner. Recent productions of the play abound. The Irish Classical Theater Co. in Buffalo, New York, staged a well-received performance in April 2003. That same year, the celebrated British director Peter Hall chose Brenda Blethyn for the lead and his daughter Rebecca Hall for Vivie in the London West End production at the Strand Theatre. The reviews praised Blethyn and the rest of the cast, but they especially honored Shaw for attacking hypocrisy. Cherry Jones appeared as Mrs. Warren in Doug Hughes's production at the Roundabout Theatre in New York in 2010. Felicity Kendal received strong reviews as Mrs. Warren in London's Harold Pinter Theatre in 2010, after having toured the play in several English cities in 2009. These contemporary productions demonstrate the validity of Shaw's views.

BERNARD SHAW (1856–1950)

Mrs. Warren's Profession   1898

Characters

VIVIE WARREN
PRAED
MRS WARREN
SIR GEORGE CROFTS
FRANK GARDNER
REVEREND SAMUEL GARDNER

ACT I

Summer afternoon in a cottage garden on the eastern slope of a hill a little south of Haslemere in Surrey. Looking up the hill, the cottage is seen in the left hand corner of the garden, with its thatched roof and porch, and a large latticed window to the left of the porch. Farther back a little wing is built out, making an angle with the right side wall. From the end of this wing a paling curves across and forward, completely shutting in the garden, except for a gate on the right. The common rises uphill beyond the paling to the sky line. Some folded canvas garden chairs are leaning against the side bench in the porch. A lady's bicycle is propped against the wall, under the window. A little to the right of the porch a hammock is slung from two posts. A big canvas umbrella, stuck in the ground, keeps the sun off the hammock, in which a young lady lies reading and making notes, her head towards the cottage and her feet towards the gate. In front of the hammock, and within reach of her hand, is a common kitchen chair, with a pile of serious-looking books and a supply of writing paper upon it.

A gentleman walking on the common comes into sight from behind the cottage. He is hardly past middle age, with something of the artist about him, unconventionally but carefully dressed, and clean-shaven except for a moustache, with an eager, susceptible face and very amiable and considerate manners. He has silky black hair, with waves of grey and white in it. His eyebrows are white, his moustache black. He seems not certain of his way. He looks over the paling; takes stock of the place; and sees the young lady.

THE GENTLEMAN (*taking off his hat*): I beg your pardon. Can you direct me to Hindhead View—Mrs Alison's?

THE YOUNG LADY (*glancing up from her book*): This is Mrs Alison's. (*She resumes her work.*)

THE GENTLEMAN: Indeed! Perhaps—may I ask are you Miss Vivie Warren?

THE YOUNG LADY (*sharply, as she turns on her elbow to get a good look at him*): Yes.

THE GENTLEMAN (*daunted and conciliatory*): I'm afraid I appear intrusive. My name is Praed. (*Vivie at once throws her books upon the chair, and gets out of the hammock.*) Oh, pray dont let me disturb you.

VIVIE (*striding to the gate and opening it for him*): Come in, Mr Praed. (*He comes in.*) Glad to see you. (*She proffers her hand and takes his with a resolute and hearty grip. She is an attractive specimen of the sensible, able, highly educated young middle-class Englishwoman. Age 22. Prompt, strong, confident, self-possessed. Plain, business-like dress, but not dowdy. She wears a chatelaine at her belt, with a fountain pen and a paper knife among its pendants.*)

PRAED: Very kind of you indeed, Miss Warren. (*She shuts the gate with a vigorous slam: he passes in to the middle of the garden, exercising his fingers, which are slightly numbed by her greeting.*) Has your mother arrived?

VIVIE (*quickly, evidently scenting aggression*): Is she coming?

PRAED (*surprised*): Didnt you expect us?

VIVIE: No.

PRAED: Now, goodness me, I hope Ive not mistaken the day. That would be just like me, you know. Your mother arranged that she was to come down from London and that I was to come over from Horsham to be introduced to you.

VIVIE (*not at all pleased*): Did she? Hm! My mother has rather a trick of taking me by surprise—to see how I behave myself when she's away, I suppose. I fancy I shall take my mother very much by surprise one of these days, if she makes arrangements that concern me without consulting me beforehand. She hasnt come.

PRAED (*embarrassed*): I'm really very sorry.

VIVIE (*throwing off her displeasure*): It's not your fault, Mr Praed, is it? And I'm very glad youve come, believe me. You are the only one of my mother's friends I have asked her to bring to see me.

PRAED (*relieved and delighted*): Oh, now this is really very good of you, Miss Warren!

VIVIE: Will you come indoors; or would you rather sit out here whilst we talk?

PRAED: It will be nicer out here, dont you think?

VIVIE: Then I'll go and get you a chair. (*She goes to the porch for a garden chair.*)

PRAED (*following her*): Oh, pray, pray! Allow me. (*He lays hands on the chair.*)

VIVIE (*letting him take it*): Take care of your fingers: theyre rather dodgy things, those chairs. (*She goes across to the chair with the books on it; pitches them into the hammock; and brings the chair forward with one swing.*)

PRAED (*who has just unfolded his chair*): Oh, now do let me take that hard chair! I like hard chairs.

VIVIE: So do I. (*She sits down.*) Sit down, Mr Praed. (*This invitation she gives with genial peremptoriness, his anxiety to please her clearly striking her as a sign of weakness of character on his part.*)

PRAED: By the way, though, hadnt we better go to the station to meet your mother?

VIVIE (*coolly*): Why? She knows the way. (*Praed hesitates, and then sits down in the garden chair, rather disconcerted.*) Do you know, you are just like what I expected. I hope you are disposed to be friends with me.

PRAED (*again beaming*): Thank you, my dear Miss Warren: thank you. Dear me! I'm so glad your mother hasnt spoilt you!

VIVIE: How?

PRAED: Well, in making you too conventional. You know, my dear Miss Warren, I am a born anarchist. I hate authority. It spoils the relations between parent and child—even between mother and daughter. Now I was always afraid that your mother would strain her authority to make you very conventional. It's such a relief to find that she hasnt.

VIVIE: Oh! have I been behaving unconventionally?

PRAED: Oh no: oh dear no. At least not conventionally unconventionally, you understand. (*She nods. He goes on, with a cordial outburst.*) But it was so charming of you to say that you were disposed to be friends with me! You modern young ladies are splendid—perfectly splendid!

VIVIE (*dubiously*): Eh? (*Watching him with dawning disappointment as to the quality of his brains and character.*)

PRAED: When I was your age, young men and women were afraid of each other: there was no good fellowship—nothing real—only gallantry copied out of novels, and as vulgar and affected as it could be. Maidenly reserve!—gentlemanly chivalry!—always saying no when you meant yes!—simple purgatory for shy and sincere souls!

VIVIE: Yes, I imagine there must have been a frightful waste of time—especially women's time.

PRAED: Oh, waste of life, waste of everything. But things are improving. Do you know, I have been in a positive state of excitement about meeting you ever since your magnificent achievements at Cambridge—a thing unheard of in my day. It was perfectly splendid, your tieing with the third wrangler.° Just the right place, you know. The first wrangler is always a dreamy, morbid fellow, in whom the thing is pushed to the length of a disease.

VIVIE: It doesnt pay. I wouldnt do it again for the same money.

---

wrangler: An honors student in mathematics. The term also implies achievement in debate.

PRAED (*aghast*): The same money!

VIVIE: I did it for £50. Perhaps you dont know how it was. Mrs Latham, my tutor at Newnham, told my mother that I could distinguish myself in the mathematical tripos° if I went in for it in earnest. The papers were full just then of Phillipa Summers beating the senior wrangler—you remember about it; and nothing would please my mother but that I should do the same thing. I said flatly that it was not worth my while to face the grind since I was not going in for teaching; but I offered to try for fourth wrangler or thereabouts for £50. She closed with me at that, after a little grumbling; and I was better than my bargain. But I wouldnt do it again for that. £200 would have been nearer the mark.

PRAED (*much damped*): Lord bless me! Thats a very practical way of looking at it.

VIVIE: Did you expect to find me an unpractical person?

PRAED: No, no. But surely it's practical to consider not only the work these honors cost, but also the culture they bring.

VIVIE: Culture! My dear Mr Praed: do you know what the mathematical tripos means? It means grind, grind, grind for six to eight hours a day at mathematics, and nothing but mathematics. I'm supposed to know something about science; but I know nothing except the mathematics it involves. I can make calculations for engineers, electricians, insurance companies, and so on; but I know next to nothing about engineering or electricity or insurance. I dont even know arithmetic well. Outside mathematics, lawn-tennis, eating, sleeping, cycling, and walking, I'm a more ignorant barbarian than any woman could possibly be who hadnt gone in for the tripos.

PRAED (*revolted*): What a monstrous, wicked, rascally system! I knew it! I felt at once that it meant destroying all that makes womanhood beautiful.

VIVIE: I dont object to it on that score in the least. I shall turn it to very good account, I assure you.

PRAED: Pooh! In what way?

VIVIE: I shall set up in chambers in the City and work at actuarial calculations and conveyancing. Under cover of that I shall do some law, with one eye on the Stock Exchange all the time. Ive come down here by myself to read law—not for a holiday, as my mother imagines. I hate holidays.

PRAED: You make my blood run cold. Are you to have no romance, no beauty in your life?

VIVIE: I dont care for either, I assure you.

PRAED: You cant mean that.

VIVIE: Oh yes I do. I like working and getting paid for it. When I'm tired of working, I like a comfortable chair, a cigar, a little whisky, and a novel with a good detective story in it.

PRAED (*in a frenzy of repudiation*): I dont believe it. I am an artist; and I cant believe it: I refuse to believe it.

°tripos: An examination for the B.A. degree with honors at Cambridge University.

(*Enthusiastically.*) Ah, my dear Miss Warren, you havnt discovered yet, I see, what a wonderful world art can open up to you.

VIVIE: Yes I have. Last May I spent six weeks in London with Honoria Fraser. Mamma thought we were doing a round of sightseeing together; but I was really at Honoria's chambers in Chancery Lane every day, working away at actuarial calculations for her, and helping her as well as a greenhorn could. In the evenings we smoked and talked, and never dreamt of going out except for exercise. And I never enjoyed myself more in my life. I cleared all my expenses, and got initiated into the business without a fee into the bargain.

PRAED: But bless my heart and soul, Miss Warren, do you call that trying art?

VIVIE: Wait a bit. That wasnt the beginning. I went up to town on an invitation from some artistic people in Fitzjohn's Avenue: one of the girls was a Newnham chum. They took me to the National Gallery, to the Opera, and to a concert where the band played all the evening—Beethoven and Wagner and so on. I wouldnt go through that experience again for anything you could offer me. I held out for civility's sake until the third day; and then I said, plump out, that I couldnt stand any more of it, and went off to Chancery Lane. Now you know the sort of perfectly splendid modern young lady I am. How do you think I shall get on with my mother?

PRAED (*startled*): Well, I hope—er—

VIVIE: It's not so much what you hope as what you believe, that I want to know.

PRAED: Well, frankly, I am afraid your mother will be a little disappointed. Not from any shortcoming on your part—I dont mean that. But you are so different from her ideal.

VIVIE: What is her ideal like?

PRAED: Well, you must have observed, Miss Warren, that people who are dissatisfied with their own bringing up generally think that the world would be all right if everybody were to be brought up quite differently. Now your mother's life has been—er—I suppose you know—

VIVIE: I know nothing. (*Praed is appalled. His consternation grows as she continues.*) Thats exactly my difficulty. You forget, Mr Praed, that I hardly know my mother. Since I was a child I have lived in England, at school or college, or with people paid to take charge of me. I have been boarded out all my life; and my mother has lived in Brussels or Vienna and never let me go to her. I only see her when she visits England for a few days. I dont complain: it's been very pleasant; for people have been very good to me; and there has always been plenty of money to make things smooth. But dont imagine I know anything about my mother. I know far less than you do.

PRAED (*very ill at ease*): In that case—(*He stops, quite at a loss. Then, with a forced attempt at gaiety*) But what nonsense we are talking! Of course you and your mother will get on capitally. (*He rises, and looks abroad at the view.*) What a charming little place you have here!

VIVIE (*unmoved*): If you think you are doing anything but confirming my worst suspicions by changing the subject like that, you must take me for a much greater fool than I hope I am.

PRAED: Your worst suspicions! Oh, pray dont say that. Now dont.

VIVIE: Why wont my mother's life bear being talked about?

PRAED: Pray think, Miss Vivie. It is natural that I should have a certain delicacy in talking to my old friend's daughter about her behind her back. You will have plenty of opportunity of talking to her about it when she comes. (*Anxiously*) I wonder what is keeping her.

VIVIE: No: she wont talk about it either. (*Rising*) However, I wont press you. Only, mind this, Mr Praed. I strongly suspect there will be a battle royal when my mother hears of my Chancery Lane project.

PRAED (*ruefully*): I'm afraid there will.

VIVIE: I shall win the battle, because I want nothing but my fare to London to start there to-morrow earning my own living by devilling° for Honoria. Besides, I have no mysteries to keep up; and it seems she has. I shall use that advantage over her if necessary.

PRAED (*greatly shocked*): Oh no! No, pray. Youd not do such a thing.

VIVIE: Then tell me why not.

PRAED: I really cannot. I appeal to your good feeling. (*She smiles at his sentimentality.*) Besides, you may be too bold. Your mother is not to be trifled with when she's angry.

VIVIE: You cant frighten me, Mr Praed. In that month at Chancery Lane I had opportunities of taking the measure of one or two women very like my mother, who came to consult Honoria. You may back me to win. But if I hit harder in my ignorance than I need, remember that it is you who refuse to enlighten me. Now, let us drop the subject. (*She takes her chair and replaces it near the hammock with the same vigorous swing as before.*)

PRAED (*taking a desperate resolution*): One word, Miss Warren. I had better tell you. It's very difficult; but—

(*Mrs Warren and Sir George Crofts arrive at the gate. Mrs Warren is a woman between 40 and 50, good-looking, showily dressed in a brilliant hat and a gay blouse fitting tightly over her bust and flanked by fashionable sleeves. Rather spoiled and domineering, but, on the whole, a genial and fairly presentable old blackguard of a woman.*

Crofts is a tall, powerfully-built man of about 50, fashionably dressed in the style of a young man. Nasal voice, reedier than might be expected from his strong

---

°**devilling:** To aid a professional (such as a lawyer or literary person) without fee or monetary recognition. This would constitute an apprenticeship.

frame. Clean-shaven, bulldog jaws, large flat ears, and thick neck, gentlemanly combination of the most brutal types of city man, sporting man, and man about town.)

VIVIE: Here they are. (*Coming to them as they enter the garden.*) How do, mater. Mr Praed's been here this half hour, waiting for you.

MRS WARREN: Well, if youve been waiting, Praddy, it's your own fault: I thought youd have had the gumption to know I was coming by the 3:10 train. Vivie: put your hat on, dear: youll get sunburnt. Oh, I forgot to introduce you. Sir George Crofts: my little Vivie.

(*Crofts advances to Vivie with his most courtly manner. She nods, but makes no motion to shake hands.*)

CROFTS: May I shake hands with a young lady whom I have known by reputation very long as the daughter of one of my oldest friends?

VIVIE (*who has been looking him up and down sharply*): If you like. (*She takes his tenderly proffered hand and gives it a squeeze that makes him open his eyes; then turns away, and says to her mother.*) Will you come in, or shall I get a couple more chairs? (*She goes into the porch for the chairs.*)

MRS WARREN: Well, George, what do you think of her?

CROFTS (*ruefully*): She has a powerful fist. Did you shake hands with her, Praed?

PRAED: Yes: it will pass off presently.

CROFTS: I hope so. (*Vivie reappears with two more chairs. He hurries to her assistance.*) Allow me.

MRS WARREN (*patronizingly*): Let Sir George help you with the chairs, dear.

VIVIE (*almost pitching the two into his arms*): Here you are. (*She dusts her hands and turns to Mrs Warren.*) Youd like some tea, wouldnt you?

MRS WARREN (*sitting in Praed's chair and fanning herself*): I'm dying for a drop to drink.

VIVIE: I'll see about it. (*She goes into the cottage. Sir George has by this time managed to unfold a chair and plant it beside Mrs Warren, on her left. He throws the other on the grass and sits down, looking dejected and rather foolish, with the handle of his stick in his mouth. Praed, still very uneasy, fidgets about the garden on their right.*)

MRS WARREN (*to Praed, looking at Crofts*): Just look at him, Praddy: he looks cheerful, dont he? He's been worrying my life out these three years to have that little girl of mine shewn to him; and now that Ive done it, he's quite out of countenance. (*Briskly.*) Come! sit up, George; and take your stick out of your mouth. (*Crofts sulkily obeys.*)

PRAED: I think, you know—if you dont mind my saying so—that we had better get out of the habit of thinking of her as a little girl. You see she has really distinguished herself; and I'm not sure, from what I have seen of her, that she is not older than any of us.

MRS WARREN (*greatly amused*): Only listen to him, George! Older than any of us! Well, she has been stuffing you nicely with her importance.

PRAED: But young people are particularly sensitive about being treated in that way.

MRS WARREN: Yes; and young people have to get all that nonsense taken out of them, and a good deal more besides. Dont you interfere, Praddy. I know how to treat my own child as well as you do. (*Praed, with a grave shake of his head, walks up the garden with his hands behind his back. Mrs Warren pretends to laugh, but looks after him with perceptible concern. Then she whispers to Crofts*) Whats the matter with him? What does he take it like that for?

CROFTS (*morosely*): Youre afraid of Praed.

MRS WARREN: What! Me! Afraid of dear old Praddy! Why, a fly wouldnt be afraid of him.

CROFTS: Youre afraid of him.

MRS WARREN (*angry*): I'll trouble you to mind your own business, and not try any of your sulks on me. I'm not afraid of you, anyhow. If you cant make yourself agreeable, youd better go home. (*She gets up, and, turning her back on him, finds herself face to face with Praed.*) Come, Praddy, I know it was only your tender-heartedness. Youre afraid I'll bully her.

PRAED: My dear Kitty: you think I'm offended. Dont imagine that: pray dont. But you know I often notice things that escape you; and though you never take my advice, you sometimes admit afterwards that you ought to have taken it.

MRS WARREN: Well, what do you notice now?

PRAED: Only that Vivie is a grown woman. Pray, Kitty, treat her with every respect.

MRS WARREN (*with genuine amazement*): Respect! Treat my own daughter with respect! What next, pray!

VIVIE (*appearing at the cottage door and calling to Mrs Warren*): Mother: will you come up to my room and take your bonnet off before tea?

MRS WARREN: Yes, dearie. (*She laughs indulgently at Praed and pats him on the cheek as she passes him on her way to the porch. She follows Vivie into the cottage.*)

CROFTS (*furtively*): I say, Praed.

PRAED: Yes.

CROFTS: I want to ask you a rather particular question.

PRAED: Certainly. (*He takes Mrs Warren's chair and sits close to Crofts.*)

CROFTS: Thats right: they might hear us from the window. Look here: did Kitty ever tell you who that girl's father is?

PRAED: Never.

CROFTS: Have you any suspicion of who it might be?

PRAED: None.

CROFTS (*not believing him*): I know, of course, that you perhaps might feel bound not to tell if she had said anything to you. But it's very awkward to be uncertain about it now that we shall be meeting the girl every day. We dont exactly know how we ought to feel towards her.

PRAED: What difference can that make? We take her on her own merits. What does it matter who her father was?

CROFTS (*suspiciously*): Then you know who he was?

PRAED (*with a touch of temper*): I said no just now. Did you not hear me?

CROFTS: Look here, Praed. I ask you as a particular favor. If you do know (*movement of protest from Praed*)—I only say, if you know, you might at least set my mind at rest about her. The fact is, I feel attracted towards her. Oh dont be alarmed: it's quite an innocent feeling. Thats what puzzles me about it. Why, for all I know, I might be her father.

PRAED: You! Impossible! Oh no, nonsense!

CROFTS (*catching him up cunningly*): You know for certain that I'm not?

PRAED: I know nothing about it, I tell you, any more than you. But really, Crofts—oh no, it's out of the question. Theres not the least resemblance.

CROFTS: As to that, theres no resemblance between her and her mother that I can see. I suppose she's not your daughter, is she?

PRAED (*He meets the question with an indignant stare; then recovers himself with an effort and answers gently and gravely*): Now listen to me, my dear Crofts. I have nothing to do with that side of Mrs Warren's life, and never had. She has never spoken to me about it; and of course I have never spoken to her about it. Your delicacy will tell you that a handsome woman needs some friends who are not—well, not on that footing with her. The effect of her own beauty would become a torment to her if she could not escape from it occasionally. You are probably on much more confidential terms with Kitty than I am. Surely you can ask her the question yourself.

CROFTS (*rising impatiently*): I have asked her, often enough. But she's so determined to keep the child all to herself that she would deny that it ever had a father if she could. No: theres nothing to be got out of her—nothing that one can believe, anyhow. I'm thoroughly uncomfortable about it, Praed.

PRAED (*rising also*): Well, as you are, at all events, old enough to be her father, I dont mind agreeing that we both regard Miss Vivie in a parental way, as a young girl whom we are bound to protect and help. All the more, as the real father, whoever he was, was probably a black-guard. What do you say?

CROFTS (*aggressively*): I'm no older than you, if you come to that.

PRAED: Yes you are, my dear fellow: you were born old. I was born a boy: Ive never been able to feel the assurance of a grown-up man in my life.

MRS WARREN (*calling from within the cottage*): Praddee! George! Tea-ea-ea-ea!

CROFTS (*hastily*): She's calling us. (*He hurries in. Praed shakes his head bodingly, and is following slowly when he is hailed by a young gentleman who has just appeared on the common, and is making for the gate. He is a pleasant, pretty, smartly dressed, and entirely good-for-nothing young fellow, not long turned 20, with a charming voice and agreeably disrespectful manners. He carries a very light sporting magazine rifle.*)

THE YOUNG GENTLEMAN: Hallo! Praed!

PRAED: Why, Frank Gardner! (*Frank comes in and shakes hands cordially.*) What on earth are you doing here?

FRANK: Staying with my father.

PRAED: The Roman father?

FRANK: He's rector here. I'm living with my people this autumn for the sake of economy. Things came to a crisis in July: the Roman father had to pay my debts. He's stony broke in consequence; and so am I. What are you up to in these parts? Do you know the people here?

PRAED: Yes: I'm spending the day with a Miss Warren.

FRANK (*enthusiastically*): What! Do you know Vivie? Isnt she a jolly girl! I'm teaching her to shoot—you see (*shewing the rifle*)! I'm so glad she knows you: youre just the sort of fellow she ought to know. (*He smiles, and raises the charming voice almost to a singing tone as he exclaims.*) It's ever so jolly to find you here, Praed. Aint it now?

PRAED: I'm an old friend of her mother's. Mrs Warren brought me over to make her daughter's acquaintance.

FRANK: The mother! Is she here?

PRAED: Yes—inside, at tea.

MRS WARREN (*calling from within*): Prad-dee-ee-ee-eee! The tea-cake'll be cold.

PRAED (*calling*): Yes, Mrs Warren. In a moment. Ive just met a friend here.

MRS WARREN: A what?

PRAED (*louder*): A friend.

MRS WARREN: Bring him up.

PRAED: All right. (*To Frank.*) Will you accept the invitation?

FRANK (*incredulous, but immensely amused*): Is that Vivie's mother?

PRAED: Yes.

FRANK: By Jove! What a lark! Do you think she'll like me?

PRAED: Ive no doubt youll make yourself popular, as usual. Come in and try (*moving towards the house*).

FRANK: Stop a bit. (*Seriously.*) I want to take you into my confidence.

PRAED: Pray dont. It's only some fresh folly, like the barmaid at Redhill.

FRANK: It's ever so much more serious than that. You say youve only just met Vivie for the first time?

PRAED: Yes.

FRANK (*rhapsodically*): Then you can have no idea what a girl she is. Such character! Such sense! And her cleverness! Oh, my eye, Praed, but I can tell you she is clever! And the most loving little heart that—

CROFTS (*putting his head out of the window*): I say, Praed: what are you about? Do come along. (*He disappears.*)

FRANK: Hallo! Sort of chap that would take a prize at a dog show, aint he? Who's he?

PRAED: Sir George Crofts, an old friend of Mrs Warren's. I think we had better come in.

(*On their way to the porch they are interrupted by a call from the gate. Turning, they see an elderly clergyman looking over it.*)

THE CLERGYMAN (*calling*): Frank!

FRANK: Hello! (*To Praed.*) The Roman father. (*To the clergyman.*) Yes, gov'nor: all right: presently. (*To Praed.*) Look here, Praed: youd better go in to tea. I'll join you directly.

PRAED: Very good. (*He raises his hat to the clergyman, who acknowledges the salute distantly. Praed goes into the cottage. The clergyman remains stiffly outside the gate, with his hands on the top of it. The Rev. Samuel Gardner, a beneficed clergyman of the Established Church, is over 50. He is a pretentious, booming, noisy person, hopelessly asserting himself as a father and a clergyman without being able to command respect in either capacity.*)

REV. SAMUEL: Well, sir. Who are your friends here, if I may ask?

FRANK: Oh, it's all right, gov'nor! Come in.

REV. SAMUEL: No, sir; not until I know whose garden I am entering.

FRANK: It's all right. It's Miss Warren's.

REV. SAMUEL: I have not seen her at church since she came.

FRANK: Of course not: she's a third wrangler—ever so intellectual!—took a higher degree than you did; so why should she go to hear you preach?

REV. SAMUEL: Dont be disrespectful, sir.

FRANK: Oh, it dont matter: nobody hears us. Come in. (*He opens the gate, unceremoniously pulling his father with it into the garden.*) I want to introduce you to her. She and I get on rattling well together: she's charming. Do you remember the advice you gave me last July, gov'nor?

REV. SAMUEL (*severely*): Yes. I advised you to conquer your idleness and flippancy, and to work your way into an honorable profession and live on it and not upon me.

FRANK: No: thats what you thought of afterwards. What you actually said was that since I had neither brains nor money, I'd better turn my good looks to account by marrying somebody with both. Well, look here. Miss Warren has brains: you cant deny that.

REV. SAMUEL: Brains are not everything.

FRANK: No, of course not: theres the money—

REV. SAMUEL (*interrupting him austerely*): I was not thinking of money, sir. I was speaking of higher things—social position, for instance.

FRANK: I dont care a rap about that.

REV. SAMUEL: But I do, sir.

FRANK: Well, nobody wants you to marry her. Anyhow, she has what amounts to a high Cambridge degree; and she seems to have as much money as she wants.

REV. SAMUEL (*sinking into a feeble vein of humor*): I greatly doubt whether she has as much money as you will want.

FRANK: Oh, come: I havnt been so very extravagant. I live ever so quietly; I dont drink; I dont bet much; and I never go regularly on the razzle-dazzle as you did when you were my age.

REV. SAMUEL (*booming hollowly*): Silence, sir.

FRANK: Well, you told me yourself, when I was making ever such an ass of myself about the barmaid at Redhill, that you once offered a woman £50 for the letters you wrote to her when—

REV. SAMUEL (*terrified*): Sh-sh-sh, Frank, for Heaven's sake! (*He looks round apprehensively. Seeing no one within earshot he plucks up courage to boom again, but more subduedly.*) You are taking an ungentlemanly advantage of what I confided to you for your own good, to save you from an error you would have repented all your life long. Take warning by your father's follies, sir; and dont make them an excuse for your own.

FRANK: Did you ever hear the story of the Duke of Wellington and his letters?

REV. SAMUEL: No, sir; and I dont want to hear it.

FRANK: The old Iron Duke didnt throw away £50—not he. He just wrote: "My dear Jenny: Publish and be damned! Yours affectionately, Wellington." Thats what you should have done.

REV. SAMUEL (*piteously*): Frank, my boy: when I wrote those letters I put myself into that woman's power. When I told you about her I put myself, to some extent, I am sorry to say, in your power. She refused my money with these words, which I shall never forget: "Knowledge is power," she said; "and I never sell power." Thats more than twenty years ago; and she has never made use of her power or caused me a moment's uneasiness. You are behaving worse to me than she did, Frank.

FRANK: Oh yes I dare say! Did you ever preach at her the way you preach at me every day?

REV. SAMUEL (*wounded almost to tears*): I leave you, sir. You are incorrigible. (*He turns towards the gate.*)

FRANK (*utterly unmoved*): Tell them I shant be home to tea, will you, gov'nor, like a good fellow? (*He goes towards the cottage door and is met by Vivie coming out, followed by Praed, Crofts, and Mrs Warren.*)

VIVIE (*to Frank*): Is that your father, Frank? I do so want to meet him.

FRANK: Certainly. (*Calling after his father*) Gov'nor. (*The Rev Samuel turns at the gate, fumbling nervously at his hat. Praed comes down the garden on the opposite side, beaming in anticipation of civilities. Crofts prowls about near the hammock, poking it with his stick to make it swing. Mrs Warren halts on the threshold, staring hard at the clergyman.*) Let me introduce—my father: Miss Warren.

VIVIE (*going to the clergyman and shaking his hand*): Very glad to see you here, Mr Gardner. Let me introduce everybody. Mr Gardner—Mr Frank Gardner—Mr Praed—Sir George Crofts, and—(*As the men are raising their hats to one another, Vivie is interrupted by an exclamation from her mother, who swoops down on the Reverend Samuel.*)

MRS WARREN: Why, it's Sam Gardner, gone into the church! Dont you know us, Sam? This is George Crofts, as large as life and twice as natural. Dont you remember me?

REV. SAMUEL (*very red*): I really—er—

MRS WARREN: Of course you do. Why, I have a whole album of your letters still: I came across them only the other day.

REV. SAMUEL (*miserably confused*): Miss Vavasour, I believe.

MRS WARREN (*correcting him quickly in a loud whisper*): Tch! Nonsense—Mrs. Warren: dont you see my daughter there?

ACT II

(*Inside the cottage after nightfall. Looking eastward from within instead of westward from without, the latticed window, with its curtains drawn, is now seen in the middle of the front wall of the cottage, with the porch door to the left of it. In the left-hand side wall is the door leading to the wing. Farther back against the same wall is a dresser with a candle and matches on it, and Frank's rifle standing beside them, with the barrel resting in the plate-rack. In the centre a table stands with a lighted lamp on it. Vivie's books and writing materials are on a table to the right of the window, against the wall. The fireplace is on the right, with a settle: there is no fire. Two of the chairs are set right and left of the table.*

The cottage door opens, showing a fine starlit night without; and Mrs Warren, her shoulders wrapped in a shawl borrowed from Vivie, enters, followed by Frank. She has had enough of walking, and gives a gasp of relief as she unpins her hat; takes it off; sticks the pin through the crown; and puts it on the table.)

MRS WARREN: O Lord! I dont know which is the worst of the country, the walking or the sitting at home with nothing to do. I could do a whisky and soda now very well, if only they had such a thing in this place.

FRANK (*helping her to take off her shawl, and giving her shoulders the most delicate possible little caress with his fingers as he does so*): Perhaps Vivie's got some.

MRS WARREN (*glancing back at him for an instant from the corner of her eye as she detects the pressure*): Nonsense! What would a young girl like her be doing with such things! Never mind: it dont matter. (*She throws herself wearily into a chair at the table.*) I wonder how she passes her time here! I'd a good deal rather be in Vienna.

FRANK: Let me take you there. (*He folds the shawl neatly; hangs it on the back of the other chair; and sits down opposite Mrs Warren.*)

MRS WARREN: Get out! I'm beginning to think youre a chip of the old block.

FRANK: Like the gov'nor, eh?

MRS WARREN: Never you mind. What do you know about such things? Youre only a boy.

FRANK: Do come to Vienna with me? It'd be ever such larks.

MRS WARREN: No, thank you. Vienna is no place for you—at least not until youre a little older. (*She nods at him to emphasize this piece of advice. He makes a mock-piteous face, belied by his laughing eyes. She looks at him; then rises and goes to him.*) Now, look here, little boy (*taking his face in her hands and turning it up to her*): I know you through and through by your likeness to your father, better than you know yourself. Dont you go taking any silly ideas into your head about me. Do you hear?

FRANK (*gallantly wooing her with his voice*): Cant help it, my dear Mrs Warren: it runs in the family. (*She pretends to box his ears; then looks at the pretty, laughing, upturned face for a moment, tempted. At last she kisses him, and immediately turns away, out of patience with herself.*)

MRS WARREN: There! I shouldnt have done that. I am wicked. Never you mind, my dear: it's only a motherly kiss. Go and make love to Vivie.

FRANK: So I have.

MRS WARREN (*turning on him with a sharp note of alarm in her voice*): What!

FRANK: Vivie and I are ever such chums.

MRS WARREN: What do you mean? Now see here: I wont have any young scamp tampering with my little girl. Do you hear? I wont have it.

FRANK (*quite unabashed*): My dear Mrs Warren: dont you be alarmed. My intentions are honorable—ever so honorable; and your little girl is jolly well able to take care of herself. She dont need looking after half so much as her mother. She aint so handsome, you know.

MRS WARREN (*taken aback by his assurance*): Well, you have got a nice, healthy two inches thick of cheek all over you. I dont know where you got it—not from your father, anyhow. (*Voices and footsteps in the porch.*) Sh! I hear the others coming in. (*She sits down hastily.*) Remember: youve got your warning. (*The Rev. Samuel comes in, followed by Crofts.*) Well, what became of you two? And wheres Praddy and Vivie?

CROFTS (*putting his hat on the settle and his stick in the chimney corner*): They went up the hill. We went to the village. I wanted a drink. (*He sits down on the settle, putting his legs up along the seat.*)

MRS WARREN: Well, she oughtnt to go off like that without telling me. (*To Frank*) Get your father a chair, Frank: where are your manners? (*Frank springs up and gracefully offers his father his chair; then takes another from the wall and sits down at the table, in the middle, with his father on his right and Mrs Warren on his left.*) George: where are you going

to stay to-night? You cant stay here. And whats Praddy going to do?

CROFTS: Gardner'll put me up.

MRS WARREN: Oh, no doubt youve taken care of yourself! But what about Praddy?

CROFTS: Dont know. I suppose he can sleep at the inn.

MRS WARREN: Havnt you room for him, Sam?

REV. SAMUEL: Well, er—you see, as rector here, I am not free to do as I like exactly. Er—what is Mr Praed's social position?

MRS WARREN: Oh, he's all right: he's an architect. What an old stick-in-the-mud you are, Sam!

FRANK: Yes, it's all right, gov'nor. He built that place down in Monmouthshire for the Duke of Beaufort—Tintern Abbey they call it. You must have heard of it. (*He winks with lightning smartness at Mrs Warren, and regards his father blandly.*)

REV. SAMUEL: Oh, in that case, of course we shall only be too happy. I suppose he knows the Duke of Beaufort personally.

FRANK: Oh, ever so intimately! We can stick him in Georgina's old room.

MRS WARREN: Well, thats settled. Now if those two would only come in and let us have supper. Theyve no right to stay out after dark like this.

CROFTS (*aggressively*): What harm are they doing you?

MRS WARREN: Well, harm or not, I dont like it.

FRANK: Better not wait for them, Mrs Warren. Praed will stay out as long as possible. He has never known before what it is to stray over the heath on a summer night with my Vivie.

CROFTS (*sitting up in some consternation*): I say, you know. Come!

REV. SAMUEL (*startled out of his professional manner into real force and sincerity*): Frank, once for all, its out of the question. Mrs Warren will tell you that its not to be thought of.

CROFTS: Of course not.

FRANK (*with enchanting placidity*): Is that so, Mrs Warren?

MRS WARREN (*reflectively*): Well, Sam, I dont know. If the girl wants to get married, no good can come of keeping her unmarried.

REV. SAMUEL (*astounded*): But married to him!—your daughter to my son! Only think: it's impossible.

CROFTS: Of course it's impossible. Dont be a fool, Kitty.

MRS WARREN (*nettled*): Why not? Isnt my daughter good enough for your son?

REV. SAMUEL: But surely, my dear Mrs Warren, you know the reason—

MRS WARREN (*defiantly*): I know no reasons. If you know any, you can tell them to the lad, or to the girl, or to your congregation, if you like.

REV. SAMUEL (*helplessly*): You know very well that I couldnt tell anyone the reasons. But my boy will believe me when I tell him there are reasons.

FRANK: Quite right, Dad: he will. But has your boy's conduct ever been influenced by your reasons?

CROFTS: You cant marry her; and thats all about it. (*He gets up and stands on the hearth, with his back to the fireplace, frowning determinedly.*)

MRS WARREN (*turning on him sharply*): What have you got to do with it, pray?

FRANK (*with his prettiest lyrical cadence*): Precisely what I was going to ask, myself, in my own graceful fashion.

CROFTS (*to Mrs Warren*): I suppose you dont want to marry the girl to a man younger than herself and without either a profession or twopence to keep her on. Ask Sam, if you dont believe me. (*To the Rev. Samuel.*) How much more money are you going to give him?

REV. SAMUEL: Not another penny. He has had his patrimony; and he spent the last of it in July. (*Mrs Warren's face falls.*)

CROFTS (*watching her*): There! I told you. (*He resumes his place on the settle and puts up his legs on the seat again, as if the matter were finally disposed of.*)

FRANK (*plaintively*): This is ever so mercenary. Do you suppose Miss Warren's going to marry for money? If we love one another—

MRS WARREN: Thank you. Your love's a pretty cheap commodity, my lad. If you have no means of keeping a wife, that settles it: you cant have Vivie.

FRANK (*much amused*): What do you say, gov'nor, eh?

REV. SAMUEL: I agree with Mrs Warren.

FRANK: And good old Crofts has already expressed his opinion.

CROFTS (*turning angrily on his elbow*): Look here: I want none of your cheek.

FRANK (*pointedly*): I'm ever so sorry to surprise you, Crofts; but you allowed yourself the liberty of speaking to me like a father a moment ago. One father is enough, thank you.

CROFTS (*contemptuously*): Yah! (*He turns away again.*)

FRANK (*rising*): Mrs Warren: I cannot give my Vivie up, even for your sake.

MRS WARREN (*muttering*): Young scamp!

FRANK (*continuing*): And as you no doubt intend to hold out other prospects to her, I shall lose no time in placing my case before her. (*They stare at him; and he begins to declaim gracefully*)

He either fears his fate too much,
Or his deserts are small,
That dares not put it to the touch
To gain or lose it all.

(*The cottage door opens whilst he is reciting; and Vivie and Praed come in. He breaks off. Praed puts his hat on the dresser. There is an immediate improvement in the company's behaviour. Crofts takes down his legs from the settle and pulls himself together as Praed joins him at the fireplace. Mrs Warren loses her ease of manner and takes refuge in querulousness.*)

MRS WARREN: Wherever have you been, Vivie?

VIVIE (*taking off her hat and throwing it carelessly on the table*): On the hill.

MRS WARREN: Well, you shouldnt go off like that without letting me know. How could I tell what had become of you—and night coming on too!

VIVIE (*going to the door of the inner room and opening it, ignoring her mother*): Now, about supper? We shall be rather crowded in here, I'm afraid.

MRS WARREN: Did you hear what I said, Vivie?

VIVIE (*quietly*): Yes, mother. (*Reverting to the supper difficulty.*) How many are we? (*Counting.*) One, two, three, four, five, six. Well, two will have to wait until the rest are done: Mrs Allison has only plates and knives for four.

PRAED: Oh, it doesnt matter about me. I—

VIVIE: You have had a long walk and are hungry, Mr Praed: you shall have your supper at once. I can wait myself. I want one person to wait with me. Frank: are you hungry?

FRANK: Not the least in the world—completely off my peck, in fact.

MRS WARREN (*to Crofts*): Neither are you, George. You can wait.

CROFTS: Oh, hang it, Ive eaten nothing since tea-time. Cant Sam do it?

FRANK: Would you starve my poor father?

REV. SAMUEL (*testily*): Allow me to speak for myself, sir. I am perfectly willing to wait.

VIVIE (*decisively*): Theres no need. Only two are wanted. (*She opens the door of the inner room.*) Will you take my mother in, Mr Gardner. (*The Rev. Samuel takes Mrs Warren; and they pass into the next room. Praed and Crofts follow. All except Praed clearly disapprove of the arrangement, but do not know how to resist it. Vivie stands at the door looking in at them.*) Can you squeeze past to that corner, Mr Praed: it's rather a tight fit. Take care of your coat against the white-wash—thats right. Now, are you all comfortable?

PRAED (*within*): Quite, thank you.

MRS WARREN (*within*): Leave the door open, dearie. (*Frank looks at Vivie; then steals to the cottage door and softly sets it wide open.*) Oh Lor, what a draught! Youd better shut it, dear. (*Vivie shuts it promptly. Frank noiselessly shuts the cottage door.*)

FRANK (*exulting*): Aha! Got rid of em. Well, Vivvums: what do you think of my governor?

VIVIE (*preoccupied and serious*): Ive hardly spoken to him. He doesnt strike me as being a particularly able person.

FRANK: Well, you know, the old man is not altogether such a fool as he looks. You see, he's rector here; and in trying to live up to it he makes a much bigger ass of himself than he really is. No, the gov'nor aint so bad, poor old chap; and I dont dislike him as much as you might expect. He means well. How do you think youll get on with him?

VIVIE (*rather grimly*): I dont think my future life will be much concerned with him, or with any of that old circle of my mother's, except perhaps Praed. What do you think of my mother?

FRANK: Really and truly?

VIVIE: Yes, really and truly.

FRANK: Well, she's ever so jolly. But she's rather a caution, isnt she? And Crofts! Oh, my eye, Crofts!

VIVIE: What a lot, Frank!

FRANK: What a crew!

VIVIE (*with intense contempt for them*): If I thought that *I* was like that—that I was going to be a waster, shifting along from one meal to another with no purpose, and no character, and no grit in me, I'd open an artery and bleed to death without one moment's hesitation.

FRANK: Oh no, you wouldnt. Why should they take any grind when they can afford not to? I wish I had their luck. No: what I object to is their form. It isnt the thing: it's slovenly, ever so slovenly.

VIVIE: Do you think your form will be any better when youre as old as Crofts, if you dont work?

FRANK: Of course I do—ever so much better. Vivvums mustnt lecture: her little boy's incorrigible. (*He attempts to take her face caressingly in his hands.*)

VIVIE (*striking his hands down sharply*): Off with you: Vivvums is not in a humor for petting her little boy this evening.

FRANK: How unkind!

VIVIE (*stamping at him*): Be serious. I'm serious.

FRANK: Good. Let us talk learnedly. Miss Warren: do you know that all the most advanced thinkers are agreed that half the diseases of modern civilization are due to starvation of the affections in the young. Now, I—

VIVIE (*cutting him short*): You are getting tiresome. (*She opens the inner door*) Have you room for Frank there? He's complaining of starvation.

MRS WARREN (*within*): Of course there is (*clatter of knives and glasses as she moves the things on the table.*) Here: theres room now beside me. Come along, Mr Frank.

FRANK (*aside to Vivie, as he goes*): Her little boy will be ever so even with his Vivvums for this. (*He goes into the other room.*)

MRS WARREN (*within*): Here, Vivie: come on you too, child. You must be famished. (*She enters, followed by Crofts, who holds the door open for Vivie with marked deference. She goes out without looking at him; and he shuts the door after her.*) Why, George, you cant be done: youve eaten nothing.

CROFTS: Oh, all I wanted was a drink. (*He thrusts his hands in his pockets, and begins prowling about the room, restless and sulky.*)

MRS WARREN: Well, I like enough to eat. But a little of that cold beef and cheese and lettuce goes a long way. (*With a sigh of only half repletion she sits down lazily at the table.*)

CROFTS: What do you go encouraging that young pup for?

MRS WARREN (*on the alert at once*): Now see here, George: what are you up to about that girl? Ive been watching your way of looking at her. Remember: I know you and what your looks mean.

CROFTS: Theres no harm in looking at her, is there?

MRS WARREN: I'd put you out and pack you back to London pretty soon if I saw any of your nonsense. My girl's little finger is more to me than your whole body and soul. (*Crofts receives this with a sneering grin. Mrs Warren, flushing a little at her failure to impose on him in the character of a theatrically devoted mother, adds in a lower key*) Make your mind easy: the young pup has no more chance than you have.

CROFTS: Maynt a man take an interest in a girl?

MRS WARREN: Not a man like you.

CROFTS: How old is she?

MRS WARREN: Never you mind how old she is.

CROFTS: Why do you make such a secret of it?

MRS WARREN: Because I choose.

CROFTS: Well, I'm not fifty yet; and my property is as good as ever it was—

MRS WARREN (*interrupting him*): Yes; because youre as stingy as youre vicious.

CROFTS (*continuing*): And a baronet isnt to be picked up every day. No other man in my position would put up with you for a mother-in-law. Why shouldnt she marry me?

MRS WARREN: You!

CROFTS: We three could live together quite comfortably. I'd die before her and leave her a bouncing widow with plenty of money. Why not? It's been growing in my mind all the time Ive been walking with that fool inside there.

MRS WARREN (*revolted*): Yes: it's the sort of thing that would grow in your mind. (*He halts in his prowling; and the two look at one another, she steadfastly, with a sort of awe behind her contemptuous disgust: he stealthily with a carnal gleam in his eye and a loose grin, tempting her.*)

CROFTS (*suddenly becoming anxious and urgent as he sees no sign of sympathy in her*): Look here, Kitty: youre a sensible woman: you neednt put on any moral airs. I'll ask no more questions; and you need answer none. I'll settle the whole property on her; and if you want a cheque for yourself on the wedding day, you can name any figure you like—in reason.

MRS WARREN: So it's come to that with you, George, like all the other worn out old creatures!

CROFTS (*savagely*): Damn you! (*She rises and turns fiercely on him; but the door of the inner room is opened just then; and the voices of the others are heard returning. Crofts, unable to recover his presence of mind, hurries out of the cottage. The clergyman comes back.*)

REV. SAMUEL (*looking round*): Where is Sir George?

MRS WARREN: Gone out to have a pipe. (*She goes to the fireplace, turning her back on him to compose herself. The clergyman goes to the table for his hat. Meanwhile Vivie comes in, followed by Frank, who collapses into the nearest chair with an air of extreme exhaustion. Mrs Warren looks round at Vivie and says, with her affectation of maternal patronage even*) *more forced than usual.*) Well, dearie: have you had a good supper?

VIVIE: You know what Mrs Alison's suppers are. (*She turns to Frank and pets him.*) Poor Frank! was all the beef gone? did it get nothing but bread and cheese and ginger beer? (*Seriously, as if she had done quite enough trifling for one evening.*) Her butter is really awful. I must get some down from the stores.

FRANK: Do, in Heaven's name!

(*Vivie goes to the writing-table and makes a memorandum to order the butter. Praed comes in from the inner room, putting up his handkerchief, which he has been using as a napkin.*)

REV. SAMUEL: Frank, my boy: it is time for us to be thinking of home. Your mother does not know yet that we have visitors.

PRAED: I'm afraid we're giving trouble.

FRANK: Not the least in the world, Praed: my mother will be delighted to see you. She's a genuinely intellectual, artistic woman; and she sees nobody here from one year's end to another except the gov'nor; so you can imagine how jolly dull it pans out for her. (*To the Rev. Samuel.*) Youre not intellectual or artistic, are you, pater? So take Praed home at once; and I'll stay here and entertain Mrs Warren. Youll pick up Crofts in the garden. He'll be excellent company for the bull-pup.

PRAED (*taking his hat from the dresser, and coming close to Frank*): Come with us, Frank. Mrs Warren has not seen Miss Vivie for a long time; and we have prevented them from having a moment together yet.

FRANK (*quite softened, and looking at Praed with romantic admiration*): Of course: I forgot. Ever so thanks for reminding me. Perfect gentleman, Praddy. Always were—my ideal through life. (*He rises to go, but pauses a moment between the two older men, and puts his hand on Praed's shoulder.*) Ah, if you had only been my father instead of this unworthy old man! (*He puts his other hand on his father's shoulder.*)

REV. SAMUEL (*blustering*): Silence, sir, silence: you are profane.

MRS WARREN (*laughing heartily*): You should keep him in better order, Sam. Good-night. Here: take George his hat and stick with my compliments.

REV. SAMUEL (*taking them*): Good-night. (*They shake hands. As he passes Vivie he shakes hands with her also and bids her good-night. Then, in booming command, to Frank*) Come along, sir, at once. (*He goes out. Meanwhile Frank has taken his cap from the dresser and his rifle from the rack. Praed shakes hands with Mrs Warren and Vivie and goes out, Mrs Warren accompanying him idly to the door and looking out after him as he goes across the garden. Frank silently begs a kiss from Vivie; but she, dismissing him with a stern glance, takes a couple of books and some paper from the writing-table, and sits down with them at the middle table, so as to have the benefit of the lamp.*)

FRANK (*at the door, taking Mrs Warren's hand*): Goodnight, dear Mrs Warren. (*He squeezes her hand. She snatches it away, her lips tightening, and looks more than half disposed to box his ears. He laughs mischievously and runs off, clapping-to° the door behind him.*)

MRS WARREN (*coming back to her place at the table, opposite Vivie, resigning herself to an evening of boredom now that the men are gone*): Did you ever in your life hear anyone rattle on so? Isnt he a tease? (*She sits down.*) Now that I think of it, dearie, dont you go encouraging him. I'm sure he's a regular good-for-nothing.

VIVIE: Yes: I'm afraid poor Frank is a thorough good-fornothing. I shall have to get rid of him; but I shall feel sorry for him, though he's not worth it, poor lad. That man Crofts does not seem to me to be good for much either, is he?

MRS WARREN (*galled by Vivie's cool tone*): What do you know of men, child, to talk that way about them? Youll have to make up your mind to see a good deal of Sir George Crofts, as he's a friend of mine.

VIVIE (*quite unmoved*): Why? Do you expect that we shall be much together—you and I, I mean?

MRS WARREN (*staring at her*): Of course—until youre married. Youre not going back to college again.

VIVIE: Do you think my way of life would suit you? I doubt it.

MRS WARREN: Your way of life! What do you mean?

VIVIE (*cutting a page of her book with the paper knife on her chatelaine*): Has it really never occurred to you, mother, that I have a way of life like other people?

MRS WARREN: What nonsense is this youre trying to talk? Do you want to shew your independence, now that youre a great little person at school? Dont be a fool, child.

VIVIE (*indulgently*): Thats all you have to say on the subject, is it, mother?

MRS WARREN (*puzzled, then angry*): Dont you keep on asking me questions like that. (*Violently*) Hold your tongue. (*Vivie works on, losing no time, and saying nothing.*) You and your way of life, indeed! What next? (*She looks at Vivie again. No reply.*) Your way of life will be what I please, so it will. (*Another pause.*) Ive been noticing these airs in you ever since you got that tripos or whatever you call it. If you think I'm going to put up with them youre mistaken; and the sooner you find it out, the better. (*Muttering.*) All I have to say on the subject, indeed! (*Again raising her voice angrily.*) Do you know who youre speaking to, Miss?

VIVIE (*looking across at her without raising her head from her book*): No. Who are you? What are you?

MRS WARREN (*rising breathless*): You young imp!

clapping-to: Slamming.

VIVIE: Everybody knows my reputation, my social standing, and the profession I intend to pursue. I know nothing about you. What is that way of life which you invite me to share with you and Sir George Crofts, pray?

MRS WARREN: Take care. I shall do something I'll be sorry for after, and you too.

VIVIE (*putting aside her books with cool decision*): Well, let us drop the subject until you are better able to face it. (*Looking critically at her mother*) You want some good walks and a little lawn tennis to set you up. You are shockingly out of condition: you were not able to manage twenty yards uphill to-day without stopping to pant; and your wrists are mere rolls of fat. Look at mine. (*She holds out her wrists.*)

MRS WARREN (*after looking at her helplessly, begins to whimper*): Vivie—

VIVIE (*springing up sharply*): Now pray dont begin to cry. Anything but that. I really cannot stand whimpering. I will go out of the room if you do.

MRS WARREN (*piteously*): Oh, my darling, how can you be so hard on me? Have I no rights over you as your mother?

VIVIE: Are you my mother?

MRS WARREN (*appalled*): Am I your mother! Oh, Vivie!

VIVIE: Then where are our relatives—my father—our family friends? You claim the rights of a mother: the right to call me fool and child; to speak to me as no woman in authority over me at college dare speak to me; to dictate my way of life; and to force on me the acquaintance of a brute whom anyone can see to be the most vicious sort of London man about town. Before I give myself the trouble to resist such claims, I may as well find out whether they have any real existence.

MRS WARREN (*distracted, throwing herself on her knees*): Oh no, no. Stop, stop. I am your mother: I swear it. Oh, you cant mean to turn on me—my own child: it's not natural. You believe me, dont you? Say you believe me.

VIVIE: Who was my father?

MRS WARREN: You dont know what youre asking. I cant tell you.

VIVIE (*determinedly*): Oh yes you can, if you like. I have a right to know; and you know very well that I have that right. You can refuse to tell me, if you please; but if you do, you will see the last of me to-morrow morning.

MRS WARREN: Oh, it's too horrible to hear you talk like that. You wouldnt—you couldnt leave me.

VIVIE (*ruthlessly*): Yes, without a moment's hesitation, if you trifle with me about this. (*Shivering with disgust.*) How can I feel sure that I may not have the contaminated blood of that brutal waster in my veins?

MRS WARREN: No, no. On my oath it's not he, nor any of the rest that you have ever met. I'm certain of that, at least. (*Vivie's eyes fasten sternly on her mother as the significance of this flashes on her.*)

VIVIE (*slowly*): You are certain of that, at least. Ah! You mean that that is all you are certain of. (*Thoughtfully.*) I see. (*Mrs Warren buries her face in her hands.*) Dont do that, mother: you know you dont feel it

a bit. (*Mrs Warren takes down her hands and looks up deplorably at Vivie, who takes out her watch and says*) Well, that is enough for to-night. At what hour would you like breakfast? Is half-past eight too early for you?

MRS WARREN (*wildly*): My God, what sort of woman are you?

VIVIE (*coolly*): The sort the world is mostly made of, I should hope. Otherwise I dont understand how it gets its business done. Come (*taking her mother by the wrist, and pulling her up pretty resolutely*): pull yourself together. Thats right.

MRS WARREN (*querulously*): Youre very rough with me, Vivie.

VIVIE: Nonsense. What about bed? It's past ten.

MRS WARREN (*passionately*): Whats the use of my going to bed? Do you think I could sleep?

VIVIE: Why not? I shall.

MRS WARREN: You! youve no heart. (*She suddenly breaks out vehemently in her natural tongue—the dialect of a woman of the people—with all her affectations of maternal authority and conventional manners gone, and an overwhelming inspiration of true conviction and scorn in her.*) Oh, I wont bear it: I wont put up with the injustice of it. What right have you to set yourself up above me like this? You boast of what you are to me—to me, who gave you the chance of being what you are. What chance had I? Shame on you for a bad daughter and a stuck-up prude!

VIVIE (*cool and determined, but no longer confident; for her replies, which have sounded convincingly sensible and strong to her so far, now begin to ring rather woodenly and even priggishly against the new tone of her mother*): Dont think for a moment I set myself above you in any way. You attacked me with the conventional authority of a mother: I defended myself with the conventional superiority of a respectable woman. Frankly, I am not going to stand any of your nonsense; and when you drop it I shall not expect you to stand any of mine. I shall always respect your right to your own opinions and your own way of life.

MRS WARREN: My own opinions and my own way of life! Listen to her talking! Do you think I was brought up like you—able to pick and choose my own way of life? Do you think I did what I did because I liked it, or thought it right, or wouldnt rather have gone to college and been a lady if I'd had the chance?

VIVIE: Everybody has some choice, mother. The poorest girl alive may not be able to choose between being Queen of England or Principal of Newnham; but she can choose between ragpicking and flowerselling, according to her taste. People are always blaming their circumstances for what they are. I dont believe in circumstances. The people who get on in this world are the people who get up and look for the circumstances they want, and, if they cant find them, make them.

MRS WARREN: Oh, it's easy to talk, very easy, isnt it? Here!—would you like to know what my circumstances were?

VIVIE: Yes: you had better tell me. Wont you sit down?

MRS WARREN: Oh, I'll sit down: dont you be afraid. (*She plants her chair farther forward with brazen energy, and sits down. Vivie is impressed in spite of herself.*) D'you know what your gran'mother was?

VIVIE: No.

MRS WARREN: No, you dont. I do. She called herself a widow and had a fried-fish shop down by the Mint, and kept herself and four daughters out of it. Two of us were sisters: that was me and Liz; and we were both good-looking and well made. I suppose our father was a well-fed man: mother pretended he was a gentleman; but I dont know. The other two were only half sisters—undersized, ugly, starved looking, hard working, honest poor creatures: Liz and I would have half-murdered them if mother hadnt half-murdered us to keep our hands off them. They were the respectable ones. Well, what did they get by their respectability? I'll tell you. One of them worked in a white-lead factory twelve hours a day for nine shillings a week until she died of lead poisoning. She only expected to get her hands a little paralyzed; but she died. The other was always held up to us as a model because she married a Government laborer in the Deptford victualling yard, and kept his room and the three children neat and tidy on eighteen shillings a week—until he took to drink. That was worth being respectable for, wasnt it?

VIVIE (*now thoughtfully attentive*): Did you and your sister think so?

MRS WARREN: Liz didnt, I can tell you: she had more spirit. We both went to a church school—that was part of the ladylike airs we gave ourselves to be superior to the children that knew nothing and went nowhere—and we stayed there until Liz went out one night and never came back. I know the schoolmistress thought I'd soon follow her example; for the clergyman was always warning me that Lizzie'd end by jumping off Waterloo Bridge. Poor fool: that was all he knew about it! But I was more afraid of the white-lead factory than I was of the river; and so would you have been in my place. That clergyman got me a situation as scullery maid in a temperance restaurant where they sent out for anything you liked. Then I was waitress; and then I went to the bar at Waterloo station—fourteen hours a day serving drinks and washing glasses for four shillings a week and my board. That was considered a great promotion for me. Well, one cold, wretched night, when I was so tired I could hardly keep myself awake, who should come up for a half of Scotch but Lizzie, in a long fur cloak, elegant and comfortable, with a lot of sovereigns in her purse.

VIVIE (*grimly*): My aunt Lizzie!

MRS WARREN: Yes; and a very good aunt to have, too. She's living down at Winchester now, close to the cathedral, one of the most respectable ladies there—chaperones girls at the county ball, if you please. No river for Liz, thank you! You remind me of Liz a little: she was a first-rate business woman—saved money from the beginning—never let herself look too like what she was—never lost her head or threw away a chance. When she saw I'd grown up good-looking she said to me across the bar "What are you doing there, you little fool? wearing out your health and your appearance for other people's profit!" Liz was saving money then to take a house for herself in Brussels; and she thought we two could save faster than one. So she lent me some money and gave me a start; and I saved steadily and first paid her back, and then went into business with her as her partner. Why shouldnt I have done it? The house in Brussels was real high class—a much better place for a woman to be in than the factory where Anne Jane got poisoned. None of our girls were ever treated as I was treated in the scullery of that temperance place, or at the Waterloo bar, or at home. Would you have had me stay in them and become a worn out old drudge before I was forty?

VIVIE (*intensely interested by this time*): No; but why did you choose that business? Saving money and good management will succeed in any business.

MRS WARREN: Yes, saving money. But where can a woman get the money to save in any other business? Could you save out of four shillings a week and keep yourself dressed as well? Not you. Of course, if youre a plain woman and cant earn anything more; or if you have a turn for music, or the stage, or newspaper-writing: thats different. But neither Liz nor I had any turn for such things: all we had was our appearance and our turn for pleasing men. Do you think we were such fools as to let other people trade in our good looks by employing us as shopgirls, or barmaids, or waitresses, when we could trade in them ourselves and get all the profits instead of starvation wages? Not likely.

VIVIE: You were certainly quite justified—from the business point of view.

MRS WARREN: Yes; or any other point of view. What is any respectable girl brought up to do but to catch some rich man's fancy and get the benefit of his money by marrying him?—as if a marriage ceremony could make any difference in the right or wrong of the thing! Oh, the hypocrisy of the world makes me sick! Liz and I had to work and save and calculate just like other people; elseways we should be as poor as any good-for-nothing, drunken waster of a woman that thinks her luck will last for ever. (*With great energy.*) I despise such people: theyve no character; and if theres a thing I hate in a woman, it's want of character.

VIVIE: Come now, mother: frankly! Isnt it part of what you call character in a woman that she should greatly dislike such a way of making money?

MRS WARREN: Why, of course. Everybody dislikes having to work and make money; but they have to do it all the same. I'm sure Ive often pitied a poor girl, tired out and in low spirits, having to try to please some man that she doesnt care two straws for—some half-drunken fool that thinks he's making himself agreeable when he's teasing and worrying and disgusting a woman so that hardly any money could pay her for putting up with it. But she has to bear with

[RIGHT] Vivie and her mother console each other in *Mrs. Warren's Profession*, Huntington Theatre, Boston, 1999.
[BELOW] Vivie, played by Kate Goehring, listens to her mother, Mariette Hartley, reveal her secret in Bernard Shaw's *Mrs. Warren's Profession* at the Huntington Theatre, Boston 1999.

disagreeables and take the rough with the smooth, just like a nurse in a hospital or anyone else. It's not work that any woman would do for pleasure, goodness knows; though to hear the pious people talk you would suppose it was a bed of roses.

VIVIE: Still you consider it worth while. It pays.

MRS WARREN: Of course it's worth while to a poor girl, if she can resist temptation and is good-looking and well conducted and sensible. It's far better than any other employment open to her. I always thought that oughtnt to be. It cant be right, Vivie, that there shouldnt be better opportunities for women. I stick to that: it's wrong. But it's so, right or wrong; and a girl must make the best of it. But of course its not worth while for a lady. If you took to it youd be a fool; but I should have been a fool if I'd taken to anything else.

VIVIE (*more and more deeply moved*): Mother: suppose we were both as poor as you were in those wretched old days, are you quite sure that you wouldnt advise me to try the Waterloo bar, or marry a laborer, or even go into the factory?

MRS WARREN (*indignantly*): Of course not. What sort of mother do you take me for! How could you keep your self-respect in such starvation and slavery? And whats a woman worth? whats life worth? without self-respect! Why am I independent and able to give my daughter a first-rare education, when other women that had just as good opportunities are in the gutter? Because I always knew how to respect myself and control myself. Why is Liz looked up to in a cathedral town? The same reason. Where would we be now if we'd minded the clergyman's foolishness? Scrubbing floors for one and sixpence a day and nothing to look forward to but the workhouse infirmary. Dont you be led astray by people who dont know the world, my girl. The only way for a woman to provide for herself decently is for her to be good to some man that can afford to be good to her. If she's in his own station of life, let her make him marry her; but if she's far beneath him she cant expect it—why should she? It wouldnt be for her own happiness. Ask any lady in London society that has daughters; and she'll tell you the same, except that I tell you straight and she'll tell you crooked. Thats all the difference.

VIVIE (*fascinated, gazing at her*): My dear mother: you are a wonderful woman—you are stronger than all England. And are you really and truly not one wee bit doubtful—or—or—ashamed?

MRS WARREN: Well, of course, dearie, it's only good manners to be ashamed of it: it's expected from a woman. Women have to pretend to feel a great deal that they dont feel. Liz used to be angry with me for plumping out the truth about it. She used to say that when every woman could learn enough from what was going on in the world before her eyes, there was no need to talk about it to her. But then Liz was such a perfect lady! She had the true instinct of it; while I was always a bit of a vulgarian. I used to be so pleased when you sent me your photographs to see

that you were growing up like Liz: youve just her ladylike, determined way. But I cant stand saying one thing when everyone knows I mean another. Whats the use in such hypocrisy? If people arrange the world that way for women, theres no good pretending that it's arranged the other way. I never was a bit ashamed really. I consider that I had a right to be proud that we managed everything so respectably, and never had a word against us, and that the girls were so well taken care of. Some of them did very well: one of them married an ambassador. But of course now I darent talk about such things: whatever would they think of us! (*She yawns.*) Oh dear! I do believe I'm getting sleepy after all. (*She stretches herself lazily, thoroughly relieved by her explosion, and placidly ready for her night's rest.*)

VIVIE: I believe it is I who will not be able to sleep now. (*She goes to the dresser and lights the candle. Then she extinguishes the lamp, darkening the room a good deal.*) Better let in some fresh air before locking up. (*She opens the cottage door, and finds that it is broad moonlight.*) What a beautiful night! Look! (*She draws aside the curtains of the window. The landscape is seen bathed in the radiance of the harvest moon rising over Blackdown.*)

MRS WARREN (*with a perfunctory glance at the scene*): Yes, dear; but take care you dont catch your death of cold from the night air.

VIVIE (*contemptuously*): Nonsense.

MRS WARREN (*querulously*): Oh yes: everything I say is nonsense, according to you.

VIVIE (*turning to her quickly*): No: really that is not so, mother. You have got completely the better of me tonight, though I intended it to be the other way. Let us be good friends now.

MRS WARREN (*shaking her head a little ruefully*): So it has been the other way. But I suppose I must give in to it. I always got the worst of it from Liz; and now I suppose it'll be the same with you.

VIVIE: Well, never mind. Come: good-night, dear old mother. (*She takes her mother in her arms.*)

MRS WARREN (*fondly*): I brought you up well, didnt I, dearie?

VIVIE: You did.

MRS WARREN: And youll be good to your poor old mother for it, wont you?

VIVIE: I will, dear. (*Kissing her*) Good-night.

MRS WARREN (*with unction*): Blessings on my own dearie darling—a mother's blessing! (*She embraces her daughter protectingly, instinctively looking upward as if to call down a blessing.*)

ACT III

(*In the Rectory garden next morning, with the sun shining and the birds in full song. The garden wall has a five-barred wooden gate, wide enough to admit a carriage, in the middle. Beside the gate hangs a bell on a coiled spring, communicating with a pull outside. The carriage drive comes down the middle of the garden and then swerves to its left, where it ends in a little gravelled circus opposite the Rectory porch. Beyond the gate is seen the dusty high road, parallel with the wall, bounded on the farther side by a strip of turf and an unfenced pine wood. On the lawn, between the house and the drive, is a clipped yew tree with a garden bench in its shade. On the opposite side the garden is shut in by a box hedge; and there is a sundial on the turf, with an iron chair near it. A little path leads off through the box hedge, behind the sundial.*

Frank, seated on the chair near the sundial, on which he has placed the morning papers, is reading the Standard. *His father comes from the house, red-eyed and shivery, and meets Frank's eye with misgiving.*)

FRANK (*looking at his watch*): Half past eleven. Nice hour for a rector to come down to breakfast!

REV. SAMUEL: Dont mock, Frank: dont mock. I am a little—er—(*Shivering*)—

FRANK: Off colour?

REV. SAMUEL (*repudiating the expression*): No, sir: unwell this morning. Wheres your mother?

FRANK: Dont be alarmed: she's not here. Gone to town by the 11.13 with Bessie. She left several messages for you. Do you feel equal to receiving them now, or shall I wait till youve breakfasted?

REV. SAMUEL: I have breakfasted, sir. I am surprised at your mother going to town when we have people staying with us. Theyll think it very strange.

FRANK: Possibly she has considered that. At all events, if Crofts is going to stay here, and you are going to sit up every night with him until four, recalling the incidents of your fiery youth, it is clearly my mother's duty, as a prudent housekeeper, to go up to the stores and order a barrel of whisky and a few hundred siphons.

REV. SAMUEL: I did not observe that Sir George drank excessively.

FRANK: You were not in a condition to, gov'nor.

REV. SAMUEL: Do you mean to say that *I*—

FRANK (*calmly*): I never saw a beneficed clergyman less sober. The anecdotes you told about your past career were so awful that I really dont think Praed would have passed the night under your roof if it hadnt been for the way my mother and he took to one another.

REV. SAMUEL: Nonsense, sir. I am Sir George Crofts' host. I must talk to him about something; and he has only one subject. Where is Mr Praed now?

FRANK: He is driving my mother and Bessie to the station.

REV. SAMUEL: Is Crofts up yet?

FRANK: Oh, long ago. He hasnt turned a hair: he's in much better practice than you—has kept it up ever since, probably. He's taken himself off somewhere to smoke. (*Frank resumes his paper. The Rev. Samuel*

turns disconsolately towards the gate; then comes back irresolutely.)

REV. SAMUEL: Er—Frank.

FRANK: Yes.

REV. SAMUEL: Do you think the Warrens will expect to be asked here after yesterday afternoon?

FRANK: Theyve been asked already. Crofts informed us at breakfast that you told him to bring Mrs Warren and Vivie over here to-day, and to invite them to make this house their home. It was after that communication that my mother found she must go to town by the 11.13 train.

REV. SAMUEL (*with despairing vehemence*): I never gave any such invitation. I never thought of such a thing.

FRANK (*compassionately*): How do you know, gov'nor, what you said and thought last night? Hallo! heres Praed back again.

PRAED (*coming in through the gate*): Good morning.

REV. SAMUEL: Good morning. I must apologize for not having met you at breakfast. I have a touch of—of—

FRANK: Clergyman's sore throat, Praed. Fortunately not chronic.

PRAED (*changing the subject*): Well, I must say your house is in a charming spot here. Really most charming.

REV. SAMUEL: Yes: it is indeed. Frank will take you for a walk, Mr Praed, if you like. I'll ask you to excuse me: I must take the opportunity to write my sermon while Mrs Gardner is away and you are all amusing yourselves. You wont mind, will you?

PRAED: Certainly not. Dont stand on the slightest ceremony with me.

REV. SAMUEL: Thank you. I'll—er—er—(*He stammers his way to the porch and vanishes into the house.*)

PRAED (*sitting down on the turf near Frank, and hugging his ankles*): Curious thing it must be writing a sermon every week.

FRANK: Ever so curious, if he did it. He buys em. He's gone for some soda water.

PRAED: My dear boy: I wish you would be more respectful to your father. You know you can be so nice when you like.

FRANK: My dear Praddy: you forget that I have to live with the governor. When two people live together—it dont matter whether theyre father and son, husband and wife, brother and sister—they cant keep up the polite humbug which comes so easy for ten minutes on an afternoon call. Now the governor, who unites to many admirable domestic qualities the irresoluteness of a sheep and the pompousness and aggressiveness of a jackass—

PRAED: No, pray, pray, my dear Frank, remember! He is your father.

FRANK: I give him due credit for that. But just imagine his telling Crofts to bring the Warrens over here! He must have been ever so drunk. You know, my dear Praddy, my mother wouldnt stand Mrs Warren for a moment. Vivie mustnt come here until she's gone back to town.

PRAED: But your mother doesnt know anything about Mrs Warren, does she?

FRANK: I dont know. Her journey to town looks as if she did. Not that my mother would mind in the ordinary way: she has stuck like a brick to lots of women who had got into trouble. But they were all nice women. Thats what makes the real difference. Mrs Warren, no doubt, has her merits; but she's ever so rowdy; and my mother simply wouldnt put up with her. So—hallo! (*This exclamation is provoked by the reappearance of the clergyman, who comes out of the house in haste and dismay.*)

REV. SAMUEL: Frank: Mrs Warren and her daughter are coming across the heath with Crofts: I saw them from the study windows. What am I to say about your mother?

FRANK (*jumping up energetically*): Stick on your hat and go out and say how delighted you are to see them; and that Frank's in the garden; and that mother and Bessie have been called to the bedside of a sick relative, and were ever so sorry they couldnt stop; and that you hope Mrs Warren slept well; and—and—say any blessed thing except the truth, and leave the rest to Providence.

REV. SAMUEL: But how are we to get rid of them afterwards?

FRANK: Theres no time to think of that now. Here! (*He bounds into the porch and returns immediately with a clerical felt hat, which he claps on his father's head.*) Now: off with you. Praed and I'll wait here, to give the thing an unpremeditated air. (*The clergyman, dazed but obedient, hurries off through the gate. Praed gets up from the turf, and dusts himself.*)

FRANK: We must get that old lady back to town somehow, Praed. Come! honestly, dear Praddy, do you like seeing them together—Vivie and the old lady?

PRAED: Oh, why not?

FRANK (*his teeth on edge*): Dont it make your flesh creep ever so little?—that wicked old devil, up to every villainy under the sun, I'll swear, and Vivie—ugh!

PRAED: Hush pray. Theyre coming. (*The clergyman and Crofts are seen coming along the road followed by Mrs Warren and Vivie walking affectionately together.*)

FRANK: Look: she actually has her arm round the old woman's waist. It's her right arm: she began it. She's gone sentimental, by God! Ugh! ugh! Now do you feel the creeps? (*The clergyman opens the gate; and Mrs Warren and Vivie pass him and stand in the middle of the garden looking at the house. Frank, in an ecstasy of dissimulation, turns gaily to Mrs Warren, exclaiming*) Ever so delighted to see you, Mrs Warren. This quiet old rectory garden becomes you perfectly.

MRS WARREN: Well, I never! Did you hear that, George? He says I look well in a quiet old rectory garden.

REV. SAMUEL (*still holding the gate for Crofts, who loafs through it, heavily bored*): You look well everywhere, Mrs Warren.

FRANK: Bravo, gov'nor! Now look here: lets have an awful jolly time of it before lunch. First lets see the church. Everyone has to do that. It's a regular old thirteenth century church, you know: the gov'nor's ever so fond of it, because he got up a restoration fund and had it completely rebuilt six years ago. Praed will be able to show its points.

REV. SAMUEL (*mooning hospitably at them*): I shall be pleased, I'm sure, if Sir George and Mrs Warren really care about it.

MRS WARREN: Oh, come along and get it over. Itll do George good: I'll lay he doesnt trouble church much.

CROFTS (*turning back towards the gate*): Ive no objection.

REV. SAMUEL: Not that way. We go through the fields, if you dont mind. Round here. (*He leads the way by the little path through the box hedge.*)

CROFTS: Oh, all right. (*He goes with the parson. Praed follows with Mrs Warren. Vivie does not stir, but watches them until they have gone, with all the lines of purpose in her face marking it strongly.*)

FRANK: Aint you coming?

VIVIE: No. I want to give you a warning, Frank. You were making fun of my mother just now when you said that about the rectory garden. That is barred in future. Please treat my mother with as much respect as you treat your own.

FRANK: My dear Viv: she wouldnt appreciate it. She's not like my mother: the same treatment wouldnt do for both cases. But what on earth has happened to you? Last night we were perfectly agreed as to your mother and her set. This morning I find you attitudinizing sentimentally with your arm round your parent's waist.

VIVIE (*flushing*): Attitudinizing!

FRANK: That was how it struck me. First time I ever saw you do a second-rate thing.

VIVIE (*controlling herself*): Yes, Frank: there has been a change; but I dont think it a change for the worse. Yesterday I was a little prig.

FRANK: And to-day?

VIVIE (*wincing; then looking at him steadily*): To-day I know my mother better than you do.

FRANK: Heaven forbid!

VIVIE: What do you mean?

FRANK: Viv: theres a freemasonry among thoroughly immoral people that you know nothing of. Youve too much character. Thats the bond between your mother and me: thats why I know her better than youll ever know her.

VIVIE: You are wrong: you know nothing about her. If you knew the circumstances against which my mother had to struggle—

FRANK (*adroitly finishing the sentence for her*): I should know why she is what she is, shouldnt I? What difference would that make? Circumstances or no circumstances, Viv, you wont be able to stand your mother.

VIVIE (*very angry*): Why not?

FRANK: Because she's an old wretch, Viv. If you ever put your arm round her waist in my presence again, I'll shoot myself there and then as a protest against an exhibition which revolts me.

VIVIE: Must I choose between dropping your acquaintance and dropping my mother's?

FRANK (*gracefully*): That would put the old lady at ever such a disadvantage. No, Viv: your infatuated little boy will have to stick to you in any case. But he's all the more anxious that you shouldnt make mistakes. It's no use, Viv: your mother's impossible. She may be a good sort; but she's a bad lot, a very bad lot.

VIVIE (*hotly*): Frank—! (*He stands his ground. She turns away and sits down on the bench under the yew tree, struggling to recover her self-command. Then she says*) Is she to be deserted by all the world because she's what you call a bad lot? Has she no right to live?

FRANK: No fear of that, Viv: she wont ever be deserted. (*He sits on the bench beside her.*)

VIVIE: But I am to desert her, I suppose.

FRANK (*babyishly, lulling her and making love to her with his voice*): Mustnt go live with her. Little family group of mother and daughter wouldnt be a success. Spoil our little group.

VIVIE (*falling under the spell*): What little group?

FRANK: The babes in the wood: Vivie and little Frank. (*He slips his arm round her waist and nestles against her like a weary child.*) Lets go and get covered up with leaves.

VIVIE (*rythmically, rocking him like a nurse*): Fast asleep, hand in hand, under the trees.

FRANK: The wise little girl with her silly little boy.

VIVIE: The dear little boy with his dowdy little girl.

FRANK: Ever so peaceful, and relieved from the imbecility of the little boy's father and the questionableness of the little girl's—

VIVIE (*smothering the word against her breast*): Sh-sh-sh-sh! little girl wants to forget all about her mother. (*They are silent for some moments, rocking one another. Then Vivie wakes up with a shock, exclaiming*) What a pair of fools we are! Come: sit up. Gracious! your hair. (*She smooths it.*) I wonder do all grown up people play in that childish way when nobody is looking. I never did it when I was a child.

FRANK: Neither did I. You are my first playmate. (*He catches her hand to kiss it, but checks himself to look round first. Very unexpectedly, he sees Crofts emerging from the box hedge.*) Oh damn!

VIVIE: Why damn, dear?

FRANK (*whispering*): Sh! Here's this brute Crofts. (*He sits farther away from her with an unconcerned air.*)

VIVIE: Dont be rude to him, Frank. I particularly wish to be polite to him. It will please my mother. (*Frank makes a wry face.*)

CROFTS: Could I have a few words with you, Miss Vivie?

VIVIE: Certainly.

CROFTS (*to Frank*): Youll excuse me, Gardner. Theyre waiting for you in the church, if you dont mind.

FRANK (*rising*): Anything to oblige you, Crofts—except church. If you want anything, Vivie, ring the gate bell, and a domestic will appear. (*He goes into the house with unruffled suavity.*)

CROFTS (*watching him with a crafty air as he disappears, and speaking to Vivie with an assumption of being on privileged terms with her*): Pleasant young fellow that, Miss Vivie. Pity he has no money, isnt it?

VIVIE: Do you think so?

CROFTS: Well, whats he to do? No profession, no property. Whats he good for?

VIVIE: I realize his disadvantages, Sir George.

CROFTS (*a little taken aback at being so precisely interpreted*): Oh, it's not that. But while we're in this world we're in it; and money's money. (*Vivie does not answer.*) Nice day, isnt it?

VIVIE (*with scarcely veiled contempt for this effort at conversation*): Very.

CROFTS (*with brutal good humor, as if he liked her pluck*): Well, thats not what I came to say. (*Affecting frankness*) Now listen, Miss Vivie. I'm quite aware that I'm not a young lady's man.

VIVIE: Indeed, Sir George?

CROFTS: No; and to tell you the honest truth I dont want to be either. But when I say a thing I mean it; when I feel sentiment I feel it in earnest; and what I value I pay hard money for. Thats the sort of man I am.

VIVIE: It does you great credit, I'm sure.

CROFTS: Oh, I dont mean to praise myself. I have my faults, Heaven knows: no man is more sensible of that than I am. I know I'm not perfect: thats one of the advantages of being a middle-aged man; for I'm not a young man, and I know it. But my code is a simple one, and, I think, a good one. Honor between man and man; fidelity between man and woman; and no cant about this religion or that religion, but an honest belief that things are making for good on the whole.

VIVIE: (*with biting irony*): "A power, not ourselves, that makes for rightcousness," eh?

CROFTS (*taking her seriously*): Oh, certainly, not ourselves, of course. You understand what I mean. (*He sits down beside her, as one who has found a kindred spirit.*) Well, now as to practical matters. You may have an idea that Ive flung my money about; but I havnt: I'm richer to-day than when I first came into the property. Ive used my knowledge of the world to invest my money in ways that other men have overlooked; and whatever else I may be, I'm a safe man from the money point of view.

VIVIE: It's very kind of you to tell me all this.

CROFTS: Oh well, come, Miss Vivie: you neednt pretend you dont see what I'm driving at. I want to settle down with a Lady Crofts. I suppose you think me very blunt, eh?

VIVIE: Not at all: I am much obliged to you for being so definite and business-like. I quite appreciate the offer: the money, the position, Lady Crofts, and so on. But I think I will say no, if you dont mind. I'd rather not. (*She rises, and strolls across to the sundial to get out of his immediate neighborhood.*)

CROFTS (*not at all discouraged, and taking advantage of the additional room left him on the seat to spread himself comfortably, as if a few preliminary refusals were part of the inevitable routine of courtship*): I'm in no hurry. It was only just to let you know in case young Gardner should try to trap you. Leave the question open.

VIVIE (*sharply*): My no is final. I wont go back from it. (*She looks authoritatively at him. He grins; leans forward with his elbows on his knees to prod with his stick at some unfortunate insect in the grass; and looks cunningly at her. She turns away impatiently.*)

CROFTS: I'm a good deal older than you—twenty-five years—quarter of a century. I shant live for ever; and I'll take care that you shall be well off when I'm gone.

VIVIE: I am proof against even that inducement, Sir George. Dont you think youd better take your answer? There is not the slightest chance of my altering it.

CROFTS (*rising, after a final slash at a daisy, and beginning to walk to and fro*): Well, no matter. I could tell you some things that would change your mind fast enough; but I wont, because I'd rather win you by honest affection. I was a good friend to your mother: ask her whether I wasnt. She'd never have made the money that paid for your education if it hadnt been for my advice and help, not to mention the money I advanced her. There are not many men would have stood by her as I have. I put not less than £40,000 into it, from first to last.

VIVIE (*staring at him*): Do you mean to say you were my mother's business partner?

CROFTS: Yes. Now just think of all the trouble and the explanations it would save if we were to keep the whole thing in the family, so to speak. Ask your mother whether she'd like to have to explain all her affairs to a perfect stranger.

VIVIE: I see no difficulty, since I understand that the business is wound up, and the money invested.

CROFTS (*stopping short, amazed*): Wound up! Wind up a business thats paying 35 per cent in the worst years! Not likely. Who told you that?

VIVIE (*her color quite gone*): Do you mean that it is still—? (*She stops abruptly, and puts her hand on the sundial to support herself. Then she gets quickly to the iron chair and sits down.*) What business are you talking about?

CROFTS: Well, the fact is it's not what would be considered exactly a high-class business in my set—the county set, you know—our set it will be if you think better of my offer. Not that theres any mystery about it: dont think that. Of course you know by your mother's being in it that it's perfectly straight and honest. Ive known her for many years; and I can say of her that she'd cut off her hands sooner than touch anything that was not what it ought to be. I'll tell you all about it if you like. I dont know whether youve found in travelling how hard it is to find a really comfortable private hotel.

VIVIE (*sickened, averting her fate*): Yes: go on.

CROFTS: Well, thats all it is. Your mother has a genius for managing such things. We've got two in Brussels, one in Berlin, one in Vienna, and two in Buda-Pesth. Of course there are others besides ourselves in it; but we hold most of the capital; and your mother's indispensable as managing director. Youve noticed, I daresay, that she travels a good deal. But you see you cant mention such things in society. Once let out the word hotel and everybody says you keep a public-house. You wouldnt like people to say that of your mother, would you? Thats why we're so reserved about it. By the bye, youll keep it to yourself, wont you? Since it's been a secret so long, it had better remain so.

VIVIE: And this is the business you invite me to join you in?

CROFTS: Oh no. My wife shant be troubled with business. Youll not be in it more than youve always been.

VIVIE: *I* always been! What do you mean?

CROFTS: Only that youve always lived on it. It paid for your education and the dress you have on your back. Dont turn up your nose at business, Miss Vivie; where would your Newnhams and Girtons be without it?

VIVIE (*rising, almost beside herself*): Take care. I know what this business is.

CROFTS (*starting, with a suppressed oath*): Who told you?

VIVIE: Your partner—my mother.

CROFTS (*black with rage*): The old—(*Vivie looks quickly at him. He swallows the epithet and stands swearing and raging foully to himself. But he knows that his cue is to be sympathetic. He takes refuge in generous indignation.*) She ought to have had more consideration for you. *I'd* never have told you.

VIVIE: I think you would probably have told me when we were married: it would have been a convenient weapon to break me in with.

CROFTS (*quite sincerely*): I never intended that. On my word as a gentleman I didnt.

(*Vivie wonders at him. Her sense of the irony of his protest cools and braces her. She replies with contemptuous self-possession.*)

VIVIE: It does not matter. I suppose you understand that when we leave here to-day our acquaintance ceases.

CROFTS: Why? Is it for helping your mother?

VIVIE: My mother was a very poor woman who had no reasonable choice but to do as she did. You were a rich gentleman; and you did the same for the sake of 35 per cent. You are a pretty common sort of scoundrel, I think. That is my opinion of you.

CROFTS (*after a stare—not at all displeased, and much more at his ease on these frank terms than on their former ceremonious ones*): Ha, ha, ha, ha! Go it, little missie, go it: it doesnt hurt me and it amuses you. Why the devil shouldnt I invest my money that way? I take the interest on my capital like other people: I hope you dont think I dirty my own hands with the work. Come: you wouldnt refuse the acquaintance of my mother's cousin the Duke of Belgravia because some of the rents he gets are earned in queer ways. You wouldnt cut the Archbishop of Canterbury, I suppose, because the Ecclesiastical Commissioners have a few publicans and sinners among their tenants. Do you remember your Crofts scholarship at Newnham? Well, that was founded by my brother the M.P. He gets his 22 per cent out of a factory with 600 girls in it, and not one of them getting wages enough to live on. How d'ye suppose most of them manage? Ask your mother. And do you expect me to turn my back on 35 per cent when all the rest are pocketing what they can, like sensible men? No such fool! If youre going to pick and choose your acquaintances on moral principles, youd better clear out of this country, unless you want to cut yourself out of all decent society.

VIVIE (*conscience stricken*): You might go on to point out that I myself never asked where the money I spent came from. I believe I am just as bad as you.

CROFTS (*greatly reassured*): Of course you are; and a very good thing too! What harm does it do after all? (*Rallying her jocularly*) So you dont think me such a scoundrel now you come to think it over. Eh?

VIVIE: I have shared profits with you; and I admitted you just now to the familiarity of knowing what I think of you.

CROFTS (*with serious friendliness*): To be sure you did. You wont find me a bad sort; I dont go in for being superfine intellectually; but Ive plenty of honest human feeling; and the old Crofts breed comes out in a sort of instinctive hatred of anything low, in which I'm sure youll sympathize with me. Believe me, Miss Vivie, the world isnt such a bad place as the croakers make out. So long as you dont fly openly in the face of society, society doesnt ask any inconvenient questions; and it makes precious short work of the cads who do. There are no secrets better kept than the secrets that everybody guesses. In the society I can introduce you to, no lady or gentleman would so far forget themselves as to discuss my business affairs or your mother's. No man can offer you a safer position.

VIVIE (*studying him curiously*): I suppose you really think youre getting on famously with me.

CROFTS: Well, I hope I may flatter myself that you think better of me than you did at first.

VIVIE (*quietly*): I hardly find you worth thinking about at all now. (*She rises and turns towards the gate, pausing on her way to contemplate him and say almost gently, but with intense conviction*) When I think of the society that tolerates you, and the laws that protect you — when I think of how helpless nine out of ten young girls would be in the hands of you and my mother — the unmentionable woman and her capitalist bully —

CROFTS (*livid*): Damn you!

VIVIE: You need not. I am among the damned already.

(*She raises the latch of the gate to open it and go out. He follows her and puts his hand heavily on the top bar to prevent its opening.*)

CROFTS (*panting with fury*): Do you think I'll put up with this from you, you young devil, you?

VIVIE (*unmoved*): Be quiet. Some one will answer the bell. (*Without flinching a step she strikes the bell with the back of her hand. It clangs harshly; and he starts back involuntarily. Almost immediately Frank appears at the porch with his rifle.*)

FRANK (*with cheerful politeness*): Will you have the rifle, Viv; or shall I operate?

VIVIE: Frank: have you been listening?

FRANK: Only for the bell, I assure you; so that you shouldnt have to wait. I think I showed great insight into your character, Crofts.

CROFTS: For two pins I'd take that gun from you and break it across your head.

FRANK (*stalking him cautiously*): Pray dont. I'm ever so careless in handling firearms. Sure to be a fatal accident, with a reprimand from the coroner's jury for my negligence.

VIVIE: Put the rifle away, Frank: it's quite unnecessary.

FRANK: Quite right, Viv. Much more sportsmanlike to catch him in a trap. (*Crofts, understanding the insult, makes a threatening movement.*) Crofts: there are fifteen cartridges in the magazine here; and I am a dead shot at the present distance and at an object of your size.

CROFTS: Oh, you neednt be afraid. I'm not going to touch you.

FRANK: Ever so magnanimous of you under the circumstances! Thank you.

CROFTS: I'll just tell you this before I go. It may interest you, since youre so fond of one another. Allow me, Mister Frank, to introduce you to your half-sister, the eldest daughter of the Reverend Samuel Gardner. Miss Vivie: Your half-brother. Good morning. (*He goes out through the gate and along the road.*)

FRANK (*after a pause of stupefaction, raising the rifle*): Youll testify before the coroner that it's an accident, Viv. (*He takes aim at the retreating figure of Crofts. Vivie seizes the muzzle and pulls it round against her breast.*)

VIVIE: Fire now. You may.

FRANK (*dropping his end of the rifle hastily*): Stop! take care. (*She lets it go. It falls on the turf.*) Oh, youve given your little boy such a turn. Suppose it had gone off — ugh! (*He sinks on the garden seat, overcome.*)

VIVIE: Suppose it had: do you think it would not have been a relief to have some sharp physical pain tearing through me?

FRANK (*coaxingly*): Take it ever so easy, dear Viv. Remember: even if the rifle scared that fellow into telling the truth for the first time in his life, that only makes us the babes in the wood in earnest. (*He holds out his arms to her.*) Come and be covered up with leaves again.

VIVIE (*with a cry of disgust*): Ah, not that, not that. You make all my flesh creep.

FRANK: Why, whats the matter?

VIVIE: Good-bye. (*She makes for the gate.*)

FRANK (*jumping up*): Halla! Stop! Viv! Viv! (*She turns in the gateway*) Where are you going to? Where shall we find you?

VIVIE: At Honoria Fraser's chambers, 67 Chancery Lane, for the rest of my life. (*She goes off quickly in the opposite direction to that taken by Crofts.*)

FRANK: But I say—wait—dash it! (*He runs after her.*)

ACT IV

(*Honoria Fraser's chambers in Chancery Lane. An office at the top of New Stone Buildings, with a plate-glass window, distempered walls, electric light, and a patent stove. Saturday afternoon. The chimneys of Lincoln's Inn and the western sky beyond are seen through the window. There is a double writing-table in the middle of the room, with a cigar box, ash pans, and a portable electric reading lamp almost snowed up in heaps of papers and books. This table has knee holes and chairs right and left and is very untidy. The clerk's desk, closed and tidy, with its high stool, is against the wall, near a door communicating with the inner rooms. In the opposite wall is the door leading to the public corridor. Its upper panel is of opaque glass, lettered in black on the outside, "Fraser and Warren." A baize screen hides the corner between this door and the window.*

Frank, in a fashionable light-colored coaching suit, with his stick, gloves, and white hat in his hands, is pacing up and down the office. Somebody tries the door with a key.)

FRANK (*calling*): Come in. It's not locked.

(*Vivie comes in, in her hat and jacket. She stops and stares at him.*)

VIVIE (*sternly*): What are you doing here?

FRANK: Waiting to see you. Ive been here for hours. Is this the way you attend to your business? (*He puts his hat and stick on the table, and perches himself with a vault on the clerk's stool, looking at her with every appearance of being in a specially restless, teasing, flippant mood.*)

VIVIE: Ive been away exactly twenty minutes for a cup of tea. (*She takes off her hat and jacket and hangs them up behind the screen.*) How did you get in?

FRANK: The staff had not left when I arrived. He's gone to play cricket on Primrose Hill. Why dont you employ a woman, and give your sex a chance?

VIVIE: What have you come for?

FRANK (*springing off the stool and coming close to her*): Viv: lets go and enjoy the Saturday half-holiday somewhere, like the staff. What do you say to Richmond, and then a music hall, and a jolly supper?

VIVIE: Cant afford it. I shall put in another six hours work before I go to bed.

FRANK: Cant afford it, cant we? Aha! Look here. (*He takes out a handful of sovereigns and makes them chink.*) Gold, Viv, gold!

VIVIE: Where did you get it?

FRANK: Gambling, Viv, gambling. Poker.

VIVIE: Pah! It's meaner than stealing it. No: I'm not coming. (*She sits down to work at the table, with her back to the glass door, and begins turning over the papers.*)

FRANK (*remonstrating piteously*): But, my dear Viv, I want to talk to you ever so seriously.

VIVIE: Very well: sit down in Honoria's chair and talk here. I like ten minutes chat after tea. (*He murmurs.*) No use groaning: I'm inexorable. (*He takes the opposite seat disconsolately.*) Pass that cigar box, will you?

FRANK (*pushing the cigar box across*): Nasty womanly habit. Nice men dont do it any longer.

VIVIE: Yes: they object to the smell in the office; and weve had to take to cigarets. See! (*She opens the box and takes out a cigaret, which she lights. She offers him one; but he shakes his head with a wry face. She settles herself comfortably in her chair, smoking.*) Go ahead.

FRANK: Well, I want to know what youve done—what arrangements youve made.

VIVIE: Everything was settled twenty minutes after I arrived here. Honoria has found the business too much for her this year; and she was on the point of sending for me and proposing a partnership when I walked in and told her I hadnt a farthing in the world. So I installed myself and packed her off for a fortnight's holiday. What happened at Haslemere when I left?

FRANK: Nothing at all. I said youd gone to town on particular business.

VIVIE: Well?

FRANK: Well, either they were too flabbergasted to say anything, or else Crofts had prepared your mother. Anyhow, she didnt say anything; and Crofts didnt say anything; and Praddy only stared. After tea they got up and went; and Ive not seen them since.

VIVIE (*nodding placidly with one eye on a wreath of smoke*): Thats all right.

FRANK (*looking round disparagingly*): Do you intend to stick in this confounded place?

VIVIE (*blowing the wreath decisively away, and sitting straight up*): Yes. These two days have given me back all my strength and self-possession. I will never take a holiday again as long as I live.

FRANK (*with a very wry face*): Mps! You look quite happy—and as hard as nails.

VIVIE (*grimly*): Well for me that I am!

FRANK (*rising*): Look here, Viv: we must have an explanation. We parted the other day under a complete misunderstanding.

VIVIE (*putting away the cigaret*): Well: clear it up.

FRANK: You remember what Crofts said?

VIVIE: Yes.

FRANK: That revelation was supposed to bring about a complete change in the nature of our feeling for one another. It placed us on the footing of brother and sister.

VIVIE: Yes.

FRANK: Have you ever had a brother?

VIVIE: No.

FRANK: Then you dont know what being brother and sister feels like? Now I have lots of sisters: Jessie and Georgina and the rest. The fraternal feeling is quite familiar to me; and I assure you my feeling for you is not the least in the world like it. The girls will go their way; I will go mine; and we shant care if we never see one another again. Thats brother and sister. But as to you, I cant be easy if I have to pass a week without seeing you. Thats not brother and sister. It's exactly what I felt an hour before Crofts made his revelation. In short, dear Viv, it's love's young dream.

VIVIE (bitingly): The same feeling, Frank, that brought your father to my mother's feet. Is that it?

FRANK (revolted): I very strongly object, Viv, to have my feelings compared to any which the Reverend Samuel is capable of harboring; and I object still more to a comparison of you to your mother. Besides, I dont believe the story. I have taxed my father with it, and obtained from him what I consider tantamount to a denial.

VIVIE: What did he say?

FRANK: He said he was sure there must be some mistake.

VIVIE: Do you believe him?

FRANK: I am prepared to take his word as against Crofts'.

VIVIE: Does it make any difference? I mean in your imagination or conscience; for of course it makes no real difference.

FRANK (shaking his head): None whatever to me.

VIVIE: Nor to me.

FRANK (staring): But this is ever so surprising! I thought our whole relations were altered in your imagination and conscience, as you put it, the moment those words were out of that brute's muzzle.

VIVIE: No: it was not that. I didnt believe him. I only wish I could.

FRANK: Eh?

VIVIE: I think brother and sister would be a very suitable relation for us.

FRANK: You really mean that?

VIVIE: Yes. It's the only relation I care for, even if we could afford any other. I mean that.

FRANK (raising his eyebrows like one on whom a new light has dawned, and speaking with quite an effusion of chivalrous sentiment): My dear Viv: why didnt you say so before? I am ever so sorry for persecuting you. I understand, of course.

VIVIE (puzzled): Understand what?

FRANK: Oh, I'm not a fool in the ordinary sense—only in the Scriptural sense of doing all the things the wise man declared to be folly, after trying them himself on the most extensive scale. I see I am no longer Vivvum's little boy. Dont be alarmed: I shall never call you Vivvums again—at least unless you get tired of your new little boy, whoever he may be.

VIVIE: My new little boy!

FRANK (with conviction): Must be a new little boy. Always happens that way. No other way, in fact.

VIVIE: None that you know of, fortunately for you.

(Someone knocks at the door.)

FRANK: My curse upon yon caller, whoe'er he be!

VIVIE: It's Praed. He's going to Italy and wants to say good-bye. I asked him to call this afternoon. Go and let him in.

FRANK: We can continue our conversation after his departure for Italy. I'll stay him out. (He goes to the door and opens it.) How are you, Praddy. Delighted to see you. Come in. (Praed, dressed for travelling, comes in, in high spirits, excited by the beginning of his journey.)

PRAED: How do you do, Miss Warren. (She presses his hand cordially, though a certain sentimentality in his high spirits jars on her.) I start in an hour from Holborn Viaduct. I wish I could persuade you to try Italy.

VIVIE: What for?

PRAED: Why, to saturate yourself with beauty and romance, of course. (Vivie, with a shudder, turns her chair to the table, as if the work waiting for her there were a consolation and support to her. Praed sits opposite to her. Frank places a chair just behind Vivie, and drops lazily and carelessly into it, talking at her over his shoulder.)

FRANK: No use, Praddy. Viv is a little Philistine. She is indifferent to my romance, and insensible to my beauty.

VIVIE: Mr Praed: once for all, there is no beauty and no romance in life for me. Life is what it is; and I am prepared to take it as it is.

PRAED (enthusiastically): You will not say that If you come to Verona and on to Venice. You will cry with delight at living in such a beautiful world.

FRANK: This is most eloquent, Praddy. Keep it up.

PRAED: Oh, I assure you I have cried—I shall cry again, I hope—at fifty! At your age, Miss Warren, you would not need to go so far as Verona. Your spirits would absolutely fly up at the mere sight of Ostend. You would be charmed with the gaiety, the vivacity, the happy air of Brussels. (Vivie recoils) Whats the matter?

FRANK: Hallo, Viv!

VIVIE (to Praed, with deep reproach): Can you find no better example of your beauty and romance than Brussels to talk to me about?

PRAED (puzzled): Of course it's very different from Verona. I dont suggest for a moment that—

VIVIE (bitterly): Probably the beauty and romance come to much the same in both places.

PRAED (*completely sobered and much concerned*): My dear Miss Warren: I—(*looking enquiringly at Frank*) Is anything the matter?

FRANK: She thinks your enthusiasm frivolous, Praddy. She's had ever such a serious call.

VIVIE (*sharply*): Hold your tongue, Frank. Dont be silly.

FRANK (*calmly*): Do you call this good manners, Praed?

PRAED (*anxious and considerate*): Shall I take him away, Miss Warren? I feel sure we have disturbed you at your work. (*He is about to rise.*)

VIVIE: Sit down: I'm not ready to go back to work yet. You both think I have an attack of nerves. Not a bit of it. But there are two subjects I want dropped, if you dont mind. One of them (*to Frank*) is love's young dream in any shape or form: the other (*to Praed*) is the romance and beauty of life, especially as exemplified by the gaiety of Brussels. You are welcome to any illusions you may have left on these subjects: I have none. If we three are to remain friends, I must be treated as a woman of business, permanently single (*to Frank*) and permanently unromantic (*to Praed*).

FRANK: I also shall remain permanently single until you change your mind. Praddy: change the subject. Be eloquent about something else.

PRAED (*diffidently*): I'm afraid theres nothing else in the world that I can talk about. The Gospel of Art is the only one I can preach. I know Miss Warren is a great devotee of the Gospel of Getting On; but we cant discuss that without hurting your feelings, Frank, since you are determined not to get on.

FRANK: Oh, dont mind my feelings. Give me some improving advice by all means: it does me ever so much good. Have another try to make a successful man of me, Viv. Come: lets have it all: energy, thrift, foresight, self-respect, character. Dont you hate people who have no character, Viv?

VIVIE (*wincing*): Oh, stop, stop: let us have no more of that horrible cant. Mr Praed: if there are really only those two gospels in the world, we had better all kill ourselves; for the same taint is in both, through and through.

FRANK (*looking critically at her*): There is a touch of poetry about you to-day, Viv, which has hitherto been lacking.

PRAED (*remonstrating*): My dear Frank: arnt you a little unsympathetic?

VIVIE (*merciless to herself*): No: it's good for me. It keeps me from being sentimental.

FRANK (*bantering her*): Checks your strong natural propensity that way, dont it?

VIVIE (*almost hysterically*): Oh yes: go on: dont spare me. I was sentimental for one moment in my life—beautifully sentimental—by moonlight; and now—

FRANK (*quickly*): I say, Viv: take care. Dont give yourself away.

VIVIE: Oh, do you think Mr Praed does not know all about my mother? (*Turning on Praed*) You had better have told me that morning, Mr Praed. You are very old fashioned in your delicacies, after all.

PRAED: Surely it is you who are a little old fashioned in your prejudices, Miss Warren. I feel bound to tell you, speaking as an artist, and believing that the most intimate human relationships are far beyond and above the scope of the law, that though I know that your mother is an unmarried woman, I do not respect her the less on that account. I respect her more.

FRANK (*airily*): Hear, hear!

VIVIE (*staring at him*): Is that all you know?

PRAED: Certainly that is all.

VIVIE: Then you neither of you know anything. Your guesses are innocence itself compared to the truth.

PRAED (*startled and indignant, preserving his politeness with an effort*): I hope not. (*More emphatically*) I hope not, Miss Warren. (*Frank's face shows that he does not share Praed's incredulity. Vivie utters an exclamation of impatience. Praed's chivalry droops before their conviction. He adds, slowly*) If there is anything worse—that is, anything else—are you sure you are right to tell us, Miss Warren?

VIVIE: I am sure that if I had the courage I should spend the rest of my life in telling it to everybody—in stamping and branding it into them until they felt their share in its shame and horror as I feel mine. There is nothing I despise more than the wicked convention that protects these things by forbidding a woman to mention them. And yet I cant tell you. The two infamous words that describe what my mother is are ringing in my ears and struggling on my tongue; but I cant utter them: my instinct is too strong for me. (*She buries her face in her hands. The two men, astonished, stare at one another and then at her. She raises her head again desperately and takes a sheet of paper and a pen.*) Here: let me draft you a prospectus.

FRANK: Oh, she's mad. Do you hear, Viv, mad. Come: pull yourself together.

VIVIE: You shall see. (*She writes.*) "Paid up capital: not less than £40,000 standing in the name of Sir George Crofts, Baronet, the chief shareholder." What comes next?—I forget. Oh yes: "Premises at Brussels, Berlin, Vienna and Buda-Pesth. Managing director: Mrs Warren"; and now dont let us forget her qualifications: the two words. There! (*She pushes the paper to them.*) Oh, no: dont read it: dont! (*She snatches it back and tears it to pieces; then seizes her head in her hands and hides her face on the table. Frank, who has watched the writing carefully over her shoulder, and opened his eyes very widely at it, takes a card from his pocket; scribbles a couple of words; and silently hands it to Praed, who looks at it with amazement. Frank then remorsefully stoops over Vivie.*)

FRANK (*whispering tenderly*): Viv, dear: thats all right. I read what you wrote: so did Praddy. We understand. And we remain, as this leaves us at present, yours ever so devotedly. (*Vivie slowly raises her head.*)

PRAED: We do indeed, Miss Warren. I declare you are the most splendidly courageous woman I ever met.

(*This sentimental compliment braces Vivie. She throws it away from her with an impatient shake, and forces herself to stand up, though not without some support from the table.*)

FRANK: Dont stir, Viv, if you dont want to. Take it easy.

VIVIE: Thank you. You can always depend on me for two things, not to cry and not to faint. (*She moves a few steps towards the door of the inner rooms, and stops close to Praed to say*) I shall need much more courage than that when I tell my mother that we have come to the parting of the ways. Now I must go into the next room for a moment to make myself neat again, if you dont mind.

PRAED: Shall we go away?

VIVIE: No: I'll be back presently. Only for a moment.

(*She goes into the other room, Praed opening the door for her.*)

PRAED: What an amazing revelation! I'm extremely disappointed in Crofts: I am indeed.

FRANK: I'm not in the least. I feel he's perfectly accounted for at last. But what a facer for me, Praddy! I cant marry her now.

PRAED (*sternly*): Frank! (*The two look at one another, Frank unruffled, Praed deeply indignant.*) Let me tell you, Gardner, that if you desert her now you will behave very despicably.

FRANK: Good old Praddy! Ever chivalrous! But you mistake: it's not the moral aspect of the case: it's the money aspect. I really cant bring myself to touch the old woman's money now.

PRAED: And was that what you were going to marry on?

FRANK: What else? *I* havnt any money, nor the smallest turn for making it. If I married Viv now she would have to support me; and I should cost her more than I am worth.

PRAED: But surely a clever, bright fellow like you can make something by your own brains.

FRANK: Oh yes, a little. (*He takes out his money again.*) I made all that yesterday—in an hour and a half. But I made it in a highly speculative business. No, dear Praddy. even if Jessie and Georgina marry millionaires and the governor dies after cutting them off with a shilling, I shall have only four hundred a year. And he wont die until he's three score and ten: he hasnt originality enough. I shall be on short allowance for the next twenty years. No short allowance for Viv, if I can help it. I withdraw gracefully and leave the field to the gilded youth of England. So thats settled. I shant worry her about it: I'll just send her a little note after we're gone. She'll understand.

PRAED (*grasping his hand*): Good fellow, Frank! I heartily beg your pardon. But must you never see her again?

FRANK: Never see her again! Hang it all, be reasonable. I shall come along as often as possible, and be her brother. I can not understand the absurd consequences you romantic people expect from the most ordinary transactions. (*A knock at the door.*) I wonder who this is. Would you mind opening the door? If it's a client it will look more respectable than if I appeared.

PRAED: Certainly. (*He goes to the door and opens it. Frank sits down in Vivie's chair to scribble a note.*) My dear Kitty: come in, come in.

(*Mrs Warren comes in, looking apprehensively round for Vivie. She has done her best to make herself matronly and dignified. The brilliant hat is replaced by a sober bonnet, and the gay blouse covered by a costly black silk mantle. She is pitiably anxious and ill at ease—evidently panic-stricken.*)

MRS WARREN (*to Frank*): What! Youre here, are you?

FRANK (*turning in his chair from his writing, but not rising*): Here, and charmed to see you. You come like a breath of spring.

MRS WARREN: Oh, get out with your nonsense. (*In a low voice*) Wheres Vivie?

(*Frank points expressively to the door of the inner room, but says nothing.*)

MRS WARREN (*sitting down suddenly and almost beginning to cry*): Praddy: wont she see me, dont you think?

PRAED: My dear Kitty: dont distress yourself. Why should she not?

MRS WARREN: Oh, you never can see why not: youre too amiable. Mr Frank: did she say anything to you?

FRANK (*folding his note*): She must see you, if (*very expressively*) you wait until she comes in.

MRS WARREN (*frightened*): Why shouldnt I wait?

(*Frank looks quizzically at her; puts his note carefully on the ink-bottle, so that Vivie cannot fail to find it when next she dips her pen; then rises and devotes his attention entirely to her.*)

FRANK: My dear Mrs Warren: suppose you were a sparrow—ever so tiny and pretty a sparrow hopping in the roadway—and you saw a steam roller coming in your direction, would you wait for it?

MRS WARREN: Oh, dont bother me with your sparrows. What did she run away from Haslemere like that for?

FRANK: I'm afraid she'll tell you if you wait until she comes back.

MRS WARREN: Do you want me to go away?

FRANK: No. I always want you to stay. But I advise you to go away.

MRS WARREN: What! And never see her again!

FRANK: Precisely.

MRS WARREN (*crying again*): Praddy: dont let him be cruel to me. (*She hastily checks her tears and wipes her eyes.*) She'll be so angry if she sees Ive been crying.

FRANK (*with a touch of real compassion in his airy tenderness*): You know that Praddy is the soul of kindness, Mrs Warren. Praddy: what do you say? Go or stay?

PRAED (*to Mrs Warren*): I really should be very sorry to cause you unnecessary pain; but I think perhaps you had better not wait. The fact is—(*Vivie is heard at the inner door.*)

FRANK: Sh! Too late. She's coming.

MRS WARREN: Dont tell her I was crying. (*Vivie comes in. She stops gravely on seeing Mrs Warren, who greets her with hysterical cheerfulness.*) Well, dearie. So here you are at last.

VIVIE: I am glad you have come: I want to speak to you. You said you were going, Frank, I think.

FRANK: Yes. Will you come with me, Mrs Warren? What do you say to a trip to Richmond, and the theatre in the evening? There is safety in Richmond. No steam roller there.

VIVIE: Nonsense, Frank. My mother will stay here.

MRS WARREN (*scared*): I dont know: perhaps I'd better go. We're disturbing you at your work.

VIVIE (*with quiet decision*): Mr Praed: please take Frank away. Sit down, mother. (*Mrs Warren obeys helplessly.*)

PRAED: Come, Frank. Good-bye, Miss Vivie.

VIVIE (*shaking hands*): Good-bye. A pleasant trip.

PRAED: Thank you: thank you. I hope so.

FRANK (*to Mrs Warren*): Good-bye: youd ever so much better have taken my advice. (*He shakes hands with her. Then airily to Vivie*) Bye-bye, Viv.

VIVIE: Good-bye. (*He goes out gaily without shaking hands with her. Praed follows. Vivie, composed and extremely grave, sits down in Honoria's chair, and waits for her mother to speak. Mrs Warren, dreading a pause, loses no time in beginning.*)

MRS WARREN: Well, Vivie, what did you go away like that for without saying a word to me? How could you do such a thing! And what have you done to poor George? I wanted him to come with me; but he shuffled out of it. I could see that he was quite afraid of you. Only fancy: he wanted me not to come. As if (*trembling*) I should be afraid of you, dearie. (*Vivie's gravity deepens.*) But of course I told him it was all settled and comfortable between us, and that we were on the best of terms. (*She breaks down.*) Vivie: whats the meaning of this? (*She produces a paper from an envelope; comes to the table; and hands it across.*) I got it from the bank this morning.

VIVIE: It is my month's allowance. They sent it to me as usual the other day. I simply sent it back to be placed to your credit, and asked them to send you the lodgment receipt. In future I shall support myself.

MRS WARREN (*not daring to understand*): Wasnt it enough? Why didnt you tell me? (*With a cunning gleam in her eye*) I'll double it: I was intending to double it. Only let me know how much you want.

VIVIE: You know very well that that has nothing to do with it. From this time I go my own way in my own business and among my own friends. And you will go yours. (*She rises*) Good-bye.

MRS WARREN (*appalled*): Good-bye?

VIVIE: Yes: good-bye. Come: dont let us make a useless scene: you understand perfectly well. Sir George Crofts has told me the whole business.

MRS WARREN (*angrily*): Silly old—(*She swallows an epithet, and turns white at the narrowness of her escape from uttering it.*) He ought to have his tongue cut out. But I explained it all to you; and you said you didnt mind.

VIVIE (*steadfastly*): Excuse me: I do mind. You explained how it came about. That does not alter it.

(*Mrs Warren, silenced for a moment, looks forlornly at Vivie, who waits like a statue, secretly hoping that the combat is over. But the cunning expression comes back into Mrs Warren's face; and she bends across the table, sly and urgent, half whispering.*)

MRS WARREN: Vivie: do you know how rich I am?

VIVIE: I have no doubt you are very rich.

MRS WARREN: But you dont know all that that means: youre too young. It means a new dress every day; it means theatres and balls every night; it means having the pick of all the gentlemen in Europe at your feet; it means a lovely house and plenty of servants; it means the choicest of eating and drinking; it means everything you like, everything you want, everything you can think of. And what are you here? A mere drudge, toiling and moiling early and late for your bare living and two cheap dresses a year. Think over it. (*Soothingly*) Youre shocked, I know. I can enter into your feelings; and I think they do you credit; but trust me, nobody will blame you: you may take my word for that. I know what young girls are; and I know youll think better of it when youve turned it over in your mind.

VIVIE: So thats how it's done, is it? You must have said all that to many a woman, mother, to have it so pat.

MRS WARREN (*passionately*): What harm am I asking you to do? (*Vivie turns away contemptuously. Mrs Warren follows her desperately*) Vivie: listen to me: you dont understand: youve been taught wrong on purpose: you dont know what the world is really like.

VIVIE (*arrested*): Taught wrong on purpose! What do you mean?

MRS WARREN: I mean that youre throwing away all your chances for nothing. You think that people are what they pretend to be—that the way you were taught at school and college to think right and proper is the way things really are. But it's not: it's all only a pretence, to keep the cowardly, slavish common run of people quiet. Do you want to find that out, like other women, at forty, when youve thrown yourself away and lost your chances; or wont you take it in good time now from your own mother, that loves you and swears to you that it's truth—gospel truth? (*Urgently*) Vivie: the big people, the clever people, the managing people, all know it. They do as I do, and think what I think. I know plenty of them. I know them to speak to, to introduce you to, to make friends of for you. I dont mean anything wrong: thats what you dont understand: your head is full of ignorant ideas about me. What do the people that taught you know about life or about people like me? When did they ever meet me, or speak to me, or let anyone tell them about me?—the fools! Would they ever have done anything for you if I hadnt paid them? Havnt I told you that I want you to be respectable? Havnt I brought you up to be respectable? And how can you keep it up without my money and my influence and Lizzie's friends? Cant you see that youre cutting your own throat as well as breaking my heart in turning your back on me?

VIVIE: I recognise the Crofts philosophy of life, mother. I heard it all from him that day at the Gardners'.

MRS WARREN: You think I want to force that played-out old sot on you! I dont, Vivie: on my oath I dont.

VIVIE: It would not matter if you did: you would not succeed. (*Mrs Warren winces, deeply hurt by the implied indifference towards her affectionate intention. Vivie, neither understanding this nor concerning herself about it, goes on calmly*) Mother: you dont at all know the sort of person I am. I dont object to Crofts more than to any other coarsely built man of his class. To tell you the truth, I rather admire him for being strong-minded enough to enjoy himself in his own way and make plenty of money instead of living the usual shooting, hunting, dining-out, tailoring, loafing life of his set merely because all the rest do it. And I'm perfectly aware that if I'd been in the same circumstances as my aunt Liz, I'd have done exactly what she did. I dont think I'm more prejudiced or straitlaced than you: I think I'm less. I'm certain I'm less sentimental. I know very well that fashionable morality is all a pretence, and that if I took your money and devoted the rest of my life to spending it fashionably, I might be as worthless and vicious as the silliest woman could possibly want to be without having a word said to me about it. But I dont want to be worthless. I shouldnt enjoy trotting about the park to advertize my dressmaker and carriage builder, or being bored at the opera to show off a shop windowful of diamonds.

MRS WARREN (*bewildered*): But—

VIVIE: Wait a moment: Ive not done. Tell me why you continue your business now that you are independent of it. Your sister, you told me, has left all that behind her. Why dont you do the same?

MRS WARREN: Oh, it's all very easy for Liz: she likes good society, and has the air of being a lady. Imagine me in a cathedral town! Why, the very rooks in the trees would find me out even if I could stand the dulness of it. I must have work and excitement, or I should go melancholy mad. And what else is there for me to do? The life suits me: I'm fit for it and not for anything else. If I didnt do it somebody else would; so I dont do any real harm by it. And then it brings in money; and I like making money. No: it's no use: I cant give it up—not for anybody. But what need you know about it? I'll never mention it. I'll keep Crofts away. I'll not trouble you much: you see I have to be constantly running about from one place to another. Youll be quit of me altogether when I die.

VIVIE: No. I am my mother's daughter. I am like you: I must have work, and must make more money than I spend. But my work is not your work, and my way not your way. We must part. It will not make much difference to us: instead of meeting one another for perhaps a few months in twenty years, we shall never meet: thats all.

MRS WARREN (*her voice stifled in tears*): Vivie: I meant to have been more with you: I did indeed.

VIVIE: It's no use, mother: I am not to be changed by a few cheap tears and entreaties any more than you are, I dare say.

MRS WARREN (*wildly*): Oh, you call a mother's tears cheap.

VIVIE: They cost you nothing; and you ask me to give you the peace and quietness of my whole life in exchange for them. What use would my company be to you if you could get it? What have we two in common that could make either of us happy together?

MRS WARREN (*lapsing recklessly into her dialect*): We're mother and daughter. I want my daughter. Ive a right to you. Who is to care for me when I'm old? Plenty of girls have taken to me like daughters and cried at leaving me; but I let them all go because I had you to look forward to. I kept myself lonely for you. Youve no right to turn on me now and refuse to do your duty as a daughter.

VIVIE (*jarred and antagonized by the echo of the slums in her mother's voice*): My duty as a daughter! I thought we should come to that presently. Now once for all, mother, you want a daughter and Frank wants a wife. I dont want a mother; and I dont want a husband. I have spared neither Frank nor myself in sending him about his business. Do you think I will spare you?

MRS WARREN (*violently*): Oh, I know the sort you are—no mercy for yourself or anyone else. *I* know. My experience has done that for me anyhow: I can tell the pious, canting, hard, selfish woman when I meet her. Well, keep yourself to yourself: *I* dont want you. But listen to this. Do you know what I would do with you if you were a baby again—aye, as sure as there's a Heaven above us?

VIVIE: Strangle me, perhaps.

MRS WARREN: No: I'd bring you up to be a real daughter to me, and not what you are now, with your pride and your prejudices and the college education you stole from me—yes, stole: deny it if you can: what was it but stealing? I'd bring you up in my own house, so I would.

VIVIE (*quietly*): In one of your own houses.

MRS WARREN (*screaming*): Listen to her! listen to how she spits on her mother's grey hairs! Oh, may you live to have your own daughter tear and trample on you as you have trampled on me. And you will: you will. No woman ever had luck with a mother's curse on her.

VIVIE: I wish you wouldnt rant, mother. It only hardens me. Come: I suppose I am the only young woman you ever had in your power that you did good to. Dont spoil it all now.

MRS WARREN: Yes, Heaven forgive me, it's true; and you are the only one that ever turned on me. Oh, the injustice of it, the injustice, the injustice! I always wanted to be a good woman. I tried honest work; and I was slave-driven until I cursed the day I ever heard of honest work. I was a good mother; and because I made my daughter a good woman she turns me out as if I was a leper. Oh, if I only had my life to live over again! I'd talk to that lying clergyman in the school. From this time forth, so help me Heaven in my last hour, I'll do wrong and nothing but wrong. And I'll prosper on it.

VIVIE: Yes: it's better to choose your line and go through with it. If I had been you, mother, I might have done as you did; but I should not have lived one life and believed in another. You are a conventional woman at heart. That is why I am bidding you good-bye now. I am right, am I not?

MRS WARREN (*taken aback*): Right to throw away all my money!

VIVIE: No: right to get rid of you? I should be a fool not to? Isnt that so?

MRS WARREN (*sulkily*): Oh well, yes, if you come to that, I suppose you are. But Lord help the world if everybody took to doing the right thing! And now I'd better go than stay where I'm not wanted. (*She turns to the door.*)

VIVIE (*kindly*): Wont you shake hands?

MRS WARREN (*after looking at her fiercely for a moment with a savage impulse to strike her*): No, thank you. Good-bye.

VIVIE (*matter-of-factly*): Good-bye. (*Mrs Warren goes out, slamming the door behind her. The strain on Vivie's face relaxes; her grave expression breaks up into one of joyous content; her breath goes out in a half sob, half laugh of intense relief. She goes buoyantly to her place at the writing-table; pushes the electric lamp out of the way; pulls over a great sheaf of papers; and is in the act of dipping her pen in the ink when she finds Frank's note. She opens it unconcernedly and reads it quickly, giving a little laugh at some quaint turn of expression in it.*) And good-bye, Frank. (*She tears the note up and tosses the pieces into the waste-paper basket without a second thought. Then she goes at her work with a plunge, and soon becomes absorbed in her figures.*)

COMMENTARIES

BERNARD SHAW (1856–1950)

Plays Unpleasant:
Mrs. Warren's Profession 1898

Shaw included *Mrs. Warren's Profession* in a group of three plays he titled "unpleasant." In this excerpt from one of his prefaces (1898), he explains that the subjects of these plays are not to be taken lightly by an audience out for an evening of fun but are serious and meant to be considered carefully.

In *Mrs Warren's Profession* I have gone straight at the fact that, as Mrs Warren puts it, "the only way for a woman to provide for herself decently is for her to be good to some man that can afford to be good to her." There are some questions on which I am, like most Socialists, an extreme Individualist. I believe that any society which desires to found itself on a high standard of integrity of character in its units should organize itself in such a fashion as to make it possible too for all men and all women to maintain themselves in reasonable comfort by their industry without selling their affections and their convictions. At present we not only condemn women as a sex to attach themselves to "breadwinners," licitly or illicitly, on pain of heavy privation and disadvantage; but we have great prostitute classes of men: for instance, dramatists and journalists, to whom I myself belong, not to mention the legions of lawyers, doctors, clergymen, and platform politicians who are daily using their highest faculties to belie their real sentiments: a sin compared to which that of a woman who sells the use of her person for a few hours is too venial to be worth mentioning; for rich men without conviction are more dangerous in modern society than poor women without chastity. Hardly a pleasant subject this!

I must, however, warn my readers that my attacks are directed against themselves, not against my stage figures. They cannot too thoroughly understand that the guilt of defective social organization does not lie alone on the people who actually work the commercial makeshifts which the defects make inevitable, and who often, like Sartorius° and Mrs Warren, display valuable executive capacities and even high moral virtues in their administration, but with the whole body of citizens whose public opinion, public action, and public contribution as ratepayers alone can replace Sartorius's slums with decent dwellings, Charteris's° intrigues with reasonable marriage contracts, and Mrs Warren's profession with honorable industries guarded by a humane industrial code and a "moral minimum" wage.

BERNARD SHAW (1856–1950)

From the Preface to
Mrs. Warren's Profession 1902

Most of Shaw's prefaces to his plays address the issues of the plays themselves. This preface concentrates on the efforts of authorities to censor the play and prevent its production. Shaw gives us his views on censorship and on the public attitudes that viewed the play as threatening to public morality. However, he also goes on to comment on the issues of prostitution in the late nineteenth century and its relationship to the society that sustained it. As he puts it, even his supportive critics would not see themselves as responsible for the existence of the Mrs. Warrens among them.

The Author's Apology

Mrs Warren's Profession has been performed at last, after a delay of only eight years; and I have once more shared with Ibsen the triumphant amusement of startling all but the strongest-headed of the London theater critics clean out of the practice of their profession. No author who has ever known the exultation of sending the Press into an hysterical tumult of protest, of moral panic, of involuntary and frantic confession of sin, of a horror of conscience in which the power of distinguishing between the work of art on the stage and the real life of the spectator is confused and overwhelmed, will ever care for the stereotyped compliments which every successful farce or melodrama elicits from the newspapers. Give me that critic who rushed from my play to declare furiously that Sir George Crofts ought to be kicked. What a triumph for the actor, thus to reduce a jaded London journalist to the condition of the simple sailor in the Wapping gallery, who shouts execrations at Iago and

---

Sartorius: Sartorius is a slum landlord in Shaw's first successful play, *Widowers' Houses*.
Charteris's: Leonard Charteris is the protagonist in Shaw's play *The Philanderer* (1893).

warnings to Othello not to believe him! But dearer still than such simplicity is that sense of the sudden earthquake shock to the foundations of morality which sends a pallid crowd of critics into the street shrieking that the pillars of society are cracking and the ruin of the State at hand. Even the Ibsen champions of ten years ago remonstrate with me just as the veterans of those brave days remonstrated with them. Mr Grein, the hardy iconoclast who first launched my plays on the stage alongside *Ghosts* and *The Wild Ducks*, exclaims that I have shattered his ideals. Actually his ideals! What would Dr. Relling say? And Mr William Archer himself disowns me because I "cannot touch pitch without wallowing in it." Truly my play must be more needed than I knew; and yet I thought I knew how little the others know.

Do not suppose, however, that the consternation of the Press reflects any consternation among the general public. Anybody can upset the theater critics, in a turn of the wrist, by substituting for the romantic commonplaces of the stage the moral commonplaces of the pulpit, the platform, or the library. Play *Mrs Warren's Profession* to an audience of clerical members of the Christian Social Union and of women well experienced in Rescue, Temperance, and Girls' Club work, and no moral panic will arise: every man and woman present will know that as long as poverty makes virtue hideous and the spare pocket-money of rich bachelordom makes vice dazzling, their daily hand-to-hand fight against prostitution with prayer and persuasion, shelters and scanty alms, will be a losing one. There was a time when they were able to urge that though "the white-lead factory where Anne Jane was poisoned" may be a far more terrible place than Mrs Warren's house, yet hell is still more dreadful. Nowadays they no longer believe in hell; and the girls among whom they are working know that they did not believe in it, and would laugh at them if they did. So well have the rescuers learnt that Mrs Warren's defense of herself and indictment of society is the thing that most needs saying, that those who know me personally reproach me, not for writing this play, but for wasting my energies on "pleasant plays" for the amusement of frivolous people, when I can build up such excellent stage sermons on their own work. *Mrs Warren's Profession* is the one play of mine which I could submit to a censorship without doubt of the result; only, it must not be the censorship of the minor theater critic, nor of an innocent court official like the King's Reader of Plays, much less of people who consciously profit by Mrs Warren's profession, or who personally make use of it, or who hold the widely whispered view that it is an indispensable safety-valve for the protection of domestic virtue, or, above all, who are smitten with a sentimental affection for our fallen sister, and would "take her up tenderly, lift her with care, fashioned so slenderly, young, and so fair." Nor am I prepared to accept the verdict of the medical gentlemen who would compulsorily examine and register Mrs Warren, whilst leaving Mrs Warren's patrons, especially her military patrons, free to destroy her health and anybody else's without fear of reprisals. But I should be quite content to have my play judged by, say, a joint committee of the Central Vigilance Society and the Salvation Army. And the sterner moralists the members of the committee were, the better.[. . .]

I now come to those critics who, intellectually baffled by the problem in *Mrs Warren's Profession*, have made a virtue of running away from it. I will illustrate their method by a quotation from Dickens, taken from the fifth chapter of *Our Mutual Friend*.

> "Hem!" began Wegg. "This, Mr Boffin and Lady, is the first chapter of the first wollume of the *Decline and Fall of——*" here he looked hard at the book, and stopped.
>
> "What's the matter, Wegg?"

"Why, it comes into my mind, do you know, sir," said Wegg with an air of insinuating frankness (having first again looked hard at the book), "that you made a little mistake this morning, which I had meant to set you right in; only something put it out of my head. I think you said Rooshan Empire, sir?"

"It is Rooshan; ain't it, Wegg?"

"No, sir. Roman. Roman."

"What's the difference, Wegg?"

"The difference, sir?" Mr Wegg was faltering and in danger of breaking down, when a bright thought flashed upon him. "The difference, sir? There you place me in a difficulty, Mr Boffin. Suffice it to observe, that the difference is best postponed to some other occasion when Mrs Boffin does not honour us with her company. In Mrs Boffin's presence, sir, we had better drop it."

Mr Wegg thus came out of his disadvantage with quite a chivalrous air, and not only that, but by dint of repeating with a manly delicacy, "In Mrs Boffin's presence, sir, we had better drop it!" turned the disadvantage on Boffin, who felt that he had committed himself in a very painful manner.

I am willing to let Mr Wegg drop it on these terms, provided I am allowed to mention here that *Mrs Warren's Profession* is a play for women; that it was written for women; that it has been performed and produced mainly through the determination of women that it should be performed and produced; that the enthusiasm of women made its first performance excitingly successful; and that not one of these women had any inducement to support it except their belief in the timeliness and the power of the lesson the play teaches. Those who were "surprised to see ladies present" were men; and when they proceeded to explain that the journals they represented could not possibly demoralize the public by describing such a play, their editors cruelly devoted the space saved by their delicacy to an elaborate and respectful account of the progress of a young lord's attempt to break the bank at Monte Carlo. A few days sooner Mrs Warren would have been crowded out of their papers by an exceptionally abominable police case. [. . .]

My old Independent Theater manager, Mr Grein, besides that reproach to me for shattering his ideals, complains that Mrs Warren is not wicked enough, and names several romancers who would have clothed her black soul with all the terrors of tragedy. I have no doubt they would; but if you please, my dear Mr. Grein, that is just what I did not want to do. Nothing would please our sanctimonious British public more than to throw the whole guilt of Mrs Warren's profession on Mrs Warren herself. Now the whole aim of my play is to throw that guilt on the British public itself. You may remember that when he produced my first play, *Widowers' Houses*, exactly the same misunderstanding arose. When the virtuous young gentleman rose up in wrath against the slum landlord, the slum landlord very effectually shewed him that slums are the product, not of individual Harpagons, but of the indifference of virtuous young gentlemen to the condition of the city they live in, provided they live at the west end of it on money earned by somebody else's labor. The notion that prostitution is created by the wickedness of Mrs Warren is as silly as the notion — prevalent, nevertheless, to some extent in Temperance circles — that drunkenness is created by the wickedness of the publican. Mrs Warren is not a whit a worse woman than the reputable daughter who cannot endure her. Her indifference to the ultimate social consequences of her means of making money, and her discovery of that means by the ordinary method of taking the line of least resistance to getting it, are too common in English society to call for any special remark. Her vitality, her thrift, her energy, her outspokenness, her wise care of her daughter, and the managing capacity which has enabled her and her sister to climb from the fried fish shop down by the Mint to the establishments of which she boasts, are all high English social virtues. Her defense of herself is so overwhelming that it provokes the *St James's Gazette* to declare that "the tendency of the play is wholly evil" because "it contains one of the boldest and most specious defenses of an immoral life for poor women that has ever been penned." Happily the *St James's Gazette* here speaks in its haste. Mrs Warren's defense of herself is not only bold and specious, but valid and unanswerable. But it is no defense at all of the vice which she organizes. It is no defense of an immoral life to say that the alternative offered by society collectively to poor women is a miserable life, starved, overworked, fetid, ailing, ugly. Though it is quite natural and *right* for Mrs Warren to choose what is, according to her lights, the least immoral alternative, it is none the less infamous of society to offer such alternatives. For the alternatives offered are not morality and immorality, but two sorts of immorality. The man who cannot see that starvation, overwork, dirt, and disease are as immoral as prostitution—that they are the vices and crimes of a nation, and not merely its misfortunes—is (to put it as politely as possible) a hopelessly Private Person.

The notion that Mrs Warren must be a fiend is only an example of the violence and passion which the slightest reference to sex rouses in undisciplined minds, and which makes it seem natural to our lawgivers to punish silly and negligible indecencies with a ferocity unknown in dealing with, for example, ruinous financial swindling. Had my play been entitled *Mr Warren's Profession*, and Mr Warren been a bookmaker, nobody would have expected me to make him a villain as well. Yet gambling is a vice, and bookmaking an institution, for which there is absolutely nothing to be said. The moral and economic evil done by trying to get other people's money without working for it (and this is the essence of gambling) is not only enormous but uncompensated. There are no two sides to the question of gambling, no circumstances which force us to tolerate it lest its suppression lead to worse things, no consensus of opinion among responsible classes, such as magistrates and military commanders, that it is a necessity, no Athenian records of gambling made splendid by the talents of its professors, no contention that instead of violating morals it only violates a legal institution which is in many respects oppressive and unnatural, no possible plea that the instinct on which it is founded is a vital one. Prostitution can confuse the issue with all these excuses: gambling has none of them. Consequently, if Mrs Warren must needs be a demon, a bookmaker must be a cacodemon.° Well, does anybody who knows the sporting world really believe that bookmakers are worse than their neighbors? On the contrary, they have to be a good deal better; for in that world nearly everybody whose social rank does not exclude such an occupation would be a bookmaker if he could; but the strength of character required for handling large sums of money and for strict settlements and unflinching payment of losses is so rare that successful bookmakers are rare too. It may seem that at least public spirit cannot be one of a bookmaker's virtues; but I can testify from personal experience that excellent public work is done with money subscribed by bookmakers. It is true that there are abysses in bookmaking: for example, welshing. Mr Grein hints that there are abysses in Mrs Warren's profession also. So there are in every profession: the error lies in supposing that every member of them sounds these depths. I sit on a public body which prosecutes Mrs Warren zealously; and I can assure Mr Grein that she is often leniently dealt

cacodemon: Evil spirit.

with because she has conducted her business "respectably" and held herself above its vilest branches. The degrees in infamy are as numerous and as scrupulously observed as the degrees in the peerage: the moralist's notion that there are depths at which the moral atmosphere ceases is as delusive as the rich man's notion that there are no social jealousies or snobberies among the very poor. No: had I drawn Mrs Warren as a fiend in human form, the very people who now rebuke me for flattering her would probably be the first to deride me for deducing character logically from occupation instead of observing it accurately in society.

One critic is so enslaved by this sort of logic that he calls my portraiture of the Reverend Samuel Gardner an attack on religion. According to this view Subaltern Iago is an attack on the army, Sir John Falstaff an attack on knighthood, and King Claudius an attack on royalty. Here again the clamor for naturalness and human feeling, raised by so many critics when they are confronted by the real thing on the stage, is really a clamor for the most mechanical and superficial sort of logic. The dramatic reason for making the clergyman what Mrs Warren calls "an old stick-in-the-mud," whose son, in spite of much capacity and charm, is a cynically worthless member of society, is to set up a mordant contrast between him and the woman of infamous profession, with her well brought-up, straightforward, hardworking daughter. The critics who have missed the contrast have doubtless observed often enough that many clergymen are in the Church through no genuine calling, but simply because, in circles which can command preferment, it is the refuge of "the fool of the family"; and that clergymen's sons are often conspicuous reactionists against the restraints imposed on them in childhood by their father's profession. These critics must know, too, from history if not from experience, that women as unscrupulous as Mrs Warren have distinguished themselves as administrators and rulers, both commercially and politically. But both observation and knowledge are left behind when journalists go to the theater. Once in their stalls, they assume that it is "natural" for clergymen to be saintly, for soldiers to be heroic, for lawyers to be hard-hearted, for sailors to be simple and generous, for doctors to perform miracles with little bottles, and for Mrs Warren to be a beast and a demon. All this is not only not natural, but not dramatic. A man's profession only enters into the drama of his life when it comes into conflict with his nature. The result of this conflict is tragic in Mrs Warren's case, and comic in the clergyman's case (at least we are savage enough to laugh at it); but in both cases it is illogical, and in both cases natural. I repeat, the critics who accuse me of sacrificing nature to logic are so sophisticated by their profession that to them logic is nature, and nature absurdity.

The "Woman Question" in the Late Nineteenth Century

The "woman question" was central to great controversy that swept throughout Europe and the United States during the nineteenth century and brought the circumstances of women to the attention of society. Prior to the industrial revolution, women worked side by side with men in the fields or in home-based industries. With the creation of a moneyed class made possible by the fruits of factory labor, however, women similar to Ibsen's Nora Helmer sought economic independence. Although wealthy and newly middle-class women were considered "angels of the house"—responsible for managing the household, supervising the children, and supporting their husbands' efforts—eventually these women began to see the limitations of their role. As the philosopher John Stuart Mill put it, women were expected to be willing slaves, but some of them, like Nora in Ibsen's *A Doll House,* rebelled.

Ibsen's Nora Helmer and Strindberg's Miss Julie offer views into the opportunities for women in the age. Marriage is the key to Nora's sense of self and satisfaction until she realizes how little her efforts to save her husband are appreciated. For Miss Julie, romance is not synonymous with marriage, but she realizes, too, that her virtue, once spent, can no longer give her power over men such as Jean. These plays demonstrate the limits of women's power in the second half of the nineteenth century.

The limited legal status of married women was increasingly unsatisfactory to wives during the latter part of the nineteenth century, and laws were passed to help them retain control over some of their own property, keeping it distinct from their husbands' property. Because divorce was difficult or impossible, separation usually ended in the ostracism of the woman. Many women in this era worked for reform, and several of the dramas of Ibsen and other Scandinavian writers argued for better treatment of women in society.

The economic limitations imposed on women were severe. Women of the upper-middle classes were expected not to work at all, whereas women of the lower classes living in cities had few choices. Women who did factory work risked injury and disease. As Mrs. Warren eloquently explains in Shaw's *Mrs. Warren's Profession,* even late in the nineteenth century, factory women

For links to further resources,
click on *Casebook Links* at
bedfordstmartins.com/jacobus.

aged quickly, had no job security, were dispensable, and often ended badly. One alternative was the choice made by Mrs. Warren, who avoided the early death experienced by her sister Jane, victim of lead poisoning in a factory, by becoming a prostitute and then a madam.

In the Victorian era, prostitution remained an almost universal fact of life. It was licensed in some places, tolerated in others, and subject to graft in yet others. In England, the Contagious Diseases Acts, instituted between 1860 and 1870, supposedly protected sailors and other military personnel from venereal disease. The laws required all prostitutes in military regions to be examined by appointed officials. Prostitutes adjudged "sick" were confined in hospitals with little or no hope of being released. Politically active women who had been at the forefront of the equal rights movement and the quest for the vote were outraged at this unequal treatment of the participants in the act of prostitution. Eventually, their protests forced the government to repeal the Contagious Diseases Acts.

Some of the following documents point out the economic and social issues involved in prostitution in the period. Descriptions from brothel directories reveal the widely accepted "business" of running a brothel. Madams, "landladies" of the brothels, were managers who had risen from the ranks, but few women managed to do this, as Barbara Meil Hobson explains in "Successful Madams." The small number of madams who actually achieved financial independence is a point to remember when considering the achievement of Mrs. Warren in Shaw's play.

As this collection of documents attests, the debate over the "woman question" was conducted in the houses of Parliament, in the daily newspapers of many nations, and in the essays, dramas, and writings of authors such as August Strindberg. The plays of Ibsen, Strindberg, Shaw, and other writers of the period must be seen against the backdrop of the struggle for women's rights.

JOHN STUART MILL (1806–1873)

On the Subjection of Women   1869

John Stuart Mill was an important philosopher in the mid-nineteenth century. He held to a philosophy of utilitarianism, which stressed the usefulness of actions and principles. His views on the subjection of women note that the superior strength of men had been turned into principles of law and behavior as if women were meant to be subjugated. According to Mill, women have been forced into wrongful submission.

From the very earliest twilight of human society, every woman (owing to the value attached to her by men, combined with her inferiority in muscular strength) was found in a state of bondage to some man. Laws and systems of polity always begin by recognizing the relations they find already existing between individuals. They convert what was a mere physical fact into a legal right, give it the sanction of society, and principally aim at the substitution of public and organized means of asserting and protecting these rights, instead of the irregular and lawless conflict of physical strength. Those who had already been compelled to obedience became in this manner legally bound to it.

All causes, social and natural, combine to make it unlikely that women should be collectively rebellious to the power of men. They are so far in a position different from all other subject classes, that their masters require something more from them than actual service. Men do not want solely the obedience of women, they want their sentiments. All men, except the most brutish, desire to have, in the woman most nearly connected with them, not a forced slave but a willing one, not a slave merely, but a favorite. They have therefore put everything in practice to enslave their minds. The masters of all other slaves rely, for maintaining obedience, on fear; either fear of themselves, or religious fears. The masters of women wanted more than simple obedience, and they turned the whole force of education to effect their purpose. All women are brought up from the very earliest years in the belief that their ideal of character is the very opposite to that of men; not self-will, and government by self-control, but submission, and yielding to the control of others. All the moralities tell them that it is the duty of women, and all the current sentimentalities that it is their nature, to live for others; to make complete abnegation of themselves, and to have no life but in their affections. And by their affections are meant the only ones they are allowed to have—those to the men with whom they are connected, or to the children who constitute an additional and indefeasible tie between them and a man. When we put together three things—first, the natural attraction between opposite sexes; secondly, the wife's entire dependence on the husband, every privilege or pleasure she has being either his gift, or depending entirely on his will; and lastly, that the principal object of human pursuit, consideration, and all objects of social ambition, can in general be sought or obtained by her only through him, it would be a miracle if the object of being attractive to men had not become the polar star of feminine education and formation of character. And, this great means of influence over the minds of women having been acquired, an instinct of selfishness made men avail themselves of it to the utmost as a means of holding women in subjection, by representing to them meekness, submissiveness, and resignation of all individual will into the hands of a man, as an essential part of sexual attractiveness. What is now called the nature of women is an eminently artificial thing—the result of forced repression in some directions, unnatural stimulation in others.

AUGUST STRINDBERG (1849–1912)

The Woman Question: Women's Rights   1884

TRANSLATED FROM THE SWEDISH BY MARY SANDBACH

Though he eventually developed a reputation as a misogynist, the playwright August Strindberg published a forward-looking book on marriage early in his career. He was married to the actress Siri von Essen and living in Switzerland when he wrote *The Last Word on the Woman Question* (1883). But it was hardly his last word on the subject. The very next year he wrote the novel *Getting Married*. The following excerpt is from the preface to part 1 of that work. Feminism had been a growing movement in Scandinavia and elsewhere, and while Strindberg's views may seem compatible with feminist ideals, he wrote the following declaration of women's rights in a state of irritation. He was apparently sick and tired of the woman question by 1884.

Meanwhile, under present conditions, it is both impossible and harmful to detach the Woman Question from its context. Woman's desire for emancipation is identical with man's restless longing for freedom. Let us therefore liberate man from his prejudices, and we shall see that the emancipation of women will follow. But we must work together for our objective as friends, not as enemies. The woman of the future, be it a nearer or a more distant future, shall have an indisputable right to demand certain things and, in order to dispel the suspicion that I entertain reactionary ideas, I will now set these out under the following heading:

Woman's Rights

Which the laws of nature would grant her, but of which, thanks to our perverse social system (and not as a result of male tyranny), she has been deprived.

1. The right to the same education as men. I cannot too often repeat that by this I do not mean to imagine that she will be raised to man's level by learning all the unnecessary things with which he now has to stuff himself. Posterity, which will put an end to the difference between elementary and secondary schools, which will put an end to matriculation, and all other examinations, will one day feel obliged to establish a single civic examination which everyone will take, and which will replace confirmation. This examination will be the same for men and women, and will only require those examined to have a thorough knowledge of the arts of reading, writing, and arithmetic, a knowledge of the laws of their country, a knowledge of their civic rights and duties, and also of one living language. He who wants after that to learn what Cicero thought of Lucius Sulla, and what Moses intended to do with the children of Israel may do so, that is if he has time for such luxuries, for posterity will demand that every citizen shall support himself by bodily toil as nature intended.

2. Boys and girls shall attend the same schools, so that both sexes learn to know each other early in life. Things will not then be as they are today, when boys imagine that girls are angels, and girls that boys are knights. In this way we shall avoid all the silent sins of fantasy and precocity, for they are a result of the way in which the sexes are isolated.

3. The girl shall have the same freedom to "run wild" and choose what company she pleases.

4. There shall be complete equality between the sexes, which will do away with that revolting form of hypocrisy called gallantry, or politeness to ladies. A girl will not expect a boy to get up and give her his seat, for that is the hallmark of the subservient slave; and a brother will not get into the habit of expecting his sister to make his bed, or sew on his shirt buttons, for these are things he must do for himself.

5. Woman shall have the vote. In the future, when her confirmation consists of an examination in the laws that govern the community in which she lives, and when this community is obliged to present an annual report to its members, as companies do today, a woman will be just as well able to decide for whom or for what she will vote as a man.

6. Woman shall be eligible for all occupations, which should not be any more difficult to arrange under self-government than it is today when, inconsequently enough, she can become the monarch. Self-government will not be the same as government by professionals, but will be more like local government, that is a commission which can be performed in leisure moments. Is anyone wiser and better suited to govern than an old mother, who has learned through motherhood and running a household both how to rule and how to administrate? (Our forefathers had such a veneration for the wisdom of older women that they believed them to possess supernatural knowledge.)

7. This measure will mean that the moral code will become less rigid, and the law less strict, for a mother has learned to be more tolerant than anyone, and no one knows better than she how patient and how unexacting you must be with the erring children of man.

8. Woman shall be exempt from military service. Anyone who regards this as unjust should take into consideration the fact that nature exacts compensation from her in the form of heavy maternal duties. For that matter military service will not in future be regarded as particularly glorious. It will simply be a duty.

9. By a just distribution of the combined riches of nature the community of the future will ensure that all who are born receive sustenance and instruction. Marriage as a guarantee for these advantages will therefore become unnecessary. Man and wife will conclude a contract, verbal or written, for a union of any length they may decide, which they will have the right to dissolve when they please, without reference to law or gospel. It is true that this will not prevent a situation in which two males want to possess the same female, but the struggle will be less cruel, and the female will be the one to choose,—which is not the case at present—for no one in future will be obliged to marry for money or position, as neither of these things will exist. Selection will therefore be natural, and consequently the race will improve.

So much for the woman of the future and marriage. But there are things we can do to make reasonable improvements in the married state under present conditions. These are:

1. That boys and girls shall be allowed to mix more freely.

2. That the education of boys shall be simplified, so that it will not be unjust if the education of girls is simplified too.

3. The girl (like the boy) shall no longer be forced to learn so much about the past, but she shall be obliged to acquaint herself with the way in which society is governed today.

4. She may be given the vote at the earliest possible moment.

5. False gallantry will cease of itself, and men and women will associate together as men do now. But things shall not be as at present, when men have all male banquets, which end with a toast to the ladies, while the latter sit at home eating porridge and milk.

6. Civil marriage shall be introduced, and this will make divorce easier. Not that it is likely to become more frequent, but easier divorce will make the bonds feel less irksome, and will disabuse the man of the idea that he owns the woman. Children will still hold married couples together, unless the circumstances are very difficult.

Civil marriage would do away with the horrible legal ruling that necessitates warnings by the clergy, or obligatory "desertion."

7. The paragraphs in our laws about a husband's rights as a guardian shall be rescinded.

8. A woman shall come of age at eighteen without any reservations.

9. Deeds of settlement and the judicial division of property shall be obligatory on all married couples.

10. A woman (when her education is the same as that given to men) shall have the right to fill any post and practice any profession she pleases. (But if two million women were let loose on the labor market at the moment the result would be ruthless competition. Here—under present conditions—we must perhaps condescend to an inconsistency, unless by any chance, a surplus of labor accelerated the adoption of the new social system.)

11. When he marries a man shall be obliged to take out a life insurance policy, so that in the event of his death, his wife and children will not be left destitute. This is more especially his duty if he takes a woman away from a gainful occupation.

12. A woman shall keep her own name. She shall not have the right to take her husband's title in its feminine form, for a title under present conditions is a possession, often expensively acquired, and worth money. This proviso is necessary if there is to be equality, and it will prevent many women from being tempted to buy a title with their wealth. Boys shall take their father's name, and girls their mother's.

13. Separate bedrooms shall be the rule from the beginning. For a practice so offensive to "decency" as a common bedchamber brings its own punishment, and gives rise to confusion, distaste, satiety, and even worse things in a relationship. This rule will make a woman's position freer, and will give her the right to possess her own body.

14. If a woman is solely her husband's wife, and the mother of his children and has no independent occupation, she shall receive an allowance for clothes and recreation. She shall not have a salary, or receive clothes as presents, for which she has to say thank you. Moreover, she shall have the *right* to pay for her amusements herself, even when she is out with her husband, and thus be spared from always being *treated*.

15. If a married woman is gainfully occupied and does not run her own home, she shall be obliged to contribute from her earnings as much to the household as her husband does. If she also works in her home she shall be allowed to keep what she earns, for her work at home will thus come to be regarded as an extra contribution, and not as now, as the services rendered by a slave.

JOHAN THORSTEN SELLIN (1897–1994)

Marriage and Divorce in Sweden 1922

Johan Thorsten Sellin discusses the rights of Swedish women in marriage before the sweeping changes invoked by the law of 1920. Prior to that time, the wife was essentially at the mercy of her husband's decisions. She was bound to obey her husband's wishes on virtually all important issues, and her children were her husband's to educate or train as he liked. A wife's limitations were established under law.

Before the law of 1920 went into effect, the status of the wife, as far as the law was concerned, was, in spite of improvements, rather unfavorable in many respects, giving unmistakable evidence of the double standard, which the present law has succeeded in abolishing. She, first of all, followed her husband's estate in life; if he for some reason or other became poor, she was obliged to accept this fact with resignation, even though he might have been the cause of the poverty. Her husband's nationality was hers, and the choice of domicile was in his hands. Her only right to refuse to live where he determined to live depended on whether or not his decision would cause her life to be placed in jeopardy, expose her to injustice, or force her to move abroad. In the last mentioned case, she could refuse to comply with his wishes only if his business at the time of the marriage was not likely to take him abroad or if he was not appointed to some official position which necessitated foreign residence.

A wife was in duty bound to expend her energies and efforts for her family and her home, in accordance with her husband's wishes. This meant that she could not accept outside work without his permission, unless the needs of the family made it imperative. Although the law gave him no power to compel her to follow his wishes, he could refuse to support her or could ask the clergy to "warn" her, the first step toward separation from bed and board. With her husband's permission[1] she could conduct a business or engage in other profitable employment, but if he were legally disqualified to engage in business (due to official position as custom officer, public prosecutor, or tax collector) she shared his disability, even though she may have had his permission. If she failed to heed her husband's refusal, she could be fined like any other individual who conducted a business without license. When she worked lawfully, i.e., with her husband's permission, her earnings belonged to her, although it is not certain that what she purchased with these earnings became hers to do with as she chose.

A married mother had nothing to say in the bringing up of her own children, i.e., the law gave her no such right. Her husband was their guardian until they reached majority, [he] chose their life's work, and [he] gave away his daughters in marriage. If he abused his guardianship, the court could appoint someone else guardian, but in no instance could the mother be so appointed while the family remained undisrupted. She was thereby classified with "feeble-minded persons, heavy debtors, spendthrifts, enemies of the child, persons not yet twenty-five years of age, or so old and crippled that he cannot discharge his duties as guardian, etc." Only in case the husband went insane, deserted his wife, or for other reasons was unable to exercise his guardianship could she be substituted, and if he died, she took his place as guardian of her children—until she remarried. In case husband and wife belonged to different religious faiths, the former decided in which faith the children should be brought up.

As a rule, all the property of the spouses was joint, since in the majority of marriages no private property or income existed. Of this joint property the husband was the sole manager. His administrative powers extended even to his wife's private property, with the exception of her private real property. He decided upon the amount to be spent for the household expenses, for the education of the children, and even for his wife's personal needs. The latter had no right to demand anything from her husband, except necessities, even though she may have been the source of the entire family fortune. Most important of all, perhaps, was the fact that no matter how he managed the joint property, he owed his wife no accounting.

---

[1]The industrial and commercial acts of 1846 prohibited a woman to engage in business without her husband's permission and security.

RICHARD PANOFSKY (b. 1943)

A Nineteenth-Century Husband's Letter to His Wife   1844

Richard Panofsky, a professor at the University of Massachusetts at Dartmouth, provided the following translated letter, from a man named Marcus (1807–1865) to his wife Ulrike (1816–1888). The couple and their six children lived in nineteenth-century Hamburg, Germany. The letter establishes the conditions under which Marcus would take his wife back into his house after she had left him and the children. It also establishes exactly what he expects of his wife. According to Panofsky, Ulrike returned.

June 23, 1844

Dear Wife,

You have sinned greatly—and maybe I too; but this much is certain: Adam sinned after Eve had already sinned. So it is with us; you, alone, carry the guilt of all the misfortune which, however, I helped to enlarge later by my behavior. Listen now, since I still believe certain things to be necessary in order that we may have a peaceful life. If we want not only to be content for a day but forever, you will have to follow my wishes. So examine yourself and determine if you are strong enough to conquer your false ambitions and your stubbornness to submit to all the conditions, the fulfillment of which I cannot ignore. Every sensible person will tell you that all I ask of you is what is easily understood. If you insist on remaining stubborn, then do not return to my house, for you will never be happy with me; your husband, children, and the entire city threaten indifference or even contempt.

But if you decide to act *sensibly* and *correctly*, that is *justly* and *kindly*, then be certain that many in the world will envy you.

I am including here the paper which I read to you in front of the rabbi; ask anyone in your residence if the wishes expressed by me are not quite reasonable, and are of a kind to which every wife can agree for the welfare of domestic happiness. In any case, act in a way you think best.

When you decide to return, write to tell me on which day and hour you depart from Berlin and give me your itinerary whether by way of Kuestrin and Pinne or by way of Wollstein. I will then meet you at Wollstein or Pinne. I expect you will bring Solomon with you.

Don't travel unprepared. If you need money, ask your father.

May God enlighten your heart and mind.

I remain your so far unhappy,

[MARCUS]

Greetings to my parents, brothers, and sisters; also your brother. Show them what you wish, this letter, the enclosure, whatever you want. The children are fortunately healthy.

If you want to return with joy and peace, write me by return mail. In that case, I would rather send you a carriage. Maybe Madam Fraenkel will come along. . . .

[*Enclosure*]

My wife promises—for which every wife is obligated to her husband—to follow my wishes in everything and to strictly obey my orders. It is already self-evident that our marital relations have often been disturbed by the fact that my wife does not follow my wishes but believes herself to be entitled to act on her own, even if this is totally against my orders. In order not to have to remind my wife every second what my wishes are regarding homemaking and public conduct—wishes which I have often expressed—I want to make here a few rules which shall serve as a code of conduct. A home is best run if the work for each hour is planned ahead of time, if possible.

Servants get up no later than 5:00 A.M. in summer and 6:00 A.M. in winter, the children an hour later. The cook prepares breakfast. The nursemaid puts out clothes for every child, prepares water and sponge, cleans the combs, etc. The cook should stay in the kitchen unless there is time to clean the rooms. At least once a week the rooms should be cleaned whenever possible, but not all on the same day.

Every Wednesday, the people in the house should do a laundry. Every last Wednesday in the month, there shall be a large laundry with an outside washerwoman. At least every Monday, the seamstress shall come into the house to fix what is necessary.

Every Thursday or Friday, bread is baked for the week; I think it is best to buy grain and have it ground, but to knead it at home.

Every Friday special bread (Barches) should be bought for the evening meal.

The kitchen list will be prepared and discussed every Thursday evening, jointly, by me and my wife; but my wish is to be decisive.

After this, provisions are to be bought every Friday at the market. For this purpose, my wife, herself, will go to the market on Fridays, accompanied by a servant; she can substitute a special woman who does errands (*Faktorfrau*) if she wishes, but not a servant.

All expenditures have to be written down daily and punctually.

The children receive a bath every Thursday evening. The children's clothes must be kept in a specially appointed chest, with a separate compartment for each child with the child's name upon it. The boys' suits and girls' dresses are to be kept separately. To keep used laundry, there must be a hamper easily accessible. Equally important is the food storage box in which provisions are kept in order, locked and safe from vermin.

The kitchen should be kept in order. Once a week all woodwork and copper must be scoured. The lights and lamps have to be cleaned daily. Toward servants, one has to be strict and just. Therefore, one should not call them names which aren't suitable for a decent wife. One should give them enough nourishing food. Disobedience and obstinacy are to be referred to me.

My wife will never make visits in my absence. However, she should visit the synagogue every Saturday—at least once a month; also she should go for a walk with the children at least once a week.

HELEN WATTERSON MOODY (1859–1928)

What It Means to Be a Wife   1899

The *Ladies' Home Journal*, by no means a radical magazine in 1899, attempted to show wives how best to serve their husbands and themselves. Helen Watterson Moody, a frequent contributor to the *Journal*, emphasizes methods by which a wife can "Keep Love Secure."

When a woman marries she assumes two new sets of relations—those of sentiment, through which she becomes the loving, faithful companion of one man and the mother of his children, and the economic relation, through which she becomes one of the great conserving and distributing agents of the world. Since I shall speak of these last two conditions later, I will now only consider that one sentimental relation whose beauty and holiness, if rightly assumed, give foundation to all the rest—that of wifehood.

Marriage is, or should be, primarily a relation of sentiment, yet the happiness of married life is decided by quite other things than sentiment—sturdy and steady moral qualities, good sense, and fair executive ability. I think the recognition of the fact that, though love is the supreme thing in married life, love alone is not enough, always comes to a newly married couple with a sense of surprise.

The Only Way to Keep Love Secure

In the first months of married life, love is so sufficient, and loving so simple, that there seems no other need in life. But by-and-by, when care begins to shadow them, when duties present themselves, and, strangely enough, conflict with each other, when convictions clash and tastes differ, then both husband and wife begin to realize that back of love must stand what I have called "steady and sturdy moral qualities"—justice, patience, honesty, and sincerity, and magnanimity. Indeed, on these depends the very continuance of love in marriage, for it is not possible to go on loving unless that is found which is worthy of love. I say this advisedly. I know the world is full of men and women who think, either because they like to think so, or sadly, because they must, that one can love where one does not respect. It seems to me that this does not ennoble one's ideal of love. One may pity, may have an infinite yearning tenderness over what one cannot respect, but love is of royal birth and recognizes only what is as royal as itself. The way, then, to keep love secure in married life is not so much to be anxiously watching and guarding lest it should escape, or crying that love has spread its wings because the first holiday romance is replaced by graver feeling, but by living along simply and honestly and frankly together, on a high plane, looking most and always toward "whatsoever things are true, whatsoever things are honest, whatsoever things are just, whatsoever things are pure, whatsoever things are lovely, whatsoever things are of good report." Then Love will be not a captive, but a most willing guest.

Marriage Is a Serious and Steady Occupation

That is why I say that the real happiness of married life depends largely upon the personal character that is put into it. Next in importance I place sound, good sense; and I mean by this that underlying sense of proportion by which one is able to discriminate the insignificant, the passing, the unimportant, from the grave, the permanent, the important—that capacity for steady, balancing thought which keeps one from impulsive words and rash deeds. A woman who is blessed with good sense does not consider at the start that marriage is a role to be skillfully and successfully enacted, or a grand frolic of which she is to be the admired and indulged center, or a mere incident in a life crowded with other activities. She knows that marriage is a serious and steady vocation, and that the true wife is one who enters marriage not thinking how much she can get out of it, but how much she can put into it. It is this larger conception of marriage which makes women dwell by their own firesides in sweet content with what is commonly called the "narrow limits of home," knowing well that no true home is narrow since it must give cover to "the whole primal mysteries of life—food, raiment, and work to earn them withal: love and marriage, birth and death, right-doing and wrong-doing—all these commonplaces of humanity which are most divine because they are most commonplace."

The way to make home a wide place to dwell in, is to bring a wide personality to dwell in it. Any home is just as wide as the maker, and can be no wider. When a woman understands this she is able to keep her head steady and her heart undisturbed over newspaper sketches about other women, in which each one of them is made to do the most remarkable and entirely unnecessary combination of things. [. . .]

Married Women Can Find Time If They Will

When I hear a married woman lament the lack of wide opportunities in her life I find myself wondering, in a kind of daze, what she means. If I inquire particularly, I usually discover that by lack of opportunities she means either the time for study and self-cultivation which she deeply desires, or else an opportunity for public activity and recognition. Well, both of these are good in their proper places, and there are few wives who will not be able to find some hours in the week to give to either one or the other. I suspect that in the case of those women who say they actually do not get time for study or music, or for an occasional club meeting, the trouble lies in the fact that they do not want to enough. For be sure of this, that in the long run a man or a woman usually finds time in life to do the thing that he or she wants to do most. A woman may desire the opportunity for self-culture and growth, but if she in her heart really prefers an hour of neighborhood gossip, or a piece of drawn linen for her luncheon table, or a vulgar profusion in the menu she offers her guests, she will have these and not the study. If, on the other hand, the intellectual quickening that comes from communion with big and earnest minds be the one thing in life that she feels she must have, be sure that in some degree she will have it—not enough of it, possibly, to satisfy her, but enough to make her life richer, because she will make her living less complex in order that she may have it.

FLORA TRISTAN (1803–1844)

London Journal: Prostitutes in London . . . All the Streets Are Full of Them 1842

TRANSLATED FROM THE FRENCH BY JEAN HAWKES

Flora Tristan, a French feminist, visited London often. Her journal was published in France in 1840 and translated into English in 1842. Among her many observations, her comments on the prostitutes of London establish the fact of their presence in remarkable numbers. Waterloo Bridge remained a notorious site for plying the trade of prostitution, both in the late nineteenth century and afterward. Tristan's detailed account implies a deep sympathy for the women involved.

[RIGHT] Scene in a brothel, from the *National Police Gazette,* July 26, 1879. (Collection of The New-York Historical Society, negative number 67854)

[BELOW] A scene from Hogarth's *Harlot's Progress*: A madam welcomes a newly arrived woman who will soon become part of the establishment. One of her customers looks on eagerly.

There are so many prostitutes in London that one sees them everywhere at any time of day; all the streets are full of them, but at certain times they flock in from outlying districts in which most of them live, and mingle with the crowds in theaters and public places. It is rare for them to take men home; their landlords would object, and besides their lodgings are unfit. They take their "captures" to the houses reserved for their trade. . . .

Between seven and eight o'clock one evening, accompanied by two friends armed with canes, I went to take a look at the new suburb which lies on either side of the long broad thoroughfare called Waterloo Road at the end of Waterloo Bridge. This neighborhood is almost entirely inhabited by prostitutes and people who live off prostitution; it is courting danger to go there alone at night. It was a hot summer evening; in every window and doorway women were laughing and joking with their protectors. Half dressed, some of them *naked to the waist,* they were a revolting sight, and the criminal, cynical expressions of their companions filled me with apprehension. These men are for the most part very good looking— young, vigorous, and well made—but their coarse and common air marks them as animals whose sole instinct is to satisfy their appetites. . . .

We went on our way and explored all the streets in the vicinity of Waterloo Road, then we sat upon the bridge to watch the women of the neighborhood flock past, as they do every night between the hours of eight and nine, on their way to the West End, where they ply their trade all through the night and return home between eight and nine in the morning. They infest the promenades and any other place where people gather, such as the approaches to the Stock Exchange, the various public buildings and the theaters, which they invade as soon as entry is reduced to half price. . . . After the play they move on to the "finishes"; these are squalid taverns or vast resplendent gin-palaces where people go to spend what remains of the night. . . .

I had heard descriptions of the debauchery to be seen at finishes, but could never bring myself to believe them. Now I was in London for the fourth time with the firm resolve to discover everything for myself. I determined to overcome my repugnance and go in person to one of these finishes. . . . The same friends who had accompanied me to the Waterloo Road again offered to be my guides. . . .

From the outside these "gin-palaces" with their carefully fastened shutters seem to be quietly slumbering; but no sooner has the doorkeeper admitted you by the little door reserved for the initiates than you are dazzled by the light of a thousand gas lamps. Upstairs there is a spacious salon divided down the middle; in one half there is a row of tables separated one from the other by wooden screens, as in all English restaurants. . . . In the other half there is a dais where the prostitutes parade in all their finery; seeking to arouse the men with their glances and remarks. . . .

Towards midnight the regular clients begin to arrive; several finishes are frequented by men in high society, and this is where the cream of the aristocracy gather. At first the young noblemen recline on the sofas, smoking and exchanging pleasantries with the women; then, when they have drunk enough for the fumes of champagne and Madeira to go to their heads, the illustrious scions of the English nobility, the very honorable members of Parliament remove their coats, untie their cravats, take off their waistcoats and braces, and proceed to set up their private boudoir in a public place. Why not make themselves at home, since they are paying out so much money for the right to display their contempt. . . . The orgy rises to a crescendo; between four and five o'clock in the morning it reaches its height.

At this point it takes a good deal of courage to remain in one's seat, a mute spectator of all that takes place. What a worthy use these English lords make of their immense fortunes! How fine and generous they are when they have lost the use of their reason and offer fifty, even a hundred guineas to a prostitute if she will lend herself to all the obscenities that drunkenness engenders. . . .

For in a finish there is no lack of entertainment. One of the favorite sports is to *ply a woman with drink* until she falls dead drunk upon the floor, then to make her swallow a draught compounded of *vinegar, mustard, and pepper;* this invariably throws the poor creature into horrible convulsions, and her spasms and contortions provoke the *honorable company* to gales of laughter and infinite amusement. Another diversion much appreciated at these fashionable gatherings is to empty the contents of the nearest glass upon the women as they lie insensible on the ground. I have seen satin dresses of no recognizable color, only a confused mass of stains; wine, brandy, beer, tea, coffee, cream, etc. . . . daubed all over them in a thousand fantastic shapes. . . . The air is heavy with the noxious odors of food, drink, tobacco, and others more fetid still which seize you by the throat, grip your temples in a vice, and make your senses reel: it is indescribably horrible! . . . However, this life, which continues relentlessly night after night, is the prostitute's sole hope of a fortune, for she has no hold on the Englishman when he is sober. *The sober Englishman is chaste to the point of prudery.*

It is usually between seven and eight o'clock in the morning when people leave the finish. The servants go out to look for cabs, and anyone still on his feet gathers up his clothes and returns home; as for the rest, the pot-boys dress them in the first garments that come to hand, bundle them into a cab, and tell the cabman where to deliver them. Often nobody knows their address; then they are deposited in the cellar and left to sleep in the straw. This place is known as the drunkards hole, and there they stay until they have recovered their wits sufficiently to say where they wish to be taken.

A Letter to the *Times* (London) from a Prostitute 1858

After a concerted effort on the part of prominent London citizens to reduce prostitution in London, a prostitute who referred to herself as "one of that abandoned sisterhood" came forth with the following letter, filled with suggestions about how to improve the circumstances of the prostitute and her customers. She hopes to avoid the "persecution" of individuals while London attempts to deal with a vice it considers a nuisance.

Sir:

Certain Persons have, as you know, commenced a crusade against London Prostitutes, and, if one of that abandoned sisterhood may presume to address you, grant me your attention.

The precept and example set me by parents, now, thank God, in their graves; the education likewise "thrown away" upon me, and my subsequent experience as a governess in a highly respectable family, were not necessary to the conviction that the class among which I may be numbered consists of outcasts whose undisguised pursuit is an offense to the laws of God and man.

I know that we are cut off from the moral, social, and religious worlds. . . . We need not be told of our ruin and degradation, because we never "fall" without being alive to the fact. A woman seduced may forgive her wrongs . . . it is impossible for her to forget what she is; society will not permit her to do so. . . . Do not suppose, then, that I would attempt to defend what transpires nightly in the Haymarket, in Coventry Street, or wherever women of my caste congregate. I do not ask you to countenance anything of the kind. No, Sir, give "Vice its own image" and do your duty.

But, while you yourself refrain from going a step too far, pray give a warning to others. It is one thing to put down a nuisance. It is another to persecute individuals. I will anticipate much that may fairly be said, and admit that if I live avowedly in defiance of those regulations which the community has established as essential to its well being . . . I must expect to be checked in such openly vicious courses, for I believe the liberty of the subject should end where injustice to others begins. But pray tell those good gentlemen who are bent on "putting us down," that theirs is not only a delicate, but a difficult undertaking, and they should be careful lest they have more to answer for than they dream of in their philosophy.

The vice of London, Sir, is seen to float upon its surface; let it pass as the weed on its way to the ocean. If it accumulates so as to become offensive, disperse it. If it is otherwise annoying and cannot conveniently be avoided, deal with it accordingly.

Appoint commissioners who are fitted for the office, intelligent, respectable, and responsible gentlemen, and make it worth their while to devote themselves entirely to the reduction of the scandal complained of. Empower these officials to have us taken up and punished for riot or impropriety of any kind. But let not the "pelting petty officer," the ignorant constable of a few shillings a week, and it may be an unfeeling and unthinking brute, interfere with us as he will. Recollect it was man who made us what we are. It is man who pays for the finery, the rouge, and the gin . . . it is man who, when we apply ourselves to industry and honesty, employs us upon starvation wages; and if man had his way, and women's nature were not superior to his, there would be no virtue extant. Say, then, is it for man to persecute even the most profligate among us?

Pray, Sir, think of this, and tell those gentlemen whose speeches I read to act upon it. They may be husbands and fathers . . . and I allow for their parental solicitude. But if they be Christians they will imitate one who said, "Go, and sin no more," and not "move on," "anywhere, anywhere, out of the world."

Your humble servant,

ONE MORE UNFORTUNATE

BARBARA MEIL HOBSON
Successful Madams   1987

In this brief excerpt, Hobson describes prostitutes who became "successful entrepreneurs" and achieved positions similar to that of Mrs. Warren in Bernard Shaw's play. However, very few prostitutes ever became financially independent. Mrs. Warren is remarkable for her success, not for her profession.

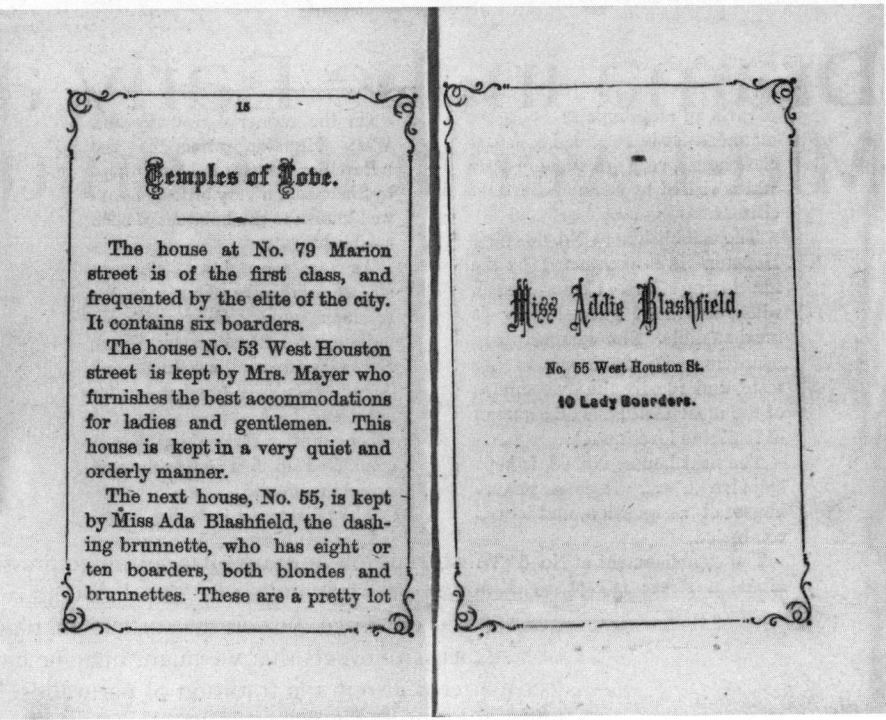

The Gentleman's Directory, Temples of Love, address listings, 1870. Published directories such as this one informed men where to find the best brothels. Even newspapers carried discreet advertisements when prostitutes changed houses so that they would not lose their regular clientele.
(Collection of The New-York Historical Society, negative number 54525)

On the other hand, the image of the prostitute as someone who accumulates savings from her trade, wisely invests her capital, and obtains a small fortune was not very realistic either. We know of some famous successful madams at the turn of the century, including the Everleigh sisters, who operated gilded palaces of vice in Chicago, and Nell Kimball, the famous "queen" of Storeyville. They were the successful entrepreneurs of the demimonde, and they even published their memoirs.

What little we know of typical prostitutes' futures suggests that few women achieved upward economic mobility through prostitution. The nineteenth-century police registers tell us that women in regulated prostitution were most likely to reenter traditional working class occupations. [...] The fees Swedish prostitutes had to pay for medical examinations, the percentages madams took for room and board, and the expenses for dress and cosmetics did not leave very much money for savings. Prostitutes in the high-class brothels in nineteenth-century American cities were paid high prices for their sexual services. But madams usually took 50 percent of a prostitute's receipts, and expenses were high. In addition, prostitutes in many of these cities had to take a cut from their earnings for police protection. Research on nineteenth-century St. Paul documents that career paths within prostitution were limited. Only four out of sixty-one brothel prostitutes listed in official records became madams, a revealing statistic in a city where prostitution was aboveboard—unofficially licensed.

Drama in the Early and Mid-Twentieth Century

The realist tradition in drama has certain expressionist qualities evident in the symbolic actions in Strindberg's *Miss Julie* and certain romantic fantasies seen in later plays of Ibsen. But on the surface the plays appear realistic, consisting of a sequence of events that we might imagine happening in real life. The subject matter is also in the tradition of naturalism because it is drawn from life and not beautified or toned down for the middle-class audience.

But in the early to mid-twentieth century, realistic drama took a new turn, incorporating distortions of reality that border on the unreal or *surreal*. From the time of Anton Chekhov in 1903 to that of Samuel Beckett in the 1950s, drama exploited the possibilities of realism, antirealism, and the poetic expansion of expressionism.

The Heritage of Realism

In the late nineteenth century, realism was often perceived as too severe for an audience that had loved melodrama. Realistic plays forced comfortable audiences to observe psychological and physical problems that their status as members of the middle class usually allowed them to avoid. Audiences often protested loudly at this painful experience.

Early in the twentieth century, Susan Glaspell (1876–1948) began writing plays for the pleasure of having them read in her own living room in Provincetown, Massachusetts. *Trifles* (1916) told the story of a murdered husband in a deadpan fashion without alluding directly to the abusive nature of the husband and the ultimate resistance of the wife. The play may be said to be realistic on the surface, but its deep structure is symbolic, and its indirectness implies an experimental attitude toward the writing of plays.

The technique of realism could, however, be adapted for many different purposes, and eventually realism was reshaped to satisfy middle-class sensibilities by commercial playwrights, who produced popular, pleasant plays. By the 1920s in Europe and the 1930s in the United States, theatergoing audiences expected plays to be realistic. Even the light comedies dominating the commercial stage were in a more or less realistic mode. Anything that disturbed the illusion of realism was thought to be a flaw.

Reactions to the comfortable use of realistic techniques were numerous, especially after World War I. One extreme reaction was that of **Dadaism**. Through the Dadaists' chief propagandist, Tristan Tzara (1896–1963), the group promoted an art that was essentially enigmatic and incoherent to the average person. That was its point. The Dadaists blamed World War I on sensible, middle-class people who were logical and well intentioned but never questioned convention. The brief plays that were performed in many Dadaist clubs in Europe often featured actors speaking simultaneously so that nothing they said could be understood. The purpose was to confound the normal expectations of theatergoers.

Other developments were also making it possible for playwrights to experiment and move away from a strict reliance on "comfortable" realism. By World War I, motion pictures had begun to make melodramatic entertainment available to most people in the world. Even when films were silent, they relied on techniques that had been common on the nineteenth-century stage. With their growing domination of popular dramatic entertainment, films provided an outlet for the expectations of middle-class audiences, freeing more imaginative playwrights to experiment and develop in different directions.

Realism and Myth

The incorporation of myth in drama offered new opportunities to expand the limits of realism. Sigmund Freud's theories of psychoanalysis at the turn of the century stimulated a new interest in myth and dreams as psychological links between people. Freud studied Greek myths for clues to the psychic state of his patients, and he published a number of commentaries on Greek plays and on *Hamlet*. (See excerpt on pp. 101–104.) The psychologist Carl Jung, a follower of Freud who eventually split with him, helped give a powerful impetus to the interest in dreams and the symbolism of myth by suggesting that all members of a culture share an inborn knowledge of the basic myths of the culture. Jung postulated a collective unconscious, a repository of mythic material in the mind that all humans inherit as part of their birthright. This theory gave credence to the power of myth in everyday life; along with Freud's theories, it was one of the most important ideas empowering drama and other art forms in the twentieth century. Playwrights who used elements of myth in their plays produced a poetic form of realism that dealt with a level of truth common to all humans.

Myth and Culture

Some non-European drama depends on interpretation of local myth in relation to the culture or cultures that produce it. Wole Soyinka's background as a Nigerian familiar with Yoruba culture and myth, along with his formal education in England, prepared him for a career that expanded the horizons of drama for both Nigerian and European audiences.

Soyinka's experimentation has spanned two traditions—modern European theater and modern ritual theater of the Yoruba people of Nigeria. Traditional Yoruba drama develops from religious celebrations and annual festivals and includes music and dance. Soyinka's plays, including *The Strong Breed* (1962), concern themselves with African traditions and issues, but they often also explore mythic forces that link European and African cultures. His plays have been produced throughout the world and have demonstrated the universality of community and the anxiety it sometimes breeds in the individual. Soyinka has also written critical studies on Yoruba tragedy and has interpreted, translated, and produced Greek tragedy.

Poetic Realism

The Abbey Theatre in Dublin, which functioned with distinction from the turn of the century, produced major works by John Millington Synge, W. B. Yeats, Sean O'Casey, and Lady Gregory. Lady Gregory's peasant plays concentrated on the charming, the amusing, and occasionally the grotesque. She tried to represent the dialect she heard in the west of Ireland, a dialect that was distinctive, poetic, and colorful. She also took advantage of local Irish myths and used some of them for her most powerful plays, such as *Dervorgilla* and *Grania,* both portraits of passionate women from Irish legend and myth.

John Millington Synge, like Lady Gregory, was interested in both myth and peasant dialects. His plays are difficult to fit into a realist mold, although they are sometimes naturalistic on the surface. Some audiences reacted violently to his portrayals of peasant life because they were unflattering. Synge's plays were sometimes directly connected with ancient Irish myth; *Deirdre of the Sorrows* (1910) concerns a willful Irish princess who runs off with a young warrior and his brothers on the eve of her wedding to an old king. The story ends sadly for Deirdre, and she is regarded as a fated heroine, assuming almost the stature of a Greek tragic figure. Synge's most popular one-act play, *Riders to the Sea* (1904), reveals his gift for emulating the Irish way of speaking English in Ireland's western county of Mayo. His creation of peasant dialogue remains one of his most important contributions to modern drama.

In the United States, Eugene O'Neill, influenced by Strindberg, experimented with realism, first by presenting stark, powerful plays that disturbed his audiences. *The Hairy Ape* (1922) portrayed a primitive coal stoker on a passenger liner who awakened base emotions in the more refined passengers. In *The Emperor Jones* (1920), O'Neill produced the first important American expressionist play. The shifting scenery, created by lighting, was dreamlike and at times frightening. The experience of the play reflected the frightening psychic experiences of the main character, Brutus Jones.

O'Neill also experimented with more poetic forms of realism. In *Desire under the Elms* (1924), he explores the myth of Phaedra—centering on her incestuous love for her husband's son—but sets it in rural New England on a rocky farm. In the tradition of realism, the play treats unpleasant themes: a son's distrust and dishonoring of his father, lust between a son and his stepmother, and the murder of a baby to "prove" love. But it is not simply realistic. Without its underpinning of myth, the play would be sordid, but the myth helps us see that fate operates even today, not in terms of messages from the gods but rather in terms of messages from our hearts and bodies. Lust is a force in nature that drives and destroys.

Meanwhile, in Fascist Spain, Federico García Lorca, also a poetic realist, was uncovering dark emotional centers of the psyche in his *House of Bernarda Alba* (1936), which explores erotic forces repressed and then set loose. Lorca was opposed to Fascism and was murdered by a Fascist agent. His plays reveal a bleakness of spirit that helps us imagine the darkness—moral and psychological—that enveloped Europe in the 1940s.

Social Realism

Ten years after *Desire under the Elms* enjoyed popularity, a taste for plays based on **social realism** developed. This was realism with a political conscience. Because the world was in the throes of a depression that had reduced many people to destitution and homelessness, drama began to aim at awakening governments to the consequences of unbridled capitalism and the depressions that freewheeling economies produced.

Plays such as Jack Kirkland's *Tobacco Road* (1933), adapted from Erskine Caldwell's novel, presented a grim portrait of rural poverty in the United States. Sidney Kingsley's *Dead End* (1935) portrayed the lives of virtually homeless boys on the Lower East Side of Manhattan. In the same year, Maxwell Anderson produced a verse tragedy, *Winterset*, with gangsters and gangsterism at its core. Also in 1935, Clifford Odets produced *Waiting for Lefty*, an openly leftist labor drama. These plays' realist credentials lay primarily in their effort to show audiences portraits of life that might shock their middle-class sensibilities.

Realism and Expressionism

O'Neill's later plays shed the underpinnings of myth and developed a powerful realistic style, as seen in *The Iceman Cometh* (1939), set in a dingy bar filled with patrons living on the edge, listening to Theodor Hickman (Hickey) and Harry Hope give their philosophy of life. During this period, O'Neill also wrote a haunting one-act play, *Hughie* (1941), set in a shabby hotel lobby late at night. In it, Erie Smith, a small-time gambler, shares his views of life with the hotel night manager, Charlie Hughes. The play is simple but intense and moving. One of O'Neill's greatest plays, *Long Day's Journey into Night*, completed in 1941 but not published or produced until 1956, took him in a new direction. For the first time, he began an analysis of his own tortured family background, which included alcoholism and drug addiction. The play was so searing and painful that O'Neill sequestered it with Random House, instructing publisher Bennett Cerf not to publish it until twenty-five years after his death. O'Neill's wife, however, broke the will and had the play produced. It has since become the vehicle for some of the best performances of the latter part of the twentieth century.

After Eugene O'Neill's experiments, later American dramatists looked for new ways to expand the resources of realism while retaining its power. The use of **expressionism**—often poetic in language and effect—was one solution that appealed to both Tennessee Williams and Arthur Miller. Expressionism developed in the first and second decades of the twentieth century. The movement began in Germany and was influenced by some of Strindberg's work. Because expressionism takes many forms, there is no simple way to define the term except as an alternative to realistic drama. Instead of having realistic sets, the stage may sometimes be barren or flooded with light or draped. Characters sometimes become symbolic; dialogue is often sharp, abrupt, enigmatic. The German theater saw its earliest developments of expressionism in the work of Frank Wedekind, whose first play, *Spring Awakening*, abandoned a naturalistic style to explore sexual repression. Wedekind's work influenced later German playwrights such as George Kaiser, Ernst Toller, Erwin Piscator, and Bertolt Brecht, whose *Three-penny Opera* (1928) incorporated some of the hallmarks of expressionism, such as a music-hall atmosphere and broadly drawn characters.

Later American playwrights modified the characteristics of expressionism; they melded expressionist elements, such as fantastic sets and highly poetic diction, with a relatively realistic style. Tennessee Williams's *The Glass Menagerie*

Figure 21. Expressionistic setting in Arthur Miller's *Death of a Salesman*.

(1944) and Arthur Miller's *Death of a Salesman* (1949) both use expressionist techniques. Williams's poetic stage directions make clear that he is drawing on nonrealistic dramatic devices. He describes the scene as "memory and . . . therefore nonrealistic." He calls for an interior "rather dim and poetic," and he uses a character who also steps outside the staged action to serve as a narrator—one who "takes whatever license with dramatic convention as is convenient to his purposes." As the narrator tells his story, the walls of the building seem to melt away, revealing the inside of a house and the lives and fantasies of his mother and sister, both caught in their own distorted visions of life.

Arthur Miller's original image for *Death of a Salesman* was the inside of Willy Loman's mind; Jo Mielziner's expressionist set represented his idea as a cross-section of Loman's house. As the action in one room concluded, lights went up to begin action in another (Figure 21). This evocative staging influenced the production of numerous plays by later writers. In the original set, a scrim, or gauze screen, was painted with branches and leaves. When this scrim was lit from the front for memory scenes, the set was transformed to evoke an earlier time when the sons were boys.

Miller used expressionist techniques to create the hallucinatory sequences when Willy talks with Ben, the man who walked into the jungle poor and walked out a millionaire, and when Biff recalls seeing Willy with the woman in Boston.

For Williams and Miller, expressionism offered a way to bring other worlds to bear on the staged action—the worlds of dream and fantasy. And although expressionism made some inroads in American theater, the techniques of realism persisted and developed. Lorraine Hansberry's *A Raisin in the Sun* (1959) uses basically realistic staging and dialogue to portray the difficulties of the members of one family in reaching for opportunity to overcome poverty. Hansberry does not use the expressionist techniques of Miller. Her only exotic touch is the visit of the African young man, Asagai, who offers a moment of cultural counterpoint. Hansberry's realism is essentially conservative.

Antirealism

Surrealism (literally, "beyond realism") in the early twentieth century was based originally on an interpretation of experience not through the lucid mind of the waking person but through the mind of the dreamer, the unconscious mind that Freud described. Surrealism augmented or, for some playwrights, supplanted realism and became a means of distorting reality for emotional purposes.

When Pirandello's six characters come onstage looking for their author in *Six Characters in Search of an Author* (1921), no one believes that they are characters rather than actors. Pirandello's play is an examination of the realities we take for granted in drama. He turns the world of expectation in drama upside down. He reminds us that what we assume to be real is always questionable: we cannot be sure of anything; we must presume that things are true, and in some cases we must take them on faith.

Pirandello's philosophy dominated his stories, plays, and novels. His questioning of the certainty of human knowledge was designed to undermine his audience's faith in an absolute reality. Modern physicists have concurred with philosophers, ancient and modern, who question everyday reality. Pirandello was influenced by the modern theories of relativity that physicists were developing, and he found in them validation of his own attack on certainty.

Epic Theater

Bertolt Brecht (1898–1956) began writing plays just after World War I. He was a political dramatist who rejected the theater of his day, which valued the realistic "well-made play," in which all the parts fit perfectly together and function almost as a machine. His feeling was that such plays were too mechanical, like a "clockwork mouse."

Exploring the style of his predecessor Irwin Piscator, Brecht developed **epic theater**. The term implies a sequence of actions or episodes of the kind found in Homer's *Iliad*. In epic theater, the sense of dramatic illusion is continually counteracted by reminders from the stage that one is watching a play. Stark, harsh lighting, blank stages, placards announcing changes of scenes, bands playing music onstage, and long, discomfiting pauses make it impossible for an audience to become totally immersed in a realistic illusion. Brecht, offering a genuine alternative to realistic drama, wanted the audience to analyze a play's thematic content rather than to sit back and be entertained. He believed that realistic drama convinced audiences that the play's vision of reality described not just things as they are but things as they must be. Such drama, Brecht asserted, helped maintain the social problems that it portrayed by reinforcing, rather than challenging, their reality.

Brecht's *Mother Courage* (written in 1939) is an antiwar drama staged early in World War II (1941). The use of song, an unreal setting, and an unusual historical perspective (the Thirty Years' War in the seventeenth century) help to achieve the "defamiliarization" that Brecht thought drama ought to produce in its audiences. The techniques of epic theater in *Galileo* (1938–1939) and *The Good Woman of Setzuan* (1943)—a study of the immoralities that prosper under capitalism—were imitated by playwrights in the 1950s. Hardly a major play from that period is free of Brecht's influence.

Absurdist Drama

The critic Martin Esslin coined the term **theater of the absurd** when describing the work of Samuel Beckett (1906–1989), the Irish playwright whose dramas often dispense with almost everything that makes a well-made play well made. Some of his plays have no actors onstage—amplified breathing is the only hint of human presence in one case. Some have little or no plot; others have no words. His theater is minimalist, offering a stage reality that seems cut to the bone, without the usual realistic devices of plot, character development, and intricate setting.

Eugène Ionesco (1909–1994) is said to have been the first of the postwar absurdist dramatists, with his production of *The Bald Soprano* and *The Lesson* (both in 1951). Ionesco called them "anti-plays" because they avoided the normal causal relationship of actions and realistic expectations of conventional drama.

The theater of the absurd assumes that the world is meaningless, that meaning is a human concept, and that individuals must create significance and not rely on institutions or traditions to provide it. The absurdist movement grew out of **existentialism**, a postwar French philosophy demanding that the individual face the emptiness of the universe and create meaning in a life that has no inherent meaning. Beckett's *Waiting for Godot* (1952) captured the modern imagination and established a landmark in absurdist drama.

In *Waiting for Godot,* two tramps, Vladimir and Estragon, meet near a tree where they expect Godot to arrive to talk with them. The play has two acts that both end with a small boy explaining that Godot cannot come today but will come tomorrow. Godot is not coming, and the tramps who wait for Godot will wait forever. While they wait, they entertain themselves with vaudeville routines and eventually are met by a rich man, Pozzo, and his slave, Lucky. Lucky, on the command "Think, pig," speaks in a stream of garbled phrases that evoke Western philosophy and religion but that remain incoherent. Pozzo and Lucky have no interest in joining Vladimir and Estragon in waiting for Godot. They leave the two alone, waiting—afraid to leave for fear of missing Godot, but uncertain that Godot will ever arrive.

Beckett seems to be saying that in an absurd world, such gestures are necessary to create the sense of significance that people need to live. His characters' awareness of an audience and his refusal to create a drama in which an audience can "lose" itself in a comfortable surface of realistic illusion are, in their own way, indebted to Brecht.

Beckett's *Krapp's Last Tape* (1958) places some extraordinary limitations on performance. Krapp is the only person onstage throughout the play, and his dialogues are with tapes of himself made many years before. The situation is absurd, but as Beckett reveals to us, the absurd has its own complexities, and situations such as Krapp's can sustain complex interpretations. Beckett expects his audience to analyze the drama, not merely to be entertained.

The illusion of reality is shed almost entirely in *Endgame* (1957). Hamm cannot move. His parents, both legless, are in trashcans onstage. Clov performs all the play's movement on a barren, cellarlike stage.

Beckett's *Happy Days* (1961) is generally thought to be his most optimistic play. Winnie, who talks almost nonstop throughout, seems mired in trivia and the details of everyday life. Yet, she can pause for philosophical observations on the nature of her existence and position herself thoughtfully in regard to the world. In the first act she is buried in a mound of earth up to her waist, and in the second act she is buried up to her neck, but her positive attitude intensifies. She is doing the best she can. Willy, her husband, hardly says a word and does not begin to act until the last minute of the play, at which time his action is ambiguous. *Happy Days*, while similar to Beckett's other absurdist plays, still intrigues audiences in the twenty-first century. It speaks to the hopeful among us, but it also offers a view of life that is far from sugar coated. It is absurd in the sense that it does not offer an easy answer to the questions raised by the limitations of Winnie's and Willy's existence.

The great plays of this period reflect the values of the cultures from which they spring. They make comments on life in the modern world and question the values that the culture takes for granted. The drama of this part of the twentieth century is a drama of examination.

The Early- and Mid-Twentieth-Century Stage

The physical stage continued its evolution into the twentieth century, although it depended on the proscenium arch and the concept of the "fourth wall" most of the time, especially in the development of the musical theater, which was, to an extent, a substitute for the nineteenth-century melodrama. With early silent films and then mid-century musicals, the popular stage was still home to melodramatic entertainment.

One of the primary aims of early-twentieth-century theater designs was to create spaces in which the audience and the actors became more intimate than in the pure proscenium theater, which treated the audience almost as voyeurs. The smaller theaters, such as the Vieux Colombier (Figure 22), opened the proscenium and extended the stage forward, making it possible for actors to be much closer to the audience and to produce a more involving experience.

In France and England, so-called little theaters developed quickly even before the first world war, taking advantage of this newfound intimacy. In the United States, the growth of "little" theaters led to the founding, in 1915, of the Provincetown Players by George Cram Cook, Eugene O'Neill, and Susan Glaspell. This company held its early performances at the end of a wharf in an old abandoned fish house in Provincetown, Massachusetts (see Figure 23).

Eventually the Provincetown Players moved to New York City, where the Provincetown Playhouse still exists, now connected with New York University. Most major cities (Boston, New York, Chicago, and Detroit) and even some smaller cities produced plays in "little" theaters, some of which still exist. The Theatre Guild formed in 1919 in the United States for the purpose of producing plays that were not likely to have a broad commercial appeal. It became one of the most distinguished theater companies of its time.

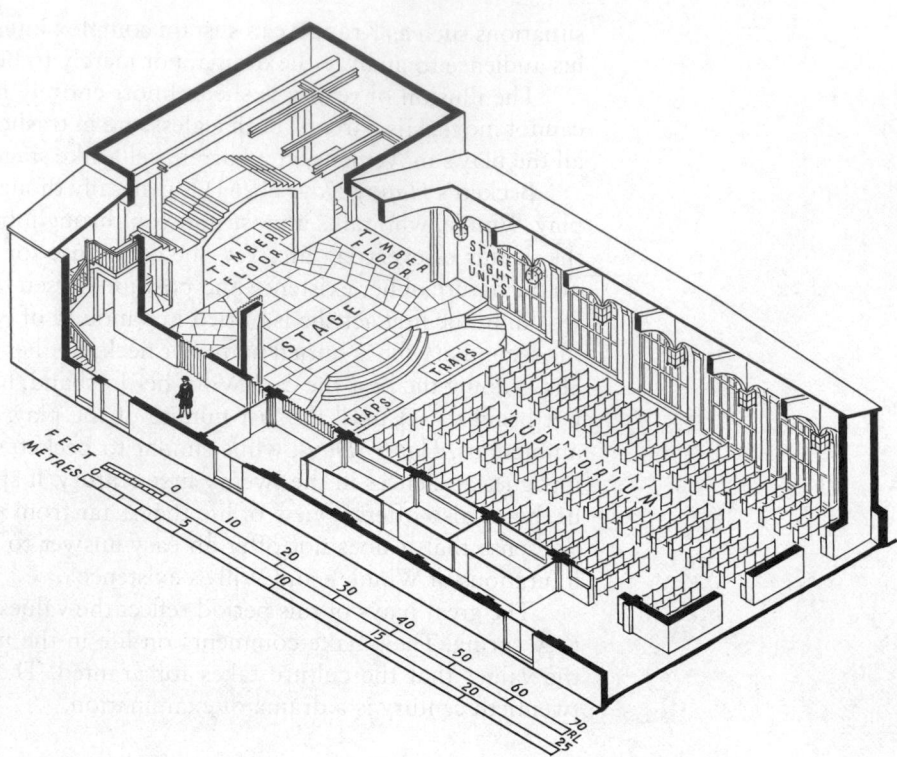

Figure 22. The Vieux Colombier, Paris, 1920.

Although he worked directly on stage in Paris for only a few years in the 1920s, Antonin Artaud (1896–1948) made a lasting impression on drama theory and theatrical space. His concept of the **theater of cruelty** helped shape the modern theater as we know it. The cruelty he prosposed was psychological in that he wanted the audience to relinquish its comfortable and privileged position in the theater and to feel the discomfort produced by facing unpleasant ideas and events. This was a complete departure from the goal of earlier melodrama, which soothed the audience with happy endings and avoided raising profound and unanswerable questions. Artaud proposed avoiding standard theaters altogether and moving drama into a barn or warehouse or similar open space. Even today, many small theater companies follow his lead and perform in such spaces as garages and storefronts.

Technical developments in larger theaters naturally continued throughout the early part of the century, with improved lighting, revolving stages, and complex arrangements of flies that lowered and then raised elaborate scenery for set changes. Some experiments in staging brought the audience to all sides of the stage so that they were virtually "involved" in such necessary activities as entrances and exits. Theater in the round developed in the 1930s, and it helped create some of the most intense experiences in the mid-century, particularly those that depended on surrealist effects. Artaud was a proponent of theater in the round because the audience could never feel separated from the action, as it would in a proscenium theater. Many of the stage settings in the larger theaters in Europe and the United States generated exciting visual designs for expressionist and surrealist plays that are still talked about as visionary productions.

Figure 23 The original theater of the Provincetown Players was a converted fishing shack on Lewis Wharf, in Provincetown, Massachusetts.

Expressionist drama, such as *Miss Julie* and other late-nineteenth-century experimental works, often attempted to examine transformations of the inner life of characters through the use of symbolism. Expressionist plays favored a certain form of abstraction, represented in their stage settings, that attempted to be emotionally representational rather than realistic in the usual sense. The stage settings for O'Neill's plays, as well as those for Elmer Rice's *The Adding Machine* (1923), have been interpreted in many interesting ways, but they are often described as symbolic. In a Queens College production of Rice's *The Adding Machine*, the primary character is Mr. Zero, who eventually kills Boss. The sets allude visually to the machine, as in Figure 24, where the interior of the machine suggests a virtual cave as Mr. Zero approaches Heaven. The play itself is a commentary on the influence of the machine on modern life, and it may be even more relevant in the twenty-first century than it was in the twentieth.

The Early- and Mid-Twentieth-Century Actor

From the Moscow Art Theater in the late 1890s to the Group Theatre in the United States in 1931, the most persistent influence on acting and acting theory was Constantin Stanislavski (1863–1938) (Figure 25). Stanislavski, a name

Figure 24. Elmer Rice's *The Adding Machine*, Queens College Drama, Theatre, and Dance Production, 1999.

adopted for the stage, was born into a prosperous Russian family but decided to make his own way acting and directing. His productions of Gorky and Chekhov were legendary, and it was while working on these plays that he developed acting techniques that actors are still using today. He wished above all to encourage a natural style of acting that would be instantly recognized as offering insight into the truth of life. Years of successful melodramas had produced an exaggerated mode of acting, both "theatrical" in the pejorative sense and rhetorical in its demand for attention. It was against this "star" system, which relied entirely on stars of the magnitude of Edwin Forrest, William Macready, Edmund Kean, Junius Brutus Booth, William Gillette, Sarah Bernhardt, and others, that Stanislavski rebelled.

Instead, Stanislavski insisted that the actor prepare for a role using a method rooted in modern psychology—searching for the subconscious energy that would inform the actor and permit him or her to understand a character's most profound feelings. Applying Stanislavski's method, the actor should first analyze the scenes carefully to establish the underlying motive of the character and then attempt to recreate within himself or herself the motivation and the emotional content of the action by reflecting on his or her own life and drawing from a personal store of emotional experience. Only then was the actor ready to go on stage and perform the scene.

Stanislavski also developed exercises for actors, some of which he discusses in *An Actor Prepares* (1936). One of the exercises on his principle of concentration of attention requires that the actor concentrate on something

Figure 25. Constantin Stanislavski as Gayev in Chekhov's *The Cherry Orchard*, 1923.

on stage—it must arrest the actor's attention and utterly absorb the actor in order to generate the closeness to truth that Stanislavski demanded from his company. As he said, "Here we are dealing with powers of observation that are subconscious in their origin. Our ordinary type of attention is not sufficiently far-reaching to carry out the process of penetrating another person's soul." Some of the most famous actors of the twentieth century, including Marlon Brando, Al Pacino, Jane Fonda, and Jack Nicholson, employed the basic principles of "The Method," which they learned as students of Lee Strasberg's Actor's Studio in New York City in the 1940s and 1950s.

Some form of naturalism was dominant on the stage in the first half of the century, but expressionist plays such as O'Neill's *The Emperor Jones* (1920), *The Hairy Ape* (1922), and *The Great God Brown* (1926) depended on a style of acting that verged on distortion and exaggeration. The characters were meant to be larger than life, so the style of acting followed suit, but it could not be described as overly theatrical in the style that Stanislavski and others condemned. Many of the best actors of the period also worked in films. Examples include Emile Jannings (1887–1950), Sir Cedric Hardwicke (1893–1964), Sibyl Thorndike (1882–1976), John Barrymore (1882–1942), and Laurette Taylor (1884–1946). Each was renowned, but much of their best work was done in film and not on the stage. Most of these distinguished actors relied on conventional acting training rather than following Stanislavski, although most of them were aware of his ideas and were, if only indirectly, affected by them.

On a theoretical level, the work of Bertolt Brecht (1898–1956) reinforced Artaud's ideas about acting and the structure of drama in Europe and elsewhere between the two world wars. Brecht's concept of epic theater and the "alienation effect" took root and influenced theaters and actors everywhere. For example, Brecht insisted on controlling the amount of empathy an actor on stage might evoke. He also wished to avoid "magic" on stage, by which he meant the creation of an illusion of reality. In this sense, he was anti-Aristotelian. He said,

> On the Epic stage, no attempt is made to create the atmosphere of a particular place (a room at evening, a street in autumn), or to generate a mood by a broken speech-rhythm. The actor does not warm the audience up by unloosing a flood of temperament, nor cast a spell over them by tightening his muscles. In short, no effort is made to put the audience into a trance and give them the illusion of witnessing natural, unrehearsed events.

Brecht's staging often was symbolic in nature, and his actors often were outfitted in oversized clothing and spoke in an unnatural fashion. His staging employed dance and/or music as needed. A Communist protesting the brutalities of the Nazis, Brecht expressed a political message between the wars, as in his extraordinary play *Galileo*, which was written in 1938 and 1939 and was first produced in Hollywood in 1947, with Charles Laughton in the title role. Galileo had been punished by the Catholic Church for his discovery that the earth revolves around the sun, not the other way around. Brecht's *Galileo* became a symbol for people resisting tyranny of all kinds. Brecht, like many other playwrights in the first half of the twentieth century, was searching for ways to express serious ideas through the medium of drama. They knew they could not rely on the ordinary realistic styles of the late nineteenth century, so they had to invent new ways to write and new ways to act.

Early- and Mid-Twentieth-Century Drama

Date	Theater	Political	Social/Cultural
1850–1900	**1853–1931:** David Belasco, American producer who uses pictorial realism in staging and creates "stars" on the New York stage	**1857:** Sepoy mutiny in India against British officers	**1853:** U.S. Navy arrives in Tokyo Bay to negotiate a trade treaty.
	1862–1928: Adolphe Appia, influential Swiss designer	**1861–1865:** Civil War in the United States	**1861:** Russia emancipates its serfs.
	1863–1938: Constantin Stanislavski, Russian actor and director	**1867:** Dominion of Canada is formed.	**1863:** U.S. Emancipation Proclamation frees slaves.
	1871–1909: John Millington Synge, Irish playwright, author of *Riders to the Sea* (1904) and *The Playboy of the Western World* (1907)	**1868–1912:** Meiji period in Japan	**1869:** The Suez Canal opens.
	1872–1966: Edward Gordon Craig, influential English theatrical designer	**1871:** Feudalism in Japan ends.	
	1873–1943: Max Reinhardt, Austrian director, producer, and theorist		
	1880–1964: Sean O'Casey, Irish playwright, author of *Juno and the Paycock* (1924) and *The Plough and the Stars* (1926)		**1876:** General George Custer's troops are destroyed at Little Big Horn by Sioux-Cheyennes.
	1887–1954: Robert Edmond Jones, revolutionary American scenic designer		**1880–1914:** All of Africa (except Ethiopia) is rapidly colonized by European and Turkish authorities.
	1888–1953: Eugene O'Neill, American playwright among whose works are *Desire under the Elms* (1924), *Mourning Becomes Electra* (1931), and *Long Day's Journey into Night* (1939–1941)	**1889:** First Japanese Constitution is enacted.	
	1896–1948: Antonin Artaud, French playwright, poet, actor, and director	**1895:** China is defeated in war by Japan. Korea becomes independent.	
	1898–1956: Bertolt Brecht, German playwright, author of *The Threepenny Opera* (1928), *Mother Courage* (1941), and *The Good Woman of Setzuan* (1943)	**1898:** Spanish-American War. Cuba is freed from Spain.	
	1898: The Irish Literary Society is founded by W. B. Yeats (1865–1939) and Lady Augusta Gregory (1852–1932). The group leads the way in creating an indigenous Irish theater.	**1899–1902:** Boer War in South Africa	

Date	Theater	Political	Social/Cultural
1900–1950	**1901–1976:** Jo Mielziner, set designer	**1900:** The Boxer Rebellion attempts to curtail Western commercial interests in China.	**1900:** Sigmund Freud (1856–1939) writes *The Interpretation of Dreams*.
	1904: The Abbey Theatre, evolved from the Irish Literary Society founded by Yeats and Lady Gregory, opens in Dublin.	**1901:** Queen Victoria of Great Britain dies and is succeeded by her son Edward VII.	**1900s:** Ragtime music becomes popular in the United States.
	1905–1984: Lillian Hellman, American playwright, author of *The Children's Hour* (1934) and *The Little Foxes* (1939). Other important American female playwrights of the period include Rachel Crothers (1878–1958), Zona Gale (1874–1938), and Susan Glaspell (1876–1948).	**1904–1905:** Russo-Japanese War. Russia is defeated, and Japan emerges as a world power.	**1901–1971:** Louis Armstrong, African American jazz trumpet player
		1905: The Sinn Fein party is founded in Dublin.	**1903:** Wilbur and Orville Wright make their first flight.
			1905–1914: More than 10 million immigrants arrive in the United States.
	1906–1989: Samuel Beckett, Irish playwright who wrote some of his plays in French, including *Waiting for Godot* (1952) and *Endgame* (1957)		**1906:** An earthquake and subsequent fire ravage San Francisco.
	1909–1994: Eugène Ionesco, playwright		**1907:** Picasso (1881–1973) paints *Les Demoiselles d'Avignon,* one of the earliest instances of the cubism movement in art.
	1911–1983: Tennessee Williams, American playwright, author of *The Glass Menagerie* (1944), *A Streetcar Named Desire* (1947), and *Cat on a Hot Tin Roof* (1955)		**1908:** Henry Ford (1863–1947) designs the Model T.
			1909: W. E. B. DuBois (1868–1963), African American civil rights leader and author, establishes the NAACP.
	1915: George Cram Cook, Eugene O'Neill, and Susan Glaspell found the Provincetown Players in Provincetown, Massachusetts.	**1912:** Sun Yat Sen is elected president of the Republic of China and founds the Kuomintang.	**1912:** The ocean liner *Titanic* sinks, killing 1,513 passengers.
	1915–2005: Arthur Miller, American playwright, among whose works are *Death of a Salesman* (1949) and *The Crucible* (1953)	**1914:** World War I begins with the assassination of Austrian Archduke Franz Ferdinand in Sarajevo.	**1913:** Niels Bohr (1885–1962) formulates his theory of atomic structure.
		1916: The Easter Rising in Ireland is suppressed by the British.	**1914:** The Panama Canal is completed.
	1917: J. L. Williams's *Why Marry?* receives the first Pulitzer Prize for drama.	**1917:** The Russian Revolution overthrows the czar and establishes Bolshevik control under V. I. Lenin.	**1915:** D. W. Griffith's film *The Birth of a Nation* is released.
	1918: The Theatre Guild is formed in New York City.	**1919:** The Treaty of Versailles formally ends World War I.	**c. 1916:** Albert Einstein (1879–1955) formulates his theory of relativity.
	1919: Actors Equity Association is officially recognized as a union in the United States.	**1920:** The Nineteenth Amendment recognizes the right of American women to vote.	**1918–1922:** Influenza epidemic kills 22 million people worldwide.
			1919: The Bauhaus, an influential school of art and architecture, is established by Walter Gropius in Germany.
	1920: Théâtre National Populaire is founded in Paris.	**1921:** Southern Ireland becomes the independent Republic of Ireland.	**1920:** Prohibition begins in the United States. It will continue until 1933.
			1920s: Jazz music evolves in New Orleans, Chicago, and New York City.

Date	Theater	Political	Social/Cultural
1900–1950 (continued)	**1921:** Italian playwright Luigi Pirandello (1867–1936) writes *Six Characters in Search of an Author*. **1923–1924:** Moscow Art Theater visits the United States for the first time. **1927:** Neil Simon is born. His plays include *The Odd Couple* (1965), *Chapter Two* (1979), and *Biloxi Blues* (1984). **1928:** Bertolt Brecht and Kurt Weill produce *The Threepenny Opera* in Berlin. **1930–1965:** Lorraine Hansberry, African American playwright, author of *A Raisin in the Sun* (1959) **1931:** The Group Theatre is founded by Harold Clurman, Cheryl Crawford, and Lee Strasberg. It will operate for ten years. **1934:** Wole Soyinka, Nigerian playwright, is born. His works include *The Strong Breed* (1962) and *A Play of Giants* (1984). **1934:** Socialist realism is declared the official artistic policy in Soviet theater.	**1921:** Ku Klux Klan activities become violent throughout the southern United States. **1921:** Sacco and Vanzetti, Italian anarchists, are sentenced to death in the United States. **1922:** Fascist dictator Benito Mussolini gains power in Italy. **1925:** Adolf Hitler reorganizes the Nazi Party and publishes volume 1 of *Mein Kampf*. **1928:** The Kellogg-Briand Pact, outlawing war, is signed in Paris by 65 states. **c. 1928:** Joseph Stalin comes to power in the Soviet Union. **1929:** The U.S. stock market crash begins the Great Depression. **1933:** New Deal economic reforms attempt to stimulate recovery from the Depression. **1933:** Adolf Hitler comes to power in Germany. German labor unions and political parties other than the Nazi Party are suppressed. Nazis erect their first concentration camp; persecution of Jews begins in Germany. **1935:** Roosevelt signs the U.S. Social Security Act. **1935:** The Nuremberg laws in Nazi Germany deprive German Jews of their citizenship and civil rights. **1935–1936:** Italy's conquest of Ethiopia **1936:** Chiang Kai-shek declares war on Japan.	**1920s:** Harlem Renaissance: African American literature, music, and art flourish in New York City. Langston Hughes (1902–1967), Zora Neale Hurston (1891–1960), Jean Toomer (1894–1967), and many others publish. **1922:** T. S. Eliot (1888–1965) publishes *The Waste Land*. **1922:** James Joyce (1882–1941) publishes *Ulysses*. **1923:** George Gershwin (1898–1937) performs *Rhapsody in Blue*. **1925:** F. Scott Fitzgerald (1896–1940) publishes *The Great Gatsby*. **1925:** Margaret Sanger (1879–1966) organizes the first international birth control conference. **1925:** John T. Scopes, schoolteacher, is tried for violating a Tennessee law that prohibits the teaching of the theory of evolution. **1926:** Ernest Hemingway (1899–1961) publishes *The Sun Also Rises*. **1926:** Duke Ellington's (1899–1974) first records appear. **1927:** *The Jazz Singer* is the first "talkie" movie. **1927:** Charles Lindbergh (1902–1974) makes the first solo nonstop transatlantic flight. **1927:** Virginia Woolf (1882–1941), English novelist, publishes *To the Lighthouse*. **1929:** William Faulkner (1897–1962) publishes *The Sound and the Fury*. **1931:** Robert Frost (1874–1963) wins the Pulitzer Prize for *Collected Poems*. **1931:** The Empire State Building in New York City is completed. **1932:** Aldous Huxley (1894–1963) publishes *Brave New World*.

Date	Theater	Political	Social/Cultural
1900–1950 (continued)	**1935:** The American plays *Dead End* by Sidney Kingsley, *Winterset* by Maxwell Anderson, and *Waiting for Lefty* by Clifford Odets are produced.	**1936–1939:** Civil War in Spain results in Generalissimo Franco's consolidation of power.	**1937:** Amelia Earhart (1897–1937), the first woman to fly across the Atlantic, vanishes over the Pacific Ocean.
	1935–1939: The Federal Theatre Project operates in the United States under the auspices of the Works Progress Administration.	**1939:** Germany invades Poland.	**1938:** Joe Louis (1914–1981), African American heavyweight boxer, defeats German Max Schmeling.
	1936: Federico García Lorca (1898–1936), Spanish playwright, writes *The House of Bernarda Alba*.	**1939:** Great Britain and France declare war on Germany and its allies.	
	1938: Antonín Artaud, French playwright and theorist, writes *The Theater and Its Double*.	**1940:** Germany invades France.	
	1940s: The era of great musical theater begins in the United States, featuring the songs of Cole Porter (1891–1964), Richard Rodgers (1902–1979), and Oscar Hammerstein (1895–1960), among many others.	**1941:** Japan attacks Pearl Harbor, and the United States enters World War II. **1942:** Germany begins killing Jews and others in gas chambers. **1942:** The U.S. Army interns Japanese Americans in prison camps.	**1943:** Penicillin is first used in the treatment of chronic diseases.
	1946: The Living Theatre is founded by Judith Malina and Julian Beck.	**1944:** Allies liberate France. **1945:** Hitler commits suicide in Berlin, and Germany surrenders. **1945:** The United States drops atomic bombs on Hiroshima and Nagasaki, Japan. **1946:** Juan Perón is elected president of Argentina.	
	1947: The Actors Studio is founded in New York City by Robert Lewis, Elia Kazan, and Cheryl Crawford. Lee Strasberg assumes control by 1948.	**1947:** India proclaims independence and is divided into Pakistan and India.	**1947:** Jackie Robinson (1919–1972) becomes the first African American to sign a contract with a major league baseball club.
	1947–1950: The regional theater movement begins in the United States. Margo Jones opens an arena theater in Dallas, Nina Vance founds the Alley Theatre in Houston, and the Arena Stage opens in Washington, D.C.	**1948:** The Republic of Israel is proclaimed by Jewish leaders in Palestine. **1948:** Indian leader Mahatma Gandhi is assassinated. **1949:** Mao Zedong announces the establishment of the People's Republic of China.	
	1949: The Berliner Ensemble is founded in East Berlin.	**1949:** The North Atlantic Treaty Organization unites Canada, Western Europe, and the United States as allies. **1949:** The apartheid system is established in South Africa.	

John Millington Synge

John Millington Synge (1871–1909) was one of the brilliant discoveries of the Irish Literary Renaissance, which was largely brought about by Lady Gregory and William Butler Yeats, the codirectors of the Abbey Theatre in Dublin. The Abbey ranks as one of the most influential and successful national theaters in European history. From 1904 to the present, it has been devoted to producing plays by Irish writers, some of whom have gone on to be ranked among the greatest of their age. Besides Synge, Bernard Shaw, Lady Gregory, Yeats, Sean O'Casey, and Brian Friel are among the many who contributed to the reputation of the Abbey.

Synge was gifted in languages and earned a degree in German from Trinity College, Dublin. Also a violinist, he went to Paris to study music and live the bohemian life of the artist. It was there, in 1896, that Yeats and Lady Gregory met Synge and persuaded him to return to Ireland and write plays for what was to become the Abbey. They convinced him to spend time in the Aran Islands, the wildest part of Ireland. Yeats believed that the Arans were an important source of the literary energy of the nation because the islanders' colorful language sounded like English filtered through Irish Gaelic.

Synge wrote a number of important plays within less than ten years. Most of them remain in the repertory of modern drama: *In the Shadow of the Glen* (1903), *Riders to the Sea* (1904), *The Well of the Saints* (1905), *The Tinker's Wedding* (1907), *The Playboy of the Western World* (1907), and *Deirdre of the Sorrows* (1910). With the exception of *The Tinker's Wedding*, which is so anticlerical that it took sixty years for it to be given a production at the Abbey, they are all still regularly produced there.

Synge was not always a popular playwright in Ireland. He believed that he faithfully represented peasant ways, but his Dublin audiences often protested that he insulted the Irish. Synge's kind of realism, though not especially harsh or critical, was an unvarnished view of the west of Ireland. The Abbey audiences wanted an idealized portrait of their countrymen and countrywomen, not straightforward and sometimes embarrassing portraits such as the one Synge offered them in *The Playboy of the Western World*. That play caused riots in the Abbey Theatre when it was first performed because of its nationalistic elements, its gritty, honest portrayal of country people, and its use of "indecent" language. Regarding this last, it is said that Synge's use of the image of "chosen females standing in their shifts"—*shifts* referring to women's slips or chemises—incensed audiences.

Synge was shocked at the uproar; he had never expected his play to stimulate such a response. The question of realism was probably not on Synge's mind at all. *Playboy* is a less realistic play than *Riders to the Sea*, and both are rooted not in any effort to force the audience to look at life as it is really lived but, rather, in the mythic and symbolic forces that underlie everyone's experiences of heroism, life, and death. The deep roots of both plays are in Irish myth and the Christian religion. Synge was amazed that audiences ignored those important aspects and focused on other, less significant issues.

Synge's early death robbed world drama of a figure who certainly would have been among the greatest writers of the century. As it is, his work is remarkable; but in his last play, *Deirdre of the Sorrows*, which he never finished, we can see the promise of a body of work that would have taken its place with the best plays of our time.

Riders to the Sea

Riders to the Sea (1904) was the first success that Synge produced for the Abbey Theatre. In some ways it is one of the most impressive plays to come out of the Irish Literary Renaissance. It is a one-act play, which the Abbey found congenial for its early programs, but its brevity in no way diminishes its power.

The play is set in the west of Ireland, the part least touched by English influence. Aran Islanders speak both Gaelic and English, but their English has a very expressive and idiosyncratic flavor, which Synge tries to replicate in this play. Synge's skill at rendering the syntax of the peasants derives from his musician's ear as well as from his having lived in an inn in Wicklow, where he eavesdropped on the conversations of the local Irish kitchen girls.

Riders to the Sea owes much of its power to the local speech and the local way of life portrayed faithfully in the play. In his preface to *The Playboy of the Western World*, Synge credits Irish writers with the advantage of being able to listen "for a few years more" to a language that is "rich as a nut." Maurya's long speeches at the end of *Riders to the Sea* are filled with the rhythms of the sea and the agony of someone who has suffered as much as the world can demand. Even the speeches of the lesser characters have an extraordinarily expressive flavor.

The drama depicts the sufferings of a superstitious peasant woman, yet it contains the same kind of intensity of dramatic action found in Greek tragedies. It maintains a unity of time, place, character, and action, as well as an intense sense of fate and impending doom. Synge may well have begun developing a new genre of folk tragedy, just as Arthur Miller later began developing a new genre of middle-class tragedy in *Death of a Salesman*. *Riders to the Sea* is permeated by a sense of fate; and Maurya, whose name is remarkably close in sound to *moira*, the Greek word for "fate," senses the inevitability of the premature death of her last son on the sea. The feeling of inevitability is heightened by the discussion between the daughters about the son Michael, who has been feared lost at sea, by their identification of his sock that was recovered from the sea, and by the willful insistence of the last son, Bartley, on riding the mares across the sea to the mainland, knowingly risking his life. (In fact, men did swim their animals from the islands to the mainland, and they often went out to meet the large boats that came near. Even today those waters are difficult, and Aran Islanders still use the same black curraghs their ancestors used to ferry themselves, their goods, and their livestock between the mainland and their homes.) Maurya's horrifying vision of Michael and Bartley on the mares confirms her premonitions and fears. It also injects an element of supernatural intensity.

For discussion questions and assignments on *Riders to the Sea,* visit **bedfordstmartins.com/jacobus**.

Perhaps because of its tragic Greek pattern, *Riders to the Sea* has a mythic force. The sense of destiny that Maurya feels is built into her life. Her resignation and deep faith help her grow in our imagination and give her a heroic dimension. Synge's approach to realism is much different from Ibsen's or Chekhov's. It is more elemental, based on the spiritual life of the folk as expressed in the eloquence of their language.

Riders to the Sea in Performance

All of Synge's plays were written for the early Abbey Theatre, founded in 1904 by Lady Gregory and W. B. Yeats to perform Irish plays. At that time all performances were in Molesworth Hall, leased facilities. Synge's *In the Shadow of the Glen* was one of the first plays to be performed by the company, then known as the Irish National Theatre. That play opened in October 1903, coinciding with the Irish holiday Samhain (pronounced *sow-in*). Although controversial, the play was a success. *Riders to the Sea* was Synge's second play, produced in Molesworth Hall in February 1904. By this time the Abbey had already attracted some excellent actors. Bartley was played by W. G. Fay, who was instrumental in shaping the Abbey. Sarah Allgood, destined to become a standard player in American films in the 1930s and 1940s, played Cathleen. The production was well received by the press and the public.

Riders to the Sea has usually been paired with other Irish plays in production. The Abbey Theatre Company still produces the play regularly and often takes it on tour. One of the most memorable tours was in 1957, when the Abbey brought the play to the tiny Theatre East in New York. Despite the theater's small size, the effect of the play, which had not been seen in an Abbey performance in the United States since 1911, was electrifying. The finest Irish actress of the age, Siobhan McKenna, played Maurya.

Ralph Vaughan Williams used Synge's play as the basis for his opera *Riders to the Sea* (1925–1932). One of the most recent productions of the opera was at the University of California at Santa Barbara Opera Theatre in February 2008. The opera explores the deep emotional valences of Synge's original.

Riders to the Sea enjoys frequent production by both high school and college students. Its brevity and power make it a strong vehicle for amateur productions.

JOHN MILLINGTON SYNGE (1871–1909)

Riders to the Sea 1904

Persons in the Play

MAURYA (*an old woman*)
BARTLEY (*her son*)
CATHLEEN (*her daughter*)
NORA (*a younger daughter*)
MEN *and* WOMEN

Scene: *An Island off the West of Ireland.*

(*Cottage kitchen, with nets, oilskins, spinning wheel, some new boards standing by the wall, etc. Cathleen, a girl of about twenty, finishes kneading cake, and puts it down in the pot-oven by the fire; then wipes her hands, and begins to spin at the wheel. Nora, a young girl, puts her head in at the door.*)

NORA (*in a low voice*): Where is she?

CATHLEEN: She's lying down, God help her, and may be sleeping, if she's able.

(*Nora comes in softly and takes a bundle from under her shawl.*)

CATHLEEN (*spinning the wheel rapidly*): What is it you have?

NORA: The young priest is after bringing them. It's a shirt and a plain stocking were got off a drowned man in Donegal.

(*Cathleen stops her wheel with a sudden movement, and leans out to listen.*)

NORA: We're to find out if it's Michael's they are, some time herself will be down looking by the sea.

CATHLEEN: How would they be Michael's, Nora? How would he go the length of that way to the far north?

NORA: The young priest says he's known the like of it. "If it's Michael's they are," says he, "you can tell herself he's got a clean burial by the grace of God, and if they're not his, let no one say a word about them, for she'll be getting her death," says he, "with crying and lamenting."

(*The door which Nora half closed is blown open by a gust of wind.*)

CATHLEEN (*looking out anxiously*): Did you ask him would he stop Bartley going this day with the horses to the Galway fair?

NORA: "I won't stop him," says he, "but let you not be afraid. Herself does be saying prayers half through the night, and the Almighty God won't leave her destitute," says he, "with no son living."

CATHLEEN: Is the sea bad by the white rocks, Nora?

NORA: Middling bad, God help us. There's a great roaring in the west, and it's worse it'll be getting when the tide's turned to the wind. (*She goes over to the table with the bundle.*) Shall I open it now?

CATHLEEN: Maybe she'd wake up on us, and come in before we'd done. (*Coming to the table.*) It's a long time we'll be, and the two of us crying.

NORA (*goes to the inner door and listens*): She's moving about on the bed. She'll be coming in a minute.

CATHLEEN: Give me the ladder, and I'll put them up in the turf-loft, the way she won't know of them at all, and maybe when the tide turns she'll be going down to see would he be floating from the east.

(*They put the ladder against the gable of the chimney; Cathleen goes up a few steps and hides the bundle in the turf-loft. Maurya comes from the inner room.*)

MAURYA (*looking up at Cathleen and speaking querulously*): Isn't it turf enough you have for this day and evening?

CATHLEEN: There's a cake baking at the fire for a short space (*throwing down the turf*) and Bartley will want it when the tide turns if he goes to Connemara.

(*Nora picks up the turf and puts it round the pot-oven.*)

MAURYA (*sitting down on a stool at the fire*): He won't go this day with the wind rising from the south and west. He won't go this day, for the young priest will stop him surely.

NORA: He'll not stop him, mother, and I heard Eamon Simon and Stephen Pheety and Colum Shawn saying he would go.

MAURYA: Where is he itself?

NORA: He went down to see would there be another boat sailing in the week, and I'm thinking it won't be long till he's here now, for the tide's turning at the green head, and the hooker's tacking from the east.

CATHLEEN: I hear some one passing the big stones.

NORA (*looking out*): He's coming now, and he in a hurry.

BARTLEY (*comes in and looks round the room. Speaking sadly and quietly*): Where is the bit of new rope, Cathleen, was bought in Connemara?

CATHLEEN (*coming down*): Give it to him, Nora; it's on a nail by the white boards. I hung it up this morning, for the pig with the black feet was eating it.

NORA (*giving him a rope*): Is that it, Bartley?

MAURYA: You'd do right to leave that rope, Bartley, hanging by the boards. (*Bartley takes the rope.*) It will be wanting in this place, I'm telling you, if Michael is washed up tomorrow morning, or the

The fateful first scene of *Riders to the Sea* in the 1998 Royal Shakespeare Company/The Other Place production directed by John Crowley. Mairead McKinley (foreground) and Aislinn Mangan (background) play the daughters, Cathleen and Nora. Stella McCusker plays their mother, Maurya.

next morning, or any morning in the week, for it's a deep grave we'll make him by the grace of God.

BARTLEY (*beginning to work with the rope*): I've no halter the way I can ride down on the mare, and I must go now quickly. This is the one boat going for two weeks or beyond it, and the fair will be a good fair for horses I heard them saying below.

MAURYA: It's a hard thing they'll be saying below if the body is washed up and there's no man in it to make the coffin, and I after giving a big price for the finest white boards you'd find in Connemara.

(*She looks round at the boards.*)

BARTLEY: How would it be washed up, and we after looking each day for nine days, and a strong wind blowing a while back from the west and south?

MAURYA: If it wasn't found itself, that wind is raising the sea, and there was a star up against the moon, and it rising in the night. If it was a hundred horses, or a thousand horses you had itself, what is the price of a thousand horses against a son where there is one son only?

BARTLEY (*working at the halter, to Cathleen*): Let you go down each day, and see the sheep aren't jumping in on the rye, and if the jobber comes you can sell the pig with the black feet if there is a good price going.

MAURYA: How would the like of her get a good price for a pig?

BARTLEY (*to Cathleen*): If the west wind holds with the last bit of the moon let you and Nora get up weed enough for another cock for the kelp. It's hard set we'll be from this day with no one in it but one man to work.

MAURYA: It's hard set we'll be surely the day you're drownd'd with the rest. What way will I live and the girls with me, and I an old woman looking for the grave?

(*Bartley lays down the halter, takes off his old coat, and puts on a newer one of the same flannel.*)

BARTLEY (*to Nora*): Is she coming to the pier?

NORA (*looking out*): She's passing the green head and letting fall her sails.

BARTLEY (*getting his purse and tobacco*): I'll have half an hour to go down, and you'll see me coming again in two days, or in three days, or maybe in four days if the wind is bad.

MAURYA (*turning round to the fire, and putting her shawl over her head*): Isn't it a hard and cruel man won't hear a word from an old woman, and she holding him from the sea?

CATHLEEN: It's the life of a young man to be going on the sea, and who would listen to an old woman with one thing and she saying it over?

BARTLEY (*taking the halter*): I must go now quickly. I'll ride down on the red mare, and the gray pony'll run behind me. . . . The blessing of God on you.

(*He goes out.*)

MAURYA (*crying out as he is in the door*): He's gone now, God spare us, and we'll not see him again. He's gone now, and when the black night is falling I'll have no son left me in the world.

CATHLEEN: Why wouldn't you give him your blessing and he looking round in the door? Isn't it sorrow enough is on every one in this house without your sending him out with an unlucky word behind him, and a hard word in his ear?

(*Maurya takes up the tongs and begins raking the fire aimlessly without looking round.*)

NORA (*turning toward her*): You're taking away the turf from the cake.

CATHLEEN (*crying out*): The Son of God forgive us, Nora, we're after forgetting his bit of bread.

(She comes over to the fire.)

NORA: And it's destroyed he'll be going till dark night, and he after eating nothing since the sun went up.

CATHLEEN (*turning the cake out of the oven*): It's destroyed he'll be, surely. There's no sense left on any person in a house where an old woman will be talking forever.

(Maurya sways herself on her stool.)

CATHLEEN (*cutting off some of the bread and rolling it in a cloth; to Maurya*): Let you go down now to the spring well and give him this and he passing. You'll see him then and the dark word will be broken, and you can say "God speed you," the way he'll be easy in his mind.

MAURYA (*taking the bread*): Will I be in it as soon as himself?

CATHLEEN: If you go now quickly.

MAURYA (*standing up unsteadily*): It's hard set I am to walk.

CATHLEEN (*looking at her anxiously*): Give her the stick, Nora, or maybe she'll slip on the big stones.

NORA: What stick?

CATHLEEN: The stick Michael brought from Connemara.

MAURYA (*taking a stick Nora gives her*): In the big world the old people do be leaving things after them for their sons and children, but in this place it is the young men do be leaving things behind for them that do be old.

(She goes out slowly. Nora goes over to the ladder.)

CATHLEEN: Wait, Nora, maybe she'd turn back quickly. She's that sorry, God help her, you wouldn't know the thing she'd do.

NORA: Is she gone round by the bush?

CATHLEEN (*looking out*): She's gone now. Throw it down quickly, for the Lord knows when she'll be out of it again.

NORA (*getting the bundle from the loft*): The young priest said he'd be passing tomorrow, and we might go down and speak to him below if it's Michael's they are surely.

CATHLEEN (*taking the bundle*): Did he say what way they were found?

NORA (*coming down*): "There were two men," says he, "and they rowing round with poteen before the cocks crowed, and the oar of one of them caught the body, and they passing the black cliffs of the north."

CATHLEEN (*trying to open the bundle*): Give me a knife, Nora, the string's perished with the salt water, and there's a black knot on it you wouldn't loosen in a week.

NORA (*giving her a knife*): I've heard tell it was a long way to Donegal.

CATHLEEN (*cutting the string*): It is surely. There was a man in here a while ago—the man sold us that knife—and he said if you set off walking from the rocks beyond, it would be seven days you'd be in Donegal.

NORA: And what time would a man take, and he floating?

(Cathleen opens the bundle and takes out a bit of a stocking. They look at them eagerly.)

CATHLEEN (*in a low voice*): The Lord spare us, Nora! isn't it a queer hard thing to say if it's his they are surely?

NORA: I'll get his shirt off the hook the way we can put the one flannel on the other. (*She looks through some clothes hanging in the corner.*) It's not with them, Cathleen, and where will it be?

CATHLEEN: I'm thinking Bartley put it on him in the morning, for his own shirt was heavy with the salt in it (*pointing to the corner*). There's a bit of a sleeve was of the same stuff. Give me that and it will do.

(Nora brings it to her and they compare the flannel.)

CATHLEEN: It's the same stuff, Nora; but if it is itself aren't there great rolls of it in the shops of Galway, and isn't it many another man may have a shirt of it as well as Michael himself?

NORA (*who has taken up the stocking and counted the stitches, crying out*): It's Michael, Cathleen, it's Michael; God spare his soul, and what will herself say when she hears this story, and Bartley on the sea?

CATHLEEN (*taking the stocking*): It's a plain stocking.

NORA: It's the second one of the third pair I knitted, and I put up three score stitches, and I dropped four of them.

CATHLEEN (*counts the stitches*): It's that number is in it. (*Crying out.*) Ah, Nora, isn't it a bitter thing to think of him floating that way to the far north, and no one to keen him but the black hags that do be flying on the sea?

NORA (*swinging herself round, and throwing out her arms on the clothes*): And isn't it a pitiful thing when there is nothing left of a man who was a great rower and fisher, but a bit of an old shirt and a plain stocking?

CATHLEEN (*after an instant*): Tell me is herself coming, Nora? I hear a little sound on the path.

NORA (*looking out*): She is, Cathleen. She's coming up to the door.

CATHLEEN: Put these things away before she'll come in. Maybe it's easier she'll be after giving her blessing to Bartley, and we won't let on we've heard anything the time he's on the sea.

NORA (*helping Cathleen to close the bundle*): We'll put them here in the corner.

(They put them into a hole in the chimney corner. Cathleen goes back to the spinning wheel.)

NORA: Will she see it was crying I was?

CATHLEEN: Keep your back to the door the way the light'll not be on you.

(Nora sits down at the chimney corner, with her back to the door. Maurya comes in very slowly, without looking at the girls, and goes over to her stool at the

other side of the fire. The cloth with the bread is still in her hand. The girls look at each other, and Nora points to the bundle of bread.)

CATHLEEN (after spinning for a moment): You didn't give him his bit of bread?

(Maurya begins to keen softly, without turning round.)

CATHLEEN: Did you see him riding down?

(Maurya goes on keening.)

CATHLEEN (a little impatiently): God forgive you; isn't it a better thing to raise your voice and tell what you seen, than to be making lamentation for a thing that's done? Did you see Bartley, I'm saying to you.

MAURYA (with a weak voice): My heart's broken from this day.

CATHLEEN (as before): Did you see Bartley?

MAURYA: I seen the fearfulest thing.

CATHLEEN (leaves her wheel and looks out): God forgive you; he's riding the mare now over the green head, and the gray pony behind him.

MAURYA (starts, so that her shawl falls back from her head and shows her white tossed hair. With a frightened voice): The gray pony behind him.

CATHLEEN (coming to the fire): What is it ails you, at all?

MAURYA (speaking very slowly): I've seen the fearfulest thing any person has seen, since the day Bride Dara seen the dead man with the child in his arms.

CATHLEEN AND NORA: Uah.

(They crouch down in front of the old woman at the fire.)

NORA: Tell us what it is you seen.

MAURYA: I went down to the spring well, and I stood there saying a prayer to myself. Then Bartley came along, and he riding on the red mare with the gray pony behind him. (She puts up her hands, as if to hide something from her eyes.) The Son of God spare us, Nora!

CATHLEEN: What is it you seen?

MAURYA: I seen Michael himself.

CATHLEEN (speaking softly): You did not, mother. It wasn't Michael you seen, for his body is after being found in the far north, and he's got a clean burial by the grace of God.

MAURYA (a little defiantly): I'm after seeing him this day, and he riding and galloping. Bartley came first on the red mare; and I tried to say "God speed you," but something choked the words in my throat. He went by quickly; and "the blessing of God on you," says he, and I could say nothing. I looked up then, and I crying, at the gray pony, and there was Michael upon it—with fine clothes on him, and new shoes on his feet.

CATHLEEN (begins to keen): It's destroyed we are from this day. It's destroyed, surely.

NORA: Didn't the young priest say the Almighty God wouldn't leave her destitute with no son living?

MAURYA (in a low voice, but clearly): It's little the like of him knows of the sea.... Bartley will be lost now, and let you call in Eamon and make me a good coffin out of the white boards, for I won't live after them. I've had a husband, and a husband's father, and six sons in this house—six fine men, though it was a hard birth I had with every one of them and they coming to the world—and some of them were found and some of them were not found, but they're gone now the lot of them.... There were Stephen, and Shawn, were lost in the great wind, and found after in the Bay of Gregory of the Golden Mouth, and carried up the two of them on the one plank, and in by that door.

(She pauses for a moment, the girls start as if they heard something through the door that is half open behind them.)

NORA (in a whisper): Did you hear that, Cathleen? Did you hear a noise in the northeast?

CATHLEEN (in a whisper): There's some one after crying out by the seashore.

MAURYA (continues without hearing anything): There was Sheamus and his father, and his own father again, were lost in a dark night, and not a stick or sign was seen of them when the sun went up. There was Patch after was drowned out of a curagh° that turned over. I was sitting here with Bartley, and he a baby, lying on my two knees, and I seen two women, and three women, and four women coming in, and they crossing themselves, and not saying a word. I looked out then, and there were men coming after them, and they holding a thing in the half of a red sail, and water dripping out of it—it was a dry day, Nora—and leaving a track to the door.

(She pauses again with her hand stretched out toward the door. It opens softly and old women begin to come in, crossing themselves on the threshold, and kneeling down in front of the stage with red petticoats over their heads.)

MAURYA (half in a dream, to Cathleen): Is it Patch or Michael, or what is it at all?

CATHLEEN: Michael is after being found in the far north, and when he is found there how could he be here in this place?

MAURYA: There does be a power of young men floating round in the sea, and what way would they know if it was Michael they had, or another man like him, for when a man is nine days in the sea, and the wind blowing, it's hard set his own mother would be to say what man was it.

CATHLEEN: It's Michael, God spare him, for they're after sending us a bit of his clothes from the far north.

(She reaches out and hands Maurya the clothes that belonged to Michael. Maurya stands up slowly and takes them in her hands. Nora looks out.)

curagh: A small boat with a hide- or tarpaulin-covered frame.

Maurya (Stella McCusker) mourns the death of her last son, Bartley (Stephen Kennedy).

NORA: They're carrying a thing among them and there's water dripping out of it and leaving a track by the big stones.

CATHLEEN (*in a whisper to the women who have come in*): Is it Bartley it is?

ONE OF THE WOMEN: It is surely, God rest his soul.

(*Two younger women come in and pull out the table. Then men carry in the body of Bartley, laid on a plank, with a bit of a sail over it, and lay it on the table.*)

CATHLEEN (*to the women, as they are doing so*): What way was he drowned?

ONE OF THE WOMEN: The gray pony knocked him into the sea, and he was washed out where there is a great surf on the white rocks.

(*Maurya has gone over and knelt down at the head of the table. The women are keening softly and swaying themselves with a slow movement. Cathleen and Nora kneel at the other end of the table. The men kneel near the door.*)

MAURYA (*raising her head and speaking as if she did not see the people around her*): They're all gone now, and there isn't anything more the sea can do to me.... I'll have no call now to be up crying and praying when the wind breaks from the south, and you can hear the surf is in the east, and the surf is in the west, making a great stir with the two noises, and they hitting one on the other. I'll have no call now to be going down and getting Holy Water in the dark nights after Samhain,° and I won't care what way

Samhain: Feast of All Saints, October 31–November 1.

the sea is when the other women will be keening. (*To Nora.*) Give me the Holy Water, Nora, there's a small sup still on the dresser.

(*Nora gives it to her.*)

MAURYA (*drops Michael's clothes across Bartley's feet, and sprinkles the Holy Water over him*): It isn't that I haven't prayed for you, Bartley, to the Almighty God. It isn't that I haven't said prayers in the dark night till you wouldn't know what I'll be saying; but it's a great rest I'll have now, and it's time surely. It's a great rest I'll have now, and great sleeping in the long nights after Samhain, if it's only a bit of wet flour we do have to eat, and maybe a fish that would be stinking.

(*She kneels down again, crossing herself, and saying prayers under her breath.*)

CATHLEEN (*to an old man*): Maybe yourself and Eamon would make a coffin when the sun rises. We have fine white boards herself bought, God help her, thinking Michael would be found, and I have a new cake you can eat while you'll be working.

THE OLD MAN (*looking at the boards*): Are there nails with them?

CATHLEEN: There are not, Colum; we didn't think of the nails.

ANOTHER MAN: It's a great wonder she wouldn't think of the nails, and all the coffins she's seen made already.

CATHLEEN: It's getting old she is, and broken.

(*Maurya stands up again very slowly and spreads out the pieces of Michael's clothes beside the body, sprinkling them with the last of the Holy Water.*)

NORA (*in a whisper to Cathleen*): She's quiet now and easy; but the day Michael was drowned you could hear her crying out from this to the spring well. It's fonder she was of Michael, and would any one have thought that?

CATHLEEN (*slowly and clearly*): An old woman will be soon tired with anything she will do, and isn't it nine days herself is after crying and keening, and making great sorrow in the house?

MAURYA (*puts the empty cup mouth downward on the table, and lays her hands together on Bartley's feet*): They're all together this time, and the end is come. May the Almighty God have mercy on Bartley's soul, and on Michael's soul, and on the souls of Sheamus and Patch, and Stephen and Shawn (*bending her head*); and may He have mercy on my soul, Nora, and on the soul of every one is left living in the world.

(*She pauses, and the keen rises a little more loudly from the women, then sinks away.*)

MAURYA (*continuing*): Michael has a clean burial in the far north, by the grace of the Almighty God. Bartley will have a fine coffin out of the white boards, and a deep grave surely. What more can we want than that? No man at all can be living forever, and we must be satisfied.

(*She kneels down again and the curtain falls slowly.*)

COMMENTARY

JOHN MILLINGTON SYNGE (1871–1909)

From The Aran Islands   1907

For several weeks a year from 1898 to 1902, Synge traveled to the Aran Islands, off the west coast of Ireland near Galway. He spent part of his time learning Gaelic and part of it keeping a journal. He wrote mostly about his experiences in this remote part of Ireland, so distant from Dublin civilization that Synge sometimes felt he was in a time warp. This excerpt, published in 1907 but written before *Riders to the Sea*, portrays the people he met on the Aran Islands. Synge said he learned how people speak on the islands in part from overhearing servant girls, such as those he describes here, talking among themselves in the kitchen beneath his room. His musical training enabled him to catch the intonations of English as it was spoken by native Gaelic speakers.

I am settled at last on Inishmaan in a small cottage with a continual drone of Gaelic coming from the kitchen that opens into my room.

Early this morning the man of the house came over for me with a four-oared curagh°—that is, a curagh with four rowers and four oars on either side, as each man uses two—and we set off a little before noon.

It gave me a moment of exquisite satisfaction to find myself moving away from civilization in this rude canvas canoe of a model that has served primitive races since men first went on the sea.

We had to stop for a moment at a hulk that is anchored in the bay, to make some arrangements for the fish-curing of the middle island, and my crew called out as

curagh: Small boat in the general shape of a canoe.

soon as we were within earshot that they had a man with them who had been in France a month from this day.

When we started again, a small sail was run up in the bow, and we set off across the sound with a leaping oscillation that had no resemblance to the heavy movement of a boat.

The sail is only used as an aid, so the men continued to row after it had gone up, and as they occupied the four cross-seats I lay on the canvas at the stern and the frame of slender laths, which bent and quivered as the waves passed under them.

When we set off it was a brilliant morning of April, and the green, glittering waves seemed to toss the canoe among themselves, yet as we drew nearer this island a sudden thunderstorm broke out behind the rocks we were approaching, and lent a momentary tumult to this still vein of the Atlantic.

We landed at a small pier, from which a rude track leads up to the village between small fields and bare sheets of rock like those in Aranmor. The youngest son of my boatman, a boy of about seventeen, who is to be my teacher and guide, was waiting for me at the pier and guided me to his house, while the men settled the curagh and followed slowly with my baggage.

My room is at one end of the cottage, with a boarded floor and ceiling, and two windows opposite each other. Then there is the kitchen with earth floor and open rafters, and two doors opposite each other opening into the open air, but no windows. Beyond it there are two small rooms of half the width of the kitchen with one window apiece.

The kitchen itself, where I will spend most of my time, is full of beauty and distinction. The red dresses of the women who cluster round the fire on their stools give a glow of almost Eastern richness, and the walls have been toned by the turf-smoke to a soft brown that blends with the grey earth-colour of the floor. Many sorts of fishing-tackle, and the nets and oilskins of the men, are hung upon the walls or among the open rafters; and right overhead, under the thatch, there is a whole cowskin from which they make pampooties.°

Every article on these islands has an almost personal character, which gives this simple life, where all art is unknown, something of the artistic beauty of medieval life. The curaghs and spinning-wheels, the tiny wooden barrels that are still much used in the place of earthenware, the homemade cradles, churns, and baskets, are all full of individuality, and being made from materials that are common here, yet to some extent peculiar to the island, they seem to exist as a natural link between the people and the world that is about them.

The simplicity and unity of the dress increases in another way the local air of beauty. The women wear red petticoats and jackets of the island wool stained with madder, to which they usually add a plaid shawl twisted round their chests and tied at the back. When it rains they throw another petticoat over their heads with the waistband round their faces, or, if they are young, they use a heavy shawl like those worn in Galway. Occasionally other wraps are worn, and during the thunderstorm I arrived in I saw several girls with men's waistcoats buttoned round their bodies. Their skirts do not come much below the knee, and show their powerful legs in the heavy indigo stockings with which they are all provided.

---

pampooties: Soft slippers of sealskin or rawhide.

The men wear three colours: the natural wool, indigo, and a grey flannel that is woven of alternate threads of indigo and the natural wool. In Aranmor many of the younger men have adopted the usual fisherman's jersey, but I have only seen one on this island.

As flannel is cheap—the women spin the yarn from the wool of their own sheep, and it is then woven by a weaver in Kilronan for fourpence a yard—the men seem to wear an indefinite number of waistcoats and woollen drawers one over the other. They are usually surprised at the lightness of my own dress, and one old man I spoke to for a minute on the pier, when I came ashore, asked me if I was not cold with "my little clothes."

As I sat in the kitchen to dry the spray from my coat, several men who had seen me walking up came in to talk to me, usually murmuring on the threshold, "The blessing of God on this place," or some similar words.

The courtesy of the old woman of the house is singularly attractive, and though I could not understand much of what she said—she has no English— I could see with how much grace she motioned each visitor to a chair, or stool, according to his age, and said a few words to him till he drifted into our English conversation.

For the moment my own arrival is the chief subject of interest, and the men who come in are eager to talk to me.

Some of them express themselves more correctly than the ordinary peasant, others use the Gaelic idioms continually and substitute "he" or "she" for "it," as the neuter pronoun is not found in modern Irish.

A few of the men have a curiously full vocabulary, others know only the commonest words in English, and are driven to ingenious devices to express their meaning. Of all the subjects we can talk of war seems their favourite, and the conflict between America and Spain° is causing a great deal of excitement. Nearly all the families have relations who have had to cross the Atlantic, and all eat of the flour and bacon that is brought from the United States, so they have a vague fear that "if anything happened to America," their own island would cease to be habitable.

Foreign languages are another favourite topic, and as these men are bilingual they have a fair notion of what it means to speak and think in many different idioms. Most of the strangers they see on the islands are philological students, and the people have been led to conclude that linguistic studies, particularly Gaelic studies, are the chief occupation of the outside world.

"I have seen Frenchmen, and Danes, and Germans," said one man, "and there does be a power of Irish books along with them, and they reading them better than ourselves. Believe me there are few rich men now in the world who are not studying the Gaelic."

They sometimes ask me the French for simple phrases, and when they have listened to the intonation for a moment, most of them are able to reproduce it with admirable precision.

No one who has not lived for weeks among these grey clouds and seas can realize the joy with which the eye rests on the red dresses of the women, especially when a number of them are to be found together, as happened early this morning.

conflict between America and Spain: Spanish-American War, 1898.

I heard that the young cattle were to be shipped for a fair on the mainland, which is to take place in a few days, and I went down on the pier, a little after dawn, to watch them.

The bay was shrouded in the greys of coming rain, yet the thinness of the cloud threw a silvery light on the sea, and an unusual depth of blue to the mountains of Connemara.

As I was going across the sandhills one dun-sailed hooker° glided slowly out to begin her voyage, and another beat up to the pier. Troops of red cattle, driven mostly by the women, were coming up from several directions, forming, with the green of the long tract of grass that separates the sea from the rocks, a new unity of colour.

The pier itself was crowded with bullocks and a great number of the people. I noticed one extraordinary girl in the throng who seemed to exert an authority on all who came near her. Her curiously-formed nostrils and narrow chin gave her a witch-like expression, yet the beauty of her hair and skin made her singularly attractive.

When the empty hooker was made fast its deck was still many feet below the level of the pier, so the animals were slung down by a rope from the mast-head, with much struggling and confusion. Some of them made wild efforts to escape, nearly carrying their owners with them into the sea, but they were handled with wonderful dexterity, and there was no mishap.

When the open hold was filled with young cattle, packed as tightly as they could stand, the owners with their wives or sisters, who go with them to prevent extravagance in Galway, jumped down on the deck, and the voyage was begun. Immediately afterwards a rickety old hooker beat up with turf° from Connemara, and while she was unlading all the men sat along the edge of the pier and made remarks upon the rottenness of her timber till the owners grew wild with rage.

The tide was now too low for more boats to come to the pier, so a move was made to a strip of sand towards the southeast, where the rest of the cattle were shipped through the surf. Here the hooker was anchored about eighty yards from the shore, and a curagh was rowed round to tow out the animals. Each bullock was caught in its turn and girded with a sling of rope by which it could be hoisted on board. Another rope was fastened to the horns and passed out to a man in the stern of the curagh. Then the animal was forced down through the surf and out of its depth before it had much time to struggle. Once fairly swimming, it was towed out to the hooker and dragged on board in a half-drowned condition.

The freedom of the sand seemed to give a stronger spirit of revolt, and some of the animals were only caught after a dangerous struggle. The first attempt was not always successful, and I saw one three-year-old lift two men with his horns, and drag another fifty yards along the sand by his tail before he was subdued.

While this work was going on a crowd of girls and women collected on the edge of the cliff and kept shouting down a confused babble of satire and praise.

When I came back to the cottage I found that among the women who had gone to the mainland was a daughter of the old woman's, and that her baby of about nine months had been left in the care of its grandmother.

hooker: A commercial fishing boat.
turf: Peat used for fuel.

As I came in she was busy getting ready my dinner, and old Pat Dirane, who usually comes at this hour, was rocking the cradle. It is made of clumsy wicker-work, with two pieces of rough wood fastened underneath to serve as rockers, and all the time I am in my room I can hear it bumping on the floor with extraordinary violence. When the baby is awake it sprawls on the floor, and the old woman sings it a variety of inarticulate lullabies that have much musical charm.

Another daughter, who lives at home, has gone to the fair also, so the old woman has both the baby and myself to take care of as well as a crowd of chickens that live in a hole beside the fire. Often when I want tea, or when the old woman goes for water, I have to take my own turn at rocking the cradle.

Susan Glaspell

Susan Glaspell (1876–1948) was already established as a novelist when she became an important figure in early-twentieth-century drama. She was born in Davenport, Iowa, graduated from Drake University in Des Moines, and went to work as a reporter on the *Des Moines Daily News* in 1899. While there she began writing short fiction and novels, and with the beginnings of publishing success, she returned to Davenport to write. Her first novel, *The Glory of the Conquered: The Story of a Great Love* (1909), earned enough for her to spend a year in Paris. *The Visioning* (1911) was set on an army base and presented a less sentimentalized world than her first book. Back in the United States in 1911, she published her book of short stories, *Lifted Masks* (1912). One of her best novels, *Fidelity*, published in 1915, tells the story of a woman who leaves her loving husband and family to run off with a married man.

In 1908, Glaspell first met her future husband, George Cram (Jig) Cook, a traveled intellectual and Harvard graduate who was teaching at Iowa University. After that initial meeting, Cook married another woman, but five years later he was divorced for the second time. Glaspell and Cook were reintroduced in 1913 by mutual friends and eventually came to believe they were fated for each other. Because the scandal of Cook's divorces made it virtually impossible for them to live in Iowa, the couple moved to New York and Provincetown, Massachusetts.

In Provincetown, Cook wanted to involve himself in a new kind of drama, and the two of them wrote *Suppressed Desires* (1915), which they first produced in their living room. They eventually relocated to a neglected fish house on a wharf, and this playhouse was a local success. *Suppressed Desires* was a satire that poked fun at the trend of using Freudian theories to explain everyday life. In a letter to the *New York Times* (February 13, 1920), Glaspell wrote that the play "is having fun with the people who went off their heads about psychoanalysis—went 'bugs'—when this subject reached the first circle in New York to know of it." *Trifles*, written entirely by Glaspell, followed in 1916. Its story line developed from a murder in Des Moines that Glaspell was familiar with from her days as a journalist.

The Provincetown Players, which Glaspell and Cook founded with Eugene O'Neill, quickly became an influential platform for a number of important American writers, such as Edna St. Vincent Millay and Eugene O'Neill, whose first play, *Bound East for Cardiff*, was produced at the Wharf Theatre in 1916. Eventually the Provincetown Players relocated to New York, where they attracted other important playwrights and produced additional plays by Glaspell and O'Neill.

Glaspell's one-act plays, including *Close the Book* (1917), *A Woman's Honor* (1918), and *Tickless Time* (1919), were collected in 1920. Her first full-length play, *Bernice* (1919), centered on interpreting the character of a dead woman. Its success led to another full-length play, *The Verge* (1921), about a woman who tries to make a new reality around herself and begins with creating new kinds of plants. Some critics saw the protagonist as an admirable new woman; others saw her as neurotic. *The Inheritors* (1921), also a full-length

For links to resources about Glaspell, click on *AuthorLinks* at **bedfordstmartins.com/jacobus**.

drama, focuses on the third-generation inheritors of a Midwestern college who clash because one family has liberal views and one has conservative views. Glaspell's last play, winner of the Pulitzer Prize, was *Alison's House* (1930), based on the life of Emily Dickinson. The latter part of Glaspell's life was spent writing fiction, especially four novels set in the Midwest that traced the struggles of women to maintain their ideals and values. *The Morning Is Near Us* sold over 100,000 copies in 1940 and was only one of her best-selling novels.

Jig Cook, a writer himself and a partner in many of Glaspell's ventures, spent the last two years of his life living in Delphi, Greece, in the manner of the peasants living on Mount Parnassus near the temple of Apollo. He died in 1924, and when Glaspell returned to the United States, she wrote a memoir of their life together called *The Road to the Temple*. In 1925, she broke with the Provincetown Players, who had moved in directions she did not approve of under the directorship of Eugene O'Neill. O'Neill tried to mollify Glaspell, but she never accepted his use of the theater company she and her husband had cofounded with him. When she died in 1948, she and O'Neill were essentially unreconciled.

Trifles

Trifles (1916) was apparently written as a companion piece for Eugene O'Neill's first produced play, the one-act *Bound East for Cardiff*. The two were performed together to make a complete evening presentation. In one sense *Trifles* is a murder mystery, but in another it is a critique of the gender-rigid attitudes of the officials whose responsibility it is to investigate the death of John Wright. Its main character, Minnie Foster Wright, is never presented but only described as a sweet woman who loved to sing when she was young but who married a man who slowly stifled her joy in living.

The setting of the play is a kitchen where the women, Mrs. Peters and Mrs. Hale, remain throughout the action. They examine the condition of the room and, by extension, the condition of Minnie Foster Wright. The men, examining the crime scene, the upstairs bedroom, spend much of the time offstage. They believe they are examining the important evidence, yet when they return with their findings, they are unable to understand what led to the death of John Wright, who to them seems quite a normal farmer.

The women, however, by examining the messy condition of the kitchen, the state of Minnie's preserves, and the quilt she was working on, begin to understand the motive behind Wright's murder. When they get to the dead body of the songbird Minnie had valued, they understand things in a way that the men cannot. The men observe that women are concerned with trifles, things of no importance. But the truth is that the women understand the fate of Minnie Foster Wright and John Wright in a way that would be almost impossible for the men, given their sense of what is significant and what is a trifle.

For discussion questions and assignments on *Trifles*, visit **bedfordstmartins.com/jacobus**.

In many ways the play is a study of gender differences and the way men's expectations and their sense of reality can distort the truth and deform a woman's life. In 1917, Glaspell wrote a short story using all the same material, called "A Jury of Her Peers," implying that the only peers of Minnie Foster Wright would be women like Mrs. Hale and Mrs. Peters. In 1917, however, women could not vote and in most states could not serve on juries.

Trifles in Performance

The original production, which may have included Eugene O'Neill among its cast members, was well received, but after Glaspell's death, most of her work fell out of fashion. *The Verge*, however, is still highly regarded in England and is often performed there. *Trifles* was neglected until the early 1960s, when feminist interest helped revive Glaspell's plays. Teacher and writer Sylvan Barnet included the play in his drama anthology, helping to bring it to the attention of contemporary viewers. Now produced most often by school and college groups, the play enjoys considerable popularity.

SUSAN GLASPELL (1876–1948)

Trifles   1916

Characters

GEORGE HENDERSON, *county attorney*
HENRY PETERS, *sheriff*
LEWIS HALE, *a neighboring farmer*
MRS. PETERS
MRS. HALE

Scene: *The kitchen in the now abandoned farmhouse of John Wright, a gloomy kitchen, and left without having been put in order — the walls covered with a faded wall paper. Down right is a door leading to the parlor. On the right wall above this door is a built-in kitchen cupboard with shelves in the upper portion and drawers below. In the rear wall at right, up two steps is a door opening onto stairs leading to the second floor. In the rear wall at left is a door to the shed and from there to the outside. Between these two doors is an old-fashioned black iron stove. Running along the left wall from the shed door is an old iron sink and sink shelf, in which is set a hand pump. Downstage of the sink is an uncurtained window. Near the window is an old wooden rocker. Center stage is an unpainted wooden kitchen table with straight chairs on either side. There is a small chair down right. Unwashed pans under the sink, a loaf of bread outside the breadbox, a dish towel on the table — other signs of incompleted work. At the rear the shed door opens and the Sheriff comes in followed by the County Attorney and Hale. The Sheriff and Hale are men in middle life, the County Attorney is a young man; all are much bundled up and go at once to the stove. They are followed by the two women — the Sheriff's wife, Mrs. Peters, first: she is a slight wiry woman, a thin nervous face. Mrs. Hale is larger and would ordinarily be called more comfortable looking, but she is disturbed now and looks fearfully about as she enters. The women have come in slowly, and stand close together near the door.*

COUNTY ATTORNEY (*at stove rubbing his hands*): This feels good. Come up to the fire, ladies.

MRS. PETERS (*after taking a step forward*): I'm not—cold.

SHERIFF (*unbuttoning his overcoat and stepping away from the stove to right of table as if to mark the beginning of official business*): Now, Mr. Hale, before we move things about, you explain to Mr. Henderson just what you saw when you came here yesterday morning.

COUNTY ATTORNEY (*crossing down to left of the table*): By the way, has anything been moved? Are things just as you left them yesterday?

SHERIFF (*looking about*): It's just about the same. When it dropped below zero last night I thought I'd better send Frank out this morning to make a fire for us — (*sits right of center table*) no use getting pneumonia with a big case on, but I told him not to touch anything except the stove—and you know Frank.

COUNTY ATTORNEY: Somebody should have been left here yesterday.

SHERIFF: Oh—yesterday. When I had to send Frank to Morris Center for that man who went crazy—I want you to know I had my hands full yesterday. I knew you could get back from Omaha by today and as long as I went over everything here myself————

COUNTY ATTORNEY: Well, Mr. Hale, tell just what happened when you came here yesterday morning.

HALE (*crossing down to above table*): Harry and I had started to town with a load of potatoes. We came along the road from my place and as I got here I said, "I'm going to see if I can't get John Wright to go in with me on a party telephone." I spoke to Wright about it once before and he put me off, saying folks talked too much anyway, and all he asked was peace and quiet—I guess you know about how much he talked himself; but I thought maybe if I went to the house and talked about it before his wife, though I said to Harry that I didn't know as what his wife wanted made much difference to John————

COUNTY ATTORNEY: Let's talk about that later, Mr. Hale. I do want to talk about that, but tell now just what happened when you got to the house.

HALE: I didn't hear or see anything; I knocked at the door, and still it was all quiet inside. I knew they must be up, it was past eight o'clock. So I knocked again, and I thought I heard someone say, "Come in." I wasn't sure, I'm not sure yet, but I opened the door—this door (*indicating the door by which the two women are still standing*) and there in that rocker—(*pointing to it*) sat Mrs. Wright. (*They all look at the rocker down left.*)

COUNTY ATTORNEY: What—was she doing?

HALE: She was rockin' back and forth. She had her apron in her hand and was kind of—pleating it.

COUNTY ATTORNEY: And how did she—look?

HALE: Well, she looked queer.

COUNTY ATTORNEY: How do you mean—queer?

HALE: Well, as if she didn't know what she was going to do next. And kind of done up.

COUNTY ATTORNEY (*takes out notebook and pencil and sits left of center table*): How did she seem to feel about your coming?

HALE: Why, I don't think she minded—one way or other. She didn't pay much attention. I said, "How do, Mrs. Wright, it's cold, ain't it?" And she said, "Is it?"—and went on kind of pleating at her apron. Well, I was surprised; she didn't ask me to come up to the stove, or to set down, but just sat there, not even looking at me, so I said, "I want to see John." And then she—laughed. I guess you would call it a laugh. I thought of Harry and the team outside, so I said a little sharp: "Can't I see John?" "No," she says, kind o' dull like. "Ain't he home?" says I. "Yes," says she, "he's home." "Then why can't I see him?" I asked her, out of patience. "'Cause he's dead," says she. "*Dead?*" says I. She just nodded her head, not getting a bit excited, but rockin' back and forth. "Why—where is he?" says I, not knowing what to say. She just pointed upstairs—like that. (*Himself pointing to the room above.*) I started for the stairs, with the idea of going up there. I walked from there to here—then I says, "Why, what did he die of?" "He died of a rope round his neck," says she, and just went on pleatin' at her apron. Well, I went out and called Harry. I thought I might—need help. We went upstairs and there he was lyin'————

COUNTY ATTORNEY: I think I'd rather have you go into that upstairs, where you can point it all out. Just go on now with the rest of the story.

HALE: Well, my first thought was to get that rope off. It looked . . . (*stops; his face twitches*) . . . but Harry, he went up to him, and he said, "No, he's dead all right, and we'd better not touch anything." So we went right back downstairs. She was still sitting that same way. "Has anybody been notified?" I asked. "No," says she, unconcerned. "Who did this, Mrs. Wright?" said Harry. He said it businesslike—and she stopped pleatin' of her apron. "I don't know," she says. "You don't *know?*" says Harry. "No," says she. "Weren't you sleepin' in the bed with him?" says Harry. "Yes," says she, "but I was on the inside." "Somebody slipped a rope round his head and strangled him and you didn't wake up?" says Harry. "I didn't wake up," she said after him. We must 'a' looked as if we didn't see how that could be, for after a minute she said, "I sleep sound." Harry was going to ask her more questions but I said maybe we ought to let her tell her story first to the coroner, or the sheriff, so Harry went fast as he could to Rivers' place, where there's a telephone.

COUNTY ATTORNEY: And what did Mrs. Wright do when she knew that you had gone for the coroner?

HALE: She moved from the rocker to that chair over there (*pointing to a small chair in the down right corner*) and just sat there with her hands held together and looking down. I got a feeling that I ought to make some conversation, so I said I had come in to see if John wanted to put in a telephone, and at that she started to laugh, and then she stopped and looked at me—scared. (*The County Attorney, who has had his notebook out, makes a note.*) I dunno, maybe it wasn't scared. I wouldn't like to say it was. Soon Harry got back, and then Dr. Lloyd came and you, Mr. Peters, and so I guess that's all I know that you don't.

COUNTY ATTORNEY (*rising and looking around*): I guess we'll go upstairs first—and then out to the barn and around there. (*To the Sheriff.*) You're convinced that there was nothing important here—nothing that would point to any motive?

SHERIFF: Nothing here but kitchen things. (*The County Attorney, after again looking around the kitchen,*

An early performance by the Provincetown Players of *Trifles* shows the small space and simple staging of the Wharf Theatre.

opens the door of a cupboard closet in right wall. He brings a small chair from right—gets on it and looks on a shelf. Pulls his hand away, sticky.)

COUNTY ATTORNEY: Here's a nice mess. (*The women draw nearer up to center.*)

MRS. PETERS (*to the other woman*): Oh, her fruit; it did freeze. (To the Lawyer.) She worried about that when it turned so cold. She said the fire'd go out and her jars would break.

SHERIFF (*rises*): Well, can you beat the woman! Held for murder and worryin' about her preserves.

COUNTY ATTORNEY (*getting down from chair*): I guess before we're through she may have something more serious than preserves to worry about. (*Crosses down right center.*)

HALE: Well, women are used to worrying over trifles. (*The two women move a little closer together.*)

COUNTY ATTORNEY (*with the gallantry of a young politician*): And yet, for all their worries, what would we do without the ladies? (*The women do not unbend. He goes below the center table to the sink, takes a dipperful of water from the pail, and pouring it into a basin, washes his hands. While he is doing this the Sheriff and Hale cross to cupboard, which they inspect. The County Attorney starts to wipe his hands on the roller towel, turns it for a cleaner place.*) Dirty towels! (*Kicks his foot against the pans under the sink.*) Not much of a housekeeper, would you say, ladies?

MRS. HALE (*stiffly*): There's a great deal of work to be done on a farm.

COUNTY ATTORNEY: To be sure. And yet (*with a little bow to her*) I know there are some Dickson County

farmhouses which do not have such roller towels. (*He gives it a pull to expose its full-length again.*)

MRS. HALE: Those towels get dirty awful quick. Men's hands aren't always clean as they might be.

COUNTY ATTORNEY: Ah, loyal to your sex, I see. But you and Mrs. Wright were neighbors. I suppose you were friends, too.

MRS. HALE (*shaking her head*): I've not seen much of her of late years. I've not been in this house—it's more than a year.

COUNTY ATTORNEY (*crossing to women up center*): And why was that? You didn't like her?

MRS. HALE: I liked her all well enough. Farmer's wives have their hands full, Mr. Henderson. And then———

COUNTY ATTORNEY: Yes———?

MRS. HALE (*looking about*): It never seemed a very cheerful place.

COUNTY ATTORNEY: No—it's not cheerful. I shouldn't say she had the homemaking instinct.

MRS. HALE: Well, I don't know as Wright had, either.

COUNTY ATTORNEY: You mean that they didn't get on very well?

MRS. HALE: No, I don't mean anything. But I don't think a place'd be any cheerfuller for John Wright's being in it.

COUNTY ATTORNEY: I'd like to talk more of that a little later. I want to get the lay of things upstairs now. (*He goes past the women to up right where the steps lead to a stair door.*)

SHERIFF: I suppose anything Mrs. Peters does'll be all right. She was to take in some clothes for her, you know, and a few little things. We left in such a hurry yesterday.

COUNTY ATTORNEY: Yes, but I would like to see what you take, Mrs. Peters, and keep an eye out for anything that might be of use to us.

MRS. PETERS: Yes, Mr. Henderson. (*The men leave by up right door to stairs. The women listen to the men's steps on the stairs, then look about the kitchen.*)

MRS. HALE (*crossing left to sink*): I'd hate to have men coming into my kitchen, snooping around and criticizing. (*She arranges the pans under sink which the lawyer had shoved out of place.*)

MRS. PETERS: Of course it's no more than their duty. (*Crosses to cupboard up right.*)

MRS. HALE: Duty's all right, but I guess that deputy sheriff that came out to make the fire might have got a little of this on. (*Gives the roller towel a pull.*) Wish I'd thought of that sooner. Seems mean to talk about her for not having things slicked up when she had to come away in such a hurry. (*Crosses right to Mrs. Peters at cupboard.*)

MRS. PETERS (*who has been looking through cupboard, lifts one end of towel that covers a pan*): She had bread set. (*Stands still.*)

MRS. HALE (*eyes fixed on a loaf of bread beside the breadbox, which is on a low shelf of the cupboard*): She was going to put this in there. (*Picks up loaf, abruptly drops it. In a manner of returning to familiar things.*) It's a shame about her fruit. I wonder if it's all gone. (*Gets up on chair and looks.*) I think there's some here that's all right, Mrs. Peters. Yes—here; (*holding it toward the window*) this is cherries, too. (*Looking again.*) I declare I believe that's the only one. (*Gets down, jar in hand. Goes to the sink and wipes it off on the outside.*) She'll feel awful bad after all her hard work in the hot weather. I remember the afternoon I put up my cherries last summer. (*She puts the jar on the big kitchen table, center of the room. With a sigh, is about to sit down in the rocking chair. Before she is seated realizes what chair it is; with a slow look at it, steps back. The chair which she has touched rocks back and forth. Mrs. Peters moves to center table and they both watch the chair rock for a moment or two.*)

MRS. PETERS (*shaking off the mood which the empty rocking chair has evoked. Now in a businesslike manner she speaks*): Well I must get those things from the front room closet. (*She goes to the door at the right but, after looking into the other room, steps back.*) You coming with me, Mrs. Hale? You could help me carry them. (*They go in the other room; reappear, Mrs. Peters carrying a dress, petticoat, and skirt, Mrs. Hale following with a pair of shoes.*) My, it's cold in there. (*She puts the clothes on the big table and hurries to the stove.*)

MRS. HALE (*right of center table examining the skirt*): Wright was close. I think maybe that's why she kept so much to herself. She didn't even belong to the Ladies' Aid. I suppose she felt she couldn't do her part, and then you don't enjoy things when you feel shabby. I heard she used to wear pretty clothes and be lively, when she was Minnie Foster, one of the town girls singing in the choir. But that—oh, that was thirty years ago. This all you want to take in?

MRS. PETERS: She said she wanted an apron. Funny thing to want, for there isn't much to get you dirty in jail, goodness knows. But I suppose just to make her feel more natural. (*Crosses to cupboard.*) She said they was in the top drawer in this cupboard. Yes, here. And then her little shawl that always hung behind the door. (*Opens stair door and looks.*) Yes, here it is. (*Quickly shuts door leading upstairs.*)

MRS. HALE (*abruptly moving toward her*): Mrs. Peters?

MRS. PETERS: Yes, Mrs. Hale? (*At up right door.*)

MRS. HALE: Do you think she did it?

MRS. PETERS (*in a frightened voice*): Oh, I don't know.

MRS. HALE: Well, I don't think she did. Asking for an apron and her little shawl. Worrying about her fruit.

MRS. PETERS (*starts to speak, glances up, where footsteps are heard in the room above. In a low voice*): Mr. Peters says it looks bad for her. Mr. Henderson is awful sarcastic in a speech and he'll make fun of her sayin' she didn't wake up.

MRS. HALE: Well, I guess John Wright didn't wake when they was slipping that rope under his neck.

MRS. PETERS (*crossing slowly to table and placing shawl and apron on table with other clothing*): No, it's strange. It must have been done awful crafty and still. They say it was such a—funny way to kill a man, rigging it all up like that.

MRS. HALE (*crossing to left of Mrs. Peters at table*): That's just what Mr. Hale said. There was a gun in the house. He says that's what he can't understand.

MRS. PETERS: Mr. Henderson said coming out that what was needed for the case was a motive; something to show anger, or—sudden feeling.

MRS. HALE (*who is standing by the table*): Well, I don't see any signs of anger around here. (*She puts her hand on the dish towel, which lies on the table, stands looking down at table, one-half of which is clean, the other half messy.*) It's wiped to here. (*Makes a move as if to finish work, then turns and looks at loaf of bread outside the breadbox. Drops towel. In that voice of coming back to familiar things.*) Wonder how they are finding things upstairs. (*Crossing below table to down right.*) I hope she had it a little more red-up° up there. You know, it seems kind of sneaking. Locking her up in town and then coming out here and trying to get her own house to turn against her!

MRS. PETERS: But, Mrs. Hale, the law is the law.

MRS. HALE: I s'pose 'tis. (*Unbuttoning her coat.*) Better loosen up your things, Mrs. Peters. You won't feel them when you go out. (*Mrs. Peters takes off her fur tippet, goes to hang it on chair back left of table, stands looking at the work basket on floor near down left window.*)

---

red-up: (slang) Ready for company

MRS. PETERS: She was piecing a quilt. (*She brings the large sewing basket to the center table and they look at the bright pieces, Mrs. Hale above the table and Mrs. Peters left of it.*)

MRS. HALE: It's a log cabin pattern. Pretty, isn't it? I wonder if she was goin' to quilt it or just knot it? (*Footsteps have been heard coming down the stairs. The Sheriff enters followed by Hale and the County Attorney.*)

SHERIFF: They wonder if she was going to quilt it or just knot it! (*The men laugh, the women look abashed.*)

COUNTY ATTORNEY (*rubbing his hands over the stove*): Frank's fire didn't do much up there, did it? Well, let's go out to the barn and get that cleared up. (*The men go outside by up left door.*)

MRS. HALE (*resentfully*): I don't know as there's anything so strange, our takin' up our time with little things while we're waiting for them to get the evidence. (*She sits in chair right of table smoothing out a block with decision.*) I don't see as it's anything to laugh about.

MRS. PETERS (*apologetically*): Of course they've got awful important things on their minds. (*Pulls up a chair and joins Mrs. Hale at the left of the table.*)

MRS. HALE (*examining another block*): Mrs. Peters, look at this one. Here, this is the one she was working on, and look at the sewing! All the rest of it has been so nice and even. And look at this! It's all over the place! Why, it looks as if she didn't know what she was about! (*After she has said this they look at each other, then start to glance back at the door. After an instant Mrs. Hale has pulled at a knot and ripped the sewing.*)

MRS. PETERS: Oh, what are you doing, Mrs. Hale?

MRS. HALE (*mildly*): Just pulling out a stitch or two that's not sewed very good. (*Threading a needle.*) Bad sewing always made me fidgety.

MRS. PETERS (*with a glance at the door, nervously*): I don't think we ought to touch things.

MRS. HALE: I'll just finish up this end. (*Suddenly stopping and leaning forward.*) Mrs. Peters?

MRS. PETERS: Yes, Mrs. Hale?

MRS. HALE: What do you suppose she was so nervous about?

MRS. PETERS: Oh—I don't know. I don't know as she was nervous. I sometimes sew awful queer when I'm just tired. (*Mrs. Hale starts to say something, looks at Mrs. Peters, then goes on sewing.*) Well, I must get these things wrapped up. They may be through sooner than we think. (*Putting apron and other things together.*) I wonder where I can find a piece of paper, and string. (*Rises.*)

MRS. HALE: In that cupboard, maybe.

MRS. PETERS (*crosses right looking in cupboard*): Why, here's a bird-cage. (*Holds it up.*) Did she have a bird, Mrs. Hale?

MRS. HALE: Why, I don't know whether she did or not—I've not been here for so long. There was a

Mrs. Hale (Sarah Einerson) and Mrs. Peters (Mary-Margaret Pyeatt) discovering the truth about the dead songbird in the 2000 Echo Theatre production of Susan Glaspell's *Trifles*, performed in Dallas, Texas, and directed by Ellen Locy. The production was an entry in Dallas's second annual Festival of Independent Theaters (FIT).

man around last year selling canaries cheap, but I don't know as she took one; maybe she did. She used to sing real pretty herself.

MRS. PETERS (*glancing around*): Seems funny to think of a bird here. But she must have had one, or why would she have a cage? I wonder what happened to it?

MRS. HALE: I s'pose maybe the cat got it.

MRS. PETERS: No, she didn't have a cat. She's got that feeling some people have about cats—being afraid of them. My cat got in her room and she was real upset and asked me to take it out.

MRS. HALE: My sister Bessie was like that. Queer, ain't it?

MRS. PETERS (*examining the cage*): Why, look at this door. It's broke. One hinge is pulled apart. (*Takes a step down to Mrs. Hale's right.*)

MRS. HALE (*looking too*): Looks as if someone must have been rough with it.

MRS. PETERS: Why, yes. (*She brings the cage forward and puts it on the table.*)

MRS. HALE (*glancing toward up left door*): I wish if they're going to find any evidence they'd be about it. I don't like this place.

MRS. PETERS: But I'm awful glad you came with me, Mrs. Hale. It would be lonesome for me sitting here alone.

MRS. HALE: It would, wouldn't it? (*Dropping her sewing.*) But I tell you what I do wish, Mrs. Peters. I wish I had come over sometimes when *she* was here. I—(*looking around the room*)—wish I had.

MRS. PETERS: But of course you were awful busy, Mrs. Hale—your house and your children.

MRS. HALE (*rises and crosses left*): I could've come. I stayed away because it weren't cheerful—and that's why I ought to have come. I—(*looking out left window*)—I've never liked this place. Maybe it's because it's down in a hollow and you don't see the road. I dunno what it is, but it's a lonesome place and always was. I wish I had come over to see Minnie Foster sometimes. I can see now—(*Shakes her head.*)

MRS. PETERS (*left of table and above it*): Well, you mustn't reproach yourself, Mrs. Hale. Somehow we just don't see how it is with other folks until—something turns up.

MRS. HALE: Not having children makes less work—but it makes a quiet house, and Wright out to work all day, and no company when he did come in. (*Turning from window.*) Did you know John Wright, Mrs. Peters?

MRS. PETERS: Not to know him; I've seen him in town. They say he was a good man.

MRS. HALE: Yes—good; he didn't drink, and kept his word as well as most, I guess, and paid his debts. But he was a hard man, Mrs. Peters. Just to pass the time of day with him—(*Shivers.*) Like a raw wind that gets to the bone. (*Pauses, her eye falling on the cage.*) I should think she would 'a' wanted a bird. But what do you suppose went with it?

MRS. PETERS: I don't know, unless it got sick and died. (*She reaches over and swings the broken door, swings it again, both women watch it.*)

MRS. HALE: You weren't raised round here, were you? (*Mrs. Peters shakes her head.*) You didn't know—her?

MRS. PETERS: Not till they brought her yesterday.

MRS. HALE: She—come to think of it, she was kind of like a bird herself—real sweet and pretty, but kind of timid and—fluttery. How—she—did—change. (*Silence: then as if struck by a happy thought and relieved to get back to everyday things. Crosses right above Mrs. Peters to cupboard, replaces small chair used to stand on to its original place down right.*) Tell you what, Mrs. Peters, why don't you take the quilt in with you? It might take up her mind.

MRS. PETERS: Why, I think that's a real nice idea, Mrs. Hale. There couldn't possibly be any objection to it could there? Now, just what would I take? I wonder if her patches are in here—and her things. (*They look in the sewing basket.*)

MRS. HALE (*crosses to right of table*): Here's some red. I expect this has got sewing things in it. (*Brings out a fancy box.*) What a pretty box. Looks like something somebody would give you. Maybe her scissors are in here. (*Opens box. Suddenly puts her hand to her nose.*) Why————(*Mrs. Peters bends nearer, then turns her face away.*) There's something wrapped up in this piece of silk.

MRS. PETERS: Why, this isn't her scissors.

MRS. HALE (*lifting the silk*): Oh, Mrs. Peters—it's———— (*Mrs. Peters bends closer.*)

MRS. PETERS: It's the bird.

MRS. HALE: But, Mrs. Peters—look at it! Its neck! Look at its neck! It's all—other side *to*.

MRS. PETERS: Somebody—wrung—its—neck. (*Their eyes meet. A look of growing comprehension, of horror. Steps are heard outside. Mrs. Hale slips box under quilt pieces, and sinks into her chair. Enter Sheriff and County Attorney. Mrs. Peters steps down left and stands looking out of window.*)

COUNTY ATTORNEY (*as one turning from serious things to little pleasantries*): Well, ladies, have you decided whether she was going to quilt it or knot it? (*Crosses to center above table.*)

MRS. PETERS: We think she was going to—knot it. (*Sheriff crosses to right of stove, lifts stove lid, and glances at fire, then stands warming hands at stove.*)

COUNTY ATTORNEY: Well, that's interesting, I'm sure. (*Seeing the bird-cage.*) Has the bird flown?

MRS. HALE (*putting more quilt pieces over the box*): We think the—cat got it.

COUNTY ATTORNEY (*preoccupied*): Is there a cat? (*Mrs. Hale glances in a quick covert way at Mrs. Peters.*)

MRS. PETERS (*turning from window takes a step in*): Well, not *now*. They're superstitious, you know. They leave.

COUNTY ATTORNEY (*to Sheriff Peters, continuing an interrupted conversation*): No sign at all of anyone having come from the outside. Their own rope. Now let's go up again and go over it piece by piece. (*They start upstairs.*) It would have to have been someone who knew just the————(*Mrs. Peters sits down left of table. The two women sit there not looking at one another, but as if peering into something and at the same time holding back. When they talk now it is in the manner of feeling their way over strange ground, as if afraid of what they are saying, but as if they cannot help saying it.*)

MRS. HALE (*hesistatively and in hushed voice*): She liked the bird. She was going to bury it in that pretty box.

MRS. PETERS (*in a whisper*): When I was a girl—my kitten—there was a boy took a hatchet, and before my eyes—and before I could get there————(*Covers her face an instant.*) If they hadn't held me back I would have—(*catches herself, looks upstairs where steps are heard, falters weakly*)—hurt him.

MRS. HALE (*with a slow look around her*): I wonder how it would seem never to have had any children around. (*Pause.*) No, Wright wouldn't like the bird—a thing that sang. She used to sing. He killed that, too.

MRS. PETERS (*moving uneasily*): We don't know who killed the bird.

MRS. HALE: I knew John Wright.

MRS. PETERS: It was an awful thing was done in this house that night, Mrs. Hale. Killing a man while he slept, slipping a rope around his neck that choked the life out of him.

MRS. HALE: His neck. Choked the life out of him. (*Her hand goes out and rests on the bird-cage.*)

MRS. PETERS (*with rising voice*): We don't know who killed him. We don't know.

MRS. HALE (*her own feelings not interrupted*): If there'd been years and years of nothing, then a bird to sing to you, it would be awful—still, after the bird was still.

MRS. PETERS (*something within her speaking*): I know what stillness is. When we homesteaded in Dakota, and my first baby died—after he was two years old, and me with no other then————

MRS. HALE (*moving*): How soon do you suppose they'll be through looking for the evidence?

MRS. PETERS: I know what stillness is. (*Pulling herself back.*) The law has got to punish crimes, Mrs. Hale.

MRS. HALE (*not as if answering that*): I wish you'd seen Minnie Foster when she wore a white dress with blue ribbons and stood up there in the choir and sang. (*A look around the room.*) Oh, I *wish* I'd come over here once in a while! That was a crime! That was a crime! Who's going to punish that?

MRS. PETERS (*looking upstairs*): We mustn't—take on.

MRS. HALE: I might have known she needed help! I know how things can be—for women. I tell you, it's queer, Mrs. Peters. We live close together and we live far apart. We all go through the same things—it's all just a different kind of the same thing. (*Brushes her eyes, noticing the jar of fruit, reaches out for it.*) If I was you I wouldn't tell her her fruit was gone. Tell her it *ain't.* Tell her it's all right. Take this in to prove it to her. She—she may never know whether it was broke or not.

MRS. PETERS (*takes the jar, looks about for something to wrap it in; takes petticoat from the clothes brought from the other room, very nervously begins winding this around the jar. In a false voice*): My, it's a good thing the men couldn't hear us. Wouldn't they just laugh! Getting all stirred up over a little thing like a—dead canary. As if that could have anything to do with—with—wouldn't they *laugh!* (*The men are heard coming downstairs.*)

MRS. HALE (*under her breath*): Maybe they would—maybe they wouldn't.

COUNTY ATTORNEY: No, Peters, it's all perfectly clear except a reason for doing it. But you know juries when it comes to women. If there was some definite thing. (*Crosses slowly to above table. Sheriff crosses down right. Mrs. Hale and Mrs. Peters remain seated at either side of table.*) Something to show—something to make a story about—a thing that would connect up with this strange way of doing it————(*The women's eyes meet for an instant. Enter Hale from outer door.*)

HALE (*remaining by door*): Well, I've got the team around. Pretty cold out there.

COUNTY ATTORNEY: I'm going to stay awhile by myself. (*To the Sheriff.*) You can send Frank out for me, can't you? I want to go over everything. I'm not satisfied that we can't do better.

SHERIFF: Do you want to see what Mrs. Peters is going to take in? (*The Lawyer picks up the apron, laughs.*)

COUNTY ATTORNEY: Oh, I guess they're not very dangerous things the ladies have picked out. (*Moves a few things about, disturbing the quilt pieces which cover the box. Steps back.*) No, Mrs. Peters doesn't need supervising. For that matter a sheriff's wife is married to the law. Ever think of it that way, Mrs. Peters?

MRS. PETERS: Not—just that way.

SHERIFF (*chuckling*): Married to the law. (*Moves to down right door to the other room.*) I just want you to come in here a minute, George. We ought to take a look at these windows.

COUNTY ATTORNEY (*scoffingly*): Oh, windows!

SHERIFF: We'll be right out, Mr. Hale. (*Hale goes outside. The Sheriff follows the County Attorney into the room. Then Mrs. Hale rises, hands tight together, looking intensely at Mrs. Peters, whose eyes make a slow turn, finally meeting Mrs. Hale's. A moment Mrs. Hale holds her, then her own eyes point the way to where the box is concealed. Suddenly Mrs. Peters throws back quilt pieces and tries to put the box in the bag she is carrying. It is too big. She opens box, starts to take bird out, cannot touch it, goes to pieces, stands there helpless. Sound of a knob turning in the other room. Mrs. Hale snatches the box and puts it in the pocket of her big coat. Enter County Attorney and Sheriff, who remains down right.*)

COUNTY ATTORNEY (*crosses to up left door facetiously*): Well, Henry, at least we found out that she was not going to quilt it. She was going to—what is it you call it, ladies?

MRS. HALE (*standing center below table facing front, her hand against her pocket*): We call it—knot it, Mr. Henderson.

COMMENTARY

CHRISTINE DYMKOWSKI (b. 1950)

On the Edge: The Plays of Susan Glaspell 1988

Christine Dymkowski sees *Trifles* as a play that occupies the edge — the marginalized space reserved for women. The male figures in the play assume that their interests are central to the murder investigation, whereas Glaspell demonstrates that the most significant issues in the investigation are on the edge of men's attention, where they can never see them.

The paradoxically central nature of the edge informs Glaspell's theatrical methods and themes. Her first play, *Trifles* (1916), illustrates its use in several ways, the irony of the title already having been noted. The plot revolves around the visit to a farmhouse by County Attorney Henderson and Sheriff Peters to investigate the murder of John Wright; they are accompanied by the farmer who discovered the murder and, almost incidentally, by the farmer's and sheriff's wives. The men's assumption is that Minnie Wright, already in custody for the crime, has killed her husband, and they are there to search the house for clues to a motive. The audience undoubtedly sees them as protagonists at the start of the play.

The stage directions immediately call attention to the women's marginality: the men, "much bundled up" against the freezing cold, "go at once to the stove" in the Wrights' kitchen, while the women who follow them in do so "slowly, and stand close together near the door." The separateness of the female and male worlds is thus immediately established visually and then reinforced by the dialogue:

> MRS. PETERS (*to the other woman*): Oh, her fruit; it did freeze. (*To the Lawyer.*) She worried about that when it turned so cold. . . .
>
> SHERIFF: Well, can you beat the women [*sic*]! Held for murder and worryin' about her preserves.
>
> COUNTY ATTORNEY: I guess before we're through she may have something more serious than preserves to worry about.
>
> HALE: Well, women are used to worrying over trifles.
> (*The two women move a little closer together.*)

Not surprisingly, the women are relegated to the kitchen, while the men's attention turns to the rest of the house, particularly the bedroom where the crime was committed: "You're convinced that there was nothing important here — nothing that would point to any motive," Henderson asks Peters, and is assured that there is "Nothing here but kitchen things." However, while the men view the kitchen as marginal to their purpose, the drama stays centered there where the women are: contrary to expectation, it becomes the central focus of the play.

929

Ironically, it is the kitchen that holds the clues to the desperation and loneliness of Minnie's life and yields the women the answers for which the men search in vain; moreover, the understanding that they do reach goes beyond the mere solving of the crime to a redefinition of what the crime was. Mrs. Hale blames herself for a failure of imagination: "Oh, I *wish* I'd come over here once in a while! That was a crime! That was a crime! Who's going to punish that? . . . I might have known she needed help! I know how things can be—for women. I tell you, it's queer, Mrs. Peters. We live close together and we live far apart. We all go through the same things—it's all just a different kind of the same thing." The empathy both women feel for Minnie leads them to suppress the evidence they have found, patiently enduring the men's condescension instead of competing with them on their own ground. Conventional moral values are overturned, just as the expected form of the murder mystery is ignored: the play differentiates between justice and law and shows that the traditional "solution" is no such thing.

Just as Glaspell sets the play in the seemingly marginal kitchen, she makes the absent Minnie Wright its focus, a tactic she was to use again in *Bernice* and *Alison's House;* although noted by critics, this use of an absent central character has not received much comment. It is yet another way in which Glaspell makes central the apparently marginal—indeed, in stage terms, the nonexistent.

Luigi Pirandello

Luigi Pirandello (1867–1936) was an Italian short-story writer and novelist, a secondary school teacher, and finally a playwright. His life was complicated by business failures that wiped out his personal income and threw his wife into a psychological depression that Pirandello quite bluntly described as madness. Out of his acquaintance with madness—he remained with his wife for fourteen years after she lost touch with reality—Pirandello claimed to have developed much of his attitude toward the shifting surfaces of appearances.

Pirandello's short stories and novels show the consistent pattern of his plays: a deep examination of what we know to be real and a questioning of our confidence in our beliefs. His novel *Shoot* (1915) questions the surfaces of cinema reality, which contemporary Italy had embraced with great enthusiasm. His relentless examination of the paradoxes of experience has given him a reputation for pessimism. He himself said, "I think of life as a very sad piece of buffoonery," and he insisted that people bear within them a deep need to deceive themselves "by creating a reality . . . which . . . is discovered to be vain and illusory."

For most of his early career, Pirandello was not a popular playwright in Italy, and therefore much of his dramatic work was first performed abroad. In 1923, he was known as an important novelist and came to the attention of Benito Mussolini (1883–1945), the Fascist dictator of Italy. Pirandello joined the Italian Fascist party as a means of establishing the National Art Theatre in Rome, which enjoyed considerable state support. When asked why he was a Fascist, he said, "I am a Fascist because I am an Italian." After Pirandello won the Nobel Prize for literature in 1934, one account has him breaking with Fascism entirely over the Italian invasion of Ethiopia, and another account has him giving over his Nobel medal to be melted down for the Ethiopian campaign. Profound uncertainties about his behavior, as well as about some of his dramas, persist to this day.

Pirandello's influence in modern theater resulted from his experimentation with the concept of realism that dominated drama from the time of Strindberg and Ibsen. The concept of the imaginary "fourth wall" of the stage through which the audience observed the action of characters in their living rooms had become the norm in theater. Pirandello, however, questioned all thought of norms by subjecting the very idea of reality to philosophical scrutiny. His questioning helped playwrights around the world expand their approaches to theater in the early part of the twentieth century. Pirandello was one of the first, and one of the best, experimentalists.

Six Characters in Search of an Author

Pirandello's play is part of a trilogy: *Six Characters in Search of an Author* (1921), *Each in His Own Way* (1924), and *Tonight We Improvise* (1930). These plays all examine the impossibility of knowing reality. There is no objective truth to know, Pirandello tells us, and what we think of as reality is totally subjective, something that each of us maintains independently of other people and that none of us can communicate. We are, in other words, apart—each of us sealed into his or her own limited world.

These ideas were hardly novel. Playwrights had dealt with them before, even during the Elizabethan age, at a time when—because of the Protestant Reformation—the absolute hold of the definitions of reality promoted by the Roman Catholic Church had crumbled. Pirandello's plays were produced during the 1920s, when people were uncertain, frightened, and still reeling in shock from the destruction of World War I. In this depressed time, Pirandello's audience saw in his work a reflection of their own dispirited, fearful selves.

In a sense, *Six Characters in Search of an Author* is about the relationship between art and life, and especially about the relationship between drama and life. The premise of the play is absurd. In the middle of a rehearsal of a Pirandello play, several characters appear and request that an author be found to cobble them into a play. The stage manager assumes that they are presenting themselves as actors to be in a play, but they explain that they are not actors. They are real characters. This implies a paradox: that characters are independent of the actors who play them (we are used to the characters being only on paper). When the characters demand actors to represent them, we know that one limit of impossibility has been reached.

The characters who appear are, in a sense, types: a father, a mother, a stepdaughter, a son, two silent figures—the boy and the child—and, finally, a milliner, Madame Pace. They share the stage with the actors of the company, who are rehearsing the Pirandello play *Mixing It Up*. The six characters have been abandoned by their creator, the author who has absconded, leaving them in search of a substitute. The stepdaughter, late in the play, surmises that their author abandoned them "in a fit of depression, of disgust for the ordinary theater as the public knows it and likes it."

Pirandello uses his characters and their situation to comment on the life of the theater in the 1920s, and he also uses them to begin a series of speculations on the relationship of a public to the actors they see in plays, the characters the actors play, and the authors who create them. To an extent, the relationship between an author and his or her characters is always a metaphor for the relationship between a creator and all creation. It is tempting to think of Samuel Beckett years later in his *Waiting for Godot* imagining an "author" having abandoned his creations because they failed to satisfy him. The six characters—or creations—who invade the stage in Pirandello's play have a firm sense of themselves and their actions. They bring with them a story—as all characters in plays do—and they invite the manager to participate in their stories, just as characters invite audiences to become one with their narratives.

One of the more amusing scenes depicts the characters' reactions to seeing actors play their parts. Since they are "real" characters, they have the utmost authority regarding how their parts should be played, and they end up laughing at the inept efforts of the actors in act 2. When the manager disputes with them, wondering why they protest so vigorously, they explain that they want to make sure the truth is told. The truth: the concept seems so simple on the

For discussion questions and assignments on *Six Characters in Search of an Author*, visit **bedfordstmartins.com/jacobus**.

surface, but in the situation that Pirandello has conceived, it is loaded with complexities that the stage manager cannot fathom.

By the time the question of truth has been raised, the manager has begun to get a sense of the poignancy of the story that these characters have to tell. He has also begun to see that he must let them continue to tell their story—except that they are not telling it, they are living it. When the climax of their story is reached in the last moments of the play, the line between what is acted and what is lived onstage has become almost completely blurred. When the play ends, it is difficult to know what has truly occurred and what has truly been acted out.

Six Characters in Search of an Author has endured because it still rings true in its examination of the relationship between art and life, illusion and reality. The very word *illusion* is rejected by the characters—as characters, they are part of the illusion of reality. They reject the thought that they are literature, asserting, "This is Life, this is passion!"

Six Characters in Search of an Author in Performance

The first production of *Six Characters in Search of an Author* in Rome in May 1921 resulted in a riot that threatened the author and his daughter. The calmer London production in March 1922 in the Kingsway Theater garnered positive reviews, and the audiences, although at times puzzled, were responsive to what the *Christian Science Monitor* called "one of the freshest and most original productions seen for a long time." The first production in New York was directed by Brock Pemberton at the Princess Theatre in October 1922 with the distinguished American actress Florence Eldridge as the stepdaughter. One newspaper critic said, "Pirandello turns a powerful microscope on the dramatist's mental workshop—the modus operandi of play production—and after having destroyed our illusion, like a prestidigitator who shows us how a trick is done, expects us to believe in him."

Pirandello directed the play in Italian in London in 1925, and despite the audience's general inability to understand the language, the New Oxford Theatre was filled for every night of its run. He brought the company to the United States after the British censor determined that the play was "unsuitable for English audiences" and closed the play in London. It was not officially licensed for performance in England again until 1928.

Revivals of the play have been numerous. Three productions in New York in the 1930s preceded revivals in 1948 and 1955. London saw productions in February 1932 and November 1950. By the 1930s audience confusion had diminished, and in 1932 one London critic declared, "Repetition cannot dull the brilliance of the play's attack on theatrical shams." In 1955, Tyrone Guthrie's Phoenix Theatre used a translation and adaptation by Guthrie and Michael Wager. The production was not successful, although critics liked the translation. Sir Ralph Richardson performed in London's West End production in 1963. Robert Brustein received extraordinary praise for his American Repertory Theater (ART) production in 1985. Instead of interrupting a Pirandello play, the six characters interrupt the rehearsal of a Molière play, *Sganarelle*, which has roots in Italian commedia dell'arte and which had been a highly successful ART production. This self-reference—in Pirandellian fashion—helped to blur the line between the realities on and off the stage. Boston critic Kevin

Kelly said of the performance, "Brustein immediately links the paradox in Pirandello's theme about reality in illusion / illusion in reality to . . . the pragmatic fantasy of theater itself." The play was revived by Brustein and ART once more in 1996 to great acclaim. The 2008 production directed by Rupert Goold in the Gielgud Theatre in London's West End had the six characters interrupt a conference of film people discussing how to finish their upcoming documentary about an English boy who successfully sought euthanasia in Norway. This production added the question of life and death to the question of appearance and reality.

LUIGI PIRANDELLO (1867–1936)

Six Characters in Search of an Author 1921

A Comedy in the Making

TRANSLATED BY EDWARD STORER

Characters of the Comedy in the Making

THE FATHER
THE MOTHER
THE STEPDAUGHTER
THE SON
THE BOY } *do not speak*
THE CHILD
MADAME PACE

Actors of the Company

THE MANAGER
LEADING LADY
LEADING MAN
SECOND LADY LEAD
L'INGÉNUE
JUVENILE LEAD
OTHER ACTORS AND ACTRESSES
PROPERTY MAN
PROMPTER
MACHINIST
MANAGER'S SECRETARY
DOOR-KEEPER
SCENE SHIFTERS

Scene: *Daytime. The stage of a theater.*

(N.B.: *The Comedy is without acts or scenes. The performance is interrupted once, without the curtain being lowered, when the Manager and the chief characters withdraw to arrange a scenario. A second interruption of the action takes place when, by mistake, the stage hands let the curtain down.*)

ACT I

(*The spectators will find the curtain raised and the stage as it usually is during the daytime. It will be half dark, and empty, so that from the beginning the public may have the impression of an impromptu performance.*)

(*Prompter's box and a small table and chair for the Manager*)

(*Two other small tables and several chairs scattered about as during rehearsals.*)

(*The Actors and Actresses of the company enter from the back of the stage: first one, then another, then two together; nine or ten in all. They are about to rehearse a Pirandello play: Mixing It Up. Some of the company move off toward their dressing rooms. The Prompter, who has the "book" under his arm, is waiting for the Manager in order to begin the rehearsal.*)

(*The Actors and Actresses, some standing, some sitting, chat and smoke. One perhaps reads a paper; another cons his part.*)

(*Finally, the Manager enters and goes to the table prepared for him. His Secretary brings him his mail, through which he glances. The Prompter takes his seat, turns on a light, and opens the "book."*)

THE MANAGER (*throwing a letter down on the table*): I can't see. (*To Property Man.*) Let's have a little light, please!

PROPERTY MAN: Yes, sir, yes, at once. (*A light comes down on to the stage.*)

THE MANAGER (*clapping his hands*): Come along! Come along! Second act of "Mixing It Up." (*Sits down.*)

(*The Actors and Actresses go from the front of the stage to the wings, all except the three who are to begin the rehearsal.*)

THE PROMPTER (*reading the "book"*): "Leo Gala's house. A curious room serving as dining-room and study."

THE MANAGER (*to Property Man*): Fix up the old red room.

PROPERTY MAN (*noting it down*): Red set. All right!

THE PROMPTER (*continuing to read from the "book"*): "Table already laid and writing desk with books and papers. Bookshelves. Exit rear to Leo's bedroom. Exit left to kitchen. Principal exit to right."

THE MANAGER (*energetically*): Well, you understand: The principal exit over there; here, the kitchen. (*Turning to actor who is to play the part of Socrates.*) You make your entrances and exits here. (*To Property Man.*) The baize doors at the rear, and curtains.

PROPERTY MAN (*noting it down*): Right!

PROMPTER (*reading as before*): "When the curtain rises, Leo Gala, dressed in cook's cap and apron, is busy beating an egg in a cup. Philip, also dressed as a cook, is beating another egg. Guidi Venanzi is seated and listening."

LEADING MAN (*to Manager*): Excuse me, but must I absolutely wear a cook's cap?

THE MANAGER (*annoyed*): I imagine so. It says so there anyway. (*Pointing to the "book."*)

LEADING MAN: But it's ridiculous!

THE MANAGER (*jumping up in a rage*): Ridiculous? Ridiculous? Is it my fault if France won't send us any more good comedies, and we are reduced to putting on Pirandello's works, where nobody understands anything, and where the author plays the fool with us all? (*The Actors grin. The Manager goes to Leading Man and shouts.*) Yes sir, you put on the cook's cap and beat eggs. Do you suppose that with all this egg-beating business you are on an ordinary stage? Get that out of your head. You represent the shell of the eggs you are beating! (*Laughter and comments among the Actors.*) Silence! and listen to my explanations, please! (*To Leading Man.*) "The empty form of reason without the fullness of instinct, which is blind."—You stand for reason, your wife is instinct.

It's a mixing up of the parts, according to which you who act your own part become the puppet of yourself. Do you understand?

LEADING MAN: I'm hanged if I do.

THE MANAGER: Neither do I. But let's get on with it. It's sure to be a glorious failure anyway. (*Confidentially.*) But I say, please face three-quarters. Otherwise, what with the abstruseness of the dialogue, and the public that won't be able to hear you, the whole thing will go to hell. Come on! come on!

PROMPTER: Pardon sir, may I get into my box? There's a bit of a draft.

THE MANAGER: Yes, yes, of course!

(*At this point, the Door-Keeper has entered from the stage door and advances toward the Manager's table, taking off his braided cap. During this maneuver, the Six Characters enter, and stop by the door at back of stage, so that when the Door-Keeper is about to announce their coming to the Manager, they are already on the stage. A tenuous light surrounds them, almost as if irradiated by them—the faint breath of their fantastic reality.*)

(*This light will disappear when they come forward toward the actors. They preserve, however, something of the dream lightness in which they seem almost suspended; but this does not detract from the essential reality of their forms and expressions.*)

(*He who is known as the Father is a man of about 50: hair, reddish in color, thin at the temples; he is not bald, however, thick mustaches, falling over his still fresh mouth, which often opens in an empty and uncertain smile. He is fattish, pale; with an especially wide forehead. He has blue, oval-shaped eyes, very clear and piercing. Wears light trousers and a dark jacket. He is alternatively mellifluous and violent in his manner.*)

(*The Mother seems crushed and terrified as if by an intolerable weight of shame and abasement. She is dressed in modest black and wears a thick widow's veil of crepe. When she lifts this, she reveals a waxlike face. She always keeps her eyes downcast.*)

(*The Stepdaughter is dashing, almost impudent, beautiful. She wears mourning too, but with great elegance. She shows contempt for the timid half-frightened manner of the wretched Boy (14 years old, and also dressed in black); on the other hand, she displays a lively tenderness for her little sister, the Child (about four), who is dressed in white, with a black silk sash at the waist.*)

(*The Son (22) is tall, severe in his attitude of contempt for the Father, supercilious and indifferent to the Mother. He looks as if he had come on the stage against his will.*)

DOOR-KEEPER (*cap in hand*): Excuse me, sir . . .

THE MANAGER (*rudely*): Eh? What is it?

DOOR-KEEPER (*timidly*): These people are asking for you, sir.

THE MANAGER (*furious*): I am rehearsing, and you know perfectly well no one's allowed to come in during rehearsals! (*Turning to the Characters.*) Who are you, please? What do you want?

THE FATHER (*coming forward a little, followed by the others who seem embarrassed*): As a matter of fact . . . we have come here in search of an author . . .

THE MANAGER (*half angry, half amazed*): An author? What author?

THE FATHER: Any author, sir.

THE MANAGER: But there's no author here. We are not rehearsing a new piece.

THE STEPDAUGHTER (*vivaciously*): So much the better, so much the better! We can be your new piece.

AN ACTOR (*coming forward from the others*): Oh, do you hear that?

THE FATHER (*to Stepdaughter*): Yes, but if the author isn't here . . . (*To Manager.*) unless you would be willing . . .

THE MANAGER: You are trying to be funny.

THE FATHER: No, for Heaven's sake, what are you saying? We bring you a drama, sir.

THE STEPDAUGHTER: We may be your fortune.

THE MANAGER: Will you oblige me by going away? We haven't time to waste with mad people.

THE FATHER (*mellifluously*): Oh sir, you know well that life is full of infinite absurdities, which, strangely enough, do not even need to appear plausible, since they are true.

THE MANAGER: What the devil is he talking about?

THE FATHER: I say that to reverse the ordinary process may well be considered a madness: that is, to create credible situations, in order that they may appear true. But permit me to observe that if this be madness, it is the sole *raison d'être*° of your profession, gentlemen. (*The Actors look hurt and perplexed.*)

THE MANAGER (*getting up and looking at him*): So our profession seems to you one worthy of madmen then?

THE FATHER: Well, to make seem true that which isn't true . . . without any need . . . for a joke as it were . . . Isn't that your mission, gentlemen: to give life to fantastic characters on the stage?

THE MANAGER (*interpreting the rising anger of the Company*): But I would beg you to believe, my dear sir, that the profession of the comedian is a noble one. If today, as things go, the playwrights give us stupid comedies to play and puppets to represent instead of men, remember we are proud to have given life to immortal works here on these very boards! (*The Actors, satisfied, applaud their Manager.*)

THE FATHER (*interrupting furiously*): Exactly, perfectly, to living beings more alive than those who breathe and wear clothes: beings less real perhaps, but truer! I agree with you entirely. (*The Actors look at one another in amazement.*)

THE MANAGER: But what do you mean? Before, you said . . .

THE FATHER: No, excuse me, I meant it for you, sir, who were crying out that you had no time to lose with madmen, while no one better than yourself knows that nature uses the instrument of human fantasy in order to pursue her high creative purpose.

raison d'être: French for "reason to exist."

THE MANAGER: Very well,—but where does all this take us?

THE FATHER: Nowhere! It is merely to show you that one is born to life in many forms, in many shapes, as tree, or as stone, as water, as butterfly, or as woman. So one may also be born a character in a play.

THE MANAGER (*with feigned comic dismay*): So you and these other friends of yours have been born characters?

THE FATHER: Exactly, and alive as you see! (*Manager and Actors burst out laughing.*)

THE FATHER (*hurt*): I am sorry you laugh, because we carry in us a drama, as you can guess from this woman here veiled in black.

THE MANAGER (*losing patience at last and almost indignant*): Oh, chuck it! Get away please! Clear out of here! (*To Property Man.*) For Heaven's sake, turn them out!

THE FATHER (*resisting*): No, no, look here, we . . .

THE MANAGER (*roaring*): We come here to work, you know.

LEADING ACTOR: One cannot let oneself be made such a fool of.

THE FATHER (*determined, coming forward*): I marvel at your incredulity, gentlemen. Are you not accustomed to see the characters created by an author spring to life in yourselves and face each other? Just because there is no "book" (*pointing to the Prompter's box*) which contains us, you refuse to believe . . .

THE STEPDAUGHTER (*advances toward Manager, smiling and coquettish*): Believe me, we are really six most interesting characters, sir; sidetracked however.

THE FATHER: Yes, that is the word! (*To Manager all at once.*) In the sense, that is, that the author who created us alive no longer wished, or was no longer able, materially to put us into a work of art. And this was a real crime, sir, because he who has had the luck to be born a character can laugh even at death. He cannot die. The man, the writer, the instrument of the creation will die, but his creation does not die. And to live for ever, it does not need to have extraordinary gifts or to be able to work wonders. Who was Sancho Panza? Who was Don Abbondio?° Yet they live eternally because—live germs as they were—they had the fortune to find a fecundating matrix, a fantasy which could raise and nourish them: make them live for ever!

THE MANAGER: That is quite all right. But what do you want here, all of you?

THE FATHER: We want to live.

THE MANAGER (*ironically*): For Eternity?

THE FATHER: No, sir, only for a moment . . . in you.

AN ACTOR: Just listen to him!

LEADING LADY: They want to live, in us . . . !

Sancho Panza . . . Don Abbondio: Memorable characters in novels: the squire in Cervantes's *Don Quixote* and the priest in Manzoni's *I Promessi Sposi* (*The Betrothed*), respectively.

JUVENILE LEAD (*pointing to the Stepdaughter*): I've no objection, as far as that one is concerned!

THE FATHER: Look here! look here! The comedy has to be made. (*To the Manager.*) But if you and your actors are willing, we can soon concert it among ourselves.

THE MANAGER (*annoyed*): But what do you want to concert? We don't go in for concerts here. Here we play dramas and comedies!

THE FATHER: Exactly! That is just why we have come to you.

THE MANAGER: And where is the "book"?

THE FATHER: It is in us! (*The Actors laugh.*) The drama is in us, and we are the drama. We are impatient to play it. Our inner passion drives us on to this.

THE STEPDAUGHTER (*disdainful, alluring, treacherous, full of impudence*): My passion, sir! Ah, if you only knew! My passion for him! (*Points to the Father and makes a pretense of embracing him. Then she breaks out into a loud laugh.*)

THE FATHER (*angrily*): Behave yourself! And please don't laugh in that fashion.

THE STEPDAUGHTER: With your permission, gentlemen, I, who am a two months orphan, will show you how I can dance and sing. (*Sings and then dances Prenez garde à Tchou-Tchin-Tchou.*)

Les chinois sont un peuple malin,
De Shangaî à Pékin,
Ils ont mis des écriteaux partout:
Prenez garde à Tchou-Tchin-Tchou.°

ACTORS AND ACTRESSES: Bravo! Well done! Tip-top!

THE MANAGER: Silence! This isn't a café concert, you know! (*Turning to the Father in consternation.*) Is she mad?

THE FATHER: Mad? No, she's worse than mad.

THE STEPDAUGHTER (*to Manager*): Worse? Worse? Listen! Stage this drama for us at once! Then you will see that at a certain moment I . . . when this little darling here. . . . (*Takes the Child by the hand and leads her to the Manager.*) Isn't she a dear? (*Takes her up and kisses her.*) Darling! Darling! (*Puts her down again and adds feelingly.*) Well, when God suddenly takes this dear little child away from that poor mother there; and this imbecile here (*seizing hold of the Boy roughly and pushing him forward*) does the stupidest things, like the fool he is, you will see me run away. Yes, gentlemen, I shall be off. But the moment hasn't arrived yet. After what has taken place between him and me (*indicates the Father with a horrible wink*) I can't remain any longer in this society, to have to witness the anguish of this mother here for that fool. . . . (*Indicates the Son.*) Look at him! Look at him! See how indifferent, how frigid he is, because he is the legitimate son. He despises me, despises him (*pointing to the Boy*), despises this baby

Prenez . . . Tchou: This French popular song is an adaptation of "Chu-Chin Chow," an old Broadway show tune. "The Chinese are a sly people; / From Shanghai to Peking, / They've stuck up warning signs: / Beware of Tchou-Tchin-Tchou." (The words are funnier in French because *chou* means "cabbage.")

here; because . . . we are bastards. (*Goes to the Mother and embraces her.*) And he doesn't want to recognize her as his mother—she who is the common mother of us all. He looks down upon her as if she were only the mother of us three bastards. Wretch! (*She says all this very rapidly, excitedly. At the word "bastards" she raises her voice, and almost spits out the final "Wretch!"*)

THE MOTHER (*to the Manager, in anguish*): In the name of these two little children, I beg you. . . . (*She grows faint and is about to fall.*) Oh God!

THE FATHER (*coming forward to support her as do some of the Actors*): Quick, a chair, a chair for this poor widow!

THE ACTORS: Is it true? Has she really fainted?

THE MANAGER: Quick, a chair! Here!

(*One of the Actors brings a chair, the others proffer assistance. The Mother tries to prevent the Father from lifting the veil which covers her face.*)

THE FATHER: Look at her! Look at her!

THE MOTHER: No, no; stop it please!

THE FATHER (*raising her veil*): Let them see you!

THE MOTHER (*rising and covering her face with her hands, in desperation*): I beg you, sir, to prevent this man from carrying out his plan which is loathsome to me.

THE MANAGER (*dumbfounded*): I don't understand at all. What is the situation? (*To the Father.*) Is this lady your wife?

THE FATHER: Yes, gentlemen: my wife!

THE MANAGER: But how can she be a widow if you are alive? (*The Actors find relief for their astonishment in a loud laugh.*)

THE FATHER: Don't laugh! Don't laugh like that, for Heaven's sake. Her drama lies just here in this: she has had a lover, a man who ought to be here.

THE MOTHER (*with a cry*): No! No!

THE STEPDAUGHTER: Fortunately for her, he is dead. Two months ago as I said. We are in mourning, as you see.

THE FATHER: He isn't here, you see, not because he is dead. He isn't here—look at her a moment and you will understand—because her drama isn't a drama of the love of two men for whom she was incapable of feeling anything except possibly a little gratitude—gratitude not for me but for the other. She isn't a woman, she is a mother, and her drama—powerful, sir, I assure you—lies, as a matter of fact, all in these four children she has had by two men.

THE MOTHER: I had them? Have you got the courage to say that I wanted them? (*To the Company.*) It was his doing. It was he who gave me that other man, who forced me to go away with him.

THE STEPDAUGHTER: It isn't true.

THE MOTHER (*startled*): Not true, isn't it?

THE STEPDAUGHTER: No, it isn't true, it just isn't true.

THE MOTHER: And what can you know about it?

THE STEPDAUGHTER: It isn't true. Don't believe it. (*To Manager.*) Do you know why she says so? For that fellow there. (*Indicates the Son.*) She tortures herself, destroys herself on account of the neglect of that son there, and she wants him to believe that if she abandoned him when he was only two years old, it was because he (*indicates the Father*) made her do so.

THE MOTHER (*vigorously*): He forced me to it, and I call God to witness it. (*To the Manager.*) Ask him (*indicates Husband*) if it isn't true. Let him speak. You (*to Daughter*) are not in a position to know anything about it.

THE STEPDAUGHTER: I know you lived in peace and happiness with my father while he lived. Can you deny it?

THE MOTHER: No, I don't deny it....

THE STEPDAUGHTER: He was always full of affection and kindness for you. (*To the Boy, angrily.*) It's true, isn't it? Tell them! Why don't you speak, you little fool?

THE MOTHER: Leave the poor boy alone. Why do you want to make me appear ungrateful, daughter? I don't want to offend your father. I have answered him that I didn't abandon my house and my son through any fault of mine, nor from any wilful passion.

THE FATHER: It is true. It was my doing.

LEADING MAN (*to the Company*): What a spectacle!

LEADING LADY: We are the audience this time.

JUVENILE LEAD: For once, in a way.

THE MANAGER (*beginning to get really interested*): Let's hear them out. Listen!

THE SON: Oh yes, you're going to hear a fine bit now. He will talk to you of the Demon of Experiment.

THE FATHER: You are a cynical imbecile. I've told you so already a hundred times. (*To the Manager.*) He tries to make fun of me on account of this expression which I have found to excuse myself with.

THE SON (*with disgust*): Yes, phrases! phrases!

THE FATHER: Phrases! Isn't everyone consoled when faced with a trouble or fact he doesn't understand, by a word, some simple word, which tells us nothing and yet calms us?

THE STEPDAUGHTER: Even in the case of remorse. In fact, especially then.

THE FATHER: Remorse? No, that isn't true. I've done more than use words to quiet the remorse in me.

THE STEPDAUGHTER: Yes, there was a bit of money too. Yes, yes, a bit of money. There were the hundred lire he was about to offer me in payment, gentlemen.... (*Sensation of horror among the Actors.*)

THE SON (*to the Stepdaughter*): This is vile.

THE STEPDAUGHTER: Vile? There they were in a pale blue envelope on a little mahogany table in the back of Madame Pace's shop. You know Madame Pace — one of those ladies who attract poor girls of good family into their ateliers, under the pretext of their selling *robes et manteaux.*°

THE SON: And he thinks he has bought the right to tyrannize over us all with those hundred lire he was going to pay; but which, fortunately — note this, gentlemen — he had no chance of paying.

robes et manteaux: French for "dresses and capes."

THE STEPDAUGHTER: It was a near thing, though, you know! (*Laughs ironically.*)

THE MOTHER (*protesting*): Shame, my daughter, shame!

THE STEPDAUGHTER: Shame indeed! This is my revenge! I am dying to live that scene ... The room ... I see it ... Here is the window with the mantles exposed, there the divan, the looking-glass, a screen, there in front of the window the little mahogany table with the blue envelope containing one hundred lire. I see it. I see it. I could take hold of it.... But you, gentlemen, you ought to turn your backs now: I am almost nude, you know. But I don't blush: I leave that to him. (*Indicating Father.*)

THE MANAGER: I don't understand this at all.

THE FATHER: Naturally enough. I would ask you, sir, to exercise your authority a little here, and let me speak before you believe all she is trying to blame me with. Let me explain.

THE STEPDAUGHTER: Ah yes, explain it in your own way.

THE FATHER: But don't you see that the whole trouble lies here? In words, words. Each one of us has within him a whole world of things, each man of us his own special world. And how can we ever come to an understanding if I put in the words I utter the sense and value of things as I see them; while you who listen to me must inevitably translate them according to the conception of things each one of you has within himself. We think we understand each other, but we never really do. Look here! This woman (*indicating the Mother*) takes all my pity for her as a specially ferocious form of cruelty.

THE MOTHER: But you drove me away.

THE FATHER: Do you hear her? I drove her away! She believes I really sent her away.

THE MOTHER: You know how to talk, and I don't but, believe me, sir (*to Manager*), after he had married me ... who knows why? ... I was a poor insignificant woman....

THE FATHER: But, good Heavens! it was just for your humility that I married you. I loved this simplicity in you. (*He stops when he sees she makes signs to contradict him, opens his arms wide in sign of desperation, seeing how hopeless it is to make himself understood.*) You see she denies it. Her mental deafness, believe me, is phenomenal, the limit: (*touches his forehead*) deaf, deaf, mentally deaf! She has plenty of feeling. Oh yes, a good heart for the children; but the brain — deaf, to the point of desperation — !

THE STEPDAUGHTER: Yes, but ask him how his intelligence has helped us.

THE FATHER: If we could see all the evil that may spring from good, what should we do? (*At this point the Leading Lady, who is biting her lips with rage at seeing the Leading Man flirting with the Stepdaughter, comes forward and speaks to the Manager.*)

LEADING LADY: Excuse me, but are we going to rehearse today?

THE MANAGER: Of course, of course; but let's hear them out.

JUVENILE LEAD: This is something quite new.

L'INGÉNUE: Most interesting!

LEADING LADY: Yes, for the people who like that kind of thing. (*Casts a glance at Leading Man.*)

THE MANAGER (*to Father*): You must please explain yourself quite clearly. (*Sits down.*)

THE FATHER: Very well then: listen! I had in my service a poor man, a clerk, a secretary of mine, full of devotion, who became friends with her. (*Indicating the Mother.*) They understood one another, were kindred souls in fact, without, however, the least suspicion of any evil existing. They were incapable even of thinking of it.

THE STEPDAUGHTER: So he thought of it—for them!

THE FATHER: That's not true. I meant to do good to them—and to myself, I confess, at the same time. Things had come to the point that I could not say a word to either of them without their making a mute appeal, one to the other, with their eyes. I could see them silently asking each other how I was to be kept in countenance, how I was to be kept quiet. And this, believe me, was just about enough of itself to keep me in a constant rage, to exasperate me beyond measure.

THE MANAGER: And why didn't you send him away then—this secretary of yours?

THE FATHER: Precisely what I did, sir. And then I had to watch this poor woman drifting forlornly about the house like an animal without a master, like an animal one has taken in out of pity.

THE MOTHER: Ah yes . . . !

THE FATHER (*suddenly turning to the Mother*): It's true about the son anyway, isn't it?

THE MOTHER: He took my son away from me first of all.

THE FATHER: But not from cruelty. I did it so that he should grow up healthy and strong by living in the country.

THE STEPDAUGHTER (*pointing to him ironically*): As one can see.

THE FATHER (*quickly*): Is it my fault if he has grown up like this? I sent him to a wet nurse in the country, a peasant, as *she* did not seem to me strong enough, though she is of humble origin. That was, anyway, the reason I married her. Unpleasant all this may be, but how can it be helped? My mistake possibly, but there we are! All my life I have had these confounded aspirations towards a certain moral sanity. (*At this point the Stepdaughter bursts into a noisy laugh.*) Oh, stop it! Stop it! I can't stand it.

THE MANAGER: Yes, please stop it, for Heaven's sake.

THE STEPDAUGHTER: But imagine moral sanity from him, if you please—the client of certain ateliers like that of Madame Pace!

THE FATHER: Fool! That is the proof that I am a man! This seeming contradiction, gentlemen, is the strongest proof that I stand here a live man before you. Why, it is just for this very incongruity in my nature that I have had to suffer what I have. I could not live by the side of that woman (*indicating the Mother*) any longer; but not so much for the boredom she inspired me with as for the pity I felt for her.

THE MOTHER: And so he turned me out—.

THE FATHER: —well provided for! Yes, I sent her to that man, gentlemen . . . to let her go free of me.

THE MOTHER: And to free himself.

THE FATHER: Yes, I admit it. It was also a liberation for me. But great evil has come of it. I meant well when I did it, and I did it more for her sake than mine. I swear it. (*Crosses his arms on his chest; then turns suddenly to the Mother.*) Did I ever lose sight of you until that other man carried you off to another town, like the angry fool he was? And on account of my pure interest in you . . . my pure interest, I repeat, that had no base motive in it . . . I watched with the tenderest concern the new family that grew up around her. She can bear witness to this. (*Points to the Stepdaughter.*)

THE STEPDAUGHTER: Oh yes, that's true enough. When I was a kiddie so so high, you know, with plaits over my shoulders and knickers longer than my skirts, I used to see him waiting outside the school for me to come out. He came to see how I was growing up.

THE FATHER: This is infamous, shameful!

THE STEPDAUGHTER: No. Why?

THE FATHER: Infamous! infamous! (*Then excitedly to Manager, explaining.*) After she (*indicating the Mother*) went away, my house seemed suddenly empty. She was my incubus, but she filled my house. I was like a dazed fly alone in the empty rooms. This boy here (*indicating the Son*) was educated away from home, and when he came back, he seemed to me to be no more mine. With no mother to stand between him and me, he grew up entirely for himself, on his own, apart, with no tie of intellect or affection binding him to me. And then—strange but true—I was driven, by curiosity at first and then by some tender sentiment, towards her family, which had come into being through my will. The thought of her began gradually to fill up the emptiness I felt all around me. I wanted to know if she were happy in living out the simple daily duties of life. I wanted to think of her as fortunate and happy because far away from the complicated torments of my spirit. And so, to have proof of this, I used to watch that child coming out of school.

THE STEPDAUGHTER: Yes, yes. True. He used to follow me in the street and smiled at me, waved his hand, like this. I would look at him with interest, wondering who he might be. I told my mother, who guessed at once. (*The Mother agrees with a nod.*) Then she didn't want to send me to school for some days; and when I finally went back, there he was again—looking so ridiculous—with a paper parcel in his hands. He came close to me, caressed me, and drew out a fine straw hat from the parcel, with a bouquet of flowers—all for me!

THE MANAGER: A bit discursive this, you know!

THE SON (*contemptuously*): Literature! Literature!

Scene from the 1985 American Repertory Theater production of *Six Characters in Search of an Author,* directed by Robert Brustein.

THE FATHER: Literature indeed! This is life, this is passion!

THE MANAGER: It may be, but it won't act.

THE FATHER: I agree. This is only the part leading up. I don't suggest this should be staged. She (*pointing to the Stepdaughter*), as you see, is no longer the flapper with plaits down her back—

THE STEPDAUGHTER:—and knickers showing below the skirt!

THE FATHER: The drama is coming now, sir; something new, complex, most interesting.

THE STEPDAUGHTER: As soon as my father died . . .

THE FATHER:—there was absolute misery for them. They came back here, unknown to me. Through her stupidity! (*Pointing to the Mother.*) It is true she can barely write her own name; but she could anyhow have got her daughter to write to me that they were in need . . .

THE MOTHER: And how was I to divine all this sentiment in him?

THE FATHER: That is exactly your mistake, never to have guessed any of my sentiments.

THE MOTHER: After so many years apart, and all that had happened . . .

THE FATHER: Was it my fault if that fellow carried you away? It happened quite suddenly, for after he had obtained some job or other, I could find no trace of them; and so, not unnaturally, my interest in them dwindled. But the drama culminated unforeseen and violent on their return, when I was impelled by my miserable flesh that still lives. . . . Ah! what misery, what wretchedness is that of the man who is alone and disdains debasing *liaisons!* Not old enough to do without women, and not young enough to go and look for one without shame. Misery? It's worse than misery; it's a horror; for no woman can any longer give him love; and when a man feels this. . . . One ought to do without, you say? Yes, yes, I know. Each of us when he appears before his fellows is clothed in a certain dignity. But every man knows what unconfessable things pass within the secrecy of his own heart. One gives way to the temptation, only to rise from it again, afterwards, with a great eagerness to reestablish one's dignity, as if it were a tombstone to place on the grave of one's shame, and a monument to hide and sign the memory of our weaknesses. Everybody's in the same case. Some folks haven't the courage to say certain things, that's all!

THE STEPDAUGHTER: All appear to have the courage to do them though.

THE FATHER: Yes, but in secret. Therefore, you want more courage to say these things. Let a man but speak these things out, and folks at once label him a cynic. But it isn't true. He is like all the others, better indeed, because he isn't afraid to reveal with the light of the intelligence the red shame of human bestiality on which most men close their eyes so as not to see it.

Woman—for example, look at her case! She turns tantalizing inviting glances on you. You seize her. No sooner does she feel herself in your grasp than she closes her eyes. It is the sign of her mission, the sign by which she says to man: "Blind yourself, for I am blind."

THE STEPDAUGHTER: Sometimes she can close them no more: when she no longer feels the need of hiding her shame to herself, but dry-eyed and dispassionately, sees only that of the man who has blinded himself without love. Oh, all these intellectual complications make me sick, disgust me—all this philosophy that uncovers the beast in man, and then seeks to save him, excuse him . . . I can't stand it, sir. When a man seeks to "simplify" life bestially, throwing aside every relic of humanity, every chaste aspiration, every pure feeling, all sense of ideality, duty, modesty, shame . . . then nothing is more revolting and nauseous than a certain kind of remorse—crocodiles' tears, that's what it is.

THE MANAGER: Let's come to the point. This is only discussion.

THE FATHER: Very good, sir! But a fact is like a sack which won't stand up when it's empty. In order that it may stand up, one has to put into it the reason and sentiment which have caused it to exist. I couldn't possibly know that after the death of that man, they had decided to return here, that they were in misery, and that she (*pointing to the Mother*) had gone to work as a modiste,° and at a shop of the type of that of Madame Pace.

THE STEPDAUGHTER: A real high-class modiste, you must know, gentlemen. In appearance, she works for the leaders of the best society; but she arranges matters so that these elegant ladies serve her purpose . . . without prejudice to other ladies who are . . . well . . . only so so.

THE MOTHER: You will believe me, gentlemen, that it never entered my mind that the old hag offered me work because she had her eye on my daughter.

THE STEPDAUGHTER: Poor mamma! Do you know, sir, what that woman did when I brought her back the work my mother had finished? She would point out to me that I had torn one of my frocks, and she would give it back to my mother to mend. It was I who paid for it, always I; while this poor creature here believed she was sacrificing herself for me and these two children here, sitting up at night sewing Madame Pace's robes.

THE MANAGER: And one day you met there . . .

THE STEPDAUGHTER: Him, him. Yes sir, an old client. There's a scene for you to play! Superb!

THE FATHER: She, the Mother arrived just then . . .

THE STEPDAUGHTER (*treacherously*): Almost in time!

THE FATHER (*crying out*): No, in time! in time! Fortunately I recognized her . . . in time. And I took them back home with me to my house. You can imagine now her position and mine; she, as you see her; and I who cannot look her in the face.

THE STEPDAUGHTER: Absurd! How can I possibly be expected—after that—to be a modest young miss, a fit person to go with his confounded aspirations for "a solid moral sanity"?

modiste: A person who makes fashionable clothing for women.

THE FATHER: For the drama lies all in this—in the conscience that I have, that each one of us has. We believe this conscience to be a single thing, but it is many-sided. There is one for this person, and another for that. Diverse consciences. So we have this illusion of being one person for all, of having a personality that is unique in all our acts. But it isn't true. We perceive this when, tragically perhaps, in something we do, we are as it were, suspended, caught up in the air on a kind of hook. Then we perceive that all of us was not in that act, and that it would be an atrocious injustice to judge us by that action alone, as if all our existence were summed up in that one deed. Now do you understand the perfidy of this girl? She surprised me in a place, where she ought not to have known me, just as I could not exist for her; and she now seeks to attach to me a reality such as I could never suppose I should have to assume for her in a shameful and fleeting moment of my life. I feel this above all else. And the drama, you will see, acquires a tremendous value from this point. Then there is the position of the others . . . his. . . . (*Indicating the Son.*)

THE SON (*shrugging his shoulders scornfully*): Leave me alone! I don't come into this.

THE FATHER: What? You don't come into this?

THE SON: I've got nothing to do with it, and don't want to have; because you know well enough I wasn't made to be mixed up in all this with the rest of you.

THE STEPDAUGHTER: We are only vulgar folk! He is the fine gentleman. You may have noticed, Mr. Manager, that I fix him now and again with a look of scorn while he lowers his eyes—for he knows the evil he has done me.

THE SON (*scarcely looking at her*): I?

THE STEPDAUGHTER: You! you! I owe my life on the streets to you. Did you or did you not deny us, with your behavior, I won't say the intimacy of home, but even that mere hospitality which makes guests feel at their ease? We were intruders who had come to disturb the kingdom of your legitimacy. I should like to have you witness, Mr. Manager, certain scenes between him and me. He says I have tyrannized over everyone. But it was just his behavior which made me insist on the reason for which I had come into the house,—this reason he calls "vile"—into his house, with my mother who is his mother too. And I came as mistress of the house.

THE SON: It's easy for them to put me always in the wrong. But imagine, gentlemen, the position of a son, whose fate it is to see arrive one day at his home a young woman of impudent bearing, a young woman who inquires for his father, with whom who knows what business she has. This young man has then to witness her return bolder than ever, accompanied by that child there. He is obliged to watch her treat his father in an equivocal and confidential manner. She asks for money of him in a way that lets one suppose he must give it to her, *must,* do you understand, because he has every obligation to do so.

THE FATHER: But I have, as a matter of fact, this obligation. I owe it to your mother.

THE SON: How should I know? When had I ever seen or heard of her? One day there arrive with her (*indicating Stepdaughter*) that lad and this baby here. I am told: "This is *your* mother too, you know." I divine from her manner (*indicating Stepdaughter again*) why it is they have come home. I had rather not say what I feel and think about it. I shouldn't even care to confess to myself. No action can therefore be hoped for from me in this affair. Believe me, Mr. Manager, I am an "unrealized" character, dramatically speaking; and I find myself not at all at ease in their company. Leave me out of it, I beg you.

THE FATHER: What? It is just because you are so that . . .

THE SON: How do you know what I am like? When did you ever bother your head about me?

THE FATHER: I admit it. I admit it. But isn't that a situation in itself? This aloofness of yours which is so cruel to me and to your mother, who returns home and sees you almost for the first time grown up, who doesn't recognize you but knows you are her son. . . . (*Pointing out the Mother to the Manager.*) See, she's crying!

THE STEPDAUGHTER (*angrily, stamping her foot*): Like a fool!

THE FATHER (*indicating Stepdaughter*): She can't stand him, you know. (*Then referring again to the Son.*) He says he doesn't come into the affair, whereas he is really the hinge of the whole action. Look at that lad who is always clinging to his mother, frightened and humiliated. It is on account of this fellow here. Possibly his situation is the most painful of all. He feels himself a stranger more than the others. The poor little chap feels mortified, humiliated at being brought into a home out of charity as it were. (*In confidence.*) He is the image of his father. Hardly talks at all. Humble and quiet.

THE MANAGER: Oh, we'll cut him out. You've no notion what a nuisance boys are on the stage. . . .

THE FATHER: He disappears soon, you know. And the baby too. She is the first to vanish from the scene. The drama consists finally in this: when that mother reenters my house, her family born outside of it, and shall we say superimposed on the original, ends with the death of the little girl, the tragedy of the boy and the flight of the elder daughter. It cannot go on, because it is foreign to its surroundings. So after much torment, we three remain: I, the mother, that son. Then, owing to the disappearance of that extraneous family, we too find ourselves strange to one another. We find we are living in an atmosphere of mortal desolation which is the revenge, as he (*indicating Son*) scornfully said of the Demon of Experiment, that unfortunately hides in me. Thus, sir, you see when faith is lacking, it becomes impossible to create certain states of happiness, for we lack the necessary humility. Vaingloriously, we try to substitute ourselves for this faith, creating thus for the rest of the world a reality which we believe after their fashion, while, actually, it doesn't exist. For each one of us has his own reality to be respected before God, even when it is harmful to one's very self.

THE MANAGER: There is something in what you say. I assure you all this interests me very much. I begin to think there's the stuff for a drama in all this, and not a bad drama either.

THE STEPDAUGHTER (*coming forward*): When you've got a character like me . . .

THE FATHER (*shutting her up, all excited to learn the decision of the Manager*): You be quiet!

THE MANAGER (*reflecting, heedless of interruption*): It's new . . . hem . . . yes. . . .

THE FATHER: Absolutely new!

THE MANAGER: You've got a nerve though, I must say, to come here and fling it at me like this . . .

THE FATHER: You will understand, sir, born as we are for the stage . . .

THE MANAGER: Are you amateur actors then?

THE FATHER: No, I say born for the stage, because . . .

THE MANAGER: Oh, nonsense. You're an old hand, you know.

THE FATHER: No sir, no. We act that role for which we have been cast, that role which we are given in life. And in my own case, passion itself, as usually happens, becomes a trifle theatrical when it is exalted.

THE MANAGER: Well, well, that will do. But you see, without an author. . . . I could give you the address of an author if you like . . .

THE FATHER: No, no. Look here! You must be the author.

THE MANAGER: I? What are you talking about?

THE FATHER: Yes, you, you! Why not?

THE MANAGER: Because I have never been an author: that's why.

THE FATHER: Then why not turn author now? Everybody does it. You don't want any special qualities. Your task is made much easier by the fact that we are all here alive before you. . . .

THE MANAGER: It won't do.

THE FATHER: What? When you see us live our drama. . . .

THE MANAGER: Yes, that's all right. But you want someone to write it.

THE FATHER: No, no. Someone to take it down, possibly, while we play it, scene by scene! It will be enough to sketch it out at first, and then try it over.

THE MANAGER: Well . . . I am almost tempted. It's a bit of an idea. One might have a shot at it.

THE FATHER: Of course. You'll see what scenes will come out of it. I can give you one, at once . . .

THE MANAGER: By Jove, it tempts me. I'd like to have a go at it. Let's try it out. Come with me to my office. (*Turning to the Actors.*) You are at liberty for a bit, but don't step out of the theater for long. In a quarter of an hour, twenty minutes, all back here again! (*To the Father.*) We'll see what can be done. Who knows if we don't get something really extraordinary out of it?

THE FATHER: There's no doubt about it. They (*indicating the Characters*) had better come with us too, hadn't they?

THE MANAGER: Yes, yes. Come on! come on! (*Moves away and then turning to the Actors.*) Be punctual, please! (*Manager and the Six Characters cross the stage and go off. The other Actors remain, looking at one another in astonishment.*)

LEADING MAN: Is he serious? What the devil does he want to do?

JUVENILE LEAD: This is rank madness.

THIRD ACTOR: Does he expect to knock up a drama in five minutes?

JUVENILE LEAD: Like the improvisers!

LEADING LADY: If he thinks I'm going to take part in a joke like this. . . .

JUVENILE LEAD: I'm out of it anyway.

FOURTH ACTOR: I should like to know who they are. (*Alludes to Characters.*)

THIRD ACTOR: What do you suppose? Madmen or rascals!

JUVENILE LEAD: And he takes them seriously!

L'INGÉNUE: Vanity! He fancies himself as an author now.

LEADING MAN: It's absolutely unheard of. If the stage has come to this . . . well I'm . . .

FIFTH ACTOR: It's rather a joke.

THIRD ACTOR: Well, we'll see what's going to happen next.

(*Thus talking, the Actors leave the stage, some going out by the little door at the back, others retiring to their dressing rooms.*)

(*The curtain remains up.*)

(*The action of the play is suspended for twenty minutes.*)

ACT II

(*The stage call-bells ring to warn the company that the play is about to begin again.*)

(*The Stepdaughter comes out of the Manager's office along with the Child and the Boy. As she comes out of the office, she cries: —*)

Nonsense! nonsense! Do it yourselves! I'm not going to mix myself up in this mess. (*Turning to the Child and coming quickly with her on to the stage.*) Come on, Rosetta, let's run!

(*The Boy follows them slowly, remaining a little behind and seeming perplexed.*)

THE STEPDAUGHTER (*stops, bends over the Child and takes the latter's face between her hands*): My little darling! You're frightened, aren't you? You don't know where we are, do you? (*Pretending to reply to a question of the Child.*) What is the stage? It's a place, baby, you know, where people play at being serious, a place where they act comedies. We've got to act a comedy now, dead serious, you know; and

you're in it also, little one. (*Embraces her, pressing the little head to her breast, and rocking the Child for a moment.*) Oh darling, darling, what a horrid comedy you've got to play! What a wretched part they've found for you! A garden . . . a fountain . . . look . . . just suppose, kiddie, it's here. Where, you say? Why, right here in the middle. It's all pretense you know. That's the trouble, my pet: it's all make-believe here. It's better to imagine it though, because if they fix it up for you, it'll only be painted cardboard, painted cardboard for the rockery, the water, the plants. . . . Ah, but I think a baby like this one would sooner have a make-believe fountain than a real one, so she could play with it. What a joke it'll be for the others! But for you, alas! not quite such a joke: you who are real, baby dear, and really play by a real fountain that is big and green and beautiful, with ever so many bamboos around it that are reflected in the water, and a whole lot of little ducks swimming about. . . . No, Rosetta, no, your mother doesn't bother about you on account of that wretch of a son there. I'm in the devil of a temper, and as for that lad. . . . (*Seizes Boy by the arm to force him to take one of his hands out of his pockets.*) What have you got there? What are you hiding? (*Pulls his hand out of his pocket, looks into it, and catches the glint of a revolver.*) Ah! where did you get this? (*The Boy, very pale in the face, looks at her, but does not answer.*) Idiot! If I'd been in your place, instead of killing myself, I'd have shot one of those two, or both of them: father and son.

(*The Father enters from the office, all excited from his work. The Manager follows him.*)

THE FATHER: Come on, come on dear! Come here for a minute! We've arranged everything. It's all fixed up.

THE MANAGER (*also excited*): If you please, young lady, there are one or two points to settle still. Will you come along?

THE STEPDAUGHTER (*following him toward the office*): Ouff! what's the good, if you've arranged everything,

(*The Father, Manager, and Stepdaughter go back into the office again [off] for a moment. At the same time, the Son, followed by the Mother, comes out.*)

THE SON (*looking at the three entering office*): Oh this is fine, fine! And to think I can't even get away!

(*The Mother attempts to look at him, but lowers her eyes immediately when he turns away from her. She then sits down. The Boy and the Child approach her. She casts a glance again at the Son, and speaks with humble tones, trying to draw him into conversation.*)

THE MOTHER: And isn't my punishment the worst of all? (*Then seeing from the Son's manner that he will not bother himself about her.*) My God! Why are you so cruel? Isn't it enough for one person to support all this torment? Must you then insist on others seeing it also?

THE SON (*half to himself, meaning the Mother to hear, however*): And they want to put it on the stage! If there was at least a reason for it! He thinks he has got at the meaning of it all. Just as if each one of us in every circumstance of life couldn't find his own explanation of it! (*Pauses.*) He complains he was discovered in a place where he ought not to have been seen, in a moment of his life which ought to have remained hidden and kept out of the reach of that convention which he has to maintain for other people. And what about my case? Haven't I had to reveal what no son ought ever to reveal: how father and mother live and are man and wife for themselves quite apart from that idea of father and mother which we give them? When this idea is revealed, our life is then linked at one point only to that man and that woman; and as such it should shame them, shouldn't it?

(*The Mother hides her face in her hands. From the dressing rooms and the little door at the back of the stage the Actors and Stage Manager return, followed by the Property Man and the Prompter. At the same moment, the Manager comes out of his office, accompanied by the Father and the Stepdaughter.*)

THE MANAGER: Come on, come on, ladies and gentlemen! Heh! you there, machinist!

MACHINIST: Yes sir?

THE MANAGER: Fix up the parlor with the floral decorations. Two wings and a drop with a door will do. Hurry up!

(*The Machinist runs off at once to prepare the scene and arranges it while the Manager talks with the Stage Manager, the Property Man, and the Prompter on matters of detail.*)

THE MANAGER (*to Property Man*): Just have a look, and see if there isn't a sofa or a divan in the wardrobe . . .

PROPERTY MAN: There's the green one.

THE STEPDAUGHTER: No no! Green won't do. It was yellow, ornamented with flowers—very large! and most comfortable!

PROPERTY MAN: There isn't one like that.

THE MANAGER: It doesn't matter. Use the one we've got.

THE STEPDAUGHTER: Doesn't matter? It's most important!

THE MANAGER: We're only trying it now. Please don't interfere. (*To Property Man.*) See if we've got a shop window—long and narrowish.

THE STEPDAUGHTER: And the little table! The little mahogany table for the pale blue envelope!

PROPERTY MAN (*to Manager*): There's that little gilt one.

THE MANAGER: That'll do fine.

THE FATHER: A mirror.

THE STEPDAUGHTER: And the screen! We must have a screen. Otherwise how can I manage?

PROPERTY MAN: That's all right, Miss. We've got any amount of them.

THE MANAGER (*to the Stepdaughter*): We want some clothes pegs too, don't we?

THE STEPDAUGHTER: Yes, several, several!

THE MANAGER: See how many we've got and bring them all.

PROPERTY MAN: All right!

(*The Property Man hurries off to obey his orders. While he is putting the things in their places, the Manager talks to the Prompter and then with the Characters and the Actors.*)

THE MANAGER (*to Prompter*): Take your seat. Look here: this is the outline of the scenes, act by act. (*Hands him some sheets of paper.*) And now I'm going to ask you to do something out of the ordinary.

PROMPTER: Take it down in shorthand?

THE MANAGER (*pleasantly surprised*): Exactly! Can you do shorthand?

PROMPTER: Yes, a little.

THE MANAGER: Good! (*Turning to a Stage Hand.*) Go and get some paper from my office, plenty, as much as you can find.

(*The Stage Hand goes off and soon returns with a handful of paper which he gives to the Prompter.*)

THE MANAGER (*to Prompter*): You follow the scenes as we play them, and try and get the points down, at any rate the most important ones. (*Then addressing the Actors.*) Clear the stage, ladies and gentlemen! Come over here (*pointing to the left*) and listen attentively.

LEADING LADY: But, excuse me, we . . .

THE MANAGER (*guessing her thought*): Don't worry! You won't have to improvise.

LEADING MAN: What have we to do then?

THE MANAGER: Nothing. For the moment you just watch and listen. Everybody will get his part written out afterwards. At present we're going to try the thing as best we can. They're going to act now.

THE FATHER (*as if fallen from the clouds into the confusion of the stage*): We? What do you mean, if you please, by a rehearsal?

THE MANAGER: A rehearsal for them. (*Points to the Actors.*)

THE FATHER: But since we are the characters . . .

THE MANAGER: All right: "characters" then, if you insist on calling yourselves such. But here, my dear sir, the characters don't act. Here the actors do the acting. The characters are there, in the "book" (*pointing toward Prompter's box*)—when there is a "book"!

THE FATHER: I won't contradict you; but excuse me, the actors aren't the characters. They want to be, they pretend to be, don't they? Now if these gentlemen here are fortunate enough to have us alive before them . . .

THE MANAGER: Oh, this is grand! You want to come before the public yourselves then?

THE FATHER: As we are. . . .

THE MANAGER: I can assure you it would be a magnificent spectacle!

LEADING MAN: What's the use of us here anyway then?

THE MANAGER: You're not going to pretend that you can act? It makes me laugh! (*The Actors laugh.*) There, you see, they are laughing at the notion. But, by the way, I must cast the parts. That won't be difficult. They cast themselves. (*To the Second Lady Lead.*) You play the Mother. (*To the Father.*) We must find her a name.

THE FATHER: Amalia, sir.

THE MANAGER: But that is the real name of your wife. We don't want to call her by her real name.

THE FATHER: Why ever not, if it is her name? ... Still, perhaps, if that lady must ... (*Makes a slight motion of the hand to indicate the Second Lady Lead.*) I see this woman here (*means the Mother*) as Amalia. But do as you like. (*Gets more and more confused.*) I don't know what to say to you. Already, I begin to hear my own words ring false, as if they had another sound ...

THE MANAGER: Don't you worry about it. It'll be our job to find the right tones. And as for her name, if you want her Amalia, Amalia it shall be; and if you don't like it, we'll find another! For the moment though, we'll call the characters in this way: (*To Juvenile Lead.*) You are the Son. (*To the Leading Lady.*) You naturally are the Stepdaughter. ...

THE STEPDAUGHTER (*excitedly*): What? what? I, that woman there? (*Bursts out laughing.*)

THE MANAGER (*angry*): What is there to laugh at?

LEADING LADY (*indignant*): Nobody has ever dared to laugh at me. I insist on being treated with respect; otherwise I go away.

THE STEPDAUGHTER: No, no, excuse me ... I am not laughing at you. ...

THE MANAGER (*to Stepdaughter*): You ought to feel honored to be played by ...

LEADING LADY (*at once, contemptuously*): "That woman there" ...

THE STEPDAUGHTER: But I wasn't speaking of you, you know. I was speaking of myself—whom I can't see at all in you! That is all. I don't know ... but ... you ... aren't in the least like me. ...

THE FATHER: True. Here's the point. Look here, sir, our temperaments, our souls. ...

THE MANAGER: Temperament, soul, be hanged! Do you suppose the spirit of the piece is in you? Nothing of the kind!

THE FATHER: What, haven't we our own temperaments, our own souls?

THE MANAGER: Not at all. Your soul or whatever you like to call it takes shape here. The actors give body and form to it, voice and gesture. And my actors—I may tell you—have given expression to much more lofty material than this little drama of yours, which may or may not hold up on the stage. But if it does, the merit of it, believe me, will be due to my actors.

THE FATHER: I don't dare contradict you, sir, but, believe me, it is a terrible suffering for us who are as we are, with these bodies of ours, these features to see. ...

THE MANAGER (*cutting him short and out of patience*): Good heavens! The make-up will remedy all that, man, the make-up. ...

THE FATHER: Maybe. But the voice, the gestures ...

THE MANAGER: Now, look here! On the stage, you as yourself, cannot exist. The actor here acts you, and that's an end to it!

THE FATHER: I understand. And now I think I see why our author who conceived us as we are, all alive, didn't want to put us on the stage after all. I haven't the least desire to offend your actors. Far from it! But when I think that I am to be acted by ... I don't know by whom. ...

LEADING MAN (*on his dignity*): By me, if you've no objection!

THE FATHER (*humbly, mellifluously*): Honored, I assure you, sir. (*Bows.*) Still, I must say that try as this gentleman may, with all his good will and wonderful art, to absorb me into himself. ...

LEADING MAN: Oh chuck it! "Wonderful art!" Withdraw that, please!

THE FATHER: The performance he will give, even doing his best with make-up to look like me. ...

LEADING MAN: It will certainly be a bit difficult! (*The Actors laugh.*)

THE FATHER: Exactly! It will be difficult to act me as I really am. The effect will be rather—apart from the make-up—according as to how he supposes I am, as he senses me—if he does sense me—and not as I inside of myself feel myself to be. It seems to me then that account should be taken of this by everyone whose duty it may become to criticize us. ...

THE MANAGER: Heavens! The man's starting to think about the critics now! Let them say what they like. It's up to us to put on the play if we can. (*Looking around.*) Come on! come on! Is the stage set? (*To the Actors and Characters.*) Stand back—stand back! Let me see, and don't let's lose any more time! (*To the Stepdaughter.*) Is it all right as it is now?

THE STEPDAUGHTER: Well, to tell the truth, I don't recognize the scene.

THE MANAGER: My dear lady, you can't possibly suppose that we can construct that shop of Madame Pace piece by piece here? (*To the Father.*) You said a white room with flowered wallpaper, didn't you?

THE FATHER: Yes.

THE MANAGER: Well then. We've got the furniture right more or less. Bring that little table a bit further forward. (*The Stage Hands obey the order. To Property Man.*) You go and find an envelope, if possible, a pale blue one; and give it to that gentleman. (*Indicates Father.*)

PROPERTY MAN: An ordinary envelope?

MANAGER AND FATHER: Yes, yes, an ordinary envelope.

PROPERTY MAN: At once, sir. (*Exit.*)

THE MANAGER: Ready, everyone! First scene—the Young Lady. (*The Leading Lady comes forward.*) No, no, you must wait. I meant her. (*Indicating the Stepdaughter.*) You just watch—

THE STEPDAUGHTER (*adding at once*): How I shall play it, how I shall live it! . . .

LEADING LADY (*offended*): I shall live it also, you may be sure, as soon as I begin!

THE MANAGER (*with his hands to his head*): Ladies and gentlemen, if you please! No more useless discussions! Scene I: the Young Lady with Madame Pace: Oh! (*Looks around as if lost.*) And this Madame Pace, where is she?

THE FATHER: She isn't with us, sir.

THE MANAGER: Then what the devil's to be done?

THE FATHER: But she is alive too.

THE MANAGER: Yes, but where is she?

THE FATHER: One minute. Let me speak! (*Turning to the Actresses.*) If these ladies would be so good as to give me their hats for a moment. . . .

THE ACTRESSES (*half surprised, half laughing, in chorus*): What? Why? Our hats? What does he say?

THE MANAGER: What are you going to do with the ladies' hats? (*The Actors laugh.*)

THE FATHER: Oh nothing. I just want to put them on these pegs for a moment. And one of the ladies will be so kind as to take off her mantle. . . .

THE ACTORS: Oh, what d'you think of that? Only the mantle? He must be mad.

SOME ACTRESSES: But why? Mantles as well?

THE FATHER: To hang them up here for a moment. Please be so kind, will you?

THE ACTRESSES (*taking off their hats, one or two also their cloaks, and going to hang them on the racks*): After all, why not? There you are! This is really funny. We've got to put them on show.

THE FATHER: Exactly; just like that, on show.

THE MANAGER: May we know why?

THE FATHER: I'll tell you. Who knows if, by arranging the stage for her, she does not come here herself, attracted by the very articles of her trade? (*Inviting the Actors to look toward the exit at back of stage.*) Look! Look!

(*The door at the back of stage opens and Madame Pace enters and takes a few steps forward. She is a fat, oldish woman with puffy oxygenated hair. She is rouged and powdered, dressed with a comical elegance in black silk. Round her waist is a long silver chain from which hangs a pair of scissors. The Stepdaughter runs over to her at once amid the stupor of the Actors.*)

THE STEPDAUGHTER (*turning toward her*): There she is! There she is!

THE FATHER (*radiant*): It's she! I said so, didn't I! There she is!

THE MANAGER (*conquering his surprise, and then becoming indignant*): What sort of a trick is this?

LEADING MAN (*almost at the same time*): What's going to happen next?

JUVENILE LEAD: Where does she come from?

L'INGÉNUE: They've been holding her in reserve, I guess.

LEADING LADY: A vulgar trick!

THE FATHER (*dominating the protests*): Excuse me, all of you! Why are you so anxious to destroy in the name of a vulgar, commonplace sense of truth, this reality which comes to birth attracted and formed by the magic of the stage itself, which has indeed more right to live here than you, since it is much truer than you—if you don't mind my saying so? Which is the actress among you who is to play Madame Pace? Well, here is Madame Pace herself. And you will allow, I fancy, that the actress who acts her will be less true than this woman here, who is herself in person. You see my daughter recognized her and went over to her at once. Now you're going to witness the scene!

(*But the scene between the Stepdaughter and Madame Pace has already begun despite the protest of the Actors and the reply of the Father. It has begun quietly, naturally, in a manner impossible for the stage. So when the Actors, called to attention by the Father, turn round and see Madame Pace, who has placed one hand under the Stepdaughter's chin to raise her head, they observe her at first with great attention, but hearing her speak in an unintelligible manner their interest begins to wane.*)

THE MANAGER: Well? well?

LEADING MAN: What does she say?

LEADING LADY: One can't hear a word.

JUVENILE LEAD: Louder! Louder please!

THE STEPDAUGHTER (*leaving Madame Pace, who smiles a Sphinx-like smile, and advancing toward the Actors*): Louder? Louder? What are you talking about? These aren't matters which can be shouted at the top of one's voice. If I have spoken them out loud, it was to shame him and have my revenge. (*Indicates Father.*) But for Madame it's quite a different matter.

THE MANAGER: Indeed? indeed? But here, you know people have got to make themselves heard, my dear. Even we who are on the stage can't hear you. What will it be when the public's in the theater? And anyway, you can very well speak up now among yourselves, since we shan't be present to listen to you as we are now. You've got to pretend to be alone in a room at the back of a shop where no one can hear you.

(*The Stepdaughter coquettishly and with a touch of malice makes a sign of disagreement two or three times with her finger.*)

THE MANAGER: What do you mean by no?

THE STEPDAUGHTER (*sotto voce,° mysteriously*): There's someone who will hear us if she (*indicating Madame Pace*) speaks out loud.

THE MANAGER (*in consternation*): What? Have you got someone else to spring on us now? (*The Actors burst out laughing.*)

THE FATHER: No, no sir. She is alluding to me. I've got to be here—there behind that door, in waiting; and

sotto voce: In a soft voice or stage whisper.

Madame Pace knows it. In fact, if you will allow me, I'll go there at once, so I can be quite ready. (*Moves away.*)

THE MANAGER (*stopping him*): No! wait! wait! We must observe the conventions of the theater. Before you are ready . . .

THE STEPDAUGHTER (*interrupting him*): No, get on with it at once! I'm just dying, I tell you, to act this scene. If he's ready, I'm more than ready.

THE MANAGER (*shouting*): But, my dear young lady, first of all, we must have the scene between you and this lady. . . . (*Indicates Madame Pace.*) Do you understand?

THE STEPDAUGHTER: Good Heavens! She's been telling me what you know already: that mama's work is badly done again, that the material's ruined; and that if I want her to continue to help us in our misery I must be patient. . . .

MADAME PACE (*coming forward with an air of great importance*): Yes indeed, sir, I no wanta take advantage of her, I no wanta be hard. . . .

(*Note: Madame Pace is supposed to talk in a jargon half Italian, half English.*)

THE MANAGER (*alarmed*): What? What? She talks like that? (*The Actors burst out laughing again.*)

THE STEPDAUGHTER (*also laughing*): Yes yes, that's the way she talks, half English, half Italian! Most comical it is!

MADAME PACE: Itta seem not verra polite gentlemen laugha atta me eeff I trya best speaka English.

THE MANAGER: *Diamine!*° Of course! Of course! Let her talk like that! Just what we want. Talk just like that, Madame, if you please! The effect will be certain. Exactly what was wanted to put a little comic relief into the crudity of the situation. Of course she talks like that! Magnificent!

THE STEPDAUGHTER: Magnificent? Certainly! When certain suggestions are made to one in language of that kind, the effect is certain, since it seems almost a joke. One feels inclined to laugh when one hears her talk about an "old signore" "who wanta talka nicely with you." Nice old signore, eh, Madame?

MADAME PACE: Not so old my dear, not so old! And even if you no like him, he won't make any scandal!

THE MOTHER (*jumping up amid the amazement and consternation of the Actors, who had not been noticing her. They move to restrain her*): You old devil! You murderess!

THE STEPDAUGHTER (*running over to calm her Mother*): Calm yourself, Mother, calm yourself! Please don't. . . .

THE FATHER (*going to her also at the same time*): Calm yourself! Don't get excited! Sit down now!

THE MOTHER: Well then, take that woman away out of my sight!

THE STEPDAUGHTER (*to Manager*): It is impossible for my mother to remain here.

THE FATHER (*to Manager*): They can't be here together. And for this reason, you see: that woman there was not with us when we came. . . . If they are on together, the whole thing is given away inevitably, as you see.

THE MANAGER: It doesn't matter. This is only a first rough sketch—just to get an idea of the various points of the scene, even confusedly. . . . (*Turning to the Mother and leading her to her chair.*) Come along, my dear lady, sit down now, and let's get on with the scene. . . .

(*Meanwhile, the Stepdaughter, coming forward again, turns to Madame Pace.*)

THE STEPDAUGHTER: Come on, Madame, come on!

MADAME PACE (*offended*): No, no, *grazie*. I do not do anything witha your mother present.

THE STEPDAUGHTER: Nonsense! Introduce this "old signore" who wants to talk nicely to me. (*Addressing the Company imperiously.*) We've got to do this scene one way or another, haven't we? Come on! (*To Madame Pace.*) You can go!

MADAME PACE: Ah yes! I go'way! I go'way! Certainly! (*Exits furious.*)

THE STEPDAUGHTER (*to the Father*): Now you make your entry. No, you needn't go over there. Come here. Let's suppose you've already come in. Like that, yes! I'm here with bowed head, modest like. Come on! Out with your voice! Say "Good morning, Miss" in that peculiar tone, that special tone. . . .

THE MANAGER: Excuse me, but are you the Manager, or am I? (*To the Father, who looks undecided and perplexed.*) Get on with it, man! Go down there to the back of the stage. You needn't go off. Then come right forward here.

(*The Father does as he is told, looking troubled and perplexed at first. But as soon as he begins to move, the reality of the action affects him, and he begins to smile and to be more natural. The Actors watch intently.*)

THE MANAGER (*sotto voce, quickly to the Prompter in his box*): Ready! ready! Get ready to write now.

THE FATHER (*coming forward and speaking in a different tone*): Good afternoon, Miss!

THE STEPDAUGHTER (*head bowed down slightly, with restrained disgust*): Good afternoon!

THE FATHER (*looks under her hat which partly covers her face. Perceiving she is very young, he makes an exclamation, partly of surprise, partly of fear lest he compromise himself in a risky adventure*): Ah . . . but . . . ah . . . I say . . . this is not the first time that you have come here, is it?

THE STEPDAUGHTER (*modestly*): No sir.

THE FATHER: You've been here before, eh? (*Then seeing her nod agreement.*) More than once? (*Waits for her to answer, looks under her hat, smiles, and then says:*) Well then, there's no need to be so shy, is there? May I take off your hat?

Diamine!: Italian for "Well, I'll be damned!"

THE STEPDAUGHTER (*anticipating him and with veiled disgust*): No sir ... I'll do it myself. (*Takes it off quickly.*)

(*The Mother, who watches the progress of the scene with the Son and the other two children who cling to her, is on thorns; and follows with varying expressions of sorrow, indignation, anxiety, and horror the words and actions of the other two. From time to time she hides her face in her hands and sobs.*)

THE MOTHER: Oh, my God, my God!

THE FATHER (*playing his part with a touch of gallantry*): Give it to me! I'll put it down. (*Takes hat from her hands.*) But a dear little head like yours ought to have a smarter hat. Come and help me choose one from the stock, won't you?

L'INGÉNUE (*interrupting*): I say ... those are our hats you know.

THE MANAGER (*furious*): Silence! silence! Don't try and be funny, if you please.... We're playing the scene now, I'd have you notice. (*To the Stepdaughter.*) Begin again, please!

THE STEPDAUGHTER (*continuing*): No thank you, sir.

THE FATHER: Oh, come now. Don't talk like that. You must take it. I shall be upset if you don't. There are some lovely little hats here; and then— Madame will be pleased. She expects it, anyway, you know.

THE STEPDAUGHTER: No, no! I couldn't wear it!

THE FATHER: Oh, you're thinking about what they'd say at home if they saw you come in with a new hat? My dear girl, there's always a way round these little matters, you know.

THE STEPDAUGHTER (*all keyed up*): No, it's not that. I couldn't wear it because I am ... as you see ... you might have noticed ...

(*Showing her black dress.*)

THE FATHER: ... in mourning! Of course: I beg your pardon: I'm frightfully sorry....

THE STEPDAUGHTER (*forcing herself to conquer her indignation and nausea*): Stop! Stop! It's I who must thank you. There's no need for you to feel mortified or specially sorry. Don't think any more of what I've said. (*Tries to smile.*) I must forget that I am dressed so....

THE MANAGER (*interrupting and turning to the Prompter*): Stop a minute! Stop! Don't write that down. Cut out that last bit. (*Then to the Father and Stepdaughter.*) Fine! it's going fine! (*To the Father only.*) And now you can go on as we arranged. (*To the Actors.*) Pretty good that scene, where he offers her the hat, eh?

THE STEPDAUGHTER: The best's coming now. Why can't we go on?

THE MANAGER: Have a little patience! (*To the Actors.*) Of course, it must be treated rather lightly.

LEADING MAN: Still, with a bit of go in it!

LEADING LADY: Of course! It's easy enough! (*To Leading Man.*) Shall you and I try it now?

LEADING MAN: Why, yes! I'll prepare my entrance. (*Exit in order to make his entrance.*)

THE MANAGER (*to Leading Lady*): See here! The scene between you and Madame Pace is finished. I'll have it written out properly after. You remain here ... oh, where are you going?

LEADING LADY: One minute. I want to put my hat on again. (*Goes over to hatrack and puts her hat on her head.*)

THE MANAGER: Good! You stay here with your head bowed down a bit.

THE STEPDAUGHTER: But she isn't dressed in black.

LEADING LADY: But I shall be, and much more effectively than you.

THE MANAGER (*to Stepdaughter*): Be quiet please, and watch! You'll be able to learn something. (*Clapping his hands.*) Come on! come on! Entrance, please!

(*The door at rear of stage opens, and the Leading Man enters with the lively manner of an old gallant. The rendering of the scene by the Actors from the very first words is seen to be quite a different thing, though it has not in any way the air of a parody. Naturally, the Stepdaughter and the Father, not being able to recognize themselves in the Leading Lady and the Leading Man, who deliver their words in different tones and with a different psychology, express, sometimes with smiles, sometimes with gestures, the impression they receive.*)

LEADING MAN: Good afternoon, Miss ...

THE FATHER (*at once unable to contain himself*): No! no!

(*The Stepdaughter, noticing the way the Leading Man enters, bursts out laughing.*)

THE MANAGER (*furious*): Silence! And you, please, just stop that laughing. If we go on like this, we shall never finish.

THE STEPDAUGHTER: Forgive me, sir but it's natural enough. This lady (*indicating Leading Lady*) stands there still; but if she is supposed to be me, I can assure you that if I heard anyone say "Good afternoon" in that manner and in that tone, I should burst out laughing as I did.

THE FATHER: Yes, yes, the manner, the tone ...

THE MANAGER: Nonsense! Rubbish! Stand aside and let me see the action.

LEADING MAN: If I've got to represent an old fellow who's coming into a house of an equivocal character ...

THE MANAGER: Don't listen to them, for Heaven's sake! Do it again! It goes fine. (*Waiting for the Actors to begin again.*) Well?

LEADING MAN: Good afternoon, Miss.

LEADING LADY: Good afternoon.

LEADING MAN (*imitating the gesture of the Father when he looked under the hat, and then expressing quite clearly first satisfaction and then fear*): Ah, but ... I say ... this is not the first time that you have come here, is it?

THE MANAGER: Good, but not quite so heavily. Like this. (*Acts himself.*) "This isn't the first time that you have come here"...(*To Leading Lady.*) And you say: "No, sir."

LEADING LADY: No, sir.

LEADING MAN: You've been here before, more than once.

THE MANAGER: No, no, stop! Let her nod "yes" first. "You've been here before, eh?" (*The Leading Lady lifts up her head slightly and closes her eyes as though in disgust. Then she inclines her head twice.*)

THE STEPDAUGHTER (*unable to contain herself*): Oh my God! (*Puts a hand to her mouth to prevent herself from laughing.*)

THE MANAGER (*turning round*): What's the matter?

THE STEPDAUGHTER: Nothing, nothing!

THE MANAGER (*to Leading Man*): Go on!

LEADING MAN: You've been here before, eh? Well then, there's no need to be so shy, is there? May I take off your hat?

(*The Leading Man says this last speech in such a tone and with such gestures that the Stepdaughter, though she has her hand to her mouth, cannot keep from laughing.*)

LEADING LADY (*indignant*): I'm not going to stop here to be made a fool of by that woman there.

LEADING MAN: Neither am I! I'm through with it!

THE MANAGER (*shouting to Stepdaughter*): Silence! for once and all, I tell you!

THE STEPDAUGHTER: Forgive me! forgive me!

THE MANAGER: You haven't any manners: that's what it is! You go too far.

THE FATHER (*endeavoring to intervene*): Yes, it's true, but excuse her...

THE MANAGER: Excuse what? It's absolutely disgusting.

THE FATHER: Yes, sir, but believe me, it has such a strange effect when...

THE MANAGER: Strange? Why strange? Where is it strange?

THE FATHER: No, sir; I admire your actors—this gentleman here, this lady; but they are certainly not us!

THE MANAGER: I should hope not. Evidently they cannot be you, if they are actors.

THE FATHER: Just so: actors! Both of them act our parts exceedingly well. But, believe me, it produces quite a different effect on us. They want to be us, but they aren't, all the same.

THE MANAGER: What is it then anyway?

THE FATHER: Something that is...that is theirs—and no longer ours...

THE MANAGER: But naturally, inevitably, I've told you so already.

THE FATHER: Yes, I understand...I understand...

THE MANAGER: Well then, let's have no more of it! (*Turning to the Actors.*) We'll have the rehearsals by ourselves, afterwards, in the ordinary way. I never could stand rehearsing with the author present. He's never satisfied! (*Turning to Father and Stepdaughter.*) Come on! Let's get on with it again; and try and see if you can't keep from laughing.

THE STEPDAUGHTER: Oh, I shan't laugh any more. There's a nice little bit coming from me now: you'll see.

THE MANAGER: Well then: when she says "Don't think any more of what I've said, I must forget, etc.," you (*addressing the Father*) come in sharp with "I understand"; and then you ask her...

THE STEPDAUGHTER (*interrupting*): What?

THE MANAGER: Why she is in mourning.

THE STEPDAUGHTER: Not at all! See here: when I told him that it was useless for me to be thinking about my wearing mourning, do you know how he answered me? "Ah well," he said, "then let's take off this little frock."

THE MANAGER: Great! Just what we want, to make a riot in the theater!

THE STEPDAUGHTER: But it's the truth!

THE MANAGER: What does that matter? Acting is our business here. Truth up to a certain point, but no further.

THE STEPDAUGHTER: What do you want to do then?

THE MANAGER: You'll see, you'll see! Leave it to me.

THE STEPDAUGHTER: No sir! What you want to do is to piece together a little romantic sentimental scene out of my disgust, out of all the reasons, each more cruel and viler than the other, why I am what I am. He is to ask me why I'm in mourning; and I'm to answer with tears in my eyes, that it is just two months since papa died. No sir, no! He's got to say to me, as he did say, "Well, let's take off this little dress at once." And I, with my two months' mourning in my heart, went there behind that screen, and with these fingers tingling with shame...

THE MANAGER (*running his hands through his hair*): For Heaven's sake! What are you saying?

THE STEPDAUGHTER (*crying out excitedly*): The truth! The truth!

THE MANAGER: It may be. I don't deny it, and I can understand all your horror; but you must surely see that you can't have this kind of thing on the stage. It won't go.

THE STEPDAUGHTER: Not possible, eh? Very well! I'm much obliged to you—but I'm off.

THE MANAGER: Now be reasonable! Don't lose your temper!

THE STEPDAUGHTER: I won't stop here! I won't! I can see you fixed it all up with him in your office. All this talk about what is possible for the stage...I understand! He wants to get at his complicated "cerebral drama," to have his famous remorses and torments acted; but I want to act my part, *my part!*

THE MANAGER (*annoyed, shaking his shoulders*): Ah! Just *your* part! But, if you will pardon me, there are other parts than yours: His (*indicating the Father*) and hers (*indicating the Mother*)! On the stage you can't have a character becoming too prominent and overshadowing all the others. The thing is to pack them all into a neat little framework and then act what is actable. I am aware of the fact that everyone has his own interior life which he wants very much to put forward. But the difficulty lies in this fact: to set out just so much as is necessary for the stage, taking the other characters into consideration, and at the same time hint at the unrevealed interior life of each. I am willing to admit, my dear young lady, that from your point of view it would be a fine idea if each character could tell the public all his troubles in a nice monologue or a regular one hour lecture. (*Good humoredly.*) You must restrain yourself, my dear, and in your own interest, too; because this fury of yours, this exaggerated disgust you show, may make a bad impression, you know. After you have confessed to me that there were others before him at Madame Pace's and more than once . . .

THE STEPDAUGHTER (*bowing her head, impressed*): It's true. But remember those others mean him for me all the same.

THE MANAGER (*not understanding*): What? The others? What do you mean?

THE STEPDAUGHTER: For one who has gone wrong, sir, he who was responsible for the first fault is responsible for all that follow. He is responsible for my faults, was, even before I was born. Look at him, and see if it isn't true!

THE MANAGER: Well, well! And does the weight of so much responsibility seem nothing to you? Give him a chance to act it, to get it over!

THE STEPDAUGHTER: How? How can he act all his "noble remorses," all his "moral torments," if you want to spare him the horror of being discovered one day—after he had asked her what he did ask her—in the arms of her, that already fallen woman, that child, sir, that child he used to watch come out of school? (*She is moved.*)

(*The Mother at this point is overcome with emotion and breaks out into a fit of crying. All are touched. A long pause.*)

THE STEPDAUGHTER (*as soon as the Mother becomes a little quieter, adds resolutely and gravely*): At present, we are unknown to the public. Tomorrow, you will act us as you wish, treating us in your own manner. But do you really want to see drama, do you want to see it flash out as it really did?

THE MANAGER: Of course! That's just what I do want, so I can use as much of it as is possible.

THE STEPDAUGHTER: Well then, ask that Mother there to leave us.

THE MOTHER (*changing her low plaint into a sharp cry*): No! No! Don't permit it, sir, don't permit it!

THE MANAGER: But it's only to try . . .

THE MOTHER: I can't bear it. I can't.

THE MANAGER: But since it has happened already . . . I don't understand!

THE MOTHER: It's taking place now. It happens all the time. My torment isn't a pretended one. I live and feel every minute of my torture. Those two children there—have you heard them speak? They can't speak anymore. They cling to me to keep my torment

actual and vivid for me. But for themselves, they do not exist, they aren't anymore. And she (*indicating the Stepdaughter*) has run away, she has left me, and is lost. If I now see her here before me, it is only to renew for me the tortures I have suffered for her too.

THE FATHER: The eternal moment! She (*indicating the Stepdaughter*) is here to catch me, fix me, and hold me eternally in the stocks for that one fleeting and shameful moment of my life. She can't give it up! And you, sir, cannot either fairly spare me . . .

THE MANAGER: I never said I didn't want to act it. It will form, as a matter of fact, the nucleus of the whole first act right up to her surprise. (*Indicates the Mother.*)

THE FATHER: Just so! This is my punishment: the passion in all of us that must culminate in her final cry.

THE STEPDAUGHTER: I can hear it still in my ears. It's driven me mad, that cry!—You can put me on as you like; it doesn't matter. Fully dressed, if you like—provided I have at least the arm bare; because, standing like this (*she goes close to the Father and leans her head on his breast*) with my head so, and my arms round his neck, I saw a vein pulsing in my arm here; and then, as if that live vein had awakened disgust in me, I closed my eyes like this, and let my head sink on his breast. (*Turning to the Mother.*) Cry out, mother! Cry out! (*Buries head in Father's breast, and with her shoulders raised as if to prevent her hearing the cry, adds in tones of intense emotion.*) Cry out as you did then!

THE MOTHER (*coming forward to separate them*): No! My daughter, my daughter! (*And after having pulled her away from him.*) You brute! you brute! She is my daughter! Don't you see she's my daughter?

THE MANAGER (*walking backward toward footlights*): Fine! fine! Damned good! And then, of course—curtain!

THE FATHER (*going toward him excitedly*): Yes, of course, because that's the way it really happened.

THE MANAGER (*convinced and pleased*): Oh, yes, no doubt about it. Curtain here, curtain!

(*At the reiterated cry of the Manager, the Machinist lets the curtain down, leaving the Manager and the Father in front of it before the footlights.*)

THE MANAGER: The darned idiot! I said "curtain" to show the act should end there, and he goes and lets it down in earnest. (*To the Father, while he pulls the curtain back to go on to the stage again.*) Yes, yes, it's all right. Effect certain! That's the right ending. I'll guarantee the first act at any rate.

ACT III

(*When the curtain goes up again, it is seen that the stage hands have shifted the bit of scenery used in the last part and have rigged up instead at the back of the stage a drop, with some trees, and one or two wings. A portion of a fountain basin is visible. The Mother is sitting on the right with the two children by her side. The Son is on the same side, but away from the others. He seems bored, angry, and full of shame. The Father and the Stepdaughter are also seated toward the right front. On the other side (left) are the Actors, much in the positions they occupied before the curtain was lowered. Only the Manager is standing up in the middle of the stage, with his hand closed over his mouth, in the act of meditating.)*

THE MANAGER (*shaking his shoulders after a brief pause*): Ah yes: the second act! Leave it to me, leave it all to me as we arranged, and you'll see! It'll go fine!

THE STEPDAUGHTER: Our entry into his house (*indicates Father*) in spite of him . . . (*Indicates the Son.*)

THE MANAGER (*out of patience*): Leave it to me, I tell you!

THE STEPDAUGHTER: Do let it be clear, at any rate, that it is in spite of my wishes.

THE MOTHER (*from her corner, shaking her head*): For all the good that's come of it . . .

THE STEPDAUGHTER (*turning toward her quickly*): It doesn't matter. The more harm done us, the more remorse for him.

THE MANAGER (*impatiently*): I understand! Good Heavens! I understand! I'm taking it into account.

THE MOTHER (*supplicatingly*): I beg you, sir, to let it appear quite plain that for conscience' sake I did try in every way . . .

THE STEPDAUGHTER (*interrupting indignantly and continuing for the Mother*): . . . to pacify me, to dissuade me from spiting him. (*To Manager.*) Do as she wants: satisfy her, because it is true! I enjoy it immensely. Anyhow, as you can see, the meeker she is, the more she tries to get at his heart, the more distant and aloof does he become.

THE MANAGER: Are we going to begin this second act or not?

THE STEPDAUGHTER: I'm not going to talk any more now. But I must tell you this: you can't have the whole action take place in the garden, as you suggest. It isn't possible!

THE MANAGER: Why not?

THE STEPDAUGHTER: Because he (*indicates the Son again*) is always shut up alone in his room. And then there's all the part of that poor dazed-looking boy there which takes place indoors.

THE MANAGER: Maybe! On the other hand, you will understand—we can't change scenes three or four times in one act.

LEADING MAN: They used to once.

THE MANAGER: Yes, when the public was up to the level of that child there.

LEADING LADY: It makes the illusion easier.

THE FATHER (*irritated*): The illusion! For Heaven's sake, don't say illusion. Please don't use that word, which is particularly painful for . . .

THE MANAGER (*astounded*): And why, if you please?

THE FATHER: It's painful, cruel, really cruel; and you ought to understand that.

THE MANAGER: But why? What ought we to say then? The illusion, I tell you, sir, which we've got to create for the audience. . . .

LEADING MAN: With our acting.

THE MANAGER: The illusion of a reality.

THE FATHER: I understand; but you, perhaps, do not understand us. Forgive me! You see . . . here for you and your actors, the thing is only—and rightly so . . . a kind of game. . . .

LEADING LADY (*interrupting indignantly*): A game! We're not children here, if you please! We are serious actors.

THE FATHER: I don't deny it. What I mean is the game, or play, of your art, which has to give, as the gentleman says, a perfect illusion of reality.

THE MANAGER: Precisely—!

THE FATHER: Now, if you consider the fact that we (*indicates himself and the other five Characters*), as we are, have no other reality outside of this illusion. . . .

THE MANAGER (*astonished, looking at his Actors, who are also amazed*): And what does that mean?

THE FATHER (*after watching them for a moment with a wan smile*): As I say, sir, that which is a game of art for you is our sole reality. (*Brief pause. He goes a step or two nearer the Manager and adds.*) But not only for us, you know, by the way. Just you think it over well. (*Looks him in the eyes.*) Can you tell me who you are?

THE MANAGER (*perplexed, half-smiling*): What? Who am I? I am myself.

THE FATHER: And if I were to tell you that that isn't true, because you and I . . . ?

THE MANAGER: I should say you were mad—! (*The Actors laugh.*)

THE FATHER: You're quite right to laugh, because we are all making believe here. (*To Manager.*) And you can therefore object that it's only for a joke that that gentleman there (*indicates the Leading Man*), who naturally is himself, has to be me, who am on the contrary myself—this thing you see here. You see I've caught you in a trap! (*The Actors laugh.*)

THE MANAGER (*annoyed*): But we've had all this over once before. Do you want to begin again?

THE FATHER: No, no! That wasn't my meaning! In fact, I should like to request you to abandon this game of art (*looking at the Leading Lady as if anticipating her*) which you are accustomed to play here with your actors, and to ask you seriously once again who are you?

THE MANAGER (*astonished and irritated, turning to his Actors*): If this fellow here hasn't got a nerve! A man who calls himself a character comes and asks me who I am!

THE FATHER (*with dignity, but not offended*): A character, sir, may always ask a man who he is. Because a character has really a life of his own, marked with his especial characteristics; for which reason he is always "somebody." But a man—I'm not speaking of you now—may very well be "nobody."

THE MANAGER: Yes, but you are asking these questions of me, the boss, the manager! Do you understand?

THE FATHER: But only in order to know if you, as you really are now, see yourself as you once were with all the illusions that were yours then, with all the things both inside and outside of you as they seemed to you—as they were then indeed for you. Well, sir, if you think of all those illusions that mean nothing to you now, of all those things which don't even *seem* to you to exist anymore, while once they *were* for you, don't you feel that—I won't say these boards—but the very earth under your feet is sinking away from you when you reflect that in the same way this *you* as you feel it today—all this present reality of yours—is fated to seem a mere illusion to you tomorrow?

THE MANAGER (*without having understood much, but astonished by the specious argument*): Well, well! And where does all this take us anyway?

THE FATHER: Oh, nowhere! It's only to show you that if we (*indicating the Characters*) have no other reality beyond the illusion, you too must not count overmuch on your reality as you feel it today, since, like that of yesterday, it may prove an illusion for you tomorrow.

THE MANAGER (*determining to make fun of him*): Ah, excellent! Then you'll be saying next that you, with this comedy of yours that you brought here to act, are truer and more real than I am.

THE FATHER (*with the greatest seriousness*): But of course, without doubt!

THE MANAGER: Ah, really?

THE FATHER: Why, I thought you'd understand that from the beginning.

THE MANAGER: More real than I?

THE FATHER: If your reality can change from one day to another. . . .

THE MANAGER: But everyone knows it can change. It is always changing, the same as anyone else's.

THE FATHER (*with a cry*): No, sir, not ours! Look here! That is the very difference! Our reality doesn't change: it can't change! It can't be other than what it is, because it is already fixed for ever. It's terrible. Ours is an immutable reality which should make you shudder when you approach us if you are really conscious of the fact that your reality is a mere transitory and fleeting illusion, taking this form today and that tomorrow, according to the conditions, according to your will, your sentiments, which in turn are controlled by an intellect that shows them to you today in one manner and tomorrow . . . who knows how? . . . Illusions of reality represented in this fatuous comedy of life that never ends, nor can ever end! Because if tomorrow it were to end . . . then why, all would be finished.

THE MANAGER: Oh for God's sake, will you *at least* finish with this philosophizing and let us try and shape this comedy which you yourself have brought me here? You argue and philosophize a bit too much, my dear sir. You know you seem to me almost, almost . . . (*Stops and looks him over from head to foot.*) Ah, by the way, I think you introduced yourself to me as a—what shall . . . we say—a "character," created by an author who did not afterward care to make a drama of his own creations.

THE FATHER: It is the simple truth, sir.

THE MANAGER: Nonsense! Cut that out, please! None of us believes it, because it isn't a thing, as you must recognize yourself, which one can believe seriously. If you want to know, it seems to me you are trying to imitate the manner of a certain author whom I heartily detest—I warn you—although I have unfortunately bound myself to put on one of his works. As a matter of fact, I was just starting to rehearse it, when you arrived. (*Turning to the Actors.*) And this is what we've gained—out of the frying-pan into the fire!

THE FATHER: I don't know to what author you may be alluding, but believe me I feel what I think; and I seem to be philosophizing only for those who do not think what they feel, because they blind themselves with their own sentiment. I know that for many people this self-blinding seems much more "human"; but the contrary is really true. For man never reasons so much and becomes so introspective as when he suffers, since he is anxious to get at the cause of his sufferings, to learn who has produced them, and whether it is just or unjust that he should have to bear them. On the other hand, when he is happy, he takes his happiness as it comes and doesn't analyze it, just as if happiness were his right. The animals suffer without reasoning about their sufferings. But take the case of a man who suffers and begins to reason about it. Oh no! it can't be allowed! Let him suffer like an animal, and then—ah yes, he is "human"!

THE MANAGER: Look here! Look here! You're off again, philosophizing worse than ever.

THE FATHER: Because I suffer, sir! I'm not philosophizing: I'm crying aloud the reason of my sufferings.

THE MANAGER (*makes brusque movement as he is taken with a new idea*): I should like to know if anyone has ever heard of a character who gets right out of his part and perorates and speechifies as you do. Have you ever heard of a case? I haven't.

THE FATHER: You have never met such a case, sir, because authors, as a rule, hide the labor of their creations. When the characters are really alive before their author, the latter does nothing but follow them in their action, in other words, in the situations which they suggest to him; and he has to will them the way they will themselves—for there's trouble if he doesn't. When a character is born, he acquires at once such an independence, even of his own author, that he can be imagined by everybody even in many other situations where the author never dreamed of placing him; and so he acquires for himself a meaning which the author never thought of giving him.

THE MANAGER: Yes, yes, I know this.

THE FATHER: What is there then to marvel at in us? Imagine such a misfortune for characters as I have described to you: to be born of an author's fantasy, and be denied life by him; and then answer me if these characters left alive, and yet without life, weren't right in doing what they did do and are doing now, after they have attempted everything in their power to persuade him to give them their stage life. We've all tried him in turn, I, she (*indicating the Stepdaughter*) and she (*indicating the Mother*).

THE STEPDAUGHTER: It's true. I too have sought to tempt him, many, many times, when he has been sitting at his writing table, feeling a bit melancholy, at the twilight hour. He would sit in his armchair too lazy to switch on the light, and all the shadows that crept into his room were full of our presence coming to tempt him. (*As if she saw herself still there by the writing table, and was annoyed by the presence of the Actors.*) Oh, if you would only go away, go away and leave us alone—mother here with that son of hers—I with that child—that boy there always alone—and then I with him (*just hints at the Father*)—and then I alone, alone . . . in those shadows! (*Makes a sudden movement as if in the vision she has of herself illuminating those shadows she wanted to seize hold of herself.*) Ah! my life! my life! Oh, what scenes we proposed to him—and I tempted him more than any of the others!

THE FATHER: Maybe. But perhaps it was your fault that he refused to give us life: because you were too insistent, too troublesome.

THE STEPDAUGHTER: Nonsense! Didn't he make me so himself? (*Goes close to the Manager to tell him as if in confidence.*) In my opinion he abandoned us in a fit of depression, of disgust for the ordinary theater as the public knows it and likes it.

THE SON: Exactly what it was, sir; exactly that!

THE FATHER: Not at all! Don't believe it for a minute. Listen to me! You'll be doing quite right to modify, as you suggest, the excesses both of this girl here, who wants to do too much, and of this young man, who won't do anything at all.

THE SON: No, nothing!

THE MANAGER: You too get over the mark occasionally, my dear sir, if I may say so.

THE FATHER: I? When? Where?

THE MANAGER: Always! Continuously! Then there's this insistence of yours in trying to make us believe you are a character. And then too, you must really argue and philosophize less, you know, much less.

THE FATHER: Well, if you want to take away from me the possibility of representing the torment of my spirit which never gives me peace, you will be suppressing me: that's all. Every true man, sir, who is a little above the level of the beasts and plants does not live for the sake of living, without knowing how to live; but he lives so as to give a meaning and a value of his own to life. For me this is *everything*. I cannot give up this, just to represent a mere fact as she (*indicating the Stepdaughter*) wants. It's all very well for

her, since her "vendetta" lies in the "fact." I'm not going to do it. It destroys my *raison d'être.*

THE MANAGER: Your *raison d'être!* Oh, we're going ahead fine! First she starts off, and then you jump in. At this rate, we'll never finish.

THE FATHER: Now, don't be offended! Have it your own way—provided, however, that within the limits of the parts you assign us each one's sacrifice isn't too great.

THE MANAGER: You've got to understand that you can't go on arguing at your own pleasure. Drama is action, sir, action and not confounded philosophy.

THE FATHER: All right. I'll do just as much arguing and philosophizing as everybody does when he is considering his own torments.

THE MANAGER: If the drama permits! But for Heaven's sake, man, let's get along and come to the scene.

THE STEPDAUGHTER: It seems to me we've got too much action with our coming into his house. (*Indicating Father.*) You said, before, you couldn't change the scene every five minutes.

THE MANAGER: Of course not. What we've got to do is to combine and group up all the facts in one simultaneous, close-knit action. We can't have it as you want, with your little brother wandering like a ghost from room to room, hiding behind doors and meditating a project which—what did you say it did to him?

THE STEPDAUGHTER: Consumes him, sir, wastes him away!

THE MANAGER: Well, it may be. And then at the same time, you want the little girl there to be playing in the garden . . . one in the house, and the other in the garden; isn't that it?

THE STEPDAUGHTER: Yes, in the sun, in the sun! That is my only pleasure: to see her happy and careless in the garden after the misery and squalor of the horrible room where we all four slept together. And I had to sleep with her—I, do you understand?—with my vile contaminated body next to hers; with her holding me fast in her loving little arms. In the garden, whenever she spied me, she would run to take me by the hand. She didn't care for the big flowers, only the little ones; and she loved to show me them and pet me.

THE MANAGER: Well then, we'll have it in the garden. Everything shall happen in the garden; and we'll group the other scenes there. (*Calls a Stage Hand.*) Here, a backcloth with trees and something to do as a fountain basin. (*Turning round to look at the back of the stage.*) Ah, you've fixed it up. Good! (*To Stepdaughter.*) This is just to give an idea, of course. The Boy, instead of hiding behind the doors, will wander about here in the garden, hiding behind the trees. But it's going to be rather difficult to find a child to do that scene with you where she shows you the flowers. (*Turning to the Boy.*) Come forward a little, will you please? Let's try it now! Come along! come along! (*Then seeing him come shyly forward, full of fear and looking lost.*) It's a nice business, this lad here. What's the matter with him? We'll have to give him a word or two to say. (*Goes close to him, puts a hand on his shoulders, and leads him behind one of the trees.*) Come on! come on! Let me see you a little! Hide here . . . yes, like that. Try and show your head just a little as if you were looking for someone. . . . (*Goes back to observe the effect, when the Boy at once goes through the action.*) Excellent! fine! (*Turning to Stepdaughter.*) Suppose the little girl there were to surprise him as he looks round, and run over to him, so we could give him a word or two to say?

THE STEPDAUGHTER: It's useless to hope he will speak, as long as that fellow there is here. . . . (*Indicates the Son.*) You must send him away first.

THE SON (*jumping up*): Delighted! Delighted! I don't ask for anything better. (*Begins to move away.*)

THE MANAGER (*at once stopping him*): No! No! Where are you going? Wait a bit!

(*The Mother gets up alarmed and terrified at the thought that he is really about to go away. Instinctively she lifts her arms to prevent him, without, however, leaving her seat.*)

THE SON (*to Manager, who stops him*): I've got nothing to do with this affair. Let me go, please! Let me go!

THE MANAGER: What do you mean by saying you've got nothing to do with this?

THE STEPDAUGHTER (*calmly, with irony*): Don't bother to stop him: he won't go away.

THE FATHER: He has to act the terrible scene in the garden with his mother.

THE SON (*suddenly resolute and with dignity*): I shall act nothing at all. I've said so from the very beginning. (*To the Manager.*) Let me go!

THE STEPDAUGHTER (*going over to the Manager*): Allow me? (*Puts down the Manager's arm which is restraining the Son.*) Well, go away then, if you want to! (*The Son looks at her with contempt and hatred. She laughs and says.*) You see, he can't, he can't go away! He is obliged to stay here, indissolubly bound to the chain. If I, who fly off when that happens which has to happen because I can't bear him—if I am still here and support that face and expression of his, you can well imagine that he is unable to move. He has to remain here, has to stop with that nice father of his, and that mother whose only son he is. (*Turning to the Mother.*) Come on, mother, come along! (*Turning to Manager to indicate her.*) You see, she was getting up to keep him back. (*To the Mother, beckoning her with her hand.*) Come on, come on! (*Then to Manager.*) You can imagine how little she wants to show these actors of yours what she really feels; but so eager is she to get near him that. . . . There, you see? She is willing to act her part. (*And in fact, the Mother approaches him; and as soon as the Stepdaughter has finished speaking, opens her arms to signify that she consents.*)

THE SON (*suddenly*): No! no! If I can't go away, then I'll stop here; but I repeat: I act nothing!

THE FATHER (*to Manager excitedly*): You can force him, sir.

THE SON: Nobody can force me.

THE FATHER: I can.

THE STEPDAUGHTER: Wait a minute, wait . . . First of all, the baby has to go to the fountain. . . . (*Runs to take the Child and leads her to the fountain.*)

THE MANAGER: Yes, yes of course; that's it. Both at the same time.

(*The Second Lady Lead and the Juvenile Lead at this point separate themselves from the group of Actors. One watches the Mother attentively; the other moves about studying the movements and manner of the Son whom he will have to act.*)

THE SON (*to Manager*): What do you mean by both at the same time? It isn't right. There was no scene between me and her. (*Indicates the Mother.*) Ask her how it was!

THE MOTHER: Yes, it's true. I had come into his room. . . .

THE SON: Into my room, do you understand? Nothing to do with the garden.

THE MANAGER: It doesn't matter. Haven't I told you we've got to group the action?

THE SON (*observing the Juvenile Lead studying him*): What do you want?

JUVENILE LEAD: Nothing! I was just looking at you.

THE SON (*turning toward the Second Lady Lead*): Ah! she's at it too: to re-act her part! (*Indicating the Mother.*)

THE MANAGER: Exactly! And it seems to me that you ought to be grateful to them for their interest.

THE SON: Yes, but haven't you yet perceived that it isn't possible to live in front of a mirror which not only freezes us with the image of ourselves, but throws our likeness back at us with a horrible grimace?

THE FATHER: That is true, absolutely true. You must see that.

THE MANAGER (*to Second Lady Lead and Juvenile Lead*): He's right! Move away from them!

THE SON: Do as you like. I'm out of this!

THE MANAGER: Be quiet, you, will you? And let me hear your mother! (*To Mother.*) You were saying you had entered. . . .

THE MOTHER: Yes, into his room, because I couldn't stand it any longer. I went to empty my heart to him of all the anguish that tortures me. . . . But as soon as he saw me come in. . . .

THE SON: Nothing happened! There was no scene. I went away, that's all! I don't care for scenes!

THE MOTHER: It's true, true. That's how it was.

THE MANAGER: Well now, we've got to do this bit between you and him. It's indispensable.

THE MOTHER: I'm ready . . . when you are ready. If you could only find a chance for me to tell him what I feel here in my heart.

THE FATHER (*going to Son in a great rage*): You'll do this for your mother, for your mother, do you understand?

THE SON (*quite determined*): I do nothing!

THE FATHER (*taking hold of him and shaking him*): For God's sake, do as I tell you! Don't you hear your mother asking you for a favor? Haven't you even got the guts to be a son?

THE SON (*taking hold of the Father*): No! No! And for God's sake stop it, or else.... (*General agitation. The Mother, frightened, tries to separate them.*)

THE MOTHER (*pleading*): Please! please!

THE FATHER (*not leaving hold of the Son*): You've got to obey, do you hear?

THE SON (*almost crying from rage*): What does it mean, this madness you've got? (*They separate.*) Have you no decency, that you insist on showing everyone our shame? I won't do it! I won't! And I stand for the will of our author in this. He didn't want to put us on the stage, after all!

THE MANAGER: Man alive! You came here ...

THE SON (*indicating Father*): *He* did! I didn't!

THE MANAGER: Aren't you here now?

THE SON: It was his wish, and he dragged us along with him. He's told you not only the things that did happen, but also things that have never happened at all.

THE MANAGER: Well, tell me then what did happen. You went out of your room without saying a word?

THE SON: Without a word, so as to avoid a scene!

THE MANAGER: And then what did you do?

THE SON: Nothing ... walking in the garden.... (*Hesitates for a moment with expression of gloom.*)

THE MANAGER (*coming closer to him, interested by his extraordinary reserve*): Well, well ... walking in the garden....

THE SON (*exasperated*): Why on earth do you insist? It's horrible!

(*The Mother trembles, sobs, and looks toward the fountain.*)

THE MANAGER (*slowly observing the glance and turning toward the Son with increasing apprehension*): The baby?

THE SON: There in the fountain....

THE FATHER (*pointing with tender pity to the Mother*): She was following him at the moment....

THE MANAGER (*to the Son anxiously*): And then you ...

THE SON: I ran over to her; I was jumping in to drag her out when I saw something that froze my blood ... the boy standing stock still, with eyes like a madman's, watching his little drowned sister, in the fountain! (*The Stepdaughter bends over the fountain to hide the Child. She sobs.*) Then.... (*A revolver shot rings out behind the trees where the Boy is hidden.*)

THE MOTHER (*with a cry of terror runs over in that direction together with several of the Actors amid general confusion*): My son! My son! (*Then amid the cries and exclamations one hears her voice.*) Help! Help!

THE MANAGER (*pushing the Actors aside while they lift up the Boy and carry him off*): Is he really wounded?

SOME ACTORS: He's dead! dead!

OTHER ACTORS: No, no, it's only make-believe, it's only pretense!

THE FATHER (*with a terrible cry*): Pretense? Reality, sir, reality!

THE MANAGER: Pretense? Reality? To hell with it all! Never in my life has such a thing happened to me. I've lost a whole day over these people, a whole day!

Federico García Lorca

"I sincerely believe that theatre is not and cannot be anything but emotion and poetry—in word, action, gesture."

–Federico García Lorca

Federico García Lorca (1898–1936) lived through some of the most troubling times modern Spain has seen. He was born in the countryside near Granada, and he maintained a lifelong love of Spanish village and country people. His father was a wealthy farmer, and his mother was a teacher who encouraged his early love of literature, art, and music. Lorca's talents were extraordinary. A fine pianist, he counted among his friends some of Spain's greatest musicians, including Manuel de Falla. Lorca painted throughout his life and maintained a close friendship with Salvador Dalí. His career at the university was not especially distinguished, but as a student he became famous for readings of his own poetry. He produced an early play, *The Butterfly's Evil Spell*, in 1920, the year before he published his first book of poems. His political leanings throughout his life were liberal and reformist, but his early years were spent living under a Spanish dictatorship. General elections ended Spain's monarchy and established the Second Spanish Republic in 1931, but Fascist leaders, notably Francisco Franco, began agitating for control. Standing for a free republic and prominent as a leftist, Lorca was killed suddenly and without explanation by Franco's forces in 1936, just two days before the start of the Spanish Civil War.

Lorca's dramatic work had developed steadily. His second play, *The Girl Who Waters the Sweet Basil Flower and the Inquisitive Prince* (1923), was a puppet show. Lorca, who especially enjoyed this form of drama, had bought his own puppet theater when he was fifteen. He designed the sets, and Manuel de Falla provided the music. Unfortunately, the manuscript for this play has been lost. Text for another puppet play of the same period, *The Billy-Club Puppets*, does exist, as do copies of some later dramatic sketches: *Buster Keaton's Promenade* (1926), which takes off on Buster Keaton's film character, and *The Public* (1933), one of several experimental surrealist plays. His first real success was *Mariana Pineda* (1927), produced in Granada. After suffering a personal crisis, perhaps connected to his growing awareness of his homosexuality, Lorca spent a year in New York, from which experience he wrote *The Poet in New York*, published—much later—in 1940.

Lorca returned to Spain and produced a number of plays in the early 1930s, such as *The Shoemaker's Prodigious Wife* (1930), *The Love of Don Perlimplín with Belisa in the Garden* (1933), and *Doña Rosita, the Spinster* (1935), the last of his plays to be produced during his lifetime. His three most important plays are generally referred to as folk tragedies: *Blood Wedding* (1933) and *Yerma* (1934) were produced in Madrid, and *The House of Bernarda Alba* (1936) was produced in Buenos Aires in 1945. These three plays were influenced by a great Spanish actress and producer, Margarita Xirgu, for whom the title role of Yerma was created.

Lorca's reputation flourished after the end of World War II, but because Spain's Fascist government continued until Franco's death in 1975, Lorca's work could not be produced in his native country until the 1980s. His gift was in combining poetry, music, original set designs, and a sense of the language of the country people who inspired his work. He had a feel for the pagan forces

For links to resources about Lorca, click on *AuthorLinks* at **bedfordstmartins.com/jacobus**.

that informed the country people and aimed to show their creative power in everyday life. He celebrated instinctive, primitive religious feeling, the joy of living, the sexual energy of the universe, and the fullness of life.

The House of Bernarda Alba

Lorca diverged from his earlier poetic style when he created *The House of Bernarda Alba*, subtitled "A Drama about Women in the Villages of Spain." He is on record as having said, "Not a drop of poetry! Reality! Realism!" Supposed to be as realistic and detailed as a "photographic document," the play pointed to some of the harsher realities of life for women in rural Spain. Indeed, only women appear in the play. Pepe el Romano, a young handsome man, betrothed to Angustias, Bernarda's eldest daughter (apparently for her money), is mentioned often but never appears. In the beginning of the third act, a stallion making loud sounds in his stall represents the symbolic force of sex in nature. Bernarda Alba demands that the stallion be freed before it brings the walls down, but at the same time she determines to keep her daughters hidden away in her house and under her thumb. The focus of the play is on Bernarda Alba's determination to preserve her dignity in her village. She wants to make sure that no one talks about her family disparagingly; she must keep up appearances even at the risk of smothering the sexual energies of her five daughters.

When the play opens, Bernarda's second husband has just died, and she declares that the household shall mourn for eight years. Her daughters will be shut in and not see a man for any of that time. However, since Angustias has her own money from her father, Bernarda's first husband, she is courted by Pepe el Romano. At the same time, Pepe secretly expresses his true affection to Angustias's sister Adela, who is much closer to him in age and who would be a more suitable wife. Bernarda, however, is adamant about the period of mourning and eventually chases Pepe away with a shotgun after discovering that he has given in to his desires.

This is a play about the tyranny of Bernarda over her daughters. It portrays her desire to be respected in the community at all costs, even the cost of living a lie. It is also a play about "women without men." Some critics have seen in the prisonlike atmosphere (note the constant reference to bars) a suggestion of the religious convent and the sexual repression it implies. The Cistercians, known as Bernardas, were an order of nuns familiar to Lorca. But Lorca is exploring a number of powerful forces in life: the power of the family and tradition, the power of religion and its strictures of moral behavior, the power of economic necessity and the way it distorts lives, and the power of a political force that maintains itself through absolute authority. Most of these forces were evident in the Spain Lorca knew throughout his life. From 1932 much of his time was spent traveling with, and writing for, a government-sponsored touring company, La Barraca, that put on classic Spanish plays in remote towns around the nation. He had plenty of opportunity to observe everyday life in rural Spain. This play reveals some of its nature.

For discussion questions and assignments on *The House of Bernarda Alba*, visit **bedfordstmartins.com/jacobus**.

The House of Bernarda Alba in Performance

The first production of the play, in 1945, was in Buenos Aires, which Lorca visited shortly before he died, impressing those he met with his genius. South America has long found his work important; Lorca's play was produced in various South American countries long before it appeared in Spain. Eric Bentley staged a minimalist production of the play at the Abbey Theatre in Dublin in 1950, with Peggy Hayes as Bernarda and Angela Newmann as Adela. He describes this production in his *In Search of Theater* (1953), saying, "Ireland and Spain are two of the remaining vestiges of Catholic-peasant civilization. Lorca's play springs from this civilization, gives it amazingly full expression, and is a bitter rejection of it."

The play was given a limited production in Paris in the Studio des Champs-Élyées in 1946, employing a fine set with stark white walls and black wrought-iron bars across the windows. A New York production at the ANTA Playhouse lasted for seventeen performances in January 1951. Bentley had earlier speculated that the play would be very difficult to communicate to 1950s London or New York audiences, and he seems to have been correct. It was produced in New York again by Teatro Hispano, directed by Max Ferra, in early 1972. Bernarda was played by the Cuban actress Ofelia González. Numerous productions in Europe followed; one of the most powerful was in 1986 at the Lyric Theatre in Hammersmith, London, directed by Nuria Espert. The sets and the lighting served to intensify the sense of overwhelming heat from the Andalusian sun. Paul Preston, in his review in the *Times Literary Supplement*, said, "Glenda Jackson's Bernarda is as stiff-back as the most humorless prison governor or mother superior, dominating her brood with snarling sarcasm and fulminating looks." Joan Plowright played a powerful Poncia, but Patricia Hayes, as Bernarda's mother, was singled out for her stunning performance: "wearing muslin rags over white flesh like a feverish and ecstatic moth" (Michael Ratcliffe in the *Observer*). The play moved into the West End (London's Broadway) to the Globe Theatre in 1987 with the same cast. Among recent productions was the 1993 production in Northern Ireland at the adventurous women's company, the Charabanc Theatre Company. Lynne Parker adapted and directed the play to exceptional reviews, and the production toured twenty towns throughout Ireland and Northern Ireland before settling in at the Project Arts Centre in Dublin. The reviews of the production celebrated its excellence and explored the women's issues in the drama. The Orange Tree Theatre in Richmond, which is billed as "London's only theatre in the round," staged a very well reviewed production in March and April 2003. Auriol Smith directed a translation that she and Rebecca Morahan had done. Lynn Farley played Bernarda Alba. The 2005 production of *The House of Bernarda Alba* at the National Theatre in London was described by Philip Fisher in the *British Theatre Guide:* "This new version by Sir David Hare is all shimmering sensuality in the massive hothouse of a room created by designer Vicki Mortimer and lighting designer Paule Constable." In June 2007, the National Asian American Theatre Company produced a very well received adaptation that was praised for capturing the intensity of Lorca's original. Clearly, this play resonates in modern times.

FEDERICO GARCÍA LORCA (1898–1936)

The House of Bernarda Alba 1936
A Drama about Women in the Villages of Spain
TRANSLATED BY JAMES GRAHAM-LUJÁN AND RICHARD L. O'CONNELL

Characters

BERNARDA (*age 60*)
MARÍA JOSEFA, *Bernarda's Mother* (*age 80*)
ANGUSTIAS, *Bernarda's Daughter* (*age 39*)
MAGDALENA, *Bernarda's Daughter* (*age 30*)
AMELIA, *Bernarda's Daughter* (*age 27*)
MARTIRIO, *Bernarda's Daughter* (*age 24*)
ADELA, *Bernarda's Daughter* (*age 20*)
A MAID (*age 50*)
LA PONCIA, *A Maid* (*age 60*)
PRUDENCIA (*age 50*)
WOMEN IN MOURNING

The writer states that these Three Acts are intended as a photographic document.

ACT 1

(*A very white room in Bernarda Alba's house. The walls are white. There are arched doorways with jute curtains tied back with tassels and ruffles. Wicker chairs. On the walls, pictures of unlikely landscapes full of nymphs or legendary kings.*

It is summer. A great brooding silence fills the stage. It is empty when the curtain rises. Bells can be heard tolling outside.)

FIRST SERVANT (*entering*): The tolling of those bells hits me right between the eyes.
PONCIA (*she enters, eating bread and sausage*): More than two hours of mumbo jumbo. Priests are here from all the towns. The church looks beautiful. At the first responsory for the dead, Magdalena fainted.
FIRST SERVANT: She's the one who's left most alone.
PONCIA: She's the only one who loved her father. Ay! Thank God we're alone for a little. I came over to eat.
FIRST SERVANT: If Bernarda sees you . . . !
PONCIA: She's not eating today so she'd just as soon we'd all die of hunger! Domineering old tyrant! But she'll be fooled! I opened the sausage crock.
FIRST SERVANT (*with an anxious sadness*): Couldn't you give me some for my little girl, Poncia?
PONCIA: Go ahead! And take a fistful of peas too. She won't know the difference today.

VOICE (*within*): Bernarda!
PONCIA: There's the grandmother! Isn't she locked up tight?
FIRST SERVANT: Two turns of the key.
PONCIA: You'd better put the cross-bar up too. She's got the fingers of a lock-picker!
VOICE (*within*): Bernarda!
PONCIA (*shouting*): She's coming! (*to the servant*) Clean everything up good. If Bernarda doesn't find things shining, she'll pull out the few hairs I have left.
SERVANT: What a woman!
PONCIA: Tyrant over everyone around her. She's perfectly capable of sitting on your heart and watching you die for a whole year without turning off that cold little smile she wears on her wicked face. Scrub, scrub those dishes!
SERVANT: I've got blood on my hands from so much polishing of everything.
PONCIA: She's the cleanest, she's the decentest, she's the highest everything! A good rest her poor husband's earned!

(*The bells stop.*)

SERVANT: Did all the relatives come?
PONCIA: Just hers. His people hate her. They came to see him dead and make the sign of the cross over him; that's all.
SERVANT: Are there enough chairs?
PONCIA: More than enough. Let them sit on the floor. When Bernarda's father died people stopped coming under this roof. She doesn't want them to see her in her "domain." Curse her!
SERVANT: She's been good to you.
PONCIA: Thirty years washing her sheets. Thirty years eating her leftovers. Nights of watching when she had a cough. Whole days peeking through a crack in the shutters to spy on the neighbors and carry her the tale. Life without secrets one from the other. But in spite of that—curse her! May the "pain of the piercing nail" strike her in the eyes.
SERVANT: Poncia!
PONCIA: But I'm a good watchdog! I bark when I'm told and bite beggars' heels when she sics me on 'em. My sons work in her fields—both of them already married, but one of these days I'll have enough.
SERVANT: And then . . . ?
PONCIA: Then I'll lock myself up in a room with her and spit in her face—a whole year. "Bernarda, here's for

this, that and the other!" Till I leave her—just like a lizard the boys have squashed. For that's what she is—she and her whole family! Not that I envy her her life. Five girls are left her, five ugly daughters—not counting Angustias the eldest, by her first husband, who has money—the rest of them, plenty of eyelets to embroider, plenty of linen petticoats, but bread and grapes when it comes to inheritance!

SERVANT: Well, *I'd* like to have what they've got!

PONCIA: All we have is our hands and a hole in God's earth.

SERVANT: And that's the only earth they'll ever leave to us—to us who have nothing!

PONCIA (*at the cupboard*): This glass has some specks.

SERVANT: Neither soap nor rag will take them off.

(*The bells toll.*)

PONCIA: The last prayer! I'm going over and listen. I certainly like the way our priest sings. In the Pater Noster his voice went up, and up—like a pitcher filling with water little by little. Of course, at the end his voice cracked, but it's glorious to hear it. No, there never was anybody like the old Sacristan—Tronchapinos. At my mother's Mass, may she rest in peace, he sang. The walls shook—and when he said "Amen," it was as if a wolf had come into the church.

(*Imitating him.*)

A-a-a-a-men!

(*She starts coughing.*)

SERVANT: Watch out—you'll strain your windpipe!

PONCIA: I'd rather strain something else!

(*Goes out laughing.*)

(*The servant scrubs. The bells toll.*)

SERVANT (*imitating the bells*): Dong, dong, dong. Dong, dong, dong. May God forgive him!

BEGGAR WOMAN (*at the door, with a little girl*): Blesséd be God!

SERVANT: Dong, dong, dong. I hope he waits many years for us! Dong, dong, dong.

BEGGAR (*loudly, a little annoyed*): Blesséd be God!

SERVANT (*annoyed*): Forever and ever!

BEGGAR: I came for the scraps.

(*The bells stop tolling.*)

SERVANT: You can go right out the way you came in. Today's scraps are for me.

BEGGAR: But you have somebody to take care of you—and my little girl and I are all alone!

SERVANT: Dogs are alone too, and they live.

BEGGAR: They always give them to me.

SERVANT: Get out of here! Who let you in anyway? You've already tracked up the place.

(*The beggar woman and little girl leave. The servant goes on scrubbing.*)

Floors finished with oil, cupboards, pedestals, iron beds—but us servants, we can suffer in silence—and live in mud huts with a plate and a spoon. I hope someday not a one will be left to tell it.

(*The bells sound again.*)

Yes, yes—ring away. Let them pelt you in a coffin with gold inlay and brocade to carry it on—you're no less dead than I'll be, so take what's coming to you, Antonio María Benavides—stiff in your broadcloth suit and your high boots—take what's coming to you! You'll never again lift my skirts behind the corral door!

(*From the rear door, two by two, women in mourning with large shawls and black skirts and fans, begin to enter. They come in slowly until the stage is full.*)

SERVANT (*breaking into a wail*): Oh, Antonio María Benavides, now you'll never see these walls, nor break bread in this house again! I'm the one who loved you most of all your servants.

(*Pulling her hair.*)

Must I live on after you've gone? Must I go on living?

(*The two hundred women finish coming in, and Bernarda and her five daughters enter. Bernarda leans on a cane.*)

BERNARDA (*to the servant*): Silence!

SERVANT (*weeping*): Bernarda!

BERNARDA: Less shrieking and more work. You should have had all this cleaner for the wake. Get out. This isn't your place.

(*The servant goes off crying.*)

The poor are like animals—they seem to be made of different stuff.

FIRST WOMAN: The poor feel their sorrows too.

BERNARDA: But they forget them in front of a plateful of peas.

FIRST GIRL (*timidly*): Eating is necessary for living.

BERNARDA: At your age one doesn't talk in front of older people.

WOMAN: Be quiet, child.

BERNARDA: I've never taken lessons from anyone. Sit down.

(*They sit down. Pause. Loudly.*)

Magdalena, don't cry. If you want to cry, get under your bed. Do you hear me?

SECOND WOMAN (*to Bernarda*): Have you started to work the fields?

BERNARDA: Yesterday.

THIRD WOMAN: The sun comes down like lead.

FIRST WOMAN: I haven't known heat like this for years.

(*Pause. They all fan themselves.*)

BERNARDA: Is the lemonade ready?

PONCIA: Yes, Bernarda.

(*She brings in a large tray full of little white jars which she distributes.*)

BERNARDA: Give the men some.

PONCIA: They're already drinking in the patio.

BERNARDA: Let them get out the way they came in. I don't want them walking through here.

A GIRL (*to Angustias*): Pepe el Romano was with the men during the service.

ANGUSTIAS: There he was.

BERNARDA: His mother was there. She saw his mother. Neither she nor I saw Pepe . . .

GIRL: I thought . . .

BERNARDA: The one who *was* there was Darajalí, the widower. Very close to your Aunt. We all of us saw him.

SECOND WOMAN (*aside, in a low voice*): Wicked, worse than wicked woman!

THIRD WOMAN: A tongue like a knife!

BERNARDA: Women in church shouldn't look at any man but the priest—and him only because he wears skirts. To turn your head is to be looking for the warmth of corduroy.

FIRST WOMAN: Sanctimonious old snake!

PONCIA (*between her teeth*): Itching for a man's warmth.

BERNARDA (*beating with her cane on the floor*): Blesséd be God!

ALL (*crossing themselves*): Forever blessed and praised.

BERNARDA: Rest in peace with holy company at your head.

ALL: Rest in peace!

BERNARDA: With the Angel Saint Michael, and his sword of justice.

ALL: Rest in peace!

BERNARDA: With the key that opens, and the hand that locks.

ALL: Rest in peace!

BERNARDA: With the most blessed, and the little lights of the field.

ALL: Rest in peace!

BERNARDA: With our holy charity, and all souls on land and sea.

ALL: Rest in peace!

BERNARDA: Grant rest to your servant, Antonio María Benavides, and give him the crown of your blesséd glory.

ALL: Amen.

BERNARDA (*she rises and chants*): *Requiem aeternam donat eis domine.*

ALL (*standing and chanting in the Gregorian fashion*): *Et lux perpetua luce ab eis.*°

(*They cross themselves.*)

FIRST WOMAN: May you have health to pray for his soul. (*They start filing out.*)

THIRD WOMAN: You won't lack loaves of hot bread.

SECOND WOMAN: Nor a roof for your daughters.

(*They are all filing in front of Bernarda and going out. Angustias leaves by the door to the patio.*)

FOURTH WOMAN: May you go on enjoying your wedding wheat.

PONCIA (*she enters, carrying a money bag*): From the men—this bag of money for Masses.

BERNAHDA: Thank them—and let them have a glass of brandy.

Requiem aeternam . . . ab eis: Eternal rest grant to him, O Lord And let perpetual light shine on him.

GIRL (*to Magdalena*): Magdalena . . .

BERNARDA (*to Magdalena, who is starting to cry*): Sh–h–h–h!

(*She beats with her cane on the floor.*)
(*All the women have gone out.*)

BERNARDA (*to the women who have just left*): Go back to your houses and criticize everything you've seen! I hope it'll be many years before you pass under the archway of my door again.

PONCIA: You've nothing to complain about. The whole town came.

BERNARDA: Yes, to fill my house with the sweat from their wraps and the poison of their tongues.

AMELIA: Mother, don't talk like that.

BERNARDA: What other way is there to talk about this cursed village with no river—this village full of wells where you drink water always fearful it's been poisoned?

PONCIA: Look what they've done to the floor!

BERNARDA: As though a herd of goats had passed through.

(*Poncia cleans the floor.*)

Adela, give me a fan.

ADELA: Take this one.

(*She gives her a round fan with green and red flowers.*)

BERNARDA (*throwing the fan on the floor*): Is that the fan to give to a widow? Give me a black one and learn to respect your father's memory.

MARTIRIO: Take mine.

BERNARDA: And you?

MARTIRIO: I'm not hot.

BERNARDA: Well, look for another, because you'll need it. For the eight years of mourning, not a breath of air will get in this house from the street. We'll act as if we'd sealed up doors and windows with bricks. That's what happened in my father's house—and in my grandfather's house. Meantime, you can all start embroidering your hope-chest linens. I have twenty bolts of linen in the chest from which to cut sheets and coverlets. Magdalena can embroider them.

MAGDALENA: It's all the same to me.

ADELA (*sourly*): If you don't want to embroider them—they can go without. That way yours will look better.

MAGDALENA: Neither mine nor yours. I know I'm not going to marry. I'd rather carry sacks to the mill. Anything except sit here day after day in this dark room.

BERNARDA: That's what a woman is for.

MAGDALENA: Cursed be all women.

BERNAHDA: In this house you'll do what I order. You can't run with the story to your father any more. Needle and thread for women. Whiplash and mules for men. That's the way it has to be for people who have certain obligations.

(*Adela goes out.*)

VOICE: Bernarda! Let me out!

BERNARDA (*calling*): Let her out now!

(*The first servant enters.*)

FIRST SERVANT: I had a hard time holding her. In spite of her eighty years, your mother's strong as an oak.

BERNARDA: It runs in the family. My grandfather was the same way.

SERVANT: Several times during the wake I had to cover her mouth with an empty sack because she wanted to shout out to you to give her dishwater to drink at least, and some dogmeat, which is what she says you feed her.

MARTIRIO: She's mean!

BERNARDA (*to servant*): Let her get some fresh air in the patio.

SERVANT: She took her rings and the amethyst earrings out of the box, put them on, and told me she wants to get married.

(*The daughters laugh.*)

BERNARDA: Go with her and be careful she doesn't get near the well.

SERVANT: You don't need to be afraid she'll jump in.

BERNARDA: It's not that—but the neighbors can see her there from their windows.

(*The servant leaves.*)

MARTIRIO: We'll go change our clothes.

BERNARDA: Yes, but don't take the kerchiefs from your heads.

(*Adela enters.*)

And Angustias?

ADELA (*meaningfully*): I saw her looking out through the cracks of the back door. The men had just gone.

BERNARDA: And you, what were *you* doing at the door?

ADELA: I went there to see if the hens had laid.

BERNARDA: But the men had already gone!

ADELA (*meaningfully*): A group of them were still standing outside.

BERNARDA (*furiously*): Angustias! Angustias!

ANGUSTIAS (*entering*): Did you want something?

BERNARDA: For what—and at whom—were you looking?

ANGUSTIAS: Nobody.

BERNARDA: Is it decent for a woman of your class to be running after a man the day of her father's funeral? Answer me! Whom were you looking at?

(*Pause.*)

ANGUSTIAS: I . . .

BERNARDA: Yes, you!

ANGUSTIAS: Nobody.

BERNARDA: Soft! Honeytongue!

(*She strikes her.*)

PONCIA (*running to her*): Bernarda, calm down!

(*She holds her. Angustias weeps.*)

BERNARDA: Get out of here, all of you!

(*They all go out.*)

PONCIA: She did it not realizing what she was doing— although it's bad, of course. It really disgusted me to see her sneak along to the patio. Then she stood at the window listening to the men's talk, which, as usual, was not the sort one should listen to.

BERNARDA: That's what they come to funerals for. (*With curiosity.*) What were they talking about?

PONCIA: They were talking about Paca la Roseta. Last night they tied her husband up in a stall, stuck her on a horse behind the saddle, and carried her away to the depths of the olive grove.

BERNARDA: And what did she do?

PONCIA: She? She was just as happy—they say her breasts were exposed and Maximiliano held on to her as if he were playing a guitar. Terrible!

BERNARDA: And what happened?

PONCIA: What had to happen. They came back almost at daybreak. Paca la Roseta with her hair loose and a wreath of flowers on her head.

BERNARDA: She's the only bad woman we have in the village.

PONCIA: Because she's not from here. She's from far away. And those who went with her are the sons of outsiders too. The men from here aren't up to a thing like that.

BERNARDA: No, but they like to see it, and talk about it, and suck their fingers over it.

PONCIA: They were saying a lot more things.

BERNARDA (*looking from side to side with a certain fear*): What things?

PONCIA: I'm ashamed to talk about them.

BERNARDA: And my daughter heard them?

PONCIA: Of course!

BERNARDA: That one takes after her Aunts: white and mealy-mouthed and casting sheep's eyes at any little barber's compliment. Oh, what one has to go through and put up with so people will be decent and not too wild!

PONCIA: It's just that your daughters are of an age when they ought to have husbands. Mighty little trouble they give you. Angustias must be much more than thirty now.

BERNARDA: Exactly thirty-nine.

PONCIA: Imagine. And she's never had a beau . . .

BERNARDA (*furiously*): None of them has ever had a beau and they've never needed one! They get along very well.

PONCIA: I didn't mean to offend you.

BERNARDA: For a hundred miles around there's no one good enough to come near them. The men in this town are not of their class. Do you want me to turn them over to the first shepherd?

PONCIA: You should have moved to another town.

BERNARDA: That's it. To sell them!

PONCIA: No, Bernarda, to change. . . . Of course, any place else, they'd be the poor ones.

BERNARDA: Hold your tormenting tongue!

PONCIA: One can't even talk to you. Do we, or do we not share secrets?

BERNARDA: We do not. You're a servant and I pay you. Nothing more.

PONCIA: But . . .

FIRST SERVANT (*entering*): Don Arturo's here. He's come to see about dividing the inheritance.

BERNARDA: Let's go. (*to the servant*) You start white-washing the patio. (*to La Poncia*) And you start putting all the dead man's clothes away in the chest.

PONCIA: We could give away some of the things.

BERNARDA: Nothing—not a button even! Not even the cloth we covered his face with.

(*She goes out slowly, leaning on her cane. At the door she turns to look at the two servants. They go out. She leaves.*)

(*Amelia and Martirio enter.*)

AMELIA: Did you take the medicine?

MARTIRIO: For all the good it'll do me.

AMELIA: But you took it?

MARTIRIO: I do things without any faith, but like clock-work.

AMELIA: Since the new doctor came you look livelier.

MARTIRIO: I feel the same.

AMELIA: Did you notice? Adelaida wasn't at the funeral.

MARTIRIO: I know. Her sweetheart doesn't let her go out even to the front doorstep. Before, she was gay. Now, not even powder on her face.

AMELIA: These days a girl doesn't know whether to have a beau or not.

MARTIRIO: It's all the same.

AMELIA: The whole trouble is all these wagging tongues that won't let us live. Adelaida has probably had a bad time.

MARTIRIO: She's afraid of our mother. Mother is the only one who knows the story of Adelaida's father and where he got his lands. Everytime she comes here, Mother twists the knife in the wound. Her father killed his first wife's husband in Cuba so he could marry her himself. Then he left her there and went off with another woman who already had one daughter, and then he took up with this other girl, Adelaida's mother, and married her after his second wife died insane.

AMELIA: But why isn't a man like that put in jail?

MARTIRIO: Because men help each other cover up things like that and no one's able to tell on them.

AMELIA: But Adelaida's not to blame for any of that.

MARTIRIO: No. But history repeats itself. I can see that everything is a terrible repetition. And she'll have the same fate as her mother and grandmother—both of them wife to the man who fathered her.

AMELIA: What an awful thing!

MARTIRIO: It's better never to look at a man. I've been afraid of them since I was a little girl. I'd see them in the yard, yoking the oxen and lifting grain sacks, shouting and stamping, and I was always afraid to grow up for fear one of them would suddenly take me in his arms. God has made me weak and ugly and has definitely put such things away from me.

AMELIA: Don't say that! Enrique Humanas was after you and he liked you.

MARTIRIO: That was just people's ideas! One time I stood in my nightgown at the window until daybreak because he let me know through his shepherd's little girl that he was going to come, and he didn't. It was all just talk. Then he married someone else who had more money than I.

AMELIA: And ugly as the devil.

MARTIRIO: What do men care about ugliness? All they care about is lands, yokes of oxen, and a submissive bitch who'll feed them.

AMELIA: Ay!

(*Magdalena enters.*)

MAGDALENA: What are you doing?

MARTIRIO: Just here.

AMELIA: And you?

MAGDALENA: I've been going through all the rooms. Just to walk a little, and look at Grandmother's needle-point pictures—the little woolen dog, and the black man wrestling with the lion—which we liked so much when we were children. Those were happier times. A wedding lasted ten days and evil tongues weren't in style. Today people are more refined. Brides wear white veils, just as in the cities, and we drink bottled wine, but we rot inside because of what people might say.

MARTIRIO: Lord knows what went on then!

AMELIA (*to Magdalena*): One of your shoelaces has come untied.

MAGDALENA: What of it?

AMELIA: You'll step on it and fall.

MAGDALENA: One less!

MARTIRIO: And Adela?

MAGDALENA: Ah! She put on the green dress she made to wear for her birthday, went out to the yard, and began shouting: "Chickens! Chickens, look at me!" I had to laugh.

AMELIA: If Mother had only seen her!

MAGDALENA: Poor little thing! She's the youngest one of us and still has her illusions. I'd give something to see her happy.

(*Pause. Angustias crosses the stage, carrying some towels.*)

ANGUSTIAS: What time is it?

MAGDALENA: It must be twelve.

ANGUSTIAS: So late?

AMELIA: It's about to strike.

(*Angustias goes out.*)

MAGDALENA (*meaningfully*): Do you know what?

(*Pointing after Angustias.*)

AMELIA: No.

MAGDALENA: Come on!

MARTIRIO: I don't know what you're talking about!

MAGDALENA: Both of you know it better than I do, always with your heads together, like two little sheep, but not letting anybody else in on it. I mean about Pepe el Romano!

MARTIRIO: Ah!

MAGDALENA (*mocking her*): Ah! The whole town's talking about it. Pepe el Romano is coming to marry Angustias. Last night he was walking around the house and I think he's going to send a declaration soon.

MARTIRIO: I'm glad. He's a good man.

AMELIA: Me too. Angustias is well off.

MAGDALENA: Neither one of you is glad.

MARTIRIO: Magdalena! What do you mean?

MAGDALENA: If he were coming because of Angustias' looks, for Angustias as a woman, I'd be glad too, but he's coming for her money. Even though Angustias is our sister, we're her family here and we know she's old and sickly, and always has been the least attractive one of us! Because if she looked like a dressed-up stick at twenty, what can she look like now, now that she's forty?

MARTIRIO: Don't talk like that. Luck comes to the one who least expects it.

AMELIA: But Magdalena's right after all! Angustias has all her father's money; she's the only rich one in the house and that's why, now that Father's dead and the money will be divided, they're coming for her.

MAGDALENA: Pepe el Romano is twenty-five years old and the best looking man around here. The natural thing would be for him to be after you, Amelia, or our Adela, who's twenty—not looking for the least likely one in this house, a woman who, like her father, talks through her nose.

MARTIRIO: Maybe he likes that!

MAGDALENA: I've never been able to bear your hypocrisy.

MARTIRIO: Heavens!

(*Adela enters.*)

MAGDALENA: Did the chickens see you?

ADELA: What did you want me to do?

AMELIA: If Mother sees you, she'll drag you by your hair!

ADELA: I had a lot of illusions about this dress. I'd planned to put it on the day we were going to eat watermelons at the well. There wouldn't have been another like it.

MARTIRIO: It's a lovely dress.

ADELA: And one that looks very good on me. It's the best thing Magdalena's ever cut.

MAGDALENA: And the chickens, what did they say to you?

ADELA: They presented me with a few fleas that riddled my legs.

(*They laugh.*)

MARTIRIO: What you can do is dye it black.

MAGDALENA: The best thing you can do is give it to Angustias for her wedding with Pepe el Romano.

ADELA (*with hidden emotion*): But Pepe el Romano . . .

AMELIA: Haven't you heard about it?

ADELA: No.

MAGDALENA: Well, now you know!

ADELA: But it can't be!

MAGDALENA: Money can do anything.

ADELA: Is that why she went out after the funeral and stood looking through the door?

(*Pause.*)

And that man would . . .

MAGDALENA: Would do anything.

(*Pause.*)

MARTIRIO: What are you thinking, Adela?

ADELA: I'm thinking that this mourning has caught me at the worst moment of my life for me to bear it.

MAGDALENA: You'll get used to it.

ADELA (*bursting out, crying with rage*): I will not get used to it! I can't be locked up. I don't want my skin to look like yours. I don't want my skin's whiteness lost in these rooms. Tomorrow I'm going to put on my green dress and go walking in the streets. I want to go out!

(*The first servant enters.*)

MAGDALENA (*in a tone of authority*): Adela!

SERVANT: The poor thing! How she misses her father. . . .

(*She goes out.*)

MARTIRIO: Hush!

AMELIA: What happens to one will happen to all of us.

(*Adela grows calm.*)

MAGDALENA: The servant almost heard you.

SERVANT (*entering*): Pepe el Romano is coming along at the end of the street.

(*Amelia, Martirio and Magdalena run hurriedly.*)

MAGDALENA: Let's go see him!

(*They leave rapidly.*)

SERVANT (*to Adela*): Aren't you going?

ADELA: It's nothing to me.

SERVANT: Since he has to turn the corner, you'll see him better from the window of your room.

(*The servant goes out. Adela is left on the stage, standing doubtfully; after a moment, she also leaves rapidly, going toward her room. Bernarda and La Poncia come in.*)

BERNARDA: Damned portions and shares.

PONCIA: What a lot of money is left to Angustias!

BERNARDA: Yes.

PONCIA: And for the others, considerably less.

BERNARDA: You've told me that three times now, when you know I don't want it mentioned! Considerably less; a lot less! Don't remind me any more.

(*Angustias comes in, her face heavily made up.*)

Angustias!

ANGUSTIAS: Mother.

BERNARDA: Have you dared to powder your face? Have you dared to wash your face on the day of your father's death?

ANGUSTIAS: He wasn't my father. Mine died a long time ago. Have you forgotten that already?

BERNARDA: You owe more to this man, father of your sisters, than to your own. Thanks to him, your fortune is intact.

ANGUSTIAS: We'll have to see about that first!

BERNARDA: Even out of decency! Out of respect!

ANGUSTIAS: Let me go out, mother!

BERNARDA: Let you go out? After I've taken that powder off your face, I will. Spineless! Painted hussy! Just like your aunts!

(*She removes the powder violently with her handkerchief.*)

Now get out!

PONCIA: Bernarda, don't be so hateful!

BERNARDA: Even though my mother is crazy, I still have my five senses and I know what I'm doing.

(*They all enter.*)

MAGDALENA: What's going on here?

BERNARDA: Nothing's "going on here"!

MAGDALENA (*to Angustias*): If you're fighting over the inheritance, you're the richest one and can hang on to it all.

ANGUSTIAS: Keep your tongue in your pocketbook!

BERNARDA (*beating on the floor*): Don't fool yourselves into thinking you'll sway me. Until I go out of this house feet first I'll give the orders for myself and for you!

(*Voices are heard and María Josefa, Bernarda's mother, enters. She is very old and has decked out her head and breast with flowers.*)

MARÍA JOSEFA: Bernarda, where is my mantilla? Nothing, nothing of what I own will be for any of you. Not my rings nor my black moiré dress. Because not a one of you is going to marry—not a one. Bernarda, give me my necklace of pearls.

BERNARDA (*to the servant*): Why did you let her get in here?

SERVANT (*trembling*): She got away from me!

MARÍA JOSEFA: I ran away because I want to marry—I want to get married to a beautiful manly man from the shore of the sea. Because here the men run from women.

BERNARDA: Hush, hush, Mother!

MARÍA JOSEFA: No, no—I won't hush. I don't want to see these single women, longing for marriage, turning their hearts to dust; and I want to go to my home town. Bernarda, I want a man to get married to and be happy with!

BERNARDA: Lock her up!

MARÍA JOSEFA: Let me go out, Bernarda!

(*The servant seizes María Josefa.*)

BERNARDA: Help her, all of you!

(*They all grab the old woman.*)

MARÍA JOSEFA: I want to get away from here! Bernarda! To get married by the shore of the sea—by the shore of the sea!

(*Quick curtain.*)

ACT 2

(*A white room in Bernarda's house. The doors on the left lead to the bedrooms. Bernarda's daughters are seated on low chairs, sewing. Magdalena is embroidering. La Poncia is with them.*)

ANGUSTIAS: I've cut the third sheet.

MARTIRIO: That one goes to Amelia.

MAGDALENA: Angustias, shall I put Pepe's initials here too?

ANGUSTIAS (*dryly*): No.

MAGDALENA (*calling, from off stage to Adela*): Adela, aren't you coming?

AMELIA: She's probably stretched out on the bed.

PONCIA: Something's wrong with that one. I find her restless, trembling, frightened—as if a lizard were between her breasts.

MARTIRIO: There's nothing, more or less, wrong with her than there is with all of us.

MAGDALENA: All of us except Angustias.

ANGUSTIAS: I feel fine, and anybody who doesn't like it can pop.

MAGDALENA: We all have to admit the nicest things about you are your figure and your tact.

ANGUSTIAS: Fortunately, I'll soon be out of this hell.

MAGDALENA: Maybe you won't get out!

MARTIRIO: Stop this talk!

ANGUSTIAS: Besides, a good dowry is better than dark eyes in one's face!

MAGDALENA: All you say just goes in one ear and out the other.

AMELIA (*to La Poncia*): Open the patio door and see if we can get a bit of a breeze.

(*La Poncia opens the door.*)

MARTIRIO: Last night I couldn't sleep because of the heat.

AMELIA: Neither could I.

MAGDALENA: I got up for a bit of air. There was a black storm cloud and a few drops even fell.

PONCIA: It was one in the morning and the earth seemed to give off fire. I got up too. Angustias was still at the window with Pepe.

MAGDALENA (*with irony*): That late? What time did he leave?

ANGUSTIAS: Why do you ask, if you saw him?

AMELIA: He must have left about one-thirty.

ANGUSTIAS: Yes. How did you know?

AMELIA: I heard him cough and heard his mare's hoofbeats.

PONCIA: But I heard him leave around four.

ANGUSTIAS: It must have been someone else!

PONCIA: No, I'm sure of it!

AMELIA: That's what it seemed to me, too.

MAGDALENA: That's very strange!

Cherry Morris as María Josefa, Penelope Wilton as Bernarda Alba, and Justine Mitchell as Magdalena in David Hare's 2005 production of *The House of Bernarda Alba* at the National Theatre, London.

(*Pause.*)

PONCIA: Listen, Angustias, what did he say to you the first time he came by your window?

ANGUSTIAS: Nothing. What should he say? Just talked.

MARTIRIO: It's certainly strange that two people who never knew each other should suddenly meet at a window and be engaged.

ANGUSTIAS: Well, I didn't mind.

AMELIA: I'd have felt very strange about it.

ANGUSTIAS: No, because when a man comes to a window he knows, from all the busybodies who come and go and fetch and carry, that he's going to be told "yes."

MARTIRIO: All right, but he'd have to ask you.

ANGUSTIAS: Of course!

AMELIA (*inquisitively*): And how did he ask you?

ANGUSTIAS: Why, no way:—"You know I'm after you. I need a good, well brought up woman, and that's you—if it's agreeable."

AMELIA: These things embarrass me!

ANGUSTIAS: They embarrass me too, but one has to go through it!

PONCIA: And did he say anything more?

ANGUSTIAS: Yes, he did all the talking.

MARTIRIO: And you?

ANGUSTIAS: I couldn't have said a word. My heart was almost coming out of my mouth. It was the first time I'd ever been alone at night with a man.

MAGDALENA: And such a handsome man.

ANGUSTIAS: He's not bad looking!

PONCIA: Those things happen among people who have an idea how to do things, who talk and say and move their hand. The first time my husband, Evaristo the Short-tailed, came to my window . . . Ha! Ha! Ha!

AMELIA: What happened?

PONCIA: It was very dark. I saw him coming along and as he went by he said, "Good evening." "Good evening," I said. Then we were both silent for more than half an hour. The sweat poured down my body. Then Evaristo got nearer and nearer as if he wanted to squeeze in through the bars and said in a very low voice—"Come here and let me feel you!"

(*They all laugh. Amelia gets up, runs, and looks through the door.*)

AMELIA: Ay, I thought mother was coming!

MAGDALENA: What she'd have done to us!

(*They go on laughing.*)

AMELIA: Sh-h-h! She'll hear us.

PONCIA: Then he acted very decently. Instead of getting some other idea, he went to raising birds, until he died. You aren't married but it's good for you to know, anyway, that two weeks after the wedding a man gives up the bed for the table, then the table for the tavern, and the woman who doesn't like it can just rot, weeping in a corner.

AMELIA: You liked it.

PONCIA: I learned how to handle him!

MARTIRIO: Is it true that you sometimes hit him?

PONCIA: Yes, and once I almost poked out one of his eyes!

MAGDALENA: All women ought to be like that!

PONCIA: I'm one of your mother's school. One time I don't know what he said to me, and then I killed all his birds—with the pestle!

(*They laugh.*)

MAGDALENA: Adela, child! Don't miss this.

AMELIA: Adela!

The National Asian American Theatre Company's 2007 production of *The House of Bernarda Alba*.

(*Pause.*)

MAGDALENA: I'll go see!

(*She goes out.*)

PONCIA: That child is sick!

MARTIRIO: Of course. She hardly sleeps!

PONCIA: What *does* she do, then?

MARTIRIO: How do I know what she does?

PONCIA: You probably know better than we do, since you sleep with just a wall between you.

ANGUSTIAS: Envy gnaws on people.

AMELIA: Don't exaggerate.

ANGUSTIAS: I can tell it in her eyes. She's getting the look of a crazy woman.

MARTIRIO: Don't talk about crazy women. This is one place you're not allowed to say that word.

(*Magdalena and Adela enter.*)

MAGDALENA: Didn't you say she was asleep?

ADELA: My body aches.

MARTIRIO (*with a hidden meaning*): Didn't you sleep well last night?

ADELA: Yes.

MARTIRIO: Then?

The women stand as witnesses in a scene from *The House of Bernarda Alba*, directed by Julia Robinson at the TOMI Theater in New York in 1987.

ADELA (*loudly*): Leave me alone. Awake or asleep, it's no affair of yours. I'll do whatever I want to with my body.

MARTIRIO: I was just concerned about you!

ADELA: Concerned?—curious! Weren't you sewing? Well, continue! I wish I were invisible so I could pass through a room without being asked where I was going!

SERVANT (*entering*): Bernarda is calling you. The man with the laces is here.

(*All but Adela and La Poncia go out, and as Martirio leaves, she looks fixedly at Adela.*)

ADELA: Don't look at me like that! If you want, I'll give you my eyes, for they're younger, and my back to improve that hump you have, but look the other way when I go by.

PONCIA: Adela, she's your sister, and the one who most loves you besides!

ADELA: She follows me everywhere. Sometimes she looks in my room to see if I'm sleeping. She won't let me breathe, and always, "Too bad about that face!" "Too bad about that body! It's going to waste!" But I won't let that happen. My body will be for whomever I choose.

PONCIA (*insinuatingly, in a low voice*): For Pepe el Romano, no?

ADELA (*frightened*): What do you mean?

PONCIA: What I said, Adela!

ADELA: Shut up!

PONCIA (*loudly*): Don't you think I've noticed?

ADELA: Lower your voice!

PONCIA: Then forget what you're thinking about!

ADELA: What do you know?

PONCIA: We old ones can see through walls. Where do you go when you get up at night?

ADELA: I wish you were blind!

PONCIA: But my head and hands are full of eyes, where something like this is concerned. I couldn't possibly guess your intentions. Why did you sit almost naked at your window, and with the light on and the window open, when Pepe passed by the second night he came to talk with your sister?

ADELA: That's not true!

PONCIA: Don't be a child! Leave your sister alone. And if you like Pepe el Romano, keep it to yourself.

(*Adela weeps.*)

Besides, who says you can't marry him? Your sister Angustias is sickly. She'll die with her first child. Narrow waisted, old—and out of my experience I can tell you she'll die. Then Pepe will do what all widowers do in these parts: he'll marry the youngest and most beautiful, and that's you. Live on that hope, forget him, anything; but don't go against God's law.

ADELA: Hush!

PONCIA: I won't hush!

ADELA: Mind your own business. Snooper, traitor!

PONCIA: I'm going to stick to you like a shadow!

ADELA: Instead of cleaning the house and then going to bed and praying for the dead, you root around like an old sow about goings on between men and women—so you can drool over them.

PONCIA: I keep watch; so people won't spit when they pass our door.

ADELA: What a tremendous affection you've suddenly conceived for my sister.

PONCIA: I don't have any affection for any of you. I want to live in a decent house. I don't want to be dirtied in my old age!

ADELA: Save your advice. It's already too late. For I'd leap not over you, just a servant, but over my mother to put out this fire I feel in my legs and my mouth. What can you possibly say about me? That I lock myself in my room and will not open the door? That I don't sleep? I'm smarter than you! See if you can catch the hare with your hands.

PONCIA: Don't defy me, Adela, don't defy me! Because I can shout, light lamps, and make bells ring.

ADELA: Bring four thousand yellow flares and set them about the walls of the yard. No one can stop what has to happen.

PONCIA: You like him that much?

ADELA: That much! Looking in his eyes I seem to drink his blood in slowly.

PONCIA: I won't listen to you.

ADELA: Well, you'll have to. I've been afraid of you. But now I'm stronger than you!

(*Angustias enters.*)

ANGUSTIAS: Always arguing!

PONCIA: Certainly. She insists that in all this heat I have to go bring her I don't know what from the store.

ANGUSTIAS: Did you buy me the bottle of perfume?

PONCIA: The most expensive one. And the face powder. I put them on the table in your room.

(*Angustias goes out.*)

ADELA: And be quiet!

PONCIA: We'll see!

(*Martirio and Amelia enter.*)

MARTIRIO (*to Adela*): Did you see the laces?

AMELIA: Angustias', for her wedding sheets, are beautiful.

ADELA (*to Martirio, who is carrying some lace*): And these?

MARTIRIO: They're for me. For a nightgown.

ADELA (*with sarcasm*): One needs a sense of humor around here!

MARTIRIO (*meaningfully*): But only for me to look at. I don't have to exhibit myself before anybody.

PONCIA: No one ever sees us in our nightgowns.

MARTIRIO (*meaningfully, looking at Adela*): Sometimes they don't! But I love nice underwear. If I were rich, I'd have it made of Holland Cloth. It's one of the few tastes I've left.

PONCIA: These laces are beautiful for babies caps and christening gowns. I could never afford them for my own. Now let's see if Angustias will use them for hers. Once she starts having children, they'll keep her running night and day.

MAGDALENA: I don't intend to sew a stitch on them.

AMELIA: And much less bring up some stranger's children. Look how our neighbors across the road are—making sacrifices for four brats.

PONCIA: They're better off than you. There at least they laugh and you can hear them fight.

MARTIRIO: Well, you go work for them, then.

PONCIA: No, fate has sent me to this nunnery!

(*Tiny bells are heard distantly as though through several thicknesses of wall.*)

MAGDALENA: It's the men going back to work.

PONCIA: It was three o'clock a minute ago.

MARTIRIO: With this sun!

ADELA (*sitting down*): Ay! If only we could go out in the fields too!

MAGDALENA (*sitting down*): Each class does what it has to!

MARTIRIO (*sitting down*): That's it!

AMELIA (*sitting down*): Ay!

PONCIA: There's no happiness like that in the fields right at this time of year. Yesterday morning the reapers arrived. Forty or fifty handsome young men.

MAGDALENA: Where are they from this year?

PONCIA: From far, far away. They came from the mountains! Happy! Like weathered trees! Shouting and throwing stones! Last night a woman who dresses in sequins and dances, with an accordion, arrived, and fifteen of them made a deal with her to take her to the olive grove. I saw them from far away. The one who talked with her was a boy with green eyes—tight knit as a sheaf of wheat.

AMELIA: Really?

ADELA: Are you sure?

PONCIA: Years ago another one of those women came here, and I myself gave my eldest son some money so he could go. Men need things like that.

ADELA: Everything's forgiven *them*.

AMELIA: To be born a woman's the worst possible punishment.

MAGDALENA: Even our eyes aren't our own.

(*A distant song is heard, coming nearer.*)

PONCIA: There they are. They have a beautiful song.

AMELIA: They're going out to reap now.

CHORUS:
*The reapers have set out
Looking for ripe wheat;
They'll carry off the hearts
Of any girls they meet.*

(*Tambourines and carrañacas are heard. Pause. They all listen in the silence cut by the sun.*)

AMELIA: And they don't mind the sun!

MARTIRIO: They reap through flames.

ADELA: How I'd like to be a reaper so I could come and go as I pleased. Then we could forget what's eating us all.

MARTIRIO: What do you have to forget?

ADELA: Each one of us has something.

MARTIRIO (*intensely*): Each one!

PONCIA: Quiet! Quiet!

CHORUS (*very distantly*):
> Throw wide your doors and windows,
> You girls who live in the town
> The reaper asks you for roses
> With which to deck his crown.

PONCIA: What a song!

MARTIRIO (*with nostalgia*):
> Throw wide your doors and windows,
> You girls who live in the town.

ADELA (*passionately*):
> The reaper asks you for roses
> With which to deck his crown.

(*The song grows more distant.*)

PONCIA: Now they're turning the corner.

ADELA: Let's watch them from the window of my room.

PONCIA: Be careful not to open the shutters too much because they're likely to give them a push to see who's looking.

(*The three leave. Martirio is left sitting on the low chair with her head between her hands.*)

AMELIA (*drawing near her*): What's wrong with you?

MARTIRIO: The heat makes me feel ill.

AMELIA: And it's no more than that?

MARTIRIO: I was wishing it were November, the rainy days, the frost—anything except this unending summertime.

AMELIA: It'll pass and come again.

MARTIRIO: Naturally.

(*Pause.*)

What time did you go to sleep last night?

AMELIA: I don't know. I sleep like a log. Why?

MARTIRIO: Nothing. Only I thought I heard someone in the yard.

AMELIA: Yes?

MARTIRIO: Very late.

AMELIA: And weren't you afraid?

MARTIRIO: No. I've heard it other nights.

AMELIA: We'd better watch out! Couldn't it have been the shepherds?

MARTIRIO: The shepherds come at six.

AMELIA: Maybe a young, unbroken mule?

MARTIRIO (*to herself, with double meaning*): That's it! That's it! An unbroken little mule.

AMELIA: We'll have to set a watch.

MARTIRIO: No. No. Don't say anything. It may be I've just imagined it.

AMELIA: Maybe.

(*Pause. Amelia starts to go.*)

MARTIRIO: Amelia!

AMELIA (*at the door*): What?

(*Pause.*)

MARTIRIO: Nothing.

(*Pause.*)

AMELIA: Why did you call me?

(*Pause.*)

MARTIRIO: It just came out. I didn't mean to.

(*Pause.*)

AMELIA: Lie down for a little.

ANGUSTIAS (*she bursts in furiously, in a manner that makes a great contrast with previous silence*): Where's that picture of Pepe I had under my pillow? Which one of you has it?

MARTIRIO: No one.

AMELIA: You'd think he was a silver St. Bartholomew.°

ANGUSTIAS: Where's the picture?

(*Poncia, Magdalena and Adela enter.*)

ADELA: What picture?

ANGUSTIAS: One of you has hidden it from me.

MAGDALENA: Do you have the effrontery to say that?

ANGUSTIAS: I had it in my room, and now it isn't there.

MARTIRIO: But couldn't it have jumped out into the yard at midnight? Pepe likes to walk around in the moonlight.

ANGUSTIAS: Don't joke with me! When he comes I'll tell him.

PONCIA: Don't do that! Because it'll turn up.

(*Looking at Adela.*)

ANGUSTIAS: I'd like to know which one of you has it.

ADELA (*looking at Martirio*): Somebody has it! But not me!

MARTIRIO (*with meaning*): Of course not you!

BERNARDA (*entering with her cane*): What scandal is this in my house in the heat's heavy silence? The neighbors must have their ears glued to the walls.

ANGUSTIAS: They've stolen my sweetheart's picture!

BERNARDA (*fiercely*): Who? Who?

ANGUSTIAS: They have!

BERNARDA: Which one of you?

(*Silence.*)

Answer me!

(*Silence.*) (*To La Poncia.*)

Search their rooms! Look in their beds. This comes of not tying you up with shorter leashes. But I'll teach you now! (*to Angustias*) Are you sure?

ANGUSTIAS: Yes.

---

silver St. Bartholomew: A medallion used for good fortune.

BERNARDA: Did you look everywhere?

ANGUSTIAS: Yes, Mother.

(*They all stand in an embarrassed silence.*)

BERNARDA: At the end of my life—to make me drink the bitterest poison a mother knows. (*to Poncia*) Did you find it?

PONCIA: Here it is.

BERNARDA: Where did you find it?

PONCIA: It was . . .

BERNARDA: Say it! Don't be afraid.

PONCIA (*wonderingly*): Between the sheets in Martirio's bed.

BERNARDA (*to Martirio*): Is that true?

MARTIRIO: It's true.

BERNARDA (*advancing on her, beating her with her cane*): You'll come to a bad end yet, you hypocrite! Trouble maker!

MARTIRIO (*fiercely*): Don't hit me, Mother!

BERNARDA: All I want to!

MARTIRIO: If I let you! You hear me? Get back!

PONCIA: Don't be disrespectful to your mother!

ANGUSTIAS (*holding Bernarda*): Let her go, please!

BERNARDA: Not even tears in your eyes.

MARTIRIO: I'm not going to cry just to please you.

BERNARDA: Why did you take the picture?

MARTIRIO: Can't I play a joke on my sister? What else would I want it for?

ADELA (*leaping forward, full of jealousy*): It wasn't a joke! You never liked to play jokes. It was something else bursting in her breast—trying to come out. Admit it openly now.

MARTIRIO: Hush, and don't make me speak; for if I should speak the walls would close together one against the other with shame.

ADELA: An evil tongue never stops inventing lies.

BERNARDA: Adela!

MAGDALENA: You're crazy.

AMELIA: And you stone us all with your evil suspicions.

MARTIRIO: But some others do things more wicked!

ADELA: Until all at once they stand forth stark naked and the river carries them along.

BERNARDA: Spiteful!

ANGUSTIAS: It's not my fault Pepe el Romano chose me!

ADELA: For your money.

ANGUSTIAS: Mother!

BERNARDA: Silence!

MARTIRIO: For your fields and your orchards.

MAGDALENA: That's only fair.

BERNARDA: Silence, I say! I saw the storm coming but I didn't think it'd burst so soon. Oh, what an avalanche of hate you've thrown on my heart! But I'm not old yet—I have five chains for you, and this house my father built, so not even the weeds will know of my desolation. Out of here!

(*They go out. Bernarda sits down desolately. La Poncia is standing close to the wall. Bernarda recovers herself, and beats on the floor.*)

I'll have to let them feel the weight of my hand! Bernarda, remember your duty!

PONCIA: May I speak?

BERNARDA: Speak. I'm sorry you heard. A stranger is always out of place in a family.

PONCIA: What I've seen, I've seen.

BERNARDA: Angustias must get married right away.

PONCIA: Certainly. We'll have to get her away from here.

BERNARDA: Not her, him!

PONCIA: Of course. He's the one to get away from here. You've thought it all out.

BERNARDA: I'm not thinking. These are things that shouldn't and can't be thought out. I give orders.

PONCIA: And you think he'll be satisfied to go away?

BERNARDA (*rising*): What are you imagining now?

PONCIA: He will, of course, marry Angustias.

BERNARDA: Speak up! I know you well enough to see that your knife's out for me.

PONCIA: I never knew a warning could be called murder.

BERNARDA: Have you some "warning" for me?

PONCIA: I'm not making any accusations, Bernarda. I'm only telling you to open your eyes and you'll see.

BERNARDA: See what?

PONCIA: You've always been smart, Bernarda. You've seen other people's sins a hundred miles away. Many times I've thought you could read minds. But, your children are your children, and now you're blind.

BERNARDA: Are you talking about Martirio?

PONCIA: Well, yes—about Martirio . . .

(*With curiosity.*)

I wonder why she hid the picture?

BERNARDA (*shielding her daughter*): After all, she says it was a joke. What else could it be?

PONCIA (*scornfully*): Do you believe that?

BERNARDA (*sternly*): I don't merely believe it. It's so!

PONCIA: Enough of this. We're talking about your family. But if we were talking about your neighbor across the way, what would it be?

BERNARDA: Now you're beginning to pull the point of the knife out.

PONCIA (*always cruelly*): No, Bernarda. Something very grave is happening here. I don't want to put the blame on your shoulders, but you've never given your daughters any freedom. Martirio is lovesick. I don't care what you say. Why didn't you let her marry Enrique Humanas? Why, on the very day he was coming to her window did you send him a message not to come?

BERNARDA (*loudly*): I'd do it a thousand times over! My blood won't mingle with the Humanas' while I live! His father was a shepherd.

PONCIA: And you see now what's happening to you with these airs!

BERNARDA: I have them because I can afford to. And you don't have them because you know where you came from!

PONCIA (*with hate*): Don't remind me! I'm old now. I've always been grateful for your protection.

BERNARDA (*emboldened*): You don't seem so!

PONCIA (*with hate, behind softness*): Martirio will forget this.

BERNARDA: And if she doesn't—the worse for her. I don't believe this is that "very grave thing" that's happening here. Nothing's happening here. It's just that you wish it would! And if it should happen one day, you can be sure it won't go beyond these walls.

PONCIA: I'm not so sure of that! There are people in town who can also read hidden thoughts, from afar.

BERNARDA: How you'd like to see me and my daughters on our way to a whorehouse!

PONCIA: No one knows her own destiny!

BERNARDA: I know my destiny! And my daughters! The whorehouse was for a certain woman, already dead....

PONCIA (*fiercely*): Bernarda, respect the memory of my mother!

BERNARDA: Then don't plague me with your evil thoughts!

(*Pause.*)

PONCIA: I'd better stay out of everything.

BERNARDA: That's what you ought to do. Work and keep your mouth shut. The duty of all who work for a living.

PONCIA: But we can't do that. Don't you think it'd be better for Pepe to marry Martirio or . . . yes! . . . Adela?

BERNARDA: No, I *don't* think so.

PONCIA (*with meaning*): Adela! She's Romano's real sweetheart!

BERNARDA: Things are never the way we want them!

PONCIA: But it's hard work to turn them from their destined course. For Pepe to be with Angustias seems wrong to me—and to other people—and even to the wind. Who knows if they'll get what they want?

BERNARDA: There you go again! Sneaking up on me— giving me bad dreams. But I won't listen to you, because if all you say should come to pass—I'd scratch your face.

PONCIA: Frighten someone else with that.

BERNARDA: Fortunately, my daughters respect me and have never gone against my will!

PONCIA: That's right! But, as soon as they break loose they'll fly to the rooftops!

BERNARDA: And I'll bring them down with stones!

PONCIA: Oh, yes! You were always the bravest one!

BERNARDA: I've always enjoyed a good fight!

PONCIA: But aren't people strange. You should see Angustias' enthusiasm for her lover, at her age! And he seems very smitten too. Yesterday my oldest son told me that when he passed by with the oxen at four-thirty in the morning they were still talking.

BERNARDA: At four-thirty?

ANGUSTIAS (*entering*): That's a lie!

PONCIA: That's what he told me.

BERNARDA (*to Angustias*): Speak up!

ANGUSTIAS: For more than a week Pepe has been leaving at one. May God strike me dead if I'm lying.

MARTIRIO (*entering*): I heard him leave at four too.

BERNARDA: But did you see him with your eyes?

MARTIRIO: I didn't want to look out. Don't you talk now through the side window?

ANGUSTIAS: We talk through my bedroom window.

(*Adela appears at the door.*)

MARTIRIO: Then . . .

BERNARDA: What's going on here?

PONCIA: If you're not careful, you'll find out! At least Pepe was at *one* of your windows—and at four in the morning too!

BERNARDA: Are you sure of that?

PONCIA: You can't be sure of anything in this life!

ADELA: Mother, don't listen to someone who wants us to lose everything we have.

BERNARDA: I know how to take care of myself! If the townspeople want to come bearing false witness against me, they'll run into a stone wall! Don't any of you talk about this! Sometimes other people try to stir up a wave of filth to drown us.

MARTIRIO: I don't like to lie.

PONCIA: So there must be something.

BERNARDA: There won't be anything. I was born to have my eyes always open. Now I'll watch without closing them 'til I die.

ANGUSTIAS: I have the right to know.

BERNARDA: You don't have any right except to obey. No one's going to fetch and carry for me. (*to La Poncia*) And don't meddle in our affairs. No one will take a step without my knowing it.

SERVANT (*entering*): There's a big crowd at the top of the street, and all the neighbors are at their doors!

BERNARDA (*to Poncia*): Run see what's happening!

(*The girls are about to run out.*)

Where are you going? I always knew you for window-watching women and breakers of your mourning. All of you, to the patio!

(*They go out. Bernarda leaves. Distant shouts are heard.*) (*Martirio and Adela enter and listen, not daring to step farther than the front door.*)

MARTIRIO: You can be thankful I didn't happen to open my mouth.

ADELA: I would have spoken too.

MARTIRIO: And what were you going to say? Wanting isn't doing!

ADELA: I do what I can and what happens to suit me. You've wanted to, but haven't been able.

MARTIRIO: You won't go on very long.
ADELA: I'll have everything!
MARTIRIO: I'll tear you out of his arms!
ADELA (*pleadingly*): Martirio, let me be!
MARTIRIO: None of us will have him!
ADELA: He wants me for his house!
MARTIRIO: I saw how he embraced you!
ADELA: I didn't want him to. It's as if I were dragged by a rope.
MARTIRIO: I'll see you dead first!

(*Magdalena and Angustias look in. The tumult is increasing. A servant enters with Bernarda. Poncia also enters from another door.*)

PONCIA: Bernarda!
BERNARDA: What's happening?
PONCIA: Librada's daughter, the unmarried one, had a child and no one knows whose it is!
ADELA: A child?
PONCIA: And to hide her shame she killed it and hid it under the rocks, but the dogs, with more heart than most Christians, dug it out and, as though directed by the hand of God, left it at her door. Now they want to kill her. They're dragging her through the streets—and down the paths and across the olive groves the men are coming, shouting so the fields shake.
BERNARDA: Yes, let them all come with olive whips and hoe handles—let them all come and kill her!
ADELA: No, not to kill her!
MARTIRIO: Yes—and let us go out too!
BERNARDA: And let whoever loses her decency pay for it!

(*Outside a woman's shriek and a great clamor is heard.*)

ADELA: Let her escape! Don't you go out!
MARTIRIO (*looking at Adela*): Let her pay what she owes!
BERNARDA (*at the archway*): Finish her before the guards come! Hot coals in the place where she sinned!
ADELA (*holding her belly*): No! No!
BERNARDA: Kill her! Kill her!

(*Curtain.*)

ACT 3

(*Four white walls, lightly washed in blue, of the interior patio of Bernarda Alba's house. The doorways, illumined by the lights inside the rooms, give a tenuous glow to the stage. At the center there is a table with a shaded oil lamp about which Bernarda and her daughters are eating. La Poncia serves them. Prudencia sits apart. When the curtain rises, there is a great silence interrupted only by the noise of plates and silverware.*)

PRUDENCIA: I'm going. I've made you a long visit.

(*She rises.*)

BERNARDA: But wait, Prudencia. We never see one another.
PRUDENCIA: Have they sounded the last call to rosary?
PONCIA: Not yet.

(*Prudencia sits down again.*)

BERNARDA: And your husband, how's he getting on?
PRUDENCIA: The same.
BERNARDA: We never see him either.
PRUDENCIA: You know how he is. Since he quarrelled with his brothers over the inheritance, he hasn't used the front door. He takes a ladder and climbs over the back wall.
BERNARDA: He's a real man! And your daughter?
PRUDENCIA: He's never forgiven her.
BERNARDA: He's right.
PRUDENCIA: I don't know what he told you. I suffer because of it.
BERNARDA: A daughter who's disobedient stops being a daughter and becomes an enemy.
PRUDENCIA: I let water run. The only consolation I've left is to take refuge in the church, but, since I'm losing my sight, I'll have to stop coming so the children won't make fun of me.

(*A heavy blow is heard against the walls.*)

What's that?
BERNARDA: The stallion. He's locked in the stall and he kicks against the wall of the house.

(*Shouting.*)

Tether him and take him out in the yard!

(*In a lower voice.*)

He must be too hot.
PRUDENCIA: Are you going to put the new mares to him?
BERNARDA: At daybreak.
PRUDENCIA: You've known how to increase your stock.
BERNARDA: By dint of money and struggling.
PONCIA (*interrupting*): And she has the best herd in these parts. It's a shame that prices are low.
BERNARDA: Do you want a little cheese and honey?
PRUDENCIA: I have no appetite.

(*The blow is heard again.*)

PONCIA: My God!
PRUDENCIA: It quivered in my chest.
BERNARDA (*rising, furiously*): Do I have to say things twice? Let him out to roll on the straw.

(*Pause. Then, as though speaking to the stableman.*)

Well then, lock the mares in the corral, but let him run free or he may kick down the walls.

(*She returns to the table and sits again.*)

Ay, what a life!

PRUDENCIA: You have to fight like a man.

BERNARDA: That's it.

(*Adela gets up from the table.*)

Where are you going?

ADELA: For a drink of water.

BERNARDA (*raising her voice*): Bring a pitcher of cool water. (*to Adela*) You can sit down. (*Adela sits down.*)

PRUDENCIA: And Angustias, when will she get married?

BERNARDA: They're coming to ask for her within three days.

PRUDENCIA: You must be happy.

ANGUSTIAS: Naturally!

AMELIA (*to Magdalena*): You've spilled the salt!

MAGDALENA: You can't possibly have worse luck than you're having.

AMELIA: It always brings bad luck.

BERNARDA: That's enough!

PRUDENCIA (*to Angustias*): Has he given you the ring yet?

ANGUSTIAS: Look at it.

(*She holds it out.*)

PRUDENCIA: It's beautiful. Three pearls. In my day, pearls signified tears.

ANGUSTIAS: But things have changed now.

ADELA: I don't think so. Things go on meaning the same. Engagement rings should be diamonds.

PONCIA: The most appropriate.

BERNARDA: With pearls or without them, things are as one proposes.

MARTIRIO: Or as God disposes.

PRUDENCIA: I've been told your furniture is beautiful.

BERNARDA: It cost sixteen thousand *reales*.°

PONCIA (*interrupting*): The best is the wardrobe with the mirror.

PRUDENCIA: I never saw a piece like that.

BERNARDA: We had chests.

PRUDENCIA: The important thing is that everything be for the best.

ADELA: And that you never know.

BERNARDA: There's no reason why it shouldn't be.

(*Bells are heard very distantly.*)

PRUDENCIA: The last call. (*to Angustias*) I'll be coming back to have you show me your clothes.

ANGUSTIAS: Whenever you like.

PRUDENCIA: Good evening—God bless you!

BERNARDA: Good-bye, Prudencia.

ALL FIVE DAUGHTERS (*at the same time*): God go with you!

(*Pause. Prudencia goes out.*)

BERNARDA: Well, we've eaten.

reales: Spanish silver coin. Sixteen thousand would have been a great sum.

(*They rise.*)

ADELA: I'm going to walk as far as the gate to stretch my legs and get a bit of fresh air.

(*Magdalena sits down in a low chair and leans against the wall.*)

AMELIA: I'll go with you.

MARTIRIO: I too.

ADELA (*with contained hate*): I'm not going to get lost!

AMELIA: One needs company at night.

(*They go out. Bernarda sits down. Angustias is clearing the table.*)

BERNARDA: I've told you once already! I want you to talk to your sister Martirio. What happened about the picture was a joke and you must forget it.

ANGUSTIAS: You know she doesn't like me.

BERNARDA: Each one knows what she thinks inside. I don't pry into anyone's heart, but I want to put up a good front and have family harmony. You understand?

ANGUSTIAS: Yes.

BERNARDA: Then that's settled.

MAGDALENA (*she is almost asleep*): Besides, you'll be gone in no time.

(*She falls asleep.*)

ANGUSTIAS: Not soon enough for me.

BERNARDA: What time did you stop talking last night?

ANGUSTIAS: Twelve-thirty.

BERNARDA: What does Pepe talk about?

ANGUSTIAS: I find him absent-minded. He always talks to me as though he were thinking of something else. If I ask him what's the matter, he answers—"We men have our worries."

BERNARDA: You shouldn't ask him. And when you're married, even less. Speak if he speaks, and look at him when he looks at you. That way you'll get along.

ANGUSTIAS: But, Mother, I think he's hiding things from me.

BERNARDA: Don't try to find out. Don't ask him, and above all, never let him see you cry.

ANGUSTIAS: I should be happy, but I'm not.

BERNARDA: It's all the same.

ANGUSTIAS: Many nights I watch Pepe very closely through the window bars and he seems to fade away—as though he were hidden in a cloud of dust like those raised by the flocks.

BERNARDA: That's just because you're not strong.

ANGUSTIAS: I hope so!

BERNARDA: Is he coming tonight?

ANGUSTIAS: No, he went into town with his mother.

BERNARDA: Good, we'll get to bed early. Magdalena!

ANGUSTIAS: She's asleep.

(*Adela, Martirio and Amelia enter.*)

AMELIA: What a dark night!

ADELA: You can't see two steps in front of you.

MARTIRIO: A good night for robbers, for anyone who needs to hide.

ADELA: The stallion was in the middle of the corral. White. Twice as large. Filling all the darkness.

AMELIA: It's true. It was frightening. Like a ghost.

ADELA: The sky has stars as big as fists.

MARTIRIO: This one stared at them till she almost cracked her neck.

ADELA: Don't you like them up there?

MARTIRIO: What goes on over the roof doesn't mean a thing to me. I have my hands full with what happens under it.

ADELA: Well, that's the way it goes with you!

BERNARDA: And it goes the same for you as for her.

ANGUSTIAS: Good night.

ADELA: Are you going to bed now?

ANGUSTIAS: Yes, Pepe isn't coming tonight.

(*She goes out.*)

ADELA: Mother, why, when a stars falls or lightning flashes, does one say:

Holy Barbara, blessed on high
May your name be in the sky
With holy water written high?

BERNARDA: The old people know many things we've forgotten.

AMELIA: I close my eyes so I won't see them.

ADELA: Not I. I like to see what's quiet and been quiet for years on end, running with fire.

MARTIRIO: But all that has nothing to do with us.

BERNARDA: And it's better not to think about it.

ADELA: What a beautiful night! I'd like to stay up till very late and enjoy the breeze from the fields.

BERNARDA: But we have to go to bed. Magdalena!

AMELIA: She's just dropped off.

BERNARDA: Magdalena!

MAGDALENA (*annoyed*): Leave me alone!

BERNARDA: To bed!

MAGDALENA (*rising, in a bad humor*): You don't give anyone a moment's peace!

(*She goes off grumbling.*)

AMELIA: Good night!

(*She goes out.*)

BERNARDA: You two get along, too.

MARTIRIO: How is it Angustias' sweetheart isn't coming tonight?

BERNARDA: He went on a trip.

MARTIRIO (*looking at Adela*): Ah!

ADELA: I'll see you in the morning!

(*She goes out. Martirio drinks some water and goes out slowly, looking at the door to the yard. La Poncia enters.*)

PONCIA: Are you still here?

BERNARDA: Enjoying this quiet and not seeing anywhere the "very grave thing" that's happening here — according to you.

PONCIA: Bernarda, let's not go any further with this.

BERNARDA: In this house there's no question of a yes or a no. My watchfulness can take care of anything.

PONCIA: Nothing's happening outside. That's true, all right. Your daughters act and are as though stuck in a cupboard. But neither you nor anyone else can keep watch inside a person's heart.

BERNARDA: My daughters breathe calmly enough.

PONCIA: That's your business, since you're their mother. I have enough to do just with serving you.

BERNARDA: Yes, you've turned quiet now.

PONCIA: I keep my place — that's all.

BERNARDA: The trouble is you've nothing to talk about. If there were grass in this house, you'd make it your business to put the neighbors' sheep to pasture here.

PONCIA: I hide more than you think.

BERNARDA: Do your sons still see Pepe at four in the morning? Are they still repeating this house's evil litany?

PONCIA: They say nothing.

BERNARDA: Because they can't. Because there's nothing for them to sink their teeth in. And all because my eyes keep constant watch!

PONCIA: Bernarda, I don't want to talk about this because I'm afraid of what you'll do. But don't you feel so safe.

BERNARDA: Very safe!

PONCIA: Who knows, lightning might strike suddenly. Who knows but what all of a sudden, in a rush of blood, your heart might stop.

BERNARDA: Nothing will happen here. I'm on guard now against all your suspicions.

PONCIA: All the better for you.

BERNARDA: Certainly, all the better!

SERVANT (*entering*): I've just finished with the dishes. Is there anything else, Bernarda?

BERNARDA (*rising*): Nothing. I'm going to get some rest.

PONCIA: What time do you want me to call you?

BERNARDA: No time. Tonight I intend to sleep well.

(*She goes out.*)

PONCIA: When you're powerless against the sea, it's easier to turn your back on it and not look at it.

SERVANT: She's so proud! She herself pulls the blindfold over her eyes.

PONCIA: I can do nothing. I tried to head things off, but now they frighten me too much. You feel this silence? — in each room there's a thunderstorm and the day it breaks, it'll sweep all of us along with it. But I've said what I had to say.

SERVANT: Bernarda thinks nothing can stand against her, yet she doesn't know the strength a man has among women alone.

PONCIA: It's not all the fault of Pepe el Romano. It's true last year he was running after Adela; and she was crazy about him — but she ought to keep her place and not lead him on. A man's a man.

SERVANT: And some there are who believe he didn't have to talk many times with Adela.

PONCIA: That's true.

(*In a low voice.*)

And some other things.

SERVANT: I don't know what's going to happen here.

PONCIA: How I'd like to sail across the sea and leave this house, this battleground, behind!

SERVANT: Bernarda's hurrying the wedding and it's possible nothing will happen.

PONCIA: Things have gone much too far already. Adela is set no matter what comes, and the rest of them watch without rest.

SERVANT: Martirio too . . . ?

PONCIA: That one's the worst. She's a pool of poison. She sees El Romano is not for her, and she'd sink the world if it were in her hand to do so.

SERVANT: How bad they all are!

PONCIA: They're women without men, that's all. And in such matters even blood is forgotten. Sh-h-h-h!

(*She listens.*)

SERVANT: What's the matter?

PONCIA (*she rises*): The dogs are barking.

SERVANT: Someone must have passed by the back door.

(*Adela enters wearing a white petticoat and corselet.*)

PONCIA: Aren't you in bed yet?

ADELA: I want a drink of water.

(*She drinks from a glass on the table.*)

PONCIA: I imagined you were asleep.

ADELA: I got thirsty and woke up. Aren't you two going to get some rest?

SERVANT: Soon now.

(*Adela goes out.*)

PONCIA: Let's go.

SERVANT: We've certainly earned some sleep. Bernarda doesn't let me rest the whole day.

PONCIA: Take the light.

SERVANT: The dogs are going mad.

PONCIA: They're not going to let us sleep.

(*They go out. The stage is left almost dark. María Josefa enters with a lamb in her arms.*)

MARÍA JOSEFA (*singing*):
Little lamb, child of mine,
Let's go to the shore of the sea,
The tiny ant will be at his doorway,
I'll nurse you and give you your bread.
Bernarda, old leopard-face,
And Magdalena, hyena-face,
Little lamb . . .
Rock, rock-a-bye,
Let's go to the palms at Bethlehem's gate.

(*She laughs.*)

Neither you nor I would want to sleep
The door will open by itself
And on the beach we'll go and hide
In a little coral cabin.
Bernarda, old leopard-face,
And Magdalena, hyena-face,
Little lamb . . .
Rock, rock-a-bye,
Let's go to the palms at Bethlehem's gate.

(*She goes off singing.*)
(*Adela enters. She looks about cautiously and disappears out the door leading to the corral. Martirio enters by another door and stands in anguished watchfulness near the center of the stage. She also is in petticoats. She covers herself with a small black scarf. María Josefa crosses before her.*)

MARTIRIO: Grandmother, where are you going?

MARÍA JOSEFA: You are going to open the door for me? Who are you?

MARTIRIO: How did you get out here?

MARÍA JOSEFA: I escaped. You, who are you?

MARTIRIO: Go back to bed.

MARÍA JOSEFA: You're Martirio. Now I see you. Martirio, face of a martyr. And when are you going to have a baby? I've had this one.

MARTIRIO: Where did you get that lamb?

MARÍA JOSEFA: I know it's a lamb. But can't a lamb be a baby? It's better to have a lamb than not to have anything. Old Bernarda, leopard-face, and Magdalena, hyena-face!

MARTIRIO: Don't shout.

MARÍA JOSEFA: It's true. Everything's very dark. Just because I have white hair you think I can't have babies, but I can — babies and babies and babies. This baby will have white hair, and I'd have *this* baby, and another, and this *one* other; and with all of us with snow white hair we'll be like the waves — one, then another, and another. Then we'll all sit down and all of us will have white heads, and we'll be seafoam. Why isn't there any seafoam here? Nothing but mourning shrouds here.

MARTIRIO: Hush, hush.

MARÍA JOSEFA: When my neighbor had a baby, I'd carry her some chocolate and later she'd bring me some, and so on — always and always and always. You'll have white hair, but your neighbors won't come. Now I have to go away, but I'm afraid the dogs will bite me. Won't you come with me as far as the fields? I don't like fields. I like houses, but open houses, and the neighbor women asleep in their beds with their little tiny tots, and the men outside sitting in their chairs. Pepe el Romano is a giant. All of you love him. But he's going to devour you because you're grains of wheat. No, not grains of wheat. Frogs with no tongues!

MARTIRIO (*angrily*): Come, off to bed with you.

(*She pushes her.*)

MARÍA JOSEFA: Yes, but then you'll open the door for me, won't you?

MARTIRIO: Of course.

MARÍA JOSEFA (*weeping*):
Little lamb, child of mine,
Let's go to the shore of the sea,
The tiny ant will be at his doorway,
I'll nurse you and give you your bread.

(*Martirio locks the door through which María Josefa came out and goes to the yard door. There she hesitates, but goes two steps farther.*)

MARTIRIO (*in a low voice*): Adela! (*Pause. She advances to the door. Then, calling.*) Adela!

(*Adela enters. Her hair is disarranged.*)

ADELA: And what are you looking for me for?

MARTIRIO: Keep away from him.

ADELA: Who are you to tell me that?

MARTIRIO: That's no place for a decent woman.

ADELA: How you wish *you'd* been there!

MARTIRIO (*shouting*): This is the moment for me to speak. This can't go on.

ADELA: This is just the beginning. I've had strength enough to push myself forward—the spirit and looks you lack. I've seen death under this roof, and gone out to look for what was mine, what belonged to me.

MARTIRIO: That soulless man came for another woman. You pushed yourself in front of him.

ADELA: He came for the money, but his eyes were always on me.

MARTIRIO: I won't allow you to snatch him away. He'll marry Angustias.

ADELA: You know better than I he doesn't love her.

MARTIRIO: I know.

ADELA: You know because you've seen—he loves me, me!

MARTIRIO (*desperately*): Yes.

ADELA (*close before her*): He loves me, *me!* He loves me, *me!*

MARTIRIO: Stick me with a knife if you like, but don't tell me that again.

ADELA: That's why you're trying to fix it so I won't go away with him. It makes no difference to you if he puts his arms around a woman he doesn't love. Nor does it to me. He could be a hundred years with Angustias, but for him to have his arms around me seems terrible to you—because you too love him! You love him!

MARTIRIO (*dramatically*): Yes! Let me say it without hiding my head. Yes! my breast's bitter, bursting like a pomegranate. I love him!

ADELA (*impulsively, hugging her*): Martirio, Martirio, I'm not to blame!

MARTIRIO: Don't put your arms around me! Don't try to smooth it over. My blood's no longer yours, and even though I try to think of you as a sister, I see you as just another woman.

(*She pushes her away.*)

ADELA: There's no way out here. Whoever has to drown—let her drown. Pepe is mine. He'll carry me to the rushes along the river bank. . . .

MARTIRIO: He won't!

ADELA: I can't stand this horrible house after the taste of his mouth. I'll be what he wants me to be. Everybody in the village against me, burning me with their fiery fingers; pursued by those who claim they're decent, and I'll wear, before them all, the crown of thorns that belongs to the mistress of a married man.

MARTIRIO: Hush!

ADELA: Yes, yes. (*In a low voice.*) Let's go to bed. Let's let him marry Angustias. I don't care any more, but I'll go off alone to a little house where he'll come to see me whenever he wants, whenever he feels like it.

MARTIRIO: That'll never happen! Not while I have a drop of blood left in my body.

ADELA: Not just weak you, but a wild horse I could force to his knees with just the strength of my little finger.

MARTIRIO: Don't raise that voice of yours to me. It irritates me. I have a heart full of a force so evil that, without my wanting to be, I'm drowned by it.

ADELA: You show us the way to love our sisters. God must have meant to leave me alone in the midst of darkness because I can see you as I've never seen you before.

(*A whistle is heard and Adela runs toward the door, but Martirio gets in front of her.*)

MARTIRIO: Where are you going?

ADELA: Get away from that door!

MARTIRIO: Get by me if you can!

ADELA: Get away!

(*They struggle.*)

MARTIRIO (*shouts*): Mother! Mother!

ADELA: Let me go!

(*Bernarda enters. She wears petticoats and a black shawl.*)

BERNARDA: Quiet! Quiet! How poor I am without even a man to help me!

MARTIRIO (*pointing to Adela*): She was with him. Look at those skirts covered with straw!

BERNARDA (*going furiously toward Adela*): That's the bed of a bad woman!

ADELA (*facing her*): There'll be an end to prison voices here! (*Adela snatches away her mother's cane and breaks it in two.*) This is what I do with the tyrant's cane. Not another step. No one but Pepe commands me!

(*Magdalena enters.*)

MAGDALENA: Adela!

(*La Poncia and Angustias enter.*)

ADELA: I'm his. (*to Angustias*) Know that—and go out in the yard and tell him. He'll be master in this house.

ANGUSTIAS: My God!
BERNARDA: The gun! Where's the gun?

(*She rushes out. La Poncia runs ahead of her. Amelia enters and looks on frightened, leaning her head against the wall. Behind her comes Martirio.*)

ADELA: No one can hold me back!

(*She tries to go out.*)

ANGUSTIAS (*holding her*): You're not getting out of here with your body's triumph! Thief! Disgrace of this house!
MAGDALENA: Let her go where we'll never see her again!

(*A shot is heard.*)

BERNARDA (*entering*): Just try looking for him now!
MARTIRIO (*entering*): That does away with Pepe el Romano.
ADELA: Pepe! My God! Pepe!

(*She runs out.*)

PONCIA: Did you kill him?
MARTIRIO: No. He raced away on his mare!
BERNARDA: It was my fault. A woman can't aim.
MAGDALENA: Then, why did you say . . . ?
MARTIRIO: For her! I'd like to pour a river of blood over her head!
PONCIA: Curse you!
MAGDALENA: Devil!
BERNARDA: Although it's better this way!

(*A thud is heard.*)

Adela! Adela!

PONCIA (*at her door*): Open this door!
BERNARDA: Open! Don't think the walls will hide your shame!
SERVANT (*entering*): All the neighbors are up!

BERNARDA (*in a low voice, but like a roar*): Open! Or I'll knock the door down!

(*Pause. Everything is silent.*)

Adela!

(*She walks away from the door.*)

A hammer!

(*La Poncia throws herself against the door. It opens and she goes in. As she enters, she screams and backs out.*)

What is it?

PONCIA (*she puts her hands to her throat*): May we never die like that!

(*The sisters fall back. The servant crosses herself. Bernarda screams and goes forward.*)

Don't go in!

BERNARDA: No, not I! Pepe, you're running now, alive in the darkness, under the trees, but another day you'll fall. Cut her down! My daughter died a virgin. Take her to another room and dress her as though she were a virgin. No one will say anything about this! She died a virgin. Tell them, so that at dawn, the bells will ring twice.
MARTIRIO: A thousand times happy she, who had him.
BERNARDA: And I want no weeping. Death must be looked at face to face. Silence!

(*To one daughter.*)

Be still, I said!

(*To another daughter.*)

Tears when you're alone! We'll drown ourselves in a sea of mourning. She, the youngest daughter of Bernarda Alba, died a virgin. Did you hear me? Silence, silence, I said. Silence!

Eugene O'Neill

Eugene O'Neill (1888–1953) is a major figure in American drama. His enormous output began in the tradition of realism established by Strindberg and Ibsen, and his early plays, such as *Anna Christie* (1921), introduced Americans to the techniques of the great European realists. Realism for Americans was a move away from the sentimental comedies and the melodramas that dominated the American stage from before the Civil War to World War I. Some of O'Neill's plays, such as *Strange Interlude* (1928) and *Dynamo* (1929), were expressionist in style, demonstrating his considerable range. O'Neill rejected the kind of theater in which his father had thrived. James O'Neill had long been a stage star, traveling across the country in his production of *The Count of Monte Cristo*, which had made him rich but had also made him a prisoner of a single role.

Eugene O'Neill won the Pulitzer Prize for drama three times in the 1920s and once posthumously in 1957 for *Long Day's Journey into Night*, which had been completed in 1941. He won the Nobel Prize for literature in 1936. Although not popular successes in his own day, his plays—including those published posthumously—are now mainstays of the American theater. Some of the finest American actors have taken a strong interest in his work, both producing his plays and acting in them on the stage and on television. From the 1950s to the 1990s, the late Colleen Dewhurst and Jason Robards, Jr., in particular, gave some magnificent performances and interpretations of O'Neill's work.

The young O'Neill was a romantic in the popular sense of the word. After a year at Princeton University, he began to travel on the sea. His jaunts took him to South America, and he once wound up virtually broke and without resources in Buenos Aires. When he returned to the United States, he studied for a year at Harvard with George Pierce Baker, the most famous drama teacher of his day. Eventually, O'Neill took up residence in Provincetown, Massachusetts, where a group of people dedicated to theater—including the playwright Susan Glaspell—began to put on plays in their living rooms. When their audiences spilled over, the group created the Provincetown Playhouse, the theater in which some of O'Neill's earliest pieces were first performed.

The subjects of many of O'Neill's plays were not especially appealing to general theater audiences. Those who hoped for light comedy and a good laugh or light melodrama and a good cry found the intensity of his dark vision of the world to be overwhelming. They came for mere entertainment, and he was providing them with frightening visions of the soul's interior. The glum and painful surroundings of *Anna Christie* (1921) and the brutality of the lower-class coal stoker in *The Hairy Ape* (1922) were foreign to the comfortable middle-class audiences who supported commercial theater in the United States. They found O'Neill's characters to be haunted by family agonies, affections never given, ambitions never realized, pains never assuaged. Despite his remarkable abilities and the power of his drama, audiences often did not know what to make of him. To a large extent, his acceptance came on waves of shock, as had the acceptance of the Scandinavian realists.

O'Neill's early work is marked by a variety of experiments with theatrical effects and moods. He tried to use the primary influences of Greek drama in such plays as *Desire under the Elms* (1924), which has been described by critics as Greek tragedy, and *Mourning Becomes Electra* (1931), based on the *Oresteia*, which took three days to perform. But many of his early plays now seem dated and strange. His most impressive plays are his later work, such as *Ah, Wilderness!* (1933), *The Iceman Cometh* (1939), *Long Day's Journey into Night* (1939–1941), *A Moon for the Misbegotten* (1943), and *A Touch of the Poet* (1935–1942), which was performed posthumously in 1957.

O'Neill's personal life had been darkened by the alcoholism of his father and brother and the drug addiction of his mother. O'Neill himself had to fight alcoholism and depression brought on by the instability of his life and family. The darkness of his dramas may or may not be related to his personal life experiences, but the dramas reflect his understanding of the human condition. His experiments with Greek concepts of fate are tempered and strengthened by his interpretation of Freud's theories about the unconscious, the ruling force of the sexual drive, and the effects of trauma on childhood. *Desire under the Elms* brings together all these elements with the influence of the land—the environment of Puritan New England—and illustrates perfectly his awareness of the limits of human free will and the power of the forces that work on us all.

Desire under the Elms

Desire under the Elms (1924) is Eugene O'Neill's first effort at writing in the style of Greek tragedy. He did not follow the Greek tradition of choosing a great figure of noble birth whose mystery the fates unravel. Rather, he was deliberately democratic, choosing a New England farmer and his family as the protagonists of his drama. Just as fate animates a Greek tragedy, the emotional forces of jealousy, resentment, lust, and incestuous love animate *Desire under the Elms*.

O'Neill set his play on typically rocky New England soil, which in many ways bears a striking resemblance to the rocky soil of Athens and the Greek coastline. The unyielding toughness of life on that land contrasts with the easy life to be made from gold mining in California. Ephraim Cabot, the seventy-five-year-old father, has been made hard and physically powerful by his work. He has just taken a third wife, the young and scheming Abbie. His youngest son, Eben, has decided to stay on the farm, whereas his two other sons plan to put New England behind them and go to California.

The sense of having been dispossessed of his farm by his new stepmother drives Eben to hate Abbie, who has married the elder Cabot merely to inherit his farm. At first the sparring between Abbie and Eben is based on calculating self-interest, but eventually their feelings overpower them. Lust turns to love, and the son they produce is passed off as old Cabot's, although the townspeople have no illusion about whose child it is.

The farm itself is a powerful presence in the play. Whenever old Cabot thinks he should give up and follow the promise of easy money in California, he feels God's presence urging him to stay. God operates for Ephraim as the oracle in *Oedipus Rex* does, giving him a message that is painful but must be

For discussion questions and assignments on *Desire under the Elms*, visit bedfordstmartins.com/jacobus.

obeyed. The rocks on the farm are unforgiving, and so is the fate that Abbie and Eben face. Theirs is an impossible love; everything they do to prove their love condemns them even more. The forces of fate center on the farm. When the play opens, Eben says of it, "God! Purty!" When the play ends, the sheriff praises the farm and says he surely would like to own it, striking a clear note of irony: the agony of the play is rooted in lust—lust for the farm that parallels the lust between Abbie and Eben.

The play is haunted by the ghost of Eben's mother, whom Ephraim married primarily for her farm. Her ghost is exorcised only after the cycle of retribution has begun. Old Cabot has committed a crime against her, and now he must become the victim.

The language of the dialogue is that of New England in the mid-nineteenth century. Living in New England, O'Neill understood the ways and the language of its people. He seems to have imagined the "downeast" flavor of Maine in the language, and he has been careful to build the proper pronunciation into the dialogue. This folksy way of speaking helps emphasize the peasantlike qualities in these New England farmers. O'Neill's careful use of language is reminiscent of Synge's masterful representation of the Irish-English speech in *Riders to the Sea*.

The language of O'Neill's characters has a rocky toughness at times. Characters are laconic—they often answer in a single word: "Ay-eh." Faithful to his vision of the simple speech of country folk, O'Neill avoids giving them elaborate poetic soliloquies. Instead, he shows how, despite their limited language, rural people feel profound emotions and act on them.

O'Neill carefully links Abbie with Queen Phaedra, who in Euripides' play *Hippolytus* and in Racine's seventeenth-century play *Phaedra* finds herself uncontrollably desiring her husband's son as a lover. Racine and his audience could easily imagine such intense emotions overwhelming a noblewoman, because they thought that members of the nobility felt and lived more intensely than ordinary people. But O'Neill is trying to make his audience see that even unlettered farm people can feel as deeply as tragic heroes of any age do. The Cabots are victims of passion. They share their fate with the great families of the Greek tragedies.

Desire under the Elms in Performance

Desire under the Elms was first performed in Greenwich Village in 1924 under the auspices of the Provincetown Players. A year later, it appeared on Broadway for thirty-six weeks, a long run for a tragedy. Its first reviewers were courteous but puzzled. They compared the play with earlier O'Neill works, remarking on its "tragic gloom and irony" and praising its language. At the Los Angeles production in 1926, the cast was arrested for "giving an obscene play." The sexual themes offended theatergoers in California, and even those who defended the play admitted that the text would be offensive to some members of the audience.

Because the English censor banned the play until 1938, its first European production was in Prague's National Theatre in 1925. Its Czech title translated as "The Farm under the Elms." The director used a highly stylized set influenced by the Moscow Art Theatre and later described as "a sort of two-storied wooden edifice . . . rather like a log cabin multiplied by four."

Other European productions followed in Moscow in 1932, in Stockholm in 1933, and finally in London in 1940. The 1952 New York revival was not successful. The 1963 revival at the Circle in the Square in New York starred George C. Scott and his wife, Colleen Dewhurst. José Quintero, a notable interpreter of O'Neill, directed. Critics complained about "awkward" echoes of Greek tragedy while admitting that the play had an uncanny power despite its flaws. It ran for 380 performances.

The play has often been revived: in Boston in 1967; at the Berkshire Theater Festival in 1974; at the Roundabout Theatre in New York, directed by Terry Schrieber, in 1984; and by numerous local theater groups. In 1978, Edward Thomas staged it at Connecticut College in New London as an opera. A creditable production, it emphasized the play's American folk qualities. Dan Wackerman directed an off-Broadway production in 1997 adding an African American character named Silent Woman. She did not speak but added the issue of race to this issue-laden play. In 2005, the American Repertory Theater staged the play under the direction of János Szász with an innovative, expressionistic set designed by Riccardo Hernandez. Brian Dennehy, who has become the most distinguished current interpreter of O'Neill, appeared as Ephraim Cabot in a production directed by Robert Falls that played at the Goodman Theatre in Chicago before moving to the St. James Theater in New York in 2009. The reviews were enthusiastic, and critic Charles Isherwood said, "Mr. Dennehy exudes the hungry malice of a jackal tearing away at a rodent."

EUGENE O'NEILL (1888–1953)

Desire under the Elms   1924

Characters

EPHRAIM CABOT
SIMEON ⎫
PETER ⎬ *his sons*
EBEN   ⎭
ABBIE PUTNAM
YOUNG GIRL, TWO FARMERS, *the* FIDDLER, *a* SHERIFF, *and other folk from the neighboring farms.*

Scene: *The action of the entire play takes place in, and immediately outside of, the Cabot farmhouse in New England, in the year 1850. The south end of the house faces front to a stone wall with a wooden gate at center opening on a country road. The house is in good condition but in need of paint. Its walls are a sickly* grayish, the green of the shutters faded. *Two enormous elms are on each side of the house. They bend their trailing branches down over the roof. They appear to protect and at the same time subdue. There is a sinister maternity in their aspect, a crushing, jealous absorption. They have developed from their intimate contact with the life of man in the house an appalling humanness. They brood oppressively over the house. They are like exhausted women resting their sagging breasts and hands and hair on its roof, and when it rains their tears trickle down monotonously and rot on the shingles.*

There is a path running from the gate around the right corner of the house to the front door. A narrow porch is on this side. The end wall facing us has two windows in its upper story, two larger ones on the floor below. The two upper are those of the father's bedroom and that of the brothers. On the left, ground floor, is the kitchen—on the right, the parlor, the shades of which are always drawn down.

PART I • Scene I

(*Exterior of the farmhouse. It is sunset of a day at the beginning of summer in the year 1850. There is no wind and everything is still. The sky above the roof is suffused with deep colors, the green of the elms glows, but the house is in shadow, seeming pale and washed out by contrast.*)

(*A door opens and Eben Cabot comes to the end of the porch and stands looking down the road to the right. He has a large bell in his hand and this he swings mechanically, awakening a deafening clangor. Then he puts his hands on his hips and stares up at the sky. He sighs with a puzzled awe and blurts out with halting appreciation.*)

EBEN: God! Purty! (*His eyes fall and he stares about him frowningly. He is twenty-five, tall and sinewy. His face is well formed, good-looking, but its expression is resentful and defensive. His defiant, dark eyes remind one of a wild animal's in captivity. Each day is a cage in which he finds himself trapped but inwardly unsubdued. There is a fierce repressed vitality about him. He has black hair, mustache, a thin curly trace of beard. He is dressed in rough farm clothes.*)

(*He spits on the ground with intense disgust, turns, and goes back into the house.*)

(*Simeon and Peter come in from their work in the fields. They are tall men, much older than their half-brother [Simeon is thirty-nine and Peter thirty-seven], built on a squarer, simpler model, fleshier in body, more bovine and homelier in face, shrewder and more practical. Their shoulders stoop a bit from years of farm work. They clump heavily along in their clumsy thick soled boots caked with earth. Their clothes, their faces, hands, bare arms, and throats are earth-stained. They smell of earth. They stand together for a moment in front of the house and, as if with the one impulse, stare dumbly up at the sky, leaning on their hoes. Their faces have a compressed, unresigned expression. As they look upward, this softens.*)

SIMEON (*grudgingly*): Purty.
PETER: Ay-eh.
SIMEON (*suddenly*): Eighteen year ago.
PETER: What?
SIMEON: Jenn. My woman. She died.
PETER: I'd fergot.
SIMEON: I rec'lect—now an' agin. Makes it lonesome. She'd hair long's a hoss' tail—an' yeller like gold!
PETER: Waal—she's gone. (*This with indifferent finality—then after a pause.*) They's gold in the West, Sim.

SIMEON (*still under the influence of sunset—vaguely*): In the sky?
PETER: Waal—in a manner o' speakin'—that's the promise. (*Growing excited.*) Gold in the sky—in the West—Golden Gate—Californi-a!—Goldest West!—fields o' gold!
SIMEON (*excited in his turn*): Fortunes layin' just atop o' the ground waitin' t' be picked! Solomon's mines, they says! (*For a moment they continue looking up at the sky—then their eyes drop.*)
PETER (*with sardonic bitterness*): Here—it's stones atop o' the ground—stones atop o' stones—makin' stone walls—year atop o' year—him 'n' yew 'n' me 'n' then Eben—makin' stone walls fur him to fence us in!
SIMEON: We've wuked. Give our strength. Give our years. Plowed 'em under in the ground—(*He stamps rebelliously.*)—rottin'—makin' soil for his crops! (*A pause.*) Waal—the farm pays good for hereabouts.
PETER: If we plowed in Californi-a, they'd be lumps o' gold in the furrow!
SIMEON: Californi-a's t'other side o' earth, a'most. We got t' calc'late—
PETER (*after a pause*): 'Twould be hard fur me, too, to give up what we've 'arned here by our sweat. (*A pause. Eben sticks his head out of the dining room window, listening.*)
SIMEON: Ay-eh. (*A pause.*) Mebbe—he'll die soon.
PETER (*doubtfully*): Mebbe.
SIMEON: Mebbe—fur all we knows—he's dead now.
PETER: Ye'd need proof.
SIMEON: He's been gone two months—with no word.
PETER: Left us in the fields an evenin' like this. Hitched up an' druv off into the West. That's plum onnateral. He hadn't never been off this farm 'ceptin' t' the village in thirty year or more, not since he married Eben's maw. (*A pause. Shrewdly.*) I calc'late we might git him declared crazy by the court.
SIMEON: He skinned 'em too slick. He got the best o' all on 'em. They'd never b'lieve him crazy. (*A pause.*) We got t' wait—till he's underground.
EBEN (*with a sardonic chuckle*): Honor thy father! (*They turn startled, and stare at him. He grins, then scowls.*) I pray he's died. (*They stare at him. He continues matter-of-factly.*) Supper's ready.
SIMEON AND PETER (*together*): Ay-eh.
EBEN (*gazing up at the sky*): Sun's downin' purty.
SIMEON AND PETER (*together*): Ay-eh. They's gold in the West.
EBEN: Ay-eh. (*Pointing.*) Yonder atop o' the hill pasture, ye mean?
SIMEON AND PETER (*together*): In Californi-a!
EBEN: Hunh? (*Stares at them indifferently for a second, then drawls.*) Waal— supper's gittin' cold. (*He turns back into kitchen.*)
SIMEON (*startled—smacks his lips*): I air hungry!
PETER (*sniffing*): I smells bacon!
SIMEON (*with hungry appreciation*): Bacon's good!
PETER (*in same tone*): Bacon's bacon! (*They turn, shouldering each other, their bodies bumping and rubbing together as they hurry clumsily to their food, like two*

Riccardo Hernandez's set model for the American Repertory Theater's 2004–2005 production of *Desire under the Elms*.

friendly oxen toward their evening meal. They disappear around the right corner of house and can be heard entering the door.)

Scene II

(The color fades from the sky. Twilight begins. The interior of the kitchen is now visible. A pine table is at center, a cook-stove in the right rear corner, four rough wooden chairs, a tallow candle on the table. In the middle of the rear wall is fastened a big advertising poster with a ship in full sail and the word "California" in big letters. Kitchen utensils hang from nails. Everything is neat and in order but the atmosphere is of a men's camp kitchen rather than that of a home.)

(Places for three are laid. Eben takes boiled potatoes and bacon from the stove and puts them on the table, also a loaf of bread and a crock of water. Simeon and Peter shoulder in, slump down in their chairs without a word. Eben joins them. The three eat in silence for a moment, the two elder as naturally unrestrained as beasts of the field, Eben picking at his food without appetite, glancing at them with a tolerant dislike.)

SIMEON (*suddenly turns to Eben*): Looky here! Ye'd oughtn't t' said that, Eben.

PETER: 'Twa'n't righteous.

EBEN: What?

SIMEON: Ye prayed he'd died.

EBEN: Waal—don't yew pray it? (*A pause.*)

PETER: He's our Paw.

EBEN (*violently*): Not mine!

SIMEON (*dryly*): Ye'd not let no one else say that about yer Maw! Ha! (*He gives one abrupt sardonic guffaw. Peter grins.*)

EBEN (*very pale*): I meant—I hain't his'n—I hain't like him—he hain't me!

PETER (*dryly*): Wait till ye've growed his age!

EBEN (*intensely*): I'm Maw—every drop o' blood! (*A pause. They stare at him with indifferent curiosity.*)

PETER (*reminiscently*): She was good t' Sim 'n' me. A good Stepmaw's scurse.

SIMEON: She was good t' everyone.

EBEN (*greatly moved, gets to his feet and makes an awkward bow to each of them—stammering*): I be thankful t' ye. I'm her—her heir. (*He sits down in confusion.*)

PETER (*after a pause—judicially*): She was good even t' him.

EBEN (*fiercely*): An' fur thanks he killed her!

SIMEON (*after a pause*): No one never kills nobody. It's allus somethin'. That's the murderer.

EBEN: Didn't he slave Maw t' death?

984

PETER: He's slaved himself t' death. He's slaved Sim 'n' me 'n' yew t' death—on'y none o' us hain't died—yit.

SIMEON: It's somethin'—drivin' him—t' drive us!

EBEN (*vengefully*): Waal—I hold him t' jedgment! (*Then scornfully.*) Somethin'! What's somethin'?

SIMEON: Dunno.

EBEN (*sardonically*): What's drivin' yew to Californi-a, mebbe? (*They look at him in surprise.*) Oh, I've heerd ye! (*Then, after a pause.*) But ye'll never go t' the gold fields!

PETER (*assertively*): Mebbe!

EBEN: Whar'll ye git the money?

PETER: We kin walk. It's an a'mighty ways—Californi-a—but if yew was t' put all the steps we've walked on this farm end t' end we'd be in the moon!

EBEN: The Injuns'll skulp ye on the plains.

SIMEON (*with grim humor*): We'll mebbe make 'em pay a hair fur a hair!

EBEN (*decisively*): But t'aint that. Ye won't never go because ye'll wait here fur yer share o' the farm, thinkin' allus he'll die soon.

SIMEON (*after a pause*): We've a right.

PETER: Two-thirds belongs t'us.

EBEN (*jumping to his feet*): Ye've no right! She wa'n't yewr Maw! It was her farm! Didn't he steal it from her? She's dead. It's my farm.

SIMEON (*sardonically*): Tell that t' Paw—when he comes! I'll bet ye a dollar he'll laugh—fur once in his life. Ha! (*He laughs himself in one single mirthless bark.*)

PETER (*amused in turn, echoes his brother*): Ha!

SIMEON (*after a pause*): What've ye got held agin us, Eben? Year arter year it's skulked in yer eye—somethin'.

PETER: Ay-eh.

EBEN: Ay-eh. They's somethin'. (*Suddenly exploding.*) Why didn't ye never stand between him 'n' my Maw when he was slavin' her to her grave—t' pay her back fur the kindness she done t' yew? (*There is a long pause. They stare at him in surprise.*)

SIMEON: Waal—the stock'd got t' be watered.

PETER: 'R they was woodin' t' do.

SIMEON: 'R plowin'.

PETER: 'R hayin'.

SIMEON: 'R spreadin' manure.

PETER: 'R weedin'.

SIMEON: 'R prunin'.

PETER: 'R milkin'.

EBEN (*breaking in harshly*): An' makin' walls—stone atop o' stone—makin' walls till yer heart's a stone ye heft up out o' the way o' growth onto a stone wall t' wall in yer heart!

SIMEON (*matter-of-factly*): We never had no time t' meddle.

PETER (*to Eben*): Yew was fifteen afore yer Maw died—an' big fur yer age. Why didn't ye never do nothin'?

EBEN (*harshly*): They was chores t' do, wasn't they? (*A pause—then slowly.*) It was on'y arter she died I come to think o' it. Me cookin'—doin' her work—that made me know her, suffer her sufferin'—she'd come back t' help—come back t' bile potatoes—come back t' fry bacon—come back t' bake biscuits—come back all cramped up t' shake the fire, an' carry ashes, her eyes weepin' an' bloody with smoke an' cinders same's they used t' be. She still comes back—stands by the stove thar in the evenin'—she can't find it nateral sleepin' an' restin' in peace. She can't git used t' bein' free—even in her grave.

SIMEON: She never complained none.

EBEN: She'd got too tired. She'd got too used t' bein' too tired. That was what he done. (*With vengeful passion.*) An' sooner'r later, I'll meddle. I'll say the thin's I didn't say then t' him! I'll yell 'em at the top o' my lungs. I'll see t' it my Maw gits some rest an' sleep in her grave! (*He sits down again, relapsing into a brooding silence. They look at him with a queer indifferent curiosity.*)

PETER (*after a pause*): Whar in tarnation d'ye s'pose he went, Sim?

SIMEON: Dunno. He druv off in the buggy, all spick an' span, with the mare all breshed an' shiny, druv off clackin' his tongue an' wavin' his whip. I remember it right well. I was finishin' plowin', it was spring an' May an' sunset, an' gold in the West, an' he druv off into it. I yells "Whar ye goin', Paw?" an' he hauls up by the stone wall a jiffy. His old snake's eyes was glitterin' in the sun like he'd been drinkin' a jugful an' he says with a mule's grin: "Don't ye run away till I come back!"

PETER: Wonder if he knowed we was wantin' fur Californi-a?

SIMEON: Mebbe. I didn't say nothin' and he says, lookin' kinder queer an' sick: "I been hearin' the hens cluckin' an' the roosters crowin' all the durn day. I been listenin' t' the cows lowin' an' everythin' else kickin' up till I can't stand it no more. It's spring an' I'm feelin' damned," he says. "Damned like an old bare hickory tree fit on'y fur burnin'," he says. An' then I calc'late I must've looked a mite hopeful, fur he adds real spry and vicious: "But don't git no fool idee I'm dead. I've sworn t' live a hundred an' I'll do it, if on'y t' spite yer sinful greed! An' now I'm ridin' out t' learn God's message t' me in the spring, like the prophets done. An' yew git back t' yer plowin'," he says. An' he druv off singin' a hymn. I thought he was drunk—'r I'd stopped him goin'.

EBEN (*scornfully*): No, ye wouldn't! Ye're scared o' him. He's stronger—inside—than both o' ye put together!

PETER (*sardonically*): An' yew—be yew Samson?°

EBEN: I'm gittin' stronger. I kin feel it growin' in me—growin' an' growin'—till it'll bust out ! (*He gets up and puts on his coat and a hat. They watch him, gradually breaking into grins. Eben avoids their eyes sheepishly.*) I'm goin' out fur a spell—up the road.

Samson: A biblical hero known for his great physical strength.

PETER: T' the village.

SIMEON: T' see Minnie?

EBEN (*defiantly*): Ay-eh!

PETER (*jeeringly*): The Scarlet Woman!

SIMEON: Lust—that's what's growin' in ye!

EBEN: Waal—she's purty!

PETER: She's been purty fur twenty year.

SIMEON: A new coat o' paint'll make a heifer out of forty.

EBEN: She hain't forty!

PETER: If she hain't, she's teeterin' on the edge.

EBEN (*desperately*): What d'yew know—

PETER: All they is . . . Sim knew her—an' then me arter—

SIMEON: An' Paw kin tell yew somethin' too! He was fust!

EBEN: D'ye mean t' say he . . . ?

SIMEON (*with a grin*): Ay-eh! We air his heirs in everythin'!

EBEN (*intensely*): That's more to it! That grows on it! It'll bust soon! (*Then violently.*) I'll go smash my fist in her face! (*He pulls open the door in rear violently.*)

SIMEON (*with a wink at Peter—drawlingly*): Mebbe—but the night's wa'm—purty—by the time ye git thar mebbe ye'll kiss her instead!

PETER: Sart'n he will! (*They both roar with coarse laughter. Eben rushes out and slams the door—then the outside front door—comes around the corner of the house and stands still by the gate, staring up at the sky.*)

SIMEON (*looking after him*): Like his Paw.

PETER: Dead spit an' image!

SIMEON: Dog'll eat dog!

PETER: Ay-eh. (*Pause. With yearning.*) Mebbe a year from now we'll be in Californi-a.

SIMEON: Ay-eh. (*A pause. Both yawn.*) Let's git t'bed. (*He blows out the candle. They go out door in rear. Eben stretches his arms up to the sky—rebelliously.*)

EBEN: Waal—thar's a star, an' somewhar's they's him, an' here's me, an' thar's Min up the road—in the same night. What if I does kiss her? She's like t'night, she's soft 'n' wa'm, her eyes kin wink like a star, her mouth's wa'm, her arms're wa'm, she smells like a wa'm plowed field, she's purty . . . Ay-eh! By God A'mighty she's purty, an' I don't give a damn how many sins she's sinned afore mine or who she's sinned 'em with, my sin's as purty as any one on 'em! (*He strides off down the road to the left.*)

Scene III

(*It is the pitch darkness just before dawn. Eben comes in from the left and goes around to the porch, feeling his way, chuckling bitterly and cursing half-aloud to himself.*)

EBEN: The cussed old miser! (*He can be heard going in the front door. There is a pause as he goes upstairs, then a loud knock on the bedroom door of the brothers.*) Wake up!

SIMEON (*startledly*): Who's thar?

EBEN (*Pushing open the door and coming in, a lighted candle in his hand. The bedroom of the brothers is revealed. Its ceiling is the sloping roof. They can stand upright only close to the center dividing wall of the upstairs. Simeon and Peter are in a double bed, front. Eben's cot is to the rear. Eben has a mixture of silly grin and vicious scowl on his face.*): I be!

PETER (*angrily*): What in hell's-fire . . . ?

EBEN: I got news fur ye! Ha! (*He gives one abrupt sardonic guffaw.*)

SIMEON (*angrily*): Couldn't ye hold it 'til we'd got our sleep?

EBEN: It's nigh sunup. (*Then explosively.*) He's gone an' married agen!

SIMEON AND PETER (*explosively*): Paw?

EBEN: Got himself hitched to a female 'bout thirty-five—an' purty, they says . . .

SIMEON (*aghast*): It's a durn lie!

PETER: Who says?

SIMEON: They been stringin' ye!

EBEN: Think I'm a dunce, do ye? The hull village says. The preacher from New Dover, he brung the news—told it t'our preacher—New Dover, that's whar the old loon got himself hitched—that's whar the woman lived—

PETER (*no longer doubting—stunned*): Waal . . . !

SIMEON (*the same*): Waal . . . !

EBEN (*sitting down on a bed—with vicious hatred*): Ain't he a devil out o' hell? It's jest t' spite us—the damned old mule!

PETER (*after a pause*): Everythin'll go t'her now.

SIMEON: Ay-eh. (*A pause—dully.*) Waal—if it's done—

PETER: It's done us. (*Pause—then persuasively.*) They's gold in the fields o' Californi-a, Sim. No good a-stayin' here now.

SIMEON: Jest what I was a-thinkin'. (*Then with decision.*) S'well fust's last! Let's light out and git this mornin'.

PETER: Suits me.

EBEN: Ye must like walkin'.

SIMEON (*sardonically*): If ye'd grow wings on us we'd fly thar!

EBEN: Ye'd like ridin' better—on a boat, wouldn't ye? (*Fumbles in his pocket and takes out a crumpled sheet of foolscap.*) Waal, if ye sign this ye kin ride on a boat. I've had it writ out an' ready in case ye'd ever go. It says fur three hundred dollars t' each ye agree yewr shares o' the farm is sold t' me. (*They look suspiciously at the paper. A pause.*)

SIMEON (*wonderingly*): But if he's hitched agen—

PETER: An' whar'd yew git that sum o' money, anyways?

EBEN (*cunningly*): I know whar it's hid. I been waitin'—Maw told me. She knew whar it lay fur years, but she was waitin' . . . It's her'n—the money he hoarded from her farm an' hid from Maw. It's my money by rights now.

PETER: Whar's it hid?

EBEN (*cunningly*): Whar yew won't never find it without me. Maw spied on him—'r she'd never knowed. (*A pause. They look at him suspiciously, and he at them.*) Waal, is it fa'r trade?

SIMEON: Dunno.

PETER: Dunno.

SIMEON (*looking at window*): Sky's grayin'.

PETER: Ye better start the fire, Eben.

SIMEON: An' fix some vittles.

EBEN: Ay-eh. (*Then with a forced jocular heartiness.*) I'll git ye a good one. If ye're startin' t' hoof it t' Californi-a ye'll need somethin' that'll stick t' yer ribs. (*He turns to the door, adding meaningly.*) But ye kin ride on a boat if ye'll swap. (*He stops at the door and pauses. They stare at him.*)

SIMEON (*suspiciously*): Whar was ye all night?

EBEN (*defiantly*): Up t' Min's. (*Then slowly.*) Walkin' thar, fust I felt 's if I'd kiss her; then I got a-thinkin' o' what ye'd said o' him an' her an' I says, I'll bust her nose fur that! Then I got t' the village an' heerd the news an' I got madder'n hell an' run all the way t' Min's not knowin' what I'd do—(*He pauses—then sheepishly but more defiantly.*) Waal—when I seen her, I didn't hit her—nor I didn't kiss her nuther—I begun t' beller like a calf an' cuss at the same time, I was so durn mad—an' she got scared—an' I jest grabbed holt an' tuk her! (*Proudly.*) Yes, sirree! I tuk her. She may've been his'n—an' your'n, too—but she's mine now!

SIMEON (*dryly*): In love, air yew?

EBEN (*with lofty scorn*): Love! I don't take no stock in sech slop!

PETER (*winking at Simeon*): Mebbe Eben's aimin' t' marry, too.

SIMEON: Min'd make a true faithful he'pmeet! (*They snicker.*)

EBEN: What do I care fur her—'ceptin' she's round an' wa'm? The p'int is she was his'n—an' now she b'longs t' me! (*He goes to the door—then turns—rebelliously.*) An' Min hain't sech a bad un. They's worse'n Min in the world, I'll bet ye! Wait'll we see this cow the Old Man's hitched t'! She'll beat Min, I got a notion! (*He starts to go out.*)

SIMEON (*suddenly*): Mebbe ye'll try t' make her your'n, too?

PETER: Ha! (*He gives a sardonic laugh of relish at this idea.*)

EBEN (*spitting with disgust*): Her—here—sleepin' with him—stealin' my Maw's farm! I'd as soon pet a skunk 'r kiss a snake! (*He goes out. The two stare after him suspiciously. A pause. They listen to his steps receding.*)

PETER: He's startin' the fire.

SIMEON: I'd like t' ride t' Californi-a—but—

PETER: Min might o' put some scheme in his head.

SIMEON: Mebbe it's all a lie 'bout Paw marryin'. We'd best wait an' see the bride.

PETER: An' don't sign nothin' till we does!

SIMEON: Nor till we've tested it's good money! (*Then with a grin.*) But if Paw's hitched we'd be sellin' Eben somethin' we'd never git nohow!

PETER: We'll wait an' see. (*Then with sudden vindictive anger.*) An' till he comes, let's yew 'n' me not wuk a lick, let Eben tend to thin's if he's a mind t', let's us jest sleep an' eat an' drink likker, an' let the hull damned farm go t' blazes!

SIMEON (*excitedly*): By God, we've 'arned a rest! We'll play rich fur a change. I hain't a-going to stir outa bed till breakfast's ready.

PETER: An' on the table!

SIMEON (*after a pause—thoughtfully*): What d'ye calc'late she'll be like—our new Maw? Like Eben thinks?

PETER: More'n' likely.

SIMEON (*vindictively*): Waal—I hope she's a she-devil that'll make him wish he was dead an' livin' in the pit o' hell fur comfort!

PETER (*fervently*): Amen!

SIMEON (*imitating his father's voice*): "I'm ridin' out t' learn God's message t' me in the spring like the prophets done," he says. I'll bet right then an' thar he knew plumb well he was goin' whorin', the stinkin' old hypocrite!

Scene IV

(*Same as scene II—shows the interior of the kitchen with a lighted candle on table. It is gray dawn outside. Simeon and Peter are just finishing their breakfast. Eben sits before his plate of untouched food, brooding frowningly.*)

PETER (*glancing at him rather irritably*): Lookin' glum don't help none.

SIMEON (*sarcastically*): Sorrowin' over his lust o' the flesh!

PETER (*with a grin*): Was she yer fust?

EBEN (*angrily*): None o'yer business. (*A pause.*) I was thinkin' o' him. I got a notion he's gittin' near—I kin feel him comin' on like yew kin feel malaria chill afore it takes ye.

PETER: It's too early yet.

SIMEON: Dunno. He'd like t' catch us nappin'—jest t' have somethin' t' boss us 'round over.

PETER (*mechanically gets to his feet. Simeon does the same.*): Waal—let's git t'wuk. (*They both plod mechanically toward the door before they realize. Then they stop short.*)

SIMEON (*grinning*): Ye're a cussed fool, Pete—and I be wuss! Let him see we hain't wukin'! We don't give a durn!

PETER (*as they go back to the table*): Not a damned durn! It'll serve t' show him we're done with him. (*They sit down again. Eben stares from one to the other with surprise.*)

SIMEON (*grins at him*): We're aimin' t' start bein' lilies o' the field.

PETER: Nary a toil 'r spin 'r lick o' wuk do we put in!

SIMEON: Ye're sole owner—till he comes—that's what ye wanted. Waal, ye got t' be sole hand, too.

PETER: The cows air bellerin'. Ye better hustle at the milkin'.

EBEN (*with excited joy*): Ye mean ye'll sign the paper?

SIMEON (*dryly*): Mebbe.

PETER: Mebbe.

SIMEON: We're considerin'. (*Peremptorily.*) Ye better git t' wuk.

EBEN (*with queer excitement*): It's Maw's farm agen! It's my farm! Them's my cows! I'll milk my durn fingers off fur cows o' mine! (*He goes out door in rear, they stare after him indifferently.*)

SIMEON: Like his Paw.

PETER: Dead spit 'n' image!

SIMEON: Waal—let dog eat dog! (*Eben comes out of front door and around the corner of the house. The sky is beginning to grow flushed with sunrise. Eben stops by the gate and stares around him with glowing, possessive eyes. He takes in the whole farm with his embracing glance of desire.*)

EBEN: It's purty! It's damned purty! It's mine! (*He suddenly throws his head back boldly and glares with hard, defiant eyes at the sky.*) Mine, d'ye hear? Mine! (*He turns and walks quickly off left, rear, toward the barn. The two brothers light their pipes.*)

SIMEON (*putting his muddy boots up on the table, tilting back his chair, and puffing defiantly*): Waal—this air solid comfort—fur once.

PETER: Ay-eh. (*He follows suit. A pause. Unconsciously they both sigh.*)

SIMEON (*suddenly*): He never was much o' a hand at milkin', Eben wa'n't.

PETER (*with a snort*): His hands air like hoofs! (*A pause.*)

SIMEON: Reach down the jug thar! Let's take a swaller. I'm feelin' kind o' low.

PETER: Good idee! (*He does so—gets two glasses—they pour out drinks of whisky.*) Here's t' the gold in Californi-a!

SIMEON: An' luck t' find it! (*They drink—puff resolutely—sigh—take their feet down from the table.*)

PETER: Likker don't pear t' sot right.

SIMEON: We hain't used t' it this early. (*A pause. They become very restless.*)

PETER: Gittin' close in this kitchen.

SIMEON (*with immense relief*): Let's git a breath o' air. (*They arise briskly and go out rear—appear around house and stop by the gate. They stare up at the sky with a numbed appreciation.*)

PETER: Purty!

SIMEON: Ay-eh. Gold's t' the East now.

PETER: Sun's startin' with us fur the Golden West.

SIMEON (*staring around the farm, his compressed face tightened, unable to conceal his emotion*): Waal—it's our last mornin'—mebbe.

PETER (*the same*): Ay-eh.

SIMEON (*stamps his foot on the earth and addresses it desperately*): Waal—ye've thirty year o' me buried in ye—spread out over ye—blood an' bone an' sweat—rotted away—fertilizin' ye—richin' yer soul—prime manure, by God, that's what I been t' ye!

PETER: Ay-eh! An' me.

SIMEON: An' yew, Peter. (*He sighs—then spits.*) Waal—no use'n cryin' over spilt milk.

PETER: They's gold in the West—an' freedom, mebbe. We been slaves t' stone walls here.

SIMEON (*defiantly*): We hain't nobody's slaves from this out—nor nothin's slaves nuther. (*A pause—restlessly.*) Speaking o' milk, wonder how Eben's managin'?

PETER: I s'pose he's managin'.

SIMEON: Mebbe we'd ought t' help—this once.

PETER: Mebbe. The cows knows us.

SIMEON: An' likes us. They don't know him much.

PETER: An' the hosses, an' pigs, an' chickens. They don't know him much.

SIMEON: They knows us like brothers—an' likes us! (*Proudly.*) Hain't we raised 'em t' be fust-rate, number one prize stock?

PETER: We hain't—not no more.

SIMEON (*dully*): I was fergittin'. (*Then resignedly.*) Waal, let's go help Eben a spell an' git waked up.

PETER: Suits me. (*They are starting off down left, rear, for the barn when Eben appears from there hurrying toward them, his face excited.*)

EBEN (*breathlessly*): Waal—har they be! The old mule an' the bride! I seen 'em from the barn down below at the turnin'.

PETER: How could ye tell that far?

EBEN: Hain't I as far-sight as he's near-sight? Don't I know the mare 'n' buggy, an' two people settin' in it? Who else . . . ? An' I tell ye I kin feel 'em a'comin', too! (*He squirms as if he had the itch.*)

PETER (*beginning to be angry*): Waal—let him do his own unhitchin'!

SIMEON (*angry in his turn*): Let's hustle in an' git our bundles an' be a-goin' as he's a-comin'. I don't want never t' step inside the door agen arter he's back. (*They both start back around the corner of the house. Eben follows them.*)

EBEN (*anxiously*): Will ye sign it afore ye go?

PETER: Let's see the color o' the old skinflint's money an' we'll sign. (*They disappear left. The two brothers clump upstairs to get their bundles. Eben appears in the kitchen, runs to window, peers out, comes back and pulls up a strip of flooring in under stove, takes out a canvas bag and puts it on table, then sets the floorboard back in place. The two brothers appear a moment after. They carry old carpetbags.*)

EBEN (*puts his hand on bag guardingly*): Have ye signed?

SIMEON (*shows paper in his hand*): Ay-eh. (*Greedily.*) Be that the money?

EBEN (*opens bag and pours out pile of twenty-dollar gold pieces*): Twenty-dollar pieces—thirty of 'em. Count 'em. (*Peter does so, arranging them in stacks of five, biting one or two to test them.*)

PETER: Six hundred. (*He puts them in bag and puts it inside his shirt carefully.*)

SIMEON (*handing paper to Eben*): Har ye be.

EBEN (*after a glance, folds it carefully and hides it under his shirt—gratefully*): Thank yew.

PETER: Thank yew fur the ride.

SIMEON: We'll send ye a lump o' gold fur Christmas. (*A pause. Eben stares at them and they at him.*)

PETER (*awkwardly*): Waal—we're a-goin'.

SIMEON: Comin' out t' the yard?

EBEN: No. I'm waitin' in here a spell. (*Another silence. The brothers edge awkwardly to door in rear—then turn and stand.*)

SIMEON: Waal—good-by.

PETER: Good-by.

EBEN: Good-by. (*They go out. He sits down at the table, faces the stove and pulls out the paper. He looks from it to the stove. His face, lighted up by the shaft of sunlight from the window, has an expression of trance. His lips move. The two brothers come out to the gate.*)

PETER (*looking off toward barn*): Thar he be—unhitchin'.

SIMEON (*with a chuckle*): I'll bet ye he's riled!

PETER: An thar she be.

SIMEON: Let's wait 'n' see what our new Maw looks like.

PETER (*with a grin*): An' give him our partin' cuss!

SIMEON (*grinning*): I feel like raisin' fun. I feel light in my head an' feet.

PETER: Me, too. I feel like laffin' till I'd split up the middle.

SIMEON: Reckon it's the likker?

PETER: No. My feet feel itchin' t' walk an' walk—an' jump high over thin's—an'....

SIMEON: Dance? (*A pause.*)

PETER (*puzzled*): It's plumb onnateral.

SIMEON (*a light coming over his face*): I calc'late it's 'cause school's out. It's holiday. Fur once we're free!

PETER (*dazedly*): Free?

SIMEON: The halter's broke—the harness is busted—the fence bars is down—the stone walls air crumblin' an' tumblin'! We'll be kickin' up an' tearin' away down the road!

PETER (*drawing a deep breath—oratorically*): Anybody that wants this stinkin' old rock-pile of a farm kin hev it. T'ain't our'n, no sirree!

SIMEON (*takes the gate off its hinges and puts it under his arm*): We harby 'bolishes shet gates, an' open gates, an' all gates, by thunder!

PETER: We'll take it with us fur luck an' let 'er sail free down some river.

SIMEON (*as a sound of voices comes from left, rear*): Har they comes! (*The two brothers congeal into two stiff, grim-visaged statues. Ephraim Cabot and Abbie Putnam come in. Cabot is seventy-five, tall and gaunt, with great, wiry, concentrated power, but stoop-shouldered from toil. His face is as hard as if it were hewn out of a boulder, yet there is a weakness in it, a petty pride in its own narrow strength. His eyes are small, close together, and extremely near-sighted, blinking continually in the effort to focus on objects, their stare having a straining, ingrowing quality. He is dressed in his dismal black Sunday suit. Abbie is thirty-five, buxom, full of vitality. Her round face is pretty but marred by its rather gross sensuality. There is strength and obstinacy in her jaw, a hard determination in her eyes, and about her whole personality the same unsettled, untamed, desperate quality which is so apparent in Eben.*)

CABOT (*as they enter—a queer strangled emotion in his dry cracking voice*): Har we be t' hum, Abbie.

ABBIE (*with lust for the word*): Hum! (*Her eyes gloating on the house without seeming to see the two stiff figures at the gate.*) It's purty—purty! I can't b'lieve it's r'ally mine.

CABOT (*sharply*): Yewr'n? Mine! (*He stares at her penetratingly. She stares back. He adds relentingly.*) Our'n—mebbe! It was lonesome too long. I was growin' old in the spring. A hum's got t' hev a woman.

ABBIE (*her voice taking possession*): A woman's got t' hev a hum!

CABOT (*nodding uncertainly*): Ay-eh. (*Then irritably.*) Whar be they? Ain't thar nobody about—'r wukin'—'r nothin'?

ABBIE (*Sees the brothers. She returns their stare of cold appraising contempt with interest—slowly.*): Thar's two men loafin' at the gate an' starin' at me like a couple o' strayed hogs.

CABOT (*straining his eyes*): I kin see 'em—but I can't make out....

SIMEON: It's Simeon.

PETER: It's Peter.

CABOT (*exploding*): Why hain't ye wukin'?

SIMEON (*dryly*): We're waitin' t' welcome ye hum—yew an' the bride!

CABOT (*confusedly*): Huh? Waal—this be yer new Maw, boys. (*She stares at them and they at her.*)

SIMEON (*turns away and spits contemptuously*): I see her!

PETER (*spits also*): An I see her!

ABBIE (*with the conqueror's conscious superiority*): I'll go in an' look at *my* house. (*She goes slowly around to porch.*)

SIMEON (*with a snort*): Her house!

PETER (*calls after her*): Ye'll find Eben inside. Ye better not tell him it's *yewr* house.

ABBIE (*mouthing the name*): Eben. (*Then quietly.*) I'll tell Eben.

CABOT (*with a contemptuous sneer*): Ye needn't heed Eben. Eben's a dumb fool—like his Maw—soft an' simple!

SIMEON (*with his sardonic burst of laughter*): Ha! Eben's a chip o' yew—spit 'n' image—hard 'n' bitter's a hickory tree! Dog'll eat dog. He'll eat ye yet, old man!

CABOT (*commandingly*): Ye git t' wuk.

SIMEON (*as Abbie disappears in house—winks at Peter and says tauntingly*): So that thar's our new Maw, be it? Whar in hell did ye dig her up? (*He and Peter laugh.*)

PETER: Ha! Ye'd better turn her in the pen with the other sows. (*They laugh uproariously, slapping their thighs.*)

CABOT (*so amazed at their effrontery that he stutters in confusion*): Simeon! Peter! What's come over ye? Air ye drunk?

SIMEON: We're free, old man—free o' yew an' the hull damned farm! (*They grow more and more hilarious and excited.*)

PETER: An' we're startin' out fur the gold fields o' Californi-a!

SIMEON: Ye kin take this place an' burn it!

PETER: An' bury it—fur all we cares!

SIMEON: We're free, old man! (*He cuts a caper.*)

PETER: Free! (*He gives a kick in the air.*)

SIMEON (*in a frenzy*): Whoop!

PETER: Whoop! (*They do an absurd Indian war dance about the old man who is petrified between rage and the fear that they are insane.*)

SIMEON: We're free as Injuns! Lucky we don't skulp ye!

PETER: An' burn yer barn an' kill the stock!

SIMEON: An' rape yer new woman! Whoop! (*He and Peter stop their dance, holding their sides, rocking with wild laughter.*)

CABOT (*edging away*): Lust fur gold—fur the sinful, easy gold o' Californi-a! It's made ye mad!

SIMEON (*tauntingly*): Wouldn't ye like us to send ye back some sinful gold, ye old sinner?

PETER: They's gold besides what's in Californi-a! (*He retreats back beyond the vision of the old man and takes the bag of money and flaunts it in the air above his head, laughing.*)

SIMEON: And sinfuller, too!

PETER: We'll be voyagin' on the sea! Whoop! (*He leaps up and down.*)

SIMEON: Livin' free! Whoop! (*He leaps in turn.*)

CABOT (*suddenly roaring with rage*): My cuss on ye!

SIMEON: Take our'n in trade fur it! Whoop!

CABOT: I'll hev ye both chained up in the asylum!

PETER: Ye old skinflint! Good-by!

SIMEON: Ye old blood sucker! Good-by!

CABOT: Go afore I . . . !

PETER: Whoop! (*He picks a stone from the road. Simeon does the same.*)

SIMEON: Maw'll be in the parlor.

PETER: Ay-eh! One! Two!

CABOT (*frightened*): What air ye . . . ?

PETER: Three! (*They both throw, the stones hitting the parlor window with a crash of glass, tearing the shade.*)

SIMEON: Whoop!

PETER: Whoop!

CABOT (*in a fury now, rushing toward them*): If I kin lay hands on ye—I'll break yer bones fur ye! (*But they beat a capering retreat before him, Simeon with the*

gate still under his arm. Cabot comes back, panting with impotent rage. Their voices as they go off take up the song of the gold-seekers to the old tune of "Oh, Susannah!")

"I jumped aboard the Liza ship,
And traveled on the sea,
And every time I thought of home
I wished it wasn't me!
Oh! Californi-a,
That's the land fur me!
I'm off to Californi-a!
With my wash bowl on my knee."

(*In the meantime, the window of the upper bedroom on right is raised and Abbie sticks her head out. She looks down at Cabot—with a sigh of relief.*)

ABBIE: Waal—that's the last o' them two, hain't it? (*He doesn't answer. Then in possessive tones.*) This here's a nice bedroom, Ephraim. It's a r'al nice bed. Is it my room, Ephraim?

CABOT (*grimly—without looking up*): Our'n! (*She cannot control a grimace of aversion and pulls back her head slowly and shuts the window. A sudden horrible thought seems to enter Cabot's head.*) They been up to somethin'! Mebbe—mebbe they've pizened the stock—'r somethin'! (*He almost runs off down toward the barn. A moment later the kitchen door is slowly pushed open and Abbie enters. For a moment she stands looking at Eben. He does not notice her at first. Her eyes take him in penetratingly with a calculating appraisal of his strength as against hers. But under this her desire is dimly awakened by his youth and good looks. Suddenly he becomes conscious of her presence and looks up. Their eyes meet. He leaps to his feet, glowering at her speechlessly.*)

ABBIE (*in her most seductive tones which she uses all through this scene*): Be you—Eben? I'm Abbie—(*She laughs.*) I mean, I'm yer new Maw.

EBEN (*viciously*): No, damn ye!

ABBIE (*as if she hadn't heard—with a queer smile*): Yer Paw's spoke a lot o' yew. . . .

EBEN: Ha!

ABBIE: Ye mustn't mind him. He's an old man. (*A long pause. They stare at each other.*) I don't want t' pretend playin' Maw t' ye, Eben. (*Admiringly.*) Ye're too big an' too strong fur that. I want t' be frens with ye. Mebbe with me fur a fren ye'd find ye'd like livin' here better. I kin make it easy fur ye with him, mebbe. (*With a scornful sense of power.*) I calc'late I kin git him t' do most anythin' fur me.

EBEN (*with bitter scorn*): Ha! (*They stare again, Eben obscurely moved, physically attracted to her—in forced stilted tones.*) Yew kin go t' the devil!

ABBIE (*calmly*): If cussin' me does ye good, cuss all ye've a mind t'. I'm all prepared t' have ye agin me—at fust. I don't blame ye nuther. I'd feel the same at any stranger comin' t' take my Maw's place. (*He shudders. She is watching him carefully.*) Yew must've cared a lot fur yewr Maw, didn't ye? My Maw died afore I'd growed. I don't remember her none. (*A pause.*) But yew won't hate me long, Eben. I'm not the wust in the world—an' yew an' me've got a lot in common. I kin tell that by lookin' at ye. Waal—I've had a hard life, too—oceans o' trouble an' nuthin' but wuk fur reward. I was a orphan early an' had t' wuk fur others in other folks' hums. Then I married an' he turned out a drunken spreer an' so he had to wuk fur others an' me too agen in other folks' hums, an' the baby died, an' my husband got sick an' died too, an' I was glad sayin' now I'm free fur once, on'y I diskivered right away all I was free fur was t'wuk agen in other folks' hums, doin' other folks' wuk till I'd most give up hope o' ever doin' my own wuk in my own hum, an' then your Paw come ... (*Cabot appears returning from the barn. He comes to the gate and looks down the road the brothers have gone. A faint strain of their retreating voices is heard: "Oh, Californi-a! That's the place for me." He stands glowering, his fist clenched, his face grim with rage.*)

EBEN (*fighting against his growing attraction and sympathy—harshly*): An' bought yew—like a harlot! (*She is stung and flushes angrily. She has been sincerely moved by the recital of her troubles. He adds furiously.*) An' the price he's payin' ye—this farm—was my Maw's, damn ye!

ABBIE (*with a cool laugh of confidence*): Yewr'n? We'll see 'bout that! (*Then strongly.*) Waal—what if I did need a hum? What else'd I marry an old man like him fur?

EBEN (*maliciously*): I'll tell him ye said that!

ABBIE (*smiling*): I'll say ye're lyin' a-purpose—an' he'll drive ye off the place!

EBEN: Ye devil!

ABBIE (*defying him*): This be my farm—this be my hum—this be my kitchen—!

EBEN (*furiously, as if he were going to attack her*): Shut up, damn ye!

ABBIE (*walks up to him—a queer coarse expression of desire in her face and body—slowly*): An' upstairs—that be my bedroom—an' my bed! (*He stares into her eyes, terribly confused and torn. She adds softly.*) I hain't bad nor mean—'ceptin' fur an enemy—but I got t' fght fur what's due me out o' life, if I ever 'spect t' git it. (*Then putting her hand on his arm—seductively.*) Let's yew 'n' me be frens, Eben.

EBEN (*stupidly—as if hypnotized*): Ay-eh. (*Then furiously flinging off her arm.*) No, ye durned old witch! I hate ye! (*He rushes out the door.*)

ABBIE (*looks after him smiling satisfiedly—then half to herself, mouthing the word*): Eben's nice. (*She looks at the table, proudly.*) I'll wash up *my* dishes now. (*Eben appears outside, slamming the door behind him. He comes around corner, stops on seeing his father, and stands staring at him with hate.*)

CABOT (*raising his arms to heaven in the fury he can no longer control*): Lord God o' Hosts, smite the undutiful sons with Thy wust cuss!

EBEN (*breaking in violently*): Yew 'n' yewr God! Allus cussin' folks—allus naggin' 'em!

CABOT (*oblivious to him—summoningly*): God o' the old! God o' the lonesome!

EBEN (*mockingly*): Naggin' His sheep t' sin! T' hell with yewr God! (*Cabot turns. He and Eben glower at each other.*)

CABOT (*harshly*): So it's yew. I might've knowed it. (*Shaking his finger threateningly at him.*) Blasphemin' fool! (*Then quickly.*) Why hain't ye t' wuk?

EBEN: Why hain't yew? They've went. I can't wuk it all alone.

CABOT (*contemptuously*): Nor noways! I'm wuth ten o' ye yit, old's I be! Ye'll never be more'n half a man! (*Then, matter-of-factly.*) Waal—let's git t' the barn. (*They go. A last faint note of the "Californi-a" song is heard from the distance. Abbie is washing her dishes.*)

PART II • Scene I

(*The exterior of the farmhouse, as in part I—a hot Sunday afternoon two months later. Abbie, dressed in her best, is discovered sitting in a rocker at the end of the porch. She rocks listlessly, enervated by the heat, staring in front of her with bored, half-closed eyes.*)

(*Eben sticks his head out of his bedroom window. He looks around furtively and tries to see—or hear—if anyone is on the porch, but although he has been careful to make no noise, Abbie has sensed his movement. She stops rocking, her face grows animated and eager, she waits attentively. Eben seems to feel her presence, he scowls back his thoughts of her and spits with exaggerated disdain—then withdraws back into the room. Abbie waits, holding her breath as she listens with passionate eagerness for every sound within the house.*)

(*Eben comes out. Their eyes meet; his falter. He is confused, he turns away and slams the door resentfully. At this gesture, Abbie laughs tantalizingly, amused but at the same time piqued and irritated. He scowls, strides off the porch to the path and starts to walk past her to the road with a grand swagger of ignoring her existence. He is dressed in his store suit, spruced up, his face shines from soap and water. Abbie leans forward on her chair, her eyes hard and angry now, and, as he passes her, gives a sneering, taunting chuckle.*)

EBEN (*stung—turns on her furiously*): What air yew cacklin' 'bout?

ABBIE (*triumphant*): Yew!

EBEN: What about me?

ABBIE: Ye look all slicked up like a prize bull.

EBEN (*with a sneer*): Waal—ye hain't so durned purty yerself, be ye? (*They stare into each other's eyes, his held by hers in spite of himself, hers glowingly possessive. Their physical attraction becomes a palpable force quivering in the hot air.*)

ABBIE (*softly*): Ye don't mean that, Eben. Ye may think ye mean it, mebbe, but ye don't. Ye can't. It's agin nature, Eben. Ye been fightin' yer nature ever since the day I come—tryin' t' tell yerself I hain't purty t'ye. (*She laughs a low humid laugh without taking her eyes from his. A pause—her body squirms desirously—she murmurs languorously.*) Hain't the sun strong an' hot? Ye kin feel it burnin' into the earth—Nature—makin' thin's grow—bigger 'n' bigger—burnin' inside ye—makin' ye want t' grow—into somethin' else—till ye're jined with it—an' it's your'n—but it owns ye, too—ant makes ye grow bigger—like a tree—like them elums—(*She laughs again softly, holding his eyes. He takes a step toward her, compelled against his will.*) Nature'll beat ye, Eben. Ye might's well own up t' it fust 's last.

EBEN (*trying to break from her spell—confusedly*): If Paw'd hear ye goin' on.... (*Resentfully.*) But ye've made such a damned idjit out o' the old devil...! (*Abbie laughs.*)

ABBIE: Waal—hain't it easier fur yew with him changed softer?

EBEN (*defiantly*): No. I'm fightin' him—fightin' yew—fightin' fur Maw's rights t' her hum! (*This breaks her spell for him. He glowers at her.*) An' I'm onto ye. Ye hain't foolin' me a mite. Ye're aimin' t' swaller up everythin' an' make it your'n. Waal, you'll find I'm a heap sight bigger hunk nor yew kin chew! (*He turns from her with a sneer.*)

ABBIE (*trying to regain her ascendancy—seductively*): Eben!

EBEN: Leave me be! (*He starts to walk away.*)

ABBIE (*more commandingly*): Eben!

EBEN (*stops—resentfully*): What d'ye want?

ABBIE (*trying to conceal a growing excitement*): Whar air ye goin'?

EBEN (*with malicious nonchalance*): Oh—up the road a spell.

ABBIE: T' the village?

EBEN (*airily*): Mebbe.

ABBIE (*excitedly*): T' see that Min, I s'pose?

EBEN: Mebbe.

ABBIE (*weakly*): What d'ye want t' waste time on her fur?

EBEN (*revenging himself now—grinning at her*): Ye can't beat Nature, didn't ye say? (*He laughs and again starts to walk away.*)

ABBIE (*bursting out*): An ugly old hake!

EBEN (*with a tantalizing sneer*): She's purtier'n yew be!

ABBIE: That every wuthless drunk in the country has....

EBEN (*tauntingly*): Mebbe—but she's better'n yew. She owns up fa'r 'n' squar' t' her doin's.

ABBIE (*furiously*): Don't ye dare compare....

EBEN: She don't go sneakin' an' stealin'—what's mine.

ABBIE (*savagely seizing on his weak point*): Your'n? Yew mean—my farm?

EBEN: I mean the farm yew sold yerself fur like any other old whore—my farm!

ABBIE (*stung—fiercely*): Ye'll never live t' see the day when even a stinkin' weed on it'll belong t' ye! (*Then in a scream.*) Git out o' my sight! Go on t' yer slut—disgracin' yer Paw 'n' me! I'll git yer Paw t' horsewhip ye off the place if I want t'! Ye're only livin'

here 'cause I tolerate ye! Git along! I hate the sight o' ye! (*She stops, panting and glaring at him.*)

EBEN (*returning her glance in kind*): An' I hate the sight o' yew! (*He turns and strides off up the road. She follows his retreating figure with concentrated hate. Old Cabot appears coming up from the barn. The hard, grim expression of his face has changed. He seems in some queer way softened, mellowed. His eyes have taken on a strange, incongruous dreamy quality. Yet there is no hint of physical weakness about him—rather he looks more robust and younger. Abbie sees him and turns away quickly with unconcealed aversion. He comes slowly up to her.*)

CABOT (*mildly*): War yew an' Eben quarrelin' agen?

ABBIE (*shortly*): No.

CABOT: Ye was talkin' a 'mighty loud. (*He sits down on the edge of porch.*)

ABBIE (*snappishly*): If ye heerd us they hain't no need askin' questions.

CABOT: I didn't hear what ye said.

ABBIE (*relieved*): Waal—it wa'n't nothin' t' speak on.

CABOT (*after a pause*): Eben's queer.

ABBIE (*bitterly*): He's the dead spit 'n' image o' yew!

CABOT (*queerly interested*): D'ye think so, Abbie? (*After a pause, ruminatingly.*) Me 'n' Eben's allus fit 'n' fit. I never could b'ar him noways. He's so thunderin' soft—like his Maw.

ABBIE (*scornfully*): Ay-eh! 'Bout as soft as yew be!

CABOT (*as if he hadn't heard*): Mebbe I been too hard on him.

ABBIE (*jeeringly*): Waal—ye're gittin' soft now—soft as slop! That's what Eben was sayin'.

CABOT (*his face instantly grim and ominous*): Eben was sayin'? Waal, he'd best not do nothin' t' try me 'r he'll soon diskiver.... (*A pause. She keeps her face turned away. His gradually softens. He stares up at the sky.*) Purty, hain't it?

ABBIE (*crossly*): I don't see nothin' purty.

CABOT: The sky. Feels like a wa'm field up thar.

ABBIE (*sarcastically*): Air yew aimin' t' buy up over the farm too? (*She snickers contemptuously.*)

CABOT (*strangely*): I'd like t' own my place up thar. (*A pause.*) I'm gittin' old, Abbie. I'm gittin' ripe on the bough. (*A pause. She stares at him mystified. He goes on.*) It's allus lonesome cold in the house—even when it's bilin' hot outside. Hain't yew noticed?

ABBIE: No.

CABOT: It's wa'm down t' the barn—nice smellin' an' warm—with the cows. (*A pause.*) Cows is queer.

ABBIE: Like yew?

CABOT: Like Eben. (*A pause.*) I'm gittin' t' feel resigned t' Eben—jest as I got t' feel 'bout his Maw. I'm gittin' t' learn to b'ar his softness—jest like her'n. I calc'late I c'd a'most take t' him—if he wa'n't sech a dumb fool! (*A pause.*) I s'pose it's old age a-creepin' in my bones.

ABBIE (*indifferently*): Waal—ye hain't dead yet.

CABOT (*roused*): No, I hain't, yew bet—not by a hell of a sight—I'm sound 'n' tough as hickory! (*Then moodily.*) But arter three score and ten the Lord warns ye t' prepare. (*A pause.*) That's why Eben's come in my head. Now that his cussed sinful brothers is gone their path t' hell, they's no one left but Eben.

ABBIE (*resentfully*): They's me, hain't they? (*Agitatedly.*) What's all this sudden likin' ye've tuk to Eben? Why don't ye say nothin' 'bout me? Hain't I yer lawful wife?

CABOT (*simply*): Ay-eh. Ye be. (*A pause—he stares at her desirously—his eyes grow avid—then with a sudden movement he seizes her hands and squeezes them, declaiming in a queer camp meeting preacher's tempo.*) Yew air my Rose o' Sharon! Behold, yew air fair; yer eyes air doves; yer lips air like scarlet; yer two breasts air like two fawns; yer navel be like a round goblet; yer belly be like a heap o' wheat.... (*He covers her hand with kisses. She does not seem to notice. She stares before her with hard angry eyes.*)

ABBIE (*jerking her hands away—harshly*): So ye're plannin' t' leave the farm t' Eben, air ye?

CABOT (*dazedly*): Leave...? (*Then with resentful obstinacy.*) I hain't a-givin' it t' no one!

ABBIE (*remorselessly*): Ye can't take it with ye.

CABOT (*thinks a moment—then reluctantly*): No, I calc'late not. (*After a pause—with a strange passion.*) But if I could, I would, by the Eternal! 'R if I could, in my dyin' hour, I'd set it afire an' watch it burn—this house an' every ear o' corn an' every tree down t' the last blade o' hay! I'd sit an' know it was all a-dying with me an' no one else'd ever own what was mine, what I'd made out o' nothin' with my own sweat 'n' blood! (*A pause—then he adds with a queer affection.*) 'Ceptin' the cows. Them I'd turn free.

ABBIE (*harshly*): An' me?

CABOT (*with a queer smile*): Ye'd be turned free, too.

ABBIE (*furiously*): So that's the thanks I git fur marryin' ye—t' have ye change kind to Eben who hates ye, an' talk o' turnin' me out in the road.

CABOT (*hastily*): Abbie! Ye know I wa'n't....

ABBIE (*vengefully*): Just let me tell ye a thing or two 'bout Eben! Whar's he gone? T' see that harlot, Min! I tried fur t' stop him. Disgracin' yew an' me—on the Sabbath, too!

CABOT (*rather guiltily*): He's a sinner—nateral-born. It's lust eatin' his heart.

ABBIE (*enraged beyond endurance—wildly vindictive*): An' his lust fur me! Kin ye find excuses fur that?

CABOT (*stares at her—after a dead pause*): Lust—fur yew?

ABBIE (*defiantly*): He was tryin' t' make love t' me—when ye heerd us quarrelin'.

CABOT (*stares at her—then a terrible expression of rage comes over his face—he springs to his feet shaking all over*): By the A'mighty God—I'll end him!

ADDIE (*frightened now for Eben*): No! Don't ye!

CABOT (*violently*): I'll git the shotgun an' blow his soft brains t' the top o' them elums!

ABBIE (*throwing her arms around him*): No, Ephraim!

CABOT (*pushing her away violently*): I will, by God!

ABBIE (*in a quieting tone*): Listen, Ephraim. 'Twa'n't nothin' bad—on'y a boy's foolin'—'twa'n't meant serious—jest jokin' an' teasin'....

CABOT: Then why did ye say—lust?

ABBIE: It must hev sounded wusser'n I meant. An' I was mad at thinkin'—ye'd leave him the farm.

CABOT (*quieter but still grim and cruel*): Waal then, I'll horsewhip him off the place if that much'll content ye.

ABBIE (*reaching out and taking his hand*): No. Don't think o' me! Ye mustn't drive him off. 'Tain't sensible. Who'll ye get to help ye on the farm? They's no one hereabouts.

CABOT (*considers this—then nodding his appreciation*): Ye got a head on ye. (*Then irritably.*) Waal, let him stay. (*He sits down on the edge of the porch. She sits beside him. He murmurs contemptuously.*) I oughtn't t' git riled so—at that 'ere fool calf. (*A pause.*) But har's the p'int. What son o' mine'll keep on here t' the farm—when the Lord does call me? Simeon an' Peter air gone t' hell—an' Eben's follerin' 'em.

ABBIE: They's me.

CABOT: Ye're on'y a woman.

ABBIE: I'm yewr wife.

CABOT: That hain't me. A son is me—my blood—mine. Mine ought t' git mine. An' then it's still mine—even though I be six foot under. D'ye see?

ABBIE (*giving him a look of hatred*): Ay-eh. I see. (*She becomes very thoughtful, her face growing shrewd, her eyes studying Cabot craftily.*)

CABOT: I'm gittin' old—ripe on the bough. (*Then with a sudden forced reassurance.*) Not but what I hain't a hard nut t' crack even yet—an' fur many a year t' come! By the Eternal, I kin break most o' the young fellers' backs at any kind o' work any day o' the year!

ABBIE (*suddenly*): Mebbe the Lord'll give *us* a son.

CABOT (*turns and stares at her eagerly*): Ye mean—a son—t' me 'n' yew?

ABBIE (*with a cajoling smile*): Ye're a strong man yet, hain't ye? 'Tain't noways impossible, be it? We know that. Why d'ye stare so? Hain't ye never thought o' that afore? I been thinkin' o' it all along. Ay-eh—an' I been prayin' it'd happen, too.

CABOT (*his face growing full of joyous pride and a sort of religious ecstasy*): Ye been prayin', Abbie?—fur a son?—t' us?

ABBIE: Ay-eh. (*With a grim resolution.*) I want a son now.

CABOT (*excitedly clutching both of her hands in his*): It'd be the blessin' o' God, Abbie—the blessin' o' God A'mighty on me—in my old age—in my lonesomeness! They hain't nothin' I wouldn't do fur ye then, Abbie. Ye'd hev on'y t' ask it—anythin' ye'd a mind t'!

ABBIE (*interrupting*): Would ye will the farm t' me then—t' me an' it...?

CABOT (*vehemently*): I'd do anythin' ye axed, I tell ye! I swar it! May I be everlastin' damned t' hell if I wouldn't! (*He sinks to his knees pulling her down* *with him. He trembles all over with the fervor of his hopes.)* Pray t' the Lord agen, Abbie. It's the Sabbath! I'll jine ye! Two prayers air better nor one. "An' God hearkened unto Rachel"! An' God hearkened unto Abbie! Pray, Abbie! Pray fur him to hearken! *(He bows his head, mumbling. She pretends to do likewise but gives him a side glance of scorn and triumph.)*

Scene II

(About eight in the evening. The interior of the two bedrooms on the top floor is shown. Eben is sitting on the side of his bed in the room on the left. On account of the heat he has taken off everything but his undershirt and pants. His feet are bare. He faces front, brooding moodily, his chin propped on his hands, a desperate expression on his face.)

(In the other room Cabot and Abbie are sitting side by side on the edge of their bed, an old four-poster with feather mattress. He is in his nightshirt, she in her nightdress. He is still in the queer, excited mood into which the notion of a son has thrown him. Both rooms are lighted dimly and flickeringly by tallow candles.)

CABOT: The farm needs a son.

ABBIE: I need a son.

CABOT: Ay-eh. Sometimes ye air the farm an' sometimes the farm be yew. That's why I clove t'ye in my lonesomeness. *(A pause. He pounds his knee with his fist.)* Me an' the farm has got t' beget a son!

ABBIE: Ye'd best go t' sleep. Ye're gittin' thin's all mixed.

CABOT *(with an impatient gesture)*: No, I hain't. My mind's clear's a well. Ye don't know me, that's it. *(He stares hopelessly at the floor.)*

ABBIE *(indifferently)*: Mebbe. *(In the next room Eben gets up and paces up and down distractedly. Abbie hears him. Her eyes fasten on the intervening wall with concentrated attention. Eben stops and stares. Their hot glances seem to meet through the wall. Unconsciously he stretches out his arms for her and she half rises. Then aware, he mutters a curse at himself and flings himself face downward on the bed, his clenched fists above his head, his face buried in the pillow. Abbie relaxes with a faint sigh but her eyes remain fixed on the wall; she listens with all her attention for some movement from Eben.)*

CABOT *(suddenly raises his head and looks at her—scornfully)*: Will ye ever know me—'r will any man 'r woman? *(Shaking his head.)* No. I calc'late wa'n't t' be. *(He turns away. Abbie looks at the wall. Then, evidently unable to keep silent about his thoughts, without looking at his wife, he puts out his hand and clutches her knee. She starts violently, looks at him, sees he is not watching her, concentrates again on the wall, and pays no attention to what he says.)* Listen, Abbie. When I come here fifty odd year ago—I was jest twenty an' the strongest an' hardest ye ever

seen—ten times as strong an' fifty times as hard as Eben. Waal—this place was nothin' but fields o' stones. Folks laughed when I tuk it. They couldn't know what I knowed. When ye kin make corn sprout out o' stones, God's livin' in yew! They wa'n't strong enuf fur that! They reckoned God was easy. They laughed. They don't laugh no more. Some died hereabouts. Some went West an' died. They're all underground—fur follerin' arter an easy God. God hain't easy. *(He shakes his head slowly.)* An' I growed hard. Folks kept allus sayin' he's a hard man like 'twas sinful t' be hard, so's at last I said back at 'em: Waal then, by thunder, ye'll git me hard an' see how ye like it! *(Then suddenly.)* But I give in t' weakness once. 'Twas arter I'd been here two year. I got weak—despairful—they was so many stones. They was a party leavin', givin' up, goin' West. I jined 'em. We tracked on 'n' on. We come t' broad medders, plains, whar the soil was black an' rich as gold. Nary a stone. Easy. Ye'd on'y to plow an' sow an' then set an' smoke yer pipe an' watch thin's grow. I could o' been a rich man—but somethin' in me fit me an' fit me—the voice o' God sayin': "This hain't wuth nothin' t' Me. Git ye back t' hum!" I got afeerd o' that voice an' I lit out back t' hum here, leavin' my claim an' crops t' whoever'd a mind t' take 'em. Ay-eh. I actoolly give up what was rightful mine! God's hard, not easy! God's in the stones! Build my church on a rock—out o' stones an' I'll be in them! That's what He meant t' Peter! *(He sighs heavily—a pause.)* Stones. I picked 'em up an' piled 'em into walls. Ye kin read the years of my life in them walls, every day a hefted stone, climbin' over the hills up and down, fencin' in the fields that was mine, whar I'd made thin's grow out o' nothin'—like the will o' God, like the servant o' His hand. It wa'n't easy. It was hard an' He made me hard fur it. *(He pauses.)* All the time I kept gittin' lonesomer. I tuk a wife. She bore Simeon an' Peter. She was a good woman. She wuked hard. We was married twenty year. She never knowed me. She helped but she never knowed what she was helpin'. I was allus lonesome. She died. After that it wa'n't so lonesome fur a spell. *(A pause.)* I lost count o' the years. I had no time t' fool away countin' 'em. Sim an' Peter helped. The farm growed. It was all mine! When I thought o' that I didn't feel lonesome. *(A pause.)* But ye can't hitch yer mind t' one thin' day an' night. I tuk another wife—Eben's Maw. Her folks was contestin' me at law over my deeds t' the farm—my farm! That's why Eben keeps a-talkin' his fool talk o' this bein' his Maw's farm. She bore Eben. She was purty—but soft. She tried t' be hard. She couldn't. She never knowed me nor nothin'. It was lonesomer 'n hell with her. After a matter o' sixteen odd years, she died. *(A pause.)* I lived with the boys. They hated me 'cause I was hard. I hated them 'cause they was soft. They coveted the farm without knowin' what it meant. It made me bitter 'n wormwood. It aged me—them coveting what I'd made fur

Abbie in the 1988 Pushkin Theatre (Moscow) production of *Desire under the Elms*, directed by Mark Lamos of the Hartford Stage Company.

mine. Then this spring the call come—the voice o' God cryin' in my wilderness, in my lonesomeness—t' go out an' seek an' find! (*Turning to her with strange passion.*) I sought ye an' I found ye! Yew air my Rose o' Sharon! Yer eyes air like. . . . (*She has turned a blank face, resentful eyes to his. He stares at her for a moment—then harshly.*) Air ye any the wiser fur all I've told ye?

ABBIE (*confusedly*): Mebbe.

CABOT (*pushing her away from him angrily*): Ye don't know nothin'—nor never will. If ye don't hev a son t' redeem ye. . . . (*This in a tone of cold threat.*)

ABBIE (*resentfully*): I've prayed, hain't I?

CABOT (*bitterly*): Pray agen—fur understandin'!

ABBIE (*a veiled threat in her tone*): Ye'll have a son out o' me, I promise ye.

CABOT: How kin ye promise?

ABBIE: I got second-sight mebbe. I kin foretell. (*She gives a queer smile.*)

CABOT: I believe ye have. Ye give me the chills sometimes. (*He shivers.*) It's cold in this house. It's oneasy. They's thin's pokin' about in the dark—in the corners. (*He pulls on his trousers, tucking in his nightshirt, and pulls on his boots.*)

ABBIE (*surprised*): Whar air ye goin'?

CABOT (*queerly*): Down whar it's restful—whar it's warm—down t' the barn. (*Bitterly.*) I kin talk t' the cows. They know. They know the farm an' me. They'll give me peace. (*He turns to go out the door.*)

ABBIE (*a bit frightenedly*): Air ye ailin' tonight, Ephraim?

CABOT: Growin'. Growin' ripe on the bough. (*He turns and goes, his boots clumping down the stairs. Eben sits up with a start, listening. Abbie is conscious of his movement and stares at the wall. Cabot comes out of the house around the corner and stands by the gate, blinking at the sky. He stretches up his hands in a tortured gesture.*) God A'mighty, call from the dark! (*He listens as if expecting an answer. Then his arms drop, he shakes his head and plods off toward the barn. Eben and Abbie stare at each other through the wall. Eben sighs heavily and Abbie echoes it. Both become terribly nervous, uneasy. Finally Abbie gets up and listens, her ear to the wall. He acts as if he saw every move she was making, he becomes resolutely still. She seems driven into a decision—goes out the door in rear determinedly. His eyes follow her. Then as the door of his room is opened softly, he turns away, waits in an attitude of strained fixity. Abbie stands for a second staring at him, her eyes burning with desire. Then with a little cry she runs over and throws her arms about his neck, she pulls his head back and covers his mouth with kisses. At first, he submits dumbly; then he puts his arms about her neck and returns her kisses, but finally, suddenly aware of his hatred, he hurls her away from him, springing to his feet. They stand speechless and breathless, panting like two animals.*)

ABBIE (*at last—painfully*): Ye shouldn't, Eben—ye shouldn't—I'd make ye happy!

EBEN (*harshly*): I don't want t' be happy—from yew!

ABBIE (*helplessly*): Ye do, Eben! Ye do! Why d'ye lie?

EBEN (*viciously*): I don't take t'ye, I tell ye! I hate the sight o' ye!

ABBIE (*with an uncertain troubled laugh*): Waal, I kissed ye anyways—an' ye kissed back—yer lips was burnin'—ye can't lie 'bout that! (*Intensely.*) If ye don't care, why did ye kiss me back—why was yer lips burnin'?

EBEN (*wiping his mouth*): It was like pizen on 'em. (*Then tauntingly.*) When I kissed ye back, mebbe I thought 'twas someone else.

ABBIE (*wildly*): Min?

EBEN: Mebbe.

ABBIE (*torturedly*): Did ye go t' see her? Did ye r'ally go? I thought ye mightn't. Is that why ye throwed me off jest now?

EBEN (*sneeringly*): What if it be?

ABBIE (*raging*): Then ye're a dog, Eben Cabot!

EBEN (*threateningly*): Ye can't talk that way t' me!

ABBIE (*with a shrill laugh*): Can't I? Did ye think I was in love with ye—a weak thin' like yew? Not much! I on'y wanted ye fur a purpose o' my own—an' I'll hev ye fur it yet 'cause I'm stronger'n yew be!

EBEN (*resentfully*): I knowed well it was on'y part o' yer plan t' swaller everythin'!

ABBIE (*tauntingly*): Mebbe!

EBEN (*furious*): Git out o' my room!

ABBIE: This air my room an' ye're on'y hired help!

EBEN (*threateningly*): Git out afore I murder ye!

ABBIE (*quite confident now*): I hain't a mite afeerd. Ye want me, don't ye? Yes, ye do! An' yer Paw's son'll never kill what he wants! Look at yer eyes! They's lust fur me in 'em, burnin' 'em up! Look at yer lips now! They're tremblin' an' longin' t' kiss me, an' yer teeth t' bite! (*He is watching her now with a horrible fascination. She laughs a crazy triumphant laugh.*) I'm a-goin' t' make all o' this hum my hum! They's one room hain't mine yet, but it's a-goin' t' be tonight. I'm a-goin' down now an' light up! (*She makes him a mocking bow.*) Won't ye come courtin' me in the best parlor, Mister Cabot?

EBEN (*staring at her—horribly confused—dully*): Don't ye dare! It hain't been opened since Maw died an' was laid out thar! Don't ye . . . ! (*But her eyes are fixed on his so burningly that his will seems to wither before hers. He stands swaying toward her helplessly.*)

ABBIE (*holding his eyes and putting all her will into her words as she backs out the door*): I'll expect ye afore long, Eben.

EBEN (*Stares after her for a while, walking toward the door. A light appears in the parlor window. He murmurs.*): In the parlor? (*This seems to arouse connotations, for he comes back and puts on his white shirt, collar, half ties the tie mechanically, puts on*

coat, takes his hat, stands barefooted looking about him in bewilderment, mutters wonderingly.*) Maw! Whar air yew? (*Then goes slowly toward the door in rear.*)

Scene III

(*A few minutes later. The interior of the parlor is shown. A grim, repressed room like a tomb in which the family has been interred alive. Abbie sits on the edge of the horsehair sofa. She has lighted all the candles and the room is revealed in all its preserved ugliness. A change has come over the woman. She looks awed and frightened now, ready to run away.*)

(*The door is opened and Eben appears. His face wears an expression of obsessed confusion. He stands staring at her, his arms hanging disjointedly from his shoulders, his feet bare, his hat in his hand.*)

ABBIE (*after a pause—with a nervous, formal politeness*): Won't ye set?

EBEN (*dully*): Ay-eh. (*Mechanically he places his hat carefully on the floor near the door and sits stiffly beside her on the edge of the sofa. A pause. They both remain rigid, looking straight ahead with eyes full of fear.*)

ABBIE: When I fust come in—in the dark—they seemed somethin' here.

EBEN (*simply*): Maw.

ABBIE: I kin still feel—somethin'. . . .

EBEN: It's Maw.

ABBIE: At fust I was feered o' it. I wanted t' yell an' run. Now—since yew come—seems like it's growin' soft an' kind t' me. (*Addressing the air—queerly.*) Thank yew.

EBEN: Maw allus loved me.

ABBIE: Mebbe it knows I love yew, too. Mebbe that makes it kind t' me.

EBEN (*dully*): I dunno. I should think she'd hate ye.

ABBIE (*with certainty*): No. I kin feel it don't—not no more.

EBEN: Hate ye fur stealin' her place—here in her hum—settin' in her parlor whar she was laid—(*He suddenly stops, staring stupidly before him.*)

ABBIE: What is it, Eben?

EBEN (*in a whisper*): Seems like Maw didn't want me t' remind ye.

ABBIE (*excitedly*): I knowed, Eben! It's kind t' me! It don't b'ar me no grudges fur what I never knowed an' couldn't help!

EBEN: Maw b'ars him a grudge.

ABBIE: Waal, so does all o' us.

EBEN: Ay-eh. (*With passion.*) I does, by God!

ABBIE (*taking one of his hands in hers and patting it*): Thar! Don't git riled thinkin' o' him. Think o' yer Maw who's kind t' us. Tell me about yer Maw, Eben.

Raymond J. Barry and Amelia Campbell in the American Repertory Theater's 2004–2005 production of *Desire under the Elms*, directed by János Szász.

EBEN: They hain't nothin' much. She was kind. She was good.

ADDIE (*Putting one arm over his shoulder. He does not seem to notice—passionately.*): I'll be kind an' good t' ye!

EBEN: Sometimes she used t' sing fur me.

ABBIE: I'll sing fur ye!

EBEN: This was her hum. This was her farm.

ABBIE: This is my hum! This is my farm!

EBEN: He married her t' steal 'em. She was soft an' easy. He couldn't 'preciate her.

ABBIE: He can't 'preciate me!

EBEN: He murdered her with his hardness.

ABBIE: He's murderin' me!

EBEN: She died. (*A pause.*) Sometimes she used to sing fur me. (*He bursts into a fit of sobbing.*)

ABBIE (*both her arms around him—with wild passion*): I'll sing fur ye! I'll die fur ye! (*In spite of her overwhelming desire for him, there is a sincere maternal love in her manner and voice—a horribly frank mixture of lust and mother love.*) Don't cry, Eben! I'll take yer Maw's place! I'll be everythin' she was t' ye! Let me kiss ye, Eben! (*She pulls his head around. He makes a bewildered pretense of resistance. She is tender.*) Don't be afeered! I'll kiss ye pure, Eben—same 's if I was a Maw t' ye—an' ye kin kiss me back 's if yew was my son—my boy—sayin' good-night t' me! Kiss me, Eben. (*They kiss in restrained fashion. Then suddenly wild passion overcomes her. She kisses him lustfully again and again and he flings his arms about her and returns her kisses. Suddenly, as in the bedroom, he frees himself from her violently and springs to his feet. He is trembling all over, in a strange state of terror. Abbie strains her arms toward him with fierce pleading.*) Don't ye leave me, Eben! Can't ye see it hain't enuf—lovin' ye like a Maw—can't ye see it's got t' be that an' more—much more—a hundred times more—fur me t' be happy—fur yew t' be happy?

EBEN (*to the presence he feels in the room*): Maw! Maw! What d'ye want? What air ye tellin' me?

ABBIE: She's tellin' ye t' love me. She knows I love ye an' I'll be good t' ye. Can't ye feel it? Don't ye know? She's tellin' ye t' love me, Eben!

EBEN: Ay-eh. I feel—mebbe she—but—I can't figger out—why—when ye've stole her place—here in her hum—in the parlor whar she was

ABBIE (*fiercely*): She knows I love ye!

EBEN (*his face suddenly lighting up with a fierce, triumphant grin*): I see it! I sees why. It's her vengeance on him—so's she kin rest quiet in her grave!

ABBIE (*wildly*): Vengeance o' God on the hull o' us! What d'we give a durn? I love ye, Eben! God knows I love ye! (*She stretches out her arms for him.*)

EBEN (*throws himself on his knees beside the sofa and grabs her in his arms—releasing all his pent-up passion*): An' I love ye, Abbie!—now I kin say it! I been dyin' fur want o' ye—every hour since ye come! I love ye! (*Their lips meet in a fierce, bruising kiss.*)

Scene IV

(*Exterior of the farmhouse. It is just dawn. The front door at right is opened and Eben comes out and walks around to the gate. He is dressed in his working clothes. He seems changed. His face wears a bold and confident expression, he is grinning to himself with evident satisfaction. As he gets near the gate, the window of the parlor is heard opening and the shutters are flung back and Abbie sticks her head out. Her hair tumbles over her shoulders in disarray, her face is flushed, she looks at Eben with tender, languorous eyes and calls softly.*)

ABBIE: Eben. (*As he turns—playfully.*) Jest one more kiss afore ye go. I'm goin' to miss ye fearful all day.

EBEN: An' me yew, ye kin bet! (*He goes to her. They kiss several times. He draws away, laughingly.*) Thar. That's enuf, hain't it? Ye won't hev none left fur next time.

ABBIE: I got a million o' 'em left fur yew! (*Then a bit anxiously.*) D'ye r'ally love me, Eben?

EBEN (*emphatically*): I like ye better'n any gal I ever knowed! That's gospel!

ABBIE: Likin' hain't lovin'.

EBEN: Waal then—I love ye. Now air yew satisfied?

ABBIE: Ay-eh, I be. (*She smiles at him adoringly.*)

EBEN: I better git t' the barn. The old critter's liable t' come sneakin' up.

ABBIE (*with a confident laugh*): Let him! I kin allus pull the wool over his eyes. I'm goin' t' leave the shutters open and let in the sun 'n' air. This room's been dead long enuf. Now it's goin' t' be my room!

EBEN (*frowning*): Ay-eh.

ABBIE (*hastily*): I meant—our room.

EBEN: Ay-eh.

ABBIE: We made it our'n last night, didn't we? We give it life—our lovin' did. (*A pause.*)

EBEN (*with a strange look*): Maw's gone back t' her grave. She kin sleep now.

ABBIE: May she rest in peace! (*Then tenderly rebuking.*) Ye oughtn't t' talk o' sad thin's—this mornin'.

EBEN: It jest come up in my mind o' itself.

ABBIE: Don't let it. (*He doesn't answer. She yawns.*) Waal, I'm a-goin' t' steal a wink o' sleep. I'll tell the Old Man I hain't feelin' pert. Let him git his own vittles.

EBEN: I see him comin' from the barn. Ye better look smart an' git upstairs.

ABBIE: Ay-eh. Good-by. Don't ferget me. (*She throws him a kiss. He grins—then squares his shoulders and awaits his father confidently. Cabot walks slowly up from the left, staring up at the sky with a vague face.*)

EBEN (*jovially*): Mornin', Paw. Star-gazin' in daylight?

CABOT: Purty, hain't it?

EBEN (*looking around him possessively*): It's a durned purty farm.

CABOT: I mean the sky.

EBEN (*grinning*): How d'ye know? Them eyes o' your'n can't see that fur. (*This tickles his humor and he slaps his thigh and laughs.*) Ho-ho! That's a good un!

CABOT (*grimly sarcastic*): Ye're feelin' right chipper, hain't ye? Whar'd ye steal the likker?

EBEN (*good-naturedly*): 'Tain't likker. Jest life. (*Suddenly holding out his hand—soberly.*) Yew 'n' me is quits. Let's shake hands.

CABOT (*suspiciously*): What's come over ye?

EBEN: Then don't. Mebbe it's jest as well. (*A moment's pause.*) What's come over me? (*Queerly.*) Didn't ye feel her passin'—goin' back t' her grave?

CABOT (*dully*): Who?

EBEN: Maw. She kin rest now an' sleep content. She's quit with ye.

CABOT (*confusedly*): I rested. I slept good—down with the cows. They know how t' sleep. They're teachin' me.

EBEN (*suddenly jovial again*): Good fur the cows! Waal—ye better git t' work.

CABOT (*grimly amused*): Air yew bossin' me, ye calf?

EBEN (*beginning to laugh*): Ay-eh! I'm bossin' yew! Ha-ha-ha! See how ye like it! Ha-ha-ha! I'm the prize rooster o' this roost. Ha-ha-ha! (*He goes off toward the barn laughing.*)

CABOT (*looks after him with scornful pity*): Soft-headed. Like his Maw. Dead spit 'n' image. No hope in him! (*He spits with contemptuous disgust.*) A born fool! (*Then matter-of-factly.*) Waal—I'm gittin' peckish. (*He goes toward door.*)

PART III • Scene I

(*A night in late spring the following year. The kitchen and the two bedrooms upstairs are shown. The two bedrooms are dimly lighted by a tallow candle in each. Eben is sitting on the side of the bed in his room, his chin propped on his fists, his face a study of the struggle he is making to understand his conflicting emotions. The noisy laughter and music from below where a kitchen dance is in progress annoy and distract him. He scowls at the floor.*)

(*In the next room a cradle stands beside the double bed.*)

(*In the kitchen all is festivity. The stove has been taken down to give more room to the dancers. The chairs, with wooden benches added, have been pushed back against the walls. On these are seated, squeezed in tight against one another, farmers and their wives and their young folks of both sexes from the neighboring farms. They are all chattering and laughing loudly. They evidently have some secret joke in common. There is no end of winking, of nudging, of meaning nods of the head toward Cabot who, in a state of extreme hilarious excitement increased by the amount he has drunk, is standing near the rear door where there is a small keg of whisky and serving drinks to all the men. In the left corner, front, dividing the attention with her husband, Abbie is sitting in a rocking chair, a shawl wrapped about her shoulders. She is very pale, her face is thin and drawn, her eyes are fixed anxiously on the open door in rear as if waiting for someone.*)

(*The musician is tuning up his fiddle, seated in the far right corner. He is a lanky young fellow with a long, weak face. His pale eyes blink incessantly and he grins about him slyly with a greedy malice.*)

ABBIE (*suddenly turning to a young girl on her right*): Whar's Eben?

YOUNG GIRL (*eyeing her scornfully*): I dunno, Mrs. Cabot. I hain't seen Eben in ages. (*Meaningly.*) Seems like he's spent most o' his time t' hum since yew come.

ABBIE (*vaguely*): I tuk his Maw's place.

YOUNG GIRL: Ay-eh. So I've heerd. (*She turns away to retail this bit of gossip to her mother sitting next to her. Abbie turns to her left to a big stoutish middle-aged man whose flushed face and starting eyes show the amount of "likker" he has consumed.*)

ABBIE: Ye hain't seen Eben, hev ye?

MAN: No, I hain't. (*Then he adds with a wink.*) If yew hain't, who would?

ABBIE: He's the best dancer in the county. He'd ought t' come an' dance.

MAN (*with a wink*): Mebbe he's doin' the dutiful an' walkin' the kid t' sleep. It's a boy, hain't it?

ABBIE (*nodding vaguely*): Ay-eh—born two weeks back—purty's a picter.

MAN: They all is—t' their Maws. (*Then in a whisper, with a nudge and a leer.*) Listen, Abbie—if ye ever git tired o' Eben, remember me! Don't fergit now! (*He looks at her uncomprehending face for a second—then grunts disgustedly.*) Waal—guess I'll likker agin. (*He goes over and joins Cabot who is arguing noisily with an old farmer over cows. They all drink.*)

ABBIE (*this time appealing to nobody in particular*): Wonder what Eben's a-doin'? (*Her remark is repeated down the line with many a guffaw and titter until it reaches the fiddler. He fastens his blinking eyes on Abbie.*)

FIDDLER (*raising his voice*): Bet I kin tell ye, Abbie, what Eben's doin'! He's down t' the church offerin' up prayers o' thanksgivin'. (*They all titter expectantly.*)

A MAN: What fur? (*Another titter.*)

FIDDLER: 'Cause unto him a—(*He hesitates just long enough.*) brother is born! (*A roar of laughter. They all look from Abbie to Cabot. She is oblivious, staring at the door. Cabot, although he hasn't heard the words, is irritated by the laughter and steps forward, glaring about him. There is an immediate silence.*)

CABOT: What're ye all bleatin' about—like a flock o' goats? Why don't ye dance, damn ye? I axed ye here t' dance—t' eat, drink an' be merry—an' thar ye set cacklin' like a lot o' wet hens with the pip! Ye've swilled my likker an' guzzled my vittles like hogs, hain't ye? Then dance fur me, can't ye? That's fa'r an' squar', hain't it? (*A grumble of resentment goes around but they are all evidently in too much awe of him to express it openly.*)

FIDDLER (*slyly*): We're waitin' fur Eben. (*A suppressed laugh.*)

CABOT (*with a fierce exultation*): T'hell with Eben! Eben's done fur now! I got a new son! (*His mood switching with drunken suddenness.*) But ye needn't t' laugh at Eben, none o' ye! He's my blood, if he be a dumb fool. He's better nor any o' yew! He kin do a day's work a'most up t' what I kin—an' that'd put any o' yew pore critters t' shame!

FIDDLER: An' he kin do a good night's work, too! (*A roar of laughter.*)

CABOT: Laugh, ye damn fools! Ye're right jist the same, Fiddler. He kin work day an' night too, like I kin, if need be!

OLD FARMER (*from behind the keg where he is weaving drunkenly back and forth—with great simplicity*): They hain't many t' touch ye, Ephraim—a son at seventy-six. That's a hard man fur ye! I be on'y sixty-eight an' I couldn't do it. (*A roar of laughter in which Cabot joins uproariously.*)

CABOT (*slapping him on the back*): I'm sorry fur ye, Hi. I'd never suspicion sech weakness from a boy like yew!

OLD FARMER: An' I never reckoned yew had it in ye nuther, Ephraim. (*There is another laugh.*)

CABOT (*suddenly grim*): I got a lot in me—a hell of a lot—folks don't know on. (*Turning to the fiddler.*) Fiddle 'er up, durn ye! Give 'em somethin' t' dance t'! What air ye, an ornament? Hain't this a celebration? Then grease yer elbow an' go it!

FIDDLER (*seizes a drink which the Old Farmer holds out to him and downs it*): Here goes! (*He starts to fiddle "Lady of the Lake." Four young fellows and four girls form in two lines and dance a square dance. The Fiddler shouts directions for the different movements, keeping his words in the rhythm of the music and interspersing them with jocular personal remarks to the dancers themselves. The people seated along the walls stamp their feet and clap their hands in unison. Cabot is especially active in this respect. Only Abbie remains apathetic, staring at the door as if she were alone in a silent room.*)

FIDDLER: Swing your partner t' the right! That's it, Jim! Give her a b'ar hug. Her Maw hain't lookin'. (*Laughter.*) Change partners! That suits ye, don't it, Essie, now ye got Reub afore ye? Look at her redden up, will ye? Waal, life is short an' so's love, as the feller says. (*Laughter.*)

CABOT (*excitedly, stamping his foot*): Go it, boys! Go it, gals!

FIDDLER (*with a wink at the others*): Ye're the spryest seventy-six ever I sees, Ephraim! Now if ye'd on'y good eyesight . . . ! (*Suppressed laughter. He gives Cabot no chance to retort but roars.*) Promenade! Ye're walkin' like a bride down the aisle, Sarah! Waal, while they's life they's allus hope, I've heerd tell. Swing your partner to the left! Gosh A'mighty, look at Johnny Cook high-steppin'! They hain't goin' t' be much strength left fur howin' in the corn lot t'morrow. (*Laughter.*)

CABOT: Go it! Go it! (*Then suddenly, unable to restrain himself any longer, he prances into the midst of the dancers, scattering them, waving his arms about wildly.*) Ye're all hoofs! Git out o' my road! Give me room! I'll show ye dancin'. Ye're all too soft! (*He pushes them roughly away. They crowd back toward the walls, muttering, looking at him resentfully.*)

FIDDLER (*jeeringly*): Go it, Ephraim! Go it! (*He starts "Pop, Goes the Weasel," increasing the tempo with every verse until at the end he is fiddling crazily as fast as he can go.*)

CABOT (*Starts to dance, which he does very well and with tremendous vigor. Then he begins to improvise, cuts incredibly grotesque capers, leaping up and cracking his heels together, prancing around in a circle with body bent in an Indian war dance, then suddenly straightening up and kicking as high as he can with both legs. He is like a monkey on a string. And all the while he intersperses his antics with shouts and derisive comments.*): Whoop! Here's dancin' fur ye! Whoop! See that! Seventy-six, if I'm a day! Hard as iron yet! Beatin' the young 'uns like I allus done! Look at me! I'd invite ye t' dance on my hundredth birthday on'y ye'll all be dead by then. Ye're a sickly generation! Yer hearts air pink, not red! Yer veins is full o' mud an' water! I be the on'y man in the county! Whoop! See that! I'm a Injun! I've killed Injuns in the West afore ye was born—an' skulped 'em too! They's a arrer wound on my backside I c'd show ye! The hull tribe chased me. I outrun 'em all—with the arrer stuck in me! An' I tuk vengeance on 'em. Ten eyes fur an eye, that was my motter! Whoop! Look at me! I kin kick the ceilin' off the room! Whoop!

FIDDLER (*stops playing—exhaustedly*): God A'mighty, I got enuf. Ye got the devil's strength in ye.

CABOT (*delightedly*): Did I beat yew, too? Waal, ye played smart. Hev a swig. (*He pours whisky for himself and Fiddler. They drink. The others watch Cabot silently with cold, hostile eyes. There is a dead pause. The Fiddler rests. Cabot leans against the keg, panting, glaring around him confusedly. In the room above, Eben gets to his feet and tiptoes out the door in rear, appearing a moment later in the other bedroom. He moves silently, even frightenedly, toward the cradle and stands there looking down at the baby. His face is as vague as his reactions are confused, but there is a trace of tenderness, of interested discovery. At the same moment that he reaches the cradle, Abbie seems to sense something. She gets up weakly and goes to Cabot.*)

ABBIE: I'm goin' up t' the baby.

CABOT (*with real solicitation*): Air ye able fur the stairs? D'ye want me t' help ye, Abbie?

ABBIE: No. I'm able. I'll be down agen soon.

CABOT: Don't ye git wore out! He needs ye, remember—our son does! (*He grins affectionately, patting her on the back. She shrinks from his touch.*)

ABBIE (*dully*): Don't—tech me. I'm goin'—up. (*She goes. Cabot looks after her. A whisper goes around the room. Cabot turns. It ceases. He wipes his forehead streaming with sweat. He is breathing pantingly.*)

CABOT: I'm a-goin' out t' git fresh air. I'm feelin' a mite dizzy. Fiddle up thar! Dance, all o' ye! Here's likker fur them as wants it. Enjoy yerselves. I'll be back. (*He goes, closing the door behind him.*)

FIDDLER (*sarcastically*): Don't hurry none on our account! (*A suppressed laugh. He imitates Abbie.*) Whar's Eben? (*More laughter.*)

A WOMAN (*loudly*): What's happened in this house is plain as the nose on yer face! (*Abbie appears in the doorway upstairs and stands looking in surprise and adoration at Eben who does not see her.*)

A MAN: Ssshh! He's li'ble t' be listenin' at the door. That'd be like him. (*Their voices die to an intensive whispering. Their faces are concentrated on this gossip. A noise as of dead leaves in the wind comes from the room. Cabot has come out from the porch and stands by the gate, leaning on it, staring at the sky blinkingly. Abbie comes across the room silently. Eben does not notice her until quite near.*)

EBEN (*starting*): Abbie!

ABBIE: Ssshh! (*She throws her arms around him. They kiss—then bend over the cradle together.*) Ain't he purty?—dead spit 'n' image o' yew!

EBEN (*pleased*): Air he? I can't tell none.

ABBIE: E-zactly like!

EBEN (*frowningly*): I don't like this. I don't like lettin' on what's mine's his'n. I been doin' that all my life. I'm gittin' t' the end o' b'arin' it!

ABBIE (*putting her finger on his lips*): We're doin' the best we kin. We got t' wait. Somethin's bound t' happen. (*She puts her arms around him.*) I got t' go back.

EBEN: I'm goin' out. I can't b'ar it with the fiddle playin' an' the laughin'.

ABBIE: Don't git feelin' low. I love ye, Eben. Kiss me. (*He kisses her. They remain in each other's arms.*)

CABOT (*at the gate, confusedly*): Even the music can't drive it out—somethin'. Ye kin feel it droppin' off the elums, climbin' up the roof, sneakin' down the chimney, pokin' in the corners! They's no peace in houses, they's no rest livin' with folks. Somethin's always livin' with ye. (*With a deep sigh.*) I'll go t' the barn an' rest a spell. (*He goes wearily toward the barn.*)

FIDDLER (*tuning up*): Let's celebrate the old skunk gittin' fooled! We kin have some fun now he's went. (*He starts to fiddle "Turkey in the Straw." There is real merriment now. The young folks get up to dance.*)

Scene II

(*A half hour later—exterior—Eben is standing by the gate looking up at the sky, an expression of dumb pain bewildered by itself on his face. Cabot appears, returning from the barn, walking wearily, his eyes on the ground. He sees Eben and his whole mood immediately changes. He becomes excited, a cruel, triumphant grin comes to his lips, he strides up and slaps Eben on the back. From within comes the whining of the fiddle and the noise of stamping feet and laughing voices.*)

CABOT: So har ye be!

EBEN (*startled, stares at him with hatred for a moment—then dully*): Ay-eh.

CABOT (*surveying him jeeringly*): Why hain't ye been in t' dance? They was all axin' fur ye.

EBEN: Let 'em ax!

CABOT: They's a hull passel o' purty gals.

EBEN: T' hell with 'em!

CABOT: Ye'd ought t' be marryin' one o' 'em soon.

EBEN: I hain't marryin' no one.

CABOT: Ye might 'arn a share o' a farm that way.

EBEN (*with a sneer*): Like yew did, ye mean? I hain't that kind.

CABOT (*stung*): Ye lie! 'Twas yer Maw's folks aimed t' steal my farm from me.

EBEN: Other folks don't say so. (*After a pause—defiantly.*) An' I got a farm, anyways!

CABOT (*derisively*): Whar?

EBEN (*stamps a foot on the ground*): Har!

CABOT (*throws his head back and laughs coarsely*): Ho-ho! Ye hev, hev ye? Waal, that's a good un!

EBEN (*controlling himself—grimly*): Ye'll see!

CABOT (*stares at him suspiciously, trying to make him out—a pause—then with scornful confidence*): Ay-eh. I'll see. So'll ye. It's ye that's blind—blind as a mole underground. (*Eben suddenly laughs, one short sardonic bark: "Ha." A pause. Cabot peers at him with renewed suspicion.*) What air ye hawin' 'bout? (*Eben turns away without answering. Cabot grows angry.*) God A'mighty, yew air a dumb dunce! They's nothin' in that thick skull o' your'n but noise—like a empty keg it be! (*Eben doesn't seem to hear. Cabot's rage grows.*) Yewr farm! God A'mighty! If ye wa'n't a born donkey ye'd know ye'll never own stick nor stone on it, specially now arter him bein' born. It's his'n, I tell ye—his'n arter I die—but I'll live a hundred jest t' fool ye all—an' he'll be growed then—yewr age a'most! (*Eben laughs again his sardonic "Ha." This drives Cabot into a fury.*) Ha? Ye think ye kin git 'round that someways, do ye? Waal, it'll be her'n, too—Abbie's—ye won't git 'round her—she knows yer tricks—she'll be too much fur ye—she wants the farm her'n—she was afeerd o' ye—she told me ye was sneakin' 'round tryin' t' make love t' her t' git her on yer side . . . ye . . . ye mad fool, ye! (*He raises his clenched fists threateningly.*)

EBEN (*is confronting him, choking with rage*): Ye lie, ye old skunk! Abbie never said no sech thing!

CABOT (*suddenly triumphant when he sees how shaken Eben is*): She did. An' I says, I'll blow his brains t' the top o' them elums—an' she says no that hain't sense, who'll ye git t'help ye on the farm in his place—an' then she says yew'n me ought t' have a son—I know we kin, she says—an' I says, if we do, ye kin have anythin' I've got ye've a mind t'. An' she says, I wants Eben cut off so's this farm'll be mine when ye die! (*With terrible gloating.*) An' that's what's happened, hain't it? An' the farm's her'n! An' the dust o' the road—that's you'rn! Ha! Now who's hawin'?

EBEN (*has been listening, petrified with grief and rage—suddenly laughs wildly and brokenly*): Ha-ha-ha! So that's her sneakin' game—all along!—like I suspicioned at fust—t' swaller it all—an' me, too . . . ! (*Madly.*) I'll murder her! (*He springs toward the porch but Cabot is quicker and gets in between.*)

CABOT: No, ye don't!

EBEN: Git out o' my road! (*He tries to throw Cabot aside. They grapple in what becomes immediately a murderous struggle. The old man's concentrated strength is too much for Eben. Cabot gets one hand on his throat and presses him back across the stone wall. At the same moment, Abbie comes out on the porch. With a stifled cry she runs toward them.*)

ABBIE: Eben! Ephraim! (*She tugs at the hand on Eben's throat.*) Let go, Ephraim! Ye're chokin' him!

CABOT (*Removes his hand and flings Eben sideways full length on the grass, gasping and choking. With a cry, Abbie kneels beside him, trying to take his head on her lap, but he pushes her away. Cabot stands looking down with fierce triumph.*): Ye needn't t've fret, Abbie, I wa'n't aimin' t' kill him. He hain't wuth hangin' fur—not by a hell of a sight! (*More and more triumphantly.*) Seventy-six an' him not thirty yit—an' look whar he be fur thinkin' his Paw was easy! No, by God, I hain't easy! An' him upstairs, I'll raise him t' be like me! (*He turns to leave them.*) I'm goin' in an' dance!—sing an' celebrate! (*He walks to the porch—then turns with a great grin.*) I don't calc'late it's left in him, but if he gits pesky, Abbie, ye jest sing out. I'll come a-runnin' an' by the Etarnal, I'll put him across my knee an' birch him! Ha-ha-ha! (*He goes into the house laughing. A moment later his loud "whoop" is heard.*)

ABBIE (*tenderly*): Eben. Air ye hurt? (*She tries to kiss him but he pushes her violently away and struggles to a sitting position.*)

EBEN (*gaspingly*): T'hell—with ye!

ABBIE (*not believing her ears*): It's me, Eben—Abbie—don't ye know me?

EBEN (*glowering at her with hatred*): Ay-eh—I know ye—now! (*He suddenly breaks down, sobbing weakly.*)

ABBIE (*fearfully*): Eben—what's happened t' ye—why did ye look at me 's if ye hated me?

EBEN (*violently, between sobs and gasps*): I do hate ye! Ye're a whore—a damn trickin' whore!

ABBIE (*shrinking back horrified*): Eben! Ye don't know what ye're sayin'!

EBEN (*scrambling to his feet and following her—accusingly*): Ye're nothin' but a stinkin' passel o' lies! Ye've been lyin' t' me every word ye spoke, day an' night, since we fust—done it. Ye've kept sayin' ye loved me. . . .

ABBIE (*frantically*): I do love ye! (*She takes his hand but he flings hers away.*)

EBEN (*unheeding*): Ye've made a fool o' me—a sick, dumb fool—a-purpose! Ye've been on'y playin' yer sneakin', stealin' game all along—gittin' me t' lie with ye so's ye'd hev a son he'd think was his'n, an' makin' him promise he'd give ye the farm and let me eat dust, if ye did git him a son! (*Staring at her with anguished, bewildered eyes.*) They must be a devil livin' in ye! T'ain't human t' be as bad as that be!

ABBIE (*stunned—dully*): He told yew . . . ?

EBEN: Hain't it true? It hain't no good in yew lyin'.

ABBIE (*pleadingly*): Eben, listen—ye must listen—it was long ago—afore we done nothin'—yew was scornin' me—goin' t' see Min—when I was lovin' ye—an' I said it t' him t' git vengeance on ye!

EBEN (*Unheedingly. With tortured passion.*): I wish ye was dead! I wish I was dead along with ye afore this come! (*Ragingly.*) But I'll git my vengeance too! I'll pray Maw t' come back t' help me—t' put her cuss on yew an' him!

ABBIE (*brokenly*): Don't ye, Eben! Don't ye! (*She throws herself on her knees before him, weeping.*) I didn't mean t' do bad t'ye! Fergive me, won't ye?

EBEN (*not seeming to hear her—fiercely*): I'll git squar' with the old skunk—an' yew! I'll tell him the truth 'bout the son he's so proud o'! Then I'll leave ye here t' pizen each other—with Maw comin' out o' her grave at nights—an' I'll go t' the gold fields o' Californi-a whar Sim an' Peter be!

ABBIE (*terrified*): Ye won't—leave me? Ye can't!

EBEN (*with fierce determination*): I'm a-goin', I tell ye! I'll git rich thar an' come back an' fight him fur the farm he stole—an' I'll kick ye both out in the road—t' beg an' sleep in the woods—an' yer son along with ye—t' starve an' die! (*He is hysterical at the end.*)

ABBIE (*with a shudder—humbly*): He's yewr son, too, Eben.

EBEN (*torturedly*): I wish he never was born! I wish he'd die this minit! I wish I'd never sot eyes on him! It's him—yew havin' him—a-purpose t' steal—that's changed everythin'!

ABBIE (*gently*): Did ye believe I loved ye—afore he come?

EBEN: Aye-eh—like a dumb ox!

ABBIE: An' ye don't believe no more?

EBEN: B'lieve a lyin' thief! Ha!

ABBIE (*shudders—then humbly*): An' did ye r'ally love me afore?

EBEN (*brokenly*): Ay-eh—an' ye was trickin' me!

ABBIE: An' ye don't love me now!

EBEN (*violently*): I hate ye, I tell ye!

ABBIE: An' ye're truly goin' West—goin' t' leave me—all account o' him being born?

EBEN: I'm a-goin' in the mornin'—or may God strike me t' hell!

ABBIE (*after a pause—with a dreadful cold intensity—slowly*): If that's what his comin's done t' me—killin' yewr love—takin' yew away—my on'y joy—the on'y joy I ever knowed—like heaven t' me—purtier'n heaven—then I hate him, too, even if I be his Maw!

EBEN (*bitterly*): Lies! Ye love him! He'll steal the farm fur ye! (*Brokenly.*) But t'ain't the farm so much—not no more—it's yew foolin' me—gittin' me t' love ye—lyin' yew loved me—jest t' git a son t' steal!

ABBIE (*distractedly*): He won't steal! I'd kill him fust! I do love ye! I'll prove t' ye . . . !

EBEN (*harshly*): T'ain't no use lyin' no more. I'm deaf t' ye! (*He turns away.*) I hain't seein' ye agen. Good-by!

ABBIE (*pale with anguish*): Hain't ye even goin' t' kiss me—not once—arter all we loved?

EBEN (*in a hard voice*): I hain't wantin' t' kiss ye never agen! I'm wantin' t' forgit I ever sot eyes on ye!

ABBIE: Eben!—ye mustn't—wait a spell—I want t' tell ye. . . .

EBEN: I'm a-goin' in t' git drunk. I'm a-goin' t' dance.

ABBIE (*clinging to his arm—with passionate earnestness*): If I could make it—'s if he'd never come up between us—if I could prove t' ye I wa'n't schemin' t' steal from ye—so's everythin' could be jest the same with us, lovin' each other jest the same, kissin' an' happy the same's we've been happy afore he come—if I could do it—ye'd love me agen, wouldn't ye? Ye'd kiss me agen? Ye wouldn't never leave me, would ye?

EBEN (*moved*): I calc'late not. (*Then shaking her hand off his arm—with a bitter smile.*) But ye hain't God, be ye?

ABBIE (*exultantly*): Remember ye've promised! (*Then with strange intensity.*) Mebbe I kin take back one thin' God does!

EBEN (*peering at her*): Ye're gittin' cracked, hain't ye? (*Then going toward door.*) I'm a-goin' t' dance.

ABBIE (*calls after him intensely*): I'll prove t' ye! I'll prove I love ye better'n. . . . (*He goes in the door, not seeming to hear. She remains standing where she is, looking after him—then she finishes desperately.*) Better'n everythin' else in the world!

Scene III

(*Just before dawn in the morning—shows the kitchen and Cabot's bedroom. In the kitchen, by the light of a tallow candle on the table, Eben is sitting, his chin propped on his hands, his drawn face blank and expressionless. His carpetbag is on the floor beside him. In the bedroom, dimly lighted by a small whale-oil lamp, Cabot lies asleep. Abbie is bending over the cradle, listening, her face full of terror yet with an undercurrent of desperate triumph. Suddenly, she breaks down and sobs, appears about to throw herself on her knees beside the cradle, but the old man turns restlessly, groaning in his sleep, and she controls herself, and, shrinking away from the cradle with a gesture of horror, backs swiftly toward the door in rear and goes out. A moment later she comes into the kitchen and, running to Eben, flings her arms about his neck and kisses him wildly. He hardens himself, he remains unmoved and cold, he keeps his eyes straight ahead.*)

ABBIE (*hysterically*): I done it, Eben! I told ye I'd do it! I've proved I love ye—better'n everythin'—so's ye can't never doubt me no more!

EBEN (*dully*): Whatever ye done, it hain't no good now.

ABBIE (*wildly*): Don't ye say that! Kiss me, Eben, won't ye? I need ye t' kiss me arter what I done! I need ye t' say ye love me!

EBEN (*kisses her without emotion—dully*): That's fur good-by. I'm a-goin' soon.

ABBIE: No! No! Ye won't go—not now!

EBEN (*going on with his own thoughts*): I been a-thinkin'—an' I hain't goin' t' tell Paw nothin'. I'll leave Maw t' take vengeance on ye. If I told him, the old skunk'd jest be stinkin' mean enuf to take it out on that baby. (*His voice showing emotion in spite of him.*) An' I don't want nothin' bad t' happen t' him. He hain't t' blame fur yew. (*He adds with a certain queer pride.*) An' he looks like me! An' by God, he's mine! An' some day I'll be a-comin' back an' . . . !

ABBIE (*too absorbed in her own thoughts to listen to him—pleadingly*): They's no cause fur ye t' go now—they's no sense—it's all the same's it was—they's nothin' come b'tween us now—arter what I done!

EBEN (*Something in her voice arouses him. He stares at her a bit frightenedly.*): Ye look mad, Abbie. What did ye do?

ABBIE: I—I killed him, Eben.

EBEN (*amazed*): Ye killed him?

ABBIE (*dully*): Ay-eh.

EBEN (*recovering from his astonishment—savagely*): An' serves him right! But we got t' do somethin' quick t' make it look s'if the old skunk'd killed himself when he was drunk. We kin prove by 'em all how drunk he got.

ABBIE (*wildly*): No! No! Not him! (*Laughing distractedly.*) But that's what I ought t' done, hain't it? I oughter killed him instead! Why didn't ye tell me?

EBEN (*appalled*): Instead? What d'ye mean?

ABBIE: Not him.

EBEN (*his face grown ghastly*): Not—not that baby!

ABBIE (*dully*): Ay-eh!

EBEN (*falls to his knees as if he'd been struck—his voice trembling with horror*): Oh, God A'mighty! A'mighty God! Maw, whar was ye, why didn't ye stop her?

ABBIE (*simply*): She went back t' her grave that night we fust done it, remember? I hain't felt her about since. (*A pause. Eben hides his head in his hands, trembling all over as if he had the ague. She goes on dully.*) I left the piller over his little face. Then he killed himself. He stopped breathin' (*She begins to weep softly.*)

EBEN (*rage beginning to mingle with grief*): He looked like me. He was mine, damn ye!

ABBIE (*slowly and brokenly*): I didn't want t' do it I hated myself fur doin' it. I loved him. He was so purty—dead spit 'n' image o' yew. But I loved yew more—an' yew was goin' away—far off whar I'd never see ye agen, never kiss ye, never feel ye pressed agin me agen—an' ye said ye hated me fur havin' him—ye said ye hated him an' wished he was dead—ye said if it hain't been fur him comin' it'd been the same's afore between us.

EBEN (*unable to endure this, springs to his feet in a fury, threatening her, his twitching fingers seeming to reach out for her throat*): Ye lie! I never said—I never dreamed ye'd—I'd cut off my head afore I'd hurt his finger!

ABBIE (*piteously, sinking on her knees*): Eben, don't ye look at me like that—hatin' me—not after what I done fur ye—fur us—so's we could be happy agen—

EBEN (*furiously now*): Shut up, or I'll kill ye! I see yer game now—the same old sneakin' trick—ye're aimin' t' blame me fur the murder ye done!

ABBIE (*moaning—putting her hands over her ears*): Don't ye, Eben! Don't ye! (*She grasps his legs.*)

EBEN (*his mood suddenly changing to horror, shrinks away from her*): Don't ye tech me! Ye're pizen! How could ye—t' murder a pore little critter—Ye must've swapped yer soul t' hell! (*Suddenly raging.*) Ha! I kin see why ye done it! Not the lies ye jest told—but 'cause ye wanted t' steal agen—steal the last thin' ye'd left me—my part o' him—no, the hull o' him—ye saw he looked like me—ye knowed he was all mine—an' ye couldn't b'ar it—I know ye! Ye killed him fur bein' mine! (*All this has driven him almost insane. He makes a rush past her for the door—then turns—shaking both fists at her, violently.*) But I'll take vengeance now! I'll git the Sheriff! I'll tell him everythin'! Then I'll sing "I'm off to Californi-a!" an' go—gold—Golden Gate—gold sun—fields o' gold in the West! (*This last he half shouts, half croons incoherently, suddenly breaking off passionately.*) I'm a-goin' fur the Sheriff t' come an' git ye! I want ye tuk away, locked up from me! I can't stand t' luk at ye! Murderer an' thief 'r not, ye still tempt me! I'll give ye up t' the Sheriff! (*He turns and runs out, around the corner of house, panting and sobbing, and breaks into a swerving sprint down the road.*)

ABBIE (*struggling to her feet, runs to the door, calling after him*): I love ye, Eben! I love ye! (*She stops at the door weakly, swaying, about to fall.*) I don't care what ye do—if ye'll on'y love me agen—(*She falls limply to the floor in a faint.*)

Scene IV

(*About an hour later. Same as scene III. Shows the kitchen and Cabot's bedroom. It is after dawn. The sky is brilliant with the sunrise. In the kitchen, Abbie sits at the table, her body limp and exhausted, her head bowed down over her arms, her face hidden. Upstairs, Cabot is still asleep but awakens with a start. He looks toward the window and gives a snort of surprise and irritation—throws back the covers and begins hurriedly pulling on his clothes. Without looking behind him, he begins talking to Abbie whom he supposes beside him.*)

CABOT: Thunder 'n' lightin', Abbie! I hain't slept this late in fifty year! Looks 's if the sun was full riz a'most. Must've been the dancin' an' likker. Must be gittin' old. I hope Eben's t' wuk. Ye might've tuk the trouble t' rouse me, Abbie. (*He turns—sees no one there—surprised.*) Waal—whar air she? Gittin' vittles, I calc'late. (*He tiptoes to the cradle and peers down—proudly.*) Mornin', sonny. Purty's a picter! Sleepin' sound. He don't beller all night like most o' 'em. (*He goes quietly out the door in rear—a few*

Paolo Schreiber (left) and Brian Dennehy play father and son, and Carla Gugino the father's new wife, in the production of *Desire under the Elms* directed by Robert Falls at the St. James Theater, 2009.

moments later enters kitchen—sees Abbie—with satisfaction.) So thar ye be. Ye got any vittles cooked?

ABBIE (*without moving*): No.

CABOT (*coming to her, almost sympathetically*): Ye feelin' sick?

ABBIE: No.

CABOT (*Pats her on shoulder. She shudders.*): Ye'd best lie down a spell. (*Half jocularly.*) Yer son'll be needin' ye soon. He'd ought t' wake up with a gnashin' appetite, the sound way he's sleepin'.

ABBIE (*shudders—then in a dead voice*): He hain't never goin' t' wake up.

CABOT (*jokingly*): Takes after me this mornin'. I hain't slept so late in . . .

ABBIE: He's dead.

CABOT (*stares at her—bewilderedly*): What. . . .

ABBIE: I killed him.

CABOT (*stepping back from her—aghast*): Air ye drunk—'r crazy—'r . . . ?

ABBIE (*suddenly lifts her head and turns on him—wildly*): I killed him, I tell ye! I smothered him. Go up an' see if ye don't b'lieve me!

(*Cabot stares at her a second, then bolts out the rear door, can be heard bounding up the stairs, and rushes into the bedroom and over to the cradle. Abbie has sunk back lifelessly into her former position. Cabot puts his hand down on the body in the crib. An expression of fear and horror comes over his face.*)

CABOT (*shrinking away—tremblingly*): God A'mighty! God A'mighty. (*He stumbles out the door—in a short while returns to the kitchen—comes to Abbie, the stunned expression still on his face—hoarsely.*) Why did ye do it? Why? (*As she doesn't answer, he grabs her violently by the shoulder and shakes her.*) I ax ye why ye done it! Ye'd better tell me 'r . . . !

ABBIE (*gives him a furious push which sends him staggering back and springs to her feet—with wild rage and hatred*): Don't ye dare tech me! What right hev ye t' question me 'bout him? He wa'n't yewr son! Think I'd have a son by yew? I'd die fust! I hate the sight o' ye an' allus did! It's yew I should've murdered, if I'd had good sense! I hate ye! I love Eben. I did from the fust. An' he was Eben's son—mine an' Eben's—not your'n!

CABOT (*stands looking at her dazedly—a pause—finding his words with an effort—dully*): That was it—what I felt—pokin' round the corners—while ye lied—holdin' yerself from me—sayin' ye'd already conceived—(*He lapses into crushed silence—then with a strange emotion.*) He's dead, sart'n. I felt his heart. Pore little critter! (*He blinks back one tear, wiping his sleeve across his nose.*)

ABBIE (*hysterically*): Don't ye! Don't ye! (*She sobs unrestrainedly.*)

CABOT (*with a concentrated effort that stiffens his body into a rigid line and hardens his face into a stony mask—through his teeth to himself*): I got t' be—like a stone—a rock o' jedgment! (*A pause. He gets complete control over himself—harshly*.) If he was Eben's, I be glad he air gone! An' mebbe I suspicioned it all along. I felt they was somethin' onnateral— somewhars—the house got so lonesome—an' cold— drivin' me down t' the barn—t' the beasts o' the field.... Ay-eh. I must've suspicioned—somethin'. Ye didn't fool me—not altogether, leastways—I'm too old a bird—growin' ripe on the bough.... (*He becomes aware he is wandering, straightens again, looks at Abbie with a cruel grin*.) So ye'd liked t' hev murdered me 'steed o' him, would ye? Waal, I'll live to a hundred! I'll live t' see ye hung! I'll deliver ye up t' the jedgment o' God an' the law! I'll git the Sheriff now. (*Starts for the door*.)

ABBIE (*dully*): Ye needn't. Eben's gone fur him.

CABOT (*amazed*): Eben—gone fur the Sheriff?

ABBIE: Ay-eh.

CABOT: T' inform agen ye?

ABBIE: Ay-eh.

CABOT (*considers this—a pause—then in a hard voice*): Waal, I'm thankful fur him savin' me the trouble. I'll git t' wuk. (*He goes to the door—then turns—in a voice full of strange emotion*.) He'd ought t' been my son, Abbie. Ye'd ought t' loved me. I'm a man. If ye'd loved me, I'd never told no Sheriff on ye no matter what ye did, if they was t' brile me alive!

ABBIE (*defensively*): They's more to it nor yew know, makes him tell.

CABOT (*dryly*): Fur yewr sake, I hope they be. (*He goes out—comes around to the gate—stares up at the sky. His control relaxes. For a moment he is old and weary. He murmurs despairingly*.) God A'mighty, I be lonesomer'n ever! (*He hears running footsteps from the left, immediately is himself again. Eben runs in, panting exhaustedly, wild-eyed and mad looking. He lurches through the gate. Cabot grabs him by the shoulder. Eben stares at him dumbly*.) Did ye tell the Sheriff?

EBEN (*nodding stupidly*): Ay-eh.

CABOT (*gives him a push away that sends him sprawling—laughing with withering contempt*): Good fur ye! A prime chip o' yer Maw ye be! (*He goes toward the barn, laughing harshly. Eben scrambles to his feet. Suddenly Cabot turns—grimly threatening*.) Git off this farm when the Sheriff takes her—or, by God, he'll have t' come back an' git me fur murder, too! (*He stalks off. Eben does not appear to have heard him. He runs to the door and comes into the kitchen. Abbie looks up with a cry of anguished joy. Eben stumbles over and throws himself on his knees beside her sobbing brokenly*.)

EBEN: Fergive me!

ABBIE (*happily*): Eben! (*She kisses him and pulls his head over against her breast*.)

EBEN: I love ye! Fergive me!

ABBIE (*ecstatically*): I'd fergive ye all the sins in hell fur sayin' that! (*She kisses his head, pressing it to her with a fierce passion of possession*.)

EBEN (*brokenly*): But I told the Sheriff. He's comin' fur ye!

ABBIE: I kin b'ar what happens t' me—now!

EBEN: I woke him up. I told him. He says, wait 'til I git dressed. I was waiting. I got to thinkin' o' yew. I got to thinkin' how I'd loved ye. It hurt like somethin' was bustin' in my chest an' head. I got t' cryin'. I knowed sudden I loved ye yet, an' allus would love ye!

ABBIE (*caressing his hair—tenderly*): My boy, hain't ye?

EBEN: I begun t' run back. I cut across the fields an' through the woods. I thought ye might have time t' run away—with me—an' ...

ABBIE (*shaking her head*): I got t' take my punishment— t' pay fur my sin.

EBEN: Then I want t' share it with ye.

ABBIE: Ye didn't do nothin'.

EBEN: I put it in yer head. I wisht he was dead! I as much as urged ye t' do it!

ABBIE: No. It was me alone!

EBEN: I'm as guilty as yew be! He was the child o' our sin.

ABBIE (*lifting her head as if defying God*): I don't repent that sin! I hain't askin' God t' fergive that!

EBEN: Nor me—but it led up t' the other—an' the murder ye did, ye did 'count o' me—an' it's my murder, too, I'll tell the Sheriff—an' if ye deny it, I'll say we planned it t'gether—an' they'll all b'lieve me, fur they suspicion everythin' we've done, an' it'll seem likely an' true to 'em. An' it is true—way down. I did help ye—somehow.

ABBIE (*laying her head on his—sobbing*): No! I don't want yew t' suffer!

EBEN: I got t' pay fur my part o' the sin! An' I'd suffer wuss leavin' ye, goin' West, thinkin' o' ye day an' night, bein' out when yew was in—(*lowering his voice*) 'r bein' alive when yew was dead. (*A pause*.) I want t' share with ye, Abbie—prison 'r death 'r hell 'r anythin'! (*He looks into her eyes and forces a trembling smile*.) If I'm sharin' with ye, I won't feel lonesome, leastways.

ABBIE (*weakly*): Eben! I won't let ye! I can't let ye!

EBEN (*kissing her—tenderly*): Ye can't he'p yerself. I got ye beat fur once!

ABBIE (*forcing a smile—adoringly*): I hain't beat— s'long's I got ye!

EBEN (*hears the sound of feet outside*): Ssshh! Listen! They've come t' take us!

ABBIE: No, it's him. Don't give him no chance to fight ye, Eben. Don't say nothin'—no matter what he says. An' I won't neither. (*It is Cabot. He comes up from the barn in a great state of excitement and strides into the house and then into the kitchen. Eben is kneeling beside Abbie, his arm around her, hers around him. They stare straight ahead*.)

CABOT (*Stares at them, his face hard. A long pause— vindictively*.): Ye make a slick pair o' murderin' turtle doves! Ye'd ought t' be both hung on the same limb an' left thar t' swing in the breeze an' rot—a warnin' t' old fools like me t' b'ar their lonesomeness alone—an' fur young fools like ye t' hobble their lust.

(*A pause. The excitement returns to his face, his eyes snap, he looks a bit crazy.*) I couldn't work today. I couldn't take no interest. T' hell with the farm! I'm leavin' it! I've turned the cows an' other stock loose! I've druv 'em into the woods whar they kin be free! By freein' 'em, I'm freein' myself! I'm quittin' here today! I'll set fire t' house an' barn an' watch 'em burn, an' I'll leave yer Maw t' haunt the ashes, an' I'll will the fields back t' God, so that nothin' human kin never touch 'em! I'll be a-goin' to Californi-a—t' jine Simeon an' Peter—true sons o' mine if they be dumb fools—an' the Cabots'll find Solomon's Mines t'gether! (*He suddenly cuts a mad caper.*) Whoop! What was the song they sung? "Oh, Californi-a! That's the land fur me." (*He sings this—then gets on his knees by the floorboard under which the money was hid.*) An' I'll sail thar on one o' the finest clippers I kin find! I've got the money! Pity ye didn't know whar this was hidden so's ye could steal. . . . (*He has pulled up the board. He stares—feels—stares again. A pause of dead silence. He slowly turns, slumping into a sitting position on the floor, his eyes like those of a dead fish, his face the sickly green of an attack of nausea. He swallows painfully several times—forces a weak smile at last.*) So—ye did steal it!

EBEN (*emotionlessly*): I swapped it t' Sim an' Peter fur their share o' the farm—t' pay their passage t' Californi-a.

CABOT (*with one sardonic*): Ha! (*He begins to recover. Gets slowly to his feet—strangely.*) I calc'late God give it to 'em—not yew! God's hard, not easy! Mebbe they's easy gold in the West but it hain't God's gold. It hain't fur me. I kin hear His voice warnin' me agen t' be hard an' stay on my farm. I kin see his hand usin' Eben t' steal t' keep me from weakness. I kin feel I be in the palm o' His hand, His fingers guidin' me. (*A pause—then he mutters sadly.*) It's a-goin' t' be lonesomer now than ever it war afore—an' I'm gittin'

old, Lord—ripe on the bough. . . . (*Then stiffening.*) Waal—what d'ye want? God's lonesome, hain't He? God's hard an' lonesome! (*A pause. The Sheriff with two men comes up the road from the left. They move cautiously to the door. The Sheriff knocks on it with the butt of his pistol.*)

SHERIFF: Open in the name o' the law! (*They start.*)

CABOT: They've come fur ye. (*He goes to the rear door.*) Come in, Jim! (*The three men enter. Cabot meets them in doorway.*) Jest a minit, Jim. I got 'em safe here. (*The Sheriff nods. He and his companions remain in the doorway.*)

EBEN (*suddenly calls*): I lied this mornin', Jim. I helped her to do it. Ye kin take me, too.

ABBIE (*brokenly*): No!

CABOT: Take 'em both. (*He comes forward—stares at Eben with a trace of grudging admiration.*) Purty good—fur yew! Waal, I got t' round up the stock. Good-by.

EBEN: Good-by.

ABBIE: Good-by. (*Cabot turns and strides past the men—comes out and around the corner of the house, his shoulders squared, his face stony, and stalks grimly toward the barn. In the meantime the Sheriff and men have come into the room.*)

SHERIFF (*embarrassedly*): Waal—we'd best start.

ABBIE: Wait. (*Turns to Eben.*) I love ye, Eben.

EBEN: I love ye, Abbie. (*They kiss. The three men grin and shuffle embarrassedly. Eben takes Abbie's hand. They go out the door in rear, the men following, and come from the house, walking hand in hand to the gate. Eben stops there and points to the sunrise sky.*) Sun's a-rizin'. Purty, hain't it?

ABBIE: Ay-eh. (*They both stand for a moment looking up raptly in attitudes strangely aloof and devout.*)

SHERIFF (*looking around at the farm enviously—to his companions*): It's a jim-dandy farm, no denyin'. Wished I owned it!

COMMENTARY

ROGER ASSELINEAU 1915–2002

The Quest for God in *Desire Under the Elms* 1969

Roger Asselineau was a professor of American literature at the Sorbonne in Paris. In this excerpt from his essay "*Desire Under the Elms*: A Phase of Eugene O'Neill's Philosophy," he explores the play as "a philosophical tragedy" about the relationship between man and God.

Though to all appearances O'Neill was primarily a playwright and an experimenter with dramatic forms who never considered himself a thinker, he was in fact desperately trying to express "something" in all his plays. He chose drama as a medium, but, for all his interest in technique, he never considered it an end in itself, but rather a means to live by proxy a certain number of problems which obsessed him. In *Lazarus Laughed*, he speaks of men as "those haunted heroes." Actually this is less a definition of mankind than a description of himself. He composed plays because he *had* to write in order to liberate himself and exorcise ghosts. It was a compulsion. The result was plays because of his environment, because his father was an actor and he was an "enfant de la balle," but it might have been novels just as well, and he would probably have written better novels than plays, for he was constantly hampered by the limitations of the stage. In his case literary creation was not a gratuitous activity, but an intense imaginative experience, an "*Erlebnis.*" He lived it. It was a passionate answer to the problems which tormented him with excruciating strength. This is no mere figure of speech. He roamed the world for years in search of a solution, trying to find a remedy for his fundamental despair, giving up the comfort and security of family life and nearly losing his health and life in the process.

After his wandering years, his *Wanderjahre,* when his health broke down and he was obliged to bring his restless comings-and-goings to a close, he went on exploring the world in imagination, not as a dilettante or a tourist in the realms of thought, but as a passionate pilgrim in quest of a shrine at which to worship. Though brought up a Roman Catholic, he lost his faith as an adolescent. Yet his nature abhorred this spiritual vacuum and he ardently looked for a substitute ever after. His religious faith was killed by rationalism and scientific materialism, but the restlessness and violence of his quest for a personal religion sprang from no coldly rational intellect.

Each of his plays is thus not only an experiment in craftsmanship, but also an attempt to find God or at least some justification for the flagrant inconsistencies of the human condition. His interest was less in psychology than in metaphysics. He said so himself in a letter to Joseph Wood Krutch: "Most modern plays are concerned with the relation between man and man, but that does not interest me at all. I am interested only in the relation between man and God."

In spite of its apparent dramatic directness therefore, *Desire Under the Elms* is essentially, like his other plays, a philosophical tragedy about man and God rather than a naturalistic chunk of life depicting the mores of a bunch of clumsy New England rustics.

Animal Nature of Man

Reduced to essentials in this very primitive setting man appears primarily as an animal. The first specimens whom we have a chance to observe when the curtain rises, Eben and especially Simeon and Peter, look like oxen, eat, work and behave like a team of oxen, and feel tied up to the other animals of the farm by bonds of brotherhood: ". . . the cows knows us . . . An' the hosses, an' pigs, an' chickens . . . They knows us like brothers—and likes us" (Part I, scene 4). They obey their instincts blindly and think only of drinking, eating and fornicating. Their lust is quite literally bestial as is shown by Eben's account of his visit to Min: "I begun t'beller like a calf an' cuss at the same time . . . an' she got scared, an' I just grabbled holt an' tuk her" (Part I, scene 3). When Abbie courts Eben, the scene is not much different.

She kisses him greedily and at first he submits dumbly, but soon, after returning her kisses he hurls her away from him and, O'Neill tells us, "they stand speechless and breathless, panting like two animals" (Part II, scene 2).

These inarticulate, animal-like creatures differ from their dumb brothers in only one respect (but it is hardly an improvement): they are possessed with the mania of owning things, whether gold or land. They all crave for money or title-deeds. In short, they bear a strong family likeness to Swift's Yahoos. They have only one redeeming feature: an embryonic sense of beauty which makes them exclaim "purty" in a rather monotonous manner whenever they notice the beauty of their surroundings. The only exception is the sheriff, who at the very end of the play passes very matter-of-fact and anti-climactic comments on the salable value of the farm while Eben and Abbie admire the beauty of the sunrise.

Man Trapped by Circumstance

Far from being a free agent, man is thus by and large the slave of his instincts and O'Neill here revives the old Calvinistic dogma of predestination. As early as his very first play, *The Web*, of the transparent title, he attempted to show that man is caught in a web of circumstances, a web that is not of his own weaving. At the end of *The Web*, O'Neill tells us that Rose, the prostitute, "seems to be aware of something in the room which none of the others can see—perhaps the personification of the ironic life force that has crushed her." In *Desire Under the Elms* Eben feels trapped in exactly the same way: "Each day," the stage directions inform us, "is a cage in which he finds himself trapped." He is indeed trapped by circumstances—tied up to that bleak New England farm which he somehow considers part of his mother, and he is also psychologically trapped by an all-powerful mother-complex which unknown to him determines his whole behavior towards his father as well as towards women in general. His temperament is wholly determined by his heredity: it is a combination of his mother's softness and lack of will, as his father again and again points out, and of his father's aggressiveness and obstinacy, as his two elder brothers repeatedly tell us: "he is a chip off the old block, the spitting image of his father. . . ."

As to Abbie, she is just as trapped as he is. When she enters the stage, we are warned that she has "the same unsettled, untamed, desperate quality which is so apparent in Eben." And shortly afterwards we learn that she "was a orphan early an' had t'wuk fur others in other folks' hums" and her first husband "turned out a drunken spreer" and got sick and died. She then felt free again only to discover that all she was free for was to work again "in other folks' hums, doin' other folks' wuk" till she had almost given up hope of ever doing her own work in her own home (Part I, scene 4).

Ephraim Cabot himself, for all his will-power and vigor, is caught in the same web as the others. His whole behavior is conditioned by his Puritan upbringing. He cannot think of anything but work, hard work on a barren New England farm. "*Laborare est orare*," Carlyle claimed, "work is worship." Ephraim Cabot is a degenerate Puritan. Work has ceased to be a form of worship for him, yet he believes in its virtue and absolute value because he has been brought up that way. He once tried to escape this self-imposed serfdom. Like many other New Englanders, he went West and in the broad meadows of the central plains found black soil as rich as gold, without a stone. He had only to plough and sow and then sit and smoke his pipe and watch things grow. He could have become a rich man and led an easy and idle life, but he preferred to give it up and return to his New England farm and to hard work on a stony soil, which proves the extraordinary strength of his Puritan compulsions. They practically deprived him of his freedom of choice.

So, at the start at least, the three major characters of *Desire Under the Elms* are not free. They bear psychological or moral chains. Consequently, they cannot be held responsible for their actions, and Simeon with his peasant shrewdness is perfectly aware of it. When Eben accuses his father of killing his "Maw," Simeon retorts: "No one never kills nobody. It's allus somethin' that's the murderer" (Part I, scene 2). "Somethin'," that is to say one of those mysterious things which impel men to act this way or that, whether they like it or not, whether they are aware of it or not. This is a modified form of Puritan pessimism: all men are sinners in the clutches of Satan—or of God who is always "nagging his sheep to sin" (Part I, scene 4), the better to punish them afterwards, always ready to smite his undutiful sons with his worst curse.

The Redeeming Power of Passion

How can a man save his soul under such circumstances? Though, theoretically, O'Neill's approach is strictly nontheological and he is not concerned with the problem of salvation, he is constantly obsessed with it all the same and in this particular play, he gives it a Nietzschean answer: passion. Passion alone, he suggests, can enable man to transcend his animal nature. He repeatedly exalts the purity and transfiguring power of love. Eben's passion for Abbie which at first is mere lust soon becomes love—and there is a difference in kind between the two. The passage from lust to love is similar to the transmutation of lead into gold. Whereas lust, which is tied to the body, is finite and transient, love, which transcends the body, is infinite and eternal. Abbie kills her infant son to prove her love to Eben, and at the end of scene 3 of Part III proclaims that her love for Eben will never change, whatever he does to her. The play ends on an apotheosis of love. The two lovers stand "looking up raptly in attitudes strangely aloof and devout" at the "purty" rising sun, which contrasts with the pallid setting sun that lit up the opening of the play, at a time when everything took place on the plane of coarse material things and lust.

Man can thus be redeemed by a great passion and save his soul and attain grandeur. The farm under the elms, which looked so sordid when the curtain rose, witnesses a sublime *dénouement* and at the end almost becomes one of those places where the spirit bloweth.

The reason for this extraordinary change is that, in Hamlet's words:

There are more things in heaven and earth ...
Than are dreamt of in all [our] philosophy,

as Cabot again and again feels, for all his hardness and insensitivity: "They's thin's pokin' about in the dark—in the corners" (Part II, scene 2). "Even the music can't drive it out—somethin'. Ye kin feel it droppin' off the elums, climbin' up the roof, sneakin' down the chimney, pokin' in the corners. They's no peace in houses, they's no rest livin' with folks. Somethin's always livin' with ye ..." (Part III, scene 2).

God in Nature

What is that "somethin'" whose presence disturbs him? It is the "Desire" of the title—an irresistible life-force (somewhat similar to G. B. Shaw's), which flows through the elms and through old Cabot himself sometimes, as when it makes him leave his farm in spring and go in search of a new wife. But it is especially powerful in Eben and Abbie. It is that thing which makes Eben look like a wild animal in captivity when he enters the stage and feel "inwardly unsubdued." It is quite impersonal and Eben refers to it in the neuter: "I kin feel it growin' in me—growin' an' growin'—till it'll bust out" (Part I, scene 2). It is the magnetic force which draws Eben to Abbie through walls and partitions (Part II, scene 2). It is Nature—and Abbie intones a hymn to her—or it—in her own inarticulate way when she presses Eben to yield to his passion: "Hain't the sun strong an' hot? Ye kin feel it burnin' into the earth—Nature—makin' thin's grow—bigger 'n' bigger—burnin' inside ye—makin' ye want t'grow—into somethin' else—till ye are jined with it—an' it's your'n—but it owns ye—too—an' makes ye grow bigger—like a tree—like them elums" (Part II, scene 1).

In short, the "Desire" which flows through the elms and drips from them and pervades everything under them is God—though the word is never used. It is not, however, the God of the Christians, but rather a dynamic, impersonal, pantheistic or panpsychistic deity present in all things, whether animate or inanimate, breaking barriers between individuals as in the case of Eben and Abbie, dissolving their lonesomeness and making them feel one. In a way it is a pagan God, a Dionysian deity, for it partly manifests itself in the form of carnal desire. Under its influence, Eben and Cabot become inspired poets (in prose) and sing woman, the lovely incarnation of the soft and warm goddess of fertility and life: "She's like t'night, she's soft 'n' warm, her eyes kin wink like a star, her mouth's wa'm, her arms're wa'm. She smells like a wa'm plowed field, she's purty" (Part I, scene 2). "Yew air my Rose o' Sharon! Behold! yew air fair; yer eyes air doves; yer lips air like scarlet; yer two breasts air like two fawns; yer navel be like a round goblet; yer belly be like a heap o' wheat," exclaims old Cabot echoing chapters 4 and 7 of the Song of Solomon.

This omnipresent God is fundamentally a cosmic sexual urge, spontaneous, beautiful, unselfish and amoral. In this perspective the notion of sin becomes meaningless. "He was the child of our sin," says Eben of the baby, but Abbie proudly answers "as if defying God" (the God of the Christians): "I don't repent that sin. I ain't askin' God t'fergive that" (Part III, scene 4). The two lovers have gone back to the Garden of Eden from which Adam and Eve were expelled. They have become "Children of Adam," to take up Walt Whitman's phrase.

The life-force, the desire which circulates through the elms as well as through the *dramatis personae* is the very reverse of the God worshipped by Ephraim Cabot, which has the hardness and immobility of a stone—and the sterility of one (Part II, scene 2). His God is the God of repression and lonesomeness and hard work—the God humorously called up by Robert Frost in "Of the Stones of the Place" and to some extent a duplicate of Robinson Jeffers's anti-human God.

Abbie, on the contrary, recommends to yield to the life impulse, to let Nature speak at every hazard "without check with original energy." It is against nature, it is impious, she claims, to resist its will: "It's agin nature, Eben. Ye been fightin' yer nature ever since the day I come. . . ." (Part II, scene 1).

This is a combination of Nietzsche's Dionysian philosophy and Freudianism and in *Desire Under the Elms* it leads—in spite of the Dostoevskian quality of the *Crime and Punishment* situation at the end of the play—to an optimistic conclusion: the couple Eben-Abbie is not crushed by adverse circumstances. They have fulfilled themselves, they have fully lived and, far from being driven to despair by their trials, they are full of a strange "hopeless hope" when the curtain falls.

Bertolt Brecht

"Whenever I teach
playwriting I use
Mother Courage."

–Tony Kushner

Among the most inventive and influential of modern playwrights, Bertolt Brecht (1898–1956) left a legacy of important plays and theories about how those plays should be produced. Throughout most of his career, he believed that drama should inform and awaken sensibilities, not just entertain or anesthetize an audience. Most of his plays concern philosophical and political issues, and some of them so threatened the Nazi regime that his works were burned publicly in Germany during the Third Reich.

At nineteen, Brecht worked as an orderly in a hospital during the last months of World War I. Seeing so much carnage and misery in the medical wards made him a lifelong pacifist. After the war, while a student in Munich, he began writing plays. His first successes in the Munich theater took the form of commentary on returned war veterans and on the questions of duty and heroism—two concepts that Brecht viewed negatively. His rejection of spiritual concepts was influenced by his reading of Hegel and of Marx's doctrine of dialectical materialism. Marx's theories predicted class struggles and based most social values in economic realities. Brecht eventually moved to Berlin, the theatrical center of Germany, and by 1926 was on his way to becoming a Communist.

Finding the political pressures in early Nazi Germany too frightening and dangerous for his writing, Brecht went into exile in 1933. He lived for a time in Scandinavia and later in the United States. After World War II Brecht and his wife returned to Berlin where, in 1949, he founded the Berliner Ensemble, which produced most of his later work. Brecht chose East Berlin as his home, in part because he believed his work could best be understood in a Communist setting. One irony is that his work has been even more widely appreciated and accepted in the West than in the countries of the former Communist eastern bloc.

In 1928 Brecht wrote his most popular play, a musical on which he collaborated with the German composer Kurt Weill: *The Threepenny Opera*. The model for this play, the English writer John Gay's 1728 ballad opera *The Beggar's Opera*, provided Brecht with a perfect platform for commenting satirically on the political and economic circumstances in Germany two hundred years after Gay wrote. The success of the Brecht–Weill collaboration—the work is still performed regularly—is due in part to Brecht's capacity to create appealing underworld characters such as Polly Peachum and Macheath, known as Mack the Knife. Brecht's wife, Helene Weigel, played Mrs. Peachum, the madam of the brothel in which the action takes place. Kurt Weill's second wife, Lotte Lenya, was an overnight sensation in the part of Jenny. She had a highly acclaimed reprise in New York almost twenty-five years after the play's premiere.

Brecht's most successful plays are *Galileo* (1938–1939), *Mother Courage and Her Children* (1941), *The Good Woman of Setzuan* (1943), *The Private Lives of the Master Race* (1945), and *The Caucasian Chalk Circle* (1948). But these represent only a tiny fraction of a mass of work that includes plays, poetry, criticism, and fiction. Brecht's output is extraordinary in volume and quality. It includes plays adapted from the work not only of Gay but also of Sophocles, Molière, Gorky, Shakespeare, and John Webster, among others.

For links to resources about
Brecht, click on
AuthorLinks at
bedfordstmartins.com/jacobus.

Brecht developed a number of theories regarding drama. He used the term *epic theater* to distinguish his own theater from traditional Aristotelian drama. Brecht expected his audience to observe critically, to draw conclusions, and to participate in an intellectual argument with the work at hand. The confrontational relationship he intended was designed to engage the audience in analyzing what they saw rather than in identifying with the main characters or in enjoying a wash of sentimentality or emotion.

One of the ways Brecht achieved his ends was by making a production's props, lights, sets, and equipment visible, thereby reminding the members of the audience that they were seeing a play. He used the term **alienation** to define the effect he wanted his theater to have on an audience. He hoped that by alienating his audience from the drama, he would keep them emotionally detached and intellectually alert. Brecht's theater was political. He saw a connection between an audience that could analyze theater critically and an audience that could analyze reality critically—and see that social, political, and economic conditions were not "natural" or fixed immutably but could (and should) be changed.

Brecht's theories produced interesting results and helped stimulate audiences that expected to be entertained by realistic or sentimental plays. His style spread rapidly throughout the world of theater, and it is still being used and developed by contemporary playwrights such as Suzan-Lori Parks and Tony Kushner.

Mother Courage and Her Children

Since *Mother Courage and Her Children* was first produced in 1941 in Zurich, it has become a classic of modern theater, performed successfully in the United States and most other Western countries. Brecht conceived of the drama as a powerful antiwar play. He set it in Germany during the Thirty Years' War, in which German Protestants, supported by countries such as France, Denmark, and England, fought against the Hapsburg empire, which was allied with the Holy Roman Empire and the German Catholic princes. The war was actually a combination of many wars fought during the period of thirty years. It was bloody and seemingly interminable, devastating Germany's towns and citizenry as well as its agriculture and commerce. The armies fought to control territory and economic markets; also underlying the war were longstanding religious differences between German Lutherans and Roman Catholics.

Brecht was not interested in the immediate causes of the Thirty Years' War. He was making a case against war entirely, regardless of its cause. To do this, he deliberately avoided making his play realistic. The stage setting is essentially barren, and the play is structured in scenes that are very intense but that avoid any sense of continuity of action. Audiences cannot become involved in unfolding action; they must always remain conscious of themselves as audience.

For discussion questions and assignments on *Mother Courage,* visit **bedfordstmartins.com/jacobus**.

Moreover, the lighting is high-intensity, almost cruel at times, spotlighting the action in a way that is completely unnatural. In the early productions, Brecht included slide projections of the headings that accompany each of the twelve scenes so that the audience was always reminded of the presence of the playwright and the fact that they were seeing a play. These headings provided yet another break in the continuity of the action.

Although the printed text does not convey it, the play as Brecht produced it employed long silences, some of which were unsettling to the audience. When Swiss Cheese, Mother Courage's "honest son," has a moment of rest in scene 3, he is in an intense ring of stage light as he comments on sitting in the sun in his shirtsleeves. As Swiss Cheese relaxes for the last time, the intense light becomes an ironic device; it seems to expose him as a thief, and he is dragged off to his death. Although he is Mother Courage's "honest son," circumstances make it seem that he has been corrupted by the war, like everyone else.

Mother Courage herself lives off the war by selling goods to the soldiers. She and her children haul their wagon across the battlefields with no concern for who is winning, who is losing, or even where they are. Her only ambition is to stock her wagon, sell her goods, and make sure she does not get stuck with any useless inventory. When the chaplain tells her that peace has broken out, she laments their condition—without war the family has no livelihood.

As Mother Courage continues to pull her wagon across field after field, she learns how to survive. But she also loses her children, one by one, to the war. Eilif, seduced into joining the army by a recruitment officer, is led into battle thinking that war is a heroic adventure. Swiss Cheese thinks he has found a good deal in a paymaster's uniform. Both are wrong; there is no security in war, and they eventually perish.

Kattrin, the daughter, is likewise a victim of the violence of war. Having been violated by a Swedish soldier, she becomes mute. Near the end of the play she is treated violently again, and the terrible scar on her face leaves her unmarriageable. At the end Kattrin dies while sounding an alarm to warn the sleeping town of an imminent attack.

Finally, Mother Courage is left alone. She picks up her wagon and finds that she can maneuver it herself. The play ends as she circles the stage, with everything around her consumed by war.

Brecht's stated intentions were somewhat thwarted by the reactions of the play's first audiences. They were struck by the power of Brecht's characterization of Mother Courage and treated her with immense sympathy. They saw her as an indomitable woman whose strength in the face of adversity was so great that she could not be overwhelmed. But Brecht intended the audience to analyze Mother Courage further and to see in her a reflection of society's wrong values. She conducts business on the field of battle, paying no attention to the moral question of war itself. She makes her living from the war but cannot see that it is the war that causes her anguish.

In response to audiences' sympathetic reactions, Brecht revised the play, adding new lines to help audiences see the venality of Mother Courage's motives. But subsequent audiences have continued to treat her as a survivor—almost a biblical figure. Brecht's German critics saw her as one whose endurance of all the terrors of war testifies to the resilience of humankind. No matter how one decides to interpret her, Mother Courage remains one of the most unusual and haunting characters in modern drama.

Mother Courage and Her Children in Performance

Brecht wrote *Mother Courage* in three months, beginning in September 1939, while he and Helene Weigel were in Sweden, in exile from Nazi Germany. Its first production was on April 19, 1941, in Zurich, Switzerland, while Brecht waited in Sweden for entry papers to the United States. Brecht and Weigel returned to Europe after the war. In 1948 they went to East Berlin to work with a new theater group explicitly to produce *Mother Courage* with Helene Weigel in the title role; the production opened in January 1949. In October 1950 Brecht directed Thérèsa Giehse as Courage in Munich. Other productions were staged in provincial German towns and in other European cities, such as Rotterdam and Paris, both in 1951.

Brecht's productions are sometimes regarded as "canonical," although contemporary directors often modify his original plans. He usually began the performance with a half-curtain and a four-person orchestra playing an overture. Next, an unseen record player played a song associated with Courage; as Courage came on stage, she sang the second verse of her song herself. The stage had only a **cyclorama**, a large curved curtain used as a backdrop, and a circle marked on the floor. This defined the space that was Mother Courage's world, and various sets were placed on the circle to accommodate successive scenes. The circle itself was a revolving turntable on which the wagon moved, going essentially nowhere. Brecht used placards to signal changes in time and place as well as to indicate events in the life of Mother Courage and her children. The lighting was generally bright, and the effect was lively and colorful.

Brecht's plays were not widely produced in the West during the cold war, but Leon Epp directed *Mother Courage* at the Volkstheater in Vienna in 1963. In the same year Jerome Robbins produced the play at the Martin Beck Theatre on Broadway, with sets by Ming Cho Lee. Anne Bancroft played Mother Courage, and Zohra Lampert was Kattrin. The reviews praised Bancroft for achievhing a "lonely magnificence" at the end of the play and maintained that Brecht generated a considerable emotional intensity despite his theoretical distaste for such effects.

The next year Joseph Slowik produced the play in the Goodman Theatre in Chicago with students playing some of the roles and the distinguished Eugenie Leontovich as Mother Courage. In England *Mother Courage* was produced twice in the 1950s in London. In 1961 and 1965 it was produced by the Old Vic. Numerous local theaters put on the play in the late 1960s and 1970s. In 1980 Ntozake Shange adapted the play for its second New York production, resetting it in the period after the American Civil War; Gloria Foster and Morgan Freeman had the major roles. Frank Rich praised the acting and the energy of the play but feared that Brecht's original vision had been altered almost beyond recognition: Mother Courage becomes "an innocent victim of an entire system," which is exactly what Brecht argued against.

The Royal Shakespeare Company produced the play in London in 1984 with Judi Dench as Courage and Zoë Wanamaker as Kattrin. Both received fine reviews, as did the production itself. Diana Rigg was Mother Courage in the production at the Olivier Theatre in London (November 1995–January 1996), which featured a new colloquial translation by the playwright David Hare and reset the play in the period of World War I. Like all productions of the play, this one maintained the circular set that Brecht had originally used and experimented with Brecht's theories of alienation and distancing.

Gwendolyn Mulamba played Mother Courage in the Classical Theatre of Harlem's production in New York City in February 2004. Christopher McElroen directed. In the summer of 2006, Kevin Kline and Meryl Streep starred in George Wolfe's production of *Mother Courage* at Shakespeare in the Park Public Theater, based on a new translation of the play by Tony Kushner. Clearly, Brecht's play speaks to all of us in the twenty-first century.

BERTOLT BRECHT (1898–1956)

Mother Courage and Her Children   1941
A Chronicle of the Thirty Years' War

TRANSLATED BY TONY KUSHNER

Characters

MOTHER COURAGE
KATTRIN, *her mute daughter*
EILIF, *her oldest son*
SWISS CHEESE, *her youngest son*
THE SERGEANT *in Scene One*
THE ARMY RECRUITER
THE COOK
THE GENERAL
THE CHAPLAIN
THE QUARTERMASTER
YVETTE POTTIER
THE ONE WITH THE EYEPATCH
THE COLONEL
THE SERGEANT *in Scene Three*
THE CLERK
THE YOUNG SOLDIER
THE OLDER SOLDIER
THE FARMER *in Scene Five*
THE FARMER'S WIFE *in Scene Five*
THE REGIMENTAL SECRETARY
THE OLD WOMAN
THE YOUNG MAN
THE VOICE INSIDE
THE LIEUTENANT
THE FARMER *in Scene Eleven*
THE FARMER'S WIFE *in Scene Eleven*
THE FARMER'S SON
SOLDIERS

ONE

Spring 1624. The Protestant King of Sweden invades Catholic Poland. Recruiters for the Swedish General Oxenstjerna° search in Dalarna° for soldiers. The merchant, Anna Fierling, who goes by the name Mother Courage, loses a son.

A road outside of town.

A Sergeant and an Army Recruiter stand waiting, shivering.

THE ARMY RECRUITER: How's a recruiter going to find recruits in a place like this? Orders from the General Staff, *four fresh companies* in two weeks time! I contemplate suicide, Sergeant. And the people here are so lacking in fundamental decency they've given me insomnia! Imagine if you will some jerk, concave chest, veiny legs, a total zero. I buy him beers till he's shit-faced, he signs up, and then: I'm paying the tab, he's off to take a leak, he says, I try to keep an eye on him because I've learned the smell of rat, and sure enough, zzzzzzzip! Jump up and fled like a louse flees louse-powder. A handshake's meaningless, honour and duty

---

Oxenstjerna: Axel Oxenstierna (1583–1654) was Governor-General of Prussia during the Thirty Years' War (1618–1648), which was largely a war between Catholics and Protestants and resulted in the destruction of more lives per capita than any war since.   **Dalarna:** A province of Sweden.

are empty words. A place like this, you lose your conviction in the Inner Goodness of Man, Sergeant.

THE SERGEANT: The problem with these people is they haven't had enough war. Where else do morals come from? War! Everything rots in peacetime. People turn into carefree rutting animals and nobody fucking cares. Everyone overeats, whatever they want, 'Oh I'll just sit down now and eat a big cheese and fatback sandwich on fluffy white bread.' Think these people know how many young men and horses they've got? Why count? It's peacetime! I've been in some towns that've gone seventy years without any war whatsoever, people hadn't even bothered naming their children, no one knew whose was whose. You need a bit of butchery to get them counting and listing and naming: big piles of empty boots, corn bagged for portage, man and cow alike stamped and mobilised. War makes order, order makes war.

THE ARMY RECRUITER: Amen.

THE SERGEANT: It isn't easy, starting a war, but nothing worthwhile is easy. And once you're in, you're hooked like a gambler, you can't afford to walk away from the crapshoot once you're deep into it. You become as afraid of peace as you ever were of war, no one really wants the fighting to end. You just have to get people used to the idea. Everyone's scared of anything changing.

THE ARMY RECRUITER: Heads up, a wagon. Two boys appropriate age. Tell 'em to pull over. If this goes bust I'm packing it in, I'm kissing the April wind goodbye.

(*A Jew's harp offstage. A canteen wagon comes down the road. It's pulled by two young men, Eilif and Swiss Cheese. In the wagon, driving it, Mother Courage; seated beside her, playing the Jew's harp, her mute daughter Kattrin.*)

MOTHER COURAGE: Morning, Sergeant.

(*The Sergeant blocks the wagon.*)

THE SERGEANT: Morning, people. Declare yourselves!

MOTHER COURAGE: Retail!

(*She sings:*)
To feed a war you have to pillage,
But let your soldiers rest a bit:
For what they need, here's Mother Courage,
With woolen coats and boots that fit!
Their heads ablaze with lice and liquor,
The boys are marching to the beat!
I guarantee they'll step it quicker
With boots upon their blistered feet!

MOTHER COURAGE AND HER SONS (*singing*):
Now Spring has come, and Winter's dead.
The snow has gone, so draw a breath!
Let Christian souls crawl out of bed,
Pull on their socks and conquer death!

MOTHER COURAGE (*singing*):
Unless his belly's full of porridge,
A soldier's sure to turn and run.
Buy him some grub from Mother Courage—
So he'll know where to point his gun.
They fight for God and legal tender,
I'll see them clothed, and feed them well,

And bless the boys, in all their splendour,
As they march down the road to hell.

MOTHER COURAGE AND HER SONS (*singing*):
Now Spring has come, and Winter's dead.
The snow has gone, so draw a breath!
Let Christian souls crawl out of bed,
Pull on their socks and conquer death!

(*The wagon starts to roll again. Again the Sergeant blocks it.*)

THE SERGEANT: Hang on a minute, garbage. What's your regiment?

EILIF: Second Finnish.

THE SERGEANT: Paperwork!

MOTHER COURAGE: Paperwork?

SWISS CHEESE: She's Mother Courage.

THE SERGEANT: I never heard of her. Why's she called 'Courage'?

MOTHER COURAGE: They called me Courage because I was scared of financial ruin, Sergeant, so I drove my wagon straight through the cannon fire at Riga, with fifty loaves of bread turning mouldy—I didn't see that I had a choice.

THE SERGEANT: Fascinating, now I know your life's story, gimme your paperwork.

(*Mother Courage reaches behind her, finds a battered tin box, removes a big stack of tattered paper. She climbs down off the wagon.*)

MOTHER COURAGE: Here's paper, all I possess. A prayer book I bought in Alt-Ötting,° I use the pages to wrap pickles, and a map of Moravia, will I ever get to Moravia? God knows. If I don't the map's for the cat to shit on. And here, official proof my horse doesn't have hoof-and-mouth disease, which is swell except the horse is dead, poor thing, fifteen guilders she cost, although praise Jesus, not *my* fifteen guilders. I have more paper if you want it.

THE SERGEANT: What I want is, I want your licence to sell. You want my boot up your ass?

MOTHER COURAGE: Excuse me but you may not discuss my ass in front of my children, that's disgusting. And my ass is not for you. The Second Finnish Regiment never required any licence besides my patent honesty which, if you had a better character, you could read off my face.

THE ARMY RECRUITER: Sergeant, I think this woman's insubordinate. The King's army needs discipline.

MOTHER COURAGE: And sausages!

THE SERGEANT: Name.

MOTHER COURAGE: Anna Fierling.

THE SERGEANT: And these others are Fierlings?

MOTHER COURAGE: Who? I'm Fierling. Not them.

THE SERGEANT: They're your children.

MOTHER COURAGE: They are. What's your problem? (*Pointing to her elder son.*) Take him for example, he's Finnish, he's Eilif Nojocki, why? His father was Kojocki or Mojocki so I split the difference. The boy's got fond memories of his father, only it's not actually his father he remembers but a French guy with

Alt-Ötting: A small town in Bavaria, Germany.

a goatee. Regardless, he inherited the Kojocki or Mojocki brains; that man could steal a farmer's socks without removing the boots first. None of us has the same name.

THE SERGEANT: None of you?

MOTHER COURAGE: Four points on the compass and I've been pricked in every direction.

THE SERGEANT (*pointing at the youngest son*): I bet. Was his father Chinese?

MOTHER COURAGE: Bad guess. Swiss.

THE SERGEANT: He came along after the French guy?

MOTHER COURAGE: French guy? I never knew any French guys, try to follow or we'll be here till night falls. His father was Swiss, as in Switzerland, but *his* name's Fejos because he's not named after his father, who built fortresses, drunk.

(*Swiss Cheese smiles proudly, nodding. Kattrin hides a laugh.*)

THE SERGEANT: Then who was Fejos?

MOTHER COURAGE: I don't mean to be rude, but you're entirely devoid of imagination, aren't you? I more or less had to call him Fejos because when he came out I was with a Hungarian. He couldn't care less, the Hungarian, he was dying, his kidneys shrivelled up even though he was abstemious. A nice man, the boy looks just like him.

THE SERGEANT: But he wasn't the father.

MOTHER COURAGE: Nevertheless. His big talent is pulling the wagon, so I call him Swiss Cheese. (*Pointing to her daughter.*) She's Kattrin Haupt. Half-German.

THE SERGEANT: Jesus. A nice wholesome family.

MOTHER COURAGE: We are. I've crossed the wide world in this wagon.

THE SERGEANT: You're Bavarian. I'm guessing Bamberg. What're you doing in Sweden?

MOTHER COURAGE: There's no war in Bamberg, is there? Was I supposed to wait?

THE ARMY RECRUITER: So, Jacob and Esau Ox.° Does she ever unstrap the rig and turn you loose to graze?

EILIF: Mama, can I punch this asshole in the mouth? Please?

MOTHER COURAGE: Can you stay where you are and keep quiet, please? Now, Officers, how's about a good pistol, or a belt buckle? Sergeant, your buckle's all bent.

THE SERGEANT: How's about you tell me instead why these two boys who are solid as birch trees with chests and legs like Arabian chargers aren't in the army.

MOTHER COURAGE (*quick*): Drop it, Sergeant, my kids aren't suited for war work.

THE ARMY RECRUITER: They look suitable to me. Make a little money, get famous. Selling shoes, that's for women. (*To Eilif.*) Come here. You talk big. But maybe you're a chicken.

MOTHER COURAGE: He is. He's a chicken. Look at him cross-eyed, he'll faint.

THE ARMY RECRUITER: I'm crossing my eyes, he still looks good to me!

(*The Army Recruiter gestures to Eilif to follow him.*)

MOTHER COURAGE: He's mine, not yours.

Jacob and Esau Ox: A reference to brothers working together.

THE ARMY RECRUITER: He called me an asshole. I invite him to accompany me to the field over there so I can clobber him.

EILIF: Glad to. Don't fret, Mama, I'll be right back.

MOTHER COURAGE: Don't you move, you brawling lump! (*To the Army Recruiter, pointing at Eilif.*) Watch out, he's got a knife sheathed in his boot!

THE ARMY RECRUITER: A knife, huh? I'll extract it easy as a baby tooth. This way, baby boy.

MOTHER COURAGE (*to the Sergeant*): You listen to me, your Captain has been ogling my daughter, and I'm going to tell him you're making her unhappy and he'll clap you in the stocks.

THE SERGEANT (*to the Army Recruiter*): No fighting, OK? (*To Mother Courage.*) What's so terrible about a job in the army? Bet his daddy was a soldier! Died a hero or something?

MOTHER COURAGE: Or something, dead at any rate, and (*pointing at Eilif*) he's just a child! I know your kind, you'll get a five-guilder fee and he'll get slaughtered!

THE ARMY RECRUITER: We'll give him a soldier's snazzy hat and brand new regulation boots when he signs.

EILIF: I don't want you to give me shit.

MOTHER COURAGE: Hey hey hey, I got a fun idea, let's you and me go fishing said the fisherman to the worm. (*To Swiss Cheese.*) Run tell the Captain they're stealing your brother! (*She pulls a knife.*)

He's mine! He's not going to war! I'll poke your eyes out first, you cannibals. We're merchants, we sell ham and shirts and we're friendly people.

THE SERGEANT: Yeah, you look friendly. Put up the knife, you old cunt. If there's a war, there have to be soldiers, right?

MOTHER COURAGE: Somebody else's kids, not mine.

THE SERGEANT: And there it is, your brood gets fat off the war but you think it's a one-way transaction. Maybe your sons have courage even if you don't.

EILIF: The war doesn't scare me.

THE SERGEANT: Why would it? See any bruises on me? I joined at seventeen!

MOTHER COURAGE: Let's see how close you get to seventy.

THE SERGEANT: What're you insinuating? I'm gonna get killed?

MOTHER COURAGE: You look marked to me. What if you're just a cadaver who hasn't heard the bad news, hmm?

SWISS CHEESE: She can see things, everyone knows that, she sees into the future.

THE ARMY RECRUITER: Tell the Sergeant his future then. He likes a good laugh.

THE SERGEANT: That's crap. Seeing things.

MOTHER COURAGE: Give me your helmet.

(*He does.*)

THE SERGEANT: Whatever you're doing, it means as much as dried turds in dead grass. (*Mother Courage looks at him, asking if she should continue.*)

Go ahead, it'll make a good story.

(*She tears a piece of paper in two.*)

MOTHER COURAGE: Eilif, Swiss Cheese, Kattrin, we'll all be torn to scrap like this, if we let the war pull us in too deeply. (*To the Sergeant.*) For a friend I do it for free. I make a black cross on the paper. Black is death.

SWISS CHEESE: And see the other piece of paper's empty.

MOTHER COURAGE: I fold them, I tumble 'em together, topsy turvy as we all tumble together, the marked and unremarkable, from mother love onward, and now draw and now you'll know.

(*The Sergeant hesitates.*)

THE ARMY RECRUITER (*to Eilif*): I'm the pickiest recruiter in the Swedish Army, most don't come close to making the cut but maybe you've got the grit, the beans, that special fire.

(*The Sergeant reaches in the helmet.*)

THE SERGEANT: It's all gobbledegook, oooh, the scales are falling from my eyes!

(*He draws a piece of paper, unfolds it.*)

SWISS CHEESE: Uh-oh! The black cross! He's going away!

THE ARMY RECRUITER: There are more soldiers than bullets. Don't let them scare you.

THE SERGEANT (*hoarse*): You cheated me.

MOTHER COURAGE: You did that to yourself the day you enlisted. Now we'll get going, it isn't every day there's a war on, we don't want to miss out on the fun.

THE SERGEANT: Hell and the Devil, you cheated me, bitch, but you'll be sorry you did! Your bastard's a soldier now!

EILIF: I wanna go with them, Mama.

MOTHER COURAGE: Shut your mouth, nasty!

EILIF: Swiss Cheese too, he wants to be a soldier too!

MOTHER COURAGE: You think so? Says who? Draw your own papers from the helmet, all three of you, then we'll see what's what.

(*She goes behind the wagon, where she tears paper and marks slips with crosses.*)

THE ARMY RECRUITER (*to Eilif*): And I've heard the enemy propaganda, in the Swedish Army it's Bible study and hymn singing night and day, but between us, the army's the army and once you're in you're washed clean of sin, and you can sing any song you like.

(*Mother Courage returns with the helmet.*)

MOTHER COURAGE: Time to abandon mother, huh, my two terrors? War is irresistible to young knuckleheads like you. Draw, draw and see what a welcome the world has in store. You bet I'm terrified, Sergeant, you would be too if you'd given birth to 'em, each one has a horrible personality defect. (*To Eilif.*) Here. Fish out your ticket. (*Eilif picks a slip of paper. She snatches it from him and unfolds it.*)

Oh I'm an unlucky mother! My womb only ever gave me grief after grief after grief! So young, into the army and then rotting in the ground, grass waving over him, it's hideously clear. You see, you see! A cross! Marked! Your father was a brazen idiot, like you, but you learned from me: think or die. Just like the paper shows. (*She flattens Eilif.*)

ARE YOU GOING TO THINK???!!!

EILIF: Sure, why not?

MOTHER COURAGE: And if they laugh and call you a chicken just cluck at them, who cares?

THE ARMY RECRUITER: If you've crapped your pants we can take your brother instead.

MOTHER COURAGE: Cluck! Cluck! Laugh right back! (*To Swiss Cheese.*) Now you, Swiss Cheese, fish for it. I'm not much worried about you, honest as you are. (*Swiss Cheese draws a slip from the helmet. He stares at it.*)

It's empty, isn't it? It can't be you pulled a black cross, that I'm losing you too, can't be. (*She takes the slip from him.*)

A cross! I guess because he's the simple son? Swiss Cheese, you're also going down unless you're always honest, like I taught you when you were a tiny kid—always bring back exact change from the baker. Otherwise you're lost. See, Sergeant, a black cross, yeah?

THE SERGEANT: Yeah. But I don't get it. I stay back, I never go near the fighting, why'd I get one? (*To the Army Recruiter.*) She's not a swindler, even her own kids get marked.

SWISS CHEESE: Even I'm marked. But I get it, I'm obedient.

MOTHER COURAGE (*to Kattrin*): You're safe, I know it, you won't draw a cross because you are the cross I bear: your good heart. (*She holds the helmet up to Kattrin, but she snatches the slip out herself before Kattrin has a chance.*)

I'm completely desperate. Something's wrong, maybe the way I stirred them. You can't be so kind, Kattrin, not any more, a cross stands athwart the road for you too. Stay quiet always, that should be easy for a mute. So now you all know, safety first, all of you. Back to the wagon and let's get far away from here.

(*Mother Courage hands the Sergeant his helmet and climbs back up on the wagon.*)

THE ARMY RECRUITER (*to the Sergeant*): Do something!

THE SERGEANT: I feel funny.

THE ARMY RECRUITER: You have to wear your hat in wind like this, now you're getting sick. Catch her up in some haggling. (*Loud.*) At least take a look at the merchandise, Sergeant, these nice people have to make a living, right? Wait a minute, lady, the Sergeant here wants a buckle.

MOTHER COURAGE: A half-guilder. Though buckles like mine are worth two guilders easy.

(*She climbs down from the wagon, pulls out a box of belt buckles.*)

THE SERGEANT: It looks like it was chewed on. I'm shivering with this wind, let me look it over back here.

(*He goes behind the wagon.*)

MOTHER COURAGE: Doesn't seem windy to me.

THE SERGEANT: A half-guilder, maybe, it's silver.

MOTHER COURAGE (*going behind the wagon*): Solid six ounces.

THE ARMY RECRUITER (*to Eilif*): And now let's go get drunk, you and me, man to man, I have a pocket full of change.

(*Eilif hesitates, undecided.*)

MOTHER COURAGE: OK, a half-guilder, done deal.

THE SERGEANT: I just don't get it. I stay in the rear, I find a safe place, a sergeant's prerogative, I let the others go for the glory. Now I won't manage to keep my lunch down, I can tell, I'm queasy all of a sudden.

MOTHER COURAGE: Don't let it ruin your appetite. Here, take a slug of schnapps, man, and stick to the rear.

(*She gives him a drink. The Army Recruiter has taken Eilif's arm and is leading him away.*)

THE ARMY RECRUITER: Ten guilders up front, and you're a brave warrior for the King, and all the women go for you. And you can punch me in the mouth for insulting you.

(*They go out. Dumb Kattrin jumps down from the wagon and starts making wild loud noises.*)

MOTHER COURAGE: Wait Kattrin, wait a minute. The Sergeant's paying. (*She bites the half-guilder the Sergeant's given her.*)

I've been burned, Sergeant, never learned to trust money. And now—where's Eilif?

SWISS CHEESE: With the recruiter. Gone.

MOTHER COURAGE (*stands frozen, then*): You're simplicity itself, you are. (*To Kattrin.*) I know, I know, you can't speak, it isn't your fault.

THE SERGEANT: Give yourself a little schnapps, Mama. So goes the world. It's not so terrible, a soldier's life.

MOTHER COURAGE: You have to help your brother pull. Kattrin.

(*Side by side, brother and sister harness themselves to the wagon and pull it away. Mother Courage walks alongside. They exit.*)

THE SERGEANT (*watching them leave*):

If off the war you hope to live,
Take what you can. You'll also give.

TWO

From 1625 to 1626 Mother Courage follows the Swedish Army as it crosses Poland. Near the fort at Wallhof she sees her son again. The lucky sale of a chicken and a great day for the brave son.

The General's tent.

Beside the tent, the kitchen. Cannon fire in the distance. The Cook argues with Mother Courage who hopes to sell him a chicken.

THE COOK: Sixty hellers for that scraggly hen?

MOTHER COURAGE: Scraggly? This fat beast? What, your General, who can outeat anyone from Sweden to Poland and back again, and woe unto the cook who serves him up a skimpy table, he can't up sixty little hellers?

THE COOK: For ten hellers on any street corner I can fetch a dozen birds better looking than that.

MOTHER COURAGE: Sure, sure you can get a fat chicken like this on a street corner with everyone from miles about all withered and skeletal. You'll fetch a rat from the fields, maybe, *maybe,* if you can find one, they've all been eaten, I saw five men chase one rat for hours. Fifty hellers for this, this, what, would you call it, well it's practically a turkey, it's so big. And in the middle of a siege.

THE COOK: We're not in the middle of a siege, it's them up in the fort that are in the middle of the siege, we're the besiegers. Try to keep it straight.

MOTHER COURAGE: Why bother, the besiegers have less food than the besieged. They hauled all the crops and cattle up to the fort before they locked themselves in.

I hear they're swimming in sauce and beer up there. Down here, well, I've been to the farms. Grim. Zilch.

THE COOK: They've got it, the farmers. They hide it.

MOTHER COURAGE (*playing her trump*): They've got nothing, starving, I've seen them, digging roots up out of the ground and sucking their fingers after a meal of boiled leather. And I'm supposed to sell a gourmet capon for forty hellers.

THE COOK: I offered thirty, not forty.

MOTHER COURAGE: This isn't any workaday chicken. He was musically gifted, he'd eat only to the tune of his favorite marches, and he could do arithmetic. All that for forty hellers. If you don't have something to serve him, your General's liable to eat your head.

THE COOK: Know why I'm not worried? (*He spears a piece of beef with his knife and lifts it up.*)

A roast for roasting. I've tendered you my final offer.

MOTHER COURAGE: Roast it, but hurry, it's been dead three weeks and it stinks.

THE COOK: I saw it running across the fields yesterday.

MOTHER COURAGE: Praise Jesus, a dead dog, running around. It's a miracle.

THE COOK: It was a cow, not a dog, and after two hours in a stewpot, it'll be tender as a tit.

MOTHER COURAGE: After five hours, it'll be glue, but say a prayer if the general comes hungry, and keep the pepper handy, I'm telling you, it stinks.

(*The General, a Chaplain and Eilif enter the General's tent. The General claps Eilif's shoulder.*)

THE GENERAL: Come on, son, sit at the right hand of your General. You're a hero and a real Christian and this is a war for God and what's done is done because God wants it done and you did it and I feel fantastic! When we take the goddamned fort I'm going to give you a gold bracelet. We come to set their souls free, and what do they do, these farmers who've happily let centuries of their beefsteak disappear down the gullets of fat Polish priests? They decide to turn their livestock loose so we can't eat. Savages. Ingrates. Stinky little shitpeople. But they'll remember what they learned from you, boy! (*He pours wine into two tin cups, then offers one to Eilif.*)

Here's a can of my best red, we'll bolt it down together. (*Eilif and General gulp down the wine.*)

Chaplain can lap up the dregs, like the suffering Christ he is. Now what's for lunch, heart of my hearts?

EILIF: Umm . . . steak!

THE GENERAL (*screaming to the kitchen*): Cook! Meat!

THE COOK: He knows we're out of everything so he brings guests.

(*Mother Courage gestures to him to be silent, so she can hear what's happening in the tent.*)

EILIF: You really work up an appetite, butchering peasants.

MOTHER COURAGE: Jesus, it's my Eilif.

THE COOK: Who?

MOTHER COURAGE: My eldest. Haven't laid eyes on him for two years, stolen from me on the open road, and he must be in great good favour with the General, his special lunch guest, and what're you going to feed them, nothing! You heard the General: meat! My advice: buy the chicken. Price: one hundred hellers.

THE GENERAL: Lunch, Lamb, you beast-who-barely-learned-to-cook, or I'll hook and gut you!

THE COOK: Oh hell, give it, it's blackmail.

MOTHER COURAGE: This shabby bird?

THE COOK: Just give it to me, it's a sin, fifty hellers for scraggle like that.

MOTHER COURAGE: I said a hundred, one whole guilder. Nothing's too nice for my eldest, the General's special guest.

(*The Cook gives her the money.*)

THE COOK: Plucking included. While I get the fire up.

MOTHER COURAGE (*sitting down, plucking*): The look on his face when he sees it's me! He's my brave, clever boy. I've got another one, stupid but honest. The girl's nothing. At least she's quiet, at least there's that.

(*The General pours another drink. They keep drinking, getting drunker.*)

THE GENERAL: Have another, son, a lip-smacking Falernian,° only one or maybe two kegs left, but I don't begrudge my best for my true believers. Who act! Not like this watery-eyed old simp of a soul-shepherd, he preaches sunup to sundown till the whole church is out cold and snoring but we still haven't taken the goddamned fort and don't ask him how to do it, or how to do anything. You, Eilif, my son, on the other hand, you showed an initiative which eventuated in the requisitioning of twenty head of cattle from some farmers. Which will arrive soon I hope.

EILIF: By morning.

MOTHER COURAGE: That's thoughtful of my Eilif, delivering the oxen tomorrow, otherwise I doubt my chicken would've had such an enthusiastic reception.

THE GENERAL: Regale us!

EILIF: Yep, well, this is the way it went: I heard the farmers were sneaking out at night all hush-hush to round up these cows they were hiding in a woods. They'd arranged a sale of the cows with the people up in the fort. I held back, let the farmers do all the work rounding up the cows—they're good at herding, saved me the work. Meanwhile I got my men good and ready, for two days I fed them only bread and water, so they got crazy for meat, they'd drool if they just heard the word 'meat', if they even heard a word beginning with 'M', like . . . um . . . 'meat'!

THE GENERAL: You're smart.

EILIF: I dunno. After that it was basically one-two-three. Except the farmers had huge clubs and they outnumbered us three to one and when they saw we wanted their cows they came after us like murder. Four of them got me backed up against a thornbush and one of them clouted the sword from out of my hand and they were hollering 'give up' and I thought right, I give up and you pound me to paste.

THE GENERAL: What'd you do?

EILIF: I started laughing.

THE GENERAL: What?

Falernian: A highly valued wine.

EILIF: I laughed. So then they wanted to discuss that. So I start bargaining: 'You're fucking kidding, twenty guilders for that ox? More like fifteen tops!' Like we're doing business. Which confuses them, they're scratching their heads. And that's when I picked up my cutlass and I cut their heads off, HUH! HUH! HUH! HUH! All four of them. Necessity trumps the commandments. Right?

THE GENERAL: Want to rule on that, you pious pedant?

THE CHAPLAIN: There's no such exemption in the Bible, in the literal sense, but back then Our Lord could take five loaves of bread and make five hundred, so there was no necessity per se. You can command people to love their neighbours and if they're full of bread they may comply. That was then and this is now.

THE GENERAL (*laughing*): You can say that again. Here, you need to whet your whistle after that, Pharisee.°

(*He pours the Chaplain a glass of wine.*)

(*To Eilif.*) You massacred the farmers and now my brave boys'll bite down on a bit of real red meat, and how could God gripe about that? Doesn't His Holy Writ say 'Whateversoever thou dost for the least of My brethren is done for Me'? It'll be like in the old days again, a bit of beef, a gulp of wine and then fight for God.

EILIF: I snatched up my sword and I split their skulls in two!

THE GENERAL: You're a Caesar in the making. You ought to meet His Majesty.

EILIF: I saw him once, distantly. He kind of gives off light. I want to be just like him.

THE GENERAL: You already are. I treasure you, Eilif, brave soldier boy, you're my own son, that's how I'll handle you. (*He leads Eilif to a big map.*)

Here's the picture, Eilif, the whole campaign. So much to do.

(*In the kitchen, Courage stops eavesdropping and resumes plucking the chicken, furious.*)

MOTHER COURAGE: That's one lousy General.

THE COOK: No he's not, he eats to excess but he's good at what he does.

MOTHER COURAGE: If he knew what he was doing he wouldn't need brave soldiers, he could make do with ordinary soldiers. It's when the General's a moron the soldiers have to be brave. It's when the King's pinching his pennies and doesn't hire enough soldiers, every soldier has to be hard-working. You only need brave hard-working patriot soldiers when the country's coming unglued. In a decent country that's properly managed with decent kings and generals, people can be just what people are, common and of middling intelligence and for all I care every one of them a shivering coward. In a decent country that's properly managed.

THE GENERAL: A man like you was born a soldier.

EILIF: My daddy was. A soldier. My mother taught me a song about it.

THE GENERAL: Sing it for me! (*Hollering.*) Where's my goddamn food?!

EILIF: It's called 'The Song about the Soldier and His Wife'.

Pharisee: Used to imply that the chaplain is a hypocrite.

(*He sings, doing a sabre dance:*)
'Your gun is precise, and your bayonet's nice—
But the ice on the river won't hold you.
You'll drown in a trice if you march on the ice.
And lonely cold death shall enfold you!'

Thus spoke his wife, as he whetted his knife;
Hoisting his pack he said, 'Marching's my life!
When you're marching no woman can scold you.
When you're marching no woman can scold you.
We're marching into Poland,
Then we're marching off to Spain!
With your bayonet sharpened—
With your sharp bayonet you've no need to explain!
No woman ever controlled you!'

Oh bitter her tears, she was younger in years,
But wiser than he, so she told him.
March off if he must, it will all come to dust—
For only a coffin shall hold him.
Off goes her man, he will write when he can,
And women have wept since the world first began,
And her weeping has often consoled him.
The sound of her sorrow consoled him.

With the moon on the shingles,
Icy white on the snow,
Wave goodbye to your husband!
So long to your husband and then back home you go,
Where you'll wait for the fate you foretold him!
(*Mother Courage, in the kitchen, takes up his song,
beating time on a pot with spoon.*)
MOTHER COURAGE (*singing*):
It isn't a joke. Your life is like smoke.
And someday you'll wish you had tarried.
Oh, how quickly you'll fall. Oh God. Help us all.
Soldiers should never get married.
EILIF: Who's that?
MOTHER COURAGE (*singing*):
He tumbled the dice and he soon paid the price:
They gave him his orders to march on the ice.
And the water rose up all around him,
And the water rose up and it drowned him.
Through Poland, through Spain, his poor wife
    searched in vain.
But he'd vanished, and she never found him.
He was gone and his wife never found him.
THE GENERAL: Who told them they could sing in my
    kitchen?
(*Eilif goes into the kitchen. He sees his mother. He embraces her.*)
EILIF: I missed you! Where's everybody else?
(*Mother Courage stays in his embrace.*)
MOTHER COURAGE: Everyone's fine, stout as trout in a
    brook. Swiss Cheese is paymaster for the Second
    Regiment; that keeps him away from fighting, even if
    I couldn't keep him out of the army.
EILIF: How are your feet?
MOTHER COURAGE: Too swollen for shoes in the morning.
(*The General has joined them.*)

Lotte Lenya as Mother Courage, pulling her wagon in Brecht's 1979 Berliner Ensemble production of his play.

THE GENERAL: So you're his mother! Got any more sons
    like this one?
EILIF: That's what my luck's like. You happen to be sitting
    in the kitchen so you can hear your son called a hero.
MOTHER COURAGE: You're goddamned right I heard.
(*She slaps Eilif.*)
EILIF (*holding his cheek*): For taking the oxen?
MOTHER COURAGE: For not surrendering! Four peasants!?
    Are you nuts?! I taught you always to watch out for
    yourself! You brazen sticky-fingered fork-tongued
    son of a Finn!
(*The General and the Chaplain laugh.*)

THREE

*Three years later, Mother Courage and the Remnants of
the Second Finnish Regiment, still in Poland, are made
prisoners of war. Her daughter is saved, and also her
wagon, but her honest son dies.*
    The army camp.

Afternoon. The regimental flag hangs from a flag-pole. A clothes line stretches from Mother Courage's wagon to the pole, and a variety of merchandise is hanging from it. Near the wagon is a large cannon, on which laundry has been draped for drying. Mother Courage is simultaneously folding clothes that have dried with Kattrin and negotiating the purchase of a sack of bullets with a Quartermaster. Swiss Cheese, in his paymaster's uniform, is watching all this.

Yvette Pottier, a pretty woman, sits nearby drinking brandy and sewing vivid things to her hat. She's in her stocking feet, her red high-heeled shoes lying nearby.

THE QUARTERMASTER: Two guilders. That's cheap for bullets, but I need money now, the Colonel's been on a two-day bender, celebrating with his staff, they drank us dry and where am I supposed to get money for more liquor?

MOTHER COURAGE: Not from me. That's official ammunition, they catch me holding a bag of that, I'll be court-martialled and shot. You crooks sell the soldiers' ammo out from under them, in the thick of battle what're they supposed to do? Throw rocks?

THE QUARTERMASTER: What am I supposed to do when he wants his wine, serve rainwater?

MOTHER COURAGE: It's immoral. I don't want army ammunition. Not for two guilders.

THE QUARTERMASTER: Two little guilders, come on, buy them from me then sell them to the Fourth Regiment's quartermaster, the Fourth's clean out of bullets, he'll give you five guilders for them, eight guilders if you make him out a receipt says he paid twelve guilders, and one hand washes the other and who isn't happy?

MOTHER COURAGE: Go to the Fourth's quartermaster on your own, why do you need me?

THE QUARTERMASTER: I don't trust him and he doesn't trust me, we've been friends for years.

MOTHER COURAGE: Give. (*She takes the sack and gives it to Kattrin.*)

(*To Kattrin*): Stow this in the back and give the man one and a half guilders. (*The Quartermaster starts to complain; she stops him.*)

No more discussion. (*Kattrin drags the sack behind the wagon. The Quartermaster follows her.*)

(*To Swiss Cheese*): Here's your woolens, look after them, it's October and frosty soon, at any rate it should be, who knows, you can't expect anything with any certainty, not even fall following summer. Only one thing must be as must be: and that's your regimental cash box, whatever else is awry, you keep their cash pin-tidy. Is it pin-tidy?

SWISS CHEESE: Yes, Mama.

MOTHER COURAGE: They made you paymaster because you're honest, you're not brave like your brother, they like it that you're too feeble-minded to get your mind around the idea of stealing it. Which puts my mind at ease. Cash in the cash box and where do the woolies go?

SWISS CHEESE: Under my mattress, Mama, except when I'm wearing 'em.

(*He starts to go.*)

THE QUARTERMASTER: Wait for me, paymaster, I'll go with you.

MOTHER COURAGE: Don't teach him your tricks. (*The Quartermaster walks off with Swiss Cheese. Yvette waves to the Quartermaster as he leaves. He doesn't wave back.*)

YVETTE: Whatever happened to 'So long, nice to meet you'?

MOTHER COURAGE (*to Yvette*): I don't want my Swiss Cheese consorting with people like him, I don't even like to see them walking together, it makes me worry, though in general everything's OK, the war's going well, every other day fresh countries are joining in, it'll last four or five years easily. Thinking ahead and no impulsive moves, I can build a good business. And you, with your disease, don't you know you should lay off the booze?

YVETTE: What disease, it's a lie, who says so?

MOTHER COURAGE: Everybody does.

YVETTE: Everybody lies. I'm panicked, Mother Courage, customers avoid me like the plague, it's like I hung a sign over my cootch saying 'Remember you must die.' Why the hell am I stitching new crap to this fucking hat? (*She throws it to the ground.*)

I never used to drink in the morning, it gives you crow's feet, but so what? Pride isn't for people like us. If you can't learn to eat shit and like it, down you go.

MOTHER COURAGE: Here it comes, the why-oh-why and woe-is-me, your Piping Pieter and how he done you dirt. Just don't start your filthy yowling where my innocent daughter can hear you.

YVETTE: Let her listen, she should learn what it's like to lose a man and spend ten bad years looking everywhere for him, never finding him, she should learn what love is.

MOTHER COURAGE: That's something they never learn.

YVETTE: Then I'll talk just for the relief of talking, I need some relief. It started in Flanders because I was a girl there, if I'd been a girl someplace else I wouldn't have seen him that day, Dutch, blond and thin, and now I'm in Poland just because he cooked for the army, a thin cook. What I didn't know then, Kattrin, is stay away from the thin boys, and also I didn't know he had another girlfriend or that they called him Piping Pieter because even when he did it, he kept his pipe in his mouth, with him doing it was just a casual thing.

(*Yvette sings 'The Song of Fraternisation'.*)
We hated the soldiers,
Their army took our town.
I was sixteen. The foreign occupier
Grinned as he loosened my nightgown.
     May mornings are so bright.
     But comes the dark May night . . .
     The Captain shouts 'You're all dismissed!'
     Then boys with mischief in their eyes
     Will find the girls who fraternise.
     How could I hate him when we kissed?

The foreign occupation
Brought sorrows—and a cook!
By day I would despise him, then when night fell,

I loved the liberties that he took!
   May mornings are so bright.
   But comes the dark May night . . .
   The Captain shouts 'Boys, hit the hay!'
   But one with something on his mind
   Knows just the kind of girl to find.
   We fraternised till day.

My oppressor and my lover
For me were one and the same.
Everyone said, 'Her love's just convenient.'
What we agreed on was my shame.
   A cloud that hid the sun
   Announced my joy was done.
   You have your fun but troops move on.
   You wait all night. Where can he be?
   Your lover and your enemy?
   His army's marching, and he's . . . gone.

(*She stumbles back behind the wagon. As she goes:*)

MOTHER COURAGE: Your hat.

YVETTE: Anyone wants it, be my guest.

(*She goes behind the wagon.*)

MOTHER COURAGE: You heard, Kattrin? Don't start up with soldiers. He tells you he wants to kiss the ground over which your delicate feet have trod—and did you wash your delicate feet yesterday, as long as we're talking about feet—and bang, you're his goat cow mule and whatever else he's itching after. Be happy you're a mute, when you've finally got a husband you'll never contradict yourself or bite your tongue because you told the truth, it's a blessing from God, being dumb. And here comes the General's cook, what brought him?

(*The Cook and the Chaplain enter.*)

THE CHAPLAIN: I bring a message from your son, Eilif, and the cook wanted to accompany me, you've made an impression.

THE COOK: I accompanied you for the exercise and air.

MOTHER COURAGE: Air's free so breathe all you want, just mind your manners, and if you forget, I'm ready for you. (*To the Chaplain.*) So what's Eilif want? I have no extra money.

THE CHAPLAIN: Truth to be told the message is for his brother, Mr Paymaster.

MOTHER COURAGE: He isn't his brother's paymaster. And he's gone, so he can't get led into temptation by bright ideas. (*She takes money from her money belt and hands it to the Chaplain.*)
   Give this to him, it's a sin, calculating on maternal instinct and he should be ashamed of himself.

THE COOK: His regiment's marching out, who knows, maybe off to die. Add a little to that pittance, lady, or later on you'll regret. You women come on hard, but later on, you regret. A guy pleads for a glass of brandy, but you're not feeling generous, so the brandy isn't flowing, and he goes off dry, next thing he's dead under the green green ground in some place far away and, oh, you wish you could serve him that brandy now, but forget it, he's gone where you'll never claw him up.

THE CHAPLAIN: Any soldier who falls in a religious war will go straight to heaven, where he can have all the brandy he wants.

THE COOK: Point taken, though still the woman who turns him away without a little brandy to burn his belly should burn with shame, and not because he's a holy kind of soldier—she shouldn't turn him away unrefreshed even if he was just your normal undistinguished infidel infantryman off to meet St Peter with all his venality, shooting and looting, and don't forget a rape here and there, completely unexculpated by virtue of his having done all those things but in the service of his Protestant faith. Thirsty's thirsty is my point.

THE CHAPLAIN (*to Mother Courage, indicating the Cook*): I didn't want him to come with me but he says he's dreaming about you.

THE COOK (*lighting his pipe*): Brandy poured by a slender hand, nothing contemptible on my mind.

MOTHER COURAGE: Who'd say no to a drink?

THE CHAPLAIN: Temptation! shrieked the Bishop, and fell. (*Looking at Kattrin.*) And who is this comely young lady?

MOTHER COURAGE: She isn't comely, she's stay-at-homely and I don't want clergy sniffing up my daughter.

THE COOK: Keep a gimlet eye on this dirty dog, you oughta hear his jokes! Revolting!

(*The Chaplain and the Cook go behind the wagon with Mother Courage. Kattrin watches them leave, then she leaves her washing and goes to Yvette's hat. She puts it on, then sits and puts on the red shoes. From behind the wagon Mother Courage is heard talking politics with the Chaplain and the Cook.*)

MOTHER COURAGE: What's the news from the front?

THE COOK: Nobody knows where that is.

MOTHER COURAGE: It's a mess. It was a nice peaceful invasion, the Swedish king rolled in with his troops and horses and wagons, waving the Protestant flag, he rolled here, he rolled there, he's ready to roll back to Sweden and now, now the Poles break the peace and look, blood's poured down on their heads.

THE COOK: The way I see it is, I knew you'd serve exquisite brandy, I never misread a face.

THE CHAPLAIN: All our King ever wanted was to set Poland free from the tyranny of the Pope and his crony the Kaiser.

(*In front of the wagon, Kattrin, checking to make sure she's not being seen, wearing the hat and shoes, begins imitating Yvette's provocative walk. As she continues she abandons the imitation; she becomes more confident, more mature, a pretty young woman. She even dances a little. The talk behind the wagon is continuous.*)

THE COOK: Absolutely. Liberty! Everybody craves liberty, the human body needs it like it needs water or bread or salt. Who knows why we need liberty? What humans need is a mystery. Who knows why we need salt? We need what we need.

THE CHAPLAIN: Amen.

THE COOK: But it's expensive, liberty, especially when you start exporting it to other countries, so the King has to levy a tax on salt back home in Sweden, so his own subjects are free but they can't afford salt, or, well, the poor can't afford it, the rich can afford anything, even when it's taxed and pricey, and even better, the rich get tax exemptions!

THE CHAPLAIN: You shouldn't mock liberty. It's —

THE COOK: Who's mocking?

MOTHER COURAGE: He isn't mocking anything, he's a cook, cooks have an intellectual bent, not like preachers.

THE COOK: I'm talking about the human body.

MOTHER COURAGE: Right.

THE COOK: A lovely thing, the human body.

THE CHAPLAIN: Created in God's image.

THE COOK: You bet. Given half a chance, it'll do a little jig. It's stubborn, though. The body. Or is that the soul? Preacher I get confused.

THE CHAPLAIN: I'm sure you do.

THE COOK: It's the wanting that makes 'em stubborn, is my point. So sometimes you have to torture the people — which by the way adds to the cost of the war, since contrary to expectations the Poles have preferred to remain unliberated, the King's tried everything, the rack and the screw and prisons are expensive, and when the King discovered they didn't want to be free, even after torture, he stopped having any fun. But God told our King to fight, He didn't say it'd be fun, and it isn't much fun, is it, though since I cook for the General I have table salt at least, and the rest of it's beyond me, what bodies want and what bodies get, and it's a good thing the King's got God going for him. Or else people might suspect that he's just in it for what he can take out of it. But he's always had his principles, our King, and with his clear conscience he doesn't get depressed.

MOTHER COURAGE: Long live Gustavus Adolphus, the Hero-King. About whom a certain kind of talk is unhealthy.

THE CHAPLAIN (to the Cook): You eat his bread.

THE COOK: I don't eat it, I bake it.

MOTHER COURAGE: The King will never be defeated, and why, his people believe in him, and why? Precisely because everyone knows he's in the war to make a profit. If he wasn't, little people like me would smell disaster in the war and steer away from it. If it's business, it makes sense.

THE COOK: Here's to the little people like you.

THE CHAPLAIN: Hey, Dutchman, it would be advisable to cast a glance at the Swedish flag that's flying overhead before sharing your opinions so liberally.

MOTHER COURAGE: No harm done. Nobody here but us Protestants! Alley-oop!

(They toast and drink, we hear the clink of their glasses. Suddenly cannon thunder and rifle shots are heard. Mother Courage, the Cook and the Chaplain rush around from behind the wagon, the Cook and Chaplain with brandy glasses in hand.)

MOTHER COURAGE: What's happened? (The Quartermaster and a Soldier rush in and begin to wheel the cannon away, clothes hanging all over it.)
    I have to take the laundry down first, you idiots.

(She scrambles to retrieve her laundry.)

THE QUARTERMASTER: The Catholics! Attacking! There wasn't any warning, I don't know if we have time to — (An increase in the sound of fighting, drums and alarms.)
    (To the soldier.) Do something about the cannon!

(The Quartermaster runs away. The Soldier tries with all his might to move the cannon, which won't budge.)

THE COOK: Better get back to my General, if they haven't shot him he'll be screaming for dinner. Look for me, Courage, I'll be back for more political debate.

(He starts to leave.)

MOTHER COURAGE: You're leaving your pipe!

THE COOK (exiting): Keep it for me, I'll need it.

MOTHER COURAGE: Of course, just when we're starting to clear a profit the sky falls in.

THE CHAPLAIN: I'll be making tracks myself, if the enemy breaks through there's apt to be serious trouble. Blessed are the peaceable, that's my battle cry. I need a big cloak for camouflage.

MOTHER COURAGE: I'm not lending cloaks or anything else, not if it costs your life. I've gone that route before.

THE CHAPLAIN: But my religious calling puts me in particular jeopardy.

(She hands him a cloak.)

MOTHER COURAGE: This rubs against my better impulses. Now get lost.

THE CHAPLAIN: Many thanks, it's big-hearted of you, but on further consideration it might be better to settle here for a bit.

MOTHER COURAGE (turning to the Soldier struggling with the cannon): Drop it you donkey, who's paying you to do that? I'll watch it for you, it's not worth your life.

THE SOLDIER (running away): You can tell them I tried!

MOTHER COURAGE: I'll swear on the Bible. (She sees her daughter with Yvette's hat.)
    What're you doing in that hooker's hat? Take that off, are you cracked? Now, with the enemy coming? (She tears the hat off Kattrin's head.)
    You want them stumbling across you and making you their whore? And you've put on the shoes too, haven't you, you scarlet Babylonian?! Take 'em off, now now now! (Courage tries to yank the shoes off Kattrin's feet. Then she turns to the Chaplain.)
    Jesus, help me, Pastor, get her shoes off. I'll be back in a minute.

(She runs to the wagon. Yvette comes in, powdering herself.)

YVETTE: Is it the Catholics? Oh please God let it be the Catholics! Where's my hat? (She sees the hat on the ground.) Who stomped on it? I can't run around in that, not if it's Catholics, they're finnicky about costumes. I gotta get to a mirror. And where are the shoes? (She looks around for them, not seeing them, because Kattrin has hidden her feet under her skirt.)
    They were here when I left them. I'll have to walk back to my tent barefoot. It's mortifying. (To the Chaplain.) What do you think? Too heavy with the make-up?

THE CHAPLAIN: You're perfect.

(*Yvette leaves. Swiss Cheese runs in, carrying a metal cash box. Mother Courage comes out of the wagon, her hands full of soot.*)

MOTHER COURAGE (*to Kattrin*): Here. Soot. For you. (*To Swiss Cheese.*) What're you lugging there?

SWISS CHEESE: It's the regimental cash box.

MOTHER COURAGE: Get rid of that! You're not the pay-master any more.

SWISS CHEESE: I am. It's my responsibility.

(*He goes behind the wagon.*)

MOTHER COURAGE (*to the Chaplain*): Take off your clerical get-up, Pastor, they'll see it under the cloak. (*She rubs soot all over Kattrin's face.*)

Hold still! A little filth, a little bit safer. What a disaster! Bet the sentries guarding the camp got drunk. Hide your light under a bushel, just like they say. A soldier sees a girl with a clean face, watch out! When he's done raping her, he calls for his buddies. (*Looking at Kattrin's face.*) That oughta do it. Let me look. Not bad. Like you've been rolling in shit. Don't shiver. Now nothing will happen to you. (*To Swiss Cheese.*) Where'd you leave the cash box?

SWISS CHEESE: I figured it should go in the wagon.

MOTHER COURAGE (*horrified*): In my wagon? Of all the godforsaken blockheadedness. If I don't watch every second! They'll hang us, all three of us!

SWISS CHEESE: Then I'll put it someplace else, or I could take it and run away.

MOTHER COURAGE: Stay here, too late for that.

(*The Chaplain, changing his clothes, notices the regimental flag.*)

THE CHAPLAIN: Oh my goodness, the flag!

(*Mother Courage takes down the flag.*)

MOTHER COURAGE: Holy crap! Blinded by habit! I've flown it for twenty-five years. (*The cannons' thunder gets louder.*)

(*Mid-morning, three days later. The cannon that had been next to the wagon is gone. Mother Courage, Kattrin, Swiss Cheese and the Chaplain, nervous, burdened, eating together.*)

SWISS CHEESE: It's three days now and I'm wasting time sitting around and the Sergeant, who was always nice to me even when I made mistakes, has finally got to be asking himself: where's that Swiss Cheese gone with the regimental cash box?

MOTHER COURAGE: Just be glad they haven't come sniffing around here.

THE CHAPLAIN: Amen. Unobjectionable is our only hope. He whose heart is full of woe must sing out loud, as they say, but God and all the apostles forfend I should start singing now! I don't know any Latin hymns.

MOTHER COURAGE: One's got his cash box and the other's got an ecclesiastical sense of humour and I'm stuck between the two and I don't know which is worse.

THE CHAPLAIN: Even now God's watching over us.

MOTHER COURAGE: Which explains why I'm not sleeping well. God and your cash box keep me awake. I think I've straightened my own position out. I told them

I was a good Catholic and adamantly opposed to Satan, I'd seen him, Satan, he's a Swede with ram's horns. I stopped to ask if they knew where I could buy votive candles. I've got that churchy talk down pat. I know they knew I was lying but they don't have any commissary wagons, so they squint a little. It could still work out well for us. We're prisoners, but so are head lice.

THE CHAPLAIN: It's good milk. Albeit available only in small quantities, we may have to curb our Swedish appetites. Since we're defeated.

MOTHER COURAGE: Victory, defeat, depends on your perspective. Defeat is frequently profitable for underdogs. Honour's lost, but what's that? What works out best for us is what they call paralysis, a shot here, a shot there, one step forward, one back, and troops going no place needing provisions. (*To Swiss Cheese.*) Eat!

SWISS CHEESE: I don't want to eat. How's the Sergeant going to pay the soldiers?

MOTHER COURAGE: They're retreating, they don't get paid when they're retreating.

SWISS CHEESE: If they don't get paid to do it they shouldn't retreat.

MOTHER COURAGE: Swiss Cheese, your conscientiousness is terrifying. Since you're stupid I decided to raise you to be honest but really it's getting out of hand. Now I'm taking the Chaplain to buy a Catholic flag and some meat. Nobody noses out good meat like the Chaplain, when there's good meat anywhere in the area you can tell because there are little spit bubbles in the corners of his mouth and his lips get shiny. Everything's going to be all right as long as they let me do business. Protestant pants cover your ass same as any other.

THE CHAPLAIN: Martin Luther met a priest who was begging for alms by the side of the road. Luther said to the beggar priest, 'After I turn the world inside out we won't need priests!' 'Maybe not,' said the priest, 'but you'll still need beggars,' and he went on his way. (*Mother Courage has gone into the wagon.*)

That cash box is weighing on her. Everyone thinks we all belong to the wagon, but how long before they come to investigate?

SWISS CHEESE: I can take it someplace else.

THE CHAPLAIN: That could mean trouble for us all if they catch you doing it. They've got spies everywhere. Yesterday morning I was relieving myself in an open-air latrine. I'd just started to squat when a spy jumped up! Right out of the latrine!

SWISS CHEESE: He was in the latrine?

THE CHAPLAIN: Yes! *In* the latrine!

SWISS CHEESE: Why was he in the latrine?

THE CHAPLAIN: Sniffing out Protestants! Probably sleeps down there. This one was a little stump of a man with a patch over his eye. I screamed and almost ejaculated a prayer in Swedish, which would have been the end of me.

(*Mother Courage climbs down from the wagon with a basket.*)

MOTHER COURAGE: And what have I found, you shameless nothing? (*In triumph she holds up the red shoes.*) Yvette's red shoes! She's a cold-blooded thief! (*To the*

Chaplain.) You led her straight into this, telling her she was comely! (*Putting the shoes in her basket.*) I'm returning them. Stealing Yvette's shoes! She does what she does to make a living, I understand that. But you'll give it for nothing, hoping for a little fun. But until peace comes you have no business having hopes, you hear me? None!

THE CHAPLAIN: Everyone's entitled to have hopes.

MOTHER COURAGE: Not her! I'm her mother, not you! Let her be like a stone in Darlarna. One grey stone among many grey stones as far as the eye can see, and all silent, that's how I want it with her. That way nothing ever happens to her. (*To Swiss Cheese.*) Listen up you, leave that cash box right where it is. And keep a close eye on your sister, she needs watching. Raising kids! It'd be easier turning weasels into house pets.

(*She leaves with the Chaplain. Kattrin clears the dishes from their meal.*)

SWISS CHEESE: Not many days left when people can sit out in the sun in their shirtsleeves. (*Kattrin points to a tree.*)

That's what I mean, the leaves turned yellow. (*Kattrin gestures to ask him if he wants something to drink.*)

I won't drink. I have to think. (*Pause.*)

She said she isn't sleeping. I should take the cash box someplace else, I found a secret place for it. All right, now I will have a drink. (*Kattrin goes behind the wagon.*)

There are mole rills down by the river, I'll stick it down into one, then I'll fetch it back. Maybe tonight just before morning and I'll take it to the regiment. It's been three days, how far have they retreated? The Sergeant's eyes are going to bug out of his head. 'Swiss Cheese, I am pleasantly disappointed,' is what he's going to say. 'I trusted you would take care of the regimental cash box and you did.'

(*Kattrin is coming from behind the wagon with a glass of brandy when she runs into two men suddenly standing there. One is a Sergeant, and the other, bowing, sweeps the ground before him with his hat. He wears an eyepatch over one eye.*)

THE ONE WITH THE EYEPATCH: Nominy dominy, pretty girlie. Seen anyone around here from the HQ of the Second Finnish Regiment?

(*Kattrin, badly frightened, runs to Swiss Cheese at the front of the wagon, spilling brandy, making gestures, including something about an eyepatch. The two men look at one another and, after seeing Swiss Cheese, they disappear.*)

SWISS CHEESE (*startled out of a reverie*): You spilled half of it. Why are you being silly? Did you stab yourself in the eye? I don't understand. I have to go someplace else, I decided, that's what I have to do. (*He stands to leave. She frantically tries to explain the danger to him, to stop him. He gets around her.*)

I wish I knew what you mean. It's something important, you poor mutt, you just can't explain what. Don't worry about the brandy, I'm sure I'll have lots of chances to drink brandy, a little spilt brandy, so what? (*He goes into the wagon and returns with the cash box, which he stuffs under his jacket. Kattrin grabs him.*)

I'll be back in two shakes. Don't hold on to me, or else I'll have to pinch you. Probably you mean something important. I wish you could talk.

(*He kisses her and pulls himself away. He leaves. Kattrin runs back and forth, gesticulating frantically, grunting, trying to make words. The Chaplain and Mother Courage return. Kattrin storms around her mother.*)

MOTHER COURAGE: What then, what then? You're falling into pieces. Did somebody do something to you? Where's Swiss Cheese? (*Trying to calm her.*) One thing, and then the next thing, Kattrin, not all jumbled. Your mother understands you. The biscuit-brains took the money box? I'll twist his ears right off him! Slow down and stop all this flurry, use your hands, I hate it when you moan like a dog, what's the pastor going to think? You'll make his skin crawl. There was a one-eyed man?

THE CHAPLAIN: The one with one eye, he's a spy. They arrested Swiss Cheese? (*Kattrin nods 'yes'.*)

It's over.

(*Mother Courage takes the Catholic flag out of her basket.*)

MOTHER COURAGE: Raise the new flag!

(*The Chaplain affixes it to the flagpole.*)

THE CHAPLAIN (*bitterly*): Good Catholics now, root and branches.

(*Voices are heard. The two men drag in Swiss Cheese.*)

SWISS CHEESE: Let me go, I'm not carrying anything. Stop yanking on my shoulder, I didn't do anything wrong.

THE SERGEANT: He came from here. You know each other.

MOTHER COURAGE: We do? From where?

SWISS CHEESE: I don't know them. Who knows who they are? I don't know anything about them. I bought my lunch from them, ten hellers it cost me. Maybe you saw me sitting here, too salty to boot.

THE SERGEANT: Who are you, huh?

MOTHER COURAGE: Ordinary people. It's just like he said, he bought lunch. For him it was oversalted.

THE SERGEANT: You want me to believe you don't know each other?

MOTHER COURAGE: Why should I know him? I don't know everyone. I don't ask names or if someone's a heathen; if you pay up, you're not a heathen. (*To Swiss Cheese.*) Are you a heathen?

SWISS CHEESE: Not at all.

THE CHAPLAIN: He was an orderly customer and he never opened his mouth, except when he ate. Then you more or less have to.

THE SERGEANT: And who are you?

MOTHER COURAGE: He serves my liquor. And you're thirsty, he'll fetch you a glass of brandy, you've got to be parched and melting.

THE SERGEANT: No booze when we're working. (*To Swiss Cheese.*) You had something with you. You hid it near the river. Your shirt was all puffed out when you left here.

MOTHER COURAGE: You're sure it was him?

SWISS CHEESE: Must've been somebody else. I saw a guy run away from here in a big puffy shirt. But that wasn't me.

MOTHER COURAGE: I agree with him, you're confused, that can happen. I know a good person when I see one, I'm Courage, you've probably heard of me, everybody knows me, and I'm telling you, he seems honest to me.

THE SERGEANT: We're after the cash box of the Second Finnish Regiment. And we know what he looks like, the guy responsible for it. We've been looking for him for two days. You're it.

SWISS CHEESE: I'm not it.

THE SERGEANT: And if you don't hand it over you're dead, you know that. Where is it?

MOTHER COURAGE (*urgent*): Of course he'd give it to you if he knew his life depended on it. Right here, he'd say, I have it, you're stronger than me. He's not that dumb. Do it already, you goose, the Sergeant here is trying to help you.

SWISS CHEESE: If I don't have it.

THE SERGEANT: Let's go, then. We'll help you find it.

(*The two men drag Swiss Cheese away.*)

MOTHER COURAGE (*calling after them*): He'd tell you. He's not that stupid. And don't wrench his shoulder like that! (*She runs after them.*)

(*Evening of the same day. The Chaplain and dumb Kattrin are washing glasses and polishing knives.*)

THE CHAPLAIN: These traps into which one falls, they're not unfamiliar from our Devotional tales. It reminds me a little of the Passion of our Lord and Saviour. There's a very old song about that.

(*He sings the 'Song of the Hours'.*)
In the first hour of the day
Our Lord finally knows that
Like a murderer he'll be judged by
Heathen Pontius Pilate.

Pilate shall refuse the blame
Wash his hands in water
Then the innocent condemned
Sent off to the slaughter.

In the third hour God's own son
Flails and scourges flayed him
On his head a thorny crown
That the soldiers made him.

Dressed in rags and mockery
They beat him and deride him
And the cross of his own death
He'll drag along beside him.

In the sixth hour, naked, cold
On the cross they staved him
As his blood spilled down he prayed
For his father to save him.

One thief laughed and one thief wept
As he died beside them
While the sun withdrew its light
Hoping thus to hide them.

Jesus screamed by hour nine
Why does God forsake him
In his mouth a bitter gall
Vinegar to slake him.

At last he gave up the ghost
Mountains disassembled
Temple veils were rent in twain
And the whole world trembled.

Dark and sudden night time fell
The mocking crowd was scattered
Jesus's sides were torn by spears
The two thieves' bones were shattered.

Still the blood and water flows
Sill their mocking laughter
Thus befell the Son of Man
And many people after.

(*Mother Courage comes in, very worried, upset.*)

MOTHER COURAGE: He's strung up between life and death. But the Sergeant's still open to talking. And taking. Only we can't let on that Swiss Cheese is ours, they'll say we helped him. It's just about money. But where are we going to get money? Yvette's snagged herself a colonel, maybe he's interested in getting her started selling merchandise. Where is she? She said she'd hurry.

THE CHAPLAIN: You're going to sell her the wagon?

MOTHER COURAGE: How else get the money the Sergeant's demanding?

THE CHAPLAIN: How will you make a living?

MOTHER COURAGE: That's it, isn't it?

(*Yvette comes in with a decrepit Colonel. She embraces Mother Courage.*)

YVETTE: Courage, my love, long time no see! (*Whispering.*) It's a go. (*Loud again.*) This is my dear pal and business advisor, Poldi. Poldi, Courage. I hear you're looking to sell your wagon owing to exigent circumstances. It got me thinking.

MOTHER COURAGE: Pawn it, not sell it, don't trip over yourself, it's not so easy to find a good wagon in war time. Two hundred guilders.

YVETTE (*disappointed*): Pawn? I thought it was for sale. (*To the Colonel.*) What's your opinion?

THE COLONEL: Your opinion's my opinion, honey.

MOTHER COURAGE: It's only up for pawning.

YVETTE: I thought you needed the money.

MOTHER COURAGE (*decisively*): No way around it, the wagon's our life. This is a good thing for you, Yvette, who knows when something like this'll come your way again? You front me the money and when I redeem the pawn, you pocket a tidy profit, you never made such easy money, your nice old pal there agrees with me. (*To the Colonel.*) I'm right, huh? What's his name? Mouldy?

YVETTE: Poldi. And he thinks we should keep looking for something we can buy. Don't you, Poldi?

THE COLONEL: That's what I think.

MOTHER COURAGE: You keep looking then, maybe you'll find something you want, two or three weeks of looking is all it should take, just pray Poldi holds up, but you better hurry, he looks wobbly to me.

YVETTE: I'm happy shopping with you, Poldi. You don't mind looking around for a few weeks, do you, so long as we're always together? There are lots of places to look.

THE COLONEL (*to Mother Courage*): Well, baby girl, my knees go all stiff in this weather, I—

MOTHER COURAGE: I'll pay it back, quick as possible, with interest.

YVETTE: I'm all confused, Poldi, *chéri*, advise me. (*She takes the Colonel aside.*)
   We should give her the cash, let her pawn it, we'll own the wagon outright in the end, where's she gonna get two hundred guilders from to redeem it? I don't have two hundred guilders, but I can get money from that young blond lieutenant with the enormous feet. Know who I mean, Poldi? He's always waving it at me!

THE COLONEL: You don't need him, I told you I'd buy it for you, didn't I, baby bunny?

YVETTE: Oh, but it's indecent taking money from someone you love when you aren't married to him, though if in your opinion the lieutenant is inclined to exploit a situation, I'll let you do it.

THE COLONEL: I insist.

YVETTE: I'll find some way to pay you back.

THE COLONEL: I hate that lieutenant!

YVETTE: I know. (*She goes back to Mother Courage.*)
   My friend advises me to accept. Write out a receipt that the wagon's mine, after two weeks, and everything in it. I'll bring your two hundred guilders straight away. (*To the Colonel.*) Run back to the camp, I'll be right behind you. I just want to take stock so nothing'll go missing from my wagon. (*She kisses the Colonel and he leaves. She climbs up into the wagon.*)
   (*Inside the wagon.*) You've got boots, but not many.

MOTHER COURAGE: Yvette, there's no time for that! You have to go talk to that Sergeant, tell him the money's coming, there's not a minute to spare.

YVETTE (*inside the wagon*): Let me just take a second count of these linen shirts.

(*Mother Courage grabs hold of Yvette's skirt and pulls her down from the wagon.*)

MOTHER COURAGE: Leave it for now, jackal, or it's over for Swiss Cheese. And not a word who's making this offer. It came from your lover, swear that on God's good name, otherwise we'll all be implicated, his accomplices, we sheltered him.

YVETTE: Calm down, I'll take care of it, One-Eye's meeting me behind those trees, over there.

THE CHAPLAIN: And when you make your first offer, it doesn't have to be the whole two hundred up front, start with one hundred and fifty, that's perfectly ample.

MOTHER COURAGE (*to the Chaplain*): It's your money? Please, butt out. You'll still get your soup, now go haggle somewhere else, this is his life.

(*She shoos Yvette on her way.*)

THE CHAPLAIN: Apologies for interfering, but if you give them the full two hundred, how are you going to live, to earn money? With your unemployable daughter hanging around your neck.

MOTHER COURAGE: I'm counting on that regimental cash box, genius. When Swiss Cheese is free he'll bring it back to us, we can take out money to cover expenses.

I'll redeem the pawn, we'll get the wagon back when we get the cash box. (*To Kattrin.*) You, polish the knives, use the pumice stone. (*To the Chaplain.*) And you, leave off posing like Christ on Mount Olive, wash the glasses, by evening we'll have fifty suppers to serve. Thank God they're corrupt. They aren't wolves, they're just men after money. Corruption is the human equivalent of God's Mercy. As long as someone's on the take you can buy lighter sentences, so even the innocent have a shot at justice.

(*Yvette enters, winded.*)

YVETTE: Two hundred even. I'll go get the money from my Colonel, fast, soon it'll be too late, already he's sentenced to die. They used the thumbscrews, he confessed that he had the cash box. He told them when he saw he was being followed he threw it in the river.

MOTHER COURAGE: The cash box? He threw it in the . . .

YVETTE: It's gone. I'm gonna run and get the money from my Colonel.

MOTHER COURAGE: But if the cash box is gone, how will I get back my two hundred guilders?

YVETTE: Oh, of course, damn I'm stupid, you were hoping to take it outa that cash box! I shoulda known you'd find an angle. Well, give that up, you'll have to pay if you want Swiss Cheese back, or maybe you want to forget the whole deal, and you can keep your wagon?

MOTHER COURAGE: I hadn't anticipated this. Don't panic, you'll get the wagon, it's lost, I had it seventeen years. I need more time to think, what to do, I can't do two hundred, you should've bargained them down. If I'm left without anything, any stranger who wants to can have me in a ditch. Go and tell them I can't do two hundred, I'll give them a hundred twenty guilders, the wagon's lost regardless.

YVETTE: They're not going to agree. One-Eye's rushing me, he keeps looking with that one eye to see if someone's watching. He's scared. I have to offer the whole two hundred!

MOTHER COURAGE (*despairing*): I can't! I worked thirty years. She's twenty-five and she hasn't got a husband. She's mine as well. Stop tearing at me, I know what I'm doing. Tell them a hundred twenty and that's that.

YVETTE: Your choice.

(*She leaves. Mother Courage, avoiding looking at the Chaplain or her daughter, sits and helps Kattrin with the knives.*)

MOTHER COURAGE (*to the Chaplain*): Don't break any glasses, they don't belong to us now. (*To Kattrin.*) Pay attention, you'll cut yourself. Swiss Cheese will be back, I'll pay the two hundred if that's the only way. You'll get your brother back. With eighty guilders we can provision a rucksack with goods and start over. It's same game everywhere, you want to cook, you cook with water.

THE CHAPLAIN: The Lord will steer us right, as they say.

MOTHER COURAGE: Dry them carefully.

(*They scour the knives, silent. Suddenly Kattrin bursts into tears, hurries behind the wagon. Yvette runs in.*)

YVETTE: They said no deal. I warned you. One-Eye wants to drop the whole business, he says it's nearly over, in a minute we're going to hear the drums, the rifles are loaded. I went up to one hundred fifty. He didn't budge, not a flicker. I begged him to wait till I talked to you.

MOTHER COURAGE: Tell him I'll pay two hundred. Run. (*Yvette runs out. They sit in silence. The Chaplain has stopped cleaning the glasses.*)

Seems to me, I haggled too long.

(*Drums are heard in the distance. The Chaplain stands and goes behind the wagon. Courage remains seated. It gets dark. The drumroll stops. Then it gets light again. Mother Courage sits, motionless. Yvette enters, ashen.*)

YVETTE: Look what you've done with your haggling and hanging on. He got eleven bullets, eleven bullets, it was enough. It's not worth it, worrying about the likes of you. But they don't believe he threw the cash box in the river. They suspect it's been here all along, that you were working with him. So they're bringing him here, maybe you'll give yourself away when you see him. I warn you, you don't know him, or you're all dead. Should I take Kattrin away?

(*Mother Courage shakes her head 'no'.*)

MOTHER COURAGE: She knows. Fetch her.

(*Yvette gets Kattrin, who goes to her mother and stands beside her. Mother Courage takes her hand. Two soldiers enter with a stretcher on which something is lying, covered with a sheet. The Sergeant follows. They put the stretcher on the ground.*)

THE SERGEANT: Here's somebody, we don't know his name. It's got to be entered in the record, everything in its place. He bought a meal from you. Look and see if you know him. (*He takes the sheet away.*)

Know him? (*Mother Courage shakes her head.*)

You never saw him before you served him supper? (*Mother Courage shakes her head.*)

Lift him up. Throw him in the pit. He's got no one who knows him. (*They carry him away.*)

FOUR

Mother Courage sings 'The Song of the Great Capitulation'.

In front of an officer's tent. Mother Courage is waiting. A Clerk looks out from inside the tent.

THE CLERK: I know you. You're the one who was hiding that Protestant paymaster. Think twice before you make any complaints.

MOTHER COURAGE: I'm making a complaint. I hid nobody, and if I just take what they did to me it'll look like I think I'm guilty of something. They cut my wagon and my entire inventory to ribbons with their sabres, and then they charged me a five thaler fine, and all for having done nothing, less than nothing.

THE CLERK: Listen to what I'm telling you, it's for your own good: we don't have many merchandise wagons, so we'll let you stay in business, provided you assuage your guilty conscience by paying the necessary fines. And keep your mouth shut.

MOTHER COURAGE: I want to make a complaint.

THE CLERK: Be my guest. Wait here for the Captain's convenience.

(*He goes back into the tent. A Young Soldier enters, furious. An Older Soldier is running after him.*)

THE YOUNG SOLDIER: By the Holy Virgin's Flowerbush where's that goddamned sonofabitch of a Captain who withheld my bonus and then spent it on his whores' bar tab? Time to pay up!

THE OLDER SOLDIER: Aw Jesus, they're gonna slam you in the stocks!

THE YOUNG SOLDIER: Come out, you crook! I'm gonna butcher you! Refusing me my bonus after I was the only one willing to swim that river, the only one in the whole battalion, and I can't even buy a beer for myself. I'm not letting myself get fucked like this. You come outside now and let me cut your fucking head off!

(*The Older Soldier restrains the Young Soldier, who's trying to get into the tent.*)

THE OLDER SOLDIER: Sweet Christ, he's gonna mess everything up for himself.

MOTHER COURAGE: They screwed him out of his bonus?

THE YOUNG SOLDIER: Let go of me or I'll murder you too, he's gonna get hung out to dry, it's gotta happen.

THE OLDER SOLDIER: He rescued the Colonel's horse but then they didn't give the bonus like they're supposed to. He's young, he hasn't learned.

MOTHER COURAGE: Let him loose, he's not a dog, a man doesn't have to be put on a leash. A bonus is a bonus and it's perfectly reasonable to expect to be paid. Why else bother being brave?

THE YOUNG SOLDIER: He's drinking in there! You all shit yourselves for fear of him. I stepped up and stood out and now I get my bonus pay!

MOTHER COURAGE: Don't bark at me, son. I've got problems of my own, and anyway you should spare your big fine voice—if all you can do is whisper when the Captain comes out, he won't haul your ass to the stocks. People who shout the way you're shouting are hoarse in half an hour and so exhausted anyone can sing them to sleep.

THE YOUNG SOLDIER: I'm not exhausted and who could sleep this hungry? The bread's made out of acorn mash and hemp seed and now they're cutting back on that. He spent my bonus on whores and I'm starving. He's gonna pay!

MOTHER COURAGE: I get it, you're hungry. I remember last year when your general ordered you guys to march back and forth across the cornfields—I could've sold boots for ten guilders a pair if I'd had any boots to sell. He planned to be elsewhere by now, but here he is, a year later, bogged down, and there's no corn and everyone's starving. I get it, you're angry.

THE YOUNG SOLDIER: Stop talking to me, I don't give a shit about any of that, I won't let myself be treated unfairly.

MOTHER COURAGE: How long? How long will you refuse to be treated unfairly? An hour, two? See, never occurs to you to ask yourself that, and that's the first thing you should ask, 'cause it's no good figuring it out later, after all the skin on your back has been flayed off with the whipping you'll get for insubordination, after the whip's blistered all the skin off you and you're raw and bleeding, in chains praying for death it hurts so bad, then it's a little late to realise that maybe, on second thoughts, actually you can live with being treated unfairly.

THE YOUNG SOLDIER: Why am I listening to you? By the Holy Mother's Bush! CAPTAIN!

MOTHER COURAGE: I'll tell you why you're listening: I'm right and you know it, your fury's just a lightning bolt that splits the air, bright, noisy, then BANG!—all over. It was short-lived anger, when what you needed was long-burning rage, but where would you get something like that?

THE YOUNG SOLDIER: You're saying I don't have a right to get paid what I'm owed?

MOTHER COURAGE: Just the opposite. You have a right, but you have a short-lived anger and that'll never get you what you want. If you had long-lasting rage, I'd cheer you on. Hack the sonofabitch to death, I'm right behind you, but what if you cool down smack in the middle of it, and he doesn't get hacked up, because your hard-on's gone all of a sudden? There I am, standing there, you've slunk off and the Captain blames me.

THE OLDER SOLDIER: You're right, he'll settle down, he just went a little crazy.

THE YOUNG SOLDIER: You'll see, I'm gonna cut his throat. (*He draws his sword.*)

   As soon as he sets his foot out here I'm gonna do it. (*The Clerk comes out.*)

THE CLERK: The Captain'll be out soon. Sit.

(*The Young Soldier sits.*)

MOTHER COURAGE: They say sit, he sits. Like I said. Sitting pretty. They know us so well, what makes us tick. Sit! And we sit. And sitting people don't make trouble. (*The Young Soldier starts to stand.*)

   Better not stand up again, you won't be standing the way you did before. (*He sits back down.*)

   Hope you're not embarrassed on my account, I'm not better than you, worse if anything. We had gumption. They bought it, all of it. Why kick, might hurt business. It's called the Great Capitulation.

(*She sings 'The Song of the Great Capitulation'.*)
Back when I was young, fresh as grass and innocent,
Any day, I'd fly away on butterfly wings.

(*Speaking.*) Not just a peddler's daughter, me with my good looks and my talent and my longing for a better life!

(*Singing.*)
If my soup was cold, or the meat they served me
   wasn't succulent,
Back it went, it's worth the wait for nicer things.

(*Speaking.*) All or nothing, next best is no good at all, everyone makes her own luck, I don't take orders from anyone.

(*Singing.*)
Birdsong up above:
Push comes to shove.

Soon you fall down from the grandstand
And join the players in the band
Who tootle out that melody:
Wait, wait and see.
And then: it's all downhill.
Your fall was God's will.
Better let it be.

But within a year, I would eat what I was served.
And I learned, you smile and take your medicine.

(*Speaking.*) Two kids hanging on my neck and the price of bread and everything it takes from you.

(*Singing.*)
I'd accepted that I only got the shit that I deserved
On my ass, or on my knees, I took it with a grin.

(*Speaking.*) You have to learn to make deals with people, one hand washes the other one, your head's not hard enough to knock over a wall.

(*Singing.*)
Birdsong from above:
Push comes to shove.
Soon you fall down from your grandstand
And join the players in the band
Who tootle out that melody:
Wait, wait and see.
And then: it's all downhill.
Your fall was God's will.
Better let it be.

Many folk I've known planned to scale the highest peak.
Off they go, the starry sky high overhead.

(*Speaking.*) To the victor the spoils, where there's a will there's a way, at least act like you own the store.

(*Singing.*)
Stone by stone you climb, but your efforts only
   leave you worn and weak,
Broken down, you barely make it back to bed.

(*Speaking.*) If the shoe fits, wear it.

(*Singing.*)
From the God of Love:
Push comes to shove.
And you fall down from that grandstand
And join the players in the band
Who tootle out that melody:
Wait, wait and see.
And then; it just goes downhill,
Who knows? It's God's will.
Best to leave it be.

(*Speaking, to the Young Soldier.*) Stay here with your sword ready if your anger is great enough, because you're in the right, I know you are, but if your anger's only a flash, better to run away.

THE YOUNG SOLDIER: Go fuck yourself in hell.

(*He stumbles out, the Older Soldier following him. The Clerk sticks his head out of the tent.*)

THE CLERK: The Captain's ready. You can make your complaint now.

MOTHER COURAGE: I've thought it over. I'm not complaining. (*She leaves.*)

Interval.

FIVE

Two years have gone by. The war has expanded over ever wider territory. Mother Courage's little wagon travels ceaselessly, crossing Poland, Moravia, Bavaria, Italy, and Bavaria again. 1631. Tilly's victory at Magdeburg costs Mother Courage four officers' shirts.

Mother Courage's wagon has set up in a village that's been wrecked by cannon fire. Military marches sound in the distance. Two Soldiers stand at the wagon's bar, served by Kattrin and Mother Courage. One of the Soldiers has a woman's fur coat draped over his shoulders.

MOTHER COURAGE: Why can't you pay? No money, no schnapps. If I'm hearing a victory march, the soldiers ought to have enough back pay to pay a bar tab.

SOLDIER: C'mon, schnapps! I was delayed and I missed the looting. The general only allowed one hour of looting, one hour for a whole city! It'd be inhuman to allow more, he said; the city must've bribed him, the treacherous fuck.

(*The Chaplain stumbles in.*)

THE CHAPLAIN: In the farmyard, they're lying there. A family. Somebody help me. I need linen.

(*The Second Soldier goes with him. Kattrin, agitated, beseeches her mother to bring out linen.*)

MOTHER COURAGE: I'm out. I sold every bandage in stock to the regiment. What should I do, tear up good officers' shirts to bandage farmers?

THE CHAPLAIN (*calling from offstage*): I said I need linen.

(*Mother Courage sits on the steps to the wagon so Kattrin can't go in.*)

MOTHER COURAGE: I'm giving nothing. They'll never pay and here's why, because they've got nothing.

(*The Chaplain is bent over a woman he's carried from the yard.*)

THE CHAPLAIN (*to the woman*): Why did you stay after the shooting started?

THE FARMER'S WIFE (*very weak*): Farm.

MOTHER COURAGE: Them let go of what's theirs? Oh no never! And I should be left holding the bill. Not me, no way.

FIRST SOLDIER: Too bad they wouldn't convert.

MOTHER COURAGE: They would have if anyone'd asked. They'd whistle any tune you wanted. The farm's everything to farmers.

SECOND SOLDIER: Anyway, not a one of them is Protestant. These are Catholics, same as us.

FIRST SOLDIER: That's the trouble with artillery shells, they're indiscriminate.

(*The Chaplain has carried the Farmer from the yard.*)

FARMER: My arm's ripped open.

THE CHAPLAIN: Where's the linen?

(*Everyone looks at Mother Courage who doesn't move.*)

MOTHER COURAGE: Taxes, tolls, penalties and payoffs! I can't spare a thing. (*Growling, Kattrin picks up a plank and threatens her mother with it.*)

Have you snapped your tether? You put that plank down now or I'll slap your face off you, you cramp! I'm giving nothing, no one can make me, I've got myself to think about. (*The Chaplain lifts her off the steps and puts her on the ground. He goes into the wagon and comes out with linen shirts, which he proceeds to tear into strips.*)

Oh not my shirts! That's half a guilder I paid per. I'm ruined!

(*A baby is heard screaming in terror inside the house.*)

THE FARMER: Baby's still inside!

(*Kattrin rushes into the house. The Farmer's Wife tries to sit up, the Chaplain restrains her.*)

THE CHAPLAIN (*to the Farmer's Wife*): Stay, stay, they've gone in to get it.

MOTHER COURAGE: Stop her, the roof might collapse.

THE CHAPLAIN: I'm not going in there again.

MOTHER COURAGE: Leave off my poor linen, you jackass.

(*Kattrin emerges from the rubble, carrying an infant.*)

Oh what luck, who's found herself another suckling to haul around? You give it back to its mother one-two-three before you get attached and I have to spend hours pulling it away, you hear me? (*To the Second Soldier.*) Stop gawping, go tell them they can stop that music, I don't need to hear about it, I can see they've had a victory. I've had only losses from your victory.

(*The Chaplain is bandaging wounds.*)

THE CHAPLAIN: This isn't stopping the bleeding.

(*Kattrin rocks the baby, singing a cradle song in her thick inarticulate way.*)

MOTHER COURAGE: Look at her, joy sitting in the midst of misery, now give it back, its mother's coming to. (*She grabs the First Soldier, who's been pouring himself drinks and is now trying to get away with the whole bottle.*)

Pay up, pig, no victories for you here animal! Pay up.

FIRST SOLDIER: With what?

(*She tears the fur coat off his shoulders.*)

MOTHER COURAGE: Leave me the coat, which anyway you stole somewhere.

THE CHAPLAIN: Someone's still inside.

SIX

Near the Bavarian city of Ingolstadt Mother Courage observes the funeral of the fallen Imperial Field Marshal Tilly. Discussions take place regarding war heroes and the duration of the war. The Chaplain complains that he's wasting his talents, and dumb Kattrin gets the red shoes. The year's recorded: 1632.

Inside a canteen tent Mother Courage has set up. A bar in the back is open to serve people outside. Rain. Drumrolls and sad music in the distance. The Chaplain

and the Regimental Secretary are playing a board game.
Mother Courage and her daughter are taking stock.

THE CHAPLAIN: The funeral cortege has set forth.

MOTHER COURAGE: Too bad about the Field Marshal—
twenty-two pairs of socks—he was up at the front
before the battle, inspiring yet another regiment,
don't fear death and that sort of thing, then he
headed back to HQ but there was fog on the meadows and he got turned around and ended up in the
middle of the slaughter and he caught a musket ball
in the gut—we've only got four lanterns left. (*Some-*
one outside whistles and Mother Courage goes to
tend the bar.)
    You guys are shameless, he was your Field Mar-
shal and you're skipping his funeral!

(*She serves them drinks.*)

THE REGIMENTAL SECRETARY: It was a mistake, paying
them before the funeral. Now instead of attending,
they're all getting soused.

THE CHAPLAIN (*to the Regimental Secretary*): Shouldn't
you be at the funeral?

THE REGIMENTAL SECRETARY: I wanted to go but it's raining.

MOTHER COURAGE: You've got an excuse, the rain'd ruin
your uniform. They're saying they wanted to ring
church bells for the funeral, the way you ought to, but
the Field Marshal blew up every steeple in Ingolstadt,
so no bells for the poor bastard as his coffin's dropped
down to the worms. They'll fire off the cannons, just
to keep it from getting too sober seventeen bullet belts.

(*Calls from outside, men at the bar:*)

VOICES OUTSIDE: COME ON! SERVICE! BRANDY!!

MOTHER COURAGE: Show me your money first. And no
one comes inside, you're not mucking up my tent
with your filthy boots. You'll drink outside, rain rain
go away. (*To the Regimental Secretary.*) Only commissioned officers get in. On a memorable occasion
such as this you want classier company.

(*A funeral march. Everyone looks outside.*)

THE CHAPLAIN: They're filing past the estimable corpse.

MOTHER COURAGE: It grieves me in a special way when
it's a field marshal or a king who dies, someone who
dreamed of doing things that'll still be talked about
ages hence, whose strivings fell flat all because big
dreamers need common people to do the sweaty work,
and common people have no aspirations, a cold mug
of beer in some friendly saloon and they're happy.
Look at those men out there, drinking brandy in the
rain. It's pathetic is what it is, that tiny-mindedness.

THE CHAPLAIN: Oh, they're not so bad. Soldiers. They do
what they're told. They'll fight for a hundred more
years if they're ordered to. Two hundred years. Tell
'em to do it and they'll fight for ever.

MOTHER COURAGE: Think the war will end now?

THE CHAPLAIN: Why? Because a field marshal died? Don't
be silly. Food's scarce, not field marshals.

MOTHER COURAGE: Seriously, for me it's not a casual
question, I could really beef up the inventory, I've got
cash and prices are low, but then if the war ends, no
demand, I'll be sunk.

THE CHAPLAIN: Very well then, my earnest opinion. There
are always people who run around and say, 'Some day
the war will end.' I say no one can say whether the
war will end. There will of course be brief pauses, intermissions if you will. The war might meet with an
accident, same as the Field Marshal. There are risks in
every enterprise, the earth is under heaven and nothing's perfect upon it. Wars get stuck in ruts, no one
saw it coming, no one can think of everything, maybe
there's been short-sighted planning and all at once
your war's a big mess. But the Emperor or the King
or the Pope reliably provides what's necessary to get
it going again. This war's got no significant worries as
far as I can see, a long life lies ahead of it.

(*A soldier is singing at the bar.*)

THE SOLDIER (*singing*):
    A schnapps, landlord, and fast!
    A soldier's never last!
    His fists are even faster!

(*Speaking.*) Make mine a double, today's a holiday!

MOTHER COURAGE: I must be getting tired, or it's the
rain or the funeral or something, uncertainty's never
bothered me before.

THE CHAPLAIN: What's uncertain? What will ever stop the
war?

THE SOLDIER (*singing*):
    Your tits, girl, show 'em fast!
    A soldier's heart is vast!
    But please don't tell the pastor!

THE REGIMENTAL SECRETARY (*abruptly*): And peace, whatever happened to that? I'm from Bohemia and I want
to go home.

THE CHAPLAIN: Oh, yes, peace indeed. It's the hole in the
cheese, we search high and low for it after we've eaten.

THE SOLDIER (*singing*):
    Your cards, comrades, and fast!
    A soldier's not tight-assed!
    He smiles at disaster!

    Your prayer, good priest, and fast!
    A soldier's die is cast!
    He's mincemeat for his master!

THE REGIMENTAL SECRETARY: People can't live without
peace.

THE CHAPLAIN: True, but just because there's war doesn't
mean there's no peace, war has its moments of peace.
War satisfies every human need, even for peace, it's got
to or why else would we have wars? You can take a
dump in wartime exactly as you do when things are
peaceful, and between one battle and the next have a
beer. Even when you're dog weary on the march you
can prop your head up on your elbows and catch a nap
in a ditch. While it's true that in the thick of battle you
can't play cards, you can't do that in the thick of peacetime either, when you're ploughing furrows in the field,
hour by hour day after day—after a battle, at least,
if you win, there are possibilities. Your leg's shot up,
maybe, and first thing you scream, then you calm down,
then a glass of schnapps, then in the end you're hopping about like a regular flea and the war's still the war,

unperturbed by your misadventure. And what's to stop you from multiplying in the midst of slaughter, behind a barn or anyplace, breeding like maggots in raw meat, nothing stops that, and then the war takes the kids you produce and on and on it goes on and on and on. No, war always finds a way. Why should it ever end?

(*Kattrin has stopped working. She's holding a basket full of bottles and is staring at the Chaplain.*)

MOTHER COURAGE: OK, I'm buying more goods. On your say-so. (*Kattrin suddenly throws the basket to the ground and runs off.*)

　　　　Kattrin! (*Laughing.*) Jesus, she's waiting for peace. I promised her she'd get a husband when peace arrives.

(*Mother Courage runs after her. The Regimental Secretary stands up.*)

THE REGIMENTAL SECRETARY: While you chattered I paid attention to the game. I win. Pay up.

(*Mother Courage returns with Kattrin.*)

MOTHER COURAGE: A little more war, a little more money, peace'll be sweeter for the wait. You go to town, ten minutes' walk, get our package at the Golden Lion, the pricey things, the rest we'll pick up with the wagon. They expect you, and the Regimental Secretary here will accompany you. Most everyone's at the Field Marshal's funeral, nothing can happen to you. Hang tight to the package, anyone says they'll help carry it no thanks, think about your trousseau.

(*Kattrin covers her head with a scarf and leaves with the Regimental Secretary.*)

THE CHAPLAIN: You think it's a good idea, letting her go with him?

MOTHER COURAGE: She should be so pretty that a man like him pays attention to her.

THE CHAPLAIN: Often I sit back and watch you, amazed. Your quick mind, your indomitable spirit, it's the right name for you, Courage.

MOTHER COURAGE: You're talkative today. I'm not courageous. Only poor people need courage. Why, because they're hopeless. To get out of bed each morning, or plough a potato field in wartime, or bring kids with no prospects into the world—to live poor, that takes courage. Consider how easily and often they murder each other, they need courage just to look one another in the face. They trudge along, uncomplainingly carrying the Emperor and his heavy throne and the Pope and his stone cathedral, they stagger, starving, bearing the whole thundering weight of the great wealth of the wealthy on their broad stupid backs, and is that courage? Must be, but it's perverted courage, because what they carry on their backs will cost them their lives. (*She sits, takes a small pipe from a pocket, lights it and smokes.*)

　　　　You could be chopping up kindling.

(*The Chaplain reluctantly takes off his coat, picks up a hatchet and a bundle of branches, and starts chopping kindling, standing over a chopping block, hacking the branches into smaller sticks.*)

THE CHAPLAIN: I'm a pastor, not a woodcutter.

MOTHER COURAGE: I don't have a soul so I don't need a pastor. I have a stove, and it needs firewood.

THE CHAPLAIN: Where'd you get that stubby little pipe?

MOTHER COURAGE: It's a pipe, who knows?

THE CHAPLAIN: It's not a pipe, or rather not just a pipe, it's special.

MOTHER COURAGE: Is it?

THE CHAPLAIN: It's the stubby little pipe of the cook from the Oxenstjerna Regiment.

MOTHER COURAGE: If you know, why're you asking, hypocrite?

THE CHAPLAIN: Because I don't know whether you pay attention to what you smoke. Could be you just fish around in your pockets like some people do and any stumpy grubby snub of a pipe your fingers come across, you'll pop it in your mouth from sheer absent-mindedness.

MOTHER COURAGE: As long as I can suck smoke out of it, I'm not fussy.

THE CHAPLAIN: Perhaps, only I don't think so. Not you. You know what you're smoking.

MOTHER COURAGE: This is going somewhere?

THE CHAPLAIN: Listen to me, Courage. It's my obligation as your minister. It's hardly likely you'll meet up with that character again, and you know what character I mean, but that's luck not loss.

MOTHER COURAGE: Seemed nice enough to me. Who cares what you think?

THE CHAPLAIN: Good, you think he was nice, I think he wasn't, I think he's maybe not actually evil, but nice, definitely not. A Don Juan, exceedingly well-oiled. Take a look at that pipe, it exposes him, his personality.

MOTHER COURAGE: I'm looking at it.

THE CHAPLAIN: The stem of which has been half chewed through. As if a rat had attacked it. The gnawed-upon pipe of a boorish violent rat of a man, you can see it for yourself if you haven't lost your last lick of horse sense.

MOTHER COURAGE: You're really going to town with that hatchet.

THE CHAPLAIN: I'm not trained to do this, I'm trained to preach. I went to divinity school. My gifts, my abilities are squandered on physical activity. It's an inappropriate application of God-given talents. Which is sinful. You never heard me preach. I can so intoxicate a battalion they think the enemy army's a grazing flock of fine fat mutton. When I preach, a soldier's life's no more to him than an old *fershtunkeneh*° footwrap he casts away as he marches off to glory. God gave me a mighty tongue. When I preach people fall dumb and go blind.

MOTHER COURAGE: Jesus, that's sort of terrifying.

THE CHAPLAIN: Courage, I've been waiting for this opportunity to talk to you.

MOTHER COURAGE: Maybe if we're quiet we'll hear more funeral music.

THE CHAPLAIN: Beneath your customarily brusque and businesslike manner you're human, a woman, you need warmth.

---

fershtunkeneh: Used.

MOTHER COURAGE: I'm warm, and all it takes is a steady supply of chopped wood.

THE CHAPLAIN: Kindling aside, Courage, shouldn't we make our relationship a closer one? I mean, consider how the whirligig of war has whirled us two together.

MOTHER COURAGE: I think we've whirled close as we're ever going to get. I cook, you eat what I cook, you do this and that and when you feel like it you chop kindling.

(*The Chaplain moves towards her.*)

THE CHAPLAIN: You know perfectly well that when I use the word 'close' I don't mean cooking or eating or kindling.

MOTHER COURAGE: Don't come at me waving that axe.

THE CHAPLAIN: I'm not a figure of fun. You make me a figure of fun. I'm a man with his dignity and I'm tendering you a considered, legitimate proposal. I'm proposing! Respond to my proposal!

MOTHER COURAGE: Give it a rest, Pastor. We get along, don't make me dunk your head in a pail. I want nothing more than for me and my children to get through all this with our wagon. I have nothing to give anyone, and anyway there's no room inside me for private dramas. It's drama enough, stocking up with the Field Marshal fallen and everyone talking about peace. If my business folds, where would you be? Look, you hesitate, you don't know. If you make kindling we'll be warm come evening, and that's a lot, these days. (*She stands up.*) What's that? (*Kattrin enters, a large cut across her forehead and over an eye. She carries many packages, leather goods, a drum and other things as well.*)

What, what, did somebody attack you? On your way back? Someone attacked her on the way back! Bet it was that soldier who was getting drunk! I shouldn't have sent you. Drop those things! It's not so terrible, a bad scratch. I'll bandage you up and in a week you're healed. They're not human, none of 'em, every one of them's swine.

(*She bandages Kattrin's wounds.*)

THE CHAPLAIN: Blame the ones who start the wars. They don't rape back home.

MOTHER COURAGE: I'll blame who I want and the hell they don't. Why didn't the Regimental Secretary walk you back? Probably he figured an upstanding person such as yourself wouldn't get bothered by anyone. The wound's not deep, it won't leave a mark. Done and done, wrapped tight. You just rest, calm yourself. I've got a secret something to show you, you'll see. (*She gets a sack from which she takes Yvette's red shoes.*)

All right, look! See? You've been dreaming about them. They're yours. Put them on quick, before I have second thoughts. You won't be scarred, though there are worse things than that. If you're pretty you've got to be afraid of what's hiding behind every bush, your life's a nightmare. It's the ones no one warns who manage to have a life, like with trees, the tall beautiful trees get felled for roof beams, but the crippled and crooked trees get overlooked and go on living.

You have to know how to recognise good luck. The shoes are ready to be worn, I've been shining them on the sly.

(*Kattrin leaves the shoes and crawls into the wagon.*)

THE CHAPLAIN: Hopefully she won't be disfigured.

MOTHER COURAGE: It'll scar. Peace will never come for her.

THE CHAPLAIN: She didn't let them take your merchandise.

MOTHER COURAGE: I shouldn't have made such a fuss about that maybe. I wish I knew what it looked like inside her head! She stayed out all night just once in all these years. After that she stumped around the way she does, only she started to work herself till she dropped, every day. She'd never tell me about it, what adventures she'd had. I clubbed my forehead with my fists for a long time over that one. (*She picks up the goods Kattrin dropped and angrily inspects them.*)

War! A great way to make a living!

(*Cannon fire.*)

THE CHAPLAIN: Now they're burying the Field Marshal. A moment in history.

MOTHER COURAGE: The only history I know is today's the day they hit my daughter in the eye. She's more than halfway to done-for now, no husband for her now, and her such a great fool for children, she's mute because of the war, that too, when she was little a soldier stuffed something in her mouth. I'll never see Swiss Cheese again, and where Eilif is only God knows. It's a curse, this fucking war.

SEVEN

Mother Courage at the height of her business career.

A highway. The Chaplain and Kattrin are pulling the wagon, festooned with new wares. Mother Courage walks alongside, wearing a necklace made of silver thalers.

MOTHER COURAGE: I won't let you knock the war. Everyone says the weak are exterminated, but the weak don't fare any better in peacetime. War feeds its people better.

(*She sings:*)
It overwhelms all opposition,
it needs to grow or else it dies.
What else is war but competition,
A profit-building enterprise?

(*Speaking.*) You can't hide from it. The ones who hide are the first it finds.

War isn't nice, you hope to shirk it,
You hope you'll find someplace to hide.
But if you've courage you can work it,
And put a tidy sum aside.
The refugees? Oh sure, I've seen 'em,
the thousands fleeing from the war!
They've not a scrap of bread between 'em.
I wonder what they're running for?
The Spring has come, and Winter's dead.

The snow has gone, so draw a breath!
Let Christian souls crawl out of bed,
    pull on their socks and conquer death!
(*They keep pulling.*)

EIGHT

*In the same year the Swedish king, Gustavus Adolphus,
falls in the battle of Lutzen. Peace threatens to ruin
Mother Courage's business. Her brave son does one heroic deed too many and comes to an ignominious end.*

*An army camp. A summer's morning. Outside the
wagon, an Old Woman and a Young Man, her son, are
waiting. The son is carrying a heavy mattress.*

MOTHER COURAGE'S VOICE (*inside the wagon*): Does it
have to be so goddamned early?

THE YOUNG MAN: We've been walking all night, twenty
miles, we have to get back today.

MOTHER COURAGE'S VOICE (*inside the wagon*): Who's buying mattresses? People don't have houses.

THE YOUNG MAN: Come look at it.

THE OLD WOMAN: She doesn't want it, no one does. Let's
go home.

THE YOUNG MAN: Home's forfeit if we can't pay the taxes.
She'll give us at least three guilders for the bed if we
include your crucifix. (*Bells start ringing.*)
        Listen, Mama!

OFFSTAGE VOICES: Peace! The Swedish King is dead!

(*Mother Courage sticks her head out of the wagon. Her
hair's an uncombed mess.*)

MOTHER COURAGE: What's with the bells? It's Wednesday!

(*The Chaplain crawls out from under the wagon.*)

THE CHAPLAIN: What's the shouting about?

MOTHER COURAGE: Don't tell me peace has broken out.
I've just replenished my entire stock.

THE CHAPLAIN (*shouting to the rear*): Is it peace?

A VOICE: The war was over three weeks ago, they're saying, it took three weeks for the news to get here!

ANOTHER VOICE: In town, a whole heap of Lutherans arrived in their carts, they brought the news with them.

THE YOUNG MAN: Ma, it's peace! (*The Old Woman collapses. Her son rushes to her.*)
        Ma? MA!

(*Mother Courage goes back inside the wagon.*)

MOTHER COURAGE: Mary and Joseph! Kattrin, it's peace!
Put your black dress on! We'll go find a Protestant
church. We should pray for Swiss Cheese. I can't believe it!

THE YOUNG MAN: They wouldn't be saying it if it wasn't true.
They made peace. (*To his mother.*) Can you stand up?

(*The Old Woman stands.*)

I'll start making saddles again, I'll open up the
shop. I promise you. Everything will go back to what
it was. We'll bring back Daddy's bedding. Can you
walk? (*To the Chaplain.*) It hit her hard. The news. She
decided long ago the war would last for ever. (*To his
mother.*) Daddy always said otherwise. Let's get home.

(*The mother and son leave.*)

MOTHER COURAGE (*inside the wagon*): Give the old
woman a schnapps!

THE CHAPLAIN: Gone. Gone.

MOTHER COURAGE (*inside the wagon*): What're they up
to in the camp?

THE CHAPLAIN: There's a huge crowd. I'll go over. Think I
should put on my evangelical garb?

MOTHER COURAGE (*inside the wagon*): If it was me, I'd
inquire a little more precisely as to the state of things
before I went into a Catholic army camp dressed as
the Antichrist. I'm so happy it's peace, I don't care if
I'm ruined. At least two of my children survived the
war, I saw to that. Bet I'll see my Eilif soon.

(*The Cook enters, haggard, carrying a bundle.*)

THE CHAPLAIN: And look what peace already dragged in.
It's the General's cook!

THE COOK: What's this apparition I see before me? The
Holy Ghost? No, it's the General's chaplain, same as
ever, pale as a snail's sticky underbelly!

THE CHAPLAIN: Courage, a visitor!

(*Mother Courage climbs down from the wagon.*)

MOTHER COURAGE: The General's cook. After all these
years.

THE COOK: At the first opportunity, as promised, a visit,
a little intelligent conversation, some unforgettable
brandy, Mrs Fierling, a man's only as good as his word.

MOTHER COURAGE: Where's Eilif, my eldest?

THE COOK: He left before I did, on his way here same as
me. Funny he isn't here yet, he's so robust.

THE CHAPLAIN: I'm putting on my pastoral vestements,
don't say anything interesting till I get back.

(*He goes behind the wagon.*)

MOTHER COURAGE: He's robust but he dawdles. He'll
show up any minute, I can feel it! (*Calling into the
wagon.*) Kattrin, Eilif's coming! Bring the cook a
glass of brandy, Kattrin! (*Kattrin doesn't come out.*)
        (*Calling into the wagon.*) Comb your bangs down
over it, it's enough already! Mr Lamb isn't a stranger.
(*She gets the brandy herself.*)
        She won't come out, what does peace mean to
her? It took its time coming and it came too late.
They hit her, right above the eye, you can barely see
the scar now, but to her mind people stare.

THE COOK: War.

(*They sit.*)

MOTHER COURAGE: You're showing up at an unlucky
moment for me, Cook. Ruined. I took the Chaplain's
advice and I've overstocked, forked over all my cash
for goods I'll be sitting on, the troops'll be packing
up and heading home.

THE COOK: A woman your age listening to a preacher? For
shame. I meant to warn you back when to give that
dried-up-twig of a chaplain a wide berth but there
wasn't time, and you—you fell for his big words.

MOTHER COURAGE: I fell for nothing. He's chief dish-
washer and assistant drayhorse and that's it.

THE COOK: You must be hard up for drayhorses. He
tell you any of his sideways jokes, he's sort of got a

careless opinion of women, I tried to use my influence for moral improvements but in vain, the man's absolutely unsolid.

MOTHER COURAGE: You're solid, huh?

THE COOK: If I'm anything, I'm solid. (*Toasting her.*) *Skol!*

MOTHER COURAGE: *Prosit!*°

THE COOK: *A votre santé!*°

MOTHER COURAGE: Mud in yer eye. I've only been with one solid man, thank God. Soon as spring arrived for a little extra pocket money he stripped the blankets from the kids' beds, then he told me my harmonica wasn't a Christian instrument.

THE COOK: I like a woman who knows how to handle a harmonica.

MOTHER COURAGE: Maybe later, if the mood strikes me, I might play a snatch.

THE COOK: Here we sit, together again, and the bells are chiming peace, peace peace . . . And then there's your indelible brandy, your unimpeachable hospitality.

MOTHER COURAGE: Did you get paid before you deserted?

THE COOK (*hesitantly*): Not exactly, no, they've been out of cash all year. So I didn't desert, non-payment of our salaries inspired us to dissolve our regiment on our own authority.

MOTHER COURAGE: You're broke.

THE COOK: Oh really you know, they could stop that fucking din. I'm not broke, I'm between money, looking for something to which I can apply these capable hands, I've lost my appetite as it were for army cooking, they give me roots and boots for the soup pot then they throw the consequences piping hot in my face. I begged to be transferred to the infantry, and now, peacetime. (*The Chaplain appears in his pastor's coat.*) (*To Mother Courage.*) Later.

THE CHAPLAIN: Apart from the occasional moth hole, it's perfectly presentable.

THE COOK: But not worth the effort, putting it on. No more soldiers to inflame. And I have another chicken to pluck with you, if you've the time, because thanks to you this lady purchased surplus goods under the illusion you peddled her that the war will go on eternally.

THE CHAPLAIN (*heatedly*): I'm going to have to ask you how this is any concern of yours?

THE COOK: It's unscrupulous, what you did! Interfering in the way other people manage their affairs with unasked-for advice.

THE CHAPLAIN: I interfered? Who says I interfered? (*To Mother Courage.*) Did you say I interfered?

MOTHER COURAGE: Don't get excited, the Cook's entitled to his personal opinion.

THE CHAPLAIN: I didn't know you owed him perusal of your accounts.

MOTHER COURAGE: I owe him quatsch, and I owe you quatsch, and his point is your war was a bust, and he's got a point. You ruined me.

THE CHAPLAIN: The way you talk about peace, Courage, it's a sin. You're a hyena of the battlefields.

Prosit!: "Cheers."   *A votre santé!*: "To your health."

MOTHER COURAGE: I'm what?

THE COOK: He who insults my friend deals with me.

THE CHAPLAIN: I wasn't talking to you. You have transparent intentions. (*To Mother Courage.*) But when I see you picking up peace disdainfully betwixt your thumb and forefinger as if it were a, a, a snot-rag, my humanity's affronted; I see you as you are, a woman who hates peace and loves war, as long as you can make money off it, but don't forget the old saying, 'If you want to dine with the Devil bring a long spoon!'

MOTHER COURAGE: I didn't ask the war to linger and it didn't linger any longer than it wanted to. And anybody calls me a hyena is looking for a divorce.

THE CHAPLAIN: The whole world's finally, finally able to draw a deep breath and you alone, you, carping about peace because, because what, because of that load of tattery antiquated crap in your wagon?!

MOTHER COURAGE: My wares aren't crap, and I survived by selling them, and you survived by leeching off me.

THE CHAPLAIN: By leeching off war! My point! Right!

THE COOK (*to the Chaplain*): Adults should neither give nor receive advice, according to someone or other. Who probably knew what he was talking about. (*To Mother Courage.*) Sell quick before prices fall much farther. Dress up and get going, there isn't a second to spare!

MOTHER COURAGE: Sharp thinking. I like it, I'll do it.

THE CHAPLAIN: On his say-so?

MOTHER COURAGE: Better his than yours! Anyone asks, I'm off to the market.

(*She goes into the wagon.*)

THE COOK: Score one for me, Pastor. You don't think quick on your feet. You should have said, 'When did I ever advise you? A little political hypothesising was all it was!' You're outflanked. Cockfighting doesn't suit men who're dressed like that.

THE CHAPLAIN: If you don't shut up, whether or not it suits my clothes, I'm going to murder you.

(*The Cook takes his shoes off and unwinds the rags wrapped around his feet.*)

THE COOK: If the war hadn't turned you into the secular wreck I see before me, you could've found a parsonage to settle in, what with peace and all. No one needs a cook when there's no food, but folks still believe in things they can't see, nothing changes that.

THE CHAPLAIN: Mr Lamb, please, I'm asking you, don't push me out. I am a wreck, you're right, I've been brought low, humiliated, debased. But I . . . I like myself better now. Even if you handed me a nice metropolitan pulpit with a sinecure, I don't think I could preach. Washing bottles is better work than saving souls, the bottles come clean. Tell her to keep me.

(*Yvette comes in, dressed in black, but bedizened, walking with a cane. She's much older, fatter, and she wears gobs of make-up. A serving man walks behind her. The Cook turns away and busies himself with something.*)

YVETTE: Hey hey, everyone! Is this Mother Courage's?

THE CHAPLAIN: Is, was, and always will be.

YVETTE: Where's Courage? Could you please announce that she has a guest, Madame Colonel Starhemberg.

THE CHAPLAIN (*calling into the wagon*): Madame Colonel Starhemberg wants to speak with you!

MOTHER COURAGE (*from inside*): Be right out!

YVETTE: I'm Yvette!

MOTHER COURAGE (*excited, from inside*): Aaaaccchh! Yvette!

YVETTE: Popped over to see what's up! (*The Cook turns around.*)
Pieter!

THE COOK: Yvette!

YVETTE: Holy shit! Since when! How come you're here?

THE COOK: As opposed to where?

THE CHAPLAIN: How well do you know each other?

YVETTE: Too well! (*She gives the Cook the once-over.*)
Fat!

THE COOK: You've been slimmer yourself.

YVETTE: You're fat and I'm fat and how-de-do, you scalded hog. How many years has it been I've been waiting to tell you what I think of you?

THE CHAPLAIN: Many, many years, from the look of it, but if you could wait just a minute longer and start telling him when Courage is here.

(*Mother Courage comes out of the wagon, hauling merchandise.*)

MOTHER COURAGE: Yvette! (*They embrace.*)
You're in mourning?

YVETTE: Looks nice, huh? My husband the Colonel died a few years back.

MOTHER COURAGE: The old guy who wanted to buy you my wagon?

YVETTE: No, his father!

MOTHER COURAGE: You look nice all right, not bad, not bad at all! At least somebody got something out of the war.

YVETTE: Touch and go, that's how I do it, up and down and up and down and etcetera.

MOTHER COURAGE: Yeah, but you hooked a colonel and we have to hand it those colonels, they made hay.

THE CHAPLAIN (*to the Cook*): Heaven forfend I offer advice, but you might want to consider getting back in your boots. (*To Yvette.*) Madame Colonel, you had something you were about to say about this barefoot man.

THE COOK: Don't make a stink, Yvette.

MOTHER COURAGE: Yvette, let me introduce you to a friend of mine.

YVETTE: No, no, let me introduce you! Courage, meet Piping Pieter.

MOTHER COURAGE (*laughing*): Piping Pieter!

THE COOK: An old nickname, forget it.

MOTHER COURAGE: Who made the girls throw their skirts over their heads!

THE COOK: My name's Lamb.

MOTHER COURAGE: Look, I hung on to your pipe.

THE CHAPLAIN: Rarely took it out of her mouth.

YVETTE: Fling his poxy pipe away, Courage, this is the nastiest fish ever to wash up on the Flanders shore. Every one of his fingers has brought misery to a different miserable girl.

THE COOK: Years ago. A man can change.

YVETTE: Stand up when a lady talks to you, poodle. God how I loved this man!

THE COOK: I was the best thing ever happened to you, I helped you find your calling.

YVETTE: Shut your mouth, you tragic disaster! (*To Mother Courage.*) After he disappeared and left me, um, broken-hearted, I found four other girls in town in a similar condition and it was a very small town! Maybe you're thinking time and dissipation has ground down his teeth and horns, but you listen to me, be careful, there's danger in the ruins. If he's here hoping to hitch a ride on your wagon, show him the highway and bless his scabby backside with your boot!

MOTHER COURAGE (*to Yvette*): You come with me to the market, I've got to unload this stuff before the prices hit bottom. You must know the whole regiment, tell me who to talk to. (*Calling into the wagon.*) Never mind church, Kattrin. I am going to market. As soon as Eilif shows, give him something to drink.

(*She leaves with Yvette. As they go, Yvette says:*)

YVETTE: It amazes me, a picked-over carcass of man like you was enough to overturn my apple cart. I've got my lucky star to thank, I got every fucking apple back, and then some! I've saved this woman from the catastrophe of your company, and that'll go down to my credit in the world to come. And now at very long last, Piping Pieter, you can kiss my ass!

(*They leave.*)

THE CHAPLAIN: I suddenly find my tongue freed, I can sermonise again! I take as our text today: 'The mills of God grind slowly. And they grind small.'

THE COOK: I never had a lucky star. It's just . . . well, I'd hoped there might be a warm meal. I'm starving. I haven't had food in two days. Now they're cluckling about me, and she'll form a more-or-less completely false impression. It discombobulates me, a woman's cold shoulder. I'll leave before she's back.

THE CHAPLAIN: Better part of valour. Amen.

THE COOK: Peace is as heavy as a millstone. I miss the General, you know, God knows where he is, I could be basting a fat roasted capon with mustard sauce, served with yellow carrots.

THE CHAPLAIN: Red cabbage. Red cabbage with a capon.

THE COOK: I know, I know, but he insisted on carrots.

THE CHAPLAIN: The man was an appalling ignoramus.

THE COOK: You never mentioned that when you were sitting next to him stuffing your face.

THE CHAPLAIN: I swallowed my pride.

THE COOK: You swallowed more than that. Who knew we'd long for those days?

THE CHAPLAIN: Nostalgic for the war. Peace seems less hospitable, somehow.

THE COOK: You're finished here same as me, you called her a hyena. You—what are you staring at?

THE CHAPLAIN: I think it's Eilif. (*A grim contingent of Soldiers with pikes leading Eilif, whose hands are tied. He's chalk-white.*)
What's happened?

EILIF: Where's my mother?

THE CHAPLAIN: In town.

EILIF: I heard she was here. They let me come to see her.

THE COOK (*to the Soldiers*): Where are you taking him?

A SOLDIER: Noplace good.

THE CHAPLAIN: What did he do?

THE SOLDIER: He broke into a farmhouse. The wife— (*Gestures to indicate she's dead.*)

THE CHAPLAIN: You did that? How could you do that?

EILIF: Same as I've always done.

THE COOK: But it's peacetime. You can't—

EILIF: Shut up. Can I sit till she comes back?

THE SOLDIER: We don't have time for that.

THE CHAPLAIN: During the war he got medals for things like this, he was fearless, they said, brave, he was summoned to sit at the General's right hand. Couldn't we talk to your commander?

THE SOLDIER: Why bother? Stealing some farmer's cow, that's brave?

THE COOK: It was idiotic!

EILIF: If I was an idiot I'd have starved long before this, you asshole.

THE COOK: So you used your brains and now they're going to cut your head off.

THE CHAPLAIN: At least let's get Kattrin.

EILIF: No! Don't! Leave her. Give me a taste of schnapps.

THE SOLDIER: You don't have time for that, come on!

THE CHAPLAIN: What should we tell your mother?

EILIF: Tell her it wasn't different. Tell her it was the same. Or don't tell her anything.

(*The Soldiers shove him and he starts to walk.*)

THE CHAPLAIN: I'll walk with you on your hard path.

EILIF: I don't need you, black crow.

THE CHAPLAIN: You don't know what you may need.

(*The Soldiers shove Eilif again and they leave. The Chaplain follows them.*)

THE COOK (*calling after the Chaplain*): I have to tell her, she'll want to see him!

THE CHAPLAIN: Better not say anything. Or he was here and he'll be back, tomorrow possibly. When I get back I'll find some way to explain.

(*The Chaplain runs off after them. The Cook watches them leave, shakes his head, then finally goes to the wagon. He calls in.*)

THE COOK: Hey! Don't you want to come out? I understand you, I think, peace comes and you crawl under the rug. Me too. It's terrifying. I was the General's cook, remember? I'm asking myself if maybe there's a scrap left over from your breakfast, just to tide me over till your mother returns? A little ham or some bread, we might have a bit of a wait. (*He looks inside.*) She's thrown the blanket over her head.

(*In the distance, cannonfire. Mother Courage runs in, still carrying all her wares, out of breath.*)

MOTHER COURAGE: Cook! Peace is finished! The war's been back on three whole days. I was just about to sell at a loss when I heard the news! Thank God! In town they're shooting at the Lutherans and the Lutherans are shooting back. We've got to get on our way with the wagon. Kattrin, pack! (*To the Cook.*) Look me in the eye. What's the matter?

THE COOK: Nothing.

MOTHER COURAGE: Bullshit, it's something, something's wrong.

THE COOK: War's started up, maybe that's it. And it'll probably be tomorrow evening before I get hot food in my stomach.

MOTHER COURAGE: You're lying, Cook.

THE COOK: Eilif was here. He couldn't stay.

MOTHER COURAGE: He was here? Then we'll find him on the march. From now on I'm pulling right behind the soldiers, like I was official, it's safer. Did he look all right?

THE COOK: As always.

MOTHER COURAGE: He's always the same as always, smart. That one the war couldn't take from me. Help me pack? (*She starts packing. The Cook helps.*) Did he have any news? Is he still the General's favourite? Any more heroism?

THE COOK (*grim*): Yes, apparently, only recently.

MOTHER COURAGE: Tell me about it once we're under way. (*Kattrin comes out of the wagon and takes her place at the axle shaft, ready to pull.*) Peace is already over, Kattrin. We're on the move again. (*To the Cook.*) And you?

THE COOK: Find my regiment, sign up.

MOTHER COURAGE: You could do that I guess or . . . Where's his Holiness?

THE COOK: He went towards town with Eilif.

MOTHER COURAGE: Come along, Lamb, for a bit. I need a helper.

THE COOK: All that stuff Yvette was saying . . .

MOTHER COURAGE: Didn't do you discredit in my eyes. The opposite. I've always admired vitality; don't worry as much as I used to over the shape it chooses to take. Interested?

THE COOK: I'm not saying no.

MOTHER COURAGE: The Twelfth Regiment's already headed out. Take hold and pull. Here's a slice of bread. We'll have to go the long way around to catch up with the Lutherans. I might see Eilif this very night. I love him best of all. It was a short peace. Let's get going.

(*Kattrin and the Cook in harness start to pull the wagon while Mother Courage sings:*)
From Ulm to Metz . . .

THE COOK (*singing*):
. . . from Metz to Maähren!

MOTHER COURAGE (*singing*):
The goddamned army's on its feet!
What if the land is burnt and barren?

THE COOK (*singing*):
The war needs men, and men must eat!

MOTHER COURAGE (*singing*):
The war will feed you steel and fire
If you sign up for bloody deeds!
It's only blood that wars require!
So come and feed it what it needs!

NINE

The Great War of Religion has been going on for six-teen years. Over half the inhabitants of Germany have perished. Widespread plague kills those the war spares. In once fertile countries, famine. Wolves prowl through the burnt-out cities. In the autumn of 1634 we meet Courage in the German mountains called Fichtelbirge, off the route of the Swedish Army. Winter this year has come early and is severe. Business is terrible, and beg-ging is all that remains. The Cook gets a letter from Utrecht and is bid farewell.

Outside a half-ruined parsonage. Grey morning in early winter. Wind is blasting. Mother Courage and the Cook in ratty sheepskins, the wagon nearby.

THE COOK: It's pitch black, nobody's up.

MOTHER COURAGE: It's a parsonage. The bells will have to be rung and the Father's got to crawl to it. Then he'll have hot soup.

THE COOK: You're talking nonsense, the village was burnt to the ground.

MOTHER COURAGE: Someone's living here, there was a dog barking.

THE COOK: If the parson's got anything, he won't give it away.

MOTHER COURAGE: Maybe if we sing something.

THE COOK: I've had more than my share of this. (*He takes a letter from his pocket.*) A letter from Utrecht, my mother's dead from cholera, her inn belongs to me now. Read the letter if you don't believe me. (*He proffers the letter, Mother Courage reaches to take it, he snatches it back.*)

From my aunt, the handwriting's a little primitive. But . . . there's stuff about what a wretched little bas-tard I always was, that's family matters, skip that, read here, the salient part.

(*He hands her the letter, which she takes and reads. She stops reading, looks at him.*)

MOTHER COURAGE: Lamb, I can't take the open road any more either. Look at us begging. My whole life, I never begged before. I feel like a slaughterhouse dog, red meat for paying customers but nothing for me. I have nothing to sell any more and no one has anything to pay with. In Saxony one of those raggedy beggars offered me a parcel of precious books wrapped in greaseproof parchment, just for two eggs, and for a little bag of salt in Würtenburg they wanted to give me their plough. What's the use of ploughing? Nothing grows but nettles. In Pomerania I've heard there's vil-lagers so ravenous they've eaten little children.

THE COOK: The world's dying.

MOTHER COURAGE: Sometimes I see myself pulling that wagon through the streets of hell, selling burning pitch. Or making a living in purgatory, offering my wares to the wandering souls till the last trumpet blast. If me and my children could find a place where no one's shooting, I wouldn't mind a few years' rest, a few years of calm.

THE COOK: We could make a go of it at the inn. Give it serious consideration, Anna. Last night I made my final decision, I'm going to Utrecht with you or alone, today.

MOTHER COURAGE: I have to talk it over with Kattrin. It's a little abrupt, and I'm usually averse to making big decisions when I'm freezing and there's nothing in my belly. Kattrin! (*Kattrin climbs down from the wagon.*)

Kattrin, we have to talk about something. The Cook and I want to go to Utrecht. He's inherited an inn. You'd have a home, make acquaintances. There are many men who'd want a competent somebody who helped run an inn, good looks aren't everything. It's a good deal. The Cook and I get along. I will say this about him: he tucks his head between his shoulders and goes about his business. We'd know where our next meal came from, and when to expect it, that'd be a change, huh, nice? And your own bed, you'd sleep better, right? Finally, life on the road isn't life. Look at us, you're fall-ing apart. Lice are eating you alive. We have to decide, all right, Utrecht or, or we could just keep on, go where the Swede soldiers are, the army up north. (*She gestures vaguely to the left.*) We could go find the army again, but . . . I think we'll go with cook, Kattrin.

THE COOK: Anna, I have to talk to you alone.

MOTHER COURAGE: Go back in the wagon, Kattrin.

(*Kattrin climbs back into the wagon.*)

THE COOK: I interrupted you because you didn't under-stand me. I thought I was clear but I guess I wasn't, so: you can't bring her. I think that's clear enough.

(*Kattrin positions herself inside so she can listen.*)

MOTHER COURAGE: What do you mean, leave Kattrin?

THE COOK: Think. There's not enough room for her. It's not a big place. If we screw our hind legs to the floor we might keep it open and running, but three people, the inn can't support that. Kattrin can take over the wagon.

MOTHER COURAGE: I was thinking she'd find a husband in Utrecht.

THE COOK: That's a laugh! Dumb, a scarred face, and old as she is?

MOTHER COURAGE: Don't talk so loud!

THE COOK: What is, is, loud or soft. And come to think of it, there's the paying guests at the inn, who'd want to look up from supper and see that waiting to clear the table? How do you think this could work?

MOTHER COURAGE: I said shut up, I said don't talk so loud.

THE COOK: Someone's lit a candle in the parsonage. Let's sing.

MOTHER COURAGE: Cook, how'd she pull that wagon on her own? She's frightened by the war. She couldn't manage. The dreams she must have! I hear her groaning nights. After battles especially. What she sees in those dreams, I can't imagine. She suffers because she pities. A few days back I found a hedgehog we'd killed, the wagon, an ac-cident. She'd hidden it in her blanket.

THE COOK: The inn's too small. (*Shouting.*) Worthy gentle-men, servants, and all who dwell within! In the hope of procuring a little leftover food, we will now give you a lecture in the form of a song, the Song of Solomon,

Julius Caesar and other men possessed of a gigantic spirit, which proved to be of little use to them. All of this so you can see that we're decent obedient people and we are having a hard time getting by, especially this winter!

(*He sings:*)
No doubt you've heard of Solomon,
The wisest man on earth!
He saw with perfect clarity,
He would spit on the cursed hour of his birth
And say that all was vanity.
How deep and wise was Solomon!
And see, before the night descends,
He longed to taste oblivion!
He started wise but as a fool he ends.
Oh, wisdom's fine; we're glad we've none.

(*Shouting.*) All virtues are dangerous in a world like this, as our beautiful song shows, you're better off having an easy life and breakfast, in our opinion, hot soup. I for instance, I've got none and I'd like some, I'm a soldier, but what use was it to me, my bravery in all those battles, nix, nil, starvation, and if I'd stayed home shitting myself I'd be better off. This is why:

(*Sings:*)
Then Julius Caesar, mighty one,
Raised high his royal rod,
So brave he tore the world apart,
So they voted and changed their Caesar to a God,
Then drove a dagger through his heart.
How loud he screamed: 'You too, my son!'
And see, before the night descends,
His reign had only just begun,
So brave, but screaming out in fear he ends.
Brave hearts are grand! We're fine with none.

(*Muttering.*) They're hiding in there, the bastards. (*Shouting.*) Worthy gentlemen, servants and the whole household! You aren't responding, you're sitting in there by your fire, and maybe you're saying to yourself sure, bravery's not much when you need a hot meal, I agree, but maybe if you were honest you wouldn't be so bad off! Maybe if you were honest someone would feed you or at least not leave you completely sober.
   Let's test this proposition!

(*Sings:*)
And Socrates, that paragon,
Who always told the truth—
They mixed a bitter poison drink
Made of hemlock; they said he's done things to our
   youth
And now we hate the way they think!
His truth was a phenomenon.
And see, before his night descends,
No longer dazzled by the sun,
He pays his bills and with a sip, he ends.
Truths are lovely; we know none.

(*Shouting.*) You still don't want to give, and it's not surprising, who wants to give anyone anything? Sure, they tell us to give unto others, but what if you've got nothing to give? And the ones who give are left empty-handed, and that can't feel very good either, and that's why sacrifice is the rarest of all the virtues, because in the end it makes everyone feel like crap.

(*Sings:*)
St Martin° sang his benison,
His pity flowereth.
He met a man lost in the snows
Who was freezing, so Martin shared with him his
   clothes.
Of course the two men froze to death.
The pearly gates no doubt he won!
And see, before the night descends,
So kind beyond comparison!
Warm-hearted but beneath the ice he ends.
Oh, pity's great; thank God we've none.

(*Shouting.*) And that's how it is with us! Law-abiding people, loyal to each other, we don't steal, murder or burn down houses! And like the song says, down we're going, deeper in the hole, and soup's a rare commodity, and if we were thieves and murderers we might eat! So if you've no food for us you better pray our patience holds out, because we know! It's not virtue that pays in this world, but wickedness, that's how the world is and it shouldn't be that way!

(*Sings:*)
At last our final yarn's been spun.
We ask you, gentle souls,
What use our loving heaven's been?
While you sit safe and soft within,
We stand without, with empty bowls.
God's love has left us here, undone.
And see, before the night descends
The way the meek are overrun.
Our virtues led us to our wretched ends.
And folk do better who have none.

A VOICE FROM ABOVE (*inside the house*): You out there! Come inside! We'll give you some hot marrow stew.

MOTHER COURAGE: I'd choke on anything I tried to swallow now, Lamb. I can't argue with anything you've said but is it your final word? We've always had a good understanding.

THE COOK: My last word. Take some time to decide.

MOTHER COURAGE: I don't need it. I'm not leaving her here.

THE COOK: That's pure senselessness, but nothing I can do about it. I'm not a monster, it's a small inn. Let's go inside before there's no more soup, we'll have sung in the cold in vain.

MOTHER COURAGE: I'll get Kattrin.

THE COOK: Come get it and bring it out to her. If it's three of us tramping in, they might get scared.

(*They go into the house. Kattrin climbs down from the wagon, carrying a bundle. She looks to make sure the others have gone in. She drapes, over a wheel of the wagon where it can't be missed, one of her mother's*

St Martin: The patron saint of soldiers (316–397).

skirts, and then atop the skirt, an old pair of the cook's pants. As she's leaving with her bundle, Mother Courage comes out of the house, carrying a bowl of hot soup.)

MOTHER COURAGE: Kattrin! Wait! Kattrin! Stop! What's the bundle and where are you off to? Have you turned your back on God and all his angels? (She grabs the bundle away from Kattrin and opens it.)

She's packed her belongings! You heard? I told him to fuck himself, with the shitty tiny tavern and Utrecht, what would we do in Utrecht? We don't know anything about innkeeping. The war's still got a great deal in store for us. (She sees the skirt and pants.)

You're an idiot. What do you think I'd have done, seeing that and you just gone? (Kattrin tries to go, but Mother Courage won't let her.)

Don't be so quick, it wasn't for your sake I handed him his walking papers. It's the wagon. I'm never giving up that wagon. It's mine, it's what I'm used to, it's not about you in the least. We'll go now, we'll go the opposite direction of Utrecht and find the army and leave the cook's stuff here where he'll trip over it, the stupid man. (She climbs up and then throws out a few things to lie near the trousers.)

There, the partnership's dissolved, and I'm not taking anyone else into the business ever. We'll both go on. The winter will be over some day, like all the other winters. Get in the harness, snow's coming.

(They strap themselves into the harnesses, turn the wagon in another direction and pull it away. The Cook comes out of the house. He sees his things on the ground. And stands there, dumbstruck.)

TEN

The entire year 1635 Mother Courage and her daughter Kattrin pull across central German highways, following behind ever more ragged armies.

A highway. Mother Courage and Kattrin are pulling the wagon. They come to a small farmhouse. Someone inside is singing. Mother Courage and Kattrin stop to listen.

A VOICE INSIDE (singing):
We've got a rosebush glowing
Within our garden wall.
When April winds come calling
They set the blossoms blowing
And petals will go falling,
All white and red the petals fall
When April winds come calling.

When wild geese go flying
Before the winter storm,
The autumn roses dying,
Our roof's in need of fixing!
Of moss and straw we're mixing
The stuff to keep the parlour warm
For when wild geese go flying.

(Mother Courage and Kattrin start to pull again.)

ELEVEN

January 1636. Imperial troops threaten the Protestant city of Halle. The stone begins to speak. Mother Courage loses her daughter and continues alone. The war goes on, no sign that it will end.

The wagon, beaten up, stands forlornly alongside a farmhouse with a huge thatched roof which leans against a cliff. It's night. A Lieutenant and three Soldiers in heavy armour step out of the nearby woods.

THE LIEUTENANT: I don't want any noise. Somebody even looks like shouting, gut 'em.

(One of the Soldiers knocks on the door of the house. A farm woman comes out. He covers her mouth with his hand. The other two Soldiers go into the house. They come out with the farmer and his son. Kattrin has put her head out of the wagon to see what's happening. The Lieutenant points at her.)

THE LIEUTENANT: There's someone else. (One of the Soldiers pulls Kattrin out of the wagon.) Who else lives here?

THE FARMER: That's our son.

THE FARMER'S WIFE: She's a dumb girl.

THE FARMER: Her mother's marketing in town.

THE FARMER'S WIFE: For their provisioning business, salespeople, people are fleeing and they're hunting bargains.

THE FARMER: They're migrants.

THE LIEUTENANT: All right enough, you have to stay quiet all of you, the first noise from any of you I'm going to tell my boys to shove bayonets through your thick stupid country-ass heads. I need one of you to show us the path into town. (Pointing to the Farmer's Son.) You.

THE FARMER'S SON: I don't know where the path is.

SECOND SOLDIER (grinning): Doesn't know where his dick is. Fucking peasants.

THE FARMER'S SON: There's no path for Catholics.

THE LIEUTENANT (to the Second Soldier): You gonna take that from him?

(The Soldiers force the Farmer's Son to his knees and the Second Soldier holds a bayonet to his throat.)

THE FARMER'S SON: Cut my throat. I won't help you.

FIRST SOLDIER (to his comrades): Watch this. (The First Soldier goes to the barn door and looks in.) Two cows and an ox. Before the army I was a butcher's apprentice.

THE FARMER'S SON: Don't!

THE FARMER'S WIFE (crying): Captain, please, leave our animals alone.

THE LIEUTENANT: Help us out or we'll eat your ox. (Indicating the Farmer's Son.) Hope you didn't raise stubborn children.

FIRST SOLDIER: Wish I'd brought my bone saw. Here goes.

THE FARMER'S SON (to his father): What do I do? (The Farmer's Wife looks at her son.)

(To the Soldiers.) All right, all right. Let's go.

THE FARMER'S WIFE: And many thanks, Captain, for not butchering them, for ever and amen.

(The Farmer stops his wife from continuing to thank the Lieutenant.)

FIRST SOLDIER: It's the ox before everything, then the cows, then their kid, farm priorities.

(*The Lieutenant and the Soldiers leave, led by the Farmer's Son.*)

THE FARMER: What're they planning? Nothing good.

THE FARMER'S WIFE: Probably they're just scouting around— (*The Farmer has got a ladder and is propping it against the wall of the house.*)

What in God's name?

THE FARMER: I want to see how many. (*He climbs up to the roof.*) The woods are full of 'em. To the quarry. I can see armoured men in the clearing, and there's cannons, it's more than a regiment. God help the city and everyone in it.

THE FARMER'S WIFE: Any lights on?

THE FARMER: None. Everyone's sleeping. (*He climbs down.*) They'll kill everyone.

THE FARMER'S WIFE: The town sentries.

THE FARMER: Probably killed the men in the watchtower in the cliffs, or else we'd have heard their horns.

THE FARMER'S WIFE: If we had a few more of us . . .

THE FARMER: More than just us all the way up here, us and this cripple.

THE FARMER'S WIFE: What should we do then? Anything?

THE FARMER: Nothing.

THE FARMER'S WIFE: Even if we dared to, it's night and we couldn't run.

THE FARMER: They're all over the hill like ants.

THE FARMER'S WIFE: So there's no way to signal?

THE FARMER: Not unless you want to get killed.

THE FARMER'S WIFE (*to Kattrin*): Pray, you poor dumb beast, pray. We can't stop the slaughter, but we can pray to God and maybe because you're a cripple He'll listen better. (*They all kneel. Kattrin kneels behind the farm couple.*)

Our Father who art in heaven, don't let them murder the people in the city, who're asleep and don't know that death's come so near, at least wake them up, Father, so they can see the spears and rifles and the siege engines and fires, the enemy in the night. (*Nodding towards Kattrin.*) Remember her mother, Lord, who's gone there and remember to keep the night watchman wakeful, maybe he'll sound the alarm, and remember and protect my brother-in-law and the four kids my late sister's left him, may her soul rest, poor thing, save the four kids who never did nothing wrong. (*Kattrin groans.*)

The little one isn't two yet, the eldest only seven. (*Kattrin stands, very upset. As the Farmer's Wife keeps praying, Kattrin moves quietly to the wagon, takes something from it, goes to the ladder and climbs to the roof.*)

We have no defence but you, Lord. In your wisdom you saw fit to leave us helpless and now we ask you to show us mercy, save our son and save our animals and the crops and the sleeping people in the town, the little children and old people especially, death's come in the night, Heavenly Father, and all your children are in dreadful need.

THE FARMER: And we hope to be forgiven our sins as we try to forgive them who sin against us. Amen.

(*On the roof, Kattrin starts banging the drum she's taken from the wagon.*)

THE FARMER'S WIFE: Jesus what is she doing?

THE FARMER: Lost her wits!

THE FARMER'S WIFE: Drag her down from there, quick! (*The Farmer moves towards the ladder, but Kattrin pulls it up on the roof and resumes her drumming.*)

Oh, this is disastrous!

THE FARMER: Stop that pounding, you cripple!

THE FARMER'S WIFE: The Kaiser's whole army's going to come crashing down on us! (*Kattrin keeps drumming, looking towards the city.*)

(*To her husband.*) I warned you about letting gypsies put up here, think they care if the soldiers take our last cow?

(*The Lieutenant and his Soldiers and the Farmer's Son run in.*)

THE LIEUTENANT: I'll fucking murder you!

THE FARMER'S WIFE: Mr Officer sir, please, it's not us, she—

FIRST SOLDIER: Jesus Christ.

SECOND SOLDIER: Fucking hell.

THE LIEUTENANT: Where's the ladder? Where's the goddamn—

THE FARMER: It's on the roof, with her.

FIRST SOLDIER: She— (*To the Second Soldier.*) Get the— get the gun, do you—

THIRD SOLDIER: You told me not to, it's heavy, you—fuck, listen to her.

THE FARMER'S WIFE: She got up there without our noticing.

FIRST SOLDIER: Hey girl, get down or we're gonna come up and get you!

SECOND SOLDIER: Yeah, get down here and suck my—

THE LIEUTENANT (*to Kattrin*): All right, all right, stay calm, stay calm, this is—

THE FARMER'S WIFE: She's a total stranger.

THE LIEUTENANT: Shut up! This is an order! Throw the drum down. (*Kattrin keeps drumming.*)

(*To the Farmer.*) You planned this, you're responsible, if she—

THE FARMER: There's some tall pine trees they cut down in the woods.

THE LIEUTENANT: So what?

THE FARMER: I dunno, maybe if somehow we could . . . you know, we could hoist one of the tall tree trunks somehow and use one end to sort of shove her off and—

FIRST SOLDIER (*to the Lieutenant*): Can I try something sir? (*The Lieutenant nods. The First Soldier calls to Kattrin:*) Hey! Girl! We wanna make a deal with you, friends, right?

SECOND SOLDIER: They're gonna hear that, they're bound to—kill the bitch.

THIRD SOLDIER: Should I go back and get the—

FIRST SOLDIER (*to the Third Soldier*): QUIET, goddamn it! (*To Kattrin.*) You, you listening?

SECOND SOLDIER: Hey! Hey you, listen to him, he's trying to—

FIRST SOLDIER: We're friends, we . . . Get down, right, if you get down we'll take you with us, we promise we won't touch you—

SECOND SOLDIER: Who'd want to touch an ugly fucking—

FIRST SOLDIER: We'll take you into town with us and you point out your mother and she won't get hurt.

(*Kattrin keeps drumming. The Lieutenant shoves the First Soldier aside.*)

THE LIEUTENANT (*calling up to Kattrin*): You don't believe him, you aren't stupid, you know we're not friends and anyway, who'd trust someone with a face like his? But will you believe me if I give you my word as an officer of His Majesty the Emperor's army? My sacred word?

(*Kattrin drums harder.*)

THIRD SOLDIER (*muttering*): Well that was effective. Jesus Christ.

FIRST SOLDIER: You better do something, sir.

SECOND SOLDIER: They're gonna hear that in town.

THE LIEUTENANT: We've gotta—

THIRD SOLDIER: Torch the house!

THE LIEUTENANT: Make some sort of noise!

SECOND SOLDIER: You told us not to make any noise, we—

THE LIEUTENANT: Drown out the—

FIRST SOLDIER: I thought we weren't supposed to make any—

THE LIEUTENANT: Drown out the drumming, a, a normal noise, you goddamned imbecile, a peacetime sound, like—

THE FARMER: Wood chopping!

THE LIEUTENANT: Good, do it, start chopping! (*The Farmer takes up his axe and starts chopping at a log lying on the ground.*)

Can't you chop any harder than that? (*Kattrin drums a little softer, distracted by the chopping sound, but then she realises what's happening and starts drumming all the harder.*)

(*To the Farmer.*) Louder dammit! (*To the First Soldier.*) You too! Start chopping!

THE FARMER: There's just the one axe.

THE LIEUTENANT: Torch it, torch the house.

(*The Farmer stops chopping.*)

THE FARMER: They'll see the fire in town, that's a bad idea.

(*Kattrin, still drumming, laughs.*)

THE LIEUTENANT: That does it, she's laughing at us. Get the gun, shoot her down, I don't care, shoot her!

(*Two of the Soldiers run out. Kattrin drums harder.*)

THE FARMER'S WIFE: That wagon over there's all they have. Take the axe to that and she'll have to stop.

(*The Lieutenant hands the axe to the Farmer's Son.*)

THE LIEUTENANT: Do it, you heard your mother, chop that wagon to splinters. (*To Kattrin.*) You want him to take an axe to your wagon? Then stop!

(*The Lieutenant signals to the Farmer's Son, who hits the wagon with the axe, a few tepid blows.*)

THE FARMER'S WIFE (*screaming up to Kattrin*): STOP IT YOU DUMB COW!

(*As the boy hits the wagon, Kattrin watches with a stricken expression, making a few low groaning sounds. But she doesn't stop drumming.*)

THE LIEUTENANT: Where are those lazy cunts with the rifle?

FIRST SOLDIER: LISTEN! (*Everyone, including Kattrin, stops and listens. Silence.*)

They're not hearing her in town, there'd be alarm bells if they did.

THE LIEUTENANT (*to Kattrin*): Nobody's hearing you, it's not working, and now you're going to get shot and killed for nothing. One last time: throw down that drum!

(*The Farmer's Son throws the axe down and calls out abruptly:*)

THE FARMER'S SON: Keep drumming! They'll kill them all! Drum! Drum! Drum!

(*Kattrin resumes her drumming. The First Soldier knocks the Farmer's Son to the ground and clubs him brutally, with the butt end of his spear. Kattrin starts crying but keeps drumming.*)

THE FARMER'S WIFE: Oh God, please stop hitting him in the back, you're killing him!

(*The Soldiers run in with a large musket on a tripod.*)

SECOND SOLDIER: The Colonel's foaming at the mouth, Lieutenant. We're gonna get court-martialled.

THE LIEUTENANT: Set it up! Hurry! (*They set up the musket. The Lieutenant calls up to Kattrin while this is being done:*)

All right this is the final warning: Stop drumming! (*Kattrin is crying and drumming as hard as she can.*) STOP IT! STOP IT! STOP THE— (*He turns to his Soldiers.*) Fire! (*The Soldiers fire. Kattrin is hit. She strikes the drum weakly a few more times, then collapses, slowly.*)

No more noise.

(*From the city, a cannon's shot answers Kattrin's last drumbeat. Alarm bells and cannonfire sounding all together is heard in the distance.*)

FIRST SOLDIER: Listen. It worked. She did it.

TWELVE

Night, nearly dawn. Trumpets and drums and fifes, an army departing.

Alongside the wagon, Mother Courage sits, bent down over her daughter. The farm couple stand nearby.

THE FARMER (*angrily*): You have to go now, lady. Only one last regiment left and then that's it. You wanna travel alone?

MOTHER COURAGE: Maybe she's sleeping.

(*Sings:*)
Eia popeia,°
Who sleeps in the hay?
The neighbour's brat's crying
While my children play.
The neighbour's kid's shabby
But my kids look nice,
With shirts like the angels wear
In paradise.

Neighbour can't feed 'em
But mine shall have cake,

Eia popeia: Lullaby.

The sweetest and choicest
The baker can bake.

Eia popeia,
I see your eyes close.
One kid lies in Poland.
The other — well, who knows?

(*Speaking*) You should never have told her about your brother-in-law's children.

THE FARMER: You had to go to town to hunt for bargains, maybe if you'd been here none of this would have happened.

MOTHER COURAGE: Now she's sleeping.

THE FARMER'S WIFE: She isn't sleeping, stop saying that and look, she's gone.

THE FARMER: And you have to go too. There are wolves around here, and people who're worse than the wolves.

MOTHER COURAGE: Yes.

(*She goes to the wagon and brings out a sheet.*)

THE FARMER'S WIFE: Do you have anyone left? Anyone you could go to?

MOTHER COURAGE: One left. Eilif.

(*She uses the sheet to wrap Kattrin's body.*)

THE FARMER: You've got to go find him then. We'll take care of her, she'll have a decent burial. Don't worry.

MOTHER COURAGE: Here's money for what it costs.

(*She gives the Farmer some money. The Farmer and his son shake her hand and carry Kattrin's body away. The Farmer's Wife follows them. She turns as she leaves and says to Mother Courage:*)

THE FARMER'S WIFE: Hurry.

(*She leaves.*)

MOTHER COURAGE (*harnessing herself to the wagon*): Hopefully I'll manage to pull the wagon alone. I bet I can do it, not much in it any more. I have to get back in business.

(*The fife and drums of another regiment marching by. Soldiers are singing in the distance. As they sing, Mother Courage begins to pull her wagon, pursuing them.*)

SOLDIERS (*offstage, singing*):
Sometimes there's luck, and always worry.
The war goes on, and perseveres!
For war is never in a hurry,
And it can last a thousand years.

The day of wrath will come like thunder
But who has time to make amends?
You march in line, but never wonder
How it began and where it ends.

The Spring has come, and Winter's dead!

MOTHER COURAGE (*over the singing*): Take me with you!

SOLDIERS (*singing over her, offstage*):
The snow has gone, so draw a breath!
Let Christian souls crawl out of bed,
Pull on their socks and conquer death!

The world will end, and time will cease!
And while we live we buy and sell!
And in our graves we shall find peace —
Unless the war goes on in Hell!

COMMENTARIES

BERTOLT BRECHT (1898–1956)

The Alienation Effect   1964

TRANSLATED BY JOHN WILLETT

In this short description, Brecht explains some of his theories of staging and acting. His alienation effect (A-effect) reminds the audience that the characters on stage are dramatic constructs, not real people suffering real emotions. As he explains, the A-effect is the opposite of traditional acting, which is designed to produce an empathy between actor and audience. The A-effect rejects that empathy.

What follows represents an attempt to describe a technique of acting which was applied in certain theaters with a view to taking the incidents portrayed and alienating them from the spectator. The aim of this technique, known as the alienation effect, was to make the spectator adopt an attitude of inquiry and criticism in his approach to the incident. The means were artistic.

The first condition for the A-effect's application to this end is that stage and auditorium must be purged of everything "magical" and that no "hypnotic tensions" should be set up. This ruled out any attempt to make the stage convey the flavor of a particular place (a room at evening, a road in the autumn), or to create atmosphere by relaxing the tempo of the conversation. The audience was not "worked up" by a display of temperament or "swept away" by acting with tautened muscles; in short, no attempt was made to put it in a trance and give it the illusion of watching an ordinary unrehearsed event. As will be seen presently, the audience's tendency to plunge into such illusions has to be checked by specific artistic means.

The first condition for the achievement of the A-effect is that the actor must invest what he has to show with a definite gest of showing. It is of course necessary to drop the assumption that there is a fourth wall cutting the audience off from the stage and the consequent illusion that the stage action is taking place in reality and without an audience. That being so, it is possible for the actor in principle to address the audience directly.

It is well known that contact between audience and stage is normally made on the basis of empathy. Conventional actors devote their efforts so exclusively to bringing about this psychological operation that they may be said to see it as the principal aim of their art. Our introductory remarks will already have made it clear that the technique which produces an A-effect is the exact opposite of that which aims at empathy. The actor applying it is bound not to try to bring about the empathy operation.

Yet in his efforts to reproduce particular characters and show their behavior he need not renounce the means of empathy entirely. He uses these means just as any normal person with no particular acting talent would use them if he wanted to portray someone else, i.e., show how he behaves. This showing of other people's behavior happens time and again in ordinary life (witnesses of an accident demonstrating to newcomers how the victim behaved, a facetious person imitating a friend's walk, etc.), without those involved making the least effort to subject their spectators to an illusion. At the same time they do feel their way into their characters' skins with a view to acquiring their characteristics.

As has already been said, the actor too will make use of this psychological operation. But whereas the usual practice in acting is to execute it during the actual performance, in the hope of stimulating the spectator into a similar operation, he will achieve it only at an earlier stage, at some time during rehearsals.

To safeguard against an unduly "impulsive," frictionless and uncritical creation of characters and incidents, more reading rehearsals can be held than usual. The actor should refrain from living himself into the part prematurely in any way, and should go on functioning as long as possible as a reader (which does not mean a reader-aloud). An important step is memorizing one's first impressions.

When reading his part the actor's attitude should be one of a man who is astounded and contradicts. Not only the occurrence of the incidents, as he reads about them, but the conduct of the man he is playing, as he experiences it, must be weighed up by him and their peculiarities understood; none can be taken as given, as something that "was bound to turn out that way," that was "only to be expected from a character like that." Before memorizing the words he must memorize what he felt astounded at and where he felt impelled to contradict. For these are dynamic forces that he must preserve in creating his performance.

When he appears on the stage, besides what he actually is doing he will at all essential points discover, specify, imply what he is not doing; that is to say he will act in such a way that the alternative emerges as clearly as possible, that his acting allows the other possibilities to be inferred and only represents one out of the possible variants. He will say for instance "You'll pay for that," and not say "I forgive you." He detests his children; it is not the case that he loves them. He moves down stage left and not up stage right. Whatever he doesn't do must be contained and conserved in what he does. In this way every sentence and every gesture signifies a decision; the character remains under observation and is tested. The technical term for this procedure is "fixing the 'not . . . but.'"

The actor does not allow himself to become completely transformed on the stage into the character he is portraying. He is not Lear, Harpagon, Schweik; he shows them. He reproduces their remarks as authentically as he can; he puts forward their way of behaving to the best of his abilities and knowledge of men; but he never tries to persuade himself (and thereby others) that this amounts to a complete transformation. Actors will know what it means if I say that a typical kind of acting without this complete transformation takes place when a producer or colleague shows one how to play a particular passage. It is not his own part, so he is not completely transformed; he underlines the technical aspect and retains the attitude of someone just making suggestions.

Once the idea of total transformation is abandoned the actor speaks his part not as if he were improvising it himself but like a quotation. At the same time he obviously has to render all the quotation's overtones, the remark's full human and concrete shape; similarly the gesture he makes must have the full substance of a human gesture even though it now represents a copy.

Given this absence of total transformation in the acting there are three aids which may help to alienate the actions and remarks of the characters being portrayed:

1. Transposition into the third person.
2. Transposition into the past.
3. Speaking the stage directions out loud.

Using the third person and the past tense allows the actor to adopt the right attitude of detachment. In addition he will look for stage directions and remarks that comment on his lines, and speak them aloud at rehearsal ("He stood up and exclaimed angrily, not having eaten: . . . ," or "He had never been told so before, and didn't know if it was true or not," or "He smiled, and said with forced nonchalance: . . ."). Speaking the stage directions out loud in the third person results in a clash between two tones of voice, alienating the second of them, the text proper. This style of acting is further alienated by taking place on the stage after having already been outlined and announced in words. Transposing it into the past gives the speaker a standpoint from which he can look back at his sentence. The sentence too is thereby alienated without the speaker adopting an unreal point of view; unlike the spectator, he has read the play right through and is better placed to judge the sentence in accordance with the ending, with its consequences, than the former, who knows less and is more of a stranger to the sentence.

This composite process leads to an alienation of the text in the rehearsals which generally persists in the performance too. The directness of the relationship with the audience allows and indeed forces the actual speech delivery to be varied in accordance with the greater or smaller significance attaching to the sentences. Take the case of witnesses addressing a court. The underlinings, the characters' insistence on their remarks, must be developed as a piece of effective virtuosity. If the actor turns to the audience it must be a whole-hearted turn rather than the asides and soliloquizing technique of the old-fashioned theater. To get the full A-effect from the poetic medium the actor should start at rehearsal by paraphrasing the verse's content in vulgar prose, possibly accompanying this by the gestures designed for the verse. A daring and beautiful handling of verbal media will alienate the text. (Prose can be alienated by translation into the actor's native dialect.)

Gesture will be dealt with below, but it can at once be said that everything to do with the emotions has to be externalized; that is to say, it must be developed into a gesture. The actor has to find a sensibly perceptible outward expression for his character's emotions, preferably some action that gives away what is going on inside him. The emotion in question must be brought out, must lose all its restrictions so that it can be treated on a big scale. Special elegance, power and grace of gesture bring about the A-effect.

A masterly use of gesture can be seen in Chinese acting. The Chinese actor achieves the A-effect by being seen to observe his own movements.

Whatever the actor offers in the way of gesture, verse structure, etc., must be finished and bear the hallmarks of something rehearsed and rounded-off. The impression to be given is one of ease, which is at the same time one of difficulties overcome. The actor must make it possible for the audience to take his own art, his mastery of technique, lightly too. He puts an incident before the spectator with perfection and as he thinks it really happened or might have happened. He does not conceal the fact that he has rehearsed it, any more than an acrobat conceals his training, and he emphasizes that it is his own (actor's) account, view, version of the incident.

Because he doesn't identify himself with him he can pick a definite attitude to adopt towards the character whom he portrays, can show what he thinks of him and invite the spectator, who is likewise not asked to identify himself, to criticize the character portrayed.

The attitude which he adopts is a socially critical one. In his exposition of the incidents and in his characterization of the person he tries to bring out those features which come within society's sphere. In this way his performance becomes a discussion (about social conditions) with the audience he is addressing. He prompts the spectator to justify or abolish these conditions according to what class he belongs to.

The object of the A-effect is to alienate the social gest underlying every incident. By social gest is meant the mimetic and gestural expression of the social relationships prevailing between people of a given period.

It helps to formulate the incident for society, and to put it across in such a way that society is given the key, if titles are thought up for the scenes. These titles must have a historical quality.

This brings us to a crucial technical device: historicization.

The actor must play the incidents as historical ones. Historical incidents are unique, transitory incidents associated with particular periods. The conduct of the persons involved in them is not fixed and "universally human"; it includes elements that have been or may be overtaken by the course of history, and is subject to criticism from the immediately following period's point of view. The conduct of those born before us is alienated[1] from us by an incessant evolution.

[1]*Entfremdet.*

It is up to the actor to treat present-day events and modes of behavior with the same detachment as the historian adopts with regard to those of the past. He must alienate these characters and incidents from us.

Characters and incidents from ordinary life, from our immediate surroundings, being familiar, strike us as more or less natural. Alienating them helps to make them seem remarkable to us. Science has carefully developed a technique of getting irritated with the everyday, "self-evident," universally accepted occurrence, and there is no reason why this infinitely useful attitude should not be taken over by art. It is an attitude which arose in science as a result of the growth in human productive powers. In art the same motive applies.

As for the emotions, the experimental use of the A-effect in the epic theater's German productions indicated that this way of acting too can stimulate them, though possibly a different class of emotion is involved from those of the orthodox theater. A critical attitude on the audience's part is a thoroughly artistic one. Nor does the actual practice of the A-effect seem anything like so unnatural as its description. Of course it is a way of acting that has nothing to do with stylization as commonly practiced. The main advantage of the epic theater with its A-effect, intended purely to show the world in such a way that it becomes manageable, is precisely its quality of being natural and earthly, its humor and its renunciation of all the mystical elements that have stuck to the orthodox theater from the old days.

BERTOLT BRECHT

Notes for *Mother Courage*, Scene 12   1949

TRANSLATED BY ERIC BENTLEY AND HUGO SCHMIDT

For some of his work, Brecht produced booklets that supply a great deal of background information that does not appear in the text of the plays. Brecht's manner of producing his plays was important to him. Although he did not expect every successive production to adhere strictly to the standards he established in commentaries such as this, he hoped his intentions would be substantially respected.

Twelfth Scene

Courage Moves On

The peasants have to convince Courage that Kattrin is dead. Kattrin's lullaby. Mother Courage pays for Kattrin's funeral and receives the expressions of sympathy of the peasants. Mother Courage harnesses herself to her empty covered wagon. Still hoping to get back into business, she follows the tattered army.

Basic Arrangement

The wagon stands on the empty stage. Mother Courage holds dead Kattrin's head in her lap. The peasants stand at the foot of the dead girl, huddled together and hostile. Courage talks as if her daughter were only sleeping, and deliberately overhears the reproach of the peasants that she was to blame for Kattrin's death.

Kattrin's lullaby. The mother's face is bent low over the face of the daughter. The song does not conciliate those who listen.

Mother Courage pays for Kattrin's funeral and receives expressions of sympathy from the peasants. After she has realized that her last child is dead, Courage gets up laboriously and hobbles around the corpse (right), along the footlights, behind the wagon. She returns with a tent cloth, and answers over her shoulder the peasant's question whether she had no one to turn to: "Oh yes, one. Eilif." And places the cloth over the body, with her back toward the footlights. At the head of the corpse, she pulls the cloth all the way over the face, then again takes her place behind the corpse. The peasant and his son shake hands with her and bow ceremoniously before carrying the body out (to the right). The peasant woman, too, shakes hands with Courage, walks to the right and stops once more, undecided. The two women exchange a few words, then the peasant woman exits.

Mother Courage harnesses herself to her empty covered wagon. Still hoping to get back into business, she follows the tattered army. Slowly, the old woman walks to the wagon, rolls up the rope which Dumb Kattrin had been pulling to this point, takes a stick, looks at it, slips it through the sling of the second rope, tucks the stick under her arm, and starts pulling. The turntable begins to move, and Courage circles the stage once. The curtain closes when she is upstage right for the second time.

The Peasants

The attitude of the peasants toward Courage is hostile. She got them into difficulties, and they will be saddled with her if she does not catch up with the regiments. Besides, she is to blame for the accident herself, in their opinion. And moreover the canteen woman is not part of the resident population, and now, in time of war, she belongs to the fleecers, cutthroats, and marauders in the wake of the armies. When they condole with her by shaking her hand, they merely follow custom.

The Bow

During this entire scene, Weigel, as Courage, showed an almost animal indifference. All the more beautiful was the deep bow that she made when the body was carried away.

The Lullaby

The lullaby must be sung without sentimentality and without the desire to arouse sentimentality. Otherwise, its significance does not get across. The thought that is the basis of this song is a murderous one: the child of this mother was supposed to be better off than other children of other mothers. Through a slight stress on the "you," Weigel revealed the treacherous hope of Courage to get her child, and perhaps only hers, through the war alive. The child to whom the most common things were denied was promised the uncommon.

Paying for the Funeral

Even when paying for the funeral, Weigel gave another hint at the character of Courage. She fished a few coins from her leather purse, put one back, and gave the rest to the peasant. The overpowering impression she gave of having been destroyed was not in the least diminished by this.

The Last Verse

While Courage slowly harnessed herself to her wagon, the last verse of her song was sung from the box in which the band had been placed. It expresses one more time her undestroyed hope to get something out of war anyway. It becomes more impressive in that it does not aim at the illusion that the song is actually sung by army units moving past in the distance.

Giehse in the Role of Courage

When covering up the body, Giehse put her head under the cloth, looking at her daughter one more time, before finally dropping it over her face.

Before she began pulling away her covered wagon—another beautiful variant—she looked into the distance, to figure out where to go, and before she started pulling, she blew her nose with her index finger.

Take Your Time

At the end of the play it is necessary that one see the wagon roll away. Naturally, the audience gets the idea when the wagon starts. If the movement is extended, a moment of irritation arises ("that's long enough, now"). If it is prolonged even further, deeper understanding sets in.

Pulling the Wagon in the Last Scene

For the 12th scene, farm house and stable with roof (of the 11th scene) were cleared away, and only the wagon and Dumb Kattrin's body were left. The act of dragging the wagon off—the large letters "Saxony" were pulled up (out of sight) when the music begins—took place on a completely empty stage: whereby one remembered the setting of the first scene. Courage and her wagon moved in a complete circle on the revolving stage. She passed the footlights once more. As usual, the stage was bathed in light.

Discoveries of the Realists

Wherein lies the effectiveness of Weigel's gesture when she mechanically puts one coin back into her purse, after having fished her money out, as she hands the peasant the funeral money for dead Kattrin? She shows that this tradeswoman, in all her grief, does not completely forget to count, since money is so hard to come by. And she shows this as a discovery about human nature that is shaped by certain conditions. This little feature has the power and the suddenness of a discovery. The art of the realists consists of digging out the truth from under the rubble of the evident, of connecting the particular with the general, of pinning down the unique within the larger process.

A Change of Text

After "I'll manage, there isn't much in it now," Courage added, in the Munich and then also in the Berlin production: "I must start up again in business."

Mother Courage Learns Nothing

In the last scene, Weigel's Courage appeared like an eighty-year-old woman. And she comprehends nothing. She reacts only to the statements that are connected with war, such as that one must not remain behind. She overhears the crude reproach of the peasants that Kattrin's death was her fault.

Courage's inability to learn from the unproductiveness of war was a prophecy in the year 1938 when the play was written. At the Berlin production in 1948 the desire was voiced that Courage should at least come to a realization in the play. To make it possible for the spectator to get something out of this realistic play, i.e., to make the spectator learn a lesson, theaters have to arrive at an acting style that does not seek an identification of the spectator with the protagonist.

Judging on the basis of reports of spectators and newspaper reviews, the Zurich world premiere—although artistically on a high level—presented only the image of war as a natural catastrophe and an inevitable fate, and thereby it underscored to the middle-class spectator in the orchestra his own indestructibility, his ability to survive. But even to the likewise middle-class Courage, the decision "Join in or don't join in" was always left open in the play. The production, it seems, must also have presented Courage's business dealings, profiteering, willingness to take risks, as quite natural, "eternally human" behavior, so that she had no other choice. Today, it is true, the man of the middle class can no longer stay out of war, as Courage could have. To him, a production of the play can probably teach nothing but a real hatred of war, and a certain insight into the fact that the big deals of which war consists are not made by the little people. In that sense, the play is more of a lesson than reality is, because here in the play the situation of war is more of an experimental situation, made for the sake of insights. I.e., the spectator attains the attitude of a student—as long as the acting style is correct. The part of the audience that belongs to the proletariat, i.e., the class that actually can struggle against and overcome war, should be given insight into the connection between business and war (again provided the acting style is correct): the proletariat as a class can do away with war by doing away with capitalism. Of course, as far as the proletarian part of the audience is concerned, one must also take into consideration the fact that this class is busy drawing its own conclusions—inside as well as outside the theater.

The Epic Element

The Epic element was certainly visible in the production at the Deutsches Theater—in the arrangement, in the presentation of the characters, in the minute execution of details, and in the pacing of the entire play. Also, contradictory elements were not eliminated but stressed, and the parts, visible as such, made a convincing whole. However, the goal of Epic Theater was not reached. Much became clear, but clarification was in the end absent. Only in a few recasting-rehearsals did it clearly emerge, for then the actors were only "pretending," i.e., they only showed to the newly added colleague the positions and intonations, and then the whole thing received that preciously loose, unlabored, non-urgent element that incites the spectator to have his own independent thoughts and feelings.

That the production did not have an Epic foundation was never remarked, however: which was probably the reason the actors did not dare provide one.

Concerning the Notes Themselves

We hope that the present notes, offering various explanations and inventions essential to the production of a play, will not have an air of spurious seriousness. It is admittedly hard to establish the lightness and casualness that are of the essence of theater. The arts, even when they are instructive, are forms of amusement.

Tennessee Williams

Tennessee Williams (1911–1983) was one of a handful of post–World War II American playwrights to achieve an international reputation. He was born Thomas Lanier Williams in Columbus, Mississippi, the first son of a traveling shoe salesman who eventually moved the family to a dark and dreary tenement in St. Louis. A precocious child, Williams was given a typewriter by his mother when he was eleven years old. The instrument helped him create fantasy worlds that seemed more real, more important to him than the dark and sometimes threatening world in which he lived. His parents, expecting a third child, their son Dakin, moved out of the tenement and bought a house whose gloominess depressed virtually everyone in it. His mother and father found themselves arguing, and his older sister, Rose, took refuge from the real world by closeting herself with a collection of glass animals.

Both Rose and Tennessee responded badly to their environment, and both had breakdowns. Tennessee was so ill that he suffered a partial paralysis of his legs, a disorder that made him a victim of bullies at school and a disappointment to his father at home. He could never participate in sports and was always somewhat frail; however, he was very advanced intellectually and published his first story when he was sixteen.

His education was sporadic. He attended the University of Missouri but, failing ROTC because of his physical limitations, soon dropped out to work in a shoe company. He then went to Washington University in St. Louis but dropped out again. Finally, he earned a bachelor's degree in playwriting at the State University of Iowa when he was twenty-four. During this time he was writing plays, some of which were produced at Washington University. Two years after he graduated, the Theatre Guild produced his first commercial play, *Battle of Angels* (1940), in Boston. It was such a distinct failure that he feared his fledgling career was stunted, but he kept writing and managed to live for a few years on foundation grants. It was not until the production of *The Glass Menagerie* (1944 in Chicago, 1945 in New York) that he achieved the kind of notice he knew he deserved. His first real success, the play was given the New York Drama Critics' Circle Award, the sign of his having achieved a measure of professional recognition and financial independence.

Having tried several jobs that did not work out, including an unsuccessful attempt at screenwriting, Williams had no more worries about work after *The Glass Menagerie* ran on Broadway for 561 performances. In 1947, his second success, *A Streetcar Named Desire,* starring the then-unknown Marlon Brando, was an even bigger box-office smash. It ran for 855 performances and won the Pulitzer Prize. By the time Tennessee Williams was thirty-six, he was regarded as one of the most important playwrights in the United States.

Williams followed these successes with a number of plays that were not all as well received as his first works. *Summer and Smoke* (1948), *The Rose Tattoo* (1951), and *Camino Real* (1953) were met with measured enthusiasm from the public, although the critics thought highly of Williams's work. These plays were followed by another success, *Cat on a Hot Tin Roof*, the saga of a southern family, which won all the major drama prizes in 1955, including the Pulitzer.

Williams's energy was unfailing over the next several years. He authored a screenplay, *Baby Doll,* with the legendary director Elia Kazan, in 1956. In 1958 he wrote a one-act play, *Suddenly Last Summer,* and in 1959 *Sweet Bird of Youth.* Some of his later plays are *The Night of the Iguana* (1961), *The Milk Train Doesn't Stop Here Anymore* (1963), and *Small Craft Warnings* (1972). He also wrote a novel and several volumes of short stories, establishing himself as an important writer in many genres. His sudden death in 1983 was a blow to the theater world.

Cat on a Hot Tin Roof

For discussion questions and assignments on *Cat on a Hot Tin Roof,* visit **bedfordstmartins.com/jacobus.**

The title *Cat on a Hot Tin Roof* comes from an offhand remark made by Tennessee Williams's father, Cornelius Williams, who told his wife that she sometimes made him "as nervous as a cat on a hot tin roof." In speaking about the play's first production, Williams said that he saw his father in the character of Big Daddy. Reminiscence and family memory are as apparent in this play as in most of Williams's work. The secret ingredient in the play, the secret that haunts Brick and torments Maggie, is homosexuality and Brick's relationship with his now-dead friend Skipper. Maggie seduced Skipper to find out what his relation with Brick was, and when he was unable to perform sexually with her, she felt she knew the truth. The theme of homosexuality extends to the previous inhabitants of Maggie and Brick's bedroom, the bachelors Jack Straw and Peter Ochello, the original owners of the plantation. Williams's note that the two "shared this room all their lives together" implies that their relationship was that of lovers. Williams had already become fully aware of his own homosexuality, although he revealed that personal element only obliquely, in works such as *Cat on a Hot Tin Roof,* until he "came out" during a television interview with David Frost in 1970.

Williams said in his *Memoirs* that this play was his favorite: "I believe that in *Cat* I reached beyond myself, in the second act, to a kind of crude eloquence of expression in Big Daddy that I have managed to give no other character of my creation." Critics have said that one reason Williams liked the play is that he was able to observe the unities of time, place, and action. Brick is confined to his room because he has broken his ankle in a drunken competition at the high school track. The central action of the play, the celebration of Big Daddy's sixty-fifth birthday, is thus brought to the bedroom, which is also at the center of one of the principal tensions in the play.

Big Daddy owns a cotton plantation, and both his sons are a disappointment to him. Gooper, with his ambitious wife and his five "no-neck monsters," is weak and unappealing. Even though Gooper has become a lawyer and produced children in an effort to please his father, Big Daddy sees him as possessing none of the masculine qualities he expects in his heir. Brick, a former football player and Big Daddy's favorite, slipped into debilitating alcoholism after Skipper's death. At the time of the play, he has no career and few prospects. Maggie sees that the only way she can secure Big Daddy's blessing in the form of Brick's inheritance is by having a child. And with Brick keeping a sexual distance from her, she has to find a way to help him overcome his grief.

Because Williams made Brick's homosexuality more or less ambiguous, some critics asserted that the play's structure was inconclusive. For example, they reasoned that one sexual failure did not prove anything about Skipper's sexual preference. They also pointed out that Maggie and Brick's sexual efforts after the curtain falls on the last act may not be successful at all.

Williams's original version of the play — before it was performed — differed from his final version. Originally, Big Daddy did not appear after act 2, and Maggie and Brick did not vow to have a child or to get together at all. The play was changed because its first director, Elia Kazan, believed that Big Daddy was too brilliant a character to leave out of act 3. He argued with Williams until, against his will, Williams revised act 3 to imply a more positive ending, to bring back Big Daddy — who tells an elephant joke that caused the censor to complain in 1955 — and to make Maggie a softer, less acerbic, and much more appealing character. Williams later said that he agreed that the revision made the play stronger, although he preferred his original ending. He later published the play with two versions of act 3 so that regional and other theaters could choose the ending they preferred.

Cat on a Hot Tin Roof in Performance

The play premiered at the Morosco Theatre in New York in March 1955 with Burl Ives, then known best as a folk singer, as Big Daddy, Barbara Bel Geddes as Maggie, Ben Gazzara as Brick, and Mildred Dunnock as Big Mama. This powerful cast made the play a huge success. After 694 performances in New York, the play toured for another 268 performances. It won Williams his second Pulitzer Prize and his third Drama Critics' Circle Award for best play of the season. Elia Kazan not only directed the play but worked hard to help Williams alter his conception. Williams believed that the play should have a realistic production, since in his mind it was a realistic play. Kazan saw it otherwise and introduced soft lighting and a dreamy setting that established the play as moderately expressionistic.

London theaters were forbidden to put on the play as written, but a theater club produced it to mixed reviews in 1956. The film version originally was to have Grace Kelly as Maggie, but Elizabeth Taylor got the role, and Paul Newman played Brick. The film version removed all suggestions of homosexuality, focusing instead on Brick's immaturity and his need to grow up to the responsibilities of marriage. It was a highly successful film for its time.

Numerous revivals of the play have appeared in many countries, including a production in Tokyo in 1970. Williams revised the ending once more — putting back the elephant joke — for a restaging of the play in 1974 in Stratford, Connecticut, and then took it to New York for twenty weeks with Elizabeth Ashley as Maggie and Keir Dullea as Brick. That version (which we use in this book) was made into a television production in 1984 with Rip Torn as Big Daddy, Kim Stanley as Big Mama, Tommy Lee Jones as Brick, and Jessica Lange as Maggie. TV critic Richard Zoglin said, "The net effect is to retain the beefed-up dimensions of Maggie and Big Daddy from Broadway, but to leave Brick, at the end, a little more stuck in what Williams describes as a 'state of spiritual despair.'" Kathleen Turner was nominated for a Tony Award for her acclaimed performance as Maggie in the 1990 revival of the play at the Eugene O'Neill Theatre on Broadway. Polly Holliday won the Tony for her portrayal of Big Mama. But theater critic Frank Rich said the play would be best remembered for the performance of Charles Durning as Big Daddy.

Ned Beatty, as Big Daddy, and Margo Martindale, as Big Mama, were both praised in reviews for their performances in the 2003 revival at the Music Box Theatre on Broadway. Ashley Judd as Maggie and Jason Patric as Brick also got strong reviews for their performances. In 2004, the play was performed at the Kennedy Center in Washington, D.C., with George Grizzard as Big Daddy, Dana Ivey as Big Mama, and Mary Stuart Masterson as Maggie. Both of these productions were successful and much anticipated. Debbie Allen's 2008 Broadway production featured an all African American cast, including Anika Noni Rose as Maggie, James Earl Jones as Big Daddy, Terrence Howard as Brick, and Phylicia Rashad as Big Mama. The production was well heralded but not warmly reviewed in New York. However, when it moved to London, where it featured Sanaa Lathan as Maggie and Adrian Lester as Brick, the reviews were excellent. Jones was described as leaving "the critics breathless." In 2011, Vienna's English Theatre in Austria produced the play in celebration of Williams's one-hundredth birthday.

TENNESSEE WILLIAMS (1911–1983)

Cat on a Hot Tin Roof   1955

Characters

MARGARET
BRICK
MAE, *sometimes called Sister Woman*
BIG MAMA
DIXIE, *a little girl*
BIG DADDY
REVEREND TOOKER
GOOPER, *sometimes called Brother Man*
DOCTOR BAUGH, *pronounced "Baw"*
LACEY, *a Negro servant*
SOOKEY, *another*
CHILDREN

Notes for the Designer: *The set is the bed-sitting-room of a plantation home in the Mississippi Delta. It is along an upstairs gallery which probably runs around the entire house; it has two pairs of very wide doors opening onto the gallery, showing white balustrades against a fair summer sky that fades into dusk and night during the course of the play, which occupies* precisely *the time of its performance, excepting, of course, the fifteen minutes of intermission.*

Perhaps the style of the room is not what you would expect in the home of the Delta's biggest cotton planter. It is Victorian with a touch of the Far East. It hasn't changed much since it was occupied by the original owners of the place, Jack Straw and Peter Ochello, a pair of old bachelors who shared this room all their lives together. In other words, the room must evoke some ghosts; it is gently and poetically haunted by a relationship that must have involved a tenderness which was uncommon. This may be irrelevant or unnecessary, but I once saw a reproduction of a faded photograph of the verandah of Robert Louis Stevenson's home on that Samoan Island where he spent his last years, and there was a quality of tender light on weathered wood, such as porch furniture made of bamboo and wicker, exposed to tropical suns and tropical rains, which came to mind when I thought about the set for this play, bringing also to mind the grace and comfort of light, the reassurance it gives, on a late and fair afternoon in summer, the way that no matter what, even dread of death, is gently touched and soothed by it. For the set is the back-ground for a play that deals with human extremities of emotion, and it needs that softness behind it.

The bathroom door, showing only pale-blue tile and silver towel racks, is in one side wall; the hall door in the opposite wall. Two articles of furniture need mention: a big double bed which staging should make a functional part of the set as often as suitable, the surface of which should be slightly raked to make figures on it seen more easily; and against the wall space between the two huge double doors upstage: a monumental monstrosity peculiar to our times, a huge console combination of radio-phonograph (hi-fi with three speakers), TV set, and liquor cabinet, bearing and containing many glasses and bottles, all in one piece, which is a composition of muted silver tones, and the opalescent tones of reflecting glass, a chromatic link, this thing, between the sepia (tawny gold) tones of the interior and the cool (white and blue) tones of the gallery and sky. This piece of furniture (?!), this monu-ment, is a very complete and compact little shrine to virtually all the comforts and illusions behind which we hide from such things as the characters in the play are faced with. . . .

The set should be far less realistic than I have so far implied in this description of it. I think the walls below the ceiling should dissolve mysteriously into air; the set should be roofed by the sky; stars and moon suggested by traces of milky pallor, as if they were observed through a telescope lens out of focus.

Anything else I can think of? Oh, yes, fanlights (transoms shaped like an open glass fan) above all the doors in the set, with panes of blue and amber, and above all, the designer should take as many pains to give the actors room to move about freely (to show their restlessness, their passion for breaking out) as if it were a set for a ballet.

An evening in summer. The action is continuous with two intermissions.

ACT 1

(At the rise of the curtain someone is taking a shower in the bathroom, the door of which is half open. A pretty young woman, with anxious lines in her face, enters the bedroom and crosses to the bathroom door.)

MARGARET *(shouting above roar of water)*: One of those no-neck monsters hit me with a hot buttered biscuit so I have t' change!

(Margaret's voice is both rapid and drawling. In her long speeches she has the vocal tricks of a priest deliv-ering a liturgical chant, the lines are almost sung, always continuing a little beyond her breath so she has

to gasp for another. Sometimes she intersperses the lines with a little wordless singing, such as "Da-da-daaaa!")

(Water turns off and Brick calls out to her, but is still unseen. A tone of politely feigned interest, masking indifference, or worse, is characteristic of his speech with Margaret.)

BRICK: Wha'd you say, Maggie? Water was on s' loud I couldn't hearya. . . .

MARGARET: Well, I!—just remarked that!—one of th' no-neck monsters messed up m' lovely lace dress so I got t'—cha-a-ange. . . .

(She opens and kicks shut drawers of the dresser.)

BRICK: Why d'ya call Gooper's kiddies no-neck monsters?

MARGARET: Because they've got no necks! Isn't that a good enough reason?

BRICK: Don't they have any necks?

MARGARET: None visible. Their fat little heads are set on their fat little bodies without a bit of connection.

BRICK: That's too bad.

MARGARET: Yes, it's too bad because you can't wring their necks if they've got no necks to wring! Isn't that right, honey?

(She steps out of her dress, stands in a slip of ivory satin and lace.)

Yep, they're no-neck monsters, all no-neck people are monsters . . .

(Children shriek downstairs.)

Hear them? Hear them screaming? I don't know where their voice boxes are located since they don't have necks. I tell you I got so nervous at that table tonight I thought I would throw back my head and utter a scream you could hear across the Arkansas border an' parts of Louisiana an' Tennessee. I said to your charming sister-in-law, Mae, honey, couldn't you feed those precious little things at a separate table with an oilcloth cover? They make such a mess an' the lace cloth looks *so* pretty! She made enor-mous eyes at me and said, "Ohhh, noooooo! On Big Daddy's birthday? Why, he would never forgive me!" Well, I want you to know, Big Daddy hadn't been at the table two minutes with those five no-neck mon-sters slobbering and drooling over their food before he threw down his fork an' shouted, "Fo' God's sake, Gooper, why don't you put them pigs at a trough in th' kitchen?"—Well, I swear, I simply could have di-ieed!

Think of it, Brick, they've got five of them and number six is coming. They've brought the whole bunch down here like animals to display at a county fair. Why, they have those children doin' tricks all the time! "Junior, show Big Daddy how you do this, show Big Daddy how you do that, say your little piece fo' Big Daddy, Sister. Show your dimples, Sugar. Brother, show Big Daddy how you stand on your head!"—It goes on all the time, along with constant little remarks and innuendos about the fact that you and I have not produced any children, are totally childless and therefore totally useless!—Of course it's comical but it's also disgusting since it's so obvious what they're up to!

BRICK (*without interest*): What are they up to, Maggie?

MARGARET: Why you know what they're up to!

BRICK (*appearing*): No, I don't know what they're up to.

(*He stands there in the bathroom doorway drying his hair with a towel and hanging onto the towel rack because one ankle is broken, plastered and bound. He is still slim and firm as a boy. His liquor hasn't started tearing him down outside. He has the additional charm of that cool air of detachment that people have who have given up the struggle. But now and then, when disturbed, something flashes behind it, like lightning in a fair sky, which shows that at some deeper level he is far from peaceful. Perhaps in a stronger light he would show some signs of deliquescence, but the fading, still warm light from the gallery treats him gently.*)

MARGARET: I'll tell you what they're up to, boy of mine!—They're up to cutting you out of your father's estate, and—

(*She freezes momentarily before her next remark. Her voice drops as if it were somehow a personally embarrassing admission.*)

—Now we know that Big Daddy's dyin' of—*cancer.* . . .

(*There are voices on the lawn below: long-drawn calls across distance. Margaret raises her lovely bare arms and powders her armpits with a light sigh.*)

(*She adjusts the angle of a magnifying mirror to straighten an eyelash, then rises fretfully saying:*)

There's so much light in the room it—

BRICK (*softly but sharply*): Do we?

MARGARET: Do we what?

BRICK: Know Big Daddy's dyin' of cancer?

MARGARET: Got the report today.

BRICK: Oh . . .

MARGARET (*letting down bamboo blinds which cast long, gold-fretted shadows over the room*): Yep, got th' report just now . . . it didn't surprise me, Baby. . . .

(*Her voice has range, and music; sometimes it drops low as a boy's and you have a sudden image of her playing boy's games as a child.*)

I recognized the symptoms soon's we got here last spring and I'm willin' to bet you that Brother Man and his wife were pretty sure of it, too. That more than likely explains why their usual summer migration to the coolness of the Great Smokies was passed up this summer in favor of—hustlin' down here

ev'ry whipstitch with their whole screamin' tribe! And why so many allusions have been made to Rainbow Hill lately. You know what Rainbow Hill is? Place that's famous for treatin' alcoholics an' dope fiends in the movies!

BRICK: I'm not in the movies.

MARGARET: No, and you don't take dope. Otherwise you're a perfect candidate for Rainbow Hill, Baby, and that's where they aim to ship you—over my dead body! Yep, over my dead body they'll ship you there, but nothing would please them better. Then Brother Man could get a-hold of the purse strings and dole out remittances to us, maybe get power of attorney and sign checks for us and cut off our credit wherever, whenever he wanted! Son-of-a-bitch!—How'd you like that, Baby?—Well, you've been doin' just about ev'rything in your power to bring it about, you've just been doin' ev'rything you can think of to aid and abet them in this scheme of theirs! Quittin' work, devoting yourself to the occupation of drinkin'!—Breakin' your ankle last night on the high school athletic field: doin' what? Jumpin' hurdles? At two or three in the morning? Just fantastic! Got in the paper. *Clarksdale Register* carried a nice little item about it, human interest story about a well-known former athlete stagin' a one-man track meet on the Glorious Hill High School athletic field last night, but was slightly out of condition and didn't clear the first hurdle! Brother Man Gooper claims he exercised his influence t' keep it from goin' out over AP or UP or every goddamn "P."

But, Brick? You still have one big advantage!

(*During the above swift flood of words, Brick has reclined with contrapuntal leisure on the snowy surface of the bed and has rolled over carefully on his side or belly.*)

BRICK (*wryly*): Did you *say* something, Maggie?

MARGARET: Big Daddy dotes on you, honey. And he can't stand Brother Man and Brother Man's wife, that monster of fertility, Mae. Know how I know? By little expressions that flicker over his face when that woman is holding fo'th on one of her choice topics such as—how she refused twilight sleep!°—when the twins were delivered! Because she feels motherhood's an experience that a woman ought to experience fully!—in order to fully appreciate the wonder and beauty of it! HAH!—and how she made Brother Man come in an' stand beside her in the delivery room so he would not miss out on the "wonder and beauty" of it either!—producin' those no-neck monsters. . . .

(*A speech of this kind would be antipathetic from almost anybody but Margaret; she makes it oddly funny, because her eyes constantly twinkle and*

twilight sleep: Anesthesia.

her voice shakes with laughter which is basically indulgent.)

—Big Daddy shares my attitude toward those two! As for me, well—I give him a laugh now and then and he tolerates me. In fact!—I sometimes suspect that Big Daddy harbors a little unconscious "lech" fo' me. . . .

BRICK: What makes you think that Big Daddy has a lech for you, Maggie?

MARGARET: Way he always drops his eyes down my body when I'm talkin' to him, drops his eyes to my boobs an' licks his old chops! Ha ha!

BRICK: That kind of talk is disgusting.

MARGARET: Did anyone ever tell you that you're an ass-aching Puritan, Brick?

I think it's mighty fine that that ole fellow, on the doorstep of death, still takes in my shape with what I think is deserved appreciation!

And you wanta know something else? Big Daddy didn't know how many little Maes and Goopers had been produced! "How many kids have you got?" he asked at the table, just like Brother Man and his wife were new acquaintances to him! Big Mama said he was jokin', but that ole boy wasn't jokin', Lord, no!

And when they infawmed him that they had five already and were turning out number six!—the news seemed to come as a sort of unpleasant surprise . . .

(Children yell below.)

Scream, monsters!

(Turns to Brick with a sudden, gay, charming smile which fades as she notices that he is not looking at her but into fading gold space with a troubled expression.)

(It is constant rejection that makes her humor "bitchy.")

Yes, you should of been at that supper-table, Baby.

(Whenever she calls him "baby" the word is a soft caress.)

Y'know, Big Daddy, bless his ole sweet soul, he's the dearest ole thing in the world, but he does hunch over his food as if he preferred not to notice anything else. Well, Mae an' Gooper were side by side at the table, direckly across from Big Daddy, watchin' his face like hawks while they jawed an' jabbered about the cuteness an' brilliance of th' no-neck monsters!

(She giggles with a hand fluttering at her throat and her breast and her long throat arched.)

(She comes downstage and recreates the scene with voice and gesture.)

And the no-neck monsters were ranged around the table, some in high chairs and some on th' *Books of Knowledge,* all in fancy little paper caps in honor of Big Daddy's birthday, and all through dinner, well, I want you to know that Brother Man an' his partner never once, for one moment, stopped exchanging pokes an' pinches an' kicks an' signs an' signals!—Why, they were like a couple of cardsharps fleecing a sucker.—Even Big Mama, bless her ole sweet soul, she isn't th' quickest an' brightest thing in the world, she finally noticed, at last, an' said to Gooper, "Gooper, what are you an' Mae makin' all these signs at each other about?"—I swear t' goodness, I nearly choked on my chicken!

(Margaret, back at the dressing table, still doesn't see Brick. He is watching her with a look that is not quite definable—Amused? shocked? contemptuous?—part of those and part of something else.)

Y'know—your brother Gooper still cherishes the illusion he took a giant step up on the social ladder when he married Miss Mae Flynn of the Memphis Flynns.

But I have a piece of Spanish news for Gooper. The Flynns never had a thing in this world but money and they lost that, they were nothing at all but fairly successful climbers. Of course, Mae Flynn came out in Memphis eight years before I made my debut in Nashville, but I had friends at Ward-Belmont who came from Memphis and they used to come to see me and I used to go to see them for Christmas and spring vacations, and so I know who rates an' who doesn't rate in Memphis society. Why, y'know ole Papa Flynn, he barely escaped doing time in the Federal pen for shady manipulations on th' stock market when his chain stores crashed, and as for Mae having been a cotton carnival queen, as they remind us so often, lest we forget, well, that's one honor that I don't envy her for!—Sit on a brass throne on a tacky float an' ride down Main Street, smilin', bowin', and blowin' kisses to all the trash on the street—

(She picks out a pair of jeweled sandals and rushes to the dressing table.)

Why, year before last, when Susan McPheeters was singled out fo' that honor, y'know what happened to her? Y'know what happened to poor little Susie McPheeters?

BRICK *(absently)*: No. What happened to little Susie McPheeters?

MARGARET: Somebody spit tobacco juice in her face.

BRICK *(dreamily)*: Somebody spit tobacco juice in her face?

MARGARET: That's right, some old drunk leaned out of a window in the Hotel Gayoso and yelled, "Hey, Queen, hey, hey, there, Queenie!" Poor Susie looked up and flashed him a radiant smile and he shot out a squirt of tobacco juice right in poor Susie's face.

BRICK: Well, what d'you know about that.

MARGARET (*gaily*): What do I know about it? I was there, I saw it!

BRICK (*absently*): Must have been kind of funny.

MARGARET: Susie didn't think so. Had hysterics. Screamed like a banshee. They had to stop th' parade an' remove her from her throne an' go on with—

(*She catches sight of him in the mirror, gasps slightly, wheels about to face him. Count ten.*)

—Why are you looking at me like that?

BRICK (*whistling softly, now*): Like what, Maggie?

MARGARET (*intensely, fearfully*): The way y' were lookin' at me just now, befo' I caught your eye in the mirror and you started t' whistle! I don't know how t' describe it but it froze my blood!—I've caught you lookin' at me like that so often lately. What are you thinkin' of when you look at me like that?

BRICK: I wasn't conscious of lookin' at you, Maggie.

MARGARET: Well, I was conscious of it! What were you thinkin'?

BRICK: I don't remember thinking of anything, Maggie.

MARGARET: Don't you think I know that—? Don't you—?—Think I know that—?

BRICK (*cooly*): Know *what*, Maggie?

MARGARET (*struggling for expression*): That I've gone through this—*hideous!*—*transformation*, become—hard! Frantic!

(*Then she adds, almost tenderly:*)

—cruel!!

That's what you've been observing in me lately. How could y' help but observe it? That's all right. I'm not—thin-skinned any more, can't afford t' be thin-skinned any more.

(*She is now recovering her power.*)

—But Brick? Brick?

BRICK: Did you say something?

MARGARET: I was goin t' say something: that I get—lonely. Very!

BRICK: Ev'rybody gets that . . .

MARGARET: Living with someone you love can be lonelier—than living entirely *alone!*—if the one that y' love doesn't love you. . . .

(*There is a pause. Brick hobbles downstage and asks, without looking at her:*)

BRICK: Would you like to live alone, Maggie?

(*Another pause: then—after she has caught a quick, hurt breath:*)

MARGARET: *No!*—God!—I wouldn't!

(*Another gasping breath. She forcibly controls what must have been an impulse to cry out. We see her deliberately, very forcibly, going all the way back to the world in which you can talk about ordinary matters.*)

Did you have a nice shower?

BRICK: Uh-huh.

MARGARET: Was the water cool?

BRICK: No.

MARGARET: But it made y' feel fresh, huh?

BRICK: Fresher. . . .

MARGARET: I know something would make y' feel *much* fresher!

BRICK: What?

MARGARET: An alcohol rub. Or cologne, a rub with cologne!

BRICK: That's good after a workout but I haven't been workin' out, Maggie.

MARGARET: You've kept in good shape, though.

BRICK: (*indifferently*): You think so, Maggie?

MARGARET: I always thought drinkin' men lost their looks, but I was plainly mistaken.

BRICK (*wryly*): Why, thanks, Maggie.

MARGARET: You're the only drinkin' man I know that it never seems t' put fat on.

BRICK: I'm gettin' softer, Maggie.

MARGARET: Well, sooner or later it's bound to soften you up. It was just beginning to soften up Skipper when

(*She stops short.*)

I'm sorry. I never could keep my fingers off a sore—I wish you *would* lose your looks. If you did it would make the martyrdom of Saint Maggie a little more bearable. But no such goddamn luck. I actually believe you've gotten better looking since you've gone on the bottle. Yeah, a person who didn't know you would think you'd never had a tense nerve in your body or a strained muscle.

(*There are sounds of croquet on the lawn below: the click of mallets, light voices, near and distant.*)

Of course, you always had that detached quality as if you were playing a game without much concern over whether you won or lost, and now that you've lost the game, not lost but just quit playing, you have that rare sort of charm that usually only happens in very old or hopelessly sick people, the charm of the defeated.—You look so cool, so cool, so enviably cool.

REVEREND TOOKER (*offstage right*): Now looka here, boy, lemme show you how to get outa that!

MARGARET: They're playing croquet. The moon has appeared and it's white, just beginning to turn a little bit yellow. . . .

You were a wonderful lover. . . .

Such a wonderful person to go to bed with, and I think mostly because you were really indifferent to it. Isn't that right? Never had any anxiety about it, did it naturally, easily, slowly, with absolute confidence and perfect calm, more like opening a door for a lady or seating her at a table than giving expression to any longing for her. Your indifference made you wonderful at lovemaking—*strange?*—but true. . . .

REVEREND TOOKER: Oh! That's a beauty.

DOCTOR BAUGH: Yeah. I got you boxed.

MARGARET: You know, if I thought you would never, never, *never* make love to me again—I would go downstairs to the kitchen and pick out the longest and sharpest knife I could find and stick it straight into my heart, I swear that I would!

REVEREND TOOKER: Watch out, you're gonna miss it.

DOCTOR BAUGH: You just don't know me, boy!

MARGARET: But one thing I don't have is the charm of the defeated, my hat is still in the ring, and I am determined to win!

(*There is the sound of croquet mallets hitting croquet balls.*)

REVEREND TOOKER: Mmm—You're too slippery for me.

MARGARET:—What is the victory of a cat on a hot tin roof?—I wish I knew. . . .
Just staying on it, I guess, as long as she can. . . .

DOCTOR BAUGH: Jus' like an eel, boy, jus' like an eel!

(*More croquet sounds.*)

MARGARET: Later tonight I'm going to tell you I love you an' maybe by that time you'll be drunk enough to believe me. Yes, they're playing croquet. . . .
Big Daddy is dying of cancer. . . .
What were you thinking of when I caught you looking at me like that? Were you thinking of Skipper?

(*Brick takes up his crutch, rises.*)

Oh, excuse me, forgive me, but laws of silence don't work! No, laws of silence don't work. . . .

(*Brick crosses to the bar, takes a quick drink, and rubs his head with a towel.*)

Laws of silence don't work. . . .
When something is festering in your memory or your imagination, laws of silence don't work, it's just like shutting a door and locking it on a house on fire in hope of forgetting that the house is burning. But not facing a fire doesn't put it out. Silence about a thing just magnifies it. It grows and festers in silence, becomes malignant. . . .

(*He drops his crutch.*)

BRICK: Give me my crutch.

(*He has stopped rubbing his hair dry but still stands hanging onto the towel rack in a white towel-cloth robe.*)

MARGARET: Lean on me.

BRICK: No, just give me my crutch.

MARGARET: Lean on my shoulder.

BRICK: *I don't want to lean on your shoulder, I want my crutch!*

(*This is spoken like sudden lightning.*)

Are you going to give me my crutch or do I have to get down on my knees on the floor and—

MARGARET: *Here, here, take it, take it!*

(*She has thrust the crutch at him.*)

BRICK (*hobbling out*): Thanks . . .

MARGARET: We mustn't scream at each other, the walls in this house have ears. . . .

(*He hobbles directly to liquor cabinet to get a new drink.*)

—but that's the first time I've heard you raise your voice in a long time, Brick. A crack in the wall?—Of composure?
—I think that's a good sign. . . .
A sign of nerves in a player on the defensive!

(*Brick turns and smiles at her coolly over his fresh drink.*)

BRICK: It just hasn't happened yet, Maggie.

MARGARET: What?

BRICK: The click I get in my head when I've had enough of this stuff to make me peaceful. . . .
Will you do me a favor?

MARGARET: Maybe I will. What favor?

BRICK: Just, just keep your voice down!

MARGARET (*in a hoarse whisper*): I'll do you that favor, I'll speak in a whisper, if not shut up completely, if *you* will do *me* a favor and make that drink your last one till after the party.

BRICK: What party?

MARGARET: Big Daddy's birthday party.

BRICK: Is this Big Daddy's birthday?

MARGARET: You know this is Big Daddy's birthday!

BRICK: No, I don't, I forgot it.

MARGARET: Well, I remembered it for you . . .

(*They are both speaking as breathlessly as a pair of kids after a fight, drawing deep exhausted breaths and looking at each other with faraway eyes, shaking and panting together as if they had broken apart from a violent struggle.*)

BRICK: Good for you, Maggie.

MARGARET: You just have to scribble a few lines on this card.

BRICK: You scribble something, Maggie.

MARGARET: It's got to be your handwriting; it's your present, I've given him my present; it's got to be your handwriting!

(*The tension between them is building again, the voices becoming shrill once more.*)

BRICK: I didn't get him a present.

MARGARET: I got one for you.

BRICK: All right. You write the card, then.

MARGARET: And have him know you didn't remember his birthday?

BRICK: I didn't remember his birthday.

MARGARET: You don't have to prove you didn't!

BRICK: I don't want to fool him about it.

MARGARET: Just write "Love, Brick!" for God's—

BRICK: No.

MARGARET: You've *got* to!

BRICK: I don't have to do anything I don't want to do. You keep forgetting the conditions on which I agreed to stay on living with you.

MARGARET (*out before she knows it*): I'm not living with you. We occupy the same cage.

BRICK: You've got to remember the conditions agreed on.

SONNY (*offstage*): Mommy, give it to me. I had it first.

MAE: Hush.

MARGARET: They're impossible conditions!

BRICK: Then why don't you—?

SONNY: I want it, I want it!

MAE: Get away!

MARGARET: HUSH! Who is out there? Is somebody at the door?

(*There are footsteps in hall.*)

MAE (*outside*): May I enter a moment?

MARGARET: Oh, *you!* Sure. Come in, Mae.

(*Mae enters bearing aloft the bow of a young lady's archery set.*)

MAE: Brick, is this thing yours?

MARGARET: Why, Sister Woman—that's my Diana Trophy. Won it at the intercollegiate archery contest on the Ole Miss campus.

MAE: It's a mighty dangerous thing to leave exposed round a house full of nawmal rid-blooded children attracted t'weapons.

MARGARET: "Nawmal rid-blooded children attracted t'weapons" ought t'be taught to keep their hands off things that don't belong to them.

MAE: Maggie, honey, if you had children of your own you'd know how funny that is. Will you please lock this up and put the key out of reach?

MARGARET: Sister Woman, nobody is plotting the destruction of your kiddies.—Brick and I still have our special archers' license. We're goin' deer-huntin' on Moon Lake as soon as the season starts. I love to run with dogs through chilly woods, run, run leap over obstructions—

(*She goes into the closet carrying the bow.*)

MAE: How's the injured ankle, Brick?

BRICK: Doesn't hurt. Just itches.

MAE: Oh, my! Brick—Brick, you should've been downstairs after supper! Kiddies put on a show. Polly played the piano, Buster an' Sonny drums, an' then they turned out the lights an' Dixie an' Trixie puhfawmed a toe dance in fairy costume with *spahkluhs!* Big Daddy just beamed! He just beamed!

MARGARET (*from the closet with a sharp laugh*): Oh, I bet. It breaks my heart that we missed it!

(*She reenters.*)

But Mae? Why did y'give dawgs' names to all your kiddies?

MAE: *Dogs'* names?

MARGARET (*sweetly*): Dixie, Trixie, Buster, Sonny, Polly!—Sounds like four dogs and a parrot . . .

MAE: Maggie?

(*Margaret turns with a smile.*)

Why are you so catty?

MARGARET: Cause I'm a cat! But why can't *you* take a joke, Sister Woman?

MAE: Nothin' pleases me more than a joke that's funny. You know the real names of our kiddies. Buster's real name is Robert. Sonny's real name is Saunders. Trixie's real name is Marlene and Dixie's—

(*Gooper downstairs calls for her. "Hey, Mae! Sister Woman, intermission is over!"—She rushes to door, saying:*)

Intermission is over! See ya later!

MARGARET: I wonder what Dixie's real name is?

BRICK: Maggie, being catty doesn't help things any . . .

MARGARET: I know! *WHY!*—Am I so catty?—Cause I'm consumed with envy an' eaten up with longing?— Brick, I'm going to lay out your beautiful Shantung silk suit from Rome and one of your monogrammed silk shirts. I'll put your cuff links in it, those lovely star sapphires I get you to wear so rarely. . . .

BRICK: I can't get trousers on over this plaster cast.

MARGARET: Yes, you can, I'll help you.

BRICK: I'm not going to get dressed, Maggie.

MARGARET: Will you just put on a pair of white silk pajamas?

BRICK: Yes, I'll do that, Maggie.

MARGARET: *Thank* you, thank you so *much!*

BRICK: Don't mention it.

MARGARET: *Oh, Brick!* How long does it have t' go on? This punishment? Haven't I done time enough, haven't I served my term, can't I apply for a—pardon?

BRICK: Maggie, you're spoiling my liquor. Lately your voice always sounds like you'd been running upstairs to warn somebody that the house was on fire!

MARGARET: Well, no wonder, no wonder. Y'know what I feel like, Brick?

I feel all the time like a cat on a hot tin roof!

BRICK: Then jump off the roof, jump off it, cats can jump off roofs and land on their four feet uninjured!

MARGARET: Oh, yes!

BRICK: Do it!—fo' God's sake, do it . . .

MARGARET: Do what?

BRICK: Take a lover!

MARGARET: I can't see a man but you! Even with my eyes closed, I just see you! Why don't you get ugly, Brick, why don't you please get fat or ugly or something so I could stand it?

Maggie (Barbara Bel Geddes) and Brick (Ben Gazzara) in the original 1955 Broadway production of *Cat on a Hot Tin Roof*.

Barbara Bel Geddes as Maggie.

Maggie (Anika Noni Rose) attempts to seduce Brick (Terrence Howard) in the 2008 New York production of *Cat on a Hot Tin Roof*, directed by Debbie Allen.

(*She rushes to hall door, opens it, listens.*)

The concert is still going on! Bravo, no-necks, bravo!

(*She slams and locks door fiercely.*)

BRICK: What did you lock the door for?
MARGARET: To give us a little privacy for a while.
BRICK: You know better, Maggie.
MARGARET: No, I don't know better. . . .

(*She rushes to gallery doors, draws the rose-silk drapes across them.*)

BRICK: Don't make a fool of yourself.
MARGARET: I don't mind makin' a fool of myself over you!
BRICK: I mind, Maggie. I feel embarrassed for you.
MARGARET: Feel embarrassed! But don't continue my torture. I can't live on and on under these circumstances.
BRICK: You agreed to—
MARGARET: I know but—
BRICK:—Accept that condition!
MARGARET: I CAN'T! CAN'T! CAN'T!

(*She seizes his shoulder.*)

BRICK: Let go!

(*He breaks away from her and seizes the small boudoir chair and raises it like a lion-tamer facing a big circus cat.*)
(*Count five. She stares at him with her fist pressed to her mouth, then bursts into shrill, almost hysterical*

laughter. *He remains grave for a moment, then grins and puts the chair down.*)
(*Big Mama calls through closed door.*)

BIG MAMA: Son? Son? Son?
BRICK: What is it, Big Mama?
BIG MAMA (*outside*): Oh, son! We got the most wonderful news about Big Daddy. I just had t' run up an' tell you right this—

(*She rattles the knob.*)

—What's this door doin', locked, faw? You all think there's robbers in the house?
MARGARET: Big Mama, Brick is dressin', he's not dressed yet.
BIG MAMA: That's all right, it won't be the first time I've seen Brick not dressed. Come on, open this door!

(*Margaret, with a grimace, goes to unlock and open the hall door, as Brick hobbles rapidly to the bathroom and kicks the door shut. Big Mama has disappeared from the hall.*)

MARGARET: Big Mama?

(*Big Mama appears through the opposite gallery doors behind Margaret, huffing and puffing like an old bulldog. She is a short, stout woman; her sixty years and 170 pounds have left her somewhat breathless most of the time; she's always tensed like a boxer, or rather, a*

Japanese wrestler. Her "family" was maybe a little superior to Big Daddy's, but not much. She wears a black or silver lace dress and at least half a million in flashy gems. She is very sincere.)

BIG MAMA (*loudly, startling Margaret*): Here—I come through Gooper's and Mae's gall'ry door. Where's Brick? *Brick*—Hurry on out of there son, I just have a second and want to give you the news about Big Daddy.—I hate locked doors in a house . . .

MARGARET (*with affected lightness*): I've noticed you do, Big Mama, but people have got to have *some* moments of privacy, don't they?

BIG MAMA: No, ma'am, not in *my* house. (*Without pause.*) Whacha took off you' dress faw? I thought that little lace dress was so sweet on yuh, honey.

MARGARET: I thought it looked sweet on me, too, but one of m' cute little table-partners used it for a napkin so—!

BIG MAMA (*picking up stockings on floor*): What?

MARGARET: You know, Big Mama, Mae and Gooper's so touchy about those children—thanks, Big Mama . . .

(*Big Mama has thrust the picked-up stockings in Margaret's hand with a grunt.*)

—that you just don't dare to suggest there's any room for improvement in their—

BIG MAMA: Brick, hurry out!—Shoot, Maggie, you just don't like children.

MARGARET: I do SO like children! Adore them!—well brought up!

BIG MAMA (*gentle—loving*): Well, why don't you have some and bring them up well, then, instead of all the time pickin' on Gooper's an' Mae's?

GOOPER (*shouting up the stairs*): Hey, hey, Big Mama, Betsy an' Hugh got to go, waitin' t' tell yuh g'by!

BIG MAMA: Tell 'em to hold their hawses, I'll be right down in a jiffy!

GOOPER: Yes ma'am!

(*She turns to the bathroom door and calls out.*)

BIG MAMA: Son? Can you hear me in there?

(*There is a muffled answer.*)

We just got the full report from the laboratory at the Ochsner Clinic, completely negative, son, ev'rything negative, right on down the line! Nothin' a-tall's wrong with him but some little functional thing called a spastic colon. Can you hear me, son?

MARGARET: He can hear you, Big Mama.

BIG MAMA: Then why don't he say something? God Almighty, a piece of news like that should make him shout. It made *me* shout, I can tell you. I shouted and sobbed and fell right down on my knees!—Look!

(*She pulls up her skirt.*)

See the bruises where I hit my kneecaps? Took both doctors to haul me back on my feet!

(*She laughs—she always laughs like hell at herself.*)

Big Daddy was furious with me! But ain't that wonderful news?

(*Facing bathroom again, she continues:*)

After all the anxiety we been through to git a report like that on Big Daddy's birthday? Big Daddy tried to hide how much of a load that news took off his mind, but didn't fool *me*. He was mighty close to crying about it *himself!*

(*Good-byes are shouted downstairs, and she rushes to door.*)

GOOPER: Big Mama!

BIG MAMA: *Hold those people down there, don't let them go!*—Now, git dressed we're all comin' up to this room fo' Big Daddy's birthday party because of your ankle.—How's his ankle, Maggie?

MARGARET: Well, he broke it, Big Mama.

BIG MAMA: I know he broke it.

(*A phone is ringing in hall. A Negro voice answers: "Mistuh Polly's res'dence."*)

I mean does it hurt him much still.

MARGARET: I'm afraid I can't give you that information, Big Mama. You'll have to ask Brick if it hurts much still or not.

SOOKEY (*in the hall*): It's Memphis, Mizz Polly, it's Miss Sally in Memphis.

BIG MAMA: Awright, Sookey.

(*Big Mama rushes into the hall and is heard shouting on the phone:*)

Hello, Miss Sally. How are you, Miss Sally?—Yes, well, I was just gonna call you about it. *Shoot!*—

MARGARET: Brick, don't!

(*Big Mama raises her voice to a bellow.*)

BIG MAMA: *Miss Sally? Don't ever call me from the Gayoso Lobby, too much talk goes on in that hotel lobby, no wonder you can't hear me!* Now listen, Miss Sally. They's nothin' serious wrong with Big Daddy. We got the report just now, they's nothin' wrong but a thing called a—spastic! *SPASTIC!*—colon . . .

(*She appears at the hall door and calls to Margaret.*)

—Maggie, come out here and talk to that fool on the phone. I'm shouted breathless!

MARGARET (*goes out and is heard sweetly at phone*): Miss Sally? This is Brick's wife, Maggie. So nice to hear your voice. Can you hear *mine?* Well, *good!*—Big Mama just wanted you to know that they've got the report from the Ochsner Clinic and what Big Daddy has is a spastic colon. Yes. Spastic colon, Miss Sally. That's right, spastic colon. G'bye, Miss Sally, hope I'll see you real soon!

(*Hangs up a little before Miss Sally was probably ready to terminate the talk. She returns through the hall door.*)

She heard me perfectly. I've discovered with deaf people the thing to do is not shout at them but just enunciate clearly. My rich old Aunt Cornelia was deaf as the dead but I could make her hear me just by sayin' each word slowly, distinctly, close to her ear. I read her the *Commercial Appeal* ev'ry night, read her the classified ads in it, even, she never missed a word of it. But was she a mean ole thing! Know what I got when she died? Her unexpired subscriptions to five magazines and the Book-of-the-Month Club and a LIBRARY full of ev'ry dull book ever written! All else went to her hellcat of a sister . . . meaner than she was, even!

(*Big Mama has been straightening things up in the room during this speech.*)

BIG MAMA (*closing closet door on discarded clothes*): Miss Sally sure is a case! Big Daddy says she's always got her hand out fo' something. He's not mistaken. That poor ole thing always has her hand out fo' somethin'. I don't think Big Daddy gives her as much as he should.

GOOPER: Big Mama! Come on now! Betsy and Hugh can't wait no longer!

BIG MAMA (*shouting*): I'm comin'!

(*She starts out. At the hall door, turns and jerks a forefinger, first toward the bathroom door, then toward the liquor cabinet, meaning: "Has Brick been drinking?" Margaret pretends not to understand, cocks her head and raises her brows as if the pantomimic performance was completely mystifying to her.*)

(*Big Mama rushes back to Margaret:*)

Shoot! Stop playin' so dumb!—I mean has he been drinkin' that stuff much yet?

MARGARET (*with a little laugh*): Oh! I think he had a highball after supper.

BIG MAMA: Don't laugh about it!—Some single men stop drinkin' when they git married and others start! Brick never touched liquor before he—!

MARGARET (*crying out*): THAT'S NOT FAIR!

BIG MAMA: Fair or not fair I want to ask you a question, one question: D'you make Brick happy in bed?

MARGARET: Why don't you ask if he makes *me* happy in bed?

BIG MAMA: Because I know that—

MARGARET: *It works both ways!*

BIG MAMA: Something's not right! You're childless and my son drinks!

GOOPER: Come on, Big Mama!

(*Gooper has called her downstairs and she has rushed to the door on the line above. She turns at the door and points at the bed.*)

—When a marriage goes on the rocks, the rocks are *there*, right *there*!

MARGARET: *That's*—

(*Big Mama has swept out of the room and slammed the door.*)

—not—*fair* . . .

(*Margaret is alone, completely alone, and she feels it. She draws in, hunches her shoulders, raises her arms with fists clenched, shuts her eyes tight as a child about to be stabbed with a vaccination needle. When she opens her eyes again, what she sees is the long oval mirror and she rushes straight to it, stares into it with a grimace and says: "Who are you?"—Then she crouches a little and answers herself in a different voice which is high, thin, mocking: "I am Maggie the Cat!"—Straightens quickly as bathroom door opens a little and Brick calls out to her.*)

BRICK: Has Big Mama gone?

MARGARET: She's gone.

(*He opens the bathroom door and hobbles out, with his liquor glass now empty, straight to the liquor cabinet. He is whistling softly. Margaret's head pivots on her long, slender throat to watch him.*)

(*She raises a hand uncertainly to the base of her throat, as if it was difficult for her to swallow, before she speaks:*)

You know, our sex life didn't just peter out in the usual way, it was cut off short, long before the natural time for it to, and it's going to revive again, just as sudden as that. I'm confident of it. That's what I'm keeping myself attractive for. For the time when you'll see me again like other men see me. Yes, like other men see me. They still see me, Brick, and they like what they see. Uh-huh. Some of them would give their—

Look, Brick!

(*She stands before the long oval mirror, touches her breast and then her hips with her two hands.*)

How high my body stays on me!—Nothing has fallen on me—not a fraction. . . .

(*Her voice is soft and trembling: a pleading child's. At this moment as he turns to glance at her—a look which is like a player passing a ball to another player, third down and goal to go—she has to capture the audience in a grip so tight that she can hold it till the first intermission without any lapse of attention.*)

Other men still want me. My face looks strained, sometimes, but I've kept my figure as well as you've kept yours, and men admire it. I still turn heads on the street. Why, last week in Memphis everywhere that I went men's eyes burned holes in my clothes, at the country club and in restaurants and department stores, there wasn't a man I met or walked by that didn't just eat me up with his eyes and turn around when I passed him and look back at me. Why, at Alice's party for her New York cousins, the best-lookin' man in the crowd—followed me upstairs and tried to force his way in the powder room with me, followed me to the door and tried to force his way in!

BRICK: Why didn't you let him, Maggie?

MARGARET: Because I'm not that common, for one thing. Not that I wasn't almost tempted to. You like to know who it was? It was Sonny Boy Maxwell, that's who!

BRICK: Oh, yeah, Sonny Boy Maxwell, he was a good end-runner but had a little injury to his back and had to quit.

MARGARET: He has no injury now and has no wife and still has a lech for me!

BRICK: I see no reason to lock him out of a powder room in that case.

MARGARET: And have someone catch me at it? I'm not that stupid. Oh, I might sometime cheat on you with someone, since you're so insultingly eager to have me do it! —But if I do, you can be damned sure it will be in a place and a time where no one but me and the man could possibly know. Because I'm not going to give you any excuse to divorce me for being unfaithful or anything else....

BRICK: Maggie, I wouldn't divorce you for being unfaithful or anything else. Don't you know that? Hell. I'd be relieved to know that you'd found yourself a lover.

MARGARET: Well, I'm taking no chances. No, I'd rather stay on this hot tin roof.

BRICK: A hot tin roof's 'n uncomfo'table place t' stay on....

(*He starts to whistle softly.*)

MARGARET (*through his whistle*): Yeah, but I can stay on it just as long as I have to.

BRICK: You could leave me, Maggie.

(*He resumes whistle. She wheels about to glare at him.*)

MARGARET: *Don't want to and will not!* Besides if I did, you don't have a cent to pay for it but what you get from Big Daddy and he's dying of cancer!

(*For the first time a realization of Big Daddy's doom seems to penetrate to Brick's consciousness, visibly, and he looks at Margaret.*)

BRICK: Big Mama just said he *wasn't,* that the report was okay.

MARGARET: That's what she thinks because she got the same story that they gave Big Daddy. And was just as taken in by it as he was, poor ole things....

But tonight they're going to tell her the truth about it. When Big Daddy goes to bed, they're going to tell her that he is dying of cancer.

(*She slams the dresser drawer.*)

—It's malignant and it's terminal.

BRICK: Does Big Daddy know it?

MARGARET: Hell, do they *ever* know it? Nobody says, "You're dying." You have to fool them. They have to fool *themselves.*

BRICK: Why?

MARGARET: *Why?* Because human beings dream of life everlasting, that's the reason! But most of them want it on earth and not in heaven.

(*He gives a short, hard laugh at her touch of humor.*)

Well.... (*She touches up her mascara.*) That's how it is, anyhow.... (*She looks about.*) Where did I put down my cigarette? Don't want to burn up the home-place, at least not with Mae and Gooper and their five monsters in it!

(*She has found it and sucks at it greedily. Blows out smoke and continues:*)

So this is Big Daddy's last birthday. And Mae and Gooper, they know it, oh, *they* know it, all right. They got the first information from the Ochsner Clinic. That's why they rushed down here with their no-neck monsters. Because. Do you know something? Big Daddy's made no will? Big Daddy's never made out any will in his life, and so this campaign's afoot to impress him, forcibly as possible, with the fact that you drink and I've borne no children!

(*He continues to stare at her a moment, then mutters something sharp but not audible and hobbles rather rapidly out onto the long gallery in the fading, much faded, gold light.*)

MARGARET (*continuing her liturgical chant*): Y'know, I'm *fond* of Big Daddy, I am genuinely fond of that old man, I really *am,* you know....

BRICK (*faintly, vaguely*): Yes, I know you are....

MARGARET: I've always sort of admired him in spite of his coarseness, his four-letter words and so forth. Because Big Daddy *is* what he *is,* and he makes no bones about it. He hasn't turned gentleman farmer, he's still a Mississippi redneck, as much of a redneck as he must have been when he was just overseer here on the old Jack Straw and Peter Ochello place. But he got hold of it an' built it into th' biggest an' finest plantation in the Delta.—I've always *liked* Big Daddy....

(*She crosses to the proscenium.*)

Well, this is Big Daddy's last birthday. I'm sorry about it. But I'm facing the facts. It takes money to take care of a drinker and that's the office that I've been elected to lately.

BRICK: You don't have to take care of me.

MARGARET: Yes, I do. Two people in the same boat have got to take care of each other. At least you want money to buy more Echo Spring when this supply is exhausted, or will you be satisfied with a ten-cent beer?

Mae an' Gooper are plannin' to freeze us out of Big Daddy's estate because you drink and I'm childless. But we can defeat that plan. We're *going* to defeat that plan!

Brick, y'know, I've been so God damn disgustingly poor all my life!—That's the *truth,* Brick!

BRICK: I'm not sayin' it isn't.

MARGARET: Always had to suck up to people I couldn't stand because they had money and I was poor as

Job's turkey. You don't know what that's like. Well, I'll tell you, it's like you would feel a thousand miles away from Echo Spring!—And had to get back to it on that broken ankle . . . without a crutch!

That's how it feels to be as poor as Job's turkey and have to suck up to relatives that you hated because they had money and all you had was a bunch of hand-me-down clothes and a few old moldy three-percent government bonds. My daddy loved his liquor, he fell in love with his liquor the way you've fallen in love with Echo Spring!—And my poor Mama, having to maintain some semblance of social position, to keep appearances up, on an income of one hundred and fifty dollars a month on those old government bonds!

When I came out, the year that I made my debut, I had just two evening dresses! One Mother made me from a pattern in *Vogue*, the other a hand-me-down from a snotty rich cousin I hated!

—The dress that I married you in was my grandmother's weddin' gown. . . .

So that's why I'm like a cat on a hot tin roof!

(*Brick is still on the gallery. Someone below calls up to him in a warm Negro voice, "Hiya, Mistuh Brick, how yuh feelin'?" Brick raises his liquor glass as if that answered the question.*)

MARGARET: You can be young without money, but you can't be old without it. You've got to be old *with* money because to be old without it is just too awful, you've got to be one or the other, either *young* or *with money,* you can't be old and *without* it.—That's the *truth,* Brick. . . .

(*Brick whistles softly, vaguely.*)

Well, now I'm dressed, I'm all dressed, there's nothing else for me to do.

(*Forlornly, almost fearfully.*)

I'm dressed, all dressed, nothing else for me to do . . .

(*She moves about restlessly, aimlessly, and speaks, as if to herself.*)

What am I—? Oh!—my bracelets. . . .

(*She starts working a collection of bracelets over her hands onto her wrists, about six on each, as she talks.*)

I've thought a whole lot about it and now I know when I made my mistake. Yes, I made my mistake when I told you the truth about that thing with Skipper. Never should have confessed it, a fatal error, tellin' you about that thing with Skipper.

BRICK: Maggie, shut up about Skipper. I mean it, Maggie; you got to shut up about Skipper.

MARGARET: You ought to understand that Skipper and I—

BRICK: You don't think I'm serious, Maggie? You're fooled by the fact that I am saying this quiet? Look, Maggie. What you're doing is a dangerous thing to do. You're—you're—you're—foolin' with something that—nobody ought to fool with.

MARGARET: This time I'm going to finish what I have to say to you. Skipper and I made love, if love you could call it, because it made both of us feel a little bit closer to you. You see, you son of a bitch, you asked too much of people, of me, of him, of all the unlucky poor damned sons of bitches that happen to love you, and there was a whole pack of them, yes, there was a pack of them besides me and Skipper, you asked too goddamn much of people that loved you, you—superior creature!—you godlike being!—And so we made love to each other to dream it was you, both of us! Yes, yes, yes! Truth, truth! What's so awful about it? I like it, I think the truth is—yeah! I shouldn't have told you. . . .

BRICK (*holding his head unnaturally still and uptilted a bit*): It was Skipper that told me about it. Not you, Maggie.

MARGARET: I told you!

BRICK: After he told me!

MARGARET: What does it matter who—?

DIXIE: I got your mallet, I got your mallet.

TRIXIE: Give it to me, give it to me. IT's mine.

(*Brick turns suddenly out upon the gallery and calls:*)

BRICK: Little girl! Hey, little girl!

LITTLE GIRL (*at a distance*): What, Uncle Brick?

BRICK: Tell the folks to come up!—Bring everybody upstairs!

TRIXIE: It's mine, it's mine.

MARGARET: I can't stop myself! I'd go on telling you this in front of them all, if I had to!

BRICK: Little girl! Go on, go on, will you? Do what I told you, call them!

DIXIE: Okay.

MARGARET: Because it's got to be told and you, you!—you never let me!

(*She sobs, then controls herself, and continues almost calmly.*)

It was one of those beautiful, ideal things they tell about in the Greek legends, it couldn't be anything else, you being you, and that's what made it so sad, that's what made it so awful, because it was love that never could be carried through to anything satisfying or even talked about plainly.

BRICK: Maggie, you gotta stop this.

MARGARET: Brick, I tell you, you got to believe me, Brick, I *do* understand all about it! I—I think it was—*noble!* Can't you tell I'm sincere when I say I respect it? My only point, the only point that I'm making, is life has got to be allowed to continue even after the *dream* of life is—all—over. . . .

(*Brick is without his crutch. Leaning on furniture, he crosses to pick it up as she continues as if possessed by a will outside herself:*)

Why I remember when we double-dated at college, Gladys Fitzgerald and I and you and Skipper, it was more like a date between you and Skipper. Gladys and I were just sort of tagging along as if it was necessary to chaperone you!—to make a good public impression—

BRICK (*turns to face her, half lifting his crutch*): Maggie, you want me to hit you with this crutch? Don't you know I could kill you with this crutch?

MARGARET: Good Lord, man, d' you think I'd care if you did?

BRICK: One man has one great good true thing in his life. One great good thing which is true!—I had friendship with Skipper.—You are naming it dirty!

MARGARET: I'm not naming it dirty! I am naming it clean.

BRICK: Not love with you, Maggie, but friendship with Skipper was that one great true thing, and you are naming it dirty!

MARGARET: Then you haven't been listenin', not understood what I'm saying! I'm naming it so damn clean that it killed poor Skipper!—You two had something that had to be kept on ice, yes, incorruptible, yes!—and death was the only icebox where you could keep it....

BRICK: I married you, Maggie. Why would I marry you, Maggie, if I was—?

MARGARET: Brick, let me finish!—I know, believe me I know, that it was only Skipper that harbored even any *unconscious* desire for anything not perfectly pure between you two!—Now let me skip a little. You married me early that summer we graduated out of Ole Miss, and we were happy, weren't we, we were blissful, yes, hit heaven together ev'ry time that we loved! But that fall you an' Skipper turned down wonderful offers of jobs in order to keep on bein' football heroes—pro-football heroes. You organized the Dixie Stars that fall, so you could keep on bein' teammates forever! But somethin' was not right with it!—*Me included!*—between you. Skipper began hittin' the bottle...you got a spinal injury—couldn't play the Thanksgivin' game in Chicago, watched it on TV from a traction bed in Toledo. I joined Skipper. The Dixie Stars lost because poor Skipper was drunk. We drank together that night all night in the bar of the Blackstone and when cold day was comin' up over the Lake an' we were comin' out drunk to take a dizzy look at it, I said, "SKIPPER! STOP LOVIN' MY HUSBAND OR TELL HIM HE'S GOT TO LET YOU ADMIT IT TO HIM!"—one way or another!

HE SLAPPED ME HARD ON THE MOUTH!—then turned and ran without stopping once, I am sure, all the way back into his room at the Blackstone....

—When I came to his room that night, with a little scratch like a shy little mouse at his door, he made that pitiful, ineffectual little attempt to prove that what I had said wasn't true....

(*Brick strikes at her with crutch, a blow that shatters the gemlike lamp on the table.*)

—In this way, I destroyed him, by telling him truth that he and his world which he was born and raised in, yours and his world, had told him could not be told?

—From then on Skipper was nothing at all but a receptacle for liquor and drugs....

—Who shot cock robin? I with my—

(*She throws back her head with tight shut eyes.*)

—merciful arrow!

(*Brick strikes at her; misses.*)

Missed me!—Sorry,—I'm not tryin' to whitewash my behavior, Christ, no! Brick, I'm not good. I don't know why people have to pretend to be good, nobody's good. The rich or the well-to-do can afford to respect moral patterns, conventional moral patterns, but I could never afford to, yeah, but—I'm honest! Give me credit for just that, will you *please?*—Born poor, raised poor, expect to die poor unless I manage to get us something out of what Big Daddy leaves when he dies of cancer! But Brick?!—*Skipper is dead! I'm alive!* Maggie the cat is—

(*Brick hops awkwardly forward and strikes at her again with his crutch.*)

—alive! I am alive, alive! I am...

(*He hurls the crutch at her, across the bed she took refuge behind, and pitches forward on the floor as she completes her speech.*)

—alive!

(*A little girl, Dixie, bursts into the room, wearing an Indian war bonnet and firing a cap pistol at Margaret and shouting: "Bang, bang, bang!"*)

(*Laughter downstairs floats through the open hall door. Margaret had crouched gasping to bed at child's entrance. She now rises and says with cool fury:*)

Little girl, your mother or someone should teach you—(*gasping*)—to knock at a door before you come into a room. Otherwise people might think that you—lack—good breeding....

DIXIE: Yanh, yanh, yanh, what is Uncle Brick doin' on th' floor?

BRICK: I tried to kill your Aunt Maggie, but I failed—and I fell. Little girl, give me my crutch so I can get up off th' floor.

MARGARET: Yes, give your uncle his crutch, he's a cripple, honey, he broke his ankle last night jumping hurdles on the high school athletic field!

DIXIE: What were you jumping hurdles for, Uncle Brick?

BRICK: Because I used to jump them, and people like to do what they used to do, even after they've stopped being able to do it....

MARGARET: That's right, that's your answer, now go away, little girl.

(*Dixie fires cap pistol at Margaret three times.*)

    Stop, you stop that, monster! You little no-neck monster!

(*She seizes the cap pistol and hurls it through gallery doors.*)

DIXIE (*with a precocious instinct for the cruelest thing*): You're *jealous!*—You're just jealous because you can't have babies!

(*She sticks out her tongue at Margaret as she sashays past her with her stomach stuck out, to the gallery. Margaret slams the gallery doors and leans panting against them. There is a pause. Brick has replaced his spilt drink and sits, faraway, on the great four-poster bed.*)

MARGARET: You see?—they gloat over us being childless, even in front of their five little no-neck monsters!

(*Pauses. Voices approach on the stairs.*)

    Brick?—I've been to a doctor in Memphis, a—a gynecologist....

    I've been completely examined, and there is no reason why we can't have a child whenever we want one. And this is my time by the calendar to conceive. Are you listening to me? Are you? Are you LISTENING TO ME!

BRICK: Yes. I hear you, Maggie.

(*His attention returns to her inflamed face.*)

    —But how in hell on earth do you imagine—that you're going to have a child by a man that can't stand you?

MARGARET: That's a problem that I will have to work out.

(*She wheels about to face the hall door.*)

MAE (*offstage left*): Come on, Big Daddy. We're all goin' up to Brick's room.

(*From offstage left, voices: Reverend Tooker, Doctor Baugh, Mae.*)

MARGARET: *Here they come!*

(*The lights dim.*)

ACT 2

(*There is no lapse of time. Margaret and Brick are in the same positions they held at the end of act 1.*)

MARGARET (*at door*): *Here they come!*

(*Big Daddy appears first, a tall man with a fierce, anxious look, moving carefully not to betray his weakness even, or especially, to himself.*)

GOOPER: I read in the *Register* that you're getting a new memorial window.

(*Some of the people are approaching through the hall, others along the gallery: voices from both directions. Gooper and Reverend Tooker become visible outside gallery doors, and their voices come in clearly.*)
(*They pause outside as Gooper lights a cigar.*)

REVEREND TOOKER (*vivaciously*): Oh, but St. Paul's in Grenada has three memorial windows, and the latest one is a Tiffany stained-glass window that cost twenty-five hundred dollars, a picture of Christ the Good Shepherd with a Lamb in His arms.

MARGARET: Big Daddy.

BIG DADDY: Well, Brick.

BRICK: Hello Big Daddy.—Congratulations!

BIG DADDY:—Crap....

GOOPER: Who give that window, Preach?

REVEREND TOOKER: Clyde Fletcher's widow. Also presented St. Paul's with a baptismal font.

GOOPER: Y'know what somebody ought t' give your church is a *coolin'* system, Preach.

MAE (*almost religiously*):—Let's see now, they've had their *tyyy*-phoid shots, and their tetanus shots, their diphtheria shots and their hepatitis shots and their polio shots, they got *those* shots every month from May through September, and— Gooper? Hey! Gooper!— What all have the kiddies been shot faw?

REVEREND TOOKER: Yes, siree, Bob! And y'know what Gus Hamma's family gave in his memory to the church at Two Rivers? A complete new stone parish-house with a basketball court in the basement and a—

BIG DADDY (*uttering a loud barking laugh which is far from truly mirthful*): Hey, Preach! What's all this talk about memorials, Preach? Y' think somebody's about t' kick off around here? 'S that it?

(*Startled by this interjection, Reverend Tooker decides to laugh at the question almost as loud as he can.*)
(*How he would answer the question we'll never know, as he's spared that embarrassment by the voice of Gooper's wife, Mae, rising high and clear as she appears with "Doc" Baugh, the family doctor, through the hall door.*)

MARGARET (*overlapping a bit*): Turn on the hi-fi, Brick! Let's have some music t' start off th' party with!

BRICK: You turn it on, Maggie.

(*The talk becomes so general that the room sounds like a great aviary of chattering birds. Only Brick remains unengaged, leaning upon the liquor cabinet with his faraway smile, an ice cube in a paper napkin with which he now and then rubs his forehead. He doesn't respond to Margaret's command. She bounds forward and stoops over the instrument panel of the console.*)

GOOPER: We gave 'em that thing for a third anniversary present, got three speakers in it.

(*The room is suddenly blasted by the climax of a Wagnerian opera or a Beethoven symphony.*)

BIG DADDY: *Turn that damn thing off!*

(*Almost instant silence, almost instantly broken by the shouting charge of Big Mama, entering through hall door like a charging rhino.*)

BIG MAMA: *Wha's my Brick, wha's mah precious baby!!*
BIG DADDY: *Sorry! Turn it back on!*

(*Everyone laughs very loud. Big Daddy is famous for his jokes at Big Mama's expense, and nobody laughs louder at these jokes than Big Mama herself, though sometimes they're pretty cruel and Big Mama has to pick up or fuss with something to cover the hurt that the loud laugh doesn't quite cover.*)

(*On this occasion, a happy occasion because the dread in her heart has also been lifted by the false report on Big Daddy's condition, she giggles, grotesquely, coyly, in Big Daddy's direction and bears down upon Brick, all very quick and alive.*)

BIG MAMA: Here he is, here's my precious baby! What's that you've got in your hand? You put that liquor down, son, your hand was made fo' holdin' somethin' better than that!
GOOPER: Look at Brick put it down!

(*Brick has obeyed Big Mama by draining the glass and handing it to her. Again everyone laughs, some high, some low.*)

BIG MAMA: Oh, you bad boy, you, you're my bad little boy. Give Big Mama a kiss, you bad boy, you!—Look at him shy away, will you? Brick never liked bein' kissed or made a fuss over, I guess because he's always had too much of it!
Son, you turn that thing off!

(*Brick has switched on the TV set.*)

I can't stand TV, radio was bad enough but TV has gone it one better, I mean—(*plops wheezing in chair*)—one worse, ha ha! Now what'm I sittin' down here faw? I want t' sit next to my sweetheart on the sofa, hold hands with him and love him up a little!

(*Big Mama has on a black and white figured chiffon. The large irregular patterns, like the markings of some massive animal, the luster of her great diamonds and many pearls, the brilliants set in the silver frames of her glasses, her riotous voice, booming laugh, have dominated the room since she entered. Big Daddy has been regarding her with a steady grimace of chronic annoyance.*)

BIG MAMA (*still louder*): Preacher, Preacher, hey, Preach! Give me you' hand an' help me up from this chair!
REVEREND TOOKER: None of your tricks, Big Mama!
BIG MAMA: What tricks? You give me you' hand so I can get up an'—

(*Reverend Tooker extends her his hand. She grabs it and pulls him into her lap with a shrill laugh that spans an octave in two notes.*)

Ever seen a preacher in a fat lady's lap? Hey, hey, folks! Ever seen a preacher in a fat lady's lap?

(*Big Mama is notorious throughout the Delta for this sort of inelegant horseplay. Margaret looks on with indulgent humor, sipping Dubonnet "on the rocks" and watching Brick, but Mae and Gooper exchange signs of humorless anxiety over these antics, the sort of behavior which Mae thinks may account for their failure to quite get in with the smartest young married set in Memphis, despite all. One of the Negroes, Lacey or Sookey, peeks in, cackling. They are waiting for a sign to bring in the cake and champagne. But Big Daddy's not amused. He doesn't understand why, in spite of the infinite mental relief he's received from the doctor's report, he still has these same old fox teeth in his guts. "This spastic condition is something else," he says to himself, but aloud he roars at Big Mama:*)

BIG DADDY: *BIG MAMA, WILL YOU QUIT HORSIN'?*—You're too old an' too fat fo' that sort of crazy kid stuff an' besides a woman with your blood pressure—she had two hundred last spring!—is riskin' a stroke when you mess around like that. . . .

(*Mae blows on a pitch pipe.*)

BIG MAMA: Here comes Big Daddy's birthday!

(*Negroes in white jackets enter with an enormous birthday cake ablaze with candles and carrying buckets of champagne with satin ribbons about the bottle necks.*)

(*Mae and Gooper strike up song, and everybody, including the Negroes and Children, joins in. Only Brick remains aloof.*)

EVERYONE: Happy birthday to you.
Happy birthday to you.
Happy birthday, Big Daddy—

(*Some sing: "Dear, Big Daddy!"*)

Happy birthday to you.

(*Some sing: "How old are you?"*)

(*Mae has come down center and is organizing her children like a chorus. She gives them a barely audible: "One, two, three!" and they are off in the new tune.*)

CHILDREN: Skinamarinka—dinka—dink
Skinamarinka—do
We love you.
Skinamarinka—dinka—dink
Skinamarinka—do.

(*All together, they turn to Big Daddy.*)

Big Daddy, you!

(*They turn back front, like a musical comedy chorus.*)

We love you in the morning;
We love you in the night.

James Earl Jones as Big Daddy and Phylicia Rashad as Big Mama in Debbie Allen's production at the Novello Theatre in London, 2009.

We love you when we're with you,
And we love you out of sight.
Skinamarinka—dinka—dink
Skinamarinka—do.

(*Mae turns to Big Mama.*)

Big Mama, too!

(*Big Mama bursts into tears. The Negroes leave.*)

BIG DADDY: Now Ida, what the hell is the matter with you?
MAE: She's just so happy.
BIG MAMA: I'm just so happy, Big Daddy, I have to cry or something.

(*Sudden and loud in the hush:*)

Brick, do you know the wonderful news that Doc Baugh got from the clinic about Big Daddy? Big Daddy's one hundred percent!
MARGARET: Isn't that wonderful?
BIG MAMA: He's just one hundred percent. Passed the examination with flying colors. Now that we know there's nothing wrong with Big Daddy but a spastic colon, I can tell you something. I was worried sick half out of my mind, for fear that Big Daddy might have a thing like—

(*Margaret cuts through this speech, jumping up and exclaiming shrilly:*)

MARGARET: Brick, honey, aren't you going to give Big Daddy his birthday present?

(*Passing by him, she snatches his liquor glass from him.*)
(*She picks up a fancily wrapped package.*)

Here it is, Big Daddy, this is from Brick!
BIG MAMA: This is the biggest birthday Big Daddy's ever had, a hundred presents and bushels of telegrams from—
MAE (*at same time*): What is it, Brick?
GOOPER: I bet 500 to 50 that Brick don't *know* what it is.
BIG MAMA: The fun of presents is not knowing what they are till you open the package. Open your present, Big Daddy.
BIG DADDY: Open it you'self. I want to ask Brick somethin! Come here, Brick.
MARGARET: Big Daddy's callin' you, Brick.

(*She is opening the package.*)

BRICK: Tell Big Daddy I'm crippled.
BIG DADDY: I see you're crippled. I want to know how you got crippled.
MARGARET (*making diversionary tactics*): Oh, look, oh, look, why, it's a cashmere robe!

(*She holds the robe up for all to see.*)

MAE: You sound surprised, Maggie.
MARGARET: I never saw one before.
MAE: That's funny.—Hah!
MARGARET (*turning on her fiercely, with a brilliant smile*): Why is it funny? All my family ever had was family—and luxuries such as cashmere robes still surprise me!

BIG DADDY (*ominously*): Quiet!

MAE (*heedless in her fury*): I don't see how you could be so surprised when you bought it yourself at Loewenstein's in Memphis last Saturday. You know how I know?

BIG DADDY: I said, Quiet!

MAE: —I know because the salesgirl that sold it to you waited on me and said, Oh, Mrs. Pollitt, your sister-in-law just bought a cashmere robe for your husband's father!

MARGARET: Sister Woman! Your talents are wasted as a housewife and mother, you really ought to be with the FBI or—

BIG DADDY: QUIET!

(*Reverend Tooker's reflexes are slower than the others'. He finishes a sentence after the bellow.*)

REVEREND TOOKER (*to Doc Baugh*): —the Stork and the Reaper are running neck and neck!

(*He starts to laugh gaily when he notices the silence and Big Daddy's glare. His laugh dies falsely.*)

BIG DADDY: Preacher, I hope I'm not butting in on more talk about memorial stained-glass windows, am I, Preacher?

(*Reverend Tooker laughs feebly, then coughs dryly in the embarrassed silence.*)

Preacher?

BIG MAMA: Now, Big Daddy, don't you pick on Preacher!

BIG DADDY (*raising his voice*): You ever hear that expression all hawk and no spit? You bring that expression to mind with that little dry cough of yours, all hawk an' no spit. . . .

(*The pause is broken only by a short startled laugh from Margaret, the only one there who is conscious of and amused by the grotesque.*)

MAE (*raising her arms and jangling her bracelets*): I wonder if the mosquitoes are active tonight?

BIG DADDY: What's that, Little Mama? Did you make some remark?

MAE: Yes, I said I wondered if the mosquitoes would eat us alive if we went out on the gallery for a while.

BIG DADDY: Well, if they do, I'll have your bones pulverized for fertilizer!

BIG MAMA (*quickly*): Last week we had an airplane spraying the place and I think it done some good, at least I haven't had a—

BIG DADDY (*cutting her speech*): Brick, they tell me, if what they tell me is true, that you done some jumping last night on the high school athletic field?

BIG MAMA: Brick, Big Daddy is talking to you, son.

BRICK (*smiling vaguely over his drink*): What was that, Big Daddy?

BIG DADDY: They said you done some jumping on the high school track field last night.

BRICK: That's what they told me, too.

BIG DADDY: Was it jumping or humping that you were doing out there? What were you doing out there at three A.M., layin' a woman on that cinder track?

BIG MAMA: Big Daddy, you are off the sick-list, now, and I'm not going to excuse you for talkin' so—

BIG DADDY: Quiet!

BIG MAMA: —*nasty* in front of Preacher and—

BIG DADDY: *QUIET!*—I ast you, Brick, if you was cut-in' you'self a piece o' poon-tang last night on that cinder track? I thought maybe you were chasin' poon-tang on that track an' tripped over something in the heat of the chase—'sthat it?

(*Gooper laughs, loud and false, others nervously following suit. Big Mama stamps her foot, and purses her lips, crossing to Mae and whispering something to her as Brick meets his father's hard, intent, grinning stare with a slow, vague smile that he offers all situations from behind the screen of his liquor.*)

BRICK: No, sir, I don't think so. . . .

MAE (*at the same time, sweetly*): Reverend Tooker, let's you and I take a stroll on the widow's walk.

(*She and the preacher go out on the gallery as Big Daddy says:*)

BIG DADDY: Then what the hell were you doing out there at three o'clock in the morning?

BRICK: Jumping the hurdles, Big Daddy, runnin' and jumpin' the hurdles, but those high hurdles have gotten too high for me, now.

BIG DADDY: Cause you was drunk?

BRICK (*his vague smile fading a little*): Sober I wouldn't have tried to jump the *low* ones. . . .

BIG MAMA (*quickly*): Big Daddy, blow out the candles on your birthday cake!

MARGARET (*at the same time*): I want to propose a toast to Big Daddy Pollitt on his sixty-fifth birthday, the biggest cotton planter in—

BIG DADDY (*bellowing with fury and disgust*): *I told you to stop it, now stop it, quit this*—!

BIG MAMA (*coming in front of Big Daddy with the cake*): Big Daddy, I will not allow you to talk that way, not even on your birthday, I—

BIG DADDY: I'll talk like I want to on my birthday, Ida, or any other goddamn day of the year and anybody here that don't like it knows what they can do!

BIG MAMA: You don't mean that!

BIG DADDY: What makes you think I don't mean it?

(*Meanwhile various discreet signals have been exchanged and Gooper has also gone out on the gallery.*)

BIG MAMA: I just know you don't mean it.

BIG DADDY: You don't know a goddamn thing and you never did!

BIG MAMA: Big Daddy, you don't mean that.

BIG DADDY: Oh, yes, I do, oh, yes, I do, I mean it! I put up with a whole lot of crap around here because I thought I was dying. And you thought I was dying and you started taking over, well, you can stop taking over now, Ida, because I'm not gonna die, you can just stop now this business of taking over because you're not taking over because I'm not dying, I went through the laboratory and the goddamn exploratory operation and there's nothing wrong with me but a spastic colon. And I'm not dying of cancer which you thought I was dying of. Ain't that so? Didn't you think that I was dying of cancer, Ida?

(*Almost everybody is out on the gallery but the two old people glaring at each other across the blazing cake.*)

(*Big Mama's chest heaves and she presses a fat fist to her mouth.*)

(*Big Daddy continues, hoarsely:*)

Ain't that so, Ida? Didn't you have an idea I was dying of cancer and now you could take control of this place and everything on it? I got that impression, I seemed to get that impression. Your loud voice everywhere, your fat old body butting in here and there!

BIG MAMA: Hush! The Preacher!

BIG DADDY: Fuck the goddamn preacher!

(*Big Mama gasps loudly and sits down on the sofa which is almost too small for her.*)

Did you hear what I said? I said fuck the goddamn preacher!

(*Somebody closes the gallery doors from outside just as there is a burst of fireworks and excited cries from the children.*)

BIG MAMA: I never seen you act like this before and I can't think what's got in you!

BIG DADDY: I went through all that laboratory and operation and all just so I would know if you or me was boss here! Well, now it turns out that I am and you ain't—and that's my birthday present—and my cake and champagne!—because for three years now you been gradually taking over. Bossing. Talking. Sashaying your fat old body around the place I made! I made this place! I was overseer on it! I was the overseer on the old Straw and Ochello plantation. I quit school at ten! I quit school at ten years old and went to work like a nigger in the fields. And I rose to be overseer of the Straw and Ochello plantation. And old Straw died and I was Ochello's partner and the place got bigger and bigger and bigger and bigger and bigger! I did all that myself with no goddamn help from you, and now you think you're just about to take over. Well, I am just about to tell you that you are not just about to take over, you are not just about to take over a God damn thing. Is that clear to you, Ida? Is that very plain to you, now? Is that understood completely? I been through the laboratory from A to Z. I've had the goddamn exploratory operation, and nothing is wrong with me but a spastic colon—made spastic, I guess, by *disgust!* By all the goddamn lies and liars that I have had to put up with and all the goddamn hypocrisy

that I lived with all these forty years that we been livin' together!

Hey! Ida!! Blow out the candles on the birthday cake! Purse up your lips and draw a deep breath and blow out the goddamn candles on the cake!

BIG MAMA: Oh, Big Daddy, oh, oh, oh, Big Daddy!

BIG DADDY: What's the matter with you?

BIG MAMA: *In all these years you never believed that I loved you??*

BIG DADDY: Huh?

BIG MAMA: *And I did, I did so much, I did love you!*—I even loved your hate and your hardness, Big Daddy!

(*She sobs and rushes awkwardly out onto the gallery.*)

BIG DADDY (*to himself*): *Wouldn't it be funny if that was true. . . .*

(*A pause is followed by a burst of light in the sky from the fireworks.*)

BRICK! HEY, BRICK!

(*He stands over his blazing birthday cake.*)

(*After some moments, Brick hobbles in on his crutch, holding his glass.*)

(*Margaret follows him with a bright, anxious smile.*)

I didn't call you, Maggie. I called Brick.

MARGARET: I'm just delivering him to you.

(*She kisses Brick on the mouth which he immediately wipes with the back of his hand. She flies girlishly back out. Brick and his father are alone.*)

BIG DADDY: Why did you do that?

BRICK: Do what, Big Daddy?

BIG DADDY: Wipe her kiss off your mouth like she'd spit on you.

BRICK: I don't know. I wasn't conscious of it.

BIG DADDY: That woman of yours has a better shape on her than Gooper's but somehow or other they got the same look about them.

BRICK: What sort of look is that, Big Daddy?

BIG DADDY: I don't know how to describe it but it's the same look.

BRICK: They don't look peaceful, do they?

BIG DADDY: No, they sure in hell don't.

BRICK: They look nervous as cats?

BIG DADDY: That's right, they look nervous as cats.

BRICK: Nervous as a couple of cats on a hot tin roof?

BIG DADDY: That's right, boy, they look like a couple of cats on a hot tin roof. It's funny that you and Gooper being so different would pick out the same type of woman.

BRICK: Both of us married into society, Big Daddy.

BIG DADDY: Crap . . . I wonder what gives them both that look?

BRICK: Well. They're sittin' in the middle of a big piece of land, Big Daddy, twenty-eight thousand acres is a pretty big piece of land and so they're squaring off on it, each determined to knock off a bigger piece of it than the other whenever you let it go.

BIG DADDY: I got a surprise for those women. I'm not gonna let it go for a long time yet if that's what they're waiting for.

BRICK: That's right, Big Daddy. You just sit tight and let them scratch each other's eyes out. . . .

BIG DADDY: You bet your life I'm going to sit tight on it and let those sons of bitches scratch their eyes out, ha ha ha. . . .

But Gooper's wife's a good breeder, you got to admit she's fertile. Hell, at supper tonight she had them all at the table and they had to put a couple of extra leafs in the table to make room for them, she's got five head of them, now, and another one's comin'.

BRICK: Yep, number six is comin' . . .

BIG DADDY: Six hell, she'll probably drop a litter next time. Brick, you know, I swear to God, I don't know the way it happens.

BRICK: The way what happens, Big Daddy?

BIG DADDY: You git you a piece of land, by hook or crook, an' things start growin' on it, things accumulate on it, and the first thing you know it's completely out of hand, completely out of hand!

BRICK: Well, they say nature hates a vacuum, Big Daddy.

BIG DADDY: That's what they say, but sometimes I think that a vacuum is a hell of a lot better than some of the stuff that nature replaces it with.

Is someone out there by that door?

GOOPER: Hey Mae.

BRICK: Yep.

BIG DADDY: Who?

(*He has lowered his voice.*)

BRICK: Someone int'rested in what we say to each other.

BIG DADDY: Gooper?—GOOPER!

(*After a discreet pause, Mae appears in the gallery door.*)

MAE: Did you call Gooper, Big Daddy?

BIG DADDY: Aw, it was you.

MAE: Do you want Gooper, Big Daddy?

BIG DADDY: No, and I don't want you. I want some privacy here, while I'm having a confidential talk with my son Brick. Now it's too hot in here to close them doors, but if I have to close those fuckin' doors in order to have a private talk with my son Brick, just let me know and I'll close 'em. Because I hate eavesdroppers, I don't like any kind of sneakin' an' spyin'.

MAE: Why, Big Daddy—

BIG DADDY: You stood on the wrong side of the moon, it threw your shadow!

MAE: I was just—

BIG DADDY: You was just nothing but *spyin'* an' you *know* it!

MAE (*begins to sniff and sob*): Oh, Big Daddy, you're so unkind for some reason to those that really love you!

BIG DADDY: Shut up, shut up, shut up! I'm going to move you and Gooper out of that room next to this! It's none of your goddamn business what goes on in here at night between Brick an' Maggie. You listen at night like a couple of rutten peekhole spies and

go and give a report on what you hear to Big Mama an' she comes to me and says they say such and such and so and so about what they heard goin' on between Brick an' Maggie, and Jesus, it makes me sick. I'm goin' to move you an' Gooper out of that room, I can't stand sneakin' an' spyin', it makes me puke. . . .

(*Mae throws back her head and rolls her eyes heavenward and extends her arms as if invoking God's pity for this unjust martyrdom; then she presses a handkerchief to her nose and flies from the room with a loud swish of skirts.*)

BRICK (*now at the liquor cabinet*): They listen, do they?

BIG DADDY: Yeah. They listen and give reports to Big Mama on what goes on in here between you and Maggie. They say that—

(*He stops as if embarrassed.*)

—You won't sleep with her, that you sleep on the sofa. Is that true or not true? If you don't like Maggie, get rid of Maggie!—What are you doin' there now?

BRICK: Fresh'nin' up my drink.

BIG DADDY: Son, you know you got a real liquor problem?

BRICK: Yes, sir, yes, I know.

BIG DADDY: Is that why you quit sports-announcing, because of this liquor problem?

BRICK: Yes, sir, yes, sir, I guess so.

(*He smiles vaguely and amiably at his father across his replenished drink.*)

BIG DADDY: Son, don't guess about it, it's too important.

BRICK (*vaguely*): Yes, sir.

BIG DADDY: And listen to me, don't look at the damn chandelier. . . .

(*Pause. Big Daddy's voice is husky.*)

—Somethin' else we picked up at th' big fire-sale in Europe.

(*Another pause.*)

Life is important. There's nothing else to hold onto. A man that drinks is throwing his life away. Don't do it, hold onto your life. There's nothing else to hold onto. . . .

Sit down over here so we don't have to raise our voices, the walls have ears in this place.

BRICK (*hobbling over to sit on the sofa beside him*): All right, Big Daddy.

BIG DADDY: Quit!—how'd that come about? Some disappointment?

BRICK: I don't know. Do you?

BIG DADDY: I'm askin' you, God damn it! How in hell would I know if you don't?

BRICK: I just got out there and found that I had a mouth full of cotton. I was always two or three beats behind what was goin' on on the field and so I—

BIG DADDY: Quit!

BRICK (*amiably*): Yes, quit.

BIG DADDY: Son?

BRICK: Huh?

BIG DADDY (*inhales loudly and deeply from his cigar; then bends suddenly a little forward, exhaling loudly and raising a hand to his forehead*):—Whew!—ha ha!—I took in too much smoke, it made me a little lightheaded. . . .

(*The mantel clock chimes.*)

Why is it so damn hard for people to talk?

BRICK: Yeah. . . .

(*The clock goes on sweetly chiming till it has completed the stroke of ten.*)

—Nice peaceful-soundin' clock, I like to hear it all night. . . .

(*He slides low and comfortable on the sofa; Big Daddy sits up straight and rigid with some unspoken anxiety. All his gestures are tense and jerky as he talks. He wheezes and pants and sniffs through his nervous speech, glancing quickly, shyly, from time to time, at his son.*)

BIG DADDY: We got that clock the summer we wint to Europe, me an' Big Mama on that damn Cook's Tour, never had such an awful time in my life, I'm tellin' you, son, those gooks over there, they gouge your eyeballs out in their grand hotels. And Big Mama bought more stuff than you could haul in a couple of boxcars, that's no crap. Everywhere she wint on this whirlwind tour, she bought, bought, bought. Why, half that stuff she bought is still crated up in the cellar, under water last spring!

(*He laughs.*)

That Europe is nothin' on earth but a great big auction, that's all it is, that bunch of old worn-out places, it's just a big fire-sale, the whole fuckin' thing, an' Big Mama wint wild in it, why, you couldn't hold that woman with a mule's harness! Bought, bought, bought!—lucky I'm a rich man, yes siree, Bob, an' half that stuff is mildewin' in th' basement. It's lucky I'm a rich man, it sure is lucky, well, I'm a rich man, Brick, yep, I'm a mighty rich man.

(*His eyes light up for a moment.*)

Y'know how much I'm worth? Guess, Brick! Guess how much I'm worth!

(*Brick smiles vaguely over his drink.*)

Close on ten million in cash an' blue-chip stocks, outside, mind you, of twenty-eight thousand acres of the richest land this side of the valley Nile!

But a man can't buy his life with it, he can't buy back his life with it when his life has been spent, that's one thing not offered in the Europe fire-sale or in the American markets or any markets on earth, a man can't buy his life with it, he can't buy back his life when his life is finished. . . .

That's a sobering thought, a very sobering thought, and that's a thought that I was turning over in my head, over and over and over—until today. . . .

I'm wiser and sadder, Brick, for this experience which I just gone through. They's one thing else that I remember in Europe.

BRICK: What is that, Big Daddy?

BIG DADDY: The hills around Barcelona in the country of Spain and the children running over those bare hills in their bare skins beggin' like starvin' dogs with howls and screeches, and how fat the priests are on the streets of Barcelona, so many of them and so fat and so pleasant, ha ha!—Y'know I could feed that country? I got money enough to feed that goddamn country, but the human animal is a selfish beast and I don't reckon the money I passed out there to those howling children in the hills around Barcelona would more than upholster the chairs in this room, I mean pay to put a new cover on this chair!

Hell, I threw them money like you'd scatter feed corn for chickens, I threw money at them just to get rid of them long enough to climb back into th' car and—drive away. . . .

And then in Morocco, them Arabs, why, I remember one day in Marrakech, that old walled Arab city, I set on a broken-down wall to have a cigar, it was fearful hot there and this Arab woman stood in the road and looked at me till I was embarrassed, she stood stock still in the dusty hot road and looked at me till I was embarrassed. But listen to this. She had a naked child with her, a little naked girl with her, barely able to toddle, and after a while she set this child on the ground and give her a push and whispered something to her.

This child come toward me, barely able t' walk, come toddling up to me and—

Jesus, it makes you sick t' remember a thing like this! It stuck out its hand and tried to unbutton my trousers!

That child was not yet five! Can you believe me? Or do you think that I am making this up? I wint back to the hotel and said to Big Mama, Git packed! We're clearing out of this country. . . .

BRICK: Big Daddy, you're on a talkin' jag tonight.

BIG DADDY (*ignoring this remark*): Yes, sir, that's how it is, the human animal is a beast that dies but the fact that he's dying don't give him pity for others, no, sir, it—

—Did you say something?

BRICK: Yes.

BIG DADDY: What?

BRICK: Hand me over that crutch so I can get up.

BIG DADDY: Where you goin'?

BRICK: I'm takin' a little short trip to Echo Spring.

BIG DADDY: To where?

BRICK: Liquor cabinet. . . .

BIG DADDY: Yes, sir, boy—

(*He hands Brick the crutch.*)

—the human animal is a beast that dies and if he's got money he buys and buys and buys and I think the reason he buys everything he can buy is that in the back of his mind he has the crazy hope that one of his purchases will be life everlasting!— Which it never can be. . . . The human animal is a beast that—

BRICK (*at the liquor cabinet*): Big Daddy, you sure are shootin' th' breeze here tonight.

(*There is a pause and voices are heard outside.*)

BIG DADDY: I been quiet here lately, spoke not a word, just sat and stared into space. I had something heavy weighing on my mind but tonight that load was took off me. That's why I'm talking.—The sky looks diff'rent to me. . . .

BRICK: You know what I like to hear most?

BIG DADDY: What?

BRICK: Solid quiet. Perfect unbroken quiet.

BIG DADDY: Why?

BRICK: Because it's more peaceful.

BIG DADDY: Man, you'll hear a lot of that in the grave.

(*He chuckles agreeably.*)

BRICK: Are you through talkin' to me?

BIG DADDY: Why are you so anxious to shut me up?

BRICK: Well, sir, ever so often you say to me, Brick, I want to have a talk with you, but when we talk, it never materializes. Nothing is said. You sit in a chair and gas about this and that and I look like I listen. I try to look like I listen, but I don't listen, not much. Communication is—awful hard between people an'—somehow between you and me, it just don't—happen.

BIG DADDY: Have you ever been scared? I mean have you ever felt downright terror of something?

(*He gets up.*)

Just one moment.

(*He looks off as if he were going to tell an important secret.*)

Brick?

BRICK: What?

BIG DADDY: Son, I thought I had it!

BRICK: Had what? Had what, Big Daddy?

BIG DADDY: Cancer!

BRICK: Oh . . .

BIG DADDY: I thought the old man made out of bones had laid his cold and heavy hand on my shoulder!

BRICK: Well, Big Daddy, you kept a tight mouth about it.

BIG DADDY: A pig squeals. A man keeps a tight mouth about it, in spite of a man not having a pig's advantage.

BRICK: What advantage is that?

BIG DADDY: Ignorance—of mortality—is a comfort. A man don't have that comfort, he's the only living thing that conceives of death, that knows what it is. The others go without knowing, which is the way that anything living should go, go without knowing, without any knowledge of it, and yet a pig squeals, but a man sometimes, he can keep a tight mouth about it. Sometimes he—

(*There is a deep, smoldering ferocity in the old man.*)

—can keep a tight mouth about it. I wonder if—

BRICK: What, Big Daddy?

BIG DADDY: A whiskey highball would injure this spastic condition?

BRICK: No, sir, it might do it good.

BIG DADDY (*grins suddenly, wolfishly*): Jesus, I can't tell you! The sky is open! Christ, it's open again! It's open, boy, it's open!

(*Brick looks down at his drink.*)

BRICK: You feel better, Big Daddy?

BIG DADDY: Better? Hell! I can breathe!—All of my life I been like a doubled up fist. . . .

(*He pours a drink.*)

—Poundin', smashin', drivin'!—now I'm going to loosen these doubled-up hands and touch things *easy* with them. . . .

(*He spreads his hands as if caressing the air.*)

You know what I'm contemplating?

BRICK (*vaguely*): No, sir. What are you contemplating?

BIG DADDY: Ha ha!—*Pleasure!*—pleasure with *women!*

(*Brick's smile fades a little but lingers.*)

—Yes, boy. I'll tell you something that you might not guess. I still have desire for women and this is my sixty-fifth birthday.

BRICK: I think that's mighty remarkable, Big Daddy.

BIG DADDY: Remarkable?

BRICK: *Admirable*, Big Daddy.

BIG DADDY: You're damn right it is, remarkable and admirable both. I realize now that I never had me enough. I let many chances slip by because of scruples about it, scruples, convention—crap. . . . All that stuff is bull, bull, bull!—It took the shadow of death to make me see it. Now that shadow's lifted, I'm going to cut loose and have, what is it they call it, have me a—ball!

BRICK: A ball, huh?

BIG DADDY: That's right, a ball, a ball! Hell!—I slept with Big Mama till, let's see, five years ago, till I was sixty and she was fifty-eight, and never even liked her, never did!

(*The phone has been ringing down the hall. Big Mama enters, exclaiming:*)

BIG MAMA: Don't you men hear that phone ring? I heard it way out on the gall'ry.

BIG DADDY: There's five rooms off this front gall'ry that you could go through. Why do you go through this one?

(*Big Mama makes a playful face as she bustles out the hall door.*)

Hunh!—Why, when Big Mama goes out of a room, I can't remember what that woman looks like—

BIG MAMA: Hello.

BIG DADDY: —But when Big Mama comes back into the room, boy, then I see what she looks like, and I wish I didn't!

(*Bends over laughing at this joke till it hurts his guts and he straightens with a grimace. The laugh subsides to a chuckle as he puts the liquor glass a little distrustfully down on the table.*)

BIG MAMA: Hello, Miss Sally.

(*Brick has risen and hobbled to the gallery doors.*)

BIG DADDY: Hey! Where you goin'?

BRICK: Out for a breather.

BIG DADDY: Not yet you ain't. Stay here till this talk is finished, young fellow.

BRICK: I thought it was finished, Big Daddy.

BIG DADDY: It ain't even begun.

BRICK: My mistake. Excuse me. I just wanted to feel that river breeze.

BIG DADDY: Set back down in that chair.

(*Big Mama's voice rises, carrying down the hall.*)

BIG MAMA: Miss Sally, you're a case! You're a caution, Miss Sally.

BIG DADDY: Jesus, she's talking to my old maid sister again.

BIG MAMA: Why didn't you give me a chance to explain it to you?

BIG DADDY: Brick, this stuff burns me.

BIG MAMA: Well, good-bye, now, Miss Sally. You come down real soon. Big Daddy's dying to see you.

BIG DADDY: Crap!

BIG MAMA: Yaiss, good-bye, Miss Sally. . . .

(*She hangs up and bellows with mirth. Big Daddy groans and covers his ears as she approaches.*)

(*Bursting in:*)

Big Daddy, that was Miss Sally callin' from Memphis again! You know what she done, Big Daddy? She called her doctor in Memphis to git him to tell her what that spastic thing is! Ha-*HAAAA!*—And called back to tell me how relieved she was that—Hey! Let me in!

(*Big Daddy has been holding the door half closed against her.*)

BIG DADDY: Naw I ain't. I told you not to come and go through this room. You just back out and go through those five other rooms.

BIG MAMA: Big Daddy? Big Daddy? Oh, Big Daddy!—You didn't mean those things you said to me, did you?

(*He shuts door firmly against her but she still calls.*)

Sweetheart? Sweetheart? Big Daddy? You didn't mean those awful things you said to me?—I know you didn't. I know you didn't mean those things in your heart. . . .

(*The childlike voice fades with a sob and her heavy footsteps retreat down the hall. Brick has risen once more on his crutches and starts for the gallery again.*)

BIG DADDY: All I ask of that woman is that she leave me alone. But she can't admit to herself that she makes me sick. That comes of having slept with her too many years. Should of quit much sooner but that old woman she never got enough of it—and I was good in bed . . . I never should of wasted so much of it on her. . . . They say you got just so many and each one is numbered. Well, I got a few left in me, a few, and I'm going to pick me a good one to spend 'em on! I'm going to pick me a choice one, I don't care how much she costs, I'll smother her in—minks! Ha ha! I'll strip her naked and smother her in minks and choke her with diamonds! Ha ha! I'll strip her naked and choke her with diamonds and smother her with minks and hump her from hell to breakfast. *Ha aha ha ha ha!*

MAE: (*gaily at door*): Who's that laughin' in there?

GOOPER: Is Big Daddy laughin' in there?

BIG DADDY: Crap!—them two—*drips. . . .*

(*He goes over and touches Brick's shoulder.*)

Yes, son. Brick, boy.—I'm—*happy!* I'm happy, son, I'm happy!

(*He chokes a little and bites his under lip, pressing his head quickly, shyly against his son's head and then, coughing with embarrassment, goes uncertainly back to the table where he set down the glass. He drinks and makes a grimace as it burns his guts. Brick sighs and rises with effort.*)

What makes you so restless? Have you got ants in your britches?

BRICK: Yes, sir . . .

BIG DADDY: Why?

BRICK: —Something—hasn't happened. . . .

BIG DADDY: Yeah? What is that!

BRICK (*sadly*): —the click. . . .

BIG DADDY: Did you say click?

BRICK: Yes, click.

BIG DADDY: What click?

BRICK: A click that I get in my head that makes me peaceful.

BIG DADDY: I sure in hell don't know what you're talking about, but it disturbs me.

BRICK: It's just a mechanical thing.

BIG DADDY: What is a mechanical thing?

BRICK: This click that I get in my head that makes me peaceful. I got to drink till I get it. It's just a mechanical thing, something like a—like a—like a—

BIG DADDY: Like a—

BRICK: Switch clicking off in my head, turning the hot light off and the cool night on and—

(*He looks up, smiling sadly.*)

—all of a sudden there's—peace!

BIG DADDY (*whistles long and soft with astonishment; he goes back to Brick and clasps his son's two shoulders*): Jesus! I didn't know it had gotten that bad with you. Why, boy, you're—*alcoholic!*

BRICK: That's the truth, Big Daddy. I'm alcoholic.

BIG DADDY: This shows how I—let things go!

BRICK: I have to hear that little click in my head that makes me peaceful. Usually I hear it sooner than this, sometimes as early as—noon, but—

—Today it's—dilatory....

I just haven't got the right level of alcohol in my bloodstream yet!

(*This last statement is made with energy as he freshens his drink.*)

BIG DADDY: Uh—huh. Expecting death made me blind. I didn't have no idea that a son of mine was turning into a drunkard under my nose.

BRICK (*gently*): Well, now you do, Big Daddy, the news has penetrated.

BIG DADDY: UH-huh, yes, now I do, the news has—penetrated....

BRICK: And so if you'll excuse me—

BIG DADDY: No, I won't excuse you.

BRICK: —I'd better sit by myself till I hear that click in my head, it's just a mechanical thing but it don't happen except when I'm alone or talking to no one....

BIG DADDY: You got a long, long time to sit still, boy, and talk to no one, but now you're talkin' to me. At least I'm talking to you. And you set there and listen until I tell you the conversation is over!

BRICK: But this talk is like all the others we've ever had together in our lives! It's nowhere, nowhere!—it's—it's *painful*, Big Daddy....

BIG DADDY: All right, then let it be painful, but don't you move from that chair!—I'm going to remove that crutch....

(*He seizes the crutch and tosses it across room.*)

BRICK: I can hop on one foot, and if I fall, I can crawl!

BIG DADDY: If you ain't careful you're gonna crawl off this plantation and then, by Jesus, you'll have to hustle your drinks along Skid Row!

BRICK: That'll come, Big Daddy.

BIG DADDY: Naw, it won't. You're my son and I'm going to straighten you out; now that *I'm* straightened out, I'm going to straighten out you!

BRICK: Yeah?

BIG DADDY: Today the report come in from Ochsner Clinic. Y'know what they told me?

(*His face glows with triumph.*)

The only thing that they could detect with all the instruments of science in that great hospital is a little spastic condition of the colon! And nerves torn to pieces by all that worry about it.

(*A little girl bursts into room with a sparkler clutched in each fist, hops and shrieks like a monkey gone mad and rushes back out again as Big Daddy strikes at her.*)

(*Silence. The two men stare at each other. A woman laughs gaily outside.*)

I want you to know I breathed a sigh of relief almost as powerful as the Vicksburg tornado!

(*There is laughter outside, running footsteps, the soft, plushy sound and light of exploding rockets.*)

(*Brick stares at him soberly for a long moment; then makes a sort of startled sound in his nostrils and springs up on one foot and hops across the room to grab his crutch, swinging on the furniture for support. He gets the crutch and flees as if in horror for the gallery. His father seizes him by the sleeve of his white silk pajamas.*)

Stay here, you son of a bitch!—till I say go!

BRICK: I can't.

BIG DADDY: You sure in hell will, God damn it.

BRICK: No, I can't. We talk, you talk, in—circles! We get no where, no where! It's always the same, you say you want to talk to me and don't have a fuckin' thing to say to me!

BIG DADDY: Nothin' to say when I'm tellin' you I'm going to live when I thought I was dying?!

BRICK: Oh—*that!*—Is that what you have to say to me?

BIG DADDY: Why, you son of a bitch! Ain't that, ain't that—*important?!*

BRICK: Well, you said that, that's said, and now I—

BIG DADDY: Now you set back down.

BRICK: You're all balled up, you—

BIG DADDY: I ain't balled up!

BRICK: You are, you're all balled up!

BIG DADDY: Don't tell me what I am, you drunken whelp! I'm going to tear this coat sleeve off if you don't set down!

BRICK: Big Daddy—

BIG DADDY: Do what I tell you! I'm the boss here, now! I want you to know I'm back in the driver's seat now!

(*Big Mama rushes in, clutching her great heaving bosom.*)

BIG MAMA: Big Daddy!

BIG DADDY: What in hell do you want in here, Big Mama?

BIG MAMA: Oh, Big Daddy! Why are you shouting like that? I just cain't *stainnnnnnnd*—it....

BIG DADDY (*raising the back of his hand above his head*): GIT!—outa here.

(*She rushes back out, sobbing.*)

BRICK (*softly, sadly*): Christ....

BIG DADDY (*fiercely*): Yeah! Christ!—is right....

(*Brick breaks loose and hobbles toward the gallery.*)

(*Big Daddy jerks his crutch from under Brick so he steps with the injured ankle. He utters a hissing cry of anguish, clutches a chair and pulls it over on top of him on the floor.*)

Son of a—tub of—hog fat. . . .

BRICK: Big Daddy! Give me my crutch.

(*Big Daddy throws the crutch out of reach.*)

Give me that crutch, Big Daddy.

BIG DADDY: Why do you drink?

BRICK: Don't know, give me my crutch!

BIG DADDY: You better think why you drink or give up drinking!

BRICK: Will you please give me my crutch so I can get up off this floor?

BIG DADDY: First you answer my question. Why do you drink? Why are you throwing your life away, boy, like somethin' disgusting you picked up on the street?

BRICK (*getting onto his knees*): Big Daddy, I'm in pain, I stepped on that foot.

BIG DADDY: Good! I'm glad you're not too numb with the liquor in you to feel some pain!

BRICK: You—spilled my—drink . . .

BIG DADDY: I'll make a bargain with you. You tell me why you drink and I'll hand you one. I'll pour you the liquor myself and hand it to you.

BRICK: Why do I drink?

BIG DADDY: Yea! Why?

BRICK: Give me a drink and I'll tell you.

BIG DADDY: Tell me first!

BRICK: I'll tell you in one word.

BIG DADDY: What word?

BRICK: DISGUST!

(*The clock chimes softly, sweetly. Big Daddy gives it a short, outraged glance.*)

Now how about that drink?

BIG DADDY: What are you disgusted with? You got to tell me that, first. Otherwise being disgusted don't make no sense!

BRICK: Give me my crutch.

BIG DADDY: You heard me, you got to tell me what I asked you first.

BRICK: I told you, I said to kill my disgust!

BIG DADDY: DISGUST WITH WHAT!

BRICK: You strike a hard bargain.

BIG DADDY: What are you disgusted with?—an' I'll pass you the liquor.

BRICK: I can hop on one foot, and if I fall, I can crawl.

BIG DADDY: You want liquor that bad?

BRICK (*dragging himself up, clinging to bedstead*): Yeah, I want it that bad.

BIG DADDY: If I give you a drink, will you tell me what it is you're disgusted with, Brick?

BRICK: Yes, sir, I will try to.

(*The old man pours him a drink and solemnly passes it to him.*)

(*There is silence as Brick drinks.*)

Have you ever heard the word "mendacity"?

BIG DADDY: Sure. Mendacity is one of them five dollar words that cheap politicians throw back and forth at each other.

BRICK: You know what it means?

BIG DADDY: Don't it mean lying and liars?

BRICK: Yes, sir, lying and liars.

BIG DADDY: Has someone been lying to you?

CHILDREN (*chanting in chorus offstage*):
We want Big Dad-dee!
We want Big Dad-dee!

(*Gooper appears in the gallery door.*)

GOOPER: Big Daddy, the kiddies are shouting for you out there.

BIG DADDY (*fiercely*): Keep out, Gooper!

GOOPER: 'Scuse me!

(*Big Daddy slams the doors after Gooper.*)

BIG DADDY: Who's been lying to you, has Margaret been lying to you, has your wife been lying to you about something, Brick?

BRICK: Not her. That wouldn't matter.

BIG DADDY: Then who's been lying to you, and what about?

BRICK: No one single person and no one lie. . . .

BIG DADDY: Then what, what then, for Christ's sake?

BRICK: —The whole, the whole—thing. . . .

BIG DADDY: Why are you rubbing your head? You got a headache?

BRICK: No, I'm tryin' to—

BIG DADDY: —Concentrate, but you can't because your brain's all soaked with liquor, is that the trouble? Wet brain!

(*He snatches the glass from Brick's hand.*)

What do you know about this mendacity thing? Hell! I could write a book on it! Don't you know that? I could write a book on it and still not cover the subject? Well, I could, I could write a goddamn book on it and still not cover the subject anywhere near enough!!—Think of all the lies I got to put up with!—Pretenses! Ain't that mendacity? Having to pretend stuff you don't think or feel or have any idea of? Having for instance to act like I care for Big Mama!—I haven't been able to stand the sight, sound, or smell of that woman for forty years now!—even when I *laid* her!—regular as a piston. . . .

Pretend to love that son of a bitch of a Gooper and his wife Mae and those five same screechers out there like parrots in a jungle? Jesus! Can't stand to look at 'em!

Church!—it bores the bejesus out of me but I go!—I go an' sit there and listen to the fool preacher!

Clubs!—Elks! Masons! Rotary!—*crap!*

(*A spasm of pain makes him clutch his belly. He sinks into a chair and his voice is softer and hoarser.*)

You I *do* like for some reason, did always have some kind of real feeling for—affection—respect—yes, always. . . .

You and being a success as a planter is all I ever had any devotion to in my whole life!—and that's the truth. . . .

I don't know why, but it is!

I've lived with mendacity!—Why can't *you* live with it? Hell, you *got* to live with it, there's nothing *else* to *live* with except mendacity, is there?

BRICK: Yes, sir. Yes, sir there is something else that you can live with!

BIG DADDY: What?

BRICK (*lifting his glass*): This!—Liquor. . . .

BIG DADDY: That's not living, that's dodging away from life.

BRICK: I want to dodge away from it.

BIG DADDY: Then why don't you kill yourself, man?

BRICK: I like to drink. . . .

BIG DADDY: Oh, God, I can't talk to you. . . .

BRICK: I'm sorry, Big Daddy.

BIG DADDY: Not as sorry as I am. I'll tell you something. A little while back when I thought my number was up—

(*This speech should have torrential pace and fury.*)

—before I found out it was just this—spastic—colon. I thought about you. Should I or should I not, if the jig was up, give you this place when I go—since I hate Gooper an' Mae an' know that they hate me, and since all five same monkeys are little Maes an' Goopers.—And I thought, No!—Then I thought, Yes!—I couldn't make up my mind. I hate Gooper and his five same monkeys and that bitch Mae! Why should I turn over twenty-eight thousand acres of the richest land this side of the valley Nile to not my kind?—But why in hell, on the other hand, Brick—should I subsidize a goddamn fool on the bottle?—Liked or not liked, well, maybe even—*loved!*—Why should I do that?—Subsidize worthless behavior? Rot? Corruption?

BRICK (*smiling*): I understand.

BIG DADDY: Well, if you do, you're smarter than I am, God damn it, because I don't understand. And this I will tell you frankly. I didn't make up my mind at all on that question and still to this day I ain't made out no will!—Well, now I don't *have* to. The pressure is gone. I can just wait and see if you pull yourself together or if you don't.

BRICK: That's right, Big Daddy.

BIG DADDY: You sound like you thought I was kidding.

BRICK (*rising*): No, sir, I know you're not kidding.

BIG DADDY: But you don't care—?

BRICK (*hobbling toward the gallery door*): No, sir, I don't care. . . .

(*He stands in the gallery doorway as the night sky turns pink and green and gold with successive flashes of light.*)

BIG DADDY: *WAIT!*—Brick. . . .

(*His voice drops. Suddenly there is something shy, almost tender, in his restraining gesture.*)

Don't let's—leave it like this, like them other talks we've had, we've always—talked around things, we've—just talked around things for some fuckin' reason, I don't know what, it's always like something was left not spoken, something avoided because neither of us was honest enough with the—other. . . .

BRICK: I never lied to you, Big Daddy.

BIG DADDY: Did I ever to *you?*

BRICK: No, sir. . . .

BIG DADDY: Then there is at least two people that never lied to each other.

BRICK: But we've never *talked* to each other.

BIG DADDY: We can *now.*

BRICK: Big Daddy, there don't seem to be anything much to say.

BIG DADDY: You say that you drink to kill your disgust with lying.

BRICK: You said to give you a reason.

BIG DADDY: Is liquor the only thing that'll kill this disgust?

BRICK: Now. Yes.

BIG DADDY: But not once, huh?

BRICK: Not when I was still young an' believing. A drinking man's someone who wants to forget he isn't still young an' believing.

BIG DADDY: Believing what?

BRICK: Believing. . . .

BIG DADDY: Believing *what?*

BRICK (*stubbornly evasive*): Believing. . . .

BIG DADDY: I don't know what the hell you mean by believing and I don't think you know what you mean by believing, but if you still got sports in your blood, go back to sports announcing and—

BRICK: Sit in a glass box watching games I can't play? Describing what I can't do while players do it? Sweating out their disgust and confusion in contests I'm not fit for? Drinkin' a coke, half bourbon, so I can stand it? That's no goddamn good any more, no help—time just outran me, Big Daddy—got there first . . .

BIG DADDY: I think you're passing the buck.

BRICK: You know many drinkin' men?

BIG DADDY (*with a slight, charming smile*): I have known a fair number of that species.

BRICK: Could any of them tell you why he drank?

BIG DADDY: Yep, you're passin' the buck to things like time and disgust with "mendacity" and—crap!—if you got to use that kind of language about a thing, it's ninety-proof bull, and I'm not buying any.

BRICK: I had to give you a reason to get a drink!

BIG DADDY: You started drinkin' when your friend Skipper died.

(*Silence for five beats. Then Brick makes a startled movement, reaching for his crutch.*)

BRICK: What are you suggesting?
BIG DADDY: I'm suggesting nothing.

(*The shuffle and clop of Brick's rapid hobble away from his father's steady, grave attention.*)

　　—But Gooper an' Mae suggested that there was something not right exactly in your—
BRICK (*stopping short downstage as if backed to a wall*): "Not right"?
BIG DADDY: Not, well, exactly *normal* in your friendship with—
BRICK: They suggested that, too? I thought that was Maggie's suggestion.

(*Brick's detachment is at last broken through. His heart is accelerated; his forehead sweat-beaded; his breath becomes more rapid and his voice hoarse. The thing they're discussing, timidly and painfully on the side of Big Daddy, fiercely, violently on Brick's side, is the inadmissible thing that Skipper died to disavow between them. The fact that if it existed it had to be disavowed to "keep face" in the world they lived in, may be at the heart of the "mendacity" that Brick drinks to kill his disgust with. It may be the root of his collapse. Or maybe it is only a single manifestation of it, not even the most important. The bird that I hope to catch in the net of this play is not the solution of one man's psychological problem. I'm trying to catch the true quality of experience in a group of people, that cloudy, flickering, evanescent—fiercely charged!—interplay of live human beings in the thundercloud of a common crisis. Some mystery should be left in the revelation of character in a play, just as a great deal of mystery is always left in the revelation of character in life, even in one's own character to himself. This does not absolve the playwright of his duty to observe and probe as clearly and deeply as he legitimately can: But it should steer him away from "pat" conclusions, facile definitions which make a play just a play, not a snare for the truth of human experience.*)
　　(*The following scene should be played with great concentration, with most of the power leashed but palpable in what is left unspoken.*)

　　Who else's suggestion is it, is it *yours*? How many others thought that Skipper and I were—
BIG DADDY (*gently*): Now, hold on, hold on a minute, son.—I knocked around in my time.
BRICK: What's that got to do with—
BIG DADDY: I said "Hold on!"—I bummed, I bummed this country till I was—
BRICK: Whose suggestion, who else's suggestion is it?
BIG DADDY: Slept in hobo jungles and railroad Y's and flophouses in all cities before I—
BRICK: Oh, *you* think so, too, you call me your son and a queer. Oh! Maybe that's why you put Maggie and me in this room that was Jack Straw's and Peter

Ochello's, in which that pair of old sisters slept in a double bed where both of 'em died!
BIG DADDY: *Now just don't go throwing rocks at*—

(*Suddenly Reverend Tooker appears in the gallery doors, his head slightly, playfully, fatuously cocked, with a practiced clergyman's smile, sincere as a birdcall blown on a hunter's whistle, the living embodiment of the pious, conventional lie.*)
　　(*Big Daddy gasps a little at this perfectly timed, but incongruous, apparition.*)

　　—What're you lookin' for, preacher?
REVEREND TOOKER: The gentleman's lavatory, ha ha!—heh, heh . . .
BIG DADDY (*with strained courtesy*):—Go back out and walk down to the other end of the gallery, Reverend Tooker, and use the bathroom connected with my bedroom, and if you can't find it, ask them where it is!
REVEREND TOOKER: Ah, thanks.

(*He goes out with a deprecatory chuckle.*)

BIG DADDY: It's hard to talk in this place . . .
BRICK: Son of a—!
BIG DADDY (*leaving a lot unspoken*):—I seen all things and understood a lot of them, till 1910. Christ, the year that—I had worn my shoes through, hocked my—I hopped off a yellow dog freight car half a mile down the road, slept in a wagon of cotton outside the gin—Jack Straw an' Peter Ochello took me in. Hired me to manage this place which grew into this one.—When Jack Straw died—why, old Peter Ochello quit eatin' like a dog does when its master's dead, and died, too!
BRICK: Christ!
BIG DADDY: I'm just saying I understand such—
BRICK (*violently*): Skipper is dead. I have not quit eating!
BIG DADDY: No, but you started drinking.

(*Brick wheels on his crutch and hurls his glass across the room shouting.*)

BRICK: YOU THINK SO, TOO?

(*Footsteps run on the gallery. There are women's calls.*)
　　(*Big Daddy goes toward the door.*)
　　(*Brick is transformed, as if a quiet mountain blew suddenly up in volcanic flame.*)

BRICK: You think so, too? You think so, too? You think me an' Skipper did, did, did!—*sodomy!*—together?
BIG DADDY: Hold —!
BRICK: That what you—
BIG DADDY:—*ON*—a minute!
BRICK: You think we did dirty things between us, Skipper an'—
BIG DADDY: Why are you shouting like that? Why are you—

BRICK:—Me, is that what you think of Skipper, is that—

BIG DADDY:—so excited? I don't think nothing. I don't know nothing. I'm simply telling you what—

BRICK: You think that Skipper and me were a pair of dirty old men?

BIG DADDY: Now that's—

BRICK: Straw? Ochello? A couple of—

BIG DADDY: Now just—

BRICK:—fucking sissies? Queers? Is that what you—

BIG DADDY: Shhh.

BRICK:—think?

(He loses his balance and pitches to his knees without noticing the pain. He grabs the bed and drags himself up.)

BIG DADDY: Jesus!—Whew. . . .Grab my hand!

BRICK: Naw, I don't want your hand. . . .

BIG DADDY: Well, I want yours. Git up!

(He draws him up, keeps an arm about him with concern and affection.)

You broken out in a sweat! You're panting like you'd run a race with—

BRICK *(freeing himself from his father's hold)*: Big Daddy, you shock me, Big Daddy, you, you—*shock* me! Talkin' so—

(He turns away from his father.)

—casually!—about a—thing like that . . .

—Don't you know how people *feel* about things like that? How, how *disgusted* they are by things like that? Why, at Ole Miss when it was discovered a pledge to our fraternity, Skipper's and mine, did a, *attempted* to do a, unnatural thing with—

We not only dropped him like a hot rock!—We told him to git off the campus, and he did, he got!—All the way to—

(He halts, breathless.)

BIG DADDY:—Where?

BRICK:—North Africa, last I heard!

BIG DADDY: Well, I have come back from further away than that, I have just now returned from the other side of the moon, death's country, son, and I'm not easy to shock by anything here.

(He comes downstage and faces out.)

Always, anyhow, lived with too much space around me to be infected by ideas of other people. One thing you can grow on a big place more important than cotton!—is *tolerance!*—I grown it.

(He returns toward Brick.)

BRICK: Why can't exceptional friendship, *real, real, deep, deep friendship!* between two men be respected as something clean and decent without being thought of as—

BIG DADDY: It can, it is, for God's sake.

BRICK:—*Fairies.* . . .

(In his utterance of this word, we gauge the wide and profound reach of the conventional mores he got from the world that crowned him with early laurel.)

BIG DADDY: I told Mae an' Gooper—

BRICK: Frig Mae and Gooper, frig all dirty lies and liars!—Skipper and me had a clean, true thing between us!—had a clean friendship, practically all our lives, till Maggie got the idea you're talking about. Normal? No!—It was too rare to be normal, any true thing between two people is too rare to be normal. Oh, once in a while he put his hand on my shoulder or I'd put mine on his, oh, maybe even, when we were touring the country in pro-football an' shared hotel rooms we'd reach across the space between the two beds and shake hands to say goodnight, yeah, one or two times we—

BIG DADDY: Brick, nobody thinks that that's not normal!

BRICK: Well, they're mistaken, it was! It was a pure an' true thing an' that's not normal.

MAE *(offstage)*: Big Daddy, they're startin' the fireworks.

(They both stare straight at each other for a long moment. The tension breaks and both turn away as if tired.)

BIG DADDY: Yeah, it's—hard t'—talk. . . .

BRICK: All right, then, let's—let it go. . . .

BIG DADDY: Why did Skipper crack up? Why have you?

(Brick looks back at his father again. He has already decided, without knowing that he has made this decision, that he is going to tell his father that he is dying of cancer. Only this could even the score between them: one inadmissible thing in return for another.)

BRICK *(ominously)*: All right. You're asking for it, Big Daddy. We're finally going to have that real true talk you wanted. It's too late to stop it, now, we got to carry it through and cover every subject.

(He hobbles back to the liquor cabinet.)

Uh-huh.

(He opens the ice bucket and picks up the silver tongs with slow admiration of their frosty brightness.)

Maggie declares that Skipper and I went into pro-football after we left Ole Miss because we were scared to grow up . . .

(He moves downstage with the shuffle and clop of a cripple on a crutch. As Margaret did when her speech became "recitative," he looks out into the house, commanding its attention by his direct, concentrated gaze—a broken, "tragically elegant" figure telling simply as much as he knows of "the Truth":)

—Wanted to—keep on tossing—those long, long!—high, high!—passes that—couldn't be intercepted except by time, the aerial attack that made us famous! And so we did, we did, we kept it up for one season, that aerial attack, we held it high!—Yeah, but—

    —that summer, Maggie, she laid the law down to me, said, Now or never, and so I married Maggie....

BIG DADDY: How was Maggie in bed?

BRICK (*wryly*): Great! the greatest!

(*Big Daddy nods as if he thought so.*)

She went on the road that fall with the Dixie Stars. Oh, she made a great show of being the world's best sport. She wore a—wore a—tall bearskin cap! A shako, they call it, a dyed moleskin coat, a moleskin coat dyed red!—Cut up crazy! Rented hotel ballrooms for victory celebrations, wouldn't cancel them when it—turned out—defeat....

    MAGGIE THE CAT! Ha ha!

(*Big Daddy nods.*)

—But Skipper, he had some fever which came back on him which doctors couldn't explain and I got that injury— turned out to be just a shadow on the X-ray plate—and a touch of bursitis....

    I lay in a hospital bed, watched our games on TV, saw Maggie on the bench next to Skipper when he was hauled out of a game for stumbles, fumbles!—Burned me up the way she hung on his arm!—Y'know, I think that Maggie had always felt sort of left out because she and me never got any closer together than two people just get in bed, which is not much closer than two cats on a—fence humping....

    So! She took this time to work on poor dumb Skipper. He was a less than average student at Ole Miss, you know that, don't you?!—Poured in his mind the dirty, false idea that what we were, him and me, was a frustrated case of that ole pair of sisters that lived in this room, Jack Straw and Peter Ochello!—He, poor Skipper, went to bed with Maggie to prove it wasn't true, and when it didn't work out, he thought it *was* true!—Skipper broke in two like a rotten stick—nobody ever turned so fast to a lush—or died of it so quick....

    —Now are you satisfied?

(*Big Daddy has listened to this story, dividing the grain from the chaff. Now he looks at his son.*)

BIG DADDY: Are *you* satisfied?

BRICK: With what?

BIG DADDY: That half-ass story!

BRICK: What's half-ass about it?

BIG DADDY: Something's left out of that story. What did you leave out?

(*The phone has started ringing in the hall.*)

GOOPER (*offstage*): Hello.

(*As if it reminded him of something, Brick glances suddenly toward the sound and says:*)

BRICK: Yes!—I left out a long-distance call which I had from Skipper—

GOOPER: Speaking, go ahead.

BRICK: —In which he made a drunken confession to me and on which I hung up!

GOOPER: No.

BRICK: —Last time we spoke to each other in our lives ...

GOOPER: No, sir.

BIG DADDY: You musta said something to him before you hung up.

BRICK: What could I say to him?

BIG DADDY: Anything. Something.

BRICK: Nothing.

BIG DADDY: Just hung up?

BRICK: Just hung up.

BIG DADDY: Uh-huh. Anyhow now!—we have tracked down the lie with which you're disgusted and which you are drinking to kill your disgust with, Brick. You been passing the buck. This disgust with mendacity is disgust with yourself.

    You!—dug the grave of your friend and kicked him in it!—before you'd face truth with him!

BRICK: *His* truth, not *mine!*

BIG DADDY: His truth, okay! But you wouldn't face it with him!

BRICK: Who *can* face truth? Can *you?*

BIG DADDY: Now don't start passin' the rotten buck again, boy!

BRICK: How about these birthday congratulations, these many, many happy returns of the day, when ev'rybody knows there won't be any except you!

(*Gooper, who has answered the hall phone, lets out a high, shrill laugh; the voice becomes audible saying: "No, no, you got it all wrong! Upside down! Are you crazy?"*)

(*Brick suddenly catches his breath as he realizes that he has made a shocking disclosure. He hobbles a few paces, then freezes, and without looking at his father's shocked face says:*)

Let's, let's—go out, now, and—watch the fireworks. Come on, Big Daddy.

(*Big Daddy moves suddenly forward and grabs hold of the boy's crutch like it was a weapon for which they were fighting for possession.*)

BIG DADDY: Oh, no, no! No one's going out! What did you start to say?

BRICK: I don't remember.

BIG DADDY: "Many happy returns when they know there won't be any"?

BRICK: Aw, hell, Big Daddy, forget it. Come on out on the gallery and look at the fireworks they're shooting off for your birthday....

BIG DADDY: First you finish that remark you were makin' before you cut off. "Many happy returns when they know there won't be any"?—Ain't that what you just said?

BRICK: Look, now. I can get around without that crutch if I have to but it would be a lot easier on the furniture an' glassware if I didn't have to go swinging along like Tarzan of th'—

BIG DADDY: FINISH! WHAT YOU WAS SAYIN'!

(*An eerie green glow shows in sky behind him.*)

BRICK (*sucking the ice in his glass, speech becoming thick*): Leave th' place to Gooper and Mae an' their five little same little monkeys. All I want is—

BIG DADDY: "LEAVE TH' PLACE," did you say?

BRICK (*vaguely*): All twenty-eight thousand acres of the richest land this side of the valley Nile.

BIG DADDY: Who said I was "leaving the place" to Gooper or anybody? This is my sixty-fifth birthday! I got fifteen years or twenty years left in me! I'll outlive *you!* I'll bury you an' have to pay for your coffin!

BRICK: Sure. Many happy returns. Now let's go watch the fireworks, come on, let's—

BIG DADDY: Lying, have they been lying? About the report from th'—clinic? Did they, did they—find something?—*Cancer.* Maybe?

BRICK: Mendacity is a system that we live in. Liquor is one way out an' death's the other. . . .

(*He takes the crutch from Big Daddy's loose grip and swings out on the gallery leaving the doors open.*)
(*A song, "Pick a Bale of Cotton," is heard.*)

MAE (*appearing in door*): Oh, Big Daddy, the field hands are singin' fo' you!

BRICK: I'm sorry, Big Daddy. My head don't work any more and it's hard for me to understand how anybody could care if he lived or died or was dying or cared about anything but whether or not there was liquor left in the bottle and so I said what I said without thinking. In some ways I'm no better than the others, in some ways worse because I'm less alive. Maybe it's being alive that makes them lie, and being almost *not* alive makes me sort of accidentally truthful—I don't know but—anyway—we've been friends . . .
—And being friends is telling each other the truth. . . .

(*There is a pause.*)

You told *me!* I told *you!*

BIG DADDY (*slowly and passionately*): CHRIST—DAMN—

GOOPER (*offstage*): Let her go!

(*Fireworks offstage right.*)

BIG DADDY:—ALL—LYING SONS OF—LYING BITCHES!

(*He straightens at last and crosses to the inside door. At the door he turns and looks back as if he had some*

desperate question he couldn't put into words. Then he nods reflectively and says in a hoarse voice:*)

Yes, all liars, all liars, all lying dying liars!

(*This is said slowly, slowly, with a fierce revulsion. He goes on out.*)

—Lying! Dying! Liars!

(*Brick remains motionless as the lights dim out and the curtain falls.*)

ACT 3

(*There is no lapse of time. Big Daddy is seen leaving as at the end of act 2.*)

BIG DADDY: ALL LYIN'—DYIN'!—LIARS! LIARS!—LIARS!

(*Margaret enters.*)

MARGARET: Brick, what in the name of God was goin' on in this room?

(*Dixie and Trixie enter through the doors and circle around Margaret shouting. Mae enters from the lower gallery window.*)

MAE: Dixie, Trixie, you quit that!

(*Gooper enters through the doors.*)

Gooper, will y' please get these kiddies to bed right now!

GOOPER: Mae, you seen Big Mama?

MAE: Not yet.

(*Gooper and kids exit through the doors. Reverend Tooker enters through the windows.*)

REVEREND TOOKER: Those kiddies are so full of vitality. I think I'll have to be starting back to town.

MAE: Not yet, Preacher. You know we regard you as a member of this family, one of our closest an' dearest, so you just got t' be with us when Doc Baugh gives Big Mama th' actual truth about th' report from the clinic.

MARGARET: Where do you think you're going?

BRICK: Out for some air.

MARGARET: Why'd Big Daddy shout "Liars"?

MAE: Has Big Daddy gone to bed, Brick?

GOOPER (*entering*): Now where is that old lady?

REVEREND TOOKER: I'll look for her.

(*He exits to the gallery.*)

MAE: Cain'tcha find her, Gooper?

GOOPER: She's avoidin' this talk.

MAE: I think she senses somethin'.

MARGARET (*going out on the gallery to Brick*): Brick, they're goin' to tell Big Mama the truth about Big Daddy and she's goin' to need you.

DOCTOR BAUGH: This is going to be painful.

MAE: Painful things caint always be avoided.

REVEREND TOOKER: I see Big Mama.

GOOPER: Hey, Big Mama, come here.

MAE: Hush, Gooper, don't holler.

BIG MAMA (*entering*): Too much smell of burnt fireworks makes me feel a little bit sick at my stomach.—Where is Big Daddy?

MAE: That's what I want to know, where has Big Daddy gone?

BIG MAMA: He must have turned in, I reckon he went to baid . . .

GOOPER: Well, then, now we can talk.

BIG MAMA: What *is* this talk, *what* talk?

(*Margaret appears on the gallery, talking to Doctor Baugh.*)

MARGARET (*musically*): My family freed their slaves ten years before abolition. My great-great-grandfather gave his slaves their freedom five years before the War between the States started!

MAE: Oh, for God's sake! Maggie's climbed back up in her family tree!

MARGARET (*sweetly*): What, Mae?

(*The pace must be very quick: great Southern animation.*)

BIG MAMA (*addressing them all*): I think Big Daddy was just worn out. He loves his family, he loves to have them around him, but it's a strain on his nerves. He wasn't himself tonight, Big Daddy wasn't himself, I could tell he was all worked up.

REVEREND TOOKER: I think he's remarkable.

BIG MAMA: Yaisss! Just remarkable. Did you all notice the food he ate at that table? Did you all notice the supper he put away? Why he ate like a hawss!

GOOPER: I hope he doesn't regret it.

BIG MAMA: What? Why that man—ate a huge piece of cawn bread with molasses on it! Helped himself twice to hoppin' John.

MARGARET: Big Daddy loves hoppin' John.—We had a real country dinner.

BIG MAMA (*overlapping Margaret*): Yaiss, he simply adores it! an' candied yams? Son? That man put away enough food at that table to stuff a *field* hand!

GOOPER (*with grim relish*): I hope he don't have to pay for it later on . . .

BIG MAMA (*fiercely*): What's *that*, Gooper?

MAE: Gooper says he hopes Big Daddy doesn't suffer tonight.

BIG MAMA: Oh, shoot, Gooper says, Gooper says! Why should Big Daddy suffer for satisfying a normal appetite? There's nothin' wrong with that man but nerves, he's sound as a dollar! And now he knows he is an' that's why he ate such a supper. He had a big load off his mind, knowin' he wasn't doomed t'—what he thought he was doomed to . . .

MARGARET (*sadly and sweetly*): Bless his old sweet soul . . .

BIG MAMA (*vaguely*): Yais, bless his heart, where's Brick?

MAE: Outside.

GOOPER:—Drinkin' . . .

BIG MAMA: I know he's drinkin'. Caint I see he's drinkin' without you continually tellin' me that boy's drinkin'?

MARGARET: Good for you, Big Mama!

(*She applauds.*)

BIG MAMA: Other people *drink* and *have* drunk an' will *drink,* as long as they make that stuff an' put it in bottles.

MARGARET: That's the truth. I never trusted a man that didn't drink.

BIG MAMA: *Brick? Brick!*

MARGARET: He's still on the gall'ry. I'll go bring him in so we can talk.

BIG MAMA (*worriedly*): I don't know what this mysterious family conference is about.

(*Awkward silence. Big Mama looks from face to face, then belches slightly and mutters, "Excuse me . . ." She opens an ornamental fan suspended about her throat. A black lace fan to go with her black lace gown, and fans her wilting corsage, sniffing nervously and looking from face to face in the uncomfortable silence as Margaret calls "Brick?" and Brick sings to the moon on the gallery.*)

MARGARET: Brick, they're gonna tell Big Mama the truth an' she's gonna need you.

BIG MAMA: I don't know what's wrong here, you all have such long faces! Open that door on the hall and let some air circulate through here, will you please, Gooper?

MAE: I think we'd better leave that door closed, Big Mama, till after the talk.

MARGARET: Brick!

BIG MAMA: Reveren' Tooker, will you please open that door?

REVEREND TOOKER: I sure will, Big Mama.

MAE: I just didn't think we ought t' take any chance of Big Daddy hearin' a word of this discussion.

BIG MAMA: *I swan!* Nothing's going to be said in Big Daddy's house that he caint hear if he want to!

GOOPER: Well, Big Mama, it's—

(*Mae gives him a quick, hard poke to shut him up. He glares at her fiercely as she circles before him like a burlesque ballerina, raising her skinny bare arms over her head, jangling her bracelets, exclaiming:*)

MAE: *A breeze! A breeze!*

REVEREND TOOKER: I think this house is the coolest house in the Delta.—Did you all know that Halsey Banks's widow put air-conditioning units in the church and rectory at Friar's Point in memory of Halsey?

(*General conversation has resumed; everybody is chatting so that the stage sounds like a bird cage.*)

GOOPER: Too bad nobody cools your church off for you. I bet you sweat in that pulpit these hot Sundays, Reverend Tooker.

REVEREND TOOKER: Yes, my vestments are drenched. Last Sunday the gold in my chasuble faded into the purple.

GOOPER: Reveren', you musta been preachin' hell's fire last Sunday.

MAE (*at the same time to Doctor Baugh*): You reckon those vitamin B12 injections are what they're cracked up t' be, Doc Baugh?

DOCTOR BAUGH: Well, if you want to be stuck with something I guess they're as good to be stuck with as anything else.

BIG MAMA (*at the gallery door*): Maggie, Maggie, aren't you comin' with Brick?

MAE (*suddenly and loudly, creating a silence*): I have a strange feeling, I have a peculiar feeling!

BIG MAMA (*turning from the gallery*): What feeling?

MAE: That Brick said somethin' he shouldn't of said t' Big Daddy.

BIG MAMA: Now what on earth could Brick of said t' Big Daddy that he shouldn't say?

GOOPER: Big Mama, there's somethin'—

MAE: NOW, WAIT!

(*She rushes up to Big Mama and gives her a quick hug and kiss. Big Mama pushes her impatiently off.*)

DOCTOR BAUGH: In my day they had what they call the Keeley cure for heavy drinkers.

BIG MAMA: Shoot!

DOCTOR BAUGH: But now I understand they just take some kind of tablets.

GOOPER: They call them "Annie Bust" tablets.

BIG MAMA: Brick don't need to take *nothin'*.

(*Brick and Margaret appear in gallery doors, Big Mama unaware of his presence behind her.*)

That boy is just broken up over Skipper's death. You know how poor Skipper died. They gave him a big, big dose of that sodium amytal stuff at his home and then they called the ambulance and give him another big, big dose of it at the hospital and that and all of the alcohol in his system fo' months an' months just proved too much for his heart . . . I'm scared of needles! I'm more scared of a needle than the knife . . . I think more people have been needled out of this world than—

(*She stops short and wheels about.*)

Oh—here's Brick! My precious baby—

(*She turns upon Brick with short, fat arms extended, at the same time uttering a loud, short sob, which is both comic and touching. Brick smiles and bows slightly, making a burlesque gesture of gallantry for Margaret to pass before him into the room. Then he hobbles on his crutch directly to the liquor cabinet and there is absolute silence, with everybody looking at Brick as everybody has always looked at Brick when he spoke or moved or appeared. One by one he drops ice cubes in his glass, then suddenly, but not quickly, looks back over his shoulder with a wry, charming smile, and says:*)

BRICK: I'm sorry! Anyone else?

BIG MAMA (*sadly*): No, son. I *wish* you wouldn't!

BRICK: I wish I didn't have to, Big Mama, but I'm still waiting for that click in my head which makes it all smooth out!

BIG MAMA: Ow, Brick, you—BREAK MY HEART!

MARGARET (*at same time*): Brick, go sit with Big Mama!

BIG MAMA: I just cain't staiiiiii-nnnnnnnd-it . . .

(*She sobs.*)

MAE: Now that we're all assembled—

GOOPER: We kin talk . . .

BIG MAMA: Breaks my heart . . .

MARGARET: Sit with Big Mama, Brick, and hold her hand.

(*Big Mama sniffs very loudly three times, almost like three drumbeats in the pocket of silence.*)

BRICK: You do that, Maggie. I'm a restless cripple. I got to stay on my crutch.

(*Brick hobbles to the gallery door; leans there as if waiting.*)

(*Mae sits beside Big Mama, while Gooper moves in front and sits on the end of the couch, facing her. Reverend Tooker moves nervously into the space between them; on the other side, Doctor Baugh stands looking at nothing in particular and lights a cigar. Margaret turns away.*)

BIG MAMA: Why're you all *surroundin'* me—like this? Why're you all starin' at me like this an' makin' signs at each other?

(*Reverend Tooker steps back startled.*)

MAE: Calm yourself, Big Mama.

BIG MAMA: Calm you'self, *you'self*, Sister Woman. How could I calm myself with everyone starin' at me as if big drops of blood had broken out on m'face? What's this all about, annh! What?

(*Gooper coughs and takes a center position.*)

GOOPER: Now, Doc Baugh.

MAE: Doc Baugh?

GOOPER: Big Mama wants to know the complete truth about the report we got from the Ochsner Clinic.

MAE (*eagerly*): —on Big Daddy's condition!

GOOPER: Yais, on Big Daddy's condition, we got to face it.

DOCTOR BAUGH: Well . . .

BIG MAMA (*terrified, rising*): Is there? Something? Something that I? Don't—know?

(*In these few words, this startled, very soft, question, Big Mama reviews the history of her forty-five years with Big Daddy, her great, almost embarrassingly true-hearted and simple-minded devotion to Big Daddy, who must have had something Brick has, who made himself loved so much by the "simple expedient" of not loving enough to disturb his charming detachment, also once coupled, like Brick, with virile beauty.)*

(Big Mama has a dignity at this moment; she almost stops being fat.)

DOCTOR BAUGH *(after a pause, uncomfortably)*: Yes?—Well—

BIG MAMA: I!!!—want to—*knowwwwww* . . .

(Immediately she thrusts her fist to her mouth as if to deny that statement. Then for some curious reason, she snatches the withered corsage from her breast and hurls it on the floor and steps on it with her short, fat feet.)

Somebody must be lyin'!—I want to know!

MAE: Sit down, Big Mama, sit down on this sofa.

MARGARET: Brick, go sit with Big Mama.

BIG MAMA: *What is it, what is it?*

DOCTOR BAUGH: I never have seen a more thorough examination than Big Daddy Pollitt was given in all my experience with the Ochsner Clinic.

GOOPER: It's one of the best in the country.

MAE: It's THE best in the country—bar *none!*

(For some reason she gives Gooper a violent poke as she goes past him. He slaps at her hand without removing his eyes from his mother's face.)

DOCTOR BAUGH: Of course they were ninety-nine and nine-tenths percent sure before they even started.

BIG MAMA: Sure of what, sure of what, sure of—*what?—what?*

(She catches her breath in a startled sob. Mae kisses her quickly. She thrusts Mae fiercely away from her, staring at the Doctor.)

MAE: Mommy, be a brave girl!

BRICK *(in the doorway, softly)*: "By the light, by the light, Of the sil-ve-ry mo-oo-n . . ."

GOOPER: Shut up!—Brick

BRICK: Sorry . . .

(He wanders out on the gallery.)

DOCTOR BAUGH: But now, you see, Big Mama, they cut a piece of this growth, a specimen of the tissue and—

BIG MAMA: Growth? You told Big Daddy—

DOCTOR BAUGH: Now wait.

BIG MAMA *(fiercely)*: You told me and Big Daddy there wasn't a thing wrong with him but—

MAE: Big Mama, they always—

GOOPER: Let Doc Baugh talk, will yuh?

BIG MAMA: —little spastic condition of—

(Her breath gives out in a sob.)

DOCTOR BAUGH: Yes, that's what we told Big Daddy. But we had this bit of tissue run through the laboratory and I'm sorry to say the test was positive on it. It's—well—malignant . . .

(Pause.)

BIG MAMA: —Cancer?! Cancer?!

(Doctor Baugh nods gravely. Big Mama gives a long gasping cry.)

MAE AND GOOPER: Now, now, now, Big Mama, you had to know . . .

BIG MAMA: WHY DIDN'T THEY CUT IT OUT OF HIM? HANH? HANH?

DOCTOR BAUGH: Involved too much, Big Mama, too many organs affected.

MAE: Big Mama, the liver's affected and so's the kidneys, both! It's gone way past what they call a—

GOOPER: A surgical risk.

MAE: —Uh-huh . . .

(Big Mama draws a breath like a dying gasp.)

REVEREND TOOKER: Tch, tch, tch, tch, tch!

DOCTOR BAUGH: Yes it's gone past the knife.

MAE: *That's why he's turned yellow, Mommy!*

BIG MAMA: *Git away from me, git away from me, Mae!*

(She rises abruptly.)

I want Brick! Where's Brick? Where is my only son?

MAE: Mama! Did she say *"only son"?*

GOOPER: What does that make *me?*

MAE: A sober responsible man with five precious children!—*Six!*

BIG MAMA: I want Brick to tell me! Brick! Brick!

MARGARET *(rising from her reflections in a corner)*: Brick was so upset he went back out.

BIG MAMA: *Brick!*

MARGARET: Mama, let *me* tell you!

BIG MAMA: No, no, leave me alone, you're not my blood!

GOOPER: *Mama, I'm your son!* Listen to *me!*

MAE: Gooper's your son, he's your first-born!

BIG MAMA: Gooper never liked Daddy.

MAE *(as if terribly shocked)*: *That's not TRUE!*

(There is a pause. The minister coughs and rises.)

REVEREND TOOKER *(to Mae)*: I think I'd better slip away at this point.

(Discreetly.)

Good night, good night, everybody, and God bless you all . . . on this place . . .

(He slips out.)

(Mae coughs and points at Big Mama.)

GOOPER: Well, Big Mama . . .

(He sighs.)

BIG MAMA: It's all a mistake, I know it's just a bad dream.

DOCTOR BAUGH: We're gonna keep Big Daddy as comfortable as we can.

BIG MAMA: Yes, it's just a bad dream, that's all it is, it's just an awful dream.

GOOPER: In my opinion Big Daddy is having some pain but won't admit that he has it.

BIG MAMA: Just a dream, a bad dream.

DOCTOR BAUGH: That's what lots of them do, they think if they don't admit they're having the pain they can sort of escape the fact of it.

GOOPER (*with relish*): Yes, they get sly about it, they get real sly about it.

MAE: Gooper and I think—

GOOPER: Shut up, Mae! Big Mama, I think—Big Daddy ought to be started on morphine.

BIG MAMA: Nobody's going to give Big Daddy morphine.

DOCTOR BAUGH: Now, Big Mama, when that pain strikes it's going to strike mighty hard and Big Daddy's going to need the needle to bear it.

BIG MAMA: I tell you, nobody's going to give him morphine.

MAE: Big Mama, you don't want to see Big Daddy suffer, you know you—

(*Gooper, standing beside her, gives her a savage poke.*)

DOCTOR BAUGH (*placing a package on the table*): I'm leaving this stuff here, so if there's a sudden attack you all won't have to send out for it.

MAE: I know how to give a hypo.

BIG MAMA: Nobody's gonna give Big Daddy morphine.

GOOPER: Mae took a course in nursing during the war.

MARGARET: Somehow I don't think Big Daddy would want Mae to give him a hypo.

MAE: You think he'd want *you* to do it?

DOCTOR BAUGH: Well . . .

(*Doctor Baugh rises.*)

GOOPER: Doctor Baugh is goin'.

DOCTOR BAUGH: Yes, I got to be goin'. Well, keep your chin up, Big Mama.

GOOPER (*with jocularity*): She's gonna keep *both* chins up, aren't you, Big Mama?

(*Big Mama sobs.*)

Now stop that, Big Mama.

GOOPER (*at the door with Doctor Baugh*): Well, Doc, we sure do appreciate all you done. I'm telling you, we're surely obligated to you for—

(*Doctor Baugh has gone out without a glance at him.*)

—I guess that doctor has got a lot on his mind but it wouldn't hurt him to act a little more human . . .

(*Big Mama sobs.*)

Now be a brave girl, Mommy.

BIG MAMA: It's not true, I know that it's just not true!

GOOPER: Mama, those tests are infallible!

BIG MAMA: Why are you so determined to see your father daid?

MAE: Big Mama!

MARGARET (*gently*): I know what Big Mama means.

MAE (*fiercely*): Oh, do you?

MARGARET (*quietly and very sadly*): Yes, I think I do.

MAE: For a newcomer in the family you sure do show a lot of understanding.

MARGARET: Understanding is needed on this place.

MAE: I guess you must have needed a lot of it in your family, Maggie, with your father's liquor problem and now you've got Brick with his!

MARGARET: Brick does not have a liquor problem at all. Brick is devoted to Big Daddy. This thing is a terrible strain on him.

BIG MAMA: Brick is Big Daddy's boy, but he drinks too much and it worries me and Big Daddy, and, Margaret, you've got to cooperate with us, you've got to cooperate with Big Daddy and me in getting Brick straightened out. Because it will break Big Daddy's heart if Brick don't pull himself together and take hold of things.

MAE: Take hold of *what* things, Big Mama?

BIG MAMA: The place.

(*There is a quick violent look between Mae and Gooper.*)

GOOPER: Big Mama, you've had a shock.

MAE: Yais, we've all had a shock, but . . .

GOOPER: Let's be realistic—

MAE: —Big Daddy would never, would *never*, be foolish enough to—

GOOPER: —put this place in irresponsible hands!

BIG MAMA: Big Daddy ain't going to leave the place in anybody's hands; Big Daddy is *not* going to die. I want you to get that in your heads, all of you!

MAE: Mommy, Mommy, Big Mama, we're just as hopeful an' optimistic as you are about Big Daddy's prospects, we have faith in *prayer*—but nevertheless there are certain matters that have to be discussed an' dealt with, because otherwise—

GOOPER: Eventualities have to be considered and now's the time . . . Mae, will you please get my brief case out of our room?

MAE: Yes, honey.

(*She rises and goes out through the hall door.*)

GOOPER (*standing over Big Mama*): Now, Big Mom. What you said just now was not at all true and you know it. I've always loved Big Daddy in my own quiet way. I never made a show of it, and I know that Big Daddy has always been fond of me in a quiet way, too, and he never made a show of it neither.

(*Mae returns with Gooper's brief case.*)

MAE: Here's your brief case, Gooper, honey.

GOOPER (*handing the brief case back to her*): Thank you . . . Of cou'se, my relationship with Big Daddy is different from Brick's.

MAE: You're eight years older'n Brick an' always had t' carry a bigger load of th' responsibilities than Brick ever had t' carry. He never carried a thing in his life but a football or a highball.

GOOPER: Mae, will y' let me talk, please?

MAE: Yes, honey.

GOOPER: Now, a twenty-eight-thousand-acre plantation's a mighty big thing t' run.

MAE: Almost singlehanded.

(Margaret has gone out onto the gallery and can be heard calling softly to Brick.)

BIG MAMA: You never had to run this place! What are you talking about? As if Big Daddy was dead and in his grave, you had to run it? Why, you just helped him out with a few business details and had your law practice at the same time in Memphis!

MAE: Oh, Mommy, Mommy, Big Mommy! Let's be fair!

MARGARET: Brick!

MAE: Why, Gooper has given himself body and soul to keeping this place up for the past five years since Big Daddy's health started failing.

MARGARET: Brick!

MAE: Gooper won't say it, Gooper never thought of it as a duty, he just did it. And what did Brick do? Brick kept living in his past glory at college! Still a football player at twenty-seven!

MARGARET *(returning alone)*: Who are you talking about now? Brick? A football player? He isn't a football player and you know it. Brick is a sports announcer on TV and one of the best-known ones in the country!

MAE: I'm talking about what he was.

MARGARET: Well, I wish you would just stop talking about my husband.

GOOPER: I've got a right to discuss my brother with other members of MY OWN family, which don't include *you*. Why don't you go out there and drink with Brick?

MARGARET: I've never seen such malice toward a brother.

GOOPER: How about his for me? Why, he can't stand to be in the same room with me!

MARGARET: This is a deliberate campaign of vilification for the most disgusting and sordid reason on earth, and I know what it is! It's *avarice, avarice, greed, greed!*

BIG MAMA: *Oh, I'll scream! I will scream in a moment unless this stops!*

(Gooper has stalked up to Margaret with clenched fists at his sides as if he would strike her. Mae distorts her face again into a hideous grimace behind Margaret's back.)

BIG MAMA *(sobs)*: Margaret. Child. Come here. Sit next to Big Mama.

MARGARET: Precious Mommy. I'm sorry, I'm sorry, I—!

(She bends her long graceful neck to press her forehead to Big Mama's bulging shoulder under its black chiffon.)

MAE: How beautiful, how touching, this display of devotion! Do you know why she's childless? She's childless because that big beautiful athlete husband of hers won't go to bed with her!

GOOPER: You jest won't let me do this in a nice way, will yah? Aw right—I don't give a goddamn if Big Daddy likes me or don't like me or did or never did or will or will never! I'm just appealing to a sense of common decency and fair play. I'll tell you the truth. I've resented Big Daddy's partiality to Brick ever since Brick was born, and the way I've been

treated like I was just barely good enough to spit on and sometimes not even good enough for that. Big Daddy is dying of cancer, and it's spread all through him and it's attacked all his vital organs including the kidneys and right now he is sinking into uremia, and you all know what uremia is, it's poisoning of the whole system due to the failure of the body to eliminate its poisons.

MARGARET *(to herself, downstage, hissingly)*: Poisons, poisons! Venomous thoughts and words! In hearts and minds!—That's poisons!

GOOPER *(overlapping her)*: I am asking for a square deal, and, by God, I expect to get one. But if I don't get one, if there's any peculiar shenanigans going on around here behind my back, well, I'm not a corporation lawyer for nothing, I know how to protect my own interests.

(Brick enters from the gallery with a tranquil, blurred smile, carrying an empty glass with him.)

BRICK: Storm coming up.

GOOPER: Oh! A late arrival!

MAE: Behold the conquering hero comes!

GOOPER: The fabulous Brick Pollitt! Remember him?— Who could forget him!

MAE: He looks like he's been injured in a game!

GOOPER: Yep, I'm afraid you'll have to warm the bench at the Sugar Bowl this year, Brick!

(Mae laughs shrilly.)

Or was it the Rose Bowl that he made that famous run in?—

(Thunder.)

MAE: The punch bowl, honey. It was in the punch bowl, the cut-glass punch bowl!

GOOPER: Oh, that's right, I'm getting the bowls mixed up!

MARGARET: Why don't you stop venting your malice and envy on a sick boy?

BIG MAMA: *Now you two hush, I mean it, hush, all of you, hush!*

DAISY, SOOKEY: Storm! Storm comin'! Storm! Storm!

LACEY: Brightie, close them shutters.

GOOPER: Lacey, put the top up on my Cadillac, will yuh?

LACEY: Yes, suh, Mistah Pollitt!

GOOPER *(at the same time)*: Big Mama, you know it's necessary for me t' go back to Memphis in th' mornin' t' represent the Parker estate in a lawsuit.

(Mae sits on the bed and arranges papers she has taken from the brief case.)

BIG MAMA: Is it, Gooper?

MAE: Yaiss.

GOOPER: That's why I'm forced to—to bring up a problem that—

MAE: Somethin' that's too important t' be put off!

GOOPER: If Brick was sober, he ought to be in on this.

MARGARET: Brick is present; we're present.

GOOPER: Well, good. I will now give you this outline my partner, Tom Bullitt, an' me have drawn up—a sort of dummy—trusteeship.

MARGARET: Oh, that's it! You'll be in charge an' dole out remittances, will you?

GOOPER: This we did as soon as we got the report on Big Daddy from th' Ochsner Laboratories. We did this thing, I mean we drew up this dummy outline with the advice and assistance of the Chairman of the Boa'd of Directors of th' Southern Plantahs Bank and Trust Company in Memphis, C. C. Bellowes, a man who handles estates for all th' prominent fam'lies in West Tennessee and th' Delta.

BIG MAMA: Gooper?

GOOPER (*crouching in front of Big Mama*): Now this is not—not final, or anything like it. This is just a preliminary outline. But it does provide a basis—a design—a—possible, feasible—*plan!*

MARGARET: Yes, I'll bet it's a plan.

(*Thunder.*)

MAE: It's a plan to protect the biggest estate in the Delta from irresponsibility an'—

BIG MAMA: Now you listen to me, all of you, you listen here! They's not goin' to be any more catty talk in my house! And Gooper, you put that away before I grab it out of your hand and tear it right up! I don't know what the hell's in it, and I don't want to know what the hell's in it. I'm talkin' in Big Daddy's language now; I'm his *wife*, not his *widow*, I'm still his *wife!* And I'm talkin' to you in his language an'—

GOOPER: Big Mama, what I have here is—

MAE (*at the same time*): Gooper explained that it's just a plan . . .

BIG MAMA: I don't care what you got there. Just put it back where it came from, an' don't let me see it again, not even the outside of the envelope of it! Is that understood? Basis! Plan! Preliminary! Design! I say—what is it Big Daddy always says when he's disgusted?

BRICK (*from the bar*): Big Daddy says "crap" when he's disgusted.

BIG MAMA (*rising*): That's right—CRAP! I say CRAP too, like Big Daddy!

(*Thunder.*)

MAE: Coarse language doesn't seem called for in this—

GOOPER: Somethin' in me is *deeply outraged* by hearin' you talk like this.

BIG MAMA: *Nobody's goin' to take nothin'!*—till Big Daddy lets go of it—maybe, just possibly, not—not even then! No, not even then!

(*Thunder.*)

MAE: Sookey, hurry up an' git that po'ch furniture covahed; want th' paint to come off?

GOOPER: Lacey, put mah car away!

LACEY: Caint, Mistah Pollitt, you got the keys!

GOOPER: Naw, you got 'em, man. Where th' keys to th' car, honey?

MAE: You got 'em in your pocket!

BRICK: "You can always hear me singin' this song, Show me the way to go home."

(*Thunder distantly.*)

BIG MAMA: Brick! Come here, Brick, I need you. Tonight Brick looks like he used to look when he was a little boy, just like he did when he played wild games and used to come home when I hollered myself hoarse for him, all sweaty and pink cheeked and sleepy, with his—red curls shining . . .

(*Brick draws aside as he does from all physical contact and continues the song in a whisper, opening the ice bucket and dropping in the ice cubes one by one as if he were mixing some important chemical formula.*)
(*Distant thunder.*)

Time goes by so fast. Nothin' can outrun it. Death commences too early—almost before you're half acquainted with life—you meet the other . . . Oh, you know we just got to love each other an' stay together, all of us, just as close as we can, especially now that such a *black* thing has come and moved into this place without invitation.

(*Awkwardly embracing Brick, she presses her head to his shoulder.*)
(*A dog howls offstage.*)

Oh, Brick, son of Big Daddy, Big Daddy does so love you. Y'know what would be his fondest dream come true? If before he passed on, if Big Daddy has to pass on . . .

(*A dog howls.*)

. . . you give him a child of yours, a grandson as much like his son as his son is like Big Daddy . . .

MARGARET: I know that's Big Daddy's dream.

BIG MAMA: That's his dream.

MAE: Such a pity that Maggie and Brick can't oblige.

BIG DADDY (*off downstage right on the gallery*): Looks like the wind was takin' liberties with this place.

SERVANT (*offstage*): Yes, sir, Mr. Pollitt.

MARGARET (*crossing to the right door*): Big Daddy's on the gall'ry.

(*Big Mama has turned toward the hall door at the sound of Big Daddy's voice on the gallery.*)

BIG MAMA: I can't stay here. He'll see somethin' in my eyes.

(*Big Daddy enters the room from upstage right.*)

BIG DADDY: Can I come in?

(*He puts his cigar in an ash tray.*)

MARGARET: Did the storm wake you up, Big Daddy?

BIG DADDY: Which stawm are you talkin' about—th' one outside or th' hullballoo in here?

(*Gooper squeezes past Big Daddy.*)

GOOPER: 'Scuse me.

(*Mae tries to squeeze past Big Daddy to join Gooper, but Big Daddy puts his arm firmly around her.*)

BIG DADDY: I heard some mighty loud talk. Sounded like somethin' important was bein' discussed. What was the powwow about?

MAE (*flustered*): Why—nothin', Big Daddy . . .

BIG DADDY (*crossing to extreme left center, taking Mae with him*): What is that pregnant-lookin' envelope you're puttin' back in your brief case, Gooper?

GOOPER (*at the foot of the bed, caught, as he stuffs papers into envelope*): That? Nothin', suh—nothin' much of anythin' at all . . .

BIG DADDY: Nothin'? It looks like a whole lot of nothin'!

(*He turns upstage to the group.*)

You all know th' story about th' young married couple—

GOOPER: Yes, sir!

BIG DADDY: Hello, Brick—

BRICK: Hello, Big Daddy.

(*The group is arranged in a semicircle above Big Daddy, Margaret at the extreme right, then Mae and Gooper, then Big Mama, with Brick at the left.*)

BIG DADDY: Young married couple took Junior out to th' zoo one Sunday, inspected all of God's creatures in their cages, with satisfaction.

GOOPER: Satisfaction.

BIG DADDY (*crossing to upstage center, facing front*): This afternoon was a warm afternoon in spring an' that ole elephant had somethin' else on his mind which was bigger'n peanuts. You know this story, Brick?

(*Gooper nods.*)

BRICK: No, sir, I don't know it.

BIG DADDY: Y'see, in th' cage adjoinin' they was a young female elephant in heat!

BIG MAMA (*at Big Daddy's shoulder*): Oh, Big Daddy!

BIG DADDY: What's the matter, preacher's gone, ain't he? All right. That female elephant in the next cage was permeatin' the atmosphere about her with a powerful and excitin' odor of female fertility! Huh! Ain't that a nice way to put it, Brick?

BRICK: Yes, sir, nothin' wrong with it.

BIG DADDY: Brick says th's nothin' wrong with it!

BIG MAMA: Oh, Big Daddy!

BIG DADDY (*crossing to downstage center*): So this ole bull elephant still had a couple of fornications left in him. He reared back his trunk an' got a whiff of that elephant lady next door!—began to paw at the dirt in his cage an' butt his head against the separatin' partition and, first thing y'know, there was a conspicuous change in his *profile*—very *conspicuous*! Ain't I tellin' this story in decent language, Brick?

BRICK: Yes, sir, too fuckin' decent!

BIG DADDY: So, the little boy pointed at it and said, "What's that?" His mama said, "Oh, that's—nothin'!"—His papa said, "She's spoiled!"

(*Big Daddy crosses to Brick at left.*)

You didn't laugh at that story, Brick.

(*Big Mama crosses to downstage right crying. Margaret goes to her. Mae and Gooper hold upstage right center.*)

BRICK: No, sir, I didn't laugh at that story.

BIG DADDY: What is the smell in this room? Don't you notice it, Brick? Don't you notice a powerful and obnoxious odor of mendacity in this room?

BRICK: Yes, sir, I think I do, sir.

GOOPER: Mae, Mae . . .

BIG DADDY: There is nothing more powerful. Is there, Brick?

BRICK: No, sir. No, sir, there isn't, an' nothin' more obnoxious.

BIG DADDY: Brick agrees with me. The odor of mendacity is a powerful and obnoxious odor an' the stawm hasn't blown it away from this room yet. You notice it, Gooper?

GOOPER: What, sir?

BIG DADDY: How about you, Sister Woman? You notice the unpleasant odor of mendacity in this room?

MAE: Why, Big Daddy, I don't even know what that is.

BIG DADDY: You can smell it. Hell it smells like death!

(*Big Mama sobs. Big Daddy looks toward her.*)

What's wrong with that fat woman over there, loaded with diamonds? Hey, what's-you-name, what's the matter with you?

MARGARET (*crossing toward Big Daddy*): She had a slight dizzy spell, Big Daddy.

BIG DADDY: You better watch that, Big Mama. A stroke is a bad way to go.

MARGARET (*crossing to Big Daddy at center*): Oh, Brick, Big Daddy has on your birthday present to him, Brick, he has on your cashmere robe, the softest material I have ever felt.

BIG DADDY: Yeah, this is my soft birthday, Maggie . . . Not my gold or my silver birthday, but my soft birthday, everything's got to be soft for Big Daddy on this soft birthday.

(*Maggie kneels before Big Daddy at center.*)

MARGARET: Big Daddy's got on his Chinese slippers that I gave him, Brick. Big Daddy, I haven't given you my big present yet, but now I will, now's the time for me to present it to you! I have an announcement to make!

MAE: What? What kind of announcement?

GOOPER: A sports announcement, Maggie?

MARGARET: Announcement of life beginning! A child is coming, sired by Brick, and out of Maggie the Cat! I have Brick's child in my body, an' that's my birthday present to Big Daddy on this birthday!

(*Big Daddy looks at Brick who crosses behind Big Daddy to downstage portal, left.*)

BIG DADDY: Get up, girl, get up off your knees, girl.

(*Big Daddy helps Margaret to rise. He crosses above her, to her right, bites off the end of a fresh cigar, taken from his bathrobe pocket, as he studies Margaret.*)

   Uh-huh, this girl has life in her body, that's no lie!
BIG MAMA: BIG DADDY'S DREAM COME TRUE!
BRICK: JESUS!
BIG DADDY (*crossing right below wicker stand*): Gooper, I want my lawyer in the mornin'.
BRICK: Where are you goin', Big Daddy?
BIG DADDY: Son, I'm goin' up on the roof, to the belvedere on th' roof to look over my kingdom before I give up my kingdom—twenty-eight thousand acres of th' richest land this side of the valley Nile!

(*He exits through right doors, and down right on the gallery.*)

BIG MAMA (*following*): Sweetheart, sweetheart, sweetheart—can I come with you?

(*She exits downstage right.*)
   (*Margaret is downstage center in the mirror area. Mae has joined Gooper and she gives him a fierce poke, making a low hissing sound and a grimace of fury.*)

GOOPER (*pushing her aside*): Brick, could you possibly spare me one small shot of that liquor?
BRICK: Why, help yourself, Gooper boy.
GOOPER: I will.
MAE (*shrilly*): Of course we know that this is—a lie.
GOOPER: *Be still, Mae.*
MAE: I won't be still! I know she's made this up!
GOOPER: Goddamn it, I said shut up!
MARGARET: Gracious! I didn't know that my little announcement was going to provoke such a storm!
MAE: *That* woman isn't *pregnant!*
GOOPER: Who said she was?
MAE: *She* did.
GOOPER: The doctor didn't. Doc Baugh didn't.
MARGARET: I haven't gone to Doc Baugh.
GOOPER: Then who'd you go to, Maggie?
MARGARET: One of the best gynecologists in the South.
GOOPER: Uh huh, uh huh!—I see . . .

(*He takes out a pencil and notebook.*)

   —May we have his name, please?
MARGARET: No, you may not, Mister Prosecuting Attorney!
MAE: He doesn't have any name, he doesn't exist!
MARGARET: Oh, he exists all right, and so does my child, Brick's baby!
MAE: You can't conceive a child by a man that won't sleep with you unless you think you're—

(*Brick has turned on the phonograph. A scat song cuts Mae's speech.*)

GOOPER: *Turn that off!*
MAE: We know it's a lie because we hear you in here; he won't sleep with you, we hear you! So don't imagine you're going to put a trick over on us, to fool a dying man with a—

(*A long drawn cry of agony and rage fills the house. Margaret turns the phonograph down to a whisper. The cry is repeated.*)

MAE: Did you hear that, Gooper, did you hear that?
GOOPER: Sounds like the pain has struck.
MAE: Go see, Gooper!
GOOPER: Come along and leave these lovebirds together in their nest!

(*He goes out first. Mae follows but turns at the door, contorting her face and hissing at Margaret.*)

MAE: *Liar!*

(*She slams the door.*)
   (*Margaret exhales with relief and moves a little unsteadily to catch hold of Brick's arm.*)

MARGARET: Thank you for—keeping still . . .
BRICK: O.K., Maggie.
MARGARET: It was gallant of you to save my face!

(*He now pours down three shots in quick succession and stands waiting, silent. All at once he turns with a smile and says:*)

BRICK: *There!*
MARGARET: What?
BRICK: The *click* . . .

(*His gratitude seems almost infinite as he hobbles out on the gallery with a drink. We hear his crutch as he swings out of sight. Then, at some distance, he begins singing to himself a peaceful song. Margaret holds the big pillow forlornly as if it were her only companion, for a few moments, then throws it on the bed. She rushes to the liquor cabinet, gathers all the bottles in her arms, turns about undecidedly, then runs out of the room with them, leaving the door ajar on the dim yellow hall. Brick is heard hobbling back along the gallery, singing his peaceful song. He comes back in, sees the pillow on the bed, laughs lightly, sadly, picks it up. He has it under his arm as Margaret returns to the room. Margaret softly shuts the door and leans against it, smiling softly at Brick.*)

MARGARET: Brick, I used to think that you were stronger than me and I didn't want to be overpowered by you. But now, since you've taken to liquor—you know what?—I guess it's bad, but now I'm stronger than you and I can love you more truly! Don't move that pillow. I'll move it right back if you do!—Brick?

(*She turns out all the lamps but a single rose-silk-shaded one by the bed.*)

I really have been to a doctor and I know what to do and—Brick?—this is my time by the calendar to conceive?

BRICK: Yes, I understand, Maggie. But how are you going to conceive a child by a man in love with his liquor?

MARGARET: By locking his liquor up and making him satisfy my desire before I unlock it!

BRICK: Is that what you've done, Maggie?

MARGARET: Look and see. That cabinet's mighty empty compared to before!

BRICK: Well, I'll be a son of a—

(*He reaches for his crutch but she beats him to it and rushes out on the gallery, hurls the crutch over the rail, and comes back in, panting.*)

MARGARET: And so tonight we're going to make the lie true, and when that's done, I'll bring the liquor back here and we'll get drunk together, here, tonight, in this place that death has come into . . .—What do you say?

BRICK: I don't say anything. I guess there's nothing to say.

MARGARET: Oh, you weak people, you weak, beautiful people!—who give up with such grace. What you want is someone to—

(*She turns out the rose-silk lamp.*)

—take hold of you.—Gently, gently with love hand your life back to you, like somethin' gold you let go of. I *do* love you, Brick, I *do!*

BRICK (*smiling with charming sadness*): Wouldn't it be funny if that was true?

COMMENTARIES

TENNESSEE WILLIAMS (1911–1983)

From Memoirs   1972

Tennessee Williams published *Memoirs* in 1972, after establishing himself as one of the most successful American playwrights. The excerpts included here concern his feelings about *Cat on a Hot Tin Roof* and his feelings about being a writer.

Well, now, about plays, what about them? Plays are written and then, if they are lucky, they are performed, and if their luck still holds, which is not too frequently the case, their performance is so successful that both audience and critics at the first night are aware that they are being offered a dramatic work which is both honest and entertaining and also somehow capable of engaging their aesthetic appreciation.

I have never liked to talk about the professional side of my life. Am I afraid that it is a bird that will be startled away by discussion, as by a hawk's shadow? Something like that, I suppose.

People are always asking me, at those symposia to which I've been subjected in recent years, which is my favorite among the plays I have written, the number of which eludes my recollection, and I either say to them, "Always the latest" or I succumb to my instinct for the truth and say, "I suppose it must be the published version of *Cat on a Hot Tin Roof.*"

That play comes closest to being both a work of art and a work of craft. It is really very well put together, in my opinion, and all its characters are amusing and credible and touching. Also it adheres to the valuable edict of Aristotle that a tragedy must have unity of time and place and magnitude of theme.

The set in *Cat* never changes and its running time is exactly the time of its action, meaning that one act, timewise, follows directly upon the other, and I know of no other modern American play in which this is accomplished.

However my reasons for liking *Cat* best are deeper than that. I believe that in *Cat* I reached beyond myself, in the second act, to a kind of crude eloquence of expression in Big Daddy that I have managed to give no other character of my creation.

The story of *Cat's* production in 1954 and the disaster that followed upon its enormous success must be told now.

[Director Elia] Kazan immediately shared Audrey's [Wood, Williams's agent] enthusiasm for *Cat* but he said that it was faulty in one act. I assumed that he meant the first act, but no, it was the third act. He wanted a more admirable heroine than the Maggie offered in the original script.

Inwardly I disagreed. I thought that in Maggie I had presented a very true and moving portrait of a young woman whose frustration in love and whose practicality drove her to the literal seduction of an unwilling young man. Seduction is too soft a word. Brick was literally forced back to bed by Maggie, when she confiscated his booze . . .

Then I also had to violate my own intuition by having Big Daddy re-enter the stage in Act Three. I saw nothing for him to do in that act when he re-entered and I did not think that it was dramatically proper that he should re-enter. Consequently I had him tell "the elephant story." This was assaulted by censors. I was told it must be removed. The material which I then had to put in its place was always offensive to me.

I would not tell you this except for the consequences to me as a writer after *Cat* had received its Critics' Award and its Pulitzer.

Even though I always go crazy on opening nights, the New York opening of *Cat* was particularly dreadful. I thought it was a failure, a distortion of what I had intended. After the show was over I thought I had heard coughs all during the performance. I suppose there weren't that many, probably the usual number. And it did become my biggest, my longest-running play. But after the show was over on opening night, Kazan said, "Let's go to my apartment until the reviews are out." He was totally confident that it would be a hit. I met Audrey Wood outside, and at the time I was totally dependent on her for any creative confidence; and so I said, "Audrey, we're all going up to the Kazans' to wait for the notices." She said, "Oh no, I have other plans." I was hurt, and said something mean. . . .

What is it like being a writer? I would say it is like being free.

I know that some writers aren't free, they are professionally employed, which is quite a different thing.

Professionally, they are probably better writers in the conventional sense of "better." They have an ear to the ground of best-seller demands: They please their publishers and presumably their public as well.

But they are not free and so they are not what I regard a true writer as being.

To be free is to have achieved your life.

It means any number of freedoms.

It means the freedom to stop when you please, to go where and when you please, it means to be voyager here and there, one who flees many hotels, sad or happy, without obstruction and without much regret.

It means the freedom of being. And someone has wisely observed, if you can't be yourself, what's the point of being anything at all?

I am not a frequent reader nor quoter of Scriptures and yet I love a piece of advice which occurs among them:

"Let thy light so shine among men that they see thy good works and glorify thy Father which is in heaven."

There is a New Journalism, there is a New Criticism, there is a new look and style of cinema and theater, of practically everything that we live with, but what I think we most need is a New Morality.

And I think we've arrived at a point where that is a necessity of continued and bearable existence.

BRENDA MURPHY (b. 1950)

Tennessee Williams and Elia Kazan Collaborate on *Cat* 1991

Theater is a collaborative art, and numerous plays have been altered because of suggestions of a director or actor. The collaboration of Tennessee Williams and director Elia Kazan was special because both were powerful personalities and each respected the other. The *Cat on a Hot Tin Roof* that we know is much different from the one that Williams first wrote. He was willing to make many of the creative changes suggested by Kazan.

[Director Elia Kazan's] imagination stimulated by Big Daddy's rhetorical power, Kazan developed the production around the impetus of direct communication between the characters and the audience. At the beginning of Act 2, for example, he made a note to himself to have Big Daddy come downstage facing the audience and talk straight out to them while the others remained way upstage, even out on the gallery. Williams agreed with Kazan about the power of Big Daddy's character and the centrality of words in the play. In *Memoirs* he wrote, "In *Cat* I reached beyond myself, in the second act, to a kind of crude eloquence of expression in Big Daddy that I have managed to give no other character of my creation."[1]

Although Williams had incorporated the idea of addressing the audience in the "recitative" speeches of Maggie and Brick in the early scripts, he had not counted on what was in 1955 the radical concept that Kazan devised for the production. As Kazan noted in a later interview, the conventions of representational realism were so entrenched in the Broadway theater of the fifties that foregrounding the production's theatricality to the extent of having the characters address the audience directly had been considered anathema for many years. The last time he could remember it being done was in the production of *Our Town*° in 1938.[2]

---

[1]Tennessee Williams, *Memoirs* (Garden City: Doubleday, 1975).
[2]Michel Ciment, *Kazan on Kazan* (New York: Viking, 1974) 47.
Our Town: In this play the Stage Manager speaks to the audience.

Kazan's pride in this rejection of realistic convention and his continuing interest in subjectifying theatrical experience were evident in an interview he gave in the early sixties:

> I was busting out of the goddamned proscenium theater uptown. In *Cat on a Hot Tin Roof* I had everybody address the audience continually. Every time they had one of those long speeches they'd turn and say it to the audience. Nobody thought anything of it once we opened. But there was a hell of a lot of bitching about it before. . . . The whole second act of *Cat* was a long address by Burl Ives to the audience. I had him address various members of the audience . . . "what would *you* do?" is implicit in this kind of staging. It sucks the audience into the experience and emotion of that moment.[3]

Kazan wrote in his autobiography that he had to convince Williams to accept his notion of how Burl Ives would play the part of Big Daddy. When Kazan said he was going to bring Ives right down to the edge of the forestage, have him "look the audience right in the eye, and speak it directly to them," Williams protested that *Cat* was a realistic play, and should be kept within the representational conventions. When pressed by Kazan to say whether old cotton planters actually talked that eloquently and that long without interruption, Williams replied that they did. After all, who would dare interrupt them?[4] Nonetheless Kazan pursued his concept for the production in the face of Williams's skepticism, if not his opposition.

The Design

When the central dynamic of the production had been established as direct communication between the characters and the audience, it had to imbue all the elements of the stage language. Here Kazan reports that he did run into opposition from Williams, who had a clear idea of what he thought the set should be like, an image that had evolved as he had revised the play. In the notes for the designer he prepared for the script preceding the November pre-rehearsal version, Williams described the basic plan of the set that was eventually used for the production: a bed–sitting room in a Mississippi Delta plantation, opening onto an upstairs gallery and showing white balustrades against a fair summer sky that fades into dusk and night during the course of the play. This is what is needed to support the action of the play which, as Williams was fond of pointing out, observed the unities of time and place, the action of the play being confined to the single set and occupying exactly the amount of time it took to enact on stage. The lighting was obviously crucial for this play, to show the passage of time that is a central thematic concern as well as a structural one.

Beyond this, however, Williams's original image of the set was strikingly different from the set Kazan and Jo Mielziner eventually devised between them. Williams described the room as Victorian, with a touch of the Far East, and poetically haunted by the tender relationship of Jack Straw and Peter Ochello. He noted that the room should not have changed much since Straw and Ochello's time. To suggest the style for the design, Williams referred the designer to the reproduction he had seen of a faded photograph of the verandah of Robert Louis Stevenson's home in Samoa: "There was a quality of tender light on weathered wood, such as porch-furniture made of bamboo and wicker, exposed to tropical suns and tropical rains,

[3] Quoted in Richard Schechner and Theodore Hoffman, " 'Look, There's the American Theatre': An Interview with Elia Kazan," *Tulane Drama Review,* 9 (Winter 1964): 71.
[4] Elia Kazan, *Elia Kazan: A Life* (New York: Knopf, 1988) 541–42.

which came to mind when I thought about the set for this play" (RV xiii).° The photograph, he wrote, also brought to mind "the grace and comfort of light, the reassurance it gives, on a late and fair afternoon in summer, the way that no matter what, even dread of death, is gently touched and soothed by it. For the set is the background for a play that deals with human extremities of emotion and needs that softness behind it" (RV xiii).

Williams described in detail the big, slightly raked, double bed and the "entertainment center" that were the most significant objects in the set, and then he cautioned the designer, lest he feel that the previous description confined him to literal realism. As in the published "Note for the Designer," Williams envisioned that "the set should be far less realistic than I have so far implied in this description of it": The walls should dissolve mysteriously into the air below the ceiling; the set should be roofed by the sky; stars and moon suggested by traces of milky pallor, as if they were observed through a telescope lens out of focus (RV xiv). The original note, however, added the idea that a spiral nebula might be faintly suggested in order to suggest the "mystery of the cosmos," which Williams thought should be a visible presence in the play, almost as present as an actor in it. He also thought that the cloud effects and the sound effects for the windstorm in Act 3 should be as unrealistic as the set. As he revised the script, however, Williams began to reconceptualize the set as well. In November he sent off a rewrite of the scene description suggesting that the room should appear to have been remodeled since Straw and Ochello's time, and now had an open, Japanese effect. The canopied bed, he suggested, could appear to have been removed from an Italian renaissance palazzo when Big Daddy and Big Mama raided Europe a few years previously.

When Kazan and Mielziner began talking about the design, their concept of a production that foregrounded the characters' rhetorical appeals to the audience became the central element in their discussion. Kazan has written:

> Jo Mielziner and I had read the play in the same way; we saw its great merit was its brilliant rhetoric and its theatricality. Jo didn't see the play as realistic any more than I did. If it was to be done realistically, I would have to contrive stage business to keep the old man talking those great second-act speeches turned out front and pretend that it was just another day in the life of the Pollitt family. This would, it seemed to me, amount to an apology to the audience for the glory of the author's language. It didn't seem like just another day in the life of a cotton planter's family to Jo or to me; it seemed like the best kind of theater, the kind we were interested in encouraging, the theater theatrical, not pretending any longer that an audience wasn't out there to be addressed but having a performer as great as Burl Ives acknowledge their presence at all times and even make eye contact with individuals.[5]

Accordingly, Kazan wrote, "I caused Jo to design our setting as I wished, a large, triangular platform, tipped toward the audience and holding only one piece of furniture, an ornate bed. This brought the play down to its essentials and made it impossible for it to be played any way except as I preferred."[6]

The set was not quite so spare as Kazan remembered it, but the central point of his statement, that the presentational impulse was the dominant aesthetic factor in

---

[5]Kazan 542–43.
[6]Kazan 543.
RV: The reading version of the play (New York: New American Library, 1958), which has both versions of the third act.

creating the design, has been fully corroborated by Mielziner. In his memoir, Mielziner described their discussion about the design much as Kazan did. Asked how he thought the "elephant story" should be handled proxemically, Mielziner told Kazan that he thought it should receive as much emphasis as possible: "I suggested that we have an area of the stage on which Big Daddy could come down close to the audience and deliver the lines with dramatic force." Mielziner wrote that Kazan was delighted with his answer, and "from this discussion grew the idea of creating a stage within the stage. It would be steeply raked toward the audience with one corner actually jutting out over the footlights. In its final form it turned out to be a sort of thrust stage."[7]

Mielziner's design was a departure from the subjective realism he had employed in *Menagerie, Streetcar,* and *Summer and Smoke,* in that he did not try to suggest through the material elements of the stage language that the events unfolding on stage were filtered through the mind of one of the characters. Instead, the design of the set projected the action out toward the audience, forcing it to become involved as though it were one of the characters. Extremely spare, the set was composed of two platforms, a large diamond-shaped one, a corner of which projected beyond the proscenium, and a smaller rectangle a foot lower at stage right. There were no doors, such actions as opening doors and looking into the mirror being mimed in this production. The only items of furniture Mielziner drew in his sketches were the primary material signifiers: the large bed, which signified both Maggie and Brick's failing marriage and the lingering memory of Straw and Ochello; the entertainment center, which signified both Brick's immediate goal of escape from reality and the vacuous materialism that Williams saw in the fifties; and the daybed, which signified Brick's withdrawal from Maggie, their marriage, and life in general. The actual set, however, also held a wicker night table and a large wicker armchair which could accommodate either Burl Ives or two of the other actors. The overall effect was of a large playing space down front where the actors could address the audience as if from a bare platform.

The lines of the design contributed to this effect. The perspective was such that the corner of the ceiling came down to a point slightly to the left of upstage center, helping to focus the audience's attention on the point of the diamond where the characters addressed the audience. Mielziner took Williams's hints to give lighting a central function in the play, running a scrim from floor to ceiling along two sides of the set with strips of black velour indicating the lines of the columns outside the windows of the room when the light of the moon was projected through them. To signify sunlight, slide projections of blinds were thrown on the scrims, while the gallery and the lawn beyond the windows were blocked out. When characters on the gallery or the lawn were to be seen, the lights behind the scrim were brought up, making the actors visible to the audience, as had been done with *Streetcar.*

Two follow-spots were used in the production. One, on the audience's left, highlighted Maggie throughout Act 1 and picked up Big Mama, Maggie, and Brick in Act 2, as they were in turn nominally being addressed by Big Daddy, who was downstage talking to the audience. In Act 3 the light again shone on Maggie almost without interruption. The follow-spot on the audience's right highlighted the characters Maggie was addressing in Act 1, chiefly Brick, as she had her turn at "recitative." It shone on Big Daddy throughout Act 2 and picked up Brick, Big Mama,

[7]*Designing for Theatre: A Memoir and a Portfolio* (New York: Bram Hall House, 1965) 183.

Gooper, Mae, and Maggie at various times during Act 3, emphasizing a significant entrance or a significant reaction indexically as it occurred. Contributing to the generally "golden" look of the production's lighting, the follow-spots were amber except when a character went out onto the gallery, when they were changed to blue. The follow-spots not only helped to avoid confusion by focusing the audience's attention where Kazan wanted it to be, they also contributed to the foregrounding of the theatricality in the production by "framing" specific characters and pieces of action. Kazan stylized the composition of his stage picture in *Cat*, and encoded a great deal of meaning through gesture, movement, and pose in the production. Using the follow-spots to highlight these formal compositions emphasized that what was happening onstage was not real life but theater.

In designing the furniture, both Kazan and Mielziner took their cue from Williams's earlier description of the set, emphasizing the qualities he had seen in the Robert Louis Stevenson photograph. Kazan had underlined elements of this description in his copy of the script. Listed together, they indicate quite well the direction Mielziner took with the design after their conferences:

> Delta's biggest cotton planter
> Far East
> The room must evoke some ghosts
> Gently . . . poetically haunted by a relationship . . . a tenderness which was uncommon
> Samoan Island
> tender light on weathered wood
> Bamboo . . . wicker
> [the entertainment center] monument . . . very complete . . . compact little shrine . . . all the comforts . . . illusions . . . hide [written in the margin, "Brick hides"] such things as the characters in the play are faced with (RV xii-xiv)

From these suggestions came the old wicker headboard with its huge and fantastically shaped design of two cornucopias, the matching wicker furniture, the carpet with its lushly fertile design of oversized flowers and vines, and the one object in the room that competed with the fertility symbol of the bed for the audience's attention, the oversized bar, hi-fi, radio, and television with its sleekly modern fifties lines. This object realized Williams's description of a compact modern shrine to all the comforts and illusions of contemporary life and signified Brick's retreat from human contact.

Kazan has said more than once that Williams did not like the set that Mielziner finally developed for *Cat* because he thought his play should be performed realistically. Kazan has also indicated that the set was a material signifier of his aesthetic vision in opposition to Williams's:

> I had the setting I'd asked for; Jo had given me what I wanted. Tennessee had approved of it earlier, when he was ready to approve of damn near anything I asked for, because I was the director he wanted. Now the setting was up onstage, too late to change, and on that setting there was only one way for any human to conduct himself: "out front" it's called. Dear Tennessee was stuck with my vision, like it or not.[8]

---

[8] Kazan 543.

Arthur Miller

Arthur Miller (1915–2005) was the dean of American playwrights after the opening of *Death of a Salesman* in 1949. His steady output as a writer and a playwright began with his first publications after college in 1939, when he worked in the New York Federal Theatre Project, a branch of the Works Progress Administration (WPA), Franklin D. Roosevelt's huge Depression-era effort to put Americans back to work.

Miller, the son of a Jewish immigrant, was born in the Harlem section of Manhattan and raised first there and later in Brooklyn, after his father's business failed. In high school Miller thought of himself more as an athlete than as a student, and he had trouble getting teachers' recommendations for college. After considerable struggle and waiting, he entered the University of Michigan, where his talent as a playwright emerged under the tutelage of Kenneth Rowe, his playwriting professor. His undergraduate plays won important university awards, and he became noticed by the Theatre Guild, a highly respected theater founded to present excellent plays (not necessarily commercial successes). His career was under way.

From 1939 to 1947 Miller wrote radio plays, screenplays, articles, stories, and a novel. His work covered a wide range of material, much of it growing out of his childhood memories of a tightly knit and somewhat eccentric family that provided him with a large gallery of characters. But he also dealt with political issues and problems of anti-Semitism, which was widespread in the 1930s and 1940s. Miller's political concerns were a presence in his work throughout his career.

All My Sons (1947) was his first successful play. It ran on Broadway for three hundred performances, a remarkable record for a serious drama. The story centers on a man who knowingly produces defective parts for airplanes and then blames the subsequent crashes on his business partner, who is ruined and imprisoned. When the guilty man's son finds out the truth, he confronts his father and rebukes him. Ultimately, the man realizes not only that he has lost his son because of his deceit but that the dead pilots were also "all my sons." The play won the New York Drama Critics' Circle Award.

Miller's next play, *Death of a Salesman* (1949), was written in eight weeks. Focusing on the American ideal of business success, the play in its conclusions challenged standard American business values. Willy Loman, first performed by Lee J. Cobb, was intended to be a warning for Americans in the postwar period of the cost of growing wealth and affluence.

Miller's next play, *The Crucible* (1953), portrayed witch hunts of seventeenth-century New England, but most people recognized the subtext: it was about contemporary anti-Communist witch hunts. In the late 1940s and early 1950s, the House Un-American Activities Committee (HUAC) held hearings to uncover suspected Communists in all areas of American life, particularly the arts. Many writers, artists, and performers came under close, often unfair, scrutiny by HUAC for their own political views and allegiances and were asked to testify against their friends. Many were blacklisted (prevented from working in commercial theaters and movie companies), some were imprisoned for not testifying at others' trials, and some had their reputations and careers destroyed.

Arthur Miller was fearless in facing down HUAC, and he was convicted of contempt of court for not testifying against his friends. For a time he too was

For links to resources about Miller, click on *AuthorLinks* at **bedfordstmartins.com/jacobus**.

blacklisted, but his contempt citation was reversed, and he was not imprisoned. Given his personal political stance during that dangerous time, it is not a surprise that he usually wrote about matters of social concern.

In the 1990s, Miller became the darling of the London stage, while at the same time being somewhat neglected in the United States. One full-scale play, *Broken Glass* (1994), played in regional theater before a brief run on Broadway and then a longer run in London's West End. The play concerns a woman who becomes paralyzed in response to *Kristallnacht* ("night of broken glass"), a night of violent rampages against Jews and Jewish property in Germany that resulted in 91 Jewish dead, hundreds injured, and 7,500 businesses and 177 synagogues gutted. After November 9, 1938, it was clear that Jews were no longer safe in Hitler's Germany. The subject of Miller's play is intense, significant, and still timely.

The Ride Down Mount Morgan had its premiere in London in 1991; it then took seven years to open in New York in 1998. Its protagonist, Lyman Felt, played by Patrick Stewart in New York, was conceived as a Reaganite go-getter of the late 1980s: economically rapacious, sexually voracious, and amoral. When Felt's Porsche crashes on a ride down Mount Morgan, his two wives discover each other at the hospital. The play proceeds from there, examining the ethical values that permit Felt to live as he does. George Wolfe produced the play at the Joseph Papp Public Theater. The Broadway production opened at the Ambassador Theater in April 2000, again with Patrick Stewart. The play was nominated for a Tony Award.

Death of a Salesman

Death of a Salesman (1949) was a hit from its first performances and has remained at the center of modern American drama ever since. Everywhere this play has touched the hearts and minds of its audiences. The success of this American drama has been phenomenal.

The play was first performed in an experimental environment. Miller had originally conceived of a model of a man's head as the stage setting. He said, "The first image that occurred to me which was to result in *Death of a Salesman* was of an enormous face the height of the proscenium arch which would appear and then open up, and we would see the inside of a man's head. In fact, *The Inside of His Head* was the first title." This technique was not used, but when Miller worked with the director and producer of the first production, he helped develop a setting that became a model for the "American style" in drama. The multilevel set permitted the play to shift from Willy Loman and his wife, Linda, having a conversation in their kitchen to their sons' bedroom on the second level of the house. The set permitted portions of the stage to be reserved for Willy's visions of his brother, Ben, and for scenes outside the house, such as Willy's interlude with the woman in Boston.

In a way, the setup of the stage respected Miller's original plan, but instead of portraying a cross section of Willy's head, it presented a metaphor for a cross section of his life. The audience was looking in not on just a living room, as in the nineteenth-century Ibsenist approach, but on an entire house and an entire life.

Using a cross section of a house as a metaphor was an especially important device in this play because of the play's allusions to Greek tragedy. The great

For discussion questions and assignments on *Death of a Salesman*, visit **bedfordstmartins.com/jacobus**.

Greek tragedies usually portray the destruction of a house—such as the house of Atreus—in which "house" stands for a whole family, not a building. When Shakespeare's Hamlet dies, for example, his entire line—his house—dies with him. The death in *Death of a Salesman* implies the destruction of a family holding certain beliefs that have been wrong from the start.

The life of the salesman has given Willy a sense of dignity and worth, and he imagines that the modern world has corrupted that sense by robbing salesmen of the value of their personality. He thinks that the modern world has failed him, but he is wrong. His original belief—that what counts is not *what* you know but *whom* you know and how well you are liked—lies at the heart of his failure. When the play opens, he already has failed at the traveling salesman's job because he can no longer drive to his assigned territory. He cannot sell what he needs to sell.

Willy has inculcated his beliefs in his sons, Happy and Biff, and both are as ineffectual as their father. Willy doted on Biff and encouraged him to become a high school football star at the expense of his studies. But when Biff cannot pass an important course, and his plans to make up the work are subverted by his disillusionment in his father, his dreams of a college football career vanish. He cannot change and recover from this defeat. Happy, like his father, builds castles in the air and assumes somehow that he will be successful, though he has nothing with which to back up this assumption. He wants the glory—and he spends time in fanciful imaginings, as Willy does—but he cannot do the basic work that makes it possible to achieve glory. Ironically, it is the "anemic" Bernard—who studies hard, stresses personal honesty and diligence, and never brags—who is successful.

Linda supports Willy's illusions, allowing him to be a fraud by sharing—or pretending to believe—in his dream. Willy has permitted himself to believe that integrity, honesty, and fidelity are not as important as being well liked.

The play ends with Willy still unable to face the deceptions he has perpetuated. He commits suicide, believing that his sons will be able to follow in his footsteps and succeed where he did not; he thinks that his insurance money will save the house and the family. What he does not realize is that his sons are no more capable than he is. They have been corrupted by his thinking, his values, his beliefs. And they cannot solve the problems that overwhelmed him.

Death of a Salesman has been given a privileged position in American drama because it is a modern tragedy. Aristotle believed that only characters of noble birth could be tragic heroes, but Miller confounds this theory, as Eugene O'Neill did, by showing the human integrity in even the most humble characters. Miller's Willy Loman is not a peasant, nor is he noble. In fact, Miller took a frightening risk in creating a character whom we find hard to like. Willy wants to be well liked, but as an audience we find it difficult to like a person who whines, complains, and accepts petty immorality as a normal way of life. Despite his character, we are awed by his fate.

One Chinese commentator said, after seeing Miller's Chinese production of the play in 1983, that China is filled with such dreamers as Willy. Certainly the United States has been filled with them. Willy stands as an aspect of our culture, commercial and otherwise, that is at the center of our reflection of ourselves. Perhaps we react so strongly to Willy because we are afraid that we might easily become a Willy Loman if we are not vigilant about our moral views, our psychological well-being, and the limits of our commitment to success. Willy Loman has mesmerized U.S. audiences under many different economic circumstances: prosperity, recession, rapid growth, and cautious development. No matter what those circumstances, we have looked at the play as if looking in a mirror. What we have seen has always involved us, although it has not always made us pleased with ourselves.

Death of a Salesman in Performance

Death of a Salesman opened on Broadway on February 10, 1949, and won virtually every prize available for drama, including the Pulitzer Prize and the New York Drama Critics' Circle Award for best play. It ran on Broadway for an incredible 742 performances. Elia Kazan, director, was instrumental in establishing the play's innovative staging. Lee J. Cobb was cast as Willy, Mildred Dunnock as Linda, Arthur Kennedy as Biff, and Cameron Mitchell as Happy. Robert Coleman said of the New York production: "An explosion of emotional dynamite was set off last evening in the Morosco [Theatre]. . . . In fashioning *Death of a Salesman* for them, author Arthur Miller and director Elia Kazan have collaborated on as exciting and devastating a theatrical blast as the nerves of modern playgoers can stand." Of Cobb, Howard Barnes said, "Cobb contributes a mammoth and magnificent portrayal of the central character. In his hands the salesman's frustration and final suicide are a matter of tremendous import."

The London production in July 1949, with Paul Muni as Willy and Kevin McCarthy as Biff, lasted 204 performances. An all-black production was directed by Lee Sankowich in Baltimore in 1972. Miller, in the audience on that production's opening night, commented that the play had been well received in "many countries and cultures" and that the Baltimore production further underscored the universality of the play. George C. Scott was praised for the power of his performance as Willy in New York's Circle in the Square production in 1975. A Chinese production directed by Arthur Miller was enormously successful in 1983. In the most celebrated revival of the play, Dustin Hoffman portrayed Willy, John Malkovich played Biff, and Michael Rudman directed at the Broadhurst Theatre in New York in 1984. The critic Benedict Nightingale said of that production, "Somewhere at the core of him [Willy] an elaborate battle is being fought between dishonesty and honesty, glitter and substance, appearance and reality, between the promises or supposed promises of society and the claims of the self, between what Willy professes to value and what, perhaps without knowing it, he actually does value." In 1985, Dustin Hoffman brought his production of Miller's play to television, where it was viewed by an estimated twenty-five million people.

On February 10, 1999, exactly fifty years to the day from its original opening, a major production opened with Brian Dennehy as Willy Loman. The production was conceived in Chicago by the Goodman Theatre Company, and Dennehy was praised by critics and theater-goers alike for presenting a powerful portrayal of Willy Loman for a new generation. With Claire Higgins as Linda, Dennehy brought the play to London's Lyric Theatre in 2005 to resounding reviews. Critics praised the timelessness of the drama— ultimately crowning it an American classic.

The 2012 revival of the play at the Ethel Barrymore Theatre in New York featured Philip Seymour Hoffman as Willy Loman in Mike Nichols's production. In his review in the *New York Times*, Ben Brantley described it as "an immaculate monument to a great American play." Nichols, who saw the play in 1949, tried to honor the designs of Jo Mielziner and the spirit of the original production.

ARTHUR MILLER (1915–2005)

Death of a Salesman   1949

Certain Private Conversations in Two Acts and a Requiem

Characters

WILLY LOMAN	UNCLE BEN
LINDA	HOWARD WAGNER
BIFF	JENNY
HAPPY	STANLEY
BERNARD	MISS FORSYTHE
THE WOMAN	LETTA
CHARLEY	

The action takes place in Willy Loman's house and yard and in various places he visits in the New York and Boston of today.

(Throughout the play, in the stage directions, left and right mean stage left and stage right.)

ACT I

(A melody is heard, played upon a flute. It is small and fine, telling of grass and trees and the horizon. The curtain rises.)

(Before us is the Salesman's house. We are aware of towering, angular shapes behind it, surrounding it on all sides. Only the blue light of the sky falls upon the house and forestage; the surrounding area shows an angry glow of orange. As more light appears, we see a solid vault of apartment houses around the small, fragile-seeming home. An air of the dream clings to the place, a dream rising out of reality. The kitchen at center seems actual enough, for there is a kitchen table with three chairs, and a refrigerator. But no other fixtures are seen. At the back of the kitchen there is a draped entrance, which leads to the living room. To the right of the kitchen, on a level raised two feet, is a bedroom furnished only with a brass bedstead and a straight chair. On a shelf over the bed a silver athletic trophy stands. A window opens onto the apartment house at the side.)

(Behind the kitchen, on a level raised six and a half feet, is the boys' bedroom, at present barely visible. Two beds are dimly seen, and at the back of the room a dormer window. [This bedroom is above the unseen living room.] At the left a stairway curves up to it from the kitchen.)

(The entire setting is wholly or, in some places, partially transparent. The roofline of the house is one-dimensional; under and over it we see the apartment buildings. Before the house lies an apron, curving beyond the forestage into the orchestra. This forward area serves as the back yard as well as the locale of all Willy's imaginings and of his city scenes. Whenever the action is in the present the actors observe the imaginary wall-lines, entering the house only through its door at the left. But in the scenes of the past these boundaries are broken, and characters enter or leave a room by stepping "through" a wall onto the forestage.)

(From the right, Willy Loman, the Salesman, enters, carrying two large sample cases. The flute plays on. He hears but is not aware of it. He is past sixty years of age, dressed quietly. Even as he crosses the stage to the doorway of the house, his exhaustion is apparent. He unlocks the door, comes into the kitchen, and thankfully lets his burden down, feeling the soreness of his palms. A word-sigh escapes his lips—it might be "Oh, boy, oh, boy." He closes the door then carries his cases out into the living room, through the draped kitchen doorway.)

(Linda, his wife, has stirred in her bed at the right. She gets out and puts on a robe, listening. Most often jovial, she has developed an iron repression of her exceptions to Willy's behavior—she more than loves him, she admires him, as though his mercurial nature, his temper, his massive dreams and little cruelties, served her only as sharp reminders of the turbulent longings within him, longings which she shares but lacks the temperament to utter and follow to their end.)

LINDA (*hearing Willy outside the bedroom, calls with some trepidation*): Willy!

WILLY: It's all right. I came back.

LINDA: Why? What happened? (*Slight pause.*) Did something happen, Willy?

WILLY: No, nothing happened.

LINDA: You didn't smash the car, did you?

WILLY (*with casual irritation*): I said nothing happened. Didn't you hear me?

LINDA: Don't you feel well?

WILLY: I'm tired to the death. (*The flute has faded away. He sits on the bed beside her, a little numb.*) I couldn't make it. I just couldn't make it, Linda.

LINDA (*very carefully, delicately*): Where were you all day? You look terrible.

WILLY: I got as far as a little above Yonkers. I stopped for a cup of coffee. Maybe it was the coffee.

LINDA: What?

WILLY (*after a pause*): I suddenly couldn't drive anymore. The car kept going off onto the shoulder, y'know?

LINDA (*helpfully*): Oh. Maybe it was the steering again. I don't think Angelo knows the Studebaker.

WILLY: No, it's me, it's me. Suddenly I realize I'm goin' sixty miles an hour and I don't remember the last five minutes. I'm—I can't seem to—keep my mind to it.

LINDA: Maybe it's your glasses. You never went for your new glasses.

WILLY: No, I see everything. I came back ten miles an hour. It took me nearly four hours from Yonkers.

LINDA (*resigned*): Well, you'll just have to take a rest, Willy, you can't continue this way.

WILLY: I just got back from Florida.

LINDA: But you didn't rest your mind. Your mind is overactive, and the mind is what counts, dear.

WILLY: I'll start out in the morning. Maybe I'll feel better in the morning. (*She is taking off his shoes.*) These goddam arch supports are killing me.

LINDA: Take an aspirin. Should I get you an aspirin? It'll soothe you.

WILLY (*with wonder*): I was driving along, you understand? And I was fine. I was even observing the scenery. You can imagine, me looking at scenery, on the road every week of my life. But it's so beautiful up there, Linda, the trees are so thick, and the sun is warm. I opened the windshield and just let the warm air bathe over me. And then all of a sudden I'm goin' off the road! I'm tellin' ya, I absolutely forgot I was driving. If I'd've gone the other way over the white line I might've killed somebody. So I went on again—and five minutes later I'm dreamin' again, and I nearly—(*He presses two fingers against his eyes.*) I have such thoughts, I have such strange thoughts.

LINDA: Willy, dear. Talk to them again. There's no reason why you can't work in New York.

WILLY: They don't need me in New York. I'm the New England man. I'm vital in New England.

LINDA: But you're sixty years old. They can't expect you to keep traveling every week.

WILLY: I'll have to send a wire to Portland. I'm supposed to see Brown and Morrison tomorrow morning at ten o'clock to show the line. Goddammit, I could sell them! (*He starts putting on his jacket.*)

LINDA (*taking the jacket from him*): Why don't you go down to the place tomorrow and tell Howard you've simply got to work in New York? You're too accommodating, dear.

WILLY: If old man Wagner was alive I'd a been in charge of New York now! That man was a prince, he was a masterful man. But that boy of his, that Howard, he don't appreciate. When I went north the first time, the Wagner Company didn't know where New England was!

LINDA: Why don't you tell those things to Howard, dear?

WILLY (*encouraged*): I will, I definitely will. Is there any cheese?

LINDA: I'll make you a sandwich.

WILLY: No, go to sleep. I'll take some milk. I'll be up right away. The boys in?

LINDA: They're sleeping. Happy took Biff on a date tonight.

WILLY (*interested*): That so?

LINDA: It was so nice to see them shaving together, one behind the other, in the bathroom. And going out together. You notice? The whole house smells of shaving lotion.

WILLY: Figure it out. Work a lifetime to pay off a house. You finally own it, and there's nobody to live in it.

LINDA: Well, dear, life is a casting off. It's always that way.

WILLY: No, no, some people—some people accomplish something. Did Biff say anything after I went this morning?

LINDA: You shouldn't have criticized him, Willy, especially after he just got off the train. You mustn't lose your temper with him.

WILLY: When the hell did I lose my temper? I simply asked him if he was making any money. Is that a criticism?

LINDA: But, dear, how could he make any money?

WILLY (*worried and angered*): There's such an undercurrent in him. He became a moody man. Did he apologize when I left this morning?

LINDA: He was crestfallen, Willy. You know how he admires you. I think if he finds himself, then you'll both be happier and not fight any more.

WILLY: How can he find himself on a farm? Is that a life? A farmhand? In the beginning, when he was young, I thought, well, a young man, it's good for him to tramp around, take a lot of different jobs. But it's more than ten years now and he has yet to make thirty-five dollars a week!

LINDA: He's finding himself, Willy.

WILLY: Not finding yourself at the age of thirty-four is a disgrace!

LINDA: Shh!

WILLY: The trouble is he's lazy, goddammit!

LINDA: Willy, please!

WILLY: Biff is a lazy bum!

LINDA: They're sleeping. Get something to eat. Go on down.

WILLY: Why did he come home? I would like to know what brought him home.

LINDA: I don't know. I think he's still lost, Willy. I think he's very lost.

WILLY: Biff Loman is lost. In the greatest country in the world a young man with such—personal attractiveness, gets lost. And such a hard worker. There's one thing about Biff—he's not lazy.

LINDA: Never.

WILLY (*with pity and resolve*): I'll see him in the morning; I'll have a nice talk with him. I'll get him a job selling. He could be big in no time. My God! Remember how they used to follow him around in high school? When he smiled at one of them their faces lit up. When he walked down the street . . . (*He loses himself in reminiscences.*)

LINDA (*trying to bring him out of it*): Willy, dear, I got a new kind of American-type cheese today. It's whipped.

WILLY: Why do you get American when I like Swiss?

LINDA: I just thought you'd like a change—

WILLY: I don't want a change! I want Swiss cheese. Why am I always being contradicted?

LINDA (*with a covering laugh*): I thought it would be a surprise.

WILLY: Why don't you open a window in here, for God's sake?

LINDA (*with infinite patience*): They're all open, dear.

WILLY: The way they boxed us in here. Bricks and windows, windows and bricks.

LINDA: We should've bought the land next door.

WILLY: The street is lined with cars. There's not a breath of fresh air in the neighborhood. The grass don't grow anymore, you can't raise a carrot in the back yard. They should've had a law against apartment houses. Remember those two beautiful elm trees out there? When I and Biff hung the swing between them?

LINDA: Yeah, like being a million miles from the city.

WILLY: They should've arrested the builder for cutting those down. They massacred the neighborhood. (*Lost.*) More and more I think of those days, Linda. This time of year it was lilac and wisteria. And then the peonies would come out, and the daffodils. What fragrance in this room!

LINDA: Well, after all, people had to move somewhere.

WILLY: No, there's more people now.

LINDA: I don't think there's more people. I think—

WILLY: There's more people! That's what's ruining this country! Population is getting out of control. The competition is maddening! Smell the stink from that apartment house! And another one on the other side . . . How can they whip cheese?

(*On Willy's last line, Biff and Happy raise themselves up in their beds, listening.*)

LINDA: Go down, try it. And be quiet.

WILLY (*turning to Linda, guiltily*): You're not worried about me, are you, sweetheart?

BIFF: What's the matter?

HAPPY: Listen!

LINDA: You've got too much on the ball to worry about.

WILLY: You're my foundation and my support, Linda.

LINDA: Just try to relax, dear. You make mountains out of molehills.

WILLY: I won't fight with him any more. If he wants to go back to Texas, let him go.

LINDA: He'll find his way.

WILLY: Sure. Certain men just don't get started till later in life. Like Thomas Edison, I think. Or B. F. Goodrich. One of them was deaf. (*He starts for the bedroom doorway.*) I'll put my money on Biff.

LINDA: And Willy—if it's warm Sunday we'll drive in the country. And we'll open the windshield, and take lunch.

WILLY: No, the windshields don't open on the new cars.

LINDA: But you opened it today.

WILLY: Me? I didn't. (*He stops.*) Now isn't that peculiar! Isn't that a remarkable—(*He breaks off in amazement and fright as the flute is heard distantly.*)

LINDA: What, darling?

WILLY: That is the most remarkable thing.

LINDA: What, dear?

WILLY: I was thinking of the Chevvy. (*Slight pause.*) Nineteen twenty-eight . . . when I had that red Chevvy—(*Breaks off.*) That funny? I coulda sworn I was driving that Chevvy today.

LINDA: Well, that's nothing. Something must've reminded you.

WILLY: Remarkable. Ts. Remember those days? The way Biff used to simonize that car? The dealer refused to believe there was eighty thousand miles on it. (*He shakes his head.*) Heh! (*To Linda.*) Close your eyes, I'll be right up. (*He walks out of the bedroom.*)

HAPPY (*to Biff*): Jesus, maybe he smashed up the car again!

LINDA (*calling after Willy*): Be careful on the stairs, dear! The cheese is on the middle shelf! (*She turns, goes over to the bed, takes his jacket, and goes out of the bedroom.*)

(*Light has risen on the boys' room. Unseen, Willy is heard talking to himself, "Eighty thousand miles," and a little laugh. Biff gets out of bed, comes downstage a bit, and stands attentively. Biff is two years older than his brother Happy, well built, but in these days bears a worn air and seems less self-assured. He has succeeded less, and his dreams are stronger and less acceptable than Happy's. Happy is tall, powerfully made. Sexuality is like a visible color on him, or a scent that many women have discovered. He, like his brother, is lost, but in a different way, for he has never allowed himself to turn his face toward defeat and is thus more confused and hard-skinned, although seemingly more content.*)

HAPPY (*getting out of bed*): He's going to get his license taken away if he keeps that up. I'm getting nervous about him, y'know, Biff?

BIFF: His eyes are going.

HAPPY: No, I've driven with him. He sees all right. He just doesn't keep his mind on it. I drove into the city with him last week. He stops at a green light and then it turns red and he goes. (*He laughs.*)

BIFF: Maybe he's color-blind.

HAPPY: Pop? Why he's got the finest eye for color in the business. You know that.

BIFF (*sitting down on his bed*): I'm going to sleep.

HAPPY: You're not still sour on Dad, are you, Biff?

BIFF: He's all right, I guess.

WILLY (*underneath them, in the living room*): Yes, sir, eighty thousand miles—eighty-two thousand!

BIFF: You smoking?

HAPPY (*holding out a pack of cigarettes*): Want one?

BIFF (*taking a cigarette*): I can never sleep when I smell it.

WILLY: What a simonizing job, heh!

HAPPY (*with deep sentiment*): Funny, Biff, y'know? Us sleeping in here again? The old beds. (*He pats his bed affectionately.*) All the talk that went across those two beds, huh? Our whole lives.

BIFF: Yeah. Lotta dreams and plans.

HAPPY (*with a deep and masculine laugh*): About five hundred women would like to know what was said in this room.

(*They share a soft laugh.*)

BIFF: Remember that big Betsy something—what the hell was her name—over on Bushwick Avenue?

HAPPY (*combing his hair*): With the collie dog!

BIFF: That's the one. I got you in there, remember?

HAPPY: Yeah, that was my first time—I think. Boy, there was a pig. (*They laugh, almost crudely.*) You taught me everything I know about women. Don't forget that.

BIFF: I bet you forgot how bashful you used to be. Especially with girls.

HAPPY: Oh, I still am, Biff.

BIFF: Oh, go on.

HAPPY: I just control it, that's all. I think I got less bashful and you got more so. What happened, Biff? Where's the old humor, the old confidence? (*He shakes Biff's knee. Biff gets up and moves restlessly about the room.*) What's the matter?

BIFF: Why does Dad mock me all the time?

HAPPY: He's not mocking you, he—

BIFF: Everything I say there's a twist of mockery on his face. I can't get near him.

HAPPY: He just wants you to make good, that's all. I wanted to talk to you about Dad for a long time, Biff. Something's—happening to him. He—talks to himself.

BIFF: I noticed that this morning. But he always mumbled.

HAPPY: But not so noticeable. It got so embarrassing I sent him to Florida. And you know something? Most of the time he's talking to you.

BIFF: What's he say about me?

HAPPY: I can't make it out.

BIFF: What's he say about me?

HAPPY: I think the fact that you're not settled, that you're still kind of up in the air . . .

BIFF: There's one or two other things depressing him, Happy.

HAPPY: What do you mean?

BIFF: Never mind. Just don't lay it all to me.

HAPPY: But I think if you just got started—I mean—is there any future for you out there?

BIFF: I tell ya, Hap, I don't know what the future is. I don't know—what I'm supposed to want.

HAPPY: What do you mean?

BIFF: Well, I spent six or seven years after high school trying to work myself up. Shipping clerk, salesman, business of one kind or another. And it's a measly manner of existence. To get on that subway on the hot mornings in summer. To devote your whole life to keeping stock, or making phone calls, or selling or buying. To suffer fifty weeks of the year for the sake of a two-week vacation, when all you really desire is to be outdoors, with your shirt off. And always to have to get ahead of the next fella. And still—that's how you build a future.

HAPPY: Well, you really enjoy it on a farm? Are you content out there?

BIFF (*with rising agitation*): Hap, I've had twenty or thirty different kinds of jobs since I left home before the war, and it always turns out the same. I just realized it lately. In Nebraska when I herded cattle, and the Dakotas, and Arizona, and now in Texas. It's why I came home now, I guess, because I realized it. This farm I work on, it's spring there now, see? And they've got about fifteen new colts. There's nothing more inspiring or—beautiful than the sight of a mare and a new colt. And it's cool there now, see? Texas is cool now, and it's spring. And whenever spring comes to where I am, I suddenly get the feeling, my God, I'm not gettin' anywhere! What the hell am I doing, playing around with horses, twenty-eight dollars a week! I'm thirty-four years old, I oughta be makin' my future. That's when I come running home. And now, I get here, and I don't know what to do with myself. (*After a pause.*) I've always made a point of not wasting my life, and every time I come back here I know that all I've done is to waste my life.

HAPPY: You're a poet, you know that, Biff? You're a—you're an idealist!

BIFF: No, I'm mixed up very bad. Maybe I oughta get married. Maybe I oughta get stuck into something. Maybe that's my trouble. I'm like a boy. I'm not married, I'm not in business, I just—I'm like a boy. Are you content, Hap? You're a success, aren't you? Are you content?

HAPPY: Hell, no!

BIFF: Why? You're making money, aren't you?

HAPPY (*moving about with energy, expressiveness*): All I can do now is wait for the merchandise manager to die. And suppose I get to be merchandise manager? He's a good friend of mine, and he just built a terrific estate on Long Island. And he lived there about two months and sold it, and now he's building another one. He can't enjoy it once it's finished. And I know that's just what I would do. I don't know what the hell I'm workin' for. Sometimes I sit in my apartment—all alone. And I think of the rent I'm paying. And it's crazy. But then, it's what I always wanted. My own apartment, a car, and plenty of women. And still, goddammit, I'm lonely.

BIFF (*with enthusiasm*): Listen, why don't you come out West with me?

HAPPY: You and I, heh?

BIFF: Sure, maybe we could buy a ranch. Raise cattle, use our muscles. Men built like we are should be working out in the open.

HAPPY (*avidly*): The Loman Brothers, heh?

BIFF (*with vast affection*): Sure, we'd be known all over the counties!

HAPPY (*enthralled*): That's what I dream about, Biff. Sometimes I want to just rip my clothes off in the middle of the store and outbox that goddam merchandise manager. I mean I can outbox, outrun and outlift anybody in that store, and I have to take orders from those common, petty sons-of-bitches till I can't stand it anymore.

BIFF: I'm tellin' you, kid, if you were with me I'd be happy out there.

HAPPY (*enthused*): See, Biff, everybody around me is so false that I'm constantly lowering my ideals . . .

BIFF: Baby, together we'd stand up for one another, we'd have someone to trust.

HAPPY: If I were around you—

BIFF: Hap, the trouble is we weren't brought up to grub for money. I don't know how to do it.

HAPPY: Neither can I!

BIFF: Then let's go!

HAPPY: The only thing is—what can you make out there?

BIFF: But look at your friend. Builds an estate and then hasn't the peace of mind to live in it.

HAPPY: Yeah, but when he walks into the store the waves part in front of him. That's fifty-two thousand dollars a year coming through the revolving door, and I got more in my pinky finger than he's got in his head.

BIFF: Yeah, but you just said—

HAPPY: I gotta show some of those pompous, self-important executives over there that Hap Loman can make the grade. I want to walk into the store the way he walks in. Then I'll go with you, Biff. We'll be together yet, I swear. But take those two we had tonight. Now weren't they gorgeous creatures?

BIFF: Yeah, yeah, most gorgeous I've had in years.

HAPPY: I get that any time I want, Biff. Whenever I feel disgusted. The only trouble is, it gets like bowling or something. I just keep knockin' them over and it doesn't mean anything. You still run around a lot?

BIFF: Naa. I'd like to find a girl—steady, somebody with substance.

HAPPY: That's what I long for.

BIFF: Go on! You'd never come home.

HAPPY: I would! Somebody with character, with resistance! Like Mom, y'know? You're gonna call me a bastard when I tell you this. That girl Charlotte I was with tonight is engaged to be married in five weeks. (*He tries on his new hat.*)

BIFF: No kiddin'!

HAPPY: Sure, the guy's in line for the vice-presidency of the store. I don't know what gets into me, maybe I just have an overdeveloped sense of competition or something, but I went and ruined her, and furthermore I can't get rid of her. And he's the third executive I've done that to. Isn't that a crummy characteristic? And to top it all, I go to their weddings! (*Indignantly, but laughing.*) Like I'm not supposed to take bribes. Manufacturers offer me a hundred-dollar bill now and then to throw an order their way. You know how honest I am, but it's like this girl, see. I hate myself for it. Because I don't want the girl, and, still, I take it and—I love it!

BIFF: Let's go to sleep.

HAPPY: I guess we didn't settle anything, heh?

BIFF: I just got one idea that I think I'm going to try.

HAPPY: What's that?

BIFF: Remember Bill Oliver?

HAPPY: Sure, Oliver is very big now. You want to work for him again?

BIFF: No, but when I quit he said something to me. He put his arm on my shoulder, and he said, "Biff, if you ever need anything, come to me."

HAPPY: I remember that. That sounds good.

BIFF: I think I'll go to see him. If I could get ten thousand or even seven or eight thousand dollars I could buy a beautiful ranch.

HAPPY: I bet he'd back you. 'Cause he thought highly of you, Biff. I mean, they all do. You're well liked, Biff. That's why I say to come back here, and we both have the apartment. And I'm tellin' you, Biff, any babe you want . . .

BIFF: No, with a ranch I could do the work I like and still be something. I just wonder though. I wonder if Oliver still thinks I stole that carton of basketballs.

HAPPY: Oh, he probably forgot that long ago. It's almost ten years. You're too sensitive. Anyway, he didn't really fire you.

BIFF: Well, I think he was going to. I think that's why I quit. I was never sure whether he knew or not. I know he thought the world of me, though. I was the only one he'd let lock up the place.

WILLY (*below*): You gonna wash the engine, Biff?

HAPPY: Shh!

(*Biff looks at Happy, who is gazing down, listening. Willy is mumbling in the parlor.*)

HAPPY: You hear that?

(*They listen. Willy laughs warmly.*)

BIFF (*growing angry*): Doesn't he know Mom can hear that?

WILLY: Don't get your sweater dirty, Biff!

(*A look of pain crosses Biff's face.*)

HAPPY: Isn't that terrible? Don't leave again, will you? You'll find a job here. You gotta stick around. I don't know what to do about him, it's getting embarrassing.

WILLY: What a simonizing job!

BIFF: Mom's hearing that!

WILLY: No kiddin', Biff, you got a date? Wonderful!

HAPPY: Go on to sleep. But talk to him in the morning, will you?

BIFF (*reluctantly getting into bed*): With her in the house. Brother!

HAPPY (*getting into bed*): I wish you'd have a good talk with him.

(*The light on their room begins to fade.*)

BIFF (*to himself in bed*): That selfish, stupid . . .

HAPPY: Sh . . . Sleep, Biff.

(*Their light is out. Well before they have finished speaking, Willy's form is dimly seen below in the darkened kitchen. He opens the refrigerator, searches in there, and takes out a bottle of milk. The apartment houses are fading out, and the entire house and surroundings become covered with leaves. Music insinuates itself as the leaves appear.*)

WILLY: Just wanna be careful with those girls, Biff, that's all. Don't make any promises. No promises of any kind. Because a girl, y'know, they always believe what you tell 'em, and you're very young, Biff, you're too young to be talking seriously to girls.

(*Light rises on the kitchen. Willy, talking, shuts the refrigerator door and comes downstage to the kitchen table. He pours milk into a glass. He is totally immersed in himself, smiling faintly.*)

WILLY: Too young entirely, Biff. You want to watch your schooling first. Then when you're all set, there'll be plenty of girls for a boy like you. (*He smiles broadly at a kitchen chair.*) That so? The girls pay for you? (*He laughs.*) Boy, you must really be makin' a hit.

(*Willy is gradually addressing—physically—a point offstage, speaking through the wall of the kitchen, and his voice has been rising in volume to that of a normal conversation.*)

WILLY: I been wondering why you polish the car so careful. Ha! Don't leave the hubcaps, boys. Get the chamois to the hubcaps. Happy, use newspaper on the windows, it's the easiest thing. Show him how to do it, Biff! You see, Happy? Pad it up, use it like a pad. That's it, that's it, good work. You're doin' all right, Hap. (*He pauses, then nods in approbation for a few seconds, then looks upward.*) Biff, first thing we gotta do when we get time is clip that big branch over the house. Afraid it's gonna fall in a storm and hit the roof. Tell you what. We get a rope and sling her around, and then we climb up there with a couple of saws and take her down. Soon as you finish the car, boys, I wanna see ye. I got a surprise for you, boys.

BIFF (*offstage*): Whatta ya got, Dad?

WILLY: No, you finish first. Never leave a job till you're finished—remember that. (*Looking toward the "big trees."*) Biff, up in Albany I saw a beautiful hammock. I think I'll buy it next trip, and we'll hang it right between those two elms. Wouldn't that be something! Just swingin' there under those branches. Boy, that would be . . .

(*Young Biff and Young Happy appear from the direction Willy was addressing. Happy carries rags and a pail of water. Biff, wearing a sweater with a block "S," carries a football.*)

BIFF (*pointing in the direction of the car offstage*): How's that, Pop, professional?

WILLY: Terrific. Terrific job, boys. Good work, Biff.

HAPPY: Where's the surprise, Pop?

WILLY: In the back seat of the car.

HAPPY: Boy! (*He runs off.*)

BIFF: What is it, Dad? Tell me, what'd you buy?

WILLY (*laughing, cuffs him*): Never mind, something I want you to have.

BIFF (*turns and starts off*): What is it, Hap?

HAPPY (*offstage*): It's a punching bag!

BIFF: Oh, Pop!

WILLY: It's got Gene Tunney's signature on it!

(*Happy runs onstage with a punching bag.*)

BIFF: Gee, how'd you know we wanted a punching bag?

WILLY: Well, it's the finest thing for the timing.

HAPPY (*lies down on his back and pedals with his feet*): I'm losing weight, you notice, Pop?

WILLY (*to Happy*): Jumping rope is good too.

BIFF: Did you see the new football I got?

WILLY (*examining the ball*): Where'd you get a new ball?

BIFF: The coach told me to practice my passing.

WILLY: That so? And he gave you the ball, heh?

BIFF: Well, I borrowed it from the locker room. (*He laughs confidentially.*)

WILLY (*laughing with him at the theft*): I want you to return that.

HAPPY: I told you he wouldn't like it!

BIFF (*angrily*): Well, I'm bringing it back!

WILLY (*stopping the incipient argument, to Happy*): Sure, he's gotta practice with a regulation ball, doesn't he? (*To Biff.*) Coach'll probably congratulate you on your initiative!

BIFF: Oh, he keeps congratulating my initiative all the time, Pop.

WILLY: That's because he likes you. If somebody else took that ball there'd be an uproar. So what's the report, boys, what's the report?

BIFF: Where'd you go this time, Dad? Gee we were lonesome for you.

WILLY (*pleased, puts an arm around each boy and they come down to the apron*): Lonesome, heh?

BIFF: Missed you every minute.

WILLY: Don't say? Tell you a secret, boys. Don't breathe it to a soul. Someday I'll have my own business, and I'll never have to leave home anymore.

HAPPY: Like Uncle Charley, heh?

WILLY: Bigger than Uncle Charley! Because Charley is not liked. He's liked, but he's not—well liked.

BIFF: Where'd you go this time, Dad?

WILLY: Well, I got on the road, and I went north to Providence. Met the Mayor.

BIFF: The Mayor of Providence!

WILLY: He was sitting in the hotel lobby.

BIFF: What'd he say?

WILLY: He said, "Morning!" And I said, "You got a fine city here, Mayor." And then he had coffee with me. And then I went to Waterbury. Waterbury is a fine city. Big clock city, the famous Waterbury clock. Sold a nice bill there. And then Boston—Boston is the cradle of the Revolution. A fine city. And a couple of other towns in Mass., and on to Portland and Bangor and straight home!

BIFF: Gee, I'd love to go with you sometime, Dad.

WILLY: Soon as summer comes.

HAPPY: Promise?

WILLY: You and Hap and I, and I'll show you all the towns. America is full of beautiful towns and fine, upstanding people. And they know me, boys, they

Biff (Kevin Anderson), Willy (Brian Dennehy), and Happy (Ted Koch) in a bright moment in Robert Falls's 1999 Broadway revival of *Death of a Salesman.*

know me up and down New England. The finest people. And when I bring you fellas up, there'll be open sesame for all of us, 'cause one thing, boys: I have friends. I can park my car in any street in New England, and the cops protect it like their own. This summer, heh?

BIFF AND HAPPY (*together*): Yeah! You bet!

WILLY: We'll take our bathing suits.

HAPPY: We'll carry your bags, Pop!

WILLY: Oh, won't that be something! Me comin' into the Boston stores with you boys carryin' my bags. What a sensation!

(*Biff is prancing around, practicing passing the ball.*)

WILLY: You nervous, Biff, about the game?

BIFF: Not if you're gonna be there.

WILLY: What do they say about you in school, now that they made you captain?

HAPPY: There's a crowd of girls behind him every time the classes change.

BIFF (*taking Willy's hand*): This Saturday, Pop, this Saturday—just for you, I'm going to break through for a touchdown.

HAPPY: You're supposed to pass.

BIFF: I'm takin' one play for Pop. You watch me, Pop, and when I take off my helmet, that means I'm breakin' out. Then you watch me crash through that line!

WILLY (*kisses Biff*): Oh, wait'll I tell this in Boston!

(*Bernard enters in knickers. He is younger than Biff, earnest and loyal, a worried boy.*)

BERNARD: Biff, where are you? You're supposed to study with me today.

WILLY: Hey, looka Bernard. What're you lookin' so anemic about, Bernard?

BERNARD: He's gotta study, Uncle Willy. He's got Regents next week.

HAPPY (*tauntingly, spinning Bernard around*): Let's box, Bernard!

BERNARD: Biff! (*He gets away from Happy.*) Listen, Biff, I heard Mr. Birnbaum say that if you don't start studyin' math he's gonna flunk you, and you won't graduate. I heard him!

WILLY: You better study with him, Biff. Go ahead now.

BERNARD: I heard him!

BIFF: Oh, Pop, you didn't see my sneakers! (*He holds up a foot for Willy to look at.*)

WILLY: Hey, that's a beautiful job of printing!

BERNARD (*wiping his glasses*): Just because he printed University of Virginia on his sneakers doesn't mean they've got to graduate him, Uncle Willy!

WILLY (*angrily*): What're you talking about? With scholarships to three universities they're gonna flunk him?

BERNARD: But I heard Mr. Birnbaum say—

WILLY: Don't be a pest, Bernard! (*To his boys.*) What an anemic!

BERNARD: Okay, I'm waiting for you in my house, Biff.

(*Bernard goes off. The Lomans laugh.*)

WILLY: Bernard is not well liked, is he?

BIFF: He's liked, but he's not well liked.

HAPPY: That's right, Pop.

WILLY: That's just what I mean. Bernard can get the best marks in school, y'understand, but when he gets out in the business world, y'understand, you are going to be five times ahead of him. That's why I thank Almighty God you're both built like Adonises. Because the man who makes an appearance in the business world, the man who creates personal interest, is the man who gets ahead. Be liked and you will never want. You take me, for instance. I never have to wait in line to see a buyer. "Willy Loman is here!" That's all they have to know, and I go right through.

BIFF: Did you knock them dead, Pop?

WILLY: Knocked 'em cold in Providence, slaughtered 'em in Boston.

HAPPY (*on his back, pedaling again*): I'm losing weight, you notice, Pop?

(*Linda enters as of old, a ribbon in her hair, carrying a basket of washing.*)

LINDA (*with youthful energy*): Hello, dear!

WILLY: Sweetheart!

LINDA: How'd the Chevvy run?

WILLY: Chevrolet, Linda, is the greatest car ever built. (*To the boys.*) Since when do you let your mother carry wash up the stairs?

BIFF: Grab hold there, boy!

HAPPY: Where to, Mom?

LINDA: Hang them up on the line. And you better go down to your friends, Biff. The cellar is full of boys. They don't know what to do with themselves.

BIFF: Ah, when Pop comes home they can wait!

WILLY (*laughs appreciatively*): You better go down and tell them what to do, Biff.

BIFF: I think I'll have them sweep out the furnace room.

WILLY: Good work, Biff.

BIFF (*goes through wall-line of kitchen to doorway at back and calls down*): Fellas! Everybody sweep out the furnace room! I'll be right down!

VOICES: All right! Okay, Biff.

BIFF: George and Sam and Frank, come out back! We're hangin' up the wash! Come on, Hap, on the double! (*He and Happy carry out the basket.*)

LINDA: The way they obey him!

WILLY: Well, that's training, the training. I'm tellin' you, I was sellin' thousands and thousands, but I had to come home.

LINDA: Oh, the whole block'll be at that game. Did you sell anything?

WILLY: I did five hundred gross in Providence and seven hundred gross in Boston.

LINDA: No! Wait a minute, I've got a pencil. (*She pulls pencil and paper out of her apron pocket.*) That makes your commission ... Two hundred—my God! Two hundred and twelve dollars!

WILLY: Well, I didn't figure it yet, but ...

LINDA: How much did you do?

WILLY: Well, I—I did—about a hundred and eighty gross in Providence. Well, no—it came to—roughly two hundred gross on the whole trip.

LINDA (*without hesitation*): Two hundred gross. That's ... (*She figures.*)

WILLY: The trouble was that three of the stores were half-closed for inventory in Boston. Otherwise I woulda broke records.

LINDA: Well, it makes seventy dollars and some pennies. That's very good.

WILLY: What do we owe?

LINDA: Well, on the first there's sixteen dollars on the refrigerator—

WILLY: Why sixteen?

LINDA: Well, the fan belt broke, so it was a dollar eighty.

WILLY: But it's brand new.

LINDA: Well, the man said that's the way it is. Till they work themselves in, y'know.

(*They move through the wall line into the kitchen.*)

WILLY: I hope we didn't get stuck on that machine.

LINDA: They got the biggest ads of any of them!

WILLY: I know, it's a fine machine. What else?

LINDA: Well, there's nine-sixty for the washing machine. And for the vacuum cleaner there's three and a half due on the fifteenth. Then the roof, you got twenty-one dollars remaining.

WILLY: It don't leak, does it?

LINDA: No, they did a wonderful job. Then you owe Frank for the carburetor.

WILLY: I'm not going to pay that man! That goddam Chevrolet, they ought to prohibit the manufacture of that car!

LINDA: Well, you owe him three and a half. And odds and ends, comes to around a hundred and twenty dollars by the fifteenth.

WILLY: A hundred and twenty dollars! My God, if business don't pick up I don't know what I'm gonna do!

LINDA: Well, next week you'll do better.

WILLY: Oh, I'll knock 'em dead next week. I'll go to Hartford. I'm very well liked in Hartford. You know, the trouble is, Linda, people don't seem to take to me.

(*They move onto the forestage.*)

LINDA: Oh, don't be foolish.

WILLY: I know it when I walk in. They seem to laugh at me.

LINDA: Why? Why would they laugh at you? Don't talk that way, Willy.

(*Willy moves to the edge of the stage. Linda goes into the kitchen and starts to darn stockings.*)

WILLY: I don't know the reason for it, but they just pass me by. I'm not noticed.

LINDA: But you're doing wonderful, dear. You're making seventy to a hundred dollars a week.

WILLY: But I gotta be at it ten, twelve hours a day. Other men—I don't know—they do it easier. I don't know why—I can't stop myself—I talk too much. A man oughta come in with a few words. One thing about Charley. He's a man of few words, and they respect him.

LINDA: You don't talk too much, you're just lively.

WILLY (*smiling*): Well, I figure, what the hell, life is short, a couple of jokes. (*To himself.*) I joke too much! (*The smile goes.*)

LINDA: Why? You're—

WILLY: I'm fat. I'm very—foolish to look at, Linda. I didn't tell you, but Christmas time I happened to be calling on F. H. Stewarts, and a salesman I know, as I was going in to see the buyer I heard him say something about—walrus. And I—I cracked him right across the face. I won't take that. I simply will not take that. But they do laugh at me. I know that.

LINDA: Darling . . .

WILLY: I gotta overcome it. I know I gotta overcome it. I'm not dressing to advantage, maybe.

LINDA: Willy, darling, you're the handsomest man in the world—

WILLY: Oh, no, Linda.

LINDA: To me you are. (*Slight pause.*) The handsomest.

(*From the darkness is heard the laughter of a woman. Willy doesn't turn to it, but it continues through Linda's lines.*)

LINDA: And the boys, Willy. Few men are idolized by their children the way you are.

(*Music is heard as behind a scrim, to the left of the house, The Woman, dimly seen, is dressing.*)

WILLY (*with great feeling*): You're the best there is, Linda, you're a pal, you know that? On the road—on the road I want to grab you sometimes and just kiss the life outa you.

(*The laughter is loud now, and he moves into a brightening area at the left, where The Woman has come from behind the scrim and is standing, putting on her hat, looking into a "mirror" and laughing.*)

WILLY: 'Cause I get so lonely—especially when business is bad and there's nobody to talk to. I get the feeling that I'll never sell anything again, that I won't make a living for you, or a business, a business for the boys. (*He talks through The Woman's subsiding laughter; The Woman primps at the "mirror."*) There's so much I want to make for—

THE WOMAN: Me? You didn't make me, Willy. I picked you.

WILLY (*pleased*): You picked me?

THE WOMAN (*who is quite proper-looking, Willy's age*): I did. I've been sitting at that desk watching all the salesmen go by, day in, day out. But you've got such a sense of humor, and we do have such a good time together, don't we?

WILLY: Sure, sure. (*He takes her in his arms.*) Why do you have to go now?

THE WOMAN: It's two o'clock . . .

WILLY: No, come on in! (*He pulls her.*)

THE WOMAN: . . . my sisters'll be scandalized. When'll you be back?

WILLY: Oh, two weeks about. Will you come up again?

THE WOMAN: Sure thing. You do make me laugh. It's good for me. (*She squeezes his arm, kisses him.*) And I think you're a wonderful man.

WILLY: You picked me, heh?

THE WOMAN: Sure. Because you're so sweet. And such a kidder.

WILLY: Well, I'll see you next time I'm in Boston.

THE WOMAN: I'll put you right through to the buyers.

WILLY (*slapping her bottom*): Right. Well, bottoms up!

THE WOMAN (*slaps him gently and laughs*): You just kill me, Willy. (*He suddenly grabs her and kisses her roughly.*) You kill me. And thanks for the stockings. I love a lot of stockings. Well, good night.

WILLY: Good night. And keep your pores open!

THE WOMAN: Oh, Willy!

(*The Woman bursts out laughing, and Linda's laughter blends in. The Woman disappears into the dark. Now the area at the kitchen table brightens. Linda is sitting where she was at the kitchen table, but now is mending a pair of her silk stockings.*)

LINDA: You are, Willy. The handsomest man. You've got no reason to feel that—

WILLY (*coming out of The Woman's dimming area and going over to Linda*): I'll make it all up to you, Linda, I'll—

LINDA: There's nothing to make up, dear. You're doing fine, better than—

WILLY (*noticing her mending*): What's that?

LINDA: Just mending my stockings. They're so expensive—

WILLY (*angrily, taking them from her*): I won't have you mending stockings in this house! Now throw them out!

(*Linda puts the stockings in her pocket.*)

BERNARD (*entering on the run*): Where is he? If he doesn't study!

WILLY (*moving to the forestage, with great agitation*): You'll give him the answers!

BERNARD: I do, but I can't on a Regents! That's a state exam! They're liable to arrest me!

WILLY: Where is he? I'll whip him, I'll whip him!

LINDA: And he'd better give back that football, Willy, it's not nice.

WILLY: Biff! Where is he? Why is he taking everything?

LINDA: He's too rough with the girls, Willy. All the mothers are afraid of him!

WILLY: I'll whip him!

BERNARD: He's driving the car without a license!

(*The Woman's laugh is heard.*)

WILLY: Shut up!

LINDA: All the mothers—

WILLY: Shut up!

BERNARD (*backing quietly away and out*): Mr. Birnbaum says he's stuck up.

WILLY: Get outa here!

BERNARD: If he doesn't buckle down he'll flunk math! (*He goes off.*)

LINDA: He's right, Willy, you've gotta—

WILLY (*exploding at her*): There's nothing the matter with him! You want him to be a worm like Bernard? He's got spirit, personality . . .

(*As he speaks, Linda, almost in tears, exits into the living room. Willy is alone in the kitchen, wilting and staring. The leaves are gone. It is night again, and the apartment houses look down from behind.*)

WILLY: Loaded with it. Loaded! What is he stealing? He's giving it back, isn't he? Why is he stealing? What did I tell him? I never in my life told him anything but decent things.

(*Happy in pajamas has come down the stairs; Willy suddenly becomes aware of Happy's presence.*)

HAPPY: Let's go now, come on.

WILLY (*sitting down at the kitchen table*): Huh! Why did she have to wax the floors herself? Everytime she waxes the floors she keels over. She knows that!

HAPPY: Shh! Take it easy. What brought you back tonight?

WILLY: I got an awful scare. Nearly hit a kid in Yonkers. God! Why didn't I go to Alaska with my brother Ben that time! Ben! That man was a genius, that man was success incarnate! What a mistake! He begged me to go.

HAPPY: Well, there's no use in—

WILLY: You guys! There was a man started with the clothes on his back and ended up with diamond mines!

HAPPY: Boy, someday I'd like to know how he did it.

WILLY: What's the mystery? The man knew what he wanted and went out and got it! Walked into a jungle, and comes out, the age of twenty-one, and he's rich! The world is an oyster, but you don't crack it open on a mattress!

HAPPY: Pop, I told you I'm gonna retire you for life.

WILLY: You'll retire me for life on seventy goddam dollars a week? And your women and your car and your apartment, and you'll retire me for life! Christ's sake, I couldn't get past Yonkers today! Where are you guys, where are you? The woods are burning! I can't drive a car!

(*Charley has appeared in the doorway. He is a large man, slow of speech, laconic, immovable. In all he says, despite what he says, there is pity, and, now, trepidation. He has a robe over pajamas, slippers on his feet. He enters the kitchen.*)

CHARLEY: Everything all right?

HAPPY: Yeah, Charley, everything's . . .

WILLY: What's the matter?

CHARLEY: I heard some noise. I thought something happened. Can't we do something about the walls? You sneeze in here, and in my house hats blow off.

HAPPY: Let's go to bed, Dad. Come on.

(*Charley signals to Happy to go.*)

WILLY: You go ahead, I'm not tired at the moment.

HAPPY (*to Willy*): Take it easy, huh? (*He exits.*)

WILLY: What're you doin' up?

CHARLEY (*sitting down at the kitchen table opposite Willy*): Couldn't sleep good. I had a heartburn.

WILLY: Well, you don't know how to eat.

CHARLEY: I eat with my mouth.

WILLY: No, you're ignorant. You gotta know about vitamins and things like that.

CHARLEY: Come on, let's shoot. Tire you out a little.

WILLY (*hesitantly*): All right. You got cards?

CHARLEY (*taking a deck from his pocket*): Yeah, I got them. Someplace. What is it with those vitamins?

WILLY (*dealing*): They build up your bones. Chemistry.

CHARLEY: Yeah, but there's no bones in a heartburn.

WILLY: What are you talkin' about? Do you know the first thing about it?

CHARLEY: Don't get insulted.

WILLY: Don't talk about something you don't know anything about.

(*They are playing. Pause.*)

CHARLEY: What're you doin' home?

WILLY: A little trouble with the car.

CHARLEY: Oh. (*Pause.*) I'd like to take a trip to California.

WILLY: Don't say.

CHARLEY: You want a job?

WILLY: I got a job, I told you that. (*After a slight pause.*) What the hell are you offering me a job for?

CHARLEY: Don't get insulted.

WILLY: Don't insult me.

CHARLEY: I don't see no sense in it. You don't have to go on this way.

WILLY: I got a good job. (*Slight pause.*) What do you keep comin' in here for?

CHARLEY: You want me to go?

WILLY (*after a pause, withering*): I can't understand it. He's going back to Texas again. What the hell is that?

CHARLEY: Let him go.

WILLY: I got nothin' to give him, Charley, I'm clean, I'm clean.

CHARLEY: He won't starve. None a them starve. Forget about him.

WILLY: Then what have I got to remember?

CHARLEY: You take it too hard. To hell with it. When a deposit bottle is broken you don't get your nickel back.

WILLY: That's easy enough for you to say.

CHARLEY: That ain't easy for me to say.

WILLY: Did you see the ceiling I put up in the living room?

CHARLEY: Yeah, that's a piece of work. To put up a ceiling is a mystery to me. How do you do it?

WILLY: What's the difference?

CHARLEY: Well, talk about it.

WILLY: You gonna put up a ceiling?

CHARLEY: How could I put up a ceiling?

WILLY: Then what the hell are you bothering me for?

CHARLEY: You're insulted again.

WILLY: A man who can't handle tools is not a man. You're disgusting.

CHARLEY: Don't call me disgusting, Willy.

(*Uncle Ben, carrying a valise and an umbrella, enters the forestage from around the right corner of the house. He is a stolid man, in his sixties, with a mustache and an authoritative air. He is utterly certain of his destiny, and there is an aura of far places about him. He enters exactly as Willy speaks.*)

WILLY: I'm getting awfully tired, Ben.

(*Ben's music is heard. Ben looks around at everything.*)

CHARLEY: Good, keep playing; you'll sleep better. Did you call me Ben?

(*Ben looks at his watch.*)

WILLY: That's funny. For a second there you reminded me of my brother Ben.

BEN: I only have a few minutes. (*He strolls, inspecting the place. Willy and Charley continue playing.*)

CHARLEY: You never heard from him again, heh? Since that time?

WILLY: Didn't Linda tell you? Couple of weeks ago we got a letter from his wife in Africa. He died.

CHARLEY: That so.

BEN (*chuckling*): So this is Brooklyn, eh?

CHARLEY: Maybe you're in for some of his money.

WILLY: Naa, he had seven sons. There's just one opportunity I had with that man . . .

BEN: I must make a train, William. There are several properties I'm looking at in Alaska.

WILLY: Sure, sure! If I'd gone with him to Alaska that time, everything would've been totally different.

CHARLIE: Go on, you'd froze to death up there.

WILLY: What're you talking about?

BEN: Opportunity is tremendous in Alaska, William. Surprised you're not up there.

WILLY: Sure, tremendous.

CHARLEY: Heh?

WILLY: There was the only man I ever met who knew the answers.

CHARLEY: Who?

BEN: How are you all?

WILLY (*taking a pot, smiling*): Fine, fine.

CHARLEY: Pretty sharp tonight.

BEN: Is Mother living with you?

WILLY: No, she died a long time ago.

CHARLEY: Who?

BEN: That's too bad. Fine specimen of a lady, Mother.

WILLY (*to Charley*): Heh?

BEN: I'd hoped to see the old girl.

CHARLEY: Who died?

BEN: Heard anything from Father, have you?

WILLY (*unnerved*): What do you mean, who died?

CHARLEY (*taking a pot*): What're you talkin' about?

BEN (*looking at his watch*): William, it's half-past eight!

WILLY (*as though to dispel his confusion he angrily stops Charley's hand*): That's my build!

CHARLEY: I put the ace—

WILLY: If you don't know how to play the game I'm not gonna throw my money away on you!

CHARLEY (*rising*): It was my ace, for God's sake!

WILLY: I'm through, I'm through!

BEN: When did Mother die?

WILLY: Long ago. Since the beginning you never knew how to play cards.

CHARLEY (*picks up the cards and goes to the door*): All right! Next time I'll bring a deck with five aces.

WILLY: I don't play that kind of game!

CHARLEY (*turning to him*): You ought to be ashamed of yourself!

WILLY: Yeah?

CHARLEY: Yeah! (*He goes out.*)

WILLY (*slamming the door after him*): Ignoramus!

BEN (*as Willy comes toward him through the wall-line of the kitchen*): So you're William.

WILLY (*shaking Ben's hand*): Ben! I've been waiting for you so long! What's the answer? How did you do it?

BEN: Oh, there's a story in that.

(*Linda enters the forestage, as of old, carrying the wash basket.*)

LINDA: Is this Ben?

BEN (*gallantly*): How do you do, my dear.

LINDA: Where've you been all these years? Willy's always wondered why you—

WILLY (*pulling Ben away from her impatiently*): Where is Dad? Didn't you follow him? How did you get started?

BEN: Well, I don't know how much you remember.

WILLY: Well, I was just a baby, of course, only three or four years old—

BEN: Three years and eleven months.

WILLY: What a memory, Ben!

BEN: I have many enterprises, William, and I have never kept books.

WILLY: I remember I was sitting under the wagon in—was it Nebraska?

BEN: It was South Dakota, and I gave you a bunch of wild flowers.

WILLY: I remember you walking away down some open road.

BEN (*laughing*): I was going to find Father in Alaska.

WILLY: Where is he?

BEN: At that age I had a very faulty view of geography, William. I discovered after a few days that I was heading due south, so instead of Alaska, I ended up in Africa.

LINDA: Africa!

WILLY: The Gold Coast!

BEN: Principally diamond mines.

LINDA: Diamond mines!

BEN: Yes, my dear. But I've only a few minutes—

WILLY: No! Boys! Boys! (*Young Biff and Happy appear.*) Listen to this. This is your Uncle Ben, a great man! Tell my boys, Ben!

BEN: Why, boys, when I was seventeen I walked into the jungle, and when I was twenty-one I walked out. (*He laughs.*) And by God I was rich.

WILLY (*to the boys*): You see what I been talking about? The greatest things can happen!

BEN (*glancing at his watch*): I have an appointment in Ketchikan Tuesday week.

WILLY: No, Ben! Please tell about Dad. I want my boys to hear. I want them to know the kind of stock they spring from. All I remember is a man with a big beard, and I was in Mamma's lap, sitting around a fire, and some kind of high music.

BEN: His flute. He played the flute.

WILLY: Sure, the flute, that's right!

(*New music is heard, a high, rollicking tune.*)

BEN: Father was a very great and a very wild-hearted man. We would start in Boston, and he'd toss the whole family into the wagon, and then he'd drive the team right across the country; through Ohio, and Indiana, Michigan, Illinois, and all the Western states. And we'd stop in the towns and sell the flutes that he'd made on the way. Great inventor Father. With one gadget he made more in a week than a man like you could make in a lifetime.

WILLY: That's just the way I'm bringing them up, Ben— rugged, well liked, all-around.

BEN: Yeah? (*To Biff.*) Hit that, boy—hard as you can. (*He pounds his stomach.*)

BIFF: Oh, no, sir!

BEN (*taking boxing stance*): Come on, get to me! (*He laughs.*)

WILLY: Go to it, Biff! Go ahead, show him!

BIFF: Okay! (*He cocks his fists and starts in.*)

LINDA (*to Willy*): Why must he fight, dear?

BEN (*sparring with Biff*): Good boy! Good boy!

WILLY: How's that, Ben, heh?

HAPPY: Give him the left, Biff!

LINDA: Why are you fighting?

BEN: Good boy! (*Suddenly comes in, trips Biff, and stands over him, the point of his umbrella poised over Biff's eye.*)

LINDA: Look out, Biff!

BIFF: Gee!

BEN (*patting Biff's knee*): Never fight fair with a stranger, boy. You'll never get out of the jungle that way. (*Taking Linda's hand and bowing.*) It was an honor and a pleasure to meet you, Linda.

LINDA (*withdrawing her hand coldly, frightened*): Have a nice—trip.

BEN (*to Willy*): And good luck with your—what do you do?

WILLY: Selling.

BEN: Yes. Well . . . (*He raises his hand in farewell to all.*)

WILLY: No, Ben, I don't want you to think . . . (*He takes Ben's arm to show him.*) It's Brooklyn, I know, but we hunt too.

BEN: Really, now.

WILLY: Oh, sure, there's snakes and rabbits and—that's why I moved out here. Why, Biff can fell any one of these trees in no time! Boys! Go right over to where they're building the apartment house and get some sand. We're gonna rebuild the entire front stoop right now! Watch this, Ben!

BIFF: Yes, sir! On the double, Hap!

HAPPY (*as he and Biff run off*): I lost weight, Pop, you notice?

(*Charley enters in knickers, even before the boys are gone.*)

CHARLEY: Listen, if they steal any more from that building the watchman'll put the cops on them!

LINDA (*to Willy*): Don't let Biff . . .

(*Ben laughs lustily.*)

WILLY: You shoulda seen the lumber they brought home last week. At least a dozen six-by-tens worth all kinds a money.

CHARLEY: Listen, if that watchman—

WILLY: I gave them hell, understand. But I got a couple of fearless characters there.

CHARLEY: Willy, the jails are full of fearless characters.

BEN (*clapping Willy on the back, with a laugh at Charley*): And the stock exchange, friend!

WILLY (*joining in Ben's laughter*): Where are the rest of your pants?

CHARLEY: My wife bought them.

WILLY: Now all you need is a golf club and you can go upstairs and go to sleep. (*To Ben.*) Great athlete! Between him and his son Bernard they can't hammer a nail!

BERNARD (*rushing in*): The watchman's chasing Biff!

WILLY (*angrily*): Shut up! He's not stealing anything!

LINDA (*alarmed, hurrying off left*): Where is he? Biff, dear! (*She exits.*)

WILLY (*moving toward the left, away from Ben*): There's nothing wrong. What's the matter with you?

BEN: Nervy boy. Good!

WILLY (*laughing*): Oh, nerves of iron, that Biff!

CHARLEY: Don't know what it is. My New England man comes back and he's bleedin', they murdered him up there.

WILLY: It's contacts, Charley, I got important contacts!

CHARLEY (*sarcastically*): Glad to hear it, Willy. Come in later, we'll shoot a little casino. I'll take some of your Portland money. (*He laughs at Willy and exits.*)

WILLY (*turning to Ben*): Business is bad, it's murderous. But not for me, of course.

BEN: I'll stop by on my way back to Africa.

WILLY (*longingly*): Can't you stay a few days? You're just what I need, Ben, because I—I have a fine position here, but I—well, Dad left when I was such a baby and I never had a chance to talk to him and I still feel—kind of temporary about myself.

BEN: I'll be late for my train.

(*They are at opposite ends of the stage.*)

WILLY: Ben, my boys—can't we talk? They'd go into the jaws of hell for me, see, but I—

BEN: William, you're being first-rate with your boys. Outstanding, manly chaps!

WILLY (*hanging on to his words*): Oh, Ben, that's good to hear! Because sometimes I'm afraid that I'm not teaching them the right kind of—Ben, how should I teach them?

BEN (*giving great weight to each word, and with a certain vicious audacity*): William, when I walked into the jungle, I was seventeen. When I walked out I was twenty-one. And, by God, I was rich! (*He goes off into darkness around the right corner of the house.*)

WILLY: . . . was rich! That's just the spirit I want to imbue them with! To walk into a jungle! I was right! I was right! I was right!

(*Ben is gone, but Willy is still speaking to him as Linda, in nightgown and robe, enters the kitchen, glances around for Willy, then goes to the door of the house, looks out and sees him. Comes down to his left. He looks at her.*)

LINDA: Willy, dear? Willy?

WILLY: I was right!

LINDA: Did you have some cheese? (*He can't answer.*) It's very late, darling. Come to bed, heh?

WILLY (*looking straight up*): Gotta break your neck to see a star in this yard.

LINDA: You coming in?

WILLY: Whatever happened to that diamond watch fob? Remember? When Ben came from Africa that time? Didn't he give me a watch fob with a diamond in it?

LINDA: You pawned it, dear. Twelve, thirteen years ago. For Biff's radio correspondence course.

WILLY: Gee, that was a beautiful thing. I'll take a walk.

LINDA: But you're in your slippers.

WILLY (*starting to go around the house at the left*): I was right! I was! (*Half to Linda, as he goes, shaking his head.*) What a man! There was a man worth talking to. I was right!

LINDA (*calling after Willy*): But in your slippers, Willy!

(*Willy is almost gone when Biff, in his pajamas, comes down the stairs and enters the kitchen.*)

BIFF: What is he doing out there?

LINDA: Sh!

BIFF: God Almighty, Mom, how long has he been doing this?

LINDA: Don't, he'll hear you.

BIFF: What the hell is the matter with him?

LINDA: It'll pass by morning.

BIFF: Shouldn't we do anything?

LINDA: Oh, my dear, you should do a lot of things, but there's nothing to do, so go to sleep.

(*Happy comes down the stair and sits on the steps.*)

HAPPY: I never heard him so loud, Mom.

LINDA: Well, come around more often, you'll hear him. (*She sits down at the table and mends the lining of Willy's jacket.*)

BIFF: Why didn't you ever write me about this, Mom?

LINDA: How would I write to you? For over three months you had no address.

BIFF: I was on the move. But you know I thought of you all the time. You know that, don't you, pal?

LINDA: I know, dear, I know. But he likes to have a letter. Just to know that there's still a possibility for better things.

BIFF: He's not like this all the time, is he?

LINDA: It's when you come home he's always the worst.

BIFF: When I come home?

LINDA: When you write you're coming, he's all smiles and talks about the future, and—he's just wonderful. And then the closer you seem to come, the more shaky he gets, and then, by the time you get here, he's arguing, and he seems angry at you. I think it's just that maybe he can't bring himself to—to open up to you. Why are you so hateful to each other? Why is that?

BIFF (*evasively*): I'm not hateful, Mom.

LINDA: But you no sooner come in the door than you're fighting!

BIFF: I don't know why. I mean to change. I'm tryin', Mom, you understand?

LINDA: Are you home to stay now?

BIFF: I don't know. I want to look around, see what's goin'.

LINDA: Biff, you can't look around all your life, can you?

BIFF: I just can't take hold, Mom. I can't take hold of some kind of a life.

LINDA: Biff, a man is not a bird, to come and go with the springtime.

BIFF: Your hair . . . (*He touches her hair.*) Your hair got so gray.

LINDA: Oh, it's been gray since you were in high school. I just stopped dyeing it, that's all.

BIFF: Dye it again, will ye? I don't want my pal looking old. (*He smiles.*)

LINDA: You're such a boy! You think you can go away for a year and . . . You've got to get it into your head now that one day you'll knock on this door and there'll be strange people here—

BIFF: What are you talking about? You're not even sixty, Mom.

LINDA: But what about your father?

BIFF (*lamely*): Well, I meant him too.

HAPPY: He admires Pop.

LINDA: Biff, dear, if you don't have any feeling for him, then you can't have any feeling for me.

BIFF: Sure I can, Mom.

LINDA: No. You can't just come to see me, because I love him. (*With a threat, but only a threat, of tears.*) He's the dearest man in the world to me, and I won't have anyone making him feel unwanted and low and blue. You've got to make up your mind now, darling, there's no leeway any more. Either he's your father and you pay him that respect, or else you're not to come here. I know he's not easy to get along with—nobody knows that better than me—but . . .

WILLY (*from the left, with a laugh*): Hey, hey, Biffo!

BIFF (*starting to go out after Willy*): What the hell is the matter with him? (*Happy stops him.*)

LINDA: Don't—don't go near him!

BIFF: Stop making excuses for him! He always, always wiped the floor with you. Never had an ounce of respect for you.

HAPPY: He's always had respect for—

BIFF: What the hell do you know about it?

HAPPY (*surlily*): Just don't call him crazy!

BIFF: He's got no character—Charley wouldn't do this. Not in his own house—spewing out that vomit from his mind.

HAPPY: Charley never had to cope with what he's got to.

BIFF: People are worse off than Willy Loman. Believe me, I've seen them!

LINDA: Then make Charley your father, Biff. You can't do that, can you? I don't say he's a great man. Willy Loman never made a lot of money. His name was never in the paper. He's not the finest character that ever lived. But he's a human being, and a terrible thing is happening to him. So attention must be paid. He's not to be allowed to fall into his grave like an old dog. Attention, attention must be finally paid to such a person. You called him crazy—

BIFF: I didn't mean—

LINDA: No, a lot of people think he's lost his—balance. But you don't have to be very smart to know what his trouble is. The man is exhausted.

HAPPY: Sure!

LINDA: A small man can be just as exhausted as a great man. He works for a company thirty-six years this March, opens up unheard-of territories to their trademark, and now in his old age they take his salary away.

HAPPY (*indignantly*): I didn't know that, Mom.

LINDA: You never asked, my dear! Now that you get your spending money someplace else you don't trouble your mind with him.

HAPPY: But I gave you money last—

LINDA: Christmas time, fifty dollars! To fix the hot water it cost ninety-seven fifty! For five weeks he's been on straight commission, like a beginner, an unknown!

BIFF: Those ungrateful bastards!

LINDA: Are they any worse than his sons? When he brought them business, when he was young, they were glad to see him. But now his old friends, the old buyers that loved him so and always found some order to hand him in a pinch—they're all dead, retired. He used to be able to make six, seven calls a day in Boston. Now he takes his valises out of the car and puts them back and takes them out again and he's exhausted. Instead of walking he talks now. He

drives seven hundred miles, and when he gets there no one knows him anymore, no one welcomes him. And what goes through a man's mind, driving seven hundred miles home without having earned a cent? Why shouldn't he talk to himself? Why? When he has to go to Charley and borrow fifty dollars a week and pretend to me that it's his pay? How long can that go on? How long? You see what I'm sitting here and waiting for? And you tell me he has no character? The man who never worked a day but for your benefit? When does he get the medal for that? Is this his reward—to turn around at the age of sixty-three and find his sons, who he loved better than his life, one a philandering bum—

HAPPY: Mom!

LINDA: That's all you are, my baby! (*To Biff.*) And you! What happened to the love you had for him? You were such pals! How you used to talk to him on the phone every night! How lonely he was till he could come home to you!

BIFF: All right, Mom. I'll live here in my room, and I'll get a job. I'll keep away from him, that's all.

LINDA: No, Biff. You can't stay here and fight all the time.

BIFF: He threw me out of this house, remember that.

LINDA: Why did he do that? I never knew why.

BIFF: Because I know he's a fake and he doesn't like anybody around who knows!

LINDA: Why a fake? In what way? What do you mean?

BIFF: Just don't lay it all at my feet. It's between me and him—that's all I have to say. I'll chip in from now on. He'll settle for half my pay check. He'll be all right. I'm going to bed. (*He starts for the stairs.*)

LINDA: He won't be all right.

BIFF (*turning on the stairs, furiously*): I hate this city and I'll stay here. Now what do you want?

LINDA: He's dying, Biff.

(*Happy turns quickly to her, shocked.*)

BIFF (*after a pause*): Why is he dying?

LINDA: He's been trying to kill himself.

BIFF (*with great horror*): How?

LINDA: I live from day to day.

BIFF: What're you talking about?

LINDA: Remember I wrote you that he smashed up the car again? In February?

BIFF: Well?

LINDA: The insurance inspector came. He said that they have evidence. That all these accidents in the last year—weren't—weren't—accidents.

HAPPY: How can they tell that? That's a lie.

LINDA: It seems there's a woman . . . (*She takes a breath as*)

BIFF (*sharply but contained*): ⎫ What woman?
LINDA (*simultaneously*): ⎬ . . . and this woman . . .

LINDA: What?

BIFF: Nothing. Go ahead.

LINDA: What did you say?

BIFF: Nothing. I just said what woman?

HAPPY: What about her?

LINDA: Well, it seems she was walking down the road and saw his car. She says that he wasn't driving fast at all, and that he didn't skid. She says he came to that little bridge, and then deliberately smashed into the railing, and it was only the shallowness of the water that saved him.

BIFF: Oh, no, he probably just fell asleep again.

LINDA: I don't think he fell asleep.

BIFF: Why not?

LINDA: Last month . . . (*With great difficulty.*) Oh, boys, it's so hard to say a thing like this! He's just a big stupid man to you, but I tell you there's more good in him than in many other people. (*She chokes, wipes her eyes.*) I was looking for a fuse. The lights blew out, and I went down the cellar. And behind the fuse box—it happened to fall out—was a length of rubber pipe—just short.

HAPPY: No kidding!

LINDA: There's a little attachment on the end of it. I knew right away. And sure enough, on the bottom of the water heater there's a new little nipple on the gas pipe.

HAPPY (*angrily*): That—jerk.

BIFF: Did you have it taken off?

LINDA: I'm—I'm ashamed to. How can I mention it to him? Every day I go down and take away that little rubber pipe. But, when he comes home, I put it back where it was. How can I insult him that way? I don't know what to do. I live from day to day, boys. I tell you, I know every thought in his mind. It sounds so old-fashioned and silly, but I tell you he put his whole life into you and you've turned your backs on him. (*She is bent over in the chair, weeping, her face in her hands.*) Biff, I swear to God! Biff, his life is in your hands!

HAPPY (*to Biff*): How do you like that damned fool!

BIFF (*kissing her*): All right, pal, all right. It's all settled now. I've been remiss. I know that, Mom. But now I'll stay, and I swear to you, I'll apply myself. (*Kneeling in front of her, in a fever of self-reproach.*) It's just—you see, Mom, I don't fit in business. Not that I won't try. I'll try, and I'll make good.

HAPPY: Sure you will. The trouble with you in business was you never tried to please people.

BIFF: I know, I—

HAPPY: Like when you worked for Harrison's. Bob Harrison said you were tops, and then you go and do some damn fool thing like whistling whole songs in the elevator like a comedian.

BIFF (*against Happy*): So what? I like to whistle sometimes.

HAPPY: You don't raise a guy to a responsible job who whistles in the elevator!

LINDA: Well, don't argue about it now.

HAPPY: Like when you'd go off and swim in the middle of the day instead of taking the line around.

BIFF (*his resentment rising*): Well, don't you run off? You take off sometimes, don't you? On a nice summer day?

HAPPY: Yeah, but I cover myself!

LINDA: Boys!

HAPPY: If I'm going to take a fade the boss can call any number where I'm supposed to be and they'll swear to him that I just left. I'll tell you something that I hate to say, Biff, but in the business world some of them think you're crazy.

BIFF (*angered*): Screw the business world!

HAPPY: All right, screw it! Great, but cover yourself!

LINDA: Hap, Hap!

BIFF: I don't care what they think! They've laughed at Dad for years, and you know why? Because we don't belong in this nuthouse of a city! We should be mixing cement on some open plain, or—or carpenters. A carpenter is allowed to whistle!

(*Willy walks in from the entrance of the house, at left.*)

WILLY: Even your grandfather was better than a carpenter. (*Pause. They watch him.*) You never grew up. Bernard does not whistle in the elevator, I assure you.

BIFF (*as though to laugh Willy out of it*): Yeah, but you do, Pop.

WILLY: I never in my life whistled in an elevator! And who in the business world thinks I'm crazy?

BIFF: I didn't mean it like that, Pop. Now don't make a whole thing out of it, will ye?

WILLY: Go back to the West! Be a carpenter, a cowboy, enjoy yourself!

LINDA: Willy, he was just saying—

WILLY: I heard what he said!

HAPPY (*trying to quiet Willy*): Hey, Pop, come on now . . .

WILLY (*continuing over Happy's line*): They laugh at me, heh? Go to Filene's, go to the Hub, go to Slattery's, Boston. Call out the name Willy Loman and see what happens! Big shot!

BIFF: All right, Pop.

WILLY: Big!

BIFF: All right!

WILLY: Why do you always insult me?

BIFF: I didn't say a word. (*To Linda.*) Did I say a word?

LINDA: He didn't say anything, Willy.

WILLY (*going to the doorway of the living room*): All right, good night, good night.

LINDA: Willy, dear, he just decided . . .

WILLY (*to Biff*): If you get tired hanging around tomorrow, paint the ceiling I put up in the living room.

BIFF: I'm leaving early tomorrow.

HAPPY: He's going to see Bill Oliver, Pop.

WILLY (*interestedly*): Oliver? For what?

BIFF (*with reserve, but trying, trying*): He always said he'd stake me. I'd like to go into business, so maybe I can take him up on it.

LINDA: Isn't that wonderful?

WILLY: Don't interrupt. What's wonderful about it? There's fifty men in the City of New York who'd stake him. (*To Biff.*) Sporting goods?

BIFF: I guess so. I know something about it and—

WILLY: He knows something about it! You know sporting goods better than Spalding, for God's sake! How much is he giving you?

BIFF: I don't know, I didn't even see him yet, but—

WILLY: Then what're you talkin' about?

BIFF (*getting angry*): Well, all I said was I'm gonna see him, that's all!

WILLY (*turning away*): Ah, you're counting your chickens again.

BIFF (*starting left for the stairs*): Oh, Jesus, I'm going to sleep!

WILLY (*calling after him*): Don't curse in this house!

BIFF (*turning*): Since when did you get so clean?

HAPPY (*trying to stop them*): Wait a . . .

WILLY: Don't use that language to me! I won't have it!

HAPPY (*grabbing Biff, shouts*): Wait a minute! I got an idea. I got a feasible idea. Come here, Biff, let's talk this over now, let's talk some sense here. When I was down in Florida last time, I thought of a great idea to sell sporting goods. It just came back to me. You and I, Biff—we have a line, the Loman Line. We train a couple of weeks, and put on a couple of exhibitions, see?

WILLY: That's an idea!

HAPPY: Wait! We form two basketball teams, see? Two water polo teams. We play each other. It's a million dollars' worth of publicity. Two brothers, see? The Loman Brothers. Displays in the Royal Palms—all the hotels. And banners over the ring and the basketball court: "Loman Brothers." Baby, we could sell sporting goods!

WILLY: That is a one-million-dollar idea!

LINDA: Marvelous!

BIFF: I'm in great shape as far as that's concerned.

HAPPY: And the beauty of it is, Biff, it wouldn't be like a business. We'd be out playin' ball again . . .

BIFF (*enthused*): Yeah, that's . . .

WILLY: Million-dollar . . .

HAPPY: And you wouldn't get fed up with it, Biff. It'd be the family again. There'd be the old honor, and comradeship, and if you wanted to go off for a swim or somethin'—well, you'd do it! Without some smart cooky gettin' up ahead of you!

WILLY: Lick the world! You guys together could absolutely lick the civilized world.

BIFF: I'll see Oliver tomorrow. Hap, if we could work that out . . .

LINDA: Maybe things are beginning to—

WILLY (*wildly enthused, to Linda*): Stop interrupting! (*To Biff.*) But don't wear sport jacket and slacks when you see Oliver.

BIFF: No, I'll—

WILLY: A business suit, and talk as little as possible, and don't crack any jokes.

BIFF: He did like me. Always liked me.

LINDA: He loved you!

WILLY (*to Linda*): Will you stop! (*To Biff.*) Walk in very serious. You are not applying for a boy's job. Money is to pass. Be quiet, fine, and serious. Everybody likes a kidder, but nobody lends him money.

HAPPY: I'll try to get some myself, Biff. I'm sure I can.

WILLY: I see great things for you kids, I think your troubles are over. But remember, start big and you'll end big. Ask for fifteen. How much you gonna ask for?

BIFF: Gee, I don't know—

WILLY: And don't say "Gee." "Gee" is a boy's word. A man walking in for fifteen thousand dollars does not say "Gee!"

BIFF: Ten, I think, would be top though.

WILLY: Don't be so modest. You always started too low. Walk in with a big laugh. Don't look worried. Start off with a couple of your good stories to lighten things up. It's not what you say, it's how you say it—because personality always wins the day.

LINDA: Oliver always thought the highest of him—

WILLY: Will you let me talk?

BIFF: Don't yell at her, Pop, will ye?

WILLY (*angrily*): I was talking, wasn't I?

BIFF: I don't like you yelling at her all the time, and I'm tellin' you, that's all.

WILLY: What're you, takin' over this house?

LINDA: Willy—

WILLY (*turning to her*): Don't take his side all the time, goddammit!

BIFF (*furiously*): Stop yelling at her!

WILLY (*suddenly pulling on his cheek, beaten down, guilt ridden*): Give my best to Bill Oliver—he may remember me. (*He exits through the living room doorway.*)

LINDA (*her voice subdued*): What'd you have to start that for? (*Biff turns away.*) You see how sweet he was as soon as you talked hopefully? (*She goes over to Biff.*) Come up and say good night to him. Don't let him go to bed that way.

HAPPY: Come on, Biff, let's buck him up.

LINDA: Please, dear. Just say good night. It takes so little to make him happy. Come. (*She goes through the living room doorway, calling upstairs from within the living room.*) Your pajamas are hanging in the bathroom, Willy!

HAPPY (*looking toward where Linda went out*): What a woman! They broke the mold when they made her. You know that, Biff?

BIFF: He's off salary. My God, working on commission!

HAPPY: Well, let's face it: he's no hot-shot selling man. Except that sometimes, you have to admit, he's a sweet personality.

BIFF (*deciding*): Lend me ten bucks, will ye? I want to buy some new ties.

HAPPY: I'll take you to a place I know. Beautiful stuff. Wear one of my striped shirts tomorrow.

BIFF: She got gray. Mom got awful old. Gee, I'm gonna go in to Oliver tomorrow and knock him for a—

HAPPY: Come on up. Tell that to Dad. Let's give him a whirl. Come on.

BIFF (*steamed up*): You know, with ten thousand bucks, boy!

HAPPY (*as they go into the living room*): That's the talk, Biff, that's the first time I've heard the old confidence out of you! (*From within the living room, fading off.*) You're gonna live with me, kid, and any babe you want just say the word . . . (*The last lines are hardly heard. They are mounting the stairs to their parents' bedroom.*)

LINDA (*entering her bedroom and addressing Willy, who is in the bathroom. She is straightening the bed for him.*): Can you do anything about the shower? It drips.

WILLY (*from the bathroom*): All of a sudden everything falls to pieces. Goddam plumbing, oughta be sued, those people. I hardly finished putting it in and the thing . . . (*His words rumble off.*)

LINDA: I'm just wondering if Oliver will remember him. You think he might?

WILLY (*coming out of the bathroom in his pajamas*): Remember him? What's the matter with you, you crazy? If he'd've stayed with Oliver he'd be on top by now! Wait'll Oliver gets a look at him. You don't know the average caliber any more. The average young man today—(*he is getting into bed*)—is got a caliber of zero. Greatest thing in the world for him was to bum around.

(*Biff and Happy enter the bedroom. Slight pause.*)

WILLY (*stops short, looking at Biff*): Glad to hear it, boy.

HAPPY: He wanted to say good night to you, sport.

WILLY (*to Biff*): Yeah. Knock him dead, boy. What'd you want to tell me?

BIFF: Just take it easy, Pop. Good night. (*He turns to go.*)

WILLY (*unable to resist*): And if anything falls off the desk while you're talking to him—like a package or something—don't you pick it up. They have office boys for that.

LINDA: I'll make a big breakfast—

WILLY: Will you let me finish? (*To Biff.*) Tell him you were in the business in the West. Not farm work.

BIFF: All right, Dad.

LINDA: I think everything—

WILLY (*going right through her speech*): And don't undersell yourself. No less than fifteen thousand dollars.

BIFF (*unable to bear him*): Okay. Good night, Mom. (*He starts moving.*)

WILLY: Because you got a greatness in you, Biff, remember that. You got all kinds of greatness . . . (*He lies back, exhausted. Biff walks out.*)

LINDA (*calling after Biff*): Sleep well, darling!

HAPPY: I'm gonna get married, Mom. I wanted to tell you.

LINDA: Go to sleep, dear.

HAPPY (*going*): I just wanted to tell you.

WILLY: Keep up the good work. (*Happy exits.*) God . . . remember that Ebbets Field game? The championship of the city?

LINDA: Just rest. Should I sing to you?

WILLY: Yeah. Sing to me. (*Linda hums a soft lullaby.*) When that team came out—he was the tallest, remember?

LINDA: Oh, yes. And in gold.

(*Biff enters the darkened kitchen, takes a cigarette, and leaves the house. He comes downstage into a golden pool of light. He smokes, staring at the night.*)

WILLY: Like a young god. Hercules—something like that. And the sun, the sun all around him. Remember how he waved to me? Right up from the field, with the representatives of three colleges standing by? And the buyers I brought, and the cheers when he came out—Loman, Loman, Loman! God Almighty, he'll be great yet. A star like that, magnificent, can never really fade away!

(*The light on Willy is fading. The gas heater begins to glow through the kitchen wall, near the stairs, a blue flame beneath red coils.*)

LINDA (*timidly*): Willy dear, what has he got against you?

WILLY: I'm so tired. Don't talk anymore.

(*Biff slowly returns to the kitchen. He stops, stares toward the heater.*)

LINDA: Will you ask Howard to let you work in New York?

WILLY: First thing in the morning. Everything'll be all right.

(*Biff reaches behind the heater and draws out a length of rubber tubing. He is horrified and turns his head toward Willy's room, still dimly lit, from which the strains of Linda's desperate but monotonous humming rise.*)

WILLY (*staring through the window into the moonlight*): Gee, look at the moon moving between the buildings!

(*Biff wraps the tubing around his hand and quickly goes up the stairs.*)

ACT II

(*Music is heard, gay and bright. The curtain rises as the music fades away. Willy, in shirt sleeves, is sitting at the kitchen table, sipping coffee, his hat in his lap. Linda is filling his cup when she can.*)

WILLY: Wonderful coffee. Meal in itself.

LINDA: Can I make you some eggs?

WILLY: No. Take a breath.

LINDA: You look so rested, dear.

WILLY: I slept like a dead one. First time in months. Imagine, sleeping till ten on a Tuesday morning. Boys left nice and early, heh?

LINDA: They were out of here by eight o'clock.

WILLY: Good work!

LINDA: It was so thrilling to see them leaving together. I can't get over the shaving lotion in this house!

WILLY (*smiling*): Mmm—

LINDA: Biff was very changed this morning. His whole attitude seemed to be hopeful. He couldn't wait to get downtown to see Oliver.

WILLY: He's heading for a change. There's no question, there simply are certain men that take longer to get—solidified. How did he dress?

LINDA: His blue suit. He's so handsome in that suit. He could be a—anything in that suit!

(*Willy gets up from the table. Linda holds his jacket for him.*)

WILLY: There's no question, no question at all. Gee, on the way home tonight I'd like to buy some seeds.

LINDA (*laughing*): That'd be wonderful. But not enough sun gets back there. Nothing'll grow any more.

WILLY: You wait, kid, before it's all over we're gonna get a little place out in the country, and I'll raise some vegetables, a couple of chickens . . .

LINDA: You'll do it yet, dear.

(*Willy walks out of his jacket. Linda follows him.*)

WILLY: And they'll get married, and come for a weekend. I'd build a little guest house. 'Cause I got so many fine tools, all I'd need would be a little lumber and some peace of mind.

LINDA (*joyfully*): I sewed the lining . . .

WILLY: I could build two guest houses, so they'd both come. Did he decide how much he's going to ask Oliver for?

LINDA (*getting him into the jacket*): He didn't mention it, but I imagine ten or fifteen thousand. You going to talk to Howard today?

WILLY: Yeah. I'll put it to him straight and simple. He'll just have to take me off the road.

LINDA: And Willy, don't forget to ask for a little advance, because we've got the insurance premium. It's the grace period now.

WILLY: That's a hundred . . . ?

LINDA: A hundred and eight, sixty-eight. Because we're a little short again.

WILLY: Why are we short?

LINDA: Well, you had the motor job on the car . . .

WILLY: That goddam Studebaker!

LINDA: And you got one more payment on the refrigerator . . .

WILLY: But it just broke again!

LINDA: Well, it's old, dear.

WILLY: I told you we should've bought a well-advertised machine. Charley bought a General Electric and it's twenty years old and it's still good, that son-of-a-bitch.

LINDA: But, Willy—

WILLY: Whoever heard of a Hastings refrigerator? Once in my life I would like to own something outright before it's broken! I'm always in a race with the junkyard! I just finished paying for the car and it's on its last legs. The refrigerator consumes belts like a goddamn maniac. They time those things. They time them so when you finally paid for them, they're used up.

LINDA (*buttoning up his jacket as he unbuttons it*): All told, about two hundred dollars would carry us, dear. But that includes the last payment on the mortgage. After this payment, Willy, the house belongs to us.

WILLY: It's twenty-five years!

LINDA: Biff was nine years old when we bought it.

WILLY: Well, that's a great thing. To weather a twenty-five year mortgage is—

LINDA: It's an accomplishment.

WILLY: All the cement, the lumber, the reconstruction I put in this house! There ain't a crack to be found in it anymore.

LINDA: Well, it served its purpose.

WILLY: What purpose? Some stranger'll come along, move in, and that's that. If only Biff would take this house, and raise a family . . . (*He starts to go.*) Goodby, I'm late.

LINDA (*suddenly remembering*): Oh, I forgot! You're supposed to meet them for dinner.

WILLY: Me?

LINDA: At Frank's Chop House on Forty-eighth near Sixth Avenue.

WILLY: Is that so! How about you?

LINDA: No, just the three of you. They're gonna blow you to a big meal!

WILLY: Don't say! Who thought of that?

LINDA: Biff came to me this morning, Willy, and he said, "Tell Dad, we want to blow him to a big meal." Be there six o'clock. You and your two boys are going to have dinner.

WILLY: Gee whiz! That's really somethin'. I'm gonna knock Howard for a loop, kid. I'll get an advance, and I'll come home with a New York job. Goddammit, now I'm gonna do it!

LINDA: Oh, that's the spirit, Willy!

WILLY: I will never get behind a wheel the rest of my life!

LINDA: It's changing, Willy, I can feel it changing!

WILLY: Beyond a question. G'by, I'm late. (*He starts to go again.*)

LINDA (*calling after him as she runs to the kitchen table for a handkerchief*): You got your glasses?

WILLY (*feels for them, then comes back in*): Yeah, yeah, got my glasses.

LINDA (*giving him the handkerchief*): And a handkerchief.

WILLY: Yeah, handkerchief.

LINDA: And your saccharine?

WILLY: Yeah, my saccharine.

LINDA: Be careful on the subway stairs.

(*She kisses him, and a silk stocking is seen hanging from her hand. Willy notices it.*)

WILLY: Will you stop mending stockings? At least while I'm in the house. It gets me nervous. I can't tell you. Please.

(*Linda hides the stocking in her hand as she follows Willy across the forestage in front of the house.*)

LINDA: Remember, Frank's Chop House.

WILLY (*passing the apron*): Maybe beets would grow out there.

LINDA (*laughing*): But you tried so many times.

WILLY: Yeah. Well, don't work hard today. (*He disappears around the right corner of the house.*)

LINDA: Be careful!

(*As Willy vanishes, Linda waves to him. Suddenly the phone rings. She runs across the stage and into the kitchen and lifts it.*)

LINDA: Hello? Oh, Biff! I'm so glad you called, I just . . . Yes, sure, I just told him. Yes, he'll be there for dinner at six o'clock, I didn't forget. Listen, I was just dying to tell you. You know that little rubber pipe I told you about? That he connected to the gas heater? I finally decided to go down the cellar this morning and take it away and destroy it. But it's gone! Imagine? He took it away himself, it isn't there! (*She listens.*) When? Oh, then you took it. Oh—nothing, it's just that I'd hoped he'd taken it away himself. Oh, I'm not worried, darling, because this morning he left in such high spirits, it was like the old days! I'm not afraid any more. Did Mr. Oliver see you? . . . Well, you wait there then. And make a nice impression on him, darling. Just don't perspire too much before you see him. And have a nice time with Dad. He may have big news too! . . . That's right, a New York job. And be sweet to him tonight, dear. Be loving to him. Because he's only a little boat looking for a harbor. (*She is trembling with sorrow and joy.*) Oh, that's wonderful, Biff, you'll save his life. Thanks, darling. Just put your arm around him when he comes into the restaurant. Give him a smile. That's the boy . . . Good-by, dear. . . . You got your comb? . . . That's fine. Good-by, Biff dear.

(*In the middle of her speech, Howard Wagner, thirty-six, wheels in a small typewriter table on which is a wire-recording machine and proceeds to plug it in. This is on the left forestage. Light slowly fades on Linda as it rises on Howard. Howard is intent on threading the machine and only glances over his shoulder as Willy appears.*)

WILLY: Pst! Pst!

HOWARD: Hello, Willy, come in.

WILLY: Like to have a little talk with you, Howard.

HOWARD: Sorry to keep you waiting. I'll be with you in a minute.

WILLY: What's that, Howard?

HOWARD: Didn't you ever see one of these? Wire recorder.

WILLY: Oh. Can we talk a minute?

HOWARD: Records things. Just got delivery yesterday. Been driving me crazy, the most terrific machine I ever saw in my life. I was up all night with it.

WILLY: What do you do with it?

HOWARD: I bought it for dictation, but you can do anything with it. Listen to this. I had it home last night. Listen to what I picked up. The first one is my daughter. Get this. (*He flicks the switch and "Roll out the Barrel" is heard being whistled.*) Listen to that kid whistle.

WILLY: That is lifelike, isn't it?

HOWARD: Seven years old. Get that tone.

WILLY: Ts, ts. Like to ask a little favor if you . . .

(*The whistling breaks off, and the voice of Howard's daughter is heard.*)

HIS DAUGHTER: Now you, Daddy.

HOWARD: She's crazy for me! (*Again the same song is whistled.*) That's me! Ha! (*He winks.*)

WILLY: You're very good!

(*The whistling breaks off again. The machine runs silent for a moment.*)

HOWARD: Sh! Get this now, this is my son.

HIS SON: "The capital of Alabama is Montgomery; the capital of Arizona is Phoenix; the capital of Arkansas is Little Rock; the capital of California is Sacramento . . ." (*and on, and on.*)

HOWARD (*holding up five fingers*): Five years old, Willy!

WILLY: He'll make an announcer some day!

HIS SON (*continuing*): "The capital . . ."

HOWARD: Get that—alphabetical order! (*The machine breaks off suddenly.*) Wait a minute. The maid kicked the plug out.

WILLY: It certainly is a—

HOWARD: Sh, for God's sake!

HIS SON: "It's nine o'clock, Bulova watch time. So I have to go to sleep."

WILLY: That really is—

HOWARD: Wait a minute! The next is my wife.

(*They wait.*)

HOWARD'S VOICE: "Go on, say something." (*Pause.*) "Well, you gonna talk?"

HIS WIFE: "I can't think of anything."

HOWARD'S VOICE: "Well, talk—it's turning."

HIS WIFE (*shyly, beaten*): "Hello." (*Silence.*) "Oh, Howard, I can't talk into this . . ."

HOWARD (*snapping the machine off*): That was my wife.

WILLY: That is a wonderful machine. Can we—

HOWARD: I tell you, Willy, I'm gonna take my camera, and my bandsaw, and all my hobbies, and out they go. This is the most fascinating relaxation I ever found.

WILLY: I think I'll get one myself.

HOWARD: Sure, they're only a hundred and a half. You can't do without it. Supposing you wanna hear Jack Benny, see? But you can't be at home at that hour. So you tell the maid to turn the radio on when Jack Benny comes on, and this automatically goes on with the radio . . .

WILLY: And when you come home you . . .

HOWARD: You can come home twelve o'clock, one o'clock, any time you like, and you get yourself a Coke and sit yourself down, throw the switch, and there's Jack Benny's program in the middle of the night!

WILLY: I'm definitely going to get one. Because lots of times I'm on the road, and I think to myself, what I must be missing on the radio!

HOWARD: Don't you have a radio in the car?

WILLY: Well, yeah, but who ever thinks of turning it on?

HOWARD: Say, aren't you supposed to be in Boston?

WILLY: That's what I want to talk to you about, Howard. You got a minute? (*He draws a chair in from the wing.*)

HOWARD: What happened? What're you doing here?

WILLY: Well . . .

HOWARD: You didn't crack up again, did you?

WILLY: Oh, no. No . . .

HOWARD: Geez, you had me worried there for a minute. What's the trouble?

WILLY: Well, tell you the truth, Howard. I've come to the decision that I'd rather not travel anymore.

HOWARD: Not travel! Well, what'll you do?

WILLY: Remember, Christmas time, when you had the party here? You said you'd try to think of some spot for me here in town.

HOWARD: With us?

WILLY: Well, sure.

HOWARD: Oh, yeah, yeah. I remember. Well, I couldn't think of anything for you, Willy.

WILLY: I tell ya, Howard. The kids are all grown up, y'know. I don't need much anymore. If I could take home—well, sixty-five dollars a week, I could swing it.

HOWARD: Yeah, but Willy, see I—

WILLY: I tell ya why, Howard. Speaking frankly and between the two of us, y'know—I'm just a little tired.

HOWARD: Oh, I could understand that, Willy. But you're a road man, Willy, and we do a road business. We've only got a half-dozen salesmen on the floor here.

WILLY: God knows, Howard, I never asked a favor of any man. But I was with the firm when your father used to carry you in here in his arms.

HOWARD: I know that, Willy, but—

WILLY: Your father came to me the day you were born and asked me what I thought of the name Howard, may he rest in peace.

HOWARD: I appreciate that, Willy, but there just is no spot here for you. If I had a spot I'd slam you right in, but I just don't have a single solitary spot.

(*He looks for his lighter. Willy has picked it up and gives it to him. Pause.*)

WILLY (*with increasing anger*): Howard, all I need to set my table is fifty dollars a week.

HOWARD: But where am I going to put you, kid?

WILLY: Look, it isn't a question of whether I can sell merchandise, is it?

HOWARD: No, but it's business, kid, and everybody's gotta pull his own weight.

WILLY (*desperately*): Just let me tell you a story, Howard—

HOWARD: 'Cause you gotta admit, business is business.

WILLY (*angrily*): Business is definitely business, but just listen for a minute. You don't understand this. When I was a boy—eighteen, nineteen—I was already on the road. And there was a question in my mind as to whether selling had a future for me. Because in those days I had a yearning to go to Alaska. See, there were three gold strikes in one month in Alaska, and I felt like going out. Just for the ride, you might say.

HOWARD (*barely interested*): Don't say.

WILLY: Oh, yeah, my father lived many years in Alaska. He was an adventurous man. We've got quite a little streak of self-reliance in our family. I thought I'd go out with my older brother and try to locate him, and maybe settle in the North with the old man. And I was almost decided to go, when I met a salesman in the Parker House. His name was Dave Singleman. And he was eighty-four years old, and he'd drummed merchandise in thirty-one states. And old Dave, he'd go up to his room, y'understand, put on his green velvet slippers—I'll never forget—and pick up his phone and call the buyers, and without ever leaving his room, at the age of eighty-four, he made his living. And when I saw that, I realized that selling was the greatest career a man could want. 'Cause what could be more satisfying than to be able to go, at the age of eighty-four, into twenty or thirty different cities, and pick up a phone, and be remembered and loved and helped by so many different people? Do you know? When he died—and by the way he died the death of a salesman, in his green velvet slippers in the smoker of the New York, New Haven and Hartford, going into Boston—when he died, hundreds of salesmen and buyers were at his funeral. Things were sad on a lotta trains for months after that. (*He stands up. Howard has not looked at him.*) In those days there was personality in it, Howard. There was respect and comradeship, and gratitude in it. Today, it's all cut and dried, and there's no chance for bringing friendship to bear—or personality. You see what I mean? They don't know me any more.

HOWARD (*moving away, to the right*): That's just the thing, Willy.

WILLY: If I had forty dollars a week—that's all I'd need. Forty dollars, Howard.

HOWARD: Kid, I can't take blood from a stone, I—

WILLY (*desperation is on him now*): Howard, the year Al Smith was nominated, your father came to me and—

HOWARD (*starting to go off*): I've got to see some people, kid.

WILLY (*stopping him*): I'm talking about your father! There were promises made across this desk! You mustn't tell me you've got people to see—I put thirty-four years into this firm, Howard, and now I can't pay my insurance! You can't eat the orange and throw the peel away—a man is not a piece of fruit! (*After a pause.*) Now pay attention. Your father—in 1928 I had a big year. I averaged a hundred and seventy dollars a week in commissions.

HOWARD (*impatiently*): Now, Willy, you never averaged—

WILLY (*banging his hand on the desk*): I averaged a hundred and seventy dollars a week in the year of 1928! And your father came to me—or rather I was in the office here—it was right over this desk—and he put his hand on my shoulder—

HOWARD (*getting up*): You'll have to excuse me, Willy, I gotta see some people. Pull yourself together. (*Going out.*) I'll be back in a little while.

(*On Howard's exit, the light on his chair grows very bright and strange.*)

WILLY: Pull myself together! What the hell did I say to him? My God, I was yelling at him! How could I? (*Willy breaks off, staring at the light, which occupies the chair, animating it. He approaches this chair, standing across the desk from it.*) Frank, Frank, don't you remember what you told me that time? How you put your hand on my shoulder, and Frank . . . (*He leans on the desk and as he speaks the dead man's name he accidentally switches on the recorder, and instantly)*

HOWARD'S SON: "...of New York is Albany. The capital of Ohio is Cincinnati, the capital of Rhode Island is..." *(The recitation continues.)*

WILLY *(leaping away with fright, shouting)*: Ha! Howard! Howard! Howard!

HOWARD *(rushing in)*: What happened?

WILLY *(pointing at the machine, which continues nasally, childishly, with the capital cities)*: Shut it off! Shut it off!

HOWARD *(pulling the plug out)*: Look, Willy...

WILLY *(pressing his hands to his eyes)*: I gotta get myself some coffee. I'll get some coffee...

(Willy starts to walk out. Howard stops him.)

HOWARD *(rolling up the cord)*: Willy, look...

WILLY: I'll go to Boston.

HOWARD: Willy, you can't go to Boston for us.

WILLY: Why can't I go?

HOWARD: I don't want you to represent us. I've been meaning to tell you for a long time now.

WILLY: Howard, are you firing me?

HOWARD: I think you need a good long rest, Willy.

WILLY: Howard—

HOWARD: And when you feel better, come back, and we'll see if we can work something out.

WILLY: But I gotta earn money, Howard. I'm in no position to—

HOWARD: Where are your sons? Why don't your sons give you a hand?

WILLY: They're working on a very big deal.

HOWARD: This is no time for false pride, Willy. You go to your sons and you tell them that you're tired. You've got two great boys, haven't you?

WILLY: Oh, no question, no question, but in the meantime...

HOWARD: Then that's that, heh?

WILLY: All right, I'll go to Boston tomorrow.

HOWARD: No, no.

WILLY: I can't throw myself on my sons. I'm not a cripple!

HOWARD: Look, kid, I'm busy this morning.

WILLY *(grasping Howard's arm)*: Howard, you've got to let me go to Boston!

HOWARD *(hard, keeping himself under control)*: I've got a line of people to see this morning. Sit down, take five minutes, and pull yourself together, and then go home, will ya? I need the office, Willy. *(He starts to go, turns, remembering the recorder, starts to push off the table holding the recorder.)* Oh, yeah. Whenever you can this week, stop by and drop off the samples. You'll feel better, Willy, and then come back and we'll talk. Pull yourself together, kid, there's people outside.

(Howard exits, pushing the table off left. Willy stares into space, exhausted. Now the music is heard—Ben's music—first distantly, then closer, closer. As Willy speaks, Ben enters from the right. He carries valise and umbrella.)

WILLY: Oh, Ben, how did you do it? What is the answer? Did you wind up the Alaska deal already?

BEN: Doesn't take much time if you know what you're doing. Just a short business trip. Boarding ship in an hour. Wanted to say good-by.

WILLY: Ben, I've got to talk to you.

BEN *(glancing at his watch)*: Haven't the time, William.

WILLY *(crossing the apron to Ben)*: Ben, nothing's working out. I don't know what to do.

BEN: Now, look here, William. I've bought timberland in Alaska and I need a man to look after things for me.

WILLY: God, timberland! Me and my boys in those grand outdoors!

BEN: You've a new continent at your doorstep, William. Get out of these cities, they're full of talk and time payments and courts of law. Screw on your fists and you can fight for a fortune up there.

WILLY: Yes, yes! Linda, Linda!

(Linda enters as of old, with the wash.)

LINDA: Oh, you're back?

BEN: I haven't much time.

WILLY: No, wait! Linda, he's got a proposition for me in Alaska.

LINDA: But you've got—*(To Ben.)* He's got a beautiful job here.

WILLY: But in Alaska, kid, I could—

LINDA: You're doing well enough, Willy!

BEN *(to Linda)*: Enough for what, my dear?

LINDA *(frightened of Ben and angry at him)*: Don't say those things to him! Enough to be happy right here, right now. *(To Willy, while Ben laughs.)* Why must everybody conquer the world? You're well liked, and the boys love you, and someday—*(To Ben)*—why, old man Wagner told him just the other day that if he keeps it up he'll be a member of the firm, didn't he, Willy?

WILLY: Sure, sure. I am building something with this firm, Ben, and if a man is building something he must be on the right track, mustn't he?

BEN: What are you building? Lay your hand on it. Where is it?

WILLY *(hesitantly)*: That's true, Linda, there's nothing.

LINDA: Why? *(To Ben.)* There's a man eighty-four years old—

WILLY: That's right, Ben, that's right. When I look at that man I say, what is there to worry about?

BEN: Bah!

WILLY: It's true, Ben. All he has to do is go into any city, pick up the phone, and he's making his living and you know why?

BEN *(picking up his valise)*: I've got to go.

WILLY *(holding Ben back)*: Look at this boy!

(Biff, in his high school sweater, enters carrying suitcase. Happy carries Biff's shoulder guards, gold helmet, and football pants.)

WILLY: Without a penny to his name, three great universities are begging for him, and from there the sky's the limit, because it's not what you do, Ben. It's who you know and the smile on your face! It's contacts, Ben, contacts! The whole wealth of Alaska passes over the lunch table at the Commodore Hotel, and that's the wonder, the wonder of this country, that a man can end with diamonds here on the basis of being liked! (*He turns to Biff.*) And that's why when you get out on that field today it's important. Because thousands of people will be rooting for you and loving you. (*To Ben, who has again begun to leave.*) And Ben! when he walks into a business office his name will sound out like a bell and all the doors will open to him! I've seen it, Ben, I've seen it a thousand times! You can't feel it with your hand like timber, but it's there!

BEN: Good-by, William.

WILLY: Ben, am I right? Don't you think I'm right? I value your advice.

BEN: There's a new continent at your doorstep, William. You could walk out rich. Rich! (*He is gone.*)

WILLY: We'll do it here, Ben! You hear me? We're gonna do it here!

(*Young Bernard rushes in. The gay music of the Boys is heard.*)

BERNARD: Oh, gee, I was afraid you left already!

WILLY: Why? What time is it?

BERNARD: It's half-past one!

WILLY: Well, come on, everybody! Ebbets Field next stop! Where's the pennants? (*He rushes through the wall-line of the kitchen and out into the living room.*)

LINDA (*to Biff*): Did you pack fresh underwear?

BIFF (*who has been limbering up*): I want to go!

BERNARD: Biff, I'm carrying your helmet, ain't I?

HAPPY: No, I'm carrying the helmet.

BERNARD: Oh, Biff, you promised me.

HAPPY: I'm carrying the helmet.

BERNARD: How am I going to get in the locker room?

LINDA: Let him carry the shoulder guards. (*She puts her coat and hat on in the kitchen.*)

BERNARD: Can I, Biff? 'Cause I told everybody I'm going to be in the locker room.

HAPPY: In Ebbets Field it's the clubhouse.

BERNARD: I meant the clubhouse. Biff!

HAPPY: Biff!

BIFF (*grandly, after a slight pause*): Let him carry the shoulder guards.

HAPPY (*as he gives Bernard the shoulder guards*): Stay close to us now.

(*Willy rushes in with the pennants.*)

WILLY (*handing them out*): Everybody wave when Biff comes out on the field. (*Happy and Bernard run off.*) You set now, boy?

(*The music has died away.*)

BIFF: Ready to go, Pop. Every muscle is ready.

WILLY (*at the edge of the apron*): You realize what this means?

BIFF: That's right, Pop.

WILLY (*feeling Biff's muscles*): You're comin' home this afternoon captain of the All-Scholastic Championship Team of the City of New York.

BIFF: I got it, Pop. And remember, pal, when I take off my helmet, that touchdown is for you.

WILLY: Let's go! (*He is starting out, with his arm around Biff, when Charley enters, as of old, in knickers.*) I got no room for you, Charley.

CHARLEY: Room? For what?

WILLY: In the car.

CHARLEY: You goin' for a ride? I wanted to shoot some casino.

WILLY (*furiously*): Casino! (*Incredulously.*) Don't you realize what today is?

LINDA: Oh, he knows, Willy. He's just kidding you.

WILLY: That's nothing to kid about!

CHARLEY: No, Linda, what's goin' on?

LINDA: He's playing in Ebbets Field.

CHARLEY: Baseball in this weather?

WILLY: Don't talk to him. Come on, come on! (*He is pushing them out.*)

CHARLEY: Wait a minute, didn't you hear the news?

WILLY: What?

CHARLEY: Don't you listen to the radio? Ebbets Field just blew up.

WILLY: You go to hell! (*Charley laughs. Pushing them out.*) Come on, come on! We're late.

CHARLEY (*as they go*): Knock a homer, Biff, knock a homer!

WILLY (*the last to leave, turning to Charley*): I don't think that was funny, Charley. This is the greatest day of his life.

CHARLEY: Willy, when are you going to grow up?

WILLY: Yeah, heh? When this game is over, Charley, you'll be laughing out of the other side of your face. They'll be calling him another Red Grange. Twenty-five thousand a year.

CHARLEY (*kidding*): Is that so?

WILLY: Yeah, that's so.

CHARLEY: Well, then, I'm sorry, Willy. But tell me something.

WILLY: What?

CHARLEY: Who is Red Grange?

WILLY: Put up your hands. Goddam you, put up your hands!

(*Charley, chuckling, shakes his head and walks away, around the left corner of the stage. Willy follows him. The music rises to a mocking frenzy.*)

WILLY: Who the hell do you think you are, better than everybody else? You don't know everything, you big, ignorant, stupid . . . Put up your hands!

(*Light rises, on the right side of the forestage, on a small table in the reception room of Charley's office. Traffic sounds are heard. Bernard, now mature, sits whistling to himself. A pair of tennis rackets and an overnight bag are on the floor beside him.*)

WILLY (*offstage*): What are you walking away for? Don't walk away! If you're going to say something say it to my face! I know you laugh at me behind my

back. You'll laugh out of the other side of your goddam face after this game. Touchdown! Touchdown!
Eighty thousand people! Touchdown! Right between
the goal posts.

(*Bernard is a quiet, earnest, but self-assured young
man. Willy's voice is coming from right upstage now.
Bernard lowers his feet off the table and listens. Jenny,
his father's secretary, enters.*)

JENNY (*distressed*): Say, Bernard, will you go out in the
hall?

BERNARD: What is that noise? Who is it?

JENNY: Mr. Loman. He just got off the elevator.

BERNARD (*getting up*): Who's he arguing with?

JENNY: Nobody. There's nobody with him. I can't deal
with him anymore, and your father gets all upset everytime he comes. I've got a lot of typing to do, and
your father's waiting to sign it. Will you see him?

WILLY (*entering*): Touchdown! Touch—(*He sees Jenny.*)
Jenny, Jenny, good to see you. How're ya? Workin'?
Or still honest?

JENNY: Fine. How've you been feeling?

WILLY: Not much any more, Jenny. Ha, ha! (*He is surprised to see the rackets.*)

BERNARD: Hello, Uncle Willy.

WILLY (*almost shocked*): Bernard! Well, look who's here!
(*He comes quickly, guiltily, to Bernard and warmly
shakes his hand.*)

BERNARD: How are you? Good to see you.

WILLY: What are you doing here?

BERNARD: Oh, just stopped by to see Pop. Get off my
feet till my train leaves. I'm going to Washington in
a few minutes.

WILLY: Is he in?

BERNARD: Yes, he's in his office with the accountant. Sit
down.

WILLY (*sitting down*): What're you going to do in Washington?

BERNARD: Oh, just a case I've got there, Willy.

WILLY: That so? (*Indicating the rackets.*) You going to
play tennis there?

BERNARD: I'm staying with a friend who's got a court.

WILLY: Don't say. His own tennis court. Must be fine
people, I bet.

BERNARD: They are, very nice. Dad tells me Biff's in town.

WILLY (*with a big smile*): Yeah, Biff's in. Working on a
very big deal, Bernard.

BERNARD: What's Biff doing?

WILLY: Well, he's been doing very big things in the West.
But he decided to establish himself here. Very big.
We're having dinner. Did I hear your wife had a boy?

BERNARD: That's right. Our second.

WILLY: Two boys! What do you know!

BERNARD: What kind of a deal has Biff got?

WILLY: Well, Bill Oliver—very big sporting-goods
man—he wants Biff very badly. Called him in from
the West. Long distance, carte blanche, special deliver-
ies. Your friends have their own private tennis court?

BERNARD: You still with the old firm, Willy?

WILLY (*after a pause*): I'm—I'm overjoyed to see how
you made the grade, Bernard, overjoyed. It's an
encouraging thing to see a young man really—
really—Looks very good for Biff—very—(*He
breaks off, then.*) Bernard—(*He is so full of emotion,
he breaks off again.*)

BERNARD: What is it, Willy?

WILLY (*small and alone*): What—what's the secret?

BERNARD: What secret?

WILLY: How—how did you? Why didn't he ever catch on?

BERNARD: I wouldn't know that, Willy.

WILLY (*confidentially, desperately*): You were his friend,
his boyhood friend. There's something I don't understand about it. His life ended after that Ebbets Field
game. From the age of seventeen nothing good ever
happened to him.

BERNARD: He never trained himself for anything.

WILLY: But he did, he did. After high school he took so
many correspondence courses. Radio mechanics;
television; God knows what, and never made the
slightest mark.

BERNARD (*taking off his glasses*): Willy, do you want to
talk candidly?

WILLY (*rising, faces Bernard*): I regard you as a very brilliant man, Bernard. I value your advice.

BERNARD: Oh, the hell with the advice, Willy. I couldn't
advise you. There's just one thing I've always wanted
to ask you. When he was supposed to graduate, and
the math teacher flunked him—

WILLY: Oh, that son-of-a-bitch ruined his life.

BERNARD: Yeah, but, Willy, all he had to do was go to
summer school and make up that subject.

WILLY: That's right, that's right.

BERNARD: Did you tell him not to go to summer school?

WILLY: Me? I begged him to go. I ordered him to go!

BERNARD: Then why wouldn't he go?

WILLY: Why? Why! Bernard, that question has been
trailing me like a ghost for the last fifteen years. He
flunked the subject, and laid down and died like a
hammer hit him!

BERNARD: Take it easy, kid.

WILLY: Let me talk to you—I got nobody to talk to.
Bernard, Bernard, was it my fault? Y'see? It keeps going around in my mind, maybe I did something to
him. I got nothing to give him.

BERNARD: Don't take it so hard.

WILLY: Why did he lay down? What is the story there?
You were his friend!

BERNARD: Willy, I remember, it was June, and our grades
came out. And he'd flunked math.

WILLY: That son-of-a-bitch!

BERNARD: No, it wasn't right then. Biff just got very angry, I remember, and he was ready to enroll in summer school.

WILLY (*surprised*): He was?

BERNARD: He wasn't beaten by it at all. But then, Willy,
he disappeared from the block for almost a month.
And I got the idea that he'd gone up to New England
to see you. Did he have a talk with you then?

(*Willy stares in silence.*)

BERNARD: Willy?

WILLY (*with a strong edge of resentment in his voice*): Yeah, he came to Boston. What about it?

BERNARD: Well, just that when he came back—I'll never forget this, it always mystifies me. Because I'd thought so well of Biff, even though he'd always taken advantage of me. I loved him, Willy, y'know? And he came back after that month and took his sneakers—remember those sneakers with "University of Virginia" printed on them? He was so proud of those, wore them every day. And he took them down in the cellar, and burned them up in the furnace. We had a fist fight. It lasted at least half an hour. Just the two of us, punching each other down the cellar, and crying right through it. I've often thought of how strange it was that I knew he'd given up his life. What happened in Boston, Willy?

(*Willy looks at him as at an intruder.*)

BERNARD: I just bring it up because you asked me.

WILLY (*angrily*): Nothing. What do you mean, "What happened?" What's that got to do with anything?

BERNARD: Well, don't get sore.

WILLY: What are you trying to do, blame it on me? If a boy lays down is that my fault?

BERNARD: Now, Willy, don't get—

WILLY: Well, don't—don't talk to me that way! What does that mean, "What happened?"

(*Charley enters. He is in his vest, and he carries a bottle of bourbon.*)

CHARLEY: Hey, you're going to miss that train. (*He waves the bottle.*)

BERNARD: Yeah, I'm going. (*He takes the bottle.*) Thanks, Pop. (*He picks up his rackets and bag.*) Good by, Willy, and don't worry about it. You know, "If at first you don't succeed . . ."

WILLY: Yes, I believe in that.

BERNARD: But sometimes, Willy, it's better for a man just to walk away.

WILLY: Walk away?

BERNARD: That's right.

WILLY: But if you can't walk away?

BERNARD (*after a slight pause*): I guess that's when it's tough. (*Extending his hand.*) Good-by, Willy.

WILLY (*shaking Bernard's hand*): Good-by, boy.

CHARLEY (*an arm on Bernard's shoulder*): How do you like this kid? Gonna argue a case in front of the Supreme Court.

BERNARD (*protesting*): Pop!

WILLY (*genuinely shocked, pained, and happy*): No! The Supreme Court!

BERNARD: I gotta run. 'By, Dad!

CHARLEY: Knock 'em dead, Bernard!

(*Bernard goes off.*)

WILLY (*as Charley takes out his wallet*): The Supreme Court! And he didn't even mention it!

CHARLEY (*counting out money on the desk*): He don't have to—he's gonna do it.

WILLY: And you never told him what to do, did you? You never took any interest in him.

CHARLEY: My salvation is that I never took any interest in anything. There's some money—fifty dollars. I got an accountant inside.

WILLY: Charley, look . . . (*With difficulty.*) I got my insurance to pay. If you can manage it—I need a hundred and ten dollars.

(*Charley doesn't reply for a moment; merely stops moving.*)

WILLY: I'd draw it from my bank but Linda would know, and I . . .

CHARLEY: Sit down, Willy.

WILLY (*moving toward the chair*): I'm keeping an account of everything, remember. I'll pay every penny back. (*He sits.*)

CHARLEY: Now listen to me, Willy.

WILLY: I want you to know I appreciate . . .

CHARLEY (*sitting down on the table*): Willy, what're you doin'? What the hell is goin' on in your head?

WILLY: Why? I'm simply . . .

CHARLEY: I offered you a job. You make fifty dollars a week. And I won't send you on the road.

WILLY: I've got a job.

CHARLEY: Without pay? What kind of a job is a job without pay? (*He rises.*) Now, look, kid, enough is enough. I'm no genius but I know when I'm being insulted.

WILLY: Insulted!

CHARLEY: Why don't you want to work for me?

WILLY: What's the matter with you? I've got a job.

CHARLEY: Then what're you walkin' in here every week for?

WILLY (*getting up*): Well, if you don't want me to walk in here—

CHARLEY: I'm offering you a job.

WILLY: I don't want your goddam job!

CHARLEY: When the hell are you going to grow up?

WILLY (*furiously*): You big ignoramus, if you say that to me again I'll rap you one! I don't care how big you are! (*He's ready to fight.*)

(*Pause.*)

CHARLEY (*kindly, going to him*): How much do you need, Willy?

WILLY: Charley, I'm strapped. I'm strapped. I don't know what to do. I was just fired.

CHARLEY: Howard fired you?

WILLY: That snotnose. Imagine that? I named him. I named him Howard.

CHARLEY: Willy, when're you gonna realize that them things don't mean anything? You named him Howard, but you can't sell that. The only thing you got in this world is what you can sell. And the funny thing is that you're a salesman, and you don't know that.

WILLY: I've always tried to think otherwise, I guess. I always felt that if a man was impressive, and well liked, that nothing—

CHARLEY: Why must everybody like you? Who liked J. P. Morgan?° Was he impressive? In a Turkish bath he'd look like a butcher. But with his pockets on he was very well liked. Now listen, Willy, I know you don't like me, and nobody can say I'm in love with you, but I'll give you a job because—just for the hell of it, put it that way. Now what do you say?

WILLY: I—I just can't work for you, Charley.

CHARLEY: What're you, jealous of me?

WILLY: I can't work for you, that's all, don't ask me why.

CHARLEY (*angered, takes out more bills*): You been jealous of me all your life, you dammed fool! Here, pay your insurance. (*He puts the money in Willy's hand.*)

WILLY: I'm keeping strict accounts.

CHARLEY: I've got some work to do. Take care of yourself. And pay your insurance.

WILLY (*moving to the right*): Funny, y'know? After all the highways, and the trains, and the appointments, and the years, you end up worth more dead than alive.

CHARLEY: Willy, nobody's worth nothin' dead. (*After a slight pause.*) Did you hear what I said?

(*Willy stands still, dreaming.*)

CHARLEY: Willy!

WILLY: Apologize to Bernard for me when you see him. I didn't mean to argue with him. He's a fine boy. They're all fine boys, and they'll end up big—all of them. Someday they'll all play tennis together. Wish me luck, Charley. He saw Bill Oliver today.

CHARLEY: Good luck.

WILLY (*on the verge of tears*): Charley, you're the only friend I got. Isn't that a remarkable thing? (*He goes out.*)

CHARLEY: Jesus!

(*Charley stares after him a moment and follows. All light blacks out. Suddenly raucous music is heard, and a red glow rises behind the screen at right. Stanley, a young waiter, appears, carrying a table, followed by Happy, who is carrying two chairs.*)

STANLEY (*putting the table down*): That's all right, Mr. Loman, I can handle it myself. (*He turns and takes the chairs from Happy and places them at the table.*)

HAPPY (*glancing around*): Oh, this is better.

STANLEY: Sure, in the front there you're in the middle of all kinds of noise. Whenever you got a party, Mr. Loman, you just tell me and I'll put you back here. Y'know, there's a lotta people they don't like it private, because when they go out they like to see a lotta action around them because they're sick and tired to stay in the house by theirself. But I know you, you ain't from Hackensack. You know what I mean?

HAPPY (*sitting down*): So how's it coming, Stanley?

STANLEY: Ah, it's a dog life. I only wish during the war they'd a took me in the Army. I coulda been dead by now.

HAPPY: My brother's back, Stanley.

STANLEY: Oh, he come back, heh? From the Far West.

HAPPY: Yeah, big cattle man, my brother, so treat him right. And my father's coming too.

STANLEY: Oh, your father too!

HAPPY: You got a couple of nice lobsters?

STANLEY: Hundred percent, big.

HAPPY: I want them with the claws.

STANLEY: Don't worry, I don't give you no mice. (*Happy laughs.*) How about some wine? It'll put a head on the meal.

HAPPY: No. You remember, Stanley, that recipe I brought you from overseas? With the champagne in it?

STANLEY: Oh, yeah, sure. I still got it tacked up yet in the kitchen. But that'll have to cost a buck apiece anyways.

HAPPY: That's all right.

STANLEY: What'd you, hit a number or somethin'?

HAPPY: No, it's a little celebration. My brother is—I think he pulled off a big deal today. I think we're going into business together.

STANLEY: Great! That's the best for you. Because a family business, you know what I mean?—that's the best.

HAPPY: That's what I think.

STANLEY: 'Cause what's the difference? Somebody steals? It's in the family. Know what I mean? (*Sotto voce.*°) Like this bartender here. The boss is goin' crazy what kinda leak he's got in the cash register. You put it in but it don't come out.

HAPPY (*raising his head*): Sh!

STANLEY: What?

HAPPY: You notice I wasn't lookin' right or left, was I?

STANLEY: No.

HAPPY: And my eyes are closed.

STANLEY: So what's the—?

HAPPY: Strudel's comin'.

STANLEY (*catching on, looks around*): Ah, no, there's no—

(*He breaks off as a furred, lavishly dressed girl enters and sits at the next table. Both follow her with their eyes.*)

STANLEY: Geez, how'd ya know?

HAPPY: I got radar or something. (*Staring directly at her profile.*) Oooooooo . . . Stanley.

STANLEY: I think that's for you, Mr. Loman.

HAPPY: Look at that mouth. Oh, God. And the binoculars.

STANLEY: Geez, you got a life, Mr. Loman.

HAPPY: Wait on her.

STANLEY (*going to the girl's table*): Would you like a menu, ma'am?

GIRL: I'm expecting someone, but I'd like a—

HAPPY: Why don't you bring her—excuse me, miss, do you mind? I sell champagne, and I'd like you to try my brand. Bring her a champagne, Stanley.

GIRL: That's awfully nice of you.

HAPPY: Don't mention it. It's all company money. (*He laughs.*)

GIRL: That's a charming product to be selling, isn't it?

HAPPY: Oh, gets to be like everything else. Selling is selling, y'know.

J. P. Morgan: Wealthy financier and art collector (1837–1913), whose money was made chiefly in banking, railroads, and steel.

Sotto voce: In a soft voice or stage whisper.

GIRL: I suppose.

HAPPY: You don't happen to sell, do you?

GIRL: No, I don't sell.

HAPPY: Would you object to a compliment from a stranger? You ought to be on a magazine cover.

GIRL (*looking at him a little archly*): I have been.

(*Stanley comes in with a glass of champagne.*)

HAPPY: What'd I say before, Stanley? You see? She's a cover girl.

STANLEY: Oh, I could see, I could see.

HAPPY (*to the Girl*): What magazine?

GIRL: Oh, a lot of them. (*She takes the drink.*) Thank you.

HAPPY: You know what they say in France, don't you? "Champagne is the drink of the complexion"—Hya, Biff!

(*Biff has entered and sits with Happy.*)

BIFF: Hello, kid. Sorry I'm late.

HAPPY: I just got here. Uh, Miss—?

GIRL: Forsythe.

HAPPY: Miss Forsythe, this is my brother.

BIFF: Is Dad here?

HAPPY: His name is Biff. You might've heard of him. Great football player.

GIRL: Really? What team?

HAPPY: Are you familiar with football?

GIRL: No, I'm afraid I'm not.

HAPPY: Biff is quarterback with the New York Giants.

GIRL: Well, that is nice, isn't it? (*She drinks.*)

HAPPY: Good health.

GIRL: I'm happy to meet you.

HAPPY: That's my name. Hap. It's really Harold, but at West Point they called me Happy.

GIRL (*now really impressed*): Oh, I see. How do you do? (*She turns her profile.*)

BIFF: Isn't Dad coming?

HAPPY: You want her?

BIFF: Oh, I could never make that.

HAPPY: I remember the time that idea would never come into your head. Where's the old confidence, Biff?

BIFF: I just saw Oliver—

HAPPY: Wait a minute. I've got to see that old confidence again. Do you want her? She's on call.

BIFF: Oh, no. (*He turns to look at the Girl.*)

HAPPY: I'm telling you. Watch this. (*Turning to the Girl*): Honey? (*She turns to him.*) Are you busy?

GIRL: Well, I am . . . but I could make a phone call.

HAPPY: Do that, will you, honey? And see if you can get a friend. We'll be here for a while. Biff is one of the greatest football players in the country.

GIRL (*standing up*): Well, I'm certainly happy to meet you.

HAPPY: Come back soon.

GIRL: I'll try.

HAPPY: Don't try, honey, try hard.

(*The Girl exits. Stanley follows, shaking his head in bewildered admiration.*)

HAPPY: Isn't that a shame now? A beautiful girl like that? That's why I can't get married. There's not a good woman in a thousand. New York is loaded with them, kid!

BIFF: Hap, look—

HAPPY: I told you she was on call!

BIFF (*strangely unnerved*): Cut it out, will ya? I want to say something to you.

HAPPY: Did you see Oliver?

BIFF: I saw him all right. Now look, I want to tell Dad a couple of things and I want you to help me.

HAPPY: What? Is he going to back you?

BIFF: Are you crazy? You're out of your goddam head, you know that?

HAPPY: Why? What happened?

BIFF (*breathlessly*): I did a terrible thing today, Hap. It's been the strangest day I ever went through. I'm all numb, I swear.

HAPPY: You mean he wouldn't see you?

BIFF: Well, I waited six hours for him, see? All day. Kept sending my name in. Even tried to date his secretary so she'd get me to him, but no soap.

HAPPY: Because you're not showin' the old confidence Biff. He remembered you, didn't he?

BIFF (*stopping Happy with a gesture*): Finally, about five o'clock, he comes out. Didn't remember who I was or anything. I felt like such an idiot, Hap.

HAPPY: Did you tell him my Florida idea?

BIFF: He walked away. I saw him for one minute. I got so mad I could've torn the walls down! How the hell did I ever get the idea I was a salesman there? I even believed myself that I'd been a salesman for him! And then he gave me one look and—I realized what a ridiculous lie my whole life has been! We've been talking in a dream for fifteen years. I was a shipping clerk.

HAPPY: What'd you do?

BIFF (*with great tension and wonder*): Well, he left, see. And the secretary went out. I was all alone in the waiting room. I don't know what came over me, Hap. The next thing I know I'm in his office—paneled walls, everything. I can't explain it. I—Hap, I took his fountain pen.

HAPPY: Geez, did he catch you?

BIFF: I ran out. I ran down all eleven flights. I ran and ran and ran.

HAPPY: That was an awful dumb—what'd you do that for?

BIFF (*agonized*): I don't know, I just—wanted to take something, I don't know. You gotta help me, Hap. I'm gonna tell Pop.

HAPPY: You crazy? What for?

BIFF: Hap, he's got to understand that I'm not the man somebody lends that kind of money to. He thinks I've been spiting him all these years and it's eating him up.

HAPPY: That's just it. You tell him something nice.

BIFF: I can't.

HAPPY: Say you got a lunch date with Oliver tomorrow.

BIFF: So what do I do tomorrow?

HAPPY: You leave the house tomorrow and come back at night and say Oliver is thinking it over. And he thinks it over for a couple of weeks, and gradually it fades away and nobody's the worse.

BIFF: But it'll go on forever!

HAPPY: Dad is never so happy as when he's looking forward to something!

(*Willy enters.*)

HAPPY: Hello, scout!

WILLY: Gee, I haven't been here in years!

(*Stanley has followed Willy in and sets a chair for him. Stanley starts off but Happy stops him.*)

HAPPY: Stanley!

(*Stanley stands by, waiting for an order.*)

BIFF (*going to Willy with guilt, as to an invalid*): Sit down, Pop. You want a drink?

WILLY: Sure, I don't mind.

BIFF: Let's get a load on.

WILLY: You look worried.

BIFF: N-no. (*To Stanley.*) Scotch all around. Make it doubles.

STANLEY: Doubles, right. (*He goes.*)

WILLY: You had a couple already, didn't you?

BIFF: Just a couple, yeah.

WILLY: Well, what happened, boy? (*Nodding affirmatively, with a smile.*) Everything go all right?

BIFF (*takes a breath, then reaches out and grasps Willy's hand*): Pal . . . (*He is smiling bravely, and Willy is smiling too.*) I had an experience today.

HAPPY: Terrific, Pop.

WILLY: That so? What happened?

BIFF (*high, slightly alcoholic, above the earth*): I'm going to tell you everything from first to last. It's been a strange day. (*Silence. He looks around, composes himself as best he can, but his breath keeps breaking the rhythm of his voice.*) I had to wait quite a while for him, and—

WILLY: Oliver?

BIFF: Yeah, Oliver. All day, as a matter of cold fact. And a lot of—instances—facts, Pop, facts about my life came back to me. Who was it, Pop? Who ever said I was a salesman with Oliver?

WILLY: Well, you were.

BIFF: No, Dad, I was a shipping clerk.

WILLY: But you were practically—

BIFF (*with determination*): Dad, I don't know who said it first, but I was never a salesman for Bill Oliver.

WILLY: What're you talking about?

BIFF: Let's hold on to the facts tonight, Pop. We're not going to get anywhere bullin' around. I was a shipping clerk.

WILLY (*angrily*): All right, now listen to me—

BIFF: Why don't you let me finish?

WILLY: I'm not interested in stories about the past or any crap of that kind because the woods are burning, boys, you understand? There's a big blaze going on all around. I was fired today.

BIFF (*shocked*): How could you be?

WILLY: I was fired, and I'm looking for a little good news to tell your mother, because the woman has waited and the woman has suffered. The gist of it is that I haven't got a story left in my head, Biff. So don't give me a lecture about facts and aspects. I am not interested. Now what've you got to say to me?

(*Stanley enters with three drinks. They wait until he leaves.*)

WILLY: Did you see Oliver?

BIFF: Jesus, Dad!

WILLY: You mean you didn't go up there?

HAPPY: Sure he went up there.

BIFF: I did. I—saw him. How could they fire you?

WILLY (*on the edge of his chair*): What kind of a welcome did he give you?

BIFF: He won't even let you work on commission?

WILLY: I'm out! (*Driving.*) So tell me, he gave you a warm welcome?

HAPPY: Sure, Pop, sure!

BIFF (*driven*): Well, it was kind of—

WILLY: I was wondering if he'd remember you. (*To Happy.*) Imagine, man doesn't see him for ten, twelve years and gives him that kind of a welcome!

HAPPY: Damn right!

BIFF (*trying to return to the offensive*): Pop, look—

WILLY: You know why he remembered you, don't you? Because you impressed him in those days.

BIFF: Let's talk quietly and get this down to the facts, huh?

WILLY (*as though Biff had been interrupting*): Well, what happened? It's great news, Biff. Did he take you into his office or'd you talk in the waiting room?

BIFF: Well, he came in, see, and—

WILLY (*with a big smile*): What'd he say? Betcha he threw his arm around you.

BIFF: Well, he kinda—

WILLY: He's a fine man. (*To Happy.*) Very hard man to see, y'know.

HAPPY (*agreeing*): Oh, I know.

WILLY (*to Biff*): Is that where you had the drinks?

BIFF: Yeah, he gave me a couple of—no, no!

HAPPY (*cutting in*): He told him my Florida idea.

WILLY: Don't interrupt. (*To Biff.*) How'd he react to the Florida idea?

BIFF: Dad, will you give me a minute to explain?

WILLY: I've been waiting for you to explain since I sat down here! What happened? He took you into his office and what?

BIFF: Well—I talked. And—and he listened, see.

WILLY: Famous for the way he listens, y'know. What was his answer?

BIFF: His answer was—(*He breaks off, suddenly angry.*) Dad, you're not letting me tell you what I want to tell you!

WILLY (*accusing, angered*): You didn't see him, did you?

BIFF: I did see him!

WILLY: What'd you insult him or something? You insulted him, didn't you?

BIFF: Listen, will you let me out of it, will you just let me out of it!

HAPPY: What the hell!

WILLY: Tell me what happened!

BIFF (*to Happy*): I can't talk to him!

(*A single trumpet note jars the ear. The light of green leaves stains the house, which holds the air of night and a dream. Young Bernard enters and knocks on the door of the house.*)

YOUNG BERNARD (*frantically*): Mrs. Loman, Mrs. Loman!

HAPPY: Tell him what happened!

BIFF (*to Happy*): Shut up and leave me alone!

WILLY: No, no! You had to go and flunk math!

BIFF: What math? What're you talking about?

YOUNG BERNARD: Mrs. Loman, Mrs. Loman!

(*Linda appears in the house, as of old.*)

WILLY (*wildly*): Math, math, math!

BIFF: Take it easy, Pop!

YOUNG BERNARD: Mrs. Loman!

WILLY (*furiously*): If you hadn't flunked you'd've been set by now!

BIFF: Now, look, I'm gonna tell you what happened, and you're going to listen to me.

YOUNG BERNARD: Mrs. Loman!

BIFF: I waited six hours—

HAPPY: What the hell are you saying?

BIFF: I kept sending in my name but he wouldn't see me. So finally he . . . (*He continues unheard as light fades low on the restaurant.*)

YOUNG BERNARD: Biff flunked math!

LINDA: No!

YOUNG BERNARD: Birnbaum flunked him! They won't graduate him!

LINDA: But they have to. He's gotta go to the university. Where is he? Biff! Biff!

YOUNG BERNARD: No, he left. He went to Grand Central.

LINDA: Grand—You mean he went to Boston!

YOUNG BERNARD: Is Uncle Willy in Boston?

LINDA: Oh, maybe Willy can talk to the teacher. Oh, the poor, poor boy!

(*Light on house area snaps out.*)

BIFF (*at the table, now audible, holding up a gold fountain pen*): . . . so I'm washed up with Oliver, you understand? Are you listening to me?

WILLY (*at a loss*): Yeah, sure. If you hadn't flunked—

BIFF: Flunked what? What're you talking about?

WILLY: Don't blame everything on me! I didn't flunk math—you did! What pen?

HAPPY: That was awful dumb, Biff, a pen like that is worth—

WILLY (*seeing the pen for the first time*): You took Oliver's pen?

BIFF (*weakening*): Dad, I just explained it to you.

WILLY: You stole Bill Oliver's fountain pen!

BIFF: I didn't exactly steal it! That's just what I've been explaining to you!

HAPPY: He had it in his hand and just then Oliver walked in, so he got nervous and stuck it in his pocket!

WILLY: My God, Biff!

BIFF: I never intended to do it, Dad!

OPERATOR'S VOICE: Standish Arms, good evening!

WILLY (*shouting*): I'm not in my room!

BIFF (*frightened*): Dad, what's the matter? (*He and Happy stand up.*)

OPERATOR: Ringing Mr. Loman for you!

WILLY: I'm not there, stop it!

BIFF (*horrified, gets down on one knee before* Willy): Dad, I'll make good, I'll make good. (*Willy tries to get to his feet. Biff holds him down.*) Sit down now.

WILLY: No, you're no good, you're no good for anything.

BIFF: I am, Dad, I'll find something else, you understand? Now don't worry about anything. (*He holds up Willy's face.*) Talk to me, Dad.

OPERATOR: Mr. Loman does not answer. Shall I page him?

WILLY (*attempting to stand, as though to rush and silence the Operator*): No, no, no!

HAPPY: He'll strike something, Pop.

WILLY: No, no . . .

BIFF (*desperately, standing over* Willy): Pop, listen! Listen to me! I'm telling you something good. Oliver talked to his partner about the Florida idea. You listening? He—he talked to his partner, and he came to me . . . I'm going to be all right, you hear? Dad, listen to me, he said it was just a question of the amount!

WILLY: Then you . . . got it?

HAPPY: He's gonna be terrific, Pop!

WILLY (*trying to stand*): Then you got it, haven't you? You got it! You got it!

BIFF (*agonized, holds* Willy *down*): No, no. Look, Pop. I'm supposed to have lunch with them tomorrow. I'm just telling you this so you'll know that I can still make an impression, Pop. And I'll make good somewhere, but I can't go tomorrow, see?

WILLY: Why not? You simply—

BIFF: But the pen, Pop!

WILLY: You give it to him and tell him it was an oversight!

HAPPY: Sure, have lunch tomorrow!

BIFF: I can't say that—

WILLY: You were doing a crossword puzzle and accidentally used his pen!

BIFF: Listen, kid, I took those balls years ago, now I walk in with his fountain pen? That clinches it, don't you see? I can't face him like that! I'll try elsewhere.

PAGE'S VOICE: Paging Mr. Loman!

WILLY: Don't you want to be anything?

BIFF: Pop, how can I go back?

WILLY: You don't want to be anything, is that what's behind it?

BIFF (*now angry at* Willy *for not crediting his sympathy*): Don't take it that way! You think it was easy walking into that office after what I'd done to him? A team of horses couldn't have dragged me back to Bill Oliver!

WILLY: Then why'd you go?

BIFF: Why did I go? Why did I go! Look at you! Look at what's become of you!

(*Off left, The Woman laughs.*)

WILLY: Biff, you're going to go to that lunch tomorrow, or—

BIFF: I can't go. I've got no appointment!

HAPPY: Biff, for . . . !

WILLY: Are you spiting me?

BIFF: Don't take it that way! Goddammit!

WILLY (*strikes Biff and falters away from the table*): You rotten little louse! Are you spiting me?

THE WOMAN: Someone's at the door, Willy!

BIFF: I'm no good, can't you see what I am?

HAPPY (*separating them*): Hey, you're in a restaurant! Now cut it out, both of you! (*The girls enter.*) Hello, girls, sit down.

(*The Woman laughs, off left.*)

MISS FORSYTHE: I guess we might as well. This is Letta.

THE WOMAN: Willy, are you going to wake up?

BIFF (*ignoring Willy*): How're ya, miss, sit down. What do you drink?

MISS FORSYTHE: Letta might not be able to stay long.

LETTA: I gotta get up very early tomorrow. I got jury duty. I'm so excited! Were you fellows ever on a jury?

BIFF: No, but I been in front of them! (*The girls laugh.*) This is my father.

LETTA: Isn't he cute? Sit down with us, Pop.

HAPPY: Sit him down, Biff!

BIFF (*going to him*): Come on, slugger, drink us under the table. To hell with it! Come on, sit down, pal.

(*On Biff's last insistence, Willy is about to sit.*)

THE WOMAN (*now urgently*): Willy, are you going to answer the door!

(*The Woman's call pulls Willy back. He starts right, befuddled.*)

BIFF: Hey, where are you going?

WILLY: Open the door.

BIFF: The door?

WILLY: The washroom . . . the door . . . where's the door?

BIFF (*leading Willy to the left*): Just go straight down.

(*Willy moves left.*)

THE WOMAN: Willy, Willy, are you going to get up, get up, get up, get up?

(*Willy exits left.*)

LETTA: I think it's sweet you bring your daddy along.

MISS FORSYTHE: Oh, he isn't really your father!

BIFF (*at left, turning to her resentfully*): Miss Forsythe, you've just seen a prince walk by. A fine, troubled prince. A hard-working, unappreciated prince. A pal, you understand? A good companion. Always for his boys.

LETTA: That's so sweet.

HAPPY: Well, girls, what's the program? We're wasting time. Come on, Biff. Gather round. Where would you like to go?

BIFF: Why don't you do something for him?

HAPPY: Me!

BIFF: Don't you give a damn for him, Hap?

HAPPY: What're you talking about? I'm the one who—

BIFF: I sense it, you don't give a good goddam about him. (*He takes the rolled-up hose from his pocket and puts it on the table in front of Happy.*) Look what I found in the cellar, for Christ's sake. How can you bear to let it go on?

HAPPY: Me? Who goes away? Who runs off and—

BIFF: Yeah, but he doesn't mean anything to you. You could help him—I can't! Don't you understand what I'm talking about? He's going to kill himself, don't you know that?

HAPPY: Don't I know it! Me!

BIFF: Hap, help him! Jesus . . . help him . . . Help me, help me, I can't bear to look at his face! (*Ready to weep, he hurries out, up right.*)

HAPPY (*starting after him*): Where are you going?

MISS FORSYTHE: What's he so mad about?

HAPPY: Come on, girls, we'll catch up with him.

MISS FORSYTHE (*as Happy pushes her out*): Say, I don't like that temper of his!

HAPPY: He's just a little overstrung, he'll be all right!

WILLY (*off left, as The Woman laughs*): Don't answer! Don't answer!

LETTA: Don't you want to tell your father—

HAPPY: No, that's not my father. He's just a guy. Come on, we'll catch Biff, and, honey, we're going to paint this town! Stanley, where's the check! Hey, Stanley!

(*They exit. Stanley looks toward left.*)

STANLEY (*calling to Happy indignantly*): Mr. Loman! Mr. Loman!

(*Stanley picks up a chair and follows them off. Knocking is heard off left. The Woman enters, laughing. Willy follows her. She is in a black slip; he is buttoning his shirt. Raw, sensuous music accompanies their speech.*)

WILLY: Will you stop laughing? Will you stop?

THE WOMAN: Aren't you going to answer the door? He'll wake the whole hotel.

WILLY: I'm not expecting anybody.

THE WOMAN: Whyn't you have another drink, honey, and stop being so damn self-centered?

WILLY: I'm so lonely.

THE WOMAN: You know you ruined me, Willy? From now on, whenever you come to the office, I'll see that you go right through to the buyers. No waiting at my desk anymore, Willy. You ruined me.

WILLY: That's nice of you to say that.

THE WOMAN: Gee, you are self-centered! Why so sad? You are the saddest, self-centeredest soul I ever did see-saw. (*She laughs. He kisses her.*) Come on inside, drummer boy. It's silly to be dressing in the middle of the night. (*As knocking is heard.*) Aren't you going to answer the door?

WILLY: They're knocking on the wrong door.

THE WOMAN: But I felt the knocking. And he heard us talking in here. Maybe the hotel's on fire!

WILLY (*his terror rising*): It's a mistake.

THE WOMAN: Then tell him to go away!

WILLY: There's nobody there.

THE WOMAN: It's getting on my nerves, Willy. There's somebody standing out there and it's getting on my nerves!

WILLY (*pushing her away from him*): All right, stay in the bathroom here, and don't come out. I think there's a law in Massachusetts about it, so don't come out. It may be that new room clerk. He looked very mean. So don't come out. It's a mistake, there's no fire.

(*The knocking is heard again. He takes a few steps away from her, and she vanishes into the wing. The light follows him, and now he is facing Young Biff, who carries a suitcase. Biff steps toward him. The music is gone.*)

BIFF: Why didn't you answer?

WILLY: Biff! What are you doing in Boston?

BIFF: Why didn't you answer? I've been knocking for five minutes, I called you on the phone—

WILLY: I just heard you. I was in the bathroom and had the door shut. Did anything happen home?

BIFF: Dad—I let you down.

WILLY: What do you mean?

BIFF: Dad . . .

WILLY: Biffo, what's this about? (*Putting his arm around Biff.*) Come on, let's go downstairs and get you a malted.

BIFF: Dad, I flunked math.

WILLY: Not for the term?

BIFF: The term. I haven't got enough credits to graduate.

WILLY: You mean to say Bernard wouldn't give you the answers?

BIFF: He did, he tried, but I only got a sixty-one.

WILLY: And they wouldn't give you four points?

BIFF: Birnbaum refused absolutely. I begged him, Pop, but he won't give me those points. You gotta talk to him before they close the school. Because if he saw the kind of man you are, and you just talked to him in your way, I'm sure he'd come through for me. The class came right before practice, see, and I didn't go enough. Would you talk to him? He'd like you, Pop. You know the way you could talk.

WILLY: You're on. We'll drive right back.

BIFF: Oh, Dad, good work! I'm sure he'll change it for you!

WILLY: Go downstairs and tell the clerk I'm checkin' out. Go right down.

BIFF: Yes, sir! See, the reason he hates me, Pop—one day he was late for class so I got up at the blackboard and imitated him. I crossed my eyes and talked with a lithp.

WILLY (*laughing*): You did? The kids like it?

BIFF: They nearly died laughing!

WILLY: Yeah? What'd you do?

BIFF: The thquare root of thixthy twee is . . . (*Willy bursts out laughing; Biff joins.*) And in the middle of it he walked in!

(*Willy laughs and The Woman joins in offstage.*)

WILLY (*without hesitation*): Hurry downstairs and—

BIFF: Somebody in there?

WILLY: No, that was next door.

(*The Woman laughs offstage.*)

BIFF: Somebody got in your bathroom!

WILLY: No, it's the next room, there's a party—

THE WOMAN (*enters, laughing. She lisps this.*): Can I come in? There's something in the bathtub, Willy, and it's moving!

(*Willy looks at Biff, who is staring open-mouthed and horrified at The Woman.*)

WILLY: Ah—you better go back to your room. They must be finished painting by now. They're painting her room so I let her take a shower here. Go back, go back . . . (*He pushes her.*)

THE WOMAN (*resisting*): But I've got to get dressed, Willy, I can't—

WILLY: Get out of here! Go back, go back . . . (*Suddenly striving for the ordinary.*) This is Miss Francis, Biff, she's a buyer. They're painting her room. Go back, Miss Francis, go back . . .

THE WOMAN: But my clothes, I can't go out naked in the hall!

WILLY (*pushing her offstage*): Get outa here! Go back, go back!

(*Biff slowly sits down on his suitcase as the argument continues offstage.*)

THE WOMAN: Where's my stockings? You promised me stockings, Willy!

WILLY: I have no stockings here!

THE WOMAN: You had two boxes of size nine sheers for me, and I want them!

WILLY: Here, for God's sake, will you get outa here!

THE WOMAN (*enters holding a box of stockings*): I just hope there's nobody in the hall. That's all I hope. (*To Biff.*) Are you football or baseball?

BIFF: Football.

THE WOMAN (*angry, humiliated*): That's me too. G'night. (*She snatches her clothes from Willy, and walks out.*)

WILLY (*after a pause*): Well, better get going. I want to get to the school first thing in the morning. Get my suits out of the closet. I'll get my valise. (*Biff doesn't move.*) What's the matter! (*Biff remains motionless, tears falling.*) She's a buyer. Buys for J. H. Simmons. She lives down the hall—they're painting. You don't imagine—(*He breaks off. After a pause.*) Now listen, pal, she's just a buyer. She sees merchandise in her room and they have to keep it looking just so . . . (*Pause. Assuming command.*) All right, get my suits. (*Biff doesn't move.*) Now stop crying and do as I say. I gave you an order. Biff, I gave you an order! Is that what you do when I give you an order? How dare you cry! (*Putting his arm around Biff.*) Now look, Biff, when you grow up you'll understand about these things. You mustn't—you mustn't overemphasize a thing like this. I'll see Birnbaum first thing in the morning.

BIFF: Never mind.

WILLY (*getting down beside Biff*): Never mind! He's going to give you those points. I'll see to it.

BIFF: He wouldn't listen to you.

WILLY: He certainly will listen to me. You need those points for the U. of Virginia.

BIFF: I'm not going there.

WILLY: Heh? If I can't get him to change that mark you'll make it up in summer school. You've got all summer to—

BIFF (*his weeping breaking from him*): Dad . . .

WILLY (*infected by it*): Oh, my boy . . .

BIFF: Dad . . .

WILLY: She's nothing to me, Biff. I was lonely, I was terribly lonely.

BIFF: You—you gave her Mama's stockings! (*His tears break through and he rises to go.*)

WILLY (*grabbing for Biff*): I gave you an order!

BIFF: Don't touch me, you—liar!

WILLY: Apologize for that!

BIFF: You fake! You phony little fake! You fake! (*Overcome, he turns quickly and weeping fully goes out with his suitcase. Willy is left on the floor on his knees.*)

WILLY: I gave you an order! Biff, come back here or I'll beat you! Come back here! I'll whip you!

(*Stanley comes quickly in from the right and stands in front of Willy.*)

WILLY (*shouts at Stanley*): I gave you an order . . .

STANLEY: Hey, let's pick it up, pick it up, Mr. Loman. (*He helps Willy to his feet.*) Your boys left with the chippies. They said they'll see you home.

(*A second waiter watches some distance away.*)

WILLY: But we were supposed to have dinner together.

(*Music is heard, Willy's theme.*)

STANLEY: Can you make it?

WILLY: I'll—sure, I can make it. (*Suddenly concerned about his clothes.*) Do I—I look all right?

STANLEY: Sure, you look all right. (*He flicks a speck off Willy's lapel.*)

WILLY: Here—here's a dollar.

STANLEY: Oh, your son paid me. It's all right.

WILLY (*putting it in Stanley's hand*): No, take it. You're a good boy.

STANLEY: Oh, no, you don't have to . . .

WILLY: Here—here's some more, I don't need it anymore. (*After a slight pause.*) Tell me—is there a seed store in the neighborhood?

STANLEY: Seeds? You mean like to plant?

(*As Willy turns, Stanley slips the money back into his jacket pocket.*)

WILLY: Yes. Carrots, peas . . .

STANLEY: Well, there's hardware stores on Sixth Avenue, but it may be too late now.

WILLY (*anxiously*): Oh, I'd better hurry. I've got to get some seeds. (*He starts off to the right.*) I've got to get some seeds, right away. Nothing's planted. I don't have a thing in the ground.

(*Willy hurries out as the light goes down. Stanley moves over to the right after him, watches him off. The other waiter has been staring at Willy.*)

STANLEY (*to the waiter*): Well, whatta you looking at?

(*The waiter picks up the chairs and moves off right. Stanley takes the table and follows him. The light fades on this area. There is a long pause, the sound of the flute coming over. The light gradually rises on the kitchen, which is empty. Happy appears at the door of the house, followed by Biff. Happy is carrying a large bunch of long-stemmed roses. He enters the kitchen, looks around for Linda. Not seeing her, he turns to Biff, who is just outside the house door, and makes a gesture with his hands, indicating "Not here, I guess." He looks into the living room and freezes. Inside, Linda, unseen, is seated, Willy's coat on her lap. She rises ominously and quietly and moves toward Happy, who backs up into the kitchen, afraid.*)

HAPPY: Hey, what're you doing up? (*Linda says nothing but moves toward him implacably.*) Where's Pop? (*He keeps backing to the right, and now Linda is in full view in the doorway to the living room.*) Is he sleeping?

LINDA: Where were you?

HAPPY (*trying to laugh it off*): We met two girls, Mom, very fine types. Here, we brought you some flowers. (*Offering them to her.*) Put them in your room, Ma.

(*She knocks them to the floor at Biff's feet. He has now come inside and closed the door behind him. She stares at Biff, silent.*)

HAPPY: Now what'd you do that for? Mom, I want you to have some flowers—

LINDA (*cutting Happy off, violently to Biff*): Don't you care whether he lives or dies?

HAPPY (*going to the stairs*): Come upstairs, Biff.

BIFF (*with a flare of disgust, to Happy*): Go away from me! (*To Linda.*) What do you mean, lives or dies? Nobody's dying around here, pal.

LINDA: Get out of my sight! Get out of here!

BIFF: I wanna see the boss.

LINDA: You're not going near him!

BIFF: Where is he? (*He moves into the living room and Linda follows.*)

LINDA (*shouting after Biff*): You invite him for dinner. He looks forward to it all day—(*Biff appears in his parents' bedroom, looks around, and exits*)—and then you desert him there. There's no stranger you'd do that to!

HAPPY: Why? He had a swell time with us. Listen, when I—(*Linda comes back into the kitchen*)—desert him I hope I don't outlive the day!

LINDA: Get out of here!

HAPPY: Now look, Mom . . .

LINDA: Did you have to go to women tonight? You and your lousy rotten whores!

(*Biff reenters the kitchen.*)

HAPPY: Mom, all we did was follow Biff around trying to cheer him up! (*To Biff.*) Boy, what a night you gave me!

LINDA: Get out of here, both of you, and don't come back! I don't want you tormenting him any more. Go on now, get your things together! (*To Biff.*) You can sleep in his apartment. (*She starts to pick up the flowers and stops herself.*) Pick up this stuff, I'm not your maid anymore. Pick it up, you bum, you!

(*Happy turns his back to her in refusal. Biff slowly moves over and gets down on his knees, picking up the flowers.*)

LINDA: You're a pair of animals! Not one, not another living soul would have had the cruelty to walk out on that man in a restaurant!

BIFF (*not looking at her*): Is that what he said?

LINDA: He didn't have to say anything. He was so humiliated he nearly limped when he came in.

HAPPY: But, Mom, he had a great time with us—

BIFF (*cutting him off violently*): Shut up!

(*Without another word, Happy goes upstairs.*)

LINDA: You! You didn't even go in to see if he was all right!

BIFF (*still on the floor in front of Linda, the flowers in his hand; with self-loathing*): No. Didn't. Didn't do a damned thing. How do you like that, heh? Left him babbling in a toilet.

LINDA: You louse. You . . .

BIFF: Now you hit it on the nose! (*He gets up, throws the flowers in the wastebasket.*) The scum of the earth, and you're looking at him!

LINDA: Get out of here!

BIFF: I gotta talk to the boss, Mom. Where is he?

LINDA: You're not going near him. Get out of this house!

BIFF (*with absolute assurance, determination*): No. We're gonna have an abrupt conversation, him and me.

LINDA: You're not talking to him.

(*Hammering is heard from outside the house, off right. Biff turns toward the noise.*)

LINDA (*suddenly pleading*): Will you please leave him alone?

BIFF: What's he doing out there?

LINDA: He's planting the garden!

BIFF (*quietly*): Now? Oh, my God!

(*Biff moves outside, Linda following. The light dies down on them and comes up on the center of the apron as Willy walks into it. He is carrying a flashlight, a hoe, and a handful of seed packets. He raps the top of the hoe sharply to fix it firmly, and then moves to the left, measuring off the distance with his foot. He holds the flashlight to look at the seed packets, reading off the instructions. He is in the blue of night.*)

WILLY: Carrots . . . quarter-inch apart. Rows . . . one-foot rows. (*He measures it off.*) One foot. (*He puts down a package and measures off.*) Beets. (*He puts down another package and measures again.*) Lettuce. (*He reads the package, puts it down.*) One foot—(*He breaks off as Ben appears at the right and moves slowly down to him.*) What a proposition, ts, ts. Terrific, terrific. 'Cause she's suffered, Ben, the woman has suffered. You understand me? A man can't go out the way he came in, Ben, a man has got to add up to something. You can't, you can't—(*Ben moves toward him as though to interrupt.*) You gotta consider, now. Don't answer so quick. Remember, it's a guaranteed twenty-thousand-dollar proposition. Now look, Ben, I want you to go through the ins and outs of this thing with me. I've got nobody to talk to, Ben, and the woman has suffered, you hear me?

BEN (*standing still, considering*): What's the proposition?

WILLY: It's twenty thousand dollars on the barrelhead. Guaranteed, gilt-edged, you understand?

BEN: You don't want to make a fool of yourself. They might not honor the policy.

WILLY: How can they dare refuse? Didn't I work like a coolie to meet every premium on the nose? And now they don't pay off? Impossible!

BEN: It's called a cowardly thing, William.

WILLY: Why? Does it take more guts to stand here the rest of my life ringing up a zero?

BEN (*yielding*): That's a point, William. (*He moves, thinking, turns.*) And twenty thousand—that is something one can feel with the hand, it is there.

WILLY (*now assured, with rising power*): Oh, Ben, that's the whole beauty of it! I see it like a diamond, shining in the dark, hard and rough, that I can pick up and touch in my hand. Not like—like an appointment! This would not be another damned-fool appointment, Ben, and it changes all the aspects. Because he thinks I'm nothing, see, and so he spites me. But the funeral—(*Straightening up.*) Ben, that funeral will be massive! They'll come from Maine, Massachusetts, Vermont, New Hampshire! All the old-timers with the strange license plates—that boy will be thunderstruck, Ben, because he never realized—I am known! Rhode Island, New York, New Jersey—I am known, Ben and he'll see it with his eyes once and for all. He'll see what I am, Ben! He's in for a shock, that boy!

BEN (*coming down to the edge of the garden*): He'll call you a coward.

WILLY (*suddenly fearful*): No, that would be terrible.

BEN: Yes. And a damned fool.

WILLY: No, no, he mustn't, I won't have that! (*He is broken and desperate.*)

BEN: He'll hate you, William.

(*The gay music of the Boys is heard.*)

WILLY: Oh, Ben, how do we get back to all the great times? Used to be so full of light, and comradeship, the sleigh-riding in winter, and the ruddiness on his cheeks. And always some kind of good news coming up, always something nice coming up ahead. And never even let me carry the valises in the house, and simonizing, simonizing that little red car! Why, why can't I give him something and not have him hate me?

BEN: Let me think about it. (*He glances at his watch.*) I still have a little time. Remarkable proposition, but you've got to be sure you're not making a fool of yourself.

(*Ben drifts off upstage and goes out of sight. Biff comes down from the left.*)

WILLY (*suddenly conscious of Biff, turns and looks up at him, then begins picking up the packages of seeds in confusion*): Where the hell is that seed? (*Indignantly.*) You can't see nothing out here! They boxed in the whole goddam neighborhood!

BIFF: There are people all around here. Don't you realize that?

WILLY: I'm busy. Don't bother me.

BIFF (*taking the hoe from Willy*): I'm saying good-by to you, Pop. (*Willy looks at him, silent, unable to move.*) I'm not coming back any more.

WILLY: You're not going to see Oliver tomorrow?

BIFF: I've got no appointment, Dad.

WILLY: He put his arm around you, and you've got no appointment?

BIFF: Pop, get this now, will you? Everytime I've left it's been a fight that sent me out of here. Today I realized something about myself and I tried to explain it to you and I—I think I'm just not smart enough to make any sense out of it for you. To hell with whose fault it is or anything like that. (*He takes Willy's arm.*) Let's just wrap it up, heh? Come on in, we'll tell Mom. (*He gently tries to pull Willy to left.*)

WILLY (*frozen, immobile, with guilt in his voice*): No, I don't want to see her.

BIFF: Come on! (*He pulls again, and Willy tries to pull away.*)

WILLY (*highly nervous*): No, no, I don't want to see her.

BIFF (*tries to look into Willy's face, as if to find the answer there*): Why don't you want to see her?

WILLY (*more harshly now*): Don't bother me, will you?

BIFF: What do you mean, you don't want to see her? You don't want them calling you yellow, do you? This isn't your fault; it's me, I'm a bum. Now come inside! (*Willy strains to get away.*) Did you hear what I said to you?

(*Willy pulls away and quickly goes by himself into the house. Biff follows.*)

LINDA (*to Willy*): Did you plant, dear?

BIFF (*at the door, to Linda*): All right, we had it out. I'm going and I'm not writing any more.

LINDA (*going to Willy in the kitchen*): I think that's the best way, dear. 'Cause there's no use drawing it out, you'll just never get along.

(*Willy doesn't respond.*)

BIFF: People ask where I am and what I'm doing, you don't know, and you don't care. That way it'll be off your mind and you can start brightening up again. All right? That clears it, doesn't it? (*Willy is silent, and Biff goes to him.*) You gonna wish me luck, scout? (*He extends his hand.*) What do you say?

LINDA: Shake his hand, Willy.

WILLY (*turning to her, seething with hurt*): There's no necessity to mention the pen at all, y'know.

BIFF (*gently*): I've got no appointment, Dad.

WILLY (*erupting fiercely*): He put his arm around . . . ?

BIFF: Dad, you're never going to see what I am, so what's the use of arguing? If I strike oil I'll send you a check. Meantime forget I'm alive.

WILLY (*to Linda*): Spite, see?

BIFF: Shake hands, Dad.

WILLY: Not my hand.

BIFF: I was hoping not to go this way.

WILLY: Well, this is the way you're going. Good-by.

(*Biff looks at him a moment, then turns sharply and goes to the stairs.*)

WILLY (*stops him with*): May you rot in hell if you leave this house!

BIFF (*turning*): Exactly what is it that you want from me?

WILLY: I want you to know, on the train, in the mountains, in the valleys, wherever you go, that you cut down your life for spite!

BIFF: No, no.

WILLY: Spite, spite, is the word of your undoing! And when you're down and out, remember what did it. When you're rotting somewhere beside the railroad tracks, remember, and don't you dare blame it on me!

BIFF: I'm not blaming it on you!

WILLY: I won't take the rap for this, you hear?

(*Happy comes down the stairs and stands on the bottom step, watching.*)

BIFF: That's just what I'm telling you!

WILLY (*sinking into a chair at a table, with full accusation*): You're trying to put a knife in me—don't think I don't know what you're doing!

BIFF: All right, phony! Then let's lay it on the line. (*He whips the rubber tube out of his pocket and puts it on the table.*)

HAPPY: You crazy . . .

LINDA: Biff! (*She moves to grab the hose, but Biff holds it down with his hand.*)

BIFF: Leave it there! Don't move it!

WILLY (*not looking at it*): What is that?

BIFF: You know goddam well what that is.

WILLY (*caged, wanting to escape*): I never saw that.

BIFF: You saw it. The mice didn't bring it into the cellar! What is this supposed to do, make a hero out of you? This supposed to make me sorry for you?

WILLY: Never heard of it.

BIFF: There'll be no pity for you, you hear it? No pity!

WILLY (*to Linda*): You hear the spite!

BIFF: No, you're going to hear the truth—what you are and what I am!

LINDA: Stop it!

WILLY: Spite!

HAPPY (*coming down toward Biff*): You cut it now!

BIFF (*to Happy*): The man don't know who we are! The man is gonna know! (*To Willy.*) We never told the truth for ten minutes in this house!

Dustin Hoffman as Willy Loman in the 1985 television version of *Death of a Salesman*.

HAPPY: We always told the truth!

BIFF (*turning on him*): You big blow, are you the assistant buyer? You're one of the two assistants to the assistant, aren't you?

HAPPY: Well, I'm practically . . .

BIFF: You're practically full of it! We all are! and I'm through with it. (*To Willy.*) Now hear this, Willy, this is me.

WILLY: I know you!

BIFF: You know why I had no address for three months? I stole a suit in Kansas City and I was in jail. (*To Linda, who is sobbing.*) Stop crying. I'm through with it.

(*Linda turns away from them, her hands covering her face.*)

WILLY: I suppose that's my fault!

BIFF: I stole myself out of every good job since high school!

WILLY: And whose fault is that?

BIFF: And I never got anywhere because you blew me so full of hot air I could never stand taking orders from anybody! That's whose fault it is!

WILLY: I hear that!

LINDA: Don't, Biff!

BIFF: It's goddam time you heard that! I had to be boss big shot in two weeks, and I'm through with it!

WILLY: Then hang yourself! For spite, hang yourself!

BIFF: No! Nobody's hanging himself, Willy! I ran down eleven flights with a pen in my hand today. And suddenly I stopped, you hear me? And in the middle of that office building, do you hear this? I stopped in the middle of that building and I saw—the sky. I saw the things that I love in this world. The work and the food and time to sit and smoke. And I looked at the pen and said to myself, what the hell am I grabbing this for? Why am I trying to become what I don't want to be? What am I doing in an office, making a contemptuous begging fool of myself, when all I want is out there, waiting for me the minute I say I know who I am! Why can't I say that, Willy? (*He tries to make Willy face him, but Willy pulls away and moves to the left.*)

WILLY (*with hatred, threateningly*): The door of your life is wide open!

BIFF: Pop! I'm a dime a dozen, and so are you!

WILLY (*turning on him now in an uncontrolled outburst*): I am not a dime a dozen! I am Willy Loman, and you are Biff Loman!

(*Biff starts for Willy, but is blocked by Happy. In his fury, Biff seems on the verge of attacking his father.*)

BIFF: I am not a leader of men, Willy, and neither are you. You were never anything but a hard-working drummer who landed in the ash can like all the rest of them! I'm one dollar an hour, Willy! I tried seven states and couldn't raise it. A buck an hour! Do you gather my meaning? I'm not bringing home any prizes any more, and you're going to stop waiting for me to bring them home!

WILLY (*directly to Biff*): You vengeful, spiteful mutt!

(*Biff breaks from Happy. Willy, in fright, starts up the stairs. Biff grabs him.*)

BIFF (*at the peak of his fury*): Pop, I'm nothing! I'm nothing, Pop. Can't you understand that? There's no spite in it any more. I'm just what I am, that's all.

(*Biff's fury has spent itself and he breaks down, sobbing, holding on to Willy, who dumbly fumbles for Biff's face.*)

WILLY (*astonished*): What're you doing? What're you doing? (*To Linda.*) Why is he crying?

BIFF (*crying, broken*): Will you let me go, for Christ's sake? Will you take that phony dream and burn it before something happens? (*Struggling to contain himself he pulls away and moves to the stairs.*) I'll go in the morning. Put him—put him to bed. (*Exhausted, Biff moves up the stairs to his room.*)

WILLY (*after a long pause, astonished, elevated*): Isn't that—isn't that remarkable? Biff—he likes me!

LINDA: He loves you, Willy!

HAPPY (*deeply moved*): Always did, Pop.

WILLY: Oh, Biff! (*Staring wildly.*) He cried! Cried to me. (*He is choking with his love, and now cries out his promise.*) That boy—that boy is going to be magnificent!

(*Ben appears in the light just outside the kitchen.*)

BEN: Yes, outstanding, with twenty thousand behind him.

LINDA (*sensing the racing of his mind, fearfully, carefully*): Now come to bed, Willy. It's all settled now.

WILLY (*finding it difficult not to rush out of the house*): Yes, we'll sleep. Come on. Go to sleep, Hap.

BEN: And it does take a great kind of a man to crack the jungle.

(*In accents of dread, Ben's idyllic music starts up.*)

HAPPY (*his arm around Linda*): I'm getting married, Pop, don't forget it. I'm changing everything. I'm gonna run that department before the year is up. You'll see, Mom. (*He kisses her.*)

BEN: The jungle is dark but full of diamonds, Willy.

(*Willy turns, moves, listening to Ben.*)

LINDA: Be good. You're both good boys, just act that way, that's all.

HAPPY: 'Night, Pop. (*He goes upstairs.*)

LINDA (*to Willy*): Come, dear.

BEN (*with greater force*): One must go in to fetch a diamond out.

WILLY (*to Linda, as he moves slowly along the edge of kitchen, toward the door*): I just want to get settled down, Linda. Let me sit alone for a little.

LINDA (*almost uttering her fear*): I want you upstairs.

WILLY (*taking her in his arms*): In a few minutes, Linda. I couldn't sleep right now. Go on, you look awful tired. (*He kisses her.*)

BEN: Not like an appointment at all. A diamond is rough and hard to the touch.

WILLY: Go on now. I'll be right up.

LINDA: I think this is the only way, Willy.

WILLY: Sure, it's the best thing.

BEN: Best thing!

WILLY: The only way. Everything is gonna be—go on, kid, get to bed. You look so tired.

LINDA: Come right up.

WILLY: Two minutes.

(*Linda goes into the living room, then reappears in her bedroom. Willy moves just outside the kitchen door.*)

WILLY: Loves me. (*Wonderingly.*) Always loved me. Isn't that a remarkable thing? Ben, he'll worship me for it!

BEN (*with promise*): It's dark there, but full of diamonds.

WILLY: Can you imagine that magnificence with twenty thousand dollars in his pocket?

LINDA (*calling from her room*): Willy! Come up!

WILLY (*calling into the kitchen*): Yes! yes. Coming! It's very smart, you realize that, don't you, sweetheart? Even Ben sees it. I gotta go, baby. 'By! 'By! (*Going*

Biff (Kevin Anderson) and Willy (Brian Dennehy) try to console each other in Robert Falls's 1999 production of *Death of a Salesman.*

over to Ben, almost dancing.) Imagine? When the mail comes he'll be ahead of Bernard again!

BEN: A perfect proposition all around.

WILLY: Did you see how he cried to me? Oh, if I could kiss him, Ben!

BEN: Time, William, time!

WILLY: Oh, Ben, I always knew one way or another we were gonna make it, Biff and I!

BEN (*looking at his watch*): The boat. We'll be late. (*He moves slowly off into the darkness.*)

WILLY (*elegiacally, turning to the house*): Now when you kick off, boy, I want a seventy-yard boot, and get right down the field under the ball, and when you hit, hit low and hit hard, because it's important, boy. (*He swings around and faces the audience.*) There's all kinds of important people in the stands, and the first thing you know . . . (*Suddenly realizing he is alone.*) Ben! Ben, where do I . . . ? (*He makes a sudden movement of search.*) Ben, how do I . . . ?

LINDA (*calling*): Willy, you coming up?

WILLY (*uttering a gasp of fear, whirling about as if to quiet her*): Sh! (*He turns around as if to find his way; sounds, faces, voices, seem to be swarming in upon him and he flicks at them, crying, Sh! Sh! Suddenly music, faint and high, stops him. It rises in intensity, almost to an unbearable scream. He goes up and down on his toes, and rushes off around the house.*) Shhh!

LINDA: Willy?

(*There is no answer. Linda waits. Biff gets up off his bed. He is still in his clothes. Happy sits up. Biff stands listening.*)

LINDA (*with real fear*): Willy, answer me! Willy!

(*There is the sound of a car starting and moving away at full speed.*)

LINDA: No!

BIFF (*rushing down the stairs*): Pop!

(*As the car speeds off, the music crashes down in a frenzy of sound, which becomes the soft pulsation of a single cello string. Biff slowly returns to his bedroom. He and Happy gravely don their jackets. Linda slowly walks out of her room. The music has developed into a dead march. The leaves of day are appearing over everything. Charley and Bernard, somberly dressed, appear and knock on the kitchen door. Biff and Happy slowly descend the stairs to the kitchen as Charley and Bernard enter. All stop a moment when Linda, in clothes of mourning, bearing a little bunch of roses, comes through the draped doorway into the kitchen. She goes to Charley and takes his arm. Now all move toward the audience, through the wall-line of the kitchen. At the limit of the apron, Linda lays down the flowers, kneels, and sits back on her heels. All stare down at the grave.*)

REQUIEM

CHARLEY: It's getting dark, Linda.

(*Linda doesn't react. She stares at the grave.*)

BIFF: How about it, Mom? Better get some rest, heh? They'll be closing the gate soon.

(*Linda makes no move. Pause.*)

HAPPY (*deeply angered*): He had no right to do that. There was no necessity for it. We would've helped him.

CHARLEY (*grunting*): Hmmm.

BIFF: Come along, Mom.

LINDA: Why didn't anybody come?

CHARLEY: It was a very nice funeral.

LINDA: But where are all the people he knew? Maybe they blame him.

CHARLEY: Naa. It's a rough world, Linda. They wouldn't blame him.

LINDA: I can't understand it. At this time especially. First time in thirty-five years we were just about free and clear. He only needed a little salary. He was even finished with the dentist.

CHARLEY: No man only needs a little salary.

LINDA: I can't understand it.

BIFF: There were a lot of nice days. When he'd come home from a trip; or on Sundays, making the stoop; finishing the cellar; putting on the new porch; when he built the extra bathroom; and put up the garage. You know something, Charley, there's more of him in that front stoop than in all the sales he ever made.

CHARLEY: Yeah. He was a happy man with a batch of cement.

LINDA: He was so wonderful with his hands.

BIFF: He had the wrong dreams. All, all, wrong.

HAPPY (*almost ready to fight Biff*): Don't say that!

BIFF: He never knew who he was.

CHARLEY (*stopping Happy's movement and reply. To Biff*): Nobody dast blame this man. You don't understand: Willy was a salesman. And for a salesman, there is no rock bottom to the life. He don't put a bolt to a nut, he don't tell you the law or give you medicine. He's a man way out there in the blue, riding on a smile and a shoeshine. And when they start not smiling back—that's an earthquake. And then you get yourself a couple of spots on your hat, and you're finished. Nobody dast blame this man. A salesman is got to dream, boy. It comes with the territory.

BIFF: Charley, the man didn't know who he was.

HAPPY (*infuriated*): Don't say that!

BIFF: Why don't you come with me, Happy?

HAPPY: I'm not licked that easily. I'm staying right in this city, and I'm gonna beat this racket! (*He looks at Biff, his chin set.*) The Loman Brothers!

BIFF: I know who I am, kid.

HAPPY: All right, boy. I'm gonna show you and everybody else that Willy Loman did not die in vain. He had a good dream. It's the only dream you can have—to come out number-one man. He fought it out here, and this is where I'm gonna win it for him.

BIFF (*with a hopeless glance at Happy, bends toward his mother*): Let's go, Mom.

LINDA: I'll be with you in a minute. Go on, Charley. (*He hesitates.*) I want to, just for a minute. I never had a chance to say good-by.

(*Charley moves away, followed by Happy. Biff remains a slight distance up and left of Linda. She sits there, summoning herself. The flute begins, not far away, playing behind her speech.*)

LINDA: Forgive me, dear. I can't cry. I don't know what it is, but I can't cry. I don't understand it. Why did you ever do that? Help me, Willy, I can't cry. It seems to me that you're just on another trip. I keep expecting you. Willy, dear, I can't cry. Why did you do it? I search and search and I search, and I can't understand it, Willy. I made the last payment on the house today. Today, dear. And there'll be nobody home. (*A sob rises in her throat.*) We're free and clear. (*Sobbing more fully, released.*) We're free. (*Biff comes slowly toward her.*) We're free . . . We're free . . .

(*Biff lifts her to her feet and moves out up right with her in his arms. Linda sobs quietly. Bernard and Charley come together and follow them, followed by Happy. Only the music of the flute is left on the darkening stage as over the house the hard towers of the apartment buildings rise into sharp focus, and the curtain falls.*)

COMMENTARY

ARTHUR MILLER (1915–2005)

Tragedy and the Common Man 1949

One of the curious debates that arose around *Death of a Salesman* was the question of whether it was a genuine tragedy. One of the traditional requirements for tragedy is that the hero be of noble birth. Miller countered that notion with a clear statement of modern purpose regarding tragedy.

In this age few tragedies are written. It has often been held that the lack is due to a paucity of heroes among us, or else that modern man has had the blood drawn out of his organs of belief by the skepticism of science, and the heroic attack on life cannot feed on an attitude of reserve and circumspection. For one reason or another, we are often held to be below tragedy—or tragedy above us. The inevitable conclusion is, of course, that the tragic mode is archaic, fit only for the very highly placed, the kings or the kingly, and where this admission is not made in so many words it is most often implied.

I believe that the common man is as apt a subject for tragedy in its highest sense as kings were. On the face of it this ought to be obvious in the light of modern psychiatry, which bases its analysis upon classic formulations, such as the Oedipus and Orestes complexes, for instance, which were enacted by royal beings, but which apply to everyone in similar emotional situations.

More simply, when the question of tragedy in art is not at issue, we never hesitate to attribute to the well-placed and the exalted the very same mental processes as the lowly. And finally, if the exaltation of tragic action were truly a property of the high-bred character alone, it is inconceivable that the mass of mankind should cherish tragedy above all other forms, let alone be capable of understanding it.

As a general rule, to which there may be exceptions unknown to me, I think the tragic feeling is evoked in us when we are in the presence of a character who is ready to lay down his life, if need be, to secure one thing—his sense of personal dignity. From Orestes to Hamlet, Medea to Macbeth, the underlying struggle is that of the individual attempting to gain his "rightful" position in his society.

Sometimes he is one who has been displaced from it, sometimes one who seeks to attain it for the first time, but the fateful wound from which the inevitable events spiral is the wound of indignity, and its dominant force is indignation. Tragedy, then, is the consequence of a man's total compulsion to evaluate himself justly.

In the sense of having been initiated by the hero himself, the tale always reveals what has been called his "tragic flaw," a failing that is not peculiar to grand or elevated characters. Nor is it necessarily a weakness. The flaw, or crack in the character, is really nothing—and need be nothing—but his inherent unwillingness to remain passive in the face of what he conceives to be a challenge to his dignity, his image of his rightful status. Only the passive, only those who accept their lot without active retaliation, are "flawless." Most of us are in that category.

But there are among us today, as there always have been, those who act against the scheme of things that degrades them, and in the process of action everything we have accepted out of fear or insensitivity or ignorance is shaken before us and examined, and from this total onslaught by an individual against the seemingly stable cosmos surrounding us—from this total examination of the "unchangeable" environment—comes the terror and the fear that is classically associated with tragedy.

More important, from this total questioning of what has previously been unquestioned, we learn. And such a process is not beyond the common man. In revolutions around the world, these past thirty years, he has demonstrated again and again this inner dynamic of all tragedy.

Insistence upon the rank of the tragic hero, or the so-called nobility of his character, is really but a clinging to the outward forms of tragedy. If rank or nobility of character was indispensable, then it would follow that the problems of those with rank were the particular problems of tragedy. But surely the right of one monarch to capture the domain from another no longer raises our passions, nor are our concepts of justice what they were to the mind of an Elizabethan king.

The quality in such plays that does shake us, however, derives from the underlying fear of being displaced, the disaster inherent in being torn away from our chosen image of what and who we are in this world. Among us today this fear is as strong, and perhaps stronger, than it ever was. In fact, it is the common man who knows this fear best.

Now, if it is true that tragedy is the consequence of a man's total compulsion to evaluate himself justly, his destruction in the attempt posits a wrong or an evil in his environment. And this is precisely the morality of tragedy and its lesson. The discovery of the moral law, which is what the enlightenment of tragedy consists of, is not the discovery of some abstract or metaphysical quantity.

The tragic right is a condition of life, a condition in which the human personality is able to flower and realize itself. The wrong is the condition which suppresses man, perverts the flowing out of his love and creative instinct. Tragedy enlightens—and it must, in that it points the heroic finger at the enemy of man's freedom. The thrust for freedom is the quality in tragedy which exalts. The revolutionary questioning of the stable environment is what terrifies. In no way is the common man debarred from such thoughts or such actions.

Seen in this light, our lack of tragedy may be partially accounted for by the turn which modern literature has taken toward the purely psychiatric view of life, or the purely sociological. If all our miseries, our indignities, are born and bred within our minds, then all action, let alone the heroic action, is obviously impossible.

And if society alone is responsible for the cramping of our lives, then the protagonist must needs be so pure and faultless as to force us to deny his validity as a character. From neither of these views can tragedy derive, simply because neither represents a balanced concept of life. Above all else, tragedy requires the finest appreciation by the writer of cause and effect.

No tragedy can therefore come about when its author fears to question absolutely everything, when he regards any institution, habit, or custom as being either everlasting, immutable, or inevitable. In the tragic view the need of man to wholly realize himself is the only fixed star, and whatever it is that hedges his nature and lowers it is ripe for attack and examination. Which is not to say that tragedy must preach revolution.

The Greeks could probe the very heavenly origin of their ways and return to confirm the rightness of laws. And Job could face God in anger, demanding his right, and end in submission. But for a moment everything is in suspension, nothing is accepted, and in this stretching and tearing apart of the cosmos, in the very action of so doing, the character gains "size," the tragic stature which is spuriously attached to the royal or the highborn in our minds. The commonest of men may take on that stature to the extent of his willingness to throw all he has into the contest, the battle to secure his rightful place in his world.

There is a misconception of tragedy with which I have been struck in review after review, and in many conversations with writers and readers alike. It is the idea that tragedy is of necessity allied to pessimism. Even the dictionary says nothing more about the word than that it means a story with a sad or unhappy ending. This impression is so firmly fixed that I almost hesitate to claim that in truth tragedy implies more optimism in its author than does comedy, and that its final result ought to be the reinforcement of the onlooker's brightest opinions of the human animal.

For, if it is true to say that in essence the tragic hero is intent upon claiming his whole due as a personality, and if this struggle must be total and without reservation, then it automatically demonstrates the indestructible will of man to achieve his humanity.

The possibility of victory must be there in tragedy. Where pathos rules, where pathos is finally derived, a character has fought a battle he could not possibly have won. The pathetic is achieved when the protagonist is, by virtue of his witlessness, his insensitivity, or the very air he gives off, incapable of grappling with a much superior force.

Pathos truly is the mode for the pessimist. But tragedy requires a nicer balance between what is possible and what is impossible. And it is curious, although edifying, that the plays we revere, century after century, are the tragedies. In them, and in them alone, lies the belief—optimistic, if you will—in the perfectibility of man.

It is time, I think, that we who are without kings, took up this bright thread of our history and followed it to the only place it can possibly lead in our time—the heart and spirit of the average man.

Death of a Salesman

The original staging of *Death of a Salesman* presented enormous challenges to everyone involved with the production. In many ways the play was radical in conception. Not only was the theory of tragedy challenged by the choice of a traveling salesman as the hero, but the approach to the drama itself—the sense that one needed to get inside Willy Loman's head—made the first production quite different from what theatergoers in 1949 would have expected. Arthur Miller's original title for the play, *The Inside of His Head,* was a rough guide to staging problems. The final production designs bestowed a novel transparency on the Lomans' house, so that the audience was not just looking through a fourth wall, as in conventional stagings, but looking through a small world.

The designer for the stage, Jo Mielziner (1901–1976), was committed to innovation in stage design even before he was given the chance to work with director Elia Kazan on this project. In his notes, he discusses the ways in which the illusional realistic theater seemed to be limited in spite of extraordinary technical resources—the use of projections, film (or video), and multilevel staging—all of which could achieve effects that could only be suggested previously. He approached the problems of the play enthusiastically, as his journal excerpts reveal. While working on *Death of a Salesman,* he was approached by Josh Logan to work on *South Pacific,* an upbeat and timeless American musical that must have provided Mielziner with an emotional relief of sorts while he dealt with the complexities of Miller's dark play.

It is perhaps unfair to refer to the play as dark, but when Miller sent the script to Elia Kazan, already a distinguished director, Kazan called him and said, "What a sad play." Miller thought that Kazan was rejecting the play. At that time Miller was famous as the author of *All My Sons,* but he was not at all confident that his new play would be acceptable for the stage. However, Kazan, whose voice sounded almost funereal, went on to talk about his own father; Miller later said Kazan was the first of many people who saw their own fathers in Willy Loman. The conversation with Kazan ended with a commitment to produce the play within the year. Kazan's "Directing

Death of a Salesman" essay offers an overview of his experience as the play's director.

The problem of finding the right actor to play Willy Loman naturally challenged Kazan, who had Lee J. Cobb in mind right away, even though Miller believed that the actor who played the part should be small in stature. Cobb was so large a man that Miller referred to him as "the walrus," and for a very long time Miller had no confidence in Cobb's ability to play the part. Deep into rehearsals, Cobb internalized the role and shocked Miller into seeing him as perfect. From the beginning, Cobb was convinced that this play was a masterpiece and that it would alter theater history.

Casting for the play involved a great deal of thought and agreement between the author and the director. Arthur Miller, in his essay "The American Theater," gives us some interesting insights into the complexities and challenges that both actors and producers face. He includes an engrossing description of the way Mildred Dunnock, a distinguished and well-known actress, kept coming back for auditions even after being told she was not right for the role of Linda. What this demonstrates is that minds can be changed even when firm decisions have been made—and that people can misjudge the ability of actors to do the work that needs to be done. As it turned out, Mildred Dunnock was perfect for the part and breathed life into it as few actresses have done since.

As June Schlueter and James K. Flanagan point out, Willy Loman might well be the most memorable character in modern theater. Consequently, it is no surprise that a great variety of significant actors have played the role of Willy. Dustin Hoffman was notable as Willy and, because of his small size, close to what Miller had originally intended. Interestingly, Hoffman played Bernard in 1965, with Lee J. Cobb as Willy, when they produced a long-playing-record version of the play. Hume Cronyn and Brian Dennehy were both important in the part also, although Cronyn was almost *too* small in stature. Arthur Miller describes Ying Ruocheng, who translated the play into Chinese for Miller's 1983 production in Beijing, as a "brilliant" Willy.

All-black productions of the play, as well as versions in which some of the characters were played by black actors, presented their own issues. Brenda Murphy considers some of the questions that those renditions raised in her essay "Racial Consciousness in Casting *Death of a Salesman.*" Any view that sees Willy Loman as restricted to a specific place and time seems to have been contradicted by the remarkable range of productions and producers, all of which have faced considerable problems in staging and casting.

Some of the interesting questions concerning the universality of the play were answered in the Asian productions, which have been enthusiastically received. One such production was the Taiwanese production reviewed by professor and director Catherine Diamond. The Beijing production was especially exciting because it came at a time when China's attitude toward capitalism was beginning to shift.

Perhaps the only generalization that can really be made is that the challenges the play presents seem to have inspired a boundless upswelling of creativity.

JO MIELZINER (1901–1976)

Designing a Play: *Death of a Salesman* 1948–1949

A seasoned and already respected set designer when he began work on the play, Jo Mielziner reveals the detailed and demanding work that went into making the innovative designs for the first production of *Death of a Salesman*. The late nights; the collaboration with electricians and carpenters, not to mention those with the director and the producer; and all the worries and difficulties of conception — all these are revealed in the journal Mielziner kept as a record of his work on the play.

Figure 26. Jo Mielziner's early sketch for the design of the original 1949 production of *Death of a Salesman*.

Figure 27. Jo Mielziner's painting of the original set, showing the backdrop of apartment buildings.

December 15, 1948

During my midweek check-up of unfinished *Salesman* chores, I realized that a large number of basic decisions still had to be made about the small scenes outside Willy Loman's house. Since rehearsals were due to start a couple of days after Christmas, I appealed to Kazan for a good long session.

During the previous weeks I had been receiving from Arthur Miller, scene by scene, the final version of the rehearsal script. Although he had done the basic rewriting, he had made no attempt to say how the transitions from one scene to another would be made. This was a problem for the director and the designer to work out together as we studied the model, the ground plan, and the cut-out cardboard symbols representing the props.

I pointed out to Kazan how difficult it would be in an office scene, for instance, to remove two desks, two chairs, and a hat rack (which the present script called for) and at the same time have an actor walk quickly across the stage and appear in "a hotel room in Boston where he meets a girl." I urged him to do even more cutting, not in the text but in the props called for in this latest version of the script. We finally got the office pared down to one desk and one chair. Then I suggested going so far as to use the same desk for both office scenes—first in Heiser's office and then, with a change of other props, in Charley's office. As usual, Kazan's imagination rose to the suggestion. He replied, "Sure, let's cut this down to the bone—we can play on practically anything." This is effective abstraction, giving the spectator the opportunity to "fill in."

I had felt from the outset that the cemetery scene at the end of the play would be done on the forestage, and I had actually drawn up a design for a trick trapdoor out of which would rise the small gravestone that we had thought necessary for this scene. I had shown Kazan the working drawing for the gravestone, explained how

Figure 28. Mildred Dunnock (Linda), Lee J. Cobb (Willy), Arthur Kennedy (Biff), and Cameron Mitchell (Happy) on the original set of *Death of a Salesman* in 1949.

it would operate, and mentioned that because of union rules the man operating this mechanism would be doing this and nothing else, thereby adding a member to the crew for the sake of one effect. I had also mentioned that since the trap would be very close to the audience the sound of its opening might disturb the solemnity of the scene.

With some malice aforethought, I had also done a drawing showing the Salesman's widow sitting on the step leading to the forestage, with her two sons standing behind her, their heads bowed; on the floor at her feet was a small bouquet of flowers. The whole scene was bathed in a magic-lantern projection of autumn leaves. Here, again, leaves were symbolic. With this kind of lighting I thought I could completely obliterate the house in the background and evoke a sense of sadness and finality that might enable us to eliminate the gravestone itself.

My hints were not lost. "I get your point," Kazan said. "Let's do it without the gravestone. No matter how quietly you move it into place, everybody nearby is going to be so busy thinking, 'How is that done?' that they'll miss the mood of the scene."

I felt that this extreme simplicity would be the best theatre possible, and later, in dress rehearsal, it proved to be the right answer.

Kazan and I went over all the prop problems, especially the small hand props—who would bring them on, what actors would be handling them, were stagehands necessary on the set, how long could we black out the stage successfully for the changes?

A blackout is always difficult. As a rule, only a few seconds are permissible for a well-rehearsed stagehand to cross the stage in the darkness, pick up a prop, and exit without being seen by the audience. The eyes of those seated close to the stage soon become used to the sudden change of light, and figures onstage can be observed after six or eight seconds of the dark; gradually, everyone in the theatre can make them out. Stage blackouts are never complete anyway because there are masked and dimmed lights in the wings that must stay on for the control of the switchboard, the stage manager's desk with its telephones and master cue sheets, and the prop tables where the master property man gives hand props to actors waiting for entrance cues.

When we came to the scene in the Boston hotel room, Kazan said, "I don't need anything; just give me the feeling of a hotel room." I showed him a sketch of a panel of cheap wallpaper which I planned to project from the theatre balcony onto a background that was really a section of the trellis at one side of the Salesman's house. Projected images used in conjunction with scenery can be very valuable. In this case, the associations evoked by faded old wallpaper gave the audience a complete picture. Both the house and the exterior trellis faded away. The audience saw the Salesman in that cheap hotel room with that woman. I stress the phrase "in that room." Actors should never play against a scenic background but within the setting.

Kazan felt that the right actress cast in the role of the girl who visits Willy Loman in the hotel room, dressed in the right costume, plus the visual image of the wallpaper, would be enough to make this short scene come alive. There is no question that when a good actor is backed up by simple scenic treatment, his strong qualities are stressed. Of course, this can work in reverse, but Arthur Miller was lucky in the casting of *Salesman;* even the bit roles were played by vivid actors.

During these last weeks before rehearsals began, the producer's office was finishing the always difficult financing of the production, arranging details in preparation for the tryout and the New York run, organizing theatre parties, completing the casting. Arthur Miller was correcting and polishing the rehearsal version of the script. And Kazan was in constant communication with the author as well as the technical staff. I was busy enough myself. Although my wife and children were enjoying Christmas vacation in the country, I wasn't to join them until the day before Christmas.

January 19, 1949

This day was all mine. The stage was ready for me to set the lighting levels for the entire production. Backstage, property men were still unpacking and arranging hand props, and carpenters were finishing the masking of light leaks and cleaning up the paraphernalia; the acting company was still in New York for final run-throughs and costume fittings. The production stage manager had come down to Philadelphia to make notes from my lighting cues and to take over running the crew backstage; one of his assistants stayed in New York to be with Kazan and the company. The company manager was already in Philadelphia and had reported happily that advance sales were promising.

I had asked Del Hughes, the production stage manager, to enlist a couple of local drama students as volunteer stand-ins for my lighting rehearsal. For this process, without the company on hand, I always try to have someone on the set each time I set a light. It is easy to become so absorbed in lighting an empty stage that you wind up illuminating the scenery for its own sake; if I have stand-ins, not only can I see exactly what they themselves look like in the acting light, but I have figures in the foreground to give perspective when I am lighting the background.

I began by taking out every light in the theatre except those over the fire exits. We had to find out how much light the electricians needed on their boards, how much the fly men needed in the fly loft, and how much the property man needed in the wings; with these necessities as a base, I would know how much light there was to start with. Then, with my assistant sitting in back of me, the complete blueprint in my hands which showed the number of each pipe and area, and a speaker in front of me, I called out to Richard Raven, the chief electrician, "Light first pipe playing area right, blue circuit."

As the process went on, I could judge two things: what my predetermined color would look like on the set, and how well my assistant and the crew had angled the units. One by one, I looked at every group of lamps, every individual spot, every color, and every circuit. Then I looked at each projection individually.

The next phase was to create the mood of the background. For the opening of the play I had decided to start with lights behind the drop, which would illuminate the windows of the neighboring buildings painted on the face of the drop. I always start by telling my electrician, "When I call for something, don't bring it on full power, but start with it low on the dimmer." Dimmer controls have markings from one to ten, one being full power, nine and ten being lowest intensity. In this case, I said on the intercom, "Bring the tenth pipe amber up slowly from the bottom." When it reached about halfway, I said, "Hold it." Then I went to the lights on the face of the drop; for this we had two pipes of border lights. I had planned one to cover the top half of the drop; the other was to pick up and carry the bottom half. Each of these pipes contained three colors; one color at a time, I brought the lights up to a certain level, blending the three elements. In this way I gradually established the mood for the opening scene.

I next worked with a series of light pipes that gave a blue backlighting to the Loman house; this brought out the plastic element in that part of the set which was built three-dimensionally. When I had established these, I called backstage on the intercom to the chief electrician, "Mark it up carefully." It takes patience to sit in the dark of the auditorium and wait for what seems an endless time; but the boys on the switchboard, in this case three of them, have to look at each one of the many dimmer handles and mark meticulously at just what point I had called out to hold. This has to be checked and double-checked and then written down on each one of their cue sheets.

Because of the refusal of theatre owners to provide modern electronic lighting systems, almost all of the professional theatres in America are still forced to use the same manual switchboards that were in use fifty and more years ago. While university theatres and community playhouses throughout the country are decades ahead, the professional theatre still hauls in antiquated, heavy (even if serviceable) manual boards. All this, of course, means extra money for the management of a play. In this respect a theatrical producer is not unlike a person who might rent an expensive Fifth Avenue apartment and find a kitchen with an outlet plug for a stove and a refrigerator, but no stove or refrigerator. In most of the New York theatres even the outlets are inadequate in power for modern lighting. Many a time, not only in New York but in try out on the road, I have had every fuse in the place blow out because the electric service was being taxed beyond the limit.

I welcomed the chief electrician's voice on the intercom, saying, "O.K., Mr. M., we're all marked up; what next?" I was ready now for the playing areas, and the stage manager brought on the two young people who were going to stand in for the actors. I placed them first in the bedroom. The opening scene occurs late at night when the Salesman arrives home; I wanted just enough glow to bring out the forms in bed. I then traced through the entrance of Willy Loman and had the electricians mark down the "pre-set," the lights that can be set behind the curtain before it rises. When this was done, I planned the "follow-up"; this is the next cue, which the stage manager gives when he sees that the house curtain is all the way up and the lights in the auditorium can be brought up; these lights, of course, cannot be pre-set, since their beams would hit the house curtain when it was down, creating ugly patterns on its surface.

I had to be careful to judge the effect of light on the faces of people who were not in make-up and costume. For instance, the young lady stand-in had appeared in a white blouse, and I had borrowed a throw from the bed to put around her shoulders. The mere presence of that much white would have given me the illusion that I was getting much more light than was actually there. When I finished with a scene and was waiting for it to be noted on the electricians' cue sheets, I had the property man bring out the props that went with the scene at hand; this gave me a chance to see them not only in terms of distance but also in relationship to their surroundings. The color of the "oilcloth" on the kitchen table, for example, proved to be satisfactory on the surfaces facing the audience but too light on the top surface, where the bounce from the overhead spotlights brought it into competition with the actors' faces. This was swiftly remedied by spraying down the table top.

Knowing that we had about a hundred and fifty light cues to set, we decided to work straight through the night until we had at least a basic scheme and a basic cue for every part of the production. There was no time for polishing or for going back to rehearse the timing of cues, things I usually have been able to do on this day. As it was, we worked until midnight, sent out for coffee and sandwiches for all, and didn't finish the final scene until 4:30 in the morning. This added up to twenty and a half hours of pretty intense work, and the week had just begun.

During the afternoon Alex North and the musicians had arrived from New York, and I used what little time I had, while waiting for the electrical crew to do their mark-ups, to work out some details about the music. I checked to see that the dressing room which was to be the "sound studio" was properly equipped with microphones and a communication system. We had to put blankets on the floor and on the walls before North was satisfied with the quality of the sound as it came into the auditorium over the speaker system. At the same time the assistant electrician rigged a signal-and-sound system for the musicians so that the stage manager's voice announcing cue warnings and cues would be clear and unmistakable.

The process of lighting a musical is basically the same as for a play like *Death of a Salesman,* but there is less refinement in the musical because the picture is broader and the contrasts greater; less subtlety is needed, more vitality desired. Another difference is that in a legitimate play, with the acting areas more limited and the sets fewer, there is much greater need for extreme control of lighting equipment. During this day of setting the lighting for *Salesman* I occasionally had the two follow-spot men turn on their new and beautifully engineered lights, and the effect was fascinating. In the opening scene, for instance, when the Salesman makes his tiptoe entrance carrying his bags, we dimmed the follow-spot far down and played the beam just on the face of the stand-in. The effect was magical; there was so little light that there was no shadow behind him, and yet there was enough warmth in it so that the face stood out in the gray-blue night light. I was sure that this new experiment would come through very serviceably indeed.

How different this subtle and complex lighting was from earlier times! When I designed *Of Thee I Sing* in 1931 for Sam Harris, he was disturbed that I was not willing to use the 1900 type of stage lighting that had characterized his previous productions. This consisted of border lights, footlights, and old-fashioned flood-lights for what were known as "entrances." There was no control of any segment of the stage, only a system of dimming and raising lights for the total acting area, with all people, all objects, and all scenery treated alike.

After Harris had finally agreed to let me try out "modern lighting," I was busy one day with the electrician, who had laid out several dozen new spotlights on the stage in preparation for hanging them. Harris walked on, gave a quizzical glance at the equipment, started to leave, and then turned and said, "You know, kid, my name is Sam Harris, not Uncle Sam." But the lighting stayed in and Harris' productions started to look like their contemporaries.

January 24, 1949

At last: Opening Night. Nerves take over backstage on this night of nights, and it is the rare actor or stage manager who isn't in a cold sweat until the performance moves into high gear. But from the very beginning of my career I have been favored. As I sit out front, I become fatalistic: I've done what I've done; good, bad, or indifferent, there it stands. I can no longer do anything about it. If something goes wrong, I may cringe, but I rarely get up to go backstage.

One of the fascinating aspects of theatre is the feeling I get when I am watching a familiar performance as a member of an audience for the first time. I do not mean an audience of fellow professionals or the people with whom I have been working for weeks on the production, but an audience of ordinary theatre-goers who are seeing the show for the first time. I become intensely aware of their response, and my own reactions, both intellectual and emotional, change completely from what they were the night before when only my fellow workers were around me. I become part of a community of 800 people, and my responses reflect the communal atmosphere.

The first public performance of *Death of a Salesman* gave us all the feeling that the play had it. There were scenes that didn't go well; others seemed a little long, and would later be cut or changed. But from the very beginning, long before any applause, there was a sense that the play really held the audience. There is nothing esoteric about being able to make a fairly reliable verdict on whether a show is going to be a hit after seeing an out-of-town performance. If there are serious doubts, the chances are that the play will not succeed. Of course, some plays received coolly out of town can become moderate successes on Broadway, but out of the more than 250 productions I have designed I cannot remember one really first-rate show that did not reveal its strength on first exposure.

ELIA KAZAN (1909–2003)

Directing *Death of a Salesman*   1988

Kazan speaks very personally about his involvement with *Death of a Salesman*, beginning with his first reading of the script. He explains that the experience was like that of a brother speaking to him, someone who had shared his life experiences. And although he had directed the plays of Tennessee Williams and films such as *On the Waterfront*, *Death of a Salesman* was his favorite. The way in which he internalized the play may well parallel the responses of many readers and theater-goers, who might go home and wonder, as Kazan did, "Was I a good father? No? Why hadn't I done better?"

Of all the plays I've directed, *Death of a Salesman* is my favorite. When I read it again recently, it hit me as hard as it had when I read it the first time, thirty-eight years ago—just as hard and in the same place, immediately, on page two! I am a man who has trained himself to let no pain show, but I felt tears coming as I turned that page. I suppose the play revives the memory, long at rest, of my father, a salesman of another product, of his hopes for his sons in this new country and the gently twisted Anatolian° smile on his face when he'd ask me, a muddle-headed kid of sixteen, "Who going support me my old age? Hey, you Elia, what you saying to that?" When I had nothing to say to that, but looked away, feeling

---

Anatolian: Of the main portion of Turkey, in western Asia. Kazan was born Elia Kazanjoglous to a Greek family in Istanbul, then the capital of the multiethnic Turkish Ottoman Empire.

threatened, he'd shrug and mutter—I'd hear it—"Hopeh-less case." That and more from those years of my life, as well as other memories, without words or faces, lying in wait with their burden of sadness, swarmed up when I read that damned disturbing play last week, just as they had when Art Miller, the day after he finished it in 1948, gave it to me.

After I'd read it that first time, I didn't wait for the next morning to see if I'd have a more "balanced" judgment, didn't delay as I generally did in those years to hear what Molly° might say about it, but called Art as I turned the back cover and told him his play had "killed" me. "I wrote it in eight weeks," he replied.

When I say this was my favorite play, I don't mean it was the best play. I am not a critic, and I do believe Williams wrote better. They were both Puritans, they were both concerned with morality—Tennessee more open about his "sins" and his problems, Miller more guarded. Still *Salesman* is the play that got to me most deeply. It's as if a brother was speaking of our common experience, a man who'd been through precisely the same life with his family that I had with mine. Art does an extraordinary thing there; he shows us a man who represents everything Art believes to be misguided about the system we live in, then goes on to make us feel affection and concern, pity and even love for this man. Then he goes deeper and we are aware of a tragic weight. Is it for the Salesman? Is it for ourselves? And along with arousing this sympathetic pain, his horrendous hero is able to make us laugh. He is ridiculous and he is tragic all at once. How is that accomplished? I don't know any other play in any other language that does all these things at the same time. But Arthur Miller did them all—that one time and never again.

I believe the reason he was able to do this was not that he was more understanding than anyone else about his fellow Americans and the system we live in, or knew better than the rest of us what was wrong with our civilization. It was because of his uncle. I remember—and I hope I remember correctly— that he derived Willy Loman from his uncle, "a very small man," the original stage direction reads, "who wears little shoes and little vests . . . " and "His emotions, in a word, are mercurial." Which is the way Art expected the part would be cast, not with Lee Cobb, certainly not great lumbering Leo Jacob Cobb. Art had this most ambivalent feeling about an actual person, thought him completely wrongheaded, believed he'd misguided his family and that everything he said that was meant to be serious was rubbish, but he still felt great affection for him and enjoyed his company and relished his passionate, nonsensical talk. The man made Art laugh, and Art likes to laugh. In short, he had the living model with that impossible combination of qualities in his own family, and he was smart enough, Art was, and talented enough to recognize that he had a character who could arouse affection and pity at the same time he evoked total condemnation and that both these reactions were significant separately, but together, in the same person, they were much more meaningful; together they could be tragic; together they were all of us.

Studying the play, as I was preparing to direct it, I began to see my father differently; I stopped being angry at him. I was ready at last to forget what I'd considered tyrannical and appreciate what he'd done for me. To gain an understanding of the play, one of the first things I did was sum up the similarities of my father to

Molly: His wife, Molly Day Thatcher (1907–1963).

Willy Loman. George Kazan was a man full of violence that he dared release only at home, where it was safe to be angry. But the possibility that he might blow up at any time kept us all in terrible fear.

He also had about him, my father along with Willy, the euphoria of a salesman. When it came time to seduce a customer, he was expressive to a theatrical degree. "Feel it!" I remember him shouting at a buyer, as he lifted the end of a large Kashan carpet and thrust it into the man's hand. "Go on, take it in your hand. Give yourself the pleasure. No charge. Like butter, right? Eh? What you say? Like sweet butter! Tell me where you find piece goods like this piece goods, tell me that much." And so on. People in the trade said he was a great salesman. But when I watched these mercantile revels, they embarrassed me.

"Baba" dressed as a salesman and had his shoes shined every day. Even when he went to my aunt's apple farm in the Catskills for a weekend's vacation, he'd bring along other rug merchants, to talk about prices and the market and the sources "on the other side," then to play poker or pinochle most of the night. Sundays, when he would supervise the shish-ke-bab, bending over the hot wood coals and carefully turning the spits thrust through the cubes of well-marinated lamb leg, he wore a hard collar and a bow tie. Sometimes he even wore the jacket of his business suit and a flat-brimmed straw hat. In the Catskills on a Sunday, he was a merchant waiting for Monday.

It's the essence of the salesman's philosophy that your success or failure depends on your impressing others not only with the goods you have for sale but with yourself. You must gain their approval of your personality, make them believe that anything you say is true, even when you know it's grossly exaggerated or even totally false. That is how my father lived, by saying with the passion of unqualified conviction what was useful in winning a customer. Come to think of it, it was not different from what actors do on stage; they must make an audience believe the poetry and the nonsense, even when they don't believe it themselves. They are rewarded not with a sale but with applause.

Like Willy, my father considered his eldest son a special failure and oh, God, this hurt him! And me! But how could I blame him for what he expected of me and didn't get? Obviously what his wife had produced for him, this silent, secretive, mysteriously sullen son, was not going to rally to his side and sell rugs, not any to anyone, ever. Father preferred his next two boys: one was bound to study medicine—Father already called him "the doctor"—and the other actually did show, for a time, an interest in the business that had been my father's life. But he was afraid to tell himself the truth about his eldest son, the truth being that I didn't give a damn about the Oriental rug trade and, despite his persisting hopes, would never go into it; and if I did, would soon defect; and if I stayed, be no damn good. But just as Willy did, George Kazan kept pumping up hope, and the burden of that hope was on my back.

Willy had Linda, ever-faithful, fiercely devoted Linda; my father had my mother, Athena. She'd stand behind him every night as he gulped the dinner she'd spent the day preparing, would sit to eat her own meal only after he'd moved to the sofa; typically Anatolian that, taking a quick nap after his *yehmek*.° Old lions sleep after eating what the lioness provides.

There is an unarticulated tragedy when a woman discovers that the man she married is not what she hoped he was when she married him. Both Linda and

yehmek: Meal.

Willy's best friend, Charley, saw through him but still loved him. Like Linda, my mother would not tolerate any criticism of my father from me; not while he was alive. If I indicated some disaffection, she'd turn on me and tell me he was a good man; "he never goes to other woman," she'd say, and someday I'd come to appreciate what he'd done for us all. He'd brought her to America, you see, not found her here, and she appreciated this. She protected him until the day he died; but when he was finally quiet in the grave, she surprised me one day by saying, "Your father was a stupid man." And soon afterward she said, "These years"—those following his death—"are best years of my life."

Art's play had such deep value for me because it forced me to understand my parents better. Even recently, when I read the play again, it made me wonder about the way I was treating my youngest son, ask myself if I was being as understanding of him as I should be. It disturbed me that I'd discovered my father's traits—even his facial expressions!—in myself. It disturbed me greatly when my youngest son told me that for years he'd lived in terror of my anger. I was repeating the pressure patterns of my father, and I was ashamed when I read Art's play and realized this. That damned play cut me where I was most vulnerable: Was I a good father? No? Why hadn't I done better?

I know it did this for many men; it was the only play I ever directed where men in the audience cried. I recall hearing sobs at the end of a performance, and they were mostly from men.

All the critics rushed to nail down the theme of the play, and Miller helped them with what's in the dialogue: "The man didn't know who he was," spoken over the grave, and a line even closer to the meaning, "He had the wrong dream," which is stated and restated. But it seemed to me that I, as the director, had to take another step and ask what that "wrong dream" was. I came to believe that the point was far more lethal than anything Art put into words. It's in the very fabric of the work, in the legend itself, which is where a theme should be. The Christian faith of this God-fearing civilization says we should love our brother as ourselves. Miller's story tells us that actually—as we have to live—we live by an opposite law, by which the purpose of life is to get the better of your brother, destroying him if necessary, yes, by in effect killing him. Even sex becomes a kind of aggression—to best your boss by taking his woman! That contrast between the ideal and the practice specific to our time is the sense in which the play is a "social drama," and this theme, so shameful and so final, permeates the work's fabric and is projected through the example of human behavior so there can be no avoiding it. Here is an antisystem play that is not "agitprop." We are out of the thirties at last—the audience does not have to suffer instruction or correction. The essence of our society, the capitalist system, is being destroyed not by rhetoric but by that unchallengeable vocabulary, action between people, which makes you believe that the terrible things that happen are true, are inevitable, and concern us all. Furthermore, the conflict we watch is between people who have every traditional reason to love each other. Miller makes us reach out for the lesson; it is not thrust down our throats. The question remains: Why do we live by that law when we know—and Art shows us this—that the result is so humanly destructive?

Art was trained first of all by Henrik Ibsen. The play has a strong structure. The viewer is immediately made aware, first by the title, then by Willy's revealing that he found himself driving off the road, that we are gathered together to watch the course of a suicide. That promise of terror and tragedy lies under every scene in the action that follows and makes the tension continuous. You wait in anxiety as you watch this ridiculous, tragic, misguided, frantically obsessed man — whether Cobb plays him, or the actor is a smaller man like Miller's uncle, doesn't matter. What you watch is yourself, struggling against the fate you've made for yourself.

This production became the other half (with *Streetcar*)° of a theatre legend. The fascinating game of what is fact and what is public relations buildup began to be played. In the accounts of the production and in the remeasuring of the people involved, what had actually happened was replaced by what a hungry press needed — good copy! — and what the imaginations of the people who saw the production were prepared to believe. Furthermore, within each of the people involved there was a swell of confidence. We became convinced of our ability to do anything we chose to do. Success seemed the natural course for us all, the inevitable reward of our efforts. The great success of the play certified our worth. Truth was soon out of sight; we all puffed up. Our producers, Bloomgarden and Fried, Lee Cobb, Arthur Miller, and Elia Kazan were never the same again.

The play became, to the surprise of many theatre people, including its producers, a great success, selling out immediately. Kermit Bloomgarden, an excellent "line" producer, who had the ability to see to it that everything necessary for mounting a show arrived on time and in good working order, was now offered to the public as something more, the leading producer of "class" plays that no one else dared produce on Broadway. His pressman immediately set about creating an enlarged reputation. But how Kermit was able to acquire *Death of a Salesman* and what he thought of it is more interesting than this "puff." Daring is not a feature of the true story; luck is.

At the end of the triumphant opening night performance, Eddie Kook, who'd provided the equipment for lighting the show, was sitting behind Cheryl Crawford, listening to the applause storm. Eddie noticed tears in Cheryl's eyes and commented on the play's power. "That's not why I'm crying," she said. "I had this play and let it get away." This was true. When Art and I weren't sure which producer to entrust it to, I suggested we give it to Cheryl. To my surprise, the force it would have with an audience did not strike her. She hesitated; the time allowed for hesitation in the theatre is brief. Cheryl seemed especially dubious about the play's commercial potential. She'd given it to friends to read; they hadn't been sure either. Since a lively enthusiasm is a necessity for a successful ride through the obstacle course of a Broadway production, and Cheryl didn't show any, I told her to forget the play.

Now luck was loose. Art and I decided to pass the script on to another good friend, Kermit, and his associate, Walter Fried. They'd accepted the play for production, but, as had been the case with Cheryl, they were not sure of its box office strength. Kermit told me he'd consulted theatre owners and box office treasurers, and everyone had cautioned him that the word "Death" in a title invited death to the ticket window; this had been proven time and again, so they maintained.

Streetcar: *A Streetcar Named Desire* by Tennessee Williams, which Kazan directed earlier in 1947. It was still running when *Death of a Salesman* opened.

One morning when I was in Kermit's side office, working on casting, he burst in and declared that he was convinced the title of the play had to be changed. He said there was an "upbeat" phrase in the play that would make a fine title, commercial as well as meaningful. Fried and he were determined that *Free and Clear* should be our title. When my reaction was negative, then obdurate, then — when they persisted — scornful, they asked if I'd mind if they talked to Miller without me there. I don't know why I was so damned gracious, because my emotions were violently hostile, but I did say, "Go ahead," and they summoned the author quickly for consultation. Art had to pass the small office where I was waiting with the door open. When he came by, I pulled him in, and without telling him what their proposal was, I said, "They want to talk to you about something I'm dead against. Don't you dare say yes." Art went in, they talked without me; our title was not changed.

But Kermit was a man who made it a matter of pride that he never changed his mind. Perhaps he thought that I, along with others who knew his original concerns about Miller's title, might think him weak if he altered his stand. Kermit had a horror of appearing weak. On opening night, he was cornered by Irving Hoffman, who wrote theatre reviews for the *Hollywood Reporter,* and although Irving didn't ask him what he thought of the title, Kermit volunteered, "I still don't like the title, but it's Arthur Miller's play and he wants the title we have and that's all right with me." Perhaps Kermit was throwing up a defense for himself in case Hoffman didn't like the title either. His anxiety about what Hoffman might think was not altogether unfounded. The "head" of the review in the *Hollywood Reporter* read: "Tragically We Roll Along."

The imaginative qualities of Art's play, the nonrealistic aspects, worked successfully on stage and added a great deal to the force of the theme. They were indeed innovative, and Art deserved all the praise he's been given. How they came to be in the production, however, is a story that brings credit to the theatre as an institution, as well as confirming a string of influences. As Tennessee Williams admired and was stirred by *All My Sons* ("It has the kind of eloquence we need now," he'd written me), so did Art benefit from *A Streetcar Named Desire.* I remember the night he came to see *Streetcar.* After the performance he appeared to be full of wonder at the theatre's expressive possibilities. He told me he was amazed at how simply and successfully the nonrealistic elements in the play — "*Flores! Flores para los muertos!*"° — blended with the realistic ones. These two men, completely different humans who never mixed socially, influenced each other's work and owed each other a debt.

After *Death of a Salesman* had made theatre history, it was published, and the sentence that follows "The Curtain rises" on the first printed pages is: "Before us is the Salesman's home . . . an air of a dream clings to the place, a dream rising out of reality." However, the stage direction in the original manuscript that Art gave me to read directly he'd finished it does not mention a home as a scenic element. It reads: "A pinpoint travelling spot lights a small area on stage left. The Salesman is revealed. He takes out his keys and opens an invisible door." It was a play waiting for a directorial solution.

Flores! . . . muertos!: Flowers! Flowers for the dead!

The concept of a house standing like a specter behind all the scenes of the play, always present as it might be always present in Willy's mind, wherever his travels take him, even behind the office he visits, even behind the Boston hotel room and above his grave plot, is not even suggested in the original script. Although the spectral home is a directorial vision, it was not my idea any more than it was Art's. It was urged on us by the scenic designer, Jo Mielziner. I went for it—it solved many problems for me—and when we took it to Miller, he approved of it. In this production, it was the single most critically important contribution and the key to the way I directed the play. Both Miller and I were praised for what Jo had conceived; he never got the credit he deserved. Art rewrote his stage direction for the book based on Jo's design. A published play is often the record of a collaboration: The director's stage directions are incorporated, as are some of the contributions of others working on the show—actors' "business," designer's solutions, and so on. The theatre is not an exclusively literary form. Although the playscript is the essentially important element, after that is finished, actors, designers, directors, technicians "write" the play together.

Lee J. Cobb became the great star of that season; people marveled at his power and his brilliance. This adulation may have done him more harm than good. When I recommended that we cast Cobb as Willy, I knew him well from our days in the Group° and a road tour we'd played of *Golden Boy*. Our friendship had started close, but like many actors' friendships, it thinned out. I knew him for a mass of contradictions: loving and hateful, anxious yet still supremely pleased with himself, smug but full of doubt, guilty and arrogant, fiercely competitive but very withdrawn, publicly private, suspicious but always reaching for trust, boastful with a modest air, begging for total acceptance no matter what he did to others. In other words, the part was him; I knew that Willy was in Cobb, there to be pulled out.

When he received his fabulous notices, Lee awarded himself a status even higher than any the theatre world gave him. He was great as Willy Loman until he was told he was great and believed it—then he was less great. He was at his best during the last week of the tryout in Philadelphia, before his New York triumph. After we opened on Broadway, he began to share the audience's admiration for his performance and their pity for the character he played. Life on Broadway would not, because it could not, satisfy this man's hunger for unqualified recognition. He withdrew from our play before he should have, claiming that he was dangerously exhausted—which we might have appreciated except that we all saw he was dramatizing it beyond its measure. He said he was on the verge of a breakdown and demanded that I consult with his analyst. I did; we had a bad scene. I still don't know how serious Lee's trouble was; he was a very good actor and determined to prove that he had to leave the show.

Once he was "available" again, no more parts like Willy came his way. He began to masquerade as a martyr to an unappreciative theatre. Something pouting in his character waited for "justice," meaning that a role of great worth was his due and had to come soon. He'd certainly be the Lear of our time, he boasted. Friends agreed. But the theatre is no more just than life, and nothing came along that he found acceptable. Today, Cobb is remembered for Willy Loman and that is all; it became the story of his life.

Group: The Group Theatre was founded in New York in 1931.

Many actors are remembered because of a single great performance, but this comfort from history did not satisfy Cobb. When another season's crop of new plays came along with nothing for him, he decided to return west and to films. I brought him back east to my "location" in Hoboken, to play the corrupt labor boss in *Waterfront,* and he did well, even had an Academy Award nomination. But after that the roles offered him in films were beneath his talent. He felt aggrieved and insulted, and found that the people who dominated the film community were no less arrogant than I. To save his pride, he responded with arrogance. To release his tensions, he gambled more frequently and more seriously. I know only what I heard, the outside of the story. He disappeared from my view. Then suddenly he was dead, too young and—I agree—insufficiently rewarded. What a waste!

Thinkers who think about the theatre have said that success is a problem more difficult than failure—an astonishing thought to anyone who'd been hungry for recognition as long as I'd been. I didn't find success a problem; I was not uncomfortable sitting on a peak. I was credited with all kinds of magic and became the coy object of artistic temptation and commercial seduction. Every play of worth intended for Broadway was offered me first. I had to shrug them off. In films it was only a matter of what I wanted to do, name it. I could see no limit to what I might accomplish. I began to make notes on ambitious future projects, those I'd once only dreamed of. Now they were within reach; all I had to do was extend my hand. And work! That was easy; I had perfect health and boundless energy. I enjoyed the devotion and the intimate friendship of the two best playwrights of the day; one was writing a play, the other a film, both intended for me. I didn't have an enemy, not that I knew of; no, nothing but admiring followers. I was so successful there was no reason for anyone to be jealous of me: I was too far ahead of the pack. I was certain all this would endure—why would it not?—sure that my success would swell, my friendships deepen, my creative associations become richer. No longer suffering from self-doubt, I quit my analyst.

In time I had to confront some facts. I am a mediocre director except when a play or a film touches a part of my life's experience. Other times my cleverness and facility will not overcome my inadequacies. When I rely on mechanics, I do only what a good stage manager should be able to do. I am not catholic in my tastes. I dislike Beckett—his work. I am not an intellectual. I don't have great range. I am no good with music or with spectacles. The classics are beyond me. I enjoy humor and the great clowns, but I can't make up jokes or amusing bits of byplay and visual humor. What I need I steal. I have no ear for poetry. I have a pretty good eye but not a great eye. I do have courage, even some daring. I am able to talk to actors; I don't fear them and their questions. I've been able to arouse them to better work. I have strong, even violent, feelings, and they are assets. I am not shy about ripping the cover-guard off my own experiences; this encourages actors to overcome their inhibitions. I enjoy working with performers; they sense this and have been happy as well as successful with me. This is useful.

Molly used to say that I was too hard on myself. But I don't feel the above is inaccurate. I prefer this measure to the pumped-up state of fame I had after *Death of a Salesman* and *A Streetcar Named Desire.* It took me some years to face what I was as a director; in fact, it took a painful defeat at the Lincoln Center Repertory Theatre. At the time I'm writing about, I was mired in media mud; I'm afraid that for a time I believed what I read. When I see my photographs from that period, I don't like what I see. For three years I was on the very top, then life twisted, as it will; by surviving a great deal of pain and trouble, I became a different person. But that's looking too far ahead.

ARTHUR MILLER (1915–2005)

From "The American Theater"   1978

Reflecting on the process of casting both the main character, Willy, and Willy's wife, Linda, Miller considers some of the reasons for choosing one actor over another. He reminds us that the choices that producers and directors make are usually sound and sensible. Some actors have a great track record and recommend themselves in terms of their recent successes. Others have a quality that a director remembers and sees as appropriate for a part. In addition, there are actors who see themselves as the only viable choice for the part they want; their job, perhaps the most difficult, is to persuade the decision makers that they are the right choice.

The basis upon which actors are hired or not hired is sometimes quite sound; for example, they may have been seen recently in a part which leads the director to believe they are right for the new role; but quite as often a horde of applicants is waiting beyond the door of the producer's private office and neither he nor the director nor the author has the slightest knowledge of any of them. It is at this point that things become painful, for the strange actor sits before them, so nervous and frightened that he either starts talking and can't stop, and sometimes says he can't stop, or is unable to say anything at all and says that. During the casting of one of my plays there entered a middle-aged woman who was so frightened she suddenly started to sing. The play being no musical, this was slightly beside the point, but the producer, the director, and myself, feeling so guilty ourselves, sat there and heard her through.

To further complicate matters there is each year the actor or actress who suddenly becomes what they call "hot." A hot performer is one not yet well-known, but who, for some mysterious reason, is generally conceded to be a coming star. It is possible, naturally, that a hot performer really has talent, but it is equally possible, and much more likely, that she or he is not a whit more attractive or more talented than a hundred others. Nevertheless, there comes a morning when every producer in these five blocks—some of them with parts the performer could never play—simply has to have him or her. Next season, of course, nobody hears about the new star and it starts all over again with somebody else.

All that is chancy in life, all that is fortuitous, is magnified to the bursting point at casting time; and that, I suspect, is one of the attractions of this whole affair, for it makes the ultimate winning of a part so much more zesty. It is also, to many actors, a most degrading process and more and more of them refuse to submit to these interviews until after the most delicate advances of friendship and hospitality are made to them. And their use of agents as intermediaries is often an attempt to soften the awkwardness of their applying for work.

The theatrical agents, in keeping with the unpredictable lunacy of the business, may be great corporations like the Music Corporation of America, which has an entire building on Madison Avenue, and will sell you anything from a tap dancer to a movie star, a symphony orchestra, saxophonists, crooners, scene designers, actors, and playwrights, to a movie script complete with cast; or they may be like Jane Broder, who works alone and can spread out her arms and touch both walls of her office. They may even be like Carl Cowl, who lives around the corner from me in Brooklyn. Carl is an ex-seaman who still ships out when he has no likely scripts on hand to sell, and when things get too nerve-racking he stays up all night playing Mozart on his flute. MCA has antique desks, English eighteenth-century prints, old broken clocks and inoperative antique barometers hanging on its paneled walls, but Carl Cowl had a hole in his floor that the cat got into, and when he finally got the landlord to repair it he was happy and sat down to play his flute again; but he heard meowing, and they had to rip the floor open again to let out the cat. Still, Carl is not incapable of landing a hit play and neither more nor less likely than MCA to get it produced, and that is another handicraft aspect of this much publicized small business, a quality of opportunity which keeps people coming into it. The fact is that theatrical agents do not sell anyone or anything in the way one sells merchandise. Their existence is mainly due to the need theater people have for a home, some semblance of order in their lives, some sense of being wanted during the long periods when they have nothing to do. To have an agent is to have a kind of reassurance that you exist. The actor is hired, however, mainly because he is wanted for the role.

By intuition, then, by rumor, on the recommendation of an agent—usually heartfelt; out of sheer exhaustion, and upsurge of sudden hope or what not, several candidates for each role are selected in the office of the producer, and are called for readings on the stage of a theater.

It is here that the still unsolved mystery begins, the mystery of what makes a stage performer. There are persons who, in an office, seem exciting candidates for a role, but as soon as they step onto a stage the observers out front—if they are experienced—know that the blessing was not given them. For myself, I know it when, regardless of how well the actor is reading, my eyes begin to wander up to the brick wall back of the stage. Conversely, there are many who make little impression in an office, but once on the stage it is impossible to take one's attention from them. It is a question neither of technique nor of ability, I think, but some quality of surprise inherent in the person.

For instance, when we were searching for a woman to play Linda, the mother in *Death of a Salesman*, a lady came in whom we all knew but could never imagine in the part. We needed a woman who looked as though she had lived in a house dress all her life, even somewhat coarse and certainly less than brilliant. Mildred Dunnock insisted she was that woman, but she was frail, delicate, not long ago a teacher in a girl's college, and a cultivated citizen who probably would not be out of place in a cabinet post. We told her this, in effect, and she understood, and left.

And the next day the line of women formed again in the wings, and suddenly there was Milly again. Now she had padded herself from neck to hem line to look a bit bigger, and for a moment none of us recognized her, and she read again. As soon as she spoke we started to laugh at her ruse; but we saw, too, that she *was* a little more worn now, and seemed less well-maintained, and while she was not quite ordinary, she reminded you of women who were. But we all agreed, when she was finished reading, that she was not right, and she left.

Next day she was there again in another getup, and the next and the next, and each day she agreed with us that she was wrong; and to make a long story short when it came time to make the final selection it had to be Milly, and she turned out to be magnificent. But in this case we had known her work; there was no doubt that she was an excellent actress. The number of talented applicants who are turned down because they are unknown is very large. Such is the crap-shooting chanciness of the business, its chaos, and part of its charm. In a world where one's fate so often seems machined and standardized, and unlikely to suddenly change, these five blocks are like a stockade inside which are people who insist that the unexpected, the sudden chance, must survive. And to experience it they keep coming on all the trains.

But to understand its apparently deathless lure for so many it is necessary, finally, to have participated in the first production of a new play. When a director takes his place at the beaten-up wooden table placed at the edge of the stage, and the cast for the first time sit before him in a semicircle, and he gives the nod to the actor who has the opening lines, the world seems to be filling with a kind of hope, a kind of regeneration that, at the time, anyway, makes all the sacrifices worth while.

The production of a new play, I have often thought, is like another chance in life, a chance to emerge cleansed of one's imperfections. Here, as when one was very young, it seems possible again to attain even greatness, or happiness, or some otherwise unattainable joy. And when production never loses that air of hope through all its three-and-a-half-week rehearsal period, one feels alive as at no other imaginable occasion. At such a time, it seems to all concerned that the very heart of life's mystery is what must be penetrated. They watch the director and each other and they listen with the avid attention of deaf mutes who have suddenly learned to speak and hear. Above their heads there begins to form a tantalizing sort of cloud, a question, a challenge to penetrate the mystery of why men move and speak and act.

It is a kind of glamour that can never be reported in a newspaper column, and yet it is the center of all the lure theater has. It is a kind of soul-testing that ordinary people rarely experience except in the greatest emergencies. The actor who has always regarded himself as a strong spirit discovers now that his vaunted power somehow sounds querulous, and he must look within himself to find his strength. The actress who has made her way on her charm discovers that she appears not charming so much as shallow now, and must evaluate herself all over again, and create anew what she always took for granted. And the great performers are merely those who have been able to face themselves without remorse.

In the production of a good play with a good cast and a knowing director a kind of banding together occurs; there is formed a fraternity whose members share a mutual sense of destiny. In these five blocks, where the rapping of the tap-dancer's feet and the bawling of the phonographs in the record-shop doorways mix with the roar of the Broadway traffic; where the lonely, the perverted, and the lost wander like the souls in Dante's hell and the life of the spirit seems impossible, there are still little circles of actors in the dead silence of empty theaters, with a director in their center, and a new creation of life taking place.

There are always certain moments in such rehearsals, moments of such wonder that the memory of them serves to further entrap all who witness them into this most insecure of all professions. Remembering such moments the resolution to leave and get a "real" job vanishes, and they are hooked again.

I think of Lee Cobb, the greatest dramatic actor I ever saw, when he was creating the role of Willy Loman in *Death of a Salesman*. When I hear people scoffing at actors as mere exhibitionists, when I hear them ask why there must be a theater if it cannot support itself as any business must, when I myself grow sick and weary of the endless waste and the many travesties of this most abused of all arts, I think then of Lee Cobb making that role and I know that the theater can yet be one of the chief glories of mankind.

He sat for days on the stage like a great lump, a sick seal, a mourning walrus. When it came his time to speak lines, he whispered meaninglessly. Kazan, the director, pretended certainty, but from where I sat he looked like an ant trying to prod an elephant off his haunches. Ten days went by. The other actors were by now much further advanced: Milly Dunnock, playing Linda, was already creating a role; Arthur Kennedy as Biff had long since begun to reach for his high notes; Cameron Mitchell had many scenes already perfected; but Cobb stared at them, heavy-eyed, morose, even persecuted, it seemed.

And then, one afternoon, there on the stage of the New Amsterdam way up on top of a movie theater on Forty-second Street (this roof theater had once been Ziegfeld's private playhouse in the gilded times, and now was barely heated and misty with dust), Lee rose from his chair and looked at Milly Dunnock and there was a silence. And then he said, "I was driving along, you understand, and then all of a sudden I'm going off the road. . . . "

And the theater vanished. The stage vanished. The chill of an age-old recognition shuddered my spine; a voice was sounding in the dimly lit air up front, a created spirit, an incarnation, a Godlike creation was taking place; a new human being was being formed before all our eyes, born for the first time on this earth, made real by an act of will, by an artist's summoning up of all his memories and his intelligence; a birth was taking place above the meaningless traffic below; a man was here transcending the limits of his body and his own history. Through the complete concentration of his mind he had even altered the stance of his body, which now was strangely not the body of Lee Cobb (he was thirty-seven then) but of a sixty-year-old salesman; a mere glance of his eye created a window beside him, with the gentle touch of his hand on this empty stage a bed appeared, and when he glanced up at the emptiness above him a ceiling was there, and there was even a crack in it where his stare rested.

I knew then that something astounding was being made here. It would have been almost enough for me without even opening the play. The actors, like myself and Kazan and the producer, were happy, of course, that we might have a hit; but there was a good deal more. There was a new fact of life, there was an alteration of history for all of us that afternoon.

There is a certain immortality involved in theater, not created by monuments and books, but through the knowledge the actor keeps to his dying day that on a certain afternoon, in an empty and dusty theater, he cast a shadow of a being that was not himself but the distillation of all he had ever observed; all the unsingable heartsong the ordinary man may feel but never utter, he gave voice to. And by that he somehow joins the ages.

And that is the glamour that remains, but it will not be found in the gossip columns. And it is enough, once discovered, to make people stay with the theater, and others to come seeking it.

I think also that people keep coming into these five blocks because the theater is still so simple, so old-fashioned. And that is why, however often its obsequies are intoned, it somehow never really dies. Because underneath our shiny fronts of stone, our fascination with gadgets, and our new toys that can blow the earth into a million stars, we are still outside the doorway through which the great answers wait. Not all the cameras in Christendom nor all the tricky lights will move us one step closer to a better understanding of ourselves, but only, as it always was, the truly written word, the profoundly felt gesture, the naked and direct contemplation of man which is the enduring glamour of the stage.

BRENDA MURPHY (b. 1950)

Racial Consciousness in Casting
Death of a Salesman 1995

A number of interesting issues came to the surface when the 1972 Baltimore production of *Death of a Salesman* cast all black actors. Race-blind casting had been common with other classic American plays and often with Shakespeare and other European plays. This play provided unexpected surprises, however, as Murphy explains.

The Center Stage production in 1972 brought to the fore the issue of race and ethnicity in casting the play. Although it was the first professional production cast with African-Americans, it was not the first to raise the color issue. As early as 1960, Miller had turned down a request from Terry Carter to do a "Negro version" of *Salesman* Off-Broadway. Although Carter assured Miller that care would be taken to avoid interracial casting that might "distort" the play—the entire Loman family, as well as The Woman, Miss Forsythe, and Letta were to be played by black actors—the request was refused, presumably because of Miller's ban on professional productions in New York.[1] According to Miller, however, he approved a production in New York during the sixties that would have featured African-American Frederick O'Neal as Willy, although the production never materialized.[2] O'Neal had played Willy in a 1962 production directed by Esther Merle Jackson at Clark College in Atlanta with an all-black cast.

The Center Stage production featured Richard Ward, who had been a hit in *Ceremonies of Dark Old Men* at the theatre in the previous year. Miller attended the opening night of the all-black production, and contributed a note to the program, saying:

> I have felt for many years that particularly with this play, which has been so well received in so many countries and cultures, the black actor would have an opportunity, if indeed that is needed anymore, to demonstrate to all his common humanity and his talent.[3]

[1]Unpublished letter from Terry Carter to Kay Brown, January 1960, HRHRC. [Harry Ransom Humanities Research Center]

[2]Unpublished letter from Arthur Miller to George [C. Scott], 28 April 1975, HRHRC.

[3]Quoted in Mel Gussow, "Stage: Black *Salesman*," *New York Times*, 9 April 1972: 69.

The production was not particularly successful, chiefly because some inexperienced actors were cast in the minor roles. In several interviews, Ward made it clear that he had wanted to do the play with an integrated cast, particularly with Charley played by a white man, showing that "a white man and a black man can live next door to each other and care for each other . . . their children can grow up together and love each other."[4] Miller also was quoted as saying he would like to see the play done with an integrated cast, just because it would allow a greater selection of players.[5] The producers reported that they had thought about an integrated cast, but decided that it "might be an attempt to make a statement that's not in the play." They had wanted to make Charley white, "but some black leaders in Baltimore pointed out that the neighbor ends up success[ful], and that a 'be white, be a success' message might come across."[6]

Not surprisingly, the production was analyzed almost exclusively in terms of the race issue. Mel Gussow asserted in the *New York Times* that "Black time has caught up to *Salesman*," and contended that "what makes this more than just an intriguing experiment, but an exciting concept, is not only what it tells us about *Death of a Salesman*, but what it tells us about the black experience."[7] In Gussow's view, "Willy Loman's values are white values—the elevation of personality, congeniality, conformity, salesmanship in the sense of selling oneself, so that in the context of an all-black production, Willy becomes a black man embracing the white world as an example to be emulated."[8] Hollie West of the *Washington Post* found the concept less revealing. Putting black actors "in roles written for whites," she contended, required the actors to "shed the badge of their color. Without the nuances of black dialogue and a consciousness reflecting the unique customs and traditions of black life, such actors may ask the question: Am I playing a white black man?"[9] West did not think the production succeeded in transferring the circumstances of the lower-middle-class white family in New York during the 1930s and 1940s to "the black circumstances of the same period."[10] Although she found Ward's performance as Willy entirely convincing, she found historical and social reality impinging on the dramatic illusion of the other characters: "Have black women been willing to play secondary roles when their husbands were failing, as in the case of Mrs. Loman?" she asked. "Would Biff have been considered an outcast among thousands of similar black men a generation ago?"[11]

Despite his support for Richard Ward's desire for interracial casting in the Baltimore production, Miller made it clear three years later that he found the question of race in casting an extremely complex one. A year after taking over the direction of the Philadelphia Drama Guild production from Scott, Miller approved an Off-Broadway revival of *Salesman* at the Circle in the Square Theatre that Scott was to direct, with himself in the title role. When he learned that Scott was planning to cast a black actor as Charley, Miller wrote him a four-page single-spaced

[4]Quoted in Carl Schoettler, "Actor in *Death of a Salesman* Went on Stage at Age 13," Baltimore *Evening Sun*, 3 April 1972: C6. See also Larry Siddons, "A Black Willy Loman Talks of *Salesman*'s Soul," *New York Post*, 4 April 1972: 60.

[5]Quoted in Siddons, "A Black Willy Loman."

[6]*Ibid.*

[7]Gussow, "Black *Salesman*."

[8]*Ibid.*

[9]Hollie I. West, "*Death of a Salesman*," *Washington Post*, 14 April 1972: D1.

[10]*Ibid.*, D7.

[11]*Ibid.*

letter, warning him to consider carefully what the implications of this casting would be. So-called color-blind casting, he believed, only worked when it was entirely color-blind, with Biff black and Happy white, for example. This, however, took the play out of the realm of realism, and made its relation to the social reality it depicted purely metaphorical, a conception which needed to be thoroughly thought through.[12]

In 1975, casting one "white" role with a black actor immediately foregrounded the issue of race. In the case of Charley, Miller did not think this would work. It would suggest that Willy, in daring to have a black man for his best friend during the thirties, would have it in him to rebel against accepted social values and prejudices, a quality antithetical to his character. It would also take away the sense that Charley is fundamentally the same as Willy, except for Willy's ruling passion, which destroys him. Miller felt that Charley should face the same conditions in life that Willy does, that he should be a representative of the American system when it functions as it should. He felt that adding the issue of race to this relationship would distort its dynamics as he had intended them to work.

JUNE SCHLUETER (b. 1948) and JAMES K. FLANAGAN

Memorable Willy 1987

The authors contend that there may be no more memorable character on the modern stage than Willy Loman. To an extent they base their statement on the effect that Willy has on the audience's imagination. Audiences in the 1970s and 1980s seem to have been affected by Willy Loman even more than the original 1949 audience. The society had changed in a direction that made Willy's values seem less connected with the Depression of the 1930s and more connected with the affluence of the 1970s.

When Walter Goodman reviewed the 1975 revival of *Death of a Salesman*, in which George C. Scott replaced Lee J. Cobb as the self-deluded drummer, he claimed that the play, though applauded in 1949 as the great American tragedy, might well mean more in 1975. Goodman argues that the sympathetic reception of so unmitigated a failure as Willy Loman could be expected from a people who had lived through the Great Depression and World War II, but identification with this loser of a salesman could not have lasted beyond the two-hour life of the play. For this audience was on its way to becoming the Affluent Society; in 1949, Willy Loman was "an anachronism, a relic of a Depression mentality." By 1975, however, America had again become a society ready to acknowledge that "attention must be paid," even to this unlikable, inept failure, whose condition rather than personality was moving. For the 1975 audience had lived through an unpopular, unnecessary war, which brought none of the enthusiasm or the nationalism of World War II; and it was disillusioned with two decades of an

---

[12]Unpublished letter from Arthur Miller to George [C. Scott], 28 April 1975, HRHRC.

energetic prosperity that could not pause for failures nor accommodate a man who yearned to plant seeds or look at the moon.[1]

In 1984, Willy Loman appeared once again on the Broadway stage, this time a bit thinner and a bit smaller—more like the original "shrimp" Miller had created than the "walrus" into which Willy was metamorphosed when Lee J. Cobb was cast. Dustin Hoffman's portrayal of Willy was powerful and convincing, suggesting that the method actor had clearly found some coincidence between himself and the character that enabled him to create the role. But where America was in the mid-1980s did not seem to concern the critics. *Death of a Salesman* was no longer being viewed as time-bound commentary on capitalism and its victims, and audience response was not being judged in terms of economic or social circumstance. Miller's play had clearly earned its author's description of it as a play that raises "questions . . . whose answers define humanity,"[2] a description dramatically endorsed in 1983 when the play opened at the Beijing People's Art Theatre in China.

That production, the first in China of an American play directed by an American, challenged the assumption that *Salesman* was culture-bound, meeting with enthusiastic responses in a country where peasants constitute 90 percent of the population and where there are no salesmen. Speaking of the opening in "*Salesman*" *in Beijing*, Miller noticed the odd laughs, the cruel laughs, beneath which he sensed "a comprehension of Willy's character, a recognition. Which I suppose means they share these embarrassing weaknesses?"[3] Harry Moses, producer of the Bill Moyers show on PBS, which ran a special program on the production of *Death of a Salesman* in Beijing, told Miller the day after opening night that the last shot on the program would be of a young Chinese who spoke English, saying that "China was full of Willys, dreamers of the dream."[4]

But the problem with Willy—aside from his self-delusion, his ineptness, his self-pity, his misplaced pride, and his fraudulent morality—is that he has dreamed the wrong dream. About to be fired from his job, Willy cries out to the young upstart Howard, "You can't eat the orange and throw the peel away—a man is not a piece of fruit!" Though only the peel of Willy's dream remains, he refuses to discard it, deluding himself into believing that the dream of being a salesman with green velvet slippers, who was not only liked but well liked by the hundreds who mourned his death, was right for him.

There may well be no character in modern drama more memorable than Willy Loman. The image of the tired salesman, valise in hand, shoulders sloping, suit jacket hanging loosely about his weary frame, which appeared on the jacket of the Viking edition of the play for years, has sustained its power in the imagination of the theatergoing public. It has become a symbol of the pursuer of the American—and the universal—dream who met with the harsh consequences of not being able to keep up. Willy Loman is indeed a low man; no tragic hero of high degree, he is circumstantially and psychologically down. Surrounded by high-rise apartment buildings that deflect the sun from the backyard, Willy's little house

[1]Walter Goodman, "Miller's *Salesman*, Created in 1949, May Mean More to 1975." *New York Times*, June 15, 1975, pp. 1, 5.

[2]Arthur Miller, introduction to *Arthur Miller's Collected Plays* (New York: Viking Press, 1957), p. 32.

[3]Arthur Miller, "*Salesman*" *in Beijing* (New York: Viking Press, 1984), p. 238.

[4]Miller, "*Salesman*" *in Beijing*, p. 245.

in Brooklyn stands as a symbol of time past, when the world still had room for vegetable gardens and for salesmen who carried on their trade on the strength of a smile. There is a collective guilt in Willy's failure in which every theatergoer participates; it is a guilt occasioned by the knowledge that society cannot accommodate its failures in a system that relentlessly demands success.

CATHERINE DIAMOND (b. 1951)

Death of a Salesman in Taipei   1993

Diamond, who is a professor and director of the only English-language theater in Taiwan, asserts that a 1992 Taiwanese production of *Death of a Salesman* reflected Chinese values almost as much as it did American values. The political complexities of the production give some indication of the difficulties that the National Theater of Taipei had to overcome in order to produce the play. Diamond points to some of the interesting cultural differences that might be invisible to an American audience but that would be of considerable importance to the Chinese.

DEATH OF A SALESMAN. By Arthur Miller. The Performance Workshop. The National Theater, Taipei, Taiwan, Republic of China. 18–26 April 1992.

In 1987, Yang Shipeng, director of the Hong Kong Repertory Theatre, was invited to direct a play at Taiwan's new National Theater. He requested permission from Arthur Miller to use a Taiwanese translation of *Death of a Salesman* because he could not use the Ying Ruocheng translation Miller used in Beijing. Miller initially gave his permission with the caveat that the translation be used only in Taiwan. The production was postponed and later, Yang heard from Miller's agent that only the Ying Ruocheng translation was acceptable. The reason for this change of mind has never been clearly determined, but the Taiwan press put the blame on Miller, insinuating his pro-communist sympathies. On the other hand, perhaps Miller, irritated that Taiwan's refusal of the mainland translation was based purely on political rather than artistic grounds, revoked his initial permission.

In 1991, Yang again wrote to Miller, asking whether he could use the Ying Ruocheng translation with some of his own emendations. Miller answered affirmatively. In both his alteration of the translation, in which he substituted Taipei idiom for the original Beijing idiom, and in his directing style, Yang strove for what he believed would appear most natural to the Taipei audience, neither emphasizing the play's Americanisms nor trying to adapt the story to a Taiwanese locale.

The actors played the essence of relationships rather than their specifically American manifestations. However, there were some fundamental differences in social values that made it difficult for the audience to comprehend Willy's character and to sympathize with him. For example, virtually no Chinese father harbors aspirations for his son to become a professional sportsman, but desires instead for him to go to university—an American school preferably—and become a professor, doctor, manager, or lawyer. As an actor in Miller's *Salesman in Beijing* expressed it: "Every man wants his son to be a dragon." The audience clearly understood

Figure 29. The 1992 Chinese production of *Death of a Salesman,* at the National Theater in Taipei, Taiwan, directed by Yang Shipeng.

Willy's hopes for Biff and his ensuing disappointment, but since Taiwanese society so clearly admires the path taken by Willy's neighbor, the successful businessman Charley and his bookish son Bernard, people laughed at Willy's delusions, often failing to empathize with his particular dreams of success.

Despite some confusion caused by Willy's highly individualized character, other aspects of the play were almost written for modern day Taipei. The similarities between the United States in the wheeling-dealing 1920s and laissez faire capitalism in 1990s Taiwan are uncanny. Out-of-town extramarital affairs, children suffering from parental expectations, the high cost of housing, overcrowding, disappearance of green spaces, job obsolescence, increasing competition for jobs, and the struggle to maintain the esteem of others while facing failure are well-known phenomena in the postindustrial, newly wealthy metropolis of Taipei. Yet the production did not challenge the audience to reflect upon these problems or the social values that cause them.

Director Yang had a clearcut goal of presenting an American play without any concessions to the Chinese actors or the Chinese audience, yet certain changes were inevitable. In the translation itself, the flavor of individual characters' speech gets attenuated, especially Happy's, which is slangy.

Another significant difference was in acting style. Modern Chinese stage acting tends to be broad, exaggerated and emphatic. This has roots in the traditional drama and is reinforced by television dramas which tend to be either contemporary soap operas or historical melodramas. Consequently the male actors in particular engaged in a great deal of demonstrative acting—pointing, waving their hands around, and touching each other to get attention. Seasoned stage actor Li Lichun played Willy's poignant scenes with admirable restraint, but Deng Chenghui, as the loyal wife Linda, evoked more sympathy. Her voice never broke until her last line at Willy's grave: "We're free . . . we're free," and, because she held back her tears until the very end, the audience wept with her, moved more by her devotion than Willy's fall and final sacrifice.

In his Beijing production, Miller initially felt apprehensive that his play might be reduced to a political message—an indictment of American capitalism. This aspect was wholly absent from the Taipei production, where it might have been more justified. Instead, both director and actors stressed the pathos of the Loman family. Yang Shipeng wanted to move the audience, but to what end, his production never made clear.

Eugène Ionesco

Eugène Ionesco (1909–1994) was born in Slatina, a small town in Romania not far from Bucharest, to a Romanian father and a French mother. In 1911 the family moved to Paris, where Ionesco's father studied law, and from 1917 to 1919 Ionesco and his sister attended boarding school in the country village of La Chapelle-Anthenaise. Early in his life his parents were separated and his father presumed dead. Then his father reappeared, only to divorce his mother secretly in Romania and take Eugène and his sister to live with him and his new wife. The move left Eugène very unhappy, because he was more attached to his mother than to his father, who was a domineering and sometimes violent man. Eugène eventually left home when he was seventeen, while his sister, unable to tolerate their stepmother, rejoined their mother.

Ionesco studied French at the University of Bucharest. There he began his writing career and was noticed by a number of Romanian writers. Ionesco's first volume of poetry, *Elegies for Minuscule Creatures,* was published in 1931, but he later disowned it as the musings of an immature writer. He married in 1936, three months before his mother died, and taught high school French in Romania until 1939, when he returned to France. Although he and his wife were forced to return to Romania when World War II began, Ionesco was permitted to teach in Bucharest. He made his way to Marseilles in 1942 and weathered the rest of the war virtually in hiding and in relative poverty.

After the war, Ionesco and his family (a daughter was born in 1944) moved back to Paris. While working as a proofreader, he also used textbooks to teach himself English. His amusement at the essential nonsense of the phrases and expressions he encountered in the books led him to write his first play, *The Bald Soprano* (1950). In the play, he employs the kinds of clichéd expressions that appear in such books. Ultimately, as the critics have said, the play is about the certainty of a failure of communication.

Failure of communication is present in many of Ionesco's plays, and some commentators have pointed to the problems of his childhood as the source of his anxiety. Ionesco's journals of his early years record a tumultuous family life in which his mother appears as a virtual household slave. Some recurrent issues in his plays—including females as victims or as robotic extensions of the husband's will and masculine figures as dark, tyrannical, and threatening—have led critics to credit Ionesco's childhood experiences with having colored the main lines of his drama.

From the first performance of *The Bald Soprano,* soon linked with *The Lesson* (1951), Ionesco was considered a leader in a new wave of postwar drama. The first performance of *The Bald Soprano* entertained an audience of three, but all three were influential literary people in Paris, and the resultant word-of-mouth praise soon brought more people into the theater. In a short time, Ionesco became associated with the absurdist writers, and his plays were thought to be the beginning of absurdist drama.

Ionesco was more comfortable with the term *anti-play,* which is what he applied to *The Bald Soprano.* His theory was that realistic theater was dead, or certainly backward-looking. As an experimenter in avant-garde drama, Ionesco created fantasies that avoided realistic limitation and instead used symbol and language to convey a deeper level of meaning. He was not interested in the contemporary realistic drama or in the light entertainment of his day. He was also uninterested in the experiments of directors who tried to shock audiences. Instead, he intended the language in his plays to produce insight.

The ultimate success of *The Bald Soprano* and *The Lesson* has been remarkable. The plays established Ionesco as a powerful force in absurdist drama, along with Samuel Beckett. In Ionesco's next play, *The Chairs* (1952), Old Woman and Old Man hire an Orator to deliver their message to the world. Instead of an audience, they draw only a collection of empty chairs. After they throw themselves out a window, calling, "Long live the Emperor!" the Orator steps forward to reveal that he can speak only gibberish. As an absurdist play, *The Chairs* remains a classic.

Among Ionesco's other important plays are *Rhinoceros* (1959), *Exit the King* (1962), *Killing Game* (1970), and *Macbett* (1972). His later plays seem to move away from the stark experimentation of the early drama, a disappointment to some of his fans. However, audiences have disagreed. *Rhinoceros*, about people who mutate into animals, is one of the best received of Ionesco's plays among general theatergoers. In the last twenty years of his life, Ionesco wrote several prose works and concentrated on painting and lithography.

The Bald Soprano

For discussion questions and assignments on *The Bald Soprano*, visit **bedfordstmartins.com/jacobus**.

Ionesco's first produced play, or "anti-play," was inspired by his efforts to learn English from a French primer. He realized that the phrases used to illustrate the use of the English language were filled with simple but important insights that, fractured though they were in the exercises he studied, contained their own logic. But when he wrote *The Bald Soprano*, Ionesco was not so much interested in the logic implied in specific phrases as in the way language communicated or failed to communicate ideas. His experimentation in this play involves language, both as it seems to make sense and as it totally breaks down into gibberish. As a dramatic experiment, the play is determinedly nonrepresentational and stubbornly non-Aristotelian. The audience is not asked to become emotionally involved in the lives of the Smiths and the Martins. Nor is the audience led to assume that the action on stage represents real life. Instead, the audience's experience is that of seeing a play about how language and logic work, while always knowing that they are seeing a play.

The Bald Soprano is the opposite of the well-made play designed to delight the bourgeois audience. Yet the characters, the Smiths and the Martins, are absolute stereotypes of the English bourgeoisie. The set for the play usually relies on middle-class wallpaper designs, appropriate overstuffed chairs or sofas, and chintzy decorations. The irony of the contrast between the set, the characters, and the language is part of the play's strength. And even though Ionesco said that the play has no psychology (meaning that the characters are not developed), the Smiths and the Martins, who seem to have no clear function in life other than to attend each other's dinners, are distinct from the maid Mary and the Fire Chief, who both have jobs and functions in society that distinguish them from the bourgeoisie. Thus when the latter two characters meet, they recognize each other through their useful purposes in life.

Mary at one point calls herself Sherlock Holmes, the famous fictional detective who solved cases by a process of deduction, examining evidence and events until an inevitable conclusion emerged. The Martins, when they arrive at the Smiths', perform an act of deduction when they look at one another and try to figure out how they know each other. They begin by retracing their steps, one by one, as they traveled to the Smiths' home. At each instance of discovering they have both had the same experience, they marvel, until, finally, they identify themselves as sharing the same bed and having a child with one white eye and one red eye. They then realize who they are. However, Mary points out that they are wrong. The red and white eyes are actually reversed left from right from what the Martins say they are, and thus the extensive deductive process they just developed proves inconclusive. In other words, there is no guarantee that logic will reveal the truth, and the failure of logic is demonstrated over and over again throughout the play.

Ionesco experiments here with absurdism. Logic fails, language is slippery and undependable, and even the daily signs we rely on—the bells of the clocks and the bell of the door—are unreliable. The play breaks all the normal rules of drama and even of daily life. The very title, *The Bald Soprano,* seems absurd in view of the fact that there is no bald soprano in the play and the expression is used just once by the Fire Chief as a throwaway line.

The Bald Soprano in Performance

The first performance was given in 1951 in a small theater in Paris and directed by Nicolas Bataille. In February 1957, Bataille moved the production to the Théâtre de la Huchette, where it has played with many of the same cast ever since, making it the longest-running play in the world! It has usually been performed with Ionesco's *The Lesson,* which may make a similar claim to longevity. Again and again, audiences seem to find that these plays resonate with their own time. The Théâtre de la Huchette has used the same set for all these years. In 1987, the Cubiculo Theater in New York produced the play, with John Turturro as Mr. Smith, to excellent reviews. Joseph Chaikin, a major figure in American drama, directed. Christopher Isherwood praised the Atlantic Theater Company's 2004 production in New York, in part by relating the language of the play to the upcoming elections, which he described as "always a joy for students of the uses and abuses of language." In a well-received production at the Shakespeare Theatre of New Jersey in August 2007, designer Mimi Lien placed the living room in a giant wooden packing case. In his review, Robert Daniels said, "One need only observe the picture frames on the wall that echo the chintzy flowery print of the wallpaper to be coaxed into the insanity that follows."

EUGÈNE IONESCO (1909–1994)

The Bald Soprano   1950
Anti-Play

TRANSLATED BY DONALD M. ALLEN

The Characters

MR. SMITH
MRS. SMITH
MR. MARTIN
MRS. MARTIN
MARY, *the maid*
THE FIRE CHIEF

Scene: *A middle-class English interior, with English armchairs. An English evening. Mr. Smith, an Englishman, seated in his English armchair and wearing English slippers, is smoking his English pipe and reading an English newspaper, near an English fire. He is wearing English spectacles and a small gray English mustache. Beside him, in another English armchair, Mrs. Smith, an Englishwoman, is darning some English socks. A long moment of English silence. The English clock strikes 17 English strokes.*

MRS. SMITH: There, it's nine o'clock. We've drunk the soup, and eaten the fish and chips, and the English salad. The children have drunk English water. We've eaten well this evening. That's because we live in the suburbs of London and because our name is Smith.

MR. SMITH [*continues to read, clicks his tongue.*]

MRS. SMITH: Potatoes are very good fried in fat; the salad oil was not rancid. The oil from the grocer at the corner is better quality than the oil from the grocer across the street. It is even better than the oil from the grocer at the bottom of the street. However, I prefer not to tell them that their oil is bad.

MR. SMITH [*continues to read, clicks his tongue.*]

MRS. SMITH: However, the oil from the grocer at the corner is still the best.

MR. SMITH [*continues to read, clicks his tongue.*]

MRS. SMITH: Mary did the potatoes very well, this evening. The last time she did not do them well. I do not like them when they are well done.

MR. SMITH [*continues to read, clicks his tongue.*]

MRS. SMITH: The fish was fresh. It made my mouth water. I had two helpings. No, three helpings. That made me go to the w.c. You also had three helpings. However, the third time you took less than the first two times, while as for me, I took a great deal more. I eat better than you this evening. Why is that? Usually, it is you who eats more. It is not appetite you lack.

MR. SMITH [*clicks his tongue.*]

MRS. SMITH: But still, the soup was perhaps a little too salt. It was saltier than you. Ha, ha, ha. It also had too many leeks and not enough onions. I regret I didn't advise Mary to add some aniseed stars. The next time I'll know better.

MR. SMITH [*continues to read, clicks his tongue.*]

MRS. SMITH: Our little boy wanted to drink some beer; he's going to love getting tiddly. He's like you. At table did you notice how he stared at the bottle? But I poured some water from the jug into his glass. He was thirsty and he drank it. Helen is like me: she's a good manager, thrifty, plays the piano. She never asks to drink English beer. She's like our little daughter who drinks only milk and eats only porridge. It's obvious that she's only two. She's named Peggy. The quince and bean pie was marvelous. It would have been nice, perhaps, to have had a small glass of Australian Burgundy with the sweet, but I did not bring the bottle to the table because I did not wish to set the children a bad example of gluttony. They must learn to be sober and temperate.

MR. SMITH [*continues to read, clicks his tongue.*]

MRS. SMITH: Mrs. Parker knows a Rumanian grocer by the name of Popesco Rosenfeld, who has just come from Constantinople.° He is a great specialist in yogurt. He has a diploma from the school of yogurt-making in Adrianople.° Tomorrow I shall buy a large pot of native Rumanian yogurt from him. One doesn't often find such things here in the suburbs of London.

MR. SMITH [*continues to read, clicks his tongue.*]

MRS. SMITH: Yogurt is excellent for the stomach, the kidneys, the appendicitis, and apotheosis. It was Doctor Mackenzie-King who told me that, he's the one who takes care of the children of our neighbors, the Johns. He's a good doctor. One can trust him. He never prescribes any medicine that he's not tried out on himself first. Before operating on Parker, he had his own liver operated on first, although he was not the least bit ill.

MR. SMITH: But how does it happen that the doctor pulled through while Parker died?

Constantinople: Major city in Turkey that was once the capital of the Roman empire.   **Adrianople:** City in Turkey named after the Emperor Hadrian. It was renamed Edirne in 1918.

MRS. SMITH: Because the operation was successful in the doctor's case and it was not in Parker's.

MR. SMITH: Then Mackenzie is not a good doctor. The operation should have succeeded with both of them or else both should have died.

MRS. SMITH: Why?

MR. SMITH: A conscientious doctor must die with his patient if they can't get well together. The captain of a ship goes down with his ship into the briny deep, he does not survive alone.

MRS. SMITH: One cannot compare a patient with a ship.

MR. SMITH: Why not? A ship has its diseases too; moreover, your doctor is as hale as a ship; that's why he should have perished at the same time as his patient, like the captain and his ship.

MRS. SMITH: Ah! I hadn't thought of that . . . Perhaps it is true . . . And then, what conclusion do you draw from this?

MR. SMITH: All doctors are quacks. And all patients too. Only the Royal Navy is honest in England.

MRS. SMITH: But not sailors.

MR. SMITH: Naturally [*A pause. Still reading his paper:*] Here's a thing I don't understand. In the newspaper they always give the age of deceased persons but never the age of the newly born. That doesn't make sense.

MRS. SMITH: I never thought of that!

[*Another moment of silence. The clock strikes seven times. Silence. The clock strikes three times. Silence. The clock doesn't strike.*]

MR. SMITH [*still reading his paper*]: Tsk, it says here that Bobby Watson died.

MRS. SMITH: My God, the poor man! When did he die?

MR. SMITH: Why do you pretend to be astonished? You know very well that he's been dead these past two years. Surely you remember that we attended his funeral a year and a half ago.

MRS. SMITH: Oh yes, of course I do remember. I remembered it right away, but I don't understand why you yourself were so surprised to see it in the paper.

MR. SMITH: It wasn't in the paper. It's been three years since his death was announced. I remembered it through an association of ideas.

MRS. SMITH: What a pity! He was so well preserved.

MR. SMITH: He was the handsomest corpse in Great Britain. He didn't look his age. Poor Bobby, he'd been dead for four years and he was still warm. A veritable living corpse. And how cheerful he was!

MRS. SMITH: Poor Bobby.

MR. SMITH: Which poor Bobby do you mean?

MRS. SMITH: It is his wife that I mean. She is called Bobby too, Bobby Watson. Since they both had the same name, you could never tell one from the other when you saw them together. It was only after his death that you could really tell which was which. And there are still people today who confuse her with the deceased and offer their condolences to him. Do you know her?

MR. SMITH: I only met her once, by chance, at Bobby's burial.

MRS. SMITH: I've never seen her. Is she pretty?

MR. SMITH: She has regular features and yet one cannot say that she is pretty. She is too big and stout. Her features are not regular but still one can say that she is very pretty. She is a little too small and too thin. She's a voice teacher.

[*The clock strikes five times. A long silence.*]

MRS. SMITH: And when do they plan to be married, those two?

MR. SMITH: Next spring, at the latest.

MRS. SMITH: We shall have to go to their wedding, I suppose.

MR. SMITH: We shall have to give them a wedding present. I wonder what?

MRS. SMITH: Why don't we give them one of the seven silver salvers° that were given us for our wedding and which have never been of any use to us? [*Silence.*]

MRS. SMITH: How sad for her to be left a widow so young.

MR. SMITH: Fortunately, they had no children.

MRS. SMITH: That was all they needed! Children! Poor woman, how could she have managed!

MR. SMITH: She's still young. She might very well remarry. She looks so well in mourning.

MRS. SMITH: But who would take care of the children? You know very well that they have a boy and a girl. What are their names?

MR. SMITH: Bobby and Bobby like their parents. Bobby Watson's uncle, old Bobby Watson, is a rich man and very fond of the boy. He might very well pay for Bobby's education.

MRS. SMITH: That would be proper. And Bobby Watson's aunt, old Bobby Watson, might very well, in her turn, pay for the education of Bobby Watson, Bobby Watson's daughter. That way Bobby, Bobby Watson's mother, could remarry. Has she anyone in mind?

MR. SMITH: Yes, a cousin of Bobby Watson's.

MRS. SMITH: Who? Bobby Watson?

MR. SMITH: Which Bobby Watson do you mean?

MRS. SMITH: Why, Bobby Watson, the son of old Bobby Watson, the late Bobby Watson's other uncle.

MR. SMITH: No, it's not that one, it's someone else. It's Bobby Watson, the son of old Bobby Watson, the late Bobby Watson's aunt.

MRS. SMITH: Are you referring to Bobby Watson the commercial traveler?

MR. SMITH: All the Bobby Watsons are commercial travelers.

MRS. SMITH: What a difficult trade! However, they do well at it.

MR. SMITH: Yes, when there's no competition.

MRS. SMITH: And when is there no competition?

MR. SMITH: On Tuesdays, Thursdays, and Tuesdays.

MRS. SMITH: Ah! Three days a week? And what does Bobby Watson do on those days?

MR. SMITH: He rests, he sleeps.

salvers: Silver trays for carrying calling cards or drinks.

MRS. SMITH: But why doesn't he work those three days if there's no competition?

MR. SMITH: I don't know everything. I can't answer all your idiotic questions!

MRS. SMITH [offended]: Oh! Are you trying to humiliate me?

MR. SMITH [all smiles]: You know very well that I'm not.

MRS. SMITH: Men are all alike! You sit there all day long, a cigarette in your mouth, or you powder your nose and rouge your lips, fifty times a day, or else you drink like a fish.

MR. SMITH: But what would you say if you saw men acting like women do, smoking all day long, powdering, rouging their lips, drinking whisky?

MRS. SMITH: It's nothing to me! But if you're only saying that to annoy me . . . I don't care for that kind of joking, you know that very well!

[She hurls the socks across the stage and shows her teeth. She gets up.]

MR. SMITH [also getting up and going towards his wife, tenderly]: Oh, my little ducky daddles, what a little spitfire you are! You know that I only said it as a joke! [He takes her by the waist and kisses her.] What a ridiculous pair of old lovers we are! Come, let's put out the lights and go bye-byes.

MARY [entering]: I'm the maid. I have spent a very pleasant afternoon. I've been to the cinema with a man and I've seen a film with some women. After the cinema, we went to drink some brandy and milk and then read the newspaper.

MRS. SMITH: I hope that you've spent a pleasant afternoon, that you went to the cinema with a man and that you drank some brandy and milk.

MR. SMITH: And the newspaper.

MARY: Mr. and Mrs. Martin, your guests, are at the door. They were waiting for me. They didn't dare come in by themselves. They were supposed to have dinner with you this evening.

MRS. SMITH: Oh, yes. We were expecting them. And we were hungry. Since they didn't put in an appearance, we were going to start dinner without them. We've had nothing to eat all day. You should not have gone out!

MARY: But it was you who gave me permission.

MR. SMITH: We didn't do it on purpose.

MARY [bursts into laughter, then she bursts into tears. Then she smiles]: I bought me a chamber pot.

MRS. SMITH: My dear Mary, please open the door and ask Mr. and Mrs. Martin to step in. We will change quickly. [Mr. and Mrs. Smith exit right. Mary opens the door at the left by which Mr. and Mrs. Martin enter.]

MARY: Why have you come so late! You are not very polite. People should be punctual. Do you understand? But sit down there, anyway, and wait now that you're here.

[She exits. Mr. and Mrs. Martin sit facing each other, without speaking. They smile timidly at each other. The dialogue which follows must be spoken in voices that are drawling, monotonous, a little singsong, without nuances.]

MR. MARTIN: Excuse me, madam, but it seems to me, unless I'm mistaken, that I've met you somewhere before.

MRS. MARTIN: I, too, sir. It seems to me that I've met you somewhere before.

MR. MARTIN: Was it, by any chance, at Manchester that I caught a glimpse of you, madam?

MRS. MARTIN: That is very possible. I am originally from the city of Manchester. But I do not have a good memory, sir. I cannot say whether it was there that I caught a glimpse of you or not!

MR. MARTIN: Good God, that's curious! I, too, am originally from the city of Manchester, madam!

MRS. MARTIN: That is curious!

MR. MARTIN: Isn't that curious! Only, I, madam, I left the city of Manchester about five weeks ago.

MRS. MARTIN: That is curious! What a bizarre coincidence! I, too, sir, I left the city of Manchester about five weeks ago.

MR. MARTIN: Madam, I took the 8:30 morning train which arrives in London at 4:45.

MRS. MARTIN: That is curious! How very bizarre! And what a coincidence! I took the same train, sir, I too.

MR. MARTIN: Good Lord, how curious! Perhaps then, madam, it was on the train that I saw you?

MRS. MARTIN: It is indeed possible; that is, not unlikely. It is plausible and, after all, why not!—But I don't recall it, sir!

MR. MARTIN: I traveled second class, madam. There is no second class in England, but I always travel second class.

MRS. MARTIN: That is curious! How very bizarre! And what a coincidence! I, too, sir, I traveled second class.

MR. MARTIN: How curious that is! Perhaps we did meet in second class, my dear lady!

MRS. MARTIN: That is certainly possible, and it is not at all unlikely. But I do not remember very well, my dear sir!

MR. MARTIN: My seat was in coach No. 8, compartment 6, my dear lady.

MRS. MARTIN: How curious that is! My seat was also in coach No. 8, compartment 6, my dear sir!

MR. MARTIN: How curious that is and what a bizarre coincidence! Perhaps we met in compartment 6, my dear lady?

MRS. MARTIN: It is indeed possible, after all! But I do not recall it, my dear sir!

MR. MARTIN: To tell the truth, my dear lady, I do not remember it either, but it is possible that we caught a glimpse of each other there, and as I think of it, it seems to me even very likely.

MRS. MARTIN: Oh! truly, of course, truly, sir!

MR. MARTIN: How curious it is! I had seat No. 3, next to the window, my dear lady.

MRS. MARTIN: Oh, good Lord, how curious and bizarre! I had seat No. 6, next to the window, across from you, my dear sir.

MR. MARTIN: Good God, how curious that is and what a coincidence! We were then seated facing each other, my dear lady! It is there that we must have seen each other!

MRS. MARTIN: How curious it is! It is possible, but I do not recall it, sir!

MR. MARTIN: To tell the truth, my dear lady, I do not remember it either. However, it is very possible that we saw each other on that occasion.

MRS. MARTIN: It is true, but I am not at all sure of it, sir.

MR. MARTIN: Dear madam, were you not the lady who asked me to place her suitcase in the luggage rack and who thanked me and gave me permission to smoke?

MRS. MARTIN: But of course, that must have been I, sir. How curious it is, how curious it is, and what a coincidence!

MR. MARTIN: How curious it is, how bizarre, what a coincidence! And well, well, it was perhaps at that moment that we came to know each other, madam?

MRS. MARTIN: How curious it is and what a coincidence! It is indeed possible, my dear sir! However, I do not believe that I recall it.

MR. MARTIN: Nor do I, madam. [*A moment of silence. The clock strikes twice, then once.*] Since coming to London, I have resided in Bromfield Street, my dear lady.

MRS. MARTIN: How curious that is, how bizarre! I, too, since coming to London, I have resided in Bromfield Street, my dear sir.

MR. MARTIN: How curious that is, well then, well then, perhaps we have seen each other in Bromfield Street, my dear lady.

MRS. MARTIN: How curious that is, how bizarre! It is indeed possible, after all! But I do not recall it, my dear sir.

MR. MARTIN: I reside at No. 19, my dear lady.

MRS. MARTIN: How curious that is. I also reside at No. 19, my dear sir.

MR. MARTIN: Well then, well then, well then, well then, perhaps we have seen each other in that house, dear lady.

MRS. MARTIN: It is indeed possible but I do not recall it, dear sir.

MR. MARTIN: My flat is on the fifth floor, No. 8, my dear lady.

MRS. MARTIN: How curious it is, good Lord, how bizarre! And what a coincidence! I too reside on the fifth floor, in flat No. 8, dear sir!

MR. MARTIN [*musing*]: How curious it is, how curious it is, how curious it is, and what a coincidence! You know, in my bedroom there is a bed, and it is covered with a green eiderdown. This room, with the bed and the green eiderdown, is at the end of the corridor between the w.c. and the bookcase, dear lady!

MRS. MARTIN: What a coincidence, good Lord, what a coincidence! My bedroom, too, has a bed with a green eiderdown and is at the end of the corridor, between the w.c., dear sir, and the bookcase!

MR. MARTIN: How bizarre, curious, strange! Then, madam, we live in the same room and we sleep in the same bed, dear lady. It is perhaps there that we have met!

MRS. MARTIN: How curious it is and what a coincidence! It is indeed possible that we have met there, and perhaps even last night. But I do not recall it, dear sir!

MR. MARTIN: I have a little girl, my little daughter, she lives with me, dear lady. She is two years old, she's blonde, she has a white eye and a red eye, she is very pretty, her name is Alice, dear lady.

MRS. MARTIN: What a bizarre coincidence! I, too, have a little girl. She is two years old, has a white eye and a red eye, she is very pretty, and her name is Alice, too, dear sir!

MR. MARTIN [*in the same drawling, monotonous voice*]: How curious it is and what a coincidence! And bizarre! Perhaps they are the same, dear lady!

MRS. MARTIN: How curious it is! It is indeed possible, dear sir. [*A rather long moment of silence. The clock strikes 29 times.*]

MR. MARTIN [*after having reflected at length, gets up slowly and, unhurriedly, moves toward Mrs. Martin, who, surprised by his solemn air, has also gotten up very quietly. Mr. Martin, in the same flat, monotonous voice, slightly singsong*]: Then, dear lady, I believe that there can be no doubt about it, we have seen each other before and you are my own wife . . . Elizabeth, I have found you again!

[*Mrs. Martin approaches Mr. Martin without haste. They embrace without expression. The clock strikes once, very loud. This striking of the clock must be so loud that it makes the audience jump. The Martins do not hear it.*]

MRS. MARTIN: Donald, it's you, darling!

[*They sit together in the same armchair, their arms around each other, and fall asleep. The clock strikes several more times. Mary, on tiptoe, a finger to her lips, enters quietly and addresses the audience.*]

MARY: Elizabeth and Donald are now too happy to be able to hear me. I can therefore let you in on a secret. Elizabeth is not Elizabeth, Donald is not Donald. And here is the proof: the child that Donald spoke of is not Elizabeth's daughter, they are not the same person. Donald's daughter has one white eye and one red eye like Elizabeth's daughter. Whereas Donald's child has a white right eye and a red left eye, Elizabeth's child has a red right eye and a white left eye! Thus all of Donald's system of deduction collapses when it comes up against this last obstacle which destroys his whole theory. In spite of the extraordinary coincidences which seem to be definitive proofs, Donald and Elizabeth, not being the parents of the same child, are not Donald and Elizabeth. It is in vain that he thinks he is Donald, it is in vain that she thinks she is Elizabeth. He believes in vain that she is Elizabeth. She believes in vain that he is Donald—they are sadly deceived. But who is the true Donald? Who is the true Elizabeth? Who has any interest in prolonging this confusion? I don't know. Let's not try to know. Let's leave things as they are. [*She takes several steps toward the door, then returns and says to the audience:*] My real name is Sherlock Holmes. [*She exits.*]

Scene from the Cubiculo Theater's 1987 production of *The Bald Soprano*, starring John Turturro as Mr. Smith.

[*The clock strikes as much as it likes. After several seconds, Mr. and Mrs. Martin separate and take the chairs they had at the beginning.*]

MR. MARTIN: Darling, let's forget all that has not passed between us, and, now that we have found each other again, let's try not to lose each other any more, and live as before.

MRS. MARTIN: Yes, darling.

[*Mr. and Mrs. Smith enter from the right, wearing the same clothes.*]

MRS. SMITH: Good evening, dear friends! Please forgive us for having made you wait so long. We thought that we should extend you the courtesy to which you are entitled and as soon as we learned that you had been kind enough to give us the pleasure of coming to see us without prior notice we hurried to dress for the occasion.

MR. SMITH [*furious*]: We've had nothing to eat all day. And we've been waiting four whole hours for you. Why have you come so late?

[*Mr. and Mrs. Smith sit facing their guests. The striking of the clock underlines the speeches, more or less strongly, according to the case. The Martins, particularly Mrs. Martin, seem embarrassed and timid. For this reason the conversation begins with difficulty and the words are uttered, at the beginning, awkwardly. A long embarrassed silence at first, then other silences and hesitations follow.*]

MR. SMITH: Hm. [*Silence.*]

MRS. SMITH: Hm, hm. [*Silence.*]

MRS. MARTIN: Hm, hm, hm. [*Silence.*]

MR. MARTIN: Hm, hm, hm, hm. [*Silence.*]

MRS. MARTIN: Oh, but definitely. [*Silence.*]

MR. MARTIN: We all have colds. [*Silence.*]

MR. SMITH: Nevertheless, it's not chilly. [*Silence.*]

MRS. SMITH: There's no draft. [*Silence.*]

MR. MARTIN: Oh no, fortunately. [*Silence.*]

MR. SMITH: Oh dear, oh dear, oh dear. [*Silence.*]

MR. MARTIN: Don't you feel well? [*Silence.*]

MRS. SMITH: No, he's wet his pants. [*Silence.*]

MRS. MARTIN: Oh, sir, at your age, you shouldn't. [*Silence.*]

MR. SMITH: The heart is ageless. [*Silence.*]

MR. MARTIN: That's true. [*Silence.*]

MRS. SMITH: So they say. [*Silence.*]

MRS. MARTIN: They also say the opposite. [*Silence.*]

MR. SMITH: The truth lies somewhere between the two. [*Silence.*]

MR. MARTIN: That's true. [*Silence.*]

MRS. SMITH [*to the Martins*]: Since you travel so much, you must have many interesting things to tell us.

MR. MARTIN [*to his wife*]: My dear, tell us what you've seen today.

MRS. MARTIN: It's scarcely worth the trouble, for no one would believe me.

MR. SMITH: We're not going to question your sincerity!

MRS. SMITH: You will offend us if you think that.

MR. MARTIN [*to his wife*]: You will offend them, my dear, if you think that . . .

MRS. MARTIN [*graciously*]: Oh well, today I witnessed something extraordinary. Something really incredible.

MR. MARTIN: Tell us quickly, my dear.

MR. SMITH: Oh, this is going to be amusing.

MRS. SMITH: At last.

MRS. MARTIN: Well, today, when I went shopping to buy some vegetables, which are getting to be dearer and dearer . . .

MRS. SMITH: Where is it all going to end!

MR. SMITH: You shouldn't interrupt, my dear, it's very rude.

John Turturro as Mr. Smith in the Cubiculo Theater production, 1987.

MRS. MARTIN: In the street, near a café, I saw a man, properly dressed, about fifty years old, or not even that, who . . .

MR. SMITH: Who, what?

MRS. SMITH: Who, what?

MR. SMITH [to his wife]: Don't interrupt, my dear, you're disgusting.

MRS. SMITH: My dear, it is you who interrupted first, you boor.

MR. SMITH [to his wife]: Hush. [To Mrs. Martin:] What was this man doing?

MRS. MARTIN: Well, I'm sure you'll say that I'm making it up—he was down on one knee and he was bent over.

MR. MARTIN, MR. SMITH, MRS. SMITH: Oh!

MRS. MARTIN: Yes, bent over.

MR. SMITH: Not possible.

MRS. MARTIN: Yes, bent over. I went near him to see what he was doing . . .

MR. SMITH: And?

MRS. MARTIN: He was tying his shoe lace which had come undone.

MR. MARTIN, MR. SMITH, MRS. SMITH: Fantastic!

MR. SMITH: If someone else had told me this, I'd not believe it.

MR. MARTIN: Why not? One sees things even more extraordinary every day, when one walks around. For instance, today in the Underground I myself saw a man, quietly sitting on a seat, reading his newspaper.

MRS. SMITH: What a character!

MR. SMITH: Perhaps it was the same man!

[The doorbell rings.]

MR. SMITH: Goodness, someone is ringing.

MRS. SMITH: There must be somebody there. I'll go and see. [She goes to see, she opens the door and closes it, and comes back.] Nobody. [She sits down again.]

MR. MARTIN: I'm going to give you another example . . .

[Doorbell rings again.]

MR. SMITH: Goodness, someone is ringing.

MRS. SMITH: There must be somebody there. I'll go and see. [She goes to see, opens the door, and comes back.] No one. [She sits down again.]

MR. MARTIN [who has forgotten where he was]: Uh . . .

MRS. MARTIN: You were saying that you were going to give us another example.

MR. MARTIN: Oh, yes . . .

[Doorbell rings again.]

MR. SMITH: Goodness, someone is ringing.

MRS. SMITH: I'm not going to open the door again.

MR. SMITH: Yes, but there must be someone there!

MRS. SMITH: The first time there was no one. The second time, no one. Why do you think that there is someone there now?

MR. SMITH: Because someone has rung!

MRS. MARTIN: That's no reason.

The Shakespeare Theatre of New Jersey's August 2007 performance of *The Bald Soprano*, starring Kelly McAndrew and Mathew Floyd Miller and featuring set designer Mimi Lien's wooden packing case [RIGHT], which contained the living room [BELOW]. (Photo by Andrew Murad.)

MR. MARTIN: What? When one hears the doorbell ring, that means someone is at the door ringing to have the door opened.

MRS. MARTIN: Not always. You've just seen otherwise!

MR. MARTIN: In most cases, yes.

MR. SMITH: As for me, when I go to visit someone, I ring in order to be admitted. I think that everyone does the same thing and that each time there is a ring there must be someone there.

MRS. SMITH: That is true in theory. But in reality things happen differently. You have just seen otherwise.

MRS. MARTIN: Your wife is right.

MR. MARTIN: Oh! You women! You always stand up for each other.

MRS. SMITH: Well, I'll go and see. You can't say that I am obstinate, but you will see that there's no one there! [*She goes to look, opens the door and closes it.*] You see, there's no one there. [*She returns to her seat.*]

MRS. SMITH: Oh, these men who always think they're right and who's always wrong!

[*The doorbell rings again.*]

MR. SMITH: Goodness, someone is ringing. There must be someone there.

MRS. SMITH [*in a fit of anger*]: Don't send me to open the door again. You've seen that it was useless. Experience teaches us that when one hears the doorbell ring it is because there is never anyone there.

MRS. MARTIN: Never.

MR. MARTIN: That's not entirely accurate.

MR. SMITH: In fact it's false. When one hears the doorbell ring it is because there is someone there.

MRS. SMITH: He won't admit he's wrong.

MRS. MARTIN: My husband is very obstinate, too.

MR. SMITH: There's someone there.

MR. MARTIN: That's not impossible.

MRS. SMITH [*to her husband*]: No.

MR. SMITH: Yes.

MRS. SMITH: I tell you *no*. In any case you are not going to disturb me again for nothing. If you wish to know, go and look yourself!

MR. SMITH: I'll go.

[*Mrs. Smith shrugs her shoulders. Mrs. Martin tosses her head.*]

MR. SMITH [*opening the door*]: Oh! how do you do. [*He glances at Mrs. Smith and the Martins, who are all surprised.*] It's the Fire Chief!

FIRE CHIEF [*he is of course in uniform and is wearing an enormous shining helmet*]: Good evening, ladies and gentlemen. [*The Smiths and the Martins are still slightly astonished. Mrs. Smith turns her head away, in a temper, and does not reply to his greeting.*] Good evening, Mrs. Smith. You appear to be angry.

MRS. SMITH: Oh!

MR. SMITH: You see it's because my wife is a little chagrined at having been proved wrong.

MR. MARTIN: There's been an argument between Mr. and Mrs. Smith, Mr. Fire Chief.

MRS. SMITH [*to Mr. Martin*]: This is no business of yours! [*To Mr. Smith:*] I beg you not to involve outsiders in our family arguments.

MR. SMITH: Oh, my dear, this is not so serious. The Fire Chief is an old friend of the family. His mother courted me, and I knew his father. He asked me to give him my daughter in marriage if ever I had one. And he died waiting.

MR. MARTIN: That's neither his fault, nor yours.

FIRE CHIEF: Well, what is it all about?

MRS. SMITH: My husband was claiming . . .

MR. SMITH: No, it was you who was claiming.

MR. MARTIN: Yes, it was she.

MRS. MARTIN: No, it was he.

FIRE CHIEF: Don't get excited. You tell me, Mrs. Smith.

MRS. SMITH: Well, this is how it was. It is difficult for me to speak openly to you, but a fireman is also a confessor.

FIRE CHIEF: Well then?

MRS. SMITH: We were arguing because my husband said that each time the doorbell rings there is always someone there.

MR. MARTIN: It is plausible.

MRS. SMITH: And I was saying that each time the doorbell rings there is never anyone there.

MRS. MARTIN: It might seem strange.

MRS. SMITH: But it has been proved, not by theoretical demonstrations, but by facts.

MR. SMITH: That's false, since the Fire Chief is here. He rang the bell, I opened the door, and there he was.

MRS. MARTIN: When?

MR. MARTIN: But just now.

MRS. SMITH: Yes, but it was only when you heard the doorbell ring the fourth time that there was someone there. And the fourth time does not count.

MRS. MARTIN: Never. It is only the first three times that count.

MR. SMITH: Mr. Fire Chief, permit me in my turn to ask you several questions.

FIRE CHIEF: Go right ahead.

MR. SMITH: When I opened the door and saw you, it was really you who had rung the bell?

FIRE CHIEF: Yes, it was I.

MR. MARTIN: You were at the door? And you rang in order to be admitted?

FIRE CHIEF: I do not deny it.

MR. SMITH [*to his wife, triumphantly*]: You see? I was right. When you hear the doorbell ring, that means someone rang it. You certainly cannot say that the Fire Chief is not someone.

MRS. SMITH: Certainly not. I repeat to you that I was speaking of only the first three times, since the fourth time does not count.

MRS. MARTIN: And when the doorbell rang the first time, was it you?

FIRE CHIEF: No, it was not I.

MRS. MARTIN: You see? The doorbell rang and there was no one there.

MR. MARTIN: Perhaps it was someone else?

MR. SMITH: Were you standing at the door for a long time?

FIRE CHIEF: Three-quarters of an hour.

MR. SMITH: And you saw no one?

FIRE CHIEF: No one. I am sure of that.

MRS. MARTIN: And did you hear the bell when it rang the second time?

FIRE CHIEF: Yes, and that wasn't I either. And there was still no one there.

MRS. SMITH: Victory! I was right.

MR. SMITH [*to his wife*]: Not so fast. [*To the Fire Chief:*] And what were you doing at the door?

FIRE CHIEF: Nothing. I was just standing there. I was thinking of many things.

MR. MARTIN [*to the Fire Chief*]: But the third time—it was not you who rang?

FIRE CHIEF: Yes, it was I.

MR. SMITH: But when the door was opened nobody was in sight.

FIRE CHIEF: That was because I had hidden myself—as a joke.

MRS. SMITH: Don't make jokes, Mr. Fire Chief. This business is too sad.

MR. MARTIN: In short, we still do not know whether, when the doorbell rings, there is someone there or not!

MRS. SMITH: Never anyone.

MR. SMITH: Always someone.

FIRE CHIEF: I am going to reconcile you. You both are partly right. When the doorbell rings, sometimes there is someone, other times there is no one.

MR. MARTIN: This seems logical to me.

MRS. MARTIN: I think so too.

FIRE CHIEF: Life is very simple, really. [*To the Smiths:*] Go on and kiss each other.

MRS. SMITH: We just kissed each other a little while ago.

MR. MARTIN: They'll kiss each other tomorrow. They have plenty of time.

MRS. SMITH: Mr. Fire Chief, since you have helped us settle this, please make yourself comfortable, take off your helmet and sit down for a moment.

FIRE CHIEF: Excuse me, but I can't stay long. I should like to remove my helmet, but I haven't time to sit down. [*He sits down, without removing his helmet.*] I must admit that I have come to see you for another reason. I am on official business.

MRS. SMITH: And what can we do for you, Mr. Fire Chief?

FIRE CHIEF: I must beg you to excuse my indiscretion [*terribly embarrassed*] . . . uhm [*He points a finger at the Martins*] . . . you don't mind . . . in front of them . . .

MRS. MARTIN: Say whatever you like.

MR. MARTIN: We're old friends. They tell us everything.

MR. SMITH: Speak.

FIRE CHIEF: Eh, well—is there a fire here?

MRS. SMITH: Why do you ask us that?

FIRE CHIEF: It's because—pardon me—I have orders to extinguish all the fires in the city.

MRS. MARTIN: All?

FIRE CHIEF: Yes, all.

MRS. SMITH [*confused*]: I don't know . . . I don't think so. Do you want me to go and look?

MR. SMITH [*sniffing*]: There can't be one here. There's no smell of anything burning.

FIRE CHIEF [*aggrieved*]: None at all? You don't have a little fire in the chimney, something burning in the attic or in the cellar? A little fire just starting, at least?

MRS. SMITH: I am sorry to disappoint you but I do not believe there's anything here at the moment. I promise that I will notify you when we do have something.

FIRE CHIEF: Please don't forget, it would be a great help.

MRS. SMITH: That's a promise.

FIRE CHIEF [*to the Martins*]: And there's nothing burning at your house either?

MRS. MARTIN: No, unfortunately.

MR. MARTIN [*to the Fire Chief*]: Things aren't going so well just now.

FIRE CHIEF: Very poorly. There's been almost nothing, a few trifles—a chimney, a barn. Nothing important. It doesn't bring in much. And since there are no returns, the profits on output are very meager.

MR. SMITH: Times are bad. That's true all over. It's the same this year with business and agriculture as it is with fires, nothing is prospering.

MR. MARTIN: No wheat, no fires.

FIRE CHIEF: No floods either.

MRS. SMITH: But there is some sugar.

MR. SMITH: That's because it is imported.

MRS. MARTIN: It's harder in the case of fires. The tariffs are too high!

FIRE CHIEF: All the same, there's an occasional asphyxiation by gas, but that's unusual too. For instance, a young woman asphyxiated herself last week—she had left the gas on.

MRS. MARTIN: Had she forgotten it?

FIRE CHIEF: No, but she thought it was her comb.

MR. SMITH: These confusions are always dangerous!

MRS. SMITH: Did you go to see the match dealer?

FIRE CHIEF: There's nothing doing there. He is insured against fires.

MR. MARTIN: Why don't you go see the Vicar of Wakefield, and use my name?

FIRE CHIEF: I don't have the right to extinguish clergymen's fires. The Bishop would get angry. Besides they extinguish their fires themselves, or else they have them put out by vestal virgins.

MR. SMITH: Go see the Durands.

FIRE CHIEF: I can't do that either. He's not English. He's only been naturalized. And naturalized citizens have the right to have houses, but not the right to have them put out if they're burning.

MRS. SMITH: Nevertheless, when they set fire to it last year, it was put out just the same.

FIRE CHIEF: He did that all by himself. Clandestinely. But it's not I who would report him.

MR. SMITH: Neither would I.

MRS. SMITH: Mr. Fire Chief, since you are not too pressed, stay a little while longer. You would be doing us a favor.

FIRE CHIEF: Shall I tell you some stories?

MRS. SMITH: Oh, by all means, how charming of you. [*She kisses him.*]

MR. SMITH, MRS. MARTIN, MR. MARTIN: Yes, yes, some stories, hurrah!

[*They applaud.*]

MR. SMITH: And what is even more interesting is the fact that firemen's stories are all true, and they're based on experience.

FIRE CHIEF: I speak from my own experience. Truth, nothing but the truth. No fiction.

MR. MARTIN: That's right. Truth is never found in books, only in life.

MRS. SMITH: Begin!

MR. MARTIN: Begin!

MRS. MARTIN: Be quiet, he is beginning.

FIRE CHIEF [*coughs slightly several times*]: Excuse me, don't look at me that way. You embarrass me. You know that I am shy.

MRS. SMITH: Isn't he charming! [*She kisses him.*]

FIRE CHIEF: I'm going to try to begin anyhow. But promise me that you won't listen.

MRS. MARTIN: But if we don't listen to you we won't hear you.

FIRE CHIEF: I didn't think of that!

MRS. SMITH: I told you, he's just a boy.

MR. MARTIN, MR. SMITH: Oh, the sweet child! [*They kiss him.*]

MRS. MARTIN: Chin up!

FIRE CHIEF: Well, then! [*He coughs again in a voice shaken by emotion:*] "The Dog and the Cow," an experimental fable. Once upon a time another cow asked another dog: "Why have you not swallowed your trunk?" "Pardon me," replied the dog, "it is because I thought that I was an elephant."

MRS. MARTIN: What is the moral?

FIRE CHIEF: That's for you to find out.

MR. SMITH: He's right.

MRS. SMITH [*furious*]: Tell us another.

FIRE CHIEF: A young calf had eaten too much ground glass. As a result, it was obliged to give birth. It brought forth a cow into the world. However, since the calf was male, the cow could not call him Mamma. Nor could she call him Papa, because the calf was too little. The calf was then obliged to get married and the registry office carried out all the details completely à la mode.

MR. SMITH: À la mode de Caen.

MR. MARTIN: Like tripes.

FIRE CHIEF: You've heard that one?

MRS. SMITH: It was in all the papers.

MRS. MARTIN: It happened not far from our house.

FIRE CHIEF: I'll tell you another: "The Cock." Once upon a time, a cock wished to play the dog. But he had no luck because everyone recognized him right away.

MRS. SMITH: On the other hand, the dog that wished to play the cock was never recognized.

MR. SMITH: I'll tell you one: "The Snake and the Fox." Once upon a time, a snake came up to a fox and said: "It seems to me that I know you!" The fox replied to him: "Me too." "Then," said the snake, "give me some money." "A fox doesn't give money," replied

the tricky animal, who, in order to escape, jumped down into a deep ravine full of strawberries and chicken honey. But the snake was there waiting for him with a Mephistophelean° laugh. The fox pulled out his knife, shouting: "I'm going to teach you how to live!" Then he took to flight, turning his back. But he had no luck. The snake was quicker. With a well-chosen blow of his fist, he struck the fox in the middle of his forehead, which broke into a thousand pieces, while he cried: "No! No! Four times no! I'm not your daughter."

MRS. MARTIN: It's interesting.

MRS. SMITH: It's not bad.

MR. MARTIN [*shaking Mr. Smith's hand*]: My congratulations.

FIRE CHIEF [*jealous*]: Not so good. And anyway, I've heard it before.

MR. SMITH: It's terrible.

MRS. SMITH: But it wasn't even true.

MRS. MARTIN: Yes, unfortunately.

MR. MARTIN [*to Mrs. Smith*]: It's your turn, dear lady.

MRS. SMITH: I only know one. I'm going to tell it to you. It's called "The Bouquet."

MR. SMITH: My wife has always been romantic.

MR. MARTIN: She's a true Englishwoman.

MRS. SMITH: Here it is: Once upon a time, a fiancé gave a bouquet of flowers to his fiancée, who said, "Thanks"; but before she had said, "Thanks," he, without saying a single word, took back the flowers he had given her in order to teach her a good lesson, and he said, "I take them back." He said, "Goodbye," and took them back and went off in all directions.

MR. MARTIN: Oh, charming! [*He either kisses or does not kiss Mrs. Smith.*]

MRS. MARTIN: You have a wife, Mr. Smith, of whom all the world is jealous.

MR. SMITH: It's true. My wife is intelligence personified. She's even more intelligent than I. In any case, she is much more feminine, everyone says so.

MRS. SMITH [*to the Fire Chief*]: Let's have another, Mr. Fire Chief.

FIRE CHIEF: Oh, no, it's too late.

MR. MARTIN: Tell us one, anyway.

FIRE CHIEF: I'm too tired.

MR. SMITH: Please do us a favor.

MR. MARTIN: I beg you.

FIRE CHIEF: No.

MRS. MARTIN: You have a heart of ice. We're sitting on hot coals.

MRS. SMITH [*falls on her knees sobbing, or else she does not do this*]: I implore you!

FIRE CHIEF: Righto.

MR. SMITH [*in Mrs. Martin's ear*]: He agrees! He's going to bore us again.

MRS. MARTIN: Shh.

MRS. SMITH: No luck. I was too polite.

Mephistophelean: Devilish, controlling; after Mephistopheles in Christopher Marlowe's *Doctor Faustus*.

FIRE CHIEF: "The Headcold." My brother-in law had, on the paternal side, a first cousin whose maternal uncle had a father-in-law whose paternal grandfather had married as his second wife a young native whose brother he had met on one of his travels, a girl of whom he was enamored and by whom he had a son who married an intrepid lady pharmacist who was none other than the niece of an unknown fourth-class petty officer of the Royal Navy and whose a-dopted father had an aunt who spoke Spanish fluently and who was, perhaps, one of the granddaughters of an engineer who died young, himself the grandson of the owner of a vineyard which produced mediocre wine, but who had a second cousin, a stay-at-home, a sergeant-major, whose son had married a very pretty young woman, a divorcée, whose first husband was the son of a loyal patriot who, in the hope of making his fortune, had managed to bring up one of his daughters so that she could marry a footman who had known Rothshild, and whose brother, after having changed his trade several times, married and had a daughter whose stunted great-grandfather wore spectacles which had been given him by a cousin of his, the brother-in-law of a man from Portugal, natural son of a miller, not too badly off, whose foster-brother had married the daughter of a former country doctor, who was himself a foster-brother of the son of a forrester, himself the natural son of another country doctor, married three times in a row, whose third wife . . .

MR. MARTIN: I knew that third wife, if I'm not mistaken. She ate chicken sitting on a hornet's nest.

FIRE CHIEF: It's not the same one.

MRS. SMITH: Shh!

FIRE CHIEF: As I was saying . . . whose third wife was the daughter of the best midwife in the region and who, early left a widow . . .

MR. SMITH: Like my wife.

FIRE CHIEF: . . . Had married a glazier who was full of life and who had had, by the daughter of a station master, a child who had burned his bridges . . .

MRS. SMITH: His britches?

MR. MARTIN: No his bridge game.

FIRE CHIEF: And had married an oyster woman, whose father had a brother, mayor of a small town, who had taken as his wife a blonde schoolteacher, whose cousin, a fly fisherman . . .

MR. MARTIN: A fly by night?

FIRE CHIEF: . . . Had married another blonde school-teacher, named Marie, too, whose brother was married to another Marie, also a blonde schoolteacher . . .

MR. SMITH: Since she's blonde, she must be Marie.

FIRE CHIEF: . . . And whose father had been reared in Canada by an old woman who was the niece of a priest whose grandmother, occasionally in the winter, like everyone else, caught a cold.

MRS. SMITH: A curious story. Almost unbelievable.

MR. MARTIN: If you catch a cold, you should get yourself a colt.

MR. SMITH: It's a useless precaution, but absolutely necessary.

MRS. MARTIN: Excuse me, Mr. Fire Chief, but I did not follow your story very well. At the end, when we got to the grandmother of the priest, I got mixed up.

MR. SMITH: One always gets mixed up in the hands of a priest.

MRS. SMITH: Oh yes, Mr. Fire Chief, begin again. Everyone wants to hear.

FIRE CHIEF: Ah, I don't know whether I'll be able to. I'm on official business. It depends on what time it is.

MRS. SMITH: We don't have the time, here.

FIRE CHIEF: But the clock?

MR. SMITH: It runs badly. It is contradictory, and always indicates the opposite of what the hour really is.

[Enter Mary.]

MARY: Madam . . . sir . . .

MRS. SMITH: What do you want?

MR. SMITH: What have you come in here for?

MARY: I hope, madam and sir will excuse me . . . and these ladies and gentlemen too . . . I would like . . . I would like . . . to tell you a story, myself.

MRS. MARTIN: What is she saying?

MR. MARTIN: I believe that our friends' maid is going crazy . . . she wants to tell us a story, too.

FIRE CHIEF: Who does she think she is? [He looks at her.] Oh!

MRS. SMITH: Why are you butting in?

MR. SMITH: This is really uncalled for, Mary . . .

FIRE CHIEF: Oh! But it is she! Incredible!

MR. SMITH: And you?

MARY: Incredible! Here!

MRS. SMITH: What does all this mean?

MR. SMITH: You know each other?

FIRE CHIEF: And how!

[Mary throws herself on the neck of the Fire Chief.]

MARY: I'm so glad to see you again . . . at last!

MR. AND MRS. SMITH: Oh!

MR. SMITH: This is too much, here, in our home, in the suburbs of London.

MRS. SMITH: It's not proper! . . .

FIRE CHIEF: It was she who extinguished my first fires.

MARY: I'm your little firehose.

MR. MARTIN: If that is the case . . . dear friends . . . these emotions are understandable, human, honorable . . .

MRS. MARTIN: All that is human is honorable.

MRS. SMITH: Even so, I don't like to see it . . . here among us . . .

MR. SMITH: She's not been properly brought up . . .

FIRE CHIEF: Oh, you have too many prejudices.

MRS. MARTIN: What I think is that a maid, after all—even though it's none of my business—is never anything but a maid . . .

MR. MARTIN: Even if she can sometimes be a rather good detective.

FIRE CHIEF: Let me go.

MARY: Don't be upset! . . . They're not so bad really.

MR. SMITH: Hm . . . hm . . . you two are very touching, but at the same time, a little . . . a little . . .

MR. MARTIN: Yes, that's exactly the word.

MR. SMITH: . . . A little too exhibitionistic . . .

MR. MARTIN: There is a native British modesty—forgive me for attempting, yet again, to define my thought—not understood by foreigners, even by specialists, thanks to which, if I may thus express myself . . . of course, I don't mean to refer to you . . .

MARY: I was going to tell you . . .

MR. SMITH: Don't tell us anything . . .

MARY: Oh yes!

MRS. SMITH: Go, my little Mary, go quietly to the kitchen and read your poems before the mirror . . .

MR. MARTIN: You know, even though I'm not a maid, I also read poems before the mirror.

MRS. MARTIN: This morning when you looked at yourself in the mirror you didn't see yourself.

MR. MARTIN: That's because I wasn't there yet . . .

MARY: All the same, I could, perhaps, recite a little poem for you.

MRS. SMITH: My little Mary, you are frightfully obstinate.

MARY: I'm going to recite a poem, then, is that agreed? It is a poem entitled "The Fire" in honor of the Fire Chief:

The Fire

The polypoids were burning in the wood
A stone caught fire
The castle caught fire
The forest caught fire
The men caught fire
The women caught fire
The birds caught fire
The fish caught fire
The water caught fire
The sky caught fire
The ashes caught fire
The smoke caught fire
The fire caught fire
Everything caught fire
Caught fire, caught fire.

[*She recites the poem while the Smiths are pushing her offstage.*]

MRS. MARTIN: That sent chills up my spine . . .

MR. MARTIN: And yet there's a certain warmth in those lines . . .

FIRE CHIEF: I thought it was marvelous.

MRS. SMITH: All the same . . .

MR. SMITH: You're exaggerating . . .

FIRE CHIEF: Just a minute . . . I admit . . . all this is very subjective . . . but this is my conception of the world. My world. My dream. My ideal . . . And now this reminds me that I must leave. Since you don't have the time here, I must tell you that in exactly three-quarters of an hour and sixteen minutes, I'm having a fire at the other end of the city. Consequently, I must hurry. Even though it will be quite unimportant.

MRS. SMITH: What will it be? A little chimney fire?

FIRE CHIEF: Oh, not even that. A straw fire and a little heartburn.

MR. SMITH: Well, we're sorry to see you go.

MRS. SMITH: You have been very entertaining.

MRS. MARTIN: Thanks to you, we have passed a truly Cartesian quarter of an hour.

FIRE CHIEF [*moving towards the door, then stopping*] Speaking of that—the bald soprano? [*General silence, embarrassment.*]

MRS. SMITH: She always wears her hair in the same style.

FIRE CHIEF: Ah! Then goodbye, ladies and gentlemen.

MR. MARTIN: Good luck, and a good fire!

FIRE CHIEF: Let's hope so. For everybody.

[*Fire Chief exits. All accompany him to the door and then return to their seats.*]

MRS. MARTIN: I can buy a pocketknife for my brother, but you can't buy Ireland for your grandfather.

MR. SMITH: One walks on his feet, but one heats with electricity or coal.

MR. MARTIN: He who sells an ox today, will have an egg tomorrow.

MRS. SMITH: In real life, one must look out of the window.

MRS. MARTIN: One can sit down on a chair, when the chair doesn't have any.

MR. SMITH: One must always think of everything.

MR. MARTIN: The ceiling is above, the floor is below.

MRS. SMITH: When I say yes, it's only a manner of speaking.

MRS. MARTIN: To each his own.

MR. SMITH: Take a circle, caress it, and it will turn vicious.

MRS. SMITH: A schoolmaster teaches his pupils to read, but the cat suckles her young when they are small.

MRS. MARTIN: Nevertheless, it was the cow that gave us tails.

MR. SMITH: When I'm in the country, I love the solitude and the quiet.

MR. MARTIN: You are not old enough yet for that.

MRS. SMITH: Benjamin Franklin was right; you are more nervous than he.

MRS. MARTIN: What are the seven days of the week?

MR. SMITH: Monday, Tuesday, Wednesday, Thursday, Friday, Saturday, Sunday.

MR. MARTIN: Edward is a clerk; his sister Nancy is a typist, and his brother William a shop-assistant.

MRS. SMITH: An odd family!

MRS. MARTIN: I prefer a bird in the bush to a sparrow in a barrow.

MR. SMITH: Rather a steak in a chalet than gristle in a castle.

MR. MARTIN: An Englishman's home is truly his castle.

MRS. SMITH: I don't know enough Spanish to make myself understood.

MRS. MARTIN: I'll give you my mother-in-law's slippers if you'll give me your husband's coffin.

MR. SMITH: I'm looking for a monophysite priest to marry to our maid.

MR. MARTIN: Bread is a staff, whereas bread is also a staff, and an oak springs from an oak every morning at dawn.

MRS. SMITH: My uncle lives in the country, but that's none of the midwife's business.

MR. MARTIN: Paper is for writing, the cat's for the rat. Cheese is for scratching.

MRS. SMITH: The car goes very fast, but the cook beats batter better.

MR. SMITH: Don't be turkeys; rather kiss the conspirator.

MR. MARTIN: Charity begins at home.

MRS. SMITH: I'm waiting for the aqueduct to come and see me at my windmill.

MR. MARTIN: One can prove that social progress is definitely better with sugar.

MR. SMITH: To hell with polishing!

[*Following this last speech of Mr. Smith's, the others are silent for a moment, stupefied. We sense that there is a certain nervous irritation. The strokes of the clock are more nervous too. The speeches which follow must be said, at first, in a glacial, hostile tone. The hostility and the nervousness increase. At the end of this scene, the four characters must be standing very close to each other, screaming their speeches, raising their fists, ready to throw themselves upon each other.*]

MR. MARTIN: One doesn't polish spectacles with black wax.

MRS. SMITH: Yes, but with money one can buy anything.

MR. MARTIN: I'd rather kill a rabbit than sing in the garden.

MR. SMITH: Cockatoos, cockatoos, cockatoos, cockatoos, cockatoos, cockatoos, cockatoos, cockatoos, cockatoos.

MRS. SMITH: Such caca, such caca, such caca, such caca, such caca, such caca, such caca, such caca, such caca.

MR. MARTIN: Such cascades of cacas, such cascades of cacas, such cascades of cacas, such cascades of cacas, such cascades of cacas, such cascades of cacas, such cascades of cacas, such cascades of cacas.

MR. SMITH: Dogs have fleas, dogs have fleas.

MRS. MARTIN: Cactus, coccyx! crocus! cockaded! cockroach!

MRS. SMITH: Incasker, you incask us.

MR. MARTIN: I'd rather lay an egg in a box than go and steal an ox.

MRS. MARTIN [*opening her mouth very wide*]: Ah! oh! ah! oh! Let me gnash my teeth.

MR. SMITH: Crocodile!

MR. MARTIN: Let's go and slap Ulysses.

MR. SMITH: I'm going to live in my cabana among my cacao trees.

MRS. MARTIN: Cacao trees on cacao farms don't bear coconuts, they yield cocoa! Cacao trees on cacao farms don't bear coconuts, they yield cocoa! Cacao trees on cacao farms don't bear coconuts, they yield cocoa.

MRS. SMITH: Mice have lice, lice haven't mice.

MRS. MARTIN: Don't ruche my brooch!

MR. MARTIN: Don't smooch the brooch!

MR. SMITH: Groom the goose, don't goose the groom.

MRS. MARTIN: The goose grooms.

MRS. SMITH: Groom your tooth.

MR. MARTIN: Groom the bridegroom, groom the bridegroom.

MR. SMITH: Seducer seduced!

MRS. MARTIN: Scaramouche!°

MRS. SMITH: Sainte-Nitouche!°

MR. SMITH: Go take a douche.

MR. SMITH: I've been goosed.

MRS. MARTIN: Sainte-Nitouche stoops to my cartouche.

MRS. SMITH: "Who'd stoop to blame? . . . and I never choose to stoop."

MR. MARTIN: Robert!

MR. SMITH: Browning!°

MRS. MARTIN, MR. SMITH: Rudyard.

MRS. SMITH, MR. MARTIN: Kipling.°

MRS. MARTIN, MR. SMITH: Robert Kipling!

MRS. SMITH, MR. MARTIN: Rudyard Browning.

MRS. MARTIN: Silly gobblegobblers, silly gobblegobblers.

MR. MARTIN: Marietta, spot the pot!

MRS. SMITH: Krishnamurti,° Krishnamurti, Krishnamurti!

MR. SMITH: The pope elopes! The pope's got no horoscope. The horoscope's bespoke.

MRS. MARTIN: Bazaar, Balzac, bazooka!

MR. MARTIN: Bizarre, beaux-arts, brassieres!

MR. SMITH: A, e, i, o, u, a, e, i, o, u, a, e, i, o, u, i!

MRS. MARTIN: B, c, d, f, g, l, m, n, p, r, s, t, v, w, x, z!

MR. MARTIN: From sage to stooge, from stage to serge!

MRS. SMITH [*imitating a train*]: Choo, choo, choo, choo, choo, choo, choo, choo, choo, choo, choo!

MR. SMITH: It's!

MRS. MARTIN: Not!

MR. MARTIN: That!

MRS. SMITH: Way!

MR. SMITH: It's!

MRS. MARTIN: O!

MR. MARTIN: Ver!

MRS. SMITH: Here!

[*All together, completely infuriated, screaming in each other's ears. The light is extinguished. In the darkness we hear, in an increasingly rapid rhythm:*]

ALL TOGETHER: It's not that way, it's over here, it's not that way, it's over here, it's not that way, it's over here, it's not that way, it's over here!

[*The words cease abruptly. Again, the lights come on. Mr. and Mrs. Martin are seated like the Smiths at the beginning of the play. The play begins again with the Martins, who say exactly the same lines as the Smiths in the first scene, while the curtain softly falls.*]

Scaramouche: A novel by Rafael Sabatini about the French Revolution. **Sainte-Nitouche:** A poem by Edward Arlington Robinson about a burial. **Robert Browning:** British poet (1812–1899), once England's most popular poet. **Rudyard Kipling:** British novelist and poet (1865–1936), popular patriotic writer. **Krishnamurti:** Indian figure associated with a spiritual organization.

COMMENTARY

EUGÈNE IONESCO (1909–1994)

The Tragedy of Language   1960
How an English Primer Became My First Play

TRANSLATED BY JACK UNDANK

Eugène Ionesco comments on his inspiration for writing *The Bald Soprano*, reminiscing about his efforts to learn English from a French-English primer. What he eventually learned was not the English language but insights about language itself. These are what he put to work in his play.

In 1948, before writing my first play, *The Bald Soprano*, I had no idea of becoming a playwright. My only ambition, quite simply, was to learn English. The study of English does not necessarily lead to play writing. On the contrary, it was because I had no luck with English that I turned to the stage. Nor did I write these plays to avenge my failure, although some have said that my *Bald Soprano* was a satire of the English bourgeoisie. If I had wanted to learn Italian, Russian, or Turkish and not succeeded, they would have claimed, by the same token, that the play resulting from that futile effort was a satire of Italian, Russian, or Turkish society. Perhaps I ought to explain. Here is what happened: nine or ten years ago, in order to learn English conversation, I bought a French-English Primer. I set to work. Conscientiously, I copied whole sentences from my Primer with the purpose of memorizing them. Rereading them attentively, I learned not English, but some astonishing truths: that, for example, there are seven days in the week, something, moreover, I already knew; that the floor is down, the ceiling up, things I already knew as well perhaps, but which I had never seriously thought about or had forgotten and which seemed to me, suddenly, as stupefying as they were indisputably true.

I probably have enough of a philosophical bent to have realized that what I was copying into my notebook were not simple English sentences in French translation, but fundamental truths, profound observations. I didn't give up English quite yet. Fortunately so, because, after universal truths, the author of the Primer went on to disclose private ones; probably inspired by the Platonic method, he expressed them by means of dialogue. From the third lesson onward, two characters were presented whose real or fictive existence I am still not sure of: Mr. and Mrs. Smith, an English couple. To my great astonishment, Mrs. Smith informed her husband that they had several children, that they lived in the vicinity of London, that their name was Smith, that Mr. Smith was a clerk, that they had a servant, Mary, English like themselves, that for the past twenty years they have had friends by the name of Mr. and Mrs. Martin, that their house was a palace, for "the home of an Englishman is his true palace."

I really supposed that Mr. Smith was probably somewhat abreast of all this, but can one be sure; there are people that absent-minded. Moreover, it is wise to remind our fellow men of things they may forget or of which they are insufficiently conscious. Besides these permanent, private truths, there were other truths, truths of the moment, which became apparent: for example, the fact that the Smiths had just finished their dinner and that it was nine o'clock at night, according to the clock—English time.

I should like to point out the irrefutable, perfectly axiomatic character of Mrs. Smith's assertions as well as the entirely Cartesian manner of the author of my English Primer, for what was truly remarkable about it was its eminently methodical procedure in its quest for truth. In the fifth lesson, the Smiths' friends, the Martins, arrive; the four of them begin to chat, and, starting from basic axioms, they build more complex truths: "the country is quieter than the big city," some of them contend; "yes, but the city is more heavily populated and there are also more shops," the others reply—which is equally true and proves, moreover, that opposing truths can very well coexist.

It was then that my idea came to me. Perfecting my knowledge of English was now out of the question. To concentrate on enriching my English vocabulary, to learn words, to translate into another language what I could just as well say in French, without bearing in mind the "content" of those words, what they revealed, would have been to stumble into that sin of formalism which our thought-directors of today rightly condemn. My ambition had become greater: to communicate to my contemporaries the essential truths of which the French-English Primer had made me aware. And what is more, the dialogues of the Smiths, the Martins, the Smiths and the Martins, were really theater, theater and dialogue being one and the same thing. I had only to put it into a play. That is how I came to write *The Bald Soprano*, a pointedly didactic, theatrical work. And why is this work called *The Bald Soprano* and not *English Without Toil*, the title I first thought of giving it, or *The English Hour*, a title I thought of subsequently? That is too long a story: one of the reasons why *The Bald Soprano* has its present title is that no soprano, bald or otherwise, appears in it. That ought to be sufficient comment. A good part of the play is composed of sentence fragments drawn from my English Primer and set end to end. The Smiths and Martins of the Primer are the Smiths and Martins of my play; they are one and the same, mouth the same maxims, perform the same actions or the same "inactions." In all "didactic theater," you are not supposed to be original, to say what you yourself think: that would be a serious mishandling of objective *truth*; you have only to transmit, humbly, the instruction that has been transmitted to you, ideas that have been handed down. How could I take the slightest liberty with words expressing absolute truth in so edifying a fashion? My play, *authentically* didactic, was not meant to be original nor intended to show my talent to advantage.

. . . Nevertheless, the text of *The Bald Soprano* was a lesson (and an act of plagiarism) only at the start. A strange phenomenon took place, I don't know how: the text began imperceptibly to change before my eyes, and in spite of me. The very simple, luminously clear statements I had copied diligently into my schoolboy's notebook, left to themselves, fermented after a while, became denatured, expanded and overflowed. The repartee which I had, in careful and precise succession, copied from the Primer, became a jumble. Which is what happened to that certain, irrefutable truth: "the floor is down, the ceiling is up." Assertions—as categorical as they were solid: the seven days of the week are Monday, Tuesday, Wednesday, Thursday,

Friday, Saturday, Sunday—collapsed, and Mr. Smith, my hero, now proposed that the week consisted of three days, namely: Tuesday, Thursday, and Tuesday. My characters, my good bourgeois, the Martins, husband and wife, were suddenly afflicted with amnesia: although they continued to speak to and see one another every day, they no longer recognized each other. Other alarming things happened: the Smiths now told of the death of a certain Bobby Watson whose identity was unrecognizable because, as they mentioned elsewhere, three quarters of the town's inhabitants, men, women, children, cats, and pseudo-philosophers were named Bobby Watson. A fifth character now unexpectedly burst upon the scene and added to the confusion of the couples' peaceable domesticity: the Fire Chief, who told stories which had something to do with a young bull supposedly giving birth to an enormous heifer, with a mouse giving birth to a mountain—then, the fireman went off to catch a fire which he had foreseen three days in advance (he had marked it on his calendar) and which was scheduled to break out at the other end of town. Whereupon the Smiths resumed their conversation. Alas! the wise and fundamental truths they exchanged, each carefully linked to the next, had gone wild, their language had become disjointed; the characters disintegrated: their words became meaningless absurdities; the entire cast ended up quarreling. It was impossible to grasp my heroes' motives in this quarrel. They didn't fling retorts at one another, not even sentence fragments or words; all they spoke were syllables, consonants and vowels! . . .

. . . It represented, for me, a kind of collapse of reality. Words had become empty, noisy shells without meaning; the characters as well, of course, had become psychologically empty. Everything appeared to me in an unfamiliar light, people moving in a timeless time, in a spaceless space . . .

While writing the play (for it had become a kind of play or anti-play, that is, a parody of a play, a comedy of comedy), I felt sick, dizzy, nauseous. I had to interrupt my work from time to time and, wondering all the while what demon was prodding me on, lie down on my couch for fear of seeing my work sink into nothingness, and me with it. All the same, once I had finished, I was very proud. I fancied myself having written something like *the tragedy of language*! . . . When it was staged, I was almost amazed to hear the audience laugh; they took it lightly (and still do), believing that it was a comedy, if not an outright farce. Some people (Jean Pouillon among them), those who sensed the uneasiness in it, were not fooled. Others noticed that I was poking fun at Bernstein's theater and his actors. Nicolas Bataille's troupe was the first to notice this; they acted out the play (especially in its initial performances) as though it were a melodrama.

Serious and learned critics, analyzing the work later on, interpreted it as no more than a criticism of the Théâtre de Boulevard (popular theater). I have just said that I believe that interpretation valid; however, in my mind, it is not a satire of petty bourgeois mentality associated with any particular society. It is, above all, concerned with a kind of universal petty bourgeoisie, the petty bourgeoisie being the personification of accepted ideas and slogans, the ubiquitous conformist. His automatic use of language is, of course, what gives him away. The text of *The Bald Soprano* or of the English (or Russian or Portuguese) Primer, composed of ready-made expressions and the most tired clichés, made me aware of the automatic quality of language and human behavior, "empty talk," speaking because there is nothing personal to say, the absence of inner life, the mechanical aspect of daily existence, man bathing in his social environment, becoming an indistinguishable part of it. The Smiths, the Martins, can no longer talk because they can no longer think; they can no longer think *because they can no longer be moved, can no longer feel passions*; they can no longer be, they can "become" anybody, anything, for, having lost their identity, they assume the identity of others, become part of the world of the impersonal; they are interchangeable: you can put Martin in place of Smith and vice versa, no one will notice. The tragic character does not change, he is crushed; he is himself, he is *real*. Comic characters, fools, are people who do not exist.

Samuel Beckett

Samuel Beckett (1906–1989) was born in Dublin to an upper-middle-class Protestant family. After a privileged education at the Portora Royal School, he went to Trinity College, Dublin, where he studied French and Italian. He was an exceptionally good student and, in 1928 after graduation, taught English at the École Normale Supérieure in Paris.

Beckett early on straddled two literary cultures: Irish and Anglo-Irish. Most of the literary energy in Ireland in the 1920s and 1930s was split between the essentially conservative Anglo-Irish Protestants, such as W. B. Yeats and Lady Gregory, and the more avant-garde Catholics, such as James Joyce, with whom Beckett formed an enduring personal and literary friendship in Paris. Although much younger than Joyce, Beckett developed a close artistic sympathy with him. Beckett's first published work (1929) was one of the earliest critical essays on Joyce's most radical literary composition, the not-yet-published *Finnegans Wake*.

When he was first in France, Beckett's reading of French philosophers, especially Descartes, exerted a strong influence on his work. Beckett's earliest writings appeared in Eugene Jolas's avant-garde literary journal *transition*, which put him in the center of Parisian literary activity in the late 1920s. After 1930, his series of short stories published under the title *More Pricks Than Kicks* (1934) established him as an important writer. After settling in Paris in 1937, Beckett wrote the novel *Murphy* (1938), on a recognizably Irish theme of economic impoverishment, alienation, and inward meditation and spiritual complexity.

When World War II began in 1939, Beckett took up the cause of the French Resistance. After his activity caught the eye of the Gestapo, for two years he lay low in unoccupied France by working as a farmhand and also writing another novel, *Watt* (written in 1944 but published in 1953). After the war, he took up residence again in Paris and began writing most of his work in French. His greatest novels were written in the five years after the war, and they are often referred to as his trilogy: *Molloy, Malone Dies,* and *The Unnamable*. These three novels are about men who have become disaffected with society and who have strange and compelling urgencies to be alone and to follow exacting and repetitive patterns of behavior. In a sense, they are archetypes of the kinds of protagonists that Beckett created in most of his work.

Beckett's first published play, *Waiting for Godot* (1952), was produced in Paris (1953), in London (1955), and in Miami (1956). From the first, its repetitive, whimsical, and sometimes nonsensical style established the play as a major postwar statement. In a barren setting, Vladimir and Estragon, two tramps who echo the comic vision of Charlie Chaplin, wait for Godot to come. They amuse themselves by doing vaudeville routines, but their loneliness and isolation are painfully apparent to the audience. Godot has promised to come, and as they wait, Vladimir and Estragon speculate on whether or not he will.

The comic moments in the play, along with the enigma of Vladimir and Estragon's fruitless waiting, combined to capture the imagination of audiences and the press. They saw the play as a modern statement about the condition

For links to resources about Beckett, click on *AuthorLinks* at **bedfordstmartins.com/jacobus.**

of humankind, although there was never any agreement on just what the statement was. Godot sends a boy to say that he will indeed come, but when the play ends, he has not arrived. The implication seems to be that he will never arrive. Most audiences saw Godot as a metaphor for God. Despite the critics' constant inquiries, Beckett never confirmed the view that Godot was God and kept Godot's identity open-ended.

The play itself was open-ended, as Beckett had hoped, and therefore could be interpreted in many ways. One interpretation was to see the play as a commentary on the futility of religion; another was to suggest that the play underscored the loneliness of humankind in an empty universe; yet a third implied that it was up to individuals, represented by the hapless Vladimir and Estragon, to shape the significance of their own lives, and their waiting represented that effort.

Many of the themes in *Waiting for Godot* are apparent in Beckett's later plays. The radio play *All That Fall* (1957) was followed by the very successful *Krapp's Last Tape* (1958). Also in 1957, *Endgame,* a play on the theme of the end of the world, was produced, followed in 1961 by *Happy Days.* Beckett experimented with minimalist approaches to drama, including minimalism in setting, props, and — in mime plays such as *Act without Words I* and *Act without Words II* — even words.

Beckett's plays reveal the deep influence of French postwar philosophers such as Albert Camus and Jean-Paul Sartre, both existentialists. Their philosophy declares that people are not essentially good, bad, kind, or anything else but are what they make of themselves. Beckett's adaptation of existentialism sometimes borders on pessimism, because his vision seems to negate many of the consolations of religious and secular philosophy. His style is antirealist, but the search for beliefs that are reasonable and plausible in a fundamentally absurd world and the plight of individuals who must make their own meanings are central to most of his work.

Beckett's view of the world is not cheerful. But his vision is consistent, honest, and sympathetic to the persistence of his characters, who endure even in the face of apparent defeat. The significance of Beckett's achievements was recognized in 1969 when he was awarded the Nobel Prize for literature.

Endgame

For discussion questions and assignments on *Endgame,* visit **bedfordstmartins.com/jacobus**.

The title *Endgame* derives from the game of chess, which has three different strategies to mark the opening, the middle game, and the endgame. The strategy of the endgame focuses on the protection of the king and depends on very few pieces being left on the board — the king and sometimes a rook and a pawn. The moves in the endgame are always restricted, often repetitive, and limited by the fact that the king, if it can move at all, cannot move more than one space at a time. In Beckett's *Endgame,* Hamm is the king and the central character in the drama; however, he cannot move or even stand by himself. Beckett described Hamm as "a king in the chess game lost from the start." Hamm's parents, Nagg and Nell, stuck immobile in ashcans, resemble rooks, who protect the king by controlling spaces forward, backward, and side to side but have little reason themselves to move. Clov, who most closely resembles a pawn, cannot sit down and is the only character in the play who can move. He is also the only means by which Hamm can move.

World politics in 1957, when the play was written, were dominated by the threat of nuclear war and the possible extinction of the human race. The circumstances of *Endgame* suggest that the play portrays a version of the end of the world. Clov's description of the world outside the window implies desolation and grief. At one point as Clov looks out the window, Hamm tells him to use his "glass" (his telescope) and to report back to him. Clov says all is "Zero," and Hamm asks, "All is what?" "In a word?" says Clov. "Is that what you want to know?" And in a moment he reports his one word: "Corpsed."

Unlike Hamm and Clov, who seem rooted only in the present, Nagg and Nell have a past. They remember rowing on Lake Como on an April afternoon after they were engaged. Nell remembers it as a moment in which she was happy. But they also remember the day they crashed on their tandem bicycle and lost their legs. Nagg recalls it was in the Ardennes forest on the road to Sedan. Beckett is alluding to the French forest at Ardennes, site of the most appalling and murderous fighting in World War I, and to the French town of Sedan, the place where Napoleon III surrendered to the Germans in a battle during the Franco-Prussian war.

Ruby Cohn and other critics have noted that the characters' names have associations with hammers and nails: Nell is a homophone for *nail*; Hamm is a shortened form of *hammer*; Nagg is from the German *nagel,* for *nail*; and Clov is from the French *clou,* also for *nail.* The characters thus seem to be equipped to rebuild their society, but they refuse to do so. By using English, French, and German versions of *nail,* Beckett alludes to the principal combatants of modern European wars.

Some critics have observed that Beckett's drama often focuses on elements of play. Plays are play; life is play. In chess an endgame is played. In Beckett's drama, characters' actions seem to be performed as if they were part of a game. Clov exercises great precision, for example, in placing Hamm exactly where he wishes to be. When Clov has done the rounds and moved Hamm's chair back to its position, Hamm says, "I feel a little too far to the left. Now I feel a little too far to the right." In a game of chess, it would matter if he were too far to the left or right. In an endgame the king might move to one square and then move back again and again. The movements of Hamm and Clov are repetitious and meaningful only within the "system" of the drama and its space, just as all moves in an endgame are meaningful only within the "system" of the game of chess. Clov continually enters and exits with his ladder and looks out the windows, only to find that nothing has changed. He picks up the lids of Nagg and Nell's ashcans and replaces them several times. He pushes Hamm's chair along the wall, making minute adjustments, for no apparent reason, when he returns the chair to the center of the room. His moves are part of an endgame, and *Endgame* is a play.

Beckett critic Ted Estess said that "in Beckett's literature 'existence is play,'" implying absurdity of the kind Martin Esslin talks about in his discussion of theater of the absurd. (See the commentary on p. 1220.) The absurd implies nonmeaning, such as the meaningless movements of Hamm by Clov. The meaning of those moves is in the action itself, which strikes those in the audience as absurd. Beckett's use of the absurd helps him move away from the well-made play with its clearly marked beginning, middle, and end. In the process he pokes fun at that concept by embedding the end in the beginning of *Endgame*. As the lights go up and Clov removes the sheets from the ashcans and from Hamm in his chair, he intones to the audience: "Finished." The audience is meant to sense this irony. It is the endgame when the action—and the play—are expected to stop, but as Hamm says: "The end is in the beginning and yet you go on."

Endgame in Performance

Endgame was first produced in 1957. The year before, *Waiting for Godot* had been produced in Miami and New York, establishing Beckett as an important figure in modern absurdist drama. *Endgame,* his next major play, satisfied the critics but baffled the public. The first London production was in French, at the Royal Court Theatre, which was known for producing experimental plays. Roger Blin directed. The first Paris production began three weeks later, April 26, 1957, in the Studio des Champs-Élysées. The New York production, directed by Beckett's friend and interpreter Alan Schneider, opened on January 28, 1958. A number of important revivals of the play have attested to its continuing power. In 1964, *Endgame* was produced at The Royal Shakespeare Company's Aldwych Theatre. Beckett himself directed the play at the Schiller Theatre in Berlin in September 1967. In the 1970 Open Theater Production at the Loeb Theater in Cambridge, Massachusetts, Joseph Chaikin as Hamm created a richly nuanced performance:

> Joseph Chaikin as the chairbound Hamm throws an eerie light over the play.... He is sensual, domineering, crafty, and infinitely tender; he prattles and tells macabre stories and his dominion over the dwindling lives of his family is like the last hoarse gasp of King Lear over the strangled body of Cordelia.   (Samuel Hirsch, *Herald Traveler*, Boston, May 13, 1970)

Andre Gregory directed the play at the Manhattan Project in 1973. Clive Barnes noted the unusual staging of this production:

> Mr. Gregory has built himself a strange, bullring of a theater. It is hexagonal, and the audience is on two levels. The audience is placed in cubicles—each holding four chairs. Each cubicle is insulated from the stage and from the world by chicken wire.   (*New York Times*, February 9, 1973)

The Royal Court presented *Endgame* in English during its Beckett Festival in 1976. Beckett directed the play again in London at the Young Vic in January 1980 and then in Chicago's Goodman Theater with the San Quentin Workshop in September 1980. In 1984, JoAnn Akalaitis staged a controversial *Endgame* at the American Repertory Theater in Cambridge, Massachusetts. She set the play in a burned-out subway tunnel and commissioned an eerie musical score by minimalist composer Philip Glass. Grove Press, Beckett's representative, complained that the production disregarded "the playwright's sparse, rigorous scenic demands" and added uncalled-for music. The production was allowed to continue after the American Repertory Theater agreed to include a program insert, signed by Beckett, "decrying the interpretation."

The 2008 production directed by Andrei Belgrader at the Brooklyn Academy of Music starred John Turturro as Hamm, Max Casella as Clov, Elaine

Stritch as Nell, and Alvin Epstein as Nagg. It followed Beckett's stage directions carefully. Mark Rylance played Hamm in a warmly reviewed London production at the Duchess Theatre in October 2009; Simon McBurney directed and played the role of Clov. Again, Beckett's stage directions were adhered to in every detail. Clearly, audiences of recent productions here and abroad identify with the anxiety that inspired the first production.

SAMUEL BECKETT (1906–1989)

Endgame   1957
A Play in One Act

The Characters

NAGG	HAMM
NELL	CLOV

(*Bare interior.*)
   (*Gray light.*)
   (*Left and right back, high up, two small windows, curtains drawn.*)
   (*Front right, a door. Hanging near door, its face to wall, a picture.*)
   (*Front left, touching each other, covered with an old sheet, two ashbins.°*)
   (*Center, in an armchair on casters, covered with an old sheet, Hamm.*)
   (*Motionless by the door, his eyes fixed on Hamm, Clov. Very red face.*)
   (*Brief tableau.*)

(*Clov goes and stands under window left. Stiff, staggering walk. He looks up at window left. He turns and looks at window right. He goes and stands under window right. He looks up at window right. He turns and looks at window left. He goes out, comes back immediately with a small stepladder, carries it over and sets it down under window left, gets up on it, draws back curtain. He gets down, takes six steps (for example) towards window right, goes back for ladder, carries it over and sets it down under window right, gets up on it, draws back curtain. He gets down, takes three steps towards window left, goes back for ladder, carries it over and sets it down under window left, gets up on it, looks out of window. Brief laugh. He gets down, takes one step towards window right, goes back for ladder, carries it over and sets it down under window right, gets the*

---

ashbins: Trash cans.

---

ladder and carries it out. Pause. Hamm stirs. He yawns under the handkerchief. He removes the handkerchief from his face. Very red face. Black glasses.)

HAMM: Me—(*he yawns*)—to play.

(*He holds the handkerchief spread out before him.*)

   Old Stancher!°

(*He takes off his glasses, wipes his eyes, his face, the glasses, puts them on again, folds the handkerchief and puts it back neatly in the breast pocket of his dressing gown. He clears his throat, joins the tips of his fingers.*)

   Can there be misery—(*he yawns*)—loftier than mine? No doubt. Formerly. But now?

(*Pause.*)

   My father?

(*Pause.*)

   My mother?

(*Pause.*)

   My . . . dog?

(*Pause.*)

   Oh I am willing to believe they suffer as much as such creatures can suffer. But does that mean their sufferings equal mine? No doubt.

(*Pause.*)

   No, all is a—(*he yawns*)—bsolute, (*proudly*) the bigger a man is the fuller he is.

(*Pause. Gloomily.*)

---

stancher: Item that stops, or stanches, the flow of blood.

And the emptier.

(*He sniffs.*)

Clov!

(*Pause.*)

No, alone.

(*Pause.*)

What dreams! Those forests!

(*Pause.*)

Enough, it's time it ended, in the shelter too.

(*Pause.*)

And yet I hesitate, I hesitate to . . . to end. Yes there it is, it's time it ended and yet I hesitate to—(*he yawns*)—to end.

(*Yawns.*)

God, I'm tired, I'd be better off in bed.

(*He whistles. Enter Clov immediately. He halts beside the chair.*)

You pollute the air!

(*Pause.*)

Get me ready, I'm going to bed.

CLOV: I've just got you up.

HAMM: And what of it?

CLOV: I can't be getting you up and putting you to bed every five minutes, I have things to do.

(*Pause.*)

HAMM: Did you ever see my eyes?

CLOV: No.

HAMM: Did you never have the curiosity, while I was sleeping, to take off my glasses and look at my eyes?

CLOV: Pulling back the lids?

(*Pause.*)

No.

HAMM: One of these days I'll show them to you.

(*Pause.*)

It seems they've gone all white.

(*Pause.*)

What time is it?

CLOV: The same as usual.

HAMM (*gesture towards window right*): Have you looked?

CLOV: Yes.

HAMM: Well?

CLOV: Zero.

HAMM: It'd need to rain.

CLOV: It won't rain.

(*Pause.*)

HAMM: Apart from that, how do you feel?

CLOV: I don't complain.

HAMM: You feel normal?

CLOV (*irritably*): I tell you I don't complain.

HAMM: I feel a little queer.

(*Pause.*)

Clov!

CLOV: Yes.

HAMM: Have you not had enough?

CLOV: Yes!

(*Pause.*)

Of what?

HAMM: Of this . . . this . . . thing.

CLOV: I always had.

(*Pause.*)

Not you?

HAMM (*gloomily*): Then there's no reason for it to change.

CLOV: It may end.

(*Pause.*)

All life long the same questions, the same answers.

HAMM: Get me ready.

(*Clov does not move.*)

Go and get the sheet.

(*Clov does not move.*)

Clov!

CLOV: Yes.

HAMM: I'll give you nothing more to eat.

CLOV: Then we'll die.

HAMM: I'll give you just enough to keep you from dying. You'll be hungry all the time.

CLOV: Then we won't die.

(*Pause.*)

I'll go and get the sheet.

(*He goes towards the door.*)

HAMM: No!

(*Clov halts.*)

I'll give you one biscuit per day.

(*Pause.*)

One and a half.

(*Pause.*)

Why do you stay with me?

CLOV: Why do you keep me?

HAMM: There's no one else.

CLOV: There's nowhere else.

(*Pause.*)

HAMM: You're leaving me all the same.

CLOV: I'm trying.

HAMM: You don't love me.

CLOV: No.

HAMM: You loved me once.

CLOV: Once!

HAMM: I've made you suffer too much.

(*Pause.*)

    Haven't I?

CLOV: It's not that.

HAMM (*shocked*): I haven't made you suffer too much?

CLOV: Yes!

HAMM (*relieved*): Ah you gave me a fright!

(*Pause. Coldly.*)

    Forgive me.

(*Pause. Louder.*)

    I said, Forgive me.

CLOV: I heard you.

(*Pause.*)

    Have you bled?

HAMM: Less.

(*Pause.*)

    Is it not time for my painkiller?

CLOV: No.

(*Pause.*)

HAMM: How are your eyes?

CLOV: Bad.

HAMM: How are your legs?

CLOV: Bad.

HAMM: But you can move.

CLOV: Yes.

HAMM (*violently*): Then move!

(*Clov goes to back wall, leans against it with his forehead and hands.*)

    Where are you?

CLOV: Here.

HAMM: Come back!

(*Clov returns to his place beside the chair.*)

    Where are you?

CLOV: Here.

HAMM: Why don't you kill me?

CLOV: I don't know the combination of the cupboard.

(*Pause.*)

HAMM: Go and get two bicycle wheels.

CLOV: There are no more bicycle wheels.

HAMM: What have you done with your bicycle?

CLOV: I never had a bicycle.

HAMM: The thing is impossible.

CLOV: When there were still bicycles I wept to have one. I crawled at your feet. You told me to go to hell. Now there are none.

HAMM: And your rounds? When you inspected my paupers. Always on foot?

CLOV: Sometimes on horse.

(*The lid of one of the bins lifts and the hands of Nagg appear, gripping the rim. Then his head emerges. Nightcap. Very white face. Nagg yawns, then listens.*)

    I'll leave you, I have things to do.

HAMM: In your kitchen?

CLOV: Yes.

HAMM: Outside of here it's death.

(*Pause.*)

    All right, be off.

(*Exit Clov. Pause.*)

    We're getting on.

NAGG: Me pap!

HAMM: Accursed progenitor!

NAGG: Me pap!

HAMM: The old folks at home! No decency left! Guzzle, guzzle, that's all they think of.

(*He whistles. Enter Clov. He halts beside the chair.*)

    Well! I thought you were leaving me.

CLOV: Oh not just yet, not just yet.

NAGG: Me pap!

HAMM: Give him his pap.

CLOV: There's no more pap.

HAMM (*to Nagg*): Do you hear that? There's no more pap. You'll never get any more pap.

NAGG: I want me pap!

HAMM: Give him a biscuit.

(*Exit Clov.*)

    Accursed fornicator! How are your stumps?

NAGG: Never mind me stumps.

(*Enter Clov with biscuit.*)

CLOV: I'm back again, with the biscuit.

(*He gives biscuit to Nagg who fingers it, sniffs it.*)

NAGG (*plaintively*): What is it?

CLOV: Spratt's medium.

NAGG (*as before*): It's hard! I can't!

HAMM: Bottle him!

(*Clov pushes Nagg back into the bin, closes the lid.*)

CLOV (*returning to his place beside the chair*): If age but knew!

HAMM: Sit on him!

CLOV: I can't sit.

HAMM: True. And I can't stand.

CLOV: So it is.

HAMM: Every man his speciality.

(*Pause.*)

    No phone calls?

(*Pause.*)

    Don't we laugh?

CLOV (*after reflection*): I don't feel like it.

HAMM (*after reflection*): Nor I.

(*Pause.*)

    Clov!

CLOV: Yes.

HAMM: Nature has forgotten us.

CLOV: There's no more nature.

HAMM: No more nature! You exaggerate.

CLOV: In the vicinity.

HAMM: But we breathe, we change! We lose our hair, our teeth! Our bloom! Our ideals!

CLOV: Then she hasn't forgotten us.

HAMM: But you say there is none.

CLOV (*sadly*): No one that ever lived ever thought so crooked as we.

HAMM: We do what we can.

CLOV: We shouldn't.

(*Pause.*)

HAMM: You're a bit of all right, aren't you?

CLOV: A smithereen.

(*Pause.*)

HAMM: This is slow work.

(*Pause.*)

Is it not time for my painkiller?

CLOV: No.

(*Pause.*)

I'll leave you, I have things to do.

HAMM: In your kitchen?

CLOV: Yes.

HAMM: What, I'd like to know.

CLOV: I look at the wall.

HAMM: The wall! And what do you see on your wall? Mene, mene?° Naked bodies?

CLOV: I see my light dying.

HAMM: Your light dying! Listen to that! Well, it can die just as well here, *your* light. Take a look at me and then come back and tell me what you think of *your* light.

(*Pause.*)

CLOV: You shouldn't speak to me like that.

(*Pause.*)

HAMM (*coldly*): Forgive me.

(*Pause. Louder.*)

I said, Forgive me.

CLOV: I heard you.

(*The lid of Nagg's bin lifts. His hands appear, gripping the rim. Then his head emerges. In his mouth the biscuit. He listens.*)

HAMM: Did your seeds come up?

CLOV: No.

HAMM: Did you scratch round them to see if they had sprouted?

CLOV: They haven't sprouted.

HAMM: Perhaps it's still too early.

CLOV: If they were going to sprout they would have sprouted.

(*Violently.*)

They'll never sprout!

(*Pause. Nagg takes biscuit in his hand.*)

HAMM: This is not much fun.

Mene, mene: The handwriting on the wall in Daniel 5:25 indicating the end of King Belshazzar's reign: "MENE, MENE, TEKEL, and PARSIN."

(*Pause.*)

But that's always the way at the end of the day, isn't it, Clov?

CLOV: Always.

HAMM: It's the end of the day like any other day, isn't it, Clov?

CLOV: Looks like it.

(*Pause.*)

HAMM (*anguished*): What's happening, what's happening?

CLOV: Something is taking its course.

(*Pause.*)

HAMM: All right, be off.

(*He leans back in his chair, remains motionless. Clov does not move, heaves a great groaning sigh. Hamm sits up.*)

I thought I told you to be off.

CLOV: I'm trying.

(*He goes to door, halts.*)

Ever since I was whelped.

(*Exit Clov.*)

HAMM: We're getting on.

(*He leans back in his chair, remains motionless. Nagg knocks on the lid of the other bin. Pause. He knocks harder. The lid lifts and the hands of Nell appear, gripping the rim. Then her head emerges. Lace cap. Very white face.*)

NELL: What is it, my pet?

(*Pause.*)

Time for love?

NAGG: Were you asleep?

NELL: Oh no!

NAGG: Kiss me.

NELL: We can't.

NAGG: Try.

(*Their heads strain towards each other, fail to meet, fall apart again.*)

NELL: Why this farce, day after day?

(*Pause.*)

NAGG: I've lost me tooth.

NELL: When?

NAGG: I had it yesterday.

NELL (*elegiac*): Ah yesterday!

(*They turn painfully towards each other.*)

NAGG: Can you see me?

NELL: Hardly. And you?

NAGG: What?

NELL: Can you see me?

NAGG: Hardly.

NELL: So much the better, so much the better.

NAGG: Don't say that.

(*Pause.*)

Our sight has failed.

NELL: Yes.

(*Pause. They turn away from each other.*)

From left, Elaine Stritch (Nell), Alvin Epstein (Nagg), and John Turturro (Hamm) in the Brooklyn Academy of Music production of *Endgame* in 2008.

NAGG: Can you hear me?
NELL: Yes. And you?
NAGG: Yes.

(*Pause.*)

Our hearing hasn't failed.
NELL: Our what?
NAGG: Our hearing.
NELL: No.

(*Pause.*)

Have you anything else to say to me?
NAGG: Do you remember —
NELL: No.
NAGG: When we crashed on our tandem and lost our shanks.

(*They laugh heartily.*)

NELL: It was in the Ardennes.

(*They laugh less heartily.*)

NAGG: On the road to Sedan.

(*They laugh still less heartily.*)

Are you cold?
NELL: Yes, perished. And you?
NAGG:

(*Pause.*)

I'm freezing.

(*Pause.*)

Do you want to go in?
NELL: Yes.
NAGG: Then go in.

(*Nell does not move.*)

Why don't you go in?
NELL: I don't know.

(*Pause.*)

NAGG: Has he changed your sawdust?
NELL: It isn't sawdust.

(*Pause. Wearily.*)

Can you not be a little accurate, Nagg?
NAGG: Your sand then. It's not important.
NELL: It is important.

(*Pause.*)

NAGG: It was sawdust once.
NELL: Once!
NAGG: And now it's sand.

(*Pause.*)

From the shore.

(*Pause. Impatiently.*)

Now it's sand he fetches from the shore.

1199

NELL: Now it's sand.
NAGG: Has he changed yours?
NELL: No.
NAGG: Nor mine.

(*Pause.*)

I won't have it!

(*Pause. Holding up the biscuit.*)

Do you want a bit?
NELL: No.

(*Pause.*)

Of what?
NAGG: Biscuit. I've kept you half.

(*He looks at the biscuit. Proudly.*)

Three quarters. For you. Here.

(*He proffers the biscuit.*)

No?

(*Pause.*)

Do you not feel well?
HAMM (*wearily*): Quiet, quiet, you're keeping me awake.

(*Pause.*)

Talk softer.

(*Pause.*)

If I could sleep I might make love. I'd go into the woods. My eyes would see . . . the sky, the earth. I'd run, run, they wouldn't catch me.

(*Pause.*)

Nature!

(*Pause.*)

There's something dripping in my head.

(*Pause.*)

A heart, a heart in my head.

(*Pause.*)

NAGG (*soft*): Do you hear him? A heart in his head!

(*He chuckles cautiously.*)

NELL: One mustn't laugh at those things, Nagg. Why must you always laugh at them?
NAGG: Not so loud!
NELL (*without lowering her voice*): Nothing is funnier than unhappiness, I grant you that. But—
NAGG (*shocked*): Oh!
NELL: Yes, yes, it's the most comical thing in the world. And we laugh, we laugh, with a will, in the beginning. But it's always the same thing. Yes, it's like the funny story we have heard too often, we still find it funny, but we don't laugh anymore.

(*Pause.*)

Have you anything else to say to me?

NAGG: No.
NELL: Are you quite sure?

(*Pause.*)

Then I'll leave you.
NAGG: Do you not want your biscuit?

(*Pause.*)

I'll keep it for you.

(*Pause.*)

I thought you were going to leave me.
NELL: I am going to leave you.
NAGG: Could you give me a scratch before you go?
NELL: No.

(*Pause.*)

Where?
NAGG: In the back.
NELL: No.

(*Pause.*)

Rub yourself against the rim.
NAGG: It's lower down. In the hollow.
NELL: What hollow?
NAGG: The hollow!

(*Pause.*)

Could you not?

(*Pause.*)

Yesterday you scratched me there.
NELL (*elegiac*): Ah yesterday!
NAGG: Could you not?

(*Pause.*)

Would you like me to scratch you?

(*Pause.*)

Are you crying again?
NELL: I was trying.

(*Pause.*)

HAMM: Perhaps it's a little vein.

(*Pause.*)

NAGG: What was that he said?
NELL: Perhaps it's a little vein.
NAGG: What does that mean?

(*Pause.*)

That means nothing.

(*Pause.*)

Will I tell you the story of the tailor?
NELL: No.

(*Pause.*)

What for?

NAGG: To cheer you up.
NELL: It's not funny.
NAGG: It always made you laugh.

(*Pause.*)

The first time I thought you'd die.
NELL: It was on Lake Como.

(*Pause.*)

One April afternoon.

(*Pause.*)

Can you believe it?
NAGG: What?
NELL: That we once went out rowing on Lake Como.

(*Pause.*)

One April afternoon.
NAGG: We had got engaged the day before.
NELL: Engaged!
NAGG: You were in such fits that we capsized. By rights we should have been drowned.
NELL: It was because I felt happy.
NAGG (*indignant*): It was not, it was not, it was my story and nothing else. Happy! Don't you laugh at it still? Every time I tell it. Happy!
NELL: It was deep, deep. And you could see down to the bottom. So white. So clean.
NAGG: Let me tell it again.

(*Raconteur's voice.*)

An Englishman, needing a pair of striped trousers in a hurry for the New Year festivities, goes to his tailor who takes his measurements.

(*Tailor's voice.*)

"That's the lot, come back in four days, I'll have it ready." Good. Four days later.

(*Tailor's voice.*)

"So sorry, come back in a week, I've made a mess of the seat." Good, that's all right, a neat seat can be very ticklish. A week later.

(*Tailor's voice.*)

"Frightfully sorry, come back in ten days, I've made a hash of the crotch." Good, can't be helped, a snug crotch is always a teaser. Ten days later.

(*Tailor's voice.*)

"Dreadfully sorry, come back in a fortnight, I've made a balls of the fly." Good, at a pinch, a smart fly is a stiff proposition.

(*Pause. Normal voice.*)

I never told it worse.

(*Pause. Gloomy.*)

I tell this story worse and worse.

(*Pause. Raconteur's voice.*)

Well, to make it short, the bluebells are blowing and he ballockses the buttonholes.

(*Customer's voice.*)

"God damn you to hell, Sir, no, it's indecent, there are limits! In six days, do you hear me, six days, God made the world. Yes Sir, no less Sir, the WORLD! And you are not bloody well capable of making me a pair of trousers in three months!"

(*Tailor's voice, scandalized.*)

"But my dear Sir, my dear Sir, look—(*disdainful gesture, disgustedly*)—at the world—(*pause*) and look—(*loving gesture, proudly*)—at my TROUSERS!"

(*Pause. He looks at Nell who has remained impassive, her eyes unseeing, breaks into a high forced laugh, cuts it short, pokes his head towards Nell, launches his laugh again.*)

HAMM: Silence!

(*Nagg starts, cuts short his laugh.*)

NELL: You could see down to the bottom.
HAMM (*exasperated*): Have you not finished? Will you never finish?

(*With sudden fury.*)

Will this never finish?

(*Nagg disappears into his bin, closes the lid behind him. Nell does not move. Frenziedly.*)

My kingdom for a nightman!

(*He whistles. Enter Clov.*)

Clear away this muck! Chuck it in the sea!

(*Clov goes to bins, halts.*)

NELL: So white.
HAMM: What? What's she blathering about?

(*Clov stoops, takes Nell's hand, feels her pulse.*)

NELL (*to Clov*): Desert!

(*Clov lets go her hand, pushes her back in the bin, closes the lid.*)

CLOV (*returning to his place beside the chair*): She has no pulse.
HAMM: What was she driveling about?
CLOV: She told me to go away, into the desert.
HAMM: Damn busybody! Is that all?
CLOV: No.
HAMM: What else?
CLOV: I didn't understand.
HAMM: Have you bottled her?
CLOV: Yes.
HAMM: Are they both bottled?

CLOV: Yes.
HAMM: Screw down the lids.

(*Clov goes towards door.*)

Time enough.

(*Clov halts.*)

My anger subsides, I'd like to pee.
CLOV (*with alacrity*): I'll go and get the catheter.

(*He goes towards door.*)

HAMM: Time enough.

(*Clov halts.*)

Give me my painkiller.
CLOV: It's too soon.

(*Pause.*)

It's too soon on top of your tonic, it wouldn't act.
HAMM: In the morning they brace you up and in the evening
they calm you down. Unless it's the other way round.

(*Pause.*)

That old doctor, he's dead naturally?
CLOV: He wasn't old.
HAMM: But he's dead?
CLOV: Naturally.

(*Pause.*)

You ask *me* that?

(*Pause.*)

HAMM: Take me for a little turn.

(*Clov goes behind the chair and pushes it forward.*)

Not too fast!

(*Clov pushes chair.*)

Right round the world!

(*Clov pushes chair.*)

Hug the walls, then back to the center again.

(*Clov pushes chair.*)

I was right in the center, wasn't I?
CLOV (*pushing*): Yes.
HAMM: We'd need a proper wheelchair. With big wheels.
Bicycle wheels!

(*Pause.*)

Are you hugging?
CLOV (*pushing*): Yes.
HAMM (*groping for wall*): It's a lie! Why do you lie to me?
Clov (*bearing closer to wall*): There! There!
HAMM: Stop!

(*Clov stops chair close to back wall. Hamm lays
his hand against wall.*)

Old wall!

(*Pause.*)

Beyond is the . . . other hell.

(*Pause. Violently.*)

Closer! Closer! Up against!
CLOV: Take away your hand.

(*Hamm withdraws his hand. Clov rams chair against
wall.*)

There!

(*Hamm leans towards wall, applies his ear to it.*)

HAMM: Do you hear?

(*He strikes the wall with his knuckles.*)

Do you hear? Hollow bricks!

(*He strikes again.*)

All that's hollow!

(*Pause. He straightens up. Violently.*)

That's enough. Back!
CLOV: We haven't done the round.
HAMM: Back to my place!

(*Clov pushes chair back to center.*)

Is that my place?
CLOV: Yes, that's your place.
HAMM: Am I right in the center?
CLOV: I'll measure it.
HAMM: More or less! More or less!
CLOV (*moving chair slightly*): There!
HAMM: I'm more or less in the center?
CLOV: I'd say so.
HAMM: You'd say so! Put me right in the center!
CLOV: I'll go and get the tape.
HAMM: Roughly! Roughly!

(*Clov moves chair slightly.*)

Bang in the center!
CLOV: There!

(*Pause.*)

HAMM: I feel a little too far to the left.

(*Clov moves chair slightly.*)

Now I feel a little too far to the right.

(*Clov moves chair slightly.*)

I feel a little too far forward.

(*Clov moves chair slightly.*)

Now I feel a little too far back.

(*Clov moves chair slightly.*)

Don't stay there (*i.e., behind the chair*), you give me
the shivers.

(*Clov returns to his place beside the chair.*)

CLOV: If I could kill him I'd die happy.

(*Pause.*)

HAMM: What's the weather like?
CLOV: As usual.
HAMM: Look at the earth.
CLOV: I've looked.
HAMM: With the glass?
CLOV: No need of the glass.
HAMM: Look at it with the glass.
CLOV: I'll go and get the glass.

(*Exit Clov.*)

HAMM: No need of the glass!

(*Enter Clov with telescope.*)

CLOV: I'm back again, with the glass.

(*He goes to window right, looks up at it.*)

I need the steps.
HAMM: Why? Have you shrunk?

(*Exit Clov with telescope.*)

I don't like that, I don't like that.

(*Enter Clov with ladder, but without telescope.*)

CLOV: I'm back again, with the steps.

(*He sets down ladder under window right, gets up on it, realizes he has not the telescope, gets down.*)

I need the glass.

(*He goes towards door.*)

HAMM (*violently*): But you have the glass!
CLOV (*halting, violently*): No, I haven't the glass!

(*Exit Clov.*)

HAMM: This is deadly.

(*Enter Clov with telescope. He goes towards ladder.*)

CLOV: Things are livening up.

(*He gets up on ladder, raises the telescope, lets it fall.*)

I did it on purpose.

(*He gets down, picks up the telescope, turns it on auditorium.*)

I see . . . a multitude . . . in transports . . . of joy.

(*Pause.*)

That's what I call a magnifier.

(*He lowers the telescope, turns towards Hamm.*)

Well? Don't we laugh?
HAMM (*after reflection*): I don't.
CLOV (*after reflection*): Nor I.

(*He gets up on ladder, turns the telescope on the without.*)

Let's see.

(*He looks, moving the telescope.*)

Zero . . . (*he looks*) . . . zero . . . (*he looks*) . . . and zero.
HAMM: Nothing stirs. All is—
CLOV: Zer—
HAMM (*violently*): Wait till you're spoken to!

(*Normal voice.*)

All is . . . all is . . . all is what?

(*Violently.*)

All is what?
CLOV: What all is? In a word? Is that what you want to know? Just a moment.

(*He turns the telescope on the without, looks, lowers the telescope, turns towards Hamm.*)

Corpsed.

(*Pause.*)

Well? Content?
HAMM: Look at the sea.
CLOV: It's the same.
HAMM: Look at the ocean!

(*Clov gets down, takes a few steps towards window left, goes back for ladder, carries it over and sets it down under window left, gets up on it, turns the telescope on the without, looks at length. He starts, lowers the telescope, examines it, turns it again on the without.*)

CLOV: Never seen anything like that!
HAMM (*anxious*): What? A sail? A fin? Smoke?
CLOV (*looking*): The light is sunk.
HAMM (*relieved*): Pah! We all knew that.
CLOV (*looking*): There was a bit left.
HAMM: The base.
CLOV (*looking*): Yes.
HAMM: And now?
CLOV (*looking*): All gone.
HAMM: No gulls?
CLOV (*looking*): Gulls!
HAMM: And the horizon? Nothing on the horizon?
CLOV (*lowering the telescope, turning towards Hamm, exasperated*): What in God's name could there be on the horizon?

(*Pause.*)

HAMM: The waves, how are the waves?
CLOV: The waves?

(*He turns the telescope on the waves.*)

Lead.
HAMM: And the sun?
CLOV (*looking*): Zero.
HAMM: But it should be sinking. Look again.
CLOV (*looking*): Damn the sun.
HAMM: Is it night already then?
CLOV (*looking*): No.

HAMM: Then what is it?
CLOV (*looking*): Gray.

(*Lowering the telescope, turning towards Hamm, louder.*)

   Gray!

(*Pause. Still louder.*)

   GRRAY!

(*Pause. He gets down, approaches Hamm from behind, whispers in his ear.*)

HAMM (*starting*): Gray! Did I hear you say gray?
CLOV: Light black. From pole to pole.
HAMM: You exaggerate.

(*Pause.*)

   Don't stay there, you give me the shivers.

(*Clov returns to his place beside the chair.*)

CLOV: Why this farce, day after day?
HAMM: Routine. One never knows.

(*Pause.*)

   Last night I saw inside my breast. There was a big sore.
CLOV: Pah! You saw your heart.
HAMM: No, it was living.

(*Pause. Anguished.*)

   Clov!
CLOV: Yes.
HAMM: What's happening?
CLOV: Something is taking its course.

(*Pause.*)

HAMM: Clov!
CLOV (*impatiently*): What is it?
HAMM: We're not beginning to . . . to . . . mean something?
CLOV: Mean something! You and I, mean something!

(*Brief laugh.*)

   Ah that's a good one!
HAMM: I wonder.

(*Pause.*)

   Imagine if a rational being came back to earth, wouldn't he be liable to get ideas into his head if he observed us long enough.

(*Voice of rational being.*)

   Ah, good, now I see what it is, yes, now I understand what they're at!

(*Clov starts, drops the telescope and begins to scratch his belly with both hands. Normal voice.*)

   And without going so far as that, we ourselves . . .(*with emotion*) . . . we ourselves . . . at certain moments . . .

(*Vehemently.*)

   To think perhaps it won't all have been for nothing!
CLOV (*anguished, scratching himself*): I have a flea!

HAMM: A flea! Are there still fleas?
CLOV: On me there's one.

(*Scratching.*)

   Unless it's a crablouse.
HAMM (*very perturbed*): But humanity might start from there all over again! Catch him, for the love of God!
CLOV: I'll go and get the powder.

(*Exit Clov.*)

HAMM: A flea! This is awful! What a day!

(*Enter Clov with a sprinkling tin.*)

CLOV: I'm back again, with the insecticide.
HAMM: Let him have it!

(*Clov loosens the top of his trousers, pulls it forward and shakes powder into the aperture. He stoops, looks, waits, starts, frenziedly shakes more powder, stoops, looks, waits.*)

CLOV: The bastard!
HAMM: Did you get him?
CLOV: Looks like it.

(*He drops the tin and adjusts his trousers.*)

   Unless he's laying doggo.°
HAMM: Laying! Lying you mean. Unless he's *lying* doggo.
CLOV: Ah? One says lying? One doesn't say laying?
HAMM: Use your head, can't you. If he was laying we'd be bitched.
CLOV: Ah.

(*Pause.*)

   What about that pee?
HAMM: I'm having it.
CLOV: Ah that's the spirit, that's the spirit!

(*Pause.*)

HAMM (*with ardor*): Let's go from here, the two of us! South! You can make a raft and the currents will carry us away, far away, to other . . . mammals!
CLOV: God forbid!
HAMM: Alone, I'll embark alone! Get working on that raft immediately. Tomorrow I'll be gone forever.
CLOV (*hastening towards door*): I'll start straight away.
HAMM: Wait!

(*Clov halts.*)

   Will there be sharks, do you think?
CLOV: Sharks? I don't know. If there are there will be.

(*He goes towards door.*)

HAMM: Wait!

(*Clov halts.*)

   Is it not yet time for my painkiller?
CLOV (*violently*): No!

(*He goes towards door.*)

doggo: In hiding.

HAMM: Wait!

(*Clov halts.*)

How are your eyes?
CLOV: Bad.
HAMM: But you can see.
CLOV: All I want.
HAMM: How are your legs?
CLOV: Bad.
HAMM: But you can walk.
CLOV: I come . . . and go.
HAMM: In my house.

(*Pause. With prophetic relish.*)

One day you'll be blind, like me. You'll be sitting there, a speck in the void, in the dark, forever, like me.

(*Pause.*)

One day you'll say to yourself, I'm tired, I'll sit down, and you'll go and sit down. Then you'll say, I'm hungry, I'll get up and get something to eat. But you won't get up. You'll say, I shouldn't have sat down, but since I have I'll sit on a little longer, then I'll get up and get something to eat. But you won't get up and you won't get anything to eat.

(*Pause.*)

You'll look at the wall a while, then you'll say, I'll close my eyes, perhaps have a little sleep, after that I'll feel better, and you'll close them. And when you open them again there'll be no wall anymore.

(*Pause.*)

Infinite emptiness will be all around you, all the resurrected dead of all the ages wouldn't fill it, and there you'll be like a little bit of grit in the middle of the steppe.

(*Pause.*)

Yes, one day you'll know what it is, you'll be like me, except that you won't have anyone with you, because you won't have had pity on anyone and because there won't be anyone left to have pity on.

(*Pause.*)

CLOV: It's not certain.

(*Pause.*)

And there's one thing you forget.
HAMM: Ah?
CLOV: I can't sit down.
HAMM (*impatiently*): Well you'll lie down then, what the hell! Or you'll come to a standstill, simply stop and stand still, the way you are now. One day you'll say, I'm tired, I'll stop. What does the attitude matter?

(*Pause.*)

CLOV: So you all want me to leave you.
HAMM: Naturally.
CLOV: Then I'll leave you.

HAMM: You can't leave us.
CLOV: Then I won't leave you.

(*Pause.*)

HAMM: Why don't you finish us?

(*Pause.*)

I'll tell you the combination of the cupboard if you promise to finish me.
CLOV: I couldn't finish you.
HAMM: Then you won't finish me.

(*Pause.*)

CLOV: I'll leave you, I have things to do.
HAMM: Do you remember when you came here?
CLOV: No. Too small, you told me.
HAMM: Do you remember your father?
CLOV (*wearily*): Same answer.

(*Pause.*)

You've asked me these questions millions of times.
HAMM: I love the old questions.

(*With fervor.*)

Ah the old questions, the old answers, there's nothing like them!

(*Pause.*)

It was I was a father to you.
CLOV: Yes.

(*He looks at Hamm fixedly.*)

You were that to me.
HAMM: My house a home for you.
CLOV: Yes.

(*He looks about him.*)

This was that for me.
HAMM (*proudly*): But for me (*gesture towards himself*), no father. But for Hamm (*gesture towards surroundings*), no home.

(*Pause.*)

CLOV: I'll leave you.
HAMM: Did you ever think of one thing?
CLOV: Never.
HAMM: That here we're down in a hole.

(*Pause.*)

But beyond the hills? Eh? Perhaps it's still green. Eh?

(*Pause.*)

Flora! Pomona!

(*Ecstatically.*)

Ceres!°

(*Pause.*)

Flora . . . Ceres: Three Roman goddesses—Flora, of flowers; Pomona, of fruit; Ceres, of agriculture.

Perhaps you won't need to go very far.

CLOV: I can't go very far.

(*Pause.*)

I'll leave you.

HAMM: Is my dog ready?

CLOV: He lacks a leg.

HAMM: Is he silky?

CLOV: He's a kind of Pomeranian.

HAMM: Go and get him.

CLOV: He lacks a leg.

HAMM: Go and get him!

(*Exit Clov.*)

We're getting on.

(*Enter Clov holding by one of its three legs a black toy dog.*)

CLOV: Your dogs are here.

(*He hands the dog to Hamm who feels it, fondles it.*)

HAMM: He's white, isn't he?

CLOV: Nearly.

HAMM: What do you mean, nearly? Is he white or isn't he?

CLOV: He isn't.

(*Pause.*)

HAMM: You've forgotten the sex.

CLOV (*vexed*): But he isn't finished. The sex goes on at the end.

(*Pause.*)

HAMM: You haven't put on his ribbon.

CLOV (*angrily*): But he isn't finished, I tell you! First you finish your dog and then you put on his ribbon!

(*Pause.*)

HAMM: Can he stand?

CLOV: I don't know.

HAMM: Try.

(*He hands the dog to Clov who places it on the ground.*)

Well?

CLOV: Wait!

(*He squats down and tries to get the dog to stand on its three legs, fails, lets it go. The dog falls on its side.*)

HAMM (*impatiently*): Well?

CLOV: He's standing.

HAMM (*groping for the dog*): Where? Where is he?

(*Clov holds up the dog in a standing position.*)

CLOV: There.

(*He takes Hamm's hand and guides it towards the dog's head.*)

HAMM (*his hand on the dog's head*): Is he gazing at me?

CLOV: Yes.

HAMM (*proudly*): As if he were asking me to take him for a walk?

CLOV: If you like.

HAMM (*as before*): Or as if he were begging me for a bone.

(*He withdraws his hand.*)

Leave him like that, standing there imploring me.

(*Clov straightens up. The dog falls on its side.*)

CLOV: I'll leave you.

HAMM: Have you had your visions?

CLOV: Less.

HAMM: Is Mother Pegg's light on?

CLOV: Light! How could anyone's light be on?

HAMM: Extinguished!

CLOV: Naturally it's extinguished. If it's not on it's extinguished.

HAMM: No, I mean Mother Pegg.

CLOV: But naturally she's extinguished!

(*Pause.*)

What's the matter with you today?

HAMM: I'm taking my course.

(*Pause.*)

Is she buried?

CLOV: Buried! Who would have buried her?

HAMM: You.

CLOV: Me! Haven't I enough to do without burying people?

HAMM: But you'll bury me.

CLOV: No I won't bury you.

(*Pause.*)

HAMM: She was bonny once, like a flower of the field.

(*With reminiscent leer.*)

And a great one for the men!

CLOV: We too were bonny—once. It's a rare thing not to have been bonny—once.

(*Pause.*)

HAMM: Go and get the gaff.

(*Clov goes to door, halts.*)

CLOV: Do this, do that, and I do it. I never refuse. Why?

HAMM: You're not able to.

CLOV: Soon I won't do it anymore.

HAMM: You won't be able to anymore.

(*Exit Clov.*)

Ah the creatures, the creatures, everything has to be explained to them.

(*Enter Clov with gaff.*)

CLOV: Here's your gaff. Stick it up.

(*He gives the gaff to Hamm who, wielding it like a puntpole,° tries to move his chair.*)

HAMM: Did I move?
CLOV: No.

(*Hamm throws down the gaff.*)

HAMM: Go and get the oilcan.
CLOV: What for?
HAMM: To oil the casters.
CLOV: I oiled them yesterday.
HAMM: Yesterday! What does that mean? Yesterday!
CLOV (*violently*): That means that bloody awful day, long ago, before this bloody awful day. I use the words you taught me. If they don't mean anything anymore, teach me others. Or let me be silent.

(*Pause.*)

HAMM: I once knew a madman who thought the end of the world had come. He was a painter—and engraver. I had a great fondness for him. I used to go and see him, in the asylum. I'd take him by the hand and drag him to the window. Look! There! All that rising corn! And there! Look! The sails of the herring fleet! All that loveliness!

(*Pause.*)

He'd snatch away his hand and go back into his corner. Appalled. All he had seen was ashes.

(*Pause.*)

He alone had been spared.

(*Pause.*)

Forgotten.

(*Pause.*)

It appears the case is . . . was not so . . . so unusual.
CLOV: A madman? When was that?
HAMM: Oh way back, way back, you weren't in the land of the living.
CLOV: God be with the days!

(*Pause. Hamm raises his toque.*)

HAMM: I had a great fondness for him.

(*Pause. He puts on his toque again.*)

He was a painter—and engraver.
CLOV: There are so many terrible things.
HAMM: No, no, there are not so many now.

(*Pause.*)

Clov!
CLOV: Yes.
HAMM: Do you not think this has gone on long enough?
CLOV: Yes!

(*Pause.*)

What?
HAMM: This . . . this . . . thing.
CLOV: I've always thought so.

(*Pause.*)

You not?
HAMM (*gloomily*): Then it's a day like any other day.
CLOV: As long as it lasts.

(*Pause.*)

All life long the same inanities.
HAMM: I can't leave you.
CLOV: I know. And you can't follow me.

(*Pause.*)

HAMM: If you leave me how shall I know?
CLOV (*briskly*): Well you simply whistle me and if I don't come running it means I've left you.

(*Pause.*)

HAMM: You won't come and kiss me good-bye?
CLOV: Oh I shouldn't think so.

(*Pause.*)

HAMM: But you might be merely dead in your kitchen.
CLOV: The result would be the same.
HAMM: Yes, but how would I know, if you were merely dead in your kitchen?
CLOV: Well . . . sooner or later I'd start to stink.
HAMM: You stink already. The whole place stinks of corpses.
CLOV: The whole universe.
HAMM (*angrily*): To hell with the universe.

(*Pause.*)

Think of something.
CLOV: What?
HAMM: An idea, have an idea.

(*Angrily.*)

A bright idea!
CLOV: Ah good.

(*He starts pacing to and fro, his eyes fixed on the ground, his hands behind his back. He halts.*)

The pains in my legs! It's unbelievable! Soon I won't be able to think anymore.
HAMM: You won't be able to leave me.

(*Clov resumes his pacing.*)

What are you doing?
CLOV: Having an idea.

(*He paces.*)

Ah!

(*He halts.*)

HAMM: What a brain!

puntpole: A pole used to propel a punt, a flat-bottomed boat, through the water.

(*Pause.*)

    Well?

CLOV: Wait!

(*He meditates. Not very convinced.*)

    Yes . . .

(*Pause. More convinced.*)

    Yes!

(*He raises his head.*)

    I have it! I set the alarm.

(*Pause.*)

HAMM: This is perhaps not one of my bright days, but
    frankly—

CLOV: You whistle me. I don't come. The alarm rings. I'm
    gone. It doesn't ring. I'm dead.

(*Pause.*)

HAMM: Is it working?

(*Pause. Impatiently.*)

    The alarm, is it working?

CLOV: Why wouldn't it be working?

HAMM: Because it's worked too much.

CLOV: But it's hardly worked at all.

HAMM (*angrily*): Then because it's worked too little!

CLOV: I'll go and see.

(*Exit Clov. Brief ring of alarm off. Enter Clov with
alarm clock. He holds it against Hamm's ear and
releases alarm. They listen to it ringing to the end.
Pause.*)

    Fit to wake the dead! Did you hear it?

HAMM: Vaguely.

CLOV: The end is terrific!

HAMM: I prefer the middle.

(*Pause.*)

    Is it not time for my painkiller?

CLOV: No!

(*He goes to door, turns.*)

    I'll leave you.

HAMM: It's time for my story. Do you want to listen to
    my story?

CLOV: No.

HAMM: Ask my father if he wants to listen to my story.

(*Clov goes to bins, raises the lid of Nagg's, stoops,
looks into it. Pause. He straightens up.*)

CLOV: He's asleep.

HAMM: Wake him.

(*Clov stoops, wakes Nagg with the alarm. Unintelligible words. Clov straightens up.*)

CLOV: He doesn't want to listen to your story.

HAMM: I'll give him a bonbon.

(*Clov stoops. As before.*)

CLOV: He wants a sugarplum.

HAMM: He'll get a sugarplum.

(*Clov stoops. As before.*)

CLOV: It's a deal.

(*He goes towards door. Nagg's hands appear, gripping
the rim. Then the head emerges. Clov reaches door,
turns.*)

    Do you believe in the life to come?

HAMM: Mine was always that.

(*Exit Clov.*)

    Got him that time!

NAGG: I'm listening.

HAMM: Scoundrel! Why did you engender me?

NAGG: I didn't know.

HAMM: What? What didn't you know?

NAGG: That it'd be you.

(*Pause.*)

    You'll give me a sugarplum?

HAMM: After the audition.

NAGG: You swear?

HAMM: Yes.

NAGG: On what?

HAMM: My honor.

(*Pause. They laugh heartily.*)

NAGG: Two.

HAMM: One.

NAGG: One for me and one for—

HAMM: One! Silence!

(*Pause.*)

    Where was I?

(*Pause. Gloomily.*)

    It's finished, we're finished.

(*Pause.*)

    Nearly finished.

(*Pause.*)

    There'll be no more speech.

(*Pause.*)

    Something dripping in my head, ever since the
    fontanelles.°

(*Stifled hilarity of Nagg.*)

    Splash, splash, always on the same spot.

(*Pause.*)

    Perhaps it's a little vein.

since the fontanelles: Since soft membranes linked the incom-
pletely developed skull bones in his infant head.

(*Pause.*)

A little artery.

(*Pause. More animated.*)

Enough of that, it's story time, where was I?

(*Pause. Narrative tone.*)

The man came crawling towards me, on his belly. Pale, wonderfully pale and thin, he seemed on the point of—

(*Pause. Normal tone.*)

No, I've done that bit.

(*Pause. Narrative tone.*)

I calmly filled my pipe—the meerschaum, lit it with . . . let us say a vesta,° drew a few puffs. Aah!

(*Pause.*)

Well, what is it *you* want?

(*Pause.*)

It was an extraordinarily bitter day, I remember, zero by the thermometer. But considering it was Christmas Eve there was nothing . . . extraordinary about that. Seasonable weather, for once in a way.

(*Pause.*)

Well, what ill wind blows you my way? He raised his face to me, black with mingled dirt and tears.

(*Pause. Normal tone.*)

That should do it.

(*Narrative tone.*)

No no, don't look at me, don't look at me. He dropped his eyes and mumbled something, apologies I presume.

(*Pause.*)

I'm a busy man, you know, the final touches, before the festivities, you know what it is.

(*Pause. Forcibly.*)

Come on now, what is the object of this invasion?

(*Pause.*)

It was a glorious bright day, I remember, fifty by the heliometer,° but already the sun was sinking down into the . . . down among the dead.

(*Normal tone.*)

Nicely put, that.

(*Narrative tone.*)

Come on now, come on, present your petition and let me resume my labors.

(*Pause. Normal tone.*)

There's English for you. Ah well . . .

(*Narrative tone.*)

It was then he took the plunge. It's my little one, he said. Tsstss, a little one, that's bad. My little boy, he said, as if the sex mattered. Where did he come from? He named the hole. A good half-day, on horse. What are you insinuating? That the place is still inhabited? No, no, not a soul, except himself and the child— assuming he existed. Good. I inquired about the situation at Kov, beyond the gulf. Not a sinner. Good. And you expect me to believe you have left your little one back there, all alone, and alive into the bargain? Come now!

(*Pause.*)

It was a howling wild day, I remember, a hundred by the anemometer.° The wind was tearing up the dead pines and sweeping them . . . away.

(*Pause. Normal tone.*)

A bit feeble, that.

(*Narrative tone.*)

Come on, man, speak up, what is it you want from me, I have to put up my holly.

(*Pause.*)

Well to make it short it finally transpired that what he wanted from me was . . . bread for his brat? Bread? But I have no bread, it doesn't agree with me. Good. Then perhaps a little corn?

(*Pause. Normal tone.*)

That should do it.

(*Narrative tone.*)

Corn, yes, I have corn, it's true, in my granaries. But use your head. I give you some corn, a pound, a pound and a half, you bring it back to your child and you make him—if he's still alive—a nice pot of porridge, (*Nagg reacts*) a nice pot and a half of porridge, full of nourishment. Good. The colors come back into his little cheeks—perhaps. And then?

(*Pause.*)

I lost patience.

---

vesta: Wooden match.   **heliometer:** A telescope for measuring the apparent diameter of the sun.

anemometer: An instrument for measuring wind speed.

(*Violently.*)

Use your head, can't you, use your head, you're on earth, there's no cure for that!

(*Pause.*)

It was an exceedingly dry day, I remember, zero by the hygrometer.° Ideal weather, for my lumbago.

(*Pause. Violently.*)

But what in God's name do you imagine? That the earth will awake in spring? That the rivers and seas will run with fish again? That there's manna in heaven still for imbeciles like you?

(*Pause.*)

Gradually I cooled down, sufficiently at least to ask him how long he had taken on the way. Three whole days. Good. In what condition he had left the child. Deep in sleep.

(*Forcibly.*)

But deep in what sleep, deep in what sleep already?

(*Pause.*)

Well to make it short I finally offered to take him into my service. He had touched a chord. And then I imagined already that I wasn't much longer for this world.

(*He laughs. Pause.*)

Well?

(*Pause.*)

Well? Here if you were careful you might die a nice natural death, in peace and comfort.

(*Pause.*)

Well?

(*Pause.*)

In the end he asked me would I consent to take in the child as well—if he were still alive.

(*Pause.*)

It was the moment I was waiting for.

(*Pause.*)

Would I consent to take in the child . . .

(*Pause.*)

I can see him still, down on his knees, his hands flat on the ground, glaring at me with his mad eyes, in defiance of my wishes.

(*Pause. Normal tone.*)

hygrometer: Device for measuring humidity.

I'll soon have finished with this story.

(*Pause.*)

Unless I bring in other characters.

(*Pause.*)

But where would I find them?

(*Pause.*)

Where would I look for them?

(*Pause. He whistles. Enter Clov.*)

Let us pray to God.
NAGG: Me sugarplum!
CLOV: There's a rat in the kitchen!
HAMM: A rat! Are there still rats?
CLOV: In the kitchen there's one.
HAMM: And you haven't exterminated him?
CLOV: Half. You disturbed us.
HAMM: He can't get away?
CLOV: No.
HAMM: You'll finish him later. Let us pray to God.
CLOV: Again!
NAGG: Me sugarplum!
HAMM: God first!

(*Pause.*)

Are you right?
CLOV (*resigned*): Off we go.
HAMM (*to Nagg*): And you?
NAGG (*clasping his hands, closing his eyes, in a gabble*): Our Father which art—
HAMM: Silence! In silence! Where are your manners?

(*Pause.*)

Off we go.

(*Attitudes of prayer. Silence. Abandoning his attitude, discouraged.*)

Well?
CLOV (*abandoning his attitude*): What a hope! And you?
HAMM: Sweet damn all!

(*To Nagg.*)

And you?
NAGG: Wait!

(*Pause. Abandoning his attitude.*)

Nothing doing!
HAMM: The bastard! He doesn't exist!
CLOV: Not yet.
NAGG: Me sugarplum!
HAMM: There are no more sugarplums!

(*Pause.*)

NAGG: It's natural. After all I'm your father. It's true if it hadn't been me it would have been someone else. But that's no excuse.

(*Pause.*)

Turkish Delight,° for example, which no longer exists, we all know that, there is nothing in the world I love more. And one day I'll ask you for some, in return for a kindness, and you'll promise it to me. One must live with the times.

(*Pause.*)

Whom did you call when you were a tiny boy, and were frightened, in the dark? Your mother? No. Me. We let you cry. Then we moved you out of earshot, so that we might sleep in peace.

(*Pause.*)

I was asleep, as happy as a king, and you woke me up to have me listen to you. It wasn't indispensable, you didn't really need to have me listen to you.

(*Pause.*)

I hope the day will come when you'll really need to have me listen to you, and need to hear my voice, any voice.

(*Pause.*)

Yes, I hope I'll live till then, to hear you calling me like when you were a tiny boy, and were frightened, in the dark, and I was your only hope.

(*Pause. Nagg knocks on lid of Nell's bin. Pause.*)

Nell!

(*Pause. He knocks louder. Pause. Louder.*)

Nell!

(*Pause. Nagg sinks back into his bin, closes the lid behind him. Pause.*)

HAMM: Our revels now are ended.

(*He gropes for the dog.*)

The dog's gone.
CLOV: He's not a real dog, he can't go.
HAMM (*groping*): He's not there.
CLOV: He's lain down.
HAMM: Give him up to me.

(*Clov picks up the dog and gives it to Hamm. Hamm holds it in his arms. Pause. Hamm throws away the dog.*)

Dirty brute!

(*Clov begins to pick up the objects lying on the ground.*)

What are you doing?
CLOV: Putting things in order.

(*He straightens up. Fervently.*)

I'm going to clear everything away!

(*He starts picking up again.*)

HAMM: Order!

Turkish Delight: Gummy candy.

CLOV (*straightening up*): I love order. It's my dream. A world where all would be silent and still and each thing in its last place, under the last dust.

(*He starts picking up again.*)

HAMM (*exasperated*): What in God's name do you think you are doing?
CLOV (*straightening up*): I'm doing my best to create a little order.
HAMM: Drop it!

(*Clov drops the objects he has picked up.*)

CLOV: After all, there or elsewhere.

(*He goes towards door.*)

HAMM (*irritably*): What's wrong with your feet?
CLOV: My feet?
HAMM: Tramp! Tramp!
CLOV: I must have put on my boots.
HAMM: Your slippers were hurting you?

(*Pause.*)

CLOV: I'll leave you.
HAMM: No!
CLOV: What is there to keep me here?
HAMM: The dialogue.

(*Pause.*)

I've got on with my story.

(*Pause.*)

I've got on with it well.

(*Pause. Irritably.*)

Ask me where I've got to.
CLOV: Oh, by the way, your story?
HAMM (*surprised*): What story?
CLOV: The one you've been telling yourself all your days.
HAMM: Ah you mean my chronicle?
CLOV: That's the one.

(*Pause.*)

HAMM (*angrily*): Keep going, can't you, keep going!
CLOV: You've got on with it, I hope.
HAMM (*modestly*): Oh not very far, not very far.

(*He sighs.*)

There are days like that, one isn't inspired.

(*Pause.*)

Nothing you can do about it, just wait for it to come.

(*Pause.*)

No forcing, no forcing, it's fatal.

(*Pause.*)

I've got on with it a little all the same.

(*Pause.*)

Technique, you know.

(*Pause. Irritably.*)

I say I've got on with it a little all the same.

CLOV (*admiringly*): Well I never! In spite of everything you were able to get on with it!

HAMM (*modestly*): Oh not very far, you know, not very far, but nevertheless, better than nothing.

CLOV: Better than nothing! Is it possible?

HAMM: I'll tell you how it goes. He comes crawling on his belly—

CLOV: Who?

HAMM: What?

CLOV: Who do you mean, he?

HAMM: Who do I mean! Yet another.

CLOV: Ah him! I wasn't sure.

HAMM: Crawling on his belly, whining for bread for his brat. He's offered a job as gardener. Before—

(*Clov bursts out laughing.*)

What is there so funny about that?

CLOV: A job as gardener!

HAMM: Is that what tickles you?

CLOV: It must be that.

HAMM: It wouldn't be the bread?

CLOV: Or the brat.

(*Pause.*)

HAMM: The whole thing is comical, I grant you that. What about having a good guffaw the two of us together?

CLOV (*after reflection*): I couldn't guffaw again today.

HAMM (*after reflection*): Nor I.

(*Pause.*)

I continue then. Before accepting with gratitude he asks if he may have his little boy with him.

CLOV: What age?

HAMM: Oh tiny.

CLOV: He would have climbed the trees.

HAMM: All the little odd jobs.

CLOV: And then he would have grown up.

HAMM: Very likely.

(*Pause.*)

CLOV: Keep going, can't you, keep going!

HAMM: That's all. I stopped there.

(*Pause.*)

CLOV: Do you see how it goes on.

HAMM: More or less.

CLOV: Will it not soon be the end?

HAMM: I'm afraid it will.

CLOV: Pah! You'll make up another.

HAMM: I don't know.

(*Pause.*)

I feel rather drained.

(*Pause.*)

The prolonged creative effort.

(*Pause.*)

If I could drag myself down to the sea! I'd make a pillow of sand for my head and the tide would come.

CLOV: There's no more tide.

(*Pause.*)

HAMM: Go and see is she dead.

(*Clov goes to bins, raises the lid of Nell's, stoops, looks into it. Pause.*)

CLOV: Looks like it.

(*He closes the lid, straightens up. Hamm raises his toque. Pause. He puts it on again.*)

HAMM (*with his hand to his toque*): And Nagg?

(*Clov raises lid of Nagg's bin, stoops, looks into it. Pause.*)

CLOV: Doesn't look like it.

(*He closes the lid, straightens up.*)

HAMM (*letting go his toque*): What's he doing?

(*Clov raises lid of Nagg's bin, stoops, looks into it. Pause.*)

CLOV: He's crying.

(*He closes lid, straightens up.*)

HAMM: Then he's living.

(*Pause.*)

Did you ever have an instant of happiness?

CLOV: Not to my knowledge.

(*Pause.*)

HAMM: Bring me under the window.

(*Clov goes towards chair.*)

I want to feel the light on my face.

(*Clov pushes chair.*)

Do you remember, in the beginning, when you took me for a turn? You used to hold the chair too high. At every step you nearly tipped me out.

(*With senile quaver.*)

Ah great fun, we had, the two of us, great fun.

(*Gloomily.*)

And then we got into the way of it.

(*Clov stops the chair under window right.*)

There already?

(*Pause. He tilts back his head.*)

Is it light?

CLOV: It isn't dark.

HAMM (*angrily*): I'm asking you is it light.

CLOV: Yes.

(*Pause.*)

HAMM: The curtain isn't closed?

CLOV: No.

HAMM: What window is it?

CLOV: The earth.

HAMM: I knew it!

(*Angrily.*)

But there's no light there! The other!

(*Clov pushes chair towards window left.*)

The earth!

(*Clov stops the chair under window left. Hamm tilts back his head.*)

That's what I call light!

(*Pause.*)

Feels like a ray of sunshine.

(*Pause.*)

No?

CLOV: No.

HAMM: It isn't a ray of sunshine I feel on my face?

CLOV: No.

(*Pause.*)

HAMM: Am I very white?

(*Pause. Angrily.*)

I'm asking you am I very white!

CLOV: Not more so than usual.

(*Pause.*)

HAMM: Open the window.

CLOV: What for?

HAMM: I want to hear the sea.

CLOV: You wouldn't hear it.

HAMM: Even if you opened the window?

CLOV: No.

HAMM: Then it's not worthwhile opening it?

CLOV: No.

HAMM (*violently*): Then open it!

(*Clov gets up on the ladder, opens the window. Pause.*)

Have you opened it?

CLOV: Yes.

(*Pause.*)

HAMM: You swear you've opened it?

CLOV: Yes.

(*Pause.*)

HAMM. Well . . . !

(*Pause.*)

It must be very calm.

(*Pause. Violently.*)

I'm asking you is it very calm!

CLOV: Yes.

HAMM: It's because there are no more navigators.

(*Pause.*)

You haven't much conversation all of a sudden. Do you not feel well?

CLOV: I'm cold.

HAMM: What month are we?

(*Pause.*)

Close the window, we're going back.

(*Clov closes the window, gets down, pushes the chair back to its place, remains standing behind it, head bowed.*)

Don't stay there, you give me the shivers!

(*Clov returns to his place beside the chair.*)

Father!

(*Pause. Louder.*)

Father!

(*Pause.*)

Go and see did he hear me.

(*Clov goes to Nagg's bin, raises the lid, stoops. Unintelligible words. Clov straightens up.*)

CLOV: Yes.

HAMM: Both times?

(*Clov stoops. As before.*)

CLOV: Once only.

HAMM: The first time or the second?

(*Clov stoops. As before.*)

CLOV: He doesn't know.

HAMM: It must have been the second.

CLOV: We'll never know.

(*He closes lid.*)

HAMM: Is he still crying?

CLOV: No.

HAMM: The dead go fast.

(*Pause.*)

What's he doing?

CLOV: Sucking his biscuit.

HAMM: Life goes on.

(*Clov returns to his place beside the chair.*)

Give me a rug,° I'm freezing.

CLOV: There are no more rugs.

(*Pause.*)

HAMM: Kiss me.

(*Pause.*)

Will you not kiss me?

CLOV: No.

HAMM: On the forehead.

CLOV: I won't kiss you anywhere.

(*Pause.*)

HAMM (*holding out his hand*): Give me your hand at least.

(*Pause.*)

Will you not give me your hand?

CLOV: I won't touch you.

rug: A small blanket to cover the lap, legs, and feet.

(*Pause.*)

HAMM: Give me the dog.

(*Clov looks round for the dog.*)

    No!

CLOV: Do you not want your dog?

HAMM: No.

CLOV: Then I'll leave you.

HAMM (*head bowed, absently*): That's right.

(*Clov goes to door, turns.*)

CLOV: If I don't kill that rat he'll die.

HAMM (*as before*): That's right.

(*Exit Clov. Pause.*)

    Me to play.

(*He takes out his handkerchief, unfolds it, holds it spread out before him.*)

    We're getting on.

(*Pause.*)

    You weep, and weep, for nothing, so as not to laugh, and little by little . . . you begin to grieve.

(*He folds the handkerchief, puts it back in his pocket, raises his head.*)

    All those I might have helped.

(*Pause.*)

    Helped!

(*Pause.*)

    Saved.

(*Pause.*)

    Saved!

(*Pause.*)

    The place was crawling with them!

(*Pause. Violently.*)

    Use your head, can't you, use your head, you're on earth, there's no cure for that!

(*Pause.*)

    Get out of here and love one another! Lick your neighbor as yourself!

(*Pause. Calmer.*)

    When it wasn't bread they wanted it was crumpets.

(*Pause. Violently.*)

    Out of my sight and back to your petting parties!

(*Pause.*)

    All that, all that!

(*Pause.*)

    Not even a real dog!

(*Calmer.*)

    The end is in the beginning and yet you go on.

(*Pause.*)

    Perhaps I could go on with my story, end it and begin another.

(*Pause.*)

    Perhaps I could throw myself out on the floor.

(*He pushes himself painfully off his seat, falls back again.*)

    Dig my nails into the cracks and drag myself forward with my fingers.

(*Pause.*)

    It will be the end and there I'll be, wondering what can have brought it on and wondering what can have . . . (*he hesitates*) . . . why it was so long coming.

(*Pause.*)

    There I'll be, in the old shelter, alone against the silence and . . . (*he hesitates*) . . . the stillness. If I can hold my peace, and sit quiet, it will be all over with sound, and motion, all over and done with.

(*Pause.*)

    I'll have called my father and I'll have called my . . . (*he hesitates*) . . . my son. And even twice, or three times, in case they shouldn't have heard me, the first time, or the second.

(*Pause.*)

    I'll say to myself, He'll come back.

(*Pause.*)

    And then?

(*Pause.*)

    And then?

(*Pause.*)

    He couldn't, he has gone too far.

(*Pause.*)

    And then?

(*Pause. Very agitated.*)

    All kinds of fantasies! That I'm being watched! A rat! Steps! Breath held and then . . .

(*He breathes out.*)

    Then babble, babble, words, like the solitary child who turns himself into children, two, three, so as to be together, and whisper together, in the dark.

(*Pause.*)

Moment upon moment, pattering down, like the millet grains of . . . (*he hesitates*) . . . that old Greek, and all life long you wait for that to mount up to a life.

(*Pause. He opens his mouth to continue, renounces.*)

Ah let's get it over!

(*He whistles. Enter Clov with alarm clock. He halts beside the chair.*)

What? Neither gone nor dead?
CLOV: In spirit only.
HAMM: Which?
CLOV: Both.
HAMM: Gone from me you'd be dead.
CLOV: And vice versa.
HAMM: Outside of here it's death!

(*Pause.*)

And the rat?
CLOV: He's got away.
HAMM: He can't go far.

(*Pause. Anxious.*)

Eh?
CLOV: He doesn't need to go far.

(*Pause.*)

HAMM: Is it not time for my painkiller?
CLOV: Yes.
HAMM: Ah! At last! Give it to me! Quick!

(*Pause.*)

CLOV: There's no more painkiller.

(*Pause.*)

HAMM (*appalled*): Good . . . !

(*Pause.*)

No more painkiller!
CLOV: No more painkiller. You'll never get any more painkiller.

(*Pause.*)

HAMM: But the little round box. It was full!
CLOV: Yes. But now it's empty.

(*Pause. Clov starts to move about the room. He is looking for a place to put down the alarm clock.*)

HAMM (*soft*): What'll I do?

(*Pause. In a scream.*)

What'll I do?

(*Clov sees the picture, takes it down, stands it on the floor with its face to the wall, hangs up the alarm clock in its place.*)

What are you doing?
CLOV: Winding up.
HAMM: Look at the earth.
CLOV: Again!
HAMM: Since it's calling to you.
CLOV: Is your throat sore?

(*Pause.*)

Would you like a lozenge?

(*Pause.*)

Simon McBurney as Clov and Mark Rylance as Hamm in the production directed by McBurney at the Duchess Theatre in London, 2009.

No.

(*Pause.*)

Pity.

(*Clov goes, humming, towards window right, halts before it, looks up at it.*)

HAMM: Don't sing.

CLOV (*turning towards Hamm*): One hasn't the right to sing anymore?

HAMM: No.

CLOV: Then how can it end?

HAMM: You want it to end?

CLOV: I want to sing.

HAMM: I can't prevent you.

(*Pause. Clov turns towards window right.*)

CLOV: What did I do with that steps?

(*He looks around for ladder.*)

You didn't see that steps?

(*He sees it.*)

Ah, about time.

(*He goes towards window left.*)

Sometimes I wonder if I'm in my right mind. Then it passes over and I'm as lucid as before.

(*He gets up on ladder, looks out of window.*)

Christ, she's under water!

(*He looks.*)

How can that be?

(*He pokes forward his head, his hand above his eyes.*)

It hasn't rained.

(*He wipes the pane, looks. Pause.*)

Ah what a fool I am! I'm on the wrong side!

(*He gets down, takes a few steps towards window right.*)

Under water!

(*He goes back for ladder.*)

What a fool I am!

(*He carries ladder towards window right.*)

Sometimes I wonder if I'm in my right senses. Then it passes off and I'm as intelligent as ever.

(*He sets down ladder under window right, gets up on it, looks out of window. He turns towards Hamm.*)

Any particular sector you fancy? Or merely the whole thing?

HAMM: Whole thing.

CLOV: The general effect? Just a moment.

(*He looks out of window. Pause.*)

HAMM: Clov.

CLOV (*absorbed*): Mmm.

HAMM: Do you know what it is?

CLOV (*as before*): Mmm.

HAMM: I was never there.

(*Pause.*)

Clov!

CLOV (*turning towards Hamm, exasperated*): What is it?

HAMM: I was never there.

CLOV: Lucky for you.

(*He looks out of window.*)

HAMM: Absent, always. It all happened without me. I don't know what's happened.

(*Pause.*)

Do you know what's happened?

(*Pause.*)

Clov!

CLOV (*turning towards Hamm, exasperated*): Do you want me to look at this muckheap, yes or no?

HAMM: Answer me first.

CLOV: What?

HAMM: Do you know what's happened?

CLOV: When? Where?

HAMM (*violently*): When! What's happened? Use your head, can't you! What has happened?

CLOV: What for Christ's sake does it matter?

(*He looks out of window.*)

HAMM: I don't know.

(*Pause. Clov turns towards Hamm.*)

CLOV (*harshly*): When old Mother Pegg asked you for oil for her lamp and you told her to get out to hell, you knew what was happening then, no?

(*Pause.*)

You know what she died of, Mother Pegg? Of darkness.

HAMM (*feebly*): I hadn't any.

CLOV (*as before*): Yes, you had.

(*Pause.*)

HAMM: Have you the glass?

CLOV: No, it's clear enough as it is.

HAMM: Go and get it.

(*Pause. Clov casts up his eyes, brandishes his fists. He loses balance, clutches on to the ladder. He starts to get down, halts.*)

CLOV: There's one thing I'll never understand.

(*He gets down.*)

Why I always obey you. Can you explain that to me?

HAMM: No. . . . Perhaps it's compassion.

Clov (Max Casella) strikes Hamm (John Turturro) in the Brooklyn Academy of Music production, 2008.

(*Pause.*)

A kind of great compassion.

(*Pause.*)

Oh you won't find it easy, you won't find it easy.

(*Pause. Clov begins to move about the room in search of the telescope.*)

CLOV: I'm tired of our goings on, very tired.

(*He searches.*)

You're not sitting on it?

(*He moves the chair, looks at the place where it stood, resumes his search.*)

HAMM (*anguished*): Don't leave me there!

(*Angrily Clov restores the chair to its place.*)

Am I right in the center?

CLOV: You'd need a microscope to find this—

(*He sees the telescope.*)

Ah, about time.

(*He picks up the telescope, gets up on the ladder, turns the telescope on the without.*)

HAMM: Give me the dog.

CLOV (*looking*): Quiet!

HAMM (*angrily*): Give me the dog!

(*Clov drops the telescope, clasps his hands to his head. Pause. He gets down precipitately, looks for the dog, sees it, picks it up, hastens towards Hamm and strikes him violently on the head with the dog.*)

CLOV: There's your dog for you!

(*The dog falls to the ground. Pause.*)

HAMM: He hit me!

CLOV: You drive me mad, I'm mad!

HAMM: If you must hit me, hit me with the axe.

(*Pause.*)

Or with the gaff, hit me with the gaff. Not with the dog. With the gaff. Or with the axe.

(*Clov picks up the dog and gives it to Hamm who takes it in his arms.*)

CLOV (*imploringly*): Let's stop playing!

HAMM: Never!

(*Pause.*)

Put me in my coffin.

CLOV: There are no more coffins.

HAMM: Then let it end!

(*Clov goes towards ladder.*)

With a bang!

(*Clov gets up on ladder, gets down again, looks for telescope, sees it, picks it up, gets up ladder, raises telescope.*)

Of darkness! And me? Did anyone ever have pity on me?

CLOV (*lowering the telescope, turning towards Hamm*): What?

(*Pause.*)

Is it me you're referring to?

HAMM (*angrily*): An aside, ape! Did you never hear an aside before?

(*Pause.*)

I'm warming up for my last soliloquy.

CLOV: I warn you. I'm going to look at this filth since it's an order. But it's the last time.

(*He turns the telescope on the without.*)

Let's see.

(*He moves the telescope.*)

Nothing . . . nothing . . . good . . . good . . . nothing . . . goo—

(*He starts, lowers the telescope, examines it, turns it again on the without. Pause.*)

Bad luck to it!

HAMM: More complications!

(*Clov gets down.*)

Not an underplot, I trust.

(*Clov moves ladder nearer window, gets up on it, turns telescope on the without.*)

CLOV (*dismayed*): Looks like a small boy!

HAMM (*sarcastic*): A small . . . boy!

CLOV: I'll go and see.

(*He gets down, drops the telescope, goes towards door, turns.*)

I'll take the gaff.

(*He looks for the gaff, sees it, picks it up, hastens towards door.*)

HAMM: No!

(*Clov halts.*)

CLOV: No? A potential procreator?

HAMM: If he exists he'll die there or he'll come here. And if he doesn't . . .

(*Pause.*)

CLOV: You don't believe me? You think I'm inventing?

(*Pause.*)

HAMM: It's the end, Clov, we've come to the end. I don't need you anymore.

(*Pause.*)

CLOV: Lucky for you.

(*He goes towards door.*)

HAMM: Leave me the gaff.

(*Clov gives him the gaff, goes towards door, halts, looks at alarm clock, takes it down, looks round for a better place to put it, goes to bins, puts it on lid of Nagg's bin. Pause.*)

CLOV: I'll leave you.

(*He goes towards door.*)

HAMM: Before you go . . .

(*Clov halts near door.*)

. . . say something.

CLOV: There is nothing to say.

HAMM: A few words . . . to ponder . . . in my heart.

CLOV: Your heart!

HAMM: Yes.

(*Pause. Forcibly.*)

Yes!

(*Pause.*)

With the rest, in the end, the shadows, the murmurs, all the trouble, to end up with.

(*Pause.*)

Clov. . . . He never spoke to me. Then, in the end, before he went, without my having asked him, he spoke to me. He said . . .

CLOV (*despairingly*): Ah . . . !

HAMM: Something . . . from your heart.

CLOV: My heart!

HAMM: A few words . . . from your heart.

(*Pause.*)

CLOV (*fixed gaze, tonelessly, towards auditorium*): They said to me, That's love, yes, yes, not a doubt, now you see how—

HAMM: Articulate!

CLOV (*as before*): How easy it is. They said to me, That's friendship, yes, yes, no question, you've found it. They said to me, Here's the place, stop, raise your head and look at all that beauty. That order! They said to me, Come now, you're not a brute beast, think upon these things and you'll see how all becomes clear. And simple! They said to me, What skilled attention they get, all these dying of their wounds.

HAMM: Enough!

CLOV (*as before*): I say to myself—sometimes, Clov, you must learn to suffer better than that if you want them to weary of punishing you—one day. I say to myself—sometimes, Clov, you must be there better than that if you want them to let you go—one day. But I feel too old, and too far, to form new habits. Good, it'll never end, I'll never go.

(*Pause.*)

Then one day, suddenly, it ends, it changes, I don't understand, it dies, or it's me, I don't understand, that either. I ask the words that remain—sleeping, waking, morning, evening. They have nothing to say.

(*Pause.*)

I open the door of the cell and go. I am so bowed I only see my feet, if I open my eyes, and between my legs a little trail of black dust. I say to myself that the earth is extinguished, though I never saw it lit.

(*Pause.*)

It's easy going.

(*Pause.*)

When I fall I'll weep for happiness.

(*Pause. He goes towards door.*)

HAMM: Clov!
(*Clov halts, without turning.*)
  Nothing.

(*Clov moves on.*)

  Clov!

(*Clov halts, without turning.*)

CLOV: This is what we call making an exit.
HAMM: I'm obliged to you, Clov. For your services.
CLOV (*turning, sharply*): Ah pardon, it's I am obliged to you.
HAMM: It's we are obliged to each other.

(*Pause. Clov goes towards door.*)

  One thing more.

(*Clov halts.*)

  A last favor.

(*Exit Clov.*)

  Cover me with the sheet.

(*Long pause.*)

  No? Good.

(*Pause.*)

  Me to play.

(*Pause. Wearily.*)

  Old endgame lost of old, play and lose and have done with losing.

(*Pause. More animated.*)

  Let me see.

(*Pause.*)

  Ah yes!

(*He tries to move the chair, using the gaff as before. Enter Clov, dressed for the road. Panama hat, tweed coat, raincoat over his arm, umbrella, bag. He halts by*

the door and stands there, impassive and motionless, his eyes fixed on Hamm, till the end. Hamm gives up.)

  Good.

(*Pause.*)

  Discard.

(*He throws away the gaff, makes to throw away the dog, thinks better of it.*)

  Take it easy.

(*Pause.*)

  And now?

(*Pause.*)

  Raise hat.

(*He raises his toque.*)

  Peace to our . . . arses.

(*Pause.*)

  And put on again.

(*He puts on his toque.*)

  Deuce.

(*Pause. He takes off his glasses.*)

  Wipe.

(*He takes out his handkerchief and, without unfolding it, wipes his glasses.*)

  And put on again.

(*He puts on his glasses, puts back the handkerchief in his pocket.*)

  We're coming. A few more squirms like that and I'll call.

(*Pause.*)

  A little poetry.

(*Pause.*)

  You prayed—

(*Pause. He corrects himself.*)

  You CRIED for night; it comes—

(*Pause. He corrects himself.*)

  It FALLS: now cry in darkness.

(*He repeats, chanting.*)

  You cried for night; it falls: now cry in darkness.

(*Pause.*)

  Nicely put, that.

(*Pause.*)

  And now?

(*Pause.*)

Moments for nothing, now as always, time was never and time is over, reckoning closed and story ended.

(*Pause. Narrative tone.*)

If he could have his child with him. . . .

(*Pause.*)

It was the moment I was waiting for.

(*Pause.*)

You don't want to abandon him? You want him to bloom while you are withering? Be there to solace your last million last moments?

(*Pause.*)

He doesn't realize, all he knows is hunger, and cold, and death to crown it all. But you! You ought to know what the earth is like, nowadays. Oh I put him before his responsibilities!

(*Pause. Normal tone.*)

Well, there we are, there I am, that's enough.

(*He raises the whistle to his lips, hesitates, drops it. Pause.*)

Yes, truly!

(*He whistles. Pause. Louder. Pause.*)

Good.

(*Pause.*)

Father!

(*Pause. Louder.*)

Father!

(*Pause.*)

Good.

(*Pause.*)

We're coming.

(*Pause.*)

And to end up with?

(*Pause.*)

Discard.

(*He throws away the dog. He tears the whistle from his neck.*)

With my compliments.

(*He throws whistle towards auditorium. Pause. He sniffs. Soft.*)

Clov!

(*Long pause.*)

No? Good.

(*He takes out the handkerchief.*)

Since that's the way we're playing it . . . (*he unfolds handkerchief*) . . . let's play it that way . . . (*he unfolds*) . . . and speak no more about it . . . (*he finishes unfolding*) . . . speak no more.

(*He holds handkerchief spread out before him.*)

Old stancher!

(*Pause.*)

You . . . remain.

(*Pause. He covers his face with handkerchief, lowers his arms to armrests, remains motionless.*)

(*Brief tableau.*)

COMMENTARY

MARTIN ESSLIN (1918–2002)

The Theater of the Absurd   1960

Martin Esslin was a drama critic whose work has had wide currency. He was the first to write extensively about the theater of the absurd, and with this essay he defined the term that has come to describe the plays of Samuel Beckett and a number of other post–World War II playwrights such as Eugène Ionesco and Harold Pinter. The essay tries to establish the character of absurd drama, its limits, and its importance.

Audiences were certainly baffled by Beckett's work, starting with his very successful *Waiting for Godot* and including *Krapp's Last Tape* and *Happy Days*. All these plays are restricted in space and in action. Their very essence is restriction. Esslin shows the possible range of significance in Beckett's plays and explains that if we see the plays properly, we can understand how they interpret experience. The question of what use playwrights make of the absurd and why it is an appropriate term to reflect Beckett's achievement is explored briefly in this excerpt.

The Theater of the Absurd shows the world as an incomprehensible place. The spectators see the happenings on the stage entirely from the outside, without ever understanding the full meaning of these strange patterns of events, as newly arrived visitors might watch life in a country of which they have not yet mastered the language. The confrontation of the audience with characters and happenings which they are not quite able to comprehend makes it impossible for them to share the aspirations and emotions depicted in the play. Brecht's famous "Verfremdungs-effekt" (alienation effect), the inhibition of any identification between spectator and actor, which Brecht could never successfully achieve in his own highly rational theater, really comes into its own in the Theater of the Absurd. It is impossible to identify oneself with characters one does not understand or whose motives remain a closed book, and so the distance between the public and the happenings on the stage can be maintained. Emotional identification with the characters is replaced by a puzzled, critical attention. For while the happenings on the stage are absurd, they yet remain recognizable as somehow related to real life with *its* absurdity, so that eventually the spectators are brought face to face with the irrational side of their existence. Thus, the absurd and fantastic goings-on of the Theater of the Absurd will, in the end, be found to reveal the irrationality of the human condition and the illusion of what we thought was its apparent logical structure.

If the dialogue in these plays consists of meaningless clichés and the mechanical, circular repetition of stereotyped phrases—how many meaningless clichés and stereotyped phrases do we use in our day-to-day conversation? If the characters change their personality halfway through the action, how consistent and truly integrated are the people we meet in our real life? And if people in these plays appear as mere marionettes, helpless puppets without any will of their own, passively at the mercy of blind fate and meaningless circumstance, do we, in fact, in our overorganized world, still possess any genuine initiative or power to decide our own destiny? The spectators of the Theater of the Absurd are thus confronted with a grotesquely heightened picture of their own world: a world without faith, meaning, and genuine freedom of will. In this sense, the Theater of the Absurd is the true theater of our time.

The theater of most previous epochs reflected an accepted moral order, a world whose aims and objectives were clearly present to the minds of all its public, whether it was the audience of the medieval mystery plays with their solidly accepted faith in the Christian world order or the audience of the drama of Ibsen, Shaw, or Hauptmann with their unquestioned belief in evolution and progress. To such audiences, right and wrong were never in doubt, nor did they question the then accepted goals of human endeavor. Our own time, at least in the Western world, wholly lacks such a generally accepted and completely integrated world picture. The decline of religious faith, the destruction of the belief in automatic social and biological progress, the discovery of vast areas of irrational and unconscious forces within the human psyche, the loss of a sense of control over rational human development in an age of totalitarianism and weapons of mass destruction, have all contributed to the erosion of the basis for a dramatic convention in which the action proceeds within a fixed and self-evident framework of generally accepted values. Faced with the vacuum left by the destruction of a universally accepted and unified set of beliefs, most serious playwrights have felt the need to fit their work into the frame of values and objectives expressed in one of the contemporary ideologies: Marxism, psychoanalysis, aestheticism, or nature worship. But these, in the eyes of a writer like Adamov, are nothing but superficial rationalizations which try to hide the depth of man's predicament, his loneliness and his anxiety. Or, as Ionesco puts it:

> As far as I am concerned, I believe sincerely in the poverty of the poor, I deplore it; it is real; it can become a subject for the theatre; I also believe in the anxieties and serious troubles the rich may suffer from; but it is neither in the misery of the former nor in the melancholia of the latter, that I, for one, find my dramatic subject matter. Theatre is for me the outward projection onto the stage of an inner world; it is in my dreams, in my anxieties, in my obscure desires, in my internal contradictions that I, for one, reserve for myself the right of finding my dramatic subject matter. As I am not alone in the world, as each of us, in the depth of his being, is at the same time part and parcel of all others, my dreams, my desires, my anxieties, my obsessions do not belong to me alone. They form part of an ancestral heritage, a very ancient storehouse which is a portion of the common property of all mankind. It is this, which, transcending their outward diversity, reunites all human beings and constitutes our profound common patrimony, the universal language.[1]

In other words, the commonly acceptable framework of beliefs and values of former epochs which has now been shattered is to be replaced by the community of dreams and desires of a collective unconscious. And, to quote Ionesco again:

> ... the new dramatist is one ... who tries to link up with what is most ancient; new language and subject matter in a dramatic structure which aims at being clearer, more stripped of inessentials and more purely theatrical; the rejection of traditionalism to rediscover tradition; a synthesis of knowledge and invention, of the real and imaginary, of the particular and the universal, or as they say now, of the individual and the collective. ... By expressing my deepest obsessions, I express my deepest humanity. I become one with all others, spontaneously, over and above all the barriers of caste and different psychologies. I express my solitude and become one with all other solitudes.[2]

What is the tradition with which the Theater of the Absurd—at first sight the most revolutionary and radically new movement—is trying to link itself? It is in fact a very ancient and a very rich tradition, nourished from many and varied sources: the verbal exuberance and extravagant inventions of Rabelais, the age-old clowning of the Roman mimes and the Italian *Commedia dell'Arte*, the knockabout humor of circus clowns like Grock; the wild, archetypal symbolism of English nonsense verse, the baroque horror of Jacobean dramatists like Webster or Tourneur, the harsh, incisive and often brutal tones of the German drama of Grabbe, Büchner, Kleist, and Wedekind with its delirious language and grotesque inventiveness; and the Nordic paranoia of the dreams and persecution fantasies of Strindberg.

[1] Eugène Ionesco, "L'Impromptu de l'Alma," *Théâtre II*, Paris, 1958.
[2] Ionesco, "The Avant-Garde Theatre," *World Theatre*, 8.3 (Autumn 1959).

Lorraine Hansberry

Lorraine Hansberry (1930–1965), like John Millington Synge, died tragically young. The loss to the American stage is incalculable; her successes were only beginning, and at her death she seemed on the verge of a remarkable career.

Hansberry grew up in a middle-class black family in Chicago. Her father, who was successful in real estate, founded one of the first banks in Chicago to solicit black patronage. However, he spent much of his life vainly trying to find a way to make a decent life for himself and his family. He eventually gave up on the United States, and when he died in 1945, he was scouting for a place in Mexico where he and his family could move to live comfortably.

Lorraine Hansberry went to college after her father died, and her first ambition was to become a visual artist. She attended the Art Institute of Chicago and numerous other schools before moving to New York. Once there, she became interested in some drama groups and soon married the playwright Howard Nemiroff. She began writing, sharing parts of her first play with friends in her own living room. They helped raise money to stage the play, and, with black director Lloyd Richards and little-known Sidney Poitier as Walter Lee Younger, *A Raisin in the Sun* (1959) thrust Hansberry into the drama spotlight.

In 1959, only twenty-nine years old, Hansberry was the most promising woman writing for the American stage. She was also the first black American to win the New York Drama Critics' Circle Award for the best play of the year. She died of cancer the day her second produced play, *The Sign in Sidney Brustein's Window,* closed. She had finished a third play, *Les Blancs,* which was brought to Broadway by Nemiroff in 1970. Neither of her other plays was as popular as *Raisin,* but the two later plays demonstrate a deepening concern for and understanding of some of the key issues of racial and sexual politics that interested her throughout her career.

The hero in *The Sign in Sidney Brustein's Window* is a Jewish intellectual in the 1950s in Greenwich Village. Believing that all the gains of radical struggle of the 1930s have been lost, he agitates for personal involvement, for emotional and intellectual action. This idealistic play anticipates the political agitation in the United States during the mid-1960s and early 1970s. *Les Blancs* takes as its central character a black African intellectual, Tshembe, and explores his relationship to both Europe and Africa. In his uneasiness with both cultures he discovers that he cannot live outside his own history. *Les Blancs* reveals some of Hansberry's deep interest in Pan-Africanism and the search for a personal heritage.

A posthumous work was put together by Howard Nemiroff from Hansberry's notes, letters, and early writings. Titled *To Be Young, Gifted, and Black* (1971), it has helped solidify her achievements. Although we will never know just how Hansberry's career would have developed had she lived, her gifts were so remarkable that we can only lament that she is not writing for the stage today.

For links to resources about Hansberry, click on *AuthorLinks* at bedfordstmartins.com/jacobus.

A Raisin in the Sun

When produced on Broadway in 1959, *A Raisin in the Sun* was somewhat prophetic. Lorraine Hansberry's themes of blacks pressing forward with legitimate demands and expressing interest in their African heritage were to become primary themes of black culture in the 1960s, in the 1970s, and, indeed, to this day. The title of her play is from a poem by Langston Hughes, one of the poets of the Harlem Renaissance. The poem warns of the social explosions that might occur if society permits blacks to remain unequal and unfree.

Hansberry's work appeared at the beginning of renewed political activity on the part of African Americans; it reveals its historical position in the use of the word *Negro,* which black activists rejected in the 1960s as an enslaving euphemism. This play illustrates the American dream as it is understood not just by African Americans but by all Americans: if you work hard, save your money, are honorable, and hope, then you can one day buy your own home and have the kind of space and privacy that permit people to live with dignity. Yet this very theme has plagued the play from the beginning: its apparent emphasis on middle-class, bourgeois values. On the surface, it seems to celebrate a mild form of consumerism—the desire for the house in the suburbs with the TV set inside to anesthetize its occupants. Hansberry was shocked when such criticisms, from black critics as well as white, were leveled at the play. She had written it very carefully to explore just those issues in a context that demonstrated that black families' needs paralleled those of white families, while also having a different dimension that most white families could not understand.

Hansberry was quick to admit that Walter Lee Younger was affected by the same craziness influencing all Americans who lusted after possessions and the power they might confer. Walter wants to take his father's insurance money to buy a liquor store in partnership with a con man. Lena Younger argues against her son's plan as a profanation of her husband's memory as well as an abuse of the American dream: she believes that the product of a liquor store will further poison the community. What she wants is not a consumer product but the emblem of identity and security that she feels her family deserves.

Hansberry is painfully honest in this play. Walter Lee's weaknesses are recognizable. His male chauvinistic behavior undoes him. He is caught up in the old, failing pattern of male dominance over women. But none of the women in his life will tolerate his behavior. Hansberry also admits the social distinctions among African Americans. George Murchison is a young man from a wealthy black family, and when Beneatha tells Lena that she will not marry George, she says, "The only people in the world who are more snobbish than rich white people are rich colored people." Beneatha's desire to be a doctor is obviously not rooted in consumerism any more than in the middle-class need to be comfortable and rich.

The confusion caused in the family by a native African, Asagai, is realistically portrayed. In the early days of the Pan-African movement in the 1960s, blacks were often bemused by the way Africans presented themselves.

For a Drama in Depth tutorial on *A Raisin in the Sun*, click on *VirtualLit Drama Tutorials* at **bedfordstmartins.com/jacobus.**

Interest in Africa on the part of American blacks was distorted by Tarzan movies and *National Geographic* articles, none of which presented black Africans as role models. Therefore, the adjustment to black African pride, though it was made swiftly, was not without difficulties. The Youngers are presented as no more sophisticated about black Africans than the rest of black society would be.

The dignity of the Younger family finally triumphs. When Walter Lee stands up for himself, he is asserting not macho domination but black manhood—a manhood that needs no domination over women. He is expressing not a desire for a big house—as he had done when he reflected on the possessions of his rich employer—but a desire to demonstrate to members of the Clybourne Park Improvement Association that the Youngers are their social equals and that they have a right to live wherever they choose.

A Raisin in the Sun in Performance

Lloyd Richards directed the first production at the Ethel Barrymore Theater in New York on March 11, 1959. The play won major prizes, and Sidney Poitier as a passionate Walter Lee Younger was a signal success. *New York Times* critic Brooks Atkinson said, "Since the performance is also honest and since Sidney Poitier is a candid actor, *A Raisin in the Sun* has vigor as well as veracity and is likely to destroy the complacency of any one who sees it." Critics were astonished that a first play could have the sophistication and depth they saw onstage.

The Theatre Guild staged the play in 1960 in Boston with a different cast, but the production received similar reviews. The film version, with most of the New York cast, was directed by Daniel Petrie in 1961. A revival in Chicago in 1983 at the Art Institute of Chicago—Hansberry's alma mater—was not altogether successful, but critics agreed the text held up well. The Chicago revival, like the 1985 Merrimack Repertory Theater revival in Lowell, Massachusetts, demonstrated that the play needs strong actors to have the desired impact. A twenty-fifth-anniversary production was directed by Lloyd Richards at the Yale Repertory Theatre in 1983. This production was taken to New York in 1986 and enjoyed a successful run. The setting was a realistic interior, emphasizing the play's realistic style. Critic Mel Gussow asserted that the revival demonstrated that the play is "an enduring work of contemporary theater." The production also revealed that Hansberry's language had not become dated, nor had the social issues of the play become any less critical and important twenty-five years later. In fact, a production starring hip-hop artist and fashion mogul Sean "P. Diddy" Combs and Audra McDonald during the 2004 season in New York City got good reviews. This production was shown on television in 2008 in a version that gained the play a brand-new audience. Like the proletarian plays of Sean O'Casey, who inspired Lorraine Hansberry, this play continues to move us because the problems it examines are serious and still remain with us.

LORRAINE HANSBERRY (1930–1965)

A Raisin in the Sun 1959

Harlem (*A Dream Deferred*)

What happens to a dream deferred?

Does it dry up
like a raisin in the sun?
Or fester like a sore —
And then run?
Does it stink like rotten meat?

Or crust and sugar over —
like a syrupy sweet?

Maybe it just sags
like a heavy load.

Or does it explode?   — LANGSTON HUGHES

Characters

RUTH YOUNGER
TRAVIS YOUNGER
WALTER LEE YOUNGER (*brother*)
BENEATHA YOUNGER
LENA YOUNGER (*Mama*)
JOSEPH ASAGAI
GEORGE MURCHISON
MRS. JOHNSON
KARL LINDNER
BOBO
MOVING MEN

The action of the play is set in Chicago's Southside,
sometime between World War II and the present.

Act I

Scene I: *Friday morning.*
Scene II: *The following morning.*

Act II

Scene I: *Later, the same day.*
Scene II: *Friday night, a few weeks later.*
Scene III: *Moving day, one week later.*

Act III

An hour later.

ACT I • Scene I

(*The Younger living room would be a comfortable
and well-ordered room if it were not for a number of
indestructible contradictions to this state of being. Its
furnishings are typical and undistinguished and their
primary feature now is that they have clearly had to
accommodate the living of too many people for too
many years — and they are tired. Still, we can see that
at some time, a time probably no longer remembered
by the family [except perhaps for Mama], the furnishings of this room were actually selected with care and
love and even hope — and brought to this apartment
and arranged with taste and pride.*)

(*That was a long time ago. Now the once loved
pattern of the couch upholstery has to fight to show
itself from under acres of crocheted doilies and couch
covers which have themselves finally come to be more
important than the upholstery. And here a table or a
chair has been moved to disguise the worn places in the
carpet; but the carpet has fought back by showing its
weariness, with depressing uniformity, elsewhere on its
surface.*)

(*Weariness has, in fact, won in this room. Everything has been polished, washed, sat on, used, scrubbed
too often. All pretenses but living itself have long since
vanished from the very atmosphere of this room.*)

(*Moreover, a section of this room, for it is not really
a room unto itself, though the landlord's lease would
make it seem so, slopes backward to provide a small
kitchen area, where the family prepares the meals that
are eaten in the living room proper, which must also
serve as dining room. The single window that has
been provided for these "two" rooms is located in this
kitchen area. The sole natural light the family may
enjoy in the course of a day is only that which fights its
way through this little window.*)

(*At left, a door leads to a bedroom which is shared by
Mama and her daughter, Beneatha. At right, opposite, is
a second room [which in the beginning of the life of this
apartment was probably a breakfast room] which serves
as a bedroom for Walter and his wife, Ruth.*)

(*Time: Sometime between World War II and the
present.*)

(*Place: Chicago's Southside.*)

(*At rise: It is morning dark in the living room. Travis
is asleep on the make-down bed at center. An alarm
clock sounds from within the bedroom at right, and
presently Ruth enters from that room and closes the
door behind her. She crosses sleepily toward the window.*

As she passes her sleeping son she reaches down and shakes him a little. At the window she raises the shade and a dusky Southside morning light comes in feebly. She fills a pot with water and puts it on to boil. She calls to the boy, between yawns, in a slightly muffled voice.)

(Ruth is about thirty. We can see that she was a pretty girl, even exceptionally so, but now it is apparent that life has been little that she expected, and disappointment has already begun to hang in her face. In a few years, before thirty-five even, she will be known among her people as a "settled woman.")

(She crosses to her son and gives him a good, final, rousing shake.)

RUTH: Come on now, boy, it's seven thirty! (*Her son sits up at last, in a stupor of sleepiness.*) I say hurry up, Travis! You ain't the only person in the world got to use a bathroom! (*The child, a sturdy, handsome little boy of ten or eleven, drags himself out of the bed and almost blindly takes his towels and "today's clothes" from drawers and a closet and goes out to the bathroom, which is in an outside hall and which is shared by another family or families on the same floor. Ruth crosses to the bedroom door at right and opens it and calls in to her husband.*) Walter Lee! . . . It's after seven thirty! Lemme see you do some waking up in there now! (*She waits.*) You better get up from there, man! It's after seven thirty I tell you. (*She waits again.*) All right, you just go ahead and lay there and next thing you know Travis be finished and Mr. Johnson'll be in there and you'll be fussing and cussing round here like a madman! And be late too! (*She waits, at the end of patience.*) Walter Lee—it's time for you to GET UP!

(She waits another second and then starts to go into the bedroom, but is apparently satisfied that her husband has begun to get up. She stops, pulls the door to, and returns to the kitchen area. She wipes her face with a moist cloth and runs her fingers through her sleep-disheveled hair in a vain effort and ties an apron around her housecoat. The bedroom door at right opens and her husband stands in the doorway in his pajamas, which are rumpled and mismated. He is a lean, intense young man in his middle thirties, inclined to quick nervous movements and erratic speech habits—and always in his voice there is a quality of indictment.)

WALTER: Is he out yet?

RUTH: What you mean *out?* He ain't hardly got in there good yet.

WALTER (*wandering in, still more oriented to sleep than to a new day*): Well, what was you doing all that yelling for if I can't even get in there yet? (*Stopping and thinking.*) Check coming today?

RUTH: They *said* Saturday and this is just Friday and I hopes to God you ain't going to get up here first thing this morning and start talking to me 'bout no money—'cause I 'bout don't want to hear it.

WALTER: Something the matter with you this morning?

RUTH: No—I'm just sleepy as the devil. What kind of eggs you want?

WALTER: Not scrambled. (*Ruth starts to scramble eggs.*) Paper come? (*Ruth points impatiently to the rolled up Tribune on the table, and he gets it and spreads it out and vaguely reads the front page.*) Set off another bomb yesterday.

RUTH (*maximum indifference*): Did they?

WALTER (*looking up*): What's the matter with you?

RUTH: Ain't nothing the matter with me. And don't keep asking me that this morning.

WALTER: Ain't nobody bothering you. (*Reading the news of the day absently again.*) Say Colonel McCormick is sick.

RUTH (*affecting tea-party interest*): Is he now? Poor thing.

WALTER (*sighing and looking at his watch*): Oh, me. (*He waits.*) Now what is that boy doing in that bathroom all this time? He just going to have to start getting up earlier. I can't be being late to work on account of him fooling around in there.

RUTH (*turning on him*): Oh, no he ain't going to be getting up no earlier no such thing! It ain't his fault that he can't get to bed no earlier nights 'cause he got a bunch of crazy good-for-nothing clowns sitting up running their mouths in what is supposed to be his bedroom after ten o'clock at night . . .

WALTER: That's what you mad about, ain't it? The things I want to talk about with my friends just couldn't be important in your mind, could they?

(He rises and finds a cigarette in her handbag on the table and crosses to the little window and looks out, smoking and deeply enjoying this first one.)

RUTH (*almost matter of factly, a complaint too automatic to deserve emphasis*): Why you always got to smoke before you eat in the morning?

WALTER (*at the window*): Just look at 'em down there . . . Running and racing to work . . . (*He turns and faces his wife and watches her a moment at the stove, and then, suddenly.*) You look young this morning, baby.

RUTH (*indifferently*): Yeah?

WALTER: Just for a second—stirring them eggs. Just for a second it was—you looked real young again. (*He reaches for her; she crosses away. Then, drily.*) It's gone now—you look like yourself again!

RUTH: Man, if you don't shut up and leave me alone.

WALTER (*looking out to the street again*): First thing a man ought to learn in life is not to make love to no colored woman first thing in the morning. You all some eeeevil people at eight o'clock in the morning.

(Travis appears in the hall doorway, almost fully dressed and quite wide awake now, his towels and pajamas across his shoulders. He opens the door and signals for his father to make the bathroom in a hurry.)

TRAVIS (*watching the bathroom*): Daddy, come on!

(Walter gets his bathroom utensils and flies out to the bathroom.)

RUTH: Sit down and have your breakfast, Travis.

TRAVIS: Mama, this is Friday. (*Gleefully.*) Check coming tomorrow, huh?

RUTH: You get your mind off money and eat your breakfast.

TRAVIS (*eating*): This is the morning we supposed to bring the fifty cents to school.

RUTH: Well, I ain't got no fifty cents this morning.

TRAVIS: Teacher say we have to.

RUTH: I don't care what teacher say. I ain't got it. Eat your breakfast, Travis.

TRAVIS: I *am* eating.

RUTH: Hush up now and just eat!

(*The boy gives her an exasperated look for her lack of understanding and eats grudgingly.*)

TRAVIS: You think Grandmama would have it?

RUTH: No! And I want you to stop asking your grandmother for money, you hear me?

TRAVIS (*outraged*): Gaaaleee! I don't ask her, she just gimme it sometimes!

RUTH: Travis Willard Younger—I got too much on me this morning to be—

TRAVIS: Maybe Daddy—

RUTH: *Travis!*

(*The boy hushes abruptly. They are both quiet and tense for several seconds.*)

TRAVIS (*presently*): Could I maybe go carry some groceries in front of the supermarket for a little while after school then?

RUTH: Just hush, I said. (*Travis jabs his spoon into his cereal bowl viciously and rests his head in anger upon his fists.*) If you through eating, you can get over there and make up your bed.

(*The boy obeys stiffly and crosses the room, almost mechanically, to the bed and more or less folds the bedding into a heap, then angrily gets his books and cap.*)

TRAVIS (*sulking and standing apart from her unnaturally*): I'm gone.

RUTH (*looking up from the stove to inspect him automatically*): Come here. (*He crosses to her and she studies his head.*) If you don't take this comb and fix this here head, you better! (*Travis puts down his books with a great sigh of oppression and crosses to the mirror. His mother mutters under her breath about his "slubbornness."*) 'Bout to march out of here with that head looking just like chickens slept in it! I just don't know where you get your slubborn ways . . . And get your jacket, too. Looks chilly out this morning.

TRAVIS (*with conspicuously brushed hair and jacket*): I'm gone.

RUTH: Get carfare and milk money—(*waving one finger*)—and not a single penny for no caps, you hear me?

TRAVIS (*with sullen politeness*): Yes'm.

(*He turns in outrage to leave. His mother watches after him as in his frustration he approaches the door almost comically. When she speaks to him, her voice has become a very gentle tease.*)

RUTH (*mocking; as she thinks he would say it*): Oh, Mama makes me so mad sometimes, I don't know what to do! (*She waits and continues to his back as he stands stock-still in front of the door.*) I wouldn't kiss that woman good-bye for nothing in this world this morning! (*The boy finally turns around and rolls his eyes at her, knowing the mood has changed and he is vindicated; he does not, however, move toward her yet.*) Not for nothing in this world! (*She finally laughs aloud at him and holds out her arms to him and we see that it is a way between them, very old and practiced. He crosses to her and allows her to embrace him warmly but keeps his face fixed with masculine rigidity. She holds him back from her presently and looks at him and runs her fingers over the features of his face. With utter gentleness—*) Now—whose little old angry man are you?

TRAVIS (*the masculinity and gruffness start to fade at last*): Aw gaalee—Mama . . .

RUTH (*mimicking*): Aw—gaaaaalleeeee, Mama! (*She pushes him, with rough playfulness and finality, toward the door.*) Get on out of here or you going to be late.

TRAVIS (*in the face of love, new aggressiveness*): Mama, could I *please* go carry groceries?

RUTH: Honey, it's starting to get so cold evenings.

WALTER (*coming in from the bathroom and drawing a make-believe gun from a make-believe holster and shooting at his son*): What is it he wants to do?

RUTH: Go carry groceries after school at the supermarket.

WALTER: Well, let him go . . .

TRAVIS (*quickly, to the ally*): I have to—she won't gimme the fifty cents . . .

WALTER (*to his wife only*): Why not?

RUTH (*simply, and with flavor*): 'Cause we don't have it.

WALTER (*to Ruth only*): What you tell the boy things like that for? (*Reaching down into his pants with a rather important gesture.*) Here, son—

(*He hands the boy the coin, but his eyes are directed to his wife's. Travis takes the money happily.*)

TRAVIS: Thanks, Daddy.

(*He starts out. Ruth watches both of them with murder in her eyes. Walter stands and stares back at her with defiance and suddenly reaches into his pocket again on an afterthought.*)

WALTER (*without even looking at his son, still staring hard at his wife*): In fact, here's another fifty cents . . . Buy yourself some fruit today—or take a taxicab to school or something!

TRAVIS: Whoopee—

(*He leaps up and clasps his father around the middle with his legs, and they face each other in mutual appreciation; slowly Walter Lee peeks around the boy*) *to catch the violent rays from his wife's eyes and draws his head back as if shot.*)

WALTER: You better get down now—and get to school, man.

TRAVIS (*at the door*): O.K. Good-bye.

(*He exits.*)

WALTER (*after him, pointing with pride*): That's my boy. (*She looks at him in disgust and turns back to her work.*) You know what I was thinking 'bout in the bathroom this morning?

RUTH: No.

WALTER: How come you always try to be so pleasant!

RUTH: What is there to be pleasant 'bout!

WALTER: You want to know what I was thinking 'bout in the bathroom or not!

RUTH: I know what you thinking 'bout.

WALTER (*ignoring her*): 'Bout what me and Willy Harris was talking about last night.

RUTH (*immediately—a refrain*): Willy Harris is a good-for-nothing loudmouth.

WALTER: Anybody who talks to me has got to be a good-for-nothing loudmouth, ain't he? And what you know about who is just a good-for-nothing loudmouth? Charlie Atkins was just a "good-for-nothing loudmouth" too, wasn't he! When he wanted me to go in the dry-cleaning business with him. And now—he's grossing a hundred thousand a year. A hundred thousand dollars a year! You still call *him* a loudmouth!

RUTH (*bitterly*): Oh, Walter Lee . . .

(*She folds her head on her arms over the table.*)

WALTER (*rising and coming to her and standing over her*): You tired, ain't you? Tired of everything. Me, the boy, the way we live—this beat-up hole—everything. Ain't you? (*She doesn't look up, doesn't answer.*) So tired—moaning and groaning all the time, but you wouldn't do nothing to help, would you? You couldn't be on my side that long for nothing, could you?

RUTH: Walter, please leave me alone.

WALTER: A man needs for a woman to back him up . . .

RUTH: Walter—

WALTER: Mama would listen to you. You know she listen to you more than she do me and Bennie. She think more of you. All you have to do is just sit down with her when you drinking your coffee one morning and talking 'bout things like you do and—(*He sits down beside her and demonstrates graphically what he thinks her methods and tone should be.*)—you just sip your coffee, see, and say easy like that you been thinking 'bout that deal Walter Lee is so interested in, 'bout the store and all, and sip some more coffee, like what you saying ain't really that important to you—And the next thing you know, she be listening good and asking you questions and when I come home—I can tell her the details. This ain't no fly-by-night proposition, baby. I mean we figured it out, me and Willy and Bobo.

RUTH (*with a frown*): Bobo?

WALTER: Yeah. You see, this little liquor store we got in mind cost seventy-five thousand and we figured the initial investment on the place be 'bout thirty thousand, see. That be ten thousand each. Course, there's a couple of hundred you got to pay so's you don't spend your life just waiting for them clowns to let your license get approved—

RUTH: You mean graft?

WALTER (*frowning impatiently*): Don't call it that. See there, that just goes to show you what women understand about the world. Baby, don't *nothing* happen for you in this world 'less you pay *somebody* off!

RUTH: Walter, leave me alone! (*She raises her head and stares at him vigorously—then says, more quietly.*) Eat your eggs, they gonna be cold.

WALTER (*straightening up from her and looking off*): That's it. There you are. Man say to his woman: I got me a dream. His woman say: Eat your eggs. (*Sadly, but gaining in power.*) Man say: I got to take hold of this here world, baby! And a woman will say: Eat your eggs and go to work. (*Passionately now.*) Man say: I got to change my life, I'm choking to death, baby! And his woman say—(*in utter anguish as he brings his fists down on his thighs*)—Your eggs is getting cold!

RUTH (*softly*): Walter, that ain't none of our money.

WALTER (*not listening at all or even looking at her*): This morning, I was lookin' in the mirror and thinking about it . . . I'm thirty-five years old; I been married eleven years and I got a boy who sleeps in the living room—(*very, very quietly*)—and all I got to give him is stories about how rich white people live . . .

RUTH: Eat your eggs, Walter.

WALTER (*slams the table and jumps up*):—DAMN MY EGGS—DAMN ALL THE EGGS THAT EVER WAS!

RUTH: Then go to work.

WALTER (*looking up at her*): See—I'm trying to talk to you 'bout myself—(*shaking his head with the repetition*)—and all you can say is eat them eggs and go to work.

RUTH (*wearily*): Honey, you never say nothing new. I listen to you every day, every night and every morning, and you never say nothing new. (*Shrugging.*) So you would rather *be* Mr. Arnold than be his chauffeur. So—I would *rather* be living in Buckingham Palace.

WALTER: That is just what is wrong with the colored woman in this world . . . Don't understand about building their men up and making 'em feel like they somebody. Like they can do something.

RUTH (*drily, but to hurt*): There *are* colored men who do things.

WALTER: No thanks to the colored woman.

RUTH: Well, being a colored woman, I guess I can't help myself none.

(*She rises and gets the ironing board and sets it up and attacks a huge pile of rough-dried clothes, sprinkling them in preparation for the ironing and then rolling them into tight fat balls.*)

WALTER (*mumbling*): We one group of men tied to a race of women with small minds!

(*His sister Beneatha enters. She is about twenty, as slim and intense as her brother. She is not as pretty as her sister-in-law, but her lean, almost intellectual face has a handsomeness of its own. She wears a bright red flannel nightie, and her thick hair stands wildly about her head. Her speech is a mixture of many things; it is different from the rest of the family's insofar as education has permeated her sense of English—and perhaps the Midwest rather than the South has finally—at last—won out in her inflection; but not altogether, because over all of it is a soft slurring and transformed use of vowels which is the decided influence of the Southside. She passes through the room without looking at either Ruth or Walter and goes to the outside door and looks, a little blindly, out to the bathroom. She sees that it has been lost to the Johnsons. She closes the door with a sleepy vengeance and crosses to the table and sits down a little defeated.*)

BENEATHA: I am going to start timing those people.

WALTER: You should get up earlier.

BENEATHA (*Her face in her hands. She is still fighting the urge to go back to bed.*): Really—would you suggest dawn? Where's the paper?

WALTER (*pushing the paper across the table to her as he studies her almost clinically, as though he has never seen her before*): You a horrible-looking chick at this hour.

BENEATHA (*drily*): Good morning, everybody.

WALTER (*senselessly*): How is school coming?

BENEATHA (*in the same spirit*): Lovely. Lovely. And you know, biology is the greatest. (*Looking up at him.*) I dissected something that looked just like you yesterday.

WALTER: I just wondered if you've made up your mind and everything.

BENEATHA (*gaining in sharpness and impatience*): And what did I answer yesterday morning—and the day before that?

RUTH (*from the ironing board, like someone disinterested and old*): Don't be so nasty, Bennie.

BENEATHA (*still to her brother*): And the day before that and the day before that!

WALTER (*defensively*): I'm interested in you. Something wrong with that? Ain't many girls who decide—

WALTER AND BENEATHA (*in unison*): —"to be a doctor."

(*Silence.*)

WALTER: Have we figured out yet just exactly how much medical school is going to cost?

RUTH: Walter Lee, why don't you leave that girl alone and get out of here to work?

BENEATHA (*exits to the bathroom and bangs on the door*): Come on out of there, please!

(*She comes back into the room.*)

WALTER (*looking at his sister intently*): You know the check is coming tomorrow.

BENEATHA (*turning on him with a sharpness all her own*): That money belongs to Mama, Walter, and it's for her to decide how she wants to use it. I don't care if she wants to buy a house or a rocketship or just nail it up somewhere and look at it. It's hers. Not ours—*hers.*

WALTER (*bitterly*): Now ain't that fine! You just got your mother's interest at heart, ain't you, girl? You such a nice girl—but if Mama got that money she can always take a few thousand and help you through school too—can't she?

BENEATHA: I have never asked anyone around here to do anything for me!

WALTER: No! And the line between asking and just accepting when the time comes is big and wide—ain't it!

BENEATHA (*with fury*): What do you want from me, Brother—that I quit school or just drop dead, which!

WALTER: I don't want nothing but for you to stop acting holy 'round here. Me and Ruth done made some sacrifices for you—why can't you do something for the family?

RUTH: Walter, don't be dragging me in it.

WALTER: You are in it—Don't you get up and go work in somebody's kitchen for the last three years to help put clothes on her back?

RUTH: Oh, Walter—that's not fair . . .

WALTER: It ain't that nobody expects you to get on your knees and say thank you, Brother; thank you, Ruth; thank you, Mama—and thank you, Travis, for wearing the same pair of shoes for two semesters—

BENEATHA (*dropping to her knees*): Well—I *do*—all right?—thank everybody! And forgive me for ever wanting to be anything at all! (*Pursuing him on her knees across the floor.*) FORGIVE ME, FORGIVE ME, FORGIVE ME!

RUTH: Please stop it! Your mama'll hear you.

WALTER: Who the hell told you you had to be a doctor? If you so crazy 'bout messing 'round with sick people—then go be a nurse like other women—or just get married and be quiet . . .

BENEATHA: Well—you finally got it said . . . It took you three years but you finally got it said. Walter, give up; leave me alone—it's Mama's money.

WALTER: *He was my father, too!*

BENEATHA: So what? He was mine, too—and Travis' grandfather—but the insurance money belongs to Mama. Picking on me is not going to make her give it to you to invest in any liquor stores—(*under breath, dropping into a chair*)—and I for one say, God bless Mama for that!

WALTER (*to Ruth*): See—did you hear? Did you hear!

RUTH: Honey, please go to work.

WALTER: Nobody in this house is ever going to understand me.

BENEATHA: Because you're a nut.

WALTER: Who's a nut?

BENEATHA: You—you are a nut. Thee is mad, boy.

Claudia McNeil as Lena
(Mama) and Sidney Poitier as
Walter in the 1961 film version
of *A Raisin in the Sun.*

WALTER (*looking at his wife and his sister from the door, very sadly*): The world's most backward race of people, and that's a fact.

BENEATHA (*turning slowly in her chair*): And then there are all those prophets who would lead us out of the wilderness—(*Walter slams out of the house.*)—into the swamps!

RUTH: Bennie, why you always gotta be pickin' on your brother? Can't you be a little sweeter sometimes? (*Door opens. Walter walks in. He fumbles with his cap, starts to speak, clears throat, looks everywhere but at Ruth. Finally.*)

WALTER (*to Ruth*): I need some money for carfare.

RUTH (*looks at him, then warms; teasing, but tenderly*): Fifty cents? (*She goes to her bag and gets money.*) Here—take a taxi!

(*Walter exits. Mama enters. She is a woman in her early sixties, full-bodied and strong. She is one of those women of a certain grace and beauty who wear it so unobtrusively that it takes a while to notice. Her dark brown face is surrounded by the total whiteness of her hair, and, being a woman who has adjusted to many things in life and overcome many more, her face is full of strength. She has, we can see, wit and faith of a kind that keep her eyes lit and full of interest and expectancy. She is, in a word, a beautiful woman. Her bearing is perhaps most like the noble bearing of the women of the Hereros of Southwest Africa—rather as if she imagines that as she walks she still bears a basket or a vessel upon her head. Her speech, on the other hand, is*) *as careless as her carriage is precise—she is inclined to slur everything—but her voice is perhaps not so much quiet as simply soft.*)

MAMA: Who that 'round here slamming doors at this hour?

(*She crosses through the room, goes to the window, opens it, and brings in a feeble little plant growing doggedly in a small pot on the window sill. She feels the dirt and puts it back out.*)

RUTH: That was Walter Lee. He and Bennie was at it again.

MAMA: My children and they tempers. Lord, if this little old plant don't get more sun than it's been getting it ain't never going to see spring again. (*She turns from the window.*) What's the matter with you this morning, Ruth? You looks right peaked. You aiming to iron all them things? Leave some for me. I'll get to 'em this afternoon. Bennie honey, it's too drafty for you to be sitting 'round half dressed. Where's your robe?

BENEATHA: In the cleaners.

MAMA: Well, go get mine and put it on.

BENEATHA: I'm not cold, Mama, honest.

MAMA: I know—but you so thin . . .

BENEATHA (*irritably*): Mama, I'm not cold.

MAMA (*seeing the make-down bed as Travis has left it*): Lord have mercy, look at that poor bed. Bless his heart—he tries, don't he?

(*She moves to the bed Travis has sloppily made up.*)

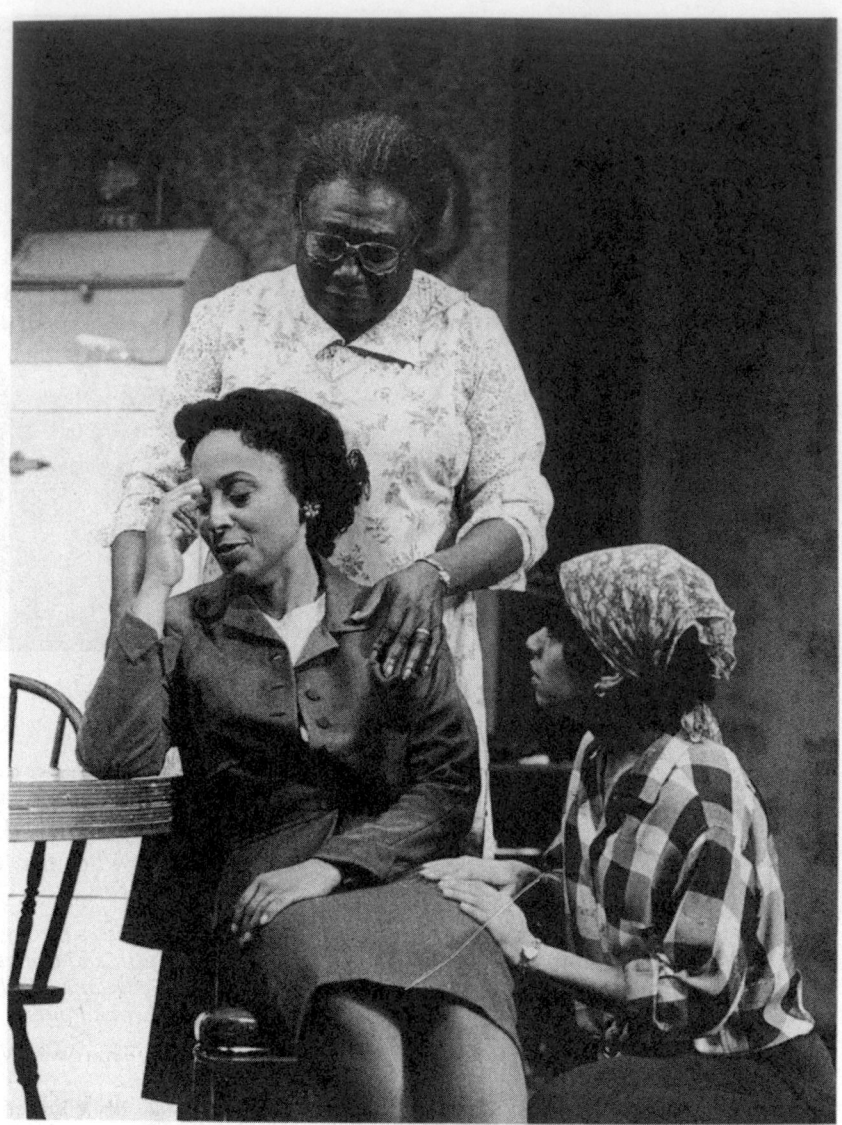

Ester Rolle as Lena Younger comforts her daughter-in-law Ruth in the Huntington Theatre Company's 1994 production of *A Raisin in the Sun*. Also in the scene are Marguerite Hannah as Ruth and B. W. Gonzalez as Beneatha.

RUTH: No—he don't half try at all 'cause he knows you going to come along behind him and fix everything. That's just how come he don't know how to do nothing right now—you done spoiled that boy so.

MAMA (*folding bedding*): Well—he's a little boy. Ain't supposed to know 'bout housekeeping. My baby, that's what he is. What you fix for his breakfast this morning?

RUTH (*angrily*): I feed my son, Lena!

MAMA: I ain't meddling—(*Under breath; busybodyish.*) I just noticed all last week he had cold cereal, and when it starts getting this chilly in the fall a child ought to have some hot grits or something when he goes out in the cold—

RUTH (*furious*): I gave him hot oats—is that all right!

MAMA: I ain't meddling. (*Pause.*) Put a lot of nice butter on it? (*Ruth shoots her an angry look and does not reply.*) He likes lots of butter.

RUTH (*exasperated*): Lena—

MAMA (*To Beneatha. Mama is inclined to wander conversationally sometimes.*): What was you and your brother fussing 'bout this morning?

BENEATHA: It's not important, Mama.

(*She gets up and goes to look out at the bathroom, which is apparently free, and she picks up her towels and rushes out.*)

MAMA: What was they fighting about?

RUTH: Now you know as well as I do.

MAMA (*shaking her head*): Brother still worrying hisself sick about that money?

RUTH: You know he is.

MAMA: You had breakfast?

RUTH: Some coffee.

MAMA: Girl, you better start eating and looking after yourself better. You almost thin as Travis.

RUTH: Lena—

MAMA: Un-hunh?

RUTH: What are you going to do with it?

MAMA: Now don't you start, child. It's too early in the morning to be talking about money. It ain't Christian.

RUTH: It's just that he got his heart set on that store—

MAMA: You mean that liquor store that Willy Harris want him to invest in?

RUTH: Yes—

MAMA: We ain't no business people, Ruth. We just plain working folks.

RUTH: Ain't nobody business people till they go into business. Walter Lee say colored people ain't never going to start getting ahead till they start gambling on some different kinds of things in the world— investments and things.

MAMA: What done got into you, girl? Walter Lee done finally sold you on investing.

RUTH: No. Mama, something is happening between Walter and me. I don't know what it is—but he needs something—something I can't give him anymore. He needs this chance, Lena.

MAMA (*frowning deeply*): But liquor, honey—

RUTH: Well—like Walter say—I spec people going to always be drinking themselves some liquor.

MAMA: Well—whether they drinks it or not ain't none of my business. But whether I go into business selling it to 'em *is*, and I don't want that on my ledger this late in life. (*Stopping suddenly and studying her daughter-in-law.*) Ruth Younger, what's the matter with you today? You look like you could fall over right there.

RUTH: I'm tired.

MAMA: Then you better stay home from work today.

RUTH: I can't stay home. She'd be calling up the agency and screaming at them, "My girl didn't come in today—send me somebody! My girl didn't come in!" Oh, she just have a fit . . .

MAMA: Well, let her have it. I'll just call her up and say you got the flu—

RUTH (*laughing*): Why the flu?

MAMA: 'Cause it sounds respectable to 'em. Something white people get, too. They know 'bout the flu. Otherwise they think you been cut up or something when you tell 'em you sick.

RUTH: I got to go in. We need the money.

MAMA: Somebody would of thought my children done all but starved to death the way they talk about money here late. Child, we got a great big old check coming tomorrow.

RUTH (*sincerely, but also self-righteously*): Now that's your money. It ain't got nothing to do with me. We all feel like that—Walter and Bennie and me—even Travis.

MAMA (*thoughtfully, and suddenly very far away*): Ten thousand dollars—

RUTH: Sure is wonderful.

MAMA: Ten thousand dollars.

RUTH: You know what you should do, Miss Lena? You should take yourself a trip somewhere. To Europe or South America or someplace—

MAMA (*throwing up her hands at the thought*): Oh, child!

RUTH: I'm serious. Just pack up and leave! Go on away and enjoy yourself some. Forget about the family and have yourself a ball for once in your life—

MAMA (*drily*): You sound like I'm just about ready to die. Who'd go with me? What I look like wandering 'round Europe by myself?

RUTH: Shoot—these here rich white women do it all the time. They don't think nothing of packing up they suitcases and piling on one of them big steamships and—swoosh!—they gone, child.

MAMA: Something always told me I wasn't no rich white woman.

RUTH: Well—what are you going to do with it then?

MAMA: I ain't rightly decided. (*Thinking. She speaks now with emphasis.*) Some of it got to be put away for Beneatha and her schoolin'—and ain't nothing going to touch that part of it. Nothing. (*She waits several seconds, trying to make up her mind about something, and looks at Ruth a little tentatively before going on.*) Been thinking that we maybe could meet the notes on a little old two-story somewhere, with a yard where Travis could play in the summertime, if we use part of the insurance for a down payment and everybody kind of pitch in. I could maybe take on a little day work again, few days a week—

RUTH (*studying her mother-in-law furtively and concentrating on her ironing, anxious to encourage without seeming to*): Well, Lord knows, we've put enough rent into this here rat trap to pay for four houses by now . . .

MAMA (*looking up at the words "rat trap" and then looking around and leaning back and sighing—in a suddenly reflective mood—*): "Rat trap"—yes, that's all it is. (*Smiling.*) I remember just as well the day me and Big Walter moved in here. Hadn't been married but two weeks and wasn't planning on living here no more than a year. (*She shakes her head at the dissolved dream.*) We was going to set away, little by little, don't you know, and buy a little place out in Morgan Park. We had even picked out the house. (*Chuckling a little.*) Looks right dumpy today. But Lord, child, you should know, all the dreams I had 'bout buying that house and fixing it up and making me a little garden in the back—(*She waits and stops smiling.*) And didn't none of it happen.

(*Dropping her hands in a futile gesture.*)

RUTH (*keeps her head down, ironing*): Yes, life can be a barrel of disappointments, sometimes.

MAMA: Honey, Big Walter would come in here some nights back then and slump down on that couch there and just look at the rug, and look at me and look at the rug and then back at me—and I'd know he was down then . . . really down. (*After a second very long and thoughtful pause; she is seeing back to times that only she can see.*) And then, Lord, when I lost that baby—little Claude—I almost thought I was going to lose Big Walter too. Oh, that man grieved hisself! He was one man to love his children.

RUTH: Ain't nothin' can tear at you like losin' your baby.

MAMA: I guess that's how come that man finally worked hisself to death like he done. Like he was fighting his own war with this here world that took his baby from him.

RUTH: He sure was a fine man, all right. I always liked Mr. Younger.

MAMA: Crazy 'bout his children! God knows there was plenty wrong with Walter Younger—hard-headed, mean, kind of wild with women—plenty wrong with him. But he sure loved his children. Always wanted them to have something—be something. That's where Brother gets all these notions, I reckon. Big Walter used to say, he'd get right wet in the eyes sometimes, lean his head back with the water standing in his eyes and say, "Seem like God didn't see fit to give the black man nothing but dreams—but He did give us children to make them dreams seem worthwhile." (*She smiles.*) He could talk like that, don't you know.

RUTH: Yes, he sure could. He was a good man, Mr. Younger.

MAMA: Yes, a fine man—just couldn't never catch up with his dreams, that's all.

(*Beneatha comes in, brushing her hair and looking up to the ceiling, where the sound of a vacuum cleaner has started up.*)

BENEATHA: What could be so dirty on that woman's rugs that she has to vacuum them every single day?

RUTH: I wish certain young women 'round here who I could name would take inspiration about certain rugs in a certain apartment I could also mention.

BENEATHA (*shrugging*): How much cleaning can a house need, for Christ's sakes.

MAMA (*not liking the Lord's name used thus*): Bennie!

RUTH: Just listen to her—just listen!

BENEATHA: Oh, God!

MAMA: If you use the Lord's name just one more time—

BENEATHA (*a bit of a whine*): Oh, Mama—

RUTH: Fresh—just fresh as salt, this girl!

BENEATHA (*drily*): Well—if the salt loses its savor—

MAMA: Now that will do. I just ain't going to have you 'round here reciting the scriptures in vain—you hear me?

BENEATHA: How did I manage to get on everybody's wrong side by just walking into a room?

RUTH: If you weren't so fresh—

BENEATHA: Ruth, I'm twenty years old.

MAMA: What time you be home from school today?

BENEATHA: Kind of late. (*With enthusiasm.*) Madeline is going to start my guitar lessons today.

(*Mama and Ruth look up with the same expression.*)

MAMA: Your *what* kind of lessons?

BENEATHA: Guitar.

RUTH: Oh, Father!

MAMA: How come you done taken it in your mind to learn to play the guitar?

BENEATHA: I just want to, that's all.

MAMA (*smiling*): Lord, child, don't you know what to do with yourself? How long it going to be before you get tired of this now—like you got tired of that little play-acting group you joined last year? (*Looking at Ruth.*) And what was it the year before that?

RUTH: The horseback-riding club for which she bought that fifty-five-dollar riding habit that's been hanging in the closet ever since!

MAMA (*to Beneatha*): Why you got to flit so from one thing to another, baby?

BENEATHA (*sharply*): I just want to learn to play the guitar. Is there anything wrong with that?

MAMA: Ain't nobody trying to stop you. I just wonders sometimes why you has to flit so from one thing to another all the time. You ain't never done nothing with all that camera equipment you brought home—

BENEATHA: I don't flit! I—I experiment with different forms of expression—

RUTH: Like riding a horse?

BENEATHA: —People have to express themselves one way or another.

MAMA: What is it you want to express?

BENEATHA (*angrily*): Me! (*Mama and Ruth look at each other and burst into raucous laughter.*) Don't worry—I don't expect you to understand.

MAMA (*to change the subject*): Who you going out with tomorrow night?

BENEATHA (*with displeasure*): George Murchison again.

MAMA (*pleased*): Oh—you getting a little sweet on him?

RUTH: You ask me, this child ain't sweet on nobody but herself—(*Under breath.*) Express herself!

(*They laugh.*)

BENEATHA: Oh—I like George all right, Mama. I mean I like him enough to go out with him and stuff, but—

RUTH (*for devilment*): What does *and stuff* mean?

BENEATHA: Mind your own business.

MAMA: Stop picking at her now, Ruth. (*She chuckles—then a suspicious sudden look at her daughter as she turns in her chair for emphasis.*) What DOES it mean?

BENEATHA (*wearily*): Oh, I just mean I couldn't ever really be serious about George. He's—he's so shallow.

RUTH: Shallow—what do you mean he's shallow? He's *Rich!*

MAMA: Hush, Ruth.

BENEATHA: I know he's rich. He knows he's rich, too.

RUTH: Well—what other qualities a man got to have to satisfy you, little girl?

BENEATHA: You wouldn't even begin to understand. Anybody who married Walter could not possibly understand.

MAMA (*outraged*): What kind of way is that to talk about your brother?

BENEATHA: Brother is a flip—let's face it.

MAMA (*to Ruth, helplessly*): What's a flip?

RUTH (*glad to add kindling*): She's saying he's crazy.

BENEATHA: Not crazy. Brother isn't really crazy yet—he—he's an elaborate neurotic.

MAMA: Hush your mouth!

BENEATHA: As for George. Well. George looks good—he's got a beautiful car and he takes me to nice places and, as my sister-in-law says, he is probably the richest boy I will ever get to know and I even like him sometimes—but if the Youngers are sitting around waiting to see if their little Bennie is going to tie up the family with the Murchisons, they are wasting their time.

RUTH: You mean you wouldn't marry George Murchison if he asked you someday? That pretty, rich thing? Honey, I knew you was odd—

BENEATHA: No I would not marry him if all I felt for him was what I feel now. Besides, George's family wouldn't really like it.

MAMA: Why not?

BENEATHA: Oh, Mama—The Murchisons are honest-to-God-real-*live*-rich colored people, and the only people in the world who are more snobbish than rich white people are rich colored people. I thought everybody knew that. I've met Mrs. Murchison. She's a scene!

MAMA: You must not dislike people 'cause they well off, honey.

BENEATHA: Why not? It makes just as much sense as disliking people 'cause they are poor, and lots of people do that.

RUTH (*A wisdom-of-the-ages manner. To Mama.*): Well, she'll get over some of this—

BENEATHA: Get over it? What are you talking about, Ruth? Listen, I'm going to be a doctor. I'm not worried about who I'm going to marry yet—if I ever get married.

MAMA AND RUTH: *If!*

MAMA: Now, Bennie—

BENEATHA: Oh, I probably will . . . but first I'm going to be a doctor, and George, for one, still thinks that's pretty funny. I couldn't be bothered with that. I am going to be a doctor and everybody around here better understand that!

MAMA (*kindly*): 'Course you going to be a doctor, honey, God willing.

BENEATHA (*drily*): God hasn't got a thing to do with it.

MAMA: Beneatha—that just wasn't necessary.

BENEATHA: Well—neither is God. I get sick of hearing about God.

MAMA: Beneatha!

BENEATHA: I mean it! I'm just tired of hearing about God all the time. What has He got to do with anything? Does he pay tuition?

MAMA: You 'bout to get your fresh little jaw slapped!

RUTH: That's just what she needs, all right!

BENEATHA: Why? Why can't I say what I want to around here, like everybody else?

MAMA: It don't sound nice for a young girl to say things like that—you wasn't brought up that way. Me and your father went to trouble to get you and Brother to church every Sunday.

BENEATHA: Mama, you don't understand. It's all a matter of ideas, and God is just one idea I don't accept. It's not important. I am not going out and be immoral or commit crimes because I don't believe in God. I don't even think about it. It's just that I get tired of Him getting credit for all the things the human race achieves through its own stubborn effort. There simply is no blasted God—there is only man and it is *he* who makes miracles!

(*Mama absorbs this speech, studies her daughter and rises slowly and crosses to Beneatha and slaps her powerfully across the face. After, there is only silence and the daughter drops her eyes from her mother's face, and Mama is very tall before her.*)

MAMA: Now—you say after me, in my mother's house there is still God. (*There is a long pause and Beneatha stares at the floor wordlessly. Mama repeats the phrase with precision and cool emotion.*) In my mother's house there is still God.

BENEATHA: In my mother's house there is still God.

(*A long pause.*)

MAMA (*Walking away from Beneatha, too disturbed for triumphant posture. Stopping and turning back to her daughter.*): There are some ideas we ain't going to have in this house. Not long as I am at the head of this family.

BENEATHA: Yes, ma'am.

(*Mama walks out of the room.*)

RUTH (*almost gently, with profound understanding*): You think you a woman, Bennie—but you still a little girl. What you did was childish—so you got treated like a child.

BENEATHA: I see. (*Quietly.*) I also see that everybody thinks it's all right for Mama to be a tyrant. But all the tyranny in the world will never put a God in the heavens!

(*She picks up her books and goes out. Pause.*)

RUTH (*goes to Mama's door*): She said she was sorry.

MAMA (*coming out, going to her plant*): They frightens me, Ruth. My children.

RUTH: You got good children, Lena. They just a little off sometimes—but they're good.

MAMA: No—there's something come down between me and them that don't let us understand each other and

I don't know what it is. One done almost lost his mind thinking 'bout money all the time and the other done commence to talk about things I can't seem to understand in no form or fashion. What is it that's changing, Ruth?

RUTH (*soothingly, older than her years*): Now . . . you taking it all too seriously. You just got strong-willed children and it takes a strong woman like you to keep 'em in hand.

MAMA (*looking at her plant and sprinkling a little water on it*): They spirited all right, my children. Got to admit they got spirit—Bennie and Walter. Like this little old plant that ain't never had enough sunshine or nothing—and look at it . . .

(*She has her back to Ruth, who has had to stop ironing and lean against something and put the back of her hand to her forehead.*)

RUTH (*trying to keep Mama from noticing*): You . . . sure . . . loves that little old thing, don't you? . . .

MAMA: Well, I always wanted me a garden like I used to see sometimes at the back of the houses down home. This plant is close as I ever got to having one. (*She looks out of the window as she replaces the plant.*) Lord, ain't nothing as dreary as the view from this window on a dreary day, is there? Why ain't you singing this morning, Ruth? Sing that "No Ways Tired." That song always lifts me up so—(*She turns at last to see that Ruth has slipped quietly to the floor, in a state of semiconsciousness.*) Ruth! Ruth honey—what's the matter with you . . . Ruth!

Scene II

(*It is the following morning; a Saturday morning, and house cleaning is in progress at the Youngers'. Furniture has been shoved hither and yon and Mama is giving the kitchen-area walls a washing down. Beneatha, in dungarees, with a handkerchief tied around her face, is spraying insecticide into the cracks in the walls. As they work, the radio is on and a Southside disk jockey program is inappropriately filling the house with a rather exotic saxophone blues. Travis, the sole idle one, is leaning on his arms, looking out of the window.*)

TRAVIS: Grandmama, that stuff Bennie is using smells awful. Can I go downstairs, please?

MAMA: Did you get all them chores done already? I ain't seen you doing much.

TRAVIS: Yes'm—finished early. Where did Mama go this morning?

MAMA (*looking at Beneatha*): She had to go on a little errand.

(*The phone rings. Beneatha runs to answer it and reaches it before Walter, who has entered from bedroom.*)

TRAVIS: Where?

MAMA: To tend to her business.

BENEATHA: Haylo . . . (*Disappointed.*) Yes, he is. (*She tosses the phone to Walter, who barely catches it.*) It's Willie Harris again.

WALTER (*as privately as possible under Mama's gaze*): Hello, Willie. Did you get the papers from the lawyer? . . . No, not yet. I told you the mailman doesn't get here till ten-thirty . . . No, I'll come there . . . Yeah! Right away. (*He hangs up and goes for his coat.*)

BENEATHA: Brother, where did Ruth go?

WALTER (*as he exits*): How should I know!

TRAVIS: Aw come on, Grandma. Can I go outside?

MAMA: Oh, I guess so. You stay right in front of the house, though, and keep a good lookout for the postman.

TRAVIS: Yes'm. (*He darts into bedroom for stickball and bat, reenters, and sees Beneatha on her knees spraying under sofa with behind upraised. He edges closer to the target, takes aim, and lets her have it. She screams.*) Leave them poor little cockroaches alone, they ain't bothering you none! (*He runs as she swings the spraygun at him viciously and playfully.*) Grandma! Grandma!

MAMA: Look out there, girl, before you be spilling some of that stuff on that child!

TRAVIS (*safely behind the bastion of Mama*): That's right—look out, now! (*He exits.*)

BENEATHA (*drily*): I can't imagine that it would hurt him—it has never hurt the roaches.

MAMA: Well, little boys' hides ain't as tough as Southside roaches. You better get over there behind the bureau. I seen one marching out of there like Napoleon yesterday.

BENEATHA: There's really only one way to get rid of them, Mama—

MAMA: How?

BENEATHA: Set fire to this building! Mama, where did Ruth go?

MAMA (*looking at her with meaning*): To the doctor, I think.

BENEATHA: The doctor? What's the matter? (*They exchange glances.*) You don't think—

MAMA (*with her sense of drama*): Now I ain't saying what I think. But I ain't never been wrong 'bout a woman neither.

(*The phone rings.*)

BENEATHA (*at the phone*): Hay-lo . . . (*Pause, and a moment of recognition.*) Well—when did you get back! . . . And how was it? . . . Of course I've missed you—in my way . . . This morning? No . . . house cleaning and all that and Mama hates it if I let people come over when the house is like this . . . You *have?* Well, that's different . . . What is it—Oh, what the hell, come on over . . . Right, see you then. *Arrivederci.*

(*She hangs up.*)

MAMA (*who has listened vigorously, as is her habit*): Who is that you inviting over here with this house looking like this? You ain't got the pride you was born with!

BENEATHA: Asagai doesn't care how houses look, Mama—he's an intellectual.

MAMA: *Who?*

BENEATHA: Asagai—Joseph Asagai. He's an African boy I met on campus. He's been studying in Canada all summer.

MAMA: What's his name?

BENEATHA: Asagai, Joseph. Ah-sah-guy . . . He's from Nigeria.

MAMA: Oh, that's the little country that was founded by slaves way back . . .

BENEATHA: No, Mama—that's Liberia.

MAMA: I don't think I never met no African before.

BENEATHA: Well, do me a favor and don't ask him a whole lot of ignorant questions about Africans. I mean, do they wear clothes and all that—

MAMA: Well, now, I guess if you think we so ignorant 'round here maybe you shouldn't bring your friends here—

BENEATHA: It's just that people ask such crazy things. All anyone seems to know about when it comes to Africa is Tarzan—

MAMA (*indignantly*): Why should I know anything about Africa?

BENEATHA: Why do you give money at church for the missionary work?

MAMA: Well, that's to help save people.

BENEATHA: You mean save them from *heathenism*—

MAMA (*innocently*): Yes.

BENEATHA: I'm afraid they need more salvation from the British and the French.

(*Ruth comes in forlornly and pulls off her coat with dejection. They both turn to look at her.*)

RUTH (*dispiritedly*): Well, I guess from all the happy faces—everybody knows.

BENEATHA: You pregnant?

MAMA: Lord have mercy, I sure hope it's a little old girl. Travis ought to have a sister.

(*Beneatha and Ruth give her a hopeless look for this grandmotherly enthusiasm.*)

BENEATHA: How far along are you?

RUTH: Two months.

BENEATHA: Did you mean to? I mean did you plan it or was it an accident?

MAMA: What do you know about planning or not planning?

BENEATHA: Oh, Mama.

RUTH (*wearily*): She's twenty years old, Lena.

BENEATHA: Did you plan it, Ruth?

RUTH: Mind your own business.

BENEATHA: It is my business—where is he going to live, on the *roof*? (*There is silence following the remark as the three women react to the sense of it.*) Gee—I

didn't mean that, Ruth, honest. Gee, I don't feel like that at all. I—I think it is wonderful.

RUTH (*dully*): Wonderful.

BENEATHA: Yes—really.

MAMA (*looking at Ruth, worried*): Doctor say everything going to be all right?

RUTH (*far away*): Yes—she says everything is going to be fine . . .

MAMA (*immediately suspicious*): "She"—What doctor you went to?

(*Ruth folds over, near hysteria.*)

MAMA (*worriedly hovering over Ruth*): Ruth honey— what's the matter with you—you sick?

(*Ruth has her fists clenched on her thighs and is fighting hard to suppress a scream that seems to be rising in her.*)

BENEATHA: What's the matter with her, Mama?

MAMA (*working her fingers in Ruth's shoulders to relax her*): She be all right. Women gets right depressed sometimes when they get her way. (*Speaking softly, expertly, rapidly.*) Now you just relax. That's right . . . just lean back, don't think 'bout nothing at all . . . nothing at all—

RUTH: I'm all right . . .

(*The glassy-eyed look melts and then she collapses into a fit of heavy sobbing. The bell rings.*)

BENEATHA: Oh, my God—that must be Asagai.

MAMA (*to Ruth*): Come on now, honey. You need to lie down and rest awhile . . . then have some nice hot food.

(*They exit, Ruth's weight on her mother-in-law. Beneatha, herself profoundly disturbed, opens the door to admit a rather dramatic-looking young man with a large package.*)

ASAGAI: Hello, Alaiyo—

BENEATHA (*holding the door open and regarding him with pleasure*): Hello . . . (*Long pause.*) Well—come in. And please excuse everything. My mother was very upset about my letting anyone come here with the place like this.

ASAGAI (*coming into the room*): You look disturbed too . . . Is something wrong?

BENEATHA (*still at the door, absently*): Yes . . . we've all got acute ghetto-itus. (*She smiles and comes toward him, finding a cigarette and sitting.*) So—sit down! No! Wait! (*She whips the spraygun off the sofa where she had left it and puts the cushions back. At last perches on arm of sofa. He sits.*) So, how was Canada?

ASAGAI (*a sophisticate*): Canadian.

BENEATHA (*looking at him*): Asagai, I'm very glad you are back.

ASAGAI (*looking back at her in turn*): Are you really?

BENEATHA: Yes—very.

ASAGAI: Why?—you were quite glad when I went away. What happened?

BENEATHA: You went away.

ASAGAI: Ahhhhhhhh.

BENEATHA: Before—you wanted to be so serious before there was time.

ASAGAI: How much time must there be before one knows what one feels?

BENEATHA (*Stalling this particular conversation. Her hands pressed together, in a deliberately childish gesture.*): What did you bring me?

ASAGAI (*handing her the package*): Open it and see.

BENEATHA (*eagerly opening the package and drawing out some records and the colorful robes of a Nigerian woman*): Oh, Asagai! . . . You got them for me! . . . How beautiful . . . and the records too! (*She lifts out the robes and runs to the mirror with them and holds the drapery up in front of herself.*)

ASAGAI (*coming to her at the mirror*): I shall have to teach you how to drape it properly. (*He flings the material about her for the moment and stands back to look at her.*) Ah—Oh-pay-gay-day, oh-gbah-mu-shay. (*A Yoruba exclamation for admiration.*) You wear it well . . . very well . . . mutilated hair and all.

BENEATHA (*turning suddenly*): My hair—what's wrong with my hair?

ASAGAI (*shrugging*): Were you born with it like that?

BENEATHA (*reaching up to touch it*): No . . . of course not.

(*She looks back to the mirror, disturbed.*)

ASAGAI (*smiling*): How then?

BENEATHA: You know perfectly well how . . . as crinkly as yours . . . that's how.

ASAGAI: And it is ugly to you that way?

BENEATHA (*quickly*): Oh, no—not ugly . . . (*More slowly, apologetically.*) But it's so hard to manage when it's, well—raw.

ASAGAI: And so to accommodate that—you mutilate it every week?

BENEATHA: It's not mutilation!

ASAGAI (*laughing aloud at her seriousness*): Oh . . . please! I am only teasing you because you are so very serious about these things. (*He stands back from her and folds his arms across his chest as he watches her pulling at her hair and frowning in the mirror.*) Do you remember the first time you met me at school? . . . (*He laughs.*) You came up to me and you said—and I thought you were the most serious little thing I had ever seen—you said: (*He imitates her.*) "Mr. Asagai—I want very much to talk with you. About Africa. You see, Mr. Asagai, I am looking for my *identity!*"

(*He laughs.*)

BENEATHA (*turning to him, not laughing*): Yes—

(*Her face is quizzical, profoundly disturbed.*)

ASAGAI (*still teasing and reaching out and taking her face in his hands and turning her profile to him*): Well . . . it is true that this is not so much a profile of a Hollywood queen as perhaps a queen of the Nile—(*A mock dismissal of the importance of the question.*) But what does it matter? Assimilationism is so popular in your country.

BENEATHA (*wheeling, passionately, sharply*): I am not an assimilationist!

ASAGAI (*the protest hangs in the room for a moment and Asagai studies her, his laughter fading*): Such a serious one. (*There is a pause.*) So—you like the robes? You must take excellent care of them—they are from my sister's personal wardrobe.

BENEATHA (*with incredulity*): You—you sent all the way home—for me?

ASAGAI (*with charm*): For you—I would do much more . . . Well, that is what I came for. I must go.

BENEATHA: Will you call me Monday?

ASAGAI: Yes . . . We have a great deal to talk about. I mean about identity and time and all that.

BENEATHA: Time?

ASAGAI: Yes. About how much time one needs to know what one feels.

BENEATHA: You see! You never understood that there is more than one kind of feeling which can exist between a man and a woman—or, at least, there should be.

ASAGAI (*shaking his head negatively but gently*): No. Between a man and a woman there need be only one kind of feeling. I have that for you . . . Now even . . . right this moment . . .

BENEATHA: I know—and by itself—it won't do. I can find that anywhere.

ASAGAI: For a woman it should be enough.

BENEATHA: I know—because that's what it says in all the novels that men write. But it isn't. Go ahead and laugh—but I'm not interested in being someone's little episode in America or—(*with feminine vengeance*)—one of them! (*Asagai has burst into laughter again.*) That's funny as hell, huh!

ASAGAI: It's just that every American girl I have known has said that to me. White—black—in this you are all the same. And the same speech, too!

BENEATHA (*angrily*): Yuk, yuk, yuk!

ASAGAI: It's how you can be sure that the world's most liberated women are not liberated at all. You all talk about it too much!

(*Mama enters and is immediately all social charm because of the presence of a guest.*)

BENEATHA: Oh—Mama—this is Mr. Asagai.

MAMA: How do you do?

ASAGAI (*total politeness to an elder*): How do you do, Mrs. Younger. Please forgive me for coming at such an outrageous hour on a Saturday.

MAMA: Well, you are quite welcome. I just hope you understand that our house don't always look like this. (*Chatterish.*) You must come again. I would love to hear all about—(*not sure of the name*)—your country. I think it's so sad the way our American Negroes don't know nothing about Africa 'cept Tarzan and all that. And all that money they pour into these churches when they ought to be helping you people over there drive out them French and Englishmen done taken away your land.

(*The mother flashes a slightly superior look at her daughter upon completion of the recitation.*)

ASAGAI (*taken aback by this sudden and acutely unrelated expression of sympathy*): Yes . . . yes . . .

MAMA (*smiling at him suddenly and relaxing and looking him over*): How many miles is it from here to where you come from?

ASAGAI: Many thousands.

MAMA (*looking at him as she would Walter*): I bet you don't half look after yourself, being away from your mama either. I spec you better come 'round here from time to time to get yourself some decent home-cooked meals . . .

ASAGAI (*moved*): Thank you. Thank you very much. (*They are all quiet, then*—) Well . . . I must go. I will call you Monday, Alaiyo.

MAMA: What's that he call you?

ASAGAI: Oh—"Alaiyo." I hope you don't mind. It is what you would call a nickname, I think. It is a Yoruba word. I am a Yoruba.

MAMA (*looking at Beneatha*): I—I thought he was from—(*Uncertain.*)

ASAGAI (*understanding*): Nigeria is my country. Yoruba is my tribal origin—

BENEATHA: You didn't tell us what Alaiyo means . . . for all I know, you might be calling me Little Idiot or something . . .

ASAGAI: Well . . . let me see . . . I do not know how just to explain it . . . The sense of a thing can be so different when it changes languages.

BENEATHA: You're evading.

ASAGAI: No—really it is difficult . . . (*Thinking.*) It means . . . it means One for Whom Bread—Food—Is Not Enough. (*He looks at her.*) Is that all right?

BENEATHA (*understanding, softly*): Thank you.

MAMA (*looking from one to the other and not understanding any of it*): Well . . . that's nice . . . You must come see us again—Mr.——

ASAGAI: Ah-sah guy . . .

MAMA: Yes . . . Do come again.

ASAGAI: Good-bye.

(*He exits.*)

MAMA (*after him*): Lord, that's a pretty thing just went out here! (*Insinuatingly, to her daughter.*) Yes, I guess I see why we done commence to get so interested in Africa 'round here. Missionaries my aunt Jenny!

(*She exits.*)

BENEATHA: Oh, Mama! . . .

(*She picks up the Nigerian dress and holds it up to her in front of the mirror again. She sets the headdress on haphazardly and then notices her hair again and clutches at it and then replaces the headdress and frowns at herself. Then she starts to wriggle in front of*

the mirror as she thinks a Nigerian woman might. Travis enters and stands regarding her.*)

TRAVIS: What's the matter, girl, you cracking up?

BENEATHA: Shut up.

(*She pulls the headdress off and looks at herself in the mirror and clutches at her hair again and squinches her eyes as if trying to imagine something. Then, suddenly, she gets her raincoat and kerchief and hurriedly prepares for going out.*)

MAMA (*coming back into the room*): She's resting now. Travis, baby, run next door and ask Miss Johnson to please let me have a little kitchen cleanser. This here can is empty as Jacob's kettle.

TRAVIS: I just came in.

MAMA: Do as you told. (*He exits and she looks at her daughter.*) Where you going?

BENEATHA (*halting at the door*): To become a queen of the Nile!

(*She exits in a breathless blaze of glory. Ruth appears in the bedroom doorway.*)

MAMA: Who told you to get up?

RUTH: Ain't nothing wrong with me to be lying in no bed for. Where did Bennie go?

MAMA (*drumming her fingers*): Far as I could make out—to Egypt. (*Ruth just looks at her.*) What time is it getting to?

RUTH: Ten twenty. And the mailman going to ring that bell this morning just like he done every morning for the last umpteen years.

(*Travis comes in with the cleanser can.*)

TRAVIS: She say to tell you that she don't have much.

MAMA (*angrily*): Lord, some people I could name sure is tight-fisted! (*Directing her grandson.*) Mark two cans of cleanser down on the list there. If she that hard up for kitchen cleanser, I sure don't want to forget to get her none!

RUTH: Lena—maybe the woman is just short on cleanser—

MAMA (*not listening*):—Much baking powder as she done borrowed from me all these years, she could of done gone into the baking business!

(*The bell sounds suddenly and sharply and all three are stunned—serious and silent—mid-speech. In spite of all the other conversations and distractions of the morning, this is what they have been waiting for, even Travis, who looks helplessly from his mother to his grandmother. Ruth is the first to come to life again.*)

RUTH (*to Travis*): Get down them steps, boy!

(*Travis snaps to life and flies out to get the mail.*)

MAMA (*her eyes wide, her hand to her breast*): You mean it done really come?

RUTH (*excited*): Oh, Miss Lena!

MAMA (*collecting herself*): Well . . . I don't know what we all so excited about 'round here for. We known it was coming for months.

RUTH: That's a whole lot different from having it come and being able to hold it in your hands . . . a piece of paper worth ten thousand dollars . . . (*Travis bursts back into the room. He holds the envelope high above his head, like a little dancer, his face is radiant and he is breathless. He moves to his grandmother with sudden slow ceremony and puts the envelope into her hands. She accepts it, and then merely holds it and looks at it.*) Come on! Open it . . . Lord have mercy, I wish Walter Lee was here!

TRAVIS: Open it, Grandmama!

MAMA (*staring at it*): Now you all be quiet. It's just a check.

RUTH: Open it . . .

MAMA (*still staring at it*): Now don't act silly . . . We ain't never been no people to act silly 'bout no money—

RUTH (*swiftly*): We ain't never had none before—OPEN IT!

(*Mama finally makes a good strong tear and pulls out the thin blue slice of paper and inspects it closely. The boy and his mother study it raptly over Mama's shoulders.*)

MAMA: *Travis!* (*She is counting off with doubt.*) Is that the right number of zeros.

TRAVIS: Yes'm . . . ten thousand dollars. Gaalee, Grandmama, you rich.

MAMA (*She holds the check away from her, still looking at it. Slowly her face sobers into a mask of unhappiness.*): Ten thousand dollars. (*She hands it to Ruth.*) Put it away somewhere, Ruth. (*She does not look at Ruth; her eyes seem to be seeing something somewhere very far off.*) Ten thousand dollars they give you. Ten thousand dollars.

TRAVIS (*to his mother, sincerely*): What's the matter with Grandmama—don't she want to be rich?

RUTH (*distractedly*): You go on out and play now, baby. (*Travis exits. Mama starts wiping dishes absently, humming intently to herself. Ruth turns to her, with kind exasperation.*) You've gone and got yourself upset.

MAMA (*not looking at her*): I spec if it wasn't for you all . . . I would just put that money away or give it to the church or something.

RUTH: Now what kind of talk is that. Mr. Younger would just be plain mad if he could hear you talking foolish like that.

MAMA (*stopping and staring off*): Yes . . . he sure would. (*Sighing.*) We got enough to do with that money, all right. (*She halts then, and turns and looks at her daughter-in-law hard; Ruth avoids her eyes and Mama wipes her hands with finality and starts to speak firmly to Ruth.*) Where did you go today, girl?

RUTH: To the doctor.

MAMA (*impatiently*): Now, Ruth . . . you know better than that. Old Doctor Jones is strange enough in his way but there ain't nothing 'bout him make somebody slip and call him "she"—like you done this morning.

RUTH: Well, that's what happened—my tongue slipped.

MAMA: You went to see that woman, didn't you?

RUTH (*defensively, giving herself away*): What woman you talking about?

MAMA (*angrily*): That woman who—

(*Walter enters in great excitement.*)

WALTER: Did it come?

MAMA (*quietly*): Can't you give people a Christian greeting before you start asking about money?

WALTER (*to Ruth*): Did it come? (*Ruth unfolds the check and lays it quietly before him, watching him intently with thoughts of her own. Walter sits down and grasps it close and counts off the zeros.*) Ten thousand dollars—(*He turns suddenly, frantically to his mother and draws some papers out of his breast pocket.*) Mama—look. Old Willy Harris put everything on paper—

MAMA: Son—I think you ought to talk to your wife . . . I'll go on out and leave you alone if you want—

WALTER: I can talk to her later—Mama, look—

MAMA: Son—

WALTER: WILL SOMEBODY PLEASE LISTEN TO ME TODAY!

MAMA (*quietly*): I don't 'low no yellin' in this house, Walter Lee, and you know it—(*Walter stares at them in frustration and starts to speak several times.*) And there ain't going to be no investing in no liquor stores.

WALTER: But, Mama, you ain't even looked at it.

MAMA: I don't aim to have to speak on that again.

(*A long pause.*)

WALTER: You ain't looked at it and you don't aim to have to speak on that again? You ain't even looked at it and *you* have decided—(*Crumpling his papers.*) Well, *you* tell that to my boy tonight when you put him to sleep on the living room couch . . . (*Turning to Mama and speaking directly to her.*) Yeah—and tell it to my wife, Mama, tomorrow when she has to go out of here to look after somebody else's kids. And tell it to *me*, Mama, every time we need a new pair of curtains and I have to watch *you* go out and work in somebody's kitchen. Yeah, you tell me then!

(*Walter starts out.*)

RUTH: Where you going?

WALTER: I'm going out!

RUTH: Where?

WALTER: Just out of this house somewhere—

RUTH (*getting her coat*): I'll come too.

WALTER: I don't want you to come!

RUTH: I got something to talk to you about, Walter.

WALTER: That's too bad.

MAMA (*still quietly*): Walter Lee—(*She waits and he finally turns and looks at her.*) Sit down.

WALTER: I'm a grown man, Mama.

MAMA: Ain't nobody said you wasn't grown. But you still in my house and my presence. And as long as you are—you'll talk to your wife civil. Now sit down.

RUTH (*suddenly*): Oh, let him go on out and drink himself to death! He makes me sick to my stomach! (*She flings her coat against him and exits to bedroom.*)

WALTER (*violently flinging the coat after her*): And you turn mine too, baby! (*The door slams behind her.*) That was my biggest mistake—

MAMA (*still quietly*): Walter, what is the matter with you?

WALTER: Matter with me? Ain't nothing the matter with *me!*

MAMA: Yes there is. Something eating you up like a crazy man. Something more than me not giving you this money. The past few years I been watching it happen to you. You get all nervous acting and kind of wild in the eyes—(*Walter jumps up impatiently at her words.*) I said sit there now, I'm talking to you!

WALTER: Mama—I don't need no nagging at me today.

MAMA: Seem like you getting to a place where you always tied up in some kind of knot about something. But if anybody ask you 'bout it you just yell at 'em and bust out the house and go out and drink somewheres. Walter Lee, people can't live with that. Ruth's a good, patient girl in her way—but you getting to be too much. Boy, don't make the mistake of driving that girl away from you.

WALTER: Why—what she do for me?

MAMA: She loves you.

WALTER: Mama—I'm going out. I want to go off somewhere and be by myself for a while.

MAMA: I'm sorry 'bout your liquor store, son. It just wasn't the thing for us to do. That's what I want to tell you about—

WALTER: I got to go out, Mama—

(*He rises.*)

MAMA: It's dangerous, son.

WALTER: What's dangerous?

MAMA: When a man goes outside his home to look for peace.

WALTER (*beseechingly*): Then why can't there never be no peace in this house then?

MAMA: You done found it in some other house?

WALTER: No—there ain't no woman! Why do women always think there's a woman somewhere when a man gets restless. (*Picks up the check.*) Do you know what this money means to me? Do you know what this money can do for us? (*Puts it back.*) Mama—Mama—I want so many things . . .

MAMA: Yes, son—

WALTER: I want so many things that they are driving me kind of crazy . . . Mama—look at me.

MAMA: I'm looking at you. You a good-looking boy. You got a job, a nice wife, a fine boy and—

WALTER: A job. (*Looks at her.*) Mama, a job? I open and close car doors all day long. I drive a man around in his limousine and I say, "Yes, sir; no, sir; very good, sir; shall I take the Drive, sir?" Mama, that ain't no kind of job . . . that ain't nothing at all. (*Very quietly.*) Mama, I don't know if I can make you understand.

MAMA: Understand what, baby?

WALTER (*quietly*): Sometimes it's like I can see the future stretched out in front of me—just plain as day. The future, Mama. Hanging over there at the edge of my days. Just waiting for me—a big, looming blank space—full of *nothing*. Just waiting for *me*. But it don't have to be. (*Pause. Kneeling beside her chair.*) Mama—sometimes when I'm downtown and I pass them cool, quiet-looking restaurants where them white boys are sitting back and talking 'bout things . . . sitting there turning deals worth millions of dollars . . . sometimes I see guys don't look much older than me—

MAMA: Son—how come you talk so much 'bout money?

WALTER (*with immense passion*): Because it is life, Mama!

MAMA (*quietly*): Oh—(*Very quietly.*) So now it's life. Money is life. Once upon a time freedom used to be life—now it's money. I guess the world really do change . . .

WALTER: No—it was always money, Mama. We just didn't know about it.

MAMA: No . . . something has changed. (*She looks at him.*) You something new, boy. In my time we was worried about not being lynched and getting to the North if we could and how to stay alive and still have a pinch of dignity too . . . Now here come you and Beneatha—talking 'bout things we ain't never even thought about hardly, me and your daddy. You ain't satisfied or proud of nothing we done. I mean that you had a home, that we kept you out of trouble till you was grown, that you don't have to ride to work on the back of nobody's streetcar—You my children—but how different we done become.

WALTER (*A long beat. He pats her hand and gets up.*): You just don't understand, Mama, you just don't understand.

MAMA: Son—do you know your wife is expecting another baby? (*Walter stands, stunned, and absorbs what his mother has said.*) That's what she wanted to talk to you about. (*Walter sinks down into a chair.*) This ain't for me to be telling—but you ought to know. (*She waits.*) I think Ruth is thinking 'bout getting rid of that child.

WALTER (*slowly understanding*): —No—no—Ruth wouldn't do that.

MAMA: When the world gets ugly enough—a woman will do anything for her family. *The part that's already living.*

WALTER: You don't know Ruth, Mama, if you think she would do that.

(*Ruth opens the bedroom door and stands there a little limp.*)

RUTH (*beaten*): Yes I would too, Walter. (*Pause.*) I gave her a five-dollar down payment.

(*There is total silence as the man stares at his wife and the mother stares at her son.*)

MAMA (*presently*): Well—(*Tightly.*) Well—son, I'm waiting to hear you say something . . . (*She waits.*) I'm waiting to hear how you be your father's son. Be the man he was . . . (*Pause. The silence shouts.*) Your wife says she going to destroy your child. And I'm waiting to hear you talk like him and say we a people who give children life, not who destroys them—(*She rises.*) I'm waiting to see you stand up and look like your daddy and say we done give up one baby to poverty and that we ain't going to give up nary another one . . . I'm waiting.

WALTER: Ruth—(*He can say nothing.*)

MAMA: If you a son of mine, tell her! (*Walter picks up his keys and his coat and walks out. She continues, bitterly.*) You . . . you are a disgrace to your father's memory. Somebody get me my hat!

ACT II • Scene I

(*Time: Later the same day.*)

(*At rise: Ruth is ironing again. She has the radio going. Presently Beneatha's bedroom door opens and Ruth's mouth falls and she puts down the iron in fascination.*)

RUTH: What have we got on tonight!

BENEATHA (*emerging grandly from the doorway so that we can see her thoroughly robed in the costume Asagai brought*): You are looking at what a well-dressed Nigerian woman wears—(*She parades for Ruth, her hair completely hidden by the headdress; she is coquettishly fanning herself with an ornate oriental fan, mistakenly more like Butterfly° than any Nigerian that ever was.*) Isn't it beautiful? (*She promenades to the radio and, with an arrogant flourish, turns off the good loud blues that is playing.*) Enough of this assimilationist junk! (*Ruth follows her with her eyes as she goes to the phonograph and puts on a record and turns and waits ceremoniously for the music to come up. Then, with a shout—*) OCOMOGOSIAY!

(*Ruth jumps. The music comes up, a lovely Nigerian melody. Beneatha listens, enraptured, her eyes far away—"back to the past." She begins to dance. Ruth is dumfounded.*)

RUTH: What kind of dance is that?

BENEATHA: A folk dance.

RUTH (*Pearl Bailey*): What kind of folks do that, honey?

BENEATHA: It's from Nigeria. It's a dance of welcome.

RUTH: Who you welcoming?

BENEATHA: The men back to the village.

RUTH: Where they been?

BENEATHA: How should I know—out hunting or something. Anyway, they are coming back now . . .

RUTH: Well, that's good.

BENEATHA (*with the record*): Alundi, alundi
Alundi alunya
Jop pu a jeepua
Ang gu sooooooooooo

Ai yai yue . . .
Ayehaye—alundi . . .

Butterfly: Madame Butterfly, the title character in the opera by Puccini, set in Japan.

(*Walter comes in during this performance; he has obviously been drinking. He leans against the door heavily and watches his sister, at first with distaste. Then his eyes look off— "back to the past"—as he lifts both his fists to the roof, screaming.*)

WALTER: YEAH . . . AND ETHIOPIA STRETCH FORTH HER HANDS AGAIN! . . .

RUTH (*drily, looking at him*): Yes—and Africa sure is claiming her own tonight. (*She gives them both up and starts ironing again.*)

WALTER (*all in a drunken, dramatic shout*): Shut up! . . . I'm digging them drums . . . them drums move me! . . . (*He makes his weaving way to his wife's face and leans in close to her.*) In my *heart of hearts*—(*he thumps his chest*)—I am much warrior!

RUTH (*without even looking up*): In your heart of hearts you are much drunkard.

WALTER (*coming away from her and starting to wander around the room, shouting*): Me and Jomo . . . (*Intently, in his sister's face. She has stopped dancing to watch him in this unknown mood.*) That's my man, Kenyatta. (*Shouting and thumping his chest.*) FLAMING SPEAR! HOT DAMN! (*He is suddenly in possession of an imaginary spear and actively spearing enemies all over the room.*) OCOMOGOSIAY . . .

BENEATHA (*to encourage Walter, thoroughly caught up with this side of him*): OCOMOGOSIAY, FLAMING SPEAR!

WALTER: THE LION IS WAKING . . . OWIMOWEH! (*He pulls his shirt open and leaps up on the table and gestures with his spear.*)

BENEATHA: OWIMOWEH!

WALTER (*On the table, very far gone, his eyes pure glass sheets. He sees what we cannot, that he is a leader of his people, a great chief, a descendant of Chaka, and that the hour to march has come.*): Listen, my black brothers—

BENEATHA: OCOMOGOSIAY!

WALTER:—Do you hear the waters rushing against the shores of the coastlands—

BENEATHA: OCOMOGOSIAY!

WALTER:—Do you hear the screeching of the cocks in yonder hills beyond where the chiefs meet in council for the coming of the mighty war—

BENEATHA: OCOMOGOSIAY!

(*And now the lighting shifts subtly to suggest the world of Walter's imagination, and the mood shifts from pure comedy. It is the inner Walter speaking: the Southside chauffeur has assumed an unexpected majesty.*)

WALTER:—Do you hear the beating of the wings of the birds flying low over the mountains and the low places of our land—

BENEATHA: OCOMOGOSIAY!

WALTER:—Do you hear the singing of the women singing the war songs of our fathers to the babies in the great houses? Singing the sweet war songs! (*The doorbell rings.*) OH, DO YOU HEAR, MY *BLACK* BROTHERS!

Sean "P. Diddy" Combs as Walter in the 2004 Broadway production of *A Raisin in the Sun* at the Royale Theater.

BENEATHA (*completely gone*): We hear you, Flaming Spear—

(*Ruth shuts off the phonograph and opens the door. George Murchison enters.*)

WALTER: Telling us to prepare for the GREATNESS OF THE TIME! (*Lights back to normal. He turns and sees George.*) Black Brother!

(*He extends his hand for the fraternal clasp.*)

GEORGE: Black Brother, hell!

RUTH (*having had enough, and embarrassed for the family*): Beneatha, you got company—what's the matter with you? Walter Lee Younger, get down off that table and stop acting like a fool . . .

(*Walter comes down off the table suddenly and makes a quick exit to the bathroom.*)

RUTH: He's had a little to drink . . . I don't know what her excuse is.

GEORGE (*to Beneatha*): Look honey, we're going *to* the theater—we're not going to be *in* it . . . so go change, huh?

(*Beneatha looks at him and slowly, ceremoniously, lifts her hands and pulls off the headdress. Her hair is close-cropped and unstraightened. George freezes mid-sentence and Ruth's eyes all but fall out of her head.*)

GEORGE: What in the name of—

RUTH (*touching Beneatha's hair*): Girl, you done lost your natural mind? Look at your head!

GEORGE: What have you done to your head—I mean your hair!

BENEATHA: Nothing—except cut it off.

RUTH: Now that's the truth—it's what ain't been done to it! You expect this boy to go out with you with your head all nappy like that?

BENEATHA (*looking at George*): That's up to George. If he's ashamed of his heritage—

GEORGE: Oh, don't be so proud of yourself, Bennie—just because you look eccentric.

BENEATHA: How can something that's natural be eccentric?

GEORGE: That's what being eccentric means—being natural. Get dressed.

BENEATHA: I don't like that, George.

RUTH: Why must you and your brother make an argument out of everything people say?

BENEATHA: Because I hate assimilationist Negroes!

RUTH: Will somebody please tell me what assimila-whoever means!

GEORGE: Oh, it's just a college girl's way of calling people Uncle Toms—but that isn't what it means at all.

RUTH: Well, what does it mean?

BENEATHA (*cutting George off and staring at him as she replies to Ruth*): It means someone who is willing to give up his own culture and submerge himself completely in the dominant, and in this case *oppressive* culture!

GEORGE: Oh, dear, dear, dear! Here we go! A lecture on the African past! On our Great West African Heritage! In one second we will hear all about the great Ashanti empires; the great Songhay civilizations; and the great sculpture of Benin—and then some poetry in the Bantu—and the whole monologue will end with the word *heritage*! (*Nastily.*) Let's face it, baby, your heritage is nothing but a bunch of raggedy-assed spirituals and some grass huts!

BENEATHA: GRASS HUTS! (*Ruth crosses to her and forcibly pushes her toward the bedroom.*) See there . . . you are standing there in your splendid ignorance talking about people who were the first to smelt iron on the face of the earth! (*Ruth is pushing her through the door.*) The Ashanti were performing surgical operations when the English—(*Ruth pulls the door to, with Beneatha on the other side, and smiles graciously at George. Beneatha opens the door and shouts the end of the sentence defiantly at George*)—were still tatooing themselves with blue dragons! (*She goes back inside.*)

RUTH: Have a seat, George. (*They both sit. Ruth folds her hands rather primly on her lap, determined to demonstrate the civilization of the family.*) Warm, ain't it? I mean for September. (*Pause.*) Just like they always say about Chicago weather: If it's too hot or cold for you, just wait a minute and it'll change. (*She smiles happily at this cliché of clichés.*) Everybody say it's got to do with them bombs and things they keep setting off. (*Pause.*) Would you like a nice cold beer?

GEORGE: No, thank you. I don't care for beer. (*He looks at his watch.*) I hope she hurries up.

RUTH: What time is the show?

GEORGE: It's an eight-thirty curtain. That's just Chicago, though. In New York standard curtain time is eight forty.

(*He is rather proud of this knowledge.*)

RUTH (*properly appreciating it*): You get to New York a lot?

GEORGE (*offhand*): Few times a year.

RUTH: Oh—that's nice. I've never been to New York.

(*Walter enters. We feel he has relieved himself, but the edge of unreality is still with him.*)

WALTER: New York ain't got nothing Chicago ain't. Just a bunch of hustling people all squeezed up together—being "Eastern."

(*He turns his face into a screw of displeasure.*)

GEORGE: Oh—you've been?

WALTER: *Plenty* of times.

RUTH (*shocked at the lie*): Walter Lee Younger!

WALTER (*staring her down*): Plenty! (*Pause.*) What we got to drink in this house? Why don't you offer this man some refreshment. (*To George.*) They don't know how to entertain people in this house, man.

GEORGE: Thank you—I don't really care for anything.

WALTER (*feeling his head; sobriety coming*): Where's Mama?

RUTH: She ain't come back yet.

WALTER (*looking Murchison over from head to toe, scrutinizing his carefully casual tweed sports jacket over cashmere V-neck sweater over soft eyelet shirt and tie, and soft slacks, finished off with white buckskin shoes*): Why all you college boys wear them faggoty-looking white shoes?

RUTH: Walter Lee!

(*George Murchison ignores the remark.*)

WALTER (*to Ruth*): Well, they look crazy as hell—white shoes, cold as it is.

RUTH (*crushed*): You have to excuse him—

WALTER: No he don't! Excuse me for what? What you always excusing me for! I'll excuse myself when I needs to be excused! (*A pause.*) They look as funny as them black knee socks Beneatha wears out of here all the time.

RUTH: It's the college *style*, Walter.

WALTER: Style, hell. She looks like she got burnt legs or something!

RUTH: Oh, Walter—

WALTER (*an irritable mimic*): Oh, Walter! Oh, Walter! (*To Murchison.*) How's your old man making out? I understand you all going to buy that big hotel on the Drive? (*He finds a beer in the refrigerator, wanders over to Murchison, sipping and wiping his lips with the back of his hand, and straddling a chair backward to talk to the other man.*) Shrewd move. Your old man is all right, man. (*Tapping his head and half winking for emphasis.*) I mean he knows how to operate. I mean he thinks *big*, you know what I mean, I mean for a *home*, you know? But I think he's kind of running out of ideas now. I'd like to talk to him. Listen, man, I got some plans that could turn this city upside down. I mean think like he does. *Big*. Invest big, gamble big, hell, lose *big* if you have to, you know what I mean. It's hard to find a man on this whole Southside who understands my kind of thinking—you dig? (*He scrutinizes Murchison again, drinks his beer, squints his eyes, and leans in close, confidential, man to man.*) Me and you ought to sit down and talk sometimes, man. Man, I got me some ideas . . .

MURCHISON (*with boredom*): Yeah—sometimes we'll have to do that, Walter.

WALTER (*understanding the indifference, and offended*): Yeah—well, when you get the time, man. I know you a busy little boy.

RUTH: Walter, please—

WALTER (*bitterly, hurt*): I know ain't nothing in this world as busy as you colored college boys with your fraternity pins and white shoes . . .

RUTH (*covering her face with humiliation*): Oh, Walter Lee—

WALTER: I see you all all the time—with the books tucked under your arms—going to your (*British A—a mimic*) "clahsses." And for what! What the hell you learning over there? Filling up your heads—(*counting off on his fingers*)—with the sociology and the psychology—but they teaching you how to be a man? How to take over and run the world? They teaching you how to run a rubber plantation or a steel mill? Naw—just to talk proper and read books and wear them faggoty-looking white shoes . . .

GEORGE (*looking at him with distaste, a little above it all*): You're all wacked up with bitterness, man.

WALTER (*intently, almost quietly, between the teeth, glaring at the boy*): And you—ain't you bitter, man? Ain't you just about had it yet? Don't you see no stars gleaming that you can't reach out and grab? You happy?—You contented son-of-a-bitch—you happy? You got it made? Bitter? Man, I'm a volcano. Bitter? Here I am a giant—surrounded by ants! Ants who can't even understand what it is the giant is talking about.

RUTH (*passionately and suddenly*): Oh, Walter—ain't you with nobody!

WALTER (*violently*): No! 'Cause ain't nobody with me! Not even my own mother!

RUTH: Walter, that's a terrible thing to say!

(*Beneatha enters, dressed for the evening in a cocktail dress and earrings, hair natural.*)

GEORGE: Well—hey—(*Crosses to Beneatha; thoughtful, with emphasis, since this is a reversal.*) You look great!

WALTER (*seeing his sister's hair for the first time*): What's the matter with your head?

BENEATHA (*tired of the jokes now*): I cut it off, Brother.

WALTER (*coming close to inspect it and walking around her*): Well, I'll be damned. So that's what they mean by the African bush . . .

BENEATHA: Ha ha. Let's go, George.

GEORGE (*looking at her*): You know something? I like it. It's sharp. I mean it really is. (*Helps her into her wrap.*)

RUTH: Yes—I think so, too. (*She goes to the mirror and starts to clutch at her hair.*)

WALTER: Oh no! You leave yours alone, baby. You might turn out to have a pin-shaped head or something!

BENEATHA: See you all later.

RUTH: Have a nice time.

GEORGE: Thanks. Good night. (*Half out the door, he reopens it. To Walter.*) Good night, Prometheus!°

(*Beneatha and George exit.*)

WALTER (*to Ruth*): Who is Prometheus?

RUTH: I don't know. Don't worry about it.

WALTER (*in fury, pointing after George*): See there—they get to a point where they can't insult you man to man—they got to go talk about something ain't nobody never heard of!

RUTH: How do you know it was an insult? (*To humor him.*) Maybe Prometheus is a nice fellow.

WALTER: Prometheus! I bet there ain't even no such thing! I bet that simple-minded clown—

RUTH: Walter—

(*She stops what she is doing and looks at him.*)

WALTER (*yelling*): Don't start!

RUTH: Start what?

WALTER: Your nagging! Where was I? Who was I with? How much money did I spend?

RUTH (*plaintively*): Walter Lee—why don't we just try to talk about it . . .

WALTER (*not listening*): I been out talking with people who understand me. People who care about the things I got on my mind.

RUTH (*wearily*): I guess that means people like Willy Harris.

WALTER: Yes, people like Willy Harris.

RUTH (*with a sudden flash of impatience*): Why don't you all just hurry up and go into the banking business and stop talking about it!

WALTER: Why? You want to know why? 'Cause we all tied up in a race of people that don't know how to do nothing but moan, pray, and have babies!

Prometheus: Defiantly inventive Titan who stole fire from the gods and gave it to humans.

(*The line is too bitter even for him and he looks at her and sits down.*)

RUTH: Oh, Walter . . . (*Softly.*) Honey, why can't you stop fighting me?

WALTER (*without thinking*): Who's fighting you? Who even cares about you?

(*This line begins the retardation of his mood.*)

RUTH: Well—(*She waits a long time, and then with resignation starts to put away her things.*) I guess I might as well go on to bed . . . (*More or less to herself.*) I don't know where we lost it . . . but we have . . . (*Then, to him.*) I—I'm sorry about this new baby, Walter. I guess maybe I better go on and do what I started . . . I guess I just didn't realize how bad things was with us . . . I guess I just didn't really realize—(*She starts out to the bedroom and stops.*) You want some hot milk?

WALTER: Hot milk?

RUTH: Yes—hot milk.

WALTER: Why hot milk?

RUTH: 'Cause after all that liquor you come home with you ought to have something hot in your stomach.

WALTER: I don't want no milk.

RUTH: You want some coffee then?

WALTER: No, I don't want no coffee. I don't want nothing hot to drink. (*Almost plaintively.*) Why you always trying to give me something to eat?

RUTH (*standing and looking at him helplessly*): What else can I give you, Walter Lee Younger?

(*She stands and looks at him and presently turns to go out again. He lifts his head and watches her going away from him in a new mood which began to emerge when he asked her "Who cares about you?"*)

WALTER: It's been rough, ain't it, baby? (*She hears and stops but does not turn around and he continues to her back.*) I guess between two people there ain't never as much understood as folks generally thinks there is. I mean like between me and you—(*She turns to face him.*) How we gets to the place where we scared to talk softness to each other. (*He waits, thinking hard himself.*) Why you think it got to be like that? (*He is thoughtful, almost as a child would be.*) Ruth, what is it gets into people ought to be close?

RUTH: I don't know, honey. I think about it a lot.

WALTER: On account of you and me, you mean? The way things are with us. The way something done come down between us.

RUTH: There ain't so much between us, Walter . . . Not when you come to me and try to talk to me. Try to be with me . . . a little even.

WALTER (*total honesty*): Sometimes . . . sometimes . . . I don't even know how to try.

RUTH: Walter—

WALTER: Yes?

RUTH (*coming to him, gently and with misgiving, but coming to him*): Honey . . . life don't have to be like this. I mean sometimes people can do things so that things are better . . . You remember how we used to talk when Travis was born . . . about the way we were going to live . . . the kind of house . . . (*She is stroking his head.*) Well, it's all starting to slip away from us . . .

(*He turns her to him and they look at each other and kiss, tenderly and hungrily. The door opens and Mama enters—Walter breaks away and jumps up. A beat.*)

WALTER: Mama, where have you been?

MAMA: My—them steps is longer than they used to be. Whew! (*She sits down and ignores him.*) How you feeling this evening, Ruth?

(*Ruth shrugs, disturbed at having been interrupted and watching her husband knowingly.*)

WALTER: Mama, where have you been all day?

MAMA (*still ignoring him and leaning on the table and changing to more comfortable shoes*): Where's Travis?

RUTH: I let him go out earlier and he ain't come back yet. Boy, is he going to get it!

WALTER: Mama!

MAMA (*as if she has heard him for the first time*): Yes, son?

WALTER: Where did you go this afternoon?

MAMA: I went downtown to tend to some business that I had to tend to.

WALTER: What kind of business?

MAMA: You know better than to question me like a child, Brother.

WALTER (*rising and bending over the table*): Where were you, Mama? (*Bringing his fists down and shouting.*) Mama, you didn't go do something with that insurance money, something crazy?

(*The front door opens slowly, interrupting him, and Travis peeks his head in, less than hopefully.*)

TRAVIS (*to his mother*): Mama, I—

RUTH: "Mama I" nothing! You're going to get it, boy! Get on in that bedroom and get yourself ready!

TRAVIS: But I—

MAMA: Why don't you all never let the child explain hisself.

RUTH: Keep out of it now, Lena.

(*Mama clamps her lips together, and Ruth advances toward her son menacingly.*)

RUTH: A thousand times I have told you not to go off like that—

MAMA (*holding out her arms to her grandson*): Well—at least let me tell him something. I want him to be the first one to hear . . . Come here, Travis. (*The boy obeys, gladly.*) Travis—(*she takes him by the shoulder and looks into his face*)—you know that money we got in the mail this morning?

TRAVIS: Yes'm—

MAMA: Well—what you think your grandmama gone and done with that money?

TRAVIS: I don't know, Grandmama.

MAMA (*putting her finger on his nose for emphasis*): She went out and she bought you a house! (*The explosion comes from Walter at the end of the revelation and he jumps up and turns away from all of them in a fury. Mama continues, to Travis.*) You glad about the house? It's going to be yours when you get to be a man.

TRAVIS: Yeah—I always wanted to live in a house.

MAMA: All right, gimme some sugar then—(*Travis puts his arms around her neck as she watches her son over the boy's shoulder. Then, to Travis, after the embrace.*) Now when you say your prayers tonight, you thank God and your grandfather—'cause it was him who give you the house—in his way.

RUTH (*taking the boy from Mama and pushing him toward the bedroom*): Now you get out of here and get ready for your beating.

TRAVIS: Aw, Mama—

RUTH: Get on in there—(*Closing the door behind him and turning radiantly to her mother-in-law.*) So you went and did it!

MAMA (*quietly, looking at her son with pain*): Yes, I did.

RUTH (*raising both arms classically*): PRAISE GOD! (*Looks at Walter a moment, who says nothing. She crosses rapidly to her husband.*) Please, honey—let me be glad . . . you be glad too. (*She has laid her hands on his shoulders, but he shakes himself free of her roughly, without turning to face her.*) Oh, Walter . . . a home . . . a home. (*She comes back to Mama.*) Well—where is it? How big is it? How much it going to cost?

MAMA: Well—

RUTH: When we moving?

MAMA (*smiling at her*): First of the month.

RUTH (*throwing back her head with jubilance*): Praise God!

MAMA (*tentatively, still looking at her son's back turned against her and Ruth*): It's—it's a nice house too . . . (*She cannot help speaking directly to him. An imploring quality in her voice, her manner, makes her almost like a girl now.*) Three bedrooms—nice big one for you and Ruth . . . Me and Beneatha still have to share our room, but Travis have one of his own and (*with difficulty*) I figure if the—new baby—is a boy, we could get one of them double-decker outfits . . . And there's a yard with a little patch of dirt where I could maybe get to grow me a few flowers . . . And a nice big basement . . .

RUTH: Walter honey, be glad—

MAMA (*still to his back, fingering things on the table*): 'Course I don't want to make it sound fancier than it is . . . It's just a plain little old house—but it's made good and solid—and it will be *ours*. Walter Lee—it makes a difference in a man when he can walk on floors that belong to *him* . . .

RUTH: Where is it?

MAMA (*frightened at this telling*): Well—well—it's out there in Clybourne Park—

(*Ruth's radiance fades abruptly, and Walter finally turns slowly to face his mother with incredulity and hostility.*)

RUTH: Where?

MAMA (*matter-of-factly*): Four o six Clybourne Street, Clybourne Park.

RUTH: Clybourne Park? Mama, there ain't no colored people living in Clybourne Park.

MAMA (*almost idiotically*): Well, I guess there's going to be some now.

WALTER (*bitterly*): So that's the peace and comfort you went out and bought for us today!

MAMA (*raising her eyes to meet his finally*): Son—I just tried to find the nicest place for the least amount of money for my family.

RUTH (*trying to recover from the shock*): Well—well—'course I ain't one never been 'fraid of no crackers,° mind you—but—well, wasn't there no other houses nowhere?

MAMA: Them houses they put up for colored in them areas way out all seem to cost twice as much as other houses. I did the best I could.

RUTH (*struck senseless with the news, in its various degrees of goodness and trouble, she sits a moment, her fists propping her chin in thought, and then she starts to rise, bringing her fists down with vigor, the radiance spreading from cheek to cheek again*): Well—well—All I can say is—if this is my time in life—MY TIME—to say good-bye—(*and she builds with momentum as she starts to circle the room with an exuberant, almost tearfully happy release*)—to these Goddamned cracking walls!—(*she pounds the walls*)—and these marching roaches!—(*she wipes at an imaginary army of marching roaches*)—and this cramped little closet which ain't now or never was no kitchen! . . . then I say it loud and good, HALLELU-JAH! AND GOOD-BYE MISERY . . . I DON'T NEVER WANT TO SEE YOUR UGLY FACE AGAIN! (*She laughs joyously, having practically destroyed the apartment, and flings her arms up and lets them come down happily, slowly, reflectively, over her abdomen, aware for the first time perhaps that the life therein pulses with happiness and not despair.*) Lena?

MAMA (*moved, watching her happiness*): Yes, honey?

RUTH (*looking off*): Is there—is there a whole lot of sunlight?

MAMA (*understanding*): Yes, child, there's a whole lot of sunlight.

(*Long pause.*)

RUTH (*collecting herself and going to the door of the room Travis is in*): Well—I guess I better see 'bout Travis. (*To Mama.*) Lord, I sure don't feel like whipping nobody today!

(*She exits.*)

crackers: White people, often used to refer disparagingly to poor whites.

MAMA (*the mother and son are left alone now and the mother waits a long time, considering deeply, before she speaks*): Son—you—you understand what I done, don't you? (*Walter is silent and sullen.*) I—I just seen my family falling apart today . . . just falling to pieces in front of my eyes . . . We couldn't of gone on like we was today. We was going backwards 'stead of forwards—talking 'bout killing babies and wishing each other was dead . . . When it gets like that in life—you just got to do something different, push on out and do something bigger . . . (*She waits.*) I wish you say something, son . . . I wish you'd say how deep inside you you think I done the right thing—

WALTER (*crossing slowly to his bedroom door and finally turning there and speaking measuredly*): What you need me to say you done right for? *You* the head of this family. You run our lives like you want to. It was your money and you did what you wanted with it. So what you need for me to say it was all right for? (*Bitterly, to hurt her as deeply as he knows is possible.*) So you butchered up a dream of mine—you—who always talking 'bout your children's dreams . . .

MAMA: Walter Lee—

(*He just closes the door behind him. Mama sits alone, thinking heavily.*)

Scene II

(*Time: Friday night. A few weeks later.*)

(*At rise: Packing crates mark the intention of the family to move. Beneatha and George come in, presumably from an evening out again.*)

GEORGE: O.K. . . . O.K., whatever you say . . . (*They both sit on the couch. He tries to kiss her. She moves away.*) Look, we've had a nice evening; let's not spoil it, huh? . . .

(*He again turns her head and tries to nuzzle in and she turns away from him, not with distaste but with momentary lack of interest; in a mood to pursue what they were talking about.*)

BENEATHA: I'm *trying* to talk to you.

GEORGE: We always talk.

BENEATHA: Yes—and I love to talk.

GEORGE (*exasperated; rising*): I know it and I don't mind it sometimes . . . I want you to cut it out, see—The moody stuff, I mean. I don't like it. You're a nice-looking girl . . . all over. That's all you need, honey, forget the atmosphere. Guys aren't going to go for the atmosphere—they're going to go for what they see. Be glad for that. Drop the Garbo routine. It doesn't go with you. As for myself, I want a nice—(*groping*)—simple (*thoughtfully*)—sophisticated girl . . . not a poet—O.K.?

(*He starts to kiss her, she rebuffs him again, and he jumps up.*)

BENEATHA: Why are you angry, George?

GEORGE: Because this is stupid! I don't go out with you to discuss the nature of "quiet desperation" or to hear all about your thoughts—because the world will go on thinking what it thinks regardless—

BENEATHA: Then why read books? Why go to school?

GEORGE (*with artificial patience, counting on his fingers*): It's simple. You read books—to learn facts—to get grades—to pass the course—to get a degree. That's all—it has nothing to do with thoughts.

(*A long pause.*)

BENEATHA: I see. (*He starts to sit.*) Good night, George.

(*George looks at her a little oddly and starts to exit. He meets Mama coming in.*)

GEORGE: Oh—hello, Mrs. Younger.

MAMA: Hello, George, how you feeling?

GEORGE: Fine—fine, how are you?

MAMA: Oh, a little tired. You know them steps can get you after a day's work. You all have a nice time tonight?

GEORGE: Yes—a fine time. A fine time.

MAMA: Well, good night.

GEORGE: Good night. (*He exits. Mama closes the door behind her.*)

MAMA: Hello, honey. What you sitting like that for?

BENEATHA: I'm just sitting.

MAMA: Didn't you have a nice time?

BENEATHA: No.

MAMA: No? What's the matter?

BENEATHA: Mama, George is a fool—honest. (*She rises.*)

MAMA (*Hustling around unloading the packages she has entered with. She stops.*): Is he, baby?

BENEATHA: Yes.

(*Beneatha makes up Travis's bed as she talks.*)

MAMA: You sure?

BENEATHA: Yes.

MAMA: Well—I guess you better not waste your time with no fools.

(*Beneatha looks up at her mother, watching her put groceries in the refrigerator. Finally she gathers up her things and starts into the bedroom. At the door she stops and looks back at her mother.*)

BENEATHA: Mama—

MAMA: Yes, baby—

BENEATHA: Thank you.

MAMA: For what?

BENEATHA: For understanding me this time.

(*She exits quickly and the mother stands, smiling a little, looking at the place where Beneatha just stood. Ruth enters.*)

RUTH: Now don't you fool with any of this stuff, Lena—

MAMA: Oh, I just thought I'd sort a few things out. Is Brother here?

RUTH: Yes.

MAMA (*with concern*): Is he—

RUTH (*reading her eyes*): Yes.

(*Mama is silent and someone knocks on the door. Mama and Ruth exchange weary and knowing glances and Ruth opens it to admit the neighbor, Mrs. Johnson,° who is a rather squeaky wide-eyed lady of no particular age, with a newspaper under her arm.*)

MAMA (*changing her expression to acute delight and a ringing cheerful greeting*): Oh—hello there, Johnson.

JOHNSON (*this is a woman who decided long ago to be enthusiastic about* EVERYTHING *in life and she is inclined to wave her wrist vigorously at the height of her exclamatory comments*): Hello there, yourself! H'you this evening, Ruth?

RUTH (*not much of a deceptive type*): Fine, Mis' Johnson, h'you?

JOHNSON: Fine. (*Reaching out quickly, playfully, and patting Ruth's stomach.*) Ain't you starting to poke out none yet! (*She mugs with delight at the overfamiliar remark and her eyes dart around looking at the crates and packing preparation; Mama's face is a cold sheet of endurance.*) Oh, ain't we getting ready round here, though! Yessir! Lookathere! I'm telling you the Youngers is really getting ready to "move on up a little higher!"—Bless God!

MAMA (*a little drily, doubting the total sincerity of the Blesser*): Bless God.

JOHNSON: He's good, ain't He?

MAMA: Oh yes, He's good.

JOHNSON: I mean sometimes He works in mysterious ways . . . but He works, don't He!

MAMA (*the same*): Yes, he does.

JOHNSON: I'm just sooooo happy for y'all. And this here child—(*about Ruth*) looks like she could just pop open with happiness, don't she. Where's all the rest of the family?

MAMA: Bennie's gone to bed—

JOHNSON: Ain't no . . . (*the implication is pregnancy*) sickness done hit you—I hope . . . ?

MAMA: No—she just tired. She was out this evening.

JOHNSON (*all is a coo, an emphatic coo*): Aw—ain't that lovely. She still going out with the little Murchison boy?

MAMA (*drily*): Ummmm huh.

JOHNSON: That's lovely. You sure got lovely children, Younger. Me and Isaiah talks all the time 'bout what fine children you was blessed with. We sure do.

MAMA: Ruth, give Mis' Johnson a piece of sweet potato pie and some milk.

JOHNSON: Oh honey, I can't stay hardly a minute—I just dropped in to see if there was anything I could

---

Mrs. Johnson: This character and the scene of her visit were cut from the original production and early editions of the play.

do. (*Accepting the food easily.*) I guess y'all seen the news what's all over the colored paper this week . . .

MAMA: No—didn't get mine yet this week.

JOHNSON (*lifting her head and blinking with the spirit of catastrophe*): You mean you ain't read 'bout them colored people that was bombed out their place out there?

(*Ruth straightens with concern and takes the paper and reads it. Johnson notices her and feeds commentary.*)

JOHNSON: Ain't it something how bad these here white folks is getting here in Chicago! Lord, getting so you think you right down in Mississippi! (*With a tremendous and rather insincere sense of melodrama.*) 'Course I thinks it's wonderful how our folks keeps on pushing out. You hear some of these Negroes round here talking 'bout how they don't go where they ain't wanted and all that—but not me, honey! (*This is a lie.*) Wilhemenia Othella Johnson goes anywhere, any time she feels like it! (*With head movement for emphasis.*) Yes I do! Why if we left it up to these here crackers the poor niggers wouldn't have nothing   (*She clasps her hand over her mouth.*) Oh, I always forgets you don't 'low that word in your house.

MAMA (*quietly, looking at her*): No—I don't 'low it.

JOHNSON (*vigorously again*): Me neither! I was just telling Isaiah yesterday when he come using it in front of me—I said, "Isaiah, it's just like Mis' Younger says all the time—"

MAMA: Don't you want some more pie?

JOHNSON: No—no thank you; this was lovely. I got to get on over home and have my midnight coffee. I hear some people say it don't let them sleep but I finds I can't close my eyes right lessen I done had that laaaast cup of coffee . . . (*She waits. A beat. Undaunted.*) My Good-night coffee, I calls it!

MAMA (*with much eye-rolling and communication between herself and Ruth*): Ruth, why don't you give Mis' Johnson some coffee.

(*Ruth gives Mama an unpleasant look for her kindness.*)

JOHNSON (*accepting the coffee*): Where's Brother tonight?

MAMA: He's lying down.

JOHNSON: Mmmmmmm, he sure gets his beauty rest, don't he? Good-looking man. Sure is a good-looking man! (*Reaching out to pat Ruth's stomach again.*) I guess that's how come we keep on having babies around here. (*She winks at Mama.*) One thing 'bout Brother, he always know how to have a *good* time. And soooooo ambitious! I bet it was his idea y'all moving out to Clybourne Park. Lord—I bet this time next month y'all's names will have been in the papers plenty—(*Holding up her hands to mark off each word of the headline she can see in front of her.*) "NEGROS INVADE CLYBOURNE PARK—BOMBED!"

MAMA (*she and Ruth look at the woman in amazement*): We ain't exactly moving out there to get bombed.

JOHNSON: Oh, honey—you know I'm praying to God every day that don't nothing like that happen! But you have to think of life like it is—and these here Chicago peckerwoods is some baaaad peckerwoods.

MAMA (*wearily*): We done thought about all that Mis' Johnson.

(*Beneatha comes out of the bedroom in her robe and passes through to the bathroom. Mrs. Johnson turns.*)

JOHNSON: Hello there, Bennie!

BENEATHA (*crisply*): Hello, Mrs. Johnson.

JOHNSON: How is school?

BENEATHA (*crisply*): Fine, thank you. (*She goes out.*)

JOHNSON (*insulted*): Getting so she don't have much to say to nobody.

MAMA: The child was on her way to the bathroom.

JOHNSON: I know—but sometimes she act like ain't got time to pass the time of day with nobody ain't been to college. Oh—I ain't criticizing her none. It's just—you know how some of our young people gets when they get a little education, (*Mama and Ruth say nothing, just look at her.*) Yes—well. Well, I guess I better get on home. (*Unmoving.*) 'Course I can understand how she must be proud and everything—being the only one in the family to make something of herself. I know just being a chauffeur ain't never satisfied Brother none. He shouldn't feel like that, though. Ain't nothing wrong with being a chauffeur.

MAMA: There's plenty wrong with it.

JOHNSON: What?

MAMA: Plenty. My husband always said being any kind of a servant wasn't a fit thing for a man to have to be. He always said a man's hands was made to make things, or to turn the earth with—not to drive nobody's car for 'em—or—(*she looks at her own hands*) carry they slop jars. And my boy is just like him—he wasn't meant to wait on nobody.

JOHNSON (*rising, somewhat offended*): Mmmmmmmmm. The Youngers is too much for me! (*She looks around.*) You sure one proud-acting bunch of colored folks. Well—I always thinks like Booker T. Washington said that time—"Education has spoiled many a good plow hand"—

MAMA: Is that what old Booker T. said?

JOHNSON: He sure did.

MAMA: Well, it sounds just like him. The fool.

JOHNSON (*indignantly*): Well—he was one of our great men.

MAMA: Who said so?

JOHNSON (*nonplussed*): You know, me and you ain't never agreed about some things, Lena Younger. I guess I better be going—

RUTH (*quickly*): Good night.

JOHNSON: Good night. Oh—(*Thrusting it at her.*) You can keep the paper! (*With a trill.*) 'Night.

MAMA: Good night, Mis' Johnson.

(*Mrs. Johnson exits.*)

RUTH: If ignorance was gold . . .

MAMA: Shush. Don't talk about folks behind their backs.

RUTH: You do.

MAMA: I'm old and corrupted. (*Beneatha enters.*) You was rude to Mis' Johnson, Beneatha, and I don't like it at all.

BENEATHA (*at her door*): Mama, if there are two things we, as a people, have got to overcome, one is the Klu Klux Klan—and the other is Mrs. Johnson. (*She exits.*)

MAMA: Smart aleck.

(*The phone rings.*)

RUTH: I'll get it.

MAMA: Lord, ain't this a popular place tonight.

RUTH (*at the phone*): Hello—Just a minute. (*Goes to door.*) Walter, it's Mrs. Arnold. (*Waits. Goes back to the phone. Tense.*) Hello. Yes, this is his wife speaking . . . He's lying down now. Yes . . . well, he'll be in tomorrow. He's been very sick. Yes—I know we should have called, but we were so sure he'd be able to come in today. Yes—yes, I'm very sorry. Yes . . . Thank you very much. (*She hangs up. Walter is standing in the doorway of the bedroom behind her.*) That was Mrs. Arnold.

WALTER (*indifferently*): Was it?

RUTH: She said if you don't come in tomorrow that they are getting a new man . . .

WALTER: Ain't that sad—ain't that crying sad.

RUTH: She said Mr. Arnold has had to take a cab for three days . . . Walter, you ain't been to work for three days! (*This is a revelation to her.*) Where you been, Walter Lee Younger? (*Walter looks at her and starts to laugh.*) You're going to lose your job.

WALTER: That's right . . . (*He turns on the radio.*)

RUTH: Oh, Walter, and with your mother working like a dog every day—

(*A steamy, deep blues pours into the room.*)

WALTER: That's sad too—Everything is sad.

MAMA: What you been doing for these three days, son?

WALTER: Mama—you don't know all the things a man what got leisure can find to do in this city . . . What's this—Friday night? Well—Wednesday I borrowed Willy Harris's car and I went for a drive . . . just me and myself and I drove and drove . . . Way out . . . way past South Chicago, and I parked the car and I sat and looked at the steel mills all day long. I just sat in the car and looked at them big black chimneys for hours. Then I drove back and I went to the Green Hat. (*Pause.*) And Thursday—Thursday I borrowed the car again and I got in it and I pointed it the other way and I drove the other way—for hours—way, way up to Wisconsin, and I looked at the farms. I just drove and looked at the farms. Then I drove back and I went to the Green Hat. (*Pause.*) And today—today I didn't get the car. Today I just walked. All over the Southside. And I looked at the Negroes and they looked at me and finally I just sat down on the curb at Thirty-ninth and South Parkway and I just sat there and watched the Negroes go by. And then I went to the Green Hat. You all sad? You all depressed? And you know where I am going right now—

(*Ruth goes out quietly.*)

MAMA: Oh, Big Walter, is this the harvest of our days?

WALTER: You know what I like about the Green Hat? I like this little cat they got there who blows a sax . . . He blows. He talks to me. He ain't but 'bout five feet tall and he's got a conked head and his eyes is always closed and he's all music—

MAMA (*rising and getting some papers out of her handbag*): Walter—

WALTER: And there's this other guy who plays the piano . . . and they got a sound. I mean they can work on some music . . . They got the best little combo in the world in the Green Hat . . . You can just sit there and drink and listen to them three men play and you realize that don't nothing matter worth a damn, but just being there—

MAMA: I've helped do it to you, haven't I, son? Walter I been wrong.

WALTER: Naw—you ain't never been wrong about nothing, Mama.

MAMA: Listen to me, now. I say I been wrong, son. That I been doing to you what the rest of the world been doing to you. (*She turns off the radio.*) Walter—(*She stops and he looks up slowly at her and she meets his eyes pleadingly.*) What you ain't never understood is that I ain't got nothing, don't own nothing, ain't never really wanted nothing that wasn't for you. There ain't nothing as precious to me . . . There ain't nothing worth holding on to, money, dreams, nothing else—if it means—if it means it's going to destroy my boy. (*She takes an envelope out of her handbag and puts it in front of him and he watches her without speaking or moving.*) I paid the man thirty-five hundred dollars down on the house. That leaves sixty-five hundred dollars. Monday morning I want you to take this money and take three thousand dollars and put it in a savings account for Beneatha's medical schooling. The rest you put in a checking account—with your name on it. And from now on any penny that come out of it or that go in it is for you to look after. For you to decide. (*She drops her hands a little helplessly.*) It ain't much, but it's all I got in the world and I'm putting it in your hands. I'm telling you to be the head of this family from now on like you supposed to be.

WALTER (*stares at the money*): You trust me like that, Mama?

MAMA: I ain't never stop trusting you. Like I ain't never stop loving you.

(*She goes out, and Walter sits looking at the money on the table. Finally, in a decisive gesture, he gets up and, in mingled joy and desperation, picks up the money. At the same moment, Travis enters for bed.*)

TRAVIS: What's the matter, Daddy? You drunk?

WALTER (*sweetly, more sweetly than we have ever known him*): No, Daddy ain't drunk. Daddy ain't going to never be drunk again . . .

TRAVIS: Well, good night, Daddy.

(*The father has come from behind the couch and leans over, embracing his son.*)

WALTER: Son, I feel like talking to you tonight.

TRAVIS: About what?

WALTER: Oh, about a lot of things. About you and what kind of man you going to be when you grow up. . . . Son—son, what do you want to be when you grow up?

TRAVIS: A bus driver.

WALTER (*laughing a little*): A what? Man, that ain't nothing to want to be!

TRAVIS: Why not?

WALTER: 'Cause, man—it ain't big enough—you know what I mean.

TRAVIS: I don't know then. I can't make up my mind. Sometimes Mama asks me that too. And sometimes when I tell her I just want to be like you—she says she don't want me to be like that and sometimes she says she does. . . .

WALTER (*gathering him up in his arms*): You know what, Travis? In seven years you going to be seventeen years old. And things is going to be very different with us in seven years Travis. . . . One day when you are seventeen I'll come home—home from my office downtown somewhere—

TRAVIS: You don't work in no office, Daddy.

WALTER: No—but after tonight. After what your daddy gonna do tonight, there's going to be offices—a whole lot of offices. . . .

TRAVIS: What you gonna do tonight, Daddy?

WALTER: You wouldn't understand yet, son, but your daddy's gonna make a transaction . . . a business transaction that's going to change our lives. . . . That's how come one day when you 'bout seventeen years old I'll come home and I'll be pretty tired, you know what I mean, after a day of conferences and secretaries getting things wrong the way they do . . . 'cause an executive's life is hell man—(*The more he talks the farther away he gets.*) And I'll pull the car up on the driveway . . . just a plain black Chrysler, I think, with white walls—no—black tires. More elegant. Rich people don't have to be flashy . . . though I'll have to get something a little sportier for Ruth—maybe a Cadillac convertible to do her shopping in. . . . And I'll come up the steps to the house and the gardener will be clipping away at the hedges and he'll say, "Good evening, Mr. Younger." And I'll say, "Hello, Jefferson, how are you this evening?" And I'll go inside and Ruth will come downstairs and meet me at the door and we'll kiss each other and she'll take my arm and we'll go up to your room to see you sitting on the floor with the catalogues of all the great schools in America around you. . . . All the

great schools in the world! And—and I'll say, all right son—it's your seventeenth birthday, what is it you've decided? . . . Just tell me where you want to go to school and you'll go. Just tell me, what it is you want to be—and you'll *be* it. . . . Whatever you want to be—Yessir! (*He holds his arms open for Travis.*) You just name it, son . . . (*Travis leaps into them*) and I hand you the world!

(*Walter's voice has risen in pitch and hysterical promise and on the last line he lifts Travis high.*)

Scene III

(*Time: Saturday, moving day, one week later.*)

(*Before the curtain rises, Ruth's voice, a strident, dramatic church alto, cuts through the silence.*)

(*It is, in the darkness, a triumphant surge, a penetrating statement of expectation: "Oh, Lord, I don't feel no ways tired! Children, oh, glory hallelujah!"*)

(*As the curtain rises we see that Ruth is alone in the living room, finishing up the family's packing. It is moving day. She is nailing crates and tying cartons. Beneatha enters, carrying a guitar case, and watches her exuberant sister-in-law.*)

RUTH: Hey!

BENEATHA (*putting away the case*): Hi.

RUTH (*pointing at a package*): Honey—look in that package there and see what I found on sale this morning at the South Center. (*Ruth gets up and moves to the package and draws out some curtains.*) Lookahere—hand-turned hems!

BENEATHA: How do you know the window size out there?

RUTH (*who hadn't thought of that*): Oh—Well, they bound to fit something in the whole house. Anyhow, they was too good a bargain to pass up. (*Ruth slaps her head, suddenly remembering something.*) Oh, Bennie—I meant to put a special note on that carton over there. That's your mama's good china and she wants 'em to be very careful with it.

BENEATHA: I'll do it.

(*Beneatha finds a piece of paper and starts to draw large letters on it.*)

RUTH: You know what I'm going to do soon as I get in that new house?

BENEATHA: What?

RUTH: Honey—I'm going to run me a tub of water up to here . . . (*With her fingers practically up to her nostrils.*) And I'm going to get in it—and I am going to sit . . . and sit . . . and sit in that hot water and the first person who knocks to tell *me* to hurry up and come out—

BENEATHA: Gets shot at sunrise.

RUTH (*laughing happily*): You said it, sister! (*Noticing how large Beneatha is absent-mindedly making the note.*) Honey, they ain't going to read that from no airplane.

BENEATHA (*laughing herself*): I guess I always think things have more emphasis if they are big, somehow.

RUTH (*looking up at her and smiling*): You and your brother seem to have that as a philosophy of life. Lord, that man—done changed so 'round here. You know—you know what we did last night? Me and Walter Lee?

BENEATHA: What?

RUTH (*smiling to herself*): We went to the movies. (*Looking at Beneatha to see if she understands.*) We went to the movies. You know the last time me and Walter went to the movies together?

BENEATHA: No.

RUTH: Me neither. That's how long it been. (*Smiling again.*) But we went last night. The picture wasn't much good, but that didn't seem to matter. We went—and we held hands.

BENEATHA: Oh, Lord!

RUTH: We held hands—and you know what?

BENEATHA: What?

RUTH: When we come out of the show it was late and dark and all the stores and things was closed up . . . and it was kind of chilly and there wasn't many people on the streets . . . and we was still holding hands, me and Walter.

BENEATHA: You're killing me.

(*Walter enters with a large package. His happiness is deep in him; he cannot keep still with his newfound exuberance. He is singing and wiggling and snapping his fingers. He puts his package in a corner and puts a phonograph record which he has brought in with him, on the record player. As the music, soulful and sensuous, comes up he dances over to Ruth and tries to get her to dance with him. She gives in at last to his raunchiness and in a fit of giggling allows herself to be drawn into his mood. They dip and she melts into his arms in a classic, body-melding "slow drag."*)

BENEATHA (*regarding them a long time as they dance, then drawing in her breath for a deeply exaggerated comment which she does not particularly mean*): Talk about—olddddddddddd—fashioneddddddddd—Negroes!

WALTER (*stopping momentarily*): What kind of Negroes?

(*He says this in fun. He is not angry with her today, nor with anyone. He starts to dance with his wife again.*)

BENEATHA: Old-fashioned.

WALTER (*as he dances with Ruth*): You know, when these *New Negroes* have their convention—(*pointing at his sister*)—that is going to be the chairman of the Committee on Unending Agitation. (*He goes on dancing, then stops.*) Race, race, race! . . . Girl, I do believe you are the first person in the history of the entire human race to successfully brainwash yourself. (*Beneatha breaks up and he goes on dancing. He stops again, enjoying his tease.*) Damn, even

the N double A C P takes a holiday sometimes! (*Beneatha and Ruth laugh. He dances with Ruth some more and starts to laugh and stops and pantomimes someone over an operating table.*) I can just see that chick someday looking down at some poor cat on an operating table and before she starts to slice him, she says . . . (*pulling his sleeves back maliciously*) "By the way, what are your views on civil rights down there? . . ."

(*He laughs at her again and starts to dance happily. The bell sounds.*)

BENEATHA: Sticks and stones may break my bones but . . . words will never hurt me!

(*Beneatha goes to the door and opens it as Walter and Ruth go on with the clowning. Beneatha is somewhat surprised to see a quiet-looking middle-aged white man in a business suit holding his hat and a briefcase in his hand and consulting a small piece of paper.*)

MAN: Uh—how do you do, miss. I am looking for a Mrs.—(*he looks at the slip of paper*) Mrs. Lena Younger? (*He stops short, struck dumb at the sight of the oblivious Walter and Ruth.*)

BENEATHA (*smoothing her hair with slight embarrassment*): Oh—yes, that's my mother. Excuse me. (*She closes the door and turns to quiet the other two.*) Ruth! Brother! (*Enunciating precisely but soundlessly: "There's a white man at the door!" They stop dancing, Ruth cuts off the phonograph, Beneatha opens the door. The man casts a curious quick glance at all of them.*) Uh—come in please.

MAN (*coming in*): Thank you.

BENEATHA: My mother isn't here just now. Is it business?

MAN: Yes . . . well, of a sort.

WALTER (*freely, the Man of the House*): Have a seat. I'm Mrs. Younger's son. I look after most of her business matters.

(*Ruth and Beneatha exchange amused glances.*)

MAN (*regarding Walter, and sitting*): Well—My name is Karl Lindner . . .

WALTER (*stretching out his hand*): Walter Younger. This is my wife—(*Ruth nods politely*)—and my sister.

LINDNER: How do you do.

WALTER (*amiably, as he sits himself easily on a chair, leaning forward on his knees with interest and looking expectantly into the newcomer's face*): What can we do for you, Mr. Lindner!

LINDNER (*some minor shuffling of the hat and briefcase on his knees*): Well—I am a representative of the Clybourne Park Improvement Association—

WALTER (*pointing*): Why don't you sit your things on the floor?

LINDNER: Oh—yes. Thank you. (*He slides the briefcase and hat under the chair.*) And as I was saying—I am from the Clybourne Park Improvement Association and we have had it brought to our attention at the last meeting that you people—or at least your mother—has bought a piece of residential property at—(*he digs for the slip of paper again*)— four o six Clybourne Street . . .

WALTER: That's right. Care for something to drink? Ruth, get Mr. Lindner a beer.

LINDNER (*upset for some reason*): Oh—no, really. I mean thank you very much, but no thank you.

RUTH: (*innocently*): Some coffee?

LINDNER: Thank you, nothing at all.

(*Beneatha is watching the man carefully.*)

LINDNER: Well, I don't know how much you folks know about our organization. (*He is a gentle man; thoughtful and somewhat labored in his manner.*) It is one of these community organizations set up to look after—oh, you know, things like block upkeep and special projects and we also have what we call our New Neighbors Orientation Committee . . .

BENEATHA (*drily*): Yes—and what do they do?

LINDNER (*turning a little to her and then returning the main force to Walter*): Well—it's what you might call a sort of welcoming committee, I guess. I mean they, we—I'm the chairman of the committee—go around and see the new people who move into the neighborhood and sort of give them the lowdown on the way we do things out in Clybourne Park.

BENEATHA (*with appreciation of the two meanings, which escape Ruth and Walter*): Un-huh.

LINDNER: And we also have the category of what the association calls—(*he looks elsewhere*)—uh—special community problems . . .

BENEATHA: Yes—and what are some of those?

WALTER: Girl, let the man talk.

LINDNER (*with understated relief*): Thank you. I would sort of like to explain this thing in my own way. I mean I want to explain to you in a certain way.

WALTER: Go ahead.

LINDNER: Yes. Well. I'm going to try to get right to the point. I'm sure we'll all appreciate that in the long run.

BENEATHA: Yes.

WALTER: Be still now!

LINDNER: Well—

RUTH (*still innocently*): Would you like another chair—you don't look comfortable.

LINDNER (*more frustrated than annoyed*): No, thank you very much. Please. Well—to get right to the point I—(*a great breath, and he is off at last*) I am sure you people must be aware of some of the incidents which have happened in various parts of the city when colored people have moved into certain areas—(*Beneatha exhales heavily and starts tossing a piece of fruit up and down in the air.*) Well—because we have what I think is going to be a unique type of organization in American community life—not only do we deplore that kind of thing—but we are trying to do something about it. (*Beneatha stops tossing and turns with a new and quizzical interest to the*

man.) We feel—(*gaining confidence in his mission because of the interest in the faces of the people he is talking to*)—we feel that most of the trouble in this world, when you come right down to it—(*he hits his knee for emphasis*)—most of the trouble exists because people just don't sit down and talk to each other.

RUTH (*nodding as she might in church, pleased with the remark*): You can say that again, mister.

LINDNER (*more encouraged by such affirmation*): That we don't try hard enough in this world to understand the other fellow's problem. The other guy's point of view.

RUTH: Now that's right.

(*Beneatha and Walter merely watch and listen with genuine interest.*)

LINDNER: Yes—that's the way we feel out in Clybourne Park. And that's why I was elected to come here this afternoon and talk to you people. Friendly like, you know, the way people should talk to each other and see if we couldn't find some way to work this thing out. As I say, the whole business is a matter of *caring* about the other fellow. Anybody can see that you are a nice family of folks, hard-working and honest I'm sure. (*Beneatha frowns slightly, quizzically, her head tilted regarding him.*) Today everybody knows what it means to be on the outside of *something*. And of course, there is always somebody who is out to take advantage of people who don't always understand.

WALTER: What do you mean?

LINDNER: Well—you see our community is made up of people who've worked hard as the dickens for years to build up that little community. They're not rich and fancy people; just hard-working, honest people who don't really have much but those little homes and a dream of the kind of community they want to raise their children in. Now, I don't say we are perfect and there is a lot wrong in some of the things they want. But you've got to admit that a man, right or wrong, has the right to want to have the neighborhood he lives in a certain kind of way. And at the moment the overwhelming majority of our people out there feel that people get along better, take more of a common interest in the life of the community, when they share a common background. I want you to believe me when I tell you that race prejudice simply doesn't enter into it. It is a matter of the people of Clybourne Park believing, rightly or wrongly, as I say, that for the happiness of all concerned that our Negro families are happier when they live in their own communities.

BENEATHA (*with a grand and bitter gesture*): This, friends, is the Welcoming Committee!

WALTER (*dumfounded, looking at Lindner*): Is this what you came marching all the way over here to tell us?

LINDNER: Well, now we've been having a fine conversation. I hope you'll hear me all the way through.

WALTER (*tightly*): Go ahead, man.

LINDNER: You see—in the face of all the things I have said, we are prepared to make your family a very generous offer . . .

BENEATHA: Thirty pieces and not a coin less!

WALTER: Yeah!

LINDNER (*putting on his glasses and drawing a form out of the briefcase*): Our association is prepared, through the collective effort of our people, to buy the house from you at a financial gain to your family.

RUTH: Lord have mercy, ain't this the living gall!

WALTER: All right, you through?

LINDNER: Well, I want to give you the exact terms of the financial arrangement—

WALTER: We don't want to hear no exact terms of no arrangements. I want to know if you got any more to tell us 'bout getting together?

LINDNER (*taking off his glasses*): Well—I don't suppose that you feel . . .

WALTER: Never mind how I feel—you got any more to say 'bout how people ought to sit down and talk to each other? . . . Get out of my house, man.

(*He turns his back and walks to the door.*)

LINDNER (*looking around at the hostile faces and reaching and assembling his hat and briefcase*): Well—I don't understand why you people are reacting this way. What do you think you are going to gain by moving into a neighborhood where you just aren't wanted and where some elements—well—people can get awful worked up when they feel that their whole way of life and everything they've ever worked for is threatened.

WALTER: Get out.

LINDNER (*at the door, holding a small card*): Well—I'm sorry it went like this.

WALTER: Get out.

LINDNER (*almost sadly regarding Walter*): You just can't force people to change their hearts, son.

(*He turns and puts his card on a table and exits. Walter pushes the door to with stinging hatred, and stands looking at it. Ruth just sits and Beneatha just stands. They say nothing. Mama and Travis enter.*)

MAMA: Well—this all the packing got done since I left out of here this morning. I testify before God that my children got all the energy of the *dead!* What time the moving men due?

BENEATHA: Four o'clock. You had a caller, Mama.

(*She is smiling, teasingly.*)

MAMA: Sure enough—who?

BENEATHA (*her arms folded saucily*): The Welcoming Committee.

(*Walter and Ruth giggle.*)

MAMA (*innocently*): Who?

BENEATHA: The Welcoming Committee. They said they're sure going to be glad to see you when you get there.

WALTER (*devilishly*): Yeah, they said they can't hardly wait to see your face.

(*Laughter.*)

MAMA (*sensing their facetiousness*): What's the matter with you all?

WALTER: Ain't nothing the matter with us. We just telling you 'bout the gentleman who came to see you this afternoon. From the Clybourne Park Improvement Association.

MAMA: What he want?

RUTH (*in the same mood as Beneatha and Walter*): To welcome you, honey.

WALTER: He said they can't hardly wait. He said the one thing they don't have, that they just *dying* to have out there is a fine family of fine colored people! (*To Ruth and Beneatha.*) Ain't that right!

RUTH (*mockingly*): Yeah! He left his card—

BENEATHA (*handing card to Mama*): In case.

(*Mama reads and throws it on the floor—understanding and looking off as she draws her chair up to the table on which she has put her plant and some sticks and some cord.*)

MAMA: Father, give us strength. (*Knowingly—and without fun.*) Did he threaten us?

BENEATHA: Oh—Mama—they don't do it like that anymore. He talked Brotherhood. He said everybody ought to learn how to sit down and hate each other with good Christian fellowship.

(*She and Walter shake hands to ridicule the remark.*)

MAMA (*sadly*): Lord, protect us . . .

RUTH: You should hear the money those folks raised to buy the house from us. All we paid and then some.

BENEATHA: What they think we going to do—eat 'em?

RUTH: No, honey, marry 'em.

MAMA (*shaking her head*): Lord, Lord, Lord . . .

RUTH: Well—that's the way the crackers crumble. (*A beat.*) Joke.

BENEATHA (*laughingly noticing what her mother is doing*): Mama, what are you doing?

MAMA: Fixing my plant so it won't get hurt none on the way . . .

BENEATHA: Mama, you going to take *that* to the new house?

MAMA: Un-huh—

BENEATHA: That raggedy-looking old thing?

MAMA (*stopping and looking at her*): It expresses ME!

RUTH (*with delight, to Beneatha*): So there, Miss Thing!

(*Walter comes to Mama suddenly and bends down behind her and squeezes her in his arms with all his strength. She is overwhelmed by the suddenness of it and, though delighted, her manner is like that of Ruth and Travis.*)

MAMA: Look out now, boy! You make me mess up my thing here!

WALTER (*his face lit, he slips down on his knees beside her, his arms still about her*): Mama . . . you know what it means to climb up in the chariot?

MAMA (*gruffly, very happy*): Get on away from me now . . .

RUTH (*near the gift-wrapped package, trying to catch Walter's eye*): Psst—

WALTER: What the old song say, Mama . . .

RUTH: Walter—Now?

(*She is pointing at the package.*)

WALTER (*speaking the lines, sweetly, playfully, in his mother's face*): I got wings . . . you got wings . . . All God's Children got wings . . .

MAMA: Boy—get out of my face and do some work . . .

WALTER: When I get to heaven gonna put on my wings, Gonna fly all over God's heaven . . .

BENEATHA (*teasingly, from across the room*): Everybody talking 'bout heaven ain't going there!

WALTER (*to Ruth, who is carrying the box across to them*): I don't know, you think we ought to give her that . . . Seems to me she ain't been very appreciative around here.

MAMA (*eyeing the box, which is obviously a gift*): What is that?

WALTER (*taking it from Ruth and putting it on the table in front of Mama*): Well—what you all think? Should we give it to her?

RUTH: Oh—she was pretty good today.

MAMA: I'll good you—

(*She turns her eyes to the box again.*)

BENEATHA: Open it, Mama.

(*She stands up, looks at it, turns, and looks at all of them, and then presses her hands together and does not open the package.*)

WALTER (*sweetly*): Open it, Mama. It's for you. (*Mama looks in his eyes. It is the first present in her life without its being Christmas. Slowly she opens her package and lifts out, one by one, a brand-new sparkling set of gardening tools. Walter continues, prodding.*) Ruth made up the note—read it . . .

MAMA (*picking up the card and adjusting her glasses*): "To our own Mrs. Miniver—Love from Brother, Ruth and Beneatha." Ain't that lovely . . .

TRAVIS (*tugging at his father's sleeve*): Daddy, can I give her mine now?

WALTER: All right, son. (*Travis flies to get his gift.*)

MAMA: Now I don't have to use my knives and forks no more . . .

WALTER: Travis didn't want to go in with the rest of us, Mama. He got his own. (*Somewhat amused.*) We don't know what it is . . .

TRAVIS (*racing back in the room with a large hatbox and putting it in front of his grandmother*): Here!

MAMA: Lord have mercy, baby. You done gone and bought your grandmother a hat?

TRAVIS (*very proud*): Open it!

(*She does and lifts out an elaborate, but very elaborate, wide gardening hat, and all the adults break up at the sight of it.*)

RUTH: Travis, honey, what is that?

TRAVIS (*who thinks it is beautiful and appropriate*): It's a gardening hat! Like the ladies always have on in the magazines when they work in their gardens.

BENEATHA (*giggling fiercely*): Travis—we were trying to make Mama Mrs. Miniver—not Scarlett O'Hara!

MAMA (*indignantly*): What's the matter with you all! This here is a beautiful hat! (*Absurdly.*) I always wanted me one just like it!

(*She pops it on her head to prove it to her grandson, and the hat is ludicrous and considerably oversized.*)

RUTH: Hot dog! Go, Mama!

WALTER (*doubled over with laughter*): I'm sorry, Mama—but you look like you ready to go out and chop you some cotton sure enough!

(*They all laugh except Mama, out of deference to Travis's feelings.*)

MAMA (*gathering the boy up to her*): Bless your heart—this is the prettiest hat I ever owned—(*Walter, Ruth, and Beneatha chime in—noisily, festively, and insincerely congratulating Travis on his gift.*) What are we all standing around here for? We ain't finished packin' yet. Bennie, you ain't packed one book.

(*The bell rings.*)

BENEATHA: That couldn't be the movers . . . it's not hardly two good yet—

(*Beneatha goes into her room. Mama starts for door.*)

WALTER (*turning, stiffening*): Wait—wait—I'll get it.

(*He stands and looks at the door.*)

MAMA: You expecting company, son?

WALTER (*just looking at the door*): Yeah—yeah . . .

(*Mama looks at Ruth, and they exchange innocent and unfrightened glances.*)

MAMA (*not understanding*): Well, let them in, son.

BENEATHA (*from her room*): We need some more string.

MAMA: Travis—you run to the hardware and get me some string cord.

(*Mama goes out and Walter turns and looks at Ruth. Travis goes to a dish for money.*)

RUTH: Why don't you answer the door, man?

WALTER (*suddenly bounding across the floor to embrace her*): 'Cause sometimes it hard to let the future begin! (*Stooping down in her face.*)

I got wings! You got wings!

All God's children got wings!

(*He crosses to the door and throws it open. Standing there is a very slight little man in a not too prosperous business suit and with haunted frightened eyes and a hat pulled down tightly, brim up, around his forehead. Travis passes between the men and exits. Walter leans deep in the man's face, still in his jubilance.*) When I get to heaven gonna put on my wings, Gonna fly all over

God's heaven . . . (*The little man just stares at him.*) Heaven—(*Suddenly he stops and looks past the little man into the empty hallway.*) Where's Willy, man?

BOBO: He ain't with me.

WALTER (*not disturbed*): Oh—come on in. You know my wife.

BOBO (*dumbly, taking off his hat*): Yes—h'you, Miss Ruth.

RUTH (*quietly, a mood apart from her husband already, seeing Bobo*): Hello, Bobo.

WALTER: You right on time today . . . Right on time. That's the way! (*He slaps Bobo on his back.*) Sit down . . . lemme hear.

(*Ruth stands stiffly and quietly in back of them, as though somehow she senses death, her eyes fixed on her husband.*)

BOBO (*his frightened eyes on the floor, his hat in his hands*): Could I please get a drink of water, before I tell you about it, Walter Lee?

(*Walter does not take his eyes off the man. Ruth goes blindly to the tap and gets a glass of water and brings it to Bobo.*)

WALTER: There ain't nothing wrong, is there?

BOBO: Lemme tell you—

WALTER: Man—didn't nothing go wrong?

BOBO: Lemme tell you—Walter Lee. (*Looking at Ruth and talking to her more than to Walter.*) You know how it was. I got to tell you how it was. I mean first I got to tell you how it was all the way . . . I mean about the money I put in, Walter Lee . . .

WALTER (*with taut agitation now*): What about the money you put in?

BOBO: Well—it wasn't much as we told you—me and Willy—(*He stops.*) I'm sorry, Walter. I got a bad feeling about it. I got a real bad feeling about it . . .

WALTER: Man, what you telling me about all this for? . . . Tell me what happened in Springfield . . .

BOBO: Springfield.

RUTH (*like a dead woman*): What was supposed to happen in Springfield?

BOBO (*to her*): This deal that me and Walter went into with Willy—Me and Willy was going to go down to Springfield and spread some money 'round so's we wouldn't have to wait so long for the liquor license . . . That's what we were going to do. Everybody said that was the way you had to do, you understand, Miss Ruth?

WALTER: Man—what happened down there?

BOBO (*a pitiful man, near tears*): I'm trying to tell you, Walter.

WALTER (*screaming at him suddenly*): THEN TELL ME, GODDAMMIT . . . WHAT'S THE MATTER WITH YOU?

BOBO: Man . . . I didn't go to no Springfield, yesterday.

WALTER (*halted, life hanging in the moment*): Why not?

BOBO (*the long way, the hard way to tell*): 'Cause I didn't have no reasons to . . .

WALTER: Man, what are you talking about!

BOBO: I'm talking about the fact that when I got to the train station yesterday morning—eight o'clock like we planned . . . Man—*Willy didn't never show up.*

WALTER: Why . . . where was he . . . where is he?

BOBO: That's what I'm trying to tell you . . . I don't know . . . I waited six hours . . . I called his house . . . and I waited . . . six hours . . . I waited in that train station six hours . . . (*Breaking into tears.*) That was all the extra money I had in the world . . . (*Looking up at Walter with the tears running down his face.*) Man, *Willy is gone.*

WALTER: Gone, what you mean Willy is gone? Gone where? You mean he went by himself. You mean he went off to Springfield by himself—to take care of getting the license—(*Turns and looks anxiously at Ruth.*) You mean maybe he didn't want too many people in on the business down there? (*Looks to Ruth again, as before.*) You know Willy got his own ways. (*Looks back to Bobo.*) Maybe you was late yesterday and he just went on down there without you. Maybe—maybe—he's been callin' you at home tryin' to tell you what happened or something. Maybe—maybe—he just got sick. He's somewhere—he's got to be somewhere. We just got to find him—me and you got to find him. (*Grabs Bobo senselessly by the collar and starts to shake him.*) We got to!

BOBO (*in sudden angry, frightened agony*): What's the matter with you, Walter! *When a cat take off with your money he don't leave you no road maps!*

WALTER (*turning madly, as though he is looking for Willy in the very room*): Willy! . . . Willy . . . don't do it . . . Please don't do it . . . Man, not with that money . . . Man, please, not with that money . . . Oh, God . . . Don't let it be true . . . (*He is wandering around, crying out for Willy and looking for him or perhaps for help from God.*) Man . . . I trusted you . . . Man, I put my life in your hands . . . (*He starts to crumple down on the floor as Ruth just covers her face in horror. Mama opens the door and comes into the room, with Beneatha behind her.*) Man . . . (*He starts to pound the floor with his fists, sobbing wildly.*) THAT MONEY IS MADE OUT MY FATHER'S FLESH——

BOBO (*standing over him helplessly*): I'm sorry, Walter . . . (*Only Walter's sobs reply. Bobo puts on his hat.*) I had my life staked on this deal, too . . .

(*He exits.*)

MAMA (*to Walter*): Son—(*She goes to him, bends down to him, talks to his bent head.*) Son . . . Is it gone? Son, I gave you sixty-five hundred dollars. Is it gone? All of it? Beneatha's money too?

WALTER (*lifting his head slowly*): Mama . . . I never . . . went to the bank at all . . .

MAMA (*not wanting to believe him*): You mean . . . your sister's school money . . . you used that too . . . Walter? . . .

WALTER: Yessss! All of it . . . It's all gone . . .

(*There is total silence. Ruth stands with her face covered with her hands; Beneatha leans forlornly against a wall, fingering a piece of red ribbon from the mother's gift. Mama stops and looks at her son without recognition and then, quite without thinking about it, starts to beat him senselessly in the face. Beneatha goes to them and stops it.*)

BENEATHA: Mama!

(*Mama stops and looks at both of her children and rises slowly and wanders vaguely, aimlessly away from them.*)

MAMA: I seen . . . him . . . night after night . . . come in . . . and look at that rug . . . and then look at me . . . the red showing in his eyes . . . the veins moving in his head . . . I seen him grow thin and old before he was forty . . . working and working and working like somebody's old horse . . . killing himself . . . and you—you give it all away in a day—(*She raises her arms to strike him again.*)

BENEATHA: Mama—

MAMA: Oh, God . . . (*She looks up to Him.*) Look down here—and show me the strength.

BENEATHA: Mama—

MAMA (*folding over*): Strength . . .

BENEATHA (*plaintively*): Mama . . .

MAMA: Strength!

ACT III

(*An hour later.*)

(*At curtain, there is a sullen light of gloom in the living room, gray light not unlike that which began the first scene of act I. At left we can see Walter within his room, alone with himself. He is stretched out on the bed, his shirt out and open, his arms under his head. He does not smoke, he does not cry out, he merely lies there, looking up at the ceiling, much as if he were alone in the world.*)

(*In the living room Beneatha sits at the table, still surrounded by the now almost ominous packing crates. She sits looking off. We feel that this is a mood struck perhaps an hour before, and it lingers now, full of the empty sound of profound disappointment. We see on a line from her brother's bedroom the sameness of their attitudes. Presently the bell rings and Beneatha rises without ambition or interest in answering. It is Asagai, smiling broadly, striding into the room with energy and happy expectation and conversation.*)

ASAGAI: I came over . . . I had some free time. I thought I might help with the packing. Ah, I like the look of packing crates! A household in preparation for a journey! It depresses some people . . . but for me . . . it is another feeling. Something full of the flow of life, do you understand? Movement, progress . . . It makes me think of Africa.

BENEATHA: Africa!

ASAGAI: What kind of a mood is this? Have I told you how deeply you move me?

BENEATHA: He gave away the money, Asagai . . .

ASAGAI: Who gave away what money?

BENEATHA: The insurance money. My brother gave it away.

ASAGAI: Gave it away?

BENEATHA: He made an investment! With a man even Travis wouldn't have trusted with his most worn-out marbles.

ASAGAI: And it's gone?

BENEATHA: Gone!

ASAGAI: I'm very sorry . . . And you, now?

BENEATHA: Me? . . . Me? . . . Me, I'm nothing . . . Me. When I was very small . . . we used to take our sleds out in the wintertime and the only hills we had were the ice-covered stone steps of some houses down the street. And we used to fill them in with snow and make them smooth and slide down them all day . . . and it was very dangerous, you know . . . far too steep . . . and sure enough one day a kid named Rufus came down too fast and hit the sidewalk and we saw his face just split open right there in front of us . . . And I remember standing there looking at his bloody open face thinking that was the end of Rufus. But the ambulance came and they took him to the hospital and they fixed the broken bones and they sewed it all up . . . and the next time I saw Rufus he just had a little line down the middle of his face . . . I never got over that . . .

ASAGAI: What?

BENEATHA: That that was what one person could do for another, fix him up—sew up the problem, make him all right again. That was the most marvelous thing in the world . . . I wanted to do that. I always thought it was the one concrete thing in the world that a human being could do. Fix up the sick, you know—and make them whole again. This was truly being God . . .

ASAGAI: You wanted to be God?

BENEATHA: No—I wanted to cure. It used to be so important to me. I wanted to cure. It used to matter. I used to care. I mean about people and how their bodies hurt . . .

ASAGAI: And you've stopped caring?

BENEATHA: Yes—I think so.

ASAGAI: Why?

BENEATHA (*bitterly*): Because it doesn't seem deep enough, close enough to what ails mankind! It was a child's way of seeing things—or an idealist's.

ASAGAI: Children see things very well sometimes—and idealists even better.

BENEATHA: I know that's what you think. Because you are still where I left off. You with all your talk and dreams about Africa! You still think you can patch up the world. Cure the Great Sore of Colonialism—(*loftily, mocking it*) with the Penicillin of Independence—!

ASAGAI: Yes!

BENEATHA: Independence *and then what?* What about all the crooks and thieves and just plain idiots who will come into power and steal and plunder the same as before—only now they will be black and do it in the name of the new Independence—WHAT ABOUT THEM?!

ASAGAI: That will be the problem for another time. First we must get there.

BENEATHA: And where does it end?

ASAGAI: End? Who even spoke of an end? To life? To living?

BENEATHA: An end to misery! To stupidity! Don't you see there isn't any real progress, Asagai, there is only one large circle that we march in, around and around, each of us with our own little picture in front of us—our own little mirage that we think is the future.

ASAGAI: That is the mistake.

BENEATHA: What?

ASAGAI: What you just said—about the circle. It isn't a circle—it is simply a long line—as in geometry, you know, one that reaches into infinity. And because we cannot see the end—we also cannot see how it changes. And it is very odd but those who see the changes—who dream, who will not give up—are called idealists . . . and those who see only the circle—we call *them* the "realists"!

BENEATHA: Asagai, while I was sleeping in that bed in there, people went out and took the future right out of my hands! And nobody asked me, nobody consulted me—they just went out and changed my life!

ASAGAI: Was it your money?

BENEATHA: What?

ASAGAI: Was it your money he gave away?

BENEATHA: It belonged to all of us.

ASAGAI: But did you earn it? Would you have had it at all if your father had not died?

BENEATHA: No.

ASAGAI: Then isn't there something wrong in a house—in a world—where all dreams, good or bad, must depend on the death of a man? I never thought to see *you* like this, Alaiyo. You! Your brother made a mistake and you are grateful to him so that now you can give up the ailing human race on account of it! You talk about what good is struggle, what good is anything! Where are we all going and why are we bothering!

BENEATHA: AND YOU CANNOT ANSWER IT!

ASAGAI (*shouting over her*): I LIVE THE ANSWER! (*Pause.*) In my village at home it is the exceptional man who can even read a newspaper . . . or who ever sees a book at all. I will go home and much of what I will have to say will seem strange to the people of my village. But I will teach and work and things will happen, slowly and swiftly. At times it will seem that nothing changes at all . . . and then again the sudden dramatic events which make history leap into the future. And then quiet again. Retrogression even. Guns, murder, revolution. And I even will have moments when I

wonder if the quiet was not better than all that death and hatred. But I will look about my village at the illiteracy and disease and ignorance and I will not wonder long. And perhaps . . . perhaps I will be a great man . . . I mean perhaps I will hold on to the substance of truth and find my way always with the right course . . . and perhaps for it I will be butchered in my bed some night by the servants of empire . . .

BENEATHA: *The martyr!*

ASAGAI (*he smiles*): . . . or perhaps I shall live to be a very old man, respected and esteemed in my new nation . . . And perhaps I shall hold office and this is what I'm trying to tell you, Alaiyo: Perhaps the things I believe now for my country will be wrong and outmoded, and I will not understand and do terrible things to have things my way or merely to keep my power. Don't you see that there will be young men and women—not British soldiers then, but my own black countrymen—to step out of the shadows some evening and slit my then useless throat? Don't you see they have always been there . . . that they always will be. And that such a thing as my own death will be an advance? They who might kill me even . . . actually replenish all that I was.

BENEATHA: Oh, Asagai, I know all that.

ASAGAI: Good! Then stop moaning and groaning and tell me what you plan to do.

BENEATHA: Do?

ASAGAI: I have a bit of a suggestion.

BENEATHA: What?

ASAGAI (*rather quietly for him*): That when it is all over—that you come home with me—

BENEATHA (*staring at him and crossing away with exasperation*): Oh—Asagai—at this moment you decide to be romantic!

ASAGAI (*quickly understanding the misunderstanding*): My dear, young creature of the New World—I do not mean across the city—I mean across the ocean: home—to Africa.

BENEATHA (*slowly understanding and turning to him with murmured amazement*): To Africa?

ASAGAI: Yes! . . . (*Smiling and lifting his arms playfully.*) Three hundred years later the African Prince rose up out of the seas and swept the maiden back across the middle passage over which her ancestors had come—

BENEATHA (*unable to play*): To—to Nigeria?

ASAGAI: Nigeria. Home. (*Coming to her with genuine romantic flippancy.*) I will show you our mountains and our stars; and give you cool drinks from gourds and teach you the old songs and the ways of our people—and, in time, we will pretend that—(*very softly*)—you have only been away for a day. Say that you'll come—(*He swings her around and takes her full in his arms in a kiss which proceeds to passion.*)

BENEATHA (*pulling away suddenly*): You're getting me all mixed up—

ASAGAI: Why?

BENEATHA: Too many things—too many things have happened today. I must sit down and think. I don't know what I feel about anything right this minute.

(*She promptly sits down and props her chin on her fist.*)

ASAGAI (*charmed*): All right, I shall leave you. No—don't get up. (*Touching her, gently, sweetly.*) Just sit awhile and think . . . Never be afraid to sit awhile and think. (*He goes to door and looks at her.*) How often I have looked at you and said, "Ah—so this is what the New World hath finally wrought . . ."

(*He exits. Beneatha sits on alone. Presently Walter enters from his room and starts to rummage through things, feverishly looking for something. She looks up and turns in her seat.*)

BENEATHA (*hissingly*): Yes—just look at what the New World hath wrought! . . . Just look! (*She gestures with bitter disgust.*) There he is! *Monsieur le petit bourgeois noir*° —himself! There he is—Symbol of a Rising Class! Entrepreneur! Titan° of the system! (*Walter ignores her completely and continues frantically and destructively looking for something and hurling things to the floor and tearing things out of their place in his search. Beneatha ignores the eccentricity of his actions and goes on with the monologue of insult.*) Did you dream of yachts on Lake Michigan, Brother? Did you see yourself on that Great Day sitting down at the Conference Table, surrounded by all the mighty bald-headed men in America? All halted, waiting, breathless, waiting for your pronouncements on industry? Waiting for you—Chairman of the Board! (*Walter finds what he is looking for—a small piece of white paper—and pushes it in his pocket and puts on his coat and rushes out without ever having looked at her. She shouts after him.*) I look at you and I see the final triumph of stupidity in the world!

(*The door slams and she returns to just sitting again. Ruth comes quickly out of Mama's room.*)

RUTH: Who was that?
BENEATHA: Your husband.
RUTH: Where did he go?
BENEATHA: Who knows—maybe he has an appointment at U.S. Steel.
RUTH (*anxiously, with frightened eyes*): You didn't say nothing bad to him, did you?
BENEATHA: Bad? Say anything bad to him? No—I told him he was a sweet boy and full of dreams and everything is strictly peachy keen, as the ofay° kids say!

(*Mama enters from her bedroom. She is lost, vague, trying to catch hold, to make some sense of her former command of the world, but it still eludes her. A sense*

Monsieur . . . noir: Mr. Black Lower Middle Class. **Titan:** Person of great power; originally, a god. **ofay:** White person, usually used disparagingly.

of waste overwhelms her gait; a measure of apology rides on her shoulders. She goes to her plant, which has remained on the table, looks at it, picks it up and takes it to the window sill and sits it outside, and she stands and looks at it a long moment. Then she closes the window, straightens her body with effort, and turns around to her children.*)

MAMA: Well—ain't it a mess in here, though? (*A false cheerfulness, a beginning of something.*) I guess we all better stop moping around and get some work done. All this unpacking and everything we got to do. (*Ruth raises her head slowly in response to the sense of the line; and Beneatha in similar manner turns very slowly to look at her mother.*) One of you all better call the moving people and tell 'em not to come.

RUTH: Tell 'em not to come?
MAMA: Of course, baby. Ain't no need in 'em coming all the way here and having to go back. They charges for that too. (*She sits down, fingers to her brow, thinking.*) Lord, ever since I was a little girl, I always remembers people saying, "Lena—Lena Eggleston, you aims too high all the time. You needs to slow down and see life a little more like it is. Just slow down some." That's what they always used to say down home—"Lord, that Lena Eggleston is a high-minded thing. She'll get her due one day!"

RUTH: No, Lena . . .
MAMA: Me and Big Walter just didn't never learn right.
RUTH: Lena, no! We gotta go. Bennie—tell her . . . (*She rises and crosses to Beneatha with her arms outstretched. Beneatha doesn't respond.*) Tell her we can still move . . . the notes ain't but a hundred and twenty-five a month. We got four grown people in this house—we can work . . .
MAMA (*to herself*): Just aimed too high all the time—
RUTH (*turning and going to Mama fast—the words pouring out with urgency and desperation*): Lena—I'll work . . . I'll work twenty hours a day in all the kitchens in Chicago . . . I'll strap my baby on my back if I have to and scrub all the floors in America and wash all the sheets in America if I have to—but we got to MOVE! We got to get OUT OF HERE!!

(*Mama reaches out absently and pats Ruth's hand.*)

MAMA: No—I sees things differently now. Been thinking 'bout some of the things we could do to fix this place up some. I seen a second-hand bureau over on Maxwell Street just the other day that could fit right there. (*She points to where the new furniture might go. Ruth wanders away from her.*) Would need some new handles on it and then a little varnish and it look like something brand-new. And we can put up them new curtains in the kitchen . . . Why this place be looking fine. Cheer us all up so that we forget trouble ever come . . . (*To Ruth.*) And you could get some nice screens to put up in your room round the baby's bassinet . . . (*She looks at both of them, pleadingly.*)

Sometimes you just got to know when to give up some things . . . and hold on to what you got. . . .

(*Walter enters from the outside, looking spent and leaning against the door, his coat hanging from him.*)

MAMA: Where you been, son?

WALTER (*breathing hard*): Made a call.

MAMA: To who, son?

WALTER: To The Man. (*He heads for his room.*)

MAMA: What man, baby?

WALTER (*stops in the door*): The Man, Mama. Don't you know who The Man is?

RUTH: Walter Lee?

WALTER: *The Man.* Like the guys in the streets say—The Man. Captain Boss—Mistuh Charley . . . Old Cap'n Please Mr. Bossman . . .

BENEATHA (*suddenly*): Lindner!

WALTER: That's right! That's good. I told him to come right over.

BENEATHA (*fiercely, understanding*): For what? What do you want to see him for!

WALTER (*looking at his sister*): We going to do business with him.

MAMA: What you talking 'bout, son?

WALTER: Talking 'bout life, Mama. You all always telling me to see life like it is. Well—I laid in there on my back today . . . and I figured it out. Life just like it is. Who gets and who don't get. (*He sits down with his coat on and laughs.*) Mama, you know it's all divided up. Life is. Sure enough. Between the takers and the "tooken." (*He laughs.*) I've figured it out finally. (*He looks around at them.*) Yeah. Some of us always getting "tooken." (*He laughs.*) People like Willy Harris, they don't never get "tooken." And you know why the rest of us do? 'Cause we all mixed up. Mixed up bad. We get to looking 'round for the right and the wrong; and we worry about it and cry about it and stay up nights trying to figure out 'bout the wrong and the right of things all the time . . . And all the time, man, them takers is out there operating, just taking and taking. Willy Harris? Shoot—Willy Harris don't even count. He don't even count in the big scheme of things. But I'll say one thing for old Willy Harris . . . he's taught me something. He's taught me to keep my eye on what counts in this world. Yeah—(*Shouting out a little.*) Thanks, Willy!

RUTH: What did you call that man for, Walter Lee?

WALTER: Called him to tell him to come on over to the show. Gonna put on a show for the man. Just what he wants to see. You see, Mama, the man came here today and he told us that them people out there where you want us to move—well they so upset they willing to pay us *not* to move! (*He laughs again.*) And—and oh, Mama—you would of been proud of the way me and Ruth and Bennie acted. We told him to get out . . . Lord have mercy! We told the man to get out! Oh, we was some proud folks this afternoon, yeah. (*He lights a cigarette.*) We were still full of that old-time stuff . . .

RUTH (*coming toward him slowly*): You talking 'bout taking them people's money to keep us from moving in that house?

WALTER: I ain't just talking 'bout it, baby—I'm telling you that's what's going to happen!

BENEATHA: Oh, God! Where is the bottom! Where is the real honest-to-God bottom so he can't go any farther!

WALTER: See—that's the old stuff. You and that boy that was here today. You all want everybody to carry a flag and a spear and sing some marching songs, huh? You wanna spend your life looking into things and trying to find the right and the wrong part, huh? Yeah. You know what's going to happen to that boy someday—he'll find himself sitting in a dungeon, locked in forever—and the takers will have the key! Forget it, baby! There ain't no causes—there ain't nothing but taking in this world, and he who takes most is smartest—and it don't make a damn bit of difference *how.*

MAMA: You making something inside me cry, son. Some awful pain inside me.

WALTER: Don't cry, Mama. Understand. That white man is going to walk in that door able to write checks for more money than we ever had. It's important to him and I'm going to help him . . . I'm going to put on the show, Mama.

MAMA: Son—I come from five generations of people who was slaves and sharecroppers—but ain't nobody in my family never let nobody pay 'em no money that was a way of telling us we wasn't fit to walk the earth. We ain't never been that poor. (*Raising her eyes and looking at him.*) We ain't never been that—dead inside.

BENEATHA: Well—we are dead now. All the talk about dreams and sunlight that goes on in this house. It's all dead now.

WALTER: What's the matter with you all! I didn't make this world! It was give to me this way! Hell, yes, I want me some yachts someday! Yes, I want to hang some real pearls 'round my wife's neck. Ain't she supposed to wear no pearls? Somebody tell me—tell me, who decides which women is suppose to wear pearls in this world. I tell you I am a *man*—and I think my wife should wear some pearls in this world!

(*This last line hangs a good while and Walter begins to move about the room. The word "Man" has penetrated his consciousness; he mumbles it to himself repeatedly between strange agitated pauses as he moves about.*)

MAMA: Baby, how you going to feel on the inside?

WALTER: Fine! . . . Going to feel fine . . . a man . . .

MAMA: You won't have nothing left then, Walter Lee.

WALTER (*coming to her*): I'm going to feel fine, Mama. I'm going to look that son-of-a-bitch in the eyes and say—(*he falters*)—and say, "All right, Mr. Lindner—(*he falters even more*)—that's *your* neighborhood out there! You got the right to keep it like you want! You got the right to have it like you want! Just write the check and—the house is yours." And—and

I am going to say—(*His voice almost breaks.*) "And you—you people just put the money in my hand and you won't have to live next to this bunch of stinking niggers! . . ." (*He straightens up and moves away from his mother, walking around the room.*) And maybe—maybe I'll just get down on my black knees . . . (*He does so; Ruth and Bennie and Mama watch him in frozen horror.*) "Captain, Mistuh, Bossman—(*Groveling and grinning and wringing his hands in profoundly anguished imitation of the slow-witted movie stereotype.*) A-hee-hee-hee! Oh, yassuh boss! Yassssssuh! Great white—(*voice breaking, he forces himself to go on*)—Father, just gi' us-sen de money, fo' God's sake, and we's—we's ain't gwine come out deh and dirty up yo' white folks neighborhood . . ." (*He breaks down completely.*) And I'll feel fine! Fine! fine! (*He gets up and goes into the bedroom.*)

BENEATHA: That is not a man. That is nothing but a toothless rat.

MAMA: Yes—death done come in this here house. (*She is nodding, slowly, reflectively.*) Done come walking in my house on the lips of my children. You what supposed to be my beginning again. You—what supposed to be my harvest. (*To Beneatha.*) You—you mourning your brother?

BENEATHA: He's no brother of mine.

MAMA: What you say?

BENEATHA: I said that that individual in that room is no brother of mine.

MAMA: That's what I thought you said. You feeling like you better than he is today? (*Beneatha does not answer.*) Yes? What you tell him a minute ago? That he wasn't a man? Yes? You give him up for me? You done wrote his epitaph too—like the rest of the world? Well, who give you the privilege?

BENEATHA: Be on my side for once! You saw what he just did, Mama! You saw him—down on his knees. Wasn't it you who taught me to despise any man who would do that? Do what he's going to do?

MAMA: Yes—I taught you that. Me and your daddy. But I thought I taught you something else too . . . I thought I taught you to love him.

BENEATHA: Love him? There is nothing left to love.

MAMA: There is *always* something left to love. And if you ain't learned that, you ain't learned nothing. (*Looking at her.*) Have you cried for that boy today? I don't mean for yourself and for the family 'cause we lost the money. I mean for him: what he been through and what it done to him. Child, when do you think is the time to love somebody the most? When they done good and made things easy for everybody? Well then, you ain't through learning—because that ain't the time at all. It's when he's at his lowest and can't believe in hisself 'cause the world done whipped him so! When you starts measuring somebody, measure him right, child, measure him right. Make sure you done taken into account what hills and valleys he come through before he got to wherever he is.

(*Travis bursts into the room at the end of the speech, leaving the door open.*)

TRAVIS: Grandmama—the moving men are downstairs! The truck just pulled up.

MAMA (*turning and looking at him*): Are they, baby? They downstairs?

(*She sighs and sits. Lindner appears in the doorway. He peers in and knocks lightly, to gain attention, and comes in. All turn to look at him.*)

LINDNER (*hat and briefcase in hand*): Uh—hello . . .

(*Ruth crosses mechanically to the bedroom door and opens it and lets it swing open freely and slowly as the lights come up on Walter within, still in his coat, sitting at the far corner of the room. He looks up and out through the room to Lindner.*)

RUTH: He's here.

(*A long minute passes and Walter slowly gets up.*)

LINDNER (*coming to the table with efficiency, putting his briefcase on the table and starting to unfold papers and unscrew fountain pens*): Well, I certainly was glad to hear from you people. (*Walter has begun the trek out of the room, slowly and awkwardly, rather like a small boy, passing the back of his sleeve across his mouth from time to time.*) Life can really be so much simpler than people let it be most of the time. Well—with whom do I negotiate? You, Mrs. Younger, or your son here? (*Mama sits with her hands folded on her lap and her eyes closed as Walter advances. Travis goes closer to Lindner and looks at the papers curiously.*) Just some official papers, sonny.

RUTH: Travis, you go downstairs—

MAMA (*opening her eyes and looking into Walter's*): No. Travis, you stay right here. And you make him understand what you doing, Walter Lee. You teach him good. Like Willy Harris taught you. You show where our five generations done come to. (*Walter looks from her to the boy, who grins at him innocently.*) Go ahead, son—(*She folds her hands and closes her eyes.*) Go ahead.

WALTER (*at last crosses to Lindner, who is reviewing the contract*): Well, Mr. Lindner. (*Beneatha turns away.*) We called you—(*there is a profound, simple groping quality in his speech*)—because, well, me and my family (*he looks around and shifts from one foot to the other*) Well—we are very plain people . . .

LINDNER: Yes—

WALTER: I mean—I have worked as a chauffeur most of my life—and my wife here, she does domestic work in people's kitchens. So does my mother. I mean—we are plain people . . .

LINDNER: Yes, Mr. Younger—

WALTER (*really like a small boy, looking down at his shoes and then up at the man*): And—uh—well, my father, well, he was a laborer most of his life. . . .

LINDNER (*absolutely confused*): Uh, yes—yes, I understand. (*He turns back to the contract.*)

WALTER (*a beat; staring at him*): And my father—(*With sudden intensity.*) My father almost *beat a man to death* once because this man called him a bad name or something, you know what I mean?

LINDNER (*looking up, frozen*): No, no, I'm afraid I don't—

WALTER (*A beat. The tension hangs; then Walter steps back from it.*): Yeah. Well—what I mean is that we come from people who had a lot of *pride.* I mean—we are very proud people. And that's my sister over there and she's going to be a doctor—and we are very proud—

LINDNER: Well—I am sure that is very nice, but—

WALTER: What I am telling you is that we called you over here to tell you that we are very proud and that this—(*Signaling to Travis.*) Travis, come here. (*Travis crosses and Walter draws him before him facing the man.*) This is my son, and he makes the sixth generation of our family in this country. And we have all thought about your offer—

LINDNER: Well, good . . . good—

WALTER: And we have decided to move into our house because my father—my father—he earned it for us brick by brick. (*Mama has her eyes closed and is rocking back and forth as though she were in church, with her head nodding the Amen yes.*) We don't want to make no trouble for nobody or fight no causes, and we will try to be good neighbors. And that's *all* we got to say about that. (*He looks the man absolutely in the eyes.*) We don't want your money. (*He turns and walks away.*)

LINDNER (*looking around at all of them*): I take it then—that you have decided to occupy . . .

BENEATHA: That's what the man said.

LINDNER (*to Mama in her reverie*): Then I would like to appeal to you, Mrs. Younger. You are older and wiser and understand things better I am sure . . .

MAMA: I am afraid you don't understand. My son said we was going to move and there ain't nothing left for me to say. (*Briskly.*) You know how these young folks is nowadays, mister. Can't do a thing with 'em! (*As he opens his mouth, she rises.*) Goodbye.

LINDNER (*folding up his materials*): Well—if you are that final about it . . . there is nothing left for me to say. (*He finishes, almost ignored by the family, who are concentrating on Walter Lee. At the door Lindner halts and looks around.*) I sure hope you people know what you're getting into.

(*He shakes his head and exits.*)

RUTH (*looking around and coming to life*): Well, for God's sake—if the moving men are here—LET'S GET THE HELL OUT OF HERE!

MAMA (*into action*): Ain't it the truth! Look at all this here mess. Ruth, put Travis's good jacket on him . . . Walter Lee, fix your tie and tuck your shirt in, you look like somebody's hoodlum! Lord have mercy, where is my plant? (*She flies to get it amid the general bustling of the family, who are deliberately trying to ignore the nobility of the past moment.*) You all start on down . . . Travis child, don't go empty-handed . . . Ruth, where did I put that box with my skillets in it? I want to be in charge of it myself . . . I'm going to make us the biggest dinner we ever ate tonight . . . Beneatha, what's the matter with them stockings? Pull them things up, girl . . .

(*The family starts to file out as two moving men appear and begin to carry out the heavier pieces of furniture, bumping into the family as they move about.*)

BENEATHA: Mama, Asagai asked me to marry him today and go to Africa—

MAMA (*in the middle of her getting-ready activity*): He did? You ain't old enough to marry nobody—(*Seeing the moving men lifting one of her chairs precariously.*) Darling, that ain't no bale of cotton, please handle it so we can sit in it again! I had that chair twenty-five years . . .

(*The movers sigh with exasperation and go on with their work.*)

BENEATHA (*girlishly and unreasonably trying to pursue the conversation*): To go to Africa, Mama—be a doctor in Africa . . .

MAMA (*distracted*): Yes, baby—

WALTER: *Africa!* What he want you to go to Africa for?

BENEATHA: To practice there . . .

WALTER: Girl, if you don't get all them silly ideas out your head! You better marry yourself a man with some loot . . .

BENEATHA (*angrily, precisely as in the first scene of the play*): What have you got to do with who I marry!

WALTER: Plenty. Now I think George Murchison—

BENEATHA: *George Murchison!* I wouldn't marry him if he was Adam and I was Eve!

(*Walter and Beneatha go out yelling at each other vigorously and the anger is loud and real till their voices diminish. Ruth stands at the door and turns to Mama and smiles knowingly.*)

MAMA (*fixing her hat at last*): Yeah—they something all right, my children . . .

RUTH: Yeah—they're something. Let's go, Lena.

MAMA (*stalling, starting to look around at the house*): Yes—I'm coming. Ruth—

RUTH: Yes?

MAMA (*quietly, woman to woman*): He finally come into his manhood today, didn't he? Kind of like a rainbow after the rain . . .

RUTH (*biting her lip lest her own pride explode in front of Mama*): Yes, Lena.

(*Walter's voice calls for them raucously.*)

WALTER (*offstage*): Y'all come on! These people charges by the hour you know!

MAMA (*waving Ruth out vaguely*): All right, honey—go on down. I be down directly.

(*Ruth hesitates, then exits. Mama stands, at last alone in the living room, her plant on the table before her as the lights start to come down. She looks around at all the walls and ceilings and suddenly, despite herself,* while the children call below, a great heaving thing rises in her and she puts her fist to her mouth to stifle it, takes a final desperate look, pulls her coat about her, pats her hat, and goes out. The lights dim down. The door opens and she comes back in, grabs her plant, and goes out for the last time.)

Wole Soyinka

Wole Soyinka (b. 1934), winner of the Nobel Prize for literature in 1986, is one of several important Nigerian writers who have achieved international fame. His work includes novels, poems, and plays, but he admits that "there is no question at all that I think the Nobel Prize is for my drama."

Soyinka studied at University College, Ibadan, Nigeria, and began his literary career as an undergraduate, publishing poetry in the distinguished African literary magazine *Black Orpheus*. His work, especially his drama, has been an investigation of political, religious, and other forces in Nigerian culture. *The Swamp Dwellers* (1958) is a powerful play condemning African superstition. *The Lion and the Jewel* (1959) offers a comic view of Nigerian attitudes toward European values left over from the colonial period. Among his other plays are *The Trials of Brother Jero* (1960), about a corrupt evangelist, and *Kongi's Harvest* (1964). *A Dance of the Forests* (1960) was written to celebrate Nigerian independence, but it also alerted people to Nigeria's past violence and warned against its return.

Nigeria went through a bitter civil war in 1967, and Soyinka's political sympathies led to a term in prison, where he was placed in solitary confinement. He continued writing, smuggling poems out of prison to give hope to his political allies. He even criticized his own tribe, the Yoruba, for murdering members of the Ibo during the war against Biafra.

Soyinka studied at the University of Leeds after his schooling in Ibadan. He has been chair of the drama department at Ife University as well as of his own University College, Ibadan. He has also lectured in Cambridge, England, and at universities in North America. Most of his writing is in English, but he still writes some of his poetry in his tribal language, Yoruba. He has recommended Swahili as the national language of Nigeria. Soyinka has spoken out against cultural parochialism, including its manifestation in the negritude movement, which rejects Western culture as a form of pollution. He expressed his philosophy to another great African writer, Leopold Senghor: "A tiger is not forever shouting about his tigritude"; a duiker antelope does not have to "prove his duikertude; you will know him by his elegant leap." One of his works, *A Play of Giants* (1984), is a scathing attack on abuse of power, indicting African tyrants such as Idi Amin and Jean-Bedel Bokassa.

For all of his criticism of Nigerian politics, Soyinka has rooted his work in the religion and folklore of the Yoruba people. Ifa, the Yoruba religion, depends on a complex cosmology that sees experience as layered in interactive animal, mineral, and vegetable spheres. African critic Femi Osofisan has described Yoruba cosmology as holding "coeval the three historical, actual, and prospective planes of entity; . . . the animal and vegetable essences are correspondent; . . . the acknowledged deities are both anthropomorphic and symbiotic, each fusing in his personality a series of antinomies." Osofisan also notes "the comprehensive union of religious and secular intuition in the traditional Yoruba." Ifa plays a role in *The Strong Breed*, but the play is nonetheless understandable to those not familiar with the religion. Soyinka must be thought of as a traditional dramatist, writing in the tradition of his Yoruba people but reaching a worldwide audience.

The Strong Breed

The Strong Breed (1962), written at a time of political uncertainty in Nigeria, examines the interrelationship of ritual and community in African culture, describing one process by which a society renews itself. The "strong breed" are those men capable of the sacrifice needed annually to purify the community of its sins and to allow it to start over again. The community's sacrifice signals the beginning of a new year.

As the new year approaches, the elders of the community, Jaguna and Oroge, search for the appropriate "carrier" who can bear the burden of the community's guilt. The tradition in their community is to choose a stranger. Despite the elders' reluctance, Eman, one of the strong breed who has exiled himself from his own community, seems a logical choice until another outsider, the idiot Ifada, comes on the scene. Ifada seems heaven-sent to serve the community, but when he is chosen, he protests in terrified confusion. Eman explains to Jaguna and Oroge that no community should force a carrier to perform unwillingly. If he is unwilling, the guilt will not be carried away. Eman then offers himself as a willing sacrifice in Ifada's place.

The mythic pattern of sacrifice and renewal is basic to much Yoruba myth. Part of the tradition of Yoruba ritual drama is the reenactment of myths that resemble Eman's willing sacrifice. These are celebrated annually on the feast day of Obatala, the god of creation. *The Strong Breed* has also been connected to ritual tragedies enacted in honor of Ogun, who suffers greatly for the good of the community.

The Strong Breed is informed by Soyinka's studies of Greek tragedy. Like Greek tragic figures, Soyinka's strong breed are genetically linked: they are fathers and sons who inherit their fathers' power. Soyinka's *The Bacchae of Euripides* (1973) deals with inspiration, intoxication, and mass hysteria. *Death and the King's Horseman* (1976), centering on death, also explores Greek themes of fate and inevitability. Soyinka demonstrates the universality of Greek themes in both European and African experience.

Certain patterns link Eman with Oedipus. Once Eman is identified by his father as one of the strong breed, he prepares himself for his mission by leaving his community. Like Oedipus, he goes to another community, not knowing he ultimately will be sacrificed there. Eman also resembles Christ: he is a teacher and healer; he refuses to exploit those around him; he lifts up the weak and has empathy for everyone, including the idiot Ifada. And, as in the case of Christ, those for whom he sacrifices himself do not hold him in high regard.

Despite its Greek and Christian overtones, the story is grounded in Yoruba tradition, with its initiation rites and concepts of heredity, community, and sacrifice. Soyinka's stagecraft includes traditional Yoruba music and dance as well as traditional Yoruba images, such as the effigy—the carrier doll—and the

For discussion questions and assignments on *The Strong Breed*, visit bedfordstmartins.com/jacobus.

appearance of the human carrier in the form of Ifada. Soyinka demonstrates that everything in the past is part of the present by overlaying the ghosts of Omae (the woman Eman was to marry), his father (the Old Man), his tutor, and the priest. The past shapes the present just as his father's blood runs in his veins and shapes everything he does as a man.

The play leaves us wondering if Eman's sacrifice was wasteful or redeeming. Is the community led by Jaguna and Oroge worth dying for? Will Eman's death benefit Sunma, Ifada, and the Girl who betrayed him to his killers? Or does Eman die only because he is one of the strong breed, whose mission is to serve as the sacrifice for the community? Even the latter interpretation might imply a positive ending for the play, although it would be a different ending than the one suggesting that Eman has died *for* this village and thus secured its renewal. Yoruba tradition implies that even if the community is unworthy, it shares in purification by the sacrifice of the willing. The subtlety of the issues in this play invites multiple interpretations.

The Strong Breed in Performance

In Ibadan in 1963, Soyinka created a twenty-five-minute version of *The Strong Breed* that omitted the flashbacks at the end of the play when Eman's past returns to him. This abbreviated version, done for Esso World Theatre, was included in the film *Culture in Transition*. The play was produced in its full-length version in 1964 at the Greenwich Mews Theatre in New York, and it has been performed by theater groups in several African nations. An African university theater group produced the play in its full-length version in Malawi in 1976 with Anthony Nazombe as Eman. In September 2002, Ahmed Yerima directed the Nigerian National Theater in an interpreted version at the Muson Center in Lagos. That was followed by another performance in October at the French Cultural Center, also in Lagos. Yerima stressed the cultural significance of the play and the appropriateness of this production at a time of political uncertainty and reconciliation. Another production, in Durban, South Africa, at the University of Natal, took place in November 2003. African directors insist on interpreting passages through mime and dance, thus imparting an emotional valence to the play.

WOLE SOYINKA (b. 1934)

The Strong Breed   1962

Characters

EMAN, *a stranger*
SUNMA, *Jaguna's daughter*
IFADA, *an idiot*
A GIRL
JAGUNA
OROGE

ATTENDANT STALWARTS, *the villagers*
From Eman's past:
OLD MAN, *his father*
OMAE, *his betrothed*
TUTOR
PRIEST
ATTENDANTS, *the villagers*

The scenes are described briefly, but very often a dark-ened stage with lit areas will not only suffice but is necessary. Except for the one indicated place, there can be no break in the action. A distracting scene change would be ruinous.

(A mud house, with space in front of it. Eman, in light buba and trousers stands at the window, looking out. Inside, Sunma is clearing the table of what looks like a modest clinic, putting the things away in a cupboard. Another rough table in the room is piled with exer-cise books, two or three worn textbooks, etc. Sunma appears agitated. Outside, just below the window crouches Ifada. He looks up with a shy smile from time to time, waiting for Eman to notice him.)

SUNMA (*hesitant*): You will have to make up your mind soon, Eman. The lorry leaves very shortly.

(As Eman does not answer, Sunma continues her work, more nervously. Two villagers, obvious travelers, pass hurriedly in front of the house, the man has a small raffia sack, the woman a cloth-covered basket, the man enters first, turns and urges the woman who is just emerging to hurry.)

SUNMA (*seeing them, her tone is more intense*): Eman, are we going or aren't we? You will leave it till too late.

EMAN (*quietly*): There is still time—if you want to go.

SUNMA: If I want to go . . . and you?

(Eman makes no reply.)

SUNMA (*bitterly*): You don't really want to leave here. You never want to go away—even for a minute.

(Ifada continues his antics. Eman eventually pats him on the head and the boy grins happily. Leaps up suddenly and returns with a basket of oranges which he offers to Eman.)

EMAN: My gift for today's festival enh?

(Ifada nods, grinning.)

EMAN: They look ripe—that's a change.

SUNMA (*she has gone inside the room. Looks round the door*): Did you call me?

EMAN: No. (*She goes back.*) And what will you do tonight, Ifada? Will you take part in the dancing? Or perhaps you will mount your own masquerade?

(Ifada shakes his head, regretfully.)

EMAN: You won't? So you haven't any? But you would like to own one.

(Ifada nods eagerly.)

EMAN: Then why don't you make your own?

(Ifada stares, puzzled by this idea.)

EMAN: Sunma will let you have some cloth you know. And bits of wool . . .

SUNMA (*coming out*): Who are you talking to, Eman?

EMAN: Ifada. I am trying to persuade him to join the young maskers.

SUNMA (*losing control*): What does he want here? Why is he hanging round us?

EMAN (*amazed*): What . . . ? I said Ifada, Ifada.

SUNMA: Just tell him to go away. Let him go and play somewhere else!

EMAN: What is this? Hasn't he always played here?

SUNMA: I don't want him here. (*Rushes to the window.*) Get away, idiot. Don't bring your foolish face here anymore, do you hear? Go on, go away from here . . .

EMAN (*restraining her*): Control yourself, Sunma. What on earth has got into you?

(Ifada, hurt and bewildered, backs slowly away.)

SUNMA: He comes crawling round here like some hor-rible insect. I never want to lay my eyes on him again.

EMAN: I don't understand. It *is* Ifada you know. Ifada! The unfortunate one who runs errands for you and doesn't hurt a soul.

SUNMA: I cannot bear the sight of him.

EMAN: You can't do what? It can't be two days since he last fetched water for you.

SUNMA: What else can he do except that? He is useless. Just because we have been kind to him . . . Others would have put him in an asylum.

EMAN: You are not making sense. He is not a madman, he is just a little more unlucky than other children. (*Looks keenly at her.*) But what is the matter?

SUNMA: It's nothing. I only wish we had sent him off to one of those places for creatures like him.

EMAN: He is quite happy here. He doesn't bother anyone and he makes himself useful.

SUNMA: Useful! Is that one of any use to anybody? Boys of his age are already earning a living but all he can do is hang around and drool at the mouth.

EMAN: But he does work. You know he does a lot for you.

SUNMA: Does he? And what about the farm you started for him! Does he ever work on it? Or have you for-gotten that it was really for Ifada you cleared that bush. Now you have to go and work it yourself. You spend all your time on it and you have no room for anything else.

EMAN: That wasn't his fault. I should first have asked him if he was fond of farming.

SUNMA: Oh, so he can choose? As if he shouldn't be thankful for being allowed to live.

EMAN: Sunma!

SUNMA: He does not like farming but he knows how to feast his dumb mouth on the fruits.

EMAN: But I want him to. I encourage him.

SUNMA: Well keep him. I don't want to see him anymore.

EMAN (*after some moments*): But why? You cannot be telling all the truth. What has he done?

SUNMA: The sight of him fills me with revulsion.

EMAN (*goes to her and holds her*): What really is it? (*Sunma avoids his eyes.*) It is almost as if you are forcing yourself to hate him. Why?

SUNMA: That is not true. Why should I?

EMAN: Then what is the secret? You've even played with him before.

SUNMA: I have always merely tolerated him. But I cannot anymore. Suddenly my disgust won't take him anymore. Perhaps . . . perhaps it is the new year. Yes, yes, it must be the new year.

EMAN: I don't believe that.

SUNMA: It must be. I am a woman, and these things matter. I don't want a misshape near me. Surely for one day in the year, I may demand some wholesomeness.

EMAN: I do not understand you. (*Sunma is silent.*) It was cruel of you. And to Ifada who is so helpless and alone. We are the only friends he has.

SUNMA: No, just you. I have told you, with me it has always been only an act of kindness. And now I haven't any pity left for him.

EMAN: No. He is not a wholesome being.

(*He turns back to looking through the window.*)

SUNMA (*half-pleading*): Ifada can rouse your pity. And yet if anything, I need more kindness from you. Every time my weakness betrays me, you close your mind against me . . . Eman . . . Eman . . .

(*A Girl comes in view, dragging an effigy° by a rope attached to one of its legs. She stands for a while gazing at Eman. Ifada, who has crept back shyly to his accustomed position, becomes somewhat excited when he sees the effigy. The Girl is unsmiling. She possesses in fact a kind of inscrutability which does not make her hard but is unsettling.*)

GIRL: Is the teacher in?

EMAN (*smiling*): No.

GIRL: Where is he gone?

EMAN: I don't really know. Shall I ask?

GIRL: Yes, do.

EMAN (*turning slightly*): Sunma, a girl outside wants to know . . .

(*Sunma turns away, goes into the inside room.*)

EMAN: Oh. (*Returns to the Girl, but his slight gaiety is lost.*) There is no one at home who can tell me.

GIRL: Why are you not in?

EMAN: I don't really know. Maybe I went somewhere.

GIRL: All right. I will wait until you get back.

(*She pulls the effigy to her, sits down.*)

EMAN (*slowly regaining his amusement*): So you are all ready for the new year.

GIRL (*without turning round*): I am not going to the festival.

EMAN: Then why have you got that?

GIRL: Do you mean my carrier? I am unwell you know. My mother says it will take away my sickness with the old year.

EMAN: Won't you share the carrier with your playmates?

GIRL: Oh, no. Don't you know I play alone? The other children won't come near me. Their mothers would beat them.

effigy: A figure or likeness in human shape.

EMAN: But I have never seen you here. Why don't you come to the clinic?

GIRL: My mother said No.

(*Gets up, begins to move off.*)

EMAN: You are not going away?

GIRL: I must not stay talking to you. If my mother caught me . . .

EMAN: All right, tell me what you want before you go.

GIRL (*stops. For some moments she remains silent*): I must have some clothes for my carrier.

EMAN: Is that all? You wait a moment.

(*Sunma comes out as he takes down a buba from the wall. She goes to the window and glares almost with hatred at the Girl. The Girl retreats hastily, still impassive.*)

By the way, Sunma, do you know who that girl is?

SUNMA: I hope you don't really mean to give her that.

EMAN: Why not? I hardly ever use it.

SUNMA: Just the same, don't give it to her. She is not a child. She is as evil as the rest of them.

EMAN: What has got into you today?

SUNMA: All right, all right. Do what you wish.

(*She withdraws. Baffled, Eman returns to the window.*)

EMAN: Here . . . will this do? Come and look at it.

GIRL: Throw it.

EMAN: What is the matter? I am not going to eat you.

GIRL: No one lets me come near them.

EMAN: But I am not afraid of catching your disease.

GIRL: Throw it.

(*Eman shrugs and tosses the buba. She takes it without a word and slips it on the effigy, completely absorbed in the task. Eman watches for a while, then joins Sunma in the inner room.*)

GIRL (*after a long, cool survey of Ifada*): You have a head like a spider's egg, and your mouth dribbles like a roof. But there is no one else. Would you like to play?

(*Ifada nods eagerly, quite excited.*)

GIRL: You will have to get a stick.

(*Ifada rushes around, finds a big stick, and whirls it aloft, bearing down on the carrier.*)

GIRL: Wait. I don't want you to spoil it. If it gets torn I shall drive you away. Now, let me see how you are going to beat it.

(*Ifada hits it gently.*)

GIRL: You may hit harder than that. As long as there is something left to hang at the end. (*She appraises him up and down.*) You are not very tall . . . will you be able to hang it from a tree?

(*Ifada nods, grinning happily.*)

GIRL: You will hang it up and I will set fire to it. (*Then, with surprising venom.*) But just because you are helping me, don't think it is going to cure you. I am the one who will get well at midnight, do you understand? It is my carrier and it is for me alone. (*She pulls at the rope to make sure that it is well attached to the leg.*) Well don't stand there drooling. Let's go.

(*She begins to walk off, dragging the effigy in the dust. Ifada remains where he is for some moments, seemingly puzzled. Then his face breaks into a large grin and he leaps after the procession, belaboring the effigy with all his strength. The stage remains empty for some moments. Then the horn of a lorry is sounded and Sunma rushes out. The hooting continues for some time with a rhythmic pattern. Eman comes out.*)

EMAN: I am going to the village . . . I shan't be back before nightfall.

SUNMA (*blankly*): Yes.

EMAN (*hesitates*): Well what do you want me to do?

SUNMA: The lorry was hooting just now.

EMAN: I didn't hear it.

SUNMA: It will leave in a few minutes. And you did promise we could go away.

EMAN: I promised nothing. Will you go home by yourself or shall I come back for you?

SUNMA: You don't even want me here?

EMAN: But you have to go home haven't you?

SUNMA: I had hoped we would watch the new year together—in some other place.

EMAN: Why do you continue to distress yourself?

SUNMA: Because you will not listen to me. Why do you continue to stay where nobody wants you?

EMAN: That is not true.

SUNMA: It is. You are wasting your life on people who really want you out of their way.

EMAN: You don't know what you are saying.

SUNMA: You think they love you? Do you think they care at all for what you—or I—do for them?

EMAN: *Them?* These are your own people. Sometimes you talk as if you were a stranger too.

SUNMA: I wonder if I really sprang from here. I know they are evil and I am not. From the oldest to the smallest child, they are nourished in evil and unwholesomeness in which I have no part.

EMAN: You knew this when you returned?

SUNMA: You reproach me then for trying at all?

EMAN: I reproach you with nothing. But you must leave me out of your plans. I can have no part in them.

SUNMA (*nearly pleading*): Once I could have run away. I would have gone and never looked back.

EMAN: I cannot listen when you talk like that.

SUNMA: I swear to you, I do not mind what happens afterwards. But you must help me tear myself away from here. I can no longer do it by myself . . . It is only a little thing. And we have worked so hard this past year . . . surely we can go away for a week . . . even a few days would be enough.

EMAN: I have told you, Sunma . . .

SUNMA (*desperately*): Two days, Eman. Only two days.

EMAN (*distressed*): But I tell you I have no wish to go.

SUNMA (*suddenly angry*): Are you so afraid then?

EMAN: Me? Afraid of what?

SUNMA: You think you will not want to come back.

EMAN (*pitying*): You cannot dare me that way.

SUNMA: Then why won't you leave here, even for an hour? If you are so sure that your life is settled here, why are you afraid to do this thing for me? What is so wrong that you will not go into the next town for a day or two?

EMAN: I don't want to. I do not have to persuade you or myself about anything. I simply have no desire to go away.

SUNMA (*his quiet confidence appears to incense her*): You are afraid. You accuse me of losing my sense of mission, but you are afraid to put yours to the test.

EMAN: You are wrong, Sunma. I have no sense of mission. But I have found peace here and I am content with that.

SUNMA: I haven't. For a while I thought that too, but I found there could be no peace in the midst of so much cruelty. Eman, tonight at least, the last night of the old year . . .

EMAN: No, Sunma. I find this too distressing; you should go home now.

SUNMA: It is the time for making changes in one's life, Eman. Let's breathe in the new year away from here.

EMAN: You are hurting yourself.

SUNMA: Tonight. Only tonight. We will come back tomorrow, as early as you like. But let us go away for this one night. Don't let another year break on me in this place . . . you don't know how important it is to me, and I will tell you, I will tell you on the way . . . but we must not be here today, Eman, do this one thing for me.

EMAN (*sadly*): I cannot.

SUNMA (*suddenly calm*): I was a fool to think it would be otherwise. The whole village may use you as they will but for me there is nothing. Sometimes I think you believe that doing anything for me makes you unfaithful to some part of your life. If it was a woman then I pity her for what she must have suffered.

(*Eman winces and hardens slowly. Sunma notices nothing.*)

Keeping faith with so much is slowly making you inhuman. (*Seeing the change in Eman.*) Eman. Eman. What is it?

(*As she goes toward him, Eman goes into the house.*)

SUNMA (*apprehensive, follows him*): What did I say? Eman, forgive me, forgive me please. (*Eman remains facing into the slow darkness of the room. Sunma, distressed, cannot decide what to do.*) I swear I didn't know . . . I would not have said it for all the world.

(*A lorry is heard taking off somewhere nearby. The sound comes up and slowly fades away into the distance. Sunma starts visibly, goes slowly to the window.*)

SUNMA (*as the sound dies off, to herself*): What happens now?

EMAN (*joining her at the window*): What did you say?

SUNMA: Nothing.

EMAN: Was that not the lorry going off?

SUNMA: It was.

EMAN: I am sorry I couldn't help you.

(*Sunma, about to speak, changes her mind.*)

EMAN: I think you ought to go home now.

SUNMA: No, don't send me away. It's the least you can do for me. Let me stay here until all the noise is over.

EMAN: But are you not needed at home? You have a part in the festival.

SUNMA: I have renounced it; I am Jaguna's eldest daughter only in name.

EMAN: Renouncing one's self is not so easy—surely you know that.

SUNMA: I don't want to talk about it. Will you at least let us be together tonight?

EMAN: But . . .

SUNMA: Unless you are afraid my father will accuse you of harboring me.

EMAN: All right, we will go out together.

SUNMA: Go out? I want us to stay here.

EMAN: When there is so much going on outside?

SUNMA: Someday you will wish that you went away when I tried to make you.

EMAN: Are we going back to that?

SUNMA: No. I promise you I will not recall it again. But you must know that it was also for your sake that I tried to get us away.

EMAN: For me? How?

SUNMA: By yourself you can do nothing here. Have you not noticed how tightly we shut out strangers? Even if you lived here for a lifetime, you would remain a stranger.

EMAN: Perhaps that is what I like. There is peace in being a stranger.

SUNMA: For a while perhaps. But they would reject you in the end. I tell you it is only I who stand between you and contempt. And because of this you have earned their hatred. I don't know why I say this now, except that somehow, I feel that it no longer matters. It is only I who have stood between you and much humiliation.

EMAN: Think carefully before you say any more. I am incapable of feeling indebted to you. This will make no difference at all.

SUNMA: I ask for nothing. But you must know it all the same. It is true I hadn't the strength to go by myself. And I must confess this now, if you had come with me, I would have done everything to keep you from returning.

EMAN: I know that.

SUNMA: You see, I bare myself to you. For days I had thought it over, this was to be a new beginning for us. And I placed my fate wholly in your hands. Now the thought will not leave me, I have a feeling which will not be shaken off, that in some way, you have tonight totally destroyed my life.

EMAN: You are depressed, you don't know what you are saying.

SUNMA: Don't think I am accusing you. I say all this only because I cannot help it.

EMAN: We must not remain shut up here. Let us go and be part of the living.

SUNMA: No. Leave them alone.

EMAN: Surely you don't want to stay indoors when the whole town is alive with rejoicing.

SUNMA: Rejoicing! Is that what it seems to you? No, let us remain here. Whatever happens I must not go out until all this is over.

(*There is silence. It has grown much darker.*)

EMAN: I shall light the lamp.

SUNMA (*eager to do something*): No, let me do it.

(*She goes into the inner room.*)

(*Eman paces the room, stops by a shelf and toys with the seeds in an "ayo" board, takes down the whole board and places it on a table, playing by himself.*)

(*The Girl is now seen coming back, still dragging her "carrier." Ifada brings up the rear as before. As he comes round the corner of the house two men emerge from the shadows. A sack is thrown over Ifada's head, the rope is pulled tight rendering him instantly helpless. The Girl has reached the front of the house before she turns round at the sound of scuffle. She is in time to see Ifada thrown over the shoulders and borne away. Her face betraying no emotion at all, the Girl backs slowly away, turns and flees, leaving the "carrier" behind. Sunma enters, carrying two kerosene lamps. She hangs one up from the wall.*)

EMAN: One is enough.

SUNMA: I want to leave one outside.

(*She goes out, hangs the lamp from a nail just above the door. As she turns she sees the effigy and gasps. Eman rushes out.*)

EMAN: What is it? Oh, is that what frightened you?

SUNMA: I thought . . . I didn't really see it properly.

(*Eman goes towards the object, stoops to pick it up.*)

EMAN: It must belong to that sick girl.

SUNMA: Don't touch it.

EMAN: Let's keep it for her.

SUNMA: Leave it alone. Don't touch it, Eman.

EMAN (*shrugs and goes back*): You are very nervous.

SUNMA: Let's go in.

EMAN: Wait. (*He detains her by the door, under the lamp.*) I know there is something more than you've told me. What are you afraid of tonight?

SUNMA: I was only scared by that thing. There is nothing else.

EMAN: I am not blind, Sunma. It is true I would not run away when you wanted me to, but that doesn't mean I do not feel things. What does tonight really mean that it makes you so helpless?

SUNMA: It is only a mood. And your indifference to me . . . let's go in.

(*Eman moves aside and she enters; he remains there for a moment and then follows.*)

(*She fiddles with the lamp, looks vaguely round the room, then goes and shuts the door, bolting it. When she turns, it is to meet Eman's eyes, questioning.*)

SUNMA: There is a cold wind coming in.

(*Eman keeps his gaze on her.*)

SUNMA: It *was* getting cold.

(*She moves guiltily to the table and stands by the "ayo" board, rearranging the seeds. Eman remains where he is a few moments, then brings a stool and sits opposite her. She sits down also and they begin to play in silence.*)

SUNMA: What brought you here at all, Eman? And what makes you stay?

(*There is another silence.*)

SUNMA: I am not trying to share your life. I know you too well by now. But at least we have worked together since you came. Is there nothing at all I deserve to know?

EMAN: Let me continue a stranger—especially to you. Those who have much to give fulfill themselves only in total loneliness.

SUNMA: Then there is no love in what you do.

EMAN: There is. Love comes to me more easily with strangers.

SUNMA: That is unnatural.

EMAN: Not for me. I know I find consummation only when I have spent myself for a total stranger.

SUNMA: It seems unnatural to me. But then I am a woman. I have a woman's longings and weaknesses. And the ties of blood are very strong in me.

EMAN (*smiling*): You think I have cut loose from all these—ties of blood.

SUNMA: Sometimes you are so inhuman.

EMAN: I don't know what that means. But I am very much my father's son.

(*They play in silence. Suddenly Eman pauses, listening.*)

EMAN: Did you hear that?

SUNMA (*quickly*): I heard nothing . . . it's your turn.

EMAN: Perhaps some of the mummers are coming this way.

(*Eman, about to play, leaps up suddenly.*)

SUNMA: What is it? Don't you want to play anymore?

(*Eman moves to the door.*)

SUNMA: No. Don't go out, Eman.

EMAN: If it's the dancers, I want to ask them to stay. At least we won't have to miss everything.

SUNMA: No, no. Don't open the door. Let us keep out everyone tonight.

(*A terrified and disordered figure bursts suddenly round the corner, past the window, and begins hammering at the door. It is Ifada. Desperate with terror, he pounds madly at the door, dumb-moaning all the while.*)

EMAN: Isn't that Ifada?

SUNMA: They are only fooling about. Don't pay any attention.

EMAN (*looks round the window*): That is Ifada. (*Begins to unbolt the door.*)

SUNMA (*pulling at his hands*): It is only a trick they are playing on you. Don't take any notice, Eman.

EMAN: What are you saying? The boy is out of his senses with fear.

SUNMA: No, no. Don't interfere, Eman. For God's sake, don't interfere.

EMAN: Do you know something of this then?

SUNMA: You are a stranger here, Eman. Just leave us alone and go your own way. There is nothing you can do.

EMAN (*he tries to push her out of the way but she clings fiercely to him*): Have you gone mad? I tell you the boy must come in.

SUNMA: Why won't you listen to me, Eman? I tell you it's none of your business. For your own sake, do as I say.

(*Eman pushes her off, unbolts the door. Ifada rushes in, clasps Eman round the knees, dumb-moaning against his legs.*)

EMAN (*manages to rebolt the door*): What is it, Ifada? What is the matter?

(*Shouts and voices are heard coming nearer the house.*)

SUNMA: Before it's too late, let him go. For once, Eman, believe what I tell you. Don't harbor him or you will regret it all your life.

(*Eman tries to calm Ifada who becomes more and more abject as the outside voices get nearer.*)

EMAN: What have they done to him? At least tell me that. What is going on, Sunma?

SUNMA (*with sudden venom*): Monster! Could you not take yourself somewhere else?

EMAN: Stop talking like that.

SUNMA: He could have run into the bush couldn't he? Toad! Why must he follow us with his own disasters!

VOICES OUTSIDE: It's here . . . Round the back . . . Spread, spread . . . this way . . . no, head him off . . . use the bush path and head him off . . . get some more lights . . .

(*Eman listens. Lifts Ifada bodily and carries him into the inner room. Returns at once, shutting the door behind him.*)

SUNMA (*slumps into a chair, resigned*): You always follow your own way.

JAGUNA (*comes round the corner followed by Oroge and three men, one bearing a torch*): I knew he would come here.

OROGE: I hope our friend won't make trouble.

JAGUNA: He had better not. You, recall all the men and tell them to surround the house.

OROGE: But he may not be in the house after all.

JAGUNA: I know he is here . . . (to the men) . . . go on, do as I say. (He bangs on the door.) Teacher, open your door . . . you two, stay by the door. If I need you I will call you.

(Eman opens the door.)

JAGUNA (speaks as he enters): We know he is here.

EMAN: Who?

JAGUNA: Don't let us waste time. We are grown men, teacher. You understand me and I understand you. But we must take back the boy.

EMAN: This is my house.

JAGUNA: Daughter, you'd better tell your friend. I don't think he quite knows our ways. Tell him why he must give up the boy.

SUNMA: Father, I . . .

JAGUNA: Are you going to tell him or aren't you?

SUNMA: Father, I beg you, leave us alone tonight . . .

JAGUNA: I thought you might be a hindrance. Go home then if you will not use your sense.

SUNMA: But there are other ways . . .

JAGUNA (turning to the men): See that she gets home. I no longer trust her. If she gives trouble carry her. And see that the women stay with her until all this is over.

(Sunma departs, accompanied by one of the men.)

JAGUNA: Now, teacher . . .

OROGE (restrains him): You see, Mister Eman, it is like this. Right now, nobody knows that Ifada has taken refuge here. No one except us and our men—and they know how to keep their mouths shut. We don't want to have to burn down the house you see, but if the word gets around, we would have no choice.

JAGUNA: In fact, it may be too late already. A carrier should end up in the bush, not in a house. Anyone who doesn't guard his door when the carrier goes by has himself to blame. A contaminated house should be burnt down.

OROGE: But we are willing to let it pass. Only, you must bring him out quickly.

EMAN: All right. But at least you will let me ask you something.

JAGUNA: What is there to ask? Don't you understand what we have told you?

EMAN: Yes. But why did you pick on a helpless boy. Obviously he is not willing.

JAGUNA: What is the man talking about? Ifada is a godsend. Does he have to be willing?

EMAN: In my home, we believe that a man should be willing.

OROGE: Mister Eman, I don't think you quite understand. This is not a simple matter at all. I don't know what you do, but here, it is not a cheap task for anybody. No one in his senses would do such a job. Why do you think we give refuge to idiots like him? We don't know where he came from. One morning, he is simply there, just like that. From nowhere at all. You see, there is a purpose in that.

JAGUNA: We only waste time.

OROGE: Jaguna, be patient. After all, the man has been with us for some time now and deserves to know. The evil of the old year is no light thing to load on any man's head.

EMAN: I know something about that.

OROGE: You do? (Turns to Jaguna who snorts impatiently.) You see I told you so didn't I? From the moment you came I saw you were one of the knowing ones.

JAGUNA: Then let him behave like a man and give back the boy.

EMAN: It is you who are not behaving like men.

JAGUNA (advances aggressively): That is a quick mouth you have . . .

OROGE: Patience, Jaguna . . . if you want the new year to cushion the land there must be no deeds of anger. What did you mean, my friend?

EMAN: It is a simple thing. A village which cannot produce its own carrier contains no men.

JAGUNA: Enough. Let there be no more talk or this business will be ruined by some rashness. You . . . come inside. Bring the boy out, he must be in the room there.

EMAN: Wait.

(The men hesitate.)

JAGUNA (hitting the nearer one and propelling him forward): Go on. Have you changed masters now that you listen to what he says?

OROGE (sadly): I am sorry you would not understand, Mister Eman. But you ought to know that no carrier may return to the village. If he does, the people will stone him to death. It has happened before. Surely it is too much to ask a man to give up his own soil.

EMAN: I know others who have done more.

(Ifada is brought out, abjectly dumb-moaning.)

EMAN: You can see him with your own eyes. Does it really have meaning to use one as unwilling as that.

OROGE (smiling): He shall be willing. Not only willing but actually joyous. I am the one who prepares them all, and I have seen worse. This one escaped before I began to prepare him for the event. But you will see him later tonight, the most joyous creature in the festival. Then perhaps you will understand.

EMAN: Then it is only a deceit. Do you believe the spirit of a new year is so easily fooled?

JAGUNA: Take him out. (The men carry out Ifada.) You see, it is so easy to talk. You say there are no men in this village because they cannot provide a willing carrier. And yet I heard Oroge tell you we only use strangers. There is only one other stranger in the village, but I have not heard him offer himself (spits). It is so easy to talk is it not? (He turns his back on him.)

(*They go off, taking Ifada with them, limp and silent. The only sign of life is that he strains his neck to keep his eyes on Eman till the very moment that he disappears from sight. Eman remains where they left him, staring after the group.*)

(*A blackout lasting no more than a minute. The lights come up slowly and Ifada is seen returning to the house. He stops at the window and looks in. Seeing no one, he bangs on the sill. Appears surprised that there is no response. He slithers down on his favorite spot, then sees the effigy still lying where the Girl had dropped it in her flight. After some hesitation, he goes towards it, begins to strip it of the clothing. Just then the Girl comes in.*)

GIRL: Hey, leave that alone. You know it's mine.

(*Ifada pauses, then speeds up his action.*)

GIRL: I said it is mine. Leave it where you found it.

(*She rushes at him and begins to struggle for possession of the carrier.*)

GIRL: Thief! Thief! Let it go, it is mine. Let it go. You animal, just because I let you play with it. Idiot! Idiot!

(*The struggle becomes quite violent. The Girl is hanging on the effigy and Ifada lifts her with it, flinging her all about. The Girl hangs on grimly.*)

GIRL: You are spoiling it . . . why don't you get your own? Thief! Let it go, you thief!

(*Sunma comes in walking very fast, throwing apprehensive glances over her shoulder. Seeing the two children, she becomes immediately angry. Advances on them.*)

SUNMA: So you've made this place your playground. Get away, you untrained pigs. Get out of here.

(*Ifada flees at once, the Girl retreats also, retaining possession of the "carrier."*)

(*Sunma goes to the door. She has her hand on the door when the significance of Ifada's presence strikes her for the first time. She stands rooted to the spot, then turns slowly round.*)

SUNMA: Ifada! What are you doing here? (*Ifada is bewildered. Sunma turns suddenly and rushes into the house, flying into the inner room and out again.*) Eman! Eman! Eman! (*She rushes outside.*) Where did he go? Where did they take him? (*Ifada distressed, points. Sunma seizes him by the arm, drags him off.*) Take me there at once. God help you if we are too late. You loathsome thing, if you have let him suffer . . .

(*Her voice fades into other shouts, running footsteps, banged tins, bells, dogs, etc., rising in volume.*)

(*It is a narrow passageway between two mud houses. At the far end one man after another is seen running across the entry, the noise dying off gradually.*)

(*About halfway down the passage, Eman is crouching against the wall, tense with apprehension. As the noise dies off, he seems to relax, but the alert hunted look is still in his eyes, which are ringed in a reddish color. The rest of his body has been whitened with a floury substance. He is naked down to the waist, wears a baggy pair of trousers, calf-length, and around both feet are bangles.*)

EMAN: I will simply stay here till dawn. I have done enough.

(*A window is thrown open and a woman empties some slop from a pail. With a startled cry Eman leaps aside to avoid it and the woman puts out her head.*)

WOMAN: Oh, my head. What have I done! Forgive me, neighbor. . . . Eh, it's the carrier!

(*Very rapidly she clears her throat and spits on him, flings the pail at him, and runs off, shouting.*)

He's here. The carrier is hiding in the passage. Quickly, I have found the carrier!

(*The cry is taken up and Eman flees down the passage. Shortly afterwards his pursuers come pouring down the passage in full cry. After the last of them come Jaguna and Oroge.*)

OROGE: Wait, wait. I cannot go so fast.

JAGUNA: We will rest a little then. We can do nothing anyway.

OROGE: If only he had let me prepare him.

JAGUNA: They are the ones who break first, these fools who think they were born to carry suffering like a hat. What are we to do now?

OROGE: When they catch him I must prepare him.

JAGUNA: He? It will be impossible now. There can be no joy left in that one.

OROGE: Still, it took him by surprise. He was not expecting what he met.

JAGUNA: Why then did he refuse to listen? Did he think he was coming to sit down to a feast? He had not even gone through one compound before he bolted. Did he think he was taken round the people to be blessed? A woman, that is all he is.

OROGE: No, no. He took the beating well enough. I think he is the kind who would let himself be beaten from night till dawn and not utter a sound. He would let himself be stoned until he dropped dead.

JAGUNA: Then what made him run like a coward?

OROGE: I don't know. I don't really know. It is a night of curses, Jaguna. It is not many unprepared minds will remain unhinged under the load.

JAGUNA: We must find him. It is a poor beginning for a year when our own curses remain hovering over our homes because the carrier refused to take them.

(*They go. The scene changes. Eman is crouching beside some shrubs, torn and bleeding.*)

EMAN: They are even guarding my house . . . as if I would go there, but I need water . . . they could at least grant me that . . . I can be thirsty too . . . (*He pricks his ears.*) . . . there must be a stream nearby . . . (*As he looks round him, his eyes widen at a scene he encounters.*)

(*An Old Man, short and vigorous looking, is seated on a stool. He also is wearing calf-length baggy trousers, white. On his head, a white cap. An attendant is engaged in rubbing his body with oil. Round his eyes, two white rings have already been marked.*)

OLD MAN: Have they prepared the boat?
ATTENDANT: They are making the last sacrifice.
OLD MAN: Good. Did you send for my son?
ATTENDANT: He's on his way.
OLD MAN: I have never met the carrying of the boat with such a heavy heart. I hope nothing comes of it.
ATTENDANT: The gods will not desert us on that account.
OLD MAN: A man should be at his strongest when he takes the boat, my friend. To be weighed down inside and out is not a wise thing. I hope when the moment comes I shall have found my strength.

(*Enter Eman, a wrapper round his waist and a danski° over it.*)

OLD MAN: I meant to wait until after my journey to the river, but my mind is so burdened with my own grief and yours I could not delay it. You know I must have all my strength. But I sit here, feeling it all eaten slowly away by my unspoken grief. It helps to say it out. It even helps to cry sometimes.

(*He signals to the attendant to leave them.*)

Come nearer . . . we will never meet again, son. Not on this side of the flesh. What I do not know is whether you will return to take my place.
EMAN: I will never come back.
OLD MAN: Do you know what you are saying? Ours is a strong breed, my son. It is only a strong breed that can take this boat to the river year after year and wax stronger on it. I have taken down each year's evils for over twenty years. I hoped you would follow me.
EMAN: My life here died with Omae.
OLD MAN: Omae died giving birth to your child and you think the world is ended. Eman, my pain did not begin when Omae died. Since you sent her to stay with me, son, I lived with the burden of knowing that this child would die bearing your son.
EMAN: Father . . .
OLD MAN: Don't you know it was the same with you? And me? No woman survives the bearing of the strong ones. Son, it is not the mouth of the boaster that says he belongs to the strong breed. It is the tongue that is red with pain and black with sorrow. Twelve years you were away my son, and for those twelve years I knew the love of an old man for his daughter and the pain of a man helplessly awaiting his loss.

danski: A brief Yoruba garment.

EMAN: I wish I had stayed away. I wish I never came back to meet her.
OLD MAN: It had to be. But you know now what slowly ate away my strength. I awaited your return with love and fear. Forgive me then if I say that your grief is light. It will pass. This grief may drive you now from home. But you must return.
EMAN: You do not understand. It is not grief alone.
OLD MAN: What is it then? Tell me, I can still learn.
EMAN: I was away twelve years. I changed much in that time.
OLD MAN: I am listening.
EMAN: I am unfitted for your work, father. I wish to say no more. But I am totally unfitted for your call.
OLD MAN: It is only time you need, son. Stay longer and you will answer the urge of your blood.
EMAN: That I stayed at all was because of Omae. I did not expect to find her waiting. I would have taken her away, but hard as you claim to be, it would have killed you. And I was a tired man. I needed peace. Because Omae was peace, I stayed. Now nothing holds me here.
OLD MAN: Other men would rot and die doing this task year after year. It is strong medicine which only we can take. Our blood is strong like no other. Anything you do in life must be less than this, son.
EMAN: That is not true, father.
OLD MAN: I tell you it is true. Your own blood will betray you, son, because you cannot hold it back. If you make it do less than this, it will rush to your head and burst it open. I say what I know, my son.
EMAN: There are other tasks in life, father. This one is not for me. There are even greater things you know nothing of.
OLD MAN: I am very sad. You only go to give to others what rightly belongs to us. You will use your strength among thieves. They are thieves because they take what is ours, they have no claim of blood to it. They will even lack the knowledge to use it wisely. Truth is my companion at this moment, my son. I know everything I say will surely bring the sadness of truth.
EMAN: I am going, father.
OLD MAN: Call my attendant. And be with me in your strength for this last journey. A-ah, did you hear that? It came out without my knowing it; this is indeed my last journey. But I am not afraid.

(*Eman goes out. A few moments later, the attendant enters.*)

ATTENDANT: The boat is ready.
OLD MAN: So am I.

(*He sits perfectly still for several moments. Drumming begins somewhere in the distance, and the Old Man sways his head almost imperceptibly. Two men come in bearing a miniature boat, containing an indefinable mound. They rush it in and set it briskly down near the Old Man, and stand well back. The Old Man gets up slowly, the Attendant watching him keenly. He signs to the men, who lift the boat quickly onto the Old Man's head. As soon as it touches his head, he holds it down with both hands and runs off, the men give him a start, then follow at a trot.)*

(As the last man disappears Oroge limps in and comes face to face with Eman—as carrier—who is now seen still standing beside the shrubs, staring into the scene he has just witnessed. Oroge, struck by the look on Eman's face, looks anxiously behind him to see what has engaged Eman's attention. Eman notices him then, and the pair stare at each other. Jaguna enters, sees him and shouts, "Here he is," rushes at Eman who is whipped back to the immediate and flees, Jaguna in pursuit. Three or four others enter and follow them. Oroge remains where he is, thoughtful.)

JAGUNA (*reenters*): They have closed in on him now, we'll get him this time.

OROGE: It is nearly midnight.

JAGUNA: You were standing there looking at him as if he was some strange spirit. Why didn't you shout?

OROGE: You shouted didn't you? Did that catch him?

JAGUNA: Don't worry. We have him now. But things have taken a bad turn. It is no longer enough to drive him past every house. There is too much contamination about already.

OROGE (*not listening*): He saw something. Why may I not know what it was?

JAGUNA: What are you talking about?

OROGE: Hm. What is it?

JAGUNA: I said there is too much harm done already. The year will demand more from this carrier than we thought.

OROGE: What do you mean?

JAGUNA: Do we have to talk with the full mouth?

OROGE: S-sh . . . look!

(Jaguna turns just in time to see Sunma fly at him, clawing at his face like a crazed tigress.)

SUNMA: Murderer! What are you doing to him. Murderer! Murderer!

(Jaguna finds himself struggling really hard to keep off his daughter; he succeeds in pushing her off and striking her so hard on the face that she falls to her knees. He moves on her to hit her again.)

OROGE (*comes between*): Think what you are doing, Jaguna, she is your daughter.

JAGUNA: My daughter! Does this one look like my daughter? Let me cripple the harlot for life.

OROGE: That is a wicked thought, Jaguna.

JAGUNA: Don't come between me and her.

OROGE: Nothing in anger—do you forget what tonight is?

JAGUNA: Can you blame me for forgetting?

(Draws his hand across his cheek—it is covered with blood.)

OROGE: This is an unhappy night for us all. I fear what is to come of it.

JAGUNA: Let's go. I cannot restrain myself in this creature's presence. My own daughter . . . and for a stranger . . .

(They go off, Ifada, who came in with Sunma and had stood apart, horror-stricken, comes shyly forward. He helps Sunma up. They go off, he holding Sunma bent and sobbing.)

(Enter Eman—as carrier. He is physically present in the bounds of this next scene, a side of a round thatched hut. A young girl, about fourteen, runs in, stops beside the hut. She looks carefully to see that she is not observed, puts her mouth to a little hole in the wall.)

OMAE: Eman . . . Eman . . .

(Eman—as carrier—responds, as he does throughout the scene, but they are unaware of him.)

EMAN (*from inside*): Who is it?

OMAE: It is me, Omae.

EMAN: How dare you come here!

(Two hands appear at the hole and pushing outwards, create a much larger hole through which Eman puts out his head. It is Eman as a boy, the same age as the girl.)

Go away at once. Are you trying to get me into trouble!

OMAE: What is the matter?

EMAN: You. Go away.

OMAE: But I came to see you.

EMAN: Are you deaf? I say I don't want to see you. Now go before my tutor catches you.

OMAE: All right. Come out.

EMAN: Do what!

OMAE: Come out.

EMAN: You must be mad.

OMAE (*sits on the ground*): All right, if you don't come out I shall simply stay here until your tutor arrives.

EMAN (*about to explode, thinks better of it and the head disappears. A moment later he emerges from behind the hut*): What sort of a devil has got into you?

OMAE: None. I just wanted to see you.

EMAN (*his mimicry is nearly hysterical*): "None. I just wanted to see you." Do you think this place is the stream where you can go and molest innocent people?

OMAE (*coyly*): Aren't you glad to see me?

EMAN: I am not.

OMAE: Why?

EMAN: Why? Do you really ask me why? Because you are a woman and a most troublesome woman. Don't you know anything about this at all. We are not meant to see any woman. So go away before more harm's done.

OMAE (*flirtatious*): What is so secret about it anyway? What do they teach you?

EMAN: Nothing any woman can understand.

OMAE: Ha ha. You think we don't know eh? You've all come to be circumcised.

EMAN: Shut up. You don't know anything.

OMAE: Just think, all this time you haven't been circumcised, and you dared make eyes at us women.

EMAN: Thank you—woman. Now go.

OMAE: Do they give you enough to eat?

EMAN (*testily*): No. We are so hungry that when silly girls like you turn up, we eat them.

OMAE (*feigning tears*): Oh, oh, oh, he's abusing me. He's abusing me.

EMAN (*alarmed*): Don't try that here. Go quickly if you are going to cry.

OMAE: All right, I won't cry.

EMAN: Cry or no cry, go away and leave me alone. What do you think will happen if my tutor turns up now?

OMAE: He won't.

EMAN (*mimicking*): "He won't." I suppose you are his wife and he tells you where he goes. In fact this is just the time he comes round to our huts. He could be at the next hut this very moment.

OMAE: Ha-ha. You're lying. I left him by the stream, pinching the girls' bottoms. Is that the sort of thing he teaches you?

EMAN: Don't say anything against him or I shall beat you. Isn't it you loose girls who tease him, wiggling your bottoms under his nose?

OMAE (*going tearful again*): A-ah, so I am one of the loose girls eh?

EMAN: Now don't start accusing me of things I didn't say.

OMAE: But you said it. You said it.

EMAN: I didn't. Look, Omae, someone will hear you and I'll be in disgrace. Why don't you go before anything happens.

OMAE: It's all right. My friends have promised to hold your old rascal tutor till I get back.

EMAN: Then you go back right now. I have work to do. (*Going in.*)

OMAE (*runs after and tries to hold him. Eman leaps back, genuinely scared*): What is the matter? I was not going to bite you.

EMAN: Do you know what you nearly did? You almost touched me!

OMAE: Well?

EMAN: Well! Isn't it enough that you let me set my eyes on you? Must you now totally pollute me with your touch? Don't you understand anything?

OMAE: Oh, that.

EMAN (*nearly screaming*): It is not "oh that." Do you think this is only a joke or a little visit like spending the night with your grandmother? This is an important period of my life. Look, these huts, we built them with our own hands. Every boy builds his own. We learn things, do you understand? And we spend much time just thinking. At least, I do. It is the first time I have had nothing to do except think. Don't you see, I am becoming a man. For the first time, I understand that I have a life to fulfill. Has that thought ever worried you?

OMAE: You are frightening me.

EMAN: There. That is all you can say. And what use will that be when a man finds himself alone—like that? (*Points to the hut.*) A man must go on his own, go where no one can help him, and test his strength. Because he may find himself one day sitting alone in a wall as round as that. In there, my mind could hold no other thought. I may never have such moments again to myself. Don't dare to come and steal any more of it.

OMAE (*this time, genuinely tearful*): Oh, I know you hate me. You only want to drive me away.

EMAN (*impatiently*): Yes, yes, I know I hate you—but go.

OMAE (*going, all tears. Wipes her eyes, suddenly all mischief*): Eman.

EMAN: What now?

OMAE: I only want to ask one thing . . . do you promise to tell me?

EMAN: Well, what is it?

OMAE (*gleefully*): Does it hurt?

(*She turns instantly and flees, landing straight into the arms of the returning tutor.*)

TUTOR: Te-he-he . . . what have we here? What little mouse leaps straight into the beak of the wise old owl eh?

(*Omae struggles to free herself, flies to the opposite side, grimacing with distaste.*)

TUTOR: I suppose you merely came to pick some fruits eh? You did not sneak here to see any of my children.

OMAE: Yes, I came to steal your fruits.

TUTOR: Te-he-he . . . I thought so. And that dutiful son of mine over there. He saw you and came to chase you off my fruit trees didn't he? Te-he-he . . . I'm sure he did, isn't that so, my young Eman?

EMAN: I was talking to her.

TUTOR: Indeed you were. Now be good enough to go into your hut until I decide your punishment. (*Eman withdraws.*) Te-he-he . . . now now, my little daughter, you need not be afraid of me.

OMAE (*spiritedly*): I am not.

TUTOR: Good. Very good. We ought to be friendly. (*His voice becomes leering.*) Now this is nothing to worry you, my daughter . . . a very small thing indeed. Although of course if I were to let it slip that your young Eman had broken a strong taboo, it might go hard on him you know. I am sure you would not like that to happen, would you?

OMAE: No.

TUTOR: Good. You are sensible, my girl. Can you wash clothes?

OMAE: Yes.

TUTOR: Good. If you will come with me now to my hut, I shall give you some clothes to wash, and then we will forget all about this matter eh? Well, come on.

OMAE: I shall wait here. You go and bring the clothes.

TUTOR: Eh? What is that? Now now, don't make me angry. You should know better than to talk back at your elders. Come now.

(*He takes her by the arm and tries to drag her off.*)

OMAE: No no, I won't come to your hut. Leave me. Leave me alone, you shameless old man.

TUTOR: If you don't come I shall disgrace the whole family of Eman, and yours too.

(*Eman reenters with a small bundle.*)

EMAN: Leave her alone. Let us go, Omae.

TUTOR: And where do you think you are going?

EMAN: Home.

TUTOR: Te-he-he . . . As easy as that eh? You think you can leave here any time you please? Get right back inside that hut!

(*Eman takes Omae by the arm and begins to walk off.*)

TUTOR: Come back at once.

(*He goes after him and raises his stick. Eman catches it, wrenches it from him, and throws it away.*)

OMAE (*hopping delightedly*): Kill him. Beat him to death.

TUTOR: Help! Help! He is killing me! Help!

(*Alarmed, Eman clamps his hand over his mouth.*)

EMAN: Old tutor, I don't mean you any harm, but you mustn't try to harm me either. (*He removes his hand.*)

TUTOR: You think you can get away with your crime. My report shall reach the elders before you ever get into town.

EMAN: You are afraid of what I will say about you? Don't worry. Only if you try to shame me, then I will speak. I am not going back to the village anyway. Just tell them I have gone, no more. If you say one word more than that I shall hear of it the same day and I shall come back.

TUTOR: You are telling me what to do? But don't think to come back next year because I will drive you away. Don't think to come back here even ten years from now. And don't send your children.

(*Goes off with threatening gestures.*)

EMAN: I won't come back.

OMAE: Smoked vulture! But Eman, he says you cannot return next year. What will you do?

EMAN: It is a small thing one can do in the big towns.

OMAE: I thought you were going to beat him that time. Why didn't you crack his dirty hide?

EMAN: Listen carefully, Omae . . . I am going on a journey.

OMAE: Come on. Tell me about it on the way.

EMAN: No, I go that way. I cannot return to the village.

OMAE: Because of that wretched man? Anyway you will first talk to your father.

EMAN: Go and see him for me. Tell him I have gone away for some time. I think he will know.

OMAE: But, Eman . . .

EMAN: I haven't finished. You will go and live with him till I get back. I have spoken to him about you. Look after him!

OMAE: But what is this journey? When will you come back?

EMAN: I don't know. But this is a good moment to go. Nothing ties me down.

OMAE: But, Eman, you want to leave me.

EMAN: Don't forget all I said. I don't know how long I will be. Stay in my father's house as long as you remember me. When you become tired of waiting, you must do as you please. You understand? You must do as you please.

OMAE: I cannot understand anything, Eman. I don't know where you are going or why. Suppose you never came back! Don't go, Eman. Don't leave me by myself.

EMAN: I must go. Now let me see you on your way.

OMAE: I shall come with you.

EMAN: Come with me! And who will look after you? Me? You will only be in my way, you know that! You will hold me back and I shall desert you in a strange place. Go home and do as I say. Take care of my father and let him take care of you.

(*He starts going but Omae clings to him.*)

OMAE: But, Eman, stay the night at least. You will only lose your way. Your father, Eman, what will he say? I won't remember what you said . . . come back to the village . . . I cannot return alone, Eman . . . come with me as far as the crossroads.

(*His face set, Eman strides off and Omae loses balance as he increases his pace. Falling, she quickly wraps her arms around his ankle, but Eman continues unchecked, dragging her along.*)

OMAE: Don't go, Eman . . . Eman, don't leave me, don't leave me . . . don't leave your Omae . . . don't go, Eman . . . don't leave your Omae . . .

(*Eman—as carrier—makes a nervous move as if he intends to go after the vanished pair. He stops but continues to stare at the point where he last saw them. There is stillness for a while. Then the Girl enters from the same place and remains looking at Eman. Startled, Eman looks apprehensively round him. The Girl goes nearer but keeps beyond arm's length.*)

GIRL: Are you the carrier?

EMAN: Yes. I am Eman.

GIRL: Why are you hiding?

EMAN: I really came for a drink of water . . . er . . . is there anyone in front of the house?

GIRL: No.

EMAN: But there might be people in the house. Did you hear voices?

GIRL: There is no one here.

EMAN: Good. Thank you. (*He is about to go, stops suddenly.*) Er . . . would you . . . you will find a cup on the table. Could you bring me the water out here? The water pot is in a corner.

(*The Girl goes. She enters the house, then, watching Eman carefully, slips out and runs off.*)

EMAN (*sitting*): Perhaps they have all gone home. It will be good to rest. (*He hears voices and listens hard.*) Too late. (*Moves cautiously nearer the house.*) Quickly, girl, I can hear people coming. Hurry up. (*Looks through the window.*) Where are you? Where is she? (*The truth dawns on him suddenly and he moves off, sadly.*)

(*Enter Jaguna and Oroge, led by the Girl.*)

GIRL (*pointing*): He was there.

JAGUNA: Ay, he's gone now. He is a sly one is your friend. But it won't save him forever.

OROGE: What was he doing when you saw him?

GIRL: He asked me for a drink of water.

JAGUNA:⎫
OROGE:⎭ Ah! (*They look at each other.*)

OROGE: We should have thought of that.

JAGUNA: He is surely finished now. If only we had thought of it earlier.

OROGE: It is not too late. There is still an hour before midnight.

JAGUNA: We must call back all the men. Now we need only wait for him—in the right place.

OROGE: Everyone must be told. We don't want anyone heading him off again.

JAGUNA: And it works so well. This is surely the help of the gods themselves, Oroge. Don't you know at once what is on the path to the stream?

OROGE: The sacred trees.

JAGUNA: I tell you it is the very hand of the gods. Let us go.

(*An overgrown part of the village. Eman wanders in, aimlessly, seemingly uncaring of discovery. Beyond him, an area lights up, revealing a group of people clustered round a spot, all the heads are bowed. One figure stands away and separate from them. Even as Eman looks, the group breaks up and the people disperse, coming down and past him. Only three people are left, a man [Eman] whose back is turned, the village priest, and the isolated one. They stand on opposite sides of the grave, the man on the mound of earth. The Priest walks round to the man's side and lays a hand on his shoulder.*)

PRIEST: Come.

EMAN: I will. Give me a few moments here alone.

PRIEST: Be comforted.

(*They fall silent.*)

EMAN: I was gone twelve years but she waited. She whom I thought had too much of the laughing child in her. Twelve years I was a pilgrim, seeking the vain shrine of secret strength. And all the time, strange knowledge, this silent strength of my child-woman.

PRIEST: We all saw it. It was a lesson to us; we did not know that such goodness could be found among us.

EMAN: Then why? Why the wasted years if she had to perish giving birth to my child? (*They are both silent.*) I do not really know for what great meaning I searched. When I returned, I could not be certain I had found it. Until I reached my home and I found her a full-grown woman, still a child at heart. When I grew to believe it, I thought, this, after all, is what I sought. It was here all the time. And I threw away my new-gained knowledge. I buried the part of me that was formed in strange places. I made a home in my birthplace.

PRIEST: That was as it should be.

EMAN: Any truth of that was killed in the cruelty of her brief happiness.

PRIEST (*looks up and sees the figure standing away from them, the child in his arms. He is totally still*): Your father—he is over there.

EMAN: I knew he would come. Has he my son with him?

PRIEST: Yes.

EMAN: He will let no one take the child. Go and comfort him, priest. He loved Omae like a daughter, and you all know how well she looked after him. You see how strong we really are. In his heart of hearts the old man's love really awaited a daughter. Go and comfort him. His grief is more than mine.

(*The Priest goes. The Old Man has stood well away from the burial group. His face is hard and his gaze unswerving from the grave. The Priest goes to him, pauses, but sees that he can make no dent in the man's grief. Bowed, he goes on his way.*)

(*Eman, as carrier, walking towards the graveside, the other Eman having gone. His feet sink into the mound and he breaks slowly onto his knees, scooping up the sand in his hands and pouring it on his head. The scene blacks out slowly.*)

(*Enter Jaguna and Oroge.*)

OROGE: We have only a little time.

JAGUNA: He will come. All the wells are guarded. There is only the stream left him. The animal must come to drink.

OROGE: You are sure it will not fail—the trap, I mean.

JAGUNA: When Jaguna sets the trap, even elephants pay homage—their trunks downwards and one leg up in the sky. When the carrier steps on the fallen twigs, it is up in the sacred trees with him.

OROGE: I shall breathe again when this long night is over.

(*They go out.*)

(*Enter Eman—as carrier—from the same direction as the last two entered. In front of him is a still figure, the Old Man as he was, carrying the dwarf boat.*)

EMAN (*joyfully*): Father.

(*The figure does not turn round.*)

EMAN: It is your son, Eman. (*He moves nearer.*) Don't you want to look at me? It is I, Eman. (*He moves nearer still.*)

OLD MAN: You are coming too close. Don't you know what I carry on my head?

EMAN: But, Father, I am your son.

OLD MAN: Then go back. We cannot give the two of us.

EMAN: Tell me first where you are going.

OLD MAN: Do *you* ask that? Where else but to the river?

EMAN (*visibly relieved*): I only wanted to be sure. My throat is burning. I have been looking for the stream all night.

OLD MAN: It is the other way.

EMAN: But you said . . .

OLD MAN: I take the longer way, you know how I must do this. It is quicker if you take the other way. Go now.

EMAN: No, I will only get lost again. I shall go with you.

OLD MAN: Go back, my son. Go back.

EMAN: Why? Won't you even look at me?

OLD MAN: Listen to your father. Go back.

EMAN: But, father!

(*He makes to hold him. Instantly the old man breaks into a rapid trot. Eman hesitates, then follows, his strength nearly gone.*)

EMAN: Wait, father. I am coming with you . . . wait . . . wait for me, father . . .

(*There is a sound of twigs breaking, of a sudden trembling in the branches. Then silence.*)

(*The front of Eman's house. The effigy is hanging from the sheaves. Enter Sunma, still supported by Ifada, she stands transfixed as she sees the hanging figure. Ifada appears to go mad, rushes at the object, and tears it down. Sunma, her last bit of will gone, crumbles against the wall. Some distance away from them, partly hidden, stands the Girl, impassively watching. Ifada hugs the effigy to him, stands above Sunma. The Girl remains where she is, observing.*)

(*Almost at once, the villagers begin to return, subdued and guilty.*)

(*They walk across the front, skirting the house as widely as they can. No word is exchanged. Jaguna and Oroge eventually appear. Jaguna, who is leading, sees Sunma as soon as he comes in view. He stops at once, retreating slightly.*)

OROGE (*almost whispering*): What is it?

JAGUNA: The viper.

(*Oroge looks cautiously at the woman.*)

OROGE: I don't think she will even see you.

JAGUNA: Are you sure? I am in no frame of mind for another meeting with her.

OROGE: Let's go home.

JAGUNA: I am sick to the heart of the cowardice I have seen tonight.

OROGE: That is the nature of men.

JAGUNA: Then it is a sorry world to live in. We did it for them. It was all for their own common good. What did it benefit me whether the man lived or died. But did you see them? One and all they looked up at the man and words died in their throats.

OROGE: It was no common sight.

JAGUNA: Women could not have behaved so shamefully. One by one they crept off like sick dogs. Not one could raise a curse.

OROGE: It was not only him they fled. Do you see how unattended we are?

JAGUNA: There are those who will pay for this night's work!

OROGE: Ay, let us go home.

(*They go off. Sunma, Ifada, and the Girl remain as they are, the light fading slowly on them.*)

COMMENTARY

LEWIS NKOSI (1936–2010)

Interview with Wole Soyinka   1962

This early interview with Soyinka was taped in Lagos, Nigeria, in August 1962, while *The Strong Breed* was very fresh in his mind. In fact, it had not yet been published in Nigeria; that occurred in 1963. Nkosi in the interview highlights the impact of Bertolt Brecht's theater on Soyinka's writing.

NKOSI: Well, Wole Soyinka, could you tell us what set you off on this road to writing?

SOYINKA: I suppose that requires really going back a bit. I would say I began writing seriously, or rather taking myself seriously, taking my *writing* seriously about three, four years ago, but I can only presume that I have always been interested in writing. In school I wrote the usual little sketches for production, the occasional verse, you know, the short story, etc., and I think about 1951 I had the great excitement of having a short story of mine broadcast on the Nigerian Broadcasting Service and that was sort of my first public performance.

NKOSI: What schools did you attend?

SOYINKA: I went to Government School, Ibadan; after that I spent a couple of years in the University College, Ibadan.

NKOSI: You have now published drama, or rather, you've had some plays produced?

SOYINKA: Yes, "produced" is the correct word. I haven't had any plays published although some are in print right now and will come out shortly.

NKOSI: Could you tell us what those plays are?

SOYINKA: There is *The Lion and the Jewel*, which was the first play I wrote.

NKOSI: No, the second.

SOYINKA: The first one I sent up, I suppose like most people do, is the *A Dance of Forests*, which I wrote in 1960 and timed it for the Independence Celebrations; there is the *House of Banigeji* which has never been performed. And I have written about four one-acts including *The Trials of Brother Jero* which was done quite recently in Nigeria.

NKOSI: The *A Dance of the Forests* won you a prize, didn't it?

SOYINKA: Yes, Nigerian Independence competition prize 1960.

NKOSI: Have you got any particular authors that have influenced you most?

SOYINKA: This is a very difficult question for me because I am not aware of any conscious influence on my work, but I can say that if I wanted to aim at any particular kind of theater, I think, however subconsciously, I might aim at Brecht's kind of theater, which I admire tremendously, just his complete freedom with the medium of the theater.

NKOSI: In your last play, *A Dance of the Forests*, which caused a lot of people a tremendous amount of agony trying to figure out just exactly what it was trying to do—they felt that there were some hidden meanings contained in lots of symbolism which they couldn't gather. Now, as you're the author, we are lucky to have you here, and we think that you probably might enlighten us about just what you were trying to say in that work of yours.

SOYINKA: Well, let me say first of all that I think that my prime duty as a playwright is to provide excellent theater; in other words, I think that I have only one commitment to the public, and that is to my audience and that is to make sure they do not leave the theater bored. I don't believe that I have any obligation to enlighten, to instruct, to teach: I don't possess that sense of duty or didacticism—very much unlike Brecht for instance, for, you see, what I like in Brecht is his sort of theater, its liveliness and freedom, not so much his purpose or intentions. I believe my primary duty is just to see that I provide excellent theater for the audience. But inevitably, it is just common sense to say that one just cannot write about just nothing. In *A Dance of the Forests*, I was very much conscious of all the potentialities of existing theatrical idioms in Nigeria and I only know that there was one thing which motivated, maybe, guided the form and the shape of the play or the eventual fate of the characters. I use this word "motivated" quite cautiously because I do not think I consciously tried to preach or bring out, you know, a series of symbolisms at all, but the main thing was the realization that human beings are just destructive all over the world. I think this is it—I have thought about this again and again but during the production—I produced it myself—and in trying to see the play take shape on the stage, I find that the main thing is my own personal conviction or observation that human beings are simply cannibals all over the world so that their main preoccupation seems to be eating up one another. This I think is the main thing I would say was in the back of my mind when I wrote it.

NKOSI: Yes, that sounds very much like Tennessee Williams's idea of the world conscious of the evil.

SOYINKA: Well, I don't sort of regard it so much as . . .

NKOSI: The ferocity of human beings.

SOYINKA: Yes, the carnivorous nature of. . . .

NKOSI: Yes, I wonder whether now—have you pursued this theme in the other plays or are the other plays different?

SOYINKA: . . . Fundamentally, I think they're different. I think that sort of semi-consciously the moment I realize I'm pursuing a theme again, it seems to ring a bell warning that I have preceded myself somewhere; I have such a feeling about this that I shirk from it but I would say there are traces of it in my other plays—in, for instance, my favorite one-act play which is *The Strong Breed*. I think this one is also very much mixed up with the whole element of sacrifice, so contrasting the idea of selfishness with willing self-sacrifice as opposed to the other general cannibalism of human beings.

Contemporary Drama

The experimentation in drama that flourished in the first half of the twentieth century has continued in contemporary drama. In fact, the achievements of Tennessee Williams, Arthur Miller, Samuel Beckett, and other midcentury playwrights encouraged later playwrights to experiment more daringly with mixing media such as film, video, opera, rock, and other music with live actors. Mixed-media approaches are still options for playwrights in the twenty-first century, but most contemporary plays celebrated by critics and audiences have been relatively traditional. They build on the achievements of nineteenth-century realism and twentieth-century expressionism.

Experimentation

Most of the interesting late-twentieth-century experimental theater was done in groups such as Richard Schechner's Performance Group, which created what Schechner called **environmental theater** in New York City in the late 1960s, and Jerzy Grotowski's Polish Laboratory Theatre in Wroclaw, Poland, during the same period. Ensembles like the Bread and Puppet Theater, the San Francisco Mime Troupe, and Luis Valdez's El Teatro Campesino on the West Coast combined a radical political message with theatrical experimentation. The work of these groups is effective primarily at the performance level; their texts are not representative of their impact on audiences.

Theater of Cruelty

The ensembles of the 1960s and 1970s were strongly influenced by the work of Antonin Artaud (1896–1948), a French actor, director, and theorist of theater. In creating what came to be known as the **theater of cruelty**, he insisted on removing the comforting distance between actors and audience. Thus the audience was involved in a direct, virtually physical fashion with the dramatic action. Artaud designed theater to be a total experience—a sensational spectacle that did not depend on coherent plot or development. He concentrated on what he called total theater, which emphasized movement, gesture, music, sound, light, and other nonverbal elements to intensify the experience.

Artaud's manifestos, collected in a work entitled *The Theater and Its Double* (1938), inspired some of the most important twentieth-century theater practitioners, including Peter Brook and Robert Wilson. Artaud's notion of a "serious" theater is at the root of his influence:

> Our long habit of seeking diversion has made us forget the idea of a serious theater, which, overturning all our preconceptions, inspires us with the fiery magnetism of its images and acts upon us like a spiritual therapeutics whose touch can never be forgotten.
>
> Everything that acts is a cruelty. It is upon this idea of extreme action, pushed beyond all limits, that theater must be rebuilt.

Artaud compared the theater artist he envisioned to a victim "burnt at the stake, signaling through the flames."

Environmental Theater

Richard Schechner's most famous production, based on Euripides' *The Bacchae*, was *Dionysus in 69* (1968), in which Pentheus is torn to pieces in an impassioned frenzy. Part of the point of Schechner's production was to inspire the audience so much that they would take to the stage, becoming indistinguishable from the actors. *Dionysus in 69* was an effort to draw on the same spiritual energies tapped by Greek drama by connecting with the feasts of Dionysus, god of wine and ecstasy. The play was a spontaneous and partly improvised performance piece rather than a text meant to be read. At one point the audience and actors disrobed in a simulation of a Greek religious orgy, and Schechner's goal of involving audience and actors in a pagan ritual was realized night after night during the run.

In a similar way Julian Beck and Judith Malina's Living Theatre maintained a special relationship with the audience. Beck's plays were designed to break down the absolutes of dramatic space and audience space by having the actors roam through the audience and interact apparently at random with audience members. *Paradise Now* (1968) is his best-known play. Like Schechner's *Dionysus in 69*, it was essentially a performance piece. Certain segments were improvised; therefore, as a reading text, it has relatively little power.

"Poor Theater"

Jerzy Grotowski called his work "poor theater" because it was meant to contrast with the "rich theater" of the commercial stage, with its expensive lighting, decorated stages, rich costumes, numerous props, and elaborate settings. Grotowski's Laboratory Theatre, begun in 1959, relied on preexisting texts but interpreted them broadly through a total reconception of their meaning. For example, Grotowski's *Akropolis* (1962; revised frequently from 1963 to 1975) adapted an older Polish drama by Stanislaw Wyspiański (1904) and reset it in modern times in Auschwitz with the actors, dressed in ragged sackcloth prison uniforms, looking wretched and starving. At the end of the play the prisoners follow a headless puppet-corpse, Christ, into an afterlife. They march in an eerie ritual procession offstage into the waiting prison camp ovens.

Grotowski's theater has been influential worldwide. When the Polish government clamped down on the Solidarity° movement in the late 1970s, Grotowski left Poland. After 1970 Grotowski shifted his focus from public performances to small, intense group workshops and to the ritual performances of cultures from all over the world. The first phase of his work with the Laboratory Theatre has remained the most influential. One of his actors, Richard Cieslak, traveled widely, training people in Grotowski's methods.

Theater of Images

Robert Wilson experimented from the 1970s through the 1990s with repetitive narratives that sometimes take eight hours to perform. His multimedia dramas involve huge casts and ordinarily cover an immense historical range (Figure 30). One of his most extraordinary successes was *Einstein on the Beach* (1976), an opera written in collaboration with composer Philip Glass. Eight hours long, it was originally produced in a conventional theater, but it uses dramatic techniques that involve extensive patterns of repetition, the creation of enigmatic and evocative images, and characters who are cartoonlike caricatures of historical people. The overall effect is hypnotic; one of the points of Wilson's work seems to be to induce a trancelike state in his audience. One of his multimedia productions, *CIVIL warS* (1983), continued to develop this concept of massive theater that transcends conventional dramatic boundaries. In 1994 Wilson produced a monologue version of *Hamlet* that received some acclaim.

Gay and Lesbian Theater and Other New Ensembles

Some of the most energetic theater of the late twentieth century came from groups that were excluded for long periods from representation in mainstream theater. Gay, lesbian, African American, Hispanic American, and Native American groups have been virtually ignored by commercial theater and as a result have formed their own collectives and groups.

Through the 1970s, 1980s, and 1990s, numerous black theatrical groups developed in many parts of the world. An important Afro-Caribbean theater group was formed in the Keskidee Centre in North London, with Edgar White (b. 1947) as one of its directors. White's plays are often centered in Caribbean mystical experiences, including Rastafarianism. *The Nine Night* (1983), produced in London, focuses on a Jamaican funeral tradition designed to help the deceased enter the gates of heaven.

One reason for the development of gay theater in the United States and Great Britain in the 1960s was the decriminalization of homosexuality, beginning in 1967 in Boston. The first openly gay play was Mart Crowley's *The Boys in the Band* (1968), a popular success produced just after the repeal of a New York law prohibiting homosexuality from being represented on stage. Depiction of homosexual love onstage waited even longer, until the Gay Workshop began producing plays in London in 1976.

The Ridiculous Theatrical Company, founded by Charles Ludlam (1940–1987) in 1969, produced a formidable body of work rooted in the experiences of the homosexual community of New York. Its influence spread to many parts of the world. One of Ludlam's catchphrases was "plays without the stink of art." His plays were often ridiculously funny. *Bluebeard* (1970),

---

Solidarity: A labor-organizing movement in Communist Poland led by Lech Walesa.

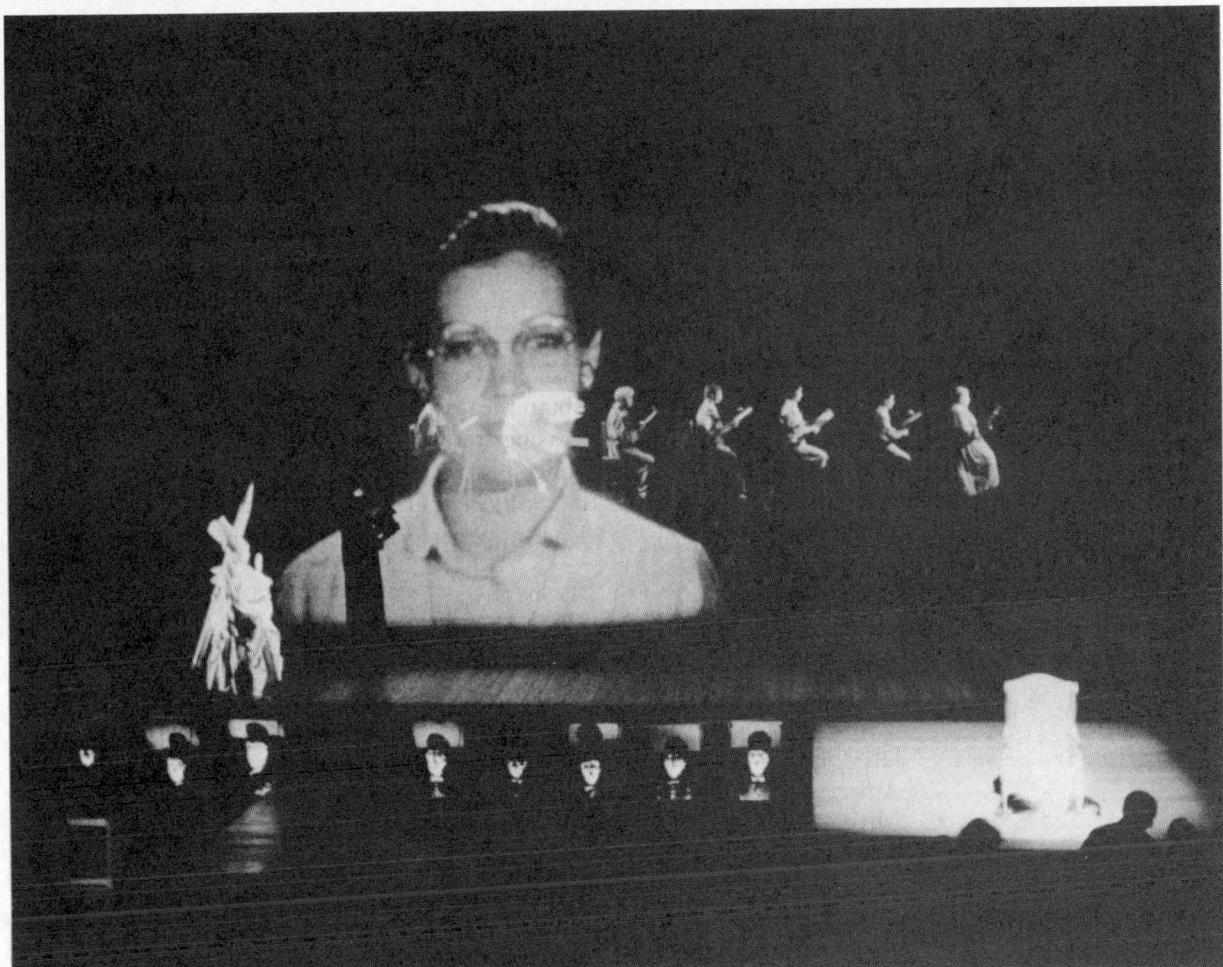

Figure 30. Multimedia effects in Robert Wilson's *CIVIL warS*.

for example, focused on creating a third gender by inventing a third genital. *Camille* (1973), starring Ludlam himself in the title role, hilariously spoofed not only Dumas's play but most of the "Hallmark card" conventions about romantic love. A gifted female impersonator, Ludlam played Hedda Gabler at the American Ibsen Theater in Pittsburgh. For a few years, under the direction of Ludlam's partner, Everett Quinton, the Ridiculous Theatrical Company continued to produce Ludlam's plays as well as new plays in his tradition.

Some of the most highly praised plays of the 1980s and 1990s addressed the issues of AIDS and its ravaging of the gay community. Harvey Fierstein's *Torch Song Trilogy* (1982) was named best play of the year and appeared several years later on television. *As Is* by William M. Hoffman (1985) has been described by Don Shewey as the "best gay play anyone has written on AIDS yet." Tony Kushner dazzled New York with *Angels in America Part One: Millennium Approaches* (1992) and *Part Two: Perestroika* (1992). This two-part drama approached the problems of gay life in America on both a personal and a public, political level. The plays are called a "fantasia" and use a free-form, nonrealistic style of presentation. In late 2003, HBO produced an award-winning version for television starring Al Pacino and Meryl Streep.

Lesbian theatrical groups have sprung up in the United States and Great Britain. They often merge with women's theater groups and address issues such as male violence, societal restrictions on women, and women's opportunities. A number of important collectives, such as the Rhode Island Women's Theater and At the Foot of the Mountain in Minneapolis, treated general women's issues in the 1970s. Groups such as Medusa's Revenge (founded 1976) and Atlanta's Red Dyke Theater (1974) centered more on lesbian experience. These last two groups disbanded after a few years of successful productions. Megan Terry's Omaha Magic Theatre, founded with Jo Ann Schmidman, has been a long-lasting theater focusing on women's issues. Other groups such as Spiderwoman, consisting of three Native American sisters, and the highly successful Split Britches consider WOW Cafe Theatre in New York's East Village to be the home of lesbian theater. Gay and lesbian theater groups have often been concerned with erasing stereotypes while also celebrating gay and lesbian lifestyles. Plays that once played only to gay and lesbian audiences— such as Martin Sherman's (b. 1939) *Bent* (1977) and Larry Kramer's (b. 1935) *The Normal Heart* (1985)—are now performed in theaters worldwide.

Contemporary Women Playwrights

The contemporary female writers whose plays appear in this collection are among a throng of powerful playwrights who have helped shape theater in the twenty-first century. María Irene Fornés's *Fefu and Her Friends* (1977) is a sprawling play featuring women in roles traditionally reserved for men. Her later play, *Conduct of Life* (1985), is a cruel parody of macho values in a Latin American dictatorship. Caryl Churchill's *Cloud Nine* (1979) critiques colonialism and gender stereotyping. *Top Girls* (1982), one of her most successful plays, centers on an employment agency for women but has as its premise the introduction of famous women from the past of several cultures. *Fen* (1983), a verse play called *Serious Money* (1987), and *The Skriker* (1994) have solidified Churchill's reputation as an experimental, powerful dramatist. Suzan-Lori Parks's *Topdog/Underdog* (2001) won the Pulitzer Prize for drama, the first for an African American female playwright. Her earlier plays, *The Death of the Last Black Man in the Whole Entire World* (1990), *The American Play* (1993), *Venus* (1996), and *In the Blood* (1999), are all powerful pieces that are frequently revived.

Lynn Nottage's *Crumbs from the Table of Joy* (1995), *Intimate Apparel* (2004), and *Ruined* (2010) have established her as one of the most important modern African American playwrights. Sarah Ruhl's plays *Eurydice* (2003), *The Clean House* (2004), and *In the Next Room: or, The Vibrator Play* (2009) have been international successes. Paula Vogel, author of *How I Learned to Drive* (1997), is not only a distinguished playwright but also a remarkable teacher who has been a mentor to both Nottage and Ruhl.

Of course, there are many exceptional contemporary female writers whose work is not included here. Among the most distinguished is Marsha Norman, author of the prison drama *Getting Out* (1977); *'night Mother* (1982), about a daughter who says goodnight to her mother and commits suicide; and *The Secret Garden* (1991). Emily Mann's *Execution of Justice* (1984) retells the trial of Dan White, who murdered Harvey Milk, an openly gay San Francisco city councilman. Irish playwright Anne Devlin's *Ourselves Alone* (1986) is set against the background of an Irish hunger strike. Lynn Siefert's *Coyote Ugly* (1986), about a painfully and comically dysfunctional Southwestern family, may have spawned a similarly named bar in New York. Anna Deveare Smith produces one-woman dramas that are *tours de force;* she personates as many as forty different characters in plays such as *Fires in the Mirror: Crown Heights, Brooklyn and Other Identities* (1991), about ethnic disturbances after a child is killed in Crown Heights; *Twilight: Los Angeles 1992* (1992), about the riots in Los Angeles following the trial of police officers charged in the beating of Rodney King; and *Let Me Down Easy* (2011), a critique of the current medical establishment. All of these playwrights have enhanced the stature of women in contemporary theater.

Experimentation within the Tradition

Much of the powerful and lasting drama of the 1980s, 1990s, and early years of the twenty-first century has been achieved in a proscenium theater, using traditional methods of **dramaturgy** (the craft or techniques of dramatic composition). Contemporary dramatists are by no means shy about experimentation, but they are also sensitive to the continuing resources of the traditional stage as it was conceived by Chekhov and Ibsen and Miller. Marsha Norman, who wrote *'night, Mother,* has said that her plays are "wildly traditional. I'm a purist about structure. Plays are like plane rides. You [the audience] buy the ticket and you have to get where the ticket takes you. Or else you've been had."

Drama in the United States

Sam Shepard (b. 1943), one of the most prolific modern playwrights in the United States, experiments with his material, much of which premiered in small theaters in Greenwich Village, such as the La Mama Experimental Theatre Club. But his most widely known plays, among them *Buried Child* (1978), are produced easily on conventional stages. Shepard's work is wide-ranging and challenging. His language is coarse, a representation of the way real people speak, and the violence he portrays onstage is strong enough to alienate many in the audience. Shepard, important as he is, has not found a popular commercial audience for his plays. At root, his work is always experimental.

Although she claims to be a traditionalist, Marsha Norman (b. 1947) has written experimental plays, including her first success, *Getting Out* (1977), which portrays the same character at two periods in her life—as an adolescent and as an adult—on separate parts of the stage at the same time. Norman's *'night, Mother* is a more traditionally structured play. It respects the Aristotelian unities of time, place, and action, and it is confrontational. Thelma and her daughter, Jessie, are in a power struggle over Jessie's right to commit suicide. The technique is naturalistic, and the play's subject matter, like that of Strindberg and Ibsen, is discomforting to contemporary audiences.

August Wilson's (1945–2005) Pittsburgh Cycle treats the subject of black life in modern America. He completed this series of ten plays just before he died in 2005, and each of the first four won the New York Drama Critics' Circle Award for best play of the year. All of Wilson's plays have explored how the heritage of blacks enables them to live intelligently in the present, with understanding and dignity. People in his plays have lost touch with the past and, for that reason, risk a loss of self-understanding. Wilson's plays also show the pain endured by blacks in a country that is supposedly the land of opportunity. Like Arthur Miller in *Death of a Salesman* and Lorraine Hansberry in *A Raisin in the Sun,* Wilson explores the nature and consequences of the American dream, especially for those effectively excluded from this dream. Blacks' frustration, exploitation, and suffering are presented through Wilson's powerful characters, such as Troy Maxson in *Fences* (1985). Troy is a garbage collector who was a star baseball player at a time when blacks could not play in the major leagues. The play centers on Maxson's anger, his pride in his family, and his concerns for his son, who is growing up into a world in which he must empower himself to achieve what he most wants for himself. Cory, Troy's son, does not see the same kind of discrimination and has not felt the unfairness that was Troy's primary experience in growing up. Showing the world as Troy Maxson sees it is one of the functions of the play.

Wilson's plays have a naturalistic surface, but they also allude to the supernatural, as in *The Piano Lesson* (1990). Some of the roots of this tradition are in the black church and some in African religion, a source shared by Soyinka and Wilson, among others.

Among current playwrights is David Henry Hwang (b. 1957), who has been active in writing for both stage and film. His work often centers on Chinese Americans and the problems they encounter in their experiences in the United States. Hwang has sensitized audiences to subjects about which playwrights had hitherto been silent. His first success, *FOB* (1980), focused on how new immigrants were viewed by Chinese Americans who had already assimilated. The play's title is an acronym for "fresh off the boat." Hwang's most successful play, *M. Butterfly* (1987), is about a romance between a French diplomat and a transvestite Chinese opera singer. *Yellow Face* (2009) is his most personal play, with a protagonist named DHH fuming about the choice of a white actor for the main Eurasian character in *Miss Saigon. Yellow Face* exposes David Henry Hwang's shortcomings as explicitly as it exposes the stresses caused by ethnic categories in contemporary theater.

Since his short but intense *The Zoo Story* (1958) came out, Edward Albee (b. 1928) has been a powerful force in American theater. He has won three Pulitzer Prizes for drama: for *A Delicate Balance* (1966), *Seascape* (1974), and *Three Tall Women* (1991). He is better known for *Who's Afraid of Virginia Woolf?* (1961), however, a portrait of a violent, alcohol-filled marriage between academics George and Martha, portrayed memorably by Richard Burton and Elizabeth Taylor in Mike Nichols's 1966 film version. Not all of Albee's plays have been successful, but throughout his career he has maintained a reputation as an important experimentalist. His Tony Award–winning play *The Goat, or Who Is Sylvia?* (2002) is a complex portrait of a prize-winning architect who falls in love with a goat. Albee thus pushes beyond the questions of heterosexuality and homosexuality into the taboo of bestiality. Beneath the surface, however, he presses the issues of tragedy as it is expressed in a modern situation.

David Mamet (b. 1947) responds to a social situation in *Oleanna* (1992). The characters, a male college professor and a female student, at first adopt an ordinary teacher-student relationship; eventually, though, that relationship alters. Mamet explores questions of power and issues of sexual harassment. As the lines he draws shift back and forth, the audience never knows exactly how clear the lines are meant to be. The issues in the play are thus subject to a number of different interpretations. Widely considered Mamet's best play, *Glengarry Glen Ross* (1983) offers a savage portrait of the masculine world of salesmanship. Deception, competition, and outright theft dominate the play, demonstrating a failure of values of the main characters, all of whom feel justified in their willingness to push property on those who do not want or need it. Mamet's language carries the weight of a philosophy that scorns the get-ahead attitude of the salesman.

Tony Kushner's two-part drama *Angels in America: Millennium Approaches* (1992) and *Perestroika* (1992) explores issues in modern American history, with an emphasis on religion, politics, and a variety of hysterias. The plays explore homophobia, red-baiting politics, and the impact of AIDS on contemporary society. The open, dynamic structure of the work is enormously powerful. The entire drama lasts six and a half hours and has been seen not only in San Francisco, where it opened, but also in New York, London, other European cities, and regional theaters throughout the United States. The Golden Globe Award–winning 2003 HBO production introduced the play to many millions of viewers and expanded some of Kushner's vision for the drama. His *Homebody/Kabul* (2001), which examines the political circumstances in Afghanistan in 1998 after U.S. bombing raids, reflects his continuing interest in exploring contemporary historical events; his chamber opera *Caroline, or Change* (2003) considers racial issues in Louisiana in 1963.

In the late 1990s, young men and women made important contributions to theater. José Rivera (b. 1955) presented two plays that drew on the tradition of magic realism that is prominent in Latin American fiction. *Marisol* (1992) and *Cloud Tectonics* (1995) are visually and emotionally impressive pieces that work counter to the Ibsenist tradition of realism. As especially theatrical pieces, they give the director a considerable degree of freedom in staging. Rivera's *Boleros for the Disenchanted,* staged at the Yale Repertory Theatre in May 2008, treats the subjects of love, aging, and marriage.

Paula Vogel (b. 1951) created a portrait of an adolescent girl, Li'l Bit, involved with an incestuous Uncle Peck in *How I Learned to Drive* (1997). The play won the 1998 Pulitzer Prize and established Vogel as one of the most important American playwrights. Her play *The Long Christmas Ride Home* (2003) continued her experimentation in the realm of puppet theater. The effect recalls techniques of Japanese Bunraku theater.

Nilo Cruz (b. 1961) won the Pulitzer Prize in 2003 for *Anna in the Tropics.* He was the first Hispanic Pulitzer winner in drama. Among his many plays is *Lorca in a Green Dress* (2003); it and *Beauty of the Father* (2007) are experiments in literary allusion.

Moisés Kaufman's Tectonic Theater Project began *The Laramie Project* in 1998, after Matthew Shepard, a young gay man, was brutally beaten, tied to a fence, and left to die in Laramie, Wyoming. The group conducted interviews of townspeople for a year and a half and presented the play, which is in some ways a portrait of the community, in Laramie in 2000. It has been televised and seen across the country.

Doug Wright (b. 1962) created a play called *I Am My Own Wife,* about Charlotte von Mahlsdorf, a transvestite who survived the Nazis and the Russians in Berlin. Directed by Moisés Kaufman, *I Am My Own Wife* won every major award in 2004, including the Pulitzer. The single actor on stage, Jefferson Mays, played dozens of characters, all convincingly.

Neil LaBute (b. 1963) makes films as well as writing plays. His *The Shape of Things* (2001) uses a highly experimental approach to language in which silences play a profound role as he explores the dark side of femininity and the complexities of art.

John Patrick Shanley (b. 1950) won the Pulitzer Prize in 2005 for *Doubt,* a play about a Catholic nun's suspicions about the behavior of a priest who befriends a young boy. The staging of the play was traditional, but the subject matter struck a painful note for some audiences.

Rolin Jones's (b. 1972) experimental and enormously entertaining *The Intelligent Design of Jenny Chow* (2006) resembles a video game, with Jenny creating a robotic other who crosses continents. Suzan-Lori Parks's (b. 1963) extraordinary experiment *365 Days/365 Plays* involved her writing a play every day for a year. She has permitted groups to stage the plays without paying royalties, and projects have been established to produce the plays across the country.

Rajiv Joseph (b. 1974) spent several years with the Peace Corps in Senegal; his best-known play is *Bengal Tiger at the Baghdad Zoo* (2009), starring Robin Williams as the tiger. A powerful political drama set in Iraq, it was a finalist for the Pulitzer Prize. Aditi Brennan Kapil's *Agnes under the Big Top: A Tall Tale* (2011) addresses the pain of immigrants in the United States and features a subway train driven by a former Bulgarian ringmaster. Much of the play is dark, set in a subway with a remarkable variety of ethnic and handicapped characters.

Katori Hall (b. 1981) has had a remarkable first success with *The Mountaintop* (2011), which portrays a very human Dr. Martin Luther King on the night before he was assassinated. Amy Herzog (b. 1978) has written *After the Revolution* (2010), which portrays a family of aging lefties holding on to earlier ideals, and *Belleville* (2011), about an expatriate couple in Paris whose marriage falls apart when their deceptions catch up with them. Quiara Alegría Hudes (b. 1977) was nominated for a Pulitzer Prize for the book of the musical *In the Heights* (2008) and won the prize for her 2011 play, *Water by the Spoonful,* which focuses on the return of Iraq veterans. These and many other excellent playwrights are making contemporary American drama a powerful force all over the globe.

Drama in Europe: England, Ireland, and France

English playwright Harold Pinter's (1930–2008) distinctive style, developed in the late 1950s and early 1960s, was connected with some of the absurdist experiments in drama. His dialogue was acerbic, repetitive, sometimes apparently aimless. However, he was able to produce intense emotional situations, such as in *The Dumb Waiter* (1957), in which two "hit men" wait for instructions in a basement room. *The Caretaker* (1960) and *The Homecoming* (1965), Pinter's first commercial successes, established him as a major figure in modern theater. He was also a screenwriter for such films as *The Quiller Memorandum* (1966), *The French Lieutenant's Woman* (1981), and *The Handmaid's Tale* (1990). His experiments with time and sequence in his full-length play *Betrayal* (1978), for which he also wrote the screenplay, have inspired other playwrights, such as Paula Vogel, to experiment with the backward movement of action.

Some of Caryl Churchill's (b. 1938) plays, emphasizing themes of socialism, colonialism, and feminism, were developed in workshops and collaborations with actors and directors. Early in the first stages of writing a play, Churchill experiments by spending time in the environments her play depicts. When she was working on *Top Girls* (1982), she came up with the idea of setting the action in an employment agency after she had talked with many people who work in the business world. For *Serious Money* (1987), she and the group developing the play spent time at the London Stock Exchange, absorbing the atmosphere of frenetic buying and selling.

Jez Butterworth's (b. 1969) *Jerusalem* (2009) opened to impressive reviews in London and in New York. Mark Rylance starred as a wildly eccentric "lord of misrule" trying to keep a piece of land away from the local town council, whose aim was to clean up the area, evict him, and erect new dwellings.

Irish playwright Brian Friel (b. 1929) began his career as an experimentalist in *Philadelphia, Here I Come!* (1964), in which Gar O'Donnell, the main character, appears both as his public self, represented by one actor, and as his private self, represented by another actor. This experimental drama ran for 326 performances on Broadway. Friel's political drama *Freedom of the City* (1974) addresses the "troubles" in Northern Ireland at a time of bombings and threats. *Translations* (1980) experiments with language—having Irish-speaking characters speak Irish to one another to baffle the British characters, while we "listen in" as if the Irish were being translated for us. *Faith Healer* (1979) presents characters onstage one at a time—with no interaction—telling us their stories in a powerful way. Throughout his career, Friel has been on the cutting edge of experimentation.

Marina Carr (b. 1964) is one of Ireland's most respected playwrights. *Portia Coughlan* (1996), which opened in Dublin and London, won the Susan Smith Blackburn Prize; *By the Bog of Cats* (1998) is a retelling of the story of Medea; *On Raftery's Hill* (2000) is a tale of madness and incest in Ireland's isolating west country. Another Irish playwright, Moira Buffini (b. 1965), wrote *Silence* (1999), which won the Susan Smith Blackburn Prize for best play by a woman. Buffini's *Welcome to Thebes* (2010) echoes Greek drama in a play about African political instability in which a political cadre of men comes to a ravaged nation now in the hands of women and tries to tell them how they must run their government. A stunning production, with a huge cast, was mounted at the enormous Olivier Theatre on London's South Bank.

Martin McDonagh (b. 1970) startled the London theater scene with his Leenane trilogy: *The Beauty Queen of Leenane* (1996), *A Skull in Connemara* (1997), and *The Lonesome West* (1997). These three plays and his *The Cripple of Inishmaan* (1996) were produced at the same time in London, a record for a twenty-seven-year-old playwright. His *The Lieutenant of Inishmore* (2003) is a brutal farce centering on IRA terrorism. His 2003 play *The Pillowman* had pedophilia as its subject. McDonagh is one of the most productive modern playwrights.

French playwright Yasmina Reza (b. 1959) had great success in France, England, the United States, and many other nations with her award-winning comedy *"Art,"* which raises unexpected questions about taste and friendship. *God of Carnage* (2006) has also been produced in many countries, solidifying her stature as a major modern playwright. Both of these plays have been made into films, and both are startling in part because they seem so normal at first and then develop in shocking ways.

Drama in Asia and Africa

China's most distinguished modern playwright, Gao Xingjian (b. 1940), now lives and writes in Paris, after having lived through the Cultural Revolution of the 1960s, when all his plays and manuscripts were destroyed and he was forced to work as a laborer for several years. His work has been banned in China because it is seen as critical of the communist system in that country. Having lived in France since 1987, Gao has been influenced by playwrights such as Samuel Beckett and Bertolt Brecht. His *Bus Stop* (1983) resembles Beckett's *Waiting for Godot* in that the characters wait patiently for the bus to come—a symbol of a positive change in their lives—but it never arrives. *The Other Shore* (1986) explores the religious aspirations of the characters from a perspective of Pure Land Buddhism, the other shore being the land of the dead, a world with ambiguous virtues. Gao is also a novelist and wrote *Soul Mountain* (1989), a best-seller in its English translation (1999). Gao won the Nobel Prize for literature in 2000.

Athol Fugard (b. 1932), a South African, writes powerful plays that work well on conventional proscenium stages. Like Shepard's, his subject matter is not the kind that permits an audience to sit back, relax, and appreciate the drama with a sense of detachment. Instead, the plays usually disturb audiences. His primary subject matter is the devastation—for blacks and whites—caused by apartheid in South Africa. Fugard's work with black actors in South Africa produced a vital experimental theater out of which his best early work grew. Fugard's *The Blood Knot* (1961) and *Boesman and Lena* (1969), part of a trilogy on South Africa, are based on the theme of racial discrimination. But other plays, such as *A Lesson from Aloes* (1978) and *My Children! My Africa!* (1989), highlight the problems of individuals in relation to their political world. Fugard is in many ways a traditional playwright, except for his subject matter. His characters are thoroughly developed, but with great economy. In *"MASTER HAROLD" . . . and the boys,* for example, we are given a deep understanding of Hally and Sam, whose relationship, past, present, and future, is the center of the play. Fugard is not writing the well-made play, any more than the other contemporary playwrights in this collection are. There is nothing "mechanical" in Fugard's work; rather, it conveys a sense of organic growth, of actions arising from perceptible conditions and historical circumstances. These contribute to the sense of integrity that his plays communicate. Fugard's three recent plays, *Coming Home* (2009), *Have You Seen Us* (2009), and *The Train Driver* (2010), take us from Capetown to Los Angeles, but they remain powerful statements of political and social reality in the tradition of most of his work. His plays have been performed in South Africa, Europe, and North and South America.

The plays of Nobel Prize winner Wole Soyinka (b. 1934) have enjoyed international celebrity far from his native Nigeria. *The Strong Breed* (1964), *Madmen and Specialists* (1971), *The Bacchae of Euripides* (1973), and *Death and the King's Horseman* (1975) are all extraordinary by virtue of Soyinka's inclusion of African themes and Yoruba rituals as well as his emphasis on the African sense of community. He has demonstrated the universality of his characters and their circumstances.

Just as Soyinka reinterpreted Euripides' *The Bacchae*, Aimé Césaire (1913–2008), from Martinique, completely reinterpreted Shakespeare's *Tempest* into his own *A Tempest* (1993), using Shakespeare's characters and an ending that satisfied him much more than the original. Césaire produced a remarkable body of work including drama, poetry, and essays. *A Season in the Congo* (1990) is only one of his pointedly political plays.

Bernard Dadié (b. 1916), from the Ivory Coast, is also interested in political drama. His *Monsieur Thôgô-gnini* (1970) is a satire on political oppression featuring an African king in 1840. The name means "one who will stop at nothing," and the play begins ironically with the sound of "Old Man River," as a white trader enters to begin doing business. Most of Dadié's plays were written originally in French. He is famous for a poem that begins, "Thank God for creating me black."

The range of African drama has been extraordinary and continues to challenge theater spaces throughout the world.

The Contemporary Theater

In the major cities of the world, most theaters comparable to those on Broadway and London's West End are compatible with the needs of nineteenth-century realist plays, many of which still entertain a wide range of audiences. However, modern theaters are not limited to large urban centers, and those that have been built since the 1950s recognize the needs of experimental drama as well as traditional drama.

Theater in the round, which seats audience members on all sides of the actors, has been exceptionally powerful for certain plays. Peter Weiss's *The Persecution and Assassination of Jean-Paul Marat as Performed by the Inmates of the Asylum of Charenton under the Direction of the Marquis de Sade* (1964) was especially effective in this format. Many contemporary theaters attempt to accommodate the needs of theater in the round, the thrust theater (which is virtually in the round), and the proscenium theater, all in one place. Such a theater is illustrated in Figure 31: the Questors Theatre in Ealing, London, built in 1964.

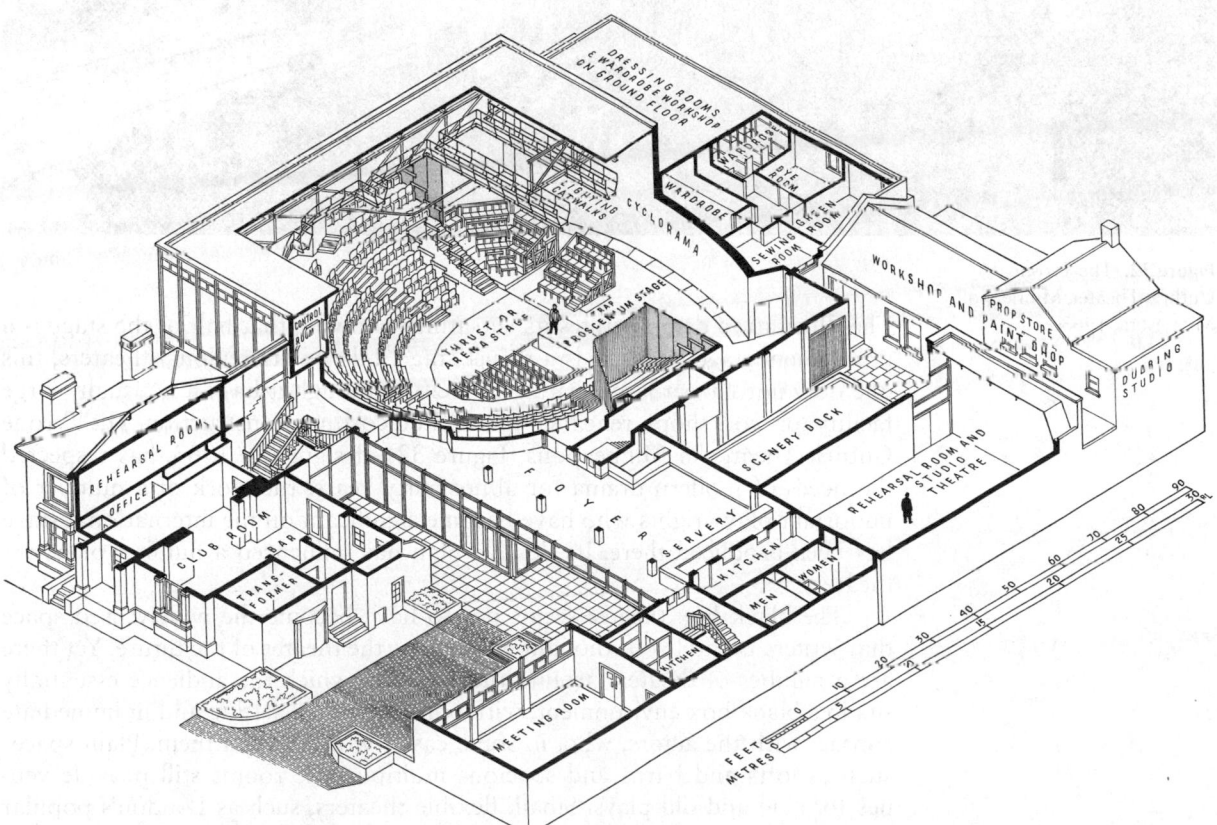

Figure 31. The Questors Theatre, Ealing, London, 1964.

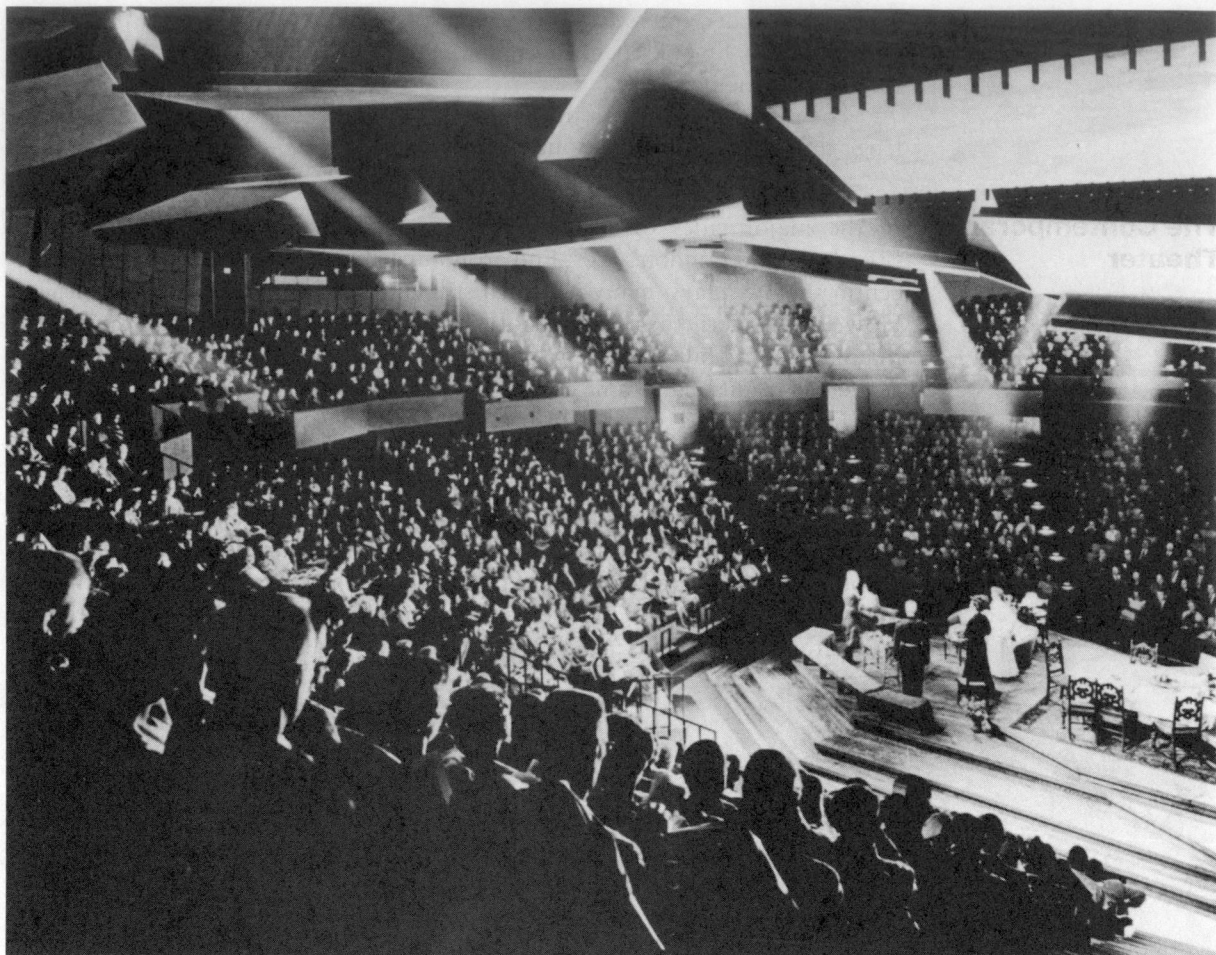

Figure 32. The Tyrone
Guthrie Theater, Minneapolis,
Minnesota, 1963.

The illustration demonstrates its versatility, showing that half of the stage is a
proscenium stage and half is a thrust stage. Like many regional theaters, this
one does not have a large seating capacity, although it has an unusually large
facility for workshops, rehearsal spaces, and costume construction. The Tyrone
Guthrie Theater in Minneapolis (Figure 32), designed in 1963, has respected
the needs of modern drama for almost fifty years; the work of a number of
important playwrights who have become significant on the international stage
has been produced there. Its flexible plan has influenced a number of newer
theaters.

The black box theater seems not to have become the widely used space
that writers in the 1960s thought it might, as the theater of the future. Yet there
are a number of theaters around the world in which the audience essentially
sits in a black box environment, with only a minimal setting and in immediate
contact with the actors, who, in some cases, work around them. Plain spaces
such as lofts and barns and spacious multipurpose rooms still provide venues for new and old plays. Small, flexible theaters, such as London's popular

Cottlesloe, seat three hundred at most; their intimacy intensifies the effect of the drama.

Other theatrical experiments have explored the power of spaces one would not have thought appropriate for drama. For example, Wladimir Pereira Cardoso designed an elaborate welded-steel set for a production of Jean Genet's *The Balcony* in the Ruth Escobar Theater in São Paulo, Brazil. The set was a huge suspended cone, in which people sat looking inward at the actors, who were suspended in the spherical space before them. The production was first staged in 1969 and was seen through 1971 and most of 1972 by many thousands of people. The set was constructed of eighty tons of iron assembled like a trellis and requiring 500,000 welds. The entire inside of the theater was torn out to accommodate the new set. The audience of 250 was seated on circular platforms, and the actors moved through the space on ramps, on suspended cables, and on moving platforms. The same theater produced *The Voyage,* an adaptation of the epic poem *The Lusiads,* about the origin of the Portuguese people. That set used open welded platforms suggesting ships' decks. In Dubrovnik, Croatia, a replica of Columbus's *Santa Maria*—built much larger than the original—was used to stage Miroslav Krleza's expressionist play *Christopher Columbus,* written in 1917. The ship was docked in Dubrovnik Harbor for the performances.

Richard Foreman's (b. 1937) Ontological-Hysteric Theater performs in a loft in New York City with all audience members facing in the same direction. This is not fundamentally different from the traditional proscenium theater, but the open loft space and the visible movements of actors offstage create a new relationship to the action. Foreman's work, such as *Sophia = (Wisdom)* (1970 and later), which has been performed in many parts, offers none of the usually accepted narrative clues to its action. Rather, it explores hitherto hidden aspects of experience, such as sexual taboos and unorthodox relationships. The relationship of the author to the performance is also experimental in Foreman's theater, since he directs his actors as if they were extensions of his will, often using a loud buzzer. His work, begun in the 1960s, continues to this day. He collaborated in the staging of Suzan-Lori Parks's *Venus* (1996).

Proscenium theaters probably make up the largest number of dramatic spaces even today, because of the large number of restored theaters whose designs generally date to the era of the Drury Lane Theatre renovations in the late eighteenth and early nineteenth centuries. Many technical innovations, such as portable microphones, elaborate methods for allowing actors to fly (Figure 33), and stage effects such as fog and stage flooding, have made it possible for audiences in larger theaters to feel closely connected with the dramatic action. Techniques that create a striking effect—such as the simulation of heavy rainfall in Sarah Ruhl's *Eurydice* when Eurydice, and later Orpheus, descending to the underworld, arrives in a stunning downpour in an elevator—would have been difficult, if not impossible, in earlier centuries.

Music and dance are central to some contemporary dramas that are not considered musicals, such as Wole Soyinka's *The Lion and the Jewel* (1963). Sound systems in modern theaters can accommodate the most difficult audio challenges. Video, too, is common in contemporary theater, whether in the

Figure 33. Visual effects and technical apparatus featured prominently in the rock musical *Spider-Man: Turn Off the Dark* (2011). In this scene, Spider-Man and the Green Goblin fly over the audience.

form of projections on scrims or working television sets in living rooms or bedrooms on stage. Complex lighting and shifting scene changes can be made convincingly realistic. What Aristotle called "spectacle" has been available in most ages in the theater, but the technology of the digital age provides resources never before possible. Even so, a great many successful dramatists insist on the simplest of dramatic effects and the simplest of theatrical spaces.

The Contemporary Actor

For the most part, the ambition of eighteenth-century British actor David Garrick to create a style of acting that is as natural as everyday life has been the goal for most contemporary actors. Marlon Brando put Stanislavski's theories of acting to work in Tennessee Williams's *A Streetcar Named Desire* and became celebrated as a Method actor. He studied at the Actors Studio, which was founded by Elia Kazan and others but later run and developed by Lee Strasberg with other important teachers such as Sanford Meisner. The modern Method involved relaxation techniques, memory exercises, and a great deal of self-analysis. The point, as Stanislavski said, was to re-create in oneself the life of the character on stage.

Marlon Brando became the first widely celebrated Method actor, and his particular style, of mumbling lines or moodily half-articulating them, became associated unfairly with Method acting. James Dean, who was a film star rather than a stage star, emulated him and made it seem all the more certain that Brando's style was that of the Method actor. But other Method

Figure 34. Al Pacino as salesman Erie Smith in Eugene O'Neill's *Hughie* (1996) at Circle in the Square Theatre.

actors, such as Al Pacino (Figure 34), who has done some important stage work, particularly in Eugene O'Neill's *Hughie* in 1996, also studied with Lee Strasberg. Pacino can be seen online in a video on YouTube reading and discussing the play.

Among the great actors to have worked in the Actors Studio, Lee J. Cobb is one who seems to have influenced a number of later actors, such as George C. Scott in the 1960s. Robert de Niro, Ellen Burstyn, Jane Fonda, Paul Newman, Joanne Woodward, Maureen Stapleton, Rod Steiger, Christopher Walken, Mickey Rourke, Julia Roberts, Harvey Keitel, Sidney Poitier, Jack Nicholson, Steve McQueen, and Marilyn Monroe were all products of the Actors Studio. The influence of the Method is still present in contemporary drama.

In England, however, the traditional training of actors continues. Whereas Method acting concentrates on the inner potential of the actor's psyche, the Royal Academy of Dramatic Arts in London and the London Academy of Music and Dramatic Arts train actors in the traditional basics, such as dance and movement, voice and projection, analysis of texts, and the study of the techniques of the best historical actors. John Gielgud, Laurence Olivier, Jeremy Irons, and Judi Dench (Figure 35) are products of such training. Sometimes their techniques are described as being external—they are "applied" outwardly as a means of creating the character on stage—as opposed to the internal process

Figure 35. Judi Dench as Viola with Gordon Reid as Sebastian in the 1969 production of *Twelfth Night* at the Royal Shakespeare Theatre.

of the Method actor. Both techniques work well on the modern stage, and some actors (such as Johnny Depp and Julianne Moore) use them both.

The purpose of the actor is to create character in the hope that we will believe the character rather than the actor. And in the dramas that disregard psychological realism, the purpose of the actor is to stimulate the audience into a recognition of the power of the drama itself and to interpret the action in an authentic and honest fashion.

Timeline Contemporary Drama

Date	Theater	Political	Social/Cultural
1950–1960	**1950:** Anna Deavere Smith, African American playwright and actress, is born. Among her works are *Fires in the Mirror* (1991) and *Twilight: Los Angeles, 1992* (1992). **1951:** Lee Strasberg becomes artistic director of the Actors Studio in New York. **1954:** Joseph Papp founds the New York Shakespeare festival. **1956:** John Osborne's *Look Back in Anger* is produced in London. **1956:** Tony Kushner, American playwright, is born. He is best known for the plays *Angels in America, Parts One and Two* (1992). **1959:** Jerzy Grotowski establishes the Laboratory Theatre in Poland. In 1968 he publishes *Towards a Poor Theatre*.	**1950:** U.S. Senator Joseph McCarthy begins his war on Communism by investigating the alleged "un-American activities" of hundreds of U.S. citizens. **1951:** The USSR explodes its first atomic bomb. **1953:** Joseph Stalin dies. **1954:** *Brown v. Board of Education* finds school segregation unconstitutional. **1954:** Senator Joseph McCarthy's witch hunt for Communist infiltration in the United States ends. **1955:** Communist Eastern European allies sign the Warsaw Pact. **1955:** Montgomery, Alabama, bus boycott **1958:** Fidel Castro begins total war against Batista in Cuba; in 1959 he becomes premier. **1958–1969:** Charles de Gaulle is president of France.	**1952:** Ralph Ellison (1914–1994), African American novelist, publishes *Invisible Man*. **1953:** The English translation of French author Simone de Beauvoir's *The Second Sex* (1949) is published in the United States. **1954:** Elvis Presley (1935–1977) makes his first recording at Sun Studios. **1957:** Jack Kerouac (1922–1969) publishes *On the Road*.
1960–1970	**1960s:** Off-off-Broadway flourishes with the formation of such groups as Café Cino (1958), La Mama ETC (1962), the Open Theatre (1963), and the Performance Group (1967). **1962:** Peter Schumann founds the Bread and Puppet Theater, an influential political ensemble, in New York City. **1963:** The National Theatre is established in London under the direction of Laurence Olivier. **1964:** Ariane Mnouchkine forms the Théâtre du Soleil in Paris. **1964:** Peter Brook's production of Peter Weiss's *Marat/Sade* opens at the Royal Shakespeare Company.	**1960:** The Belgian Congo is granted independence. **1961:** The Berlin Wall blocks movement to and from East and West Germany. **1962:** The cold war reaches one of its tensest moments when the United States confronts the USSR over Soviet nuclear missile bases in Cuba. **1962:** The first U.S. combat troops are sent to fight in South Vietnam. **1963:** President John F. Kennedy is assassinated in Dallas. **1965:** Malcolm X is assassinated in New York.	**1962:** James Watson and Francis Crick share the Nobel Prize for defining the 3-D molecular structure of DNA. **1962:** César Chávez (1927–1993) organizes California migrant farm workers. **1962:** Alexander Solzhenitsyn's *One Day in the Life of Ivan Denisovich* describes life in the Soviet gulag. **1964:** The Beatles appear on *The Ed Sullivan Show*. **1965:** The National Endowment for the Arts is established by the U.S. government.

Timeline Contemporary Drama *(continued)*

Date	Theater	Political	Social/Cultural
1960–1970 (continued)	**1968:** The Negro Ensemble Company is established in the United States under the direction of Douglas Turner Ward. **1968:** The Living Theatre produces its highly influential experimental work *Paradise Now*. **1968:** Theatrical censorship, in place since the Licensing Act of 1737, is finally abolished in England. **1968:** *Hair!*, the first rock musical, hits Broadway; it is followed by *Jesus Christ Superstar* in 1971. **1968:** The Performance Group produces *Dionysus in 69* under the direction of Richard Schechner.	**1967:** In the Six-Day War, Israel responds to Arab provocation by capturing territory from Egypt, Syria, and Jordan. **1967:** Thurgood Marshall (1908–1993) is the first African American appointed to the U.S. Supreme Court. **1968:** The American civil rights leader Martin Luther King Jr. is assassinated. **1968:** Students demonstrate throughout France.	**1966:** The National Organization for Women (NOW) is established to end discrimination against women. **1967:** Dr. Christiaan N. Barnard performs the world's first human heart transplant operation in South Africa. **1969:** U.S. astronaut Neil Armstrong walks on the moon. **1969:** New York City police raid the Stonewall Inn, a gay bar, and the resulting three-day protest becomes a symbol for the emerging gay rights movement.
1970–1980	**1970:** Peter Brook's acclaimed production of *A Midsummer Night's Dream* opens at the Royal Shakespeare Company. **1971:** Peter Stein, influential German director, produces *Peer Gynt*. **1975:** Michael Bennett's musical *A Chorus Line* opens on Broadway and runs until 1990. **1977:** María Irene Fornés's *Fefu and Her Friends* is produced. **1978:** Harold Pinter's *Betrayal* premieres at the National Theatre in London.	**1970–1975:** Civil war is fought in Cambodia; Communist leader Pol Pot takes power in 1975 and begins genocidal campaign. **1972:** U.S. President Richard Nixon and Soviet leader Leonid Brezhnev sign the Strategic Arms Limitation Treaty (SALT). **1972:** Philippine President Ferdinand Marcos declares martial law and assumes dictatorial powers. **1973:** U.S. troops are withdrawn from Vietnam. **1974:** President Nixon resigns from office as a result of the Watergate scandal. **1975:** The Spanish dictator Francisco Franco dies. **1976:** The Chinese Communist leader Mao Zedong dies. Deng Xiaoping emerges as the new Chinese leader in 1978. **1976:** Waves of violence against apartheid in Cape Town, Soweto, and Johannesburg, South Africa	**1970:** First celebration of Earth Day in the United States **1973:** In *Roe v. Wade,* the U.S. Supreme Court legalizes abortion. **1976:** The Episcopal Church approves the ordination of women to be priests and bishops.

Date	Theater	Political	Social/Cultural
1970–1980 (continued)	**1979:** Caryl Churchill's *Cloud Nine* premieres. **1979:** Stephen Sondheim's *Sweeney Todd* opens on Broadway. Other musicals by the prolific composer include *Sunday in the Park with George* (1984), *Into the Woods* (1987), and *Passion* (1995).	**1979:** After the overthrow of Shah Mohammad Reza Pahlavi, the Ayatollah Khomeini establishes the Islamic Republic of Iran.	
1980–1990	**1980:** Sam Shepard's *True West* premieres. **1982:** Athol Fugard's *"MASTER HAROLD" . . . and the boys* premieres at the Yale Repertory Theatre. **1983:** Marsha Norman's *'night, Mother* opens at New York's Golden Theatre and wins the Pulitzer Prize. **1985:** August Wilson's *Fences* premieres at the Yale Repertory Theatre and wins the Pulitzer Prize in 1987. **1987:** The immensely popular Broadway adaptation of Victor Hugo's *Les Misérables* opens, ultimately closing in March 2003.	**1980:** The Iran-Iraq War begins when Iraq invades Iran; the war lasts for eight years. **1981:** General Idi Amin begins his eight-year reign of terror in Uganda. **1981:** Egyptian leader Anwar Sadat is assassinated by Muslim extremists. **1985:** Mikhail Gorbachev becomes the leader of the Soviet Union and institutes a policy of *glasnost* (openness). **1989:** A student demonstration in Beijing's Tiananmen Square results in bloodshed **1989:** Communism crumbles in Eastern Europe, and the Berlin Wall is torn down.	**1981:** Sandra Day O'Connor becomes the first woman appointed to the U.S. Supreme Court. **1981:** IBM markets its first personal computer. **1982:** Wisconsin becomes the first state to protect gays and lesbians under civil rights legislation. **1986:** In *Bowers v. Hardwick*, the U.S. Supreme Court upholds the constitutionality of the Georgia state law against sodomy. **1986:** The U.S. space shuttle *Challenger* explodes seconds after liftoff, killing all seven on board.
1990–2000	**1990s:** In a proliferation of Shakespeare on film, new versions of *Hamlet, Henry V, Much Ado about Nothing, Othello*, and *Richard III* are released.	**1990:** Iraq invades Kuwait, which leads to the Gulf War in 1991. **1990:** East and West Germany reunite after 45 years of separation. **1990:** The South African nationalist leader Nelson Mandela is released from prison. **1990–1991:** South Africa repeals its apartheid laws. **1991:** The Soviet Union collapses. U.S. President George H. W. Bush officially recognizes the twelve new countries created as a result.	**1990:** Octavio Paz, Mexican poet, receives the Nobel Prize for literature. **1990:** The National Endowment for the Arts is attacked when controversial awards are publicized.

Date	Theater	Political	Social/Cultural
1990–2000 (continued)	**1992:** David Mamet's *Oleanna* premieres off-Broadway and runs for over 250 performances.	**1991:** Yugoslavia dissolves. Croatia, Slovenia, Bosnia-Herzegovina, and Macedonia declare independence, and bitter fighting ensues for several years.	**1993:** Toni Morrison (b. 1931), African American novelist, is awarded the Nobel Prize for literature.
		1994: Nelson Mandela is elected the first black president of South Africa after that nation's first multiracial elections.	**mid-1990s:** *Internet* and *World Wide Web* become household words.
		1994: Chechnya declares independence from Russia, and Russian troops invade the republic. Russia invades again in 1999.	
	1996: Jonathan Larson's *Rent,* a musical based on Puccini's *La Bohème,* wins the Pulitzer Prize.	**1995:** The Israeli leader Yitzhak Rabin is assassinated.	**1995:** Shannon Faulkner is the first woman to be admitted to the Citadel military academy.
	1997: Martin McDonagh, at age 27, has four plays running simultaneously in London.	**1997:** Hong Kong is returned to China after 156 years as a British colony.	**1995:** The National Endowment for the Arts budget is slashed by the newly elected Republican Congress. The Public Broadcasting Corporation and the National Endowment for the Humanities also come under fire.
	1998: Paula Vogel's play *How I Learned to Drive* wins the Pulitzer Prize.	**1998:** Asian nations face a dramatic recession after economic booms of the 1980s and early 1990s.	
	1998: Yasmina Reza's *"Art"* wins a Tony Award for best play.	**1999:** Congress impeaches President Clinton for his improper conduct in the White House, but the president remains in office.	**1996:** In *Rome v. Evans,* the U.S. Supreme Court rules that the equal protection clause of the Constitution applies to lesbians and gay men.
		1999: U.N. troops keep a tentative peace between ethnic Albanians and Serbian Albanians in Kosovo.	**1997:** Scottish scientist Ian Wilmot clones a sheep.
		1999: The United States transfers the Panama Canal to Panama.	
2000–present	**2000:** Lee Blessing's *Cobb* makes a political statement about baseball.	**2000:** Boris Yeltsin resigns as president of Russia.	**2000:** Gao Xingjian wins the Nobel Prize for literature.
	2002: Suzan-Lori Parks's *Topdog/Underdog* wins the Pulitzer Prize.	**2001:** On September 11, Al Qaeda terrorists destroy the World Trade Center with two airliners. A third plane damages the Pentagon, and a fourth crashes in Pennsylvania.	**2001:** The human genome is decoded.
	2002: Edward Albee's *The Goat, or Who Is Sylvia?* wins the Drama Desk Award for best play.	**2002:** U.S. attacks Taliban forces in Afghanistan.	**2003:** A law barring "partial-birth" abortions comes under fire with legal challenges.
	2003: Nilo Cruz's *Anna in the Tropics* wins the Pulitzer Prize.	**2003:** U.S. attacks Saddam Hussein in Iraq, bringing down his government.	**2004:** *Spirit* and *Rover* explore the surface of Mars, sending back 3-D images.
	2004: Doug Wright's *I Am My Own Wife* wins the Pulitzer Prize.		**2007:** China launches its first lunar orbiter in preparation for sending an astronaut to the moon in 2020.
	2007: David Lindsay-Abaire's *Rabbit Hole* wins the Pulitzer Prize.		

Date	Theater	Political	Social/Cultural
2000–present (continued)	**2008:** Conor McPherson's *The Seafarer* is produced on Broadway.	**2008:** America's first black president, Barack Obama (b. 1961), is elected.	**2008:** Housing bubble bursts in United States; global economy is in recession.
	2008: Tracy Letts's *August: Osage County* wins the Pulitzer Prize.	**2009:** The Tea Party movement gains popularity in the United States.	**2009:** Barack Obama wins the Nobel Peace Prize.
	2009: Lynn Nottage's *Ruined* wins the Pulitzer Prize.		**2010:** Apple introduces the iPad line of tablet computers.
	2009: Rajiv Joseph's *Bengal Tiger at the Baghdad Zoo* and Sarah Ruhl's *In the Next Room: or, The Vibrator Play* are produced.		
	2011: Bruce Norris's *Clybourne Park* wins the Pulitzer Prize.	**2011:** The Arab Spring, a wave of pro-democracy demonstrations, overthrows the governments of Tunisia, Egypt, and Libya; Syria reaches the brink of civil war.	**2011:** *Time* magazine names "The Protester" its "Person of the Year."
		2011: Osama bin Laden, leader of Al Qaeda, is killed by the United States military.	**2011:** Facebook has more than 840 million users.
		2011: Euro-zone debt crisis escalates.	

Harold Pinter

Harold Pinter (1930–2008) wrote plays for the commercial stage, radio, and television as well as film scripts used by some of the best directors of his time. Pinter was born into relatively humble circumstances in East London, but his early accomplishments in school distinguished him, and he eventually enrolled in London's prestigious Royal Academy of Dramatic Arts to study acting. When he finished his studies, he joined a company, toured for several years, and began to write for the stage. His previous writing efforts had been prose: short stories and a long novel called *The Dwarfs* (1956), purportedly autobiographical but never finished and not published until 1990. Produced as a radio play in 1960, *The Dwarfs* expresses some of the themes of Pinter's best work: the disintegration of a mind and the cruelty of people to their fellow beings.

In 1957 Pinter wrote three important plays, the one-act *The Room* and *The Dumb Waiter* and the full-length *The Birthday Party* (finished in 1958). All were well received. They established his method in dialogue and, to a large extent, the style that dominated his work. The critic Martin Esslin, who coined the term "theater of the absurd," saw in Pinter's work an absurdist strain, especially in the nihilism—the belief in nothing—that sometimes shows up. Pinter's characters usually reveal no spiritual awareness and no longing for spiritual values.

Pinter's dialogue sometimes has qualities of aimlessness, at least on the surface. But the dialogue always penetrates the unconsciousness of the audience and reveals the nature of the characters and their situation. Even the repetitious dialogue makes the audience more aware of the limitations and the pain of the circumstances in which Pinter's characters find themselves.

Early reaction to the plays sometimes saw the aimless dialogue and the absurdist qualities as shortcomings rather than as indictments of the social order from which the plays arose. Yet the brutality of his characters to one another, their lack of sympathy for one another, and their demands for dominance all became hallmarks of late-twentieth-century life.

The first of Pinter's plays to catch the attention of the general theater public was the commercially produced *The Caretaker* (1960), a play about two brothers, one of whom, Aston, invites a bewildered and all but mentally destroyed tramp, Davies, to become a caretaker in his room. Davies hardly knows who he is. His identity is essentially reduced to nothing by his soul-destroying life, and he speaks in broken language, especially when he is trying to explain that he left his identity papers in his beloved Sidcup—some fifteen years before—and that if they could find those papers, he would know where he was born and who he was. At the end of the play, the younger brother, Mick, torments Davies, demanding that he leave, twisting his arm, verbally abusing him, but then relenting. The play ends with the shards of a life, as Davies says: "Listen...if I...go down...if I was to...get my papers...would you...would you let...would you...if I got down...and got my...(*Long silence.*)"

Pinter's *The Homecoming* (1965) has a brutal, shocking quality. A professor returns to England from the United States with his wife, and it becomes clear that he plans to return to the United States but that his wife will stay on as a mistress to his father and his brothers. The matter-of-factness with which the situation is treated and the way the relationships are portrayed contribute to the play's shock value. *The Homecoming* established Pinter as a major playwright.

In 1968 his play *Landscape* was censored for the use of obscenities, but it and another short play, *Silence,* were produced in London in 1969 and in New York in 1970. *Old Times* was produced in London and in New York in 1971. Throughout the 1970s Pinter directed many plays by other playwrights and acted in films and on stage. *The Hothouse,* which was revived in 1995, was first produced in Hampstead in 1980. Pinter later directed himself in the play in Providence, Rhode Island. He wrote the screenplay for *Betrayal* in 1982; he also wrote the screenplay for *The French Lieutenant's Woman* (1981), which received an Academy Award nomination for best film. In 1992 he adapted Kazuo Ishiguro's novel *Remains of the Day* for the screen and wrote the screenplay for Franz Kafka's *The Trial.*

Later plays include the full-length *Moonlight* (1993) and the short play *Ashes to Ashes* (1996). *Celebration* (2000) is a short play that was paired at the Almeida Theatre in London with *The Room* (1957), his first play. Ordinarily, Pinter did not let his short plays be paired with other pieces. Even *Mountain Language* (1988), which lasted only twenty minutes, was produced alone by the Royal National Theatre in its Lyttelton Theatre. In 2005 Pinter won the Noble Prize for literature.

In addition to playwriting, Pinter continued acting, appearing as Sir Thomas Bertram in Patricia Rozema's film of Jane Austen's novel *Mansfield Park* (1999). In 2006 he played Krapp in Beckett's *Krapp's Last Tape.*

The Homecoming

For discussion questions and assignments on *The Homecoming,* visit **bedfordstmartins.com/jacobus.**

The shock value of *The Homecoming* was much more pronounced in 1965 than it is today, partly because the idea of the dysfunctional family was less common then than it is now. Playwrights such as Sam Shepard in the United States and Edward Bond in England—among many other writers exploring the inner workings of the family—have made the themes in *The Homecoming* more intelligible today than they were in 1965. Moreover, the impact of absurdist drama has been absorbed over the years, and audience expectations are less rigid now than in 1965. However, Pinter's play still sets the bar for portraying not only dysfunctional but also brutal, irrational, and ironic forces at work in a family of men.

The very title is ironic. Ordinarily, a homecoming brings to mind images of a warm and loving family filled with delight at receiving back into its bosom a wandering child. Homecomings are reasons for celebrations, for joyous gatherings. Norman Rockwell images of homecomings graced magazine covers for years and helped to establish our understanding of the expression. Pinter destroys that image with his own portrait, one that tears away any veneer of social acceptability. He forces us to look at a picture of hostility, anger, envy, and lust.

Beginning with the father Max's intimidation of his son Lenny, and then moving to Max's brother Sam, the limousine driver who gets no respect, we see from the start of the play that there is no pretense of geniality or even reasonable manners in this family. The characters sound pathological, even deep within their tangled language. Soon we learn that Max is a butcher, concerned with flesh and dead animals. Indeed, he cuts through everything, including the basics of family civility.

Pinter's use of silences, pauses, and a variety of rhythms within the dialogue helps us parse the emotional lives of the characters—at least insofar as they understand their own situations. We are not necessarily meant to see these characters as "realistic" in the nineteenth-century sense of the term. Rather, they are force fields that are brought to bear against one another; thus, they have abstract power in the drama without actually being symbols. They are themselves, unique—and horrifying. This is not the comfortable theater of the popular stage.

The very act of coming home takes place at night. Teddy and Ruth have been married for six years, yet people at "home" know nothing about the marriage or about the fact that there are three grandchildren. Teddy has not called ahead to let his father get ready for a celebration. He and Ruth essentially sneak into the house after everyone has gone to bed. Teddy finds that his room upstairs is still as he left it, but Ruth does not wish to sleep just yet. They have come from a vacation in Venice, usually a romantic place to visit. Because of Ruth's restlessness, the family members are slowly roused and, one by one, come to see who has entered the house.

Immediately, the men living here with no woman begin to initiate a sexual dynamic. Accusing Ruth of being a whore and a slut, Max demands that she leave. After a few moments of brutality, in which Max punches another son, Joey, a demolition worker, in the stomach and spouts abuse at everyone present, he turns and offers to embrace Teddy, the philosophy professor who has come home. Tellingly, no embrace occurs as the first act ends.

Some commentators have interpreted Ruth's decision to stay with Max and his sons and brother as a metaphor for marriage as a form of prostitution. Teddy explains what a pleasant life he has in the United States teaching at the university and entertaining intelligent friends. But Ruth never comments on her life with Teddy. Instead, she listens to the plans that Max and his sons have worked out, which include Ruth occupying her own apartment, making her own money through prostitution, and then looking after the men. Her terms are exorbitant, yet the men give in quickly. She establishes her needs, her limits, and her demands. Critics have seen this as an instance in which the woman turns the tables on the men and dominates them with her sexual power so that the play ends with her in the ascendant position.

The Homecoming in Performance

The first performance was directed by Peter Hall and produced by the Royal Shakespeare Company at the Aldwych in London's West End in 1965. The play had toured extensively before coming to London, but it was still a powerful shocker for most of the audience. Even Peter Hall, in an interview with Irving Wardle, said, "It's not a pleasant play. It's a play that's uncomfortable." He went on to compare the family with a human jungle. Paul Rogers played Max as a total bully, and Vivian Merchant played a seductive Ruth. Pinter wrote the play for the Aldwych, where his earlier work had been performed. His instructions to the set designer were to put nothing on the stage except what was absolutely required. The large stage with very little furniture was itself a powerful image of brutality. The New York performance followed in 1967, and Walter Kerr, the *Times* critic, complained that Pinter was holding too much back for too long. His review was anything but positive. By the 1990 Cambridge, Massachusetts, production at the American Repertory Theater, the play had been performed often in the United States and abroad. The reviews of the ART performance not only praised the play but also read numerous subtleties into it and even considered it to have theological implications. One reviewer said that it "is perfect, simply, devastatingly perfect." Ian Holm, who had played Lenny in the premiere, returned to play Max in the 2001 Dublin Gate Theatre production that eventually toured and played at the Lincoln Center Festival in New York City. In early 2007, Pinter himself played Max in a radio production in London. The 2007 production at the Cort Theatre in New York City starred Ian McShane as Max. McShane, fresh from his performance as a foul-mouthed brute on HBO's *Deadwood*, seemed ideally suited to the part. Ben Brantley, in the *New York Times*, said of the production that on its fortieth anniversary, the play is universal and "lives up to its reputation."

HAROLD PINTER (1930–2008)

The Homecoming   1965

Characters

MAX, *a man of seventy*
LENNY, *a man in his early thirties*
SAM, *a man of sixty-three*
JOEY, *a man in his middle twenties*
TEDDY, *a man in his middle thirties*
RUTH, *a woman in her early thirties*

Summer.
  An old house in North London.
  A large room, extending the width of the stage.
  The back wall, which contained the door, has been removed.
  A square arch shape remains. Beyond it, the hall. In the hall a staircase, ascending U.L., well in view. The front door U.R.

  A coatstand, hooks, etc.
  In the room a window, R. Odd tables, chairs. Two large armchairs. A large sofa, L. Against R. wall a large sideboard, the upper half of which contains a mirror. U.L., a radiogram.

ACT 1

Evening.
  Lenny is sitting on the sofa with a newspaper, a pencil in his hand. He wears a dark suit. He makes occasional marks on the back page.
  Max comes in, from the direction of the kitchen. He goes to sideboard, opens top drawer, rummages in it, closes it.

*He wears an old cardigan and a cap, and carries a
stick.*
He walks downstage, stands, looks about the room.

MAX: What have you done with the scissors?

(*Pause.*)

I said I'm looking for the scissors. What have you
done with them?

(*Pause.*)

Did you hear me? I want to cut something out of the
paper.

LENNY: I'm reading the paper.

MAX: Not that paper. I haven't even read that paper. I'm
talking about last Sunday's paper. I was just having a
look at it in the kitchen.

(*Pause.*)

Do you hear what I'm saying? I'm talking to you!
Where's the scissors?

LENNY (*looking up, quietly*): Why don't you shut up, you
daft prat?

(*Max lifts his stick and points it at him.*)

MAX: Don't you talk to me like that. I'm warning you.

(*He sits in large armchair.*)

There's an advertisement in the paper about flannel
vests. Cut price. Navy surplus. I could do with a few
of them.

(*Pause.*)

I think I'll have a fag. Give me a fag.

(*Pause.*)

I just asked you to give me a cigarette.

(*Pause.*)

Look what I'm lumbered with.

(*He takes a crumpled cigarette from his pocket.*)

I'm getting old, my word of honor.

(*He lights it.*)

You think I wasn't a tearaway? I could have taken
care of you, twice over. I'm still strong. You ask your
Uncle Sam what I was. But at the same time I always
had a kind heart. Always.

(*Pause.*)

I used to knock about with a man called MacGregor.
I called him Mac. You remember Mac? Eh?

(*Pause.*)

Huhh! We were two of the worst hated men in the
West End of London. I tell you, I still got the scars.
We'd walk into a place, the whole room'd stand up,
they'd make way to let us pass. You never heard such

silence. Mind you, he was a big man, he was over six
foot tall. His family were all MacGregors, they came
all the way from Aberdeen, but he was the only one
they called Mac.

(*Pause.*)

He was very fond of your mother, Mac was. Very
fond. He always had a good word for her.

(*Pause.*)

Mind you, she wasn't such a bad woman. Even
though it made me sick just to look at her rotten
stinking face, she wasn't such a bad bitch. I gave her
the best bleeding years of my life, anyway.

LENNY: Plug it, will you, you stupid sod, I'm trying to
read the paper.

MAX: Listen! I'll chop your spine off, you talk to me like
that! You understand? Talking to your lousy filthy
father like that!

LENNY: You know what, you're getting demented.

(*Pause.*)

What do you think of Second Wind for the three-
thirty?

MAX: Where?

LENNY: Sandown Park.

MAX: Don't stand a chance.

LENNY: Sure he does.

MAX: Not a chance.

LENNY: He's the winner.

(*Lenny ticks the paper.*)

MAX: He talks to me about horses.

(*Pause.*)

I used to live on the course. One of the loves of my
life. Epsom? I knew it like the back of my hand. I was
one of the best-known faces down at the paddock.
What a marvelous open-air life.

(*Pause.*)

He talks to me about horses. You only read their
names in the papers. But I've stroked their manes,
I've held them, I've calmed them down before a big
race. I was the one they used to call for. Max, they'd
say, there's a horse here, he's highly strung, you're
the only man on the course who can calm him. It
was true. I had a . . . I had an instinctive understanding of animals. I should have been a trainer. Many
times I was offered the job—you know, a proper
post, by the Duke of . . . I forget his name . . . one of
the Dukes. But I had family obligations, my family
needed me at home.

(*Pause.*)

The times I've watched those animals thundering
past the post. What an experience. Mind you, I didn't
lose, I made a few bob out of it, and you know why?
Because I always had the smell of a good horse.

I could smell him. And not only the colts but the fillies. Because the fillies are more highly strung than
the colts, they're more unreliable, did you know that?
No, what do you know? Nothing. But I was always
able to tell a good filly by one particular trick. I'd
look her in the eye. You see? I'd stand in front of
her and look her straight in the eye, it was a kind of
hypnotism, and by the look deep down in her eye I
could tell whether she was a stayer or not. It was a
gift. I had a gift.

(*Pause.*)

And he talks to me about horses.

LENNY: Dad, do you mind if I change the subject?

(*Pause.*)

I want to ask you something. That dinner we had
before, what was the name of it? What do you call it?

(*Pause.*)

Why don't you buy a dog? You're a dog cook. Honest. You think you're cooking for a lot of dogs.

MAX: If you don't like it get out.

LENNY: I am going out. I'm going out to buy myself a
proper dinner.

MAX: Well, get out! What are you waiting for?

(*Lenny looks at him.*)

LENNY: What did you say?

MAX: I said shove off out of it, that's what I said.

LENNY: You'll go before me, Dad, if you talk to me in that
tone of voice.

MAX: Will I, you bitch?

(*Max grips his stick.*)

LENNY: Oh, Daddy, you're not going to use your stick on
me, are you? Eh? Don't use your stick on me, Daddy.
No, please. It wasn't my fault, it was one of the others. I haven't done anything wrong, Dad, honest.
Don't clout me with that stick, Dad.

(*Silence.*)
(*Max sits hunched. Lenny reads the paper.*)
(*Sam comes in the front door. He wears a chauffeur's
uniform.*)
(*He hangs his hat on a hook in the hall and comes into
the room. He goes to a chair, sits in it and sighs.*)

Hullo, Uncle Sam.

SAM: Hullo.

LENNY: How are you, Uncle?

SAM: Not bad. A bit tired.

LENNY: Tired? I bet you're tired. Where you been?

SAM: I've been to London Airport.

LENNY: All the way up to London Airport? What, right
up the M4?

SAM: Yes, all the way up there.

LENNY: Tch, tch, tch. Well, I think you're entitled to be
tired, Uncle.

SAM: Well, it's the drivers.

LENNY: I know. That's what I'm talking about. I'm talking about the drivers.

SAM: Knocks you out.

(*Pause.*)

MAX: I'm here, too, you know.

(*Sam looks at him.*)

I said I'm here, too. I'm sitting here.

SAM: I know you're here.

(*Pause.*)

SAM: I took a Yankee out there today . . . to the Airport.

LENNY: Oh, a Yankee, was it?

SAM: Yes, I been with him all day. Picked him up at the
Savoy at half past twelve, took him to the Caprice
for his lunch. After lunch I picked him up again,
took him down to a house in Eaton Square—he
had to pay a visit to a friend there—and then round
about tea-time I took him right the way out to
the Airport.

LENNY: Had to catch a plane there, did he?

SAM: Yes. Look what he gave me. He gave me a box of
cigars.

(*Sam takes a box of cigars from his pocket.*)

MAX: Come here. Let's have a look at them.

(*Sam shows Max the cigars. Max takes one from the
box, pinches it and sniffs it.*)

It's a fair cigar.

SAM: Want to try one?

(*Max and Sam light cigars.*)

You know what he said to me? He told me I was the
best chauffeur he'd ever had. The best one.

MAX: From what point of view?

SAM: Eh?

MAX: From what point of view?

LENNY: From the point of view of his driving, Dad, and
his general sense of courtesy, I should say.

MAX: Thought you were a good driver, did he, Sam? Well,
he gave you a first-class cigar.

SAM: Yes, he thought I was the best he'd ever had. They
all say that, you know. They won't have anyone else,
they only ask for me. They say I'm the best chauffeur
in the firm.

LENNY: I bet the other drivers tend to get jealous, don't
they, Uncle?

SAM: They do get jealous. They get very jealous.

MAX: Why?

(*Pause.*)

SAM: I just told you.

MAX: No, I just can't get it clear, Sam. Why do the other
drivers get jealous?

SAM: Because (a) I'm the best driver, and because . . . (b)
I don't take liberties.

(*Pause.*)

I don't press myself on people, you see. These big businessmen, men of affairs, they don't want the driver jawing all the time, they like to sit in the back, have a bit of peace and quiet. After all, they're sitting in a Humber° Super Snipe, they can afford to relax. At the same time, though, this is what really makes me special . . . I do know how to pass the time of day when required.

(*Pause.*)

For instance, I told this man today I was in the second world war. Not the first. I told him I was too young for the first. But I told him I fought in the second.

(*Pause.*)

So did he, it turned out.

(*Lenny stands, goes to the mirror and straightens his tie.*)

LENNY: He was probably a colonel, or something, in the American Air Force.

SAM: Yes.

LENNY: Probably a navigator, or something like that, in a Flying Fortress. Now he's most likely a high executive in a worldwide group of aeronautical engineers.

SAM: Yes.

LENNY: Yes, I know the kind of man you're talking about.

(*Lenny goes out, turning to his right.*)

SAM: After all, I'm experienced. I was driving a dust cart at the age of nineteen. Then I was in long-distance haulage. I had ten years as a taxi-driver and I've had five as a private chauffeur.

MAX: It's funny you never got married, isn't it? A man with all your gifts.

(*Pause.*)

Isn't it? A man like you?

SAM: There's still time.

MAX: Is there?

(*Pause.*)

SAM: You'd be surprised.

MAX: What you been doing, banging away at your lady customers, have you?

SAM: Not me.

MAX: In the back of the Snipe? Been having a few crafty reefs in a layby, have you?

SAM: Not me.

MAX: On the back seat? What about the armrest, was it up or down?

SAM: I've never done that kind of thing in my car.

MAX: Above all that kind of thing, are you, Sam?

Humber: An elegant British automobile.

SAM: Too true.

MAX: Above having a good bang on the back seat, are you?

SAM: Yes, I leave that to others.

MAX: You leave it to others? What others? You paralyzed prat!

SAM: I don't mess up my car! Or my . . . my boss's car! Like other people.

MAX: Other people? What other people?

(*Pause.*)

What other people?

(*Pause.*)

SAM: Other people.

(*Pause.*)

MAX: When you find the right girl, Sam, let your family know, don't forget, we'll give you a number one send-off, I promise you. You can bring her to live here, she can keep us all happy. We'd take it in turns to give her a walk round the park.

SAM: I wouldn't bring her here.

MAX: Sam, it's your decision. You're welcome to bring your bride here, to the place where you live, or on the other hand you can take a suite at the Dorchester. It's entirely up to you.

SAM: I haven't got a bride.

(*Sam stands, goes to the sideboard, takes an apple from the bowl, bites into it.*)

Getting a bit peckish.

(*He looks out of the window.*)

Never get a bride like you had, anyway. Nothing like your bride . . . going about these days. Like Jessie.

(*Pause.*)

After all, I escorted her once or twice, didn't I? Drove her round once or twice in my cab. She was a charming woman.

(*Pause.*)

All the same, she was your wife. But still . . . they were some of the most delightful evenings I've ever had. Used to just drive her about. It was my pleasure.

MAX (*softly, closing his eyes*): Christ.

SAM: I used to pull up at a stall and buy her a cup of coffee. She was a very nice companion to be with.

(*Silence.*)

(*Joey comes in the front door. He walks into the room, takes his jacket off, throws it on a chair and stands.*)

(*Silence.*)

JOEY: Feel a bit hungry.

SAM: Me, too.

MAX: Who do you think I am, your mother? Eh? Honest. They walk in here every time of the day and night like bloody animals. Go and find yourself a mother.

(*Lenny walks into the room, stands.*)

JOEY: I've been training down at the gym.

SAM: Yes, the boy's been working all day and training all night.

MAX: What do you want, you bitch? You spend all the day sitting on your arse at London Airport, buy yourself a jamroll. You expect me to sit here waiting to rush into the kitchen the moment you step in the door? You've been living sixty-three years, why don't you learn to cook?

SAM: I can cook.

MAX: Well, go and cook!

(*Pause.*)

LENNY: What the boys want, Dad, is your own special brand of cooking, Dad. That's what the boys look forward to. The special understanding of food, you know, that you've got.

MAX: Stop calling me Dad. Just stop all that calling me Dad, do you understand?

LENNY: But I'm your son. You used to tuck me up in bed every night. He tucked you up, too, didn't he, Joey?

(*Pause.*)

He used to like tucking up his sons.

(*Lenny turns and goes towards the front door.*)

MAX: Lenny.

LENNY (*turning*): What?

MAX: I'll give you a proper tuck up one of these nights, son. You mark my word.

(*They look at each other.*)
(*Lenny opens the front door and goes out.*)
(*Silence.*)

JOEY: I've been training with Bobby Dodd.

(*Pause.*)

And I had a good go at the bag as well.

(*Pause.*)

I wasn't in bad trim.

MAX: Boxing's a gentleman's game.

(*Pause.*)

I'll tell you what you've got to do. What you've got to do is you've got to learn how to defend yourself, and you've got to learn how to attack. That's your only trouble as a boxer. You don't know how to defend yourself, and you don't know how to attack.

(*Pause.*)

Once you've mastered those arts you can go straight to the top.

(*Pause.*)

JOEY: I've got a pretty good idea . . . of how to do that.

(*Joey looks round for his jacket, picks it up, goes out of the room and up the stairs.*)
(*Pause.*)

MAX: Sam . . . why don't you go, too, eh? Why don't you just go upstairs? Leave me quiet. Leave me alone.

SAM: I want to make something clear about Jessie, Max. I want to. I do. When I took her out in the cab, round the town, I was taking care of her, for you. I was looking after her for you, when you were busy, wasn't I? I was showing her the West End.

(*Pause.*)

You wouldn't have trusted any of your other brothers. You wouldn't have trusted Mac, would you? But you trusted me. I want to remind you.

(*Pause.*)

Old Mac died a few years ago, didn't he? Isn't he dead?

(*Pause.*)

He was a lousy stinking rotten loudmouth. A bastard uncouth sodding runt. Mind you, he was a good friend of yours.

(*Pause.*)

MAX: Eh, Sam . . .

SAM: What?

MAX: Why do I keep you here? You're just an old grub.

SAM: Am I?

MAX: You're a maggot.

SAM: Oh yes?

MAX: As soon as you stop paying your way here, I mean when you're too old to pay your way, you know what I'm going to do? I'm going to give you the boot.

SAM: You are, eh?

MAX: Sure. I mean, bring in the money and I'll put up with you. But when the firm gets rid of you you can flake off.

SAM: This is my house as well, you know. This was our mother's house.

MAX: One lot after the other. One mess after the other.

SAM: Our father's house.

MAX: Look what I'm lumbered with. One cast-iron bunch of crap after another. One flow of stinking pus after another.

(*Pause.*)

Our father? I remember him. Don't worry. You kid yourself. He used to come over to me and look down at me. My old man did. He'd bend right over me, then he'd pick me up. I was only that big. Then he'd dandle me. Give me the bottle. Wipe me clean. Give me a smile. Pat me on the bum. Pass me around, pass me from hand to hand. Toss me up in the air. Catch me coming down. I remember my father.

(*Blackout.*
Lights up.
Night.
Teddy and Ruth stand at the threshold of the room.
They are both well dressed in light summer suits and
light raincoats.
Two suitcases are by their side.
They look at the room. Teddy tosses the key in his
hand, smiles.)

TEDDY: Well, the key worked.

(*Pause.*)

They haven't changed the lock.

(*Pause.*)

RUTH: No one's here.
TEDDY (*looking up*): They're asleep.

(*Pause.*)

RUTH: Can I sit down?
TEDDY: Of course.
RUTH: I'm tired.

(*Pause.*)

TEDDY: Then sit down.

(*She does not move.*)

That's my father's chair.
RUTH: That one?
TEDDY (*smiling*): Yes, that's it. Shall I go up and see if my
    room's still there?
RUTH: It can't have moved.
TEDDY: No, I mean if my bed's still there.
RUTH: Someone might be in it.
TEDDY: No. They've got their own beds.

(*Pause.*)

RUTH: Shouldn't you wake someone up? Tell them you're
    here?
TEDDY: Not at this time of night. It's too late.

(*Pause.*)

Shall I go up?

(*He goes into the hall, looks up the stairs, comes back.*)

Why don't you sit down?

(*Pause.*)

I'll just go up . . . have a look.

(*He goes up the stairs, stealthily.*)
(*Ruth stands, then slowly walks across the room.*)
(*Teddy returns.*)

It's still there. My room. Empty. The bed's there.
What are you doing?

(*She looks at him.*)

Blankets, no sheets. I'll find some sheets. I could hear
snores. Really. They're all still here, I think. They're
all snoring up there. Are you cold?
RUTH: No.
TEDDY: I'll make something to drink, if you like. Some-
    thing hot.
RUTH: No, I don't want anything.

(*Teddy walks about.*)

TEDDY: What do you think of the room? Big, isn't it? It's
a big house. I mean, it's a fine room, don't you think?
Actually there was a wall, across there . . . with a
door. We knocked it down . . . years ago . . . to make
an open living area. The structure wasn't affected,
you see. My mother was dead.

(*Ruth sits.*)

Tired?
RUTH: Just a little.
TEDDY: We can go to bed if you like. No point in waking
    anyone up now. Just go to bed. See them all in the
    morning . . . see my father in the morning. . . .

(*Pause.*)

RUTH: Do you want to stay?
TEDDY: Stay?

(*Pause.*)

We've come to stay. We're bound to stay . . . for a few
days.
RUTH: I think . . . the children . . . might be missing us.
TEDDY: Don't be silly.
RUTH: They might.
TEDDY: Look, we'll be back in a few days, won't we?

(*He walks about the room.*)

Nothing's changed. Still the same.

(*Pause.*)

Still, he'll get a surprise in the morning, won't he?
The old man. I think you'll like him very much. Honestly. He's a . . . well, he's old, of course. Getting on.

(*Pause.*)

I was born here, do you realize that?
RUTH: I know.

(*Pause.*)

TEDDY: Why don't you go to bed? I'll find some sheets. I
    feel . . . wide awake, isn't it odd? I think I'll stay up
    for a bit. Are you tired?
RUTH: No.
TEDDY: Go to bed. I'll show you the room.
RUTH: No, I don't want to.
TEDDY: You'll be perfectly all right up there without me.
    Really you will. I mean, I won't be long. Look, it's
    just up there. It's the first door on the landing. The

bathroom's right next door. You . . . need some rest, you know.

(*Pause.*)

I just want to . . . walk about for a few minutes. Do you mind?

RUTH: Of course I don't.

TEDDY: Well . . . Shall I show you the room?

RUTH: No, I'm happy at the moment.

TEDDY: You don't have to go to bed. I'm not saying you have to. I mean, you can stay up with me. Perhaps I'll make a cup of tea or something. The only thing is we don't want to make too much noise, we don't want to wake anyone up.

RUTH: I'm not making any noise.

TEDDY: I know you're not.

(*He goes to her.*)

(*Gently.*) Look, it's all right, really. I'm here. I mean . . . I'm with you. There's no need to be nervous. Are you nervous?

RUTH: No.

TEDDY: There's no need to be.

(*Pause.*)

They're very warm people, really. Very warm. They're my family. They're not ogres.

(*Pause.*)

Well, perhaps we should go to bed. After all, we have to be up early, see Dad. Wouldn't be quite right if he found us in bed, I think. (*He chuckles.*) Have to be up before six, come down, say hullo.

(*Pause.*)

RUTH: I think I'll have a breath of air.

TEDDY: Air?

(*Pause.*)

What do you mean?

RUTH (*standing*): Just a stroll.

TEDDY: At this time of night? But we've . . . only just got here. We've got to go to bed.

RUTH: I just feel like some air.

TEDDY: But I'm going to bed.

RUTH: That's all right.

TEDDY: But what am I going to do?

(*Pause.*)

The last thing I want is a breath of air. Why do you want a breath of air?

RUTH: I just do.

TEDDY: But it's late.

RUTH: I won't go far. I'll come back.

(*Pause.*)

TEDDY: I'll wait up for you.

RUTH: Why?

TEDDY: I'm not going to bed without you.

RUTH: Can I have the key?

(*He gives it to her.*)

Why don't you go to bed?

(*He puts his arms on her shoulders and kisses her.*)
(*They look at each other, briefly. She smiles.*)

I won't be long.

(*She goes out of the front door.*)
(*Teddy goes to the window, peers out after her, half turns from the window, stands, suddenly chews his knuckles.*)
(*Lenny walks into the room from U.L. He stands. He wears pajamas and dressing-gown. He watches Teddy.*)
(*Teddy turns and sees him.*)
(*Silence.*)

TEDDY: Hullo, Lenny.

LENNY: Hullo, Teddy.

(*Pause.*)

TEDDY: I didn't hear you come down the stairs.

LENNY: I didn't.

(*Pause.*)

I sleep down here now. Next door. I've got a kind of study, workroom cum bedroom next door now, you see.

TEDDY: Oh. Did I . . . wake you up?

LENNY: No. I just had an early night tonight. You know how it is. Can't sleep. Keep waking up.

(*Pause.*)

TEDDY: How are you?

LENNY: Well, just sleeping a bit restlessly, that's all. Tonight, anyway.

TEDDY: Bad dreams?

LENNY: No, I wouldn't say I was dreaming. It's not exactly a dream. It's just that something keeps waking me up. Some kind of tick.

TEDDY: A tick?

LENNY: Yes.

TEDDY: Well, what is it?

LENNY: I don't know.

(*Pause.*)

TEDDY: Have you got a clock in your room?

LENNY: Yes.

TEDDY: Well, maybe it's the clock.

LENNY: Yes, could be, I suppose.

(*Pause.*)

Well, if it's the clock I'd better do something about it. Stifle it in some way, or something.

(*Pause.*)

TEDDY: I've . . . just come back for a few days.

LENNY: Oh yes? Have you?

(*Pause.*)

TEDDY: How's the old man?
LENNY: He's in the pink.

(*Pause.*)

TEDDY: I've been keeping well.
LENNY: Oh, have you?

(*Pause.*)

Staying the night then, are you?
TEDDY: Yes.
LENNY: Well, you can sleep in your old room.
TEDDY: Yes, I've been up.
LENNY: Yes, you can sleep there.

(*Lenny yawns.*)

Oh well.
TEDDY: I'm going to bed.
LENNY: Are you?
TEDDY: Yes, I'll get some sleep.
LENNY: Yes, I'm going to bed, too.

(*Teddy picks up the cases.*)

I'll give you a hand.
TEDDY: No, they're not heavy.

(*Teddy goes into the hall with the cases.*)
(*Lenny turns out the light in the room.*)
(*The light in the hall remains on.*)
(*Lenny follows into the hall.*)

LENNY: Nothing you want?
TEDDY: Mmmm?
LENNY: Nothing you might want, for the night? Glass of water, anything like that?
TEDDY: Any sheets anywhere?
LENNY: In the sideboard in your room.
TEDDY: Oh, good.
LENNY: Friends of mine occasionally stay there, you know, in your room, when they're passing through this part of the world.

(*Lenny turns out the hall light and turns on the first landing light.*)
(*Teddy begins to walk up the stairs.*)

TEDDY: Well, I'll see you at breakfast, then.
LENNY: Yes, that's it. Ta-ta.

(*Teddy goes upstairs.*)
(*Lenny goes off L.*)
(*Silence.*)
(*The landing light goes out.*)
(*Slight night light in the hall and room.*)
(*Lenny comes back into the room, goes to the window and looks out.*)
(*He leaves the window and turns on a lamp.*)
(*He is holding a small clock.*)
(*He sits, places the clock in front of him, lights a cigarette and sits.*)
(*Ruth comes in the front door.*)

(*She stands still. Lenny turns his head, smiles. She walks slowly into the room.*)

LENNY: Good evening.
RUTH: Morning, I think.
LENNY: You're right there.

(*Pause.*)

My name's Lenny. What's yours?
RUTH: Ruth.

(*She sits, puts her coat collar around her.*)

LENNY: Cold?
RUTH: No.
LENNY: It's been a wonderful summer, hasn't it? Remarkable.

(*Pause.*)

Would you like something? Refreshment of some kind? An aperitif, anything like that?
RUTH: No, thanks.
LENNY: I'm glad you said that. We haven't got a drink in the house. Mind you, I'd soon get some in, if we had a party or something like that. Some kind of celebration . . . you know.

(*Pause.*)

You must be connected with my brother in some way. The one who's been abroad.
RUTH: I'm his wife.
LENNY: Eh listen, I wonder if you can advise me. I've been having a bit of a rough time with this clock. The tick's been keeping me up. The trouble is I'm not all that convinced it was the clock. I mean there are lots of things which tick in the night, don't you find that? All sorts of objects, which, in the day, you wouldn't call anything else but commonplace. They give you no trouble. But in the night any given one of a number of them is liable to start letting out a bit of a tick. Whereas you look at these objects in the day and they're just commonplace. They're as quiet as mice during the daytime. So . . . all things being equal . . . this question of me saying it was the clock that woke me up, well, that could very easily prove something of a false hypothesis.

(*He goes to the sideboard, pours from a jug into a glass, takes the glass to Ruth.*)

Here you are. I bet you could do with this.
RUTH: What is it?
LENNY: Water.

(*She takes it, sips, places the glass on a small table by her chair.*)
(*Lenny watches her.*)

Isn't it funny? I've got my pajamas on and you're fully dressed?

(*He goes to the sideboard and pours another glass of water.*)

Mind if I have one? Yes, it's funny seeing my old brother again after all these years. It's just the sort of tonic my Dad needs, you know. He'll be chuffed to his bollocks in the morning, when he sees his eldest son. I was surprised myself when I saw Teddy, you know. Old Ted. I thought he was in America.

RUTH: We're on a visit to Europe.

LENNY: What, both of you?

RUTH: Yes.

LENNY: What, you sort of live with him over there, do you?

RUTH: We're married.

LENNY: On a visit to Europe, eh? Seen much of it?

RUTH: We've just come from Italy.

LENNY: Oh, you went to Italy first, did you? And then he brought you over here to meet the family, did he? Well, the old man'll be pleased to see you, I can tell you.

RUTH: Good.

LENNY: What did you say?

RUTH: Good.

(*Pause.*)

LENNY: Where'd you go to in Italy?

RUTH: Venice.

LENNY: Not dear old Venice? Eh? That's funny. You know, I've always had a feeling that if I'd been a soldier in the last war—say in the Italian campaign—I'd probably have found myself in Venice. I've always had that feeling. The trouble was I was too young to serve, you see. I was only a child, I was too small, otherwise I've got a pretty shrewd idea I'd probably have gone through Venice. Yes, I'd almost certainly have gone through it with my battalion. Do you mind if I hold your hand?

RUTH: Why?

LENNY: Just a touch.

(*He stands and goes to her.*)

Just a tickle

RUTH: Why?

(*He looks down at her.*)

LENNY: I'll tell you why.

(*Slight pause.*)

One night, not too long ago, one night down by the docks, I was standing alone under an arch, watching all the men jibbing the boom, out in the harbor, and playing about with the yardarm, when a certain lady came up to me and made me a certain proposal. This lady had been searching for me for days. She'd lost track of my whereabouts. However, the fact was she eventually caught up with me, and when she caught up with me she made me this certain proposal. Well, this proposal wasn't entirely out of order and normally I would have subscribed to it. I mean I would have subscribed to it in the normal course of events. The only trouble was she was falling apart with the pox. So I turned it down. Well, this lady was very

insistent and started taking liberties with me down under this arch, liberties which by any criterion I couldn't be expected to tolerate, the facts being what they were, so I clumped her one. It was on my mind at the time to do away with her, you know, to kill her, and the fact is, that as killings go, it would have been a simple matter, nothing to it. Her chauffeur, who had located me for her, he'd popped round the corner to have a drink, which just left this lady and myself, you see, alone, standing underneath this arch, watching all the steamers steaming up, no one about, all quiet on the Western Front, and there she was up against this wall—well, just sliding down the wall, following the blow I'd given her. Well, to sum up, everything was in my favor, for a killing. Don't worry about the chauffeur. The chauffeur would never have spoken. He was an old friend of the family. But . . . in the end I thought . . . Aaah, why go to all the bother . . . you know, getting rid of the corpse and all that, getting yourself into a state of tension. So I just gave her another belt in the nose and a couple of turns of the boot and sort of left it at that.

RUTH: How did you know she was diseased?

LENNY: How did I know?

(*Pause.*)

I decided she was.

(*Silence.*)

You and my brother are newly-weds, are you?

RUTH: We've been married six years.

LENNY: He's always been my favorite brother, old Teddy. Do you know that? And my goodness we are proud of him here, I can tell you. Doctor of Philosophy and all that . . . leaves quite an impression. Of course, he's a very sensitive man, isn't he? Ted. Very. I've often wished I was as sensitive as he is.

RUTH: Have you?

LENNY: Oh yes. Oh yes, very much so. I mean, I'm not saying I'm not sensitive. I am. I could just be a bit more so, that's all.

RUTH: Could you?

LENNY: Yes, just a bit more so, that's all.

(*Pause.*)

I mean, I am very sensitive to atmosphere, but I tend to get desensitized, if you know what I mean, when people make unreasonable demands on me. For instance, last Christmas I decided to do a bit of snow-clearing for the Borough Council, because we had a heavy snow over here that year in Europe. I didn't have to do this snow-clearing—I mean I wasn't financially embarrassed in any way—it just appealed to me, it appealed to something inside me. What I anticipated with a good deal of pleasure was the brisk cold bite in the air in the early morning. And I was right. I had to get my snowboots on and I had to stand on a corner, at about five-thirty in the morning, to wait for the lorry to pick me up, to take me to the allotted area. Bloody freezing. Well, the lorry came, I jumped on the tailboard, headlights on, dipped, and off we went. Got there, shovels up, fags on, and off we went, deep into the December snow, hours before cockcrow. Well, that morning, while I was having my midmorning cup of tea in a neighboring cafe, the shovel standing by my chair, an old lady approached me and asked me if I would give her a hand with her iron mangle. Her brother-in-law, she said, had left it for her, but he'd left it in the wrong room, he'd left it in the front room. Well, naturally, she wanted it in the back room. It was a present he'd given her, you see, a mangle, to iron out the washing. But he'd left it in the wrong room, he'd left it in the front room, well that was a silly place to leave it, it couldn't stay there. So I took time off to give her a hand. She only lived up the road. Well, the only trouble was when I got there I couldn't move this mangle. It must have weighed about half a ton. How this brother-in-law got it up there in the first place I can't even begin to envisage. So there I was, doing a bit of shoulders on with the mangle, risking a rupture, and this old lady just standing there, waving me on, not even lifting a little finger to give me a helping hand. So after a few minutes I said to her, now look, why don't you stuff this iron mangle up your arse? Anyway, I said, they're out of date, you want to get a spin drier. I had a good mind to give her a workover there and then, but as I was feeling jubilant with the snow-clearing I just gave her a short-arm jab to the belly and jumped on a bus outside. Excuse me, shall I take this ashtray out of your way?

RUTH: It's not in my way.

LENNY: It seems to be in the way of your glass. The glass was about to fall. Or the ashtray. I'm rather worried about the carpet. It's not me, it's my father. He's obsessed with order and clarity. He doesn't like mess. So, as I don't believe you're smoking at the moment, I'm sure you won't object if I move the ashtray.

(*He does so.*)

And now perhaps I'll relieve you of your glass.

RUTH: I haven't quite finished.

LENNY: You've consumed quite enough, in my opinion.

RUTH: No, I haven't.

LENNY: Quite sufficient, in my own opinion.

RUTH: Not in mine, Leonard.

(*Pause.*)

LENNY: Don't call me that, please.

RUTH: Why not?

LENNY: That's the name my mother gave me.

(*Pause.*)

Just give me the glass.

RUTH: No.

(*Pause.*)

LENNY: I'll take it, then.

RUTH: If you take the glass . . . I'll take you.

(*Pause.*)

LENNY: How about me taking the glass without you taking me?

RUTH: Why don't I just take you?

(*Pause.*)

LENNY: You're joking.

(*Pause.*)

You're in love, anyway, with another man. You've had a secret liaison with another man. His family didn't even know. Then you come here without a word of warning and start to make trouble.

(*She picks up the glass and lifts it towards him.*)

RUTH: Have a sip. Go on. Have a sip from my glass.

(*He is still.*)

Sit on my lap. Take a long cool sip.

(*She pats her lap. Pause.*)
(*She stands, moves to him with the glass.*)

Put your head back and open your mouth.

LENNY: Take that glass away from me.

RUTH: Lie on the floor. Go on. I'll pour it down your throat.

LENNY: What are you doing, making me some kind of proposal?

(*She laughs shortly, drains the glass.*)

RUTH: Oh, I was thirsty.

(*She smiles at him, puts the glass down, goes into the hall and up the stairs.*)
(*He follows into the hall and shouts up the stairs.*)

LENNY: What was that supposed to be? Some kind of proposal?

(*Silence.*)
(*He comes back into the room, goes to his own glass, drains it.*)
(*A door slams upstairs.*)
(*The landing light goes on.*)
(*Max comes down the stairs, in pajamas and cap. He comes into the room.*)

MAX: What's going on here? You drunk?

(*He stares at Lenny.*)

What are you shouting about? You gone mad?

(*Lenny pours another glass of water.*)

Prancing about in the middle of the night shouting your head off. What are you, a raving lunatic?

LENNY: I was thinking aloud.

MAX: Is Joey down here? You been shouting at Joey?

LENNY: Didn't you hear what I said, Dad? I said I was thinking aloud.

MAX: You were thinking so loud you got me out of bed.

LENNY: Look, why don't you just . . . pop off, eh?

MAX: Pop off? He wakes me up in the middle of the night, I think we got burglars here, I think he's got a knife stuck in him, I come down here, he tells me to pop off.

(*Lenny sits down.*)

He was talking to someone. Who could he have been talking to? They're all asleep. He was having a conversation with someone. He won't tell me who it was. He pretends he was thinking aloud. What are you doing, hiding someone here?

LENNY: I was sleepwalking. Get out of it, leave me alone, will you?

MAX: I want an explanation, you understand? I asked you who you got hiding here.

(*Pause.*)

LENNY: I'll tell you what, Dad, since you're in the mood for a bit of a . . . chat, I'll ask you a question. It's a question I've been meaning to ask you for some time. That night . . . you know . . . the night you got me . . . that night with Mum, what was it like? Eh? When I was just a glint in your eye. What was it like? What was the background to it? I mean, I want to know the real facts about my background. I mean, for instance, is it a fact that you had me in mind all the time, or is it a fact that I was the last thing you had in mind?

(*Pause.*)

I'm only asking this in a spirit of inquiry, you understand that, don't you? I'm curious. And there's lots of people of my age share that curiosity, you know that, Dad? They often ruminate, sometimes singly, sometimes in groups, about the true facts of that particular night—the night they were made in the image of those two people *at it*. It's a question long overdue, from my point of view, but as we happen to be passing the time of day here tonight I thought I'd pop it to you.

(*Pause.*)

MAX: You'll drown in your own blood.

LENNY: If you prefer to answer the question in writing I've got no objection.

(*Max stands.*)

I should have asked my dear mother. Why didn't I ask my dear mother? Now it's too late. She's passed over to the other side.

(*Max spits at him.*)

(*Lenny looks down at the carpet.*)

Now look what you've done. I'll have to Hoover that in the morning, you know.

(*Max turns and walks up the stairs.*)

(*Lenny sits still.*)

(*Blackout.*)

(*Lights up.*)

(*Morning.*)

(*Joey in front of the mirror. He is doing some slow limbering-up exercises. He stops, combs his hair, carefully. He then shadowboxes, heavily, watching himself in the mirror.*)

(*Max comes in from U.L.*)

(*Both Max and Joey are dressed. Max watches Joey in silence. Joey stops shadowboxing, picks up a newspaper and sits.*)

(*Silence.*)

MAX: I hate this room.

(*Pause.*)

It's the kitchen I like. It's nice in there. It's cosy.

(*Pause.*)

But I can't stay in there. You know why? Because he's always washing up in there, scraping the plates, driving me out of the kitchen, that's why.

JOEY: Why don't you bring your tea in here?

MAX: I don't want to bring my tea in here. I hate it here. I want to drink my tea in there.

(*He goes into the hall and looks towards the kitchen.*)

What's he doing in there?

(*He returns.*)

What's the time?

JOEY: Half past six.

MAX: Half past six.

(*Pause.*)

I'm going to see a game of football this afternoon. You want to come?

(*Pause.*)

I'm talking to you.

JOEY: I'm training this afternoon. I'm doing six rounds with Blackie.

MAX: That's not till five o'clock. You've got time to see a game of football before five o'clock. It's the first game of the season.

JOEY: No, I'm not going.

MAX: Why not?

(*Pause.*)

(*Max goes into the hall.*)

Sam! Come here!

(*Max comes back into the room.*)

(*Sam enters with a cloth.*)

SAM: What?

MAX: What are you doing in there?

SAM: Washing up.

MAX: What else?

SAM: Getting rid of your leavings.

MAX: Putting them in the bin, eh?

SAM: Right in.

MAX: What point you trying to prove?

SAM: No point.

MAX: Oh yes, you are. You resent making my breakfast, that's what it is, isn't it? That's why you bang
round the kitchen like that, scraping the frying-pan,
scraping all the leavings into the bin, scraping all the
plates, scraping all the tea out of the teapot . . . that's
why you do that, every single stinking morning. I
know. Listen, Sam. I want to say something to you.
From my heart.

(*He moves closer.*)

I want you to get rid of these feelings of resentment
you've got towards me. I wish I could understand
them. Honestly, have I ever given you cause? Never.
When Dad died he said to me, Max, look after your
brothers. That's exactly what he said to me.

SAM: How could he say that when he was dead?

MAX: What?

SAM: How could he speak if he was dead?

(*Pause.*)

MAX: Before he died, Sam. Just before. They were his last
words. His last sacred words, Sammy. A split second
after he said those words . . . he was a dead man.
You think I'm joking? You think when my father
spoke—on his death-bed—I wouldn't obey his words
to the last letter? You hear that, Joey? He'll stop at
nothing. He's even prepared to spit on the memory of
our Dad. What kind of a son were you, you wet wick?
You spent half your time doing crossword puzzles! We
took you into the butcher's shop, you couldn't even
sweep the dust off the floor. We took MacGregor into
the shop, he could run the place by the end of a week.
Well, I'll tell you one thing. I respected my father not
only as a man but as a number one butcher! And to
prove it I followed him into the shop. I learned to
carve a carcass at his knee. I commemorated his name
in blood. I gave birth to three grown men! All on my
own bat. What have you done?

(*Pause.*)

What have you done? You tit!

SAM: Do you want to finish the washing up? Look, here's
the cloth.

MAX: So try to get rid of these feelings of resentment,
Sam. After all, we are brothers.

SAM: Do you want the cloth? Here you are. Take it.

(*Teddy and Ruth come down the stairs. They walk
across the hall and stop just inside the room.*)
(*The others turn and look at them. Joey stands.*)
(*Teddy and Ruth are wearing dressing-gowns.*)
(*Silence.*)
(*Teddy smiles.*)

TEDDY: Hullo . . . Dad . . . We overslept.

(*Pause.*)

What's for breakfast?

(*Silence.*)
(*Teddy chuckles.*)

Huh. We overslept.

(*Max turns to Sam.*)

MAX: Did you know he was here?

SAM: No.

(*Max turns to Joey.*)

MAX: Did you know he was here?

(*Pause.*)

I asked you if you knew he was here.

JOEY: No.

MAX: Then who knew?

(*Pause.*)

Who knew?

(*Pause.*)

I didn't know.

TEDDY: I was going to come down, Dad, I was going
to . . . be here, when you came down.

(*Pause.*)

How are you?

(*Pause.*)

Uh . . . look, I'd . . . like you to meet . . .

MAX: How long you been in this house?

TEDDY: All night.

MAX: All night? I'm a laughing-stock. How did you get
in?

TEDDY: I had my key.

(*Max whistles and laughs.*)

MAX: Who's this?

TEDDY: I was just going to introduce you.

MAX: Who asked you to bring tarts in here?

TEDDY: Tarts?

MAX: Who asked you to bring dirty tarts into this
house?

TEDDY: Listen, don't be silly —

MAX: You been here all night?

TEDDY: Yes, we arrived from Venice—

MAX: We've had a smelly scrubber in my house all night.
We've had a stinking pox-ridden slut in my house
all night.

TEDDY: Stop it! What are you talking about?

MAX: I haven't seen the bitch for six years, he comes
home without a word, he brings a filthy scrubber off
the street, he shacks up in my house!

TEDDY: She's my wife! We're married!

(*Pause.*)

MAX: I've never had a whore under this roof before.
Ever since your mother died. My word of honor.

(*To Joey.*) Have you ever had a whore here? Has Lenny ever had a whore here? They come back from America, they bring the slopbucket with them. They bring the bedpan with them. (*To Teddy.*) Take that disease away from me. Get her away from me.

TEDDY: She's my wife.

MAX (*to Joey*): Chuck them out.

(*Pause.*)

A Doctor of Philosophy. Sam, you want to meet a Doctor of Philosophy? (*To Joey.*) I said chuck them out.

(*Pause.*)

What's the matter? You deaf?

JOEY: You're an old man. (*To Teddy.*) He's an old man.

(*Lenny walks into the room, in a dressing-gown.*)
(*He stops.*)
(*They all look round.*)
(*Max turns back, hits Joey in the stomach with all his might.*)
(*Joey contorts, staggers across the stage. Max, with the exertion of the blow, begins to collapse. His knees buckle.*)
(*He clutches his stick.*)
(*Sam moves forward to help him.*)
(*Max hits him across the head with his stick. Sam sits, head in hands.*)
(*Joey, hands pressed to his stomach, sinks down at the feet of Ruth.*)
(*She looks down at him.*)
(*Lenny and Teddy are still.*)
(*Joey slowly stands. He is close to Ruth. He turns from Ruth, looks round at Max.*)
(*Sam clutches his head.*)
(*Max breathes heavily, very slowly gets to his feet.*)
(*Joey moves to him.*)
(*They look at each other.*)
(*Silence.*)
(*Max moves past Joey, walks towards Ruth. He gestures with his stick.*)

MAX: Miss.

(*Ruth walks towards him.*)

RUTH: Yes?

(*He looks at her.*)

MAX: You a mother?

RUTH: Yes.

MAX: How many you got?

RUTH: Three.

(*He turns to Teddy.*)

MAX: All yours, Ted?

(*Pause.*)

Teddy, why don't we have a nice cuddle and kiss, eh? Like the old days? What about a nice cuddle and kiss, eh?

TEDDY: Come on, then.

(*Pause.*)

MAX: You want to kiss your old father? Want a cuddle with your old father?

TEDDY: Come on, then.

(*Teddy moves a step towards him.*)

Come on.

(*Pause.*)

MAX: You still love your old Dad, eh?

(*They face each other.*)

TEDDY: Come on, Dad. I'm ready for the cuddle.

(*Max begins to chuckle, gurgling.*)
(*He turns to the family and addresses them.*)

MAX: He still loves his father!

Curtain

ACT 2

Afternoon.

Max, Teddy, Lenny, and Sam are about the stage, lighting cigars.

Joey comes in from U.L. with a coffee tray, followed by Ruth. He puts the tray down. Ruth hands coffee to all the men. She sits with her cup. Max smiles at her.

RUTH: That was a very good lunch.

MAX: I'm glad you liked it. (*To the others.*) Did you hear that? (*To Ruth.*) Well, I put my heart and soul into it, I can tell you. (*He sips.*) And this is a lovely cup of coffee.

RUTH: I'm glad.

(*Pause.*)

MAX: I've got the feeling you're a first-rate cook.

RUTH: I'm not bad.

MAX: No, I've got the feeling you're a number one cook. Am I right, Teddy?

TEDDY: Yes, she's a very good cook.

(*Pause.*)

MAX: Well, it's a long time since the whole family was together, eh? If only your mother was alive. Eh, what do you say, Sam? What would Jessie say if she was alive? Sitting here with her three sons. Three fine grown-up lads. And a lovely daughter-in-law. The only shame is her grandchildren aren't here. She'd have petted them and cooed over them, wouldn't she, Sam? She'd have fussed over them and played with them, told them stories, tickled them— I tell you she'd have been hysterical. (*To Ruth.*) Mind you, she taught those boys everything they know.

She taught them all the morality they know. I'm telling you. Every single bit of the moral code they live by—was taught to them by their mother. And she had a heart to go with it. What a heart. Eh, Sam? Listen, what's the use of beating round the bush? That woman was the backbone to this family. I mean, I was busy working twenty-four hours a day in the shop, I was going all over the country to find meat, I was making my way in the world, but I left a woman at home with a will of iron, a heart of gold and a mind. Right, Sam?

(*Pause.*)

What a mind.

(*Pause.*)

Mind you, I was a generous man to her. I never left her short of a few bob. I remember one year I entered into negotiations with a top-class group of butchers with continental connections. I was going into association with them. I remember the night I came home, I kept quiet. First of all I gave Lenny a bath, then Teddy a bath, then Joey a bath. What fun we used to have in the bath, eh, boys? Then I came downstairs and I made Jessie put her feet up on a pouffe—what happened to that pouffe, I haven't seen it for years—she put her feet up on the pouffe and I said to her, Jessie, I think our ship is going to come home, I'm going to treat you to a couple of items, I'm going to buy you a dress in pale corded blue silk, heavily encrusted in pearls, and for casual wear, a pair of pantaloons in lilac flowered taffeta. Then I gave her a drop of cherry brandy. I remember the boys came down, in their pajamas, all their hair shining, their faces pink, it was before they started shaving, and they knelt down at our feet, Jessie's and mine. I tell you, it was like Christmas.

(*Pause.*)

RUTH: What happened to the group of butchers?
MAX: The group? They turned out to be a bunch of criminals like everyone else.

(*Pause.*)

This is a lousy cigar.

(*He stubs it out.*)
(*He turns to Sam.*)

What time you going to work?
SAM: Soon.
MAX: You've got a job on this afternoon, haven't you?
SAM: Yes, I know.
MAX: What do you mean, you know? You'll be late. You'll lose your job? What are you trying to do, humiliate me?
SAM: Don't worry about me.
MAX: It makes the bile come up in my mouth. The bile—you understand? (*To Ruth.*) I worked as a butcher all my life, using the chopper and the slab,

the slab, you know what I mean, the chopper and the slab! To keep my family in luxury. Two families! My mother was bedridden, my brothers were all invalids. I had to earn the money for the leading psychiatrists. I had to read books! I had to study the disease, so that I could cope with an emergency at every stage. A crippled family, three bastard sons, a slutbitch of a wife—don't talk to me about the pain of childbirth—I suffered the pain, I've still got the pangs—when I give a little cough my back collapses—and here I've got a lazy idle bugger of a brother won't even get to work on time. The best chauffeur in the world. All his life he's sat in the front seat giving lovely hand signals. You call that work? This man doesn't know his gearbox from his arse!

SAM: You go and ask my customers! I'm the only one they ever ask for.
MAX: What do the other drivers do, sleep all day?
SAM: I can only drive one car. They can't all have me at the same time.
MAX: Anyone could have you at the same time. You'd bend over for half a dollar on Blackfriars Bridge.
SAM: Me!
MAX: For two bob and a toffee apple.
SAM: He's insulting me. He's insulting his brother. I'm driving a man to Hampton Court at four forty-five.
MAX: Do you want to know who could drive? MacGregor! MacGregor was a driver.
SAM: Don't you believe it.

(*Max points his stick at Sam.*)

MAX: He didn't even fight in the war. This man didn't even fight in the bloody war!
SAM: I did!
MAX: Who did you kill?

(*Silence.*)
(*Sam gets up, goes to Ruth, shakes her hand and goes out of the front door.*)
(*Max turns to Teddy.*)

Well, how you been keeping, son?
TEDDY: I've been keeping very well, Dad.
MAX: It's nice to have you with us, son.
TEDDY: It's nice to be back, Dad.

(*Pause.*)

MAX: You should have told me you were married, Teddy. I'd have sent you a present. Where was the wedding, in America?
TEDDY: No. Here. The day before we left.
MAX: Did you have a big function?
TEDDY: No, there was no one there.
MAX: You're mad. I'd have given you a white wedding. We'd have had the cream of the cream here. I'd have been only too glad to bear the expense, my word of honor.

(*Pause.*)

TEDDY: You were busy at the time. I didn't want to bother you.

MAX: But you're my own flesh and blood. You're my first born. I'd have dropped everything. Sam would have driven you to the reception in the Snipe, Lenny would have been your best man, and then we'd have all seen you off on the boat. I mean, you don't think I disapprove of marriage, do you? Don't be daft. (*To Ruth.*) I've been begging my two youngsters for years to find a nice feminine girl with proper credentials—it makes life worth living. (*To Teddy.*) Anyway, what's the difference, you did it, you made a wonderful choice, you've got a wonderful family, a marvelous career . . . so why don't we let bygones be bygones?

(*Pause.*)

You know what I'm saying? I want you both to know that you have my blessing.

TEDDY: Thank you.

MAX: Don't mention it. How many other houses in the district have got a Doctor of Philosophy sitting down drinking a cup of coffee?

(*Pause.*)

RUTH: I'm sure Teddy's very happy . . . to know that you're pleased with me.

(*Pause.*)

I think he wondered whether you would be pleased with me.

MAX: But you're a charming woman.

(*Pause.*)

RUTH: I was . . .

MAX: What?

(*Pause.*)

What she say?

(*They all look at her.*)

RUTH: I was . . . different . . . when I met Teddy . . . first.

TEDDY: No you weren't. You were the same.

RUTH: I wasn't.

MAX: Who cares? Listen, live in the present, what are you worrying about? I mean, don't forget the earth's about five thousand million years old, at least. Who can afford to live in the past?

(*Pause.*)

TEDDY: She's a great help to me over there. She's a wonderful wife and mother. She's a very popular woman. She's got lots of friends. It's a great life, at the University . . . you know . . . it's a very good life. We've got a lovely house . . . we've got all . . . we've got everything we want. It's a very stimulating environment.

(*Pause.*)

My department . . . is highly successful.

(*Pause.*)

We've got three boys, you know.

MAX: All boys? Isn't that funny, eh? You've got three, I've got three. You've got three nephews, Joey. Joey! You're an uncle, do you hear? You could teach them how to box.

(*Pause.*)

JOEY (*to Ruth*): I'm a boxer. In the evenings, after work. I'm in demolition in the daytime.

RUTH: Oh?

JOEY: Yes. I hope to be full time, when I get more bouts.

MAX (*to Lenny*): He speaks so easily to his sister-in-law, do you notice? That's because she's an intelligent and sympathetic woman.

(*He leans to her.*)

Eh, tell me, do you think the children are missing their mother?

(*She looks at him.*)

TEDDY: Of course they are. They love her. We'll be seeing them soon.

(*Pause.*)

LENNY (*to Teddy*): Your cigar's gone out.

TEDDY: Oh, yes.

LENNY: Want a light?

TEDDY: No. No.

(*Pause.*)

So has yours.

LENNY: Oh, yes.

(*Pause.*)

Eh, Teddy, you haven't told us much about your Doctorship of Philosophy. What do you teach?

TEDDY: Philosophy.

LENNY: Well, I want to ask you something. Do you detect a certain logical incoherence in the central affirmations of Christian theism?

TEDDY: That question doesn't fall within my province.

LENNY: Well, look at it this way . . . you don't mind my asking you some questions, do you?

TEDDY: If they're within my province.

LENNY: Well, look at it this way. How can the unknown merit reverence? In other words, how can you revere that of which you're ignorant? At the same time, it would be ridiculous to propose that what we *know* merits reverence. What we know merits any one of a number of things, but it stands to reason reverence isn't one of them. In other words, apart from the known and the unknown, what else is there?

(*Pause.*)

TEDDY: I'm afraid I'm the wrong person to ask.

LENNY: But you're a philosopher. Come on, be frank. What do you make of all this business of being and not-being?

TEDDY: What do you make of it?

LENNY: Well, for instance, take a table. Philosophically speaking. What is it?

TEDDY: A table.

LENNY: Ah. You mean it's nothing else but a table. Well, some people would envy your certainty, wouldn't they, Joey? For instance, I've got a couple of friends of mine, we often sit round the Ritz Bar having a few liqueurs, and they're always saying things like that, you know, things like: Take a table, take it. All right, I say, *take* it, *take* a table, but once you've taken it, what you going to do with it? Once you've got hold of it, where you going to take it?

MAX: You'd probably sell it.

LENNY: You wouldn't get much for it.

JOEY: Chop it up for firewood.

(*Lenny looks at him and laughs.*)

RUTH: Don't be too sure though. You've forgotten something. Look at me. I . . . move my leg. That's all it is. But I wear . . . underwear . . . which moves with me . . . it . . . captures your attention. Perhaps you misinterpret. The action is simple. It's a leg . . . moving. My lips move. Why don't you restrict . . . your observations to that? Perhaps the fact that they move is more significant . . . than the words which come through them. You must bear that . . . possibility . . . in mind.

(*Silence.*)
(*Teddy stands.*)

I was born quite near here.

(*Pause.*)

Then . . . six years ago, I went to America.

(*Pause.*)

It's all rock. And sand. It stretches . . . so far . . . everywhere you look. And there's lots of insects there.

(*Pause.*)

And there's lots of insects there.

(*Silence.*)
(*She is still.*)
(*Max stands.*)

MAX: Well, it's time to go to the gym. Time for your workout, Joey.

LENNY (*standing*): I'll come with you.

(*Joey sits looking at Ruth.*)

MAX: Joe.

(*Joey stands. The three go out.*)
(*Teddy sits by Ruth, holds her hand.*)
(*She smiles at him.*)
(*Pause.*)

TEDDY: I think we'll go back. Mmnn?

(*Pause.*)

Shall we go home?

RUTH: Why?

TEDDY: Well, we were only here for a few days, weren't we? We might as well . . . cut it short, I think.

RUTH: Why? Don't you like it here?

TEDDY: Of course I do. But I'd like to go back and see the boys now.

(*Pause.*)

RUTH: Don't you like your family?

TEDDY: Which family?

RUTH: Your family here.

TEDDY: Of course I like them. What are you talking about?

(*Pause.*)

RUTH: You don't like them as much as you thought you did?

TEDDY: Of course I do. Of course I . . . like them. I don't know what you're talking about.

(*Pause.*)

Listen. You know what time of the day it is there now, do you?

RUTH: What?

TEDDY: It's morning. It's about eleven o'clock.

RUTH: Is it?

TEDDY: Yes, they're about six hours behind us . . . I mean . . . behind the time here. The boys'll be at the pool . . . now . . . swimming. Think of it. Morning over there. Sun. We'll go anyway, mmnn? It's so clean there.

RUTH: Clean.

TEDDY: Yes.

RUTH: Is it dirty here?

TEDDY: No, of course not. But it's cleaner there.

(*Pause.*)

Look, I just brought you back to meet the family, didn't I? You've met them, we can go. The fall semester will be starting soon.

RUTH: You find it dirty here?

TEDDY: I didn't say I found it dirty here.

(*Pause.*)

I didn't say that.

(*Pause.*)

Look. I'll go and pack. You rest for a while. Will you? They won't be back for at least an hour. You can sleep. Rest. Please.

(*She looks at him.*)

You can help me with my lectures when we get back. I'd love that. I'd be so grateful for it, really. We can bathe till October. You know that. Here, there's nowhere to bathe, except the swimming bath down

the road. You know what it's like? It's like a urinal.
A filthy urinal!

(*Pause.*)

You liked Venice, didn't you? It was lovely, wasn't it?
You had a good week. I mean . . . I took you there. I
can speak Italian.

RUTH: But if I'd been a nurse in the Italian campaign I
would have been there before.

(*Pause.*)

TEDDY: You just rest. I'll go and pack.

(*Teddy goes out and up the stairs.*)
(*She closes her eyes.*)
(*Lenny appears from U.L.*)
(*He walks into the room and sits near her.*)
(*She opens her eyes.*)
(*Silence.*)

LENNY: Well, the evenings are drawing in.
RUTH: Yes, it's getting dark.

(*Pause.*)

LENNY: Winter'll soon be upon us. Time to renew one's
wardrobe.

(*Pause.*)

RUTH: That's a good thing to do.
LENNY: What?

(*Pause.*)

RUTH: I always . . .

(*Pause.*)

Do you like clothes?
LENNY: Oh, yes. Very fond of clothes.

(*Pause.*)

RUTH: I'm fond . . .

(*Pause.*)

What do you think of my shoes?
LENNY: They're very nice.
RUTH: No, I can't get the ones I want over there.
LENNY: Can't get them over there, eh?
RUTH: No . . . you don't get them there.

(*Pause.*)

I was a model before I went away.
LENNY: Hats?

(*Pause.*)

I bought a girl a hat once. We saw it in a glass case, in
a shop. I tell you what it had. It had a bunch of daffodils on it, tied with a black satin bow, and then it
was covered with a cloche of black veiling. A cloche.
I'm telling you. She was made for it.
RUTH: No . . . I was a model for the body. A photographic
model for the body.

LENNY: Indoor work?
RUTH: That was before I had . . . all my children.

(*Pause.*)

No, not always indoors.

(*Pause.*)

Once or twice we went to a place in the country,
by train. Oh, six or seven times. We used to pass
a . . . a large white water tower. This place . . . this
house . . . was very big . . . the trees . . . there was a
lake, you see . . . we used to change and walk down
towards the lake . . . we went down a path . . . on
stones . . . there were . . . on this path. Oh, just . . .
wait . . . yes . . . when we changed in the house we
had a drink. There was a cold buffet.

(*Pause.*)

Sometimes we stayed in the house but . . . most often . . . we walked down to the lake . . . and did our
modeling there.

(*Pause.*)

Just before we went to America I went down there. I
walked from the station to the gate and then I walked
up the drive. There were lights on . . . I stood in the
drive . . . the house was very light.

(*Teddy comes down the stairs with the cases. He puts
them down, looks at Lenny.*)

TEDDY: What have you been saying to her?

(*He goes to Ruth.*)

Here's your coat.

(*Lenny goes to the radiogram and puts on a record of
slow jazz.*)

Ruth. Come on. Put it on.
LENNY (*to Ruth*): What about one dance before you go?
TEDDY: We're going.
LENNY: Just one.
TEDDY: No. We're going.
LENNY: Just one dance, with her brother-in-law, before
she goes.

(*Lenny bends to her.*)

Madam?

(*Ruth stands. They dance, slowly.*)
(*Teddy stands, with Ruth's coat.*)
(*Max and Joey come in the front door and into the
room.*)
(*They stand.*)
(*Lenny kisses Ruth. They stand, kissing.*)

JOEY: Christ, she's wide open. Dad, look at that.

(*Pause.*)

She's a tart.

(*Pause.*)

Old Lenny's got a tart in here.

(*Joey goes to them. He takes Ruth's arm. He smiles at Lenny. He sits with Ruth on the sofa, embraces and kisses her.*)
(*He looks up at Lenny.*)

Just up my street.

(*He leans her back until she lies beneath him. He kisses her.*)
(*He looks up at Teddy and Max.*)

It's better than a rubdown, this.

(*Lenny sits on the arm of the sofa. He caresses Ruth's hair as Joey embraces her.*)
(*Max comes forward, looks at the cases.*)

MAX: You going, Teddy? Already?

(*Pause.*)

Well, when you coming over again, eh? Look, next time you come over, don't forget to let us know beforehand whether you're married or not. I'll always be glad to meet the wife. Honest. I'm telling you.

(*Joey lies heavily on Ruth.*)
(*They are almost still.*)
(*Lenny caresses her hair.*)

Listen, you think I don't know why you didn't tell me you were married? I know why. You were ashamed. You thought I'd be annoyed because you married a woman beneath you. You should have known me better. I'm broadminded. I'm a broadminded man.

(*He peers to see Ruth's face under Joey, turns back to Teddy.*)

Mind you, she's a lovely girl. A beautiful woman. And a mother too. A mother of three. You've made a happy woman out of her. It's something to be proud of. I mean, we're talking about a woman of quality. We're talking about a woman of feeling.

(*Joey and Ruth roll off the sofa onto the floor.*)
(*Joey clasps her. Lenny moves to stand above them. He looks down on them. He touches Ruth gently with his foot.*)
(*Ruth suddenly pushes Joey away.*)
(*She stands up.*)
(*Joey gets to his feet, stares at her.*)

RUTH: I'd like something to eat. (*To Lenny.*) I'd like a drink. Did you get any drink?
LENNY: We've got drink.
RUTH: I'd like one, please.
LENNY: What drink?
RUTH: Whisky.
LENNY: I've got it.

(*Pause.*)

RUTH: Well, get it.

(*Lenny goes to the sideboard, takes out bottle and glasses.*)
(*Joey moves towards her.*)

Put the record off.

(*He looks at her, turns, puts the record off.*)

I want something to eat.

(*Pause.*)

JOEY: I can't cook. (*Pointing to Max.*) He's the cook.

(*Lenny brings her a glass of whisky.*)

LENNY: Soda on the side?
RUTH: What's this glass? I can't drink out of this. Haven't you got a tumbler?
LENNY: Yes.
RUTH: Well, put it in a tumbler.

(*He takes the glass back, pours whisky into a tumbler, brings it to her.*)

LENNY: On the rocks? Or as it comes?
RUTH: Rocks? What do you know about rocks?
LENNY: We've got rocks. But they're frozen stiff in the fridge.

(*Ruth drinks.*)
(*Lenny looks round at the others.*)

Drinks all round?

(*He goes to the sideboard and pours drinks.*)
(*Joey moves closer to Ruth.*)

JOEY: What food do you want?

(*Ruth walks round the room.*)

RUTH (*to Teddy*): Have your family read your critical works?
MAX: That's one thing I've never done. I've never read one of his critical works.
TEDDY: You wouldn't understand them.

(*Lenny hands drinks all round.*)

JOEY: What sort of food do you want? I'm not the cook, anyway.
LENNY: Soda, Ted? Or as it comes?
TEDDY: You wouldn't understand my works. You wouldn't have the faintest idea of what they were about. You wouldn't appreciate the points of reference. You're way behind. All of you. There's no point in my sending you my works. You'd be lost. It's nothing to do with the question of intelligence. It's a way of being able to look at the world. It's a question of how far you can operate on things and not in things. I mean it's a question of your capacity to ally the two, to relate the two, to balance the two. To see, to be able to *see*! I'm the one who can see. That's why I can write my critical works. Might do you good . . . have

a look at them...see how certain people can view...things...how certain people can maintain...intellectual equilibrium. Intellectual equilibrium. You're just objects. You just...move about. I can observe it. I can see what you do. It's the same as I do. But you're lost in it. You won't get me being...I won't be lost in it.

(*Blackout.*)
(*Lights up.*)
(*Evening.*)
(*Teddy sitting, in his coat, the cases by him. Sam.*)
(*Pause.*)

SAM: Do you remember MacGregor, Teddy?
TEDDY: Mac?
SAM: Yes.
TEDDY: Of course I do.
SAM: What did you think of him? Did you take to him?
TEDDY: Yes. I liked him. Why?

(*Pause.*)

SAM: You know, you were always my favorite, of the lads. Always.

(*Pause.*)

When you wrote to me from America I was very touched, you know. I mean you'd written to your father a few times but you'd never written to me. But then, when I got that letter from you...well, I was very touched. I never told him. I never told him I'd heard from you.

(*Pause.*)

(*Whispering.*) Teddy, shall I tell you something? You were always your mother's favorite. She told me. It's true. You were always the...you were always the main object of her love.

(*Pause.*)

Why don't you stay for a couple more weeks, eh? We could have a few laughs.

(*Lenny comes in the front door and into the room.*)

LENNY: Still here, Ted? You'll be late for your first seminar.

(*He goes to the sideboard, opens it, peers in it, to the right and the left, stands.*)

Where's my cheese-roll?

(*Pause.*)

Someone's taken my cheese-roll. I left it there. (*To Sam.*) You been thieving?
TEDDY: I took your cheese-roll, Lenny.

(*Silence.*)
(*Sam looks at them, picks up his hat and goes out of the front door.*)
(*Silence.*)

LENNY: You took my cheese-roll?

TEDDY: Yes.
LENNY: I made that roll myself. I cut it and put the butter on. I sliced a piece of cheese and put it in between. I put it on a plate and I put it in the sideboard. I did all that before I went out. Now I come back and you've eaten it.
TEDDY: Well, what are you going to do about it?
LENNY: I'm waiting for you to apologize.
TEDDY: But I took it deliberately, Lenny.
LENNY: You mean you didn't stumble on it by mistake?
TEDDY: No, I saw you put it there. I was hungry, so I ate it.

(*Pause.*)

LENNY: Barefaced audacity.

(*Pause.*)

What led you to be so...vindictive against your own brother? I'm bowled over.

(*Pause.*)

Well, Ted, I would say this is something approaching the naked truth, isn't it? It's a real cards on the table stunt. I mean, we're in the land of no holds barred now. Well, how else can you interpret it? To pinch your younger brother's specially made cheese-roll when he's out doing a spot of work, that's not equivocal, it's unequivocal.

(*Pause.*)

Mind you, I will say you do seem to have grown a bit sulky during the last six years. A bit sulky. A bit inner. A bit less forthcoming. It's funny, because I'd have thought that in the United States of America, I mean with the sun and all that, the open spaces, on the old campus, in your position, lecturing, in the center of all the intellectual life out there, on the old campus, all the social whirl, all the stimulation of it all, all your kids and all that, to have fun with, down by the pool, the Greyhound buses and all that, tons of iced water, all the comfort of those Bermuda shorts and all that, on the old campus, no time of the day or night you can't get a cup of coffee or a Dutch gin, I'd have thought you'd have grown more forthcoming, not less. Because I want you to know that you set a standard for us, Teddy. Your family looks up to you, boy, and you know what it does? It does its best to follow the example you set. Because you're a great source of pride to us. That's why we were so glad to see you come back, to welcome you back to your birthplace. That's why.

(*Pause.*)

No, listen, Ted, there's no question that we live a less rich life here than you do over there. We live a closer life. We're busy, of course. Joey's busy with his boxing, I'm busy with my occupation, Dad still plays a good game of poker, and he does the cooking as well, well up to his old standard, and Uncle Sam's the best chauffeur in the firm. But nevertheless we do make up a unit, Teddy, and you're an integral part of it. When we all sit round the backyard having a quiet gander at the night sky, there's always an empty chair standing in the circle, which is in fact yours. And so when you at length return to us, we do expect a bit of grace, a bit of je ne sais quoi,° a bit of generosity of mind, a bit of liberality of spirit, to reassure us. We do expect that. But do we get it? Have we got it? Is that what you've given us?

(*Pause.*)

TEDDY: Yes.

(*Joey comes down the stairs and into the room, with a newspaper.*)

LENNY (*to Joey*): How'd you get on?
JOEY: Er . . . not bad.
LENNY: What do you mean?

(*Pause.*)

  What do you mean?
JOEY: Not bad.
LENNY: I want to know what you *mean*—by not bad.
JOEY: What's it got to do with you?
LENNY: Joey, you tell your brother everything.

(*Pause.*)

JOEY: I didn't get all the way.
LENNY: You didn't get all the way?

(*Pause.*)

  (*With emphasis.*) You didn't get all the way?
  But you've had her up there for two hours.
JOEY: Well?
LENNY: You didn't get all the way and you've had her up there for two hours!
JOEY: What about it?

(*Lenny moves closer to him.*)

LENNY: What are you telling me?
JOEY: What do you mean?
LENNY: Are you telling me she's a tease?

(*Pause.*)

  She's a tease!

(*Pause.*)

  What do you think of that, Ted? Your wife turns out to be a tease. He's had her up there for two hours and he didn't go the whole hog.
JOEY: I didn't say she was a tease.
LENNY: Are you joking? It sounds like a tease to me, don't it to you, Ted?
TEDDY: Perhaps he hasn't got the right touch.
LENNY: Joey? Not the right touch? Don't be ridiculous.

je ne sais quoi: French for "I don't know what."

He's had more dolly than you've had cream cakes. He's irresistible. He's one of the few and far between. Tell him about the last bird you had, Joey.

(*Pause.*)

JOEY: What bird?
LENNY: The last bird! When we stopped the car . . .
JOEY: Oh, that . . . yes . . . well, we were in Lenny's car one night last week . . .
LENNY: The Alfa.
JOEY: And er . . . bowling down the road . . .
LENNY: Up near the Scrubs.
JOEY: Yes, up over by the Scrubs . . .
LENNY: We were doing a little survey of North Paddington.
JOEY: And er . . . it was pretty late, wasn't it?
LENNY: Yes, it was late. Well?

(*Pause.*)

JOEY: And then we . . . well, by the curb, we saw this parked car . . . with a couple of girls in it.
LENNY: And their escorts.
JOEY: Yes, there were two geezers in it. Anyway . . .

(*Pause.*)

  What we do then?
LENNY: We stopped the car and got out!
JOEY: Yes . . . we got out . . . and we told the . . . two escorts . . . to go away . . . which they did . . . and then we . . . got the girls out of the car . . .
LENNY: We didn't take them over the Scrubs.
JOEY: Oh, no. Not over the Scrubs. Well, the police would have noticed us there . . . you see. We took them over a bombed site.
LENNY: Rubble. In the rubble.
JOEY: Yes, plenty of rubble.

(*Pause.*)

  Well . . . you know . . . then we had them.
LENNY: You've missed out the best bit. He's missed out the best bit!
JOEY: What bit?
LENNY (*to Teddy*): His bird says to him, I don't mind, she says, but I've got to have some protection. I've got to have some contraceptive protection. I haven't got any contraceptive protection, old Joey says to her. In that case I won't do it, she says. Yes you will, says Joey, never mind about the contraceptive protection.

(*Lenny laughs.*)

  Even my bird laughed when she heard that. Yes, even she gave out a bit of a laugh. So you can't say old Joey isn't a bit of a knockout when he gets going, can you? And here he is upstairs with your wife for two hours and he hasn't even been the whole hog. Well, your wife sounds like a bit of a tease to me, Ted. What do you make of it, Joey? You satisfied? Don't tell me you're satisfied without going the whole hog?

(*Pause.*)

JOEY: I've been the whole hog plenty of times. Sometimes . . . you can be happy . . . and not go the whole hog. Now and again . . . you can be happy . . . without going any hog.

(*Lenny stares at him.*)
(*Max and Sam come in the front door and into the room.*)

MAX: Where's the whore? Still in bed? She'll make us all animals.

LENNY: The girl's a tease.

MAX: What?

LENNY: She's had Joey on a string.

MAX: What do you mean?

TEDDY: He had her up there for two hours and he didn't go the whole hog.

(*Pause.*)

MAX: My Joey? She did that to my boy?

(*Pause.*)

To my youngest son? Tch, tch, tch, tch. How you feeling, son? Are you all right?

JOEY: Sure I'm all right.

MAX (*to Teddy*): Does she do that to you, too?

TEDDY: No.

LENNY: He gets the gravy.

MAX: You think so?

JOEY: No he don't.

(*Pause.*)

SAM: He's her lawful husband. She's his lawful wife.

JOEY: No he don't! He don't get no gravy! I'm telling you. I'm telling all of you. I'll kill the next man who says he gets the gravy.

MAX: Joey . . . what are you getting so excited about? (*To Lenny.*) It's because he's frustrated. You see what happens?

JOEY: Who is?

MAX: Joey. No one's saying you're wrong. In fact everyone's saying you're right.

(*Pause.*)
(*Max turns to the others.*)

You know something? Perhaps it's not a bad idea to have a woman in the house. Perhaps it's a good thing. Who knows? Maybe we should keep her.

(*Pause.*)

Maybe we'll ask her if she wants to stay.

(*Pause.*)

TEDDY: I'm afraid not, Dad. She's not well, and we've got to get home to the children.

MAX: Not well? I told you, I'm used to looking after people who are not so well. Don't worry about that. Perhaps we'll keep her here.

(*Pause.*)

SAM: Don't be silly.

MAX: What's silly?

SAM: You're talking rubbish.

MAX: Me?

SAM: She's got three children.

MAX: She can have more! Here. If she's so keen.

TEDDY: She doesn't want any more.

MAX: What do you know about what she wants, eh, Ted?

TEDDY (*smiling*): The best thing for her is to come home with me, Dad. Really. We're married, you know.

(*Max walks about the room, clicks his fingers.*)

MAX: We'd have to pay her, of course. You realize that? We can't leave her walking about without any pocket money. She'll have to have a little allowance.

JOEY: Of course we'll pay her. She's got to have some money in her pocket.

MAX: That's what I'm saying. You can't expect a woman to walk about without a few bob to spend on a pair of stockings.

(*Pause.*)

LENNY: Where's the money going to come from?

MAX: Well, how much is she worth? What we talking about, three figures?

LENNY: I asked you where the money's going to come from. It'll be an extra mouth to feed. It'll be an extra body to clothe. You realize that?

JOEY: I'll buy her clothes.

LENNY: What with?

JOEY: I'll put in a certain amount out of my wages.

MAX: That's it. We'll pass the hat round. We'll make a donation. We're all grown-up people, we've got a sense of responsibility. We'll all put a little in the hat. It's democratic.

LENNY: It'll come to a few quid, Dad.

(*Pause.*)

I mean, she's not a woman who likes walking around in second-hand goods. She's up to the latest fashion. You wouldn't want her walking about in clothes which don't show her off at her best, would you?

MAX: Lenny, do you mind if I make a little comment? It's not meant to be critical. But I think you're concentrating too much on the economic considerations. There are other considerations. There are the human considerations. You understand what I mean? There are the human considerations. Don't forget them.

LENNY: I won't.

MAX: Well don't.

(*Pause.*)

Listen, we're bound to treat her in something approximating, at least, to the manner in which she's accustomed. After all, she's not someone off the street, she's my daughter-in-law!

JOEY: That's right.

MAX: There you are, you see. Joey'll donate, Sam'll donate . . . .

(*Sam looks at him.*)

I'll put in a few bob out of my pension, Lenny'll cough up. We're laughing. What about you, Ted? How much you going to put in the kitty?

TEDDY: I'm not putting anything in the kitty.

MAX: What? You won't even help to support your own wife? I thought he was a son of mine. You lousy stinkpig. Your mother would drop dead if she heard you take that attitude.

LENNY: Eh, Dad.

(*Lenny walks forward.*)

I've got a better idea.

MAX: What?

LENNY: There's no need for us to go to all this expense. I know these women. Once they get started they ruin your budget. I've got a better idea. Why don't I take her up with me to Greek Street?

(*Pause.*)

MAX: You mean put her on the game?

(*Pause.*)

We'll put her on the game. That's a stroke of genius, that's a marvelous idea. You mean she can earn the money herself—on her back?

LENNY: Yes.

MAX: Wonderful. The only thing is, it'll have to be short hours. We don't want her out of the house all night.

LENNY: I can limit the hours.

MAX: How many?

LENNY: Four hours a night.

MAX (*dubiously*): Is that enough?

LENNY: She'll bring in a good sum for four hours a night.

MAX: Well, you should know. After all, it's true, the last thing we want to do is wear the girl out. She's going to have her obligations this end as well. Where you going to put her in Greek Street?

LENNY: It doesn't have to be right in Greek Street, Dad. I've got a number of flats all around that area.

MAX: You have? Well, what about me? Why don't you give me one?

LENNY: You're sexless.

JOEY: Eh, wait a minute, what's all this?

MAX: I know what Lenny's saying. Lenny's saying she can pay her own way. What do you think, Teddy? That'll solve all our problems.

JOEY: Eh, wait a minute. I don't want to share her.

MAX: What did you say?

JOEY: I don't want to share her with a lot of yobs!

MAX: Yobs! You arrogant git! What arrogance. (*To Lenny.*) Will you be supplying her with yobs?

LENNY: I've got a very distinguished clientele, Joey. They're more distinguished than you'll ever be.

MAX: So you can count yourself lucky we're including you in.

JOEY: I didn't think I was going to have to share her!

MAX: Well, you *are* going to have to share her! Otherwise she goes straight back to America. You understand?

(*Pause.*)

It's tricky enough as it is, without you shoving your oar in. But there's something worrying me. Perhaps she's not so up to the mark. Eh? Teddy, you're the best judge. Do you think she'd be up to the mark?

(*Pause.*)

I mean what about all this teasing? Is she going to make a habit of it? That'll get us nowhere.

(*Pause.*)

TEDDY: It was just love play . . . I suppose . . . that's all I suppose it was.

MAX: Love play? Two bleeding hours? That's a bloody long time for love play!

LENNY: I don't think we've got anything to worry about on that score, Dad.

MAX: How do you know?

LENNY: I'm giving you a professional opinion.

(*Lenny goes to Teddy.*)

LENNY: Listen, Teddy, you could help us, actually. If I were to send you some cards, over to America . . . you know, very nice ones, with a name on, and a telephone number, very discreet, well, you could distribute them . . . to various parties, who might be making a trip over here. Of course, you'd get a little percentage out of it.

MAX: I mean, you needn't tell them she's your wife.

LENNY: No, we'd call her something else. Dolores, or something.

MAX: Or Spanish Jacky.

LENNY: No, you've got to be reserved about it, Dad. We could call her something nice . . . like Cynthia . . . or Gillian.

(*Pause.*)

JOEY: Gillian.

(*Pause.*)

LENNY: No, what I mean, Teddy, you must know lots of professors, heads of departments, men like that. They pop over here for a week at the Savoy, they need somewhere they can go to have a nice quiet poke. And of course you'd be in a position to give them inside information.

MAX: Sure. You can give them proper data. You know, the kind of thing she's willing to do. How far she'd be prepared to go with their little whims and fancies. Eh, Lenny? To what extent she's various. I mean if you don't know who does?

(*Pause.*)

I bet you before two months we'd have a waiting list.

LENNY: You could be our representative in the States.

MAX: Of course. We're talking in international terms! By the time we've finished Pan American'll give us a discount.

(*Pause.*)

TEDDY: She'd get old . . . very quickly.

MAX: No . . . not in this day and age! With the health service? Old! How could she get old? She'll have the time of her life.

(*Ruth comes down the stairs, dressed.*)
(*She comes into the room.*)
(*She smiles at the gathering, and sits.*)
(*Silence.*)

TEDDY: Ruth . . . the family have invited you to stay, for a little while longer. As a . . . as a kind of guest. If you like the idea I don't mind. We can manage very easily at home . . . until you come back.

RUTH: How very nice of them.

(*Pause.*)

MAX: It's an offer from our heart.

RUTH: It's very sweet of you.

MAX: Listen . . . it would be our pleasure.

(*Pause.*)

RUTH: I think I'd be too much trouble.

MAX: Trouble? What are you talking about? What trouble? Listen, I'll tell you something. Since poor Jessie died, eh, Sam? we haven't had a woman in the house. Not one. Inside this house. And I'll tell you why. Because their mother's image was so dear any other woman would have . . . tarnished it. But

you . . . Ruth . . . you're not only lovely and beautiful, but you're kin. You're kith. You belong here.

(*Pause.*)

RUTH: I'm very touched.

MAX: Of course you're touched. I'm touched.

(*Pause.*)

TEDDY: But Ruth, I should tell you . . . that you'll have to pull your weight a little, if you stay. Financially. My father isn't very well off.

RUTH (*to Max*): Oh, I'm sorry.

MAX: No, you'd just have to bring in a little, that's all. A few pennies. Nothing much. It's just that we're waiting for Joey to hit the top as a boxer. When Joey hits the top . . . well . . .

(*Pause.*)

TEDDY: Or you can come home with me.

LENNY: We'd get you a flat.

(*Pause.*)

RUTH: A flat?

LENNY: Yes.

RUTH: Where?

LENNY: In town.

(*Pause.*)

But you'd live here, with us.

MAX: Of course you would. This would be your home. In the bosom of the family.

LENNY: You'd just pop up to the flat a couple of hours a night, that's all.

Ian Hart as Lenny, Lia Williams as Ruth, and Ian Holm as Max in the Dublin Gate Theatre's 2001 production of *The Homecoming*.

Ian McShane as Max, Raul
Esparza as Lenny, Eve Best as
Ruth, and Gareth Saxe as Joey
in the 2007 Cort Theatre
production, New York.

MAX: Just a couple of hours, that's all. That's all.
LENNY: And you make enough money to keep you going here.

(*Pause.*)

RUTH: How many rooms would this flat have?
LENNY: Not many.
RUTH: I would want at least three rooms and a bathroom.
LENNY: You wouldn't need three rooms and a bathroom.
MAX: She'd need a bathroom.
LENNY: But not three rooms.

(*Pause.*)

RUTH: Oh, I would. Really.
LENNY: Two would do.
RUTH: No. Two wouldn't be enough.

(*Pause.*)

I'd want a dressing-room, a rest-room, and a bed-room.

(*Pause.*)

LENNY: All right, we'll get you a flat with three rooms and a bathroom.
RUTH: With what kind of conveniences?
LENNY: All conveniences.
RUTH: A personal maid?
LENNY: Of course.

(*Pause.*)

We'd finance you, to begin with, and then, when you were established, you could pay us back, in installments.

RUTH: Oh, no, I wouldn't agree to that.
LENNY: Oh, why not?
RUTH: You would have to regard your original outlay simply as a capital investment.

(*Pause.*)

LENNY: I see. All right.
RUTH: You'd supply my wardrobe, of course?
LENNY: We'd supply everything. Everything you need.
RUTH: I'd need an awful lot. Otherwise I wouldn't be content.
LENNY: You'd have everything.
RUTH: I would naturally want to draw up an inventory of everything I would need, which would require your signatures in the presence of witnesses.
LENNY: Naturally.
RUTH: All aspects of the agreement and conditions of employment would have to be clarified to our mutual satisfaction before we finalized the contract.
LENNY: Of course.

(*Pause.*)

RUTH: Well, it might prove a workable arrangement.
LENNY: I think so.
MAX: And you'd have the whole of your daytime free, of course. You could do a bit of cooking here if you wanted to.
LENNY: Make the beds.
MAX: Scrub the place out a bit.
TEDDY: Keep everyone company.

(*Sam comes forward.*)

SAM (*in one breath*): MacGregor had Jessie in the back of my cab as I drove them along.

(*He croaks and collapses.*)
(*He lies still.*)
(*They look at him.*)

MAX: What's he done? Dropped dead?
LENNY: Yes.
MAX: A corpse? A corpse on my floor? Get him out of here! Clear him out of here!

(*Joey bends over Sam.*)

JOEY: He's not dead.
LENNY: He probably was dead, for about thirty seconds.
MAX: He's not even dead!

(*Lenny looks down at Sam.*)

LENNY: Yes, there's still some breath there.
MAX (*pointing at Sam*): You know what that man had?
LENNY: Has.
MAX: Has! A diseased imagination.

(*Pause.*)

RUTH: Yes, it sounds a very attractive idea.
MAX: Do you want to shake on it now, or do you want to leave it till later?
RUTH: Oh, we'll leave it till later.

(*Teddy stands.*)
(*He looks down at Sam.*)

TEDDY: I was going to ask him to drive me to London Airport.

(*He goes to the cases, picks one up.*)

Well, I'll leave your case, Ruth. I'll just go up the road to the Underground.
MAX: Listen, if you go the other way, first left, first right, you remember, you might find a cab passing there.
TEDDY: Yes, I might do that.
MAX: Or you can take the tube to Piccadilly Circus, won't take you ten minutes, and pick up a cab from there out to the Airport.
TEDDY: Yes, I'll probably do that.
MAX: Mind you, they'll charge you double fare. They'll charge you for the return trip. It's over the six-mile limit.
TEDDY: Yes. Well, bye-bye, Dad. Look after yourself.

(*They shake hands.*)

MAX: Thanks, son. Listen. I want to tell you something. It's been wonderful to see you.

(*Pause.*)

TEDDY: It's been wonderful to see you.
MAX: Do your boys know about me? Eh? Would they like to see a photo, do you think, of their grandfather?
TEDDY: I know they would.

(*Max brings out his wallet.*)

MAX: I've got one on me. I've got one here. Just a minute. Here you are. Will they like that one?
TEDDY (*taking it*): They'll be thrilled.

(*He turns to Lenny.*)

Good-bye, Lenny.

(*They shake hands.*)

LENNY: Ta-ta, Ted. Good to see you. Have a good trip.
TEDDY: Bye-bye, Joey.

(*Joey does not move.*)

JOEY: Ta-ta.

(*Teddy goes to the front door.*)

RUTH: Eddie.

(*Teddy turns.*)
(*Pause.*)

Don't become a stranger.

(*Teddy goes, shuts the front door.*)
(*Silence.*)
(*The three men stand.*)
(*Ruth sits relaxed in her chair.*)
(*Sam lies still.*)
(*Joey walks slowly across the room.*)
(*He kneels at her chair.*)
(*She touches his head, lightly.*)
(*He puts his head in her lap.*)
(*Max begins to move above them, backwards and forwards.*)
(*Lenny stands still.*)
(*Max turns to Lenny.*)

MAX: I'm too old, I suppose. She thinks I'm an old man.

(*Pause.*)

I'm not such an old man.

(*Pause.*)

(*To Ruth.*) You think I'm too old for you?

(*Pause.*)

Listen. You think you're just going to get that big slag all the time? You think you're just going to have him ... you're going to just have him all the time? You're going to have to work! You'll have to take them on, you understand?

(*Pause.*)

Does she realize that?

(*Pause.*)

Lenny, do you think she understands ...

(*He begins to stammer.*)

What ... what ... what ... we're getting at? What ... we've got in mind? Do you think she's got it clear?

(*Pause.*)

I don't think she's got it clear.

(*Pause.*)

You understand what I mean? Listen, I've got a funny idea she'll do the dirty on us, you want to bet? She'll use us, she'll make use of us, I can tell you! I can smell it! You want to bet?

(*Pause.*)

She won't ... be adaptable!

(*He falls to his knees, whimpers, begins to moan and sob.*)
(*He stops sobbing, crawls past Sam's body round her chair, to the other side of her.*)

I'm not an old man.

(*He looks up at her.*)

Do you hear me?

(*He raises his face to her.*)

Kiss me.

(*She continues to touch Joey's head, lightly.*)
(*Lenny stands, watching.*)

Curtain

María Irene Fornés

Born in Havana, Cuba, in 1930, Fornés was fifteen when she arrived in the United States. Originally a painter and a designer of textiles, Fornés was encouraged to begin writing and become a playwright when she lived with the critic Susan Sontag. Fornés has won six Obies for her plays in off-Broadway theaters. Despite her fame and status as a cult figure among women's groups, she has yet to achieve a major position in contemporary theater comparable to, say, that of August Wilson, because most of her work remains experimental and outside the mainstream of popular theater.

Fornés's first success was *Promenade* (1965), a musical that garnered her the first of her nine Obie awards. The play was described by reviewer Phyllis Mael as a zany satire focusing on "unrequited love, the abuse of power, the injustice of those who are supposed to uphold the law, and the illogical and random nature of life." The play, like many of Fornés's pieces, lacks a standard plot and therefore has been criticized for having a "thin" story line. But *New York Times* critic Clive Barnes asserted that there would be many in the audience who would "glory in the show's dexterity, wit and compassion."

Fefu and Her Friends (1977) was the first of Fornés's works to find a major audience. Between these two plays, Fornés worked steadily, producing plays in the Judson Poets' Theatre, at La Mama Experimental Theatre in New York, and in theaters in London, Havana, and San Francisco. *Fefu* is a feminist play that has no definite plot line, but it does have a mordant humor and a relentless pace. It is structured in short, intense scenes, moving from indoor to outdoor locations, with a second act that takes place in four different places simultaneously. In production the audience moves physically to each of these locations to watch the scenes. The effect is unsettling on the one hand, but expansive on the other. The play's focus is on the uneven treatment of women in a society dominated by men. The play has a cartoonlike quality but also a seriousness that may make some in the audience uncomfortable.

Mud (1983), produced at the Padua Hills Festival in Claremont, California, focuses on a domestic triangle with an abused woman. It is a dark, unsettling play, with a violent ending involving a gun. Fornés makes use of guns in many of her plays, including *Fefu*; some critics see the gun as an important emblem in her work. Among her later plays are *The Trial of Joan of Arc on a Matter of Faith* (1986), *The Mothers* (1986), *Abingdon Square* (1987), and *And What of the Night?* (1990).

The renowned Signature Theatre in New York devoted its entire 1999–2000 season to Fornés's work. Included were productions of *Mud*; *Drowning* (1983), based on a Chekhov story; *Enter the Night* (1999), about a man who fears he has given his lover AIDS; and the world premiere of *Letters from Cuba* (2000), for which Fornés won an Obie award. She based this play on some 200 letters she had received from her older brother Rafael, who remained in Cuba when the rest of the family came to the United States.

While Fornés has never been a mainstream playwright, her influence has been pervasive. As playwright Lanford Wilson said, "She's one of the very, very best. Expect the unexpected. She's the most original of us all."

Fefu and Her Friends

The play begins with Fefu, Stephany Beckmann, gathering a group of women to her house in New England to prepare for a charity event aimed at reforms in art and education. In 1977, when the play was written and first produced, the feminist movement was central in importance to the author and audience, but the time of the play, 1935, is distinctly prior to any thoughts of feminist independence. Indeed, while Fefu's husband Phillip is only alluded to, his influence is heavy. The gun that Fefu fires in Part I is used in a game that Phillip and Fefu play, and the threat is that Phillip may one day put a real bullet in the chamber. Moreover, much of the women's early conversation centers on men and, by implication, on their dominance.

In Part I Fefu delivers a long speech praising the camaraderie of men: "They are well together. Women are not." She tells Christina and Cindy that she likes "men better than women.—I envy them." In a later section of the play, Fornés discusses the women's sense of inadequacy, inculcated by masculine dominance. To an extent, this idea is revealed in Julia's paralysis and her hallucinatory experiences. The references to hallucinations and to dreams imply an awareness of the influence of psychiatry and Sigmund Freud, whose theories of the unconscious and the significance of dreams were powerful in the 1930s. Freudian psychology focused on sexual issues, especially the repression of sexual desire.

The first part of the play, essentially the first act, takes place in the morning and is devoted to introducing the women: Cindy, Christina, Julia, Emma, Paula, Sue, and Cecilia. Fefu explains her game of shooting at her husband when he comes home, and how he falls, pretending to die. The women find it very odd, especially when they realize that someday the gun might not be loaded with blanks. Fefu discourses on men and fixes her toilet—implying that she understands plumbing and is self-sufficient. Julia's psychosomatic injury, resulting from a hunting accident, has put her in a wheelchair, and Emma goes for a ride on her lap, as if she does not believe Julia is handicapped.

Part II, set in the afternoon, experiments by separating the space in which the actors engage the audience into four settings: the lawn, the study, the bedroom, and the kitchen. The audience itself must split up and move to each setting, much like the audiences in some medieval Corpus Christi plays. In the first setting, "On the Lawn," Emma and Fefu discuss genitals and sexuality in relation to the rewards in the after-life: "it's the angels who judge our sexual life." The scene ends with a soliloquy by Emma, who recites Shakespeare's Sonnet 14. (This and other references led critic Lynn Trenning to refer to the play as "Chickspeare" because it is heavy on ideas and has a passing resemblance to *Love's Labors Lost*.) In the study, Cindy and Christina discuss Cindy's frightening dream about men trying to kill her, while Fefu looks in and suggests a game of croquet. In the bedroom, Julia hallucinates violently, seemingly slapped repeatedly by an invisible hand. All the while, she discusses gender issues, stating, "The human being is of the masculine gender." In the kitchen, Sue and Paula decide that "A love affair lasts seven years and three months." Their discussion soon reveals that they were lovers once, but "Now we look at each other as strangers."

In Part III, set in the evening, the women gather to practice speeches suggesting reforms in education to an unnamed public group. Emma has the most powerful speech, taken literally from the Prologue to Emma Sheridan Fry's *Educational Dramatics,* published in 1917. The essence of her speech is that "Society restricts us" and that school and civilization, poverty and wealth, all hinder our development as individuals; social institutions stifle our sensory world and force women to repress natural desires and natural responses. Emma urges a reunion with the environment, the surrounding world that speaks directly to our senses. As an illustration of natural desires, the women, filled with enthusiasm for their sense of community, engage in an all-out water fight, laughing and running about and providing a bit of comic relief. But that relief is short-lived because Julia delivers a long speech in which she says, "I feel we are constantly threatened by death." Then a Freudian note is introduced with the example of the student, Gloria Schuman, who was so brilliant the faculty refused to believe she did her own work and demanded she see a psychiatrist who "almost drove her crazy."

The play is not realistic, despite its social commentary, and it is not clearly allegorical. The notes to the Red Rabbit Theatre Company's production in Kensington, Perth, Australia, in 2011 include this comment: "It is a work which cannot be categorized. It revels in the theatre of the absurd, slap stick, surrealism, and dealing in themes which include self-discovery, alienation, miscommunication, self-revelation, fear and loathing." Fornés's early experiences in the theater included Ibsenist realism and Beckettian absurdism. *Fefu and Her Friends* portrays powerful women, but in absurdist fashion, which is why the play has both baffled and excited many audiences and readers.

For discussion questions and assignments on *Fefu and Her Friends,* visit **bedfordstmartins.com/jacobus.**

Fefu and Her Friends in Performance

Fefu and Her Friends was first produced by the New York Theatre Strategy at the Relativity Media Lab in 1977, with the author directing. It was produced by the American Place Theatre in New York in 1978, when Fornés won the Obie for best off-Broadway show. Since then it has been produced frequently, both in professional theaters and in university and college theaters in the United States and abroad. Rhonda Gelfand's Los Angeles Theatre Collective production in 1989 prompted reviewer Robert Koehler to suggest a connection to Pirandello. One of the most lavish productions was given by the Yale Repertory Theatre in New Haven, featuring Julianna Margulies, in 1992. Reviews praised the production but seemed uncertain about the play's significance. Krissy Smith directed the play at the Off-Tryon Theatre in Charlotte, North Carolina, in 2001, and Christopher Scully directed the Industrial Theatre production at the Old Leverett Library in 2002 in Cambridge, Massachusetts. Reviewers in both cases found the play difficult to understand. Jillian Johnson directed the 2010 Center for Performance Research production in Brooklyn, New York.

MARÍA IRENE FORNÉS (b. 1930)

Fefu and Her Friends   1977

Author's Note: Fefu is pronounced Feh-foo.

Original cast:

FEFU
CINDY
CHRISTINA
JULIA
EMMA
PAULA
SUE
CECILIA

New England, Spring 1935.

Part I: Noon. The living room. The entire audience watches from the main auditorium.

Part II: Afternoon. The lawn, the study, the bedroom, the kitchen. The audience is divided into four groups. Each group is led to the spaces. These scenes are performed simultaneously. When the scenes are completed the audience moves to the next space and the scenes are performed again. This is repeated four times until each group has seen all four scenes. Then the audience is led back to the main auditorium.

Part III: Evening. The living room. The entire audience watches from the main auditorium.

PART I

(The living room of a country house in New England. The decor is a tasteful mixture of styles. To the right is the foyer and the main door. To the left, French doors leading to a terrace, the lawn and a pond. At the rear, there are stairs that lead to the upper floor, the entrance to the kitchen, and the entrance to other rooms on the ground floor. A couch faces the audience. There is a coffee table, two chairs on each side of the table. Upstage right there is a piano. Against the right wall there is an open liquor cabinet. Besides bottles of liquor there are glasses, an ice bucket, and a seltzer bottle. A double barrel shotgun leans on the wall near the French doors. On the table there is a dish with chocolates. On the couch there is a throw. Fefu stands on the landing. Cindy lies on the couch. Christina sits on the chair to the right.)

FEFU: My husband married me to have a constant reminder of how loathsome women are.

CINDY: What?

FEFU: Yup.

CINDY: That's just awful.

FEFU: No, it isn't.

CINDY: It isn't awful?

FEFU: No.

CINDY: I don't think anyone would marry for that reason.

FEFU: He did.

CINDY: Did he say so?

FEFU: He tells me constantly.

CINDY: Oh, dear.

FEFU: I don't mind. I laugh when he tells me.

CINDY: You laugh?

FEFU: I do.

CINDY: How can you?

FEFU: It's funny.—And it's true. That's why I laugh.

CINDY: What is true?

FEFU: That women are loathsome.

CINDY: . . . Fefu!

FEFU: That shocks you.

CINDY: It does. I don't feel loathsome.

FEFU: I don't mean that you are loathsome.

CINDY: You don't mean that I'm loathsome.

FEFU: No . . . It's something to think about. It's a thought.

CINDY: It's a hideous thought.

FEFU: I take it all back.

CINDY: Isn't she incredible?

FEFU: Cindy, I'm not talking about anyone in particular. It's something to think about.

CINDY: No one in particular, just women.

FEFU: Yes.

CINDY: In that case I am relieved. I thought you were referring to us.

FEFU: *(Affectionately.)* You are being stupid.

CINDY: Stupid and loathsome. *(To Christina.)* Have you ever heard anything so outrageous.

CHRISTINA: I am speechless.

FEFU: Why are you speechless?

CHRISTINA: I think you are outrageous.

FEFU: Don't be offended. I don't take enough care to be tactful. I know I don't. But don't be offended. Cindy is not offended. She pretends to be, but she isn't really. She understands what I mean.

CINDY: I do not.

FEFU: Yes, you do.—I like exciting ideas. They give me energy.

CHRISTINA: And how is women being loathsome an exciting idea?

FEFU: *(With mischief.)* It revolts me.

CHRISTINA: You find revulsion exciting?

FEFU: Don't you?

CHRISTINA: No.

FEFU: I do. It's something to grapple with.—What do you do with revulsion?

CHRISTINA: I avoid anything that's revolting to me.

FEFU: Hmmm. (*To Cindy.*) You too?

CINDY: Yes.

FEFU: Hmm. Have you ever turned a stone over in damp soil?

CHRISTINA: Ahm.

FEFU: And when you turn it there are worms crawling on it?

CHRISTINA: Ahm.

FEFU: And it's damp and full of fungus?

CHRISTINA: Ahm.

FEFU: Were you revolted?

CHRISTINA: Yes.

FEFU: Were you fascinated?

CHRISTINA: I was.

FEFU: There you have it! You too are fascinated with revulsion.

CHRISTINA: Hmm.

FEFU: You see, that which is exposed to the exterior . . . is smooth and dry and clean. That which is not . . . underneath, is slimy and filled with fungus and crawling with worms. It is another life that is parallel to the one we manifest. It's there. The way worms are underneath the stone. If you don't recognize it . . . (*Whispering.*) it eats you. That is my opinion. Well, who is ready for lunch?

CINDY: I'll have some fried worms with lots of pepper.

FEFU: (*To Christina.*) You?

CHRISTINA: I'll have mine in a sandwich with mayonnaise.

FEFU: And to drink?

CHRISTINA: Just some dirty dishwater in a tall glass with ice.

(*Fefu looks at Cindy.*)

CINDY: That sounds fine.

FEFU: I'll go dig them up. (*Fefu walks to the French doors. Beckoning Christina.*) Pst! (*Fefu gets the gun as Christina goes to the French doors.*) You haven't met Phillip. Have you?

CHRISTINA: No.

FEFU: That's him.

CHRISTINA: Which one?

FEFU: (*Aims and shoots.*) That one!

(*Christina and Cindy scream. Fefu smiles proudly. She blows on the mouth of the barrel. She puts down the gun and looks out again.*)

CINDY: Christ, Fefu.

FEFU: There he goes. He's up. It's a game we play. I shoot and he falls. Whenever he hears the blast he falls. No matter where he is, he falls. One time he fell in a puddle of mud and his clothes were a mess. (*She looks out.*) It's not too bad. He's just dusting off some stuff. (*She waves to Phillip and starts to go upstairs.*) He's all right. Look.

CINDY: A drink?

CHRISTINA: Yes.

(*Cindy goes to the liquor cabinet.*)

CINDY: What would you like?

CHRISTINA: Bourbon and soda . . . (*Cindy puts ice and bourbon in a glass. As she starts to squirt the soda . . .*) lots of soda. Just soda. (*Cindy starts with a fresh glass. She starts to squirt soda just as Christina speaks.*) Wait. (*Cindy stops squirting, but not soon enough.*) I'll have an ice cube with a few drops of bourbon. (*Cindy starts with a fresh glass.*)

CINDY: One or two ice cubes?

CHRISTINA: One. Something to suck on.

CINDY: She's unique. There's no one like her.

CHRISTINA: Thank God.

(*Cindy gives the drink to Christina.*)

CINDY: But she is lovely you know. She really is.

CHRISTINA: She's crazy.

CINDY: A little. She has a strange marriage.

CHRISTINA: Strange? It's revolting.—What is he like?

CINDY: He's crazy too. They drive each other crazy. They are not crazy really. They drive each other crazy.

CHRISTINA: Why do they stay together?

CINDY: They love each other.

CHRISTINA: Love?

CINDY: It's love.

CHRISTINA: Who are the other two men?

CINDY: Fefu's younger brother, John. And the gardener. His name is Tom.—The gun is not loaded.

CHRISTINA: How do you know?

CINDY: It's not. Why should it be loaded?

CHRISTINA: It seemed to be loaded a moment ago.

CINDY: That was just a blank.

CHRISTINA: It sounded like a cannon shot.

CINDY: That was just gun powder. There's no bullet in a blank.

CHRISTINA: The blast alone could kill you. One can die of fright, you know.

CINDY: True.

CHRISTINA: My heart is still beating.

CINDY: That's just fright. You're being a scaredy cat.

CHRISTINA: Of course it's just fright. It's fright.

CINDY: I mean, you were just scared. You didn't get hurt.

CHRISTINA: Just scared. I guess I was lucky I didn't get shot.

CINDY: Fefu won't shoot you. She only shoots Phillip.

CHRISTINA: That's nice of her. Put the gun away, I don't like looking at it.

FEFU: (*As she appears on the landing.*) I just fixed the toilet in your bathroom.

CINDY: You did?

FEFU: I did. The water stopper didn't work. It drained. I adjusted it. I'm waiting for the tank to fill up. Make sure it all works.

CHRISTINA: You do your own plumbing?

FEFU: I just had to bend the metal that supports the rubber stopper so it falls right over the hole. What happened was it fell to the side so the water wouldn't stop running into the bowl. (*Fefu sits near Cindy.*)

He scared me this time, you know. He looked like he was really hurt.

CINDY: I thought the guns were not loaded.

FEFU: I'm never sure.

CHRISTINA: What?

CINDY: Fefu, what do you mean?

FEFU: He told me one day he'll put real bullets in the guns. He likes to make me nervous. (*There is a moment's silence.*) I have upset you . . . I don't mean to upset you. That's the way we are with each other. We always go to extremes but it's not anything to be upset about.

CHRISTINA: You scare me.

FEFU: That's all right. I scare myself too, sometimes. But there's nothing wrong with being scared . . . it makes you stronger.—It does me.—He won't put real bullets in the guns.—It suits our relationship . . . the game, I mean. If I didn't shoot him with blanks, I might shoot him for real. Do you see the sense of it?

CHRISTINA: I think you're crazy.

FEFU: I'm not. I'm sane.

CHRISTINA: (*Gently.*) You're very stupid.

FEFU: I'm not. I'm very bright.

CHRISTINA: (*Gently.*) You depress me.

FEFU: Don't be depressed. Laugh at me if you don't agree with me. Say I'm ridiculous. I know I'm ridiculous. Come on, laugh. I hate to think I'm depressing to you.

CHRISTINA: All right. I'll laugh.

FEFU: I'll make you a drink.

CHRISTINA: No, I'm just sucking on the ice.

FEFU: Don't you feel well?

CHRISTINA: I'm all right.

FEFU: What are you drinking?

CHRISTINA: Bourbon.

FEFU: (*Getting Christina's glass and going to the liquor cabinet.*) Would you like some more? I'll get you some.

CHRISTINA: Just a drop.

FEFU: (*With great care pours a single drop of bourbon on the ice cube.*) Like that?

CHRISTINA: Yes, thank you.

FEFU: (*Gives Christina the drink and watches her put the cube to her lips.*) That's the cutest thing I've ever seen. It's cold. (*Christina nods.*) You need a stick in the ice, like a popsicle stick. You hold the stick and your fingers won't get cold. I have some sticks. I'll do some for you.

CHRISTINA: Don't trouble yourself.

FEFU: It won't be any trouble. You might want some later.—I'm strange, Christina. But I am fortunate in that I don't mind being strange. It's hard on others sometimes. But not that hard. Is it, Cindy? Those who love me, love me precisely because I am the way I am. (*To Cindy.*) Isn't that so? (*Cindy smiles and nods.*)

CINDY: I would love you even if you weren't the way you are.

FEFU: You wouldn't know it was me if I weren't the way I am.

CINDY: I would still know it was you underneath.

FEFU: (*To Christina.*) You see?—There are some good things about me.—I'm never angry, for example.

CHRISTINA: But you make everyone else angry.

(*Fefu thinks a moment.*)

FEFU: No.

CHRISTINA: You've made me furious.

FEFU: I know. And I might make you angry again. Still I would like it if you liked me.—You think it's unlikely.

CHRISTINA: I don't know.

FEFU: . . . We'll see. (*Fefu goes to the doors. She stands there briefly and speaks reflectively.*) I still like men better than women.—I envy them. I like being like a man. Thinking like a man. Feeling like a man.—They are well together. Women are not. Look at them. They are checking the new grass mower. . . . Out in the fresh air and the sun, while we sit here in the dark. . . . Men have natural strength. Women have to find their strength, and when they do find it, it comes forth with bitterness and it's erratic. . . . Women are restless with each other. They are like live wires . . . either chattering to keep themselves from making contact, or else, if they don't chatter, they avert their eyes . . . like Orpheus° . . . as if a god once said "and if they shall recognize each other, the world will be blown apart." They are always eager for the men to arrive. When they do, they can put themselves at rest, tranquilized and in a mild stupor. With the men they feel safe. The danger is gone. That's the closest they can be to feeling wholesome. Men are muscle that cover the raw nerve. They are the insulators. The danger is gone, but the price is the mind and the spirit. . . . High price.—I've never understood it. Why?—What is feared?—Hmm. Well . . .—Do you know? Perhaps the heavens would fall.—Have I offended you again?

CHRISTINA: No. I too have wished for that trust men have for each other. The faith the world puts in them and they in turn put in the world. I know I don't have it.

FEFU: Hmm. Well, I have to see how my toilet is doing. (*Fefu goes to the landing and exits. She puts her head out. She smiles.*) Plumbing is more important than you think.

(*Christina falls off her chair in a mock faint. Cindy goes to her.*)

CINDY: What do you think?

CHRISTINA: Think? I hurt. I'm all shreds inside.

CINDY: Anything I can do?

CHRISTINA: Sing.

(*Cindy sings "Winter Wonderland." Christina harmonizes. There is the sound of a horn. Fefu enters.*)

Orpheus: In Greek myth, Orpheus descended into the underworld to rescue Eurydice but lost her when he ignored Pluto's warning and turned back to look at her.

FEFU: It's Julia. (*To Christina, who is on the floor.*) Are you all right?

CHRISTINA: Yes. (*Fefu exits through the foyer.*) Darn it! (*Christina starts to stand.*)

FEFU: (*Off-stage.*) Julia . . . let me help you.

JULIA: I can manage. I'm much stronger now.

FEFU: There you go.

JULIA: You have my bag.

FEFU: Yes.

(*Julia and Fefu enter. Julia is in a wheelchair.*)

JULIA: Hello Cindy.

CINDY: Hello darling. How are you?

JULIA: I'm very well now. I'm driving now. You must see my car. It's very clever the way they worked it all out. You might want to drive it. It's not hard at all. (*Turning to Christina.*) Christina.

CHRISTINA: Hello Julia.

JULIA: I'm glad to see you.

FEFU: I'll take this to your room. You're down here, if you want to wash up.

(*Fefu exits through the upstage exit. Julia follows her.*)

CINDY: I can't get used to it.

CHRISTINA: She's better. Isn't she?

CINDY: Not really.

CHRISTINA: Was she actually hit by the bullet?

CINDY: No . . . I was with her.

CHRISTINA: I know.

CINDY: I thought the bullet hit her, but it didn't.—How do you know if a person is hit by a bullet?

CHRISTINA: Cindy . . . there's a wound and . . . there's a bullet.

CINDY: Well, the hunter aimed . . . at the deer. He shot.

CHRISTINA: He?

CINDY: Yes.

CHRISTINA: (*Pointing in the direction of Fefu.*) It wasn't . . . ?

CINDY: Fefu? . . . No. She wasn't even there. She used to hunt but she doesn't hunt any more. She loves animals.

CHRISTINA: Go on.

CINDY: He shot. Julia and the deer fell. The deer was dead . . . dying. Julia was unconscious. She had convulsions . . . like the deer. He died and she didn't. I screamed for help and the hunter came and examined Julia. He said, "She is not hurt." Julia's forehead was bleeding. He said, "It is a surface wound. I didn't hurt her." I know it wasn't he who hurt her. It was someone else. He went for help and Julia started talking. She was delirious.—Apparently there was a spinal nerve injury. She hit her head and she suffered a concussion. She blanks out and that is caused by the blow on the head. It's a scar in the brain. It's called the petit mal.

(*Fefu enters.*)

CHRISTINA: What was it she said?

CINDY: Hmm? . . .

CHRISTINA: When she was delirious.

CINDY: When she was delirious? That she was persecuted.— That they tortured her. . . . That they had tried her and that the shot was her execution. That she recanted because she wanted to live. . . . That if she talked about it . . . to anyone . . . she would be tortured further and killed. And I have not mentioned this before because . . . I fear for her.

CHRISTINA: It doesn't make any sense, Cindy.

CINDY: It makes sense to me. You heard? (*Fefu goes to Cindy and holds her.*)

FEFU: Who hurt her?

CINDY: I don't know.

FEFU: (*To Christina.*) Did you know her?

CHRISTINA: I met her once years ago.

FEFU: You remember her then as she was. . . . She was afraid of nothing. . . . Have you ever met anyone like that? . . . She knew so much. She was so young and yet she knew so much. . . . How did she learn all that? . . . (*To Cindy.*) Did you ever wonder? Well, I still haven't checked my toilet. Can you believe that. I still haven't checked it. (*Fefu goes upstairs.*)

CHRISTINA: How long ago was the accident?

CINDY: A year . . . a little over a year.

CHRISTINA: Is she in pain?

CINDY: I don't think so.

CHRISTINA: We are made of putty. Aren't we?

(*There is the sound of a car. Car doors opening and closing. A house window opening.*)

FEFU: (*Off-stage.*) Emma! What is that you're wearing. You look marvelous.

EMMA: (*Off-stage.*) I got it in Turkey.

FEFU: Hi Paula, Sue.

PAULA: Hi.

SUE: Hi.

(*Cindy goes out to greet them. Julia enters. She wheels herself to the downstage area.*)

FEFU: I'll be right down! Hey, my toilet works.

EMMA: Stephany. Mine does too.

FEFU: Don't be funny.

EMMA: Come down.

(*Fefu enters as Emma, Sue, and Paula enter. Emma and Fefu embrace.*)

FEFU: How are you?

EMMA: Good . . . good . . . good . . . (*Still embracing Fefu, Emma sees Julia.*) Julia! (*She runs to Julia and sits on her lap.*)

FEFU: Emma!

JULIA: It's all right.

EMMA: Take me for a ride. (*Julia wheels the chair in a circle. Emma waves as they ride.*) Hi, Cindy, Paula, Sue, Fefu.

JULIA: Do you know Christina?

EMMA: How do you do.

CHRISTINA: How do you do.

EMMA: (*Pointing.*) Sue . . . Paula . . .

SUE: Hello.

PAULA: Hello.

CHRISTINA: Hello.

PAULA: (*To Fefu.*) I liked your talk at Flossie Crit.

FEFU: Oh god, don't remind me. I thought I was awful. Come, I'll show you your rooms. (*She starts to go up.*)

PAULA: I thought you weren't. I found it very stimulating.

EMMA: When was that? . . . What was it on?

FEFU: Aviation.

PAULA: It wasn't on aviation. It was on Voltairine de Cleyre.°

JULIA: I wish I had known.

FEFU: It wasn't important.

JULIA: I would have gone, Fefu.

FEFU: Really, it wasn't worth the trouble.

EMMA: Now you'll have to tell Julia and me all about Voltairine de Cleyre.

FEFU: You know all about Voltairine de Cleyre.

EMMA: I don't.

FEFU: I'll tell you at lunch.

EMMA: I had lunch.

JULIA: You can sit and listen while we eat.

EMMA: I will. When do we start our meeting?

FEFU: After lunch. We'll have something to eat and then we'll have our meeting. Who's ready for lunch?

(*The following lines are said almost simultaneously.*)

CINDY: I am.

JULIA: I'm not really hungry.

CHRISTINA: I could eat now.

PAULA: I'm ready.

SUE: I'd rather wait.

EMMA: I'll have coffee.

FEFU: . . . Well . . . we'll take a vote later.

CINDY: What are we doing exactly?

FEFU: About lunch?

CINDY: That too, but I meant the agenda.

SUE: Well, I thought we should first discuss what each of us is going to talk about, so we don't duplicate what someone else is saying, and then we have a review of it, a sort of rehearsal, so we know in what order we should speak and how long it's going to take.

EMMA: We should do a rehearsal in costume. What color should each wear. It matters. Do you know what you're wearing?

PAULA: I haven't thought about it. What color should I wear?

EMMA: Red.

PAULA: Red!

EMMA: Cherry red or white.

SUE: And I?

EMMA: Dark green.

CINDY: The treasurer should wear green.

EMMA: It suits her too.

SUE: And then we'll speak in order of color.

EMMA: Right. Who else wants to know? (*Cindy and Julia raise their hands. To Cindy.*) For you lavender. (*To

Voltairine de Cleyre: A prominent American anarchist (1866–1912) who began as an individualist but became a communitarian.

Julia.) Purpurra. (*Fefu raises her hand.*) For you, all the gold in Persia.

FEFU: There is no gold in Persia.

EMMA: In Peru. I brought my costume. I'll put it on later.

FEFU: You're not in costume?

EMMA: No. This is just a dress. My costume is . . . dramatic. I won't tell you any more about it. You'll see it.

SUE: I had no idea we were going to do theatre.

EMMA: Life is theatre. Theatre is life. If we're showing what life is, can be, we must do theatre.

SUE: Will I have to act?

EMMA: It's not acting. It's being. It's springing forth with the powers of the spirit. It's breathing.

JULIA: I'll do a dance.

EMMA: I'll stage a dance for you.

JULIA: Sitting?

EMMA: On a settee.

JULIA: I'm game.

EMMA: (*Takes a deep breath and walks through the French doors.*) Phillip! What are you doing?— Hello.—Hello, John.—What? I'm staging a dance for Julia!

FEFU: We'll never see her again.—Come.

(*Fefu, Paula, and Sue go upstairs. Julia goes to the gun, takes it and smells the mouth of the barrel. She looks at Cindy.*)

CINDY: It's a blank.

(*Julia takes the remaining slug out of the gun. She lets it fall on the floor.*)

JULIA: She's hurting herself. (*Julia looks blank and is motionless. Cindy picks up the slug. She notices Julia's condition.*)

CINDY: Julia. (*To Christina.*) She's absent.

CHRISTINA: What do we do?

CINDY: Nothing, she'll be all right in a moment. (*She takes the gun from Julia. Julia comes to.*)

JULIA: It's a blank . . .

CINDY: It is.

JULIA: She's hurting herself. (*Julia lets out a strange whimper. She goes to the coffee table, takes a piece of chocolate, puts it in her mouth and goes toward her room. After she crosses the threshold, she stops.*) I must lie down a while.

CINDY: Call me if you need anything.

JULIA: I will. (*She exits. Cindy tries to put the slug in the rifle. There is the sound of a car, a car door opening, closing.*)

CINDY: Do you know how to do this?

CHRISTINA: Of course not.

(*Cindy succeeds in putting the slug in the gun. Cecilia stands in the threshold of the foyer.*)

CECILIA: I am Cecilia Johnson. Do I have the right place?

CINDY: Yes.

(*Cindy locks the gun. Lights fade all around Cecilia. Only her head is lit. The light fades.*)

PART II • On the Lawn

(*There is a bench or a tree stump. Fefu and Emma bring boxes of potatoes, carrots, beets, winter squash, and other vegetables from a root cellar and put them in a small wagon. Fefu wears a hat and gardening gloves.*)

EMMA: (*Re-enters carrying a box as Fefu exits.*) Do you think about genitals all the time?

FEFU: Genitals? No, I don't think about genitals all the time.

EMMA: (*Starting to exit.*) I do, and it drives me crazy. Each person I see in the street, anywhere at all . . . I keep thinking of their genitals, what they look like, what position they are in. I think it's odd that everyone has them. Don't you?

FEFU: (*Crossing Emma.*) No, I think it'd be odder if they didn't have them.

(*Emma laughs. Fefu re-enters.*)

EMMA: I mean, people act as if they don't have genitals.

FEFU: How do people with genitals act?

EMMA: I mean, how can business men and women stand in a room and discuss business without even one reference to their genitals. I mean everybody has them. They just pretend they don't.

FEFU: I see. (*Shifting her glance from left to right with a fiendish look.*) You mean they should do this all the time.

(*Emma laughs.*)

EMMA: No, I don't mean that. Think of it. Don't you think I'm right?

FEFU: Yes, I think you're right. (*Fefu sits.*) Oh, Emma, EmmaEmmaEmma.

EMMA: That's m'name.—Well, you see, it's generally believed that you go to heaven if you are good. If you are bad you go to hell. That is correct. However, in heaven they don't judge goodness the way we think. They don't. They have a divine registry of sexual performance. In that registry they mark down every little sexual activity in your life. If your faith is not entirely in it, if you just perform as an obligation and you don't feel the most profound devotion, if your spirit, your heart, and your flesh is not religiously delivered to it, you are condemned. They put you down in the black list and you don't go to heaven. Heaven is populated with divine lovers. And in hell live the duds.

FEFU: That's probably true.

EMMA: I knew you'd see it that way.

FEFU: Oh, I do. I do. You see, on earth we are judged by public acts, and sex is a private act. The partner cannot be said to be the public, since both partners are engaged. So naturally, it stands to reason that it's angels who judge our sexual life.

EMMA: Naturally.

(*Pause.*)

FEFU: You always bring joy to me.

EMMA: Thank you.

FEFU: I thank you. (*Fefu becomes distressed. She sits.*) I am in constant pain. I don't want to give in to it. If I do I am afraid I will never recover. . . . It's not physical, and it's not sorrow. It's very strange Emma, I can't describe it, and it's very frightening. . . . It is as if normally there is a lubricant . . . not in the body . . . a spiritual lubricant . . . it's hard to describe . . . and without it, life is a nightmare, and everything is distorted.—A black cat started coming to my kitchen. He's awfully mangled and big. He is missing an eye and his skin is diseased. At first I was repelled by him, but then, I thought, this is a monster that has been sent to me and I must feed him. And I fed him. One day he came and shat all over my kitchen. Foul diarrhea. He still comes and I still feed him.—I am afraid of him. (*Emma kisses Fefu.*) How about a little lemonade?

EMMA: Yes.

FEFU: How about a game of croquet?

EMMA: Fine.

(*Fefu exits. Emma improvises an effigy of Fefu. She puts Fefu's hat and gloves on it.*)

> Not from the stars do I my judgment pluck.
> And yet methinks I have astronomy;
> But not to tell of good or evil luck,
> Of plagues, of dearths, or seasons' quality;
> Nor can I fortune to brief minutes tell,
> Pointing to each his thunder, rain, and wind,
> Or say with princes if it shall go well
> By oft predict that I in heaven find.
> But from thine eyes my knowledge I derive.
> And, constant stars, in them I read such art
> As truth and beauty shall together thrive
> If from thyself to store thou wouldst convert:
> > Or else of thee this I prognosticate,
> > Thy end is truth's and beauty's doom and date.

(*If Fefu's entrance is delayed, Emma will sing a popular song of the period. Fefu re-enters with a pitcher and two glasses.*)

In the Study

(*There are books on the walls, a desk, Victorian chairs, a rug on the floor. Christina sits behind the desk. She reads a French text book. She mumbles French sentences. Cindy sits to the left of the desk with her feet up on a chair. She looks at a magazine. A few moments pass.*)

CHRISTINA: (*Practicing.*) Etes-vous externe ou demi-pensionnaire?° La cuisine de votre cantine est-elle bonne, passable ou mauvaise? (*She continues reading almost inaudibly. A moment passes.*)

Etes-vous . . . : These are expressions from a French language textbook. "Do you go home for lunch or have lunch at school?" "Is the food in your cafeteria good, mediocre, or bad?" "Does your teacher often question the students?"

CINDY: (*Reading.*) A lady in Africa divorced her husband because he was a cheetah.

CHRISTINA: Oh, dear. (*They laugh. They go back to their reading. A moment passes.*) Est-ce que votre professeur interroge souvent les eleves? (*They go back to their reading. A moment passes.*)

CINDY: I suppose . . . when a person is swept off their feet . . . the feet remain and the person goes off . . . with the broom.

CHRISTINA: No . . . when a person is swept off their feet . . . there is no broom.

CINDY: What does the sweeping?

CHRISTINA: An emotion . . . a feeling.

CINDY: Then emotions have bristles?

CHRISTINA: Yes.

CINDY: Now I understand. Do the feet remain?

CHRISTINA: No, the feet fly also . . . but separate from the body. At the end of the leap, just before the landing, they join the ankles and one is complete again.

CINDY: Oh, that sounds nice.

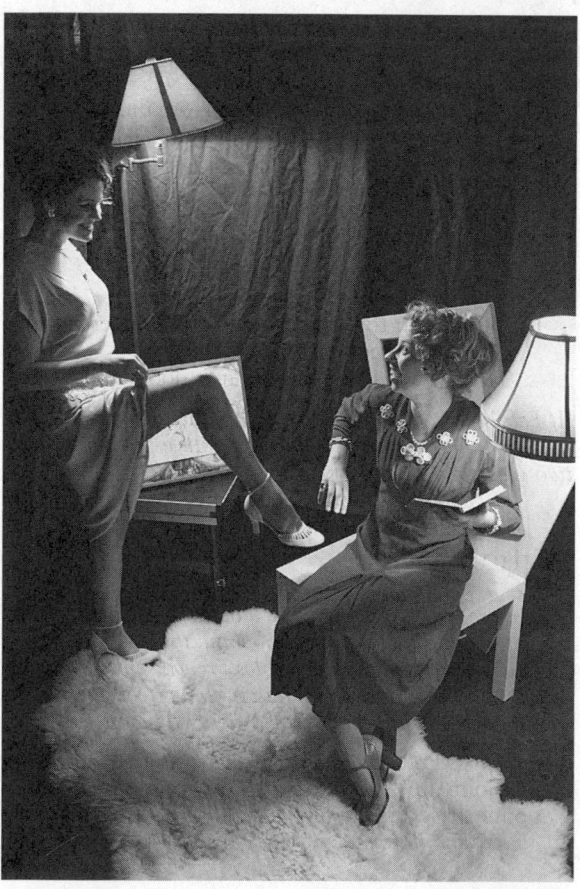

From a performance of *Fefu and Her Friends* by Tin Lily Productions at the Center for Performance Research in Brooklyn, New York, 2010.

CHRISTINA: It is. Being swept off your feet is nice. Anything else?

CINDY: Not for now. (*They go back to their reading. A moment passes.*) Are you having a good time?

CHRISTINA: Yes, I'm very glad I came.

CINDY: Do you like everybody?

CHRISTINA: Yes.

CINDY: Do you like Fefu?

CHRISTINA: I do . . . She confuses me a little.—I try to be honest . . . and I wonder if she is . . . I don't mean that she doesn't tell the truth. I know she does. I mean a kind of integrity. I know she has integrity too. . . . But I don't know if she's careful with life . . . something bigger than the self . . . I suppose I don't mean with life but more with convention. I think she is an adventurer in a way. Her mind is adventurous. I don't know if there is dishonesty in that. But in adventure there is taking chances and risks, and then one has to, somehow, have less regard or respect for things as they are. That is, regard for a kind of convention, I suppose. I am probably ultimately a conformist, I think. And I suppose I do hold back for fear of being disrespectful or destroying something—and I admire those who are not. But I also feel they are dangerous to me. I don't think they are dangerous to the world; they are more useful than I am, more important, but I feel some of my life is endangered by their way of thinking. Do you understand?

CINDY: Yes, I do.

CHRISTINA: I guess I am proud and I don't like thinking that I am thoughtful of things that have no value.—I like her.

CINDY: I had a terrible dream last night.

CHRISTINA: What was it?

CINDY: I was at a dance. And there was a young doctor I had seen in connection with my health. We all danced in a circle and he identified himself and said that he had spoken to Mike about me, but that it was all right, that he had put it so that it was all right. I was puzzled as to why Mike would mind and why he had spoken to him. Then, suddenly everybody sat down on the floor and pretended they were having singing lessons and one person was practicing Italian. The singing professor was being tested by two secret policemen. They were having him correct the voice of someone they had brought. He apparently didn't know how to do it. Then, one of the policemen put his hands on his vocal cords and kicked him out the door. Then he grabbed me and felt my throat from behind with his thumbs while he rubbed my nipples with his pinkies. Then, he pushed me out the door. Then, the young doctor started cursing me. His mouth moved like the mouth of a horse. I was on an upper level with a railing and I said to him, "Stop and listen to me." I said it so strongly that he stopped. Everybody turned to me in admiration because I had made him stop. Then, I said to him, "Restrain yourself." I wanted to say respect me. I wasn't sure whether the words coming out of my mouth were what I wanted to say. I turned to ask my sister. The young man was bending over and trembling in mad rage. Another man told me to run before the young man tried to kill me. Meg and I ran downstairs. She asked me if I wanted to go to her place. We grabbed a taxi, but before the taxi got enough speed he came out and ran to the taxi and was on the verge of opening the door when I woke up.

(*The door opens. Fefu looks in. Her entrance may interrupt Cindy's speech at any point according to how long it takes her to reach the kitchen.*)

FEFU: Who's for a game of croquet?
CINDY: In a little while.
FEFU: See you outside.
CHRISTINA: That was quite a dream.
CINDY: What do you think it means?
CHRISTINA: I think it means you should go to a different doctor.
CINDY: He's not my doctor. I never saw him before.
CHRISTINA: Well good. I'm sure he's not a good doctor.

(*At the end of the fourth repeat, when Fefu invites them for croquet, Cindy says, "Oh let's play croquet" and they follow Fefu.*)

In the Bedroom

(*A plain unpainted room. Perhaps a room that was used for storage and was set up as a sleeping place for Julia. There is a mattress on the floor. To the right of the mattress there is a small table, to the left is Julia's wheelchair. There is a sink on the wall. There are dry leaves on the floor although the time is not fall. The sheets are linen. Julia lies in bed covered to her shoulders. She wears a white hospital gown. Julia hallucinates. However, her behavior should not be the usual behavior attributed to a mad person. It should be rather still and luminous. There will be aspects of her hallucination that frighten her, but hallucinating itself does not.*)

JULIA: They clubbed me. They broke my head. They broke my will. They broke my hands. They tore my eyes out. They took my voice away. They didn't do anything to my heart because I didn't bring my heart with me. They clubbed me again, but my head did not fall off in pieces. That was because they were so good and they felt sorry for me. The judges. You didn't know the judges?—I was good and quiet. I never dropped my smile. I smiled to everyone. If I stopped smiling I would get clubbed because they love me. They say they love me. I go along with that because if I don't . . .

(*With her finger she indicates her throat being cut and makes the sound that usually accompanies that gesture.*)

I told them the stinking parts of the body are the important ones: the genitals, the anus, the mouth, the armpit. All important parts except the armpits. And who knows, maybe the armpits are important too. That's what I said. (*Her voice becomes gravelly and tight in imitation of the judges.*) He said that all those parts must be kept clean and put away. He said that women's entrails are heavier than anything on earth and to see a woman running creates a disparate and incongruous image in the mind. It's anti-aesthetic. Therefore women should not run. Instead they should strike positions that take into account the weight of their entrails. Only if they do, can they be aesthetic. He said, for example, Goya's Maja.° He said Rubens's women° are not aesthetic. Flesh. He said that a woman's bottom should be in a cushion, otherwise it's revolting. He said there are exceptions. Ballet dancers are exceptions. They can run and lift their legs because they have no entrails. Isadora Duncan° had entrails, that's why she should not have danced. But she danced and for this reason became crazy. (*Her voice is back to normal.*) She wasn't crazy.

(*She moves her hand as if guarding from a blow.*)

She was. He said that I had to be punished because I was getting too smart. I'm not smart. I never was. Neither is Fefu smart. They are after her too. Well, she's still walking!

(*She guards from a blow. Her eyes close.*)

Wait! I'll say my prayers. I'm saying it.

(*She mumbles. She opens her eyes with caution.*)

You don't think I'm going to argue with them, do you? I repented. I told them exactly what they wanted to hear. They killed me. I was dead. The bullet didn't hit me. It hit the deer. But I died. He didn't. Then I repented and the deer died and I lived. (*With a gravelly voice.*) They said, "Live but crippled. And if you tell . . ."

(*She repeats the throat cutting gesture.*)

Why do you have to kill Fefu, for she's only a joker? (*With a gravelly voice.*) "Not kill, cure. Cure her." Will it hurt?

(*She whimpers.*)

Oh, dear, dear, my dear, they want your light. Your light my dear. Your precious light. Oh dear, my dear.

(*Her head moves as if slapped.*)

Not cry. I'll say my prayer. I'll say it. Right now. Look.

Goya's Maja: Francisco Goya (1746–1828) painted the same woman twice, clothed and nude. The identity of the Maja has never been established.   **Rubens's women:** Peter Paul Rubens (1577–1640) painted large, fleshy women.   **Isadora Duncan:** American (1877–1927) who revolutionized theater dance and became famous internationally in the 1920s.

(*She sits up as if pulled by an invisible force.*)

The human being is of the masculine gender. The human being is a boy as a child and grown up he is a man. Everything on earth is for the human being, which is man. To nourish him.—There are evil things on earth, and noxious things. Evil and noxious things are on earth for man also. For him to fight with, and conquer and turn its evil into good. So that it too can nourish him.—There are Evil Plants, Evil Animals, Evil Minerals, and Women are Evil.—Woman is not a human being. She is: 1—A mystery. 2—Another species. 3—As yet undefined. 4—Unpredictable; therefore wicked and gentle and evil and good which is evil.—If a man commits an evil act, he must be pitied. The evil comes from outside him, through him and into the act. Woman generates the evil herself.—God gave man no other mate but woman. The oxen is good but it is not a mate for man. The sheep is good but it is not a mate for man. The mate for man is woman and that is the cross man must bear.—Man is not spiritually sexual, he therefore can enjoy sexuality. His sexuality is physical which means his spirit is pure. Women's spirit is sexual. That is why after coitus they dwell in nefarious feelings. Because that is their natural habitat. That is why it is difficult for them to return to the human world. Their sexual feelings remain with them till they die. And they take those feelings with them to the afterlife where they corrupt the heavens, and they are sent to hell where through suffering they may shed those feelings and return to earth as man.

(*Her head moves as if slapped.*)

Don't hit me. Didn't I just say my prayer?

(*A smaller slap.*)

I believe it.

(*She lies back.*)

They say when I believe the prayer I will forget the judges. And when I forget the judges I will believe the prayer. They say both happen at once. And all women have done it. Why can't I?

(*Sue enters with a bowl of soup on a tray.*)

SUE: Julia, are you asleep?

(*Short pause.*)

JULIA: No.
SUE: I brought your soup.
JULIA: Put it down. I'm getting up in a moment.

(*Sue puts the soup down.*)

SUE: Do you want me to help you?
JULIA: No, I can manage. Thank you, Sue.

(*Sue goes to the door.*)

SUE: You're all right?
JULIA: Yes.

SUE: I'll see you later.
JULIA: Thank you, Sue.

(*Sue exits. Julia closes her eyes. As soon as each audience group leaves, the tray is removed, if possible through a back door.*)

In the Kitchen

(*A fully equipped kitchen. There is a table and chairs and a high cutting table. On a counter next to the stove there is a tray with a soup dish and a spoon. There is also a ladle. On the cutting table there are two empty glasses. Soup is heating on a burner. A kettle with water sits on an unlit burner. In the refrigerator there is an ice tray with wooden sticks in each cube. The sticks should rest on the edge of the tray forming two parallel rows, like a caterpillar lying on its back. In the refrigerator there are also two pitchers, one with water, one with lemonade. Paula sits at the table. She is writing on a pad. Sue waits for the soup to heat.*)

PAULA: I have it all figured out.
SUE: What?
PAULA: A love affair lasts seven years and three months.
SUE: It does?
PAULA: (*Reading.*) 3 months of love. 1 year saying: It's all right. This is just a passing disturbance. 1 year trying to understand what's wrong. 2 years knowing the end had come. 1 year finding the way to end it. After the separation, 2 years trying to understand what happened. 7 years, 3 months. (*No longer reading.*) At any point the sequence might be interrupted by another love affair that has the same sequence. That is, it's not really interrupted, the new love affair relegates the first one to a second plane and both continue their sequence at the same time.

(*Sue looks over Paula's shoulder.*)

SUE: You really added it up.
PAULA: Sure.
SUE: What do you want to drink?
PAULA: Water. The old love affair may fade, so you are not aware the process goes on. A year later it may surface and you might find yourself figuring out what's wrong with the new one while trying to end the old one.
SUE: So how do you solve the problem?
PAULA: Celibacy?
SUE: (*Going to the refrigerator.*) Celibacy doesn't solve anything.
PAULA: That's true.
SUE: (*Taking out the ice tray with the sticks.*) What's this? (*Paula shakes her head.*) Dessert. (*Paula shrugs her shoulders. Sue takes an ice cube and places it against her forehead.*) For a headache. (*She takes another cube and moves her arms in a Judo style.*) Eskimo wrestling. (*She places one stick behind her

ear.) Brain cooler. That's when you're thinking too much. You could use one. (*She tries to put the ice cube behind Paula's ear. They wrestle and laugh. She puts the stick in her own mouth. She takes it out to speak.*) This is when you want to keep chaste. No one will kiss you. (*She puts it back in to demonstrate. Then takes it out.*) That's good for celibacy. If you walk around with one of these in your mouth for seven years you can keep all your sequences straight. Finish one before you start the other. (*She puts the ice cube in the tray and looks at it.*) A frozen caterpillar. (*She puts the tray away.*)

PAULA: You're leaving that ice cube in there?

SUE: I'm clean. (*Looking at the soup.*) So what else do you have on love? (*Sue places a bowl and spoon on the table and sits as she waits for the soup to heat.*)

PAULA: Well, the break-up takes place in parts. The brain, the heart, the body, mutual things, shared things. The mind leaves but the heart is still there. The heart has left but the body wants to stay. The body leaves but the things are still at the apartment. You must come back. You move everything out of the apartment but the mind stays behind. Memory lingers in the place. Seven years later, perhaps seven years later, it doesn't matter any more. Perhaps it takes longer. Perhaps it never ends.

SUE: It depends.

PAULA: Yup. It depends.

SUE: (*Pouring soup in the bowl.*) Something's bothering you.

PAULA: No.

SUE: (*Taking the tray.*) I'm going to take this to Julia.

PAULA: Go ahead.

(*As Sue exits, Cecilia enters.*)

CECILIA. May I come in?

PAULA: Yes . . . Would you like something to eat?

CECILIA: No, I ate lunch.

PAULA: I didn't eat lunch. I wasn't very hungry.

CECILIA: I know.

PAULA: Would you like some coffee?

CECILIA: I'll have tea.

PAULA: I'll make some.

CECILIA: No, you sit. I'll make it. (*Cecilia looks for tea.*)

PAULA: Here it is. (*She gets the tea and gives it to Cecilia.*)

CECILIA: (*As she lights the burner.*) I've been meaning to call you.

PAULA: It doesn't matter. I know you're busy.

CECILIA: Still I would have called you but I really didn't find the time.

PAULA: Don't worry.

CECILIA: I wanted to see you again. I want to see you often.

PAULA: There's no hurry. Now we know we can see each other.

CECILIA: Yes, I'm glad we can.

PAULA: I have thought a great deal about my life since I saw you. I have questioned my life. I can't help doing that. It's been many years and I wondered how you see me now.

CECILIA: You're the same.

PAULA: I felt small in your presence . . . I haven't done all that I could have. All I wanted to do. Our lives have gone in such different directions I cannot help but review what those years have been for me. I gave up, almost gave up. I have missed you in my life. . . . I became lazy. I lost the drive. You abandoned me and I kept going. But after a while I didn't know how to. I didn't know how to go on. I knew why when I was with you. To give you pleasure. So we could laugh together. So we could rejoice together. To bring beauty to the world. . . . Now we look at each other like strangers. We are guarded. I speak and you don't understand my words. I remember every day.

(*Fefu enters. She takes the lemonade pitcher from the refrigerator and two glasses from the top of the refrigerator.*)

FEFU: Emma and I are going to play croquet. You want to join us? . . . No. You're having a serious conversation.

PAULA: Very serious. (*Paula smiles at Cecilia in a conciliatory manner.*) Too serious.

FEFU: (*As she exits.*) Come.

PAULA: I'm sorry. Let's go play croquet.—I'm not reproaching you.

CECILIA: (*Reaching for Paula's hand.*) I know. I've missed you too.

(*They exit. As soon as the audience leaves the props are reset.*)

PART III

(*The living room. It is dusk. As the audience enters, two or three of the women are around the piano playing and singing Schubert's "Who Is Silvia?"[9] They exit. Emma enters, checks the lights in the room on her hand, looks around the room and goes upstairs. The rest enter through the rear. Cecilia enters speaking.*)

CECILIA: Well, we each have our own system of receiving information, placing it, responding to it. (*She sits in the center of the couch; the rest sit around her.*) That system can function with such a bias that it could take any situation and translate it into one formula. That is, I think, the main reason for stupidity or even madness, not being able to tell the difference between things.

SUE: Like?

CECILIA: Like . . . this person is screaming at me. He's a bully. I don't like being screamed at. Another person or the same person screams in a different situation. But you know you have done something that provokes him to scream. He has a good reason. They are two different things, the screaming of one and the

---

Who Is Silvia?: A song by Shakespeare from *Two Gentlemen of Verona*, set to music by Franz Schubert (1797–1828).

screaming of the other. Often that distinction is not made. We cannot survive in a vacuum. We must be part of a community, perhaps 10, 100, 1000. It depends on how strong you are. But even the strongest will need a dozen, three, even one who sees, thinks, and feels as he does. The greater the need for that kind of reassurance, the greater the number that he needs to identify with. Some need to identify with the whole nation. Then, the greater the number the more limited the number of responses and thoughts. A common denominator must be reached. Thoughts, emotions that fit all, have to be limited to a small number. That is, I feel, the concern of the educator—to teach how to be sensitive to the differences in ourselves as well as outside ourselves, not to supervise the memorization of facts. (*Emma's head appears in the doorway to the stairs.*) Otherwise the unusual in us will perish. As we grow we feel we are strange and fear any thought that is not shared with everyone.

JULIA: As I feel I am perishing. My hallucinations are madness, of course, but I wish I could be with others who hallucinate also. I would still know I am mad but I would not feel so isolated.—Hallucinations are real, you know. They are not like dreams. They are as real as all of you here. I have actually asked to be hospitalized so I could be with other nuts. But the doctors don't want to. They can't diagnose me. That makes me even more isolated. (*There is a moment's silence.*) You see, right now, it's an awful moment because you don't know what to say or do. If I were with other people who hallucinate, they would say, "Oh yeah. Sure. It's awful. Those dummies, they don't see anything." (*The others begin to relax.*) It's not so bad, really. I can laugh at it. . . . Emma is ready. We should start. (*The others are hesitant. Julia speaks to Fefu.*) Come on.

FEFU: Sure. (*Fefu begins to move the table. Others help move the table and enough furniture to clear a space in the center. They sit in a semicircle downstage on the floor facing upstage. Cecilia sits on a chair to the left of the semicircle.*) All right. I start. Right?

CINDY: Right.

(*Fefu goes to center and faces the others. Emma sits on the steps. Only her head and legs are visible.*)

FEFU: I talk about the stifling conditions of primary school education, etc. . . . etc. . . . The project . . . I know what I'm going to say but I don't want to bore you with it. We all know it by heart. Blah blah blah blah. And so on and so on. And so on and so on. Then I introduce Emma . . . And now Miss Emma Blake. (*They applaud. Emma shakes her head.*) What.

EMMA: Paula goes next.

FEFU: Does it matter?

EMMA: Of course it matters. Dra-ma-tics. It has to build! I'm in costume.

FEFU: Oh. And now, ladies and gentlemen, Miss Paula Cori will speak on Art as a Tool for Learning. And I tell them the work you have done at the Institute, community centers, essays, etc. Miss Paula Cori.

(*They applaud. Paula goes to center.*)

PAULA: Ladies and gentlemen, I, like my fellow educator and colleague, Stephany Beckmann . . .

FEFU: I am not an educator.

PAULA: What are you?

FEFU: . . . a do gooder, a girl scout.

PAULA: . . . Well, I, like my fellow girl scout Stephany Beckmann say blah blah blah blah, blah blah blah and I offer the jewels of my wisdom and experience, which I will write down and memorize, otherwise I would just stand there and stammer and go blank. And even after I memorize it I'm sure I will just stand there and stammer and go blank.

EMMA: I'll work with you on it.

PAULA: However, after our other colleague Miss Emma Blake works with me on it . . . (*In imitation of Emma she brings her hands together and opens her arms as she moves her head back and speaks.*) My impulses will burst forth through a symphony of eloquence.

EMMA: Breathe . . . in . . . (*Paula inhales slowly.*) And bow. (*Paula bows. They applaud.*)

PAULA: (*Coming up from the bow.*) Oh, I liked that. (*She sits.*)

EMMA: Good . . .

(*They applaud.*)

FEFU: And now, ladies and gentlemen, the one and only, the incomparable, our precious, dear Emma Blake.

(*Emma walks to center. She wears a robe which hangs from her arms to the floor.*)

EMMA: From the prologue to "The Science of Educational Dramatics" by Emma Sheridan Fry.° (*She takes a dramatic pose and starts. The whole speech is dramatized by interpretive gestures and movements that cover the stage area.*)

> Environment knocks at the gateway of the senses. A rain of summons beats upon us day and night. . . . We do not answer. Everything around us shouts against our deafness, struggles with our unwillingness, batters our walls, flashes into our blindness, strives to sieve through us at every pore, begging, fighting, insisting. It shouts, "Where are you? Where are you?" But we are deaf. The signals do not reach us.
>
> Society restricts us, school straight jackets us, civilization submerges us, privation wrings us, luxury feather-beds us. The Divine Urge is checked. The Winged Horse balks on the road, and we, discouraged, defeated, dismount and burrow into ourselves. The gates are closed and Divine Urge is imprisoned at Center. Thus we are taken by indifference that is death.

Emma Sheridan Fry: Fry taught acting to children at The Educational Alliance in New York from 1903 to 1909. In 1917, her book *Educational Dramatics* was published by Lloyd Adams Noble. The text of Emma's speech is taken from the prologue.

Environment finding the gates closed tries to break in. Turned away, it comes another way. Kept back, it stretches its hands to us. Always scheming to reach us. Never was suitor more insistent than Environment, seeking admission, claiming recognition, signaling to be seen, shouting to be heard. And through the ages we sit inside ourselves deaf, dumb and blind, and will not stir . . . .

. . . Maybe you are not deaf. . . . Perhaps signals reach you. Maybe you stir. . . . The gates give. . . . Eternal Urge pushes through the stupor of our senses, making paths to meet the challenging suitor, windows through which to see him, ears through which to hear him. Environment shouting, "Where are you?" and Center battering at the inner side of the wall crying, "Here I am," and dragging down bars, wrenching gates, prying at port-holes. Listening at cracks, reaching everywhere, and demanding that sense gates be flung open. The gates are open! Eternal Urge stands at the threshold signaling with venturous flag. An imperious instinct lets us know that "all" is ours, and that whatever anyone has ever known, or may ever have or know, we will call and claim. A sense of life universal surges through our life individual. We attack the feast of this table with an insatiable appetite that cries for all.

What are we? A creation of God's consciousness coming now slowly and painfully into recognition of ourselves.

What is Personality? A small part of us. The whole of us is behind that hungry rush at the gates of Senses.

What is Civilization? A circumscribed order in which the whole has not entered.

What is Environment? Our mate, our true mate that clamors for our reunion.

We will meet him. We will seize all, learn all, know all here, that we may fare further on the great quest! The task of Now is only a step toward the task of the Whole! Let us then seek the laws governing real life forces, that coming into their own, they may create, develop and reconstruct. Let us awaken life dormant! Let us, boldly, seizing the star of our intent, lift it as the lantern of our necessity, and let it shine over the darkness of our compliance. Come! The light shines. Come! It brightens our way. Come! Don't let its glorious light pass you by! Come! The day has come!

(*Emma throws herself on the couch. Paula embraces her.*) Oh, it's so beautiful.

JULIA: It is, Emma. It is.

(*They applaud.*)

CINDY: Encore! Encore!

(*Emma stands.*)

EMMA: Environment knocks at the gateway . . . (*She laughs and joins the others in the semi-circle. Paula remains seated on the couch.*) What's next.

FEFU: (*Going center.*) I introduce Cecilia. I don't think I should introduce Cecilia. She should just come after Emma. Now things don't need introduction. (*Imitating Emma as she goes to her seat.*) They are happening.

EMMA: Right!

(*Cecilia goes to center.*)

CECILIA: Well, as we say in the business, that's a very hard act to follow.

EMMA: Not *very* hard. It's a hard act to follow.

CECILIA: Right. I should say my name first.

FEFU: Yes.

CECILIA: I should breathe too. (*She takes a breath. All except Paula start singing "Cecilia." Cecilia is perplexed and walks backwards till she sits on the couch. She is next to Paula. Unaware of who she is next to, she puts her hand on Paula's leg. At the end of the song Cecilia realizes she is next to Paula and stands.*) I should go before Emma. I don't think anyone should speak after Emma.

CINDY: Right. It should be Fefu, Paula, Cecilia, then Emma, and then Sue explaining the finances and asking for pledges. And the money should roll in. It's very good. (*They applaud.*) Sue . . . (*Sue goes to center.*)

SUE: Yes, blahblahblahblah, pledges and money. (*She does a few balletic moves and bows. They applaud.*)

FEFU: (*As Sue returns to her seat.*) Who's ready for coffee?

CINDY: (*As she stands.*) And dishes.

CHRISTINA: (*As she stands.*) I'll help.

EMMA: (*As she stands.*) Me too.

FEFU: Don't all come. Sit. Sit. You have done enough, relax.

(*They put the furniture back as Emma and Sue jump over the couch making loud warlike sounds. As they exit to the kitchen, Sue tries to get ahead of Emma. Emma speeds ahead of her. All except Julia jump over the couch. All except Cindy and Julia exit.*)

JULIA: I should go do the dishes. I haven't done anything.

CINDY: You can do them tomorrow.

JULIA: True.—So how have you been?

CINDY: Hmm.

JULIA: Let me see. I can tell by looking at your face. Not so bad.

CINDY: Not so bad.

(*There is the sound of laughter from the kitchen. Christina runs in.*)

CHRISTINA: They're having a water fight over who's going to do the dishes.

CINDY: Emma?

CHRISTINA: And Paula, and Sue, all of them. Fefu was getting into it when I left. Cecilia got out the back door.

(*Christina walks back to the kitchen with some caution. She runs back and lies on the couch covering her head with the throw. Emma enters with a pan of water in her hand. She is wet. Cindy and Julia point to the lawn. Emma runs to the lawn. There is the sound of knocking from upstairs. While the following conversation goes on, Emma, Sue, Cindy, and Julia engage in water fights in and out of the living room. The screams, laughter, and water splashing may drown the words.)*

PAULA: Open up.

FEFU: There's no one here.

PAULA: Open up you coward.

FEFU: I can't. I'm busy.

PAULA: What are you doing?

FEFU: I have a man here. Ah ah ah ah ah.

PAULA: O.K. I'll wait. Take your time.

FEFU: It's going to take quite a while.

PAULA: It's all right. I'll wait.

FEFU: Do me a favor?

PAULA: Sure. Open up and I'll do you a favor.

(There is the sound of a pot falling, a door slamming.)

FEFU: Fill it up for me.

PAULA: O.K.

FEFU: Thank you.

PAULA: Here's water. Open up.

FEFU: Leave it there. I'll come out in a minute.

PAULA: O.K. Here it is. I'm leaving now.

(Loud steps. Paula comes down with a filled pan. Emma hides by the entrance to the steps. Emma splashes water on Paula. Paula splashes water on Emma. Sue appears with a full pan.)

PAULA: Truce!

SUE: Who's the winner?

PAULA: You are. You do the dishes.

SUE: I'm the winner. You do the dishes.

FEFU: *(From the landing.)* Line up!

SUE: Psst. *(Paula and Emma look. Sue splashes water on them.)* Gotcha!

EMMA: Please don't.

PAULA: Truce. Truce.

FEFU: O.K. Line up. *(Pointing to the kitchen.)* Get in there! *(They all go to the kitchen.)* Start doing those dishes. *(There is a moment's pause.)*

JULIA: It's over.

CINDY: We're safe.

JULIA: *(To Christina.)* You can come up now. *(Christina stays down.)* You rather wait a while. *(Christina nods.)*

CHRISTINA: *(Playful.)* I feel danger lurking.

CINDY: She's been hiding all day.

(Fefu enters. She is wet.)

FEFU: I won. I got them working.

JULIA: I thought the fight was over who'd do the dishes.

FEFU: Yes. *(Starting to go.)* I have to change. I'm soaked.

CHRISTINA: They forgot what the fight was about.

FEFU: We did?

JULIA: That's usually the way it is.

FEFU: *(Going to Christina and lifting the cover from her face.)* Are you ready for an ice cube?

(Fefu exits upstairs. Christina runs upstairs. There is silence.)

CINDY: So.—And how have you been?

JULIA: All right. I've been taking care of myself.

CINDY: You look well.

JULIA: I do not. . . . Have you seen Mike?

CINDY: No, not since Christmas.

JULIA: I'm sorry.

CINDY: I'm O.K.—And how's your love life?

JULIA: Far away. . . . I have no need for it.

CINDY: I'm sorry.

JULIA: Don't be. I'm very morbid these days. I think of death all the time.

PAULA: *(Standing in the doorway.)* Anyone for coffee? *(They raise their hands.)* Anyone take milk? *(They raise their hands.)*

JULIA: Should we go in?

PAULA: I'll bring it out. *(Paula exits.)*

JULIA: I feel we are constantly threatened by death, every second, every instant, it's there. And every moment something rescues us. Something rescues us from death every moment of our lives. For every moment we live we have to thank something. We have to be grateful to something that fights for us and saves us. I have felt lifeless and in the face of death. Death is not anything. It's being lifeless and I have felt lifeless sometimes for a brief moment, but I have been rescued by these . . . guardians. I am not sure who these guardians are. I only know they exist because I have felt their absence. I think we have come to know them as life, and we have become familiar with certain forms they take. Our sight is a form they take. That is why we take pleasure in seeing things, and we find some things beautiful. The sun is a guardian. Those things we take pleasure in are usually guardians. We enjoy looking at the sunlight when it comes through the window. Don't we? We, as people, are guardians to each other when we give love. And then of course we have white cells and antibodies protecting us. Those moments when I feel lifeless have occurred, and I am afraid one day the guardians won't come in time and I will be defenseless. I will die . . . for no apparent reason.

(Pause. Paula stands in the doorway with a bottle of milk.)

PAULA: *(In a low-keyed manner.)* Anyone take rotten milk? *(Pause.)* I'm kidding. This one is no good but there's more in there . . . *(Remaining in good spirits.)* Forget it. It's not a good joke.

JULIA: It's good.

PAULA: In there it seemed funny but here it isn't. (*As she exits and shrugging her shoulders.*) It's a kitchen joke. Bye.

JULIA: (*After her.*) It is funny, Paula. (*To Cindy.*) It was funny.

CINDY: It's all right, Paula doesn't mind.

JULIA: I'm sure she minds. I'll go see . . . (*Julia starts to go. Paula appears in the doorway.*)

PAULA: (*In a low-keyed manner.*) Hey, who was that lady I saw you with?—That was no lady. That was my rotten wife. That one wasn't good either, was it? (*Exiting.*) Emma. . . . That one was no good either.

(*Sue starts to enter carrying a tray with sugar, milk, and two cups of coffee. She stops at the doorway to look at Paula and Emma who are behind the wall.*)

SUE: (*Whispering.*) What are you doing?—What?— O.K., O.K. (*She enters whispering. Sue puts the tray down.*) They're plotting something.

(*Paula appears in the doorway.*)

PAULA: (*In a low-keyed manner.*) Ladies and gentlemen. Ladies, since our material is too shocking and avant-garde, we have decided to uplift our subject matter so it's more palatable to the sensitive public. (*Paula takes a pose. Emma enters. She lifts an imaginary camera to her face.*)

EMMA: Say cheese.

PAULA: Cheese. (*They both turn front and smile. The others applaud.*) Ah, success, success. Make it clean and you'll succeed.—Coffee's in the kitchen.

SUE: Oh, I brought theirs out.

PAULA: Oh, shall we all have it here?

JULIA: We can all go in the kitchen. (*They each take their coffee and go to the kitchen. Sue takes the tray to the kitchen. The sugar remains on the table.*)

PAULA: Either here or there. (*She sits on the couch.*) I'm exhausted.

(*Cecilia enters from the lawn.*)

CECILIA: Is the war over?

PAULA: Yes.

CECILIA: It's nice out. (*Paula nods in agreement.*) Where's everybody?

PAULA: In the kitchen, having coffee.

CECILIA: We must talk. (*Paula starts to speak.*) Not now. I'll call you. (*Cecilia starts to go.*)

PAULA: When?

CECILIA: I don't know.

PAULA: I don't want you, you know.

CECILIA: I know.

PAULA: No, you don't. I'm not lusting after you.

CECILIA: I know that. (*She starts to go.*) I'll call you.

PAULA: When?

CECILIA: As soon as I can.

PAULA: I won't be home then.

CECILIA: When will you be home?

PAULA: I'll check my book and let you know.

CECILIA: Do that.—I'll be leaving after coffee. I'll say goodbye now.

PAULA: Goodbye. (*Cecilia goes towards the kitchen. Paula starts towards the steps. Fefu comes down the steps.*)

FEFU: You're still wet.

PAULA: I'm going to change now.

FEFU: Do you need anything?

PAULA: No, I have something I can change to. Thank you.

(*As Paula goes upstairs, Fefu comes down the steps. She is downcast. The lights shift to an eerie tone. Fefu hallucinates the following: Julia enters in slow motion, walking. She goes to the coffee table, gets the sugar bowl, lifts it in Fefu's direction, takes the cover off, puts it back on and walks to the kitchen. As soon as Julia exits, Sue's voice is heard speaking the following lines. Immediately after, Julia re-enters wheeled by Sue. Cindy, Christina, Emma, and Cecilia are with them, On the arms of the wheelchair rests a tray with a coffee pot and cups. As they reach the couch and chairs they sit. Sue puts the tray on the table. Fefu stares at Julia.*)

SUE: I was terribly exhausted and run down. I lived on coffee so I could stay up all night and do my work. And they used to give us these medical check-ups all the time. But all they did was ask how we felt and we'd say "Fine," and they'd check us out. In the meantime I looked like a ghost. I was all bones. Remember Susan Austin? She was very naive and when they asked her how she felt, she said she was nervous and she wasn't sleeping well. So she had to see a psychiatrist from then on.

EMMA: Well, she was crazy.

(*Fefu exits.*)

SUE: No, she wasn't.—Oh god, those were awful days. . . . Remember Julie Brooks?

EMMA: Sure.

SUE: She was a beautiful girl.

EMMA: Ah yes, she was gorgeous.

(*Paula comes down the stairs as soon as she has changed. She sits on the steps half way down.*)

SUE: At the end of the first semester they called her in because she had been out with 28 men and they thought that was awful. And the worst thing was that after that, she thought there was something wrong with her.

CINDY: (*Jokingly.*) She was a nymphomaniac, that's all.

SUE: She was not. She was just very beautiful so all the boys wanted to go out with her. And if a boy asked her to go have a cup of coffee she'd sign out and write in the name of the boy. None of us did of course. All she did was go for coffee or go to a movie. She was really very innocent.

EMMA: And Gloria Schuman? She wrote a psychology paper the faculty decided she didn't write and they called her in to try to make her admit she hadn't written it. She insisted she wrote it and they sent her to a psychiatrist also.

JULIA: Everybody ended going to the psychiatrist.

(*Fefu enters through the foyer.*)

EMMA: After a few visits the psychiatrist said: Don't you think you know me well enough now that you can tell me the truth about the paper? He almost drove her crazy. They just couldn't believe she was so smart.

SUE: Those were difficult times.

PAULA: We were young. That's why it was difficult. On my first year I thought you were all very happy. I had been so deprived in my childhood that I believed the rich were all happy. During the summer you spent your vacations in Europe or the Orient. I went to work and I resented that. But then I realized that many lives are ruined by poverty and many lives are ruined by wealth. I was always able to manage. And I think I enjoyed myself as much when I went to Revere Beach on my day off as you did when you visited the Taj Mahal. (*Cecilia enters from the foyer. She stands there and listens. Paula doesn't acknowledge her.*) Then, when I stopped feeling envy, I started noticing the waste. I began feeling contempt for those who, having everything a person can ask for, make such a mess of it. I resented them because they were not better than the poor. If you have all you need you should be generous. If you can afford to go to school your mind should be better. If you didn't have to fight for your place on earth you should be nobler. But I saw them cheating and grabbing like the kids in the slums, or wasting away with self-indulgence. And I saw them be plain stupid. If there is a reason why some are rich while others starve it must be so they put everything they have at the service of others. They should take the responsibility of everything that happens in the world. They are the only ones who can influence things. The poor don't have the power to change things. I think we should teach the poor and let the rich take care of themselves. I'm sorry, I know that's what we're doing. That's what Emma has been doing. I'm sorry . . . I guess I feel it's not enough. (*Paula sobs.*) I'll wash my face. I'll be right back. (*She starts to go towards the kitchen.*) I think highly of all of you. (*Cecilia follows her. Paula turns. Cecilia opens her arms and puts them around Paula, engulfing her. She kisses Paula on the lips. Paula steps back. She is fearful. Cecilia follows her. Fefu enters from the lawn.*)

FEFU: Have you been out? The sky is full of stars.

(*Emma, Sue, Christina, and Cindy exit.*)

JULIA: What's the matter?

(*Fefu shakes her head. Julia starts to go toward the door.*)

FEFU: Stay a moment, will you?

JULIA: Of course.

FEFU: Did you have enough coffee?

JULIA: Yes.

FEFU: Did you find the sugar?

JULIA: Yes. There was sugar in the kitchen. What's the matter?

FEFU: Can you walk? (*Julia is hurt. She opens her arms implying she hides nothing.*) I am sorry, my dear.

JULIA: What is the matter?

FEFU: I don't know, Julia. Every breath is painful for me. I don't know. (*Fefu turns Julia's head to look into her eyes.*) I think you know.

(*Julia breaks away from Fefu.*)

JULIA: (*Avoiding Fefu's glance.*) No, I don't know. I haven't seen much of you lately. I have thought of you a great deal. I always think of you. Cindy tells me how you are. I always ask her. How is Phillip? Things are not well with Phillip?

FEFU: No.

JULIA: What's wrong?

FEFU: A lot is wrong.

JULIA: He loves you.

FEFU: He can't stand me.

JULIA: He loves you.

FEFU: He's left me. His body is here but the rest is gone. I exhaust him. I torment him and I torment myself. I need him, Julia.

JULIA: I know you do.

FEFU: I need his touch. I need his kiss. I need the person he is. I can't give him up. (*She looks into Julia's eyes.*) I look into your eyes and I know what you see. (*Julia closes her eyes.*) It's death. (*Julia shakes her head.*) Fight!

JULIA: I can't.

FEFU: I saw you walking.

JULIA: No. I can't walk.

FEFU: You came for sugar, Julia. You came for sugar. Walk!

JULIA: You know I can't walk.

FEFU: Why not? Try! Get up! Stand up!

JULIA: What is wrong with you?

FEFU: You have given up!

JULIA: I get tired! I get exhausted! I am exhausted!

FEFU: What is it you see? (*Julia doesn't answer.*) What is it you see! Where is it you go that tires you so?

JULIA: I can't spend time with others! I get tired!

FEFU: What is it you see!

JULIA: You want to see it too?

FEFU: No, I don't. You're nuts, and willingly so.

JULIA: You know I'm not.

FEFU: And you're contagious. I'm going mad too.

JULIA: I try to keep away from you.

FEFU: Why?

JULIA: I might be harmful to you.

FEFU: Why?

JULIA: I am contagious. I can't be what I used to be.

FEFU: You have no courage.

JULIA: You're being cruel.

FEFU: I want to rest, Julia. How does a person rest? I want to put my mind at rest. I am frightened. (*Julia looks at*

Fefu.) Don't look at me. (*She covers Julia's eyes with her hand.*) I lose my courage when you look at me.
JULIA: May no harm come to your head.
FEFU: Fight!
JULIA: May no harm come to your will.
FEFU: Fight, Julia!

(*Fefu starts shaking the wheelchair and pulling Julia off the wheelchair.*)

JULIA: I have no life left.
FEFU: Fight, Julia!
JULIA: May no harm come to your hands.
FEFU: I need you to fight.
JULIA: May no harm come to your eyes.
FEFU: Fight with me!
JULIA: May no harm come to your voice.
FEFU: Fight with me!
JULIA: May no harm come to your heart.

(*Christina enters. Fefu sees Christina, releases Julia. To Christina.*)

FEFU: Now I have done it. Haven't I. You think I'm a monster. (*She turns to Julia and speaks to her with kindness.*) Forgive me if you can. (*Julia nods.*)
JULIA: I forgive you.

(*Fefu gets the gun.*)

CHRISTINA: What in the world are you doing with that gun!
FEFU: I'm going to clean it!
CHRISTINA: I think you better not!
FEFU: You're silly!

(*Cecilia appears on the landing.*)

CHRISTINA: I don't care if you shoot yourself! I just don't like the mess you're making!

(*Fefu starts to go to the lawn and turns.*)

FEFU: I enjoy betting it won't be a real bullet! You want to bet!
CHRISTINA: No! (*Fefu exits. Christina goes to Julia.*) Are you all right?
JULIA: Yes.
CHRISTINA: Can I get you anything?
JULIA: Water. (*Cecilia goes to the liquor cabinet for water.*) Put some sugar in it. Could I have a damp cloth for my forehead? (*Christina goes toward the kitchen. Julia speaks front.*) I didn't tell her anything. Did I? I didn't.
CECILIA: (*Going to Julia with the water.*) About what?
JULIA: She knew.

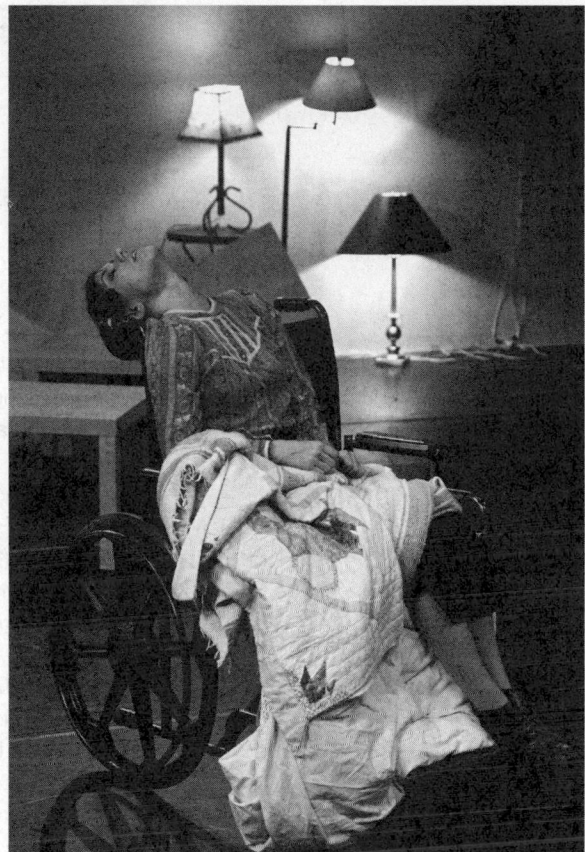

Julia in Part III of *Fefu and Her Friends,* from a performance by Tin Lily Productions at the Center for Performance Research in Brooklyn, New York, 2010.

(*There is the sound of a shot. Christina and Cecilia run out. Julia puts her hand to her forehead. Her hand goes down slowly. There is blood on her forehead. Her head falls back. Fefu enters holding a dead white rabbit.*)

FEFU: I killed it . . . I just shot . . . and killed it. . . . Julia . . .

(*Dropping the rabbit, Fefu walks to Julia and stands behind the chair as she looks at Julia. Sue and Cindy enter from the foyer, Emma and Paula from the kitchen, Christina and Cecilia from the lawn. They surround Julia. The lights fade.*)

COMMENTARY

RUBY COHN (1922–2011)

Maria Irene Fornés' Plays

Ruby Cohn taught at the University of California, Davis, and established herself as a Beckett scholar after attending the first performance of *Waiting for Godot* in 1953 in Paris. Her commentaries and critical essays on modern playwrights made her a champion of experimental dramatists such as Fornés.

[...] Maria Irene Fornés [...] endows the Off-Off-Broadway scene with several talents. Of Cuban birth (in 1930), she is doubly trilingual; her formal languages are Spanish, English, French, and her artistic languages are designing, directing, playwriting. Her single volume of published plays shows meticulous attention to visual as well as verbal detail. Slight on the surface, they are surprisingly memorable. Floating away from realism, they offer an oblique critique of reality.

Her first play announces the incisive thrust of her light touch. Although developed traditionally for the Actor's Workshop of San Francisco, *Tango Palace* (1961) displays her concern with acting rather than plot or character development. The tango palace designates the habitat and shrine of Isidore, "an androgynous clown," into which is born an earnest youth Leopold, crawling out of a sack in a business suit. Leopold is a rationalist, seeking logic and sequence, but inventive Isidore moves by caprice, and among his movements is the titular tango. The action of *Tango Palace* pivots on the duel of Isidore and Leopold, with the former highly conscious of the articulation of that duel. "Each time Isidore feels he has said something important, he takes a card from his pocket or from a drawer and flips it across the room in any direction." By the end of the play their battle-ground, the tango palace, is strewn with cards. When Leopold threatens to burn them, Isidore warns him that he will die. When Leopold actually sets fire to a card, Isidore trips him and exclaims: "There! You died."—the play's first title. But Leopold does not die. He pleads for cessation of cards, for egress from the room. Isidore regales him (and us) with a parable of a rat slain by the man who loved him, of a beetle with dirt inside him. Leopold counters with a tale of a crawling snake, as he himself crawls. Leopold refuses to continue their duel. He plunges a sword into Isidore, who promptly appears as an angel, still carrying cards. The play ends when "Leopold walks through the door slowly, but with determination. He is ready for the next stage of their battle."

Fornés' next play, *The Successful Life of 3* (1965), was created with the Open Theatre, thriving on humour and spurning psychology in an extended pun on an eternal triangle. He and She are a couple, and a rival, 3, vies for She's love. The play traces their intertwined lives from first meeting in a doctor's office where She is a nurse, through the marriage of He and She, the desertion of He by She, She's return to a household of He and 3, He as detective arresting 3 as thief, 3's adventures with police and bodyguards, and a final joyous reunion of the three. As compared to Noel Coward's *Design for Living*, Fornés' play is an *Un*design for living a successful life of three—successful because of its inventiveness. Like Bergman's *Scenes from a Marriage*, these scenes from a triangle, arbitrary as to time and place, are emblematic of sexual affinities in our culture.

Promenade was written soon after *The Successful Life of 3*, and even the revised published version shows its proximity. This time the play presents the zany adventures of two triangles—the prisoners 105 and 106 and their mother, on the one hand, and the same men with a female companion, on the other. Digging their way out of prison, the two men attend a banquet, where they steal everything portable, including a woman whom they drape in their loot. Suddenly, they are joined by their mother to comfort soldiers on a battlefield. Then they are imprisoned again, along with mother and woman. Finally alone in jail, they sing: "All is well in the city. . . . And for those who have no cake, / There's plenty of bread."

With *Dr Kheal* (1968) Fornés' satire becomes more overt. Like Dr Kheal's predecessors, Ionesco's teacher in *The Lesson* and Adamov's Professor Taranne, Fornés' professor takes a stance of omniscience, which is shaken in the play's action. Unlike his forerunners, however, Dr Kheal unbalances his *own* omniscience, with the self-contradiction implicit in his name that contains "heal" and "kill": "[Reality] is opposites, Contradictions compressed so that you don't know where one stops and the other begins." As Fornés' Isidore consigned his wisdom to cards, Dr Kheal consigns his wisdom to the blackboard, where he expounds on Poetry, Balance, Ambition, Energy, Speech, Truth, Beauty, Love, Hope, and anticlimactically, Cooking. Illustrating with figures and drawings, he arrives at ignorance rather than knowledge: "Man is the rational animal." And that is his undoing.

In *Molly's Dream* (1968) Fornés for the first time presents a rational structure for her surreal associations. The action is set in an old-fashioned saloon where waitress Molly looks at a Young Man. She leans her head on a table, falls asleep, and dreams most of the rest of the play, which gradually narrows down to herself and the young man as Jim. Actually, he leaves the saloon before she awakens. She opens her eyes and gazes at the spot where he sat—now empty of the several whimsical characters of popular culture. Less successful are characters of popular culture in an anti-war play *The Red Burning Light of Mission XQ 3* (1969).

During the 1970s Fornés' administrative work for Theatre Strategy left her reduced time for playwriting. Of three plays of these years—*The Curse of the Langston House* (1972), *Aurora* (1973), *and Fefu and her Friends* (1977), only the last has been published. In it the audience moves with the actresses through the rooms of a New England country house: living room to lawn to study to bedroom to kitchen and back to living room, there to watch scenes between Fefu, nickname for Stephany Beckmann, and her seven women friends. Unlike Fornés' earlier plays activated by actors, this subtly feminist drama appears to be activated by shifting environments.

Although Fornés has called the play plotless, a nuanced plot is traceable through the several groupings of these eight women who meet in Fefu's house on a spring day in 1935. Aside from hostess Fefu (married to Phillip, who never appears), there is Julia in her wheelchair, the pair Christina and Cindy, histrionic Emma, ex-lovers Paula and Cecilia, and Sue who is least individualized. Fefu has been toying with a gun before her guests arrive. The purpose of the women's meeting is to raise funds for supporting art as a tool of learning, with actual quotations from "The Science of Educational Dramatics" by Emma Sheridan Fry. After the fund drive rehearsal, a few women go to the kitchen ostensibly to make coffee, but they actually engage in a water-fight. Fefu is quite suddenly brutal to Julia, insisting that she can walk, that she can combat the deadly forces that she hallucinates. Interrupted by Christina, Fefu takes her gun outside. A shot is soon heard, and Julia bleeds from her forehead. Fefu re-enters with a dead rabbit, stands behind bleeding Julia, and utters the play's closing line: "I killed it . . . I just shot . . . and killed it . . . Julia." The others surround Julia as the light fades.

Wounded though she is, Julia triumphs over Fefu whose hesitancies cast doubt on her ability to kill "it." Although the innovative staging calls for the audience participation that was a tenet of the 1960s, the play is true to Fornés' own major theme—the triumph of the irrational. Through another environment, Fefu and Julia continue the duel of Leopold and Isidore of *Tango Palace* into "the next stage of their battle."

Sam Shepard

Samuel Shepard Rogers VII was born in Illinois in 1943, but his father was a career man in the army, and like most "army brats," Shepard found himself repeatedly uprooted, moving from base to base around the country. If he has roots as a writer, they are clearly in the American West, but not necessarily the West created by writers of westerns, comic books, and second-rate movies. Shepard's plays often have a surreal quality, as though set in a world of the imagination rather than a real place like Paris, Texas.

Shepard has won numerous awards, including ten Obie Awards (given to off-Broadway plays) between 1966 and 1979, an Obie Award for sustained achievement in 1980, the New York Drama Critics' Circle Award for *A Lie of the Mind* in 1985, and a Pulitzer Prize for *Buried Child* in 1979. His work has been produced primarily in the experimental theater of downtown New York (in places such as La Mama) and in regional theaters throughout the United States known for artistic integrity but not for reaching a broad spectrum of theatergoers. In his way, Shepard has been an underground playwright who has won the respect of most theater people, including the best playwrights.

Shepard's love for and frustrations with music have found their way into his plays and represent a major theme of his work. He plays drums and guitar and has never realized an early desire for a career in rock music. But the subversive qualities of rock and jazz—their implicit critique of middle-class life—appear in his plays in his analyses of the middle-class family. His primary themes center on the family and its complications, the nature of the person alone, and the myth of the Old West. In each theme Shepard expresses a deep sense of longing and of loss, emotions that his audiences have found significant.

Because his father began to drink and family life became intolerable, Shepard left home after a year at college and began to tour with the Bishops Company Repertory Players. At nineteen he wound up in New York working in one of the best jazz clubs of the day, the Village Gate. During this time in Greenwich Village he began to write one-act plays with extraordinary energy. Like Jack Kerouac, he almost never revised his work. He wrote it in a burst of energy and then had it performed for audiences whose admiration grew.

In the 1970s Shepard began acting in major motion pictures. One of the ironies of his life is that he became a matinee idol after appearing in movies such as *The Right Stuff, Fool for Love, Country,* and *Crimes of the Heart.* The critic Harry Haun said of him, "He is the Recluse as Superstar, the man who has arrived on his own terms, carefully sculpting a special myth for himself."

Shepard's output for the stage has been prodigious, including dozens of one-act plays. He has a central body of work that has gained him an enviable reputation. *Operation Sidewinder* (1970) was performed at the Vivian Beaumont Theater—a public theater at Lincoln Center in New York City—to mixed reviews. The play, set in the West, involves a giant mechanical snake designed to make contact with travelers from outer space and also features Hopi snake dances and military scenes. *The Tooth of Crime* (1972) is about turf wars between an aging rock star and an up-and-coming young star. Its brutality and directness make it intense, exciting, and revealing of the California rock 'n' roll scene in the early 1970s.

Curse of the Starving Class (1977) and *Buried Child* (1978) both helped solidify Shepard's reputation. *Suicide in B-Flat* (1976) and *True West* (1980) only made it clearer that his work was developing a consistent vein of black humor and dark criticism of the sanctity of family life. *A Lie of the Mind* (1985), like *Buried Child,* is about disturbed family life. It is filled with secrets: incest, murder, and sin. *New York Times* critic Mel Gussow said that it explores "the damage that one does to filial, fraternal, and marital bonds." Incest—or potential incest—is also a theme in *Fool for Love* (1983), in which Shepard starred on film. The play is set in the West and contains all the themes for which his work is known.

Shepard continued to write plays even while directing and acting in films. His late plays have not had quite the impact of his earlier work, but they have been produced in the United States and abroad. *States of Shock* (1991), *Simpatico* (1994), *When the World Was Green* (1996), *Eyes for Consuela* (1998), and *The Late Henry Moss* (2000) all preceded *The God of Hell* (2004), which introduced midwestern characters from Wisconsin. The political content of Shepard's late plays is evident in this play: A dairy farmer and his wife take in Greg Haynes, a radioactive man on the run who worked in a plutonium-producing plant. Then Welch, a salesman pursuing Haynes, shows up selling patriotic pins and mementos and ends up terrorizing the family. Randy Quaid played the farmer and Tim Roth played Welch for the production in Westbeth, New York.

The Abbey Theatre in Dublin produced Shepard's *Kicking a Dead Horse* (2007), which he wrote for the actor Stephen Rae. The set included a dead horse that the character Hobart Struther, a New York art dealer who has given up the city to live in the West, kicks now and then while he is digging what seems to be the horse's grave. The play shows us one man's search for "authenticity" in his life, while at the same time deromanticizing the life of the cowboy. One critic saw a connection with "the U.S. kicking a dead horse" in Iraq. *Kicking a Dead Horse* was produced at the Public Theater of New York at the end of the 2007–2008 season.

Shepard began his work with a sense of the West drawn from popular literature, reshaped it, and reproduced it in a new form. Shepard is partly responsible for the way we now see the American West, a vision that replaced its mythicization in the dime novel and John Wayne's movies.

Buried Child

For discussion questions and assignments on *Buried Child*, visit bedfordstmartins.com/jacobus.

Buried Child won the Pulitzer Prize for drama in 1979. The play was developed in an intense collaborative effort with cast, crew, director, and playwrights using a process of give-and-take that Shepard has generally found fruitful. In some cases he has turned down offers of major commercial productions of his plays because they would preclude that kind of collaborative atmosphere.

Critics have seen this play as loosely related to *Curse of the Starving Class* (1977) and *True West* (1980), forming a "family" trilogy. The three plays are very different in style, but they all offer a view of the American family that is painfully distant from the sentimental idealism of popular magazines of the 1940s and 1950s. Shepard emphasizes the rootlessness of the family, its emotional chill, and its capacity for violence.

Buried Child is beguilingly ordinary at first glance. The simple interior is dominated by a television set and an old sofa. Vince's girlfriend Shelly, who is visiting for the first time, had imagined that the house would resemble a Norman Rockwell painting—that is, a stereotypical American home. It falls short of that, but the living room is nonetheless a recognizable, low-key, ordinary room that might be found anywhere in middle America. However, beginning with the ordinariness of the setting, the ordinariness of Tilden's walking in with an armful of corn, and Dodge's wracking cough, Shepard builds a portrait of an extraordinary family.

Dodge's one-track alcoholic mind seems a minor aberration at first. And Halie's nagging seems relatively normal. Even Tilden's distant relationship with his father seems close to ordinary. But when Vince and Shelly walk in and Vince identifies himself first to his grandfather and then to his father—whom he does not expect to find here—we begin to see that something is odd and that the situation is anything but ordinary. Neither grandfather nor father recognizes Vince. Eventually, as we watch Shepard explore the family relationships, we begin to sense that the surface ordinariness hides a deeper structure, one that is built on myth.

The play draws on agricultural myth similar to that in *Oedipus Rex,* which begins with a curse on the land. The crops have failed and there has been no rain. Yet Tilden walks in with an armful of corn, which Halie thinks he must have stolen. Critics have compared Tilden with the corn god, a symbol of renewal. Shepard adds to that the sense of doom visited upon the family as if its genes carried destruction. As in Wole Soyinka's *The Strong Breed,* responsibility is transmitted from father to son. Those who are of the strong breed do not escape their fate. It is not clear how responsibility is transmitted in Shepard's family until we begin to see that Vince assumes the role of Tilden and Halie's offspring, the child of incest who is buried on the arid land. In the terms of *The Strong Breed,* Vince can be thought of as a "carrier," willing or unwilling. When Dodge bequeaths the house to Vince, he seals Vince's fate.

Certainly during the course of the play we begin to see that a change is at hand. The rains have come. Halie, who doubted the existence of the corn, calls down at the end of the play: "It's like a paradise out there, Dodge. You oughta' take a look. A miracle." But the "old king," Dodge, is dead. Vince has come to take his place.

Buried Child in Performance

Buried Child was first produced at the Magic Theatre in San Francisco in June 1978. Later that year it was transferred to the Theater for the New City in Greenwich Village. In May 1979 it was awarded the Pulitzer Prize.

About the Yale Repertory Theatre production of 1979, *New York Times* critic Mel Gussow said, "The tone of the play is almost surrealistic. Like a figure out of Ionesco, the father brings in armloads of fresh vegetables from a garden that has been barren for years." In commenting on the New York and Yale productions of the play, he said they ended with "a dirge for the decline of traditional values, a wake for the American dream."

In 1980 the Trinity Repertory Company in Providence produced the play, directed by Adrian Hall, who had directed the Yale production. The Trinity production contrasted with the New York production in that the sets and lighting were "slicker," more detailed, and more subtle. One critic labeled the first production of *Buried Child* a "Gothic comedy," and that description has affected subsequent productions. For example, the MIT student production in 1985 aimed at Gothic effects: dark colors, suspense, and other staple ingredients of horror films. *Buried Child* finally made it to Broadway in 1996 when it was performed at the Brooks Atkinson Theatre. Gary Sinise directed the play in a production that was originally mounted in Chicago at the Steppenwolf Theatre Company, in which Ethan Hawke played Vince. Ben Brantley said that the play "has the intangible spookiness of nightmares." A 2006 production at the American Theatre of Actors in New York was cited as introducing an ironic touch of the Norman Rockwell image of an American family, echoing Shelly's line when she first sees the family home: "It's like a Norman Rockwell cover or something." Productions of that sort remind us that on one level, at least, this play is about a haunted house. The year 2010 saw productions in Austin, Texas; Fullerton, California; and Pittsburgh, Pennsylvania. Christopher Rawson praised the Playhouse Rep's Pittsburgh production, writing, "I think we can say the play is an American classic." *Buried Child* has become a favorite of university and college theaters.

SAM SHEPARD (b. 1943)

Buried Child   1978

While the rain of your fingertips falls,
while the rain of your bones falls,
and your laughter and marrow fall down,
you come flying.   —PABLO NERUDA

Characters

DODGE, *in his seventies*
HALIE, *his wife, mid-sixties*
TILDEN, *their oldest son*
BRADLEY, *their next oldest son, an amputee*
VINCE, *Tilden's son*
SHELLY, *Vince's girlfriend*
FATHER DEWIS, *a Protestant minister*

ACT 1

Scene: *Day. Old wooden staircase down left with pale, frayed carpet laid down on the steps. The stairs lead offstage left up into the wings with no landing. Up right is an old, dark green sofa with the stuffing coming out in spots. Stage right of the sofa is an upright lamp with a faded yellow shade and a small night table with several small bottles of pills on it. Down right of the sofa, with the screen facing the sofa, is a large, old-fashioned brown TV. A flickering blue light comes from the screen, but no image, no sound. In the dark, the light of the* lamp and the TV slowly brighten in the black space. The space behind the sofa, upstage, is a large, screened-in porch with a board floor. A solid interior door to stage right of the sofa, leading into the room onstage; and another screen door up left, leading from the porch to the outside. Beyond that are the shapes of dark elm trees.

Gradually the form of Dodge is made out, sitting on the couch, facing the TV, the blue light flickering on his face. He wears a well-worn T-shirt, suspenders, khaki work pants, and brown slippers. He's covered himself in an old brown blanket. He's very thin and sickly looking, in his late seventies. He just stares at the TV. More light fills the stage softly. The sound of light rain. Dodge slowly tilts his head back and stares at the ceiling for a while, listening to the rain. He lowers his head again and stares at the TV. He turns his head slowly to the left and stares at the cushion of the sofa next to the one he's sitting on. He pulls his left arm out from under the blanket, slides his hand under the cushion, and pulls out a bottle of whiskey. He looks down left toward the staircase, listens, then uncaps the bottle, takes a long swig, and caps it again. He puts the bottle back under the cushion and stares at the TV. He starts to cough slowly and softly. The coughing gradually builds. He holds one hand to his mouth and tries to stifle it. The coughing gets louder, then suddenly stops when he hears the sound of his wife's voice coming from the top of the staircase.

HALIE'S VOICE: Dodge?

(Dodge just stares at the TV. Long pause. He stifles two short coughs.)

HALIE'S VOICE: Dodge! You want a pill, Dodge?

(He doesn't answer. Takes the bottle out again and takes another long swig. Puts the bottle back, stares at TV, pulls blanket up around his neck.)

HALIE'S VOICE: You know what it is, don't you? It's the rain! Weather. That's it. Every time. Every time you get like this, it's the rain. No sooner does the rain start then you start. *(Pause.)* Dodge?

(He makes no reply. Pulls a pack of cigarettes out from his sweater and lights one. Stares at TV. Pause.)

HALIE'S VOICE: You should see it coming down up here. Just coming down in sheets. Blue sheets. The bridge is pretty near flooded. What's it like down there? Dodge?

(Dodge turns his head back over his left shoulder and takes a look out through the porch. He turns back to the TV.)

DODGE *(to himself)*: Catastrophic.
HALIE'S VOICE: What? What'd you say, Dodge?
DODGE *(louder)*: It looks like rain to me! Plain old rain!
HALIE'S VOICE: Rain? Of course it's rain! Are you having a seizure or something! Dodge? *(Pause.)* I'm coming down there in about five minutes if you don't answer me!
DODGE: Don't come down.
HALIE'S VOICE: What!
DODGE *(louder)*: Don't come down!

(He has another coughing attack. Stops.)

HALIE'S VOICE: You should take a pill for that! I don't see why you just don't take a pill. Be done with it once and for all. Put a stop to it.

(He takes bottle out again. Another swig. Returns bottle.)

HALIE'S VOICE: It's not Christian, but it works. It's not necessarily Christian, that is. We don't know. There's some things the ministers can't even answer. I, personally, can't see anything wrong with it. Pain is pain. Pure and simple. Suffering is a different matter. That's entirely different. A pill seems as good an answer as any. Dodge? *(Pause.)* Dodge, are you watching baseball?
DODGE: No.
HALIE'S VOICE: What?
DODGE *(louder)*: No!
HALIE'S VOICE: What're you watching? You shouldn't be watching anything that'll get you excited! No horse racing!

DODGE: They don't race on Sundays.
HALIE'S VOICE: What?
DODGE *(louder)*: They don't race on Sundays!
HALIE'S VOICE: Well they shouldn't race on Sundays.
DODGE: Well they don't!
HALIE'S VOICE: Good. I'm amazed they still have that kind of legislation. That's amazing.
DODGE: Yeah, it's amazing.
HALIE'S VOICE: What?
DODGE *(louder)*: It is amazing!
HALIE'S VOICE: It is. It truly is. I would've thought these days they'd be racing on Christmas even. A big flashing Christmas tree right down at the finish line.
DODGE *(shakes his head)*: No.
HALIE'S VOICE: They used to race on New Year's! I remember that.
DODGE: They never raced on New Year's!
HALIE'S VOICE: Sometimes they did.
DODGE: They never did!
HALIE'S VOICE: Before we were married they did!

(Dodge waves his hand in disgust at the staircase. Leans back in sofa. Stares at TV.)

HALIE'S VOICE: I went once. With a man.
DODGE *(mimicking her)*: Oh, a "man."
HALIE'S VOICE: What?
DODGE: Nothing!
HALIE'S VOICE: A wonderful man. A breeder.
DODGE: A what?
HALIE'S VOICE: A breeder! A horse breeder! Thoroughbreds.
DODGE: Oh, thoroughbreds. Wonderful.
HALIE'S VOICE: That's right. He knew everything there was to know.
DODGE: I bet he taught you a thing or two, huh? Gave you a good turn around the old stable!
HALIE'S VOICE: Knew everything there was to know about horses. We won bookoos of money that day.
DODGE: What?
HALIE'S VOICE: Money! We won every race I think.
DODGE: Bookoos?
HALIE'S VOICE: Every single race.
DODGE: Bookoos of money?
HALIE'S VOICE: It was one of those kind of days.
DODGE: New Year's!
HALIE'S VOICE: Yes! It might've been Florida. Or California! One of those two.
DODGE: Can I take my pick?
HALIE'S VOICE: It was Florida!
DODGE: Aha!
HALIE'S VOICE: Wonderful! Absolutely wonderful! The sun was just gleaming. Flamingos. Bougainvilleas. Palm trees.
DODGE *(to himself, mimicking her)*: Bougainvilleas. Palm trees.
HALIE'S VOICE: Everything was dancing with life! There were all kinds of people from everywhere. Everyone was dressed to the nines. Not like today. Not like they dress today.
DODGE: When was this anyway?

HALIE'S VOICE: This was long before I knew you.

DODGE: Must've been.

HALIE'S VOICE: Long before. I was escorted.

DODGE: To Florida?

HALIE'S VOICE: Yes. Or it might've been California. I'm not sure which.

DODGE: All that way you were escorted?

HALIE'S VOICE: Yes.

DODGE: And he never laid a finger on you, I suppose? (*Long silence.*) Halie?

(*No answer. Long pause.*)

HALIE'S VOICE: Are you going out today?

DODGE (*gesturing toward rain*): In this?

HALIE'S VOICE: I'm just asking a simple question.

DODGE: I rarely go out in the bright sunshine, why would I go out in this?

HALIE'S VOICE: I'm just asking because I'm not doing any shopping today. And if you need anything you should ask Tilden.

DODGE: Tilden's not here!

HALIE'S VOICE: He's in the kitchen.

(*Dodge looks toward stage left, then back toward TV.*)

DODGE: All right.

HALIE'S VOICE: What?

DODGE (*louder*): All right!

HALIE'S VOICE: Don't scream. It'll only get your coughing started.

DODGE: All right.

HALIE'S VOICE: Just tell Tilden what you want and he'll get it. (*Pause.*) Bradley should be over later.

DODGE: Bradley?

HALIE'S VOICE: Yes. To cut your hair.

DODGE: My hair? I don't need my hair cut!

HALIE'S VOICE: It won't hurt!

DODGE: I don't need it!

HALIE'S VOICE: It's been more than two weeks, Dodge.

DODGE: I don't need it!

HALIE'S VOICE: I have to meet Father Dewis for lunch.

DODGE: You tell Bradley that if he shows up here with those clippers, I'll kill him!

HALIE'S VOICE: I won't be very late. No later than four at the very latest.

DODGE: You tell him! Last time he left me almost bald! And I wasn't even awake! I was sleeping! I woke up and he'd already left!

HALIE'S VOICE: That's not my fault!

DODGE: You put him up to it!

HALIE'S VOICE: I never did!

DODGE: You did too! You had some fancy, stupid meeting planned! Time to dress up the corpse for company! Lower the ears a little! Put up a little front! Surprised you didn't tape a pipe to my mouth while you were at it! That woulda' looked nice! Huh? A pipe? Maybe a bowler hat! Maybe a copy of the *Wall Street Journal* casually placed on my lap!

HALIE'S VOICE: You always imagine the worst things of people!

DODGE: That's not the worst! That's the least of the worst!

HALIE'S VOICE: I don't need to hear it! All day long I hear things like that and I don't need to hear more.

DODGE: You better tell him!

HALIE'S VOICE: You tell him yourself! He's your own son. You should be able to talk to your own son.

DODGE: Not while I'm sleeping! He cut my hair while I was sleeping!

HALIE'S VOICE: Well, he won't do it again.

DODGE: There's no guarantee.

HALIE'S VOICE: I promise he won't do it without your consent.

DODGE (*after pause*): There's no reason for him to even come over here.

HALIE'S VOICE: He feels responsible.

DODGE: For my hair?

HALIE'S VOICE: For your appearance.

DODGE: My appearance is out of his domain! It's even out of mine! In fact, it's disappeared! I'm an invisible man!

HALIE'S VOICE: Don't be ridiculous.

DODGE: He better not try it. That's all I've got to say.

HALIE'S VOICE: Tilden will watch out for you.

DODGE: Tilden won't protect me from Bradley!

HALIE'S VOICE: Tilden's the oldest. He'll protect you.

DODGE: Tilden can't even protect himself!

HALIE'S VOICE: Not so loud! He'll hear you. He's right in the kitchen.

DODGE (*yelling off left*): Tilden!

HALIE'S VOICE: Dodge, what are you trying to do?

DODGE (*yelling off left*): Tilden, get in here!

HALIE'S VOICE: Why do you enjoy stirring things up?

DODGE: I don't enjoy anything!

HALIE'S VOICE: That's a terrible thing to say.

DODGE: Tilden!

HALIE'S VOICE: That's the kind of statement that leads people right to the end of their rope.

DODGE: Tilden!

HALIE'S VOICE: It's no wonder people turn to Christ!

DODGE: TILDEN!!

HALIE'S VOICE: It's no wonder the messengers of God's word are shouted down in public places!

DODGE: TILDEN!!!!

(*Dodge goes into a violent, spasmodic coughing attack as Tilden enters from stage left, his arms loaded with fresh ears of corn. Tilden is Dodge's oldest son, late forties, wears heavy construction boots, covered with mud, dark green work pants, a plaid shirt, and a faded brown windbreaker. He has a butch haircut, wet from the rain. Something about him is profoundly burned out and displaced. He stops center stage with the ears of corn in his arms and just stares at Dodge until he slowly finishes his coughing attack. Dodge looks up at him slowly. He stares at the corn. Long pause as they watch each other.*)

HALIE'S VOICE: Dodge, if you don't take that pill nobody's going to force you.

(*The two men ignore the voice.*)

DODGE (*to Tilden*): Where'd you get that?
TILDEN: Picked it.
DODGE: You picked all that?

(*Tilden nods.*)

DODGE: You expecting company?
TILDEN: No.
DODGE: Where'd you pick it from?
TILDEN: Right out back.
DODGE: Out back where!
TILDEN: Right out in back.
DODGE: There's nothing out there!
TILDEN: There's corn.
DODGE: There hasn't been corn out there since about nineteen thirty-five! That's the last time I planted corn out there!
TILDEN: It's out there now.
DODGE (*yelling at stairs*): Halie!
HALIE'S VOICE: Yes dear!
DODGE: Tilden's brought a whole bunch of corn in here! There's no corn out in back is there?
TILDEN (*to himself*): There's tons of corn.
HALIE'S VOICE: Not that I know of!
DODGE: That's what I thought.
HALIE'S VOICE: Not since about nineteen thirty-five!
DODGE (*to Tilden*): That's right. Nineteen thirty-five.
TILDEN: It's out there now.
DODGE: You go and take that corn back to wherever you got it from!
TILDEN (*after pause, staring at Dodge*): It's picked. I picked it all in the rain. Once it's picked you can't put it back.
DODGE: I haven't had trouble with neighbors here for fifty-seven years. I don't even know who the neighbors are! And I don't wanna know! Now go put that corn back where it came from!

(*Tilden stares at Dodge, then walks slowly over to him and dumps all the corn on Dodge's lap and steps back. Dodge stares at the corn, then back to Tilden. Long pause.*)

DODGE: Are you having trouble here, Tilden? Are you in some kind of trouble?
TILDEN: I'm not in any trouble.
DODGE: You can tell me if you are. I'm still your father.
TILDEN: I know you're still my father.
DODGE: I know you had a little trouble back in New Mexico. That's why you came out here.
TILDEN: I never had any trouble.
DODGE: Tilden, your mother told me all about it.
TILDEN: What'd she tell you?

(*Tilden pulls some chewing tobacco out of his jacket and bites off a plug.*)

DODGE: I don't have to repeat what she told me! She told me all about it!
TILDEN: Can I bring my chair in from the kitchen?

DODGE: What?
TILDEN: Can I bring in my chair from the kitchen?
DODGE: Sure. Bring your chair in.

(*Tilden exits left. Dodge pushes all the corn off his lap onto the floor. He pulls the blanket off angrily and tosses it at one end of the sofa, pulls out the bottle and takes another swig. Tilden enters again from left with a milking stool and a pail. Dodge hides the bottle quickly under the cushion before Tilden sees it. Tilden sets the stool down by the sofa, sits on it, puts the pail in front of him on the floor. Tilden starts picking up the ears of corn one at a time and husking them. He throws the husks and silk in the center of the stage and drops the ears into the pail each time he cleans one. He repeats this process as they talk.*)

DODGE (*after pause*): Sure is nice looking corn.
TILDEN: It's the best.
DODGE: Hybrid?
TILDEN: What?
DODGE: Some kinda fancy hybrid?
TILDEN: You planted it. I don't know what it is.
DODGE (*pause*): Tilden, look, you can't stay here forever. You know that, don't you?
TILDEN (*spits in spittoon*): I'm not.
DODGE: I know you're not. I'm not worried about that. That's not the reason I brought it up.
TILDEN: What's the reason?
DODGE: The reason is I'm wondering what you're gonna do.
TILDEN: You're not worried about me, are you?
DODGE: I'm not worried about you.
TILDEN: You weren't worried about me when I wasn't here. When I was in New Mexico.
DODGE: No, I wasn't worried about you then either.
TILDEN: You shoulda worried about me then.
DODGE: Why's that? You didn't do anything down there, did you?
TILDEN: I didn't do anything.
DODGE: Then why should I have worried about you?
TILDEN: Because I was lonely.
DODGE: Because you were lonely?
TILDEN: Yeah. I was more lonely than I've ever been before.
DODGE: Why was that?
TILDEN (*pause*): Could I have some of that whiskey you've got?
DODGE: What whiskey? I haven't got any whiskey.
TILDEN: You've got some under the sofa.
DODGE: I haven't got anything under the sofa! Now mind your own damn business! Jesus God, you come into the house outa the middle of nowhere, haven't heard or seen you in twenty years and suddenly you're making accusations.
TILDEN: I'm not making accusations.
DODGE: You're accusing me of hoarding whiskey under the sofa!
TILDEN: I'm not accusing you.
DODGE: You just got through telling me I had whiskey under the sofa!

HALIE'S VOICE: Dodge?

DODGE (*to Tilden*): Now she knows about it!

TILDEN: She doesn't know about it.

HALIE'S VOICE: Dodge, are you talking to yourself down there?

DODGE: I'm talking to Tilden!

HALIE'S VOICE: Tilden's down there?

DODGE: He's right here!

HALIE'S VOICE: What?

DODGE (*louder*): He's right here!

HALIE'S VOICE: What's he doing?

DODGE (*to Tilden*): Don't answer her.

TILDEN (*to Dodge*): I'm not doing anything wrong.

DODGE: I know you're not.

HALIE'S VOICE: What's he doing down there!

DODGE (*to Tilden*): Don't answer.

TILDEN: I'm not.

HALIE'S VOICE: Dodge!

(*The men sit in silence. Dodge lights a cigarette. Tilden keeps husking corn, spits tobacco now and then in spittoon.*)

HALIE'S VOICE: Dodge! He's not drinking anything, is he? You see to it that he doesn't drink anything! You've gotta watch out for him. It's our responsibility. He can't look after himself anymore, so we have to do it. Nobody else will do it. We can't just send him away somewhere. If we had lots of money we could send him away. But we don't. We never will. That's why we have to stay healthy. You and me. Nobody's going to look after us. Bradley can't look after us. Bradley can hardly look after himself. I was always hoping that Tilden would look out for Bradley when they got older. After Bradley lost his leg. Tilden's the oldest. I always thought he'd be the one to take responsibility. I had no idea in the world that Tilden would be so much trouble. Who would've dreamed. Tilden was an All-American, don't forget. Don't forget that. Fullback. Or quarterback. I forget which.

TILDEN (*to himself*): Fullback. (*Still husking.*)

HALIE'S VOICE: Then when Tilden turned out to be so much trouble, I put all my hopes on Ansel. Of course Ansel wasn't as handsome, but he was smart. He was the smartest probably. I think he probably was. Smarter than Bradley, that's for sure. Didn't go and chop his leg off with a chain saw. Smart enough not to go and do that. I think he was smarter than Tilden too. Especially after Tilden got in all that trouble. Doesn't take brains to go to jail. Anybody knows that. Course then when Ansel died that left us all alone. Same as being alone. No different. Same as if they'd all died. He was the smartest. He could've earned lots of money. Lots and lots of money.

(*Halie enters slowly from the top of the staircase as she continues talking. Just her feet are seen at first as she makes her way down the stairs, a step at a time.*)

She appears dressed completely in black, as though in mourning. Black handbag, hat with a veil, and pulling on elbow-length black gloves. She is about sixty-five with pure white hair. She remains absorbed in what she's saying as she descends the stairs and doesn't really notice the two men who continue sitting there as they were before she came down, smoking and husking.)

HALIE: He would've took care of us, too. He would've seen to it that we were repaid. He was like that. He was a hero. Don't forget that. A genuine hero. Brave. Strong. And very intelligent. Ansel could've been a great man. One of the greatest. I only regret that he didn't die in action. It's not fitting for a man like that to die in a motel room. A soldier. He could've won a medal. He could've been decorated for valor. I've talked to Father Dewis about putting up a plaque for Ansel. He thinks it's a good idea. He agrees. He knew Ansel when he used to play basketball. Went to every game. Ansel was his favorite player. He even recommended to the City Council that they put up a statue of Ansel. A big, tall statue with a basketball in one hand and a rifle in the other. That's how much he thinks of Ansel.

(*Halie reaches the stage and begins to wander around, still absorbed in pulling on her gloves, brushing lint off her dress, and continuously talking to herself as the men just sit.*)

HALIE: Of course, he'd still be alive today if he hadn't married into the Catholics. The Mob. How in the world he never opened his eyes to that is beyond me. Just beyond me. Everyone around him could see the truth. Even Tilden. Tilden told him time and again. Catholic women are the Devil incarnate. He wouldn't listen. He was blind with love. Blind. I knew. Everyone knew. The wedding was more like a funeral. You remember? All those Italians. All that horrible black, greasy hair. The smell of cheap cologne. I think even the priest was wearing a pistol. When he gave her the ring I knew he was a dead man. I knew it. As soon as he gave her the ring. But then it was the honeymoon that killed him. The honeymoon. I knew he'd never come back from the honeymoon. I kissed him and he felt like a corpse. All white. Cold. Icy blue lips. He never used to kiss like that. Never before. I knew then that she'd cursed him. Taken his soul. I saw it in her eyes. She smiled at me with that Catholic sneer of hers. She told me with her eyes that she'd murder him in his bed. Murder my son. She told me. And there was nothing I could do. Absolutely nothing. He was going with her, thinking he was free. Thinking it was love. What could I do? I couldn't tell him she was a witch. I couldn't tell him that. He'd have turned on me. Hated me. I couldn't stand him hating me and then dying before he ever saw me again. Hating me in his death bed. Hating me and loving her! How could I do that? I had to let him go. I had to. I watched him leave. I watched him throw gardenias as he helped her into the limousine. I watched his face disappear behind the glass.

(*She stops abruptly and stares at the corn husks. She looks around the space as though just waking up. She turns and looks hard at Tilden and Dodge who continue sitting calmly. She looks again at the corn husks.*)

HALIE (*pointing to the husks*): What's this in my house! (*Kicks husks.*) What's all this!

(*Tilden stops husking and stares at her.*)

HALIE (*to Dodge*): And you encourage him!

(*Dodge pulls blanket over him again.*)

DODGE: You're going out in the rain?
HALIE: It's not raining.

(*Tilden starts husking again.*)

DODGE: Not in Florida it's not.
HALIE: We're not in Florida!
DODGE: It's not raining at the race track.
HALIE: Have you been taking those pills? Those pills always make you talk crazy. Tilden, has he been taking those pills?
TILDEN: He hasn't took anything.
HALIE (*to Dodge*): What've you been taking?
DODGE: It's not raining in California or Florida or the race track. Only in Illinois. This is the only place it's raining. All over the rest of the world it's bright golden sunshine.

(*Halie goes to the night table next to the sofa and checks the bottle of pills.*)

HALIE: Which ones did you take? Tilden, you must've seen him take something.
TILDEN: He never took a thing.
HALIE: Then why's he talking crazy?
TILDEN: I've been here the whole time.
HALIE: Then you've both been taking something!
TILDEN: I've just been husking the corn.
HALIE: Where'd you get that corn anyway? Why is the house suddenly full of corn?
DODGE: Bumper crop!
HALIE (*moving center*): We haven't had corn here for over thirty years.
TILDEN: The whole back lot's full of corn. Far as the eye can see.
DODGE (*to Halie*): Things keep happening while you're upstairs, ya know. The world doesn't stop just because you're upstairs. Corn keeps growing. Rain keeps raining.
HALIE: I'm not unaware of the world around me! Thank you very much. It so happens that I have an overall view from the upstairs. The back yard's in plain view of my window. And there's no corn to speak of. Absolutely none!
DODGE: Tilden wouldn't lie. If he says there's corn, there's corn.
HALIE: What's the meaning of this corn, Tilden!

TILDEN: It's a mystery to me. I was out in back there. And the rain was coming down. And I didn't feel like coming back inside. I didn't feel the cold so much. I didn't mind the wet. So I was just walking. I was muddy but I didn't mind the mud so much. And I looked up. And I saw this stand of corn. In fact I was standing in it. So, I was standing in it.
HALIE: There isn't any corn outside, Tilden! There's no corn! Now, you must've either stolen this corn or you bought it.
DODGE: He doesn't have any money.
HALIE (*to Tilden*): So you stole it!
TILDEN: I didn't steal it. I don't want to get kicked out of Illinois. I was kicked out of New Mexico and I don't want to get kicked out of Illinois.
HALIE: You're going to get kicked out of this house, Tilden, if you don't tell me where you got that corn!

(*Tilden starts crying softly to himself but keeps husking corn. Pause.*)

DODGE (*to Halie*): Why'd you have to tell him that? Who cares where he got the corn? Why'd you have to go and tell him that?
HALIE (*to Dodge*): It's your fault you know! You're the one that's behind all this! I suppose you thought it'd be funny! Some joke! Cover the house with corn husks. You better get this cleaned up before Bradley sees it.
DODGE: Bradley's not getting in the front door!
HALIE (*kicking husks, striding back and forth*): Bradley's going to be very upset when he sees this. He doesn't like to see the house in disarray. He can't stand it when one thing is out of place. The slightest thing. You know how he gets.
DODGE: Bradley doesn't even live here!
HALIE: It's his home as much as ours. He was born in this house!
DODGE: He was born in a hog wallow.
HALIE: Don't you say that! Don't you ever say that!
DODGE: He was born in a goddamn hog wallow! That's where he was born and that's where he belongs! He doesn't belong in this house!
HALIE (*she stops*): I don't know what's come over you, Dodge. I don't know what in the world's come over you. You've become an evil man. You used to be a good man.
DODGE: Six of one, a half dozen of another.
HALIE: You sit here day and night, festering away! Decomposing! Smelling up the house with your putrid body! Hacking your head off till all hours of the morning! Thinking up mean, evil, stupid things to say about your own flesh and blood!
DODGE: He's not my flesh and blood! My flesh and blood's buried in the back yard!

(*They freeze. Long pause. The men stare at her.*)

HALIE (*quietly*): That's enough, Dodge. That's quite enough. I'm going out now. I'm going to have lunch with Father Dewis. I'm going to ask him about a monument. A statue. At least a plaque.

(*She crosses to the door up right. She stops.*)

HALIE: If you need anything, ask Tilden. He's the oldest. I've left some money on the kitchen table.
DODGE: I don't need anything.
HALIE: No, I suppose not. (*She opens the door and looks out through porch.*) Still raining. I love the smell just after it stops. The ground. I won't be too late.

(*She goes out door and closes it. She's still visible on the porch as she crosses toward stage left screen door. She stops in the middle of the porch, speaks to Dodge but doesn't turn to him.*)

HALIE: Dodge, tell Tilden not to go out in the back lot anymore. I don't want him back there in the rain.
DODGE: You tell him. He's sitting right here.
HALIE: He never listens to me, Dodge. He's never listened to me in the past.
DODGE: I'll tell him.
HALIE: We have to watch him just like we used to now. Just like we always have. He's still a child.
DODGE: I'll watch him.
HALIE: Good.

(*She crosses to screen door, left, takes an umbrella off a hook, and goes out the door. The door slams behind her. Long pause. Tilden husks corn, stares at pail. Dodge lights a cigarette, stares at TV.*)

TILDEN (*still husking*): You shouldn't a told her that.
DODGE (*staring at TV*): What?
TILDEN: What you told her. You know.
DODGE: What do you know about it?
TILDEN: I know. I know all about it. We all know.
DODGE: So what difference does it make? Everybody knows, everybody's forgot.
TILDEN: She hasn't forgot.
DODGE: She should've forgot.
TILDEN: It's different for a woman. She couldn't forget that. How could she forget that?
DODGE: I don't want to talk about it!
TILDEN: What do you want to talk about?
DODGE: I don't want to talk about anything! I don't want to talk about troubles or what happened fifty years ago or thirty years ago or the race track or Florida or the last time I seeded the corn! I don't want to talk!
TILDEN: You don't wanna die, do you?
DODGE: No, I don't wanna die either.
TILDEN: Well, you gotta talk or you'll die.
DODGE: Who told you that?
TILDEN: That's what I know. I found that out in New Mexico. I thought I was dying but I just lost my voice.
DODGE: Were you with somebody?
TILDEN: I was alone. I thought I was dead.
DODGE: Might as well have been. What'd you come back here for?
TILDEN: I didn't know where to go.

DODGE: You're a grown man. You shouldn't be needing your parents at your age. It's unnatural. There's nothing we can do for you now anyway. Couldn't you make a living down there? Couldn't you find some way to make a living? Support yourself? What'd'ya come back here for? You expect us to feed you forever?
TILDEN: I didn't know where else to go.
DODGE: I never went back to my parents. Never. Never even had the urge. I was independent. Always independent. Always found a way.
TILDEN: I didn't know what to do. I couldn't figure anything out.
DODGE: There's nothing to figure out. You just forge ahead. What's there to figure out?

(*Tilden stands.*)

TILDEN: I don't know.
DODGE: Where are you going?
TILDEN: Out back.
DODGE: You're not supposed to go out there. You heard what she said. Don't play deaf with me!
TILDEN: I like it out there.
DODGE: In the rain?
TILDEN: Especially in the rain. I like the feeling of it. Feels like it always did.
DODGE: You're supposed to watch out for me. Get me things when I need them.
TILDEN: What do you need?
DODGE: I don't need anything! But I might. I might need something any second. Any second now. I can't be left alone for a minute!

(*Dodge starts to cough.*)

TILDEN: I'll be right outside. You can just yell.
DODGE (*between coughs*): No! It's too far! You can't go out there! It's too far! You might not ever hear me!
TILDEN (*moving to pills*): Why don't you take a pill? You want a pill?

(*Dodge coughs more violently, throws himself back against sofa, clutches his throat. Tilden stands by helplessly.*)

DODGE: Water! Get me some water!

(*Tilden rushes off left. Dodge reaches out for the pills, knocking some bottles to the floor, coughing in spasms. He grabs a small bottle, takes out pills, and swallows them. Tilden rushes back on with a glass of water. Dodge takes it and drinks, his coughing subsides.*)

TILDEN: You all right now?

(*Dodge nods. Drinks more water. Tilden moves in closer to him. Dodge sets glass of water on the night table. His coughing is almost gone.*)

TILDEN: Why don't you lay down for a while? Just rest a little.

(*Tilden helps Dodge lay down on the sofa. Covers him with blanket.*)

DODGE: You're not going outside, are you?

TILDEN: No.

DODGE: I don't want to wake up and find you not here.

TILDEN: I'll be here.

(*Tilden tucks blanket around Dodge.*)

DODGE: You'll stay right here?

TILDEN: I'll stay in my chair.

DODGE: That's not a chair. That's my old milking stool.

TILDEN: I know.

DODGE: Don't call it a chair.

TILDEN: I won't.

(*Tilden tries to take Dodge's baseball cap off.*)

DODGE: What're you doing! Leave that on me! Don't take that offa me! That's my cap!

(*Tilden leaves the cap on Dodge.*)

TILDEN: I know.

DODGE: Bradley'll shave my head if I don't have that on. That's my cap.

TILDEN: I know it is.

DODGE: Don't take my cap off.

TILDEN: I won't.

DODGE: You stay right here now.

TILDEN (*sits on stool*): I will.

DODGE: Don't go outside. There's nothing out there.

TILDEN: I won't.

DODGE: Everything's in here. Everything you need. Money's on the table. TV. Is the TV on?

TILDEN: Yeah.

DODGE: Turn it off! Turn the damn thing off! What's it doing on?

TILDEN (*shuts off TV, light goes out*): You left it on.

DODGE: Well, turn it off.

TILDEN (*sits on stool again*): It's off.

DODGE: Leave it off.

TILDEN: I will.

DODGE: When I fall asleep you can turn it on.

TILDEN: Okay.

DODGE: You can watch the ball game. Red Sox. You like the Red Sox don't you?

TILDEN: Yeah.

DODGE: You can watch the Red Sox. Pee Wee Reese. Pee Wee Reese. You remember Pee Wee Reese?

TILDEN: No.

DODGE: Was he with the Red Sox?

TILDEN: I don't know.

DODGE: Pee Wee Reese. (*Falling asleep.*) You can watch the Cardinals. You remember Stan Musial.

TILDEN: No.

DODGE: Stan Musial. (*Falling into sleep.*) Bases loaded. Top a' the sixth. Bases loaded. Runner on first and third. Big fat knuckle ball. Floater. Big as a blimp. Cracko! Ball just took off like a rocket. Just pulverized. I marked it. Marked it with my eyes. Straight between the clock and the Burma Shave ad. I was the first kid out there. First kid. I had to fight hard for that ball. I wouldn't give it up. They almost tore the ears right off me. But I wouldn't give it up.

(*Dodge falls into deep sleep. Tilden just sits staring at him for a while. Slowly he leans toward the sofa, checking to see if Dodge is well asleep. He reaches slowly under the cushion and pulls out the bottle of booze. Dodge sleeps soundly. Tilden stands quietly, staring at Dodge as he uncaps the bottle and takes a long drink. He caps the bottle and sticks it in his hip pocket. He looks around at the husks on the floor and then back to Dodge. He moves center stage and gathers an armload of corn husks then crosses back to the sofa. He stands holding the husks over Dodge and looking down at him he gently spreads the corn husks over the whole length of Dodge's body. He stands back and looks at Dodge. Pulls out bottle, takes another drink, returns bottle to his hip pocket. He gathers more husks and repeats the procedure until the floor is clean of corn husks and Dodge is completely covered in them except for his head. Tilden takes another long drink, stares at Dodge sleeping, then quietly exits stage left. Long pause as the sound of rain continues. Dodge sleeps on. The figure of Bradley appears up left, outside the screen porch door. He holds a wet newspaper over his head as a protection from the rain. He seems to be struggling with the door, then slips and almost falls to the ground. Dodge sleeps on, undisturbed.*)

BRADLEY: Sonuvabitch! Sonuvagoddamnbitch!

(*Bradley recovers his footing and makes it through the screen door onto the porch. He throws the newspaper down, shakes the water out of his hair, and brushes the rain off of his shoulders. He is a big man dressed in a gray sweatshirt, black suspenders, baggy dark blue pants, and black janitor's shoes. His left leg is wooden, having been amputated above the knee. He moves with an exaggerated, almost mechanical limp. The squeaking sounds of leather and metal accompany his walk coming from the harness and hinges of the false leg. His arms and shoulders are extremely powerful and muscular due to a lifetime dependency on the upper torso doing all the work for the legs. He is about five years younger than Tilden. He moves laboriously to the stage right door and enters, closing the door behind him. He doesn't notice Dodge at first. He moves toward the staircase.*)

BRADLEY (*calling to upstairs*): Mom!

(*He stops and listens. Turns upstage and sees Dodge sleeping. Notices corn husks. He moves slowly toward sofa. Stops next to pail and looks into it. Looks at husks. Dodge stays asleep. Talks to himself.*)

BRADLEY: What in the hell is this?

(*He looks at Dodge's sleeping face and shakes his head in disgust. He pulls out a pair of black electric hair clippers from his pocket. Unwinds the cord and crosses to the lamp. He jabs his wooden leg behind the knee, causing it to bend at the joint and awkwardly kneels to plug the cord into a floor outlet. He pulls himself to his feet again by using the sofa as leverage. He moves to Dodge's head and again jabs his false leg. Goes down*)

on one knee. He violently knocks away some of the
corn husks, and then jerks off Dodge's baseball cap
and throws it down center stage. Dodge stays asleep.
Bradley switches on the clippers. Lights start dimming.
Bradley cuts Dodge's hair while he sleeps. Lights dim
slowly to black with the sound of clippers and rain.)

ACT 2

*Scene: Same set as act 1. Night. Sound of rain. Dodge
still asleep on sofa. His hair is cut extremely short and
in places the scalp is cut and bleeding. His cap is still
center stage. All the corn and husks, pail and milking
stool have been cleared away. The lights come up to
the sound of a young girl laughing offstage left. Dodge
remains asleep. Shelly and Vince appear up left outside
the screen porch door sharing the shelter of Vince's
overcoat above their heads. Shelly is about nineteen,
black hair, very beautiful. She wears tight jeans, high
heels, purple T-shirt, and a short rabbit fur coat. Her
makeup is exaggerated and her hair has been curled.
Vince is Tilden's son, about twenty-two, wears a plaid
shirt, jeans, dark glasses, cowboy boots and carries a
black saxophone case. They shake the rain off themselves as they enter the porch through the screen door.*

SHELLY (*laughing, gesturing to house*): This is it? I don't
    believe this is it!
VINCE: This is it.
SHELLY: This is the house?
VINCE: This is the house.
SHELLY: I don't believe it!
VINCE: How come?
SHELLY: It's like a Norman Rockwell cover or something.
VINCE: What's a' matter with that? It's American.
SHELLY: Where's the milkman and the little dog? What's
    the little dog's name? Spot. Spot and Jane. Dick and
    Jane and Spot.
VINCE: Knock it off.
SHELLY: Dick and Jane and Spot and Mom and Dad and
    Junior and Sissy!

(*She laughs. Slaps her knee.*)

VINCE: Come on! It's my heritage. What dya' expect?

(*She laughs more hysterically, out of control.*)

SHELLY: "And Tuffy and Toto and Dooda and Bonzo all
    went down one day to the corner grocery store to buy
    a big bag of licorice for Mr. Marshall's pussy cat!"

(*She laughs so hard she falls to her knees holding her
stomach. Vince stands there looking at her.*)

VINCE: Shelly, will you get up!

(*She keeps laughing. Staggers to her feet. Turning in
circles holding her stomach.*)

SHELLY (*continuing her story in kid's voice*): "Mr.
    Marshall was on vacation. He had no idea that the

four little boys had taken such a liking to his little
    kitty cat."
VINCE: Have some respect, would ya'!
SHELLY (*trying to control herself*): I'm sorry.
VINCE: Pull yourself together.
SHELLY (*salutes him*): Yes, sir.

(*She giggles.*)

VINCE: Jesus Christ, Shelly.
SHELLY (*pause, smiling*): And Mr. Marshall—
VINCE: Cut it out.

(*She stops. Stands there staring at him. Stifles a giggle.*)

VINCE (*after pause*): Are you finished?
SHELLY: Oh brother!
VINCE: I don't wanna go in there with you acting like an
    idiot.
SHELLY: Thanks.
VINCE: Well, I don't.
SHELLY: I won't embarrass you. Don't worry.
VINCE: I'm not worried.
SHELLY: You are too.
VINCE: Shelly, look, I just don't wanna go in there with
    you giggling your head off. They might think some-
    thing's wrong with you.
SHELLY: There is.
VINCE: There is not!
SHELLY: Something's definitely wrong with me.
VINCE: There is not!
SHELLY: There's something wrong with you too.
VINCE: There's nothing wrong with me either!
SHELLY: You wanna know what's wrong with you?
VINCE: What?

(*Shelly laughs.*)

VINCE (*crosses back left toward screen door*): I'm
    leaving!
SHELLY (*stops laughing*): Wait! Stop. Stop! (*Vince stops.*)
    What's wrong with you is that you take the situation
    too seriously.
VINCE: I just don't want to have them think that I've
    suddenly arrived out of the middle of nowhere com-
    pletely deranged.
SHELLY: What do you want them to think then?
VINCE (*pause*): Nothing. Let's go in.

(*He crosses porch toward stage right interior door.
Shelly follows him. The stage right door opens slowly.
Vince sticks his head in, doesn't notice Dodge sleeping.
Calls out toward staircase.*)

VINCE: Grandma!

(*Shelly breaks into laughter, unseen behind Vince. Vince
pulls his head back outside and pulls door shut. We
hear their voices again without seeing them.*)

SHELLY'S VOICE (*stops laughing*): I'm sorry. I'm sorry,
    Vince. I really am. I really am sorry. I won't do it
    again. I couldn't help it.
VINCE'S VOICE: It's not all that funny.

SHELLY'S VOICE: I know it's not. I'm sorry.

VINCE'S VOICE: I mean this is a tense situation for me! I haven't seen them for over six years. I don't know what to expect.

SHELLY'S VOICE: I know. I won't do it again.

VINCE'S VOICE: Can't you bite your tongue or something?

SHELLY'S VOICE: Just don't say "Grandma," okay? (*She giggles, stops.*) I mean if you say "Grandma," I don't know if I can stop myself.

VINCE'S VOICE: Well try!

SHELLY'S VOICE: Okay. Sorry.

(*Door opens again. Vince sticks his head in then enters. Shelly follows behind him. Vince crosses to staircase, sets down saxophone case and overcoat, looks up staircase. Shelly notices Dodge's baseball cap. Crosses to it. Picks it up and puts it on her head. Vince goes up the stairs and disappears at the top. Shelly watches him, then turns and sees Dodge on the sofa. She takes off the baseball cap.*)

VINCE'S VOICE (*from above stairs*): Grandma!

(*Shelly crosses over to Dodge slowly and stands next to him. She stands at his head, reaches out slowly, and touches one of the cuts. The second she touches his head, Dodge jerks up to a sitting position on the sofa, eyes open. Shelly gasps. Dodge looks at her, sees his cap in her hands, quickly puts his hand to his bare head. He glares at Shelly, then whips the cap out of her hands and puts it on. Shelly backs away from him. Dodge stares at her.*)

SHELLY: I'm uh—with Vince.

(*Dodge just glares at her.*)

SHELLY: He's upstairs.

(*Dodge looks at the staircase, then back to Shelly.*)

SHELLY (*calling upstairs*): Vince!

VINCE'S VOICE: Just a second!

SHELLY: You better get down here!

VINCE'S VOICE: Just a minute! I'm looking at the pictures.

(*Dodge keeps staring at her.*)

SHELLY (*to Dodge*): We just got here. Pouring rain on the freeway so we thought we'd stop by. I mean Vince was planning on stopping anyway. He wanted to see you. He said he hadn't seen you in a long time.

(*Pause. Dodge just keeps staring at her.*)

SHELLY: We were going all the way through to New Mexico. To see his father. I guess his father lives out there. We thought we'd stop by and see you on the way. Kill two birds with one stone, you know? (*She laughs, Dodge stares, she stops laughing.*) I mean Vince has this thing about his family now. I guess it's a new thing with him. I kind of find it hard to relate to. But he feels it's important. You know. I mean he feels he wants to get to know you all again. After all this time.

(*Pause. Dodge just stares at her. She moves nervously to staircase and yells up to Vince.*)

SHELLY: Vince, will you come down here please!

(*Vince comes halfway down the stairs.*)

VINCE: I guess they went out for a while.

(*Shelly points to sofa and Dodge. Vince turns and sees Dodge. He comes all the way down staircase and crosses to Dodge. Shelly stays behind near staircase, keeping her distance.*)

VINCE: Grandpa?

(*Dodge looks up at him, not recognizing him.*)

DODGE: Did you bring the whiskey?

(*Vince looks back at Shelly, then back to Dodge.*)

VINCE: Grandpa, it's Vince. I'm Vince. Tilden's son. You remember?

(*Dodge stares at him.*)

DODGE: You didn't do what you told me. You didn't stay here with me.

VINCE: Grandpa, I haven't been here until just now. I just got here.

DODGE: You left. You went outside like we told you not to do. You went out there in back. In the rain.

(*Vince looks back at Shelly. She moves slowly toward sofa.*)

SHELLY: Is he okay?

VINCE: I don't know. (*Takes off his shades.*) Look, Grandpa, don't you remember me? Vince. Your Grandson.

(*Dodge stares at him, then takes off his baseball cap.*)

DODGE (*points to his head*): See what happens when you leave me alone? See that? That's what happens.

(*Vince looks at his head. Vince reaches out to touch his head. Dodge slaps his hand away with the cap and puts it back on his head.*)

VINCE: What's going on, Grandpa? Where's Halie?

DODGE: Don't worry about her. She won't be back for days. She says she'll be back but she won't be. (*He starts laughing.*) There's life in the old girl yet! (*Stops laughing.*)

VINCE: How did you do that to your head?

DODGE: I didn't do it! Don't be ridiculous!

VINCE: Well, who did then?

(*Pause. Dodge stares at Vince.*)

DODGE: Who do you think did it? Who do you think?

(*Shelly moves toward Vince.*)

SHELLY: Vince, maybe we oughta' go. I don't like this. I mean this isn't my idea of a good time.

VINCE (*to Shelly*): Just a second. (*To Dodge.*) Grandpa, look, I just got here. I just now got here. I haven't

been here for six years. I don't know anything that's
happened.

(*Pause. Dodge stares at him.*)

DODGE: You don't know anything?

VINCE: No.

DODGE: Well, that's good. That's good. It's much better
not to know anything. Much, much better.

VINCE: Isn't there anybody here with you?

(*Dodge turns slowly and looks off to stage left.*)

DODGE: Tilden's here.

VINCE: No, Grandpa, Tilden's in New Mexico. That's
where I was going. I'm going out there to see him.

(*Dodge turns slowly back to Vince.*)

DODGE: Tilden's here.

(*Vince backs away and joins Shelly. Dodge stares at
them.*)

SHELLY: Vince, why don't we spend the night in a motel and come back in the morning? We could have
breakfast. Maybe everything would be different.

VINCE: Don't be scared. There's nothing to be scared of.
He's just old.

SHELLY: I'm not scared!

DODGE: You two are not my idea of the perfect couple!

SHELLY (*after pause*): Oh really? Why's that?

VINCE: Shh! Don't aggravate him.

DODGE: There's something wrong between the two of
you. Something not compatible.

VINCE: Grandpa, where did Halie go? Maybe we should
call her.

DODGE: What are you talking about? Do you know what
you're talking about? Are you just talking for the
sake of talking? Lubricating the gums?

VINCE: I'm trying to figure out what's going on here!

DODGE: Is that it?

VINCE: Yes. I mean I expected everything to be different.

DODGE: Who are you to expect anything? Who are you
supposed to be?

VINCE: I'm Vince! Your Grandson!

DODGE: Vince. My Grandson.

VINCE: Tilden's son.

DODGE: Tilden's son, Vince.

VINCE: You haven't seen me for a long time.

DODGE: When was the last time?

VINCE: I don't remember.

DODGE: You don't remember?

VINCE: No.

DODGE: You don't remember. How am I supposed to remember if you don't remember?

SHELLY: Vince, come on. This isn't going to work out.

VINCE (*to Shelly*): Just take it easy.

SHELLY: I'm taking it easy! He doesn't even know who
you are!

VINCE (*crossing toward Dodge*): Grandpa, look—

DODGE: Stay where you are! Keep your distance!

(*Vince stops. Looks back at Shelly, then to Dodge.*)

SHELLY: Vince, this is really making me nervous. I mean
he doesn't even want us here. He doesn't even like us.

DODGE: She's a beautiful girl.

VINCE: Thanks.

DODGE: Very Beautiful Girl.

SHELLY: Oh my God.

DODGE (*to Shelly*): What's your name?

SHELLY: Shelly.

DODGE: Shelly. That's a man's name isn't it?

SHELLY: Not in this case.

DODGE (*to Vince*): She's a smart-ass too.

SHELLY: Vince! Can we go?

DODGE: She wants to go. She just got here and she wants
to go.

VINCE: This is kind of strange for her.

DODGE: She'll get used to it. (*To Shelly.*) What part of the
country do you come from?

SHELLY: Originally?

DODGE: That's right. Originally. At the very start.

SHELLY: L.A.

DODGE: L.A. Stupid country.

SHELLY: I can't stand this, Vince! This is really
unbelievable!

DODGE: It's stupid! L.A. is stupid! So is Florida! All those
Sunshine States. They're all stupid! Do you know
why they're stupid?

SHELLY: Illuminate me.

DODGE: I'll tell you why. Because they're full of smart-
asses! That's why.

(*Shelly turns her back to Dodge, crosses to staircase,
and sits on bottom step.*)

DODGE (*to Vince*): Now she's insulted.

VINCE: Well, you weren't very polite.

DODGE: She's insulted! Look at her! In my house she's
insulted! She's over there sulking because I insulted
her!

SHELLY (*to Vince*): This is really terrific. This is wonderful. And you were worried about me making the right
first impression!

DODGE (*to Vince*): She's a fireball, isn't she? Regular fireball. I had some a' them in my day. Temporary stuff.
Never lasted more than a week.

VINCE: Grandpa—

DODGE: Stop calling me Grandpa will ya'! It's sickening.
"Grandpa." I'm nobody's Grandpa!

(*Dodge starts feeling around under the cushion for the
bottle of whiskey. Shelly gets up from the staircase.*)

SHELLY (*to Vince*): Maybe you've got the wrong house.
Did you ever think of that? Maybe this is the wrong
address!

VINCE: It's not the wrong address! I recognize the yard.

SHELLY: Yeah, but do you recognize the people? He says
he's not your Grandfather.

DODGE (*digging for bottle*): Where's that bottle!

VINCE: He's just sick or something. I don't know what's
happened to him.

DODGE: Where's my goddamn bottle!

(Dodge gets up from sofa and starts tearing the cushions off it and throwing them downstage, looking for the whiskey.)

SHELLY: Can't we just drive on to New Mexico? This is terrible, Vince! I don't want to stay here. In this house. I thought it was going to be turkey dinners and apple pie and all that kinda stuff.

VINCE: Well, I hate to disappoint you!

SHELLY: I'm not disappointed! I'm fuckin' terrified! I wanna' go!

(Dodge yells toward stage left.)

DODGE: Tilden! Tilden!

(Dodge keeps ripping away at the sofa looking for his bottle, he knocks over the night stand with the bottles. Vince and Shelly watch as he starts ripping the stuffing out of the sofa.)

VINCE *(to Shelly)*: He's lost his mind or something. I've got to try to help him.

SHELLY: You help him! I'm leaving!

(Shelly starts to leave. Vince grabs her. They struggle as Dodge keeps ripping away at the sofa and yelling.)

DODGE: Tilden! Tilden, get your ass in here! Tilden!

SHELLY: Let go of me!

VINCE: You're not going anywhere! You're going to stay right here!

SHELLY: Let go of me, you sonuvabitch! I'm not your property!

(Suddenly Tilden walks on from stage left just as he did before. This time his arms are full of carrots. Dodge, Vince, and Shelly stop suddenly when they see him. They all stare at Tilden as he crosses slowly center stage with the carrots and stops. Dodge sits on sofa, exhausted.)

DODGE *(panting, to Tilden)*: Where in the hell have you been?

TILDEN: Out back.

DODGE: Where's my bottle?

TILDEN: Gone.

(Tilden and Vince stare at each other. Shelly backs away.)

DODGE *(to Tilden)*: You stole my bottle!

VINCE *(to Tilden)*: Dad?

(Tilden just stares at Vince.)

DODGE: You had no right to steal my bottle! No right at all!

VINCE *(to Tilden)*: It's Vince. I'm Vince.

(Tilden stares at Vince, then looks at Dodge, then turns to Shelly.)

TILDEN *(after pause)*: I picked these carrots. If anybody wants any carrots, I picked 'em.

SHELLY *(to Vince)*: This is your father?

VINCE *(to Tilden)*: Dad, what're you doing here?

(Tilden just stares at Vince, holding carrots. Dodge pulls the blanket back over himself.)

DODGE *(to Tilden)*: You're going to have to get me another bottle! You gotta get me a bottle before Halie comes back! There's money on the table. *(Points to stage left kitchen.)*

TILDEN *(shaking his head)*: I'm not going down there. Into town.

(Shelly crosses to Tilden. Tilden stares at her.)

SHELLY *(to Tilden)*: Are you Vince's father?

TILDEN *(to Shelly)*: Vince?

SHELLY *(pointing to Vince)*: This is supposed to be your son! Is he your son? Do you recognize him? I'm just along for the ride here. I thought everybody knew each other!

(Tilden stares at Vince. Dodge wraps himself up in the blanket and sits on sofa staring at the floor.)

TILDEN: I had a son once but we buried him.

(Dodge quickly looks at Tilden. Shelly looks to Vince.)

DODGE: You shut up about that! You don't know anything about that!

VINCE: Dad, I thought you were in New Mexico. We were going to drive down there and see you.

TILDEN: Long way to drive.

DODGE *(to Tilden)*: You don't know anything about that! That happened before you were born! Long before!

VINCE: What's happened, Dad? What's going on here? I thought everything was all right. What's happened to Halie?

TILDEN: She left.

SHELLY *(to Tilden)*: Do you want me to take those carrots for you?

(Tilden stares at her. She moves in close to him. Holds out her arms. Tilden stares at her arms then slowly dumps the carrots into her arms. Shelly stands there holding the carrots.)

TILDEN *(to Shelly)*: You like carrots?

SHELLY: Sure. I like all kinds of vegetables.

DODGE *(to Tilden)*: You gotta get me a bottle before Halie comes back!

(Dodge hits sofa with his fist. Vince crosses up to Dodge and tries to console him. Shelly and Tilden stay facing each other.)

TILDEN *(to Shelly)*: Back yard's full of carrots. Corn. Potatoes.

SHELLY: You're Vince's father, right?

TILDEN: All kinds of vegetables. You like vegetables?

SHELLY *(laughs)*: Yeah. I love vegetables.

TILDEN: We could cook these carrots, ya' know. You could cut 'em up and we could cook 'em.

SHELLY: All right.

TILDEN: I'll get you a pail and a knife.

SHELLY: Okay.

TILDEN: I'll be right back. Don't go.

(*Tilden exits offstage left. Shelly stands center, arms full of carrots. Vince stands next to Dodge. Shelly looks toward Vince, then down at the carrots.*)

DODGE (*to Vince*): You could get me a bottle. (*Pointing off left.*) There's money on the table.

VINCE: Grandpa, why don't you lay down for a while?

DODGE: I don't wanna lay down for a while! Every time I lay down something happens! (*Whips off his cap, points at his head.*) Look what happens! That's what happens! (*Pulls his cap back on.*) You go lie down and see what happens to you! See how you like it! They'll steal your bottle! They'll cut your hair! They'll murder your children! That's what'll happen.

VINCE: Just relax for a while.

DODGE (*pause*): You could get me a bottle, ya' know. There's nothing stopping you from getting me a bottle.

SHELLY: Why don't you get him a bottle, Vince? Maybe it would help everybody identify each other.

DODGE (*pointing to Shelly*): There, see? She thinks you should get me a bottle.

(*Vince crosses to Shelly.*)

VINCE: What're you doing with those carrots?

SHELLY: I'm waiting for your father.

DODGE: She thinks you should get me a bottle!

VINCE: Shelly, put the carrots down, will ya'! We gotta deal with the situation here! I'm gonna need your help.

SHELLY: I'm helping.

VINCE: You're only adding to the problem! You're making things worse! Put the carrots down!

(*Vince tries to knock the carrots out of her arms. She turns away from him, protecting the carrots.*)

SHELLY: Get away from me! Stop it!

(*Vince stands back from her. She turns to him still holding the carrots.*)

VINCE (*to Shelly*): Why are you doing this! Are you trying to make fun of me? This is my family, you know!

SHELLY: You coulda' fooled me! I'd just as soon not be here myself. I'd just as soon be a thousand miles from here. I'd rather be anywhere but here. You're the one who wants to stay. So I'll stay. I'll stay and I'll cut the carrots. And I'll cook the carrots. And I'll do whatever I have to do to survive. Just to make it through this.

VINCE: Put the carrots down, Shelly.

(*Tilden enters from left with pail, milking stool, and a knife. He sets the stool and pail center stage for Shelly. Shelly looks at Vince, then sits down on stool, sets the carrots on the floor, and takes the knife from Tilden. She looks at Vince again, then picks up a carrot, cuts the ends off, scrapes it, and drops it in pail. She repeats this; Vince glares at her. She smiles.*)

DODGE: She could get me a bottle. She's the type a' girl that could get me a bottle. Easy. She'd go down there.

Slink up to the counter. They'd probably give her two bottles for the price of one. She could do that.

(*Shelly laughs. Keeps cutting carrots. Vince crosses up to Dodge, looks at him. Tilden watches Shelly's hands. Long pause.*)

VINCE (*to Dodge*): I haven't changed that much. I mean physically. Physically I'm just about the same. Same size. Same weight. Everything's the same.

(*Dodge keeps staring at Shelly while Vince talks to him.*)

DODGE: She's a beautiful girl. Exceptional.

(*Vince moves in front of Dodge to block his view of Shelly. Dodge keeps craning his head around to see her as Vince demonstrates tricks from his past.*)

VINCE: Look. Look at this. Do you remember this? I used to bend my thumb behind my knuckles. You remember? I used to do it at the dinner table.

(*Vince bends a thumb behind his knuckles for Dodge and holds it out to him. Dodge takes a short glance then looks back at Shelly. Vince shifts position and shows him something else.*)

VINCE: What about this?

(*Vince curls his lips back and starts drumming on his teeth with his fingernails making little tapping sounds. Dodge watches awhile. Tilden turns toward the sound. Vince keeps it up. He sees Tilden taking notice and crosses to Tilden as he drums on his teeth. Dodge turns TV on, watches it.*)

VINCE: You remember this, Dad?

(*Vince keeps on drumming for Tilden. Tilden watches awhile, fascinated, then turns back to Shelly. Vince keeps up the drumming on his teeth, crosses back to Dodge doing it. Shelly keeps working on carrots, talking to Tilden.*)

SHELLY (*to Tilden*): He drives me crazy with that sometimes.

VINCE (*to Dodge*): I know! Here's one you'll remember. You used to kick me out of the house for this one.

(*Vince pulls his shirt out of his belt and holds it tucked under his chin with his stomach exposed. He grabs the flesh on either side of his belly button and pushes it in and out to make it look like a mouth talking. He watches his belly button and makes a deep sounding cartoon voice to synchronize with the movement. He demonstrates it to Dodge, then crosses down to Tilden doing it. Both Dodge and Tilden take short, uninterested glances then ignore him.*)

VINCE (*deep cartoon voice*): "Hello. How are you? I'm fine. Thank you very much. It's so good to see you looking well this fine Sunday morning. I was going down to the hardware store to fetch a pail of water."

SHELLY: Vince, don't be pathetic, will ya!

Ethan Hawke as Vince and
James Gammon as Dodge in
the Steppenwolf Theatre
Company's 1995 production
of *Buried Child*.

(*Vince stops. Tucks his shirt back in.*)

SHELLY: Jesus Christ. They're not gonna play. Can't you see that?

(*Shelly keeps cutting carrots. Vince slowly moves toward Tilden. Tilden keeps watching Shelly. Dodge watches TV.*)

VINCE (*to Shelly*): I don't get it. I really don't get it. Maybe it's me. Maybe I forgot something.

DODGE (*from sofa*): You forgot to get me a bottle! That's what you forgot. Anybody in this house could get me a bottle. Anybody! But nobody will. Nobody understands the urgency! Peelin carrots is more important. Playin piano on your teeth! Well I hope you all remember this when you get up in years. When you find yourself immobilized. Dependent on the whims of others.

(*Vince moves up toward Dodge. Pause as he looks at him.*)

VINCE: I'll get you a bottle.
DODGE: You will?
VINCE: Sure.

(*Shelly stands holding knife and carrot.*)

SHELLY: You're not going to leave me here, are you?
VINCE (*moving to her*): You suggested it! You said, "Why don't I go get him a bottle?" So I'll go get him a bottle!
SHELLY: But I can't stay here.
VINCE: What is going on! A minute ago you were ready to cut carrots all night!
SHELLY: That was only if you stayed. Something to keep me busy, so I wouldn't be so nervous. I don't want to stay here alone.

DODGE: Don't let her talk you out of it! She's a bad influence. I could see it the minute she stepped in here.
SHELLY (*to Dodge*): You were asleep!
TILDEN (*to Shelly*): Don't you want to cut carrots anymore?
SHELLY: Sure. Sure I do.

(*Shelly sits back down on stool and continues cutting carrots. Pause. Vince moves around, stroking his hair, staring at Dodge and Tilden. Vince and Shelly exchange glances. Dodge watches TV.*)

VINCE: Boy! This is amazing. This is truly amazing. (*Keeps moving around.*) What is this anyway? Am I in a time warp or something? Have I committed an unpardonable offense? It's true, I'm not married. (*Shelly looks at him, then back to carrots.*) But I'm also not divorced. I have been known to plunge into sinful infatuation with the Alto Saxophone. Sucking on number 5 reeds deep into the wee wee hours.
SHELLY: Vince, what are you doing that for? They don't care about any of that. They just don't recognize you, that's all.
VINCE: How could they not recognize me! How in the hell could they not recognize me! I'm their son!
DODGE (*watching TV*): You're no son of mine. I've had sons in my time and you're not one of 'em.

(*Long pause. Vince stares at Dodge, then looks at Tilden. He turns to Shelly.*)

VINCE: Shelly, I gotta go out for a while. I just gotta go out. I'll get a bottle and I'll come right back. You'll be okay here. Really.

SHELLY: I don't know if I can handle this, Vince.

VINCE: I just gotta think or something. I don't know. I gotta put this all together.

SHELLY: Can't we just go?

VINCE: No! I gotta find out what's going on.

SHELLY: Look, you think you're bad off, what about me? Not only don't they recognize me but I've never seen them before in my life. I don't know who these guys are. They could be anybody!

VINCE: They're not anybody!

SHELLY: That's what you say.

VINCE: They're my family for Christ's sake! I should know who my own family is! Now give me a break. It won't take that long. I'll just go out and I'll come right back. Nothing'll happen. I promise.

(*Shelly stares at him. Pause.*)

SHELLY: All right.

VINCE: Thanks. (*He crosses up to Dodge.*) I'm gonna go out now, Grandpa, and I'll pick you up a bottle. Okay?

DODGE: Change of heart huh? (*Pointing off left.*) Money's on the table. In the kitchen.

(*Vince moves toward Shelly.*)

VINCE (*to Shelly*): You be all right?

SHELLY (*cutting carrots*): Sure. I'm fine. I'll just keep real busy while you're gone.

(*Vince looks at Tilden who keeps staring down at Shelly's hands.*)

DODGE: Persistence, see? That's what it takes. Persistence. Persistence, fortitude, and determination. Those are the three virtues. You stick with those three and you can't go wrong.

VINCE (*to Tilden*): You want anything, Dad?

TILDEN (*looks up at Vince*): Me?

VINCE: From the store? I'm gonna get Grandpa a bottle.

TILDEN: He's not supposed to drink. Halie wouldn't like it.

VINCE: He wants a bottle.

TILDEN: He's not supposed to drink.

DODGE (*to Vince*): Don't negotiate with him! Don't make any transactions until you've spoken to me first! He'll steal you blind!

VINCE (*to Dodge*): Tilden says you're not supposed to drink.

DODGE: Tilden's lost his marbles! Look at him! He's around the bend. Take a look at him.

(*Vince stares at Tilden. Tilden watches Shelly's hands as she keeps cutting carrots.*)

DODGE: Now look at me. Look here at me!

(*Vince looks back to Dodge.*)

DODGE: Now, between the two of us, who do you think is more trustworthy? Him or me? Can you trust a man who keeps bringing in vegetables from out of nowhere? Take a look at him.

(*Vince looks back at Tilden.*)

SHELLY: Go get the bottle, Vince.

VINCE (*to Shelly*): You sure you'll be all right?

SHELLY: I'll be fine. I feel right at home now.

VINCE: You do?

SHELLY: I'm fine. Now that I've got the carrots everything is all right.

VINCE: I'll be right back.

(*Vince crosses stage left.*)

DODGE: Where are you going?

VINCE: I'm going to get the money.

DODGE: Then where are you going?

VINCE: Liquor store.

DODGE: Don't go anyplace else. Don't go off some place and drink. Come right back here.

VINCE: I will.

(*Vince exits stage left.*)

DODGE (*calling after Vince*): You've got responsibility now! And don't go out the back way either! Come out through this way! I wanna' see you when you leave! Don't go out the back!

VINCE'S VOICE (*off left*): I won't!

(*Dodge turns and looks at Tilden and Shelly.*)

DODGE: Untrustworthy. Probably drown himself if he went out the back. Fall right in a hole. I'd never get my bottle.

SHELLY: I wouldn't worry about Vince. He can take care of himself.

DODGE: Oh he can, huh? Independent.

(*Vince comes on again from stage left with two dollars in his hand. He crosses stage right past Dodge.*)

DODGE (*to Vince*): You got the money?

VINCE: Yeah. Two bucks.

DODGE: Two bucks. Two bucks is two bucks. Don't sneer.

VINCE: What kind do you want?

DODGE: Whiskey! Gold Star Sour Mash. Use your own discretion.

VINCE: Okay.

(*Vince crosses to stage right door. Opens it. Stops when he hears Tilden.*)

TILDEN (*to Vince*): You drove all the way from New Mexico?

(*Vince turns and looks at Tilden. They stare at each other. Vince shakes his head, goes out the door, crosses porch, and exits out screen door. Tilden watches him go. Pause.*)

SHELLY: You really don't recognize him? Either one of you?

(*Tilden turns again and stares at Shelly's hands as she cuts carrots.*)

DODGE (*watching TV*): Recognize who?

SHELLY: Vince.
DODGE: What's to recognize?

(*Dodge lights a cigarette, coughs slightly, and stares at TV.*)

SHELLY: It'd be cruel if you recognized him and didn't tell him. Wouldn't be fair.

(*Dodge just stares at TV, smoking.*)

TILDEN: I thought I recognized him. I thought I recognized something about him.
SHELLY: You did?
TILDEN: I thought I saw a face inside his face.
SHELLY: Well, it was probably that you saw what he used to look like. You haven't seen him for six years.
TILDEN: I haven't?
SHELLY: That's what he says.

(*Tilden moves around in front of her as she continues with carrots.*)

TILDEN: Where was it I saw him last?
SHELLY: I don't know. I've only known him for a few months. He doesn't tell me everything.
TILDEN: He doesn't?
SHELLY: Not stuff like that.
TILDEN: What does he tell you?
SHELLY: You mean in general?
TILDEN: Yeah.

(*Tilden moves around behind her.*)

SHELLY: Well, he tells me all kinds of things.
TILDEN: Like what?
SHELLY: I don't know! I mean I can't just come right out and tell you how he feels.
TILDEN: How come?

(*Tilden keeps moving around her slowly in a circle.*)

SHELLY: Because it's stuff he told me privately!
TILDEN: And you can't tell me?
SHELLY: I don't even know you!
DODGE: Tilden, go out in the kitchen and make me some coffee! Leave the girl alone.
SHELLY (*to Dodge*): He's all right.

(*Tilden ignores Dodge, keeps moving around Shelly. He stares at her hair and coat. Dodge stares at TV.*)

TILDEN: You mean you can't tell me anything?
SHELLY: I can tell you some things. I mean we can have a conversation.
TILDEN: We can?
SHELLY: Sure. We're having a conversation right now.
TILDEN: We are?
SHELLY: Yes. That's what we're doing.
TILDEN: But there's certain things you can't tell me, right?
SHELLY: Right.
TILDEN: There's certain things I can't tell you either.
SHELLY: How come?
TILDEN: I don't know. Nobody's supposed to hear it.

SHELLY: Well, you can tell me anything you want to.
TILDEN: I can?
SHELLY: Sure.
TILDEN: It might not be very nice.
SHELLY: That's all right. I've been around.
TILDEN: It might be awful.
SHELLY: Well, can't you tell me anything nice?

(*Tilden stops in front of her and stares at her coat. Shelly looks back at him. Long pause.*)

TILDEN (*after pause*): Can I touch your coat?
SHELLY: My coat? (*She looks at her coat then back to Tilden.*) Sure.
TILDEN: You don't mind?
SHELLY: No. Go ahead.

(*Shelly holds her arm out for Tilden to touch. Dodge stays fixed on TV. Tilden moves in slowly toward Shelly, staring at her arm. He reaches out very slowly and touches her arm, feels the fur gently, then draws his hand back. Shelly keeps her arm out.*)

SHELLY: It's rabbit.
TILDEN: Rabbit.

(*He reaches out again very slowly and touches the fur on her arm then pulls back his hand again. Shelly drops her arm.*)

SHELLY: My arm was getting tired.
TILDEN: Can I hold it?
SHELLY (*pause*): The coat? Sure.

(*Shelly takes off her coat and hands it to Tilden. Tilden takes it slowly, feels the fur, then puts it on. Shelly watches as Tilden strokes the fur slowly. He smiles at her. She goes back to cutting carrots.*)

SHELLY: You can have it if you want.
TILDEN: I can?
SHELLY: Yeah. I've got a raincoat in the car. That's all I need.
TILDEN: You've got a car?
SHELLY: Vince does.

(*Tilden walks around stroking the fur and smiling at the coat. Shelly watches him when he's not looking. Dodge sticks with TV, stretches out on sofa wrapped in blanket.*)

TILDEN (*as he walks around*): I had a car once! I had a white car! I drove. I went everywhere. I went to the mountains. I drove in the snow.
SHELLY: That must've been fun.
TILDEN (*still moving, feeling coat*): I drove all day long sometimes. Across the desert. Way out across the desert. I drove past towns. Anywhere. Past palm trees. Lightning. Anything. I would drive through it. I would drive through it and I would stop and I would look around and I would drive on. I would get back in and drive! I loved to drive. There was nothing I loved more. Nothing I dreamed of was better than driving.

DODGE (*eyes on TV*): Pipe down, would ya'!

(*Tilden stops. Stares at Shelly.*)

SHELLY: Do you do much driving now?

TILDEN: Now? Now? I don't drive now.

SHELLY: How come?

TILDEN: I'm grown up now.

SHELLY: Grown up?

TILDEN: I'm not a kid.

SHELLY: You don't have to be a kid to drive.

TILDEN: It wasn't driving then.

SHELLY: What was it?

TILDEN: Adventure. I went everywhere.

SHELLY: Well, you can still do that.

TILDEN: Not now.

SHELLY: Why not?

TILDEN: I just told you. You don't understand anything.
If I told you something you wouldn't understand it.

SHELLY: Told me what?

TILDEN: Told you something that's true.

SHELLY: Like what?

TILDEN: Like a baby. Like a little tiny baby.

SHELLY: Like when you were little?

TILDEN: If I told you you'd make me give your coat back.

SHELLY: I won't. I promise. Tell me.

TILDEN: I can't. Dodge won't let me.

SHELLY: He won't hear you. It's okay.

(*Pause. Tilden stares at her. Moves slightly toward her.*)

TILDEN: We had a baby. (*Motioning to Dodge.*) He did.
Dodge did. Could pick it up with one hand. Put it in
the other. Little baby. Dodge killed it.

(*Shelly stands.*)

TILDEN: Don't stand up. Don't stand up!

(*Shelly sits again. Dodge sits up on sofa and looks at
them.*)

TILDEN: Dodge drowned it.

SHELLY: Don't tell me anymore! Okay?

(*Tilden moves closer to her. Dodge takes more interest.*)

DODGE: Tilden? You leave that girl alone!

TILDEN (*pays no attention*): Never told Halie. Never told
anybody. Just drowned it.

DODGE (*shuts off TV*): Tilden!

TILDEN: Nobody could find it. Just disappeared. Cops
looked for it. Neighbors. Nobody could find it.

(*Dodge struggles to get up from sofa.*)

DODGE: Tilden, what're you telling her! Tilden!

(*Dodge keeps struggling until he's standing.*)

TILDEN: Finally everybody just gave up. Just stopped
looking. Everybody had a different answer. Kidnap.
Murder. Accident. Some kind of accident.

(*Dodge struggles to walk toward Tilden and falls.
Tilden ignores him.*)

DODGE: Tilden, you shut up! You shut up about it!

(*Dodge starts coughing on the floor. Shelly watches
him from the stool.*)

TILDEN: Little tiny baby just disappeared. It's not hard.
It's so small. Almost invisible.

(*Shelly makes a move to help Dodge. Tilden firmly
pushes her back down on the stool. Dodge keeps
coughing.*)

TILDEN: He said he had his reasons. Said it went a long
way back. But he wouldn't tell anybody.

DODGE: Tilden! Don't tell her anything! Don't tell her!

TILDEN: He's the only one who knows where it's buried.
The only one. Like a secret buried treasure. Won't tell
any of us. Won't tell me or mother or even Bradley.
Especially Bradley. Bradley tried to force it out of him
but he wouldn't tell. Wouldn't even tell why he did it.
One night he just did it.

(*Dodge's coughing subsides. Shelly stays on stool staring
at Dodge. Tilden slowly takes Shelly's coat off and holds
it out to her. Long pause. Shelly sits there trembling.*)

TILDEN: You probably want your coat back now.

(*Shelly stares at coat but doesn't move to take it. The
sound of Bradley's leg squeaking is heard off left. The
others on stage remain still. Bradley appears up left
outside the screen door wearing a yellow rain slicker.
He enters through screen door, crosses porch to stage
right door and enters stage. Closes door. Takes off rain
slicker and shakes it out. He sees all the others and
stops. Tilden turns to him. Bradley stares at Shelly.
Dodge remains on floor.*)

BRADLEY: What's going on here? (*Motioning to Shelly.*)
Who's that?

(*Shelly stands, moves back away from Bradley as he
crosses toward her. He stops next to Tilden. He sees
coat in Tilden's hand and grabs it away from him.*)

BRADLEY: Who's she supposed to be?

TILDEN: She's driving to New Mexico.

(*Bradley stares at her. Shelly is frozen. Bradley limps
over to her with the coat in his fist. He stops in front
of her.*)

BRADLEY (*to Shelly, after pause*): Vacation?

(*Shelly shakes her head "no," trembling.*)

BRADLEY (*to Shelly, motioning to Tilden*): You taking
him with you?

(*Shelly shakes her head "no." Bradley crosses back to
Tilden.*)

BRADLEY: You oughta'. No use leaving him here. Doesn't
do a lick a' work. Doesn't raise a finger. (*Stopping, to
Tilden.*) Do ya'. (*To Shelly.*) 'Course he used to be an
All-American. Quarterback or fullback or somethin'.
He tell you that?

(*Shelly shakes her head "no."*)

BRADLEY: Yeah, he used to be a big deal. Wore letter-men's sweaters. Had medals hanging all around his neck. Real purty. Big deal. (*He laughs to himself, notices Dodge on floor, crosses to him, stops.*) This one too. (*To Shelly.*) You'd never think it to look at him, would ya'? All bony and wasted away.

(*Shelly shakes her head again. Bradley stares at her, crosses back to her, clenching the coat in his fist. He stops in front of Shelly.*)

BRADLEY: Women like that kinda' thing, don't they?
SHELLY: What?
BRADLEY: Importance. Importance in a man?
SHELLY: I don't know.
BRADLEY: Yeah. You know, you know. Don't give me that. (*Moves closer to Shelly.*) You're with Tilden?
SHELLY: No.
BRADLEY (*turning to Tilden*): Tilden! She with you?

(*Tilden doesn't answer. Stares at floor.*)

BRADLEY: Tilden!

(*Tilden suddenly bolts and runs off up stage left. Bradley laughs. Talks to Shelly. Dodge starts moving his lips silently as though talking to someone invisible on the floor.*)

BRADLEY (*laughing*): Scared to death! He was always scared!

(*Bradley stops laughing. Stares at Shelly.*)

BRADLEY: You're scared too, right? (*Laughs again.*) You're scared and you don't even know me. (*Stops laughing.*) You don't gotta be scared.

(*Shelly looks at Dodge on the floor.*)

SHELLY: Can't we do something for him?
BRADLEY (*looking at Dodge*): We could shoot him (*Laughs.*) We could drown him! What about drown-ing him?
SHELLY: Shut up!

(*Bradley stops laughing. Moves in closer to Shelly. She freezes. Bradley speaks slowly and deliberately.*)

BRADLEY: Hey! Missus. Don't talk to me like that. Don't talk to me in that tone a' voice. There was a time when I had to take that tone a' voice from pretty near everyone. (*Motioning to Dodge.*) Him, for one! Him and that half brain that just ran outa' here. They don't talk to me like that now. Not anymore. Everything's turned around now. Full circle. Isn't that funny?
SHELLY: I'm sorry.
BRADLEY: Open your mouth.
SHELLY: What?
BRADLEY (*motioning for her to open her mouth*): Open up.

(*She opens her mouth slightly.*)

BRADLEY: Wider.

(*She opens her mouth wider.*)

BRADLEY: Keep it like that.

(*She does. Stares at Bradley. With his free hand he puts his fingers into her mouth. She tries to pull away.*)

BRADLEY: Just stay put!

(*She freezes. He keeps his fingers in her mouth. Stares at her. Pause. He pulls his hand out. She closes her mouth, keeps her eyes on him. Bradley smiles. He looks at Dodge on the floor and crosses over to him. Shelly watches him closely. Bradley stands over Dodge and smiles at Shelly. He holds her coat up in both hands over Dodge, keeps smiling at Shelly. He looks down at Dodge, then drops the coat so that it lands on Dodge and covers his head. Bradley keeps his hands up in the position of holding the coat, looks over at Shelly, and smiles. The lights black out.*)

ACT 3

Scene: *Same set. Morning. Bright sun. No sound of rain. Everything has been cleared up again. No sign of carrots. No pail. No stool. Vince's saxophone case and overcoat are still at the foot of the staircase. Bradley is asleep on the sofa under Dodge's blanket. His head toward stage left. Bradley's wooden leg is leaning against the sofa right by his head. The shoe is left on it. The harness hangs down. Dodge is sitting on the floor, propped up against the TV set facing stage left wearing his baseball cap. Shelly's rabbit fur coat covers his chest and shoulders. He stares off toward stage left. He seems weaker and more disoriented. The lights rise slowly to the sound of birds and remain for a while in silence on the two men. Bradley sleeps very soundly. Dodge hardly moves. Shelly appears from stage left with a big smile, slowly crossing toward Dodge balancing a steaming cup of broth in a saucer. Dodge just stares at her as she gets close to him.*

SHELLY (*as she crosses*): This is going to make all the dif-ference in the world, Grandpa. You don't mind me calling you Grandpa, do you? I mean I know you minded when Vince called you that but you don't even know him.
DODGE: He skipped town with my money, ya' know. I'm gonna hold you as collateral.
SHELLY: He'll be back. Don't you worry.

(*She kneels down next to Dodge and puts the cup and saucer in his lap.*)

DODGE: It's morning already! Not only didn't I get my bottle but he's got my two bucks!
SHELLY: Try to drink this, okay? Don't spill it.
DODGE: What is it?
SHELLY: Beef bouillon. It'll warm you up.

DODGE: Bouillon! I don't want any goddamn bouillon! Get that stuff away from me!

SHELLY: I just got through making it.

DODGE: I don't care if you just spent all week making it! I ain't drinking it!

SHELLY: Well, what am I supposed to do with it then? I'm trying to help you out. Besides, it's good for you.

DODGE: Get it away from me!

(*Shelly stands up with cup and saucer.*)

DODGE: What do you know what's good for me anyway?

(*She looks at Dodge, then turns away from him, crossing to staircase, sits on bottom step, and drinks the bouillon. Dodge stares at her.*)

DODGE: You know what'd be good for me?

SHELLY: What?

DODGE: A little massage. A little contact.

SHELLY: Oh no. I've had enough contact for a while. Thanks anyway.

(*She keeps sipping bouillon, stays sitting. Pause as Dodge stares at her.*)

DODGE: Why not? You got nothing better to do. That fella's not gonna be back here. You're not expecting him to show up again, are you?

SHELLY: Sure. He'll show up. He left his horn here.

DODGE: His horn? (*Laughs.*) You're his horn?

SHELLY: Very funny.

DODGE: He's run off with my money! He's not coming back here.

SHELLY: He'll be back.

DODGE: You're a funny chicken, you know that?

SHELLY: Thanks.

DODGE: Full of faith. Hope. Faith and hope. You're all alike, you hopers. If it's not God then it's a man. If it's not a man then it's a woman. If it's not a woman then it's the land or the future of some kind. Some kind of future.

(*Pause.*)

SHELLY (*looking toward porch*): I'm glad it stopped raining.

DODGE (*looks toward porch then back to her*): That's what I mean. See, you're glad it stopped raining. Now you think everything's gonna be different. Just 'cause the sun comes out.

SHELLY: It's already different. Last night I was scared.

DODGE: Scared a' what?

SHELLY: Just scared.

DODGE: Bradley? (*Looks at Bradley.*) He's a pushover. 'Specially now. All ya' gotta do is take his leg and throw it out the back door. Helpless. Totally helpless.

(*Shelly turns and stares at Bradley's wooden leg, then looks at Dodge. She sips bouillon.*)

SHELLY: You'd do that?

DODGE: Me? I've hardly got the strength to breathe.

SHELLY: But you'd actually do it if you could?

DODGE: Don't be so easily shocked, girlie. There's nothing a man can't do. You dream it up and he can do it. Anything.

SHELLY: You've tried I guess.

DODGE: Don't sit there sippin' your bouillon and judging me! This is my house!

SHELLY: I forgot.

DODGE: You forgot? Whose house did you think it was?

SHELLY: Mine.

(*Dodge just stares at her. Long pause. She sips from cup.*)

SHELLY: I know it's not mine but I had that feeling.

DODGE: What feeling?

SHELLY: The feeling that nobody lives here but me. I mean everybody's gone. You're here, but it doesn't seem like you're supposed to be. (*Pointing to Bradley.*) Doesn't seem like he's supposed to be here either. I don't know what it is. It's the house or something. Something familiar. Like I know my way around here. Did you ever get that feeling?

(*Dodge stares at her in silence. Pause.*)

DODGE: No. No, I never did.

(*Shelly gets up. Moves around space holding cup.*)

SHELLY: Last night I went to sleep up there in that room.

DODGE: What room?

SHELLY: That room up there with all the pictures. All the crosses on the wall.

DODGE: Halie's room?

SHELLY: Yeah. Whoever "Halie" is.

DODGE: She's my wife.

SHELLY: So you remember her?

DODGE: Whad'ya mean! 'Course I remember her! She's only been gone for a day—half a day. However long it's been.

SHELLY: Do you remember her when her hair was bright red? Standing in front of an apple tree?

DODGE: What is this, the third degree or something! Who're you to be askin' me personal questions about my wife!

SHELLY: You never look at those pictures up there?

DODGE: What pictures!

SHELLY: Your whole life's up there hanging on the wall. Somebody who looks just like you. Somebody who looks just like you used to look.

DODGE: That isn't me! That never was me! This is me. Right here. This is it. The whole shootin' match, sittin' right in front of you.

SHELLY: So the past never happened as far as you're concerned?

DODGE: The past? Jesus Christ. The past. What do you know about the past?

SHELLY: Not much. I know there was a farm.

(*Pause.*)

DODGE: A farm?

SHELLY: There's a picture of a farm. A big farm. A bull. Wheat. Corn.

DODGE: Corn?

SHELLY: All the kids are standing out in the corn. They're all waving these big straw hats. One of them doesn't have a hat.

DODGE: Which one was that?

SHELLY: There's a baby. A baby in a woman's arms. The same woman with the red hair. She looks lost standing out there. Like she doesn't know how she got there.

DODGE: She knows! I told her a hundred times it wasn't gonna' be the city! I gave her plenty a' warning.

SHELLY: She's looking down at the baby like it was somebody else's. Like it didn't even belong to her.

DODGE: That's about enough outa' you! You got some funny ideas. Some damn funny ideas. You think just because people propagate they have to love their offspring? You never seen a bitch eat her puppies? Where are you from anyway?

SHELLY: L.A. We already went through that.

DODGE: That's right, L.A. I remember.

SHELLY: Stupid country.

DODGE: That's right! No wonder.

(*Pause.*)

SHELLY: What's happened to this family anyway?

DODGE: You're in no position to ask! What do you care? You some kinda' Social Worker?

SHELLY: I'm Vince's friend.

DODGE: Vince's friend! That's rich. That's really rich. "Vince"! "Mr. Vince"! "Mr. Thief" is more like it! His name doesn't mean a hoot in hell to me. Not a tinkle in the well. You know how many kids I've spawned? Not to mention Grand kids and Great Grand kids and Great Great Grand kids after them?

SHELLY: And you don't remember any of them?

DODGE: What's to remember? Halie's the one with the family album. She's the one you should talk to. She'll set you straight on the heritage if that's what you're interested in. She's traced it all the way back to the grave.

SHELLY: What do you mean?

DODGE: What do you think I mean? How far back can you go? A long line of corpses! There's not a living soul behind me. Not a one. Who's holding me in their memory? Who gives a damn about bones in the ground?

SHELLY: Was Tilden telling the truth?

(*Dodge stops short. Stares at Shelly. Shakes his head. He looks off stage left.*)

SHELLY: Was he?

(*Dodge's tone changes drastically.*)

DODGE: Tilden? (*Turns to Shelly, calmly.*) Where is Tilden?

SHELLY: Last night. Was he telling the truth about the baby?

(*Pause.*)

DODGE (*turns toward stage left*): What's happened to Tilden? Why isn't Tilden here?

SHELLY: Bradley chased him out.

DODGE (*looking at Bradley asleep*): Bradley? Why is he on my sofa? (*Turns back to Shelly.*) Have I been here all night? On the floor?

SHELLY: He wouldn't leave. I hid outside until he fell asleep.

DODGE: Outside? Is Tilden outside? He shouldn't be out there in the rain. He'll get himself into trouble. He doesn't know his way around here anymore. Not like he used to. He went out West and got himself into trouble. Got himself into bad trouble. We don't want any of that around here.

SHELLY: What did he do?

(*Pause.*)

DODGE (*quietly stares at Shelly*): Tilden? He got mixed up. That's what he did. We can't afford to leave him alone. Not now.

(*Sound of Halie laughing comes from off left. Shelly stands, looking in direction of voice, holding cup and saucer, doesn't know whether to stay or run.*)

DODGE (*motioning to Shelly*): Sit down! Sit back down!

(*Shelly sits. Sound of Halie's laughter again.*)

DODGE (*to Shelly in a heavy whisper, pulling coat up around him*): Don't leave me alone now! Promise me? Don't go off and leave me alone. I need somebody here with me. Tilden's gone now and I need someone. Don't leave me! Promise!

SHELLY (*sitting*): I won't.

(*Halie appears outside the screen porch door, up left with Father Dewis. She is wearing a bright yellow dress, no hat, white gloves and her arms are full of yellow roses. Father Dewis is dressed in traditional black suit, white clerical collar, and shirt. He is a very distinguished gray-haired man in his sixties. They are both slightly drunk and feeling giddy. As they enter the porch through the screen door, Dodge pulls the rabbit fur coat over his head and hides. Shelly stands again. Dodge drops the coat and whispers intensely to Shelly. Neither Halie nor Father Dewis are aware of the people inside the house.*)

DODGE (*to Shelly in a strong whisper*): You promised!

(*Shelly sits on stairs again. Dodge pulls coat back over his head. Halie and Father Dewis talk on the porch as they cross toward stage right interior door.*)

HALIE: Oh, Father! That's terrible! That's absolutely terrible. Aren't you afraid of being punished?

(*She giggles.*)

DEWIS: Not by the Italians. They're too busy punishing each other.

(They both break out in giggles.)

HALIE: What about God?

DEWIS: Well, prayerfully, God only hears what he wants
to. That's just between you and me of course. In our
heart of hearts we know we're every bit as wicked as
the Catholics.

(They giggle again and reach the stage right door.)

HALIE: Father, I never heard you talk like this in Sunday
sermon.

DEWIS: Well, I save all my best jokes for private company.
Pearls before swine, you know.

*(They enter the room laughing and stop when they
see Shelly. Shelly stands. Halie closes the door behind
Father Dewis. Dodge's voice is heard under the coat,
talking to Shelly.)*

DODGE *(under coat, to Shelly)*: Sit down, sit down! Don't
let 'em buffalo you!

*(Shelly sits on stair again. Halie looks at Dodge on the
floor, then looks at Bradley asleep on sofa and sees his
wooden leg. She lets out a shriek of embarrassment for
Father Dewis.)*

HALIE: Oh my gracious! What in the name of Judas Priest
is going on in this house!

(She hands over the roses to Father Dewis.)

HALIE: Excuse me, Father.

*(Halie crosses to Dodge, whips the coat off him, and
covers the wooden leg with it. Bradley stays asleep.)*

HALIE: You can't leave this house for a second without
the Devil blowing in through the front door!

DODGE: Gimme back that coat! Gimme back that goddamn coat before I freeze to death!

HALIE: You're not going to freeze! The sun's out in case
you hadn't noticed!

DODGE: Gimme back that coat! That coat's for live flesh
not dead wood!

*(Halie whips the blanket off Bradley and throws it on
Dodge. Dodge covers his head again with blanket.
Bradley's amputated leg can be faked by having half of it
under a cushion of the sofa. He's fully clothed. Bradley
sits up with a jerk when the blanket comes off him.)*

HALIE *(as she tosses blanket)*: Here! Use this! It's yours
anyway! Can't you take care of yourself for once!

BRADLEY *(yelling at Halie)*: Gimme that blanket! Gimme
back that blanket! That's my blanket!

*(Halie crosses back toward Father Dewis who just
stands there with the roses. Bradley thrashes helplessly
on the sofa trying to reach blanket. Dodge hides himself deeper in blanket. Shelly looks on from staircase,
still holding cup and saucer.)*

HALIE: Believe me, Father, this is not what I had in mind
when I invited you in.

DEWIS: Oh, no apologies please. I wouldn't be in the ministry if I couldn't face real life.

*(He laughs self-consciously. Halie notices Shelly again
and crosses over to her. Shelly stays sitting. Halie stops
and stares at her.)*

BRADLEY: I want my blanket back! Gimme my blanket!

(Halie turns toward Bradley and silences him.)

HALIE: Shut up, Bradley! Right this minute! I've had
enough!

*(Bradley slowly recoils, lies back down on sofa, turns
his back toward Halie and whimpers softly. Halie
directs her attention to Shelly again. Pause.)*

HALIE *(to Shelly)*: What're you doing with my cup and
saucer?

SHELLY *(looking at cup, back to Halie)*: I made some
bouillon for Dodge.

HALIE: For Dodge?

SHELLY: Yeah.

HALIE: Well, did he drink it?

SHELLY: No.

HALIE: Did you drink it?

SHELLY: Yes.

*(Halie stares at her. Long pause. She turns abruptly
away from Shelly and crosses back to Father Dewis.)*

HALIE: Father, there's a stranger in my house. What would
you advise? What would be the Christian thing?

DEWIS *(squirming)*: Oh, well. . . . I . . . . I really—

HALIE: We still have some whiskey, don't we?

*(Dodge slowly pulls the blanket down off his head and
looks toward Father Dewis. Shelly stands.)*

SHELLY: Listen, I don't drink or anything. I just—

(Halie turns toward Shelly viciously.)

HALIE: You sit back down!

(Shelly sits again on stair. Halie turns again to Dewis.)

HALIE: I think we have plenty of whiskey left! Don't we,
Father?

DEWIS: Well, yes. I think so. You'll have to get it. My
hands are full.

*(Halie giggles. Reaches into Dewis's pockets, searching
for bottle. She smells the roses as she searches. Dewis
stands stiffly. Dodge watches Halie closely as she looks
for bottle.)*

HALIE: The most incredible things, roses! Aren't they
incredible, Father?

DEWIS: Yes. Yes, they are.

HALIE: They almost cover the stench of sin in this house.
Just magnificent! The smell. We'll have to put some at
the foot of Ansel's statue. On the day of the unveiling.

*(Halie finds a silver flask of whiskey in Dewis's vest
pocket. She pulls it out. Dodge looks on eagerly. Halie
crosses to Dodge, opens the flask, and takes a sip.)*

HALIE (*to Dodge*): Ansel's getting a statue, Dodge. Did you know that? Not a plaque but a real live statue. A full bronze. Tip to toe. A basketball in one hand and a rifle in the other.

BRADLEY (*his back to Halie*): He never played basketball!

HALIE: You shut up, Bradley! You shut up about Ansel! Ansel played basketball better than anyone! And you know it! He was an All-American! There's no reason to take the glory away from others.

(*Halie turns away from Bradley, crosses back toward Dewis, sipping on the flask and smiling.*)

HALIE (*to Dewis*): Ansel was a great basketball player. One of the greatest.

DEWIS: I remember Ansel.

HALIE: Of course! You remember. You remember how he could play. (*She turns toward Shelly.*) Of course, nowadays they play a different brand of basketball. More vicious. Isn't that right, dear?

SHELLY: I don't know.

(*Halie crosses to Shelly, sipping on flask. She stops in front of Shelly.*)

HALIE: Much, much more vicious. They smash into each other. They knock each other's teeth out. There's blood all over the court. Savages.

(*Halie takes the cup from Shelly and pours whiskey into it.*)

HALIE: They don't train like they used to. Not at all. They allow themselves to run amuck. Drugs and women. Women mostly.

(*Halie hands the cup of whiskey back to Shelly slowly. Shelly takes it.*)

HALIE: Mostly women. Girls. Sad, pathetic little girls. (*She crosses back to Father Dewis.*) It's just a reflection of the times, don't you think, Father? An indication of where we stand?

DEWIS: I suppose so, yes.

HALIE: Yes. A sort of bad omen. Our youth becoming monsters.

DEWIS: Well, I uh—

HALIE: Oh you can disagree with me if you want to, Father. I'm open to debate. I think argument only enriches both sides of the question don't you? (*She moves toward Dodge.*) I suppose, in the long run, it doesn't matter. When you see the way things deteriorate before your very eyes. Everything running downhill. It's kind of silly to even think about youth.

DEWIS: No, I don't think so. I think it's important to believe in certain things.

HALIE: Yes. Yes, I know what you mean. I think that's right. I think that's true. (*She looks at Dodge.*) Certain basic things. We can't shake certain basic things. We might end up crazy. Like my husband. You can see it in his eyes. You can see how mad he is.

(*Dodge covers his head with the blanket again. Halie takes a single rose from Dewis and moves slowly over to Dodge.*)

HALIE: We can't not believe in something. We can't stop believing. We just end up dying if we stop. Just end up dead.

(*Halie throws the rose gently onto Dodge's blanket. It lands between his knees and stays there! Long pause as Halie stares at the rose. Shelly stands suddenly. Halie doesn't turn to her but keeps staring at rose.*)

SHELLY (*to Halie*): Don't you wanna' know who I am! Don't you wanna know what I'm doing here! I'm not dead!

(*Shelly crosses toward Halie. Halie turns slowly toward her.*)

HALIE: Did you drink your whiskey?

SHELLY: No! And I'm not going to either!

HALIE: Well, that's a firm stand. It's good to have a firm stand.

SHELLY: I don't have any stand at all. I'm just trying to put all this together.

(*Halie laughs and crosses back to Dewis.*)

HALIE (*to Dewis*): Surprises, surprises! Did you have any idea we'd be returning to this?

SHELLY: I came here with your grandson for a little visit! A little innocent friendly visit.

HALIE: My grandson?

SHELLY: Yes! That's right. The one no one remembers.

HALIE (*to Dewis*): This is getting a little far-fetched.

SHELLY: I told him it was stupid to come back here. To try to pick up from where he left off.

HALIE: Where was that?

SHELLY: Wherever he was when he left here! Six years ago! Ten years ago! Whenever it was. I told him nobody cares.

HALIE: Didn't he listen?

SHELLY: No! No, he didn't. We had to stop off at every tiny little meatball town that he remembered from his boyhood! Every stupid little donut shop he ever kissed a girl in. Every drive-in. Every drag strip. Every football field he ever broke a bone on.

HALIE (*suddenly alarmed, to Dodge*): Where's Tilden?

SHELLY: Don't ignore me!

HALIE: Dodge! Where's Tilden gone?

(*Shelly moves violently toward Halie.*)

SHELLY (*to Halie*): I'm talking to you!

(*Bradley sits up fast on the sofa, Shelly backs away.*)

BRADLEY (*to Shelly*): Don't you yell at my mother!

HALIE: Dodge! (*She kicks Dodge.*) I told you not to let Tilden out of your sight! Where's he gone to?

DODGE: Gimme a drink and I'll tell ya'.

DEWIS: Halie, maybe this isn't the right time for a visit.

(*Halie crosses back to Dewis.*)

HALIE (*to Dewis*): I never should've left. I never, never should've left! Tilden could be anywhere by now! Anywhere! He's not in control of his faculties. Dodge knew that. I told him when I left here. I told him specifically to watch out for Tilden.

(*Bradley reaches down, grabs Dodge's blanket, and yanks it off him. He lays down on sofa and pulls the blanket over his head.*)

DODGE: He's got my blanket again! He's got my blanket!

HALIE (*turning to Bradley*): Bradley! Bradley, put that blanket back!

(*Halie moves toward Bradley. Shelly suddenly throws the cup and saucer against the stage right door. Dewis ducks. The cup and saucer smash into pieces. Halie stops, turns toward Shelly. Everyone freezes. Bradley slowly pulls his head out from under blanket, looks toward stage right door, then to Shelly. Shelly stares at Halie. Dewis cowers with roses. Shelly moves slowly toward Halie. Long pause. Shelly speaks softly.*)

SHELLY (*to Halie*): I don't like being ignored. I don't like being treated like I'm not here. I didn't like it when I was a kid and I still don't like it.

BRADLEY (*sitting up on sofa*): We don't have to tell you anything, girl. Not a thing. You're not the police, are you? You're not the government. You're just some prostitute that Tilden brought in here.

HALIE: Language! I won't have that language in my house!

SHELLY (*to Bradley*): You stuck your hand in my mouth and you call me a prostitute!

HALIE: Bradley! Did you put your hand in her mouth? I'm ashamed of you. I can't leave you alone for a minute.

BRADLEY: I never did. She's lying!

DEWIS: Halie, I think I'll be running along now. I'll just put the roses in the kitchen.

(*Dewis moves toward stage left. Halie stops him.*)

HALIE: Don't go now, Father! Not now.

BRADLEY: I never did anything, Mom! I never touched her! She propositioned me! And I turned her down. I turned her down flat!

(*Shelly suddenly grabs her coat off the wooden leg and takes both the leg and coat downstage, away from Bradley.*)

BRADLEY: Mom! Mom! She's got my leg! She's taken my leg! I never did anything to her! She's stolen my leg!

(*Bradley reaches pathetically in the air for his leg. Shelly sets it down for a second, puts on her coat fast, and picks the leg up again. Dodge starts coughing softly.*)

HALIE (*to Shelly*): I think we've had about enough of you, young lady. Just about enough. I don't know where you came from or what you're doing here but you're no longer welcome in this house.

SHELLY (*laughs, holds leg*): No longer welcome!

BRADLEY: Mom! That's my leg! Get my leg back! I can't do anything without my leg.

(*Bradley keeps making whimpering sounds and reaching for his leg.*)

HALIE: Give my son back his leg. Right this very minute!

(*Dodge starts laughing softly to himself in between coughs.*)

HALIE (*to Dewis*): Father, do something about this, would you! I'm not about to be terrorized in my own house!

BRADLEY: Gimme back my leg!

HALIE: Oh, shut up, Bradley! Just shut up! You don't need your leg now! Just lay down and shut up!

(*Bradley whimpers. Lays down and pulls blanket around him. He keeps one arm outside blanket, reaching out toward his wooden leg. Dewis cautiously approaches Shelly with the roses in his arms. Shelly clutches the wooden leg to her chest as though she's kidnapped it.*)

DEWIS (*to Shelly*): Now, honestly dear, wouldn't it be better to try to talk things out? Try to use some reason?

SHELLY: There isn't any reason here! I can't find a reason for anything.

DEWIS: There's nothing to be afraid of. These are all good people. All righteous people.

SHELLY: I'm not afraid!

DEWIS: But this isn't your house. You have to have some respect.

SHELLY: You're the strangers here, not me.

HALIE: This has gone far enough!

DEWIS: Halie, please. Let me handle this.

SHELLY: Don't come near me! Don't anyone come near me. I don't need any words from you. I'm not threatening anybody. I don't even know what I'm doing here. You all say you don't remember Vince, okay, maybe you don't. Maybe it's Vince that's crazy. Maybe he's made this whole family thing up. I don't even care anymore. I was just coming along for the ride. I thought it'd be a nice gesture. Besides, I was curious. He made all of you sound familiar to me. Every one of you. For every name, I had an image. Every time he'd tell me a name, I'd see the person. In fact, each of you was so clear in my mind that I actually believed it was you. I really believed when I walked through that door that the people who lived here would turn out to be the same people in my imagination. But I don't recognize any of you. Not one. Not even the slightest resemblance.

DEWIS: Well, you can hardly blame others for not fulfilling your hallucination.

SHELLY: It was no hallucination! It was more like a prophecy. You believe in prophecy, don't you?

HALIE: Father, there's no point in talking to her any further. We're just going to have to call the police.

BRADLEY: No! Don't get the police in here. We don't want the police in here. This is our home.

SHELLY: That's right. Bradley's right. Don't you usually settle your affairs in private? Don't you usually take them out in the dark? Out in the back?

BRADLEY: You stay out of our lives! You have no business interfering!

SHELLY: I don't have any business period. I got nothing to lose.

(*She moves around, staring at each of them.*)

BRADLEY: You don't know what we've been through. You don't know anything!

SHELLY: I know you've got a secret. You've all got a secret. It's so secret in fact, you're all convinced it never happened.

(*Halie moves to Dewis.*)

HALIE: Oh, my God, Father!

DODGE (*laughing to himself*): She thinks she's going to get it out of us. She thinks she's going to uncover the truth of the matter. Like a detective or something.

BRADLEY: I'm not telling her anything! Nothing's wrong here! Nothin's ever been wrong! Everything's the way it's supposed to be! Nothing ever happened that's bad! Everything is all right here! We're all good people!

DODGE: She thinks she's gonna suddenly bring everything out into the open after all these years.

DEWIS (*to Shelly*): Can't you see that these people want to be left in peace? Don't you have any mercy? They haven't done anything to you.

DODGE: She wants to get to the bottom of it. (*To Shelly.*) That's it, isn't it? You'd like to get right down to bedrock? You want me to tell ya'? You want me to tell ya' what happened? I'll tell ya'. I might as well.

BRADLEY: No! Don't listen to him. He doesn't remember anything!

DODGE: I remember the whole thing from start to finish. I remember the day he was born.

(*Pause.*)

HALIE: Dodge, if you tell this thing—if you tell this, you'll be dead to me. You'll be just as good as dead.

DODGE: That won't be such a big change, Halie. See this girl, this girl here, she wants to know. She wants to know something more. And I got this feeling that it doesn't make a bit a' difference. I'd sooner tell it to a stranger than anybody else.

BRADLEY (*to Dodge*): We made a pact! We made a pact between us! You can't break that now!

DODGE: I don't remember any pact.

BRADLEY (*to Shelly*): See, he doesn't remember anything. I'm the only one in the family who remembers. The only one. And I'll never tell you!

SHELLY: I'm not so sure I want to find out now.

DODGE (*laughing to himself*): Listen to her! Now she's runnin' scared!

SHELLY: I'm not scared!

(*Dodge stops laughing, long pause. Dodge stares at her.*)

DODGE: You're not, huh? Well, that's good. Because I'm not either. See, we were a well-established family once. Well-established. All the boys were grown. The farm was producing enough milk to fill Lake Michigan twice over. Me and Halie here were pointed toward what looked like the middle part of our life. Everything was settled with us. All we had to do was ride it out. Then Halie got pregnant again. Outa' the middle a' nowhere, she got pregnant. We weren't planning on havin' any more boys. We had enough boys already. In fact, we hadn't been sleepin' in the same bed for about six years.

HALIE (*moving toward stairs*): I'm not listening to this! I don't have to listen to this!

DODGE (*stops Halie*): Where are you going! Upstairs! You'll just be listenin' to it upstairs! You go outside, you'll be listenin' to it outside. Might as well stay here and listen to it.

(*Halie stays by stairs.*)

BRADLEY: If I had my leg you wouldn't be saying this. You'd never get away with it if I had my leg.

DODGE (*pointing to Shelly*): She's got your leg. (*Laughs.*) She's gonna keep your leg too. (*To Shelly.*) She wants to hear this. Don't you?

SHELLY: I don't know.

DODGE: Well even if ya' don't I'm gonna' tell ya'. (*Pause.*) Halie had this kid. This baby boy. She had it. I let her have it on her own. All the other boys I had had the best doctors, best nurses, everything. This one I let her have by herself. This one hurt real bad. Almost killed her, but she had it anyway. It lived, see. It lived. It wanted to grow up in this family. It wanted to be just like us. It wanted to be a part of us. It wanted to pretend that I was its father. She wanted me to believe in it. Even when everyone around us knew. Everyone. All our boys knew. Tilden knew.

HALIE: You shut up! Bradley, make him shut up!

BRADLEY: I can't.

DODGE: Tilden was the one who knew. Better than any of us. He'd walk for miles with that kid in his arms. Halie let him take it. All night sometimes. He'd walk all night out there in the pasture with it. Talkin' to it. Singin' to it. Used to hear him singing to it. He'd make up stories. He'd tell that kid all kinds a' stories. Even when he knew it couldn't understand him. Couldn't understand a word he was sayin'. Never would understand him. We couldn't let a thing like that continue. We couldn't allow that to grow up right in the middle of our lives. It made everything we'd accomplished look like it was nothin'. Everything was canceled out by this one mistake. This one weakness.

SHELLY: So you killed him?

DODGE: I killed it. I drowned it. Just like the runt of a litter. Just drowned it.

(*Halie moves toward Bradley.*)

HALIE (*to Bradley*): Ansel would've stopped him! Ansel would've stopped him from telling these lies! He was a hero! A man! A whole man! What's happened to the men in this family! Where are the men!

(*Suddenly Vince comes crashing through the screen porch door up left, tearing it off its hinges. Everyone but Dodge and Bradley back away from the porch and stare at Vince who has landed on his stomach on the porch in a drunken stupor. He is singing loudly to himself and hauls himself slowly to his feet. He has a paper shopping bag full of empty booze bottles. He takes them out one at a time as he sings and smashes them at the opposite end of the porch, behind the solid interior door, stage right. Shelly moves slowly toward stage right, holding wooden leg and watching Vince.*)

VINCE (*singing loudly as he hurls bottles*): "From the Halls of Montezuma to the Shores of Tripoli. We will fight our country's battles on the land and on the sea."

(*He punctuates the words "Montezuma," "Tripoli," "battles," and "sea" with a smashed bottle each. He stops throwing for a second, stares toward stage right of the porch, shades his eyes with his hand as though looking across to a battlefield, then cups his hands around his mouth and yells across the space of the porch to an imaginary army. The others watch in terror and expectation.*)

VINCE (*to imagined army*): Have you had enough over there! 'Cause there's a lot more here where that came from! (*Pointing to paper bag full of bottles.*) A helluva lot more! We got enough over here to blow ya' from here to Kingdomcome!

(*He takes another bottle, makes high whistling sound of a bomb, and throws it toward stage right porch. Sound of bottle smashing against wall. This should be the actual smashing of bottles and not tape sound. He keeps yelling and heaving bottles one after another.*)
   (*Vince stops for a while, breathing heavily from exhaustion. Long silence as the others watch him. Shelly approaches tentatively in Vince's direction, still holding Bradley's wooden leg.*)

SHELLY (*after silence*): Vince?

(*Vince turns toward her. Peers through screen.*)

VINCE: Who? What? Vince who? Who's that in there?

(*Vince pushes his face against the screen from the porch and stares in at everyone.*)

DODGE: Where's my goddamn bottle!

VINCE (*looking in at Dodge*): What? Who is that?

DODGE: It's me! Your Grandfather! Don't play stupid with me! Where's my two bucks!

VINCE: Your two bucks?

(*Halie moves away from Dewis, upstage, peers out at Vince, trying to recognize him.*)

HALIE: Vincent? Is that you, Vincent?

(*Shelly stares at Halie, then looks out at Vince.*)

VINCE (*from porch*): Vincent who? What is this! Who are you people?

SHELLY (*to Halie*): Hey, wait a minute. Wait a minute! What's going on?

HALIE (*moving closer to porch screen*): We thought you were a murderer or something. Barging in through the door like that.

VINCE: I am a murderer! Don't underestimate me for a minute! I'm the Midnight Strangler! I devour whole families in a single gulp!

(*Vince grabs another bottle and smashes it on the porch. Halie backs away.*)

SHELLY (*approaching Halie*): You mean you know who he is?

HALIE: Of course I know who he is! That's more than I can say for you.

BRADLEY (*sitting up on sofa*): You get off our front porch, you creep! What're you doing out there breaking bottles? Who are these foreigners anyway! Where did they come from?

VINCE: Maybe I should come in there and break them!

HALIE (*moving toward porch*): Don't you dare! Vincent, what's got into you! Why are you acting like this?

VINCE: Maybe I should come in there and usurp your territory!

(*Halie turns back toward Dewis and crosses to him.*)

HALIE (*to Dewis*): Father, why are you just standing around here when everything's falling apart? Can't you rectify this situation?

(*Dodge laughs, coughs.*)

DEWIS: I'm just a guest here, Halie. I don't know what my position is exactly. This is outside my parish anyway.

(*Vince starts throwing more bottles as things continue.*)

BRADLEY: If I had my leg I'd rectify it! I'd rectify him all over the goddamn highway! I'd pull his ears out if I could reach him!

(*Bradley sticks his fist through the screening of the porch and reaches out for Vince, grabbing at him and missing. Vince jumps away from Bradley's hand.*)

VINCE: Aaaah! Our lines have been penetrated! Tentacled animals! Beasts from the deep!

(*Vince strikes out at Bradley's hand with a bottle. Bradley pulls his hand back inside.*)

SHELLY: Vince! Knock it off, will ya'! I want to get out of here!

(*Vince pushes his face against screen, looks in at Shelly.*)

VINCE (*to Shelly*): Have they got you prisoner in there, dear? Such a sweet young thing too. All her life in front of her. Nipped in the bud.

SHELLY: I'm coming out there, Vince! I'm coming out there and I want us to get in the car and drive away from here. Anywhere. Just away from here.

(*Shelly moves toward Vince's saxophone case and overcoat. She sets down the wooden leg, downstage left, and picks up the saxophone case and overcoat. Vince watches her through the screen.*)

VINCE (*to Shelly*): We'll have to negotiate. Make some kind of a deal. Prisoner exchange or something. A few of theirs for one of ours. Small price to pay if you ask me.

(*Shelly crosses toward stage right door with overcoat and case.*)

SHELLY: Just go and get the car! I'm coming out there now. We're going to leave.

VINCE: Don't come out here! Don't you dare come out here!

(*Shelly stops short of the door, stage right.*)

SHELLY: How come?

VINCE: Off limits! Verboten! This is taboo territory. No man or woman has ever crossed the line and lived to tell the tale!

SHELLY: I'll take my chances.

(*Shelly moves to stage right door and opens it. Vince pulls out a big folding hunting knife and pulls open the blade. He jabs the blade into the screen and starts cutting a hole big enough to climb through. Bradley cowers in a corner of the sofa as Vince rips at the screen.*)

VINCE (*as he cuts screen*): Don't come out here! I'm warning you! You'll disintegrate!

(*Dewis takes Halie by the arm and pulls her toward staircase.*)

DEWIS: Halie, maybe we should go upstairs until this blows over.

HALIE: I don't understand it. I just don't understand it. He was the sweetest little boy!

(*Dewis drops the roses beside the wooden leg at the foot of the staircase, then escorts Halie quickly up the stairs. Halie keeps looking back at Vince as they climb the stairs.*)

HALIE: There wasn't a mean bone in his body. Everyone loved Vincent. Everyone. He was the perfect baby.

DEWIS: He'll be all right after a while. He's just had a few too many that's all.

HALIE: He used to sing in his sleep. He'd sing. In the middle of the night. The sweetest voice. Like an angel. (*She stops for a moment.*) I used to lie awake listening to it. I used to lie awake thinking it was all right if I died. Because Vincent was an angel. A guardian angel. He'd watch over us. He'd watch over all of us.

(*Dewis takes her all the way up the stairs. They disappear above. Vince is now climbing through the porch screen onto the sofa. Bradley crashes off the sofa, holding tight to his blanket, keeping it wrapped around him. Shelly is outside on the porch. Vince holds the knife in his teeth once he gets the hole wide enough to climb through. Bradley starts crawling slowly toward his wooden leg, reaching out for it.*)

DODGE (*to Vince*): Go ahead! Take over the house! Take over the whole goddamn house! You can have it! It's yours. It's been a pain in the neck ever since the very

first mortgage. I'm gonna die any second now. Any second. You won't even notice. So I'll settle my affairs once and for all.

(*As Dodge proclaims his last will and testament, Vince climbs into the room, knife in mouth, and strides slowly around the space, inspecting his inheritance. He casually notices Bradley as he crawls toward his leg. Vince moves to the leg and keeps pushing it with his foot so that it's out of Bradley's reach, then goes on with his inspection. He picks up the roses and carries them around smelling them. Shelly can be seen outside on the porch, moving slowly center and staring in at Vince. Vince ignores her.*)

DODGE: The house goes to my Grandson, Vincent. All the furnishings, accoutrements, and paraphernalia therein. Everything tacked to the walls or otherwise resting under this roof. My tools—namely my band saw, my skill saw, my drill press, my chain saw, my lathe, my electric sander, all go to my eldest son, Tilden. That is, if he ever shows up again. My shed and gasoline powered equipment, namely my tractor, my dozer, my hand tiller plus all the attachments and riggings for the above mentioned machinery, namely my spring tooth harrow, my deep plows, my disk plows, my automatic fertilizing equipment, my reaper, my swathe, my seeder, my John Deere Harvester, my post hole digger, my jackhammer, my lathe—(*to himself*) Did I mention my lathe? I already mentioned my lathe—my Bennie Goodman records, my harnesses, my bits, my halters, my brace, my rough rasp, my forge, my welding equipment, my shoeing nails, my levels and bevels, my milking stool—no, not my milking stool—my hammers and chisels, my hinges, my cattle gates, my barbed wire, self-tapping augers, my horse hair ropes, and all related materials are to be pushed into a gigantic heap and set ablaze in the very center of my fields. When the blaze is at its highest, preferably on a cold, windless night, my body is to be pitched into the middle of it and burned till nothing remains but ash.

(*Pause. Vince takes the knife out of his mouth and smells the roses. He's facing toward audience and doesn't turn around to Shelly. He folds up knife and pockets it.*)

SHELLY (*from porch*): I'm leaving, Vince. Whether you come or not, I'm leaving.

VINCE (*smelling roses*): Just put my horn on the couch there before you take off.

SHELLY (*moving toward hole in screen*): You're not coming?

(*Vince stays downstage, turns, and looks at her.*)

VINCE: I just inherited a house.

SHELLY (*through hole, from porch*): You want to stay here?

VINCE (*as he pushes Bradley's leg out of reach*): I've gotta carry on the line. I've gotta see to it that things keep rolling.

(*Bradley looks up at him from floor, keeps pulling himself toward his leg. Vince keeps moving it.*)

SHELLY: What happened to you, Vince? You just disappeared.

VINCE (*pause, delivers speech front*): I was gonna run last night. I was gonna run and keep right on running. I drove all night. Clear to the Iowa border. The old man's two bucks sitting right on the seat beside me. It never stopped raining the whole time. Never stopped once. I could see myself in the windshield. My face. My eyes. I studied my face. Studied everything about it. As though I was looking at another man. As though I could see his whole race behind him. Like a mummy's face. I saw him dead and alive at the same time. In the same breath. In the windshield, I watched him breathe as though he was frozen in time. And every breath marked him. Marked him forever without him knowing. And then his face changed. His face became his father's face. Same bones. Same eyes. Same nose. Same breath. And his father's face changed to his grandfather's face. And it went on like that. Changing. Clear on back to faces I'd never seen before but still recognized. Still recognized the bones underneath. The eyes. The breath. The mouth. I followed my family clear into Iowa. Every last one. Straight into the Corn Belt and further. Straight back as far as they'd take me. Then it all dissolved. Everything dissolved.

(*Shelly stares at him for a while then reaches through the hole in the screen and sets the saxophone case and Vince's overcoat on the sofa. She looks at Vince again.*)

SHELLY: Bye, Vince.

(*She exits left off the porch. Vince watches her go. Bradley tries to make a lunge for his wooden leg. Vince quickly picks it up and dangles it over Bradley's head like a carrot. Bradley keeps making desperate grabs at the leg. Dewis comes down the staircase and stops halfway, staring at Vince and Bradley. Vince looks up at Dewis and smiles. He keeps moving backwards with the leg toward upstage left as Bradley crawls after him.*)

VINCE (*to Dewis as he continues torturing Bradley*): Oh, excuse me, Father. Just getting rid of some of the vermin in the house. This is my house now, ya' know? All mine. Everything. Except for the power tools and stuff. I'm gonna get all new equipment anyway. New plows, new tractor, everything. All brand new. (*Vince teases Bradley closer to the up left corner of the stage.*) Start right off on the ground floor.

(*Vince throws Bradley's wooden leg far offstage left. Bradley follows his leg offstage, pulling himself along on the ground, whimpering. As Bradley exits, Vince pulls the blanket off him and throws it over his own shoulder. He crosses toward Dewis with the blanket and smells the roses. Dewis comes to the bottom of the stairs.*)

DEWIS: You'd better go up and see your Grandmother.

VINCE (*looking up stairs, back to Dewis*): My Grandmother? There's nobody else in this house. Except for you. And you're leaving, aren't you?

(*Dewis crosses toward stage right door. He turns back to Vince.*)

DEWIS: She's going to need someone. I can't help her. I don't know what to do. I don't know what my position is. I just came in for some tea. I had no idea there was any trouble. No idea at all.

(*Vince just stares at him. Dewis goes out the door, crosses porch, and exits left. Vince listens to him leaving. He smells roses, looks up the staircase, then smells roses again. He turns and looks upstage at Dodge. He crosses up to him and bends over looking at Dodge's open eyes. Dodge is dead. His death should have come completely unnoticed by the audience. Vince covers Dodge's body with the blanket, then covers his head. He sits on the sofa, smelling roses and staring at Dodge's body. Long pause. Vince places the roses on Dodge's chest, then lays down on the sofa, arms folded behind his head, staring at the ceiling. His body is in the same relationship to Dodge's. After a while Halie's voice is heard coming from above the staircase. The lights start to dim almost imperceptibly as Halie speaks. Vince keeps staring at the ceiling.*)

HALIE'S VOICE: Dodge? Is that you, Dodge? Tilden was right about the corn, you know. I've never seen such corn. Have you taken a look at it lately? Tall as a man already. This early in the year. Carrots too. Potatoes. Peas. It's like a paradise out there, Dodge. You oughta' take a look. A miracle. I've never seen it like this. Maybe the rain did something. Maybe it was the rain.

(*As Halie keeps talking offstage, Tilden appears from stage left, dripping with mud from the knees down. His arms and hands are covered with mud. In his hands he carries the corpse of a small child at chest level, staring down at it. The corpse mainly consists of bones wrapped in muddy, rotten cloth. He moves slowly downstage toward the staircase, ignoring Vince on the sofa. Vince keeps staring at the ceiling as though Tilden wasn't there. As Halie's voice continues, Tilden slowly makes his way up the stairs. His eyes never leave the corpse of the child. The lights keep fading.*)

HALIE'S VOICE: Good hard rain. Takes everything straight down deep to the roots. The rest takes care of itself. You can't force a thing to grow. You can't interfere with it. It's all hidden. It's all unseen. You just gotta wait till it pops up out of the ground. Tiny little shoot. Tiny little white shoot. All hairy and fragile. Strong though. Strong enough to break the earth even. It's a miracle, Dodge. I've never seen a crop like this in my whole life. Maybe it's the sun. Maybe that's it. Maybe it's the sun.

(*Tilden disappears above. Silence. Lights go to black.*)

Caryl Churchill

Caryl Churchill (b. 1938) is in many ways a conventional middle-class woman. She was born in London to a comfortable family; her father was a political cartoonist and her mother a model. During World War II, her family emigrated to Canada, and much of her growing up was done in Montreal. She returned to England for college, receiving her degree in English literature at Oxford.

Churchill says that through all these years she did all the right things. She was a proper intellectual, a proper student, a proper person. She began writing plays at Oxford, where they were produced by students. After college, she married David Harter, also from Oxford, who became a lawyer in London. She raised three sons and at the same time tried to keep alive her dream of being a writer. Most of her early work was written for radio, and many of the plays were short. With so many children in the house, she says, it was difficult to sustain a long project.

Churchill's social conscience has been a significant part of her playwriting and her life. She found herself sometimes depressed by the dullness of the middle-class life demanded of the wife of a lawyer, and much of her early drama is satire directed at what many people thought was an enviable lifestyle.

Her husband left a very lucrative law practice in the early 1970s and has since devoted himself to helping the poor at a nearby legal aid center. Churchill has become involved in theater groups, among them a group of women called Monstrous Regiment. She is closely aligned with the Royal Court Theatre in London, noted for producing satiric, biting, experimental drama with a punch.

Churchill's first play staged at the Royal Court Theatre was a farcical but serious drama called *Owners* (1972). It attacks the way the concept of ownership destroys potential relationships. Churchill's basic socialist views are very apparent in the play, which is a critique of the values that most capitalists take for granted: being aggressive, getting ahead, doing well. Although this play is not explicitly feminist, Churchill combines socialism and feminism in most of her plays, thus often producing an unusual approach to her subject matter. *Owners* has been criticized for its Brechtian use of disconnected scenes and its loose plot, but when it was produced off Broadway in 1973, it marked Churchill as a serious playwright.

After a year as a playwright in residence at the Royal Court Theatre, Churchill produced *Objections to Sex and Violence* (1975). The play was not immensely successful, but it introduced themes of feminism into her work, among other themes. The play examines in depth the domination of women by men and the relationship of violence to sex roles.

In 1976 Churchill produced *Vinegar Tom*, a play about witch hunts set in the seventeenth century. After researching witch trials, Churchill concluded that women were convenient scapegoats for men when times became difficult. A companion play also set in the seventeenth century is *Light Shining in Buckinghamshire*, which studies revolutions. The play was developed by the Joint Stock Theatre Group and produced at the Royal Court Theatre to uniformly positive reviews.

Churchill's first play to receive wide notice was *Cloud Nine* (1979). It treats several themes simultaneously, among them colonization. The first act is set in the Victorian era in a British colony in Africa. The play is broadly satirical, involving farcical moments in the relationships of colonizer and native, master and servant, and man and woman. Churchill cast certain parts of the play in a cross-gender fashion: A woman plays a sensitive schoolboy, and a man plays an unfulfilled wife. The effect is both comic and instructive, since one of Churchill's most important purposes is to cast some light on gender distinctions. She said that she saw "parallels between the way colonizers treat the colonized and the way men tended to treat women in our own society." *Cloud Nine* was produced in the Lucille Lortel Theatre, where it ran for two years off Broadway and won an Obie award.

Top Girls (1982) played at the Royal Court Theatre in London and at the Public Theater in New York, where the reviews were mixed. The play, essentially feminist in theme, was praised in England for being "the best British play ever from a woman dramatist." *Fen* (1983) was warmly praised by critics and audiences alike. A study of the effects of poverty on women, the play was developed with the Joint Stock Theatre Group and set in the area of England called the Fens, a flat country prone to flooding, where women work the fields and most of the people are poor.

Churchill's *Serious Money* (1987) is a verse play (like her first Oxford play) about the London stock market. It ran on Broadway to exceptional acclaim, partly because it played just after the stock market crash of October 1987. The play is a satiric study of those for whom only greed and getting ahead matter.

Churchill has written a number of plays for radio and television, such as *Lovesick, Abortive, Not Not Not Not Not Enough Oxygen, Schreber's Nervous Illness, The Hospital at the Time of the Revolution,* and *The Judge's Wife.* These are gathered in a volume called *Shorts* (1990). *The Skriker* (1994) is an experiment in fantasy, with a spirit world that parallels the real world. *Blue Heart* (1999) consists of two one-act plays: *Heart's Desire* and *Blue Kettle.* These are relatively realistic domestic dramas. *Heart's Desire* is a satire set in a sparkling kitchen where Alice and Brian wait, with Brian's sister Maisie, for the return of their daughter from Australia. Their peaceful setting is invaded by alcoholics and terrorists, among others, and yet the play has been described as "achingly, aggressively funny." *Blue Kettle* features a young man who searches for women who have given up children for adoption and then claims to be their lost son. It is a somber play that deals with the failure of language.

Among Churchill's later plays, *Far Away* (2000) is a dark piece on the subject of modern life and modern politics as seen in the context of the millennium. *A Number* (2002) treats the relationship of fathers and sons in a remarkably unusual way. A man has his son cloned twenty-one times and, in this play, interacts with two of those clones. *A Dream Play* (2005) is an adaptation of a Strindberg play with the addition of Freudian implications. *Drunk Enough to Say I Love You?* (2006) focuses on world domination, torture, and war, but from the perspective of a computer game. Jack (Union Jack), a British man, goes to the United States to live with Sam (Uncle Sam), and the two plot to control the world. One review said simply that it was the best value in London theater during its run. Churchill's ten-minute play *Seven Jewish Children* (2009), a very brief history of Israel, was written to give support to Palestinians living in Gaza. A very controversial political play, it has been released to any theater group that wishes to produce it, as long as it gathers funds for those living in Gaza. Churchill is one of the most prolific of modern playwrights and continues to stir audiences all over the world.

Cloud Nine

Cloud Nine (1979) was commissioned by London's Joint Stock Theatre Group and developed with the help of director Max Stafford-Clark, who ran the Royal Court Theatre, one of London's most exciting experimental theaters. Many of Churchill's later plays were also developed at the Royal Court, and they helped establish it as one of the centers of new drama in England. The central subject of *Cloud Nine* is sex, but the drama draws us into the worlds of politics, gender definition, and social mores.

The play is divided into two acts that are more disconnected than unified. Some of the same characters appear in both acts, but the actors trade parts in act 2. Such a disjunction is so striking—especially to the first audiences who saw the play in 1979—that we realize Churchill is telling us something radical about the psychological continuity of characters and thus about psychological realism. Also, the first act is set in British imperial Africa in the 1870s, while the second act is set in London in the 1970s, so it seems reasonable that different actors should play these characters in view of the time difference.

But there is more. The characters in act 1 play recognizable types. Clive is the patriarch of a Victorian family who rules his environment, sometimes with a whip. His wife Betty is played in both acts by a man, implying that in the Victorian world of act 1 the British woman was really a male ideal or in fact a male and was expected to act as one, while in the contemporary London of act 2 gender liberation is within the realm of possibility. Act 1 is a study of the world of Victorian sexual repression and the system of gender expectations—the social construction of conventional gender behavior. Such expectations are spoofed by nine-year-old Edward, played by a grown woman, who holds his two-year-old sister's doll for safekeeping. He wants the doll for himself but tells his parents that he is "minding" his sister's doll, not playing with it. His merely holding the doll, however, unsettles his father, who insists that Edward do something more manly, such as riding with Harry Bagley, the mythic adventurer. Harry Bagley turns out to be bisexual and involved with the black servant, who is played by a white actor.

Part of the social comment of act 1 involves a critique of British colonial rule. Joshua, the servant, regards himself as inferior, while Clive, the representative of British authority, comports himself with no thought for the feelings of the "natives." British rule is intentionally oppressive. The sound of native drums implies a threatening "jungle" environment with the potential for an uprising. The situation is self-consciously developed as a cliché in a conventional romantic mode—typical of thrillers of the Victorian period.

But in addition to a commentary on the colonial ethos of the British, the play offers a critique of Victorian repression. Clive and others are sexually promiscuous. His relationship with Mrs. Saunders is conducted almost farcically. Other characters engage in homosexual relationships in secret. All sexuality is essentially relegated to secret hideaways, while on the surface society maintains total conventionality. Churchill includes moments of comic relief, as when Ellen and Betty are attracted to each other, and Betty instructs her son Edward to go and play with Uncle Harry, whom the audience knows is a pederast. That such sexual relationships occurred in 1870s England is now well known, but the image that survives of the period is one of absolute moral rectitude.

For discussion questions and assignments on *Cloud Nine*, visit bedfordstmartins.com/jacobus.

When act 2 introduces us to the sexual mores of 1970s London, it becomes clear that the period's usual reputation for sexual liberation is no more accurate than the official version we have of Victorian England. Two mothers, Victoria and Lin, introduce us to the modern world. Their children play with guns while Victoria remarks that in Sweden such toys are banned. Lin replies that she will give her daughter, Cathy, a rifle for Christmas with the suggestion that she shoot Victoria's son, Tommy. Victoria hardly hears when Lin says that she is a lesbian and has left her husband or notices her making sexual advances. At the end of the first scene Victoria and Lin may or may not have sex with each other.

Scene 2 reveals a casual sexual encounter between two men, Edward and Gerry, on the train from Victoria to Clapham (two coded destinations that imply the distance from Victorian England to the modern world). Sex is casual, and Martin tells Victoria and Betty that he's ready for almost anything: "Whatever you want to do, I'll be delighted." The comedy reaches an amusing moment at the end of scene 2 when Edward decides he is probably a lesbian because he thinks he likes women more than men.

Scene 3 looks further back into history at ancient cults, many of whose priestesses allegedly were interested in unusual sexual relationships. It is as if Churchill is suggesting that the more things change the more they remain the same. In the play the sexual liberation of the 1970s appears to be less radical and novel than it once seemed.

Cloud Nine in Performance

The first production of *Cloud Nine* was in the Dartington College of Arts in February 1979. The play quickly went on tour and then to the Royal Court Theatre in London. The earliest versions of the play were revised based on contributions from the director and actors, and Churchill revised the text even after its first publication in 1979. The current version reflects changes made in performance and development until at least 1984.

Although much of the play is serious in tone, most productions have emphasized its burlesque elements. Some productions have approached the drama as if it were farce, using a broad comic style and producing much laughter. Segments of act 1 have been compared with sketches by Monty Python, some of whose purposes may have been similar to Churchill's.

The cross-casting—men playing women, women playing men, and adults playing children—was one of the striking elements of the earliest performances. The first act has been played with pith helmets and other emblems of the British empire. In one version a rhinoceros horn was positioned on the wall in such a way as to appear to be a phallic symbol. The 1979 production in the Royal Court Theatre established the play as a significant part of the modern English repertory.

Eighteen years later, after performances in many countries around the world, Peter Hall included *Cloud Nine* in a series of seven classic plays at the Old Vic in London. He believed the play ranked with Shakespeare's *King Lear* and Chekhov's *The Seagull*. Not everyone agreed with him, but the Old Vic production in 1997 demonstrated that the play was still timely and potentially powerful. Theater critic Alastair Macaulay said of the second act: "It is shot through with mystery, it proceeds with dreamlike fluency, and, most beautifully, it allows each character, even while he or she grows more complex and more poignant, to remain an unanswered question." *Cloud Nine* remains a popular play, having been produced in Philadelphia at the Wilma Theater in 2006, in London at the Almeida Theatre in 2007, and in Los Angeles, Seattle, and Chicago in 2011. It has proven to be a durable and important play, just as Churchill has proven to be one of contemporary theater's most important playwrights.

CARYL CHURCHILL (b. 1938)

Cloud Nine   1979

Characters

(*Act One*)
CLIVE, *a colonial administrator*
BETTY, *his wife, played by a man*
JOSHUA, *his black servant, played by a white*
EDWARD, *his son, played by a woman*
VICTORIA, *his daughter, a dummy*
MAUD, *his mother-in-law*
ELLEN, *Edward's governess*
HARRY BAGLEY, *an explorer*
MRS. SAUNDERS, *a widow*

(*Act Two*)
BETTY
EDWARD, *her son*
VICTORIA, *her daughter*
MARTIN, *Victoria's husband*
LIN
CATHY, *Lin's daughter age 5, played by a man*
GERRY, *Edward's lover*

(*Except for Cathy, characters in Act Two are played by actors of their own sex.*)
(*Act One takes place in a British colony in Africa in Victorian times.*)
(*Act Two takes place in London in 1979. But for the characters it is twenty-five years later.*)

ACT ONE • Scene One

(*Low bright sun. Verandah. Flagpole with Union Jack. The Family—Clive, Betty, Edward, Victoria, Maud, Ellen, Joshua.*)

ALL (*sing*): Come gather, sons of England, come gather in your pride.
   Now meet the world united, now face it side by side;

Ye who the earth's wide corners, from veldt to prairie, roam.
   From bush and jungle muster all who call old England "home."
   Then gather round for England,
   Rally to the flag,
   From North and South and East and West
   Come one and all for England!
CLIVE: This is my family. Though far from home
   We serve the Queen wherever we may roam
   I am a father to the natives here,
   And father to my family so dear.

(*He presents Betty. She is played by a man.*)

   My wife is all I dreamt a wife should be,
   And everything she is she owes to me.
BETTY: I live for Clive. The whole aim of my life
   Is to be what he looks for in a wife.
   I am a man's creation as you see,
   And what men want is what I want to be.

(*Clive presents Joshua. He is played by a white.*)

CLIVE: My boy's a jewel. Really has the knack.
   You'd hardly notice that the fellow's black.
JOSHUA: My skin is black but oh my soul is white.
   I hate my tribe. My master is my light.
   I only live for him. As you can see,
   What white men want is what I want to be.

(*Clive presents Edward. He is played by a woman.*)

CLIVE: My son is young. I'm doing all I can
   To teach him to grow up to be a man.
EDWARD: What father wants I'd dearly like to be.
   I find it rather hard as you can see.

(*Clive presents Victoria, who is a dummy, Maud, and Ellen.*)

CLIVE: No need for any speeches by the rest.
   My daughter, mother-in-law, and governess.

The casts of *Cloud Nine* from [TOP] the Panasonic Theatre in Toronto in 2010 and [BOTTOM] the Almeida Theatre in London in 2007.

ALL (*sing*): O'er countless numbers she, our Queen,
Victoria reigns supreme;
O'er Afric's sunny plains, and o'er
Canadian frozen stream;
The forge of war shall weld the chains of brother-
hood secure;
So to all time in ev'ry clime our Empire shall endure.

Then gather round for England,
Rally to the flag,
From North and South and East and West
Come one and all for England!

(*All go except Betty. Clive comes.*)

BETTY: Clive?
CLIVE: Betty. Joshua!

(*Joshua comes with a drink for Clive.*)

BETTY: I thought you would never come. The day's so long without you.
CLIVE: Long ride in the bush.
BETTY: Is anything wrong? I heard drums.
CLIVE: Nothing serious. Beauty is a damned good mare. I must get some new boots sent from home. These ones have never been right. I have a blister.
BETTY: My poor dear foot.
CLIVE: It's nothing.
BETTY: Oh but it's sore.
CLIVE: We are not in this country to enjoy ourselves. Must have ridden fifty miles. Spoke to three different headmen who would all gladly chop off each other's heads and wear them round their waists.
BETTY: Clive!
CLIVE: Don't be squeamish, Betty, let me have my joke. And what has my little dove done today?
BETTY: I've read a little.
CLIVE: Good. Is it good?
BETTY: It's poetry.
CLIVE: You're so delicate and sensitive.
BETTY: And I played the piano. Shall I send for the children?
CLIVE: Yes, in a minute. I've a piece of news for you.
BETTY: Good news?
CLIVE: You'll certainly think it's good. A visitor.
BETTY: From home?
CLIVE: No. Well of course originally from home.
BETTY: Man or woman?
CLIVE: Man.
BETTY: I can't imagine.
CLIVE: Something of an explorer. Bit of a poet. Odd chap but brave as a lion. And a great admirer of yours.
BETTY: What do you mean? Whoever can it be?
CLIVE: With an H and a B. And does conjuring tricks for little Edward.
BETTY: That sounds like Mr. Bagley.
CLIVE: Harry Bagley.
BETTY: He certainly doesn't admire me, Clive, what a thing to say. How could I possibly guess from that. He's hardly explored anything at all, he's just been up a river, he's done nothing at all compared to what

you do. You should have said a heavy drinker and a bit of a bore.
CLIVE: But you like him well enough. You don't mind him coming?
BETTY: Anyone at all to break the monotony.
CLIVE: But you have your mother. You have Ellen.
BETTY: Ellen is a governess. My mother is my mother.
CLIVE: I hoped when she came to visit she would be company for you.
BETTY: I don't think mother is on a visit. I think she lives with us.
CLIVE: I think she does.
BETTY: Clive you are so good.
CLIVE: But are you bored my love?
BETTY: It's just that I miss you when you're away. We're not in this country to enjoy ourselves. If I lack society that is my form of service.
CLIVE: That's a brave girl. So today has been all right? No fainting? No hysteria?
BETTY: I have been very tranquil.
CLIVE: Ah what a haven of peace to come home to. The coolth, the calm, the beauty.
BETTY: There is one thing, Clive, if you don't mind.
CLIVE: What can I do for you, my dear?
BETTY: It's about Joshua.
CLIVE: I wouldn't leave you alone here with a quiet mind if it weren't for Joshua.
BETTY: Joshua doesn't like me.
CLIVE: Joshua has been my boy for eight years. He has saved my life. I have saved his life. He is devoted to me and to mine. I have said this before.
BETTY: He is rude to me. He doesn't do what I say. Speak to him.
CLIVE: Tell me what happened.
BETTY: He said something improper.
CLIVE: Well, what?
BETTY: I don't like to repeat it.
CLIVE: I must insist.
BETTY: I had left my book inside on the piano. I was in the hammock. I asked him to fetch it.
CLIVE: And did he not fetch it?
BETTY: Yes, he did eventually.
CLIVE: And what did he say?
BETTY: Clive —
CLIVE: Betty.
BETTY: He said Fetch it yourself. You've got legs under that dress.
CLIVE: Joshua!

(*Joshua comes.*)

Joshua, madam says you spoke impolitely to her this afternoon.
JOSHUA: Sir?
CLIVE: When she asked you to pass her book from the piano.
JOSHUA: She has the book, sir.
BETTY: I have the book now, but when I told you —
CLIVE: Betty, please, let me handle this. You didn't pass it at once?

JOSHUA: No sir, I made a joke first.

CLIVE: What was that?

JOSHUA: I said my legs were tired, sir. That was funny because the book was very near, it would not make my legs tired to get it.

BETTY: That's not true.

JOSHUA: Did madam hear me wrong?

CLIVE: She heard something else.

JOSHUA: What was that, madam?

BETTY: Never mind.

CLIVE: Now Joshua, it won't do you know. Madam doesn't like that kind of joke. You must do what madam says, just do what she says and don't answer back. You know your place, Joshua. I don't have to say any more.

JOSHUA: No sir.

BETTY: I expect an apology.

JOSHUA: I apologise, madam.

CLIVE: There now. It won't happen again, my dear. I'm very shocked Joshua, very shocked.

(*Clive winks at Joshua, unseen by Betty. Joshua goes.*)

CLIVE: I think another drink, and send for the children, and isn't that Harry riding down the hill? Wave, wave. Just in time before dark. Cuts it fine, the blighter. Always a hothead, Harry.

BETTY: Can he see us?

CLIVE: Stand further forward. He'll see your white dress. There, he waved back.

BETTY: Do you think so? I wonder what he saw. Sometimes sunset is so terrifying I can't bear to look.

CLIVE: It makes me proud. Elsewhere in the empire the sun is rising.

BETTY: Harry looks so small on the hillside.

(*Ellen comes.*)

ELLEN: Shall I bring the children?

BETTY: Shall Ellen bring the children?

CLIVE: Delightful.

BETTY: Yes, Ellen, make sure they're warm. The night air is deceptive. Victoria was looking pale yesterday.

CLIVE: My love.

(*Maud comes from inside the house.*)

MAUD: Are you warm enough Betty?

BETTY: Perfectly.

MAUD: The night air is deceptive.

BETTY: I'm quite warm. I'm too warm.

MAUD: You're not getting a fever, I hope? She's not strong, you know, Clive. I don't know how long you'll keep her in this climate.

CLIVE: I look after Her Majesty's domains. I think you can trust me to look after my wife.

(*Ellen comes carrying Victoria, age 2. Edward, aged 9, lags behind.*)

BETTY: Victoria, my pet, say good evening to papa.

(*Clive takes Victoria on his knee.*)

CLIVE: There's my sweet little Vicky. What have we done today?

BETTY: She wore Ellen's hat.

CLIVE: Did she wear Ellen's big hat like a lady? What a pretty.

BETTY: And Joshua gave her a piggy back. Tell papa. Horsy with Joshy?

ELLEN: She's tired.

CLIVE: Nice Joshy played horsy. What a big strong Joshy. Did you have a gallop? Did you make him stop and go? Not very chatty tonight are we?

BETTY: Edward, say good evening to papa.

CLIVE: Edward my boy. Have you done your lessons well?

EDWARD: Yes papa.

CLIVE: Did you go riding?

EDWARD: Yes papa.

CLIVE: What's that you're holding?

BETTY: It's Victoria's doll. What are you doing with it, Edward?

EDWARD: Minding her.

BETTY: Well I should give it to Ellen quickly. You don't want papa to see you with a doll.

CLIVE: No, we had you with Victoria's doll once before, Edward.

ELLEN: He's minding it for Vicky. He's not playing with it.

BETTY: He's not playing with it, Clive. He's minding it for Vicky.

CLIVE: Ellen minds Victoria, let Ellen mind the doll.

ELLEN: Come, give it to me.

(*Ellen takes the doll.*)

EDWARD: Don't pull her about. Vicky's very fond of her. She likes me to have her.

BETTY: He's a very good brother.

CLIVE: Yes, it's manly of you Edward, to take care of your little sister. We'll say no more about it. Tomorrow I'll take you riding with me and Harry Bagley. Would you like that?

EDWARD: Is he here?

CLIVE: He's just arrived. There Betty, take Victoria now. I must go and welcome Harry.

(*Clive tosses Victoria to Betty, who gives her to Ellen.*)

EDWARD: Can I come, papa?

BETTY: Is he warm enough?

EDWARD: Am I warm enough?

CLIVE: Never mind the women, Ned. Come and meet Harry.

(*They go. The women are left. There is a silence.*)

MAUD: I daresay Mr. Bagley will be out all day and we'll see nothing of him.

BETTY: He plays the piano. Surely he will sometimes stay at home with us.

MAUD: We can't expect it. The men have their duties and we have ours.

BETTY: He won't have seen a piano for a year. He lives a very rough life.

ELLEN: Will it be exciting for you, Betty?

MAUD: Whatever do you mean, Ellen?

ELLEN: We don't have very much society.

BETTY: Clive is my society.

MAUD: It's time Victoria went to bed.

ELLEN: She'd like to stay up and see Mr. Bagley.

MAUD: Mr. Bagley can see her tomorrow.

(Ellen goes.)

MAUD: You let that girl forget her place, Betty.

BETTY: Mother, she is governess to my son. I know what her place is. I think my friendship does her good. She is not very happy.

MAUD: Young women are never happy.

BETTY: Mother, what a thing to say.

MAUD: Then when they're older they look back and see that comparatively speaking they were ecstatic.

BETTY: I'm perfectly happy.

MAUD: You are looking very pretty tonight. You were such a success as a young girl. You have made a most fortunate marriage. I'm sure you will be an excellent hostess to Mr. Bagley.

BETTY: I feel quite nervous at the thought of entertaining.

MAUD: I can always advise you if I'm asked.

BETTY: What a long time they're taking. I always seem to be waiting for the men.

MAUD: Betty you have to learn to be patient. I am patient. My mama was very patient.

(Clive approaches, supporting Caroline Saunders.)

CLIVE: It is a pleasure. It is an honor. It is positively your duty to seek my help. I would be hurt, I would be insulted by any show of independence. Your husband would have been one of my dearest friends if he had lived. Betty, look who has come, Mrs. Saunders. She has ridden here all alone, amazing spirit. What will you have? Tea or something stronger? Let her lie down, she is overcome. Betty, you will know what to do.

(Mrs. Saunders lies down.)

MAUD: I knew it. I heard drums. We'll be killed in our beds.

CLIVE: Now, please, calm yourself.

MAUD: I am perfectly calm. I am just outspoken. If it comes to being killed I shall take it as calmly as anyone.

CLIVE: There is no cause for alarm. Mrs. Saunders has been alone since her husband died last year, amazing spirit. Not surprisingly, the strain has told. She has come to us as her nearest neighbors.

MAUD: What happened to make her come?

CLIVE: This is not an easy country for a woman.

MAUD: Clive, I heard drums. We are not children.

CLIVE: Of course you heard drums. The tribes are constantly at war, if the term is not too grand to grace their squabbles. Not unnaturally Mrs. Saunders would like the company of white women. The piano. Poetry.

BETTY: We are not her nearest neighbors.

CLIVE: We are among her nearest neighbors and I was a dear friend of her late husband. She knows that she will find a welcome here. She will not be disappointed. She will be cared for.

MAUD: Of course we will care for her.

BETTY: Victoria is in bed. I must go and say goodnight. Mother, please, you look after Mrs. Saunders.

CLIVE: Harry will be here at once.

(Betty goes.)

MAUD: How rash to go out after dark without a shawl.

CLIVE: Amazing spirit. Drink this.

MRS. SAUNDERS: Where am I?

MAUD: You are quite safe.

MRS. SAUNDERS: Clive? Clive? Thank God. This is very kind. How do you do? I am sorry to be a nuisance. Charmed. Have you a gun? I have a gun.

CLIVE: There is no need for guns I hope. We are all friends here.

MRS. SAUNDERS: I think I will lie down again.

(Harry Bagley and Edward have approached.)

MAUD: Ah, here is Mr. Bagley.

EDWARD: I gave his horse some water.

CLIVE: You don't know Mrs. Saunders, do you Harry? She has at present collapsed, but she is recovering thanks to the good offices of my wife's mother who I think you've met before. Betty will be along in a minute. Edward will go home to school shortly. He is quite a young man since you saw him.

HARRY: I hardly knew him.

MAUD: What news have you for us, Mr. Bagley?

CLIVE: Do you know Mrs. Saunders, Harry? Amazing spirit.

EDWARD: Did you hardly know me?

HARRY: Of course I knew you. I mean you have grown.

EDWARD: What do you expect?

HARRY: That's quite right, people don't get smaller.

MAUD: Edward. You should be in bed.

EDWARD: No, I'm not tired, I'm not tired am I Uncle Harry?

HARRY: I don't think he's tired.

CLIVE: He is overtired. It is past his bedtime. Say goodnight.

EDWARD: Goodnight, sir.

CLIVE: And to your grandmother.

EDWARD: Goodnight, grandmother.

(Edward goes.)

MAUD: Shall I help Mrs. Saunders indoors? I'm afraid she may get a chill.

CLIVE: Shall I give her an arm?

MAUD: How kind of you Clive. I think I am strong enough.

(Maud helps Mrs. Saunders into the house.)

CLIVE: Not a word to alarm the women.

HARRY: Absolutely.

CLIVE: I did some good today I think. Kept up some alliances. There's a lot of affection there.

HARRY: They're affectionate people. They can be very cruel of course.

CLIVE: Well they are savages.

HARRY: Very beautiful people many of them.

CLIVE: Joshua! *(To Harry.)* I think we should sleep with guns.

HARRY: I haven't slept in a house for six months. It seems extremely safe.

(Joshua comes.)

CLIVE: Joshua, you will have gathered there's a spot of bother. Rumors of this and that. You should be armed I think.

JOSHUA: There are many bad men, sir. I pray about it. Jesus will protect us.

CLIVE: He will indeed and I'll also get you a weapon. Betty, come and keep Harry company. Look in the barn, Joshua, every night.

(*Clive and Joshua go. Betty comes.*)

HARRY: I wondered where you were.

BETTY: I was singing lullabies.

HARRY: When I think of you I always think of you with Edward in your lap.

BETTY: Do you think of me sometimes then?

HARRY: You have been thought of where no white woman has ever been thought of before.

BETTY: It's one way of having adventures. I suppose I will never go in person.

HARRY: That's up to you.

BETTY: Of course it's not. I have duties.

HARRY: Are you happy, Betty?

BETTY: Where have you been?

HARRY: Built a raft and went up the river. Stayed with some people. The king is always very good to me. They have a lot of skulls around the place but not white men's I think. I made up a poem one night. If I should die in this forsaken spot, There is a loving heart without a blot, Where I will live—and so on.

BETTY: When I'm near you it's like going out into the jungle. It's like going up the river on a raft. It's like going out in the dark.

HARRY: And you are safety and light and peace and home.

BETTY: But I want to be dangerous.

HARRY: Clive is my friend.

BETTY: I am your friend.

HARRY: I don't like dangerous women.

BETTY: Is Mrs. Saunders dangerous?

HARRY: Not to me. She's a bit of an old boot.

(*Joshua comes, unobserved.*)

BETTY: Am I dangerous?

HARRY: You are rather.

BETTY: Please like me.

HARRY: I worship you.

BETTY: Please want me.

HARRY: I don't want to want you. Of course I want you.

BETTY: What are we going to do?

HARRY: I should have stayed on the river. The hell with it.

(*He goes to take her in his arms, she runs away into the house. Harry stays where he is. He becomes aware of Joshua.*)

HARRY: Who's there?

JOSHUA: Only me sir.

HARRY: Got a gun now have you?

JOSHUA: Yes sir.

HARRY: Where's Clive?

JOSHUA: Going round the boundaries sir.

HARRY: Have you checked there's nobody in the barns?

JOSHUA: Yes sir.

HARRY: Shall we go in a barn and fuck? It's not an order.

JOSHUA: That's all right, yes.

(*They go off.*)

Scene Two

(*An open space some distance from the house. Mrs. Saunders alone, breathless. She is carrying a riding crop. Clive arrives.*)

CLIVE: Why? Why?

MRS. SAUNDERS: Don't fuss, Clive, it makes you sweat.

CLIVE: Why ride off now? Sweat, you would sweat if you were in love with somebody as disgustingly capricious as you are. You will be shot with poisoned arrows. You will miss the picnic. Somebody will notice I came after you.

MRS. SAUNDERS: I didn't want you to come after me. I wanted to be alone.

CLIVE: You will be raped by cannibals.

MRS. SAUNDERS: I just wanted to get out of your house.

CLIVE: My God, what women put us through. Cruel, cruel. I think you are the sort of woman who would enjoy whipping somebody. I've never met one before.

MRS. SAUNDERS: Can I tell you something, Clive?

CLIVE: Let me tell you something first. Since you came to the house I have had an erection twenty-four hours a day except for ten minutes after the time we had intercourse.

MRS. SAUNDERS: I don't think that's physically possible.

CLIVE: You are causing me appalling physical suffering. Is this the way to treat a benefactor?

MRS. SAUNDERS: Clive, when I came to your house the other night I came because I was afraid. The cook was going to let his whole tribe in through the window.

CLIVE: I know that, my poor sweet. Amazing—

MRS. SAUNDERS: I came to you although you are not my nearest neighbor—

CLIVE: Rather than to the old major of seventy-two.

MRS. SAUNDERS: Because the last time he came to visit me I had to defend myself with a shotgun and I thought you would take no for an answer.

CLIVE: But you've already answered yes.

MRS. SAUNDERS: I answered yes once. Sometimes I want to say no.

CLIVE: Women, my God. Look the picnic will start, I have to go to the picnic. Please Caroline—

MRS. SAUNDERS: I think I will have to go back to my own house.

CLIVE: Caroline, if you were shot with poisoned arrows do you know what I'd do? I'd fuck your dead body and poison myself. Caroline, you smell amazing. You terrify me. You are dark like this continent. Mysterious. Treacherous. When you rode to me through the night. When you fainted in my arms. When I came to you in your bed, when I lifted the mosquito netting, when I said let me in, let me in. Oh don't shut me out, Caroline, let me in.

(*He has been caressing her feet and legs. He disappears completely under her skirt.*)

MRS. SAUNDERS: Please stop. I can't concentrate. I want to go home. I wish I didn't enjoy the sensation because I don't like you, Clive. I do like living in your house where there's plenty of guns. But I don't like you at all. But I do like the sensation. Well I'll have it then. I'll have it, I'll have it—

(*Voices are heard singing* The First Noël.)

Don't stop. Don't stop.

(*Clive comes out from under her skirt.*)

CLIVE: The Christmas picnic. I came.
MRS. SAUNDERS: I didn't.
CLIVE: I'm all sticky.
MRS. SAUNDERS: What about me? Wait.
CLIVE: All right, are you? Come on. We mustn't be found.
MRS. SAUNDERS: Don't go now.
CLIVE: Caroline, you are so voracious. Do let go. Tidy yourself up. There's a hair in my mouth.

(*Clive and Mrs. Saunders go off. Betty and Maud come, with Joshua carrying hamper.*)

MAUD: I never would have thought a guinea fowl could taste so like a turkey.
BETTY: I had to explain to the cook three times.
MAUD: You did very well dear.

(*Joshua sits apart with gun. Edward and Harry with Victoria on his shoulder, singing* The First Noël. *Maud and Betty are unpacking the hamper. Clive arrives separately.*)

MAUD: This tablecloth was one of my mama's.
BETTY: Uncle Harry playing horsy.
EDWARD: Crackers crackers.
BETTY: Not yet, Edward.
CLIVE: And now the moment we have all been waiting for.

(*Clive opens champagne. General acclaim.*)

CLIVE: Oh dear, stained my trousers, never mind.
EDWARD: Can I have some?
MAUD: Oh no Edward, not for you.
CLIVE: Give him half a glass.
MAUD: If your father says so.
CLIVE: All rise please. To Her Majesty Queen Victoria, God bless her, and her husband and all her dear children.
ALL: The Queen.
EDWARD: Crackers crackers.

(*General cracker pulling, hats. Clive and Harry discuss champagne.*)

HARRY: Excellent, Clive, wherever did you get it?
CLIVE: I know a chap in French Equatorial Africa.
EDWARD: I won, I won mama.

(*Ellen arrives.*)

BETTY: Give a hat to Joshua, he'd like it.

(*Edward takes hat to Joshua. Betty takes a ball from the hamper and plays catch with Ellen. Murmurs of surprise and congratulations from the men whenever they catch the ball.*)

EDWARD: Mama, don't play. You know you can't catch a ball.

BETTY: He's perfectly right. I can't throw either.

(*Betty sits down. Ellen has the ball.*)

EDWARD: Ellen, don't you play either. You're no good. You spoil it.

(*Edward takes Victoria from Harry and gives her to Ellen. He takes the ball and throws it to Harry. Harry, Clive, and Edward play ball.*)

BETTY: Ellen come and sit with me. We'll be spectators and clap.

(*Edward misses the ball.*)

CLIVE: Butterfingers.
EDWARD: I'm not.
HARRY: Throw straight now.
EDWARD: I did, I did.
CLIVE: Keep your eye on the ball.
EDWARD: You can't throw.
CLIVE: Don't be a baby.
EDWARD: I'm not, throw a hard one, throw a hard one
CLIVE: Butterfingers. What will Uncle Harry think of you?
EDWARD: It's your fault. You can't throw. I hate you.

(*He throws the ball wildly in the direction of Joshua.*)

CLIVE: Now you've lost the ball. He's lost the ball.
EDWARD: It's Joshua's fault. Joshua's butterfingers.
CLIVE: I don't think I want to play any more. Joshua, find the ball will you?
EDWARD: Yes, please play. I'll find the ball. Please play.
CLIVE: You're so silly and you can't catch. You'll be no good at cricket.
MAUD: Why don't we play hide and seek?
EDWARD: Because it's a baby game.
BETTY: You've hurt Edward's feelings.
CLIVE: A boy has no business having feelings.
HARRY: Hide and seek. I'll be it. Everybody must hide. This is the base, you have to get home to base.
EDWARD: Hide and seek, hide and seek.
HARRY: Can we persuade the ladies to join us?
MAUD: I'm playing. I love games.
BETTY: I always get found straight away.
ELLEN: Come on, Betty, do. Vicky wants to play.
EDWARD: You won't find me ever.

(*They all go except Clive, Harry, Joshua.*)

HARRY: It is safe, I suppose?
CLIVE: They won't go far. This is very much my territory and it's broad daylight. Joshua will keep an open eye.
HARRY: Well I must give them a hundred. You don't know what this means to me, Clive. A chap can only go on so long alone. I can climb mountains and go down rivers, but what's it for? For Christmas and England and games and women singing. This is the empire, Clive. It's not me putting a flag in new lands. It's you. The empire is one big family. I'm one of its black sheep, Clive. And I know you think my life is rather dashing. But I want you to know I admire you. This is the empire, Clive, and I serve it. With all my heart.

CLIVE: I think that's about a hundred.

HARRY: Ready or not, here I come!

> (*He goes.*)

CLIVE: Harry Bagley is a fine man, Joshua. You should be proud to know him. He will be in history books.

JOSHUA: Sir, while we are alone.

CLIVE: Joshua of course, what is it? You always have my ear. Any time.

JOSHUA: Sir, I have some information. The stable boys are not to be trusted. They whisper. They go out at night. They visit their people. Their people are not my people. I do not visit my people.

CLIVE: Thank you, Joshua. They certainly look after Beauty. I'll be sorry to have to replace them.

JOSHUA: They carry knives.

CLIVE: Thank you, Joshua.

JOSHUA: And, sir.

CLIVE: I appreciate this, Joshua, very much.

JOSHUA: Your wife.

CLIVE: Ah, yes?

JOSHUA: She also thinks Harry Bagley is a fine man.

CLIVE: Thank you, Joshua.

JOSHUA: Are you going to hide?

CLIVE: Yes, yes I am. Thank you. Keep your eyes open Joshua.

JOSHUA: I do, sir.

(*Clive goes. Joshua goes. Harry and Betty race back to base.*)

BETTY: I can't run, I can't run at all.

HARRY: There, I've caught you.

BETTY: Harry, what are we going to do?

HARRY: It's impossible, Betty.

BETTY: Shall we run away together?

(*Maud comes.*)

MAUD: I give up. Don't catch me. I have been stung.

HARRY: Nothing serious I hope.

MAUD: I have ointment in my bag. I always carry ointment. I shall just sit down and rest. I am too old for all this fun. Hadn't you better be seeking, Harry?

(*Harry goes. Maud and Betty are alone for some time. They don't speak. Harry and Edward race back.*)

EDWARD: I won, I won, you didn't catch me.

HARRY: Yes I did.

EDWARD: Mama, who was first?

BETTY: I wasn't watching. I think it was Harry.

EDWARD: It wasn't Harry. You're no good at judging. I won, didn't I grandma?

MAUD: I expect so, since it's Christmas.

EDWARD: I won, Uncle Harry. I'm better than you.

BETTY: Why don't you help Uncle Harry look for the others?

EDWARD: Shall I?

HARRY: Yes, of course.

BETTY: Run along then. He's just coming.

> (*Edward goes.*)

Harry, I shall scream.

HARRY: Ready or not, here I come.

> (*Harry runs off.*)

BETTY: Why don't you go back to the house, mother, and rest your insect-bite?

MAUD: Betty, my duty is here. I don't like what I see. Clive wouldn't like it, Betty. I am your mother.

BETTY: Clive gives you a home because you are my mother.

(*Harry comes back.*)

HARRY: I can't find anyone else. I'm getting quite hot.

BETTY: Sit down a minute.

HARRY: I can't do that. I'm he. How's your sting?

MAUD: It seems to be swelling up.

BETTY: Why don't you go home and rest? Joshua will go with you. Joshua!

HARRY: I could take you back.

MAUD: That would be charming.

BETTY: You can't go. You're he.

(*Joshua comes.*)

BETTY: Joshua, my mother wants to go back to the house. Will you go with her please.

JOSHUA: Sir told me I have to keep an eye.

BETTY: I am telling you to go back to the house. Then you can come back here and keep an eye.

MAUD: Thank you Betty. I know we have our little differences, but I always want what is best for you.

> (*Joshua and Maud go.*)

HARRY: Don't give way. Keep calm.

BETTY: I shall kill myself.

HARRY: Betty, you are a star in my sky. Without you I would have no sense of direction. I need you, and I need you where you are, I need you to be Clive's wife. I need to go up rivers and know you are sitting here thinking of me.

BETTY: I want more than that. Is that wicked of me?

HARRY: Not wicked, Betty. Silly.

(*Edward calls in the distance.*)

EDWARD: Uncle Harry, where are you?

BETTY: Can't we ever be alone?

HARRY: You are a mother. And a daughter. And a wife.

BETTY: I think I shall go and hide again.

(*Betty goes. Harry goes. Clive chases Mrs. Saunders across the stage. Edward and Harry call in the distance.*)

EDWARD: Uncle Harry!

HARRY: Edward!

(*Edward comes.*)

EDWARD: Uncle Harry!

(*Harry comes.*)

There you are. I haven't found anyone, have you?

HARRY: I wonder where they all are.

EDWARD: Perhaps they're lost forever. Perhaps they're dead. There's trouble going on isn't there, and nobody says because of not frightening the women and children.

HARRY: Yes, that's right.

EDWARD: Do you think we'll be killed in our beds?

HARRY: Not very likely.

EDWARD: I can't sleep at night. Can you?

HARRY: I'm not used to sleeping in a house.

EDWARD: If I'm awake at night can I come and see you? I won't wake you up. I'll only come in if you're awake.

HARRY: You should try to sleep.

EDWARD: I don't mind being awake because I make up adventures. Once we were on a raft going down to the rapids. We've lost the paddles because we used them to fight off the crocodiles. A crocodile comes at me and I stab it again and again and the blood is everywhere and it tips up the raft and it has you by the leg and it's biting your leg right off and I take my knife and stab it in the throat and rip open its stomach and it lets go of you but it bites my hand but it's dead. And I drag you onto the river bank and I'm almost fainting with pain and we lie there in each other's arms.

HARRY: Have I lost my leg?

EDWARD: I forgot about the leg by then.

HARRY: Hadn't we better look for the others?

EDWARD: Wait. I've got something for you. It was in mama's box but she never wears it.

(*Edward gives Harry a necklace.*)

You don't have to wear it either but you might like it to look at.

HARRY: It's beautiful. But you'll have to put it back.

EDWARD: I wanted to give it to you.

HARRY: You did. It can go back in the box. You still gave it to me. Come on now, we have to find the others.

EDWARD: Harry, I love you.

HARRY: Yes I know. I love you too.

EDWARD: You know what we did when you were here before. I want to do it again. I think about it all the time. I try to do it to myself but it's not as good. Don't you want to any more?

HARRY: I do, but it's a sin and a crime and it's also wrong.

EDWARD: But we'll do it anyway won't we?

HARRY: Yes of course.

EDWARD: I wish the others would all be killed. Take it out now and let me see it.

HARRY: No.

EDWARD: Is it big now?

HARRY: Yes.

EDWARD: Let me touch it.

HARRY: No.

EDWARD: Just hold me.

HARRY: When you can't sleep.

EDWARD: We'd better find the others then. Come on.

HARRY: Ready or not, here we come.

(*They go out with whoops and shouts. Betty and Ellen come.*)

BETTY: Ellen, I don't want to play any more.

ELLEN: Nor do I, Betty.

BETTY: Come and sit here with me. Oh Ellen, what will become of me?

ELLEN: Betty, are you crying? Are you laughing?

BETTY: Tell me what you think of Harry Bagley.

ELLEN: He's a very fine man.

BETTY: No, Ellen, what you really think.

ELLEN: I think you think he's very handsome.

BETTY: And don't you think he is? Oh Ellen, you're so good and I'm so wicked.

ELLEN: I'm not so good as you think.

(*Edward comes.*)

EDWARD: I've found you.

ELLEN: We're not hiding Edward.

EDWARD: But I found you.

ELLEN: We're not playing, Edward, now run along.

EDWARD: Come on, Ellen, do play. Come on, mama.

ELLEN: Edward, don't pull your mama like that.

BETTY: Edward, you must do what your governess says. Go and play with Uncle Harry.

EDWARD: Uncle Harry!

(*Edward goes.*)

BETTY: Ellen, can you keep a secret?

ELLEN: Oh yes, yes please.

BETTY: I love Harry Bagley. I want to go away with him. There, I've said it, it's true.

ELLEN: How do you know you love him?

BETTY: I kissed him.

ELLEN: Betty.

BETTY: He held my hand like this. Oh I want him to do it again. I want him to stroke my hair.

ELLEN: Your lovely hair. Like this, Betty?

BETTY: I want him to put his arm around my waist.

ELLEN: Like this, Betty?

BETTY: Yes, oh I want him to kiss me again.

ELLEN: Like this Betty?

(*Ellen kisses Betty.*)

BETTY: Ellen, whatever are you doing? It's not a joke.

ELLEN: I'm sorry, Betty. You're so pretty. Harry Bagley doesn't deserve you. You wouldn't really go away with him?

BETTY: Oh Ellen, you don't know what I suffer. You don't know what love is. Everyone will hate me, but it's worth it for Harry's love.

ELLEN: I don't hate you, Betty, I love you.

BETTY: Harry says we shouldn't go away. But he says he worships me.

ELLEN: I worship you Betty.

BETTY: Oh Ellen, you are my only friend.

(*They embrace. The others have all gathered together. Maud has rejoined the party, and Joshua.*)

CLIVE: Come along everyone, you mustn't miss Harry's conjuring trick.

(*Betty and Ellen go to join the others.*)

MAUD: I didn't want to spoil the fun by not being here.

Harry pulls the British flag from his sleeve in the 2010 production of *Cloud Nine* at the Panasonic Theatre in Toronto, Canada.

HARRY: What is it that flies all over the world and is up my sleeve?

(*Harry produces a Union Jack from up his sleeve. General acclaim.*)

CLIVE: I think we should have some singing now. Ladies, I rely on you to lead the way.

ELLEN: We have a surprise for you. I have taught Joshua a Christmas carol. He has been singing it at the piano but I'm sure he can sing it unaccompanied, can't you, Joshua?

JOSHUA: In the deep midwinter
Frosty wind made moan,
Earth stood hard as iron,
Water like a stone.
Snow had fallen snow on snow
Snow on snow,
In the deep midwinter
Long long ago.

What can I give him
Poor as I am?
If I were a shepherd
I would bring a lamb.
If I were a wise man
I would do my part
What I can I give him,
Give my heart.

Scene Three

(*Inside the house. Betty, Mrs. Saunders, Maud with Victoria. The blinds are down so the light isn't bright though it is day outside. Clive looks in.*)

CLIVE: Everything all right? Nothing to be frightened of.
                              (*Clive goes. Silence.*)
MAUD: Clap hands, daddy comes, with his pockets full of plums. All for Vicky.

(*Silence.*)

MRS. SAUNDERS: Who actually does the flogging?

MAUD: I don't think we want to imagine.

MRS. SAUNDERS: I imagine Joshua.

BETTY: Yes I think it would be Joshua. Or would Clive do it himself?

MRS. SAUNDERS: Well we can ask them afterwards.

MAUD: I don't like the way you speak of it, Mrs. Saunders.

MRS. SAUNDERS: How should I speak of it?

MAUD: The men will do it in the proper way, whatever it is. We have our own part to play.

MRS. SAUNDERS: Harry Bagley says they should just be sent away. I don't think he likes to see them beaten.

BETTY: Harry is so tender hearted. Perhaps he is right.

MAUD: Harry Bagley is not altogether—He has lived in this country a long time without any responsibilities. It is part of his charm but it hasn't improved his judgment. If the boys were just sent away they would go back to the village and make more trouble.

MRS. SAUNDERS: And what will they say about us in the village if they've been flogged?

BETTY: Perhaps Clive should keep them here.

MRS. SAUNDERS: That is never wise.

BETTY: Whatever shall we do?

MAUD: I don't think it is up to us to wonder. The men don't tell us what is going on among the tribes, so how can we possibly make a judgment?

MRS. SAUNDERS: I know a little of what is going on.

BETTY: Tell me what you know. Clive tells me nothing.

MAUD: You would not want to be told about it, Betty. It is enough for you that Clive knows what is happening. Clive will know what to do. Your father always knew what to do.

BETTY: Are you saying you would do something different, Caroline?

MRS. SAUNDERS: I would do what I did at my own home. I left. I can't see any way out except to leave. I will leave here. I will keep leaving everywhere I suppose.

MAUD: Luckily this household has a head. I am squeamish myself. But luckily Clive is not.

BETTY: You are leaving here then, Caroline?

MRS. SAUNDERS: Not immediately. I'm sorry.

(*Silence.*)

MRS. SAUNDERS: I wonder if it's over.

(*Edward comes in.*)

BETTY: Shouldn't you be with the men, Edward?

EDWARD: I didn't want to see any more. They got what they deserved. Uncle Harry said I could come in.

MRS. SAUNDERS: I never allowed the servants to be beaten in my own house. I'm going to find out what's happening.

(*Mrs. Saunders goes out.*)

BETTY: Will she go and look?

MAUD: Let Mrs. Saunders be a warning to you, Betty. She is alone in the world. You are not, thank God. Since your father died, I know what it is to be unprotected. Vicky is such a pretty little girl. Clap hands, daddy comes, with his pockets full of plums. All for Vicky.

(*Edward, meanwhile, has found the doll and is playing clap hands with her.*)

BETTY: Edward, what have you got there?

EDWARD: I'm minding her.

BETTY: Edward, I've told you before, dolls are for girls.

MAUD: Where is Ellen? She should be looking after Edward. (*She goes to the door.*) Ellen! Betty, why do you let that girl mope about in her own room? That's not what she's come to Africa for.

BETTY: You must never let the boys at school know you like dolls. Never, never. No one will talk to you, you won't be on the cricket team, you won't grow up to be a man like your papa.

EDWARD: I don't want to be like papa. I hate papa.

MAUD: Edward! Edward!

BETTY: You're a horrid wicked boy and papa will beat you. Of course you don't hate him, you love him. Now give Victoria her doll at once.

EDWARD: She's not Victoria's doll, she's my doll. She doesn't love Victoria and Victoria doesn't love her. Victoria never even plays with her.

MAUD: Victoria will learn to play with her.

EDWARD: She's mine and she loves me and she won't be happy if you take her away, she'll cry, she'll cry, she'll cry.

(*Betty takes the doll away, slaps him, bursts into tears. Ellen comes in.*)

BETTY: Ellen, look what you've done. Edward's got the doll again. Now, Ellen, will you please do your job.

ELLEN: Edward, you are a wicked boy. I am going to lock you in the nursery until supper time. Now go upstairs this minute.

(*She slaps Edward, who bursts into tears and goes out.*)

I do try to do what you want. I'm so sorry.

(*Ellen bursts into tears and goes out.*)

MAUD: There now, Vicky's got her baby back. Where did Vicky's naughty baby go? Shall we smack her? Just a little smack. (*Maud smacks the doll hard.*) There, now she's a good baby. Clap hands, daddy comes, with his pockets full of plums. All for Vicky's baby. When I was a child we honored our parents. My mama was an angel.

(*Joshua comes in. He stands without speaking.*)

BETTY: Joshua?

JOSHUA: Madam?

BETTY: Did you want something?

JOSHUA: Sent to see the ladies are all right, madam.

(*Mrs. Saunders comes in.*)

MRS. SAUNDERS: We're very well thank you, Joshua, and how are you?

JOSHUA: Very well thank you, Mrs. Saunders.

MRS. SAUNDERS: And the stable boys?

JOSHUA: They have had justice, madam.

MRS. SAUNDERS: So I saw. And does your arm ache?

MAUD: This is not a proper conversation, Mrs. Saunders.

MRS. SAUNDERS: You don't mind beating your own people?

JOSHUA: Not my people, madam.

MRS. SAUNDERS: A different tribe?

JOSHUA: Bad people.

(*Harry and Clive come in.*)

CLIVE: Well this is all very gloomy and solemn. Can we have the shutters open? The heat of the day has gone, we could have some light, I think. And cool drinks on the verandah, Joshua. Have some lemonade yourself. It is most refreshing.

(*Sunlight floods in as the shutters are opened. Edward comes.*)

EDWARD: Papa, papa, Ellen tried to lock me in the nursery. Mama is going to tell you of me. I'd rather tell you myself. I was playing with Vicky's doll again and I know it's very bad of me. And I said I didn't want to be like you and I said I hated you. And it's not true and I'm sorry, I'm sorry and please beat me and forgive me.

CLIVE: Well there's a brave boy to own up. You should always respect and love me, Edward, not for myself, I may not deserve it, but as I respected and loved my own father, because he was my father. Through our father we love our Queen and our God, Edward. Do you understand? It is something men understand.

EDWARD: Yes papa.

CLIVE: Then I forgive you and shake you by the hand. You spend too much time with the women. You may spend more time with me and Uncle Harry, little man.

EDWARD: I don't like women. I don't like dolls. I love you, papa, and I love you, Uncle Harry.

CLIVE: There's a fine fellow. Let us go out onto the verandah.

(*They all start to go. Edward takes Harry's hand and goes with him. Clive draws Betty back. They embrace.*)

BETTY: Poor Clive.

CLIVE: It was my duty to have them flogged. For you and Edward and Victoria, to keep you safe.

BETTY: It is terrible to feel betrayed.

CLIVE: You can tame a wild animal only so far. They revert to their true nature and savage your hand. Sometimes I feel the natives are the enemy. I know that is wrong. I know I have a responsibility towards them, to care for them and bring them all to be like Joshua. But there is something dangerous. Implacable. This whole continent is my enemy. I am pitching my whole mind and will and reason and spirit against it to tame it, and I sometimes feel it will break over me and swallow me up.

BETTY: Clive, Clive, I am here. I have faith in you.

CLIVE: Yes, I can show you my moments of weakness, Betty, because you are my wife and because I trust you. I trust you, Betty, and it would break my heart if you did not deserve that trust. Harry Bagley is my friend. It would break my heart if he did not deserve my trust.

BETTY: I'm sorry, I'm sorry. Forgive me. It is not Harry's fault, it is all mine. Harry is noble. He has rejected me. It is my wickedness, I get bored, I get restless, I imagine things. There is something so wicked in me, Clive.

CLIVE: I have never thought of you having the weakness of your sex, only the good qualities.

BETTY: I am bad, bad, bad—

CLIVE: You are thoughtless, Betty, that's all. Women can be treacherous and evil. They are darker and more dangerous than men. The family protects us from that, you protect me from that. You are not that sort of woman. You are not unfaithful to me, Betty. I can't believe you are. It would hurt me so much to cast you off. That would be my duty.

BETTY: No, no, no.

CLIVE: Joshua has seen you kissing.

BETTY: Forgive me.

CLIVE: But I don't want to know about it. I don't want to know. I wonder of course, I wonder constantly. If Harry Bagley was not my friend I would shoot him. If I shot you every British man and woman would applaud me. But no. It was a moment of passion such as women are too weak to resist. But you must resist it, Betty, or it will destroy us. We must fight against it. We must resist this dark female lust, Betty, or it will swallow us up.

BETTY: I do, I do resist. Help me. Forgive me.

CLIVE: Yes I do forgive you. But I can't feel the same about you as I did. You are still my wife and we still have duties to the household.

(*They go out arm in arm. As soon as they have gone Edward sneaks back to get the doll, which has been dropped on the floor. He picks it up and comforts it. Joshua comes through with a tray of drinks.*)

JOSHUA: Baby. Sissy. Girly.

(*Joshua goes. Betty calls from off.*)

BETTY: Edward?

(*Betty comes in.*)

BETTY: There you are, my darling. Come, papa wants us all to be together. Uncle Harry is going to tell how he caught a crocodile. Mama's sorry she smacked you.

(*They embrace. Joshua comes in again, passing through.*)

BETTY: Joshua, fetch me some blue thread from my sewing box. It is on the piano.

JOSHUA: You've got legs under that skirt.

BETTY: Joshua.

JOSHUA: And more than legs.

BETTY: Edward, are you going to stand there and let a servant insult your mother?

EDWARD: Joshua, get my mother's thread.

JOSHUA: Oh little Eddy, playing at master. It's only a joke.

EDWARD: Don't speak to my mother like that again.

JOSHUA: Ladies have no sense of humor. You like a joke with Joshua.

EDWARD: You fetch her sewing at once, do you hear me? You move when I speak to you, boy.

JOSHUA: Yes sir, master Edward sir.

(*Joshua goes.*)

BETTY: Edward, you were wonderful.

(*She goes to embrace him but he moves away.*)

EDWARD: Don't touch me.

SONG (*"A Boy's Best Friend"—All*): While plodding on
    our way, the toilsome road of life,
How few the friends that daily there we meet.
Not many will stand in trouble and in strife,
With counsel and affection ever sweet.
But there is one whose smile will ever on us beam,
Whose love is dearer far than any other;
And wherever we may turn
This lesson we will learn
A boy's best friend is his mother.

Then cherish her with care
And smooth her silv'ry hair,
When gone you will never get another.
And wherever we may turn
This lesson we shall learn,
A boy's best friend is his mother.

Scene Four

The verandah as in Scene One. Early morning. Nobody there. Joshua comes out of the house slowly and stands for some time doing nothing. Edward comes out.

EDWARD: Tell me another bad story, Joshua. Nobody else is even awake yet.

JOSHUA: First there was nothing and then there was the great goddess. She was very large and she had golden eyes and she made the stars and the sun and the earth. But soon she was miserable and lonely and she cried like a great waterfall and her tears made all the rivers in the world. So the great spirit sent a terrible monster, a tree with hundreds of eyes and a long green tongue, and it came chasing after her and she jumped into a lake and the tree jumped in after her, and she jumped right up into the sky. And the tree couldn't follow, he was stuck in the mud. So he picked up a big handful of mud and he threw it at her, up among the stars, and hit her on the head. And she fell down onto the earth into his arms and the ball of mud is the moon in the sky. And then they had children which is all of us.

EDWARD: It's not true, though.

JOSHUA: Of course it's not true. It's a bad story. Adam and Eve is true. God made man white like him and gave him the bad woman who liked the snake and gave us all this trouble.

(Clive and Harry come out.)

CLIVE: Run along now, Edward. No, you may stay. You mustn't repeat anything you hear to your mother or your grandmother or Ellen.

EDWARD: Or Mrs. Saunders?

CLIVE: Mrs. Saunders is an unusual woman and does not require protection in the same way. Harry, there was trouble last night where we expected it. But it's all over now. Everything is under control but nobody should leave the house today I think.

HARRY: Casualties?

CLIVE: No, none of the soldiers hurt thank God. We did a certain amount of damage, set a village on fire and so forth.

HARRY: Was that necessary?

CLIVE: Obviously, it was necessary, Harry, or it wouldn't have happened. The army will come and visit, no doubt. You'll like that, eh, Joshua, to see the British army? And a treat for you, Edward, to see the soldiers. Would you like to be a soldier?

EDWARD: I'd rather be an explorer.

CLIVE: Ah, Harry, like you, you see. I didn't know an explorer at his age. Breakfast, I think, Joshua.

(Clive and Joshua go in. Harry is following.)

EDWARD: Uncle.

(Harry stops.)

EDWARD: Harry, why won't you talk to me?

HARRY: Of course I'll talk to you.

EDWARD: If you won't be nice to me I'll tell father.

HARRY: Edward, no, not a word, never, not to your mother, nobody, please. Edward, do you understand? Please.

EDWARD: I won't tell. I promise I'll never tell. I've cut my finger and sworn.

HARRY: There's no need to get so excited Edward. We can't be together all the time. I will have to leave soon anyway, and go back to the river.

EDWARD: You can't, you can't go. Take me with you.

ELLEN: Edward!

HARRY: I have my duty to the Empire.

(Harry goes in. Ellen comes out.)

ELLEN: Edward, breakfast time. Edward.

EDWARD: I'm not hungry.

ELLEN: Betty, please come and speak to Edward.

(Betty comes.)

BETTY: Why what's the matter?

ELLEN: He won't come in for breakfast.

BETTY: Edward, I shall call your father.

EDWARD: You can't make me eat.

(He goes in. Betty is about to follow.)

ELLEN: Betty.

(Betty stops.)

ELLEN: Betty, when Edward goes to school will I have to leave?

BETTY: Never mind, Ellen dear, you'll get another place. I'll give you an excellent reference.

ELLEN: I don't want another place, Betty. I want to stay with you forever.

BETTY: If you go back to England you might get married, Ellen. You're quite pretty, you shouldn't despair of getting a husband.

ELLEN: I don't want a husband. I want you.

BETTY: Children of your own, Ellen, think.

ELLEN: I don't want children, I don't like children. I just want to be alone with you, Betty, and sing for you and kiss you because I love you, Betty.

BETTY: I love you too, Ellen. But women have their duty as soldiers have. You must be a mother if you can.

ELLEN: Betty, Betty, I love you so much. I want to stay with you forever, my love for you is eternal, stronger than death. I'd rather die than leave you, Betty.

BETTY: No you wouldn't, Ellen, don't be silly. Come, don't cry. You don't feel what you think you do. It's the loneliness here and the climate is very confusing. Come and have breakfast, Ellen dear, and I'll forget all about it.

(Ellen goes, Clive comes.)

BETTY: Clive, please forgive me.

CLIVE: Will you leave me alone?

(*Betty goes back into the house. Harry comes.*)

CLIVE: Women, Harry. I envy you going into the jungle, a man's life.

HARRY: I envy you.

CLIVE: Harry, I know you do. I have spoken to Betty.

HARRY: I assure you, Clive—

CLIVE: Please say nothing about it.

HARRY: My friendship for you—

CLIVE: Absolutely. I know the friendship between us, Harry, is not something that could be spoiled by the weaker sex. Friendship between men is a fine thing. It is the noblest form of relationship.

HARRY: I agree with you.

CLIVE: There is the necessity of reproduction. The family is all important. And there is the pleasure. But what we put ourselves through to get that pleasure, Harry. When I heard about our fine fellows last night fighting those savages to protect us I thought yes, that is what I aspire to. I tell you Harry, in confidence, I suddenly got out of Mrs. Saunders' bed and came out here on the verandah and looked at the stars.

HARRY: I couldn't sleep last night either.

CLIVE: There is something dark about women, that threatens what is best in us. Between men that light burns brightly.

HARRY: I didn't know you felt like that.

CLIVE: Women are irrational, demanding, inconsistent, treacherous, lustful, and they smell different from us.

HARRY: Clive—

CLIVE: Think of the comradeship of men, Harry, sharing adventures, sharing danger, risking their lives together.

(*Harry takes hold of Clive.*)

CLIVE: What are you doing?

HARRY: Well, you said—

CLIVE: I said what?

HARRY: Between men.

(*Clive is speechless.*)

I'm sorry, I misunderstood, I would never have dreamt, I thought—

CLIVE: My God, Harry, how disgusting.

HARRY: You will not betray my confidence.

CLIVE: I feel contaminated.

HARRY: I struggle against it. You cannot imagine the shame. I have tried everything to save myself.

CLIVE: The most revolting perversion. Rome fell, Harry, and this sin can destroy an empire.

HARRY: It is not a sin, it is a disease.

CLIVE: A disease more dangerous than diphtheria. Effeminacy is contagious. How I have been deceived. Your face does not look degenerate. Oh Harry, how did you sink to this?

HARRY: Clive, help me, what am I to do?

CLIVE: You have been away from England too long.

HARRY: Where can I go except into the jungle to hide?

CLIVE: You don't do it with the natives, Harry? My God, what a betrayal of the Queen.

HARRY: Clive, I am like a man born crippled. Please help me.

CLIVE: You must repent.

HARRY: I have thought of killing myself.

CLIVE: That is a sin too.

HARRY: There is no way out. Clive, I beg of you, do not betray my confidence.

CLIVE: I cannot keep a secret like this. Rivers will be named after you, it's unthinkable. You must save yourself from depravity. You must get married. You are not unattractive to women. What a relief that you and Betty were not after all—good God, how disgusting. Now Mrs. Saunders. She's a woman of spirit, she could go with you on your expeditions.

HARRY: I suppose getting married wouldn't be any worse than killing myself.

CLIVE: Mrs. Saunders! Mrs. Saunders! Ask her now, Harry. Think of England.

(*Mrs. Saunders comes. Clive withdraws. Harry goes up to Mrs. Saunders.*)

HARRY: Mrs. Saunders, will you marry me?

MRS. SAUNDERS: Why?

HARRY: We are both alone.

MRS. SAUNDERS: I choose to be alone, Mr. Bagley. If I can look after myself, I'm sure you can. Clive, I have something important to tell you. I've just found Joshua putting earth on his head. He tells me his parents were killed last night by the British soldiers. I think you owe him an apology on behalf of the Queen.

CLIVE: Joshua! Joshua!

MRS. SAUNDERS: Mr. Bagley, I could never be a wife again. There is only one thing about marriage that I like.

(*Joshua comes.*)

CLIVE: Joshua, I am horrified to hear what has happened. Good God!

MRS. SAUNDERS: His father was shot. His mother died in the blaze.

(*Mrs. Saunders goes.*)

CLIVE: Joshua, do you want a day off? Do you want to go to your people?

JOSHUA: Not my people, sir.

CLIVE: But you want to go to your parents' funeral?

JOSHUA: No sir.

CLIVE: Yes, Joshua, yes, your father and mother. I'm sure they were loyal to the crown. I'm sure it was all a terrible mistake.

JOSHUA: My mother and father were bad people.

CLIVE: Joshua, no.

JOSHUA: You are my father and mother.

CLIVE: Well really. I don't know what to say. That's very decent of you. Are you sure there's nothing I can do? You can have the day off you know.

(*Betty comes out followed by Edward.*)

BETTY: What's the matter? What's happening?

CLIVE: Something terrible has happened. No, I mean some relatives of Joshua's met with an accident.

JOSHUA: May I go sir?

CLIVE: Yes, yes of course. Good God, what a terrible thing. Bring us a drink will you Joshua?

(*Joshua goes.*)

EDWARD: What? What?

BETTY: Edward, go and do your lessons.

EDWARD: What is it, Uncle Harry?

HARRY: Go and do your lessons.

ELLEN: Edward, come in here at once.

EDWARD: What's happened, Uncle Harry?

(*Harry has moved aside, Edward follows him. Ellen comes out.*)

HARRY: Go away. Go inside. Ellen!

ELLEN: Go inside, Edward. I shall tell your mother.

BETTY: Go inside, Edward at once. I shall tell your father.

CLIVE: Go inside, Edward. And Betty you go inside too.

(*Betty, Edward, and Ellen go. Maud comes out.*)

CLIVE: Go inside. And Ellen, you come outside.

(*Ellen comes out.*)

Mr. Bagley has something to say to you.

HARRY: Ellen. I don't suppose you would marry me?

ELLEN: What if I said yes?

CLIVE: Run along now, you two want to be alone.

(*Harry and Ellen go out. Joshua brings Clive a drink.*)

JOSHUA: The governess and your wife, sir.

CLIVE: What's that, Joshua?

JOSHUA: She talks of love to your wife, sir. I have seen them. Bad women.

CLIVE: Joshua, you go too far. Get out of my sight.

Scene Five

(*The verandah. A table with a white cloth. A wedding cake and a large knife. Bottles and glasses. Joshua is putting things on the table. Edward has the doll. Joshua sees him with it. He holds out his hand. Edward gives him the doll. Joshua takes the knife and cuts the doll open and shakes the sawdust out of it. Joshua throws the doll under the table.*)

MAUD: Come along Edward, this is such fun.

(*Everyone enters, triumphal arch for Harry and Ellen.*)

MAUD: Your mama's wedding was a splendid occasion, Edward. I cried and cried.

(*Ellen and Betty go aside.*)

ELLEN: Betty, what happens with a man? I don't know what to do.

BETTY: You just keep still.

ELLEN: And what does he do?

BETTY: Harry will know what to do.

ELLEN: And is it enjoyable?

BETTY: Ellen, you're not getting married to enjoy yourself.

ELLEN: Don't forget me, Betty.

(*Ellen goes.*)

BETTY: I think my necklace has been stolen Clive. I did so want to wear it at the wedding.

EDWARD: It was Joshua. Joshua took it.

CLIVE: Joshua?

EDWARD: He did, he did, I saw him with it.

HARRY: Edward, that's not true.

EDWARD: It is, it is.

HARRY: Edward, I'm afraid you took it yourself.

EDWARD: I did not.

HARRY: I have seen him with it.

CLIVE: Edward, is that true? Where is it? Did you take your mother's necklace? And to try and blame Joshua, good God.

(*Edward runs off.*)

BETTY: Edward, come back. Have you got my necklace?

HARRY: I should leave him alone. He'll bring it back.

BETTY: I wanted to wear it. I wanted to look my best at your wedding.

HARRY: You always look your best to me.

BETTY: I shall get drunk.

(*Mrs. Saunders comes.*)

MRS. SAUNDERS: The sale of my property is completed. I shall leave tomorrow.

CLIVE: That's just as well. Whose protection will you seek this time?

MRS. SAUNDERS: I shall go to England and buy a farm there. I shall introduce threshing machines.

CLIVE: Amazing spirit.

(*He kisses her. Betty launches herself on Mrs. Saunders. They fall to the ground.*)

CLIVE: Betty—Caroline—I don't deserve this—Harry, Harry.

(*Harry and Clive separate them. Harry holding Mrs. Saunders, Clive Betty.*)

CLIVE: Mrs. Saunders, how can you abuse my hospitality? How dare you touch my wife? You must leave here at once.

BETTY: Go away, go away. You are a wicked woman.

MAUD: Mrs. Saunders, I am shocked. This is your hostess.

CLIVE: Pack your bags and leave the house this instant.

MRS. SAUNDERS: I was leaving anyway. There's no place for me here. I have made arrangements to leave tomorrow, and tomorrow is when I will leave. I wish you joy, Mr. Bagley.

(*Mrs. Saunders goes.*)

CLIVE: No place for her anywhere I should think. Shocking behavior.
BETTY: Oh Clive, forgive me, and love me like you used to.
CLIVE: Were you jealous my dove? My own dear wife!
MAUD: Ah, Mr. Bagley, one flesh, you see.

(*Edward comes back with the necklace.*)

CLIVE: Good God, Edward, it's true.
EDWARD: I was minding it for mama because of the troubles.
CLIVE: Well done, Edward, that was very manly of you. See Betty? Edward was protecting his mama's jewels from the rebels. What a hysterical fuss over nothing. Well done, little man. It is quite safe now. The bad men are dead. Edward, you may do up the necklace for mama.

(*Edward does up Betty's necklace, supervised by Clive, Joshua is drinking steadily. Ellen comes back.*)

MAUD: Ah, here's the bride. Come along, Ellen, you don't cry at your own wedding, only at other people's.
CLIVE: Now, speeches, speeches. Who is going to make a speech? Harry, make a speech.
HARRY: I'm no speaker. You're the one for that.
ALL: Speech, speech.
HARRY: My dear friends—what can I say—the empire—the family—the married state to which I have always aspired—your shining example of domestic bliss—my great good fortune in winning Ellen's love—happiest day of my life.

(*Applause.*)

CLIVE: Cut the cake, cut the cake.

(*Harry and Ellen take the knife to cut the cake. Harry steps on the doll under the table.*)

HARRY: What's this?
ELLEN: Oh look.
BETTY: Edward.
EDWARD: It was Joshua. It was Joshua. I saw him.
CLIVE: Don't tell lies again.

(*He hits Edward across the side of the head.*)

Unaccustomed as I am to public speaking—

(*Cheers.*)

Harry, my friend. So brave and strong and supple.
Ellen, from neath her veil so shyly peeking.
I wish you joy. A toast—the happy couple.
Dangers are past. Our enemies are killed.
—Put your arm round her, Harry, have a kiss—

All murmuring of discontent is stilled.
Long may you live in peace and joy and bliss.

(*While he is speaking Joshua raises his gun to shoot Clive. Only Edward sees. He does nothing to warn the others. He puts his hands over his ears.*)
(*Black.*)

ACT TWO • Scene One

(*Winter afternoon. Inside the hut of a one o'clock club, a children's playcenter in a park, Victoria and Lin, mothers. Cathy, Lin's daughter, age 5, played by a man, clinging to Lin. Victoria reading a book.*)

CATHY: Yum yum bubblegum.
　　Stick it up your mother's bum.
　　When it's brown
　　Pull it down
　　Yum yum bubblegum.
LIN: Like your shoes, Victoria.
CATHY: Jack be nimble, Jack be quick,
　　Jack jump over the candlestick.
　　Silly Jack, he should jump higher,
　　Goodness gracious, great balls of fire.
LIN: Cathy, do stop. Do a painting.
CATHY: You do a painting.
LIN: You do a painting.
CATHY: What shall I paint?
LIN: Paint a house.
CATHY: No.
LIN: Princess.
CATHY: No.
LIN: Pirates.
CATHY: Already done that.
LIN: Spacemen.
CATHY: I never paint spacemen. You know I never.
LIN: Paint a car crash and blood everywhere.
CATHY: No, don't tell me. I know what to paint.
LIN: Go on then. You need an apron, where's an apron. Here.
CATHY: Don't want an apron.
LIN: Lift up your arms. There's a good girl.
CATHY: I don't want to paint.
LIN: Don't paint. Don't paint.
CATHY: What shall I do? You paint. What shall I do mum?
VICTORIA: There's nobody on the big bike, Cathy, quick.

(*Cathy goes out. Victoria is watching the children playing outside.*)

VICTORIA: Tommy, it's Jimmy's gun. Let him have it. What the hell.

(*She goes on reading. She reads while she talks.*)

LIN: I don't know how you can concentrate.
VICTORIA: You have to or you never do anything.

LIN: Yeh, well. It's really warm in here, that's one thing. It's better than standing out there. I got chilblains last winter.

VICTORIA: It is warm.

LIN: I suppose Tommy doesn't let you read much. I expect he talks to you while you're reading.

VICTORIA: Yes, he does.

LIN: I didn't get very far with that book you lent me.

VICTORIA: That's all right.

LIN: I was glad to have it, though. I sit with it on my lap while I'm watching telly. Well, Cathy's off. She's frightened I'm going to leave her. It's the baby-minder didn't work out when she was two, she still remembers. You can't get them used to other people if you're by yourself. It's no good blaming me. She clings round my knees every morning up the nursery and they don't say anything but they make you feel you're making her do it. But I'm desperate for her to go to school. I did cry when I left her the first day. You wouldn't, you're too fucking sensible. You'll call the teacher by her first name. I really fancy you.

VICTORIA: What?

LIN: Put your book down will you for five minutes. You didn't hear a word I said.

VICTORIA: I don't get much time to myself.

LIN: Do you ever go to the movies?

VICTORIA: Tommy's very funny who he's left with. My mother babysits sometimes.

LIN: Your husband could babysit.

VICTORIA: But then we couldn't go to the movies.

LIN: You could go to the movies with me.

VICTORIA: Oh I see.

LIN: Couldn't you?

VICTORIA: Well yes, I could.

LIN: Friday night?

VICTORIA: What film are we talking about?

LIN: Does it matter what film?

VICTORIA: Of course it does.

LIN: You choose then. Friday night.

(*Cathy comes in with gun, shoots them saying Kiou kiou kiou, and runs off again.*)

Not in a foreign language, ok. You don't go in the movies to read.

(*Lin watches the children playing outside.*)

Don't hit him, Cathy, kill him. Point the gun, kiou, kiou, kiou. That's the way.

VICTORIA: They've just banned war toys in Sweden.

LIN: The kids'll just hit each other more.

VICTORIA: Well, psychologists do differ in their opinions as to whether or not aggression is innate.

LIN: Yeh?

VICTORIA: I'm afraid I do let Tommy play with guns and just hope he'll get it out of his system and not end up in the army.

LIN: I've got a brother in the army.

VICTORIA: Oh I'm sorry. Whereabouts is he stationed?

LIN: Belfast.

VICTORIA: Oh dear.

LIN: I've got a friend who's Irish and we went on a Troops Out march. Now my dad won't speak to me.

VICTORIA: I don't get on too well with my father either.

LIN: And your husband? How do you get on with him?

VICTORIA: Oh, fine. Up and down. You know. Very well. He helps with the washing up and everything.

LIN: I left mine two years ago. He let me keep Cathy and I'm grateful for that.

VICTORIA: You shouldn't be grateful.

LIN: I'm a lesbian.

VICTORIA: You still shouldn't be grateful.

LIN: I'm grateful he didn't hit me harder than he did.

VICTORIA: I suppose I'm very lucky with Martin.

LIN: Don't get at me about how I bring up Cathy, ok?

VICTORIA: I didn't.

LIN: Yes you did. War toys. I'll give her a rifle for Christmas and blast Tommy's pretty head off for a start.

(*Victoria goes back to her book.*)

LIN: I hate men.

VICTORIA: You have to look at it in a historical perspective in terms of learnt behavior since the industrial revolution.

LIN: I just hate the bastards.

VICTORIA: Well it's a point of view.

(*By now Cathy has come back in and started painting in many colors, without an apron. Edward comes in.*)

EDWARD: Victoria, mother's in the park. She's walking round all the paths very fast.

VICTORIA: By herself?

EDWARD: I told her you were here.

VICTORIA: Thanks.

EDWARD: Come on.

VICTORIA: Ten minutes talking to my mother and I have to spend two hours in a hot bath.

(*Victoria goes out.*)

LIN: Shit, Cathy, what about an apron. I don't mind you having paint on your frock but if it doesn't wash off just don't tell me you can't wear your frock with paint on, ok?

CATHY: Ok.

LIN: You're gay, aren't you?

EDWARD: I beg your pardon?

LIN: I really fancy your sister. I thought you'd understand. You do but you can go on pretending you don't, I don't mind. That's lovely Cathy, I like the green bit.

EDWARD: Don't go around saying that. I might lose my job.

LIN: The last gardener was ever so straight. He used to flash at all the little girls.

EDWARD: I wish you hadn't said that about me. It's not true.

LIN: It's not true and I never said it and I never thought it and I never will think it again.

EDWARD: Someone might have heard you.

LIN: Shut up about it then.

(*Betty and Victoria come up.*)

BETTY: It's quite a nasty bump.

VICTORIA: He's not even crying.

BETTY: I think that's very worrying. You and Edward always cried. Perhaps he's got concussion.

VICTORIA: Of course he hasn't mummy.

BETTY: That other little boy was very rough. Should you speak to somebody about him?

VICTORIA: Tommy was hitting him with a spade.

BETTY: Well he's a real little boy. And so brave not to cry. You must watch him for signs of drowsiness. And nausea. If he's sick in the night, phone an ambulance. Well, you're looking very well darling, a bit tired, a bit peaky. I think the fresh air agrees with Edward. He likes the open air life because of growing up in Africa. He misses the sunshine, don't you, darling? We'll soon have Edward back on his feet. What fun it is here.

VICTORIA: This is Lin. And Cathy.

BETTY: Oh Cathy what a lovely painting. What is it? Well I think it's a house on fire. I think all that red is a fire. Is that right? Or do I see legs, is it a horse? Can I have the lovely painting or is it for mummy? Children have such imagination, it makes them so exhausting. (*To Lin.*) I'm sure you're wonderful, just like Victoria. I had help with my children. One does need help. That was in Africa of course so there wasn't the servant problem. This is my son Edward. This is—

EDWARD: Lin.

BETTY: Lin, this is Lin. Edward is doing something such fun, he's working in the park as a gardener. He does look exactly like a gardener.

EDWARD: I am a gardener.

BETTY: He's certainly making a stab at it. Well it will be a story to tell. I expect he will write a novel about it, or perhaps a television series. Well what a pretty child Cathy is. Victoria was a pretty child just like a little doll—you can't be certain how they'll grow up. I think Victoria's very pretty but she doesn't make the most of herself, do you darling, it's not the fashion I'm told but there are still women who dress out of *Vogue,* well we hope that's not what Martin looks for, though in many ways I wish it was, I don't know what it is Martin looks for and nor does he I'm afraid poor Martin. Well I am rattling on. I like your skirt dear but your shoes won't do at all. Well do they have lady gardeners, Edward, because I'm going to leave your father and I think I might need to get a job, not a gardener really of course. I haven't got green fingers I'm afraid, everything I touch shrivels straight up. Vicky gave me a poinsettia last Christmas and the leaves all fell off on Boxing Day. Well good heavens, look what's happened to that lovely painting.

(*Cathy has slowly and carefully been going over the whole sheet with black paint. She has almost finished.*)

LIN: What you do that for silly? It was nice.

CATHY: I like your earrings.

VICTORIA: Did you say you're leaving Daddy?

BETTY: Do you darling? Shall I put them on you? My ears aren't pierced, I never wanted that, they just clip on the lobe.

LIN: She'll get paint on you, mind.

BETTY: There's a pretty girl. It doesn't hurt does it? Well you'll grow up to know you have to suffer a little bit for beauty.

CATHY: Look mum I'm pretty, I'm pretty, I'm pretty.

LIN: Stop showing off Cathy.

VICTORIA: It's time we went home. Tommy, time to go home. Last go then, all right.

EDWARD: Mum did I hear you right just now?

CATHY: I want my ears pierced.

BETTY: Ooh, not till you're big.

CATHY: I know a girl got her ears pierced and she's three. She's got real gold.

BETTY: I don't expect she's English, darling. Can I give her a sweety? I know they're not very good for the teeth, Vicky gets terribly cross with me. What does mummy say?

LIN: Just one, thank you very much.

CATHY: I like your beads.

BETTY: Yes they are pretty. Here you are.

(*It is the necklace from Act One.*)

CATHY: Look at me, look at me. Vicky, Vicky, Vicky look at me.

LIN: You look lovely, come on now.

CATHY: And your hat, and your hat.

LIN: No, that's enough.

BETTY: Of course she can have my hat.

CATHY: Yes, yes, hat, hat. Look look look.

LIN: That's enough, please, stop it now. Hat off, bye bye hat.

CATHY: Give me my hat.

LIN: Bye bye beads.

BETTY: It's just fun.

LIN: It's very nice of you.

CATHY: I want my beads.

LIN: Where's the other earring?

CATHY: I want my beads.

(*Cathy has the other earring in her hand. Meanwhile Victoria and Edward look for it.*)

EDWARD: Is it on the floor?

VICTORIA: Don't step on it.

EDWARD: Where?

CATHY: I want my beads. I want my beads.

LIN: You'll have a smack.

(*Lin gets the earring from Cathy.*)

CATHY: I want my beads.

BETTY: Oh dear oh dear. Have you got the earring? Thank you darling.

CATHY: I want my beads, you're horrid, I hate you, mum, you smell.

BETTY: This is the point you see where one had help. Well it's been lovely seeing you dears and I'll be off again on my little walk.

VICTORIA: You're leaving him? Really?

BETTY: Yes you hear aright, Vicky, yes. I'm finding a little flat, that will be fun.

(Betty goes.)

Bye bye Tommy, granny's going now. Tommy don't hit that little girl, say goodbye to granny.

VICTORIA: Fucking hell.

EDWARD: Puking Jesus.

LIN: That was news was it, leaving your father?

EDWARD: They're going to want so much attention.

VICTORIA: Does everybody hate their mothers?

EDWARD: Mind you, I wouldn't live with him.

LIN: Stop snivelling, pigface. Where's your coat? Be quiet now and we'll have doughnuts for tea and if you keep on we'll have dogshit on toast.

(Cathy laughs so much she lies on the floor.)

VICTORIA: Tommy, you've had two last goes. Last last last last go.

LIN: Not that funny, come on, coat on.

EDWARD: Can I have your painting?

CATHY: What for?

EDWARD: For a friend of mine.

CATHY: What's his name?

EDWARD: Gerry.

CATHY: How old is he?

EDWARD: Thirty-two.

CATHY: You can if you like. I don't care. Kiou kiou kiou kiou.

(Cathy goes out. Edward takes the painting and goes out.)

LIN: Will you have sex with me?

VICTORIA: I don't know what Martin would say. Does it count as adultery with a woman?

LIN: You'd enjoy it.

Scene Two

(Spring. Swing, bench, pond nearby. Edward is gardening. Gerry sitting on a bench.)

EDWARD: I sometimes pretend we don't know each other. And you've come to the park to eat your sandwiches and look at me.

GERRY: That would be more interesting, yes. Come and sit down.

EDWARD: If the superintendent comes I'll be in trouble. It's not my dinner time yet. Where were you last night? I think you owe me an explanation. We always do tell each other everything.

GERRY: Is that a rule?

EDWARD: It's what we agreed.

GERRY: It's a habit we've got into. Look, I was drunk. I woke up at 4 o'clock on somebody's floor. I was sick. I hadn't any money for a cab. I went back to sleep.

EDWARD: You could have phoned.

GERRY: There wasn't a phone.

EDWARD: Sorry.

GERRY: There was a phone and I didn't phone you. Leave it alone, Eddy, I'm warning you.

EDWARD: What are you going to do to me, then?

GERRY: I'm going to the pub.

EDWARD: I'll join you in ten minutes.

GERRY: I didn't ask you to come. *(Edward goes.)* Two years I've been with Edward. You have to get away sometimes or you lose sight of yourself. The train from Victoria to Clapham still has those compartments without a corridor. As soon as I got on the platform I saw who I wanted. Slim hips, tense shoulders, trying not to look at anyone. I put my hand on my packet just long enough so that he couldn't miss it. The train came in. You don't want to get in too fast or some straight dumbo might get in with you. I sat by the window. I couldn't see where the fuck he'd got to. Then just as the whistle went he got in. Great. It's a six-minute journey so you can't start anything you can't finish. I stared at him and he unzipped his flies. Then he stopped. So I stood up and took my cock out. He took me in his mouth and shut his eyes tight. He was sort of mumbling it about as if he wasn't sure what to do, so I said, "A bit tighter son" and he said "Sorry" and then got on with it. He was jerking off with his left hand, and I could see he'd got a fairsized one. I wished he'd keep still so I could see his watch. I was getting really turned on. What if we pulled into Clapham Junction now. Of course by the time we sat down again the train was just slowing up. I felt wonderful. Then he started talking. It's better if nothing is said. Once you find he's a librarian in Walthamstow with a special interest in science fiction and lives with his aunt, then forget it. He said I hope you don't think I do this all the time. I said I hope you will from now on. He said he would if I was on the train, but why don't we go out for a meal? I opened the door before the train stopped. I told him I live with somebody, I don't want to know. He was jogging sideways to keep up. He said "What's your phone number, you're my ideal physical type, what sign of the zodiac are you? Where do you live? Where are you going now?" It's not fair, I saw him at Victoria a couple of months later and I went straight down to the end of the platform and I picked up somebody really great who never said a word, just smiled.

(Cathy is on the swing.)

CATHY: Batman and Robin
Had a batmobile.
Robin done a fart
And paralyzed the wheel.
The wheel couldn't take it,
The engine fell apart,
All because of Robin
And his supersonic fart.

(*Cathy goes. Martin, Victoria and Betty walking slowly.*)

MARTIN: Tom!

BETTY: He'll fall in.

VICTORIA: No he won't.

MARTIN: Don't go too near the edge Tom. Throw the bread from there. The ducks can get it.

BETTY: I'll never be able to manage. If I can't even walk down the street by myself. Everything looks so fierce.

VICTORIA: Just watch Tommy feeding the ducks.

BETTY: He's going to fall in. Make Martin make him move back.

VICTORIA: He's not going to fall in.

BETTY: It's since I left your father.

VICTORIA: Mummy, it really was the right decision.

BETTY: Everything comes at me from all directions. Martin despises me.

VICTORIA: Of course he doesn't, mummy.

BETTY: Of course he does.

MARTIN: Throw the bread. That's the way. The duck can get it. Quack quack quack quack quack.

BETTY: I don't want to take pills. Lin says you can't trust doctors.

VICTORIA: You're not taking pills. You're doing very well.

BETTY: But I'm so frightened.

VICTORIA: What are you frightened of?

BETTY: Victoria, you always ask that as if there was suddenly going to be an answer.

VICTORIA: Are you all right sitting there?

BETTY: Yes, yes. Go and be with Martin.

(*Victoria joins Martin, Betty stays sitting on the bench.*)

MARTIN: You take the job, you go to Manchester. You turn it down, you stay in London. People are making decisions like this every day of the week. It needn't be for more than a year. You get long vacations. Our relationship might well stand the strain of that, and if it doesn't we're better out of it. I don't want to put any pressure on you. I'd just like to know so we can sell the house. I think we're moving into an entirely different way of life if you go to Manchester because it won't end there. We could keep the house as security for Tommy but he might as well get used to the fact that life nowadays is insecure. You should ask your mother what she thinks and then do the opposite. I could just take that room in Barbara's house, and then we could babysit for each other. You think that means I want to fuck Barbara. I don't. Well, I do, but I won't. And even if I did, what's a fuck between friends? What are we meant to do it with, strangers? Whatever you want to do, I'll be delighted. If you could just let me know what it is I'm to be delighted about. Don't cry again, Vicky, I'm not the sort of man who makes women cry.

(*Lin has come in and sat down with Betty, Cathy joins them. She is wearing a pink dress and carrying a rifle.*)

LIN: I've bought her three new frocks. She won't wear jeans to school any more because Tracy and Mandy called her a boy.

CATHY: Tracy's got a perm.

LIN: You should have shot them.

CATHY: They're coming to tea and we've got to have trifle. Not trifle you make, trifle out of a packet. And you've got to wear a skirt. And tights.

LIN: Tracy's mum wears jeans.

CATHY: She does not. She wears velvet.

BETTY: Well I think you look very pretty. And if that gun has caps in it please take it a long way away.

CATHY: It's got red caps. They're louder.

MARTIN: Do you think you're well enough to do this job? You don't have to do it. No one's going to think any the less of you if you stay here with me. There's no point being so liberated you make yourself cry all the time. You stay and we'll get everything sorted out. What it is about sex, when we talk while it's happening I get to feel it's like a driving lesson. Left, right, a little faster, carry on, slow down—

(*Cathy shoots Victoria.*)

CATHY: You're dead Vicky.

VICTORIA: Aaaargh.

CATHY: Fall over.

VICTORIA: I'm not falling over, the ground's wet.

CATHY: You're dead.

VICTORIA: Yes, I'm dead.

CATHY: The Dead Hand Gang fall over. They said I had to fall over in the mud or I can't play. That duck's a mandarin.

MARTIN: Which one? Look, Tommy.

CATHY: That's a diver. It's got a yellow eye and it dives. That's a goose. Tommy doesn't know it's a goose, he thinks it's a duck. The babies get eaten by weasels. Kiou kiou.

(*Cathy goes.*)

MARTIN: So I lost my erection last night not because I'm not prepared to talk, it's just that taking in technical information is a different part of the brain and also I don't like to feel that you do it better to yourself. I have read the Hite report. I do know that women have to learn to get their pleasure despite our clumsy attempts at expressing undying devotion and ecstasy, and that what we spent our adolescence thinking was an animal urge we had to suppress is in fact a fine art we have to acquire. I'm not like whatever percentage of American men have become impotent as a direct result of women's liberation, which I am totally in favor of, more I sometimes think than you are yourself. Nor am I one of your villains who sticks it in, bangs away, and falls asleep. My one aim is to give you pleasure. My one aim is to give you rolling orgasms like I do other women. So why the hell don't you have them? My analysis for what it's worth is that despite all my efforts you still feel dominated by me. I in fact think it's very sad that you don't feel able to take that job. It makes me feel very guilty. I don't want you to do it just because I encourage you to do it. But don't you think you'd feel better if you did take the job? You're the one who's talked about freedom. You're the one who's experimenting with bisexuality, and I don't stop you, I think women have something to give each other. You seem to need the mutual support. You find me too overwhelming. So follow it through, go away, leave me and Tommy alone for a bit, we can manage perfectly well without you. I'm not putting any pressure on you but I don't think you're being a whole person. God knows I do everything I can to make you stand on your own two feet. Just be yourself. You don't seem to realize how insulting it is to me that you can't get yourself together.

(Martin and Victoria go.)

BETTY: You must be very lonely yourself with no husband. You don't miss him?

LIN: Not really, no.

BETTY: Maybe you like being on your own.

LIN: I'm seeing quite a lot of Vicky. I don't live alone. I live with Cathy.

BETTY: I would have been frightened when I was your age. I thought, the poor children, their mother all alone.

LIN: I've a lot of friends.

BETTY: I find when I'm making tea I put out two cups. It's strange not having a man in the house. You don't know who to do things for.

LIN: Yourself.

BETTY: Oh, that's very selfish.

LIN: Have you any women friends?

BETTY: I've never been so short of men's company that I've had to bother with women.

LIN: Don't you like women?

BETTY: They don't have such interesting conversations as men. There has never been a woman composer of genius. They don't have a sense of humor. They spoil things for themselves with their emotions. I can't say I do like women very much, no.

LIN: But you're a woman.

BETTY: There's nothing says you have to like yourself.

LIN: Do you like me?

BETTY: There's no need to take it personally, Lin.

(Martin and Victoria come back.)

MARTIN: Did you know if you put cocaine on your prick you can keep it up all night? The only thing is of course it goes numb so you don't feel anything. But you would, that's the main thing. I just want to make you happy.

BETTY: Vicky, I'd like to go home.

VICTORIA: Yes, mummy, of course.

BETTY: I'm sorry, dear.

VICTORIA: I think Tommy would like to stay out a bit longer.

LIN: Hello, Martin. We do keep out of each other's way.

MARTIN: I think that's the best thing to do.

BETTY: Perhaps you'd walk home with me, Martin. I do feel safer with a man. The park is so large the grass seems to tilt.

MARTIN: Yes, I'd like to go home and do some work. I'm writing a novel about women from the women's point of view.

(Martin and Betty go. Lin and Victoria are alone. They embrace.)

VICTORIA: Why the hell can't he just be a wife and come with me? Why does Martin make me tie myself in knots? No wonder we can't just have a simple fuck. No, not Martin, why do I make myself tie myself in knots. It's got to stop, Lin. I'm not like that with you. Would you love me if I went to Manchester?

LIN: Yes.

VICTORIA: Would you love me if I went on a climbing expedition in the Andes mountains?

LIN: Yes.

VICTORIA: Would you love me if my teeth fell out?

LIN: Yes.

VICTORIA: Would you love me if I loved ten other people?

LIN: And me?

VICTORIA: Yes.

LIN: Yes.

VICTORIA: And I feel apologetic for not being quite so subordinate as I was. I am more intelligent than him. I am brilliant.

LIN: Leave him Vic. Come and live with me.

VICTORIA: Don't be silly.

LIN: Silly, Christ, don't then. I'm not asking because I need to live with someone. I'd enjoy it, that's all, we'd both enjoy it. Fuck you. Cathy, for fuck's sake stop throwing stones at the ducks. The man's going to get you.

VICTORIA: What man? Do you need a man to frighten your child with?

LIN: My mother said it.

VICTORIA: You're so inconsistent, Lin.

LIN: I've changed who I sleep with, I can't change everything.

VICTORIA: Like when I had to stop you getting a job in a boutique and collaborating with sexist consumerism.

LIN: I should have got that job, Cathy would have liked it. Why shouldn't I have some decent clothes? I'm sick of dressing like a boy, why can't I look sexy, wouldn't you love me?

VICTORIA: Lin, you've no analysis.

LIN: No but I'm good at kissing aren't I? I give Cathy guns, my mum didn't give me guns. I dress her in jeans, she wants to wear dresses. I don't know. I can't work it out, I don't want to. You read too many books, you get at me all the time, you're worse to me than Martin is to you, you piss me off, my brother's been killed. I'm sorry to win the argument that way but there it is.

VICTORIA: What do you mean win the argument?

LIN: I mean be nice to me.

VICTORIA: In Belfast?

LIN: I heard this morning. Don't don't start. I've hardly seen him for two years. I rung my father. You'd think I'd shot him myself. He doesn't want me to go to the funeral.

(Cathy approaches.)

VICTORIA: What will you do?

LIN: Go of course.

CATHY: What is it? Who's killed? What?

LIN: It's Bill. Your uncle. In the army. Bill that gave you the blue teddy.

CATHY: Can I have his gun?

LIN: It's time we went home. Time you went to bed.

CATHY: No it's not.

LIN: We go home and you have tea and you have a bath and you go to bed.

CATHY: Fuck off.

LIN: Cathy, shut up.

VICTORIA: It's only half past five, why don't we—

LIN: I'll tell you why she has to go to bed—

VICTORIA: She can come home with me.

LIN: Because I want her out of the fucking way.

VICTORIA: She can come home with me.

CATHY: I'm not going to bed.

LIN: I want her home with me not home with you, I want her in bed, I want today over.

CATHY: I'm not going to bed.

(*Lin hits Cathy, Cathy cries.*)

LIN: And shut up or I'll give you something to cry for.

CATHY: I'm not going to bed.

VICTORIA: Cathy—

LIN: You keep out of it.

VICTORIA: Lin for God's sake.

(*They are all shouting. Cathy runs off. Lin and Victoria are silent. Then they laugh and embrace.*)

LIN: Where's Tommy?

VICTORIA: What? Didn't he go with Martin?

LIN: Did he?

VICTORIA: God oh God.

LIN: Cathy! Cathy!

VICTORIA: I haven't thought about him. How could I not think about him? Tommy!

LIN: Cathy! Come on, quick, I want some help.

VICTORIA: Tommy! Tommy!

(*Cathy comes back.*)

LIN: Where's Tommy? Have you seen him? Did he go with Martin? Do you know where he is?

CATHY: I showed him the goose. We went in the bushes.

LIN: Then what?

CATHY: I came back on the swing.

VICTORIA: And Tommy? Where was Tommy?

CATHY: He fed the ducks.

LIN: No that was before.

CATHY: He did a pee in the bushes. I helped him with his trousers.

VICTORIA: And after that?

CATHY: He fed the ducks.

VICTORIA: No no.

CATHY: He liked the ducks. I expect he fell in.

LIN: Did you see him fall in?

VICTORIA: Tommy! Tommy!

LIN: What's the last time you saw him?

CATHY: He did a pee.

VICTORIA: Mummy said he would fall in. Oh God, Tommy!

LIN: We'll go round the pond. We'll go opposite ways round the pond.

ALL (*shout*): Tommy!

(*Victoria and Lin go off opposite sides. Cathy climbs the bench.*)

CATHY: Georgie Best, superstar
Walks like a woman and wears a bra.
There he is! I see him! Mum! Vicky! There he is! He's in the bushes.

(*Lin comes back.*)

LIN: Come on Cathy love, let's go home.

CATHY: Vicky's got him.

LIN: Come on.

CATHY: Is she cross?

LIN: No. Come on.

CATHY: I found him.

LIN: Yes. Come on.

(*Cathy gets off the bench. Cathy and Lin hug.*)

CATHY: I'm watching telly.

LIN: Ok.

CATHY: After the news.

LIN: Ok.

CATHY: I'm not going to bed.

LIN: Yes you are.

CATHY: I'm not going to bed now.

LIN: Not now but early.

CATHY: How early?

LIN: Not late.

CATHY: How not late?

LIN: Early.

CATHY: How early?

LIN: Not late.

(*They go off together. Gerry comes on. He waits. Edward comes.*)

EDWARD: I've got some fish for dinner. I thought I'd make a cheese sauce.

GERRY: I won't be in.

EDWARD: Where are you going?

GERRY: For a start I'm going to a sauna. Then I'll see.

EDWARD: All right. What time will you be back? We'll eat then.

GERRY: You're getting like a wife.

EDWARD: I don't mind that.

GERRY: Why don't I do the cooking sometime?

EDWARD: You can if you like. You're just not so good at it that's all. Do it tonight.

GERRY: I won't be in tonight.

EDWARD: Do it tomorrow. If we can't eat it we can always go to a restaurant.

GERRY: Stop it.

EDWARD: Stop what?

GERRY: Just be yourself.

EDWARD: I don't know what you mean. Everyone's always tried to stop me being feminine and now you are too.

GERRY: You're putting it on.

EDWARD: I like doing the cooking. I like being fucked. You do like me like this really.

GERRY: I'm bored, Eddy.

EDWARD: Go to the sauna.

GERRY: And you'll stay home and wait up for me.

EDWARD: No, I'll go to bed and read a book.

GERRY: Or knit. You could knit me a pair of socks.

EDWARD: I might knit. I like knitting.

GERRY: I don't mind if you knit. I don't want to be married.

EDWARD: I do.

GERRY: Well I'm divorcing you.

EDWARD: I wouldn't want to keep a man who wants his freedom.

GERRY: Eddy, do stop playing the injured wife, it's not funny.

EDWARD: I'm not playing. It's true.

GERRY: I'm not the husband so you can't be the wife.

EDWARD: I'll always be here, Gerry, if you want to come back. I know you men like to go off by yourselves. I don't think I could love deeply more than once. But I don't think I can face life on my own so don't leave it too long or it may be too late.

GERRY: What are you trying to turn me into?

EDWARD: A monster, darling, which is what you are.

GERRY: I'll collect my stuff from the flat in the morning.

(*Gerry goes. Edward sits on the bench. It gets darker. Victoria comes.*)

VICTORIA: Tommy dropped a toy car somewhere, you haven't seen it? It's red. He says it's his best one. Oh the hell with it. Martin's reading him a story. There, isn't it quiet?

(*They sit on the bench, holding hands.*)

EDWARD: I like women.

VICTORIA: That should please mother.

EDWARD: No listen Vicky. I'd rather be a woman. I wish I had breasts like that, I think they're beautiful. Can I touch them?

VICTORIA: What, pretending they're yours?

EDWARD: No, I know it's you.

VICTORIA: I think I should warn you I'm enjoying this.

EDWARD: I'm sick of men.

VICTORIA: I'm sick of men.

EDWARD: I think I'm a lesbian.

Scene Three

(*The park. Summer night. Victoria, Lin, and Edward drunk.*)

LIN: Where are you?

VICTORIA: Come on.

EDWARD: Do we sit in a circle?

VICTORIA: Sit in a triangle.

EDWARD: You're good at mathematics. She's good at mathematics.

VICTORIA: Give me your hand. We all hold hands.

EDWARD: Do you know what to do?

LIN: She's making it up.

VICTORIA: We start off by being quiet.

EDWARD: What?

LIN: Hush.

EDWARD: Will something appear?

VICTORIA: It was your idea.

EDWARD: It wasn't my idea. It was your book.

LIN: You said call up the goddess.

EDWARD: I don't remember saying that.

LIN: We could have called her on the telephone.

EDWARD: Don't be so silly, this is meant to be frightening.

LIN: Kiss me.

VICTORIA: Are we going to do it?

LIN: We're doing it.

VICTORIA: A ceremony.

LIN: It's very sexy, you said it is. You said the women were priests in the temples and fucked all the time. I'm just helping.

VICTORIA: As long as it's sacred.

LIN: It's very sacred.

VICTORIA: Innin, Innana, Nana, Nut, Anat, Anahita, Istar, Isis.

LIN: I can't remember all that.

VICTORIA: Lin! Innin, Innana, Nana, Nut, Anat, Anahita, Istar, Isis.

(*Lin and Edward join in and continue the chant under Victoria's speech.*)

Goddess of many names, oldest of the old, who walked in chaos and created life, hear us calling you back through time, before Jehovah, before Christ, before men drove you out and burnt your temples, hear us, Lady, give us back what we were, give us the history we haven't had, make us the women we can't be.

ALL: Innin, Innana, Nana, Nut, Anat, Anahita, Istar, Isis.

(*Chant continues under other speeches.*)

LIN: Come back, goddess.

VICTORIA: Goddess of the sun and the moon her brother, little goddess of Crete with snakes in your hands.

LIN: Goddess of breasts.

VICTORIA: Goddess of cunts.

LIN: Goddess of fat bellies and babies. And blood blood blood.

(*Chant continues.*)

I see her.

EDWARD: What?

(*They stop chanting.*)

LIN: I see her. Very tall. Snakes in her hands. Light light light—look out! Did I give you a fright?

EDWARD: I was terrified.

VICTORIA: Don't spoil it Lin.

LIN: It's all out of a book.

VICTORIA: Innin Innana—I can't do it now. I was really enjoying myself.

LIN: She won't appear with a man here.

VICTORIA: They had men, they had sons and lovers.

EDWARD: They had eunuchs.

LIN: Don't give us ideas.

VICTORIA: There's Attis and Tammuz, they're torn to pieces.

EDWARD: Tear me to pieces, Lin.

VICTORIA: The priestess chose a lover for a year and he was king because she chose him and then he was killed at the end of the year.

EDWARD: Hurray.

VICTORIA: And the women had the children and nobody knew it was done by fucking so they didn't know about fathers and nobody cared who the father was and the property was passed down through the maternal line—

LIN: Don't turn it into a lecture, Vicky, it's meant to be an orgy.

VICTORIA: It never hurts to understand the theoretical background. You can't separate fucking and economics.

LIN: Give us a kiss.

EDWARD: Shut up, listen.

LIN: What?

EDWARD: There's somebody there.

LIN: Where?

EDWARD: There.

VICTORIA: The priestesses used to make love to total strangers.

LIN: Go on then, I dare you.

EDWARD: Go on, Vicky.

VICTORIA: He won't know it's a sacred rite in honor of the goddess.

EDWARD: We'll know.

LIN: We can tell him.

EDWARD: It's not what he thinks, it's what we think.

LIN: Don't tell him till after, he'll run a mile.

VICTORIA: Hello. We're having an orgy. Do you want me to suck your cock?

(*The stranger approaches. It is Martin.*)

MARTIN: There you are. I've been looking everywhere. What the hell are you doing? Do you know what the time is? You're all pissed out of your minds.

(*They leap on Martin, pull him down and start to make love to him.*)

MARTIN: Well that's all right. If all we're talking about is having a lot of sex there's no problem. I was all for the sixties when liberation just meant fucking.

(*Another stranger approaches.*)

LIN: Hey you, come here. Come and have sex with us.

VICTORIA: Who is it?

(*The stranger is a soldier.*)

LIN: It's my brother.

EDWARD: Lin, don't.

LIN: It's my brother.

VICTORIA: It's her sense of humor, you get used to it.

LIN: Shut up Vicky, it's my brother. Isn't it? Bill?

SOLDIER: Yes it's me.

LIN: And you are dead.

SOLDIER: Fucking dead all right yeh.

LIN: Have you come back to tell us something?

SOLDIER: No I've come for a fuck. That was the worst thing in the fucking army. Never fucking let out. Can't fucking talk to Irish girls. Fucking bored out of my fucking head. That or shit scared. For five minutes I'd be glad I wasn't bored, then I was fucking scared. Then we'd come in and I'd be glad I wasn't scared and then I was fucking bored. Spent the day reading fucking porn and the fucking night wanking. Man's fucking life in the fucking army? No fun when the fucking kids hate you. I got so I fucking wanted to kill someone and I got fucking killed myself and I want a fuck.

LIN: I miss you. Bill. Bill.

(*Lin collapses. Soldier goes. Victoria comforts Lin.*)

EDWARD: Let's go home.

LIN: Victoria, come home with us. Victoria's coming to live with me and Edward.

MARTIN: Tell me about it in the morning.

LIN: It's true.

VICTORIA: It is true.

MARTIN: Tell me when you're sober.

(*Edward, Lin, Victoria go off together. Martin goes off alone. Gerry comes on.*)

GERRY: I come here sometimes at night and pick somebody up. Sometimes I come here at night and don't pick anybody up. I do also enjoy walking about at night. There's never any trouble finding someone. I can have sex any time. You might not find the type you most fancy every day of the week, but there's plenty of people about who just enjoy having a good time. I quite like living alone. If I live with someone I get annoyed with them. Edward always put on Capital radio when he got up. The silence gets wasted. I wake up at four o'clock sometimes. Birds. Silence. If I bring somebody home I never let them stay the night. Edward! Edward!

(*Edward from Act One comes on.*)

EDWARD: Gerry I love you.

GERRY: Yes, I know. I love you, too.

EDWARD: You know what we did? I want to do it again. I think about it all the time. Don't you want to any more?

GERRY: Yes, of course.

SONG ("*Cloud Nine*"—*All*):

It'll be fine when you reach Cloud Nine.

Mist was rising and the night was dark.
Me and my baby took a walk in the park.
He said Be mine and you're on Cloud Nine.

Better watch out when you're on Cloud Nine.

Smoked some dope on the playground swings
Higher and higher on true love's wings
He said Be mine and you're on Cloud Nine.

Twenty-five years on the same Cloud Nine.

Who did she meet on her first blind date?
The guys were no surprise but the lady was great
They were women in love, they were on Cloud Nine.

Two the same, they were on Cloud Nine.

The bride was sixty-five, the groom was seventeen,
They fucked in the back of the black limousine.
It was divine in their silver Cloud Nine.

Simply divine in their silver Cloud Nine.

The wife's lover's children and my lover's wife,
Cooking in my kitchen, confusing my life.
And it's upside down when you reach Cloud Nine.

Upside down when you reach Cloud Nine.

Scene Four

(*The park. Afternoon in late summer. Martin, Cathy, Edward.*)

CATHY: Under the bramble bushes,
Under the sea boom boom boom,
True love for you my darling,
True love for me my darling,
When we are married,
We'll raise a family.
Boy for you, girl for me,
Boom tiddley oom boom
SEXY.

EDWARD: You'll have Tommy and Cathy tonight then ok? Tommy's still on antibiotics, do make him finish the bottle, he takes it in Ribena. It's no good in orange, he spits it out. Remind me to give you Cathy's swimming things.

CATHY: I did six strokes, didn't I Martin? Did I do a width? How many strokes is a length? How many miles is a swimming pool? I'm going to take my bronze and silver and gold and diamond.

MARTIN: Is Tommy still wetting the bed?

EDWARD: Don't get angry with him about it.

MARTIN: I just need to go to the launderette so I've got a spare sheet. Of course I don't get fucking angry,

Eddy, for God's sake. I don't like to say he is my son but he is my son. I'm surprised I'm not wetting the bed myself.

CATHY: I don't wet the bed ever. Do you wet the bed Martin?

MARTIN: No.

CATHY: You said you did.

(*Betty comes.*)

BETTY: I do miss the sun living in England but today couldn't be more beautiful. You appreciate the weekend when you're working. Betty's been at work this week, Cathy. It's terrible tiring, Martin, I don't know how you've done it all these years. And the money, I feel like a child with the money, Clive always paid everything but I do understand it perfectly well. Look Cathy let me show you my money.

CATHY: I'll count it. Let me count it. What's that?

BETTY: Five pounds, Five and five is—?

CATHY: One two three—

BETTY: Five and five is ten, and five—

CATHY: If I get it right can I have one?

EDWARD: No you can't.

(*Cathy goes on counting the money.*)

BETTY: I never like to say anything, Martin, or you'll think I'm being a mother-in-law.

EDWARD: Which you are.

BETTY: Thank you, Edward, I'm not talking to you. Martin, I think you're being wonderful. Vicky will come back. Just let her stay with Lin till she sorts herself out. It's very nice for a girl to have a friend; I had friends at school, that was very nice. But I'm sure Lin and Edward don't want her with them all the time. I'm not at all shocked that Lin and Edward aren't married and she already has a child, we all know first marriages don't always work out. But really Vicky must be in the way. And poor little Tommy. I hear he doesn't sleep properly and he's had a cough.

MARTIN: No, he's fine, Betty, thank you.

CATHY: My bed's horrible. I want to sleep in the big bed with Lin and Vicky and Eddy and I do get in if I've got a bad dream, and my bed's got a bump right in my back. I want to sleep in a tent.

BETTY: Well Tommy has got a nasty cough, Martin, whatever you say.

EDWARD: He's over that. He's got some medicine.

MARTIN: He takes it in Ribena.

BETTY: Well I'm glad to hear it. Look what a lot of money, Cathy, and I sit behind a desk of my own and I answer the telephone and keep the doctor's appointment book and it really is great fun.

CATHY: Can we go camping, Martin, in a tent? We could take the Dead Hand Gang.

BETTY: Not those big boys, Cathy? They're far too big and rough for you. They climb back into the park after dark. I'm sure mummy doesn't let you play with them, does she Edward? Well I don't know.

(*Ice cream bells.*)

CATHY: Ice cream. Martin you promised. I'll have a double ninety-nine. No I'll have a shandy lolly. Betty, you have a shandy lolly and I'll have a lick. No, you have a double ninety-nine and I'll have the chocolate.

(*Martin, Cathy, and Betty go, leaving Edward. Gerry comes.*)

GERRY: Hello, Eddy. Thought I might find you here.
EDWARD: Gerry.
GERRY: Not working today then?
EDWARD: I don't work here any more.
GERRY: Your mum got you into a dark suit?
EDWARD: No of course not. I'm on the dole. I am working, though, I do housework.
GERRY: Whose wife are you now then?
EDWARD: Nobody's. I don't think like that any more. I'm living with some women.
GERRY: What women?
EDWARD: It's my sister, Vic, and her lover. They go out to work and I look after the kids.
GERRY: I thought for a moment you said you were living with women.
EDWARD: We do sleep together, yes.
GERRY: I was passing the park anyway so I thought I'd look in. I was in the sauna the other night and I saw someone who looked like you but it wasn't. I had sex with him anyway.
EDWARD: I do go to the sauna sometimes.

(*Cathy comes, gives Edward an ice cream, goes.*)

GERRY: I don't think I'd like living with children. They make a lot of noise don't they?
EDWARD: I tell them to shut up and they shut up. I wouldn't want to leave them at the moment.
GERRY: Look why don't we go for a meal sometime?
EDWARD: Yes I'd like that. Where are you living now?
GERRY: Same place.
EDWARD: I'll come round for you tomorrow night about 7:30.
GERRY: Great.

(*Edward goes. Harry comes. Harry and Gerry pick each other up. They go off. Betty comes back.*)

BETTY: No, the ice cream was my treat, Martin. Off you go. I'm going to have a quiet sit in the sun.

(*Maud comes.*)

MAUD: Let Mrs. Saunders be a warning to you, Betty. I know what it is to be unprotected.
BETTY: But mother, I have a job. I earn money.
MAUD: I know we have our little differences but I always want what is best for you.

(*Ellen comes.*)

ELLEN: Betty, what happens with a man?
BETTY: You just keep still.
ELLEN: And is it enjoyable? Don't forget me, Betty.
                                            (*Maud and Ellen go.*)

BETTY: I used to think Clive was the one who liked sex. But then I found I missed it. I used to touch myself when I was very little, I thought I'd invented something wonderful. I used to do it to go to sleep with or to cheer myself up, and one day it was raining and I was under the kitchen table, and my mother saw me with my hand under my dress rubbing away, and she dragged me out so quickly I hit my head and it bled and I was sick, and nothing was said, and I never did it again till this year. I thought if Clive wasn't looking at me there wasn't a person there. And one night in bed in my flat I was so frightened I started touching myself. I thought my hand might go through space. I touched my face, it was there, my arm, my breast, and my hand went down where I thought it shouldn't, and I thought well there is somebody there. It felt very sweet, it was a feeling from very long ago, it was very soft, just barely touching, and I felt myself gathering together more and more and I felt angry with Clive and angry with my mother and I went on and on defying them, and there was this vast feeling growing in me and all round me and they couldn't stop me and no one could stop me and I was there and coming and coming. Afterwards I thought I'd betrayed Clive. My mother would kill me. But I felt triumphant because I was a separate person from them. And I cried because I didn't want to be. But I don't cry about it any more. Sometimes I do it three times in one night and it really is great fun.

(*Victoria and Lin come in.*)

VICTORIA: So I said to the professor, I don't think this is an occasion for invoking the concept of structural causality—oh hello mummy.
BETTY: I'm going to ask you a question, both of you. I have a little money from your grandmother. And the three of you are living in that tiny flat with two children. I wonder if we could get a house and all live in it together? It would give you more room.
VICTORIA: But I'm going to Manchester anyway.
LIN: We'd have a garden, Vicky.
BETTY: You do seem to have such fun all of you.
VICTORIA: I don't want to.
BETTY: I didn't think you would.
LIN: Come on, Vicky, she knows we sleep together, and Eddy.
BETTY: I think I've known for quite a while but I'm not sure. I don't usually think about it, so I don't know if I know about it or not.
VICTORIA: I don't want to live with my mother.
LIN: Don't think of her as your mother, think of her as Betty.
VICTORIA: But she thinks of herself as my mother.
BETTY: I am your mother.
VICTORIA: But mummy we don't even like each other.
BETTY: We might begin to.

(*Cathy comes on howling with a nosebleed.*)

LIN: Oh Cathy what happened?
BETTY: She's been assaulted.

VICTORIA: It's a nosebleed.
CATHY: Took my ice cream.
LIN: Who did?
CATHY: Took my money.

(*Martin comes.*)

MARTIN: Is everything all right?
LIN: I thought you were looking after her.
CATHY: They hit me. I can't play. They said I'm a girl.
BETTY: Those dreadful boys, the gang, the Dead Hand.
MARTIN: What do you mean you thought I was looking after her?
LIN: Last I saw her she was with you getting an ice cream. It's your afternoon.
MARTIN: Then she went off to play. She goes off to play. You don't keep an eye on her every minute.
LIN: She doesn't get beaten up when I'm looking after her.
CATHY: Took my money.
MARTIN: Why the hell should I look after your child anyway? I just want Tommy. Why should he live with you and Vicky all week?
LIN: I don't mind if you don't want to look after her but don't say you will and then this happens.
VICTORIA: When I get to Manchester everything's going to be different anyway, Lin's staying here, and you're staying here, we're all going to have to sit down and talk it through.
MARTIN: I'd really enjoy that.
CATHY: Hit me on the face.
LIN: You were the one looking after her and look at her now, that's all.
MARTIN: I've had enough of you telling me.
LIN: Yes you know it all.
MARTIN: Now stop it. I work very hard at not being like this, I could do with some credit.
LIN: Ok you're quite nice, try and enjoy it. Don't make me sorry for you, Martin, it's hard for me too. We've better things to do than quarrel. I've got to go and sort those little bastards out for a start. Where are they, Cathy?
CATHY: Don't kill them, mum, hit them. Give them a nosebleed, mum.

(*Lin goes.*)

VICTORIA: Tommy's asleep in the pushchair. We'd better wake him up or he won't sleep tonight.
MARTIN: Sometimes I keep him up watching television till he falls asleep on the sofa so I can hold him. Come on, Cathy, we'll get another ice cream.
CATHY: Chocolate sauce and nuts.
VICTORIA: Betty, would you like an ice cream?
BETTY: No thank you, the cold hurts my teeth, but what a nice thought, Vicky, thank you.

(*Victoria goes. Betty alone. Gerry comes.*)

BETTY: I think you used to be Edward's flatmate.
GERRY: You're his mother. He's talked about you.
BETTY: Well never mind. Children are always wrong about their parents. It's a great problem knowing where to live and who to share with. I live by myself just now.

GERRY: Good. So do I. You can do what you like.
BETTY: I don't really know what I like.
GERRY: You'll soon find out.
BETTY: What do you like?
GERRY: Waking up at four in the morning.
BETTY: I like listening to music in bed and sometimes for supper I just have a big piece of bread and dip it in very hot lime pickle. So you don't get lonely by yourself? Perhaps you have a lot of visitors. I've been thinking I should have some visitors, I could give a little dinner party. Would you come? There wouldn't just be bread and lime pickle.
GERRY: Thank you very much.
BETTY: Or don't wait to be asked to dinner. Just drop in informally. I'll give you the address shall I? I don't usually give strange men my address but then you're not a strange man, you're a friend of Edward's. I suppose I seem a different generation to you but you are older than Edward. I was married for so many years it's quite hard to know how to get acquainted. But if there isn't a right way to do things you have to invent one. I always thought my mother was far too old to be attractive but when you get to an age yourself it feels quite different.
GERRY: I think you could be quite attractive.
BETTY: If what?
GERRY: If you stop worrying.
BETTY: I think when I do more about things I worry about them less. So perhaps you could help me do more.
GERRY: I might be going to live with Edward again.
BETTY: That's nice, but I'm rather surprised if he wants to share a flat. He's rather involved with a young woman he lives with, or two young women, I don't understand Edward but never mind.
GERRY: I'm very involved with him.
BETTY: I think Edward did try to tell me once but I didn't listen. So what I'm being told now is that Edward is "gay" is that right? And you are too. And I've been making rather a fool of myself. But Edward does also sleep with women.
GERRY: He does, yes, I don't.
BETTY: Well people always say it's the mother's fault but I don't intend to start blaming myself. He seems perfectly happy.
GERRY: I could still come and see you.
BETTY: So you could, yes. I'd like that. I've never tried to pick up a man before.
GERRY: Not everyone's gay.
BETTY: No, that's lucky isn't it.

(*Gerry goes. Clive comes.*)

CLIVE: You are not that sort of woman, Betty. I can't believe you are. I can't feel the same about you as I did. And Africa is to be communist I suppose. I used to be proud to be British. There was a high ideal. I came out onto the verandah and looked at the stars.

(*Clive goes. Betty from Act One comes. Betty and Betty embrace.*)

Athol Fugard

Athol Fugard (b. 1932) was an actor before becoming a playwright. Fugard's wife, the actress Sheila Meiring, stimulated his interest in theater, and in 1956 he began working with a theater group called the Serpent Company in Cape Town, South Africa. The group included both black and white actors at a time when racial mixing was illegal, and it went on to make a notable contribution to world drama.

Fugard, who is white, met Zakes Mokae (1934–2009), a black musician and actor, in the early days of the Serpent players, and the two collaborated on several works. Mokae said that the tradition in Africa was not so much for a solitary playwright to compose a work that others would act out as it was for people to develop a communal approach to drama, crafting a dramatic piece through their interaction. To some extent, Fugard in his early efforts did just that. He worked with actors, watched the developments among them, and then shaped the drama accordingly.

In 1960 Fugard began to write a two-person play called *The Blood Knot* while he was in England trying to establish a theater group there. This play was part of a trilogy called *The Family,* with *Hello and Goodbye* (1965) and *Boesman and Lena* (1969). *The Blood Knot* was given its first performance in Dorkay House in Johannesburg, South Africa, late in 1961. As Fugard has said, the entire production, which starred Fugard and Mokae, was put together so quickly that the government never had time to stop it. The play is about two brothers, one black and the other light-skinned enough to pass for white. It is exceptionally powerful, and the play's first performances in Johannesburg were a sensation. It toured South Africa and had a revival in New Haven and in New York in 1984 and 1985.

While they toured South Africa, Fugard and Mokae were victims of the country's apartheid policies. They could not travel in the same train car: Fugard went first class, and Mokae had to go in special cars for blacks. After *The Blood Knot*'s success, the government passed laws making it all but impossible for black and white actors to work together on the stage.

Fugard has had a considerable number of plays produced in New York and London over the years. *Sizwe Banzi Is Dead* (1972), written with black actors John Kani and Winston Ntshona, is about a man who exchanges identities with a corpse as a way of avoiding the racial laws of South Africa; it was well received. *The Island* (1975), also written with Kani and Ntshona, starred the latter two, who have become associated with Fugard and his work. They portray prisoners who, while putting on *Antigone,* become immersed in the political themes of the play, seeing it as an example of the political repression they experience in their own lives. A revival in New York in April 2003, with Kani and Ntshona in a mildly revised version, received excellent reviews.

Fugard's plays *A Lesson from Aloes* (1978) and *The Road to Mecca* (1984) were successful in their first U.S. productions at the Yale Repertory Theatre and on Broadway. Fugard's works are not always concerned with racial problems, but they usually center on political issues and the stress that individuals feel in trying to be themselves in an intolerant society.

The situation in South Africa has improved since "*MASTER HAROLD*" . . . *and the boys* was first produced in 1982. Apartheid has been abolished, and the government is in the hands of the African National Congress. The shift has been more successful than white South Africans expected, although political tensions still exist. Fugard's attachment and commitment to South Africa remain deep. He has been criticized by black writers for dealing with themes they believe belong to them, while also being criticized by whites for his sympathies toward blacks. In the new South Africa some of these problems have begun to sort themselves out. *Valley Song* (1996), produced at London's Royal Court Theatre, explores the problems and the promise of the new South Africa.

In May 1998, *The Captain's Tiger* was directed by Fugard, who also acted in the role of Tiger, a character on board a ship. Fugard himself had left university to work on ships around Africa. In May 2001, Fugard directed *Sorrows and Rejoicing*, a play about a man whose white wife and colored mistress meet at his funeral. Fugard's *Exits and Entrances* (2004) was written for the Fountain Theatre in Los Angeles; it is a one-act meditation on Fugard's life in the theater. Another play, *The Abbess* (2000), is based on the life of Saint Hildegard of Bingen (1098–1179), a Benedictine abbess known for her correspondence, for her work in medicine, and for her music, poems, writing, and drama. The Long Wharf Theatre in New Haven, Connecticut, premiered Fugard's three most recent plays: *Coming Home* (2009) tells of Veronica, a hopeful young African who, after failing in her singing career, returns to her pre-apartheid family home in South Africa to raise her son; *Have You Seen Us* (2009) is set in southern California, where Fugard now lives, and focuses on anti-Semitism; *The Train Driver* (2010) tells the story of a white South African train driver who feels guilty after seeing an African woman and her child step in front of his train. All of these plays continue Fugard's concern for the welfare of those who are marginalized in one way or another.

"MASTER HAROLD" . . . and the boys

For discussion questions and assignments on "*MASTER HAROLD*" . . . *and the boys,* visit **bedfordstmartins.com/jacobus.**

Athol Fugard has said that "*MASTER HAROLD*" . . . *and the boys* (1982) is a very personal play in which he exorcises personal guilt. As a white South African (Fugard's entire name is Harold Athol Lannigan Fugard), he has written numerous plays that represent the racial circumstances of life in that troubled nation. This play won international distinction and made a reputation for its stars, especially Zakes Mokae, with whom Fugard worked for more than forty years.

Hally, the teenage son, reveals throughout the play (which is set in 1950) that he is more attached emotionally to Sam, the black waiter who has befriended him, than he is even to his own parents, owners of the restaurant where Sam works. His attitude toward his father is complicated by his father's alcoholism and confinement. At that time in South Africa, even a white alcoholic was considered superior to a black man such as Sam, even though Sam is intelligent, quick, thoughtful, and generous. When Hally reveals his anxiety about his father, Sam warns him that it is dishonorable to treat one's father the way he does, and Sam's presumption in admonishing Hally triggers Hally's meanspirited outburst toward him.

Zakes Mokae, who created the role of Sam in the first performance of the play at the Yale Repertory Theatre, commented extensively about his role and the character of Sam. He observed that some black audience members called out during a performance that he should beat up Hally the minute Hally demands that Sam call him Master Harold. But other black audience members spoke with him after the performance and agreed that, because Sam had never taken that kind of stand against Harold or his father, he was getting what he deserved. Mokae himself pointed out that Sam is probably not living in Port Elizabeth legally and that to have taken action, even if he had wanted to, would have ended with his ejection from the town into exile.

Zakes Mokae understood the character from his perspective as a black South African, and he realized Sam's limits. But he said that in his version of the play, Sam would give Hally a beating and "suffer the consequences." He pointed out, however, that, as an urban South African, unlike Sam, he had an attitude quite different from anything that Sam would have understood. As an urban black, Mokae could not have been sent into exile, although he could certainly have been punished, for beating a white boy.

On the question of whether the play made a positive contribution to white-black relations in South Africa, Mokae pointed out that a play cannot change people's minds. Audiences were not likely to seek to change the government of South Africa simply because they had seen a play. At the same time, however, he believed that it was productive to talk about apartheid and racial distrust in South Africa.

Unfortunately, the government of South Africa decided the play was too inflammatory for performance in that country, and it was banned briefly from performance in Johannesburg and other theatrical centers in South Africa. This suggests that although Zakes Mokae did not believe one play would have much impact on injustices in South Africa, the government feared otherwise.

In an important way, *"MASTER HAROLD" . . . and the boys* is a personal statement by Fugard that establishes the extent to which apartheid damages even a person sympathetic to black rights. It is astonishing in retrospect to think, as one interviewer, Heinrich von Staden, once said, that Hally could grow up to be Athol himself. If this is true, then it is also true that the play is hopeful.

One sign of hope is that the violence in the play is restrained. Sam does not beat Hally for humiliating him, although he probably would like to. And no one in the play makes a move to be physically threatening to Sam. However faint, these are signs of hope. And as Zakes Mokae said about the situation in his homeland, "One is always optimistic. It can't go on forever." He was right. On June 5, 1991, Parliament abandoned apartheid, and South Africa had a new beginning.

"MASTER HAROLD" . . . and the boys in Performance

The world premiere of *"MASTER HAROLD" . . . and the boys* was at the Yale Repertory Theatre in March 1982. Fugard himself directed the play, with Zakes Mokae as Sam, Danny Glover as Willie, and Željko Ivanek as Hally. It was the first of Fugard's plays to premiere outside South Africa. Fugard chose New Haven, Connecticut, in part because the play's setting was so personal that he feared it might disturb his brother and sister if it were produced first in

South Africa. The setting was a bright tea room—a restaurant that serves light meals—interpreted to look like the tea room Fugard's mother actually ran in Port Elizabeth when he was a child. The space was open, the walls a whitish hue, everything simple and plain in decoration.

New York Times critic Frank Rich reviewed the premiere, saying, "*'MASTER HAROLD' . . . and the boys* is only an anecdote, really, and it's often as warm and musical as the men's dance. But somewhere along the way it rises up and breaks over the audience like a storm." Alan Stern of the *Boston Phoenix* linked the play with Greek tragedy:

> One reason for the play's potency is that, as in Greek tragedy, the events seem preordained—they're the by-product of social forces and human nature. Even as he spits in Sam's face, Hally realizes the magnitude of his action, that he is the one who will be harmed by it. And yet he can't help himself. Power corrupts, and in a society that sanctions the domination of one man—or set of men—over another, all relationships, even the promising ones, are poisoned.

Zakes Mokae and Danny Glover starred in the Broadway production in May 1982. After a brief period in which it was banned, the play was produced in Johannesburg, South Africa, in March 1983 with a South African cast. Joseph Lelyveld, in the *New York Times*, said of that production, "Athol Fugard's confessional drama about a white adolescent's initiation in the uses of racial power has come home to South Africa, and it left its multiracial audience . . . visibly shaken and stunned. . . . Many, blacks and whites, were crying."

The play was televised in 1984 with Matthew Broderick as Hally. It has been revived several times: in 1985 by the Trinity Repertory Company in Providence, in 1986 by the Boston Shakespeare Company, and in 1987 at the American Stage Festival in Milford, New Hampshire. These productions, although without Fugard's direction and without a "star" cast, had the same effect on their audiences as the major productions in New York and Johannesburg. Clifford Gallo in the *Boston Globe* called the American Stage Festival production "a devastating look at the loss of racial innocence in a nation where political and social inequality are the norm." Danny Glover revived the play in June 2003 in New York's Royale Theatre. This time he played Sam, whereas twenty years before he had played Willie. In the 2010 production at the TimeLine Theatre in Chicago, the play was presented together with *The Island* and *Sizwe Banzi Is Dead,* directed by O. J. Parson. The Dayton Playhouse in Cincinnati produced "*MASTER HAROLD*" in November 2011. Its production by the Palm Beach Dramaworks in April 2012 indicates that the durability of this play is remarkable, and its appearance on regional stages here and abroad makes us aware that its message is universal.

ATHOL FUGARD (b. 1932)

"Master Harold" . . . and the boys   1982

Characters

WILLIE

SAM

HALLY

The St. George's Park Tea Room on a wet and windy Port Elizabeth afternoon.

Tables and chairs have been cleared and are stacked on one side except for one which stands apart with a single chair. On this table a knife, fork, spoon and side plate in anticipation of a simple meal, together with a pile of comic books.

Other elements: a serving counter with a few stale cakes under glass and a not very impressive display of sweets, cigarettes and cool drinks, etc.; a few cardboard advertising handouts — Cadbury's Chocolate, Coca-Cola — and a blackboard on which an untrained hand has chalked up the prices of Tea, Coffee, Scones, Milkshakes — all flavors — and Cool Drinks; a few sad ferns in pots; a telephone; an old-style jukebox.

There is an entrance on one side and an exit into a kitchen on the other.

Leaning on the solitary table, his head cupped in one hand as he pages through one of the comic books, is Sam. A black man in his mid-forties. He wears the white coat of a waiter. Behind him on his knees, mopping down the floor with a bucket of water and a rag, is Willie. Also black and about the same age as Sam. He has his sleeves and trousers rolled up.

The year: 1950.

WILLIE (*singing as he works*): "She was scandalizin'
    my name,
She took my money
She called me honey
But she was scandalizin' my name.
Called it love but was playin' a game. . . . "

(*He gets up and moves the bucket. Stands thinking for a moment, then, raising his arms to hold an imaginary partner, he launches into an intricate ballroom dance step. Although a mildly comic figure, he reveals a reasonable degree of accomplishment.*)

Hey, Sam.

(*Sam, absorbed in the comic book, does not respond.*)

Hey, Boet° Sam!

(*Sam looks up.*)

Boet: Brother.

I'm getting it. The quickstep. Look now and tell me. (*He repeats the step.*) Well?

SAM (*encouragingly*): Show me again.

WILLIE: Okay, count for me.

SAM: Ready?

WILLIE: Ready.

SAM: Five, six, seven, eight. . . . (*Willie starts to dance.*) A-n-d one two three four . . . and one two three four. . . . (*Ad libbing as Willie dances.*) Your shoulders, Willie . . . your shoulders! Don't look down! Look happy, Willie! Relax, Willie!

WILLIE (*desperate but still dancing*): I am relax.

SAM: No, you're not.

WILLIE (*he falters*): Ag no man, Sam! Mustn't talk. You make me make mistakes.

SAM: But you're stiff.

WILLIE: Yesterday I'm not straight . . . today I'm too stiff!

SAM: Well, you are. You asked me and I'm telling you.

WILLIE: Where?

SAM: Everywhere. Try to glide through it.

WILLIE: Glide?

SAM: Ja, make it smooth. And give it more style. It must look like you're enjoying yourself.

WILLIE (*emphatically*): I wasn't.

SAM: Exactly.

WILLIE: How can I enjoy myself? Not straight, too stiff and now it's also glide, give it more style, make it smooth. . . . Haai! Is hard to remember all those things, Boet Sam.

SAM: That's your trouble. You're trying too hard.

WILLIE: I try hard because it *is* hard.

SAM: But don't let me see it. The secret is to make it look easy. Ballroom must look happy, Willie, not like hard work. It must. . . . Ja! . . . it must look like romance.

WILLIE: Now another one! What's romance?

SAM: Love story with happy ending. A handsome man in tails, and in his arms, smiling at him, a beautiful lady in evening dress!

WILLIE: Fred Astaire, Ginger Rogers.

SAM: You got it. Tapdance or ballroom, it's the same. Romance. In two weeks' time when the judges look at you and Hilda, they must see a man and a woman who are dancing their way to a happy ending. What I saw was you holding her like you were frightened she was going to run away.

WILLIE: Ja! Because that is what she wants to do! I got no romance left for Hilda anymore, Boet Sam.

SAM: Then pretend. When you put your arms around Hilda, imagine she is Ginger Rogers.

WILLIE: With no teeth? You try.

SAM: Well, just remember, there's only two weeks left.

WILLIE: I know, I know! (*To the jukebox.*) I do it better with music. You got sixpence for Sarah Vaughan?

SAM: That's a slow foxtrot. You're practicing the quickstep.

WILLIE: I'll practice slow foxtrot.

SAM (*shaking his head*): It's your turn to put money in the jukebox.

WILLIE: I only got bus fare to go home. (*He returns disconsolately to his work.*) Love story and happy ending! She's doing it all right, Boet Sam, but is not me she's giving happy endings. Fuckin' whore! Three nights now she doesn't come practice. I wind up gramophone, I get record ready and I sit and wait. What happens? Nothing. Ten o'clock I start dancing with my pillow. You try and practice romance by yourself, Boet Sam. Struesgod, she doesn't come tonight I take back my dress and ballroom shoes and I find me new partner. Size twenty-six. Shoes size seven. And now she's also making trouble for me with the baby again. Reports me to Child Wellfed, that I'm not giving her money. She lies! Every week I am giving her money for milk. And how do I know is my baby? Only his hair looks like me. She's fucking around all the time I turn my back. Hilda Samuels is a bitch! (*Pause.*) Hey, Sam!

SAM: Ja.

WILLIE: You listening?

SAM: Ja.

WILLIE: So what you say?

SAM: About Hilda?

WILLIE: Ja.

SAM: When did you last give her a hiding?

WILLIE (*reluctantly*): Sunday night.

SAM: And today is Thursday.

WILLIE (*he knows what's coming*): Okay.

SAM: Hiding on Sunday night, then Monday, Tuesday, and Wednesday she doesn't come to practice . . . and you are asking me why?

WILLIE: I said okay, Boet Sam!

SAM: You hit her too much. One day she's going to leave you for good.

WILLIE: So? She makes me the hell-in too much.

SAM (*emphasizing his point*): *Too* much and *too* hard. You had the same trouble with Eunice.

WILLIE: Because she also make the hell-in, Boet Sam. She never got the steps right. Even the waltz.

SAM: Beating her up every time she makes a mistake in the waltz? (*Shaking his head.*) No, Willie! That takes the pleasure out of ballroom dancing.

WILLIE: Hilda is not too bad with the waltz, Boet Sam. Is the quickstep where the trouble starts.

SAM (*teasing him gently*): How's your pillow with the quickstep?

WILLIE (*ignoring the tease*): Good! And why? Because it got no legs. That's her trouble. She can't move them quick enough, Boet Sam. I start the record and before halfway Count Basie is already winning. Only time we catch up with him is when gramophone runs down. (*Sam laughs.*) Haaikona, Boet Sam, is not funny.

SAM (*snapping his fingers*): I got it! Give her a handicap.

WILLIE: What's that?

SAM: Give her a ten-second start and then let Count Basie go. Then I put my money on her. Hot favorite in the Ballroom Stakes: Hilda Samuels ridden by Willie Malopo.

WILLIE (*turning away*): I'm not talking to you no more.

SAM (*relenting*): Sorry, Willie. . . .

WILLIE: It's finish between us.

SAM: Okay, okay . . . I'll stop.

WILLIE: You can also fuck off.

SAM: Willie, listen! I want to help you!

WILLIE: No more jokes?

SAM: I promise.

WILLIE: Okay. Help me.

SAM (*his turn to hold an imaginary partner*): Look and learn. Feet together. Back straight. Body relaxed. Right hand placed gently in the small of her back and wait for the music. Don't start worrying about making mistakes or the judges or the other competitors. It's just you, Hilda and the music, and you're going to have a good time. What Count Basie do you play?

WILLIE: "You the cream in my coffee, you the salt in my stew."

SAM: Right. Give it to me in strict tempo.

WILLIE: Ready?

SAM: Ready.

WILLIE: A-n-d . . . (*Singing.*)

"You the cream in my coffee.
You the salt in my stew.
You will always be my necessity.
I'd be lost without you. . . ." (*etc.*)

(*Sam launches into the quickstep. He is obviously a much more accomplished dancer than Willie. Hally enters. A seventeen-year-old white boy. Wet raincoat and school case. He stops and watches Sam. The demonstration comes to an end with a flourish. Applause from Hally and Willie.*)

HALLY: Bravo! No question about it. First place goes to Mr. Sam Semela.

WILLIE (*in total agreement*): You was gliding with style, Boet Sam.

HALLY (*cheerfully*): How's it, chaps?

SAM: Okay, Hally.

WILLIE (*springing to attention like a soldier and saluting*): At your service, Master Harold!

HALLY: Not long to the big event, hey!

SAM: Two weeks.

HALLY: You nervous?

SAM: No.

HALLY: Think you stand a chance?

SAM: Let's just say I'm ready to go out there and dance.

HALLY: It looked like it. What about you, Willie?

(*Willie groans.*)

What's the matter?

SAM: He's got leg trouble.

HALLY (*innocently*): Oh, sorry to hear that, Willie.

WILLIE: Boet Sam! You promised. (*Willie returns to his work.*)

(*Hally deposits his school case and takes off his raincoat. His clothes are a little neglected and untidy: black blazer with school badge, gray flannel trousers in need of an ironing, khaki shirt and tie, black shoes. Sam has fetched a towel for Hally to dry his hair.*)

HALLY: God, what a lousy bloody day. It's coming down cats and dogs out there. Bad for business, chaps. . . . (*Conspiratorial whisper.*) . . . but it also means we're in for a nice quiet afternoon.

SAM: You can speak loud. Your Mom's not here.

HALLY: Out shopping?

SAM: No. The hospital.

HALLY: But it's Thursday. There's no visiting on Thursday afternoons. Is my Dad okay?

SAM: Sounds like it. In fact, I think he's going home.

HALLY (*stopped short by Sam's remark*): What do you mean?

SAM: The hospital phoned.

HALLY: To say what?

SAM: I don't know. I just heard your Mom talking.

HALLY: So what makes you say he's going home?

SAM: It sounded as if they were telling her to come and fetch him.

(*Hally thinks about what Sam has said for a few seconds.*)

HALLY: When did she leave?

SAM: About an hour ago. She said she would phone you. Want to eat?

(*Hally doesn't respond.*)

Hally, want your lunch?

HALLY: I suppose so. (*His mood has changed.*) What's on the menu? . . . as if I don't know.

SAM: Soup, followed by meat pie and gravy.

HALLY: Today's?

SAM: No.

HALLY: And the soup?

SAM: Nourishing pea soup.

HALLY: Just the soup. (*The pile of comic books on the table.*) And these?

National Theatre of London's 1983 production of *"MASTER HAROLD"* . . . *and the boys* with (from left to right) Ramolao Makhene as Willie, Duart Sylwain as Hally, and John Kani as Sam.

SAM: For your Dad. Mr. Kempston brought them.

HALLY: You haven't been reading them, have you?

SAM: Just looking.

HALLY (*examining the comics*): Jungle Jim . . . Batman and Robin . . . Tarzan . . . God, what rubbish! Mental pollution. Take them away.

(*Sam exits waltzing into the kitchen. Hally turns to Willie.*)

HALLY: Did you hear my Mom talking on the telephone, Willie?

WILLIE: No, Master Hally. I was at the back.

HALLY: And she didn't say anything to you before she left?

WILLIE: She said I must clean the floors.

HALLY: I mean about my Dad.

WILLIE: She didn't say nothing to me about him, Master Hally.

HALLY (*with conviction*): No! It can't be. They said he needed at least another three weeks of treatment. Sam's definitely made a mistake. (*Rummages through his school case, finds a book and settles down at the table to read.*) So, Willie!

WILLIE: Yes, Master Hally! Schooling okay today?

HALLY: Yes, okay. . . . (*He thinks about it.*) . . . No, not really. Ag, what's the difference? I don't care. And Sam says you've got problems.

WILLIE: Big problems.

HALLY: Which leg is sore?

(*Willie groans.*)

Both legs.

WILLIE: There is nothing wrong with my legs. Sam is just making jokes.

HALLY: So then you *will* be in the competition.

WILLIE: Only if I can find a partner.

HALLY: But what about Hilda?

SAM (*returning with a bowl of soup*): She's the one who's got trouble with her legs.

HALLY: What sort of trouble, Willie?

SAM: From the way he describes it, I think the lady has gone a bit lame.

HALLY: Good God! Have you taken her to see a doctor?

SAM: I think a vet would be better.

HALLY: What do you mean?

SAM: What do you call it again when a racehorse goes very fast?

HALLY: Gallop?

SAM: That's it!

WILLIE: Boet Sam!

HALLY: "A gallop down the homestretch to the winning post." But what's that got to do with Hilda?

SAM: Count Basie always gets there first.

(*Willie lets fly with his slop rag. It misses Sam and hits Hally.*)

HALLY (*furious*): For Christ's sake, Willie! What the hell do you think you're doing?

WILLIE: Sorry, Master Hally, but it's him. . . .

HALLY: Act your bloody age! (*Hurls the rag back at Willie.*) Cut out the nonsense now and get on with your work. And you too, Sam. Stop fooling around.

(*Sam moves away.*)

No. Hang on. I haven't finished! Tell me exactly what my Mom said.

SAM: I have. "When Hally comes, tell him I've gone to the hospital and I'll phone him."

HALLY: She didn't say anything about taking my Dad home?

SAM: No. It's just that when she was talking on the phone. . . .

HALLY (*interrupting him*): No, Sam. They can't be discharging him. She would have said so if they were. In any case, we saw him last night and he wasn't in good shape at all. Staff nurse even said there was talk about taking more X-rays. And now suddenly today he's better? If anything, it sounds more like a bad turn to me . . . which I sincerely hope it isn't. Hang on . . . how long ago did you say she left?

SAM: Just before two . . . (*His wrist watch.*) . . . hour and a half.

HALLY: I know how to settle it. (*Behind the counter to the telephone. Talking as he dials.*) Let's give her ten minutes to get to the hospital, ten minutes to load him up, another ten, at the most, to get home, and another ten to get him inside. Forty minutes. They should have been home for at least half an hour already. (*Pause—he waits with the receiver to his ear.*) No reply, chaps. And you know why? Because she's at his bedside in hospital helping him pull through a bad turn. You definitely heard wrong.

SAM: Okay.

(*As far as Hally is concerned, the matter is settled. He returns to his table, sits down, and divides his attention between the book and his soup. Sam is at his school case and picks up a textbook.*)

Modern Graded Mathematics for Standards Nine and Ten. (*Opens it at random and laughs at something he sees.*) Who is this supposed to be?

HALLY: Old fart-face Prentice.

SAM: Teacher?

HALLY: Thinks he is. And believe me, that is not a bad likeness.

SAM: Has he seen it?

HALLY: Yes.

SAM: What did he say?

HALLY: Tried to be clever, as usual. Said I was no Leonardo da Vinci and that bad art had to be punished. So, six of the best, and his are bloody good.

SAM: On your bum?

HALLY: Where else? The days when I got them on my hands are gone forever, Sam.

SAM: With your trousers down!

HALLY: No. He's not quite that barbaric.

SAM: That's the way they do it in jail.

HALLY (*flicker of morbid interest*): Really?

164 SAM: Ja. When the magistrate sentences you to "strokes with a light cane."

165 HALLY: Go on.

166 SAM: They make you lie down on a bench. One policeman pulls down your trousers and holds your ankles, another one pulls your shirt over your head and holds your arms . . .

167 HALLY: Thank you! That's enough.

168 SAM: . . . and the one that gives you the strokes talks to you gently and for a long time between each one. (*He laughs.*)

169 HALLY: I've heard enough, Sam! Jesus! It's a bloody awful world when you come to think of it. People can be real bastards.

170 SAM: That's the way it is, Hally.

171 HALLY: It doesn't *have* to be that way. There is something called progress, you know. We don't exactly burn people at the stake anymore.

172 SAM: Like Joan of Arc.

173 HALLY: Correct. If she was captured today, she'd be given a fair trial.

174 SAM: And then the death sentence.

175 HALLY (*a world-weary sigh*): I know, I know! I oscillate between hope and despair for this world as well, Sam. But things will change, you wait and see. One day somebody is going to get up and give history a kick up the backside and get it going again.

176 SAM: Like who?

177 HALLY (*after thought*): They're called social reformers. Every age, Sam, has got its social reformer. My history book is full of them.

178 SAM: So where's ours?

179 HALLY: Good question. And I hate to say it, but the answer is: I don't know. Maybe he hasn't even been born yet. Or is still only a babe in arms at his mother's breast. God, what a thought.

180 SAM: So we just go on waiting.

181 HALLY: Ja, looks like it. (*Back to his soup and the book.*)

182 SAM (*reading from the textbook*): "Introduction: In some mathematical problems only the magnitude . . ." (*He mispronounces the word "magnitude."*)

183 HALLY (*correcting him without looking up*): Magnitude.

184 SAM: What's it mean?

185 HALLY: How big it is. The size of the thing.

186 SAM (*reading*): " . . . magnitude of the quantities is of importance. In other problems we need to know whether these quantities are negative or positive. For example, whether there is a debit or credit bank balance . . ."

187 HALLY: Whether you're broke or not.

188 SAM: " . . . whether the temperature is above or below Zero. . . ."

189 HALLY: Naught degrees. Cheerful state of affairs! No cash and you're freezing to death. Mathematics won't get you out of that one.

190 SAM: "All these quantities are called . . ." (*spelling the word*): . . . s-c-a-l . . .

191 HALLY: Scalars.

192 SAM: Scalars! (*Shaking his head with a laugh.*) You understand all that?

193 HALLY (*turning a page*): No. And I don't intend to try.

194 SAM: So what happens when the exams come?

195 HALLY: Failing a maths exam isn't the end of the world, Sam. How many times have I told you that examination results don't measure intelligence?

196 SAM: I would say about as many times as you've failed one of them.

197 HALLY (*mirthlessly*): Ha, ha, ha.

198 SAM (*simultaneously*): Ha, ha, ha.

199 HALLY: Just remember Winston Churchill didn't do particularly well at school.

200 SAM: You've also told me that one many times.

201 HALLY: Well, it just so happens to be the truth.

202 SAM (*enjoying the word*): Magnitude! Magnitude! Show me how to use it.

203 HALLY (*after thought*): An intrepid social reformer will not be daunted by the magnitude of the task he has undertaken.

204 SAM (*impressed*): Couple of jaw-breakers in there!

205 HALLY: I gave you three for the price of one. Intrepid, daunted, and magnitude. I did that once in an exam. Put five of the words I had to explain in one sentence. It was half a page long.

206 SAM: Well, I'll put my money on you in the English exam.

207 HALLY: Piece of cake. Eighty percent without even trying.

208 SAM (*another textbook from Hally's case*): And history?

209 HALLY: So-so. I'll scrape through. In the fifties if I'm lucky.

210 SAM: You didn't do too badly last year.

211 HALLY: Because we had World War One. That at least has some action. You try to find that in the South African Parliamentary system.

212 SAM (*reading from the history textbook*): "Napoleon and the principle of equality." Hey! This sounds interesting. "After concluding peace with Britain in 1802, Napoleon used a brief period of calm to in-sti-tute . . ."

213 HALLY: Introduce.

214 SAM: " . . . many reforms. Napoleon regarded all people as equal before the law and wanted them to have equal opportunities for advancement. All ves-ti-ges of the feu-dal sys-tem with its oppression of the poor were abol-ished." Vestiges, feudal system, and abolished. I'm all right on oppression.

215 HALLY: I'm thinking. He swept away . . . abol-ished . . . the last remains . . . vestiges . . . of the bad old days . . . feudal system.

216 SAM: Ha! There's the social reformer we're waiting for. He sounds like a man of some magnitude.

217 HALLY: I'm not so sure about that. It's a damn good title for a book, though. A man of magnitude!

218 SAM: He sounds pretty big to me, Hally.

219 HALLY: Don't confuse historical significance with greatness. But maybe I'm being a bit prejudiced. Have a look in there and you'll see he's two chapters long. And hell! . . . has he only got dates, Sam, all of which you've got to remember! This campaign and that

campaign, and then, because of all the fighting, the next thing is we get Peace Treaties all over the place. And what's the end of the story? Battle of Waterloo, which he loses. Wasn't worth it. No, I don't know about him as a man of magnitude.

220 SAM: Then who would you say was?

221 HALLY: To answer that, we need a definition of greatness, and I suppose that would be somebody who . . . somebody who benefited all mankind.

222 SAM: Right. But like who?

223 HALLY (*he speaks with total conviction*): Charles Darwin. Remember him? That big book from the library. *The Origin of the Species.*

224 SAM: Him?

225 HALLY: Yes. For his Theory of Evolution.

226 SAM: You didn't finish it.

227 HALLY: I ran out of time. I didn't finish it because my two weeks was up. But I'm going to take it out again after I've digested what I read. It's safe. I've hidden it away in the Theology section. Nobody ever goes in there. And anyway who are you to talk? You hardly even looked at it.

228 SAM: I tried. I looked at the chapters in the beginning and I saw one called "The Struggle for an Existence." Ah ha, I thought. At last! But what did I get? Something called the mistletoe which needs the apple tree and there's too many seeds and all are going to die except one . . . ! No, Hally.

229 HALLY (*intellectually outraged*): What do you mean, No! The poor man had to start somewhere. For God's sake, Sam, he revolutionized science. Now we know.

230 SAM: What?

231 HALLY: Where we come from and what it all means.

232 SAM: And that's a benefit to mankind? Anyway, I still don't believe it.

233 HALLY: God, you're impossible. I showed it to you in black and white.

234 SAM: Doesn't mean I got to believe it.

235 HALLY: It's the likes of you that kept the Inquisition in business. It's called bigotry. Anyway, that's my man of magnitude. Charles Darwin! Who's yours?

236 SAM (*without hesitation*): Abraham Lincoln.

237 HALLY: I might have guessed as much. Don't get sentimental, Sam. You've never been a slave, you know. And anyway we freed your ancestors here in South Africa long before the Americans. But if you want to thank somebody on their behalf, do it to Mr. William Wilberforce.° Come on. Try again. I want a real genius.

(*Now enjoying himself, and so is Sam. Hally goes behind the counter and helps himself to a chocolate.*)

238 SAM: William Shakespeare.

239 HALLY (*no enthusiasm*): Oh. So you're also one of them, are you? You're basing that opinion on only one play,

Mr. William Wilberforce: British statesman (1759–1833) who supported a bill outlawing the slave trade and suppressing slavery in the British Empire.

you know. You've only read my *Julius Caesar* and even I don't understand half of what they're talking about. They should do what they did with the old Bible: bring the language up to date.

240 SAM: That's all you've got. It's also the only one *you've* read.

241 HALLY: I know. I admit it. That's why I suggest we reserve our judgment until we've checked up on a few others. I've got a feeling, though, that by the end of this year one is going to be enough for me, and I can give you the names of twenty-nine other chaps in the Standard Nine class of the Port Elizabeth Technical College who feel the same. But if you want him, you can have him. My turn now. (*Pacing.*) This is a damned good exercise, you know! It started off looking like a simple question and here it's got us really probing into the intellectual heritage of our civilization.

242 SAM: So who is it going to be?

243 HALLY: My next man . . . and he gets the title on two scores: social reform and literary genius . . . is Leo Nikolaevich Tolstoy.

244 SAM: That Russian.

245 HALLY: Correct. Remember the picture of him I showed you?

246 SAM: With the long beard.

247 HALLY (*trying to look like Tolstoy*): And those burning, visionary eyes. My God, the face of a social prophet if ever I saw one! And remember my words when I showed it to you? Here's a *man*, Sam!

248 SAM: Those were words, Hally.

249 HALLY: Not many intellectuals are prepared to shovel manure with the peasants and then go home and write a "little book" called *War and Peace.* Incidentally, Sam, he was somebody else who, to quote, " . . . did not distinguish himself scholastically."

250 SAM: Meaning?

251 HALLY: He was also no good at school.

252 SAM: Like you and Winston Churchill.

253 HALLY (*mirthlessly*): Ha, ha, ha.

254 SAM (*simultaneously*): Ha, ha, ha.

255 HALLY: Don't get clever, Sam. That man freed his serfs of his own free will.

256 SAM: No argument. He was a somebody, all right. I accept him.

257 HALLY: I'm sure Count Tolstoy will be very pleased to hear that. Your turn. Shoot. (*Another chocolate from behind the counter.*) I'm waiting, Sam.

258 SAM: I've got him.

259 HALLY: Good. Submit your candidate for examination.

260 SAM: Jesus.

261 HALLY (*stopped dead in his tracks*): Who?

262 SAM: Jesus Christ.

263 HALLY: Oh, come on, Sam!

264 SAM: The Messiah.

265 HALLY: Ja, but still . . . No, Sam. Don't let's get started on religion. We'll just spend the whole afternoon arguing again. Suppose I turn around and say Mohammed?

266 SAM: All right.

267 HALLY: You can't have them both on the same list!

268 SAM: Why not? You like Mohammed, I like Jesus.

269 HALLY: I *don't* like Mohammed. I never have. I was merely being hypothetical. As far as I'm concerned, the Koran is as bad as the Bible. No. Religion is out! I'm not going to waste my time again arguing with you about the existence of God. You know perfectly well I'm an atheist . . . and I've got homework to do.

270 SAM: Okay, I take him back.

271 HALLY: You've got time for one more name.

272 SAM (*after thought*): I've got one I know we'll agree on. A simple straightforward great Man of Magnitude . . . and no arguments. And *he* really *did* benefit all mankind.

273 HALLY: I wonder. After your last contribution I'm beginning to doubt whether anything in the way of an intellectual agreement is possible between the two of us. Who is he?

274 SAM: Guess.

275 HALLY: Socrates? Alexandre Dumas? Karl Marx? Dostoevsky? Nietzsche?

(*Sam shakes his head after each name.*)

Give me a clue.

276 SAM: The letter *P* is important . . .

277 HALLY: Plato!

278 SAM: . . . and his name begins with an *F*.

279 HALLY: I've got it. Freud and Psychology.

280 SAM: No. I didn't understand him.

281 HALLY: That makes two of us.

282 SAM: Think of moldy apricot jam.

283 HALLY (*after a delighted laugh*): Penicillin and Sir Alexander Fleming! And the title of the book: *The Microbe Hunters*. (*Delighted.*) Splendid, Sam! Splendid. For once we are in total agreement. The major breakthrough in medical science in the Twentieth Century. If it wasn't for him, we might have lost the Second World War. It's deeply gratifying, Sam, to know that I haven't been wasting my time in talking to you. (*Strutting around proudly.*) Tolstoy may have educated his peasants, but I've educated you.

284 SAM: Standard Four to Standard Nine.

285 HALLY: Have we been at it as long as that?

286 SAM: Yep. And my first lesson was geography.

287 HALLY (*intrigued*): Really? I don't remember.

288 SAM: My room there at the back of the old Jubilee Boarding House. I had just started working for your Mom. Little boy in short trousers walks in one afternoon and asks me seriously: "Sam, do you want to see South Africa?" Hey man! Sure I wanted to see South Africa!

289 HALLY: Was that me?

290 SAM: . . . So the next thing I'm looking at a map you had just done for homework. It was your first one and you were very proud of yourself.

291 HALLY: Go on.

292 SAM: Then came my first lesson. "Repeat after me, Sam: Gold in the Transvaal, mealies in the Free State, sugar in Natal, and grapes in the Cape." I still know it!

293 HALLY: Well, I'll be buggered. So that's how it all started.

294 SAM: And your next map was one with all the rivers and the mountains they came from. The Orange, the Vaal, the Limpopo, the Zambezi. . . .

295 HALLY: You've got a phenomenal memory!

296 SAM: You should be grateful. That is why you started passing your exams. You tried to be better than me.

(*They laugh together. Willie is attracted by the laughter and joins them.*)

297 HALLY: The old Jubilee Boarding House. Sixteen rooms with board and lodging, rent in advance and one week's notice. I haven't thought about it for donkey's years . . . and I don't think that's an accident. God, was I glad when we sold it and moved out. Those years are not remembered as the happiest ones of an unhappy childhood.

298 WILLIE (*knocking on the table and trying to imitate a woman's voice*): "Hally, are you there?"

299 HALLY: Who's that supposed to be?

300 WILLIE: "What you doing in there, Hally? Come out at once!"

301 HALLY (*to Sam*): What's he talking about?

302 SAM: Don't you remember?

303 WILLIE: "Sam, Willie . . . is he in there with you boys?"

304 SAM: Hiding away in our room when your mother was looking for you.

305 HALLY (*another good laugh*): Of course! I used to crawl and hide under your bed! But finish the story, Willie. Then what used to happen? You chaps would give the game away by telling her I was in there with you. So much for friendship.

306 SAM: We couldn't lie to her. She knew.

307 HALLY: Which meant I got another rowing for hanging around the "servants' quarters." I think I spent more time in there with you chaps than anywhere else in that dump. And do you blame me? Nothing but bloody misery wherever you went. Somebody was always complaining about the food, or my mother was having a fight with Micky Nash because she'd caught her with a petty officer in her room. Maud Meiring was another one. Remember those two? They were prostitutes, you know. Soldiers and sailors from the troopships. Bottom fell out of the business when the war ended. God, the flotsam and jetsam that life washed up on our shores! No joking, if it wasn't for your room, I would have been the first certified ten-year-old in medical history. Ja, the memories are coming back now. Walking home from school and thinking: "What can I do this afternoon?" Try out a few ideas, but sooner or later I'd end up in there with you fellows. I bet you I could still find my way to your room with my eyes closed. (*He does exactly that.*) Down the corridor . . . telephone on the right, which my Mom keeps locked because somebody is using it on the sly and not paying . . . past the kitchen and unappetizing cooking smells . . . around the corner into the backyard, hold

my breath again because there are more smells coming when I pass your lavatory, then into that little passageway, first door on the right and into your room. How's that?

SAM: Good. But, as usual, you forgot to knock.

HALLY: Like that time I barged in and caught you and Cynthia . . . at it. Remember? God, was I embarrassed! I didn't know what was going on at first.

SAM: Ja, that taught you a lesson.

HALLY: And about a lot more than knocking on doors, I'll have you know, and I don't mean geography either. Hell, Sam, couldn't you have waited until it was dark?

SAM: No.

HALLY: Was it that urgent?

SAM: Yes, and if you don't believe me, wait until your time comes.

HALLY: No, thank you. I am not interested in girls. (*Back to his memories. . . . Using a few chairs he re-creates the room as he lists the items.*) A gray little room with a cold cement floor. Your bed against that wall . . . and I now know why the mattress sags so much! . . . Willie's bed . . . it's propped up on bricks because one leg is broken . . . that wobbly little table with the washbasin and jug of water . . . Yes! . . . stuck to the wall above it are some pin-up pictures from magazines. Joe Louis . . . .

WILLIE: Brown Bomber. World Title. (*Boxing pose.*) Three rounds and knockout.

HALLY: Against who?

SAM: Max Schmeling.

HALLY: Correct. I can also remember Fred Astaire and Ginger Rogers, and Rita Hayworth in a bathing costume which always made me hot and bothered when I looked at it. Under Willie's bed is an old suitcase with all his clothes in a mess, which is why I never hide there. Your things are neat and tidy in a trunk next to your bed, and on it there is a picture of you and Cynthia in your ballroom clothes, your first silver cup for third place in a competition and an old radio which doesn't work anymore. Have I left out anything?

SAM: No.

HALLY: Right, so much for the stage directions. Now the characters. (*Sam and Willie move to their appropriate positions in the bedroom.*) Willie is in bed, under his blankets with his clothes on, complaining nonstop about something, but we can't make out a word of what he's saying because he's got his head under the blankets as well. You're on your bed trimming your toenails with a knife—not a very edifying sight—and as for me . . . . What am I doing?

SAM: You're sitting on the floor giving Willie a lecture about being a good loser while you get the checkerboard and pieces ready for a game. Then you go to Willie's bed, pull off the blankets and make him play with you first because you know you're going to win, and that gives you the second game with me.

HALLY: And you certainly were a bad loser, Willie!

WILLIE: Haai!

HALLY: Wasn't he, Sam? And so slow! A game with you almost took the whole afternoon. Thank God I gave up trying to teach you how to play chess.

WILLIE: You and Sam cheated.

HALLY: I never saw Sam cheat, and mine were mostly the mistakes of youth.

WILLIE: Then how is it you two was always winning?

HALLY: Have you ever considered the possibility, Willie, that it was because we were better than you?

WILLIE: Every time better?

HALLY: Not every time. There were occasions when we deliberately let you win a game so that you would stop sulking and go on playing with us. Sam used to wink at me when you weren't looking to show me it was time to let you win.

WILLIE: So then you two didn't play fair.

HALLY: It was for your benefit, Mr. Malopo, which is more than being fair. It was an act of self-sacrifice. (*To Sam.*) But you know what my best memory is, don't you?

SAM: No.

HALLY: Come on, guess. If your memory is so good, you must remember it as well.

SAM: We got up to a lot of tricks in there, Hally.

HALLY: This one was special, Sam.

SAM: I'm listening.

HALLY: It started off looking like another of those useless nothing-to-do afternoons. I'd already been down to Main Street looking for adventure, but nothing had happened. I didn't feel like climbing trees in the Donkin Park or pretending I was a private eye and following a stranger . . . so as usual: See what's cooking in Sam's room. This time it was you on the floor. You had two thin pieces of wood and you were smoothing them down with a knife. It didn't look particularly interesting, but when I asked you what you were doing, you just said, "Wait and see, Hally. Wait . . . and see" . . . in that secret sort of way of yours, so I knew there was a surprise coming. You teased me, you bugger, by being deliberately slow and not answering my questions!

(*Sam laughs.*)

And whistling while you worked away! God, it was infuriating! I could have brained you! It was only when you tied them together in a cross and put that down on the brown paper that I realized what you were doing. "Sam is making a kite?" And when I asked you and you said, "Yes" . . . ! (*Shaking his head with disbelief.*) The sheer audacity of it took my breath away. I mean, seriously, what the hell does a black man know about flying a kite? I'll be honest with you, Sam, I had no hopes for it. If you think I was excited and happy, you got another guess coming. In fact, I was shit-scared that we were going to make fools of ourselves. When we left the boarding house to go up onto the hill, I was praying quietly that there wouldn't be any other kids around to laugh at us.

340 SAM (*enjoying the memory as much as Hally*): Ja, I could see that.

341 HALLY: I made it obvious, did I?

342 SAM: Ja. You refused to carry it.

343 HALLY: Do you blame me? Can you remember what the poor thing looked like? Tomato-box wood and brown paper! Flour and water for glue! Two of my mother's old stockings for a tail, and then all those bits and pieces of string you made me tie together so that we could fly it! Hell, no, that was now only asking for a miracle to happen.

344 SAM: Then the big argument when I told you to hold the string and run with it when I let go.

345 HALLY: I was prepared to run, all right, but straight back to the boarding house.

346 SAM (*knowing what's coming*): So what happened?

347 HALLY: Come on, Sam, you remember as well as I do.

348 SAM: I want to hear it from you.

(*Hally pauses. He wants to be as accurate as possible.*)

349 HALLY: You went a little distance from me down the hill, you held it up ready to let it go. . . . "This is it," I thought. "Like everything else in my life, here comes another fiasco." Then you shouted, "Go, Hally!" and I started to run. (*Another pause.*) I don't know how to describe it, Sam. Ja! The miracle happened! I was running, waiting for it to crash to the ground, but instead suddenly there was something alive behind me at the end of the string, tugging at it as if it wanted to be free. I looked back . . . (*Shakes his head.*) . . . I still can't believe my eyes. It was flying! Looping around and trying to climb even higher into the sky. You shouted to me to let it have more string. I did, until there was none left and I was just holding that piece of wood we had tied it to. You came up and joined me. You were laughing.

350 SAM: So were you. And shouting, "It works, Sam! We've done it!"

351 HALLY: And we had! I was so proud of us! It was the most splendid thing I had ever seen. I wished there were hundreds of kids around to watch us. The part that scared me, though, was when you showed me how to make it dive down to the ground and then just when it was on the point of crashing, swoop up again!

352 SAM: You didn't want to try yourself.

353 HALLY: Of course not! I would have been suicidal if anything had happened to it. Watching you do it made me nervous enough. I was quite happy just to see it up there with its tail fluttering behind it. You left me after that, didn't you? You explained how to get it down, we tied it to the bench so that I could sit and watch it, and you went away. I wanted you to stay, you know. I was a little scared of having to look after it by myself.

354 SAM (*quietly*): I had work to do, Hally.

355 HALLY: It was sort of sad bringing it down, Sam. And it looked sad again when it was lying there on the ground. Like something that had lost its soul. Just tomato-box wood, brown paper and two of my mother's old stockings! But, hell, I'll never forget that first moment when I saw it up there. I had a stiff neck the next day from looking up so much.

(*Sam laughs. Hally turns to him with a question he never thought of asking before.*)

Why did you make that kite, Sam?

356 SAM (*evenly*): I can't remember.

357 HALLY: Truly?

358 SAM: Too long ago, Hally.

359 HALLY: Ja, I suppose it was. It's time for another one, you know.

360 SAM: Why do you say that?

361 HALLY: Because it feels like that. Wouldn't be a good day to fly it, though.

362 SAM: No. You can't fly kites on rainy days.

363 HALLY (*He studies Sam. Their memories have made him conscious of the man's presence in his life.*): How old are you, Sam?

364 SAM: Two score and five.

365 HALLY: Strange, isn't it?

366 SAM: What?

367 HALLY: Me and you.

368 SAM: What's strange about it?

369 HALLY: Little white boy in short trousers and a black man old enough to be his father flying a kite. It's not every day you see that.

370 SAM: But why strange? Because the one is white and the other black?

371 HALLY: I don't know. Would have been just as strange, I suppose, if it had been me and my Dad . . . cripple man and a little boy! Nope! There's no chance of me flying a kite without it being strange. (*Simple statement of fact—no self-pity.*) There's a nice little short story there. "The Kite-Flyers." But we'd have to find a twist in the ending.

372 SAM: Twist?

373 HALLY: Yes. Something unexpected. The way it ended with us was too straightforward . . . me on the bench and you going back to work. There's no drama in that.

374 WILLIE: And me?

375 HALLY: You?

376 WILLIE: Yes me.

377 HALLY: You want to get into the story as well, do you? I got it! Change the title: "Afternoons in Sam's Room" . . . expand it and tell all the stories. It's on its way to being a novel. Our days in the old Jubilee. Sad in a way that they're over. I almost wish we were still in that little room.

378 SAM: We're still together.

379 HALLY: That's true. It's just that life felt the right size in there . . . not too big and not too small. Wasn't so hard to work up a bit of courage. It's got so bloody complicated since then.

(The telephone rings. Sam answers it.)

SAM: St. George's Park Tea Room . . . Hello, Madam . . . Yes, Madam, he's here. . . . Hally, it's your mother.

HALLY: Where is she phoning from?

SAM: Sounds like the hospital. It's a public telephone.

HALLY *(relieved)*: You see! I told you. *(The telephone.)* Hello, Mom . . . Yes . . . Yes no fine. Everything's under control here. How's things with poor old Dad? . . . Has he had a bad turn? . . . What? . . . Oh, God! . . . Yes, Sam told me, but I was sure he'd made a mistake. But what's this all about, Mom? He didn't look at all good last night. How can he get better so quickly? . . . Then very obviously you must say no. Be firm with him. You're the boss. . . . You know what it's going to be like if he comes home. . . . Well then, don't blame me when I fail my exams at the end of the year. . . . Yes! How am I expected to be fresh for school when I spend half the night massaging his gammy leg? . . . So am I! . . . So tell him a white lie. Say Dr. Colley wants more X-rays of his stump. Or bribe him. We'll sneak in double tots of brandy in future. . . . What? . . . Order him to get back into bed at once! If he's going to behave like a child, treat him like one. . . . All right, Mom! I was just trying to . . . I'm sorry. . . . I said I'm sorry. . . . Quick, give me your number. I'll phone you back. *(He hangs up and waits a few seconds.)* Here we go again! *(He dials.)* I'm sorry, Mom. . . . Okay. . . . But now listen to me carefully. All it needs is for you to put your foot down. Don't take no for an answer. . . . Did you hear me? And whatever you do, don't discuss it with him. . . . Because I'm frightened you'll give in to him. . . . Yes, Sam gave me lunch. . . . I ate all of it! . . . No, Mom not a soul. It's still raining here. . . . Right, I'll tell them. I'll just do some homework and then lock up. . . . But remember now, Mom. Don't listen to anything he says. And phone me back and let me know what happens. . . . Okay. Bye, Mom. *(He hangs up. The men are staring at him.)* My Mom says that when you're finished with the floors you must do the windows. *(Pause.)* Don't misunderstand me, chaps. All I want is for him to get better. And if he was, I'd be the first person to say: "Bring him home." But he's not, and we can't give him the medical care and attention he needs at home. That's what hospitals are there for. *(Brusquely.)* So don't just stand there! Get on with it!

(Sam clears Hally's table.)

You heard right. My Dad wants to go home.

SAM: Is he better?

HALLY *(sharply)*: No! How the hell can he be better when last night he was groaning with pain? This is not an age of miracles!

SAM: Then he should stay in hospital.

HALLY *(seething with irritation and frustration)*: Tell me something I don't know, Sam. What the hell do you think I was saying to my Mom? All I can say is fuck-it-all.

SAM: I'm sure he'll listen to your Mom.

HALLY: You don't know what she's up against. He's already packed his shaving kit and pajamas and is sitting on his bed with his crutches, dressed and ready to go. I know him when he gets in that mood. If she tries to reason with him, we've had it. She's no match for him when it comes to a battle of words. He'll tie her up in knots. *(Trying to hide his true feelings.)*

SAM: I suppose it gets lonely for him in there.

HALLY: With all the patients and nurses around? Regular visits from the Salvation Army? Balls! It's ten times worse for him at home. I'm at school and my mother is here in the business all day.

SAM: He's at least got you at night.

HALLY *(before he can stop himself)*: And we've got him! Please! I don't want to talk about it anymore. *(Unpacks his school case, slamming down books on the table.)* Life is just a plain bloody mess, that's all. And people are fools.

SAM: Come on, Hally.

HALLY: Yes, they are! They bloody well deserve what they get.

SAM: Then don't complain.

HALLY: Don't try to be clever, Sam. It doesn't suit you. Anybody who thinks there's nothing wrong with this world needs to have his head examined. Just when things are going along all right, without fail someone or something will come along and spoil everything. Somebody should write that down as a fundamental law of the Universe. The principle of perpetual disappointment. If there is a God who created this world, he should scrap it and try again.

SAM: All right, Hally, all right. What you got for homework?

HALLY: Bullshit, as usual. *(Opens an exercise book and reads.)* "Write five hundred words describing an annual event of cultural or historical significance."

SAM: That should be easy enough for you.

HALLY: And also plain bloody boring. You know what he wants, don't you? One of their useless old ceremonies. The commemoration of the landing of the 1820 Settlers, or if it's going to be culture, Carols by Candlelight every Christmas.

SAM: It's an impressive sight. Make a good description, Hally. All those candles glowing in the dark and the people singing hymns.

HALLY: And it's called religious hysteria. *(Intense irritation.)* Please, Sam! Just leave me alone and let me get on with it. I'm not in the mood for games this afternoon. And remember my Mom's orders . . . you're to help Willie with the windows. Come on now, I don't want any more nonsense in here.

SAM: Okay, Hally, okay.

(Hally settles down to his homework; determined preparations . . . pen, ruler, exercise book, dictionary, another cake . . . all of which will lead to nothing.)

(*Sam waltzes over to Willie and starts to replace tables and chairs. He practices a ballroom step while doing so. Willie watches. When Sam is finished, Willie tries.*)

Good! But just a little bit quicker on the turn and only move in to her after she's crossed over. What about this one?

(*Another step. When Sam is finished, Willie again has a go.*)

Much better. See what happens when you just relax and enjoy yourself? Remember that in two weeks' time and you'll be all right.

WILLIE: But I haven't got partner, Boet Sam.

SAM: Maybe Hilda will turn up tonight.

WILLIE: No, Boet Sam. (*Reluctantly.*) I gave her a good hiding.

SAM: You mean a bad one.

WILLIE: Good bad one.

SAM: Then you mustn't complain either. Now you pay the price for losing your temper.

WILLIE: I also pay two pounds ten shilling entrance fee.

SAM: They'll refund you if you withdraw now.

WILLIE (*appalled*): You mean, don't dance?

SAM: Yes.

WILLIE: No! I wait too long and I practice too hard. If I find me new partner, you think I can be ready in two weeks? I ask Madam for my leave now and we practice every day.

SAM: Quickstep nonstop for two weeks. World record, Willie, but you'll be mad at the end.

WILLIE: No jokes, Boet Sam.

SAM: I'm not joking.

WILLIE: So then what?

SAM: Find Hilda. Say you're sorry and promise you won't beat her again.

WILLIE: No.

SAM: Then withdraw. Try again next year.

WILLIE: No.

SAM: Then I give up.

WILLIE: Haaikona, Boet Sam, you can't.

SAM: What do you mean, I can't? I'm telling you: I give up.

WILLIE (*adamant*): No! (*Accusingly.*) It was you who start me ballroom dancing.

SAM: So?

WILLIE: Before that I use to be happy. And is you and Miriam who bring me to Hilda and say here's partner for you.

SAM: What are you saying, Willie?

WILLIE: You!

SAM: But me what? To blame?

WILLIE: Yes.

SAM: Willie . . . ? (*Bursts into laughter.*)

WILLIE: And now all you do is make jokes at me. You wait. When Miriam leaves you is my turn to laugh. Ha! Ha! Ha!

SAM (*he can't take Willie seriously any longer*): She can leave me tonight! I know what to do. (*Bowing before an imaginary partner.*) May I have the pleasure? (*He dances and sings.*)
"Just a fellow with his pillow . . .
Dancin' like a willow . . .
In an autumn breeze. . . . "

WILLIE: There you go again!

(*Sam goes on dancing and singing.*)

Boet Sam!

SAM: There's the answer to your problem! Judges' announcement in two weeks' time: "Ladies and gentlemen, the winner in the open section . . . Mr. Willie Malopo and his pillow!"

(*This is too much for a now really angry Willie. He goes for Sam, but the latter is too quick for him and puts Hally's table between the two of them.*)

HALLY (*exploding*): For Christ's sake, you two!

WILLIE (*still trying to get at Sam*): I donner you, Sam! Struesgod!

SAM (*still laughing*): Sorry, Willie . . . Sorry. . . .

HALLY: Sam! Willie! (*Grabs his ruler and gives Willie a vicious whack on the bum.*) How the hell am I supposed to concentrate with the two of you behaving like bloody children!

WILLIE: Hit him too!

HALLY: Shut up, Willie.

WILLIE: He started jokes again.

HALLY: Get back to your work. You too, Sam. (*His ruler.*) Do you want another one, Willie?

(*Sam and Willie return to their work. Hally uses the opportunity to escape from his unsuccessful attempt at homework. He struts around like a little despot, ruler in hand, giving vent to his anger and frustration.*)

Suppose a customer had walked in then? Or the Park Superintendent. And seen the two of you behaving like a pair of hooligans. That would have been the end of my mother's license, you know. And your jobs? Well, this is the end of it. From now on there will be no more of your ballroom nonsense in here. This is a business establishment, not a bloody New Brighton dancing school. I've been far too lenient with the two of you. (*Behind the counter for a green cool drink and a dollop of ice cream. He keeps up his tirade as he prepares it.*) But what really makes me bitter is that I allow you chaps a little freedom in here when business is bad and what do you do with it? The foxtrot! Specially you, Sam. There's more to life than trotting around a dance floor and I thought at least you knew it.

SAM: It's a harmless pleasure, Hally. It doesn't hurt anybody.

HALLY: It's also a rather simple one, you know.

SAM: You reckon so? Have you ever tried?

HALLY: Of course not.

SAM: Why don't you? Now.

HALLY: What do you mean? Me dance?

453 SAM: Yes. I'll show you a simple step—the waltz—then you try it.

454 HALLY: What will that prove?

455 SAM: That it might not be as easy as you think.

456 HALLY: I didn't say it was easy. I said it was simple—like in simple-minded, meaning mentally retarded. You can't exactly say it challenges the intellect.

457 SAM: It does other things.

458 HALLY: Such as?

459 SAM: Make people happy.

460 HALLY (*the glass in his hand*): So do American cream sodas with ice cream. For God's sake, Sam, you're not asking me to take ballroom dancing serious, are you?

461 SAM: Yes.

462 HALLY (*sigh of defeat*): Oh, well, so much for trying to give you a decent education. I've obviously achieved nothing.

463 SAM: You still haven't told me what's wrong with admiring something that's beautiful and then trying to do it yourself.

464 HALLY: Nothing. But we happen to be talking about a foxtrot, not a thing of beauty.

465 SAM: But that is just what I'm saying. If you were to see two champions doing, two masters of the art . . . !

466 HALLY: Oh God, I give up. So now it's also art!

467 SAM: Ja.

468 HALLY: There's a limit, Sam. Don't confuse art and entertainment.

469 SAM: So then what is art?

470 HALLY: You want a definition?

471 SAM: Ja.

472 HALLY (*He realizes he has got to be careful. He gives the matter a lot of thought before answering.*): Philosophers have been trying to do that for centuries. What is Art? What is Life? But basically I suppose it's . . . the giving of meaning to matter.

473 SAM: Nothing to do with beautiful?

474 HALLY: It goes beyond that. It's the giving of form to the formless.

475 SAM: Ja, well, maybe it's not art, then. But I still say it's beautiful.

476 HALLY: I'm sure the word you mean to use is entertaining.

477 SAM (*adamant*): No. Beautiful. And if you want proof come along to the Centenary Hall in New Brighton in two weeks' time.

(*The mention of the Centenary Hall draws Willie over to them.*)

478 HALLY: What for? I've seen the two of you prancing around in here often enough.

479 SAM (*he laughs*): This isn't the real thing, Hally. We're just playing around in here.

480 HALLY: So? I can use my imagination.

481 SAM: And what do you get?

482 HALLY: A lot of people dancing around and having a so-called good time.

483 SAM: That all?

484 HALLY: Well, basically it is that, surely.

485 SAM: No, it isn't. Your imagination hasn't helped you at all. There's a lot more to it than that. We're getting ready for the championships, Hally, not just another dance. There's going to be a lot of people, all right, and they're going to have a good time, but they'll only be spectators, sitting around and watching. It's just the competitors out there on the dance floor. Party decorations and fancy lights all around the walls! The ladies in beautiful evening dresses!

486 HALLY: My mother's got one of those, Sam, and, quite frankly, it's an embarrassment every time she wears it.

487 SAM (*undeterred*): Your imagination left out the excitement.

(*Hally scoffs.*)

Oh, yes. The finalists are not going to be out there just to have a good time. One of those couples will be the 1950 Eastern Province Champions. And your imagination left out the music.

488 WILLIE: Mr. Elijah Gladman Guzana and his Orchestral Jazzonions.

489 SAM: The sound of the big band, Hally. Trombone, trumpet, tenor and alto sax. And then, finally, your imagination also left out the climax of the evening when the dancing is finished, the judges have stopped whispering among themselves and the Master of Ceremonies collects their scorecards and goes up onto the stage to announce the winners.

490 HALLY: All right. So you make it sound like a bit of a do. It's an occasion. Satisfied?

491 SAM (*victory*): So you admit that!

492 HALLY: Emotionally yes, intellectually no.

493 SAM: Well, I don't know what you mean by that, all I'm telling you is that it is going to be *the* event of the year in New Brighton. It's been sold out for two weeks already. There's only standing room left. We've got competitors coming from Kingwilliamstown, East London, Port Alfred.

(*Hally starts pacing thoughtfully.*)

494 HALLY: Tell me a bit more.

495 SAM: I thought you weren't interested . . . intellectually.

496 HALLY (*mysteriously*): I've got my reasons.

497 SAM: What do you want to know?

498 HALLY: It takes place every year?

499 SAM: Yes. But only every third year in New Brighton. It's East London's turn to have the championships next year.

500 HALLY: Which, I suppose, makes it an even more significant event.

501 SAM: Ah ha! We're getting somewhere. Our "occasion" is now a "significant event."

502 HALLY: I wonder.

503 SAM: What?

504 HALLY: I wonder if I would get away with it.

505 SAM: But what?

506 HALLY (*to the table and his exercise book*): "Write five hundred words describing an annual event of

cultural or historical significance." Would I be stretching poetic license a little too far if I called your ballroom championships a cultural event?

507 SAM: You mean . . . ?

508 HALLY: You think we could get five hundred words out of it, Sam?

509 SAM: Victor Sylvester has written a whole book on ballroom dancing.

510 WILLIE: You going to write about it, Master Hally?

511 HALLY: Yes, gentlemen, that is precisely what I am considering doing. Old Doc Bromely—he's my English teacher—is going to argue with me, of course. He doesn't like natives. But I'll point out to him that in strict anthropological terms the culture of a primitive black society includes its dancing and singing. To put my thesis in a nutshell: The war-dance has been replaced by the waltz. But it still amounts to the same thing: the release of primitive emotions through movement. Shall we give it a go?

512 SAM: I'm ready.

513 WILLIE: Me also.

514 HALLY: Ha! This will teach the old bugger a lesson. (*Decision taken.*) Right. Let's get ourselves organized. (*This means another cake on the table. He sits.*) I think you've given me enough general atmosphere, Sam, but to build the tension and suspense I need facts. (*Pencil poised.*)

515 WILLIE: Give him facts, Boet Sam.

516 HALLY: What you called the climax . . . how many finalists?

517 SAM: Six couples.

518 HALLY (*making notes*): Go on. Give me the picture.

519 SAM: Spectators seated right around the hall. (*Willie becomes a spectator.*)

520 HALLY: . . . and it's a full house.

521 SAM: At one end, on the stage, Gladman and his Orchestral Jazzonions. At the other end is a long table with the three judges. The six finalists go onto the dance floor and take up their positions. When they are ready and the spectators have settled down, the Master of Ceremonies goes to the microphone. To start with, he makes some jokes to get people laughing. . . .

522 HALLY: Good touch. (*As he writes.*) ". . . creating a relaxed atmosphere which will change to one of tension and drama as the climax is approached."

523 SAM (*onto a chair to act out the M.C.*): "Ladies and gentlemen, we come now to the great moment you have all been waiting for this evening . . . The finals of the 1950 Eastern Province Open Ballroom Dancing Championships. But first let me introduce the finalists! Mr. and Mrs. Welcome Tchabalala from Kingwilliamstown . . ."

524 WILLIE (*he applauds after every name*): Is when the people clap their hands and whistle and make a lot of noise, Master Hally.

525 SAM: "Mr. Mulligan Njikelane and Miss Nomhle Nkonyeni of Grahamstown; Mr. and Mrs. Norman Nchinga from Port Alfred; Mr. Fats Bokolane and Miss Dina Plaatjies from East London; Mr. Sipho

Danny Glover, who played Willie in the 1982 Broadway production, played the older waiter, Sam, in the 2003 New York revival of *"MASTER HAROLD"* . . . *and the boys,* directed by Lonny Price.

Dugu and Mrs. Mable Magada from Peddie; and from New Brighton our very own Mr. Willie Malopo and Miss Hilda Samuels."

(*Willie can't believe his ears. He abandons his role as spectator and scrambles into position as a finalist.*)

526 WILLIE: Relaxed and ready to romance!

527 SAM: The applause dies down. When everybody is silent, Gladman lifts up his sax, nods at the Orchestral Jazzonions. . . .

528 WILLIE: Play the jukebox please, Boet Sam!

529 SAM: I also only got bus fare, Willie.

530 HALLY: Hold it, everybody. (*Heads for the cash register behind the counter.*) How much is in the till, Sam?

531 SAM: Three shillings. Hally . . . Your Mom counted it before she left.

(*Hally hesitates.*)

532 HALLY: Sorry, Willie. You know how she carried on the last time I did it. We'll just have to pool our

combined imaginations and hope for the best. (*Returns to the table.*) Back to work. How are the points scored, Sam?

SAM: Maximum of ten points each for individual style, deportment, rhythm, and general appearance.

WILLIE: Must I start?

HALLY: Hold it for a second, Willie. And penalties?

SAM: For what?

HALLY: For doing something wrong. Say you stumble or bump into somebody . . . do they take off any points?

SAM (*aghast*): Hally . . . !

HALLY: When you're dancing. If you and your partner collide into another couple.

(*Hally can get no further. Sam has collapsed with laughter. He explains to Willie.*)

SAM: If me and Miriam bump into you and Hilda . . . .

(*Willie joins him in another good laugh.*)

Hally, Hally . . . !

HALLY (*perplexed*): Why? What did I say?

SAM: There's no collisions out there, Hally. Nobody trips or stumbles or bumps into anybody else. That's what that moment is all about. To be one of those finalists on that dance floor is like . . . like being in a dream about a world in which accidents don't happen.

HALLY (*genuinely moved by Sam's image*): Jesus, Sam! That's beautiful!

WILLIE (*can endure waiting no longer*): I'm starting!

(*Willie dances while Sam talks.*)

SAM: Of course it is. That's what I've been trying to say to you all afternoon. And it's beautiful because that is what we want life to be like. But instead, like you said, Hally, we're bumping into each other all the time. Look at the three of us this afternoon. I've bumped into Willie, the two of us have bumped into you, you've bumped into your mother, she bumping into your Dad. . . . None of us knows the steps and there's no music playing. And it doesn't stop with us. The whole world is doing it all the time. Open a newspaper and what do you read? America has bumped into Russia, England is bumping into India, rich man bumps into poor man. Those are big collisions, Hally. They make for a lot of bruises. People get hurt in all that bumping, and we're sick and tired of it now. It's been going on for too long. Are we never going to get it right? . . . Learn to dance life like champions instead of always being just a bunch of beginners at it?

HALLY (*deep and sincere admiration of the man*): You've got a vision, Sam!

SAM: Not just me. What I'm saying to you is that everybody's got it. That's why there's only standing room left for the Centenary Hall in two weeks' time. For as long as the music lasts, we are going to see six couples get it right, the way we want life to be.

HALLY: But is that the best we can do, Sam . . . watch six finalists dreaming about the way it should be?

SAM: I don't know. But it starts with that. Without the dream we won't know what we're going for. And anyway I reckon there are a few people who have got past just dreaming about it and are trying for something real. Remember that thing we read once in the paper about the Mahatma Gandhi? Going without food to stop those riots in India?

HALLY: You're right. He certainly was trying to teach people to get the steps right.

SAM: And the Pope.

HALLY: Yes, he's another one. Our old General Smuts° as well, you know. He's also out there dancing. You know, Sam, when you come to think of it, that's what the United Nations boils down to . . . a dancing school for politicians!

SAM: And let's hope they learn.

HALLY (*a little surge of hope*): You're right. We mustn't despair. Maybe there's some hope for mankind after all. Keep it up, Willie. (*Back to his table with determination.*) This is a lot bigger than I thought. So what have we got? Yes, our title: "A World Without Collisions."

SAM: That sounds good! "A World Without Collisions."

HALLY: Subtitle: "Global Politics on the Dance Floor." No. A bit too heavy, hey? What about "Ballroom Dancing as a Political Vision"?

(*The telephone rings. Sam answers it.*)

SAM: St. George's Park Tea Room . . . Yes, Madam . . . Hally, it's your Mom.

HALLY (*back to reality*): Oh, God, yes! I'd forgotten all about that. Shit! Remember my words, Sam? Just when you're enjoying yourself, someone or something will come along and wreck everything.

SAM: You haven't heard what she's got to say yet.

HALLY: Public telephone?

SAM: No.

HALLY: Does she sound happy or unhappy?

SAM: I couldn't tell. (*Pause.*) She's waiting, Hally.

HALLY (*to the telephone*): Hello, Mom . . . No, everything is okay here. Just doing my homework. . . . What's your news? . . . You've what? . . . (*Pause. He takes the receiver away from his ear for a few seconds. In the course of Hally's telephone conversation, Sam and Willie discreetly position the stacked tables and chairs. Hally places the receiver back to his ear.*) Yes, I'm still here. Oh, well, I give up now. Why did you do it, Mom? . . . Well, I just hope you know what you've let us in for. . . . (*Loudly.*) I said I hope you know what you've let us in for! It's the end of the peace and quiet we've been having. (*Softly.*) Where is he? (*Normal voice.*) He can't hear us from in there. But for God's

General Smuts: South African statesman (1870–1950), who fought the British in the Boer War in 1899, was instrumental in forming the Union of South Africa in 1910, and was active in the creation of the United Nations.

sake, Mom, what happened? I told you to be firm with him. . . . Then you and the nurses should have held him down, taken his crutches away. . . . I know only too well he's my father! . . . I'm not being disrespectful, but I'm sick and tired of emptying stinking chamber pots full of phlegm and piss. . . . Yes, I do! When you're not there, he asks *me* to do it. . . . If you really want to know the truth, that's why I've got no appetite for my food. . . . Yes! There's a lot of things you don't know about. For your information, I still haven't got that science textbook I need. And you know why? He borrowed the money you gave me for it. . . . Because I didn't want to start another fight between you two. . . . He says that every time. . . . All right, Mom! (*Viciously.*) Then just remember to start hiding your bag away again, because he'll be at your purse before long for money for booze. And when he's well enough to come down here, you better keep an eye on the till as well, because that is also going to develop a leak. . . . Then don't complain to me when he starts his old tricks. . . . Yes, you do. I get it from you on one side and from him on the other, and it makes life hell for me. I'm not going to be the peacemaker anymore. I'm warning you now: when the two of you start fighting again, I'm leaving home. . . . Mom, if you start crying, I'm going to put down the receiver. . . . Okay. . . . (*Lowering his voice to a vicious whisper.*) Okay, Mom. I heard you. (*Desperate.*) No. . . . Because I don't want to. I'll see him when I get home! Mom! . . . (*Pause. When he speaks again, his tone changes completely. It is not simply pretense. We sense a genuine emotional conflict.*) Welcome home, chum! . . . What's that? . . . Don't be silly, Dad. You being home is just about the best news in the world. . . . I bet you are. Bloody depressing there with everybody going on about their ailments, hey! . . . How you feeling? . . . Good. . . . Here as well, pal. Coming down cats and dogs. . . . That's right. Just the day for a kip° and a toss in your old Uncle Ned. . . . Everything's just hunky-dory on my side, Dad. . . . Well, to start with, there's a nice pile of comics for you on the counter. . . . Yes, old Kemple brought them in. *Batman and Robin, Submariner* . . . just your cup of tea. . . . I will. . . . Yes, we'll spin a few yarns tonight. . . . Okay, chum, see you in a little while. . . . No, I promise. I'll come straight home. . . . (*Pause—his mother comes back on the phone.*) Mom? Okay. I'll lock up now. . . . What? . . . Oh, the brandy . . . Yes, I'll remember! . . . I'll put it in my suitcase now, for God's sake. I know well enough what will happen if he doesn't get it. . . . (*Places a bottle of brandy on the counter.*) I *was* kind to him, Mom. I didn't say anything nasty! . . . All right. Bye. (*End of telephone conversation. A desolate Hally doesn't move. A strained silence.*)

kip: Nap.

SAM (*quietly*): That sounded like a bad bump, Hally.

HALLY (*Having a hard time controlling his emotions. He speaks carefully.*): Mind your own business, Sam.

SAM: Sorry. I wasn't trying to interfere. Shall we carry on? Hally? (*He indicates the exercise book. No response from Hally.*)

WILLIE (*also trying*): Tell him about when they give out the cups, Boet Sam.

SAM: Ja! That's another big moment. The presentation of the cups after the winners have been announced. You've got to put that in.

(*Still no response from Hally.*)

WILLIE: A big silver one, Master Hally, called floating trophy for the champions.

SAM: We always invite some big-shot personality to hand them over. Guest of honor this year is going to be His Holiness Bishop Jabulani of the All African Free Zionist Church.

(*Hally gets up abruptly, goes to his table, and tears up the page he was writing on.*)

HALLY: So much for a bloody world without collisions.

SAM: Too bad. It was on its way to being a good composition.

HALLY: Let's stop bullshitting ourselves, Sam.

SAM: Have we been doing that?

HALLY: Yes! That's what all our talk about a decent world has been . . . just so much bullshit.

SAM: We did say it was still only a dream.

HALLY: And a bloody useless one at that. Life's a fuckup and it's never going to change.

SAM: Ja, maybe that's true.

HALLY: There's no maybe about it. It's a blunt and brutal fact. All we've done this afternoon is waste our time.

SAM: Not if we'd got your homework done.

HALLY: I don't give a shit about my homework, so, for Christ's sake, just shut up about it. (*Slamming books viciously into his school case.*) Hurry up now and finish your work. I want to lock up and get out of here. (*Pause.*) And then go where? Home-sweet-fucking-home. Jesus, I hate that word.

(*Hally goes to the counter to put the brandy bottle and comics in his school case. After a moment's hesitation, he smashes the bottle of brandy. He abandons all further attempts to hide his feelings. Sam and Willie work away as unobtrusively as possible.*)

Do you want to know what is really wrong with your lovely little dream, Sam? It's not just that we are all bad dancers. That does happen to be perfectly true, but there's more to it than just that. You left out the cripples.

SAM: Hally!

HALLY (*now totally reckless*): Ja! Can't leave them out, Sam. That's why we always end up on our backsides on the dance floor. They're also out there dancing . . . like a bunch of broken spiders trying to do the quickstep! (*An ugly attempt at laughter.*) When you come to think of it, it's a bloody comical sight. I mean, it's bad enough on two legs . . . but one and a pair of crutches! Hell, no, Sam. That's guaranteed to turn that dance floor into a shambles. Why you shaking your head? Picture it, man. For once this afternoon let's use our imaginations sensibly.

SAM: Be careful, Hally.

HALLY: Of what? The truth? I seem to be the only one around here who is prepared to face it. We've had the pretty dream, it's time now to wake up and have a good long look at the way things really are. Nobody knows the steps, there's no music, the cripples are also out there tripping up everybody and trying to get into the act, and it's all called the All-Comers-How-to-Make-a-Fuckup-of-Life Championships. (*Another ugly laugh.*) Hang on, Sam! The best bit is still coming. Do you know what the winner's trophy is? A beautiful big chamber pot with roses on the side, and it's full to the brim with piss. And guess who I think is going to be this year's winner.

SAM (*almost shouting*): Stop now!

HALLY (*suddenly appalled by how far he has gone*): Why?

SAM: Hally? It's your father you're talking about.

HALLY: So?

SAM: Do you know what you've been saying?

(*Hally can't answer. He is rigid with shame. Sam speaks to him sternly.*)

No, Hally, you mustn't do it. Take back those words and ask for forgiveness! It's a terrible sin for a son to mock his father with jokes like that. You'll be punished if you carry on. Your father is your father, even if he is a . . . cripple man.

WILLIE: Yes, Master Hally. Is true what Sam say.

SAM: I understand how you are feeling, Hally, but even so. . . .

HALLY: No, you don't!

SAM: I think I do.

HALLY: And I'm telling you you don't. Nobody does. (*Speaking carefully as his shame turns to rage at Sam.*) It's your turn to be careful, Sam. Very careful! You're treading on dangerous ground. Leave me and my father alone.

SAM: I'm not the one who's been saying things about him.

HALLY: What goes on between me and my Dad is none of your business!

SAM: Then don't tell me about it. If that's all you've got to say about him, I don't want to hear.

(*For a moment Hally is at loss for a response.*)

HALLY: Just get on with your bloody work and shut up.

SAM: Swearing at me won't help you.

HALLY: Yes, it does! Mind your own fucking business and shut up!

SAM: Okay. If that's the way you want it, I'll stop trying.

(*He turns away. This infuriates Hally even more.*)

HALLY: Good. Because what you've been trying to do is meddle in something you know nothing about. All

that concerns you in here, Sam, is to try and do what you get paid for—keep the place clean and serve the customers. In plain words, just get on with your job. My mother is right. She's always warning me about allowing you to get too familiar. Well, this time you've gone too far. It's going to stop right now.

(*No response from Sam.*)

You're only a servant in here, and don't forget it.

(*Still no response. Hally is trying hard to get one.*)

And as far as my father is concerned, all you need to remember is that he is your boss.

SAM (*needled at last*): No, he isn't. I get paid by your mother.

HALLY: Don't argue with me, Sam!

SAM: Then don't say he's my boss.

HALLY: He's a white man and that's good enough for you.

SAM: I'll try to forget you said that.

HALLY: Don't! Because you won't be doing me a favor if you do. I'm telling you to remember it.

(*A pause. Sam pulls himself together and makes one last effort.*)

SAM: Hally, Hally . . . ! Come on now. Let's stop before it's too late. You're right. We *are* on dangerous ground. If we're not careful, somebody is going to get hurt.

HALLY: It won't be me.

SAM: Don't be so sure.

HALLY: I don't know what you're talking about, Sam.

SAM: Yes, you do.

HALLY (*furious*): Jesus, I wish you would stop trying to tell me what I do and what I don't know.

(*Sam gives up. He turns to Willie.*)

SAM: Let's finish up.

HALLY: Don't turn your back on me! I haven't finished talking.

(*He grabs Sam by the arm and tries to make him turn around. Sam reacts with a flash of anger.*)

SAM: Don't do that, Hally! (*Facing the boy.*) All right, I'm listening. Well? What do you want to say to me?

HALLY (*pause as Hally looks for something to say*): To begin with, why don't you also start calling me Master Harold, like Willie.

SAM: Do you mean that?

HALLY: Why the hell do you think I said it?

SAM: And if I don't?

HALLY: You might just lose your job.

SAM (*quietly and very carefully*): If you make me say it once, I'll never call you anything else again.

HALLY: So? (*The boy confronts the man.*) Is that meant to be a threat?

SAM: Just telling you what will happen if you make me do that. You must decide what it means to you.

HALLY: Well, I have. It's good news. Because that is exactly what Master Harold wants from now on.

Think of it as a little lesson in respect, Sam, that's long overdue, and I hope you remember it as well as you do your geography. I can tell you now that somebody who will be glad to hear I've finally given it to you will be my Dad. Yes! He agrees with my Mom. He's always going on about it as well. "You must teach the boys to show you more respect, my son."

SAM: So now you can stop complaining about going home. Everybody is going to be happy tonight.

HALLY: That's perfectly correct. You see, you mustn't get the wrong idea about me and my Dad, Sam. We also have our good times together. Some bloody good laughs. He's got a marvelous sense of humor. Want to know what our favorite joke is? He gives out a big groan, you see, and says: "It's not fair, is it, Hally?" Then I have to ask: "What, chum?" And then he says: "A nigger's arse" . . . and we both have a good laugh.

(*The men stare at him with disbelief.*)

What's the matter, Willie? Don't you catch the joke? You always were a bit slow on the uptake. It's what is called a pun. You see, fair means both light in color and to be just and decent. (*He turns to Sam.*) I thought *you* would catch it, Sam.

SAM: Oh ja, I catch it all right.

HALLY: But it doesn't appeal to your sense of humor.

SAM: Do you really laugh?

HALLY: Of course.

SAM: To please him? Make him feel good?

HALLY: No, for heavens sake! I laugh because I think it's a bloody good joke.

SAM: You're really trying hard to be ugly, aren't you? And why drag poor old Willie into it? He's done nothing to you except show you the respect you want so badly. That's also not being fair, you know . . . and I mean just or decent.

WILLIE: It's all right, Sam. Leave it now.

SAM: It's me you're after. You should just have said "Sam's arse" . . . because that's the one you're trying to kick. Anyway, how do you know it's not fair? You've never seen it. Do you want to? (*He drops his trousers and underpants and presents his backside for Hally's inspection.*) Have a good look. A real Basuto arse . . . which is about as nigger as they can come. Satisfied? (*Trousers up.*) Now you can make your Dad even happier when you go home tonight. Tell him I showed you my arse and he is quite right. It's not fair. And if it will give him an even better laugh next time, I'll also let *him* have a look. Come, Willie, let's finish up and go.

(*Sam and Willie start to tidy up the tea room. Hally doesn't move. He waits for a moment when Sam passes him.*)

HALLY (*quietly*): Sam . . .

(*Sam stops and looks expectantly at the boy. Hally spits in his face. A long and heartfelt groan from Willie. For a few seconds Sam doesn't move.*)

SAM (*taking out a handkerchief and wiping his face*): It's all right, Willie.

(*To Hally.*)

Ja, well, you've done it . . . Master Harold. Yes, I'll start calling you that from now on. It won't be difficult anymore. You've hurt yourself, Master Harold. I saw it coming. I warned you, but you wouldn't listen. You've just hurt yourself *bad*. And you're a coward, Master Harold. The face you should be spitting in is your father's . . . but you used mine, because you think you're safe inside your fair skin . . . and this time I don't mean just or decent. (*Pause, then moving violently toward Hally.*) Should I hit him, Willie?

WILLIE (*stopping Sam*): No, Boet Sam.

SAM (*violently*): Why not?

WILLIE: It won't help, Boet Sam.

SAM: I don't want to help! I want to hurt him.

WILLIE: You also hurt yourself.

SAM: And if he had done it to you, Willie?

WILLIE: Me? Spit at me like I was a dog? (*A thought that had not occurred to him before. He looks at Hally.*) Ja. Then I want to hit him. I want to hit him hard!

(*A dangerous few seconds as the men stand staring at the boy. Willie turns away, shaking his head.*)

But maybe all I do is go cry at the back. He's little boy, Boet Sam. Little *white* boy. Long trousers now, but he's still little boy.

SAM (*his violence ebbing away into defeat as quickly as it flooded*): You're right. So go on, then: groan again, Willie. You do it better than me. (*To Hally.*) You don't know all of what you've just done . . . Master Harold. It's not just that you've made me feel dirtier than I've ever been in my life . . . I mean, how do I wash off yours and your father's filth? . . . I've also failed. A long time ago I promised myself I was going to try and do something, but you've just shown me . . . Master Harold . . . that I've failed. (*Pause.*) I've also got a memory of a little white boy when he was still wearing short trousers and a black man, but they're not flying a kite. It was the old Jubilee days, after dinner one night. I was in my room. You came in and just stood against the wall, looking down at the ground, and only after I'd asked you what you wanted, what was wrong, I don't know how many times, did you speak and even then so softly I almost didn't hear you. "Sam, please help me to go and fetch my Dad." Remember? He was dead drunk on the floor of the Central Hotel Bar. They'd phoned for your Mom, but you were the only one at home. And do you remember how we did it? You went in first by yourself to ask permission for me to go into the bar. Then I loaded him onto my back like a baby and carried him back to the boarding house with you following behind carrying his crutches. (*Shaking his head as he remembers.*) A crowded Main Street with all the people watching a little white boy following his drunk father on a nigger's back! I felt for that little boy . . . Master Harold. I felt for him. After that we still had to clean him up, remember? He'd messed in his trousers, so we had to clean him up and get him into bed.

HALLY (*great pain*): I love him, Sam.

SAM: I know you do. That's why I tried to stop you from saying these things about him. It would have been so simple if you could have just despised him for being a weak man. But he's your father. You love him and you're ashamed of him. You're ashamed of so much! . . . And now that's going to include yourself. That was the promise I made to myself: to try and stop that happening. (*Pause.*) After we got him to bed you came back with me to my room and sat in a corner and carried on just looking down at the ground. And for days after that! You hadn't done anything wrong, but you went around as if you owed the world an apology for being alive. I didn't like seeing that! That's not the way a boy grows up to be a man! . . . But the one person who should have been teaching you what that means was the cause of your shame. If you really want to know, that's why I made you that kite. I wanted you to look up, be proud of something, of yourself . . . (*bitter smile at the memory*) . . . and you certainly were that when I left you with it up there on the hill. Oh, ja . . . something else! . . . If you ever do write it as a short story, there *was* a twist in our ending. I couldn't sit down there and stay with you. It was a "Whites Only" bench. You were too young, too excited to notice then. But not anymore. If you're not careful . . . Master Harold . . . you're going to be sitting up there by yourself for a long time to come, and there won't be a kite in the sky. (*Sam has got nothing more to say. He exits into the kitchen, taking off his waiter's jacket.*)

WILLIE: Is bad. Is all bad in here now.

HALLY (*books into his school case, raincoat on*): Willie . . . (*It is difficult to speak.*) Will you lock up for me and look after the keys?

WILLIE: Okay.

(*Sam returns. Hally goes behind the counter and collects the few coins in the cash register. As he starts to leave . . . .*)

SAM: Don't forget the comic books.

(*Hally returns to the counter and puts them in his case. He starts to leave again.*)

SAM (*to the retreating back of the boy*): Stop . . . Hally. . . .

(*Hally stops, but doesn't turn to face him.*)

Hally . . . I've got no right to tell you what being a man means if I don't behave like one myself, and I'm not doing so well at that this afternoon. Should we try again, Hally?

HALLY: Try what?

SAM: Fly another kite, I suppose. It worked once, and this time I need it as much as you do.

HALLY: It's still raining, Sam. You can't fly kites on rainy days, remember.

SAM: So what do we do? Hope for better weather tomorrow?

HALLY (*helpless gesture*): I don't know. I don't know anything anymore.

SAM: You sure of that, Hally? Because it would be pretty hopeless if that was true. It would mean nothing has been learnt in here this afternoon, and there was a hell of a lot of teaching going on . . . one way or the other. But anyway, I don't believe you. I reckon there's one thing you know. You don't *have* to sit up there by yourself. You know what that bench means now, and you can leave it any time you choose. All you've got to do is stand up and walk away from it.

(*Hally leaves. Willie goes up quietly to Sam.*)

WILLIE: Is okay, Boet Sam. You see. Is . . . (*he can't find any better words*) . . . is going to be okay tomorrow. (*Changing his tone.*) Hey, Boet Sam! (*He is trying hard.*) You right. I think about it and you right. Tonight I find Hilda and say sorry. And make promise I won't beat her no more. You hear me, Boet Sam?

SAM: I hear you, Willie.

WILLIE: And when we practice I relax and romance with her from beginning to end. Nonstop! You watch! Two weeks' time: "First prize for promising newcomers: Mr. Willie Malopo and Miss Hilda Samuels." (*Sudden impulse.*) To hell with it! I walk home. (*He goes to the jukebox, puts in a coin and selects a record. The machine comes to life in the gray twilight, blushing its way through a spectrum of soft, romantic colors.*) How did you say it, Boet Sam? Let's dream. (*Willie sways with the music and gestures for Sam to dance.*)

(*Sarah Vaughan sings.*)

"Little man you're crying,
I know why you're blue,
Someone took your kiddy car away;
Better go to sleep now,
Little man you've had a busy day." (*etc., etc.*)
You lead. I follow.

(*The men dance together.*)

"Johnny won your marbles,
Tell you what we'll do;
Dad will get you new ones right away;
Better go to sleep now,
Little man you've had a busy day."

COMMENTARY

ATHOL FUGARD (b. 1932)

From Notebooks 1960–1977   1983

Like most playwrights, Athol Fugard is a journal writer. His notebooks contain scraps of memories that have special meaning to him. In one entry for March 1961, long before he began to write *"MASTER HAROLD"... and the boys* (1982), he describes one of his childhood memories. It concerns the real-life Sam, and it recounts — very painfully — the personal crime that Fugard's play deals with. His gesture of contempt for the man who was like a grandfather to him became a demon that had to be exorcised.

Sam Semela — Basuto — with the family fifteen years. Meeting him again when he visited Mom set off string of memories.

The kite which he produced for me one day during those early years when Mom ran the Jubilee Hotel and he was a waiter there. He had made it himself: brown paper, its ribs fashioned from thin strips of tomato-box plank which he had smoothed down, a paste of flour and water for glue. I was surprised and bewildered that he had made it for me.

I vaguely recall shyly "haunting" the servants' quarters in the well of the hotel — cold, cement-gray world — the pungent mystery of the dark little rooms — a world I didn't understand. Frightened to enter any of the rooms. Sam, broad-faced, broader based — he smelled of woodsmoke. The "kaffir smell" of South Africa is the smell of poverty — wood smoke and sweat.

Later, when he worked for her at the Park café, Mom gave him the sack: "... he became careless. He came late for work. His work went to hell. He didn't seem to care no more." I was about thirteen and served behind the counter while he waited on table.

Realize now he was the most significant — the only — friend of my boyhood years. On terrible windy days when no one came to swim or walk in the park, we would sit together and talk. Or I was reading — Introductions to Eastern Philosophy or Plato and Socrates — and when I had finished he would take the book back to New Brighton.

Can't remember now what precipitated it, but one day there was a rare quarrel between Sam and myself. In a truculent silence we closed the café, Sam set off home to New Brighton on foot and I followed a few minutes later on my bike. I saw him walking ahead of me and, coming out of a spasm of acute loneliness, as I rode up behind him I called his name, he turned in mid-stride to look back and, as I cycled past, I spat in his face. Don't suppose I will ever deal with the shame that overwhelmed me the second after I had done that.

Now he is thin. We had a long talk. He told about the old woman ("Ma") whom he and his wife have taken in to look after their house while he goes to work — he teaches ballroom dancing. "Ma" insists on behaving like a domestic — making Sam feel guilty and embarrassed. She brings him an early morning cup of coffee. Sam: "No, Ma, you mustn't, man." Ma: "I must." Sam: "Look, Ma, if I want it, I can make it." Ma: "No, I must."

Occasionally, when she is doing something, Sam feels like a cup of tea but is too embarrassed to ask her, and daren't make one for himself. Similarly, with his washing. After three days or a week away in other towns, giving dancing lessons, he comes back with underclothes that are very dirty. He is too shy to give them out to be washed so washes them himself. When Ma sees this she goes and complains to Sam's wife that he doesn't trust her, that it's all wrong for him to do the washing.

Of tsotsis,° he said: "They grab a old man, stick him with a knife, and ransack him. And so he must go to hospital and his kids is starving with hungry." Of others: "He's got some little moneys. So he is facing starvation for the weekend."

Of township snobs, he says there are the educational ones: "If you haven't been to the big school, like Fort Hare, what you say isn't true." And the money ones: "If you aren't selling shops or got a business or a big car, man, you're nothing."

Sam's incredible theory about the likeness of those "with the true seed of love." Starts with Plato and Socrates—they were round. "Man is being shrinking all the time. An Abe Lincoln, him too, taller, but that's because man is shrinking." Basically, those with the true seed of love look the same—"It's in the eyes."

He spoke admiringly of one man, a black lawyer in East London, an educated man—university background—who was utterly without snobbery, looking down on no one—any man, educated or ignorant, rich or poor, was another *man* to him, another human being, to be respected, taken seriously, to be talked to, listened to.

"They" won't allow Sam any longer to earn a living as a dancing teacher. "You must get a job!" One of his fellow teachers was forced to work at Fraser's Quarries.

---

tsotsis: Gang members.

David Mamet

The title of one of David Mamet's plays, *A Life in the Theatre* (1977), may have been autobiographically inspired. Mamet has spent his life—from high school onward—in the theater, as actor, director, playwright, and screenwriter. Born in Chicago in 1947, he graduated with an English major from Goddard College in Vermont, where he wrote several plays, including his undergraduate thesis, *Camel* (1968). *Sexual Perversity in Chicago* (1975), Mamet's first resounding commercial success, was first drafted when he was at Goddard. In 1975, *American Buffalo* premiered in the Goodman Theatre in Chicago, launching a series of productions around the country. The Broadway production was not especially well received, but *American Buffalo* was the first American play produced at London's new National Theatre in 1978. After a 1980 revival at New Haven's Long Wharf Theatre with Al Pacino as Teach, it moved to Circle in the Square in New York in 1981 and then to Broadway in 1983. A study of petty thieves living a darkly comic underground life, *American Buffalo* has become one of Mamet's most highly regarded plays.

In the early 1970s, Mamet was involved in Chicago's St. Nicholas Theatre Company, a group that gathered to produce a variety of plays, including some of his own. William H. Macy, Steven Schacter, and Patricia Cox were the principal actors, and others joined with them. Soon, however, Mamet's responsibilities as a writer and his occasional stints as a university professor at Goddard and elsewhere led him to leave Chicago and settle in New York.

His much-acclaimed *Glengarry Glen Ross* (1983) premiered in London at the National Theatre, then moved to Broadway the following year, when it won the Pulitzer Prize and many other awards. This tale of scheming real estate salesmen derives in part from Mamet's experience working in a real estate office as a young man. The portrait of avarice and deceit is an indictment of one aspect of American business. *Glengarry Glen Ross* was eventually revised for film.

In the 1980s and 1990s, Mamet wrote many stage plays, radio plays, and film scripts. He adapted Chekhov's *The Cherry Orchard* (1985), wrote *Goldberg Street* for radio performance, and wrote the screenplays for *The Untouchables* (1987), *House of Games* (1987, nominated for a Golden Globe Award), *Things Change* (1988), and *Homicide* (1991). *Speed the Plow* (1988) opened on Broadway with Madonna playing a secretary from a temp agency. The play draws on Mamet's experience in the film industry and explores the insecurities and double-dealing of those who make decisions about producing movies. *Oleanna* (1992), set in a professor's office and dealing with issues of sexual harassment and political correctness, remains one of Mamet's most controversial plays. *The Cryptogram* (1994) was produced first in London in June 1994, then at the American Repertory Theater in Boston in February 1995; the New York production was at the Westside Arts Theatre in March 1995. *Boston Marriage* (1999) examines a lesbian relationship between Victorian blue bloods, a novel subject for Mamet, who is sometimes criticized as being misogynistic. His courtroom farce *Romance* (2005) opened at the Atlantic Theater in New York to disappointing reviews. To an extent, it was a study in ethnic slurs. Mamet directed the production of *Race* (2009), starring James Spader and David Alan Grier, at New York's Ethel Barrymore Theatre. The play portrays lawyers struggling to come up with a strategy to deal with their client, a white man accused of raping a black woman. Reviewers criticized the play for soft-peddling the touchy subject for the largely white audience, but the performances of Spader and Grier were soundly praised.

Mamet continues to be a prolific writer of plays, screenplays, and prose.

For links to resources about Mamet, click on *AuthorLinks* at bedfordstmartins.com/jacobus.

Glengarry Glen Ross

Mamet's examination of the world of sleazy real estate salesmen in *Glengarry Glen Ross* is at once comic and savage. The level of deceit that pervades the play is so deep that one almost begins to accept the views of Shelly "the Machine" Levene, who, as he ages, loses his credibility as a sales "closer" but continues to deceive himself and anyone who will listen into thinking he can still "do the job" and sell the way he once did. Of course, with Shelly it is difficult to know what to believe. Perhaps he once was a top-notch salesman, but then again, his ability to fabricate stories about himself is so advanced that it is possible he was never actually "on top." In the opening scene in the Chinese restaurant, he reveals himself to Williamson, the office manager who seems to be the "nephew of somebody," as a man willing to exaggerate his achievements and explain away his defeats as things beyond his control.

Whether or not Shelly Levene is a sympathetic character may depend on the point of view of the individual reader or audience member. Although he does not project the image of a man who was once useful and is now being cast aside because of age, he may be seen as a remote likeness of Willy Loman in *Death of a Salesman*. On the other hand, like Willy, he seems to have consistently chosen values that would ultimately doom him as a man. The language of the play repeatedly reminds us that these salesmen are men. MEN in capital letters, men who seem to be comparable to yesterday's warriors. In act 2, Roma tells us that only men can do this job because it takes a man, by which he suggests that there is something noble, something daring about going out and selling property to people who may not even want it. Roma, almost aware of Mamet's judgment, says, "it's not a world of men, Machine . . . it's a world of clock watchers, bureaucrats, officeholders . . . what it is, it's a fucked-up world . . . there's no adventure *to* it." Mamet's imagery often reverts to a revelation of male homosocial behavior, implying a brutal world built of conflict and survival, a world of predatory behavior resembling that of primitive hunters. Yet in actuality, these men are more like con men than like hunters.

In act 2, Roma sets up a con when Mr. Lingk comes into the office to ask for his money back. Lingk knows that he has three days in which to make up his mind to get a refund, and Roma tries to con him into thinking that he can wait four days. One important detail is that the "deal" they make occurs casually between Roma and Lingk in a restaurant in scene 3 of act 1. They begin their casual conversation sitting in different booths. They are just guys having a conversation. However, because one of the guys, Roma, is a skilled salesman, he is able to take the relatively untutored Lingk into his confidence and sell him property. In a marvelous twist, Lingk comes back in act 2 in the middle of a robbery investigation at the insistence of his wife. He reveals that it is not

For discussion questions and assignments on *Glengarry Glen Ross*, visit

bedfordstmartins.com/jacobus.

his decision to ask for his money back, but his wife's. She demands that he get their check back or she will go to the attorney general. She is the force behind his request, and it is she who undoes all of Roma's macho posturing, despite his trying everything he can think of, including having Levene masquerade as a very important customer who has "purchased" a great deal of property. In a sense, Roma is trying to "rob" Lingk of both his money and his will to resist. Simultaneously, the actual robbery of the real estate office is under investigation, further bewildering Lingk. Shelly Levene has let himself be drawn into a ridiculous scheme to steal leads—the names and addresses of people with enough resources to be potential buyers—and sell them to a competing firm. The entire scheme is self-defeating in the long run, but it produces immediate cash. Levene is so unsuccessful as a salesman that he has no money and sees this scheme as a temporary way out. In the process, as if displaying his lack of awareness, Levene seems to have skimmed off one of the leads and then had a "sit" with Bruce and Harriett Nyborg and "sold" them $82,000 worth of property. Near the end of the play, Williamson is astonished at Levene's naïveté: "They're nuts . . . they used to call in every week." The Nyborgs just like to talk to people—they are not legitimate customers, and Levene has allowed himself to be conned by them.

Levene is delusional when he tells Williamson that although he has committed a crime, it has taught him something: "What it taught me, that you've got to get *out* there. Big deal. So I wasn't cut out to be a thief. I was cut out to be a salesman." In Mamet's play, there is not much of a distinction.

Glengarry Glen Ross in Performance

The play premiered at the 300-seat Cottesloe Theatre in London, part of the South Bank group of National Theatres, on September 21, 1983. Derek Newark played Levene and Jack Shepherd played Roma. The American premiere followed on February 6, 1984, in Chicago at the Goodman Theatre, with Robert Prosky as Levene, Joe Mantegna as Roma, and Mike Nussbaum as Aaronow. J. T. Walsh played Williamson. Both productions were well received by reviewers and audiences alike, and the play won the Pulitzer Prize in 1984. Numerous productions have followed both regionally and abroad. The film version (1992), with Jack Lemmon as Levene and Al Pacino as Roma, was not a box-office success but has since become a cult classic. The first major theatrical revival was at the McCarter Theatre in Princeton, New Jersey, on February 18, 2000, with Scott Zigler directing. Charles Durning played Levene, Daniel Benzali played Moss, and Ruben Santiago-Hudson played Roma. Daniel L. Lewis in *Variety* said, "David Mamet's scorching 1984 drama *Glengarry Glen Ross* has lost none of its bite or blistering dramatic thrust in director Scott Zigler's McCarter Theatre production." Amy Morton directed the play at Steppenwolf Theatre in Chicago in November 2001–January 2002. In her production, Mike Nussbaum, who had played Aaronow in 1984, played Shelly Levene. The reviews noted that, even without any recognizable "stars" in the performance, the play still had power and verve. A 2005 revival had plenty of stars. Alan Alda, Liev Schreiber, Jeffrey Tambor, and Gordon Clapp garnered excellent reviews in Joe Mantello's production at the Royale Theatre in New York. Schreiber was cited for his powerful portrayal of Roma, and Santo Loquasto's stage design was especially effective.

DAVID MAMET (b. 1947)

Glengarry Glen Ross   1983

Always be closing. — PRACTICAL SALES MAXIM

The Characters

WILLIAMSON
BAYLEN
ROMA
LINGK
} *Men in their early forties.*

LEVENE
MOSS
AARONOW
} *Men in their fifties.*

The Scene: *The three scenes of Act One take place in a Chinese restaurant.*

Act Two takes place in a real estate office.

ACT ONE • Scene One

A booth at a Chinese restaurant, Williamson and Levene are seated at the booth.

LEVENE: John . . . John . . . John. Okay. John. John. Look (*Pause.*) The Glengarry Highland's leads, you're sending Roma out. Fine. He's a good man. We know what he is. He's fine. All I'm saying, you look at the *board,* he's throwing . . . wait, wait, wait, he's throwing them *away,* he's throwing the leads away. All that I'm saying, that you're wasting leads. I don't want to tell you your *job.* All that I'm saying, things get *set,* I know they do, you get a certain *mindset* . . . .guy gets a reputation. We know how this . . . all I'm saying, put a *closer* on the job. There's more than one man for the . . . Put a . . . wait a second, put a *proven man out* . . . and you watch, now *wait* a second—and you watch your *dollar* volumes. . . . You start closing them for *fifty* 'stead of *twenty-five* . . . you put a *closer* on the . . .

WILLIAMSON: Shelly, you blew the last . . .

LEVENE: No. John. No. Let's wait, let's back up here, I did . . . will you please? Wait a second. Please. I didn't "blow" them. No. I didn't "blow" them. No. One kicked *out,* one I closed . . .

WILLIAMSON: . . . you didn't close . . .

LEVENE: . . . I, if you'd *listen* to me. Please. I *closed* the cocksucker. His *ex,* John, his *ex, I* didn't know he was married . . . he, the *judge* invalidated the . . .

WILLIAMSON: Shelly . . .

LEVENE: . . . and what is that, John? What? Bad *luck.* That's all it is. I pray in your *life* you will never find it runs in streaks. That's what it does, that's all it's doing. Streaks. I pray it misses you. That's all I want to say.

WILLIAMSON (*Pause*): What about the other two?

LEVENE: What two?

WILLIAMSON: Four. You had four leads. One kicked out, one the *judge,* you say . . .

LEVENE: . . . you want to see the court records? John? Eh? You want to go down . . .

WILLIAMSON: . . . no . . .

LEVENE: . . . do you want to go down*town* . . . ?

WILLIAMSON: . . . no . . .

LEVENE: . . . then . . .

WILLIAMSON: . . . I only . . .

LEVENE: . . . then what is this "you *say*" shit, what is that? (*Pause.*) What is that . . . ?

WILLIAMSON: All that I'm saying . . .

LEVENE: What is this "you *say*"? A deal kicks out . . . I got to *eat. Shit,* Williamson, *shit.* You . . . Moss . . . Roma . . . look at the *sheets* . . . look at the *sheets.* Nineteen *eighty,* eighty-*one* . . . eighty-*two* . . . six months of eighty-two . . . who's there? Who's up there?

WILLIAMSON: Roma.

LEVENE: Under him?

WILLIAMSON: Moss.

LEVENE: Bullshit. John. Bull*shit.* April, September 1981. It's *me.* It isn't *fucking* Moss. Due respect, he's an *order* taker, John. He *talks,* he talks a good game, look at the *board,* and it's *me,* John, it's me . . .

WILLIAMSON: Not lately it isn't.

LEVENE: Lately kiss my ass lately. That isn't how you build an org . . . talk, talk to Murray. Talk to Mitch. When we were on Peterson, who paid for his fucking *car?* You talk to him. The *Seville* . . . ? He came in, "You bought that for me Shelly." Out of *what?* Cold *calling. Nothing.* Sixty-*five,* when we were there, with Glen *Ross* Farms? You call 'em downtown. What was that? *Luck?* That was "luck"? *Bull*shit, John. You're burning my ass, I can't get a fucking *lead* . . . you think that was luck. My stats for those years? Bull*shit* . . . over that period of time . . . ? Bull*shit.* It wasn't luck. It was *skill.* You want to throw that away, John . . . ? You want to throw that away?

WILLIAMSON: It isn't me . . .

LEVENE: . . . it isn't you . . . ? Who *is* it? Who is this I'm talking to? I need the *leads* . . .

WILLIAMSON: . . . after the thirtieth . . .

LEVENE: Bull*shit* the thirtieth, I don't get on the board the thirtieth, they're going to can my ass. I need the leads. I need them now. Or I'm gone, and you're going to miss me, John, I swear to you.

WILLIAMSON: Murray . . .

LEVENE: . . . you *talk* to Murray . . .

WILLIAMSON: I have. And my job is to marshal those leads . . .

LEVENE: Marshal the leads . . . marshal the leads? What the fuck, what bus did *you* get off of, we're here to fucking *sell. Fuck* marshaling the leads. What the fuck talk is that? What the fuck talk is that? Where did you learn that? In school? (*Pause.*) That's "talk," my friend, that's "talk." Our job is to *sell.* I'm the *man* to sell. I'm getting garbage. (*Pause.*) You're giving it to me, and what I'm saying is it's *fucked.*

WILLIAMSON: You're saying that I'm fucked.

LEVENE: Yes. (*Pause.*) I am. I'm sorry to antagonize you.

WILLIAMSON: Let me . . .

LEVENE: . . . and I'm going to get bounced and you're . . .

WILLIAMSON: . . . let me . . . are you listening to me . . . ?

LEVENE: Yes.

WILLIAMSON: Let me tell you something, Shelly. I do what I'm hired to do. I'm . . . wait a second. I'm *hired* to watch the leads. I'm given . . . hold on, I'm given a *policy. My* job is to *do that.* What I'm *told.* That's it. You, wait a second, *anybody* falls below a certain mark I'm not *permitted* to give them the premium leads.

LEVENE: Then how do they come up above that mark? With *dreck* . . . ? That's *nonsense.* Explain this to me. 'Cause it's a waste, and it's a stupid waste. I want to tell you something . . .

WILLIAMSON: You know what those leads cost?

LEVENE: The premium leads. Yes. I know what they cost. John. Because I, *I* generated the dollar revenue sufficient to *buy* them. Nineteen senny-*nine,* you know what I made? Senny-*nine?* Ninety-six thousand dollars. John? For *Murray* . . . For *Mitch* . . . look at the sheets . . .

WILLIAMSON: Murray said . . .

LEVENE: *Fuck* him. *Fuck* Murray. John? You know? You tell him I said so. What does *he* fucking know? He's going to have a "sales" contest . . . you know what our sales contest used to be? *Money.* A *fortune.* Money lying on the ground. Murray? When was the last time *he* went out on a sit? Sales contest? It's *laughable.* It's cold out there now, John. It's tight. Money is *tight.* This ain't sixty-five. It ain't. It just ain't. See? See? Now, I'm a good *man*—but I need a . . .

WILLIAMSON: Murray said . . .

LEVENE: John. John . . .

WILLIAMSON: Will you please wait a second. Shelly. Please. Murray told me: the hot leads . . .

LEVENE: . . . ah, *fuck* this . . .

WILLIAMSON: The . . . Shelly? (*Pause.*) The hot leads are assigned according to the board. During the contest. *Period.* Anyone who beats fifty per . . .

LEVENE: That's fucked. That's fucked. You don't look at the fucking *percentage.* You look at the *gross.*

WILLIAMSON: Either way. You're out.

LEVENE: I'm out.

WILLIAMSON: Yes.

LEVENE: I'll tell you why I'm out. I'm *out,* you're giving me toilet paper. John. I've *seen* those leads. I saw them when I was at Homestead, we pitched those cocksuckers Rio Rancho nineteen sixty-*nine* they wouldn't buy. They couldn't buy a fucking *toaster.* They're *broke,* John. They're cold. They're deadbeats, you can't judge on that. Even so. Even so. Alright. Fine. Fine. Even so. I go in, FOUR FUCKING LEADS they got their money in a *sock.* They're fucking *Polacks,* John. Four leads. I close two. *Two.* Fifty per . . .

WILLIAMSON: . . . they kicked out.

LEVENE: They *all* kick out. You run in *streaks,* pal. *Streaks.* I'm . . . I'm . . . don't look at the *board,* look at *me.* Shelly Levene. *Anyone. Ask* them on Western. Ask Getz at Homestead. Go ask Jerry Graff. You know who I am . . . I NEED A SHOT. I got to get on the fucking board. Ask them. *Ask* them. Ask them who ever picked up a check I was flush. Moss, Jerry Graff, Mitch himself . . . Those guys *lived* on the business I brought in. They *lived* on it . . . and so did Murray, John. You were here you'd of benefited from it too. And now I'm saying this. Do I want charity? Do I want *pity?* I want *sits.* I want leads don't come right out of a *phone book.* Give me a lead hotter than that, I'll go in and close it. Give me a chance. That's all I want. I'm going to *get* up on that fucking board and all I want is a chance. It's a *streak* and I'm going to turn it around. (*Pause.*) I need your help. (*Pause.*)

WILLIAMSON: I can't do it, Shelly. (*Pause.*)

LEVENE: Why?

WILLIAMSON: The leads are assigned randomly . . .

LEVENE: *Bullshit, bullshit,* you assign them. . . . What are you *telling* me?

WILLIAMSON: . . . apart from the top men on the contest board.

LEVENE: Then put me on the board.

WILLIAMSON: You start closing again, you'll *be* on the board.

LEVENE: I can't close these leads, John. No one can. It's a joke. John, look, just give me a hot lead. Just give me two of the premium leads. As a "test," alright? As a "test" and I promise you . . .

WILLIAMSON: I can't do it, Shel. (*Pause.*)

LEVENE: I'll give you ten percent. (*Pause.*)

WILLIAMSON: Of what?

LEVENE: Of my end what I close.

WILLIAMSON: And what if you don't close.

LEVENE: I *will* close.

WILLIAMSON: What if you *don't* close . . . ?

LEVENE: I *will* close.

WILLIAMSON: What if you *don't?* Then I'm *fucked.* You see . . . ? Then it's *my* job. That's what I'm *telling* you.

LEVENE: I *will* close. John, John, ten percent. I can get hot. You *know* that . . .

WILLIAMSON: Not lately you can't . . .

LEVENE: Fuck that. That's defeatist. Fuck that. Fuck it. . . . Get on my side. *Go* with me. Let's *do* something. You want to run this office, *run* it.

WILLIAMSON: Twenty percent. (*Pause.*)

LEVENE: Alright.

WILLIAMSON: And fifty bucks a lead.

LEVENE: John. (*Pause.*) Listen. I want to talk to you. Permit me to do this a second. I'm older than you. A man acquires a reputation. On the street. What he does when he's *up,* what he does otherwise. . . . I said "ten," you said "no." You said "twenty." I said "fine," I'm not going to fuck with you, how can I beat that, you tell me? . . . Okay. Okay. We'll . . . Okay. Fine. We'll . . . Alright, twenty percent, and fifty bucks a lead. That's fine. For now. That's fine. A month or two we'll talk. A month from now. Next month. After the thirtieth. (*Pause.*) We'll talk.

WILLIAMSON: What are we going to say?

LEVENE: No. You're right. That's for later. We'll talk in a month. What have you got? I want two sits. Tonight.

WILLIAMSON: I'm not sure I have two.

LEVENE: I saw the board. You've got *four* . . .

WILLIAMSON (*Snaps*): I've got *Roma.* Then I've got Moss . . .

LEVENE: *Bullshit.* They ain't been in the office yet. Give 'em some stiff. We have a deal or not? Eh? Two sits. The Des Plaines. Both of 'em, six and ten, you can do it . . . six and ten . . . eight and eleven, I don't give a shit, you set 'em up? Alright? The two sits in Des Plaines.

WILLIAMSON: Alright.

LEVENE: Good. Now we're talking. (*Pause.*)

WILLIAMSON: A hundred bucks. (*Pause.*)

LEVENE: Now? (*Pause.*) Now?

WILLIAMSON: Now. (*Pause.*) Yes . . . When?

LEVENE: Ah, *shit,* John. (*Pause.*)

WILLIAMSON: I wish I could.

LEVENE: You fucking asshole. (*Pause.*) I haven't got it. (*Pause.*) I haven't got it, John. (*Pause.*) I'll pay you tomorrow. (*Pause.*) I'm coming in here with the sales, I'll pay you *tomorrow.* (*Pause.*) I haven't got it, when I pay, the gas . . . I get back the hotel, I'll bring it in tomorrow.

WILLIAMSON: Can't do it.

LEVENE: I'll give you thirty on them now, I'll bring the rest tomorrow. I've got it at the hotel. (*Pause.*) John? (*Pause.*) We do that, for chrissake?

WILLIAMSON: No.

LEVENE: I'm asking you. As a favor to me? (*Pause.*) John. (*Long pause.*) John: my *daughter* . . .

WILLIAMSON: I can't do it, Shelly.

LEVENE: Well, I want to tell you something, fella, wasn't long I could pick up the phone, call *Murray* and I'd have your job. You know that? Not too *long* ago. For what? For *nothing.* "Mur, this new kid burns my ass." "Shelly, he's out." You're gone before I'm back from lunch. I bought him a trip to Bermuda once . . .

WILLIAMSON: I have to go . . . (*Gets up.*)

LEVENE: Wait. Alright. Fine. (*Starts going in pocket for money.*) The one. Give me the lead. Give me the one lead. The best one you have.

WILLIAMSON: I can't split them. (*Pause.*)

LEVENE: Why?

WILLIAMSON: Because I say so.

LEVENE (*Pause*): Is that it? Is that *it?* You want to do business that way . . . ?

Williamson gets up, leaves money on the table.

LEVENE: You want to do business that way . . . ? Alright. Alright. Alright. Alright. What is there on the other list . . . ?

WILLIAMSON: You want something off the B list?

LEVENE: *Yeah.* Yeah.

WILLIAMSON: Is that what you're saying?

LEVENE: That's what I'm saying. Yeah. (*Pause.*) I'd like something off the other list. Which, very least, that I'm entitled to. If I'm still *working* here, which for the moment I guess that I am. (*Pause.*) What? I'm sorry I spoke harshly to you.

WILLIAMSON: That's alright.

LEVENE: The deal still stands, our other thing.

Williamson shrugs. Starts out of the booth.

LEVENE: Good. Mmm. I, you know, I left my wallet back at the hotel.

Scene Two

A booth at the restaurant. Moss and Aaronow seated. After the meal.

MOSS: Polacks and deadbeats.

AARONOW: . . . Polacks . . .

MOSS: Deadbeats *all.*

AARONOW: . . . they hold on to their money . . .

MOSS: All of 'em. They, *hey*: it happens to us all.

AARONOW: Where am I going to work?

MOSS: You have to cheer up, George, you aren't out yet.

AARONOW: I'm *not?*

MOSS: You missed a fucking sale. Big deal. A deadbeat Polack. Big deal. How you going to sell 'em in the *first* place . . . ? Your mistake, you shoun'a took the lead.

AARONOW: I had to.

MOSS: You had to, yeah. Why?

AARONOW: To get on the . . .

MOSS: To get on the board. Yeah. How you goan'a get on the board sell'n a Polack? And I'll tell you, I'll tell you what *else.* You listening? I'll tell you what else: don't ever try to sell an Indian.

AARONOW: I'd never try to sell an Indian.

MOSS: You get those names come up, you ever get 'em, "Patel"?

AARONOW: Mmm . . .

MOSS: You ever get 'em?

AARONOW: Well, I think I had one once.

MOSS: You did?

AARONOW: I . . . I don't know.

MOSS: You had one you'd know it. *Patel*. They keep coming up. I don't know. They like to talk to salesmen. (*Pause.*) They're *lonely*, something. (*Pause.*) They like to feel *superior*, I don't know. Never bought a fucking thing. You're sitting down "The Rio Rancho *this*, the blah blah blah," "The Mountain View—" "Oh yes. My brother told me that . . . ." They got a grapevine. Fuckin' Indians, George. Not my cup of tea. Speaking of which I want to tell you something: (*Pause*) I never got a cup of tea with them. You see them in the restaurants. A supercilious race. What is this *look* on their face all the time? I don't know. (*Pause.*) I don't know. Their broads all look like they just got fucked with a dead *cat*, I don't know. (*Pause.*) I don't know. I don't like it. Christ . . .

AARONOW: What?

MOSS: The whole fuckin' thing . . . The pressure's just too great. You're ab . . . you're absolu . . . they're too important. All of them. You go in the door. I . . . "I got to *close* this fucker, or I don't eat lunch," "or I don't win the *Cadillac*. . . ." We fuckin' work too hard. You work too hard. We all, I remember when we were at Platt . . . huh? Glen Ross Farms . . . *didn't* we sell a bunch of that . . . ?

AARONOW: They came in and they, you know . . .

MOSS: Well, they fucked it up.

AARONOW: They did.

MOSS: They killed the goose.

AARONOW: They did.

MOSS: And now . . .

AARONOW: We're stuck with *this* . . .

MOSS: We're stuck with *this* fucking shit . . .

AARONOW: . . . *this* shit . . .

MOSS: It's too . . .

AARONOW: It is.

MOSS: Eh?

AARONOW: It's too . . .

MOSS: You get a bad month, all of a . . .

AARONOW: You're on this . . .

MOSS: All of, they got you on this "board . . . "

AARONOW: I, I . . . I . . .

MOSS: Some *contest* board . . .

AARONOW: I . . .

MOSS: It's not right.

AARONOW: It's not.

MOSS: No. (*Pause.*)

AARONOW: And it's not right to the *customers*.

MOSS: I know it's not. I'll tell you, you got, you know, you got . . . what did I learn as a kid on Western? Don't sell a guy one car. Sell him *five* cars over fifteen years.

AARONOW: That's right?

MOSS: Eh . . . ?

AARONOW: That's right?

MOSS: Goddamn right, that's right. Guys come on: "Oh, the blah blah blah, *I* know what I'll do: I'll go in and rob everyone blind and go to Argentina cause nobody ever *thought* of this before."

AARONOW: . . . that's right . . .

MOSS: Eh?

AARONOW: No. That's absolutely right.

MOSS: And so they kill the goose. I, I, I'll . . . and a fuckin' *man*, worked all his *life* has got to . . .

AARONOW: . . . that's right . . .

MOSS: . . . cower in his boots . . .

AARONOW (*simultaneously with "boots"*): Shoes, boots, yes . . .

MOSS: For some fuckin' "Sell ten thousand and you win the steak knives . . ."

AARONOW: For some *sales* pro . . .

MOSS: . . . sales promotion, "You *lose*, then we fire your . . ." No. It's *medieval* . . . it's wrong. "Or we're going to fire your ass." It's wrong.

AARONOW: Yes.

MOSS: Yes, it is. And you know who's responsible?

AARONOW: Who?

MOSS: You know who it is. It's Mitch. And Murray. 'Cause it doesn't have to be this way.

AARONOW: No.

MOSS: Look at Jerry Graff. He's *clean*, he's doing business for *himself*, he's got his, that *list* of his with the *nurses* . . . see? You see? That's *thinking*. Why take ten percent? A ten percent comm . . . why are we giving the rest away? What are we giving ninety per . . . for *nothing*. For some jerk sit in the office tell you "Get out there and close." "Go win the Cadillac." Graff. He goes out and *buys*. He pays top dollar for the . . . you see?

AARONOW: Yes.

MOSS: That's *thinking*. Now, he's got the leads, he goes in business for *himself*. He's . . . that's what I . . . that's *thinking*! "Who? Who's got a steady *job*, a couple bucks nobody's touched, who?"

AARONOW: Nurses.

MOSS: So Graff buys a fucking list of nurses, one grand—if he paid two I'll eat my hat—four, five thousand nurses, and he's going *wild* . . .

AARONOW: He is?

MOSS: He's doing *very* well.

AARONOW: I heard that they were running cold.

MOSS: The nurses?

AARONOW: Yes.

MOSS: You hear a *lot* of things. . . . He's doing very well. He's doing *very* well.

AARONOW: With River Oaks?

MOSS: River Oaks, Brook Farms. *All* of that shit. Somebody told me, you know what he's clearing *himself*? Fourteen, fifteen grand a *week*.

AARONOW: Himself?

MOSS: That's what I'm *saying*. Why? The *leads*. He's got the good leads . . . what are we, we're sitting in the shit here. Why? We have to go to *them* to *get* them. Huh. Ninety percent our sale, we're *paying* to the *office* for the *leads*.

AARONOW: The leads, the overhead, the telephones, there's *lots* of things.

MOSS: What do you need? A *telephone*, some broad to say "Good morning," nothing . . . nothing . . .

AARONOW: No, it's not that simple, Dave . . .

MOSS: *Yes.* It *is.* It *is* simple, and you know what the hard part is?

AARONOW: What?

MOSS: Starting up.

AARONOW: What hard part?

MOSS: Of doing the thing. The dif . . . the difference. Between me and Jerry Graff. Going to business for yourself. The hard part is . . . you know what it is?

AARONOW: What?

MOSS: Just the *act.*

AARONOW: What act?

MOSS: To say "I'm going on my own." 'Cause what you do, George, let me tell you what you do: you find yourself in *thrall* to someone else. And we *enslave* ourselves. To *please.* To win some fucking *toaster* . . . to . . . to . . . and the guy who got there first made *up* those . . .

AARONOW: That's right . . .

MOSS: He made *up* those rules, and we're working for *him.*

AARONOW: That's the truth . . .

MOSS: That's the *God's* truth. And it gets me depressed. I *swear* that it does. At MY AGE. To see a goddamn: "Somebody wins the Cadillac this month. P.S. Two guys get fucked."

AARONOW: *Huh.*

MOSS: You don't *ax* your sales force.

AARONOW: No.

MOSS: You . . .

AARONOW: You . . .

MOSS: You *build* it!

AARONOW: That's what I . . .

MOSS: You fucking *build* it! Men come . . .

AARONOW: Men come *work* for you . . .

MOSS: . . . you're absolutely right.

AARONOW: They . . .

MOSS: They have . . .

AARONOW: When they . . .

MOSS: Look look look look, when they *build* your business, then you can't fucking turn around, *enslave* them, treat them like *children,* fuck them up the ass, leave them to fend for themselves . . . no. (*Pause.*) No. (*Pause.*) You're absolutely right, and I want to tell you something.

AARONOW: What?

MOSS: I want to tell you what somebody should do.

AARONOW: What?

MOSS: Someone should stand up and strike *back.*

AARONOW: What do you mean?

MOSS: *Somebody* . . .

AARONOW: Yes . . . ?

MOSS: Should do something to *them.*

AARONOW: What?

MOSS: Something. To pay them back. (*Pause.*) Someone, someone should hurt them. Murray and Mitch.

AARONOW: Someone should hurt them.

MOSS: Yes.

AARONOW (*Pause.*): How?

MOSS: How? Do something to hurt them. Where they live.

AARONOW: What? (*Pause.*)

MOSS: Someone should rob the office.

AARONOW: Huh.

MOSS: That's what I'm *saying.* We were, if we were that kind of guys, to knock it off, and *trash* the joint, it looks like robbery, and *take* the fuckin' leads out of the files . . . go to Jerry Graff. (*Long pause.*)

AARONOW: What could somebody get for them?

MOSS: What could we *get* for them? I don't know. Buck a *throw* . . . buck-a-half a throw . . . I don't know. . . . Hey, who knows what they're worth, what do they *pay* for them? All told . . . must be, I'd . . . three bucks a throw . . . *I* don't know.

AARONOW: How many leads have we got?

MOSS: The *Glengarry* . . . the premium leads . . . ? I'd say we got five thousand. Five. Five thousand leads.

AARONOW: And you're saying a fella could take and sell these leads to Jerry Graff.

MOSS: Yes.

AARONOW: How do you know he'd buy them?

MOSS: Graff? Because I worked for him.

AARONOW: You haven't talked to him.

MOSS: No. What do you mean? Have I talked to him about *this*? (*Pause.*)

AARONOW: Yes. I mean are you actually *talking* about this, or are we just . . .

MOSS: No, we're just . . .

AARONOW: We're just *"talking"* about it.

MOSS: We're just *speaking* about it. (*Pause.*) As an *idea.*

AARONOW: As an idea.

MOSS: Yes.

AARONOW: We're not actually *talking* about it.

MOSS: No.

AARONOW: Talking about it as a . . .

MOSS: *No.*

AARONOW: As a *robbery.*

MOSS: As a "robbery"?! No.

AARONOW: *Well.* Well . . .

MOSS: *Hey.* (*Pause.*)

AARONOW: So all this, um, you didn't, actually, you didn't actually go talk to Graff.

MOSS: Not actually, no. (*Pause.*)

AARONOW: You didn't?

MOSS: No. Not actually.

AARONOW: Did you?

MOSS: What did I say?

AARONOW: What did you say?

MOSS: Yes. (*Pause.*) I said, "Not actually." The fuck *you* care, George? We're just *talking* . . .

AARONOW: We are?

MOSS: Yes. (*Pause.*)

AARONOW: Because, because, you know, it's a *crime.*

MOSS: That's right. It's a crime. It is a crime. It's also very safe.

AARONOW: You're actually *talking* about this?

MOSS: That's right. (*Pause.*)

AARONOW: You're going to steal the leads?

MOSS: Have I said that? (*Pause.*)

AARONOW: Are you? (*Pause.*)

MOSS: Did I say that?

AARONOW: Did you talk to Graff?

MOSS: Is that what I said?

AARONOW: What did he say?

MOSS: What did he say? He'd *buy* them. (*Pause.*)

AARONOW: You're going to steal the leads and sell the leads to him? (*Pause.*)

MOSS: Yes.

AARONOW: What will he pay?

MOSS: A buck a shot.

AARONOW: For five thousand?

MOSS: However they are, that's the deal. A buck a throw. Five thousand dollars. Split it half and half.

AARONOW: You're saying "me."

MOSS: Yes. (*Pause.*) Twenty-five hundred apiece. One night's work, and the job with Graff. Working the premium leads. (*Pause.*)

AARONOW: A job with Graff.

MOSS: Is that what I said?

AARONOW: He'd give me a job.

MOSS: He would take you on. Yes. (*Pause.*)

AARONOW: Is that the truth?

MOSS: Yes. It is, George. (*Pause.*) Yes. It's a big decision. (*Pause.*) And it's a big reward. (*Pause.*) It's a big reward. For one night's work. (*Pause.*) But it's got to be tonight.

AARONOW: What?

MOSS: What? What? The *leads*.

AARONOW: You have to steal the leads tonight?

MOSS: That's *right,* the guys are moving them downtown. After the thirtieth. Murray and Mitch. After the contest.

AARONOW: You're, you're saying so you have to go in there tonight and . . .

MOSS: *You . . .*

AARONOW: I'm sorry?

MOSS: *You.* (*Pause.*)

AARONOW: Me?

MOSS: *You* have to go in. (*Pause.*) *You* have to get the leads. (*Pause.*)

AARONOW: I do?

MOSS: Yes.

AARONOW: I . . .

MOSS: It's not something for nothing, George, I took you in on this, you have to go. That's your thing. I've made the deal with Graff. I can't go. I can't go in, I've spoken on this too much. I've got a big mouth. (*Pause.*) "The fucking leads" et cetera, blah blah blah " . . . the fucking tight ass company . . . "

AARONOW: They'll know when you go over to Graff . . .

MOSS: What will they know? That I stole the leads? I *didn't* steal the leads, I'm going to the *movies* tonight with a friend, and then I'm going to the Como Inn. Why did I go to Graff? I got a better deal. *Period.* Let 'em prove something. They can't prove anything that's not the case. (*Pause.*)

AARONOW: *Dave.*

MOSS: Yes.

AARONOW: You want me to break into the office tonight and steal the leads?

MOSS: Yes. (*Pause.*)

AARONOW: No.

MOSS: Oh, yes, George.

AARONOW: What does that mean?

MOSS: Listen to this. I have an alibi, I'm going to the Como Inn, why? Why? The place gets robbed, they're going to come looking for *me.* Why? Because I probably did it. Are you going to turn me in? (*Pause.*) George? Are you going to turn me in?

AARONOW: What if you don't get caught?

MOSS: They come to you, you going to turn me in?

AARONOW: Why would they come to me?

MOSS: They're going to come to *everyone.*

AARONOW: Why would I *do* it?

MOSS: You wouldn't, George, that's why I'm talking to you. Answer me. They come to you. You going to turn me in?

AARONOW: No.

MOSS: Are you sure?

AARONOW: Yes. I'm sure.

MOSS: Then listen to this: I have to get those leads tonight. That's something I have to do. If I'm not at the *movies* . . . if I'm not eating over at the inn . . . If you don't do this, then *I* have to come in here . . .

AARONOW: . . . you don't have to come in . . .

MOSS: . . . and *rob* the place . . .

AARONOW: . . . I thought that we were only talking . . .

MOSS: . . . they *take* me, then. They're going to ask me who were my accomplices.

AARONOW: *Me?*

MOSS: Absolutely.

AARONOW: That's ridiculous.

MOSS: Well, to the law, you're an accessory. Before the fact.

AARONOW: I didn't ask to be.

MOSS: Then tough luck, George, because you are.

AARONOW: Why? *Why,* because you only *told* me about it?

MOSS: That's right.

AARONOW: Why are you doing this to me, Dave. Why are you talking this way to me? I don't understand. Why are you doing this at *all* . . . ?

MOSS: That's none of your fucking business . . .

AARONOW: Well, well, well, *talk* to me, we sat down to eat *dinner,* and here I'm a *criminal* . . .

MOSS: You *went* for it.

AARONOW: In the abstract . . .

MOSS: So I'm making it concrete.

AARONOW: Why?

MOSS: Why? Why *you* going to give me five grand?

AARONOW: Do you need five grand?

MOSS: Is that what I just said?

AARONOW: You need money? Is that the . . .

MOSS: Hey, hey, let's just keep it simple, what I need is not the . . . what do *you* need . . . ?

AARONOW: What is the five grand? (*Pause.*) What is the, you said that we were going to *split* five . . .

MOSS: I lied. (*Pause.*) Alright? My end is *my* business. Your end's twenty-five. In or out. You tell me, you're out you take the consequences.

AARONOW: I do?

MOSS: Yes. (*Pause.*)

AARONOW: And why is that?

MOSS: Because you listened.

Scene Three

The restaurant. Roma is seated alone at the booth. Lingk is at the booth next to him. Roma is talking to him.

ROMA: . . . all train compartments smell vaguely of shit. It gets so you don't mind it. That's the worst thing that I can confess. You know how long it took me to get there? A long time. When you *die* you're going to regret the things you don't do. You think you're *queer* . . . ? I'm going to tell you something: we're *all* queer. You think that you're a *thief*? So *what*? You get befuddled by a middle-class morality . . . ? Get *shut* of it. Shut it out. You cheated on your wife . . . ? You *did* it, *live* with it. (*Pause.*) You fuck little girls, so *be* it. There's an absolute morality? May *be*. And *then* what? If you *think* there is, then *be* that thing. Bad people go to hell? I don't *think* so. If you think that, act that way. A hell exists on earth? Yes. I won't live in it. That's *me*. You ever take a dump made you feel you'd just slept for twelve hours . . . ?

LINGK: Did I . . . ?

ROMA: Yes.

LINGK: I don't know.

ROMA: Or a *piss* . . . ? A great meal fades in reflection. Everything else gains. You know why? 'Cause it's only food. This shit we eat, it keeps us going. But it's only food. The great fucks that you may have had. What do you remember about them?

LINGK: What do I . . . ?

ROMA: Yes.

LINGK: Mmmm . . .

ROMA: I don't know. For *me*, I'm saying, what it is, it's probably not the orgasm. Some broads, forearms on your neck, something her *eyes* did. There was a *sound* she made . . . or, me, lying in the, I'll tell you: me lying in bed; the next day she brought me café au lait. She gives me a cigarette, my balls feel like concrete. Eh? What I'm saying, what is our life? (*Pause.*) It's looking forward or it's looking back. And that's our life. That's *it*. Where is the *moment*? (*Pause.*) And what is it that we're afraid of? Loss. What else? (*Pause.*) The *bank* closes. We get *sick*, my wife died on a plane, the stock market collapsed . . . the house burnt down . . . what of these happen . . . ? None of 'em. We worry anyway. What does this mean? I'm not *secure*. How can I be secure? (*Pause.*) Through amassing wealth beyond all measure? No. And what's beyond all measure? That's a sickness. That's a trap. There is no measure. Only greed. How can we act? The right way, we would say,

to deal with this: "There is a one-in-a-million chance that so and so will happen. . . . *Fuck* it, it won't happen to *me*. . . ." No. We know that's not the right way I think. (*Pause.*) We say the *correct* way to deal with this is "There is a one-in-so-and-so chance this will happen . . . God *protect* me. I am powerless, let it not happen to me. . . ." But no to *that*. I say. There's something else. What is it? "If it happens, AS IT MAY for that is not within our powers, I will *deal* with it, just as I do *today* with what draws my concern today." I say *this* is how we must act. I do those things which seem correct to me *today*. I trust myself. And if security concerns me, I do that which *today* I think will make me secure. And every day I *do* that, when that day *arrives* that I need a reserve, (a) odds are that I have it, and (b) the *true* reserve that I have is the strength that I have of *acting each day* without fear. (*Pause.*) According to the dictates of my mind. (*Pause.*) Stocks, bonds, objects of art, real estate. Now: what are they? (*Pause.*) An opportunity. To what? To make money? Perhaps. To *lose* money? Perhaps. To "indulge" and to "learn" about ourselves? Perhaps. *So fucking what?* What *isn't*? They're an *opportunity*. That's all. They're an *event*. A guy comes up to you, you make a call, you send in a brochure, it doesn't matter, "There're these *properties* I'd like for you to see." What does it mean? What you *want* it to mean. (*Pause.*) Money? (*Pause.*) If that's what it signifies to you. Security? (*Pause.*) Comfort? (*Pause.*) All it is is THINGS THAT HAPPEN TO YOU. (*Pause.*) That's all it is. How are they different? (*Pause.*) Some poor newly married guy gets run down by a cab. Some *busboy* wins the lottery. (*Pause.*) All it is, it's a carnival. What's special . . . what *draws* us? (*Pause.*) We're all different. (*Pause.*) We're not the same. (*Pause.*) We are not the same. (*Pause.*) Hmmm. (*Pause. Sighs.*) It's been a long day. (*Pause.*) What are you drinking?

LINGK: Gimlet.

ROMA: Well, let's have a couple more. My name is Richard Roma, what's yours?

LINGK: Lingk. James Lingk.

ROMA: James. I'm glad to meet you. (*They shake hands.*) I'm glad to meet you, James. (*Pause.*) I want to show you something. (*Pause.*) It might mean *nothing* to you . . . and it might not. I don't know. I don't know anymore. (*Pause. He takes out a small map and spreads it on a table.*) What is that? Glengarry Highlands. Florida. "Florida. *Bullshit.*" And maybe that's true; and that's what *I* said: but look *here*: what is this? This is a piece of land. Listen to what I'm going to tell you now:

ACT TWO

The real estate office. Ransacked. A broken plate-glass window boarded up, glass all over the floor. Aaronow and Williamson standing around, smoking.

Pause.

AARONOW: People used to say that there are numbers of such magnitude that multiplying them by two made no difference. (*Pause.*)

WILLIAMSON: Who used to say that?

AARONOW: In school. (*Pause.*)

Baylen, a detective, comes out of the inner office.

BAYLEN: Alright . . . ?

Roma enters from the street.

ROMA: *Williamson . . . Williamson,* they stole the *contracts* . . . ?

BAYLEN: Excuse me, sir . . .

ROMA: Did they get my contracts?

WILLIAMSON: They got . . .

BAYLEN: Excuse me, fella.

ROMA: . . . did they . . .

BAYLEN: Would you excuse us, please . . . ?

ROMA: Don't *fuck* with me, fella. I'm talking about a fuckin' Cadillac car that you owe me . . .

WILLIAMSON: They didn't get your contract. I filed it before I left.

ROMA: They didn't get my contracts?

WILLIAMSON: They—excuse me . . . (*He goes back into inner room with the Detective.*)

ROMA: Oh, *fuck. Fuck.* (*He starts kicking the desk.*) FUCK FUCK FUCK! WILLIAMSON!!! WILLIAMSON!!! (*Goes to the door Williamson went into, tries the door; it's locked.*) OPEN THE FUCKING . . . WILLIAMSON . . .

BAYLEN (*coming out*): Who are you?

Williamson comes out.

WILLIAMSON: They didn't get the contracts.

ROMA: Did they . . .

WILLIAMSON: They got, listen to me . . .

ROMA: Th . . .

WILLIAMSON: Listen to me: They got *some* of them.

ROMA: Some of them . . .

BAYLEN: Who told you . . . ?

ROMA: Who told me wh . . . ? You've got a fuckin', you've . . . a . . . who is this . . . ? You've got a board up on the window. . . . *Moss* told me.

BAYLEN (*Looking back toward the inner office.*): Moss . . . Who told him?

ROMA: How the fuck do *I* know? (*To Williamson:*) *What* . . . *talk* to me.

WILLIAMSON: They took *some* of the con . . .

ROMA: . . . some of the contracts . . . Lingk. James Lingk. I closed . . .

WILLIAMSON: You closed him yesterday.

ROMA: *Yes.*

WILLIAMSON: It went down. I filed it.

ROMA: You did?

WILLIAMSON: Yes.

ROMA: Then I'm over the fucking top and you owe me a Cadillac.

WILLIAMSON: I . . .

ROMA: And I don't want any fucking shit and I don't give a shit, Lingk puts me over the top, you filed it, that's fine, any other shit kicks out *you* go back. You . . . *you* reclose it, 'cause I *closed* it and you . . . you owe me the car.

BAYLEN: Would you excuse us, please.

AARONOW: I, um, and may . . . maybe they're in . . . they're in . . . you should, John, if we're ins . . .

WILLIAMSON: I'm sure that we're insured, George . . . (*Going back inside.*)

ROMA: Fuck insured. You owe me a car.

BAYLEN (*Stepping back into the inner room*): Please don't leave. I'm going to talk to you. What's your name?

ROMA: Are you talking to me? (*Pause.*)

BAYLEN: Yes. (*Pause.*)

ROMA: My name is Richard Roma.

Baylen goes back into the inner room.

AARONOW: I, you know, they should be insured.

ROMA: What do *you* care . . . ?

AARONOW: Then, you know, they wouldn't be so ups . . .

ROMA: Yeah. That's swell. Yes. You're right. (*Pause.*) How are you?

AARONOW: I'm fine. You mean the *board*? You mean the *board* . . . ?

ROMA: I don't . . . yes. Okay, the board.

AARONOW: I'm, I'm, I'm, I'm fucked on the board. *You.* You see how . . . I . . . (*Pause.*) I can't . . . my mind must be in other places. 'Cause I can't do any . . .

ROMA: *What?* You can't do any *what?* (*Pause.*)

AARONOW: I can't close 'em.

ROMA: Well, they're old. I saw the shit that they were giving you.

AARONOW: Yes.

ROMA: Huh?

AARONOW: Yes. They are old.

ROMA: They're ancient.

AARONOW: Clear . . .

ROMA: Clear Meadows. That shit's dead. (*Pause.*)

AARONOW: It *is* dead.

ROMA: It's a waste of time.

AARONOW: Yes. (*Long pause.*) I'm no fucking good.

ROMA: That's . . .

AARONOW: Everything I . . . *you* know . . .

ROMA: That's not . . . Fuck that shit, George. You're a, *hey,* you had a bad month. You're a good man, George.

AARONOW: I am?

ROMA: You hit a bad streak. We've all . . . look at this: fifteen units Mountain View, the fucking things get stole.

AARONOW: He said he filed . . .

ROMA: He filed half of them, he filed the *big* one. All the little ones, I have, I have to go back and . . . ah, *fuck,* I got to go out like a fucking schmuck hat in my hand and reclose the . . . (*Pause.*) I mean, talk about a bad streak. That would sap *anyone's* self confi . . . I got to go out and reclose all my . . . Where's the phones?

AARONOW: They stole . . .

ROMA: They stole the . . .

AARONOW: What. What kind of outfit are we running where . . . where anyone . . .

ROMA (*To himself*): They stole the phones.

AARONOW: Where criminals can come in here . . . they take the . . .

ROMA: They stole the phones. They stole the leads. They're . . . *Christ.* (*Pause.*) What am I going to do this month? Oh, *shit* . . . (*Starts for the door.*)

AARONOW: You think they're going to catch . . . where are you going?

ROMA: Down the street.

WILLIAMSON (*Sticking his head out of the door*): Where are you going?

ROMA: To the restaura . . . what do you fucking . . . ?

WILLIAMSON: Aren't you going out today?

ROMA: With what? (*Pause.*) With what, John, they took the leads . . .

WILLIAMSON: I have the stuff from last year's . . .

ROMA: Oh. Oh. Oh, your "nostalgia" file, that's fine. No. Swell. 'Cause I don't have to . . .

WILLIAMSON: . . . you want to go out today . . . ?

ROMA: 'Cause I don't have to *eat* this month. No. Okay. Give 'em to me . . . (*To himself:*) Fucking Mitch and Murray going to shit a br . . . what am I going to *do* all . . .

Williamson starts back into the office. He is accosted by Aaronow.

AARONOW: Were the leads . . .

ROMA: . . . what am I going to *do* all month . . . ?

AARONOW: Were the leads insured?

WILLIAMSON: I don't know, George, why?

AARONOW: 'Cause, you know, 'cause they weren't, I know that Mitch and Murray uh . . . (*Pause.*)

WILLIAMSON: What?

AARONOW: That they're going to be upset.

WILLIAMSON: That's right. (*Going back into his office. Pause. To Roma:*) You want to go out today . . . ?

Pause. Williamson returns to his office.

AARONOW: He said we're all going to have to go talk to the guy.

ROMA: What?

AARONOW: He said we . . .

ROMA: To the cop?

AARONOW: Yeah.

ROMA: Yeah. That's swell. *Another* waste of time.

AARONOW: A waste of time? Why?

ROMA: *Why?* 'Cause they aren't going to find the guy.

AARONOW: The cops?

ROMA: Yes. The cops. No.

AARONOW: They aren't?

ROMA: No.

AARONOW: Why don't you think so?

ROMA: Why? Because they're *stupid.* "Where were you last night . . . "

AARONOW: Where were you?

ROMA: Where was *I*?

AARONOW: Yes.

ROMA: I was at home, where were *you*?

AARONOW: At home.

ROMA: *See* . . . ? Were you the guy who broke in?

AARONOW: Was I?

ROMA: Yes.

AARONOW: No.

ROMA: Then don't sweat it, George, you know why?

AARONOW: No.

ROMA: You have nothing to hide.

AARONOW (*Pause*): When I talk to the police, I get nervous.

ROMA: Yeah. You know who doesn't?

AARONOW: No, who?

ROMA: Thieves.

AARONOW: Why?

ROMA: They're inured to it.

AARONOW: You think so?

ROMA: Yes. (*Pause.*)

AARONOW: But what should I *tell* them?

ROMA: The truth, George. Always tell the truth. It's the easiest thing to remember.

Williamson comes out of the office with leads. Roma takes one, reads it.

ROMA: *Patel?* Ravidam *Patel?* How am I going to make a living on these deadbeat *wogs?* Where did you get this, from the *morgue?*

WILLIAMSON: If you don't want it, give it back.

ROMA: I don't "want" it, if you catch my drift.

WILLIAMSON: I'm giving you *three* leads. You . . .

ROMA: What's the fucking point in *any* case . . . ? What's the *point.* I got to argue with *you*, I got to knock heads with the *cops*, I'm busting my *balls*, sell you *dirt* to fucking *deadbeats* money in the *mattress*, I come back you can't even manage to keep the contracts safe, I have to go back and close them *again* . . . .What the fuck am I wasting my time, fuck this shit. I'm going out and reclose last week's . . .

WILLIAMSON: The word from Murray is: leave them alone. If we need a new signature he'll go out himself, he'll be the *president*, just come *in*, from out of *town* . . .

ROMA: Okay, okay, okay, gimme this shit. Fine. (*Takes the leads.*)

WILLIAMSON: Now, I'm giving you three . . .

ROMA: Three? I count *two.*

WILLIAMSON: Three.

ROMA: Patel? Fuck *you.* Fuckin' *Shiva* handed him a million dollars, told him "sign the deal," he wouldn't sign. And Vishnu, too. Into the bargain. Fuck *that*, John. You know your business, I know mine. Your business is being an *asshole*, and I find out whose fucking *cousin* you are, I'm going to go to him and figure out a way to have your *ass* . . . fuck you—I'll wait for the new leads.

Shelly Levene enters.

Alan Alda as Shelly Levene,
Tom Wopat as James Lingk,
and Liev Schreiber as Richard
Roma in the 2005 revival
at the Royale Theatre,
New York.

Charles Durning as Shelly
Levene in director Scott
Zigler's 2000 production of
Glengarry Glen Ross at the
McCarter Theatre in
Princeton, New Jersey.

LEVENE: Get the *chalk*. Get the *chalk* . . . get the *chalk*! I closed 'em! I *closed* the cocksucker. Get the chalk and put me on the *board*. I'm going to Hawaii! Put me on the Cadillac board, Williamson! Pick up the fuckin' chalk. Eight units. Mountain View . . .

ROMA: You sold eight Mountain View?

LEVENE: You bet your ass. Who wants to go to lunch? Who wants to go to lunch? I'm buying. (*Slaps contract down on Williamson's desk.*) Eighty-two fucking grand. And twelve grand in commission. John. (*Pause.*) On fucking deadbeat magazine subscription leads.

WILLIAMSON: Who?

LEVENE (*Pointing to contract*): *Read* it. Bruce and Harriett Nyborg. (*Looking around.*) What happened here?

AARONOW: Fuck. I had them on River Glen.

Levene looks around.

LEVENE: What happened?

WILLIAMSON: Somebody broke in.

ROMA: Eight units?

LEVENE: That's right.

ROMA: *Shelly* . . . !

LEVENE: Hey, big fucking deal. Broke a bad streak . . .

AARONOW: Shelly, the Machine, Levene.

LEVENE: You . . .

AARONOW: That's great.

LEVENE: Thank you, George.

Baylen sticks his head out of the room; calls in, "Aaronow." Aaronow goes into the side room.

LEVENE: Williamson, get on the phone, call Mitch . . .

ROMA: They took the phones . . .

LEVENE: They . . .

BAYLEN: *Aaronow* . . .

ROMA: They took the typewriters, they took the leads, they took the cash, they took the *contracts* . . .

LEVENE: Wh . . . wh . . . Wha . . . ?

AARONOW: We had a robbery. (*Goes into the inner room.*)

LEVENE (*Pause.*): When?

ROMA: Last night, this morning. (*Pause.*)

LEVENE: They took the leads?

ROMA: Mmm.

Moss comes out of the interrogation.

MOSS: Fuckin' asshole.

ROMA: What, they beat you with a rubber bat?

MOSS: Cop couldn't find his dick two hands and a map. Anyone talks to this guy's an *asshole* . . .

ROMA: You going to turn State's?

MOSS: Fuck you, Ricky. I ain't going out today. I'm going home. I'm going home because nothing's *accomplished* here. . . . Anyone *talks* to this guy is . . .

ROMA: Guess what the Machine did?

MOSS: Fuck the Machine.

ROMA: Mountain View. Eight units.

MOSS: Fuckin' cop's got no right talk to me that way. I didn't rob the place . . .

ROMA: You hear what I said?

MOSS: Yeah. He closed a deal.

ROMA: Eight units. Mountain View.

MOSS (*To Levene*): You did that?

LEVENE: Yeah. (*Pause.*)

MOSS: Fuck you.

ROMA: Guess who?

MOSS: When . . .

LEVENE: Just now.

ROMA: Guess who?

MOSS: You just this morning . . .

ROMA: Harriett and blah blah Nyborg.

MOSS: You did that?

LEVENE: Eighty-two thousand dollars. (*Pause.*)

MOSS: Those fuckin' *deadbeats* . . .

LEVENE: My ass. I told 'em. (*To Roma:*) Listen to this: I said . . .

MOSS: Hey, I don't want to hear your fucking war stories . . .

ROMA: Fuck *you*, Dave . . .

LEVENE: "You have to believe in your*self* . . . you"—look—"alright . . . ?"

MOSS (*To Williamson*): Give me some leads. I'm going out . . . I'm getting out of . . .

LEVENE: " . . . you have to believe in your*self* . . ."

MOSS: Na, fuck the leads, I'm going home.

LEVENE: "Bruce, Harriett . . . Fuck *me*, believe in your*self* . . ."

ROMA: We haven't got a lead . . .

MOSS: Why not?

ROMA: They took 'em . . .

MOSS: Hey, they're fuckin' garbage any case. . . . This whole goddamn . . .

LEVENE: " . . . You look around, you say, 'This one has so-and-so, and I have nothing . . .'"

MOSS: *Shit.*

LEVENE: "'*Why?* Why don't I get the opportunities . . . ?'"

MOSS: And did they steal the contracts . . . ?

ROMA: Fuck *you* care . . . ?

LEVENE: "I want to tell you something, Harriett . . ."

MOSS: . . . the fuck is *that* supposed to mean . . . ?

LEVENE: Will you shut up, I'm telling you this . . .

Aaronow sticks his head out.

AARONOW: Can we get some coffee . . . ?

MOSS: How ya doing? (*Pause.*)

AARONOW: Fine.

MOSS: Uh-huh.

AARONOW: If anyone's going, I could use some coffee.

LEVENE: "You *do* get the . . ." (*To Roma:*) Huh? Huh?

MOSS: *Fuck* is that supposed to mean?

LEVENE: "You *do* get the opportunity. . . . You *get* them. As *I* do, as *anyone* does . . ."

MOSS: Ricky? . . . That I don't care they stole the contracts? (*Pause.*)

LEVENE: I got 'em in the kitchen. I'm eating her crumb cake.

MOSS: What does that mean?

ROMA: It *means*, Dave, you haven't closed a good one in a month, none of my business, you want to push me to answer you. (*Pause.*) And so you haven't got a contract to get stolen or so forth.

MOSS: You have a mean streak in you, Ricky, you know that . . . ?

LEVENE: Rick. Let me tell you. Wait, we're in the . . .

MOSS: Shut the fuck up. (*Pause.*) Ricky. You have a mean streak in you. . . . (*To Levene:*) And what the fuck are *you* babbling about . . . ? (*To Roma:*) Bring that shit up. Of my volume. You were on a bad one and I brought it up to *you* you'd harbor it. (*Pause.*) You'd harbor it a long long while. And you'd be right.

ROMA: Who said "Fuck the Machine"?

MOSS: *"Fuck the Machine"? "Fuck the Machine"?* What is this. *Courtesy* class . . . ? You're *fucked*, Rick — are you fucking *nuts*? You're hot, so you think you're the *ruler* of this place . . . ?! You want to . . .

LEVENE: Dave . . .

MOSS: . . . Shut up. Decide who should be dealt with how? Is that the thing? I come into the fuckin' office today, I get humiliated by some jagoff cop. I get accused of . . . I get this *shit* thrown in my face by you, you genuine shit, because you're top name on the board . . .

ROMA: Is that what I did? Dave? I humiliated you? My *God* . . . I'm *sorry* . . .

MOSS: Sittin' on top of the *world*, sittin' on top of the *world*, everything's fucking *peach*fuzz . . .

ROMA: Oh, and I don't get a moment to spare for a bust-out *humanitarian* down on his luck lately. Fuck *you*, Dave, you know you got a big *mouth*, and *you* make a close the whole *place* stinks with your *farts* for a week. "How much you just ingested," what a big *man* you are, "Hey, let me buy you a pack of gum. I'll show you how to *chew* it." Your *pal* closes, all that comes out of your mouth is *bile*, how fucked *up* you are . . .

MOSS: *Who's* my pal . . . ? And what are you, Ricky, huh, what are you, Bishop *Sheean*? Who the fuck are *you*, Mr. Slick . . . ? What are you, friend to the *working-man*? Big deal. Fuck *you*, you got the memory a fuckin' *fly*. I never liked you.

ROMA: What is this, your farewell speech?

MOSS: I'm going home.

ROMA: Your farewell to the troops?

MOSS: I'm not going home. I'm going to Wis*cons*in.

ROMA: Have a good trip.

MOSS (*Simultaneously with "trip"*): And fuck *you*. Fuck the *lot* of you. Fuck you *all*.

Moss exits. Pause.

ROMA (*To Levene*): You were saying? (*Pause.*) Come on. Come on, you got them in the kitchen, you got the stats spread out, you're in your shirt-sleeves, you can *smell* it. Huh? Snap out of it, you're eating her *crumb* cake. (*Pause.*)

LEVENE: I'm eating her *crumb* cake . . .

ROMA: How was it . . . ?

LEVENE: From the store.

ROMA: Fuck *her* . . .

LEVENE: "What we have to do is *admit* to ourself that we see that opportunity . . . and *take* it. (*Pause.*) And that's it." And we *sit* there. (*Pause.*) I got the pen out . . .

ROMA: "Always be closing . . ."

LEVENE: That's what I'm *saying*. The *old* ways. The *old* ways . . . convert the motherfucker . . . *sell* him . . . *sell* him . . . *make him sign the check*. (*Pause.*) The . . . Bruce, Harriett . . . the kitchen, blah: they got their money in *government* bonds. . . . I say *fuck* it, we're going to go the whole route. I plat it out eight units. Eighty-two grand. I tell them. "This is now. This is that *thing* that you've been dreaming of, you're going to find that suitcase on the train, the guy comes in the door, the bag that's full of money. This is it, *Harriett* . . ."

ROMA (*Reflectively*): Harriett . . .

LEVENE: *Bruce* . . . "I don't want to fuck *around* with you. I don't want to go *round* this, and *pussyfoot* around the thing, you have to look back on this. I do, too. I came here to do good for you and me. For *both* of us. Why take an interim position? *The only arrangement I'll accept* is full investment. Period. The whole eight units. I know that you're saying 'be safe,' I know what you're saying. I know if I left you to yourselves, you'd say 'come back tomorrow,' and when I walked out that door, you'd make a cup of *coffee* . . . you'd sit *down* . . . and you'd think 'let's be safe . . .' and not to disappoint me you'd go *one* unit or maybe two, because you'd become scared because you'd met possi*bi*lity. But this won't do, and that's not the subject. . . ." Listen to this, I actually said this. "That's not the subject of our *evening* together." Now I handed them the pen. I held it in my hand. I turned the contract, eight units eighty-two grand. "Now I want you to sign." (*Pause.*) I sat there. Five minutes. Then, I sat there, Ricky, *twenty-two minutes* by the kitchen clock. (*Pause.*) Twenty-two minutes by the kitchen clock. Not a *word*, not a *motion*. What am I thinking? "My arm's getting tired?" *No.* I *did* it. I *did* it. Like in the *old* days, Ricky. Like I was taught . . . Like, like, like I *used* to do . . . I did it.

ROMA: Like you taught me . . .

LEVENE: Bullshit, you're . . . No. That's raw . . . well, if I *did,* then I'm *glad* I did. I, *well.* I locked on them. All on them, nothing on me. All my thoughts are on them. I'm holding the last thought that I spoke: "Now is the time." (*Pause.*) They signed, Ricky. It was *great.* It was fucking great. It was like they wilted all at once. No *gesture* . . . nothing. Like together. They, I swear to God, they both kind of *imperceptibly slumped.* And he reaches and takes the pen and signs, he passes it to her, she signs. It was so fucking solemn. I just let it sit. I nod like this. I nod again. I grasp his hands. I shake his hands. I grasp *her* hands. I nod at her like this. "Bruce . . . Harriett . . ." I'm beaming at them. I'm nodding like this. I point back in the living room, back to the side-board. (*Pause.*) *I didn't fucking know there was a sideboard there!!* He goes back, he brings us a drink. Little shot glasses. A pattern in 'em. And we toast. In silence. (*Pause.*)

ROMA: That was a great sale, Shelly. (*Pause.*)

LEVENE: Ah, fuck. Leads! Leads! Williamson! (*Williamson sticks his head out of the office.*) Send me *out*! Send me *out*!

WILLIAMSON: The leads are coming.

LEVENE: *Get* 'em to me!

WILLIAMSON: I talked to Murray and Mitch an hour ago. They're coming in, you understand they're a bit *upset* over this morning's . . .

LEVENE: Did you tell 'em my sale?

WILLIAMSON: How could I tell 'em your sale? Eh? I don't have a tel . . . I'll tell 'em your sale when they bring in the leads. Alright? Shelly. Alright? We had a little . . . You closed a deal. You made a good sale. Fine.

LEVENE: It's better than a good sale. It's a . . .

WILLIAMSON: Look: I have a lot of things on my mind, they're coming in, alright, they're very upset, I'm try-ing to make some *sense* . . .

LEVENE: All that I'm *telling* you: that one thing you can tell them it's a remarkable sale.

WILLIAMSON: The only thing remarkable is who you made it to.

LEVENE: What does *that* fucking mean?

WILLIAMSON: That if the sale sticks, it will be a miracle.

LEVENE: Why should the sale not stick? Hey, *fuck* you. That's what I'm saying. You have no idea of your job. A man's his job and you're *fucked* at yours. You hear what I'm saying to you? Your "end of month board . . ." You can't run an office. I don't care. You don't know what it *is*, you don't have the *sense*, you don't have the *balls*. You ever been on a sit? *Ever*? Has this cocksucker ever been . . . you ever sit down with a cust . . .

WILLIAMSON: I were you, I'd calm down, Shelly.

LEVENE: *Would* you? *Would* you . . . ? Or you're gonna *what*, fire me?

WILLIAMSON: It's not impossible.

LEVENE: On an eighty-thousand dollar *day*? And it ain't even *noon*.

ROMA: You closed 'em today?

LEVENE: Yes. I did. This *morning*. (*To Williamson:*) What I'm *saying* to you: things can *change*. You *see*? This is where you fuck *up*, because this is something you don't *know*. You can't look down the *road*. And see what's *coming*. Might be someone *else*, John. It might be someone *new*, eh? Someone *new*. And you can't look *back*. 'Cause you don't know *history*. You ask them. When we were at Rio Rancho, who was top man? A month . . . ? Two months . . . ? Eight months in twelve for three years in a row. You know what that means? You know what that means? Is that *luck*? Is that some, some, some purloined leads? That's *skill*. That's *talent*, that's, that's . . .

ROMA: . . . *yes* . . .

LEVENE: . . . and you don't *remember*. 'Cause you weren't *around*. That's cold *calling*. Walk up to the door. I don't even know their *name*. I'm selling something they don't even *want*. You talk about soft sell . . . before we had a name for it . . . before we called it anything, we did it.

ROMA: That's right, Shel.

LEVENE: And, and, and, I *did* it. And I put a kid through *school*. She . . . and . . . Cold *calling*, fella. Door to door. But you don't know. You don't know. You never heard of a *streak*. You never heard of "mar-shaling your sales force. . . ." What are you, you're a *secretary*, John. Fuck *you*. That's my message to you. Fuck you and kiss my ass. You don't like it, I'll go talk to Jerry Graff. Period. Fuck you. Put me on the board. And I want three worthwhile leads today and I don't want any bullshit about them and I want 'em close together 'cause I'm going to hit them all today. That's all I have to say to you.

ROMA: He's right, Williamson.

Williamson goes into a side office. Pause.

LEVENE: It's not right. I'm sorry, and I'll tell you who's to blame is Mitch and Murray.

Roma sees something outside the window.

ROMA (*Sotto*): Oh, Christ.

LEVENE: The hell with him. We'll go to lunch, the leads won't be up for . . .

ROMA: You're a client. I just sold you five waterfront Glengarry Farms. I rub my head, throw me the cue "Kenilworth."

LEVENE: What is it?

ROMA: Kenilw . . .

Lingk enters the office.

ROMA (*To Levene*): I own the property, my *mother* owns the property, I put her *into* it. I'm going to show you on the plats. You look when you get home A–3 through A–14 and 26 through 30. You take your time and if you still feel.

LEVENE: No, Mr. Roma. I don't need the time, I've made a lot of *investments* in the last . . .

LINGK: I've got to talk to you.

ROMA (*Looking up*): Jim! What are you doing here? Jim Lingk, D. Ray Morton . . .

LEVENE: Glad to meet you.

ROMA: I just put Jim into Black Creek . . . are you acquainted with . . .

LEVENE: No . . . Black *Creek*. Yes. In *Florida*?

ROMA: Yes.

LEVENE: I wanted to *speak* with you about . . .

ROMA: Well, we'll do that this weekend.

LEVENE: My *wife* told me to look into . . .

ROMA: *Beautiful*. Beautiful rolling land. I was telling Jim and Jinny, Ray, I want to tell you something. (*To Levene:*) You, Ray, you eat in a lot of restaurants. I know you do. . . . (*To Lingk:*) Mr. Morton's with

American Express . . . he's . . . (*To Levene:*) I can tell Jim what you do . . . ?

LEVENE: Sure.

ROMA: Ray is director of all European sales and services for American Ex . . . (*To Levene:*) But I'm saying you haven't had a *meal* until you've tasted . . . I was at the Lingks' last . . . as a matter of fact, what was that service feature you were talking about . . . ?

LEVENE: Which . . .

ROMA: "Home Cooking" . . . what did you call it, you said it . . . it was a tag phrase that you had . . .

LEVENE: Uh . . .

ROMA: Home . . .

LEVENE: Home cooking . . .

ROMA: The monthly interview . . . ?

LEVENE: Oh! For the *magazine* . . .

ROMA: Yes. Is this something that I can talk ab . . .

LEVENE: Well, it isn't coming *out* until the February iss . . . *sure.* Sure, go ahead, Ricky.

ROMA: You're sure?

LEVENE (*nods*): Go ahead.

ROMA: Well, Ray was eating at one of his company's men's home in France . . . the man's French, isn't he?

LEVENE: No, his *wife* is.

ROMA: Ah. Ah, his wife is. Ray: what *time* do you have . . . ?

LEVENE: Twelve-fifteen.

ROMA: Oh! My God . . . I've got to get you on the *plane*!

LEVENE: Didn't I say I was taking the two o' . . .

ROMA: No. You said the one. That's why you said we couldn't talk till Kenilworth.

LEVENE: Oh, my God, you're right! I'm on the one. . . . (*Getting up.*) Well, let's *scoot* . . .

LINGK: I've got to talk to you . . .

ROMA: I've got to get Ray to O'Hare . . . (*To Levene:*) Come on, let's hustle. . . . (*Over his shoulder:*) John! Call American Express in *Pittsburgh* for Mr. Morton, will you, tell them he's on the one o'clock. (*To Lingk:*) I'll see you. . . . Christ, I'm sorry you came all the way in. . . . I'm running Ray over to O'Hare. . . . You wait here, I'll . . . no. (*To Levene:*) I'm meeting your man at the bank. . . . (*To Lingk:*) I wish you'd phoned. . . . I'll tell you, wait: are you and Jinny going to be home tonight? (*Rubs forehead.*)

LINGK: I . . .

LEVENE: Rick.

ROMA: What?

LEVENE: *Kenilworth* . . . ?

ROMA: I'm sorry . . . ?

LEVENE: *Kenilworth.*

ROMA: Oh, God . . . Oh, God . . . (*Roma takes Lingk aside, sotto*) Jim, excuse me. . . . Ray, I told you, who he is is *the* senior vice-president American Express. His family owns 32 per. . . . Over the past years I've sold him . . . I can't tell you the dollar amount, but *quite* a lot of land. I promised five *weeks* ago that I'd go to the wife's birthday party in Kenilworth tonight. (*Sighs.*) I *have* to go. You understand. They treat me

like a member of the family, so I have to go. It's funny, you know, you get a picture of the Corporation-Type Company Man, all business . . . this man, *no.* We'll go out to his home sometime. Let's see. (*He checks his datebook.*) Tomorrow. No. Tomorrow, I'm in L.A. . . . *Monday* . . . I'll take you to lunch, where would you like to go?

LINGK: My wife . . . (*Roma rubs his head.*)

LEVENE (*Standing in the door*): Rick . . . ?

ROMA: I'm sorry, Jim. I can't talk now. I'll call you tonight . . . I'm sorry. I'm coming, Ray. (*Starts for the door.*)

LINGK: My wife said I have to cancel the deal.

ROMA: It's a common reaction, Jim. I'll tell you what it is, and I know that that's why you married her. One of the reasons is *prudence.* It's a sizable investment. One thinks *twice* . . . it's also something *women* have. It's just a reaction to the size of the investment. *Monday,* if you'd invite me for dinner again . . . (*To Levene:*) This woman can *cook* . . .

LEVENE (*Simultaneously*): I'm sure she can . . .

ROMA (*To Lingk*): We're going to talk. I'm going to *tell* you something. Because (*Sotto:*) there's something about your acreage I want you to know. I can't talk about it now. I really shouldn't. And, in fact, by *law,* I . . . (*Shrugs, resigned.*) The man next to you, he bought his lot at forty-*two,* he phoned to say that he'd *already* had an offer . . . (*Roma rubs his head.*)

LEVENE: Rick . . . ?

ROMA: I'm coming, Ray . . . what a day! I'll call you this evening, Jim. I'm sorry you had to come in . . . Monday, lunch.

LINGK: My wife . . .

LEVENE: Rick, we really have to go.

LINGK: My wife . . .

ROMA: Monday.

LINGK: She called the consumer . . . the attorney, I don't know. The attorney gen . . . they said we have three days . . .

ROMA: *Who* did she call?

LINGK: I don't know, the attorney gen . . . the . . . some consumer office, umm . . .

ROMA: Why did she do *that,* Jim?

LINGK: I don't know. (*Pause.*) They said we have three days. (*Pause.*) They said we have three days.

ROMA: Three days.

LINGK: To . . . you know. (*Pause.*)

ROMA: No, I don't know. *Tell* me.

LINGK: To change our minds.

ROMA: Of *course* you have three days. (*Pause.*)

LINGK: So we can't talk *Monday.* (*Pause.*)

ROMA: Jim, Jim, you saw my book . . . I *can't,* you saw my book . . .

LINGK: But we have to *before* Monday. To get our money ba . . .

ROMA: Three *business* days. They mean three *business* days.

LINGK: Wednesday, Thursday, Friday.

ROMA: I don't understand.

Kevin Spacey as Williamson (left) and Jack Lemmon as Levene (right) in the 1992 film version of *Glengarry Glen Ross* (New Line Cinema), directed by James Foley.

The premiere production of *Glengarry Glen Ross* in 1983 at the Cottesloe Theatre in London, directed by Bill Bryden, with Jack Shepherd as Roma (left) and Tony Haygarth as Lingk (right).

LINGK: That's what they are. Three business . . . if I wait till Monday, my time limit runs out.

ROMA: You don't count Saturday.

LINGK: I'm not.

ROMA: No, I'm saying you don't include Saturday . . . in your three days. It's not a *business* day.

LINGK: But I'm not *counting* it. (*Pause.*) Wednesday. Thursday. Friday. So it would have elapsed.

ROMA: What would have elapsed?

LINGK: If we wait till Mon . . .

ROMA: When did you write the check?

LINGK: Yest . . .

ROMA: What was yesterday?

LINGK: Tuesday.

ROMA: And when was that check cashed?

LINGK: I don't know.

ROMA: What was the *earliest* it could have been cashed? (*Pause.*)

LINGK: I don't know.

ROMA: *Today.* (*Pause.*) *Today.* Which, in any case, it was not, as there were a couple of points on the agreement I wanted to go over with you in any case.

LINGK: The check wasn't cashed?

ROMA: I just called downtown, and it's on their desk.

LEVENE: Rick . . .

ROMA: One moment, I'll be right with you. (*To Lingk:*) In fact, a . . . one point, which I spoke to you of which (*Looks around.*) I can't talk to you about here.

Detective puts his head out of the doorway.

BAYLEN: Levene!!!

LINGK: I, I . . .

ROMA: Listen to me, the *statute*, it's for your protection. I have no complaints with that, in fact, I was a member of the board when we *drafted* it, so quite the *opposite*. It *says* that you can change your mind three working days from the time the deal is closed.

BAYLEN: Levene!

ROMA: Which, wait a second, which is not until the check is cashed.

BAYLEN: Levene!!

Aaronow comes out of the Detective's office.

AARONOW: I'm *through*, with *this* fucking meshugaas. No one should talk to a man that way. How are you *talking* to me that . . . ?

BAYLEN: Levene! (*Williamson puts his head out of the office.*)

AARONOW: . . . how can you *talk* to me that . . . that . . .

LEVENE (*To Roma*): Rick, I'm going to flag a cab.

AARONOW: I didn't rob . . .

Williamson sees Levene.

WILLIAMSON: Shelly: get in the office.

AARONOW: *I* didn't . . . why should *I* . . . "Where were you last . . ." Is anybody listening to me . . . ? Where's Moss . . . ? Where . . . ?

BAYLEN: Levene? (*To Williamson:*) Is this Lev . . . (*Baylen accosts Lingk.*)

LEVENE (*Taking Baylen into the office*): Ah. Ah. Perhaps I can advise you on that . . . . (*To Roma and Lingk, as he exits:*) *Excuse* us, will you . . . ?

AARONOW (*Simultaneous with Levene's speech above*): . . . Come in here . . . I *work* here, I don't come in here to be *mistreated* . . .

WILLIAMSON: Go to *lunch*, will you . . .

AARONOW: I want to *work* today, that's why I came . . .

WILLIAMSON: The leads come in, I'll let . . .

AARONOW: . . . that's why I came in. I thought I . . .

WILLIAMSON: Just go to lunch.

AARONOW: I don't *want* to go to lunch.

WILLIAMSON: Go to lunch, George.

AARONOW: Where does he get off to talk that way to a working man? It's not . . .

WILLIAMSON (*Buttonholes him*): Will you take it outside, we have people trying to do *business* here . . .

AARONOW: That's what, that's what, that's what *I* was trying to do. (*Pause.*) That's why I came *in* . . . I meet *gestapo* tac . . .

WILLIAMSON (*Going back into his office*): Excuse me . . .

AARONOW: I meet *gestapo* tactics . . . I meet *gestapo* tactics. . . . That's not right. . . . No man has the right to . . . "Call an attorney," that means you're guilt . . . you're under sus . . . "Co . . . ," he says, "cooperate" or we'll go downtown. *That's* not . . . as long as I've . . .

WILLIAMSON (*Bursting out of his office*): Will you get out of here. Will you get *out* of here. Will you. I'm trying to run an *office* here. Will you go to lunch? Go to lunch. Will you go to lunch? (*Retreats into office.*)

ROMA (*To Aaronow*): Will you excuse . . .

AARONOW: Where did Moss . . . ? I . . .

ROMA: Will you excuse us please?

AARONOW: Uh, uh, did he go to the restaurant? (*Pause.*) I . . . I . . . (*Exits.*)

ROMA: I'm *very* sorry, Jimmy. I apologize to you.

LINGK: It's not me, it's my wife.

ROMA (*Pause.*): What is?

LINGK: I told you.

ROMA: Tell me again.

LINGK: What's going on here?

ROMA: Tell me again. Your wife.

LINGK: I told you.

ROMA: You tell me again.

LINGK: She wants her money back.

ROMA: We're going to speak to her.

LINGK: No. She told me "right now."

ROMA: We'll speak to her, Jim . . .

LINGK: She won't listen.

Detective sticks his head out.

BAYLEN: *Roma.*

LINGK: She told me if not, I have to call the State's attorney.

ROMA: No, no. That's just something she "said." We don't have to do that.

LINGK: She told me I *have* to.

ROMA: No, Jim.

LINGK: I *do*. If I don't get my *money* back . . .

(*Williamson points out Roma to Baylen.*)

BAYLEN: Roma! (*To Roma:*) I'm talking to you . . .

ROMA: I've . . . look. (*Generally:*) Will someone get this guy off my back.

BAYLEN: You have a problem?

ROMA: Yes, I have a problem. Yes, I *do*, my fr . . . It's not me that ripped the joint off, I'm doing *business*. I'll be with you in a *while*. You got it . . . ? (*Looks back. Lingk is heading for the door.*) Where are you going?

LINGK: I'm . . .

ROMA: Where are you going . . . ? This is *me*. . . . This is Ricky, Jim. Jim, anything you *want*, you *want* it, you *have* it. You understand? This is *me*. Something *upset* you. Sit down, now sit down. You tell me what it is. (*Pause.*) Am I going to help you fix it? You're god-damned right I am. Sit down. Tell you something . . . ? *Sometimes* we need someone from *outside*. It's . . . no, sit down. . . . Now *talk* to me.

LINGK: I can't negotiate.

ROMA: What does that mean?

LINGK: That . . .

ROMA: . . . what, what, *say* it. Say it to me . . .

LINGK: I . . .

ROMA: What . . . ?

LINGK: I . . . .

ROMA: What . . . ? Say the words.

LINGK: I don't have the *power*. (*Pause.*) I said it.

ROMA: What power?

LINGK: The power to negotiate.

ROMA: To negotiate what? (*Pause.*) To negotiate what?

LINGK: *This*.

ROMA: What, "this"? (*Pause.*)

LINGK: The deal.

ROMA: The "deal," *forget* the deal. *Forget* the deal, you've got something on your mind, Jim, what is it?

LINGK (*rising*): I can't talk to you, you met my wife, I . . . (*Pause.*)

ROMA: What? (*Pause.*) What? (*Pause.*) What, Jim: I tell you what, let's get out of here . . . let's go get a drink.

LINGK: She told me not to talk to you.

ROMA: Let's . . . no one's going to know, let's go around the *corner* and we'll get a drink.

LINGK: She told me I had to get back the check or call the State's att . . .

ROMA: *Forget* the deal, Jimmy. (*Pause.*) *Forget* the deal . . . you know me. The deal's *dead*. Am I talking about the *deal*? That's *over*. Please. Let's talk about *you*. Come on. (*Pause. Roma rises and starts walking toward the front door.*) Come on. (*Pause.*) Come on, Jim. (*Pause.*) I want to tell you something. Your life is your own. You have a contract with your wife. You have certain things you do *jointly*, you have a *bond* there . . . and there are *other* things. Those things are yours. You needn't feel *ashamed*, you needn't feel that you're being *untrue* . . . or that she would aban-don you if she knew. This is your life. (*Pause.*) Yes.

Now I want to *talk* to you because you're obviously upset and that *concerns* me. Now let's go. Right now.

Lingk gets up and they start for the door.

BAYLEN (*Sticks his head out of the door*): Roma . . .

LINGK: . . . and . . . and . . . (*Pause.*)

ROMA: What?

LINGK: And the check is . . .

ROMA: What did I *tell* you? (*Pause.*) What did I say about the three days . . . ?

BAYLEN: Roma, would you, I'd like to get some lunch . . .

ROMA: I'm talking with Mr. Lingk. If you please, I'll be back in. (*Checks watch.*) I'll be back in a while. . . . I told you, check with Mr. Williamson.

BAYLEN: The people downtown said . . .

ROMA: You call them again. Mr. Williamson . . . !

WILLIAMSON: Yes.

ROMA: Mr. Lingk and I are going to . . .

WILLIAMSON: Yes. Please. Please. (*To Lingk:*) The police (*Shrugs.*) can be . . .

LINGK: What are the police doing?

ROMA: It's nothing.

LINGK: What are the *police* doing here . . . ?

WILLIAMSON: We had a slight burglary last night.

ROMA: It was nothing . . . I was assuring Mr. Lingk . . .

WILLIAMSON: Mr. Lingk. James Lingk. Your contract went out. Nothing to . . .

ROMA: John . . .

WILLIAMSON: Your contract went out to the bank.

LINGK: You cashed the check?

WILLIAMSON: We . . .

ROMA: . . . Mr. Williamson . . .

WILLIAMSON: Your check was cashed yesterday after-noon. And we're completely insured, as you know, in *any* case. (*Pause.*)

LINGK (*To Roma*): You cashed the check?

ROMA: Not to my knowledge, no . . .

WILLIAMSON: I'm sure we can . . .

LINGK: Oh, Christ . . . (*Starts out the door.*) Don't follow me. . . . Oh, Christ. (*Pause. To Roma.*) I know I've let you down. I'm sorry. For . . . Forgive . . . for . . . I don't know anymore. (*Pause.*) Forgive me. (*Lingk exits. Pause.*)

ROMA (*To Williamson*): You stupid fucking cunt. *You*, Williamson . . . I'm talking to *you*, shithead. . . . You just cost me *six thousand dollars*. (*Pause.*) Six thou-sand dollars. And one Cadillac. That's right. What are you going to do about it? What are you going to do about it, asshole. You fucking *shit*. Where did you learn your *trade*. You stupid fucking *cunt*. You *idiot*. Whoever told you you could work with *men*?

BAYLEN: Could I . . .

ROMA: I'm going to have your *job*, shithead. I'm going *downtown* and talk to Mitch and Murray, and I'm going to Lemkin. I don't care *whose* nephew you are, who you know, whose dick you're sucking on. You're going *out*, I swear to you, you're going . . .

BAYLEN: Hey, fella, let's get this done . . .

ROMA: Anyone in this office lives on their *wits*.... (*To Baylen:*) I'm going to be with you in a second. (*To Williamson:*) What you're hired for is to *help* us—does that seem clear to you? To *help* us. Not to fuck us up ... to help *men* who are going *out* there to try to earn a *living.* You *fairy.* You company man ... I'll tell you something else. I hope you knocked the joint off, I can tell our friend here something might help him catch you. (*Starts into the room.*) You want to learn the first rule you'd know if you ever spent a day in your life ... you never open your mouth till you know what the shot is. (*Pause.*) You fucking *child* ... (*Roma goes to the inner room.*)

LEVENE: You *are* a shithead, Williamson ... (*Pause.*)

WILLIAMSON: Mmm.

LEVENE: You can't think on your feet you should keep your mouth closed. (*Pause.*) You hear me? I'm *talking* to you. Do you hear me ...?

WILLIAMSON: Yes. (*Pause.*) I hear you.

LEVENE: You can't learn that in an office. Eh? He's right. You have to learn it on the streets. You can't *buy* that. You have to *live* it.

WILLIAMSON: Mmm.

LEVENE: *Yes.* Mmm. *Yes. Precisely. Precisely.* 'Cause your partner *depends* on it. (*Pause.*) I'm *talking* to you, I'm trying to tell you something.

WILLIAMSON: You are?

LEVENE: Yes, I am.

WILLIAMSON: What are you trying to tell me?

LEVENE: What Roma's trying to tell you. What I told you yesterday. Why you don't belong in this business.

WILLIAMSON: Why I don't ...

LEVENE: You listen to me, someday you might say, "Hey ..." No, fuck that, you just listen what I'm going to say: your partner *depends* on you. Your partner ... a man who's your "partner" *depends* on you ... you have to go *with* him and *for* him ... or you're shit, you're *shit,* you can't exist alone ...

WILLIAMSON (*Brushing past him*): Excuse me ...

LEVENE: ... excuse you, *nothing,* you be as cold as you want, but you just fucked a good man out of six thousand dollars and his goddamn bonus 'cause you didn't know the *shot,* if you can do that and you aren't man enough that it gets you, then I don't know what, if you can't take *some thing* from that ... (*Blocking his way.*) you're *scum,* you're fucking white-bread. You be as cold as you want. A *child* would know it, he's right. (*Pause.*) You're going to make something up, be sure it will *help* or keep your mouth closed. (*Pause.*)

WILLIAMSON: Mmm. (*Levene lifts up his arm.*)

LEVENE: Now I'm done with you. (*Pause.*)

WILLIAMSON: How do you know I made it up?

LEVENE (*Pause*): What?

WILLIAMSON: How do you know I made it up?

LEVENE: What are you talking about?

WILLIAMSON: You said, "You don't make something up unless it's sure to help." (*Pause.*) How did you know that I made it up?

LEVENE: What are you talking about?

WILLIAMSON: I told the customer that his contracts had gone to the bank.

LEVENE: Well, hadn't it?

WILLIAMSON: No. (*Pause.*) It hadn't.

LEVENE: Don't *fuck* with me, John, don't *fuck* with me ... what are you saying?

WILLIAMSON: Well, I'm saying this, Shel: usually I take the contracts to the bank. Last night I didn't. How did you know that? One night in a year I left a contract on my desk. Nobody knew that but *you.* Now how did you know that? (*Pause.*) You want to talk to me, you want to talk to someone *else* ... because this is *my* job. This is my job on the line, and you are going to *talk* to me. Now how did you know that contract was on my desk?

LEVENE: You're so full of shit.

WILLIAMSON: You robbed the office.

LEVENE (*Laughs*): Sure! I robbed the office. Sure.

WILLIAMSON: What'd you do with the leads? (*Pause. Points to the Detective's room.*) You want to go in there? I tell him what I know, he's going to dig up *something.* ... You got an alibi last night? You better have one. What did you do with the leads? If you tell me what you did with the leads, we can talk.

LEVENE: I don't know what you are saying.

WILLIAMSON: If you tell me where the leads are, I won't turn you in. If you *don't,* I am going to tell the cop you stole them, Mitch and Murray will see that you go to jail. Believe me they will. Now, what did you do with the leads? I'm walking in that door—you have five seconds to tell me: or you are going to jail.

LEVENE: I ...

WILLIAMSON: I don't care. You understand? *Where are the leads?* (*Pause.*) Alright. (*Williamson goes to open the office door.*)

LEVENE: I sold them to Jerry Graff.

WILLIAMSON: How much did you get for them? (*Pause.*) How much did you get for them?

LEVENE: Five thousand. I kept half.

WILLIAMSON: Who kept the other half? (*Pause.*)

LEVENE: Do I have to tell you? (*Pause. Williamson starts to open the door.*) Moss.

WILLIAMSON: *That* was easy, *wasn't* it? (*Pause.*)

LEVENE: It was his idea.

WILLIAMSON: *Was* it?

LEVENE: I ... I'm sure he got more than the five, actually.

WILLIAMSON: Uh-huh?

LEVENE: He told me my share was twenty-five.

WILLIAMSON: Mmm.

LEVENE: Okay: I ... look: I'm going to make it worth your while. I am. I turned this thing around. I closed the *old* stuff, I can do it again. *I'm* the one's going to close 'em. *I* am! *I* am! 'Cause I turned this thing a ... I can do *that,* I can do *anyth* ... last night. I'm going to tell you, I was ready to Do the Dutch. Moss gets me, "Do this, we'll get well...." Why not. Big fuckin' deal. I'm halfway hoping to get caught. To put me out of my ... (*Pause.*) But it *taught* me something. What it taught me, that you've got to get *out* there. Big deal. So I wasn't cut out to be a thief. I was cut out to be a salesman. And now I'm back, and I got my *balls* back ... and, you know, John, you have the *advantage* on me now. Whatever it takes to make it right, we'll make it right. We're going to make it right.

WILLIAMSON: I want to tell you something, Shelly. You have a big mouth. (*Pause.*)

LEVENE: What?

WILLIAMSON: You've got a big mouth, and now I'm going to show you an even bigger one. (*Starts toward the Detective's door.*)

LEVENE: Where are you going, John? ... you can't do that, you don't want to do that ... hold, hold on ... hold on ... wait ... wait ... wait ... (*Pulls money out of his pockets.*) Wait ... uh, look ... (*Starts splitting money.*) Look, twelve, twenty, two, twen ... twenty-five hundred, it's ... take it. (*Pause.*) Take it all. ... (*Pause.*) Take it!

WILLIAMSON: No, I don't think so, Shel.

LEVENE: I ...

WILLIAMSON: No, I think I don't want your money. I think you fucked up my office. And I think you're going away.

LEVENE: I ... what? Are you, are you, that's why ... ? Are you nuts? I'm ... I'm going to *close* for you, I'm going to ... (*Thrusting money at him.*) Here, here, I'm going to *make* this office ... I'm going to be back there Number One.... Hey, hey, hey! This is only the beginning. List ... list ... listen. Listen. Just one moment. List ... here's what ... here's what we're going to do. Twenty percent. I'm going to give you twenty percent of my sales. ... (*Pause.*) Twenty percent. (*Pause.*) For as long as I am with the firm. (*Pause.*) Fifty percent. (*Pause.*) You're going to be my partner. (*Pause.*) Fifty percent. Of all my sales.

WILLIAMSON: What sales?

LEVENE: What sales ... ? I just *closed* eighty-two grand.... Are you fuckin' ... I'm *back* ... I'm *back*, this is only the beginning.

WILLIAMSON: Only the beginning ...

LEVENE: Abso ...

WILLIAMSON: Where have you been, Shelly? Bruce and Harriett Nyborg. Do you want to see the *memos* ... ? They're nuts ... they used to call in every week. When I was with Webb. And we were selling Arizona ... they're nuts ... did you see how they were *living*? How can you delude yours ...

LEVENE: I've got the check ...

WILLIAMSON: Forget it. Frame it. It's worthless. (*Pause.*)

LEVENE: The check's no good?

WILLIAMSON: You stick around I'll pull the memo for you. (*Starts for the door.*) I'm busy now ...

LEVENE: Their check's no good? They're nuts ... ?

WILLIAMSON: Call up the bank. *I* called them.

LEVENE: You did?

WILLIAMSON: I called them when we had the lead ... four months ago. (*Pause.*) The people are insane. They just like talking to salesmen. (*Williamson starts for door.*)

LEVENE: Don't.

WILLIAMSON: I'm sorry.

LEVENE: *Why?*

WILLIAMSON: Because I don't like you.

LEVENE: John: John: ... my *daughter* ...

WILLIAMSON: Fuck you. (*Roma comes out of the Detective's door. Williamson goes in.*)

ROMA (*To Baylen*): Asshole ... (*To Levene:*) Guy couldn't find his fuckin' couch the *living room* ... Ah, Christ ... what a day, what a day ... I haven't even had a cup of *coffee*.... Jagoff John opens his mouth he blows my Cadillac.... (*Sighs.*) I swear ... it's not a world of men ... it's not a world of men, Machine ... it's a world of clock watchers, bureaucrats, officeholders ... what it is, it's a fucked-up world ... there's no adventure *to* it. (*Pause.*) Dying breed. Yes it is. (*Pause.*) We are the members of a dying breed. That's ... that's ... that's why we have to stick together. Shel: I want to talk to you. I've wanted to talk to you for some time. For a long time, actually. I said, "The Machine, there's a man I would work with. There's a man...." You know? I never said a thing. I should have, don't know why I didn't. And that shit you were slinging on my guy today was *so* good ... it ... it was, and, excuse me, 'cause it isn't even my place to say it. It was admirable ... it was the old stuff. Hey, I've been on a hot streak, so *what*? There's things that I could learn from you. You eat today?

LEVENE: Me.

ROMA: Yeah.

LEVENE: Mm.

ROMA: Well, you want to swing by the Chinks, watch me eat, we'll talk?

LEVENE: I think I'd better stay here for a while.

Baylen sticks his head out of the room:

BAYLEN: Mr. *Levene* ... ?

ROMA: You're done, come down and let's ...

BAYLEN: Would you come in here, please?

ROMA: And let's put this together. Okay? Shel? Say okay. (*Pause.*)

LEVENE (*Softly, to himself*): Huh.

BAYLEN: Mr. Levene, I think we have to talk.

ROMA: I'm going to the Chinks. You're done, come down, we're going to smoke a cigarette.

LEVENE: I ...

BAYLEN (*Comes over*): ... Get in the room.

ROMA: Hey, hey, hey, *easy* friend, that's the "Machine." That is Shelly "The Machine" Lev ...

BAYLEN: Get in the goddamn room. (*Baylen starts man-handling Shelly into the room.*)

LEVENE: Ricky, I ...

ROMA: Okay, okay, I'll be at the resta ...

LEVENE: Ricky ...

BAYLEN: "Ricky" can't help you, pal.

LEVENE: ... I only want to ...

BAYLEN: Yeah. What do you want? You want to *what*? (*He pushes Levene into the room, closes the door behind him. Pause.*)

ROMA: Williamson, listen to me: when the *leads* come in . . . listen to me: when the *leads* come in I want my top two off the list. For *me*. My usual two. Anything you give *Levene* . . .

WILLIAMSON: . . . I wouldn't worry about it.

ROMA: Well I'm *going* to worry about it, and so are you, so shut up and *listen*. (*Pause.*) I GET HIS ACTION. My stuff is *mine*, whatever *he* gets for himself, I'm taking half. You put me in with him.

Aaronow enters.

AARONOW: Did they . . . ?

ROMA: You understand?

AARONOW: Did they catch . . . ?

ROMA: Do you understand? My stuff is mine, his stuff is ours. I'm taking half of his commissions—now, *you* work it out.

WILLIAMSON: Mmm.

AARONOW: Did they find the guy who broke into the office yet?

ROMA: No. *I* don't know. (*Pause.*)

AARONOW: Did the leads come in yet?

ROMA: No.

AARONOW (*Settling into a desk chair*): Oh, God, I hate this job.

ROMA (*Simultaneous with "job," exiting the office*): I'll be at the restaurant.

August Wilson

August Wilson (1945–2005) was born in Pittsburgh, the son of a white father who abandoned his family and a black mother who had come from North Carolina to a Pittsburgh slum, where she worked to keep her family together. Wilson's early childhood was spent in an environment very similar to that of his play *Fences*, and Troy Maxson seems to be patterned somewhat on Wilson's stepfather.

Wilson's writing is rooted to a large extent in music, specifically the blues. As a poet, writing over several years, Wilson became interested in the speech patterns and rhythms that were familiar to him from black neighborhoods, but the value of those patterns became clearer to him when he grew older and moved from Pittsburgh to Minneapolis. From a distance, he was able to see more clearly what had attracted him to the language and begin to use it more fully in his work.

In the 1960s and 1970s, Wilson became involved in the civil rights movement and began to describe himself as a black nationalist, a term he said he felt comfortable with. He began writing plays in the 1960s in Pittsburgh and then took a job in St. Paul writing dramatic skits for the Science Museum of Minnesota. He founded the Playwrights Center in Minneapolis and wrote a play, *Jitney*, about a gypsy cab station. *Jitney* was first produced in 1982; a revised version was staged in New York in April 2000 at the Second Stage Theatre. *Fullerton Street*, about Pittsburgh, was another play written in this early period. Wilson's first commercial success, *Ma Rainey's Black Bottom*,

August Wilson in a portrait by David Cooper made in 2004, just one year before Wilson's untimely death.

premiered at the Yale Repertory Theatre in 1984 and then went to Broadway, where it enjoyed 275 performances and won the New York Drama Critics' Circle Award.

Ma Rainey's Black Bottom was the first of a planned sequence of ten plays based on the black American experience. As Wilson said, "I think the black Americans have the most dramatic story of all mankind to tell." The concept of such a vast project echoes Eugene O'Neill's projected group of eleven plays based on the Irish American experience. Unfortunately, O'Neill destroyed all but three of the plays (*A Touch of the Poet, More Stately Mansions,* and part of *Calms of Capricorn*) in his series. Wilson's project, however, was completed and produced some of the most successful plays in the recent American theater.

Ma Rainey is about the legendary black blues singer, who preceded Bessie Smith and Billie Holiday. The play is about the ways in which Rainey was exploited by white managers and recording executives and how she dealt with her exploitation. In the cast of the play are several black musicians in the backup band. Levee, the trumpet player, has a dream of leading his own band and establishing himself as an important jazz musician. But he is haunted by memories of seeing his mother raped by a gang of white men when he was a boy. He wants to "improve" the session he's playing by making the old jazz tune "Black Bottom" swing in the new jazz style, but Ma Rainey keeps him in tow and demands that they play the tune in the old way. Levee finally cracks under the pressure, and the play ends painfully.

Fences opened at the Yale Repertory Theatre in 1985 and in New York in early 1987, where it won the Pulitzer Prize as well as the New York Drama Critics' Circle Award. This long-running success firmly established Wilson as an important writer. *Joe Turner's Come and Gone* opened at the Yale Repertory Theatre in late 1986 and moved to New York in early 1988, where it too was hailed as an important play, winning its author another New York Drama Critics' Circle Award. Set in a rooming house in Pittsburgh in 1911, *Joe Turner* is a study of the children of former slaves. They have come north to look for work, and some of them have been found by the legendary bounty hunter Joe Turner. As a study of a people in transition, the play is a quiet masterpiece. It incorporates a number of important African traditions, especially religious rituals of healing as performed by Bynum, the "bone man," a seer and a medicine man. In this play and others, Wilson makes a special effort to highlight the elements of African heritage that white society strips away from blacks.

The next play in Wilson's series, *The Piano Lesson,* which premiered at the Yale Repertory Theatre in 1987, also portrays the complexity of black attitudes toward the past and black heritage. The piano represents two kinds of culture: the white culture that produced the musical instrument and the black culture, in the form of Papa Boy Willie, who carved into it images from black Africa. The central question in the play is whether Boy Willie should sell the piano and use the money for a down payment on land and therefore on the future. Or should he follow his sister Berniece's advice and keep it because it is too precious to sell? The conflict is deep, and the play ultimately focuses on a profound moment of spiritual exorcism. How one exorcises the past — how one lives with it or without it—is a central theme in Wilson's work.

His next play, *Two Trains Running,* is set in 1969, in the decade that saw the Vietnam War, racial and political riots, and the assassinations of John and Robert Kennedy, Malcolm X, and Martin Luther King Jr. The play premiered at the Yale Repertory Theatre in 1990 and opened on Broadway at the Walter Kerr Theatre in April 1992, directed by Lloyd Richards. The characters remain in Memphis Lee's diner—scheduled for demolition—throughout the play. The two trains in the title are heading to Africa and to the old South, but the characters are immobile and seem indifferent to both of them. Wilson moved away from the careful structure of the well-made play in this work and produced an open-ended conclusion, leaving the racial and philosophical tensions unresolved.

Seven Guitars (1995) takes place in a backyard in Pittsburgh in 1948 on the eve of the landmark boxing match between Joe Louis and "Jersey" Joe Walcott. The play focuses on a blues musician, Floyd Barton, who hopes to regain his lost love, put his band back together, and move to Chicago to make his second recording. *Seven Guitars* emphasizes the blues, especially in its long first act, with Barton's friends gathered in his backyard to mourn his death and the loss of his talent. People did much the same when Joe Louis, the "Brown Bomber," lost his fight, a loss that punctuated the end of an era. The second act focuses on Hedley, a West Indian boarder, whom critic Margo Jefferson describes as "half madman and half prophet." Hedley recites a litany of racial injustices and gives voice to a torrent of wrongs. Hedley's voice is a counterpoint to the blues; he gives us a powerful range of responses to the condition of being black in Pittsburgh in the late 1940s.

King Hedley II (1999), set in 1985, picks up some of the characters of *Seven Guitars,* including Hedley, and develops further the experience of living in the Hill District of Pittsburgh. Wilson described the play as focusing on "the breakdown of the black community's extended-family structure." Wilson, then living in Seattle, returned to his hometown for the December 1999 premiere of *King Hedley II*, the first play produced in the new O'Reilly Theater by the Pittsburgh Public Theater. It moved to the Seattle Repertory Theatre in 2000 and to Broadway in 2001.

At this point, the sequence of plays detailing the African American experience for each decade of the twentieth century needed only the first and last decades' plays. *Gem of the Ocean,* set in 1904, introduced Aunt Ester, who had been alluded to in earlier plays. Her birthday, more than 280 years before, coincides with the introduction of African slaves into the United States. She has a healing power that helps cleanse some of the characters of their sense of guilt. The production, directed by Marion McClinton, featured Phylicia Rashad as Aunt Ester and won the Tony Award for best play of 2005. It ran for 72 performances. The final play in the cycle is *Radio Golf,* which premiered at Yale Repertory Theatre before Wilson's death in 2005 and then moved to the Cort Theatre on Broadway in April 2007. It too won a Tony, for best play of 2007, but it ran for only 64 performances. The play is set in 1997 and focuses on the Bedford Hills Redevelopment company, a storefront on Centre Street in Pittsburgh. This company's project involves the total demolition and reconstruction of the Hill District, including the destruction of Aunt Ester's home, the setting of *Gem of the Ocean*. The struggle between doing what is right and doing what is profitable and practicable is central to the drama. Wilson died of liver cancer, knowing his project was complete.

For links to resources about Wilson, click on *AuthorLinks* at **bedfordstmartins.com/jacobus**.

Fences

For discussion questions and assignments on *Fences*, visit bedfordstmartins.com/jacobus.

Fences (1985), like most of August Wilson's plays, was directed by Lloyd Richards, who also directed the first production of Lorraine Hansberry's *A Raisin in the Sun*. Richards was, until 1991, the dean of the School of Drama at Yale University and ran the Yale Repertory Theatre, where he directed the first several of the plays Wilson wrote in his ten-play cycle about black American life.

Fences presents a slice of life in a black tenement in Pittsburgh in the 1950s. Its main character, Troy Maxson, is a garbage collector who has taken great pride in keeping his family together and providing for them. When the play opens, he and his friend Bono are talking about Troy's challenge to the company and the union about blacks' ability to do the same "easy" work that whites do. Troy's rebellion and frustration set the tone for the entire play; he is looking for his rights, and, at age fifty-three, he has missed many opportunities to get what he deserves.

Troy's struggle for fairness becomes virtually mythic as he describes his wrestling with death during a bout of pneumonia in 1941. He describes a three-day struggle in which he eventually overcame his foe. Troy—a good baseball player who was relegated to the Negro leagues—sees death as nothing but a fastball, and he could always deal with a fastball. Both Bono and Troy's wife, Rose, show an intense admiration for him as he describes his ordeal.

The father-son relationship that begins to take a central role in the drama is complicated by strong feelings of pride and independence on both sides. Troy's son Cory wants to play football, and Troy wants him to work on the fence he's mending. Cory's youthful enthusiasm probably echoes Troy's own youthful innocence, but Troy resents it in Cory, seeing it as partly responsible for his own predicament. Cory cannot see his father's point of view and believes that he is exempt from the kind of prejudice his father suffered.

The agony of the father-son relationship and their misperceptions of each other persist through the play. Rose's capacity to cope with the deepest of Troy's anxieties—his fear of death—is one of her most important achievements in the play. At the end of the play, Rose demands that Cory give Troy the respect he deserves, although Cory's anger and inexperience make it all but impossible for him to see his father as anything other than an oppressor. Cory thinks that he must say no to his father once, but Rose will not let him deny his father. When the play ends with Gabriel's fantastic ritualistic dance, the audience feels a sense of closure, of spiritual finish.

Fences in Performance

Like many of the best American plays, *Fences* began in a workshop production. Its first version was performed as a reading, rather than as a full production—no sets, no full lighting, actors working "on book" instead of fully memorizing the play—in the summer of 1983 at the Eugene O'Neill Center in Waterford, Connecticut. This early version was four hours long.

Once Wilson found the focus of his play, it premiered in 1985 at the Yale Repertory Theatre in New Haven. Lloyd Richards, then dean of Yale Drama School, directed this as well as the New York production. The New York opening on March 27, 1987, starred Mary Alice, James Earl Jones, and Ray Aranha, the cast from New Haven. Frank Rich at the *New York Times* praised James Earl Jones, congratulating him on finding "what may be the best role of his career." Rich also said, "*Fences* leaves no doubt that Mr. Wilson is a major writer, combining a poet's ear for vernacular with a robust sense of humor (political and sexual), a sure instinct for crackling dramatic incident and a passionate commitment to a great subject." The play ran for 575 performances.

From the first, *Fences* was recognized as an important play. It won four Tony Awards: best play, best actor, best actress in a supporting role, and best director. It also won the New York Drama Critics' Circle Award for best play and the Pulitzer Prize. Before the New York production, it had traveled to Chicago, San Francisco, and Seattle. It has been performed numerous times since. The most recent major production, in April 2010, featured Denzel Washington as Troy Maxson and Viola Davis as Rose at the Cort Theatre on Broadway. Reviewers reminded audiences that Washington is physically much smaller than James Earl Jones and therefore less imposing, but they admitted that he had built a powerful Troy Maxson "brick by brick." Denzel Washington and Viola Davis won Tony Awards for best actor and best actress, and the play won the Tony for best revival. The production was nominated for ten Tony Awards in all.

AUGUST WILSON (1945–2005)

Fences   1987

Characters

TROY MAXSON
JIM BONO, *Troy's friend*
ROSE, *Troy's wife*
LYONS, *Troy's oldest son by previous marriage*
GABRIEL, *Troy's brother*
CORY, *Troy and Rose's son*
RAYNELL, *Troy's daughter*

Setting: *The setting is the yard which fronts the only entrance to the Maxson household, an ancient two-story brick house set back off a small alley in a big-city neighborhood. The entrance to the house is gained by two or three steps leading to a wooden porch badly in need of paint.*

A relatively recent addition to the house and running its full width, the porch lacks congruence. It is a sturdy porch with a flat roof. One or two chairs of dubious value sit at one end where the kitchen window opens onto the porch. An old-fashioned icebox stands silent guard at the opposite end.

The yard is a small dirt yard, partially fenced, except for the last scene, with a wooden sawhorse, a pile of lumber, and other fence-building equipment set off to the side. Opposite is a tree from which hangs a ball made of rags. A baseball bat leans against the tree. Two oil drums serve as garbage receptacles and sit near the house at right to complete the setting.

The Play: *Near the turn of the century, the destitute of Europe sprang on the city with tenacious claws and an honest and solid dream. The city devoured them. They swelled its belly until it burst into a thousand furnaces and sewing machines, a thousand butcher shops and bakers' ovens, a thousand churches and hospitals and funeral parlors and money-lenders. The city grew. It nourished itself and offered each man a partnership limited only by his talent, his guile, and his willingness and capacity for hard work. For the immigrants of Europe, a dream dared and won true.*

The descendants of African slaves were offered no such welcome or participation. They came from places called the Carolinas and the Virginias, Georgia, Alabama, Mississippi, and Tennessee. They came strong, eager, searching. The city rejected them and they fled and settled along the riverbanks and under bridges in shallow, ramshackle houses made of sticks and tar-paper. They collected rags and wood. They sold the use of their muscles and their bodies. They cleaned houses and washed clothes, they shined shoes, and in quiet desperation and vengeful pride, they stole, and lived in pursuit of their own dream. That they could breathe free, finally, and stand to meet life with the force of dignity and whatever eloquence the heart could call upon.

By 1957, the hard-won victories of the European immigrants had solidified the industrial might of America. War had been confronted and won with new energies that used loyalty and patriotism as its fuel. Life was rich, full, and flourishing. The Milwaukee Braves won the World Series, and the hot winds of change that would make the sixties a turbulent, racing, dangerous, and provocative decade had not yet begun to blow full.

ACT I • Scene I

(It is 1957. Troy and Bono enter the yard, engaged in conversation. Troy is fifty-three years old, a large man with thick, heavy hands; it is this largeness that he strives to fill out and make an accommodation with. Together with his blackness, his largeness informs his sensibilities and the choices he has made in his life.)

(Of the two men, Bono is obviously the follower. His commitment to their friendship of thirty-odd years is rooted in his admiration of Troy's honesty, capacity for hard work, and his strength, which Bono seeks to emulate.)

(It is Friday night, payday, and the one night of the week the two men engage in a ritual of talk and drink. Troy is usually the most talkative and at times he can be crude and almost vulgar, though he is capable of rising to profound heights of expression. The men carry lunch buckets and wear or carry burlap aprons and are dressed in clothes suitable to their jobs as garbage collectors.)

BONO: Troy, you ought to stop that lying!

TROY: I ain't lying! The nigger had a watermelon this big.

(He indicates with his hands.)

Talking about . . . "What watermelon, Mr. Rand?" I liked to fell out! "What watermelon, Mr. Rand?" . . . And it sitting there big as life.

BONO: What did Mr. Rand say?

TROY: Ain't said nothing. Figure if the nigger too dumb to know he carrying a watermelon, he wasn't gonna get much sense out of him. Trying to hide that great big old watermelon under his coat. Afraid to let the white man see him carry it home.

BONO: I'm like you . . . I ain't got no time for them kind of people.

TROY: Now what he look like getting mad cause he see the man from the union talking to Mr. Rand?

BONO: He come to me talking about . . . "Maxson gonna get us fired." I told him to get away from me with that. He walked away from me calling you a trouble-maker. What Mr. Rand say?

TROY: Ain't said nothing. He told me to go down the Commissioner's office next Friday. They called me down there to see them.

BONO: Well, as long as you got your complaint filed, they can't fire you. That's what one of them white fellows tell me.

TROY: I ain't worried about them firing me. They gonna fire me cause I asked a question? That's all I did. I went to Mr. Rand and asked him, "Why? Why you got the white mens driving and the colored lifting?" Told him "what's the matter, don't I count? You think only white fellows got sense enough to drive a truck. That ain't no paper job! Hell, anybody can drive a truck. How come you got all whites driving and the colored lifting?" He told me "take it to the union." Well, hell, that's what I done! Now they wanna come up with this pack of lies.

BONO: I told Brownie if the man come and ask him any questions . . . just tell the truth! It ain't nothing but something they done trumped up on you cause you filed a complaint on them.

TROY: Brownie don't understand nothing. All I want them to do is change the job description. Give everybody a chance to drive the truck. Brownie can't see that. He ain't got that much sense.

BONO: How you figure he be making out with that gal be up at Taylors' all the time . . . that Alberta gal?

TROY: Same as you and me. Getting just as much as we is. Which is to say nothing.

BONO: It is, huh? I figure you doing a little better than me . . . and I ain't saying what I'm doing.

TROY: Aw, nigger, look here . . . I know you. If you had got anywhere near that gal, twenty minutes later you be looking to tell somebody. And the first one you gonna tell . . . that you gonna want to brag to . . . is gonna be me.

BONO: I ain't saying that. I see where you be eyeing her.

TROY: I eye all the women. I don't miss nothing. Don't never let nobody tell you Troy Maxson don't eye the women.

BONO: You been doing more than eyeing her. You done bought her a drink or two.

TROY: Hell yeah, I bought her a drink! What that mean? I bought you one, too. What that mean cause I buy her a drink? I'm just being polite.

BONO: It's all right to buy her one drink. That's what you call being polite. But when you wanna be buying two or three . . . that's what you call eyeing her.

TROY: Look here, as long as you known me . . . you ever known me to chase after women?

BONO: Hell yeah! Long as I done known you. You forgetting I knew you when.

TROY: Naw, I'm talking about since I been married to Rose?

BONO: Oh, not since you been married to Rose. Now, that's the truth, there. I can say that.

TROY: All right then! Case closed.

BONO: I see you be walking up around Alberta's house. You supposed to be at Taylors' and you be walking up around there.

TROY: What you watching where I'm walking for? I ain't watching after you.

BONO: I seen you walking around there more than once.

TROY: Hell, you liable to see me walking anywhere! That don't mean nothing cause you see me walking around there.

BONO: Where she come from anyway? She just kinda showed up one day.

TROY: Tallahassee. You can look at her and tell she one of them Florida gals. They got some big healthy women down there. Grow them right up out the ground. Got a little bit of Indian in her. Most of them niggers down in Florida got some Indian in them.

BONO: I don't know about that Indian part. But she damn sure big and healthy. Woman wear some big stockings. Got them great big old legs and hips as wide as the Mississippi River.

TROY: Legs don't mean nothing. You don't do nothing but push them out of the way. But them hips cushion the ride!

BONO: Troy, you ain't got no sense.

TROY: It's the truth! Like you riding on Goodyears!

(Rose enters from the house. She is ten years younger than Troy, her devotion to him stems from her recognition of the possibilities of her life without him: a succession of abusive men and their babies, a life of partying and running the streets, the Church, or aloneness with its attendant pain and frustration. She recognizes Troy's spirit as a fine and illuminating one and she either ignores or forgives his faults, only some of which she recognizes. Though she doesn't drink, her presence is an integral part of the Friday night rituals. She alternates between the porch and the kitchen, where supper preparations are under way.)

ROSE: What you all out here getting into?

TROY: What you worried about what we getting into for? This is men talk, woman.

ROSE: What I care what you all talking about? Bono, you gonna stay for supper?

BONO: No, I thank you, Rose. But Lucille say she cooking up a pot of pigfeet.

TROY: Pigfeet! Hell, I'm going home with you! Might even stay the night if you got some pigfeet. You got something in there to top them pigfeet, Rose?

ROSE: I'm cooking up some chicken. I got some chicken and collard greens.

TROY: Well, go on back in the house and let me and Bono finish what we was talking about. This is men talk. I got some talk for you later. You know what kind of talk I mean. You go on and powder it up.

ROSE: Troy Maxson, don't you start that now!

TROY *(puts his arm around her)*: Aw, woman . . . come here. Look here, Bono . . . when I met this woman . . . I got out that place, say, "Hitch up my pony, saddle up my mare . . . there's a woman out there for me somewhere. I looked here. Looked there. Saw Rose and latched on to her." I latched on to her and told her—I'm gonna tell you the truth—I told her, "Baby, I don't wanna marry, I just wanna be your man." Rose told me . . . tell him what you told me, Rose.

ROSE: I told him if he wasn't the marrying kind, then move out the way so the marrying kind could find me.

TROY: That's what she told me. "Nigger, you in my way. You blocking the view! Move out the way so I can

find me a husband." I thought it over two or three days. Come back—

ROSE: Ain't no two or three days nothing. You was back the same night.

TROY: Come back, told her . . . "Okay, baby . . . but I'm gonna buy me a banty rooster and put him out there in the backyard . . . and when he see a stranger come, he'll flap his wings and crow . . . " Look here, Bono, I could watch the front door by myself . . . it was that back door I was worried about.

ROSE: Troy, you ought not talk like that. Troy ain't doing nothing but telling a lie.

TROY: Only thing is . . . when we first got married . . . forget the rooster . . . we ain't had no yard!

BONO: I hear you tell it. Me and Lucille was staying down there on Logan Street. Had two rooms with the outhouse in the back. I ain't mind the outhouse none. But when that goddamn wind blow through there in the winter . . . that's what I'm talking about! To this day I wonder why in the hell I ever stayed down there for six long years. But see, I didn't know I could do no better. I thought only white folks had inside toilets and things.

ROSE: There's a lot of people don't know they can do no better than they doing now. That's just something you got to learn. A lot of folks still shop at Bella's.

TROY: Ain't nothing wrong with shopping at Bella's. She got fresh food.

ROSE: I ain't said nothing about if she got fresh food. I'm talking about what she charge. She charge ten cents more than the A&P.

TROY: The A&P ain't never done nothing for me. I spends my money where I'm treated right. I go down to Bella, say, "I need a loaf of bread, I'll pay you Friday." She give it to me. What sense that make when I got money to go and spend it somewhere else and ignore the person who done right by me? That ain't in the Bible.

ROSE: We ain't talking about what's in the Bible. What sense it make to shop there when she overcharge?

TROY: You shop where you want to. I'll do my shopping where the people been good to me.

ROSE: Well, I don't think it's right for her to overcharge. That's all I was saying.

BONO: Look here . . . I got to get on. Lucille going be raising all kind of hell.

TROY: Where you going, nigger? We ain't finished this pint. Come here, finish this pint.

BONO: Well, hell, I am . . . if you ever turn the bottle loose.

TROY *(hands him the bottle)*: The only thing I say about the A&P is I'm glad Cory got that job down there. Help him take care of his school clothes and things. Gabe done moved out and things getting tight around here. He got that job. . . . He can start to look out for himself.

ROSE: Cory done went and got recruited by a college football team.

TROY: I told that boy about that football stuff. The white man ain't gonna let him get nowhere with that football. I told him when he first come to me with it. Now you come telling me he done went and got more tied up in it. He ought to go and get recruited in how to fix cars or something where he can make a living.

ROSE: He ain't talking about making no living playing football. It's just something the boys in school do. They gonna send a recruiter by to talk to you. He'll tell you he ain't talking about making no living playing football. It's a honor to be recruited.

TROY: It ain't gonna get him nowhere. Bono'll tell you that.

BONO: If he be like you in the sports . . . he's gonna be all right. Ain't but two men ever played baseball as good as you. That's Babe Ruth and Josh Gibson.° Them's the only two men ever hit more home runs than you.

TROY: What it ever get me? Ain't got a pot to piss in or a window to throw it out of.

ROSE: Times have changed since you was playing baseball, Troy. That was before the war. Times have changed a lot since then.

TROY: How in hell they done changed?

ROSE: They got lots of colored boys playing ball now. Baseball and football.

BONO: You right about that, Rose. Times have changed, Troy. You just come along too early.

TROY: There ought not never have been no time called too early! Now you take that fellow . . . what's that fellow they had playing right field for the Yankees back then? You know who I'm talking about, Bono. Used to play right field for the Yankees.

ROSE: Selkirk?

TROY: Selkirk! That's it! Man batting .269, understand? .269. What kind of sense that make? I was hitting .432 with thirty-seven home runs! Man batting .269 and playing right field for the Yankees! I saw Josh Gibson's daughter yesterday. She walking around with raggedy shoes on her feet. Now I bet you Selkirk's daughter ain't walking around with raggedy shoes on her feet! I bet you that!

ROSE: They got a lot of colored baseball players now. Jackie Robinson was the first. Folks had to wait for Jackie Robinson.

TROY: I done seen a hundred niggers play baseball better than Jackie Robinson. Hell, I know some teams Jackie Robinson couldn't even make! What you talking about Jackie Robinson. Jackie Robinson wasn't nobody. I'm talking about if you could play ball then they ought to have let you play. Don't care what color you were. Come telling me I come along too early. If you could play . . . then they ought to have let you play.

(*Troy takes a long drink from the bottle.*)

ROSE: You gonna drink yourself to death. You don't need to be drinking like that.

Josh Gibson: Powerful black baseball player (1911–1947) known in the 1930s as the Babe Ruth of the Negro leagues.

TROY: Death ain't nothing. I done seen him. Done wrassled with him. You can't tell me nothing about death. Death ain't nothing but a fastball on the outside corner. And you know what I'll do to that! Lookee here, Bono . . . am I lying? You get one of them fastballs, about waist high, over the outside corner of the plate where you can get the meat of the bat on it . . . and good god! You can kiss it goodbye. Now, am I lying?

BONO: Naw, you telling the truth there. I seen you do it.

TROY: If I'm lying . . . that 450 feet worth of lying!

(*Pause.*)

That's all death is to me. A fastball on the outside corner.

ROSE: I don't know why you want to get on talking about death.

TROY: Ain't nothing wrong with talking about death. That's part of life. Everybody gonna die. You gonna die, I'm gonna die. Bono's gonna die. Hell, we all gonna die.

ROSE: But you ain't got to talk about it. I don't like to talk about it.

TROY: You the one brought it up. Me and Bono was talking about baseball . . . you tell me I'm gonna drink myself to death. Ain't that right, Bono? You know I don't drink this but one night out of the week. That's Friday night. I'm gonna drink just enough to where I can handle it. Then I cuts it loose. I leave it alone. So don't you worry about me drinking myself to death. 'Cause I ain't worried about Death. I done seen him. I done wrestled with him.

Look here, Bono . . . I looked up one day and Death was marching straight at me. Like Soldiers on Parade! The Army of Death was marching straight at me. The middle of July, 1941. It got real cold just like it be winter. It seem like Death himself reached out and touched me on the shoulder. He touch me just like I touch you. I got cold as ice and Death standing there grinning at me.

ROSE: Troy, why don't you hush that talk.

TROY: I say . . . What you want, Mr. Death? You be wanting me? You done brought your army to be getting me? I looked him dead in the eye. I wasn't fearing nothing. I was ready to tangle. Just like I'm ready to tangle now. The Bible say be ever vigilant. That's why I don't get but so drunk. I got to keep watch.

ROSE: Troy was right down there in Mercy Hospital. You remember he had pneumonia? Laying there with a fever talking plumb out of his head.

TROY: Death standing there staring at me . . . carrying that sickle in his hand. Finally he say, "You want bound over for another year?" See, just like that . . . "You want bound over for another year?" I told him, "Bound over hell! Let's settle this now!"

It seem like he kinda fell back when I said that, and all the cold went out of me. I reached down and grabbed that sickle and threw it just as far as I could throw it . . . and me and him commenced to wrestling.

We wrestled for three days and three nights. I can't say where I found the strength from. Every time it seemed like he was gonna get the best of me, I'd reach way down deep inside myself and find the strength to do him one better.

ROSE: Every time Troy tell that story he find different ways to tell it. Different things to make up about it.

TROY: I ain't making up nothing. I'm telling you the facts of what happened. I wrestled with Death for three days and three nights and I'm standing here to tell you about it.

(*Pause.*)

All right. At the end of the third night we done weakened each other to where we can't hardly move. Death stood up, throwed on his robe . . . had him a white robe with a hood on it. He throwed on that robe and went off to look for his sickle. Say, "I'll be back." Just like that. "I'll be back." I told him, say, "Yeah, but . . . you gonna have to find me!" I wasn't no fool. I wan't going looking for him. Death ain't nothing to play with. And I know he's gonna get me. I know I got to join his army . . . his camp followers. But as long as I keep my strength and see him coming . . . as long as I keep up my vigilance . . . he's gonna have to fight to get me. I ain't going easy.

BONO: Well, look here, since you got to keep up your vigilance . . . let me have the bottle.

TROY: Aw hell, I shouldn't have told you that part. I should have left out that part.

ROSE: Troy be talking that stuff and half the time don't even know what he be talking about.

TROY: Bono know me better than that.

BONO: That's right. I know you. I know you got some Uncle Remus° in your blood. You got more stories than the devil got sinners.

TROY: Aw hell, I done seen him too! Done talked with the devil.

ROSE: Troy, don't nobody wanna be hearing all that stuff.

(*Lyons enters the yard from the street. Thirty-four years old, Troy's son by a previous marriage, he sports a neatly trimmed goatee, sport coat, white shirt, tieless and buttoned at the collar. Though he fancies himself a musician, he is more caught up in the rituals and "idea" of being a musician than in the actual practice of the music. He has come to borrow money from Troy, and while he knows he will be successful, he is uncertain as to what extent his lifestyle will be held up to scrutiny and ridicule.*)

LYONS: Hey, Pop.

TROY: What you come "Hey, Popping" me for?

LYONS: How you doing, Rose?

(*He kisses her.*)

Mr. Bono. How you doing?

Uncle Remus: Black storyteller who recounts traditional African American tales in the book by Joel Chandler Harris.

BONO: Hey, Lyons . . . how you been?

TROY: He must have been doing all right. I ain't seen him around here last week.

ROSE: Troy, leave your boy alone. He come by to see you and you wanna start all that nonsense.

TROY: I ain't bothering Lyons.

(*Offers him the bottle.*)

Here . . . get you a drink. We got an understanding. I know why he come by to see me and he know I know.

LYONS: Come on, Pop . . . I just stopped by to say hi . . . see how you was doing.

TROY: You ain't stopped by yesterday.

ROSE: You gonna stay for supper, Lyons? I got some chicken cooking in the oven.

LYONS: No, Rose . . . thanks. I was just in the neighborhood and thought I'd stop by for a minute.

TROY: You was in the neighborhood all right, nigger. You telling the truth there. You was in the neighborhood cause it's my payday.

LYONS: Well, hell, since you mentioned it . . . let me have ten dollars.

TROY: I'll be damned! I'll die and go to hell and play blackjack with the devil before I give you ten dollars.

BONO: That's what I wanna know about . . . that devil you done seen.

LYONS: What . . . Pop done seen the devil? You too much, Pops.

TROY: Yeah, I done seen him. Talked to him too!

ROSE: You ain't seen no devil. I done told you that man ain't had nothing to do with the devil. Anything you can't understand, you want to call it the devil.

TROY: Look here, Bono . . . I went down to see Hertzberger about some furniture. Got three rooms for two-ninety-eight. That what it say on the radio. "Three rooms . . . two-ninety-eight." Even made up a little song about it. Go down there . . . man tell me I can't get no credit. I'm working every day and can't get no credit. What to do? I got an empty house with some raggedy furniture in it. Cory ain't got no bed. He's sleeping on a pile of rags on the floor. Working every day and can't get no credit. Come back here—Rose'll tell you—madder than hell. Sit down . . . try to figure what I'm gonna do. Come a knock on the door. Ain't been living here but three days. Who know I'm here? Open the door . . . devil standing there bigger than life. White fellow . . . got on good clothes and everything. Standing there with a clipboard in his hand. I ain't had to say nothing. First words come out of his mouth was . . . "I understand you need some furniture and can't get no credit." I liked to fell over. He say, "I'll give you all the credit you want, but you got to pay the interest on it." I told him, "Give me three rooms worth and charge whatever you want." Next day a truck pulled up here and two men unloaded them three rooms. Man what drove the truck give me a book. Say send ten dollars, first of every month to the address in the book and everything will be all right. Say if I miss a payment the devil was coming back and it'll be hell to pay. That was fifteen years ago. To this day . . . the first of the month I send my ten dollars, Rose'll tell you.

ROSE: Troy lying.

TROY: I ain't never seen that man since. Now you tell me who else that could have been but the devil? I ain't sold my soul or nothing like that, you understand. Naw, I wouldn't have truck with the devil about nothing like that. I got my furniture and pays my ten dollars the first of the month just like clockwork.

BONO: How long you say you been paying this ten dollars a month?

TROY: Fifteen years!

BONO: Hell, ain't you finished paying for it yet? How much the man done charged you.

TROY: Ah hell, I done paid for it. I done paid for it ten times over! The fact is I'm scared to stop paying it.

ROSE: Troy lying. We got that furniture from Mr. Glickman. He ain't paying no ten dollars a month to nobody.

TROY: Aw hell, woman. Bono know I ain't that big a fool.

LYONS: I was just getting ready to say . . . I know where there's a bridge for sale.

TROY: Look here, I'll tell you this . . . it don't matter to me if he was the devil. It don't matter if the devil give credit. Somebody has got to give it.

ROSE: It ought to matter. You going around talking about having truck with the devil . . . God's the one you gonna have to answer to. He's the one gonna be at the Judgment.

LYONS: Yeah, well, look here, Pop . . . let me have that ten dollars. I'll give it back to you. Bonnie got a job working at the hospital.

TROY: What I tell you, Bono? The only time I see this nigger is when he wants something. That's the only time I see him.

LYONS: Come on, Pop, Mr. Bono don't want to hear all that. Let me have the ten dollars. I told you Bonnie working.

TROY: What that mean to me? "Bonnie working." I don't care if she working. Go ask her for the ten dollars if she working. Talking about "Bonnie working." Why ain't you working?

LYONS: Aw, Pop, you know I can't find no decent job. Where am I gonna get a job at? You know I can't get no job.

TROY: I told you I know some people down there. I can get you on the rubbish if you want to work. I told you that the last time you came by here asking me for something.

LYONS: Naw, Pop . . . thanks. That ain't for me. I don't wanna be carrying nobody's rubbish. I don't wanna be punching nobody's time clock.

TROY: What's the matter, you too good to carry people's rubbish? Where you think that ten dollars you talking about come from? I'm just supposed to haul people's rubbish and give my money to you cause you too lazy to work. You too lazy to work and wanna know why you ain't got what I got.

ROSE: What hospital Bonnie working at? Mercy?

LYONS: She's down at Passavant working in the laundry.

TROY: I ain't got nothing as it is. I give you that ten dollars and I got to eat beans the rest of the week. Naw . . . you ain't getting no ten dollars here.

LYONS: You ain't got to be eating no beans. I don't know why you wanna say that.

TROY: I ain't got no extra money. Gabe done moved over to Miss Pearl's paying her the rent and things done got tight around here. I can't afford to be giving you every payday.

LYONS: I ain't asked you to give me nothing. I asked you to loan me ten dollars. I know you got ten dollars.

TROY: Yeah, I got it. You know why I got it? Cause I don't throw my money away out there in the streets. You living the fast life . . . wanna be a musician . . . running around in them clubs and things . . . then, you learn to take care of yourself. You ain't gonna find me going and asking nobody for nothing. I done spent too many years without.

LYONS: You and me is two different people, Pop.

TROY: I done learned my mistake and learned to do what's right by it. You still trying to get something for nothing. Life don't owe you nothing. You owe it to yourself. Ask Bono. He'll tell you I'm right.

LYONS: You got your way of dealing with the world . . . I got mine. The only thing that matters to me is the music.

TROY: Yeah, I can see that! It don't matter how you gonna eat . . . where your next dollar is coming from. You telling the truth there.

LYONS: I know I got to eat. But I got to live too. I need something that gonna help me to get out of the bed in the morning. Make me feel like I belong in the world. I don't bother nobody. I just stay with my music cause that's the only way I can find to live in the world. Otherwise there ain't no telling what I might do. Now I don't come criticizing you and how you live. I just come by to ask you for ten dollars. I don't wanna hear all that about how I live.

TROY: Boy, your mamma did a hell of a job raising you.

LYONS: You can't change me, Pop. I'm thirty-four years old. If you wanted to change me, you should have been there when I was growing up. I come by to see you . . . ask for ten dollars and you want to talk about how I was raised. You don't know nothing about how I was raised.

ROSE: Let the boy have ten dollars, Troy.

TROY (*to Lyons*): What the hell you looking at me for? I ain't got no ten dollars. You know what I do with my money.

(*To Rose.*)

Give him ten dollars if you want him to have it.

ROSE: I will. Just as soon as you turn it loose.

TROY (*handing Rose the money*): There it is. Seventy-six dollars and forty-two cents. You see this, Bono? Now, I ain't gonna get but six of that back.

ROSE: You ought to stop telling that lie. Here, Lyons.

(*She hands him the money.*)

LYONS: Thanks, Rose. Look . . . I got to run . . . I'll see you later.

TROY: Wait a minute. You gonna say, "thanks, Rose" and ain't gonna look to see where she got that ten dollars from? See how they do me, Bono?

LYONS: I know she got it from you, Pop. Thanks. I'll give it back to you.

TROY: There he go telling another lie. Time I see that ten dollars . . . he'll be owing me thirty more.

LYONS: See you, Mr. Bono.

BONO: Take care, Lyons!

LYONS: Thanks, Pop. I'll see you again.

(*Lyons exits the yard.*)

TROY: I don't know why he don't go and get him a decent job and take care of that woman he got.

BONO: He'll be all right, Troy. The boy is still young.

TROY: The *boy* is thirty-four years old.

ROSE: Let's not get off into all that.

BONO: Look here . . . I got to be going. I got to be getting on. Lucille gonna be waiting.

TROY (*puts his arm around Rose*): See this woman, Bono? I love this woman. I love this woman so much it hurts. I love her so much . . . I done run out of ways of loving her. So I got to go back to basics. Don't you come by my house Monday morning talking about time to go to work . . . 'cause I'm still gonna be stroking!

ROSE: Troy! Stop it now!

BONO: I ain't paying him no mind, Rose. That ain't nothing but gin-talk. Go on, Troy. I'll see you Monday.

TROY: Don't you come by my house, nigger! I done told you what I'm gonna be doing.

(*The lights go down to black.*)

Scene II

(*The lights come up on Rose hanging up clothes. She hums and sings softly to herself. It is the following morning.*)

ROSE (*sings*): Jesus, be a fence all around me every day
Jesus, I want you to protect me as I travel on my way.
Jesus, be a fence all around me every day.

(*Troy enters from the house.*)

Jesus, I want you to protect me
As I travel on my way.

(*To Troy.*) 'Morning. You ready for breakfast? I can fix it soon as I finish hanging up these clothes.

TROY: I got the coffee on. That'll be all right. I'll just drink some of that this morning.

ROSE: That 651 hit yesterday. That's the second time this month. Miss Pearl hit for a dollar . . . seem like those that need the least always get lucky. Poor folks can't get nothing.

TROY: Them numbers don't know nobody. I don't know why you fool with them. You and Lyons both.

ROSE: It's something to do.

TROY: You ain't doing nothing but throwing your money away.

ROSE: Troy, you know I don't play foolishly. I just play a nickel here and a nickel there.

TROY: That's two nickels you done thrown away.

ROSE: Now I hit sometimes . . . that makes up for it. It always comes in handy when I do hit. I don't hear you complaining then.

TROY: I ain't complaining now. I just say it's foolish. Trying to guess out of six hundred ways which way the number gonna come. If I had all the money niggers, these Negroes, throw away on numbers for one week—just one week—I'd be a rich man.

ROSE: Well, you wishing and calling it foolish ain't gonna stop folks from playing numbers. That's one thing for sure. Besides . . . some good things come from playing numbers. Look where Pope done bought him that restaurant off of numbers.

TROY: I can't stand niggers like that. Man ain't had two dimes to rub together. He walking around with his shoes all run over bumming money for cigarettes. All right. Got lucky there and hit the numbers . . .

ROSE: Troy, I know all about it.

TROY: Had good sense, I'll say that for him. He ain't throwed his money away. I seen niggers hit the numbers and go through two thousand dollars in four days. Man bought him that restaurant down there . . . fixed it up real nice . . . and then didn't want nobody to come in it! A Negro go in there and can't get no kind of service. I seen a white fellow come in there and order a bowl of stew. Pope picked all the meat out the pot for him. Man ain't had nothing but a bowl of meat! Negro come behind him and ain't got nothing but the potatoes and carrots. Talking about what numbers do for people, you picked a wrong example. Ain't done nothing but make a worser fool out of him than he was before.

ROSE: Troy, you ought to stop worrying about what happened at work yesterday.

TROY: I ain't worried. Just told me to be down there at the Commissioner's office on Friday. Everybody think they gonna fire me. I ain't worried about them firing me. You ain't got to worry about that.

(*Pause.*)

Where's Cory? Cory in the house? (*Calls.*) Cory?

ROSE: He gone out.

TROY: Out, huh? He gone out 'cause he know I want him to help me with this fence. I know how he is. That boy scared of work.

(*Gabriel enters. He comes halfway down the alley and, hearing Troy's voice, stops.*)

TROY (*continues*): He ain't done a lick of work in his life.

ROSE: He had to go to football practice. Coach wanted them to get in a little extra practice before the season start.

TROY: I got his practice . . . running out of here before he get his chores done.

ROSE: Troy, what is wrong with you this morning? Don't nothing set right with you. Go on back in there and go to bed . . . get up on the other side.

TROY: Why something got to be wrong with me? I ain't said nothing wrong with me.

ROSE: You got something to say about everything. First it's the numbers . . . then it's the way the man runs his restaurant . . . then you done got on Cory. What's it gonna be next? Take a look up there and see if the weather suits you . . . or is it gonna be how you gonna put up the fence with the clothes hanging in the yard.

TROY: You hit the nail on the head then.

ROSE: I know you like I know the back of my hand. Go on in there and get you some coffee . . . see if that straighten you up. 'Cause you ain't right this morning.

(*Troy starts into the house and sees Gabriel. Gabriel starts singing. Troy's brother, he is seven years younger than Troy. Injured in World War II, he has a metal plate in his head. He carries an old trumpet tied around his waist and believes with every fiber of his being that he is the Archangel Gabriel. He carries a chipped basket with an assortment of discarded fruits and vegetables he has picked up in the strip district and which he attempts to sell.*)

GABRIEL (*singing*): Yes, ma'am, I got plums
    You ask me how I sell them
    Oh ten cents apiece
    Three for a quarter
    Come and buy now
    'Cause I'm here today
    And tomorrow I'll be gone

(*Gabriel enters.*)

    Hey, Rose!

ROSE: How you doing, Gabe?

GABRIEL: There's Troy . . . Hey, Troy!

TROY: Hey, Gabe.

(*Exit into kitchen.*)

ROSE (*to Gabriel*): What you got there?

GABRIEL: You know what I got, Rose. I got fruits and vegetables.

ROSE (*looking in basket*): Where's all these plums you talking about?

GABRIEL: I ain't got no plums today, Rose. I was just singing that. Have some tomorrow. Put me in a big order for plums. Have enough plums tomorrow for St. Peter and everybody.

(*Troy reenters from kitchen, crosses to steps.*)
(*To Rose.*)

    Troy's mad at me.

TROY: I ain't mad at you. What I got to be mad at you about? You ain't done nothing to me.

GABRIEL: I just moved over to Miss Pearl's to keep out from in your way. I ain't mean no harm by it.

TROY: Who said anything about that? I ain't said anything about that.

GABRIEL: You ain't mad at me, is you?

TROY: Naw . . . I ain't mad at you, Gabe. If I was mad at you I'd tell you about it.

GABRIEL: Got me two rooms. In the basement. Got my own door too. Wanna see my key?

(*He holds up a key.*)

    That's my own key! Ain't nobody else got a key like that. That's my key! My two rooms!

TROY: Well, that's good, Gabe. You got your own key . . . that's good.

ROSE: You hungry, Gabe? I was just fixing to cook Troy his breakfast.

GABRIEL: I'll take some biscuits. You got some biscuits? Did you know when I was in heaven . . . every morning me and St. Peter would sit down by the gate and eat some big fat biscuits? Oh, yeah! We had us a good time. We'd sit there and eat us them biscuits and then St. Peter would go off to sleep and tell me to wake him up when it's time to open the gates for the judgment.

ROSE: Well, come on . . . I'll make up a batch of biscuits.

(*Rose exits into the house.*)

GABRIEL: Troy . . . St. Peter got your name in the book. I seen it. It say . . . Troy Maxson. I say . . . I know him! He got the same name like what I got. That's my brother!

TROY: How many times you gonna tell me that, Gabe?

GABRIEL: Ain't got my name in the book. Don't have to have my name. I done died and went to heaven. He got your name though. One morning St. Peter was looking at his book . . . marking it up for the judgment . . . and he let me see your name. Got it in there under M. Got Rose's name . . . I ain't seen it like I seen yours . . . but I know it's in there. He got a great big book. Got everybody's name what was ever been born. That's what he told me. But I seen your name. Seen it with my own eyes.

TROY: Go on in the house there. Rose going to fix you something to eat.

GABRIEL: Oh, I ain't hungry. I done had breakfast with Aunt Jemimah. She come by and cooked me up a whole mess of flapjacks. Remember how we used to eat them flapjacks?

TROY: Go on in the house and get you something to eat now.

GABRIEL: I got to go sell my plums. I done sold some tomatoes. Got me two quarters. Wanna see?

(He shows Troy his quarters.)

> I'm gonna save them and buy me a new horn so St. Peter can hear me when it's time to open the gates.

(Gabriel stops suddenly. Listens.)

> Hear that? That's the hellhounds. I got to chase them out of here. Go on get out of here! Get out!

(Gabriel exits singing.)

> Better get ready for the judgment
> Better get ready for the judgment
> My Lord is coming down

(Rose enters from the house.)

TROY: He gone off somewhere.

GABRIEL *(offstage):* Better get ready for the judgment
> Better get ready for the judgment morning
> Better get ready for the judgment
> My God is coming down

ROSE: He ain't eating right. Miss Pearl say she can't get him to eat nothing.

TROY: What you want me to do about it, Rose? I done did everything I can for the man. I can't make him get well. Man got half his head blown away . . . what you expect?

ROSE: Seem like something ought to be done to help him.

TROY: Man don't bother nobody. He just mixed up from that metal plate he got in his head. Ain't no sense for him to go back into the hospital.

ROSE: Least he be eating right. They can help him take care of himself.

TROY: Don't nobody wanna be locked up, Rose. What you wanna lock him up for? Man go over there and fight the war . . . messin' around with them Japs, get half his head blown off . . . and they give him a lousy three thousand dollars. And I had to swoop down on that.

ROSE: Is you fixing to go into that again?

TROY: That's the only way I got a roof over my head . . . cause of that metal plate.

ROSE: Ain't no sense you blaming yourself for nothing. Gabe wasn't in no condition to manage that money. You done what was right by him. Can't nobody say you ain't done what was right by him. Look how long you took care of him . . . till he wanted to have his own place and moved over there with Miss Pearl.

TROY: That ain't what I'm saying, woman! I'm just stating the facts. If my brother didn't have that metal plate in his head . . . I wouldn't have a pot to piss in or a window to throw it out of. And I'm fifty-three years old. Now see if you can understand that!

(Troy gets up from the porch and starts to exit the yard.)

ROSE: Where you going off to? You been running out of here every Saturday for weeks. I thought you was gonna work on this fence.

TROY: I'm gonna walk down to Taylors'. Listen to the ball game. I'll be back in a bit. I'll work on it when I get back.

(He exits the yard. The lights go to black.)

Scene III

(The lights come up on the yard. It is four hours later. Rose is taking down the clothes from the line. Cory enters carrying his football equipment.)

ROSE: Your daddy like to had a fit with you running out of here this morning without doing your chores.

CORY: I told you I had to go to practice.

ROSE: He say you were supposed to help him with this fence.

CORY: He been saying that the last four or five Saturdays, and then he don't never do nothing but go down to Taylors'. Did you tell him about the recruiter?

ROSE: Yeah, I told him.

CORY: What he say?

ROSE: He ain't said nothing too much. You get in there and get started on your chores before he gets back. Go on and scrub down them steps before he gets back here hollering and carrying on.

CORY: I'm hungry. What you got to eat, Mama?

ROSE: Go on and get started on your chores. I got some meat loaf in there. Go on and make you a sandwich . . . and don't leave no mess in there.

(Cory exits into the house. Rose continues to take down the clothes. Troy enters the yard and sneaks up and grabs her from behind.)

> Troy! Go on, now. You liked to scared me to death. What was the score of the game? Lucille had me on the phone and I couldn't keep up with it.

TROY: What I care about the game? Come here, woman. *(He tries to kiss her.)*

ROSE: I thought you went down Taylors' to listen to the game. Go on, Troy! You supposed to be putting up this fence.

TROY *(attempting to kiss her again):* I'll put it up when I finish with what is at hand.

ROSE: Go on, Troy. I ain't studying you.

TROY *(chasing after her):* I'm studying you . . . fixing to do my homework!

ROSE: Troy, you better leave me alone.

TROY: Where's Cory? That boy brought his butt home yet?

ROSE: He's in the house doing his chores.

TROY *(calling):* Cory! Get your butt out here, boy!

(Rose exits into the house with the laundry. Troy goes over to the pile of wood, picks up a board, and starts sawing. Cory enters from the house.)

TROY: You just now coming in here from leaving this morning?

CORY: Yeah, I had to go to football practice.

TROY: Yeah, what?

CORY: Yessir.

TROY: I ain't but two seconds off you noway. The garbage sitting in there overflowing . . . you ain't done none of your chores . . . and you come in here talking about "Yeah."

CORY: I was just getting ready to do my chores now, Pop . . .

TROY: Your first chore is to help me with this fence on Saturday. Everything else come after that. Now get that saw and cut them boards.

(*Cory takes the saw and begins cutting the boards. Troy continues working. There is a long pause.*)

CORY: Hey, Pop . . . why don't you buy a TV?

TROY: What I want with a TV? What I want one of them for?

CORY: Everybody got one. Earl, Ba Bra . . . Jesse!

TROY: I ain't asked you who had one. I say what I want with one?

CORY: So you can watch it. They got lots of things on TV. Baseball games and everything. We could watch the World Series.

TROY: Yeah . . . and how much this TV cost?

CORY: I don't know. They got them on sale for around two hundred dollars.

TROY: Two hundred dollars, huh?

CORY: That ain't that much, Pop.

TROY: Naw, it's just two hundred dollars. See that roof you got over your head at night? Let me tell you something about that roof. It's been over ten years since that roof was last tarred. See now . . . the snow come this winter and sit up there on that roof like it is . . . and it's gonna seep inside. It's just gonna be a little bit . . . ain't gonna hardly notice it. Then the next thing you know, it's gonna be leaking all over the house. Then the wood rot from all that water and you gonna need a whole new roof. Now, how much you think it cost to get that roof tarred?

CORY: I don't know.

TROY: Two hundred and sixty-four dollars . . . cash money. While you thinking about a TV, I got to be thinking about the roof . . . and whatever else go wrong around here. Now if you had two hundred dollars, what would you do . . . fix the roof or buy a TV?

CORY: I'd buy a TV. Then when the roof started to leak . . . when it needed fixing . . . I'd fix it.

TROY: Where you gonna get the money from? You done spent it for a TV. You gonna sit up and watch the water run all over your brand new TV.

CORY: Aw, Pop. You got money. I know you do.

TROY: Where I got it at, huh?

CORY: You got it in the bank.

TROY: You wanna see my bankbook? You wanna see that seventy-three dollars and twenty-two cents I got sitting up in there?

CORY: You ain't got to pay for it all at one time. You can put a down payment on it and carry it on home with you.

TROY: Not me. I ain't gonna owe nobody nothing if I can help it. Miss a payment and they come and snatch it right out your house. Then what you got? Now, soon as I get two hundred dollars clear, then I'll buy a TV. Right now, as soon as I get two

hundred and sixty-four dollars, I'm gonna have this roof tarred.

CORY: Aw . . . Pop!

TROY: You go on and get you two hundred dollars and buy one if ya want it. I got better things to do with my money.

CORY: I can't get no two hundred dollars. I ain't never seen two hundred dollars.

TROY: I'll tell you what . . . you get you a hundred dollars and I'll put the other hundred with it.

CORY: All right, I'm gonna show you.

TROY: You gonna show me how you can cut them boards right now.

(*Cory begins to cut the boards. There is a long pause.*)

CORY: The Pirates won today. That makes five in a row.

TROY: I ain't thinking about the Pirates. Got an all-white team. Got that boy . . . that Puerto Rican boy . . . Clemente. Don't even half-play him. That boy could be something if they give him a chance. Play him one day and sit him on the bench the next.

CORY: He gets a lot of chances to play.

TROY: I'm talking about playing regular. Playing every day so you can get your timing. That's what I'm talking about.

CORY: They got some white guys on the team that don't play every day. You can't play everybody at the same time.

TROY: If they got a white fellow sitting on the bench . . . you can bet your last dollar he can't play! The colored guy got to be twice as good before he get on the team. That's why I don't want you to get all tied up in them sports. Man on the team and what it get him? They got colored on the team and don't use them. Same as not having them. All them teams the same.

CORY: The Braves got Hank Aaron and Wes Covington. Hank Aaron hit two home runs today. That makes forty-three.

TROY: Hank Aaron ain't nobody. That's what you supposed to do. That's how you supposed to play the game. Ain't nothing to it. It's just a matter of timing . . . getting the right follow-through. Hell, I can hit forty-three home runs right now!

CORY: Not off no major-league pitching, you couldn't.

TROY: We had better pitching in the Negro leagues. I hit seven home runs off of Satchel Paige.° You can't get no better than that!

CORY: Sandy Koufax. He's leading the league in strikeouts.

TROY: I ain't thinking of no Sandy Koufax.

CORY: You got Warren Spahn and Lew Burdette. I bet you couldn't hit no home runs off of Warren Spahn.

TROY: I'm through with it now. You go on and cut them boards.

(*Pause.*)

Satchel Paige: Legendary black pitcher (1906–1982) in the Negro leagues.

Your mama tell me you done got recruited by a college football team? Is that right?

CORY: Yeah. Coach Zellman say the recruiter gonna be coming by to talk to you. Get you to sign the permission papers.

TROY: I thought you supposed to be working down there at the A&P. Ain't you suppose to be working down there after school?

CORY: Mr. Stawicki say he gonna hold my job for me until after the football season. Say starting next week I can work weekends.

TROY: I thought we had an understanding about this football stuff? You suppose to keep up with your chores and hold that job down at the A&P. Ain't been around here all day on a Saturday. Ain't none of your chores done . . . and now you telling me you done quit your job.

CORY: I'm gonna be working weekends.

TROY: You damn right you are! And ain't no need for nobody coming around here to talk to me about signing nothing.

CORY: Hey, Pop . . . you can't do that. He's coming all the way from North Carolina.

TROY: I don't care where he coming from. The white man ain't gonna let you get nowhere with that football noway. You go on and get your book-learning so you can work yourself up in that A&P or learn how to fix cars or build houses or something, get you a trade. That way you have something can't nobody take away from you. You go on and learn how to put your hands to some good use. Besides hauling people's garbage.

CORY: I get good grades, Pop. That's why the recruiter wants to talk with you. You got to keep up your grades to get recruited. This way I'll be going to college. I'll get a chance . . .

TROY: First you gonna get your butt down there to the A&P and get your job back.

CORY: Mr. Stawicki done already hired somebody else 'cause I told him I was playing football.

TROY: You a bigger fool than I thought . . . to let somebody take away your job so you can play some football. Where you gonna get your money to take out your girlfriend and whatnot? What kind of foolishness is that to let somebody take away your job?

CORY: I'm still gonna be working weekends.

TROY: Naw . . . naw. You getting your butt out of here and finding you another job.

CORY: Come on, Pop! I got to practice. I can't work after school and play football too. The team needs me. That's what Coach Zellman say . . .

TROY: I don't care what nobody else say. I'm the boss . . . you understand? I'm the boss around here. I do the only saying what counts.

CORY: Come on, Pop!

TROY: I asked you . . . did you understand?

CORY: Yeah . . .

TROY: What?!

Lynn Thigpen and James Earl Jones in the 1987 production of *Fences*.

CORY: Yessir.

TROY: You go on down there to that A&P and see if you can get your job back. If you can't do both . . . then you quit the football team. You've got to take the crookeds with the straights.

CORY: Yessir.

(*Pause.*)

Can I ask you a question?

TROY: What the hell you wanna ask me? Mr. Stawicki the one you got the questions for.

CORY: How come you ain't never liked me?

TROY: Liked you? Who the hell say I got to like you? What law is there say I got to like you? Wanna stand up in my face and ask a damn fool-ass question like that. Talking about liking somebody. Come here, boy, when I talk to you.

(*Cory comes over to where Troy is working. He stands slouched over and Troy shoves him on his shoulder.*)

Straighten up, goddammit! I asked you a question . . . what law is there say I got to like you?

CORY: None.

TROY: Well, all right then! Don't you eat every day?

(*Pause.*)

    Answer me when I talk to you! Don't you eat every day?

CORY: Yeah.

TROY: Nigger, as long as you in my house, you put that sir on the end of it when you talk to me!

CORY: Yes . . . sir.

TROY: You eat every day.

CORY: Yessir!

TROY: Got a roof over your head.

CORY: Yessir!

TROY: Got clothes on your back.

CORY: Yessir.

TROY: Why you think that is?

CORY: Cause of you.

TROY: Ah, hell I know it's 'cause of me . . . but why do you think that is?

CORY (*hesitant*): Cause you like me.

TROY: Like you? I go out of here every morning . . . bust my butt . . . putting up with them crackers° every day . . . cause I like you? You about the biggest fool I ever saw.

(*Pause.*)

    It's my job. It's my responsibility! You understand that? A man got to take care of his family. You live

crackers: White people (derogatory).

[ABOVE] James Earl Jones as Troy Maxson in *Fences*. [RIGHT] Jones and Courtney Vance as his son Cory.

in my house . . . sleep you behind on my bed-clothes . . . fill you belly up with my food . . . cause you my son. You my flesh and blood. Not 'cause I like you! Cause it's my duty to take care of you. I owe a responsibility to you! Let's get this straight right here . . . before it go along any further . . . I ain't got to like you. Mr. Rand don't give me my money come payday cause he likes me. He gives me cause he owe me. I done give you everything I had to give you. I gave you your life! Me and your mama worked that out between us. And liking your black ass wasn't part of the bargain. Don't you try and go through life worrying about if somebody like you or not. You best be making sure they doing right by you. You understand what I'm saying, boy?

CORY: Yessir.

TROY: Then get the hell out of my face, and get on down to that A&P.

(*Rose has been standing behind the screen door for much of the scene. She enters as Cory exits.*)

ROSE: Why don't you let the boy go ahead and play football, Troy? Ain't no harm in that. He's just trying to be like you with the sports.

TROY: I don't want him to be like me! I want him to move as far away from my life as he can get. You the only decent thing that ever happened to me. I wish him that. But I don't wish him a thing else from my life. I decided seventeen years ago that boy wasn't getting involved in no sports. Not after what they did to me in the sports.

ROSE: Troy, why don't you admit you was too old to play in the major leagues? For once . . . why don't you admit that?

TROY: What do you mean too old? Don't come telling me I was too old. I just wasn't the right color. Hell, I'm fifty-three years old and can do better than Selkirk's .269 right now!

ROSE: How's was you gonna play ball when you were over forty? Sometimes I can't get no sense out of you.

TROY: I got good sense, woman. I got sense enough not to let my boy get hurt over playing no sports. You been mothering that boy too much. Worried about if people like him.

ROSE: Everything that boy do . . . he do for you. He wants you to say "Good job, son." That's all.

TROY: Rose, I ain't got time for that. He's alive. He's healthy. He's got to make his own way. I made mine. Ain't nobody gonna hold his hand when he get out there in that world.

ROSE: Times have changed from when you was young, Troy. People change. The world's changing around you and you can't even see it.

TROY (*slow, methodical*): Woman . . . I do the best I can do. I come in here every Friday. I carry a sack of potatoes and a bucket of lard. You all line up at the door with your hands out. I give you the lint from my pockets. I give you my sweat and my blood. I ain't got no tears. I done spent them. We go upstairs in that room at night . . . and I fall down on you and try to blast a hole into forever. I get up Monday morning . . . find my lunch on the table. I go out. Make my way. Find my strength to carry me through to the next Friday.

(*Pause.*)

That's all I got, Rose. That's all I got to give. I can't give nothing else.

(*Troy exits into the house. The lights go down to black.*)

Scene IV

(*It is Friday. Two weeks later. Cory starts out of the house with his football equipment. The phone rings.*)

CORY (*calling*): I got it!

(*He answers the phone and stands in the screen door talking.*)

Hello? Hey, Jesse. Naw . . . I was just getting ready to leave now.

ROSE (*calling*): Cory!

CORY: I told you, man, them spikes is all tore up. You can use them if you want, but they ain't no good. Earl got some spikes.

ROSE (*calling*): Cory!

CORY (*calling to Rose*): Mam? I'm talking to Jesse.

(*Into phone.*)

When she say that? (*Pause.*) Aw, you lying, man. I'm gonna tell her you said that.

ROSE (*calling*): Cory, don't you go nowhere!

CORY: I got to go to the game, Ma!

(*Into the phone.*)

Yeah, hey, look, I'll talk to you later. Yeah, I'll meet you over Earl's house. Later. Bye, Ma.

(*Cory exits the house and starts out the yard.*)

ROSE: Cory, where you going off to? You got that stuff all pulled out and thrown all over your room.

CORY (*in the yard*): I was looking for my spikes. Jesse wanted to borrow my spikes.

ROSE: Get up there and get that cleaned up before your daddy get back in here.

CORY: I got to go to the game! I'll clean it up *when I get back*.

(*Cory exits.*)

ROSE: That's all he need to do is see that room all messed up.

(*Rose exits into the house. Troy and Bono enter the yard. Troy is dressed in clothes other than his work clothes.*)

BONO: He told him the same thing he told you. Take it to the union.

TROY: Brownie ain't got that much sense. Man wasn't thinking about nothing. He wait until I confront them on it . . . then he wanna come crying seniority.

(*Calls.*)

Hey, Rose!

BONO: I wish I could have seen Mr. Rand's face when he told you.

TROY: He couldn't get it out of his mouth! Liked to bit his tongue! When they called me down there to the Commissioner's office . . . he thought they was gonna fire me. Like everybody else.

BONO: I didn't think they was gonna fire you. I thought they was gonna put you on the warning paper.

TROY: Hey, Rose!

(*To Bono.*)

Yeah, Mr. Rand like to bit his tongue.

(*Troy breaks the seal on the bottle, takes a drink, and hands it to Bono.*)

BONO: I see you run right down to Taylors' and told that Alberta gal.

TROY (*calling*): Hey, Rose! (*To Bono.*) I told everybody. Hey, Rose! I went down there to cash my check.

ROSE (*entering from the house*): Hush all that hollering, man! I know you out here. What they say down there at the Commissioner's office?

TROY: You supposed to come when I call you, woman. Bono'll tell you that.

(*To Bono.*)

Don't Lucille come when you call her?

ROSE: Man, hush your mouth. I ain't no dog . . . talk about "come when you call me."

TROY (*puts his arm around Rose*): You hear this Bono? I had me an old dog used to get uppity like that. You say, "C'mere, Blue!" . . . and he just lay there and look at you. End up getting a stick and chasing him away trying to make him come.

ROSE: I ain't studying you and your dog. I remember you used to sing that old song.

TROY (*he sings*): Hear it ring! Hear it ring! I had a dog his name was Blue.

ROSE: Don't nobody wanna hear you sing that old song.

TROY (*sings*): You know Blue was mighty true.

ROSE: Used to have Cory running around here singing that song.

BONO: Hell, I remember that song myself.

TROY (*sings*): You know Blue was a good old dog.
Blue treed a possum in a hollow log.

That was my daddy's song. My daddy made up that song.

ROSE: I don't care who made it up. Don't nobody wanna hear you sing it.

TROY (*makes a song like calling a dog*): Come here, woman.

ROSE: You come in here carrying on, I reckon they ain't fired you. What they say down there at the Commissioner's office?

TROY: Look here, Rose . . . Mr. Rand called me into his office today when I got back from talking to them people down there . . . it come from up top . . . he called me in and told me they was making me a driver.

ROSE: Troy, you kidding!

TROY: No I ain't. Ask Bono.

ROSE: Well, that's great, Troy. Now you don't have to hassle them people no more.

(*Lyons enters from the street.*)

TROY: Aw hell, I wasn't looking to see you today. I thought you was in jail. Got it all over the front page of the *Courier* about them raiding Sefus' place . . . where you be hanging out with all them thugs.

LYONS: Hey, Pop . . . that ain't got nothing to do with me. I don't go down there gambling. I go down there to sit in with the band. I ain't got nothing to do with the gambling part. They got some good music down there.

TROY: They got some rogues . . . is what they got.

LYONS: How you been, Mr. Bono? Hi, Rose.

BONO: I see where you playing down at the Crawford Grill tonight.

ROSE: How come you ain't brought Bonnie like I told you. You should have brought Bonnie with you, she ain't been over in a month of Sundays.

LYONS: I was just in the neighborhood . . . thought I'd stop by.

TROY: Here he come . . .

BONO: Your daddy got a promotion on the rubbish. He's gonna be the first colored driver. Ain't got to do nothing but sit up there and read the paper like them white fellows.

LYONS: Hey, Pop . . . if you knew how to read you'd be all right.

BONO: Naw . . . naw . . . you mean if the nigger knew how to *drive* he'd be all right. Been fighting with them people about driving and ain't even got a license. Mr. Rand know you ain't got no driver's license?

TROY: Driving ain't nothing. All you do is point the truck where you want it to go. Driving ain't nothing.

BONO: Do Mr. Rand know you ain't got no driver's license? That's what I'm talking about. I ain't asked if driving was easy. I asked if Mr. Rand know you ain't got no driver's license.

TROY: He ain't got to know. The man ain't got to know my business. Time he find out, I have two or three driver's licenses.

LYONS (*going into his pocket*): Say, look here, Pop . . .

TROY: I knew it was coming. Didn't I tell you, Bono? I know what kind of "Look here, Pop" that was.

The nigger fixing to ask me for some money. It's Friday night. It's my payday. All them rogues down there on the avenue . . . the ones that ain't in jail . . . and Lyons is hopping in his shoes to get down there with them.

LYONS: See, Pop . . . if you give somebody else a chance to talk sometime, you'd see that I was fixing to pay you back your ten dollars like I told you. Here . . . I told you I'd pay you when Bonnie got paid.

TROY: Naw . . . you go ahead and keep that ten dollars. Put it in the bank. The next time you feel like you wanna come by here and ask me for something . . . you go on down there and get that.

LYONS: Here's your ten dollars, Pop. I told you I don't want you to give me nothing. I just wanted to borrow ten dollars.

TROY: Naw . . . you go on and keep that for the next time you want to ask me.

LYONS: Come on, Pop . . . here go your ten dollars.

ROSE: Why don't you go on and let the boy pay you back, Troy?

LYONS: Here you go, Rose. If you don't take it I'm gonna have to hear about it for the next six months.

(*He hands her the money.*)

ROSE: You can hand yours over here too, Troy.

TROY: You see this, Bono. You see how they do me.

BONO: Yeah, Lucille do me the same way.

(*Gabriel is heard singing offstage. He enters.*)

GABRIEL: Better get ready for the Judgment! Better get ready for . . . Hey! . . . Hey! . . . There's Troy's boy!

LYONS: How are you doing, Uncle Gabe?

GABRIEL: Lyons . . . The King of the Jungle! Rose . . . hey, Rose. Got a flower for you.

(*He takes a rose from his pocket.*)

Picked it myself. That's the same rose like you is!

ROSE: That's right nice of you, Gabe.

LYONS: What you been doing, Uncle Gabe?

GABRIEL: Oh, I been chasing hellhounds and waiting on the time to tell St. Peter to open the gates.

LYONS: You been chasing hellhounds, huh? Well . . . you doing the right thing, Uncle Gabe. Somebody got to chase them.

GABRIEL: Oh, yeah . . . I know it. The devil's strong. The devil ain't no pushover. Hellhounds snipping at everybody's heels. But I got my trumpet waiting on the judgment time.

LYONS: Waiting on the Battle of Armageddon, huh?

GABRIEL: Ain't gonna be too much of a battle when God get to waving that Judgment sword. But the people's gonna have a hell of a time trying to get into heaven if them gates ain't open.

LYONS (*putting his arm around Gabriel*): You hear this, Pop. Uncle Gabe, you all right!

GABRIEL (*laughing with Lyons*): Lyons! King of the Jungle.

ROSE: You gonna stay for supper, Gabe. Want me to fix you a plate?

GABRIEL: I'll take a sandwich, Rose. Don't want no plate. Just wanna eat with my hands. I'll take a sandwich.

ROSE: How about you, Lyons? You staying? Got some short ribs cooking.

LYONS: Naw, I won't eat nothing till after we finished playing.

(*Pause.*)

You ought to come down and listen to me play, Pop.

TROY: I don't like that Chinese music. All that noise.

ROSE: Go on in the house and wash up, Gabe . . . I'll fix you a sandwich.

GABRIEL (*to Lyons, as he exits*): Troy's mad at me.

LYONS: What you mad at Uncle Gabe for, Pop.

ROSE: He thinks Troy's mad at him cause he moved over to Miss Pearl's.

TROY: I ain't mad at the man. He can live where he want to live at.

LYONS: What he move over there for? Miss Pearl don't like nobody.

ROSE: She don't mind him none. She treats him real nice. She just don't allow all that singing.

TROY: She don't mind that rent he be paying . . . that's what she don't mind.

ROSE: Troy, I ain't going through that with you no more. He's over there cause he want to have his own place. He can come and go as he please.

TROY: Hell, he could come and go as he please here. I wasn't stopping him. I ain't put no rules on him.

ROSE: It ain't the same thing, Troy. And you know it.

(*Gabriel comes to the door.*)

Now, that's the last I wanna hear about that. I don't wanna hear nothing else about Gabe and Miss Pearl. And next week . . .

GABRIEL: I'm ready for my sandwich, Rose.

ROSE: And next week . . . when that recruiter come from that school . . . I want you to sign that paper and go on and let Cory play football. Then that'll be the last I have to hear about that.

TROY (*to Rose as she exits into the house*): I ain't thinking about Cory nothing.

LYONS: What . . . Cory got recruited? What school he going to?

TROY: That boy walking around here smelling his piss . . . thinking he's grown. Thinking he's gonna do what he want, irrespective of what I say. Look here, Bono . . . I left the Commissioner's office and went down to the A&P . . . that boy ain't working down there. He lying to me. Telling me he got his job back . . . telling me he working weekends . . . telling me he working after school . . . Mr. Stawicki tell me he ain't working down there at all!

LYONS: Cory just growing up. He's just busting at the seams trying to fill out your shoes.

TROY: I don't care what he's doing. When he get to the point where he wanna disobey me . . . then it's time for him to move on. Bono'll tell you that. I bet he ain't never disobeyed his daddy without paying the consequences.

BONO: I ain't never had a chance. My daddy came on through . . . but I ain't never knew him to see him . . . or what he had on his mind or where he went. Just moving on through. Searching out the New Land. That's what the old folks used to call it. See a fellow moving around from place to place . . . woman to woman . . . called it searching out the New Land. I can't say if he ever found it. I come along, didn't want no kids. Didn't know if I was gonna be in one place long enough to fix on them right as their daddy. I figured I was going searching too. As it turned out I been hooked up with Lucille near about as long as your daddy been with Rose. Going on sixteen years.

TROY: Sometimes I wish I hadn't known my daddy. He ain't cared nothing about no kids. A kid to him wasn't nothing. All he wanted was for you to learn how to walk so he could start you to working. When it come time for eating . . . he ate first. If there was anything left over, that's what you got. Man would sit down and eat two chickens and give you the wing.

LYONS: You ought to stop that, Pop. Everybody feed their kids. No matter how hard times is . . . everybody care about their kids. Make sure they have something to eat.

TROY: The only thing my daddy cared about was getting them bales of cotton in to Mr. Lubin. That's the only thing that mattered to him. Sometimes I used to wonder why he was living. Wonder why the devil hadn't come and got him. "Get them bales of cotton in to Mr. Lubin" and find out he owe him money . . .

LYONS: He should have just went on and left when he saw he couldn't get nowhere. That's what I would have done.

TROY: How he gonna leave with eleven kids? And where he gonna go? He ain't knew how to do nothing but farm. No, he was trapped and I think he knew it. But I'll say this for him . . . he felt a responsibility toward us. Maybe he ain't treated us the way I felt he should have . . . but without that responsibility he could have walked off and left us . . . made his own way.

BONO: A lot of them did. Back in those days what you talking about . . . they walk out their front door and just take on down one road or another and keep on walking.

LYONS: There you go! That's what I'm talking about.

BONO: Just keep on walking till you come to something else. Ain't you never heard of nobody having the walking blues? Well, that's what you call it when you just take off like that.

TROY: My daddy ain't had them walking blues! What you talking about? He stayed right there with his family. But he was just as evil as he could be. My mama couldn't stand him. Couldn't stand that evilness. She run off when I was about eight. She sneaked off one night after he had gone to sleep. Told me she was coming back for me. I ain't never seen her no more. All his women run off and left him. He wasn't good for nobody.

When my turn come to head out, I was fourteen and got to sniffing around Joe Canewell's daughter. Had us an old mule we called Greyboy. My daddy sent me out to do some plowing and I tied up Greyboy and went to fooling around with Joe Canewell's daughter. We done found us a nice little spot, got real cozy with each other. She about thirteen and we done figured we was grown anyway . . . so we down there enjoying ourselves . . . ain't thinking about nothing. We didn't know Greyboy had got loose and wandered back to the house and my daddy was looking for me. We down there by the creek enjoying ourselves when my daddy come up on us. Surprised us. He had them leather straps off the mule and commenced to whupping me like there was no tomorrow. I jumped up, mad and embarrassed. I was scared of my daddy. When he commenced to whupping on me . . . quite naturally I run to get out of the way.

(*Pause.*)

Now I thought he was mad cause I ain't done my work. But I see where he was chasing me off so he could have the gal for himself. When I see what the matter of it was, I lost all fear of my daddy. Right there is where I become a man . . . at fourteen years of age.

(*Pause.*)

Now it was my turn to run him off. I picked up them same reins that he had used on me. I picked up them reins and commenced to whupping on him. The gal jumped up and run off . . . and when my daddy turned to face me, I could see why the devil had never come to get him . . . cause he was the devil himself. I don't know what happened. When I woke up, I was laying right there by the creek, and Blue . . . this old dog we had . . . was licking my face. I thought I was blind. I couldn't see nothing. Both my eyes were swollen shut. I layed there and cried. I didn't know what I was gonna do. The only thing I knew was the time had come for me to leave my daddy's house. And right there the world suddenly got big. And it was a long time before I could cut it down to where I could handle it.

Part of that cutting down was when I got to the place where I could feel him kicking in my blood and knew that the only thing that separated us was the matter of a few years.

(*Gabriel enters from the house with a sandwich.*)

LYONS: What you got there, Uncle Gabe?

GABRIEL: Got me a ham sandwich. Rose gave me a ham sandwich.

TROY: I don't know what happened to him. I done lost touch with everybody except Gabriel. But I hope he's dead. I hope he found some peace.

LYONS: That's a heavy story, Pop. I didn't know you left home when you was fourteen.

TROY: And didn't know nothing. The only part of the world I knew was the forty-two acres of Mr. Lubin's land. That's all I knew about life.

LYONS: Fourteen's kinda young to be out on your own. (*Phone rings.*) I don't even think I was ready to be out on my own at fourteen. I don't know what I would have done.

TROY: I got up from the creek and walked on down to Mobile. I was through with farming. Figured I could do better in the city. So I walked the two hundred miles to Mobile.

LYONS: Wait a minute . . . you ain't walked no two hundred miles, Pop. Ain't nobody gonna walk no two hundred miles. You talking about some walking there.

BONO: That's the only way you got anywhere back in them days.

LYONS: Shhh. Damn if I wouldn't have hitched a ride with somebody!

TROY: Who you gonna hitch it with? They ain't had no cars and things like they got now. We talking about 1918.

ROSE (*entering*): What you all out here getting into?

TROY (*to Rose*): I'm telling Lyons how good he got it. He don't know nothing about this I'm talking.

ROSE: Lyons, that was Bonnie on the phone. She say you supposed to pick her up.

LYONS: Yeah, okay, Rose.

TROY: I walked on down to Mobile and hitched up with some of them fellows that was heading this way. Got up here and found out . . . not only couldn't you get a job . . . you couldn't find no place to live. I thought I was in freedom. Shhh. Colored folks living down there on the riverbanks in whatever kind of shelter they could find for themselves. Right down there under the Brady Street Bridge. Living in shacks made of sticks and tarpaper. Messed around there and went from bad to worse. Started stealing. First it was food. Then I figured, hell, if I steal money I can buy me some food. Buy me some shoes too! One thing led to another. Met your mama. I was young and anxious to be a man. Met your mama and had you. What I do that for? Now I got to worry about feeding you and her. Got to steal three times as much. Went out one day looking for somebody to rob . . . that's what I was, a robber. I'll tell you the truth. I'm ashamed of it today. But it's the truth. Went to rob this fellow . . . pulled out my knife . . . and he pulled out a gun. Shot me in the chest. It felt just like somebody had taken a hot branding iron and laid it on me. When he shot me I jumped at him with my knife. They told me I killed him and they put me in the penitentiary and locked me up for fifteen years. That's where I met Bono. That's where I learned how to play baseball. Got out that place and your mama had taken you and went on to make life without me. Fifteen years was a long time for her to wait. But that fifteen years cured me of that robbing stuff. Rose'll tell you. She asked me when I met her if I had gotten all that foolishness out of my system. And I told her, "Baby, it's you and baseball all what count with me." You hear me, Bono? I meant it too. She say "Which one comes first?" I told her, "Baby, ain't no doubt it's baseball . . . but you stick and get old with me and we'll both outlive this baseball." Am I right, Rose? And it's true.

ROSE: Man, hush your mouth. You ain't said no such thing. Talking about, "Baby, you know you'll always be number one with me." That's what you was talking.

TROY: You hear that, Bono. That's why I love her.

BONO: Rose'll keep you straight. You get off the track, she'll straighten you up.

ROSE: Lyons, you better get on up and get Bonnie. She waiting on you.

LYONS (*gets up to go*): Hey, Pop, why don't you come on down to the Grill and hear me play?

TROY: I ain't going down there. I'm too old to be sitting around in them clubs.

BONO: You got to be good to play down at the Grill.

LYONS: Come on, Pop . . .

TROY: I got to get up in the morning.

LYONS: You ain't got to stay long.

TROY: Naw, I'm gonna get my supper and go on to bed.

LYONS: Well, I got to go. I'll see you again.

TROY: Don't you come around my house on my payday.

ROSE: Pick up the phone and let somebody know you coming. And bring Bonnie with you. You know I'm always glad to see her.

LYONS: Yeah, I'll do that, Rose. You take care now. See you, Pop. See you, Mr. Bono. See you, Uncle Gabe.

GABRIEL: Lyons! King of the Jungle!

(*Lyons exits.*)

TROY: Is supper ready, woman? Me and you got some business to take care of. I'm gonna tear it up too.

ROSE: Troy, I done told you now!

TROY (*puts his arm around Bono*): Aw hell, woman . . . this is Bono. Bono like family. I done known this nigger since . . . how long I done know you?

BONO: It's been a long time.

TROY: I done known this nigger since Skippy was a pup. Me and him done been through some times.

BONO: You sure right about that.

TROY: Hell, I done know him longer than I known you. And we still standing shoulder to shoulder. Hey, look here, Bono . . . a man can't ask for no more than that.

(*Drinks to him.*)

I love you, nigger.

BONO: Hell, I love you too . . . but I got to get home see my woman. You got yours in hand. I got to go get mine.

(*Bono starts to exit as Cory enters the yard, dressed in his football uniform. He gives Troy a hard, uncompromising look.*)

CORY: What you do that for, Pop?

(*He throws his helmet down in the direction of Troy.*)

ROSE: What's the matter? Cory . . . what's the matter?

CORY: Papa done went up to the school and told Coach Zellman I can't play football no more. Wouldn't even let me play the game. Told him to tell the recruiter not to come.

ROSE: Troy . . .

TROY: What you Troying me for. Yeah, I did it. And the boy know why I did it.

CORY: Why you wanna do that to me? That was the one chance I had.

ROSE: Ain't nothing wrong with Cory playing football, Troy.

TROY: The boy lied to me. I told the nigger if he wanna play football . . . to keep up his chores and hold down that job at the A&P. That was the conditions. Stopped down there to see Mr. Stawicki . . .

CORY: I can't work after school during the football season, Pop! I tried to tell you that Mr. Stawicki's holding my job for me. You don't never want to listen to nobody. And then you wanna go and do this to me!

TROY: I ain't done nothing to you. You done it to yourself.

CORY: Just cause you didn't have a chance! You just scared I'm gonna be better than you, that's all.

TROY: Come here.

ROSE: Troy . . .

(*Cory reluctantly crosses over to Troy.*)

TROY: All right! See. You done made a mistake.

CORY: I didn't even do nothing!

TROY: I'm gonna tell you what your mistake was. See . . . you swung at the ball and didn't hit it. That's strike one. See, you in the batter's box now. You swung and you missed. That's strike one. Don't you strike out!

(*Lights fade to black.*)

ACT II • Scene I

(*The following morning. Cory is at the tree hitting the ball with the bat. He tries to mimic Troy, but his swing is awkward, less sure. Rose enters from the house.*)

ROSE: Cory, I want you to help me with this cupboard.

CORY: I ain't quitting the team. I don't care what Poppa say.

ROSE: I'll talk to him when he gets back. He had to go see about your Uncle Gabe. The police done arrested him. Say he was disturbing the peace. He'll be back directly. Come on in here and help me clean out the top of this cupboard.

(*Cory exits into the house. Rose sees Troy and Bono coming down the alley.*)

Troy . . . what they say down there?

TROY: Ain't said nothing. I give them fifty dollars and they let him go. I'll talk to you about it. Where's Cory?

ROSE: He's in there helping me clean out these cupboards.

TROY: Tell him to get his butt out here.

(*Troy and Bono go over to the pile of wood. Bono picks up the saw and begins sawing.*)

TROY (*to Bono*): All they want is the money. That makes six or seven times I done went down there and got him. See me coming they stick out their *hands*.

BONO: Yeah. I know what you mean. That's all they care about . . . that money. They don't care about what's right.

(*Pause.*)

Nigger, why you got to go and get some hard wood? You ain't doing nothing but building a little old fence. Get you some soft pine wood. That's all you need.

TROY: I know what I'm doing. This is outside wood. You put pine wood inside the house. Pine wood is inside wood. This here is outside wood. Now you tell me where the fence is gonna be?

BONO: You don't need this wood. You can put it up with pine wood and it'll stand as long as you gonna be here looking at it.

TROY: How you know how long I'm gonna be here, nigger? Hell, I might just live forever. Live longer than old man Horsely.

BONO: That's what Magee used to say.

TROY: Magee's a damn fool. Now you tell me who you ever heard of gonna pull their own teeth with a pair of rusty pliers.

BONO: The old folks . . . my granddaddy used to pull his teeth with pliers. They ain't had no dentists for the colored folks back then.

TROY: Get clean pliers! You understand? Clean pliers! Sterilize them! Besides we ain't living back then. All Magee had to do was walk over to Doc Goldblum's.

BONO: I see where you and that Tallahassee gal . . . that Alberta . . . I see where you all done got tight.

TROY: What you mean "got tight"?

BONO: I see where you be laughing and joking with her all the time.

TROY: I laughs and jokes with all of them, Bono. You know me.

BONO: That ain't the kind of laughing and joking I'm talking about.

(*Cory enters from the house.*)

CORY: How you doing, Mr. Bono?

TROY: Cory? Get that saw from Bono and cut some wood. He talking about the wood's too hard to cut. Stand back there, Jim, and let that young boy show you how it's done.

BONO: He's sure welcome to it.

(*Cory takes the saw and begins to cut the wood.*)

Whew-e-e! Look at that. Big old strong boy. Look like Joe Louis. Hell, must be getting old the way I'm watching that boy whip through that wood.

CORY: I don't see why Mama want a fence around the yard noways.

TROY: Damn if I know either. What the hell she keeping out with it? She ain't got nothing nobody want.

BONO: Some people build fences to keep people out . . . and other people build fences to keep people in. Rose wants to hold on to you all. She loves you.

TROY: Hell, nigger, I don't need nobody to tell me my wife loves me, Cory . . . go on in the house and see if you can find that other saw.

CORY: Where's it at?

TROY: I said find it! Look for it till you find it!

(*Cory exits into the house.*)

What's that supposed to mean? Wanna keep us in?

BONO: Troy . . . I done known you seem like damn near my whole life. You and Rose both. I done know both of you all for a long time. I remember when you met Rose. When you was hitting them baseball out the park. A lot of them old gals was after you then. You had the pick of the litter. When you picked Rose, I was happy for you. That was the first time I knew you had any sense. I said . . . My man Troy knows what he's doing . . . I'm gonna follow this nigger . . . he might take me somewhere. I been following you too. I done learned a whole heap of things about life watching you. I done learned how to tell where the shit lies. How to tell it from the alfalfa. You done learned me a lot of things. You showed me how to not make the same mistakes . . . to take life as it comes along and keep putting one foot in front of the other.

(*Pause.*)

Rose a good woman, Troy.

TROY: Hell, nigger, I know she a good woman. I been married to her for eighteen years. What you got on your mind, Bono?

BONO: I just say she a good woman. Just like I say anything. I ain't got to have nothing on my mind.

TROY: You just gonna say she a good woman and leave it hanging out there like that? Why you telling me she a good woman?

BONO: She loves you, Troy. Rose loves you.

TROY: You saying I don't measure up. That's what you trying to say. I don't measure up cause I'm seeing this other gal. I know what you trying to say.

BONO: I know what Rose means to you, Troy. I'm just trying to say I don't want to see you mess up.

TROY: Yeah, I appreciate that, Bono. If you was messing around on Lucille I'd be telling you the same thing.

BONO: Well, that's all I got to say. I just say that because I love you both.

TROY: Hell, you know me . . . I wasn't out there looking for nothing. You can't find a better woman than Rose. I know that. But seems like this woman just stuck onto me where I can't shake her loose. I done wrestled with it, tried to throw her off me . . . but she just stuck on tighter. Now she's stuck on for good.

BONO: You's in control . . . that's what you tell me all the time. You responsible for what you do.

TROY: I ain't ducking the responsibility of it. As long as it sets right in my heart . . . then I'm okay. Cause that's all I listen to. It'll tell me right from wrong every time. And I ain't talking about doing Rose no bad turn. I love Rose. She done carried me a long ways and I love and respect her for that.

BONO: I know you do. That's why I don't want to see you hurt her. But what you gonna do when she find out? What you got then? If you try and juggle both of them . . . sooner or later you gonna drop one of them. That's common sense.

TROY: Yeah, I hear what you saying, Bono. I been trying to figure a way to work it out.

BONO: Work it out right, Troy. I don't want to be getting all up between you and Rose's business . . . but work it so it come out right.

TROY: Ah hell, I get all up between you and Lucille's business. When you gonna get that woman that refrigerator she been wanting? Don't tell me you ain't got no money now. I know who your banker is. Mellon don't need that money bad as Lucille want that refrigerator. I'll tell you that.

BONO: Tell you what I'll do . . . when you finish building this fence for Rose . . . I'll buy Lucille that refrigerator.

TROY: You done stuck your foot in your mouth now!

(*Troy grabs up a board and begins to saw. Bono starts to walk out the yard.*)

Hey, nigger . . . where you going?

BONO: I'm going home. I know you don't expect me to help you now. I'm protecting my money. I wanna see you put that fence up by yourself. That's what I want to see. You'll be here another six months without me.

TROY: Nigger, you ain't right.

BONO: When it comes to my money . . . I'm right as fireworks on the Fourth of July.

TROY: All right, we gonna see now. You better get out your bankbook.

(*Bono exits, and Troy continues to work. Rose enters from the house.*)

ROSE: What they say down there? What's happening with Gabe?

TROY: I went down there and got him out. Cost me fifty dollars. Say he was disturbing the peace. Judge set up a hearing for him in three weeks. Say to show cause why he shouldn't be recommitted.

ROSE: What was he doing that cause them to arrest him?

TROY: Some kids was teasing him and he run them off home. Say he was howling and carrying on. Some folks seen him and called the police. That's all it was.

ROSE: Well, what's you say? What'd you tell the judge?

TROY: Told him I'd look after him. It didn't make no sense to recommit the man. He stuck out his big greasy palm and told me to give him fifty dollars and take him on home.

ROSE: Where's he at now? Where'd he go off to?

TROY: He's gone on about his business. He don't need nobody to hold his hand.

ROSE: Well, I don't know. Seem like that would be the best place for him if they did put him into the hospital. I know what you're gonna say. But that's what I think would be best.

TROY: The man done had his life ruined fighting for what? And they wanna take and lock him up. Let him be free. He don't bother nobody.

ROSE: Well, everybody got their own way of looking at it I guess. Come on and get your lunch. I got a bowl of lima beans and some cornbread in the oven. Come on get something to eat. Ain't no sense you fretting over Gabe.

(*Rose turns to go into the house.*)

TROY: Rose . . . got something to tell you.

ROSE: Well, come on . . . wait till I get this food on the table.

TROY: Rose!

(*She stops and turns around.*)

I don't know how to say this.

(*Pause.*)

I can't explain it none. It just sort of grows on you till it gets out of hand. It starts out like a little bush . . . and the next thing you know it's a whole forest.

ROSE: Troy . . . what is you talking about?

TROY: I'm talking, woman, let me talk. I'm trying to find a way to tell you . . . I'm gonna be a daddy. I'm gonna be somebody's daddy.

ROSE: Troy . . . you're not telling me this? You're gonna be . . . what?

TROY: Rose . . . now . . . see . . .

ROSE: You telling me you gonna be somebody's daddy? You telling your *wife* this?

(*Gabriel enters from the street. He carries a rose in his hand.*)

GABRIEL: Hey, Troy! Hey, Rose!

ROSE: I have to wait eighteen years to hear something like this.

GABRIEL: Hey, Rose . . . I got a flower for you.

(*He hands it to her.*)

That's a rose. Same rose like you is.

ROSE: Thanks, Gabe.

GABRIEL: Troy, you ain't mad at me is you? Them bad mens come and put me away. You ain't mad at me is you?

TROY: Naw, Gabe, I ain't mad at you.

ROSE: Eighteen years and you wanna come with this.

GABRIEL (*takes a quarter out of his pocket*): See what I got? Got a brand new quarter.

TROY: Rose . . . it's just . . .

ROSE: Ain't nothing you can say, Troy. Ain't no way of explaining that.

GABRIEL: Fellow that give me this quarter had a whole mess of them. I'm gonna keep this quarter till it stop shining.

ROSE: Gabe, go on in the house there. I got some watermelon in the frigidaire. Go on and get you a piece.

GABRIEL: Say, Rose . . . you know I was chasing hellhounds and them bad mens come and get me and take me away. Troy helped me. He come down there and told them they better let me go before he beat them up. Yeah, he did!

ROSE: You go on and get you a piece of watermelon, Gabe. Them bad mens is gone now.

GABRIEL: Okay, Rose . . . gonna get me some watermelon. The kind with the stripes on it.

(*Gabriel exits into the house.*)

ROSE: Why, Troy? Why? After all these years to come dragging this in to me now. It don't make no sense at your age. I could have expected this ten or fifteen years ago, but not now.

TROY: Age ain't got nothing to do with it, Rose.

ROSE: I done tried to be everything a wife should be. Everything a wife could be. Been married eighteen years and I got to live to see the day you tell me you been seeing another woman and done fathered a child by her. And you know I ain't never wanted no half nothing in my family. My whole family is half. Everybody got different fathers and mothers . . . my two sisters and my brother. Can't hardly tell who's who. Can't never sit down and talk about Papa and Mama. It's your papa and your mama and my papa and my mama . . .

TROY: Rose . . . stop it now.

ROSE: I ain't never wanted that for none of my children. And now you wanna drag your behind in here and tell me something like this.

TROY: You ought to know. It's time for you to know.

ROSE: Well, I don't want to know, goddamn it!

TROY: I can't just make it go away. It's done now. I can't wish the circumstance of the thing away.

ROSE: And you don't want to either. Maybe you want to wish me and my boy away. Maybe that's what you want? Well, you can't wish us away. I've got eighteen years of my life invested in you. You ought to have stayed upstairs in my bed where you belong.

TROY: Rose . . . now listen to me . . . we can get a handle on this thing. We can talk this out . . . come to an understanding.

ROSE: All of a sudden it's "we." Where was "we" at when you was down there rolling around with some godforsaken woman? "We" should have come to an understanding before you started making a damn fool of yourself. You're a day late and a dollar short when it comes to an understanding with me.

TROY: It's just . . . She gives me a different idea . . . a different understanding about myself. I can step out of this house and get away from the pressures and problems . . . be a different man. I ain't got to wonder how I'm gonna pay the bills or get the roof fixed. I can just be a part of myself that I ain't never been.

ROSE: What I want to know . . . is do you plan to continue seeing her. That's all you can say to me.

TROY: I can sit up in her house and laugh. Do you understand what I'm saying. I can laugh out loud . . . and it feels good. It reaches all the way down to the bottom of my shoes.

(*Pause.*)

Rose, I can't give that up.

ROSE: Maybe you ought to go on and stay down there with her . . . if she's a better woman than me.

TROY: It ain't about nobody being a better woman or nothing. Rose, you ain't the blame. A man couldn't ask for no woman to be a better wife than you've been. I'm responsible for it. I done locked myself into a pattern trying to take care of you all that I forgot about myself.

ROSE: What the hell was I there for? That was my job, not somebody else's.

TROY: Rose, I done tried all my life to live decent . . . to live a clean . . . hard . . . useful life. I tried to be a good husband to you. In every way I knew how. Maybe I come into the world backwards, I don't know. But . . . you born with two strikes on you before you come to the plate. You got to guard it closely . . . always looking for the curve ball on the inside corner. You can't afford to let none get past you. You can't afford a call strike. If you going down . . . you going down swinging. Everything lined up against you. What you gonna do. I fooled them, Rose. I bunted. When I found you and Cory and a halfway decent job . . . I was safe. Couldn't nothing touch me. I wasn't gonna strike out no more. I wasn't going back to the penitentiary. I wasn't gonna lay in the streets with a bottle of wine. I was safe. I had me a family. A job. I wasn't gonna get that last strike. I was on first looking for one of them boys to knock me in. To get me home.

ROSE: You should have stayed in my bed, Troy.

TROY: Then when I saw that gal . . . she firmed up my backbone. And I got to thinking that if I tried . . . I just might be able to steal second. Do you understand after eighteen years I wanted to steal second.

ROSE: You should have held me tight. You should have grabbed me and held on.

TROY: I stood on first base for eighteen years and I thought . . . well, goddamn it . . . go on for it!

ROSE: We're not talking about baseball! We're talking about you going off to lay in bed with another woman . . . and then bring it home to me. That's what we're talking about. We ain't talking about no baseball.

TROY: Rose, you're not listening to me. I'm trying the best I can to explain it to you. It's not easy for me to admit that I been standing in the same place for eighteen years.

ROSE: I been standing with you! I been right here with you, Troy. I got a life too. I gave eighteen years of my life to stand in the same spot with you. Don't you think I ever wanted other things? Don't you think I had dreams and hopes? What about my life? What about me? Don't you think it ever crossed my mind to want to know other men? That I wanted to lay up somewhere and forget about my responsibilities? That I wanted someone to make me laugh so I could feel good? You not the only one who's got wants and needs. But I held on to you, Troy. I took all my feelings, my wants and needs, my dreams . . . and I buried them inside you. I planted a seed and watched and prayed over it. I planted myself inside you and waited to bloom. And it didn't take me no eighteen years to find out the soil was hard and rocky and it wasn't never gonna bloom.

But I held on to you, Troy. I held you tighter. You was my husband. I owed you everything I had. Every part of me I could find to give you. And upstairs in that room . . . with the darkness falling in on me . . . I gave everything I had to try and erase the doubt that you wasn't the finest man in the world. And wherever you was going . . . I wanted to be there with you. Cause you was my husband. Cause that's the only way I was gonna survive as your wife. You always talking about what you give . . . and what you don't have to give. But you take too. You take . . . and don't even know nobody's giving!

(*Rose turns to exit into the house; Troy grabs her arm.*)

TROY: You say I take and don't give!

ROSE: Troy! You're hurting me!

TROY: You say I take and don't give.

ROSE: Troy . . . you're hurting my arm! Let go!

TROY: I done give you everything I got. Don't you tell that lie on me.

ROSE: Troy!

TROY: Don't you tell that lie on me!

(*Cory enters from the house.*)

CORY: Mama!

ROSE: Troy. You're hurting me.

TROY: Don't you tell me about no taking and giving.

(*Cory comes up behind Troy and grabs him. Troy, surprised, is thrown off balance just as Cory throws a glancing blow that catches him on the chest and knocks him down. Troy is stunned, as is Cory.*)

ROSE: Troy. Troy. No!

(*Troy gets to his feet and starts at Cory.*)

Troy . . . no. Please! Troy!

(*Rose pulls on Troy to hold him back. Troy stops himself.*)

TROY (*to Cory*): All right. That's strike two. You stay away from around me, boy. Don't you strike out. You living with a full count. Don't you strike out.

(*Troy exits out the yard as the lights go down.*)

Scene II

(It is six months later, early afternoon. Troy enters from the house and starts to exit the yard. Rose enters from the house.)

ROSE: Troy, I want to talk to you.

TROY: All of a sudden, after all this time, you want to talk to me, huh? You ain't wanted to talk to me for months. You ain't wanted to talk to me last night. You ain't wanted no part of me then. What you wanna talk to me about now?

ROSE: Tomorrow's Friday.

TROY: I know what day tomorrow is. You think I don't know tomorrow's Friday? My whole life I ain't done nothing but look to see Friday coming and you got to tell me it's Friday.

ROSE: I want to know if you're coming home.

TROY: I always come home, Rose. You know that. There ain't never been a night I ain't come home.

ROSE: That ain't what I mean . . . and you know it. I want to know if you're coming straight home after work.

TROY: I figure I'd cash my check . . . hang out at Taylors' with the boys . . . maybe play a game of checkers . . .

ROSE: Troy, I can't live like this. I won't live like this. You livin' on borrowed time with me. It's been going on six months now you ain't been coming home.

TROY: I be here every night. Every night of the year. That's 365 days.

ROSE: I want you to come home tomorrow after work.

TROY: Rose . . . I don't mess up my pay. You know that now. I take my pay and I give it to you. I don't have no money but what you give me back. I just want to have a little time to myself . . . a little time to enjoy life.

ROSE: What about me? When's my time to enjoy life?

TROY: I don't know what to tell you, Rose. I'm doing the best I can.

ROSE: You ain't been home from work but time enough to change your clothes and run out . . . and you wanna call that the best you can do?

TROY: I'm going over to the hospital to see Alberta. She went into the hospital this afternoon. Look like she might have the baby early. I won't be gone long.

ROSE: Well, you ought to know. They went over to Miss Pearl's and got Gabe today. She said you told them to go ahead and lock him up.

TROY: I ain't said no such thing. Whoever told you that is telling a lie. Pearl ain't doing nothing but telling a big fat lie.

ROSE: She ain't had to tell me. I read it on the papers.

TROY: I ain't told them nothing of the kind.

ROSE: I saw it right there on the papers.

TROY: What it say, huh?

ROSE: It said you told them to take him.

TROY: Then they screwed that up, just the way they screw up everything. I ain't worried about what they got on the paper.

ROSE: Say the government send part of his check to the hospital and the other part to you.

TROY: I ain't got nothing to do with that if that's the way it works. I ain't made up the rules about how it work.

ROSE: You did Gabe just like you did Cory. You wouldn't sign the paper for Cory . . . but you signed for Gabe. You signed that paper.

(The telephone is heard ringing inside the house.)

TROY: I told you I ain't signed nothing, woman! The only thing I signed was the release form. Hell, I can't read, I don't know what they had on that paper! I ain't signed nothing about sending Gabe away.

ROSE: I said send him to the hospital . . . you said let him be free . . . now you done went down there and signed him to the hospital for half his money. You went back on yourself, Troy. You gonna have to answer for that.

TROY: See now . . . you been over there talking to Miss Pearl. She done got mad cause she ain't getting Gabe's rent money. That's all it is. She's liable to say anything.

ROSE: Troy, I seen where you signed the paper.

TROY: You ain't seen nothing I signed. What she doing got papers on my brother anyway? Miss Pearl telling a big fat lie. And I'm gonna tell her about it too! You ain't seen nothing I signed. Say . . . you ain't seen nothing I signed.

(Rose exits into the house to answer the telephone. Presently she returns.)

ROSE: Troy . . . that was the hospital. Alberta had the baby.

TROY: What she have? What is it?

ROSE: It's a girl.

TROY: I better get on down to the hospital to see her.

ROSE: Troy . . .

TROY: Rose . . . I got to go see her now. That's only right . . . what's the matter . . . the baby's all right, ain't it?

ROSE: Alberta died having the baby.

TROY: Died . . . you say she's dead? Alberta's dead?

ROSE: They said they done all they could. They couldn't do nothing for her.

TROY: The baby? How's the baby?

ROSE: They say it's healthy. I wonder who's gonna bury her.

TROY: She had family, Rose. She wasn't living in the world by herself.

ROSE: I know she wasn't living in the world by herself.

TROY: Next thing you gonna want to know if she had any insurance.

ROSE: Troy, you ain't got to talk like that.

TROY: That's the first thing that jumped out your mouth. "Who's gonna bury her?" Like I'm fixing to take on that task for myself.

ROSE: I am your wife. Don't push me away.

TROY: I ain't pushing nobody away. Just give me some space. That's all. Just give me some room to breathe.

(*Rose exits into the house. Troy walks about the yard.*)

TROY (*with a quiet rage that threatens to consume him*): All right . . . Mr. Death. See now . . . I'm gonna tell you what I'm gonna do. I'm gonna take and build me a fence around this yard. See? I'm gonna build me a fence around what belongs to me. And then I want you to stay on the other side. See? You stay over there until you're ready for me. Then you come on. Bring your army. Bring your sickle. Bring your wrestling clothes. I ain't gonna fall down on my vigilance this time. You ain't gonna sneak up on me no more. When you ready for me . . . when the top of your list say Troy Maxson . . . that's when you come around here. You come up and knock on the front door. Ain't nobody else got nothing to do with this. This is between you and me. Man to man. You stay on the other side of that fence until you ready for me. Then you come up and knock on the front door. Anytime you want. I'll be ready for you.

(*The lights go down to black.*)

Scene III

(*The lights come up on the porch. It is late evening three days later. Rose sits listening to the ball game waiting for Troy. The final out of the game is made and Rose switches off the radio. Troy enters the yard carrying an infant wrapped in blankets. He stands back from the house and calls.*)

(*Rose enters and stands on the porch. There is a long, awkward silence, the weight of which grows heavier with each passing second.*)

TROY: Rose . . . I'm standing here with my daughter in my arms. She ain't but a wee bittie little old thing. She don't know nothing about grownups' business. She innocent . . . and she ain't got no mama.

ROSE: What you telling me for, Troy?

(*She turns and exits into the house.*)

TROY: Well . . . I guess we'll just sit out here on the porch.

(*He sits down on the porch. There is an awkward indelicateness about the way he handles the baby. His largeness engulfs and seems to swallow it. He speaks loud enough for Rose to hear.*)

A man's got to do what's right for him. I ain't sorry for nothing I done. It felt right in my heart.

(*To the baby.*)

What you smiling at? Your daddy's a big man. Got these great big old hands. But sometimes he's scared. And right now your daddy's scared cause we sitting out here and ain't got no home. Oh, I been homeless before. I ain't had no little baby with me. But I been homeless. You just be out on the road by your lonesome and you see one of them trains coming and you just kinda go like this . . .

(*He sings as a lullaby.*)

Please, Mr. Engineer let a man ride the line
Please, Mr. Engineer let a man ride the line
I ain't got no ticket please let me ride the blinds

(*Rose enters from the house. Troy hearing her steps behind him, stands and faces her.*)

She's my daughter, Rose. My own flesh and blood. I can't deny her no more than I can deny them boys.

(*Pause.*)

You and them boys is my family. You and them and this child is all I got in the world. So I guess what I'm saying is . . . I'd appreciate it if you'd help me take care of her.

ROSE: Okay, Troy . . . you're right. I'll take care of your baby for you . . . cause . . . like you say . . . she's innocent . . . and you can't visit the sins of the father upon the child. A motherless child has got a hard time.

(*She takes the baby from him.*)

From right now . . . this child got a mother. But you a womanless man.

(*Rose turns and exits into the house with the baby. Lights go down to black.*)

Scene IV

(*It is two months later. Lyons enters from the street. He knocks on the door and calls.*)

LYONS: Hey, Rose! (*Pause.*) Rose!

ROSE (*from inside the house*): Stop that yelling. You gonna wake up Raynell. I just got her to sleep.

LYONS: I just stopped by to pay Papa this twenty dollars I owe him. Where's Papa at?

ROSE: He should be here in a minute. I'm getting ready to go down to the church. Sit down and wait on him.

LYONS: I got to go pick up Bonnie over her mother's house.

ROSE: Well, sit it down there on the table. He'll get it.

LYONS (*enters the house and sets the money on the table*): Tell Papa I said thanks. I'll see you again.

ROSE: All right, Lyons. We'll see you.

(*Lyons starts to exit as Cory enters.*)

CORY: Hey, Lyons.

LYONS: What's happening, Cory. Say man, I'm sorry I missed your graduation. You know I had a gig and couldn't get away. Otherwise, I would have been there, man. So what you doing?

CORY: I'm trying to find a job.

LYONS: Yeah I know how that go, man. It's rough out here. Jobs are scarce.

CORY: Yeah, I know.

LYONS: Look here, I got to run. Talk to Papa . . . he know some people. He'll be able to help get you a job. Talk to him . . . see what he say.

CORY: Yeah . . . all right, Lyons.

LYONS: You take care. I'll talk to you soon. We'll find some time to talk.

(*Lyons exits the yard. Cory wanders over to the tree, picks up the bat, and assumes a batting stance. He studies an imaginary pitcher and swings. Dissatisfied with the result, he tries again. Troy enters. They eye each other for a beat. Cory puts the bat down and exits the yard. Troy starts into the house as Rose exits with Raynell. She is carrying a cake.*)

TROY: I'm coming in and everybody's going out.

ROSE: I'm taking this cake down to the church for the bake sale. Lyons was by to see you. He stopped by to pay you your twenty dollars. It's laying in there on the table.

TROY (*going into his pocket*): Well . . . here go this money.

ROSE: Put it in there on the table, Troy. I'll get it.

TROY: What time you coming back?

ROSE: Ain't no use in you studying me. It don't matter what time I come back.

TROY: I just asked you a question, woman. What's the matter . . . can't I ask you a question?

ROSE: Troy, I don't want to go into it. Your dinner's in there on the stove. All you got to do is heat it up. And don't you be eating the rest of them cakes in there. I'm coming back for them. We having a bake sale at the church tomorrow.

(*Rose exits the yard. Troy sits down on the steps, takes a pint bottle from his pocket, opens it, and drinks. He begins to sing.*)

TROY: Hear it ring! Hear it ring!
    Had an old dog his name was Blue
    You know Blue was mighty true
    You know Blue as a good old dog
    Blue trees a possum in a hollow log
    You know from that he was a good old dog

(*Bono enters the yard.*)

BONO: Hey, Troy.

TROY: Hey, what's happening, Bono?

BONO: I just thought I'd stop by to see you.

TROY: What you stop by and see me for? You ain't stopped by in a month of Sundays. Hell, I must owe you money or something.

BONO: Since you got your promotion I can't keep up with you. Used to see you every day. Now I don't even know what route you working.

TROY: They keep switching me around. Got me out in Greentree now . . . hauling white folks' garbage.

BONO: Greentree, huh? You lucky, at least you ain't got to be lifting them barrels. Damn if they ain't getting heavier. I'm gonna put in my two years and call it quits.

TROY: I'm thinking about retiring myself.

BONO: You got it easy. You can *drive* for another five years.

TROY: It ain't the same, Bono. It ain't like working the back of the truck. Ain't got nobody to talk to . . . feel like you working by yourself. Naw, I'm thinking about retiring. How's Lucille?

BONO: She all right. Her arthritis get to acting up on her sometime. Saw Rose on my way in. She going down to the church, huh?

TROY: Yeah, she took up going down there. All them preachers looking for somebody to fatten their pockets.

(*Pause.*)

    Got some gin here.

BONO: Naw, thanks. I just stopped by to say hello.

TROY: Hell, nigger . . . you can take a drink. I ain't never known you to say no to a drink. You ain't got to work tomorrow.

BONO: I just stopped by. I'm fixing to go over to Skinner's. We got us a domino game going over his house every Friday.

TROY: Nigger, you can't play no dominoes. I used to whup you four games out of five.

BONO: Well, that learned me. I'm getting better.

TROY: Yeah? Well, that's all right.

BONO: Look here . . . I got to be getting on. Stop by sometime, huh?

TROY: Yeah, I'll do that, Bono. Lucille told Rose you bought her a new refrigerator.

BONO: Yeah, Rose told Lucille you had finally built your fence . . . so I figured we'd call it even.

TROY: I knew you would.

BONO: Yeah . . . okay. I'll be talking to you.

TROY: Yeah, take care, Bono. Good to see you. I'm gonna stop over.

BONO: Yeah. Okay, Troy.

(*Bono exits. Troy drinks from the bottle.*)

TROY: Old Blue died and I dig his grave
    Let him down with a golden chain
    Every night when I hear old Blue bark
    I know Blue treed a possum in Noah's Ark.
    Hear it ring! Hear it ring!

(*Cory enters the yard. They eye each other for a beat. Troy is sitting in the middle of the steps. Cory walks over.*)

CORY: I got to get by.

TROY: Say what? What's you say?

CORY: You in my way. I got to get by.

TROY: You got to get by where? This is my house. Bought and paid for. In full. Took me fifteen years. And if you wanna go in my house and I'm sitting on the steps . . . you say excuse me. Like your mama taught you.

CORY: Come on, Pop . . . I got to get by.

(*Cory starts to maneuver his way past Troy. Troy grabs his leg and shoves him back.*)

TROY: You just gonna walk over top of me?

CORY: I live here too!

TROY (*advancing toward him*): You just gonna walk over top of me in my own house?

CORY: I ain't scared of you.

TROY: I ain't asked if you was scared of me. I asked you if you was fixing to walk over top of me in my own house? That's the question. You ain't gonna say excuse me? You just gonna walk over top of me?

CORY: If you wanna put it like that.

TROY: How else am I gonna put it?

CORY: I was walking by you to go into the house cause you sitting on the steps drunk, singing to yourself. You can put it like that.

TROY: Without saying excuse me???

(*Cory doesn't respond.*)

I asked you a question. Without saying excuse me???

CORY: I ain't got to say excuse me to you. You don't count around here no more.

TROY: Oh, I see ... I don't count around here no more. You ain't got to say excuse me to your daddy. All of a sudden you done got so grown that your daddy don't count around here no more ... Around here in his own house and yard that he done paid for with the sweat of his brow. You done got so grown to where you gonna take over. You gonna take over my house. Is that right? You gonna wear my pants. You gonna go in there and stretch out on my bed. You ain't got to say excuse me cause I don't count around here no more. Is that right?

CORY: That's right. You always talking this dumb stuff. Now, why don't you just get out my way.

TROY: I guess you got someplace to sleep and something to put in your belly. You got that, huh? You got that? That's what you need. You got that, huh?

CORY: You don't know what I got. You ain't got to worry about what I got.

TROY: You right! You one hundred percent right! I done spent the last seventeen years worrying about what you got. Now it's your turn, see? I'll tell you what to do. You grown ... we done established that. You a man. Now, let's see you act like one. Turn your behind around and walk out this yard. And when you get out there in the alley ... you can forget about this house. See? 'Cause this is my house. You go on and be a man and get your own house. You can forget about this. 'Cause this is mine. You go on and get yours 'cause I'm through with doing for you.

CORY: You talking about what you did for me ... what'd you ever give me?

TROY: Them feet and bones! That pumping heart, nigger! I give you more than anybody else is ever gonna give you.

CORY: You ain't never gave me nothing! You ain't never done nothing but hold me back. Afraid I was gonna be better than you. All you ever did was try and make me scared of you. I used to tremble every time you called my name. Every time I heard your footsteps in the house. Wondering all the time ... what's Papa gonna say if I do this? ... What's he gonna say if I do that? ... What's Papa gonna say if I turn on the radio? And Mama, too ... she tries ... but she's scared of you.

TROY: You leave your mama out of this. She ain't got nothing to do with this.

CORY: I don't know how she stand you ... after what you did to her.

TROY: I told you to leave your mama out of this!

(*He advances toward Cory.*)

CORY: What you gonna do ... give me a whupping? You can't whup me no more. You're too old. You just an old man.

TROY (*shoves him on his shoulder*): Nigger! That's what you are. You just another nigger on the street to me!

CORY: You crazy! You know that?

TROY: Go on now! You got the devil in you. Get on away from me!

CORY: You just a crazy old man ... talking about I got the devil in me.

TROY: Yeah, I'm crazy! If you don't get on the other side of that yard ... I'm gonna show you how crazy I am! Go on ... get the hell out of my yard.

CORY: It ain't your yard. You took Uncle Gabe's money he got from the army to buy this house and then you put him out.

TROY (*Troy advances on Cory*): Get your black ass out of my yard!

(*Troy's advance backs Cory up against the tree. Cory grabs up the bat.*)

CORY: I ain't going nowhere! Come on ... put me out! I ain't scared of you.

TROY: That's my bat!

CORY: Come on!

TROY: Put my bat down!

CORY: Come on, put me out.

(*Cory swings at Troy, who backs across the yard.*)

What's the matter? You so bad ... put me out!

(*Troy advances toward Cory.*)

CORY (*backing up*): Come on! Come on!

TROY: You're gonna have to use it! You wanna draw that bat back on me ... you're gonna have to use it.

CORY: Come on! ... Come on!

(*Cory swings the bat at Troy a second time. He misses. Troy continues to advance toward him.*)

TROY: You're gonna have to kill me! You wanna draw that bat back on me. You're gonna have to kill me.

(*Cory, backed up against the tree, can go no farther. Troy taunts him. He sticks out his head and offers him a target.*)

Come on! Come on!

(*Cory is unable to swing the bat. Troy grabs it.*)

TROY: Then I'll show you.

(*Cory and Troy struggle over the bat. The struggle is fierce and fully engaged. Troy ultimately is the stronger and takes the bat from Cory and stands over him ready to swing. He stops himself.*)

Go on and get away from around my house.

(*Cory, stung by his defeat, picks himself up, walks slowly out of the yard and up the alley.*)

CORY: Tell Mama I'll be back for my things.
TROY: They'll be on the other side of that fence.

(*Cory exits.*)

TROY: I can't taste nothing. Helluljah! I can't taste nothing no more. (*Troy assumes a batting posture and begins to taunt Death, the fastball on the outside corner.*) Come on! It's between you and me now! Come on! Anytime you want! Come on! I be ready for you . . . but I ain't gonna be easy.

(*The lights go down on the scene.*)

Scene V

(*The time is 1965. The lights come up in the yard. It is the morning of Troy's funeral. A funeral plaque with a light hangs beside the door. There is a small garden plot off to the side. There is noise and activity in the house as Rose, Gabriel, and Bono have gathered. The door opens and Raynell, seven years old, enters dressed in a flannel nightgown. She crosses to the garden and pokes around with a stick. Rose calls from the house.*)

ROSE: Raynell!
RAYNELL: Mam?
ROSE: What you doing out there?
RAYNELL: Nothing.

(*Rose comes to the door.*)

ROSE: Girl, get in here and get dressed. What you doing?
RAYNELL: Seeing if my garden growed.
ROSE: I told you it ain't gonna grow overnight. You got to wait.
RAYNELL: It don't look like it never gonna grow. Dag!
ROSE: I told you a watched pot never boils. Get in here and get dressed.
RAYNELL: This ain't even no pot, Mama.
ROSE: You just have to give it a chance. It'll grow. Now you come on and do what I told you. We got to be getting ready. This ain't no morning to be playing around. You hear me?
RAYNELL: Yes, mam.

(*Rose exits into the house. Raynell continues to poke at her garden with a stick. Cory enters. He is dressed in a Marine corporal's uniform, and carries a duffel bag. His posture is that of a military man, and his speech has a clipped sternness.*)

CORY (*to Raynell*): Hi.

(*Pause.*)

I bet your name is Raynell.
RAYNELL: Uh huh.
CORY: Is your mama home?

(*Raynell runs up on the porch and calls through the screen door.*)

RAYNELL: Mama . . . there's some man out here. Mama?

(*Rose comes to the door.*)

ROSE: Cory? Lord have mercy! Look here, you all!

(*Rose and Cory embrace in a tearful reunion as Bono and Lyons enter from the house dressed in funeral clothes.*)

BONO: Aw, looka here . . .
ROSE: Done got all grown up!
CORY: Don't cry, Mama. What you crying about?
ROSE: I'm just so glad you made it.
CORY: Hey Lyons. How you doing, Mr. Bono.

(*Lyons goes to embrace Cory.*)

LYONS: Look at you, man. Look at you. Don't he look good, Rose. Got them Corporal stripes.
ROSE: What took you so long.
CORY: You know how the Marines are, Mama. They got to get all their paperwork straight before they let you do anything.
ROSE: Well, I'm sure glad you made it. They let Lyons come. Your Uncle Gabe's still in the hospital. They don't know if they gonna let him out or not. I just talked to them a little while ago.
LYONS: A Corporal in the United States Marines.
BONO: Your daddy knew you had it in you. He used to tell me all the time.
LYONS: Don't he look good, Mr. Bono?
BONO: Yeah, he remind me of Troy when I first met him.

(*Pause.*)

Say, Rose, Lucille's down at the church with the choir. I'm gonna go down and get the pallbearers lined up. I'll be back to get you all.
ROSE: Thanks, Jim.
CORY: See you, Mr. Bono.
LYONS (*with his arm around Raynell*): Cory . . . look at Raynell. Ain't she precious? She gonna break a whole lot of hearts.
ROSE: Raynell, come and say hello to your brother. This is your brother, Cory. You remember Cory.
RAYNELL: No, Mam.
CORY: She don't remember me, Mama.
ROSE: Well, we talk about you. She heard us talk about you. (*To Raynell.*) This is your brother, Cory. Come on and say hello.
RAYNELL: Hi.
CORY: Hi. So you're Raynell. Mama told me a lot about you.
ROSE: You all come on into the house and let me fix you some breakfast. Keep up your strength.

CORY: I ain't hungry, Mama.

LYONS: You can fix me something, Rose. I'll be in there in a minute.

ROSE: Cory, you sure you don't want nothing. I know they ain't feeding you right.

CORY: No, Mama . . . thanks. I don't feel like eating. I'll get something later.

ROSE: Raynell . . . get on upstairs and get that dress on like I told you.

(*Rose and Raynell exit into the house.*)

LYONS: So . . . I hear you thinking about getting married.

CORY: Yeah, I done found the right one, Lyons. It's about time.

LYONS: Me and Bonnie been split up about four years now. About the time Papa retired. I guess she just got tired of all them changes I was putting her through.

(*Pause.*)

I always knew you was gonna make something out yourself. Your head was always in the right direction. So . . . you gonna stay in . . . make it a career . . . put in your twenty years?

CORY: I don't know. I got six already, I think that's enough.

LYONS: Stick with Uncle Sam and retire early. Ain't nothing out here. I guess Rose told you what happened with me. They got me down the workhouse. I thought I was being slick cashing other people's checks.

CORY: How much time you doing?

LYONS: They give me three years. I got that beat now. I ain't got but nine more months. It ain't so bad. You learn to deal with it like anything else. You got to take the crookeds with the straights. That's what Papa used to say. He used to say that when he struck out. I seen him strike out three times in a row . . . and the next time up he hit the ball over the grandstand. Right out there in Homestead Field. He wasn't satisfied hitting in the seats . . . he want to hit it over everything! After the game he had two hundred people standing around waiting to shake his hand. You got to take the crookeds with the straights. Yeah, Papa was something else.

CORY: You still playing?

LYONS: Cory . . . you know I'm gonna do that. There's some fellows down there we got us a band . . . we gonna try and stay together when we get out . . . but yeah, I'm still playing. It still helps me to get out of bed in the morning. As long as it do that I'm gonna be right there playing and trying to make some sense out of it.

ROSE (*calling*): Lyons, I got these eggs in the pan.

LYONS: Let me go on and get these eggs, man. Get ready to go bury Papa.

(*Pause.*)

How you doing? You doing all right?

(*Cory nods. Lyons touches him on the shoulder and they share a moment of silent grief. Lyons exits into the house. Cory wanders about the yard. Raynell enters.*)

RAYNELL: Hi.

CORY: Hi.

RAYNELL: Did you used to sleep in my room?

CORY: Yeah . . . that used to be my room.

RAYNELL: That's what Papa call it. "Cory's room." It got your football in the closet.

(*Rose comes to the door.*)

ROSE: Raynell, get in there and get them good shoes on.

RAYNELL: Mama, can't I wear these. Them other one hurt my feet.

ROSE: Well, they just gonna have to hurt your feet for a while. You ain't said they hurt your feet when you went down to the store and got them.

RAYNELL: They didn't hurt then. My feet done got bigger.

ROSE: Don't you give me no backtalk now. You get in there and get them shoes on.

(*Raynell exits into the house.*)

Ain't too much changed. He still got that piece of rag tied to that tree. He was out here swinging that bat. I was just ready to go back in the house. He swung that bat and then he just fell over. Seem like he swung it and stood there with this grin on his face . . . and then he just fell over. They carried him on down to the hospital, but I knew there wasn't no need . . . why don't you come on in the house?

CORY: Mama . . . I got something to tell you. I don't know how to tell you this . . . but I've got to tell you . . . I'm not going to Papa's funeral.

ROSE: Boy, hush your mouth. That's your daddy you talking about. I don't want hear that kind of talk this morning. I done raised you to come to this? You standing there all healthy and grown talking about you ain't going to your daddy's funeral?

CORY: Mama . . . listen . . .

ROSE: I don't want to hear it, Cory. You just get that thought out of your head.

CORY: I can't drag Papa with me everywhere I go. I've got to say no to him. One time in my life I've got to say no.

ROSE: Don't nobody have to listen to nothing like that. I know you and your daddy ain't seen eye to eye, but I ain't got to listen to that kind of talk this morning. Whatever was between you and your daddy . . . the time has come to put it aside. Just take it and set it over there on the shelf and forget about it. Disrespecting your daddy ain't gonna make you a man, Cory. You got to find a way to come to that on your own. Not going to your daddy's funeral ain't gonna make you a man.

CORY: The whole time I was growing up . . . living in his house . . . Papa was like a shadow that followed you everywhere. It weighed on you and sunk into your flesh. It would wrap around you and lay there until you couldn't tell which one was you anymore. That shadow digging in your flesh. Trying to crawl in. Trying to live through you. Everywhere I looked, Troy Maxson was staring back at me . . . hiding under the bed . . . in the closet. I'm just saying I've got to find a way to get rid of that shadow, Mama.

ROSE: You just like him. You got him in you good.

CORY: Don't tell me that, Mama.

ROSE: You Troy Maxson all over again.

CORY: I don't want to be Troy Maxson. I want to be me.

ROSE: You can't be nobody but who you are, Cory. That shadow wasn't nothing but you growing into yourself. You either got to grow into it or cut it down to fit you. But that's all you got to make life with. That's all you got to measure yourself against that world out there. Your daddy wanted you to be everything he wasn't . . . and at the same time he tried to make you into everything he was. I don't know if he was right or wrong . . . but I do know he meant to do more good than he meant to do harm. He wasn't always right. Sometimes when he touched he bruised. And sometimes when he took me in his arms he cut.

When I first met your daddy I thought . . . Here is a man I can lay down with and make a baby. That's the first thing I thought when I seen him. I was thirty years old and had done seen my share of men. But when he walked up to me and said "I can dance a waltz that'll make you dizzy," I thought, Rose Lee, here is a man that you can open yourself up to and be filled to bursting. Here is a man that can fill all them empty spaces you been tipping around the edges of. One of them empty spaces was being somebody's mother.

I married your daddy and settled down to cooking his supper and keeping clean sheets on the bed. When your daddy walked through the house he was so big he filled it up. That was my first mistake. Not to make him leave some room for me. For my part in the matter. But at that time I wanted that. I wanted a house that I could sing in. And that's what your daddy gave me. I didn't know to keep up his strength I had to give up little pieces of mine. I did that. I took on his life as mine and mixed up the pieces so that you couldn't hardly tell which was which anymore. It was my choice. It was my life and I didn't have to live it like that. But that's what life offered me in the way of being a woman and I took it. I grabbed hold of it with both hands.

By the time Raynell came into the house, me and your daddy had done lost touch with one another. I didn't want to make my blessing off of nobody's misfortune . . . but I took on to Raynell like she was all them babies I had wanted and never had.

(*The phone rings.*)

Like I'd been blessed to relive a part of my life. And if the Lord see fit to keep up my strength . . . I'm gonna do her just like your daddy did you . . . I'm gonna give her the best of what's in me.

RAYNELL (*entering, still with her old shoes*): Mama . . . Reverend Tollivier on the phone.

(*Rose exits into the house.*)

RAYNELL: Hi.

CORY: Hi.

RAYNELL: You in the Army or the Marines?

CORY: Marines.

RAYNELL: Papa said it was the Army. Did you know Blue?

CORY: Blue? Who's Blue?

RAYNELL: Papa's dog what he sing about all the time.

CORY (*singing*): Hear it ring! Hear it ring!
  I had a dog his name was Blue
  You know Blue was mighty true
  You know Blue was a good old dog
  Blue treed a possum in a hollow log
  You know from that he was a good old dog.
  Hear it ring! Hear it ring!

(*Raynell joins in singing.*)

CORY AND RAYNELL: Blue treed a possum out on a limb
  Blue looked at me and I looked at him
  Grabbed that possum and put him in a sack
  Blue stayed there till I came back
  Old Blue's feets was big and round
  Never allowed a possum to touch the ground.

  Old Blue died and I dug his grave
  I dug his grave with a silver spade
  Let him down with a golden chain
  And every night I call his name
  Go on Blue, you good dog you
  Go on Blue, you good dog you

RAYNELL: Blue laid down and died like a man
  Blue laid down and died . . .

BOTH: Blue laid down and died like a man
  Now he's treeing possums in the Promised Land
  I'm gonna tell you this to let you know
  Blue's gone where the good dogs go
  When I hear old Blue bark
  When I hear old Blue bark
  Blue treed a possum in Noah's Ark
  Blue treed a possum in Noah's Ark.

(*Rose comes to the screen door.*)

ROSE: Cory, we gonna be ready to go in a minute.

CORY (*to Raynell*): You go on in the house and change them shoes like Mama told you so we can go to Papa's funeral.

RAYNELL: Okay, I'll be back.

(*Raynell exits into the house. Cory gets up and crosses over to the tree. Rose stands in the screen door watching him. Gabriel enters from the alley.*)

GABRIEL (*calling*): Hey, Rose!

ROSE: Gabe?

GABRIEL: I'm here, Rose. Hey Rose, I'm here!

(*Rose enters from the house.*)

ROSE: Lord . . . Look here, Lyons!

LYONS: See, I told you, Rose . . . I told you they'd let him come.

CORY: How you doing, Uncle Gabe?

LYONS: How you doing, Uncle Gabe?

GABRIEL: Hey, Rose. It's time. It's time to tell St. Peter to open the gates. Troy, you ready? You ready, Troy. I'm gonna tell St. Peter to open the gates. You get ready now.

(*Gabriel, with great fanfare, braces himself to blow. The trumpet is without a mouthpiece. He puts the end of it into his mouth and blows with great force, like a man who has been waiting some twenty-odd years for this single moment. No sound comes out of the trumpet. He braces himself and blows again with the same result. A third time he blows. There is a weight of impossible description that falls away and leaves him bare and exposed to a frightful realization. It is a trauma that a sane and normal mind would be unable to withstand. He begins to dance. A slow, strange dance, eerie and life-giving. A dance of atavistic signature and ritual. Lyons attempts to embrace him. Gabriel pushes Lyons away. He begins to howl in what is an attempt at song, or perhaps a song turning back into itself in an attempt at speech. He finishes his dance and the gates of heaven stand open as wide as God's closet.*)

That's the way that go!

COMMENTARY

JOAN HERRINGTON (b. 1960)

The Development of *Fences*   1998

Among the interesting things we know about Wilson's decision to write *Fences* is the fact that he was struck by some of the criticism of *Ma Rainey's Black Bottom* for its unusual structure. With *Fences* Wilson decided to write a play that respected the unities of time, place, and action. He also wanted to write a play about family, and in the process he chose baseball and its attendant mythologies as the all-American game. Wilson struggled with clarifying the relationship of Troy Maxson with his sons and their differing needs. He also struggled with Troy's relationship with his wife through many stages of revision. Herrington gives us a good view of what was involved in the writing of the play.

Troy's relationship with his second son, Cory, is a vital part of the play as Wilson examines Troy's attempt to guide the boy into a responsible life. A high school senior, Cory has been recruited to play college football. But Troy will not sign the papers to permit this.

Although Wilson presents Cory's position sympathetically, he supports Troy's decision. "Blacks who received sports scholarships to go to school were exploited. Very few got an education. Troy makes the right choice when he tells his son that football won't lead anywhere. He's telling his son to get a job so he won't have to carry garbage."

Despite Wilson's implicit endorsement of Troy's decision, he fully understands its negative impact on his son. And as Wilson worked on *Fences*, he continually labored over his portrayal of their relationship. In the first version of the play, there is an extended scene between Cory and Troy in which they discuss the purchase of a new television set. Cory doesn't understand why they cannot buy a TV, and Troy tries to explain the financial management of a household. The scene concludes with Troy offering to pay half if Cory can come up with the other half. Here we have an opportunity to see father and son interact in a nonconfrontational manner, and also to see Troy exercising a fatherly concern for his son beyond feeding and clothing him. During work at the O'Neill Conference, this section was effectively moved from the second to the first half of the play, where it serves as groundwork to inform the later conflicts between Troy and Cory.

At the Yale Rep, however, the entire section was dropped in an effort to shorten the work. But the omission of the exchange between Troy and Cory left too large a gap in the portrayal of Troy's exercise of familial responsibility. At the conclusion of the play, in all the drafts, Cory complains of a lack of understanding and emotional support from Troy, and he provokes Troy by asking him what he ever gave to his son. Troy responds: "Them feet and bones. That pumping heart. I give you more than anybody else is ever gonna give you."

Troy is angry with Cory's implication that he has somehow failed the boy, for he believes that he has fulfilled his obligation to his son. With the long scene about the television having been cut, however, we can see only that Troy has provided Cory the bare bones. But Wilson wanted the audience to know that Troy has, in fact, provided more—more guidance, more support, more sympathy—and he restored the television scene in the final version.

While doing so, Wilson also gave Troy the opportunity to explain more fully his attitude toward Cory's college recruitment. In earlier drafts, Troy had challenged Cory, in anger, to give up football: "You go on and get your book learning where you can learn to do something besides carry people's garbage." In Wilson's final revision, Troy is more patient, more loving and concerned, and his speech has a more inspirational quality. Wilson moved Troy from an expression of bitterness over his own life to an expression of a positive dream for his son.

> You go on and get your book learning so you can work yourself up in that A&P or learn how to fix cars or build houses or something, get you a trade. That way you have something can't nobody take away from you. You go on and learn how to put your hands to some good use. Besides hauling people's garbage.

It is important to see that Troy has good intentions even as the play reveals his failings. As a younger man, Troy pursued his personal destiny in baseball at the cost of his family. Now, later in life, he professes to have made responsibility to others his priority. But Troy's efforts are neither wholehearted nor entirely successful, and Wilson uses Cory to make this point. As he revised the play, Wilson gave Cory a more mature understanding of the workings and failings of his family, particularly his father.

In early drafts, Cory was angry at his father and revealed his emotions in naive, sophomoric outbursts: "I hate your blood in me." As the drafts progressed, Cory challenges Troy on substantive issues. At the play's close, in the final draft, Cory upbraids Troy for his mistreatment of Rose, "I don't know how [Rose] stand you . . . after what you did to her." Although Cory's understanding of the issue is not complete, it goes straight to the core of Troy's view of himself as a responsible man, forcing him to come to terms with the fact that he put himself, his own fulfillment, before his responsibility to his wife.

The structure of the play leads to a dramatic confrontation, both physical and emotional, between Troy and Cory. Recognizing the flaws in his father and needing to make his own choices, Cory has become a man. There isn't room in the house for two men, and a simple argument about Troy moving over on the steps so that Cory can pass into the house blows up into the final exchange between them.

In early drafts, this final scene was potentially more violent. In the first versions, at the height of the confrontation, when Cory picks up Troy's baseball bat, Troy brings out a gun, points it at his son, and the stage directions read that he cocks the trigger. Wilson dropped this detail before the Yale Rep production when he read that Marvin Gaye° had been shot by his father. In the later drafts, the only weapon in the scene is the baseball bat, symbolically more powerful in its meaning to Troy, and dramatically more powerful, too, since it can be used as a weapon only when two people are in close physical proximity to each other.

The conflict between father and son continued to change in other ways, too. In the production at the Yale Rep, Cory swings the bat once and then retreats into the alley as Troy continues to approach. The conflict is interrupted by the arrival of Rose, prompting Cory to leave the yard.

Wilson realized that the interruption left the conflict unresolved. Thus, in the final version, Rose does not enter, and the climax of the play is more meaningful as the complex relationship between father and son is more intricately explored. Cory swings the bat once and misses. Then he swings again and misses. Troy offers him the chance to swing a third time, having positioned himself as a target impossible to miss. Now, Cory cannot swing. The two men struggle for the bat, and Troy takes it away. Troy prepares to swing, but he stops himself. Defeated, Cory leaves the yard and does not return until after Troy's death, years later. In this final version the anger between Cory and Troy is the most visceral. And yet it is in this version where we clearly see that neither one can intentionally injure the other.

Whether Cory becomes like his father or learns to be different is explored by Wilson in the final "interaction" between the two. The play concludes after a passage of eight years and the death of Troy. The issue of Cory's sense of responsibility is explored one last time through his indecision about whether to attend Troy's funeral. Wilson, like his character, changed his mind many times about whether Cory would go.

In the first draft, Cory does not attend his father's funeral. He expresses his continued bitterness to Lyons in an extensive exchange. Then, as a casualty of Wilson's feeling that the exchange between the half-brothers did not ring true, as well as his concern for the running time of the show, this long discussion was cut before the first performance at the O'Neill Conference. Cory merely wanders away during a discussion between Lyons and Rose and does not return. Dissatisfied with Cory's disrespectful choice, the audience responded negatively. For the second O'Neill performance, Cory's discussion with Lyons and his subsequent departure were dropped, leaving the implication that Cory does attend the funeral.

Both of these versions were unsatisfactory to Wilson. So, in the Yale Rep version, Cory tells Rose that he is not going to the funeral and Rose, playing the role Wilson had previously assigned to Lyons, urges Cory to attend. Wilson also rearranged the scene so that the entire family surrounds the young man at the moment of his decision. Cory knows he must go to the funeral, and in this final draft, Wilson

---

Marvin Gaye: Popular American songwriter killed April 1, 1984.

provides Cory a subtle acknowledgment of his choice as he says to his half-sister Raynell, "You go on in the house and change them shoes like Mama told you so we can go to Papa's funeral."

Rose, having survived the most damaging kind of betrayal from Troy, is a powerful spokesperson for remaining true to one's commitments even without the expectation of reciprocity. In progressive drafts, Wilson carefully refined her character so that as she moved toward greater forgiveness and understanding, Troy's betrayal appeared all the more dramatic.

The most significant change in Rose was in her day-to-day relationship with Troy and how this, in turn, affects his relationship with Alberta. In the early version of the play, Rose is much more a nagging wife. She bothers Troy constantly about his drinking (which is considerably greater in the early drafts). She reprimands Troy for his neglect of Cory, and when she is tired of Troy's shouting, she tells him to go shout somewhere else. Although certainly none of these faults warrants Troy's infidelity, they perhaps provide him an excuse. As the versions progress, this side of Rose almost completely disappears, and Troy's affair seems less excusable, more stark a violation of his marital responsibility.

But Rose is tolerant—more and more so as the drafts of the play progressed. In the early versions of the play, Troy's announcement that he will be a father comes as a complete surprise to Rose. In later versions of the play, Rose suspects that he is having an affair as she catches inconsistencies in his explanations of his whereabouts, but she says nothing.

When Troy finally tells his wife about Alberta, Rose preaches the bible of familial responsibility.

> I gave eighteen years of my life to stand in the same spot with you. Don't you think I ever wanted things? Don't you think I had dreams and hopes? . . . Don't you think it ever crossed my mind to want to know other men? That I wanted to lay up somewhere and forget about my responsibilities? . . . But I held on to you, Troy . . . I took all my feelings, my wants and needs, my dreams . . . and I buried them inside you . . . I held on to you, Troy.

In the second, third, and fourth drafts of the script, there is no further mention of the affair until Troy brings home the baby. But in the final version, Wilson chose to extend the duration of Rose's tolerance by reinserting an original scene which had been cut to shorten the script. Here, six months after Rose learns of Troy's infidelity, she confronts him about his continuing attention to Alberta, telling him he's living on "borrowed time" with her. Rose retains her composure and her emotional charge as she points out the fallacy in Troy's theory that his physical presence in bed at the end of every night fulfills his obligation to his household regardless of where he has been up to that time.

As Rose grows more philosophical, even under the burden of a betrayal that she understands to be ongoing, our sympathy for her becomes stronger. And Rose's eventual decision to accept Troy's bastard child but to sexually renounce its father—the same in all drafts of the play—makes more sense as the action of a woman who, over time, has come to recognize the impossibility of change in her husband.

Rose stands in the center of the play as a model of responsibility but also as an example of the cost of responsibility to others at the expense of self. In response to Troy's explanation of his affair, Rose responds that she also has needs and wants not satisfied at home. But ultimately she sees no options for herself simply because, as she explains to Troy, "You my husband."

Rose's selflessness moves toward an ultimate commitment outside of herself—that is, to the church. In successive versions of the play, Rose becomes more involved with the church, participates more in its events, sings more of its hymns, and ends the final version of the play completely engrossed in the institution.

Troy remains independent, somehow able to reconcile to his own satisfaction a complex range of conflicting needs and desires. Wilson performed a complicated balancing act of his own to get the audience to be sympathetic to the choices Troy makes, even to support them. He accomplished this through careful selection of the details, choosing those that would highlight Troy's concern with personal autonomy, dignity, self-realization.

Tony Kushner

Tony Kushner was born in 1956 in New York City, but his family soon moved to Louisiana, where his father ran the family lumberyard. His parents were classical musicians, and their home was filled with art. Kushner dates his interest in theater to early memories of seeing his mother onstage. He also recollects from childhood "fairly clear memories of being gay since I was six." He did not, however, "come out" until after he had tried psychotherapy to change his sexual orientation.

After finishing his undergraduate education at Columbia University, Kushner studied directing in graduate school at New York University, partly because he was not confident of his chances to become a playwright. Among his early plays are *Yes, Yes, No, No* (1985), a children's play produced in St. Louis; *Stella* (1987), an adaptation from Goethe produced in New York; *A Bright Room Called Day* (1987), produced in San Francisco; and *The Illusion* (1988), adapted from Corneille, produced in New York and then in Hartford in 1990. He worked with Argentinian playwright Ariel Dorfman to adapt Dorfman's *Widows*, produced in Los Angeles in 1991. *A Bright Room Called Day*, about left-wing politics in Nazi Germany, was not well reviewed on its New York production in 1991. Frank Rich, for example, said that it was "an early front-runner for the most infuriating play of 1991." But some people saw in it the power that was to show up later in Kushner's work. The Eureka Theatre in San Francisco commissioned him to write a play that ultimately turned out to be *Angels in America: A Gay Fantasia on National Themes* (1992), the play that catapulted him to international prominence.

Among Kushner's projects is a series of three plays that he describes as having money as its subject—meaning, in part, the effects of economic status, both poverty and wealth, on individuals. The first of these plays, titled *Henry Box Brown* (1997), centers on the true story of a black American who escaped slavery by being smuggled out of the South in a crate. Brown eventually made his way to England, where he joined with a number of other former slaves in producing dramatic "panoramas" intended to discourage the English from buying slave-picked cotton, on which their textile industry largely relied. Kushner has said, "I've always been drawn to writing historical characters. . . . The best stories are the ones you find in history."

Kushner's play *Homebody/Kabul* (2001) seems connected with history, too. It is set in London and Afghanistan in 1998, after a U.S. bombing raid. Some of the dialogue is in Pashto. It was described by Paul Taylor, a London critic, as "a deeply felt expansively ruminative drama."

Among Kushner's many projects is a chamber opera about a black maid working for a Jewish family in Louisiana, *Caroline, or Change* (2003), written in collaboration with Jeanine Tesori and performed at the Joseph Papp Public Theater in New York.

In June 2006, Opera Unlimited produced *Angels in America* at the Calderwood Pavilion in the Boston Center for the Arts. The music was written by Peter Eotvos and the libretto was by Mari Mezei. In another interesting development, Kushner translated Brecht's *Mother Courage* for an August

2006 production at the Public Theater at the Delacorte Theater Central Park, New York. Meryl Streep was an extraordinarily energetic Mother Courage, Kevin Kline was the cook, and Austin Pendleton was the chaplain. Kushner's activism and energy have helped fuel anticipation of his next contribution to contemporary drama.

Angels in America: Millennium Approaches

Kushner began work on *Angels in America* shortly after Oskar Eustis of the Eureka Theatre commissioned a two-and-a-half-hour play with songs. Once Kushner had developed a presentable version, he showed it to Eustis and realized that, even incomplete, it was already longer than a one-evening play. Eventually, *Millennium Approaches* and *Perestroika*, the second part of *Angels* (not included here), grew to be more than seven hours long. Although the two parts are thematically linked and contain many of the same characters, both parts of *Angels* stand on their own as complete plays. Kushner said that he never expected to see his play produced anywhere but in a small theater in San Francisco; certainly he never expected it to be a smash hit on Broadway. It won the 1993 Pulitzer Prize for drama, another surprise.

Angels in America has epic, Brechtian proportions. Kushner has said that he set out to write a play on "AIDS, Mormons, and Roy Cohn." He chose AIDS because it is a scourge that has destroyed large numbers of the gay community. He chose Mormons because he saw in them a group that valued goodness and godliness but that could not tolerate gays. He chose Roy Cohn because, when Cohn was an aide to Senator Joseph McCarthy during the anti-Communist hysteria of the 1950s, he persecuted gays even though he was himself a closeted homosexual. His homosexuality did not become public until he contracted AIDS and died in 1986. In Cohn, Kushner had found a villain whose rapacious individualism and unquenchable thirst for power helped symbolize the selfishness of the 1980s. In the New York production of *Angels*, Ron Liebman was an overbearingly powerful Cohn, shouting orders and raising hypocrisy to an art form, with depths of contempt matching a profound love of power.

Kushner indicated that his play was a "fantasia on national themes," and it certainly lives up to its title. Kushner set his play in 1985, during the second presidential term of Ronald Reagan. He critiques the values of the Reagan years and politics in general. Jews, WASPs, and Mormons all suffer under Kushner's scrutiny. Moreover, he goes beyond national themes and introduces cosmological themes, notably with the introduction of an angel descending through the ceiling at the end of *Millennium Approaches*.

The play also focuses on problems of individuals. Cohn's friend and protégé Joe Pitt works for the Reagan administration and struggles with his growing awareness that he is gay. A conservative Mormon, Joe faces these complex, threatening feelings honestly and painfully. Harper, Joe's wife, relies on pills,

For discussion questions and assignments on *Angels in America*, visit **bedfordstmartins.com/jacobus**.

listens all day to talk shows, and has no job but thinks of herself as part of a traditional marriage and fights to hold on to it. Louis Ironson, a liberal but not especially political gay man, is in a relationship with Prior Walter, who is dying from AIDS. Louis has hidden his sexuality from his family and finds it impossible to stay with Prior as his lover's illness worsens. Kushner makes sure that we see all these sets of people interrelated throughout the play, despite their distinctness and the unlikelihood of their ever knowing one another.

Though the scope of the play is enormous, its focus is essentially on politics. Kushner's own views contrast sharply with Cohn's conservative politics, and he is surprised that both conservatives and liberals found the play rewarding, because he constructed it to be a pointed attack on conservative values.

Angels in America in Performance

The 1991 premiere of *Millennium Approaches* was in a workshop version at the Eureka Theatre in San Francisco. Its first full-scale production came in July 1992 at London's Royal National Theatre, where it was a sensation. Some reviewers speculated that in London the political theater of Caryl Churchill and other playwrights such as David Hare and David Edgar prepared the way for this play. The audiences were enormously enthusiastic, and the positive reviews the play received attracted attention in the United States. Despite Kushner's relatively unknown status, the two parts of the drama (over seven hours long) were staged in the Mark Taper Forum in Los Angeles in 1992, directed by Oskar Eustis and Tony Taccone. *Millennium Approaches* appeared on Broadway in April 1993 at the Walter Kerr Theatre, directed by George C. Wolfe. Frank Rich gave it a strong, positive review in the *New York Times*, saying "When first seen a year or so ago, the play seemed defined by its anger at the reigning political establishment, which tended to reward the Roy Cohns and ignore the Prior Walters. Mr. Kushner has not revised the text since — a crony of Cohn's still boasts of a Republican lock on the White House until the year 2000 — but the shift in Washington has had the subliminal effect of making *Angels in America* seem more focused on what happens next than on the past."

The second part of the work, *Perestroika*, arrived on Broadway in November 1993. Frank Rich in the *New York Times* said it was "also a true millennial work of art, uplifting, hugely comic and pantheistically religious in a very American style." After its Broadway run, the play moved to regional theaters, touring throughout the United States. The staging of the drama includes moments that may be described as magic realism, featuring ghosts, hallucinations, and other illusions. But Kushner has said, "The play benefits from a pared-down style of presentation, with minimal scenery and scene shifts done rapidly (no blackouts!), employing the cast as well as stagehands — which makes for an actor-driven event, as this must be." He said that it was not a problem if "wires showed," "but the magic should at the same time be thoroughly amazing."

One of Kushner's signal successes in 2003 was seeing *Angels in America* air in a six-part production over two evenings on Home Box Office (HBO) cable television, directed by Mike Nichols and starring Al Pacino in the role of Roy Cohn, Meryl Streep as both Hannah Pitt and Ethel Rosenberg, and Emma Thompson as the Angel. The production was beautifully done and won a Golden Globe Award. Kushner made more inroads into television with the 2004 HBO production of *Homebody/Kabul* (2001). The Signature Theatre Company's production of *Angels in America* in 2010 at the Peter Norton Space in New York was directed by Michael Greif. It was successful, but reviewers admitted that the shock value of the original production was inevitably lost despite the imaginative theatrical effects.

TONY KUSHNER (b. 1956)

Angels in America: Millennium Approaches 1992

A Gay Fantasia on National Themes

In a murderous time
  the heart breaks and breaks
    and lives by breaking. — STANLEY KUNITZ, "THE TESTING-TREE"

Characters

ROY M. COHN, *a successful New York lawyer and unofficial power broker*

JOSEPH PORTER PITT, *chief clerk for Justice Theodore Wilson of the Federal Court of Appeals, Second Circuit*

HARPER AMATY PITT, *Joe's wife, an agoraphobic with a mild Valium addiction*

LOUIS IRONSON, *a word processor working for the Second Circuit Court of Appeals*

PRIOR WALTER, *Louis's boyfriend. Occasionally works as a club designer or caterer, otherwise lives very modestly but with great style off a small trust fund.*

HANNAH PORTER PITT, *Joe's mother, currently residing in Salt Lake City, living off her deceased husband's army pension*

BELIZE, *a former drag queen and former lover of Prior's. A registered nurse. Belize's name was originally Norman Arriaga; Belize is a drag name that stuck.*

THE ANGEL, *four divine emanations, Fluor, Phosphor, Lumen and Candle; manifest in One: the Continental Principality of America. She has magnificent steel-gray wings.*

Other Characters in Part One:

RABBI ISIDOR CHEMELWITZ, *an orthodox Jewish rabbi, played by the actor playing Hannah*

MR. LIES, *Harper's imaginary friend, a travel agent, who in style of dress and speech suggests a jazz musician; he always wears a large lapel badge emblazoned "IOTA" (The International Order of Travel Agents). He is played by the actor playing Belize.*

THE MAN IN THE PARK, *played by the actor playing Prior*

THE VOICE, *the voice of The Angel*

HENRY, *Roy's doctor, played by the actor playing Hannah*

EMILY, *a nurse, played by the actor playing The Angel*

MARTIN HELLER, *a Reagan Administration Justice Department flackman, played by the actor playing Harper*

SISTER ELLA CHAPTER, *a Salt Lake City real-estate saleswoman, played by the actor playing The Angel*

PRIOR 1, *the ghost of a dead Prior Walter from the 13th century, played by the actor playing Joe. He is a blunt, gloomy medieval farmer with a guttural Yorkshire accent.*

PRIOR 2, *the ghost of a dead Prior Walter from the 17th century, played by the actor playing Roy. He is a Londoner, sophisticated, with a High British accent.*

THE ESKIMO, *played by the actor playing Joe*

THE WOMAN IN THE SOUTH BRONX, *played by the actor playing The Angel*

ETHEL ROSENBERG, *played by the actor playing Hannah*

Playwright's Notes

A Disclaimer: Roy M. Cohn, the character, is based on the late Roy M. Cohn (1927–1986), who was all too real; for the most part the acts attributed to the character Roy, such as his illegal conferences with Judge Kaufmann during the trial of Ethel Rosenberg, are to be found in the historical record. But this Roy is a work of dramatic fiction; his words are my invention, and liberties have been taken.

A Note about the Staging: The play benefits from a pared-down style of presentation, with minimal scenery and scene shifts done rapidly (no blackouts!), employing the cast as well as stagehands—which makes for an actor-driven event, as this must be. The moments of magic—the appearance and disappearance of Mr. Lies and the ghosts, the Book hallucination, and the ending—are to be fully realized, as bits of wonderful theatrical illusion—which means it's OK if the wires show, and maybe it's good that they do, but the magic should at the same time be thoroughly amazing.

ACT 1
BAD NEWS •
October–November 1985

Scene 1

(*The last days of October. Rabbi Isidor Chemelwitz alone onstage with a small coffin. It is a rough pine box with two wooden pegs, one at the foot and one at the head, holding the lid in place. A prayer shawl embroidered with a Star of David is draped over the lid, and by the head a yarzheit candle is burning.*)

RABBI ISIDOR CHEMELWITZ (*he speaks sonorously, with a heavy Eastern European accent, unapologetically consulting a sheet of notes for the family names*): Hello and good morning. I am Rabbi Isidor Chemelwitz of the Bronx Home for Aged Hebrews. We are here this morning to pay respects at the passing of Sarah Ironson, devoted wife of Benjamin Ironson, also deceased, loving and caring mother of her sons Morris, Abraham, and Samuel, and her daughters Esther and Rachel; beloved grandmother of Max, Mark, Louis, Lisa, Maria . . . uh . . . Lesley, Angela, Doris, Luke and Eric. (*Looks more closely at paper.*) Eric? This is a Jewish name? (*Shrugs.*) Eric. A large and loving family. We assemble that we may mourn collectively this good and righteous woman.

(*He looks at the coffin.*)

This woman. I did not know this woman. I cannot accurately describe her attributes, nor do justice to her dimensions. She was . . . . Well, in the Bronx Home of Aged Hebrews are many like this, the old, and to many I speak but not to be frank with this one. She preferred silence. So I do not know her and yet I know her. She was . . .

(*he touches the coffin*)

. . . not a person but a whole kind of person, the ones who crossed the ocean, who brought with us to America the villages of Russia and Lithuania—and how we struggled, and how we fought, for the family, for the Jewish home, so that you would not grow up *here*, in this strange place, in the melting pot where nothing melted. Descendants of this immigrant woman, you do not grow up in America, you and your children and their children with the goyische names. You do not live in America. No such place exists. Your clay is the clay of some Litvak shtetl, your air the air of the steppes—because she carried the old world on her back across the ocean, in a boat, and she put it down on Grand Concourse Avenue, or in Flatbush, and she worked that earth into your bones, and you pass it to your children, this ancient, ancient culture and home.

(*Little pause.*)

You can never make that crossing that she made, for such Great Voyages in this world do not any more exist. But every day of your lives the miles that voyage between that place and this one you cross. Every day. You understand me? In you that journey is.

So . . .

She was the last of the Mohicans, this one was. Pretty soon . . . all the old will be dead.

Scene 2

(*Same day. Roy and Joe in Roy's office. Roy at an impressive desk, bare except for a very elaborate phone system, rows and rows of flashing buttons which bleep and beep and whistle incessantly, making chaotic music underneath Roy's conversations. Joe is sitting, waiting. Roy conducts business with great energy, impatience and sensual abandon: gesticulating, shouting, cajoling, crooning, playing the phone, receiver and hold button with virtuosity and love.*)

ROY (*hitting a button*): Hold. (*To Joe.*) I wish I was an octopus, a fucking octopus. Eight loving arms and all those suckers. Know what I mean?

JOE: No, I . . .

ROY (*gesturing to a deli platter of little sandwiches on his desk*): You want lunch?

JOE: No, that's OK really I just . . .

ROY (*hitting a button*): Ailene? Roy Cohn. Now what kind of a greeting is . . . . I thought we were friends, Ai. . . . Look Mrs. Soffer you don't have to get . . . . You're upset. You're yelling. You'll aggravate your condition, you shouldn't yell, you'll pop little blood vessels in your face if you yell. . . . No that was a joke, Mrs. Soffer, I was joking. . . . I already apologized sixteen times for that, Mrs. Soffer, you . . . (*While she's fulminating, Roy covers the mouthpiece with his hand and talks to Joe.*) This'll take a minute, *eat* already, what is this tasty sandwich here it's—(*He takes a bite of a sandwich.*) Mmmmm, liver or some . . . . Here.

(*He pitches the sandwich to Joe, who catches it and returns it to the platter.*)

ROY (*back to Mrs. Soffer*): Uh huh, uh huh. . . . No, I already told you, it wasn't a vacation, it was business, Mrs. Soffer, I have clients in Haiti, Mrs. Soffer,

I . . . . Listen, Ailene, YOU THINK I'M THE ONLY GODDAM LAWYER IN HISTORY EVER MISSED A COURT DATE? Don't make such a big fucking . . . . Hold. (*He hits the hold button.*) You HAG!

JOE: If this is a bad time . . .

ROY: *Bad* time? This is a *good* time! (*Button.*) Baby doll, get me . . . . Oh fuck, wait . . . (*Button, button.*) Hello? Yah. Sorry to keep you holding, Judge Hollins, I . . . . Oh *Mrs.* Hollins, sorry dear deep voice you got. Enjoying your visit? (*Hand over mouthpiece again, to Joe.*) She sounds like a truckdriver and he sounds like Kate Smith, very confusing. Nixon appointed him, all the geeks are Nixon appointees . . . (*To Mrs. Hollins.*) Yeah yeah right good so how many tickets dear? Seven. For what, *Cats, 42nd Street*, what? No you wouldn't like *La Cage*, trust me, I know. Oh for godsake. . . . Hold. (*Button, button.*) Baby doll, seven for *Cats* or something, anything hard to get, I don't give a fuck what and neither will they. (*Button; to Joe.*) You see *La Cage*?

JOE: No, I . . .

ROY: Fabulous. Best thing on Broadway. Maybe ever. (*Button.*) Who? Aw, Jesus H. Christ, Harry, *no*, Harry, Judge John Francis Grimes, Manhattan Family Court. Do I have to do every goddam thing myself? *Touch* the bastard, Harry, and don't call me on this line again, I told you not to . . .

JOE (*starting to get up*): Roy, uh, should I wait outside or . . .

ROY (*to Joe*): Oh sit. (*To Harry.*) You hold. I pay you to hold fuck you Harry you jerk. (*Button.*) Half-wit dick-brain. (*Instantly philosophical.*) I see the universe, Joe, as a kind of sandstorm in outer space with winds of mega-hurricane velocity, but instead of grains of sand it's shards and splinters of glass. You ever feel that way? Ever have one of those days?

JOE: I'm not sure I . . .

ROY: So how's life in Appeals? How's the Judge?

JOE: He sends his best.

ROY: He's a good man. Loyal. Not the brightest man on the bench, but he has manners. And a nice head of silver hair.

JOE: He gives me a lot of responsibility.

ROY: Yeah, like writing his decisions and signing his name.

JOE: Well . . .

ROY: He's a nice guy. And you cover admirably.

JOE: Well, thanks, Roy, I . . .

ROY (*button*): Yah? Who is *this*? Well who the fuck are *you*? Hold—(*button*) Harry? Eighty-seven grand, something like that. Fuck him. Eat me. New Jersey, chain of porno film stores in, uh, Weehawken. That's—Harry, that's the beauty of the law. (*Button.*) So, baby doll, what? *Cats*? Bleah. (*Button.*) *Cats*! It's about cats. Singing cats, you'll love it. Eight o'clock, the theatre's always at eight. (*Button.*) Fucking tourists. (*Button, then to Joe.*) Oh live a little, Joe, *eat* something for Christ sake—

JOE: Um, Roy, could you . . .

ROY: What? (*To Harry.*) Hold a minute. (*Button.*) Mrs. Soffer? Mrs. . . . (*Button.*) God-fucking-dammit to hell, where is . . .

JOE (*overlapping*): Roy, I'd really appreciate it if . . .

ROY (*overlapping*): Well she was here a minute ago, baby doll, see if . . .

(*The phone starts making three different beeping sounds, all at once.*)

ROY (*smashing buttons*): Jesus fuck this goddam thing . . .

JOE (*overlapping*): I really wish you wouldn't . . .

ROY (*overlapping*): Baby doll? Ring the *Post* get me Suzy see if . . .

(*The phone starts whistling loudly.*)

ROY: CHRIST!

JOE: *Roy.*

ROY (*into receiver*): Hold. (*Button; to Joe.*) What?

JOE: Could you please not take the Lord's name in vain

(*Pause.*)

I'm sorry. But please. At least while I'm . . .

ROY (*laughs, then*): Right. Sorry. Fuck. Only in America. (*Punches a button.*) Baby doll, tell 'em all to fuck off. Tell 'em I died. You handle Mrs. Soffer. Tell her it's on the way. Tell her I'm schtupping the judge. I'll call her back. I *will* call her. I *know* how much I borrowed. She's got four hundred times that stuffed up her . . . . Yeah, tell her I said that. (*Button. The phone is silent.*) So, Joe.

JOE: I'm sorry Roy, I just . . .

ROY: No no no no, principles count, I respect principles, I'm not religious but I like God and God likes me. Baptist, Catholic?

JOE: Mormon.

ROY: Mormon. Delectable. Absolutely. Only in America. So, Joe. Whattya think?

JOE: It's . . . well . . .

ROY: Crazy life.

JOE: Chaotic.

ROY: Well but God bless chaos. Right?

JOE: Ummm . . .

ROY: Huh. Mormons. I knew Mormons, in, um, Nevada.

JOE: Utah, mostly.

ROY: No, these Mormons were in Vegas.

So. So, how'd you like to go to Washington and work for the Justice Department?

JOE: Sorry?

ROY: How'd you like to go to Washington and work for the Justice Department? All I gotta do is pick up the phone, talk to Ed, and you're in.

JOE: In . . . what, exactly?

ROY: Associate Assistant Something Big. Internal Affairs, heart of the woods, something nice with clout.

JOE: Ed . . . ?

ROY: Meese. The Attorney General.

JOE: Oh.

ROY: I just have to pick up the phone . . .

JOE: I have to think.

ROY: Of course.

> (*Pause.*)
>
> It's a great time to be in Washington, Joe.

JOE: Roy, it's incredibly exciting . . .

ROY: And it would mean something to me. You understand?

(*Little pause.*)

JOE: I . . . can't say how much I appreciate this Roy, I'm sort of . . . well, stunned, I mean . . . . Thanks, Roy. But I have to give it some thought. I have to ask my wife.

ROY: Your wife. Of course.

JOE: But I really appreciate . . .

ROY: Of course. Talk to your wife.

Scene 3

(*Later that day. Harper at home, alone. She is listening to the radio and talking to herself, as she often does. She speaks to the audience.*)

HARPER: People who are lonely, people left alone, sit talking nonsense to the air, imagining . . . beautiful systems dying, old fixed orders spiraling apart . . .

When you look at the ozone layer, from outside, from a spaceship, it looks like a pale blue halo, a gentle, shimmering aureole encircling the atmosphere encircling the earth. Thirty miles above our heads, a thin layer of three-atom oxygen molecules, product of photosynthesis, which explains the fussy vegetable preference for visible light, its rejection of darker rays and emanations. Danger from without. It's a kind of gift, from God, the crowning touch to the creation of the world: guardian angels, hands linked, make a spherical net, a blue-green nesting orb, a shell of safety for life itself. But everywhere, things are collapsing, lies surfacing, systems of defense giving way. . . . This is why, Joe, this is why I shouldn't be left alone.

> (*Little pause.*)

I'd like to go traveling. Leave you behind to worry. I'll send postcards with strange stamps and tantalizing messages on the back. "Later maybe." "Nevermore . . . "

(*Mr. Lies, a travel agent, appears.*)

HARPER: Oh! You startled me!

MR. LIES: Cash, check or credit card?

HARPER: I remember you. You're from Salt Lake. You sold us the plane tickets when we flew here. What are you doing in Brooklyn?

MR. LIES: You said you wanted to travel . . .

HARPER: And here you are. How thoughtful.

MR. LIES: Mr. Lies. Of the International Order of Travel Agents. We mobilize the globe, we set people adrift, we stir the populace and send nomads eddying across the planet. We are adepts of motion, acolytes of the flux. Cash, check or credit card. Name your destination.

HARPER: Antarctica, maybe. I want to see the hole in the ozone. I heard on the radio . . .

MR. LIES (*he has a computer terminal in his briefcase*): I can arrange a guided tour. Now?

HARPER: Soon. Maybe soon. I'm not safe here you see. Things aren't right with me. Weird stuff happens . . .

MR. LIES: Like?

HARPER: Well, like you, for instance. Just appearing. Or last week . . . well never mind.

People are like planets, you need a thick skin. Things get to me, Joe stays away and now . . . . Well look. My dreams are talking back to me.

MR. LIES: It's the price of rootlessness. Motion sickness. The only cure: to keep moving.

HARPER: I'm undecided. I feel . . . that something's going to give. It's 1985. Fifteen years till the third millennium. Maybe Christ will come again. Maybe seeds will be planted, maybe there'll be harvests then, maybe early figs to eat, maybe new life, maybe fresh blood, maybe companionship and love and protection, safety from what's outside, maybe the door will hold, or maybe . . . maybe the troubles will come, and the end will come, and the sky will collapse and there will be terrible rains and showers of poison light, or maybe my life is really fine, maybe Joe loves me and I'm only crazy thinking otherwise, or maybe not, maybe it's even worse than I know, maybe . . . I want to know, maybe I don't. The suspense, Mr. Lies, it's killing me.

MR. LIES: I suggest a vacation.

HARPER (*hearing something*): That was the elevator. Oh God, I should fix myself up, I . . . . You have to go, you shouldn't be here . . . you aren't even real.

MR. LIES: Call me when you decide . . .

HARPER: Go!

(*The Travel Agent vanishes as Joe enters.*)

JOE: Buddy?

Buddy? Sorry I'm late. I was just . . . out. Walking. Are you mad?

HARPER: I got a little anxious.

JOE: Buddy kiss.

(*They kiss.*)

JOE: Nothing to get anxious about.

So. So how'd you like to move to Washington?

Scene 4

(*Same day. Louis and Prior outside the funeral home, sitting on a bench, both dressed in funereal finery, talking. The funeral service for Sarah Ironson has just concluded and Louis is about to leave for the cemetery.*)

LOUIS: My grandmother actually saw Emma Goldman speak. In Yiddish. But all Grandma could remember was that she spoke well and wore a hat.

     What a weird service. That rabbi . . .

PRIOR: A definite find. Get his number when you go to the graveyard. I want him to bury me.

LOUIS: Better head out there. Everyone gets to put dirt on the coffin once it's lowered in.

PRIOR: Oooh. Cemetery fun. Don't want to miss that.

LOUIS: It's an old Jewish custom to express love. Here, Grandma, have a shovelful. Latecomers run the risk of finding the grave completely filled.

     She was pretty crazy. She was up there in that home for ten years, talking to herself. I never visited. She looked too much like my mother.

PRIOR (*hugs him*): Poor Louis. I'm sorry your grandma is dead.

LOUIS: Tiny little coffin, huh?

     Sorry I didn't introduce you to . . . . I always get so closety at these family things.

PRIOR: Butch. You get butch. (*Imitating.*) "Hi Cousin Doris, you don't remember me I'm Lou, Rachel's boy." Lou, not Louis, because if you say Louis they'll hear the sibilant S.

LOUIS: I don't have a . . .

PRIOR: I don't blame you, hiding. Bloodlines. Jewish curses are the worst. I personally would dissolve if anyone ever looked me in the eye and said "Feh." Fortunately WASPs don't say "Feh." Oh and by the way, darling, cousin Doris is a dyke.

LOUIS: No.

     Really?

PRIOR: You don't notice anything. If I hadn't spent the last four years fellating you I'd swear you were straight.

LOUIS: You're in a pissy mood. Cat still missing?

(*Little pause.*)

PRIOR: Not a furball in sight. It's your fault.

LOUIS: It is?

PRIOR: I warned you, Louis. Names are important. Call an animal "Little Sheba" and you can't expect it to stick around. Besides, it's a dog's name.

LOUIS: I wanted a dog in the first place, not a cat. He sprayed my books.

PRIOR: He was a female cat.

LOUIS: Cats are stupid, high-strung predators. Babylonians sealed them up in bricks. Dogs have brains.

PRIOR: Cats have intuition.

LOUIS: A sharp dog is as smart as a really dull two-year-old child.

PRIOR: Cats know when something's wrong.

LOUIS: Only if you stop feeding them.

PRIOR: They know. That's why Sheba left, because she knew.

LOUIS: Knew what?

(*Pause.*)

PRIOR: I did my best Shirley Booth this morning, floppy slippers, housecoat, curlers, can of Little Friskies; "Come back, Little Sheba, come back. . . . " To no avail. Le chat, elle ne reviendra jamais, jamais . . . °

     (*He removes his jacket, rolls up his sleeve, shows Louis a dark-purple spot on the underside of his arm near the shoulder.*)

     See.

LOUIS: That's just a burst blood vessel.

PRIOR: Not according to the best medical authorities.

LOUIS: What?

     (*Pause.*)

     Tell me.

PRIOR: K.S., baby. Lesion number one. Lookit. The wine-dark kiss of the angel of death.

LOUIS (*very softly, holding Prior's arm*): Oh please . . .

PRIOR: I'm a lesionnaire. The Foreign Lesion. The American Lesion. Lesionnaire's disease.

LOUIS: Stop.

PRIOR: My troubles are lesion

LOUIS: Will you *stop*.

PRIOR: Don't you think I'm handling this well?

     I'm going to die.

LOUIS: Bullshit.

PRIOR: Let go of my arm.

LOUIS: No.

PRIOR: Let go.

LOUIS (*grabbing Prior, embracing him ferociously*): No.

PRIOR: I can't find a way to spare you baby. No wall like the wall of hard scientific fact. K.S. Wham. Bang your head on that.

LOUIS: Fuck you. (*Letting go.*) Fuck you fuck you fuck you.

PRIOR: Now that's what I like to hear. A mature reaction.

     Let's go see if the cat's come home.

     Louis?

LOUIS: When did you find this?

PRIOR: I couldn't tell you.

LOUIS: Why?

PRIOR: I was scared, Lou.

LOUIS: Of what?

PRIOR: That you'll leave me.

LOUIS: Oh.

(*Little pause.*)

PRIOR: Bad timing, funeral and all, but I figured as long as we're on the subject of death . . .

LOUIS: I have to go bury my grandma.

PRIOR: Lou?

     (*Pause.*)

     Then you'll come home?

LOUIS: Then I'll come home.

Le chat . . . jamais: The cat will never ever return.

Scene 5

(*Same day, later on. Split scene: Joe and Harper at home; Louis at the cemetery with Rabbi Isidor Chemelwitz and the little coffin.*)

HARPER: Washington?

JOE: It's an incredible honor, buddy, and . . .

HARPER: I have to think.

JOE: Of course.

HARPER: Say no.

JOE: You said you were going to think about it.

HARPER: I don't want to move to Washington.

JOE: Well I do.

HARPER: It's a giant cemetery, huge white graves and mausoleums everywhere.

JOE: We could live in Maryland. Or Georgetown.

HARPER: We're happy here.

JOE: That's not really true, buddy, we . . .

HARPER: Well happy enough! Pretend-happy. That's better than nothing.

JOE: It's time to make some changes, Harper.

HARPER: No changes. Why?

JOE: I've been chief clerk for four years. I make twenty-nine thousand dollars a year. That's ridiculous. I graduated fourth in my class and I make less than anyone I know. And I'm . . . I'm tired of being a clerk, I want to go where something good is happening.

HARPER: Nothing good happens in Washington. We'll forget church teachings and buy furniture at . . . at *Conran's* and become yuppies. I have too much to do here.

JOE: Like what?

HARPER: I *do* have things . . .

JOE: What things?

HARPER: I have to finish painting the bedroom.

JOE: You've been painting in there for over a year.

HARPER: I know, I . . . . It just isn't done because I never get time to finish it.

JOE: Oh that's . . . that doesn't make sense. You have all the time in the world. You could finish it when I'm at work.

HARPER: I'm afraid to go in there alone.

JOE: Afraid of what?

HARPER: I heard someone in there. Metal scraping on the wall. A man with a knife, maybe.

JOE: There's no one in the bedroom, Harper.

HARPER: Not now.

JOE: Not this morning either.

HARPER: How do you know? You were at work this morning. There's something creepy about this place. Remember *Rosemary's Baby*?

JOE: *Rosemary's Baby*?

HARPER: Our apartment looks like that one. Wasn't that apartment in Brooklyn?

JOE: No, it was . . .

HARPER: Well, it looked like this. It did.

JOE: Then let's move.

HARPER: Georgetown's worse. *The Exorcist* was in Georgetown.

JOE: The devil, everywhere you turn, huh, buddy.

HARPER: Yeah. Everywhere.

JOE: How many pills today, buddy?

HARPER: None. One. Three. Only three.

LOUIS (*pointing at the coffin*): Why are there just two little wooden pegs holding the lid down?

RABBI ISIDOR CHEMELWITZ: So she can get out easier if she wants to.

LOUIS: I hope she stays put.

I pretended for years that she was already dead. When they called to say she had died it was a surprise. I abandoned her.

RABBI ISIDOR CHEMELWITZ: "Sharfer vi di tson fun a shlang iz an umdankbar kind!"

LOUIS: I don't speak Yiddish.

RABBI ISIDOR CHEMELWITZ: Sharper than the serpent's tooth is the ingratitude of children. Shakespeare. *King Lear.*

LOUIS: Rabbi, what does the Holy Writ say about someone who abandons someone he loves at a time of great need?

RABBI ISIDOR CHEMELWITZ: Why would a person do such a thing?

LOUIS: Because he has to. Maybe because this person's sense of the world, that it will change for the better with struggle, maybe a person who has this neo-Hegelian positivist sense of constant historical progress towards happiness or perfection or something, who feels very powerful because he feels connected to these forces, moving uphill all the time . . . maybe that person can't, um, incorporate sickness into his sense of how things are supposed to go. Maybe vomit . . . and sores and disease . . . really frighten him, maybe . . . he isn't so good with death.

RABBI ISIDOR CHEMELWITZ: The Holy Scriptures have nothing to say about such a person.

LOUIS: Rabbi, I'm afraid of the crimes I may commit.

RABBI ISIDOR CHEMELWITZ: Please, mister. I'm a sick old rabbi facing a long drive home to the Bronx. You want to confess, better you should find a priest.

LOUIS: But I'm not a Catholic, I'm a Jew.

RABBI ISIDOR CHEMELWITZ: Worse luck for you, bubbulah. Catholics believe in forgiveness. Jews believe in Guilt. (*He pats the coffin tenderly.*)

LOUIS: You just make sure those pegs are in good and tight.

RABBI ISIDOR CHEMELWITZ: Don't worry, mister. The life she had, she'll stay put. She's better off.

JOE: Look, I know this is scary for you. But try to understand what it means to me. Will you try?

HARPER: Yes.

JOE: Good. Really try.

I think things are starting to change in the world.

HARPER: But I don't want . . .

JOE: Wait. For the good. Change for the good. America has rediscovered itself. Its sacred position among nations. And people aren't ashamed of that like they used to be. This is a great thing. The truth restored. Law restored. That's what President Reagan's done, Harper. He says "Truth exists and can be spoken proudly." And the country responds to him. We become better. More good. I need to be a part of that, I need something big to lift me up. I mean, six years ago the world seemed in decline, horrible, hopeless, full of unsolvable problems and crime and confusion and hunger and . . .

HARPER: But it still seems that way. More now than before. They say the ozone layer is . . .

JOE: Harper . . .

HARPER: And today out the window on Atlantic Avenue there was a schizophrenic traffic cop who was making these . . .

JOE: Stop it! I'm trying to make a point.

HARPER: So am I.

JOE: You aren't even making sense, you . . .

HARPER: My point is the world seems just as . . .

JOE: It only seems that way to you because you never go out in the world, Harper, and you have emotional problems.

HARPER: I do so get out in the world.

JOE: You don't. You stay in all day, fretting about imaginary . . .

HARPER: I get out. I do. You don't know what I do.

JOE: You don't stay in all day.

HARPER: No.

JOE: Well. . . . Yes you do.

HARPER: That's what you think.

JOE: Where do you go?

HARPER: Where do you go? When you walk.

(*Pause, then angrily.*) And I DO NOT have emotional problems.

JOE: I'm sorry.

HARPER: And if I do have emotional problems it's from living with you. Or . . .

JOE: I'm sorry buddy, I didn't mean to . . .

HARPER: Or if you do think I do then you should never have married me. You have all these secrets and lies.

JOE: I want to be married to you, Harper.

HARPER: You shouldn't. You never should.

(*Pause.*)

Hey buddy. Hey buddy.

JOE: Buddy kiss . . .

(*They kiss.*)

HARPER: I heard on the radio how to give a blowjob.

JOE: What?

HARPER: You want to try?

JOE: You really shouldn't listen to stuff like that.

HARPER: Mormons can give blowjobs.

JOE: *Harper.*

HARPER (*imitating his tone*): Joe.

It was a little Jewish lady with a German accent. This is a good time. For me to make a baby.

(*Little pause. Joe turns away.*)

HARPER: Then they went on to a program about holes in the ozone layer. Over Antarctica. Skin burns, birds go blind, icebergs melt. The world's coming to an end.

Scene 6

(*First week of November. In the men's room of the offices of the Brooklyn Federal Court of Appeals; Louis is crying over the sink; Joe enters.*)

JOE: Oh, um. . . . Morning.

LOUIS: Good morning, counselor.

JOE (*he watches Louis cry*): Sorry, I . . . I don't know your name.

LOUIS: Don't bother. Word processor. The lowest of the low.

JOE (*holding out hand*): Joe Pitt. I'm with Justice Wilson . . .

LOUIS: Oh, I know that. Counselor Pitt. Chief Clerk.

JOE: Were you . . . are you OK?

LOUIS: Oh, yeah. Thanks. What a nice man.

JOE: Not so nice.

LOUIS: What?

JOE: Not so nice. Nothing. You sure you're . . .

LOUIS: Life sucks shit. Life . . . just sucks shit.

JOE: What's wrong?

LOUIS: Run in my nylons.

JOE: Sorry . . . ?

LOUIS: Forget it. Look, thanks for asking.

JOE: Well . . .

LOUIS: I mean it really is nice of you.

(*He starts crying again.*)

Sorry, sorry, sick friend . . .

JOE: Oh, I'm sorry.

LOUIS: Yeah, yeah, well, that's sweet.

Three of your colleagues have preceded you to this baleful sight and you're the first one to ask. The others just opened the door, saw me, and fled. I hope they had to pee real bad.

JOE (*handing him a wad of toilet paper*): They just didn't want to intrude.

LOUIS: Hah. Reaganite heartless macho asshole lawyers.

JOE: Oh, that's unfair.

LOUIS: What is? Heartless? Macho? Reaganite? Lawyer?

JOE: I voted for Reagan.

LOUIS: You did?

JOE: Twice.

LOUIS: Twice? Well, oh boy. A Gay Republican.

JOE: Excuse me?

LOUIS: Nothing.

JOE: I'm not . . .

Forget it.

LOUIS: Republican? Not Republican? Or . . .

JOE: What?

LOUIS: What?

JOE: Not gay. I'm not gay.

LOUIS: Oh. Sorry.
      (*Blows his nose loudly.*) It's just . . .
JOE: Yes?
LOUIS: Well, sometimes you can tell from the way a person sounds that . . . I mean you *sound* like a . . .
JOE: No I don't. Like what?
LOUIS: Like a Republican.

(*Little pause. Joe knows he's being teased; Louis knows he knows. Joe decides to be a little brave.*)

JOE (*making sure no one else is around*): Do I? Sound like a . . . ?
LOUIS: What? Like a . . . ? Republican, or . . . ? Do I?
JOE: Do you what?
LOUIS: Sound like a . . . ?
JOE: Like a . . . ?
      I'm . . . confused.
LOUIS: Yes.
      My name is Louis. But all my friends call me Louise. I work in Word Processing. Thanks for the toilet paper.

(*Louis offers Joe his hand, Joe reaches, Louis feints and pecks Joe on the cheek, then exits.*)

Scene 7

(*A week later. Mutual dream scene. Prior is at a fantastic makeup table, having a dream, applying the face. Harper is having a pill-induced hallucination. She has these from time to time. For some reason, Prior has appeared in this one. Or Harper has appeared in Prior's dream. It is bewildering.*)

PRIOR (*alone, putting on makeup, then examining the results in the mirror; to the audience*): "I'm ready for my closeup, Mr. DeMille."
      One wants to move through life with elegance and grace, blossoming infrequently but with exquisite taste, and perfect timing, like a rare bloom, a zebra orchid. . . . One wants . . . . But one so seldom gets what one wants, does one? No. One does not. One gets fucked. Over. One . . . dies at thirty, robbed of . . . decades of majesty.
      Fuck this shit. Fuck this shit.
      (*He almost crumbles; he pulls himself together; he studies his handiwork in the mirror.*)
      I look like a corpse. A corpsette. Oh my queen; you know you've hit rock-bottom when even drag is a drag.

(*Harper appears.*)

HARPER: Are you . . . . Who are you?
PRIOR: Who are you?
HARPER: What are you doing in my hallucination?
PRIOR: I'm not in your hallucination. You're in my dream.
HARPER: You're wearing makeup.
PRIOR: So are you.

HARPER: But you're a man.
PRIOR (*feigning dismay, shock, he mimes slashing his throat with his lipstick and dies, fabulously tragic. Then*): The hands and feet give it away.
HARPER: There must be some mistake here. I don't recognize you. You're not . . . . Are you my . . . some sort of imaginary friend?
PRIOR: No. Aren't you too old to have imaginary friends?
HARPER: I have emotional problems. I took too many pills. Why are you wearing makeup?
PRIOR: I was in the process of applying the face, trying to make myself feel better—I swiped the new fall colors at the Clinique counter at Macy's. (*Showing her.*)
HARPER: You stole these?
PRIOR: I was out of cash; it was an emotional emergency!
HARPER: Joe will be so angry. I promised him. No more pills.
PRIOR: These pills you keep alluding to?
HARPER: Valium. I take Valium. Lots of Valium.
PRIOR: And you're dancing as fast as you can.
HARPER: I'm not *addicted*. I don't believe in addiction, and I never . . . well, I never drink. And I *never* take drugs.
PRIOR: Well, smell *you*, Nancy Drew.
HARPER: Except Valium.
PRIOR: Except Valium; in wee fistfuls.
HARPER: It's terrible. Mormons are not supposed to be addicted to anything. I'm a Mormon.
PRIOR: I'm a homosexual.
HARPER: Oh! In my church we don't believe in homosexuals.
PRIOR: In my church we don't believe in Mormons.
HARPER: What church do . . . oh! (*She laughs.*) I get it.
      I don't understand this. If I didn't ever see you before and I don't think I did then I don't think you should be here, in this hallucination, because in my experience the mind, which is where hallucinations come from, shouldn't be able to make up anything that wasn't there to start with, that didn't enter it from experience, from the real world. Imagination can't create anything new, can it? It only recycles bits and pieces from the world and reassembles them into visions. . . . Am I making sense right now?
PRIOR: Given the circumstances, yes.
HARPER: So when we think we've escaped the unbearable ordinariness and, well, untruthfulness of our lives, it's really only the same old ordinariness and falseness rearranged into the appearance of novelty and truth. Nothing unknown is knowable. Don't you think it's depressing?
PRIOR: The limitations of the imagination?
HARPER: Yes.
PRIOR: It's something you learn after your second theme party: It's All Been Done Before.
HARPER: The world. Finite. Terribly, terribly . . . . Well . . .

This is the most depressing hallucination I've ever had.

PRIOR: Apologies. I do try to be amusing.

HARPER: Oh, well, don't apologize, you . . . . I can't expect someone who's really sick to entertain me.

PRIOR: How on earth did you know . . .

HARPER: Oh that happens. This is the very threshold of revelation sometimes. You can see things . . . how sick you are. Do you see anything about me?

PRIOR: Yes.

HARPER: What?

PRIOR: You are amazingly unhappy.

HARPER: Oh big deal. You meet a Valium addict and you figure out she's unhappy. That doesn't count. Of course I . . . . Something else. Something surprising.

PRIOR: Something surprising.

HARPER: Yes.

PRIOR: Your husband's a homo.

(*Pause.*)

HARPER: Oh, ridiculous.
  (*Pause, then very quietly.*)
  Really?

PRIOR (*shrugs*): Threshold of revelation.

HARPER: Well I don't like your revelations. I don't think you intuit well at all. Joe's a very normal man, he . . .
  Oh God. Oh God. He . . . . Do homos take, like, lots of long walks?

PRIOR: Yes. We do. In stretch pants with lavender coifs. I just looked at you, and there was . . .

HARPER: A sort of blue streak of recognition.

PRIOR: Yes.

HARPER: Like you knew me incredibly well.

PRIOR: Yes.

HARPER: Yes.
  I have to go now, get back, something just . . . fell apart.
  Oh God, I feel so sad . . .

PRIOR: I . . . I'm sorry. I usually say, "Fuck the truth," but mostly, the truth fucks you.

HARPER: I see something else about you . . .

PRIOR: Oh?

HARPER: Deep inside you, there's a part of you, the most inner part, entirely free of disease. I can see that.

PRIOR: Is that . . . . That isn't true.

HARPER: Threshold of revelation.
  Home . . .

(*She vanishes.*)

PRIOR: People come and go so quickly here . . .
  (*To himself in the mirror.*) I don't think there's any uninfected part of me. My heart is pumping polluted blood. I feel dirty.

(*He begins to wipe makeup off with his hands, smearing it around. A large gray feather falls from up above. Prior stops smearing the makeup and looks at the feather. He goes to it and picks it up.*)

A VOICE (*it is an incredibly beautiful voice*): Look up!

PRIOR (*looking up, not seeing anyone*): Hello?

A VOICE: Look up!

PRIOR: Who is that?

A VOICE: Prepare the way!

PRIOR: I don't see any . . .

(*There is a dramatic change in lighting, from above.*)

A VOICE: Look up, look up,
  prepare the way
  the infinite descent
  A breath in air
  floating down
  Glory to . . .

(*Silence.*)

PRIOR: Hello? Is that it? Helloooo!
  What the fuck . . . ? (*He holds himself.*)
  Poor me. Poor poor me. Why me? Why poor poor me? Oh I don't feel good right now. I really don't.

Scene 8

(*That night. Split scene: Harper and Joe at home; Prior and Louis in bed.*)

HARPER: Where were you?

JOE: Out.

HARPER: Where?

JOE: Just out. Thinking.

HARPER: It's late.

JOE: I had a lot to think about.

HARPER: I burned dinner.

JOE: Sorry.

HARPER: Not my dinner. My dinner was fine. Your dinner. I put it back in the oven and turned everything up as high as it could go and I watched till it burned black. It's still hot. Very hot. Want it?

JOE: You didn't have to do that.

HARPER: I know. It just seemed like the kind of thing a mentally deranged sex-starved pill-popping housewife would do.

JOE: Uh huh.

HARPER: So I did it. Who knows anymore what I have to do?

JOE: How many pills?

HARPER: A bunch. Don't change the subject.

JOE: I won't talk to you when you . . .

HARPER: No. No. Don't do that! I'm . . . I'm fine, pills are not the problem, not our problem, I WANT TO KNOW WHERE YOU'VE BEEN! I WANT TO KNOW WHAT'S GOING ON!

JOE: Going on with what? The job?

HARPER: Not the job.

JOE: I said I need more time.

HARPER: Not the job!

JOE: Mr. Cohn, I talked to him on the phone, he said I had to hurry . . .

HARPER: Not the . . .

JOE: But I can't get you to talk sensibly about anything so . . .

HARPER: SHUT UP!

JOE: Then what?

HARPER: Stick to the subject.

JOE: I don't know what that is. You have something you want to ask me? Ask me. Go.

HARPER: I . . . can't. I'm scared of you.

JOE: I'm tired, I'm going to bed.

HARPER: Tell me without making me ask. Please.

JOE: This is crazy, I'm not . . .

HARPER: When you come through the door at night your face is never exactly the way I remembered it. I get surprised by something . . . mean and hard about the way you look. Even the weight of you in the bed at night, the way you breathe in your sleep seems unfamiliar.

You terrify me.

JOE (*cold*): I know who you are.

HARPER: Yes. I'm the enemy. That's easy. That doesn't change.

You think you're the only one who hates sex; I do; I hate it with you; I do. I dream that you batter away at me till all my joints come apart, like wax, and I fall into pieces. It's like a punishment. It was wrong of me to marry you. I knew you . . . (*She stops herself.*) It's a sin, and it's killing us both.

JOE: I can always tell when you've taken pills because it makes you red-faced and sweaty and frankly that's very often why I don't want to . . .

HARPER: Because . . .

JOE: Well, you aren't pretty. Not like this.

HARPER: I have something to ask you.

JOE: Then ASK! ASK! What in hell are you . . .

HARPER: Are you a homo?

(*Pause.*)

Are you? If you try to walk out right now I'll put your dinner back in the oven and turn it up so high the whole building will fill with smoke and everyone in it will asphyxiate. So help me God I will.

Now answer the question.

JOE: What if I . . .

(*Small pause.*)

HARPER: Then tell me, please. And we'll see.

JOE: No. I'm not.

I don't see what difference it makes.

LOUIS: Jews don't have any clear textual guide to the afterlife; even that it exists. I don't think much about it. I see it as a perpetual rainy Thursday afternoon in March. Dead leaves.

PRIOR: Eeeugh. Very Greco-Roman.

LOUIS: Well for us it's not the verdict that counts, it's the act of judgment. That's why I could never be a lawyer. In court all that matters is the verdict.

PRIOR: You could never be a lawyer because you are oversexed. You're too distracted.

LOUIS: Not distracted; *ab*stracted. I'm trying to make a point:

PRIOR: Namely:

LOUIS: It's the judge in his or her chambers, weighing, books open, pondering the evidence, ranging freely over categories: good, evil, innocent, guilty; the judge in the chamber of circumspection, not the judge on the bench with the gavel. The shaping of the law, not its execution.

PRIOR: The point, dear, the point . . .

LOUIS: That it should be the questions and shape of a life, its total complexity gathered, arranged and considered, which matters in the end, not some stamp of salvation or damnation which disperses all the complexity in some unsatisfying little decision—the balancing of the scales . . .

PRIOR: I like this; very zen; it's . . . reassuringly incomprehensible and useless. We who are about to die thank you.

LOUIS: You are not about to die.

PRIOR: It's not going well, really . . . two new lesions. My leg hurts. There's protein in my urine, the doctor says, but who knows what the fuck that portends. Anyway it shouldn't be there, the protein. My butt is chapped from diarrhea and yesterday I shat blood.

LOUIS: I really hate this. You don't tell me . . .

PRIOR: You get too upset, I wind up comforting you. It's easier . . .

LOUIS: Oh thanks.

PRIOR: If it's bad I'll tell you.

LOUIS: Shitting blood sounds bad to me.

PRIOR: And I'm telling you.

LOUIS: And I'm handling it.

PRIOR: Tell me some more about justice.

LOUIS: I *am* handling it.

PRIOR: Well Louis you win Trooper of the Month.

(*Louis starts to cry.*)

PRIOR: I take it back. You aren't Trooper of the Month. This isn't working . . .

Tell me some more about justice.

LOUIS: You are not about to die.

PRIOR: Justice . . .

LOUIS: . . . is an immensity, a confusing vastness. Justice is God.

Prior?

PRIOR: Hmmm?

LOUIS: You love me.

PRIOR: Yes.

LOUIS: What if I walked out on this? Would you hate me forever?

(*Prior kisses Louis on the forehead.*)

PRIOR: Yes.

JOE: I think we ought to pray. Ask God for help. Ask him together . . .

HARPER: God won't talk to me. I have to make up people to talk to me.

JOE: You have to keep asking.

HARPER: I forgot the question.

Oh yeah. God, is my husband a . . .

JOE (*scary*): Stop it. Stop it. I'm warning you.

Does it make any difference? That I might be one thing deep within, no matter how wrong or ugly that thing is, so long as I have fought, with everything I have, to kill it. What do you want from me? What do you want from me, Harper? More than that? For God's sake, there's nothing left, I'm a shell. There's nothing left to kill.

As long as my behavior is what I know it has to be. Decent. Correct. That alone in the eyes of God.

HARPER: No, no, not that, that's Utah talk, Mormon talk, I hate it, Joe, tell me, say it . . .

JOE: All I will say is that I am a very good man who has worked very hard to become good and you want to destroy that. You want to destroy me, but I am not going to let you do that.

(*Pause.*)

HARPER: I'm going to have a baby.

JOE: Liar.

HARPER: You liar.

A baby born addicted to pills. A baby who does not dream but who hallucinates, who stares up at us with big mirror eyes and who does not know who we are.

(*Pause.*)

JOE: Are you really . . .

HARPER: No. Yes. No. Yes. Get away from me.

Now we both have a secret.

PRIOR: One of my ancestors was a ship's captain who made money bringing whale oil to Europe and returning with immigrants—Irish mostly, packed in tight, so many dollars per head. The last ship he captained foundered off the coast of Nova Scotia in a winter tempest and sank to the bottom. He went down with the ship—la Grande Geste—but his crew took seventy women and kids in the ship's only longboat, this big, open rowboat, and when the weather got too rough, and they thought the boat was overcrowded, the crew started lifting people up and hurling them into the sea. Until they got the ballast right. They walked up and down the longboat, eyes to the water-line, and when the boat rode low in the water they'd grab the nearest passenger and throw them into the sea. The boat was leaky, see; seventy people; they arrived in Halifax with nine people on board.

LOUIS: Jesus.

PRIOR: I think about that story a lot now. People in a boat, waiting, terrified, while implacable, unsmiling men, irresistibly strong, seize . . . maybe the person next to you, maybe you, and with no warning at all, with time only for a quick intake of air you are pitched into freezing, turbulent water and salt and darkness to drown.

I like your cosmology, baby. While time is running out I find myself drawn to anything that's suspended, that lacks an ending—but it seems to me that it lets you off scot-free.

LOUIS: What do you mean?

PRIOR: No judgment, no guilt or responsibility.

LOUIS: For me.

PRIOR: For anyone. It was an editorial "you."

LOUIS: Please get better. Please.

Please don't get any sicker.

Scene 9

(*Third week in November. Roy and Henry, his doctor, in Henry's office.*)

HENRY: Nobody knows what causes it. And nobody knows how to cure it. The best theory is that we blame a retrovirus, the Human Immunodeficiency Virus. Its presence is made known to us by the useless antibodies which appear in reaction to its entrance into the bloodstream through a cut, or an orifice. The antibodies are powerless to protect the body against it. Why, we don't know. The body's immune system ceases to function. Sometimes the body even attacks itself. At any rate it's left open to a whole horror house of infections from microbes which it usually defends against.

Like Kaposi's sarcomas. These lesions. Or your throat problem. Or the glands.

We think it may also be able to slip past the blood-brain barrier into the brain. Which is of course very bad news.

And it's fatal in we don't know what percent of people with suppressed immune responses.

(*Pause.*)

ROY: This is very interesting, Mr. Wizard, but why the fuck are you telling me this?

(*Pause.*)

HENRY: Well, I have just removed one of three lesions which biopsy results will probably tell us is a Kaposi's sarcoma lesion. And you have a pronounced swelling of glands in your neck, groin, and armpits—lymphadenopathy is another sign. And you have oral candidiasis and maybe a little more fungus under the fingernails of two digits on your right hand. So that's why . . .

ROY: This disease . . .

HENRY: Syndrome.

ROY: Whatever. It afflicts mostly homosexuals and drug addicts.

HENRY: Mostly. Hemophiliacs are also at risk.

ROY: Homosexuals and drug addicts. So why are you implying that I . . .

(*Pause.*)

What are you implying, Henry?

HENRY: I don't . . .

ROY: I'm not a drug addict.

HENRY: Oh come on Roy.

ROY: What, what, come on Roy what? Do you think I'm a junkie, Henry, do you see tracks?

HENRY: This is absurd.

ROY: Say it.

HENRY: Say what?

ROY: Say, "Roy Cohn, you are a . . . "

HENRY: Roy.

ROY: "You are a . . . . " Go on. Not "Roy Cohn you are a drug fiend." "Roy Marcus Cohn, you are a . . . "
Go on, Henry, it starts with an "H."

HENRY: Oh I'm not going to . . .

ROY: *With an "H,"* Henry, and it isn't "Hemophiliac." Come on . . .

HENRY: What are you doing, Roy?

ROY: No, say it. I mean it. Say: "Roy Cohn, you are a homosexual."
(*Pause.*)
And I will proceed, systematically, to destroy your reputation and your practice and your career in New York State, Henry. Which you know I can do.

(*Pause.*)

HENRY: Roy, you have been seeing me since 1958. Apart from the facelifts I have treated you for everything from syphilis . . .

ROY: From a whore in Dallas.

HENRY: From syphilis to venereal warts. In your rectum. Which you may have gotten from a whore in Dallas, but it wasn't a female whore.

(*Pause.*)

ROY: So say it.

HENRY: Roy Cohn, you are . . .
You have had sex with men, many many times, Roy, and one of them, or any number of them, has made you very sick. You have AIDS.

ROY: AIDS.
Your problem, Henry, is that you are hung up on words, on labels, that you believe they mean what they seem to mean. AIDS. Homosexual. Gay. Lesbian. You think these are names that tell you who someone sleeps with, but they don't tell you that.

HENRY: No?

ROY: No. Like all labels they tell you one thing and one thing only: where does an individual so identified fit in the food chain, in the pecking order? Not ideology, or sexual taste, but something much simpler: clout. Not who I fuck or who fucks me, but who will pick up the phone when I call, who owes me favors. This is what a label refers to. Now to someone who does not understand this, homosexual is what I am because I have sex with men. But really this is wrong. Homosexuals are not men who sleep with other men. Homosexuals are men who in fifteen years of trying cannot get a pissant antidiscrimination bill through City Council. Homosexuals are men who know nobody and who nobody knows. Who have zero clout. Does this sound like me, Henry?

HENRY: No.

ROY: No. I have clout. A lot. I can pick up this phone, punch fifteen numbers, and you know who will be on the other end in under five minutes, Henry?

HENRY: The President.

ROY: Even better, Henry. His wife.

HENRY: I'm impressed.

ROY: I don't want you to be impressed. I want you to understand. This is not sophistry. And this is not hypocrisy. This is reality. I have sex with men. But unlike nearly every other man of whom this is true, I bring the guy I'm screwing to the White House and President Reagan smiles at us and shakes his hand. Because *what* I am is defined entirely by *who* I am. Roy Cohn is not a homosexual. Roy Cohn is a heterosexual man, Henry, who fucks around with guys.

HENRY: OK, Roy.

ROY: And what is my diagnosis, Henry?

HENRY: You have AIDS, Roy.

ROY: No, Henry, no. AIDS is what homosexuals have. I have liver cancer.

(*Pause.*)

HENRY: Well, whatever the fuck you have, Roy, it's very serious, and I haven't got a damn thing for you. The NIH in Bethesda has a new drug called AZT with a two-year waiting list that not even I can get you onto. So get on the phone, Roy, and dial the fifteen numbers, and tell the First Lady you need in on an experimental treatment for liver cancer, because you can call it any damn thing you want, Roy, but what it boils down to is very bad news.

ACT 2
IN VITRO •
December 1985–January 1986

Scene 1

(*Night, the third week in December. Prior alone on the floor of his bedroom; he is much worse.*)

PRIOR: Louis, Louis, please wake up, oh God.

(*Louis runs in.*)

PRIOR: I think something horrible is wrong with me I can't breathe . . .

LOUIS (*starting to exit*): I'm calling the ambulance.

PRIOR: No, wait, I . . .

LOUIS: *Wait?* Are you fucking crazy? Oh God you're on fire, your head is on fire.

PRIOR: It hurts, it hurts . . .

LOUIS: I'm calling the ambulance.

PRIOR: I don't want to go to the hospital, I don't want to go to the hospital please let me lie here, just . . .

LOUIS: No, no, God, Prior, stand up . . .

PRIOR: DON'T TOUCH MY LEG!

LOUIS: We have to . . . oh God this is so crazy.

PRIOR: I'll be OK if I just lie here Lou, really, if I can only sleep a little . . .

(*Louis exits.*)

PRIOR: Louis?

    NO! NO! Don't call, you'll send me there and I won't come back, please, please Louis I'm begging, baby, please . . .

    (*Screams.*) LOUIS!!

LOUIS (*from off; hysterical*): WILL YOU SHUT THE FUCK UP!

PRIOR (*trying to stand*): Aaaah. I have . . . to go to the bathroom. Wait. Wait, just . . . oh. Oh God. (*He shits himself.*)

LOUIS (*entering*): Prior? They'll be here in . . .

    Oh my God.

PRIOR: I'm sorry, I'm sorry.

LOUIS: What did . . . ? What?

PRIOR: I had an accident.

(*Louis goes to him.*)

LOUIS: This is blood.

PRIOR: Maybe you shouldn't touch it . . . me. . . . I . . . (*He faints.*)

LOUIS (*quietly*): Oh help. Oh help. Oh God oh God oh God help me I can't I can't I can't.

Scene 2

(*Same night. Harper is sitting at home, all alone, with no lights on. We can barely see her. Joe enters, but he doesn't turn on the lights.*)

JOE: Why are you sitting in the dark? Turn on the light.

HARPER: No. I heard the sounds in the bedroom again. I know someone was in there.

JOE: No one was.

HARPER: Maybe actually in the bed, under the covers with a knife.

    Oh, boy. Joe. I, um, I'm thinking of going away. By which I mean: I think I'm going off again. You . . . you know what I mean?

JOE: Please don't. Stay. We can fix it. I pray for that. This is my fault, but I can correct it. You have to try too . . .

(*He turns on the light. She turns it off again.*)

HARPER: When you pray, what do you pray for?

JOE: I pray for God to crush me, break me up into little pieces and start all over again.

HARPER: Oh. Please. Don't pray for that.

JOE: I had a book of Bible stories when I was a kid. There was a picture I'd look at twenty times every day: Jacob wrestles with the angel. I don't really remember the story, or why the wrestling—just the picture. Jacob is young and very strong. The angel is . . . a beautiful man, with golden hair and wings, of course. I still dream about it. Many nights. I'm . . . . It's me. In that struggle. Fierce, and unfair. The angel is not human, and it holds nothing back, so how could anyone human win, what kind of a fight is that? It's not just. Losing means your soul thrown down in the dust, your heart torn out from God's. But you can't not lose.

HARPER: In the whole entire world, you are the only person, the only person I love or have ever loved. And I love you terribly. Terribly. That's what's so awfully, irreducibly real. I can make up anything but I can't dream that away.

JOE: Are you . . . are you really going to have a baby?

HARPER: It's my time, and there's no blood. I don't really know. I suppose it wouldn't be a great thing. Maybe I'm just not bleeding because I take too many pills. Maybe I'll give birth to a pill. That would give a new meaning to pill-popping, huh?

    I think you should go to Washington. Alone. Change, like you said.

JOE: I'm not going to leave you, Harper.

HARPER: Well maybe not. But I'm going to leave you.

Scene 3

(*One AM, the next morning. Louis and a nurse, Emily, are sitting in Prior's room in the hospital.*)

EMILY: He'll be all right now.

LOUIS: No he won't.

EMILY: No. I guess not. I gave him something that makes him sleep.

LOUIS: Deep asleep?

EMILY: Orbiting the moons of Jupiter.

LOUIS: A good place to be.

EMILY: Anyplace better than here. You his . . . uh?

LOUIS: Yes. I'm his uh.

EMILY: This must be hell for you.

LOUIS: It is. Hell. The After Life. Which is not at all like a rainy afternoon in March, by the way, Prior. A lot more vivid than I'd expected. Dead leaves, but the crunchy kind. Sharp, dry air. The kind of long, luxurious dying feeling that breaks your heart.

EMILY: Yeah, well we all get to break our hearts on this one.

    He seems like a nice guy. Cute.

LOUIS: Not like this.

    Yes, he is. Was. Whatever.

EMILY: Weird name. Prior Walter. Like, "The Walter before this one."

LOUIS: Lots of Walters before this one. Prior is an old old family name in an old old family. The Walters go back to the Mayflower and beyond. Back to the Norman Conquest. He says there's a Prior Walter stitched into the Bayeux tapestry.

EMILY: Is that impressive?

LOUIS: Well, it's old. Very old. Which in some circles equals impressive.

EMILY: Not in my circle. What's the name of the tapestry?

LOUIS: The Bayeux tapestry. Embroidered by La Reine Mathilde.

EMILY: I'll tell my mother. She embroiders. Drives me nuts.

LOUIS: Manual therapy for anxious hands.

EMILY: Maybe you should try it.

LOUIS: Mathilde stitched while William the Conqueror was off to war. She was capable of . . . more than loyalty. Devotion.

> She waited for him, she stitched for years. And if he had come back broken and defeated from war, she would have loved him even more. And if he had returned mutilated, ugly, full of infection and horror, she would still have loved him; fed by pity, by a sharing of pain, she would love him even more, and even more, and she would never, never have prayed to God, please let him die if he can't return to me whole and healthy and able to live a normal life. . . . If he had died, she would have buried her heart with him.
> So what the fuck is the matter with me?
> (*Little pause.*)
> Will he sleep through the night?

EMILY: At least.

LOUIS: I'm going.

EMILY: It's one A.M. Where do you have to go at . . .

LOUIS: I know what time it is. A walk. Night air, good for the . . . . The park.

EMILY: Be careful.

LOUIS: Yeah. Danger.

> Tell him, if he wakes up and you're still on, tell him goodbye, tell him I had to go.

Scene 4

(*An hour later. Split scene. Joe and Roy in a fancy [straight] bar; Louis and a Man in the Rambles in Central Park. Joe and Roy are sitting at the bar; the place is brightly lit. Joe has a plate of food in front of him but he isn't eating. Roy occasionally reaches over the table and forks small bites off Joe's plate. Roy is drinking heavily, Joe not at all. Louis and the Man are eyeing each other, each alternating interest and indifference.*)

JOE: The pills were something she started when she miscarried or . . . no, she took some before that. She had a really bad time at home, when she was a kid, her home was really bad. I think a lot of drinking and physical stuff. She doesn't talk about that, instead she talks about . . . the sky falling down, people with knives hiding under sofas. Monsters. Mormons. Everyone thinks Mormons don't come from homes like that, we aren't supposed to behave that way, but we do. It's not lying, or being two-faced. Everyone tries very hard to live up to God's strictures, which are very . . . um . . .

ROY: Strict.

JOE: I shouldn't be bothering you with this.

ROY: No, please. Heart to heart. Want another . . . . What is that, seltzer?

JOE: The failure to measure up hits people very hard. From such a strong desire to be good they feel very far from goodness when they fail.

> What scares me is that maybe what I really love in her is the part of her that's farthest from the light, from God's love; maybe I was drawn to that in the first place. And I'm keeping it alive because I need it.

ROY: Why would you need it?

JOE: There are things . . . . I don't know how well we know ourselves. I mean, what if? I know I married her because she . . . because I loved it that she was always wrong, always doing something wrong, like one step out of step. In Salt Lake City that stands out. I never stood out, on the outside, but inside, it was hard for me. To pass.

ROY: Pass?

JOE: Yeah.

ROY: Pass as what?

JOE: Oh. Well. . . . As someone cheerful and strong. Those who love God with an open heart unclouded by secrets and struggles are cheerful; God's easy simple love for them shows in how strong and happy they are. The saints.

ROY: But you had secrets? Secret struggles . . .

JOE: I wanted to be one of the elect, one of the Blessed. You feel you ought to be, that the blemishes are yours by choice, which of course they aren't. Harper's sorrow, that really deep sorrow, she didn't choose that. But it's there.

ROY: You didn't put it there.

JOE: No.

ROY: You sound like you think you did.

JOE: I am responsible for her.

ROY: Because she's your wife.

JOE: That. And I do love her.

ROY: Whatever. She's your wife. And so there are obligations. To her. But also to yourself.

JOE: She'd fall apart in Washington.

ROY: Then let her stay here.

JOE: She'll fall apart if I leave her.

ROY: Then bring her to Washington.

JOE: I just can't, Roy. She needs me.

ROY: Listen, Joe. I'm the best divorce lawyer in the business.

(*Little pause.*)

JOE: Can't Washington wait?

ROY: You do what you need to do, Joe. What *you* need. *You.* Let her life go where it wants to go. You'll both be better for that. *Somebody* should get what they want.

MAN: What do you want?

LOUIS: I want you to fuck me, hurt me, make me bleed.

MAN: I want to.

LOUIS: Yeah?

MAN: I want to hurt you.

LOUIS: Fuck me.

MAN: Yeah?

LOUIS: Hard.

MAN: Yeah? You been a bad boy?

(*Pause. Louis laughs, softly.*)

LOUIS: Very bad. Very bad.

MAN: You need to be punished, boy?

LOUIS: Yes. I do.

MAN: Yes what?

(*Little pause.*)

LOUIS: Um, I . . .

MAN: Yes *what*, boy?

LOUIS: Oh. Yes sir.

MAN: I want you to take me to your place, boy.

LOUIS: No, I can't do that.

MAN: No *what*?

LOUIS: No sir, I can't, I . . .
I don't live alone, sir.

MAN: Your lover know you're out with a man tonight, boy?

LOUIS: No sir, he . . .
My lover doesn't know.

MAN: Your lover know you . . .

LOUIS: Let's change the subject, OK? Can we go to your place?

MAN: I live with my parents.

LOUIS: Oh.

ROY: Everyone who makes it in this world makes it because somebody older and more powerful takes an interest. The most precious asset in life, I think, is the ability to be a good son. You have that, Joe. Somebody who can be a good son to a father who pushes them farther than they would otherwise go. I've had many fathers, I owe my life to them, powerful, powerful men. Walter Winchell, Edgar Hoover. Joe McCarthy most of all. He valued me because I am a good lawyer, but he loved me because I was and am a good son. He was a very difficult man, very guarded and cagey; I brought out something tender in him. He would have died for me. And me for him. Does this embarrass you?

JOE: I had a hard time with my father.

ROY: Well sometimes that's the way. Then you have to find other fathers, substitutes, I don't know. The father-son relationship is central to life. Women are for birth, beginning, but the father is continuance. The son offers the father his life as a vessel for carrying forth his father's dream. Your father's living?

JOE: Um, dead.

ROY: He was . . . what? A difficult man?

JOE: He was in the military. He could be very unfair. And cold.

ROY: But he loved you.

JOE: I don't know.

ROY: No, no, Joe, he did, I know this. Sometimes a father's love has to be very, very hard, unfair even, cold to make his son grow strong in a world like this. This isn't a good world.

MAN: Here, then.

LOUIS: I . . . . Do you have a rubber?

MAN: I don't use rubbers.

LOUIS: You should. (*He takes one from his coat pocket.*) Here.

MAN: I don't use them.

LOUIS: Forget it, then. (*He starts to leave.*)

MAN: No, wait.
Put it on me. Boy.

LOUIS: Forget it, I have to get back. Home. I must be going crazy.

MAN: Oh come on please he won't find out.

LOUIS: It's cold. Too cold.

MAN: It's never too cold, let me warm you up. Please?

(*They begin to fuck.*)

MAN: Relax.

LOUIS (*a small laugh*): Not a chance.

MAN: It . . .

LOUIS: What?

MAN: I think it broke. The rubber. You want me to keep going? (*Little pause.*) Pull out? Should I . . .

LOUIS: Keep going.
Infect me.
I don't care. I don't care.

(*Pause. The Man pulls out.*)

MAN: I . . . um, look, I'm sorry, but I think I want to go.

LOUIS: Yeah.
Give my best to mom and dad.

(*The Man slaps him.*)

LOUIS: Ow!

(*They stare at each other.*)

LOUIS: It was a joke.

(*The Man leaves.*)

ROY: How long have we known each other?

JOE: Since 1980.

ROY: Right. A long time. I feel close to you, Joe. Do I advise you well?

JOE: You've been an incredible friend, Roy, I . . .

ROY: I want to be family. Familia, as my Italian friends call it. La Familia. A lovely word. It's important for me to help you, like I was helped.

JOE: I owe practically everything to you, Roy.

ROY: I'm dying, Joe. Cancer.

JOE: Oh my God.

ROY: Please. Let me finish.
Few people know this and I'm telling you this only because . . . . I'm not afraid of death. What can death bring that I haven't faced? I've lived; life is the worst. (*Gently mocking himself.*) Listen to me, I'm a philosopher.
Joe. You must do this. You must must must. Love; that's a trap. Responsibility; that's a trap too. Like a father to a son I tell you this: Life is full of horror; nobody escapes, nobody; save yourself. Whatever

pulls on you, whatever needs from you, threatens you. Don't be afraid; people are so afraid; don't be afraid to live in the raw wind, naked, alone. . . . Learn at least this: What you are capable of. Let nothing stand in your way.

Scene 5

(*Three days later. Prior and Belize in Prior's hospital room. Prior is very sick but improving. Belize has just arrived.*)

PRIOR: Miss Thing.

BELIZE: Ma cherie bichette.

PRIOR: Stella.

BELIZE: Stella for star. Let me see. (*Scrutinizing Prior.*) You look like shit, why yes indeed you do, comme la merde!°

PRIOR: Merci.

BELIZE (*taking little plastic bottles from his bag, handing them to Prior*): Not to despair, Belle Reeve. Lookie! Magic goop!

PRIOR (*opening a bottle, sniffing*): Pooh! What kinda crap is that?

BELIZE: Beats me. Let's rub it on your poor blistered body and see what it does.

PRIOR: This is not Western medicine, these bottles . . .

BELIZE: Voodoo cream. From the botanica° 'round the block.

PRIOR: And you a registered nurse.

BELIZE (*sniffing it*): Beeswax and cheap perfume. Cut with Jergen's Lotion. Full of good vibes and love from some little black Cubana witch in Miami.

PRIOR: Get that trash away from me, I am immune-suppressed.

BELIZE: I *am* a health professional. I *know* what I'm doing.

PRIOR: It stinks. Any word from Louis?

(*Pause. Belize starts giving Prior a gentle massage.*)

PRIOR: Gone.

BELIZE: He'll be back. I know the type. Likes to keep a girl on edge.

PRIOR: It's been . . .

(*Pause.*)

BELIZE (*trying to jog his memory*): How long?

PRIOR: I don't remember.

BELIZE: How long have you been here?

PRIOR (*getting suddenly upset*): I don't remember, I don't give a fuck. I want Louis. I want my fucking boyfriend, where the fuck is he? I'm dying, I'm dying, where's Louis?

BELIZE: Shhhh, shhh . . .

PRIOR: This is a very strange drug, this drug. Emotional lability, for starters.

---

comme la merde: Like shit.   botanica: Shop that sells magic charms and herbs.

BELIZE: Save a tab or two for me.

PRIOR: Oh no, not this drug, ce n'est pas pour la joyeux noël et la bonne année, this drug she is serious poisonous chemistry, ma pauvre bichette.°

And not just disorienting. I hear things. Voices.

BELIZE: Voices.

PRIOR: A voice.

BELIZE: Saying what?

(*Pause.*)

PRIOR: I'm not supposed to tell.

BELIZE: You better tell the doctor. Or I will.

PRIOR: No no don't. Please. I want the voice; it's wonderful. It's all that's keeping me alive. I don't want to talk to some intern about it.

You know what happens? When I hear it, I get hard.

BELIZE: Oh my.

PRIOR: Comme ça. (*He uses his arm to demonstrate.*) And you know I am slow to rise.

BELIZE: My jaw aches at the memory.

PRIOR: And would you deny me this little solace—betray my concupiscence to Florence Nightingale's storm troopers?

BELIZE: Perish the thought, ma bébé.°

PRIOR: They'd change the drug just to spoil the fun.

BELIZE: You and your boner can depend on me.

PRIOR: Je t'adore, ma belle nègre.°

BELIZE: All this girl-talk shit is politically incorrect, you know. We should have dropped it back when we gave up drag.

PRIOR: I'm sick, I get to be politically incorrect if it makes me feel better. You sound like Lou.

(*Little pause.*)

Well, at least I have the satisfaction of knowing he's in anguish somewhere. I loved his anguish. Watching him stick his head up his asshole and eat his guts out over some relatively minor moral conundrum—it was the best show in town. But Mother warned me: if they get overwhelmed by the little things . . .

BELIZE: They'll be belly-up bustville when something big comes along.

PRIOR: Mother warned me.

BELIZE: And they do come along.

PRIOR: But I didn't listen.

BELIZE: No. (*Doing Hepburn.*) Men are beasts.

PRIOR (*also Hepburn*): The absolute lowest.

BELIZE: I have to go. If I want to spend my whole lonely life looking after white people I can get underpaid to do it.

PRIOR: You're just a Christian martyr.

BELIZE: Whatever happens, baby, I will be here for you.

PRIOR: Je t'aime.°

---

ce n'est pas . . . bichette: This drug isn't for a merry Christmas or a happy New Year . . . my poor little bitch.   ma bébé: My baby.   Je t'adore . . . nègre: I adore you, my beautiful negro.   Je t'aime: I love you.

BELIZE: Je t'aime. Don't go crazy on me, girlfriend, I already got enough crazy queens for one lifetime. For two. I can't be bothering with dementia.

PRIOR: I promise.

BELIZE (*touching him; softly*): Ouch.

PRIOR: Ouch. Indeed.

BELIZE: Why'd they have to pick on you?

And eat more, girlfriend, you really do look like shit.

(*Belize leaves.*)

PRIOR (*after waiting a beat*): He's gone.

Are you still . . .

VOICE: I can't stay. I will return.

PRIOR: Are you one of those "Follow me to the other side" voices?

VOICE: No. I am no nightbird. I am a messenger . . .

PRIOR: You have a beautiful voice, it sounds . . . like a viola, like a perfectly tuned, tight string, balanced, the truth. . . . Stay with me.

VOICE: Not now. Soon I will return, I will reveal myself to you; I am glorious, glorious; my heart, my countenance and my message. You must prepare.

PRIOR: For what? I don't want to . . .

VOICE: No death, no:

A marvelous work and a wonder we undertake,
an edifice awry we sink plumb and straighten, a great
Lie we abolish, a great error correct, with the rule,
sword and broom of Truth!

PRIOR: What are you talking about, I . . .

VOICE: I am on my way; when I am manifest, our Work begins:

Prepare for the parting of the air,
The breath, the ascent,
Glory to . . .

Scene 6

(*The second week of January. Martin, Roy and Joe in a fancy Manhattan restaurant.*)

MARTIN: It's a revolution in Washington, Joe. We have a new agenda and finally a real leader. They got back the Senate but we have the courts. By the nineties the Supreme Court will be block-solid Republican appointees, and the Federal bench—Republican judges like land mines, everywhere, everywhere they turn. Affirmative action? Take it to court. Boom! Land mine. And we'll get our way on just about everything: abortion, defense, Central America, family values, a live investment climate. We have the White House locked till the year 2000. And beyond. A permanent fix on the Oval Office? It's possible. By '92 we'll get the Senate back, and in ten years the South is going to give us the House. It's really the end of Liberalism. The end of New Deal Socialism. The end of ipso facto secular humanism. The dawning of a genuinely American political personality. Modeled on Ronald Wilson Reagan.

JOE: It sounds great, Mr. Heller.

MARTIN: Martin. And Justice is the hub. Especially since Ed Meese took over. He doesn't specialize in Fine Points of the Law. He's a flatfoot, a cop. He reminds me of Teddy Roosevelt.

JOE: I can't wait to meet him.

MARTIN: Too bad, Joe, he's been dead for sixty years!

(*There is a little awkwardness. Joe doesn't respond.*)

MARTIN: Teddy Roosevelt. You said you wanted to . . . . Little joke. It reminds me of the story about the . . .

ROY (*smiling, but nasty*): Aw shut the fuck up Martin.

(*To Joe.*) You see that? Mr. Heller here is one of the mighty, Joseph, in D.C. he sitteth on the right hand of the man who sitteth on the right hand of The Man. And yet I can say "shut the fuck up" and he will take no offense. Loyalty. He . . .

Martin?

MARTIN: Yes, Roy?

ROY: Rub my back.

MARTIN: Roy . . .

ROY: No no really, a sore spot, I get them all the time now, these . . . . Rub it for me darling, would you do that for me?

(*Martin rubs Roy's back. They both look at Joe.*)

ROY (*to Joe*): How do you think a handful of Bolsheviks turned St. Petersburg into Leningrad in one afternoon? *Comrades.* Who do for each other. Marx and Engels. Lenin and Trotsky. Josef Stalin and Franklin Delano Roosevelt.

(*Martin laughs.*)

ROY: *Comrades,* right Martin?

MARTIN: This man, Joe, is a Saint of the Right.

JOE: I know, Mr. Heller, I . . .

ROY: And you see what I mean, Martin? He's special, right?

MARTIN: Don't embarrass him, Roy.

ROY: Gravity, decency, smarts! His strength is as the strength of ten because his heart is pure! And he's a Royboy, one hundred percent.

MARTIN: We're on the move, Joe. On the move.

JOE: Mr. Heller, I . . .

MARTIN (*ending backrub*): We can't wait any longer for an answer.

(*Little pause.*)

JOE: Oh. Um, I . . .

ROY: Joe's a married man, Martin.

MARTIN: Aha.

ROY: With a wife. She doesn't care to go to D.C., and so Joe cannot go. And keeps us dangling. We've seen that kind of thing before, haven't we? These men and their wives.

MARTIN: Oh yes. Beware.

JOE: I really can't discuss this under . . .

MARTIN: Then *don't* discuss. Say yes, Joe.

ROY: Now.

MARTIN: Say yes I will.

ROY: Now.

Now. I'll hold my breath till you do, I'm turning blue waiting. . . . *Now*, goddammit!

MARTIN: Roy, calm down, it's not . . .

ROY: Aw, fuck it. (*He takes a letter from his jacket pocket, hands it to Joe.*)
Read. Came today.

(*Joe reads the first paragraph, then looks up.*)

JOE: Roy. This is . . . Roy, this is terrible.

ROY: You're telling me.

A letter from the New York State Bar Association, Martin.

They're gonna try and disbar me.

MARTIN: Oh my.

JOE: Why?

ROY: Why, Martin?

MARTIN: Revenge.

ROY: The whole Establishment. Their little rules. Because I know no rules. Because I don't see the Law as a dead and arbitrary collection of antiquated dictums, thou shall, thou shalt not, because, because I know the Law's a pliable, breathing, sweating . . . *organ*, because, because . . .

MARTIN: Because he borrowed half a million from one of his clients.

ROY: Yeah, well, there's that.

MARTIN: *And* he forgot to *return* it.

JOE: Roy, that's . . . . You borrowed money from a client?

ROY: I'm deeply ashamed.

(*Little pause.*)

JOE (*very sympathetic*): Roy, you know how much I admire you. Well I mean I know you have unorthodox ways, but I'm sure you only did what you thought at the time you needed to do. And I have faith that . . .

ROY: Not so damp, please. I'll deny it was a loan. She's got no paperwork. Can't prove a fucking thing.

(*Little pause. Martin studies the menu.*)

JOE (*handing back the letter, more official in tone*): Roy I really appreciate your telling me this, and I'll do whatever I can to help.

ROY (*holding up a hand, then, carefully*): I'll tell you what you can do.

I'm about to be tried, Joe, by a jury that is not a jury of my peers. The disbarment committee: genteel gentleman Brahmin lawyers, country-club men. I offend them, to these men . . . I'm what, Martin, some sort of filthy little Jewish troll?

MARTIN: Oh well, I wouldn't go so far as . . .

ROY: Oh well I would.

Very fancy lawyers, these disbarment committee lawyers, fancy lawyers with fancy corporate clients and complicated cases. Antitrust suits. Deregulation.

Environmental control. Complex cases like these need Justice Department cooperation like flowers need the sun. Wouldn't you say that's an accurate assessment, Martin?

MARTIN: I'm not here, Roy. I'm not hearing any of this.

ROY: No. Of course not.

Without the light of the sun, Joe, these cases, and the fancy lawyers who represent them, will wither and die.

A well-placed friend, someone in the Justice Department, say, can turn off the sun. Cast a deep shadow on my behalf. Make them shiver in the cold. If they overstep. They would fear that.

(*Pause.*)

JOE: Roy. I don't understand.

ROY: You do.

(*Pause.*)

JOE: You're not asking me to . . .

ROY: Sssshhhh. Careful.

JOE (*a beat, then*): Even if I said yes to the job, it would be illegal to interfere. With the hearings. It's unethical. No. I can't.

ROY: Un-ethical.

Would you excuse us, Martin?

MARTIN: Excuse you?

ROY: Take a walk, Martin. For real.

(*Martin leaves.*)

ROY: Un-ethical. Are you trying to embarrass me in front of my friend?

JOE: Well it is unethical, I can't . . .

ROY: Boy, you are really something. What the fuck do you think this is, Sunday School?

JOE: No, but Roy this is . . .

ROY: This is . . . this is gastric juices churning, this is enzymes and acids, this is intestinal is what this is, bowel movement and blood-red meat—this stinks, this is *politics*, Joe, the game of being alive. And you think you're . . . . What? Above that? Above alive is what? Dead! In the clouds! You're on earth, goddammit! Plant a foot, stay a while.

I'm sick. They smell I'm weak. They want blood this time. I must have eyes in Justice. In Justice you will protect me.

JOE: Why can't Mr. Heller . . .

ROY: Grow up, Joe. The administration can't get involved.

JOE: But I'd be part of the administration. The same as him.

ROY: Not the same. Martin's Ed's man. And Ed's Reagan's man. So Martin's Reagan's man.

And you're mine.

(*Little pause. He holds up the letter.*)

This will never be. Understand me?

(*He tears the letter up.*)

I'm gonna be a lawyer, Joe, I'm gonna be a lawyer, Joe, I'm gonna be a goddam motherfucking legally licensed member of the bar lawyer, just like my daddy was, till my last bitter day on earth, Joseph, until the day I die.

(*Martin returns.*)

ROY: Ah, Martin's back.
MARTIN: So are we agreed?
ROY: Joe?

(*Little pause.*)

JOE: I will think about it.
    (*To Roy.*) I will.
ROY: Huh.
MARTIN: It's the fear of what comes after the doing that makes the doing hard to do.
ROY: Amen.
MARTIN: But you can almost always live with the consequences.

Scene 7

(*That afternoon. On the granite steps outside the Hall of Justice, Brooklyn. It is cold and sunny. A Sabrett wagon is selling hot dogs. Louis, in a shabby overcoat, is sitting on the steps contemplatively eating one. Joe enters with three hot dogs and a can of Coke.*)

JOE: Can I . . . ?
LOUIS: Oh sure. Sure. Crazy cold sun.
JOE (*sitting*): Have to make the best of it.
    How's your friend?
LOUIS: My . . . ? Oh. He's worse. My friend is worse.
JOE: I'm sorry.
LOUIS: Yeah, well. Thanks for asking. It's nice. You're nice. I can't believe you voted for Reagan.
JOE: I hope he gets better.
LOUIS: Reagan?
JOE: Your friend.
LOUIS: He won't. Neither will Reagan.
JOE: Let's not talk politics, OK?
LOUIS (*pointing to Joe's lunch*): You're eating *three* of those?
JOE: Well . . . I'm . . . hungry.
LOUIS: They're really terrible for you. Full of rat-poo and beetle legs and wood shavings 'n' shit.
JOE: Huh.
LOUIS: And . . . um . . . irridium, I think. Something toxic.
JOE: You're eating one.
LOUIS: Yeah, well, the shape, I can't help myself, plus I'm *trying* to commit suicide, what's your excuse?
JOE: I don't have an excuse. I just have Pepto-Bismol.

(*Joe takes a bottle of Pepto-Bismol and chugs it. Louis shudders audibly.*)

JOE: Yeah I know but then I wash it down with Coke.

(*He does this. Louis mimes barfing in Joe's lap. Joe pushes Louis's head away.*)

JOE: Are you *always* like this?
LOUIS: I've been worrying a lot about his kids.
JOE: Whose?
LOUIS: Reagan's. Maureen and Mike and little orphan Patti and Miss Ron Reagan Jr., the you-should-pardon-the-expression heterosexual.
JOE: Ron Reagan Jr. is *not* . . . . You shouldn't just make these assumptions about people. How do you know? About him? What he is? You don't know.
LOUIS (*doing Tallulah*): Well darling he never sucked *my* cock but . . .
JOE: Look, if you're going to get vulgar . . .
LOUIS: No no really I mean . . . . What's it like to be the child of the Zeitgeist? To have the American Animus as your dad? It's not really a *family*, the Reagans, I read *People*, there aren't any connections there, no love, they don't ever even speak to each other except through their agents. So what's it like to be Reagan's kid? Enquiring minds want to know.
JOE: You can't believe everything you . . .
LOUIS (*looking away*): But . . . I think we all know what that's like. Nowadays. No connections. No responsibilities. All of us . . . falling through the cracks that separate what we owe to our selves and . . . and what we owe to love.
JOE: You just . . . . Whatever you feel like saying or doing, you don't care, you just . . . do it.
LOUIS: Do what?
JOE: It. Whatever. Whatever it is you want to do.
LOUIS: Are you trying to tell me something?

(*Little pause, sexual. They stare at each other. Joe looks away.*)

JOE: No, I'm just observing that you . . .
LOUIS: Impulsive.
JOE: Yes, I mean it must be scary, you . . .
LOUIS (*shrugs*): Land of the free. Home of the brave. Call me irresponsible.
JOE: It's kind of terrifying.
LOUIS: Yeah, well, freedom is. Heartless, too.
JOE: Oh you're not heartless.
LOUIS: You don't know.
    Finish your weenie.

(*He pats Joe on the knee, starts to leave.*)

JOE: Um . . .

(*Louis turns, looks at him. Joe searches for something to say.*)

JOE: Yesterday was Sunday but I've been a little unfocused recently and I thought it was Monday. So I came here like I was going to work. And the whole place was empty. And at first I couldn't figure out why, and I had this moment of incredible . . . fear and also . . . . It just flashed through my mind: The whole Hall of Justice, it's empty, it's deserted, it's gone out of business. Forever. The people that make it run have up and abandoned it.
LOUIS (*looking at the building*): Creepy.

JOE: Well yes but. I felt that I was going to scream. Not because it was creepy, but because the emptiness felt so *fast*.

And . . . well, good. A . . . happy scream.

I just wondered what a thing it would be . . . if overnight everything you owe anything to, justice, or love, had really gone away. Free.

It would be . . . heartless terror. Yes. Terrible, and . . .

Very great. To shed your skin, every old skin, one by one and then walk away, unencumbered, into the morning.

(*Little pause. He looks at the building.*)

I can't go in there today.

LOUIS: Then don't.

JOE (*not really hearing Louis*): I can't go in, I need . . .

(*He looks for what he needs. He takes a swig of Pepto-Bismol.*)

I can't *be* this anymore. I need . . . a change, I should just . . .

LOUIS (*not a come-on, necessarily; he doesn't want to be alone*): Want some company? For whatever?

(*Pause. Joe looks at Louis and looks away, afraid. Louis shrugs.*)

LOUIS: Sometimes, even if it scares you to death, you have to be willing to break the law. Know what I mean?

(*Another little pause.*)

JOE: Yes.

(*Another little pause.*)

LOUIS: I moved out. I moved out on my . . .

I haven't been sleeping well.

JOE: Me neither.

(*Louis goes up to Joe, licks his napkin and dabs at Joe's mouth.*)

LOUIS: Antacid moustache.

(*Points to the building.*) Maybe the court won't convene. Ever again. Maybe we are free. To do whatever.

Children of the new morning, criminal minds. Selfish and greedy and loveless and blind. Reagan's children.

You're scared. So am I. Everybody is in the land of the free. God help us all.

Scene 8

(*Late that night. Joe at a payphone phoning Hannah at home in Salt Lake City.*)

JOE: Mom?

HANNAH: Joe?

JOE: Hi.

HANNAH: You're calling from the street. It's . . . it must be four in the morning. What's happened?

JOE: Nothing, nothing, I . . .

HANNAH: It's Harper. Is Harper . . . . Joe? Joe?

JOE: Yeah, hi. No, Harper's fine. Well, no, she's . . . not fine. How are you, Mom?

HANNAH: What's happened?

JOE: I just wanted to talk to you. I, uh, wanted to try something out on you.

HANNAH: Joe, you haven't . . . have you been drinking, Joe?

JOE: Yes ma'am. I'm drunk.

HANNAH: That isn't like you.

JOE: No. I mean, who's to say?

HANNAH: Why are you out on the street at four A.M.? In that crazy city. It's dangerous.

JOE: Actually, Mom, I'm not on the street. I'm near the boathouse in the park.

HANNAH: What park?

JOE: Central Park.

HANNAH: CENTRAL PARK! Oh my Lord. What on earth are you doing in Central Park at this time of night? Are you . . .

Joe, I think you ought to go home right now. Call me from home.

(*Little pause.*)

Joe?

JOE: I come here to watch, Mom. Sometimes. Just to watch.

HANNAH: Watch what? What's there to watch at four in the . . .

JOE: Mom, did Dad love me?

HANNAH: What?

JOE: Did he?

HANNAH: You ought to go home and call from there.

JOE: Answer.

HANNAH: Oh now really. This is maudlin. I don't like this conversation.

JOE: Yeah, well, it gets worse from here on.

(*Pause.*)

HANNAH: Joe?

JOE: Mom. Momma. I'm a homosexual, Momma.

Boy, did that come out awkward.

(*Pause.*)

Hello? Hello?

I'm a homosexual.

(*Pause.*)

Please, Momma. Say something.

HANNAH: You're old enough to understand that your father didn't love you without being ridiculous about it.

JOE: What?

HANNAH: You're ridiculous. You're being ridiculous.

JOE: I'm . . .

What?

HANNAH: You really ought to go home now to your wife. I need to go to bed. This phone call . . . . We will just forget this phone call.

JOE: Mom.

HANNAH: No more talk. Tonight. This . . .

(*Suddenly very angry.*) Drinking is a sin! A sin! I raised you better than that. (*She hangs up.*)

Scene 9

(*The following morning, early. Split scene: Harper and Joe at home; Louis and Prior in Prior's hospital room. Joe and Louis have just entered. This should be fast and obviously furious; overlapping is fine; the proceedings may be a little confusing but not the final results.*)

HARPER: Oh God. Home. The moment of truth has arrived.

JOE: Harper.

LOUIS: I'm going to move out.

PRIOR: The fuck you are.

JOE: Harper. Please listen. I still love you very much. You're still my best buddy; I'm not going to leave you.

HARPER: No, I don't like the sound of this. I'm leaving.

LOUIS: I'm leaving.
I already have.

JOE: Please listen. Stay. This is really hard. We have to talk.

HARPER: We are talking. Aren't we. Now please shut up. OK?

PRIOR: Bastard. Sneaking off while I'm flat out here, that's low. If I could get up now I'd beat the holy shit out of you.

JOE: Did you take pills? How many?

HARPER: No pills. Bad for the . . . (*Pats stomach.*)

JOE: You aren't pregnant. I called your gynecologist.

HARPER: I'm seeing a new gynecologist.

PRIOR: You have no right to do this.

LOUIS: Oh, that's ridiculous.

PRIOR: No right. It's criminal.

JOE: Forget about that. Just listen. You want the truth. This is the truth.
I knew this when I married you. I've known this I guess for as long as I've known anything, but . . . I don't know, I thought maybe that with enough effort and will I could change myself . . . but I can't . . .

PRIOR: Criminal.

LOUIS: There oughta be a law.

PRIOR: There is a law. You'll see.

JOE: I'm losing ground here, I go walking, you want to know where I walk, I . . . go to the park, or up and down 53rd Street, or places where . . . . And I keep swearing I won't go walking again, but I just can't.

LOUIS: I need some privacy.

PRIOR: That's new.

LOUIS: Everything's new, Prior.

JOE: I try to tighten my heart into a knot, a snarl, I try to learn to live dead, just numb, but then I see someone I want, and it's like a nail, like a hot spike right through my chest, and I know I'm losing.

PRIOR: Apartment too small for three? Louis and Prior comfy but not Louis and Prior and Prior's disease?

LOUIS: Something like that.
I won't be judged by you. This isn't a crime, just—the inevitable consequence of people who run out of—whose limitations . . . .

PRIOR: Bang bang bang. The court will come to order.

LOUIS: I mean let's talk practicalities, schedules; I'll come over if you want, spend nights with you when I can, I can . . .

PRIOR: Has the jury reached a verdict?

LOUIS: I'm doing the best I can.

PRIOR: Pathetic. Who cares?

JOE: My whole life has conspired to bring me to this place, and I can't despise my whole life. I think I believed when I met you I could save you, you at least if not myself, but . . .
I don't have any sexual feelings for you, Harper. And I don't think I ever did.

(*Little pause.*)

HARPER: I think you should go.

JOE: Where?

HARPER: Washington. Doesn't matter.

JOE: What are you talking about?

HARPER: Without me.
Without me, Joe. Isn't that what you want to hear?

(*Little pause.*)

JOE: Yes.

LOUIS: You can love someone and fail them. You can love someone and not be able to . . .

PRIOR: You *can*, theoretically, yes. A person can, maybe an editorial "you" can love, Louis, but not *you*, specifically you, I don't know, I think you are excluded from that general category.

HARPER: You were going to save me, but the whole time you were spinning a lie. I just don't understand that.

PRIOR: A person could theoretically love and maybe many do but we both know now you can't.

LOUIS: I do.

PRIOR: You can't even say it.

LOUIS: I love you, Prior.

PRIOR: I repeat. Who cares?

HARPER: This is so scary, I want this to stop, to go back . . .

PRIOR: We have reached a verdict, your honor. This man's heart is deficient. He loves, but his love is worth nothing.

JOE: Harper . . .

HARPER: Mr. Lies, I want to get away from here. Far away. Right now. Before he starts talking again. Please, please . . .

JOE: As long as I've known you Harper you've been afraid of . . . Of men hiding under the bed, men hiding under the sofa, men with knives.

PRIOR (*shattered; almost pleading; trying to reach him*): I'm dying! You stupid fuck! Do you know what that is! Love! Do you know what love means? We lived together four-and-a-half years, you animal, you idiot.

LOUIS: I have to find some way to save myself.

JOE: Who are these men? I never understood it. Now I know.

HARPER: What?

JOE: It's me.

HARPER: It is?

PRIOR: GET OUT OF MY ROOM!

JOE: I'm the man with the knives.

HARPER: You are?

PRIOR: If I could get up now I'd kill you. I would. Go away. Go away or I'll scream.

HARPER: Oh God . . .

JOE: I'm sorry . . .

HARPER: It is you.

LOUIS: Please don't scream.

PRIOR: Go.

HARPER: I recognize you now.

LOUIS: Please . . .

JOE: Oh. Wait, I . . . . Oh!

> (*He covers his mouth with his hand, gags, and removes his hand, red with blood.*)
> I'm bleeding.

(*Prior screams.*)

HARPER: Mr. Lies.

MR. LIES (*appearing, dressed in antarctic explorer's apparel*): Right here.

HARPER: I want to go away. I can't see him anymore.

MR. LIES: Where?

HARPER: Anywhere. Far away.

MR. LIES: Absolutamento.

(*Harper and Mr. Lies vanish. Joe looks up, sees that she's gone.*)

PRIOR (*closing his eyes*): When I open my eyes you'll be gone.

(*Louis leaves.*)

JOE: Harper?

PRIOR (*opening his eyes*): Huh. It worked.

JOE (*calling*): Harper?

PRIOR: I hurt all over. I wish I was dead.

Scene 10

(*The same day, sunset. Hannah and Sister Ella Chapter, a real-estate saleswoman, Hannah Pitt's closest friend, in front of Hannah's house in Salt Lake City.*)

SISTER ELLA CHAPTER: Look at that view! A view of heaven. Like the living city of heaven, isn't it, it just fairly glimmers in the sun.

HANNAH: Glimmers.

SISTER ELLA CHAPTER: Even the stone and brick it just glimmers and glitters like heaven in the sunshine. Such a nice view you get, perched up on a canyon rim. Some kind of beautiful place.

HANNAH: It's just Salt Lake, and you're selling the house *for* me, not *to* me.

SISTER ELLA CHAPTER: I like to work up an enthusiasm for my properties.

HANNAH: Just get me a good price.

SISTER ELLA CHAPTER: Well, the market's off.

HANNAH: At least fifty.

SISTER ELLA CHAPTER: Forty'd be more like it.

HANNAH: Fifty.

SISTER ELLA CHAPTER: Wish you'd wait a bit.

HANNAH: Well I can't.

SISTER ELLA CHAPTER: Wish you would. You're about the only friend I got.

HANNAH: Oh well now.

SISTER ELLA CHAPTER: Know why I decided to like you? I decided to like you 'cause you're the only unfriendly Mormon I ever met.

HANNAH: Your wig is crooked.

SISTER ELLA CHAPTER: Fix it.

(*Hannah straightens Sister Ella's wig.*)

SISTER ELLA CHAPTER: New York City. All they got there is tiny rooms.

> I always thought: People ought to stay put. That's why I got my license to sell real estate. It's a way of saying: Have a house! Stay put! It's a way of saying traveling's no good. Plus I needed the cash. (*She takes a pack of cigarettes out of her purse, lights one, offers pack to Hannah.*)

HANNAH: Not out here, anyone could come by.

> There's been days I've stood at this ledge and thought about stepping over.
> It's a hard place, Salt Lake: baked dry. Abundant energy; not much intelligence. That's a combination that can wear a body out. No harm looking someplace else. I don't need much room.
> My sister-in-law Libby thinks there's radon gas in the basement.

SISTER ELLA CHAPTER: Is there gas in the . . .

HANNAH: Of course not. Libby's a fool.

SISTER ELLA CHAPTER: 'Cause I'd have to include that in the description.

HANNAH: There's no gas, Ella. (*Little pause.*) Give a puff. (*She takes a furtive drag of Ella's cigarette.*) Put it away now.

SISTER ELLA CHAPTER: So I guess it's goodbye.

HANNAH: You'll be all right, Ella, I wasn't ever much of a friend.

SISTER ELLA CHAPTER: I'll say something but don't laugh, OK?

> This is the home of saints, the godliest place on earth, they say, and I think they're right. That mean there's no evil here? No. Evil's everywhere. Sin's everywhere. But this . . . is the spring of sweet water in the desert, the desert flower. Every step a Believer takes away from here is a step fraught with peril. I fear for you, Hannah Pitt, because you are my friend. Stay put. This is the right home of saints.

HANNAH: Latter-day saints.

SISTER ELLA CHAPTER: Only kind left.

HANNAH: But still. Late in the day . . . for saints and everyone. That's all. That's all.

Fifty thousand dollars for the house, Sister Ella Chapter; don't undersell. It's an impressive view.

ACT 3
NOT-YET-CONSCIOUS, FORWARD DAWNING • January 1986

Scene 1

(*Late night, three days after the end of act 2. The stage is completely dark. Prior is in bed in his apartment, having a nightmare. He wakes up, sits up and switches on a nightlight. He looks at his clock. Seated by the table near the bed is a man dressed in the clothing of a 13th-century British squire.*)

PRIOR (*terrified*): Who are you?

PRIOR 1: My name is Prior Walter.

(*Pause.*)

PRIOR: My name is Prior Walter.

PRIOR 1: I know that.

PRIOR: Explain.

PRIOR 1: You're alive. I'm not. We have the same name. What do you want me to explain?

PRIOR: A ghost?

PRIOR 1: An ancestor.

PRIOR: Not *the* Prior Walter? The Bayeux tapestry Prior Walter?

PRIOR 1: His great-great grandson. The fifth of the name.

PRIOR: I'm the thirty-fourth, I think.

PRIOR 1: Actually the thirty-second.

PRIOR: Not according to Mother.

PRIOR 1: She's including the two bastards, then; I say leave them out. I say no room for bastards. The little things you swallow . . .

PRIOR: Pills.

PRIOR 1: Pills. For the pestilence. I too . . .

PRIOR: Pestilence. . . . You too what?

PRIOR 1: The pestilence in my time was much worse than now. Whole villages of empty houses. You could look outdoors and see Death walking in the morning, dew dampening the ragged hem of his black robe. Plain as I see you now.

PRIOR: You died of the plague.

PRIOR 1: The spotty monster. Like you, alone.

PRIOR: I'm not alone.

PRIOR 1: You have no wife, no children.

PRIOR: I'm gay.

PRIOR 1: So? Be gay, dance in your altogether for all I care, what's that to do with not having children?

PRIOR: Gay homosexual, not bonny, blithe and . . . never mind.

PRIOR 1: I had twelve. When I died.

(*The second ghost appears, this one dressed in the clothing of an elegant 17th-century Londoner.*)

PRIOR 1 (*pointing to Prior 2*): And I was three years younger than him.

(*Prior sees the new ghost, screams.*)

PRIOR: Oh God another one.

PRIOR 2: Prior Walter. Prior to you by some seventeen others.

PRIOR 1: He's counting the bastards.

PRIOR: Are we having a convention?

PRIOR 2: We've been sent to declare her fabulous incipience. They love a well-paved entrance with lots of heralds, and . . .

PRIOR 1: The messenger come. Prepare the way. The infinite descent, a breath in air . . .

PRIOR 2: They chose us, I suspect, because of the mortal affinities. In a family as long-descended as the Walters there are bound to be a few carried off by plague.

PRIOR 1: The spotty monster.

PRIOR 2: Black Jack. Came from a water pump, half the city of London, can you imagine? His came from fleas. Yours, I understand, is the lamentable consequence of venery . . .

PRIOR 1: Fleas on rats, but who knew that?

PRIOR: Am I going to die?

PRIOR 2: We aren't allowed to discuss . . .

PRIOR 1: When you do, you don't get ancestors to help you through it. You may be surrounded by children but you die alone.

PRIOR: I'm afraid.

PRIOR 1: You should be. There aren't even torches, and the path's rocky, dark and steep.

PRIOR 2: Don't alarm him. There's good news before there's bad.

We two come to strew rose petal and palm leaf before the triumphal procession. Prophet. Seer. Revelator. It's a great honor for the family.

PRIOR 1: He hasn't got a family.

PRIOR 2: I meant for the Walters, for the family in the larger sense.

PRIOR (*singing*): All I want is a room somewhere,
Far away from the cold night air . . .

PRIOR 2 (*putting a hand on Prior's forehead*): Calm, calm, this is no brain fever . . .

(*Prior calms down, but keeps his eyes closed. The lights begin to change. Distant Glorious Music.*)

PRIOR 1 (*low chant*): Adonai, Adonai,
Olam ha-yichud,
Zefirot, Zazahot,
Ha-adam, ha-gadol
Daughter of Light,
Daughter of Splendors,
Fluor! Phosphor!
Lumen! Candle!

PRIOR 2 (*simultaneously*): Even now,
From the mirror-bright halls of heaven,

Across the cold and lifeless infinity of space,
The Messenger comes
Trailing orbs of light,
Fabulous, incipient,
Oh Prophet,
To you . . .

PRIOR 1 AND PRIOR 2: Prepare, prepare,
The Infinite Descent,
A breath, a feather,
Glory to . . .

(*They vanish.*)

Scene 2

(*The next day. Split scene. Louis and Belize in a coffee shop. Prior is at the outpatient clinic at the hospital with Emily, the nurse; she has him on a pentamidine IV drip.*)

LOUIS: Why has democracy succeeded in America? Of course by succeeded I mean comparatively, not literally, not in the present, but what makes for the prospect of some sort of radical democracy spreading outward and growing up? Why does the power that was once so carefully preserved at the top of the pyramid by the original framers of the Constitution seem drawn inexorably downward and outward in spite of the best effort of the Right to stop this? I mean it's the really hard thing about being Left in this country, the American Left can't help but trip over all these petrified little fetishes: freedom, that's the worst; you know, *Jeane Kirkpatrick*° for God's sake will go on and on about freedom and so what does that mean, the word freedom, when she talks about it, or human rights; you have Bush talking about human rights, and so what are these people talking about, they might as well be talking about the mating habits of Venusians, these people don't begin to know what, ontologically, freedom is or human rights, like they see these bourgeois property-based Rights-of-Man-type rights but that's not enfranchisement, not democracy, not what's implicit, what's potential within the idea, not the idea with blood in it. That's just liberalism, the worst kind of liberalism, really, bourgeois tolerance, and what I think is that what AIDS shows us is the limits of tolerance, that it's not enough to be tolerated, because when the shit hits the fan you find out how much tolerance is worth. Nothing. And underneath all the tolerance is intense, passionate hatred.

BELIZE: Uh huh.

LOUIS: Well don't you think that's true?

BELIZE: Uh huh. It is.

Jeane Kirkpatrick: Ardent anti-Communist (1920–2006) and former U.S. ambassador to the United Nations.

LOUIS: *Power* is the object, not being tolerated. Fuck assimilation. But I mean in spite of all this the thing about America, I think, is that ultimately we're different from every other nation on earth, in that, with people here of every race, we can't . . . . Ultimately what defines us isn't race, but politics. Not like any European country where there's an insurmountable fact of a kind of racial, or ethnic, monopoly, or monolith, like all Dutchmen, I mean Dutch people, are well, Dutch, and the Jews of Europe were never Europeans, just a small problem. Facing the monolith. But here there are so many small problems, it's really just a collection of small problems, the monolith is missing. Oh, I mean, of course I suppose there's the monolith of White America. White Straight Male America.

BELIZE: Which is not unimpressive, even among monoliths.

LOUIS: Well, no, but when the race thing gets taken care of, and I don't mean to minimalize how major it is, I mean I know it is, this is a really, really incredibly racist country but it's like, well, the British. I mean, all these blue-eyed pink people. And it's just weird, you know, I mean I'm not all that Jewish-looking, or . . . well, maybe I am but, you know, in New York, everyone is . . . well, not everyone, but so many are but so but in England, in London I walk into bars and I feel like Sid the Yid, you know I mean like Woody Allen in *Annie Hall*, with the payess and the gabardine coat, like never, never anywhere so much—I mean, not actively despised, not like they're Germans, who I think are still terribly anti-Semitic, and racist too, I mean black-racist, they pretend otherwise but, anyway, in London, there's just . . . and at one point I met this black gay guy from Jamaica who talked with a lilt but he said his family'd been living in London since before the Civil War—the American one—and how the English never let him forget for a minute that he wasn't blue-eyed and pink and I said yeah, me too, these people are anti-Semites and he said yeah but the British Jews have the clothing business all sewed up and blacks there can't get a foothold. And it was an incredibly awkward moment of just . . . . I mean there we were, in this bar that was gay but it was a *pub*, you know, the beams and the plaster and those horrible little, like, two-day-old fish and egg sandwiches—and just so British, so *old*, and I felt, well, there's no way out of this because both of us are, right now, too much immersed in this history, hope is dissolved in the sheer age of this place, where race is what counts and there's no real hope of change—it's the racial destiny of the Brits that matters to them, not their political destiny, whereas in America . . .

BELIZE: Here in America race doesn't count.

LOUIS: No, no, that's not . . . . I mean you *can't* be hearing that . . .

BELIZE: I . . .

LOUIS: It's—look, race, yes, but ultimately race here is a political question, right? Racists just try to use race here as a tool in a political struggle. It's not really about race. Like the spiritualists try to use that stuff, are you enlightened, are you centered, channeled, whatever, this reaching out for a spiritual past in a country where no indigenous spirits exist—only the Indians, I mean Native American spirits and we killed them off so now, there are no gods here, no ghosts and spirits in America, there are no angels in America, no spiritual past, no racial past, there's only the political, and the decoys and the ploys to maneuver around the inescapable battle of politics, the shifting downwards and outwards of political power to the people . . .

BELIZE: POWER to the People! AMEN! (*Looking at his watch.*) *OH MY GOODNESS!* Will you look at the time, I gotta . . .

LOUIS: Do you . . . . You think this is, what, racist or naive or something?

BELIZE: Well it's certainly *something*. Look, I just remembered I have an appointment . . .

LOUIS: What? I mean I really don't want to, like, speak from some position of privilege and . . .

BELIZE: I'm sitting here, thinking, eventually he's *got* to run out of steam, so I let you rattle on and on saying about maybe seven or eight things I find really offensive.

LOUIS: What?

BELIZE: But I know you, Louis, and I know the guilt fueling this peculiar tirade is obviously already swollen bigger than your hemorrhoids.

LOUIS: I don't have hemorrhoids.

BELIZE: I hear different. May I finish?

LOUIS: Yes, but I don't have hemorrhoids.

BELIZE: So finally, when I . . .

LOUIS: Prior told you, he's an asshole, he shouldn't have . . .

BELIZE: You promised, Louis. Prior is not a subject.

LOUIS: You brought him up.

BELIZE: I brought up hemorrhoids.

LOUIS: So it's indirect. Passive-aggressive.

BELIZE: Unlike, I suppose, banging me over the head with your theory that America doesn't have a race problem.

LOUIS: Oh be fair I never said that.

BELIZE: Not exactly, but . . .

LOUIS: I said . . .

BELIZE: . . . but it was close enough, because if it'd been that blunt I'd've just walked out and . . .

LOUIS: You deliberately misinterpreted! I . . .

BELIZE: Stop interrupting! I haven't been able to . . .

LOUIS: Just let me . . .

BELIZE: NO! What, *talk*? You've been running your mouth nonstop since I got here, yaddadda yaddadda blah blah blah, up the hill, down the hill, playing with your MONOLITH . . .

LOUIS (*overlapping*): Well, you could have joined in at any time instead of . . .

BELIZE (*continuing over Louis*): . . . and girlfriend it is truly an *awesome* spectacle but I got better things to

do with my time than sit here listening to this racist bullshit just because I feel sorry for you that . . .

LOUIS: I am not a racist!

BELIZE: Oh come on . . .

LOUIS: So maybe I am a racist but . . .

BELIZE: Oh I really hate that! It's no fun picking on you Louis; you're so guilty, it's like throwing darts at a glob of jello, there's no satisfying hits, just quivering, the darts just blop in and vanish.

LOUIS: I just think when you are discussing lines of oppression it gets very complicated and . . .

BELIZE: Oh is that a fact? You know, we black drag queens have a rather intimate knowledge of the complexity of the lines of . . .

LOUIS: *Ex*-black drag queen.

BELIZE: Actually ex-ex.

LOUIS: You're doing drag again?

BELIZE: I don't . . . . Maybe. I don't have to tell you. Maybe.

LOUIS: I think it's sexist.

BELIZE: I didn't ask you.

LOUIS: Well it is. The gay community, I think, has to adopt the same attitude towards drag as black women have to take towards black women blues singers.

BELIZE: Oh my we *are* walking dangerous tonight.

LOUIS: Well, it's all internalized oppression, right, I mean the masochism, the stereotypes, the . . .

BELIZE: Louis, are you deliberately trying to make me hate you?

LOUIS: No, I . . .

BELIZE: I mean, are you deliberately transforming yourself into an arrogant, sexual-political Stalinist-slash-racist flag-waving thug for my benefit?

(*Pause.*)

LOUIS: You know what I think?

BELIZE: What?

LOUIS: You hate me because I'm a Jew.

BELIZE: I'm leaving.

LOUIS: It's true.

BELIZE: You have no basis except your . . .
  Louis, it's good to know you haven't changed; you are still an honorary citizen of the Twilight Zone, and after your pale, pale white polemics on behalf of racial insensitivity you have a flaming *fuck* of a lot of nerve calling me an anti-Semite. Now I really gotta go.

LOUIS: You called me Lou the Jew.

BELIZE: That was a joke.

LOUIS: I didn't think it was funny. It was hostile.

BELIZE: It was three years ago.

LOUIS: So?

BELIZE: You just called yourself Sid the Yid.

LOUIS: That's not the same thing.

BELIZE: Sid the Yid is different from Lou the Jew.

LOUIS: Yes.

BELIZE: Someday you'll have to explain that to me, but right now . . .
  You hate me because you hate black people.

LOUIS: I do not. But I do think most black people are anti-Semitic.

BELIZE: "Most black people." *That's* racist, Louis, and *I* think most Jews . . .

LOUIS: Louis Farrakhan.

BELIZE: Ed Koch.

LOUIS: Jesse Jackson.

BELIZE: Jackson. Oh really, Louis, this is . . .

LOUIS: Hymietown! Hymietown!

BELIZE: Louis, you voted for Jesse Jackson. You send checks to the Rainbow Coalition.

LOUIS: I'm ambivalent. The checks bounced.

BELIZE: All your checks bounce, Louis; you're ambivalent about everything.

LOUIS: What's that supposed to mean?

BELIZE: You may be dumber than shit but I refuse to believe you can't figure it out. Try.

LOUIS: I was never ambivalent about Prior. I love him. I do. I really do.

BELIZE: Nobody said different.

LOUIS: Love and ambivalence are . . . . Real love isn't ambivalent.

BELIZE: "Real love isn't ambivalent." I'd swear that's a line from my favorite bestselling paperback novel, *In Love with the Night Mysterious*, except I don't think you ever read it.

(*Pause.*)

LOUIS: I never read it, no.

BELIZE: You ought to. Instead of spending the rest of your life trying to get through *Democracy in America*. It's about this white woman whose Daddy owns a plantation in the Deep South in the years before the Civil War—the American one—and her name is Margaret, and she's in love with her Daddy's number-one slave, and his name is Thaddeus, and she's married but her white slave-owner husband has AIDS: Antebellum Insufficiently Developed Sex-organs. And there's a lot of hot stuff going down when Margaret and Thaddeus can catch a spare torrid ten under the cotton-picking moon, and then of course the Yankees come, and they set the slaves free, and the slaves string up old Daddy, and so on. Historical fiction. Somewhere in there I recall Margaret and Thaddeus find the time to discuss the nature of love; her face is reflecting the flames of the burning plantation—you know, the way white people do—and his black face is dark in the night and she says to him, "Thaddeus, real love isn't ever ambivalent."

(*Little pause. Emily enters and turns off IV drip.*)

BELIZE: Thaddeus looks at her; he's contemplating her thesis; and he isn't sure he agrees.

EMILY (*removing IV drip from Prior's arm*): Treatment number . . . (*consulting chart*) four.

PRIOR: Pharmaceutical miracle. Lazarus breathes again.

LOUIS: Is he . . . . How bad is he?

BELIZE: You want the laundry list?

EMILY: Shirt off, let's check the . . .

(*Prior takes his shirt off. She examines his lesions.*)

BELIZE: There's the weight problem and the shit problem and the morale problem.

EMILY: Only six. That's good. Pants.

(*He drops his pants. He's naked. She examines.*)

BELIZE: And. He thinks he's going crazy.

EMILY: Looking good. What else?

PRIOR: Ankles sore and swollen, but the leg's better. The nausea's mostly gone with the little orange pills. BM's pure liquid but not bloody anymore, for now, my eye doctor says everything's OK, for now, my dentist says "Yuck!" when he sees my fuzzy tongue, and now he wears little condoms on his thumb and forefinger. And a mask. So what? My dermatologist is in Hawaii and my mother . . . well leave my mother out of it. Which is usually where my mother is, out of it. My glands are like walnuts, my weight's holding steady for week two, and a friend died two days ago of bird tuberculosis; bird tuberculosis; that scared me and I didn't go to the funeral today because he was an Irish Catholic and it's probably open casket and I'm afraid of . . . something, the bird TB or seeing him or . . . . So I guess I'm doing OK. Except for of course I'm going nuts.

EMILY: We ran the toxoplasmosis series and there's no indication . . .

PRIOR: I know, I know, but I feel like something terrifying is on its way, you know, like a missile from outer space, and it's plummeting down towards the earth, and I'm ground zero, and . . . I am generally known where I am known as one cool, collected queen. And I am ruffled.

EMILY: There's really nothing to worry about. I think that shochen bamromim hamtzeh menucho nechono al kanfey haschino.

PRIOR: What?

EMILY: Everything's fine. Bemaalos k'doshim ut'horim kezohar horokeea mazhirim . . .

PRIOR: Oh I don't understand what you're . . .

EMILY: Es nishmas Prior sheholoch leolomoh, baavur she-nodvoo z'dokoh b'ad hazkoras nishmosoh.

PRIOR: Why are you doing that?! Stop it! Stop it!

EMILY: Stop what?

PRIOR: You were just . . . weren't you just speaking in Hebrew or something.

EMILY: *Hebrew?* (*Laughs.*) I'm basically Italian-American. No. I didn't speak in Hebrew.

PRIOR: Oh no, oh God please I really think I . . .

EMILY: Look, I'm sorry, I have a waiting room full of . . . . I think you're one of the lucky ones, you'll live for years, probably—you're pretty healthy for someone with no immune system. Are you seeing someone? Loneliness is a danger. A therapist?

PRIOR: No, I don't need to see anyone, I just . . .

EMILY: Well think about it. You aren't going crazy. You're just under a lot of stress. No wonder . . . (*She starts to write in his chart.*)

(*Suddenly there is an astonishing blaze of light, a huge chord sounded by a gigantic choir, and a great book with steel pages mounted atop a molten-red pillar pops up from the stage floor. The book opens; there is a large Aleph inscribed on its pages, which bursts into flames. Immediately the book slams shut and disappears instantly under the floor as the lights become normal again. Emily notices none of this, writing. Prior is agog.*)

EMILY (*laughing, exiting*): Hebrew . . .

(*Prior flees.*)

LOUIS: Help me.

BELIZE: I beg your pardon?

LOUIS: You're a nurse, give me something, I . . . don't know what to do anymore, I . . . . Last week at work I screwed up the Xerox machine like permanently and so I . . . then I tripped on the subway steps and my glasses broke and I cut my forehead, here, see, and now I can't see much and my forehead . . . it's like the Mark of Cain,° stupid, right, but it won't heal and every morning I see it and I think, Biblical things, Mark of Cain, Judas Iscariot° and his silver and his noose, people who . . . in betraying what they love betray what's truest in themselves, I feel . . . nothing but cold for myself, just cold, and every night I miss him, I miss him so much but then . . . those sores, and the smell and . . . where I thought it was going. . . . I could be . . . I could be . . . sick too, maybe I'm sick too. I don't know.

    Belize. Tell him I love him. Can you do that?

BELIZE: I've thought about it for a very long time, and I still don't understand what love is. Justice is simple. Democracy is simple. Those things are unambivalent. But love is very hard. And it goes bad for you if you violate the hard law of love.

LOUIS: I'm dying.

BELIZE: He's dying. You just wish you were.

    Oh cheer up, Louis. Look at that heavy sky out there.

LOUIS: Purple.

BELIZE: *Purple?* Boy, what kind of a homosexual are you, anyway? That's not purple, Mary, that color up there is (*very grand*) mauve.

    All day today it's felt like Thanksgiving. Soon, this . . . ruination will be blanketed white. You can smell it—can you smell it?

LOUIS: Smell what?

BELIZE: Softness, compliance, forgiveness, grace.

LOUIS: No . . .

BELIZE: I can't help you learn that. I can't help you, Louis. You're not my business. (*He exits.*)

(*Louis puts his head in his hands, inadvertently touching his cut forehead.*)

Mark of Cain: In Genesis, Cain murdered his brother Abel and subsequently was marked on his forehead by God. **Judas Iscariot:** An apostle who betrayed Jesus for thirty pieces of silver.

LOUIS: Ow FUCK! (*He stands slowly, looks towards where Belize exited.*) Smell what?

    (*He looks both ways to be sure no one is watching, then inhales deeply, and is surprised.*) Huh. Snow.

Scene 3

(*Same day. Harper in a very white, cold place, with a brilliant blue sky above; a delicate snowfall. She is dressed in a beautiful snowsuit. The sound of the sea, faint.*)

HARPER: Snow! Ice! Mountains of ice! Where am I? I . . .

    I feel better, I do, I . . . feel better. There are ice crystals in my lungs, wonderful and sharp. And the snow smells like cold, crushed peaches. And there's something . . . some current of blood in the wind, how strange, it has that iron taste.

MR. LIES: Ozone.

HARPER: Ozone! Wow! Where am I?

MR. LIES: The Kingdom of Ice, the bottommost part of the world.

HARPER (*looking around, then realizing*): Antarctica. This is Antarctica!

MR. LIES: Cold shelter for the shattered. No sorrow here, tears freeze.

HARPER: Antarctica, Antarctica, oh boy oh boy, LOOK at this, I . . . . Wow, I must've really snapped the tether, huh?

MR. LIES: Apparently

HARPER: That's great. I want to stay here forever. Set up camp. Build things. Build a city, an enormous city made up of frontier forts, dark wood and green roofs and high gates made of pointed logs and bonfires burning on every street corner. I should build by a river. Where are the forests?

MR. LIES: No timber here. Too cold. Ice, no trees.

HARPER: Oh details! I'm sick of details! I'll plant them and grow them. I'll live off caribou fat, I'll melt it over the bonfires and drink it from long, curved goat-horn cups. It'll be great. I want to make a new world here. So that I never have to go home again.

MR. LIES: As long as it lasts. Ice has a way of melting . . .

HARPER: No. Forever. I can have anything I want here—maybe even companionship, someone who has . . . desire for me. You, maybe.

MR. LIES: It's against the by-laws of the International Order of Travel Agents to get involved with clients. Rules are rules. Anyway, I'm not the one you really want.

HARPER: There isn't anyone . . . maybe an Eskimo. Who could ice-fish for food. And help me build a nest for when the baby comes.

MR. LIES: There are no Eskimo in Antarctica. And you're not really pregnant. You made that up.

HARPER: Well all of this is made up. So if the snow feels cold I'm pregnant. Right? Here, I can be pregnant. And I can have any kind of a baby I want.

MR. LIES: This is a retreat, a vacuum, its virtue is that it lacks everything; deep-freeze for feelings. You can be numb and safe here, that's what you came for. Respect the delicate ecology of your delusions.

HARPER: You mean like no Eskimo in Antarctica.

MR. LIES: Correcto. Ice and snow, no Eskimo. Even hallucinations have laws.

HARPER: Well then who's that?

(*The Eskimo appears.*)

MR. LIES: An Eskimo.

HARPER: An antarctic Eskimo. A fisher of the polar deep.

MR. LIES: There's something wrong with this picture.

(*The Eskimo beckons.*)

HARPER: I'm going to like this place. It's my own National Geographic Special! Oh! Oh! (*She holds her stomach.*) I think . . . I think I felt her kicking. Maybe I'll give birth to a baby covered with thick white fur, and that way she won't be cold. My breasts will be full of hot cocoa so she doesn't get chilly. And if it gets really cold, she'll have a pouch I can crawl into. Like a marsupial. We'll mend together. That's what we'll do; we'll mend.

Scene 4

(*Same day. An abandoned lot in the South Bronx. A homeless Woman is standing near an oil drum in which a fire is burning. Snowfall. Trash around. Hannah enters dragging two heavy suitcases.*)

HANNAH: Excuse me? I said excuse me? Can you tell me where I am? Is this Brooklyn? Do you know a Pineapple Street? Is there some sort of bus or train or . . . ?

I'm lost, I just arrived from Salt Lake. City. Utah? I took the bus that I was told to take and I got off—well it was the very last stop, so I had to get off, and I *asked* the driver was this Brooklyn, and he nodded yes but he was from one of those foreign countries where they think it's good manners to nod at everything even if you have no idea what it is you're nodding at, and in truth I think he spoke no English at all, which I think would make him ineligible for employment on public transportation. The public being English-speaking, mostly. Do you speak English?

(*The Woman nods.*)

HANNAH: I was supposed to be met at the airport by my son. He didn't show and I don't wait more than three and three-quarters hours for *anyone*. I should have been patient, I guess, I . . . . Is this . . .

WOMAN: Bronx.

HANNAH: Is that . . . . The *Bronx*? Well how in the name of Heaven did I get to the Bronx when the bus driver said . . .

WOMAN (*talking to herself*): Slurp slurp slurp will you STOP that disgusting slurping! YOU DISGUSTING SLURPING FEEDING ANIMAL! Feeding yourself, just feeding yourself, what would it matter, to you or to ANYONE, if you just stopped. Feeding. And DIED?

(*Pause.*)

HANNAH: Can you just tell me where I . . .

WOMAN: Why was the Kosciusko Bridge named after a Polack?

HANNAH: I don't know what you're . . .

WOMAN: That was a joke.

HANNAH: Well what's the punchline?

WOMAN: I don't know.

HANNAH (*looking around desperately*): Oh for pete's sake, is there anyone else who . . .

WOMAN (*again, to herself*): Stand further off you fat loathsome whore, you can't have any more of this soup, slurp slurp slurp you animal, and the—I know you'll just go pee it all away and where will you do that? Behind what bush? It's FUCKING COLD out here and I . . .

Oh that's right, because it was supposed to have been a tunnel!

That's not very funny.

Have you read the prophecies of Nostradamus?

HANNAH: Who?

WOMAN: Some guy I went out with once somewhere, Nostradamus. Prophet, outcast, eyes like . . . . Scary shit, he . . .

HANNAH: Shut up. Please. Now I want you to stop jabbering for a minute and pull your wits together and tell me how to get to Brooklyn. Because you know! And you are going to tell me! Because there is no one else around to tell me and I am wet and cold and I am very angry! So I am sorry you're psychotic but just make the effort—take a deep breath—DO IT!

(*Hannah and the Woman breathe together.*)

HANNAH: That's good. Now exhale.

(*They do.*)

HANNAH: Good. Now how do I get to Brooklyn?

WOMAN: Don't know. Never been. Sorry. Want some soup?

HANNAH: Manhattan? Maybe you know . . . I don't suppose you know the location of the Mormon Visitor's . . .

WOMAN: 65th and Broadway.

HANNAH: How do you . . .

WOMAN: Go there all the time. Free movies. Boring, but you can stay all day.

HANNAH: Well. . . . So how do I.

WOMAN: Take the D Train. Next block make a right.

HANNAH: Thank you.

WOMAN: Oh yeah. In the new century I think we will all be insane.

Scene 5

(*Same day. Joe and Roy in the study of Roy's brown-stone. Roy is wearing an elegant bathrobe. He has made a considerable effort to look well. He isn't well, and he hasn't succeeded much in looking it.*)

JOE: I can't. The answer's no. I'm sorry.

ROY: Oh, well, apologies . . .

I can't see that there's anyone asking for apologies.

(*Pause.*)

JOE: I'm sorry, Roy.

ROY: Oh, well, apologies.

JOE: My wife is missing, Roy. My mother's coming from Salt Lake to . . . to help look, I guess. I'm supposed to be at the airport now, picking her up but . . . . I just spent two days in a hospital, Roy, with a bleeding ulcer, I was spitting up blood.

ROY: Blood, huh? Look, I'm very busy here and . . .

JOE: It's just a job.

ROY: A job? A *job*? *Washington*! Dumb Utah Mormon hick shit!

JOE: Roy . . .

ROY: *WASHINGTON!* When Washington called me I was younger than you, you think I said "Aw fuck no I can't go I got two fingers up my asshole and a little moral nosebleed to boot!" When Washington calls you my pretty young punk friend you go or you can go fuck yourself sideways 'cause the train has pulled out of the station, and you are *out*, nowhere, out in the cold. Fuck you, Mary Jane, get outta here.

JOE: Just let me . . .

ROY: Explain? Ephemera. You broke my heart. Explain that. Explain that.

JOE: I love you. Roy.

There's so much that I want, to be . . . what you see in me, I want to be a participant in the world, in your world, Roy, I want to be capable of that, I've tried, really I have but . . . I can't do this. Not because I don't believe in you, but because I believe in you so much, in what you stand for, at heart, the order, the decency. I would give anything to protect you, but . . . . There are laws I can't break. It's too ingrained. It's not me. There's enough damage I've already done.

Maybe you were right, maybe I'm dead.

ROY: You're not dead, boy, you're a sissy.

You love me; that's moving, I'm moved. It's nice to be loved. I warned you about her, didn't I, Joe? But you don't listen to me, why, because you say Roy is smart and Roy's a friend but Roy . . . well, he isn't nice, and you wanna be nice. Right? A nice, nice man!

(*Little pause.*)

You know what my greatest accomplishment was, Joe, in my life, what I am able to look back on and be proudest of? And I have helped make Presidents and unmake them and mayors and more goddam judges than anyone in NYC ever—AND several million dollars, tax-free—and what do you think means the most to me?

You ever hear of Ethel Rosenberg? Huh, Joe, huh?

JOE: Well, yeah, I guess I . . . . Yes.

ROY: Yes. Yes. You have heard of Ethel Rosenberg. Yes. Maybe you even read about her in the history books.

If it wasn't for me, Joe, Ethel Rosenberg would be alive today, writing some personal-advice column for *Ms.* magazine. She isn't. Because during the trial, Joe, I was on the phone every day, talking with the judge . . .

JOE: Roy . . .

ROY: Every day, doing what I do best, talking on the telephone, making sure that timid Yid nebbish on the bench did his duty to America, to history. That sweet unprepossessing woman, two kids, boo-hoo-hoo, reminded us all of our little Jewish mamas—she came this close to getting life; I pleaded till I wept to put her in the chair. Me. I did that. I would have fucking pulled the switch if they'd have let me. Why? Because I fucking hate traitors. Because I fucking hate communists. Was it legal? Fuck legal. Am I a nice man? Fuck nice. They say terrible things about me in the *Nation*. Fuck the *Nation*. You want to be Nice, or you want to be Effective? Make the law, or subject to it. Choose. Your wife chose. A week from today, she'll be back. SHE knows how to get what SHE wants. Maybe I ought to send *her* to Washington.

JOE: I don't believe you.

ROY: Gospel.

JOE: You can't possibly mean what you're saying.

Roy, you were the Assistant United States Attorney on the Rosenberg case, ex-parte communication with the judge during the trial would be . . . censurable, at least, probably conspiracy and . . . in a case that resulted in execution, it's . . .

ROY: What? Murder?

JOE: You're not well is all.

ROY: What do you mean, not well? Who's not well?

(*Pause.*)

JOE: You said . . .

ROY: No I didn't. I said what?

JOE: Roy, you have cancer.

ROY: No I don't.

(*Pause.*)

JOE: You told me you were dying.

ROY: What the fuck are you talking about, Joe? I never said that. I'm in perfect health. There's not a goddam thing wrong with me.

(*He smiles.*)

Shake?

(*Joe hesitates. He holds out his hand to Roy. Roy pulls Joe into a close, strong clinch.*)

ROY (*more to himself than to Joe*): It's OK that you hurt me because I love you, baby Joe. That's why I'm so rough on you.

(*Roy releases Joe. Joe backs away a step or two.*)

ROY: Prodigal son. The world will wipe its dirty hands all over you.

JOE: It already has, Roy.

ROY: Now go.

(*Roy shoves Joe, hard. Joe turns to leave. Roy stops him, turns him around.*)

ROY (*smoothing Joe's lapels, tenderly*): I'll always be here, waiting for you . . .
(*Then again, with sudden violence, he pulls Joe close, violently.*)
What did you want from me, what was all this, what do you want, treacherous ungrateful little . . .

(*Joe, very close to belting Roy, grabs him by the front of his robe, and propels him across the length of the room. He holds Roy at arm's length, the other arm ready to hit.*)

ROY (*laughing softly, almost pleading to be hit*): Transgress a little, Joseph.

(*Joe releases Roy.*)

ROY: There are so many laws; find one you can break.

(*Joe hesitates, then leaves, backing out. When Joe has gone, Roy doubles over in great pain, which he's been hiding throughout the scene with Joe.*)

ROY: Ah, Christ . . .
Andy! Andy! Get in here! Andy!

(*The door opens, but it isn't Andy. A small Jewish Woman dressed modestly in a fifties hat and coat stands in the doorway. The room darkens.*)

ROY: Who the fuck are you? The new nurse?

(*The figure in the doorway says nothing. She stares at Roy. A pause. Roy looks at her carefully, gets up, crosses to her. He crosses back to the chair, sits heavily.*)

ROY: Aw, fuck. Ethel.

ETHEL ROSENBERG (*her manner is friendly, her voice is ice-cold*): You don't look good, Roy.

ROY: Well, Ethel. I don't feel good.

ETHEL ROSENBERG: But you lost a lot of weight. That suits you. You were heavy back then. Zaftig, mit hips.

ROY: I haven't been that heavy since 1960. We were all heavier back then, before the body thing started. Now I look like a skeleton. They stare.

ETHEL ROSENBERG: The shit's really hit the fan, huh, Roy?

(*Little pause. Roy nods.*)

ETHEL ROSENBERG: Well the fun's just started.

ROY: What is this, Ethel, Halloween? You trying to scare me?

(*Ethel says nothing.*)

ROY: Well you're wasting your time! I'm scarier than you any day of the week! So beat it, Ethel! BOOO!

BETTER DEAD THAN RED! Somebody trying to shake me up? HAH HAH! From the throne of God in heaven to the belly of hell, you can all fuck yourselves and then go jump in the lake because I'M NOT AFRAID OF YOU OR DEATH OR HELL OR ANYTHING!

ETHEL ROSENBERG: Be seeing you soon, Roy. Julius sends his regards.

ROY: Yeah, well send this to Julius!

(*He flips the bird in her direction, stands and moves towards her. Halfway across the room he slumps to the floor, breathing laboriously, in pain.*)

ETHEL ROSENBERG: You're a very sick man, Roy.

ROY: Oh God . . . ANDY!

Ron Liebman as Roy Cohn in the Broadway production of *Angels in America: Millennium Approaches.*

ETHEL ROSENBERG: Hmmm. He doesn't hear you, I guess. We should call the ambulance.

(*She goes to the phone.*)

Hah! Buttons! Such things they got now. What do I dial, Roy?

(*Pause. Roy looks at her, then:*)

ROY: 911.

ETHEL ROSENBERG (*dials the phone*): It sings!

(*Imitating dial tones.*) La la la . . .

Huh.

Yes, you should please send an ambulance to the home of Mister Roy Cohn, the famous lawyer. What's the address, Roy?

ROY (*a beat, then*): 244 East 87th.

ETHEL ROSENBERG: 244 East 87th Street. No apartment number, he's got the whole building.

My name? (*A beat.*) Ethel Greenglass Rosenberg.

(*Small smile.*) Me? No I'm not related to Mr. Cohn. An old friend.

(*She hangs up.*)

They said a minute.

ROY: I have all the time in the world.

ETHEL ROSENBERG: You're immortal.

ROY: I'm immortal. Ethel. (*He forces himself to stand.*) I have *forced* my way into history. I ain't never gonna die.

ETHEL ROSENBERG (*a little laugh, then*): History is about to crack wide open. Millennium approaches.

Scene 6

(*Late that night. Prior's bedroom. Prior 1 watching Prior in bed, who is staring back at him, terrified. Tonight Prior 1 is dressed in weird alchemical robes*

Scene from the end of *Angels in America: Millennium Approaches.*

and hat over his historical clothing and he carries a long palm-leaf bundle.)

PRIOR 1: Tonight's the night! Aren't you excited? Tonight she arrives! Right through the roof! Ha-adam, Ha-gadol . . .

PRIOR 2 (*appearing, similarly attired*): Lumen! Phosphor! Fluor! Candle! An unending billowing of scarlet and . . .

PRIOR: Look. Garlic. A mirror. Holy water. A crucifix. FUCK OFF! Get the fuck out of my room! GO!

PRIOR 1 (*to Prior 2*): Hard as a hickory knob, I'll bet.

PRIOR 2: We all tumesce when they approach. We wax full, like moons.

PRIOR 1: Dance.

PRIOR: Dance?

PRIOR 1: Stand up, dammit, give us your hands, dance!

PRIOR 2: Listen . . .

(*A lone oboe begins to play a little dance tune.*)

PRIOR 2: Delightful sound. Care to dance?

PRIOR: Please leave me alone, please just let me sleep . . .

PRIOR 2: Ah, he wants someone familiar. A partner who knows his steps. (*To Prior.*) Close your eyes. Imagine . . .

PRIOR: I don't . . .

PRIOR 2: Hush. Close your eyes.

(*Prior does.*)

PRIOR 2: Now open them.

(*Prior does. Louis appears. He looks gorgeous. The music builds gradually into a full-blooded, romantic dance tune.*)

PRIOR: Lou.

LOUIS: Dance with me.

PRIOR: I can't, my leg, it hurts at night . . .
Are you . . . a ghost, Lou?

LOUIS: No. Just spectral. Lost to myself. Sitting all day on cold park benches. Wishing I could be with you. Dance with me, babe . . .

(*Prior stands up. The leg stops hurting. They begin to dance. The music is beautiful.*)

PRIOR 1 (*to Prior 2*): Hah. Now I see why he's got no children. He's a sodomite.

PRIOR 2: Oh be quiet, you medieval gnome, and let them dance.

PRIOR 1: I'm not interfering, I've done my bit. Hooray, hooray, the messenger's come, now I'm blowing off. I don't like it here.

(*Prior 1 vanishes.*)

PRIOR 2: The twentieth century. Oh dear, the world has gotten so terribly, terribly old.

(*Prior 2 vanishes. Louis and Prior waltz happily. Lights fade back to normal. Louis vanishes.*
Prior dances alone.
Then suddenly, the sound of wings fills the room.*)

Scene 7

(*Split scene. Prior alone in his apartment; Louis alone in the park.*
Again, a sound of beating wings.*)

PRIOR: Oh don't come in here don't come in . . . LOUIS!!
No. My name is Prior Walter, I am . . . the scion of an ancient line, I am . . . abandoned I . . . no, my name is . . . is . . . Prior and I live . . . *here and now*, and . . . in the dark, in the dark, the Recording Angel opens its hundred eyes and snaps the spine of the Book of Life and . . . hush! Hush!
I'm talking nonsense, I . . .
No more mad scene, hush, hush.

(*Louis in the park on a bench. Joe approaches, stands at a distance. They stare at each other, then Louis turns away.*)

LOUIS: Do you know the story of Lazarus?

JOE: Lazarus?

LOUIS: Lazarus. I can't remember what happens, exactly.

JOE: I don't. . . . Well, he was dead, Lazarus, and Jesus breathed life into him. He brought him back from death.

LOUIS: Come here often?

JOE: No. Yes. Yes.

LOUIS: Back from the dead. You believe that really happened?

JOE: I don't know anymore what I believe.

LOUIS: This is quite a coincidence. Us meeting.

JOE: I followed you.
From work. I . . . followed you here.

(*Pause.*)

LOUIS: You followed me.
You probably saw me that day in the washroom and thought: there's a sweet guy, sensitive, cries for friends in trouble.

JOE: Yes.

LOUIS: You thought maybe I'll cry for you.

JOE: Yes.

LOUIS: Well I fooled you. Crocodile tears. Nothing . . .
(*He touches his heart, shrugs.*)

(*Joe reaches tentatively to touch Louis's face.*)

LOUIS (*pulling back*): What are you doing? Don't do that.

JOE (*withdrawing his hand*): Sorry. I'm sorry.

LOUIS: I'm . . . just not . . . I think, if you touch me, your hand might fall off or something. Worse things have happened to people who have touched me.

JOE: Please.
Oh, boy . . .
Can I . . .
I . . . want . . . to touch you. Can I please just touch you . . . um, here?
(*He puts his hand on one side of Louis's face. He holds it there.*)
I'm going to hell for doing this.

LOUIS: Big deal. You think it could be any worse than New York City?

(*He puts his hand on Joe's hand. He takes Joe's hand away from his face, holds it for a moment, then:*) Come on.

JOE: Where?

LOUIS: Home. With me.

JOE: This makes no sense. I mean I don't know you.

LOUIS: Likewise.

JOE: And what you do know about me you don't like.

LOUIS: The Republican stuff?

JOE: Yeah, well for starters.

LOUIS: I don't not like that. I *hate* that.

JOE: So why on earth should we . . .

(*Louis goes to Joe and kisses him.*)

LOUIS: Strange bedfellows. I don't know. I never made it with one of the damned before.

I would really rather not have to spend tonight alone.

JOE: I'm a pretty terrible person, Louis.

LOUIS: Lou.

JOE: No, I really really am. I don't think I deserve being loved.

LOUIS: There? See? We already have a lot in common.

(*Louis stands, begins to walk away. He turns, looks back at Joe. Joe follows. They exit.*)

(*Prior listens. At first no sound, then once again, the sound of beating wings, frighteningly near.*)

PRIOR: That sound, that sound, it . . . . What is that, like birds or something, like a *really* big bird, I'm frightened, I . . . no, no fear, find the anger, find the . . . anger, my blood is clean, my brain is fine, I can handle pressure, I am a gay man and I am used to pressure, to trouble, I am tough and strong and . . . . Oh. Oh my goodness. I . . . (*He is washed over by an intense sexual feeling.*) Ooohhhh. . . . I'm hot, I'm . . . so . . . aw Jeez what is going on here I . . . must have a fever I . . .

(*The bedside lamp flickers wildly as the bed begins to roll forward and back. There is a deep bass creaking and groaning from the bedroom ceiling, like the timbers of a ship under immense stress, and from above a fine rain of plaster dust.*)

PRIOR: OH!

PLEASE, OH PLEASE! Something's coming in here, I'm scared, I don't like this at all, something's approaching and I . . . . OH!

(*There is a great blaze of triumphal music, heralding. The light turns an extraordinary harsh, cold, pale blue, then a rich, brilliant warm golden color, then a hot, bilious green, and then finally a spectacular royal purple. Then silence.*)

PRIOR (*an awestruck whisper*): God almighty . . .
Very Steven Spielberg.

(*A sound, like a plummeting meteor, tears down from very, very far above the earth, hurtling at an incredible velocity towards the bedroom; the light seems to be sucked out of the room as the projectile approaches; as the room reaches darkness, we hear a terrifying CRASH as something immense strikes earth; the whole building shudders and a part of the bedroom ceiling, lots of plaster and lathe and wiring, crashes to the floor. And then in a shower of unearthly white light, spreading great opalescent gray-silver wings, the Angel descends into the room and floats above the bed.*)

ANGEL: Greetings, Prophet;
The Great Work begins:
The Messenger has arrived.

(*Blackout.*)

COMMENTARY

ANDREA BERNSTEIN

Interview with Tony Kushner   1995

Andrea Bernstein, a freelance cultural critic, engaged Tony Kushner in a discussion of the politics in his plays. Kushner's responses to her questions establish his credentials as a left-thinking critic of contemporary political life. His discussion of his work is centered much more in political reality than it is in dramatic technique or concern for theater. Yet Kushner is able to zero in on the dramatic moment and present contemporary politics as a dialectical struggle.

Tony Kushner, a gay Jewish socialist who was raised in Louisiana, won a Pulitzer Prize and two Tony Awards for his two-part, seven-hour Broadway production of *Angels in America: A Gay Fantasia on National Themes.* Other plays, *A Bright Room Called Day* (1985) and *Slavs!* (1994), are also concerned with the moral responsibilities of people in politically repressive times. Such concerns may be especially relevant in America today, where, as he observes: "What used to be called liberal is now called radical, what used to be called radical is now called insane, what used to be called reactionary is now called moderate, and what used to be called insane is now called solid conservative thinking."

Q: *Angels in America* opened on Broadway just months after the Clinton inauguration. It ends with a very hopeful speech about healing. Do you still feel that hope?

A: You have to have hope. It's irresponsible to give *false* hope, which I think a lot of playwrights are guilty of. But I also think it's irresponsible to simply be a nihilist, which quite a lot of playwrights, especially playwrights younger than me, have become guilty of. I don't believe you would bother to write a play if you really had no hope. That passage was one of the very first things I ever wrote when I was working on *Angels.* I read it to the woman who I was originally writing the part of the angel for, who died of breast cancer before the play was finished. In one of my last conversations with her, she told me that she thought about that image a lot and that she hoped I would include it in the play. I think I wouldn't have included it otherwise, but I'm glad I did now.

Q: *Angels in America* was a political play—and that's something Americans and critics frequently resist. How did you overcome that resistance?

A: What I found in the audience response is a huge hunger for political issues and political discussion. So I always wonder: Is it that Americans don't like politics, or is it that so much theater that is political isn't well done? One of the things I learned in *Slavs!* is that it's much easier to talk about being gay than it is to talk about being a socialist. People are afraid of socialism, and plays that deal with economics are scarier to them. I'll learn more about that—my next three plays are all about money.

Also, *Angels* is very entertaining. It does things formally that are new, and people were excited by the size and the scope. It's a good play and that makes all the difference.

Thelma and Louise, for instance, is a really terrific movie, and genuinely left in its political sensibilities. It's well-made, so the fact that it is unquestionably coming from a feminist perspective didn't make it absolutely marginal the way you would expect such a film to be. It had guns—that probably helped.

Q: People loved *Forrest Gump,* too.

A: People shouldn't trust artists and they shouldn't trust art. Part of the fun of art is that it invites you to interpret it.

There's a very complicated relationship between form and content and between aesthetics and politics. Good politics will produce good aesthetics, really good politics will produce really good aesthetics, and really good aesthetics, if somebody's really asking the hard questions and answering them honestly, they'll probably produce truth, which is to say progressive politics.

Q: Is it hard to write characters that are not caricatures and to overcome the barrier that people have about listening to politics from a character on stage?

A: I think that a character's politics have to live in the same sort of relationship to the character's psyche that people's politics live in relationship to their own psyches. People are never consistent. People will always do surprising things, both good and bad, and the way that people surprise themselves and their audience are the most interesting moments of human behavior. The space between what we'd like to be and what we actually are is where you find out the most interesting things.

Q: Do you see your plays as part of a political movement?

A: I do. I would hate to write anything that wasn't. I would like my plays to be of use to progressive people. I think preaching to the converted is exactly what art ought to do.

I am happiest when people who are politically engaged in the world say, "Your play meant a lot to me; it helped me think about something, or made me feel like I wasn't the only person who felt this way."

It's the way you feel when you go to a demo, which is the only way to keep sane a lot of the time. You need to remind yourself there are many bodies who are as angry about something as you are.

When I teach writing, I always tell my students you should assume that the audience you're writing for is smarter than you. You can't write if you don't think they're on your side, because then you start to yell at them or preach down to them.

Q: The character Prelapsarianov—the "world's oldest living Bolshevik"—gives the same speech in both *Angels* and *Slavs!*: "How are we to proceed without theory? Is it enough to reject the past, is it wise to move forward in this blind fashion, without the cold brilliant light of theory to guide the way? . . . You who live in this sour little age cannot imagine the sheer grandeur of the prospect we gazed upon."

A: In both *Perestroika* [part two of *Angels*] and *Slavs!*, the whole play proceeds from the question: If you don't know where you're going, can you move? And do you even have a choice, or do you just dive in and work it out as you're going?

That speech came out of a fight I had with my friend Oskar Eustis about Gorbachev. Oskar's point, which became the basis of Prelapsarianov's speech, is that if you don't have a theory to start with—Gorbachev pretended to be about democratic socialism but actually sort of was and sort of wasn't; he was also sort of about preserving the Communist Party power elite—what do you do? It's one of those big conundrums.

Q: So what *do* you do?

A: You can't stay back. The fundamental question is: Are we made by history or do we make history—and the answer is yes. I was rereading Marx's *Eighteenth Brumaire of Louis Bonaparte* recently. The whole tradition in socialist struggle is looking to the past for an antecedent form upon which the present revolutionary response is to be modeled. We may need to stop doing that.

Q: Why does the play *Slavs!* end with the question: "What is to be done?"

A: I wanted someone to ask the question: What if this really is the end of history? What if there really is literally nothing to be done, and we're simply stuck with capitalism—although I don't really think it is a possibility.

I still believe in a dialectical ordering of the universe. There is a dynamic principle at work—it isn't always mechanically moving things toward the good, but there's always either some sort of progress or decay. And there's too much misery in the world. That is not something that can hold.

Q: What do you think is to be done?

A: I'm 38 now. One of the painful rites of passage that everyone on the left goes through is to realize it's a lifelong struggle. What we're dealing with from Nixon on as a counter-reaction to the '60s is a very widespread, long-term historical trend. It's going to take many years and probably a few decades to reverse. People need to be willing to take an issue that they feel passionately about, address themselves to it as extensively as they are capable of and build common cause between issue groups.

Everybody on the left needs to start talking about how to create, first on local levels and eventually on a national level, a third party or at least a party that could establish some kind of position in Congress. That's the eternal dream of the left.

Q: You think there's no hope for revitalizing the Democratic Party?

A: It's a waste of time at this point. There's a famous story about Paul Wellstone refusing to shake Jesse Helms' hand and being chastised by everyone in the Senate because he wouldn't do it—he was told this is a gentlemen's club where we're all colleagues. That's what's wrong.

Q: One of the characters in *A Bright Room Called Day* keeps saying—as Nazism progressively snatches power and the Weimar Republic falls—that each turn for the worse would be the essential spur for people to rise up and oppose fascism. That didn't happen. Do you see parallels today?

A: You don't want to be opportunistic about it and say, "Oh, goody, millions of people are going to be thrown out of their homes—now we'll really get things cooking." It's like people saying the AIDS epidemic helped organize the gay and lesbian community.

Q: Speaking of which, there's a lot of discussion now about the second wave of the AIDS epidemic, and about gay men not practicing safer sex. Where do you weigh in?

A: It's very difficult to ask people to abstain from pleasure indefinitely, especially sexual erotic pleasure, which is so incredibly important to human beings and the enjoyment of which among homosexuals is so much of a political battlefield. There is absolutely no question that safer sex is not as gratifying and that given all the despair and the unbelievably imponderable weight of loss that the community has had to deal with, self-destructive behaviors are going to be engaged in.

Q: Do you think the gay community should be discussing this publicly?

A: Of course it's going to be discussed publicly. But you have to be smart. When you make a public utterance you are responsible for being responsible. We're still an embattled community, and if you're stupid about it you'll give aid to the enemy.

Q: Do you have that conundrum as a playwright?

A: You have to say: What am I feeding into? I think you should ask yourself that question and then make the decision based on the answers you come up with. I regret having made the only black person in *Angels* a nurse; that was an inept thing to do.

I was very scared about writing a play where there's a couple, one has AIDS and the other walks out. I thought, this is transgressive and scary and am I going to become public enemy number one in the gay community for having written a character like Louis?

On the other hand, you have to be willing to scare the horses. You have to be interesting and you have to be daring and you have to be willing to write things that shock. Shock is part of art. Art that's polite is not much fun.

Tom Stoppard

Tom Stoppard (b. 1937) was born in Czechoslovakia, but because of World War II he began a remarkable journey that ended eventually in immigration to England. To avoid the Nazis, his parents, Martha and Eugen Straussler, both Jewish, were relocated by Eugen's employer to Singapore in 1939. Tom's father, a medical doctor volunteering with the British forces, died when the Japanese invaded, but Tom and his mother found their way to Darjeeling, India. Stoppard's mother married an English major, Kenneth Stoppard, and in 1946 the family moved to Bristol, England, where Tom went to school and where English became his first language.

Instead of going on to university, in 1954 Stoppard became a journalist, writing columns and freelancing, before beginning to write short plays in 1960. For a time he became a London theater critic; he managed to see more than one hundred plays in seven months. His first major playwriting success was a one-act version of *Rosencrantz and Guildenstern Are Dead* (1966), which premiered in a minor space at the Edinburgh Fringe Festival, where its importance was recognized by an influential critic. Its subsequent performance at the Old Vic in London established Stoppard as a major playwright. Like most of his plays, it is filled with witty dialogue and contains many allusions to literature and literary figures.

Many of the plays that followed are performed regularly in university and provincial theaters as well as in commercial revivals. *The Real Inspector Hound* (1968), *After Magritte* (1970), *Jumpers* (1972), and *Travesties* (1974) are all successful plays. *Travesties* imagines the interactions among three historical figures who were living in Zurich in 1917: James Joyce, Tristan Tzara, and Vladimir Lenin. The dialogue among these characters centers on art and politics, but the play maintains a high comic profile. It has been revived frequently over the years.

Stoppard has said that much about playwriting is uncomfortable for him. He most enjoys writing dialogue and least enjoys writing plot. For that reason he has adapted a number of works, such as *On the Razzle* (1981), adapted from a play by Viennese writer Johann Nestroy (1801–1862), and *Dalliance* (1986), adapted from a play by Arthur Schnitzler (1862–1931). *On the Razzle* premiered at the Strand Theatre in London as a high-voltage comic romp featuring Felicity Kendal, a well-known actor on the British stage. She also starred in *The Real Thing* (1982), an original and brilliantly complicated play in which characters play themselves but also play actors whose roles resemble their own real-life roles. *The Real Thing* was successful on Broadway in 1984 with Glenn Close and Jeremy Irons, who both won Tony Awards for best actor. The theme of infidelity may have reflected issues in Stoppard's own life, since his affair with Felicity Kendal later ended his twenty-year marriage. The merging of the real and the artistic worlds is almost irresistible to Stoppard, whose work is frequently philosophical and intellectual.

Stoppard is also noted for his numerous television scripts and his radio plays, one of which, *In the Native State* (1991), became a stage play, *Indian Ink* (1995), about the end of the British empire. He wrote the screenplays for several enormously popular films, such as *Brazil* (1985), *Empire of the Sun* (1987), *The Russia House* (1990), and *Shakespeare in Love* (1998).

Arcadia (1993), probably Stoppard's best play, has been critically praised for Stoppard's ability to merge the intellectual with the emotional. *Arcadia*'s characters inhabit two worlds, the world of historical time and the world of the present. The audience's level of awareness of the eventual outcome of the hopes of the historical characters contrasts with that of the present-day researchers, who study the clues left behind in 1809.

Stoppard again demonstrated his ability to integrate the intellectual qualities of his drama with the emotional effects on his audience in *The Invention of Love* (1997), which tells the story of the poet and classical scholar A. E. Housman, who begins the play as a dead man standing by the river Styx, waiting for Charon the boatman to ferry him to the Underworld. While he waits, he imagines scenes from his life as an Oxford undergraduate and later as a don, or teacher. His central concern is his unrequited love for a classmate, Moses Jackson, and while he thinks of him and other people he knew, Housman quotes important Latin poets and writers whose work casts light on his own life. *The Invention of Love* won prestigious awards in both London and New York.

The Coast of Utopia (2002) includes three plays: *Voyage, Shipwreck,* and *Salvage.* The nine-hour trilogy is set in Russia during 1833–1866, a period filled with political uncertainty and great change. By 1861 the serfs had been given their freedom and the future of the Russian aristocracy was in doubt. These three plays are essentially philosophical dialogues—or debates—about the future of Russia. *The Coast of Utopia* was given lukewarm reviews in London, but when it came to Broadway in 2007 it was nominated for ten Tony Awards and won seven, setting a record at that time.

Stoppard, knighted by Queen Elizabeth II, continues to be a major figure in modern drama.

For links to resources about Stoppard, click on *AuthorLinks* at **bedfordstmartins.com/jacobus**.

Arcadia

Arcadia is filled with doublings and contrasts of many sorts—of time, of setting, of characters, and of ideas. The play takes place in two time periods, 1809 and the present, in the same room at Sidley Park, an English country estate. Characters such as Thomasina and Septimus in 1809 parallel Hannah and Bernard in the present. Science, in the person of Valentine, contrasts with liberal arts in the persons of Bernard and Hannah; however, in 1809 science and art were much less exclusive of each other, and they merge in Septimus and Thomasina. Classicism and Romanticism are among the scholarly concerns of the modern characters, while Newtonian determinism and the obvious, to Thomasina, effects of chaos and entropy interest the nineteenth-century characters. When Thomasina demonstrates by mixing her jam with her rice pudding that the process goes in only one direction—the jam cannot be un-mixed—Septimus reminds her that time goes in only one direction. Yet Stoppard undoes this idea by having us move forward in time in scenes 1 and 2 and then backward in time in scene 3. It is not until scene 7 that characters from 1809 and the present are on the set at the same time and, unaware of each other, behave like jam swirling into rice pudding, almost melding with each other.

Entropy, the measure of randomness in a system, shows up in Thomasina's understanding that the steam engine being used to landscape Sidley Park cannot put out as much energy as it consumes. Such an insight demonstrates her precocity; Thomasina's mother already thinks she is over-educated for her age, making her almost ineligible for marriage. Thomasina realizes that, like tea, which cannot stay heated, we ourselves will all sometime revert to "room temperature," thus illustrating entropy. Thomasina's extraordinary promise, in addition to her innocence, endears her to the audience.

The play begins appropriately with a lesson in mathematics that soon turns to a discussion of a "carnal embrace," for which Thomasina demands an explanation. Septimus dodges the question at first, but then learns that the servants have spread the word about his own carnal involvement with Mrs. Chater, wife of a poet whose work Septimus has panned in an obscure journal. Thus, he must provide a bit of unintended sex education for his student, who at the end of the play is clearly in love with him. What we learn later is that the mathematics that Thomasina is working with on her own is revolutionary in that it proposes a feedback system, another form of doubling, that—when computers perform the task today—produces images of a fractal geometry. One such famous image is that of a leaf, represented in the play by the leaf attached to an apple. Thomasina promises to "plot the leaf and deduce its equation."

The apple itself implies Arcadia, the classical idea of the perfect natural world, a form of paradise similar to Eden, in which an apple figures importantly. The Arcadian world is represented by Sidley Park, the Croom estate, which in 1809 is being reshaped into the picturesque style by the landscaper Noakes with ruins, romantic grottoes, a hermitage, and a ha ha (a ditch designed to keep cows off the park-like lawns). Lady Croom says that Sidley Park is "nature as God intended." Prior to Noakes, Lancelot "Capability" Brown had planned the landscape in a form consistent with the Age of Reason, which rejected complicated gardens, patterned plantings, and many of the artificial effects of an earlier age while promoting a clear, more natural setting for a home. Lady Croom alludes to Poussin's painting showing shepherds uncovering a tombstone marked "Et in Arcadia Ego," which translates as "I [meaning Death] am also in Arcadia." Lady Croom happily mistranslates it: "I can say with the painter . . . 'Here I am in Arcadia.'"

A visit by Lord Byron, the great Romantic poet, to Sidley Park recorded in the Game Book adds a special dimension to the world of 1809 in the play. When the poet Chater demands satisfaction from Septimus for the offense against his wife, we discover that Byron also enjoyed Mrs. Chater's favors and might himself have been called to account. While death threatened to appear in Arcadia in the form of a duel that did not occur despite the appearance of the dueling pistols, it definitely did arrive later when Thomasina died in a fire before she turned seventeen. The discovery of this event is one source of the emotional response that informs the audience late in the play.

Bernard Nightingale, the don (or university lecturer), arrives in Sidley Park seeking an opportunity to make a discovery that will improve his reputation. He examines the evidence that he and Hannah, a novelist and landscape historian with an interest in the Romantic age, have found in going through the holdings of the estate. Stoppard alludes to scholars reading books, manuscripts, and letters in the holdings of aristocratic households throughout England and takes the opportunity to inject a bit of satire. That Bernard is something of a peacock is underlined by his holding a letter from Thomas Love Peacock (1785–1866) and alluding to *Headlong Hall* (1815), a novel that ironically echoes many of the details of Stoppard's *Arcadia*.

Because the audience has seen Ezra Chater, Septimus, and Captain Brice and knows that Brice took the Chaters off to Martinique, Stoppard is able to have a great deal of fun by letting the audience watch Bernard and Hannah argue, citing dates, letters, reviews, and their own suppositions, about whether or not Lord Byron fled England in 1809 because he had killed a rival poet. Bernard is so certain of his reasoning that he publishes his findings and has the experience of seeing headlines in the papers celebrating his "discovery." Only then does he realize, on the basis of Hannah's reading from the garden books of Lady Croom, that Ezra Chater died from being bitten by a monkey in Martinique, not from being hit by a bullet in Sidley Park.

Earlier, Valentine's speech that "from Newton's laws you could predict everything to come" becomes a comment on Bernard's presumption that things must have happened as he thought. But the chaos theories that Thomasina had earlier proposed were actually in effect. It seemed as if Chater had fought a duel, and it seemed as if Byron had killed him, but "everything including us is just a lot of atoms bouncing off each other like billiard balls" and there was no way for Bernard to know the truth without, as he said, "being there."

For discussion questions and assignments on *Arcadia*, visit bedfordstmartins.com/jacobus.

Arcadia in Performance

The first performance of *Arcadia* was directed by Trevor Nunn in London's National Theatre in April 1993, with Felicity Kendal as Hannah and Bill Nighy as Bernard. The success of the play was almost instant. The National Theatre Bookshop was said to have sold 6,000 copies of the play in the first three weeks of performance, something never achieved before. In the following spring, the play transferred to the Haymarket, one of the largest theaters in London's West End. In total, it ran for 431 performances. The reviews, with only a few exceptions, were enthusiastic, many calling this Stoppard's best play and most praising him for adding an emotional quotient to his usually intellectual productions. The play won the 1994 Olivier Award for best play. The first New York production was in 1995 at the Vivian Beaumont Theater in Lincoln Center, with Billy Crudup as Septimus and Victor Garber as Bernard. David Leveaux directed the London revival in 2009 at the Duke of York's Theatre, then directed the Broadway revival at the Ethel Barrymore Theatre in New York in March 2011. The production was well reviewed and was nominated for a Tony for best revival of a play.

TOM STOPPARD (b. 1937)

Arcadia 1993

Characters

(in order of appearance)

THOMASINA COVERLY, *aged thirteen, later sixteen*
SEPTIMUS HODGE, *her tutor, aged twenty-two,*
    later twenty-five
JELLABY, *a butler, middle-aged*
EZRA CHATER, *a poet, aged thirty-one*
RICHARD NOAKES, *a landscape architect,*
    middle-aged
LADY CROOM, *middle thirties*
CAPT. BRICE, RN, *middle thirties*
HANNAH JARVIS, *an author, late thirties*
CHLOË COVERLY, *aged eighteen*
BERNARD NIGHTINGALE, *a don, late thirties*
VALENTINE COVERLY, *aged twenty-five to thirty*
GUS COVERLY, *aged fifteen*
AUGUSTUS COVERLY, *aged fifteen*

ACT ONE • Scene One

A room on the garden front of a very large country house in Derbyshire in April 1809. Nowadays, the house would be called a stately home. The upstage wall is mainly tall, shapely, uncurtained windows, one or more of which work as doors. Nothing much need be said or seen of the exterior beyond. We come to learn that the house stands in the typical English park of the time. Perhaps we see an indication of this, perhaps only light and air and sky.

    The room looks bare despite the large table which occupies the centre of it. The table, the straight-backed chairs and, the only other item of furniture, the architect's stand or reading stand, would all be collectable pieces now but here, on an uncarpeted wood floor, they have no more pretension than a schoolroom, which is indeed the main use of this room at this time. What elegance there is, is architectural, and nothing is impressive but the scale. There is a door in each of the side walls. These are closed, but one of the French windows is open to a bright but sunless morning.

    There are two people, each busy with books and paper and pen and ink, separately occupied. The pupil is Thomasina Coverly, aged 13. The tutor is Septimus Hodge, aged 22. Each has an open book. Hers is a slim mathematics primer. His is a handsome thick quarto, brand new, a vanity production, with little tapes to tie when the book is closed. His loose papers, etc. are kept in a stiff-backed portfolio which also ties up with tapes.

    Septimus has a tortoise which is sleepy enough to serve as a paperweight.

    Elsewhere on the table there is an old-fashioned theodolite° and also some other books stacked up.

THOMASINA: Septimus, what is carnal embrace?
SEPTIMUS: Carnal embrace is the practice of throwing one's arms around a side of beef.
THOMASINA: Is that all?
SEPTIMUS: No . . . a shoulder of mutton, a haunch of venison well hugged, an embrace of grouse . . . *caro, carnis;* feminine; flesh.
THOMASINA: Is it a sin?
SEPTIMUS: Not necessarily, my lady, but when carnal embrace is sinful it is a sin of the flesh, QED. We had *caro* in our Gallic Wars—'The Britons live on milk and meat'—'*lacte et carne vivunt*'. I am sorry that the seed fell on stony ground.
THOMASINA: That was the sin of Onan,° wasn't it, Septimus?
SEPTIMUS: Yes. He was giving his brother's wife a Latin lesson and she was hardly the wiser after it than before. I thought you were finding a proof for Fermat's last theorem.°
THOMASINA: It is very difficult, Septimus. You will have to show me how.
SEPTIMUS: If I knew how, there would be no need to ask *you.* Fermat's last theorem has kept people busy for a hundred and fifty years, and I hoped it would keep *you* busy long enough for me to read Mr Chater's poem in praise of love with only the distraction of its own absurdities.
THOMASINA: Our Mr Chater has written a poem?
SEPTIMUS: He believes he has written a poem, yes. I can see that there might be more carnality in your algebra than in Mr Chater's 'Couch of Eros'.°
THOMASINA: Oh, it was not my algebra. I heard Jellaby telling cook that Mrs Chater was discovered in carnal embrace in the gazebo.

---

theodolite: Surveying instrument. **Onan:** In Genesis 38:8–10, Onan refused carnal embrace with his brother's widow and "spilled his seed." **Fermat's last theorem:** The last theorem of Pierre de Fermat (1601–1665), a French lawyer and mathematician, was proved in 1993. **Eros:** Venus, classical goddess of love.

SEPTIMUS: (*Pause*) Really? With whom, did Jellaby happen to say?

(*Thomasina considers this with a puzzled frown.*)

THOMASINA: What do you mean, with whom?

SEPTIMUS: With what? Exactly so. The idea is absurd. Where did this story come from?

THOMASINA: Mr Noakes.

SEPTIMUS: Mr Noakes!

THOMASINA: Papa's landskip gardener. He was taking bearings in the garden when he saw—through his spyglass—Mrs Chater in the gazebo in carnal embrace.

SEPTIMUS: And do you mean to tell me that Mr Noakes told the butler?

THOMASINA: No. Mr Noakes told Mr Chater. *Jellaby* was told by the groom, who overheard Mr Noakes telling Mr Chater, in the stable yard.

SEPTIMUS: Mr Chater being engaged in closing the stable door.

THOMASINA: What do you mean, Septimus?

SEPTIMUS: So, thus far, the only people who know about this are Mr Noakes the landskip architect, the groom, the butler, the cook and, of course, Mrs Chater's husband, the poet.

THOMASINA: And Arthur who was cleaning the silver, and the bootboy. And now you.

SEPTIMUS: Of course. What else did he say?

THOMASINA: Mr Noakes?

SEPTIMUS: No, not Mr Noakes. Jellaby. You heard Jellaby telling the cook.

THOMASINA: Cook hushed him almost as soon as he started. Jellaby did not see that I was being allowed to finish yesterday's upstairs' rabbit pie before I came to my lesson. I think you have not been candid with me, Septimus. A gazebo is not, after all, a meat larder.

SEPTIMUS: I never said my definition was complete.

THOMASINA: Is carnal embrace kissing?

SEPTIMUS: Yes.

THOMASINA: And throwing one's arms around Mrs Chater?

SEPTIMUS: Yes. Now, Fermat's last theorem—

THOMASINA: I thought as much. I hope you are ashamed.

SEPTIMUS: I, my lady?

THOMASINA: If *you* do not teach me the true meaning of things, who will?

SEPTIMUS: Ah. Yes, I am ashamed. Carnal embrace is sexual congress, which is the insertion of the male genital organ into the female genital organ for purposes of procreation and pleasure. Fermat's last theorem, by contrast, asserts that when x, y and z are whole numbers each raised to power of n, the sum of the first two can never equal the third when n is greater than 2.

(*Pause.*)

THOMASINA: Eurghhh!

SEPTIMUS: Nevertheless, that is the theorem.

THOMASINA: It is disgusting and incomprehensible. Now when I am grown to practise it myself I shall never do so without thinking of you.

SEPTIMUS: Thank you very much, my lady. Was Mrs Chater down this morning?

THOMASINA: No. Tell me more about sexual congress.

SEPTIMUS: There is nothing more to be said about sexual congress.

THOMASINA: Is it the same as love?

SEPTIMUS: Oh no, it is much nicer than that.

(*One of the side doors leads to the music room. It is the other side door which now opens to admit Jellaby, the butler.*)

I am teaching, Jellaby.

JELLABY: Beg your pardon, Mr Hodge, Mr Chater said it was urgent you receive his letter.

SEPTIMUS: Oh, very well. (*Septimus takes the letter.*) Thank you. (*And to dismiss Jellaby.*) Thank you.

JELLABY: (*Holding his ground*) Mr Chater asked me to bring him your answer.

SEPTIMUS: My answer?

(*He opens the letter. There is no envelope as such, but there is a 'cover' which, folded and sealed, does the same service. Septimus tosses the cover negligently aside and reads.*)

Well, my answer is that as is my custom and my duty to his lordship I am engaged until a quarter to twelve in the education of his daughter. When I am done, and if Mr Chater is still there, I will be happy to wait upon him in—(*he checks the letter*)—in the gunroom.

JELLABY: I will tell him so, thank you, sir.

(*Septimus folds the letter and places it between the pages of 'The Couch of Eros'.*)

THOMASINA: What is for dinner, Jellaby?

JELLABY: Boiled ham and cabbages, my lady, and a rice pudding.

THOMASINA: Oh, goody.

(*Jellaby leaves.*)

SEPTIMUS: Well, so much for Mr Noakes. He puts himself forward as a gentleman, a philosopher of the picturesque, a visionary who can move mountains and cause lakes, but in the scheme of the garden he is as the serpent.

THOMASINA: When you stir your rice pudding, Septimus, the spoonful of jam spreads itself round making red trails like the picture of a meteor in my astronomical atlas. But if you stir backward, the jam will not come together again. Indeed, the pudding does not notice and continues to turn pink just as before. Do you think this is odd?

SEPTIMUS: No.

THOMASINA: Well, I do. You cannot stir things apart.

SEPTIMUS: No more you can, time must needs run backward, and since it will not, we must stir our way onward mixing as we go, disorder out of disorder into disorder until pink is complete, unchanging and unchangeable, and we are done with it for ever. This is known as free will or self-determination.

(*He picks up the tortoise and moves it a few inches as though it had strayed, on top of some loose papers, and admonishes it.*)

Sit!

THOMASINA: Septimus, do you think God is a Newtonian?°

SEPTIMUS: An Etonian?° Almost certainly, I'm afraid. We must ask your brother to make it his first enquiry.

THOMASINA: No, Septimus, a Newtonian. Septimus! Am I the first person to have thought of this?

SEPTIMUS: No.

THOMASINA: I have not said yet.

SEPTIMUS: 'If everything from the furthest planet to the smallest atom of our brain acts according to Newton's law of motion, what becomes of free will?'

THOMASINA: No.

SEPTIMUS: God's will.

THOMASINA: No.

SEPTIMUS: Sin.

THOMASINA: (*Derisively*) No!

SEPTIMUS: Very well.

THOMASINA: If you could stop every atom in its position and direction, and if your mind could comprehend all the actions thus suspended, then if you were really, *really* good at algebra you could write the formula for all the future; and although nobody can be so clever as to do it, the formula must exist just as if one could.

SEPTIMUS: (*Pause*) Yes. (*Pause.*) Yes, as far as I know, you are the first person to have thought of this. (*Pause. With an effort.*) In the margin of his copy of *Arithmetica*, Fermat wrote that he had discovered a wonderful proof of his theorem but, the margin being too narrow for his purpose, did not have room to write it down. The note was found after his death, and from that day to this—

THOMASINA: Oh! I see now! The answer is perfectly obvious.

SEPTIMUS: This time you may have overreached yourself.

(*The door is opened, somewhat violently. Chater enters.*)

Mr Chater! Perhaps my message miscarried. I will be at liberty at a quarter to twelve, if that is convenient.

CHATER: It is not convenient, sir. My business will not wait.

SEPTIMUS: Then I suppose you have Lord Croom's opinion that your business is more important than his daughter's lesson.

CHATER: I do not, but, if you like, I will ask his lordship to settle the point.

SEPTIMUS: (*Pause*) My lady, take Fermat into the music room. There will be an extra spoonful of jam if you find his proof.

THOMASINA: There is no proof, Septimus. The thing that is perfectly obvious is that the note in the margin was a joke to make you all mad.

(*Thomasina leaves.*)

SEPTIMUS: Now, sir, what is this business that cannot wait?

CHATER: I think you know it, sir. You have insulted my wife.

SEPTIMUS: Insulted her? That would deny my nature, my conduct, and the admiration in which I hold Mrs Chater.

CHATER: I have heard of your admiration, sir! You insulted my wife in the gazebo yesterday evening!

SEPTIMUS: You are mistaken. I made love to your wife in the gazebo. She asked me to meet her there, I have her note somewhere, I dare say I could find it for you, and if someone is putting it about that I did not turn up, by God, sir, it is a slander.

CHATER: You damned lecher! You would drag down a lady's reputation to make a refuge for your cowardice. It will not do! I am calling you out!

SEPTIMUS: Chater! Chater, Chater, Chater! My dear friend!

CHATER: You dare to call me that. I demand satisfaction!

SEPTIMUS: Mrs Chater demanded satisfaction and now you are demanding satisfaction. I cannot spend my time day and night satisfying the demands of the Chater family. As for your wife's reputation, it stands where it ever stood.

CHATER: You blackguard!

SEPTIMUS: I assure you. Mrs Chater is charming and spirited, with a pleasing voice and a dainty step, she is the epitome of all the qualities society applauds in her sex—and yet her chief renown is for a readiness that keeps her in a state of tropical humidity as would grow orchids in her drawers in January.

CHATER: Damn you, Hodge, I will not listen to this! Will you fight or not?

SEPTIMUS: (*Definitively*) Not! There are no more than two or three poets of the first rank now living, and I will not shoot one of them dead over a perpendicular poke in a gazebo with a woman whose reputation could not be adequately defended with a platoon of musketry deployed by rota.

CHATER: Ha! You say so! Who are the others? In your opinion?—no—no—!—this goes very ill, Hodge. I will not be flattered out of my course. You say so, do you?

SEPTIMUS: I do. And I would say the same to Milton° were he not already dead. Not the part about his wife, of course—

Newtonian: Thomasina is referring to the laws of motion of Isaac Newton (1642–1727), an English scientist whose physics and mathematics dominated science for 300 years. **Etonian:** Eton is one of England's most prestigious secondary schools, as is Harrow.

Milton: John Milton (1608–1674), author of *Paradise Lost*; the mention of Milton here is an indirect allusion to the Garden of Eden.

CHATER: But among the living? Mr Southey?°

SEPTIMUS: Southey I would have shot on sight.

CHATER: (*Shaking his head sadly*) Yes, he has fallen off. I admired 'Thalaba' *quite*, but 'Madoc', (*he chuckles*) oh dear me!—but we are straying from the business here—you took advantage of Mrs Chater, and if that were not bad enough, it appears every stableboy and scullery maid on the strength—

SEPTIMUS: Damn me! Have you not listened to a word I said?

CHATER: I have heard you, sir, and I will not deny I welcome your regard, God knows one is little appreciated if one stands outside the coterie of hacks and placemen who surround Jeffrey° and the *Edinburgh*—

SEPTIMUS: My dear Chater, they judge a poet by the seating plan of Lord Holland's table!

CHATER: By heaven, you are right! And I would very much like to know the name of the scoundrel who slandered my verse drama 'The Maid of Turkey' in the *Piccadilly Recreation*, too!

SEPTIMUS: 'The Maid of Turkey'! I have it by my bedside! When I cannot sleep I take up 'The Maid of Turkey' like an old friend!

CHATER: (*Gratified*) There you are! And the scoundrel wrote he would not give it to his dog for dinner were it covered in bread sauce and stuffed with chestnuts. When Mrs Chater read that, she wept, sir, and would not give herself to me for a fortnight—which recalls me to my purpose—

SEPTIMUS: The new poem, however, will make your name perpetual—

CHATER: Whether it do or not—

SEPTIMUS: It is not a question, sir. No coterie can oppose the acclamation of the reading public. 'The Couch of Eros' will take the town.

CHATER: Is that your estimation?

SEPTIMUS: It is my intent.

CHATER: Is it, is it? Well, well! I do not understand you.

SEPTIMUS: You see I have an early copy—sent to me for review. I say review, but I speak of an extensive appreciation of your gifts and your rightful place in English literature.

CHATER: Well, I must say. That is certainly . . . You have written it?

SEPTIMUS: (*Crisply*) Not yet.

CHATER: Ah. And how long does . . . ?

SEPTIMUS: To be done right, it first requires a careful rereading of your book, of both your books, several readings, together with outlying works for an exhibition of deference or disdain as the case merits. I make notes, of course, I order my thoughts, and finally, when all is ready and I am *calm in my mind* . . .

CHATER: (*Shrewdly*) Did Mrs Chater know of this before she—before you—

SEPTIMUS: I think she very likely did.

Mr Southey: Robert Southey (1774–1843), minor Romantic poet and critic. **Jeffrey:** Francis Jeffrey (1773–1850), strict critic of the Romantics and founder of the *Edinburgh Review*.

CHATER: (*Triumphantly*) There is nothing that woman would not do for me! Now you have an insight to her character. Yes, by God, she is a wife to me, sir!

SEPTIMUS: For that alone, I would not make her a widow.

CHATER: Captain Brice once made the same observation!

SEPTIMUS: Captain Brice did?

CHATER: Mr Hodge, allow me to inscribe your copy in happy anticipation. Lady Thomasina's pen will serve us.

SEPTIMUS: Your connection with Lord and Lady Croom you owe to your fighting her ladyship's brother?

CHATER: No! It was all nonsense, sir—a canard! But a fortunate mistake, sir. It brought me the patronage of a captain of His Majesty's Navy and the brother of a countess. I do not think Mr Walter Scott can say as much, and here I am, a respected guest at Sidley Park.

SEPTIMUS: Well, sir, you can say you have received satisfaction.

(*Chater is already inscribing the book, using the pen and ink-pot on the table. Noakes enters through the door used by Chater. He carries rolled-up plans. Chater, inscribing, ignores Noakes. Noakes on seeing the occupants, panics.*)

NOAKES: Oh!

SEPTIMUS: Ah, Mr Noakes!—my muddy-mettled rascal! Where's your spyglass?

NOAKES: I beg your leave—I thought her ladyship—excuse me—

(*He is beating an embarrassed retreat when he becomes rooted by Chater's voice. Chater reads his inscription in ringing tones.*)

CHATER: 'To my friend Septimus Hodge, who stood up and gave his best on behalf of the Author—Ezra Chater, at Sidley Park, Derbyshire, April 10th, 1809.' (*Giving the book to Septimus.*) There, sir—something to show your grandchildren!

SEPTIMUS: This is more than I deserve, this is handsome, what do you say, Noakes?

(*They are interrupted by the appearance, outside the windows, of Lady Croom and Captain Edward Brice, RN. Her first words arrive through the open door.*)

LADY CROOM: Oh, no! Not the gazebo!

(*She enters, followed by Brice who carries a leatherbound sketch book.*)

Mr Noakes! What is this I hear?

BRICE: Not only the gazebo, but the boat-house, the Chinese bridge, the shrubbery—

CHATER: By God, sir! Not possible!

BRICE: Mr Noakes will have it so.

SEPTIMUS: Mr Noakes, this is monstrous!

LADY CROOM: I am glad to hear it from *you*, Mr Hodge.

THOMASINA: (*Opening the door from the music room*) May I return now?

SEPTIMUS: (*Attempting to close the door*) Not just yet—

LADY CROOM: Yes, let her stay. A lesson in folly is worth two in wisdom.

Brice takes the sketch book to the reading stand, where he lays it open. The sketch book is the work of Mr Noakes, who is obviously an admirer of Humphry Repton's° 'Red Books'. The pages, drawn in watercolours, show 'before' and 'after' views of the landscape, and the pages are cunningly cut to allow the latter to be superimposed over portions of the former, though Repton did it the other way round.)

BRICE: Is Sidley Park to be an Englishman's garden or the haunt of Corsican brigands?

SEPTIMUS: Let us not hyperbolize, sir.

BRICE: It is rape, sir!

NOAKES: (*Defending himself*) It is the modern style.

CHATER: (*Under the same misapprehension as Septimus*) Regrettable, of course, but so it is.

(Thomasina has gone to examine the sketch book.)

LADY CROOM: Mr Chater, you show too much submission. Mr Hodge, I appeal to you.

SEPTIMUS: Madam, I regret the gazebo, I sincerely regret the gazebo—and the boat-house up to a point—but the Chinese bridge, fantasy!—and the shrubbery I reject with contempt! Mr Chater!—would you take the word of a jumped-up jobbing gardener who sees carnal embrace in every nook and cranny of the landskip!

THOMASINA: Septimus, they are not speaking of carnal embrace, are you, Mama?

LADY CROOM: Certainly not. What do you know of carnal embrace?

THOMASINA: Everything, thanks to Septimus. In my opinion, Mr Noakes's scheme for the garden is perfect. It is a Salvator!°

LADY CROOM: What does she mean?

NOAKES: (*Answering the wrong question*) Salvator Rosa, your ladyship, the painter. He is indeed the very exemplar of the picturesque style.

BRICE: Hodge, what is this?

SEPTIMUS: She speaks from innocence not from experience.

BRICE: You call it innocence? Has he ruined you, child?

(Pause.)

SEPTIMUS: Answer your uncle!

THOMASINA: (*To Septimus*) How is a ruined child different from a ruined castle?

SEPTIMUS: On such questions I defer to Mr Noakes.

NOAKES: (*Out of his depth*) A ruined castle is picturesque, certainly.

SEPTIMUS: That is the main difference. (*To Brice*) I teach the classical authors. If I do not elucidate their meaning, who will?

BRICE: As her tutor you have a duty to keep her in ignorance.

LADY CROOM: Do not dabble in paradox, Edward, it puts you in danger of fortuitous wit. Thomasina, wait in your bedroom.

THOMASINA: (*Retiring*) Yes, mama. I did not intend to get you into trouble, Septimus. I am very sorry for it. It is plain that there are some things a girl is allowed to understand, and these include the whole of algebra, but there are others, such as embracing a side of beef, that must be kept from her until she is old enough to have a carcass of her own.

LADY CROOM: One moment.

BRICE: What is she talking about?

LADY CROOM: Meat.

BRICE: Meat?

LADY CROOM: Thomasina, you had better remain. Your knowledge of the picturesque obviously exceeds anything the rest of us can offer. Mr Hodge, ignorance should be like an empty vessel waiting to be filled at the well of truth—not a cabinet of vulgar curios. Mr Noakes—now at last it is your turn—

NOAKES: Thank you, your ladyship—

LADY CROOM: Your drawing is a very wonderful transformation. I would not have recognized my own garden but for your ingenious book—is it not?—look! Here is the Park as it appears to us now, and here as it might be when Mr Noakes has done with it. Where there is the familiar pastoral refinement of an Englishman's garden, here is an eruption of gloomy forest and towering crag, of ruins where there was never a house, of water dashing against rocks where there was neither spring nor a stone I could not throw the length of a cricket pitch. My hyacinth dell is become a haunt for hobgoblins, my Chinese bridge, which I am assured is superior to the one at Kew, and for all I know at Peking, is usurped by a fallen obelisk overgrown with briars—

NOAKES: (*Bleating*) Lord Little has one very similar—

LADY CROOM: I cannot relieve Lord Little's misfortunes by adding to my own. Pray, what is this rustic hovel that presumes to superpose itself on my gazebo?

NOAKES: That is the hermitage, madam.

LADY CROOM: I am bewildered.

BRICE: It is all irregular, Mr Noakes.

NOAKES: It is, sir. Irregularity is one of the chiefest principles of the picturesque style—

LADY CROOM: But Sidley Park is already a picture, and a most amiable picture too. The slopes are green and gentle. The trees are companionably grouped at intervals that show them to advantage. The rill is a serpentine ribbon unwound from the lake peaceably contained by meadows on which the right amount of sheep are tastefully arranged—in short, it is nature as God intended, and I can say with the painter,° 'Et in Arcadia ego!' 'Here I am in Arcadia,' Thomasina.

Repton: Humphry Repton (1752–1818), landscape designer who showed his clients a picture of the landscape he proposed for them. **Salvator:** Salvator Rosa (1615–1673), Baroque painter of wild landscapes.

painter: Nicola Poussin (1594–1665), whose painting of shepherds discovering a tombstone in Arcadia was in the Duke of Devonshire's collection, near the fictional Sidley Park.

THOMASINA: Yes, mama, if you would have it so.

LADY CROOM: Is she correcting my taste or my translation?

THOMASINA: Neither are beyond correction, mama, but it was your geography caused the doubt.

LADY CROOM: Something has occurred with the girl since I saw her last, and surely that was yesterday. How old are you this morning?

THOMASINA: Thirteen years and ten months, mama.

LADY CROOM: Thirteen years and ten months. She is not due to be pert for six months at the earliest, or to have notions of taste for much longer. Mr Hodge, I hold you accountable. Mr Noakes, back to you—

NOAKES: Thank you, my—

LADY CROOM: You have been reading too many novels by Mrs Radcliffe, that is my opinion. This is a garden for *The Castle of Otranto* or *The Mysteries of Udolpho*—

CHATER: *The Castle of Otranto,* my lady, is by Horace Walpole.°

NOAKES: (*Thrilled*) Mr Walpole the gardener?!

LADY CROOM: Mr Chater, you are a welcome guest at Sidley Park but while you are one, *The Castle of Otranto* was written by whomsoever I say it was, otherwise what is the point of being a guest or having one?

(*The distant popping of guns heard.*)

Well, the guns have reached the brow—I will speak to his lordship on the subject, and we will see by and by—(*She stands looking out.*) Ah!—your friend has got down a pigeon, Mr Hodge. (*Calls out.*) Bravo, sir!

SEPTIMUS: The pigeon, I am sure, fell to your husband or to your son, your ladyship—my schoolfriend was never a sportsman.

BRICE: (*Looking out*) Yes, to Augustus!—bravo, lad!

LADY CROOM: (*Outside*) Well, come along! Where are my troops?

(*Brice, Noakes and Chater obediently follow her, Chater making a detour to shake Septimus's hand fervently.*)

CHATER: My dear Mr Hodge!

(*Chater leaves also. The guns are heard again, a little closer.*)

THOMASINA: Pop, pop, pop . . . I have grown up in the sound of guns like the child of a siege. Pigeons and rooks in the close season, grouse on the heights from August, and the pheasants to follow—partridge, snipe, woodcock, and teal—pop—pop—pop, and the culling of the herd. Papa has no need of the recording angel, his life is written in the game book.

SEPTIMUS: A calendar of slaughter. 'Even in Arcadia, there am I!'

THOMASINA: Oh, phooey to Death!

Radcliffe, Walpole: Ann Ward Radcliffe (1764–1823) and Horace Walpole (1717–1797) wrote highly sensational Gothic novels. Radcliffe wrote *The Mysteries of Udolpho.*

(*She dips a pen and takes it to the reading stand.*)

I will put in a hermit, for what is a hermitage without a hermit? Are you in love with my mother, Septimus?

SEPTIMUS: You must not be cleverer than your elders. It is not polite.

THOMASINA: Am I cleverer?

SEPTIMUS: Yes. Much.

THOMASINA: Well, I am sorry, Septimus. (*She pauses in her drawing and produces a small envelope from her pocket.*) Mrs Chater came to the music room with a note for you. She said it was of scant importance, and that therefore I should carry it to you with the utmost safety, urgency and discretion. Does carnal embrace addle the brain?

SEPTIMUS: (*Taking the letter*) Invariably. Thank you. That is enough education for today.

THOMASINA: There. I have made him like the Baptist in the wilderness.

SEPTIMUS: How picturesque.

(*Lady Croom is heard calling distantly for Thomasina who runs off into the garden, cheerfully, an uncomplicated girl. Septimus opens Mrs Chater's note. He crumples the envelope and throws it away. He reads the note, folds it and inserts it into the pages of 'The Couch of Eros'.*)

Tom Riley as Septimus and Bel Powley as Thomasina in the 2011 revival of *Arcadia,* directed by David Leveaux at the Ethel Barrymore Theatre in New York.

Scene Two

The lights come up on the same room, on the same sort of morning, in the present day, as is instantly clear from the appearance of Hannah Jarvis; and from nothing else.

Something needs to be said about this. The action of the play shuttles back and forth between the early nineteenth century and the present day, always in this same room. Both periods must share the state of the room, without the additions and subtractions which would normally be expected. The general appearance of the room should offend neither period. In the case of props—books, paper, flowers, etc., there is no absolute need to remove the evidence of one period to make way for another. However, books, etc., used in both periods should exist in both old and new versions. The landscape outside, we are told, has undergone changes. Again, what we see should neither change nor contradict.

On the above principle, the ink and pens etc., of the first scene can remain. Books and papers associated with Hannah's research, in Scene Two, can have been on the table from the beginning of the play. And so on. During the course of the play the table collects this and that, and where an object from one scene would be an anachronism in another (say a coffee mug) it is simply deemed to have become invisible. By the end of the play the table has collected an inventory of objects.

Hannah is leafing through the pages of Mr Noakes's sketch book. Also to hand, opened and closed, are a number of small volumes like diaries (these turn out to be Lady Croom's 'garden books'). After a few moments, Hannah takes the sketch book to the windows, comparing the view with what has been drawn, and then she replaces the sketch book on the reading stand.

She wears nothing frivolous. Her shoes are suitable for the garden, which is where she goes now after picking up the theodolite from the table. The room is empty for a few moments.

One of the other doors opens to admit Chloë and Bernard. She is the daughter of the house and is dressed casually. Bernard, the visitor, wears a suit and a tie. His tendency is to dress flamboyantly, but he has damped it down for the occasion, slightly. A peacock-coloured display handkerchief boils over in his breast pocket. He carries a capacious leather bag which serves as a briefcase.

CHLOË: Oh! Well, she *was* here . . .
BERNARD: Ah . . . the French window . . .
CHLOË: Yes. Hang on.

(Chloë steps out through the garden door and disappears from view. Bernard hangs on. The second door opens and Valentine looks in.)

VALENTINE: Sod.

(Valentine goes out again, closing the door. Chloë returns, carrying a pair of rubber boots. She comes in and sits down and starts exchanging her shoes for the boots, while she talks.)

CHLOË: The best thing is, you wait here, save you tramping around. She spends a good deal of time in the garden, as you may imagine.
BERNARD: Yes. Why?
CHLOË: Well, she's writing a history of the garden, didn't you know?
BERNARD: No, I knew she was working on the Croom papers but . . .
CHLOË: Well, it's not exactly a history of the garden either. I'll let Hannah explain it. The trench you nearly drove into is all to do with it. I was going to say make yourself comfortable but that's hardly possible, everything's been cleared out, it's en route to the nearest lavatory.
BERNARD: Everything is?
CHLOË: No, this room is. They drew the line at chemical 'Ladies''.
BERNARD: Yes, I see. Did you say Hannah?
CHLOË: Hannah, yes. Will you be all right?

(She stands up wearing the boots.)

I won't be . . . (*But she has lost him.*) Mr Nightingale?
BERNARD: (*Waking up*) Yes. Thank you. Miss Jarvis is Hannah Jarvis the author?
CHLOË: Yes. Have you read her book?
BERNARD: Oh, yes. Yes.
CHLOË: I bet she's in the hermitage, can't see from here with the marquee . . .
BERNARD: Are you having a garden party?
CHLOË: A dance for the district, our annual dressing up and general drunkenness. The wrinklies won't have it in the house, there was a teapot we once had to bag back from Christie's in the nick of time, so anything that can be destroyed, stolen or vomited on has been tactfully removed; tactlessly, I should say—

(She is about to leave.)

BERNARD: Um—look—would you tell her—would you mind not mentioning my name just yet?
CHLOË: Oh. All right.
BERNARD: (*Smiling*) More fun to surprise her. Would you mind?
CHLOË: No. But she's bound to ask . . . Should I give you another name, just for the moment?
BERNARD: Yes, why not?
CHLOË: Perhaps another bird, you're not really a Nightingale.

(She leaves again. Bernard glances over the books on the table. He puts his briefcase down. There is the distant pop-pop of a shotgun. It takes Bernard vaguely to the window. He looks out. The door he entered by now opens and Gus looks into the room. Bernard turns and sees him.)

BERNARD: Hello.

(Gus doesn't speak. He never speaks. Perhaps he cannot speak. He has no composure, and faced with a stranger, he caves in and leaves again. A moment later the

other door opens again and Valentine crosses the room, not exactly ignoring Bernard and yet ignoring him.)

VALENTINE: Sod, sod, sod, sod, sod, sod . . . (*As many times as it takes him to leave by the opposite door, which he closes behind him. Beyond it, he can be heard shouting. Chlo! Chlo! Bernard's discomfort increases. The same door opens and Valentine returns. He looks at Bernard.*)

BERNARD: She's in the garden looking for Miss Jarvis.

VALENTINE: Where is everything?

BERNARD: It's been removed for the, er . . .

VALENTINE: The dance is all in the tent, isn't it?

BERNARD: Yes, but this is the way to the nearest toilet.

VALENTINE: I need the commode.

BERNARD: Oh. Can't you use the toilet?

VALENTINE: It's got all the game books in it.

BERNARD: Ah. The toilet has or the commode has?

VALENTINE: Is anyone looking after you?

BERNARD: Yes. Thank you. I'm Bernard Nigh—I've come to see Miss Jarvis. I wrote to Lord Croom but unfortunately I never received a reply, so I—

VALENTINE: Did you type it?

BERNARD: Type it?

VALENTINE: Was your letter typewritten?

BERNARD: Yes.

VALENTINE: My father never replies to typewritten letters.

(*He spots a tortoise which has been half-hidden on the table.*)

Oh! Where have you been hiding, Lightning? (*He picks up the tortoise.*)

BERNARD: So I telephoned yesterday and I think I spoke to you—

VALENTINE: To me? Ah! Yes! Sorry! You're doing a talk about—someone—and you wanted to ask Hannah—something—

BERNARD: Yes. As it turns out. I'm hoping Miss Jarvis will look kindly on me.

VALENTINE: I doubt it.

BERNARD: Ah, you know about research?

VALENTINE: I know Hannah.

BERNARD: Has she been here long?

VALENTINE: Well in possession, I'm afraid. My mother had read her book, you see. Have you?

BERNARD: No. Yes. Her book. Indeed.

VALENTINE: She's terrifically pleased with herself.

BERNARD: Well, I dare say if I wrote a bestseller—

VALENTINE: No, for reading it. My mother basically reads gardening books.

BERNARD: She must be delighted to have Hannah Jarvis writing a book about her garden.

VALENTINE: Actually it's about hermits.

(*Gus returns through the same door, and turns to leave again.*)

It's all right, Gus—what do you want?—

(*But Gus has gone again.*)

Well . . . I'll take Lightning for his run.

BERNARD: Actually, we've met before. At Sussex, a couple of years ago, a seminar . . .

VALENTINE: Oh. Was I there?

BERNARD: Yes. One of my colleagues believed he had found an unattributed short story by D. H. Lawrence,° and he analysed it on his home computer, most interesting, perhaps you remember the paper?

VALENTINE: Not really. But I often sit with my eyes closed and it doesn't necessarily mean I'm awake.

BERNARD: Well, by comparing sentence structures and so forth, this chap showed that there was a ninety per cent chance that the story had indeed been written by the same person as *Women in Love*. To my inexpressible joy, one of your maths mob was able to show that on the same statistical basis there was a ninety per cent chance that Lawrence also wrote the *Just William* books and much of the previous day's *Brighton and Hove Argus*.

VALENTINE: (*Pause*) Oh, Brighton. Yes. I was there. (*And looking out.*) Oh—here she comes, I'll leave you to talk. By the way, is yours the red Mazda?

BERNARD: Yes.

VALENTINE: If you want a tip I'd put it out of sight through the stable arch before my father comes in. He won't have anyone in the house with a Japanese car. Are you queer?

BERNARD: No, actually.

VALENTINE: Well, even so.

(*Valentine leaves, closing the door. Bernard keeps staring at the closed door. Behind him, Hannah comes to the garden door.*)

HANNAH: Mr Peacock?

(*Bernard looks round vaguely then checks over his shoulder for the missing Peacock, then recovers himself and turns on the Nightingale bonhomie.*)

BERNARD: Oh . . . hello! Hello. Miss Jarvis, of course. Such a pleasure. I was thrown for a moment—the photograph doesn't do you justice.

HANNAH: Photograph?

(*Her shoes have got muddy and she is taking them off.*)

BERNARD: On the book. I'm sorry to have brought you indoors, but Lady Chloë kindly insisted she—

HANNAH: No matter—you would have muddied your shoes.

BERNARD: How thoughtful. And how kind of you to spare me a little of your time.

(*He is overdoing it. She shoots him a glance.*)

HANNAH: Are you a journalist?

BERNARD: (*Shocked*) No!

HANNAH: (*Resuming*) I've been in the ha-ha, very squelchy.

Lawrence: D. H. Lawrence (1885–1930), modern English novelist who wrote *Women in Love*—and did *not* write the *Just William* children's books.

BERNARD: (*Unexpectedly*) Ha-*hah*!

HANNAH: What?

BERNARD: A theory of mine. Ha-hah, not ha-ha. If you were strolling down the garden and all of a sudden the ground gave way at your feet, you're not going to go 'ha-ha', you're going to jump back and go 'ha-hah!', or more probably, 'Bloody 'ell!' . . . though personally I think old Murray was up the pole on that one—in France, you know, 'ha-ha' is used to denote a strikingly ugly woman, a much more likely bet for something that keeps the cows off the lawn.

(*This is not going well for Bernard but he seems blithely unaware.*

Hannah stares at him for a moment.)

HANNAH: Mr Peacock, what can I do for you?

BERNARD: Well, to begin with, you can call me Bernard, which is my name.

HANNAH: Thank you.

(*She goes to the garden door to bang her shoes together and scrape off the worst of the mud.*)

BERNARD: The book!—the book is a revelation! To see Caroline Lamb° through your eyes is really like seeing her for the first time. I'm ashamed to say I never read her fiction, and how right you are, it's extraordinary stuff—Early Nineteenth is my period as much as anything is.

HANNAH: You teach?

BERNARD: Yes. And write, like you, like we all, though I've never done anything which has sold like *Caro*.

HANNAH: I don't teach.

BERNARD: No. All the more credit to you. To rehabilitate a forgotten writer, I suppose you could say that's the main reason for an English don.

HANNAH: Not to teach?

BERNARD: Good God, no, let the brats sort it out for themselves. Anyway, many congratulations. I expect someone will be bringing out Caroline Lamb's oeuvre now?

HANNAH: Yes, I expect so.

BERNARD: How wonderful! Bravo! Simply as a document shedding reflected light on the character of Lord Byron,° it's bound to be—

HANNAH: Bernard. You did say Bernard, didn't you?

BERNARD: I did.

HANNAH: I'm putting my shoes on again.

BERNARD: Oh. You're not going to go out?

HANNAH: No, I'm going to kick you in the balls.

BERNARD: Right. Point taken. Ezra Chater.

HANNAH: Ezra Chater.

BERNARD: Born Twickenham, Middlesex, 1778, author of two verse narratives, 'The Maid of Turkey', 1808, and 'The Couch of Eros', 1809. Nothing known after 1809, disappears from view.

HANNAH: I see. And?

BERNARD: (*Reaching for his bag*) There is a Sidley Park connection.

(*He produces 'The Couch of Eros' from the bag. He reads the inscription.*)

'To my friend Septimus Hodge, who stood up and gave his best on behalf of the Author—Ezra Chater, at Sidley Park, Derbyshire, April 10th 1809.

(*He gives her the book.*)

I am in your hands.

HANNAH: 'The Couch of Eros'. Is it any good?

BERNARD: Quite surprising.

HANNAH: You think there's a book in him?

BERNARD: No, no—a monograph perhaps for the *Journal of English Studies*. There's almost nothing on Chater, not a word in the *DNB*,° of course—by that time he'd been completely forgotten.

HANNAH: Family?

BERNARD: Zilch. There's only one other Chater in the British Library database.

HANNAH: Same period?

BERNARD: Yes, but he wasn't a poet like our Ezra, he was a botanist who described a dwarf dahlia in Martinique and died there after being bitten by a monkey.

HANNAH: And Ezra Chater?

BERNARD: He gets two references in the periodical index, one for each book, in both cases a substantial review in the *Piccadilly Recreation*, a thrice weekly folio sheet, but giving no personal details.

HANNAH: And where was this (*the book*)?

BERNARD: Private collection. I've got a talk to give next week, in London, and I think Chater is interesting, so anything on him, or this Septimus Hodge, Sidley Park, any leads at all . . . I'd be most grateful.

(*Pause.*)

HANNAH: Well! This is a new experience for me. A groveling academic.

BERNARD: Oh, I say.

HANNAH: Oh, but it is. All the academics who reviewed my book patronized it.

BERNARD: Surely not.

HANNAH: Surely yes. The Byron gang unzipped their flies and patronized all over it. Where is it you don't bother to teach, by the way?

BERNARD: Oh, well, Sussex, actually.

HANNAH: Sussex. (*She thinks a moment.*) Nightingale. Yes; a thousand words in the *Observer* to see me off the premises with a pat on the bottom. You must know him.

BERNARD: As I say, I'm in your hands.

HANNAH: Quite. Say please, then.

BERNARD: Please.

HANNAH: Sit down, do.

BERNARD: Thank you.

Caroline Lamb: A writer (1785–1828) who was once Lord Byron's lover.   **Lord Byron:** George Gordon, Lord Byron (1788–1824), one of the most notorious of the Romantic poets.

DNB: Dictionary of National Biography.

(*He takes a chair. She remains standing. Possibly she smokes; if so, perhaps now. A short cigarette-holder sounds right, too. Or brown-paper cigarillos.*)

HANNAH: How did you know I was here?

BERNARD: Oh, I didn't. I spoke to the son on the phone but he didn't mention you by name . . . and then he forgot to mention me.

HANNAH: Valentine. He's at Oxford, technically.

BERNARD: Yes, I met him. Brideshead Regurgitated.

HANNAH: My fiancé.

(*She holds his look.*)

BERNARD: (*Pause*) I'll take a chance. You're lying.

HANNAH: (*Pause*) Well done, Bernard.

BERNARD: Christ.

HANNAH: He calls me his fiancée.

BERNARD: Why?

HANNAH: It's a joke.

BERNARD: You turned him down?

HANNAH: Don't be silly, do I look like the next Countess of—

BERNARD: No, no—a freebie. The joke that consoles. My tortoise Lightning, my fiancée Hannah.

HANNAH: Oh. Yes. You have a way with you, Bernard. I'm not sure I like it.

BERNARD: What's he doing, Valentine?

HANNAH: He's a postgrad. Biology.

BERNARD: No, he's a mathematician.

HANNAH: Well, he's doing grouse.

BERNARD: Grouse?

HANNAH: Not actual grouse. Computer grouse.

BERNARD: Who's the one who doesn't speak?

HANNAH: Gus.

BERNARD: What's the matter with him?

HANNAH: I didn't ask.

BERNARD: And the father sounds like a lot of fun.

HANNAH: Ah yes.

BERNARD: And the mother is the gardener. What's going on here?

HANNAH: What do you mean?

BERNARD: I nearly took her head off—she was standing in a trench at the time.

HANNAH: Archaeology. The house had a formal Italian garden until about 1740. Lady Croom is interested in garden history. I sent her my book—it contains, as you know if you've read it—which I'm not assuming, by the way—a rather good description of Caroline's garden at Brocket Hall. I'm here now helping Hermione.

BERNARD: (*Impressed*) Hermione.

HANNAH: The records are unusually complete and they have never been worked on.

BERNARD: I'm beginning to admire you.

HANNAH: Before was bullshit?

BERNARD: Completely. Your photograph does you justice, I'm not sure the book does.

(*She considers him. He waits, confident.*)

HANNAH: Septimus Hodge was the tutor.

BERNARD: (*Quietly*) Attagirl.

HANNAH: His pupil was the Croom daughter. There was a son at Eton. Septimus lived in the house: the pay book specifies allowances for wine and candles. So, not quite a guest but rather more than a steward. His letter of self-recommendation is preserved among the papers. I'll dig it out for you. As far as I remember he studied mathematics and natural philosophy at Cambridge. A scientist, therefore, as much as anything.

BERNARD: I'm impressed. Thank you. And Chater?

HANNAH: Nothing.

BERNARD: Oh. Nothing at all?

HANNAH: I'm afraid not.

BERNARD: How about the library?

HANNAH: The catalogue was done in the 1880s. I've been through the lot.

BERNARD: Books or catalogue?

HANNAH: Catalogue.

BERNARD: Ah. Pity.

HANNAH: I'm sorry.

BERNARD: What about the letters? No mention?

HANNAH: I'm afraid not. I've been very thorough in your period because, of course, it's my period too.

BERNARD: Is it? Actually, I don't quite know what it is you're . . .

HANNAH: The Sidley hermit.

BERNARD: Ah. Who's he?

HANNAH: He's my peg for the nervous breakdown of the Romantic Imagination. I'm doing landscape and literature 1750 to 1834.

BERNARD: What happened in 1834?

HANNAH: My hermit died.

BERNARD: Of course.

HANNAH: What do you mean, of course?

BERNARD: Nothing.

HANNAH: Yes, you do.

BERNARD: No, no . . . However, Coleridge° also died in 1834.

HANNAH: So he did. What a stroke of luck. (*Softening.*) Thank you, Bernard.

(*She goes to the reading stand and opens Noakes's sketch book.*)

Look—there he is.

(*Bernard goes to look.*)

BERNARD: Mmm.

HANNAH: The only known likeness of the Sidley hermit.

BERNARD: Very biblical.

HANNAH: Drawn in by a later hand, of course. The hermitage didn't yet exist when Noakes did the drawings.

BERNARD: Noakes . . . the painter?

HANNAH: Landscape gardener. He'd do these books for his clients, as a sort of prospectus. (*She demonstrates.*) Before and after, you see. This is how it all looked until, say, 1810—smooth, undulating, serpentine—open water, clumps of trees, classical boat-house—

Coleridge: Samuel Taylor Coleridge (1772–1834), one of the most important Romantic poets.

Start

BERNARD: Lovely. The real England.

HANNAH: You can stop being silly now, Bernard. English landscape was invented by gardeners imitating foreign painters who were evoking classical authors. The whole thing was brought home in the luggage from the grand tour. Here, look—Capability Brown doing Claude, who was doing Virgil. Arcadia! And here, superimposed by Richard Noakes, untamed nature in the style of Salvator Rosa. It's the Gothic novel expressed in landscape. Everything but vampires. There's an account of my hermit in a letter by your illustrious namesake.

BERNARD: Florence?

HANNAH: What?

BERNARD: No. You go on.

HANNAH: Thomas Love Peacock.°

BERNARD: Ah yes.

HANNAH: I found it in an essay on hermits and anchorites published in the *Cornhill Magazine* in the 1860s . . . (*She fishes for the magazine itself among the books on the table, and finds it.*) . . . 1862 . . . Peacock calls him (*She quotes from memory.*) 'Not one of your village simpletons to frighten the ladies, but a savant among idiots, a sage of lunacy'.

BERNARD: An oxy-moron, so to speak.

HANNAH: (*Busy*) Yes. What?

BERNARD: Nothing.

HANNAH: (*Having found the place*) Here we are. 'A letter we have seen, written by the author of *Headlong Hall* nearly thirty years ago, tells of a visit to the Earl of Croom's estate, Sidley Park—'

BERNARD: Was the letter to Thackeray?°

HANNAH: (*Brought up short*) I don't know. Does it matter?

BERNARD: No. Sorry.

(*But the gaps he leaves for her are false promises—and she is not quick enough. That's how it goes.*)

Only, Thackeray edited the *Cornhill* until '63 when, as you know, he died. His father had been with the East India Company where Peacock, of course, had held the position of Examiner, so it's quite possible that if the essay were by Thackeray, the *letter* . . . Sorry. Go on. Of course, the East India Library in Blackfriars has most of Peacock's letters, so it would be quite easy to . . . Sorry. Can I look?

(*Silently she hands him the* Cornhill.)

Yes, it's been topped and tailed, of course. It might be worth . . . Go on. I'm listening . . .

(*Leafing through the essay, he suddenly chuckles.*)

Thomas Love Peacock: English novelist and poet (1785–1866), author of *Headlong Hall*. **Thackeray:** William Makepeace Thackeray (1811–1863), English novelist, author of *Vanity Fair* and editor of the *Cornhill Magazine*.

Oh yes, it's Thackeray all right . . .
(*He slaps the book shut.*) Unbearable . . .
(*He hands it back to her.*) What were you saying?

HANNAH: Are you always like this?

BERNARD: Like what?

HANNAH: The point is, the Crooms, of course, had the hermit under their noses for twenty years so hardly thought him worth remarking. As I'm finding out. The Peacock letter is still the main source, unfortunately. When I read this (*the magazine in her hand*) well, it was one of those moments that tell you what your next book is going to be. The hermit of Sidley Park was my . . .

BERNARD: Peg.

HANNAH: Epiphany.

BERNARD: Epiphany, that's it.

HANNAH: The hermit was *placed* in the landscape exactly as one might place a pottery gnome. And there he lived out his life as a garden ornament.

BERNARD: Did he do anything?

HANNAH: Oh, he was very busy. When he died, the cottage was stacked solid with paper. Hundreds of pages. Thousands. Peacock says he was suspected of genius. It turned out, of course, he was off his head. He'd covered every sheet with cabalistic proofs that the world was coming to an end. It's perfect, isn't it? A perfect symbol, I mean.

BERNARD: Oh, yes. Of what?

HANNAH: The whole Romantic sham, Bernard! It's what happened to Enlightenment, isn't it? A century of intellectual rigour turned in on itself. A mind in chaos suspected of genius. In a setting of cheap thrills and false emotion. The history of the garden says it all, beautifully. There's an engraving of Sidley Park in 1730 that makes you want to weep. Paradise in the age of reason. By 1760 everything had gone—the topiary, pools and terraces, fountains, an avenue of limes—the whole sublime geometry was ploughed under by Capability Brown. The grass went from the doorstep to the horizon and the best box hedge in Derbyshire was dug up for the ha-ha so that the fools could pretend they were living in God's countryside. And then Richard Noakes came in to bring God up to date. By the time he'd finished it looked like this (*the sketch book*). The decline from thinking to feeling, you see.

BERNARD: (*A judgement*) That's awfully good.

(*Hannah looks at him in case of irony but he is professional.*)

No, that'll stand up.

HANNAH: Thank you.

BERNARD: Personally I like the ha-ha. Do you like hedges?

HANNAH: I don't like sentimentality.

BERNARD: Yes, I see. Are you sure? You seem quite sentimental over geometry. But the hermit is very very good. The genius of the place.

HANNAH: (*Pleased*) That's my title!

BERNARD: Of course.

HANNAH: (*Less pleased*) Of course?

BERNARD: Of course. Who was he when he wasn't being a symbol?

HANNAH: I don't know.

BERNARD: Ah.

HANNAH: I mean, yet.

BERNARD: Absolutely. What did they do with all the paper? Does Peacock say?

HANNAH: Made a bonfire.

BERNARD: Ah, well.

HANNAH: I've still got Lady Croom's garden books to go through.

BERNARD: Account books or journals?

HANNAH: A bit of both. They're gappy but they span the period.

BERNARD: Really? Have you come across Byron at all? As a matter of interest.

HANNAH: A first edition of 'Childe Harold'° in the library, and *English Bards*,° I think.

BERNARD: Inscribed?

HANNAH: No.

BERNARD: And he doesn't pop up in the letters at all?

HANNAH: Why should he? The Crooms don't pop up in his.

BERNARD: (*Casually*) That's true, of course. But Newstead isn't so far away. Would you mind terribly if I poked about a bit? Only in the papers you've done with, of course.

(*Hannah twigs something.*)

HANNAH: Are you looking into Byron or Chater?

(*Chloë enters in stockinged feet through one of the side doors, laden with an armful of generally similar leather-covered ledgers. She detours to collect her shoes.*)

CHLOË: Sorry—just cutting through—there's tea in the pantry if you don't mind mugs—

BERNARD: How kind.

CHLOË: Hannah will show you.

BERNARD: Let me help you.

CHLOË: No, it's all right—

(*Bernard opens the opposite door for her.*)

Thank you—I've been saving Val's game books. Thanks.

(*Bernard closes the door.*)

BERNARD: Sweet girl.

HANNAH: Mmm.

BERNARD: Oh, really?

HANNAH: Oh really what?

(*Chloë's door opens again and she puts her head round it.*)

CHLOË: Meant to say, don't worry if father makes remarks about your car, Mr Nightingale, he's got a thing about—(*and the Nightingale now being out of the bag*) ooh—ah, how was the surprise?—not yet, eh? Oh, well—sorry—tea, anyway—so sorry if I—(*Embarrassed, she leaves again, closing the door. Pause.*)

HANNAH: You absolute shit.

(*She heads off to leave.*)

BERNARD: The thing is, there's a Byron connection too.

(*Hannah stops and faces him.*)

HANNAH: I don't care.

BERNARD: You should. The Byron gang are going to get their dicks caught in their zip.

HANNAH: (*Pause*) Oh really?

BERNARD: If we collaborate.

HANNAH: On what?

BERNARD: Sit down, I'll tell you.

HANNAH: I'll stand for the moment.

BERNARD: This copy of 'The Couch of Eros' belonged to Lord Byron.

HANNAH: It belonged to Septimus Hodge.

BERNARD: Originally, yes. But it was in Byron's library which was sold to pay his debts when he left England for good in 1816. The sales catalogue is in the British Library. 'Eros' was lot 74A and was bought by the bookseller and publisher John Nightingale of Opera Court, Pall Mall . . . whose name survives in the firm of Nightingale and Matlock, the present Nightingale being my cousin.

(*He pauses. Hannah hesitates and then sits down at the table.*)

I'll just give you the headlines. 1939, stock removed to Nightingale country house in Kent. 1945, stock returned to bookshop. Meanwhile, overlooked box of early nineteenth-century books languish in country house cellar until house sold to make way for the Channel Tunnel rail-link. 'Eros' discovered with sales slip from 1816 attached—photocopy available for inspection.

(*He brings this from his bag and gives it to Hannah who inspects it.*)

HANNAH: All right. It was in Byron's library.

BERNARD: A number of passages have been underlined.

(*Hannah picks up the book and leafs through it.*)

All of them, and only them—no, no, look at me, not at the book—all the underlined passages, word for word, were used as quotations in the review of 'The Couch of Eros' in the *Piccadilly Recreation* of April 30th 1809. The reviewer begins by drawing attention to his previous notice in the same periodical of 'The Maid of Turkey'.

Childe Harold: *Childe Harold's Pilgrimage* (1812), a poem that made Byron famous overnight.   **English Bards:** *English Bards and Scotch Reviewers* (1809) satirized the *Edinburgh Review*.

HANNAH: The reviewer is obviously Hodge. 'My friend Septimus Hodge who stood up and gave his best on behalf of the Author.'

BERNARD: That's the point. The *Piccadilly* ridiculed both books.

HANNAH: (*Pause.*) Do the reviews read like Byron?

BERNARD: (*Producing two photocopies from his case*) They read a damn sight more like Byron than Byron's review of Wordsworth the previous year.

(*Hannah glances over the photocopies.*)

HANNAH: I see. Well, congratulations. Possibly. Two previously unknown book reviews by the young Byron. Is that it?

BERNARD: No. Because of the tapes, three documents survived undisturbed in the book.

(*He has been carefully opening a package produced from his bag. He has the originals. He holds them carefully one by one.*)

'Sir—we have a matter to settle. I wait on you in the gun room. E. Chater, Esq.'

'My husband has sent to town for pistols. Deny what cannot be proven—for Charity's sake—I keep my room this day.' Unsigned.

'Sidley Park, April 11th 1809. Sir—I call you a liar, a lecher, a slanderer in the press and a thief of my honour. I wait upon your arrangements for giving me satisfaction as a man and a poet. E. Chater, Esq.' STOP

(*Pause.*)

HANNAH: Superb. But inconclusive. The book had seven years to find its way into Byron's possession. It doesn't connect Byron with Chater, or with Sidley Park. Or with Hodge for that matter. Furthermore, there isn't a hint in Byron's letters and this kind of scrape is the last thing he would have kept quiet about.

BERNARD: *Scrape?*

HANNAH: He would have made a comic turn out of it.

BERNARD: Comic turn, fiddlesticks! (*He pauses for effect.*) He killed Chater!

HANNAH: (*A raspberry*) Oh, really!

BERNARD: Chater was thirty-one years old. The author of two books. Nothing more is heard from him after 'Eros'. He disappears completely after April 1809. And Byron—Byron had just published his satire, *English Bards and Scotch Reviewers*, in March. He was just getting a name. Yet he sailed for Lisbon as soon as he could find a ship, and stayed abroad for two years. Hannah, *this is fame*. Somewhere in the Croom papers there will be *something*—

HANNAH: There isn't, I've looked.

BERNARD: But you were looking for something else! It's not going to jump out at you like 'Lord Byron remarked wittily at breakfast!'

HANNAH: Nevertheless his presence would be unlikely to have gone unremarked. But there is nothing to suggest that Byron was here, and I don't believe he ever was.

BERNARD: All right, but let me have a look.

HANNAH: You'll queer my pitch.

BERNARD: Dear girl, I know how to handle myself—

HANNAH: And don't call me dear girl. If I find anything on Byron, or Chater, or Hodge, I'll pass it on. Nightingale, Sussex.

(*Pause. She stands up.*)

BERNARD: Thank you. I'm sorry about that business with my name.

HANNAH: Don't mention it . . .

BERNARD: What was Hodge's college, by the way?

HANNAH: Trinity.

BERNARD: Trinity?

HANNAH: Yes. (*She hesitates.*) Yes. Byron's old college.

BERNARD: How old was Hodge?

HANNAH: I'd have to look it up but a year or two older than Byron. Twenty-two . . .

BERNARD: Contemporaries at Trinity?

HANNAH: (*Wearily*) Yes, Bernard, and no doubt they were both in the cricket eleven when Harrow played Eton at Lords!

(*Bernard approaches her and stands close to her.*)

BERNARD: (*Evenly*) Do you mean that Septimus Hodge was at school with Byron?

HANNAH: (*Falters slightly*) Yes . . . he must have been . . . as a matter of fact.

BERNARD: Well, you silly cow.

(*With a large gesture of pure happiness, Bernard throws his arms around Hannah and gives her a great smacking kiss on the cheek. Chloë enters to witness the end of this.*)

CHLOË: Oh—erm . . . I thought I'd bring it to you.

(*She is carrying a small tray with two mugs on it.*)

BERNARD: I have to go and see about my car.

HANNAH: Going to hide it?

BERNARD: Hide it? I'm going to sell it! Is there a pub I can put up at in the village?

(*He turns back to them as he is about to leave through the garden.*)

Aren't you glad I'm here?

(*He leaves.*)

CHLOË: He said he knew you.

HANNAH: He couldn't have.

CHLOË: No, perhaps not. He said he wanted to be a surprise, but I suppose that's different. I thought there was a lot of sexual energy there, didn't you?

HANNAH: What?

CHLOË: Bouncy on his feet, you see, a sure sign. Should I invite him for you?

HANNAH: To what? No.

CHLOË: You can invite him—that's better. He can come as your partner.

HANNAH: Stop it. Thank you for the tea.

CHLOË: If you don't want him, I'll have him. Is he married?

HANNAH: I haven't the slightest idea. Aren't you supposed to have a pony?

CHLOË: I'm just trying to fix you up, Hannah.

HANNAH: Believe me, it gets less important.

CHLOË: I mean for the dancing. He can come as Beau Brummel.

HANNAH: I don't want to dress up and I don't want a dancing partner, least of all Mr Nightingale. I don't dance.

CHLOË: Don't be such a prune. You were kissing him, anyway.

HANNAH: He was kissing me, and only out of general enthusiasm.

CHLOË: Well, don't say I didn't give you first chance. My genius brother will be much relieved. He's in love with you, I suppose you know.

HANNAH: (*Angry*) That's a joke!

CHLOË: It's not a joke to him.

HANNAH: Of course it is—not even a joke—how can you be so ridiculous?

(*Gus enters from the garden, in his customary silent awkwardness.*)

CHLOË: Hello, Gus, what have you got?

(*Gus has an apple, just picked, with a leaf or two still attached. He offers the apple to Hannah.*)

HANNAH: (*Surprised*) Oh! . . . Thank you!

CHLOË: (*Leaving*) Told you.

(*Chloë closes the door on herself.*)

HANNAH: Thank you. Oh dear.

Scene Three

The schoolroom. The next morning. Present are: Thomasina, Septimus, Jellaby. We have seen this composition before: Thomasina at her place at the table; Septimus reading a letter which has just arrived; Jellaby waiting, having just delivered the letter.
'The Couch of Eros' is in front of Septimus, open, together with sheets of paper on which he has been writing. His portfolio is on the table, Plautus (the tortoise) is the paperweight. There is also an apple on the table now, the same apple from all appearances.

SEPTIMUS: (*With his eyes on the letter*) Why have you stopped?

(*Thomasina is studying a sheet of paper, a 'Latin unseen' lesson. She is having some difficulty.*)

THOMASINA: *Solio insessa . . . in igne* . . . seated on a throne . . . in the fire . . . and also on a ship . . . *sedebat regina* . . . sat the queen . . .

SEPTIMUS: There is no reply, Jellaby. Thank you.

(*He folds the letter up and places it between the leaves of 'The Couch of Eros'.*)

JELLABY: I will say so, sir.

THOMASINA: . . . the wind smelling sweetly . . . *purpureis velis* . . . by, with or from purple sails—

SEPTIMUS: (*To Jellaby*) I will have something for the post, if you would be so kind.

JELLABY: (*Leaving*) Yes, sir.

THOMASINA: . . . was like as to—something—by, with or from lovers—oh, Septimus!—*musica tibiarum imperabat* . . . music of pipes commanded . . .

SEPTIMUS: 'Ruled' is better.

THOMASINA: . . . the silver oars—exciting the ocean—as if—as if—amorous—

SEPTIMUS: That is very good.

(*He picks up the apple. He picks off the twig and leaves, placing these on the table. With a pocket knife he cuts a slice of apple, and while he eats it, cuts another slice which he offers to Plautus.*)

THOMASINA: *Regina reclinabat* . . . the queen—was reclining—*praeter descriptionem*—indescribably— in a golden tent . . . like Venus and yet more—

SEPTIMUS: Try to put some poetry into it.

THOMASINA: How can I if there is none in the Latin?

SEPTIMUS: Oh, a critic!

THOMASINA: Is it Queen Dido?

SEPTIMUS: No.

THOMASINA: Who is the poet?

SEPTIMUS: Known to you.

THOMASINA: Known to me?

SEPTIMUS: Not a Roman.

THOMASINA: Mr Chater?

SEPTIMUS: Your translation is quite like Chater.

(*Septimus picks up his pen and continues with his own writing.*)

THOMASINA: I know who it is, it is your friend Byron.

SEPTIMUS: Lord Byron, if you please.

THOMASINA: Mama is in love with Lord Byron.

SEPTIMUS: (*Absorbed*) Yes. Nonsense.

THOMASINA: It is not nonsense. I saw them together in the gazebo.

(*Septimus's pen stops moving, he raises his eyes to her at last.*)

Lord Byron was reading to her from his satire, and mama was laughing, with her head in her best position.

SEPTIMUS: She did not understand the satire, and was showing politeness to a guest.

THOMASINA: She is vexed with papa for his determination to alter the park, but that alone cannot account for her politeness to a guest. She came downstairs hours before her custom. Lord Byron was amusing at breakfast. He paid you a tribute, Septimus.

SEPTIMUS: Did he?

THOMASINA: He said you were a witty fellow, and he had almost by heart an article you wrote about—well, I forget what, but it concerned a book called 'The Maid of Turkey' and how you would not give it to your dog for dinner.

SEPTIMUS: Ah. Mr Chater was at breakfast, of course.

THOMASINA: He was, not like certain lazybones.

SEPTIMUS: He does not have Latin to set and mathematics to correct.

(*He takes Thomasina's lesson book from underneath Plautus and tosses it down the table to her.*)

THOMASINA: Correct? What was incorrect in it? (*She looks into the book.*) Alpha minus? Pooh! What is the minus for?

SEPTIMUS: For doing more than was asked.

THOMASINA: You did not like my discovery?

SEPTIMUS: A fancy is not a discovery.

THOMASINA: A gibe is not a rebuttal.

(*Septimus finishes what he is writing. He folds the pages into a letter. He has sealing wax and the means to melt it. He seals the letter and writes on the cover. Meanwhile—*)

You are churlish with me because mama is paying attention to your friend. Well, let them elope, they cannot turn back the advancement of knowledge. I think it is an excellent discovery. Each week I plot your equations dot for dot, xs against ys in all manner of algebraical relation, and every week they draw themselves as commonplace geometry, as if the world of forms were nothing but arcs and angles. God's truth, Septimus, if there is an equation for a curve like a bell, there must be an equation for one like a bluebell, and if a bluebell, why not a rose? Do we believe nature is written in numbers?

SEPTIMUS: We do.

THOMASINA: Then why do your equations only describe the shapes of manufacture?

SEPTIMUS: I do not know.

THOMASINA: Armed thus, God could only make a cabinet.

SEPTIMUS: He has mastery of equations which lead into infinities where we cannot follow.

THOMASINA: What a faint-heart! We must work outward from the middle of the maze. We will start with something simple. (*She picks up the apple leaf.*) I will plot this leaf and deduce its equation. You will be famous for being my tutor when Lord Byron is dead and forgotten.

(*Septimus completes the business with his letter. He puts the letter in his pocket.*)

SEPTIMUS: (*Firmly*) Back to Cleopatra.

THOMASINA: Is it Cleopatra?—I hate Cleopatra!

SEPTIMUS: You hate her? Why?

THOMASINA: Everything is turned to love with her. New love, absent love, lost love—I never knew a heroine that makes such noodles of our sex. It only needs a Roman general to drop anchor outside the window and away goes the empire like a christening mug into a pawn shop. If Queen Elizabeth had been a Ptolemy° history would have been quite different—we would be admiring the pyramids of Rome and the great Sphinx of Verona.

SEPTIMUS: God save us.

THOMASINA: But instead, the Egyptian noodle made carnal embrace with the enemy who burned the great library of Alexandria without so much as a fine for all that is overdue. Oh, Septimus!—can you bear it? All the lost plays of the Athenians! Two hundred at least by Aeschylus, Sophocles, Euripides—thousands of poems—Aristotle's own library brought to Egypt by the noodle's ancestors! How can we sleep for grief?

SEPTIMUS: By counting our stock. Seven plays from Aeschylus, seven from Sophocles, *nineteen* from Euripides, my lady! You should no more grieve for the rest than for a buckle lost from your first shoe, or for your lesson book which will be lost when you are old. We shed as we pick up, like travellers who must carry everything in their arms, and what we let fall will be picked up by those behind. The procession is very long and life is very short. We die on the march. But there is nothing outside the march so nothing can be lost to it. The missing plays of Sophocles will turn up piece by piece, or be written again in another language. Ancient cures for diseases will reveal themselves once more. Mathematical discoveries glimpsed and lost to view will have their time again. You do not suppose, my lady, that if all of Archimedes had been hiding in the great library of Alexandria, we would be at a loss for a corkscrew? I have no doubt that the improved steam-driven heat-engine which puts Mr Noakes into an ecstasy that he and it and the modern age should all coincide, was described on papyrus. Steam and brass were not invented in Glasgow. Now, where are we? Let me see if I can attempt a free translation for you. At Harrow I was better at this than Lord Byron.

(*He takes the piece of paper from her and scrutinizes it, testing one or two Latin phrases speculatively before committing himself.*)

Yes—'The barge she sat in,° like a burnished throne ... burned on the water ... the—something—the poop was beaten gold, purple the sails, and—what's this?—oh yes,—so perfumed that—

THOMASINA: (*Catching on and furious*) Cheat!

SEPTIMUS: (*Imperturbably*) '—the winds were lovesick with them ...'

THOMASINA: Cheat!

SEPTIMUS: '... the oars were silver which to the tune of flutes kept stroke ...'

Ptolemy: Cleopatra (69–30 BCE) was queen of Egypt and was next to last in the dynasty of the Ptolemies, which ruled from 323 to 30 BCE.   **barge she sat in ...:** From Shakespeare, *Antony and Cleopatra* (II, ii, 192–206).

THOMASINA: (*Jumping to her feet*) Cheat! Cheat! Cheat!

SEPTIMUS: (*As though it were too easy to make the effort worthwhile*) '. . . and made the water which they beat to follow faster, as *amorous* of their strokes. For her own person, it beggared all description—she did lie in her pavilion—'

(*Thomasina, in tears of rage, is hurrying out through the garden.*)

THOMASINA: I hope you die!

(*She nearly bumps into Brice who is entering. She runs out of sight. Brice enters.*)

BRICE: Good God, man, what have you told her?

SEPTIMUS: Told her? Told her what?

BRICE: Hodge!

(*Septimus looks outside the door, slightly contrite about Thomasina, and sees that Chater is skulking out of view.*)

SEPTIMUS: Chater! My dear fellow! Don't hang back—come in, sir!

(*Chater allows himself to be drawn sheepishly into the room, where Brice stands on his dignity.*)

CHATER: Captain Brice does me the honour—I mean to say, sir, whatever you have to say to me, sir, address yourself to Captain Brice.

SEPTIMUS: How unusual. (*To Brice*) Your wife did not appear yesterday, sir. I trust she is not sick?

BRICE: My wife? I have no wife. What the devil do you mean, sir?

(*Septimus makes to reply, but hesitates, puzzled. He turns back to Chater.*)

SEPTIMUS: I do not understand the scheme, Chater. Whom do I address when I want to speak to Captain Brice?

BRICE: Oh, slippery, Hodge—slippery!

SEPTIMUS: (*To Chater*) By the way, Chater—(*he interrupts himself and turns back to Brice, and continues as before*) by the way, Chater, I have amazing news to tell you. Someone has taken to writing wild and whirling letters in your name. I received one not half an hour ago.

BRICE: (*Angrily*) Mr Hodge! Look to your honour, sir! If you cannot attend to me without this foolery, nominate your second who might settle the business as between gentlemen. No doubt your friend Byron would do you the service.

(*Septimus gives up the game.*)

SEPTIMUS: Oh yes, he would do me the service. (*His mood changes, he turns to Chater.*) Sir—I repent your injury. You are an honest fellow with no more malice in you than poetry.

CHATER: (*Happily*) Ah well!—that is more like the thing! (*Overtaken by doubt.*) Is he apologizing?

BRICE: There is still the injury to his conjugal property, Mrs Chater's—

CHATER: Tush, sir!

BRICE: As you will—her tush. Nevertheless—

(*But they are interrupted by Lady Croom, also entering from the garden.*)

LADY CROOM: Oh—excellently found! Mr Chater, this will please you very much. Lord Byron begs a copy of your new book. He dies to read it and intends to include your name in the second edition of his *English Bards and Scotch Reviewers*.

CHATER: *English Bards and Scotch Reviewers*, your ladyship, is a doggerel aimed at Lord Byron's seniors and betters. If he intends to include me, he intends to insult me.

LADY CROOM: Well, of course he does, Mr Chater. Would you rather be thought not worth insulting? You should be proud to be in the company of Rogers and Moore and Wordsworth°—ah! 'The Couch of Eros!' (*For she has spotted Septimus's copy of the book on the table.*)

SEPTIMUS: That is my copy, madam.

LADY CROOM: So much the better—what are a friend's books for if not to be borrowed?

(*Note: 'The Couch of Eros' now contains the three letters, and it must do so without advertising the fact. This is why the volume has been described as a substantial quarto.*)

Mr Hodge, you must speak to your friend and put him out of his affectation of pretending to quit us. I will not have it. He says he is determined on the Malta packet sailing out of Falmouth! His head is full of Lisbon and Lesbos, and his portmanteau of pistols, and I have told him it is not to be thought of. The whole of Europe is in a Napoleonic fit, all the best ruins will be closed, the roads entirely occupied with the movement of armies, the lodgings turned to billets and the fashion for godless republicanism not yet arrived at its natural reversion. He says his aim is poetry. One does not aim at poetry with pistols. At poets, perhaps. I charge you to take command of his pistols, Mr Hodge! He is not safe with them. His lameness, he confessed to me, is entirely the result of his habit from boyhood of shooting himself in the foot. What is that *noise*?

(*The noise is a badly played piano in the next room. It has been going on for some time since Thomasina left.*)

SEPTIMUS: The new Broadwood pianoforte, madam. Our music lessons are at an early stage.

LADY CROOM: Well, restrict your lessons to the *piano* side of the instrument and let her loose on the *forte* when she has learned something.

Wordsworth: Samuel Rogers (1763–1855), Thomas Moore (1779–1852), and William Wordsworth (1770–1850) were all poets of the Romantic period.

(Lady Croom, holding the book, sails out back into the garden.)

BRICE: Now! If that was not God speaking through Lady Croom, he never spoke through anyone!

CHATER: *(Awed)* Take command of Lord Byron's pistols!

BRICE: You hear Mr Chater, sir—how will you answer him?

(Septimus has been watching Lady Croom's progress up the garden. He turns back.)

SEPTIMUS: By killing him. I am tired of him.

CHATER: *(Startled)* Eh?

BRICE: *(Pleased)* Ah!

SEPTIMUS: Oh, damn your soul, Chater! Ovid would have stayed a lawyer and Virgil a farmer if they had known the bathos to which love would descend in your sportive satyrs and noodle nymphs! I am at your service with a half-ounce ball in your brain. May it satisfy you—behind the boat-house at daybreak—shall we say five o'clock? My compliments to Mrs Chater—have no fear for her, she will not want for protection while Captain Brice has a guinea in his pocket, he told her so himself.

BRICE: You lie, sir!

SEPTIMUS: No, sir. Mrs Chater, perhaps.

BRICE: You lie, or you will answer to me!

SEPTIMUS: *(Wearily)* Oh, very well—I can fit you in at five minutes after five. And then it's off to the Malta packet out of Falmouth. You two will be dead, my penurious schoolfriend will remain to tutor Lady Thomasina, and I trust everybody including Lady Croom will be satisfied!

(Septimus slams the door behind him.)

BRICE: He is all bluster and bladder. Rest assured, Chater, I will let the air out of him.

(Brice leaves by the other door. Chater's assurance lasts only a moment. When he spots the flaw . . .)

CHATER: Oh! But . . .

(He hurries out after Brice.)

Scene Four

Hannah and Valentine. She is reading aloud. He is listening. Lightning, the tortoise, is on the table and is not readily distinguishable from Plautus. In front of Valentine is Septimus's portfolio, recognizably so but naturally somewhat faded. It is open. Principally associated with the portfolio (although it may contain sheets of blank paper also) are three items: a slim maths primer; a sheet of drawing paper on which there is a scrawled diagram and some mathematical notations, arrow marks, etc.; and Thomasina's mathematics lesson book, i.e. the one she writes in, which Valentine

is leafing through as he listens to Hannah reading from the primer.

HANNAH: 'I, Thomasina Coverly, have found a truly wonderful method whereby all the forms of nature must give up their numerical secrets and draw themselves through number alone. This margin being too mean for my purpose, the reader must look elsewhere for the New Geometry of Irregular Forms discovered by Thomasina Coverly.'

(Pause. She hands Valentine the text book. Valentine looks at what she has been reading.
From the next room, a piano is heard, beginning to play quietly, unintrusively, improvisationally.)

Does it mean anything?

VALENTINE: I don't know. I don't know what it means, except mathematically.

HANNAH: I meant mathematically.

VALENTINE: *(Now with the lesson book again)* It's an iterated algorithm.

HANNAH: What's that?

VALENTINE: Well, it's . . . Jesus . . . it's an algorithm that's been . . . iterated. How'm I supposed to . . . ? *(He makes an effort.)* The left-hand pages are graphs of what the numbers are doing on the right-hand pages. But all on different scales. Each graph is a small section of the previous one, blown up. Like you'd blow up a detail of a photograph, and then a detail of the detail, and so on, forever. Or in her case, till she ran out of pages.

HANNAH: Is it difficult?

VALENTINE: The maths isn't difficult. It's what you did at school. You have some x-and-y equation. Any value for x gives you a value for y. So you put a dot where it's right for both x and y. Then you take the next value for x which gives you another value for y, and when you've done that a few times you join up the dots and that's your graph of whatever the equation is.

HANNAH: And is that what she's doing?

VALENTINE: No. Not exactly. Not at all. What she's doing is, every time she works out a value for y, she's using *that* as her next value for x. And so on. Like a feedback. She's feeding the solution back into the equation, and then solving it again. Iteration, you see.

HANNAH: And that's surprising, is it?

VALENTINE: Well, it is a bit. It's the technique I'm using on my grouse numbers, and it hasn't been around for much longer than, well, call it twenty years.

(Pause.)

HANNAH: Why would she be doing it?

VALENTINE: I have no idea.

(Pause.)

I thought you were doing the hermit.

HANNAH: I am. I still am. But Bernard, damn him . . . Thomasina's tutor turns out to have interesting connections. Bernard is going through the library like a bloodhound. The portfolio was in a cupboard.

VALENTINE: There's a lot of stuff around. Gus loves going through it. No old masters or anything . . .

HANNAH: The maths primer she was using belonged to him—the tutor; he wrote his name in it.

VALENTINE: (*Reading*) 'Septimus Hodge.'

HANNAH: Why were these things saved, do you think?

VALENTINE: Why should there be a reason?

HANNAH: And the diagram, what's it of?

VALENTINE: How would I know?

HANNAH: Why are you cross?

VALENTINE: I'm not cross. (*Pause.*) When your Thomasina was doing maths it had been the same maths for a couple of thousand years. Classical. And for a century after Thomasina. Then maths left the real world behind, just like modern art, really. Nature was classical, maths was suddenly Picassos. But now nature is having the last laugh. The freaky stuff is turning out to be the mathematics of the natural world.

HANNAH: This feedback thing?

VALENTINE: For example.

HANNAH: Well, could Thomasina have—

VALENTINE: (*Snaps*) No, of course she bloody couldn't!

HANNAH: All right, you're not cross. What did you mean you were doing the same thing she was doing? (*Pause.*) What *are* you doing?

VALENTINE: Actually I'm doing it from the other end. She started with an equation and turned it into a graph. I've got a graph—real data—and I'm trying to find the equation which would give you the graph if you used it the way she's used hers. Iterated it.

HANNAH: What for?

VALENTINE: It's how you look at population changes in biology. Goldfish in a pond, say. This year there are x goldfish. Next year there'll be y goldfish. Some get born, some get eaten by herons, whatever. Nature manipulates the x and turns it into y. Then y goldfish is your starting population for the following year. Just like Thomasina. Your value for y becomes your next value for x. The question is: what is being done to x? What is the manipulation? Whatever it is, it can be written down as mathematics. It's called an algorithm.

HANNAH: It can't be the same every year.

VALENTINE: The details change, you can't keep tabs on everything, it's not nature in a box. But it isn't necessary to know the details. When they are all put together, it turns out the population is obeying a mathematical rule.

HANNAH: The goldfish are?

VALENTINE: Yes. No. The numbers. It's not about the behaviour of fish. It's about the behaviour of numbers. This thing works for any phenomenon which eats its own numbers—measles epidemics, rainfall averages, cotton prices, it's a natural phenomenon in itself. Spooky.

HANNAH: Does it work for grouse?

VALENTINE: I don't know yet. I mean, it does undoubtedly, but it's hard to show. There's more noise with grouse.

HANNAH: Noise?

VALENTINE: Distortions. Interference. Real data is messy. There's a thousand acres of moorland that had grouse on it, always did till about 1930. But nobody counted the grouse. They shot them. So you count the grouse they shot. But burning the heather interferes, it improves the food supply. A good year for foxes interferes the other way, they eat the chicks. And then there's the weather. It's all very, very noisy out there. Very hard to spot the tune. Like a piano in the next room, it's playing your song, but unfortunately it's out of whack, some of the strings are missing, and the pianist is tone deaf and drunk—I mean, the *noise*! Impossible!

HANNAH: What do you do?

VALENTINE: You start guessing what the tune might be. You try to pick it out of the noise. You try this, you try that, you start to get something—it's half-baked but you start putting in notes which are missing or not quite the right notes . . . and bit by bit . . . (*He starts to dumdi-da to the tune of 'Happy Birthday'.*) Dumdi-dum-dum, dear Val-en-tine, dumdi-dum-dum to you—the lost algorithm!

HANNAH: (*Soberly*) Yes, I see. And then what?

VALENTINE: I publish.

HANNAH: Of course. Sorry. Jolly good.

VALENTINE: That's the theory. Grouse are bastards compared to goldfish.

HANNAH: Why did you choose them?

VALENTINE: The game books. My true inheritance. Two hundred years of real data on a plate.

HANNAH: Somebody wrote down everything that's shot?

VALENTINE: Well, that's what a game book is. I'm only using from 1870, when butts and beaters came in.

HANNAH: You mean the game books go back to Thomasina's time?

VALENTINE: Oh yes. Further. (*And then getting ahead of her thought.*) No—really. I promise you. I *promise* you. Not a schoolgirl living in a country house in Derbyshire in eighteen-something!

HANNAH: Well, what was she doing?

VALENTINE: She was just playing with the numbers. The truth is, she wasn't doing anything.

HANNAH: She must have been doing something.

VALENTINE: Doodling. Nothing she understood.

HANNAH: A monkey at a typewriter?

VALENTINE: Yes. Well, a piano.

(*Hannah picks up the algebra book and reads from it.*)

HANNAH: '. . . a method whereby all the forms of nature must give up their numerical secrets and draw themselves through number alone.' This feedback, is it a way of making pictures of forms in nature? Just tell me if it is or it isn't.

VALENTINE: (*Irritated*) To *me* it is. Pictures of turbulence — growth—change—creation—it's not a way of drawing an elephant, for God's sake!

HANNAH: I'm sorry.

(*She picks up an apple leaf from the table. She is timid about pushing the point.*)

So you couldn't make a picture of this leaf by iterating a whatsit?

VALENTINE: (*Off-hand*) Oh yes, you could do that.

HANNAH: (*Furiously*) Well, tell me! Honestly, I could kill you!

VALENTINE: If you knew the algorithm and fed it back say ten thousand times, each time there'd be a dot somewhere on the screen. You'd never know where to expect the next dot. But gradually you'd start to see this shape, because every dot will be inside the shape of this leaf. It wouldn't *be* a leaf, it would be a mathematical object. But yes. The unpredictable and the predetermined unfold together to make everything the way it is. It's how nature creates itself, on every scale, the snowflake and the snowstorm. It makes me so happy. To be at the beginning again, knowing almost nothing. People were talking about the end of physics. Relativity and quantum looked as if they were going to clean out the whole problem between them. A theory of everything. But they only explained the very big and the very small. The universe, the elementary particles. The ordinary-sized stuff which is our lives, the things people write poetry about—clouds—daffodils—waterfalls—and what happens in a cup of coffee when the cream goes in—these things are full of mystery, as mysterious to us as the heavens were to the Greeks. We're better at predicting events at the edge of the galaxy or inside the nucleus of an atom than whether it'll rain on auntie's garden party three Sundays from now. Because the problem turns out to be different. We can't even predict the next drip from a dripping tap when it gets irregular. Each drip sets up the conditions for the next, the smallest variation blows prediction apart, and the weather is unpredictable the same way, will always be unpredictable. When you push the numbers through the computer you can see it on the screen. The future is disorder. A door like this has cracked open five or six times since we got up on our hind legs. It's the best possible time to be alive, when almost everything you thought you knew is wrong.

(*Pause.*)

HANNAH: The weather is fairly predictable in the Sahara.

VALENTINE: The scale is different but the graph goes up and down the same way. Six thousand years in the Sahara looks like six months in Manchester, I bet you.

HANNAH: How much?

VALENTINE: Everything you have to lose.

HANNAH: (*Pause*) No.

VALENTINE: Quite right. That's why there was corn in Egypt. (*Hiatus. The piano is heard again.*)

HANNAH: What is he playing?

VALENTINE: I don't know. He makes it up.

HANNAH: Chloë called him 'genius'.

VALENTINE: It's what my mother calls him—only *she* means it. Last year some expert had her digging in the wrong place for months to find something or other—the foundations of Capability Brown's boathouse—and Gus put her right first go.

HANNAH: Did he ever speak?

VALENTINE: Oh yes. Until he was five. You've never asked about him. You get high marks here for good breeding.

HANNAH: Yes, I know. I've always been given credit for my unconcern.

(*Bernard enters in high excitement and triumph.*)

BERNARD: *English Bards and Scotch Reviewers*. A pencilled superscription. Listen and kiss my cycle-clips!

(*He is carrying the book. He reads from it.*)

'O harbinger of Sleep, who missed the press
And hoped his drone might thus escape redress!
The wretched Chater, bard of Eros' Couch,
For his narcotic let my pencil vouch!'
You see, *you have to turn over every page*.

HANNAH: Is it his handwriting?

BERNARD: Oh, come *on*.

HANNAH: Obviously not.

BERNARD: Christ, what do you want?

HANNAH: Proof.

VALENTINE: Quite right. Who are you talking about?

BERNARD: Proof? *Proof*? You'd have to be there, you silly bitch!

VALENTINE: (*Mildly*) I say, you're speaking of my fiancée.

HANNAH: Especially when I have a present for you. Guess what I found. (*Producing the present for Bernard.*) Lady Croom writing from London to her husband. Her brother, Captain Brice, married a Mrs Chater. In other words, one might assume, a widow.

(*Bernard looks at the letter.*)

BERNARD: I *said* he was dead. What year? 1810! Oh my God, 1810! Well *done*, Hannah! Are you going to tell me it's a different Mrs Chater?

HANNAH: Oh no. It's her all right. Note her Christian name.

BERNARD: Charity. Charity . . . 'Deny what cannot be proven for Charity's sake!'

HANNAH: Don't kiss me!

VALENTINE: She won't let anyone kiss her.

BERNARD: You see! They wrote—they scribbled—they put it on paper. It was their employment. Their diversion. Paper is what they had. And there'll be more. There is always more. We can find it!

HANNAH: Such passion. First Valentine, now you. It's moving.

Lia Williams as Hannah and
Billy Crudup as Bernard in the
2011 revival in New York.

BERNARD: The aristocratic friend of the tutor—under the same roof as the poor sod whose book he savaged—the first thing he does is seduce Chater's wife. All is discovered. There is a duel. Chater dead, Byron fled! P.s. guess what?, the widow married her ladyship's brother! Do you honestly think no one wrote a word? How could they not! It dropped from sight but we will write it again!

HANNAH: You can, Bernard. I'm not going to take any credit, I haven't done anything.

(*The same thought has clearly occurred to Bernard. He becomes instantly po-faced.*)

BERNARD: Well, that's—very fair—generous—

HANNAH: Prudent. Chater could have died of anything, anywhere.

(*The po-face is forgotten.*)

BERNARD: But he fought a duel with Byron!

HANNAH: You haven't established it was fought. You haven't established it was Byron. For God's sake, Bernard, you haven't established Byron was even here!

BERNARD: I'll tell you your problem. No guts.

HANNAH: Really?

BERNARD: By which I mean a visceral belief in yourself. Gut instinct. The part of you which doesn't reason. The certainty for which there is no back-reference. Because time is reversed. Tock, tick goes the universe and then recovers itself, but it was enough, you were in there and you bloody *know.*

VALENTINE: Are you talking about Lord Byron, the poet?

BERNARD: No, you fucking idiot, we're talking about Lord Byron the chartered accountant.

VALENTINE: (*Unoffended*) Oh well, *he* was here all right, the poet.

(*Silence.*)

HANNAH: How do you know?

VALENTINE: He's in the game book. I think he shot a hare. I read through the whole lot once when I had mumps—some quite interesting people—

HANNAH: Where's the book?

VALENTINE: It's not one I'm using—too early, of course—

HANNAH: 1809.

VALENTINE: They've always been in the commode. Ask Chloë.

(*Hannah looks to Bernard. Bernard has been silent because he has been incapable of speech. He seems to have gone into a trance, in which only his mouth tries to work. Hannah steps over to him and gives him a demure kiss on the cheek. It works. Bernard lurches out into the garden and can be heard croaking for 'Chloë . . . Chloë!'*)

VALENTINE: My mother's lent him her bicycle. Lending one's bicycle is a form of safe sex, possibly the safest there is. My mother is in a flutter about Bernard, and he's no fool. He gave her a first edition of Horace Walpole, and now she's lent him her bicycle.

(*He gathers up the three items [the primer, the lesson book and the diagram] and puts them into the portfolio.*)

Can I keep these for a while?

HANNAH: Yes, of course.

(*The piano stops. Gus enters hesitantly from the music room.*)

VALENTINE: (*To Gus*) Yes, finished ... coming now. (*To Hannah*) I'm trying to work out the diagram.

(*Gus nods and smiles, at Hannah too, but she is preoccupied.*)

HANNAH: What I don't understand is ... why nobody did this feedback thing before—it's not like relativity, you don't have to be Einstein.

VALENTINE: You couldn't see to look before. The electronic calculator was what the telescope was for Galileo.

HANNAH: Calculator?

VALENTINE: There wasn't enough time before. There weren't enough *pencils*! (*He flourishes Thomasina's lesson book.*) This took her I don't know how many days and she hasn't scratched the paintwork. Now she'd only have to press a button, the same button over and over. Iteration. A few minutes. And what I've done in a couple of months, with only a *pencil* the calculations would take me the rest of my life to do again—thousands of pages—tens of thousands! And so boring!

HANNAH: Do you mean—?

(*She stops because Gus is plucking Valentine's sleeve.*)

Do you mean—?

VALENTINE: All right, Gus, I'm coming.

HANNAH: Do you mean that was the only problem? Enough time? And paper? And the boredom?

VALENTINE: We're going to get out the dressing-up box.

HANNAH: (*Driven to raising her voice*) Val! Is that what you're saying?

VALENTINE: (*Surprised by her. Mildly*) No, I'm saying you'd have to have a reason for doing it.

(*Gus runs out of the room, upset.*)

(*Apologetically*) He hates people shouting.

HANNAH: I'm sorry.

(*Valentine starts to follow Gus.*)

But anything else?

VALENTINE: Well, the other thing is, you'd have to be insane.

(*Valentine leaves.*

Hannah stays, thoughtful. After a moment, she turns to the table and picks up the Cornhill Magazine. *She looks into it briefly, then closes it, and leaves the room, taking the magazine with her.*

The empty room.

The light changes to early morning. From a long way off, there is a pistol shot. A moment later there is the cry of dozens of crows disturbed from the unseen trees.)

ACT TWO • Scene Five

Bernard is pacing around, reading aloud from a handful of typed sheets. Valentine, Chloë and Gus are his audience. Gus sits somewhat apart, perhaps less attentive. Valentine has his tortoise and is eating a sandwich from which he extracts shreds of lettuce to offer the tortoise.

BERNARD: 'Did it happen? Could it happen? Undoubtedly it could. Only three years earlier the Irish poet Tom Moore appeared on the field of combat to avenge a review by Jeffrey of the *Edinburgh*. These affairs were seldom fatal and sometimes farcical but, potentially, the duellist stood in respect to the law no differently from a murderer. As for the murderee, a minor poet like Ezra Chater could go to his death in a Derbyshire glade as unmissed and unremembered as his contemporary and namesake, the minor botanist who died in the forests of the West Indies, lost to history like the monkey that bit him. On April 16th 1809, a few days after he left Sidley Park, Byron wrote to his solicitor John Hanson: 'If the consequences of my leaving England were ten times as ruinous as you describe, I have no alternative; there are circumstances which render it absolutely indispensable, and quit the country I must immediately.' To which, the editor's note in the Collected Letters reads as follows: 'What Byron's urgent reasons for leaving England were at this time has never been revealed.' The letter was written from the family seat, Newstead Abbey, Nottinghamshire. A long day's ride to the north-west lay Sidley Park, the estate of the Coverlys—a far grander family, raised by Charles II to the Earldom of Croom ...'

(*Hannah enters briskly, a piece of paper in her hand.*)

HANNAH: Bernard ... ! Val ...

BERNARD: Do you mind?

(*Hannah puts her piece of paper down in front of Valentine.*)

CHLOË: (*Angrily*) Hannah!

HANNAH: What?

CHLOË: She's so *rude*!

HANNAH: (*Taken aback*) What? Am I?

VALENTINE: Bernard's reading us his lecture.

HANNAH: Yes, I know. (*Then recollecting herself.*) Yes—yes—that *was* rude. I'm sorry, Bernard.

VALENTINE: (*With the piece of paper*) What is this?

HANNAH: (*To Bernard*) Spot on—the India Office Library. (*To Valentine*) Peacock's letter in holograph, I got a copy sent—

CHLOË: *Hannah*! Shut up!

HANNAH: (*Sitting down*) Yes, sorry.

BERNARD: It's all right, I'll read it to myself.

CHLOË: No.

(*Hannah reaches for the Peacock letter and takes it back.*)

HANNAH: Go on, Bernard. Have I missed anything? Sorry.

(*Bernard stares at her balefully but then continues to read.*)

BERNARD: 'The Byrons of Newstead in 1809 comprised an eccentric widow and her undistinguished son, the "lame brat", who until the age of ten when he came into the title, had been carted about the country from lodging to lodging by his vulgar hectoring monster of a mother—' (*Hannah's hand has gone up*)—overruled—'and who four months past his twenty-first birthday was master of nothing but his debts and his genius. Between the Byrons and the Coverlys there was no social equality and none to be expected. The connection, undisclosed to posterity until now, was with Septimus Hodge, Byron's friend at Harrow and Trinity College—' (*Hannah's hand goes up again*)—sustained—(*He makes an instant correction with a silver pencil.*) 'Byron's contemporary at Harrow and Trinity College, and now tutor in residence to the Croom daughter, Thomasina Coverly. Byron's letters tell us where he was on April 8th and on April 12th. He was at Newstead. But on the 10th he was at Sidley Park, as attested by the game book preserved there: "April 10th 1809—forenoon. High cloud, dry, and sun between times, wind south-easterly. Self—Augustus—Lord Byron. Fourteen pigeon, one hare (Lord B.)." But, as we know now, the drama of life and death at Sidley Park was not about pigeons but about sex and literature.'

VALENTINE: Unless you were the pigeon.

BERNARD: I don't have to do this. I'm paying you a compliment.

CHLOË: Ignore him, Bernard—go on, get to the duel.

BERNARD: Hannah's not even paying attention.

HANNAH: Yes I am, it's all going in. I often work with the radio on.

BERNARD: Oh thanks!

HANNAH: Is there much more?

CHLOË: *Hannah*!

HANNAH: No, it's fascinating. I just wondered how much more there was. I need to ask Valentine about this (*letter*)—sorry, Bernard, go on, this will keep.

VALENTINE: Yes—sorry, Bernard.

CHLOË: Please, Bernard!

BERNARD: Where was I?

VALENTINE: Pigeons.

CHLOË: Sex.

HANNAH: Literature.

BERNARD: Life and death. Right. 'Nothing could be more eloquent of that than the three documents I have quoted: the terse demand to settle a matter in private; the desperate scribble of "my husband has sent for pistols"; and on April 11th, the gauntlet thrown down by the aggrieved and cuckolded author Ezra Chater. The covers have not survived. What is certain is that all three letters were in Byron's possession when his books were sold in 1816—preserved in the pages of "The Couch of Eros" which seven years earlier at Sidley Park Byron had borrowed from Septimus Hodge.'

HANNAH: Borrowed?

BERNARD: I will be taking questions at the end. Constructive comments will be welcome. Which is indeed my reason for trying out in the provinces before my London opening under the auspices of the Byron Society prior to publication. By the way, Valentine, do you want a credit?—'the game book recently discovered by.'?

VALENTINE: It was never lost, Bernard.

BERNARD: 'As recently pointed out by.' I don't normally like giving credit where it's due, but with scholarly articles as with divorce, there is a certain cachet in citing a member of the aristocracy. I'll pop it in ad lib for the lecture, and give you a mention in the press release. How's that?

VALENTINE: Very kind.

HANNAH: Press release? What happened to the *Journal of English Studies?*

BERNARD: That comes later with the apparatus, and in the recognized tone—very dry, very modest, absolutely gloat-free, and yet unmistakably 'Eat your heart out, you dozy bastards'. But first, it's 'Media Don, book early to avoid disappointment'. Where was I?

VALENTINE: Game book.

CHLOË: Eros.

HANNAH: Borrowed.

BERNARD: Right. '—borrowed from Septimus Hodge. Is it conceivable that the letters were already in the book when Byron borrowed it?'

VALENTINE: Yes.

CHLOË: Shut up, Val.

VALENTINE: Well, it's conceivable.

BERNARD: 'Is it *likely* that Hodge would have lent Byron the book without first removing the three private letters?'

VALENTINE: Look, sorry—I only meant, Byron could have borrowed the book without asking.

HANNAH: That's true.

BERNARD: Then why wouldn't Hodge get them back?

HANNAH: I don't know, I wasn't there.

BERNARD: That's right, you bloody weren't.

CHLOË: Go on, Bernard.

BERNARD: 'It is the third document, the challenge itself, that convinces. Chater "as a man and a poet", points the finger at his "slanderer in the press". Neither as a man nor a poet did Ezra Chater cut such a figure as to be habitually slandered or even mentioned in the press. It is surely indisputable that the slander was the review of "The Maid of Turkey" in the *Piccadilly Recreation*. Did Septimus Hodge have any connection with the London periodicals? No. Did Byron? Yes! He had reviewed Wordsworth two years earlier, he was to review Spencer two years later. And do we have any clue as to Byron's opinion of Chater the poet? Yes! Who but Byron could have written the four lines pencilled into Lady Croom's copy of *English Bards and Scotch Reviewers*'—

HANNAH: Almost anybody.

BERNARD: Darling—

HANNAH: Don't call me darling.

BERNARD: Dickhead, then, is it likely that the man Chater calls his friend Septimus Hodge is the same man who screwed his wife and kicked the shit out of his last book?

HANNAH: Put it like that, almost certain.

CHLOË: (*Earnestly*) You've been deeply wounded in the past, haven't you, Hannah?

HANNAH: Nothing compared to listening to this. Why is there nothing in Byron's letters about the *Piccadilly* reviews?

BERNARD: Exactly. Because he killed the author.

HANNAH: But the first one, 'The Maid of Turkey', was the year before. Was he clairvoyant?

CHLOË: Letters get lost.

BERNARD: Thank you! Exactly! There is a platonic letter which confirms everything—lost but ineradicable, like radio voices rippling through the universe for all eternity. 'My dear Hodge—here I am in Albania and you're the only person in the whole world who knows why. Poor C! I never wished him any harm—except in the *Piccadilly*, of course—it was the woman who bade me eat, dear Hodge!—what a tragic business, but thank God it ended well for poetry. Yours ever, B.—PS. Burn this.'

STOP

VALENTINE: How did Chater find out the reviewer was Byron?

BERNARD: (*Irritated*) I don't know, I wasn't there, was I? (*Pause. To Hannah*) You wish to say something?

HANNAH: Moi?

CHLOË: I know. Byron told Mrs Chater in bed. Next day he dumped her so she grassed on him, and pleaded date rape.

BERNARD: (*Fastidiously*) Date rape? What do you mean, date rape?

HANNAH: April the tenth.

(*Bernard cracks. Everything becomes loud and overlapped as Bernard threatens to walk out and is cajoled into continuing.*)

BERNARD: Right!—forget it!

HANNAH: Sorry—

BERNARD: No—I've had nothing but sarcasm and childish interruptions—

VALENTINE: What did I do?

BERNARD: No credit for probably the most sensational literary discovery of the century—

CHLOË: I think you're jolly unfair—they're jealous, Bernard—

HANNAH: I won't say another word—

VALENTINE: Yes, go on, Bernard—we promise.

BERNARD: (*Finally*) Well, only if you stop *feeding tortoises*!

VALENTINE: Well, it's his lunch time.

BERNARD: And on condition that I am afforded the common courtesy of a scholar among scholars—

HANNAH: Absolutely mum till you're finished—

BERNARD: After which, any comments are to be couched in terms of accepted academic—

HANNAH: Dignity—you're right, Bernard.

BERNARD: —respect.

HANNAH: Respect. Absolutely. The language of scholars. Count on it.

(*Having made a great show of putting his pages away, Bernard reassembles them and finds his place, glancing suspiciously at the other three for signs of levity.*)

BERNARD: Last paragraph. 'Without question, Ezra Chater issued a challenge to *somebody*. If a duel was fought in the dawn mist of Sidley Park in April 1809, his opponent, on the evidence, was a critic with a gift for ridicule and a taste for seduction. Do we need to look far? Without question, Mrs Chater was a widow by 1810. If we seek the occasion of Ezra Chater's early and unrecorded death, do we need to look far? Without question, Lord Byron, in the very season of his emergence as a literary figure, quit the country in a cloud of panic and mystery, and stayed abroad for two years at a time when Continental travel was unusual and dangerous. If we seek his reason—*do we need to look far?*

(*No mean performer, he is pleased with the effect of his peroration. There is a significant silence.*)

HANNAH: Bollocks.

CHLOË: Well, I think it's true.

HANNAH: You've left out everything which doesn't fit. Byron had been banging on for months about leaving England—there's a letter in *February*—

BERNARD: But he didn't go, did he?

HANNAH: And then he didn't sail until the beginning of July!

BERNARD: Everything moved more slowly then. Time was different. He was two weeks in Falmouth waiting for wind or something—

HANNAH: Bernard, I don't know why I'm bothering—you're arrogant, greedy and reckless. You've gone from a glint in your eye to a sure thing in a hop, skip and a jump. You deserve what you get and I think you're mad. But I can't help myself, you're like some exasperating child pedalling its tricycle towards the edge of a cliff, and I have to do something. So listen to me. If Byron killed Chater in a duel I'm Marie of Romania. You'll end up with so much *fame* you won't leave the house without a paper bag over your head.

VALENTINE: Actually, Bernard, as a scientist, your theory is incomplete.

BERNARD: But I'm not a scientist.

VALENTINE: (*Patiently*) No, *as a scientist*—

BERNARD: (*Beginning to shout*) I have yet to hear a proper argument.

HANNAH: Nobody would kill a man and then pan his book. I mean, not in that order. So he must have borrowed the book, written the review, *posted it*, seduced Mrs Chater, fought a duel and departed, all in the space of two or three days. Who would do that?

BERNARD: Byron.

HANNAH: It's hopeless.

BERNARD: You've never understood him, as you've shown in your novelette.

HANNAH: In my what?

BERNARD: Oh, sorry—did you think it was a work of historical revisionism? Byron the spoilt child promoted beyond his gifts by the spirit of the age! And Caroline the closet intellectual shafted by a male society!

VALENTINE: I read that somewhere—

HANNAH: It's his review.

BERNARD: And bloody well said, too!

(*Things are turning a little ugly and Bernard seems in a mood to push them that way.*)

You got them backwards, darling. Caroline was Romantic waffle on wheels with no talent, and Byron was an eighteenth-century Rationalist touched by genius. And he killed Chater.

HANNAH: (*Pause*) If it's not too late to change my mind, I'd like you to go ahead.

BERNARD: I intend to. Look to the mote in your own eye!—you even had the wrong bloke on the dust-jacket!

HANNAH: Dust-jacket?

VALENTINE: What about my computer model? Aren't you going to mention it?

BERNARD: It's inconclusive.

VALENTINE: (*To Hannah*) The *Piccadilly* reviews aren't a very good fit with Byron's other reviews, you see.

HANNAH: (*To Bernard*) What do you mean, the wrong bloke?

BERNARD: (*Ignoring her*) The other reviews aren't a very good fit for each other, are they?

VALENTINE: No, but differently. The parameters—

BERNARD: (*Jeering*) Parameters! You can't stick Byron's head in your laptop! Genius isn't like your average grouse.

VALENTINE: (*Casually*) Well, it's all trivial anyway.

BERNARD: What is?

VALENTINE: Who wrote what when . . .

BERNARD: Trivial?

VALENTINE: Personalities.

BERNARD: I'm sorry—did you say trivial?

VALENTINE: It's a technical term.

BERNARD: Not where I come from, it isn't.

VALENTINE: The questions you're asking don't matter, you see. It's like arguing who got there first with the calculus. The English say Newton, the Germans say Leibnitz. But it doesn't *matter*. Personalities. What matters is the calculus. Scientific progress. Knowledge.

BERNARD: Really? Why?

VALENTINE: Why what?

BERNARD: Why does scientific progress matter more than personalities?

VALENTINE: Is he serious?

HANNAH: No, he's trivial. Bernard—

VALENTINE: (*Interrupting, to Bernard*) Do yourself a favour, you're on a loser.

BERNARD: Oh, you're going to zap me with penicillin and pesticides. Spare me that and I'll spare you the bomb and aerosols. But don't confuse progress with perfectibility. A great poet is always timely. A great philosopher is an urgent need. There's no rush for Isaac Newton. We were quite happy with Aristotle's cosmos. Personally, I preferred it. Fifty-five crystal spheres geared to God's crankshaft is my idea of a satisfying universe. I can't think of anything more trivial than the speed of light. Quarks, quasars—big bangs, black holes—who gives a shit? How did you people con us out of all that status? All that money? And why are you so pleased with yourselves?

CHLOË: Are you against penicillin, Bernard?

BERNARD: Don't feed the animals. (*Back to Valentine*) I'd push the lot of you over a cliff myself. Except the one in the wheelchair,° I think I'd lose the sympathy vote before people had time to think it through.

HANNAH: (*Loudly*) What the hell do you mean, the dust-jacket?

BERNARD: (*Ignoring her*) If knowledge isn't self-knowledge it isn't doing much, mate. Is the universe expanding? Is it contracting? Is it standing on one leg and singing 'When Father Painted the Parlour'? Leave me out. I can expand my universe without you. 'She walks in beauty, like the night of cloudless climes and starry skies, and all that's best of dark and bright meet in her aspect and her eyes.' There you are, he wrote it after coming home from a party. (*With offensive politeness.*) What is it that you're doing with grouse, Valentine, I'd love to know?

(*Valentine stands up and it is suddenly apparent that he is shaking and close to tears.*)

VALENTINE: (*To Chloë*) He's not against penicillin, and he knows I'm not against poetry. (*To Bernard*) I've given up on the grouse.

HANNAH: You haven't, Valentine!

VALENTINE: (*Leaving*) I can't do it.

HANNAH: *Why?*

---

wheelchair: The one in the wheelchair is Stephen Hawking (b. 1942), the most famous living physicist.

VALENTINE: Too much noise. There's just too much *bloody noise!*

(*On which, Valentine leaves the room. Chloë, upset and in tears, jumps up and briefly pummels Bernard ineffectually with her fists.*)

CHLOË: You bastard, Bernard!

(*She follows Valentine out and is followed at a run by Gus. Pause.*)

HANNAH: Well, I think that's everybody. You can leave now, give Lightning a kick on your way out.

BERNARD: Yes, I'm sorry about that. It's no fun when it's not among pros, is it?

HANNAH: No.

BERNARD: Oh, well . . . (*he begins to put his lecture sheets away in his briefcase, and is thus reminded . . .*) do you want to know about your book jacket? 'Lord Byron and Caroline Lamb at the Royal Academy'? Ink study by Henry Fuseli?°

HANNAH: What about it?

BERNARD: It's not them.

HANNAH: (*She explodes*) Who says!?

(*Bernard brings the* Byron Society Journal *from his briefcase.*)

BERNARD: This Fuseli expert in *Byron Society Journal*. They sent me the latest . . . as a distinguished guest speaker.

HANNAH: But of course it's them! Everyone knows—

BERNARD: Popular tradition only. (*He is finding the place in the journal.*) Here we are. 'No earlier than 1820'. He's analysed it. (*Offers it to her.*) Read at your leisure.

HANNAH: (*She sounds like Bernard jeering*) Analysed it?

BERNARD: Charming sketch, of course, but Byron was in Italy . . .

HANNAH: But, Bernard—I *know* it's them.

BERNARD: How?

HANNAH: How? It just *is.* 'Analysed it', my big toe!

BERNARD: Language!

HANNAH: He's wrong.

BERNARD: Oh, gut instinct, you mean?

HANNAH: (*Flatly*) He's wrong.

(*Bernard snaps shut his briefcase.*)

BERNARD: Well, it's all trivial, isn't it? Why don't you come?

HANNAH: Where?

BERNARD: With me.

HANNAH: To London? What for?

BERNARD: What for.

HANNAH: Oh, your lecture.

BERNARD: No, no, bugger that. Sex.

HANNAH: Oh . . . No. Thanks . . . (*then, protesting*) Bernard!

Fuseli: Henry Fuseli (1741–1825), a Swiss-born painter of fantastic Romantic scenes.

BERNARD: You should try it. It's very underrated.

HANNAH: Nothing against it.

BERNARD: Yes, you have. You should let yourself go a bit. You might have written a better book. Or at any rate the right book.

HANNAH: Sex and literature. Literature and sex. Your conversation, left to itself, doesn't have many places to go. Like two marbles rolling around a pudding basin. One of them is always sex.

BERNARD: Ah well, yes. Men all over.

HANNAH: No doubt. Einstein—relativity and sex. Chippendale—sex and furniture. Galileo—'Did the earth move?' What the hell is it with you people? Chaps sometimes wanted to marry me, and I don't know a worse bargain. Available sex against not being allowed to fart in bed. What do you mean the right book?

BERNARD: It takes a romantic to make a heroine of Caroline Lamb. You were cut out for Byron.

(*Pause.*)

HANNAH: So, cheerio.

BERNARD: Oh, I'm coming back for the dance, you know. Chloë asked me.

HANNAH: She meant well, but I don't dance.

BERNARD: No, no—I'm going with her.

HANNAH: Oh, I see. I don't, actually.

BERNARD: I'm her date. Sub rosa. Don't tell Mother.

HANNAH: She doesn't want her mother to know?

BERNARD: No—*I* don't want her mother to know. This is my first experience of the landed aristocracy. I tell you, I'm boggle-eyed.

HANNAH: Bernard!—you haven't seduced that girl?

BERNARD: Seduced her? Every time I turned round she was up a library ladder. In the end I gave in. That reminds me—I spotted something between her legs that made me think of you.

(*He instantly receives a sharp stinging slap on the face but manages to remain completely unperturbed by it. He is already producing from his pocket a small book. His voice has hardly hesitated.*)

The Peaks Traveller and Gazetteer—James Godolphin 1832—unillustrated, I'm afraid. (*He has opened the book to a marked place.*) Sidley Park in Derbyshire, property of the Earl of Croom . . .'

HANNAH: (*Numbly*) The world is going to hell in a handcart.

BERNARD: 'Five hundred acres including forty of lake—the Park by Brown and Noakes has pleasing features in the horrid style—viaduct, grotto, etc—a hermitage occupied by a lunatic since twenty years without discourse or companion save for a pet tortoise, Plautus by name, which he suffers children to touch on request.' (*He holds out the book for her.*) A tortoise. They must be a feature.

(*After a moment Hannah takes the book.*)

HANNAH: Thank you.

(*Valentine comes to the door.*)

VALENTINE: The station taxi is at the front . . .

BERNARD: Yes . . . thanks . . . Oh—did Peacock come up trumps?

HANNAH: For some.

BERNARD: Hermit's name and cv?

(*He picks up and glances at the Peacock letter.*)

'My dear Thackeray . . .' God, I'm good.

(*He puts the letter down.*)

Well, wish me luck—(*Vaguely to Valentine*) Sorry about . . . you know . . . (*and to Hannah*) and about your . . .

VALENTINE: Piss off, Bernard.

BERNARD: Right.

(*Bernard goes.*)

HANNAH: Don't let Bernard get to you. It's only performance art, you know. Rhetoric, they used to teach it in ancient times, like PT. It's not about being right, they had philosophy for that. Rhetoric was their chat show. Bernard's indignation is a sort of aerobics for when he gets on television.

VALENTINE: I don't care to be rubbished by the dustbin man. (*He has been looking at the letter.*) The what of the lunatic?

(*Hannah reclaims the letter and reads it for him.*)

HANNAH: 'The testament of the lunatic serves as a caution against French fashion . . . for it was Frenchified mathematick that brought him to the melancholy certitude of a world without light or life . . . as a wooden stove that must consume itself until ash and stove are as one, and heat is gone from the earth.'

VALENTINE: (*Amused, surprised*) Huh!

HANNAH: 'He died aged two score years and seven, hoary as Job° and meagre as a cabbage-stalk, the proof of his prediction even yet unyielding to his labours for the restitution of hope through good English algebra.'

VALENTINE: That's it?

HANNAH: (*Nods*) Is there anything in it?

VALENTINE: In what? We are all doomed? (*Casually.*) Oh yes, sure—it's called the second law of thermodynamics.°

HANNAH: Was it known about?

VALENTINE: By poets and lunatics from time immemorial.

HANNAH: Seriously.

VALENTINE: No.

---

hoary as Job: As white-haired as Job in the Old Testament, thus very old.   **thermodynamics:** The second law of thermodynamics says that hot and cold objects will always progress in one direction, to room temperature, as mentioned in the play. Some scientists have postulated that the death of the universe will occur through the loss of the heat of all stars, as described in this law. See Valentine's speech in scene 7.

HANNAH: Is it anything to do with . . . you know, Thomasina's discovery?

VALENTINE: She didn't discover anything.

HANNAH: Her lesson book.

VALENTINE: No.

HANNAH: A coincidence, then?

VALENTINE: What is?

HANNAH: (*Reading*) 'He died aged two score years and seven.' That was in 1834. So he was born in 1787. So was the tutor. He says so in his letter to Lord Croom when he recommended himself for the job: 'Date of birth—1787.' The hermit was born in the same year as Septimus Hodge.

VALENTINE: (*Pause*) Did Bernard bite you in the leg?

HANNAH: Don't you see? I thought my hermit was a perfect symbol. An idiot in the landscape. But this is better. The Age of Enlightenment banished into the Romantic wilderness! The genius of Sidley Park living on in a hermit's hut!

VALENTINE: You don't *know* that.

HANNAH: Oh, but I do. I do. Somewhere there will be *something* . . . if only I can find it.

Scene Six

The room is empty.

A reprise: early morning—a distant pistol shot—the sound of the crows.

Jellaby enters the dawn-dark room with a lamp. He goes to the windows and looks out. He sees something. He returns to put the lamp on the table, and then opens one of the French windows and steps outside.

JELLABY: (*Outside*) Mr Hodge!

(*Septimus comes in, followed by Jellaby, who closes the garden door. Septimus is wearing a greatcoat.*)

SEPTIMUS: Thank you, Jellaby. I was expecting to be locked out. What time is it?

JELLABY: Half past five.

SEPTIMUS: That is what I have. Well!—what a bracing experience!

(*He produces two pistols from inside his coat and places them on the table.*)

The dawn, you know. Unexpectedly lively. Fishes, birds, frogs . . . rabbits . . . (*he produces a dead rabbit from inside his coat*) and very beautiful. If only it did not occur so early in the day. I have brought Lady Thomasina a rabbit. Will you take it?

JELLABY: It's dead.

SEPTIMUS: Yes. Lady Thomasina loves a rabbit pie.

(*Jellaby takes the rabbit without enthusiasm. There is a little blood on it.*)

JELLABY: You were missed, Mr Hodge.
SEPTIMUS: I decided to sleep last night in the boat-house. Did I see a carriage leaving the Park?
JELLABY: Captain Brice's carriage, with Mr and Mrs Chater also.
SEPTIMUS: Gone?!
JELLABY: Yes, sir. And Lord Byron's horse was brought round at four o'clock.
SEPTIMUS: Lord Byron too!
JELLABY: Yes, sir. The house has been up and hopping.
SEPTIMUS: But I have his rabbit pistols! What am I to do with his rabbit pistols?
JELLABY: You were looked for in your room.
SEPTIMUS: By whom?
JELLABY: By her ladyship.
SEPTIMUS: In my room?
JELLABY: I will tell her ladyship you are returned.

(*He starts to leave.*)

SEPTIMUS: Jellaby! Did Lord Byron leave a book for me?
JELLABY: A book?
SEPTIMUS: He had the loan of a book from me.
JELLABY: His lordship left nothing in his room, sir, not a coin.
SEPTIMUS: Oh. Well, I'm sure he would have left a coin if he'd had one. Jellaby—here is a half-guinea for you.
JELLABY: Thank you very much, sir.
SEPTIMUS: What has occurred?
JELLABY: The servants are told nothing, sir.
SEPTIMUS: Come, come, does a half-guinea buy nothing any more?
JELLABY: (*Sighs*) Her ladyship encountered Mrs Chater during the night.
SEPTIMUS: Where?
JELLABY: On the threshold of Lord Byron's room.
SEPTIMUS: Ah. Which one was leaving and which entering?
JELLABY: Mrs Chater was leaving Lord Byron's room.
SEPTIMUS: And where was Mr Chater?
JELLABY: Mr Chater and Captain Brice were drinking cherry brandy. They had the footman to keep the fire up until three o'clock. There was a loud altercation upstairs, and—

(*Lady Croom enters the room.*)

LADY CROOM: Well, Mr Hodge.
SEPTIMUS: My lady.
LADY CROOM: All this to shoot a hare?
SEPTIMUS: A rabbit. (*She gives him one of her looks.*) No, indeed, a hare, though very rabbit-like—

(*Jellaby is about to leave.*)

LADY CROOM: My infusion.
JELLABY: Yes, my lady.

(*He leaves. Lady Croom is carrying two letters. We have not seen them before. Each has an envelope which has been opened. She flings them on the table.*)

LADY CROOM: How dare you!
SEPTIMUS: I cannot be called to account for what was written in private and read without regard to propriety.
LADY CROOM: Addressed to me!
SEPTIMUS: Left in my room, in the event of my death—
LADY CROOM: Pah!—what earthly use is a love letter from beyond the grave?
SEPTIMUS: As much, surely, as from this side of it. The second letter, however, was not addressed to your ladyship.
LADY CROOM: I have a mother's right to open a letter addressed by you to my daughter, whether in the event of your life, your death, or your imbecility. What do you mean by writing to her of rice pudding when she has just suffered the shock of violent death in our midst?
SEPTIMUS: Whose death?
LADY CROOM: Yours, you wretch!
SEPTIMUS: Yes, I see.
LADY CROOM: I do not know which is the madder of your ravings. One envelope full of rice pudding, the other of the most insolent familiarities regarding several parts of my body, but have no doubt which is the more intolerable to me.
SEPTIMUS: Which?
LADY CROOM: Oh, aren't we saucy when our bags are packed! Your friend has gone before you, and I have despatched the harlot Chater and her husband—and also my brother for bringing them here. Such is the sentence, you see, for choosing unwisely in your acquaintance. Banishment. Lord Byron is a rake and a hypocrite, and the sooner he sails for the Levant the sooner he will find society congenial to his character.
SEPTIMUS: It has been a night of reckoning.
LADY CROOM: Indeed I wish it had passed uneventfully with you and Mr Chater shooting each other with the decorum due to a civilized house. You have no secrets left, Mr Hodge. They spilled out between shrieks and oaths and tears. It is fortunate that a lifetime's devotion to the sporting gun has halved my husband's hearing to the ear he sleeps on.
SEPTIMUS: I'm afraid I have no knowledge of what has occurred.
LADY CROOM: Your trollop was discovered in Lord Byron's room.
SEPTIMUS: Ah. Discovered by Mr Chater?
LADY CROOM: Who else?
SEPTIMUS: I am very sorry, madam, for having used your kindness to bring my unworthy friend to your notice. He will have to give an account of himself to me, you may be sure.

(*Before Lady Croom can respond to this threat, Jellaby enters the room with her 'infusion'. This is quite an elaborate affair: a pewter tray on small feet on which there is a kettle suspended over a spirit lamp. There is a cup and saucer and the silver 'basket' containing the dry leaves for the tea. Jellaby places the tray on the table and is about to offer further assistance with it.*)

LADY CROOM: I will do it.

JELLABY: Yes, my lady. (*To Septimus*) Lord Byron left a letter for you with the valet, sir.

SEPTIMUS: Thank you.

(*Septimus takes the letter off the tray. Jellaby prepares to leave. Lady Croom eyes the letter.*)

LADY CROOM: When did he do so?

JELLABY: As he was leaving, your ladyship.

(*Jellaby leaves. Septimus puts the letter into his pocket.*)

SEPTIMUS: Allow me.

(*Since she does not object, he pours a cup of tea for her. She accepts it.*)

LADY CROOM: I do not know if it is proper for you to receive a letter written in my house from someone not welcome in it.

SEPTIMUS: Very improper, I agree. Lord Byron's want of delicacy is a grief to his friends, among whom I no longer count myself. I will not read his letter until I have followed him through the gates.

(*She considers that for a moment.*)

LADY CROOM: That may excuse the reading but not the writing.

SEPTIMUS: Your ladyship should have lived in the Athens of Pericles! The philosophers would have fought the sculptors for your idle hour!

LADY CROOM: (*Protesting*) Oh, really! . . . (*Protesting less.*) Oh really . . .

(*Septimus has taken Byron's letter from his pocket and is now setting fire to a corner of it using the little flame from the spirit lamp.*)

Oh . . . really . . .

(*The paper blazes in Septimus's hand and he drops it and lets it burn out on the metal tray.*)

SEPTIMUS: Now there's a thing—a letter from Lord Byron never to be read by a living soul. I will take my leave, madam, at the time of your desiring it.

LADY CROOM: To the Indies?

SEPTIMUS: The Indies! Why?

LADY CROOM: To follow the Chater, of course. She did not tell you?

SEPTIMUS: She did not exchange half-a-dozen words with me.

LADY CROOM: I expect she did not like to waste the time. The Chater sails with Captain Brice.

SEPTIMUS: Ah. As a member of the crew?

LADY CROOM: No, as wife to Mr Chater, plant-gatherer to my brother's expedition.

SEPTIMUS: I knew he was no poet. I did not know it was botany under the false colours.

LADY CROOM: He is no more a botanist. My brother paid fifty pounds to have him published, and he will pay a hundred and fifty to have Mr Chater picking flowers in the Indies for a year while the wife plays mistress of the Captain's quarters. Captain Brice has fixed his passion on Mrs Chater, and to take her on voyage he has not scrupled to deceive the Admiralty, the Linnean Society° and Sir Joseph Banks, botanist to His Majesty at Kew.

SEPTIMUS: Her passion is not as fixed as his.

LADY CROOM: It is a defect of God's humour that he directs our hearts everywhere but to those who have a right to them.

SEPTIMUS: Indeed, madam. (*Pause.*) But is Mr Chater deceived?

LADY CROOM: He insists on it, and finds the proof of his wife's virtue in his eagerness to defend it. Captain Brice is *not* deceived but cannot help himself. He would die for her.

SEPTIMUS: I think, my lady, he would have Mr Chater die for her.

LADY CROOM: Indeed, I never knew a woman worth the duel, or the other way about. Your letter to me goes very ill with your conduct to Mrs Chater, Mr Hodge. I have had experience of being betrayed before the ink is dry, but to be betrayed before the pen is even dipped, and with the village noticeboard, what am I to think of such a performance?

SEPTIMUS: My lady, I was alone with my thoughts in the gazebo, when Mrs Chater ran me to ground, and I being in such a passion, in an agony of unrelieved desire—

LADY CROOM: Oh . . . !

SEPTIMUS: —I thought in my madness that the Chater with her skirts over her head would give me the momentary illusion of the happiness to which I dared not put a face.

(*Pause.*)

LADY CROOM: I do not know when I have received a more unusual compliment, Mr Hodge. I hope I am more than a match for Mrs Chater with her head in a bucket. Does she wear drawers?

SEPTIMUS: She does.

LADY CROOM: Yes, I have heard that drawers are being worn now. It is unnatural for women to be got up like jockeys. I cannot approve.

(*She turns with a whirl of skirts and moves to leave.*)

I know nothing of Pericles or the Athenian philosophers. I can spare them an hour, in my sitting room when I have bathed. Seven o'clock. Bring a book.

(*She goes out. Septimus picks up the two letters, the ones he wrote, and starts to burn them in the flame of the spirit lamp.*)

Linnean Society: Founded in 1788 for the study of biology and botany.

Scene Seven

Valentine and Chloë are at the table. Gus is in the room.

> *Chloë is reading from two Saturday newspapers. She is wearing workaday period clothes, a Regency dress,° no hat.*
>
> *Valentine is pecking at a portable computer. He is wearing unkempt Regency clothes, too.*
>
> *The clothes have evidently come from a large wicker laundry hamper, from which Gus is producing more clothes to try on himself. He finds a Regency coat and starts putting it on.*
>
> *The objects on the table now include two geometrical solids, pyramid and cone, about twenty inches high, of the type used in a drawing lesson; and a pot of dwarf dahlias (which do not look like modern dahlias).*

CHLOË: 'Even in Arcadia—Sex, Literature and Death at Sidley Park'. Picture of Byron.

VALENTINE: Not of Bernard?

CHLOË: 'Byron Fought Fatal Duel, Says Don' . . . Valentine, do you think I'm the first person to think of this?

VALENTINE: No.

CHLOË: I haven't said yet. The future is all programmed like a computer—that's a proper theory, isn't it?

VALENTINE: The deterministic universe, yes.

CHLOË: Right. Because everything including us is just a lot of atoms bouncing off each other like billiard balls.

VALENTINE: Yes. There was someone, forget his name, 1820s, who pointed out that from Newton's laws you could predict everything to come—I mean, you'd need a computer as big as the universe but the formula would exist.

CHLOË: But it doesn't work, does it?

VALENTINE: No. It turns out the maths is different.

CHLOË: No, it's all because of sex.

VALENTINE: Really?

CHLOË: That's what I think. The universe is deterministic all right, just like Newton said, I mean it's trying to be, but the only thing going wrong is people fancying people who aren't supposed to be in that part of the plan.

VALENTINE: Ah. The attraction that Newton left out. All the way back to the apple in the garden. Yes. (*Pause.*) Yes, I think you're the first person to think of this.

(Hannah enters, carrying a tabloid paper, and a mug of tea.)

HANNAH: Have you seen this? 'Bonking Byron Shot Poet'.

CHLOË: (*Pleased*) Let's see.

(Hannah gives her the paper, smiles at Gus.)

VALENTINE: He's done awfully well, hasn't he? How did they all know?

HANNAH: Don't be ridiculous. (*To Chloë*) Your father wants it back.

CHLOË: All right.

HANNAH: What a fool.

CHLOË: Jealous. I think it's brilliant. (*She gets up to go. To Gus*) Yes, that's perfect, but not with trainers. Come on, I'll lend you a pair of flatties, they'll look period on you—

HANNAH: Hello, Gus. You all look so romantic.

(Gus following Chloë out, hesitates, smiles at her.)

CHLOË: (*Pointedly*) Are you coming?

(She holds the door for Gus and follows him out, leaving a sense of her disapproval behind her.)

HANNAH: The important thing is not to give two monkeys for what young people think about you.

(She goes to look at the other newspapers.)

VALENTINE: (*Anxiously*) You don't think she's getting a thing about Bernard, do you?

HANNAH: I wouldn't worry about Chloë, she's old enough to vote on her back. 'Byron Fought Fatal Duel, Says Don'. Or rather—(*sceptically*) 'Says Don!'

VALENTINE: It may all prove to be true.

HANNAH: It can't prove to be true, it can only not prove to be false yet.

VALENTINE: (*Pleased*) Just like science.

HANNAH: If Bernard can stay ahead of getting the rug pulled till he's dead, he'll be a success.

VALENTINE: *Just* like science . . . The ultimate fear is of posterity . . .

HANNAH: Personally I don't think it'll take that long.

VALENTINE: . . . and then there's the afterlife. An afterlife would be a mixed blessing. 'Ah—Bernard Nightingale, I don't believe you know Lord Byron.' It must be heaven up there.

HANNAH: You can't believe in an afterlife, Valentine.

VALENTINE: Oh, you're going to disappoint me at last.

HANNAH: Am I? Why?

VALENTINE: Science and religion.

HANNAH: No, no, been there, done that, boring.

VALENTINE: Oh, Hannah. Fiancée. Have pity. Can't we have a trial marriage and I'll call it off in the morning?

HANNAH: (*Amused*) I don't know when I've received a more unusual proposal.

VALENTINE: (*Interested*) Have you had many?

HANNAH: That would be telling.

VALENTINE: Well, why not? Your classical reserve is only a mannerism; and neurotic.

HANNAH: Do you want the room?

VALENTINE: You get nothing if you give nothing.

HANNAH: I ask nothing.

VALENTINE: No, stay.

Regency: From 1811 to 1830, England was ruled by the Prince of Wales as regent to his father, George III, who was insane. This was a period of high style in dress and furnishings.

(*Valentine resumes work at his computer. Hannah establishes herself among her references at 'her' end of the table. She has a stack of pocket-sized volumes, Lady Croom's 'garden books'.*)

HANNAH: What are you doing? Valentine?

VALENTINE: The set of points on a complex plane made by—

HANNAH: Is it the grouse?

VALENTINE: Oh, the grouse. The damned grouse.

HANNAH: You mustn't give up.

VALENTINE: Why? Didn't you agree with Bernard?

HANNAH: Oh, that. It's *all* trivial—your grouse, my hermit, Bernard's Byron. Comparing what we're looking for misses the point. It's wanting to know that makes us matter. Otherwise we're going out the way we came in. That's why you can't believe in the afterlife, Valentine. Believe in the after, by all means, but not the life. Believe in God, the soul, the spirit, the infinite, believe in angels if you like, but not in the great celestial get-together for an exchange of views. If the answers are in the back of the book I can wait, but what a drag. Better to struggle on knowing that failure is final. (*She looks over Valentine's shoulder at the computer screen. Reacting*) Oh!, but . . . how beautiful!

VALENTINE: The Coverly set.

HANNAH: The Coverly set! My goodness, Valentine!

VALENTINE: Lend me a finger.

(*He takes her finger and presses one of the computer keys several times.*)

See? In an ocean of ashes, islands of order. Patterns making themselves out of nothing. I can't show how deep it goes. Each picture is a detail of the previous one, blown up. And so on. For ever. Pretty nice, eh?

HANNAH: Is it important?

VALENTINE: Interesting. Publishable.

HANNAH: Well done!

VALENTINE: Not me. It's Thomasina's. I just pushed her equations through the computer a few million times further than she managed to do with her pencil.

(*From the old portfolio he takes Thomasina's lesson book and gives it to Hannah. The piano starts to be heard.*)

You can have it back now.

HANNAH: What does it mean?

VALENTINE: Not what you'd like it to.

HANNAH: Why not?

VALENTINE: Well, for one thing, she'd be famous.

HANNAH: No, she wouldn't. She was dead before she had time to be famous . . .

VALENTINE: She died?

HANNAH: . . . burned to death.

VALENTINE: (*Realizing*) Oh . . . the girl who died in the fire!

HANNAH: The night before her seventeenth birthday. You can see where the dormer doesn't match. That was her bedroom under the roof. There's a memorial in the Park.

VALENTINE: (*Irritated*) I know—it's my house.

(*Valentine turns his attention back to his computer. Hannah goes back to her chair. She looks through the lesson book.*)

HANNAH: Val, Septimus was her tutor—he and Thomasina would have—

VALENTINE: You do yours.

(*Pause. Two researchers.*

Lord Augustus, fifteen years old, wearing clothes of 1812, bursts in through the non-music room door. He is laughing. He dives under the table. He is chased into the room by Thomasina, aged sixteen and furious. She spots Augustus immediately.)

THOMASINA: You swore! You crossed your heart!

(*Augustus scampers out from under the table and Thomasina chases him around it.*)

AUGUSTUS: I'll tell mama! I'll tell mama!

THOMASINA: You beast!

(*She catches Augustus as Septimus enters from the other door, carrying a book, a decanter and a glass, and his portfolio.*)

SEPTIMUS: Hush! What is this? My lord! Order, order!

(*Thomasina and Augustus separate.*)

I am obliged.

(*Septimus goes to his place at the table. He pours himself a glass of wine.*)

AUGUSTUS: Well, good day to you, Mr Hodge!

(*He is smirking about something.*

Thomasina dutifully picks up a drawing book and settles down to draw the geometrical solids.

Septimus opens his portfolio.)

SEPTIMUS: Will you join us this morning, Lord Augustus? We have our drawing lesson.

AUGUSTUS: I am a master of it at Eton, Mr Hodge, but we only draw naked women.

SEPTIMUS: You may work from memory.

THOMASINA: Disgusting!

SEPTIMUS: We will have silence now, if you please.

(*From the portfolio Septimus takes Thomasina's lesson book and tosses it to her; returning homework. She snatches it and opens it.*)

THOMASINA: No marks?! Did you not like my rabbit equation?

SEPTIMUS: I saw no resemblance to a rabbit.

THOMASINA: It eats its own progeny.

SEPTIMUS: (*Pause*) I did not see that.

(*He extends his hand for the lesson book. She returns it to him.*)

THOMASINA: I have not room to extend it.

(*Septimus and Hannah turn the pages doubled by time. Augustus indolently starts to draw the models.*)

HANNAH: Do you mean the world is saved after all?

VALENTINE: No, it's still doomed. But if this is how it started, perhaps it's how the next one will come.

HANNAH: From good English algebra?

SEPTIMUS: It will go to infinity or zero, or nonsense.

THOMASINA: No, if you set apart the minus roots they square back to sense.

(*Septimus turns the pages.*
 Thomasina starts drawing the models.
 Hannah closes the lesson book and turns her attention to her stack of 'garden books'.)

VALENTINE: Listen—you know your tea's getting cold.

HANNAH: I like it cold.

VALENTINE: (*Ignoring that*) I'm telling you something. Your tea gets cold by itself, it doesn't get hot by itself. Do you think that's odd?

HANNAH: No.

VALENTINE: Well, it is odd. Heat goes to cold. It's a one-way street. Your tea will end up at room temperature. What's happening to your tea is happening to everything everywhere. The sun and the stars. It'll take a while but we're all going to end up at room temperature. When your hermit set up shop nobody understood this. But let's say you're right, in 18-whatever nobody knew more about heat than this scribbling nutter living in a hovel in Derbyshire.

HANNAH: He was at Cambridge—a scientist.

VALENTINE: Say he was. I'm not arguing. And the girl was his pupil, she had a genius for her tutor.

HANNAH: Or the other way round.

VALENTINE: Anything you like. But not *this*! Whatever he thought he was doing to save the world with good English algebra it wasn't this!

HANNAH: Why? Because they didn't have calculators?

VALENTINE: No. Yes. Because there's an order things can't happen in. You can't open a door till there's a house.

HANNAH: I thought that's what genius was.

VALENTINE: Only for lunatics and poets.

(*Pause.*)

HANNAH: 'I had a dream which was not all a dream.
 The bright sun was extinguished, and the stars
 Did wander darkling in the eternal space,
 Rayless, and pathless, and the icy earth
 Swung blind and blackening in the moonless air . . .'

VALENTINE: Your own?

HANNAH: Byron.

(*Pause. Two researchers again.*)

THOMASINA: Septimus, do you think that I will marry Lord Byron?

AUGUSTUS: Who is he?

THOMASINA: He is the author of 'Childe Harold's Pilgrimage', the most poetical and pathetic and bravest hero of any book I ever read before, and the most modern and the handsomest, for Harold is Lord Byron himself to those who know him, like myself and Septimus. Well, Septimus?

SEPTIMUS: (*Absorbed*) No.

(*Then he puts her lesson book away into the portfolio and picks up his own book to read.*)

THOMASINA: Why not?

SEPTIMUS: For one thing, he is not aware of your existence.

THOMASINA: We exchanged many significant glances when he was at Sidley Park. I do wonder that he has been home almost a year from his adventures and has not written to me once.

SEPTIMUS: It is indeed improbable, my lady.

AUGUSTUS: Lord Byron?!—he claimed my hare, although my shot was the earlier! He said I missed by a hare's breadth. His conversation was very facetious. But I think Lord Byron will not marry you, Thom, for he was only lame and not blind.

SEPTIMUS: Peace! Peace until a quarter to twelve. It is intolerable for a tutor to have his thoughts interrupted by his pupils.

AUGUSTUS: You are not *my* tutor, sir. I am visiting your lesson by my free will.

SEPTIMUS: If you are so determined, my lord.

(*Thomasina laughs at that, the joke is for her. Augustus, not included, becomes angry.*)

AUGUSTUS: Your peace is nothing to me, sir. You do not rule over me.

THOMASINA: (*Admonishing*) Augustus!

SEPTIMUS: I do not rule here, my lord. I inspire by reverence for learning and the exaltation of knowledge whereby man may approach God. There will be a shilling for the best cone and pyramid drawn in silence by a quarter to twelve *at the earliest*.

AUGUSTUS: You will not buy my silence for a shilling, sir. What I know to tell is worth much more than that.

(*And throwing down his drawing book and pencil, he leaves the room on his dignity, closing the door sharply. Pause. Septimus looks enquiringly at Thomasina.*)

THOMASINA: I told him you kissed me. But he will not tell.

SEPTIMUS: When did I kiss you?

THOMASINA: What! Yesterday!

SEPTIMUS: Where?

THOMASINA: On the lips!

SEPTIMUS: In which county?

THOMASINA: In the hermitage, Septimus!

SEPTIMUS: On the lips in the hermitage! That? That was not a shilling kiss! I would not give sixpence to have it back. I had almost forgot it already.

THOMASINA: Oh, cruel! Have you forgotten our compact?

SEPTIMUS: God save me! Our compact?

THOMASINA: To teach me to waltz! Sealed with a kiss, and a second kiss due when I can dance like mama!

SEPTIMUS: Ah yes. Indeed. We were all waltzing like mice in London.

THOMASINA: I must waltz, Septimus! I will be despised if I do not waltz! It is the most fashionable and gayest and boldest invention conceivable—started in Germany!

SEPTIMUS: Let them have the waltz, they cannot have the calculus.

THOMASINA: Mama has brought from town a whole book of waltzes for the Broadwood, to play with Count Zelinsky.

SEPTIMUS: I need not be told what I cannot but suffer. Count Zelinsky banging on the Broadwood without relief has me reading in waltz time.

THOMASINA: Oh, stuff! What is your book?

SEPTIMUS: A prize essay of the Scientific Academy in Paris. The author deserves your indulgence, my lady, for you are his prophet.

THOMASINA: I? What does he write about? The waltz?

SEPTIMUS: Yes. He demonstrates the equation of the propagation of heat in a solid body. But in doing so he has discovered heresy—a natural contradiction of Sir Isaac Newton.

THOMASINA: Oh!—he contradicts determinism?

SEPTIMUS: No! . . . Well, perhaps. He shows that the atoms do not go according to Newton.

(*Her interest has switched in the mercurial way characteristic of her—she has crossed to take the book.*)

THOMASINA: Let me see—oh! In French?

SEPTIMUS: Yes. Paris is the capital of France.

THOMASINA: Show me where to read.

(*He takes the book back from her and finds the page for her. Meanwhile, the piano music from the next room has doubled its notes and its emotion.*)

THOMASINA: Four handed now! Mama is in love with the Count.

SEPTIMUS: He is a Count in Poland. In Derbyshire he is a piano tuner.

(*She has taken the book and is already immersed in it. The piano music becomes rapidly more passionate, and then breaks off suddenly in mid-phrase. There is an expressive silence next door which makes Septimus raise his eyes. It does not register with Thomasina. The silence allows us to hear the distant regular thump of the steam engine which is to be a topic. A few moments later Lady Croom enters from the music room, seeming surprised and slightly flustered to find the schoolroom occupied. She collects herself, closing the door behind her. And remains watching, aimless and discreet, as though not wanting to interrupt the lesson. Septimus has stood, and she nods him back into his chair.*

Chloë, in Regency dress, enters from the door opposite the music room. She takes in Valentine and Hannah but crosses without pausing to the music room door.)

CHLOË: Oh!—where's Gus?

VALENTINE: Dunno.

(*Chloë goes into the music room.*)

LADY CROOM: (*Annoyed*) Oh!—Mr Noakes's engine!

(*She goes to the garden door and steps outside. Chloë re-enters.*)

CHLOË: Damn.

LADY CROOM: (*Calls out*) Mr Noakes!

VALENTINE: He was there not long ago . . .

LADY CROOM: Halloo!

CHLOË: Well, he has to be in the photograph—is he dressed?

HANNAH: Is Bernard back?

CHLOË: No—he's late!

(*The piano is heard again, under the noise of the steam engine. Lady Croom steps back into the room. Chloë steps outside the garden door. Shouts.*)

Gus!

LADY CROOM: I wonder you can teach against such a disturbance and I am sorry for it, Mr Hodge.

(*Chloë comes back inside.*)

VALENTINE: (*Getting up*) Stop ordering everybody about.

LADY CROOM: It is an unendurable noise.

VALENTINE: The photographer will wait.

(*But, grumbling, he follows Chloë out of the door she came in by, and closes the door behind them. Hannah remains absorbed. In the silence, the rhythmic thump can be heard again.*)

LADY CROOM: The ceaseless dull overbearing monotony of it! It will drive me distracted. I may have to return to town to escape it.

SEPTIMUS: Your ladyship could remain in the country and let Count Zelinsky return to town where you would not hear him.

LADY CROOM: I mean Mr Noakes's engine! (*Semi-aside to Septimus.*) Would you sulk? I will not have my daughter study sulking.

THOMASINA: (*Not listening*) What, mama?

(*Thomasina remains lost in her book. Lady Croom returns to close the garden door and the noise of the steam engine subsides.*

Hannah closes one of the 'garden books', and opens the next. She is making occasional notes.

The piano ceases.)

LADY CROOM: (*To Thomasina*) What are we learning today? (*Pause.*) Well, not manners.

SEPTIMUS: We are drawing today.

(*Lady Croom negligently examines what Thomasina had started to draw.*)

LADY CROOM: Geometry. I approve of geometry.

SEPTIMUS: Your ladyship's approval is my constant object.

LADY CROOM: Well, do not despair of it. (*Returning to the window impatiently.*) Where is 'Culpability' Noakes?

(*She looks out and is annoyed.*) Oh!—he has gone for his hat so that he may remove it.

(*She returns to the table and touches the bowl of dahlias. Hannah sits back in her chair, caught by what she is reading.*)

For the widow's dowry of dahlias I can almost forgive my brother's marriage. We must be thankful the monkey bit the husband. If it had bit the wife the monkey would be dead and we would not be first in the kingdom to show a dahlia. (*Hannah, still reading the garden book, stands up.*) I sent one potted to Chatsworth. The Duchess was most satisfactorily put out by it when I called at Devonshire House. Your friend was there lording it as a poet.

(*Hannah leaves through the door, following Valentine and Chloë.*
Meanwhile, Thomasina thumps the book down on the table.)

THOMASINA: Well! Just as I said! Newton's machine which would knock our atoms from cradle to grave by the laws of motion is incomplete! Determinism leaves the road at every corner, as I knew all along, and the cause is very likely hidden in this gentleman's observation.
LADY CROOM: Of what?
THOMASINA: The action of bodies in heat.
LADY CROOM: Is this geometry?
THOMASINA: This? No, I despise geometry!
LADY CROOM: (*Touching the dahlias she adds, almost to herself.*) The Chater would overthrow the Newtonian system in a weekend.
SEPTIMUS: Geometry, Hobbes° assures us in the *Leviathan,* is the only science God has been pleased to bestow on mankind.
LADY CROOM: And what does he mean by it?
SEPTIMUS: Mr Hobbes or God?
LADY CROOM: I am sure I do not know what either means by it.
THOMASINA: Oh, pooh to Hobbes! Mountains are not pyramids and trees are not cones. God must love gunnery and architecture if Euclid is his only geometry. There is another geometry which I am engaged in discovering by trial and error, am I not, Septimus?
SEPTIMUS: Trial and error perfectly describes your enthusiasm, my lady.
LADY CROOM: How old are you today?
THOMASINA: Sixteen years and eleven months, mama, and three weeks.

Hobbes: Thomas Hobbes (1588–1679), a political philosopher whose *Leviathan* (1651) proposes a society whose social contract requires a sovereign with absolute power, a king, at its head.

LADY CROOM: Sixteen years and eleven months. We must have you married before you are educated beyond eligibility.
THOMASINA: I am going to marry Lord Byron.
LADY CROOM: Are you? He did not have the manners to mention it.
THOMASINA: You have spoken to him?!
LADY CROOM: Certainly not.
THOMASINA: Where did you see him?
LADY CROOM: (*With some bitterness*) Everywhere.
THOMASINA: Did you, Septimus?
SEPTIMUS: At the Royal Academy where I had the honour to accompany your mother and Count Zelinsky.
THOMASINA: What was Lord Byron doing?
LADY CROOM: Posing.
SEPTIMUS: (*Tactfully*) He was being sketched during his visit . . . by the Professor of Painting . . . Mr Fuseli.
LADY CROOM: There was more posing *at* the pictures than *in* them. His companion likewise reversed the custom of the Academy that the ladies viewing wear more than the ladies viewed—well, enough! Let him be hanged there for a Lamb. I have enough with Mr Noakes, who is to a garden what a bull is to a china shop.

(*This as Noakes enters.*)

THOMASINA: The Emperor of Irregularity!

(*She settles down to drawing the diagram which is to be the third item in the surviving portfolio.*)

LADY CROOM: Mr Noakes!
NOAKES: Your ladyship—
LADY CROOM: What have you done to me!
NOAKES: Everything is satisfactory, I assure you. A little behind, to be sure, but my dam will be repaired within the month—
LADY CROOM: (*Banging the table*) Hush!

(*In the silence, the steam engine thumps in the distance.*)

Can you hear, Mr Noakes?
NOAKES: (*Pleased and proud*) The Improved Newcomen steam pump—the only one in England!
LADY CROOM: That is what I object to. If everybody had his own I would bear my portion of the agony without complaint. But to have been singled out by the only Improved Newcomen steam pump in England, this is hard, sir, this is not to be borne.
NOAKES: Your lady—
LADY CROOM: And for what? My lake is drained to a ditch for no purpose I can understand, unless it be that snipe and curlew have deserted three counties so that they may be shot in our swamp. What you painted as forest is a mean plantation, your greenery is mud, your waterfall is wet mud, and your mount is an opencast mine for the mud that was lacking in the dell. (*Pointing through the window.*) What is that cowshed?

NOAKES: The hermitage, my lady?

LADY CROOM: It is a cowshed.

NOAKES: Madam, it is, I assure you, a very habitable cottage, properly founded and drained, two rooms and a closet under a slate roof and a stone chimney—

LADY CROOM: And who is to live in it?

NOAKES: Why, the hermit.

LADY CROOM: Where is he?

NOAKES: Madam?

LADY CROOM: You surely do not supply a hermitage without a hermit?

NOAKES: Indeed, madam—

LADY CROOM: Come, come, Mr Noakes. If I am promised a fountain I expect it to come with water. What hermits do you have?

NOAKES: I have no hermits, my lady.

LADY CROOM: Not one? I am speechless.

NOAKES: I am sure a hermit can be found. One could advertise.

LADY CROOM: Advertise?

NOAKES: In the newspapers.

LADY CROOM: But surely a hermit who takes a newspaper is not a hermit in whom one can have complete confidence.

NOAKES: I do not know what to suggest, my lady.

SEPTIMUS: Is there room for a piano?

NOAKES: (*Baffled*) A piano?

LADY CROOM: We are intruding here—this will not do, Mr Hodge. Evidently, nothing is being learned. (*To Noakes*) Come along, sir!

THOMASINA: Mr Noakes—bad news from Paris!

NOAKES: Is it the Emperor Napoleon?

THOMASINA: No. (*She tears the page off her drawing block, with her 'diagram' on it.*) It concerns your heat engine. Improve it as you will, you can never get out of it what you put in. It repays eleven pence in the shilling at most. The penny is for this author's thoughts.

(*She gives the diagram to Septimus who looks at it.*)

NOAKES: (*Baffled again*) Thank you, my lady.

(*Noakes goes out into the garden.*)

LADY CROOM: (*To Septimus*) Do you understand her?

SEPTIMUS: No.

LADY CROOM: Then this business is over. I was married at seventeen. *Ce soir il faut qu'on parle français, je te demande*, Thomasina, as a courtesy to the Count. Wear your green velvet, please, I will send Briggs to do your hair. Sixteen and eleven months . . . !

(*She follows Noakes out of view.*)

THOMASINA: Lord Byron was with a lady?

SEPTIMUS: Yes.

THOMASINA: Huh!

(*Now Septimus retrieves his book from Thomasina. He turns the pages, and also continues to study Thomasina's diagram. He strokes the tortoise absently as he reads. Thomasina takes up pencil and paper and starts to draw Septimus with Plautus.*)

SEPTIMUS: Why does it mean Mr Noakes's engine pays eleven pence in the shilling? Where does he say it?

THOMASINA: Nowhere. I noticed it by the way. I cannot remember now.

SEPTIMUS: Nor is he interested by determinism—

THOMASINA: Oh . . . yes. Newton's equations go forwards and backwards, they do not care which way. But the heat equation cares very much, it goes only one way. That is the reason Mr Noakes's engine cannot give the power to drive Mr Noakes's engine.

SEPTIMUS: Everybody knows that.

THOMASINA: Yes, Septimus, they know it about engines!

SEPTIMUS: (*Pause. He looks at his watch.*) A quarter to twelve. For your essay this week, explicate your diagram.

THOMASINA: I cannot. I do not know the mathematics.

SEPTIMUS: Without mathematics, then.

(*Thomasina has continued to draw. She tears the top page from her drawing pad and gives it to Septimus.*)

THOMASINA: There. I have made a drawing of you and Plautus.

SEPTIMUS: (*Looking at it*) Excellent likeness. Not so good of me.

(*Thomasina laughs, and leaves the room.*
Augustus appears at the garden door. His manner cautious and diffident. Septimus does not notice him for a moment. Septimus gathers his papers together.)

AUGUSTUS: Sir . . .

SEPTIMUS: My lord . . . ?

AUGUSTUS: I gave you offence, sir, and I am sorry for it.

SEPTIMUS: I took none, my lord, but you are kind to mention it.

AUGUSTUS: I would like to ask you a question, Mr Hodge. (*Pause.*) You have an elder brother, I dare say, being a Septimus?

SEPTIMUS: Yes, my lord. He lives in London. He is the editor of a newspaper, the *Piccadilly Recreation*. (*Pause.*) Was that your question?

(*Augustus, evidently embarrassed about something, picks up the drawing of Septimus.*)

AUGUSTUS: No. Oh . . . it is you? . . . I would like to keep it. (*Septimus inclines his head in assent.*) There are things a fellow cannot ask his friends. Carnal things. My sister has told me . . . my sister believes such things as I cannot, I assure you, bring myself to repeat.

SEPTIMUS: You must not repeat them, then. The walk between here and dinner will suffice to put us straight, if we stroll by the garden. It is an easy business. And then I must rely on you to correct your sister's state of ignorance.

(*A commotion is heard outside—Bernard's loud voice in a sort of agony.*)

BERNARD: (*outside the door*) Oh no—no—no—oh, bloody hell!—

AUGUSTUS: Thank you, Mr Hodge, I will.

(*Taking the drawing with him, Augustus allows himself to be shown out through the garden door, and Septimus follows him.*

Bernard enters the room, through the door Hannah left by. Valentine comes in with him, leaving the door open and they are followed by Hannah who is holding the 'garden book'.)

BERNARD: Oh, no—no—

HANNAH: I'm sorry, Bernard.

BERNARD: Fucked by a dahlia! Do you think? Is it open and shut? Am I fucked? What does it really amount to? When all's said and done? Am I fucked? What do *you* think, Valentine? Tell me the truth.

VALENTINE: You're fucked.

BERNARD: Oh God! Does it mean that?

HANNAH: Yes, Bernard, it does.

BERNARD: I'm not sure. Show me where it says. I want to see it. No—read it—no, wait . . .

(*Bernard sits at the table. He prepares to listen as though listening were an oriental art.*)

Right.

HANNAH: (*Reading*) 'October 1st, 1810. Today under the direction of Mr Noakes, a parterre was dug on the south lawn and will be a handsome show next year, a consolation for the picturesque catastrophe of the second and third distances. The dahlia having propagated under glass with no ill effect from the sea voyage, is named by Captain Brice 'Charity' for his bride, though the honour properly belongs to the husband who exchanged beds with my dahlia, and an English summer for everlasting night in the Indies.'

(*Pause.*)

BERNARD: Well it's so round the houses, isn't it? Who's to say what it means?

HANNAH: (*Patiently*) It means that Ezra Chater of the Sidley Park connection is the same Chater who described a dwarf dahlia in Martinique in 1810 and died there, of a monkey bite.

BERNARD: (*Wildly*) Ezra wasn't a botanist! He was a poet!

HANNAH: He was not much of either, but he was both.

VALENTINE: It's not a disaster.

BERNARD: Of course it's a disaster! I was on 'The Breakfast Hour'!

VALENTINE: It doesn't mean Byron didn't fight a duel, it only means Chater wasn't killed in it.

BERNARD: Oh, pull yourself together!—do you think I'd have been on 'The Breakfast Hour' if Byron had *missed*!

HANNAH: Calm down, Bernard. Valentine's right.

BERNARD: (*Grasping at straws*) Do you think so? You mean the *Piccadilly* reviews? Yes, two completely unknown Byron essays—*and* my discovery of the lines he added to 'English Bards'. That counts for something.

HANNAH: (*Tactfully*) Very possible—persuasive, indeed.

BERNARD: Oh, bugger persuasive! I've proved Byron was here and as far as I'm concerned he wrote those lines as sure as he shot that hare. If only I hadn't somehow . . . made it all about *killing Chater*. Why didn't you stop me?! It's bound to get out, you know—I mean this—this *gloss* on my discovery—I mean how long do you think it'll be before some botanical pedant blows the whistle on me?

HANNAH: The day after tomorrow. A letter in *The Times*.

BERNARD: You wouldn't.

HANNAH: It's a dirty job but somebody—

BERNARD: Darling. Sorry. Hannah—

HANNAH: —and, after all, it is my discovery.

BERNARD: Hannah.

HANNAH: Bernard.

BERNARD: Hannah.

HANNAH: Oh, shut up. It'll be very short, very dry, absolutely gloat-free. Would you rather it were one of your friends?

BERNARD: (*Fervently*) Oh God, no!

HANNAH: And then in *your* letter to *The Times*—

BERNARD: Mine?

HANNAH: Well, of course. Dignified congratulations to a colleague, in the language of scholars, I trust.

BERNARD: Oh, eat shit, you mean?

HANNAH: Think of it as a breakthrough in dahlia studies.

(*Chloë hurries in from the garden.*)

CHLOË: Why aren't you coming?!—Bernard! And you're not dressed! How long have you been back?

(*Bernard looks at her and then at Valentine and realizes for the first time that Valentine is unusually dressed.*)

BERNARD: Why are you wearing those clothes?

CHLOË: Do be quick!

(*She is already digging into the basket and producing odd garments for Bernard.*)

Just put anything on. We're all being photographed. Except Hannah.

HANNAH: I'll come and watch.

(*Valentine and Chloë help Bernard into a decorative coat and fix a lace collar round his neck.*)

CHLOË: (*To Hannah*) Mummy says have you got the theodolite?

VALENTINE: What are you supposed to be, Chlo? Bo-Peep?

CHLOË: Jane Austen!

VALENTINE: Of course.

HANNAH: (*To Chloë*) Oh—it's in the hermitage! Sorry.

BERNARD: I thought it wasn't till this evening. What photograph?

CHLOË: The local paper of course—they always come before we start. We want a good crowd of us—Gus looks gorgeous—

BERNARD: (*Aghast*) The newspaper!

(*He grabs something like a bishop's mitre from the basket and pulls it down completely over his face.*

(*Muffled*) I'm ready!

(*And he staggers out with Valentine and Chloë, followed by Hannah.*

A light change to evening. The paper lanterns outside begin to glow. Piano music from the next room.

Septimus enters with an oil lamp. He carries Thomasina's algebra primer, and also her essay on loose sheets. He settles down to read at the table. It is nearly dark outside, despite the lanterns.

Thomasina enters, in a nightgown and barefoot, holding a candlestick. Her manner is secretive and excited.)

SEPTIMUS: My lady! What is it?

THOMASINA: Septimus! Shush!

(*She closes the door quietly.*)

Now is our chance!

SEPTIMUS: For what, dear God?

(*She blows out the candle and puts the candlestick on the table.*)

THOMASINA: Do not act the innocent! Tomorrow I will be seventeen!

(*She kisses Septimus full on the mouth.*)

There!

SEPTIMUS: Dear Christ!

THOMASINA: Now you must show me, you are paid in advance.

SEPTIMUS: (*Understanding*) Oh!

THOMASINA: The Count plays for us, it is God-given! I cannot be seventeen and not waltz.

SEPTIMUS: But your mother—

THOMASINA: While she swoons, we can dance. The house is all abed. I heard the Broadwood. Oh, Septimus, teach me now!

SEPTIMUS: Hush! I cannot now!

THOMASINA: Indeed you can, and I am come barefoot so mind my toes.

SEPTIMUS: I cannot because it is not a waltz.

Billy Crudup played Septimus in the 1995 production of *Arcadia* at Lincoln Center in New York. Jennifer Dundas was Thomasina.

THOMASINA: It is not?

SEPTIMUS: No, it is too slow for waltzing.

THOMASINA: Oh! Then we will wait for him to play quickly.

SEPTIMUS: My lady—

THOMASINA: Mr Hodge!

(*She takes a chair next to him and looks at his work.*)

Are you reading my essay? Why do you work here so late?

SEPTIMUS: To save my candles.

THOMASINA: You have my old primer.

SEPTIMUS: It is mine again. You should not have written in it.

(*She takes it, looks at the open page.*)

THOMASINA: It was a joke.

SEPTIMUS: It will make me mad as you promised. Sit over there. You will have us in disgrace.

(*Thomasina gets up and goes to the furthest chair.*)

THOMASINA: If mama comes I will tell her we only met to kiss, not to waltz.

SEPTIMUS: Silence or bed.

THOMASINA: Silence!

(*Septimus pours himself some more wine. He continues to read her essay.*

The music changes to party music from the marquee. And there are fireworks—small against the sky, distant flares of light like exploding meteors.

Hannah enters. She has dressed for the party. The difference is not, however, dramatic. She closes the door and crosses to leave by the garden door. But as she gets there, Valentine is entering. He has a glass of wine in his hand.)

HANNAH: Oh . . .

(*But Valentine merely brushes past her, intent on something, and half-drunk.*)

VALENTINE: (*To her*) Got it!

(*He goes straight to the table and roots about in what is now a considerable mess of papers, books and objects. Hannah turns back, puzzled by his manner. He finds what he has been looking for—the 'diagram'.*

Meanwhile, Septimus reading Thomasina's essay, also studies the diagram.

Septimus and Valentine study the diagram doubled by time.)

VALENTINE: It's heat.
HANNAH: Are you tight, Val?
VALENTINE: It's a diagram of heat exchange.
SEPTIMUS: So, we are all doomed!
THOMASINA: (*Cheerfully*) Yes.
VALENTINE: Like a steam engine, you see—

(*Hannah fills Septimus's glass from the same decanter, and sips from it.*)

She didn't have the maths, not remotely. She saw what things meant, way ahead, like seeing a picture.
SEPTIMUS: This is not science. This is story-telling.
THOMASINA: Is it a waltz now?
SEPTIMUS: No.

(*The music is still modern.*)

VALENTINE: Like a film.
HANNAH: What did she see?
VALENTINE: That you can't run the film backwards. Heat was the first thing which didn't work that way. Not like Newton. A film of a pendulum, or a ball falling through the air—backwards, it looks the same.
HANNAH: The ball would be going the wrong way.
VALENTINE: You'd have to know that. But with heat—friction—a ball breaking a window—
HANNAH: Yes.
VALENTINE: It won't work backwards.
HANNAH: Who thought it did?
VALENTINE: She saw why. You can put back the bits of glass but you can't collect up the heat of the smash. It's gone.
SEPTIMUS: So the improved Newtonian Universe must cease and grow cold. Dear me.
VALENTINE: The heat goes into the mix.

(*He gestures to indicate the air in the room, in the universe.*)

THOMASINA: Yes, we must hurry if we are going to dance.
VALENTINE: And everything is mixing the same way, all the time, irreversibly . . .
SEPTIMUS: Oh, we have time, I think.
VALENTINE: . . . till there's no time left. That's what time means.
SEPTIMUS: When we have found all the mysteries and lost all the meaning, we will be alone, on an empty shore.
THOMASINA: Then we will dance. Is this a waltz?
SEPTIMUS: It will serve.

(*He stands up.*)

THOMASINA: (*Jumping up*) Goody!

(*Septimus takes her in his arms carefully and the waltz lesson, to the music from the marquee, begins.*

Bernard, in unconvincing Regency dress, enters carrying a bottle.)

BERNARD: Don't mind me, I left my jacket . . .

(*He heads for the area of the wicker basket.*)

VALENTINE: Are you leaving?

(*Bernard is stripping off his period coat. He is wearing his own trousers, tucked into knee socks and his own shirt.*)

BERNARD: Yes, I'm afraid so.
HANNAH: What's up, Bernard?
BERNARD: Nothing I can go into—
VALENTINE: Should I go?
BERNARD: No, *I'm* going!

(*Valentine and Hannah watch Bernard struggling into his jacket and adjusting his clothes.*

Septimus, holding Thomasina, kisses her on the mouth. The waltz lesson pauses. She looks at him. He kisses her again, in earnest. She puts her arms round him.)

THOMASINA: Septimus . . .

(*Septimus hushes her. They start to dance again, with the slight awkwardness of a lesson.*

Chloë bursts in from the garden.)

CHLOË: I'll kill her! I'll *kill* her!
BERNARD: Oh dear.
VALENTINE: What the hell is it, Chlo?
CHLOË: (*Venomously*) Mummy!
BERNARD: (*To Valentine*) Your mother caught us in that cottage.
CHLOË: She snooped!
BERNARD: I don't think so. She was rescuing a theodolite.
CHLOË: I'll come with you, Bernard.

The final scene of David Leveaux's revival of *Arcadia* at the Duke of York's Theatre in London, 2009.

BERNARD: No, you bloody won't.

CHLOË: Don't you want me to?

BERNARD: Of course not. What for? (*To Valentine*) I'm sorry.

CHLOË: (*In furious tears*) What are you saying sorry to *him* for?

BERNARD: Sorry to you too. Sorry one and all. Sorry, Hannah—sorry, Hermione—sorry, Byron—sorry, sorry, sorry, now can I go?

(*Chloë stands stiffly, tearfully.*)

CHLOË: Well . . .

(*Thomasina and Septimus dance.*)

HANNAH: What a bastard you are, Bernard.

(*Chloë rounds on her.*)

CHLOË: And you mind your own business! What do you know about anything?

HANNAH: Nothing.

CHLOË: (*To Bernard*) It *was* worth it, though, wasn't it?

BERNARD: It was wonderful.

(*Chloë goes out, through the garden door, towards the party.*)

HANNAH: (*An echo*) Nothing.

VALENTINE: Well, you shit. I'd drive you but I'm a bit sloshed.

(*Valentine follows Chloë out and can be heard outside calling 'Chlo! Chlo!'*)

BERNARD: A scrape.

HANNAH: Oh . . . (*she gives up*) Bernard!

BERNARD: I look forward to *The Genius of the Place*. I hope you find your hermit. I think out front is the safest.

(*He opens the door cautiously and looks out.*)

HANNAH: Actually, I've got a good idea who he was, but I can't prove it.

BERNARD: (*With a carefree expansive gesture*) Publish!

(*He goes out closing the door.*

Septimus and Thomasina are now waltzing freely. She is delighted with herself.)

THOMASINA: Am I waltzing?

SEPTIMUS: Yes, my lady.

(*He gives her a final twirl, bringing them to the table where he bows to her. He lights her candlestick.*

Hannah goes to sit at the table, playing truant from the party. She pours herself more wine. The table contains the geometrical solids, the computer, decanter, glasses, tea mug, Hannah's research books, Septimus's books, the two portfolios, Thomasina's candlestick, the oil lamp, the dahlia, the Sunday papers . . .

Gus appears in the doorway. It takes a moment to realize that he is not Lord Augustus; perhaps not until Hannah sees him.)

SEPTIMUS: Take your essay, I have given it an alpha in blind faith. Be careful with the flame.

THOMASINA: I will wait for you to come.
SEPTIMUS: I cannot.
THOMASINA: You may.
SEPTIMUS: I may not.
THOMASINA: You must.
SEPTIMUS: I will not.

(*She puts the candlestick and the essay on the table.*)

THOMASINA: Then I will not go. Once more, for my birthday.

(*Septimus and Thomasina start to waltz together. Gus comes forward, startling Hannah.*)

HANNAH: Oh!—you made me jump.

(*Gus looks resplendent. He is carrying an old and somewhat tattered stiff-backed folio fastened with a tape tied in a bow. He comes to Hannah and thrusts this present at her.*)

Oh . . .

(*She lays the folio down on the table and starts to open it. It consists only of two boards hinged, containing Thomasina's drawing.*)

'Septimus holding Plautus'. (*To Gus*) I was looking for that. Thank you.

(*Gus nods several times. Then, rather awkwardly, he bows to her. A Regency bow, an invitation to dance.*)

Oh, dear, I don't really . . .

(*After a moment's hesitation, she gets up and they hold each other, keeping a decorous distance between them, and start to dance, rather awkwardly.*
Septimus and Thomasina continue to dance, fluently, to the piano.)

Paula Vogel

Paula Vogel (b. 1951) came from a Washington, D.C., working-class family and knew she would have to make it on her own if she made it at all. For her, that knowledge was essentially the best inheritance she could have had. Her early years were marred by her parents' divorce and the loss of a father whom she came to know only in later years when her closest sibling, Carl, was dying of AIDS. Her earliest efforts in playwriting also met with rejection. After losing her scholarship to Bryn Mawr College, she graduated from Catholic University in Washington, where she devoted herself to dramatic literature, but then was turned down by the Yale School of Drama. Her earliest plays were also turned down by the Eugene O'Neill National Playwright's Conference. In retrospect, Vogel believes that these were good things because they made her learn her craft in a difficult—and original—way, which led eventually to her winning the Pulitzer Prize for *How I Learned to Drive*.

Vogel's earliest exposure to theater was in Washington, D.C. She talks about having "stumbled into drama class" when she was a sophomore in high school and beginning to find her way in theater. Her high school drama teacher was gay, and Vogel thinks he must have realized that she was herself a lesbian. She resisted taking acting roles—although she coached other students—and spent her years in high school as a stage manager. As a young playwright, she found other friends who were trying to write, and they gathered together to read each other's work. They occasionally did exercises, some of which became useful teaching tools for Vogel at Brown University. For example, they wrote complete plays in forty-eight hours as a way of getting the essentials down as quickly as possible. Some of her earliest work had its origin in these experiments, including a version of *How I Learned to Drive*.

Some of her plays have startling images, such as a bizarre Groucho Marx–like doctor treating a dying AIDS patient in *The Baltimore Waltz* (which won an Obie Award for best play in 1992), a play about the death of her beloved brother Carl, who had begun his professional career as an English professor but switched to being a librarian. He was gay, and according to Vogel, homophobia hurt him more than the disease that killed him. Her plays are famous for scatological humor, jokes about the body, and extremely plain talk.

Among her early plays is one about lesbians who become parents to several little boys: *And Baby Makes Seven* (1984)—a daring excursion into territory that few playwrights have explored. Another early play, *The Oldest Profession* (1988), deals with older prostitutes. *Hot 'n' Throbbing* (1994) examines the effect of theater on its characters. *The Mineola Twins* (1996) was written before *How I Learned to Drive* but was produced later, in 1999. Vogel thinks of this play as a comedy and something of a contrast to *How I Learned to Drive,* which is, if not a tragedy, certainly serious in nature. Yet it too has moments of genuine comedy.

Paula Vogel's *The Long Christmas Ride Home* opened in June 2003 at Providence's Trinity Repertory Company. It moved into the Vineyard Theatre in New York in December 2003 to good reviews. *New York Times* critic Ben Brantley said of the June production that "*The Long Christmas Ride Home* is partly a latter-day answer to the works of Thornton Wilder, including *Our Town*, and the short pieces *The Long Christmas Dinner* and *The Happy Journey to Trenton and Camden*." The play employs half-size puppets, borrowing from the Japanese Bunraku-style theater. Vogel's use of puppets to help portray a dysfunctional family has been widely praised for producing appropriate and subtle emotional nuances. The 2004 production at Long Wharf Theatre was enormously effective and powerful theater.

Vogel's *A Civil War Christmas* (2008) is set in 1864, near the end of the war, and features close-ups of many historical figures, such as Abraham Lincoln, Mary Todd Lincoln, Walt Whitman, Clara Barton, Robert E. Lee, and Ulysses S. Grant. Because it includes music and songs of the period, it has something of the shape of a pageant. One reviewer called it "a holiday entertainment grounded in historical fact."

How I Learned to Drive

How I Learned to Drive was first produced in New York off-Broadway in 1997. It won not only the Pulitzer Prize but also the New York Drama Critics' Circle, Drama Desk, and Obie awards for best play of the year. It is published in a volume with *The Mineola Twins* called *The Mammary Plays*. Vogel explains that large-busted women remained an emblem for her in the construction of both plays. As a feminist, Vogel is interested in the fetishization of women's bodies, and both these plays move toward revealing the way both men and women in Western culture regard women's bodies, even while praising their minds.

All the characters in Li'l Bit's family are named in an unusual way. Li'l Bit explains, "In my family, if we call someone 'Big Papa,' it's not because he's tall. In my family, folks tend to get nicknamed for their genitalia. Uncle Peck, for example. My mamma's adage was 'the titless wonder.'" Even Li'l Bit was named after she was physically examined at birth. Uncle Peck, married to Li'l Bit's mother's sister Mary, is not a blood relation — a fact he repeatedly stresses to Li'l Bit — and he tells her he has loved her since she was small enough to be held in his hand. Even Big Papa chases Grandma around the house; it's an unusual and curious family.

The play is about sexual molestation — but about many other things, too. It is about families, about growing up, about becoming independent, and most of all about being a survivor. In an interview with Arthur Holmberg, literary director of the American Repertory Theater, Vogel said, "My play dramatizes the gifts we receive from the people who hurt us." When asked what gift Li'l Bit received, Vogel responded, "She received the gift of how to survive." Vogel uses learning to drive as a complex metaphor for sexual initiation. At the same time, the metaphor examines what a man expects from a close relationship with a woman and what a woman expects from a close relationship with a man. Uncle Peck is careful never to hurt Li'l Bit and always reminds her that he doesn't want her to do anything she doesn't wish to do. But at the same time, Uncle Peck "has a way" with adolescent girls, as his wife tells us. He listens to Li'l Bit and becomes her confidant, patiently waiting for her to accept him on his own terms.

For discussion questions and assignments on *How I Learned to Drive,* visit **bedfordstmartins.com/jacobus.**

Although he is a predator, Uncle Peck is not necessarily a villain in the play. He takes advantage of Li'l Bit starting at age eleven and continues until she is eighteen and in college. For Vogel, part of the learning process for Li'l Bit is, as Vogel has said, becoming "an adult looking at and understanding her complicity." Then the next step is self-forgiveness. This step is essential to moving forward in her life.

How I Learned to Drive in Performance

The Vineyard Theatre in New York produced *How I Learned to Drive* in February 1997 and moved it to the large Century Theater in April. It was reviewed warmly and received positively by audiences, eventually winning Vogel the Pulitzer Prize for drama for 1997. The play relies on an interesting device, the Greek Chorus, a character who speaks in the voice of characters alluded to but not present, such as Li'l Bit's mother, grandmother, grandfather, and aunt. Vogel wanted to have slides shown at critical moments, such as the scene in which Uncle Peck is taking photographs of Li'l Bit and the scene in which Uncle Peck rhapsodizes over 1950s automobiles, but not all directors use the slides. For example, they were not used in the original New York production. Vogel's method of writing, like that of many playwrights, is to respond to the actors' interpretation of lines during rehearsal and rewriting. *How I Learned to Drive* benefited from that method.

In 1998 *How I Learned to Drive* had twenty-six regional productions and was the most produced play in the United States. Many more regional and international productions have followed, with numerous university productions virtually every year since.

PAULA VOGEL (b. 1951)

How I Learned to Drive   1997

Characters

LI'L BIT, *A woman who ages forty-something to eleven years old.*
PECK, *Attractive man in his forties. Despite a few problems, he should be played by an actor one might cast in the role of Atticus in To Kill a Mockingbird.*
THE GREEK CHORUS, *If possible, these three members should be able to sing three-part harmony.*
   MALE GREEK CHORUS, *Plays Grandfather, Waiter, High School Boys. Thirties–forties.*

FEMALE GREEK CHORUS, *Plays Mother, Aunt Mary, High School Girls. Thirty–fifty.*
TEENAGE GREEK CHORUS, *Plays Grandmother, High School Girls, and the voice of eleven-year-old Li'l Bit. Note on the casting of this actor: I would strongly recommend casting a young woman who is "of legal age," that is, twenty-one to twenty-five years old, who can look as close to eleven as possible. The contrast with the other cast members will help. If the actor is too young, the audience may feel uncomfortable.*

(*As the house lights dim, a Voice announces:*)

Safety First — You and Driver Education.

(*Then the sound of a key turning the ignition of a car. Li'l Bit steps into a spotlight on the stage; "well-endowed," she is a softer-looking woman in the present time than she was at seventeen.*)

LI'L BIT: Sometimes to tell a secret, you first have to teach a lesson. We're going to start our lesson tonight on an early, warm summer evening.

In a parking lot overlooking the Beltsville Agricultural Farms in suburban Maryland.

Less than a mile away, the crumbling concrete of U.S. One wends its way past one-room revival churches, the porno drive-in, and boarded up motels with For Sale signs tumbling down.

Like I said, it's a warm summer evening.

Here on the land the Department of Agriculture owns, the smell of sleeping farm animals is thick on the air. The smells of clover and hay mix in with the smells of the leather dashboard. You can still imagine how Maryland used to be, before the malls took over. This countryside was once dotted with farmhouses — from their porches you could have witnessed the Civil War raging in the front fields.

Oh yes. There's a moon over Maryland tonight, that spills into the car where I sit beside a man old enough to be — did I mention how still the night is? Damp soil and tranquil air. It's the kind of night that makes a middle-aged man with a mortgage feel like a country boy again.

It's 1969. And I am very old, very cynical of the world, and I know it all. In short, I am seventeen years old, parking off a dark lane with a married man on an early summer night.

(*Lights up on two chairs facing front — or a Buick Riviera, if you will. Waiting patiently, with a smile on his face, Peck sits sniffing the night air. Li'l Bit climbs in beside him, seventeen years old and tense. Throughout the following, the two sit facing directly front. They do not touch. Their bodies remain passive. Only their facial expressions emote.*)

PECK: Ummm. I love the smell of your hair.

LI'L BIT: Uh-huh.

PECK: Oh, Lord. Ummmm. (*Beat.*) A man could die happy like this.

LI'L BIT: Well, *don't.*

PECK: What shampoo is this?

LI'L BIT: Herbal Essence.

PECK: Herbal Essence. I'm gonna buy me some. Herbal Essence. And when I'm all alone in the house, I'm going to get into the bathtub, and uncap the bottle and —

LI'L BIT: — Be good.

PECK: What?

LI'L BIT: Stop being . . . bad.

PECK: What did you think I was going to say? What do you think I'm going to do with the shampoo?

LI'L BIT: I don't want to know. I don't want to hear it.

PECK: I'm going to wash my hair. That's all.

LI'L BIT: Oh.

PECK: What did you think I was going to do?

LI'L BIT: Nothing . . . I don't know. Something . . . nasty.

PECK: With shampoo? Lord, gal — your mind!

LI'L BIT: And whose fault is it?

PECK: Not mine. I've got the mind of a boy scout.

LI'L BIT: Right. A horny boy scout.

PECK: Boy scouts are always horny. What do you think the first Merit Badge is for?

LI'L BIT: There. You're going to be nasty again.

PECK: Oh, no. I'm good. Very good.

LI'L BIT: It's getting late.

PECK: Don't change the subject. I was talking about how good I am. (*Beat.*) Are you ever gonna let me show you how good I am?

LI'L BIT: Don't go over the line now.

PECK: I won't. I'm not gonna do anything you don't want me to do.

LI'L BIT: That's right.

PECK: And I've been good all week.

LI'L BIT: You have?

PECK: Yes. All week. Not a single drink.

LI'L BIT: Good boy.

PECK: Do I get a reward? For not drinking?

LI'L BIT: A small one. It's getting late.

PECK: Just let me undo you. I'll do you back up.

LI'L BIT: All right. But be quick about it.

(*Peck pantomimes undoing Li'l Bit's brassiere with one hand.*)

You know, that's amazing. The way you can undo the hooks through my blouse with one hand.

PECK: Years of practice.

LI'L BIT: You would make an incredible brain surgeon with that dexterity.

PECK: I'll bet Clyde — what's the name of the boy taking you to the prom?

LI'L BIT: Claude Souders.

PECK: Claude Souders. I'll bet it takes him two hands, lights on, and you helping him on to get to first base.

LI'L BIT: Maybe.

(*Beat.*)

PECK: Can I . . . kiss them? Please?

LI'L BIT: I don't know.

PECK: Don't make a grown man beg.

LI'L BIT: Just one kiss.

PECK: I'm going to lift your blouse.

LI'L BIT: It's a little cold.

(*Peck laughs gently.*)

PECK: That's not why you're shivering.

(*They sit, perfectly still, for a long moment of silence. Peck makes gentle, concentric circles with his thumbs in the air in front of him.*)

How does that feel?

(*Li'l Bit closes her eyes, carefully keeps her voice calm:*)

LI'L BIT: It's . . . okay.

(*Sacred music, organ music or a boy's choir swells beneath the following.*)

PECK: I tell you, you can keep all the cathedrals of Europe. Just give me a second with these—these celestial orbs—

(*Peck bows his head as if praying. But he is kissing her nipple. Li'l Bit, eyes still closed, rears back her head on the leather Buick car seat.*)

LI'L BIT: Uncle Peck—we've got to go. I've got graduation rehearsal at school tomorrow morning. And you should get on home to Aunt Mary—
PECK:—All right, Li'l Bit.
LI'L BIT:—*Don't* call me that no more. (*Calmer.*) Any more. I'm a big girl now, Uncle Peck. As you know.

(*Li'l Bit pantomimes refastening her bra behind her back.*)

PECK: That you are. Going on eighteen. Kittens will turn into cats. (*Sighs.*) I live all week long for these few minutes with you—you know that?
LI'L BIT: I'll drive.

(*A Voice cuts in with:*)

Idling in the Neutral Gear.

(*Sound of car revving cuts off the sacred music; Li'l Bit, now an adult, rises out of the car and comes to us.*)

LI'L BIT: In most families, relatives get names like "Junior," or "Brother," or "Bubba." In my family, if we call someone "Big Papa," it's not because he's tall. In my family, folks tend to get nicknamed for their genitalia. Uncle Peck, for example. My mama's adage was "the titless wonder," and my cousin Bobby got branded for life as "B.B."

(*In unison with Greek Chorus:*)

LI'L BIT: For blue balls.   GREEK CHORUS: For blue balls.
FEMALE GREEK CHORUS (*as Mother*): And of course, we were so excited to have a baby girl that when the nurse brought you in and said, "It's a girl! It's a baby girl!" I just had to see for myself. So we whipped your diapers down and parted your chubby little legs—and right between your legs there was—

(*Peck has come over during the above and chimes along:*)

PECK: Just a little bit.   GREEK CHORUS: Just a little bit.
FEMALE GREEK CHORUS (*as Mother*): And when you were born, you were so tiny that you fit in Uncle Peck's outstretched hand.

(*Peck stretches his hand out.*)

PECK: Now that's a fact. I held you, one day old, right in this hand.

(*A traffic signal is projected of a bicycle in a circle with a diagonal red slash.*)

LI'L BIT: Even with my family background, I was sixteen or so before I realized that pedophilia did not mean people who loved to bicycle. . . .

(*A Voice intrudes:*)

Driving in First Gear.

LI'L BIT: 1969. A typical family dinner.
FEMALE GREEK CHORUS (*as Mother*): Look, Grandma. Li'l Bit's getting to be as big in the bust as you are.
LI'L BIT: Mother! Could we please change the subject?
TEENAGE GREEK CHORUS (*as Grandmother*): Well, I hope you are buying her some decent bras. I never had a decent bra, growing up in the Depression, and now my shoulders are just crippled—crippled from the weight hanging on my shoulders—the dents from my bra straps are big enough to put your finger in.—Here, let me show you—

(*As Grandmother starts to open her blouse:*)

LI'L BIT: Grandma! Please don't undress at the dinner table.
PECK: I thought the entertainment came *after* the dinner.
LI'L BIT (*to the audience*): This is how it always starts. My grandfather, Big Papa, will chime in next with—
MALE GREEK CHORUS (*as Grandfather*): Yup. If Li'l Bit gets any bigger, we're gonna haveta buy her a wheelbarrow to carry in front of her—
LI'L BIT:—Damn it—
PECK:—How about those Redskins on Sunday, Big Papa?
LI'L BIT (*to the audience*): The only sport Big Papa followed was chasing Grandma around the house—
MALE GREEK CHORUS (*as Grandfather*):—Or we could write to Kate Smith. Ask her for somma her used brassieres she don't want anymore—she could maybe give to Li'l Bit here—
LI'L BIT:—I can't stand it. I can't.
PECK: Now, honey, that's just their way—
FEMALE GREEK CHORUS (*as Mother*): I tell you, Grandma, Li'l Bit's at that age. She's so sensitive, you can't say boo—
LI'L BIT: I'd like some privacy, that's all. Okay? Some goddamn privacy—
PECK:—Well, at least she didn't use the savior's name—
LI'L BIT (*to the audience*): And Big Papa wouldn't let a dead dog lie. No sirree.
MALE GREEK CHORUS (*as Grandfather*): Well, she'd better stop being so sensitive. 'Cause five minutes before Li'l Bit turns the corner, her tits turn first—

LI'L BIT (*starting to rise from the table*):—That's it. That's it.

PECK: Li'l Bit, you can't let him get to you. Then he wins.

LI'L BIT: I hate him. *Hate* him.

PECK: That's fine. But hate him and eat a good dinner at the same time.

(*Li'l Bit calms down and sits with perfect dignity.*)

LI'L BIT: The gumbo is really good, Grandma.

MALE GREEK CHORUS (*as Grandfather*): A'course, Li'l Bit's got a big surprise coming for her when she goes to that fancy college this fall—

PECK: Big Papa—let it go.

MALE GREEK CHORUS (*as Grandfather*): What does she need a college degree for? She's got all the credentials she'll need on her chest—

LI'L BIT:—Maybe I want to learn things. Read. Rise above my cracker° background—

PECK:—Whoa, now, Li'l Bit—

MALE GREEK CHORUS (*as Grandfather*): What kind of things do you want to read?

LI'L BIT: There's a whole semester course, for example, on Shakespeare—

(*Greek Chorus, as Grandfather, laughs until he weeps.*)

MALE GREEK CHORUS (*as Grandfather*): Shakespeare. That's a good one. Shakespeare is really going to help you in life.

PECK: I think it's wonderful. And on scholarship!

MALE GREEK CHORUS (*as Grandfather*): How is Shakespeare going to help her lie on her back in the dark?

(*Li'l Bit is on her feet.*)

LI'L BIT: You're getting old, Big Papa. You are going to die—very very soon. Maybe even *tonight*. And when you get to heaven, God's going to be a beautiful black woman in a long white robe. She's gonna look at your chart and say: Uh-oh. Fornication. Dog-ugly mean with blood relatives. Oh. Uh-oh. Voted for George Wallace. Well, one last chance: If you can name the play, all will be forgiven. And then she'll quote: "The quality of mercy is not strained." Your answer? Oh, too bad—*Merchant of Venice*: Act IV, Scene iii. And then she'll send your ass to fry in hell with all the other crackers. Excuse me, please.

  (*To the audience.*) And as I left the house, I would always hear Big Papa say:

MALE GREEK CHORUS (*as Grandfather*): Lucy, your daughter's got a mouth on her. Well, no sense in wasting good gumbo. Pass me her plate, Mama.

LI'L BIT: And Aunt Mary would come up to Uncle Peck:

FEMALE GREEK CHORUS (*as Aunt Mary*): Peck, go after her, will you? You're the only one she'll listen to when she gets like this.

PECK: She just needs to cool off.

cracker: A derogatory term for a poor, southern, white person.

FEMALE GREEK CHORUS (*as Aunt Mary*): Please, honey—Grandma's been on her feet cooking all day.

PECK: All right.

LI'L BIT: And as he left the room, Aunt Mary would say:

FEMALE GREEK CHORUS (*as Aunt Mary*): Peck's so good with them when they get to be this age.

(*Li'l Bit has stormed to another part of the stage, her back turned, weeping with a teenage fury. Peck, cautiously, as if stalking a deer, comes to her. She turns away even more. He waits a bit.*)

PECK: I don't suppose you're talking to family. (*No response.*) Does it help that I'm in-law?

LI'L BIT: Don't you dare make fun of this.

PECK: I'm not. There's nothing funny about this. (*Beat.*) Although I'll bet when Big Papa is about to meet his maker, he'll remember *The Merchant of Venice*.

LI'L BIT: I've got to get away from here.

PECK: You're going away. Soon. Here, take this.

(*Peck hands her his folded handkerchief. Li'l Bit uses it, noisily. Hands it back. Without her seeing, he reverently puts it back.*)

LI'L BIT: I hate this family.

PECK: Your grandfather's ignorant. And you're right—he's going to die soon. But he's family. Family is . . . family.

LI'L BIT: Grown-ups are always saying that. Family.

PECK: Well, when you get a little older, you'll see what we're saying.

LI'L BIT: Uh-huh. So family is another acquired taste, like French kissing?

PECK: Come again?

LI'L BIT: You know, at first it really grosses you out, but in time you grow to like it?

PECK: Girl, you are . . . a handful.

LI'L BIT: Uncle Peck—you have the keys to your car?

PECK: Where do you want to go?

LI'L BIT: Just up the road.

PECK: I'll come with you.

LI'L BIT: No—please? I just need to . . . to drive for a little bit. Alone.

(*Peck tosses her the keys.*)

PECK: When can I see you alone again?

LI'L BIT: Tonight.

(*Li'l Bit crosses to center stage while the lights dim around her. A Voice directs:*)

Shifting Forward from First to Second Gear.

LI'L BIT: There were a lot of rumors about why I got kicked out of that fancy school in 1970. Some say I got caught with a man in my room. Some say as a kid on scholarship I fooled around with a rich man's daughter.

  (*Li'l Bit smiles innocently at the audience.*) I'm not talking.

But the real truth was I had a constant companion in my dorm room—who was less than discreet. Canadian V.O. A fifth a day.

1970. A Nixon recession. I slept on the floors of friends who were out of work themselves. Took factory work when I could find it. A string of dead-end jobs that didn't last very long.

What I did, most nights, was cruise the Beltway and the back roads of Maryland, where there was still country, past the battlefields and farm houses. Racing in a 1965 Mustang—and as long as I had gasoline for my car and whiskey for me, the nights would pass. Full tanked, I would speed past the churches and the trees on the bend, thinking just one notch of the steering wheel would be all it would take, and yet some . . . reflex took over. My hands on the wheel in the nine and three o'clock position—I never so much as got a ticket. He taught me well.

(*A Voice announces:*)

You and the Reverse Gear.

LI'L BIT: Back up. 1968. On the Eastern Shore. A celebration dinner.

(*Li'l Bit joins Peck at a table in a restaurant.*)

PECK: Feeling better, missy?
LI'L BIT: The bathroom's really amazing here, Uncle Peck! They have these little soaps—instead of borax or something—and they're in the shape of shells.
PECK: I'll have to take a trip to the gentleman's room just to see.
LI'L BIT: How did you know about this place?
PECK: This inn is famous on the Eastern Shore—it's been open since the seventeenth century. And I know how you like history. . . .

(*Li'l Bit is shy and pleased.*)

LI'L BIT: It's great.
PECK: And you've just done your first, legal, long-distance drive. You must be hungry.
LI'L BIT: I'm starved.
PECK: I would suggest a dozen oysters to start, and the crab imperial. . . . (*Li'l Bit is genuinely agog.*) You might be interested to know the town history. When the British sailed up this very river in the dead of night—see outside where I'm pointing?—they were going to bombard the heck out of this town. But the town fathers were ready for them. They crept up all the trees with lanterns so that the British would think they saw the town lights and they aimed their cannons too high. And that's why the inn is still here for business today.
LI'L BIT: That's a great story.
PECK (*casually*): Would you like to start with a cocktail?
LI'L BIT: You're not . . . you're not going to start drinking, are you, Uncle Peck?
PECK: Not me. I told you, as long as you're with me, I'll never drink. I asked you if *you'd* like a cocktail

before dinner. It's nice to have a little something with the oysters.
LI'L BIT: But . . . I'm not . . . legal. We could get arrested. Uncle Peck, they'll never believe I'm twenty-one!
PECK: So? Today we celebrate your driver's license—on the first try. This establishment reminds me a lot of places back home.
LI'L BIT: What does that mean?
PECK: In South Carolina, like here on the Eastern Shore, they're . . . (*Searches for the right euphemism.*) . . . "European." Not so puritanical. And very understanding if gentlemen wish to escort very attractive young ladies who might want a before-dinner cocktail. If you want one, I'll order one.
LI'L BIT: Well—sure. Just . . . one.

(*The Female Greek Chorus appears in a spot.*)

FEMALE GREEK CHORUS (*as Mother*): A Mother's Guide to Social Drinking:
    A lady never gets sloppy—she may, however, get tipsy and a little gay.
    Never drink on an empty stomach. Avail yourself of the bread basket and generous portions of butter. *Slather* the butter on your bread.
    Sip your drink, slowly, let the beverage linger in your mouth—interspersed with interesting, fascinating conversation. Sip, never . . . slurp or gulp. Your glass should always be three-quarters full when his glass is empty.
    Stay away from *ladies'* drinks: drinks like pink ladies, slow gin fizzes, piña coladas, mai tais, planter's punch, white Russians, black Russians, red Russians, melon balls, blue balls, hummingbirds, hemorrhages, and hurricanes. In short, avoid anything with sugar, or anything with an umbrella. Get your vitamin C from *fruit*. Don't order anything with Voodoo or Vixen in the title or sexual positions in the name like Dead Man Screw or the Missionary. (*She sort of titters.*)
    Believe me, they are lethal. . . . I think you were conceived after one of those.
    Drink, instead, like a man: straight up or on the rocks, with plenty of water in between.
    Oh, yes. And never mix your drinks. Stay with one all night long, like the man you came in with: bourbon, gin, or tequila till dawn, damn the torpedoes, full speed ahead!

(*As the Female Greek Chorus retreats, the Male Greek Chorus approaches the table as a Waiter.*)

MALE GREEK CHORUS (*as Waiter*): I hope you all are having a pleasant evening. Is there something I can bring you, sir, before you order?

(*Li'l Bit waits in anxious fear. Carefully, Uncle Peck says with command:*)

PECK: I'll have a plain iced tea. The lady would like a drink, I believe.

(*The Male Greek Chorus does a double take; there is a moment when Uncle Peck and he are in silent communication.*)

MALE GREEK CHORUS (*as Waiter*): Very good. What would the . . . lady like?

LI'L BIT (*a bit flushed*): Is there . . . is there any sugar in a martini?

PECK: None that I know of.

LI'L BIT: That's what I'd like then—a dry martini. And could we maybe have some bread?

PECK: A drink fit for a woman of the world.—Please bring the lady a dry martini, be generous with the olives, straight up.

(*The Male Greek Chorus anticipates a large tip.*)

MALE GREEK CHORUS (*as Waiter*): Right away. Very good, sir.

(*The Male Greek Chorus returns with an empty martini glass which he puts in front of Li'l Bit.*)

PECK: Your glass is empty. Another martini, madam?

LI'L BIT: Yes, thank you.

(*Peck signals the Male Greek Chorus, who nods.*)

So why did you leave South Carolina, Uncle Peck?

PECK: I was stationed in D.C. after the war, and decided to stay. Go North, Young Man, someone might have said.

LI'L BIT: What did you do in the service anyway?

PECK (*suddenly taciturn*): I . . . I did just this and that. Nothing heroic or spectacular.

LI'L BIT: But did you see fighting? Or go to Europe?

PECK: I served in the Pacific Theater. It's really nothing interesting to talk about.

LI'L BIT: It is to me. (*The Waiter has brought another empty glass.*) Oh, goody. I love the color of the swizzle sticks. What were we talking about?

PECK: Swizzle sticks.

LI'L BIT: Do you ever think of going back?

PECK: To the Marines?

LI'L BIT: No—to South Carolina.

PECK: Well, we do go back. To visit.

LI'L BIT: No, I mean to live.

PECK: Not very likely. I think it's better if my mother doesn't have a daily reminder of her disappointment.

LI'L BIT: Are these floorboards slanted?

PECK: Yes, the floor is very slanted. I think this is the original floor.

LI'L BIT: Oh, good.

(*The Female Greek Chorus as Mother enters swaying a little, a little past tipsy.*)

FEMALE GREEK CHORUS (*as Mother*): Don't leave your drink unattended when you visit the ladies' room. There is such a thing as white slavery; the modus operandi is to spike an unsuspecting young girl's drink with a "mickey" when she's left the room to powder her nose.

But if you feel you have had more than your sufficiency in liquor, do go to the ladies' room—often. Pop your head out of doors for a refreshing breath of the night air. If you must, wet your face and head with tap water. Don't be afraid to dunk your head if necessary. A wet woman is still less conspicuous than a drunk woman.

(*The Female Greek Chorus stumbles a little; conspiratorially.*) When in the course of human events it becomes necessary, go to a corner stall and insert the index and middle finger down the throat almost to the epiglottis. Divulge your stomach contents by such persuasion, and then wait a few moments before rejoining your beau waiting for you at your table.

Oh, no. Don't be shy or embarrassed. In the very best of establishments, there's always one or two debutantes crouched in the corner stalls, their beaded purses tossed willy-nilly, sounding like cats in heat, heaving up the contents of their stomachs.

(*The Female Greek Chorus begins to wander off.*) I wonder what is it they do in the men's rooms. . . .

LI'L BIT: So why is your mother disappointed in you, Uncle Peck?

PECK: Every mother in Horry County has Great Expectations.

LI'L BIT: —Could I have another mar-ti-ni, please?

PECK: I think this is your last one.

(*Peck signals the Waiter. The Waiter looks at Li'l Bit and shakes his head no. Peck raises his eyebrow, raises his finger to indicate one more, and then rubs his fingers together. It looks like a secret code. The Waiter sighs, shakes his head sadly, and brings over another empty martini glass. He glares at Peck.*)

LI'L BIT: The name of the county where you grew up is "Horry"? (*Li'l Bit, plastered, begins to laugh. Then she stops.*) I think your mother should be proud of you.

(*Peck signals for the check.*)

PECK: Well, missy, she wanted me to do—to *be* everything my father was not. She wanted me to amount to something.

LI'L BIT: But you have! You've amounted a lot. . . .

PECK: I'm just a very ordinary man.

(*The Waiter has brought the check and waits. Peck draws out a large bill and hands it to the Waiter. Li'l Bit is in the soppy stage.*)

LI'L BIT: I'll bet your mother loves you, Uncle Peck.

(*Peck freezes a bit. To Male Greek Chorus as Waiter:*)

PECK: Thank you. The service was exceptional. Please keep the change.

MALE GREEK CHORUS (*as Waiter, in a tone that could freeze*): Thank you, sir. Will you be needing any help?

PECK: I think we can manage, thank you.

(*Just then, the Female Greek Chorus as Mother lurches on stage; the Male Greek Chorus as Waiter escorts her off as she delivers:*)

FEMALE GREEK CHORUS (*as Mother*): Thanks to judicious planning and several trips to the ladies' loo, your mother once out-drank an entire regiment of British officers on a good-will visit to Washington! Every last man of them! Milquetoasts! How'd they ever kick Hitler's cahones, huh? No match for an American lady—I could drink every man in here under the table.

(*She delivers one last crucial hint before she is gently "bounced."*)

As a last resort, when going out for an evening on the town, be sure to wear a skin-tight girdle—so tight that only a surgical knife or acetylene torch can get it off you—so that if you do pass out in the arms of your escort, he'll end up with rubber burns on his fingers before he can steal your virtue—

(*A Voice punctures the interlude with:*)

Vehicle Failure.
Even with careful maintenance and preventive operation of your automobile, it is all too common for us to experience an unexpected breakdown. If you are driving at any speed when a breakdown occurs, you must slow down and guide the automobile to the side of the road.

(*Peck is slowly propping up Li'l Bit as they work their way to his car in the parking lot of the inn.*)

PECK: How are you doing, missy?
LI'L BIT: It's so far to the car, Uncle Peck. Like the lanterns in the trees the British fired on. . . .

(*Li'l Bit stumbles. Peck swoops her up in his arms.*)

PECK: Okay, I think we're going to take a more direct route.

(*Li'l Bit closes her eyes.*)

Dizzy?

(*She nods her head.*)

Don't look at the ground. Almost there—do you feel sick to your stomach?

(*Li'l Bit nods. They reach the "car." Peck gently deposits her on the front seat.*)

Just settle here a little while until things stop spinning.

(*Li'l Bit opens her eyes.*)

LI'L BIT: What are we doing?
PECK: We're just going to sit here until your tummy settles down.
LI'L BIT: It's such nice upholst'ry—
PECK: Think you can go for a ride, now?

LI'L BIT: Where are you taking me?
PECK: Home.
LI'L BIT: You're not taking me—upstairs? There's no room at the inn? (*Li'l Bit giggles.*)
PECK: Do you want to go upstairs?

(*Li'l Bit doesn't answer.*)

Or home?
LI'L BIT: —This isn't right, Uncle Peck.
PECK: What isn't right?
LI'L BIT: What we're doing. It's wrong. It's very wrong.
PECK: What are we doing?

(*Li'l Bit does not answer.*)

We're just going out to dinner.
LI'L BIT: You know. It's not nice to Aunt Mary.
PECK: You let me be the judge of what's nice and not nice to my wife.

(*Beat.*)

LI'L BIT: Now you're mad.
PECK: I'm not mad. It's just that I thought you . . . understood me, Li'l Bit. I think you're the only one who does.
LI'L BIT: Someone will get hurt.
PECK: Have I forced you to do anything?

(*There is a long pause as Li'l Bit tries to get sober enough to think this through.*)

LI'L BIT: . . . I guess not.
PECK: We are just enjoying each other's company. I've told you, nothing is going to happen between us until you want it to. Do you know that?
LI'L BIT: Yes.
PECK: Nothing is going to happen until you want it. (*A second more, with Peck staring ahead at the river while seated at the wheel of his car. Then, softly:*) Do you want something to happen?

(*Peck reaches over and strokes her face, very gently. Li'l Bit softens, reaches for him, and buries her head in his neck. Then she kisses him. Then she moves away, dizzy again.*)

LI'L BIT: . . . I don't know.

(*Peck smiles; this has been good news for him—it hasn't been a "no."*)

PECK: Then I'll wait. I'm a very patient man. I've been waiting for a long time. I don't mind waiting.
LI'L BIT: Someone is going to get hurt.
PECK: No one is going to get hurt. (*Li'l Bit closes her eyes.*) Are you feeling sick?
LI'L BIT: Sleepy.

(*Carefully, Peck props Li'l Bit up on the seat.*)

PECK: Stay here a second.
LI'L BIT: Where're you going?
PECK: I'm getting something from the back seat.

LI'L BIT (*scared; too loud*): What? What are you going to do?

(*Peck reappears in the front seat with a lap rug.*)

PECK: Shhh. (*Peck covers Li'l Bit. She calms down.*) There. Think you can sleep?

(*Li'l Bit nods. She slides over to rest on his shoulder. With a look of happiness, Peck turns the ignition key. Beat. Peck leaves Li'l Bit sleeping in the car and strolls down to the audience. Wagner's Flying Dutchman comes up faintly.*) (*A Voice interjects:*)

Idling in the Neutral Gear.

TEENAGE GREEK CHORUS: Uncle Peck Teaches Cousin Bobby How to Fish.

PECK: I get back once or twice a year—supposedly to visit Mama and the family, but the real truth is to fish. I miss this the most of all. There's a smell in the Low Country—where the swamp and fresh inlet join the saltwater—a scent of sand and cypress, that I haven't found anywhere yet.

I don't say this very often up North because it will just play into the stereotype everyone has, but I will tell you: I didn't wear shoes in the summertime until I was sixteen. It's unnatural down here to pen up your feet in leather. Go ahead—take 'em off. Let yourself breathe—it really will make you feel better.

We're going to aim for some pompano today—and I have to tell you, they're a very shy, mercurial fish. Takes patience, and psychology. You have to believe it doesn't matter if you catch one or not.

Sky's pretty spectacular—there's some beer in the cooler next to the crab salad I packed, so help yourself if you get hungry. Are you hungry? Thirsty? Holler if you are.

Okay. You don't want to lean over the bridge like that—pompano feed in shallow water, and you don't want to get too close—they're frisky and shy little things—wait, check your line. Yep, something's been munching while we were talking.

Okay, look: We take the sand flea and you take the hook like this—right through his little sand flea rump. Sand fleas should always keep their backs to the wall. Okay. Cast it in, like I showed you. That's great! I can taste that pompano now, sautéed with some pecans and butter, a little bourbon—now—let it lie on the bottom—now, reel, jerk, reel, jerk—

Look—look at your line. There's something calling, all right. Okay, tip the rod up—not too sharp—hook it—all right, now easy, reel and then rest—let it play. And reel—play it out, that's right—really good! I can't believe it! It's a pompano.—Good work! Way to go! You are an official fisherman now. Pompano are hard to catch. We are going to have a delicious little—

What? Well, I don't know how much pain a fish feels—you can't think of that. Oh, no, don't cry, come on now, it's just a fish—the other guys are

going to see you.—No, no, you're just real sensitive, and I think that's wonderful at your age—look, do you want me to cut it free? You do?

Okay, hand me those pliers—look—I'm cutting the hook—okay? And we're just going to drop it in—no I'm not mad. It's just for fun, okay? There—it's going to swim back to its lady friend and tell her what a terrible day it had and she's going to stroke him with her fins until he feels better, and then they'll do something alone together that will make them both feel good and sleepy. . . .

(*Peck bends down, very earnest.*) I don't want you to feel ashamed about crying. I'm not going to tell anyone, okay? I can keep secrets. You know, men cry all the time. They just don't tell anybody, and they don't let anybody catch them. There's nothing you could do that would make me feel ashamed of you. Do you know that? Okay. (*Peck straightens up, smiles.*)

Do you want to pack up and call it a day? I tell you what —I think I can still remember—there's a really neat tree house where I used to stay for days. I think it's still here—it was the last time I looked. But it's a secret place—you can't tell anybody we've gone there—least of all your mom or your sisters.—This is something special just between you and me. Sound good? We'll climb up there and have a beer and some crab salad—okay, B.B.? Bobby? Robert. . . .

(*Li'l Bit sits at a kitchen table with the two Female Greek Chorus members.*)

LI'L BIT (*to the audience*): Three women, three generations, sit at the kitchen table.
    On Men, Sex, and Women: Part I:

FEMALE GREEK CHORUS (*as Mother*): Men only want one thing.

LI'L BIT (*wide-eyed*): But what? What is it they want?

FEMALE GREEK CHORUS (*as Mother*): And once they have it, they lose all interest. So Don't Give It to Them.

TEENAGE GREEK CHORUS (*as Grandmother*): I never had the luxury of the rhythm method. Your grandfather is just a big bull. A big bull. Every morning, every evening.

FEMALE GREEK CHORUS (*as Mother, whispers to Li'l Bit*): And he used to come home for lunch every day.

LI'L BIT: My god, Grandma!

TEENAGE GREEK CHORUS (*as Grandmother*): Your grandfather only cares that I do two things: have the table set and the bed turned down.

FEMALE GREEK CHORUS (*as Mother*): And in all that time, Mother, you never have experienced—?

LI'L BIT (*to the audience*):—Now my grandmother believed in all the sacraments of the church, to the day she died. She believed in Santa Claus and the Easter Bunny until she was fifteen. But she didn't believe in—

TEENAGE GREEK CHORUS (*as Grandmother*):—Orgasm! That's just something you and Mary have made up! I don't believe you.

FEMALE GREEK CHORUS (*as Mother*): Mother, it happens to women all the time—

TEENAGE GREEK CHORUS (*as Grandmother*): —Oh, now you're going to tell me about the G force!

LI'L BIT: No, Grandma, I think that's astronauts—

FEMALE GREEK CHORUS (*as Mother*): Well, Mama, after all, you were a child bride when Big Papa came and got you—you were a married woman and you still believed in Santa Claus.

TEENAGE GREEK CHORUS (*as Grandmother*): It was legal, what Daddy and I did! I was fourteen and in those days, fourteen was a grown-up woman—

(*Big Papa shuffles in the kitchen for a cookie.*)

MALE GREEK CHORUS (*as Grandfather*): —Oh, now we're off on Grandma and the Rape of the Sa-bean Women!

TEENAGE GREEK CHORUS (*as Grandmother*): Well, you were the one in such a big hurry—

MALE GREEK CHORUS (*as Grandfather to Li'l Bit*): —I picked your grandmother out of that herd of sisters just like a lion chooses the gazelle—the plump, slow, flaky gazelle dawdling at the edge of the herd—your sisters were too smart and too fast and too scrawny—

LI'L BIT (*to the audience*): —The family story is that when Big Papa came for Grandma, my Aunt Lily was waiting for him with a broom—and she beat him over the head all the way down the stairs as he was carrying out Grandma's hope chest—

MALE GREEK CHORUS (*as Grandfather*): —And they were *mean*. 'Specially Lily.

FEMALE GREEK CHORUS (*as Mother*): Well, you were robbing the baby of the family!

TEENAGE GREEK CHORUS (*as Grandmother*): I still keep a broom handy in the kitchen! And I know how to use it! So get your hand out of the cookie jar and don't you spoil your appetite for dinner—out of the kitchen!

(*Male Greek Chorus as Grandfather leaves chuckling with a cookie.*)

FEMALE GREEK CHORUS (*as Mother*): Just one thing a married woman needs to know how to use—the rolling pin or the broom. I prefer a heavy, cast-iron fry pan—they're great on a man's head, no matter how thick the skull is.

TEENAGE GREEK CHORUS (*as Grandmother*): Yes, sir, your father is ruled by only two bosses! Mr. Gut and Mr. Peter! And sometimes, first thing in the morning, Mr. Sphincter Muscle!

FEMALE GREEK CHORUS (*as Mother*): It's true. Men are like children. Just like little boys.

TEENAGE GREEK CHORUS (*as Grandmother*): Men are bulls! Big bulls!

(*The Greek Chorus is getting aroused.*)

FEMALE GREEK CHORUS (*as Mother*): They'd still be crouched on their haunches over a fire in a cave if we hadn't cleaned them up!

TEENAGE GREEK CHORUS (*as Grandmother; flushed*): Coming in smelling of sweat—

FEMALE GREEK CHORUS (*as Mother*): —Looking at those naughty pictures like boys in a dime store with a dollar in their pockets!

TEENAGE GREEK CHORUS (*as Grandmother; raucous*): No matter to them what they smell like! They've got to have it, right then, on the spot, right there! Nasty!—

FEMALE GREEK CHORUS (*as Mother*): —Vulgar!

TEENAGE GREEK CHORUS (*as Grandmother*): Primitive!—

FEMALE GREEK CHORUS (*as Mother*): —Hot!—

LI'L BIT: And just about then, Big Papa would shuffle in with—

MALE GREEK CHORUS (*as Grandfather*): —What are you all cackling about in here?

TEENAGE GREEK CHORUS (*as Grandmother*): Stay out of the kitchen! This is just for girls!

(*As Grandfather leaves:*)

MALE GREEK CHORUS (*as Grandfather*): Lucy, you'd better not be filling Mama's head with sex! Every time you and Mary come over and start in about sex, when I ask a simple question like, "What time is dinner going to be ready?," Mama snaps my head off!

TEENAGE GREEK CHORUS (*as Grandmother*): Dinner will be ready when I'm good and ready! Stay out of this kitchen!

(*Li'l Bit steps out.*)

(*A Voice directs:*)

When Making a Left Turn, You Must Downshift While Going Forward.

LI'L BIT: 1979. A long bus trip to Upstate New York. I settled in to read, when a young man sat beside me.

MALE GREEK CHORUS (*as Young Man; voice cracking*): "What are you reading?"

LI'L BIT: He asked. His voice broke into that miserable equivalent of vocal acne, not quite falsetto and not tenor, either. I glanced a side view. He was appealing in an odd way, huge ears at a defiant angle springing forward at ninety degrees. He must have been shaving, because his face, with a peach sheen, was speckled with nicks and styptic. "I have a class tomorrow," I told him.

MALE GREEK CHORUS (*as Young Man*): "You're taking a class?"

LI'L BIT: "I'm teaching a class." He concentrated on lowering his voice.

MALE GREEK CHORUS (*as Young Man*): "I'm a senior. Walt Whitman High."

LI'L BIT: The light was fading outside, so perhaps he was—with a very high voice.

I felt his "interest" quicken. Five steps ahead of the hopes in his head, I slowed down, waited, pretended surprise, acted at listening, all the while knowing we would get off the bus, he would just then seem to think to ask me to dinner, he would chivalrously insist on walking me home, he would continue to converse in the street until I would casually invite him up to my room—and—I was only into the second moment of conversation and I could see the whole evening before me.

And dramaturgically speaking, after the faltering and slightly comical "first act," there was the very briefest of intermissions, and an extremely capable and forceful and *sustained* second act. And after the second act climax and a gentle denouement—before the post-play discussion—I lay on my back in the dark and I thought about you, Uncle Peck. Oh. Oh—this is the allure. Being older. Being the first. Being the translator, the teacher, the epicure, the already jaded. This is how the giver gets taken.

(*Li'l Bit changes her tone.*) On Men, Sex, and Women: Part II:

(*Li'l Bit steps back into the scene as a fifteen-year-old, gawky and quiet, as the gazelle at the edge of the herd.*)

TEENAGE GREEK CHORUS (*as Grandmother, to Li'l Bit*): You're being mighty quiet, missy. Cat Got Your Tongue?

LI'L BIT: I'm just listening. Just thinking.

TEENAGE GREEK CHORUS (*as Grandmother*): Oh, yes, Little Miss Radar Ears? Soaking it all in? Little Miss Sponge? Penny for your thoughts?

(*Li'l Bit hesitates to ask but she really wants to know.*)

LI'L BIT: Does it—when you do it—you know, theoretically when I do it and I haven't done it before—I mean—does it hurt?

FEMALE GREEK CHORUS (*as Mother*): Does what hurt, honey?

LI'L BIT: When a . . . when a girl does it for the first time—with a man—does it hurt?

TEENAGE GREEK CHORUS (*as Grandmother; horrified*): *That's* what you're thinking about?

FEMALE GREEK CHORUS (*as Mother; calm*): Well, just a little bit. Like a pinch. And there's a little blood.

TEENAGE GREEK CHORUS (*as Grandmother*): Don't tell her that! She's too young to be thinking those things!

FEMALE GREEK CHORUS (*as Mother*): Well, if she doesn't find out from me, where is she going to find out? In the street?

TEENAGE GREEK CHORUS (*as Grandmother*): Tell her it hurts! It's agony! You think you're going to die! Especially if you do it before marriage!

FEMALE GREEK CHORUS (*as Mother*): Mama! I'm going to tell her the truth! Unlike you, you left me and Mary completely in the dark with fairy tales and told us to go to the priest! What does an eighty-year-old priest know about lovemaking with girls!

LI'L BIT (*getting upset*): It's not fair!

FEMALE GREEK CHORUS (*as Mother*): Now, see, she's getting upset—you're scaring her.

TEENAGE GREEK CHORUS (*as Grandmother*): Good! Let her be good and scared! It hurts! You bleed like a

Tim Crowe as Uncle Peck and Annie Sullivan as Li'l Bit in the Trinity Repertory Company's production of *How I Learned to Drive.*

stuck pig! And you lay there and say, "Why, O Lord, have you forsaken me?!"

LI'L BIT: It's not fair! Why does everything have to hurt for girls? Why is there always blood?

FEMALE GREEK CHORUS (*as Mother*): It's not a lot of blood—and it feels wonderful after the pain subsides. . . .

TEENAGE GREEK CHORUS (*as Grandmother*): You're encouraging her to just go out and find out with the first drugstore joe who buys her a milkshake!

FEMALE GREEK CHORUS (*as Mother*): Don't be scared. It won't hurt you—if the man you go to bed with really loves you. It's important that he loves you.

TEENAGE GREEK CHORUS (*as Grandmother*):—Why don't you just go out and rent a motel room for her, Lucy?

FEMALE GREEK CHORUS (*as Mother*): I believe in telling my daughter the truth! We have a very close relationship! I want her to be able to ask me anything—I'm not scaring her with stories about Eve's sin and snakes crawling on their bellies for eternity and women bearing children in mortal pain—

TEENAGE GREEK CHORUS (*as Grandmother*):—If she stops and thinks before she takes her knickers off, maybe someone in this family will finish high school!

(*Li'l Bit knows what is about to happen and starts to retreat from the scene at this point.*)

FEMALE GREEK CHORUS (*as Mother*): Mother! If you and Daddy had helped me—I wouldn't have had to marry that—that no-good-son-of-a—

TEENAGE GREEK CHORUS (*as Grandmother*):—He was good enough for you on a full moon! I hold you responsible!

FEMALE GREEK CHORUS (*as Mother*):—You could have helped me! You could have told me something about the facts of life!

TEENAGE GREEK CHORUS (*as Grandmother*):—I told you what my mother told me! A girl with her skirt up can outrun a man with his pants down!

(*The Male Greek Chorus enters the fray; Li'l Bit edges farther downstage.*)

FEMALE GREEK CHORUS (*as Mother*): And when I turned to you for a little help, all I got afterwards was—

MALE GREEK CHORUS (*as Grandfather*): You Made Your Bed; Now Lie On It!

(*The Greek Chorus freezes, mouths open, argumentatively.*)

LI'L BIT (*to the audience*): Oh, please! I still can't bear to listen to it, after all these years—

(*The Male Greek Chorus "unfreezes," but out of his open mouth, as if to his surprise, comes a bass refrain from a Motown song.*)

MALE GREEK CHORUS: "Do-Bee-Do-Wah!"

(*The Female Greek Chorus member is also surprised; but she, too, unfreezes.*)

FEMALE GREEK CHORUS: "Shoo-doo-be-doo-be-doo; shoo-doo-be-doo-be-doo."

(*The Male and Female Greek Chorus members continue with their harmony, until the Teenage member of the Chorus starts in with Motown lyrics such as "Dedicated to the One I Love," or "In the Still of the Night," or "Hold Me"—any Sam Cooke will do. The three modulate down into three-part harmony, softly, until they are submerged by the actual recording playing over the radio in the car in which Uncle Peck sits in the driver's seat, waiting. Li'l Bit sits in the passenger's seat.*)

LI'L BIT: Ahh. That's better.

(*Uncle Peck reaches over and turns the volume down; to Li'l Bit:*)

PECK: How can you hear yourself think?

(*Li'l Bit does not answer.*)

(*A Voice insinuates itself in the pause:*)

Before You Drive.
Always check under your car for obstructions—broken bottles, fallen tree branches, and the bodies of small children. Each year hundreds of children are crushed beneath the wheels of unwary drivers in their own driveways. Children depend on you to watch them.

(*Pause.*)
(*The Voice continues:*)

You and the Reverse Gear.

(*In the following section, it would be nice to have slides of erotic photographs of women and cars: women posed over the hood; women draped along the sideboards; women with water hoses spraying the car; and the actress playing Li'l Bit with a Bel Air or any 1950s car one can find for the finale.*)

LI'L BIT: 1967. In a parking lot of the Beltsville Agricultural Farms. The Initiation into a Boy's First Love.

PECK (*with a soft look on his face*): Of course, my favorite car will always be the '56 Bel Air Sports Coupe. Chevy sold more '55s, but the '56!—a V-8 with Corvette option, 225 horsepower; went from zero to sixty miles per hour in 8.9 seconds.

LI'L BIT (*to the audience*): Long after a mother's tits, but before a woman's breasts:

PECK: Super-Turbo-Fire! What a Power Pack—mechanical lifters, twin four-barrel carbs, lightweight valves, dual exhausts—

LI'L BIT (*to the audience*): After the milk but before the beer:

PECK: A specific intake manifold, higher-lift camshaft, and the tightest squeeze Chevy had ever made—

LI'L BIT (*to the audience*): Long after he's squeezed down the birth canal but before he's pushed his way back in: The boy falls in love with the thing that bears his weight with speed.

PECK: I want you to know your automobile inside and out.—Are you there? Li'l Bit?

(Slides end here.)

LI'L BIT: —What?

PECK: You're drifting. I need you to concentrate.

LI'L BIT: Sorry.

PECK: Okay. Get into the driver's seat. (*Li'l Bit does.*) Okay. Now. Show me what you're going to do before you start the car.

(Li'l Bit sits, with her hands in her lap. She starts to giggle.)

LI'L BIT: I don't know, Uncle Peck.

PECK: Now, come on. What's the first thing you're going to adjust?

LI'L BIT: My bra strap?—

PECK: —Li'l Bit. What's the most important thing to have control of on the inside of the car?

LI'L BIT: That's easy. The radio. I tune the radio from Mama's old fart tunes to—

(Li'l Bit turns the radio up so we can hear a 1960s tune. With surprising firmness, Peck commands:)

PECK: —Radio off. Right now. (*Li'l Bit turns the radio off.*) When you are driving your car, with your license, you can fiddle with the stations all you want. But when you are driving with a learner's permit in my car, I want all your attention to be on the road.

LI'L BIT: Yes, sir.

PECK: Okay. Now the seat—forward and up. (*Li'l Bit pushes it forward.*) Do you want a cushion?

LI'L BIT: No—I'm good.

PECK: You should be able to reach all the switches and controls. Your feet should be able to push the accelerator, brake and clutch all the way down. Can you do that?

LI'L BIT: Yes.

PECK: Okay, the side mirrors. You want to be able to see just a bit of the right side of the car in the right mirror—can you?

LI'L BIT: Turn it out more.

PECK: Okay. How's that?

LI'L BIT: A little more. . . . Okay, that's good.

PECK: Now the left—again, you want to be able to see behind you—but the left lane—adjust it until you feel comfortable. (*Li'l Bit does so.*) Next. I want you to check the rearview mirror. Angle it so you have a clear vision of the back. (*Li'l Bit does so.*) Okay. Lock your door. Make sure all the doors are locked.

LI'L BIT (*making a joke of it*): But then I'm locked in with you.

PECK: Don't fool.

LI'L BIT: All right. We're locked in.

PECK: We'll deal with the air vents and defroster later. I'm teaching you on a manual—once you learn manual, you can drive anything. I want you to be able to

drive any car, any machine. Manual gives you *control*. In ice, if your brakes fail, if you need more power—okay? It's a little harder at first, but then it becomes like breathing. Now. Put your hands on the wheel. I never want to see you driving with one hand. Always two hands. (*Li'l Bit hesitates.*) What? What is it now?

LI'L BIT: If I put my hands on the wheel—how do I defend myself?

PECK (*softly*): Now listen. Listen up close. We're not going to fool around with this. This is serious business. I will never touch you when you are driving a car. Understand?

LI'L BIT: Okay.

PECK: Hands on the nine o'clock and three o'clock position gives you maximum control and turn.

(Peck goes silent for a while. Li'l Bit waits for more instruction.)

Okay. Just relax and listen to me, Li'l Bit, okay? I want you to lift your hands for a second and look at them.

(Li'l Bit feels a bit silly, but does it.)

Those are your two hands. When you are driving, your life is in your own two hands. Understand?

(Li'l Bit nods.)

I don't have any sons. You're the nearest to a son I'll ever have—and I want to give you something. Something that really matters to me.

There's something about driving—when you're in control of the car, just you and the machine and the road—that nobody can take from you. A power. I feel more myself in my car than anywhere else. And that's what I want to give to you.

There's a lot of assholes out there. Crazy men, arrogant idiots, drunks, angry kids, geezers who are blind—and you have to be ready for them. I want to teach you to drive like a man.

LI'L BIT: What does that mean?

PECK: Men are taught to drive with confidence—with aggression. The road belongs to them. They drive defensively—always looking out for the other guy. Women tend to be polite—to hesitate. And that can be fatal.

You're going to learn to think what the other guy is going to do before he does it. If there's an accident, and ten cars pile up, and people get killed, you're the one who's gonna steer through it, put your foot on the gas if you have to, and be the only one to walk away. I don't know how long you or I are going to live, but we're for damned sure not going to die in a car.

So if you're going to drive with me, I want you to take this very seriously.

LI'L BIT: I will, Uncle Peck. I want you to teach me to drive.

PECK: Good. You're going to pass your test on the first try. Perfect score. Before the next four weeks are over, you're going to know this baby inside and out. Treat her with respect.

LI'L BIT: Why is it a "she"?

PECK: Good question. It doesn't have to be a "she"—but when you close your eyes and think of someone who responds to your touch—someone who performs just for you and gives you what you ask for—I guess I always see a "she." You can call her what you like.

LI'L BIT (*to the audience*): I closed my eyes—and decided not to change the gender.

(*A Voice:*)

Defensive driving involves defending yourself from hazardous and sudden changes in your automotive environment. By thinking ahead, the defensive driver can adjust to weather, road conditions, and road kill. Good defensive driving involves mental and physical preparation. Are you prepared?

(*Another Voice chimes in:*)

You and the Reverse Gear.

LI'L BIT: 1966. The Anthropology of the Female Body in Ninth Grade—Or A Walk Down Mammary Lane.

(*Throughout the following, there is occasional rhythmic beeping, like a transmitter signaling. Li'l Bit is aware of it, but can't figure out where it is coming from. No one else seems to hear it.*)

MALE GREEK CHORUS: In the hallway of Francis Scott Key Middle School.

(*A bell rings; the Greek Chorus is changing classes and meets in the hall, conspiratorially.*)

TEENAGE GREEK CHORUS: She's coming!

(*Li'l Bit enters the scene; the Male Greek Chorus member has a sudden, violent sneezing and lethal allergy attack.*)

FEMALE GREEK CHORUS: Jerome? Jerome? Are you all right?

MALE GREEK CHORUS: I—don't—know. I can't breathe— get Li'l Bit—

TEENAGE GREEK CHORUS: —He needs oxygen!—

FEMALE GREEK CHORUS: —Can you help us here?

LI'L BIT: What's wrong? Do you want me to get the school nurse—

(*The Male Greek Chorus member wheezes, grabs his throat and sniffs at Li'l Bit's chest, which is beeping away.*)

MALE GREEK CHORUS: No—it's okay—I only get this way when I'm around an allergy trigger—

LI'L BIT: Golly. What are you allergic to?

MALE GREEK CHORUS (*with a sudden grab of her breast*): Foam rubber.

(*The Greek Chorus members break up with hilarity; Jerome leaps away from Li'l Bit's kicking rage with agility; as he retreats:*)

LI'L BIT: Jerome! Creep! Cretin! Cro-Magnon!

TEENAGE GREEK CHORUS: Rage is not attractive in a girl.

FEMALE GREEK CHORUS: Really. Get a Sense of Humor.

(*A Voice echoes:*)

Good defensive driving involves mental and physical preparation. **Were You Prepared?**

FEMALE GREEK CHORUS: Gym Class: In the showers.

(*The sudden sound of water; the Female Greek Chorus members and Li'l Bit, while fully clothed, drape towels across their fronts, miming nudity. They stand, hesitate, at an imaginary shower's edge.*)

LI'L BIT: Water looks hot.

FEMALE GREEK CHORUS: Yesss. . . .

(*Female Greek Chorus members are not going to make the first move. One dips a tentative toe under the water, clutching the towel around her.*)

LI'L BIT: Well, I guess we'd better shower and get out of here.

FEMALE GREEK CHORUS: Yep. You go ahead. I'm still cooling off.

LI'L BIT: Okay.—Sally? Are you gonna shower?

TEENAGE GREEK CHORUS: After you—

(*Li'l Bit takes a deep breath for courage, drops the towel and plunges in: The two Female Greek Chorus members look at Li'l Bit in the all together, laugh, gasp and high-five each other.*)

TEENAGE GREEK CHORUS: Oh my god! Can you believe—

FEMALE GREEK CHORUS: Told you! It's not foam rubber! I win! Jerome owes me fifty cents!

(*A Voice editorializes:*)

Were You Prepared?

(*Li'l Bit tries to cover up; she is exposed, as suddenly 1960s Motown fills the room and we segue into:*)

FEMALE GREEK CHORUS: The Sock Hop.

(*Li'l Bit stands up against the wall with her female classmates. Teenage Greek Chorus is mesmerized by the music and just sways alone, lip-synching the lyrics.*)

LI'L BIT: I don't know. Maybe it's just me—but—do you ever feel like you're just a walking Mary Jane joke?

FEMALE GREEK CHORUS: I don't know what you mean.

LI'L BIT: You haven't heard the Mary Jane jokes? (*Female Greek Chorus member shakes her head no.*) Okay. "Little Mary Jane is walking through the woods, when all of a sudden this man who was hiding behind a tree *jumps* out, *rips* open Mary Jane's blouse, and *plunges* his hands on her breasts. And Little Mary Jane just laughed and laughed because she knew her money was in her shoes."

(*Li'l Bit laughs; the Female Greek Chorus does not.*)

FEMALE GREEK CHORUS: You're weird.

(*In another space, in a strange light, Uncle Peck stands and stares at Li'l Bit's body. He is setting up a tripod, but he just stands, appreciative, watching her.*)

LI'L BIT: Well, don't you ever feel . . . self-conscious? Like you're being looked at all the time?

FEMALE GREEK CHORUS: That's not a problem for me.— Oh—look—Greg's coming over to ask you to dance.

(*Teenage Creek Chorus becomes attentive, flustered. Male Greek Chorus member, as Greg, bends slightly as a very short young man, whose head is at Li'l Bit's chest level. Ardent, sincere, and socially inept, Greg will become a successful gynecologist.*)

TEENAGE GREEK CHORUS (*softly*): Hi, Greg.

(*Greg does not hear. He is intent on only one thing.*)

MALE GREEK CHORUS (*as Greg, to Li'l Bit*): Good evening. Would you care to dance?

LI'L BIT (*gently*): Thank you very much, Greg—but I'm going to sit this one out.

MALE GREEK CHORUS (*as Greg*): Oh. Okay. I'll try my luck later.

(*He disappears.*)

TEENAGE GREEK CHORUS: Oohhh.

(*Li'l Bit relaxes. Then she tenses, aware of Peck's gaze.*)

FEMALE GREEK CHORUS: Take pity on him. Someone should.

LI'L BIT: But he's so short.

TEENAGE GREEK CHORUS: He can't help it.

LI'L BIT: But his head comes up to (*Li'l Bit gestures*) here. And I think he asks me on the fast dances so he can watch me—you know—jiggle.

FEMALE GREEK CHORUS: I wish I had your problems.

(*The tune changes; Greg is across the room in a flash.*)

MALE GREEK CHORUS (*as Greg*): Evening again. May I ask you for the honor of a spin on the floor?

LI'L BIT: I'm . . . very complimented, Greg. But I . . . I just don't do fast dances.

MALE GREEK CHORUS (*as Greg*): Oh. No problem. That's okay.

(*He disappears. Teenage Greek Chorus watches him go.*)

TEENAGE GREEK CHORUS: That is just so—sad.

(*Li'l Bit becomes aware of Peck waiting.*)

FEMALE GREEK CHORUS: You know, you should take it as a compliment that the guys want to watch you jiggle. They're guys. That's what they're supposed to do.

LI'L BIT: I guess you're right. But sometimes I feel like these alien life forces, these two mounds of flesh have grafted themselves onto my chest, and they're using me until they can "propagate" and take over the world and they'll just keep growing, with a mind of their own until I collapse under their weight and they suck all the nourishment out of my body and I finally just waste away while they get bigger and bigger and—(*Li'l Bit's classmates are just staring at her in disbelief.*)

FEMALE GREEK CHORUS:—You are the strangest girl I have ever met.

(*Li'l Bit's trying to joke but feels on the verge of tears.*)

LI'L BIT: Or maybe someone's implanted radio transmitters in my chest at a frequency I can't hear, that girls can't detect, but they're sending out these signals to men who get mesmerized, like sirens, calling them to dash themselves on these "rocks"—

(*Just then, the music segues into a slow dance, perhaps a Beach Boys tune like "Little Surfer," but over the music there's a rhythmic, hypnotic beeping transmitted, which both Greg and Peck hear. Li'l Bit hears it too, and in horror she stares at her chest. She, too, is almost hypnotized. In a trance, Greg responds to the signals and is called to her side—actually, her front. Like a zombie, he stands in front of her, his eyes planted on her two orbs.*)

MALE GREEK CHORUS (*as Greg*): This one's a slow dance. I hope your dance card isn't . . . filled?

(*Li'l Bit is aware of Peck; but the signals are calling her to him. The signals are no longer transmitters, but an electromagnetic force, pulling Li'l Bit to his side, where he again waits for her to join him. She must get away from the dance floor.*)

LI'L BIT: Greg—you really are a nice boy. But I don't like to dance.

MALE GREEK CHORUS (*as Greg*): That's okay. We don't have to move or anything. I could just hold you and we could just *sway* a little—

LI'L BIT:—No! I'm sorry—but I think I have to leave; I hear someone calling me—

(*Li'l Bit starts across the dance floor, leaving Greg behind. The beeping stops. The lights change, although the music does not. As Li'l Bit talks to the audience, she continues to change and prepare for the coming session. She should be wearing a tight tank top or a sheer blouse and very tight pants. To the audience:*)

In every man's home some small room, some zone in his house, is set aside. It might be the attic, or the study, or a den. And there's an invisible sign as if from the old treehouse: Girls Keep Out. Here, away from female eyes, lace doilies and crochet, he keeps his manly toys: the Vargas pinups, the tackle. A scent of tobacco and WD-40. (*She inhales deeply.*) A dash of his Bay Rum. Ahhh . . . (*Li'l Bit savors it for just a moment more.*) Here he keeps his secrets: a violin or saxophone, drum set or darkroom, and the stacks of *Playboy*. (*In a whisper.*) Here, in my aunt's home, it was the basement. Uncle Peck's turf.

(*A Voice commands:*)

You and the Reverse Gear.

LI'L BIT: 1965. The Photo Shoot.

(*Li'l Bit steps into the scene as a nervous but curious thirteen-year-old. Music, from the previous scene, continues to play, changing into something like Roy Orbison later—something seductive with a beat. Peck fiddles, all business, with his camera. As in the driving lesson, he is all competency and concentration. Li'l Bit stands awkwardly. He looks through the Leica camera on the tripod, adjusts the back lighting, etc.*)

PECK: Are you cold? The lights should heat up some in a few minutes—
LI'L BIT: —Aunt Mary is?
PECK: At the National Theatre matinee. With your mother. We have time.
LI'L BIT: But—what if—
PECK: —And so what if they return? I told them you and I were going to be working with my camera. They won't come down.

(*Li'l Bit is quiet, apprehensive.*)

Look, are you sure you want to do this?
LI'L BIT: I said I'd do it. But—
PECK: —I know. You've drawn the line.
LI'L BIT (*reassured*): That's right. No frontal nudity.
PECK: Good heavens, girl, where did you pick that up?
LI'L BIT (*defensive*): I read.

(*Peck tries not to laugh.*)

PECK: And I read *Playboy* for the interviews. Okay. Let's try some different music.

(*Peck goes to an expensive reel-to-reel and forwards. Something like "Sweet Dreams" begins to play.*)

LI'L BIT: I didn't know you listened to this.
PECK: I'm not dead, you know, I try to keep up. Do you like this song?

(*Li'l Bit nods with pleasure.*)

Good. Now listen—at professional photo shoots, they always play music for the models. Okay? I want you to just enjoy the music. Listen to it with your body, and just—respond.
LI'L BIT: Respond to the music with my . . . body?
PECK: Right. Almost like dancing. Here—let's get you on the stool, first. (*Peck comes over and helps her up.*)
LI'L BIT: But nothing showing—

(*Peck firmly, with his large capable hands, brushes back her hair, angles her face. Li'l Bit turns to him like a plant to the sun.*)

PECK: Nothing showing. Just a peek.

(*He holds her by the shoulders, looking at her critically. Then he unbuttons her blouse to the midpoint, and runs his hands over the flesh of her exposed sternum, arranging the fabric, just touching her. Deliberately, calmly. Asexually. Li'l Bit quiets, sits perfectly still, and closes her eyes.*)

Okay?
LI'L BIT: Yes.

(*Peck goes back to his camera.*)

PECK: I'm going to keep talking to you. Listen without responding to what I'm saying; you want to *listen* to the music. Sway, move just your torso or your head—I've got to check the light meter.
LI'L BIT: But—you'll be watching.
PECK: No—I'm not here—just my voice. Pretend you're in your room all alone on a Friday night with your mirror—and the music feels good—just move for me, Li'l Bit—

(*Li'l Bit closes her eyes. At first self-conscious; then she gets more into the music and begins to sway. We hear the camera start to whir. Throughout the shoot, there can be a slide montage of actual shots of the actor playing Li'l Bit—interspersed with other models à la Playboy, Calvin Klein, and Victoriana/Lewis Carroll's Alice Liddell.*)

That's it. That looks great. Okay. Just keep doing that. Lift your head up a bit more, good, good, just keep moving, that a girl—you're a very beautiful young woman. Do you know that?

(*Li'l Bit looks up, blushes. Peck shoots the camera. The audience should see this shot on the screen.*)

LI'L BIT: No. I don't know that.
PECK: Listen to the music.

(*Li'l Bit closes her eyes again.*)

Well you are. For a thirteen-year-old, you have a body a twenty-year-old woman would die for.
LI'L BIT: The boys in school don't think so.
PECK: The boys in school are little Neanderthals in short pants. You're ten years ahead of them in maturity; it's gonna take a while for them to catch up.

(*Peck clicks another shot; we see a faint smile on Li'l Bit on the screen.*)

Girls turn into women long before boys turn into men.
LI'L BIT: Why is that?
PECK: I don't know, Li'l Bit. But it's a blessing for men.

(*Li'l Bit turns silent.*)

Keep moving. Try arching your back on the stool, hands behind you, and throw your head back.

(The slide shows a Playboy model in this pose.)

Oohh, great. That one was great. Turn your head away, same position. *(Whir.)* Beautiful.

(Li'l Bit looks at him a bit defiantly.)

LI'L BIT: I think Aunt Mary is beautiful.

(Peck stands still.)

PECK: My wife is a very beautiful woman. Her beauty doesn't cancel yours out. *(More casually; he returns to the camera.)* All the women in your family are beautiful. In fact, I think all women are. You're not listening to the music. *(Peck shoots some more film in silence.)* All right, turn your head to the left. Good. Now take the back of your right hand and put it on your right cheek—your elbow angled up—now slowly, slowly, stroke your cheek, draw back your hair with the back of your hand. *(Another classic Playboy or Vargas.)* Good. One hand above and behind your head; stretch your body; smile. *(Another pose.)* Li'l Bit. I want you to think of something that makes you laugh—

LI'L BIT: I can't think of anything.

PECK: Okay. Think of Big Papa chasing Grandma around the living room.

(Li'l Bit lifts her head and laughs. Click. We should see this shot.)

Good. Both hands behind your head. Great! Hold that. *(From behind his camera.)* You're doing great work. If we keep this up, in five years we'll have a really professional portfolio.

(Li'l Bit stops.)

LI'L BIT: What do you mean in five years?

PECK: You can't submit work to *Playboy* until you're eighteen.—

(Peck continues to shoot; he knows he's made a mistake.)

LI'L BIT:—Wait a minute. You're joking, aren't you, Uncle Peck?

PECK: Heck, no. You can't get into *Playboy* unless you're the very best. And you are the very best.

LI'L BIT: I would never do that!

(Peck stops shooting. He turns off the music.)

PECK: Why? There's nothing wrong with *Playboy*—it's a very classy maga—

LI'L BIT *(more upset)*: But I thought you said I should go to college!

PECK: Wait—Li'l Bit—it's nothing like that. Very respectable women model for *Playboy*—actresses with major careers—women in college—there's an Ivy League issue every—

LI'L BIT:—I'm never doing anything like that! You'd show other people these—other *men*—what I'm doing.—Why would you do that?! Any *boy* around

here could just pick up, just go into The Stop & Go and *buy*—Why would you ever want to—to share—

PECK:—Whoa, whoa. Just stop a second and listen to me. Li'l Bit. Listen. There's nothing wrong in what we're doing. I'm very proud of you. I think you have a wonderful body and an even more wonderful mind. And of course I want other people to *appreciate* it. It's not anything shameful.

LI'L BIT *(hurt)*: But this is something—that I'm only doing for you. This is something—that you said was just between us.

PECK: It is. And if that's how you feel, five years from now, it will remain that way. Okay? I know you're not going to do anything you don't feel like doing. *(He walks back to the camera.)* Do you want to stop now? I've got just a few more shots on this roll—

LI'L BIT: I don't want anyone seeing this.

PECK: I swear to you. No one will. I'll treasure this—that you're doing this only for me.

(Li'l Bit, still shaken, sits on the stool. She closes her eyes.)

Li'l Bit? Open your eyes and look at me.

(Li'l Bit shakes her head no.)

Come on. Just open your eyes, honey.

LI'L BIT: If I look at you—if I look at the camera: You're gonna know what I'm thinking. You'll see right through me—

PECK:—No, I won't. I want you to look at me. All right, then. I just want you to listen. Li'l Bit.

(She waits.)

I love you.

(Li'l Bit opens her eyes; she is startled. Peck captures the shot. On the screen we see right through her. Peck says softly.)

Do you know that?

(Li'l Bit nods her head yes.)

I have loved you every day since the day you were born.

LI'L BIT: Yes.

(Li'l Bit and Peck just look at each other. Beat. Beneath the shot of herself on the screen, Li'l Bit, still looking at her uncle, begins to unbutton her blouse.
A neutral Voice cuts off the above scene with:)

Implied Consent.
As an individual operating a motor vehicle in the state of Maryland, you must abide by "Implied Consent." If you do not consent to take the blood alcohol content test, there may be severe penalties: a suspension of license, a fine, community service, and a possible jail sentence.

(The Voice shifts tone:)

Idling in the Neutral Gear.

MALE GREEK CHORUS (*announcing*): Aunt Mary on behalf of her husband.

(*Female Greek Chorus checks her appearance, and with dignity comes to the front of the stage and sits down to talk to the audience.*)

FEMALE GREEK CHORUS (*as Aunt Mary*): My husband was such a good man—is. Is such a good man. Every night, he does the dishes. The second he comes home, he's taking out the garbage, or doing yard work, lifting the heavy things I can't. Everyone in the neighborhood borrows Peck—it's true—women with husbands of their own, men who just don't have Peck's abilities—there's always a knock on our door for a jump start on cold mornings, when anyone needs a ride, or help shoveling the sidewalk—I look out, and there Peck is, without a coat, pitching in.

I know I'm lucky. The man works from dawn to dusk. And the overtime he does every year—my poor sister. She sits every Christmas when I come to dinner with a new stole, or diamonds, or with the tickets to Bermuda.

I know he has troubles. And we don't talk about them. I wonder, sometimes, what happened to him during the war. The men who fought World War II didn't have "rap sessions" to talk about their feelings. Men in his generation were expected to be quiet about it and get on with their lives. And sometimes I can feel him just fighting the trouble—whatever has burrowed deeper than the scar tissue—and we don't talk about it. I know he's having a bad spell because he comes looking for me in the house, and just hangs around me until it passes. And I keep my banter light—I discuss a new recipe, or sales, or gossip—because I think domesticity can be a balm for men when they're lost. We sit in the house and listen to the peace of the clock ticking in his well-ordered living room, until it passes.

(*Sharply.*) I'm not a fool. I know what's going on. I wish you could feel how hard Peck fights against it—he's swimming against the tide, and what he needs is to see me on the shore, believing in him, knowing he won't go under, he won't give up—

And I want to say this about my niece. She's a sly one, that one is. She knows exactly what she's doing; she's twisted Peck around her little finger and thinks it's all a big secret. Yet another one who's borrowing my husband until it doesn't suit her anymore.

Well. I'm counting the days until she goes away to school. And she manipulates someone else. And then he'll come back again, and sit in the kitchen while I bake, or beside me on the sofa when I sew in the evenings. I'm a very patient woman. But I'd like my husband back.

I am counting the days.

(*A Voice repeats:*)

You and the Reverse Gear.

MALE GREEK CHORUS: Li'l Bit's Thirteenth Christmas. Uncle Peck Does the Dishes. Christmas 1964.

(*Peck stands in a dress shirt and tie, nice pants, with an apron. He is washing dishes. He's in a mood we haven't seen. Quiet, brooding. Li'l Bit watches him a moment before seeking him out.*)

LI'L BIT: Uncle Peck?

(*He does not answer. He continues to work on the pots.*)

I didn't know where you'd gone to.

(*He nods. She takes this as a sign to come in.*)

Don't you want to sit with us for a while?
PECK: No. I'd rather do the dishes.

(*Pause. Li'l Bit watches him.*)

LI'L BIT: You're the only man I know who does dishes.

(*Peck says nothing.*)

I think it's really nice.
PECK: My wife has been on her feet all day. So's your grandmother and your mother.
LI'L BIT: I know. (*Beat.*) Do you want some help?
PECK: No. (*He softens a bit towards her.*) You can help by just talking to me.
LI'L BIT: Big Papa never does the dishes. I think it's nice.
PECK: I think men should be nice to women. Women are always working for us. There's nothing particularly manly in wolfing down food and then sitting around in a stupor while the women clean up.
LI'L BIT: That looks like a really neat camera that Aunt Mary got you.
PECK: It is. It's a very nice one.

(*Pause, as Peck works on the dishes and some demon that Li'l Bit intuits.*)

LI'L BIT: Did Big Papa hurt your feelings?
PECK (*tired*): What? Oh, no—it doesn't hurt me. Family is family. I'd rather have him picking on me than—I don't pay him any mind, Li'l Bit.
LI'L BIT: Are you angry with us?
PECK: No, Li'l Bit. I'm not angry.

(*Another pause.*)

LI'L BIT: We missed you at Thanksgiving. . . . I did. I missed you.
PECK: Well, there were . . . "things" going on. I didn't want to spoil anyone's Thanksgiving.
LI'L BIT: Uncle Peck? (*Very carefully.*) Please don't drink anymore tonight.
PECK: I'm not . . . overdoing it.
LI'L BIT: I know. (*Beat.*) Why do you drink so much?

(*Peck stops and thinks, carefully.*)

PECK: Well, Li'l Bit—let me explain it this way. There are some people who have a . . . a "fire" in the belly. I think they go to work on Wall Street or they run for office. And then there are people who have a "fire" in their heads—and they become writers or scientists or historians. (*He smiles a little at her.*) You. You've got a "fire" in the head. And then there are people like me.

LI'L BIT: Where do you have . . . a fire?

PECK: I have a fire in my heart. And sometimes the drinking helps.

LI'L BIT: There's got to be other things that can help.

PECK: I suppose there are.

LI'L BIT: Does it help—to talk to me?

PECK: Yes. It does. (*Quiet.*) I don't get to see you very much.

LI'L BIT: I know. (*Li'l Bit thinks.*) You could talk to me more.

PECK: Oh?

LI'L BIT: I could make a deal with you, Uncle Peck.

PECK: I'm listening.

LI'L BIT: We could meet and talk—once a week. You could just store up whatever's bothering you during the week—and then we could talk.

PECK: Would you like that?

LI'L BIT: As long as you don't drink. I'd meet you somewhere for lunch or for a walk—on the weekends—as long as you stop drinking. And we could talk about whatever you want.

PECK: You would do that for me?

LI'L BIT: I don't think I'd want Mom to know. Or Aunt Mary. I wouldn't want them to think—

PECK: —No. It would just be us talking.

LI'L BIT: I'll tell Mom I'm going to a girlfriend's. To study. Mom doesn't get home until six, so you can call me after school and tell me where to meet you.

PECK: You get home at four?

LI'L BIT: We can meet once a week. But only in public. You've got to let me—draw the line. And once it's drawn, you mustn't cross it.

PECK: Understood.

LI'L BIT: Would that help?

(*Peck is very moved.*)

PECK: Yes. Very much.

LI'L BIT: I'm going to join the others in the living room now. (*Li'l Bit turns to go.*)

PECK: Merry Christmas, Li'l Bit.

(*Li'l Bit bestows a very warm smile on him.*)

LI'L BIT: Merry Christmas, Uncle Peck.

(*A Voice dictates:*)

Shifting Forward from Second to Third Gear.

(*The Male and Female Greek Chorus members come forward.*)

MALE GREEK CHORUS: 1969. Days and Gifts: A Countdown:

FEMALE GREEK CHORUS: A note. "September 3, 1969. Li'l Bit: You've only been away two days and it feels like months. Hope your dorm room is cozy. I'm sending you this tape cassette—it's a new model—so you'll have some music in your room. Also that music you're reading about for class—*Carmina Burana*. Hope you enjoy. Only ninety days to go!—Peck."

MALE GREEK CHORUS: September 22. A bouquet of roses. A note: "Miss you like crazy. Sixty-nine days . . ."

TEENAGE GREEK CHORUS: September 25. A box of chocolates. A card: "Don't worry about the weight gain. You still look great. Got a post office box—write to me there. Sixty-six days.—Love, your candy man."

MALE GREEK CHORUS: October 16. A note: "Am trying to get through the Jane Austen you're reading—*Emma*—here's a book in return: *Liaisons Dangereuses*. Hope you're saving time for me." Scrawled in the margin the number: "47."

FEMALE GREEK CHORUS: November 16. "Sixteen days to go!—Hope you like the perfume.—Having a hard time reaching you on the dorm phone. You must be in the library a lot. Won't you think about me getting you your own phone so we can talk?"

TEENAGE GREEK CHORUS: November 18. "Li'l Bit—got a package returned to the P.O. Box. Have you changed dorms? Call me at work or write to the P.O. Am still on the wagon. Waiting to see you. Only two weeks more!"

MALE GREEK CHORUS: November 23. A letter. "Li'l Bit. So disappointed you couldn't come home for the turkey. Sending you some money for a nice dinner out—nine days and counting!"

GREEK CHORUS (*in unison*): November 25th. A letter:

LI'L BIT: "Dear Uncle Peck: I am sending this to you at work. Don't come up next weekend for my birthday. I will not be here—"

(*A Voice directs:*)

Shifting Forward from Third to Fourth Gear.

MALE GREEK CHORUS: December 10, 1969. A hotel room. Philadelphia. There is no moon tonight.

(*Peck sits on the side of the bed while Li'l Bit paces. He can't believe she's in his room, but there's a desperate edge to his happiness. Li'l Bit is furious, edgy. There is a bottle of champagne in an ice bucket in a very nice hotel room.*)

PECK: Why don't you sit?

LI'L BIT: I don't want to.—What's the champagne for?

PECK: I thought we might toast your birthday—

LI'L BIT: —I am so pissed off at you, Uncle Peck.

PECK: Why?

LI'L BIT: I mean, are you crazy?

PECK: What did I do?

LI'L BIT: You scared the holy crap out of me—sending me that stuff in the mail—

PECK:—They were gifts! I just wanted to give you some little perks your first semester—

LI'L BIT:—Well, what the hell were those numbers all about! Forty-four days to go—only two more weeks.—And then just numbers—69—68—67—like some serial killer!

PECK: Li'l Bit! Whoa! This is me you're talking to—I was just trying to pick up your spirits, trying to celebrate your birthday.

LI'L BIT: My *eighteenth* birthday. I'm not a child, Uncle Peck. You were counting down to my eighteenth birthday.

PECK: So?

LI'L BIT: So? So statutory rape is not in effect when a young woman turns eighteen. And you and I both know it.

(*Peck is walking on ice.*)

PECK: I think you misunderstand.

LI'L BIT: I think I understand all too well. I know what you want to do five steps ahead of you doing it. Defensive Driving 101.

PECK: Then why did you suggest we meet here instead of the restaurant?

LI'L BIT: I don't want to have this conversation in public.

PECK: Fine. Fine. We have a lot to talk about.

LI'L BIT: Yeah. We do.
     (*Li'l Bit doesn't want to do what she has to do.*)
     Could I . . . have some of that champagne?

PECK: Of course, madam! (*Peck makes a big show of it.*) Let me do the honors. I wasn't sure which you might prefer—Taittingers or Veuve Clicquot—so I thought we'd start out with an old standard— Perrier Jouet. (*The bottle is popped.*)
     Quick—Li'l Bit—your glass! (*Uncle Peck fills Li'l Bit's glass. He puts the bottle back in the ice and goes for a can of ginger ale.*) Let me get some of this ginger ale—my bubbly—and toast you.

(*He turns and sees that Li'l Bit has not waited for him.*)

LI'L BIT: Oh—sorry, Uncle Peck. Let me have another.

(*Peck fills her glass and reaches for his ginger ale; she stops him.*)

Uncle Peck—maybe you should join me in the champagne.

PECK: You want me—to drink?

LI'L BIT: It's not polite to let a lady drink alone.

PECK: Well, missy, if you insist. . . . (*Peck hesitates.*)—Just once. It's been a while. (*Peck fills another flute for himself.*) There. I'd like to propose a toast to you and your birthday! (*Peck sips it tentatively.*) I'm not used to this anymore.

LI'L BIT: You don't have anywhere to go tonight, do you?

(*Peck hopes this is a good sign.*)

PECK: I'm all yours.—God, it's good to see you! I've gotten so used to . . . to . . . talking to you in my head. I'm used to seeing you every week—there's so

much—I don't quite know where to begin. How's school, Li'l Bit?

LI'L BIT: I—it's hard. Uncle Peck. Harder than I thought it would be. I'm in the middle of exams and papers and—I don't know.

PECK: You'll pull through. You always do.

LI'L BIT: Maybe. I . . . might be flunking out.

PECK: You always think the worst, Li'l Bit, but when the going gets tough—

(*Li'l Bit shrugs and pours herself another glass.*)

—Hey, honey, go easy on that stuff, okay?

LI'L BIT: Is it very expensive?

PECK: Only the best for you. But the cost doesn't matter—champagne should be "sipped."

(*Li'l Bit is quiet.*)

Look—if you're in trouble in school—you can always come back home for a while.

LI'L BIT: *No*—(*Li'l Bit tries not to be so harsh.*)—Thanks, Uncle Peck, but I'll figure some way out of this.

PECK: You're supposed to get in scrapes, your first year away from home.

LI'L BIT: Right. How's Aunt Mary?

PECK: She's fine. (*Pause.*) Well—how about the new car?

LI'L BIT: It's real nice. What is it, again?

PECK: It's a Cadillac El Dorado.

LI'L BIT: Oh. Well, I'm real happy for you, Uncle Peck.

PECK: I got it for you.

LI'L BIT: What?

PECK: I always wanted to get a Cadillac—but I thought, Peck, wait until Li'l Bit's old enough—and thought maybe you'd like to drive it, too.

LI'L BIT (*confused*): Why would I want to drive your car?

PECK: Just because it's the best—I want you to have the best.

(*They are running out of "gas"; small talk.*)

| LI'L BIT: Listen, Uncle Peck, I don't know how to begin this, but— | PECK: I have been thinking of how to say this in my head, over and over— |

PECK: Sorry.

LI'L BIT: You first.

PECK: Well, your going away—has just made me realize how much I miss you. Talking to you and being alone with you. I've really come to depend on you, Li'l Bit. And it's been so hard to get in touch with you lately—the distance and—and you're never in when I call—I guess you've been living in the library—

LI'L BIT:—No—the problem is, I haven't been in the library—

PECK:—Well, it doesn't matter—I hope you've been missing me as much.

LI'L BIT: Uncle Peck—I've been thinking a lot about this—and I came here tonight to tell you that—I'm not doing very well. I'm getting very confused—I can't concentrate on my work—and now that I'm away—I've been going over and over it in my mind—and I don't want us to "see" each other anymore. Other than with the rest of the family.

PECK (*quiet*): Are you seeing other men?

LI'L BIT (*getting agitated*): I—no, that's not the reason—I—well, yes, I am seeing other—listen, it's not really anybody's business!

PECK: Are you in love with anyone else?

LI'L BIT: That's not what this is about.

PECK: Li'l Bit—you're scared. Your mother and your grandparents have filled your head with all kinds of nonsense about men—I hear them working on you all the time—and you're scared. It won't hurt you—if the man you go to bed with really loves you. (*Li'l Bit is scared. She starts to tremble.*) And I have loved you since the day I held you in my hand. And I think everyone's just gotten you frightened to death about something that is just like breathing—

LI'L BIT: Oh, my god—(*She takes a breath.*) I can't see you anymore, Uncle Peck.

(*Peck downs the rest of his champagne.*)

PECK: Li'l Bit. Listen. Listen. Open your eyes and look at me. Come on. Just open your eyes, honey. (*Li'l Bit, eyes squeezed shut, refuses.*) All right then. I just want you to listen. Li'l Bit—I'm going to ask you just this once. Of your own free will. Just lie down on the bed with me—our clothes on—just lie down with me, a man and a woman . . . and let's . . . hold one another. Nothing else. Before you say anything else. I want the chance to . . . hold you. Because sometimes the body knows things that the mind isn't listening to . . . and after I've held you, then I want you to tell me what you feel.

LI'L BIT: You'll just . . . hold me?

PECK: Yes. And then you can tell me what you're feeling.

(*Li'l Bit—half wanting to run, half wanting to get it over with, half wanting to be held by him:*)

LI'L BIT: Yes. All right. Just hold. Nothing else.

(*Peck lies down on the bed and holds his arms out to her. Li'l Bit lies beside him, putting her head on his chest. He looks as if he's trying to soak her into his pores by osmosis. He strokes her hair, and she lies very still. The Male Greek Chorus member and the Female Greek Chorus member as Aunt Mary come into the room.*)

MALE GREEK CHORUS: Recipe for a Southern Boy:

FEMALE GREEK CHORUS (*as Aunt Mary*): A drawl of molasses in the way he speaks.

Mary Louise Parker as Li'l Bit and David Morse as Uncle Peck in *How I Learned to Drive* in 1997 at the Vineyard Theatre, New York City.

MALE GREEK CHORUS: A gumbo of red and brown mixed in the cream of his skin.

(*While Peck lies, his eyes closed, Li'l Bit rises in the bed and responds to her aunt.*)

LI'L BIT: Warm brown eyes—

FEMALE GREEK CHORUS (*as Aunt Mary*): Bedroom eyes—

MALE GREEK CHORUS: A dash of Southern Baptist Fire and Brimstone—

LI'L BIT: A curl of Elvis on his forehead—

FEMALE GREEK CHORUS (*as Aunt Mary*): A splash of Bay Rum—

MALE GREEK CHORUS: A closely shaven beard that he razors just for you—

FEMALE GREEK CHORUS (*as Aunt Mary*): Large hands—rough hands—

LI'L BIT: Warm hands—

MALE GREEK CHORUS: The steel of the military in his walk—

LI'L BIT: The slouch of the fishing skiff in his walk—

MALE GREEK CHORUS: Neatly pressed khakis—

FEMALE GREEK CHORUS (*as Aunt Mary*): And under the wide leather of the belt—

LI'L BIT: Sweat of cypress and sand—

MALE GREEK CHORUS: Neatly pressed khakis—

LI'L BIT: His heart beating Dixie—

FEMALE GREEK CHORUS (*as Aunt Mary*): The whisper of the zipper—you could reach out with your hand and—

LI'L BIT: His mouth—

FEMALE GREEK CHORUS (*as Aunt Mary*): You could just reach out and—

LI'L BIT: Hold him in your hand—

FEMALE GREEK CHORUS (*as Aunt Mary*): And his mouth—

(*Li'l Bit rises above her uncle and looks at his mouth; she starts to lower herself to kiss him—and wrenches herself free. She gets up from the bed.*)

LI'L BIT. I've got to get back.

PECK: Wait—Li'l Bit. Did you . . . feel nothing?

LI'L BIT (*lying*): No. Nothing.

PECK: Do you—do you think of me?

(*The Greek Chorus whispers:*)

FEMALE GREEK CHORUS: Khakis—

MALE GREEK CHORUS: Bay Rum—

FEMALE GREEK CHORUS: The whisper of the—

LI'L BIT: —No.

(*Peck, in a rush, trembling, gets something out of his pocket.*)

PECK: I'm forty-five. That's not old for a man. And I haven't been able to do anything else but think of you. I can't concentrate on my work—Li'l Bit. You've got to—I want you to think about what I am about to ask you.

LI'L BIT: I'm listening.

(*Peck opens a small ring box.*)

PECK: I want you to be my wife.

LI'L BIT: This isn't happening.

PECK: I'll tell Mary I want a divorce. We're not blood-related. It would be legal—

LI'L BIT: —What have you been thinking! You are married to my aunt, Uncle Peck. She's my family. You have—you have gone way over the line. Family is family.

    (*Quickly, Li'l Bit flies through the room, gets her coat.*) I'm leaving. Now. I am not seeing you. Again.

(*Peck lies down on the bed for a moment, trying to absorb the terrible news. For a moment, he almost curls into a fetal position.*)

I'm not coming home for Christmas. You should go home to Aunt Mary. Go home now, Uncle Peck.

(*Peck gets control, and sits, rigid.*)

Uncle Peck?—I'm sorry but I have to go.

(*Pause.*)

Are you all right?

(*With a discipline that comes from being told that boys don't cry, Peck stands upright.*)

PECK: I'm fine. I just think—I need a real drink.

(*The Male Greek Chorus has become a bartender. At a small counter, he is lining up shots for Peck. As Li'l Bit narrates, we see Peck sitting, carefully and calmly downing shot glasses.*)

LI'L BIT (*to the audience*): I never saw him again. I stayed away from Christmas and Thanksgiving for years after.

    It took my uncle seven years to drink himself to death. First he lost his job, then his wife, and finally his driver's license. He retreated to his house, and had his bottles delivered.

(*Peck stands, and puts his hands in front of him—almost like Superman flying.*)

One night he tried to go downstairs to the basement—and he flew down the steep basement stairs. My aunt came by weekly to put food on the porch, and she noticed the mail and the papers stacked up, uncollected. They found him at the bottom of the stairs. Just steps away from his dark room.

    Now that I'm old enough, there are some questions I would have liked to have asked him. Who did it to you, Uncle Peck? How old were you? Were you eleven?

(*Peck moves to the driver's seat of the car and waits.*)

Sometimes I think of my uncle as a kind of Flying Dutchman. In the opera, the Dutchman is doomed to wander the sea; but every seven years he can come ashore, and if he finds a maiden who will love him of her own free will—he will be released.

And I see Uncle Peck in my mind, in his Chevy '56, a spirit driving up and down the back roads of Carolina—looking for a young girl who, of her own free will, will love him. Release him.

(*A Voice states:*)

You and the Reverse Gear.

LI'L BIT: The summer of 1962. On Men, Sex, and Women: Part III:

(*Li'l Bit steps, as an eleven-year-old, into:*)

FEMALE GREEK CHORUS (*as Mother*): It is out of the question. End of Discussion.

LI'L BIT: But why?

FEMALE GREEK CHORUS (*as Mother*): Li'l Bit—we are not discussing this. I said no.

LI'L BIT: But I could spend an extra week at the beach! You're not telling me why!

FEMALE GREEK CHORUS (*as Mother*): Your uncle pays entirely too much attention to you.

LI'L BIT: He listens to me when I talk. And—and he talks to me. He teaches me about things. Mama—he knows an awful lot.

FEMALE GREEK CHORUS (*as Mother*): He's a small town hick who's learned how to mix drinks from Hugh Hefner.

LI'L BIT: Who's Hugh Hefner?

(*Beat.*)

FEMALE GREEK CHORUS (*as Mother*): I am not letting an eleven-year-old girl spend seven hours alone in the car with a man. . . . I don't like the way your uncle looks at you.

LI'L BIT: For god's sake, mother! Just because you've gone through a bad time with my father—you think every man is evil!

FEMALE GREEK CHORUS (*as Mother*): Oh no, Li'l Bit—not all men. . . . We . . . we just haven't been very lucky with the men in our family.

LI'L BIT: Just because you lost your husband—I still deserve a chance at having a father! Someone! A man who will look out for me! Don't I get a chance?

FEMALE GREEK CHORUS (*as Mother*): I will feel terrible if something happens.

LI'L BIT: Mother! It's in your head! Nothing will happen! I can take care of myself. And I can certainly handle Uncle Peck.

FEMALE GREEK CHORUS (*as Mother*): All right. But I'm warning you—if anything happens, I hold you responsible.

(*Li'l Bit moves out of this scene and toward the car.*)

LI'L BIT: 1962. On the Back Roads of Carolina: The First Driving Lesson.

(*The Teenage Greek Chorus member stands apart on stage. She will speak all of Li'l Bit's lines. Li'l Bit sits beside Peck in the front seat. She looks at him closely, remembering.*)

PECK: Li'l Bit? Are you getting tired?

TEENAGE GREEK CHORUS: A little.

PECK: It's a long drive. But we're making really good time. We can take the back road from here and see . . . a little scenery. Say—I've got an idea—(*Peck checks his rearview mirror.*)

TEENAGE GREEK CHORUS: Are we stopping, Uncle Peck?

PECK: There's no traffic here. Do you want to drive?

TEENAGE GREEK CHORUS: I can't drive.

PECK: It's easy. I'll show you how. I started driving when I was your age. Don't you want to?—

TEENAGE GREEK CHORUS: —But it's against the law at my age!

PECK: And that's why you can't tell anyone I'm letting you do this—

TEENAGE GREEK CHORUS: —But—I can't reach the pedals.

PECK: You can sit in my lap and steer. I'll push the pedals for you. Did your father ever let you drive his car?

TEENAGE GREEK CHORUS: No way.

PECK: Want to try?

TEENAGE GREEK CHORUS: Okay. (*Li'l Bit moves into Peck's lap. She leans against him, closing her eyes.*)

PECK: You're just a little thing, aren't you? Okay—now think of the wheel as a big clock—I want you to put your right hand on the clock where three o'clock would be; and your left hand on the nine—

(*Li'l Bit puts one hand to Peck's face, to stroke him. Then, she takes the wheel.*)

TEENAGE GREEK CHORUS: Am I doing it right?

PECK: That's right. Now, whatever you do, don't let go of the wheel. You tell me whether to go faster or slower—

TEENAGE GREEK CHORUS: Not so fast, Uncle Peck!

PECK: Li'l Bit—I need you to watch the road—

(*Peck puts his hands on Li'l Bit's breasts. She relaxes against him, silent, accepting his touch.*)

TEENAGE GREEK CHORUS: Uncle Peck—what are you doing?

PECK: Keep driving. (*He slips his hands under her blouse.*)

TEENAGE GREEK CHORUS: Uncle Peck—please don't do this—

PECK: —Just a moment longer . . . (*Peck tenses against Li'l Bit.*)

TEENAGE GREEK CHORUS (*trying not to cry*): This isn't happening.

(*Peck tenses more, sharply. He buries his face in Li'l Bit's neck, and moans softly. The Teenage Greek Chorus exits, and Li'l Bit steps out of the car. Peck, too, disappears.*)

(*A Voice reflects:*)

Driving in Today's World.

LI'L BIT: That day was the last day I lived in my body. I retreated above the neck, and I've lived inside the "fire" in my head ever since.

And now that seems like a long, long time ago. When we were both very young.

And before you know it, I'll be thirty-five. That's getting up there for a woman. And I find myself believing in things that a younger self vowed never to believe in. Things like family and forgiveness.

I know I'm lucky. Although I still have never known what it feels like to jog or dance. Any thing that . . . "jiggles." I do like to watch people on the dance floor, or out on the running paths, just jiggling away. And I say—good for them. (*Li'l Bit moves to the car with pleasure.*)

The nearest sensation I feel—of flight in the body—I guess I feel when I'm driving. On a day like today. It's five A.M. The radio says it's going to be clear and crisp. I've got five hundred miles of highway ahead of me—and some back roads too. I filled the tank last night, and had the oil checked. Checked the tires, too. You've got to treat her . . . with respect.

First thing I do is: Check under the car. To see if any two-year-olds or household cats have crawled beneath, and strategically placed their skulls behind my back tires. (*Li'l Bit crouches.*)

Nope. Then I get in the car. (*Li'l Bit does so.*)

I lock the doors. And turn the key. Then I adjust the most important control on the dashboard—the radio—(*Li'l Bit turns the radio on: We hear all of the Greek Chorus overlapping, and static:*)

FEMALE GREEK CHORUS (*overlapping*):—"You were so tiny you fit in his hand—"

MALE GREEK CHORUS (*overlapping*):—"How is Shakespeare gonna help her lie on her back in the—"

TEENAGE GREEK CHORUS (*overlapping*):—"Am I doing it right?"

(*Li'l Bit fine-tunes the radio station. A song like "Dedicated to the One I Love" or Orbison's "Sweet Dreams" comes on, and cuts off the Greek Chorus.*)

LI'L BIT: Ahh . . . (*Beat.*) I adjust my seat. Fasten my seat belt. Then I check the right side mirror—check the left side. (*She does.*) Finally, I adjust the rearview mirror.

(*As Li'l Bit adjusts the rearview mirror, a faint light strikes the spirit of Uncle Peck, who is sitting in the back seat of the car. She sees him in the mirror. She smiles at him, and he nods at her. They are happy to be going for a long ride together. Li'l Bit slips the car into first gear; to the audience:*)

And then—I floor it.

(*Sound of a car taking off. Blackout.*)

COMMENTARY

CHRISTOPHER BIGSBY (b. 1941)

Paula Vogel   1999

In this excerpt from his discussion of Paula Vogel, English theater scholar Christopher Bigsby examines some of the complexities of *How I Learned to Drive.* He comments on the attractive qualities of Peck and the seductive qualities of Li'l Bit, while also examining the subtleties of the metaphors of driving embedded in the play. He also reminds us that for Vogel, the attraction for pedophiles is not the gender of the prey, but the age. Bigsby sees the play as a complex structure that avoids psychological cliché.

[. . .] Peck is an attractive man in his forties. He should, Vogel instructs, and despite what she calls "a few problems," be played by an actor one might cast in the role of Atticus in *To Kill a Mockingbird,* hence his name (Gregory Peck [played Atticus] in the movie). Li'l Bit is by turns a woman in her thirties or forties and a prematurely developed young girl seen at various moments from the age of eleven through her twenties. The action takes place in suburban Maryland, described by the older Li'l Bit as near the crumbling concrete of U.S. One, which "winds its way past one-room revival churches, the porno drive-in, and boarded up motels with For Sale signs tumbling down." Once there had been another Maryland, "before the Malls took over," but even then innocence had been tainted: "This countryside was once dotted with farmhouses—from their porches you could have witnessed the Civil War raging in the front fields." This is a moralized landscape, invested with the qualities of a country whose own insistent innocence had itself never been entirely plausible, never quite realized. *How I Learned to Drive,* indeed, is surely in part about an America which struggles to sustain notions of innocence, spiritual concern, and family values while flooding its consciousness with sexual titillation: a cheerleader culture of prepubescent beauty pageants, eroticized movies and advertisements, as though sex were a language in which it is necessary to become fluent as soon as possible. In such a context, moral affront at Lolita-like affairs becomes more difficult to sustain or at least more profoundly ambiguous. [. . .]

The audience's attitude to Peck, and to his relationship with Li'l Bit, is in part shaped by the fact of the play's broken chronology. The first scene finds the young girl at seventeen, "going on eighteen," allowing what Blanche DuBois (who herself conducts affairs with teenage boys) would have called "little familiarities" at the hands of a man who is, admittedly, more than twice her age. Despite the disproportion between their ages, however, this seems a relationship which if disturbing is relaxed and not overtly exploitative. Though hardly an innocent encounter it is presented as little more than a parodic teenage tryst. If the genders were reversed we would have *Tea and Sympathy*. Peck partly undresses and fondles Li'l Bit but Vogel instructs that this is to be performed in mime while the mock solemnity with which it is enacted—"Sacred music, organ music or a boys' choir" swells as she permits the intimacies—defuses its potential for affront. If anything, power seems to reside with the young woman and not the man whose behavior makes him seem younger than he is, and more dependent.

In *How I Learned to Drive* we see the effect before we understand the cause, detect the trauma before being told its root. We learn early that at eighteen Li'l Bit leaves college for a string of dead-end jobs because of her fondness for alcohol, spending the nights driving through the countryside "thinking just one notch of the steering wheel would be all it would take" to end it all. However, it takes much of the play to understand what lies behind this suicidal impulse.

Meanwhile, though Peck damages Li'l Bit, she is his lifeline, all that stops him free-falling towards death, and despite his calculated seduction of a vulnerable girl he still offers her an understanding that no one else in her family cares to do, and, ultimately, warns her against himself, thus surrendering the one thing that holds him back from despair, an action that has led Vogel to call him "heroic." As Vogel observed, "I see him as teaching her ego formation, as giving her the tools to grow up and reject him and destroy him."

Peck never forces himself on Li'l Bit, though he plots his campaign with the skill of a practiced seducer and there are suggestions that she has not been his only victim. When she storms out of the family home in a teenage fury Peck's wife, Aunt Mary, observes that "Peck's so good with them when they get to be this age," while his approach to the weeping girl is described in a stage note to be "like stalking a deer."

His method is obliquely exposed in what is one of the most disturbing scenes in the play, when he describes a fishing trip back in South Carolina with a young male cousin. His strategy with fish mirrors that which he adopts with the young woman he desires: "they're very shy, mercurial, fish. Takes patience and psychology. You have to believe it doesn't matter if you catch one or not . . . you don't want to get close—they're frisky and shy little things . . . easy, reel and then net—let it play." And when the fish is landed his comments to his young cousin are a displaced version of his relationship with the young Li'l Bit: "I don't want you to feel ashamed about crying. I'm not going to tell anyone, okay? I can keep secrets . . . There's nothing you could do that would make me feel ashamed of you . . . you can't tell anybody . . . least of all your mom or your sisters. This is something special between you and me." It is Peck's apparently genuine gentleness combined with his patient cunning that is the source of his seductive power. He is driven by his sexual need but that very need gives him an insight into the vulnerabilities of others.

For Vogel, it is clear that Peck does molest his young cousin. Indeed she saw his equal attraction to young girls and boys as a necessary counterbalance to assumptions that pedophiles are gay: "it is the age that is the attraction, not the gender." When she was invited to delete the scene she insisted on retaining it, not least because she felt she owed a debt to her gay brother to clarify what she saw as a slur on gay men. At the same time the scene had not featured in her own outline for the play. It was a product of the process of writing, but it gave her and the audience what she came to feel was a crucial sense of distance, and became a vital element in the drama.

Vogel reminds her audience of the arbitrariness of the lines drawn by society. What is legitimate at eighteen is statutory rape at the age of seventeen. As Li'l Bit's grandmother reminds her daughter, "It was legal, what Daddy and I did! I was fourteen and in those days, fourteen was a grown-up woman." As a gay writer Vogel knows all too well the capricious nature of sexual prohibitions. But, as the play progresses so she raises the stakes and the audience is forced to revise its reaction to the early scene, forced to question its liberal or sentimental response as Li'l Bit becomes first seventeen, then sixteen, then fifteen and, finally, eleven. If the line was not crossed in the opening scene then it is later and we are led, little by little, into the heart of that darkness, a darkness which Li'l Bit herself, however, eventually begins to understand or at least to find echoed in her own experience.

At the age of twenty-seven she experiences the same thrill that she imagines, in retrospect, Peck must have felt as she meets a teenage boy on a bus and seduces him, staging a drama in which she is author, director and principal actor: "dramatically speaking," she explains,

> after the faltering and slightly comical "first act," there was the very briefest of intermissions, and an extremely capable and forceful and sustained [. . .] discussion—I lay on my back in the dark and I thought about you, Uncle Peck. Oh. Oh—this is the allure. Being older. Being the first. Being the translator, the teacher, the epicure, the already jaded. This is how the giver gets taken.

In one sense this could be seen as an account of how abused becomes abuser but it is equally an attempt to understand the seductiveness of seduction, the allure of innocence, the compelling nature of power, the fascination that lies in devising a plot that will enfold another's life. And the fact that Vogel chooses a theatrical metaphor is, perhaps, not without its significance in that the playwright, too, deals in the manipulation of emotions, the seduction of others. She, too, takes her audience to places they have not been, exposes them to experiences which threaten their composure, moral assurance and, ultimately, therefore, innocence. She, too, works by stealth. The description of Peck's fishing technique could, indeed, be seen as an account of her own dramatic strategy in *How I Learned to Drive:* "reel and then rest—let it play."

As the play's title suggests, the principal metaphor is that of the driving lesson. On a literal level it is this that enables Peck to secure time alone with Li'l Bit. But beyond this it charts their developing relationship and Li'l Bit's increasing autonomy. When Peck insists that "when you are driving, your life is in your own two hands," he is offering her a lesson in responsibility for her own life. When he speaks of the power it conveys, he is explaining the necessity for her to realize her own strength. Most significantly, when he instructs her in the need to "think what the other guy is going to do before he does it," this is something more than a piece of roadcraft advice. It is, we later realize, a genuine warning against his own planned action, a moment of honesty, a proffered grace. To think ahead, he insists, is to be the only one to survive an impending disaster. Indeed it is tempting to think that perhaps Peck has summoned Li'l Bit into being, or at least forged her into a weapon against himself, precisely to be his nemesis, to punish himself for past, present and future sins. Certainly he trains her to survive without him while simultaneously struggling to hold on to her.

Throughout the play, a Voice, of "the type . . . that driver education films employ" [. . .], offers a commentary on driver skills which likewise comments, often ironically, on Li'l Bit's unfolding relationship with Peck. Thus, at this moment, it remarks that "Good defensive driving involves mental and physical preparation" and asks *"Are you prepared?"* Another Voice immediately adds: "You and the Reverse Gear." Li'l Bit does not go into reverse any more than does Peck and the drive (automotive and sexual) continues, as does the journey on which they are, apparently mutually, engaged. The question *"Are you prepared?"* however, echoes throughout the text.

The references to driving thus apply as much to Li'l Bit's relationship with Peck as to road safety awareness, and that fact is underlined by phrases which implicitly comment on the unfolding action: Idling in Neutral Gear, Shifting Forward from First Gear to Second Gear, You and the Reverse Gear (the last displayed as the action moves back into the past), *Vehicle failure* (displayed as Li'l Bit is incapacitated by drink), *Implied consent, Children depend on you to watch them.* These comments, in turn, are accompanied by projected signs with equally evident ambiguities: Slow Children, Dangerous Curves, One Way. Indeed, this parallel even infiltrates the stage directions, Vogel referring to Li'l Bit and Peck as "running out of gas," a phrase glossed as meaning "running out of small talk."

Where does responsibility lie in this relationship? Clearly with Peck, but there is a level at which Li'l Bit colludes. There is, in the words of the Voice, an "Implied consent," and this is where the play treads dangerous ground. Plainly in *Lolita* the young girl is a knowing collaborator in her own seduction. In Vogel's play she is led to such implied consent by Peck's seductive skills, but also by their shared sense of exclusion. She responds to his evident need as he in turn offers her understanding. He exploits her youth and innocence, damages her, but also, in his own terms, seeks her consent and will not transgress the terms of that consent. He indulges his own needs, subordinating hers to his, rationalizing his behavior, and yet, finally, hands her back her life at ultimate cost to himself. Nothing he does justifies his actions but his own vulnerabilities are real. There is a kind of innocence even at the center of his corrupting power, for there is no reason to doubt that at the heart of his obsession there is love, as at the heart of his love there is obsession. [. . .]

Meanwhile, beneath his practical competency, his air of quiet assurance, Peck is plainly lonely and disturbed, driven by demons he can neither name nor defeat. His wife can do nothing to address his needs. Aware of his relationship with their niece, she sees it as a temporary infatuation inspired by a manipulative girl. Yet whatever pain lies at the heart of Peck's life all she can offer is domesticity, routine and what she imagines to be a restorative banality, as if this man could settle for something as prosaic as that. She lives with a stranger and seems to understand nothing beyond the fact of his suffering. The plight of her niece, meanwhile, matters not at all. She offers less love than a baffled and frustrated attempt at understanding.

Li'l Bit, by contrast, does care for Peck. On their last encounter in a hotel we are told that she is "half wanting to run, half wanting to get it over with, half wanting to be held by him." She comes close to kissing him but tears herself away. He is destroyed. The lifeline cut, he is, finally, lost. As Li'l Bit explains: "It took my uncle seven years to drink himself to death. First he lost his job, then his wife, and finally his driver's license. He retreated to his house, and had his bottles delivered." The loss of his driver's license is simultaneously a fact and a symbol as he loses that power over his direction, that command of his life, which he had once tried to teach the young girl he both abused and loved as they sat side by side and he taught her the ambiguous lessons of life.

Nor is Li'l Bit shown as ultimately damaged. This is not an accusatory play. Indeed, it ends on a note of reconciliation. As Li'l Bit drives off in her car, in the final scene, she looks in her rearview mirror and smiles at the spirit of Peck who sits behind her. She is now in charge of the car. She did, in the end, accept his advice and anticipate the problems coming towards her. She is, as he had urged her to be, the only one to survive the accident. [. . .]

Vogel has talked of her alarm at the growth of a victim culture in the United States—the desire to shuffle off responsibility for one's life by locating some external cause for failure. "I hate the word victim," she has said. "It's a buzz word people use these days. We're all victims just by virtue of being alive."[1] Li'l Bit's education is thus not only in the occasional cruelties and disabling selfishness of others, but the knowledge and acceptance of her ultimate responsibility for her own life. She comes to recognize in herself a desire for power as well as that unfocused need which had characterized Peck, until he chose to focus it on a girl whose very innocence made her a *tabula rasa,* a place to inscribe his own desperation. [. . .] And if Li'l Bit learns from Peck how cruelly exploitative some people are she also learns their potential for something which perhaps could only be called love.

She learns that her own life consists of everything that has happened to her and that a life of blame or regret is no life at all. Ironically, she never accuses him of the crime which in truth he committed. Indeed, in some ways she devises the rules of the deeply suspect games they play. Even as a woman in her thirties (who, after all, narrates this play much as did Tom in *The Glass Menagerie*) revisiting her own past, she does so not to lay blame or make accusations but to understand her life so that she may live it without regret. As a result, the audience does not reject Peck but grants him his own pain, his own bruised dignity, his own curious courage in the face of feelings he struggles to contain. But they do so not because of the man

---

[1]Steven Druckman, "A Playwright on the Edge," *New York Times* (March 16, 1997), H6.

himself—manipulative, exploitative, dangerous but also compassionate, under-standing, self-sacrificing—but because Li'l Bit accepts him in all his confusions and moral equivocations. The man we see is the man she reconstitutes in her memory. She declines the opportunity retrospectively to invent him as pure villain and her-self as simple victim, and as a result can take her life in her hands and not, finally, cede it to another, not entomb herself in a myth that can only leave her the helpless product of circumstance, the residue of process and the result of abuse. As Vogel has said, "I had no interest in a movie-of-the-week drama about child-molesting." She wished, rather, "to see if audiences will *allow* themselves to find this erotic; otherwise, they only see victimization without empowerment."[2] To her, the essence of the play lay not simply in the fact of the relationship but its consequence. As she explained, "it seems to me that one thing that gets left out when we're talk-ing about trauma is the victim's responsibility to look the experience squarely in the eye and then to move on. That's the journey I wanted to craft here" (*Playbill*, Century Theatre).

How I Learned to Drive plays against our expectations. It seeks to go beyond the labels, the categories which do little to explain ourselves to ourselves. It is about a love affair which, if not mutual, nevertheless, and not entirely paradoxically, does have love on each side. It is about a man whose loneliness is too deep to be filled, who looks for consolation in the wrong place but loves enough eventually to release the object of that love, a man who inhabits a society that is itself deeply confused as to the role of sexuality. The music to which Vogel wrote the play and which she suggests should accompany the action, is, as she has said, "rife with pedophilia," a word she seldom uses in interviews: "Dream Baby," "You're Six-teen," "Little Surfer Girl," "This Girl Is a Woman Now," "Come Back When You Grow Up." Peck, in other words, is not some aberration, someone to be labeled and filed away. He inhabits an ambiguity that reaches out beyond the parameters of his own special need.

[2]Steven Druckman, "A Playwright on the Edge," *New York Times* (March 16, 1997), H6.

Moisés Kaufman and the Tectonic Theater Project

"Truth is more interesting than fiction."

–Moisés Kaufman

Moisés Kaufman was born in 1963 in Caracas, Venezuela, and came to the United States in 1987. His parents were Romanian and Ukrainian Jews who had left Eastern Europe. He studied at a major university where most of the students studied business. After he came to New York, he said, "Being Jewish in a Catholic country, gay in an Orthodox Jewish school, an artist in a business school, and coming to the United States and becoming a Latino has given me an outsider's perspective." He was part of the noncommercial theater community of New York for many years.

Along with Jeffrey LaHoste, Kaufman founded the Tectonic Theater Project, a collaborative group of theatrical artists who were the driving force behind *The Laramie Project* from its inception in 1998 to the play's production in 2000. The Tectonic Theater Project's first play was *Women in Beckett* (1991), an adaptation of Samuel Beckett's short plays for women: *Footfalls, Not I, Rockaby,* and *Come and Go.* The cast included women between the ages of sixty and eighty. The group went on to produce a number of experimental plays, including *Machinal,* by Sophie Treadwell, and *Marlowe's Eyes,* by Naomi Iizuka, as well as other theatrical projects. In 1994 the Tectonic Theater Project produced Franz Xaver Kroetz's *The Nest,* which won several awards in its New York production and was named one of the ten best plays of the year by the *Village Voice.* Kaufman, in addition to being a writer, also directed a number of important theater projects, such as Beckett's *Endgame* and *In the Winter of Cities* by Tennessee Williams, both in the Frederick Loewe Theatre at New York University.

The Tectonic Theater Project uses the word *tectonic* for its association with *architectonic,* which refers to principles of structure. Its projects often exhibit unusual structures, differing from conventional plays in several ways. For one thing, these projects employ many more characters than one expects from a contemporary play; *The Laramie Project* has more than sixty speaking parts. At the other extreme, the Tectonic Theater Project was instrumental in developing Doug Wright's *I Am My Own Wife,* a play with only one actor, who assumes the roles of dozens of characters. In 1994, because the Tectonic Theater Project had made a decision to emphasize the text to a greater extent than before, Moisés Kaufman developed a play that relied on transcripts from trials and brought the company international recognition. This play was called *Gross Indecency: The Three Trials of Oscar Wilde.*

The budget for *Gross Indecency* was a mere $15,000, and the production began in Greenwich House, a small Greenwich Village theater. By word of mouth its reputation grew steadily, and it moved into a larger space, the Minetta Lane Theatre, also in Greenwich Village. Once the press was lured downtown to write reviews, the play became a sensation. The play relied almost entirely on transcripts of the trials of Wilde and on other documents from 1895, when Wilde sued the Marquis of Queensbury for libel, for having accused him of being a sodomite. At the time of the trials, the Irish Oscar Wilde was 41 and the most distinguished playwright in England, with two plays—*The Importance of Being Earnest* and *An Ideal Husband*—being performed simultaneously in London's West End. As a result of the trials, Wilde was imprisoned and put to hard labor, his reputation destroyed, and his plays withdrawn. The point Kaufman was making is that a great writer was utterly destroyed by a society that could not tolerate his sexual orientation. The play itself was intense, focused, and (even with a minimal set and simple courtroom lighting) enormously involving. It ran for six hundred performances in New York and then went on to many cities in the United States and abroad.

Moisés Kaufman directed Doug Wright's Pulitzer Prize–winning *I Am My Own Wife* in December 2003, enlisting some of the techniques of the Tectonic Theater Project. In September 2007, at the Arena Theater in Washington, D.C., the Project launched Kaufman's *33 Variations,* a play based on Beethoven's decision to write the *Diabelli Variations,* a piece that may be the most extensive theme-and-variation composition for piano. The play involves an actress who, in a section devoted to Beethoven's process of composition, plays some of the variations in the order in which they were composed. The modern section of the play focuses on Katherine Brandt, a musicologist who is suffering from amyotrophic lateral sclerosis (ALS), or Lou Gehrig's disease. The two stories are told almost simultaneously as Brandt goes to Berlin to research the composition of the *Diabelli* and as she has to rely more and more on her reluctant daughter.

Moisés Kaufman and the Tectonic Theater Project continue to develop new projects, and Kaufman has won a Guggenheim Award to help sustain him in his work.

The Laramie Project

For discussion questions and assignments on *The Laramie Project,* visit **bedfordstmartins.com/jacobus.**

The Laramie Project was begun after the murder of Matthew Shepard, an openly gay, twenty-one-year-old university student who was beaten so severely by two equally young men from Laramie, Wyoming, that the medical examiner almost refused to believe the damage done to him had been perpetrated by another human being. After he was beaten, Shepard was tied to a fence on a remote road, as if crucified, and left to die. When he was discovered by a bicyclist, he was first thought to be a Hallowe'en decoration or a battered scarecrow. The beating of Shepard was so savage that residents of Laramie, a bulwark of the Western ethic of live and let live and of the conservative values of independence and hard work, were shocked, not least to think how their town would be forever remembered by the rest of the nation.

The Tectonic Theater Project—consisting of artistic director Moisés Kaufman; managing director Jeffrey LaHoste; head writer and assistant director Leigh Fondakowski; associate writers Stephen Belber, Greg Pierotti, and Stephen Wangh; and dramaturges Amanda Gronich, Sarah Lambert, John McAdams, Maude Mitchell, Andy Paris, Barbara Pitts, and Kelli Simpkins—set out in 1998 to make six visits to Laramie to talk with residents about what had happened and what their reactions and feelings about the killing were and had become. The people they spoke with urged them to respect the feelings of the town and not to exaggerate or falsify the information they gathered. The members of the company were in Laramie so frequently over a period of two years that they became well known and—ultimately—trusted.

The play, drawn from some two hundred interviews, lasts two and a half hours on stage and, as acknowledged by most of the people from Laramie who are represented on stage, as well as by the critics who first saw the play, treats Laramie with considerable sensitivity. The play naturally reveals some antigay sentiment, even among those in the clergy. But it also reveals a considerable amount of soul-searching on the part of those who had believed that nothing like this killing could happen in Laramie. Even the two young men who committed the crime—men who had been known for violence and for robbing unsuspecting young men they met in bars—were treated with a sense of compassion. Matthew Shepard's father came forth to offer forgiveness to those who had killed his son, and that went a long way toward helping the town begin the process of healing and coming to terms with what had happened.

The play is similar in subject to Thornton Wilder's *Our Town* in that it portrays small-town America at a critical time in its history. The persons speaking are the inhabitants of that town, addressing their own neighbors and reflecting on the lives they live. A narrator helps to keep the material focused, and the dialogue seems spontaneous and unrehearsed. Another playwright who has approached similar material is Anna Deavere Smith, whose best-known play *Fires in the Mirror: Crown Heights, Brooklyn and Other Identities* (1992) is part of an ongoing series of theatrical pieces called *On the Road: A Search for American Character*. Smith transcribes interviews and impersonates all the speakers in a one-woman tour de force. By contrast, *The Laramie Project* used eight actors to deliver the lines of more than sixty characters, nearly all identified by their real names and their real positions in the town. (A few who speak are not identified simply because the original interviewee did not want his or her name revealed.)

In many ways, what the play achieves is a portrait of a single town in the West, but it also signals a warning to the larger community concerning tolerance and willingness to live true to the values of honesty and justice that are supposed to inform our society.

The Laramie Project in Performance

The Laramie Project premiered on February 27, 2000, at the Ricketson Theatre; it was produced by the Denver Center Theatre Company, with help from Donovan Marley, the theater's artistic director. The stage setting, by Robert Brill, was bare: a brick back wall, a few chairs, a desk, one light, and some videos and film clips. The actors were the members of the Tectonic Theater Project who had worked on the interviews and helped organize and write the material. In May of 2000, the play moved to the Union Square Theatre in New York with the same cast. The run continued until September with "packed houses," but then it ended so that the entire group could work on the film that HBO had scheduled for production in November. The HBO production used the original eight members of the Tectonic Theater Project and added a number of well-known actors, such as Steve Buscemi, Laura Linney, Kathleen Chalfant, and Peter Fonda. In 2001 the Tectonic Theater Project went to Sydney, Australia, to perform the play at the Belvoir Street Theatre, after which it played in Tokyo and then returned to the La Jolla Playhouse in California. Rob Ruggiero produced the play at TheaterWorks in Hartford, Connecticut, from August 1 to October 7, just before the HBO television production. In 2003 the play was presented at the Artwood Theatre, Toronto, and at the Cochrane Theatre,

London, and in 2005 at London's Sound Theatre. With or without the original members of the Tectonic Theater Project, the play touches audience members deeply, both in the United States and abroad.

In 2009, Kaufman and his collaborators produced an epilogue, *The Laramie Project: Ten Years After*, a staged reading with a discussion following that has played throughout the United States and elsewhere. Among the 100 theaters showing this new piece was Lincoln Center in New York City, where it was introduced by Meryl Streep in 2011. The epilogue explores the long-term effect of the original play and the murder of Matthew Shepard. It includes follow-up interviews with some of the characters in the play as well as Matthew Shepard's mother, Judy Shepard, and Matthew's murderer, Aaron McKinney.

MOISÉS KAUFMAN (b. 1963) AND THE TECTONIC THEATER PROJECT

The Laramie Project   2000

Characters

SHERRY AANENSON, *Russell Henderson's landlord, in her forties*

ANONYMOUS, *Friend of Aaron McKinney, in his twenties; works for the railroad*

BAILIFF

BAPTIST MINISTER, *Originally from Texas, in his fifties*

BAPTIST MINISTER'S WIFE, *In her late forties*

STEPHEN BELBER, *Member of Tectonic Theater Project*

DR. CANTWAY, *Emergency room doctor at Ivinson Memorial Hospital in Laramie, in his fifties*

CATHERINE CONNOLLY, *Out lesbian professor at the university, in her forties*

MURDOCK COOPER, *Rancher, in his fifties; resident of Centennial, a nearby town*

ROB DEBREE, *Detective sergeant for the Albany County Sheriff's Department, in his forties; chief investigator of Matthew's murder*

KERRY DRAKE, *Reporter with the* Casper Star-Tribune, *in his forties*

PHILIP DUBOIS, *President of the University of Wyoming, in his forties*

TIFFANY EDWARDS, *Local reporter, in her twenties*

E-MAIL WRITER

GIL AND EILEEN ENGEN, *Ranchers; he is in his sixties; she is in her fifties*

REGGIE FLUTY, *The policewoman who responded to the 911 call and discovered Matthew at the fence, in her late thirties*

LEIGH FONDAKOWSKI, *Member of Tectonic Theater Project*

MATT GALLOWAY, *Bartender at the Fireside, in his twenties; student at the University of Wyoming*

GOVERNOR JIM GERINGER, *Republican governor of Wyoming, forty-five years old*

ANDREW GOMEZ, *Latino from Laramie, in his twenties*

AMANDA GRONICH, *Member of Tectonic Theater Project*

RUSSELL HENDERSON, *One of the perpetrators, twenty-one years old*

REBECCA HILLIKER, *Head of the theater department at the University of Wyoming, in her forties; midwestern accent*

SERGEANT HING, *Detective at the Laramie Police Department, in his forties*

JEN, *A friend of Aaron McKinney, in her early twenties*

SHERRY JOHNSON, *Administrative assistant at the university, in her forties*

STEPHEN MEAD JOHNSON, *Unitarian minister, in his fifties*

TWO JUDGES

JURORS AND FOREPERSON

MOISÉS KAUFMAN, *Member of Tectonic Theater Project*

AARON KREIFELS, *University student, nineteen years old*

PHIL LABRIE, *Friend of Matthew Shepard, in his late twenties; eastern European accent*

DOUG LAWS, *Stake Ecclesiastical leader for the Mormon Church in Laramie, in his fifties*

JEFFREY LOCKWOOD, *Laramie resident, in his forties*

AARON MCKINNEY, *One of the perpetrators, twenty-one years old*

BILL MCKINNEY, *Father of Aaron McKinney, in his forties; truck driver*

ALISON MEARS, *Volunteer for a social service agency in town, in her fifties; very good friend of Marge Murray*

MEDIA/NEWSPAPER PEOPLE

MATT MICKELSON, *Owner of the Fireside, in his thirties*

CONRAD MILLER, *Car mechanic, in his thirties*

MORMON HOME TEACHER TO RUSSELL HENDERSON, *In his sixties*

MARGE MURRAY, *Reggie Fluty's mother, in her seventies; has emphysema but continues to smoke*

DOC O'CONNOR, *Limousine driver and local entrepreneur, in his fifties*

ANDY PARIS, *Member of Tectonic Theater Project*

ROMAINE PATTERSON, *Lesbian, twenty-one years old*

JON PEACOCK, *Matthew Shepard's academic adviser, in his thirties; political science professor*

REVEREND FRED PHELPS, *Minister from Kansas, in his sixties*

GREG PIEROTTI, *Member of Tectonic Theater Project*

BARBARA PITTS, *Member of Tectonic Theater Project*

KRISTIN PRICE, *Girlfriend of Aaron McKinney, in her twenties; has a son with Aaron; Tennessee accent*

PRIEST AT THE FUNERAL

CAL RERUCHA, *Prosecuting attorney, in his fifties*

ZACKIE SALMON, *Administrator at the University of Wyoming, in her forties; lesbian; Texas accent*

FATHER ROGER SCHMIT, *Catholic priest, in his forties; very outspoken*

JEDADIAH SCHULTZ, *University student, nineteen years old*

SHADOW, *DJ at the Fireside; African American man, in his thirties*

SHANNON, *A friend of Aaron McKinney, in his early twenties*

DENNIS SHEPARD, *Father of Matthew Shepard, in his forties; Wyoming native*

APRIL SILVA, *Bisexual university student, nineteen years old*

JONAS SLONAKER, *Gay man, in his forties*

RULON STACEY, *CEO Poudre Valley Hospital in Fort Collins, Colorado, in his forties, a Mormon*

TRISH STEGER, *Romaine Patterson's sister, in her forties; owner of a shop in town*

LUCY THOMPSON, *Grandmother of Russell Henderson, in her sixties; working-class woman who provided a popular day-care service for the town*

ZUBAIDA ULA, *Muslim woman, in her twenties*

WAITRESS (DEBBIE REYNOLDS)

HARRY WOODS, *Gay Laramie resident, fifty-two years old*

NOTE: *When a character is not named (for example, friend of Aaron McKinney, "Baptist minister"), it is at the person's request.*

Place: Laramie, Wyoming, U.S.A.

Time: 1998–99

About the Staging: *The set is a performance space. There are a few tables and chairs. Costumes and props are always visible. The basic costumes are the ones worn by the company of actors. Costumes to portray*

the people of Laramie should be simple: a shirt, a pair of glasses, a hat. The desire is to suggest, not re-create. Along the same lines, this should be an actor-driven event. Costume changes, set changes, and anything else that happens on the stage should be done by the company of actors.

About the Text: *When writing this play, we used a technique I developed called moment work. It is a method to create and analyze theater from a structuralist (or tectonic) perspective. For that reason, there are no scenes in this play, only moments. A moment does not mean a change of locale or an entrance or exit of actors or characters. It is simply a unit of theatrical time that is then juxtaposed with other units to convey meaning.*

ACT I • Moment: A Definition

NARRATOR: On November 14, 1998, the members of Tectonic Theater Project traveled to Laramie, Wyoming, and conducted interviews with the people of the town. During the next year, we would return to Laramie several times and conduct over two hundred interviews. The play you are about to see is edited from those interviews, as well as from journal entries by members of the company and other found texts. Company member Greg Pierotti:

GREG PIEROTTI: My first interview was with Detective Sergeant Hing of the Laramie Police Department. At the start of the interview he was sitting behind his desk, sitting something like this (*he transforms into Sergeant Hing*):

I was born and raised here.

My family is, uh, third generation.

My grandparents moved here in the early nineteen hundreds.

We've had basically three, well, my daughter makes it fourth generation.

Quite a while.... It's a good place to live. Good people—lots of space.

Now, all the towns in southern Wyoming are laid out and spaced because of the railroad came through.

It was how far they could go before having to refuel and rewater.

And, uh, Laramie was a major stopping point.

That's why the towns are spaced so far apart.

We're one of the largest states in the country, and the least populated.

REBECCA HILLIKER: There's so much space between people and towns here, so much time for reflection.

NARRATOR: Rebecca Hilliker, head of the theater department at the University of Wyoming:

REBECCA HILLIKER: You have an opportunity to be happy in your life here. I found that people here were nicer than in the Midwest, where I used to teach, because they were happy. They were glad the sun was shining. And it shines a lot here.

SERGEANT HING: What you have is, you have your old-time traditional-type ranchers, they've been here forever—Laramie's been the hub of where they come for their supplies and stuff like that.

EILEEN ENGEN: Stewardship is one thing all our ancestors taught us.

NARRATOR: Eileen Engen, rancher:

EILEEN ENGEN: If you don't take care of the land, then you ruin it and you lose your living. So you first of all have to take care of your land and do everything you can to improve it.

DOC O'CONNOR: I love it here.

NARRATOR: Doc O'Connor, limousine driver:

DOC O'CONNOR: You couldn't put me back in that mess out there back east. Best thing about it is the climate. The cold, the wind. They say the Wyoming wind'll drive a man insane. But you know what? It don't bother me. Well, some of the times it bothers me. But most of the time it don't.

SERGEANT HING: And then you got, uh, the university population.

PHILIP DUBOIS: I moved here after living in a couple of big cities.

NARRATOR: Philip Dubois, president of the University of Wyoming:

PHILIP DUBOIS: I loved it there. But you'd have to be out of your mind to let your kids out after dark. And here, in the summertime, my kids play out at night till eleven and I don't think twice about it.

SERGEANT HING: And then you have the people who live in Laramie, basically.

ZACKIE SALMON: I moved here from rural Texas.

NARRATOR: Zackie Salmon, Laramie resident:

ZACKIE SALMON: Now, in Laramie, if you don't know a person, you will definitely know someone they know. So it can only be one degree removed at most. And for me—I love it! I mean, I love to go to the grocery store 'cause I get to visit with four or five or six people every time I go. And I don't really mind people knowing my business—'cause what's my business? I mean, my business is basically good.

DOC O'CONNOR: I like the trains, too. They don't bother me. Well, some of the times they bother me, but most times they don't. Even though one goes by every thirteen minutes out where I live. . . .

NARRATOR: Doc actually lives up in Bossier. But everybody in Laramie knows him. He's also not really a doctor.

DOC O'CONNOR: They used to carry cattle . . . them trains. Now all they carry is diapers and cars.

APRIL SILVA: I grew up in Cody, Wyoming.

NARRATOR: April Silva, university student:

APRIL SILVA: Laramie is better than where I grew up. I'll give it that.

SERGEANT HING: It's a good place to live. Good people, lots of space. Now, when the incident happened with that boy, a lot of press people came here. And one time some of them followed me out to the crime scene. And uh, well, it was a beautiful day, absolutely gorgeous day, real clear and crisp and the sky was that blue that, uh . . . you know, you'll never be able to paint, it's just sky blue—it's just gorgeous. And the mountains in the background and a little snow on 'em, and this one reporter, uh, lady . . . person, that was out there, she said . . .

REPORTER: Well, who found the boy, who was out here anyway?

SERGEANT HING: And I said, "Well, this is a really popular area for people to run, and mountain biking's really big out here, horseback riding, it's just, well, it's close to town." And she looked at me and she said:

REPORTER: Who in the hell would want to run out here?

SERGEANT HING: And I'm thinking, "Lady, you're just missing the point." You know, all you got to do is turn around, see the mountains, smell the air, listen to the birds, just take in what's around you. And they were just—nothing but the story. I didn't feel judged, I felt that they were stupid. They're, they're missing the point—they're just missing the whole point.

JEDADIAH SCHULTZ: It's hard to talk about Laramie now, to tell you what Laramie is, for us.

NARRATOR: Jedadiah Schultz:

JEDADIAH SCHULTZ: If you would have asked me before, I would have told you Laramie is a beautiful town, secluded enough that you can have your own identity. . . . A town with a strong sense of community—everyone knows everyone. . . . A town with a personality that most larger cities are stripped of. Now, after Matthew, I would say that Laramie is a town defined by an accident, a crime. We've be come Waco, we've become Jasper. We're a noun, a definition, a sign. We may be able to get rid of that . . . but it will sure take a while.

Moment: Journal Entries

NARRATOR: Journal entries—members of the company. Andy Paris:

ANDY PARIS: Moisés called saying he had an idea for his next theater project. But there was a somberness to his voice, so I asked what it was all about and he told me he wanted to do a piece about what's happening in Wyoming.

NARRATOR: Stephen Belber:

STEPHEN BELBER: Leigh told me the company was thinking of going out to Laramie to conduct interviews and that they wanted me to come. But I'm hesitant. I have no real interest in prying into a town's unraveling.

NARRATOR: Amanda Gronich:

AMANDA GRONICH: I've never done anything like this in my life. How do you get people to talk to you? What do you ask?

NARRATOR: Moisés Kaufman:

MOISÉS KAUFMAN: The company has agreed that we should go to Laramie for a week and interview people.

Am a bit afraid about taking ten people in a trip of this nature. Must make some safety rules. No one works alone. Everyone carries cell phones. Have made some preliminary contacts with Rebecca

Hilliker, head of the theater department at the University of Wyoming. She is hosting a party for us our first night in Laramie and has promised to introduce us to possible interviewees.

Moment: Rebecca Hilliker

REBECCA HILLIKER: I must tell you that when I first heard that you were thinking of coming here, when you first called me, I wanted to say, You've just kicked me in the stomach. Why are you doing this to me?

But then I thought, That's stupid, you're not doing this to me. And, more important, I thought about it and decided that we've had so much negative closure on this whole thing. And the students really need to talk. When this happened they started talking about it, and then the media descended and all dialogue stopped.

You know, I really love my students because they are free thinkers. And you may not like what they have to say, and you may not like their opinions, because they can be very redneck, but they are honest and they're truthful—so there's an excitement here, there's a dynamic here with my students that I never had when I was in the Midwest or in North Dakota, because there, there was so much Puritanism that dictated how people looked at the world that a lot of times they didn't have an opinion, you couldn't get them to express an opinion. And, quite honestly, I'd rather have opinions that I don't like—and have that dynamic in education.

There's a student I think you should talk to. His name is Jedadiah Schultz.

Moment: *Angels in America*

JEDADIAH SCHULTZ: I've lived in Wyoming my whole life. The family has been in Wyoming, well … for generations. Now when it came time to go to college, my parents can't—couldn't afford to send me to college. I wanted to study theater. And I knew that if I was going to go to college I was going to have to get on a scholarship—and so, uh, they have this competition each year, this Wyoming state high school competition. And I knew that if I didn't take first place in, uh, duets that I wasn't gonna get a scholarship. So I went to the theater department of the university looking for good scenes, and I asked one of the professors—I was like, "I need—I need a killer scene," and he was like, "Here you go, this is it." And it was from *Angels in America*.

So I read it and I knew that I could win best scene if I did a good enough job.

And when the time came I told my mom and dad so that they would come to the competition. Now you have to understand, my parents go to everything—every ball game, every hockey game—everything I've ever done.

And they brought me into their room and told me that if I did that scene, that they would not come to see

me in the competition. Because they believed that it is wrong—that homosexuality is wrong—they felt that strongly about it that they didn't want to come see their son do probably the most important thing he'd done to that point in his life. And I didn't know what to do.

I had never, ever gone against my parents' wishes. So I was kind of worried about it. But I decided to do it.

And all I can remember about the competition is that when we were done, me and my scene partner, we came up to each other and we shook hands and there was a standing ovation.

Oh, man, it was amazing! And we took first place and we won. And that's how come I can afford to be here at the university, because of that scene. It was one of the best moments of my life. And my parents weren't there. And to this day, that was the one thing that my parents didn't see me do.

And thinking back on it, I think, why did I do it? Why did I oppose my parents? 'Cause I'm not gay. So why did I do it? And I guess the only honest answer I can give is that, well (*he chuckles*) I wanted to win. It was such a good scene; it was like the best scene!

Do you know Mr. Kushner? Maybe you can tell him.

Moment: Journal Entries

NARRATOR: Company member Greg Pierotti:

GREG PIEROTTI: We arrived today in the Denver Airport and drove to Laramie. The moment we crossed the Wyoming border I swear I saw a herd of buffalo. Also, I thought it was strange that the Wyoming sign said: WYOMING—LIKE NO PLACE ON EARTH instead of WYOMING—LIKE NO PLACE ELSE ON EARTH.

NARRATOR: Company member Leigh Fondakowski:

LEIGH FONDAKOWSKI: I stopped at a local inn for a bite to eat. And my waitress said to me:

WAITRESS: Hi, my name is Debbie. I was born in nineteen fifty-four and Debbie Reynolds was big then, so, yes, there are a lot of us around, but I promise that I won't slap you if you leave your elbows on the table.

MOISÉS KAUFMAN: Today Leigh tried to explain to me to no avail what chicken fried steak was.

WAITRESS: Now, are you from Wyoming? Or are you just passing through?

LEIGH FONDAKOWSKI: We're just passing through.

NARRATOR: Company member Barbara Pitts:

BARBARA PITTS: We arrived in Laramie tonight. Just past the WELCOME TO LARAMIE sign— POPULATION 26,687—the first thing to greet us was Wal-Mart. In the dark, we could be on any main drag in America—fast-food chains, gas stations. But as we drove into the downtown area by the railroad tracks, the buildings still look like a turn-of-the-century western town. Oh, and as we passed the University Inn, on the sign where amenities such as heated pool or cable TV are usually touted, it said: HATE IS NOT A LARAMIE VALUE.

NARRATOR: Greg Pierotti:

Moment: Alison and Marge

GREG PIEROTTI: I met today with two longtime Laramie residents, Alison Mears and Marge Murray, two social service workers who taught me a thing or two.

ALISON MEARS: Well, what Laramie used to be like when Marge was growing up, well, it was mostly rural.

MARGE MURRAY: Yeah, it was. I enjoyed it, you know. My kids all had horses.

ALISON MEARS: Well, there was more land, I mean, you could keep your pet cow. Your horse. Your little chickens. You know, just have your little bit of acreage.

MARGE MURRAY: Yeah, I could run around the house in my all togethers, do the housework while the kids were in school. And nobody could see me. And if they got that close . . .

ALISON MEARS: Well, then that's their problem.

MARGE MURRAY: Yeah.

GREG PIEROTTI: I just want to make sure I got the expression right: in your all togethers?

MARGE MURRAY: Well, yeah, honey, why wear clothes?

ALISON MEARS: Now, how's he gonna use that in his play?

GREG PIEROTTI: So this was a big ranching town?

ALISON MEARS: Oh, not just ranching, this was a big railroad town at one time. Before they moved everything to Cheyenne and Green River and Omaha. So now, well, it's just a drive-through spot for the railroad—because even, what was it, in the fifties? Well, they had one big roundhouse, and they had such a shop they could build a complete engine.

MARGE MURRAY: They did, my mom worked there.

GREG PIEROTTI: Your mom worked in a roundhouse?

MARGE MURRAY: Yep. She washed engines. Her name was Minnie. We used to, you know, sing that song for her, you know that song.

GREG PIEROTTI: What song?

MARGE MURRAY: "Run for the roundhouse, Minnie, they can't corner you there."

(*They crack up.*)

ALISON MEARS: But I'll tell you, Wyoming is bad in terms of jobs. I mean, the university has the big high whoop-de-do jobs. But Wyoming, unless you're a professional, well, the bulk of the people are working minimum-wage jobs.

MARGE MURRAY: Yeah, I've been either in the service industry or bartending most of my life. Now I know everybody in town.

ALISON MEARS: And she does.

MARGE MURRAY: And I do. Now that I'll tell ya, here in Laramie there is a difference and there always has been. What it is is a class distinction. It's about the well-educated and the ones that are not. And the educated don't understand why the ones that are not don't get educated. That's why I told you before my kids had to fight because their mother was a bartender. Never mind I was the best damn bartender in town.

ALISON MEARS: And she was.

MARGE MURRAY: That's not bragging, that's fact.

ALISON MEARS: But here in Laramie, if it weren't for the university, we'd just be S.O.L.

GREG PIEROTTI: What's S.O.L.?

ALISON MEARS: Well, do I have to say it? Well, it's shit outta luck. (*She cracks up.*) Oh Lordy, you've got that on your tape. Boy, you are getting an education today.

GREG PIEROTTI: Yeah, I guess I am. So, let me just ask you—what was your response when this happened to Matthew Shepard?

MARGE MURRAY: Well, I've been close enough to the case to know many of the people. I have a daughter that's on the Sheriff's Department.

As far as the gay issue, I don't give a damn one way or the other as long as they don't bother me. And even if they did, I'd just say no thank you. And that's the attitude of most of the Laramie population. They might poke one, if they were in a bar situation, you know, they had been drinking, they might actually smack one in the mouth, but then they'd just walk away. Most of 'em, they would just say, "I don't swing that way," and whistle on about their business. Laramie is live and let live.

ALISON MEARS: I'd say that Marge probably knows a lot more except she's even willing to say, and we have to respect her for that.

MARGE MURRAY: Well, uh, where are you going with this story?

GREG PIEROTTI: Oh, well, we still haven't decided. When we've finished, we are going to try to bring it around to Laramie.

MARGE MURRAY: Okay, then, there are parts I won't tell you.

Moment: Matthew

NARRATOR: Company member Andy Paris:

ANDY PARIS: Today, for the first time, we met someone who actually knew Matthew Shepard. Trish Steger, owner of a shop in town, referred to him as Matt.

TRISH STEGER: Matt used to come into my shop—that's how I knew him.

ANDY PARIS: It was the first time I heard him referred to as Matt instead of Matthew. Did he go by Matt to everyone?

DOC O'CONNOR: Well, on the second of October, I get a phone call about, uh, ten after seven.

NARRATOR: Doc O'Connor:

DOC O'CONNOR: It was Matthew Shepard. And he said, "Can you pick me up at the corner of Third and Grand?" So, anyhow, I pull up to the corner, to see who Matthew Shepard is, you know. It's a little guy, about five-two, soakin' wet, I betcha ninety-seven pounds tops. They say he weighed a hundred and ten, but I wouldn't believe it. They also said he was five-five in the newspapers, but this man, he was really only about five-two, maybe five-one. So he walks up the window—I'm gonna try and go in steps so you can better understand the principle of this man. So he walks up to the window, and I say, "Are you Matthew Shepard?" And he says, "Yeah, I'm Matthew Shepard. But I don't want you to call me Matthew, or Mr. Shepard. I don't want you to call me anything. My name is Matt. And I want you to know, I am gay and we're going to go to a gay bar. Do you have a problem with that?" And I said, "How're you payin'?"

The fact is . . . Laramie doesn't have any gay bars . . . and for that matter neither does Wyoming . . . so he was hiring me to take him to Fort Collins, Colorado, about an hour away.

Matt was a blunt little shit, you know what I'm sayin'? But I liked him 'cause he was straightforward, you see what I'm saying? Maybe gay but straightforward, you see what I'm saying?

TRISH STEGER: I don't know, you know, how does any one person ever tell about another? You really should talk to my sister Romaine. She was a very close friend of Matthew's.

ROMAINE PATTERSON: We never called him Matthew, actually, most of the time we called him Choo-choo. You know, because we used to call him Mattchew, and then we just called him Choo-choo.

And whenever I think of Matthew, I always think of his incredible beaming smile. I mean, he'd walk in and he'd be like (*demonstrates*) you know, and he'd smile at everyone . . . he just made you feel great. . . . And he—would like stare people down in the coffee shop . . . 'cause he always wanted to sit on the end seat so that he could talk to me while I was working. And if someone was sitting in that seat, he would just sit there and stare at them. Until they left. And then he would claim his spot.

But Matthew definitely had a political side to him. . . . I mean, he really wanted to get into political affairs . . . that's all his big interest was, was watching CNN and MSNBC, I mean, that's the only TV station I ever saw his TV tuned in to. He was just really smart in political affairs, but not too smart on like commonsense things . . .

So, he moves to Laramie to go to school.

JON PEACOCK: Matthew was very shy when he first came in.

NARRATOR: Jon Peacock, Matthew Shepard's academic adviser:

JON PEACOCK: To the point of being somewhat mousy I'd almost say. He was having some difficulties adjusting, but this was home for him and he made that quite clear. And so his mousiness, his shyness gave way to a person who was excited about this track that he was going to embark on. He was just figuring out wanting to work on human rights, how he was going to do that. And when that happens this person begins to bloom a little bit. He was starting to say, "Wow, there are opportunities here. There are things I can do in this world. I can be important."

ROMAINE PATTERSON: I did hear from Matthew about forty-eight hours before his attack. And he told me

that he had joined the gay and lesbian group on campus, and he said he was enjoying it, you know, he was getting ready for Pride Week and whatnot. I mean, he was totally stoked about school—yeah, he was really happy about being there.

JON PEACOCK: And in retrospect—and I can only say this in retrospect of course—I think that's where he was heading, towards human rights. Which only adds to the irony and tragedy of this.

Moment: Who's Getting What?

DOC O'CONNOR: Let me tell you something else here. There's more gay people in Wyoming than meets the eye. I know, I know for a fact. They're not particularly, ah, the whattayou call them, the queens, the gay people, queens, you know, runaround faggot-type people. No, they're the ones that throw bales of hay, jump on horses, brand 'em, and kick ass, you see what I'm saying? As I always say, Don't fuck with a Wyoming queer, 'cause they will kick you in your fucking ass, but that's not the point of what I'm trying to say. 'Cause I know a lot of gay people in Wyoming, I know a lot of people period. I've been living up here some forty-odd years, you see what I'm saying?

And I don't think Wyoming people give a damn one way or another if you're gay or straight, that's just what I just said, doesn't matter. If there's eight men and one woman in a Wyoming bar, which is often the case, now you stop and think—who's getting what? You see what I'm saying? Now jeez, it don't take a big intelligent mind to figure that one out.

Moment: Easier Said Than Done

CATHERINE CONNOLLY: My understanding when I first came here . . .

NARRATOR: Catherine Connolly:

CATHERINE CONNOLLY: . . . is that I was the first "out" lesbian or gay faculty member on campus. And that was in nineteen ninety-two. So, that wasn't that long ago. Um, I was asked at my interview what my husband did, um, and so I came out then. . . . Do you want a funny story?

When you first get here as a new faculty member, there's all these things you have to do. And so, I was in my office and I noticed that this woman called. . . . I was expecting, you know, it was a health insurance phone call, something like that, and so I called her back. And I could hear her, she's working on her keyboard, clicking away. I said, you know, "This is Cathy Connolly returning your phone call." And she said, "Oh. It's you." And I thought, "This is bizarre." And she said, "I hear—I hear—I hear you're gay. I hear you are." I was like, "Uh huh." And she said, "I hear you came as a couple. I'm one too. Not a couple, just a person." And so—she was—a kind of lesbian who knew I was coming and she wanted to come over and meet me immediately. And she later told me that there were other lesbians that she knew who wouldn't be seen with me. That I would irreparably taint them, that just to be seen with me could be a problem.

JONAS SLONAKER: When I came here I knew it was going to be hard as a gay man.

NARRATOR: Jonas Slonaker:

JONAS SLONAKER: But I kept telling myself: People should live where they want to live. And there would be times I would go down to Denver and I would go to gay bars and, um, people would ask where I was from and I'd say, "Laramie, Wyoming." And I met so many men down there from Wyoming. So many gay men who grew up here, and they're like: "This is not a place where I can live, how can you live there, I had to get out, grrr, grrr, grrr." But every once in a while there would be a guy, "Oh gosh, I miss Laramie. I mean I really love it there, that's where I want to live." And they get this starry-eyed look and I'm like: If that's where you want to live, do it. I mean, imagine if more gay people stayed in small towns. But it's easier said than done of course.

Moment: Journal Entries

MOISÉS KAUFMAN: Today we are moving from our motel and heading for the Best Western.

NARRATOR: Moisés Kaufman:

MOISÉS KAUFMAN: My hope is that it is a better Western.

NARRATOR: Amanda Gronich:

AMANDA GRONICH: Today we divided up to go to different churches in the community. Moisés and I were given a Baptist church. We were welcomed into the services by the reverend himself standing at the entrance to the chapel. This is what I remember of his sermon that morning.

Moment: The Word

BAPTIST MINISTER: My dear brothers and sisters: I am here today to bring you the Word of the Lord. Now, I have a simple truth that I tell to my colleagues and I'm gonna tell it to you today: The word is either sufficient or it is not.

Scientists tell me that human history, that the world is five billion or six billion years old—after all, what's a billion years give or take? The Bible tells me that human history is six thousand years old.

The word is either sufficient or it is not.

STEPHEN MEAD JOHNSON: Ah, the sociology of religion in the West . . .

NARRATOR: Stephen Mead Johnson, Unitarian minister:

STEPHEN MEAD JOHNSON: Dominant religious traditions in this town: Baptist, Mormon—they're everywhere, it's not just Salt Lake, you know, they're all over—they're like jam on toast down here.

DOUG LAWS: The Mormon Church has a little different thing going that irritates some folks.

NARRATOR: Doug Laws, Stake Ecclesiastical leader for the Mormon Church:

DOUG LAWS: And that is that we absolutely believe that God still speaks to man. We don't think that it happened and some folks wrote it in the Bible. God speaks to us today, and we believe that. We believe that the prophet of the church has the authority to receive inspiration and revelation from God.

STEPHEN MEAD JOHNSON: So, the spectrum would be—uh, on the left side of that panel: So far left that I am probably sitting by myself, is me—and the Unitarian Church. Unitarians are by and large humanists, many of whom are atheists. I mean—we're, you know, we're not even sure we're a religion. And to my right on the spectrum, to his credit, Father Roger, Catholic priest, who is well-established here, and God bless him—he did not equivocate at all when this happened—he hosted the vigil for Matthew that night.

FATHER ROGER SCHMIT: I was really jolted because, you know, when we did the vigil—we wanted to get other ministers involved and we called some of them, and they were not going to get involved. And it was like, "We are gonna stand back and wait and see which way the wind is blowing." And that angered me immensely. We are supposed to stand out as leaders. I thought, "Wow, what's going on here?"

DOUG LAWS: God has set boundaries. And one of our responsibilities is to learn: What is it that God wants? So you study Scripture, you look to your leaders. Then you know what the bounds are. Now once you kinda know what the bounds are, then you sorta get a feel for what's out-of-bounds.

There is a proclamation that came out on the family. A family is defined as one woman and one man and children. That's a family. That's about as clear as you can state it. There's no sexual deviation in the Mormon Church. No—no leniency. We just think it's out-of-bounds.

BAPTIST MINISTER: I warn you: You will be mocked! You will be ridiculed for the singularity of your faith! But you let the Bible be your guide. It's in there. It's all in there.

STEPHEN MEAD JOHNSON: The Christian pastors, many of the conservative ones, were silent on this. Conservative Christians use the Bible to show the rest of the world, It says here in the Bible. And most Americans believe, and they do, that the Bible is the word of God, and how you gonna fight that?

BAPTIST MINISTER: I am a Biblicist. Which means: The Bible doesn't need me to be true. The Bible is true whether I believe it or not. The word is either sufficient or it is not.

STEPHEN MEAD JOHNSON: I arrived in Laramie on September fifteenth. I looked around—tumbleweed, cement factory—and said, "What in the hell am I doing in Wyoming?" Three weeks later, I found out what the hell I'm doing in Wyoming.

Moment: A Scarf

STEPHEN BELBER: I had breakfast this morning with a university student named Zubaida Ula. She is an Islamic feminist who likes to do things her own way.

ZUBAIDA ULA: I've lived in Laramie since I was four. Yeah. My parents are from Bangladesh. Two years ago, because I'm Muslim, I decided to start wearing a scarf. That's really changed my life in Laramie. Yeah.

Like people say things to me like, "Why do you have to wear that thing on your head?" Like when I go to the grocery store, I'm not looking to give people Islam 101, you know what I mean? So I'll be like, "Well, it's part of my religion," and they'll be— this is the worst part cuz they'll be like, "I know it's part of your religion, but why?" And it's—how am I supposed to go into the whole doctrine of physical modesty and my own spiritual relationship with the Lord, standing there with my pop and chips? You know what I mean?

STEPHEN BELBER: Yeah.

ZUBAIDA ULA: You know, it's so unreal to me that, yeah, that a group from New York would be writing a play about Laramie. And then I was picturing like you're gonna be in a play about my town. You're gonna be onstage in New York and you're gonna be acting like you're us. That's so weird.

Moment: Lifestyle 1

BAPTIST MINISTER'S WIFE: Hello?

AMANDA GRONICH: Yes, hello. My name is Amanda Gronich and I am here in Laramie working with a theater company. I went to the reverend's, your husband's church on Sunday, and I was extremely interested in talking with the reverend about some of his thoughts about recent events.

BAPTIST MINISTER'S WIFE: Well, I don't think he'll want to talk to you. He has very biblical views about homosexuality—he doesn't condone that kind of violence. But he doesn't condone that kind of lifestyle, you know what I mean? And he was just bombarded with press after this happened and the media has been just terrible about this whole thing.

AMANDA GRONICH: Oh, I know, I really understand, it must have just been terrible.

BAPTIST MINISTER'S WIFE: Oh, yes, I think we are all hoping this just goes away.

AMANDA GRONICH: Well, um, do you think maybe I could call back and speak with your husband just briefly?

BAPTIST MINISTER'S WIFE: Well, all right, you can call him back tonight at nine.

AMANDA GRONICH: Oh, thank you so much. I'll do that.

Moment: The Fireside

STEPHEN BELBER: Today Barbara and I went to the Fireside Bar, which is the last place Matthew was seen in public.

BARBARA PITTS: The Fireside—definitely feels like a college bar, with a couple of pool tables and a stage area for karaoke. Still, the few regulars in the late afternoon were hardly the college crowd.

STEPHEN BELBER: First person we talked to was Matt Mickelson, the owner.

MATT MICKELSON: My great-great-grandfather moved here in eighteen sixty-two, he owned Laramie's first opera house, it was called Old Blue Front, and in eighteen seventy Louisa Grandma Swain cast the first woman's ballot in any free election in the world, and that's why Wyoming is the Equality State, so what I want to do is reestablish my bar business as the Old Blue Front Opera House and Good Time Emporium, you know, I want to have a restaurant, I want to have a gift shop, I want to have a pool hall, and do all this shit, you know . . . every night's ladies' night . . .

So the Fireside is the first step towards the Old Blue Front Opera House and Good Time Emporium.

BARBARA PITTS: So, what about the night Matthew Shepard was here?

MATT MICKELSON: We had karaoke that night, twenty or thirty people here—Matthew Shepard came in, sitting right—right where you're sitting, just hanging out. . . . I mean, if you wanna talk to somebody, you should talk to Matt Galloway, he was the kid that was bartending that night. You'd have to meet him, his character stands for itself.

(*Calling*) Hey, is Galloway bartending tonight?

MATT GALLOWAY: Okay. I'm gonna make this brief, quick, get it over with, but it will be everything—factual. Just the facts. Here we go. Ten o'clock. I clock in, usual time, Tuesday nights. Ten-thirty—Matthew Shepard shows up—alone—sits down, orders a Heineken.

NARRATOR: Phil Labrie, friend of Matthew Shepard:

PHIL LABRIE: Matt liked to drink Heineken and nothing else. Heineken even though you have to pay nine-fifty for a six-pack. He'd always buy the same beer.

MATT GALLOWAY: So what can I tell you about Matt?

If you had a hundred customers like him it'd be the—the most perfect bar I've ever been in. Okay? And nothing to do with sexual orientation. Um, absolute mannerisms. Manners. Politeness, intelligence.

Taking care of me, as in tips. Everything—conversation, uh, dressed nice, clean-cut. Some people you just know, sits down, "Please," "Thank you"—offers intellect, you know, within—within—within their vocabulary.

Um, so, he kicks it there. Didn't seem to have any worries, or like he was looking for anyone. Just enjoy his drink and the company around.

Now approximately eleven forty-five, eleven-thirty–eleven forty-five, Aaron McKinney and Russell Henderson come in—I didn't know their names then, but they're the accused, they're the perps, they're the accused. They walked in, just very stone-faced, you know. Dirty. Grungy. Rude. "Gimme." That type of thing. They walked up to the bar, uh, and, as you know, paid for a pitcher with dimes and quarters, uh, which is something that I mean you don't forget. You don't forget that. Five-fifty in dimes and quarters. That's a freakin' nightmare.

Now Henderson and McKinney, they didn't seem intoxificated at all. They came in—they just ordered a beer, took the pitcher with them back there into the pool room, and kept to themselves. Next thing I knew, probably a half hour later, they were kind of walking around—no beer. And I remember thinking to myself that I'm not gonna ask them if they want another one, because obviously they just paid for a pitcher with dimes and quarters, I have a real good feeling they don't have any more money.

NARRATOR: Romaine Patterson:

ROMAINE PATTERSON: Money meant nothing to Matthew, because he came from a lot of it. And he would like hand over his wallet in two seconds—because money meant nothing. His—shoes—might have meant something. They can say it was robbery . . . I don't buy it. For even an iota of a second.

MATT GALLOWAY: Then a few moments later I looked over and Aaron and Russell had been talking to Matthew Shepard.

KRISTIN PRICE: Aaron said that a guy walked up to him and said that he was gay, and wanted to get with Aaron and Russ.

NARRATOR: Kristin Price, girlfriend of Aaron McKinney:

KRISTIN PRICE: And Aaron got aggravated with it and told him that he was straight and didn't want anything to do with him and walked off. He said that is when he and Russell went to the bathroom and decided to pretend they were gay and get him in the truck and rob him. They wanted to teach him a lesson not to come on to straight people.

MATT GALLOWAY: Okay, no. They stated that Matt approached them, that he came on to them. I absolutely, positively disbelieve and refute the statement one hundred percent. Refute it. I'm gonna give you two reasons why.

One. Character reference.

Why would he approach them? Why them? He wasn't approaching anybody else in the bar. They say he's gay, he was a flaming gay, he's gonna come on to people like that. Bullshit. He never came on to me. Hello?!? He came on to them? I don't believe it.

Two. Territorialism is—is—is the word I will use for this. And that's the fact that Matt was sitting there. Russell and Aaron were in the pool area. Upon their first interaction, they were in Matt's area, in the area that Matt had been seen all night. So who approached who by that?

ROMAINE PATTERSON: But Matthew was the kind of person . . . like, he would never not talk to someone for any reason. If someone started talking to him, he'd just be like, "Oh, blah, blah, blah." He never had any problem just striking up a conversation with anybody.

PHIL LABRIE: Matt did feel lonely a lot of times. Me knowing that—and knowing how gullible Matt

could be . . . he would have walked right into it. The fact that he was at the bar alone without any friends made him that much more vulnerable.

MATT GALLOWAY: So the only thing is—and this is what I'm testifying to—'cause, you know, I'm also, basically, the key eyewitness in this case, uh (pause) basically what I'm testifying is that I saw Matthew leave. I saw two individuals leave with Matthew. I didn't see their faces, but I saw the back of their heads. At the same time, McKinney and Henderson were no longer around. You do the math.

MATT MICKELSON: Actually, I think the DJ was the last one to talk to him on his way out that night . . . gave him a cigarette or something. His name is Shadow.

SHADOW: I was the last person that Matt talked to before he left the Fireside. . . . I was just bullshittin' around with my shit, and he stopped me, I stopped him actually, and he's like, "Hey, Shadow, da da da," and I was like, "What, man, you gettin' ready to leave?" he's like, "Yeah, man, and this an' that." But then I noticed them two guys and they stood outside, you could see, you could see it, they were standing there, you know, and he was looking over to them, and they were lookin' back at him. And I stood and talked to Matt for like a good ten minutes and you seen the guys with him, you seen 'em getting like, you seen 'em like worried, like, you know, anxious to leave and shit. . . . So when they took off, I seen it, when they took off, it was in a black truck, it was a small truck, and the three of them sat in the front seat and Matt sat in the middle.

And I didn't think nothin' of it, you know. I didn't figure them guys was gonna be like that.

Moment: McKinney and Henderson

NARRATOR: A friend of Aaron McKinney:

ANONYMOUS: Oh, I've known Aaron a long time. Aaron was a good kid, I liked Aaron a lot, that's why I was shocked when I heard this, I'm like . . . I know he was, he was living out far . . . at his trailer house is what he told me, with his girl . . . they just started dating last summer . . . they musta gotten pregnant as soon as they started dating, you know, 'cause they had a kid. He was only twenty-one years old, but he was running around with a kid. . . . You see, that's the kinda person Aaron was, just like he always dressed in like big clothes, you know like, in like Tommy "Hile-figer," Polo, Gucci . . .

At the time I knew him, he was just, he was just a young kid trying to, you know, he just wanted to fit in, you know, acting tough, acting cool, but, you know, you could get in his face about it and he would back down, like he was some kinda scared kid.

NARRATOR: Sherry Aanenson:

SHERRY AANENSON: Russell was just so sweet. He was the one who was the Eagle Scout. I mean, his whole presence was just quiet and sweet. So of course it doesn't make sense to me and I know people snap and whatever and like it wasn't a real intimate relationship, I was just his landlord. I did work with him at the Chuck Wagon too. And I remember like at the Christmas party he was just totally drunk out of his mind, like we all were pretty much just party-party time. . . . And he wasn't belligerent, he didn't change, his personality didn't change. He was still the same little meek Russell, I remember him coming up to me and saying, "When you get a chance, Sherry, can I have a dance?" Which we never did get around to doing that but . . . Now I just want to shake him, you know—What were you thinking? What in the hell were you thinking?

Moment: The Fence

STEPHEN MEAD JOHNSON: The fence—I've been out there four times, I've taken visitors. That place has become a pilgrimage site. Clearly that's a very powerful personal experience to go out there. It is so stark and so empty and you can't help but think of Matthew out there for eighteen hours in nearly freezing temperatures, with that view up there isolated, and, the "God, my God, why have you forsaken me" comes to mind.

NARRATOR: Company member Greg Pierotti:

GREG PIEROTTI: Phil Labrie, a friend of Matthew's, took us to the fence this morning. I broke down the minute I touched it. I feel such a strong kinship with this young man. On the way back, I made sure that no one saw me crying.

NARRATOR: Leigh Fondakowski:

LEIGH FONDAKOWSKI: Greg was crying on the way back. I couldn't bring myself to tears, but I felt the same way. I have an interview this afternoon with Aaron Kreifels. He's the boy who found Matthew out there at the fence. I don't think I'm up for it right now. I'll see if someone else can do it.

Moment: Finding Matthew Shepard

AARON KREIFELS: Well I, uh, I took off on my bicycle about five P.M. on Wednesday from my dorm. I just kinda felt like going for a ride. So I—I went up to the top of Cactus Canyon, and I'm not superfamiliar with that area, so on my way back down, I didn't know where I was going, I was just sort of picking the way to go, which now . . . it just makes me think that God wanted me to find him because there's no way that I was going to go that way.

So I was in some deep ass sand, and I wanted to turn around—but for some reason, I kept going. And, uh, I went along. And there was this rock, on the   on the ground—and I just drilled it. I went—over the handlebars and ended up on the ground.

So, uh, I got up, and I was just kind of dusting myself off, and I was looking around and I noticed something—which ended up to be Matt, and he was just lying there by a fence, and I—I just thought it was a scarecrow. I was like, Halloween's coming up, thought it was a Halloween gag, so I didn't think much of it, so I got my bike, walked it around the fence that was there, it was a buck-type fence. And, uh, got closer to him, and I noticed his hair—and that was a major key to me noticing it was a human being—was his hair. 'Cause I just thought it was a dummy, seriously, I noticed—I even noticed the chest going up and down, I still thought it was a dummy, you know. I thought it was just like some kind of mechanism.

But when I saw hair, well, I knew it was a human being.

So . . . I ran to the nearest house and—I just ran as fast as I could . . . and called the police.

REGGIE FLUTY: I responded to the call.

NARRATOR: Officer Reggie Fluty:

REGGIE FLUTY: When I got there, the first—at first the only thing I could see was partially somebody's feet, and I got out of my vehicle and raced over—I seen what appeared to be a young man, thirteen, fourteen years old because he was so tiny laying on his back and he was tied to the bottom end of a pole.

I did the best I could. The gentleman that was laying on the ground, Matthew Shepard, he was covered in dry blood all over his head, there was dry blood underneath him and he was barely breathing . . . he was doing the best he could.

I was going to breathe for him and I couldn't get his mouth open—his mouth wouldn't open for me.

He was covered in, like I said, partially dry blood and blood all over his head—the only place that he did not have any blood on him, on his face, was what appeared to be where he had been crying down his face.

His head was distorted—you know, it did not look normal—he looked as if he had a real harsh head wound.

DR. CANTWAY: I was working the emergency room the night Matthew Shepard was brought in. I don't think that any of us, ah, can remember seeing a patient in that condition for a long time—those of us who've worked in big city hospitals have seen this. Ah, but we have some people here who've not worked in a big city hospital. And, ah, it's not something you expect here.

Ah, you expect it, you expect this kind of injuries to come from a car going down a hill at eighty miles an hour. You expect to see gross injuries from something like that—this horrendous, terrible thing. Ah, but you don't expect to see that from someone doing this to another person.

The ambulance report said it was a beating, so we knew.

AARON KREIFELS: There was nothing I could do. I mean, if there was anything that I could of done to help him I would've done it but there was nothing.

And I, I was yelling at the top of my lungs at him, trying to get something outta him.

Like: "Hey, wake up," "HELLO!"

But he didn't move, he didn't flinch, he didn't anything . . .

REGGIE FLUTY: He was tied to the fence—his hands were thumbs out in what we call a cuffing position—the way we handcuff people. He was bound with a real thin white rope, it went around the bottom of the pole, about four inches up off the ground.

His shoes were missing.

He was tied extremely tight—so I used my boot knife and tried to slip it between the rope and his wrist—I had to be extremely careful not to harm Matthew any further.

DR. CANTWAY: Your first thought is . . . well, certainly you'd like to think that it's somebody from out of town, that comes through and beats somebody. I mean, things like this happen, you know, shit happens, and it happens in Laramie. But if there's been somebody who has been beaten repeatedly, ah, certainly this is something that offends us. I think that's a good word. It offends us!

REGGIE FLUTY: He was bound so tight—I finally got the knife through there—I'm sorry—we rolled him over to his left side—when we did that he quit breathing. Immediately, I put him back on his back—and that was just enough of an adjustment—it gave me enough room to cut him free there—

I seen the EMS unit trying to get to the location, once the ambulance got there we put a neck collar on him, placed him on a back board, and scooted him from underneath the fence—then Rob drove the ambulance to Ivinson Hospital's emergency room . . .

DR. CANTWAY: Now, the strange thing is, twenty minutes before Matthew came in, Aaron McKinney was brought in by his girlfriend. Now I guess he had gotten into a fight later on that night back in town, so I am workin' on Aaron and the ambulance comes in with Matthew. Now at this point I don't know that there's a connection—at all. So I tell Aaron to wait and I go and treat Matthew. So there's Aaron in one room of the ER and Matthew in another room two doors down.

Now as soon as we saw Matthew . . . It was very obvious that his care was beyond our capabilities. Called the neurosurgeon at Poudre Valley, and he was on the road in an hour and fifteen minutes, I think.

REGGIE FLUTY: They showed me a picture . . . days later I saw a picture of Matthew . . . I would have never recognized him.

DR. CANTWAY: Then two days later I found out the connection and I was . . . very . . . struck!!! They were two kids!!!!! They were both my patients and they were two kids. I took care of both of them. . . . Of both their bodies. And . . . for a brief moment I wondered if this is how God feels when he looks down at us. How we are all his kids. . . . Our bodies. . . . Our souls. . . . And I felt a great deal of compassion. . . . For both of them. . . .

ACT II • Moment: A Laramie Man

NARRATOR: This is Jon Peacock, Matthew's academic adviser.

JON PEACOCK: Well, the news reports started trickling out on Thursday, but no names were mentioned, the brutality of the crime was not mentioned. All that was mentioned was that there was a man, Laramie man, found beaten, out on the prairie basically. Later on in the evening they mentioned his name. It was like, That can't, that's not the Matthew Shepard I know, that's not my student, that's not this person who I've been meeting with.

ROMAINE PATTERSON: I was in the coffee shop.

NARRATOR: Romaine Patterson:

ROMAINE PATTERSON: And someone pulled me aside and said: "I don't know much, but they say that there's been a young man who's been beaten in Laramie. And they said his name was Matthew Shepard." And he said, "Do you think this could be our Matthew?"

And I said, "Well, yeah, it sounds like it could be our Matthew."

So I called up my sister Trish and I said, "Tell me what you know." I'm just like, "I need to know anything you know because I don't know anything."

TRISH STEGER: So I'm talking to my sister on the phone and that's when the whole story came up on Channel 5 news and it was just like *baboom*.

JON PEACOCK: And the news reports kept rolling in, young University of Wyoming student, his age, his description, it's like, "Oh my God."

TRISH STEGER: And, uh (*pause*) I—I felt sick to my stomach . . . it's just instantly sick to my stomach. And I had to tell Romaine, "Yes, it was Matthew. It was your friend."

MATT GALLOWAY: Well, I'll tell you—I'll tell you what is overwhelming.

NARRATOR: Matt Galloway:

MATT GALLOWAY: Friday morning I first find out about it. I go to class, walk out, boom there it is—in the *Branding Iron*. So immediately I drive to the nearest newsstand, buy a *Laramie Boomerang* 'cause I want more details, buy that—go home . . . before I can even open the paper, my boss calls me, he says:

MATT MICKELSON: Did you hear about what happened?

MATT GALLOWAY: I'm like, "Yeah."

MATT MICKELSON: Was he in the bar Tuesday night?

MATT GALLOWAY: I go, "Yes, yes he was."

MATT MICKELSON: You've got to get down to the bar right now, we've got to talk about this, we've got to discuss what's going to go on.

JON PEACOCK: By this time, I was starting to get upset, but still the severity wasn't out yet.

RULON STACEY: It was Thursday afternoon.

NARRATOR: Rulon Stacey at Poudre Valley Hospital:

RULON STACEY: I got a call: "We just got a kid in from Wyoming and it looks like he may be the victim of a hate crime. We have a couple of newspaper reporters here asking questions." And so, we agreed that we needed one spokesperson: As CEO, I'll do that and we'll try and gather all the information that we can.

ROMAINE PATTERSON: And then I watched the ten o'clock news that night, where they started speaking about the nature and the seriousness of it . . .

MATT GALLOWAY: So I'm on the phone with Mickelson and he's like:

MATT MICKELSON: We need to go to the arraignment so we can identify these guys, and make sure these guys were in the bar.

MATT GALLOWAY: So we go to the arraignment.

Moment: The Essential Facts

NEWSPERSON: Our focus today turns to Laramie, Wyoming, and the Albany County Courthouse, where Aaron James McKinney and Russell Arthur Henderson are being charged with the brutal beating of Matthew Shepard, a gay University of Wyoming student.

NARRATOR: Catherine Connolly:

CATHERINE CONNOLLY: The arraignment was on Friday. Right around lunchtime. And I said, "I'm just going." I just took off—it's just down the street. So I walked a few blocks and I went. Has anybody told you about the arraignment?

There were probably about a hundred people from town and probably as many news media. By that point, a lot more of the details had come out. The fact that the perpetrators were kids themselves, local kids, that everyone who's from around here has some relationship to. And what—Everyone was really I think waiting on pins and needles for what would happen when the perpetrators walked in. And what happened—there's two hundred people in the room at this point . . . they walked in in their complete orange jumpsuits and their shackles, and, you could have heard a pin drop

It was incredibly solemn.

I mean, lots of people were teary at that point. Then the judge came in and did a reading—there was a reading of the evidence that the prosecution has and—it's just a—it's a statement of facts, and the reading of the facts was . . .

JUDGE: The essential facts are that the defendants, Aaron James McKinney and Russell Arthur Henderson, met Matthew Shepard at the Fireside Bar, and after Mr. Shepard confided he was gay, the subjects deceived Mr. Shepard into leaving with them in their vehicle to a remote area. Upon arrival at said area, both subjects tied their victim to a buck fence, robbed him, tortured him, and beat him. . . . Both defendants were later contacted by officers of the Laramie Police Department, who observed inside the cab of their pickup a credit card and a pair of black patent leather shoes belonging to the victim, Matthew Shepard.

(*The Judge goes sotto voce here while Catherine Connolly speaks.*)

The subjects took the victim's credit card, wallet containing twenty dollars in cash, his shoes, and other items, and obtained the victim's address in order to later burglarize his home.

CATHERINE CONNOLLY: I don't think there was any person who was left in that courtroom who wasn't crying at the end of it. I mean it lasted—five minutes, but it kept on getting more and more horrific, ending with:

JUDGE: Said defendants left the victim begging for his life.

Moment: Live and Let Live

NARRATOR: Sergeant Hing:

SERGEANT HING: How could this happen? I—I think a lot of people just don't understand, and even I don't really understand, how someone can do something like that. We have one of the most vocal populations of gay people in the state. . . . And it's pretty much: Live and let live.

NARRATOR: Laramie resident Jeffrey Lockwood:

JEFFREY LOCKWOOD: My secret hope was that they were from somewhere else, that then of course you can create that distance: We don't grow children like that here. Well, it's pretty clear that we do grow children like that here . . .

CATHERINE CONNOLLY: So that was the arraignment, and my response—was pretty catatonic—not sleeping, not eating. Don't—you know, don't leave me alone right now.

JON PEACOCK: More and more details came in about the sheer brutality, um, motivations, how this happened. And then quite frankly the media descended and there was no time to reflect on it anymore.

Moment: The Gem City of the Plains

(*Many reporters enter the stage, followed by media crews carrying cameras, microphones, and lights. They start speaking into the cameras. Simultaneously, television monitors enter the space—in our production they flew in from above the light grid. In the monitors, one can see in live feed the reporters speaking as well as other media images. The texts overlap to create a kind of media cacophony. This moment should feel like an invasion and should be so perceived by the other actors onstage.*)

NEWSPERSON 1: Laramie, Wyoming—often called the Gem City of the Plains—is now at the eye of the storm.

(*Enter Newsperson 2. Newsperson 1 goes sotto voce.*)

The cowboy state has its rednecks and yahoos for sure, but there are no more bigots per capita in

Wyoming than there are in New York, Florida, or California. The difference is that in Wyoming there are fewer places to blend in if you're anything other than prairie stock.

NEWSPERSON 2: Aaron McKinney and his friend Russell Henderson came from the poor side of town.

(*Enter Newsperson 3. Newsperson 2 goes sotto voce.*)

Both were from broken homes and as teenagers had had run-ins with the law. They lived in trailer parks and scratched out a living working at fast-food restaurants and fixing roofs.

NEWSPERSON 3: As a gay college student lay hospitalized in critical condition after a severe beating . . . this small city, which bills itself as Wyoming's Hometown, wrestled with its attitudes toward gay men.

(*Enter Newsperson 4. Newsperson 3 goes sotto voce.*)

NEWSPERSON 4: People would like to think that what happened to Matthew was an exception to the rule, but it was an extreme version of what happens in our schools on a daily basis.

(*The voices and sounds have escalated to a high pitch. And the last text we hear is:*)

NEWSPERSON 1: It's a tough business, as Matt Shepard knew, and as his friends all know, to be gay in cowboy country.

(*These reporters continue speaking into the cameras sotto voce over the next texts.*)

JON PEACOCK: It was huge. Yeah. It was herds and — and we're talking hundreds of reporters, which makes a huge dent in this town's population. There's reporters everywhere, news trucks everywhere on campus, everywhere in the town. And we're not used to that type of attention to begin with, we're not used to that type of exposure.

NARRATOR: Tiffany Edwards, local reporter:

TIFFANY EDWARDS: These people are predators. Like this one journalist actually caught one of the judges in the bathroom at the urinal and was like asking him questions. And the judge was like, "Excuse me, can I please have some privacy?" And the journalist was like *OFFENDED* that he asked for privacy. I mean, this is not how journalism started, like the Gutenberg press, you know.

DOC O'CONNOR: I'll tell you what, when *Hard Copy* came and taped me, I taped them at the exact same time. I have every word I ever said on tape so if they ever do anything funny they better watch their fuckin' ass.

NEWSPERSON: Wyoming governor Jim Geringer, a first-term Republican up for reelection:

GOVERNOR GERINGER: I am outraged and sickened by the heinous crime committed on Matthew Shepard. I extend my most heartfelt sympathies to the family.

NEWSPERSON: Governor, you haven't pushed hate crime legislation in the past.

GOVERNOR GERINGER: I would like to urge the people of Wyoming against overreacting in a way that gives one group "special rights over others."

The 2000 Denver production of *The Laramie Project*, starring Andy Paris (forefront), John McAdams (background), and Stephen Belber (background).

James Patterson (center) and cast in the 2003 production of *The Laramie Project* at the Cochrane Theatre, London.

We will wait and see if the vicious beating and torture of Matthew Shepard was motivated by hate.

SERGEANT HING: You've got the beginning of the news story where they have the graphics in the background, and they've got: "Murder in Wyoming," and Wyoming's dripping red like it's got blood on it or something, and it's like, what's the—what is this, this is sensationalism. And . . . we're here going, "Wait a minute. We had the guys in jail in less than a day. I think that's pretty damn good."

EILEEN ENGEN: And for us to be more or less maligned.

NARRATOR: Eileen and Gil Engen:

EILEEN ENGEN: That we're not a good community and we are—The majority of people here are good people.

GIL ENGEN: You git bad apples once in a while. And I think that the gay community took this as an advantage, said this is a good time for us to exploit this.

NEWSPERSON: Bill McKinney, father of one of the accused:

BILL MCKINNEY: Had this been a heterosexual these two boys decided to take out and rob, this never would have made the national news. Now my son is guilty before he's even had a trial.

TIFFANY EDWARDS: Look, I do think that, um, the media actually made people accountable. Because they made people think. Because people were sitting in their homes, like watching TV and listening to CNN and watching Dan Rather and going, "Jesus Christ, well that's not how it is here." Well how is it here?

Moment: Medical Update

NARRATOR: Matthew Shepard update at three P.M., Saturday, October tenth.

RULON STACEY: By this point, I looked out there and where there had been two or three reporters . . . it must have been ten or fifteen still photographers, another twenty or thirty reporters, and ten video cameras. The parents had just arrived. I had barely introduced myself to them. I looked out there and I thought, "My gosh. What am I going to do?"

(*He crosses to the area where the reporters are gathered with their cameras. As he arrives, several camera flashes go off. He speaks straight into the camera. We see his image on the monitors around the stage.*)

Matthew Shepard was admitted in critical condition approximately nine-fifteen P.M., October seventh. When he arrived, he was unresponsive, and breathing support was being provided.

Matthew's major injuries upon arrival consisted of hypothermia and a fracture from behind his head to just in front of the right ear. This has caused bleeding in the brain, as well as pressure on the brain. There were also several lacerations on his head, face, and neck.

Matthew's temperature has fluctuated over the last twenty-four hours, ranging from ninety-eight to one hundred and six degrees. We have had difficulty controlling his temperature.

Matthew's parents arrived at seven P.M., October ninth, and are now at his bedside. The following is a statement from them:

First of all, we want to thank the American public for their kind thoughts about Matthew and their fond wishes for his speedy recovery. We appreciate your prayers and goodwill, and we know that they are something Matthew would appreciate, too.

We also have a special request for the members of the media. Matthew is very much in need of his family at this time, and we ask that you respect our privacy, as well as Matthew's, so we can concentrate all of our efforts, thoughts, and love on our son.

Thank you very much.

Moment: Seeing Matthew

NARRATOR: Both Aaron McKinney and Russell Henderson pled not guilty to charges. Their girlfriends, Chasity Pasley and Kristin Price, also pled not guilty after being charged as accessories after the fact. On our next trip, we spoke to the chief investigating officer on the case, Detective Rob DeBree of the Albany County Sheriff's Department.

ROB DEBREE: I guess the thing that bothered me the most was when I went down to Poudre Valley, where Matthew was, and the thing that bothered me the most is seeing him, touching him. As a homicide detective, you look at bodies. . . . This poor boy is sitting here, fighting all his life, trying to make it. I wanted it so by the book you know.

AARON KREIFELS: I keep seeing that picture in my head when I found him . . .

NARRATOR: Aaron Kreifels:

AARON KREIFELS: . . . and it's not pleasant whatsoever. I don't want it to be there. I wanna like get it out. That's the biggest part for me is seeing that picture in my head. And it's kind of unbelievable to me, you know, that—I happened to be the person who found him—because the big question with me, like with my religion, is like, Why did God want ME to find him?

CATHERINE CONNOLLY: I know how to take care of myself, and I was irrationally terrified.

NARRATOR: Catherine Connolly:

CATHERINE CONNOLLY: So what that means is, not letting my twelve-year-old son walk the streets, seeing a truck do a U-turn and thinking it's coming after me. Having to stop because I'm shaking so bad. And, in fact, the pickup truck did not come after me, but my reaction was to have my heart in my mouth.

MATT GALLOWAY: Ultimately, no matter how you dice it, I did have an opportunity.

NARRATOR: Matt Galloway:

MATT GALLOWAY: If I had—amazing hindsight of 20/20—to have stopped—what occurred . . . and I keep thinkin', "I shoulda noticed. These guys shouldn'ta been talking to this guy. I shoulda not had

my head down when I was washing dishes for those twenty seconds. Things I coulda done. What the hell was I thinking?"

ROB DEBREE: So you do a lot of studying, you spend hours and hours and hours. You study and study and study . . . talking to the officers, making sure they understand, talk to your witnesses again, and then always coming back to I get this flash of seeing Matthew. . . . I wanted it so tight that there was no way that they were gonna get out of this.

REGGIE FLUTY: One of the things that happened when I got to the fence . . .

NARRATOR: Reggie Fluty:

REGGIE FLUTY: . . . It was just such an overwhelming amount of blood . . . and we try to wear protective gloves, but we had a really cheap sheriff at the time, and he bought us shit gloves, you know, you put 'em on, you put 'em on, and they kept breaking, so finally you just ran out of gloves, you know. So, you figure, well, you know, "Don't hesitate," you know, that's what your mind tells you all the time—Don't hesitate—and so you just keep moving and you try to help Matthew and find an airway and, you know, that's what you do, you know.

MARGE MURRAY: The thing I wasn't telling you before is that Reggie is my daughter.

NARRATOR: Marge Murray:

MARGE MURRAY: And when she first told me she wanted to be a police officer, well, I thought there was not a better choice for her. She could handle whatever came her way. . . .

REGGIE FLUTY: Probably a day and a half later, the hospital called me and told me Matthew had HIV. And the doctor said, "You've been exposed, and you've had a bad exposure," because, you see, I'd been—been building—building a, uh, lean-to for my llamas, and my hands had a bunch of open cuts on 'em, so I was kinda screwed (*she laughs*) you know, and you think, "Oh, shoot," you know.

MARGE MURRAY: Would you like to talk about losing sleep?

REGGIE FLUTY: So I said to the doctor, "Okay, what do I do?" And they said, "Get up here." So, I got up there and we started the ATZ (*sic*) drugs. Immediately.

MARGE MURRAY: Now they told me that's a medication that if it's administered thirty-six hours after you've been exposed . . . it can maybe stop your getting the disease . . .

REGGIE FLUTY: That is a mean nasty medicine. Mean. I've lost ten pounds and a lot of my hair. Yeah . . .

MARGE MURRAY: And quite frankly I wanted to lash out at somebody. Not at Matthew, please understand that, not one of us was mad at Matthew. But we maybe wanted to squeeze McKinney's head off. And I think about Henderson. And, you know, two absolutely human beings cause so much grief for so many people. . . . It has been terrible for my whole family, but mostly for her and her kids.

REGGIE FLUTY: I think it brought home to my girls what their mom does for a living.

MARGE MURRAY: Well, Reggie, you know what I'm gonna tell you now.

REGGIE FLUTY: And my parents told me, you know, they both said the same damn thing.

MARGE MURRAY: You're quitting this damn job!

REGGIE FLUTY: And it's just a parent thing, you know, and they're terribly proud of you, 'cause you do a good job whether it's handling a drunk or handling a case like this, but you're, you know, they don't want you getting hurt—

MARGE MURRAY: Like I said, there's a right way, a wrong way, and then there's Reggie's way.

REGGIE FLUTY: So finally I said, "Oh, for God's sakes, lighten up, Francis!"

MARGE MURRAY: You are so stubborn!

REGGIE FLUTY: They say I'm stubborn, and I don't believe them, but I just think, you know, okay, I've heard your opinion and now here's mine. I'm thirty-nine years old, you know, what are they gonna do, spank me?

MARGE MURRAY: Reggie, don't give me any ideas.

REGGIE FLUTY: It'd look pretty funny. You know, what can they say?

MARGE MURRAY: I just hope she doesn't go before me. I just couldn't handle that.

Moment: E-Mail

NARRATOR: University of Wyoming president Philip Dubois:

PHILIP DUBOIS: Well, this is a young person—who read my statement on the *Denver Post* story, and sent me an e-mail, to me directly, and said:

E-MAIL WRITER: You and the straight people of Laramie and Wyoming are guilty of the beating of Matthew Shepard just as the Germans who looked the other way are guilty of the deaths of the Jews, the Gypsies, and the homosexuals. You have taught your straight children to hate their gay and lesbian brothers and sisters. Unless and until you acknowledge that Matt Shepard's beating is not just a random occurrence, not just the work of a couple of random crazies, you have Matthew's blood on your hands.

PHILIP DUBOIS: And uh, well, I just can't begin to tell you what that does to you. And it's like, you can't possibly know what I'm thinking, you can't possibly know what this has done to me and my family and my community.

Moment: Vigils

(*We see images of the vigils taking place around the country in the monitors as:*)

NARRATOR: That first week alone, vigils were held in Laramie, Denver, Fort Collins, and Colorado Springs. Soon after in Detroit, Chicago, San Francisco, Washington, D.C., Atlanta, Nashville, Minneapolis, and Portland, Maine, among others. In Los Angeles,

five thousand people gathered, and in New York City a political rally ended in civil disobedience and hundreds of arrests. And the Poudre Valley Hospital Web site received close to a million visitors from across the country and around the world, all expressing hope for Matthew's recovery.

Moment: Medical Update

NARRATOR: Matthew Shepard medical update at nine A.M., Sunday, October eleventh.

(*Rulon Stacey is in front of the cameras. We see him on the monitors.*)

RULON STACEY: As of nine A.M. today, Matthew Shepard remains in critical condition. The family continues to emphasize that the media respect their privacy. The family also wants to thank the American public for their kind thoughts and concern for Matthew.

Moment: Live and Let Live

JEDADIAH SCHULTZ: There are certain things when I sit in church.

NARRATOR: Jedadiah Schultz:

JEDADIAH SCHULTZ: And the reverend will tell you flat out he doesn't agree with homosexuality—and I don't know—I think right now, I'm going through changes, I'm still learning about myself and—you know I don't feel like I know enough about certain things to make a decision that says, "Homosexuality is right." When you've been raised your whole life that it's wrong—and right now, I would say that I don't agree with it—yeah, that I don't agree with it but—maybe that's just because I couldn't do it—and speaking in religious terms—I don't think that's how God intended it to happen. But I don't hate homosexuals and, I mean—I'm not going to persecute them or anything like that. At all—I mean, that's not gonna be getting in the way between me and the other person at all.

CONRAD MILLER: Well, it's preached in schools that being gay is okay.

NARRATOR: Conrad Miller:

CONRAD MILLER: And if my kids asked me, I'd set them down and I'd say, "Well, this is what gay people do. This is what animals do. Okay?" And I'd tell 'em, "This is the life, this is the lifestyle, this is what they do." And I'd say, "This is why I believe it's wrong."

MURDOCK COOPER: There's more gay people around than what you think.

NARRATOR: Murdock Cooper:

MURDOCK COOPER: It doesn't bother anybody because most of 'em that are gay or lesbian they know damn well who to talk to. If you step out of line you're asking for it. Some people are saying he made a pass at them. You don't pick up regular people. I'm not excusing their actions, but it made me feel better because it was partially Matthew Shepard's fault and partially the guys who did it . . . you know, maybe it's fifty-fifty.

ZACKIE SALMON: Yes, as a lesbian I was more concerned for my safety.

NARRATOR: Zackie Salmon:

ZACKIE SALMON: I think we all were. And I think it's because somewhere inside we know it could happen to us anytime, you know. I mean, I would be afraid to walk down the street and display any sort of physical affection for my partner. You don't do that here in Laramie.

JONAS SLONAKER: Well, there's this whole idea: You leave me alone, I leave you alone.

NARRATOR: Jonas Slonaker:

JONAS SLONAKER: And it's even in some of the western literature, you know, live and let live. That is such crap. I tell my friends that—even my gay friends bring it up sometimes. I'm like, "That is crap, you know?" I mean, basically what it boils down to: If I don't tell you I'm a fag, you won't beat the crap out of me. I mean, what's so great about that? That's a great philosophy?

Moment: It Happened Here

ZUBAIDA ULA: We went to the candle vigil.

NARRATOR: Zubaida Ula:

ZUBAIDA ULA: And it was so good to be with people who felt like shit. I kept feeling like I don't deserve to feel this bad, you know? And someone got up there and said, "C'mon, guys, let's show the world that Laramie is not this kind of a town." But it is that kind of a town. If it wasn't this kind of a town, why did this happen here? I mean, you know what I mean, like—that's a lie. Because it happened here. So how could it not be a town where this kind of thing happens? Like, that's just totally—like, looking at an Escher painting and getting all confused, like, it's just totally like circular logic like how can you even say that? And we have to mourn this and we have to be sad that we live in a town, a state, a country where shit like this happens. And I'm not going to step away from that and say, "We need to show the world this didn't happen." I mean, these are people trying to distance themselves from this crime. And we need to own this crime. I feel. Everyone needs to own it. We are like this. We ARE like this. WE are LIKE this.

Moment: Shannon and Jen

STEPHEN BELBER: I was in the Fireside one afternoon and I ran into two friends of Aaron McKinney, Shannon and Jen. (*To Shannon and Jen*) You knew Aaron well, right?

SHANNON: Yeah, we both did. When I first found out about this, I thought it was really really awful. I don't know whether Aaron was fucked up or whether he was coming down or what, but Matthew had money. Shit, he had better clothes than I did. Matthew was a little rich bitch.

JEN: You shouldn't call him a rich bitch though, that's not right.

SHANNON: Well, I'm not saying he's a bad guy either, because he was just in the wrong place at the wrong time, said the wrong things. And I don't know, I won't lie to you. There was times that I was all messed up on meth and I thought about going out and robbing. I mean, I never did. But yeah, it was there. It's easy money.

JEN: Aaron's done that thing before. They've both done it. I know one night they went to Cheyenne to go do it and they came back with probably three hundred dollars. I don't know if they ever chose like gay people as their particular targets before, but anyone that looked like they had a lot of money and that was you know, they could outnumber, or overpower, was fair game.

STEPHEN BELBER: But do you think there was any homophobia involved in this that contributed to some of it?

JEN: Probably. It probably would've pissed him off that Matthew was gay 'cause he didn't like—the gay people that I've seen him interact with, he was fine as long as, you know, they didn't hit on him. As long as it didn't come up.

SHANNON: Yeah, as long as they weren't doing it in front of him.

STEPHEN BELBER: Do you get the impression that Aaron knew other gay people?

SHANNON: I'm sure that he knew people that are gay. I mean, he worked up at KFC and there was a couple people up there that—yeah (*he laughs*)—and I'm not saying it's bad or anything 'cause I don't know, half the people I know in Laramie are gay.

STEPHEN BELBER: What would you guys say to Aaron if you saw him right now?

SHANNON: First of all, I'd ask him if he'd ever do anymore tweak.

JEN: He wouldn't I bet. If I saw Aaron now, I'd be like, "Man, why'd you fuck up like that?" But, I'd want to make sure he's doing good in there. But, I'm sure he is though. I'd probably just want to like hang out with him.

SHANNON: Smoke a bowl with him.

JEN: I bet he wants one so bad.

STEPHEN BELBER: So, you guys both went to Laramie High?

SHANNON: Yeah. Can't you tell? We're a product of our society.

Moment: Homecoming

NEWSPERSON: On a day that is traditionally given over to nothing more profound than collegiate exuberance and the fortunes of the University of Wyoming football team, this community on the high plains had a different kind of homecoming Saturday, as many searched their souls in the wake of a vicious, apparent antigay hate crime.

NARRATOR: University president Philip Dubois:

PHILIP DUBOIS: This was homecoming weekend. There were a lot of people in town, and there's a homecoming parade that was scheduled, and then the students organized to tag onto the back of it—you know, behind the banner supporting Matt, and everybody wearing the armbands that the students had created . . .

HARRY WOODS: I live in the center of town.

NARRATOR: Harry Woods:

HARRY WOODS: And my apartment has windows on two opposite streets. One goes north and one goes south. And that is exactly the homecoming parade route. Now, on the day of the parade, I had a cast on my leg because of a fall. So I was very disappointed because I really wanted to walk with the people that were marching for Matthew. But I couldn't. So I watched from my window. And it was . . . it was just . . . I'm fifty-two years old and I'm gay. I have lived here for many years and I've seen a lot. And I was very moved when I saw the tag on the end of the homecoming parade. About a hundred people walking behind a banner for Matthew Shepard.

So then the parade went down to the end of the block to make a U-turn, and I went to the other side of my apartment to wait for it to come south down the other street.

MATT GALLOWAY: I was right up in front there where they were holding the banner for Matthew, and let me tell you . . . I've never had goose bumps so long in my life. It was incredible. A mass of people. Families—mothers holding their six-year-old kids, tying these armbands around these six-year-old kids and trying to explain to them why they should wear an armband. Just amazing. I mean it was absolutely one of the most—beautiful things I've ever done in my life.

HARRY WOODS: Well, about ten minutes went by, and sure enough the parade started coming down the street. And then I noticed the most incredible thing . . . as the parade came down the street . . . the number of people walking for Matthew Shepard had grown five times. There were at least five hundred people marching for Matthew. Five hundred people. Can you imagine? The tag at the end was larger than the entire parade. And people kept joining in. And you know what? I started to cry. Tears were streaming down my face. And I thought, "Thank God that I got to see this in my lifetime." And my second thought was, "Thank you, Matthew."

Moment: One of Ours

SHERRY JOHNSON: I really haven't been all that involved, per se. My husband's a highway patrolman, so that's really the only way that I've known about it.

Now when I first found out I just thought it was horrible. I just, I can't . . . Nobody deserves that! I don't care who ya are.

But, the other thing that was not brought out—at the same time this happened that patrolman was killed. And there was nothing. Nothing. They didn't say anything about the old man that killed him. He was driving down the road and he shouldn't have been driving and killed him. It was just a little piece in the paper. And we lost one of our guys.

You know, my husband worked with him. This man was brand-new on the force. But, I mean, here's one of ours, and it was just a little piece in the paper.

And a lot of it is my feeling that the media is portraying Matthew Shepard as a saint. And making him as a martyr. And I don't think he was. I don't think he was that pure.

Now, I didn't know him, but . . . there's just so many things about him that I found out that I just, it's scary. You know about his character and spreading AIDS and a few other things, you know, being the kind of person that he was. He was, he was just a barfly, you know. And I think he pushed himself around. I think he flaunted it.

Everybody's got problems. But why they exemplified him I don't know. What's the difference if you're gay? A hate crime is a hate crime. If you murder somebody you hate 'em. It has nothing to do with if you're gay or a prostitute or whatever.

I don't understand. I don't understand.

Moment: Two Queers and a Catholic Priest

NARRATOR: Company member Leigh Fondakowski:

LEIGH FONDAKOWSKI: This is one of the last days on our second trip to Laramie. Greg and I have been conducting interviews nonstop and we are exhausted.

GREG PIEROTTI: We are to meet Father Roger at seven-thirty in the morning. I was wishing we could skip it all together, but we have to follow through to the end. So here we go: seven-thirty A.M., two queers and a Catholic priest.

FATHER ROGER SCHMIT: Matthew Shepard has served us well. You realize that? He has served us well. And I do not mean to condemn Matthew to perfection, but I cannot mention anyone who has done more for this community than Matthew Shepard.

And I'm not gonna sit here and say, "I was just this bold guy—no fear." I was scared. I was very vocal in this community when this happened—and I thought, "You know, should we, uh, should we call the bishop and ask him permission to do the vigil?" And I was like, "Hell, no, I'm not going to do that." His permission doesn't make it correct, you realize that? And I'm not knocking bishops, but what is correct is correct.

You people are just out here on a search, though. I will do this. I will trust you people that if you write a play of this, that you (*pause*) say it right, say it correct. I think you have a responsibility to do that.

Don't—don't—don't, um (*pause*) don't make matters worse. . . . You think violence is what they did to Matthew—they did do violence to Matthew—but you know, every time that you are called a fag, or you are called a you know, a lez or whatever . . .

LEIGH FONDAKOWSKI: Or a dyke.

FATHER ROGER SCHMIT: Dyke, yeah, dyke. Do you realize that is violence? That is the seed of violence. And I would resent it immensely if you use anything I said, uh, you know, to—to somehow cultivate that kind of violence, even in its smallest form. I would resent it immensely. You need to know that.

LEIGH FONDAKOWSKI: Thank you, Father, for saying that.

FATHER ROGER SCHMIT: Just deal with what is true. You know what is true. You need to do your best to say it correct.

Moment: Christmas

NARRATOR: Andrew Gomez:

ANDREW GOMEZ: I was in there, I was in jail with Aaron in December. I got thrown in over Christmas. Assault and battery, two counts. I don't wanna talk about it. But we were sittin' there eatin' our Christmas dinner, tryin' to eat my stuffing, my motherfucking bread, my little roll and whatnot, and I asked him, I was like, "Hey, homey, tell me something, tell me something please, why did you—" Okay, I'm thinking how I worded this, I was like, "Why did you kill a faggot if you're gonna be destined to BE a faggot later?" You know? I mean, think about it, he's either gonna get humped a lot or he's gonna die. So why would you do that, think about that. I don't understand that.

And you know what he told me? Honest to God, this is what he said, he goes: "He tried to grab my dick." That's what he said, man! He's dumb, dog, he don't even act like it was nothin'.

Now I heard they was auctioning those boys off. Up there in the max ward, you know, where the killers go, I heard that when they found out Aaron was coming to prison, they were auctioning those boys off. "I want him. I'll put aside five, six, seven cartons of cigarettes." Auction his ass off. I'd be scared to go to prison if I was those two boys.

Moment: Lifestyle 2

BAPTIST MINISTER: Hello.

AMANDA GRONICH: Reverend?

BAPTIST MINISTER: Yes, hello.

AMANDA GRONICH: I believe your wife told you a bit about why I'm contacting you.

BAPTIST MINISTER: Yes, she did. And let me tell you— uh—I don't know that I really want to talk to any-one about any of this incident—uh—I am somewhat involved and I just don't think—

AMANDA GRONICH: Yes, I completely understand and I don't blame you. You know, I went to your service on Sunday.

BAPTIST MINISTER: You went to the services on Sunday?

AMANDA GRONICH: Yes, I did.

BAPTIST MINISTER: On Sunday?

AMANDA GRONICH: Yes, this past Sunday.

BAPTIST MINISTER: Did I meet you?

AMANDA GRONICH: Yes, you welcomed me at the beginning, I believe.

BAPTIST MINISTER: I see, Well, let me tell you. I am not afraid to be controversial or to speak my mind, and that is not necessarily the views of my congregation per se. Now as I said, I am somewhat involved—that half the people in the case—well, the girlfriend of the accused is a member of our congregation, and one of the accused has visited.

AMANDA GRONICH: Mmmmmm.

BAPTIST MINISTER: Now, those two people, the accused, have forfeited their lives. We've been after the two I mentioned for ages, trying to get them to live right, to do right. Now, one boy is on suicide watch and I am working with him—until they put him in the chair and turn on the juice I will work for his salvation. Now I think they deserve the death penalty—I will try to deal with them spiritually.

AMANDA GRONICH: Right, I understand.

BAPTIST MINISTER: Now, as for the victim, I know that that lifestyle is legal, but I will tell you one thing: I hope that Matthew Shepard as he was tied to that fence, that he had time to reflect on a moment when someone had spoken the word of the Lord to him—and that before he slipped into a coma he had a chance to reflect on his lifestyle.

AMANDA GRONICH: Thank you, Reverend, I appreciate your speaking with me.

(*Rain begins to fall on the stage.*)

Moment: That Night

RULON STACEY: About eleven-thirty that night, I had just barely gone to bed, and Margo, our chief operating officer, called and said, "His blood pressure has started to drop." "Well, let's wait and see." She called me about ten after—he just died. So I quick got dressed and came in, and uh went into the ICU where the family was, and Judy came up and she put her arms around me and I put my arms around her and we just stood there—honestly, for about ten minutes just—'cause what else do you do?

And then we had to sit and talk about things that you just—"Dennis, it's now public knowledge.... And I'm gonna go out there now and tell the whole world that this has happened."

'Cause by this point it was clear to us that it was the world—it was the whole world.

And so Judy told me what she wanted me to say. And I went out at four A.M.

(*He crosses to the camera.*)

Moment: Medical Update

NARRATOR: Matthew Shepard medical update for four-thirty A.M., Monday, October twelfth.

RULON STACEY: At twelve midnight on Monday, October twelfth, Matthew Shepard's blood pressure began to drop. We immediately notified his family, who were already at the hospital.

At twelve fifty-three A.M. Matthew Shepard died. His family was at his bedside.

The family did release the following statement,

The family again asked me to express their sincerest gratitude to the entire world for the overwhelming response for their son.

The family was grateful that they did not have to make a decision regarding whether or not to continue life support for their son. Like a good son, he was caring to the end and removed guilt or stress from the family.

He came into the world premature and left the world premature.

Matthew's mother said:

Go home, give your kids a hug, and don't let a day go by without telling them that you love them.

Moment: Magnitude

RULON STACEY: And —I don't know *how* I let that happen—I lost it on national television, but, you now, we had been up for like seventy-two hours straight and gone home and gone to sleep for half an hour and had to get up and come in—and maybe I was just way—I don't know—but (*pause*) in a moment of complete brain-deadness, while I was out there reading that statement I thought about my own four daughters—and go home, hug your kids (*he begins to cry*) and, oh, she doesn't have her kid anymore.

And there I am and I'm thinking, "This is so lame."

Um, and then we started to get people sending us e-mails and letters. And most of them were just generally very kind. But I did get this one. This guy wrote me and said, "Do you cry like a baby on TV for all of your patients or just the faggots?" And as I told you before, homosexuality is not a lifestyle with which I agree. Um, but having been thrown into this (*pause*) I guess I didn't understand the magnitude with which some people hate. And of all the letters that we got, there were maybe two or three that were like that, most of them were, Thank you for your caring and compassion, and Matthew had caring and compassion from the moment he got here.

Moment: H-O-P-E

STEPHEN BELBER: I spoke with Doc today and told him we would soon be coming back out for the upcoming trials of Russell Henderson and Aaron McKinney, and this is what he had to say.

DOC O'CONNOR: I'll tell you what, if they put those two boys to death, that would defeat everything Matt would be thinking about on them. Because Matt would not want those two to die. He'd want to leave them with hope. (*Spelling*) H-O-P-E. Just like the whole world hoped that Matt would survive. The whole thing, you see, the whole thing, ropes around hope, H-O-P-E.

ACT III

(*The stage is now empty except for several chairs stage right. They occupy that half of the stage. They are all facing the audience and arranged in rows as if to suggest a church or a courthouse. As the lights come up, several actors are sitting there dressed in black. Some of them have umbrellas. A few beats with just this image in silence. Then Matt Galloway enters stage left. Looks at them and says:*)

Moment: Snow

MATT GALLOWAY: The day of the funeral, it was snowing so bad, big huge wet snowflakes. And when I got there, there were thousands of people in just black, with umbrellas everywhere. And there were two churches—one for the immediate family, uh, invited guests, people of that nature, and then one church for everybody else who wanted to be there. And then, still, hundreds of people outside that couldn't fit into either of the churches. And there was a big park by the church, and that's where these people were. And this park was full.

PRIEST: The liturgy today is an Easter liturgy. It finds its meaning in the Resurrection. The service invites your full participation.

PRIEST: The Lord be with you.

PEOPLE: And also with you.

PRIEST: Let us pray.

TIFFANY EDWARDS: And I guess it was like the worst storm that they have had.

NARRATOR: Tiffany Edwards:

TIFFANY EDWARDS: Like that anybody could ever tell, like trees fell down and the power went out for a couple of days because of it and I just thought, "It's like the forces of the universe at work, you know." Whatever higher spirit, you know, is like that blows storms, was blowin' this storm.

PRIEST: For our brother, Matthew, let us pray to our Lord Jesus Christ, who said, "I am the Resurrection and the Life." We pray to the Lord.

PEOPLE: HEAR US, LORD.

(*The Priest begins and goes into sotto voce.*)

PRIEST: Lord, you who consoled Martha and Mary in their distress: draw near to us who mourn for Matthew, and dry the tears of those who weep. We pray to the Lord.

PEOPLE: HEAR US, LORD.

PRIEST: You wept at the grave of Lazarus, your friend: comfort us in our sorrow. We pray to the Lord.

PEOPLE: HEAR US, LORD.

PRIEST: You raised the dead to life: give to our brother eternal life. We pray to the Lord.

PEOPLE: HEAR US, LORD.

PRIEST: You promised paradise to the thief who repented: bring our brother the joys of heaven. We pray to the Lord.

PEOPLE: HEAR US, LORD.

PRIEST: He was nourished with your Body and Blood; grant him a place at the table in your heavenly kingdom. We pray to the Lord.

PEOPLE: HEAR US, LORD.

PRIEST: Comfort us in our sorrows at the death of our brother; let our faith be our consolation, and eternal life our hope. We pray to the Lord.

KERRY DRAKE: My most striking memory from the funeral . . .

NARRATOR: Kerry Drake, *Casper Star-Tribune:*

KERRY DRAKE: . . . is seeing the Reverend Fred Phelps from Kansas . . . that scene go up in the park.

REVEREND FRED PHELPS: Do you believe the Bible? Do you believe you're supposed to separate the precious from the vile? You don't believe that part of the Bible? You stand over there ignorant of the fact that the Bible—two times for every verse it talks about God's love it talks about God's hate.

(*Reverend Fred Phelps continues sotto voce.*)

KERRY DRAKE: A bunch of high school kids who got out early came over and started yelling at some of these people in the protest—the Fred Phelps people—and across the street you had people lining up for the funeral . . . Well, I remember a guy, this skinhead coming over, and he was dressed in leather and spikes everywhere, and he came over from across the street where the protest was and he came into the crowd and I just thought, "Oh, this is gonna be a really ugly confrontation" BUT instead he came over and he started leading them in "Amazing Grace."

(*The people sing "Amazing Grace."*)

REVEREND FRED PHELPS: We wouldn't be here if this was just another murder the state was gonna deal with. The state deals with hundreds of murders every single day. But this murder is different, because the fags are bringing us out here trying to make Matthew Shepard into a poster boy for the gay lifestyle. And we're going to answer it. It's just that simple.

(*Reverend Fred Phelps continues sotto voce.*)

NARRATOR: Six months later, the company returned to Laramie for the trial of Russell Henderson, the first of the two perpetrators. It was to be a capital murder trial. When we got to the Albany County Courthouse, Fred Phelps was already there.

REVEREND FRED PHELPS: You don't like that attribute of God.

NARRATOR: But so was Romaine Patterson.

REVEREND FRED PHELPS: That perfect attribute of God. Well, WE love that attribute of God, and we're going to preach it. Because God's hatred is pure. It's a determination—it's a determination that he's gonna send some people to hell. That's God's hatred . . .

(*Continues sotto voce.*)

We're standing here with God's message. We're standing here with God's message. Is homosexuality— is being a fag okay? What do you mean it's not for you to judge? If God doesn't hate fags, why does he put 'em in hell? . . . You see the barrenness and sterility of your silly arguments when set over against some solid gospel truth? Barren and sterile. Like your lifestyle. Your silly arguments.

ROMAINE PATTERSON: After seeing Fred Phelps protesting at Matthew's funeral and finding out that he was coming to Laramie for the trial of Russell Henderson, I decided that someone needed to stand toe-to-toe with this guy and show the differences. And I think at times like this, when we're talking about hatred as much as the nation is right now, that someone needs to show that there is a better way of dealing with that kind of hatred.

So our idea is to dress up like angels. And so we have designed an angel outfit—for our wings are huge—they're like big-ass wings—and there'll be ten to twenty of us that are angels—and what we're gonna do is we're gonna encircle Phelps . . . and because of our big wings—we are gonna completely block him.

So this big-ass band of angels comes in, we don't say a fuckin' word, we just turn our backs to him and we stand there. . . . And we are a group of people bringing forth a message of peace and love and compassion. And we're calling it "Angel Action."

Yeah, this twenty-one-year-old little lesbian is ready to walk the line with him.

REVEREND FRED PHELPS: When those old preachers laid their hands on me it's called an ordination. Mine was from Isaiah fifty-eight: one—"Cry aloud. Spare not. Lift up thy voice like a trumpet and show my people their transgressions."

ROMAINE PATTERSON: And I knew that my angels were gonna be taking the brunt of everything he had to yell and say. I mean, we were gonna be blocking his view and he was gonna be liked pissed off to all hell. . . . So I went out and bought all my angels earplugs.

(*"Amazing Grace" ends.*)

Moment: Jury Selection

BAILIFF: The court is in session.

(*All stand.*)

NARRATOR: Romaine Patterson's sister, Trish Steger:

TRISH STEGER: As soon as they started jury selection, you know, everybody was coming into my shop with "I don't want to be on this trial. I hope they don't call me." Or, "Oh my God, I've been called. How do I get off?" Just wanting to get as far away from it as they could . . . very fearful that they were going to have to be part of that jury.

And then I heard . . . Henderson had to sit in the courtroom while they question the prospective jurors. And one of the questions that they ask is: Would you be willing to put this person to death?

And I understand that a lot of the comments were: "Yes, I would."

JUROR: Yes, I would, Your Honor.

JUROR: Yes, sir.

JUROR: Absolutely.

JUROR: Yes, sir!

(*Jurors continue underneath.*)

JUROR: No problem.

JUROR: Yep.

TRISH STEGER: Well, can you imagine hearing that? You know, juror after juror after juror . . .

Moment: Russell Henderson

(*"Amazing Grace" begins again.*)

JUDGE: You entered a not guilty plea earlier, Mr. Henderson. But I understand you wish to change your plea today. Is that correct?

RUSSELL HENDERSON: Yes, sir.

JUDGE: You understand, Mr. Henderson, that the recommended sentence here is two life sentences?

RUSSELL HENDERSON: Yes, sir.

JUDGE: Do you understand that those may run concurrently or they may run consecutively?

RUSSELL HENDERSON: Yes, sir.

JUDGE: Mr. Henderson, I will now ask you how you wish to plead. Guilty or not guilty?

RUSSELL HENDERSON: Guilty.

JUDGE: Before the Court decides whether the sentences will be concurrent or consecutive, I understand that there are statements to be made by at least one individual.

NARRATOR: This is an excerpt from a statement made to the court by Lucy Thompson.

MS. THOMPSON: As the grandmother and the person who raised Russell, along with my family, we have written the following statement: Our hearts ache for the pain and suffering that the Shepards have went through. We have prayed for your family since the very beginning. Many times throughout the day I have thought about Matt. And you will continue to be in our thoughts and prayers, as we know that your pain will never go away. You have showed such mercy in allowing us to have this plea, and we are so grateful that you are giving us all the opportunity to live. Your Honor, we, as a family, hope that as you sentence Russell, that you will do it concurrently two life terms. For the Russell we know and love, we humbly plead, Your Honor, to not take Russell completely out of our lives forever.

JUDGE: Thank you. Mr. Henderson, you have a constitutional right to make a statement if you would like to do so. Do you have anything you would like to say?

RUSSELL HENDERSON: Yes, I would, Your Honor. Mr. and Mrs. Shepard, there is not a moment that goes by that I don't see what happened that night. I know what I did was very wrong, and I regret greatly what I did. You have my greatest sympathy for what happened. I hope that one day you will be able to find it in your hearts to forgive me. Your Honor, I know what I did was wrong. I'm very sorry for what I did, and I'm ready to pay my debt for what I did.

JUDGE: Mr. Henderson, you drove the vehicle that took Matthew Shepard to his death. You bound him to that fence in order that he might be more savagely beaten and in order that he might not escape to tell his tale. You left him out there for eighteen hours, knowing full well that he was there, perhaps having an opportunity to save his life, and you did nothing. Mr. Henderson, this Court does not believe that you really feel any true remorse for your part in this matter. And I wonder, Mr. Henderson, whether you fully realize the gravity of what you've done.

The Court finds it appropriate, therefore, that sentence be ordered as follows: As to Count Three, that being felony murder with robbery, you are to serve a period of imprisonment for the term of your natural life. On Count One, kidnapping, that you serve a period of imprisonment for the term of your natural life. Sentencing for Count One to run consecutive to sentencing for Count Three.

NARRATOR: After the hearing, we spoke with Russell Henderson's Mormon home teacher.

MORMON HOME TEACHER: I've known Russell's family for thirty-eight years. Russell's only twenty-one, so I've known him his entire life. I ordained Russell a priest of the Mormon Church, so when this happened, you can imagine—disbelief. . . . After the sentencing . . . the church held a disciplinary council, and the result of that meeting was to excommunicate Russell from the Mormon Church. And what that means is that your name is taken off the records of the church, so you just disappear.

Russell's reaction to that was not positive, it hurt him, it hurt him to realize how serious a transgression he had committed.

But I will not desert Russell. That's a matter of my religion and my friendship with the family.

(*All exit. Lights fade on Russell, his grandmother, and his home teacher.*)

Moment: *Angels in America*

NARRATOR: Before we left Laramie, we met again with Rebecca Hilliker at the theater department. She is producing *Angels in America* this year at the university.

REBECCA HILLIKER: I think that's the focus the university has taken—is that we have a lot of work to do. That we have an obligation to find ways to reach our students. . . . And the question is, How do we move—how do we reach a whole state where there is some really deep-seated hostility toward gays? How do you reach them?

This is the beginning . . . and guess who's auditioning for the lead?

JEDADIAH SCHULTZ: MY PARENTS!

NARRATOR: Jedadiah Schultz:

JEDADIAH SCHULTZ: My parents were like, "So what plays are you doing this year at school?" And I was like, *"Angels in America,"* and I told them the whole list of plays. And they're like, *"Angels in America?* Is that . . . that play you did in high school? That scene you did in high school?" And I was like, "Yeah." And she goes: "Huh. So are you gonna audition for it?" And I was like, "Yeah." And we got in this huge argument . . . and my best, the best thing that I knew I had them on is it was just after they had seen me in a performance of *Macbeth,* and onstage like I murdered like a little kid, and Lady Macduff and these two other guys and like and she goes, "Well, you know homosexuality is a sin"—she kept saying that—and I go, "Mom, I just played a murderer tonight. And you didn't seem to have a problem with that . . ."

I tell you. I've never prepared myself this much for an audition in my life. Never ever. Not even close.

ROB DEBREE: Not having to deal that much with the gay society here in Laramie.

NARRATOR: Detective Sergeant Rob DeBree:

ROB DEBREE: Well, once we started working into the case, and actually speaking to the people that were gay and finding out what their underlying fears were, well, then it sort of hit home. This is America. You don't have the right to feel that fear.

And we're still going to have people who hold with the old ideals, and I was probably one of them fourteen months ago. I'm not gonna put up with it, and I'm not going to listen to it. And if they don't like my views on it, fine. The door goes both ways. I already lost a couple of buddies. I don't care. I feel more comfortable and I can sleep at night.

REGGIE FLUTY: Well, you're tested every three months.

NARRATOR: Reggie Fluty:

REGGIE FLUTY: And I was able to have the DNA test done. And so they got me to Fort Collins, they drew the blood there, flew it to Michigan, and did all the DNA work there and—which was—a week later . . . I knew I was negative for good.

MARGE MURRAY: I'll tell ya, we were all on our knees saying Hail Marys.

REGGIE FLUTY: You were just elated, you know, and you think, "Thank God!"

MARGE MURRAY: So what's the first thing she does?

REGGIE FLUTY: I stuck my tongue right in my husband's mouth. I was just happy, you know, you're just so happy. You think, "Yeah, I hope I did this service well," you know, I hope I did it with some kind of integrity. So, you're just really happy . . . and my daughters just bawled.

MARGE MURRAY: They were so happy.

REGGIE FLUTY: And the force . . .

MARGE MURRAY: Oh boy . . .

REGGIE FLUTY: We went out and got shitfaced.

MARGE MURRAY: (*Simultaneous*) Shitfaced.

REGGIE FLUTY: They all bought me drinks too, it was great . . . and everybody hugged and cried, and, you know, I kissed everybody who walked through the door . . .

MARGE MURRAY: Reggie, they don't need to know that.

REGGIE FLUTY: I didn't care if they were male or female, they each got a kiss on the lips.

(*Reggie and Marge exit together, arguing as they go.*)

MARGE MURRAY: Now what part of what I just said didn't you understand?

REGGIE FLUTY: Oh, get over it, Maw!

Moment: A Death Penalty Case

NARRATOR: Almost a year to the day that Matthew Shepard died, the trial for Aaron James McKinney was set to begin.

CAL RERUCHA: Probably the question that most of you have in your mind is ah, ah, how the McKinney case will proceed.

NARRATOR: Cal Rerucha, prosecuting attorney:

CAL RERUCHA: And it's the decision of the county attorney's office that that will definitely be a death penalty case.

MARGE MURRAY: Part of me wants McKinney to get it. But I'm not very proud of that. I was on and off, off and on. I can't say what I would do . . . I'm too personally involved.

ZACKIE SALMON: Oh, I believe in the death penalty one hundred percent. You know, because I want to make sure that guy's ass dies. This is one instance where I truly believe with all my heart an eye for an eye, a tooth for a tooth.

MATT MICKELSON: I don't know about the death penalty. But I don't ever want to see them ever walk out of Rawlins Penitentiary. I'll pay my nickel, or whatever, my little percentage of tax, nickel a day to make sure that his ass stays in there and never sees society again and definitely never comes into my bar again.

MATT GALLOWAY: I don't believe in the death penalty. It's too much for me. I don't believe that one person should be killed as redemption for his having killed another. Two wrongs don't make a right.

ZUBAIDA ULA: How can I protest, if the Shepards want McKinney dead? I just can't interfere in that. But on a personal level, I knew Aaron in grade school. We never called him Aaron, he was called A.J. . . . How can we put A.J. McKinney—how can we put A.J. McKinney to death?

FATHER ROGER SCHMIT: I think right now our most important teachers must be Russell Henderson and Aaron McKinney. They have to be our teachers. How did you learn? What did we as a society do to teach you that? See, I don't know if many people will let them be their teachers. I think it would be wonderful if the judge said: "In addition to your sentence, you must tell your story, you must tell your story."

BAILIFF: All rise. State of Wyoming versus Aaron James McKinney, docket number 6381. The Honorable Barton R. Voigt presiding. The Court is in session.

Moment: Aaron McKinney

NARRATOR: During the trial of Aaron McKinney, the prosecution played a tape recording of his confession.

ROB DEBREE: My name is Rob DeBree, sergeant for the Sheriff's Office. You have the right to remain silent. Anything you say can and may be used against you in a court of law.

NARRATOR: The following is an excerpt of that confession.

ROB DEBREE: Okay, so you guys, you and Russ go to the Fireside. So you're at the Fireside by yourselves, right?

AARON MCKINNEY: Yeah.

ROB DEBREE: Okay, where do you go after you leave the Fireside?

AARON MCKINNEY: Some kid wanted a ride home.

ROB DEBREE: What's he look like?

AARON MCKINNEY: Mmm, like a queer. Such a queer dude.

ROB DEBREE: He looks like a queer?

AARON MCKINNEY: Yeah, like a fag, you know?

ROB DEBREE: Okay. How did you meet him?

AARON MCKINNEY: He wanted a ride home and I just thought, well, the dude's drunk, let's just take him home.

ROB DEBREE: When did you and Russ talk about jacking him up?

AARON MCKINNEY: We kinda talked about it at the bar.

ROB DEBREE: Okay, what happened next?

AARON MCKINNEY: We drove him out past Wal-Mart. We got over there, and he starts grabbing my leg and grabbing my genitals. I was like, "Look, I'm not a fuckin' faggot. If you touch me again you're gonna get it." I don't know what the hell he was trying to do but I beat him up pretty bad. Think I killed him.

ROB DEBREE: What'd you beat him with?

AARON MCKINNEY: Blacked out. My fist. My pistol. The butt of the gun. Wondering what happened to me. I had a few beers and, I don't know. It's like I could see what was going on, but I don't know, but I don't know, it was like somebody else was doing it.

ROB DEBREE: What was the first thing that he said or that he did in the truck that made you hit him?

AARON MCKINNEY: Well, he put his hand on my leg, slid his hand like as if he was going to grab my balls.

Moment: Gay Panic

ZACKIE SALMON: When that defense team argued that McKinney did what he did because Matthew made a pass at him . . . I just wanted to vomit, because that's like saying that it's okay. It's like the "Twinkie

Defense," when the guy killed Harvey Milk and Moscone. It's the same thing.

REBECCA HILLIKER: As much as, uh, part of me didn't want the defense of them saying that it was a gay bashing or that it was gay panic, part of me is really grateful. Because I was really scared that in the trial they were going to try and say that it was a robbery, or it was about drugs. So when they used "gay panic" as their defense, I felt, this is good, if nothing else the truth is going to be told . . . the truth is coming out.

Moment: Aaron McKinney (continued)

ROB DEBREE: Did he ever try to defend himself against you or hit you back?

AARON MCKINNEY: Yeah, sort of. He tried his little swings or whatever but he wasn't very effective.

ROB DEBREE: Okay. How many times did you hit him inside the truck before you guys stopped where you left him?

AARON MCKINNEY: I'd say I hit him two or three times, probably three times with my fists and about six times with the pistol.

ROB DEBREE: Did he ask you to stop?

AARON MCKINNEY: Well, yeah. He was getting the shit kicked out of him.

ROB DEBREE: What did he say?

AARON MCKINNEY: After he asked me to stop most all he was doing was screaming.

ROB DEBREE: So Russ kinda dragged him over to the fence, I'm assuming, and tied him up?

AARON MCKINNEY: Something like that. I just remember Russ was laughing at first but then he got pretty scared.

ROB DEBREE: Was Matthew conscious when Russ tied him up?

AARON MCKINNEY: Yeah. I told him to turn around and don't look at my license plate number 'cause I was scared he would tell the police. And then I asked him what my license plate said. He read it and that's why I hit him a few more times.

ROB DEBREE: Just to be sure? (*Pause*) So obviously you don't like gay people?

AARON MCKINNEY: No, I don't.

ROB DEBREE: Would you say you hate them?

AARON MCKINNEY: Uh, I really don't hate them but, you know, when they start coming on to me and stuff like that I get pretty aggravated.

ROB DEBREE: Did he threaten you?

AARON MCKINNEY: This gay dude?

ROB DEBREE: Yeah.

AARON MCKINNEY: Not really.

ROB DEBREE: Can you answer me one thing? Why'd you guys take his shoes?

AARON MCKINNEY: I don't know. (*Pause*) Now I'm never going to see my son again.

ROB DEBREE: I don't know. You'll probably go to court sometime today.

AARON MCKINNEY: Today? So I'm gonna go in there and just plead guilty or not guilty today?

ROB DEBREE: No, no, you're just going to be arraigned today.

AARON MCKINNEY: He is gonna die for sure?

ROB DEBREE: There is no doubt that Mr. Shepard is going to die.

AARON MCKINNEY: So what are they going to give me, twenty-five to life or just the death penalty and get it over with?

ROB DEBREE: That's not our job. That's the judge's job and the jury.

Moment: The Verdict

NARRATOR: Has the jury reached a verdict?

FOREPERSON: We have, Your Honor.

We the jury, impaneled and sworn to try the above entitled case, after having well and truly tried the matter, unanimously find as follows:

As to the charge of kidnapping, we find the defendant, Aaron James McKinney, guilty.

As to the charge of aggravated robbery, we find the defendant, Aaron James McKinney, guilty.

As to the charge of first-degree felony murder (kidnapping), we find the defendant, Aaron James McKinney, guilty.

(*Verdict goes sotto voce. Narration begins.*)

As to the charge of first-degree felony murder (robbery), we find the defendant, Aaron James McKinney, guilty.

As to the charge of premeditated first-degree murder, we find the defendant, Aaron James McKinney, not guilty.

As to the lesser-included offense of second-degree murder, we find the defendant, Aaron James McKinney, guilty.

Moment: Dennis Shepard's Statement

NARRATOR: Aaron McKinney was found guilty of felony murder, which meant the jury could give him the death penalty. That evening, Judy and Dennis Shepard were approached by McKinney's defense team, who pled for their client's life. The following morning, Dennis Shepard made a statement to the Court. Here is some of what he said.

DENNIS SHEPARD: My son Matthew did not look like a winner. He was rather uncoordinated and wore braces from the age of thirteen until the day he died. However, in his all too brief life he proved that he was a winner. On October 6, 1998, my son tried to show the world that he could win again. On October 12, 1998, my firstborn son and my hero lost. On October 12, 1998, my firstborn son and my hero died, fifty days before his twenty-second birthday.

I keep wondering the same thing that I did when I first saw him in the hospital. What would he have become? How could he have changed his piece of the world to make it better?

Matt officially died in a hospital in Fort Collins, Colorado. He actually died on the outskirts of Laramie, tied to a fence. You, Mr. McKinney, with your friend Mr. Henderson left him out there by himself, but he wasn't alone. There were his lifelong friends with him, friends that he had grown up with. You're probably wondering who these friends were. First he had the beautiful night sky and the same stars and moon that we used to see through a telescope. Then he had the daylight and the sun to shine on him. And through it all he was breathing in the scent of pine trees from the snowy range. He heard the wind, the ever-present Wyoming wind, for the last time. He had one more friend with him, he had God. And I feel better knowing he wasn't alone.

Matt's beating, hospitalization, and funeral focused worldwide attention on hate. Good is coming out of evil. People have said enough is enough. I miss my son, but I am proud to be able to say that he is my son.

Judy has been quoted as being against the death penalty. It has been stated that Matt was against the death penalty. Both of these statements are wrong. Matt believed that there were crimes and incidents that justified the death penalty. I too believe in the death penalty. I would like nothing better than to see you die, Mr. McKinney. However, this is the time to begin the healing process. To show mercy to someone who refused to show any mercy. Mr. McKinney, I am going to grant you life, as hard as it is for me to do so, because of Matthew. Every time you celebrate Christmas, a birthday, the Fourth of July, remember that Matt isn't. Every time you wake up in your prison cell, remember that you had the opportunity and the ability to stop your actions that night. You robbed me of something very precious, and I will never forgive you for that. Mr. McKinney, I give you life in the memory of one who no longer lives. May you have a long life, and may you thank Matthew every day for it.

Moment: Aftermath

REGGIE FLUTY: Me and DeBree hugged and cried.... And, you know, everybody had tears in their eyes, and you're just so thankful, you know, and Mr. Shepard was cryin', and then that got me bawlin' and everybody just—

ROB DEBREE: This is all we've lived and breathed for a year. Daily. This has been my case daily. And now it's over.

REGGIE FLUTY: Maybe now we can go on and we can quit being stuck, you know?

AARON KREIFELS: It just hit me today, the minute that I got out of the courthouse. That the reason that God wanted me to find him is, for he didn't have to die out there alone, you know. And if I wouldn't of came along, they wouldn't of found him for a couple of weeks at least. So it makes me feel really good that he didn't have to die out there alone.

MATT GALLOWAY: I'm just glad it's over. I really am. Testifying in that trial was one of the hardest things I've ever done. And don't get me wrong, I love the stage, I really do, I love it. But it's tricky, because basically what you have is lawyers questioning you from this angle but the answers need to be funneling this way, to the jury. So what you have to do is establish a funneling system. And that's hard for me because I'm a natural conversationalist, so it's just natural instinct that when someone asks you a question, you look at that person to make eye contact. But it's kind of tough when you literally have to scoot over—change your position, in effect, funnel over to where the jury is. But I was able to do that several times over the course of my testimony.

(*Everyone is amused and baffled by this last text.*)

REGGIE FLUTY: It's time to move on. And I think for even the citizens are having the town painted red so to speak. They're gonna just be glad to maybe get moved on.

Moment: Epilogue

ANDY PARIS: On our last trip, I had the good fortune of seeing Jedadiah Schultz play the role of Prior in *Angels in America*. After a performance, we spoke.

JEDADIAH SCHULTZ: I didn't for the longest time let myself become personally involved in the Matthew Shepard thing. It didn't seem real, it just seemed way blown out of proportion. Matthew Shepard was just a name instead of an individual. . . .

I don't know, it's weird. It's so weird, man. I just—I just feel bad. Just for all that stuff I told you, for the person I used to be. That's why I want to hear those interviews from last year when I said all that stuff. I don't know. I just can't believe I ever said that stuff about homosexuals, you know. How did I ever let that stuff make me think that you were different from me?

NARRATOR: This is Romaine Patterson.

ROMAINE PATTERSON: Well, a year ago, I wanted to be a rock star. That was my goal. And now, um, well, now it's obviously changed in the fact that, um, throughout the last year I—I've really realized my role in, um, in taking my part. And, um, so now instead of going to school to be in music, I'm gonna go to school for communications and political science. Um, because I have a career in political activism.

Actually, I just recently found out I was gonna be honored in Washington, D.C, from the Anti-Defamation League. And whenever I think about the angels or any of the speaking that I've done, you know . . . Matthew gave me—Matthew's like guiding this little path with his light for me to walk down. And he just—every time we get to like a door, he opens it. And he just says, "Okay, next step."

And if I get to be a rock star on the side, okay.

NARRATOR: This is Jonas Slonaker.

JONAS SLONAKER: Change is not an easy thing, and I don't think people were up to it here. They got what they wanted. Those two boys got what they deserve, and we look good now. Justice has been served. The OK Corral. We shot down the villains. We sent the prostitutes on the train. The town's cleaned up, and we don't need to talk about it anymore.

You know, it's been a year since Matthew Shepard died, and they haven't passed shit in Wyoming . . . at a state level, any town, nobody anywhere, has passed any kind of laws, antidiscrimination laws or hate crime legislation, nobody has passed anything anywhere. What's come out of it? What's come out of this that's concrete or lasting?

NARRATOR: We all said we would meet again—one last time at the fence.

DOC O'CONNOR: I been up to that site in my limousine, okay? And I remembered to myself the night he and I drove around together, he said to me, "Laramie sparkles, doesn't it?" And where he was up there, if you sit exactly where he was, up there, Laramie sparkles from there, with a low-lying cloud, . . . it's the blue lights that's bouncing off the clouds from the airport, and it goes *tst tst tst tst* . . . right over the whole city. I mean, it blows you away. . . . Matt was right there in that spot, and I can just picture in his eyes, I can just picture what he was seeing. The last thing he saw on this earth was the sparkling lights.

Moment: Departure

MOISÉS KAUFMAN: We've spent the last two days packing a year's worth of materials and saying our good byes. We've been here six times and conducted over two hundred interviews. Jedadiah cried when he said good-bye.

LEIGH FONDAKOWSKI: Marge wished us luck, and when we asked her how Laramie would feel seeing a play about itself, she said:

MARGE MURRAY: I think we'd enjoy it. To show it's not the hellhole of the earth would be nice, but that is up to how you portray us. And that in turn is up to how Laramie behaves.

GREG PIEROTTI: As we were getting off the phone she said to me:

MARGE MURRAY: Now, you take care. I love you, honey.

STEPHEN BELBER: Doc asked me if I wanted to ghostwrite a book about the whole event. Galloway offered me or anyone else a place to stay if and when we come back to Laramie. He also seemed interested as to whether there'd be any open auditions for this play.

ANDY PARIS: We left Laramie at about seven in the evening. On the way to Denver, I looked in my rearview mirror to take one last look at the town.

FATHER ROGER SCHMIT: And I will speak with you, I will trust that if you write a play of this, that you say it right. You need to do your best to say it correct.

ANDY PARIS: And in the distance I could see the sparkling lights of Laramie, Wyoming.

Suzan-Lori Parks

Suzan-Lori Parks (b. 1964) was named by Mel Gussow in the *New York Times* as the "year's most promising playwright" in 1989. Currently she serves as the Master Writer Chair at the Public Theater in New York and as a visiting professor of dramatic writing at New York University's Tisch School of the Arts. Parks's work has been supported by grants from numerous foundations, including the Rockefeller and Ford Foundations and the National Endowment for the Arts, from which she has twice received a playwriting fellowship. She also received a MacArthur Award in 2001. In 2002 she became the first African American woman to win the Pulitzer Prize in drama, for *Topdog/Underdog* (2001).

Parks is the daughter of an army officer and grew up in several locations. She says, "I've heard horrible stories about twelve-step groups for army people. But I had a great childhood. My parents were really into experiencing the places we lived." She lived, for example, in a small town in Germany and attended German schools, studying in German. She went to Mt. Holyoke College and took courses at nearby Hampshire College, where she studied writing with James Baldwin. After that experience she went to London for a year to study acting. "It really made a difference in my writing. It dawned on me that a lot of people write with ideas in mind. . . . But I never really have ideas, per se. I have these movements, these gestures. Then I figure out how to put those gestures into words."

Parks is aware of being influenced by a number of important literary figures, among them Gertrude Stein, James Joyce, William Faulkner, and Samuel Beckett, but echoes of other writers such as Shakespeare and Richard Wright can be heard in *The Death of the Last Black Man in the Whole Entire World* (1990). Parks's approach to language is partly vernacular, as she attempts to reproduce speech both as it is spoken and as her audience assumes it may be spoken. But she is interested in the hypnotic and musical value of words, which accounts for much of the patterning of repetition that marks her work.

Parks's early short plays are *Betting on the Dust Commander* (1990), *Fishes* (1987), *The Sinners' Place* (1984), and *The America Play* (1994). Her full-length play *Imperceptible Mutabilities in the Third Kingdom* (1989), directed by her longtime collaborator Liz Diamond, won the Obie Award for the best off-Broadway play of 1990. One section of *Mutabilities* takes place on Emancipation Day in 1865 and is played in whiteface by African American actors. Another section, "Greeks," makes reference to her own family, with a character called Mr. Sergeant Smith. Parts of the play have been described as "like a choral poem."

Parks produced a film, *Anemone Me* (1990), that has been shown in New York. Her *Devotees in the Garden of Love* (1992) premiered at the Actors Theatre of Louisville, Kentucky. Her next play, *Venus* (1996), was a coproduction of the Joseph Papp Public Theater and Yale Repertory Theatre. It was directed by Richard Foreman, the founder of the Ontological-Hysteric Theater. The play focuses on the life of a black woman brought to England as the Venus Hottentot, a sideshow freak displaying "an intensely ugly figure, distorted beyond all European notions of beauty." The authorities put an end to the sideshow, and Parks explores this mysterious woman's life. Parks also wrote *Girl 6* (1996), a film directed by Spike Lee.

Parks has said that characters stay with her, and she feels free to create new plays on old themes. *In the Blood* (1999) focuses on Hester, a mother of five who faces poverty, the welfare system's workfare, and sterilization. The play examines attitudes toward poverty and responsibility. Hester appears again in *Fucking A* (2000), based on Nathaniel Hawthorne's novel *The Scarlet Letter* but with the A standing for abortion rather than adultery. *The America Play* (1994) features a black Lincoln impersonator, a character who later inspired *Topdog/Underdog*.

In 2003 Parks published her first novel, *Getting Mother's Body*, which was inspired by a novel by William Faulkner. She next produced a remarkably daring sequence of plays, each written in one day and each performed in one day, called *365 Days/365 Plays*. The work was performed by more than 700 theater companies and arts organizations from November 13, 2006, to November 12, 2007. *Ray Charles Live! A New Musical* (2007) won the NAACP Theatre Award in 2008 and opened on Broadway in 2010 with the title *Unchain My Heart: The Ray Charles Musical*. *Book of Grace* (2010) played in the Public Theater in New York to good reviews that likened its portrait of a dysfunctional family to a portrait of the nation at large. In 2011 Parks, with director Diane Paulus, adapted *The Gershwins' Porgy and Bess*, adding a positive ending and a number of new scenes. The first performances were at the American Repertory Theater in Boston; the musical opened on Broadway in 2012.

Parks is an energetic and carefully focused playwright with a special interest in the language of speech and the language of gesture—in almost equal measure.

Topdog/Underdog

Although Lincoln is listed as the top dog and Booth as the underdog, Parks has said they shift from moment to moment in this drama. John Wilkes Booth shot and killed Abraham Lincoln in 1865, but Booth was hunted down twelve days later and either shot or burned to death by federal troops. Lincoln is history's top dog, but the real Booth believed that Lincoln was a tyrant who needed to be put to death not only because the South lost the war but also because Lincoln planned to give blacks citizenship and voting rights in addition to their freedom. Modern historians have pointed out that Lincoln's personal views on matters of race were complex and sometimes contradictory. He believed, for example, that only very bright blacks should have voting rights. He also believed that blacks and whites would probably not be able to live together as social equals, and, as a result, he hoped that the white race would essentially be top dog in the future.

Naturally, it is a striking irony to have Lincoln, the elder brother in the play, play the part of Abraham Lincoln in an entertainment arcade, where he sits staring at a shiny metal electrical box while customers pay for the privilege of shooting him with a pistol loaded with blanks. He plays the part in whiteface and gets less pay than the previous "Lincoln," a white man. Nevertheless, he believes the job is an opportunity. He likes the work and hopes to continue and build something for himself. For Lincoln, this job represents a way out of the pattern of hustling and petty crime that has been his heritage. The fact that he is let go because of belt-tightening on the part of the arcade owners is emblematic of patterns of black hiring: "last hired, first fired."

Lincoln's younger brother, Booth, has a real gun. He carries it with him, and it remains a threatening presence throughout the play. He spends much of his time "boosting" goods from stores. He also practices the street con card game three-card monte, in which the dealer throws down three cards and then permits a "mark" to gamble on finding the ace of spades among the cards. It's a dishonest game, using sleight of hand and a number of sidekicks who act as shills, or make-believe players. Lincoln is the very best at the game, but he has left the street and wants to make a go of the "straight" life with a job that has potential and benefits. He has abandoned his game and refuses in act 1 to touch the cards. Booth, on the other hand, has no plans of going straight and pleads with Lincoln to teach him how the game works. He expects to be the best ever at three-card monte. Booth is even willing to change his name to Three-Card, and he envisions getting Lincoln's "old gang" together again to work with him.

Over the course of the play, the brothers examine their backgrounds, beginning with the fact that their parents separated and individually left them to fend for themselves when Lincoln was sixteen and Booth was thirteen. Booth points out that each of them got an inheritance from their parents of $500. The money that his mother gave Booth, we learn in act 2, is safe in a stocking that he has never opened. The final struggle in the last act seems focused on that "bequest," although it also has its roots in jealousy and brotherly competition of the kind found in the Bible's story of Cain and Abel.

The fact that they were abandoned as children weighs on both brothers, as does the fact that they were named Lincoln and Booth by their father as a joke. In other words, they were burdened by a violent history, unaware that, as the Chinese saying goes, "One's name is one's fate." In addition to reliving the personal history of Lincoln and Booth (both in the arcade and beyond it), however, they also live through the history of slavery and its aftermath. Their heritage is one of hustling and insecurity, and when Lincoln tries to emulate the virtues of his namesake—"Honest Abe"—he finds that, indeed, he likes the feeling of being honest and making an honest living. He does not want to go back to the street hustle, whereas Booth sees no hope of finding himself a role in the working world. He does not even try. In the end, however, Lincoln, having tried and temporarily succeeded, finds himself replaced because of cutbacks not by another actor, but by a wax dummy—essentially a wax machine that sits there and is shot, combined with a recording apparatus that can cry out appropriately at the proper moment.

In his review of the second New York performance in the *New York Times*, critic Ben Brantley said, "Brotherly love and hatred is translated into the terms of men who have known betrayal since their youth, when their parents walked out on them, and who will never be able entirely to trust anyone, including (and especially) each other. Implicit in their relationship is the idea that to live is to con."

Topdog/Underdog
in Performance

The first production of *Topdog/Underdog* was on July 22, 2001, at the Joseph Papp Public Theater/New York Shakespeare Festival. George C. Wolfe was the producer and director. Don Cheadle played Booth and Jeffrey Wright played Lincoln. With the success of this production, the play moved to the larger Ambassador Theater on Broadway in April 2002, with Jeffrey Wright as Lincoln and the hip-hop artist Mos Def as Booth. The reviews of the production cited the intensity and brilliance of this performance. The energy displayed by Mos Def was extraordinary, and the interplay with Jeffrey Wright was so powerful that at times one wondered how they could contain themselves to get to the end of the play. The setting, by Riccardo Hernández, suggested the gloominess of a mid-nineteenth-century rooming house, adding to the tension and darkness of the drama.

Despite the demands of the play, it has been performed to considerable acclaim in London and in regional theaters in the United States and Canada. The Canadian premiere at the Shaw Festival at Niagara-on-the-Lake in 2011 received strong reviews that cited the special power of the play in "the Obama era." It has become noticed widely as a very important play.

SUZAN-LORI PARKS (b. 1964)

Topdog/Underdog   2001

I am God in nature;
I am a weed by the wall.   — RALPH WALDO EMERSON, FROM "CIRCLES," *ESSAYS: FIRST SERIES* (1841)

The Players

LINCOLN, *the topdog*
BOOTH *(aka 3-Card), the underdog*

Author's Notes: From the "Elements of Style"

I'm continuing the use of my slightly unconventional theatrical elements. Here's a road map.

- *(Rest)*
  Take a little time, a pause, a breather; make a transition.

- A Spell
  An elongated and heightened (*Rest*). Denoted by repetition of figures' names with no dialogue. Has sort of an architectural look:

  LINCOLN
  BOOTH
  LINCOLN
  BOOTH

  This is a place where the figures experience their pure true simple state. While no action or stage business is necessary, directors should fill this moment as they best see fit.

- [Brackets in the text indicate optional cuts for production.]

- (Parentheses around dialogue indicate softly spoken passages (asides; sotto voce)).

SCENE ONE

Thursday evening, A seedily furnished rooming house room. A bed, a reclining chair, a small wooden chair, some other stuff but not much else. Booth, a black man in his early 30s, practices his 3-card monte scam on the classic setup: 3 playing cards and the cardboard playing board atop 2 mismatched milk crates. His moves and accompanying patter are, for the most part, studied and awkward.

BOOTH: Watch me close watch me close now: who-see-thuh-red-card-who-see-thuh-red-card?

I-see-thuh-red-card. Thuh-red-card-is-thuh-winner.
Pick-thuh-red-card-you-pick-uh-winner. Pick-uh-
black-card-you-pick-uh-loser. Theres-thuh-loser, yeah,
theres-thuh-black-card, theres-thuh-other-loser-and-
theres-thuh-red-card, thuh-winner.

(*Rest*)

Watch me close watch me close now: 3-Card-
throws-thuh-cards-lightning-fast. 3-Card-thats-me-
and-Ima-last. Watch-me-throw-cause-here-I-go.
One-good-pickll-get-you-in, 2-good-picks-and-you-
gone-win. See-thuh-red-card-see-thuh-red-card-who-
see-thuh-red-card?

(*Rest*)

Dont touch my cards, man, just point to thuh one you
want. You-pick-that-card-you-pick-a-loser, yeah, that-
cards-a-loser. You-pick-that-card-thats-thuh-other-
loser. You-pick-that-card-you-pick-a-winner. Follow
that card. You gotta chase that card. You-pick-thuh-
dark-deuce-thats-a-loser-other-dark-deuces-thuh-
other-loser, red-deuce, thuh-deuce-of-heartsll-win-it-all.
Follow thuh red card.

(*Rest*)

Ima show you thuh cards: 2 black cards but only one
heart. Now watch me now. Who-sees-thuh-red-card-
who-knows-where-its-at? Go on, man, point to thuh
card. Put yr money down cause you aint no clown. No?
Ah you had thuh card, but you didnt have thuh heart.

(*Rest*)

You wanna bet? 500 dollars? Shoot. You musta
been watching 3-Card real close. Ok. Lay the cash
in my hand cause 3-Cards thuh man. Thank you,
mister. This card you say?

(*Rest*)

Wrong! Sucker! Fool! Asshole! Bastard! I bet yr daddy
heard how stupid you was and drank himself to death
just cause he didnt wanna have nothing to do witchu!
I bet yr mama seen you when you comed out and she
walked away from you with thuh afterbirth still hanging from out twixt her legs, sucker! Ha Ha Ha! And
3-Card, once again, wins all thuh money!!

(*Rest*)

What? Cops looking my way? Fold up thuh game, and
walk away. Sneak outa sight. Set up on another corner.

(*Rest*)

Yeah.

(*Rest*)

*Having won the imaginary loot and dodged the imagi-
nary cops, Booth sets up his equipment and starts practicing his scam all over again. Lincoln comes in quietly.
He is a black man in his later 30s. He is dressed in an
antique frock coat and wears a top hat and fake beard,
that is, he is dressed to look like Abraham Lincoln.
He surreptitiously walks into the room to stand right*

*behind Booth, who, engrossed in his cards, does not
notice Lincoln right away.*

BOOTH: Watch me close watch me close now: who-
see-thuh-red-card-who-see-thuh-red-card?
I-see-thuh-red-card. Thuh-red-card-is-thuh-
winner. Pick-thuh-red-card-you-pick-uh-winner.
Pick-uh-black-card-you-pick-uh-loser. Theres-
thuh-loser-yeah-theres-thuh-black-card, theres-thuh-
other-loser-and-theres-thuh-red-card, thuh-winner.
Dont touch my cards, man, dont—

(*Rest*)

Dont do that shit. Dont do that shit. Dont do that shit!

*Booth, sensing someone behind him, whirls around,
pulling a gun from his pants. While the presence of
Lincoln doesnt surprise him, the Lincoln costume does.*

BOOTH: And woah, man dont *ever* be doing that shit!
Who thuh fuck you think you is coming in my shit
all spooked out and shit. You pull that one more time
I'll shoot you!
LINCOLN: I only had a minute to make the bus.
BOOTH: Bullshit.
LINCOLN: Not completely. I mean, its either bull or shit,
but not a complete lie so it aint bullshit, right?

(*Rest*)

Put yr gun away.
BOOTH: Take off the damn hat at least.

*Lincoln takes off the stovepipe hat. Booth puts his gun
away.*

LINCOLN: Its cold out there. This thing kept my head
warm.
BOOTH: I dont like you wearing that bullshit, that shit that
bull that disguise that getup that motherdisfuckinguise
anywhere in the vicinity of my humble abode.

Lincoln takes off the beard.

LINCOLN: Better?
BOOTH: Take off the damn coat too. Damn, man. Bad
enough you got to wear that shit all day you come
up in here wearing it. What my women gonna say?
LINCOLN: What women?
BOOTH: I got a date with Grace tomorrow. Shes in love with
me again but she dont know it yet. Aint no man can
love her the way I can. She sees you in that getup its
gonna reflect bad on me. She coulda seen you coming
down the street. Shit. Could be standing outside right
now taking her ring off and throwing it on the sidewalk.

Booth takes a peek out the window.

BOOTH: I got her this ring today. Diamond. Well, dia-
mond-esque, but it looks just as good as the real
thing. Asked her what size she wore. She say 7 so I
go boost a size 6 and a half, right? Show it to her and
she loves it and I shove it on her finger and its a tight
fit right, so she cant just take it off on a whim, like
she did the last one I gave her. Smooth, right?

Booth takes another peek out the window.

LINCOLN: She out there?

BOOTH: Nope. Coast is clear.

LINCOLN: You boosted a ring?

BOOTH: Yeah. I thought about spending my inheritance on it but—take off that damn coat, man, you make me nervous standing there looking like a spook, and that damn face paint, take it off. You should take all of it off at work and leave it there.

LINCOLN: I don't bring it home someone might steal it.

BOOTH: At least take it *off* there, then.

LINCOLN: Yeah.

(*Rest*)

Lincoln takes off the frock coat and applies cold cream, removing the whiteface.

LINCOLN: I was riding the bus. Really I only had a minute to make my bus and I was sitting in the arcade thinking, should I change into my street clothes or should I make the bus? Nobody was in there today anyway. Middle of week middle of winter. Not like on weekends. Weekends the place is packed. So Im riding the bus home. And this kid asked me for my autograph. I pretended I didnt hear him at first. I'd had a long day. But he kept asking. Theyd just done Lincoln in history class and he knew all about him, he'd been to the arcade but, I dunno, for some reason he was tripping cause there was Honest Abe right beside him on the bus. I wanted to tell him to go fuck hisself. But then I got a look at him. A little rich kid. Born on easy street, you know the type. So I waited until I could tell he really wanted it, the autograph, and I told him he could have it for 10 bucks. I was gonna say 5, cause of the Lincoln connection but something in me made me ask for 10.

BOOTH: But he didnt have a 10. All he had was a penny. So you took the penny.

LINCOLN: All he had was a *20*. So I took the 20 and told him to meet me on the bus tomorrow and Honest Abe would give him the change.

BOOTH: Shit.

LINCOLN: Shit is right.

(*Rest*)

BOOTH: Whatd you do with thuh 20?

LINCOLN: Bought drinks at Luckys. A round for everybody. They got a kick out of the getup.

BOOTH: You shoulda called me down.

LINCOLN: Next time, bro.

(*Rest*)

You making bookshelves? With the milk crates, you making bookshelves?

BOOTH: Yeah, big bro, Im making bookshelves.

LINCOLN: Whats the cardboard part for?

BOOTH: Versatility.

LINCOLN: Oh.

BOOTH: I was thinking we dont got no bookshelves we dont got no dining room table so Im making a sorta modular unit you put the books in the bottom and the table top on top. We can eat and store our books. We could put the photo album in there.

Booth gets the raggedy family photo album and puts it in the milk crate.

BOOTH: Youd sit there, I'd sit on the edge of the bed. Gathered around the dinner table. Like old times.

LINCOLN: We just gotta get some books but thats great, Booth, thats real great.

BOOTH: Dont be calling me Booth no more, K?

LINCOLN: You changing yr name?

BOOTH: Maybe.

LINCOLN

BOOTH

LINCOLN: What to?

BOOTH: Im not ready to reveal it yet.

LINCOLN: You already decided on something?

BOOTH: Maybe.

LINCOLN: You gonna call yrself something african? That be cool. Only pick something thats easy to spell and pronounce, man, cause you know, some of them african names, I mean, ok, Im down with the power to the people thing, but, no ones gonna hire you if they cant say yr name. And some of them fellas who got they african names, no one can say they names and they cant say they names neither. I mean, you dont want yr new handle to obstruct yr employment possibilities.

BOOTH

LINCOLN

BOOTH: You bring dinner?

LINCOLN: "Shango" would be a good name. The name of the thunder god. If you aint decided already Im just throwing it in the pot. I brought Chinese.

BOOTH: Lets try the table out.

LINCOLN: Cool.

They both sit at the new table. The food is far away near the door.

LINCOLN

BOOTH

LINCOLN: I buy it you set it up. Thats the deal. Thats the deal, right?

BOOTH: You like this place?

LINCOLN: Ssallright.

BOOTH: But a little cramped sometimes, right?

LINCOLN: You dont hear me complain. Although that recliner sometimes Booth, man—no Booth, right—man, Im too old to be sleeping in that chair.

BOOTH: Its my place. You dont got a place. Cookie, she threw you out. And you cant seem to get another woman. Yr lucky I let you stay.

LINCOLN: Every Friday you say *mi casa es su casa.*°

BOOTH: Every Friday you come home with yr paycheck. Today is Thursday and I tell you brother, its a long way from Friday to Friday. All kinds of things can happen. All kinds of bad feelings can surface and erupt while yr little brother waits for you to bring in yr share.

(*Rest*)

I got my Thursday head on, Link. Go get the food.

Lincoln doesnt budge.

---

mi . . . casa: My house is your house.

[ABOVE] Don Cheadle as Booth and Jeffrey Wright as Lincoln in the original 2001 production of *Topdog/Underdog* at the Joseph Papp Public Theater in New York, directed and produced by George C. Wolfe. [RIGHT] Mos Def as Booth, playing three-card monte in the 2002 New York production at the Ambassador Theater on Broadway.

LINCOLN: You dont got no running water in here, man.

BOOTH: So?

LINCOLN: You dont got no toilet you dont got no sink.

BOOTH: Bathrooms down the hall.

LINCOLN: You living in thuh Third World, fool! Hey, I'll get thuh food.

Lincoln goes to get the food. He sees a stray card on the floor and examines it without touching it. He brings the food over, putting it nicely on the table.

LINCOLN: You been playing cards?

BOOTH: Yeah.

LINCOLN: Solitaire?

BOOTH: Thats right. Im getting pretty good at it.

LINCOLN: Thats soup and thats sauce. I got you the meat and I got me the skrimps.

BOOTH: I wanted the skrimps.

LINCOLN: You said you wanted the meat. This morning when I left you said you wanted the meat.

(Rest)

Here man, take the skrimps. No sweat.

They eat. Chinese food, from styrofoam containers, cans of the soda, fortune cookies. Lincoln eats slowly and carefully, Booth eats ravenously.

LINCOLN: Yr getting good at solitaire?

BOOTH: Yeah. How about we play a hand after eating?

LINCOLN: Solitaire?

BOOTH: Poker or rummy or something.

LINCOLN: You know I dont touch thuh cards, man.

BOOTH: Just for fun.

LINCOLN: I dont touch thuh cards.

BOOTH: How about for money?

LINCOLN: You dont got no money. All the money you got I bring in here.

BOOTH: I got my inheritance.

LINCOLN: Thats like saying you dont got no money cause you aint never gonna do nothing with it so its like you dont got it.

BOOTH: At least I still got mines. You blew yrs.

LINCOLN

BOOTH

LINCOLN: You like the skrimps?

BOOTH: Ssallright.

LINCOLN: Whats yr fortune?

BOOTH: "Waste not want not." Whats yrs?

LINCOLN: "Your luck will change!"

Booth finishes eating. He turns his back to Lincoln and fiddles around with the cards, keeping them on the bed, just out of Lincolns sight. He mutters the 3-card patter under his breath. His moves are still clumsy. Every once and a while he darts a look over at Lincoln who does his best to ignore Booth.

((((Watch me close watch me close now: who-see-thuh-red-card who-see-thuh-red-card? I-see-thuh-red-card. Thuh-red-card-is-thuh-winner. Pick-thuh-red-card-you-pick-uh-winner.

Pick-uh-black-card-and-you-pick-uh-loser. Theres-thuh-loser, yeah, theres-thuh-black-card, theres-thuh-other-loser-and-theres-thuh-red-card, thuh-winner! Cop C, Stick, Cop C! Go on—))))

LINCOLN: ((Shit.))

BOOTH: (((((((One-good-pickll-get-you-in, 2-good-picks-and-you-gone-win. Dont touch my cards, man, just point to thuh one you want. You-pick-that-card-you-pick-uh-loser, yeah, that-cards-uh-loser, You-pick-that-card-thats-thuh-other-loser. You-pick-that-card-you-pick-uh-winner. Follow-that-card. You-gotta-chase-that-card!)))))))

LINCOLN: You wanna hustle 3-card monte, you gotta do it right, you gotta break it down. Practice it in smaller bits. Yr trying to do the whole thing at once thats why you keep fucking it up.

BOOTH: Show me.

LINCOLN: No. Im just saying you wanna do it you gotta do it right and if you gonna do it right you gotta work on it in smaller bits, thatsall.

BOOTH: You and me could team up and do it together. We'd clean up, Link.

LINCOLN: I'll clean up—bro.

Lincoln cleans up. As he clears the food, Booth goes back to using the "table" for its original purpose.

BOOTH: My new names 3-Card. 3-Card, got it? You wanted to know it so now you know it. 3-card monte by 3-Card. Call me 3-Card from here on out.

LINCOLN: 3-Card. Shit.

BOOTH: Im getting everybody to call me 3-Card. Grace likes 3-Card better than Booth. She says 3-Cards got something to it. Anybody not calling me 3-Card gets a bullet.

LINCOLN: Yr too much, man.

BOOTH: Im making a point.

LINCOLN: Point made, 3-Card. Point made.

Lincoln picks up his guitar. Plays at it.

BOOTH: Oh, come on, man, we could make money you and me. Throwing down the cards. 3 Card and Link: look out! We could clean up you and me. You would throw the cards and I'd be yr Stickman. The one in the crowd who looks like just an innocent passerby, who looks like just another player, like just another customer, but who gots intimate connections with you, the Dealer, the one throwing the cards, the main man. I'd be the one who brings in the crowd, I'd be the one who makes them want to put they money down, you do yr moves and I do mines. You turn yr head and I turn the card—

LINCOLN: It aint as easy as all that. Theres—

BOOTH: We could be a team, man. Rake in the money! Sure thered be some cats out there with fast eyes, some brothers and sisters who would watch real close and pick the right card, and so thered be some days when we would lose money, but most of the days we would come out on top! Pockets bulging, plenty of cash! And the ladies would be thrilling! You could afford to get laid! Grace would be all over me again.

LINCOLN: I thought you said she was all over you.

BOOTH: She is she is. Im seeing her tomorrow but today we gotta solidify the shit twixt you and me. Big brother Link and little brother Booth—

LINCOLN: 3-Card.

BOOTH: Yeah. Scheming and dreaming. No one throws the cards like you, Link. And with yr moves and my magic, and we get Grace and a girl for you to round out the posse. We'd be golden, bro! Am I right?

LINCOLN

BOOTH

BOOTH: Am I right?

LINCOLN: I dont touch thuh cards, 3-Card. I dont touch thuh cards no more.

LINCOLN

BOOTH

LINCOLN

BOOTH

BOOTH: You know what Mom told me when she was packing to leave? You was at school motherfucker you was at school. You got up that morning and sat down in yr regular place and read the cereal box while Dad read the sports section and Mom brought you yr dick toast and then you got on the damn school bus cause you didnt have the sense to do nothing else you was so into yr own shit that you didnt have the sense to feel nothing else going on. I had the sense to go back cause I was feeling something going on man, I was feeling something changing. So I—

LINCOLN: Cut school that day like you did almost every day—

BOOTH: She was putting her stuff in bags. She had all them nice suitcases but she was putting her stuff in bags.

(Rest)

Packing up her shit. She told me to look out for you. I told her I was the little brother and the big brother should look out after the little brother. She just said it again. That I should look out for you. Yeah. So who gonna look out for me. Not like you care. Here I am interested in an economic opportunity, willing to work hard, willing to take risks and all you can say you shiteating motherfucking pathetic limpdick uncle tom, all you can tell me is how you dont do no more what I be wanting to do. Here I am trying to earn a living and you standing in my way. YOU STANDING IN MY WAY, LINK!

LINCOLN: Im sorry.

BOOTH: Yeah, you sorry all right.

LINCOLN: I cant be hustling no more, bro.

BOOTH: What you do all day aint no hustle?

LINCOLN: Its honest work.

BOOTH: Dressing up like some crackerass white man, some dead president and letting people shoot at you sounds like a hustle to me.

LINCOLN: People know the real deal. When people know the real deal it aint a hustle.

BOOTH: We do the card game people will know the real deal. Sometimes we will win sometimes they will win. They fast they win, we faster we win.

LINCOLN: I aint going back to that, bro. I aint going back.

BOOTH: You play Honest Abe. You aint going back but you going all the way back. Back to way back then when folks was slaves and shit.

LINCOLN: Dont push me.

BOOTH

LINCOLN

BOOTH: You gonna have to leave.

LINCOLN: I'll be gone tomorrow.

BOOTH: Good. Cause this was only supposed to be a temporary arrangement.

LINCOLN: I will be gone tomorrow.

BOOTH: Good.

Booth sits on his bed. Lincoln, sitting in his easy chair with his guitar, plays and sings.

LINCOLN:

My dear mother left me, my fathers gone away
My dear mother left me and my fathers gone away
I dont got no money, I dont got no place to stay.

My best girl, she threw me out into the street
My favorite horse, they ground him into meat
Im feeling cold from my head down to my feet.

My luck was bad but now it turned to worse
My luck was bad but now it turned to worse
Dont call me up a doctor, just call me up a hearse.

BOOTH: You just made that up?

LINCOLN: I had it in my head for a few days.

BOOTH: Sounds good.

LINCOLN: Thanks.

(Rest)

Daddy told me once why we got the names we do.

BOOTH: Yeah?

LINCOLN: Yeah.

(Rest)

He was drunk when he told me, or maybe I was drunk when he told me. Anyway he told me, may not be true, but he told me. Why he named us both. Lincoln and Booth.

BOOTH: How come. How come, man?

LINCOLN: It was his idea of a joke.

Both men relax back as the lights fade.

SCENE TWO

Friday evening. The very next day. Booth comes in looking like he is bundled up against the cold. He makes sure his brother isnt home, then stands in the middle of the room. From his big coat sleeves he pulls out one new shoe then another, from another sleeve come two more shoes. He then slithers out a belt from each sleeve. He removes his coat. Underneath he wears a very nice new suit. He removes the jacket and pants revealing another new suit underneath. The suits still have the price tags on them. He takes two neckties from his pockets and two folded shirts from the back of his pants. He pulls a magazine from the front of his pants. Hes clearly had a busy day of shoplifting. He lays one suit out on Lincolns easy chair. The other he lays out on his own bed. He goes out into the hall returning with a folding screen which he sets up between the bed and the recliner creating 2 separate spaces. He takes out a bottle of whiskey and two glasses, setting them on the two stacked milk crates. He hears footsteps and sits down in the small wooden chair reading the magazine. Lincoln, dressed in street clothes, comes in.

LINCOLN: Taaaaadaaaaaaaa!

BOOTH: Lordamighty, Pa, I smells money!

LINCOLN: Sho nuff, Ma. Poppas brung home thuh bacon.

BOOTH: Bringitherebringitherebringithere.

With a series of very elaborate moves Lincoln brings the money over to Booth.

BOOTH: Put it in my hands, Pa!

LINCOLN: I want ya tuh smells it first, Ma!

BOOTH: Put it neath my nose then, Pa!

LINCOLN: Take yrself a good long whiff of thcm greenbacks.

BOOTH: Oh lordamighty Ima faint, Pa! Get me muh med-sin!

Lincoln quickly pours two large glasses of whiskey.

LINCOLN: Dont die on me, Ma!

BOOTH: Im fading fast, Pa!

LINCOLN: Thinka thuh children, Ma! Thinka thuh farm!

BOOTH: 1-2-3.

Both men gulp down their drinks simultaneously.

LINCOLN AND BOOTH: ΛAAAAAAAAAAAAAAAAAAAAH!

Lots of laughing and slapping on the backs.

LINCOLN: Budget it out man budget it out.

BOOTH: You in a hurry?

LINCOLN: Yeah. I wanna see how much we got for the week.

BOOTH: You rush in here and dont even look around. Could be a fucking A-bomb in the middle of the floor you wouldnt notice. Yr wife, Cookie—

LINCOLN: X-wife—

BOOTH: —could be in my bed you wouldnt notice—

LINCOLN: She was once—

BOOTH: Look the fuck around please.

Lincoln looks around and sees the new suit on his chair.

LINCOLN: Wow.

BOOTH: Its yrs.

LINCOLN: Shit.

BOOTH: Got myself one too.

LINCOLN: Boosted?

BOOTH: Yeah, I boosted em. Theys stole from a big-ass department store. That store takes in more money in one day than we will in our whole life. I stole and I stole generously. I got one for me and I got one for you. Shoes belts shirts ties socks in the shoes and everything. Got that screen too.

LINCOLN: You all right, man.

BOOTH: Just cause I aint good as you at cards dont mean I cant do nothing.

LINCOLN: Lets try em on.

They stand in their separate sleeping spaces. Booth near his bed, Lincoln near his recliner, and try on their new clothes.

BOOTH: Ima wear mine tonight. Gracell see me in this and *she* gonna ask me tuh marry *her.*

(Rest)

I got you the blue and I got me the brown. I walked in there and walked out and they didnt as much as bat an eye. Thats how smooth lil bro be, Link.

LINCOLN: You did good. You did real good, 3-Card.

BOOTH: All in a days work.

LINCOLN: They say the clothes make the man. All day long I wear that getup. But that dont make me who I am. Old black coat not even real old just fake old. Its got worn spots on the elbows, little raggedy places thatll break through into holes before the winters out. Shiny strips around the cuffs and the collar. Dust from the cap guns on the left shoulder where they shoot him, where they shoot mc I should say but I never feel like they shooting me. The fella who had the gig before I had it wore the same coat. When I got the job they had the getup hanging there waiting for me. Said thuh fella before me just took it off onc day and never came hack.

(Rest)

Remember how Dads clothes used to hang in the closet?

BOOTH: Until you took em outside and burned em.

(Rest)

He had some nice stuff. What he didnt spend on booze he spent on women. What he didnt spend on them two he spent on clothes. He had some nice stuff I would look at his stuff and calculate thuh how long it would take till I was big enough to fit it. Then you went and burned it all up.

LINCOLN: I got tired of looking at em without him in em.

(Rest)

They said thuh fella before me—he took off the getup one day, hung it up real nice, and never came back. And as they offered me thuh job, saying of course I would have to wear a little makeup and accept less than what they would offer a—another guy—

BOOTH: Go on, say it. "White." Theyd pay you less than theyd pay a white guy.

LINCOLN: I said to myself thats exactly what I would do: wear it out and then leave it hanging there and not come back. But until then, I would make a living at it. But it dont make me. Worn suit coat, not even worn by the fool that Im supposed to be playing, but making fools out of all those folks who come crowding in for they chance to play at something great. Fake beard. Top hat. Dont make me into no Lincoln. I was Lincoln on my own before any of that.

The men finish dressing. They style and profile.

BOOTH: Sharp, huh?

LINCOLN: Very sharp.

BOOTH: You look sharp too, man. You look like the real you. Most of the time you walking around all bedraggled and shit. You look good. Like you used to look back in thuh day when you had Cookie in love with you and all the women in the world was eating out of yr hand.

LINCOLN: This is real nice, man. I dont know where Im gonna wear it but its real nice.

BOOTH: Just wear it around. Itll make you feel good and when you feel good yll meet someone nice. Me I aint interested in meeting no one nice, I mean, I only got eyes for Grace. You think she'll go for me in this?

LINCOLN: I think thuh tie you gave me'll go better with what you got on.

BOOTH: Yeah?

LINCOLN: Grace likes bright colors dont she? My ties bright, yrs is too subdued.

BOOTH: Yeah. Gimmie yr tie.

LINCOLN: You gonna take back a gift?

BOOTH: I stole the damn thing didnt I? Gimmie yrs! I'll give you mines.

They switch neckties. Booth is pleased. Lincoln is more pleased.

LINCOLN: Do thuh budget.

BOOTH: Right. Ok lets see: we got 314 dollars. We put 100 aside for the rent. 100 a week times 4 weeks makes the rent and—

LINCOLN AND BOOTH: —we dont want thuh rent spent.

BOOTH: That leaves 214. We put aside 30 for the electric leaving 184. We put aside 50 for thuh phone leaving 134.

LINCOLN: We dont got a phone.

BOOTH: We pay our bill theyll turn it back on.

LINCOLN: We dont need no phone.

BOOTH: How you gonna get a woman if you dont got a phone? Women these days are more cautious, more whaddacallit, more circumspect. You go into a club looking like a fast daddy, you get a filly to give you her numerophono and gone is the days when she just gives you her number and dont ask for yrs.

LINCOLN: Like a woman is gonna call me.

BOOTH: She dont wanna call you she just doing a preliminary survey of the property. Shit, Link, you dont know nothin no more.

(*Rest*)

She gives you her number and she asks for yrs. You give her yr number. The phone number of yr home. Thereby telling her 3 things: 1) you got a home, that is, you aint no smooth talking smooth dressing *homeless* joe; 2) that you is in possession of a telephone and a working telephone number which is to say that you got thuh cash and thuh wherewithal to acquire for yr self the worlds most revolutionary communication apparatus and you together enough to pay yr bills!

LINCOLN: Whats 3?

BOOTH: You give her yr number you telling her that its cool to call if she should so please, that is, that you aint got no wife or wife approximation on the premises.

(*Rest*)

50 for the phone leaving 134. We put aside 40 for "med-sin."

LINCOLN: The price went up. 2 bucks more a bottle.

BOOTH: We'll put aside 50, then. That covers the bills. We got 84 left. 40 for meals together during the week leaving 44. 30 for me 14 for you. I got a woman I gotta impress tonight.

LINCOLN: You didnt take out for the phone last week.

BOOTH: Last week I was depressed. This week things is looking up. For both of us.

LINCOLN: Theyre talking about cutbacks at the arcade. I only been there 8 months, so—

BOOTH: Dont sweat it man, we'll find something else.

LINCOLN: Not nothing like this. I like the job. This is sit down, you know, easy work. I just gotta sit there all day. Folks come in kill phony Honest Abe with the phony pistol. I can sit there and let my mind travel.

BOOTH: Think of women.

LINCOLN: Sometimes.

(*Rest*)

All around the whole arcade is buzzing and popping. Thuh whirring of thuh duckshoot, baseballs smacking the back wall when someone misses the stack of cans, some woman getting happy cause her fella just won the ring toss. The Boss playing the barker talking up the fake freaks. The smell of the ocean and cotton candy and rat shit. And in thuh middle of all that, I can just sit and let my head go quiet. Make up songs, make plans. Forget.

(*Rest*)

You should come down again.

BOOTH: Once was plenty, but thanks.

(*Rest*)

Yr Best Customer, he come in today?

LINCOLN: Oh, yeah, he was there.

BOOTH: He shoot you?

LINCOLN: He shot Honest Abe, yeah.

BOOTH: He talk to you?

LINCOLN: In a whisper. Shoots on the left whispers on the right.

BOOTH: Whatd he say this time?

LINCOLN: "Does thuh show stop when no ones watching or does thuh show go on?"

BOOTH: Hes getting deep.

LINCOLN: Yeah.

BOOTH: Whatd he say, that one time? " Yr only yrself—"

LINCOLN: "—when no ones watching," yeah.

BOOTH: Thats deep shit.

(*Rest*)

Hes a brother, right?

LINCOLN: I think so.

BOOTH: He know yr a brother?

LINCOLN: I dunno. Yesterday he had a good one. He shoots me, Im playing dead, and he leans in close then goes: "God aint nothing but a parasite."

BOOTH: Hes one *deep* black brother.

LINCOLN: Yeah. He makes the day interesting.

BOOTH (*Rest*): Thats a fucked-up job you got.

LINCOLN: Its a living.

BOOTH: But you aint living.

LINCOLN: Im alive aint I?

(*Rest*)

One day I was throwing the cards. Next day Lonny died. Somebody shot him. I knew I was next, so I quit. I saved my life.

(*Rest*)

The arcade gig is the first lucky break Ive ever had. And Ive actually grown to like the work. And now theyre talking about cutting me.

BOOTH: You was lucky with thuh cards.

LINCOLN: Lucky? Aint nothing lucky about cards. Cards aint luck. Cards is work. Cards is skill. Aint never nothing lucky about cards.

(*Rest*)

I dont wanna lose my job.

BOOTH: Then you gotta jazz up yr act. Elaborate yr moves, you know. You was always too stiff with it. You cant just sit there! Maybe, when they shoot you, you know, leap up flail yr arms then fall down and wiggle around and shit so they gotta shoot you more than once. Blam Blam Blam! Blam!

LINCOLN: Help me practice. I'll sit here like I do at work and you be like one of the tourists.

BOOTH: No thanks.

LINCOLN: My paychecks on the line, man.

BOOTH: I got a date. Practice on yr own.

(*Rest*)

I got a rendezvous with Grace. Shit she so sweet she makes my teeth hurt.

(*Rest*)

Link, uh, howbout slipping me an extra 5 spot. Its the biggest night of my life.

LINCOLN

BOOTH

Lincoln gives Booth a 5er.

BOOTH: Thanks.

LINCOLN: No sweat.

BOOTH: Howabout I run through it with you when I get back. Put on yr getup and practice till then.

LINCOLN: Sure.

Booth leaves. Lincoln stands there alone. He takes off his shoes, giving them a shine. He takes off his socks and his fancy suit, hanging it neatly over the little wooden chair. He takes his getup out of his shopping bag. He puts it on, slowly, like an actor preparing for a great role: frock coat, pants, beard, top hat, necktie. He leaves his feet bare. The top hat has an elastic band which he positions securely underneath his chin. He picks up the white pancake makeup but decides against it. He sits. He pretends to get shot, flings himself on the floor and thrashes around. He gets up, considers giving the new moves another try, but instead pours himself a big glass of whiskey and sits there drinking.

SCENE THREE

Much later that same Friday evening. The recliner is reclined to its maximum horizontal position and Lincoln lies there asleep. He wakes with a start. He is horrific, bleary eyed and hungover, in his full Lincoln regalia. He takes a deep breath, realizes where he is and reclines again, going back to sleep. Booth comes in full of swagger. He slams the door trying to wake his brother who is dead to the world. He opens the door and slams it again. This time Lincoln wakes up, as hungover and horrid as before. Booth swaggers about, his moves are exaggerated, rooster-like. He walks round and round Lincoln making sure his brother sees him.

LINCOLN: You hurt yrself?

BOOTH: I had me "an evening to remember."

LINCOLN: You look like you hurt yrself.

BOOTH: Grace Grace Grace. *Grace.* She wants me back. She wants me back so bad she wiped her hand over the past where we wasnt together just so she could say we aint never been apart. She wiped her hand over our breakup. She wiped her hand over her childhood, her teenage years, her first boyfriend, just so she could say that she been mine since the dawn of time.

LINCOLN: Thats great, man.

BOOTH: And all the shit I put her through: she wiped it clean. And the women I saw while I was seeing her—

LINCOLN: Wiped clean too?

BOOTH: Mister Clean, Mister, Mister Clean!

LINCOLN: Whered you take her?

BOOTH: We was over at her place. I brought thuh food, Stopped at the best place I could find and stuffed my coat with only the best. We had candlelight, we had music we had—

LINCOLN: She let you do it?

BOOTH: Course she let me do it.

LINCOLN: She let you do it without a rubber?

BOOTH: —Yeah.

LINCOLN: Bullshit.

BOOTH: I put my foot down—and she *melted*. And she was—huh—she was something else. I dont wanna get you jealous, though.

LINCOLN: Go head, I dont mind.

BOOTH (*Rest*): Well, you know what she looks like.

LINCOLN: She walks on by and the emergency room fills up cause all the guys get whiplash from lookin at her.

BOOTH: Thats right thats right. Well—she comes to the door wearing nothing but her little nightie, eats up the food I'd brought like there was no tomorrow and then goes and eats on me.

(*Rest*)

LINCOLN: Go on.

BOOTH: I dont wanna make you feel bad, man.

LINCOLN: Ssallright. Go on.

BOOTH (*Rest*): Well, uh, you know what shes like. Wild. Goodlooking. So sweet my teeth hurt.

LINCOLN: Sexmachine.

BOOTH: Yeah.

LINCOLN: Hotsy-Totsy.

BOOTH: Yeah.

LINCOLN: Amazing Grace.

BOOTH: Amazing Grace! Yeah. Thats right. She let me do her how I wanted. And no rubber.

(*Rest*)

LINCOLN: Go on.

BOOTH: You dont wanna hear the mushy shit.

LINCOLN: Sure I do.

BOOTH: You hate mushy shit. You always hated thuh mushy shit.

LINCOLN: Ive changed. Go head. You had "an evening to remember," remember? I was just here alone sitting here. Drinking. Go head. Tell Link thuh stink.

(*Rest*)

Howd ya do her?

BOOTH: Dogstyle.

LINCOLN: Amazing Grace.

BOOTH: In front of a mirror.

LINCOLN: So you could see her. Her face her breasts her back her ass. Graces got a great ass.

BOOTH: Its all right.

LINCOLN: Amazing Grace!

Booth goes into his bed area and takes off his suit, tossing the clothes on the floor.

BOOTH: She said next time Ima have to use a rubber. She let me have my way this time but she said that next time I'd have to put my boots on.

LINCOLN: Im sure you can talk her out of it.

BOOTH: Yeah.

(*Rest*)

What kind of rubbers you use, I mean, when you was with Cookie.

LINCOLN: We didnt use rubbers. We was married, man.

BOOTH: Right. But you had other women on the side. What kind you use when you was with them?

LINCOLN: Magnums.

BOOTH: Thats thuh kind I picked up. For next time. Grace was real strict about it.

While Booth sits on his bed fiddling with his box of condoms, Lincoln sits in his chair and resumes drinking.

LINCOLN: Im sure you can talk her out of it. You put yr foot down and she'll melt.

BOOTH: She was real strict. Sides I wouldnt wanna be taking advantage of her or nothing. Putting my foot down and her melting all over thuh place.

LINCOLN: Magnums then.

(*Rest*)

Theyre for "the larger man."

BOOTH: Right. Right.

Lincoln keeps drinking as Booth, sitting in the privacy of his bedroom, fiddles with the condoms, perhaps trying to put one on.

LINCOLN: Thats right.

BOOTH: Graces real different from them fly-by-night gals I was making do with. Shes in school. Making something of herself. Studying cosmetology. You should see what she can do with a womans hair and nails.

LINCOLN: Too bad you aint a woman.

BOOTH: What?

LINCOLN: You could get yrs done for free, I mean.

BOOTH: Yeah. She got this way of sitting. Of talking. Everything she does is. Shes just so hot.

(*Rest*)

We was together 2 years. Then we broke up. I had my little employment difficulty and she needed time to think.

LINCOLN: And shes through thinking now.

BOOTH: Thats right.

LINCOLN

BOOTH

LINCOLN: Whatcha doing back there?

BOOTH: Resting. That girl wore me out.

LINCOLN: You want some med-sin?

BOOTH: No thanks.

LINCOLN: Come practice my moves with me, then.

BOOTH: Lets hit it tomorrow, K?

LINCOLN: I been waiting. I got all dressed up and you said if I waited up—come on, man, they gonna replace me with a wax dummy.

BOOTH: No shit.

LINCOLN: Thats what theyre talking about. Probably just talk, but—come on, man, I even lent you 5 bucks.

BOOTH: Im tired.

LINCOLN: You didnt get shit tonight.

BOOTH: You jealous, man. You just jail-us.

LINCOLN: You laying over there yr balls blue as my boosted suit. Laying over there waiting for me to go back to sleep or black out so I wont hear you rustling thuh pages of yr fuck book.

BOOTH: Fuck you, man.

LINCOLN: I was over there looking for something the other week and theres like 100 fuck books under yr bed and theyre matted together like a bad fro, bro, cause you spunked in the pages and didnt wipe them off.

BOOTH: Im hot. I need constant sexual release. If I wasnt taking care of myself by myself I would be out there running around on thuh town which costs cash that I dont have so I would be doing worse: I'd be out there doing who knows what, shooting people and shit. Out of a need for unresolved sexual release. I'm a hot man. I aint apologizing for it. When I dont got a woman, I gotta make do. Not like you, Link. When you dont got a woman you just sit there. Letting yr shit fester. Yr dick, if it aint failed off yet, is hanging there between yr legs, little whiteface shriveled-up blank-shooting grub worm. As goes thuh man so goes thuh mans dick. Thats what I say. Least my shits intact.

(*Rest*)

You a limp dick jealous whiteface motherfucker whose wife dumped him cause he couldnt get it up and she told me so. Came crawling to me cause she needed a man.

(*Rest*)

I gave it to Grace good tonight. So goodnight.

LINCOLN (*Rest*): Goodnight.

LINCOLN

BOOTH

LINCOLN

BOOTH

LINCOLN

BOOTH

Lincoln sitting in his chair. Booth lying in bed. Time passes. Booth pecks out to see if Lincoln is asleep. Lincoln is watching for him.

LINCOLN: You can hustle 3-card monte without me you know.

BOOTH: Im planning to.

LINCOLN: I could contact my old crew. You could work with them. Lonny aint around no more but theres the rest of them. Theyre good.

BOOTH: I can get my own crew. I dont need yr crew. Buncha has-beens. I can get my own crew.

LINCOLN: My crews experienced. We usedta pull down a thousand a day. Thats 7 G a week. That was years ago. They probably do twice, 3 times that now.

BOOTH: I got my own connections, thank you.

LINCOLN: Theyd take you on in a heartbeat. With my say. My say still counts with them. They know you from before, when you tried to hang with us but—wernt ready yet. They know you from then, but I'd talk you up. I'd say yr my bro, which they know, and I'd say youd been working the west coast. Little towns. Mexican border. Taking tourists. I'd tell them you got moves like I dreamed of having. Meanwhile youd be working out yr shit right here, right in this room, getting good and getting better every day so when I did do the reintroductions youd have some marketable skills. Youd be passable.

BOOTH: I'd be more than passable, I'd be the be all end all.

LINCOLN: Youd be the be all end all. And youd have my say. If yr interested.

BOOTH: Could do.

LINCOLN: Youd have to get a piece. They all pack pistols, bro.

BOOTH: I *got* a piece.

LINCOLN: Youd have to be packing something more substantial than that pop gun, 3-Card. These hustlers is upper echelon hustlers they pack upper echelon heat, not no Saturday night shit, now.

BOOTH: Whata you know of heat? You aint hung with those guys for 6, 7 years. You swore off em. Threw yr heat in thuh river and you "Dont touch thuh cards." I know more about heat than you know about heat.

LINCOLN: Im around guns every day. At the arcade. Theyve all been reworked so they only fire caps but I see guns every day. Lots of guns.

BOOTH: What kinds?

LINCOLN: You been there, you seen them. Shiny deadly metal each with their own deadly personality.

BOOTH: Maybe I *could* visit you over there. I'd boost one of them guns and rework it to make it shoot for real again. What kind you think would best suit my personality?

LINCOLN: You aint stealing nothing from the arcade.

BOOTH: I go in there and steal if I want to go in there and steal I go in there and steal.

LINCOLN: It aint worth it. They dont shoot nothing but blanks.

BOOTH: Yeah, like you. Shooting blanks.

(*Rest*)

(*Rest*)

You ever wonder if someones gonna come in there with a real gun? A real gun with real slugs? Someone with uh axe tuh grind or something?

LINCOLN: No.

BOOTH: Someone who hates you come in there and guns you down and gets gone before anybody finds out.

LINCOLN: I dont got no enemies.

BOOTH: Yr X.

LINCOLN: Cookie dont hate me.

BOOTH: Yr Best Customer? Some miscellaneous stranger?

LINCOLN: I cant be worrying about the actions of miscellaneous strangers.

BOOTH: But there they come day in day out for a chance to shoot Honest Abe.

(Rest)

Who are they mostly?

LINCOLN: I dont really look.

BOOTH: You must see something.

LINCOLN: Im supposed to be staring straight ahead. Watching a play, like Abe was.

BOOTH: All day goes by and you never ever take a sneak peek at who be pulling the trigger.

Pulled in by his own curiosity, Booth has come out of his bed area to stand on the dividing line between the two spaces.

LINCOLN: Its pretty dark. To keep thuh illusion of thuh whole thing.

(Rest)

But on thuh wall opposite where I sit theres a little electrical box, like a fuse box. Silver metal. Its got uh dent in it like somebody hit it with they fist. Big old dent so everything reflected in it gets reflected upside down. Like yr looking in uh spoon. And thats where I can see em. The assassins.

(Rest)

Not behind me yet but I can hear him coming. Coming in with his gun in hand, thuh gun he already picked out up front when he paid his fare. Coming on in. But not behind me yet. His dress shoes making too much noise on the carpet, the carpets too thin, Boss should get a new one but hes cheap. Not behind me yet. Not behind me yet. Cheap lightbulb just above my head.

(Rest)

And there he is. Standing behind me. Standing in position. Standing upside down. Theres some feet shapes on the floor so he knows just where he oughta stand. So he wont miss. Thuh gun is always cold. Winter or summer thuh gun is always cold. And when the gun touches me he can feel that Im warm and he knows Im alive. And if Im alive then he can shoot me dead. And for a minute, with him hanging back there behind me, its real. Me looking at him upside down and him looking at me looking like Lincoln. Then he shoots.

(Rest)

I slump down and close my eyes. And he goes out thuh other way. More come in. Uh whole day full. Bunches of kids, little good for nothings, in they

school uniforms. Businessmen smelling like two for one martinis. Tourists in they theme park t-shirts trying to catch it on film. Housewives with they mouths closed tight, shooting more than once.

(Rest)

They all get so into it. I do my best for them. And now they talking bout replacing me with uh wax dummy. Itll cut costs.

BOOTH: You just gotta show yr boss that you can do things a wax dummy cant do. You too dry with it. You gotta add spicy shit.

LINCOLN: Like what.

BOOTH: Like when they shoot you, I dunno, scream or something.

LINCOLN: Scream?

Booth plays the killer without using his gun.

BOOTH: Try it. I'll be the killer. Bang!

LINCOLN: Aaaah!

BOOTH: Thats good.

LINCOLN: A wax dummy can scream. They can put a voicebox in it and make it like its screaming.

BOOTH: You can curse. Try it. Bang!

LINCOLN: Motherfucking cocksucker!

BOOTH: Thats good, man.

LINCOLN: They aint going for that, though.

BOOTH: You practice rolling and wiggling on the floor?

LINCOLN: A little.

BOOTH: Lemmie see. Bang!

Lincoln slumps down, falls on the floor and silently wiggles around.

BOOTH: You look more like a worm on the sidewalk. Move yr arms. Good. Now scream or something.

LINCOLN: Aaaah! Aaaaah! Aaaah!

BOOTH: A little tougher than that, you sound like yr fucking.

LINCOLN: Aaaaaah!

BOOTH: Hold yr head or something, where I shotcha. Good. And look at me! I am the assassin! *I am Booth!!* Come on man this is life and death! Go all out!

Lincoln goes all out.

BOOTH: Cool, man thats cool. Thats enough.

LINCOLN: Whatdoyathink?

BOOTH: I dunno, man. Something about it. I dunno. It was looking too real or something.

LINCOLN: They dont want it looking too real. I'd scare the customers. Then I'd be out for sure. Yr trying to get me fired.

BOOTH: Im trying to help. Cross my heart.

LINCOLN: People are funny about they Lincoln shit. Its historical. People like they historical shit in a certain way. They like it to unfold the way they folded it up. Neatly like a book. Not raggedy and bloody and screaming. You trying to get me fired.

(Rest)

I am uh brother playing Lincoln. Its uh screech for anyones imagination. And it aint easy for me neither. Every day I put on that shit, I leave my own shit at the door and I put on that shit and I go out there and I make it work. I make it look easy but its hard. That shit is hard. But it works. Cause I work it. And you trying to get me fired.

(Rest)

I swore off them cards. Took nowhere jobs. Drank. Then Cookie threw me out. What thuh fuck was I gonna do? I seen that "Help Wanted" sign and I went up in there and I looked good in the getup and agreed to the whiteface and they really dug it that me and Honest Abe got the same name.

(Rest)

Its a sit down job. With benefits. I dont wanna get fired. They wont give me a good reference if I get fired.

BOOTH: Iffen you was tuh get fired, then, well—then you and me could—hustle the cards together. We'd have to support ourselves somehow.

(Rest)

Just show me how to do the hook part of the card hustle, man. The part where the Dealer looks away but somehow he sees—

LINCOLN: I couldnt remember if I wanted to.

BOOTH: Sure you could.

LINCOLN: No.

(Rest)

Night, man.

BOOTH: Yeah.

Lincoln stretches out in his recliner. Booth stands over him waiting for him to get up, to change his mind. But Lincoln is fast asleep. Booth covers him with a blanket then goes to his bed, turning off the lights as he goes. He quietly rummages underneath his bed for a girlie magazine which, as the lights fade, he reads with great interest.

SCENE FOUR

Saturday. Just before dawn. Lincoln gets up. Looks around. Booth is fast asleep, dead to the world.

LINCOLN: No fucking running water.

He stumbles around the room looking for something which he finally finds: a plastic cup, which he uses as a urinal. He finishes peeing and finds an out of the way place to stow the cup. He claws at his Lincoln getup, removing it and tearing it in the process. He strips down to his t-shirt and shorts.

LINCOLN: Hate falling asleep in this damn shit. Shit. Ripped the beard. I can just hear em tomorrow.

Busiest day of the week. They looking me over to make sure Im presentable. They got a slew of guys working but Im the only one they look over every day. "Yr beards ripped, pal. Sure, we'll getcha new one but its gonna be coming outa yr pay." Shit. I should quit right then and there. I'd yank off the beard, throw it on the ground and stomp it, then go strangle the fucking boss. Thatd be good. My hands around his neck and his bug eyes bugging out. You been ripping me off since I took this job and now Im gonna have to take it outa *yr* pay, motherfucker. Shit.

(Rest)

Sit down job. With benefits.

(Rest)

Hustling. Shit, I was good. I was great. Hell I was the be all end all. I was throwing cards like throwing cards was made for me. Made for me and me alone. I was the best anyone ever seen. Coast to coast. Everybody said so. And I never lost. Not once. Not one time. Not never. Thats how much them cards was mines. I was the be all end all. I was that good.

(Rest)

Then you woke up one day and you didnt have the taste for it no more. Like something in you knew—. Like something in you knew it was time to quit. Quit while you was still ahead. Something in you was telling you—. But hells no. Not Link thuh stink. So I went out there and threw one more time. What thuh fuck. And Lonny died.

(Rest)

Got yrself a good job. And when the arcade lets you go yll get another good job. I dont gotta spend my whole life hustling. Theres more to Link than that. More to me than some cheap hustle. More to life than cheating some idiot out of his paycheck or his life savings.

(Rest)

Like that joker and his wife from out of town. Always wanted to see the big city. I said you could see the bigger end of the big city with a little more cash. And if they was fast enough, faster than me, and here I slowed down my moves I slowed em way down and my Lonny, my right hand, my Stickman, Spanish guy who looked white and could draw a customer in like nothing else, Lonny could draw a fly from fresh shit, he could draw Adam outa Eve just with that look he had, Lonny always got folks playing.

(Rest)

Somebody shot him. They dont know who. Nobody knows nobody cares.

(Rest)

We took that man and his wife for hundreds. No, thousands. We took them for everything they had and everything they ever wanted to have. We took a father for the money he was gonna get his kids new bike with and he cried in the street while we vanished. We took a mothers welfare check, she pulled a knife on us and we ran. She threw it but her aim werent shit. People shopping. Greedy. Thinking they could take me and they got took instead.

(*Rest*)

Swore off thuh cards. Something inside me telling me—. But I was good.

LINCOLN

LINCOLN

He sees a packet of cards. He studies them like an alcoholic would study a drink. Then he reaches for them, delicately picking them up and choosing 3 cards.

LINCOLN: Still got my moves. Still got my touch. Still got my chops. Thuh feel of it. And I aint hurting no one, God. Link is just here hustling hisself.

(*Rest*)

Lets see whatcha got.

He stands over the monte setup. Then he bends over it placing the cards down and moving them around. Slowly at first, aimlessly, as if hes just making little ripples in water. But then the game draws him in. Unlike Booth, Lincolns patter and moves are deft, dangerous, electric.

LINCOLN: (((Lean in close and watch me now: who see thuh black card who see thuh black card I see thuh black card black cards thuh winner pick thuh black card thats thuh winner pick thuh red card thats thuh loser pick thuh other red card thats thuh other loser pick thuh black card you pick thuh winner. Watch me as I throw thuh cards. Here we go.)))

(*Rest*)

(((Who see thuh black card who see thuh black card? You pick thuh red card you pick a loser you pick that red card you pick a loser you pick thuh black card thuh deuce of spades you pick a winner who sees thuh deuce of spades thuh one who sees it never fades watch me now as I throw thuh cards. Red losers black winner follow thuh deuce of spades chase thuh black deuce. Dark deuce will get you thuh win.)))

Even though Lincoln speaks softly, Booth wakes and, unbeknownst to Lincoln, listens intently.

(*Rest*)

LINCOLN: ((10 will get you 20, 20 will get you 40.))

(*Rest*)

((Ima show you thuh cards: 2 red cards but only one spade. Dark winner in thuh center and thuh red losers on thuh sides. Pick uh red card you got a loser

pick thuh other red card you got a loser pick thuh black card you got a winner. One good pickll get you in, 2 good picks and you gone win. Watch me come on watch me now.))

(*Rest*)

((Who sees thuh winner who knows where its at? You do? You sure? Go on then, put yr money where yr mouth is. Put yr money down you aint no clown. No? Ah, you had thuh card but you didnt have thuh heart.))

(*Rest*)

((Watch me now as I throw thuh cards watch me real close. Ok, man, you know which card is the deuce of spades? Was you watching Links lightning fast express? Was you watching Link cause he the best? So you sure, huh? Point it out first, then place yr bet and Linkll show you yr winner.))

(*Rest*)

((500 dollars? You thuh man of thuh hour you thuh man with thuh power. You musta been watching Link real close. You must be thuh man who know thuh most. Ok. Lay the cash in my hand cause Link the man. Thank you, mister. This card you say?))

(*Rest*)

((Wrong! Ha!))

(*Rest*)

((Thats thuh show. We gotta go.))

Lincoln puts the cards down. He moves away from the monte setup. He sits on the edge of his easy chair, but he can't take his eyes off the cards.

Intermission

SCENE FIVE

Several days have passed. Its now Wednesday night. Booth is sitting in his brand-new suit. The monte setup is nowhere in sight. In its place is a table with two nice chairs. The table is covered with a lovely tablecloth and there are nice plates, silverware, champagne glasses and candles. All the makings of a very romantic dinner for two. The whole apartment in fact takes its cue from the table. Its been cleaned up considerably. New curtains on the windows, a doily-like object on the recliner. Booth sits at the table darting his eyes around, making sure everything is looking good.

BOOTH: Shit.

He notices some of his girlie magazines visible from underneath his bed. He goes over and nudges them out of sight. He sits back down. He notices that theyre still visible. He goes over and nudges them some more, kicking at them finally. Then he takes the spread from his bed and pulls it down, hiding them. He sits back

Jeffrey Wright and Mos Def in the 2002 production at the Ambassador Theater.

down. He gets up. Checks the champagne on much melted ice. Checks the food.

BOOTH: Foods getting cold, Grace!! Dont worry man, she'll get here, she'll get here.

He sits back down. He goes over to the bed. Checks it for springiness. Smoothes down the bedspread. Double-checks 2 matching silk dressing gowns, very expensive, marked "His" and "Hers." Lays the dressing gowns across the bed again. He sits back down. He cant help but notice the visibility of the girlie magazines again. He goes to the bed, kicks them fiercely, then on his hands and knees shoves them. Then he begins to get under the bed to push them, but he remembers his nice cloth-ing and takes off his jacket. After a beat he removes his pants and, in this half-dressed way, he crawls under the bed to give those telltale magazines a good and final shove. Lincoln comes in. At first Booth, still stripped down to his underwear, thinks its his date. When he realizes its his brother, he does his best to keep Lincoln from entering the apartment. Lincoln wears his frock coat and carries the rest of his getup in a plastic bag.

LINCOLN: You in the middle of it?

BOOTH: What the hell you doing here?

LINCOLN: If yr in thuh middle of it I can go. Or I can just be real quiet and just—sing a song in my head or something.

BOOTH: The casas off limits to you tonight.

LINCOLN: You know when we lived in that 2-room place with the cement backyard and the frontyard with nothing but trash in it, Mom and Pops would do it in the middle of the night and I would always hear them but I would sing in my head, cause, I dunno, I couldnt bear to listen.

BOOTH: You gotta get out of here.

LINCOLN: I would make up all kinds of songs. Oh, sorry, yr all up in it. No sweat, bro. No sweat. Hey, Grace, howyadoing?!

BOOTH: She aint here yet, man. Shes running late. And its a good thing too cause I aint all dressed yet. Yr gonna spend thuh night with friends?

LINCOLN: Yeah.

Booth waits for Lincoln to leave. Lincoln stands his ground.

LINCOLN: I lost my job.

BOOTH: Hunh.

LINCOLN: I come in there right on time like I do every day and that motherfucker gives me some song and dance about cutbacks and too many folks complaining.

BOOTH: Hunh.

LINCOLN: Showd me thuh wax dummy—hes buying it right out of a catalog.

(*Rest*)

I walked out still wearing my getup.

(*Rest*)

I could go back in tomorrow. I could tell him I'll take another pay cut. Thatll get him to take me back.

BOOTH: Link. Yr free. Dont go crawling back. Yr free at last! Now you can do anything you want. Yr not tied down by that job. You can—you can do something else. Something that pays better maybe.

LINCOLN: You mean Hustle.

BOOTH: Maybe. Hey, Graces on her way. You gotta go.

Lincoln flops into his chair. Booth is waiting for him to move. Lincoln doesnt budge.

LINCOLN: I'll stay until she gets here. I'll act nice. I wont embarrass you.

BOOTH: You gotta go.

LINCOLN: What time she coming?

BOOTH: Shes late. She could be here any second.

LINCOLN: I'll meet her. I met her years ago. I'll meet her again.

(*Rest*)

How late is she?

BOOTH: She was supposed to be here at 8.

LINCOLN: Its after 2 a.m. Shes—shes late.

(*Rest*)

Maybe when she comes you could put the blanket over me and I'll just pretend like Im not here.

(*Rest*)

I'll wait. And when she comes I'll go. I need to sit down. I been walking around all day.

BOOTH

LINCOLN

Booth goes to his bed and dresses hurriedly.

BOOTH: Pretty nice, right? The china thuh silver thuh crystal.

LINCOLN: Its great.

(*Rest*)

Boosted?

BOOTH: Yeah.

LINCOLN: Thought you went and spent yr inheritance for a minute, you had me going I was thinking shit, Booth—3-Card—that 3-Cards gone and spent his inheritance and the gal is—late.

BOOTH: Its boosted. Every bit of it.

(*Rest*)

Fuck this waiting bullshit.

LINCOLN: She'll be here in a minute. Dont sweat it.

BOOTH: Right.

Booth comes to the table. Sits. Relaxes as best he can.

BOOTH: How come I got a hand for boosting and I dont got a hand for throwing cards? Its sorta the same thing—you gotta be quick—and slick. Maybe yll show me yr moves sometime.

LINCOLN
BOOTH
LINCOLN
BOOTH

LINCOLN: Look out the window. When you see Grace coming, I'll go.

BOOTH: Cool. Cause youd jinx it, youd really jinx it. Maybe you being here has jinxed it already. Naw. Shes just a little late. You aint jinxed nothing.

Booth sits by the window, glancing out, watching for his date. Lincoln sits in his recliner. He finds the whiskey bottle, sips from it. He then rummages around, finding the raggedy photo album. He looks through it.

LINCOLN: There we are at that house. Remember when we moved in?

BOOTH: No.

LINCOLN: You were 2 or 3.

BOOTH: I was 5.

LINCOLN: I was 8. We all thought it was the best fucking house in the world.

BOOTH: Cement backyard and a frontyard full of trash, yeah, dont be going down memory lane man, yll jinx thuh vibe I got going in here. Gracell be walking in here and wrinkling up her nose cause you done jinxed up thuh joint with yr raggedy recollections.

LINCOLN: We had some great times in that house, bro. Selling lemonade on thuh corner, thuh treehouse out back, summers spent lying in thuh grass and looking at thuh stars.

BOOTH: We never did none of that shit.

LINCOLN: But we had us some good times. That row of nails I got you to line up behind Dads car so when he backed out the driveway to work—

BOOTH: He came back that night, only time I ever seen his face go red, 4 flat tires and yelling bout how thuh white man done sabotaged him again.

LINCOLN: And neither of us flinched. Neither of us let on that itd been us.

BOOTH: It was at dinner, right? What were we eating?

LINCOLN: Food.

BOOTH: We was eating pork chops, mashed potatoes and peas. I remember cause I had to look at them peas real hard to keep from letting on. And I would glance over at you, not really glancing not actually turning my head, but I was looking at you out thuh corner of my eye. I was sure he was gonna find us out and then he woulda whipped us good. But I kept glancing at yon and you was cool, man. Like nothing was going on. You was coooooool.

(*Rest*)

What time is it?

LINCOLN: After 3.

(*Rest*)

You should call her. Something mighta happened.

BOOTH: No man, Im cool. She'll be here in a minute. Patience is a virtue. She'll be here.

LINCOLN: You look sad.

BOOTH: Nope. Im just, you know, Im just—

LINCOLN: Cool.

BOOTH: Yeah. Cool.

Booth comes over, takes the bottle of whiskey and pours himself a big glassful. He returns to the window looking out and drinking.

BOOTH: They give you a severance package, at thuh job?

LINCOLN: A weeks pay.

BOOTH: Great.

LINCOLN: I blew it. Spent it all.

BOOTH: On what?

LINCOLN: —. Just spent it.

(*Rest*)

It felt good, spending it. Felt really good. Like back in thuh day when I was really making money. Throwing thuh cards all day and strutting and rutting all night. Didnt have to take no shit from no fool, didnt have to worry about getting fired in favor of some damn wax dummy. I was thuh shit and they was my fools.

(*Rest*)

Back in thuh day.

(*Rest*)

(*Rest*)

Why you think they left us, man?

BOOTH: Mom and Pops? I dont think about it too much.

LINCOLN: I dont think they liked us.

BOOTH: Naw. That aint it.

LINCOLN: I think there was something out there that they liked more than they liked us and for years they was struggling against moving towards that more liked something. Each of them had a special something that they was struggling against. Moms had hers. Pops had his. And they was struggling. We moved out of that nasty apartment into a house. A whole house. It wernt perfect but it was a house and theyd bought it and they brought us there and everything we owned, figuring we could be a family in that house and them things, them two separate things each of them was struggling against, would just leave them be. Them things would see thuh house and be impressed and just leave them be. Would see thuh job Pops had and how he shined his shoes every night before he went to bed, shining them shoes whether they needed it or not, and thuh thing he was struggling against would see all that and just let him be, and thuh thing Moms was struggling against, it would see the food on the table every night and listen to her voice when she'd read to us sometimes, the clean clothes, the buttons sewed on all right and it would just let her be. Just let us all be, just regular people living in a house. That wernt too much to ask.

BOOTH: Least we was grown when they split.

LINCOLN: 16 and 13 aint grown.

BOOTH: 16s grown. Almost. And I was ok cause you were there.

(*Rest*)

Shit man, it aint like they both one day both together packed all they shit up and left us so they could have fun in thuh sun on some tropical island and you and me would have to grub in thuh dirt forever. They didnt leave together. That makes it different. She left. 2 years go by. Then he left. Like neither of them couldnt handle it no more. She split then he split. Like thuh whole family mortgage bills going to work thing was just too much. And I dont blame them. You dont see me holding down a steady job. Cause its bullshit and I know it. I seen how it cracked them up and I aint going there.

(*Rest*)

It aint right me trying to make myself into a one woman man just because she wants me like that. One woman rubber-wearing motherfucker. Shit. Not me. She gonna walk in here looking all hot and shit trying to see how much she can get me to sweat, how much she can get me to give her before she gives me mines. Shit.

LINCOLN

BOOTH

LINCOLN: Moms told me I shouldnt never get married.

BOOTH: She told me thuh same thing.

LINCOLN: They gave us each 500 bucks then they cut out.

BOOTH: Thats what Im gonna do. Give my kids 500 bucks then cut out. Thats thuh way to do it.

LINCOLN: You dont got no kids.

BOOTH: Im gonna have kids then Im gonna cut out.

LINCOLN: Leaving each of yr offspring 500 bucks as yr splitting.

BOOTH: Yeah.

(*Rest*)

Just goes to show Mom and Pops had some agreement between them.

LINCOLN: How so.

BOOTH: Theyd stopped talking to eachother. Theyd stopped *screwing* eachother. But they had an agreement. Somewhere in there when it looked like all they had was hate they sat down and did thuh "split" budget.

(*Rest*)

When Moms splits she gives me 5 hundred-dollar bills rolled up and tied up tight in one of her nylon stockings. She tells me to put it in a safe place, to spend it only in case of an emergency, and not to tell nobody I got it, not even you. 2 years later Pops splits and before he goes —

LINCOLN: He slips me 10 fifties in a clean handkerchief: "Hide this somewheres good, dont go blowing it, dont tell no one you got it, especially that Booth."

BOOTH: Theyd been scheming together all along. They left separately but they was in agreement. Maybe they arrived at the same place at the same time, maybe they renewed they wedding vows, maybe they got another family.

LINCOLN: Maybe they got 2 new kids. 2 boys. Different than us, though. Better.

BOOTH: Maybe.

Their glasses are empty. The whiskey bottle is empty too. Booth takes the champagne bottle front the ice tub. He pops the cork and pours drinks for his brother and himself.

BOOTH: I didnt mind them leaving cause you was there. Thats why Im hooked on us working together. If we could work together it would be like old times. They split and we got that room downtown. You was done with school and I stopped going. And we had to run around doing odd jobs just to keep the lights on and the heat going and thuh child protection bitch off our backs. It was you and me against thuh world, Link. It could be like that again.

LINCOLN

BOOTH

LINCOLN

BOOTH

LINCOLN: Throwing thuh cards aint as easy as it looks.

BOOTH: I aint stupid.

LINCOLN: When you hung with us back then, you was just on thuh sidelines. Thuh perspective from thuh sidelines is thuh perspective of a customer. There was all kinds of things you didnt know nothing about.

BOOTH: Lonny would entice folks into thuh game as they walked by. Thuh 2 folks on either side of ya looked like they was playing but they was only pretending tuh play. Just tuh generate excitement. You was moving thuh cards as fast as you could hoping that yr hands would be faster than yr customers eyes. Sometimes you won sometimes you lost what else is there to know?

LINCOLN: Thuh customer is actually called the "Mark." You know why?

BOOTH: Cause hes thuh one you got yr eye on. You mark him in with yr eye.

LINCOLN

LINCOLN

BOOTH: Im right, right?

LINCOLN: Lemmie show you a few moves. If you pick up these yll have a chance.

BOOTH: Yr playing.

LINCOLN: Get thuh cards and set it up.

BOOTH: No shit.

LINCOLN: Set it up set it up.

In a flash, Booth clears away the romantic table setting by gathering it all up in the tablecloth and tossing it aside. As he does so he reveals the "table" underneath: the 2 stacked monte milk crates and the cardboard playing surface. Lincoln lays out the cards. The brothers are ready. Lincoln begins to teach Booth in earnest.

LINCOLN: Thuh deuce of spades is thuh card tuh watch.

BOOTH: I work with thuh deuce of hearts. But spades is cool.

LINCOLN: Theres thuh Dealer, thuh Stickman, thuh Sides, thuh Lookout and thuh Mark. I'll be thuh Dealer.

BOOTH: I'll be thuh Lookout. Lemmie be thuh Lookout, right? I'll keep an eye for thuh cops. I got my piece on me.

LINCOLN: You got it on you right now?

BOOTH: I always carry it.

LINCOLN: Even on a date? In yr own home?

BOOTH: You never know, man.

(Rest)

So Im thuh Lookout.

LINCOLN: Gimmie yr piece.

Booth gives Lincoln his gun. Lincoln moves the little wooden chair to face right in front of the setup. He then puts the gun on the chair.

LINCLON: We dont need nobody standing on the corner watching for cops cause there aint none.

BOOTH: I'll be thuh Stickman, then.

LINCOLN: Stickman knows the game inside out. You aint there yet. But you will be. You wanna learn good, be my Sideman. Playing along with the Dealer, moving the Mark to lay his money down. You wanna learn, right?

BOOTH: I'll be thuh Side.

LINCOLN: Good.

(Rest)

First thing you learn is what is. Next thing you learn is what aint. You dont know what is you dont know what aint, you dont know shit.

BOOTH: Right.

LINCOLN

BOOTH

BOOTH: Whatchu looking at?

LINCOLN: Im sizing you up.

BOOTH: Oh yeah?!

LINCOLN: Dealer always sizes up thuh crowd.

BOOTH: Im yr Side, Link, Im on yr team, you dont go sizing up yr own team. You save looks like that for yr Mark.

LINCOLN: Dealer always sizes up thuh crowd. Everybody out there is part of the crowd. His crew is part of the crowd, he himself is part of the crowd. Dealer always sizes up thuh crowd.

Lincoln looks Booth over some more then looks around at an imaginary crowd.

BOOTH: Then what then what?

LINCOLN: Dealer dont wanna play.

BOOTH: Bullshit man! Come on you promised!

LINCOLN: Thats thuh Dealers attitude. He *acts* like he dont wanna play. He holds back and thuh crowd, with their eagerness to see his skill and their willingness to take a chance, and their greediness to win his cash, the larceny in their hearts, all goad him on and push him to throw his cards, although of course the Dealer has been wanting to throw his cards all along. Only he dont never show it.

BOOTH: Thats some sneaky shit, Link.

LINCOLN: It sets thuh mood. You wanna have them in yr hand before you deal a hand, K?

BOOTH: Cool.—K.

LINCOLN: Right.

LINCOLN

BOOTH

BOOTH: You sizing me up again?

LINCOLN: Theres 2 parts to throwing thuh cards. Both parts are fairly complicated. Thuh moves and thuh grooves, thuh talk and thuh walk, thuh patter and thuh pitter pat, thuh flap and thuh rap: what yr doing with yr mouth and what yr doing with yr hands.

BOOTH: I got thuh words down pretty good.

LINCOLN: You need to work on both.

BOOTH: K.

LINCOLN: A goodlooking walk and a dynamite talk captivates their entire attention. The Mark focuses with 2 organs primarily: his eyes and his ears. Leave one out you lose yr shirt. Captivate both, yr golden.

BOOTH: So them times I seen you lose, them times I seen thuh Mark best you, that was a time when yr hands werent fast enough or yr patter werent right.

LINCOLN: You could say that.

BOOTH: So, there was plenty of times—

Lincoln moves the cards around.

LINCOLN: You see what Im doing? Dont look at my hands, man, look at my eyes. Know what is and know what aint.

BOOTH: What is?

LINCOLN: My eyes.

BOOTH: What aint?

LINCOLN: My hands. Look at my eyes not my hands. And you standing there thinking how thuh fuck I gonna learn how tuh throw thuh cards if I be looking in his eyes? Look into my eyes and get yr focus. Dont think about learning how tuh throw thuh cards. Dont think about nothing. Just look into my eyes. Focus.

BOOTH: Theyre red.

LINCOLN: Look into my eyes.

BOOTH: You been crying?

LINCOLN: Just look into my eyes, fool. Now. Look down at thuh cards. I been moving and moving and moving them around. Ready?

BOOTH: Yeah.

LINCOLN: Ok, Sideman, thuh Marks got his eye on you. Yr gonna show him its easy.

BOOTH: K.

LINCOLN: Pick out thuh deuce of spades. Dont pick it up just point to it.

BOOTH: This one, right?

LINCOLN: Dont ask thuh Dealer if yr right, man, point to yr card with confidence.

Booth points.

BOOTH: That one.

(Rest)

Flip it over, man.

Lincoln flips over the card. It is in fact the deuce of spades. Booth struts around gloating like a rooster. Lincoln is mildly crestfallen.

BOOTH: Am I right or am I right?! Make room for 3-Card! Here comes thuh champ!

LINCOLN: Cool. Stay focused. Now we gonna add the second element. Listen.

Lincoln moves the cards and speaks in a low hypnotic voice.

LINCOLN: Lean in close and watch me now: who see thuh black card who see thuh black card I see thuh black card black cards thuh winner pick thuh black card thats thuh winner pick thuh red card thats thuh loser pick thuh other red card thats thuh other loser pick thuh black card you pick thuh winner. Watch me as I throw thuh cards. Here we go.

(Rest)

Who see thuh black card who see thuh black card? You pick thuh red card you pick a loser you pick that red card you pick a loser you pick thuh black card thuh deuce of spades you pick a winner who sees thuh deuce of spades thuh one who sees it never fades watch me now as I throw thuh cards. Red losers black winner follow thuh deuce of spades chase thuh black deuce. Dark deuce will get you thuh win. One good pickll get you in 2 good picks you gone win. 10 will get you 20, 20 will get you 40.

(Rest)

Ima show you thuh cards: 2 red cards but only one spade. Dark winner in thuh center and thuh red losers on thuh sides. Pick uh red card you got a loser pick thuh other red card you got a loser pick thuh black card you got a winner. Watch me watch me watch me now.

(Rest)

Ok, 3-Card, you know which cards thuh deuce of spades?

BOOTH: Yeah.

LINCOLN: You sure? Yeah? You sure you sure or you just think you sure? Oh you sure you sure huh? Was you watching Links lightning fast express? Was you watching Link cause he the best? So you sure, huh? Point it out. Now, place yr bet and Linkll turn over yr card.

BOOTH: What should I bet?

LINCOLN: Dont bet nothing man, we just playing. Slap me 5 and point out thuh deuce.

Booth slaps Lincoln 5, then points out a card which Lincoln flips over. It is in fact again the deuce of spades.

BOOTH: Yeah, baby! 3-Card got thuh moves! You didnt know lil bro had thuh stuff, huh? Think again, Link, think again.

LINCOLN: You wanna learn or you wanna run yr mouth?

BOOTH: Thought you had fast hands. Wassup? What happened tuh "Links Lightning Fast Express"? Turned into uh local train looks like tuh me.

LINCOLN: Thats yr whole motherfucking problem. Yr so busy running yr mouth you aint never gonna learn nothing! You think you something but you aint shit.

BOOTH: I aint shit, I am *The* Shit. Shit. Wheres thuh dark deuce? Right there! Yes, baby!

LINCOLN: Ok, 3-Card. Cool. Lets switch. Take thuh cards and show me whatcha got. Go on. Dont touch thuh cards too heavy just—its a light touch. Like yr touching Graces skin. Or, whatever, man, just a light touch. Like uh whisper.

BOOTH: Like uh whisper.

Booth moves the cards around, in an awkward imitation of his brother.

LINCOLN: Good.

BOOTH: Yeah. All right. Look into my eyes.

Booths speech is loud and his movements are jerky. He is doing worse than when he threw the cards at the top of the play.

BOOTH: Watch-me-close-watch-me-close-now: who-see-thuh-dark-card-who-see-thuh-dark-card? I-see-thuh-dark-card. Here-it-is. Thuh-dark-card-is-thuh-winner. Pick-thuh-dark-card-and-you-pick-uh-winner. Pick-uh-red-card-and-you-pick-uh-loser. Theres-thuh-loser-yeah-theres-thuh-red-card, theres-thuh-other-loser-and-theres-thuh-black-card, thuh-winner. Watch-me-close-watch-me-close-now: 3-Card-throws-thuh-cards-lightning-fast. 3-Card-thats-me-and-Ima-last. Watch-me-throw-cause-here-I-go. See thuh black card? Yeah? Who see I see you see thuh black card?

LINCOLN: Hahahahhahahahahahahah!

Lincoln doubles over laughing. Booth puts on his coat and pockets his gun.

BOOTH: What?

LINCOLN: Nothing, man, nothing.

BOOTH: *What?!*

LINCOLN: Yr just, yr just a little wild with it. You talk like that on thuh street cards or no cards and theyll lock you up, man. Shit. Reminds me of that time when you hung with us and we let you try being thuh Stick cause you wanted to so bad. Thuh hustle was so simple. Remember? I told you that when I put my hand in my left pocket you was to get thuh Mark tuh pick thuh card on that side. You got to thinking something like Links left means my left some dyslexic shit and turned thuh wrong card. There was 800 bucks on the line and you fucked it up.

(*Rest*)

But it was cool, little bro, cause we made the money back. It worked out cool.

(*Rest*)

So, yeah, I said a light touch, little bro. Throw thuh cards light. Like uh whisper.

BOOTH: Like Graces skin.

LINCOLN: Like Graces skin.

BOOTH: What time is it?

Lincoln holds up his watch. Booth takes a look.

BOOTH: Bitch. *Bitch!* She said she was gonna show up around 8. 8-a-fucking-clock.

LINCOLN: Maybe she meant 8 *a.m.*

BOOTH: Yeah. She gonna come all up in my place talking bout how she *love* me. How she cant stop *thinking* bout me. Nother mans shit up in her nother mans thing in her nother mans dick on her breath.

LINCOLN: Maybe something happened to her.

BOOTH: Something happened to her all right. She trying to make a chump outa me. I aint her chump. I aint nobodys chump.

LINCOLN: Sit. I'll go to the payphone on the corner. I'll—

BOOTH: Thuh world puts its foot in yr face and you dont move. You tell thuh world tuh keep on stepping. But Im my own man, Link. I aint you.

Booth goes out, slamming the door behind him.

LINCOLN: You got that right.

After a moment Lincoln picks up the cards. He moves them around fast, faster, faster.

SCENE SIX

Thursday night. The room looks empty, as if neither brother is home. Lincoln comes in. Hes fairly drunk. He strides in, leaving the door slightly ajar.

LINCOLN: Taaadaaaa!

(*Rest*)

(*Rest*)

Taadaa, motherfucker. Taadaa!

(*Rest*)

Booth—uh, 3-Card—you here? Nope. Good. Just as well. HaHa *Ha Ha Ha*!

He pulls an enormous wad of money from his pocket. He counts it, slowly and luxuriously, arranging and smoothing the bills and sounding the amounts under his breath. He neatly rolls up the money, secures it with a rubber band and puts it back in his pocket. He relaxes in his chair. Then he takes the money out again, counting it all over again, but this time quickly, with the touch of an expert hustler.

LINCOLN: You didnt go back, Link, you got back, you got it back you got yr shit back in thuh saddle, man, you got back in business. Walking in Luckys and you seen how they was looking at you? Lucky starts pouring for you when you walk in. And the women. You see how they was looking at you? Bought drinks for everybody. Bought drinks for Lucky. Bought drinks for Luckys damn dog. Shit. And thuh women be hanging on me and purring. And I be feeling that old call of thuh wild calling. I got more phone numbers in my pockets between thuh time I walked out that door and thuh time I walked back in than I got in my whole life. Cause my shit is *back*. And back better than it was when it left too. Shoot. Who thuh man? Link. Thats right. Purrrrring all up on me and letting me touch them and promise them shit. 3 of them sweethearts in thuh restroom on my dick all at once and I was *there* my shit was there. And Cookie just went out of my mind which is cool which is very cool. 3 of them. Fighting over it. Shit. Cause they knew I'd been throwing thuh cards. Theyd seen me on thuh corner with thuh old crew or if they aint seed me with they own eyes theyd heard word. Links thuh stink! Theyd heard word and they seed uh sad face on some poor sucker or a tear in thuh eye of some stupid fucking tourist and they figured it was me whod just took thuh suckers last dime, it was me who had all thuh suckers loot. They knew. They knew.

Booth appears, in the room. He was standing behind the screen, unseen all this time. He goes to the door, soundlessly, just stands there.

LINCOLN: And they was all in Luckys. Shit. And they was waiting for me to come in from my last throw. Cant take too many fools in one day, its bad luck, Link, so they was all waiting in there for me to come in thuh door and let thuh liquor start flowing and thuh music start going and let thuh boys who dont have thuh balls to get nothing but a regular job and uh weekly paycheck, let them crowd around and get in somehow on thuh excitement, and make way for thuh ladies, so they can run they hands on my clothes and feel thuh magic and imagine thuh man, with plenty to go around, living and breathing underneath.

(Rest)

They all thought I was down and out! They all thought I was some NoCount HasBeen LostCause motherfucker. But I got my shit back. Thats right. They stepped on me and kept right on stepping. Not no more. Who thuh man?! Goddamnit, who thuh—

Booth closes the door.

LINCOLN
BOOTH

(Rest)

LINCOLN: Another evening to remember, huh?

BOOTH *(Rest)*: Uh—yeah, man, yeah. Thats right, thats right.
LINCOLN: Had me a memorable evening myself.
BOOTH: I got news.

(Rest)

What you been up to?
LINCOLN: Yr news first.
BOOTH: Its good.
LINCOLN: Yeah?
BOOTH: Yeah.
LINCOLN: Go head then.
BOOTH *(Rest)*: Grace got down on her knees. Down on her knees, man. Asked *me* tuh marry *her*.
LINCOLN: Shit.
BOOTH: Amazing Grace!
LINCOLN: Lucky you, man.
BOOTH: And guess where she was, I mean, while I was here waiting for her. She was over at her house watching tv. I'd told her come over Thursday and I got it all wrong and was thinking I said Wednesday and here I was sitting waiting my ass off and all she was doing was over at her house just watching tv.
LINCOLN: Howboutthat.
BOOTH: She wants to get married right away. Shes tired of waiting. Feels her clock ticking and shit. Wants to have my baby. But dont look so glum man, we gonna have a boy and we gonna name it after you.
LLNCOLN: Thats great, man. Thats really great.
BOOTH
LINCOLN
BOOTH: Whats yr news?
LINCOLN *(Rest)*: Nothing.
BOOTH: Mines good news, huh?
LINCOLN: Yeah. Real good news, bro.
BOOTH: Bad news is—well, shes real set on us living together. And she always did like this place.

(Rest)

Yr gonna have to leave. Sorry.
LINCOLN: No sweat.
BOOTH: This was only a temporary situation anyhow.
LINCOLN: No sweat man. You got a new life opening up for you, no sweat. Graces moving in today? I can leave right now.
BOOTH: I dont mean to put you out.
LINCOLN: No sweat. I'll just pack up.

Lincoln rummages around finding a suitcase and begins to pack his things.

BOOTH: Just like that, huh? "No sweat"?! Yesterday you lost yr damn job. You dont got no cash. You dont got no friends, no nothing, but you clearing out just like that and its "no sweat"?!
LINCOLN: Youve been real generous and you and Grace need me gone and its time I found my own place.
BOOTH: No sweat.
LINCOLN: No sweat.

(Rest)

K. I'll spill it. I got another job, so getting my own place aint gonna be so bad.

BOOTH: You got a new job! Doing what?

LINCOLN: Security guard.

BOOTH (*Rest*): Security guard. Howaboutthat.

Lincoln continues packing the few things he has. He picks up a whiskey bottle.

BOOTH: Go head, take thuh med-sin, bro. You gonna need it more than me. I got, you know, I got my love to keep me warm and shit.

LINCOLN: You gonna have to get some kind of work, or are you gonna let Grace support you?

BOOTH: I got plans.

LINCOLN: She might want you now but she wont want you for long if you dont get some kind of job. Shes a smart chick. And she cares about you. But she aint gonna let you treat her like some pack mule while shes out working her ass off and yr laying up in here scheming and dreaming to cover up thuh fact that you dont got no skills.

BOOTH: Grace is very cool with who I am and where Im at, thank you.

LINCOLN: It was just some advice. But, hey, yr doing great just like yr doing.

LINCOLN

BOOTH

LINCOLN

BOOTH

BOOTH: When Pops left he didnt take nothing with him. I always thought that was fucked-up.

LINCOLN: He was a drunk. Everything he did was always half regular and half fucked-up.

BOOTH: Whyd he leave his clothes though? Even drunks gotta wear clothes.

LINCOLN: Whyd he leave his clothes whyd he leave us? He was uh drunk, bro. He—whatever, right? I mean, you aint gonna figure it out by thinking about it. Just call it one of thuh great unsolved mysteries of existence.

BOOTH: Moms had a man on thuh side.

LINCOLN: Yeah? Pops had side shit going on too. More than one. He would take me with him when he went to visit them. Yeah.

(*Rest*)

Sometimes he'd let me meet the ladies. They was all very nice. Very polite. Most of them real pretty. Sometimes he'd let me watch. Most of thuh time I was just outside on thuh porch or in thuh lobby or in thuh car waiting for him but sometimes he'd let me watch.

BOOTH: What was it like?

LINCOLN: Nothing. It wasnt like nothing. He made it seem like it was this big deal this great thing he was letting me witness but it wasnt like nothing.

(*Rest*)

One of his ladies liked me, so I would do her after he'd done her. On thuh sly though. He'd be laying

there, spent and sleeping and snoring and her and me would be sneaking it.

BOOTH: Shit.

LINCOLN: It was alright.

BOOTH

LINCOLN

Lincoln takes his crumpled Abe Lincoln getup from the closet. Isnt sure what to do with it.

BOOTH: Im gonna miss you coming home in that getup. I dont even got a picture of you in it for the album.

LINCOLN (*Rest*): Hell, I'll put it on. Get thuh camera get thuh camera.

BOOTH: Yeah?

LINCOLN: What thuh fuck, right?

BOOTH: Yeah, what thuh fuck.

Booth scrambles around the apartment and finds the camera. Lincoln quickly puts on the getup, including 2 thin smears of white pancake makeup, more like war paint than whiteface.

LINCOLN: They didnt fire me cause I wasnt no good. They fired me cause they was cutting back. Me getting dismissed didnt have no reflection on my performance. And I was a damn good Honest Abe considering.

BOOTH: Yeah. You look great man, really great. Fix yr hat. Get in thuh light. Smile.

LINCOLN: Lincoln didnt never smile.

BOOTH: Sure he smiled.

LINCOLN: No he didnt, man, you seen thuh pictures of him. In all his pictures he was real serious.

BOOTH: You got a new job, yr having a good day, right?

LINCOLN: Yeah.

BOOTH: So smile.

LINCOLN: Snapshots gonna look pretty stupid with me—

Booth takes a picture.

BOOTH: Thisll look great in thuh album.

LINCOLN: Lets take one together, you and me.

BOOTH: No thanks. Save the film for the wedding.

LINCOLN: This wasnt a bad job. I just outgrew it. I could put in a word for you down there, maybe when business picks up again theyd hire you.

BOOTH: No thanks. That shit aint for me. I aint into pretending Im someone else all day.

LINCOLN: I was just sitting there in thuh getup. I wasnt pretending nothing.

BOOTH: What was going on in yr head?

LINCOLN: I would make up songs and shit.

BOOTH: And think about women.

LINCOLN: Sometimes.

BOOTH: Cookie.

LINCOLN: Sometimes.

BOOTH: And how she came over here one night looking for you.

LINCOLN: I was at Luckys.

BOOTH: She didnt know that.

LINCOLN: I was drinking.

BOOTH: All she knew was you couldnt get it up. You couldnt get it up with her so in her head you was tired of her and had gone out to screw somebody new and this time maybe werent never coming back.

(Rest)

She had me pour her a drink or 2. I didnt want to. She wanted to get back at you by having some fun of her own and when I told her to go out and have it, she said she wanted to have her fun right here. With me.

(Rest)

[And then, just like that, she changed her mind.

(Rest)

But she'd hooked me. That bad part of me that I fight down everyday. You beat yrs down and it stays there dead but mine keeps coming up for another round. And she hooked the bad part of me. And the bad part of me opened my mouth and started promising her things. Promising her things I knew she wanted and you couldnt give her. And the bad part of me took her clothing off and carried her into thuh bed and had her, Link, yr Cookie. It wasnt just thuh bad part of me it was all of me, man,] I had her. Yr damn wife. Right in that bed.

LINCOLN: I used to think about her all thuh time but I dont think about her no more.

BOOTH: I told her if she dumped you I'd marry her but I changed my mind.

LINCOLN: I dont think about her no more.

BOOTH: You dont go back.

LINCOLN: Nope.

BOOTH: Cause you cant. No matter what you do you cant get back to being who you was. Best you can do is just pretend to be yr old self.

LINCOLN: Yr outa yr mind.

BOOTH: Least Im still me!

LINCOLN: Least I work. You never did like to work. You better come up with some kinda way to bring home the bacon or Gracell drop you like a hot rock.

BOOTH: I got plans!

LINCOLN: Yeah, you gonna throw thuh cards, right?

BOOTH: Thats right!

LINCOLN: You a double left-handed motherfucker who dont stand a chance in all get out out there throwing no cards.

BOOTH: You scared.

LINCOLN: Im gone.

Lincoln goes to leave.

BOOTH: Fuck that!

LINCOLN: Yr standing in my way.

BOOTH: You scared I got yr shit.

LINCOLN: The only part of my shit you got is the part of my shit you think you got and that aint shit.

BOOTH: Did I pick right them last times? Yes. Oh, I got yr shit.

LINCOLN: Set up the cards.

BOOTH: Thought you was gone.

LINCOLN: Set it up.

BOOTH: I got yr shit and Ima go out there and be thuh man and you aint gonna be nothin.

LINCOLN: Set it up!

Booth hurriedly sets up the milk crates and cardboard top. Lincoln throws the cards.

LINCOLN: Lean in close and watch me now: who see thuh black card who see thuh black card I see thuh black card black cards thuh winner pick thuh black card thats thuh winner pick thuh red card thats thuh loser pick thuh other red card thats thuh other loser pick thuh black card you pick thuh winner. Who see thuh black card who see thuh black card? You pick thuh red card you pick a loser you pick that red card you pick a loser you pick thuh black card thuh deuce of spades you pick a winner who sees thuh deuce of spades thuh one who sees it never fades watch me now as I throw thuh cards. Red losers black winner follow thuh deuce of spades chase thuh black deuce. Dark deuce will get you thuh win. 10 will get you 20, 20 will get you 40. One good pickll get you in 2 good picks and you gone win.

(Rest)

Ok, man, wheres thuh black deuce?

Booth points to a card. Lincoln flips it over. It is the deuce of spades.

BOOTH: Who thuh man?!

Lincoln turns over the other 2 cards, looking at them confusedly.

LINCOLN: Hhhhh.

BOOTH: Who thuh man, Link?! Huh? Who thuh man, Link?!?!

LINCOLN: You thuh man, man.

BOOTH: I got yr shit down.

LINCOLN: Right.

BOOTH: "Right"? All you saying is "right"?

(Rest)

You was out on the street throwing. Just today. Werent you? You wasnt gonna tell me.

LINCOLN: Tell you what?

BOOTH: That you was out throwing.

LINCOLN: I was gonna tell you, sure. Cant go and leave my little bro out thuh loop, can I? Didnt say nothing cause I thought you heard. Did all right today but Im still rusty, I guess. But hey—yr getting good.

BOOTH: But I'll get out there on thuh street and still fuck up, wont I?

LINCOLN: You seem pretty good, bro.

BOOTH: You gotta do it for real, man.

LINCOLN: I am doing it for real. And yr getting good.

BOOTH: I dunno. It didnt feel real. Kinda felt—well it didnt feel real.

LINCOLN: We're missing the essential elements. The crowd, the street, thuh traffic sounds, all that.

BOOTH: We missing something else too, thuh thing thatll really make it real.

LINCOLN: Whassat, bro?

BOOTH: Thuh cash. Its just bullshit without thuh money. Put some money down on thuh table then itd be real, then youd do it for real, then I'd win it for real.

(*Rest*)

And dont be looking all glum like that. I know you got money. A whole pocketful. Put it down.

LINCOLN

BOOTH

BOOTH: You scared of losing it to thuh man, chump? Put it down, less you think thuh kid who got two left hands is gonna give you uh left hook. Put it down, bro, put it down.

Lincoln takes the roll of bills from his pocket and places it on the table.

BOOTH: How much you got there?

LINCOLN: 500 bucks.

BOOTH: Cool.

(*Rest*)

Ready?

LINCOLN: Does it feel real?

BOOTH: Yeah. Clean slate. Take it from the top. "One good pickll get you in 2 good picks and you gone win."

(*Rest*)

Go head.

LINCOLN: Watch me now.

BOOTH: Woah, man, woah.

(*Rest*)

You think Ima chump.

LINCOLN: No I dont.

BOOTH: You aint going full out.

LINCOLN: I was just getting started.

BOOTH: But when you got good and started you wasnt gonna go full out. Ye wasnt gonna go all out. You was gonna do thuh pussy shit, not thuh real shit.

LINCOLN: I put my money down. Money makes it real.

BOOTH: But not if I dont put no money down tuh match it.

LINCOLN: You dont got no money.

BOOTH: I got money!

LINCOLN: You aint worked in years. You dont got shit.

BOOTH: I got money.

LINCOLN: Whatcha been doing, skimming off my weekly paycheck and squirreling it away?

BOOTH: I got money.

(*Rest*)

They stand there sizing each other up. Booth breaks away, going over to his hiding place from which he gets

an old nylon stocking with money in the toe, a knot holding the money secure.

LINCOLN

BOOTH

BOOTH: You know she was putting her stuff in plastic bags? She was just putting her stuff in plastic bags not putting but shoving. She was shoving her stuff in plastic bags and I was standing in thuh doorway watching her and she was so busy shoving thuh shit she didnt see me. "I aint made of money," thats what he always saying. The guy she had on the side. I would catch them together sometimes. Thuh first time I cut school I got tired of hanging out so I goes home—figured I could tell Mom I was sick and cover my ass. Come in thuh house real slow cause Im sick and moving slow and quiet. He had her bent over. They both had all they clothes on like they was about to do something like go out dancing cause they was dressed to thuh 9s but at thuh last minute his pants had fallen down and her dress had flown up and theyd ended up doing something else.

(*Rest*)

They didnt see me come in, they didnt see me watching them, they didnt see me going out. That was uh Thursday. Something told me tuh cut school thuh next Thursday and sure enough—. He was her Thursday man. Every Thursday. Yeah. And Thursday nights she was always all cleaned up and fresh and smelling nice. Serving up dinner. And Pops would grab her cause she was all bright and she would look at me, like she didnt know that I knew but she was asking me not to tell nohow. She was asking me to—oh who knows.

(*Rest*)

She was talking with him one day, her sideman, her Thursday dude, her backdoor man, she needed some money for something, thered been some kind of problem some kind of mistake had been made some kind of mistake that needed cleaning up and she was asking Mr. Thursday for some money to take care of it. "I aint made of money," he says. He was putting his foot down. And then there she was 2 months later not showing yet, maybe she'd got rid of it maybe she hadnt maybe she'd stuffed it along with all her other things in them plastic bags while he waited outside in thuh car with thuh motor running. She musta known I was gonna walk in on her this time cause she had my payoff—my *inheritance*—she had it all ready for me. 500 dollars in a nylon stocking. Huh.

He places the stuffed nylon stocking on the table across from Lincolns money roll.

BOOTH: Now its real.

LINCOLN: Dont put that down.

BOOTH: Throw thuh cards.

LINCOLN: I dont want to play.

BOOTH: Throw thuh fucking cards, man!!

LINCOLN (*Rest*): 2 red cards but only one black. Pick thuh black you pick thuh winner. All thuh cards are face down you point out thuh cards and then you move them around. Now watch me now, now watch me real close. Put thuh winning deuce down in the center put thuh loser reds on either side then you just move thuh cards around. Move them slow or move them fast, Links thuh king he gonna last.

(*Rest*)

Wheres thuh deuce of spades?

Booth chooses a card and chooses correctly.

BOOTH: HA!

LINCOLN: One good pickll get you in 2 good picks and you gone win.

BOOTH: I know man I know.

LINCOLN: Im just doing thuh talk.

BOOTH: Throw thuh fucking cards!

Lincoln throws the cards.

LINCOLN: Lean in close and watch me now: who see thuh black card who see thuh black card I see thuh black card black cards thuh winner pick thuh black card thats thuh winner pick thuh red card thats thuh loser pick thuh other red card thats thuh other loser pick thuh black card you pick thuh winner. Watch me as I throw thuh cards. Here we go.

(*Rest*)

Ima show you thuh cards: 2 red cards but only one spade. Dark winner in thuh center and thuh red losers on thuh sides. Pick uh red card you got a loser pick thuh other red card you got a loser pick thuh black card you got a winner. Watch me watch me watch me now.

(*Rest*)

Who see thuh black card who see thuh black card? You pick thuh red card you pick a loser you pick that red card you pick a loser you pick thuh black card thuh deuce of spades you pick a winner who sees thuh deuce of spades thuh one who sees it never fades watch me now as I throw thuh cards. Red losers black winner follow thuh deuce of spades chase thuh black deuce. Dark deuce will get you thuh win.

(*Rest*)

Ok, 3-Card, you know which cards thuh deuce of spades? This is for real now, man. You pick wrong Im in yr wad and I keep mines.

BOOTH: I pick right I got yr shit.

LINCOLN: Yeah.

BOOTH: Plus I beat you for real.

LINCOLN: Yeah.

(*Rest*)

You think we're really brothers?

BOOTH: Huh?

LINCOLN: I know we *brothers,* but is we really brothers, you know, blood brothers or not, you and me, what-duhyathink?

BOOTH: I think we're brothers.

BOOTH

LINCOLN

BOOTH

LINCOLN

BOOTH

LINCOLN

LINCOLN: Go head man, wheres thuh deuce?

In a flash Booth points out a card.

LINCOLN: You sure?

BOOTH: Im sure!

LINCOLN: Yeah? Dont touch thuh cards, now.

BOOTH: Im sure.

The 2 brothers lock eyes. Lincoln turns over the card that Booth selected and Booth, in a desperate break of concentration, glances down to see that he has chosen the wrong card.

LINCOLN: Deuce of hearts, bro. Im sorry. Thuh deuce of spades was this one.

(*Rest*)

I guess all this is mines.

He slides the money toward himself.

LINCOLN: You were almost right. Better luck next time.

(*Rest*)

Aint yr fault if yr eyes aint fast. And you cant help it if you got 2 left hands, right? Throwing cards aint thuh whole world. You got other shit going for you. You got Grace.

BOOTH: Right.

LINCOLN: Whassamatter?

BOOTH: Mm.

LINCOLN: Whatsup?

BOOTH: Nothing.

LINCOLN:

(*Rest*)

It takes a certain kind of understanding to be able to play this game.

(*Rest*)

I still got thuh moves, dont I?

BOOTH: Yeah you still got thuh moves.

Lincoln cant help himself. He chuckles.

LINCOLN: I aint laughing at you, bro, Im just laughing. Shit there is so much to this game. This game is—there is just so much to it.

Lincoln, still chuckling, flops down in the easy chair. He takes up the nylon stocking and fiddles with the knot.

LINCOLN: Woah, she sure did tie this up tight, didnt she?

BOOTH: Yeah. I aint opened it since she gived it to me.

LINCOLN: Yr kidding. 500 and you aint never opened it? Shit. Sure is tied tight. She said heres 500 bucks and you didnt undo thuh knot to get a look at the cash? You aint needed to take a peek in all these years? Shit. I woulda opened it right away. Just a little peek.

BOOTH: I been saving it.

(*Rest*)

Oh, dont open it, man.

LINCOLN: How come?

BOOTH: You won it man, you dont gotta go opening it.

LINCOLN: We gotta see whats in it.

BOOTH: We *know* whats in it. Dont open it.

LINCOLN: You are a chump, bro. There could be millions in here! There could be nothing! I'll open it.

BOOTH: Dont.

LINCOLN

BOOTH

(*Rest*)

LINCOLN: Shit this knot aint coming out. I could cut it, but that would spoil the whole effect, wouldnt it? Shit. Sorry. I aint laughing at you Im just laughing. Theres so much about those cards. You think you can learn them just by watching and just by playing but there is more to them cards than that. And—. Tell me something, Mr. 3-Card, she handed you this stocking and she said there was money in it and then she split and you say you didnt open it. Howd you know she was for real?

BOOTH: She was for real.

LINCOLN: How you know? She coulda been jiving you, bro. Jiving you that there really *was* money in this thing. Jiving you big time. Its like thuh cards. And ooooh you certainly was persistent. But you was in such a hurry to learn thuh last move that you didnt bother learning thuh first one. That was yr mistake. Cause its thuh first move that separates thuh Player from thuh Played. And thuh first move is to know that there aint no winning. It may look like you got a chance but the only time yon pick right is when thuh man lets you. And when its thuh real deal, when its thuh real fucking deal, bro, and thuh moneys on thuh line, thats when thuh man wont want you picking right. He will want you picking wrong so he will make you pick wrong. Wrong wrong wrong. Ooooh, you thought you was finally happening, didnt you? You thought yr ship had come in or some shit, huh? Thought you was uh player. But I played you, bro.

BOOTH: Fuck you. Fuck you FUCK YOU *FUCK YOU*!!

LINCOLN: Whatever, man. Damn this knot is tough. Ima cut it.

Lincoln reaches in his boot, pulling out a knife. He chuckles all the while.

LINCOLN: Im not laughing at you, bro, Im just laughing.

Booth chuckles with him. Lincoln holds the knife high ready to cut the stocking.

LINCOLN: Turn yr head. You may not wanna look.

Booth turns away slightly. They both continue laughing. Lincoln brings the knife down to cut the stocking.

BOOTH: I popped her.

LINCOLN: Huh?

BOOTH: Grace. I popped her. Grace.

(*Rest*)

Who thuh fuck she think she is doing me like she done? Telling me I dont got nothing going on. I showed her what I got going on. Popped her good. Twice. 3 times. Whatever.

(*Rest*)

She aint dead.

(*Rest*)

She werent wearing my ring I gived her. Said it was too small. Fuck that. Said it hurt her. Fuck that. Said she was into bigger things. *Fuck* that. Shes alive not to worry, she aint going out that easy, shes alive shes shes—.

LINCOLN: Dead. Shes—

BOOTH: Dead.

LINCOLN: Ima give you back yr stocking, man. Here, bro—

BOOTH: Only so long I can stand that little brother shit. Can only take it so long. Im telling you—

LINCOLN: Take it back, man—

BOOTH: That little bro shit had to go—

LINCOLN: Cool—

BOOTH: Like Booth went—

LINCOLN: Here, 3-Card—

BOOTH: That Booth shit is over. 3-Cards thuh man now—

LINCOLN: Ima give you yr stocking back, 3-Card—

BOOTH: Who thuh man now, huh? Who thuh man now?! Think you can fuck with me, motherfucker think again motherfucker think again! Think you can take me like Im just some chump some two left-handed pussy dickbreath chump who you can take and then go laugh at. Aint laughing at me you was just laughing bunch uh bullshit and you know it.

LINCOLN: Here. Take it.

BOOTH: I aint gonna be needing it. Go on. You won it you open it.

LINCOLN: No thanks.

BOOTH: Open it open it open it open it. *OPEN IT!!!*

(*Rest*)

Open it up, bro.

LINCOLN

BOOTH

Lincoln brings the knife down to cut the stocking. In a flash, Booth grabs Lincoln from behind. He pulls his gun and thrusts it into the left side of Lincolns neck. They stop there poised.

LINCOLN: Dont.

Booth shoots Lincoln. Lincoln slumps forward, falling out of his chair and onto the floor. He lies there dead. Booth paces back and forth, like a panther in a cage, holding his gun.

BOOTH: Think you can take my shit? My shit. That shit was mines. I kept it. Saved it. All this while. Through thick and through thin. Through fucking thick and through fucking thin, motherfucker. And you just gonna come up in here and mock my shit and call me two lefthanded talking bout how she coulda been jiving me then go steal from me? My *inheritance*. You stole my *inheritance*, man. That aint right. That aint right and you know it. You had yr own. And you blew it. You *blew* it, motherfucker! I saved mines and you blew yrs. Thinking you all that and blew yr shit. And I *saved* mines.

(Rest)

You aint gonna be needing yr fucking money-roll no more, dead motherfucker, so I will pocket it thank you.

(Rest)

Watch me close watch me close now: Ima go out there and make a name for myself that dont have nothing to do with you. And 3-Cards gonna be in everybodys head and in everybodys mouth like Link was.

(Rest)

Ima take back my inheritance too. It was mines anyhow. Even when you stole it from me it was still mines cause she gave it to me. She didnt give it to you. And I been saving it all this while.

He bends to pick up the money-filled stocking. Then he just crumples. As he sits beside Lincolns body, the money-stocking falls away. Booth holds Lincolns body, hugging him close. He sobs.

BOOTH: *AAAAAAAAAAAAAAAAAAAAH!*

Sarah Ruhl

Although she is from Chicago, Sarah Ruhl (b. 1974) now lives in New York City and is married to a physician at New York University. She studied with Paula Vogel at Brown University and, in 2006, won a MacArthur Fellowship, which provided her with $100,000 a year for five years—freeing her to write without financial concerns. Since the production of *The Clean House* (2004), which won the Susan Smith Blackburn Award for the best play of the year by a woman and was a finalist for the 2005 Pulitzer Prize, her plays are eagerly anticipated. In almost record time, Ruhl has become a powerful force in modern theater. Paula Vogel said that her work takes us "back to the importance of theatre as myth, the importance of theatre as community."

Some of her earlier plays, such as *Melancholy Play* (2002), deal with psychological issues. Ruhl explores melancholy and sadness in this play, with a special perspective on the medication that often masks such emotions. Not all sadness is depression, she argues, and using Prozac and other such drugs to treat sadness is not necessarily valid. One need not always be "up," and moments of sadness are normal human feelings, not medical emergencies.

Late: A Cowboy Song was given a reading in 2002 in Dallas, Texas, but a full production did not occur until 2005 in Houston at Stages Repertory Theatre. Set in Pittsburgh, the play examines questions of identity and focuses on a man and woman who change their lives after a chance meeting with a cowgirl. Unfortunately, the reviews were not kind to this play. By contrast, the reviews of *Eurydice* (2003) have been overwhelmingly positive, and the staging has been praised as highly original. The play is an adaptation of the myth of Orpheus and Eurydice, in which the poet Orpheus sings so beautifully that the very rocks feel emotion.

The Clean House (2004) not only was successful in its premiere at Yale Repertory Theatre, and in its later production in New York, but also has gone on to become one of the most produced plays of the past several years. In it, Matilde is a Portuguese woman who cleans house for Lane and her husband Charles, both doctors. Matilde was born laughing and spends her time searching for the perfect joke. Secretly, she does not enjoy cleaning house. Lane's sister Virginia visits and discovers Matilde's secret, and then she creates a secret of her own by cleaning Lane's house herself without Lane's knowledge. Cleaning together, Matilde and Virginia discover that Charles is having an affair with one of his patients who is dying of cancer. The complications that arise from these circumstances are deftly woven together in such a way as to involve every character and to produce changes that surprise everyone.

Ruhl's next work, *Passion Play* (2007), developed over a period of ten years. It began when, as a student in Providence, Rhode Island, Ruhl saw a performance of the passion play and began writing an undergraduate thesis. A traditional play that has been performed for centuries in one form or another, the passion play tells the story of the crucifixion of Jesus Christ. The production in Oberammergau, Germany, has been put on regularly since the Middle Ages, and because it has changed little in all that time, it is often accused of contributing to European anti-Semitism. What Ruhl did with the play, which was produced by the Goodman Theatre in Chicago in September 2007, was to explore it in different contexts, both historically and geographically. The play is told in three parts. The first is set in England in 1571 during the reign of Queen Elizabeth, in the period during which there was a very severe crackdown on Roman Catholics, who were thought to be a threat to the English Crown. The second part is set in Germany in 1934, when Hitler especially approved of the passion play at Oberammergau because it fueled his hatred of the Jews, helped spread anti-Semitism, and made it politically easier for him to begin murdering Europe's Jews. The third part is set in Spearfish, South Dakota, in the 1980s, during Ronald Reagan's presidency, at the Black Hills passion play. This event is a huge outdoor undertaking that reenacts the last days of Jesus's life using period costumes, dozens of players, and a great deal of sophisticated technology in a pageant described as the most impressive of its kind.

Ruhl's play merges religion and politics to demonstrate the ways in which the religious material of the passion play can be molded into a political message appropriate for its time. She comments on both religion and politics at a time when they have once again merged as a force in the modern world.

Dead Man's Cell Phone (2007), commissioned by and performed at Playwrights Horizons in New York, starred Mary-Louise Parker, Kathleen Chalfant, and Anne Bogart. This play deals with moral issues and the way people connect with one another. It centers on a woman who answers a cell phone, only to discover that the owner is dead and that the man's life was strange and challenging in ways that she could never have imagined.

In the Next Room: or, The Vibrator Play premiered at the Berkeley Repertory Theatre in Berkeley, California, in February 2009, then moved to the Lyceum Theatre in New York in October, thus becoming Ruhl's first play with a Broadway opening. Michael Cerveris and Maria Dizzia starred. The play is set in the 1880s, when electricity began to be available in households. The play focuses on the assumption among some psychologists and doctors at that time that what most women suffered from could be cured by the application of the vibrator so as to produce an orgasm. What Ruhl reveals in the play is not that the doctors are prurient, but that the sexual relationships between the husbands and wives in the play are distorted by the social values of the age, when sexual issues could not be frankly discussed even by married couples. *In the Next Room: or, The Vibrator Play* was nominated for the Pulitzer Prize and a Tony Award.

Eurydice

Eurydice is about the terrible power of loss. In the myth of Orpheus and Eurydice, as told by Ovid in his *Metamorphoses,* Orpheus, the most famous musician in classical literature, has the reputation of charming even the stones when he sings. In Ovid's version, Eurydice steps on a snake in the grass at her wedding to Orpheus and dies of its bite. In another version of the myth, Eurydice attracts the attention of a satyr, who attempts to assault her. In trying to get away, she runs through tall grass and arouses a viper that gives her a fatal bite. In both versions, Orpheus, coming upon her, sings a lamentation that reduces all to tears. One of the wedding guests suggests he visit the underworld and persuade Persephone, goddess of the underworld, to return his wife. Orpheus goes to the underworld and sings so plaintively that Persephone permits

Eurydice to return on the condition that she follow Orpheus to the upper world without Orpheus's looking back at her. But when Orpheus reaches daylight, he is startled and turns around before Eurydice has also reached the upper world. She then disappears and Orpheus loses her forever. The poignancy of the myth inspired the very first opera, Monteverdi's *Orfeo* (1607), and many subsequent operas.

Ruhl focuses on the fact that Eurydice dies not once, but twice. She explores Eurydice's love for Orpheus by studying their sense of each other. Eurydice, for example, loves reading and loves books. Orpheus, in contrast, loves music and very little more. At their wedding, Eurydice expects to meet more interesting people, but she does not. Orpheus tries to teach her something about music, but she has no sense of rhythm and cannot sing on pitch.

The stranger who attracts Eurydice to his high-rise apartment with a letter from her recently deceased father seems at first to be an interesting person. But we know from the myth that he is a stand-in for the satyr in one version and the snake in another. He is a sexual predator. In the version staged by the Yale Repertory Theatre, he appears on a tricycle, which seems to foreshadow his reappearance later as a child in the underworld. Eurydice dies by falling from the high-rise apartment. In a brilliant scene (movement 2, scene 1), Eurydice arrives in the underworld in an elevator in which it is raining, carrying an umbrella. Water is an emblem throughout the play, referred to frequently in the stage directions, and this scene establishes its power. When Eurydice arrives, she must swim across Lethe, the classical river of forgetfulness. As a result, she can no longer read the works of Shakespeare, nor does she even know what to do with a book, yet she has not totally forgotten the world. She meets her father, who remembers her and tells her about the past and helps her to read. This section of the play explores the powerful bond between father and daughter, also illustrated by allusions to King Lear and Cordelia. Ruhl, in dedicating the play to her father, seems to be establishing the importance of the father-daughter relationship and the pain of their separation through death.

After Orpheus arrives in the raining elevator and has won Eurydice's release, they proceed to the upper world, but in Ruhl's version, the loss of Eurydice is not caused by Orpheus's inattention—it is caused by Eurydice's uncertainty. Throughout the last section of the play she is uncertain of her husband's name, even while being advised by her father to return to her husband. When she seems to have gone back to the upper world, her father dips himself in the river and loses the memory of the world and of his daughter. When Eurydice returns, expecting to find her father, she is cast into mourning and chastised by the stones, who have given her direction throughout her time in Hades. After writing a letter to Orpheus and his next wife, Eurydice lies down beside her father and dips herself into the river along with him.

Eurydice in Performance

The play is intentionally Greek in character, with the lines often resembling the poetic forms expected from playwrights like Euripides. Along with three principal characters and two minor characters, there is a chorus of stones. In performance, the sense of tragic intensity is very clear. The most impressive theatrical effect is achieved by the use of the elevator and the rain on the stage. An elevator (without rain) was first used in Jacques Offenbach's operetta *Orpheus in the Underworld* (1874).

The world premiere of *Eurydice* was at the Madison Repertory Theatre in 2003, directed by Richard Corley. The Berkeley Repertory Theatre in Berkeley,

California, produced the play, directed by Les Waters, in October 2004. The Yale Repertory Theatre production was in October 2006, also directed by Les Waters and starring Maria Dizzia as Eurydice. The play has been performed throughout the United States and abroad many times since then, in Denver's Curious Theatre in 2006, in London's Young Vic Theatre in 2010, and in Chicago's Filament Theatre Ensemble production and Toronto's Summer Festival in 2011. In his *New York Times* review, Charles Isherwood said of *Eurydice,* "It may just be the most moving exploration of the theme of loss that the American theater has produced since the events of September 11, 2001."

SARAH RUHL (b. 1974)

Eurydice 2003

Characters

EURYDICE
HER FATHER
ORPHEUS
A NASTY INTERESTING MAN/THE LORD OF THE UNDERWORLD
A CHORUS OF STONES:
  BIG STONE
  LITTLE STONE
  LOUD STONE

Setting: *The set contains a raining elevator,*
a water-pump,
some rusty exposed pipes,
an abstracted River of Forgetfulness,
an old-fashioned glow-in-the-dark globe.

Notes

Eurydice and Orpheus should be played as though they are a little too young and a little too in love. They should resist the temptation to be "classical."

The underworld should resemble the world of Alice in Wonderland more than it resembles Hades.

The stones might be played as though they are nasty children at a birthday party.

When people compose letters in this play they needn't actually scribble them—they can speak directly to the audience.

The play should be performed without an intermission.

FIRST MOVEMENT • Scene 1

A young man—Orpheus—
and a young woman—Eurydice.

They wear swimming outfits from the 1950s.
Orpheus makes a sweeping gesture with his arm,
indicating the sky.

EURYDICE: All those birds?

He nods.

EURYDICE: For me? Thank you.

They make a quarter turn and he makes a sweeping gesture.
He makes a gesture of giving the sea to Eurydice.

EURYDICE: And—the sea! Now?

Orpheus opens his hands.

EURYDICE: It's mine already?

Orpheus nods.

EURYDICE: Wow.

They kiss. He indicates the sky.

EURYDICE: Surely not—surely not the sky and the stars too.

Orpheus nods.

EURYDICE: That's very generous.

Orpheus nods.

EURYDICE: Perhaps too generous?

Orpheus shakes his head.

EURYDICE: Thank you.

She crawls on top of him and kisses his eyes.

EURYDICE: What are you thinking about?
ORPHEUS: Music.
EURYDICE: How can you think about music? You either hear it or you don't.
ORPHEUS: I'm hearing it then.
EURYDICE: Oh.

(*Pause.*)

I read a book today.

ORPHEUS: Did you?

EURYDICE: Yes. It was very interesting.

ORPHEUS: That's good.

EURYDICE: Don't you want to know what it was about?

ORPHEUS: Of course.

EURYDICE: There were—stories—about people's lives—how some come out well—and others come out badly.

ORPHEUS: Do you love the book?

EURYDICE: Yes—I think so.

ORPHEUS: Why?

EURYDICE: It can be interesting to see if other people—like dead people who wrote books—agree or disagree with what you think.

ORPHEUS: Why?

EURYDICE: Because it makes you—a larger part of the human community. It had very interesting arguments.

ORPHEUS: Oh. And arguments that are interesting are good arguments?

EURYDICE: Well—yes.

ORPHEUS: I didn't know an argument should be interesting. I thought it should be right or wrong.

EURYDICE: Well, these particular arguments were very interesting.

ORPHEUS: Maybe you should make up your own thoughts. Instead of reading them in a book.

EURYDICE: I do. I do think up my own thoughts.

ORPHEUS: I know you do. I love how you love books. Don't be mad.

Pause.

ORPHEUS: I made up a song for you today.

EURYDICE: Did you!?

ORPHEUS: Yup. It's not *interesting* or *not*-interesting. It just—is.

EURYDICE: Will you sing it for me?

ORPHEUS: It has too many parts.

EURYDICE: Let's go in the water.

They start walking, arm in arm,
on extensive unseen boardwalks, towards the water.

ORPHEUS: Wait—remember this melody.

He hums a bar of melody.

EURYDICE: I'm bad at remembering melodies. Why don't you remember it?

ORPHEUS: I have eleven other ones in my head, making for a total of twelve.
You have it?

EURYDICE: Yes. I think so.

ORPHEUS: Let's hear it.

She sings the melody.
She misses a few notes.
She's not the best singer in the world.

ORPHEUS: Pretty good. The rhythm's a little off. Here—clap it out.

She claps.
He claps the rhythmic sequence for her.
She tries to imitate.
She is still off.

EURYDICE: Is that right?

ORPHEUS: We'll practice.

EURYDICE: I don't need to know about rhythm. I have my books.

ORPHEUS: Don't books have rhythm?

EURYDICE: Kind of. Let's go in the water.

ORPHEUS: Will you remember my melody under the water?

EURYDICE: Yes! I WILL ALWAYS REMEMBER YOUR MELODY! It will be imprinted on my heart like wax.

ORPHEUS: Thank you.

EURYDICE: You're welcome. When are you going to play me the whole song?

ORPHEUS: When I get twelve instruments.

EURYDICE: Where are you going to get twelve instruments?

ORPHEUS: I'm going to make each strand of your hair into an instrument. Your hair will stand on end as it plays my music and become a hair orchestra. It will fly you up into the sky.

EURYDICE: I don't know if I want to be an instrument.

ORPHEUS: Why?

EURYDICE: Won't I fall down when the song ends?

ORPHEUS: That's true. But the clouds will be so moved by your music that they will fill up with water until they become heavy and you'll sit on one and fall gently down to earth. How about that?

EURYDICE: Okay.

They gaze at each other.

ORPHEUS: It's settled then.

EURYDICE: What is?

ORPHEUS: Your hair will be my orchestra and—I love you.

EURYDICE: I love you too.

ORPHEUS: How will you remember?

EURYDICE: That I love you?

ORPHEUS: Yes.

EURYDICE: That's easy. I can't help it.

ORPHEUS: You never know. I'd better tie a string around your finger to remind you.

EURYDICE: Is there string at the ocean?

ORPHEUS: I always have string. In case I come upon a broken instrument.

He takes out a string from his pocket.
He takes her left hand.

ORPHEUS: This hand.

He wraps string deliberately around her fourth finger.

ORPHEUS: Is this too tight?

EURYDICE: No—it's fine.

ORPHEUS: There—now you'll remember.

EURYDICE: That's a very particular finger.

ORPHEUS: Yes.

EURYDICE: You're aware of that?

ORPHEUS: Yes.

EURYDICE: How aware?

ORPHEUS: Very aware.

EURYDICE: Orpheus—are we?

ORPHEUS: You tell me.

EURYDICE: Yes.
    I think so.

ORPHEUS: You *think* so?

EURYDICE: I wasn't thinking.
    I mean—Yes. Just: Yes.

ORPHEUS: Yes?

EURYDICE: Yes.

ORPHEUS: Yes!

EURYDICE: Yes!

ORPHEUS: May our lives be full of music!

Music.
He picks her up and throws her into the sky.

EURYDICE: Maybe you could also get me another ring—a
    gold one—to put over the string one. You know?

ORPHEUS: Whatever makes you happy. Do you still have
    my melody?

EURYDICE: It's right here.

She points to her temple.
They look at each other. A silence.

EURYDICE: What are you thinking about?

ORPHEUS: Music.

Her face falls.

ORPHEUS: Just kidding. I was thinking about you. And
    music.

EURYDICE: Let's go in the water. I'll race you!

She puts on her swimming goggles.

ORPHEUS: I'll race *you!*

EURYDICE: I'll race *you!*

ORPHEUS: I'll race *you!*

EURYDICE: I'll race *you!*

They race towards the water.

Scene 2

The Father, dressed in a grey suit, reads from a letter.

FATHER: Dear Eurydice,

    A letter for you on your wedding day.

    There is no choice of any importance in life but the
    choosing of a beloved. I haven't met Orpheus, but he
    seems like a serious young man. I understand he's a
    musician.

    (*The father thinks—oh, dear.*)

    If I were to give a speech at your wedding I would
    start with one or two funny jokes and then I might
    offer some words of advice. I would say:

Cultivate the arts of dancing and small talk.

Everything in moderation.

Court the companionship and respect of dogs.

Grilling a fish or toasting bread without burning requires singleness of purpose, vigilance and steadfast
watching.

Keep quiet about politics, but vote for the right man.

Take care to change the light bulbs.

Continue to give yourself to others because that's the
ultimate satisfaction in life—to love, accept, honor
and help others.

As for me, this is what it's like being dead: the atmosphere smells. And there are strange high pitched
noises—like a tea kettle always boiling over. But it
doesn't seem to bother anyone. And, for the most part,
there is a pleasant atmosphere and you can work and
socialize, much like at home. I'm working in the business world and it seems that, here, you can better see
the far reaching consequences of your actions.

Also, I am one of the few dead people who still remembers how to read and write. That's a secret. If
anyone finds out, they might dip me in the River again.

I write you letters. I don't know how to get them to
you.

Love,
Your father

He drops the letter as though into a mail slot.
It falls on the ground.

Wedding music.
*In the underworld, the father walks in a straight line as
though he is walking his daughter down the aisle.*

*He is affectionate, then solemn, then glad, then solemn,
then amused, then solemn.*

*He looks at his imaginary daughter; he looks straight
ahead; he acknowledges the guests at the wedding; he
gets choked up; he looks at his daughter and smiles an
embarrassed smile for getting choked up.*

He looks straight ahead, calm.
He walks.

Suddenly, he checks his watch.
He exits, in a hurry.

Scene 3

Eurydice, by a water pump.
The noise of a party, from far off.

EURYDICE: I hate parties.
    And a wedding party is the biggest party of all.
    All the guests arrived and Orpheus is taking a shower.
    He's always taking a shower when the guests arrive
    so he doesn't have to greet them.

Then I have to greet them.

A wedding is for daughters and fathers. The mothers all dress up, trying to look like young women. But a wedding is for a father and a daughter. They stop being married to each other on that day.

I always thought there would be more interesting people at my wedding.

She drinks water from the water pump.
The Nasty Interesting Man, wearing a trench coat, appears and sees Eurydice cupping her hands full of water.

MAN: Are you a homeless person?

EURYDICE: No.

MAN: Oh. I'm on my way to a party where there are really very interesting people. Would you like to join me?

EURYDICE: No. I just left my own party.

MAN: You were giving a party and you just—left?

EURYDICE: I was thirsty.

MAN: You must be a very interesting person, to leave your own party like that.

EURYDICE: Thank you.

MAN: You mustn't care at all what other people think of you. I always say that's a mark of a really interesting person, don't you?

EURYDICE: I guess.

MAN: So would you like to accompany me to this interesting affair?

EURYDICE: No, thank you. I just got married, you see.

MAN: Oh—lots of people do that.

EURYDICE: That's true—lots of people do.

MAN: What's your name?

EURYDICE: Eurydice.

He looks at her, hungry.

MAN: Eurydice.

EURYDICE: Good-bye, then.

MAN: Good-bye.

She exits. He sits by the water pump.
He notices a letter on the ground.
He picks it up and reads it.

MAN: (*to himself*) Dear Eurydice.

Musty dripping sounds.

Scene 4

The father tries to remember how to do the jitterbug in the underworld.
He does the jitterbug with an imaginary partner.
He has fun.

Orpheus and Eurydice dance together at their wedding.
They are happy.
They have had some champagne.
They sing together.

ORPHEUS AND EURYDICE: Don't sit under the apple tree

with anyone else but me
anyone else but me
anyone else but me
no no no
Don't sit under the apple tree
with anyone else but me,
'til I come marching home . . .

On the other side of the stage,
the Father checks his watch.
He stops doing the jitterbug.
He exits, in a hurry.

EURYDICE: I'm warm; are you warm?

ORPHEUS: Yes!

EURYDICE: I'm going to get a drink of water.

ORPHEUS: Don't go.

EURYDICE: I'll be right back.

ORPHEUS: Promise?

EURYDICE: Yes.

ORPHEUS: I can't stand to let you out of my sight tonight.

EURYDICE: Silly goose.

They kiss.

Scene 5

Eurydice at the water pump,
getting a glass of water.
The Interesting Man appears.

EURYDICE: Oh—you're still here.

MAN: Yes. I forgot to tell you something. I have a letter. Addressed to Eurydice—that's you—from your father.

EURYDICE: That's not possible.

MAN: He wrote down some thoughts—for your wedding day.

EURYDICE: Let me see.

MAN: I left it at home. It got delivered to my elegant highrise apartment by mistake.

EURYDICE: Why didn't you say so before?

MAN: You left in such a hurry.

EURYDICE: From my father?

MAN: Yes.

EURYDICE: You're sure?

MAN: Yes.

EURYDICE: I knew he'd send something!

MAN: It'll just take a moment. I live around the block. What an interesting dress you're wearing.

EURYDICE: Thank you.

Scene 6

Orpheus, from the water pump.

ORPHEUS: Eurydice?
    Eurydice!

Scene 7

The sound of a door closing.
The Interesting Apartment—a giant loft space with no furniture.
Eurydice and the Man enter, panting.

MAN: Voila.

EURYDICE: You're very high up.

MAN: Yes. I am.

EURYDICE: I feel a little faint.

MAN: It'll pass.

EURYDICE: Have you ever thought about installing an elevator?

MAN: No. I prefer stairs. I think architecture is so interesting, don't you?

EURYDICE: Oh, yes. So, where's the letter?

MAN: But isn't this an interesting building?

EURYDICE: It's so—high up.

MAN: Yes.

EURYDICE: There's no one here. I thought you were having a party.

MAN: I like to celebrate things quietly. With a few other interesting people. Don't you?

She tilts her head to the side and stares at him.

Would you like some champagne?

EURYDICE: Maybe some water.

MAN: Water it is! Make yourself comfortable.

He gestures to the floor.
He switches on Brazilian mood music.
She looks around.

EURYDICE: I can't stay long!

She looks out the window. She is very high up.

EURYDICE: I can see my wedding from here!
The people are so small—they're dancing!
There's Orpheus!
He's not dancing.

MAN: (*shouting from off-stage*) So, who's this guy you're marrying?

EURYDICE: (*shouting*) His name is Orpheus.

MAN: (*as he attempts to open the champagne, off-stage*) Orpheus. Not a very interesting name. I've heard it before.

EURYDICE: (*shouting*) Maybe you've heard of him. He's kind of famous. He plays the most beautiful music in the world, actually.

MAN: I can't hear you!

EURYDICE: (*shouting*) So the letter was delivered—here—today?

MAN: That's right.

EURYDICE: Through the post?

MAN: It was—mysterious.

The sound of champagne popping.
He enters with one glass of champagne.

MAN: Voila.

He drinks the champagne.

So. Eurydice. Tell me one thing. Name me one person you find interesting.

EURYDICE: Why?

MAN: Just making conversation.

He sways a little, to the music.

EURYDICE: Right. Um—all the interesting people I know are dead or speak French.

MAN: Well, I don't speak French, Eurydice.

He takes one step toward her.
She takes one step back.

EURYDICE: I'm sorry. I have to go. There's no letter, is there?

MAN: Of course there's a letter. It's right here.

He pats his breast pocket.

MAN: Eurydice. I'm not interesting, but I'm strong. You could teach me to be interesting. I would listen. Orpheus is too busy listening to his own thoughts. There's music in his head. Try to pluck the music out and it bites you. I'll bet you had an interesting thought today, for instance.

She tilts her head to the side, quizzical.

I bet you're always having them, the way you tilt your head to the side and stare . . .

She jerks her head back up.
Musty dripping sounds.

EURYDICE: I feel dizzy all of a sudden. I want my husband. I think I'd better go now.

MAN: You're free to go, whenever you like.

EURYDICE: I know.
I think I'll go now, in fact. I'll just take my letter first, if you don't mind.

She holds out her hand for the letter.
He takes her hand.

MAN: Relax

She takes her hand away.

EURYDICE: Good-bye.

She turns to exit.
He blocks the doorway.

MAN: Wait. Eurydice. Don't go. I love you.

EURYDICE: Oh no.

MAN: You need to get yourself a real man. A man with broad shoulders like me. Orpheus has long fingers that would tremble to pet a bull or pluck a bee from a hive—

EURYDICE: How do you know about my husband's fingers?

MAN: A man who can put his big arm around your little shoulders as he leads you through the crowd, a man who answers the door at parties. . . . A man with big hands, with big stupid hands like potatoes, a man who can carry a cow in labor.

The man backs Eurydice against the wall.

MAN: My lips were meant to kiss your eyelids, that's obvious!

EURYDICE: Close your eyes, then!

He closes his eyes, expecting a kiss.
She takes the letter from his breast pocket.
She slips under him and opens the door to the stairwell.
He opens his eyes.
She looks at the letter.

EURYDICE: It's his handwriting!

MAN: Of course it is!

He reaches for her.

EURYDICE: Good-bye.

She runs for the stairs.
She wavers, off-balance, at the top of the stairwell.

MAN: Don't do that, you'll trip!

EURYDICE: Orpheus!

From the water pump:

ORPHEUS: EURYDICE!

She runs, trips and pitches down the stairs, holding her letter.
She follows the letter down, down down . . .
Blackout. A clatter. Strange sounds—xylophones, brass bands, sounds of falling, sounds of vertigo.
Sounds of breathing.

SECOND MOVEMENT

The underworld.
There is no set change.
Strange watery noises.
Drip, drip, drip.
The movement to the underworld is marked by the entrance of stones.

Scene 1

THE STONES: We are a chorus of stones.

LITTLE STONE: I'm a little stone.

BIG STONE: I'm a big stone.

LOUD STONE: I'm a loud stone.

THE STONES: We are all three stones.

LITTLE STONE: We live with the dead people in the land of the dead.

BIG STONE: Eurydice was a great musician. Orpheus was his wife.

LOUD STONE: (*correcting Big Stone*) Orpheus was a great musician. Eurydice was his wife. She died.

LITTLE STONE: Then he played the saddest music. Even we—

THE STONES: The stones—

LITTLE STONE: Cried when we heard it.

The sound of three drops of water hitting a pond.

LITTLE STONE: Oh, look,
she is coming into the land of the dead now.

BIG STONE: Oh!

LOUD STONE: Oh!

LITTLE STONE: Oh!
We might say—"Poor Eurydice"—

LOUD STONE: But stones don't feel bad for dead people.

The sound of an elevator ding.
An elevator door opens.
Inside the elevator, it is raining.
Eurydice gets rained on inside the elevator.
She carries a suitcase and an umbrella.
She is dressed in the kind of 1930s suit that women wore when they eloped.
She looks bewildered.

Ramiz Monsef as Big Stone, Gian-Murray Gianino as Loud Stone, and Carla Harting as Little Stone in the 2006 production of *Eurydice* directed by Les Waters at the Yale Repertory Theatre.

Eurydice (Ony Uhiara) arrives in the underworld in a production directed by Bijan Sheibani at the Young Vic Theatre in London, 2010.

The sound of an elevator ding.
Eurydice steps out of the elevator.
The elevator door closes.

She walks towards the audience and opens her mouth,
trying to speak.
There is a great humming noise.
She closes her mouth.
The humming noise stops.
She opens her mouth for the second time,
attempting to tell her story to the audience.
There is a great humming noise.
She closes her mouth—the humming noise stops.
She has a tantrum of despair.

STONES: Eurydice wants to speak to you.
  But she can't speak your language anymore.
  She talks in the language of dead people now.
LITTLE STONE: It's a very quiet language.
LOUD STONE: Like if the pores in your face opened up
  and talked.

BIG STONE: Like potatoes sleeping in the dirt.

The stones look at Big Stone as though that were a
dumb thing to say.

LITTLE STONE: Pretend that you understand her
  or she'll be embarrassed.
BIG STONE: Yes—pretend for a moment
  that you understand
  the language of stones.
LOUD STONE: Listen to her the way you would listen
  to your own daughter
  if she died too young
  and tried to speak to you
  across long distances.

Eurydice shakes out her umbrella.
She approaches the audience.
This time, she can speak.

EURYDICE: There was a roar, and a coldness—
  I think my husband was with me.
  What was my husband's name?

Eurydice turns to the stones.

  My husband's name? Do you know it?

The stones shrug their shoulders.

  How strange. I don't remember.
  It was horrible to see his face
  when I died. His eyes were
  two black birds
  and they flew to me.

  I said no—stay where you are—
  he needs you in order to see!

  When I got through the cold
  they made me swim in a river
  and I forgot his name.
  I forgot all the names.
  I know his name starts with my mouth
  shaped like a ball of twine—
  Oar—oar.
  I forget.
  They took me to a tiny boat.
  I only just fit inside.
  I looked at the oars
  and I wanted to cry.
  I tried to cry but I just drooled a little.
  I'll try now.

She tries to cry and finds that she can't.

EURYDICE: What happiness it would be to cry.

(She takes a breath.)

  I was not lonely
  only alone with myself
  begging myself not to leave my own body
  but I *was* leaving.

Good-bye, head—I said—
it inclined itself a little, as though to nod to me
in a solemn kind of way.

(*She turns to the stones.*)

How do you say good-bye to yourself?

They shake their heads.
A train whistle.
Eurydice steps onto a platform, surveying a large crowd.

EURYDICE: A train!
LITTLE STONE: The station is like a train but there is no train.
BIG STONE: The train has wheels that are not wheels.
LOUD STONE: There is the opposite of a wheel and the opposite of smoke and the opposite of a train.

A train pulls away.

EURYDICE: Oh! I'm waiting for someone to meet me, I think.

Eurydice's Father approaches and takes her baggage.

FATHER: Eurydice.
EURYDICE: (*to the stones*) At last, a porter to meet me!

(*to the father*) Do you happen to know where the bank is? I need money. I've just arrived. I need to exchange my money at the Bureau de Change. I didn't bring traveler's checks because I left in such a hurry. They didn't even let me pack my suitcase. There's nothing in it! That's funny, right? Funny—ha ha! I suppose I can buy new clothes here. I would *really* love a bath.
FATHER: Eurydice!
EURYDICE: What is that language you're speaking? It gives me tingles. Say it again.
FATHER: Eurydice!
EURYDICE: Oooh—it's like a fruit! Again!
FATHER: Eurydice—I'm your father!
EURYDICE: (*strangely imitating*) Eurydice—I'm your father. How funny! You remind me of something but I can't understand a word you're saying. Say it again!
FATHER: Your father.
STONES: (*to the father*) Shut up, shut up!
She doesn't understand you.
She's dead now too.
You have to speak in the language of stones.
FATHER: You're dead now. I'm dead, too.
EURYDICE: Yes, that's right. I need a reservation. For the fancy hotel.
FATHER: When you were alive, I was your father.
STONES: Father is not a word that dead people understand.
BIG STONE: He is what we call subversive.

FATHER: When you were alive, I was your tree.
EURYDICE: My tree! Yes, the tall one in the back yard! I used to sit all day in its shade!

She sits at the feet of her father.

EURYDICE: Ah—there—shade!
LITTLE STONE: There is a problem here.
EURYDICE: Is there any entertainment at the hotel? Any dancing ladies? Like with the great big fans?
FATHER: I named you Eurydice: Your mother named all the other children. But Eurydice I chose for you.
BIG STONE: Be careful, sir.
FATHER: Eurydice. I wanted to remember your name. I asked the stones. They said: Forget the names—the names make you remember.
LOUD STONE: We told you how it works!
FATHER: One day it would not stop raining.

I heard your name inside the rain—somewhere between the drops—I saw falling letters. Each letter of your name—I began to translate.

E—I remembered elephants. U—I remembered ulcers and under. R—I remembered reindeers. I saw them putting their black noses into snow. Y—youth and yellow. D—dog, dig, daughter, day. Time poured into my head. The days of the week. Hours, months. . . .
EURYDICE: The tree talks so beautifully.
STONES: Don't listen!
EURYDICE: I feel suddenly hungry! Where is the porter who met me at the station?
FATHER: Here I am.
EURYDICE: I would like a continental breakfast, please. Maybe some rolls and butter. Oh—and jam. Please take my suitcase to my room, if you would.
FATHER: I'm sorry, Miss, but there are no rooms here.
EURYDICE: What? No rooms? Where do people sleep?
FATHER: People don't sleep here.
EURYDICE: I have to say I'm very disappointed. It's been such a tiring day. I've been traveling all day—first on a river, then on an elevator that rained, then on a train . . . I thought someone would meet me at the station . . .

Eurydice is on the verge of tears.

STONES: Don't cry! Don't cry!
EURYDICE: I don't know where I am and there are all these stones and I hate them! They're horrible! I want a bath! I thought someone would meet me at the station!
FATHER: Don't be sad. I'll take your luggage to your room.
STONES: THERE ARE NO ROOMS!

He picks up her luggage.
He gives the stones a dirty look.
The sound of water in rusty pipes.

Scene 2

Orpheus writes a letter to Eurydice.

ORPHEUS: Dear Eurydice,

I miss you. No—that's not enough.

He crumples up the letter.
He writes a new letter.
He thinks.
He writes:

ORPHEUS: Dear Eurydice,
Symphony for twelve instruments.

(A pause.
He hears the music in his head.
He conducts.)

Love, Orpheus

He drops the letter as though into a mail slot.

Scene 3

The father creates a room out of string for Eurydice.

He makes four walls and a door out of string.
Time passes.
It takes time to build a room out of string.

Eurydice observes the underworld.
There isn't much to observe.
She plays hop-scotch without chalk.

Every so often,
the father looks at her,
happy to see her,
while he makes her room out of string.
She looks back at him, polite.

Scene 4

The father has completed the string room.
He gestures for Eurydice to enter.
She enters.

EURYDICE: Thank you. That will do.

She nods to her father.
He doesn't leave.

EURYDICE: Oh.
I suppose you want a tip.

He shakes his head.

EURYDICE: Would you run a bath for me?
FATHER: Yes, miss.

He exits the string room.
Eurydice opens her suitcase.
She is surprised that nothing is inside.
She sits down inside her suitcase.

Scene 5

ORPHEUS: Dear Eurydice,

I love you. I'm going to find you. I play the saddest music now that you're gone. You know I hate writing letters. I'll give this letter to a worm. I hope he finds you.

Love,
Orpheus

He drops the letter as though into a mail slot.

Scene 6

The father enters the string room with a letter on a silver tray.

FATHER: There is a letter for you, miss.
EURYDICE: A letter?

He nods.

FATHER: A letter.

He hands her the letter.

FATHER: It's addressed to you.
EURYDICE: There's dirt on it.

Eurydice wipes the dirt off the letter.
She opens it.
She scrutinizes it.
She does not know how to read it.
She puts it on the ground, takes off her shoes,
stands on the letter, and shuts her eyes.
She thinks, without language for the thought,
the melody: There's no place like home . . .

FATHER: Miss.
EURYDICE: What is it?
FATHER: Would you like me to *read* you the letter?
EURYDICE: "Read you the letter"?
FATHER: You can't do it with your feet.

(The father guides her off the letter, picks it up and begins to read.)

It's addressed to Eurydice. That's you.
EURYDICE: That's you.
FATHER: You.
It says: I love you.

EURYDICE: I love you?
FATHER: It's like your tree.
EURYDICE: Tall?

The father considers.

EURYDICE: Green?
FATHER: It's like sitting in the shade.
EURYDICE: Oh.
FATHER: It's like sitting in the shade with no clothes on.
EURYDICE: Oh!—yes.
FATHER: (*reading*) I'm going to find you. I play the sad-dest music—
EURYDICE: Music?

He whistles a note.

FATHER: It's like that.

She smiles.

EURYDICE: Go on.
FATHER: You know I hate writing letters. I'll give this letter to a worm. I hope he finds you.

    Love,
    Orpheus

EURYDICE: Orpheus?
FATHER: Orpheus.

A pause.

EURYDICE: That word!
    It's like—I can't breathe.
    Orpheus! My husband.

Eurydice looks at her father.
She recognizes him.

EURYDICE: Oh!

She embraces her father.

Scene 7

ORPHEUS: Dear Eurydice,

Last night I dreamed that we climbed Mount Olympus and we started to make love and all the strands of your hair were little faucets and water was streaming out of your head and I said, why is water coming out of your hair? And you said, gravity is very compelling.

And then we jumped off Mount Olympus and flew through the clouds and you held your knee to your chest because you skinned it on a sharp cloud and then we fell into a salty lake. Then I woke up and the window frightened me and I thought: Eurydice is dead. Then I thought—who is Eurydice? Then the whole room started to float and I thought: what are people? Then my bed clothes smiled at me with a crooked green mouth and I thought: who am I? It scares me, Eurydice. Please come back.

    Love,
    Orpheus

Scene 8

Eurydice and her Father in the string room.

FATHER: Did you get my letters?
EURYDICE: No! You wrote me letters?
FATHER: Every day.
EURYDICE: What did they say?
FATHER: Oh—nothing much. The usual stuff.
EURYDICE: Tell me the names of my mother and brothers and sisters.
FATHER: I don't think that's a good idea. It will make you sad.
EURYDICE: I want to know.
FATHER: It's a long time to be sad.
EURYDICE: I'd rather be sad.
THE STONES: Being sad is not allowed! Act like a stone.

Scene 9

Time shifts. Drops of water.
Eurydice and her father in the string room.

EURYDICE: Teach me another.
FATHER: Ostracize.
EURYDICE: What does it mean?
FATHER: To exclude. The Greeks decided who to banish. They wrote the name of the banished person on a white piece of pottery called ostrakon.
EURYDICE: Ostrakon.

    Another.

FATHER: Peripatetic. From the Greek. It means to walk slowly, speaking of weighty matters, in bare feet.
EURYDICE: Peripatetic: a learned fruit, wandering through the snow.

    Another.

FATHER: Defunct.
EURYDICE: Defunct.
FATHER: It means dead in a very abrupt way. Not the way I died, which was slowly. But all at once, in cowboy boots.
EURYDICE: Tell me a story of when you were little.
FATHER: Well, there was the time your uncle shot at me with a bee-bee gun and I was mad at him so I swallowed a nail.

Then there was the time I went to a dude ranch and I was riding a horse and I lassoed a car. The lady driving the car got out and spanked me. And your grandmother spanked me too.

EURYDICE: Remember the Christmas when she gave me a doll and I said, "If I see one more doll I'm going to throw up"?
FATHER: I think grammy was a little surprised when you said that.
EURYDICE: Tell me a story about your mother.
FATHER: The most vivid recollection I have of mother was seeing her at parties and in the house playing piano. When she was younger she was extremely animated.

She could really play the piano. She could play everything by ear. They called her Flaming Sally.

EURYDICE: I never saw grammy play the piano.

FATHER: She was never the same after my father died. My father was a very gentle man.

EURYDICE: Tell me a story about your father.

FATHER: My father and I used to duck hunt. By the Mississippi River. He would call up old Frank the night before and ask, "Where are the ducks moving tonight?" Old Frank, he could really call the ducks.

It was hard for me to kill the poor little ducks, but you get caught up in the fervor of it. You'd get as many as ten ducks.

If you went over the limit—there were only so many ducks per person—father would throw the ducks to the side of the creek we were paddling on and make sure there was no game warden. If the warden was gone, he'd run back and get the extra ducks and throw them in the back of the car. My father was never a great conversationalist—but he loved to rhapsodize about hunting. He would always say, if I ever have to die, it's in a duck pond. And he did.

EURYDICE: There was something I always wanted to ask you. A story—or someone's name—I forget.

FATHER: Don't worry. You'll remember. There's plenty of time.

Scene 10

Orpheus writes a letter.

ORPHEUS: Dear Eurydice,

I wonder if you miss reading books in the underworld.

Orpheus holds the Collected Works of Shakespeare with a long string attached.
He drops it slowly to the ground.

Scene 11

Eurydice holds the Collected Works of Shakespeare.

EURYDICE: What is this?

She opens it. She doesn't understand it.
She throws the book on the ground.

EURYDICE: What are you?

She is wary of it, as though it might bite her.
She tries to understand the book.
She tries to make the book do something.

EURYDICE: (*to the book*) What do you do?

What do you DO?!

Say something!

I hate you!

She stands on the book, trying to read it.

EURYDICE: Damn you!

She throws the book.
She lies down in the string room.
Drops of water. Time passes.
The Father picks up the book.
He brushes it off.
In the string room,
the father teaches Eurydice how to read.
She looks over his shoulder as he reads out loud from King Lear.

FATHER: We two alone will sing like birds in the cage.
When thou dost ask my blessing, I'll kneel down
And ask of thee forgiveness; so we'll live,
And pray and sing. . . .°

Scene 12

Orpheus, with a telephone.

ORPHEUS: For Eurydice—E, U, R, Y—that's right. No, there's no last name. It's not like that. What? No, I don't know the country. I don't know the city either. I don't know the street. I don't know—it probably starts with a vowel. Could you just—would you mind checking please—I would really appreciate it. You can't enter a name without a city? Why not? Well, thank you for trying. Wait—miss—it's a special case. She's dead. Well, thank you for trying. You have a nice day too.

He hangs up.

I'll find you. Don't move!

He fingers a glow-in-the-dark globe, looking for her.

Scene 13

Eurydice and her father in the string room.

EURYDICE: Tell me another story of when you were little.

FATHER: Well, there was my first piano recital. I was playing "I Got Rhythm." I played the first few chords and I couldn't remember the rest. I ran out of the room and locked myself in the bathroom.

EURYDICE: Then what happened?

FATHER: Your grandmother pulled me out of the bathroom and made me apologize to everyone in the auditorium. I never played piano after that. But I still know the first four chords—let's see—

We two alone . . . : In Shakespeare's *King Lear* (V, viii, 6–9), the mad Lear speaks these words to his still living daughter Cordelia, expecting them both to be placed in prison.

(*He plays the chords in the air with his hands*)

> Da Da *Dee* Da
> Da Da *Dee* Da
> Da Da *Dee* Da . . .

EURYDICE: What are the words?
FATHER: I can't remember.
> Let's see . . .
> Da da Dee Da
> Da da Dee da . . .

They both start singing to the tune of I Got Rhythm.

FATHER AND EURYDICE: Da da Dee Da
> Da da Dee Da
> Da da Dee Da
> Da dee da da doo dee dee da.

> Da da Da da
> Da da Da da
> Da Da da Da
> Da da da . . .

> Da da Dee Da
> Da da dee da . . .

STONES: WHAT IS THAT NOISE?
LITTLE STONE: Stop singing!
LOUD STONE: STOP SINGING!
BIG STONE: Neither of you can carry a tune.
LITTLE STONE: It's awful.
STONES: DEAD PEOPLE CAN'T SING!
EURYDICE: I'm not a very good singer.
FATHER: Neither am I.

Scene 14

The Father leaves for work.
He takes his briefcase.
He waves to Eurydice.
She waves back.
She is alone in the string room.
She touches the string.

The Lord of the Underworld enters on his red tricycle.
Music from a heavy metal band accompanies his entrance.
His clothes and his hat are too small for him.
He stops pedaling at the entrance to the string room.

CHILD: Knock, knock.
EURYDICE: Who's there?
CHILD: I am Lord of the Underworld.
EURYDICE: Very funny.
CHILD: I am.
EURYDICE: Prove it.
CHILD: I can do chin-ups inside your bones. Close your
> eyes.

She closes her eyes.

EURYDICE: Ow.
CHILD: See?
> You're pretty.

EURYDICE: You're little.
CHILD: I grow downward. Like a turnip.
EURYDICE: What do you want?
CHILD: I wanted to see if you were comfortable.
> You're not itchy?
EURYDICE: No.
CHILD: That's good. Sometimes our residents get itchy.
> Then I scratch them.
EURYDICE: I'm not itchy.
CHILD: What's all this string?
EURYDICE: It's my room.
CHILD: Rooms are not allowed!

(*To the stones.*)

> Tell her.
STONES: ROOMS ARE NOT ALLOWED!
CHILD: Who made your room?
EURYDICE: My father.
CHILD: Fathers are not allowed! Where is he?
EURYDICE: He's at work.
CHILD: We'll have to dip you in the river again and make
> sure you're good and dunked.
EURYDICE: Please, don't.
CHILD: Oooh—say that again. It's nice.
EURYDICE: Please, don't.
CHILD: Say it in my ear.
EURYDICE: (*towards his ear*) Please, don't.
CHILD: I like that.

(*A seduction:*)

> I'll huff and I'll puff and I'll blow your house down!

(*He blows on her face.*)

> I mean that in the nicest possible way.
EURYDICE: I have a husband.
CHILD: Husbands are for children. You need a lover. I'll
> be back.

(*To the stones.*)

> See that she's . . . comfortable.
STONES: We will!
CHILD: Good-bye.
EURYDICE: Good-bye.
STONES: Good-bye.
CHILD: I'm growing. Can you tell? I'm growing!

He laughs his hysterical laugh and speeds away on his
red tricycle.

Scene 15

A big storm. The sound of rain on a roof.
Orpheus in a rain slicker.

ORPHEUS: (*shouting above the storm*) If a drop of water
> enters the soil
> at a particular angle, with a particular pitch,
> what's to say a man can't ride one note
> into the earth like a fireman's pole?

He puts a bucket on the ground to catch rain falling.
He looks at the rain falling into the bucket.
He tunes his guitar, trying to make the pitch of each
note correspond with the pitch of each water drop.

Orpheus wonders if one particular pitch
might lead him to the underworld.
Orpheus wonders if the pitch
he is searching for might
correspond to the pitch of a drop
of rain, as it enters the soil.
A pitch.

ORPHEUS: Eurydice—did you hear that?

Another pitch.

Eurydice? That's the note. That one, right there.

Scene 16

Eurydice and her father in the string room.

EURYDICE: Orpheus never liked words. He had his music. He would get a funny look on his face and I would say what are you thinking about and he would always be thinking about music.

If we were in a restaurant sometimes Orpheus would look sullen and wouldn't talk to me and I thought people felt sorry for me. I should have realized that women envied me. Their husbands talked too much.

But I wanted to talk to him about my notions. I was working on a new philosophical system. It involved hats.

This is what it is to love an artist: The moon is always rising above your house. The houses of your neighbors look dull and lacking in moonlight. But he is always going away from you. Inside his head there is always something more beautiful.

Orpheus said the mind is a slide ruler. It can fit around anything. Words can mean anything. Show me your body, he said. It only means one thing.

Scene 17

ORPHEUS: Eurydice!

Before I go down there, I won't practice my music. Some say practice. But practice is a word invented by cowards. The animals don't have a word for practice. A gazelle does not run for practice. He runs because he is scared or he is hungry. A bird doesn't sing for practice. She sings because she's happy or sad. So I say: store it up. The music sounds better in my head than it does in the world. When songs are pressing against my throat, then, only then, I will go down and sing for the devils and they will cry through their parched throats.

Eurydice, don't kiss a dead man. Their lips look red and tempting but put your tongue in their mouths and it tastes like oatmeal. I know how much you hate oatmeal.

I'm going the way of death.

Here is my plan: Tonight, when I go to bed, I will turn off the light and put a straw in my mouth. When I fall asleep, I will crawl through the straw and my breath will push me like a great wind into the darkness and I will sing your name and I will arrive. I have consulted the almanacs, the footstools, and the architects, and everyone agrees: I found the right note. Wait for me.

Love,
Orpheus

Scene 18

EURYDICE: I got a letter. From Orpheus.
FATHER: What did he say?
EURYDICE: He says he's going to come find me.
FATHER: How?
EURYDICE: He's going to sing.

Scene 19

Darkness.
An unearthly light surrounds Orpheus.
He holds a straw up to his lips in slow motion.

He blows into the straw.

The sound of breath.
He disappears.

Scene 20

The sound of a knock.

LITTLE STONE: Someone is knocking!
BIG STONE: Who is it?
LOUD STONE: Who is it?

The sound of three loud knocks, insistent.

STONES: NO ONE KNOCKS AT THE DOOR OF THE DEAD!

THIRD MOVEMENT • Scene 1

Orpheus stands at the gates of hell.
He opens his mouth.

He looks like he's singing, but he's silent.
Music surrounds him.
The melody Orpheus hummed in the first scene,
repeated over and over again.

Raspberries, peaches and plums drop from the ceiling
into the River. Perhaps only in our imagination.
Orpheus keeps singing.

The stones weep.
They look at their tears, bewildered.
Orpheus keeps singing.

A child comes out of a trap door.

CHILD: Who are you?
ORPHEUS: I am Orpheus.
CHILD: I am Lord of the Underworld.
ORPHEUS: But you're so young!
CHILD: Don't be rude.
ORPHEUS: Sorry.
   Did you like my music?
CHILD: No, I prefer happy music with a nice beat.
ORPHEUS: Oh.
CHILD: You've come for Eurydice.
ORPHEUS: Yes!
CHILD: And you thought singing would get you through
   the gates of hell.
ORPHEUS: See here. I want my wife.
   What do I have to do?
CHILD: You'll have to do more than sing.
ORPHEUS: I'm not sure what you mean, sir.
CHILD: Start walking home. Your wife just might be on the
   road behind you. We make it real nice here. So people
   want to stick around. As you walk, keep your eyes fac-
   ing front. If you look back at her—poof! She's gone.
ORPHEUS: I can't look at her?
CHILD: No.
ORPHEUS: Why?
CHILD: Because.
ORPHEUS: Because?
CHILD: Because!
ORPHEUS: I look straight ahead. That's all?
CHILD: Yes.
ORPHEUS: That's easy.
CHILD: Good.

The child smiles. He exits.

Scene 2

Eurydice and her father.

EURYDICE: I hear him at the gates! That's his music! He's
   come to save me!
FATHER: Do you want to go with him?
EURYDICE: Yes, of course!

She sees that his face falls a little.

EURYDICE: Oh—you'll be lonely, won't you?
FATHER: No, no. You should go to your husband. You
   should have grandchildren. You'll all come down and
   meet me one day.
EURYDICE: Are you sure?
FATHER: You should love your family until the grapes
   grow dust on their purple faces.
   I'll take you to him.
EURYDICE: Now?
FATHER: It's for the best.

He takes her arm.
They process, arm in arm, as at a wedding.
Wedding music.
They are solemn and glad.
They walk.
They see Orpheus up ahead.

FATHER: Is that him?
EURYDICE: Yes—I think so—
FATHER: His shoulders aren't very broad. Can he take
   care of you?

Eurydice nods.

FATHER: Are you sure?
EURYDICE: Yes.
FATHER: There's one thing you need to know. If he turns
   around and sees you, you'll die a second death. Those
   are the rules. So step quietly. And don't cry out.
EURYDICE: I won't.
FATHER: Good-bye.

They embrace.

EURYDICE: I'll come back to you. I seem to keep dying.
FATHER: Don't let them dip you in the River too long, the
   second time. Hold your breath.
EURYDICE: I'll look for a tree.
FATHER: I'll write you letters.
EURYDICE: Where will I find them?
FATHER: I don't know yet. I'll think of something. Good-
   bye, Eurydice.
EURYDICE: Good-bye.

They move away.
The father waves.
She waves back,
as though on an old steamer ship.
The father exits.
Eurydice takes a deep breath. She takes a big step for-
ward towards the audience, on an unseen gangplank.
She is brave.
She takes another step forward.
She hesitates.
She is all of a sudden not so brave.
She is afraid.
SHE LOOKS BACK.
She turns in the direction of her father, her back to the
audience. He's out of sight.

EURYDICE: Wait, come back!
LITTLE STONE: You can't go back now, Eurydice.
LOUD STONE: Face forward!
BIG STONE: Keep walking.
EURYDICE: I'm afraid!
LOUD STONE: Your husband is waiting for you, Eurydice.
EURYDICE: I don't recognize him! That's a stranger!
LITTLE STONE: Go on. It's him.
EURYDICE: I want to go home! I want my father!
LOUD STONE: You're all grown up now. You have a
   husband.
STONES: TURN AROUND!
EURYDICE: Why?

STONES: BECAUSE!
EURYDICE: That's a stupid reason.
LITTLE STONE: Orpheus braved the gates of hell
  to find you.
LOUD STONE: He played the saddest music.
BIG STONE: Even we—
STONES: The stones—
LITTLE STONE: cried when we heard it.

She turns slowly, facing front.

EURYDICE: That's Orpheus?
STONES: Yes, that's him!
EURYDICE: Where's his music?
STONES: It's in your head.

*Orpheus walks slowly, in a straight line, with the focus
of a tight-rope walker.
Eurydice moves to follow him.
She follows him, several steps behind.
THEY WALK.
Eurydice follows him with precision, one step for every
step he takes.
She makes a decision.
She increases her pace.
She takes two steps for every step that Orpheus takes.
She catches up to him.*

EURYDICE: Orpheus?

*HE TURNS TOWARDS HER, STARTLED.
ORPHEUS LOOKS AT EURYDICE.
EURYDICE LOOKS AT ORPHEUS.
THE WORLD FALLS AWAY.*

ORPHEUS: You startled me.

*A small sound—ping.
They turn their faces away from each other,
matter-of-fact, compelled.
The lights turn blue.*

EURYDICE: I'm sorry
ORPHEUS: Why?
EURYDICE: I don't know.

ORPHEUS: (*syncopated*)	EURYDICE:
You always clapped your hands on the third beat you couldn't wait for the fourth. Remember— I tried to teach you—	I could never spell the word rhythm— it is such a difficult word to spell— r—y—no— there's an H in it—
you were always one step ahead of the music your sense of rhythm— it was—off—	somewhere— a breath— rhy—rhy— rhy—

ORPHEUS: I would say clap on the down-beat—
  no, the down-beat—
  It's dangerous not

to have a sense of rhythm.
  You LOSE things when you can't
  keep a simple beat—
  why'd you have to say my name—
  Eurydice—
EURYDICE: I'm sorry.
ORPHEUS: I know we used to fight—
  it seems so silly now—if—
EURYDICE: If ifs and ands were pots and pans
  there'd be no need for tinkers—
ORPHEUS: Why?

*They begin walking away from each other
on extensive unseen boardwalks,
their figures long shadows,
looking straight ahead.*

EURYDICE: If ifs and ands were pots and pans
  there'd be no need for tinkers—
ORPHEUS: Eurydice—
EURYDICE: I think I see the gates.
  The stones—the boat—
  it looks familiar—
  the stones look happy to see me—
ORPHEUS: Don't look—
EURYDICE: Wow! That's the happiest I've ever seen them!

ORPHEUS: (*syncopated*)	EURYDICE:
Think of things we did:	Everything is so grey— it looks familiar—
we went ice skating—	like home— our house was—
I wore a red sweater—	grey—with a red door— we had two cats and two dogs and two fish that died—

ORPHEUS: Will you talk to me!
EURYDICE: The train looks like
  the opposite of a train—
ORPHEUS: Eurydice!
  WE'VE KNOWN EACH OTHER FOR CENTURIES!
  I want to reminisce!
  Remember when you wanted your name in a song
  so I put your name in a song—
  When I played my music
  at the gates of hell
  I was singing your name
  over and over and over again.
  Eurydice.

*He grows quiet.
They walk away from each other on extended lines
until they are out of sight.*

Scene 3

THE STONES: Finally.
  Some peace.
LOUD STONE: And quiet.

THE STONES: Like the old days.
No music.
No conversation.
How about that.

A pause.

FATHER: With Eurydice gone it will be a second death
for me.
LITTLE STONE: Oh, please, sir—
BIG STONE: We're tired.
FATHER: Do you understand the love a father has for his
daughter?
LITTLE STONE: Love is a big, funny word.
BIG STONE: Dead people should be seen and not heard.

The father looks at the stones.
He looks at the string room.
He dismantles the string room,
matter-of-fact.
There's nothing else to do.
This can take time.
It takes time to dismantle a room made of string.
Music.
He sits down in what used to be the string room.

FATHER: How does a person remember to forget. It's
difficult.
LOUD STONE: It's not difficult.
LITTLE STONE: We told you how it works.
LOUD STONE: Dip yourself in the river.
BIG STONE: Dip yourself in the river.
LITTLE STONE: Dip yourself in the river.
FATHER: I need directions.
LOUD STONE: That's ridiculous.
BIG STONE: There are no directions.

A pause.
The father thinks.

FATHER: I remember.
Take Tri-State South—294—
to Route 88 West.
Take Route 88 West to Route 80.
You'll go over a bridge.
Go three miles and you'll come
to the exit for Middle Road.
Proceed 3 to 4 miles.
Duck Creek Park will be on the right.
Take a left on Fernwood Avenue.

Continue straight on Fernwood past
two intersections.
Fernwood will curve to the right leading
you to Forest Road.
Take a left on Forest Road.
Go two blocks.
Pass the first entrance to the alley on the right.
Take the second entrance.
You'll go about 100 yards.
A red brick house will
be on the right.
Look for Illinois license plates.

Go inside the house.
In the living room,
look out the window.
You'll see the lights on the Mississippi River.
Take off your shoes.
Walk down the hill.
You'll pass a tree good for climbing on the right.
Cross the road.
Watch for traffic.
Cross the train tracks.
Catfish are sleeping in the mud, on your left.
Roll up your jeans.
Count to ten.
Put your feet in the river
and swim.

He dips himself in the river.
A small metallic sound of forgetfulness—ping.
The sound of water.
He lies down on the ground,
curled up, asleep.

Eurydice returns and sees that her string room is gone.

EURYDICE: Where's my room?

The stones are silent.

EURYDICE: (*to the stones*) WHERE IS MY ROOM?
Answer me!
LITTLE STONE: It's none of our business.
LOUD STONE: What are you doing here?
BIG STONE: You should be with your husband.
LOUD STONE: Up there.
EURYDICE: Where's my father?

The stones point to the father.

EURYDICE: (*to the stones*) Why is he sleeping?

The stones shrug their shoulders.

EURYDICE: (*to her father*) I've come back!
LOUD STONE: He can't hear you.
LITTLE STONE: It's too late.
EURYDICE: What are you talking about?
BIG STONE: He dipped himself in the River.
EURYDICE: My father did not dip himself in the River.
STONES: He did!
We saw him!
LOUD STONE: He wanted some peace and quiet.
EURYDICE: (*to the stones*) HE DID NOT!

(*To her father.*)

Listen. I'll teach you the words. Then we'll know
each other again. Ready? We'll start with my name.
Eurydice. E U R Y . . . .
BIG STONE: He can't hear you.
LOUD STONE: He can't see you.
LITTLE STONE: He can't remember you.
EURYDICE: (*to the stones*) I hate you! I've always hated
you!
Shut up! Shut up! Shut up!

(To her father.)

Listen. I'll tell you a story.

LITTLE STONE: Try speaking in the language of stones.

LOUD STONE: It's a very quiet language.
Like if the pores in your
face opened up and wanted to talk.

EURYDICE: Stone.
Rock.
Tree. Rock. Stone.

It doesn't work.
She holds her father.

LOUD STONE: Didn't you already mourn for your father, young lady?

LITTLE STONE: Some things should be left well enough alone.

BIG STONE: To mourn twice is excessive.

LITTLE STONE: To mourn three times a sin.

LOUD STONE: Life is like a good meal.

BIG STONE: Only gluttons want more food when they finish their helping.

LITTLE STONE: Learn to be more moderate.

BIG STONE: It's weird for a dead person to be morbid.

LITTLE STONE: We don't like to watch it!

LOUD STONE: We don't like to see it!

BIG STONE: It makes me uncomfortable.

Eurydice cries.

STONES: Don't cry!
Don't cry!

BIG STONE: Learn the art of keeping busy!

EURYDICE: IT'S HARD TO KEEP BUSY WHEN YOU'RE DEAD!

STONES: It is not hard!
We keep busy
and we like it
We're busy busy busy stones
Watch us work
Keeping still
Keeping quiet
It's hard work
to be a stone
No time for crying
No no no!

EURYDICE: I HATE YOU! I'VE ALWAYS HATED YOU!

She runs towards them and tries to hit them.

STONES: Go ahead.
Try to hit us.

LITTLE STONE: You'll hurt your fist.

BIG STONE: You'll break your hand.

STONES: Ha ha ha!

Enter the child.
He has grown.
He is now at least ten feet tall.
His voice sounds suspiciously
like the Nasty Interesting Man's.

CHILD: Is there a problem here?

STONES: No, sir.

CHILD: *(to Eurydice)* You chose to stay with us, huh? Good.

(He looks her over.)

Perhaps to be my bride?

EURYDICE: I told you. You're too young.

CHILD: I'll be the judge of that.
I've grown.

EURYDICE: Yes—I see that.

CHILD: I'm ready to be a man now. I'm ready—to be—a man.

EURYDICE: Please. Leave me alone.

CHILD: I'll have them start preparing the satins and silks. You can't refuse me. I've made my choice.

EURYDICE: Can I have a moment to prepare myself?

CHILD: Don't be long. The wedding songs are already being written. They're very quiet. Inaudible, you might say. A dirt-filled orchestra for my bride. Don't trouble the songs with your music, I say. A song is two dead bodies rubbing under the covers to keep warm.

Orpheus (played by Joseph Parks) descending into the underworld in a rainy elevator in the Yale Repertory Theatre's 2006 performance of Sarah Ruhl's *Eurydice*.

He exits.

STONES: Well, well, well!
LITTLE STONE: You had better prepare yourself.
EURYDICE: There is nothing to prepare.
BIG STONE: You had better comb your hair.
LOUD STONE: You had better find a veil.
EURYDICE: I don't need a veil. I need a pen!
LITTLE STONE: Pens are forbidden here.
EURYDICE: I need a pencil then.
LOUD STONE: Pencils, too.
EURYDICE: Damn you! I'll dip you in the river!
BIG STONE: Too late, too late!
EURYDICE: There must be a pen. There are. There must be.

*She remembers the pen and paper in the breast pocket
of her father's coat.
She takes them out.
She holds the pen up to show the stones.*

EURYDICE: A pen.

She writes a letter.

EURYDICE: Dear Orpheus,

   I'm sorry. I don't know what came over me. I was afraid.
   I'm not worthy of you. But I still love you, I think. Don't
   try to find me again. You would be lonely for music. I
   want you to be happy. I want you to marry again. I am
   going to write out instructions for your next wife.

   To my Husband's Next Wife:

   Be gentle.
   Be sure to comb his hair when it's wet.
   Do not fail to notice
   that his face flushes pink
   like a bride's
   when you kiss him.

Give him lots to eat.
He forgets to eat and he gets cranky.

When he's sad,
kiss his forehead and I will thank you.
Because he is a young prince
and his robes are too heavy on him.
His crown falls down
around his ears.

I'll give this letter to a worm. I hope he finds you.

Love,
Eurydice.

*She puts the letter on the ground.
She dips herself in the river.
A small metallic sound of forgetfulness—ping.
The sound of water.
She lies down next to her father, as though asleep.*

*The sound of an elevator—ding.
Orpheus appears in the elevator.
He sees Eurydice.
He is happy.
The elevator starts raining on Orpheus.
He forgets.
He steps out of the elevator.*

*He sees the letter on the ground.
He picks it up.
He scrutinizes it.
He can't read it.
He stands on it.
He closes his eyes.
The sound of water.
Then silence.*

The end.

John Patrick Shanley

John Patrick Shanley (b. 1950) grew up in the Bronx, New York, and his experiences in school were marked by difficulties. He was expelled from kindergarten, and in St. Anthony's, a school run by the Sisters of Charity, he was restricted from the lunch program for life. At Cardinal Spellman High School, he rebelled against the strict program and was eventually asked to leave. He then attended Thomas More, a private Catholic school in New Hampshire, where his talent for writing was discovered and nurtured. He went to New York University for a semester, but was asked to leave. He then joined the Marines during the Vietnam War. After returning home, he finished his degree at New York University and began his professional writing career with his first play, *Saturday Night at the War* (1978). His academic difficulties were not an indication of a lack of intelligence—he was the valedictorian of his class at NYU—but of a certain lack of judgment that Shanley said later helped him in working out dramatic problems.

Shanley's screenwriting experience earned him an Oscar for his original script, *Moonstruck* (1988), starring Cher and Nicholas Cage. He produced several more scripts that attracted famous stars, such as Tom Hanks and Meg Ryan, but while he was writing screenplays and directing, he continued writing off-Broadway plays. Shanley has said that his four early plays are essentially one long play: *Danny and the Deep Blue Sea* (1983), *Savage in Limbo* (1984), *The Dreamer Examines His Pillow* (1985), and *Italian-American Reconciliation* (1986). While there is a great deal of humor in these plays, Shanley also works out a number of personal issues related to family and the stress of relationships. For example, *Italian-American Reconciliation*, which premiered in New York in 1988 at the Manhattan Theatre Club, starring John Turturro, explores the virtual insanity of a character who turns his back on a loving woman to attempt a reconciliation with his impossible ex-wife. Shanley has been married twice and now lives with his two adopted sons. His plays, he has hinted, come from a deep reservoir of personal experiences.

Critics have not always been kind to Shanley, and one of their early complaints was that his plays are too "talky." In his own defense, Shanley says he uses the language of his plays to discuss difficult and important issues. He makes every effort to have his characters talk the way he has heard real people talk and to be clear about the truth. He tries to avoid clichés that give people the sense that they know the truth about something when, in fact, they do not. Political slogans, for example, are a clichéd kind of shorthand for positions that are only vaguely understood, and Shanley believes that there are "middlemen"—journalists, politicians, and others—who appropriate language in such a way as to keep people confused about important issues in their lives.

One result of Shanley's Catholic education and his experience in the Marine Corps is that he developed an understanding of and respect for the nature of authority. But he also came to understand that the certainty imparted to him by his early experiences was not absolute. His desire to discover the truth about important issues in life could not be satisfied by accepting without question everything he was told.

Shanley's plays often show us wounded people in situations of stress. *Kissing Christine* (1996) introduces two differently traumatized people on a first date; *Psychopathia Sexualis* (1998) is about a man with an argyle sock fetish who wishes to marry a woman who defies their psychiatrist; and *Where's My Money?* (2001) treats sexual infidelity in marriage and the opinions people rush to in judging others. His most quoted line is from *Where's My Money?*: "Monogamy is like a 40-watt bulb. It works, but it's not enough."

The idea for *Doubt* (2004) came to Shanley as he was rehearsing another play. Fearing that it was too close to current headlines exposing child molestation in the Roman Catholic Church, he hesitated. But he knew that the idea depended on his own experience in Catholic school, and in an interview he said that when he thought of the scene in which a child's mother, Mrs. Muller, talks with Sister Aloysius, he knew that he had a real play, not a hint of journalism.

For links to resources about Shanley, click on *AuthorLinks* at **bedfordstmartins.com/jacobus**.

Doubt: A Parable

In his preface to the play, Shanley says, "We are living in a culture of extreme advocacy, of confrontation, of judgment, and of verdict." *Doubt* is, in many ways, an illustration of that statement. Sister Aloysius has arrived at a verdict with respect to Father Flynn, who she believes is molesting a young student, Donald Muller. Flynn himself delivers a sermon on the question of doubt related to the assassination of President Kennedy. He later delivers a sermon on the consequences of malicious gossip, using a simple parable to illustrate his point. Sister James is much younger than Sister Aloysius and by nature tends to be much less confrontational and judgmental. She is, as Sister Aloysius tells her, innocent, and as a result turns out to be easily led by her superior to suspect Father Flynn.

Father Flynn's first sermon arises in response to the despair people felt after the assassination of President Kennedy. Interestingly, he ends the sermon with a story about a figure on the open ocean who sets his course and then begins to doubt whether he has set it truly. Flynn likens this situation to a crisis in faith, which at that point seems to be the center of doubt for members of the church. Flynn says, "Doubt can be a bond as powerful and sustaining as certainty." The bond he refers to is a bond of a community, whether a community of two or a community of dozens. When he speaks later of the force of gossip and its effects on a community, he speaks in reference not to a public action, but to the specific action of Sister Aloysius and her attempt to destroy his reputation. In both of his sermons, Father Flynn adds a parable to his message, a practice that recalls the sermons of Jesus Christ.

The structure of the play depends on the absolute certainty of Sister Aloysius in her conviction that Father Flynn's behavior with his students is dangerous. The fact that Father Flynn takes Donald Muller under his wing is, for her, evidence of his inappropriate treatment of the student. Although she admits that there is no real evidence, nothing specific or provable that would indict Father Flynn, she insists that she knows the truth. Her personal experience, combined with her suspicions and observations, makes her totally convinced. Nothing that Father Flynn can say to her will change her mind. From her position of power she comes close to converting Sister James to her point of view. It is only in the presence of Father Flynn himself that Sister James becomes uncertain and then decides that he may not be guilty of child molestation.

When Mrs. Muller comes for a conference with Sister Aloysius, we discover additional complexities in the situation. Mrs. Muller is confounded by the fact that Sister Aloysius makes her son pay for the aberrant behavior of a priest, when she should remove the priest, not the student. Mrs. Muller explains how important this school is for her son, how he had been beaten up by students in his other school. She implies that Donald might be gay and for that reason her husband beats Donald. The fact that Father Flynn has taken an interest in Donald is for Mrs. Muller something positive. Yet her sense of what her son needs and the benefits he receives from the school do not move Sister Aloysius, who remains certain of herself.

Audience members cannot be certain why Father Flynn accepts a promotion and leaves the school, nor can they be certain why Sister Aloysius resorts to lying to Father Flynn about her phone call "investigating" his former appointments. John Patrick Shanley leaves us with doubts.

For discussion questions and assignments on *Doubt,* visit bedfordstmartins.com/jacobus.

Doubt: A Parable in Performance

Doubt premiered off-Broadway at the Manhattan Theatre Club in New York in November 2004, because Lynne Meadow, artistic director of the Manhattan Theatre Club, asked to produce it. Since Shanley had produced so many plays off-Broadway, the venue seemed a natural choice to him. The play soon transferred to the Walter Kerr Theatre on Broadway in response to intense audience approval. Doug Hughes directed in March 2005, with Brían O'Byrne as Father Flynn and Cherry Jones as Sister Aloysius. Interestingly, Shanley invited his first-grade teacher, also named Sister James, to sit with him at both openings. The critics were uniformly positive, with a great many of them naming it the number one show of the year. The play won the Tony Award for best play, the New York Drama Critics' Circle Award, the Lucille Lortel Award, and the Pulitzer Prize for drama. *Doubt* was made into a film in 2008 starring Meryl Streep, Philip Seymour Hoffman, and Amy Adams. The film received five Academy Award nominations, including one for best writing.

From 2006 to the present, the play has been performed regionally and internationally. It went on tour in the United States in 2006 and 2007. It played in the Philippines, in Paris (directed by Roman Polanski), in Poland, in Australia at the Sidney Opera House, and in many other venues throughout the world. The play has been called "actor proof" and continues to be produced in high schools as well as university theaters.

JOHN PATRICK SHANLEY (b. 1950)

Doubt   2004
A Parable

ONE

A priest, Father Flynn, in his late thirties, in green and gold vestments, gives a sermon. He is working class, from the Northeast.

FLYNN: What do you do when you're not sure? That's the topic of my sermon today. You look for God's direction and can't find it. Last year when President Kennedy was assassinated, who among us did not experience the most profound disorientation. Despair. "What now? Which way? What do I say to my kids? What do I tell myself?" It was a time of people sitting together, bound together by a common feeling of hopelessness. But think of that! Your *bond* with your fellow beings was your *despair*. It was a public experience, shared by everyone in our society. It was awful, but we were in it together! How much worse is it then for the lone man, the lone woman, stricken by a private calamity? "No one knows I'm sick. No one knows I've lost my last real friend. No one knows I've done something wrong." Imagine the isolation. You see the world as through a window. On the one side of the glass: happy, untroubled people. On the other side: you. Something has happened, you have to carry it, and it's incommunicable. For those so afflicted, only God knows their pain. Their secret. The secret of their alienating sorrow. And when such a person, as they must, howls to the sky, to God: "Help me!" What if no answer comes? Silence. I want to tell you a story. A cargo ship sank, and all her crew was drowned. Only this one sailor survived. He made a raft of some spars and, being of a nautical discipline, turned his eyes to the Heavens and read the stars. He set a course for his home and, exhausted, fell asleep. Clouds rolled in and blanketed the sky. For the next twenty nights, as he floated on the vast ocean, he could no longer see the stars. He thought he was on course, but there was no way to be certain. As the days rolled on, and he wasted away with fevers, thirst and starvation, he began to have doubts. Had he set his course right? Was he still going on towards his home? Or was he horribly lost and doomed to a terrible death? No way to know. The message of the constellations—had he imagined it because of his desperate circumstance? Or had he seen Truth once and now had to hold on to it without further reassurance? That was his dilemma on a voyage without apparent end. There are those of you in church today who know exactly the crisis of faith I describe. I want to say to you. Doubt can be a bond as powerful and sustaining as certainty. When you are lost, you are not alone. In the name of the Father, the Son, and the Holy Ghost. Amen. (*He exits.*)

TWO

The lights crossfade to a corner office in a Catholic school in the Bronx. The principal, Sister Aloysius Beauvier, sits at her desk, writing in a ledger with a fountain pen. She is in her fifties or sixties. She is watchful, reserved, unsentimental. She is of the order of the Sisters of Charity. She wears a black bonnet and floor-length black habit, rimless glasses. A knock at the door.

SISTER ALOYSIUS: Come in. (*Sister James, also of the Sisters of Charity, pokes her head in. She is in her twenties. There's a bit of sunshine in her heart, though she's reserved as well.*)
SISTER JAMES: Have you a moment, Sister Aloysius?
SISTER ALOYSIUS: Come in, Sister James. (*She enters.*) Who's watching your class?
SISTER JAMES: They're having Art.
SISTER ALOYSIUS: Art. Waste of time.
SISTER JAMES: It's only an hour a week.
SISTER ALOYSIUS: Much can be accomplished in sixty minutes.
SISTER JAMES: Yes, Sister Aloysius. I wondered if I might know what you did about William London?
SISTER ALOYSIUS: I sent him home.
SISTER JAMES: Oh dear. So he's still bleeding?
SISTER ALOYSIUS: Oh yes.
SISTER JAMES: His nose just let loose and started gushing during the Pledge of Allegiance.
SISTER ALOYSIUS: Was it spontaneous?
SISTER JAMES: What else would it be?
SISTER ALOYSIUS: Self-induced.
SISTER JAMES: You mean, you think he might've intentionally given himself a nosebleed?
SISTER ALOYSIUS: Exactly.
SISTER JAMES: No!

SISTER ALOYSIUS: You are a very innocent person, Sister James. William London is a fidgety boy and if you do not keep right on him, he will do anything to escape his chair. He would set his foot on fire for half a day out of school.

SISTER JAMES: But why?

SISTER ALOYSIUS: He has a restless mind.

SISTER JAMES: But that's good.

SISTER ALOYSIUS: No, it's not. His father's a policeman, and the last thing he wants is a rowdy boy. William London is headed for trouble. Puberty has got hold of him. He will be imagining all the wrong things, and I strongly suspect he will not graduate high school. But that's beyond our jurisdiction. We simply have to get him through, out the door, and then he's somebody else's project. Ordinarily, I assign my most experienced sisters to eighth grade, but I'm working within constraints. Are you in control of your class?

SISTER JAMES: I think so.

SISTER ALOYSIUS: Usually more children are sent down to me.

SISTER JAMES: I try to take care of things myself.

SISTER ALOYSIUS: That can be an error. You are answerable to me, I to the monsignor, he to the bishop, and so on up to the Holy Father. There's a chain of discipline. Make use of it.

SISTER JAMES: Yes, Sister.

SISTER ALOYSIUS: How's Donald Muller doing?

SISTER JAMES: Steady.

SISTER ALOYSIUS: Good. Has anyone hit him?

SISTER JAMES: No.

SISTER ALOYSIUS: Good. That girl, Linda Conte, have you seated her away from the boys?

SISTER JAMES: As far as space permits. It doesn't do much good.

SISTER ALOYSIUS: Just get her through. Intact. (*Pause, Sister Aloysius is staring absently at Sister James. A silence falls.*)

SISTER JAMES: So. Should I go? (*No answer.*) Is something the matter?

SISTER ALOYSIUS: No. Why? Is something the matter?

SISTER JAMES: I don't think so.

SISTER ALOYSIUS: Then nothing's the matter then.

SISTER JAMES: Well. Thank you, Sister. I just wanted to check on William's nose. (*She starts to go.*)

SISTER ALOYSIUS: He had a ballpoint pen.

SISTER JAMES: Excuse me, Sister?

SISTER ALOYSIUS: William London had a ballpoint pen. He was fiddling with it while he waited for his mother. He's not using it for assignments, I hope.

SISTER JAMES: No, of course not.

SISTER ALOYSIUS: I'm sorry I allowed even cartridge pens into the school. The students really should only be learning script with true fountain pens. Always the easy way out these days. What does that teach? Every easy choice today will have its consequence tomorrow. Mark my words.

SISTER JAMES: Yes, Sister.

SISTER ALOYSIUS: Ballpoints make them pr[...] when they press down, they write like [...]

SISTER JAMES: I don't allow them ballpoi[...]

SISTER ALOYSIUS: Good. Penmanship is dying all a[...] the country. You have some time. Sit down. (*Sister James hesitates and sits down.*) We might as well have a talk. I've been meaning to talk to you. I observed your lesson on the New Deal at the beginning of the term. Not bad. But I caution you. Do not idealize Franklin Delano Roosevelt. He was a good president, but he did attempt to pack the Supreme Court. I do not approve of making heroes of lay historical figures. If you want to talk about saints, do it in Religion.

SISTER JAMES: Yes, Sister.

SISTER ALOYSIUS: Also. I question your enthusiasm for History.

SISTER JAMES: But I love History!

SISTER ALOYSIUS: That is exactly my meaning. You favor History and risk swaying the children to value it over their other subjects. I think this is a mistake.

SISTER JAMES: I never thought of that. I'll try to treat my other lessons with more enthusiasm.

SISTER ALOYSIUS: No. Give them their History without putting sugar all over it. That's the point. Now. Tell me about your class. How would you characterize the condition of 8-B?

SISTER JAMES: I don't know where to begin. What do you want to know?

SISTER ALOYSIUS: Let's begin with Stephen Inzio.

SISTER JAMES: Stephen Inzio has the highest marks in the class.

SISTER ALOYSIUS: Noreen Horan?

SISTER JAMES: Second highest marks.

SISTER ALOYSIUS: Brenda McNulty?

SISTER JAMES: Third highest.

SISTER ALOYSIUS: You see I am making a point, Sister James. I know that Stephen Inzio, Noreen Horan and Brenda McNulty are one, two and three in your class. School-wide, there are forty-eight such students each grade period. I make it my business to know all forty-eight of their names. I do not say this to aggrandize myself, but to illustrate the importance of paying attention. You must pay attention as well.

SISTER JAMES: Yes, Sister Aloysius.

SISTER ALOYSIUS: I cannot be everywhere.

SISTER JAMES: Am I falling short, Sister?

SISTER ALOYSIUS: These three students with the highest marks. Are they the most intelligent children in your class?

SISTER JAMES: No, I wouldn't say they are. But they work the hardest.

SISTER ALOYSIUS: Very good! That's right! That's the ethic. What good's a gift if it's left in the box? What good is a high IQ if you're staring out the window with your mouth agape? Be hard on the bright ones, Sister James. Don't be charmed by cleverness. Not theirs. And not yours. I think you are a competent teacher, Sister James, but maybe not our best teacher.

The best teachers do not perform, they cause the students to perform.

SISTER JAMES: Do I perform?

SISTER ALOYSIUS: As if on a Broadway stage.

SISTER JAMES: Oh dear. I had no conception!

SISTER ALOYSIUS: You're showing off. You like to see yourself ten feet tall in their eyes. Another thing occurs to me. Where were you before?

SISTER JAMES: Mount St. Margaret's.

SISTER ALOYSIUS: All girls.

SISTER JAMES: Yes.

SISTER ALOYSIUS: I feel I must remind you. Boys are made of gravel, soot and tar paper. Boys are a different breed.

SISTER JAMES: I feel I know how to handle them.

SISTER ALOYSIUS: But perhaps you are wrong. And perhaps you are not working hard enough.

SISTER JAMES: Oh. (*Sister James cries a little.*)

SISTER ALOYSIUS: No tears.

SISTER JAMES: I thought you were satisfied with me.

SISTER ALOYSIUS: Satisfaction is a vice. Do you have a handkerchief?

SISTER JAMES: Yes.

SISTER ALOYSIUS: Use it. Do you think that Socrates was satisfied? Good teachers are never content. We have some three hundred and seventy-two students in this school. It is a society which requires constant educational, spiritual and human vigilance. I cannot afford an excessively innocent instructor in my eighth grade class. It's self-indulgent. Innocence is a form of laziness. Innocent teachers are easily duped. You must be canny, Sister James.

SISTER JAMES: Yes, Sister.

SISTER ALOYSIUS: When William London gets a nosebleed, be skeptical. Don't let a little blood fuddle your judgment. God gave you a brain and a heart. The heart is warm, but your wits must be cold. Liars should be frightened to lie to you. They should be uncomfortable in your presence. I doubt they are.

SISTER JAMES: I don't know. I've never thought about it.

SISTER ALOYSIUS: The children should think you see right through them.

SISTER JAMES: Wouldn't that be a little frightening?

SISTER ALOYSIUS: Only to the ones that are up to no good.

SISTER JAMES: But I want my students to feel they can talk to me.

SISTER ALOYSIUS: They're children. They can talk to each other. It's more important they have a fierce moral guardian. You stand at the door, Sister. You are the gatekeeper. If you are vigilant, they will not need to be.

SISTER JAMES: I'm not sure what you want me to do.

SISTER ALOYSIUS: And if things occur in your classroom which you sense require understanding, but you don't understand, come to me.

SISTER JAMES: Yes, Sister.

SISTER ALOYSIUS: That's why I'm here. That's why I'm the principal of this school. Do you stay when the specialty instructors come in?

SISTER JAMES: Yes.

SISTER ALOYSIUS: But you're here now while the Art class is going on.

SISTER JAMES: I was a little concerned about William's nose.

SISTER ALOYSIUS: Right. So you have Art in class.

SISTER JAMES: She comes in. Mrs. Bell. Yes.

SISTER ALOYSIUS: And you take them down to the basement for Dance with Mrs. Shields.

SISTER JAMES: On Thursdays.

SISTER ALOYSIUS: Another waste of time.

SISTER JAMES: Oh, but everyone loves the Christmas pageant.

SISTER ALOYSIUS: I don't love it. Frankly it offends me. Last year the girl playing Our Lady was wearing lipstick. I was waiting in the wings for that little jade.

SISTER JAMES: Then there's Music.

SISTER ALOYSIUS: That strange woman with the portable piano. What's wrong with her neck?

SISTER JAMES: Some kind of goiter. Poor woman.

SISTER ALOYSIUS: Yes. Mrs. Carolyn.

SISTER JAMES: That's right.

SISTER ALOYSIUS: We used to have a Sister teaching that. Not enough Sisters. What else?

SISTER JAMES: Physical Education and Religion.

SISTER ALOYSIUS: And for that we have Father Flynn. Two hours a week. And you stay for those?

SISTER JAMES: Mostly. Unless I have reports to fill out or . . .

SISTER ALOYSIUS: What do you think of Father Flynn?

SISTER JAMES: Oh, he's a brilliant man. What a speaker!

SISTER ALOYSIUS: Yes. His sermon this past Sunday was poetic.

SISTER JAMES: He's actually very good, too, at teaching basketball. I was surprised. I wouldn't think a man of the cloth the personality type for basketball, but he has a way he has, very natural with dribbling and shooting.

SISTER ALOYSIUS: What do you think that sermon was about?

SISTER JAMES: What?

SISTER ALOYSIUS: This past Sunday. What was he talking about?

SISTER JAMES: Well, Doubt. He was talking about Doubt.

SISTER ALOYSIUS: Why?

SISTER JAMES: Excuse me, Sister?

SISTER ALOYSIUS: Well, sermons come from somewhere, don't they? Is Father Flynn in Doubt, is he concerned that someone else is in Doubt?

SISTER JAMES: I suppose you'd have to ask him.

SISTER ALOYSIUS: No. That would not be appropriate. He is my superior. And if he were troubled, he should confess it to a fellow priest, or the monsignor. We do not share intimate information with priests. (*A pause.*)

SISTER JAMES: I'm a little concerned. (*Sister Aloysius leans forward.*)

SISTER ALOYSIUS: About what?

SISTER JAMES: The time. Art class will be over in a few minutes. I should go up.

SISTER ALOYSIUS: Have you noticed anything, Sister James?

SISTER JAMES: About what?

SISTER ALOYSIUS: I want you to be alert.

SISTER JAMES: I don't believe I'm following you, Sister.

SISTER ALOYSIUS: I'm sorry I'm not more forthright, but I must be careful not to create something by saying it. I can only say I am concerned, perhaps needlessly, about matters in St. Nicholas School.

SISTER JAMES: Academically?

SISTER ALOYSIUS: I wasn't inviting a guessing game. I want you to pay attention to your class.

SISTER JAMES: Well, of course I'll pay attention to my class, Sister. And I'll try not to perform. And I'll try to be less innocent. I'm sorry you're disappointed in me. Please know that I will try my best. Honestly.

SISTER ALOYSIUS: Look at you. You'd trade anything for a warm look. I'm telling you here and now, I want to see the starch in your character cultivated. If you are looking for reassurance, you can be fooled. If you forget yourself and study others, you will not be fooled. It's important. One final matter and then you really must get back. Sister Veronica is going blind.

SISTER JAMES: Oh how horrible!

SISTER ALOYSIUS: This is not generally known, and I don't want it known. If they find out in the rectory, she'll be gone. I cannot afford to lose her. But now if you see her making her way down those stone stairs into the courtyard, for the love of Heaven, lightly take her hand as if in fellowship and see that she doesn't destroy herself. All right, go.

THREE

The lights crossfade to Father Flynn, whistle around his neck, in a sweatshirt and pants, holding a basketball.

FLYNN: All right, settle down, boys. Now the thing about shooting from the foul line: It's psychological. The rest of the game you're cooperating with your teammates, you're competing against the other team. But at the foul line, it's you against yourself. And the danger is: You start to think. When you think, you stop breathing. Your body locks up. So you have to remember to relax. Take a breath, unlock your knees—this is something for you to watch, Jimmy. You stand like a parking meter. Come up with a routine of what you do. Shift your weight, move your hips . . . You think that's funny, Ralph? What's funny is you never getting a foul shot. Don't worry if you look silly. They won't think you're silly if you get the basket. Come up with a routine, concentrate on the routine, and you'll forget to get tensed up. Now on another matter, I've noticed several of you guys have dirty nails. I don't want to see that. I'm not talking about the length of your nails, I'm talking about cleanliness. See? Look at my nails. They're long, I like them a little long, but look at how clean they are. That makes it okay. There was a kid I grew up with, Timmy Mathisson, never had clean nails, and he'd stick his fingers up his nose, in his mouth.—This is a true story, learn to listen! He got spinal meningitis and died a horrible death. Sometimes it's the little things that get you. You try to talk to a girl with those filthy paws, Mr. Conroy, she's gonna take off like she's being chased by the Red Chinese! (*Reacting genially to laughter*) All right, all right. You guys, what am I gonna do with you? Get dressed, come on over to the rectory, have some Kool-Aid and cookies, we'll have a bull session. (*Blows his whistle.*) Go!

FOUR

Crossfade to a bit of garden, a bench, brick walls. Sister Aloysius, in full habit and a black shawl, is wrapping a pruned rosebush in burlap. Sister James enters.

SISTER JAMES: Good afternoon, Sister.

SISTER ALOYSIUS: Good afternoon, Sister James. Mr. McGinn pruned this bush, which was the right thing to do, but he neglected to protect it from the frost.

SISTER JAMES: Have we had a frost?

SISTER ALOYSIUS: When it comes, it's too late.

SISTER JAMES: You know about gardening?

SISTER ALOYSIUS: A little. Where is your class?

SISTER JAMES: The girls are having Music.

SISTER ALOYSIUS: And the boys?

SISTER JAMES: They're in the rectory. (*Sister James indicates the rectory, which is out of view, just on the other side of the garden.*)

SISTER ALOYSIUS: With Father Flynn.

SISTER JAMES: Yes. He's giving them a talk.

SISTER ALOYSIUS: On what subject?

SISTER JAMES: How to be a man.

SISTER ALOYSIUS: Well, if Sisters were permitted in the rectory, I would be interested to hear that talk. I don't know how to be a man. I would like to know what's involved. Have you ever given the girls a talk on how to be a woman?

SISTER JAMES: No. I wouldn't be competent.

SISTER ALOYSIUS: Why not?

SISTER JAMES: I just don't think I would. I took my vows at the beginning . . . Before . . . At the beginning.

SISTER ALOYSIUS: The founder of our order, the Blessed Mother Seton, was married and had five children before embarking on her vows.

SISTER JAMES: I've often wondered how she managed so much in one life.

SISTER ALOYSIUS: Life perhaps is longer than you think and the dictates of the soul more numerous. I was married.

SISTER JAMES: You were! (*Sister Aloysius smiles for the first time.*)

Heather Goldenhersh as Sister James and Cherry Jones as Sister Aloysius in the 2005 Broadway production of *Doubt* at the Walter Kerr Theatre in New York.

SISTER ALOYSIUS: You could at least hide your astonishment.

SISTER JAMES: I . . . didn't know.

SISTER ALOYSIUS: When one takes on the habit, one must close the door on secular things. My husband died in the war against Adolph Hitler.

SISTER JAMES: Really! Excuse me, Sister.

SISTER ALOYSIUS: But I'm like you. I'm not sure I would feel competent to lecture tittering girls on the subject of womanhood. I don't come into this garden often. What is it, forty feet across? The convent here, the rectory there. We might as well be separated by the Atlantic Ocean. I used to potter around out here, but Monsignor Benedict does his reverie at quixotic times, and we are rightly discouraged from crossing paths with priests unattended. He is seventy-nine, but nevertheless.

SISTER JAMES: The monsignor is very good, isn't he?

SISTER ALOYSIUS: Yes. But he is oblivious.

SISTER JAMES: To what?

SISTER ALOYSIUS: I don't believe he knows who's President of the United States. I mean him no disrespect of course. It's just that he's otherworldly in the extreme.

SISTER JAMES: Is it that he's innocent, Sister Aloysius?

SISTER ALOYSIUS: You have a slyness at work, Sister James. Be careful of it. How is your class? How is Donald Muller?

SISTER JAMES: He is thirteenth in class.

SISTER ALOYSIUS: I know. That's sufficient. Is he being accepted?

SISTER JAMES: He has no friends.

SISTER ALOYSIUS: That would be a lot to expect after only two months. Has anyone hit him?

SISTER JAMES: No.

SISTER ALOYSIUS: Someone will. And when it happens, send them right down to me.

SISTER JAMES: I'm not so sure anyone will.

SISTER ALOYSIUS: There is a statue of St. Patrick on one side of the church altar and a statue of St. Anthony on the other. This parish serves Irish and Italian families. Someone will hit Donald Muller.

SISTER JAMES: He has a protector.

SISTER ALOYSIUS: Who?

SISTER JAMES: Father Flynn. (*Sister Aloysius, who has been fussing with mulch, is suddenly rigid. She rises.*)

SISTER ALOYSIUS: What?

SISTER JAMES: He's taken an interest. Since Donald went on the altar boys. (*Pause.*) I thought I should tell you.

SISTER ALOYSIUS: I told you to come to me, but I hoped you never would.

SISTER JAMES: Maybe I shouldn't have.

SISTER ALOYSIUS: I knew once you did, something would be set in motion. So it's happened.

SISTER JAMES: What?! I'm not telling you that! I'm not even certain what you mean.

SISTER ALOYSIUS: Yes, you are.

SISTER JAMES: I've been trying to become more cold in my thinking as you suggested . . . I feel as if I've lost my way a little, Sister Aloysius. I had the most terrible dream last night. I want to be guided by you and responsible to the children, but I want my peace of mind. I must tell you I have been longing for the return of my peace of mind.

SISTER ALOYSIUS: You may not have it. It is not your place to be complacent. That's for the children. That's what we give them.

SISTER JAMES: I think I'm starting to understand you a little. But it's so unsettling to look at things and people with suspicion. It feels as if I'm less close to God.

SISTER ALOYSIUS: When you take a step to address wrongdoing, you are taking a step away from God, but in His service. Dealing with such matters is hard and thankless work.

SISTER JAMES: I've become more reserved in class. I feel separated from the children.

SISTER ALOYSIUS: That's as it should be.

SISTER JAMES: But I feel. Wrong. And about this other matter, I don't have any evidence. I'm not at all certain that anything's happened.

SISTER ALOYSIUS: We can't wait for that.

SISTER JAMES: But what if it's nothing?

SISTER ALOYSIUS: Then it's nothing. I wouldn't mind being wrong. But I doubt I am.

SISTER JAMES: Then what's to be done?

SISTER ALOYSIUS: I don't know.

SISTER JAMES: You'll know what to do.

SISTER ALOYSIUS: I don't know what to do. There are parameters which protect him and hinder me.

SISTER JAMES: But he can't be safe if it's established. I doubt he could recover from the shame.

SISTER ALOYSIUS: What have you seen?

SISTER JAMES: I don't know.

SISTER ALOYSIUS: What have you seen?

SISTER JAMES: He took Donald to the rectory.

SISTER ALOYSIUS: What for?

SISTER JAMES: A talk.

SISTER ALOYSIUS: Alone?

SISTER JAMES: Yes.

SISTER ALOYSIUS: When?

SISTER JAMES: A week ago.

SISTER ALOYSIUS: Why didn't you tell me?

SISTER JAMES: I didn't think there was anything wrong with it. It never came into my mind that he . . . that there could be anything wrong.

SISTER ALOYSIUS: Of all the children. Donald Muller. I suppose it makes sense.

SISTER JAMES: How does it make sense?

SISTER ALOYSIUS: He's isolated. The little sheep lagging behind is the one the wolf goes for.

SISTER JAMES: I don't know that anything's wrong!

SISTER ALOYSIUS: Our first Negro student. I thought there'd be fighting, a parent or two to deal with . . . I should've foreseen this possibility.

SISTER JAMES: How could you imagine it?

SISTER ALOYSIUS: It is my job to outshine the fox in cleverness! That's my job!

SISTER JAMES: But maybe it's nothing!

SISTER ALOYSIUS: Then why do you look like you've seen the Devil?

SISTER JAMES: It's just the way the boy acted when he came back to class.

SISTER ALOYSIUS: He said something?

SISTER JAMES: No. It was his expression. He looked frightened and . . . he put his head on the desk in the most peculiar way. (*Struggles.*) And one other thing. I think there was alcohol on his breath. There was alcohol on his breath. (*Sister Aloysius looks toward the rectory.*)

SISTER ALOYSIUS: Eight years ago at St. Boniface we had a priest who had to be stopped. But I had Monsignor Scully then . . . whom I could rely on. Here, there's no man I can go to, and men run everything. We are going to have to stop him ourselves.

SISTER JAMES: Can't you just . . . report your suspicions?

SISTER ALOYSIUS: To Monsignor Benedict? The man's guileless! He would just ask Father Flynn!

SISTER JAMES: Well, would that be such a bad idea?

SISTER ALOYSIUS: And he would believe whatever Father Flynn told him. He would think the matter settled.

SISTER JAMES: But maybe that is all that needs to be done. If it's true. If I had done something awful, and I was confronted with it, I'd be so repentant.

SISTER ALOYSIUS: Sister James, my dear, you must try to imagine a very different kind of person than yourself. A man who would do this has already denied a great deal. If I tell the monsignor and he is satisfied with Father Flynn's rebuttal, the matter is suppressed.

SISTER JAMES: Well then, tell the bishop.

SISTER ALOYSIUS: The hierarchy of the Church does not permit my going to the bishop. No. Once I tell the monsignor, it's out of my hands, I'm helpless. I'm going to have to come up with a pretext, get Father Flynn into my office. Try to force it. You'll have to be there.

SISTER JAMES: Me? No! Why? Oh no, Sister! I couldn't!

SISTER ALOYSIUS: I can't be closeted alone with a priest. Another Sister must be in attendance, and it has to be you. The circle of confidence mustn't be made any wider. Think of the boy if this gets out.

SISTER JAMES: I can't do it!

SISTER ALOYSIUS: Why not? You're squeamish?

SISTER JAMES: I'm not equipped! It's . . . I would be embarrassed. I couldn't possibly be present if the topic were spoken of!

SISTER ALOYSIUS: Please, Sister, do not indulge yourself in witless adolescent scruples. I assure you I would prefer a more seasoned confederate. But you are the one who came to me.

SISTER JAMES: You told me to!

SISTER ALOYSIUS: Would you rather leave the boy to be exploited? And don't think this will be the only story. If you close your eyes, you will be a party to all that comes after.

SISTER JAMES: You're supposed to tell the monsignor!

SISTER ALOYSIUS: That you saw a look in a boy's eye? That perhaps you smelled something on his breath? Monsignor Benedict thinks the sun rises and sets on Father Flynn. You'd be branded an hysteric and transferred.

SISTER JAMES: We can ask him.

SISTER ALOYSIUS: Who?

SISTER JAMES: The boy. Donald Muller.

SISTER ALOYSIUS: He'll deny it.

SISTER JAMES: Why?

SISTER ALOYSIUS: Shame.

SISTER JAMES: You can't know that.

SISTER ALOYSIUS: And if he does point the finger, how do you think that will be received in this community? A black child. (*No answer.*) I am going to think this through. Then I'm going to invite Father Flynn to my office on an unrelated matter. You will be there.

SISTER JAMES: But what good can I do?

SISTER ALOYSIUS: Aside from the unacceptability of a priest and nun being alone, I need a witness.

SISTER JAMES: To what?

SISTER ALOYSIUS: He may tell the truth and lie afterwards. (*Sister James looks toward the rectory.*)

SISTER JAMES: The boys are coming out of the rectory. They look happy enough.

SISTER ALOYSIUS: They look smug. Like they have a secret.

SISTER JAMES: There he is.

SISTER ALOYSIUS: If I could, Sister James, I would certainly choose to live in innocence. But innocence can only be wisdom in a world without evil. Situations arise, and we are confronted with wrongdoing and the need to act.

SISTER JAMES: I have to take the boys up to class.

SISTER ALOYSIUS: Go on, then. Take them. I will be talking to you. (*The sound of wind. Sister Aloysius pulls her shawl tightly about her and goes. After a moment, Sister James goes as well.*)

FIVE

The principal's office. A phone rings, Sister Aloysius enters with a pot of tea, walking quickly to answer the phone.

SISTER ALOYSIUS: Hello, St. Nicholas School? Oh yes, Mr. McGinn. Thank you for calling back. That was quite a windstorm we had last night. No, I didn't know there was a Great Wind in Ireland and you were there for it. That's fascinating. Yes. I was wondering if you would be so kind as to remove a tree limb that's fallen in the courtyard of the church. Sister Veronica tripped on it this morning and fell on her face. I think she's all right. She doesn't look any worse, Mr. McGinn. Thank you, Mr. McGinn. (*She hangs up the phone and looks at her watch, a bit anxious. A knock at the door.*) Come in. (*The door opens. Father Flynn is standing there in his black cassock. He doesn't come in.*)

FLYNN: Good morning, Sister Aloysius! How are you today?

SISTER ALOYSIUS: Good morning, Father Flynn. Very well. Good of you to come by. (*Father Flynn takes a step into the office.*)

FLYNN: Are we ready for the meeting?

SISTER ALOYSIUS: We're just short Sister James. (*Father Flynn steps back into the doorway.*) Did you hear that wind last night?

FLYNN: I certainly did. Imagine what it must've been like in the frontier days when a man alone in the woods sat by a fire in his buckskins and listened to a sound like that. Imagine the loneliness! The immense darkness pressing in! How frightening it must've been!

SISTER ALOYSIUS: If one lacked faith in God's protection, I suppose it would be frightening.

FLYNN: Did I hear Sister Veronica had an accident?

SISTER ALOYSIUS: Yes. Sister Veronica fell on a piece of wood this morning and practically killed herself.

FLYNN: Is she all right?

SISTER ALOYSIUS: Oh, she's fine.

FLYNN: Her sight isn't good, is it?

SISTER ALOYSIUS: Her sight is fine. Nuns fall, you know.

FLYNN: No, I didn't know that.

SISTER ALOYSIUS: It's the habit. It catches us up more often than not. What with our being in black and white, and so prone to falling, we're more like dominos than anything else. (*Sister James appears at the door, breathless.*)

SISTER JAMES: Am I past the time? (*Father Flynn takes a step into the office.*)

FLYNN: Not at all. Sister Aloysius and I were just having a nice chat.

SISTER JAMES: Good morning, Father Flynn. Good morning, Sister. I'm sorry I was delayed. Mr. McGinn has closed the courtyard to fix something so I had to go back through the convent and out the side door, and then I ran into Sister Veronica.

FLYNN: How is she?

SISTER JAMES: She has a bit of a bloody nose.

SISTER ALOYSIUS: I'm beginning to think you're punching people.

SISTER JAMES: Sister?

SISTER ALOYSIUS: Well, after the incident with . . . Never mind. Well, come in, please. Sit down. (*They come in and sit down. Father Flynn takes Sister Aloysius' chair. He's sitting at her desk. She reacts but says nothing.*) I actually have a hot pot of tea. (*Closes the door but for an inch.*) And close this but not quite, for form's sake. Would you have a cup of tea, Father?

FLYNN: I would love a cup of tea.

SISTER ALOYSIUS: Perhaps you could serve him, Sister?

SISTER JAMES: Of course.

SISTER ALOYSIUS: And yourself, of course.

SISTER JAMES: Would you like tea, Sister Aloysius?

SISTER ALOYSIUS: I've already had my cup.

FLYNN: Is there sugar?

SISTER ALOYSIUS: Sugar? Yes! (*Rummages in her desk.*) It's here somewhere. I put it in the drawer for Lent last year and never remembered to take it out.

FLYNN: It mustn't have been much to give up then.

SISTER ALOYSIUS: No, I'm sure you're right. Here it is. I'll serve you, though for want of practice, I'm . . . [clumsy] (*She's got the sugar bowl and is poised to serve him a lump of sugar with a small pair of tongs when she sees his nails.*) Your fingernails.

FLYNN: I wear them a little long. The sugar?

SISTER ALOYSIUS: Oh yes. One?

FLYNN: Three.

SISTER ALOYSIUS: Three. (*She's appalled but tries to hide it.*)

FLYNN: Sweet tooth

SISTER ALOYSIUS: One, two, three. Sister, do you take sugar? (*Sister Aloysius looks at Sister James.*)

SISTER JAMES: (*To Sister Aloysius.*) Never! (*To Father Flynn.*) Not that there's anything wrong with sugar. (*To Sister Aloysius again.*) Thank you. (*Sister Aloysius puts the sugar away in her desk.*)

SISTER ALOYSIUS: Well, thank you, Father, for making the time for us. We're at our wit's end.

FLYNN: I think it's an excellent idea to rethink the Christmas pageant. Last year's effort was a little woebegone.

SISTER JAMES: No! I loved it! (*Becomes self-conscious.*) But I love all Christmas pageants. I just love the Nativity. The birth of the Savior. And the hymns of course. "O Little Town of Bethlehem," "O Come, O Come, Emmanuel" . . .

SISTER ALOYSIUS: Thank you, Sister James. Sister James will be co-directing the pageant with Mrs. Shields this year. So what do you think, Father Flynn? Is there something new we could do?

FLYNN: Well, we all love the Christmas hymns, but it might be jolly to include a secular song.

SISTER ALOYSIUS: Secular.

FLYNN: Yes. "It's Beginning to Look a Lot Like Christmas." Something like that.

SISTER ALOYSIUS: What would be the point of performing a secular song?

FLYNN: Fun.

SISTER JAMES: Or "Frosty the Snowman."

FLYNN: That's a good one. We could have one of the boys dress as a snowman and dance around.

SISTER ALOYSIUS: Which boy?

FLYNN: We'd do tryouts.

SISTER ALOYSIUS: "Frosty the Snowman" espouses a pagan belief in magic. The snowman comes to life when an enchanted hat is put on his head. If the music were more somber, people would realize the images are disturbing and the song heretical. (*Sister James and Father Flynn exchange a look.*)

SISTER JAMES: I've never thought about "Frosty the Snowman" like that.

SISTER ALOYSIUS: It should be banned from the airwaves.

FLYNN: So. Not "Frosty the Snowman." (*Father Flynn writes something in a small notebook.*)

SISTER ALOYSIUS: I don't think so. "It's Beginning to Look a Lot Like Christmas" would be fine, I suppose. The parents would like it. May I ask what you wrote down? With that ballpoint pen.

FLYNN: Oh. Nothing. An idea for a sermon.

SISTER ALOYSIUS: You had one just now?

FLYNN: I get them all the time.

SISTER ALOYSIUS: How fortunate.

FLYNN: I forget them, so I write them down.

SISTER ALOYSIUS: What is the idea?

FLYNN: Intolerance. (*Sister James tries to break a bit of tension.*)

SISTER JAMES: Would you like a little more tea, Father?

FLYNN: Not yet. I think a message of the Second Ecumenical Council° was that the Church needs to take on a more familiar face. Reflect the local community. We should sing a song from the radio now and then. Take the kids out for ice cream.

SISTER ALOYSIUS: Ice cream.

FLYNN: Maybe take the boys on a camping trip. We should be friendlier. The children and the parents should see us as members of their family rather than emissaries from Rome. I think the pageant should be charming, like a community theatre doing a show.

SISTER ALOYSIUS: But we are not members of their family. We're different.

FLYNN: Why? Because of our vows?

SISTER ALOYSIUS: Precisely.

FLYNN: I don't think we're so different. (*To Sister James.*) You know, I would take some more tea, Sister. Thank you.

SISTER ALOYSIUS: And they think we're different. The working-class people of this parish trust us to be different.

FLYNN: I think we're getting off the subject.

SISTER ALOYSIUS: Yes, you're right, back to it. The Christmas pageant. We must be careful how Donald Muller is used in the pageant. (*Sister James shakes as she pours the tea.*)

FLYNN: Easy there, Sister, you don't spill.

SISTER JAMES: Oh, uh, yes, Father.

FLYNN: What about Donald Muller?

SISTER ALOYSIUS: We must be careful, in the pageant, that we neither hide Donald Muller nor put him forward.

FLYNN: Because of the color of his skin.

Second Ecumenical Council: The Second Vatican Council, opened by Pope John XXIII in 1962, addressed the Church's recognition of modern life and its need to respond to the contemporary world.

Sister James, Father Flynn (Brían F. O'Byrne), and Sister Aloysius meet over tea in the principal's office in the 2005 Broadway production.

SISTER ALOYSIUS: That's right.

FLYNN: Why?

SISTER ALOYSIUS: Come, Father. You're being disingenuous.

FLYNN: I think he should be treated like every other boy.

SISTER ALOYSIUS: You yourself singled the boy out for special attention. You held a private meeting with him at the rectory. (*Turning to Sister James.*) A week ago?

SISTER JAMES: Yes. (*He realizes something's up.*)

FLYNN: What are we talking about?

SISTER JAMES: Donald Muller?

SISTER ALOYSIUS: The boy acted strangely when he returned to class. (*Father Flynn turns to Sister James.*)

FLYNN: He did?

SISTER JAMES: When he returned from the rectory. A little odd, yes.

SISTER ALOYSIUS: Can you tell us why?

FLYNN: How did he act strangely?

SISTER JAMES: I'm not sure how to explain it. He laid his head on the desk . . .

FLYNN: You mean you had some impression?

SISTER JAMES: Yes.

FLYNN: And he'd come from the rectory so you're asking me if I know anything about it?

SISTER JAMES: That's it.

FLYNN: Hmmm. Did you want to discuss the pageant, is that why I'm here, or is this what you wanted to discuss?

SISTER JAMES: This.

FLYNN: Well. I feel a little uncomfortable.

SISTER ALOYSIUS: Why?

FLYNN: Why do you think? Something about your tone.

SISTER ALOYSIUS: I would prefer a discussion of fact rather than tone.

FLYNN: Well. If I had judged my conversation with Donald Muller to be of concern to you, Sister, I would have sat you down and talked to you about it. But I did not judge it to be of concern to you.

SISTER ALOYSIUS: Perhaps you are mistaken in your understanding of what concerns me. The boy is in my school, and his well-being is my responsibility.

FLYNN: His well-being is not at issue.

SISTER ALOYSIUS: I am not satisfied that that is true. He was upset when he returned to class.

FLYNN: Did he say something?

SISTER JAMES: No.

SISTER ALOYSIUS: What happened in the rectory?

FLYNN: Happened? Nothing happened. I had a talk with a boy.

SISTER ALOYSIUS: What about?

FLYNN: It was a private matter.

SISTER ALOYSIUS: He's twelve years old. What could be private?

FLYNN: I'll say it again, Sister. I object to your tone.

SISTER ALOYSIUS: This is not about my tone or your tone, Father Flynn. It's about arriving at the truth.

FLYNN: Of what?

SISTER ALOYSIUS: You know what I'm talking about. Don't you? You're controlling the expression on your face right now. Aren't you?

FLYNN: My face? You said you wanted to talk about the pageant, Sister. That's why I'm here. Am I to understand that you brought me into your office to confront me in some way? It's outrageous. I'm not answerable to you. What exactly are you accusing me of?

SISTER ALOYSIUS: I am not accusing you of anything, Father Flynn. I am asking you to tell me what happened in the rectory. (*Father Flynn stands.*)

FLYNN: I don't wish to continue this conversation at all further. And if you are dissatisfied with that, I suggest you speak to Monsignor Benedict. I can only imagine that your unfortunate behavior this morning is the result of overwork. Perhaps you need a leave of absence. I may suggest it. Have a good morning. (*To Sister James.*) Sister?

SISTER JAMES: Good morning, Father. (*Sister Aloysius' next words stop him.*)

SISTER ALOYSIUS: There was alcohol on his breath. (*He turns.*) When he returned from his meeting with you. (*He comes back and sits down. He rubs his eyes.*)

FLYNN: Alcohol.

SISTER JAMES: I did smell it on his breath.

SISTER ALOYSIUS: Well?

FLYNN: Can't you let this alone?

SISTER ALOYSIUS: No.

FLYNN: I see there's no way out of this.

SISTER JAMES: Take your time, Father. Would you like some more tea?

FLYNN: You should've let it alone.

SISTER ALOYSIUS: Not possible.

FLYNN: Donald Muller served as altar boy last Tuesday morning. After Mass, Mr. McGinn caught him in the sacristy drinking altar wine. When I found out, I sent for him. There were tears. He begged not to be removed from the altar boys. And I took pity on him.

I told him if no one else found out, I would let him stay on. (*Sister James is overjoyed. Sister Aloysius is unmoved.*)

SISTER JAMES: Oh, what a relief! That explains everything! Thanks be to God! Oh, Sister, look, it's all a mistake!

SISTER ALOYSIUS: And if I talk to Mr. McGinn?

FLYNN: Talk to Mr. McGinn by all means. But now that the boy's secret's out, I'm going to have to remove him from the altar boys. Which I think is too bad. That's what I was trying to avoid.

SISTER JAMES: You were trying to protect the boy!

FLYNN: That's right.

SISTER JAMES: I might've done the same thing! (*To Sister Aloysius.*) Is there a way Donald could stay on the altar boys?

SISTER ALOYSIUS: No. If the boy drank altar wine, he cannot continue as an altar boy.

FLYNN: Of course you're right. I'm just not the disciplinarian you are, Sister. And he is the only Negro in the school. That did affect my thinking on the matter. It will be commented on that he's no longer serving at Mass. It's a public thing. A certain ignorant element in the parish will be confirmed in their beliefs.

SISTER ALOYSIUS: He must be held to the same standard as the others.

FLYNN: Of course. Do we need to discuss the pageant or was that just . . .

SISTER ALOYSIUS: No, this was the issue.

FLYNN: Are you satisfied?

SISTER ALOYSIUS: Yes.

FLYNN: Then I'll be going. I have some writing to do.

SISTER ALOYSIUS: Intolerance.

FLYNN: That's right. (*He goes, then stops at the door.*) I'm not pleased with how you handled this, Sister. Next time you are troubled by dark ideas, I suggest you speak to the monsignor. (*He goes. After a moment, Sister James weakly launches into optimism.*)

SISTER JAMES: Well. What a relief! He cleared it all up.

SISTER ALOYSIUS: You believe him?

SISTER JAMES: Of course.

SISTER ALOYSIUS: Isn't it more that it's easier to believe him?

SISTER JAMES: But we can corroborate his story with Mr. McGinn!

SISTER ALOYSIUS: Yes. These types of people are clever. They're not so easily undone.

SISTER JAMES: Well, I'm convinced!

SISTER ALOYSIUS: You're not. You just want things to be resolved so you can have simplicity back.

SISTER JAMES: I want no further part of this.

SISTER ALOYSIUS: I'll bring him down. With or without your help.

SISTER JAMES: How can you be so sure he's lying?

SISTER ALOYSIUS: Experience.

SISTER JAMES: You just don't like him! You don't like it that he uses a ballpoint pen. You don't like it that he takes three lumps of sugar in his tea. You don't like it that he likes "Frosty the Snowman." And you're letting that convince you of something terrible, just terrible! Well, I like "Frosty the Snowman"! And it would be nice if this school weren't run like a prison! And I think it's a good thing that I love to teach History and that I might inspire my students to love it, too! And if you judge that to mean I'm not fit to be a teacher, then so be it!

SISTER ALOYSIUS: Sit down. (*Sister James does.*) In ancient Sparta, important matters were decided by who shouted loudest. Fortunately, we are not in ancient Sparta. Now. Do you honestly find the students in this school to be treated like inmates in a prison?

SISTER JAMES: (*Relenting.*) No, I don't. Actually, by and large, they seem to be fairly happy. But they're all uniformly terrified of you!

SISTER ALOYSIUS: Yes. That's how it works. Sit there. (*Sister Aloysius looks in a notebook, picks up the phone, dials.*) Hello, this is Sister Aloysius Beauvier, the principal of St. Nicholas. Is this Mrs. Muller? I'm calling about your son, Donald. I would like you and your husband to come down here for a talk. When would be convenient? (*Lights fade.*)

SIX

Father Flynn, in blue and white vestments, is at the pulpit.

FLYNN: A woman was gossiping with a friend about a man she hardly knew—I know none of you have ever done this—and that night she had a dream. A great hand appeared over her and pointed down at her. She was immediately seized with an overwhelming sense of guilt. The next day she went to confession. She got the old parish priest, Father O'Rourke, and she told him the whole thing. "Is gossiping a sin?" she asked the old man. "Was that the Hand of God Almighty pointing a finger at me? Should I be asking your absolution? Father, tell me, have I done something wrong?" (*Irish brogue.*) "Yes!" Father O'Rourke answered her. "Yes, you ignorant, badly brought-up female! You have borne false witness against your neighbor, you have played fast and loose with his reputation, and you should be heartily ashamed!" So the woman said she was sorry and asked forgiveness. "Not so fast!" says O'Rourke. "I want you to go home, take a pillow up on your roof, cut it open with a knife, and return here to me!" So she went home, took the pillow off her bed, a knife from the drawer, went up the fire escape to the roof, and stabbed the pillow. Then she went back to the old priest as instructed. "Did you gut the pillow with the knife?" he says. "Yes, Father." "And what was the result?" "Feathers," she said. "Feathers?" he repeated. "Feathers everywhere, Father!" "Now I want you to go back and gather up every last feather that flew out on the wind!" "Well," she says, "it can't be

done. I don't know where they went. The wind took them all over." "And that," said Father O'Rourke, "is gossip!" In the name of the Father, Son, and the Holy Ghost, Amen.

SEVEN

The lights crossfade to the garden. A crow caws.
Sister James sits on the bench, deep in thought. Father Flynn enters.

FLYNN: Good afternoon, Sister James.

SISTER JAMES: Good afternoon, Father.

FLYNN: What is that bird complaining about? What kind of bird is that? A starling? A grackle?

SISTER JAMES: A crow?

FLYNN: Of course it is. Are you praying? I didn't mean to interrupt.

SISTER JAMES: I'm not praying, no.

FLYNN: You seem subdued.

SISTER JAMES: Oh. I can't sleep.

FLYNN: Why not?

SISTER JAMES: Bad dreams. Actually one bad dream, and then I haven't slept right since.

FLYNN: What about?

SISTER JAMES: I looked in a mirror and there was a darkness where my face should be. It frightened me.

FLYNN: I can't sleep on occasion.

SISTER JAMES: No? Do you see that big hand pointing a finger at you?

FLYNN: Yes. Sometimes.

SISTER JAMES: Was your sermon directed at anyone in particular?

FLYNN: What do you think?

SISTER JAMES: Did you make up that story about the pillow?

FLYNN: Yes. You make up little stories to illustrate. In the tradition of the parable.

SISTER JAMES: Aren't the things that actually happen in life more worthy of interpretation than a made-up story?

FLYNN: No. What actually happens in life is beyond interpretation. The truth makes for a bad sermon. It tends to be confusing and have no clear conclusion.

SISTER JAMES: I received a letter from my brother in Maryland yesterday. He's very sick.

FLYNN: Maybe you should go and see him.

SISTER JAMES: I can't leave my class.

FLYNN: How's Donald Muller doing?

SISTER JAMES: I don't know.

FLYNN: You don't see him?

SISTER JAMES: I see him every day, but I don't know how he's doing. I don't know how to judge these things. Now.

FLYNN: I stopped speaking to him for fear of it being misunderstood. Isn't that a shame? I actually avoided him the other day when I might've passed him in the hall. He doesn't understand why. I noticed you didn't come to me for confession.

SISTER JAMES: No. I went to Monsignor Benedict. He's very kind.

FLYNN: I wasn't?

SISTER JAMES: It wasn't that. As you know. You know why.

FLYNN: You're against me?

SISTER JAMES: No.

FLYNN: You're not convinced?

SISTER JAMES: It's not for me to be convinced, one way or the other. It's Sister Aloysius.

FLYNN: Are you just an extension of her?

SISTER JAMES: She's my superior.

FLYNN: But what about you?

SISTER JAMES: I wish I knew nothing whatever about it. I wish the idea had never entered my mind.

FLYNN: How did it enter your mind?

SISTER JAMES: Sister Aloysius.

FLYNN: I feel as if my reputation has been damaged through no fault of my own. But I'm reluctant to take the steps necessary to repair it for fear of doing further harm. It's frustrating, I can tell you that.

SISTER JAMES: Is it true?

FLYNN: What?

SISTER JAMES: You know what I'm asking.

FLYNN: No, it's not true.

SISTER JAMES: Oh, I don't know what to believe.

FLYNN: How can you take sides against me?

SISTER JAMES: It doesn't matter.

FLYNN: It does matter! I've done nothing. There's no substance to any of this. The most innocent actions can appear sinister to the poisoned mind. I had to throw that poor boy off the altar. He's devastated. The only reason I haven't gone to the monsignor is I don't want to tear apart the school. Sister Aloysius would most certainly lose her position as principal if I made her accusations known. Since they're baseless, You might lose your place as well.

SISTER JAMES: Are you threatening me?

FLYNN: What do you take me for? No.

SISTER JAMES: I want to believe you.

FLYNN: Then do. It's as simple as that.

SISTER JAMES: It's not me that has to be convinced.

FLYNN: I don't have to prove anything to her.

SISTER JAMES: She's determined.

FLYNN: To what?

SISTER JAMES: Protect the boy.

FLYNN: It's me that cares about that boy, not her. Has she ever reached out a hand to that child or any child in this school? She's like a block of ice! Children need warmth, kindness, understanding! What does she give them? Rules. That black boy needs a helping hand or he's not going to make it here! But if she has her way, he'll be left to his own undoing. Why do you think he was in the sacristy drinking wine that day? He's in trouble! She sees me talk in a human way to these children and she immediately assumes there must be something wrong with it. Something dirty.

Well, I'm not going to let her keep this parish in the Dark Ages! And I'm not going to let her destroy my spirit of compassion!

SISTER JAMES: I'm sure that's not her intent.

FLYNN: I care about this congregation!

SISTER JAMES: I know you do.

FLYNN: Like you care about your class! You love them, don't you?

SISTER JAMES: Yes.

FLYNN: That's natural. How else would you relate to children? I can look at your face and know your philosophy: kindness.

SISTER JAMES: I don't know. I mean, of course.

FLYNN: What is Sister Aloysius' philosophy do you suppose? (*A pause.*)

SISTER JAMES: I don't have to suppose. She's told me. She discourages . . . warmth. She's suggested I be more . . . formal.

FLYNN: There are people who go after your humanity, Sister James, who tell you the light in your heart is a weakness. That your soft feelings betray you. I don't believe that. It's an old tactic of cruel people to kill kindness in the name of virtue. Don't believe it. There's nothing wrong with love.

SISTER JAMES: Of course not, but . . .

FLYNN: Have you forgotten that was the message of the Savior to us all. Love. Not suspicion, disapproval and judgment. Love of people. Have you found Sister Aloysius a positive inspiration?

SISTER JAMES: I don't want to misspeak, but no. She's taken away my joy of teaching. And I loved teaching more than anything. (*She cries a little. He pats her uneasily, looking around.*)

FLYNN: It's all right. You're going to be all right.

SISTER JAMES: I feel as if everything is upside down.

FLYNN: It isn't though. There are just times in life when we feel lost. You're not alone with it. It happens to many of us.

SISTER JAMES: A bond. (*Becomes self-conscious.*) I'd better go in.

FLYNN: I'm sorry your brother is ill.

SISTER JAMES: Thank you, Father. (*Starts to go, stops.*) I don't believe it!

FLYNN: You don't?

SISTER JAMES: No.

FLYNN: Thank you, Sister. That's a great relief to me. Thank you very much. (*She goes. He takes out his little black book and writes in it. The crow caws. He yells at it:*) Oh, be quiet. (*Then he opens a prayer book and walks away.*)

EIGHT

Crossfade to the principal's office. Sister Aloysius is sitting looking out the window, very still. A knock at the door. She doesn't react. A second knock, louder. She pulls a small earplug out of her ear and scurries to the door. She opens it. There stands Mrs. Muller, a black woman of about thirty-eight, in her Sunday best, dressed for church. She's on red alert.

SISTER ALOYSIUS: Mrs. Muller?

MRS. MULLER: Yes.

SISTER ALOYSIUS: Come in. (*Sister Aloysius closes the door.*) Please have a seat.

MRS. MULLER: I thought I might a had the wrong day when you didn't answer the door.

SISTER ALOYSIUS: Oh. Yes. Well, just between us, I was listening to a transistor radio with an earpiece. (*She shows Mrs. Muller a very small transistor radio.*) Look at how tiny they're making them now. I confiscated it from one of the students, and now I can't stop using it.

MRS. MULLER: You like music?

SISTER ALOYSIUS: Not really. News reports. Years ago I used to listen to all the news reports because my husband was in Italy in the war. When I came into possession of this little radio, I found myself doing it again. Though there is no war and the voices have changed.

MRS. MULLER: You were a married woman?

SISTER ALOYSIUS: Yes. But then he was killed. Is your husband coming?

MRS. MULLER: Couldn't get off work.

SISTER ALOYSIUS: I see. Of course. It was a lot to ask.

MRS. MULLER: How's Donald doing?

SISTER ALOYSIUS: He's passing his subjects. He has average grades.

MRS. MULLER: Oh. Good. He was upset about getting taken off the altar boys.

SISTER ALOYSIUS: Did he explain why?

MRS. MULLER: He said he was caught drinking wine.

SISTER ALOYSIUS: That is the reason.

MRS. MULLER: Well, that seems fair. But he's a good boy, Sister. He fell down there, but he's a good boy pretty much down the line. And he knows what an opportunity he has here. I think the whole thing was just a bit much for him.

SISTER ALOYSIUS: What do you mean, the whole thing?

MRS. MULLER: He's the only colored here. He's the first in this school. That'd be a lot for a boy.

SISTER ALOYSIUS: I suppose it is. But he has to do the work of course.

MRS. MULLER: He is doing it though, right?

SISTER ALOYSIUS: Yes. He's getting by. He's getting through. How is he at home?

MRS. MULLER: His father beat the hell out of him over that wine.

SISTER ALOYSIUS: He shouldn't do that.

MRS. MULLER: You don't tell my husband what to do. You just stand back. He didn't want Donald to come here.

SISTER ALOYSIUS: Why not?

MRS. MULLER: Thought he'd have a lot of trouble with the other boys. But that hasn't really happened as far as I can make out.

SISTER ALOYSIUS: Good.

MRS. MULLER: That priest, Father Flynn, been watching out for him.

SISTER ALOYSIUS: Yes. Have you met Father Flynn?

MRS. MULLER: Not exactly, no. I seen him on the altar, but I haven't met him face to face. No. Just, you know, heard from Donald.

SISTER ALOYSIUS: What does he say?

MRS. MULLER: You know, Father Flynn, Father Flynn. He looks up to him. The man gives him his time, which is what the boy needs. He needs that.

SISTER ALOYSIUS: Mrs. Muller, we may have a problem.

MRS. MULLER: Well, I thought you must a had a reason for asking me to come in. Principal's a big job. If you stop your day to talk to me, must be something. I just want to say though, it's just till June.

SISTER ALOYSIUS: Excuse me?

MRS. MULLER: Whatever the problem is, Donald just has to make it here till June. Then he's off into high school.

SISTER ALOYSIUS: Right.

MRS. MULLER: If Donald can graduate from here, he has a better chance of getting into a good high school. And that would mean an opportunity at college. I believe he has the intelligence. And he wants it, too.

SISTER ALOYSIUS: I don't see anything at this time standing in the way of his graduating with his class.

MRS. MULLER: Well, that's all I care about. Anything else is all right with me.

SISTER ALOYSIUS: I doubt that.

MRS. MULLER: Try me.

SISTER ALOYSIUS: I'm concerned about the relationship between Father Flynn and your son.

MRS. MULLER: You don't say. Concerned. What do you mean, concerned?

SISTER ALOYSIUS: That it may not be right.

MRS. MULLER: Uh-huh. Well, there's something wrong with everybody, isn't that so? Got to be forgiving.

SISTER ALOYSIUS: I'm concerned, to be frank, that Father Flynn may have made advances on your son.

MRS. MULLER: *May* have made.

SISTER ALOYSIUS: I can't be certain.

MRS. MULLER: No evidence?

SISTER ALOYSIUS: No.

MRS. MULLER: Then maybe there's nothing to it?

SISTER ALOYSIUS: I think there is something to it.

MRS. MULLER: Well, I would prefer not to see it that way if you don't mind.

SISTER ALOYSIUS: I can understand that this is hard to hear. I think Father Flynn gave Donald that altar wine.

MRS. MULLER: Why would he do that?

SISTER ALOYSIUS: Has Donald been acting strangely?

MRS. MULLER: No.

SISTER ALOYSIUS: Nothing out of the ordinary?

MRS. MULLER: He's been himself.

SISTER ALOYSIUS: All right.

MRS. MULLER: Look, Sister, I don't want any trouble, and I feel like you're on the march somehow.

SISTER ALOYSIUS: I'm not sure you completely understand.

MRS. MULLER: I think I understand the kind of thing you're talking about. But I don't want to get into it.

SISTER ALOYSIUS: What's that?

MRS. MULLER: Not to be disagreeing with you, but if we're talking about something floating around between this priest and my son, that ain't my son's fault.

SISTER ALOYSIUS: I'm not suggesting it is.

MRS. MULLER: He's just a boy.

SISTER ALOYSIUS: I know.

MRS. MULLER: Twelve years old. If somebody should be taking blame for anything, it should be the man, not the boy.

SISTER ALOYSIUS: I agree with you completely.

MRS. MULLER: You're agreeing with me but I'm sitting in the principal's office talking about my son. Why isn't the priest in the principal's office, if you know what I'm saying and you'll excuse my bringing it up.

SISTER ALOYSIUS: You're here because I'm concerned about Donald's welfare.

MRS. MULLER: You think I'm not?

SISTER ALOYSIUS: Of course you are.

MRS. MULLER: Let me ask you something. You honestly think that priest gave Donald that wine to drink?

SISTER ALOYSIUS: Yes, I do.

MRS. MULLER: Then how come my son got kicked off the altar boys if it was the man that gave it to him?

SISTER ALOYSIUS: The boy got caught, the man didn't.

MRS. MULLER: How come the priest didn't get kicked off the priesthood?

SISTER ALOYSIUS: He's a grown man, educated. And he knows what's at stake. It's not so easy to pin someone like that down.

MRS. MULLER: So you give my son the whole blame. No problem my son getting blamed and punished. That's easy. You know why that is?

SISTER ALOYSIUS: Perhaps you should let me talk. I think you're getting upset.

MRS. MULLER: That's because that's the way it is. You're just finding out about it, but that's the way it is and the way it's been, Sister. You're not going against no *man* in a *robe* and win, Sister. He's got the position.

SISTER ALOYSIUS: And he's got your son.

MRS. MULLER: Let him have 'im then.

SISTER ALOYSIUS: What?

MRS. MULLER: It's just till June.

SISTER ALOYSIUS: Do you know what you're saying?

MRS. MULLER: Know more about it than you.

SISTER ALOYSIUS: I believe this man is creating or has already brought about an improper relationship with your son.

MRS. MULLER: I don't know.

SISTER ALOYSIUS: I know I'm right.

MRS. MULLER: Why you need to know something like that for sure when you don't? Please, Sister. You got some kind a righteous cause going with this priest, and now you want to drag my boy into it. My son doesn't need additional difficulties. Let him take the good and leave the rest when he leaves this place in June. He knows how to do that, I taught him how to do that.

SISTER ALOYSIUS: What kind of mother are you?

MRS. MULLER: Excuse me, but you don't know enough about life to say a thing like that, Sister.

SISTER ALOYSIUS: I know enough.

MRS. MULLER: You know the rules maybe, but that don't cover it.

SISTER ALOYSIUS: I know what I won't accept!

MRS. MULLER: You accept what you gotta accept, and you work with it. That's the truth I know. Sorry to be so sharp, but you're in here in this room...

SISTER ALOYSIUS: This man is in my school.

MRS. MULLER: Well, he's gotta be somewhere, and maybe he's doing some good too. You ever think of that?

SISTER ALOYSIUS: He's after the boys.

MRS. MULLER: Well, maybe some of them boys want to get caught. Maybe what you don't know maybe is my son is ... that way. That's why his father beat him up. Not the wine. He beat Donald for being what he is.

SISTER ALOYSIUS: What are you telling me?

MRS. MULLER: I'm his mother. I'm talking about his nature now, not anything he's done. But you can't hold a child responsible for what God gave him to be.

SISTER ALOYSIUS: Listen to me with care, Mrs. Muller. I'm only interested in actions. It's hopeless to discuss a child's possible inclination. I'm finding it difficult enough to address a man's deeds. This isn't about what the boy may be, but what the man is. It's about the man.

MRS. MULLER: But there's the boy's nature.

SISTER ALOYSIUS: Let's leave that out of it.

MRS. MULLER: Forget it then. You're the one forcing people to say these things out loud. Things are in the air and you leave them alone if you can. That's what I know. My boy came to this school 'cause they were gonna kill him at the public school. So we were lucky enough to get him in here for his last year. Good. His father don't like him. He comes here, the kids don't like him. One man is good to him. This priest. Puts out a hand to the boy. Does the man have his reasons? Yes. Everybody has their reasons. *You* have your reasons. But do I ask the man why he's good to my son? No. I don't care why. My son needs some man to care about him and see him through to where he wants to go. And thank God, this educated man with some kindness in him wants to do just that.

SISTER ALOYSIUS: This will not do.

MRS. MULLER: It's just till June. Sometimes things aren't black and white.

SISTER ALOYSIUS: And sometimes they are. I'll throw your son out of this school. Make no mistake.

MRS. MULLER: But why would you do that? If nothing started with him?

SISTER ALOYSIUS: Because I will stop this whatever way I must.

MRS. MULLER: You'd hurt my son to get your way?

SISTER ALOYSIUS: It won't end with your son. There will be others, if there aren't already.

MRS. MULLER: Throw the priest out then.

SISTER ALOYSIUS: I'm trying to do just that.

MRS. MULLER: Well, what do you want from me? (*A pause.*)

SISTER ALOYSIUS: Nothing. As it turns out. I was hoping you might know something that would help me, but it seems you don't.

MRS. MULLER: Please leave my son out of this. My husband would kill that child over a thing like this.

SISTER ALOYSIUS: I'll try. (*Mrs. Muller stands up.*)

MRS. MULLER: I don't know, Sister. You may think you're doing good, but the world's a hard place. I don't know that you and me are on the same side. I'll be standing with my son and those who are good with my son. It'd be nice to see you there. Nice talking with you, Sister. Good morning. (*She goes, leaving the door open behind her. Sister Aloysius is shaken. After a moment, Father Flynn appears at the door. He's in a controlled fury.*)

FLYNN: May I come in?

SISTER ALOYSIUS: We would require a third party.

Father Flynn (Brían F. O'Byrne) confronts Sister Aloysius (Cherry Jones) in the original production of *Doubt* by the Manhattan Theatre Club in 2004.

FLYNN: What was Donald's mother doing here?

SISTER ALOYSIUS: We were having a chat.

FLYNN: About what?

SISTER ALOYSIUS: A third party is truly required, Father.

FLYNN: No Sister. No third party. You and me are due for a talk. (*He comes in and slams the door behind him. They face each other.*) You have to stop this campaign against me!

SISTER ALOYSIUS: You can stop it at any time.

FLYNN: How?

SISTER ALOYSIUS: Confess and resign.

FLYNN: You are attempting to destroy my reputation! But the result of all this is going to be your removal, not mine!

SISTER ALOYSIUS: What are you doing in this school?

FLYNN: I am trying to do good!

SISTER ALOYSIUS: Or even more to the point, what are you doing in the priesthood?

FLYNN: You are single-handedly holding this school and this parish back!

SISTER ALOYSIUS: From what?

FLYNN: Progressive education and a welcoming church.

SISTER ALOYSIUS: You can't distract me, Father Flynn. This isn't about my behavior, it's about yours.

FLYNN: It's about your unfounded suspicions.

SISTER ALOYSIUS: That's right. I have suspicions.

FLYNN: You know what I haven't understood through all this? Why do you suspect me? What have I done?

SISTER ALOYSIUS: You gave that boy wine to drink. And you let him take the blame.

FLYNN: That's completely untrue! Did you talk to Mr. McGinn?

SISTER ALOYSIUS: All McGinn knows is the boy drank wine. He doesn't how he came to drink it.

FLYNN: Did his mother have something to add to that?

SISTER ALOYSIUS: No.

FLYNN: So that's it. There's nothing there.

SISTER ALOYSIUS: I'm not satisfied.

FLYNN: Well, if you're not satisfied, ask the boy then!

SISTER ALOYSIUS: No, he'd protect you. That's what he's been doing.

FLYNN: Oh, and why would he do that?

SISTER ALOYSIUS: Because you have seduced him.

FLYNN: You're insane! You've got it in your head that I've corrupted this child after giving him wine, and nothing I say will change that.

SISTER ALOYSIUS: That's right.

FLYNN: But correct me if I'm wrong. This has nothing to do with the wine, not really. You had a fundamental mistrust of me before this incident! It was you that warned Sister James to be on the lookout, wasn't it?

SISTER ALOYSIUS: That's true.

FLYNN: So you admit it!

SISTER ALOYSIUS: Certainly.

FLYNN: Why?

SISTER ALOYSIUS: I know people.

FLYNN: That's not good enough!

SISTER ALOYSIUS: It won't have to be.

FLYNN: How's that?

SISTER ALOYSIUS: You will tell me what you've done.

FLYNN: Oh I will?

SISTER ALOYSIUS: Yes.

FLYNN: I'm not one of your truant boys, you know. Sister James is convinced I'm innocent.

SISTER ALOYSIUS: So you talked to Sister James? Well, of course you talked to Sister James.

FLYNN: Did you know that Donald's father beats him?

SISTER ALOYSIUS: Yes.

FLYNN: And might that not account for the odd behavior Sister James noticed in the boy?

SISTER ALOYSIUS: It might.

FLYNN: Then what is it? What? What did you hear, what did you see that convinced you so thoroughly?

SISTER ALOYSIUS: What does it matter?

FLYNN: I want to know.

SISTER ALOYSIUS: On the first day of the school year, I saw you touch William London's wrist. And I saw him pull away.

FLYNN: That's all?

SISTER ALOYSIUS: That was all.

FLYNN: But that's nothing. (*He writes in his book.*)

SISTER ALOYSIUS: What are you writing now?

FLYNN: You leave me no choice, I'm writing down what you say. I tend to get too flustered to remember the details of an upsetting conversation, and this may be important. When I talk to the monsignor and explain why you have to be removed as the principal of this school.

SISTER ALOYSIUS: This morning, before I spoke with Mrs. Muller, I took the precaution of calling the last parish to which you were assigned.

FLYNN: What did he say?

SISTER ALOYSIUS: Who?

FLYNN: The pastor?

SISTER ALOYSIUS: I did not speak to the pastor. I spoke to one of the nuns.

FLYNN: You should've spoken to the pastor.

SISTER ALOYSIUS: I spoke to a nun.

FLYNN: That's not the proper route for you to have taken, Sister! The Church is very clear. You're supposed to go through the pastor.

SISTER ALOYSIUS: Why? Do you have an understanding, you and he? Father Flynn, you have a history.

FLYNN: You have no right to go rummaging through my past!

SISTER ALOYSIUS: This is your third parish in five years.

FLYNN: Call the pastor and ask him why I left! It was perfectly innocent.

SISTER ALOYSIUS: I'm not calling the pastor.

FLYNN: I am a good priest! And there is nothing in my record to suggest otherwise.

SISTER ALOYSIUS: You will go after another child and another, until you are stopped.

FLYNN: What nun did you speak to?

SISTER ALOYSIUS: I won't say.

FLYNN: I've not touched a child.

SISTER ALOYSIUS: You have.

FLYNN: You have not the slightest proof of anything.

SISTER ALOYSIUS: But I have my certainty, and armed with that, I will go to your last parish, and the one before

that if necessary. I will find a parent, Father Flynn! Trust me I will. A parent who probably doesn't know that you are still working with children! And once I do that, you will be exposed. You may even be attacked, metaphorically or otherwise.

FLYNN: You have no right to act on your own! You are a member of a religious order. You have taken vows, obedience being one! You answer to us! You have no right to step outside the Church!

SISTER ALOYSIUS: I will step outside the Church if that's what needs to be done, though the door should shut behind me! I will do what needs to be done, Father, if it means I'm damned to Hell! You should understand that, or you will mistake me. Now, did you give Donald Muller wine to drink?

FLYNN: Have you never done anything wrong?

SISTER ALOYSIUS: I have.

FLYNN: Mortal sin?

SISTER ALOYSIUS: Yes.

FLYNN: And?

SISTER ALOYSIUS: I confessed it! Did you give Donald Muller wine to drink?

FLYNN: Whatever I have done, I have left in the healing hands of my confessor. As have you! We are the same!

SISTER ALOYSIUS: We are not the same! A dog that bites is a dog that bites! I do not justify what I do wrong and go on. I admit it, desist, and take my medicine. Did you give Donald Muller wine to drink?

FLYNN: No.

SISTER ALOYSIUS: Mental reservation?

FLYNN: No.

SISTER ALOYSIUS: You lie. Very well then. If you won't leave my office, I will. And once I go, I will not stop. (*She goes to the door. Suddenly, a new tone comes into his voice.*)

FLYNN: Wait!

SISTER ALOYSIUS: You will request a transfer from this parish. You will take a leave of absence until it is granted.

FLYNN: And do what for the love of God? My life is here.

SISTER ALOYSIUS: Don't.

FLYNN: Please! Are we people? Am I a person flesh and blood like you? Or are we just ideas and convictions. I can't say everything. Do you understand? There are things I can't say. Even if you can't imagine the explanation, Sister, remember that there are circumstances beyond your knowledge. Even if you feel certainty, it is an emotion and not a fact. In the spirit of charity, I appeal to you. On behalf of my life's work. You have to behave responsibly. I put myself in your hands.

SISTER ALOYSIUS: I don't want you.

FLYNN: My reputation is at stake.

SISTER ALOYSIUS: You can preserve your reputation.

FLYNN: If you say these things, I won't be able to do my work in the community.

SISTER ALOYSIUS: Your work in the community should be discontinued.

FLYNN: You'd leave me with nothing.

SISTER ALOYSIUS: That's not true. It's Donald Muller who has nothing, and you took full advantage of that.

FLYNN: I have not done anything wrong. I care about that boy very much.

SISTER ALOYSIUS: Because you smile at him and sympathize with him, and talk to him as if you were the same?

FLYNN: That child needed a friend!

SISTER ALOYSIUS: You are a cheat. The warm feeling you experienced when that boy looked at you with trust was not the sensation of virtue. It can be got by a drunkard from his tot of rum. You're a disgrace to the collar. The only reason you haven't been thrown out of the Church is the decline in vocations.

FLYNN: I can fight you.

SISTER ALOYSIUS: You will lose.

FLYNN: You can't know that.

SISTER ALOYSIUS: I know.

FLYNN: Where's your compassion?

SISTER ALOYSIUS: Nowhere you can get at it. Stay here. Compose yourself. Use the phone if you like. Good day, Father. I have no sympathy for you. I know you're invulnerable to true regret. (*Starts to go. Pause.*) And cut your nails. (*She goes, closing the door behind her. After a moment, he goes to the phone and dials.*)

FLYNN: Yes. This is Father Brendan Flynn of St. Nicholas parish. I need to make an appointment to see the bishop. (*Lights fade.*)

NINE

The lights crossfade to Sister Aloysius walking into the garden. It's a sunny day. She sits on the bench. Sister James enters.

SISTER ALOYSIUS: How's your brother?

SISTER JAMES: Better. Much better.

SISTER ALOYSIUS: I'm very glad. I prayed for him.

SISTER JAMES: It was good to get away. I needed to see my family. It had been too long.

SISTER ALOYSIUS: Then I'm glad you did it.

SISTER JAMES: And Father Flynn is gone.

SISTER ALOYSIUS: Yes.

SISTER JAMES: Where?

SISTER ALOYSIUS: St. Jerome's.

SISTER JAMES: So you did it. You got him out.

SISTER ALOYSIUS: Yes.

SISTER JAMES: Donald Muller is heartbroken that he's gone.

SISTER ALOYSIUS: Can't be helped. It's just till June.

SISTER JAMES: I don't think Father Flynn did anything wrong.

SISTER ALOYSIUS: No? He convinced you?

SISTER JAMES: Yes, he did.

SISTER ALOYSIUS: Hmmm.

SISTER JAMES: Did you ever prove it?

SISTER ALOYSIUS: What?

SISTER JAMES: That he interfered with Donald Muller?

SISTER ALOYSIUS: Did I ever prove it to whom?

SISTER JAMES: Anyone but yourself?

SISTER ALOYSIUS: No.

SISTER JAMES: But you were sure.

SISTER ALOYSIUS: Yes.

SISTER JAMES: I wish I could be like you.

SISTER ALOYSIUS: Why?

SISTER JAMES: Because I can't sleep at night anymore. Everything seems uncertain to me.

SISTER ALOYSIUS: Maybe we're not supposed to sleep so well. They've made Father Flynn the pastor of St. Jerome.

SISTER JAMES: Who?

SISTER ALOYSIUS: The bishop appointed Father Flynn the pastor of St. Jerome Church and School. It's a promotion.

SISTER JAMES: You didn't tell them?

SISTER ALOYSIUS: I told our good Monsignor Benedict. I crossed the garden and told him. He did not believe it to be true.

SISTER JAMES: Then why did Father Flynn leave? What did you say to him to make him go?

SISTER ALOYSIUS: That I had called a nun in his previous parish. That I had found out his prior history of infringements.

SISTER JAMES: So you did prove it!

SISTER ALOYSIUS: I was lying. I made no such call.

SISTER JAMES: You lied?

SISTER ALOYSIUS: Yes. But if he had no such history, the lie wouldn't have worked. His resignation was his confession. He was what I thought he was. And he's gone.

SISTER JAMES: I can't believe you lied.

SISTER ALOYSIUS: In the pursuit of wrongdoing, one steps away from God. Of course there's a price.

SISTER JAMES: I see. So now he's in another school.

SISTER ALOYSIUS: Yes. Oh, Sister James!

SISTER JAMES: What is it, Sister?

SISTER ALOYSIUS: I have doubts! I have such doubts! (*Sister Aloysius is bent with emotion. Sister James comforts her. Lights fade.*)

Conor McPherson

> "The theme of loneliness is quintessential to the evolution of Conor as a playwright."
>
> –Brian Cox, Actor

Conor McPherson, born in 1971, went through school without much success until he reached University College Dublin, where his talent for playwriting began to show in a number of plays, such as *Taking Stock* (1989), *Michelle Pfeiffer* (1990), and *Scenes Federal* (1991), which were produced locally. Because these were not developed into professional plays, McPherson went on to get his master's degree in English and philosophy, and he worked as a university tutor in ethics and moral philosophy for some two years.

Still feeling the attraction of the stage, McPherson established a theater company with some friends in Dublin. The Fly by Night Theatre Company produced many of his plays in The International Bar in Dublin, a site that had hosted a number of other developing theater groups since 1980. In 1994 his plays *Rum and Vodka* and *The Good Thief* were performed at the City Arts Center in Dublin and attracted the attention of a larger audience. The alcoholism that suffuses *Rum and Vodka* attracted the attention of critics, who interpreted the drinking and drunkenness that were central to many of McPherson's plays as a kind of trademark. These two plays exhibited another trademark quality of McPherson's work: reliance on the monologue. McPherson's early plays were largely monologues, and even his very successful later plays were often a succession of monologues told by a succession of characters. McPherson has said that he is fascinated by people who can sit down and tell a story that completely entrances him. He said, "I love it when somebody sits back and tells me story after story. . . . That's my favorite kind of relationship." Also seen in the work of Brian Friel and some other Irish playwrights, the monologue has taken on a distinctive modern Irish tone that has sometimes irritated critics.

The Good Thief (1994), *This Lime Tree Bower* (1995), and *St. Nicholas* (1997) were performed not only in Dublin but also in New York, and all three are essentially monologues or sequences of monologues. The first of these plays involves a thug who ruminates on his chosen profession and begins to think he might shift gears despite the fact that he's got an assignment to rough up a fellow he hardly knows. *This Lime Tree Bower* is a succession of three monologues, including one by an academic who has fallen far from grace. *St. Nicholas* is a sly dig at drama critics of the sort that everybody hates. The critic in this play falls into a den of vampires—also a sly bit of wit because *Dracula*, the epitome of vampire novels, was written by an Irishman.

The Weir (1997) was the play that brought McPherson great international recognition. It won the Olivier Prize for best play in London that year; although it did not win a Tony Award in New York, it had a long run and excellent reviews. The play involves four men drinking at their favorite country pub, exchanging stories about the local scene. They are interrupted by the entrance of a woman who has bought a local house, and they begin to tell her some ghost stories, as if hoping to scare her a bit. But the tables turn when she tells them a ghost story that trumps theirs! This play established McPherson's reputation and has been performed widely since its premiere.

McPherson not only wrote about alcoholism but was himself a formidable drinker even while he was working on his early plays. In 2001 he collapsed on the opening night of a new play, *Port Authority,* suffering an attack of pancreatitis, a potentially fatal disorder. He came very close to dying at the age of 29, and that experience changed him entirely. He joined Alcoholics Anonymous and stopped drinking. He began to see the world in a different light and achieved the insights he needed to begin work on his next play, *Shining City* (2004), which also reads something like a ghost story. In it a businessman, John, comes to see Ian, a psychotherapist who has just begun his practice, because John has been seeing the ghost of his wife, who died in an accident. In this play, McPherson abandons the monologue and develops a highly original type of dialogue marked by striking pauses that give a peculiar emphasis to everything that is said. The dialogue is ordinary in every way, except that it accretes significance and begins to build meaning out of what, on the surface, sounds almost commonplace. Other playwrights, such as Pinter, Mamet, and Albee, have been complimented on their oblique dialogue, and McPherson is certainly comparable to them in this play.

McPherson's penchant for the supernatural continues in his later plays. In *The Seafarer* (2006), four men sit down to play poker and a Mr. Lockhart joins them, only to slowly reveal that he is none other than the devil. *The Birds* (2009) is adapted from the Daphne Du Maurier short story that also inspired Alfred Hitchcock's 1963 film. *The Veil* (2011), McPherson's first period piece, is set in a haunted house in 1822, during a period of economic stress. McPherson is one of the most prolific of modern playwrights — an international figure whose work is always eagerly anticipated by audiences in the United States and abroad.

For links to resources about McPherson, click on *AuthorLinks* at bedfordstmartins.com/jacobus.

The Seafarer

Conor McPherson has said that he is all the characters in *The Seafarer* and that this may be the last in a series of plays that draw on autobiographical sources. The play also has a literary source in the folklore of Ireland. A game of cards has been a feature in many Irish folktales, and in some of those tales the devil makes his presence known and plays for the souls of the Irish folk. In *The Seafarer,* the characters, all men, meet at Christmas time to have a good game of cards, as they have done before. Sharky, the main character, has come back to town from his chauffeuring job to look after his recently blinded older brother Richard. Most of the characters are blind drunk much of the time, but Sharky has been sober for three days and is trying desperately to remain sober. Nicky not only is drunk, but is wearing sunglasses, and Ivan has lost his glasses, so none of them are able to see what is in front of them. Mr. Lockhart, on the other hand, not only dresses and looks different from all these men but seems almost immune to the liquor he is consuming.

Like characters in many of McPherson's plays, Sharky has secrets in his past, which Mr. Lockhart has uncovered. He confronts Sharky with the fact that they shared a prison cell twenty-five years before, when Sharky had confessed to beating a man who eventually died. Sharky seems unaware of the fact that Laurence Joyce — a very literary combination of names — died, but

Lockhart assures him it is so. Lockhart reveals himself to Sharky in a profoundly dramatic moment in act 1, stunning him with insight and forcing Sharky to his knees by simply staring at him. On stage, the action is sudden and profound, although not totally unexpected. Sharky learns that in this card game he is playing against the devil and the devil wants his soul. In the second act, Mr. Lockhart describes heaven and hell in extraordinary detail in an extensive monologue that echoes the style of McPherson's earlier plays.

During the Abbey Theatre production in 2008 in Dublin, McPherson said that Irish audiences are more likely than audiences might be in New York or London to appreciate and understand his drama. His confidence in the Irish audience has to do in part with the conventional patterns of drinking that have been apparent in Ireland for many years. Richard begins the play so hung over that when the curtain goes up, the audience cannot see him under a pile of clothes and rags. And throughout the play he continually demands another drink. He drinks beer, as do some of the other characters, but he also drinks Powers Irish whiskey, and eventually all of the characters turn to poteen, the most potent of all Irish drinks, usually distilled from potatoes and of uncertain—but always extremely high—alcohol content. The setting of *The Seafarer* is hellish in that the rooms in which the action takes place are lower than street level and the "winos" who annoy Richard so much are like minor devils causing havoc at a distance.

Behind the play is a legend associated with the nearby Wicklow hills. The Hell Fire Club, a lodge set on the crest of Montpelier Hill, was built in the eighteenth century using stones from a sacred cairn. This is said to have angered the devil, and as a result, a number of unexplained, supposedly satanic events have occurred in the region.

The old English poem "The Seafarer" is also important to the play. The poem is told by a seafarer whose story resembles a man's journey through life. He holds firm to his route through the unmarked ocean and eventually begins to praise God for his survival. It is a deeply religious poem, and McPherson's play is also religious in that it offers hope and a second chance for a man who has made many mistakes. In a sense, Sharky has a chance for redemption and a new life, particularly if he can keep to his new path and give up his past errant ways. The old poem imparts not only the experiences of a survivor who has weathered years of struggle, but the wisdom of one who understands the significance of a life well lived.

Despite the dark setting, the dingy household, and the unremitting drunkenness, *The Seafarer* is often wildly comic. McPherson lets us understand that even in the midst of the most serious events in life there is humor and, through humor, possibly relief from despair. When the play ends, we see these five characters through different eyes.

For discussion questions and assignments on *The Seafarer,* visit bedfordstmartins.com/jacobus.

The Seafarer in Performance

The first performance of *The Seafarer* was in the Cottlesloe Auditorium of the National Theatre in London in September 2006. Jim Norton won an Olivier Award for his performance as Richard, and the play was nominated for best new play in 2007. The Broadway production in New York was in December 2007 with Jim Norton, David Morse as Sharky, and Ciaran Hinds as Mr. Lockhart. Jim Norton won a Tony Award for best featured actor, and the play was nominated for several other Tonys, including best play. The play was first performed in Ireland at the Abbey Theatre in Dublin in 2008. The London, New York, and Dublin productions were directed by Conor McPherson. Productions followed in Budapest, Hungary; Mill Valley, California; and New Brunswick, New Jersey, in 2008, and at the Steppenwolf Theatre in Chicago, the Studio Theatre in Washington, D.C., the Geffen Playhouse in Los Angeles, and the Seattle Repertory in 2009. Catey Sullivan said in the *Chicago Theatre Review Examiner*, "*The Seafarer* might seem like an unlikely masterpiece. But there's no denying its power. It is spellbinding, and continues to be so long after the final curtain call."

CONOR McPHERSON (b. 1971)

The Seafarer 2006

He knows not
Who lives most easily on land, how I
Have spent my winter on the ice-cold sea
Wretched and anxious, in the paths of exile
Lacking dear friends, hung round by icicles
While hail flew past in showers . . . —ANONYMOUS, *THE SEAFARER*, C. 755 AD,
                         TRANSLATED FROM ANGLO-SAXON BY RICHARD HAMER

Characters

JAMES 'SHARKY' HARKIN, *erstwhile fisherman/van driver/ chauffeur, fifties*
RICHARD HARKIN, *his older brother, recently gone blind, late fifties/sixties*
IVAN CURRY, *old friend of the Harkins, late forties*
NICKY GIBLIN, *a friend of Richard's, late forties/fifties*
MR LOCKHART, *an acquaintance of Nicky's, fifties*

Setting: *The action takes place in a house in Baldoyle, a coastal settlement north of Dublin City. It is an old area which could hardly be called a town these days. It is rather a suburb of the city with a church and a few pubs and shops at its heart. From the coast one is looking at the north side of the Howth peninsula. Howth Head (Binn Eadair) is a hill on the peninsula which marks the northern arm of Dublin Bay. Due to its prominence it has long been the focus of myths and legends.*

Act One takes place on Christmas Eve morning and late afternoon.

Act Two takes place late on Christmas Eve night.

ACT ONE: THE DEVIL AT BINN EADAIR

Scene One

The grim living area of a house in Baldoyle in Dublin. The house seems to be built into a hill. The main entrance is down a flight of stairs from the ground floor, giving a basement feel to the room. There is a window with a net curtain and threadbare heavier curtains drawn over it. At the back wall is an opening to a passageway giving access to a yard. Off the passageway are a mostly unseen kitchen and a toilet.

The place lacks a woman's touch. It has morphed into a kind of a bar in its appearance. Those who live or pass through here are so immersed in pub culture that many artefacts in the room are originally from bars: a big mirror advertising whiskey, ashtrays, beer mats, a bar stool or two somewhere. There is a cold stove. The furniture is old and worn. An armchair, a couch, mismatched chairs, a dresser with very old mugs, cups and various chipped plates, a little table more suited for playing cards than for eating at . . .

As the play begins the room is more or less in darkness. Some light seeps through from the kitchen, from the door to the yard, from down the stairs and through the threadbare curtains. There doesn't appear to be anyone here. An old stereo plays low music. A scrawny artificial Christmas tree haunts a corner.

Sharky comes down the stairs, pausing to tap a red light under a picture of the Sacred Heart which has gone out. It flickers to life for a second but goes out again as he descends and surveys the scene. He is in mismatched pyjamas with a sweater over them and wears a pair of runners. He is not a big man, but is wiry and strong. A very tough life is etched on his face. His eyes are quick and ready. He has a small plaster at the bridge of his nose and a few plasters on the knuckles of his right hand. He opens the curtains to let in the morning light which reveals the squalor. He goes to the stereo and shuts it off. He then realises the phone is ringing. He lifts the receiver.

SHARKY: Hello? Hello?

He hangs up. As he does so, Richard, his older brother, stirs awake. He has been asleep (passed out) on the floor where we didn't notice him or took him for a bundle of rags. He wears a black suit, one slipper, an ancient baseball cap and a filthy white shirt. He is unshaven and looks terrible. He has recently gone blind. He rises up behind Sharky . . .

RICHARD: Who's that? Sharky?

SHARKY (*startled*): What are you fucking doing?!

RICHARD: What happened?

SHARKY: Nothing—I just turned off the radio. I thought you told me you'd go up to bed!

RICHARD: Yeah, I meant to, but I'd no one to help me up the stairs!

SHARKY: Where was Ivan?

RICHARD: I don't know! He must've gone home.

SHARKY: I thought you said you could feel your way up!

RICHARD: Ah, Sharky! Not when I'm jarred!°

SHARKY (*going to Richard, picking up a slipper*): For fuck's sake, Richard . . .

RICHARD: Ah, don't be at me now, I'm not able for it. What time is it?

SHARKY: It's half ten.

RICHARD: Oh God, I'm bursting . . . give us a hand, where's me stick?

Sharky, slipper in hand, looks around for Richard's stick, while Richard shakily holds on to the chair, one slipper on, one slipper off.

Sharky!

SHARKY: I'm here!

RICHARD: God, it's freezing! Where's me stick?

SHARKY: I don't know! Where did you put it?

RICHARD: If I knew where I put it, I'd have it!

SHARKY: Ah, don't fucking start, I'm looking for it, if you'd've let me bring you up to bed last night you'd have everything . . .

RICHARD: Ivan was here! What was I gonna do, leave him sitting in here on his own?

SHARKY: No, you were too busy drinking your fucking brains out.

Sharky goes towards the kitchen.

RICHARD: Hark at you! Hark at Sharky! That's a good one! 'The hypocrite's voice haunts his own den!'°

Sharky returns with the stick.

SHARKY: Here, I have it.

RICHARD: Where was it?

SHARKY: It was outside the jacks° door. Where it was yesterday as well.

Sharky gives Richard the stick and crouches to help Richard get his slipper on.

RICHARD: Would you give me a hand and bring me through!!

SHARKY: I am! What do you think I'm doing?

Sharky lifts Richard's foot into his slipper.

RICHARD: Alright! I'm just asking . . . Jaysus, who got out of bed on the wrong side this morning?

SHARKY (*helping Richard towards the passageway*): Good fuck, Richard, you absolutely stink again, do you know that?

RICHARD: Yeah, happy Christmas to you as well!

SHARKY: Would you not let me put you in the bath? I'll give you a nice shave.

RICHARD: I told you! Tomorrow! Christmas morning! What's the point doing it today? I'll only stink the place out for Santy!

SHARKY: Alright! Relax! You have me going deaf in that ear!

Sharky opens the toilet door.

Ah, Richard, who did that all over the floor?

RICHARD: Well, I don't know!

SHARKY: Come on, let me bring you upstairs I'll give you a shave, come on.

RICHARD: I said tomorrow! Would you let me do my toilet please, Sharky? For . . . Jaysus' sake will you come out of me road?

SHARKY (*off*): I am! Let me just wipe the seat . . .

RICHARD (*storming in and ejecting Sharky*): Come out of me road!

The toilet door slams. Sharky tidies up a few things, finding a bottle of Powers whiskey under a chair with about a quarter left. He goes to the stove and pokes around in there.

(*Off.*) Sharky!

SHARKY: What?

RICHARD (*off*): Is there not any jacks roll in here?

---

jarred: Drunk.

hypocrite's voice . . . den: Folk saying from unknown source.
jacks: Toilet.

SHARKY: I don't know! You're in there!

RICHARD (*off*): Well there's none on the holder and I can't feel on the floor . . .

SHARKY: Hold on!

Sharky goes into the kitchen and takes a roll of tissue paper to the toilet.

RICHARD (*off*): Don't come in!

SHARKY: Well what do you want me to do?

RICHARD (*off*): Just hand me in some!

SHARKY: There's only kitchen roll here, okay?

RICHARD (*off*): Just hand it in to me.

SHARKY: Here . . .

RICHARD (*off*): Where's your hand?

SHARKY: Here! Here!

Sharky slams the toilet door.

RICHARD (*off*): Don't slam the door!

Sharky reappears and begins laying the table for some breakfast, bringing out a bowl of mandarin oranges, and a Kellogg's variety pack of various cereals in small boxes. He goes back into the kitchen. Ivan appears at the top of the stairs. He is a big burly man with a red face and curly hair. He wears a shirt tucked into his pants, the back sticking out. He feels his way gingerly down. Sharky comes back with some milk and two bowls.

IVAN (*sheepishly*): Morning, Sharky.

SHARKY: Ivan! Did you stay over?

IVAN: Yeah, no, I couldn't get a taxi. (*Hands shaking . . .*) Oh God, I feel terrible.

SHARKY: Have some breakfast.

IVAN: Oh God, I don't know. Let me just . . . get my bearings for a minute, is that okay?

SHARKY: You don't have to ask me that, Ivan. Sure, do whatever you . . .

IVAN: Yeah, no, I . . . can't find my glasses. You didn't see them?

SHARKY (*looking*): Em . . . Where did you . . . did you get a good kip?°

IVAN: Yeah, yeah . . . I was dead to the world just then. What was all the shouting?

SHARKY: Ah, that was . . . (*He signals 'Richard'.*)

IVAN: When did you get back?

SHARKY: I got back three . . . four days ago.

IVAN: Yeah?

SHARKY: Sure, I was talking to you last night!

IVAN: Were you here last night?

SHARKY: Yeah, I made yous hot whiskeys . . .

IVAN: Oh yeah . . .

SHARKY: Do you not remember?

IVAN: No yeah, no, no I do. Just I wasn't even . . . sure I was only on my way home. I was only calling in to see if your man was alright . . . I certainly didn't mean to still fucking be here! Jaysus . . .

kip: Sleep.

SHARKY (*laughs*): Yeah, well . . . Listen, thanks for all the . . . calling in on him and . . . he's . . . eh . . .

IVAN: Yeah, yeah, no, no bother. God, I'm gonna be killed . . .

SHARKY: Are you?

IVAN: No, there's still a few Christmas bits I have to do. God, I'm gonna be killed now.

SHARKY: How is Karen keeping?

IVAN: Don't talk to me.

SHARKY: Yeah?

IVAN: Don't talk to me.

SHARKY: And the kids?

IVAN: Ah, they're great, yeah. They're grand, you know yourself.

SHARKY: Yeah, well that's . . .

IVAN: Yeah . . .

Pause.

SHARKY (*calling off*): Are you alright there, Rich?

RICHARD (*off*): What's wrong with ya?

SHARKY: No, I was just seeing if you were alright?

RICHARD (*off*): Would you leave me alone? I'm trying to go to the fucking toilet in here!

SHARKY: I'll just grab the . . . the tea . . .

IVAN: Yeah, yeah, work away.

Sharky goes into the kitchen. Ivan moves through the room a little, throwing his eye around quickly for something to drink. He can't see anything. Sharky comes back with a pot of tea and some cups then he goes to put some briquettes in the stove.

SHARKY: Here, were yous out the back last night?

IVAN: What? Oh! Yeah . . . Oh no, it was . . . (*Unsaid 'stupid'.*) Did you hear him?

SHARKY: Ah yeah, I heard him, I heard yous. I rolled over, I tried to just ignore it. Sure that's . . .

IVAN: Yeah . . .

SHARKY: . . . that's a regular . . .

IVAN: I know, mad!

SHARKY: What was it? The winos out in the lane?

IVAN: Yeah! We were sitting there at the fire and bang! Suddenly he gets up! I'm like, 'What are you doing?' He's like, 'Them winos are out in the lane again! I'm gonna kill them!' he says, waving the fucking . . . stick around!

SHARKY: I know!

IVAN: Nearly took my fucking head off with it, and out he runs, *off* on out through the back there, it was nearly like he could see! You know?

SHARKY: I know!

IVAN (*rubbing his elbow gingerly*): And I . . . fucking went over, smack! . . . on them newspapers all in the back door there, trying to stop him! And then out in the garden or . . . ! I didn't know where I was!

SHARKY: I know. He's a mad bollocks, Ivan.

IVAN: Ah no, he's alright. He's just . . . (*Beat.*) So, here, did I ask you this last night? How did you get on down in . . . Where was this you were?

SHARKY: I was down in Lahinch, in County Clare.

IVAN: Yeah?

SHARKY: Yeah, it was, it was, it was . . . it was great.

IVAN: You got on well?

SHARKY: Yeah, got on great. Down the country is great, you know . . .

IVAN: Ah, down the country's smashing. Were you on the boats or . . . ?

SHARKY: Nah . . . Can't get a job on the boats. But the people I was working for were spot on . . .

IVAN: What were you doing? Chauffeur?

SHARKY: Yeah, I was doing a bit of driving for this developer guy . . . and his wife there and eh . . . (*Short pause.*) But I had to get back up because . . .

He signals 'Richard'. They hear an attempt to flush the toilet.

IVAN: Ah yeah, no, fair play, Sharky. Oh here, Nicky Giblin was telling me, how's the . . .

They stop to listen to Richard's attempts to flush the toilet.

SHARKY (*calling*): Are you alright, Rich?

RICHARD (*off*): Ah, I can't flush this fucking thing!

SHARKY: Do you want me to do it?

RICHARD (*off*): Is that Ivan out there?

SHARKY: He's heard you.

IVAN (*going towards kitchen door*): Are you alright, Richard? Do you not want your brother?

RICHARD (*off*): No, Ivan, you're strong. Come here and give this yoke a yank, will ya?

Ivan goes off to help Richard. Sharky continues to get the breakfast and tidy up while Ivan and Richard attend to the toilet.

    (*Off.*) That's it—one more like that, Ivan . . .

IVAN (*off*): Here give us that till I stick it down the . . . hold on, come away . . .

The toilet flushes. Ivan leads Richard back out.

RICHARD: Well done, Ivan . . . sorry about that . . .

SHARKY: Lads, some breakfast.

IVAN (*unable to consider it*): Oh . . .

RICHARD: What is there?

SHARKY: There's toast, if you want, there's cereal . . .

RICHARD: What cereal?

SHARKY (*looking at variety pack*): There's Cornflakes, there's Frosties, there's Coco Pops, there's . . .

RICHARD (*gravely*): Em . . . Coco Pops . . .

SHARKY: Okay, and I've mandarin oranges, there's tea, Ivan.

RICHARD: Did you not get coffee?

SHARKY (*pouring out bowl of cereal*): No, I told you, I forgot, I'll get it today.

RICHARD: You know what I'd really like?

SHARKY: What?

RICHARD: Ivan? Irish coffee . . .

IVAN: Oh now . . .

RICHARD: Warm us up!

SHARKY: Yeah, well, we don't even have coffee so . . .

RICHARD: Well, then, we'll just have the Irish and no coffee—ha, Ivan?

SHARKY (*going to kitchen*): I'll put on some toast.

RICHARD: Well, Ivan, how's the head?

IVAN: Don't talk to me, Rich. I can't find my glasses. I'm like you, I'm feeling my way around.

RICHARD: Well they have to be here somewhere. Did you have them when you got here?

IVAN: I'm assuming I did.

Sharky comes back.

RICHARD (*of Sharky*): Hey, check out Johnny Weismuller,° off the drink for . . . what is it, Sharky? Two days?

SHARKY: What?

RICHARD: How long are you on the dry now? Two days, is it? I was just telling Ivan. The old delirium tremens° must be fairly ramping up now, ha?

Sharky ignores him.

IVAN: Yeah well, fair play. Hey Shark, I was gonna ask you, how's the nose? Nicky Giblin was telling me.

Sharky signals to him not to continue with this line of enquiry. Ivan doesn't twig it in time.

RICHARD: What's this?

IVAN: Did he not tell you?

SHARKY (*signalling to Ivan who finally sees him*): No, it was nothing . . .

RICHARD: Tell me what?

Pause.

    What? Tell me what?

IVAN: No . . . eh . . . Nicky was . . . (*Dismissively.*) Ah, you know Nicky . . .

RICHARD: I know Nicky well! What happened to you, Sharky?

SHARKY: Ah, it was nothing, it was . . .

RICHARD: What? Ivan?

IVAN: Ah . . . (*To Sharky.*) Nicky was saying, I was only asking to see if you were . . . (*To Richard.*) Nicky was saying that Sharky got in a spot of bother there off someone there outside the Elphin and I was just . . .

RICHARD: When was this?

SHARKY: Ah, it was . . . it was the other evening . . . the night I got here.

RICHARD: You kept that very quiet! What happened?

SHARKY: Ah, it was fucking . . . I got off the Dart° at Howth Junction and I was . . .

Johnny Weissmuller: Film actor (1904–1984) famous for portraying Tarzan. **delirium tremens:** Latin for shaking frenzy, a form of alcohol withdrawal. **Dart:** Dublin Area Rapid Transit.

RICHARD: What did you get off at Howth Junction for?

SHARKY: Ah, I meant to go to Bayside or Sutton Cross, and I mixed it up and I . . .

RICHARD: You blew it!

SHARKY: Yeah, well I was walking all up there, up the coast, and . . .

RICHARD: Why didn't you get a taxi?

SHARKY: I had no cash!

RICHARD: Go on out of that, you were in the Elphin!

SHARKY: No, I went into the Elphin . . .

RICHARD (*sarcastically, as though he had failed to see a big distinction*): Oh!

SHARKY: I needed to make a phone call . . . my phone was . . .

RICHARD: Go on out of that! You were jarred from the train, you got off at the wrong fucking station . . .

SHARKY: I fucking . . . ! I had two, three pints . . . (*To Ivan.*) 'cause young Cathy Wolfe was having her birthday in there and her da bought me one . . .

RICHARD: Oh . . . I see . . .

SHARKY: And then the end of the match was on and . . .

RICHARD: Ah, of course . . .

SHARKY: Ah, I'm not gonna fucking tell you if you're . . .

RICHARD: No, I'm only having you on! What happened?

Pause.

SHARKY: Ah . . . I was coming out and there was some lads messing around, sitting on the bonnet of a car out there and . . .

Pause.

RICHARD: What happened?

SHARKY: Ah, I just said, 'Come up off of that . . .' as I was kind of walking by . . .

RICHARD: What?

SHARKY: Just, only, not even that serious, you know . . .

RICHARD: You fucking eejit . . .

SHARKY: And next thing, I'm down at the corner, they're all around me! And your man is, 'What did you fucking say?' And all this. And I'm like, 'Ah lads, I was only . . .' And then, one of them . . . he just gave me this unbelievable kick in the arse, you know? And it was so . . . it was so . . . the humiliation of it, like, and I . . .

RICHARD: Ah, Sharky . . .

SHARKY: I turned around and I threw a dig and I was . . . but there was loads of them and I got an awful couple of smacks in the . . . my nose was pumping, it's alright now, but I had to leg it back into the Elphin. The fucking . . . streams of toilet roll I had stuck up my nose . . . it was so . . . The Wolfes put me in a cab, gave your man twenty euros to drop me up.

Short pause.

RICHARD: Why didn't you say anything? (*Short pause.*) You fucking eejit!

SHARKY: Yeah, well, I'll get the toast.

Sharky goes into the kitchen.

IVAN: Mmm . . .

RICHARD: I mean, what can you do with a fella like that?

IVAN: Yeah, it was . . . they were all . . . Nicky Giblin was telling me . . .

RICHARD: Yeah, well Nicky means well, I'm sure . . .

Short pause. Ivan checks to see if Sharky is in earshot.

IVAN: Does Sharky know that Eileen is with Nicky now?

RICHARD: What? Ah, yeah . . . no that's . . . Sure that's . . . she called into me here about two weeks ago, did I tell you that?

IVAN: Who, Eileen?

RICHARD: Yeah, she was here, she does a morning or two cleaning for the Franciscan monks up there in the Friary. She called in to see if I was . . . to see how I was. We had smoked cod and chips from the chipper and everything. Ah, it was great, we were talking about Head-the-ball (*Sharky*) . . . and Nicky and . . . yeah, the whole . . .

IVAN: Ah I'm kind of avoiding Nicky, to be honest with you, Dick.

RICHARD: Why?

IVAN: Ah, there's just always some fucking shite going on and I'm . . .

Ivan clams up as Sharky returns with some toast.

SHARKY: Can you see there, Ivan?

IVAN: I can just about . . .

SHARKY: Would you . . . ? (*Unsaid: 'help Richard'.*)

IVAN: Yeah, yeah, do you want some toast there, Dick?

Ivan starts to very shakily butter some toast as Sharky nips back into the kitchen to get some for himself.

RICHARD: I tell you what I'd love. I'd love a big Irish breakfast! A big fry with all white pudding and a runny egg and all . . .

Sharky returns with his own toast and a carton of orange juice.

Do you hear me, Sharky?

SHARKY: What?

RICHARD: We should be having a nice Christmassy breakfast. We have to get some decent grub in for tomorrow, Sharky, Christmas pud and the works. This is disgraceful!

SHARKY: Yeah, I'm going up now when I get dressed . . .

RICHARD: How will you go?

SHARKY: Do you have your car with you, Ivan?

Pause. Ivan looks at him blankly.

RICHARD: Do you have your car, Ivan?

IVAN: I can't . . . I don't know.

RICHARD: We'll go in a taxi.

SHARKY: Are you coming as well?

RICHARD: Ah, let me get out for a bit, for Jaysus' sake, Sharky, we might even get a Christmas pint . . .

SHARKY (*sighing*): Oh . . . well, wait now because if . . .

RICHARD: No, because we need to get a few bits in as well, Sharky, from the off-licence, in case anyone calls. We'll get a taxi back, because I want to be settled in here now for Christmas Eve . . .

SHARKY: Yeah, but wait a minute, because if I have to . . .

RICHARD (*suddenly despairing*): I have so little left to live for!

Pause.

IVAN (*reassuringly*): Ah now, Richard . . .

RICHARD: What?! Yous don't know. Yous don't know.

SHARKY: No we'll all . . . we'll all go . . . we'll get the few bits and . . .

IVAN: Sure you'll be grand, you'll have a grand Christmas here with Sharky here, and with you and all, and . . .

RICHARD (*dismally*): Yeah . . .

SHARKY: If we're going out . . . will you have a wash?

RICHARD (*shouting*): I'll have a wash tomorrow!! I told you! Now leave it!

Pause.

IVAN: God, I'll have to find my glasses. Karen'll kill me, God, what am I gonna say?

SHARKY: We'll find them, I'll have a look now in a minute before we go.

IVAN: Thanks, Sharky.

SHARKY: Tea, Rich?

RICHARD (*sheepishly*): Yeah, thanks.

Sharky brings him a cup of tea.

I just don't want to be cooped up all over the . . .

SHARKY: Yeah, I know, we'll get out, we'll get you some fresh air.

RICHARD: Yeah . . .

IVAN: Hey, any sign of your money there yet, Sharky? From the bus people?

SHARKY: What? Aw . . . Well, the . . .

RICHARD: Get this!

SHARKY: Well, no, because the solicitor fucking . . . he misdated the statement I gave him. About the . . . the actual night I fell down the stairs . . .

IVAN: What, the bus went round the wrong corner, or a different corner or something, was it?

SHARKY: Yeah, he went around the wrong corner up there at Christchurch there, he went around too early, and I was getting up to get off . . . but that's . . . no one is disputing that, but the date, you see, on the . . . affidavit, it's the wrong date and . . .

IVAN: Can you not just . . . ?

SHARKY: Nah, the courts are . . .

RICHARD: He put the wrong year on it!

SHARKY: The whole thing has been put right back now, I don't even know if . . .

IVAN: But can he not just change the . . .

RICHARD: It's a shambles . . .

IVAN: . . . the year . . .

SHARKY: No . . .

IVAN: . . . if it was just a mistake . . .

RICHARD: Ivan, the law . . . the law is the law. It has to be.

IVAN: Yeah . . .

SHARKY: So now I have to look at . . .

IVAN: Yeah, if you keep going with it . . .

SHARKY: No, if I want to start the whole thing off again . . .

IVAN: What?

RICHARD: Yeah. Seven-and-a-half years he's been . . .

SHARKY: Ah, it doesn't matter, it's too . . .

IVAN: Jaysus, that's a pain in the bollocks, isn't it?

SHARKY: Ah it's . . .

Waving it away.

IVAN: 'Cause I'd say you could've done with the few bob . . .

SHARKY: Yeah well . . .

IVAN: Nightmare . . .

RICHARD: Of course, he was using your man, that solicitor out of Kilbarrack.

SHARKY: Yeah, alright, Rich . . .

IVAN: That drinks in *The Fox & Hound*?!

RICHARD: Yeah, your man that does be falling around the car park!

SHARKY: Ah no, see it was him that . . .

RICHARD (*shaking his head*): Sharky . . .

SHARKY: I was never even gonna take a case! It was him that . . . I mean . . .

RICHARD: What a shambles . . .

SHARKY: Yeah, well . . .

IVAN: Aw well, I'm sorry to hear that, Shark. I only saw your man the other week there actually, and the Baker, and Steady Eddie and all them lads were down in Graingers, do you know what they were talking about? Do you remember Maurice Macken?

RICHARD: That used drive the milk lorry?

IVAN: Yeah, and then he got into me electrical trade. Do you remember him, Sharky?

SHARKY: The skinny fella?

IVAN: Yeah, Maurice Macken used play a lot of cards all up around Sutton and Howth, you heard what happened him?

RICHARD: Oh yeah, I heard all about that.

SHARKY: Was this in the paper?

IVAN: Yeah it was all in the paper, you would've seen it. He was electrocuted up in a house where he was working in Santry. There was a tremendous bang! Blew him right across the room, I believe. One of his fillings ended up in his ear. Somehow he survived. They let him go home out of Beaumont Hospital, and then there was a fire in his house that night! And he was gone!

RICHARD: Gobshite . . .

SHARKY: Jaysus, that's mad.

IVAN: His number was up! His number was just up and he was going to have to go, one way or the other, you know what I mean, mad! Survived the electrocution only to be burned!

RICHARD: Fucking eejit . . .

IVAN: But listen, what the lads were saying up in Grainger's—two people, two different people, now, have seen him hanging around at the off-licence serving hatch round the side near the car park.

RICHARD (*incredulously*): Come on!

IVAN: Two different people saw him, Dick, on different nights. And apparently a barman tidying up after they were closed said he heard someone shouting in the jacks—and when he went in, there was no one there.

RICHARD: That's bollocks.

IVAN: Yeah, well, apparently he looks really white. He was standing near the hatch. Big Bernard's cousin saw him. Apparently he was just standing there looking out into the car park, like he was waiting on a lift or something.

RICHARD: Go on out of that! What's he waiting on? A few cans?

He laughs.

IVAN (*to Sharky*): Spooky though, isn't it?

SHARKY: Yeah, well . . .

RICHARD (*mildly derisive*): Yeah, right . . .

Suddenly there are three loud bangs at the front door upstairs. Richard jumps with fright.

Fucking hell! Who's that?

SHARKY (*going up the stairs*): Probably the postman . . .

RICHARD: We have a letterbox! For the love of God . . .

Short pause.

IVAN (*sighing*): Yeah . . .

RICHARD: Ivan, quick, where did he put that Gold Label?

IVAN (*quickly squinting around*): I can't fucking see, Dick . . .

RICHARD: Have a look in the kitchen, go on, quick.

Ivan strides purposefully towards the kitchen.

On top of the fridge or in the press with the pots . . .

Ivan disappears into the kitchen and returns quickly with the bottle Sharky put away earlier, unscrewing the lid . . .

IVAN: Here, Rich, give us your cup.

RICHARD (*offering his cup of tea to Ivan*): Pour that out.

Ivan takes Richard's cup and wildly looks for somewhere to pour it out, deciding eventually to pour it on to the carpet nearby, bending low so as not to make a splashing sound, he then rubs the steaming carpet with

his foot and pours a big dollop of whiskey into Richard's cup, handing it to him. Richard raises it to his mouth immediately. Ivan goes to the table to look for a cup for himself, swigging a mouthful of whiskey from the neck of the bottle as he does so.

He grabs a mug and pours some whiskey, wheeling around to give Richard another shot, as Richard instinctively holds his cup out for it. Both men are retching and making faces as though their throats are burning. Their arms and legs undergo a rudimentary stretch as they seem to come alive. Ivan pours some tea on top of the whiskey in his cup and conceals the bottle while Sharky appears at the top of the stairs, descending with a tastefully gift-wrapped box.

(*Brightly.*) What was it, Shark?

SHARKY: Postman.

IVAN: Look at that!

RICHARD: What is it?

SHARKY: It's a . . . it's a present . . .

RICHARD: For who?

SHARKY: For me.

RICHARD: Who's it from?

SHARKY: Ah, the, the people I was working for down in Clare . . . His wife, Miriam, she's very . . . you know . . . (*To Ivan.*) She's a very nice lady, she's eh . . .

RICHARD: Wooooooooo! (*Childishly.*) The big birthday present!

SHARKY: It's a Christmas present, you dozy fucking eejit.

RICHARD: Oh! (*Same tone.*) A Christmas present! Anything good?

SHARKY (*handing Richard an envelope*): Here, there's a card here for you.

RICHARD: Who's it from?

SHARKY: The Department of Social Welfare.

RICHARD (*throwing it away*): Ah, that's only my balls!

Sharky opens the card that came with his present and stands there reading it. Ivan slurps his tea . . .

Well? What is it?

Sharky looks at him as though coming out of a daze . . .

SHARKY: What?

IVAN: Are you gonna open it up?

RICHARD: Yes! Cheer us all up! Presents arriving for Sharky! I mean, what next?

Sharky takes the wrapping off. . . .

What is it?

SHARKY: It's a few CDs.

IVAN: Nice one!

RICHARD (*childishly*): Wooooooo, music to put you in the mood . . . ! For getting in your nude . . . !

IVAN: Hey, she knows her stuff! Some of these are classics! Here, put one on!

RICHARD: No! Later! We have to go and get the few bits for the Christmas! Come on . . .

IVAN: I have to find my glasses!

RICHARD: Sharky'll look for them. Sharky, have a quick look for Ivan's specs, will you?

SHARKY: Where would they be, Ivan? Where did you sleep?

IVAN: Eh, in the box room.

SHARKY: There's no bed in there!

IVAN: I slept on the rug.

SHARKY: The rug?

RICHARD: Ah, Ivan . . .

IVAN: Ah, no, there was towels, and there was . . .

SHARKY: I'll have a quick look. (*Going off up the stairs.*) You should've slept in the spare room . . .

IVAN: Ah no, I was grand I was fine . . .

RICHARD: Did you just sleep on the floor? Like an animal?

IVAN: No, I slept on the rug.

RICHARD: Ah, I don't even know what you're talking about. Give us a hand, Ivan, will you?

IVAN (*helping Richard up*): I thought Sharky was in the spare room.

RICHARD: I often just go off here at the fire. (*He coughs up some deeply embedded old phlegm and rubs it into the side of his armchair.*) You should have got into my bed.

IVAN: Nah, I wouldn't do that, Dick. Here, do you want your shoes?

RICHARD: Ah, sure we'll get a taxi, my slippers is grand. I don't expect we'll be walking the street like hobos. Just get us my anorak hanging up there behind the kitchen door.

Ivan goes to the kitchen. Richard feels around for his cup. Ivan brings the anorak and starts looking for his own coat.

Is that Gold Label dead? We have to make a list. We have nothing organised. That's your man, of course. He was supposed to get up to me weeks ago. His head is arseways. You're seeing him on the dry now, that's why he's running around in here like a fly in a bottle.

Ivan finds his own coat which he puts on and goes to retrieve the bottle from whatever nook he hid it in. There is only a swig left in it.

But of course then with jar on him he's worse! Throwing digs outside the Elphin! Or getting in mills outside the chipper on Kilbarrack Road the last time he was here! Getting arrested by the Guards up in Howth! I mean what am I going to do?

As Ivan drains the last shot of whiskey straight from the bottle . . .

Here, is there a shot left in that Powers, Ivan?

IVAN: Nah, we've had it. Here do you want your anorak, Dick?

RICHARD (*sighing heavily*): Yeah . . .

Ivan helps Richard to put his coat on.

Here, if you're gonna be round tomorrow, you should drop in, do you know what I have that I've been saving? A drop of Brigid Blake's poteen,° that Big Bernard got me . . .

IVAN: Oh, look out!

RICHARD: That'll fucking . . .

He makes a high-pitched whistle, pointing to his head. Ivan laughs. Sharky descends. He has got dressed and wears his coat.

SHARKY: Ivan, I can't see your glasses anywhere.

RICHARD: Ah they have to be somewhere, Sharky!

SHARKY: Do you not have a spare pair at home'll do you till . . . ?

IVAN: Yeah, I think I . . . they're an older prescription, if I can find them . . . Oh God, Karen is gonna kill me.

RICHARD: No, no she won't! I'll ring her, I'll say I had them here, it'll be grand. Sharky, get a pen, we need to make a list. Ivan I expect we'll be seeing you over the Christmas, I'll be very disappointed if we didn't, so Sharky, Harp, what, four six packs?

SHARKY (*grabbing a pen*): Yeah, Harp . . .

IVAN: Ah, don't just do that for me, Rich. Sharky, I'll drink whatever's going.

RICHARD (*pointing imperiously*): No. Sharky.

SHARKY (*writing*): Yeah, Harp. Stout, Richard?

RICHARD: Yeah and Paddy Powers. Get three bottles.

SHARKY: Three bottles? The off-licence° is open again on Monday, Rich.

RICHARD: If we have visitors they may want a hot whiskey. It's called being festive. I know you may not comprehend it, Sharky, but some us like to be social. Ivan, Christmas? You have to!

IVAN: Ah, Christmas is great!

RICHARD: And Miller for Nicky.

SHARKY: For Nicky Giblin?

RICHARD: Nicky drinks Miller, Sharky. We all understand that you have issues with life and it's an endless struggle for you to grasp human relationships, but Nicky is a friend of mine. And a friend of Ivan's . . . and . . .

IVAN: Ah, he can be very messy, Richard.

RICHARD (*with finality*): The man is welcome here!

SHARKY (*writing*): Bottles of Miller.

RICHARD: Thank you.

SHARKY: What'll I get for tomorrow? A chicken?

RICHARD: Turkey! Turkey!

SHARKY: We won't get a turkey now at this stage, Rich . . .

IVAN: Karen is doing us a big turkey tomorrow, I could drop down with maybe a few . . .

RICHARD: No, no, Ivan we couldn't do that to you, we'll get a turkey, don't worry about it . . .

SHARKY (*sucking his pen*): I mean we might be able to get a piece of em . . .

RICHARD: Look! Let's go!

---

poteen: Homemade whiskey (pronounced "po-cheen").   **off licence:** Liquor store.

SHARKY: Do you not want to make a list?

RICHARD: Yeah, yeah, we'll get all that when we're there. We'll see all that. Ivan will you take me out the back way and we'll hail a taxi on the road, I want to check them awful fucking winos haven't been messing around at our laneway door.

Ivan is leading Richard out towards the yard.

Will you lock up, Sharky?

SHARKY: Yeah.

RICHARD: We'll see you out on the road. (*As they go.*) All the kids' presents got then, Ivan?

IVAN: Ah, yeah . . . I think they are.

RICHARD: Well, I hope so, says you!

As they leave through the back door, Sharky folds up the list and puts it in his pocket. He takes out his keys and goes to lock the back door. He comes back into the silence and picks up the card he received. He looks at it for a moment, then briskly puts it in his pocket and leaves, running up the stairs.

We hear the wind and perhaps music plays as the lights slowly change from bright morning to a dusky feel and we slide into:

Scene Two

The wind is picking up outside as the sunlight fades and the temperature drops. The music dies away as Sharky comes down the stairs with bags of shopping, mostly from the off-licence, which he takes into the kitchen. A church bell chimes solemnly somewhere off in the distance. He reappears, switches on a lamp or two, bends down under the scraggy old Christmas tree and plugs in some coloured fairy lights. He sees two little presents wrapped up there. He picks one up and looks at it for a moment, wondering about it before he puts it back. He goes back up the stairs, pausing to tap the extinguished light under the Sacred Heart. It doesn't come on and he continues up to the hall to get the rest of the shopping and reappears, carrying more bags. As he descends we hear Richard calling from off, up in the hallway.

RICHARD (*off*): What are you fucking doing?

SHARKY (*halting and turning*): What?

RICHARD (*off*): What, were you gonna just leave me up here?

SHARKY: I thought you could manage your way down!

RICHARD (*off*): Ah, not when I'm jarred, Sharky!

SHARKY: Just give me a second.

Sharky carries the bags down, leaving them at the bottom of the stairs, and makes his way back up.

RICHARD (*off*): I'm freezing!

Sharky reappears, helping Richard down.

You are in one foul humour today . . .

SHARKY: Richard, now, please don't start . . .

RICHARD (*warmly, paternally*): What's the matter with you?

SHARKY: Richard . . .

RICHARD: What . . .

SHARKY: Nothing's the matter with me.

Richard stands in the room rubbing his hands. Sharky starts clearing a few things away, taking the breakfast things on a tray into the kitchen.

RICHARD: God, it's freezing! Would you get the fire going for the love of Jaysus, Shark?

SHARKY: I am! I'm doing it! I've a million things to do here, just give me a second, would you?

RICHARD (*as though Sharky has completely overreacted*): Okay! Okay!

Sharky returns, goes to the stove, puts some peat briquettes° in and sets about lighting it.

God, I never seen such a Christmas wrecker! Would you not have left the old Kaliber° out for today and had a drink with me and Ivan . . . and . . .

SHARKY (*working at the stove*): I'm pissed *off* with you, Richard.

RICHARD: With me? Why? What did I do now?

SHARKY: What did you have to go and invite Nicky Giblin up here for?

RICHARD: When?

SHARKY: When Big Bernard let you speak to him on his mobile.

RICHARD: Ah that was only a Happy Christmas, Jimmy, come on . . .

SHARKY: You told him to call in to us . . .

RICHARD: But sure, that's what you say! That's what everybody says!

SHARKY: You told him to call in to play cards!

RICHARD: That's . . . that's just what you say! Anyway— so what?! Would you stop being such a curmudgeonly old bollocks your whole life, will you?

Pause. Sharky works . . .

(*Warmly, drunkenly conciliatory.*) Ah, Sharky . . . I only said to stick the head in if he was in the area . . .

SHARKY: You don't fucking say that to fellas like Nicky, Dick. He'll be in on top of us before you know it!

RICHARD: No he won't! He was elephants! He was down in the Brookwood Inn of all places! How the hell is he gonna rock up here? In a taxi? I don't think so! Hey, is there 'ere a Christmas drink going a-begging around here?

SHARKY: Yeah, well I saw him the other day, and he was driving my car, Richard.

RICHARD: Who?

peat briquettes: Burnable turf used to heat houses.   **Kaliber:** A brand of non-alcoholic beer.

SHARKY: Nicky Giblin!

RICHARD: Yeah, well you gave your car to Eileen!

SHARKY: I loaned it to her for the school run, Dick. I didn't ever expect to see that fucker driving around in it! I saw him pulling out of the shops down there in Bayside, and I was walking down to get the Dart in the pissing rain! And he was in my car!

RICHARD: Ah, grow up, Sharky! What do you want? Him and Eileen are together now, so get over it, 'cause that's life, okay? Now would you ever give us a Jaysus fucking drink, you're gonna blow the whole Christmas atmosphere. This is all I have! And how many do I have left? Maybe only this one! Maybe that's it for me!

SHARKY: What are you talking about?

RICHARD: Ah! It's hardly even worth it! . . . What's the point?

Richard turns away in disgust. Sharky takes the rest of the shopping into the kitchen. Richard opens his coat and makes his way unsteadily towards his armchair and sits forlornly. Sharky re-emerges with a glass of whiskey for him.

SHARKY: Here . . . Richard . . .

RICHARD: What?

SHARKY (*putting the drink in Richard's hand*): Here . . .

RICHARD: Ah, thanks, Sharky.

Sharky takes a festive-looking candle in a red glass holder from a bag. He is tearing the price and the cellophane wrapping off and bringing it to the window sill.

What's that?

SHARKY: Hmm?

RICHARD: What are you doing, there?

SHARKY: Ah, I'm just gonna put an old candle in the window.

RICHARD: Ah, that's nice. That's more like it, Sharky. I never like it when you're down. It changes the whole . . .

SHARKY: Would you like some smoked salmon and brown bread?

RICHARD: Oh, now, that sounds . . . Ah, thanks, Sharky . . . thanks. Delicious!

SHARKY: Keep us going anyway . . . Is that getting warm?

RICHARD: Oh, we're warming up now . . .

Sharky goes towards the kitchen.

Oh, Sharky. Just one . . . just one small thing, quickly, before you do that.

SHARKY: Yeah?

RICHARD: You wouldn't take a basin of hot water down out to the back door at the lane . . . ? Them filthy fucking winos have all puke and piss and everything else all down our step all up the fucking door out there . . .

SHARKY (*face dropping*): Are you serious?

RICHARD: Ah, it's absolutely disgusting. We can't leave it like that on Christmas Eve . . . It'll only take you a minute . . . Good man . . .

Sharky goes unhappily to the kitchen to boil the kettle. Richard cosily raises his shoulders as though he is snuggling down into a lovely warm bed.

Now, this is nice now. It's getting nice and Christmassy now . . .

There is a loud rapping at the front door upstairs. Richard turns to profile. Sharky steps back into the room . . .

Sharky!

SHARKY: I hear it.

RICHARD: Well, get it, will you!

SHARKY: I'm not gonna get it, I told you I don't want Nicky Giblin in here, I just don't want it.

RICHARD: What!?

There are more loud raps at the door . . .

SHARKY: I told you, Richard! Why do you have to do this to me?

RICHARD: What are you talking about? I'm not doing anything to you. Don't be a fucking child, will you, and get the door, for God's sake . . .

Sharky just stands there looking at Richard. Richard suddenly bursts up out of his chair . . .

I'll get it myself!

With surprising speed, Richard darts towards the staircase. He hits the wall, collapses, bounces up again, grabs the banister and attempts to pull himself up the stairs . . .

SHARKY: Richard! Hold on, will you?

Sharky runs across and grabs Richard. Richard stumbles and falls backwards into Sharky's arms, the two of them sinking to the ground as the doorbell rings.

RICHARD: What are you fucking doing?!

SHARKY: What are you fucking doing? Come back over here and sit down, will you?

Sharky bundles Richard towards his chair . . .

For fuck's sake . . .

RICHARD: Will you get the door?

SHARKY: Yeah, will you just sit down please?

Sharky storms angrily off up the stairs. Richard gets up and feels around for his glass which has fallen somewhere . . . We hear Sharky's voice off upstairs . . .

(*Off.*) No, no, it's no problem! Don't be silly . . . come on, come on down to Richard.

IVAN (*off*): I'm sorry, Sharky.

Sharky leads Ivan down.

I'm sorry, Richard, I'm sorry to . . .

RICHARD: Who is it? Ivan?

IVAN: Richard, I'm sorry, I'm barging in on you again . . . I'm sorry, Sharky . . .

SHARKY: No . . .

RICHARD: What's the matter with you?

IVAN: Karen's after completely doing her nut.

RICHARD: What? Why?

IVAN: Ah, even if I . . . I should've just gone straight home it might have been different. But after you left and I was gonna head, I was just standing outside Doyle's with Big Bernard having a smoke, she was coming out of the post office and I didn't have my glasses and I didn't see her and . . .

RICHARD: Did you not get your spare glasses?

IVAN: I didn't even get in the house, Dick! She fucking reefed me out of it! (*His face crumples in pain.*) The kids were there and . . . (*A sudden impassioned plea.*) I only went in to have that quick one with yous! I was on my way home! Yous know that! But sure then there was people buying me Christmas pints left and right—I couldn't even see who they were to say to say no! (*He sinks into a chair.*) This is a disaster!

RICHARD: Ah now, come on, Ivan . . .

IVAN: I hate it when the kids see us fighting and . . .

RICHARD: These things happen.

IVAN: Now I'm after ruining Christmas on them all (*Beat.*) again!

RICHARD: No, you haven't! She'll calm down . . . Just take it easy . . . Sharky, where's your manners? Will you get poor Ivan something to drink?

SHARKY: I'll tell you what. I've a nice bit of smoked salmon we were gonna have, and there's little mince pies I was gonna heat up. Will you have one, Ivan?

IVAN (*rubbing his face*): Oh, I don't know . . .

SHARKY: Ah, it'll do you good, Ivan . . .

IVAN: I suppose . . . thanks, Sharky.

RICHARD: Yeah, great, and get him a drink, will you, Sharky? Good man.

Sharky goes to the kitchen.

Now, not to worry, Ivan. The woman is being completely unreasonable, she'll come round, just you watch. And we'll be nice and cosy here now and we'll figure it out . . .

Sharky returns with some glasses, a can of Harp for Ivan, and a bottle of whiskey for Richard.

Sharky. (*A little laugh.*) Excuse me, I lost my drink in the . . . in the confusion there . . .

SHARKY: I have one here for you.

RICHARD: Ah, thanks. Hey, I know! Sharky'll go back up with you, Ivan.

Sharky impotently shoots a look at Richard.

Sharky, you'll explain! His glasses have to be here somewhere! And we can . . .

IVAN: Oh, I don't know, I wouldn't go up there now at the moment, Sharky. She absolutely now . . . she fucking reefed me out of it. There was people all standing there looking at us . . . even Bernard just went back in. It was awful. The kids were there . . .

RICHARD: No, no, we'll let her cool down, absolutely . . .

Sharky gives Ivan a glass of beer.

IVAN: Thanks, Sharky.

RICHARD: Yeah, and get the mince pies, we'll get nice and Christmassy here now.

SHARKY: Yeah, I've the oven heating up.

RICHARD: Oh and listen, don't forget to wash that auld step and the door in the lane, will you?

SHARKY: Yeah, I'll do it . . .

RICHARD: Good man, Sharky.

Sharky goes.

(*Raising his glass, brightly.*) Now! Happy Christmas!

IVAN: Yeah . . . happy Christmas . . .

RICHARD: Sure here we are, aren't we? Ha? We're having a nice Christmas drink. And we'll let the whole . . . Ivan, are you listening to me?

IVAN: Yeah. No, I am . . .

RICHARD: The whole situation will . . . (*He signals 'Settle down'.*) And we'll talk to her and . . . And we'll all be right as dodgers. Do you hear me?

IVAN: Yeah, I'm sorry, Richard.

RICHARD: No, no, no, no, no, no, no . . . Come on! When I used to clean windows all up along, all up the coast all up into Sutton, I saw every conceivable kind of men and women all shacked up in myriad . . . (*With sudden force.*) myriad, states of confusion and banjaxed relationships. Believe me, she'd have been rid of you long ago at this stage if your marriage wasn't strong enough to weather a tiny little bump every now and again . . . (*He laughs.*) It's Christmas Eve! Ivan. Ivan . . .

Ivan just looks up silently into Richard's blind eyes. The doorbell rings, a loud cutting sound. Ivan looks up and then back at Richard. Pause.

(*Calling.*) Sharky! (*Pause.*) Ah he's out the back. You wouldn't go up and answer that for us, would you, Ivan?

IVAN: Yeah, no . . .

He shoots his drink back and goes up the stairs.

RICHARD: Ah thanks, good man. (*Starts to sing tunelessly.*) 'Oh the weather outside is frightening, it's dark and there's thunder and lightning . . .'

He suddenly hunches and shudders, holding his shoulders as though someone has walked over his grave. We hear voices off and then see Nicky's legs descending. It is completely dark outside by now.

NICKY (*off*): Oh yeah, yeah, yeah, yeah, yeah, no, yeah! (*In Irish.*) 'Is mise le meas, Sean Lemass!'° (*He laughs.*) Did you see all the Christmas lights all up the . . . Aw no, no, no, no, no, no . . . We won't stay long if he's . . . Come down Mr Lockhart!

Nicky descends into the room followed by Ivan and Lockhart.

RICHARD (*rising*): Nicky!
NICKY: Happy Christmas! Happy Christmas! Happy Christmas!

Nicky Giblin has a skinny, nervy appearance. He rarely seems in bad humour. He is about Sharky's age or maybe younger. He wears a tatty-looking anorak and threadbare grey slacks that are slightly too short for him, revealing white towelling sport socks in low-cut, dark, wine-coloured slip-on shoes. Lockhart is a man in his fifties perhaps. He is well-dressed with a camel hair Crombie overcoat, a silk scarf, a fine trilby hat and an expensive-looking suit. He looks like a wealthy businessman and bon viveur. Both he and Nicky glow warmly with festive indulgence.

RICHARD: And a Happy Christmas to you, Nicky!

They embrace fondly. Nicky produces a gift-wrapped bottle of whiskey from his anorak pocket.

NICKY: And I brought you just a little . . .
RICHARD (*mildly remonstrating*): Ah, Nicky . . .
NICKY (*dismissive*): Ah, go on, would you? Sure where would you be without the old Christmas, and I was just saying to . . . Sorry, this is . . . Richard this is Mr Lockhart.
RICHARD: Mr Lockhart! Pleased to meet you. Seasons' greetings!
LOCKHART: And to you too, Mr Harkin. I hope you don't mind us crashing in on you here now . . .
RICHARD: What are you talking about? Not at all! Not at all! Of course not! Will you have a drop of . . . Nicky! We have Miller! Ivan, will you get a glass there for . . . I got Miller in especially for you, Nicky. Ivan, it's in the . . . it's probably in the kitchen there. Ask Sharky, will you?
NICKY: Is Sharky here?
RICHARD: Mr Lockhart? Will you have a drop? Is this what I think it is? Or a drop of stout or . . .
LOCKHART: I'll take a small Irish whiskey if you have it, Mr Harkin.
NICKY: And you do have it! Right there!
RICHARD: Ah, Nicky . . . And Mr Lockhart, please, call me Richard . . . Ivan, here will you . . .

He holds the bottle out.

IVAN: Ha?
RICHARD: Will you take this and . . . (*Thinks better of it.*) or actually, just bring me a glass for Mr Lockhart, and a bottle of Miller for Nicky out of the fridge there, or it should be . . . just ask Sharky. Please excuse me, Mr Lockhart. Unfortunately my sight is . . . I fell into a skip° and I . . .

I have no sight.

Ivan goes to the kitchen.

LOCKHART: God help you.
RICHARD: And this is my, this is my first Christmas here in the dark, so to speak . . . so it's eh . . .
LOCKHART: Yes. But let me say, you have a fine holy glow off you, all the same.
RICHARD: I say me prayers!
LOCKHART: I can see it.
NICKY: And the old mind burns brightly, Richard, ha?
RICHARD: Ah, well, I don't know . . .
NICKY: No, no! To me, here now, sure you seem absolutely no different at all.
RICHARD: Ah, Nicky . . .
NICKY: No, it's true! So you got out for a Christmas drink?
RICHARD: Yes! We were down in Doyle's. Ivan was there and Big Bernard and Steady Eddie and the bouncy castle fella was singing hymns and, ah, it was brilliant . . .

Ivan returns with a drink for Nicky, a glass for Lockhart and a glass for himself. The glasses are somewhat mixed and unsuitable but usable, e.g. perhaps he is using a little jug for himself . . .

NICKY (*to Ivan*): Is Sharky here?
IVAN: I think he's out in the . . .
RICHARD: Ah, don't mind him, he's off the drink—for Christmas!—and he has all our heads wrecked. So tell us, where were you? (*Proffering bottle.*) Here, Mr Lockhart!

Nicky takes the bottle from Richard to pour a drink for Lockhart.

NICKY: Where weren't we? Is the question! Good God—we've been . . . Well, what happened was, I'd a few bits to do with Eileen down in Killester, so she went off and I went into the Beachcomber— fucking nobody in it! (*To Lockhart.*) What time was that at?
LOCKHART: About twelve?
NICKY: Twelve o'clock, nobody in there. I think, 'Right, I'll just have a quick pint and head on . . .' But then I see Mr Lockhart is sitting up at the bar, who I know from up in the Marine . . . Mr Lockhart, you'd do a lot of your drinking up in the Marine Hotel . . .

Is mise . . . Lemass: Irish for Respectfully yours, Sean Lemass. Lemass was president (Taoiseach) of Ireland from 1959 to 1966.

skip: Large open-top waste bin. Richard uses the term to refer to the bin into which he fell (mentioned in act 2).

LOCKHART: I've been known to frequent the premises . . .

They all laugh.

NICKY: And we know each other from me calling up there to see my brother Eric . . . so we have a pint, but there was no atmosphere, so fuck it, we left—up to the Yacht.

LOCKHART: No, Harry Byrne's.

NICKY: Sorry no, Harry Byrne's . . .

RICHARD: Oh, very posh!

NICKY (*pouring drinks for Lockhart, Richard and Ivan*): Oh yeah, they had the fires lit and then we were in the Yacht . . . which was hopping.

RICHARD: Jaysus, yous were getting around!

NICKY: That was only the start of it! The Yacht, the Dollymount House . . .

LOCKHART: The Raheny Inn . . .

NICKY: The Raheny Inn, the Green Dolphin, the Station House, the Cedars, the Elphin—your man (*indicating Lockhart*) won't let me put my hand in my pocket—this is taxis everywhere now!

RICHARD: Very wise . . . God yous were . . .

NICKY: Then back all the way up to Edenmore, Eugene's, the Concorde . . . the bleeding Brookwood Inn! (*He laughs.*) And then up here.

RICHARD: My God, that's a right Christmas drink, Nicky!

NICKY: Yeah well, Mr Lockhart had to say happy Christmas to a few people . . . (*Suddenly to Lockhart.*) We never tracked them down!

LOCKHART: And I'm glad we didn't! Because we would never have made it up here! Anyway, as soon as a sing-along starts, I'm out of a place, that's just the way I am . . . But we're here now, and that's it!

RICHARD: Well, I'm glad you're here!

LOCKHART: Yes, and we'll say Happy Christmas—(*He raises his glass in a toast.*) and we'll have a toast . . .

NICKY (*raising glass*): Yes.

Ivan has just taken a big gulp of whiskey. His glass is empty, so he spits the whiskey back into the glass for the toast . . .

LOCKHART: To old friends and old times!

RICHARD: And new friends!

NICKY: Exactly! Cheers!

RICHARD: Happy Christmas!

NICKY: Happy Christmas!

They all drink deeply.

(*Taking the bottle to give refills.*) So where's Sharky? God, I haven't seen him in ages . . .

RICHARD: Ivan, get Sharky there, will you?

IVAN: Yeah, I'll . . .

He goes out through the kitchen.

RICHARD: There's a good man.

NICKY: How is he doing? Alright?

RICHARD: Ah, Nicky, sure you know yourself. This is my brother, Mr Lockhart. He claims he's here to look after me, but between ourselves, he's an awful useless fucking eejit, God love him. I don't know who's looking after who!

NICKY: Sure you'd be well able to look after yourself, Dick . . .

RICHARD: This is it. If they can get me one of those dogs that bring you your meals . . . or even someone just to do a tiny bit of shopping. Sure all I really need is the bit of company really.

NICKY: Well, I knew you'd up for a bit of companionship and when I mentioned to Mr Lockhart that there might be an old game of cards on the horizon, he was very, eh . . .

LOCKHART: Well, there's nothing like a game of cards at Christmas.

RICHARD: You're so right! And you're welcome, Mr Lockhart. We're only amateurs now you understand.

NICKY: Go on out of that! You'll have to watch yourself, Mr Lockhart, you'll be fleeced for Christmas!

RICHARD: Yeah, right!

LOCKHART: No fear! I'm not a big gambler myself necessarily. To be honest with you I just like the social . . . ness and the crack.°

RICHARD: Well, this is it! There's no big gamblers here, Mr Lockhart. Why can't a game of cards be just for fun? You know what I mean?

Sharky and Ivan appear from the kitchen. Sharky is wearing an apron and rubber gloves and carrying a filthy cloth. Pause.

NICKY: Ah, there you are, Sharky! Happy Christmas!

Nicky goes to him to shake hands. Sharky removes a glove to shake his hand dutifully.

SHARKY: Yeah, happy Christmas, Nicky.

NICKY: Eileen sends her regards. We hope you'll pop in over the . . .

SHARKY: Yeah, sure . . .

NICKY: This is Mr Lockhart.

LOCKHART: Sharky. A pleasure.

SHARKY: How do you do.

As they shake hands, Sharky is wondering where he knows Lockhart from.

NICKY: Mr Lockhart said he'd pop in to help us make up the old numbers for a game of cards . . .

LOCKHART: I hope you don't mind, Sharky . . .

SHARKY: No. I just didn't know we were playing cards.

NICKY: Ah, it's a tradition, Sharky! Ivan, you'll play . . .

IVAN: Well, yeah, I'll . . . No, I've no . . . I've no money on me 'cause . . .

RICHARD: Don't worry about that, Ivan. Of course he'll play, we'll all play!

---

crack: Fun, gossip.

SHARKY (*to Richard*): How will you read your cards?

RICHARD: Ivan and me'll play together! Ivan, you can read our cards and I'll bankroll us. How does that sound?

IVAN: Yeah, that's . . . that'd suit me . . .

RICHARD: And we'll split our takings fifty-fifty. Sure, I'm probably gonna have to bankroll Sharky anyway!

NICKY: Ivan'll be the eyes and Richard'll be the ears!

RICHARD: And the brains!

LOCKHART: Now, you're sure I'm not barging in on your . . .

RICHARD: Not at all! Not at all! You're welcome. We'll take all of Nicky's money. Do you have any collateral, Nicky?

NICKY: Always. Feel that.

He holds out his arm for Richard.

RICHARD: Feel what?

NICKY: You feel that fabric?

Richard feels the arm of Nicky's anorak.

RICHARD: Oh, nice!

NICKY: This is a Versace jacket.

RICHARD: Yes . . .

IVAN: Is it?

NICKY (*to Ivan*): Feel that.

RICHARD: It's nice . . .

NICKY: You feel that? It's dog's skin.

IVAN: What?

NICKY (*laughing*): No, it's not dog's skin. It's called dog's skin. It's German. Right, Mr Lockhart?

LOCKHART: Yup.

RICHARD: It's nice, Nicky.

IVAN (*incredulous*): That's a Versace jacket?

NICKY (*defensively*): Yeah . . . Well . . . no, like it needs a wash for Christmas, only 'cause I wear it all the time, but it's eh . . . yeah, you know?

RICHARD: You might tell Sharky where he'd get a nice jacket like that, Nicky.

NICKY: Jacket like this? Two, three grand, Richard.

IVAN: What?!

NICKY: Oh, big time! Oh here, Ivan, are you still driving that old orange Ford Fiesta?

IVAN: Yeah . . .

NICKY: 'Cause didn't we see, Mr Lockhart? There was a load of old winos out there sitting on it, you don't want that.

IVAN: What? Is my car here?

NICKY: Yeah. (*To Lockhart.*) Didn't I point it out to you? And I fucking said it . . .

LOCKHART: Yeah, it's parked up around the other side of the green out there sort of half up on the path on the corner.

RICHARD (*springing into action*): Them fucking winos!! Come on, we can go out this way! Ivan, give me a hand. Show us where, Nicky.

SHARKY: Richard!

Richard goes towards the kitchen, taking hold of Ivan's arm.

RICHARD: We won't be long, Mr Lockhart. The winos are always scared of me. Drinking that old meths° always has them nervy, you see. Sharky, you look after Mr Lockhart. Come on! We'll have them gone out of it now, lickity spit.

NICKY: We're not gonna be getting in a fight, are we?

RICHARD: No, no, they'll run off immediately. We'll be back in a minute. Come on, Ivan! Nicky, hit that light out there for yourselves.

NICKY: Yeah, I got it.

Nicky hits a switch as Ivan opens the back door and leads Richard out, followed by Nicky. Sharky and Lockhart are alone. Sharky shakes his head at Lockhart.

LOCKHART: I know. Family, ha?

SHARKY: Yeah, don't talk to me. Are you okay for a drink there or . . .

LOCKHART: Yeah, I'm grand. You not having a drink yourself?

SHARKY: Nah . . . I'm . . . trying to . . . not drink.

LOCKHART: If you can just beat Christmas, ha?

SHARKY (*with a little laugh*): Yeah . . .

LOCKHART: If I can just beat Christmas I can achieve anything!

SHARKY: Mmm.

LOCKHART: But it's so hard. 'Cause the old drink stops the brain cranking. Stops the mind going into the forest.

Sharky is looking at Lockhart, wondering about him.

(*Knowingly.*) Oh yes, I've seen you on your travels. You don't remember me, Sharky . . .

SHARKY (*trying to place him*): No, I . . . I do . . .

LOCKHART: Yeah, I've seen you. On your wandering ways. I've seen you going down Wicklow Street, and halfway up Dame Street, down Suffolk Street, Grafton Street, Dawson Street, round and round, back up, back down, am I right? (*Pause.*) I've seen all those hopeless thoughts, buried there, in your stupid scrunched-up face.

SHARKY: What are you talking about?

LOCKHART: Oh, come on, Sharky! You don't remember me?

SHARKY: No, I . . . I do. But where did we . . . ?

LOCKHART: We met in the Bridewell,° Sharky.

Short pause.

Remember? We were locked up in a cell together. You'd had a bit of bother the night before . . . ? You

---

meths: Methanol, a basic alcohol.   **Bridewell:** Prison, possibly in Cork City or Dublin.

were waiting to go up before the judge in the morning . . . We played cards!

SHARKY: Yeah . . . no . . . I remember you, but . . .

LOCKHART (*brightly*): So how have things been with you?

SHARKY: . . . Okay . . .

LOCKHART: Not great though . . .

Pause.

SHARKY: You've a good memory.

LOCKHART: Old as the hills, Sharky. You know I was sure I'd run into you today. (*Laughs.*) But you're off the drink! Now that completely threw me, I have to say! Do you know how many pubs I was in?

SHARKY: What, were you looking for me?

LOCKHART: Well, it's just that matter we discussed back then, in the Bridewell that night.

Short pause.

SHARKY: This has to be what? Twenty years ago!

LOCKHART: Twenty-five years ago. But I'm still surprised you don't know why I'm here.

SHARKY: Yeah, well I don't.

LOCKHART (*disappointed*): Ah, Sharky . . . We had a deal. (*Short pause.*) No?

SHARKY: Look, I don't know what's going on here, or if Nicky's put you up to this, but I have to say I don't know what you're talking about.

LOCKHART: Are you serious?

SHARKY: Do I look like I'm telling a joke?

LOCKHART: No, hold on. You're seriously standing there telling me that it's never struck you as odd, down all these years, that you just walked out of jail? After what you did? Ah, that's brilliant, Sharky!

SHARKY: What do you mean 'after what I did'?

LOCKHART: Oh, come on, now . . .

SHARKY: What? What did I . . . I can't even . . . What? I got into a fight with some wino in the back of a shebeen° up in . . . Francis Street or . . . somewhere, was it? I can hardly even remember! So what?

LOCKHART: Well no, not quite. His name was Laurence Joyce. He was sixty-one. He was a vagrant. He said he was trying to get to Cardiff . . . ? Said he had some family there . . . ? Said his wife was once the Cardiff Rose? You beat him up in the back of O'Dowd's public house in the early hours of the twenty fourth of December 1981. You killed him. (*Short pause.*) I let you out. I set you free.

Pause.

SHARKY: No, here, wait a minute . . .

LOCKHART: Come on, you remember. Remember in the morning, that moment when the guards opened the door, and told you to get your stuff and get lost?

SHARKY: . . . Yeah?

shebeen: Irish for an unlicensed liquor bar.

LOCKHART: I organised that. Because you won that hand of poker we were playing.

SHARKY: Wait a minute. That fella didn't die!

LOCKHART: Oh no. He did. What, are you trying to tell me you don't see him in your nightmares?

Pause. Sharky doesn't respond.

God, the poor old brain hasn't aged too well, has it, Sharky? Look at you. Twenty-five years on the lash° like some old borderline wino yourself. What chance haven't you fucked up? Driving the van for those English fellas? Or when you blew that nice cushy security job on the building site in Naas? You make me laugh, Sharky. Tell me, are you still in the wars with Dublin Bus about the night you were pissed and you fell down the stairs? How much are you looking for? For that twinge in your back?

Pause. Sharky is staring at Lockhart, dumbfounded.

You even blew that chauffeur job down in Lahinch! (*Darkly.*) You fancied your man's wife, didn't you?

SHARKY: Who are you?

LOCKHART: Ah, Sharky . . . don't say you don't know who I am. (*Short pause.*) Or what I want.

SHARKY: Well, I don't know!

LOCKHART: You don't remember we played cards?

SHARKY: No, I kind of do but . . .

LOCKHART: Poor Sharky. It's always a bit hazy, isn't it? (*Short pause.*) I want your soul, Sharky.

SHARKY: What?

LOCKHART: I want your soul.

SHARKY: What the hell are you talking about? Is this some kind of stupid fucking joke of Nicky's?

Lockhart just looks at him. Sharky seems to feel queasy and then enters the grip of some greater pain. It's so excruciating that he starts to sink pathetically to his knees. He tries to get a grip on something but ends up on all fours fighting the urge to pass out, so great is the agony—both physically and deep within his mind.

LOCKHART: I'm the son of the morning, Sharky. I'm the snake in the garden. I've come here for your soul this Christmas, and I've been looking for you all fucking day! We made a deal. We played cards for your freedom and you promised me, you promised me, the chance to play you again. So don't start messing me about now. (*Short pause.*) Of course, after you skipped merrily off to some early house in the morning you probably never even thought about it again, did you? Ha? You think I'm just farting around? You think you're better than me? Pig. Well, think again. Because we're gonna play for your soul and I'm gonna win and you're coming through the old hole in the wall with me tonight. Now get up.

on the lash: Drunk.

David Morse as Sharky and Ciaran Hinds as Lockhart in the 2007 Broadway production of *The Seafarer* at the Booth Theatre in New York.

Sharky is silently crying as he staggers back to his feet. Lockhart suddenly bursts towards Sharky, as though about to beat him.

No crying! Don't do a Maurice Macken on it! I'll fucking batter you! Do you hear me?

Sharky flinches backwards, blinking, a hand feebly raised. Lockhart laughs.

(*With disgust.*) Don't make me puke . . .

There is a commotion outside as Nicky helps Richard back in through the back door, followed by Ivan.

RICHARD (*on his way in*): Them friggin' winos! They do my head in!

NICKY: You should've seen it! They ran for their lives!

RICHARD: Good Jaysus, would someone please give me a drink, for the love of God?

NICKY (*grabbing the whiskey bottle to give Richard a drink*): He blew them out of it! They flew off up the coast! You should have seen it!

Ivan comes in from the kitchen with a Miller for Nicky and a can of Harp for himself.

RICHARD: But was your man there? My little friend that I fucking hate, with the navy anorak and the big black head of hair on him? He's the worst . . .

NICKY: Yeah, I think there was one like that. He fucking legged it! (*To Sharky and Lockhart.*) The roars out of this fella . . .

RICHARD: Ah, you have to . . .

NICKY: And then Ivan!

RICHARD: I have Ivan well-trained! You see, they're so shaky and nervy when they get that old meths into them, you can destroy them with a good scream. They think it's the banshee, God help them.

NICKY: Did you see that one was going to the toilet down behind the car?

IVAN: I thought I saw one down in behind . . .

NICKY: That was a woman!

IVAN: Was it?!

RICHARD (*with disgust*): Oh, don't . . . !

NICKY (*bursting out laughing*): It was all going down the back of her leg when she ran and fell over the bin!

RICHARD: Ah stop, will you? They're awful . . .

LOCKHART (*to Ivan*): Is your car alright?

IVAN: Ah . . . it . . . it wasn't my car! I don't have my car with me. I forgot I walked up here in all the excitement.

RICHARD: Ah well, all's well that ends well! Are we gonna play cards?

NICKY (*to Ivan*): Can you see to play cards?

IVAN: I can see to about here. (*He holds his hand up about ten inches from his face.*) After that, it's your guess is as good as mine!

RICHARD: Yeah, you can see the cards . . .

IVAN: I can read the cards . . .

RICHARD: Hey, Shark! Where's all the goodies you promised us that you were banging on about earlier? Get the smoked salmon and the mince pies out and all the Christmas goodies and the crisps and all . . . Are you hungry, Mr Lockhart?

LOCKHART (*looking at Sharky*): I wouldn't say no.

NICKY (*making a face and touching his stomach*): Them cocktail sausages they were handing out earlier down in Raheny were gone off . . .

RICHARD: Well, Sharky'll get the grub organised. Ivan, pull out that table into the middle, the cards is on the windowsill.

Nicky and Ivan begin to bustle about getting the table ready for cards.

Another beer, Nicky?

NICKY: I have one, I'm good, Richard . . .

RICHARD: Mr Lockhart? Another drop of Irish? Is it there? You can help yourself.

LOCKHART: I'm grand. Sharky's looking after me . . .

NICKY: I'm bursting for a slash° will I run in quickly?

RICHARD: No, run up. There's a better one, Nicky. Sharky! Is that upstairs loo in tip top condition?

SHARKY: Yeah, you know where it is, Nicky.

NICKY: Yup, end of the landing.

Nicky runs up the stairs.

RICHARD: Ivan, there's stout there if you want a stout. I think I might have a stout actually.

IVAN: Good idea.

He goes towards the kitchen.

RICHARD: And don't mind Matt Talbot° on the Kaliber there, he can look after himself. Is the table out?

LOCKHART: Here, Richard . . .

Lockhart helps Richard to the table.

RICHARD: Ah, thanks, Mr Lockhart, you're a real gent. And don't mind Sharky's bad humour, he came out backwards and his head has been arseways ever since. Here, give us the cards till I give them a shuffle.

Lockhart hands the cards to Richard. Lockhart and Sharky stand looking at each other from opposite ends of the room.

(*Shuffling cards.*) When Ivan comes back now he can cut them for me. (*Laughs.*) I don't know whether these are up or down! I'm in total space here, Mr Lockhart. Wheeee! And when Sharky has the grub for us and Nicky's back down we'll get going. God, I haven't played an old game of poker in so long! I'm really looking forward to it now, Ivan!

IVAN (*off*): Yeah?

RICHARD: Come on till we sort out this money!

IVAN (*off*): I'm coming, Dick! I'm just going to the jacks!

RICHARD: Come on, Nicky! Sit down, Mr Lockhart, sit down. Sharky! Where's Sharky? Sharky, come on! Sharky!! . . . Let's play!!

Blackout.

ACT TWO: MUSIC IN THE SUN

It is many hours later. The room is darker, seemingly lit only by a few lamps, candles and the glow from the stove. The wind is howling outside as a storm lashes the coast. The card game is in progress. Richard sits in his armchair which has been pulled nearer to the centre of the room, closer to the table. He has a big box of chocolates nearby and munches one from time to time. To his left sits Ivan, who is at the edge of the

slash: Piss. **Matt Talbot:** Irish alcoholic (1856–1925) who became a major temperance figure.

table where he can play but also turn easily away from the others to consult strategy with Richard. Sharky sits to Ivan's left and Nicky sits to Sharky's left. Lockhart sits at the far end of the table. They are coming to the end of a round of heavy betting. The biggest piles of money are in front of Ivan and Lockhart. A lot of drink has been consumed; bottles, cans and empty plates are strewn around. Ivan's intoxication is constant, he coasts along, veering neither up into euphoria nor down into depression. It is his efficient life-state, removed, yet heavily present. Nicky, on the other hand, is a euphoric drunk. His genuine love for friends and comrades is freed. While he plays cards he wears wraparound mirror shades like a poker pro. When not playing he sits them on his head. Richard, as we have seen, can lurch from sentimentality to vicious insults within seconds. But while all inhibitions may be gone, he remains alert, quick-witted and deeply interested in what goes on around him. Lockhart is a philosophical drunk, yet prone to deeper maudlin feelings. Sharky has thus far managed to remain sober . . .

IVAN: Nicky . . .

NICKY: I'm thinking. I'm thinking.

RICHARD: I know. I can hear your brain crunching in your head from over here.

NICKY: Yeah, well, don't be rushing me. What is it again?

RICHARD: Mr Lockhart raised it twenty. We're in. Sharky's bailed.

IVAN: You have to put in forty.

NICKY (*takes a long sharp inhalation and thinks*): Yeah, well, you're bluffing 'cause I saw Richard telling you . . .

RICHARD: Would you go on out of that!

NICKY: Mr Lockhart is being cautious, he raised it twenty, but he's on a roll anyway so he's battering us from a position of strength. (*To Ivan.*) You have nothing.

IVAN (*ironically*): That's right.

NICKY: You have nothing! So stop with the . . . If you didn't have that pile in front of you, I'd have your guts for garters.

RICHARD: Why, what have we got?

NICKY: You've about two hundred and fifty fucking euros in front of you there, Dick.

RICHARD: Yo ho! Santy's come early!

IVAN (*playing down their success*): We're doing alright. We're doing nicely.

NICKY: And half of that is mine. (*With sudden confidence.*) You have fuck all there, Ivan.

IVAN: Well, why don't you make sure?

NICKY: Mr Lockhart has two pair or something.

RICHARD: Well, come on then!

NICKY: I am! (*Seeing and raising.*) Here's your forty. And twenty now to show yous a statement of intent.

RICHARD: Oh ho . . .

NICKY: Now, that shook yous.

IVAN: Mr Lockhart?

LOCKHART: I'll stick around.

He sees Nicky's twenty.

The cast of *The Seafarer* in the 2007 Broadway production.

IVAN: And we'll have a look.

He sees it too. Pause. Nicky's courage seems to wane.

NICKY (*to Ivan*): What do you have?
IVAN (*to Nicky*): What do you have?
RICHARD: What do we have?
IVAN (*to Nicky*): What do you have?
NICKY (*to Lockhart*): What do you have?
LOCKHART: Threes.
NICKY: Threes of what?
LOCKHART (*shows his hand*): Three nines.
NICKY: Three nines! You stuck it out with three nines?!
LOCKHART: I enjoy playing. Isn't it worth a go?

Nicky bursts out laughing.

RICHARD: What have you got, Nicky?
NICKY: Christmas present. Full house. (*He shows his hand.*) Fives and kings.
IVAN (*showing his hand*): Kings and sevens.
NICKY: Bollocks!

Richard whoops.

Ah, that's fucking . . .
LOCKHART: Hard luck, Nicky . . .
NICKY (*to Lockhart*): What were you doing driving the pot up the wazoo with three nines?! These lads are cleaning me out here!
RICHARD: Ah, Nicky . . .
NICKY: Look at me! I'm like Sharky here. I've about thirty-five euros to me name. This is to do me all through January.

Nicky gets up and walks over to the stove, restlessly.

IVAN (*counting his winnings*): Well, Sharky had the right idea. He bailed. He knew.
RICHARD: He has no money!
IVAN: Do you want a stout, Rich?
RICHARD: Sure! Hey! You know what I have in there of course, beside the boiler? There's a drop of Brigid Blake's famous Antrim poteen in there.
IVAN: Oh ho!

RICHARD: Do you ever take a drop, Mr Lockhart?

Ivan heads towards the kitchen.

LOCKHART: I will! Why not? Sure I might as well be shit-faced as the way I am!

IVAN (*on his way into the kitchen*): Yo ho!

RICHARD: Good man!

NICKY: Yeah, well leave me out of it . . . Grab us a Miller there, Ivan, would you?

IVAN (*off*): Yeah!

NICKY: Ah, well . . . it's only a game. It's only money, that right, Rich?

RICHARD: Yeah . . . Your money!

Nicky sighs heavily looking to Lockhart in a silent appeal for understanding.

NICKY: So, Sharky! You're back! (*Drunkenly placing a hand on Sharky's shoulder.*) We've missed you! D'you know that?

He turns to Lockhart, pointing at Sharky meaninglessly then turns back to Sharky.

RICHARD (*insincerely*): Yeah . . . we've all missed you . . .

NICKY: So tell us! Where's this you were working?

SHARKY: Ah, down in Lahinch, County Clare.

NICKY: On the trawlers?

SHARKY: No.

NICKY (*surprised*): No?

SHARKY: No, I was eh . . . (*Glancing at Lockhart, who is smiling at him broadly.*) I was doing a bit of driving for a fella down there.

NICKY: Lahinch? Was I reading somewhere or where was it? That Lahinch is the gay pick-up capital of Europe?

SHARKY: What?

NICKY: So I believe . . .

Ivan returns with a whiskey bottle full of clear liquid.

SHARKY: No . . .

RICHARD: Ah Nicky, Lahinch is only a small town, how could it possibly be the gay capital of Europe?

NICKY: Well, I don't know!

RICHARD: The gay capital of Europe is Cork City!

NICKY: Is it?

RICHARD: It very probably is. Are you pouring us a drop of that Moon Juice,° Ivan?

IVAN: Will I open it?

RICHARD: Yes.

NICKY: Did you get me a Miller?

IVAN: Did you ask me for one?

NICKY: Yes!

IVAN: Oh sorry, I didn't hear you.

Ivan goes off towards the kitchen.

Moon Juice: Moonshine whisky, poteen.

NICKY: Thanks, Ivan. I wouldn't touch that brain blower now if you paid me . . . Look out, Mr Lockhart, you'll be bollixed.

RICHARD: No, he won't! It'll help him play!

NICKY: It will in my arse! Sure Steady Eddie was hallucinating that traffic wardens were coming to arrest him in the snooker club in Harmonstown one morning after he'd been skulling that shite the night before!

RICHARD: Ah, he's a child! Don't mind him, Mr Lockhart.

LOCKHART: No, I'll have a drop.

RICHARD: Good man.

NICKY: Well, I don't mind if you all start losing!

Ivan returns, making his way to the table to pour some drinks.

Thanks, Ivan. Good to see you, Shark. Of course you know I'm in a totally new line now myself?

SHARKY: What, you're not doing the babysitting?

NICKY: No, I'm out of the babysitting. I'm out of that this long weather now. Too many trust issues, essentially. Not on my part. No, I'm gone into the cheesemongering business.

SHARKY: Cheesemongering?

Ivan is pouring some poteen for Richard and Lockhart, bringing it to them.

NICKY: Yeah, I've me own counter down the back of Thrifties.

SHARKY: Have you?

NICKY: Yup. I'm only started it, but it could be a whole new empire.

SHARKY: Do you not have to study for years to do something like that?

NICKY (*incredulously*): What!?

SHARKY: I thought you had to study to do cheese and wines and all . . . to do it properly . . .

NICKY: No, you don't! Who told you that?

SHARKY: I don't know. No, I just thought . . .

NICKY: No, you don't! (*He laughs.*) Whoever told you that now is . . . Ah, poor Sharky!

SHARKY: How's the car?

NICKY: What car?

SHARKY: The Peugeot.

NICKY: Eileen's car?

SHARKY: Well, it's my old car actually.

NICKY: Oh, is it?

SHARKY: Yeah.

NICKY: Did you get a new one?

Pause.

RICHARD: No, he didn't! Sure where would Sharky get a new car? (*Raising his glass of poteen.*) Your health, Mr Lockhart!

NICKY: Say goodbye to it!

LOCKHART: No, this is smooth!

NICKY: Yeah, you think . . .

LOCKHART: You know this is the only time of the year I really enjoy? A game of cards on Christmas Eve, sure where would you get it?

RICHARD: Absolutely!

IVAN: You play a lot of cards, Mr Lockhart?

LOCKHART: Well . . . I do at Christmas! Boys, I've played cards in public houses, shebeens, hotel bar rooms, suburban boozers—anywhere! Three, four in the morning, nobody there, only a few auld lads in their shirt sleeves, tidying up while they watch some poor fucking eejit play it all away . . . Houses! Little houses . . . on Christmas Eve . . . in the . . . middle of nowhere I've played. Out on the Western seaboard, but mostly in the East. Ah, I've played everywhere! You name it! In Garda° barracks . . . Sharky. Up in amazing Georgian rooms with wonderful evocative gilt mirrors and beautiful windows towering out on to bountiful trees—in the middle of Dublin, or London, in the city, yup. A school or two I've played in. In my time. Always late. It's always so late . . . Time deepens and slows down somehow in a card game. It could be any moment. It's always the same moment . . . Where do I know you from, Ivan?

IVAN: Ha?

LOCKHART: Have we played cards?

SHARKY: No, I don't think you have . . .

IVAN: Yeah, we might of . . .

LOCKHART: You're the fella won the boat that time in a card game, Nicky was telling me . . .

NICKY: Yeah.

IVAN (modestly): Well . . .

RICHARD: No, he did, that's right.

IVAN (to Richard): Do you remember that, Dick?

RICHARD: I sure do! 'The Briquette Queen.'

NICKY: Forty grand's worth of boat, Mr Lockhart!

IVAN: Yeah, but I sold it for twelve. I didn't want it! What would I want with a fucking boat?

NICKY: It only would've cost him money anyway . . .

IVAN: I sold it for twelve grand up in the Cock tavern in Howth—Do you remember, Richard? Best Christmas ever!

RICHARD: Ah, brilliant. It was brilliant!

NICKY: You could never top that!

IVAN: I lost it all in three weeks, Mr Lockhart, betting in the bookies in Baldoyle and practically living in Doyle's Lounge. I was eating so much fish and chips and battered sausages at all weird hours and I saw fuck-all daylight . . .

NICKY: This is all true!

IVAN: . . . that I ended up getting the runs so bad and I was so dehydrated the doctor wouldn't let me out of the house for four whole days!

Richard, Nicky and Ivan are laughing . . .

It was unbelievable! It was an absolutely unbelievable Christmas. Do you remember all the stars we saw that Stephen's Night, Nicky?

NICKY (too beautiful to describe): Aw!

Garda: Police.

IVAN: Yeah, but you panic though when it starts to run right down. Oh Jaysus, if Karen had've known I'd had all that . . . Oh! (He shudders.) Had to get rid of it.

LOCKHART: Yeah, and you won it just in a card game in a house?

IVAN: Yeah, won it off a total nutcase that killed himself not long after. He drowned after driving his lorry off the end of the pier in Howth.

NICKY: 'The Briquette Queen.'

IVAN: He had a business delivering peat briquettes . . .

RICHARD: Oh, he was a nasty piece of work, Mr Lockhart . . .

NICKY: Aw, he was a real bollocks!

LOCKHART: Yeah? God, that's a great story. But you know what I was wondering, after Nicky told me about it, I wanted to ask you . . . Look at Sharky looking at me suspiciously there . . . no, I was just wondering, with the stakes so high—a forty grand boat, like—I was wondering what you had in the pot that he was betting his boat against you?

IVAN: Ha?

LOCKHART: No, just what did you have in the pot to put up against his boat? I'm assuming there couldn't have been forty grand in the pot. In a card game like the way we're playing now . . . What did you have, that he wanted . . . ?

Ivan looks at Nicky. Pause.

SHARKY: Here, look, are we gonna play here?

LOCKHART: You don't have to tell me . . .

RICHARD: It was stupid! Your man was out of it! They were all elephants!

NICKY: He was a lunatic! He was acting the bollocks. Ivan took him down fair and square and . . .

LOCKHART: It was something to do with that hotel down in Wicklow, was it?

Long pause.

SHARKY (to Lockhart): What are you doing?

LOCKHART: You told me something about that, Nicky, didn't you? About Ivan and what was it? The Ardlawn Hotel?

NICKY (guiltily): No . . .

RICHARD (disappointed): Nicky . . .

NICKY: I didn't . . .

SHARKY: Let's just play, will we? That's got nothing to do with anything.

LOCKHART: What was the name of those two families?

IVAN (in a dark place): The Murdochs and the Kavanaghs.

LOCKHART: That's right . . .

RICHARD: That was all in the news. Ivan was completely exonerated . . .

NICKY: It was inconclusive . . .

SHARKY: Yeah. Hey, look . . . Can we just get on with the . . .

Sharky takes a sharp intake of breath and puts his hand to his head in sudden, immense pain.

NICKY: Are you alright, Shark?

SHARKY (*blinking*): Yeah, no, I'm . . .

RICHARD: Leave him alone. He just needs a drink. That whole thing was an open and shut case, Mr Lockhart . . .

LOCKHART: What happened? There was a fire . . . ?

IVAN: Yeah, well . . . It was twenty odd years ago. It was more . . .

NICKY: Ancient history . . .

IVAN: I was working in the Ardlawn. I was doing a bit of portering and bit of night-portering . . .

RICHARD: Ivan was completely exonerated.

NICKY: There was no blame.

IVAN: No, they had to investigate it. I had . . . you see I had burned my hand on the ring of the cooker when I was . . . I was heating some beans . . . it was very late and . . . (*Pause.*) This was all in the papers!

LOCKHART: Yeah . . . but it can really hang over a man, something like that . . .

IVAN: Well, yeah, the . . . this fella with the boat, the briquette king. He wanted to play for . . .

NICKY: He was a wanker.°

IVAN: The bet was that he could . . . if he won, he wanted to ask me . . . about it. I don't know . . .

LOCKHART: To give him the truth.

Pause.

IVAN: Yeah . . .

NICKY: It was a ridiculous fucking bet . . . He was a sick fucking eejit and that's all that was going on. And he got his comeuppance!

RICHARD: He's gone and good luck to him. He was a bully.

LOCKHART: High stakes, Ivan . . .

IVAN: Yeah . . . well I'd a strong hand.

LOCKHART: Yeah. I knew there had to be something . . . You don't mind talking about it . . .

Pause.

NICKY: I hate that fucking poteen! The fucking smell of it, even!

RICHARD: Ah, stop giving out! Are we gonna play cards? There's too much Auld Lang Syne going on around here and not enough cards!

NICKY: Yeah, well, let's play, come on!

RICHARD: Whose deal is it? Sharky! You deal!

LOCKHART: Yes! We haven't hardly had a burst out of Sharky tonight at all!

RICHARD: Ah, Sharky could never play cards!

NICKY (*gathering up the cards to give Sharky*): I've seen Sharky win.

LOCKHART: Maybe he's preoccupied.

RICHARD: Ah, he's always preoccupied . . .

NICKY: Come on. Two euros to play. Maybe this is Sharky's hand.

---

wanker: Literally, a masturbator; the term is used as a general insult (analogous to the U.S. word "jerk").

RICHARD: Give us a drop of that holy water, Ivan, till we bless ourselves.

NICKY: Little threes is all I need.

Sharky shuffles the cards to deal. Everyone puts in two euros. Ivan puts in four, to cover himself and Richard, then he gets up to pour a drink for Richard.

IVAN: Richard . . .

RICHARD (*to Ivan*): Good man. (*Raising glass.*) Mr Lockhart?

LOCKHART: I will! Thank you, Ivan.

RICHARD: Hey, Mr Lockhart . . .

Lockhart looks at Richard who points to his head and makes a whistling sound to indicate the effect of the poteen.

LOCKHART: I know! I'm fucking slipping in and out of time zones here. I thought it was last Christmas there for a minute!

RICHARD: Yes! That's right!

Ivan goes to pour a drink for Lockhart.

NICKY: Yeah, well leave me out of it. I want to stay here in this Christmas and beat the shite out of yous now with this hand. I can feel it in me waters. Little threes there now, Sharky. Get us a Miller there, Ivan, will you?

Ivan goes to get a beer.

IVAN: Do you want another Seven-Up, Shark?

SHARKY: Nah, I'm alright . . .

RICHARD: Oh, threes is a beaut . . .

NICKY: That's my killer hand, is three threes.

RICHARD: Yeah: I love three tens. Three tens is my . . .

LOCKHART: Ah, a ten is like a shining tower. It's like the Twentieth Century. It's solid. It looms at you, yeah?

RICHARD: Absolutely.

NICKY: Well, I also like to see an eight. Give me a pair of eights for starters and I'm . . .

RICHARD (*dismissively*): Ah, eight! Eight is sneaky . . . Look at it! What is it? Eight! It's not a ten, it's almost as bad as a nine . . .

LOCKHART: Well, nine can have a certain symmetry to it.

NICKY: Oh, three threes is a lovely little hand. It's like a little grenade.

RICHARD: And seven . . .

LOCKHART: Oh, seven is deep.

NICKY (*to Ivan, who has returned with beers for Nicky and himself*): We're talking about numbers.

IVAN (*unconvinced*): Ah, seven is only my hole. Give me a four.

SHARKY: Yeah . . .

IVAN: Four is where you build your house.

They have all picked up their cards and peruse them.

LOCKHART (*to Ivan*): Do you not have two fours in front of you there?

IVAN: That's a secret, Mr Lockhart.

NICKY: Ah, nice try! Mr Lockhart is no slouch!

RICHARD: Well, neither is Ivan! How are we doing? Who's it to?

SHARKY: Ivan?

IVAN: Ah, check . . .

SHARKY: Nicky?

NICKY: Eh . . . I'll check for a minute.

SHARKY: Mr Lockhart . . .

LOCKHART: Ah, sure we'll make it interesting anyway. (*Putting in coins.*) Three euros.

RICHARD: Will we stick around for three euros, Ivan?

IVAN: We'll see what happens.

He puts in coins.

SHARKY: Nicky?

NICKY: Ah, we'll hang around.

Sees the bet.

SHARKY: And I'll have a look. (*Sees it and picks up the deck to deal.*) Ivan?

IVAN: Eh . . . Three please, Sharky.

Sharky deals him three cards.

LOCKHART: Little pair of fours there, Ivan?

RICHARD: Don't tell him nothing!

IVAN: I'm not . . .

SHARKY: Nicky.

NICKY: Eh . . . two . . .

Sharky deals him two cards. Nicky suddenly throws down one more card.

No, three . . .

SHARKY: You sure?

NICKY: Yeah, three, thanks.

SHARKY (*deals another card to Nicky*): Mr Lockhart?

LOCKHART: Just one, please, Sharky.

Reactions to this around the table. Sharky deals him a card.

RICHARD: Just the one, Mr Lockhart?

LOCKHART: Just the one . . .

NICKY: Ah, he's on a kamikaze. What is it? A run? Flush? Did you get it?

LOCKHART: Maybe it's four of a kind.

RICHARD: Maybe it's total bollocks.

LOCKHART: Maybe . . .

SHARKY: And I'll take three. To you, Mr Lockhart.

LOCKHART: Ah, we'll keep the dream alive. Sure, five euros.

Puts in money.

RICHARD: Oh, look out . . .

SHARKY: Ivan?

IVAN: Ehm . . . We'll hang on.

Sees the bet.

RICHARD: We'll hang on for a minute . . .

SHARKY: Nicky?

NICKY: Ah, we'll go along for the ride. (*He sees it.*) And we'll make it interesting. Ten euros.

He raises the bet. Reactions around the table . . .

RICHARD: Oh, now!

SHARKY: Mr Lockhart?

LOCKHART: I'll see you . . . With ten.

Raises the bet further still.

RICHARD: Oh now, here! What are we doing? Ivan!

NICKY (*to Lockhart*): You fucker . . .

Ivan leans over to whisper to Richard, who listens intently . . .

RICHARD: Ah, fold, for fuck's sake! Would you? Jaysus . . .

IVAN (*throws his hand in*): We're gone.

SHARKY: Nicky?

NICKY (*considers Lockhart*): I'll see you.

Puts in ten.

RICHARD: You're a fucking eejit . . .

NICKY: Hold your horses. Stranger things have happened at sea . . .

RICHARD (*dismissively*): Yeah, right . . .

LOCKHART: Sharky?

RICHARD: Don't be a hero now, Sharky . . .

SHARKY (*considering his hand*): So what is it?

NICKY: It's twenty-eight for you to play, Shark. And I'd advise you to tread warily against what I have here now . . .

RICHARD: Easy now, Sharky. I'm not keeping you in pocket money for the whole of next month now, right?

SHARKY: Twenty-eight. (*He sees it and reaches into his pocket, taking some money out*). With twenty-five.

RICHARD: What!?

IVAN: Ah, let him play, Rich.

LOCKHART: Brave man . . .

NICKY: To you, Mr Lockhart . . .

LOCKHART: I'm in.

He sees the bet. Nicky looks at his cards . . .

IVAN: Nicky . . .

NICKY: I'm thinking. I'm thinking. I'm thinking. I'm thinking.

RICHARD: I thought I smelled something burning . . .

NICKY: Ha ha . . . (*To Lockhart, putting money in.*) Come on! What do you have?

(*Pause.*)

LOCKHART (*showing his hand*): I've nothing.

NICKY: You bastard! What were you doing?!

LOCKHART: I'm playing the game!

NICKY (*derisively*): The game! You fucking eejit. That's that poteen. I told you . . .

IVAN: It could be yours, Nicky . . .

RICHARD: It better not be!

IVAN: Go on, Nicky! What do you have?

Pause.

NICKY: Ah, I've even less nothing. I've a hand of feet. Half a run. I knew he (*Lockhart*) had nothing. I thought it'd be too pricey for Sharky. I thought he was having us on. What have you got Shark, two pair or some fucking thing . . .

SHARKY: Not even. One pair.

NICKY: One pair?! (*He grabs Sharky's cards.*) Two fucking fours!?

IVAN: It still beats you.

LOCKHART: Nicely played, Sharky . . .

Nicky throws the cards on the table and stands up.

NICKY: A hundred euros with two fours!

He paces around, going towards the stove.

SHARKY: Your deal, Nicky . . .

Nicky kicks a pile of newspapers.

NICKY: Bollocks!

RICHARD: Oy! Oy! Nicky, don't destroy the place.

NICKY: No, no. I'm sorry, Richard.

IVAN: Nice one, Sharky . . .

NICKY (*taking money from his wallet*): What were we all doing? (*To Lockhart.*) You had nothing!? I had fuck all! And Sharky wins a hundred euros with two fucking fours!

LOCKHART: Luck of the draw.

NICKY: What were you doing raising all the time?

LOCKHART: You were raising as well.

NICKY: Ah, I was only having a go! Here, give us some change there, Ivan.

LOCKHART: It's only money . . .

Nicky goes to Ivan's pile to get some smaller denominations, throwing two twenty-euro notes down.

RICHARD: Ah, hard luck, Nicky, sure it's only a bit of fun . . .

NICKY: I won't be having much more fun at this rate . . .

RICHARD: You could never bluff, Nicky. That's just something you can't . . .

IVAN (*pointing at Sharky*): You see him? King of the bluffers.

RICHARD: Who, Sharky?

IVAN: Yeah.

RICHARD: Yeah, well, that's only because he has a recklessness in his heart which is the undoing and ruination of his whole life.

IVAN: Not tonight.

RICHARD: Yeah? Just wait. Ah, cheer up, Nicky.

NICKY: Yeah, well, give me a few minutes . . .! That's a harsh lesson there now.

LOCKHART: Only kind that works, Nicky.

IVAN: Well, Sharky's around for another few hands in anyway . . .

RICHARD: He should quit while he's ahead.

LOCKHART: Don't worry, Nicky. I'm gonna take Sharky down.

NICKY: Can I bet on it?

LOCKHART: Nothing surer.

RICHARD: Ah, would you come on and deal the cards and stop moaning. You'll probably trounce us all this time out.

NICKY (*taking the cards to give them a shuffle*): I hope so!

RICHARD (*handing box of sweets to Ivan*): Here, Ivan, pass them around.

IVAN: Oh, nice one!

A mobile phone is ringing somewhere . . .

RICHARD: What's that music?

NICKY: Oh bollocks! That's my phone!

RICHARD: Oh, here's trouble . . .

IVAN: I'm not here . . .

Nicky goes to his jacket and rummages for his phone . . .

NICKY: It's Eileen!

IVAN: Well, whoever it is, I'm not here.

They all wait as Nicky stands looking at his phone.

NICKY: I'm gonna have to answer this, Dick.

RICHARD: Well, would you answer the Jaysus thing and stop driving us all around the fucking twist!

Nicky answers it.

NICKY (*very innocently*): Hello?

The others are listening.

Hi hon. What? No! No, I'm just visiting poor Richard to see if he . . . No. No, Sharky's here. Yeah, no he's here. He's not even drinking. And I'm only . . . I'm just having a very quick bottle of Miller. No, I swear to God, he isn't! What? Yeah, no I'll be back. No, don't try lifting it down yourself . . . No, no I'll do it! (*He drifts upstage towards the staircase and upstairs out of earshot of the others.*) No, I'll be there! What's wrong with you? It's Christmas, Eileen! What? Hold on, just let me . . .

He is gone.

RICHARD: Trouble in paradise.

IVAN: Don't talk to me about trouble in paradise! Here, will I put on some music?

RICHARD: Oh yes! Good idea! Good idea!

Ivan wanders over to the stereo . . .

LOCKHART: Hey, hold on, are we not gonna . . . ? (*Unsaid 'play'.*)

RICHARD: Music to soothe the soul. What kind of music do you like, Mr Lockhart?

LOCKHART: I don't really like music.

Ivan surfs up the dial on the tuner and finds some softly-played, festive, perhaps choral, music . . .

RICHARD: How can you not like music? Any music?

LOCKHART: I don't like any music.

RICHARD: Do you hear that, Ivan? Mr Lockhart doesn't like any music!

IVAN: Sure, that's impossible.

RICHARD: That's what I would've thought.

LOCKHART: No, you see . . . I can't hear it.

IVAN: What, are you tone-deaf?

LOCKHART: No, no, I just don't like the sound. You see, to me it's just an ugly noise.

RICHARD: Dear God! That's a terrible affliction. Sure you can hardly escape music!

IVAN: What? Like, do you want me to turn it off?

LOCKHART: If you don't mind.

Ivan stands there, hoping Lockhart will relent.

That would be most agreeable.

Ivan goes and turns off the music. Pause.

RICHARD: Lordy, lordy, lordy, lordy, lordy, lordy, lordy, lordy, lordy, would you listen to that wind? God, I had an awful dream the other night. I dreamt I could see. I dreamt that I woke up and I could see and that being blind had been a dream. And I dreamt the sun was shining in through the window there, and there, just sitting on the windowsill, was a bluebottle looking at me. You ever notice about those things? The whole head is nearly their eyes. Two big black footballs on the whole two sides of their head. And I was just staring at him and he was just staring at me—as much as you can tell if he's 'looking' at you at all . . . 'What does he think of me?' I was wondering, as we were kind of . . . communing with each other there. And there was such . . . comfort, in his blank unseeing regard for me, Mr Lockhart. You just know that God is in a fly, don't you? The very existence and the amazing design in something so small and intricate as a bluebottle—it's God's revelation really, isn't it? Don't you feel that?

LOCKHART: Well . . . except that they seem to like the taste of shit so much, don't they?

RICHARD: Ah, that only adds to their intrigue . . .

LOCKHART: If you say so.

RICHARD: Well I do! I do say so! And . . . But then I had the terrible misfortune to wake up and . . . and I realised I couldn't see. And I kind of . . . I kind of panicked. I didn't know if it was night, or day, or what the hell it was or where I was. And I didn't want to call out to Sharky, because in case I woke him, his moods do be bad enough! And I . . . or turn on the radio in case I woke him, but I got my bearings. I was down here and I thought, 'If I can get a drop of whiskey, the old panic may subside.' But then, of course, I fell in the fucking kitchen door and I made such a clatter that Sharky woke up anyway! Didn't you?

SHARKY: Yeah, well, I wasn't asleep. But Jaysus . . . I thought someone was breaking in. Bottles smashing all over the floor . . .

RICHARD: Yeah! What was it? It was . . .

SHARKY: It was five o'clock in the bleeding morning.

RICHARD: Yeah, well, we were up then, weren't we?

SHARKY: Yeah.

RICHARD: Then your man (*Sharky*) wants to give me a bath! (*Pronounced 'bat'.*)

LOCKHART: A what?

Ivan goes round with the poteen topping up their drinks . . .

RICHARD: A bat! He wants to wash me! And bathe me, the fucking . . . (*Unsaid 'eejit'.*)

LOCKHART: Well, he's trying to be what's known as 'a good person'.

RICHARD: Well he should give up! (*He laughs.*) Hey, Sharky, (*Touching his groin.*) what about that . . .

SHARKY (*remembering with disgust*): Oh . . . !

RICHARD: Ivan, there was a . . . what would you call it, Sharky?

SHARKY: I don't want to talk about it.

RICHARD: It was like a lump of . . . up here at the top of me leg where the crease meets the . . .

SHARKY: Aw, would you fucking stop, Richard?

RICHARD: It was hard, now. And deeply . . . embedded in the . . .

SHARKY: Ah, Richard!

RICHARD: Like either congealed . . . or . . . The smell when Sharky started rubbing it!

Nicky descends.

SHARKY: Richard!

RICHARD: And the fucking pain of it . . . Sharky going at it with the nailbrush! And the smell!

NICKY: What's this?

RICHARD: Nicky, you'd be interested in this, I had this . . .

SHARKY: No, come on, that's it now. Jesus Christ!

RICHARD (*angrily*): Ah, I'm only trying tell a fucking story here, Jim, what's the matter with you, for Jaysus' sake?! (*Short pause, to Nicky.*) I'll tell you later . . .

Short pause.

NICKY: Well, I've got about an hour's parole, so let's get on with the cards because if I want to have any chance of . . .

There is a sudden loud bang at the back door out in the kitchen. They all fall silent, listening.

What was that?

RICHARD (*getting up*): That's them fucking winos! Where's me stick? Ivan!

SHARKY: Ah, Rich, come on . . . don't be . . .

Nicky goes into the kitchen, peering out the back door into the gloom.

RICHARD: Don't fucking start now, Sharky! You don't know what I have to live with! I'm sorry, Mr Lockhart, we have an awful problem with these winos out in the lane, come on, Ivan!

IVAN: They're probably gone, they just . . .

NICKY: I think they must have thrown something or . . .
IVAN: Put the light on out there, Nicky.

Richard has a hold of Ivan.

RICHARD: Come on, Ivan. Come on, Nicky. Open that back door for me.
NICKY: Hey, hold on, is there something I can . . . ?
RICHARD: There's an old golf club in there beside the jacks door, Nicky.
IVAN: Put the light on out there, Nicky, will you?

Nicky finds the golf club and hits a light in the back garden.

NICKY: Hold on now, Rich, now I don't see anyone.
RICHARD: Come on, we'll get them in the lane.
SHARKY: Richard, put your coat on, will you?
RICHARD: Ah, we're alright, we'll just chase them off.
IVAN: They'll be gone I'd say anyway.

Nicky opens the back door and goes out into the wind, Richard and Ivan following. Richard does a native Indian whooping sound by vibrating his open palm in front of his mouth while letting out a high-pitched shout.

RICHARD (*going*): Keep a hold of me now, Ivan!
NICKY (*off*): Hey, mind with that stick, will ya?
RICHARD (*off*): Sorry, Nicky!

The back door shuts. Sharky and Lockhart are alone. Pause.

LOCKHART: Well, Sharky. You ready to come with me?
SHARKY: You haven't beaten me yet.
LOCKHART (*getting up to pour himself more poteen*): No, not yet, I'm enjoying myself too much! I'll hammer you now in this next hand. And then I'll take you right through the old hole in the wall.°

As Lockhart pours himself a drink, he sways and steadies himself against the table.

Whoops.
SHARKY: Mind you don't fall.
LOCKHART: Well, to tell you the truth, I never drink this much.
SHARKY: Yeah, well, welcome to our house.
LOCKHART: Mmm. Your brother . . . He's a real . . . believer, isn't he?

Sharky shrugs. Lockhart stands with his drink and raises his free hand to look at it in the light.

I hate these stupid insect bodies you have. (*He switches his drink from one hand to another*). This fucker is left-handed! (*Looking down at his legs.*) I mean, what is it? What are human beings? Two balloons—that's your lungs and an annoying little

---

hole in the wall: Automatic teller machine.

---

whistle at the top where the air comes out—that's your voice . . . (*Pause. Bitterly.*) I mean what have you got that I haven't?! (*Short pause.*) I'm talking to you, Love's Young Dream! What have you got? Ha? You all age and wither before me like dead flowers in a bright window! You're nothing! Me? I live in the stars above St Anne's park! Thousands of Christmas Eves I've seen! I'm so old . . . and thousands more I'll see; maybe millions! I'm the very power that keeps us apart! Isn't that worth saving? (*Beat.*) Evidently not. No, he loves you. He loves all you insects . . . (*Lost and distant.*) Figure that one out.

Pause.

SHARKY: What'll to happen to me? If I lose.
LOCKHART: When you lose.
SHARKY: If I lose.
LOCKHART: You're going to Hell.

Short pause.

SHARKY: What is it?
LOCKHART: What's Hell? (*He gives a little laugh.*) Hell is . . . (*He stares gloomily.*) Well, you know, Sharky, when you're walking round and round the city and the street lights have all come on and it's cold. Or you're standing outside a shop where you were hanging around reading the magazines, pretending to buy one 'cause you've no money and nowhere to go and your feet are like blocks of ice in those stupid little slip-on shoes you bought for chauffeuring. And you see all the people who seem to live in another world all snuggled up together in the warmth of a tavern or a cosy little house, and you just walk and walk and walk and you're on your own and nobody knows who you are. And you don't know anyone and you're trying not to hassle people or beg, because you're trying not to drink, and you're hoping you won't meet anyone you know because of the blistering shame that rises up in your face and you have to turn away because you know you can't even deal with the thought that someone might love you, because of all the pain you always cause.

Well, that's a fraction of the self-loathing you feel in Hell, except it's worse. Because there truly is no one to love you. Not even Him. (*He points to the sky.*) He lets you go. Even He's sick of you. You're locked in a space that's smaller than a coffin. And it's lying a thousand miles down, under the bed of a vast, icy, pitch-black sea. You're buried alive in there. And it's so cold that you can feel your angry tears freezing in your eye lashes and your very bones ache with deep perpetual agony and you think, 'I must be going to die . . .'

But you never die. You never even sleep, because every few minutes you're gripped by a claustrophobic panic and you get so frightened you squirm uselessly against the stone walls and the heavy lid you've banged your head off a million times and your heart beats so fast against your ribs you think, 'I must be going to die...' But of course...you never will. Because of what you did. And what you didn't do.

Pause. Sharky stares into his bleak eternal fate.

That's where I am too, Sharky. I know you see me here in this man's clothes, but that's where I really am...Out on that sea. (*Short pause.*) Oh, you'd have loved Heaven, Sharky. It's unbelievable! Everyone feels peaceful! (*He laughs.*) Everyone feels at such peace! Simply to exist there is to know an exquisite, trance-like bliss, because your mind is at one with the infinite!

(*Darker.*) At a certain point each day, music plays. It seems to emanate from the very sun itself. Not so much a tune as a heartbreakingly beautiful vibration in the sunlight shining down on and through all the souls. It's so moving you wonder how you could ever have doubted anything as you think back on this painful life which is just a sad distant memory. Time just slips away in Heaven, Sharky. But not for you. No. You are about to find out that time is more measureless and bigger and blacker and so much more boundless than you could ever have thought possible with your puny broken mind.

Sharky looks down forlornly.

Poor old Sharky. You've really got it for her, haven't you?

SHARKY: Who?

LOCKHART (*derisively*): Who! The wife of that fella you were working for down in Lahinch.

Sharky looks away.

...That sent you all those CDs this morning! (*Derisively.*) 'Who...?' Trust you to blow it, Sharky. Trust you. That's how I know you'll be coming with me tonight. I know you'll lose this next hand. Because you always make a pig's mickey of everything.

Sharky seems to ponder his whole life for a moment, then goes to the bottle of poteen and pours himself a huge measure. He begins to drink it perfunctorily with one hand on his hip...

That's it, Sharky, good man. Drink yourself up on to the next shelf in the basement. Drink to where possibility feels infinite and your immortality feels strong.

Sharky, having drained his glass, joylessly pours another.

That's it...Genius! You poor, stupid bastard.

SHARKY: Why don't you give it a rest?

LOCKHART: The condemned man's last meal. A big glass of hooch!

SHARKY (*snapping at Lockhart*): I said, give it rest, will ya?

LOCKHART (*fumbling towards Sharky, holding out his glass*): Here, give me one.

SHARKY (*shuffling away*): Get it yourself.

LOCKHART: Oy, oy, oy oy!

Sharky drinks while Lockhart looks at him, unsure for a moment... We hear a commotion as the others return to the kitchen through the back door. They are laughing.

NICKY (*wandering in to get a drink*): They'd scarpered! They were gone!

RICHARD (*coming through with Ivan*): We chased them off! Another battle to us. The generals prevail! Ivan, would you please pour us a sharpener to warm us up? Mr Lockhart? Are you alright for a...?

LOCKHART: I don't know...This poor brain can't cope, I don't think!

RICHARD: Would you go on out of that? Have a stout! Ivan, are you alright? Ivan fell.

NICKY (*laughs*): Ivan wrecked himself!

IVAN: Ah, I walked right into the basin of dirty water Sharky left out there! Me socks are wringing!

RICHARD: You fucking eejit!

IVAN (*going towards kitchen*): Ah, I'll take these off. I'll deal with it later...

RICHARD: You gobaloon...And Sharky, what were you doing leaving a basin of water in the laneway? (*Imploring the heavens.*) Lord, I'm surrounded by ninnies! Deliver me!

NICKY: Oh, I'll tell yous, Richard's blood is up!

RICHARD: What?

NICKY: He's missed his mill with the winos!

RICHARD: Excuse me?

NICKY: You were gunning for a fight, so you were, go on out of that!

RICHARD: Yeah, right! Sure, how could I be? I'm blind, Nicky, actually, you know?

NICKY: Go on out of that! That never stopped you! (*Spies Sharky pouring a drink.*) You having a Christmas nip, Sharky?

RICHARD (*ears pricking up at this*): Ha!

Ivan falls in the kitchen door with a crash, trying to get his socks off.

NICKY: Wo! Easy there, Ivan! Are you alright?

IVAN (*off*): Yah...

RICHARD: So...Is Sharky back among the living, yeah?

LOCKHART: He's just trying to kill the pain.

RICHARD: Mr Lockhart, take it from me, Sharky will never kill all that pain. He'd have to drink Lough Derg° dry, God help him!

They all laugh except Sharky, who continues to drink perfunctorily...Ivan wanders back in, barefoot, from the kitchen, drinking a beer. Nicky brings Richard a drink.

Ah, at last! Hey, Cheers, Sharky! (*He raises his glass, needling Sharky.*) Welcome back!

Lough Derg: Third largest lake in Ireland.

Sharky just looks at Richard darkly. Nicky, Ivan and Lockhart look at Sharky.

SHARKY: Yeah, Cheers, Richard . . .

Nicky and Ivan relax but . . .

RICHARD: Ah, clink me glass, will ya?

Sharky reluctantly goes and clinks his glass against Richard's.

Good man. Drink up. Mr Lockhart, it's a well-known fact in this whole area that my brother has that rare gift which is, unfortunately, the opposite to whatever the Midas touch was.

NICKY: Ah, Richard . . .

RICHARD: No, no . . . I'm going to say something positive. I believe that Sharky has potential. Yes. I believe he can change.

LOCKHART: Ah, well, that's sweet . . . Isn't that nice, Sharky?

NICKY (*moving to the table*): Yeah, lovely. Come on, are we gonna play cards?

RICHARD: You ever see an old couple going down the street, Mr Lockhart? An old couple who've been married for a million years, going along the road to the shops or to mass, with their grey, dead faces?

LOCKHART: Yes.

RICHARD: Like some ghastly ancient brother and sister. Nothing to say to each other any more or ever again except to snap the fucking head off each other for not putting the jelly back in the fridge or some fucking shite, you ever see that? Don't tell me they were always like that! Don't tell me they haven't changed! 'Cause I won't believe it! No, I believe in Sharky. He can change. I believe that he can change back to . . .

SHARKY: Back to what?

NICKY: Will I deal?

IVAN: Yeah, go on, Nicky, deal . . .

LOCKHART: Hold on, Sharky wants to ask something . . .

RICHARD: What did you say?

SHARKY: Back to what? I can change back to what?

NICKY: Ah, lads . . .

RICHARD: Well . . . How about back to the little fella that always had a tune on his lips and had integrity, and wasn't a sneaky little fucker who broke his mother's heart. How's that for starters?

NICKY: Ah, Richard, come on . . .

RICHARD: Back to that! You see, I remember, Mr Lockhart, when it was all fields all's around here . . . all around all up to Donaghmede, all up to Sutton, all up to Howth. All fields, Mr Lockhart. All farms, Nicky.

NICKY: Yeah, well my roots are in Ballyfermot.

RICHARD: Our mother was a wonderful woman! (*He suddenly stands to attention.*) Our father was a fine man. A tough man. He was devoted to his greyhounds! He lived for them! Great with his fists.

LOCKHART: That's fascinating . . .

RICHARD: Yes. No, our mother, God rest her, she only ever had one problem in her life. Sharky. Yes . . .

NICKY: Ah, Richard, come on, that's the poteen talking. Sharky, sit down till we play . . .

RICHARD: He upset her that much, she hit him with a chair and broke it one night, Mr Lockhart. I witnessed it.

NICKY: Ah, come on, Dick, come on, Sharky . . . let's not have the yearly . . .

SHARKY: What's your point, Richard?

RICHARD: Ha?

IVAN: Come on, Shark . . .

SHARKY: What? Did you want me to stay? And live here with you and them? And all the fucking rows all the time, and all the fucking drink?

RICHARD: You never needed anyone to show you how to drink!

SHARKY: 'Cause would you have got the house then?

RICHARD: What!

NICKY: Ah, lads, for fuck's sake . . .

LOCKHART: No, wait, let Sharky finish.

SHARKY: I am finished.

RICHARD: What do you mean would I have got the house then? How dare you?

SHARKY: You think you've always got it all figured out. Look at you.

RICHARD: What do you mean 'Look at me?' Look at you!!

SHARKY: Yeah well, don't worry about it. Because you know what? You're gonna get what you want.

NICKY: Ah, lads . . .

SHARKY: 'Cause I'm leaving here tonight and I'll be gone and that'll be the end of it.

NICKY: Ah, Sharky . . .

SHARKY (*forcefully*): And you can walk into the walls and spill Paddy Powers all down your horrible filthy whiskers and sit in your own stink 'cause you don't even know what day it is or what time it is. And then they'll stick you in some home out in Blanchardstown or somewhere where you won't even get a drink, how does that sound?

RICHARD: You're being completely unreasonable!

SHARKY: Am I? Just watch!

NICKY: Come on, Sharky, you don't mean it . . .

SHARKY: Yeah? Tell them, Mr Lockhart, or whatever your fucking name is, go on, tell him! Tell him!

Nicky is on his feet, trying to pacify Sharky.

NICKY: Sharky . . . come on . . . it's alright . . .

SHARKY: Take your fucking hands off me, I'll give you such a box in the fucking head!

IVAN: Wo, wo . . . Sharky . . .

NICKY: Hey, easy, Shark . . .

SHARKY: You're only a fucking scumbag.

NICKY: What?

SHARKY: You heard me, you sponger.

Ivan is also on his feet.

IVAN: Ah, Sharky, now, come on . . .

SHARKY: Eileen is far too good for a fucking scumhead like you. Always on the mooch . . .

Sharky (David Morse) fights with Richard (Jim Norton), 2007.

NICKY: Hey! Don't be having a go at me! (*He rolls up his sleeve to show Sharky a tattoo.*) Read that! What does that say! Eileen! And that? Eileen! I look after Eileen and the kids!

IVAN: Ah, lads!

NICKY: At least I don't be getting into mills° all the time and getting barred out of pubs all over the place! At least I don't be waking up screaming and roaring at all hours of the night having bad dreams and freaking the kids out and waking the whole place up!

RICHARD: That's right!

SHARKY: What?

NICKY: Sure everybody knows! You're a nutcase, Sharky! Everybody knows!

Sharky enters an inarticulate rage and throws a punch at Nicky. Nicky defends himself, pushing Sharky backwards. Ivan manages to get a hold of Sharky and restrains him.

RICHARD: What's going on? Sharky! Calm down!

Sharky tries to escape Ivan's grip, dragging him over to Lockhart.

SHARKY (*shouting at Lockhart*): Come on! You and me! Outside! Let's finish this for once and for all!

mills: Bar fights.

IVAN: Come on, Sharky. Come on . . .

Ivan bundles Sharky towards the kitchen.

SHARKY (*turning to shout at Lockhart*): You fucking bastard!

Ivan gets him into the kitchen and shuts the door. We hear Sharky's muffled cries for a moment and Ivan's soothing voice.

LOCKHART: What did I do?

RICHARD: No, no, Mr Lockhart, you didn't do anything. What did any of us do, sure? I can only say I'm terribly sorry . . . for his behaviour . . .

LOCKHART: Not your fault, Richard.

NICKY (*picking up an overturned chair and a glass*): He's renowned for that temper. Renowned. He can't drink! He never could! He's barred out of . . . Richard?

RICHARD: Ah, he's barred out of nearly everywhere. He can't even get a job on the fishing boats anymore . . . They won't have him.

NICKY: Yeah! Like, he had a go at all of us there! You know what I mean?

RICHARD: That's what I live with! That's what we all had to live with, with him.

Nicky shakily pours them all a drink.

If our poor old ma said left, Sharky said right. If our Da said up, Sharky went down. They'd send him out on a message, maybe to get a few bottles of stout or whatever, he just wouldn't come back! He was like a stray cat in a sock, God help him. Always. And you also have to excuse that he hasn't had a drink in a couple of days, Mr Lockhart. And I don't know why he bothers. That's like running into a brick wall at full tilt there now tonight again, the fucking eejit . . . What's he drinking?

NICKY: He's drinking that fucking poteen shite you got from the North!

RICHARD: Yeah, I should have known . . . But, this is the mad thing, he'll be grand now in a minute, watch! Won't he, Nicky?

NICKY: Oh yeah, he'll calm right down now, wait till you see . . . I should probably be heading on soon anyway or we won't get a taxi . . .

RICHARD: Ah, Nicky . . .

NICKY: Fucking . . . Sharky's left hook is nothing compared to Eileen's, I'll tell you!

RICHARD: She wouldn't hit you, Nicky . . .

NICKY: It's the force of her words, Richard! Fucking pin you up against the wall . . .

They laugh. The kitchen door opens and a sheepish Sharky appears with Ivan. They are both holding cans of beer. Pause.

SHARKY: I'm sorry, Nicky.

NICKY: Yeah, no worries, Shark . . .

Pause.

SHARKY: I'm sorry, Richard.

RICHARD (*grandly*): Apology accepted.

They are silent while the wind continues to blow outside. Sharky stands near his chair. Nicky sits, Ivan sits . . .

Are you not going to apologise to Mr Lockhart?

Pause.

LOCKHART: No need. No need. No need.

RICHARD: No, Mr Lockhart, I think he should . . .

LOCKHART: No, no! I perfectly understand. It was only the old drink talking. Sure I'm full of it myself. I'll tell you what: the only reparation I'd require, if no one objects is . . . let's all finish up like friends and play the last hand and we'll call it a night. How does that sound?

NICKY: Good idea!

IVAN: Ah, I don't know if maybe this is such a — (*Unsaid 'good idea'.*)

NICKY: Yeah! It's alright for you there with a big pile of money in front of you!

RICHARD: No, no, don't worry, Nicky, we'll play, we'll play, won't we? Sharky? A last hand now and no digs flying, alright?

Pause.

LOCKHART: Okay, Sharky?

SHARKY (*looking at Lockhart*): Okay . . .

RICHARD: Will someone pour Sharky a drink there, calm him down . . .

IVAN: He has one . . .

LOCKHART: Will I deal?

He expertly shuffles the cards like a dealer in a casino.

RICHARD: Fire away, Mr Lockhart!

LOCKHART: I'll give 'em a good shuffle . . .

NICKY: You alright, Shark?

Sharky nods.

I'm sorry as well, OK?

He offers a handshake. Sharky shakes his hand, watching Lockhart shuffle. Nicky and Ivan put two euros each in the pot.

RICHARD: He's grand! Leave him alone. I live with that silence!

LOCKHART (*proffering deck to Sharky*): Cut the deck, Sharky?

A little pause before Sharky leans forward and taps the deck with his knuckle to indicate that he is satisfied with the cut.

(*Taking the cards and dealing.*) Right!

RICHARD: I feel a big win in me waters!

NICKY: That's my big win!

RICHARD: Then why am I feeling it in my waters?

NICKY: Your waters is warning you.

RICHARD: Oh, I don't know about that. I heard a little whistle from Santy down the chimney, Mr Lockhart . . .

LOCKHART: Well, last hand! I feel something's really gonna happen . . .

NICKY: Something's got to give . . .

They all collect their cards and peruse them.

Well . . .

RICHARD: Anything interesting, Nicky?

NICKY: A card or two of note . . .

RICHARD: Ivan?

IVAN: We're doing alright . . .

LOCKHART: Care to open the betting, Ivan?

IVAN: Ah, last hand, we'll open it with five euros.

He puts five euros in the pot.

NICKY: Five euros?

RICHARD: Easy now, Ivan!

NICKY: Here, wait! Who's shy?

SHARKY: Oh, sorry . . .

Sharky puts two euros in the pot . . .

LOCKHART: I'd hate for you not to be in this hand, Sharky.

SHARKY: Yeah . . .

RICHARD: So five to play, lads.

NICKY: I'll hang around.

He puts in a fiver.

LOCKHART: Sharky?

Sharky considers . . .

Ah, you're not gonna go without a fight?

RICHARD: Sharky's had more than enough fights! You should sit this one out, Shark, hang on to your few shekels and don't have me be bailing you out . . .

LOCKHART: Ah, it's the last hand . . .

RICHARD: Exactly!

SHARKY: No. I'm in. (*He puts in five and then throws in another note.*) With twenty.

The table reacts.

RICHARD: With what? Twenty? You fucking berk!

NICKY: Ah, now, here! Hello . . .

RICHARD: What are you doing?

IVAN: Let him play, Rich . . .

RICHARD: Ah, this is mad! How are we doing? What have we got?

Ivan leans over to confer with Richard, whispering in his ear.

NICKY: God, Shark! I thought we were quits . . . the punishment continues!

LOCKHART: It's only a game!

NICKY (*sarcastically*): Oh, is it?

LOCKHART: Are you in or out, Nicky?

NICKY: Ah fuck it, come on!

He puts in twenty euros.

LOCKHART: Ivan?

IVAN: We'll see it . . .

LOCKHART: And so will I.

Ivan and Lockhart put in twenty.

RICHARD: You're some bollocks, Sharky.

IVAN: Let him play, Dick.

LOCKHART: Ivan?

IVAN (*throwing a card in*): Just one please, Mr Lockhart.

LOCKHART: One . . .

He deals him a card.

NICKY (*incredulous*): One?

RICHARD: Yes, Nicky, one.

LOCKHART: Sharky?

SHARKY: One.

NICKY (*downbeat*): One as well?

RICHARD: Ah, he's having a laugh, don't mind him.

NICKY: And what are yous doing?

RICHARD: We're not messing about. We're playing for keeps.

NICKY: Great . . . Give me three.

LOCKHART (*dealing him three cards*): Three.

Nicky looks at his cards.

RICHARD: That made you go quiet.

NICKY: No, it didn't.

RICHARD: What suddenly happened?

NICKY: No, nothing . . .

RICHARD: Go on out of that. Nicky suddenly has a hand.

NICKY: Why don't you play me and find out. With your pathetic little run up to a six or whatever it is.

RICHARD: Don't worry, we will. How many did you take, Mr Lockhart?

LOCKHART: I'm happy.

NICKY: You're happy?!

LOCKHART: No cards. I'll stick with these.

NICKY: Oh bollocks.

LOCKHART: The bet's to Sharky.

RICHARD: Throw 'em in, Shark. Don't lose it all on a bluff now.

Pause. Sharky considers Lockhart.

SHARKY: Fifty.

NICKY: Oh God . . .

RICHARD: Sharky!

IVAN: No, let him play, Dick!

LOCKHART: Nicky?

NICKY: Oh God . . .

Nicky gets up and walks away from the table.

RICHARD: Where's he going?

NICKY: I'm thinking!

RICHARD: God help us!

Pause. Nicky comes back, taking some money out of his pocket.

NICKY: Come on! It's Christmas. Fifty. I'm in. And I'm fucked now.

LOCKHART: Ivan?

NICKY: Sure he (*Sharky*) has nothing.

IVAN: Yeah. (*He puts in fifty.*) Fifty.

RICHARD: Jaysus, you're very *flathulach* (*Irish for 'generous'*) with my money there now, Vano.

IVAN: Hey, I won some of this too, Rich, don't forget.

RICHARD: Yeah well, easy come . . .

LOCKHART: And I'll see Sharky's fifty. With fifty.

NICKY (*throwing in his hand, then standing up*): Ah here! If yous are . . .

RICHARD: With what?

IVAN: With fifty . . .

NICKY: 'Cause if yous are . . .

RICHARD: With fifty?!

IVAN (*trying to keep Richard committed*): No, hold on . . . hold on . . .

NICKY: This is just too expensive! I mean I can have fun for nothing, like!

RICHARD: You out, Nicky?

NICKY: I'm gone! I'm out . . .

Nicky goes and grabs his jacket.

(*Almost mumbling.*) This is fucking crazy . . .

LOCKHART: Ivan?

Ivan turns to whisper to Richard. Sharky sits watching Lockhart, who returns his gaze.

NICKY: Lads, I have to shoot. 'Cause we won't get a taxi . . .

RICHARD: Yeah, hold your horses . . .

NICKY: Yous have all me money!

RICHARD (*to Ivan*): Go on, go on . . .

IVAN: We're in.

He puts in fifty.

NICKY: Jaysus . . .

LOCKHART: Sharky.

SHARKY: Here. (*Raising.*) And whatever else this is . . . eighty . . .

LOCKHART: With eighty?

RICHARD: Sharky, what are you doing? You mad bollocks?

LOCKHART: Ivan?

NICKY: Lads . . . don't blow a good evening now . . .

IVAN: No, we'll see it . . .

RICHARD: Ivan . . .

IVAN: To you, Mr Lockhart.

LOCKHART: Well, I've no change so I'll just throw in a hundred.

IVAN: So twenty to play.

He puts in twenty to see the bet.

RICHARD: Ivan!

IVAN: We're alright, Dick.

RICHARD: Speak for yourself!

LOCKHART: Sharky?

SHARKY: Em . . .

NICKY: Sharky's busted. You're gone, Shark, you're out . . .

LOCKHART: Well, if he wants to play . . . I know he's good for it.

RICHARD: Good for it?! He is not!

SHARKY: Richard, I have it.

RICHARD: Where? Under the mattress down in Lahinch?

SHARKY: Yeah, just not . . . I have it.

RICHARD: Where?

NICKY: Ah, he's good for it, Rich.

LOCKHART: I'll play him.

RICHARD: What the fuck is this, the Credit Union? Sharky, if we win, you've to cook that coddle I been asking you for, right?

SHARKY: Yeah, alright, I'll do it!

RICHARD: With the black pudding?

SHARKY: Yeah, alright!

NICKY: He'll do it . . .

RICHARD: Yeah, but what if Mr Lockhart wins? Who's gonna pay him for Sharky?

SHARKY: I'll pay him myself.

RICHARD: With what?

IVAN: We'll give it to him!

RICHARD: We'll have nothing left!

LOCKHART: We'll go up to the hole in the wall, sure. Isn't there one up there by the off-licence?

RICHARD: The hole in the wall? (*Laughing.*) Sharky has no bank account!

SHARKY: I have it, Rich, alright? Just let me play.

RICHARD: Do you have a sneaky bank account? Are you putting all my change from the shopping in there?

SHARKY: Richard! Would you give it a rest?

RICHARD: You're gone mad!

LOCKHART: I'm happy to play him, Richard. And I'm happy to go up to the hole in the wall with him if I win.

IVAN: Let him play, Rich . . .

RICHARD: Okay! But this is . . . I give up. I fucking give up!

LOCKHART: So? We're all in? Show our hands?

NICKY: Yous probably all have nothing, have yous?

Pause. Sharky takes a long drink.

LOCKHART: Sharky?

SHARKY: I have a poker. Four eights.

Sharky and Lockhart sit watching each other.

NICKY: Four fucking eights? Bang!

IVAN: Yous are not gonna believe this . . .

RICHARD: I'm sick . . .

NICKY: What have you got, Ivan?

IVAN: We had a poker as well! Four fours!

RICHARD: Ah, this is a disaster!

NICKY: No!

IVAN: Four fours . . .

He throws his cards face down with disgust . . .

NICKY: Sharky wins! What a hand, though! Both of yous!

RICHARD: That is a total killer now . . .

LOCKHART: Well, one moment gentlemen, please . . .

Pause. He lays his hand down for them to see. Sharky closes his eyes when he sees it.

NICKY: Four tens!!! What are the chances?!

RICHARD: What?

IVAN: Four tens . . .

NICKY: Sharky . . .

RICHARD: Did Sharky blow it?

NICKY: Sharky, you're beaten . . .

RICHARD: Sharky, you fucking eejit!

NICKY: You had to play it.

RICHARD: What were you doing?

IVAN: He had to play with a hand like that, Dick, come on . . .

RICHARD (*angrily*): Ah!

NICKY: Well you certainly cleaned us all out, Mr Lockhart.

LOCKHART: A pleasure, gentlemen . . .

IVAN: Hard luck, lads . . .

NICKY: Look, I'm gonna have to see if I can grab a taxi. (*Remembering he is broke.*) Eh . . . D'you want to share one, Mr Lockhart?

LOCKHART (*rising, collecting his money*): No, I'm going to walk, Nicky.

NICKY: All the way up to Howth?

LOCKHART: I always like to savour the last few hours of dawn before the Child arrives. I never have too long, you see. Sharky'll keep me company as far as the hole in the wall anyway.

NICKY (*baffled*): Eh . . . well, whatever you want . . . I'm gonna . . .

He zips up his jacket.

LOCKHART: Sharky?

SHARKY: Yeah.

RICHARD: Here, take it from me, Mr Lockhart, what do we owe you, twenty?

SHARKY: Nah, it's alright, Dick, I'll go with him . . .

LOCKHART: I'd be happy to oblige you, Richard. But Sharky seems to feel he should pay me himself.

RICHARD (*groping for money, holding out whatever he has grabbed*): Jaysus, Sharky, I'll give it to you, alright? Happy Christmas, okay? Are you happy?

SHARKY: I have to go, Richard. I have to do it myself. I'm sorry.

RICHARD: Ah, I give up! Come straight back now, won't you?

Pause.

You promise me?

Short pause.

SHARKY: Yeah.

Nicky reappears, coming down the stairs.

NICKY: Where's Ivan? Is he coming? I have a jo! It's Mungo Mickey's brother, whats his name . . . He's on his way home, so come on! Ivan!

Ivan reappears from the toilet, wearing a big pair of spectacles.

IVAN: I found me glasses!

RICHARD: Well thank fuck for that!

NICKY: Come on, do you want to chance it, I'll bring you home?

IVAN: Oh, I don't know . . . I'm really after blowing it now sure, it's the fucking morning!

RICHARD: Look, hang on here with me, Ivan, we'll give her a ring, alright? And smooth the passage . . .

IVAN: Yeah, maybe . . . (*Defeated.*) Oh . . . Sure, I'm jarred, Nicky . . .

NICKY: Okay, well, look, I'll see yous. Good luck, Richard.

RICHARD: But we have it here! Give it to me later!

SHARKY: Nah, I should give him my own . . . what I owe him.

RICHARD: Don't be ridiculous! It's the middle of the night!

SHARKY: No, it's fine. Really . . .

RICHARD: Talk about contrary! Sharky, come on . . .

NICKY: Here, Ivan, do you want a lift if I can grab a taxi out on the street?

IVAN: Oh, I don't know if I'd be welcome now at this hour . . .

NICKY: Would you not chance it? What time is it? It's a quarter to seven?! Oh bollocks!! How did that happen?

IVAN: What? Oh God, okay, let me have a slash quickly!

Ivan jogs into the kitchen to use the toilet. Nicky runs up the stairs.

NICKY: I'll see if I can grab a jo. I doubt it though . . . Bollocks!

He is gone.

LOCKHART: Well, Richard. It was very nice to make your acquaintance.

RICHARD: Yes! Well, thank you for calling.

LOCKHART: I hope you're not too sore about losing.

RICHARD: No, I'm just annoyed that I can't see and I can't play properly for myself. Or do anything that I'd really want. But we must do it again. Are you around?

LOCKHART: Oh I'll be gone now . . . till Good Friday anyway.

RICHARD: Well, maybe around then. And please excuse my brother and his . . . behaviour. Please, let me give you the twenty euros. I'm nervous about him going off out now at this hour . . . I just . . . he's had a few drinks and you've seen that he can be . . . Sure, you'll nearly have to go all the way up to Sutton Cross! The cash machine at the shops has been empty for days now coming up to Christmas!

Nicky comes and shakes hands with Richard. Ivan sits at the table and takes a drink.

RICHARD: See ya, Nicky, me old flower!

NICKY: And I'll be in to see you now over the Christmas. And we'll have a nice, proper Christmas drink . . .

RICHARD: Absolutely. You'll have to rescue me.

NICKY: Would you go on out of that, you don't need rescuing, Dick! (*Hurrying towards stairs.*) Lads, I'll see yous. You sure yous won't take a lift?

IVAN: Here, hold on . . .

He picks up his hand from the game . . .

These is four aces!

NICKY: What? (*He goes to look.*) It is! Yous had four aces, you dozy fucking eejit!

RICHARD: What's he saying?

NICKY: Yous had four aces!

IVAN: I thought they were fours, I couldn't . . .

NICKY: Yous won it! (*Turns to Lockhart.*) They beat you, Mr Lockhart . . .

LOCKHART: No . . .

NICKY: No, they did.

LOCKHART: Let me see . . .

Nicky brings the cards to Lockhart.

IVAN: I thought they were . . . you see I fucking thought they were fours! They were aces!

RICHARD: Well, Happy Christmas!

IVAN: I just couldn't see them!

RICHARD: Here, hold on, how many other hands did you balls up on me?

NICKY: Well, that saves you an auld trip to the hole in the wall, Sharky . . .

Sharky and Lockhart look at each other.

RICHARD: Let's have a drink! I knew that hand was ours! I could feel it in me waters! I told yous! Woo hoo!

IVAN: I'm sorry about that, Mr Lockhart . . .

NICKY: Oh that's a pain in the hole, Mr Lockhart. Lads, I have to run, I can't believe none of yous is coming with me! Come on, Mr Lockhart, you might as well take a lift now . . . Come on!

Lockhart stands there looking at them, then he takes the money from his pocket and puts it on the table.

LOCKHART: Well, what can I say? Somebody's done you a big favour, Sharky.

RICHARD: Hey, this is a square house, there's no cheating or favours being done when it comes to playing cards in here!

LOCKHART: I'm not saying it was anyone here . . .

RICHARD: What in the name of God are you talking about? It was just a mistake. People make mistakes, Mr Lockhart. It's not the end of the world . . .

LOCKHART: No . . .

IVAN: I just couldn't see! They looked like fours . . . I didn't look at them properly, I'm sorry.

RICHARD: Hey, you owe me that twenty euros now, Sharky.

NICKY: Come on, Mr Lockhart, I'll drop you at Sutton Cross, you can stroll up from there. Sharky. I'll see you, right?

SHARKY: Yeah, I'll see you, Nicky.

They shake hands.

NICKY: Call in over the Christmas, say hello, won't you?

SHARKY: Yeah.

NICKY: Good man. Ivan, I'll see you up in Doyles no doubt, have a good one, right?

IVAN: Yeah. Cheers, Nicky.

NICKY: And don't spend all that wonga until you get me a pint of Miller, or three, right? I'm gone! Come on, Mr Lockhart, if we lose this lad we're goosed!

Nicky runs up the stairs.

LOCKHART: Well then . . . I'll say goodnight.

RICHARD: Yeah, good morning! Happy Christmas! I hope Santy brings you what you want!

LOCKHART (*buttoning up his coat*): I only want what yous fellas have.

RICHARD: Yeah? What's that, then?

LOCKHART (*putting on his hat*): Peace of mind.

Richard and Ivan burst out laughing.

RICHARD: What? Are you fucking joking me?

LOCKHART: No. Goodbye, Richard. Goodbye, Ivan. See you again.

IVAN (*pouring a drink for himself and Richard*): Yeah, good luck.

LOCKHART: Goodbye, Sharky.

Sharky doesn't answer him.

Perhaps we'll play again some time, when my luck changes. Or yours does.

SHARKY: Nah, you're alright.

RICHARD: Sharky!

SHARKY: I just don't want to play anymore.

LOCKHART: Well you should think about it. Somebody up there likes you, Sharky. You've got it all.

Lockhart unsteadily mounts the stairs and goes off. The light under the Sacred Heart blinks on. The first rays of dawn are seeping into the room. The front door slams.

RICHARD: Well Jaysus! That is one maudlin fucker! Talk about a poor loser!

IVAN: Where do I know him from?

RICHARD: Ah, he's one of Nicky's strays. Jesus Christ, it's freezing in here!

SHARKY: Yeah, let me just . . .

Sharky goes to the stove and puts fuel in.

RICHARD: Good man, Sharko! Hey, do yous know what we should do? The monks do have an early mass in the Friary. Do yous feel like it? Because then—this is brilliant—we'll get one of them to run you up home, Ivan, soothe Karen's temper—they love her up there—and be an honest broker. How's that for genius?

IVAN (*considers, not too convinced*): Well, I don't know . . .

RICHARD: And you know of course that they brew their own ale up there? I was there when they started doling it out one Christmas. It's strong stuff. Two or three jugs of that after mass and you'll be whistling Dixie for the whole afternoon! What do you think, Sharky?

SHARKY: Yeah, I suppose we could walk up if it's not still raining . . .

RICHARD: Hey, Sharky . . .

SHARKY: Yeah?

RICHARD: Go over to the tree.

SHARKY: What?

RICHARD: 'What?' he says! What, did you think I didn't get you anything? What do you think I am? An ogre? Hey, Ivan, check out bah humbug over here! Go on, Ivan, get yours as well. He knows what it is. He wrapped them for me, didn't you, Ivan?

Ivan lets out a loud snore . . .

SHARKY: He's having a nap.

RICHARD: Ah, leave him. Yours is there. It has your name on it. It doesn't matter. They're both the same.

SHARKY: Ah, Rich, are you serious?

RICHARD: Yeah, well you don't deserve it now after your disgraceful behaviour. But sure, it's Christmas. All is forgiven. What do you say?

Sharky goes to the tree and picks up one of the presents.

Open it, you berk!

Sharky opens the wrapping.

You see what it is? It's a mobile phone!

SHARKY: Oh yeah. Thanks Rich . . . it's . . .

RICHARD: Yeah, well, that old 088 you were using, sure that's practically obsolete! No one can ever get you! I just thought that if you were gonna get back to the driving or if I ever needed to . . . that I could get you, you know . . .

SHARKY: Yeah . . . Thanks . . .

RICHARD: What? Is something wrong?

SHARKY: No, I'm . . . I'm just . . .

RICHARD: Ah, buck up, will you, Sharky! I don't want the whole—(*A mocking, unfair impression of Sharky.*)

'Aw, life is too hard and I can't take it!' off you today now, right? Do you hear me? We all know you're
an alcoholic and your life is in tatters and you're an
awful fucking gobshite. We all know that. But you
know what? You're alive, aren't you? (*Beat.*) Aren't
you?

SHARKY: Yeah.

RICHARD: So come on! Buck up now! It's Christmas day
and I feel like going to mass, so go on and put the
kettle on! Ivan!

Ivan jumps.

IVAN: What?

RICHARD: You better get a cup of tea into you, come on,
we're gonna go up to mass. And see if we can get one
of the monks to broker a peace deal for you. (*Going
towards the stairs.*) Hey, Shark, do I have a clean shirt?

SHARKY: I left one on your bed.

RICHARD: Good man, stick on a bit of toast, will you?
Ivan, you might come up and help me get a shave in
a minute, is that alright?

IVAN: Yeah, no problem, Dick.

RICHARD (*going up*): Hey lads, we really showed that
fucker, didn't we?

IVAN: We sure did.

RICHARD: There was funny smell off him. Get Ivan a bit
of breakfast, will you, Sharky?

SHARKY: Do you want a bit of toast, Ivan?

IVAN: Oh, I don't think so. I don't think I'm quite there
yet.

SHARKY: Well, I'll put the kettle on.

RICHARD (*as he disappears*): Good man, Sharky. That's
the way.

*Sharky goes to the kitchen. Ivan wanders over to the
stereo. He takes a CD from Sharky's gift parcel.
Morning is really beginning to pour in now. The wind
has died down. The sky is clear.*

IVAN: Hey, Shark! She has good taste, your one who sent
you these . . .

Sharky comes out with a tray, tidying up.

SHARKY: What's that?

IVAN: No, I said you got some good music off your friend
down the country.

SHARKY: Yeah?

IVAN: Yeah. These are classics.

SHARKY: Stick one on.

IVAN: Will I?

SHARKY: Yeah, go on . . .

*Sharky continues to tidy up while Ivan puts on a CD.
John Martyn's 'Sweet Little Mystery' begins to play
softly. Ivan stands nodding his approval in time with the
music and then goes off up the stairs to help Richard.*

*Sharky pauses for a moment. He reaches into his
pocket and takes out the card he received in Act One.
He stands there reading, and as John Martyn sings the
sunlight seems to stream in brighter and brighter for a
moment, before it fades away with the music.*

Yasmina Reza

Yasmina Reza's (b. 1959) father, a pianist, is Russian of Iranian descent, and her mother, a violinist, is Hungarian. Her parents, who are Jewish, left the Soviet Union for Paris, where Reza was born. Reza studied at Paris X University and later at the Jacques Lecoq Drama School. She began working as an actress in France and appeared in numerous plays by contemporary authors as well as plays by Molière, Marivaux, and Sacha Guitry. In 1987 she wrote *Conversations after a Burial* for performance in France and won the prestigious Molière Award for best author, as well as many other awards. *Conversations after a Burial* reveals a deceased father's hidden secrets while also uncovering the mixed feelings of the children left behind, especially those who came to understand that their father was disappointed in them. Following the play's performance in France, it was produced in translation in Europe and South America.

Reza's French translation of Steven Berkoff's adaptation of Franz Kafka's novel *Metamorphosis*, for performance by Roman Polanski, was nominated for the 1988 Molière Award for translation. *Winter Crossing* (1990), Reza's second play, won the 1990 Molière Award for best fringe production. Set on the terrace of a hotel in the Alps, this play explores the quiet lives of people who explain themselves away by saying they are only on vacation. Reza uses her background as the daughter of musicians to create "quartets" of characters who reveal themselves in counterpoint to each other.

"*Art*" (1994), Reza's first international success, places three friends—Serge, Marc, and Yvan—in a room with a totally white painting with almost indistinguishable diagonal lines, for which Serge paid fifty thousand dollars. The friends' reactions to the painting reveal the cracks in what had been thought to be their inseparability. "*Art*" premiered in Berlin and opened in Paris in 1994, where it won the Molière Award for best author, best play, and best production. It also won prizes in London for best comedy and in Germany for best foreign play. In 1996 it was produced in London's West End, the equivalent of New York's Broadway, and one newspaper declared it "the perfect West End play." It won the Evening Standard Award for best play in 1998. The cast for the New York production on Broadway in 1998 included Alan Alda and later Judd Hirsch, George Wendt, and Joe Morton. The cast was always important, but the play, which won the Tony Award for best play, worked independently of its stars. "*Art*" has been translated into 35 languages and continues to be performed throughout the world.

The Unexpected Man (1995) is set in a railroad compartment in which a man and woman sit mostly in silence—except that they voice their inner monologues. The man, Paul Parsky, is a famous author, and the woman has his book, *The Unexpected Man*, in her bag but does not tell him because she fears embarrassing him. The tension mounts and the characters' inner stories reveal their secrets. *The Unexpected Man* was produced in London and in France and several other European countries. It was revived in 1998 by the Royal Shakespeare Company at the Barbican in London. It has also played in New York.

Reza herself starred in *Life X 3* (2000) in the French premiere at the Théâtre Antoine in Paris, winning an award for her performance. The New York production at the Circle in the Square Theater in 2003 was not well reviewed, despite the talents of John Turturro and Helen Hunt. The play offers three different views of a dinner party with two couples in an apartment at which there is very little to eat but a great deal to drink. In 2007 John Turturro directed the New York production of Reza's *A Spanish Play* (2004) at the Classic Stage Company. It is a play within a play, with five actors, who are working on a Spanish play they will perform in French, discussing the problems they have with the play, the characters in it, and each other. Much time is spent reflecting on romantic entanglements among the actors themselves.

God of Carnage (2006), which premiered in Zurich and opened in 2009 in New York, has been an international sensation, with productions from Paris to London to Hong Kong and many cities in between. It has won prizes for best play in London and New York and continues to be produced in many languages.

In addition to writing plays, Yasmina Reza has also published several novels and written screenplays. She collaborated with Roman Polanski in adapting *God of Carnage* for his film version, *Carnage* (2011), starring Jodie Foster and Kate Winslet. Her book *Dawn, Dusk or Night* (2008), an authorized "intimate bio" of French president Nicolas Sarkozy, caused a stir in France and has been translated throughout Europe and the Americas.

In the French magazine *L'Express*, Reza said, "I'm one of those writers who works on her own stuff and speaks about herself through the voice of her characters. When I write, I'm really exposing who I am, but I remain masked, and I get to choose the mask that represents me."

For links to resources about Reza, click on *AuthorLinks* at **bedfordstmartins.com/jacobus**.

God of Carnage

God of Carnage begins so slowly, and so cordially, that at first the play seems little more than a pleasant conversation among two couples such as one might meet in any metropolitan community. Its universality in Western society is underscored by the fact that it was first performed in German in Zurich, later in French in France, and then in English in England and the United States. But while the play moves slowly at first, it escalates and moves inexorably from a discussion of two eleven-year-old boys who have had a violent confrontation to a discourse on violence and ultimately an allusion to genocide.

Annette and Alan have come to the home of Veronica and Michael to discuss a fight between their sons in Cobble Hill Park, which resulted in Veronica and Michael's son losing a tooth. Near the end of the play, Veronica says something that audience members have begun to realize: "What goes on in Cobble Hill Park reflects the values of Western society." At this point we understand that the violence of the children parallels the violence not just of these parents, but of adults in general. Michael's admission that he is a Neanderthal only deepens the message by implying that human violence is in our genes, that there is no way that civilization—which is frequently referred to in the play—can totally cover over our primitive urges.

Veronica's concern for Darfur, the region of the Sudan in which more than a half million people have been killed and many more forced into refugee camps, parallels Alan's recent visit to the Congo, where violence and murder also hold sway. The world of Cobble Hill Park is set in contrast with that world, but we see that many of the same forces are at work, only more subtly and more indirectly. The forces motivating genocide in Darfur manifest on a smaller scale in Alan's annoying cell phone conversations, which reveal that he is not concerned with anything but making sure that the pharmaceutical company he represents as a lawyer can continue making a prescription drug that is damaging many thousands of people who take it. Similarly, Michael's callow treatment of his daughter's pet hamster, leaving it in the gutter to be killed and/or eaten, reveals a capacity to ignore the needs of others and to compartmentalize their pain. Annette accuses him of murdering the animal, and Michael simply does not understand her.

Even the references to art, a mark of highly civilized people, center on violence. Francis Bacon's work often displays violence in the form of flayed animals and halved carcasses along with painfully distorted human figures. Oskar Kokoschka, whose book suffers the indignity of being vomited upon in the play, was a German expressionist painter whose work, while by no means as visceral as Bacon's, is sometimes emotionally distressing. The fact that Alan is going to the Hague in Holland to appear at the International Criminal Court, where tyrants are tried for genocide, relates not only to references to Darfur, but even to references to the beautiful tulips, which come from Holland to the Korean delicatessen every week. The great scene in which Annette throws the flowers all around the room is a dramatic way of resolving her feelings about primitive violence and civilization.

In spite of the focus on violence, many details in the play evoke humor, such as the serving of clafouti, a fancy urban term for a variety of fruitcake, which is, when understood metaphorically, a comment on the people in the room. Michael's fear of rodents contrasts comically with his tough guy image—the fellow who beat up Bobby Kopecki in order to be the leader of his gang. Michael's phone conversations with his aged mother, who happens to be taking the dangerous prescription drug, ironically lead Alan to talk with her on the phone, to suavely calm her and suggest she stop taking it.

Alan, despite his high-minded view of the International Criminal Court, takes the view that children getting a beating is part of the "law of life." Late in the play, it is Alan who declares, "I believe in the god of carnage. He has ruled, uninterruptedly, since the dawn of time." By that point in the play, the audience has been given more than enough evidence to substantiate his claim.

For discussion questions and assignments on *God of Carnage*, visit bedfordstmartins.com/jacobus.

God of Carnage in Performance

The first production of *God of Carnage* was in Zurich in December 2006, followed by a major production in Paris in 2008. The English production was in the Gielgud Theatre in London's West End in March of 2008, with Ralph Fiennes and Janet McTeer. The play won the Olivier Award for the best new play of the year. The Broadway production was in March 2009 and starred Jeff Daniels as Alan, Hope Davis as Annette, Marcia Gay Harden as Veronica, and James Gandolfini as Michael. The play ran for 452 regular performances and won the Tony Award for best play. Marcia Gay Harden won the Tony for best actress.

Productions in 2011 were mounted at the Gate Theatre in Dublin, the Goodman Theatre in Chicago, the Hong Kong Cultural Centre in Hong Kong, and numerous regional theaters in the United States and overseas. The Ahmanson Theatre production in Los Angeles in April 2011 reunited the original Broadway cast and received glowing reviews.

YASMINA REZA (b. 1959)

God of Carnage 2006

TRANSLATED BY CHRISTOPHER HAMPTON

Characters

ALAN RALEIGH
ANNETTE RALEIGH
MICHAEL NOVAK
VERONICA NOVAK

All in their forties.

A living room.
No realism.
Nothing superfluous.
The Novaks and the Raleighs, sitting down, facing one another. We need to sense right away that the place belongs to the Novaks and that the two couples have just met. In the center, a coffee table, covered with art books. Two big bunches of tulips in vases. The prevailing mood is serious, friendly and tolerant.

VERONICA: So, this is our statement . . . You'll be doing your own, of course . . . At 5:30 P.M. on the third of November, in Cobble Hill Park, following a verbal altercation, Benjamin Raleigh, eleven, armed with a stick, struck our son Henry Novak in the face. This action resulted in, apart from a swelling of the upper lip, the breaking of two incisors, including injury to the nerve in the right incisor.

ALAN: Armed?

VERONICA: Armed? You don't like armed, what shall we say, Michael, furnished, equipped, furnished with a stick, is that all right?

ALAN: Furnished, yes.

MICHAEL: Furnished with a stick.

VERONICA: (*Making the correction.*) Furnished. The irony is, we've always regarded Cobble Hill Park as a haven of security, unlike Whitman Park.

MICHAEL: She's right. We've always said, Cobble Hill Park yes, Whitman Park no.

VERONICA: Absolutely. Anyway, thank you for coming. There's nothing to be gained from getting stuck down some emotional cul-de-sac.

ANNETTE: We should be thanking you. We should.

VERONICA: I don't see that any thanks are necessary. Fortunately, there is still such a thing as the art of co-existence, isn't there?

ALAN: Which the children don't appear to have mastered. At least, not ours!

ANNETTE: Yes, not ours! . . . What's going to happen to the tooth with the affected nerve? . . .

VERONICA: We don't know yet. They're being cautious about the prognosis. Apparently the nerve hasn't been totally exposed.

MICHAEL: Only a little bit of it's been exposed.

VERONICA: Yes. Some of it's been exposed and some of it's still covered. That's why they've decided not to kill the nerve just yet.

MICHAEL: They're trying to give the tooth a chance.

VERONICA: Obviously it would be best to avoid endodontic surgery.

ANNETTE: Well, yes . . .

VERONICA: So there'll be an interim period while they give the nerve a chance to recover.

MICHAEL: In the meantime, they'll be giving him ceramic crowns.

VERONICA: Whatever happens, you can't have an implant before you're eighteen.

MICHAEL: No.

VERONICA: Permanent implants can't be fitted until you finish growing.

ANNETTE: Of course. I hope . . . I hope it all works out.

VERONICA: Yes, I hope so. (*Slight pause.*)

ANNETTE: Those tulips are gorgeous.

VERONICA: They're from that little Korean deli up on Smith Street. You know, the one at the end.

ANNETTE: Oh, yes.

VERONICA: They come every morning direct from Holland, forty dollars for a bunch of fifty.

ANNETTE: Oh, really!

VERONICA: You know, the one at the end.

ANNETTE: Yes, yes.

VERONICA: You know he didn't want to identify Benjamin.

MICHAEL: No, he didn't.

VERONICA: Impressive sight, that child, face bashed in, teeth missing, still refusing to talk.

ANNETTE: I can imagine.

MICHAEL: He also didn't want to identify him for fear of looking like a tattletale in front of his friends, we have to be honest, Veronica, it was nothing more than bravado.

VERONICA: Of course, but bravado is a kind of courage, isn't it?

ANNETTE: That's right . . . So how . . . ? What I mean is how did you manage to get Benjamin's name? . . .

VERONICA: Well, we explained to Henry he wasn't helping this child by shielding him.

MICHAEL: We said to him if this child thinks he can keep on hitting people with impunity, why should he stop?

VERONICA: We said to him if we were this kid's parents, we would definitely want to be told.

ANNETTE: Absolutely.

ALAN: Yes . . . (*His cell phone vibrates.*) Excuse me . . . (*He moves away from the group; as he talks, he pulls a newspaper out of his pocket.*) Yes, Murray, thanks for calling back. Right, in today's *Times*, let me read it to you . . . According to a paper published in the *Lancet* and taken up yesterday in the *Financial Times*, two Australian researchers have revealed the neurological side effects of Antril, a hypertensive beta-blocker, manufactured at the Verenz-Pharma laboratories. These side effects range from hearing loss to ataxia . . . So who the hell is your media watchdog . . . Yes, it's very goddamn inconvenient . . . No, what's most inconvenient about it as far as I'm concerned is the annual shareholders' meeting's in two weeks. Do you have an insurance contingency to cover litigation? . . . OK . . . Oh, and Murray, Murray, ask your PR gal to find out if this story shows up anywhere else . . . Call me back. (*He hangs up.*) . . . Excuse me.

MICHAEL: So you're . . .

ALAN: A lawyer.

ANNETTE: What about you?

MICHAEL: Me, I have a wholesale company, household goods; and Veronica's a writer and works part-time in an art history bookshop.

ANNETTE: A writer?

VERONICA: I contributed to a collection on the civilization of Sheba, based on the excavations that were restarted at the end of the Ethiopian-Eritrean war. And I have a book coming out in January on the Darfur tragedy.

ANNETTE: So you specialize in Africa.

VERONICA: I'm very interested in that part of the world.

ANNETTE: Do you have any other children?

VERONICA: Henry has a nine-year-old sister, Camille. Who's furious at her father because last night her father got rid of the hamster.

ANNETTE: You got rid of the hamster?

MICHAEL: Yes. This hamster makes the most godawful racket all night, then spends the whole day fast asleep! Henry was in a lot of pain last night; he was being driven crazy by the noise that the hamster was making. And, to tell you the truth, I've been wanting to get rid of it for a long time, so I said to myself, OK, that's it, I took it and put it in the street. I thought they loved drains and gutters and all that, but I guess not, it just sat there paralyzed on the sidewalk. Well, they're not domestic animals, they're not wild animals, I don't really know where their natural habitat is. Dump them in the woods, they're probably just as unhappy, so I don't know where you're supposed to put them.

ANNETTE: You left it outside?

VERONICA: He left it there and tried to convince Camille it had run away. But she wasn't having it.

ALAN: Was the hamster gone this morning?

MICHAEL: Gone, yes.

VERONICA: And you, what field are you in?

ANNETTE: I'm in wealth management.

VERONICA: Is it at all possible . . . forgive me for putting the question so bluntly, that Benjamin might apologize to Henry?

ALAN: It'd be good if they talked.

ANNETTE: He has to apologize, Alan. He has to tell him he's sorry.

ALAN: Yes, yes. Of course.

VERONICA: But is he sorry?

ALAN: He realizes what he's done. He just doesn't understand the implications. He's eleven.

VERONICA: If you're eleven, you're not a baby any more.

MICHAEL: You're not an adult either! We haven't offered you anything, coffee, tea, is there any of that clafouti left, Ronnie? It's an extraordinary clafouti!

ALAN: I wouldn't mind an espresso.

ANNETTE: Just some water.

MICHAEL: (*To Veronica on her way out.*) Espresso for me too, sweetie, and bring the clafouti anyway. (*After a hiatus.*) What I always say is, we're a lump of potter's clay and it's up to us to fashion something out of it. Perhaps it won't take shape till the very end. Who knows?

ANNETTE: Mm.

MICHAEL: You have to taste this clafouti. Good clafouti is an endangered species.

ANNETTE: You're right.

ALAN: What is it you sell?

MICHAEL: Domestic hardware. Locks, doorknobs, soldering irons, all sorts of household goods, saucepans, frying pans . . .

ALAN: Money in that, is there?

MICHAEL: Well, you know, it's never exactly been a bonanza, it was pretty hard when we started. But if I'm out there every day pushing my product, we survive. At least it's not seasonal, like textiles. Although we do sell a lot of fondue pots around Christmastime!

ALAN: I'm sure . . .

ANNETTE: When you saw the hamster sitting there, paralyzed, why didn't you bring it back home?

MICHAEL: Because I couldn't pick it up.

ANNETTE: You put it on the sidewalk.

MICHAEL: I took it out in its cage and sort of tipped it out. I don't like to touch rodents. (*Veronica comes back with a tray. Drinks and the clafouti.*)

VERONICA: I don't know who put the clafouti in the fridge. Monica puts everything in the fridge, she won't be told. What's Benjamin said to you? Sugar?

ALAN: No, thanks. What's in the clafouti?

VERONICA: Apples and pears.

ANNETTE: Apples and pears?

VERONICA: My own little recipe. (*She cuts the clafouti and distributes slices.*) It's going to be too cold, it's a shame.

ANNETTE: Apples and pears, this is a first.

VERONICA: Apples and pears, it's pretty textbook, but there's a little trick to it.

ANNETTE: There is?

VERONICA: Pears need to be cut thicker than apples. Because pears cook faster than apples.

ANNETTE: Ah, of course.

MICHAEL: But wait, she's not telling you the real secret.

VERONICA: Let them try it.

ALAN: Very good. It's very good.

ANNETTE: Tasty.

VERONICA: . . . Gingerbread crumbs!

ANNETTE: Brilliant!

VERONICA: To be quite honest, I got it from his mother.

ALAN: Gingerbread, delicious . . . Well, at least all this has given us a new recipe.

VERONICA: I'd have preferred it if it hadn't cost my son two teeth.

ALAN: Of course, that's what I meant.

ANNETTE: Strange way of expressing it.

ALAN: Not at all, I . . . (*His cell phone vibrates, he looks at the screen.*) I have to take this . . . Yes, Murray . . . No, no, don't ask for right of reply, you'll only feed the controversy . . . Are you insured? . . . Mm, mm . . . What are these symptoms, what is ataxia? . . . What about on a standard dose? . . . How long have you known about this? . . . And all that time you never recalled it? . . . What's the gross? . . . Ah, got it. I see . . . (*He hangs up and immediately dials another number, scarfing clafouti all the while.*)

ANNETTE: Alan, do you mind joining us?

ALAN: Yes, yes, I'm coming . . . (*To the cell.*) Serge? . . . They've known about the risks for two years . . . An internal report, but it didn't formally identify any undesirable side effects . . . No, they took no precautions, they didn't insure, not a word about it in the annual report . . . Impaired motor skills, stability problems, in short you look completely retarded . . . (*He laughs along with his colleague.*) They are grossing one hundred and fifty million dollars . . . Blanket denial . . . Idiot wanted to demand a right of reply. We certainly don't want a right of reply, on the other hand if the story spreads we could put out a press release, say it's disinformation leaked two weeks before the shareholders' meeting . . . He's going to call me back . . . OK. (*He hangs up.*) I haven't had lunch.

MICHAEL: Please, help yourself, help yourself.

ALAN: Thanks. I have no manners. What were we saying?

VERONICA: That it would have been nicer to meet under different circumstances.

ALAN: Oh, yes, right. So the clafouti, it's your mother's?

MICHAEL: The recipe is my mother's, but Ronnie made this one.

VERONICA: Your mother doesn't mix pears and apples!

MICHAEL: No.

VERONICA: Poor thing has to have an operation.

ANNETTE: Really? What for?

VERONICA: Her knee.

MICHAEL: They're going to insert a rotatable prosthesis made of metal and polyethylene. She's wondering what's going to be left of it when she's cremated.

VERONICA: Don't be horrible.

MICHAEL: She refuses to be buried next to my father. She wants to be cremated and put next to her mother who's all on her own in Florida. Two urns, looking out to sea, trying to get a word in edgewise. Ha, ha! . . . (*Smiles all round. Pause.*)

ANNETTE: We're very touched by your generosity. We appreciate the fact you're trying to calm the situation down rather than exacerbate it.

VERONICA: Frankly, it's the least we can do.

MICHAEL: Yes!

ANNETTE: Not at all. How many parents standing up for their children become infantile themselves? If Henry had broken two of Benjamin's teeth, I'm afraid Alan and I would have been a lot more thin-skinned about it. I'm not certain we'd have been so broad-minded.

MICHAEL: Of course you would!

ALAN: She's right. Not at all certain.

MICHAEL: Oh, yes. Because we all know it could easily have been the other way around. (*Pause.*)

VERONICA: So what does Benjamin have to say about it? How does he view the situation?

ANNETTE: He's not saying much. I think he's still slightly in shock.

VERONICA: He understands that he's disfigured his playmate?

ALAN: No. No, he does not understand that he's disfigured his playmate.

ANNETTE: Why are you saying that? Benjamin understands very well!

ALAN: He understands he's behaved like a thug, he does not understand that he's disfigured his playmate.

VERONICA: You don't care for the word, but the word is unfortunately accurate.

ALAN: My son has not disfigured your son.

VERONICA: Your son has disfigured my son. Come back at five and have a look at his mouth and teeth.

MICHAEL: Temporarily disfigured.

ALAN: The swelling on his lip will go down, and as for his teeth, take him to the best dentist, I'm prepared to chip in . . .

MICHAEL: That's what the insurance is for. What we'd like is for the boys to make up so that this sort of thing never happens again.

ANNETTE: Let's arrange a meeting.

MICHAEL: Yes. That's the answer.

VERONICA: Should we be there?

ALAN: They don't need to be coached. Just let them do it man to man.

ANNETTE: Man to man, Alan, don't be ridiculous. Having said that, we don't necessarily have to be there. It'd probably be better if we weren't, wouldn't it?

VERONICA: The question isn't whether we should be there or not. The question is do they want to talk to one another, do they want to have a discussion?

MICHAEL: Henry wants to.

VERONICA: What about Benjamin?

ANNETTE: It's no use asking his opinion.

VERONICA: But it has to come from him.

ANNETTE: Benjamin has behaved like a hooligan, we're not interested in what mood he's in.

VERONICA: If Benjamin is forced to meet Henry in a punitive context, I can't see the results would be very positive.

ALAN: Madam, our son is a savage. To hope for any kind of spontaneous repentance would be fanciful. Right, I'm sorry, I have to get back to the office. You stay, Annette, you'll tell me what you've decided, I'm no use whichever way you cut it. Women always think you need a man, you need a father, as if they'd be any help at all. Men are a dead weight, they're clumsy and maladjusted, oh, you can see the F train, that's great!

ANNETTE: I'm so embarrassed, but I can't stay either . . . My husband has never exactly been a stroller dad! . . .

VERONICA: What a pity. It's lovely, taking the baby for a walk. And it lasts such a short time. You always enjoyed taking care of the children, didn't you, Michael, you loved pushing the stroller.

MICHAEL: Yes, I did.

VERONICA: So what have we decided?

ANNETTE: Could you come by the house with Henry about seven-thirty?

VERONICA: Seven-thirty? . . . What do you think, Michael?

MICHAEL: Well . . . Honestly . . .

ANNETTE: Go on.

MICHAEL: I think Benjamin ought to come here.

VERONICA: Yes, I agree.

MICHAEL: I don't think it's right for the victim to go traipsing around.

VERONICA: That's right.

ALAN: Personally, I can't be anywhere at seven-thirty.

ANNETTE: Since you're no use, we won't be needing you.

VERONICA: All the same, it would be better if his father were here. (*Alan's cell phone vibrates.*)

ALAN: All right, but then it can't be this evening . . . Yeah? . . . There's no mention of this in the executive report. And no risk has been formally established. There's no evidence . . . (*He hangs up.*)

VERONICA: Tomorrow?

ALAN: I'm flying to The Hague tomorrow.

VERONICA: You're working in The Hague?

ALAN: I have a case at the International Criminal Court.

ANNETTE: The main thing is that the children speak to one another. I'll bring Benjamin here at seven-thirty and we can leave them to have their discussion. No? You don't look very convinced.

VERONICA: If Benjamin is not made aware of his responsibilities, they'll just look at each other like a pair of china dogs, it'll be a catastrophe.

ALAN: What do you mean? What do you mean, made aware of his responsibilities?

VERONICA: I'm sure your son is not a savage.

ANNETTE: Of course Benjamin isn't a savage.

ALAN: Yes he is.

ANNETTE: Alan, this is absurd, why say something like that?

ALAN: He's a savage.

MICHAEL: How does he explain his behavior?

ANNETTE: He doesn't want to discuss it.

VERONICA: But he ought to discuss it.

ALAN: He ought to do any number of things. He ought to come here, he ought to discuss it, he ought to be sorry for it, clearly you have parenting skills that put us to shame, we hope to improve, but in the meantime, please bear with us.

MICHAEL: All right! This is idiotic. Let's not end up like this!

VERONICA: I'm only thinking of him, I'm only thinking of Benjamin.

ALAN: I got the message.

ANNETTE: Let's just sit down for another couple of minutes.

MICHAEL: A little more coffee?

ALAN: A coffee, okay.

ANNETTE: Then I'll have one too. Thanks.

MICHAEL: That's all right, Ronnie, I'll do it. (*Pause. Annette delicately shuffles some of the numerous art books dispersed around the coffee table.*)

ANNETTE: I see you're a great art lover.

VERONICA: Art. Photographs. To some extent it's my job.

ANNETTE: I adore Bacon.

VERONICA: Ah, yes, Bacon.

ANNETTE: (*Turning the pages.*) . . . Cruelty. Majesty.

VERONICA: Chaos. Balance.

ANNETTE: That's right . . .

VERONICA: Is Benjamin interested in art?

ANNETTE: Not as much as he should be . . . What about your children?

VERONICA: We try. We try to fill the gaps in the education system.

ANNETTE: Yes . . .

VERONICA: We try to make them read. To take them to concerts and exhibits. We're eccentric enough to believe in the soothing powers of culture!

ANNETTE: And you're right . . . (*Michael comes back with the coffee.*)

MICHAEL: So, clafouti, is it a cake or a tart? Serious question. I was just thinking in the kitchen, Linzertorte, for example, is that a tart? Come on, come on, you can't leave that one little slice.

VERONICA: Clafouti is a cake. The pastry's not rolled out, it's mixed in with the fruit.

ALAN: You really are a cook.

VERONICA: I love it. The thing about cooking is you have to love it. In my opinion, it's only the classic tart, that's to say on a pastry base, that deserves to be called a tart.

MICHAEL: What about you, do you have other children?

ALAN: A son from my first marriage.

MICHAEL: I was wondering, not that it's at all important, what started the fight. Henry won't say one single word about it.

ANNETTE: Henry refused to let Benjamin join his gang.

VERONICA: Henry has a gang?

ALAN: He also called Benjamin a snitch.

VERONICA: Did you know Henry had a gang?

MICHAEL: No. That's terrific!

VERONICA: Why is it terrific?

MICHAEL: Because I had my own gang.

ALAN: Me too.

VERONICA: And what does that entail?

MICHAEL: There are five or six kids that follow you and are ready to sacrifice themselves. Like in *Spartacus*.

ALAN: Absolutely, like in *Spartacus*!

VERONICA: Who knows about *Spartacus* these days?

ALAN: They use a different model. Spiderman.

VERONICA: Anyway, clearly you know more than we do. Benjamin hasn't been as silent as you implied. And do we know why Henry called him a snitch? No, sorry, stupid, that's a stupid question. First of all, I couldn't care less, also, it's beside the point.

ANNETTE: We can't get involved in children's quarrels.

VERONICA: And it's none of our business.

ANNETTE: No.

VERONICA: On the other hand, what is our business is what unfortunately happened. The violence, that's our business.

MICHAEL: To become the head of my gang, when I was twelve, I had to fight Bobby Kopecki, who was bigger than me, one-on-one, single combat.

VERONICA: What are you talking about, Michael? What's that got to do with it?

MICHAEL: No, you're right, it's got nothing to do with it.

VERONICA: We're not discussing single combat. The children weren't fighting.

MICHAEL: I know, I know. I just suddenly had a flashback.

ALAN: There's not that big a difference.

VERONICA: Oh, yes, there is. Excuse me, there's a very big difference.

MICHAEL: There's a very big difference.

ALAN: What?

MICHAEL: With Bobby Kopecki, we'd agreed to have a fight.

ALAN: Did you beat the shit out of him?

MICHAEL: Up to a point.

VERONICA: Alright, can we forget Bobby Kopecki? Would you allow me to speak to Benjamin?

ANNETTE: By all means!

VERONICA: I wouldn't want to do it without your permission.

ANNETTE: Speak to him. What could be more natural?

ALAN: Good luck.

ANNETTE: Stop it, Alan. I don't understand you.

ALAN: Mrs. Novak . . .

VERONICA: Veronica. We don't have to be so formal.

ALAN: Veronica, you're motivated by an educational impulse, which is very sympathetic . . .

VERONICA: If you don't want me to speak to him, I won't speak to him.

ALAN: No, speak to him, read him the riot act, do what you like.

VERONICA: I don't understand why you don't seem to care about this.

ALAN: Ma'am . . .

MICHAEL: Veronica.

ALAN: Of course I care, Veronica, enormously. My son has injured another child . . .

VERONICA: On purpose.

ALAN: See, that's the kind of remark that gets my back up. Obviously, on purpose.

VERONICA: But that makes all the difference.

ALAN: The difference between what and what? That's what we're talking about. Our son picked up a stick and hit your son. That's why we're here, isn't it?

ANNETTE: This is pointless.

MICHAEL: Yes, she's right, this kind of argument is pointless.

ALAN: Why do you feel the need to slide in on purpose? What kind of message is that supposed to be sending me?

ANNETTE: Listen, we're on a slippery slope, my husband is desperate about all kinds of other things, I'll come back this evening with Benjamin and we'll let things sort themselves out naturally.

ALAN: I'm not in the least bit desperate.

ANNETTE: Well, I am.

MICHAEL: There's nothing to be desperate about.

ANNETTE: Yes, there is. (*Alan's cell phone vibrates.*)

ALAN: . . . Don't make any statement . . . No comment . . . No, of course you can't take it off the market! If you take it off the market, you become responsible . . . The minute you take Antril off the market, you're admitting liability! There's nothing in the annual accounts. If you want to be sued for falsifying the executive report and get shitcanned in two weeks, take it off the market . . .

VERONICA: Last year, on Parents' Day, wasn't it Benjamin who was in that play . . . ?

ANNETTE: *Charley's Aunt.*

VERONICA: *Charley's Aunt.*

ALAN: We'll think about the victims later, Murray . . . let's see what the shares do after the annual meeting . . .

VERONICA: He was extraordinary.

ANNETTE: Yes . . .

ALAN: We are not going to take the medicine off the market just because two or three people are bumping into the furniture! . . . Don't make any statements for the time being . . . Yes. I'll call you back . . . (*He cuts him off and phones his colleague.*)

VERONICA: I remember him very clearly in *Charley's Aunt*. Do you remember him, Michael?

MICHAEL: Yes, yes . . .

VERONICA: He was hilarious when he was in drag.

ANNETTE: Yes . . .

ALAN: (*To his colleague.*) . . . They're panicking, they've got the media up their ass, you have to prepare a press release, not something defensive, not at all, on the contrary, go out all guns blazing, you insist that Verenz-Pharma is the victim of a destabilization attempt two weeks before its annual shareholders' meeting, where does this paper come from, why did it have to fall out of the sky right now, et cetera and so on . . . Don't say anything about health problems, just ask one question: Who's behind this report? . . . Right. (*He hangs up. Brief pause.*)

MICHAEL: They're terrible, these pharmaceutical companies. Profit, profit, profit.

ALAN: You're not supposed to be listening to my conversation.

MICHAEL: You're not obliged to have it in front of me.

ALAN: Yes, I am. I'm absolutely obliged to have it here. Not my choice, believe me.

MICHAEL: They dump any old crap on you without giving it a second thought.

ALAN: In the therapeutic field, every advance brings with it risk as well as benefit.

MICHAEL: Yes, I understand that. All the same. Funny job you have.

ALAN: Meaning?

VERONICA: Michael, this has nothing to do with us.

MICHAEL: Funny job.

ALAN: And what is it you do?

MICHAEL: I have an ordinary job.

ALAN: What is an ordinary job?

MICHAEL: I told you, I sell frying pans.

ALAN: And doorknobs.

MICHAEL: And toilet fittings. Lots of other things.

ALAN: Ah, toilet fittings. Now we're talking. That's really interesting.

ANNETTE: Alan.

ALAN: It's really interesting. I'm interested in toilet fittings.

MICHAEL: Why shouldn't you be?

ALAN: How many types are there?

MICHAEL: Two different systems. Gravity or pressure-assist.

ALAN: I see.

MICHAEL: Depending on the feed.

ALAN: Well, yes.

MICHAEL: Either the water comes down from above or up from below.

ALAN: Yes.

MICHAEL: I could introduce you to one of my stock managers who specializes in this kind of thing, if you like. You'd have to leg it out to Secaucus, though.

ALAN: You seem to be very on top of the subject.

VERONICA: Are you intending to punish Benjamin in any way? You can carry on with the plumbing in some more appropriate setting.

ANNETTE: I'm not feeling well.

VERONICA: What's the matter?

ALAN: Yes, you're very pale, sweetheart.

MICHAEL: A little pale, certainly.

ANNETTE: I feel nauseous.

VERONICA: Nauseous? . . . I have some Pepto-Bismol . . .

ANNETTE: No, no . . . It'll be all right . . .

VERONICA: What could we . . . ? Coke. Coke's very good. (*She immediately sets off in search of it.*)

ANNETTE: I'll be all right . . .

MICHAEL: Walk around a little. Take a few steps. (*She takes a few steps. Veronica comes back with the Coca-Cola.*)

ANNETTE: Really? You think so? . . .

VERONICA: Yes, yes. Small sips.

ANNETTE: Thank you . . . (*Alan has discreetly called his office.*)

ALAN: . . . Give me Serge, will you please? . . . Oh, right . . . Ask him to call me back, ask him to call me back right away . . . (*He hangs up.*) Is it good, Coca-Cola? I thought it was just supposed to be for diarrhea.

VERONICA: Not only for that. (*To Annette.*) Alright?

ANNETTE: Alright . . . Veronica, if we want to reprimand our child, we'll do it in our own way and without having to account to anybody.

MICHAEL: Absolutely.

VERONICA: What do you mean, absolutely, Michael?

MICHAEL: They can do whatever they want with their son, it's their prerogative.

VERONICA: I don't think so.

MICHAEL: What do you mean you don't think so, Ronnie?

VERONICA: I don't think it is their prerogative.

ALAN: Really? Explain. (*His cell phone vibrates.*) I'm sorry . . . (*To his colleague.*) Excellent . . . But don't forget, nothing's been proved, there's nothing definite . . . Get this straight, if anyone fucks up, Murray is a dead man in two weeks, and us with him.

ANNETTE: That's enough, Alan! That's enough now with the cell phone! Will you pay attention to what's going on here, shit!

ALAN: Yes . . . Call me back and read it to me. (*He hangs up.*) What's the matter with you, have you gone nuts, shouting like that? Serge heard everything.

ANNETTE: Good! Drives me crazy, that cell phone, endlessly!

ALAN: Listen, Annette, I'm already doing you a big favor by being here in the first place . . .

VERONICA: Extraordinary thing to say.

ANNETTE: I'm going to throw up.

ALAN: No, you're not, you are not going to throw up.

ANNETTE: Yes, I am . . .

MICHAEL: Would you like to use the bathroom?

ANNETTE: (*To Alan.*) No one's forcing you to stay.

VERONICA: No, no one's forcing him to stay.

ANNETTE: I'm feeling dizzy . . .

ALAN: Stare at a fixed point. Stare at a fixed point, Woof-woof.

ANNETTE: Go away, leave me alone.

VERONICA: She would be better off in the bathroom.

ALAN: Go to the bathroom. Go to the bathroom if you want to throw up.

MICHAEL: Give her some Pepto-Bismol.

ALAN: You don't suppose it could be the clafouti?

VERONICA: It was made yesterday!

ANNETTE: (*To Alan.*) Don't touch me! . . .

ALAN: Calm down, Woof-woof.

MICHAEL: Please, let's not get worked up about nothing.

ANNETTE: According to my husband, everything to do with house, school or garden is my department.

ALAN: No, it's not!

ANNETTE: Yes, it is. And I understand why. It's deathly, all of it. It's deathly.

VERONICA: If you think it's so deathly, why have children in the first place?

MICHAEL: Maybe Benjamin senses your lack of interest.

ANNETTE: What lack of interest?

MICHAEL: You just said . . . (*Annette vomits violently. A brutal and catastrophic spray, part of which goes over Alan. The art books on the coffee table are likewise deluged.*) Go get the dishpan, go get the dishpan! (*Veronica runs out to look for a pan and Michael hands her the coffee tray just in case. Annette retches again, but nothing comes out.*)

ALAN: You should have gone to the bathroom, Woof-woof, this is ridiculous!

MICHAEL: Looks like your suit ate most of it! (*Very soon, Veronica is back with a basin and a cloth. The basin is given to Annette.*)

VERONICA: Well, it's absolutely not the clafouti, couldn't possibly be.

MICHAEL: It's not the clafouti, it's nerves. This is pure nerves.

VERONICA: (*To Alan.*) Would you like to clean up in the restroom? Oh, no, the Kokoschka! Oh, my God! (*Annette vomits bile into the basin.*)

MICHAEL: Give her some Pepto-Bismol.

VERONICA: Not now, she can't keep anything down.

ALAN: Where's the restroom?

VERONICA: I'll show you. (*Veronica and Alan leave.*)

MICHAEL: It's nerves. It's a panic attack. You're a mom, Annette. Whether you want to be or not. I understand why you feel desperate.

ANNETTE: Mmm.

MICHAEL: What I always say is, you can't control the things that control you.

ANNETTE: Mmm . . .

MICHAEL: With me, it's the cervical vertebrae. The vertebrae seize up.

ANNETTE: Mmm . . . (*She brings up a little more bile. Veronica returns with another basin, containing a sponge.*)

VERONICA: What are we going to do about the Kokoschka?

MICHAEL: Well, I would spray it with Mr. Clean . . . the problem is how to dry it . . . Or else you could sponge it down and put a bit of perfume on it.

VERONICA: Perfume?

MICHAEL: Use my Kouros, I never wear it.

VERONICA: It'll warp.

MICHAEL: We could run the hair dryer over it and flatten it out under a pile of other books. Or iron it, like they do with money.

VERONICA: Oh, my God . . .

ANNETTE: I'll buy you another one.

VERONICA: You can't find it! It went out of print years ago!

ANNETTE: I'm so sorry . . .

MICHAEL: We'll salvage it. Let me do it, Ronnie. (*She hands him the basin of water and the sponge, disgusted. Michael gets started on cleaning up the book.*)

VERONICA: It's a reprint of the catalogue from the '53 London exhibition, more than twenty years old! . . .

MICHAEL: Go get the hair dryer. And the Kouros. In the linen closet.

VERONICA: Her husband's in the restroom.

MICHAEL: Well, he's not naked, is he? (*She goes out as he continues to clean up.*) . . . There, that's the worst of it. *The People of the Tundra* needs a bit more of a wipe . . . I'll be back. (*He goes out with the used basin. Veronica and Michael return more or less simultaneously. She has the bottle of perfume, he has the basin containing fresh water. Michael finishes cleaning up.*)

VERONICA: (*To Annette.*) Feeling better?

ANNETTE: Yes . . .

VERONICA: Can we spray now?

MICHAEL: Where's the hair dryer?

VERONICA: He's bringing it when he's finished with it.

MICHAEL: We'll wait for him. We'll put the Kouros on last thing.

ANNETTE: Can I use the bathroom as well?

VERONICA: Yes. Yes, yes. Of course.

ANNETTE: I can't tell you how sorry I am . . . (*Veronica takes her out and returns immediately.*)

VERONICA: What a nightmare! Horrible!

MICHAEL: Tell you what, he'd better not push me any further.

VERONICA: She's dreadful as well.

MICHAEL: Not as bad.

VERONICA: She's a phony.

MICHAEL: Less irritating.

VERONICA: They're both dreadful! Why do you keep siding with them? (*She sprays the tulips.*)

MICHAEL: I don't keep siding with them, what are you talking about?

VERONICA: You keep vacillating, trying to play both ends against the middle.

MICHAEL: No, I don't!

VERONICA: Yes, you do. Going on about your triumphs as a gang leader, telling them they're free to do whatever they like with their son when the child is a public menace; when a child's a public menace, it's everybody's concern, I can't believe she puked all over my books! (*She sprays the Kokoschka.*)

MICHAEL: (*Pointing.*) Put some on *The People of the Tundra* . . .

VERONICA: If you think you're about to hurl, you go to the proper place.

MICHAEL: . . . And the Foujita.

VERONICA: (*Spraying everything.*) This is disgusting.

MICHAEL: I was pushing it a little bit with the shithouse systems.

VERONICA: You were brilliant.

MICHAEL: Good answers, don't you think?

VERONICA: Brilliant. The stock manager thing was brilliant.

MICHAEL: What an asshole. And what did he call her?! . . .

VERONICA: Woof-woof.

MICHAEL: That's right, Woof-woof!

VERONICA: Woof-woof! (*They both laugh. Alan returns, hair dryer in hand.*)

ALAN: That's right, I call her Woof-woof.

VERONICA: Oh...I'm sorry, I didn't mean to be rude...It's so easy to make fun of other people's nicknames! What about us, what do we call each other, Michael? Far worse, isn't it?

ALAN: Did you want the hair dryer?

VERONICA: Thank you.

MICHAEL: Thank you. (*He takes the hair dryer.*) We call each other Darjeeling, like the tea. That's more ridiculous, if you ask me! (*Michael switches on the machine and starts drying the books. Veronica flattens out the damp pages.*) Smooth them out, smooth them out.

VERONICA: (*As she smoothes out the pages, raising her voice above the noise.*) How's the poor thing feeling, better?

ALAN: Better.

VERONICA: I reacted very badly, I'm ashamed of myself.

ALAN: Not at all.

VERONICA: I just steam-rollered her about my catalogue, I can't believe I did that.

MICHAEL: Turn the page. Stretch it out, stretch it out all the way.

ALAN: You're going to tear it.

VERONICA: You're right...He's right, Michael. That's enough, Michael, it's dry. Objects can become ridiculously important, half the time you can't even remember why. (*Michael shuts the catalogue and they both cover it with a little cairn of heavy books. Michael finishes drying the Foujita,* The People of the Tundra, *etc....*)

MICHAEL: There we are! Good as new. Where does Woof-woof come from?

ALAN: How much is that doggie in the window.

MICHAEL: I know it! I know the one! (*He hums.*) Woof-woof! Ha, ha!...Ours comes from our honeymoon in India. It's idiotic, really!

VERONICA: Shouldn't I go and see how she is?

MICHAEL: Off you go, Darjeeling.

VERONICA: Shall I?...(*Annette returns.*) Ah, Annette! I was worried about you...Are you feeling better?

ANNETTE: I think so.

ALAN: If you're not sure, stay away from the coffee table.

ANNETTE: I left the towel in the bathtub, I wasn't sure where to put it.

VERONICA: Perfect.

ANNETTE: You've cleaned it all up. I'm so sorry.

MICHAEL: Everything's great. Everything's in order.

VERONICA: Annette, forgive me, I've hardly paid any attention to you. I've been obsessed with my Kokoschka.

ANNETTE: Don't worry about it.

VERONICA: The way I reacted, very bad of me.

ANNETTE: Not at all...(*After an embarrassed pause.*) Something occurred to me in the bathroom...

VERONICA: Yes?

ANNETTE: Perhaps we skated too hastily over...I mean, what I mean is...

MICHAEL: Say it, Annette, say it.

ANNETTE: An insult is also a kind of assault.

MICHAEL: Of course it is

VERONICA: Well, that depends, Michael.

MICHAEL: Yes, it depends.

ANNETTE: Benjamin's never shown any signs of violence. He wouldn't have done that without a reason.

ALAN: He got called a snitch! (*His cell phone vibrates.*)... I'm sorry!...(*He moves to one side, making elaborately apologetic signs to Annette.*) Yes...As long as there aren't any statements from victims. We don't want any victims. I don't want you being quoted alongside victims!...A blanket denial and if necessary attack the newspaper...They'll fax you the draft of the press release, Murray. (*He hangs up.*) If anyone calls me a snitch, I'm liable to get annoyed.

MICHAEL: Unless it's true.

ALAN: What did you say?

MICHAEL: I mean, suppose it's justified?

ANNETTE: My son is a snitch?

MICHAEL: 'Course not, I was joking.

ANNETTE: Yours is as well, if that's how it's going to be.

MICHAEL: What do you mean, ours is as well?

ANNETTE: Well, he did identify Benjamin.

MICHAEL: Because we insisted!

VERONICA: Michael, this is completely beside the point.

ANNETTE: What's the difference? Whether you insisted or not, he gave you the name.

ALAN: Annette.

ANNETTE: Annette what? (*To Michael.*) You think my son is a snitch?

MICHAEL: I don't think anything.

ANNETTE: Well, if you don't think anything, don't say anything. Stop making these insinuations.

VERONICA: Let's stay calm, Annette. Michael and I are making an effort to be reasonable and moderate...

ANNETTE: Not that moderate.

VERONICA: Oh, really? What do you mean?

ANNETTE: Moderate on the surface.

ALAN: I really have to go, Woof-woof...

ANNETTE: All right, go on, be a coward.

ALAN: Annette, right now I'm risking my most important client, so this responsible parent routine...

VERONICA: My son has lost two teeth. Two incisors.

ALAN: Yes, yes, I think we all got that.

VERONICA: One of them for good.

ALAN: He'll have new ones, we'll give him new ones! Better ones! It's not as if he's burst an eardrum!

ANNETTE: We're making a mistake not to take into account the origin of the problem.

VERONICA: There's no origin. There's just an eleven-year-old child hitting someone. With a stick.

ALAN: Armed with a stick.

MICHAEL: We withdrew that word.

ALAN: You withdrew it because we objected to it.

MICHAEL: We withdrew it without any protest.

ALAN: A word deliberately designed to rule out error or clumsiness, to rule out childhood.

VERONICA: I'm not sure I'm able to take much more of this tone of voice.

ALAN: You and I have had trouble seeing eye-to-eye right from the start.

VERONICA: There's nothing more infuriating than to be attacked for something you yourself consider a mistake. The word armed was inappropriate, so we changed it. Although, if you stick to the strict definition of the word, its use is far from inaccurate.

ANNETTE: Benjamin was insulted and he reacted. If I'm attacked, I defend myself, especially if I find myself alone, confronted by a gang.

MICHAEL: Puking seems to have perked you up.

ANNETTE: Do you have any idea how crude that sounds?

MICHAEL: We all mean well. All four of us, I'm sure. Why let these minor irritants, these pointless aggravations push us over the edge? . . .

VERONICA: Oh, Michael, that's enough! Let's stop beating around the bush. If all we are is moderate on the surface, let's forget it.

MICHAEL: No, no, I refuse to allow myself to slide down that slope.

ALAN: What slope?

MICHAEL: The shitty slope those two little bastards have perched us on! There, I've said it!

ALAN: I'm not sure Ronnie has quite the same outlook.

VERONICA: Veronica!

ALAN: Sorry.

VERONICA: So now Henry's a little bastard, is he? That is the last straw!

ALAN: Right, well, I really do have to go.

ANNETTE: Me too.

VERONICA: Go on, go, I give up. (*The telephone rings.*)

MICHAEL: Hello? . . . Oh, Mom . . . No, no, we're with some friends, but tell me about it . . . do whatever the doctor wants you to do . . . They've given you Antril?! Wait a minute, Mom, wait a minute, don't go away . . . (*To Alan.*) Antril's your crap, isn't it? My mother's taking it!

ALAN: Thousands of people take it.

MICHAEL: You stop taking that stuff right now. Do you hear what I'm saying, Mom? Immediately . . . Don't argue, I'll explain later . . . Tell Dr. Perolo I'm forbidding you to take it . . . Why glow-in-the-dark? . . . That's completely ridiculous . . . All right, we'll talk about it later. Lots of love, Mom. I'll call you back. (*He hangs up.*) . . . She's rented glow-in-the-dark crutches, so she doesn't get knocked down by a truck. As if someone in her condition would be strolling down the BQE in the middle of the night. They've given her Antril for her blood pressure.

ALAN: If she takes it and stays normal, I'll have her called as a witness. Didn't I have a scarf? Ah, there it is.

MICHAEL: I don't appreciate your cynicism. If my mother displays the most minor symptom, I'll be starting a class action.

ALAN: Oh, that'll happen anyway.

MICHAEL: Well, I would hope so.

ANNETTE: Goodbye, Mr. and Mrs. Novak.

VERONICA: Behaving well gets you nowhere. Courtesy is a waste of time, it weakens you and undermines you . . .

ALAN: Right, come on, Annette, let's go, enough preaching and sermons for today.

MICHAEL: Go on, go. But can I say one thing? Having met you two, it's pretty clear that for what's-his-name, Benjamin, there are mitigating circumstances.

ANNETTE: When you murdered that hamster . . .

MICHAEL: Murdered?!

ANNETTE: Yes.

MICHAEL: I murdered the hamster?!

ANNETTE: Yes. You've done your best to make us feel guilty, but your virtue went straight out the window once you decided to be a killer.

MICHAEL: I absolutely did not murder that hamster!

ANNETTE: Worse. You left it, shivering with terror, in a hostile environment. That poor hamster is bound to have been eaten by a dog or a rat.

VERONICA: It's true! That is true!

MICHAEL: What do you mean, that is true!

VERONICA: It's true. What do you expect me to say? It's appalling what must have happened to that creature.

MICHAEL: I thought the hamster would be happy to be liberated. I thought it was going to run off down the gutter, jumping for joy!

VERONICA: Well, it didn't.

ANNETTE: And you abandoned it.

MICHAEL: I can't touch those things! For fuck's sake, Ronnie, you know very well, I'm incapable of touching that whole species!

VERONICA: He has a phobia about rodents.

MICHAEL: That's right, I'm frightened of rodents, I'm terrified of snakes, anything close to the ground, I don't want them near me. So that's the end of it!

ALAN: (*To Veronica.*) And you, why didn't you go out and look for it?

VERONICA: Because I had no idea what had happened! Michael didn't tell us, me and the children, that the hamster had escaped, till the following morning. I went out immediately, immediately, I walked around the block, I even went down to the basement.

MICHAEL: Veronica, I find it intolerable to be on trial all of a sudden for this hamster saga that you've seen fit to reveal. It's a personal matter which is nobody else's business but ours and which has nothing to do with the present situation! And I find it incomprehensible to be called a killer! In my own home!

VERONICA: What's your home got to do with it?

MICHAEL: My home, the doors of which I have opened, the doors of which I have opened wide in a spirit of reconciliation, to people who ought to be grateful to me for it!

ALAN: It's wonderful the way you keep patting yourself on the back.

ANNETTE: Don't you feel any guilt?

MICHAEL: I feel no guilt whatsoever. I've always found that creature repulsive. I'm ecstatic that it's gone.

VERONICA: Michael, that's ridiculous.

MICHAEL: What's ridiculous? Have you gone crazy as well? Their son beats up Henry, and I get shit on because of a hamster?

VERONICA: You behaved very badly with that hamster, you can't deny it.

MICHAEL: Fuck the hamster!

VERONICA: You won't be able to say that to your daughter this evening.

MICHAEL: Bring her on! I'm not going to let myself be told how to behave by some nine-year-old snot-nose.

ALAN: Hundred per cent behind you there.

VERONICA: Pathetic.

MICHAEL: Careful, Veronica, you be careful, I've been extremely restrained up to now, but I'm two inches away from crossing that line.

ANNETTE: And what about Henry?

MICHAEL: What about Henry?

ANNETTE: Isn't he upset?

MICHAEL: If you remember, Henry has other problems.

VERONICA: Henry was less attached to Nibbles.

MICHAEL: Stupid name as well!

ANNETTE: If you feel no guilt, why do you expect our son to feel any?

MICHAEL: Let me tell you something, I'm up to here with these idiotic discussions. We tried to be nice, we bought tulips, my wife passed me off as a liberal, but I can't keep this bullshit up any more. I am not a member of polite society. What I am and always have been, is a fucking Neanderthal.

ALAN: Aren't we all?

VERONICA: No. No. I'm sorry, we are not all fucking Neanderthals.

ALAN: Well, not you, obviously.

VERONICA: No, not me, thank God.

MICHAEL: Not you, Darjee, not you, you're a fully evolved woman, you're stain-resistant.

VERONICA: Why are you attacking me?

MICHAEL: I'm not attacking you. Quite the opposite.

VERONICA: Yes, you're attacking me, you know you are.

MICHAEL: You organized this little shindig, I just let myself be recruited . . .

VERONICA: You let yourself be recruited?

MICHAEL: Yes.

VERONICA: That's detestable.

MICHAEL: Not at all. You stand up for civilization, that's completely to your credit.

VERONICA: Exactly, I'm standing up for civilization! And it's lucky there are people who are prepared to do that! (*She's on the brink of tears.*) You think it's a better idea to be a fucking Neanderthal?

ALAN: Come on now, come on . . .

VERONICA: (*As above.*) Is it normal to criticize someone for not being a fucking Neanderthal? . . .

ANNETTE: No one's saying that. No one's criticizing you.

VERONICA: Yes, they are! . . . (*She bursts into tears.*)

ALAN: No, they're not!

VERONICA: What were we supposed to do? Sue you? Not speak to one another and try to slaughter each other with insurance claims?

MICHAEL: Stop it, Ronnie . . .

VERONICA: Stop what?! . . .

MICHAEL: You're blowing things out of proportion . . .

VERONICA: I don't give a shit! You force yourself to rise above petty-mindedness . . . and you finish up humiliated and completely on your own . . . (*Alan's cell phone has vibrated.*)

ALAN: . . . Yes . . . Let them prove it! . . . Prove it . . . but if you ask me, don't answer at all . . .

MICHAEL: We're always on our own! Everywhere! Who wants a little rum?

ALAN: . . . Murray, I'm in a meeting, I'll call you back from the office . . . (*He cuts the line.*)

The cast of the Broadway production of *God of Carnage* at the Bernard Jacobs Theatre in New York, March 2009: from left, James Gandolfini as Michael, Hope Davis as Annette, Marcia Gay Harden as Veronica, and Jeff Daniels as Alan.

VERONICA: So, you see! I'm living with someone who's totally negative.

ALAN: Who's negative?

MICHAEL: I am.

VERONICA: This was the worst idea! We should never have arranged this meeting!

MICHAEL: I told you.

VERONICA: You told me?

MICHAEL: Yes.

VERONICA: You told me you didn't want to have this meeting?!

MICHAEL: I didn't think it was a good idea.

ANNETTE: It was a good idea . . .

MICHAEL: Oh, please! . . . (*He raises the bottle of rum.*) Anybody? VERONICA: You told me it wasn't a good idea, Michael?!

MICHAEL: Think so.

VERONICA: You think so!

ALAN: Wouldn't mind a little drop.

ANNETTE: Didn't you have to go?

ALAN: I could manage a small glass, now that we've come this far. (*Michael pours a glass for Alan.*)

VERONICA: You look me in the eye and tell me we weren't in complete agreement about this!

ANNETTE: Calm down, Veronica, calm down, this is pointless . . .

Michael offers the bottle of rum.

VERONICA: Who stopped anyone touching the clafouti this morning? Who said, let's keep the rest of the clafouti for the Raleighs?! Who said it?!

ALAN: That was nice.

MICHAEL: What's that got to do with it?

VERONICA: What do you mean, what's that got to do with it?

MICHAEL: If you invite people, you invite people.

VERONICA: You're a liar, you're a liar! He's a liar!

ALAN: You know, speaking personally, my wife had to drag me here. When you're brought up with a kind of John Wayne-ish idea of virility, you don't want to settle this kind of problem with a lot of yakking. (*Michael laughs.*)

ANNETTE: I thought your model was Spartacus.

ALAN: Same family.

MICHAEL: Analogous.

VERONICA: Analogous! Are there no lengths you won't go to to humiliate yourself, Michael?

ANNETTE: Obviously it was pointless dragging him here.

ALAN: What were you hoping for, Woof-woof? It's true, it's a ludicrous nickname. Were you hoping for a glimpse of universal harmony? This rum is terrific.

MICHAEL: It is, isn't it? English Harbor, ten years old, direct from Antigua.

VERONICA: And the tulips, whose idea was that? I said it's a shame the tulips are finished, I didn't say rush down to the Korean deli at the crack of dawn.

ANNETTE: Don't work yourself up into this state, Veronica, it's crazy.

VERONICA: The tulips were his idea! Entirely his idea! Aren't we allowed a drink?

ANNETTE: Yes, Veronica and I would like one too. By the way, it's pretty amusing, someone descended from Spartacus and John Wayne who can't even pick up a mouse.

MICHAEL: Will you SHUT UP about that hamster! Shut up! . . . (*He gives Annette a glass of rum.*)

VERONICA: Ha, ha! You're right, it's laughable!

ANNETTE: What about her?

MICHAEL: I don't think she needs any.

VERONICA: Give me a drink, Michael.

MICHAEL: No.

VERONICA: Michael!

MICHAEL: No. (*Veronica tries to snatch the bottle out of his hands. Michael resists.*)

ANNETTE: What's the matter with you, Michael?!

MICHAEL: All right, there you are, take it. Drink, drink, who cares?

ANNETTE: Is alcohol bad for you?

VERONICA: It's wonderful. (*She slumps.*)

ALAN: Right . . . Well, I don't know . . .

VERONICA: (*To Alan.*) . . . Listen, Mr. Raleigh . . .

ANNETTE: Alan.

VERONICA: Alan, we're not exactly soulmates, you and me, but, you see, I live with a man who's decided, once and for all, that life is second-rate. It's very difficult living with a man who comforts himself with that thought, who doesn't want anything to change, who can't work up any enthusiasm about anything . . .

MICHAEL: He doesn't give a shit. He doesn't give a shit about any of that.

VERONICA: You have to believe . . . you have to believe in the possibility of improvement, don't you?

MICHAEL: He's the last person you should be telling all this.

VERONICA: I'll talk to whoever I goddamn well please! (*The telephone rings.*)

MICHAEL: Who the fuck is this now? . . . Yes, Mom . . . He's fine. I say he's fine, he's lost his teeth, but he's fine . . . Yes, he's in pain. He's in pain but it'll pass. Mom, I'm busy, I'll call you back.

ANNETTE: He's still in pain?

VERONICA: No.

ANNETTE: Then why worry your mother?

VERONICA: He can't help himself. He always has to worry her.

MICHAEL: Right, that's enough, Veronica! What is with this psychodrama?

ALAN: Veronica, are we ever interested in anything but ourselves? Of course we'd all like to believe in the possibility of improvement. Of which we could be the architect and which would be in no way self-serving. Does such a thing exist? In life, some people drag their feet, it's their strategy, others refuse to acknowledge the passing of time, and drive themselves demented, what difference does it make? People struggle until they're dead. Education, the miseries of the world . . . You're writing a book about Darfur, fine, I can understand you saying to yourself, OK, I'm going to choose a massacre, what else does history consist of, and I'm going to write about it. You do what you can to save yourself.

VERONICA: I'm not writing the book to save myself. You haven't read it, you don't know what it's about.

ALAN: It makes no difference. (*Pause.*)

VERONICA: Terrible stink of Kouros! . . .

MICHAEL: Terrible.

ALAN: You certainly laid it on.

ANNETTE: I'm sorry.

VERONICA: Not your fault. I was the one spraying like a lunatic . . . Anyway, why can't we take things more lightly, why does everything always have to be so exhausting? . . .

ALAN: You think too much. Women think too much.

ANNETTE: There's an original remark. I bet that's thrown you for a loop.

VERONICA: Think too much, I don't know what that means. And I don't see the point of existence without some kind of moral conception of the world.

MICHAEL: See what I have to live with?!

VERONICA: Shut up! Will you shut up! I detest this pathetic complicity! You disgust me.

MICHAEL: Come on, have a sense of humor.

VERONICA: I don't have a sense of humor. And I have no intention of acquiring one.

MICHAEL: What I always say is, marriage: the most terrible ordeal God can inflict on you.

ANNETTE: Great.

MICHAEL: Marriage, and children.

ANNETTE: There's no need for you to share your views with us, Michael. As a matter of fact, I find it slightly indecent.

VERONICA: That's not going to worry him.

MICHAEL: You mean you don't agree?

ANNETTE: These observations are beside the point. Alan, say something.

ALAN: He's entitled to his opinions.

ANNETTE: Yes, but he doesn't have to broadcast them.

ALAN: Well, yes, perhaps . . .

ANNETTE: We don't give a damn about their marriage. We're here to settle a problem to do with our children, we don't give a damn about their marriage.

ALAN: Yes, but . . .

ANNETTE: But what? What do you mean?

ALAN: There's a connection.

MICHAEL: There's a connection! Of course there's a connection!

VERONICA: There's a connection between Henry having his teeth broken and our marriage?!

MICHAEL: Obviously.

ANNETTE: We don't get it.

MICHAEL: Children consume our lives and then destroy them. Children drag us towards disaster; it's unavoidable. When you see those laughing couples casting off into the sea of matrimony, you say to yourself, they have no idea, poor things, they just have no idea, they're happy. No one tells you anything when you start out. I have an old school buddy who's just about to have a child with his new girlfriend. I said to him, a child, at our age, are you insane? The ten or twelve good years we have left before cancer or a stroke, and you're going to screw yourself up with some brat?

ANNETTE: You don't really believe what you're saying.

VERONICA: He does.

MICHAEL: Of course I believe it. Worse, even.

VERONICA: Yes.

ANNETTE: You're demeaning yourself, Michael.

MICHAEL: Is that right? Ha, ha!

ANNETTE: Stop crying, Veronica, you can see it only encourages him.

MICHAEL: (*To Alan, who's refilling his empty glass.*) Help yourself, help yourself, exceptional, isn't it?

ALAN: Exceptional.

MICHAEL: Could I offer you a cigar? . . .

VERONICA: No, no cigars!

ALAN: Too bad.

ANNETTE: You're not intending to smoke a cigar, Alan!

ALAN: I'll do what I like, Annette, if I feel like accepting a cigar, I'll accept a cigar. If I'm not smoking, it's because I don't want to upset Veronica, who's already completely lost it. She's right, stop sniveling, when a woman cries, a man is immediately provoked to the worst excesses. Added to which, Michael's point of view is, I'm sorry to say, entirely sound. (*His cell phone vibrates.*) . . . Yes, Serge . . . Go ahead . . . Put New York, the date . . . and the exact time . . .

ANNETTE: This is obscene!

ALAN: (*Moving aside and muffling his voice to escape her fury.*) . . . Whatever time you send it. It has to look piping-hot fresh out of the oven . . . No, not we're surprised. We condemn. Surprised is feeble . . .

ANNETTE: This goes on from morning to night, from morning to night he's glued to that cell! That cell phone makes mincemeat of our lives!

ALAN: Er . . . Just a minute . . . (*He covers the telephone.*) Annette, this is very important! . . .

ANNETTE: It's always very important. Anything happening somewhere else is always more important.

ALAN: (*Resuming.*) . . . Go ahead . . . Yes . . . Not procedure. Maneuver. A maneuver, timed for two weeks before the annual accounts, etc. . . .

ANNETTE: In the street, at dinner, he doesn't care where . . .

ALAN: . . . A paper in quotes! Put the word paper in quotes . . .

ANNETTE: I give up. Total surrender. I want to throw up again.

MICHAEL: Where's the dishpan?

VERONICA: I don't know.

ALAN: . . . You just have to quote me: "This is simply a disgraceful attempt to manipulate share prices . . ."

VERONICA: There it is. Please, help yourself.

MICHAEL: Ronnie.

VERONICA: Everything's all right. We're fully equipped.

ALAN: ". . . Share prices and to undermine my client," confirms Alan Raleigh, head counsel for the Verenz-Pharma company . . . AP, Reuters, general press, medical press, the whole nine yards . . . (*He hangs up.*)

VERONICA: She wants to throw up again.

ALAN: What's the matter with you?

ANNETTE: I'm touched by your concern.

ALAN: It's upsetting me!

ANNETTE: I am sorry. I must have misunderstood.

ALAN: Oh, Annette, please! Let's not us start now! Just because they're fighting, just because their marriage is fucked, doesn't mean we have to compete!

VERONICA: What right do you have to say our marriage is fucked? Who gave you permission? (*Alan's cell phone vibrates.*)

ALAN: . . . They just read it to me. We're sending it to you, Murray . . . Manipulation, manipulate share prices. It's on its way. (*He hangs up.*) . . . Wasn't me who said it, it was Frank.

VERONICA: Michael.

ALAN: Michael, sorry.

VERONICA: I forbid you to stand in any kind of judgment over our relationship.

ALAN: Then don't stand in judgment over my son.

VERONICA: That's got nothing to do with it! Your son injured ours!

ALAN: They're young, they're kids, kids have always given each other a good beating during recess. It's a law of life.

VERONICA: No, no, it isn't!

ALAN: Of course it is. You have to go through a kind of apprenticeship before violence gives way to what's right. Originally, let me remind you, might was right.

VERONICA: Possibly in prehistoric times. Not in our society.

ALAN: Our society? Explain our society.

VERONICA: You're exhausting me, these conversations are exhausting.

ALAN: You see, Veronica, I believe in the god of carnage. He has ruled, uninterruptedly, since the dawn of time. You're interested in Africa, aren't you? . . . (*To Annette, who retches.*) Feeling bad?

ANNETTE: Don't worry about me.

ALAN: I am worried.

ANNETTE: Everything's fine.

ALAN: As a matter of fact, I just came back from the Congo. Over there, little boys are taught to kill when they're eight years old. During their childhood, they may kill hundreds of people, with a machete, with a Kalash, with a thump gun, so you'll understand that when my son picks up a bamboo rod, hits his playmate and breaks a tooth, or even two, in Cobble Hill Park, I'm likely to be less susceptible than you are to horror and indignation.

VERONICA: You're wrong.

ANNETTE: (*Mocking.*) A thump gun! . . .

ALAN: Yes, that's what they call a grenade launcher. (*Annette spits in the basin.*)

MICHAEL: Are you all right?

ANNETTE: . . . Perfectly.

ALAN: What's the matter with you? What's the matter with her?

ANNETTE: It's just bile! It's nothing!

VERONICA: Don't lecture me about Africa. I know all about Africa's martyrdom, I've been steeped in it for months . . .

ALAN: I don't doubt it. Anyway, the ICC has already conducted an inquiry on Darfur.

VERONICA: You think I don't know about that?

MICHAEL: Don't get her started on that! For God's sake! (*Veronica throws herself at her husband and hits him several times, with an uncontrolled and irrational desperation. Alan pulls her off him.*)

ALAN: You know what, I'm starting to like you!

VERONICA: Well, I don't like you!

MICHAEL: She's a supporter of peace and stability in the world.

VERONICA: Shut up! We're living in America. We're not living in Kinshasa! We're living in America according to the principles of Western society. What goes on in Cobble Hill Park reflects the values of Western society! Of which, if it's all the same to you, I am happy to be a member.

MICHAEL: Beating up on your husband is one of those principles, is it?

VERONICA: Michael, this is going to end badly.

ALAN: She threw herself on you in such a frenzy. If I were you I'd be flattered.

VERONICA: I'll do it again in a minute.

ANNETTE: He's making fun of you, do you realize that?

VERONICA: I don't give a shit.

ALAN: I'm not making fun. On the contrary. Morality decrees we should control our impulses, but sometimes it's good not to control them. You don't want to be singing *Ave Maria* when you're fucking. Where can you find this rum?

MICHAEL: That vintage, I doubt you can.

ANNETTE: Thump gun! Ha, ha! . . .

VERONICA: (*Same tone.*) Thump gun, you're right!

ALAN: That's right. Thump gun.

ANNETTE: Why don't you just say grenade launcher?

ALAN: Because thump gun is correct. It's like you say Kalash instead of Kalashnikov.

ANNETTE: Who's this "you"?

ALAN: That's enough, Annette. That's enough.

ANNETTE: The great warriors, like my husband, you have to give them some leeway, they have trouble working up an interest in local events.

ALAN: True.

VERONICA: I don't see why. I don't see why. We're citizens of the world. I don't see why we should give up the struggle just because it's in our own backyard.

MICHAEL: Oh, Ronnie! Do stop shoving these thoughts for the day down our throat.

VERONICA: I'm going to kill him. (*Alan's cell phone has vibrated.*)

ALAN: . . . Yes, all right, take out regrettable . . . Crude. A crude attempt to . . . That's it . . .

VERONICA: You're right, this is excruciating!

ALAN: . . . Otherwise he approves the rest? . . . Fine, fine. Very good. (*He hangs up.*) . . . What were we saying? . . . Thump gun?

VERONICA: I was saying, whether my husband likes it or not, that no one place is more important than another when it comes to exercising vigilance.

ALAN: Vigilance . . . well . . . Annette, it's ridiculous to drink, the state you're in.

ANNETTE: What state? On the contrary.

ALAN: Vigilance, it's an interesting idea . . . (*His cell phone.*) Yes, no, no interviews before the circulation of the press release.

VERONICA: That's it, I insist you break off this horrendous conversation!

ALAN: . . . Absolutely not . . . the shareholders won't give a fuck . . . remind him, the shareholder is king . . . (*Annette launches herself at Alan, snatches the cell phone and, after a brief look around to see where she can put it, shoves it into the vase of tulips.*) Annette, what the . . . !

ANNETTE: So there.

VERONICA: Ha, ha! Well done!

MICHAEL: (*Horrified.*) Oh, my God!

ALAN: Are you completely insane? Fuck!!! (*He rushes towards the vase, but Michael, who has got in ahead of him, fishes out the dripping object.*)

MICHAEL: The hair dryer! Where's the hair dryer? (*He finds it and turns it on at once, directing it towards the cell phone.*)

ALAN: You need to be locked up, you poor thing! This is incomprehensible! . . . I had everything in there! . . . It's brand new, it took me hours to set up!

MICHAEL: (*To Annette; above the infernal din of the hair dryer.*) Really, I don't understand you. That was completely irresponsible.

ALAN: Everything's in there, my whole life . . .

ANNETTE: His whole life! . . .

MICHAEL: (*Still fighting the noise.*) Hang on, we might be able to fix it . . .

ALAN: Forget it! It's fucked! . . .

The cast of the Broadway production of *God of Carnage* at the Bernard Jacobs Theatre in New York, March 2009.

Annette (Hope Davis) dodges Alan after taking the cell phone from him (Jeff Daniels).

MICHAEL: We'll take out the battery and the SIM card. Can you open it? (*Alan tries to open it with no conviction.*)

ALAN: I don't know how, I just got it.

MICHAEL. Give it to me.

ALAN: It's fucked . . . And they think it's funny, they think it's funny! . . .

MICHAEL: (*Opening it easily.*) There we are. (*He goes back on the offensive with the hair dryer, having laid out the various parts.*) You, Veronica, you at least could have the manners not to laugh at this!

VERONICA: (*Laughing heartily.*) My husband will have spent his entire afternoon blow-drying!

ANNETTE: Ha, ha, ha! (*Annette makes no bones about helping herself to more rum. Michael, immune to finding any of this amusing, keeps busy, concentrating intently. For a moment, there's only the sound of the hair dryer. Alan has slumped.*)

ALAN: Leave it, pal. Leave it. There's nothing you can do. (*Michael finally switches off the hair dryer.*)

MICHAEL: We'll have to wait a minute . . . (*Pause.*) You want to use our phone? (*Alan gestures that he doesn't and that he couldn't care less.*) I have to say . . .

ANNETTE: Yes, what is it you have to say, Michael?

MICHAEL: No . . . I really can't think what to say.

ANNETTE: Well, if you ask me, everyone's feeling fine. If you ask me, everyone's feeling better. (*Pause.*) . . . Everyone's much calmer, don't you think? . . . Men are so wedded to their gadgets . . . It belittles them . . . It takes away all their authority . . . A man needs to keep his hands free . . . if you ask me. Even an attaché case is enough to put me off. There was a man, once, I found really attractive, then I saw him with a square shoulder-bag, a man's shoulder-bag, but that was it. There's nothing worse than a shoulder-bag. Although there's also nothing worse than a cell phone. A man ought to give the impression that he's alone . . . if you ask me. I mean, that he's capable of being alone . . .! I also have a John Wayne-ish idea of virility. And what was it he had? A Colt .45. A device for creating a vacuum . . . A man who can't give the impression that he's a loner has no texture . . . So, Michael, are you happy? It is somewhat fractured, our little . . . What was it you said? . . . I've forgotten the word . . . but in the end . . . everyone's feeling more or less all right . . . if you ask me.

MICHAEL: I should probably warn you, rum drives you crazy.

ANNETTE: I've never felt more normal.

MICHAEL: Right.

ANNETTE: I'm starting to feel rather pleasantly serene.

VERONICA: Ha, ha! That's wonderful! . . . Rather pleasantly serene.

MICHAEL: As for you, Darjeeling, I don't see what's to be gained by getting publicly smashed.

VERONICA: Kiss my ass. (*Michael goes to fetch the cigar box.*)

MICHAEL: Take one, Alan. Relax.

VERONICA: Cigars are not smoked in this house!

MICHAEL: These are Cuban, Cohiba, Monte Cristo number three and number four.

VERONICA: You don't smoke in a house with an asthmatic child!

ANNETTE: Who's asthmatic?

VERONICA: Our son.

MICHAEL: Didn't stop you buying a fucking hamster.

ANNETTE: It's true, if somebody has asthma, keeping animals isn't recommended.

MICHAEL: Completely unrecommended!

ANNETTE: Even a goldfish can be risky.

VERONICA: Do I have to listen to this fatuous nonsense? (*She snatches the cigar box out of Michael's hands and slams it shut brutally.*) I'm sorry, no doubt I'm the only one of us not feeling rather pleasantly serene. In fact, I've never been so unhappy. I think this is the unhappiest day of my life.

MICHAEL: Drinking always makes you unhappy.

VERONICA: Michael, every word that comes out of your mouth is destroying me. I don't drink. I drank a mouthful of this shitty rum you're waving about as if you were showing the congregation the Shroud of Turin, I don't drink and I bitterly regret it, it'd be a relief to be able to take refuge in a little drop at every minor setback.

ANNETTE: My husband's unhappy as well. Look at him. Slumped. He looks as if someone's left him by the side of the road. I think it's the unhappiest day of his life too.

ALAN: Yes.

ANNETTE: I'm so sorry, Woof-woof. (*Michael starts up the hair dryer again, directing it at the various parts of the cell phone.*)

VERONICA: Will you turn off the blow-dryer! That thing is toast. (*The telephone rings.*)

MICHAEL: Yes! Because it could kill you! That medication is poison! Someone's going to explain it to you . . . (*He hands the receiver to Alan.*) Tell her.

ALAN: Tell her what? . . .

MICHAEL: Everything you know about that crap you're peddling.

ALAN: . . . How are you, ma'am? . . .

ANNETTE: What can he tell her? He doesn't know the first thing about it!

ALAN: . . . Yes . . . And does it hurt? . . . Of course. Well, the operation will fix that . . . And the other leg, I see. No, no, I'm not an orthopedic surgeon . . . (*Aside.*) She keeps calling me "doctor" . . .

ANNETTE: Doctor, this is grotesque, hang up!

ALAN: But you . . . I mean to say, you're not having any problems with your balance? . . . Oh, no. Not at all.

Not at all. Don't listen to any of that. All the same, it'd probably be a good idea to stop taking it for the time being. Until . . . until you've had a chance to get comfortably through your operation . . . Yes, you sound as if you're in very good shape . . . (*Michael snatches the receiver from him.*)

MICHAEL: All right, Mom, is that clear, stop taking the medication, why do you always have to argue, stop taking it, do what you're told, I'll call you back . . . Lots of love, love from us all. (*He hangs up.*) She's killing me. One pain in the balls after another!

ANNETTE: Right then, what have we decided? Shall I come back this evening with Benjamin? No one seems to give a rat's ass anymore. All the same, I should point out, that's what we're here for.

VERONICA: Now I'm starting to feel nauseous. Where's the pan? (*Michael takes the bottle of rum out of Annette's reach.*)

MICHAEL: That's enough.

ANNETTE: In my mind, there are wrongs on both sides. That's it. Wrongs on both sides.

VERONICA: Are you serious?

ANNETTE: What?

VERONICA: Are you aware of what you're saying?

ANNETTE: I am. Yes.

VERONICA: Our son Henry, to whom I was obliged to give two Extra-Strength Tylenol last night, is in the wrong?

ANNETTE: He's not necessarily innocent.

VERONICA: Fuck off! I've had quite enough of you. (*She grabs Annette's handbag and hurls it towards the door.*) Fuck off!

ANNETTE: My purse! . . . (*Like a little girl.*) Alan! . . .

MICHAEL: What's going on? They've lost their shit.

ANNETTE: (*Gathering up her scattered possessions.*) Alan, help! . . .

VERONICA: "Alan, help!"

ANNETTE: Shut up! . . . She's broken my compact! And my spray bottle! (*To Alan.*) Defend me, why aren't you defending me? . . .

ALAN: We're going. (*He prepares to gather up the parts of his cell phone.*)

VERONICA: It's not as if I'm strangling her!

ANNETTE: What have I done to you?

VERONICA: There are not wrongs on both sides! Don't mix up the victims and the executioners!

ANNETTE: Executioners!

MICHAEL: You're so full of shit, Veronica, all this simplistic baloney, we're up to here with it!

VERONICA: I stand by everything I've said.

MICHAEL: Yes, yes, you stand by what you've said, you stand by what you've said, your infatuation for a bunch of Sudanese coons is bleeding into everything now.

VERONICA: I'm appalled. Why are you choosing to show yourself in this horrible light?

MICHAEL: Because I feel like it. I feel like showing myself in a horrible light.

VERONICA: One day you may understand the extreme gravity of what's going on in that part of the world and you'll be ashamed of this inertia and your repulsive nihilism.

MICHAEL: You're just wonderful, Darjeeling, you're the best of us all!

VERONICA: I am. Yes.

ANNETTE: Let's get out of here, Alan, these people are monsters! (*She drains her glass and goes to pick up the bottle.*)

ALAN: (*Preventing her.*) . . . Stop it, Annette.

ANNETTE: No, I want to drink some more, I want to get bombed out of my mind, this bitch hurls my purse across the room and no one bats an eye, I want to get drunk!

ALAN: You already are.

ANNETTE: Why are you letting them call my son an executioner? You come to their house to settle things and you get insulted and bullied and lectured on how to be a good citizen of the planet. Our son did well to clout yours and I wipe my ass with your bill of rights!

MICHAEL: A mouthful of rum and bam, the real face appears.

VERONICA: I told you! Didn't I tell you?

ALAN: What did you tell him?

VERONICA: That she was a phony. This woman is a phony. I'm sorry.

ANNETTE: (*Upset.*) Ha, ha, ha! . . .

ALAN: When did you tell him?

VERONICA: When you were in the bathroom.

ALAN: You'd known her for fifteen minutes, but you could tell she was a phony.

VERONICA: It's the kind of thing I pick up on right away.

MICHAEL: It's true.

VERONICA: I have an instinct for that kind of thing.

ALAN: And phony, what does that mean?

ANNETTE: I don't want to hear any more! Why are you putting me through this, Alan?

ALAN: Calm down, Woof-woof!

VERONICA: She's someone who tries to smooth the rough edges. Period. She doesn't care any more than you do. She's all front.

MICHAEL: It's true.

ALAN: It's true.

VERONICA: It's true! Are you saying it's true?

MICHAEL: They don't give a fuck! They haven't given a fuck since the start, it's obvious! Her too, you're right!

ALAN: And you do, I suppose? (*To Annette.*) Let me say something, honey. Explain to me in what way you care, Michael. What does the word mean in the first place? You're far more authentic when you're showing yourself in a horrible light. To tell you the truth, no one in this room cares, except for Veronica, whose integrity, it has to be said, must be acknowledged.

VERONICA: Don't acknowledge me! Don't acknowledge me!

ANNETTE: I care. I absolutely care.

ALAN: We only care about our own feelings, Annette, we're not social crusaders. (*To Veronica.*) I saw your friend Jane Fonda on TV the other day, I was inches away from joining the KKK . . .

VERONICA: What do you mean, "my friend"? What's Jane Fonda got to do with all this? . . .

ALAN: You're the same breed. You're part of the same category of woman, committed, problem-solving, that's not what we like about women, what we like about women is sensuality, wildness, hormones. Women who make a song and dance about their intuition, women who are custodians of the world depress us, even him, poor Michael, your husband, he's depressed . . .

MICHAEL: Don't speak for me!

VERONICA: Who gives a flying fuck what you like about women? Where does this lecture come from? A man like you, who could begin to give a fuck for your opinion?

ALAN: She's yelling. She's yelling like a stuck pig.

VERONICA: What about her, doesn't she yell?! When she said that little bastard had done well to clout our son?

ANNETTE: Yes, he did do well! At least he's not a sniveling little faggot!

VERONICA: Yours is a snitch, is that any better?

ANNETTE: Alan, let's go! What are we doing, staying in this dump? (*She makes to leave, then returns towards the tulips, which she lashes out at violently. Flowers fly, disintegrate and scatter all over the place.*) There, there, that's what I think of your pathetic flowers, your hideous tulips! . . . Ha, ha, ha! (*She bursts into tears.*) . . . It's the worst day of my life as well. (*Silence. A long stunned pause. Michael picks something up off the floor.*)

MICHAEL: (*To Annette.*) This yours? (*Annette takes a spectacle-case, opens it and takes out a pair of glasses.*)

ANNETTE: Thanks . . .

MICHAEL: Not broken? . . .

ANNETTE: No . . . (*Pause.*)

MICHAEL: What I always say is . . . (*Alan starts gathering up the stems and petals.*) Leave it.

ALAN: No . . . (*The telephone rings. After some hesitation, Veronica picks up the receiver.*)

VERONICA: Yes, darling . . . Oh, good . . . Will you be able to do your homework at Annabelle's? . . . No, no, darling, we haven't found her . . . Yes, I went all the way to the grocery store. But you know, my love, Nibbles is very resourceful, I think you have to have faith in her. You think she was happy in a cage? . . . Daddy's very sad, he didn't mean to upset you . . . Yes, you will, of course you'll speak to him again. Listen, darling, we're worried enough already about your brother . . . She'll eat . . . she'll eat leaves . . . acorns, horse chestnuts . . . she'll find things, she knows what food she needs . . . worms, snails, stuff that drops out of trash cans, she's like us, she's omnivorous . . . See you soon, sweetheart. (*Pause.*)

MICHAEL: Chances are that creature's probably stuffing its face as we speak.

VERONICA: No. (*Silence.*)

MICHAEL: What do we know?

Tracy Letts

Like many playwrights who seem to be overnight successes, Tracy Letts (b. 1965) has a long history of work in theater, both as an actor and as a writer. He was born in Tulsa, Oklahoma, in the general region in which his play *August: Osage County* takes place. Yet, because his father was a professor and his mother, a best-selling author, was also a college teacher, Tracy Letts moved around often. He felt much like an outsider in Durant, Oklahoma, where he went to high school and where, as he has said, "The fact that I was smart, or smart-aleck, was not valued."

After high school, Letts moved to Dallas, Texas, where he worked at odd jobs and began to find parts in plays. When he was twenty, he moved to Chicago and became part of the famed Steppenwolf Theatre Company, acting in a wide variety of plays, from *The Glass Menagerie* to *Who's Afraid of Virginia Woolf*? He also acted in a number of films, although he has said that film acting was less rewarding than being on stage, primarily because he feels a sense of community in theater that was completely absent for him in movie making. Interestingly, his father, Dennis Letts, became both a film actor and a stage actor after he retired from teaching.

Letts's first play, *Killer Joe* (1993), is set in a Texas trailer park. The Smith family (Ansel, his wife Sharla, and Ansel's son and daughter from his first marriage) hires a cop who doubles as a hit man to kill Ansel's ex-wife so that they can collect the insurance. Everything seems under control until the cop enters the trailer. Then things get interesting, when the cop decides he's sexually attracted to Ansel's daughter. The drama alarmed critics with its violence and nudity when it premiered in New York, but it went on to play in Edinburgh and London.

After *Bug* (1996) premiered at the Gate Theatre in Notting Hill, London, it played in Washington, D.C., in 2000 and off-Broadway in 2004 at the Barrow Street Theatre, a production that won the Lucille Lortel Award for outstanding play. In 2010 it played in Australia. In *Bug,* Agnes, hiding out from her violent ex-husband, befriends a paranoid veteran of the Gulf War whose belief in conspiracy theories and other delusions helps Agnes sink into a form of insanity. The play was made into a film in 2006 with Ashley Judd.

Man from Nebraska (2003) is about Ken Carpenter, a solid citizen of the Midwest who abandons his wife and family to go to London, where he had been stationed with the military forty years before. He tries to live a simple bohemian life and finds people he can live with who like him, in part because of his money. More than a dramatization of a mid-life crisis, the play is the story of a man who wants to see if he can't live a life that he once imagined for himself. The play was nominated for a Pulitzer Prize in 2004 and enjoyed a Chicago production in 2011.

Letts won the Pulitzer Prize for drama in 2008 for *August: Osage County* (2007), a wide-canvas play in three acts about a dysfunctional family that meets at a funeral for the father. Coincidentally, Letts's father acted in the play on Broadway and died of cancer after his role ended. *Superior Donuts* (2008), set in Chicago, centers on immigrants and assimilation in a much more calm and pacific setting than in anything Letts had written earlier. It premiered in

Chicago at the Steppenwolf Theatre, then opened in 2009 at the Music Box Theatre on Broadway. The *New York Times* critic compared the play to a 1970s sitcom, but he meant that as a positive review. Letts said that after writing *Superior Donuts* he felt like less of a transplant in Chicago and no longer has to say, "I'm from Oklahoma originally."

For links to resources about Letts, click on *AuthorLinks* at **bedfordstmartins.com/jacobus**.

August: Osage County

Tracy Letts's play is in the grand tradition of plays that reveal the incredible internal forces that help rupture or destroy a family. *August: Osage County* makes us think immediately of Eugene O'Neill's disguised portraits of his own family, soaked in booze and warped by drugs. We think, too, of some of Sam Shepard's Western families and their enthusiastic violence. Dysfunction in families has always been a common theme in drama; the dramatic power of the family is nowhere better displayed than in the earliest Greek tragedies. The fate of the House of Atreus, as revealed in the plays of both Aeschylus and Sophocles, reminds us that in some ways nothing is more inherently dramatic than a family that faces forces it cannot control.

August: Osage County also has a slight Shakespearean tone in the return of three daughters to the house of their father, Beverly Weston, a Lear-like patriarch who has failed as a poet and given himself over to drink. His wife, Violet, suffers from cancer of the mouth—but she continues to talk even after taking so many prescription pain killers that she is hardly intelligible. She shows herself to be the character with the most energy, the most pain, and the most understanding of all those who gather to mourn Beverly's loss. She had grown up in an era of poverty and loss and is, as a result, hardened to what she calls "life on the plains." Her daughter Barbara, the dominant sister, in the middle of a failed marriage, arrives from Colorado with her husband and their daughter Jean. Ivy, who never married, loves her feckless cousin Little Charles and resents the fact that she is the only one who lives close enough to tend to her parents. Karen, who has been unlucky in love, returns from Florida with Steve, himself so damaged as an adult that he smokes pot with the irresponsible fourteen-year-old Jean.

Letts adds to the group Mattie Fae, who is Violet's sister, and her husband Charlie. Things come to a boil among these folks at the post-funeral dinner, where so much repressed anger is concentrated in one place that the audience wonders if it might spill off the stage. Yet, with all the anger there is also plenty of humor, although it is often the darkest of black humor.

Unlike many earlier dramatists, Letts invokes a number of allusions to literary culture, film culture, and general modern culture, some of them probably not immediately recognizable to most audiences. For example, the play begins with a Prologue in which Beverly talks with Johnna, a young Cheyenne woman without a family, whom he hires to take care of the house. In the course of the conversation, he makes reference to two famous American poets, Hart Crane and John Berryman, who both killed themselves. Hart Crane, a heavy drinker, jumped into the Gulf of Mexico at the age of thirty-two; Berryman, also a heavy drinker and an Oklahoman, threw himself off a bridge into the Mississippi River when he was fifty-eight.

The third poet Beverly alludes to, one who influenced both Crane and Berryman, is T. S. Eliot, author of *The Waste Land* (1922), an iconic poem of the period between the world wars that painted a dark picture of modern civilization. In that poem, Eliot, a deeply religious thinker, includes a section entitled "IV. Death by Water," which presents Phlebas, a drowned man. Some have interpreted the drowned man as a fertility symbol, implying a rebirth and a new chance for the world. Other critics have seen him as a metaphor for Christ. What Letts does in the opening pages of his play, therefore, is to connect Beverly Weston as a poet to Crane and Berryman, with whom he shares a zeal for drink and a sense of despair, and to Eliot, with whom he shares a vision of a waste land that can be redeemed only by a commitment to a spiritual view of life. Connecting Beverly Weston to these poets makes it a bit easier for audience members to understand why he ends his life in the water as he does.

For discussion questions and assignments on *August: Osage County*, visit bedfordstmartins.com/jacobus.

August: Osage County in Performance

The first production of *August: Osage County* was in Chicago at the Steppenwolf Theatre in June 2007. It was directed by Anna Shapiro, and Dennis Letts played Beverly. The New York Broadway production was in December 2007, with the same director and most of the same cast. Critics were lavish in their praise for the play. Charles Isherwood said, "'August' is probably the most exciting new American play Broadway has seen in years. Oh, forget probably: It is, flat-out, no asterisks and without qualifications, the most exciting new American play Broadway has seen in years." The play won the Tony Award for best play and the Pulitzer Prize for 2008, and it ran for 648 performances. The London premiere was in 2008 at the National Theatre. Deanna Dunagan, who played Violet in the American productions, starred in London. She was lauded as a memorable and powerful evil mother. In 2009 the play went on tour in the United States.

TRACY LETTS (b. 1965)

August: Osage County   2007

The child comes home and the parent puts the hooks in him. The old man, or the woman, as the case may be, hasn't got anything to say to the child. All he wants is to have that child sit in a chair for a couple of hours and then go off to bed under the same roof. It's not love. I am not saying that there is not such a thing as love. I am merely pointing to something which is different from love but which sometimes goes by the name of love. It may well be that without this thing which I am talking about there would not be any love. But this thing in itself is not love. It is just something in the blood. It is a kind of blood greed, and it is the fate of a man. It is the thing which man has which distinguishes him from the happy brute creation. When you get born your father and mother lost something out of themselves, and they are going to bust a hame trying to get it back, and you are it. They know they can't get it all back but they will get as big a chunk out of you as they can. And the good old family reunion, with picnic dinner under the maples, is very much like diving into the octopus tank at the aquarium.   — ROBERT PENN WARREN, *ALL THE KING'S MEN*

Characters

The Weston Family:
BEVERLY WESTON, *sixty-nine years old*
VIOLET WESTON, *Bev's wife, sixty-five years old*
BARBARA FORDHAM, *Bev and Violet's daughter, forty-six years old*
BILL FORDHAM, *her husband, forty-nine years old*
JEAN FORDHAM, *their daughter, fourteen years old*
IVY WESTON, *Bev and Violet's daughter, forty-four years old*
KAREN WESTON, *Bev and Violet's daughter, forty years old*
MATTIE FAY AIKEN, *Violet's sister, fifty-seven years old*
CHARLIE AIKEN, *Mattie Fay's husband, sixty years old*
LITTLE CHARLES AIKEN, *their son, thirty-seven years old*

Others:
JOHNNA MONEVATA, *housekeeper, twenty-six years old*
STEVE HEIDEBRECHT, *Karen's fiancé, fifty years old*
SHERIFF DEON GILBEAU, *forty-seven years old*

Place: *A large country home outside Pawhuska, Oklahoma, sixty miles northwest of Tulsa.*

Time: *August 2007.*

PROLOGUE

A rambling country house outside Pawhuska, Oklahoma, sixty miles northwest of Tulsa. More than a century old, the house was probably built by a clan of successful Irish homesteaders. Additions, renovations and repairs have essentially modernized the house until 1972 or so, when all structural care ceased.

The First Floor:
The three main playing areas are separated by entryways. Stage right, the dining room. The Mission-style table seats eight; the matching sideboard holds the fine china. A tatty crystal-tiered chandelier hangs over the table and casts a gloomy yellow light. An archway upstage leads to a sitting room. A rotary-dial telephone rests on a small side table, beside an upholstered chair. Further upstage, a doorway leads to a hallway, off.

Downstage center, the living room. Hide-a-bed, TV, hi-fi turntable, Wurlitzer electric piano.

Left, the study. A medium-sized desk is piled with books, legal pads, manila folders, notepaper. An archway upstage leads to the house's front door, landing, and a stairway to the second floor. Further upstage, a doorway opens onto a partial view of the kitchen.

Far left, the front porch, strewn with dead grass and a few rolled-up small-town newspapers.

The Second Floor:
The stairway arrives at a landing (above the sitting room on the first floor). A cushioned window seat, a hallway leading to the bedrooms, off, and another stairway leading to . . .

The Attic:
A single chamber, center, with peaked roof and slanted walls, inexpensively modeled into a bedroom.

The house is filled with books. All the windows in the house have been covered with cheap plastic shades. Black duct tape seals the edge of the shades, effecting a complete absence of outside light.

At rise: Lit dimly by his desk lamp, Beverly Weston, drunk, nurses a glass of whiskey as he "interviews" Johnna Monevata.

BEVERLY: "Life is very long . . ."
   T. S. Eliot.° I mean . . . he's given credit for it because he bothered to write it down. He's not the first person to say it . . . certainly not the first person to think it. *Feel* it. But he wrote the words on a sheet of paper and signed it and the four-eyed prick was a genius . . . so if you say it, you have to say his name after it.
   "Life is very long": T. S. Eliot.
   Absolutely goddamn right. Especially in his case, since he lived to be seventy-six or something, a very long life, especially in those days. And he was only in his thirties when he wrote it so he must've had some inside dope.
   Give the devil his due. Very few poets could've made it through his . . . his trial and come out on the other side, brilliantined and double-breasted and Anglican. Not hard to imagine, faced with Eliot's first wife, lovely Viv, how Hart Crane or John Berryman° might've reacted, just foot-raced to the nearest bridge, Olympian Suicidalists. Not Eliot: following sufficient years of ecclesiastical guilt, plop her in the nearest asylum and get on with the day. God a-mighty. You have to admire the purity of the survivor's instinct.
   Berryman, the old goat: "The world is gradually becoming a place where I do not care to be anymore." I don't know what it says about me that I have a greater affinity with the damaged. Probably nothing good. I admire the hell out of Eliot *the poet*, but the *person?* I can't identify.
VIOLET: (*Offstage.*) . . . son-of-a-bitch . . .
BEVERLY: Violet. My wife. She takes pills, sometimes a great many. And they affect . . . among other things, her equilibrium. Fortunately, the pills she takes eliminate her *need* for equilibrium. So she falls when she rambles . . . but she doesn't ramble much.

T. S. Eliot: Important poet (1888–1965), author of *The Waste Land* (1922). His wife, Viv, became insane and was hospitalized. The first line here, "Life is very long," is from Eliot's poem "The Hollow Men," a meditation on death, the ideal, and reality.   **Crane or Berryman:** Hart Crane (1899–1932) and John Berryman (1914–1972) were ranking poets who killed themselves by drowning.

My wife takes pills and I drink. That's the bargain we've struck . . . one of the bargains, just one paragraph of our marriage contract . . . cruel covenant. She takes pills and I drink. I don't drink because she takes pills. As to whether she takes pills because I drink . . . I learned long ago not to speak for my wife. The reasons why we partake are anymore inconsequential. The facts are: My wife takes pills and I drink. And these facts have over time made burdensome the maintenance of traditional American routine: paying of bills, purchase of goods, cleaning of clothes or carpets or crappers. Rather than once more assume the mantle of guilt . . . vow abstinence with my fingers crossed in the queasy hope of righting our ship, I've chosen to turn my life over to a Higher Power . . . (*Hoists his glass.*) . . . and join the ranks of the Hiring Class.

It's not a decision with which I'm entirely comfortable. I know how to launder my dirty undies . . . done it all my life, me or my wife, but I'm finding it's getting in the way of my drinking. "Something has been said for sobriety but very little." (Berryman again.) And now you are here.

The place isn't in such bad shape, not yet. I've done all right. I've managed. And just last night, I burned an awful lot of . . . debris . . .

Y'know . . . a simple utility bill can mean so much to a living person. Once they've passed, though . . . after they've passed, the words and numbers just seem like . . . otherworldly symbols. It's only paper. Worse. Worse than blank paper. (*Johnna wipes sweat from her brow. Beverly takes a folded handkerchief from his pocket and hands it to her.*) This is clean.

JOHNNA: (*Wiping her forehead.*) Thank you.

BEVERLY: I apologize for the temperature in here. My wife is cold-blooded and not just in the metaphorical sense. She does not believe in air-conditioning . . . as if it is a thing to be disbelieved.

JOHNNA: My daddy was the same way. I'm used to it.

BEVERLY: I knew Mr. Youngbird, you know.

JOHNNA: You knew Daddy?

BEVERLY: Small town. Bought many a watermelon from his fruit stand. Some summers he sold fireworks too, right?

JOHNNA: Yes, sir.

BEVERLY: I bought Roman candles for my children. He did pass, didn't he?

JOHNNA: Yes, sir.

BEVERLY: May I ask how?

JOHNNA: He had a heart attack. Fell into a flatbed truck full of wine grapes.

BEVERLY: Wine grapes. In Oklahoma. I'm sorry.

JOHNNA: Thank you. (*He finishes his drink, pours another.*)

BEVERLY: May I ask about the name?

JOHNNA: Hm?

BEVERLY: He was Youngbird and you are . . .

JOHNNA: Monevata.

BEVERLY: "Monevata."

JOHNNA: I went back to the original language.

BEVERLY: And does it mean "young bird"?

JOHNNA: Yes.

BEVERLY: And taking the name, that was your choice?

JOHNNA: Mm-hm.

BEVERLY: (*Raising his glass.*) Cheers. (*Violet calls from offstage.*)

VIOLET: (*Offstage.*) Bev . . . ?

BEVERLY: (*To himself.*)

By night within that ancient house
Immense, black, damned, anonymous.°

(*Lights up, dimly, on the second-floor landing. Just out of bed, wearing wrinkled clothes, smoking a Winston, Violet squints down the darkened stairway.*)

VIOLET: Bev!

BEVERLY: Yes?

VIOLET: Did you pullish . . . ?

BEVERLY: What?

VIOLET: Did you . . . (*Long pause. Violet stares, waiting for an answer. Beverly stares, waiting for her to complete her question.*)

BEVERLY: What, dear?

VIOLET: Oh, goddamn it . . . did. You. Are the police here?

BEVERLY: No.

VIOLET: Is this a window? Am I looking through window? A window?

BEVERLY: Can you come here? (*Violet considers, then clomps down the stairs, into the study, nonplussed by Johnna.*)

VIOLET: Oh. (*Vaguely.*) Hello.

JOHNNA: Hello.

VIOLET: (*To Beverly.*) I didn't know you were entertaaaaaining.

BEVERLY: This is Johnna, the young woman I told you about.

VIOLET: You're tell me's a woman.

BEVERLY: Pardon?

VIOLET: A woman. Wo-man. Whoa-man.

BEVERLY: Yes, dear, the young woman I'm hiring. To watch the place.

VIOLET: Oh! You're hiring women's now the thing. I thought you meant the other woman.

BEVERLY: What other woman?

VIOLET: (*Pause; then, ugly.*) Huh?!

BEVERLY: I hope to hire her to cook and clean and take you to the clinic and to the—

VIOLET: (*Attempting to over-articulate.*) In the int'rest of . . . civil action . . . your par-tic-u-lars ways of speak-king, I thought you meant you had thought a whoa-man to be HIRED!

BEVERLY: I don't understand you.

VIOLET: (*Suddenly winsome, to Johnna.*) Hello.

JOHNNA: Hello.

By . . . anonymous: Lines from John Berryman's poem "The Curse." The preceding lines are "Only the idiot and the dead / Stand by, while who were young before / Wage insolent and guilty war."

VIOLET: I'm sorry. (*Curtsies.*) Like this.

JOHNNA: Yes, ma'am.

VIOLET: I'm Violet. What's your name?

JOHNNA: Johnna.

VIOLET: You're very pretty.

JOHNNA: Thank you.

VIOLET: Are you an Indian?

JOHNNA: Yes, ma'am.

VIOLET: What kind?

JOHNNA: Cheyenne.

VIOLET: Do you think I'm pretty?

JOHNNA: Yes, ma'am.

VIOLET: (*Curtsies again.*) Like . . . this? (*Curtsies again.*) Like this . . . (*Curtsies lower, stumbles, catches herself.*)

BEVERLY: Careful.

VIOLET: (*Still to Johnna.*) You're the house now. I'm sorry, I . . . I took some medicine for my musssss . . . muscular.

BEVERLY: Why don't you go back to bed, sweetheart?

VIOLET: Why don't you go fuck a fucking sow's ass?

BEVERLY: All right.

VIOLET: (*To Johnna.*) I'm sorry. I'll be sickly sweet. I'm soooooooooooo sweet. In-el-abrially sweet. (*She stubs out her cigarette on Beverly's desk ashtray . . . stares at Johnna as if she might say something else . . . then suddenly exits.*)

BEVERLY: I think I mentioned on the phone that Dr. Burke recommended you. He feels you're qualified to handle the needs of our household.

JOHNNA: I have a year toward my nursing certificate at Tulsa Community College, but I had to drop out when Daddy died. And I saw my mom and grandma through bad times.

BEVERLY: Dr. Burke says you've been struggling for work.

JOHNNA: I've been cleaning houses and babysitting.

BEVERLY: He did tell you we wanted a live-in.

JOHNNA: Yes, sir.

BEVERLY: We keep unusual hours here. Try not to differentiate between night and day. I doubt you'll be able to maintain any sort of a healthy routine.

JOHNNA: I need the work.

BEVERLY: The work itself . . . pretty mundane. I myself require very little personal attention. Thrive without it, in fact, sort of a human cactus. My *wife* has been diagnosed with a touch of cancer, so she'll need to be driven to Tulsa for her final chemotherapy treatments. You're welcome to use that American-made behemoth parked in the carport. You're welcome to make use of anything, everything, all this garbage we've acquired, our life's work. If you're going to live here, I want you to live here. You understand?

JOHNNA: Yes, sir.

BEVERLY: Please call me Beverly. Do you have any questions?

JOHNNA: What kind of cancer?

BEVERLY: I didn't say? My God, I nearly neglected the punch line: *mouth* cancer.

JOHNNA: What pills does she take?

BEVERLY: Valium. Vicodin. Darvon, Darvocet. Percodan, Percocet. Xanax for fun. OxyContin in a pinch. Some Black Mollies once, just to make sure I was still paying attention. And of course Dilaudid. I shouldn't forget Dilaudid. (*Beverly studies her. Finishes his drink.*)

My wife. Violet. Violet, my wife, doesn't believe she needs treatment for her habit. She has been down that road once before, and came out of it clean as a whistle . . . then chose for herself this reality instead.

You were about to ask why she isn't currently seeking treatment. Weren't you?

JOHNNA: No, sir.

BEVERLY: Oh, good, that relieves me. Now hold on a second . . . (*Beverly wobbles to his feet unsteadily, as much from weariness as drink, explores his bookshelf.*) My last refuge, my books: simple pleasures, like finding wild onions by the side of a road, or requited love. (*He takes a book from his bookshelf and gives it to Johnna.*)

JOHNNA: T. S. Eliot.

BEVERLY: Read it or not. It isn't a job requirement. That's just for your enjoyment. Feel free to read any of my books.

Here we go round the prickly pear
Prickly pear prickly pear
Here we go round the prickly pear . . .°

ACT ONE • Scene 1

Ivy, Mattie Fae and Charlie are in the living room. Mattie Fae drinks a glass of scotch. Charlie has the TV tuned to a baseball game, the sound low, and he keeps an eye on the score as he nurses a bottle of beer.

Elsewhere in the house: Violet talks on the telephone in the sitting room; Johnna cooks and cleans in the kitchen.

MATTIE FAE: Beverly's done this before.

IVY: I know.

MATTIE FAE: You remember he used to just take off, no call, nothing. You remember, Charlie?

CHARLIE: They've always had trouble

MATTIE FAE: One time, this one time, he just up and left without a word, I told Vi, I said, "You pack that son-of-a-bitch's bags and have them waiting for him on the *front porch*." And you know I always liked your father.

Here we go . . . prickly pear: These are lines from T. S. Eliot's poem "The Hollow Men." A few lines later the poem ends with "This is the way the world ends / Not with a bang, but a whimper."

IVY: I know.

MATTIE FAE: No, I always liked your father, you know that. I introduced Vi and Bev, for God's sake.

CHARLIE: You did not introduce them.

MATTIE FAE: The hell I didn't.

CHARLIE: You had a date with him and stood him up and sent your sister instead.

MATTIE FAE: *That's an introduction.* That's what an introduction is.

CHARLIE: I just don't think it's accurate to say—

MATTIE FAE: He was too old for me and anyway, Violet? "Shrinking Violet?" She couldn't meet a man on her own.

CHARLIE: No one ever called her "Shrinking Violet"—

MATTIE FAE: And Charlie and your father always got on real well. They used to go on fishing trips together.

IVY: I know.

MATTIE FAE: But when Beverly just took off like that, without saying anything, without a note even, my first obligation was to look after my sister, don'tcha know.

CHARLIE: You don't have an obligation to do anything.

MATTIE FAE: I have an obligation to look after my sister.

CHARLIE: You're not obliged to get involved in somebody else's marriage.

MATTIE FAE: Not any marriage, but when they're married to my big sister, I sure as hell do. Ivy has sisters, she knows what I mean. I told her, I said, "Vi, you pack that son-of-a-bitch's bags and put them on the front porch. You take all those goddamn books he's so fond of and you make a big pile in the front yard and you have yourself a bonfire. Take all his papers too, just everything and throw it in—"

CHARLIE: You don't burn a man's books.

MATTIE FAE: Will you stop? You keep contradicting—

CHARLIE: The man's books didn't do anything. His possessions aren't responsible.

MATTIE FAE: Well, she didn't do it, so it doesn't make any—

CHARLIE: Of course she didn't do it.

MATTIE FAE: Let me tell you something, Charlie Aiken: You ever get any ideas about just up and taking off, you better believe—

CHARLIE: I'm not going anywhere—

MATTIE FAE: I'm saying if you did, you better believe I'm gonna give you about three days to get your head straight and then it's all going up in a blaze of glory.

CHARLIE: I'm not going anywhere!

MATTIE FAE: If you did!

CHARLIE: I'm not!

MATTIE FAE: Not that Charlie has any books lying around. I don't think I've ever seen Charlie read a book in my life.

CHARLIE: Is that a criticism? Does that bother you?

MATTIE FAE: Well, I haven't. What's the last book you read?

CHARLIE: Goddamn it—

MATTIE FAE: Just tell me the last book you read.

CHARLIE: Beverly was a teacher; teachers read books. I'm in the upholstery business; people in the upholstery business—

MATTIE FAE: You can't tell me the last book you read.

CHARLIE: This girl is concerned about her daddy's whereabouts. She doesn't need to sit here and listen to us—

MATTIE FAE: I think we're all concerned about Beverly.

CHARLIE: Then what the hell are you needling me for?

MATTIE FAE: He came back though, you know, and they worked things out, and he'll come back again, I know he will.

IVY: I think this time is different.

MATTIE FAE: I think so too.

CHARLIE: Why?

MATTIE FAE: Because back then—

CHARLIE: I'm not asking you. (*To Ivy.*) Why do you think this time is different?

IVY: Because I think back then they were trying.

MATTIE FAE: (*To Charlie.*) Which is what I was gonna say. (*To Ivy.*) Beverly was a very complicated man.

IVY: I know.

CHARLIE: Stop saying "was."

MATTIE FAE: Well, he was. He is, very complicated.

CHARLIE: But in a kind-y quiet way.

IVY: Kind of like Charles.

CHARLIE: Yes, like Little Charles. Exactly—

MATTIE FAE: Oh. He's nothing like Little Charles.

CHARLIE: She just means in their sort of quiet complicated ways—

MATTIE FAE: Little Charles isn't complicated.

CHARLIE: I think—

MATTIE FAE: No, Little Charles isn't complicated, he's just unemployed.

CHARLIE: He's an observer.

MATTIE FAE: All he observes is the television.

CHARLIE: So you can't even see Ivy's point?

MATTIE FAE: No.

CHARLIE: That Little Charles and Beverly share some kind of . . . complication.

MATTIE FAE: Honey, you have to be smart to be complicated.

CHARLIE: That's our boy. Are you saying our boy isn't smart?

MATTIE FAE: Yes, that's what I'm saying.

CHARLIE: What's the matter with you? (*To Ivy.*) Your cousin is very smart.

MATTIE FAE: I'm sweating. Are you sweating?

CHARLIE: Hell, yes, I'm sweating, it's ninety degrees in here.

MATTIE FAE: Feel my back.

CHARLIE: I don't want to feel your back.

MATTIE FAE: Feel it. Sweat is just dripping down my back.

CHARLIE: I believe you.

MATTIE FAE: Feel it.

CHARLIE: No.

MATTIE FAE: Come on, put your hand here—

CHARLIE: Goddamn it—

MATTIE FAE: Sweat's just dripping—

CHARLIE: Ivy. Let me ask you something. When did this start? This business with the shades, taping the shades?

IVY: That's been a couple of years now.

MATTIE FAE: My gosh, has it been that long since we've been here?

CHARLIE: Do you know its purpose?

MATTIE FAE: You can't tell if it's night or day.

IVY: I think that's the purpose.

CHARLIE: Well, I don't know, but I don't think that's healthy.

MATTIE FAE: It's not. You need sunlight.

CHARLIE: Do you know which one of them decided on this?

IVY: I can't really see Dad taking the initiative.

CHARLIE: No, I suppose not. I don't know about you, but I find this whole setup depressing. Y'know, a person's *environment* . . . (*Points to the stereo.*) And what the hell, is that an Eric Clapton album? Vi's a *Clapton fan?* (*Mattie Fae starts to peel the tape from one of the shades.*) Don't do that.

MATTIE FAE: The body needs sunlight.

CHARLIE: It's nighttime. And this isn't your place, you can't come into somebody else's home and start changing—

MATTIE FAE: Do you believe we haven't been here in two years? (*Violet enters.*)

VIOLET: He said they checked the hospitals but no Beverly.

MATTIE FAE: This is the highway patrol?

VIOLET: No, not the highway patrol, the sheriff, the Gilbeau boy.

MATTIE FAE: Gilbeau. Don't tell me C. J. Gilbeau is the sheriff here now.

VIOLET: Not C. J., his boy Deon.

MATTIE FAE: I was gonna say—

VIOLET: He went to school with the girls, Deon did. Was he in your class, Ivy?

IVY: Barbara's class, I think.

MATTIE FAE: Is that right?

CHARLIE: Who's this now?

MATTIE FAE: C. J. Gilbeau was a boy we grew up with. Mean little son-of-a-bitch, juvenile delinquent—

VIOLET: His boy Deon's the sheriff now.

MATTIE FAE: C. J. was the preacher's son and you know—

CHARLIE: Say no more.

MATTIE FAE: —and you *know* how they are.

VIOLET: You remember he went to the penitentiary.

MATTIE FAE: Yes, I remember that, for killing what was it?

VIOLET: A boxer.

MATTIE FAE: Right, for killing this man's boxer dog.

VIOLET: His boy Deon's the sheriff. I sent you that subscription to the *Pawhuska Journal-Capital*. Don't you read it?

MATTIE FAE: No, I don't read it.

VIOLET: So you Tulsa big shots could keep up with us small-town folks.

MATTIE FAE: No, I don't read it.

VIOLET: Well, if you read it you'd know that his boy Deon is the sheriff here now.

IVY: What hospitals did they check?

VIOLET: He rattled off a bunch of them.

IVY: What else did he say?

VIOLET: The boat's missing. (*Pause.*)

IVY: Mom?

VIOLET: He sent a patrolman out to the dock to check if anybody had seen him and Beverly's pontoon boat is gone.

MATTIE FAE: Oh, no.

VIOLET: He said they've had a couple of boats stolen in the last little while so he didn't think it proved anything, but he was worried about it. (*Violet starts to ascend the stairs.*)

CHARLIE: Vi, you think there's a chance Bev loaded that boat onto his trailer and took it out of there? I mean if he was going somewhere's else.

MATTIE FAE: Trailer's out by the shed, I saw it when we pulled up. (*Violet exits. Ivy follows her. Johnna enters, occupied with housework. Charlie holds up his empty beer bottle.*)

CHARLIE: 'Scuse me, dear . . . could I trouble you for another beer?

MATTIE FAE: Goddamn it, she's not a waitress.

CHARLIE: I know that.

MATTIE FAE: Then get your own beer. (*Johnna crosses, takes the empty . . .*)

JOHNNA: I'll get it. (. . . *and goes.*)

MATTIE FAE: I don't believe you. Watchin' the baseball game and drinkin' beers. Don't you have any sense of what's going on around you? This situation is fraught.

CHARLIE: Am I supposed to sit here like a statue? You're drinking whiskey.

MATTIE FAE: I'm having a cocktail.

CHARLIE: You're drinking straight whiskey.

MATTIE FAE: Just . . . show a little class.

CHARLIE: I don't think we need to sit here crying in the dark.

MATTIE FAE: Oh well, since you got everything all figured out, let's party down.

CHARLIE: Mattie Fae—

MATTIE FAE: Get that Indian gal to whip us up some cheese Coneys and let's call a few friends.

CHARLIE: Oooh, a cheese Coney sounds good.

MATTIE FAE: It does, doesn't it? You smell something cooking?

CHARLIE: Yeah.

MATTIE FAE: Come with me to the kitchen, let's see what it is.

CHARLIE: What do you need me for? I've got the Royals on.

MATTIE FAE: Just come with me. (*She takes his hand, pulls him from the couch.*)

CHARLIE: That's not good news about that boat. (*As Charlie follows Mattie Fae to the kitchen, and intercepts his beer from Johnna, the lights crossfade to Violet and Ivy on the second-floor landing. During the following, they descend the stairs and enter the dining room.*)

VIOLET: Did you call Barb?

IVY: Yes.

VIOLET: When'd you call her?

IVY: This morning.

VIOLET: What'd she say?

IVY: She's on her way.

VIOLET: How's she getting here?

IVY: She and Bill are coming.

VIOLET: Is she driving?

IVY: I doubt it.

VIOLET: Why?

IVY: Boulder's a long way.

VIOLET: Is she bringing Jean?

IVY: I don't know.

VIOLET: When did she say she'd be here?

IVY: She didn't say. She just said she was on her way.

VIOLET: What'd you tell her?

IVY: I told her Dad was missing.

VIOLET: That's all.

IVY: Is there anything else?

VIOLET: Did you tell her how long he'd been missing?

IVY: Five days.

VIOLET: Did you tell her that?

IVY: I think so.

VIOLET: What did she say?

IVY: She said she was on her way.

VIOLET: Goddamn it, Ivy, what did she *say?* Was she irritated? Was she amused? Tell me what she said.

IVY: She said she was on her way.

VIOLET: You're hopeless. (*Takes a pill.*) Goddamn your father for putting me through this. For leaving me to handle this. You seen that office of his, all that paperwork, that mess? I can't make heads or tails of it. He hired this Indian a week ago to look after the place for some goddamn reason and now I have a stranger in my house. I don't know what to say to that girl. What's her name?

IVY: Johnna.

VIOLET: He's always paid the bills and made the phone calls and now suddenly I'm supposed to handle it? You know this house is falling apart, something about the basement or the sump pump or the foundation. I don't know anything about it. I can't do all this by myself.

IVY: I called Karen.

VIOLET: What did she say?

IVY: She said she'd try to get here.

VIOLET: She'll be a big fat help, just like you. (*Takes another pill.*) I need Barb.

IVY: I don't know what Barb's going to be able to do.

VIOLET: What did you do to your hair?

IVY: I had it straightened.

VIOLET: You had it straightened. Why would anybody do that?

IVY: I don't know.

VIOLET: Why did *you* do it?

IVY: I just wanted a change.

VIOLET: You're a pretty girl. You're the prettiest of my three girls, but you always look like such a schlub. Why don't you wear any makeup?

IVY: Do I need makeup?

VIOLET: All women need makeup. Don't let anybody tell you different. The only woman who was pretty enough to go without makeup was Elizabeth Taylor and she wore a *ton*. Sit up straight.

IVY: Mom.

VIOLET: Your shoulders are slumped and your hair's all straight and you don't wear makeup. You look like a lesbian. You're a pretty enough girl, you could get a decent man if you spruced up. A bit, that's all I'm saying.

IVY: I'm not looking for a man.

VIOLET: You should be. Everybody needs somebody.

IVY: I'm not looking for a man.

VIOLET: Listen, there are a lot of losers out there, don't think I don't know it. But just because you got a bad one doesn't mean—

IVY: Barry wasn't a loser.

VIOLET: Barry was an asshole. And I warned you from the start, didn't I? First time you brought him over here in his ridiculous little electric car, with that stupid orange beard and that turban.

IVY: It wasn't a turban—

VIOLET: I just don't understand some of the choices you make. You're forty-three years old—

IVY: Forty-four.

VIOLET: Forty-four years old. Maybe you're past the point of having children, and that's all right if you don't want them, but aren't you interested in finding a husband?

IVY: A husband. In *Pawhuska*.

VIOLET: You don't meet people where you live, you meet them where you work. You work at a college. Don't tell me there aren't people coming through the door of that library every day.

IVY: You want me to marry a student, some eighteen-year-old boy from one of these hick towns?

VIOLET: They still have teachers on the Tulsa campus, don't they? They did when your father taught there—

IVY: Barry was a teacher at TU.

VIOLET: Yeah, "Environmental Studies." Barry was a *loser*.

IVY: He wasn't a loser—

VIOLET: He dumped you, didn't he? To my mind, that makes him—

IVY: He did not dump me. It just didn't work out between us.

VIOLET: All right, yes, dear, I'm sorry. I'll get it straight. I'm sorry. But maybe it would've worked out between you if you'd worn some makeup. (*Takes another pill.*) How many was that?

IVY: I wasn't counting. (*Violet takes another pill.*) Is your mouth burning?

VIOLET: Like a son-of-a-bitch. My tongue is on fire.

IVY: Are you supposed to be smoking?

VIOLET: Is anybody supposed to smoke?

IVY: You have cancer of the mouth.

VIOLET: Ivy, I have enough to worry about right this minute without you getting on me about my smoking.

IVY: I'm not getting on you.

VIOLET: Just leave it alone.

IVY: Are you scared?

VIOLET: 'Course I'm scared. And you are a comfort, sweetheart. Thank God one of my girls stayed close to home. My generation, families stayed together.

IVY: That was a different time.

VIOLET: No kidding. Did you call Mattie Fae?

IVY: Aunt Mattie Fae's here.

VIOLET: I know that, dummy, did *you* call her?

IVY: I thought you called her.

VIOLET: I guess I did. I don't remember.

IVY: You've got a lot on your mind.

VIOLET: She means to come in here and tell *me* what's what.

IVY: I don't know how Uncle Charlie puts up with it.

VIOLET: He smokes a lot of grass.

IVY: He does?

VIOLET: He smokes a *lot* of grass. (*They laugh.*)

IVY: "Grass"? You say "grass"?

VIOLET: What do you call it?

IVY: Hey, are you into Clapton now?

VIOLET: What?

IVY: Eric Clapton, you have an Eric Clapton album.

VIOLET: I've had it forever.

IVY: I've never seen it.

VIOLET: I like it. It's got a good beat. I'm not old, you know. (*Lights down on the dining room and up on the front porch as Barbara and Bill arrive, carrying suitcases. Violet and Ivy exit and, during the following, Mattie Fae and Charlie enter from the kitchen and cross to the dining room with plates of hot apple pie.*)

BARBARA: What's Jean doing?

BILL: Smoking.

BARBARA: I wish you wouldn't encourage that.

BILL: I haven't encouraged anything.

BARBARA: I don't know, there's just something a little funny about the way you say, "smoking," like you admire her for getting hooked at fourteen.

BILL: Are you ready for this?

BARBARA: No. No way.

BILL: Well. Take a second. (*They stand, taking in the night, breathing the air.*)

BARBARA: Goddamn, it's hot.

BILL: Wimp.

BARBARA: I know it. Colorado spoiled me.

BILL: That's one of the reasons we got out of here.

BARBARA: No, it's not.

BILL: You suppose your mom's turned on the air conditioner?

BARBARA: Are you kidding? Remember the parakeets?

BILL: The parakeets.

BARBARA: I didn't tell you about the parakeets? She got a parakeet, for some insane reason, and the little fucker croaked after about two days. So she went to the pet store and raised hell and they gave her another parakeet. That one died after just one day. So she went back and they gave her a third parakeet and that one

died, too. So the chick from the pet store came out here to see just what in hell this serial parakeet killer was doing to bump off these birds.

BILL: And?

BARBARA: The heat. It was too hot. They were dying from the heat.

BILL: Jesus.

BARBARA: These are tropical birds, all right? They live in the fucking tropics. (*Beat. She looks out.*) What were these people thinking?

BILL: What people?

BARBARA: The jokers who settled this place. The Germans and the Dutch and the Irish. Who was the asshole who saw this flat hot nothing and planted his flag? I mean, we fucked the Indians for *this*?

BILL: Well, genocide always seems like such a good idea *at the time.*

BARBARA: Right, you need a little hindsight.

BILL: Anyway, if you want me to explain the creepy character of the Midwest, you're asking the wrong

BARBARA: Hey. Please. This is not the Midwest. All right? *Michigan* is the Midwest, God knows why. This is the Plains: a state of mind, right, some spiritual affliction, like the Blues.

BILL: "Are you okay?" "I'm fine. Just got the Plains." (*They laugh. He reaches up and touches her neck tenderly.*)

BARBARA: Don't. (*She pulls away. They look away from one another, an uncomfortable moment. Regarding Jean.*) What, is she smoking a fucking cigar?

BILL: She's coming. (*Jean arrives on the front porch, carrying a suitcase.*) You ready, kiddo?

JEAN: Yeah, sure.

BARBARA: All right. (*Gives Jean a quick kiss.*) You're precious. I'm having a hot flash. All right . . . here goes. (*Lights up on the entryway as Barbara, Bill and Jean enter.*) Mom?! (*Lights up on the dining room. Mattie Fae and Charlie travel from the dining room to the entryway. The following salutations are quick and overlapping, and they range from forte [Mattie Fae] to piano [Ivy].*)

MATTIE FAE: Oh my God,   BARBARA: Hi, Aunt Mattie
Barbara!—   Fae —

MATTIE FAE: You give me some sugar! (*Barbara and Mattie Fae hug. Over Barbara's shoulder.*) Hi, Bill! Look how skinny you are!

BILL: Hi, Mattie Fae.

MATTIE FAE: Oh my gosh, will you look at this one? Come here and give your Aunt Mattie Fae some sugar! (*Mattie Fae and Jean hug. Bill and Charlie shake hands.*)

BILL: Hi, Charlie.

CHARLIE: 'Lo, Bill. Man, you have dropped some weight, haven't you?

MATTIE FAE: (*Still to Jean.*) My gosh, you're so big! And look at your big boobs! They're so big! Last time I saw you, you looked just like a little boy! (*Barbara and Charlie hug.*)

CHARLIE: Hello, sweetheart.

BARBARA: Good to see you, Uncle Charlie.

CHARLIE: You too.

MATTIE FAE: Oh, I can't get over that one, she's just too much. Come here, Bill, and give me some sugar! (*Charlie mushes Jean's shoulder, kisses her on the temple.*)

CHARLIE: Lovely to see you, dear.

JEAN: Yeah, same here.

CHARLIE: (*Gently mocking.*) Same here, same here. (*Violet appears on the stairway, followed by Ivy. Violet bursts into tears, rushes to Barbara, clenches her. Ivy watches from the stairs.*)

BARBARA: It's okay, Mom. I'm here, I'm here. (*Violet weeps. The others are awkwardly respectful of the moment.*) Shhh, it's okay, I'm here.

BILL: (*To Charlie.*) No word then?

CHARLIE: No.   MATTIE FAE: No, huh-uh.

BARBARA: It's okay, Mom.

VIOLET: What am I going to do? What am I going to do?

BARBARA: Well, we can talk about that. Did you see Bill and Jean? (*Violet takes them in, disoriented.*)

VIOLET: Yes. Hi, Bill.

BILL: Hello, Violet. (*Violet and Bill kiss.*) I'm sorry you're going through this. (*Violet holds Bill, cries.*)

VIOLET: I'm just so scared. (*Mattie Fae reaches out, strokes Violet's back.*)

MATTIE FAE: Of course you are, poor thing.

VIOLET: You're too thin.

BILL: Hardly.

VIOLET: Yes, you are. (*Violet sees Jean.*) Well, look at you.

MATTIE FAE: I know, isn't she something else? Look at her boobs!

JEAN: O-kay, we've all stared at my tits now.

MATTIE FAE: They're just so darn big.

CHARLIE: Mattie Fae . . . (*Violet hugs Jean.*)

VIOLET: You're just the prettiest thing. Thank you for coming to see me.

JEAN: No problem.

BARBARA: Ivy, I didn't see you up there.

IVY: (*Descending the stairs.*) It looked crowded.

BARBARA: God, you look good. Doesn't she look good, Bill?

BILL: Yes, she does.

BARBARA: I love your hair, that looks great.

VIOLET: She had it straightened.

BARBARA: I know, it looks great. (*Ivy and Jean wave.*)

IVY: Hi, Jean.

JEAN: Hi. (*Violet pulls Barbara into the living room. The others follow.*)

VIOLET: Barbara, or Bill, it doesn't matter, I need you to go through Beverly's things and help me with some of this paperwork.

BARBARA: Well . . . we can   IVY: I was going to help
do that, Mom, we're   with that—
here for a while.

VIOLET: No, now that desk of his is such a mess and I get confused—

BILL: I'll take care of it, Violet—

BARBARA: (*To Charlie.*) Which room are you in?

MATTIE FAE: We're headed back tonight.

VIOLET: You're going back?

MATTIE FAE: We have to, Vi, we left in such a rush we didn't get anyone to take care of those damn dogs.

VIOLET: You want to drive that hour and a half tonight?

MATTIE FAE: Not the way Charlie drives. Anyway, I know you want to spend some time with these girls.

VIOLET: Can't you call someone about the dogs? Or how about Little Charles, can't he take care of them?

CHARLIE: Well, yeah, I guess he could—

MATTIE FAE: No, he can't, either. We have to get back.

CHARLIE: Maybe we should call him, Mattie Fae—

MATTIE FAE: We talked about this.

CHARLIE: I know, but—

MATTIE FAE: (*To Violet.*) You've got all these people here and not enough beds—

VIOLET: You can stay at Ivy's place.

IVY: (*Beat.*) Yeah, sure. I've got room.

MATTIE FAE: (*To Charlie.*) We talked about this.

BARBARA: You all can figure that out on your own. So, Mom? Jean can stay in the attic?

VIOLET: No, that's where what's-her-name lives.

IVY: Johnna.

BARBARA: Who's Johnna?

VIOLET: She's the Indian who lives in my attic.

BARBARA: She's the what? (*Johnna enters.*)

JOHNNA: Hi, I'm Johnna. Welcome home.

Scene 2

Barbara, Bill and Violet are in the dining room with coffee and pie. Violet's pills are starting to kick in.

Elsewhere in the house: Johnna reads a book in her attic bedroom; Jean listens to an iPod on the second-floor landing.

VIOLET: Saturday. Saturday morning. That girl, the Indian girl made us biscuits and gravy. We ate some, we . . . he walked out the door, that door right there. And that was it.

BARBARA: That was the last time you saw him.

VIOLET: I went to bed Saturday night and got up Sunday morning . . . still no Beverly. I didn't make much of it, thought he'd gone out on a bender.

BARBARA: Why would he do that? Not like he couldn't drink at home. Unless you were riding his ass.

VIOLET: I never said anything to him about his drinking, never got on him about it.

BARBARA: Really.

VIOLET: Barbara, I swear. He could drink himself into obliv-uh, obliv-en-em . . .

BARBARA: Oblivion.

BILL: So Sunday, still no sign of him . . .

VIOLET: Yes, Sunday, no sign. I started getting worried, don'tcha know, and that's when I got so worked up about that safety deposit box. We kept an awful lot of cash in that box, some jewelry, expensive jewelry.

I had a diamond ring in that box appraised at over seven thousand dollars—

BARBARA: Wait, wait, wait, I'm missing something, why do you care about the safety deposit box?

VIOLET: Well, I know what you'll say about this, but. Your father and I had a urge-ment—arrangement. If something were to ever happen to one of us, the other one would go empty that safety deposit box.

BARBARA: Be*cause* . . .

BILL: It gets rolled into the estate, then goes to *probate*.

VIOLET: Right, that's right—

BARBARA: You're such a fucking cynic.

VIOLET: I knew you would *disapprove*—

BARBARA: (*Impatient.*) Okay, fine, so what about the safety deposit box?—

VIOLET: I had to wait for the bank to open on Monday. And after I emptied that box, I called the police and reported him missing. Monday morning.

BARBARA: And you're just now calling me, today, on *Thursday*.

VIOLET: *I* didn't call you.

BARBARA: You had Ivy call me. *Five days later.*

VIOLET: I didn't want to worry you, honey—

BARBARA: *Jesus Christ.*

BILL: Vi, you sure there wasn't some event that triggered his leaving, some incident?

VIOLET: You mean like a fight.

BILL: Yes.

VIOLET: No. And we fought enough . . . you know . . . but no, he just left.

BARBARA: Maybe he just needed some time away from you.

VIOLET: That's nice of you to say.

BARBARA: Hey, that's no crime. Being married is hard.

BILL: Under the best of circumstances.

BARBARA: But nothing. Not, "See you later," or "I'm taking a walk." (*Violet shakes her head.*) Good old unfathomable Dad.

VIOLET: Oh. That man. What I first fell of with fell in love with, you know, was his mystery. I thought it was sexy as hell. You knew he was the smartest one in the room, knew if he'd just say something . . . knock you out. But he'd just stand there, little smile on his face . . . not say a word. Sexy.

BARBARA: Yeah, that "mystery" can cut both ways.

BILL: And you can't think of anything different or unusual, or—

VIOLET: He hired this woman. He didn't ask me, just hired this woman to come here and live in our house. Few days before he left.

BARBARA: You don't want her here.

VIOLET: I don't know what she's doing here. She's stranger in my house. There's an *Indian* in my house.

BILL: (*Laughing.*) You have some problem with Indians, Violet?

VIOLET: I don't know what to say to an Indian.

BARBARA: They're called Native Americans now, Mom.

VIOLET: *Who* calls them that? Who *makes* that decision?

BARBARA: It's what they like to be called.

VIOLET: They aren't any more native than me.

BARBARA: In fact, they are.

VIOLET: What's wrong with "Indian"?

BARBARA: Why is it so hard to just call people what they want?—

VIOLET: Let's just call the dinosaurs "Native Americans" while we're at it.

BARBARA: She may be an Indian, but she makes the best goddamn apple pie I ever ate in my life.

BILL: It is good, isn't it?

BARBARA: Oh, man—

VIOLET: A cook? So he hired a cook? It doesn't make any sense. We don't eat.

BARBARA: That sounds healthy.

VIOLET: We eat, cheese and saltines, or a ham sandwich. But I can't tell you the last time that stove, oh . . . turned on. Years.

BARBARA: And now you get biscuits and gravy. Kind of nice, huh?

VIOLET: Nice for you, now. But you'll be gone soon enough, never to return.

BARBARA: (*A warning.*) Mom.

VIOLET: When was the last time you were here?

BARBARA: Don't get started on that—

VIOLET: Really, I don't even remember.

BARBARA: I'm very dutiful, Mom, I call, I write, I send presents—

VIOLET: You do not *write*—

BARBARA: I send presents on birthdays and Mother's Day—

VIOLET: Because you're "dutiful."

BARBARA: Don't you quote me.

BILL: All right, now—

VIOLET: You're grown-up people, growed-ups. You go where you want—

BARBARA: I have a lot of obligations, I have a daughter starting high school in a couple of—

VIOLET: That right? Last time I saw her she's grade school—

BARBARA: I won't talk about this—

VIOLET: I don't care about you two, really. I'd just like to see my granddaughter every now and again.

BARBARA: Well, you're seeing her now.

VIOLET: But your father. You broke his heart when you moved away.

BARBARA: That is wildly unfair.

BILL: Am I going to have to separate you two?

VIOLET: You know you were Beverly's favorite; don't pretend you don't know that.

BARBARA: I don't *want* to know that. I'd prefer to think my parents loved all their children equally.

VIOLET: I'm sure you'd prefer to think that Santy Claus brought you presents at Christmas, too, but it just isn't so. If you'd had more than one child, you'd realize a parent always has favorites. Mattie Fae was my mother's favorite. Big deal. I got used to it. You were your daddy's favorite.

BARBARA: Great. Thanks. (*Pause.*)

VIOLET: Broke his heart.

BARBARA: What was I supposed to do?! Colorado offered Bill twice the money he was making at TU—

BILL: Why are you even getting into this?

BARBARA: —and they were willing to hire me, too. Daddy knew we had to take those jobs. You think he wouldn't have jumped at the chance Bill got?

VIOLET: Now you're wrong there. You never would've gotten Beverly Weston out of Oklahoma. And don't think he didn't have his opportunities, either, after *Meadowlark* came out.

BILL: I'm sure.

VIOLET: After *Meadowlark* was published, he got offers from everywhere in the country, lots better places than Colorado.

BARBARA: Now you want to knock Colorado.

VIOLET: It's not hard to do.

BILL: Barbara, Jesus—

BARBARA: Daddy's book came out forty years ago. Academia's very different now, it's extremely competitive.

VIOLET: Please, tell me all about *academia*.

BARBARA: Daddy gave me his blessing, and I didn't even ask for it.

VIOLET: 'Swhat he told *you*.

BARBARA: Now you're going to tell me the *true* story, some terrible shit Daddy said behind my back?

BILL: Hey, enough. Everybody's a little on edge—

VIOLET: Beverly didn't say terrible things behind your back—

BILL: Vi, come on—

VIOLET: He just told me he's disappointed in you because you settled.

BARBARA: Is that supposed to be a comment on Bill? Daddy never said anything like that to you—

VIOLET: Your father thought you had talent, as a writer.

BARBARA: If he thought that, and I doubt he did, he was wrong. Anyway, what difference does it make? It's my life. I can do what I want. So he was disappointed in me because I settled for a beautiful family and a teaching career, is that what you're saying? What a load of absolute horseshit.

VIOLET: Oh, horseshit, horseshit, let's all say horseshit. Say horseshit, Bill.

BILL: Horseshit. (*Bill exits to the kitchen.*)

BARBARA: Are you high?

VIOLET: No.

BARBARA: No, are you high? I mean literally. Are you taking something?

VIOLET: A muscle relaxer.

BARBARA: Listen to me: I will not go through this with you again.

VIOLET: Go through what?

BARBARA: These fucking pills.

VIOLET: They're muscle relaxers—

BARBARA: I will not do this again.

VIOLET: I don't know what you're talking about.

BARBARA: The psych ward? Calls at three A.M. about people in your backyard?

VIOLET: You're so much drama—

BARBARA: The police, all the rest of it? You *do* know what I'm talking about. You spent a goddamn fortune on these fucking pills—

VIOLET: Stop yelling at me!

BARBARA: —and then you spent another fortune getting off them.

VIOLET: It's not the same thing, I didn't have a reason.

BARBARA: So now it's okay to get hooked because you have a reason.

VIOLET: I'm not hooked on anything.

BARBARA: I don't know if you are or not, I'm just saying I won't go—

VIOLET: I'm not. I'm in pain.

BARBARA: Because of your mouth.

VIOLET: Yes, because my mouth burns from the chemotheeeahh.

BARBARA: Are you in a lot of pain?

VIOLET: (*Starting to cry.*) Yes, I'm in pain. I have got . . . gotten cancer. In my mouth. And it burns like a . . . bullshit. And Beverly's disappeared and you're yelling at me.

BARBARA: I'm not yelling at you. (*Bill returns.*)

VIOLET: You couldn't come home when I got cancer but as soon as Beverly disappeared you rushed back—

BARBARA: I'm sorry, I . . . you're right. I'm sorry. (*Violet cries. Barbara kneels in front of her, takes her hand.*) You know where I think he is? I think he got some whiskey . . . a carton of cigarettes, couple of good spy novels . . . aannnd I think he got out on the boat, steered it to a nice spot, somewhere in the shade, close to shore . . . and he's fishing, and reading, and drinking, and if the mood strikes him, maybe even writing a little. I think he's safe. And I think he'll walk through that door . . . any time. (*Lights down on the dining room, and up on the attic, where Johnna is reading. Jean has put away her iPod and now ascends the stairs.*)

JEAN: Hi.

JOHNNA: Hello.

JEAN: Am I bugging you?

JOHNNA: No, do you need something?

JEAN: No, I thought maybe you'd like to smoke a bowl with me?

JOHNNA: No, thank you.

JEAN: Okay. I didn't know. (*Jean stands, looking at her.*) Am I bugging you?

JOHNNA: No, huh-uh.

JEAN: Okay. Do you mind if I smoke a bowl?

JOHNNA: I. No, I—

JEAN: 'Cause there's no place I can go. Y'know, I'm staying right by Grandma's room, and if I go outside, they're gonna wonder—

JOHNNA: Right—

JEAN: Mom and Dad don't mind. You won't get into trouble or anything.

JOHNNA: Okay.

JEAN: Okay. You sure? (*Johnna nods. From her pocket, Jean takes a small glass pipe and a clear cigarette wrapper holding a bud of marijuana. She fixes the pipe.*) I say they don't mind. If they knew I stuck this bud under the cap of Dad's deodorant before our flight and then sat there sweating like in that movie *Maria Full of Grace*. Did you see that?

JOHNNA: I don't think so.

JEAN: I just mean they don't mind that I smoke pot. Dad doesn't. Mom kind of does. She thinks it's bad for me. I think the real reason it bugs her is 'cause Dad smokes pot, too, and she wishes he didn't. Dad's much cooler than Mom, really. Well, that's not true. He's just cooler in that way, I guess. (*Jean smokes. She offers the smoldering pipe to Johnna. Holding her breath.*) You sure?

JOHNNA: Yes. No. I'm fine.

JEAN: No, he's really not cooler. (*Exhales smoke.*) He and Mom are separated right now.

JOHNNA: I'm sorry.

JEAN: He's fucking one of his students which is pretty uncool, if you ask me. Some people would think that's cool, like those dicks who teach with him in the Humanities Department because they're all fucking their students or wish they were fucking their students. "Lo-liii-ta." I mean, I don't care and all, he can fuck whoever he wants and he's a teacher and that's who teachers meet, students. He was just a turd the way he went about it and didn't give Mom a chance to respond or anything. What sucks now is that Mom's watching me like a hawk, like, she's afraid I'll have some post-divorce freak-out and become some heroin addict or shoot everybody at school. Or God forbid, lose my virginity. I don't know what it is about Dad splitting that put Mom on hymen patrol. Do you have a boyfriend?

JOHNNA: No, not these days.

JEAN: Me neither. I did go with this boy Josh for like almost a year but he was retarded. Are your parents still together?

JOHNNA: They passed away.

JEAN: Oh. I'm sorry.

JOHNNA: That's okay. Thank you.

JEAN: Oh, fuck, no, I'm really sorry, I feel fucking terrible now.

JOHNNA: It's okay.

JEAN: Oh God. Okay. Were you close with them?

JOHNNA: Yeah.

JEAN: Okay, another stupid question there, Jean, real good. Wow. Like: "Are you close to your parents?"

JOHNNA: Not everybody is.

JEAN: Yeah, right? So that's what I meant. Thanks. (*Johnna takes a framed photograph from her nightstand and hands it to Jean.*) Oh, wow. This is them.

JOHNNA: Mm-hm, their wedding picture.

JEAN: That's sweet. Their costumes are fantastic. (*Johnna smiles. Jean hands the photograph back, walks around the room.*) This is a great room. Very *Night of the Hunter*.° This used to be my room when we'd come and stay.

Night of the Hunter: A 1955 thriller—a parable of good and evil featuring a psychopathic preacher and two threatened children.

JOHNNA: I'm sorry.

JEAN: Oh. No, I . . . it doesn't matter to me. It's just a room. (*Beat.*) What are you reading?

JOHNNA: T. S. Eliot.

JEAN: That's cool.

JOHNNA: Your grandfather loaned it to me.

JEAN: Grandpa's weird. Mom freaked when she got the call from Aunt Ivy this morning, just like . . . freaked. I've never seen her like that. I couldn't get her to calm down. It was weird. I guess it's not weird that she freaked out, but like, to see your mom freak like that, like you've never seen before, y'know? And we're real close. Did you ever see your parents freak out?

JOHNNA: They weren't really the type.

JEAN: Yeah, right? So like imagine if you did just one day see them like totally lose their shit, just like, "Whoa." (*Jean reaches, touches a beaded pouch in the shape of a turtle hanging from Johnna's neck.*) I like your necklace.

JOHNNA: Thank you.

JEAN: Did you make that?

JOHNNA: My grandma.

JEAN: It's a turtle, right?

JOHNNA: Mm-hm.

JEAN: It feels like there's something in it.

JOHNNA: My umbilical cord. (*Jean recoils, wipes her hand on her pant leg. Johnna laughs.*)

JEAN: Ewww, are you serious?

JOHNNA: Yes.

JEAN: Oh my God. That's kind of gross.

JOHNNA: It's not unsanitary.

JEAN: Why would you do that, is it some kind of . . . ?

JOHNNA: It's a Cheyenne tradition.

JEAN: You're Cheyenne.

JOHNNA: Mm-hm.

JEAN: Like that movie *Powwow Highway*. Did you see that?

JOHNNA: When a Cheyenne baby is born, their umbilical cord is dried and sewn into this pouch. Turtles for girls, lizards for boys. And we wear it for the rest of our lives.

JEAN: Wow.

JOHNNA: Because if we lose it, our souls belong nowhere and after we die our souls will walk the Earth looking for where we belong.

JEAN: Don't say anything about Mom and Dad splitting up, okay? They're trying to play this kind of low-key.

Scene 3

Barbara unfolds the hide-a-bed in the living room. Bill enters from the study, carrying a thin hardback book.

BILL: Look what I found. Isn't that great?

BARBARA: We have copies.

BILL: I don't think I remember a hardback edition. I forgot there was ever a time they published poetry in

Start

hardback. Hell, I forgot there was ever a time they published poetry at all.

BARBARA: I'm not going to be able to sleep in this heat.

BILL: I wonder if this is worth something.

BARBARA: I'm sure it's not.

BILL: You never know. First edition, hardback, mint condition? Academy Fellowship, uh . . . Wallace Stevens° Award? That's right, isn't it?

BARBARA: Mm-hm.

BILL: This book was a big deal.

BARBARA: It wasn't that big a deal.

BILL: In those circles, it was.

BARBARA: Those are small circles.

BILL: (*Reads from the book.*) "Dedicated to my Violet." That's nice. Christ . . . I can't imagine the kind of pressure he must've felt after this came out. Probably every word he wrote after this, he had to be thinking, "What are they going to say about this? Are they going to compare it to *Meadowlark*?"

BARBARA: Did Jean go to bed?

BILL: She just turned out the light. You would think, though, at some point, you just say, "To hell with this," and you write something anyway and who cares what they say about it. I mean I don't know, myself—

BARBARA: Will you please shut up about that fucking book?!

BILL: What's the matter?

BARBARA: You are just dripping with envy over these . . . thirty poems my father wrote back in the fucking sixties, for God's sake. Don't you hear yourself?

BILL: You're mistaken. I have great admiration for these poems, not envy—

BARBARA: Reciting his list of awards—

BILL: I was merely talking about the value—

BARBARA: My father didn't write anymore for a lot of reasons, but critical opinion was not one of them, hard as that may be for you to believe. I know how important that stuff is to you.

BILL: What are you attacking me for? I haven't done anything.

BARBARA: I'm sure that's what you tell *Sissy*, too, so she can comfort you, reassure you: "No, Billy, you haven't done anything."

BILL: What does that have to do—why are you bringing that up?

BARBARA: They're all symptoms of your male menopause, whether it's you struggling with the "creative question," or screwing a girl who still wears a retainer.

BILL: All right, look. I'm here for you. Because I want to be with you, in a difficult time. But I'm not going to be held hostage in this room so you can attack me—

BARBARA: I'm sorry, I didn't mean to hold you hostage. You really should go then.

BILL: I'm not going anywhere. I flew to Oklahoma to be here with you and now you're stuck with me. And her name is Cindy.

BARBARA: I know her stupid name. At least do me the courtesy of recognizing when I'm demeaning you.

BILL: Violet really has a way of putting you in attack mode, you know it?

BARBARA: She doesn't have anything to do with it.

BILL: Don't you believe it. You feel such rage for her that you can't help dishing it my direction—

BARBARA: I swear to God, you psychoanalyze me right now, I skin you.

BILL: You may not agree with my methods, but you know I'm right.

BARBARA: Your "methods." Thank you, Doctor, but I actually don't need any help from my mother to feel rage.

BILL: You want to argue? Is that what you need to do? Well, pick a subject, all right, and let me know what it is, so I can have a fighting chance—

BARBARA: The subject is me! I am the subject, you narcissistic motherfucker! I am in pain! I need help! (*Jean enters from the second-floor hallway, sits on the stairway, listens.*)

BILL: I've copped to being a narcissist. We're the products of a narcissistic generation.

BARBARA: You can't do it, can you? You can't talk about me for two seconds—

BILL: You called me a narcissist! And when I try to talk about you, you accuse me of psychoanalyzing you—!

BARBARA: You do understand that it hurts, to go from sharing a bed with you for twenty-three years to sleeping by myself.

BILL: I'm here, now.

BARBARA: Men always say shit like that, as if the past and the future don't exist.

BILL: Can we not make this a gender discussion?

BARBARA: Do men really believe that here and now is enough? It's just horseshit, to avoid talking about the things they're afraid to say.

BILL: I'm not necessarily keen on the notion of saying things that would hurt you.

BARBARA: Like what?

BILL: Don't.

BARBARA: What? Say it. You must realize there's nothing you can say that would hurt me any more than I'm already hurting. The damage is done.

BILL: I think you're wrong. I think you get in this masochistic frame of mind that actually desires to be hurt more than—

BARBARA: *What?!*

BILL: Barbara, please, we have enough on our hands with your parents right now. Let's not revisit all this.

BARBARA: *Revisit*, when did we visit this to begin with? You pulled the rug out from under me. I still don't know what happened. Do I bore you, intimidate you, disgust you? Is this just about the pleasures of young flesh, teenage pussy? I really need to know.

Wallace Stevens Award: The award named for American poet Wallace Stevens (1879–1955) has been given every year since 1994, so technically Beverly Weston could not have won the prize.

BILL: You need to know *now?* You want to have this discussion with Beverly missing, and your mother as crazy as a loon, and our daughter twenty feet away? Do you really want to do this now?

BARBARA: No. You're right. I'll just hunker down for a cozy night's sleep. Next to my husband. (*She calmly gets under the covers.*)

BILL: This discussion deserves our care. And patience. We'll both be in a better frame of mind to talk about this once your father's come home.

BARBARA: My father's dead, Bill. (*She rolls onto her side, her back to Bill.*)

Scene 4

Red and blue police flashers bounce across the exterior of the house. Sheriff Gilbeau stands on the front porch. The rest of the house is dark.

Johnna, wearing a robe, quietly knocks on the stereo cabinet in the living room.

BARBARA: Mm . . . what?

JOHNNA: Excuse me . . . it's Johnna.

BARBARA: What?

JOHNNA: Excuse me—

BARBARA: What is it?

JOHNNA: The sheriff's here.

BILL: Turn on the light. (*Johnna turns on a lamp, temporarily blinding Bill and Barbara.*)

JOHNNA: The sheriff is here. (*Pause. This sinks in. Then Bill and Barbara scramble out of bed.*) Should I wake Mrs. Weston?

BARBARA: I don't know. Bill?

BILL: Yeah, you better get her up. (*Johnna leaves the room. Jean enters the second-floor landing, bleary-eyed, as Bill and Barbara scurry into clothes. Barbara climbs the stairs.*)

JEAN: What's going on?

BARBARA: The sheriff is here.

JEAN: What?

BARBARA: Go back to bed, honey.

JEAN: Why are the police here?

BARBARA: I don't know, sweetheart, please go back to bed. (*Offstage, an attempt to alert Violet. Johnna knocks on Violet's bedroom door.*)

JOHNNA: Mrs. Weston? (*Knocks again.*) Mrs. Weston. (*Barbara knocks loudly.*)

BARBARA: Mom? . . . Mom, wake up.

VIOLET: Huh?

BARBARA: Wake up, the sheriff's here.

VIOLET: Did you call them?

BARBARA: No.

VIOLET: I dig in call them.

BARBARA: Mom. The sheriff is here. You need to wake up and come downstairs.

VIOLET: Inna esther?

BARBARA: What?

VIOLET: Inna esther broke. 'N' pays me 'em . . . sturck . . . struck.

BILL: (*From the bottom of the stairs.*) Come on.

BARBARA: (*To Bill.*) What . . . ?

BILL: Come on. Leave her there. (*Barbara halfway descends the stairs, trailed by Johnna, as Bill admits Sheriff Gilbeau, shakes hands.*) Bill Fordham, Barbara's husband.

SHERIFF GILBEAU: Hello. Hi, Barbara.

BARBARA: Oh my God, I know you. Oh my God, Deon . . .

SHERIFF GILBEAU: Yes, ma'am. I'm afraid I have some bad news for you folks.

BARBARA: Okay—

SHERIFF GILBEAU: We found your father. He's dead.

BILL: Oh dear God. (*Barbara keens immediately, sinks to her knees on the stairway. Johnna wraps one hand around Barbara's middle, places the other hand firmly on Barbara's forehead. Jean sits down on a step.*)

SHERIFF GILBEAU: I am sorry.

BILL: What happened?

SHERIFF GILBEAU: We got a call from the lake patrol a few hours ago that Mr. Weston's boat was found washed up on a sandbar. We were planning to drag the lake this morning around that area, southeast, when we got another call. Couple old boys running jug lines in the cove, uh . . . *hooked* . . . Mr. Weston. And pulled him up.

BILL: Now? This time of night?

SHERIFF GILBEAU: These guys run those lines early.

BILL: He drowned. That's how he died, from drowning.

SHERIFF GILBEAU: Yes, sir.

BILL: Is there any possibility . . . *any* possibility that it's not him?

SHERIFF GILBEAU: Given the proximity of the boat to where the body was found, we're pretty sure it's Mr. Weston. (*Barbara suddenly dries her eyes, shrugs Johnna's grasp, stands.*)

BARBARA: All right. Okay. So what happens? What do we do now?

SHERIFF GILBEAU: I need a relative to come with me to positively identify the body.

BILL: To your station house.

SHERIFF GILBEAU: No, sir, he's still at the lake.

BARBARA: Oh God, I don't think I can do this.

SHERIFF GILBEAU: I'm sorry.

BILL: I'll go. Can I go? Can I do it?

SHERIFF GILBEAU: I need a blood relative. But if Barbara is the one to identify him, I suggest you come along.

BARBARA: Bill, I can't do it.

BILL: Honey, what choice do we have?

JEAN: I can do it. I'm a blood relative.

BARBARA: No, no. No, I'll do it. I will. (*Johnna exits to the kitchen, turns on the lights, starts a pot of coffee.*)

BILL: Can we have a couple of minutes to get ready?

SHERIFF GILBEAU: Yes, sir. Barbara? (*She turns to him.*) I'm very sorry. This is the hardest part of my job. And I'm . . . to do it for someone you know . . . I'm just . . . very sorry. (*She nods.*)

BILL: What do you want to do about your mother?

BARBARA: I . . . I . . . fuck it. (*Laughs.*) Fuck it. I'll go . . . put some clothes on.

BILL: I'll be right up. Jean, help your mother, okay? (*Barbara and Jean exit down the second-floor hallway. Bill pulls Sheriff Gilbeau into the study.*) Is there any way to determine if he—I mean, is this an accident, or suicide?—

SHERIFF GILBEAU: There's really no way to tell.

BILL: What do you think happened? I mean . . . what's your guess?

SHERIFF GILBEAU: Suicide. I would guess suicide. But the official cause of death is "drowning." And that's the extent of it.

BILL: I understand.

SHERIFF GILBEAU: I should warn you. That body has been in the water for all of three days.

BILL: Right.

SHERIFF GILBEAU: I think you should try to prepare your wife, if you can.

BILL: "Prepare her . . . "

SHERIFF GILBEAU: What happens to a body. It's very bloated. It's an ugly color. And fish have eaten the eyes.

BILL: Oh Christ. How does a person jump in the water . . . and choose not to swim?

SHERIFF GILBEAU: I don't think you do unless you really mean business.

BILL: Choose not to swim. (*Lights shift to the second-floor landing as Barbara and Jean enter. Jean sits on the window seat as Barbara rakes a brush through her hair.*)

JEAN: What about Aunt Ivy?

BARBARA: I guess we'll stop there on the way back and tell her. Christ, I need to call Karen, too. What the fuck am I brushing my hair for? (*She throws the brush. She slumps on the window seat next to Jean.*) I used to go out with that boy. With that man.

JEAN: What man?

BARBARA: The sheriff.

JEAN: You did?

BARBARA: Yeah, in high school. He was my prom date.

JEAN: You're kidding.

BARBARA: The day of the prom, his father got drunk and stole his car. Stole his own son's car and went somewhere. Mexico. Deon showed up at the door, wearing this awful tuxedo. He'd been crying, I could tell. And he confessed he didn't have a way to take me to the prom. I just felt awful for him, so I told him we'd walk. About three miles. I busted a heel and we both got so sweaty and dirty. We gave up . . . got a six-pack and broke into the chapel, stayed up all night talking and kissing. And now he's here telling me . . . oh, it's just surreal. Thank God we can't tell the future. We'd never get out of bed. (*She fixes Jean with a look.*) Listen to me: Die after me, all right? I don't care what else you do, where you go, how you screw up your life, just . . . survive. Outlive me, please.

JEAN: I'll do my best. (*Bill enters.*)

Deanna Dunagan (foreground) as Violet and Amy Morton as Barbara in the Steppenwolf Theatre production directed by Anna Shapiro at the Imperial Theatre on Broadway, 2007.

BILL: You ready?

BARBARA: Give me a second. (*Lights shift to the study, where Sheriff Gilbeau waits. Violet, wearing silk pajamas, shakily descends the stairs, crosses into the study.*)

VIOLET: Izza story.

SHERIFF GILBEAU: Hello, Violet.

VIOLET: Barely's back.

SHERIFF GILBEAU: I beg your pardon?

VIOLET: Did sum Beer-ley come home?

SHERIFF GILBEAU: Ma'am. (*Violet shuffles up to Sheriff Gilbeau.*)

VIOLET: Gizza cig . . . some cigezze? Cig-zezz, cig-zizz, cig-uhzzz. (*She laughs at her own inability to speak. Sheriff Gilbeau takes a Pall Mall from his shirt pocket, hands it to her. She stands, sways, holding the cigarette in her mouth. He lights it.*) In the archa, archa-tex? I'm in the bottom. Izza bottom of them. Inna . . . ell. (*She shuffles to the stereo in the living room . . .*) His master's voice. (*. . . and plays a song: "Lay Down, Sally," by Clapton. Sheriff Gilbeau trails her into the living room.*) Mm, good beat. Right?

SHERIFF GILBEAU: Yes, ma'am. (*She does a jerky little dance, puffing on her cigarette.*)

VIOLET: Barbara?! Is Barbara here?!

SHERIFF GILBEAU: She's upstairs.

VIOLET: Barbara?! Izza time in duhh . . . izza time? What's time?!

SHERIFF GILBEAU: It's about 5:45.

VIOLET: BARB'RA! BARB'RA! (*Barbara, Bill, Jean and Johnna enter from various points in the house. Violet sees them, continues her tight little dance.*) Idn't it's good beat? Inna good beats. Mmm, I been on the music . . . pell-man onna sheriff. C.J.'s boy. Right? Donna two inna school? Armen in tandel s'lossle, s'lost? Lost?! From the day, the days. Am Beerly . . . and Beverly lost? (*Violet abandons her dance, separates invisible threads in the air. The others stand frozen, staring at her.*) And then you're here. And Barbara, and then you're here, and Beverly, and then you're here, and then you're here, and then you're here, and then you're here, and then you're here, and then you're here, and then you're here, and then you're here, and then you're here, and then you're here, and then you're here, and then you're here, and then you're here, and then you're here, and then you're here, and then you're here . . . (*Blackout.*)

ACT TWO

The house has been manifestly refreshed, presumably by Johnna's hand. The dull, dusty finish has been replaced by the transparent gleam of function.

Of note:
The study has been reorganized. Stacks of paper are neater, books are shelved. The dining room table is set with the fine china, candles, a floral centerpiece. In a corner of the dining room, a "kid's table," with seating for two, is also set. The warm, clean kitchen now bubbles and steams, redolent of collard and kale.

At rise:
Three o'clock of an eternal Oklahoma afternoon. The body of Beverly Weston has just been buried.

    Violet, relatively sober now, in a handsome modern black dress, stands in Beverly's study, a bottle of pills in her hand.

    Elsewhere in the house: Karen and Barbara are in the dining room. Johnna is in the kitchen.

VIOLET: August . . . your month. Locusts are raging. "Summer psalm become summer wrath." 'Course it's only August out there. In *here* . . . who knows? All right . . . okay. "The Carriage held but just Ourselves," dum-de-dum . . . mm, best I got . . . Emily Dickinson's° all I got . . . something something, "Horse's Heads Were Toward Eternity . . . " (*She takes a pill.*) That's for me . . . one for me . . . (*She*

Emily Dickinson: American poet (1830–1886) whose lines Violet is quoting.

picks up the hardback copy of Meadowlark, *flips to the dedication.*) "Dedicated to my Violet." Put that one in marble. (*She drops the book on the desk. She takes a pill.*) For the girls, God love 'em. That's all I can dedicate to you, sorry to say. Other than them . . . not one thing. No thing. You think I'll weep for you? Think I'll play that part, like we played the others? (*She takes a pill.*) You made your choice. You made this happen. *You* answer for this . . . not me. Not me. This is not mine. (*Lights crossfade to the dining room. Barbara and Karen, wearing black dresses, fold napkins, munch food from a relish tray, etc.*)

KAREN: The present. Today, here and now. I think I spent so much of my early life thinking about what's to come, y'know, who would I marry, would he be a lawyer or a football player, would he be dark-haired and good-looking and broad-shouldered. I spent a lot of time in that bedroom upstairs pretending my pillow was my husband and I'd ask him about his day at work and what was happening at the office, and did he like the dinner I made for him and where were we going to vacation that winter and he'd surprise me with tickets to Belize and we'd kiss—I mean I'd kiss my pillow, make out with my pillow, and then I'd tell him I'd been to the doctor that day and I'd found out I was pregnant. I know how pathetic all that sounds now, but it was innocent enough . . . Then real life takes over because it always does—

BARBARA: —uh-huh—

KAREN: —and things work out differently than you'd planned. That pillow was a better husband than any real man I'd ever met; this parade of men fails to live up to your expectations, all of them so much less than Daddy or Bill (you know I always envied you finding Bill). And you punish yourself, tell yourself it's your fault you can't find a good one, you've only deluded yourself into thinking they're better than they are. I don't know how well you remember Andrew . . .

BARBARA: No, I remember.

KAREN: That's the best example: Here's a guy I loved so intensely, and all the things he did wrong were just opportunities for me to make things right. So if he cheated on me or he called me a cunt, I'd think to myself, "No, you love him, you love him forever, and here's an opportunity to make an adjustment in the way you view the world." And I can't say when the precise moment was that I looked in the mirror and said, "Okay, moron," and walked out, but it kicked off this whole period of reflection, just swamped in this sticky recollection. How had I screwed it up, where'd I go wrong, and before you know it you can't move forward, you're just suspended there, you can't because you can't stop thinking backward, I mean, you know . . . years! Years of punishment, self-loathing. And that's when I got into all those books and discussion groups—

BARBARA: And Scientology, too, right, or something like that?—

KAREN: Yes, exactly, and finally one day, I threw it all out, I just said, "No, it's *me*. It's just *me*, here and now, with my music on the stereo and my glass of wine and Bloomers my cat, and I don't need anything else, I can live my life with myself." And I got my license, threw myself into my work, sold a lot of houses, and that's when I met Steve. That's how it happens, of course, you only really find it when you're not looking for it, suddenly you turn around and there it is. And then the things you thought were so important aren't really important. I mean, when I made out with my pillow, I never imagined Steve! Here he is, you know, this kinda country club Chamber of Commerce guy, ten years older than me, but a thinker, you know, someone who's been around, and he's just so good. He's a good man and he's good to me and he's good *for* me.

BARBARA: That's great, Karen—

KAREN: He's got this great business and it's because he has these great ideas and he's unafraid to make his ideas realities, you know, he's not afraid of *doing*. I think men on the whole are better at that than women, don't you? *Doing*, just jumping in and *doing*, right or wrong, we'll figure out what it all means later. And the best thing about him, the best thing about him for me, is that now what I think about is *now*. I live *now*. My focus, my life, my world is *now*. I don't give a care about the past anymore, the mistakes I made, the way I *thought*, I won't go back there. And I've realized you can't plan the future, because as soon as you do, you know, something happens, some terrible thing happens—

BARBARA: Like your father drowning himself.

KAREN: Exactly! Exactly, that's exactly what I mean! That's not something you plan for! There's no contingency; you take it as it comes, here and now! Steve had a very important presentation today, for some bigwig government guys who could be very important for his business, something he's been putting together for months, and as soon as we heard about Daddy, he called and canceled his meeting. He has his priorities straight. And you know what the kicker is? (*Barbara waits.*) Do you know what the kicker is?

BARBARA: What's the kicker?

KAREN: We're going to Belize on our honeymoon. (*Johnna enters from the kitchen, bringing in a pitcher of iced tea.*)

BARBARA: Sorry. Hot flash.

KAREN: I never told him my little Belize fantasy, he just up and surprised me with tickets for after the wedding.

BARBARA: (*To Johnna.*) God, that smells good, what are we having?

JOHNNA: Um . . . baked chicken, fried potatoes, green bean casserole . . . some greens . . .

BARBARA: Did Mattie Fae bring her green bean casserole?

JOHNNA: Oh. I don't know. Should I not have made it?

BARBARA: No, it's good you did, hers is inedible. (*Johnna exits.*)

KAREN: I mean, can you believe that about Belize?

BARBARA: That's terrific.

KAREN: I know you only just met him, but did you get a read off him? Did you like him?

BARBARA: We said two words to each other—

KAREN: But you still get a feel, don't you? Did you get a feel?

BARBARA: He seemed very nice, sweetheart—

KAREN: He *is*, and—

BARBARA: —but what I think about him doesn't matter. I'm not marrying him—

KAREN: You'll come to the wedding, won't you?

BARBARA: Yeah, when is it again?

KAREN: New Year's Day. One reason we chose New Year's is because I know you and Bill have a break from school and it's important to me that you're there.

BARBARA: It's in Sarasota?

KAREN: Miami. Didn't you know I moved to Miami?

BARBARA: Wait, yes, I did know that—

KAREN: That's where Steve's business—

BARBARA: —right, right.

KAREN: I guess what I'm telling you is that I'm finally happy. I've been really unhappy for most of my life, my adult life. I doubt you've been aware of that. I know our lives have led us apart, you, me and Ivy, and maybe we're not as close as we . . . as close as some families—

BARBARA: Yeah, we really need to talk about Mom, what to do about Mom—

KAREN: —but I think at least one reason for that is that I haven't wanted to live my unhappiness in full view of my family. But now I'm . . . well, I'm just really happy. And I'd really like us to maybe get to know each other a little better.

BARBARA: Yes. Yes. (*Karen wraps her arms around Barbara.*) Okay. Yes. (*They separate.*) Christ, where are they with the wine already?

KAREN: And see, there's another example, Steve doesn't know a soul here, but he jumped right in the car with Bill and Jean to go get the wine. He's family! (*Lights crossfade to the second-floor landing. Ivy enters, pursued by Violet, who carries a dress and a pair of high heels. Mattie Fae follows, rooting through a box of photographs. Like Violet, Mattie Fae wears a black dress; Ivy wears a black suit. During the following, Barbara and Karen exit to the kitchen.*)

IVY: I really don't want to.

VIOLET: It won't kill you to try it on—

MATTIE FAE: (*Regarding photographs.*) Oh, this is a sweet one, Vi—

IVY: I find all this a tidge morbid, quite frankly—

MATTIE FAE: Look at this,   VIOLET: What's morbid
Ivy—   about it?

IVY: —and I'm really not prepared to look at these photographs right now—

VIOLET: This is a beautiful dress and it's very modern.

IVY: It's not my style, Mom—

MATTIE FAE: Where was this taken?—

VIOLET: You don't have a style, that's the whole point—

MATTIE FAE: Vi?

VIOLET: (*Glancing at the photo.*) New York City. That's from the first book tour, New York—

IVY: You mean I don't have *your* style. I have a style of my own—

MATTIE FAE: "New York City, 1964"—

VIOLET: Honey, you wore a suit to your father's funeral. A woman doesn't wear a suit to a funeral—

IVY: God, you're weird; it's a black suit.

VIOLET: You look like a magician's assistant.

IVY: You know—

MATTIE FAE: Little Charles has been talking about moving to New York.

IVY: —why do you feel it necessary to—?   MATTIE FAE: Can you picture that?

VIOLET: Don't discourage him now—

MATTIE FAE: He wouldn't last a day in that city. They'd tear him apart.

IVY: Why do you feel it—?

MATTIE FAE: I could kill that kid—

IVY: Why do you feel it necessary to insult me?

VIOLET: Stop being so sensitive.

MATTIE FAE: He overslept? For my brother-in-law's funeral? A *noon* service?

IVY: I'm sure there's more to the story than—

MATTIE FAE: You shouldn't make excuses for him. That's what Charlie does, has always done. Just, "Oh, he overslept, la-di-da, I'll go pick him up at the bus station."

IVY: You're so hard on him.

MATTIE FAE: Boy's thirty-seven years old and *can't drive?*

VIOLET: He's a little different, I'll give you that.

IVY: I think you're being—

MATTIE FAE: Who *can't drive?*

IVY: I don't think you're very —

MATTIE FAE: I've seen a *chimp* drive.

VIOLET: Will you take off that cheap suit and try this on for me, please?

IVY: Cheap?! Did you call this—?!

MATTIE FAE: Is this the kind of thing you had in mind, Vi?

VIOLET: No, it's to go on the sideboard for the meal, so it should be something we easily recognize—

MATTIE FAE: You mean something big.

VIOLET: Yes, I have a frame we can—

IVY: This is the most expensive item of clothing I own.

VIOLET: I don't see what difference that makes, how much you paid for it. A suit of armor is expensive, too, but that doesn't make it appropriate—

MATTIE FAE: Well, *this* one's big, but it's of the *two* of you—

IVY: Why are you trying to give away your clothes?

MATTIE FAE: Do you mind if it's of the two of you?—

VIOLET: All this shit's going. I'm downgrading.

IVY: "Downgrading."

VIOLET: Down*sizing*, I'm downsizing.

IVY: You're "downsizing"—

MATTIE FAE: Vi, do you think this is—?

VIOLET: I'm serious, it's all going. I don't plan to spend the rest of my days walking around and looking at what used to be. I want that shit in the office gone, I want all these clothes I'm never going to wear gone, I want it all gone! I mean look at these fucking shoes. (*Holds up the high heels.*) Can you picture me in these? Even if I didn't fall on my face, can you imagine anything less attractive, my swollen ankles and varicose veins? And my toenails, good God, anymore they could dig through cement. (*Mattie Fae holds a photograph in front of Violet.*)

MATTIE FAE: Is this the idea?

VIOLET: (*Takes the photograph.*) Look at me. (*Shows the photograph to Ivy.*) Look at me.

IVY: You're beautiful, Mom.

VIOLET: I was beautiful. Not anymore.

MATTIE FAE: Oh, now—

IVY: You're still beautiful.

VIOLET: No. One of those lies we tell to give us comfort, but don't you believe it. Women are beautiful when they're young, and not after. Men can still preserve their sex appeal well into old age. I don't mean those men like you see with shorts and those little purses around their waists. Some men can maintain, if they embrace it . . . cragginess, weary masculinity. Women just get old and fat and wrinkly.

MATTIE FAE: I beg your pardon.

VIOLET: Think about what makes a young woman sexy. Think about the last time you went to the mall and saw some sweet little gal and thought, "She's a cute trick." What makes her that way? Taut skin, firm boobs, an ass above her knees—

MATTIE FAE: I'm still very sexy, thank you very much.

VIOLET: You're about as sexy as a wet cardboard box, Mattie Fae, you and me both. Don't kid yourself. Look . . . can we all just stop kidding ourselves? Wouldn't we be better off, all of us, if we stopped lying about these things and told the truth? "Women aren't sexy when they're old." I can live with that. Can you live with that?

MATTIE FAE: I can live with it, but I disagree. What about Sophia Loren? What about Lena Horne? She stayed sexy until she was eighty.

VIOLET: The world is round. Get over it. Now try this dress on.

IVY: I'm sorry, I won't.

VIOLET: Ivy.

IVY: All right, the heat in here is getting just stupid now—

VIOLET: Now listen to me: you don't know how to attract a man. I do. That's something I've always—

IVY: It's a funeral! We just buried my father, I'm not trying to attract—!

VIOLET: I'm not talking about today, dummy, this is something you can wear some—

IVY: I have a man. All right? I have a man. (*Mattie Fae turns her attention to Ivy.*)

VIOLET: You said . . . you told me you weren't looking for a man—

IVY: And I'm not. Because I have one. Okay? Now will you leave it alone? (*Pause.*)

VIOLET: No, I won't leave it alone.   MATTIE FAE: No, let's not leave it alone.

IVY: I wish you both could see the brainsick looks on your faces—

VIOLET: Who is it?

IVY: Nobody. Forget it—

VIOLET: No, no you don't, I want to know who you're—

IVY: I'm not talking about this—

MATTIE FAE: Ivy, please tell us—

IVY: No.

MATTIE FAE: Is he someone from school?

VIOLET: Tell me you're not back with Loser Barry.

IVY: No, it isn't Barry.

VIOLET: Thank you, Jesus.

MATTIE FAE: Tell us something, how old is he, what does he do?—

IVY: I'm not telling you anything, either of you, so you might as well—

MATTIE FAE: You have to tell us *something!*

IVY: No, I really don't.

VIOLET: Are you in love, Ivy?

IVY: (*Stunned.*) I . . . I don't . . . I'm . . . (*She bursts into awkward laughter and exits down the second-floor hallway. Violet and Mattie Fae squeal and follow Ivy off. Lights crossfade to the front porch as Jean zips inside. She races to the TV, turns it on, finds a channel, and sits improbably close. Bill and Steve Heidebrecht follow, dressed in dark suits and laden with paper grocery bags.*)

STEVE: No, we maintain the accounts offshore, just until we get approvals.

BILL: To get around approvals?

STEVE: To get around approvals until we *get* approvals. There's a lot of red tape, a lot of bureaucracy. I don't know how much you know about Florida, Florida politics—

BILL: Only what I read and that's—

STEVE: Right, right, and this kind of business in particular—

BILL: I'm sorry, what is the business again? I don't—

STEVE: You know, it's essentially security work. The situation in the Middle East is *perpetually* dangerous, so there's a tremendous amount of money involved—

BILL: Security work. You mean . . . mercenary? (*Barbara enters from the kitchen.*)

BARBARA: Give. Me. The wine. (*She pulls a bottle of wine from Bill's grocery bag.*)

STEVE: I think of it more like "missionary" than "mercenary."

BARBARA: (*To Jean, regarding the TV.*) Is that what you were in such a hurry to get home for?

JEAN: Yeah.

BARBARA: What the hell is on TV that's so important you can't—?

JEAN: *Phantom of the Opera*, 1925. Lon Chaney.°

BILL: Cool.

BARBARA: For God's sake, Jean, you can get it at any video store.

JEAN: No, but they're showing it with the scene in color restored.

BILL: Oh, no kidding, from the . . . what's that scene called again, sweetie? "The Masked Ball"?

JEAN: Yeah.

BARBARA: Let me make sure I've got this: when you threw a fit about going to the store with your father—hey. Look at me. (*She does.*) And you were so very distraught over the start time of your grandpa's funeral. Was this your concern? Getting back here in time to watch the *Phantom of the Fucking Opera?*

JEAN: I guess. (*Barbara gives Jean a withering look, exits.*)

BILL: (*To Steve.*) I'll take these into the kitchen.

STEVE: No, I can.

BILL: I've got it. (*Bill takes Steve's grocery bag and follows Barbara into the kitchen.*)

STEVE: Movie buff?

JEAN: Yeah.

STEVE: Right, right, me too. You ever seen this?

JEAN: Huh-uh.

STEVE: It's a great one. You know Chaney designed his own makeup.

JEAN: I know.

STEVE: Apparently very painful. He ran these fishing lines from under his nostrils and pulled them up under his—

JEAN: Yeah, I know.

STEVE: You see any of the remakes? They're pretty bad.

JEAN: I've seen the one with Claude Rains.°

STEVE: Right, right, pretty bad, right? Phantom's queer. That's a problem.

JEAN: I don't remember it so hot, I was just a kid.

STEVE: Yeah . . . (*Steve sits on the couch behind her. They watch the movie for a moment.*) You're not a kid anymore, I guess.

JEAN: What?

STEVE: I say you're not a kid anymore.

JEAN: No. I mean, *yeah.*

STEVE: How old are you, about, seventeen?

JEAN: Fifteen.

STEVE: Right, right. Fifteen. That's no kid. (*They watch TV.*) You're no kid. (*Beat.*) You know what I was doing when I was fifteen?

Lon Chaney: American actor (1883–1930) known as "the man of a thousand faces," who played the Phantom in the 1925 silent film production of *The Phantom of the Opera*, regarded as a classic.   **Claude Rains:** British actor (1889–1967) who played the Phantom in a remake of the Chaney film. While not as well respected, it won two Oscars in 1943.

JEAN: What?

STEVE: Cattle processing. You know what that is?

JEAN: It doesn't sound good.

STEVE: Slaughterhouse. Sanitation. Slaughterhouse sanitation.

JEAN: That's disgusting.

STEVE: I don't recommend it. But hey. Put food on the table. Get it? (*He sniffs the air.*) Whoa, whoa. Wait now. What's that smell?

JEAN: Food, from the kitchen.

STEVE: Nah, that's not what I'm smelling. (*He continues to sniff the air, follows his nose, until he is on the floor, above her. He smells her.*)

JEAN: What are you doing?

STEVE: Do I smell what I think I smell?

JEAN: What do you smell?

STEVE: What do you think I smell?

JEAN: I think you smell food from the kitchen.

STEVE: Guess again. (*He whiffs, hard, breathing her in.*)

JEAN: What are you—?

STEVE: Is that—is that pot?

JEAN: Oh. I don't know. (*She smells her sleeve.*)

STEVE: You smoking pot?

JEAN: No.

STEVE: You can tell me.

JEAN: No.

STEVE: Is it just me, or is it getting hot in here?

JEAN: It's hot.

STEVE: You're hot?

JEAN: Yeah . . .

STEVE: How hot are you?

JEAN: Really hot.

STEVE: Really hot.

JEAN: Yeah.

STEVE: Yeah . . . you a little dope smoker? (*No response.*) Well then you are in luck. Because I just happen to have some really tasty shit. Because I just happen to have some really good connects. And I am going to hook you up.

JEAN: That would be great 'cause I just smoked my last bowl, and I really need to get fucked up.

STEVE: You what?

JEAN: I really need to get fucked up—

STEVE: You need to get what?

JEAN: Fucked up—

STEVE: What? You need to get fucked what? (*She snort-laughs, pushes him away.*)

JEAN: You're bad.

STEVE: I'm just goofin' with you. (*Karen enters from the kitchen, finds Steve on the floor, looming over Jean.*) Hi, sweetheart.

KAREN: What are you doing?

STEVE: Goofin' with your niece.

KAREN: I think we're getting ready to eat.

STEVE: Right, right, I'm starving.

KAREN: Did you remember to get cigarettes?

STEVE: Damn it. (*To Jean.*) Didn't I ask you what I was forgetting? I knew I was forgetting something—

KAREN: I'll have to borrow from Momma.

JEAN: I've got cigarettes.

KAREN: *You've* got cigarettes.

JEAN: Camel Lights?

STEVE: She's got our brand.

KAREN: Jean, honey, you're too young to smoke.

STEVE: (*Faux stern.*) Yeah.

KAREN: (*Whacks him playfully.*) Stop it now, don't encourage her—

STEVE: Hey, she's no kid—

KAREN: Can we borrow a couple of cigarettes?

JEAN: Yep-per. (*Jean gets cigarettes from her purse.*)

STEVE: Now let's not encourage her—

KAREN: Oh, hush. (*Takes cigarettes.*) Thanks, doll. Now stop smoking. (*Jean watches TV. Karen snuggles with Steve, speaks in a baby voice.*) Hi, doodle.

STEVE: Hey, baby.

KAREN: (*In a super baby voice.*) Hi, doodle! (*Steve embraces her. They kiss. His hands wander, squeeze her ass. She giggles, then breaks it.*) Come into the backyard, I want to show you our old fort. Man, the air in here just doesn't move . . . (*She goes ahead of him. He follows, but stops . . .*)

STEVE: (*Privately, to Jean.*) Hook you up, later. (. . . *rubs his hand over the entirety of Jean's face. He exits. Lights crossfade to the front porch as Charlie and Little Charles arrive.*)

LITTLE CHARLES: I'm sorry, Dad.

CHARLIE: Stop apologizing to me. Hold on a second, comb your hair. (*Charlie gives Little Charles a comb.*)

LITTLE CHARLES: I know Mom's mad at me.

CHARLIE: Don't worry about her.

LITTLE CHARLES: What did she say?

CHARLIE: You know your mother, she says what she says.

LITTLE CHARLES: I set the alarm. I did.

CHARLIE: I know you did.

LITTLE CHARLES: I wanted to be there.

CHARLIE: You're here now.

LITTLE CHARLES: I loved Uncle Bev, you know that—

CHARLIE: Stop apologizing.

LITTLE CHARLES: The power must've gone out. I woke up and the clock was blinking noon. That means the power went out, right?

CHARLIE: It's okay.

LITTLE CHARLES: I missed his funeral!

CHARLIE: It's a ceremony. It's ceremonial. It doesn't mean anything compared to what you have in your heart.

LITTLE CHARLES: Uncle Bev must be disappointed in me.

CHARLIE: Your Uncle Bev has got bigger and better things ahead of him. He doesn't have time for spite. He wasn't that kind of man anyway— (*Little Charles weeps.*) Hey. Little Charles. Hey. It's okay. It's okay, now . . .

LITTLE CHARLES: Just . . . it's just . . . you know, I know how things are. I know how they feel about me, and when, something like this . . . you want to be there for people, and—

CHARLIE: —shhhh—

LITTLE CHARLES: —I missed Uncle Bev's funeral, and I know how they feel about me—

CHARLIE: Who, how who feels about you? Feels what about you?

LITTLE CHARLES: All of them. I know what they say.

CHARLIE: They don't say things about you—

LITTLE CHARLES: I see how they are. I don't blame them. I'm sorry I let you down, Dad.

CHARLIE: You haven't let me down. You never let me down. Now listen here . . . you're wrong about these people, they love you. Some of them haven't gotten a chance to see what I see: a fine man, very loving, with a lot to offer. Now take this . . . (*Gives Little Charles a handkerchief.*) Give me my comb. Stand up straight. Look folks in the eye. And stop being so hard on yourself.

LITTLE CHARLES: I love you, Dad.

CHARLIE: Love you too, son. (*Charlie claps Little Charles on the back as they enter the living room. Lights crossfade to the dining room as Barbara and Bill enter from the kitchen. Johnna occasionally interrupts as she moves between the kitchen and the dining room, setting the table with food.*)

BILL: Jean doesn't understand all this. You think she has any concept—?

BARBARA: *Phantom of the Opera*—

BILL: Do you remember what it was like to be fourteen?

BARBARA: She's old enough to exhibit a little character. But then I guess that's something you normally learn from your parents.

BILL: That's a shot across my bow, right? I missed something.

BARBARA: Really? Instilling character: our burden, as parents.

BILL: I got that part.

BARBARA: And you really haven't been much of a parent lately, so it's tough to expect—

BILL: Just because you and I are struggling with this Gordian knot doesn't make me any less of a—

BARBARA: Nice, "Gordian knot," but her little fourteen-year-old self might view it differently, might consider it "abandonment"—

BILL: Oh, come on—

BARBARA: Maybe she views her father as "absent," or maybe "not present," or perhaps even "a son-of-a-bitch."

BILL: Jean's a little more sophisticated than that, don't you think?

BARBARA: Pretty fucking sophisticated, the restored whatever from *Phantom of the Opera*, I know that makes your dick hard—

BILL: Barbara—

BARBARA: Precocious little shit—

BILL: I'm not defending her.

BARBARA: (*Voice rising.*) I'm not blaming her, because I don't expect her to act any differently when her father is a selfish son-of-a-bitch!

BILL: (*Voice rising.*) I'm on your side. How can we fight when I'm on your side? Barbara . . . Barbara, settle down!

BARBARA: Be a father! Help me!

BILL: I am her father, goddamn it!—

BARBARA: Her father *in absentia*, her father in name only!—

BILL: I have not forsook my responsibilities!—

BARBARA: It's "forsaken," big shot!

BILL: Actually, "forsook" is *also* an acceptable usage!—

BARBARA: Oh, "forsook" you and the horse you rode in on!

BILL: So we need to fight on your terms then: on topic one moment, and whimsical insults the next, all of it when it suits you—

BARBARA: We covered this around Year Three, Bill: that you're the Master of Space and Time and I'm a spastic Pomeranian.

BILL: That's not fair.

BARBARA: I'm sick of being fair! I've seen where being fair gets me! I'm sick of the whole notion of the enduring female. GROW UP! 'Cause while you're going through your fifth puberty, the world is falling apart and I can't handle it! More importantly, your kid can't handle it!

BILL: Our kid is just trying to deal with this goddamn madhouse you've dragged her into.

BARBARA: This madhouse is my home.

BILL: Think about that statement for a second, why don't you?

BARBARA: Jean is here with me because this is a family event.

BILL: Jean's here with you because she's a buffer between you and the shrill insanity of your mother.

BARBARA: Y'know, you'd have a lot more credibility if you had any credibility.

BILL: You can't resist, can you?

BARBARA: You're a pretty easy mark.

BILL: You're so goddamn self-righteous, you know? You're so—

BARBARA: Surely you must've known when you started porking Pippi Longstocking you were due for a little self-righteousness, just a smidgen of indignation on my part—

BILL: Maybe I split because of it.

BARBARA: Is this your confession, then, when you finally unload all—?

BILL: You're thoughtful, Barbara, but you're not open. You're passionate, but you're hard. You're a good, decent, funny, wonderful woman, and I love you, but you're a pain in the ass. (*Lights up on the entire house: Bill exits to the porch, gathers himself. Karen and Steve reenter, run into Barbara in the sitting room. Mattie Fae descends the stairs to the living room where Jean, Charlie and Little Charles watch TV. Violet and Ivy reenter the second-floor landing.*)

JOHNNA: Dinner's ready.

STEVE: I told you, smoke a cigarette and the food comes—

KAREN: (*To Barbara.*) When's the last time someone mowed the yard around here?

BARBARA: Hm?

KAREN: I just showed Steve our old fort, have you been out there?

BARBARA: No, I haven't—

STEVE: Barb, would you consider me uncouth if I removed my suit jacket?

KAREN: Are you okay?

BARBARA: Yeah, I'm fine.

STEVE: Barbara, can I . . . ?

BARBARA: Yeah, sure.

KAREN: Poor thing, you've had a long few days, haven't you?

STEVE: Sure she has.

KAREN: I know how I get during these times, I think, "I couldn't eat a bite," but then you put a plate of hot food in front of me and suddenly I'm starving.

(*A pause, as Barbara seems to take them in for the first time.*)

BARBARA: You're right. Let's eat.

STEVE: Let's eat!

(*They cross from the kitchen into the dining room.*)

MATTIE FAE: Well, look who decided to show up. I'm sorry we woke you, sweetheart.

LITTLE CHARLES: Mom, I'm so sorry—

MATTIE FAE: I'm sure you are—

CHARLIE: He's here now and that's all that matters.

MATTIE FAE: It's really not all that matters—

LITTLE CHARLES: The electricity must have gone out, I woke up and the clock—

MATTIE FAE: Don't go through it all, Little Charles. There's no need to go through all—

CHARLIE: Honey, the boy's trying to tell you he's sorry—

MATTIE FAE: Stop making excuses for him, he's thirty-seven years old—

CHARLIE: Please let's not have this argument now.

MATTIE FAE: I'm not arguing.

LITTLE CHARLES: I know I let you down, Mom—

MATTIE FAE: What else is new?

CHARLIE: You behave yourself, there's more important things—

MATTIE FAE: I'm not talking about this anymore, I'm ready to eat. Did you bring my casserole in from—?

CHARLIE: No, I'll get it now.

MATTIE FAE: You let my casserole sit for an hour inside a hot car?—

CHARLIE: I'll get it, I'll get it—

LITTLE CHARLES: *I'll* get it. (*Little Charles exits the house.*)

IVY: I'm serious, if you say anything—

VIOLET: You didn't say I couldn't tell people—

IVY: I'm telling you now.

VIOLET: Why are you so worked up? You're seeing someone, I think that's great—

IVY: Don't you dare—

VIOLET: You'd think you might be happy to tell your family some good news, on a day like today?—

IVY: It's nobody's business.

VIOLET: Folks only want what's best for you.

IVY: It's nobody's business!

VIOLET: Why should I do you any favors?

IVY: Why not? Why *wouldn't* you?

VIOLET: You wouldn't even try on my dress—

IVY: I'm not bargaining with you!

VIOLET: You're so melodramatic—

IVY: I'm going downstairs to eat now because you are impossible.

VIOLET: (*Sarcastic.*) I'm sorry to be so impossible, it's been kind of a tough day—

IVY: Tough on everybody, Mom.

(*Ivy heads downstairs, enters the living room as Mattie Fae and Charlie join Barbara, Karen, Steve and Johnna in the dining room. They gradually take their seats. Bill reenters from the porch, crosses into the living room.*)

The set of the Steppenwolf Theatre production at the Imperial Theater on Broadway, 2007.

KAREN: This just looks lovely. (*To Johnna.*) Did you do all this?

JOHNNA: Mm-hm.

MATTIE FAE: What a pretty table!

BARBARA: She does it all, this one.

STEVE: The chicken looks tasty, doesn't it?—

MATTIE FAE: Do we have enough seats?

BARBARA: I think so . . .

MATTIE FAE: This'll be fine, right here—

KAREN: Sit by me, honey.

STEVE: Okie-doke.

CHARLIE: Where do you want to sit?

BILL: Jean. Time to eat.

JEAN: I don't suppose it would be okay if I ate out here.

BILL: You suppose right.

IVY: Did I hear Little Charles?

BILL: Yeah, I think so—

JEAN: You're just gonna stick me at the kid's table anyway.

BILL: I'm not in the mood for this right now, okay?

IVY: Is he—do you know where he is?

BILL: I think he went outside for something—

BARBARA: Who gets stuck with Jean at the kid's table?

MATTIE FAE: We'll put Mr. Little Charles there.

CHARLIE: Are you serious?

KAREN: Nooo, now—

MATTIE FAE: Who else is going to sit there? Do *you* want to sit there?

CHARLIE: He's going to know you're trying to punish him—

JOHNNA: I can sit there, it's okay.

MATTIE FAE: After you went to all the trouble of cooking this fabulous meal—?

JOHNNA: I don't mind.

(*As the family continues to settle in for the meal, lights shift again: up on the front porch. Ivy greets Little Charles as he returns with Mattie Fae's casserole.*)

IVY: Hey.

LITTLE CHARLES: Hi.

IVY: Are you okay?

LITTLE CHARLES: Not really.

IVY: They said you overslept.

LITTLE CHARLES: I don't know, maybe I purposely accidentally overslept. I don't know. I'm so sorry—

IVY: Please.

LITTLE CHARLES: I know you've had one of the worst days of your life and I'm just sorry if I made it any—

IVY: Stop. We don't have to do that with each other. (*She embraces him, kisses him . . .*)

LITTLE CHARLES: You're breaking our rule.

IVY: They're on to me.

LITTLE CHARLES: What?

IVY: Not us, just me. I told them I was seeing someone. I didn't tell them who. I just wanted you to know, in case there were questions . . .

LITTLE CHARLES: All right . . . I mentioned New York to Mom. Only, you know, that I was considering a move.

IVY: She told me.

LITTLE CHARLES: She was typically approving, I bet . . .

IVY: But you know what? I think it helps, just letting them know, piece by piece. (*He stares at her.*) What? (*He stares, smiles.*) Charles . . .

LITTLE CHARLES: I adore you. (*Lights crossfade to the dining room. Seated around the table: Barbara, Bill, Mattie Fae, Charlie, Karen and Steve. Jean and Johnna sit at the kid's table. The men have all removed their suit coats.*)

MATTIE FAE: This food's going to get cold.

BARBARA: (*Calling out.*) Mom?! Let's eat.

CHARLIE: Will you pass the casserole, please?

MATTIE FAE: *My* casserole's coming.

(*Ivy exits to the front porch. Jean stomps toward the dining room. Bill stops her.*)

Why are you giving me all this attitude?

JEAN: I'm not.

BILL: You do realize your mother needs you at your best right now.

JEAN: Mom's not the one crawling up my ass.

BILL: Never mind. Wash up for dinner.

JEAN: "Wash up"? I'm not performing surgery.

(*Jean and Bill enter the dining room.*)

CHARLIE: I'll eat some of yours, too—

BILL: Can I pour anyone some wine?

KAREN: Yes, please.

STEVE: Sure, I'll have some—

(*Little Charles enters with Mattie Fae's casserole.*)

MATTIE FAE: There he is. I wanted to put you at the kid's table, but they wouldn't let me.

LITTLE CHARLES: That would've been okay. Where do you want this?

MATTIE FAE: Anywhere's fine. (*Ad-lib greetings, hugs, handshakes, Karen's introduction of Steve, etc. Ivy slips in and takes her seat. Little Charles drops Mattie Fae's casserole. It lands with a sickening "splat" on the dining room floor.*)

LITTLE CHARLES: Oh Jesus!—

BILL: Whoops.

MATTIE FAE: Goddamn it!—

BARBARA: That's too bad—

LITTLE CHARLES: Oh Jesus no!—

STEVE: O-pah!

MATTIE FAE: You *goofball!*

KAREN: Can it be saved?

(*Johnna goes to the kitchen for paper towels, a wet rag, etc.*)

MATTIE FAE: You goddamn clumsy *goofball!*

LITTLE CHARLES: Mom, I'm so sorry—

CHARLIE: All right, all right, nobody's hurt.

(*Little Charles helps Johnna clean up the mess.*)

MATTIE FAE: What about me? *I'm* hurt.

CHARLIE: You're not hurt.

LITTLE CHARLES: Mom, Jesus, I'm sorry—

IVY: It's just an accident.

MATTIE FAE: That's *my* casserole!

CHARLIE: Let it go, Mattie Fae.

STEVE: It's not a party until someone spills something.

CHARLIE: Jean, you didn't get any chicken.

BARBARA: No, she won't—   JEAN: I don't eat meat.

CHARLIE: You don't eat meat.

STEVE: Good for you.

CHARLIE: "Don't eat meat." Okay. Who wants chicken? Here, Little Charles, get some chicken.

MATTIE FAE: Just put it on his plate for him or he's liable to burn the house down.

CHARLIE: All right, Mattie Fae. (*Violet enters with the framed photograph of her and Beverly.*)

VIOLET: Barb . . . will you put this—?

BARBARA: Yeah, sure . . . (*Barbara takes the photograph, places it on the sideboard.*)

MATTIE FAE: That's nice.

KAREN: That's sweet.

STEVE: Very nice, yes.

IVY: The table's lovely.

BARBARA: Johnna did it all.

JEAN: Yayyy, Johnna—

VIOLET: I see you gentlemen have all stripped down to your shirt fronts. I thought we were having a funeral dinner, not a cockfight. (*An awkward moment. The men glumly put their suit coats back on. Taking her seat.*) Someone should probably say grace. (*All look to one another.*) Barbara? Will you . . . ?

BARBARA: No, I don't think so.

VIOLET: Oh now, it's no big—

BARBARA: Uncle Charlie should say grace. He's the patriarch around here now.

CHARLIE: I am? Oh, I guess I am.

VIOLET: By default.

CHARLIE: Okay. (*Clears his throat.*) Dear Lord . . . (*All bow their heads, clasp hands.*) We ask that you watch over this family in this sad time, O Lord . . . that you bless this good woman and keep her in your, in your . . . grace. (*A cellphone rings, playing the theme from a 1970s television show. Steve quickly digs through his pockets, finds the phone, checks the caller ID.*)

STEVE: I'm sorry, I have to take this. (*Steve hustles out to talk on the phone.*)

CHARLIE: We ask that you watch over Beverly, too, as he, as he . . . as he, as he, as he makes his journey.

   We thank thee, O Lord, that we are able to join together to pay tribute to this fine man, in his house, with his beautiful family, his three beautiful daughters. We are truly blessed in our, our fellowship, our togetherness, our . . . our fellowship.

   Thank thee for the food, O Lord, that we can share this food and replenish our bodies with . . . with nourishment. We ask that you help us . . . get better. Be better. Be better people. (*Steve reenters, snapping his phone shut.*) We recognize, now more than ever, the power, the, the . . . joy of family. And we ask that you bless and watch over this family. Amen.

MATTIE FAE: Amen.

STEVE: Amen. Sorry, folks.

BILL: Let's eat. (*They begin to eat.*)

VIOLET: Barbara, you have any use for that sideboard.

BARBARA: Hm?

VIOLET: That sideboard there, you have any interest in that?

BARBARA: This? Well . . . no. I mean, why?

VIOLET: I'm getting rid of a lot of this stuff and I thought you might want that sideboard.

BARBARA: No, Mom, I . . . I   KAREN: Really pretty. wouldn't have any way to get that to Boulder.

VIOLET: Mm. Maybe Ivy'll take it.

IVY: No, I have something like that, remember, from the—

BARBARA: What are you getting rid of?

VIOLET: All of it, I'm clearing all this stuff out of here. I want to have a brand-new everything.

BARBARA: I. I guess I'm just sort of . . . not prepared to talk about your stuff.

VIOLET: Suit yourself.

STEVE: This food is just spectacular.

KAREN: It's so good—   LITTLE CHARLES: Yes, it is—

IVY: You like your food, Mom?

VIOLET: I haven't tried much of it, yet—

BARBARA: Johnna cooked this whole meal by herself.

VIOLET: Hm? What?

BARBARA: I say Johnna cooked this whole meal by—

VIOLET: 'Swhat she's paid for. (*A silent moment.*) You all did know she's getting paid, right?

CHARLIE: Jean, so I'm curious, when you say you don't eat meat . . .

JEAN: Yeah?

CHARLIE: You mean you don't eat meat of any kind?

JEAN: Right.   BARBARA: No, she, hm-mm . . .

CHARLIE: And is that for health reasons, or . . . ?

JEAN: When you eat meat, you ingest an animal's fear.

VIOLET: Ingest what? Its fur?

JEAN: Fear.

VIOLET: (*Snickers.*) I thought she said—

CHARLIE: Its fear. How do you do that? You can't eat fear.

JEAN: Sure you can. I mean even if you don't sort of think of it spiritually, what happens to *you*, when you feel afraid? Doesn't your body produce all sorts of chemical reactions?

CHARLIE: Does it?

LITTLE CHARLES: It does.

IVY: Yes.

LITTLE CHARLES: Adrenaline, and, and—

JEAN: Your body goes through this whole chemical process when it experiences fear—

LITTLE CHARLES: —yep, and cortisol—

JEAN: —particularly like strong mortal fear, you know when you sweat and your heart races—

LITTLE CHARLES: —*oh* yeah—

CHARLIE: Okay, sure.

JEAN: Do you think an animal experiences fear?

STEVE: You bet it does.

JEAN: So when you eat an animal, you're eating all that fear it felt when it was slaughtered to make food.

CHARLIE: Wow.

STEVE: Right, right, I used to work in a processing factory and there's a lot of fear flying around that place—

CHARLIE: God, you mean I've been eating fear, what, three times a day for sixty years?

MATTIE FAE: This one won't have a meal unless there's meat in it.

CHARLIE: I guess it was the way I was raised, but it just doesn't seem like a legitimate meal unless it has some meat somewhere—

MATTIE FAE: If I make a pasta dish of some kind, he'll just be like, "Okay, that was good for an appetizer, now where's the meat?"

VIOLET: "Where's the meat?" Isn't that some TV commercial, the old lady says, "Where's the meat?"

KAREN: "Beef." "Where's the beef?"

VIOLET: (*Screeching.*) *"Where's the meat?!" "Where's the meat?!" "Where's the meat?!"* (*Everyone freezes, a little stunned.*)

CHARLIE: I sure thought the services were lovely.

KAREN: Yes, weren't they?—

STEVE: Preacher did a fine job.

VIOLET: (*Sticking her hand out, flat, waggling it back and forth.*) Ehhhhh! I give it a . . . (*Repeats gesture.*) Ehhhhh!

KAREN: Really? I thought it was—

BARBARA: Great, now we get some dramatic criticism—

VIOLET: I would've preferred an open casket.

BARBARA: That just wasn't possible, Mom.

VIOLET: That today's the send-off Bev should've got if he died around 1974. Lots of talk about poetry, teaching. Well, he hadn't written any poetry to speak of since '65 and he never liked teaching worth a damn. Nobody talked about the good stuff. Man was a world-class alcoholic, more'n fifty years. Nobody told the story about that night he got wrangled into giving a talk at a TU alumni dinner . . . (*Laughs.*) Drank a whole bottle of rum, Ron Bocoy White Rum—I don't know why I remember that—and got up to give this talk . . . and he fouled himself! Comes back to our table with this huge—

BARBARA: Yeah, I can't imagine why no one told *that* story.

VIOLET: He didn't get invited back to any more alumni dinners, I'll tell you that! (*She cracks up.*)

STEVE: You know, I don't know much about poetry, but I thought his poems were extraordinary. (*To Bill.*) And your reading was very fine.

BILL: Thank you.

VIOLET: (*To Steve.*) Who *are* you?

KAREN: Mom, this is my fiancé, Steve, I introduced you at the church.

STEVE: Steve Heidebrecht.

VIOLET: Hide-the-what?

STEVE: Heidebrecht.

VIOLET: Hide-a-burrr . . . German, you're a German.

STEVE: Well, German-Irish, really, I—

VIOLET: That's peculiar, Karen, to bring a date to your father's funeral. I know the poetry was good, but I wouldn't have really considered it date material—

BARBARA: Jesus.

KAREN: He's not a date, he's my fiancé. We're getting married on New Year's.

CHARLIE: Man, these potatoes are—

KAREN: In Miami, I hope you can make it.

VIOLET: I don't really see that happening, do you?

KAREN: I—

VIOLET: Steve. That right? *Steve?*

STEVE: Yes, ma'am.

VIOLET: You ever been married before?

KAREN: That's personal.

STEVE: I don't mind. Yes, ma'am, I have.

VIOLET: More'n once?

STEVE: Three times, actually, three times before this—

VIOLET: You should pretty much have it down by now, then.

STEVE: (*Laughs.*) Right, right—

VIOLET: (*To Mattie Fae.*) I had that one pegged, didn't I? I mean, look at him, you can tell he's been married—

KAREN: I took Steve out to show him the old fort and it's gone!

IVY: That's been gone for years.

KAREN: That made me so sad!

BILL: What is this now?

KAREN: Our old fort, where we used to play Cowboys and Indians.

IVY: Daddy said rats were getting in there—

VIOLET: Karen! Shame on you!

KAREN: Hm?

VIOLET: Don't you know not to say "Cowboys and Indians"? You played Cowboys and Native Americans. Right, Barb?

BARBARA: What'd you take?

VIOLET: Hm?

BARBARA: What did you take? What pills did you take?

VIOLET: Lemme alone— (*Charlie drops his head, appears distressed.*)

CHARLIE: Uh-oh . . .

MATTIE FAE: What is it?

CHARLIE: UH-OH!

MATTIE FAE: What's the matter? (*Rising panic . . .*)

LITTLE CHARLES: Dad—?   IVY: You okay, Uncle—?

CHARLIE: I just got a big bite of fear! (*Everyone laughs.*) I'm shakin' in my boots! (*Laughter, ad-libs, etc. Charlie digs into his plate ravenously.*) Fear never tasted so good. (*He winks at Jean.*)

STEVE: (*Laughing.*) Right, right, it's pretty good once you get used to the taste.

BARBARA: (*Teasing.*) I catch her eating a cheeseburger every now and again.

JEAN: I do not!

BARBARA: Double cheeseburger with bacon, extra fear.

JEAN: Mom, you are such a liar! (*More laughter.*)

VIOLET: (*Staring intensely at Jean.*) Y'know . . . if I ever called my mom a liar? She would've knocked my goddamn head off my shoulders. (*Silence.*) Bill, I see you've gone through much of Beverly's office.

BILL: Not all of it, but—

VIOLET: Find any hidden treasure?

BILL: Not exactly, but it appears he was working on some new poetry.

KAREN: Really?

BILL: I found a couple of notebooks that had—

VIOLET: You girls know there's a will.

BARBARA: Mom . . .

VIOLET: We took care of that some time back, but—

BARBARA: Mom, really, we don't want to talk about this now—

VIOLET: I want to talk about it. What about what I want to talk about, that count for anything?

BARBARA: It's just—

VIOLET: Bev made some good investments if you can believe it, and we had things covered for you girls, but he and I talked it over after some years passed and decided to change things, leave everything to me. We never got around to taking care of it legally, but you should know he meant to leave everything to me. Leave the money to me.

BARBARA: Okay.

VIOLET: Okay? (*Checks in with Ivy, Karen.*) Okay?

IVY: Okay.

VIOLET: Karen? Okay? (*Uncertain, Karen looks to Steve, then Barbara.*)

BARBARA: Okay.

KAREN: Okay.

VIOLET: Okay. But now some of this furniture, some of this old shit you can just have. I don't want it, got no use for it. Maybe I should have an auction.

MATTIE FAE: Sure, an auction's a fine idea—

VIOLET: Some things, though, like the silver, that's worth a pretty penny. But if you like I'll sell it to you, cheaper'n I might get in an auction.

BARBARA: Or you might never get around to the auction and then we can just have it for free after you die.

IVY: Barbara . . . (*Pause. Violet coolly studies Barbara.*)

VIOLET: You might at that.

LITTLE CHARLES: Excuse me, Bill? I'm wondering, this writing you found, these poems—?

VIOLET: Where are you living now, Bill? You want this old sideboard?

BILL: I beg your pardon.

VIOLET: You and Barbara are separated, right? Or you divorced already? (*Another silence.*)

BILL: We're separated.

VIOLET: (*To Barbara.*) Thought you could slip that one by me, didn't you?

BARBARA: What is the matter with you?

VIOLET: Nobody slips anything by me. I know what's what. Your father thought he's slipping one by me, right? No way. I'm sorry you two're having trouble . . . maybe you can work it out. Bev'n I separated a couple of times, 'course, though we didn't call it that—

The family grows concerned for Charlie in the 2007 production of *August: Osage County.*

BARBARA: Please, help us to benefit from an illustration of your storybook marriage—

VIOLET: Truth is, sweetheart, you can't compete with a younger woman, there's no way to compete. One of those unfair things in life. Is there a younger woman involved?

BARBARA: You've already said enough on this subject, I think—

BILL: Yes. There's a younger woman.

VIOLET: Ah . . . y'see? Odds're against you there, babe.

IVY: Mom believes women don't grow more attractive with age.

KAREN: Oh, I disagree, I—

VIOLET: I didn't say they "don't grow more attractive," I said they get ugly. And it's not really a matter of opinion, Karen dear. You've only just started to prove it yourself.

CHARLIE: You're in rare form today, Vi.

VIOLET: The day calls for it, doesn't it? What form would you have me in?

CHARLIE: I just don't understand why you're so adversarial.

VIOLET: I'm just truth-telling. (*Cutting her eyes to Barbara.*) Some people get antagonized by the truth.

CHARLIE: Everyone here loves you, dear.

VIOLET: You think you can *shame* me, Charlie? Blow it out your ass.

BARBARA: Three days ago . . . I had to identify my father's corpse. And now I sit here and listen to you viciously attack each and every member of this family— (*Violet rises, her voice booming.*)

VIOLET: "Attack my family"?! You ever been attacked in your sweet spoiled life?! Tell her 'bout attacks, Mattie Fae, tell her what an attack looks like!

MATTIE FAE: Vi, please—

IVY: Settle down, Mom—

VIOLET: Stop telling me to settle down, goddamn it! I'm not a goddamn invalid! I don't need to be abided, do I?! Am I already passed over?!

MATTIE FAE: Honey—

VIOLET: (*Points to Mattie Fae.*) This woman came to my rescue when one of my dear mother's many gentlemen friends was attacking me, with a claw hammer! This woman has dents in her skull from hammer blows! You think you been attacked?! What do you know about life on these Plains? What do you know about hard times?

BARBARA: I know you had a rotten childhood, Mom. Who didn't?

VIOLET: You DON'T know! You do NOT know! None of you know, 'cept this woman right here and that man we buried today! Sweet girl, sweet Barbara, my heart breaks for every time you ever felt pain. I wish I coulda shielded you from it. But if you think for a solitary second you can fathom the pain that man endured in his natural life, you got another think coming. Do you know where your father lived from age four 'til about ten? Do you? (*No one responds.*) Do you?!

BARBARA: No.

IVY: No.

VIOLET: *In a Pontiac sedan.* With his mother, his father, in a fucking car! Now what else do you want to say about your rotten childhood? That's the crux of the biscuit: We lived too hard, then rose too high. We sacrificed everything and we did it all for you. Your father and I were the first in our families to finish high school and he wound up an award-winning poet. You girls, given a college education, taken for granted no doubt, and where'd *you* wind up? (*Jabs a finger at Karen.*) Whadda *you* do? (*Jabs a finger at Ivy.*) Whadda *you* do? (*Jabs a finger at Barbara.*) Who're *you*? Jesus, you worked as hard as us, you'd all be president. You never had real problems so you got to make all your problems yourselves.

BARBARA: Why are you screaming at us?

VIOLET: Just time we had some truths told 'round here's all. Damn fine day, tell the truth.

CHARLIE: Well, the truth is . . . I'm getting full.

STEVE: Amen.

JOHNNA: There's dessert, too.

KAREN: I saw her making those pics. They looked so good. (*Little Charles suddenly stands.*)

LITTLE CHARLES: I have a truth to tell.

VIOLET: It speaks. (*Little Charles looks to Ivy.*)

IVY: (*Softly pleading.*) Nooo, nooo—

CHARLIE: What is it, son?

LITTLE CHARLES: I have a truth. (*Silence.*)

MATTIE FAE: Little Charles . . . ?

LITTLE CHARLES: I . . .

IVY: (*Almost to herself.*) Charles, not like this, please . . .

LITTLE CHARLES: The truth is, I . . . I forgot to set the clock. This morning. The power didn't go out, I just . . . forgot to set the clock. Sorry, Mom. I'm sorry, everyone. Excuse me . . . I . . . I. (*He leaves the dining room, exits the house . . . pauses on the porch, exits.*)

VIOLET: Scintillating. (*Charlie turns to Mattie Fae, confused.*)

MATTIE FAE: I gave up a long time ago . . . Little Charles is your project.

IVY: (*Near tears.*) Charles. His name is Charles. (*The family eats in silence. Violet pats Ivy's wrists.*)

VIOLET: Poor Ivy. Poor thing.

IVY: Please, Mom . . .

VIOLET: Poor baby.

IVY: Please . . .

VIOLET: She's always had a feeling for the underdog.

IVY: Don't be mean to me right now, okay?

VIOLET: Everyone's got this idea I'm mean, all of a sudden.

IVY: *Please*, Momma.

VIOLET: I told you, I'm just telling the—

BARBARA: You're a drug addict.

VIOLET: That is the truth! That's what I'm getting at! I, everybody listen . . . I am a drug addict. I am addicted to drugs, pills, 'specially downers. (*Pulls a bottle of pills from her pocket, holds them up.*) Y'see these little blue babies? These are my best fucking friends and they never let me down. Try to get 'em away from me and I'll eat you alive.

BARBARA: Gimme those goddamn pills—

VIOLET: I'll eat you alive, girl! (*Barbara lunges at the bottle of pills. She and Violet wrestle with it. Bill and Ivy try to restrain Barbara. Mattie Fae tries to restrain Violet. Others rise, ad-lib.*)

STEVE: Holy shit.

IVY: Barbara, stop it!—

CHARLIE: Hey, now, c'mon!—

KAREN: Oh God— (*Violet wins, wrests the pills away from Barbara. Bill pulls Barbara back into her seat. Violet shakes the pill bottle, taunting Barbara. Barbara snaps, screams, lunges again, grabs Violet by the hair, pulls her up, toppling chairs. They crash through the house, pursued by the family. Pandemonium. Screaming. Barbara strangles Violet. With great effort, Bill and Charlie pry the two women apart. Mattie Fae and Johnna rush to Violet, tend to her.*)

VIOLET: (*Crying.*) Goddamn you . . . goddamn you, Barb . . .

BARBARA: SHUT UP! (*To the others.*) Okay. Pill raid. Johnna, help me in the kitchen. Bill, take Ivy and Jean upstairs. (*To Ivy.*) You remember how to do this, right?

IVY: Yeah . . .

BARBARA: (*To Jean.*) Everything. Go through everything, every counter, every drawer, every shoe box. Nothing's too personal. Anything even looks suspicious, throw it in a box and we can sort it out later. You understand?

CHARLIE: What should we do?

BARBARA: Get Mom some black coffee and a wet towel and listen to her bullshit. Karen, call Dr. Burke.

KAREN: What do you want me to say?

BARBARA: Tell him we got a sick woman here.

VIOLET: You can't do this! This is *my* house! This is *my* house!

BARBARA: You don't get it, do you? (*With a burst of adrenaline, she strides to Violet, towers over her.*) I'M RUNNING THINGS NOW! (*Blackout.*)

ACT THREE • Scene 1

The window shades have all been removed. Nighttime is now free to encroach.

At rise: the three sisters in the study. They share a bottle of whiskey. An inflatable mattress, covered with a thin sheet, now lies on the study floor.

 Elsewhere in the house: a game of spades in the dining room—Charlie and Mattie Fae versus Jean and Steve. Little Charles sits by himself in the living room, watching TV. Bill sorts through paperwork on the porch. Violet, pensive, wearing a robe, her hair wrapped in a towel, sits at the window on the second-floor landing.

KAREN: The doctor really thinks she needs to go to an institution? *Does* she need to go? Did he examine her?

BARBARA: Dr. Burke says she may be brain damaged. "Slightly brain damaged." I told him he was "slightly incompetent" and I hoped some day soon he'd be "slightly dead." He claims not to know she was taking so much. That's why he's eager to put her away, he's afraid of a malpractice suit. I told him I was considering it. Irresponsible shithead—

KAREN: Why did he write so many prescriptions? Doesn't he know—?

BARBARA: It's not just him; she's got a doctor in every port—

IVY: Here's how she does it: She sees a doctor for back spasms and gets a prescription. Day or two later she goes back, says she lost her pills and he writes her another one. Then next week she pulls a muscle, more pills, then the dosage is wrong, more pills, over and over, until she makes one too many trips and he says I'm not prescribing anymore. And she pulls a sheaf of prescription receipts out of her purse and says, "I'll go to the AMA and have your ass in court for overprescribing me." She genuinely threatens these men and they give in to her.

BARBARA (*To Ivy.*): You knew this was going on again? (*Ivy shrugs.*) Different tactic today, just at her wounded best, this wilting hothouse flower. Which made me look like Bette Davis.° I tried to goad her into it, you know, "C'mon, Mom, give him your speech about the Greatest Generation. Tell him about the claw hammer." I was like that guy in the cartoon with the frog that only sings for him.

IVY: It wouldn't have done any good, Dr. Burke's part of the same generation.

BARBARA: "Greatest Generation," my ass. Are they really considering *all* the generations? Maybe there are some generations from the *Iron Age* that could compete. And what makes them so great anyway? Because they were poor and hated Nazis? Who doesn't fucking hate Nazis?! You remember when we checked her in the psych ward, that stunt she pulled?

IVY: Which time?

KAREN: I wasn't there.

BARBARA: Big speech, she's getting clean, this sacrifice she's making for her family, and—

IVY: Right, she's let her *family* down but now she wants to prove she's a good family member—

BARBARA: She smuggled Darvocet into the psych ward . . . *in her vagina.* There's your Greatest Generation for you. She made this speech to us while she was clenching a bottle of pills in her cooch, for God's sake.

KAREN: God, I've never heard that story.

IVY: Did you just say "cooch"?

BARBARA: The phrase "Mom's pussy" seems a bit gauche.

IVY: You're a little more comfortable with "cooch," are you?

Bette Davis: American actress (1908–1989) prominent over six decades, famous for her part in *Whatever Happened to Baby Jane* (1962).

BARBARA: What word should I use to describe our mother's vagina?

IVY: I don't know, but—

BARBARA: "Mom's beaver"? "Mother's box"?

IVY: Oh God—

KAREN: Barbara! (*Laughter, finally dying out.*) I'm sorry about you and Bill.

IVY: Me, too, Barb.

BARBARA: If I had my way, you never would've known.

KAREN: Do you think it's a temporary thing, or . . . ?

BARBARA: Who knows? We've been married a long time.

KAREN: That's one thing about Mom and Dad. You have to tip your cap to anyone who can stay married that long.

IVY: Karen. He killed himself.

KAREN: Yeah, but still.

BARBARA: Is there something going on between you and Little Charles?

IVY: I don't know that I'm comfortable talking about that.

BARBARA: Because you know he is our first cousin.

IVY: Give me a break.

KAREN: You know you shouldn't consider children.

IVY: I'm almost forty-five, Karen, I put those thoughts behind me a long time ago. Anyway, I had a hysterectomy year before last.

KAREN: Why?

IVY: Cervical cancer.

KAREN: I didn't know that.

BARBARA: Neither did I.

IVY: I didn't tell anyone except Charles. That's where it started between him and me.

BARBARA: Why not? Why wouldn't you tell anyone?

IVY: And hear those comments from Mom for the rest of my life? She doesn't need any more excuses to treat me like some damaged thing.

BARBARA: You might have told us.

IVY: You weren't going to tell us about you and Bill.

BARBARA: That's different.

IVY: Why? Because it's you, and not me?

BARBARA: No, because divorce is an embarrassing public admission of defeat. Cancer's fucking cancer, you can't help that. We're your sisters. We might've given you some comfort.

IVY: I just don't feel that connection very keenly.

KAREN: I feel very connected, to both of you.

IVY: (*Amused.*) We never see you, you're never around, you haven't been around for—

KAREN: But I still feel that connection!

IVY: You think if you tether yourself to this place in mind only, you don't need to actually appear.

KAREN: You know me that well.

IVY: No, and that's my point. I can't perpetuate these myths of family or sisterhood anymore. We're all just people, some of us accidentally connected by genetics, a random selection of cells. Nothing more.

BARBARA: When did you get so cynical?

IVY: That's funny coming from you.

BARBARA: Bitter, sure, but "random selection of cells"?

IVY: Maybe my cynicism flowered with the realization that the obligation of caring for our parents was mine alone.

BARBARA: Don't give me that. I participated in every goddamn—

IVY: Until you had enough and got out, you and Karen.

BARBARA: I had my own family to think about.

IVY: That's a cheap excuse. As if by having a child you were alleviated of all responsibility.

BARBARA: So now I'm being criticized for procreating.

IVY: I'm not criticizing. Do what you want. You did, Karen did.

BARBARA: And if you didn't, that's not my fault.

IVY: That's right, so don't lay this sister thing on me now, all right? I don't buy it. I haven't bought it for a long time. When I leave here and leave for good I won't feel any more guilty than you two did.

KAREN: Who says we don't?

BARBARA: Are you leaving here?

IVY: Charles and I are going to New York. (*Barbara bursts out laughing.*)

BARBARA: What the hell are you going to do in New York?

IVY: We have plans.

BARBARA: Like what?

IVY: None of your business.

BARBARA: You can't just go to New York.

IVY: This isn't whimsy. This isn't fleeting. This is unlike anything I've ever felt, for anybody. Charles and I have something rare, and extraordinary, something very few people ever have.

KAREN: Which is what?

IVY: Understanding.

BARBARA: What about Mom?

IVY: What about her?

BARBARA: You feel comfortable leaving Mom here?

IVY: Do you? (*No response.*) You think she was difficult while Dad was alive? Think about what it's going to be like now. You can't imagine the cumulative effect, after a month, after a year, after many years. You can't imagine. And even if you could, you can only imagine for yourself, for yourself, the favorite.

BARBARA: Christ, Mom pulled that on me the other day about Dad, that I was his favorite.

IVY: Well . . . that's not true. You weren't his favorite. I was. You're Mom's favorite.

BARBARA: *What?*

KAREN: Thanks, Ivy.

IVY: You don't think so? Good God, Barb, I've lived my life by that standard.

BARBARA: She said Dad was heartbroken when we moved to Boulder—

IVY: Mom was heartbroken, not Dad. She was convinced you left to get away from her.

KAREN: If you were Daddy's favorite, you must take his suicide kind of personally.

IVY: Daddy killed himself for his own reasons.

BARBARA: And what were those reasons?

IVY: I won't presume.

BARBARA: Aren't you angry with him?

IVY: No. He's accountable to no one but himself. If he's better off now, and I don't doubt he is, who are we to begrudge him that?

BARBARA: *His daughters.*

KAREN: *Yeah—*

BARBARA: And I'm fucking furious. The selfish son-of-a-bitch, his silence, his melancholy . . . he could have, for me, for us, for all of us, he could have helped us, included us, talked to us.

IVY: You might not have liked what you heard. What if the truth of the matter is that Beverly Weston never liked you? That he never liked any of us, never had any special feeling of any kind for his children?

BARBARA: You know that's not true.

IVY: Do I? How? Do *you?*

KAREN: You said you were his favorite.

IVY: Only because he recognized a kindred spirit.

BARBARA: Mm, sorry, but your little theory, your "accidental genetics," that doesn't fly, not with me. I believe he had a responsibility to something greater than himself; we *all* do.

IVY: Good luck with that.

KAREN: I just can't believe your worldview is that dark.

IVY: You live in Florida.

BARBARA: When are you and Little Charles leaving?

IVY: Weeks, if not days. And his name is Charles.

BARBARA: Are you telling Mom?

IVY: I'm trying to figure it out.

BARBARA: What about your job, your house?

IVY: I've been taking care of myself a lot longer than you've been in charge. Karen, you're going back to Miami, right?

KAREN: Yes. (*Violet descends the stairs.*)

IVY: There you go, Barb. You want to know what we're going to do about Mom? Karen and I are leaving. You want to stay and deal with her, that's your decision; if you don't like it, that's your prerogative. But nobody gets to point a finger at me. Nobody. (*Shaky but mainly lucid, Violet enters, knocking softly.*)

VIOLET: Hello? Am I interrupting anything? (*Ad-libs: "Not at all," "Come in," etc.*)

BARBARA: You had a bath?

VIOLET: Mm-hm.

BARBARA: You need something to eat, or drink?

VIOLET: No.

BARBARA: You want some more coffee?

VIOLET: No, honey, I'm fine. (*Violet sits, exhales. Karen picks up a hand cream from the bedside table, rubs it on her hands.*) You girls all together in this house. Just hearing your voices outside the door gives me a warm feeling. These walls must've heard a lot of secrets.

KAREN: I get embarrassed just thinking about it.

VIOLET: Oh . . . nothing to be embarrassed about. Secret crushes, secret schemes . . . province of teenage girls. I can't imagine anything more delicate, or bittersweet. Some part of you girls I just always identified with . . . no matter how old you get, a woman's

hard-pressed to throw off that part of herself. (*To Karen, regarding the hand cream.*) That smells good.

KAREN: Doesn't it? It's apple. You want some?

VIOLET: Yes, please. (*Karen passes the hand cream to Violet.*) I ever tell you the story of Raymond Qualls? Not much story to it. Boy I had a crush on when I was thirteen or so. Real rough-looking boy, beat-up Levis, messy hair. Terrible underbite. But he had these beautiful cowboy boots, shiny chocolate leather. He was so proud of those boots, you could tell, the way he'd strut around, all arms and elbows, puffed-up and cocksure. I decided I needed to get a girly pair of those same boots and I knew he'd ask me to go steady, convinced myself of it. He'd see me in those boots and say, "Now there's the gal for me." Found the boots in a window downtown and just went crazy: I'd stay up late in bed, praying for those boots, rehearsing the conversation I was going to have with Raymond when he saw me in my boots. Must've asked my momma a hundred times if I could get those boots. "What do you want for Christmas, Vi?" "Momma, I'll give all of it up just for those boots." Bargaining, you know? She started dropping hints about a package under the tree she had wrapped up, about the size of a boot box, real nice wrapping paper. "Now, Vi, don't you cheat and look in there before Christmas morning." Little smile on her face. Christmas morning, I was up like a shot, boy, under the tree, tearing open that box. There was a pair of boots, all right . . . men's work boots, holes in the toes, chewed-up laces, caked in mud and dog shit. Lord, my momma laughed for days. (*Silence.*)

BARBARA: Please don't tell me that's the end of that story.

VIOLET: Oh, no. That's the end.

KAREN: You never got the boots?

VIOLET: No, huh-uh.

BARBARA: Okay, well, that's the worst story I ever heard. That makes me wish for a heartwarming claw hammer story. (*Elsewhere in the house: Jean and Steve win the card game with an exclamation of triumph. The players disperse.*)

VIOLET: No, no. My momma was a nasty, mean old lady. I suppose that's where I get it from. (*An awkward moment.*)

KAREN: You're not nasty-mean. You're our mother and we love you.

VIOLET: Thank you, sweetheart. (*Karen kisses Violet's cheek.*)

BARBARA: Hey you all, I need to talk to Mom for a minute.

KAREN: Sure. (*Ivy and Karen exit.*)

BARBARA: How's your head?

VIOLET: I'm fine, Barb. Don't worry about that.

BARBARA: I'm sorry.

VIOLET: Please, honey—

BARBARA: No, it's important that I say this. I lost my temper and went too far.

VIOLET: Barbara. The day, the funeral . . . the pills. I was spoiling for a fight and you gave it to me.

BARBARA: So . . . truce?

VIOLET: (*Laughs.*) Truce.

BARBARA: What do you want to do?

VIOLET: How do you mean?

BARBARA: Don't you think you should consider a rehab center, or—?

VIOLET: Oh, no. I can't go through that. No, I can do this. I'm pretty sure I can.

BARBARA: Really?

VIOLET: Yes. Well, look, you got rid of my pills, right?

BARBARA: All we could find.

VIOLET: I don't have that many hiding places.

BARBARA: Mom, now, come on.

VIOLET: You wanna search me?

BARBARA: Uh . . . no.

VIOLET: If the pills are gone, I'll be fine. Just take me a few days to get my feet under me.

BARBARA: I can't imagine what all this must be like for you right now. I just want you to know, you're not alone in this. (*No response.*) How can I help?

VIOLET: I don't need help.

BARBARA: I want to help.

VIOLET: I don't need your help.

BARBARA: Mom.

VIOLET: I don't need your *help*. I've gotten myself through some . . . (*Stops, collects herself.*) I know how this goes: Once all the talking's through, people go back to their own nonsense. I know that. So don't you worry about me. I'll manage. I get by. (*Lights cross-fade to the living room where Little Charles watches TV. Ivy enters the room guardedly.*)

IVY: Is the coast clear?

LITTLE CHARLES: Never very.

IVY: What are you watching?

LITTLE CHARLES: Television.

IVY: Can I watch it with you?

LITTLE CHARLES: I wish you would. (*She sits beside him on the couch. They watch TV.*) I almost blew it, didn't I?

IVY: Yeah.

LITTLE CHARLES: Are you mad at me?

IVY: Nope. (*They hold hands.*)

LITTLE CHARLES: I was trying to be brave.

IVY: I know.

LITTLE CHARLES: I just . . . I want everyone to know that I got what I always wanted. And that means . . . I'm not a loser.

IVY: Hey. Hey. (*He turns to look at her.*) You're my hero. (*He considers this . . . then beams a huge smile. He goes to the electric piano, turns it on.*)

LITTLE CHARLES: Come here. You can help me push the pedals. (*She sits beside him on the piano bench.*) I wrote this for you. (*He plays, and quietly sings a gentle but quirky love song. Midway through, Mattie Fae enters from the kitchen, breaking the spell, Charlie in tow.*)

MATTIE FAE: Liberace. Get yourself together, we're heading back.

IVY: Are you all staying at   LITTLE CHARLES: Okay . . .
my place?

MATTIE FAE: No, we have to get home and take care of those damn dogs.

IVY: You know you're welcome.

MATTIE FAE: (*To Charlie.*)   CHARLIE: Thanks, Ivy.
Oh, look, honey, Little
Charles has got the
TV on.

LITTLE CHARLES: No, I was just—

MATTIE FAE: (*To Ivy.*) This one watches so much television, it's rotted his brain.

IVY: I'm sure that's not true.

MATTIE FAE: (*To Little Charles.*) What was it I caught you watching the other day?

LITTLE CHARLES: I don't   CHARLIE: Mattie Fae—
remember.

MATTIE FAE: You do so remember, some dumb game show about people swapping wives.

LITTLE CHARLES: I don't remember.

MATTIE FAE: You don't remember.

CHARLIE: C'mon, Mattie Fae—

MATTIE FAE: Too bad there isn't a job where they pay you to sit around watching television.

CHARLIE: Mattie Fae, it's been a long day.

MATTIE FAE: I suppose you wouldn't like TV then, not if watching it constituted getting a job.

CHARLIE: Mattie Fae—

MATTIE FAE: (*To Ivy.*) Did I tell you he got fired from a *shoe store*?

CHARLIE: Mattie Fae, we're gonna go get in the car right now and go home and if you say one more mean thing to that boy I'm going to kick your fat Irish ass onto the highway. You hear me? (*She wheels on Charlie, stung.*)

MATTIE FAE: What the hell did you say?—

CHARLIE: You kids go outside. (*Ivy and Little Charles exit the house. Barbara, who had started to enter during the previous exchange, stops short, unseen by Charlie or Mattie Fae.*) I don't understand this meanness. I look at you and your sister and the way you talk to people and I don't understand it. I just can't understand why folks can't be respectful of one another. I don't think there's any excuse for it. My family didn't treat each other that way.

MATTIE FAE: Well maybe that's because your family is a—

CHARLIE: You had better not say anything about my family right now. I mean it.

   We buried a man today I loved very much. And whatever faults he may have had, he was a good, kind, *decent* person. And to hear you tear into your own son on a day like today dishonors Beverly's memory.

   We've been married for thirty-eight years. I wouldn't trade them for anything. But if you can't find a generous place in your heart for your own son, we're not going to make it to thirty-nine. (*He leaves. Mattie Fae becomes aware of Barbara.*)

BARBARA: I'm sorry, I didn't mean to eavesdrop. I froze.

MATTIE FAE: That's. Do you have a cigarette, hon?

BARBARA: No, I quit years ago.

MATTIE FAE: So did I. It just sounded good to me. Barbara. I thought today at dinner . . . at that horrible dinner, it seemed like . . .

BARBARA: What?

MATTIE FAE: It seemed as if something might be going on between Ivy and Little Charles. Do you know if that's true?

BARBARA: Oh, this is . . . I'm not sure what to say here, it's—

MATTIE FAE: Look, just. Can you tell me if that's true.

BARBARA: Yes. It's true.

MATTIE FAE: Okay. That can't happen.

BARBARA: This is going to be difficult to explain. Um. You know, Ivy and Little Charles have always marched to their own—and obviously, I would expect this to be toughest on you—

MATTIE FAE: Barb—?

BARBARA: I think they're very much in love. Or at least they think they are. What's the difference, right? And I'm sure they must be terrified of you and Mom—

MATTIE FAE: Honey—

BARBARA: I realize it's pretty unorthodox for cousins to get together, at least these days—

MATTIE FAE: They're not cousins.

BARBARA: —but believe it or not, it's not as uncommon as you might—

MATTIE FAE: Barbara. Listen to me. They're not cousins.

BARBARA: Beg pardon?

MATTIE FAE: Little Charles is not your cousin. He's your brother. He's your blood brother. He is not your cousin. He is your blood brother. Half-brother. He's your father's child. Which means that he is Ivy's brother. Do you see? Little Charles and Ivy are brother and sister.

BARBARA: No, that's not—no.

MATTIE FAE: Listen— (*Karen and Steve enter.*)

BARBARA: No. Go back.

KAREN: We're just going to—

BARBARA: Go back into the kitchen. Now! Just . . . everyone stay in the kitchen! (*Karen and Steve retreat to the kitchen.*) No, that's wrong. You. Okay, well this may be—are you sure?

MATTIE FAE: Yes.

BARBARA: You and Dad.

MATTIE FAE: Yes.

BARBARA: Who knows this?

MATTIE FAE: I do. And you do.

BARBARA: Uncle Charlie doesn't suspect.

MATTIE FAE: We've never discussed it.

BARBARA: What?!

MATTIE FAE: We've never discussed it. Okay?

BARBARA: Did Dad know? (*Mattie Fae nods.*)

MATTIE FAE: Y'know, I'm not proud of this.

BARBARA: *Really.* You people amaze me. What, were you drunk? Was this just some—?

MATTIE FAE: I wasn't drunk, no. Maybe it's hard for you to believe, looking at me, knowing me the way you do, all these years. I know to you, I'm just your old fat Aunt Mattie Fae. But I'm more than that, sweetheart . . . there's more to me than that.

Charlie's right, of course. As usual. I don't know why Little Charles is such a disappointment to me. Maybe he . . . well, I don't know why. I guess I'm disappointed *for* him, more than anything.

I made a mistake, a long time ago. Well, okay. Fair enough. I've paid for it. But the mistake ends here.

BARBARA: If Ivy found out about this, it would destroy her.

MATTIE FAE: *I'm* sure as hell not gonna tell her. You have to find a way to stop it. You have to put a stop to it.

BARBARA: Why me?

MATTIE FAE: You said you were running things.

Scene 2

Giggling from the kitchen, Jean and Steve quietly scamper from the kitchen into the dining room, sharing a joint. She wears a knee-length T-shirt and white socks; he wears sweatpants and a sleeveless T-shirt.

The rest of the house is sleeping. Karen sleeps in the living room on the unfolded hide-a-bed. Bill sleeps on the mattress in the study.

STEVE: Shhh . . . (*Jean snort-laughs.*) You're gonna get me busted, you.

JEAN: I thought you weren't doing anything wrong.

STEVE: We're not, but some folks may not be crazy about me smoking pot with a girl born during the Clinton administration.

JEAN: First Bush.

STEVE: Great. Stop talking about your bush, all right? You're gonna get me hot and bothered—

JEAN: (*Laughing.*) You are sick—

STEVE: —and I won't be able to control myself.

JEAN: God, you weren't kidding, this stuff is strong.

STEVE: Florida, baby. Number one industry.

JEAN: Who cares?

STEVE: Number one, by far. You want a shotgun?

JEAN: Huh?

STEVE: You don't know what a shotgun is?

JEAN: I know what a shotgun is.

STEVE: Not that kind of shotgun—here. Just put your lips right next to mine and you inhale while I exhale.

JEAN: Okay. (*He puts the joint in his mouth, lit end first. Their lips nearly touch as he blows marijuana smoke into her mouth in a steady stream. She nearly chokes.*)

STEVE: Hold it. Don't let it out. (*She finally gasps, exhales, coughs.*)

JEAN: Whoa.

STEVE: That's a kick, huh?

JEAN: Whoa, shit, man.

STEVE: (*Laughs.*) That's what I'm talkin' about.

JEAN: Whoa, Jesus— (*She takes an off-balance step, sways. He catches her, holds her.*)

STEVE: Careful, now—

JEAN: Oh, man, what a head rush.

STEVE: You okay? You're not passing out on me, are you?

JEAN: No, I'm cool. Oh God . . . (*Coughs deeply.*) I really feel that in my chest. (*He reaches for her breasts.*)

STEVE: Here, let me feel. (*Unperturbed, she pushes him away.*)

JEAN: You're just an old perv.

STEVE: No shit. Christ, you got a great set. *How* old are you?

JEAN: I'm fifteen, perv.

STEVE: Show 'em to me.

JEAN: No, perv.

STEVE: Shhh. Yeah, show 'em to me. I won't look.

JEAN: If you won't look, there's no point in showing them to you.

STEVE: Okay, okay, I'll look then.

JEAN: (*Dumb guy voice.*) "Lemme look at your tits, little girl—"

STEVE: C'mon, we're partners!

JEAN: No!

STEVE: Aren't we amazing card partners?

JEAN: Forget it!

STEVE: I'll show you mine if you show me yours.

JEAN: I don't want to see yours.

STEVE: You ever seen one?

JEAN: Yes.

STEVE: No, you haven't.

JEAN: Yes, I have. I'm not a virgin.

STEVE: You're not?

JEAN: Not technically. Well, no *technically*, I am. I mean not theoretically.

STEVE: That changes everything. (*He moves in close to her.*)

JEAN: What are you doing?

STEVE: Nothing.

JEAN: You're gonna get us both in trouble.

STEVE: I'm white and over thirty. I don't get in trouble. (*He turns off the light. Total darkness.*)

JEAN: Hey . . .

STEVE: Shhh . . . (*Moaning, heavy breathing from Steve, in the dark. The overhead light clicks on. Johnna stands in the dining-room entryway, brandishing a cast-iron skillet. Jean and Steve, clothes in disarray, separate.*)

JEAN: Oh my God . . .

STEVE: Ho, fuck! (*Johnna approaches Steve.*) Hold up there, lady, you don't know what you're— (*Johnna swings the skillet, barely missing Steve's nose.*) Hey, goddamn it, careful— (*He reaches for the skillet. She swings again and smacks his knuckles.*) Ow, goddamn—! (*He grimaces, holds his hand in pain. She wades in with a strong swing and connects squarely with his forehead. Steve goes down. Johnna stands above him, arm cocked, watching for a recovery, but he does not*

attempt it. *Elsewhere in the house: Bill, Barbara and Karen wake in their different locations, head to the dining room. Karen sees Steve on the floor and screams:*)

KAREN: What happened?! (*Johnna and Jean share a look. Karen goes to Steve, props him up.*) Steve, what happened?! (*He groans.*) Tell me what happened.

JOHNNA: He was messing with Jean.

KAREN: Honey, you're bleeding, are you okay? (*He groans again, tries to stand. Now Bill and Barbara enter the dining room, both in their night clothes.*)

BARBARA: Jean, what are you doing up? What's going on—?

JEAN: We were, I don't know—

BARBARA: Who was? Talk to me, are you all right?

JEAN: Yeah, I'm fine.

BILL: What happened to him? Do I need to call a doctor?

KAREN: I don't know.

BARBARA: Johnna, what's going on?

JOHNNA: He was messing with Jean. So I tuned him up.

BARBARA: "Messing with," what do you mean, "messing with"?

BILL: What . . . what's that mean?

JOHNNA: He was kissing her and grabbing her. (*This information settles in . . . Then Barbara attacks Steve, who has by now gotten to his feet. Ad-libs. Karen gets between them. Bill grabs Barbara from behind, tries to pull her away. Ad-libs.*)

BARBARA: I'll murder you, you prick!

BILL: (*To Karen.*) Get him out of here!

STEVE: I didn't do anything!—

JEAN: Mom, stop it!

KAREN: Settle down!—

BILL: Get back in the living room!—

BARBARA: You know how old that girl is?!

STEVE: (*To Jean.*) Tell them I didn't do anything!—

BARBARA: She's fourteen years old!—

JEAN: Mom!

STEVE: She said she was fifteen!

BARBARA: Are you out of your goddamn mind?

KAREN: Barbara, just back off! (*Karen manages to push Steve out of the dining room, into the living room. During the following, they get dressed and pack their bags. Barbara, Bill, Jean and Johnna remain in the dining room.*)

BARBARA: Oh my God! Do you fucking believe that crazy prick?!

BILL: I know, I know, settle down.

BARBARA: "Settle down," the son-of-a-bitch is a goddamn sociopath! What the fuck is going on?

BILL: (*To Jean.*) Are you okay?

JEAN: Yes, I'm okay, what is the *matter* with you?

BARBARA: With *us*?

JEAN: Will you please stop freaking out?

BILL: Why don't you start at the beginning?

BARBARA: What are you doing out of bed?

BILL: Please, sweetheart, we need to know what went on here.

JEAN: Nothing "went on." Can we just not make a federal case out of everything? I couldn't sleep, I came to the kitchen for a drink, he came in . . . end of story.

BARBARA: That's not the end of the story. BILL: That's not the end of the story.

JEAN: We smoked pot, all right? We smoked a little pot, and we were goofing around, and then everything just went haywire.

BARBARA: What have I told you about smoking that shit?! What did I say? BILL: Then Johnna just chose to attack him with a frying pan? I don't think so.

JEAN: Look at you two, you're both so ridiculous. It's no big deal, nothing happened.

BILL: We're concerned about you.

JEAN: No, you're not. You just want to know who to punish.

BARBARA: Stop it—

JEAN: You can't tell the difference between the good guys and the bad guys, so you want me to sort it all out for you—

BARBARA: You know what, skip the lecture. Just tell me what he did!

JEAN: He didn't do anything! Even if he did, what's the big deal?

BILL: The big deal, Jean, is that you're fourteen years old.

JEAN: Which is only a few years younger than you like 'em. (*Barbara slaps Jean; Jean bursts into tears.*) I hate you!

BARBARA: Yeah, I hate you too, you little freak! (*Jean tries to exit. Bill grabs her.*)

BILL: Jean—

JEAN: Let me go! (*Jean pulls free, runs off.*)

BILL: (*To Barbara.*) What's the matter with you? (*Bill exits, pursuing Jean.*)

JOHNNA: Excuse me. (*Johnna exits, returns to her attic room. Barbara regains some composure, moves into the living room. Steve has by now dressed and exited, carrying suitcases. Karen is pulling on a sweatshirt, grabbing a few leftover items, restoring the hide-a-bed.*)

KAREN: I can do without a speech.

BARBARA: I beg your pardon?

KAREN: I'm leaving. *We're* leaving. Back to Florida, tonight, *now*. Me and Steve, together. You want to give me some grief about that?

BARBARA: Now wait just a goddamn—

KAREN: You better find out from Jean just exactly what went on in there before you start pointing fingers, that's all I'm saying. 'Cause I doubt Jean's exactly blameless in all this. And I'm not *blaming* her. Just because I said she's not blameless, that doesn't mean I've *blamed* her. I'm saying she might share in the responsibility. You understand me?

I know Steve should know better than Jean, that she's only fourteen. My point is, it's not cut and dried, black and white, good and bad. It lives where everything lives: somewhere in the middle. Where everything lives, where all the rest of us live, *everyone but you.*

BARBARA: Karen—

KAREN: I'm not defending him. He's not perfect. Just like all the rest of us, down here in the muck. I'm no angel myself. I've done some things I'm not proud of. Things you'll never know about. Know what? I may even have to do some things I'm not proud of *again.* 'Cause sometimes life puts you in a corner that way. And I am a human being, after all.

Anyway you have your own hash to settle. Before you start making speeches to the rest of us.

BARBARA: Right . . .

KAREN: Come January . . . I'll be in Belize. Doesn't that sound nice? (*Karen exits, rolling her suitcase behind her. Bill enters.*)

BILL: I'm taking Jean with me. We're heading back.

BARBARA: Fine.

BILL: She's too much for you right now.

BARBARA: Okay.

BILL: I'm sure you'll blame me for all this.

BARBARA: Yeah, well . . . (*Beat.*) I fail. As a sister, as a mother, as a wife. I fail.

BILL: No, you don't.

BARBARA: No? I've physically attacked Mom and Jean in the space of about nine hours. Stick around here much longer and I'll cut off your penis.

BILL: That's not funny.

BARBARA: I can't make it up to Jean right now. She's just going to have to wait until I come back to Boulder.

BILL: You and Jean have about forty years left to fight and make up.

BARBARA: (*Confused.*) Why, what happens in forty years?

BILL: You die.

BARBARA: Oh, right.

BILL: I mean—

BARBARA: No. Right.

BILL: If you're lucky.

BARBARA: Says you.

BILL: If *we're* lucky. (*Pause.*)

BARBARA: You're never coming back to me, are you, Bill?

BILL: Never say never, but . . .

BARBARA: But no.

BILL: But no.

BARBARA: Even if things don't work out with you and Marsha.

BILL: Cindy.

BARBARA: Cindy.

BILL: Right. Even if things don't work out.

BARBARA: And I'm never really going to understand why, am I? (*Bill struggles . . . it seems as if he might say something more, but then:*)

BILL: Probably not. (*Silence. Bill heads for the door. Barbara watches him go and sobs.*)

BARBARA: I love you . . . I love you . . . (*He stands for a moment, his back to her. He exits. Barbara stands, alone.*)

Scene 3

The study: Barbara and Johnna, in the same positions as Beverly and Johnna in the Prologue. Barbara's had a few. She nurses a glass of whiskey.

BARBARA: One of the last times I spoke with my father, we were talking about . . . I don't know, the state of the world, something . . . and he said, "You know, this country was always pretty much a whorehouse, but at least it used to have some promise. Now it's just a shithole." And I think now maybe he was talking about something else, something more specific, something more personal to him . . . this house? This family? His marriage? Himself? I don't know. But there was something sad in his voice—or no, not sad, he always sounded sad—something more hopeless than that. As if it had already happened. As if whatever was disappearing had already disappeared. As if it was too late. As if it was already over. And no one saw it go. This country, this experiment, America, this hubris:° what a lament, if no one saw it go. Here today, gone tomorrow. (*Beat.*) Dissipation is actually much worse than cataclysm.

JOHNNA: Mrs. Fordham, are you firing me?

BARBARA: Barbara. No, no. Oh, no. I'm giving you the opportunity to quit. I mean . . . there's work. And then there's work. And after all . . . I'm here. Look around. No one else is here. I mean, am I here, or am I here? I'm not saying your services aren't necessary. I just mean: *I'm* still here, goddamn it.

JOHNNA: I'm prepared to stay. I'm familiar with this job. I can do this job. I don't do it for you or Mrs. Weston. Or even for Mr. Weston. Right? I do it for me.

BARBARA: Why?

JOHNNA: I need the work. (*Barbara finishes her glass of whiskey.*)

BARBARA: Johnna . . . what did my father say to you? (*Pause.*)

JOHNNA: He talked a lot about his daughters . . . his three daughters, and his granddaughter. That was his joy.

BARBARA: Thank you. That makes me feel better. Knowing that you can lie. (*Beat.*) I want you to stay on. Don't worry about your salary. I'll take care of it. (*Johnna nods, exits. Barbara refills her whiskey glass. To herself.*) *I'm* still here, goddamn it.

Scene 4

For the first time since the shades were removed from the windows, the house is seen in morning light. Barbara and Sheriff Gilbeau stand in the living room.

hubris: Greek for the kind of pride that offends the gods.

BARBARA: Everyone just . . . vanished.

SHERIFF GILBEAU: You were the one I wanted to talk to.

BARBARA: 'Kay. Sit down. Do you want some coffee?

SHERIFF GILBEAU: No, thanks.

BARBARA: God, Deon, you look really good. You really . . . filled out. *Nicely*, I mean. You just look great.

SHERIFF GILBEAU: Thanks.

BARBARA: How 'bout me, don't I look good?

SHERIFF GILBEAU: Yes, sorry, yes. You look great, too, just great.

BARBARA: Did you want some coffee?

SHERIFF GILBEAU: Uh. No. No, thank you.

BARBARA: And you're the sheriff. Of all things. That's ironic.

SHERIFF GILBEAU: Why is that ironic?

BARBARA: It's not. It's incongruous. I think I misused "ironic." Oh, if my husband could hear *that*. Well, fuck him. No, but it is, "incongruous."

SHERIFF GILBEAU: Why's it incongruous?

BARBARA: Because of your, because of your . . . your dad.

SHERIFF GILBEAU: Oh, I see, yeah.

BARBARA: Is he still alive?

SHERIFF GILBEAU: Yeah, after a fashion. He has Alzheimer's.

BARBARA: Oh. That's awful.

SHERIFF GILBEAU: He's in a home over in Nowata.

BARBARA: I'm sorry to hear that. That's just. Married? You're married? Wow. Hot flash. I'm sorry, did you want some coffee? I asked you that already. You're married.

SHERIFF GILBEAU: Divorced.

BARBARA: Join the club.

SHERIFF GILBEAU: Really?

BARBARA: I mean, I'm joining your club. I mean looks like I'll be joining your, your club.

SHERIFF GILBEAU: Sorry to hear that.

BARBARA: Have kids?

SHERIFF GILBEAU: Three daughters.

BARBARA: Uh-huh. Look at that.

SHERIFF GILBEAU: Right, no, I can't tell you—

BARBARA: Three daughters, that's—

SHERIFF GILBEAU: —how many times I've thought about the Weston sisters over the years.

BARBARA: The Weston sisters. Been a while since I heard that. Sounds like a singing group.

SHERIFF GILBEAU: Yeah, I guess.

BARBARA: "Ladies and gentlemen . . . The Agitated Weston Sisters."

SHERIFF GILBEAU: Is your husband still here?

BARBARA: No, he left a few days ago. A week ago? Two weeks ago. Two weeks ago? Back to Colorado, with my daughter. With Jean.

SHERIFF GILBEAU: She seemed real sweet.

BARBARA: Ah, she's a nymphomaniac.

SHERIFF GILBEAU: Really.

BARBARA: "*Jean.*" That's a stupid name.

SHERIFF GILBEAU: I like it.

BARBARA: You know why we named her that? Bill's a big Jean Seberg° fan. Now *that's* ironic.

SHERIFF GILBEAU: I don't get it.

BARBARA: Jean Seberg killed herself. With a massive over-blah of . . . blah-biturates.

SHERIFF GILBEAU: Oh.

BARBARA: So. (*Silence.*)

SHERIFF GILBEAU: Barbara? Are you okay?

BARBARA: (*Softly.*) I'm fine. Just got the Plains.

SHERIFF GILBEAU: I thought . . . I thought if you were going to be staying here a while we might get some lunch someday. Catch up? Been a long time.

BARBARA: Mm.

SHERIFF GILBEAU: Would you like to get some lunch someday?

BARBARA: Mm-hm.

SHERIFF GILBEAU: The other reason I came. I got a call from a woman named Chitra Naidu, who runs the Country Squire Motel. She was throwing out some old newspapers and she saw a photo of Mr. Weston that ran with his obituary. And she recognized him as the man who stayed in Room 17 for two nights, the first two nights of his absence. (*Beat.*) She said he checked in and she didn't see him again until he checked out. He made no phone calls. She has no way of telling if he received any phone calls. But I can have a check run on the line to find out if he did.

BARBARA: Do you have a . . . cigarette?

SHERIFF GILBEAU: Yeah, sure. (*Fishes for a cigarette.*) I can check with the phone company, is what I mean. (*He lights her smoke.*)

BARBARA: That's not. No one knew where he was. I suppose he was, what . . . just trying to build up the courage to jump in the water, I guess.

SHERIFF GILBEAU: Or overcoming the courage not to.

BARBARA: Right? I don't follow that, but it doesn't matter.

SHERIFF GILBEAU: In any case. I thought you should know. (*A sad, still moment.*) So . . . I can call you sometime? About having lunch?

BARBARA: Come here.

SHERIFF GILBEAU: Barbara?

BARBARA: Sh. Come here . . . (*He does not.*) Come here . . . (*He does. She touches his face.*) Sweet . . .

SHERIFF GILBEAU: Barbara . . .

BARBARA: Mm . . . just . . . touches . . . (*She kisses him. He begins to take her arms but she moves away.*)

SHERIFF GILBEAU: Barbara.

BARBARA: I'm . . .

SHERIFF GILBEAU: I'm sorry?

BARBARA: I . . .

Jean Seberg: American film star (1938–1979) who played Joan of Arc, ostracized for being a supporter of the Black Panthers. FBI head J. Edgar Hoover spread false rumors about her and she eventually killed herself.

SHERIFF GILBEAU: Barbara? Barbara, did you say something?

BARBARA: I've forgotten what I look like.

Scene 5

Barbara, still wearing her nightgown, and Ivy, in the dining room. The house has taken on a ghostly cast. Elsewhere in the house: Johnna prepares dinner in the kitchen.

IVY: Is she clean?

BARBARA: Clean-ish.

IVY: So she's not clean.

BARBARA: The woman's got brain-damage, dummy. If you think I'm going to strip-search her every time she slurs a word—

IVY: You know the difference.

BARBARA: She's moderately clean.

IVY: "Moderately"?

BARBARA: You don't like "moderately"? Then let's say tolerably.

IVY: Is she clean, or not?

BARBARA: Back off. We're trying to get by here, okay?

IVY: I'm nervous.

BARBARA: Why? Oh, Christ, Ivy, not tonight.

IVY: Why not?

BARBARA: We're only just now settling into some kind of rhythm around here. Now you come in here with your little *issues*—

IVY: I have to tell her, don't I? We're leaving for New York tomorrow.

BARBARA: That's not a good idea.

IVY: "A good idea."

BARBARA: For you and Little Charles to take this thing any further.

IVY: Where is this coming from?

BARBARA: I just got to thinking about it, and I think it's a little weird, that's all.

IVY: It's not up to you.

BARBARA: Lot of fish in the sea. Surely you can rule out the one single man in the world you're related to.

IVY: I happen to love the man I'm related—

BARBARA: *Fuck love*, what a crock of shit. People can convince themselves they love a painted rock. (*Johnna brings food from the kitchen.*) Looks great. What is it?

JOHNNA: Catfish.

BARBARA: Bottom feeders, my favorite. (*Johnna retires to the kitchen. Violet enters from the second-floor hallway, heads slowly for the dining room.*)

IVY: You think I shouldn't tell her.

BARBARA: You should rethink the whole proposition. New York City is a ridiculous idea. You're almost fifty years old, Ivy, you can't go to New York, you'll break a hip. Eat your catfish.

IVY: You're infuriating.

BARBARA: I ain't the one fuckin' my cousin.

IVY: I have lived in this town, year in and year out, hoping against hope someone would come into my life—

BARBARA: Don't get all Carson McCullers° on me. Now wipe that tragic look off your face and eat some catfish.

IVY: Who are you to speak to me like this? (*Violet enters the dining room.*)

BARBARA: Howdy, Mom.

VIOLET: What's howdy about it?

BARBARA: Look, catfish.

VIOLET: Catfish.

BARBARA: (*Calling off.*) Johnna! (*To Violet.*) You hungry?

VIOLET: Ivy, you should smile. Like me. (*Johnna enters.*)

BARBARA: Mom needs her dinner, please. (*Johnna exits.*)

VIOLET: I'm not hungry.

BARBARA: You haven't eaten anything today. You didn't eat anything yesterday.

VIOLET: I'm not hungry.

BARBARA: You're eating. You do what I say. Everyone do what I say.

IVY: May I ask why neither of you is dressed?

BARBARA: What is it with you?

VIOLET: Yeah.

BARBARA: We're dressed. We're not sitting here naked, are we? Or did you want us to dress up?

VIOLET: Right, 'cause you're coming over for fish.

BARBARA: Right, 'cause you're coming over for fish we're supposed to dress up. (*Johnna reenters with two plates of food.*)

JOHNNA: I'll eat in my room.

BARBARA: That's fine, thank you. (*Johnna exits with her plate of food. To Violet.*) Eat.

VIOLET: No.

BARBARA: Eat it. Mom? Eat it.

VIOLET: No.

BARBARA: Eat it, you fucker. Eat that catfish.

VIOLET: Go to hell!

BARBARA: That doesn't cut any fucking ice with me. Now eat that fucking fish.

IVY: Mom. I have something to talk to you about.

BARBARA: No, you don't.

IVY: Barbara—

BARBARA: No, you don't. Shut up. Shut the fuck up.

IVY: Please—

VIOLET: What's to talk about?

IVY: Mom—

BARBARA: Forget it. Mom? Eat that fucking fish.

VIOLET: I'm not hungry.

BARBARA: Eat it.

VIOLET: NO!

IVY: Mom, I need to—!

VIOLET: NO!

IVY: Mom!

BARBARA: EAT THE FISH, BITCH!

IVY: Mom, please!

VIOLET: Barbara . . . !

BARBARA: Okay, fuck it, do what you want.

IVY: I have to tell you something.

BARBARA: Ivy's a lesbian.

VIOLET: What?

IVY: Barbara—

VIOLET: No, you're not.

IVY: No, I'm not—

BARBARA: Yes, you are. Did you eat your fish?

IVY: Barbara, stop it!

BARBARA: Eat your fish.

IVY: Barbara!

BARBARA: Eat your fish.

VIOLET: Barbara, quiet now—

IVY: Mom, please, this is important—

BARBARA: Eatyourfisheatyourfisheatyourfish— (*Ivy hurls her plate of food, smashes it.*) What the fuck—

IVY: I have something to say!

BARBARA: Are we breaking shit? (*Barbara takes a vase from the sideboard, smashes it.*) 'Cause I can break shit— (*Violet throws her plate, smashes it.*) See, we can all break shit.

IVY: Charles and I—

BARBARA: You don't want to break shit with *me*, muthah-fuckah!

IVY: Charles and I—

BARBARA: Johnna?! Little spill in here!

IVY: Barbara, stop it! Mom, Charles and I—

BARBARA: Little Charles—

IVY: Charles and I—

BARBARA: Little Charles—

IVY: Charles and I—

BARBARA: Little Charles—

IVY: Charles and I—

BARBARA: Little Charles—

IVY: Charles and I—

BARBARA: Little Charles—

IVY: Barbara—

BARBARA: You have to say "Little Charles" or she won't know who you're talking about.

IVY: Little Charles and I . . . (*Barbara relents. Ivy will finally get to say the words.*) Little Charles and I are—

VIOLET: Little Charles and you are brother and sister. I know that.

BARBARA: Oh . . . Mom.

IVY: What? *No*, listen to me, Little Charles—

VIOLET: I've always known that. I told you, no one slips anything by me.

IVY: *Mom*—

BARBARA: Don't listen to her.

VIOLET: I knew the whole time Bev and Mattie Fae were carrying on. Charlie shoulda known too, if he wasn't smoking all that grass.

BARBARA: It's the pills talking.

VIOLET: Pills can't talk.

IVY: Wait . . .

VIOLET: Your father tore himself up over it, for thirty some-odd years, but Beverly wouldn't have been Beverly if he didn't have plenty to brood about.

Carson McCullers: American writer (1917–1967) whose work is often described as Southern gothic. Her novel *The Heart Is a Lonely Hunter* (1940) championed the weak, the afflicted, and the outsider in society.

IVY: Mom, what are you . . . ?

BARBARA: Oh, honey . . .

VIOLET: It's better you girls know now, though, now you're older. Never know when someone might need a kidney. Better if everyone knows the truth.

IVY: Oh my God . . .

VIOLET: Though I can't see the benefit in Little Charles ever knowing, break his little heart. (*Tell Ivy.*) Tell me though, honey: how'd *you* find out? (*Ivy looks from Violet to Barbara . . . suddenly lurches away from the table, knocking over her chair.*)

BARBARA: Ivy?

IVY: Why did you tell me? Why in God's name did you tell me this?

VIOLET: Hey, what do *you* care?

IVY: You're monsters.

VIOLET: Come on now—

IVY: Picking the bones of the rest of us—

VIOLET: You crazy nut.

IVY: Monsters.

VIOLET: Who's the injured party here? (*Ivy staggers out of the dining room, into the living room. Barbara pursues her.*)

BARBARA: Ivy, listen—

IVY: Leave me alone!

BARBARA: Honey—

IVY: I won't let you do this to me!

BARBARA: When Mattie Fae told me, I didn't know what to do—

IVY: I won't let you change my story! (*Ivy exits. Barbara chases after her and catches her on the front porch.*)

BARBARA: Goddamn it, listen to me: I tried to protect you—

IVY: We'll go anyway. We'll still go away, and you will never see me again.

BARBARA: Don't leave me like this.

IVY: *You will never see me again.*

BARBARA: This is not my fault. I didn't tell you, *Mom* told you. It wasn't me, it was *Mom*.

IVY: There's no difference. (*Ivy exits. Barbara reenters the house. She finds Violet lighting a cigarette in the living room.*)

VIOLET: You know well's I do, we couldn't let Ivy run off with Little Charles. Just wouldn't be right. Ivy's place is right here.

BARBARA: She says she's leaving anyway.

VIOLET: Nah. She won't go. She's a sweet girl, Ivy, and I love her to death. But she isn't strong. Not like you. Or me.

BARBARA: Right. (*Beat.*) You've known about Daddy and Mattie Fae all these years.

VIOLET: Oh, sure. I never told them I knew. But your father knew. He knew I knew. He always knew I knew. But we never talked about it. I chose the higher ground.

BARBARA: Right.

VIOLET: Now if I'd had the chance, there at the end, I would've told him, "I hope this isn't about Little Charles, 'cause you know I know all about that." If

I'd reached him at the motel, I would've said, "You'd be better off if you quit sulking about this ancient history. And anyway, just 'cause you feel cast down doesn't let you off the hook."

BARBARA: If you had reached him at the motel.

VIOLET: I *called* the motel, the Country Squire Motel—

BARBARA: —the Country Squire Motel, right—

VIOLET: —but it was too late, he must've already checked out. I called over there on Monday, after I got into that safety deposit box. I told you I had to wait until Monday morning for the bank to open so I could get into that safety deposit box. I should've called him sooner, I guess, should've called the police, or Ivy, someone. But Beverly and I had an arrangement. You have to understand, for people like your father and me, who never had any money, ever, as kids, people from our generation, that money is important.

BARBARA: How'd you know where he was?

VIOLET: He left a note. Said I could call him at the Country Squire Motel. And I did, I did call him, called him on Monday.

BARBARA: After you got into your safety deposit box.

VIOLET: We had an arrangement.

BARBARA: If you could've stopped Daddy from killing himself, you wouldn't have *needed* to get into your safety deposit box.

VIOLET: Well, hindsight's twenty-twenty, isn't it.

BARBARA: Did the note say Daddy was going to kill himself? (*No response.*) Mom?

VIOLET: If I'd had my wits about me, I might've done it different. But I was, your father and me both, we were . . .

BARBARA: You were both fucked-up. (*Beat.*) You were fucked-up. (*Beat.*) You're fucked-up.

VIOLET: You had better understand this, you smug little ingrate, there is at least one reason Beverly killed himself and that's *you*. Think there's any way he would've done what he did if you were still here? No, just him and me, here in this house, in the dark, left to just ourselves, abandoned, wasted lifetimes devoted to your care and comfort. So stick that knife of judgment in me, go ahead, but make no mistake, his blood is just as much on your hands as it is on mine. (*No response. Violet enters the study. Barbara follows.*) He did this, though; this was his doing, not ours. Can you imagine anything more cruel, to make *me* responsible? And why, just to weaken me, just to make me prove my character? So no, I waited, I waited so I could get my hands on that safety deposit box, but I would have waited anyway. You want to show who's stronger, Bev? Nobody is stronger than me, goddamn it. When nothing is left, when everything is gone and disappeared, I'll be here. Who's stronger now, you son-of-a-bitch?!

BARBARA: No, you're right, Mom. You're the strong one. (*Barbara kisses her mother . . . exits the study, returns to the living room. Violet calls after her.*)

VIOLET: Barbara? (*Barbara grabs her purse, digs out rental car keys.*) Barbara? (*Barbara stands, listens to her mother.*) Barbara, please. (*Barbara exits the house.*) Please, Barbara. *Please.* (*Violet shuffles into the living room.*) Barbara? You in here? (*She crosses to the dining room.*) Ivy? Ivy, you here? Barb? (*She crosses to the kitchen.*) Barb? Ivy? (*She turns in a circle, disoriented, panicked. She crosses to the study.*) Bev? (*She reenters the living room, stumbles to the stereo, puts on Clapton . . . stares at the turntable as the album spins . . . attacks the record player, rakes the needle across the album. She looks around, terrified, disoriented.*) Johnna?! (*She reels to the stairway, crawls up the stairs on all fours.*) Johnna, Johnna, Johnna . . . (*She arrives on the second floor. Johnna puts her plate of food aside and turns toward the* stairs. *Violet, on all fours, continues up the stairs to the attic. She arrives in Johnna's room. She scrabbles into Johnna's lap. Johnna holds Violet's head, smoothes her hair, rocks her.*) And then you're gone, and Beverly, and then you're gone, and Barbara, and then you're gone, and then you're gone, and then you're gone— (*Johnna quietly sings to Violet.*)

JOHNNA: "This is the way the world ends, this is the way the world ends, this is the way the world ends . . ."° (*Blackout.*)

VIOLET: —and then you're gone, and then you're gone, and then you're gone, and then you're gone—

This is the way the world ends: The lines are from T. S. Eliot's "The Hollow Men." See the note on page 1775.

Lynn Nottage

Lynn Nottage, born in 1964 in Brooklyn, New York, was educated at Brown University and then at the Yale School of Drama, where she has served as a visiting lecturer in playwriting. After graduating from Yale, she spent four years working for Amnesty International, learning firsthand about international injustice. She left Amnesty International during the period of the Rwandan genocide, in which the Hutu and Tutsi people slaughtered each other. Her pain over this tragedy was intensified by the realization that the outside world was not going to attempt to stop the genocide. Nothing was being done, while people were dying by the hundreds of thousands throughout the country. Her interest in Africa and in injustice would infuse her later work.

One of Nottage's earliest works is also one of her most unusual. *Poof!* (1993) is a ten-minute play that was produced at the Humana Festival at the Actors Theatre of Louisville. In it an abusive husband experiences spontaneous human combustion. In this satire, Loureen begins the play by damning her husband Samuel, who then suddenly explodes and leaves a pile of ash. Loureen and her friend Florence discuss what she should do, a conversation that ultimately leads her to put off calling the police. The play is vigorous and comic but with a serious undertone. *Por'Knockers* (1995) is also a satire. The pork knockers of the title are people of mixed ethnicity who have subsisted by panning for gold in remote South American regions and who are now disappearing. The play, which was written prior to the Oklahoma City bombing, focuses on the plans and rationale of a group called the People's Diasporatic Party, who blow up a federal building that they mistakenly think is empty.

The play that brought Nottage to the attention of major critics is *Crumbs from the Table of Joy* (1995), a memory play featuring an adolescent girl, Ernestine, whose conventional African American family lives in Brooklyn in the 1950s. Ernestine's mother has died, and her aunt Lily has come to visit the family. Ermina, Ernestine's younger sister, and their father, Godfrey, take Lily in without understanding her agenda. Lily thinks that because she is the sister of Ernestine's dead mother, she has a claim on Godfrey. Lily, however, is a fast, boisterous woman who frightens Godfrey, a devotee of Father Divine, the black evangelist who was among the most popular religious figures of the 1950s. The play moves in a new direction when Godfrey brings home a white woman, a German émigrée, whom he decides to marry, thus rejecting Lily entirely. The portrait of a mixed-race marriage in this period is handled with delicacy and understanding. And although the play is not a bright and cheerful portrait of any of the characters, it is touching and significant.

Mud, River, Stone (1996) was produced in New York in 1997 at Playwrights Horizons and directed by Roger Rees. It is set in both New York and southeast Africa and concerns a hostage situation in which a white neocolonialist, an African aid worker, an African American couple, and a United Nations worker—none of whom knew one another—discuss the situation in Africa as they understand it.

In an interesting departure, Nottage's next play was *Las Meninas* (2002), a historical comedy that focuses on an illegitimate daughter of Marie Therese, the wife of Louis XIV, who had an affair with an African dwarf named Nabo. The daughter was sent off to a convent and became a nun, while Nabo was sent away. The play was produced in 2002 at the San Jose Repertory Theatre in California.

Nottage won the Drama Critics' Circle Award for best play in 2004 with *Intimate Apparel,* set in Lower Manhattan in 1905, during the building of the Panama Canal and after the Spanish-American War. In this play, Esther, a shy, virginal thirty-five-year-old seamstress who has virtually given up hope of marriage, sews beautiful intimate garments for the girls in Mrs. Dickson's rooming house who leave to get married. When Esther gets a letter from George Armstrong, a laborer on the Panama Canal, she slowly begins to see her opportunity for a truly intimate relationship.

After the opening of *Fabulation: or The Re-Education of Undine* in 2004, for which Nottage won the Obie Award for Playwriting, she traveled to Uganda with director Kate Whoriskey to search for material for a drama on the subject of the refugee women and girls who had fled the Sudan and the Democratic Republic of the Congo — women who had been raped and sometimes mutilated and who had lost virtually everything. The resulting play, *Ruined,* set in a brothel in the Congo, won the Pulitzer Prize for drama in 2009. Nottage's most recent play, *By the Way, Meet Vera Stark* (2011), tells the story of a black woman who acted in films from the 1930s on, but in somewhat demeaning roles as a maid or even a slave in plantation dramas. Both plays illustrate why Nottage is known for her sharp intelligence and her powerful narratives.

For links to resources about Nottage, click on *AuthorLinks* at **bedfordstmartins.com/jacobus.**

Ruined

After spending time in Africa interviewing women survivors of the civil war in the Democratic Republic of the Congo, Lynn Nottage returned to the United States to write about her experiences. *Ruined* focuses on the effects of brutal rape and enslavement of women by violent soldiers on both sides of a civil conflict that has been going on for years. The main character in the play is Mama Nadi, who runs a supply store and brothel that caters to local miners as well as to both Commander Osembenga, the government troop commander, and Jerome Kisembe, the leader of the rebels. Mama Nadi's shop is on the edge of a rain forest that is now being cut down by miners searching for coltan, an ore that produces tantalum, a metal used in mobile phones, DVD players, and gaming systems.

Nottage says nothing in the play about the uses of coltan, but her own view is that one of the sources of the problems that have produced the terrible military actions in the Congo is the need of the developed nations for the natural resources of Africa. Coltan is, in fact, being mined in the Congo, and the mining has had a serious effect on the cultures of the people who live near the source of the ores that are so important to China and other industrial nations. The presence in the play of the coltan mines provides the reason for the conflict between government and rebel troops in the area of Mama Nadi's business.

Mama Nadi at first seems indifferent to either side in the war. She provides what both sides need: sex and beer. Because she is a businesswoman, she attracts people like Christian, who travels with supplies and repeatedly asks her to leave everything and come away with him. Christian has a concern for the women who are in the midst of the war and brings both Salima and Sophie to Mama Nadi's. He has to persuade her to take his niece, Sophie, into her brothel even though she is "ruined," a term meaning that the soldiers have raped her so brutally and so often that she is mutilated and cannot give a man sexual satisfaction. She is ruined as a woman, but it turns out that her ability to keep the books is enough to save her. Mr. Harari, an entrepreneur and diamond merchant with contacts in the larger cities in the Congo, offers help when Mama Nadi needs it. He enjoys the pleasures of her establishment and also has earned her trust as an honest man.

The women in her house understand that they survive because of Mama Nadi's protection, based on her ability to manipulate commanders on both sides of the battle. Salima, pregnant, has been enslaved and raped repeatedly and is afraid to return to her husband because of the shame involved in being used by the soldiers. Josephine's attitude is different from Salima's. The daughter of a village chieftain, she is a survivor, like Mama Nadi, and manages to deal with the miners and the soldiers. Mama Nadi takes special care of Sophie because she is ruined. Late in the play we discover that Mama Nadi has her own secrets, which have placed her in the difficult situation she has somehow managed to take advantage of to maintain her store.

Mama Nadi has been compared with Mother in Brecht's *Mother Courage* because both businesswomen deal with warriors on both sides of the battle. Both women are damaged, but both keep on because they have survived. Yet Mama Nadi seems to have much more feeling for those around her and more of a capacity to change than Brecht's character.

For discussion questions and assignments on *Ruined,* visit bedfordstmartins.com/jacobus.

Ruined in Performance

Ruined premiered as a joint production of the Goodman Theatre and the Manhattan Theatre Club at the Goodman Theatre in Chicago in November 2008. It opened in February 2009 off-Broadway at the City Center Stage I in New York. The director of both productions was Kate Whoriskey, who had worked with Lynn Nottage earlier on *Fabulation.* Mama Nadi was played by Saidah Arrika Ekulona and Sophie by Condola Rashad, both of whom received special praise in the reviews. The play won the Pulitzer Prize for drama in 2009. *Ruined* garnered good reviews in its London production by the Almeida Theatre Company in 2010. London theater critic Philip Fisher said, "This is the kind of work that makes the supposedly civilized world understand what is going on in countries that are far too rarely featured in the media or the arts." The Arena Stage in Washington, D.C., produced *Ruined* in April 2011. In her review in the *Baltimore Sun,* Mary Carole McCauley said, "This is the first time *Ruined* has been staged in the round, and the seating arrangement has two [salutary] results: Theatergoers are brought close to the action, and a perception is created that the characters on stage are surrounded and trapped." The play has gone on to be one of the most frequently performed plays at regional theaters in recent seasons.

LYNN NOTTAGE (b. 1964)

Ruined 2008

Characters

SALIMA
JOSEPHINE
JEROME KISEMBE
MAMA NADI
SIMON
FORTUNE
CHRISTIAN
COMMANDER OSEMBENGA
MR. HARARI
LAURENT
SOPHIE
AID WORKER
SOLDIERS
MINERS

Place: *A small mining town in the Democratic Republic of the Congo.*

ACT ONE • Scene 1

A small mining town. The sounds of the tropical Ituri rain forest. Democratic Republic of the Congo.

A bar with makeshift furniture and a rundown pool table. A lot of effort has gone into making the worn bar cheerful. A stack of plastic washtubs rests in the corner. An old car battery powers the lights and audio system, a covered birdcage conspicuously sits in the corner of the room.

Mama Nadi, early forties, an attractive woman with an arrogant stride and majestic air, watches Christian, early forties, a perpetually cheerful traveling salesman, knock back a Fanta. His good looks have been worn down by hard living on the road. He wears a suit that might have been considered stylish when new, but it's now nearly ten years old and overly loved. He brushes travel dust from his clothing, and takes a generous sip of his soda.

CHRISTIAN: Ah. Cold. The only cold Fanta in twenty-five kilometers. You don't know how good this tastes. (*Mama flashes a warm, flirtatious smile, then pours herself a Primus beer.*)

MAMA: And where the hell have you been?

CHRISTIAN: It was no easy task getting here.

MAMA: I've been expecting you for the last three weeks. How am I supposed do business? No soap, no cigarettes, no condoms. Not even a half liter of petrol for the generator.

CHRISTIAN: Why are you picking a fight with me already? I didn't create this damn chaos. Nobody, and I'm telling you, nobody could get through on the main road. Every two kilometers a boy with a Kalashnikov and pockets that need filling. Toll, tax, tariff. They invent reasons to lighten your load.

MAMA: Then why does Mr. Harari always manage to get through?

CHRISTIAN: Mr. Harari doesn't bring you things you need, does he? Mr. Harari has interests that supercede his safety. Me, I still hope to have a family one day. (*Christian laughs, heartily.*)

MAMA: And my lipstick?

CHRISTIAN: Your lipstick? Aye! Did you ask me for lipstick?

MAMA: Of course, I did, you idiot!

CHRISTIAN: Look at the way you speak to me, *Chérie. Comment est-ce possible?* You should be happy I made it here in one piece. (*Christian produces a tube of lipstick from his pocket.*) Play nice or I'll give this to Josephine. She knows how to show her appreciation.

MAMA: Yes, but you always take home a little more than you ask for with Josephine. I hope you know how to use a condom. (*Christian laughs.*)

CHRISTIAN: Are you jealous?

MAMA: Leave me alone, you're too predictable. (*Mama turns away, dismissive.*)

CHRISTIAN: Where are you going? Hey, hey what are you doing? (*Teasingly.*) *Chérie*, I know you wanted me to forget, so you could yell at me, but you won't get the pleasure this time. (*Christian taunts her with the lipstick. Mama resists the urge to smile.*)

MAMA: Oh shut up and give it to me. (*He passes her the lipstick.*) Thank you, Christian.

CHRISTIAN: I didn't hear you—

MAMA: Don't press your luck. And it better be red. (*Mama grabs a sliver of a broken mirror from behind the rough hewn bar, and gracefully applies the lipstick.*)

CHRISTIAN: You don't have to say it. I know you want a husband.

MAMA: Like a hole in my head.

CHRISTIAN: (*Reciting.*)
What, is this love?
An unexpected wind,
A fluctuation,
fronting the coming of a storm.

Resolve, a thorny bush
Blown asunder and swept away
There, *Chérie*. I give you a poem in lieu of the kiss
you won't allow me. (*Christian laughs, warmly.
Mama puts out a bowl of peanuts.*)

MAMA: Here. I saved you some groundnuts, *Professor*.

CHRISTIAN: That's all you saved for me?

MAMA: Be smart, and I'll show you the door in one second. (*Mama scolds him with her eyes.*)

CHRISTIAN: Ach, ach . . . why are you wearing my Grandmama's face? (*Christian mocks her expression.
Mama laughs and downs her beer.*)

MAMA: You sure you don't want a beer?

CHRISTIAN: You know me better than that, *Chérie*,
I haven't had a drop of liquor in four years.

MAMA: (*Teasing.*) It's cold.

CHRISTIAN: Tst! (*Christian cracks open a few peanuts,
and playfully pops them into his mouth. The parrot
squawks.*) What's there? In the cage?

MAMA: Oh, that, a grey parrot. Old Papa Batunga passed.

CHRISTIAN: When?

MAMA: Last Thursday. No one wanted the damn bird. It complains too much.

CHRISTIAN: (*Amused.*) Yeah, what does it say? (*Christian
walks to the birdcage, and peers under the covering.*)

MAMA: Who the hell knows? It speaks pygmy. He . . . Old
Papa was the last of his tribe. That stupid bird was
the only thing he had left to talk to.

CHRISTIAN: (*To bird.*) Hello?

MAMA: He believed as long as the words of the forest
people were spoken the spirits would stay alive.

CHRISTIAN: For true? (*Christian pokes his finger into the
cage. To Mama.*) What are you going to do with
him?

MAMA: Sell it. I don't want it. It stinks. (*Christian pokes
at the birdcage.*)

CHRISTIAN: (*To bird.*) Hello.

MAMA: Hey, hey don't put your fingers in there.

CHRISTIAN: Look. He likes me. So Mama, you haven't
asked me what else I've brought for you? Go see.
(*Christian quickly withdraws his finger.*) Ow. Shit.
He bit me.

MAMA: Well, you shouldn't be messing with it. (*Mama
laughs.*)

CHRISTIAN: Ow, damn it.

MAMA: (*Impatiently.*) Don't be a crybaby, what did
you bring me? Well? . . . Are you going to keep me
guessing?

CHRISTIAN: Go on. Take a peek in the truck. And don't
say I don't think about you. (*Mama smiles.*)

MAMA: How many?

CHRISTIAN: Three.

MAMA: Three? But, I can't use three right now. You know
that.

CHRISTIAN: Of course you can. And I'll give you a
good price if you take all of them. (*Mama goes
to the doorway, and peers out at the offerings,
unimpressed.*)

MAMA: I don't know. They look used. Worn.

CHRISTIAN: C'mon, Mama. Take another look. A full
look. You've said it yourself business is good.
(*Mama considers, then finally.*)

MAMA: Okay, one. That one in front. (*Points into the
distance.*)

CHRISTIAN: Three. C'mon, don't make me travel back
with them.

MAMA: Just one. How much?

CHRISTIAN: Do you know how difficult it was getting
here? The road was completely washed out—

MAMA: All right, all right. I don't need the whole damn
saga. Just tell me, how much for the one?

CHRISTIAN: The same as usual plus twenty-five, because . . . because . . . You understand it wasn't easy
to get here with the—

MAMA: I'll give you fifteen.

CHRISTIAN: Ahh! Fifteen? No. That's nothing. Twenty-
two. C'mon.

MAMA: Twenty. My best offer. (*Christian mulls it over.
He's reluctant.*)

CHRISTIAN: Aye. Okay. Okay. Damn it. Yes. Yes. But I
expect another cold Fanta. One from the bottom
this time. (*Christian, defeated, exits. Mama smiles
victoriously, and retrieves another soda from the
refrigerator. She reapplies lipstick for good measure, then counts out her money. Christian reenters proudly bearing two cartons of Ugandan
cigarettes. A moment later two women in ragged
clothing step tentatively into the bar: Sophie,
a luminous beauty with an air of defiance, and
Salima, a sturdy peasant woman whose face
betrays a world weariness. They hold hands. Mama
studies the women, then—*)

MAMA: I said one. That one. (*She points to Sophie.*)

CHRISTIAN: It's been a good week, and I'll tell you what,
I'll give you two for the price of one. Why not?

MAMA: Are you deaf? No. Tst! I don't need two more
mouths to feed and pester me. (*Mama continues to
examine each woman.*)

CHRISTIAN: Take both. Feed them as one. Please, Mama,
I'll throw in the cigarettes for cost.

MAMA: But, I'll only pay for one.

CHRISTIAN: Of course. We agree, why are we arguing?

MAMA: (*Yelling.*) Josephine! Josephine! Where is that
stupid woman? (*Josephine, a sexy woman in a short
Western-style miniskirt and high heels, appears in the
beaded doorway. She surveys the new women with
obvious contempt.*) Take them out back. Get them
washed and some proper clothing.

JOSEPHINE: *Njoo.* [Come.] (*Beat.*) *Sasa.* [Quick.]
(*Josephine beckons to the women. They reluctantly
follow.*)

MAMA: Wait. (*Mama gestures to Salima, who clings to
Sophie.*) You. Come here. (*Salima doesn't move.*)
Come. (*Salima clings to Sophie, then slowly walks
toward Mama.*) What's your name?

SALIMA: (*Whispers.*) Salima.

MAMA: What?

SALIMA: Salima. (*Mama examines Salima's rough hands.*)

MAMA: Rough. (*With disdain.*) A digger. We'll have to do something about that. (*Salima yanks her hand away. Mama registers the bold gesture.*) And you, come. You're a pretty thing, what's your name?

SOPHIE: (*Gently.*) Sophie.

MAMA: Do you have a smile?

SOPHIE: Yes.

MAMA: Then let me see it. (*Sophie struggles to find a defiant smile.*) Good. Go get washed up. (*A moment.*)

JOSEPHINE: (*Snaps.*) C'mon, now! (*Salima looks to Sophie. She follows. The women follow behind Josephine. Sophie walks with some pain.*)

MAMA: Did you at least tell them this time?

CHRISTIAN: Yes. They know and they came willingly.

MAMA: And—?

CHRISTIAN: Salima is from a tiny village. No place really. She was captured by rebel soldiers, Mayi-mayi; the poor thing spent nearly five months in the bush as their concubine.

MAMA: And what of her people?

CHRISTIAN: She says her husband is a farmer, and from what I understand, her village won't have her back. Because . . . But she's a simple girl, she doesn't have much learning, I wouldn't worry about her.

MAMA: And the other?

CHRISTIAN: Sophie. Sophie is . . .

MAMA: Is what?

CHRISTIAN: . . . is . . . ruined. (*A moment.*)

MAMA: (*Enraged.*) You brought me a girl that's ruined?

CHRISTIAN: She cost you nothing.

MAMA: I paid money for her, not the other one. The other one is plain. I have a half a dozen girls like her, I don't need to feed another plain girl.

CHRISTIAN: I know this, okay, don't get worked up. Sophie is a good girl, she won't trouble you.

MAMA: How do I know that?

CHRISTIAN: (*Defensively.*) Because I am telling you. She's seen some very bad times.

MAMA: Yeah? And why is that my concern?

CHRISTIAN: Take her on, just for a month. You'll see she's a good girl. Hard worker. (*Mama gestures toward her genitals.*)

MAMA: But damaged, am I right?

CHRISTIAN: . . . Yes . . . Look, militia did ungodly things to the child, took her with . . . a bayonet and then left her for dead. And she was—

MAMA: (*Snaps.*) I don't need to hear it. Are you done?

CHRISTIAN: (*Passionately.*) Things are gonna get busy, Mama. All along the road people are talking about how this red dirt is rich with Coltan.° Suddenly everyone has a shovel, and wants to stake a claim since that boastful pygmy dug up his fortune in the reserve. I guarantee there'll be twice as many miners here by September. And you know all those bastards will be thirsty. So, take her, put her to work for you.

MAMA: And what makes you think I have any use for her?

Coltan: An ore that produces tantalum, a metal used in mobile phones and electronic gadgets.

CHRISTIAN: (*Pleads.*) The girl cooks, cleans, and she sings like an angel. And you . . . you haven't had nice music here since that one, that beauty Camille got the AIDS.

MAMA: No. A girl like this is bad luck. I can't have it. Josephine! Josephine!

CHRISTIAN: And Mama, she's pretty pretty. She'll keep the miner's eyes happy. I promise.

MAMA: Stop it already, no. You're like a hyena. Won't you shut up, now. (*Josephine enters, put-upon.*)

JOSEPHINE: Yes, Mama.

MAMA: Bring the girl, Sophie, back.

CHRISTIAN: Wait. Give us a minute, Josephine. (*Josephine doesn't move.*) Mama, please. Look, okay, I'm asking you to do me this favor. I've done many things for you over the years. And I don't ask you for a lot in return. Please. The child has no place else to go.

MAMA: I'm sorry, but I'm running a business, not a mission. Take her to the sisters in Bunia, let her weave baskets for them. Josephine, why are you standing there like a fool . . . go get the girl.

CHRISTIAN: Wait. (*Josephine addresses both of them.*)

JOSEPHINE: (*Annoyed.*) Do you want me to stay or to go?

MAMA: (*Snaps.*) Get her! (*Josephine sucks her teeth and exits.*)

CHRISTIAN: (*With a tinge of resentment.*) Tst! I remembered your lipstick and everything.

MAMA: Don't look at me that way. I open my doors, and tomorrow I'm a refugee camp overrun with suffering. Everyone has their hand open since this damned war began. I can't do it. I keep food in the mouths of eight women, when half the country's starving, so don't give me shit about taking on one more girl.

CHRISTIAN: Look. Have anything you want off of my truck. Anything! I even have some . . . some Belgian chocolate.

MAMA: You won't let up. Why are you so damn concerned with this girl? Huh?

CHRISTIAN: C'mon, Mama, please.

MAMA: Chocolate. I always ask you for chocolate, and you always tell me it turns in this heat. How many times have you refused me this year. Huh? But, she must be very very important to you. I see that. Do you want to fuck her or something? (*A moment.*)

CHRISTIAN: She's my sister's only daughter. Okay? I told my family I'd find a place for her . . . And here at least I know she'll be safe. Fed. (*He stops himself and gulps down his soda.*) And as you know the village isn't a place for a girl who has been . . . ruined. It brings shame, dishonor to the family.

MAMA: (*Ironically.*) But it's okay for her to be here, huh? I'm sorry, but, I can't. I don't have room for another broken girl.

CHRISTIAN: She eats like a bird. Nothing. (*Sophie enters.*)

SOPHIE: Madame.

MAMA: (*Defensively.*) It's Mademoiselle. (*A moment. Mama stares at Sophie, thinking, her resolve slowly softening.*) Come here. (*Sophie walks over to Mama.*) How old are you? (*Sophie meets Mama's eyes.*)

SOPHIE: Eighteen.

MAMA: Yeah? Do you have a beau?

SOPHIE: No. (*Mama's surprised by her haughtiness.*)

MAMA: Are you a student?

SOPHIE: Yes, I was to sit for the university exam.

MAMA: I bet you were good at your studies. Am I right?

SOPHIE: Yes.

MAMA: A *petit* bureaucrat in the making. (*Sophie shifts with discomfort. Her body aches, tears escape her eyes. Mama uses the cloth from her skirt to wipe Sophie's eyes.*) Did they hurt you badly?

SOPHIE: (*Whispered.*) . . . Yes.

MAMA: I bet they did. (*Mama studies Sophie. Considers, and then decides.*) Christian, go get me the chocolate.

CHRISTIAN: Does that mean . . . ?

MAMA: I'm doing this for you, 'cuz you've been good to me. (*Whispers to Christian.*) But this is the last time you bring me damaged goods. Understood? It's no good for business.

CHRISTIAN: Thank you. It's the last time. I promise. Thank you.

MAMA: You sing?

SOPHIE: (*Softly.*) Yes.

MAMA: Do you know any popular songs?

SOPHIE: Yes. A few.

CHRISTIAN: Speak up! (*Christian exits.*)

SOPHIE: Yes, Mad— (*Catching herself.*) . . . emoiselle.

MAMA: Mama. You do math? Stuff like that?

SOPHIE: Yes, Mama.

MAMA: Good. (*Mama lifts Sophie's chin with her fingers, enviously examining her face.*) Yes, you're very pretty. I can see how that caused you problems. Do you know what kind of place this is?

SOPHIE: Yes, Mama. I think so.

MAMA: Good. (*Mama carefully applies red lipstick to Sophie's mouth.*) Then we have no problems. I expect my girls to be well-behaved and clean. That's all. I provide a bed, food, and clothing. If things are good, everyone gets a little. If things are bad, then Mama eats first. Am I making myself clear? (*Sophie nods.*) Good. Red is your color. (*Sophie doesn't respond.*) Thank you, Mama.

SOPHIE: Thank you, Mama. (*Mama pours a glass of local home-brewed liquor. She holds it out.*)

MAMA: Here. It'll help the pain down below. I know it hurts, because it smells like the rot of meat. So wash good. (*Sophie takes the glass, and slowly drinks the liquor down.*) Don't get too dependent on drink. It'll make you sloppy, and I have no tolerance for sloppiness. Understood? (*Christian, put-upon, reenters with a faded, but pretty, box of chocolates.*)

CHRISTIAN: Handmade. Imported. *Très bon.* I hope you're impressed. A Belgian shopkeeper in Bunia ordered them. Real particular. I had a hell of a time trying to find these Goddamn chocolates. And then poof, she's gone. And now I'm stuck with twenty boxes. I tried to pawn them off on Pastor Robbins, but apparently he's on a diet. (*Mama opens the box, surveying the chocolates. She's in seventh heaven. She offers a piece to Sophie, who timidly selects a chocolate.*)

Mama Nadi (Saidah Arrika Ekulona) applies lipstick to Sophie (Condola Rashad) in the Manhattan Theatre Club production of *Ruined* at City Center Stage I in New York, directed by Kate Whoriskey in 2009.

SOPHIE: *Merci.* (*Mama bites into the chocolate.*)

MAMA: Mmm.

CHRISTIAN: Happy? That's what the good life in Belgium tastes like.

MAMA: Caramel. (*Savoring.*) Good God, I haven't had caramel in ages. You bastard, you've been holding out on me! Mmm. Smell 'em, the smell reminds me of my mother. She'd take me and my brothers to Kisangani. And she'd buy us each an enormous bag of caramels wrapped in that impossible plastic. You know why? So we wouldn't tell my grandfather about all of the uncles she visited in the big town. She'd sit us on the bank of the river, watching the boats and eating sweaty caramels, while she "visited with uncles." And as long as there were sweets, we didn't breathe a word, not a murmur, to old Papa. (*Sophie eats her chocolate, smiling for the first time. Christian reaches for a chocolate, but Mama quickly slaps his hand and shuts the box.*)

CHRISTIAN: What about me?

MAMA: What about you?

CHRISTIAN: Don't I get one?

MAMA: No! (*This amuses Sophie. She smiles.*)

CHRISTIAN: Why are you smiling? You're a lucky girl. You're lucky you have such a good uncle. A lot of men would've left you for dead. (*Sophie's smile disappears.*)

MAMA: Never mind him. (*To Christian.*) Go, all ready and bring the other stuff in before the vultures steal it!

CHRISTIAN: Sophie. I'm . . . you . . . you be a good girl. Don't make Mama angry.

SOPHIE: I won't, Uncle. (*Christian exits with apology in his posture. Sophie licks her chocolate-covered fingers as the lights fade.*)

Scene 2

A month later.

The bar. Josephine cranks the generator, and colorful Christmas lights flicker on. The birdcage rests in the back of the bar; periodically the bird makes a raucous squawk.

At the bar, drunk and disheveled rebel soldiers drain their beers and laugh too loudly. Salima, wearing a shiny gold midriff, a colorful traditional wrap, and mismatched yellow heels, shoots pool doing her best to ignore the occasional lustful leers of the soldiers.

Jerome Kisembe, the rebel leader dressed in military uniform, holds court. Mama, toting bowls of peanuts, wears a bright red kerchief around her neck, in recognition of the rebel leaders' colors.

Josephine dirty-dances for Mr. Harari, a handsome tipsy Lebanese mineral merchant sporting a surprisingly pristine safari suit. He is barefoot.

Sophie plows through an upbeat dance song, accompanied by a guitar and drums.

SOPHIE: (*Sings.*)
> The liquid night slowly pours in.
> Languor peels away like a curtain.
> Spirits rise, and tongues loosen
> And the weary ask to be forgiven
>
> You come here to forget,
> You say drive away all regret.
> And dance like it's the ending
> The ending of the war.
>
> The day's heavy door closes quick
> Leaving the scold of the sun behind
> Dusk ushers in the forest's music
> And your body's free to unwind

(*Josephine dances for the men.*)

> You come here to forget,
> You say drive away all regret
> And dance like it's the ending
> The ending of the war.
>
> But, can the music be all forgiving
> Purge the wear and tear of the living?
> Will the sound drown out your sorrow,
> So you'll remember nothing tomorrow?

(*A drunk rebel soldier stands and demands attention.*)

REBEL SOLDIER #1: Another! Hey!

MAMA: I hear you! I hear you!

REBEL SOLDIER #1: C'mon! Another! (*He clumsily slams the bottle on the counter, and gestures to Sophie.*) Psst! You! Psst! Psst! (*Another rebel soldier gives Sophie a cat-call. Sophie ignores him. Rebel Soldier #1 turns his attention back to Mama.*) Her! Why won't she come talk to me?

MAMA: You want to talk to her. Behave, and let me see your money. (*Jerome Kisembe, the haughty rebel leader, lets out a roar of a laugh.*)

REBEL SOLDIER #1: The damn beer drained my pocket. It cost too much! You're a fucking thief!

MAMA: Then go somewhere else, and mind your tongue. (*Mama turns away.*)

REBEL SOLDIER #1: Hey. Wait. Wait. I want her to talk to me. Mama, lookie! I have this. (*Rebel Soldier #1 proudly displays a cloth filled with little chunks of ore.*)

MAMA: What is it? Huh? Coltan? Where'd you get it?

REBEL SOLDIER #1: (*Boasting.*) From a miner on the reserve.

MAMA: He just gave it to you?

REBEL SOLDIER #1: (*Snickering.*) Yeah, he give it to me. Dirty poacher been diggin' up our forest, we run 'em off. Run them good, gangsta-style, "muthafucka run!," left 'em for the fucking scavengers. (*Rebel Soldier #1 strikes a hip-hop "gangsta-style" pose. The other rebel soldiers laugh. Mr. Harari, unamused, ever so slightly registers the conversation. Mama laughs.*)

MAMA: Coltan? Let me see. Ah, that's nothing, it's worthless, my friend. A month ago, yes, but now you can't get a handful of meal for it. Too many prospectors. Every miner that walks in here has a bucket of it. Bring me a gram of gold, then we talk.

REBEL SOLDIER #1: What do you mean? Liar! In the city this would fetch me plenty.

MAMA: This ain't the city, is it, soldier? (*He aggressively grabs Mama's wrist.*) This is a nice place for a drink. Yeah? I don't abide by bush laws. If you want to drink like a man, you drink like a man, you want to behave like a gorilla, then go back into the bush. (*The rebel soldiers laugh. He unhands Mama.*)

REBEL SOLDIER #1: C'mon Mama, this is worth plenty! Yeah? (*Again, he gestures to Sophie. He's growing increasingly belligerent.*) Bitch. Why won't she talk to me? (*Frustrated, Rebel Soldier #1 puts the cloth back in his pocket. He broods, silently watching Sophie sway to the music. Then all of sudden he collects himself, and drunkenly makes his way toward her.*) I'll teach her manners! Respect me! (*Rebel Soldier #1 pounds his chest, the other rebel soldier goads him on. Sophie stiffens. Mama quickly steps between them. The musicians stop playing.*)

MAMA: But . . . as the Coltan is all you have. I'll take it this time. Now go sit down. Sit down. Please.

REBEL SOLDIER #1: (*Excited.*) Yeah? Now, I want her to talk to me! Will she talk to me?

MAMA: Okay. Okay. Sit. (*Rebel Soldier #1 pulls out the cloth. He gently removes several pieces of the ore.*) Don't be stingy. Tst! Let me see all of it. (*Rebel Soldier #1 reluctantly relinquishes the weathered cloth to Mama. Smiling.*) Salima! Salima, come! (*Salima, disgusted, bristles at the sound of her name. She reluctantly approaches Rebel Soldier #1.*)

REBEL SOLDIER #1: What about her? (*He gestures to Sophie.*)

MAMA: Salima is a better dancer. I promise. Okay. Everyone is happy.

KISEMBE: Soldier, everyone is happy! (*Salima sizes up the drunken Rebel Soldier #1.*)

SALIMA: So, "gangsta," you wanna dance with me? (*She places his arms around her waist. He longingly looks over at Sophie, then pulls Salima close. He leads aggressively.*) Easy.

MAMA: Sophie. (*Sophie, relieved, resumes singing.*)

SOPHIE: (*Sings.*)

> Have another beer, my friend,
> Douse the fire of your fears, my friend,
> Get drunk and foolish on the moment,
> Brush aside the day's heavy judgment
>
> Yes, have another beer, my friend
> Wipe away the angry tears, my friend
> Get drunk and foolish on the moment,
> Brush aside the day's heavy judgment.
>
> 'Cuz, you come here to forget,
> You say drive away all regret.
> And dance like it's the ending
> The ending of the war.
> The ending of the war.
> The ending of the war.

(*Applause. Mama, having quenched the fire, fetches her lockbox from a hiding place beneath the counter and puts the ore inside.*)

MR. HARARI: That one, she's pretty. (*He gestures to Sophie.*)

JOSEPHINE: (*With disdain.*) Sophie?! She's broken. All of the girls think she's bad luck. (*Josephine leads Mr. Harari to the table, they sit.*)

MR. HARARI: What are you wearing? Where's the dress I bought you?

JOSEPHINE: If I had known you were coming, I'd have put it on.

MR. HARARI: Then what are you waiting for, my darling? (*Josephine exits quickly. Mama, toting her lockbox, joins Mr. Harari at his table.*)

MAMA: What happened to your shoes, Mr. Harari?

MR. HARARI: Your fucking country, some drunk child doing his best impersonation of a rebel soldier liberated my shoes. (*Laughter from pool table.*) Every time I come here I have to buy a new fucking pair of shoes.

MAMA: You're lucky he only wanted your shoes. *Santé.* Cheers. (*Rebel Soldier #1 gets too friendly with Salima. She lurches away.*)

REBEL SOLDIER #1: Hey!

KISEMBE: Ach, ach, quiet, I'm trying to play here. (*Rebel Soldier #1 grabs Salima onto his lap. Mr. Harari watches the Rebel Soldier #1 and Salima.*)

MR. HARARI: You took that poor man's Coltan. Shame on you. He probably doesn't know what he gave away for the taste of that woman. (*To Rebel Soldier #1.*) Savor it! The toll to enter that tunnel was very expensive, my friend. (*To Mama.*) We both know how much it would fetch on the market.

MAMA: Six months ago it was just more black dirt. I don't get why everyone's crawling over each other for it.

MR. HARARI: Well, my darling, in this damnable age of the mobile phone it's become quite the precious ore, no? And for whatever reason God has seen fit to bless your backward country with an abundance of it. Now, if that young man had come to me, I would've given him enough money to buy pussy for a month. Even yours. So who's the bigger thief, you or him?

MAMA: He give it to me, you saw. So, does that make me a thief or merely more clever than you. (*Mr. Harari laughs.*)

MR. HARARI: My darling, you'd do well in Kisangani.

MAMA: I do well here, and I'd get homesick in Kisangani. It's a filthy city full of bureaucrats and thieves.

MR. HARARI: Very funny, but I imagine you'd enjoy it, terribly. And I mean that as compliment.

MAMA: Do you have a minute?

MR. HARARI: Of course.

KISEMBE: Soldier! Soldier!

REBEL SOLDIER #2: Chief.

KISEMBE: Bring me my mobile! What're you, an old man? Hurry! (*Mama empties a bag containing a precious stone onto a cloth on the table.*)

MAMA: What do you think? Huh?

MR. HARARI: (*Referring to rough stones.*) Just looking, I can tell you, most of these are worthless. I'm sorry. (*Mama takes out another stone. She discreetly shows it to Mr. Harari.*)

MAMA: What about that one? (*Mr. Harari examines the diamond on the table, then meticulously places a loupe to his eye and examines the stone more closely.*)

MR. HARARI: Hm. It's a rough diamond. Where'd you get this?

MAMA: Don't you worry. I'm holding it for someone. (*Mr. Harari continues to examine the diamond.*)

MR. HARARI: Nice. Yes, you see, there. It carries the light very well.

MAMA: Yeah, yeah, but is it worth anything?

MR. HARARI: . . . Well—

MAMA: Well—

MR. HARARI: Depends. (*Mama smiles.*) It's raw, and the market—

MAMA: Yeah, yeah but, how much are we talking? A new generator or a plot of land? (*Mr. Harari chuckles.*)

MR. HARARI: Slow down, I can offer you a fairly good price. But, be reasonable, darling, I'm an independent with a family that doesn't appreciate how hard I work. (*Mama takes back the diamond.*)

MAMA: You sound like my old Papa. He was like you, Mr. Harari, work too much, always want more, no rest. He drove his farm hard, too hard. When there was famine our bananas were rotting. He used to say as long as the forest grows a man will never starve.

MR. HARARI: Yes, but does he still have the farm? (*Mama smiles to herself.*)

MAMA: You know better, Mr. Harari, you're in the Congo. Things slip from our fingers like butter. No. When I was eleven, this white man turned up with a piece of paper. It say he have rights to my family land. (*With acid.*) Just like that. Taken! And you want to hear a joke? Poor old Papa bought magic from a friend, he thought a hand full of powder would give him back his land. Everyone talk talk diamonds, but I...I want a powerful slip of paper that says I can cut down forests and dig holes and build to the moon if I choose. I don't want someone to turn up at my door, and take my life from me. Not ever again. But how does a woman get a piece of land, without having to pick up a fucking gun? (*Mr. Harari watches the soldiers.*)

MR. HARARI: I wish I could tell you, but I can't even hold onto a fucking pair of shoes. These idiots keep changing the damn rules. You file papers, and the next day the office is burned down. You buy land, and the next day the Chief's son has built a fucking house on it. I don't know why anybody bothers. Madness. And look now, a hungry pygmy digs a hole in the forest, and suddenly every two-bit militia is battling for the keys to hell.

MAMA: True, but someone must provide them with beer and distractions. (*Mr. Harari laughs. Mama scoops up the diamonds and places them back into her lockbox. Mr. Harari removes the loupe.*)

MR. HARARI: But, be careful; where will I drink if anything happens to you? (*Mr. Harari gives Mama a friendly kiss.*)

MAMA: Don't worry about me. Everything is beautiful. (*Josephine enters proudly sporting an elegant traditional dress. Mr. Harari watches Sophie.*)

JOSEPHINE: What do you think? (*Mr. Harari shifts his gaze to Josephine.*)

MR. HARARI: Such loveliness. Doesn't she look beautiful?

MAMA: Yes, very. Excuse me. *Karibu.*°

MR. HARARI: I just might have to take you home with me.

JOSEPHINE: (*Excited.*) Promise.

MR. HARARI: Of course. (*Josephine hitches up her dress, straddles Mr. Harari, and kisses him.*)

KISEMBE: (*Shouts.*) Mama! Mama!

MAMA: Okay, okay, chief, *sawa sawa.* [Okay okay.]

KISEMBE: Two more Primus.° And Mama, why can't I get mobile service in this pit?

Karibu: Welcome.   **Primus:** A brand of beer.

MAMA: You tell me, you're important, go make it happen!

MR. HARARI: Who's that?

JOSEPHINE: Him? Jerome Kisembe, leader of the rebel militia. He's very powerful. He have sorcerer that give him a charm so he can't be touched by bullet. He's fearless. He is the boss man, the government and the church and anything else he wants to be. (*Harari studies Kisembe.*) Don't look so hard at a man like that. (*Josephine grabs Mr. Harari's face and kisses him. Mama clears the beer bottles from Kisembe's table. The rebel soldier gropes at Salima, then he nips her on the neck.*)

SALIMA: Ow! You jackass. (*Salima pulls away from the rebel soldier and heads for the door. Mama races after her, catching her arm forcefully.*)

MAMA: What's your problem?

SALIMA: Did you see what he did?

MAMA: You selfish girl. Now get back to him. (*Mama shoves Salima toward the rebel soldier. Sophie, watching, walks over to Salima.*)

SOPHIE: Are you all right, Salima?

SALIMA: The dog bit me. (*Whispered.*) I'm not going back over there.

SOPHIE: You have to.

SALIMA: He's filth! It's a man like him that—

SOPHIE: Don't. Mama's looking. (*Tears well up in Salima's eyes.*)

SALIMA: Do you know what he said to me—

SOPHIE: They'll say anything to impress a lady. Half of them are lies. Dirty fucking lies! Go back, don't listen. I'll sing the song you like. (*Sophie gives Salima a kiss on the cheek. Salima's eyes shoot daggers at Mama, and she reluctantly returns to the drunken soldier. Sophie launches into. Josephine dirty-dances for Mr. Harari. Sophie sings.*)

Have another beer, my friend
Wipe away the angry tears, my friend
Get drunk and foolish on the moment,
Brush aside the day's heavy judgment.

'Cuz,
You come here to forget,
You say drive away all regret.
And dance like it's the ending,
The ending, The ending, The ending,
And dance like it's the ending.

(*Mama watches Salima like a hawk. Lights fade.*)

Scene 3

Morning.

   Living quarters behind the bar. Ragged wood and straw beds. A poster of a popular African-American pop star hangs over Josephine's bed. Sophie paints Salima's fingernails, as she peruses a worn fashion magazine. Salima shifts in place, agitated.

SALIMA: (*Impatiently.*) C'mon, c'mon, c'mon, Sophie. Finish before she comes back.

SOPHIE: Keep still, will ya. Stop moving. She's with Mr. Harari.

SALIMA: She's gonna kill me if she find out I use her nail polish.

SOPHIE: Well, keep it up, and she's gonna find out one of these days.

SALIMA: But, not today. So hurry! (*Sophie makes a mistake with Salima's nails. Salima yanks her hand away.*) Aye girl, look what you did! *Pumbafu!* [Stupid!]

SOPHIE: What's your problem?!

SALIMA: Nothing. Nothing. I'm fine. (*Salima, frustrated, stands up and walks away.*)

SOPHIE: Yeah? You've been short with me all morning? Don't turn away. I'm talking to you.

SALIMA: "Smile, Salima. Talk pretty." Them soldiers don't respect nothing. Them miners, they easy, they want drink, company, and it's over. But the soldiers, they want more of you, and—

SOPHIE: Did that man do something to hurt you?

SALIMA: You know what he say? He say fifteen Hema° men were shot dead and buried in their own mining pit, in mud so thick it swallow them right into the ground without mercy. He say, one man stuff the Coltan into his mouth to keep the soldiers from stealing his hard work, and they split his belly open with a machete. "It'll show him for stealing," he say, bragging like I should be congratulating him. And then he fucked me, and when he was finished he sat on the floor and wept. He wanted me to hold him. Comfort him.

SOPHIE: And, did you?

SALIMA: No. I'm Hema. One of those men could be my brother.

SOPHIE: Don't even say that. (*Salima is overcome by the possibility.*)

SALIMA: I . . . I . . . miss my family. My husband. My baby—

SOPHIE: Stop it! We said we wouldn't talk about it.

SALIMA: Just then I was thinking about Beatrice and how much she liked banana. I feed her like this, I squeeze banana between my fingers and let her suck them, and she'd make a funny little face. Such delight. Delight. (*Emotionally.*) Delight! Delight!

SOPHIE: Shhh! Lower your voice.

SALIMA: Please, let me say my baby's name, Beatrice.

SOPHIE: Shhh!

SALIMA: I wanna go home!

SOPHIE: Now, look at me. Look here, if you leave, where will you go? Huh? Sleep in the bush? Scrounge for food in a stinking refugee camp.

SALIMA: But I wanna—!

Hema: An ethnic group in the Congo related to the Bantu people. Their northern neighbors are the Lendu people.

SOPHIE: What? Be thrown back out there? Where will you go? Huh? Your husband? Your village? How much goodness did they show you?

SALIMA: (*Wounded.*) Why did you say that?

SOPHIE: I'm sorry, but you know it's true. There is a war going on, and it isn't safe for a woman alone. You know this! It's better this way. Here.

SALIMA: You, you don't have to be with them. Sometimes their hands are so full of rage that it hurts to be touched. This night, I look over at you singing, and you seem almost happy like a sunbird that can fly away if you reach out to touch it.

SOPHIE: Is that what you think? While I'm singing, I'm praying the pain will be gone, but what those men did to me lives inside of my body. Every step I take I feel them in me. Punishing me. And it will be that way for the rest of my life. (*Salima touches Sophie's face.*)

SALIMA: I'm pregnant.

SOPHIE: What?

SALIMA: I'm pregnant. I can't tell Mama. (*Tears fill her eyes. Sophie hugs Salima.*)

SOPHIE: No. Shh. Shh. Okay. Okay. (*Sophie breaks away from Salima.*)

SALIMA: I can't tell Mama, she'll turn me out. (*Sophie digs in a basket for a book.*) What are you doing?

SOPHIE: Shh. Be quiet. I want to show you something. Look, look. (*Sophie pulls money from between the pages of the book.*)

SALIMA: Sophie?!

SOPHIE: Shhh. This is for us. We won't be here forever. Okay.

SALIMA: Where'd you get . . . the money?

SOPHIE: Don't worry. Mama may be many things, but she don't count so good. And when there's enough we'll get a bus to Bunia. I promise. But you can't say anything, not even to Josephine. Okay?

SALIMA: But if Mama finds out that you're—

SOPHIE: Shhhh. She won't. (*Josephine, bedraggled, enters and throws herself on the bed.*)

JOSEPHINE: What you two whispering about?

SALIMA AND SOPHIE: Nothing. (*Sophie hides the nail polish and book beneath the mattress, and places the fashion magazine back on Josephine's bed.*)

JOSEPHINE: God, I'm starving. I thought you were going to save me some fufu.

SOPHIE: I did, I put it on the shelf under the cloth.

SALIMA: I bet that stupid monkey took it again. Pesky creature.

JOSEPHINE: It ain't the monkey, it's Emeline's nasty child. He's a menace. That boy's buttocks would be raw if he were mine. (*Josephine takes off her shirt revealing an enormous disfiguring black scar circumventing her stomach. She tries to hide it. Sophie's eyes are drawn to the scar. To Salima.*) But, if it's you who's been pinching my supper don't think I won't find out. I ain't the only one who's noticed that you getting fat fat off the same food we eating. (*To Sophie.*) What are you looking at? (*A moment.*) No questions. Hang up my shirt! *Sasa!* (*Sophie hangs Josephine's shirt on a nail.*)

SALIMA: Tst.

JOSEPHINE: And what's wrong with you?

SALIMA: Nothing. Tst. (*Josephine suspiciously sniffs the air. Then puts on a traditional colorful wrap. A moment. Salima sits back on the bed. Josephine notices her magazine on the bed.*)

JOSEPHINE: Hey, girl, why is my fashion magazine here? Huh?

SALIMA: I . . . I had a quick look.

JOSEPHINE: What do you want with it? Can you even read?

SALIMA: Oh shut your mouth, I like looking at the photographs.

JOSEPHINE: Oh c'mon, girl, you've seen them a dozen times. It's the same photographs that were there yesterday.

SALIMA: So why do you care if I look at them?

SOPHIE: *Atsha, makelle.* [Stop the noise.] Let her see it, Josephine. Let's not have the same argument.

JOSEPHINE: There.

SALIMA: (*Whispered.*) Bitch.

JOSEPHINE: What?

SALIMA: Thank you.

JOSEPHINE: Yeah, that's what I thought. (*Josephine tosses the magazine at Salima.*) Girl, I really should charge you for all the times your dirty fingers fuss with it. (*Josephine sucks her teeth.*)

SOPHIE: Oh, give us peace, she doesn't feel well.

JOSEPHINE: No? (*Salima moping, thumbs through the magazine doing her best to ignore Josephine.*)

SALIMA: The only reason I don't read is 'cuz my younger sister get school, and I get good husband.

JOSEPHINE: So where is he?! (*Josephine, ignoring her, turns on the portable radio hanging over her bed.*)

ANNOUNCER: (*Voiceover.*) Nous avons reçu des rapports que les bandits armés de Lendu et des groupes rivaux de Hema combattent pour la commande de la ville —°

SALIMA: What's he say?

SOPHIE: Lendu and Hema, fighting near Bunia. (*Josephine quickly turns the radio dial. American R&B music plays. She does a few quick suggestive steps, then lights a cigarette.*)

JOSEPHINE: Hey. Hey. Guess what? Guess what? I'm going to Kisangani next month.

SOPHIE: What?

JOSEPHINE: Mr. Harari is going to take me. Watch out, *Chérie,* he's promised to set me up in a high-rise apartment. Don't hate, all of this fineness belongs in the city.

SOPHIE: For true?

JOSEPHINE: What, you think I'm lying?

Nous . . . la ville: We have received reports that armed Lendu bandits and rival groups of Hema are fighting for possession of the city.

Condola Rashad as Sophie, Cherise Boothe as Josephine, and Quincy Tyler Bernstine as Salima in *Ruined,* in 2009.

SOPHIE: No, no that's real cool, Josephine. The big town. Yeah, what's it like? Have you been?

JOSEPHINE: Me? . . . No. No. (*To Salima.*) And I know you haven't.

SALIMA: How do you know? Huh? I was planning to go sometime next year. My husband—

JOSEPHINE: (*Sarcastically.*) What, he was going to sell his yams in the market?

SALIMA: I'll ask you not to mention my family.

JOSEPHINE: And if I do?

SALIMA: I'm asking you kindly this time. (*Josephine recognizes the weight of her words.*)

JOSEPHINE: I'm tired of hearing about your family. (*Josephine blows smoke at Salima.*)

SALIMA: Mention them again, and I swear to God I'll beat your ass.

JOSEPHINE: Yeah?

SALIMA: Yeah. You don't know what the hell you're talking about.

JOSEPHINE: I don't? All right. Digger! I'm stupid! I don't! You are smarter than all of us. Yeah? That's what you think, huh? *Kiwele wele.* [Dummy.] You wait, girl. I'll forgive you, I will, when you say "Josephine you were so so right."

SOPHIE: Just shut up!

JOSEPHINE: Hey, I'm done. (*Josephine blows a kiss, and throws herself across the bed. Salima, enraged, starts for the door.*)

SOPHIE: Salima, Salima.

JOSEPHINE: (*Taunting.*) Salima! (*Josephine falls on the bed laughing.*)

SOPHIE: What's wrong with you? What did Salima do to you? You make me sick. (*Sophie flicks off the radio.*)

JOSEPHINE: Hey, *jolie fille.* (*Josephine makes kissing sounds.*)

SOPHIE: Don't talk to me.

JOSEPHINE: I can't talk to you? Who put you on the top shelf? You flutter about here as if God touched only you. What you seem to forget is that this is a whorehouse, *Chérie.*

SOPHIE: Yeah, but, I'm not a whore.

JOSEPHINE: A mere trick of fate. I'm sorry, but let me say what we all know, you are something worse than a whore. So many men have had you that you're worthless. (*A moment. Sophie, wounded, turns and walks away silently.*)

JOSEPHINE: Am I wrong?

SOPHIE: . . . Yes.

JOSEPHINE: Am I wrong?

SOPHIE: Yes.

JOSEPHINE: My father was chief! (*Sophie heads for the door, Josephine blocks her.*) My father was chief! The most important man in the villages, and when the soldiers raided us, who was kind to me? Huh? Not his second wife. "There she is the chief's daughter!" Or the cowards who pretended not to know me, and did any of them bring a blanket to cover me, did anyone move to help me? NO! So you see, you ain't special! (*Lights fade.*)

Scene 4

Dusk. Generator hums. The bar bustles with activity: miners, prostitutes, and government soldiers. Laughter. Salima and Josephine sit at a table with two government soldiers. Sophie sings.

SOPHIE: (*Sings.*)
> A rare bird on a limb
> sings a song heard by a few.
> A few patient and distant listeners.
>
> Hear, its sweet call,
> a sound that haunts the forest
> A cry that tells a story,
> harmonious, but time forgotten.
>
> To be seen, is to be doomed
> It must evade capture,
> And yet the bird
> Still cries out to be heard.
>
> And yet the bird
> Still cries out to be heard.

> And yet the bird
> Still cries out to be heard.

(*Mama feeds the parrot.*)

MAMA: Hello. Talk to me. You hungry? Yes?

CHRISTIAN: Mama! (*Mama is surprised by Christian, her face lights up.*)

MAMA: Ah, Professor! (*Mama cracks open a couple of sodas. Christian places a box of chocolates and several cartons of cigarettes on the counter. The music stops, and he launches into a poem.*)

CHRISTIAN:
> The tidal dance,
> a nasty tug of war,
> two equally implacable partners
> Day fighting night . . .

And so forth and so on.

Forgive me, I bring you an early poem, but I'm afraid it's running away from my memory. I still hope one day you will hear the music and dance with me.

MAMA: (*Dismissive.*) You're a ridiculous man. (*Mama passes a cold soda to Christian. He blows a kiss to Sophie.*)

CHRISTIAN: Lovely, *Chérie.* It's what I've been waiting for.

MAMA: You're the only man I know who doesn't crave a cold beer at the end of a long drive.

CHRISTIAN: Last time I had a drink, I lost several years of my life. (*Mama hands him a list.*) What's this?

MAMA: A list of everything I know you forgot to bring me. (*Christian examines the list.*)

CHRISTIAN: What? When'd you learn to spell so good?

MAMA: Oh, close your mouth. Sophie wrote it down for me. She's a smart girl, been helping me here and there. (*Christian laughs.*)

CHRISTIAN: You see how things work out. And you, you wanted to turn her away—

MAMA: Are you finished? (*The government soldiers break into loud laughter.*) Those soldiers want a full meal, but never want to pay. Tst. (*The government soldiers laugh. Flirtatiously.*) Professor, I looked out for you on Friday. What the hell happened?

CHRISTIAN: I had to deliver supplies to the mission. Have you heard? Pastor Robbin's been missing for a couple days. (*Sophie and a government soldier laugh.*) I told them I'd ask about.

MAMA: The white preacher? I'm not surprised. He's got a big fucking mouth. The mission's better off without him, the only thing that old bastard ever did was pass out flaky aspirin and maybe a round of penicillin if you were dying.

CHRISTIAN: Well, the rumor is the pastor's been treating wounded rebel soldiers.

MAMA: (*Concerned.*) Really?

CHRISTIAN: That's what I'm hearing. Things are getting ugly over that way.

MAMA: Since when?

CHRISTIAN: Last week. The militias are battling for control of the area. It is impossible.

MAMA: What about Yaka-Yaka mine? Has the fighting scared off the miners?

CHRISTIAN: I don't know about the miners, but it's scaring me. (*Salima and miner laugh.*) I was just by Yaka-Yaka. When I was there six months ago, it was a forest filled with noisy birds, now it looks like God spooned out heaping mouthfuls of earth! And every stupid bastard is trying to get a taste of it. It's been ugly, *Chérie*, but never like this. Not here.

MAMA: No more talk. (*She's spooked, but doesn't want to show it. She signals for the musicians to play an upbeat song. ["Rare Bird."] The song plays softly. Josephine leads a government soldier to the back.*) There will always be squabbles, ancient and otherwise. Me, I thank God for deep dirty holes like Yaka-Yaka. In my house I try to keep everyone happy.

CHRISTIAN: Don't fool yourself!

MAMA: Hey, hey Professor, are you worried about me? (*Christian gently takes Mama's hand.*)

CHRISTIAN: Of course, *Chérie*. I am a family man at heart. A lover, baby. We could build a nice business together. I have friends in Kampala, I have friends in Bamako, I even have friends in Paris, the city of love. (*Mama laughs, and withdraws her hand away from Christian. His affection throws her off balance.*)

MAMA: You . . . are . . . a stupid . . . man . . . with a running tongue. And look here, I have my own business, and I'm not leaving it for a jackass who doesn't have enough sense to buy a new suit.

CHRISTIAN: You are too proud and stubborn, you know that. This is a good suit, *très chic*, so who cares if it's old? And . . . don't pretend, *Chérie*, eventually you'll grace me with . . . a dance.

MAMA: Have a cold beer, it'll flush out some of your foolishness.

CHRISTIAN: Ach, ach, woman! Liquor is not a dance partner I choose. (*Christian does a few seductive dance steps. Just then Commander Osembenga, a pompous peacock of a man in dark sunglasses, a gold chain, and a jogging suit, struts into the bar. He wears a pistol in a harness. Christian nods deferentially. He is accompanied by a government soldier in uniform.*) *Monsieur*. (*Osembenga stands erect waiting to be acknowledged. Everyone grows silent.*)

MAMA: (*Flirtatiously.*) Good evening.

OSEMBENGA: It is now. (*He gives the place a once-over.*)

MAMA: Can I get you something?

OSEMBENGA: Bring me a cold Primus. A pack of cigarettes, fresh. (*Mama produces a chair for Osembenga, then she fishes into the cooler for a beer.*)

MAMA: *Monsieur*, I must ask you to leave your bullets at the bar, otherwise you don't come in.

OSEMBENGA: And if I choose not to. (*Mama holds the cold beer in her hand.*)

MAMA: Then you don't get served. I don't want any mischief in here. Is that clear? (*Osembenga is charmed by her tenacity. He laughs with the robust authority of a man in charge.*)

OSEMBENGA: Do you know who I am?

MAMA: I'm afraid you must edify me. And then forgive me, if it makes absolutely no difference. Once you step through my door, then you're in my house. And I make the rules here. (*Osembenga laughs again.*)

OSEMBENGA: All right, Mama. Forgive me. (*Osembenga makes a show of removing the bullets from his gun and placing them on the table.*) And who said I don't respect the rule of law? (*Josephine, laughing, runs in from the back. A drunk government soldier chases her. His pants are unzipped.*)

GOVERNMENT SOLDIER #1: Commander, beg my pardon.

OSEMBENGA: Take it easy, young man. Take it easy. We're all off duty. Clean up. We're in Mama's house. (*Osembenga sits down, and unzips his jacket. Mama opens a pack of cigarettes and passes them to Osembenga.*)

MAMA: *Monsieur*, I don't recall seeing you here before.

OSEMBENGA: No. (*Mama lights Osembenga's cigarette.*)

MAMA: What brings you to *mon* hotel?

OSEMBENGA: Jerome Kisembe, the rebel leader. (*Osembenga studies her face to gauge the response.*) You know him, of course.

MAMA: I know of him. We all know of him. His name is spoken here at least several times a day. We've felt the sting of his reputation.

OSEMBENGA: So, you do know him.

MAMA: No, as I said I know of him. His men control the road east and the forest to the north of here. (*Osembenga turns his attention to everyone. Scrutiny. Suspicion.*)

OSEMBENGA: Is that so?

MAMA: Yes, but you must know that. (*Osembenga speaks to Mama, but he is clearly addressing everyone.*)

OSEMBENGA: This Jerome Kisembe is a dangerous man. You hide him and his band of renegades in your villages. Give them food, and say you're protecting your liberator. What liberator? What will he give the people? That is what I want to know. What has he given you, Mama? Hm? A new roof? Food? Peace?

MAMA: Me, I don't need a man to give me anything.

OSEMBENGA: Make a joke, but Kisembe has one goal and that is to make himself rich on your back, Mama. (*Osembenga grows loud and more forthright as he speaks. The bar grows quiet.*) He will burn your crops, steal your women, and make slaves of your men all in the name of peace and reconciliation. Don't believe him. He, and men like him, these careless militias wage a diabolical campaign. They leave stains everywhere they go. And remember the land he claims as his own, it is a national reserve, it is the people's land, our land. And yet he will tell you the government has taken everything, though we're actually paving the way for democracy.

MAMA: I know that, but the government needs to let him know that. But you, I'm only seeing you for the first time. Kisembe I hear his name every day.

OSEMBENGA: Then hear my name, Commander Prestige de Bembe Osembenga, *Banga Liwa.* [Fear death.] (*A moment. Mama absorbs the news, she seems genuinely humbled. Christian retreats to the bar.*) You will hear my name quite a bit from now on.

MAMA: Commander Osembenga, forgive me for not knowing your name. *Karibu.* [Welcome.] It's a pleasure to have such an important man in our company. Allow me to pour you a glass of our very best whiskey. From the U.S of A.

OSEMBENGA: Thank you. A clean glass.

MAMA: Of course. (*Mama fetches Osembenga a glass of whiskey. She makes a show of wiping out the cloudy glass. She pours him a generous glass of whiskey and places the bottle in front of him. Seductively.*) *Karibu!* We take good care of our visitors. And we offer very good company. Clean company, not like other places. You are safe here. If you need something, anything, while—

OSEMBENGA: You are a practical woman, I know that you have the sense to keep your doors closed to rebel dogs. Am I right?

MAMA: Of course. (*Osembenga gently takes Mama's hand. She allows the intimacy. Christian looks on. Contempt. Jealousy. A miner enters covered in mud.*) Hey, hey my friend. Wash your hands and feet in the bucket outside! (*The miner, annoyed, exits.*) These fucking miners have no respect for nothing. I have to tell that one every time. (*Christian sits at the bar, fuming. Osembenga notices him. Obsequiously.*) Anything you need.

OSEMBENGA: I will keep that in mind. (*Mama politely pulls her hand away from Osembenga. She beckons to Josephine and Salima, who join Osembenga at the table. The government soldiers groan.*)

MAMA: Ladies.

JOSEPHINE: Commander. (*Josephine places her hand on his knee.*)

MAMA: Excuse me a moment. (*Christian grabs Mama's arm as she passes.*)

CHRISTIAN: (*Whispers.*) Watch that one.

MAMA: What? It's always good to have friends in the government, no? (*Mama clears bottles from the government soldiers' tables. The miner reenters, and sits at the bar.*)

GOVERNMENT SOLDIER #1: Another.

MAMA: Show me your money. (*The government soldier holds up his money.*) Sophie! Sophie! What are you standing around for? I'm losing money as I speak. Quick. Quick. Two beers. (*Sophie cracks open two beers, and carries them over to the government soldiers. The government soldier places his money on the table. Sophie picks it up, and quickly slips it into her shirt. She doesn't realize Mama is watching her. The government soldier grabs her onto his lap. Christian protectively rises. Sophie skillfully*

extracts herself from the government soldier's lap, and exits.*)

CHRISTIAN: Are you okay?

SOPHIE: Yes. (*Christian smiles to himself, and lights a cigarette. A drunken government soldier plops down next to Christian.*)

GOVERNMENT SOLDIER #1: Ça va, Papa?°

CHRISTIAN: *Bien merci.* (*The government soldier stares down Christian.*)

GOVERNMENT SOLDIER #1: You give me a cigarette, my friend?

CHRISTIAN: (*Nervously.*) Sorry, this is my last one.

GOVERNMENT SOLDIER #1: Yeah? You, buy me cigarette.

CHRISTIAN: What?

GOVERNMENT SOLDIER #1: (*Showing off.*) Buy me cigarette!

CHRISTIAN: Sure. (*Christian reluctantly digs into his pocket, and places money on the counter. Mama places a cigarette on the counter. The government soldier scoops it up triumphantly, and walks away.*) And? *Merci?* (*The government soldier stops short, and menacingly stares down Christian.*)

OSEMBENGA: Soldier, show this good man the bush hasn't robbed you of your manners. (*A moment.*)

GOVERNMENT SOLDIER #1: *Merci.* (*Christian acknowledges Commander.*)

OSEMBENGA: Of course. (*The government soldier, embarrassed, angrily drives the miner out of his bar seat. The miner retreats. Christian thankfully acknowledges Osembenga with a nod. Osembenga smiles, and gestures to Mama.*)

MAMA: Yes, Commander.

OSEMBENGA: (*Whispered.*) Who is he?

MAMA: Passing through.

OSEMBENGA: What's his business?

MAMA: Salesman. He's nobody.

OSEMBENGA: I don't trust him.

MAMA: Does he look dangerous to you?

OSEMBENGA: Everyone looks dangerous to me, until I've shared a drink with them. (*Osembenga sizes up Christian. Deciding.*) Give him a glass of whiskey, and tell him I hope he finds success here. (*Mama pours a glass of whiskey, and walks over to Christian.*)

MAMA: Good news, you've made a friend, the Commander has bought you a drink of whiskey and hopes that you'll find prosperity.

CHRISTIAN: That's very generous, but you know I don't drink. Please, tell him thanks, but no thanks. (*A moment.*)

MAMA: The Commander is buying you a drink. (*Mama places the glass in Christian's hand.*) Raise your glass to him, and smile.

CHRISTIAN: Thank you, but I don't drink.

MAMA: (*Whispered.*) Oh you most certainly do, today. You will drink every last drop of what he offers, and when he buys you another round you'll drink that as well. You will drink until he decides you've had enough.

Ça va, Papa?: How is it going, Pop?

(*Christian looks over at the smiling Osembenga. He raises his glass to Osembenga across the room, contemplating the drink for a long hard moment.*)

OSEMBENGA: Drink up! (*The government soldiers encourage Christian.*)

CHRISTIAN: I—

MAMA: Please. (*Whispered.*) He's a very important man. So when he offers you a drink, you drink it.

CHRISTIAN: Please, Mama.

MAMA: He can help us, or he can cause us many problems. It's your decision. Remember, if you don't step on the dog's tail, he won't bite you.

OSEMBENGA: Drink up! (*Nervous, Christian slowly and with difficulty drinks back the liquor, wincing. Osembenga laughs, and signals for Mama to pour him another. She does. The government soldiers cheer Christian on.*) Good. (*Shouts.*) To health and prosperity! (*Christian looks at the second drink. Osembenga encourages him to drink up. Christian nervously knocks back the second shot of whiskey, and winces. Osembenga laughs. The soldiers cheer. Mama pours him another.*)

CHRISTIAN: Don't make—

MAMA: Trust me. (*She places the glass in his hand. Christian walks over to Osembenga's table. We aren't sure whether he's going to throw the drink in Osembenga's face or toast him. He forcefully thrusts his drink into the air.*)

Scene 5

Morning. Bar.
Sophie reads from the pages of a romance novel. Josephine and Salima sit listening, rapt.

SOPHIE: (*Reading.*) "The others had left the party, they were alone. She was now painfully aware that there was only the kiss left between them. She felt herself stiffen as he leaned into her. The hairs on her forearms stood on end, and the room suddenly grew several degrees warmer."

JOSEPHINE: Oh, kiss her!

SALIMA: Shh!

SOPHIE: "His lips met hers. She could taste him, smell him, and all at once her body was infused with—" (*Mama enters with the lockbox. Sophie protectively slips the book behind her back. Mama grabs it.*)

MAMA: What's this?

SOPHIE: . . . A romance, Uncle Christian bought it.

MAMA: A romance?

SOPHIE: Yes. (*Mama examines the book. The women's eyes plead with her not to take it.*)

MAMA: Josephine, we need water in the back, and Salima, the broom is waiting for you in the yard.

SALIMA: Ah Mama, let her finish the chapter.

MAMA: Are you giving me lip? I didn't think so. Come here. Hurry. (*Salima reluctantly walks over to Mama.*

Mama grabs her wrist and runs her hand over Salima's stomach.) You must be happy here. You're getting fat fat!

SALIMA: I didn't notice.

MAMA: Well, I have. (*Salima, petrified, isn't sure what Mama's going to do. Then.*) You did good last night.

SALIMA: Thank you. (*Mama tosses the book back to Sophie.*)

JOSEPHINE: You don't care for romance, Mama?

MAMA: Me? No, the problem is I already know how it's going to end. There'll be kissing, fucking, a betrayal, and then the woman will foolishly surrender her heart to an undeserving man. Okay. Move. Move. Ach. Ach. Sophie wait. (*Salima grabs the broom and exits.*)

JOSEPHINE: (*Gesturing to Sophie.*) What about her? How come she never has to fetch water?

MAMA: I need Sophie's help.

JOSEPHINE: Tst!

MAMA: You have a problem with that? You count good? (*Josephine stares down Sophie. Sophie isn't having it. Mama laughs. Salima pokes her head in the door.*)

SALIMA: Mama. Someone's coming around the bend.

MAMA: (*Surprised.*) So early?

JOSEPHINE: Tst! Another stupid miner looking to get his cock wet.

SALIMA: No, I think it's Mr. Harari. (*Josephine runs to the door. Salima smiles, jokingly, at Sophie.*)

JOSEPHINE: What?

SALIMA: "Come with me to the city, my darling."

JOSEPHINE: Don't hate!

SOPHIE: "I'm going to buy you a palace in Lebanon, my darling." (*This strikes a nerve. The women laugh.*)

JOSEPHINE: Hey, hey. At least I have somebody, I take care of him good. And he comes back. (*Josephine seductively approaches Sophie. She grabs her close.*) Joke, laugh, *jolie fille*, but we all know a man wants a woman who's complete.

SOPHIE: Okay, stop—

JOSEPHINE: He wants her to open up and allow him to release himself, he wants to pour the whole world into her.

SOPHIE: I said stop!

JOSEPHINE: Can you be that woman?

MAMA: Let her alone. Go get the water!

JOSEPHINE: I was firstborn child! My father was chief!

MAMA: Yeah, and my father was whoever put money in my Mama's pocket! Chief, farmer, who the hell cares? Go! (*A moment. Josephine exits. Salima follows.*) Give Josephine a good smack in the mouth, and she won't bother you no more. (*Mama places the lockbox on the table.*) Here. Count the money from last night. Let me know how we did. (*Sophie opens the lockbox and holds up. Mama skillfully funnels water into the whiskey bottle.*) I don't know where all these men are coming from, but I'm happy for it. (*Sophie pulls out the money, a worn ribbon, and then a small stone.*)

SOPHIE: Why do you keep this pebble?

MAMA: That? It doesn't look like anything. Stupid man, give it to me to hold for a one night of company and four beers not even cold enough to quench his thirst. He said he'd be back for it and he'd pay me. It's a rough diamond. It probably took him a half year of sifting through mud to dig it up, and he promised his simple wife a Chinese motor scooter and fabric from Senegal. And here it is, in my hand, some unfortunate woman's dream. (*Mama places the stone in her lockbox.*)

SOPHIE: What will you do with it? (*Mama chuckles to herself.*)

MAMA: Do? Ha! (*Mama knocks back a shot of watered-down whiskey.*) It still tastes like whiskey. I don't know, but as long as they are foolish enough to give it to me, I'll keep accepting it. My mother taught me that you can follow behind everyone and walk in the dust, or you can walk ahead through the unbroken thorny brush. You may get blood on your ankles, but you arrive first and not covered in the residue of others. This land is fertile and blessed in many regards, and the men are not the only ones entitled to its bounty.

SOPHIE: But what if the man comes back for his stone?

MAMA: A lot of people would sell it, run away. But it is my insurance policy, it is what keeps me from becoming like them. There must always be a part of you that this war can't touch. It'll be here, if he comes back. It's a damn shame, but I keep it for that stupid woman. Too many questions, how'd we do?

SOPHIE: Good. If we—

MAMA: We?

SOPHIE: Charged a little more for the beer, a few more francs, by the end of the year you'll have enough to buy a new generator.

MAMA: Yeah? A new generator? Good. You're quick with numbers. You counted everything from last night?

SOPHIE: Yes.

MAMA: Your tips?

SOPHIE: Yes.

MAMA: Yes? (*A moment. Mama grabs Sophie and reaches into her dress, producing a fold of money.*) Is this yours?

SOPHIE: Yes. I was—

MAMA: So tell me what you're planning to do with my money. (*With edge.*) 'Cuz it's my money.

SOPHIE: I—

MAMA: I, I, I . . . what?

SOPHIE: It's not what you think, Mama.

MAMA: "Take her in, give her food." Your uncle begged me. What am I supposed to do? I trust you. Everyone say, she bad luck, but I think this is a smart girl, maybe Mama won't have to do everything by herself. You read books, you speak good like white man—but is this who you want to be?

SOPHIE: I'm sorry, Mama.

MAMA: No. No. I will put you out on your ass. I will let you walk naked down that road, let every scavenger dog have a piece of you, is that what you want? What did you think you were going to do with my money?! (*Mama grabs Sophie and pulls her to the door.*)

SOPHIE: Mama! Please! . . .

MAMA: You want to be out there? Huh? Huh? Then go! Go! (*Sophie struggles, terrified.*) That's what I thought. (*A beat.*) Now tell me, what were you going to do?

SOPHIE: A woman that come in here said she can help me. She said there is an operation for girls.

MAMA: Don't you lie to me.

SOPHIE: Listen, listen, please listen, they can repair the damage. (*A moment. Mama releases Sophie.*)

MAMA: An operation?

SOPHIE: Yes, she give me this pamphlet. Look, look.

MAMA: And it can make it better?

SOPHIE: Yes. (*Mama puts the money into her lockbox.*)

MAMA: Hm. Congratulations! You're the first girl bold enough to steal from me. (*Laughs.*) Where are your books?

SOPHIE: Under my bed.

MAMA: Go bring them to me. I know you better than you think, girl. (*Lights fade.*)

Scene 6

Bar. Morning light pours in. Josephine struggles with a drunk miner. She finally manages to push him out of the bar, then exits into the back. Salima quickly sneaks food from under the counter. She stuffs fufu into her mouth. The bird squawks as if to tell on her.

SALIMA: Shh! Shh! (*Christian, winded and on edge, comes rushing into the bar.*) Professor!

CHRISTIAN: Get Mama! (*Salima exits quickly. Christian paces. Mama enters.*)

MAMA: (*She lights up.*) Professor! (*Beat.*) What, what is it?

CHRISTIAN: The white pastor's dead.

MAMA: What? (*Christian sits, then immediately stands.*)

CHRISTIAN: He was dead for over a week before anyone found his body. He was only a hundred meters from the chapel. The cook said it was Osembenga's soldiers. They accused the pastor of aiding rebels. They cut him up beyond recognition. Cut out his eyes and tongue. (*He's nauseated by the notion.*)

MAMA: The pastor? I'm sorry to hear that. (*Mama pours herself a whiskey.*)

CHRISTIAN: Can I have one of those, please?

MAMA: Are you sure?

CHRISTIAN: Just give it to me, damn it! (*Mama hesitantly pours Christian a drink. She stares at him.*) What? (*He gulps it down.*) The policeman said there were no witnesses. No one saw anything, and so there is nothing he can do. Bury him, he said. Me? I barely know the man, and people who worked with him for years were mute, no one knew anything. He was butchered, and no one knows anything.

MAMA: Take it easy.

CHRISTIAN: These ignorant country boys, who wouldn't be able to tell left from right, they put on a uniform and suddenly they're making decisions for us. *Mambo kama hayo siyawezi*, Mama! *Yani hata kidogo! Siyawezi kabisa! Kabisa!* [Things like these I can't take, Mama! Not even one bit. I can't, just can't.] Get me another.

MAMA: The Fantas are cold.

CHRISTIAN: I don't want a Fanta. (*Mama goes behind the counter, and reluctantly pours Christian another drink. His hand slightly quivers as he knocks back the liquor.*) They've killed a white man. Do you know what that means? A missionary. They won't think twice about killing us.

MAMA: A dead pastor is just another dead man, and people here see that every day. I can't think about it right now. I have ten girls to feed, and a business to run. (*Mama buries her face in her palms, overwhelmed.*)

CHRISTIAN: We'll go West where there's no trouble. Between the two of us . . . The two of us. We'll open a small place. Serve food, drink, dancing. Come with me, Mama. (*Mama isn't convinced. Christian reaches for the bottle of whiskey, Mama snatches it away. Christian slams the bar and goes to a table. Meanwhile two men, Fortune and Simon, silently enter, fatigued and ragged. They carry beat-up rifles and wear dirty, ill-fitting uniforms. Fortune also carries an iron pot. The men are very nervous, which makes Mama uneasy.*)

MAMA: Yes?

FORTUNE: Is this the place of Mama Nadi?

MAMA: Yes, that is me. What can I do for you?

FORTUNE: We'll have a meal and a beer.

MAMA: Okay, no problem. I have fish and fufu from last night.

FORTUNE: Yeah. Good. Good.

MAMA: It ain't hot.

SIMON: We'll have it. (*Mama eyes the men suspiciously. Christian glares at them.*)

MAMA: Please don't be offended, but I'll need to see your money. (*Fortune removes a pile of worn bills from his pocket. The men move to sit.*) Hey. Hey. Hey. Empty your weapons. (*The men hesitate.*)

SIMON: No, our wea—

MAMA: It's the rule. If you want to be fed. (*The men reluctantly remove their clips from their guns and hand them to Mama.*)

FORTUNE: (*To Christian.*) Good morning.

CHRISTIAN: Good morning.

SIMON: Do you have a place for us to wash up?

FORTUNE: In the back maybe. (*A moment.*)

MAMA: (*Suspicious.*) I can bring you a basin of water. (*They sit at the table. Sophie enters. She's surprised to find Christian and Simon.*)

SOPHIE: Uncle.

CHRISTIAN: *Bonjour, mon amour.*° (*She is leery of the men.*)

SOPHIE: What happened to—

Bonjour, mon amour: Good day, my love.

CHRISTIAN: Shh. I'm okay. (*Sophie notes the caution in his tone.*)

FORTUNE/SIMON: Good morning. How are you? (*The men politely rise.*)

SOPHIE: Good morning. (*The men sit.*)

MAMA: Bring some water for the basin.

FORTUNE: Please. (*Sophie exits with the basin while Mama serves the beer.*) Thank you.

MAMA: You come from the east?

FORTUNE: No.

MAMA: Farmers?

FORTUNE: NO! We're soldiers! We follow Commander Osembenga! (*Sophie returns with the full basin but Christian signals for her to leave. Christian grows increasingly nervous. He watches the men like a hawk.*)

MAMA: Easy. I don't mean to insult you, soldier. But you look like good men. Men who don't follow trouble. (*Fortune seems reluctant to speak.*)

SIMON: We are—

FORTUNE: I'm told there is a woman here named Salima. Is that true?

CHRISTIAN: There— (*Christian starts to speak, Mama cuts him off.*)

MAMA: Why? Who is looking for her?

FORTUNE: Is she here!? I asked you, is she here!?

MAMA: I'd adjust your tone, Mister.

FORTUNE: Please, I'm looking for a woman named Salima.

MAMA: I have to ask inside. (*Christian and Mama exchange a look.*)

FORTUNE: She's from Kaligili. She has a small scar on her right cheek. Just so.

MAMA: A lot of women come and go. I'll ask around. And may I say who's looking for her?

FORTUNE: Fortune, her husband. (*Christian registers this discovery.*)

MAMA: Excuse me. I'll go ask inside. (*Mama exits. Christian disappears into his drink.*)

SIMON: We'll find her, Fortune. C'mon. Drink up. When was your last cold beer?

FORTUNE: I'm not thirsty. (*Simon drinks.*)

SIMON: Ah, that's nice. It's nice, man. (*Fortune isn't interested.*)

FORTUNE: Come on, come on, where is she?

SIMON: Be patient. Man, if she's here we'll find her.

FORTUNE: Why is it taking so long?

SIMON: Take it easy.

FORTUNE: You heard it, the man on the road described Salima. It is her. (*Simon laughs.*) What? (*Fortune paces.*)

SIMON: You say that every time. Maybe it is, maybe it isn't. We've been walking for months, and in every village there is a Salima. You are certain. So please, don't— (*Mama reemerges.*)

MAMA: There is no Salima here.

FORTUNE: (*Shocked.*) What? No! She is here!

MAMA: I'm sorry, you are mistaken. You got bad information.

FORTUNE: Salima! Salima Mukengeshayi!

MAMA: I said she is not here.

FORTUNE: You lying witch! Salima!

MAMA: Call me names, but there's still no Salima here. I think maybe the woman you're looking for is dead.

FORTUNE: She is here! Goddamn you, she is here. (*Fortune flips the table. Mama grabs a machete. Christian brandishes the whiskey bottle like a weapon.*)

MAMA: Please, I said she is not here. And if you insist I will show you how serious I am.

SIMON: We don't want trouble.

MAMA: Now go. Get out! Get the hell out of here.

FORTUNE: Tell Salima, I will be back for her. (*Fortune storms out, Simon follows. The birds raise hell. Christian scolds Mama with his eyes. Blackout.*)

ACT TWO • Scene 1

Fortune in his ill-fitting uniform stands outside the bar, like a centurion guarding the gates.

    Josephine teases two drunk government soldiers and a miner. Guitar. Drums. Mama and Sophie sing a dance song. Mr. Harari and Christian watch. Festive.

MAMA: (*Sings.*)
    Hey, hey Monsieur.
    Come play, Monsieur,
    Hey, hey Monsieur.
    Come play, Monsieur,
    The Congo sky rages electric,
    As bullets fly like hell's rain,
    Wild flowers wilt, and the forest decays.
    But here we're pouring Champagne.

MAMA AND SOPHIE:
    'Cuz a warrior knows no peace,
    When a hungry lion's awake.
    But when that lion's asleep
    The warrior is free to play.

SOPHIE:
    Drape your weariness on my shoulder,
    Sweep travel dust from your heart.
    Villagers die as soldiers grow bolder.
    We party as the world falls apart.

MAMA AND SOPHIE:
    'Cuz a warrior knows no peace,
    When a hungry lion's awake.
    But when that lion's asleep
    The warrior is free to play.

(*The drum beats a furious rhythm. Josephine answers with a dance, which begins playfully, seductively, then slowly becomes increasingly frenzied. She releases her anger, her pain . . . everything. The men cheer her on, a mob growing louder and more demanding. Josephine desperately grabs at the air as if trying to hold on to something. Her dance becomes uglier, more frantic. She abruptly stops, overwhelmed. Sophie goes to her aid.*)

MAMA:
    Hey, Monsieur.
    Come play, Monsieur,

    Hey, Monsieur.
    Come play, Monsieur
    The door never closes at Mama's place.
    The door never closes at Mama's place.

(*Distant gunfire. The bar grows still. A moment.*)

    The door never closes at Mama's place.

(*Lights fade.*)

Scene 2

Back room. Josephine is asleep.
    Salima quickly pulls down her shirt hiding her pregnant stomach as Mama enters eating a mango.

MAMA: (*To Salima.*) Are you going to hang here in the shadows until forever? I have a thirsty miner with a good day in his pockets.

SALIMA: Sorry, Mama, but—

MAMA: I need one of you to go make him happy, show him his hard work isn't for naught. (*Mama clicks her tongue.*) C'mon. C'mon.

SALIMA: (*Whispered.*) But . . .

MAMA: Josephine!

JOSEPHINE: Ah! Why is it always me? (*Josephine rises, and exits in a huff, as Sophie enters from bathing. Salima nervously looks to the door.*)

SALIMA: Is Fortune still outside?

MAMA: Your husband? Yes. He's still standing there, he couldn't be more quiet than if he were a stake driven into the ground. I don't like quiet men.

SALIMA: He's always been so.

MAMA: Well, I wish he wouldn't be "so" outside of my door. (*Salima involuntarily smiles, then . . .*)

SALIMA: Why won't he go already? I don't want him to see me.

SOPHIE: He's not leaving until he sees you, Salima. (*Sophie gets dressed.*)

MAMA: Ha. What for? So he can turn his lip up at her again.

SOPHIE: No. C'mon, he's been out there for two nights. If he doesn't love you, why would he still be there.

SALIMA: Yeah?

MAMA: Tst! Both of you are so stupid. He'll see you, love will flood into his eyes, he'll tell you everything you want to hear, and then one morning, I know how it happens, he will begin to ask ugly questions, but he won't be able to hear the answers. And no matter what you say, he won't be satisfied. I know. And *Chérie*, don't look away from me, will you be able to tell him the truth? Huh? We know, don't we? The woman he loved is dead.

SOPHIE: That's not true. He—

MAMA: (*To Salima.*) He left her for dead. (*A moment. Mama's words hit home.*) See. This is your home now. Mama takes care of you. (*Mama takes Salima in her arms.*) But if you want to go back out there, go, but they, your village, your people, they won't

Saidah Arrika Ekulona as Mama Nadi and Quincy Tyler Bernstine as Salima in *Ruined*, in 2009.

understand. Oh, they'll say they will, but they won't. Because, you know, underneath everything, they will be thinking, "She's damaged. She's been had by too many men. She let them, those dirty men, touch her. She's a whore." And Salima, are you strong enough to stomach their hate? It will be worse than anything you've felt yet.

SOPHIE: But he—

MAMA: I'm not being cruel, but your simple life, the one you remember, that . . . Yeah the one you're so fond of . . . it's vapor, *Chérie*. It's gone. (*Tears flood Salima's eyes.*) Now, uh-uh, don't cry. We keep our faces pretty. I will send him away. Okay? Okay?

SALIMA: Okay.

MAMA: We'll make him go away. Yeah?

SALIMA: Okay. Good.

SOPHIE: No, Mama, please, let her at least talk to him. He wants to take her home.

MAMA: You read too many of those romance novels where everything is forgiven with a kiss. Enough, my

miner is waiting. So c'mon, one of you! (*Mama suspiciously eyes Salima's belly and exits.*)

SOPHIE: If you don't want to see him, then at least go out there and tell him. He's been sitting outside in the rain for two days, and he's not going to leave.

SALIMA: Let him sit.

SOPHIE: Go, talk to him. Maybe you'll feel differently.

SALIMA: He doesn't know that I'm pregnant. When he sees me, he'll hate me all over again.

SOPHIE: You don't know that. He came all this way. (*A moment.*)

SALIMA: Stupid man. Why did he have to come?

SOPHIE: All you ever talk about is wanting to get away from here. Go with him, Salima. Get the hell out of here! Go!

SALIMA: He called me a filthy dog, and said I tempted them. Why else would it happen? Five months in the bush, passed between the soldiers like a wash rag. Used. I was made poison by their fingers, that is what he said. He had no choice but to turn away from me, because I dishonored him.

SOPHIE: He was hurting. It was sour pride.

SALIMA: Why are you defending him!? Then you go with him!

SOPHIE: I'm not def—

SALIMA: Do you know what I was doing on that morning? I was working in our garden picking the last of the sweet tomatoes. I put Beatrice down in the shade of a frangipani tree, because my back was giving me some trouble. Forgiven? Where was Fortune? He was in town fetching a new iron pot. "Go," I said. "Go, today, man, or you won't have dinner tonight!" I had been after him for a new pot for a month. And finally on that day the damn man had to go and get it. A new pot. The sun was about to crest, but I had to put in another hour before it got too hot. It was such a clear and open sky. This splendid bird, a peacock, had come into the garden to taunt me, and was showing off its feathers. I stooped down and called to the bird, "Wssht, Wssht." And I felt a shadow cut across my back, and when I stood four men were there over me, smiling, wicked schoolboy smiles. "Yes?" I said. And the tall soldier slammed the butt of his gun into my cheek. Just like that. It was so quick, I didn't even know I'd fallen to the ground. Where did they come from? How could I not have heard them?

SOPHIE: You don't have to—

SALIMA: One of the soldiers held me down with his foot. He was so heavy, thick like an ox and his boot was cracked and weathered like it had been left out in the rain for weeks. His boot was pressing my chest and the cracks in the leather had the look of drying sorghum. His foot was so heavy and it was all I could see, as the others . . . "took" me. My baby was crying. She was a good baby. Beatrice never cried, but she was crying, screaming. "Shhh," I said. "Shhh." And right then (*Salima closes her eyes.*) a soldier stomped on her head with his boot. And she was quiet. (*A moment. Salima releases.*) Where was everybody? WHERE WAS EVERYBODY? (*Sophie hugs Salima.*)

SOPHIE: It's okay. Take a breath.

SALIMA: I fought them!

SOPHIE: I know.

SALIMA: I did!

SOPHIE: I know.

SALIMA: But they still took me from my home. They took me through the bush, raiding thieves. Fucking demons! "She is for everyone, soup to be had before dinner," that is what someone said. They tied me to a tree by my foot, and the men came whenever they wanted soup. I make fires, I cook food, I listen to their stupid songs, I carry bullets, I clean wounds, I wash blood from their clothing, and, and, and . . . I lay there as they tore me to pieces, until I was raw . . . five months. Five months. Chained like a goat. These men fighting . . . fighting for our liberation. Still I close my eyes and I see such terrible things. Things, I cannot stand to have in my head. How can men be this way? (*A moment.*) It was such a clear and open sky. So, so beautiful. How could I not hear them coming?

SOPHIE: Those men were on a path and we were there. It happened.

SALIMA: A peacock wandered into my garden, and the tomatoes were ripe beyond belief. Our fields of red sorghum were so perfect, it was going to be a fine season. Fortune thought so too, and we could finally think about planning a trip on the ferry to visit his brother. Oh God please give me back that morning. "Forget the pot, Fortune. Stay, . . . stay," that's what I would tell him. How did I get in the middle of their fight? What did I do, Sophie? I must have done something.

SOPHIE: You were picking sweet tomatoes. That's all. You didn't do anything wrong. (*Sophie kisses Salima on the cheek.*)

SALIMA: It isn't his baby. It's the child of a monster, and there's no telling what it will be. Now, he's willing to forgive me, and is it that simple, Sophie? But what happens when the baby is born, will he be able to forgive the child, will I? And, and . . . and even if I do, I don't think I'll be able to forgive him.

SOPHIE: You can't know that until you speak to him.

SALIMA: I walked into the family compound expecting wide open arms. An embrace. Five months, suffering. I suffered every single second of it. And my family gave me the back of their heads. And he, the man I loved since I was fourteen, chased me away with a green switch. He beat my ankles raw. And I dishonored him? I dishonored him?! Where was he? Buying a pot? He was too proud to bear my shame . . . but not proud enough to protect me from it. Let him sit in the rain.

SOPHIE: Is that really what you want?

SALIMA: Yes.

SOPHIE: He isn't going to leave.

SALIMA: Then I'm sorry for him. (*Lights shift to moonlight.*)

Scene 3

Rain. Moonlight. Outside of the bar.
Fortune stands in the rain. His posture is erect. Music and laughter pours out of the bar. Mama stands seductively in the doorway.

MAMA: The sky doesn't look like it's gonna let up for a long time. My mama used to say, "Careful of the cold rain it carries more men to their death than a storm of arrows."

FORTUNE: Why won't you let me see her?

MAMA: Young man, the woman you're looking for isn't here. But if you want company I have plenty of that. What do you like? (*Seductively.*) I know the challenges of a soldier's life, I hear stories from men every day. And there's nothing better than a gentle hand to pluck out the thorns, and heal the heart. (*Mama runs her hand up her thigh and laughs. Fortune turns away, disgusted. Mama smiles.*)

FORTUNE: Please, tell my wife I love her.

MAMA: Yeah. Yeah. I've heard it before. You're not the first man to come here for his wife. But soldier, are you sure this is the place you want to be looking for her?

FORTUNE: Here. Give this to her. (*Fortune lifts an iron pot.*)

MAMA: A pot? (*Mama laughs.*)

FORTUNE: Yes, please. Just give it to her.

MAMA: Very charming. A pot. Is this how you intend to woo a lady? (*Fortune shoves it into her hand. A moment. She refuses the pot.*) You're a nice-looking young man. You seem decent. Go from here. Take care of your land and your mother. (*Two tipsy government soldiers tumble out of the bar.*)

GOVERNMENT SOLDIER #2: Just one more time. One. More. Time.

GOVERNMENT SOLDIER #3: Shut up! That girl doesn't want you.

GOVERNMENT SOLDIER #2: Oh yes, she do. She don't know it, but she do. Let me go.

GOVERNMENT SOLDIER #3: I'm not touching you. (*Drunk, Government Soldier #2 crumples to the ground; the other government soldier finds it hysterically funny.*)

MAMA: (*To Fortune.*) Go home. Have I made myself clear? (*Mama goes into the bar. Fortune fumes.*)

FORTUNE: (*To Government Soldier #3.*) Idiot! Pick him up! God is watching you. (*Government Soldier #3 lifts up his friend, as Simon, out of breath, comes running up to Fortune. Josephine seductively fills the doorway.*)

JOSEPHINE: Ay! Ay! Don't leave me so soon. Where are you going?

SIMON: Fortune! Fortune! (*The two government soldiers disappear into the night.*)

JOSEPHINE: Come back! Let me show you something sweet and pretty. Come. (*Josephine laughs.*)

SIMON: Fortune! (*Simon doubles over, out of breath.*) The Commander is gathering everyone. We march out tomorrow morning. The militia is moving on the next village.

FORTUNE: What about Salima? I can't leave her.

SIMON: But we have our orders. We have to go.

JOSEPHINE: (*Seductively.*) Hello, baby. Come say hello to me. (*His face lights up.*)

SIMON: God help me, look at that sweetness. (*Simon licks his lips. Josephine does several down-and-dirty pelvic thrusts. Fortune tries not to smile.*) Quick. Let me hold some money, so I can go inside and talk to this good time girl. C'mon. C'mon . . . C'mon, Fortune. What's your name?

JOSEPHINE: Josephine. Come inside, baby.

FORTUNE: Don't let the witch tempt you.

SIMON: Let's enjoy ourselves, Man, tonight . . . At least let me have one more taste of pleasure. A little taste. Just the tip of my tongue. C'mon, man, let me hold some money. (*Simon laughs. Fortune does not respond. Josephine laughs and disappears inside. Fortune silently prays.*) How long are you gonna do this? Huh? We've been up and down the road. It's time to consider that maybe she's dead.

FORTUNE: Then leave! (*A moment. Simon, frustrated, starts to leave, then.*)

SIMON: This makes no sense. You can't stay here, the rebel militia are moving this way. And if they find you, they'll kill you. We have to go by morning, with or without her.

FORTUNE: Go!

SIMON: Are you sure? You're becoming like Emmanuel Bwiza whose wife drowned in the river when we were children. Remember, the old fool got drunk on bitterness and lost heself. Look here, Fortune, they're making a joke of you. The men are saying "Why won't the man just take another woman." "Why is he chasing a damaged girl?" (*Fortune impulsively grabs Simon around the neck. The friends struggle. Fortune turns Simon loose.*)

FORTUNE: (*Challenges.*) Say it again!

SIMON: It is not me saying it. It is the other men in the brigade.

FORTUNE: Who?

SIMON: If I tell you, are you going to fight all of them?

FORTUNE: Tell me who!

SIMON: Everyone. Every damn one of them. Okay. (*Fortune releases Simon.*) Man, *Mavi Yako!* [Shit!] It's time to forget her. I'm your cousin, and for three months I've been walking with you, right? Got dirty, got bloody with you. But now, I'm begging you, stop looking. It's time.

FORTUNE: No, I've prayed on this.

SIMON: Come out of the rain. We'll go inside and spend the last of our money, and forget her. C'mon, Fortune. Let's get stupid drunk. Huh? Huh? C'mon. (*Simon tries to drag Fortune into the bar. He resists. Fortune, fuming, raises his fist to Simon.*) If you are angry, then be angry at the men who took her. Think about how they did you, they reached right into your pocket and stole from you. I know Salima since we were children. I love her the same as you. She'd want

you to avenge her honor. That is the only way to heal your soul. (*Fortune contemplates his words.*)

FORTUNE: Kill?

SIMON: Yes. (*Fortune laughs ironically.*)

FORTUNE: We are farmers. What are we doing? They tell us shoot and we shoot. But for what are we getting? Salima? A better crop? No, man, we're moving further and further away from home. I want my wife! That's all. I want my family.

SIMON: The Commander gave us orders to kill all deserters.

FORTUNE: Are you going to kill me?

SIMON: I wouldn't have said it a month ago, but I'll say it now. She's gone. (*Simon runs into the darkness. Fortune stands outside of the bar in the pouring rain. Gunfire. A fire fight. The sounds of the forest.*)

Scene 4

The bar.
    Christian, drunk and haggard, is in the middle of an energetic story. He stands at the bar nursing a beer. Mr. Harari, Sophie, and Mama stand around listening with urgency.

CHRISTIAN: (*With urgency.*) No, no, no . . . listen, listen to me, I've just come from there, and it's true. I saw a boy take a machete to a man, sever his neck, a clean blow and lift the head in the air like a trophy. May God be my witness. Men were hollering. "We strong warriors, we taste victory. We will kill!"

MAMA: Shh, keep it down?!

CHRISTIAN: Oh shit, my hand, my hand is still shaking. This . . . this man Osembenga is evil. He plays at democracy. This word we all bandy about. Democracy, and the first opportunity we get, we spit on our neighbors and why? Because he has cattle and I don't. Because he is a fisherman and I am not. But nobody has and nobody will have, except for men like you, Mr. Harari, who have the good sense to come and go, and not give a damn.

MAMA: Oh, hush up.

CHRISTIAN: But we have to pretend that all this ugliness means nothing. We wash the blood off with buckets of frigid water, and whitewash our walls. Our leaders tell us, follow my rules your life will be better, their doctors say take this pill your life will be better, plant these seeds your life will be better, read this book your life will be better, kill your neighbor your life will be better—

MAMA: Stop. Take it outside. You know I don't allow this talk in here. My doors are open to everybody. And that way trouble doesn't settle here.

CHRISTIAN: Well, someone has to say it, otherwise what? We let it go on. Huh?

MAMA: Professor, enough! Stop it now. Leave the philosophizing and preaching to the wretched politicians. I mean it! I won't have it here!

CHRISTIAN: One day it will be at your door, Mama.

MAMA: And then I'll shut it. People come here to leave behind whatever mess they've made out there. That includes you, Professor. (*Two rebel soldiers appear from the back in various stages of undress. Josephine and Jerome Kisembe enter from the back. She buttons his shirt. He pushes her away.*) Sophie, turn on the music. (*Sophie turns on the radio. Congolese hip-hop music plays. Christian attempts to disappear behind his drink. Sophie stands behind the bar drying glasses. Mama walks over to greet the men. The parrot squawks.*) Colonel Kisembe, I hope my girls gave you good company.

KISEMBE: Very. It is good to be back, Mama. Where's everyone?

MAMA: You tell me. It's been this way for a week. I haven't seen but a handful of miners. I bake bread and it goes stale.

KISEMBE: It is Commander Osembenga. He is giving us some trouble.

CHRISTIAN: He's a crazy bastard!

KISEMBE: His men set fire to several of our mining villages, now everyone has fled deeper into the bush.

MAMA: I saw smoke over the trees.

REBEL SOLDIER #3: The mission. They're burning everything to save bullets. (*Sophie gasps and covers her mouth.*)

KISEMBE: They took machetes to anything that moves. This is their justice. (*Kisembe sits at the table. Josephine spots Mr. Harari and is torn between where to place her affection.*) Believe me, when we find Osembenga and his collaborators, he will be shown the same mercy he showed our people. It's what they deserve. (*To Christian.*) Am I right? Am I right?

CHRISTIAN: (*Reluctantly.*) You are right. But—

KISEMBE: I'm sorry. It's how it has to be. They have done this to us. I see you agree, Mama.

MAMA: Of course. (*Everyone in the bar grows uneasy, afraid of Kisembe's intense erratic energy. They're barely listening to his rhetoric, instead focused on trying not to set him off. Jerome addresses everyone with growing intensity.*)

KISEMBE: They say we are the renegades. We don't respect the rule of law . . . but how else do we protect ourselves against their aggression? Huh? How do we feed our families? Ay? They bring soldiers from Uganda, drive us from our land and make us refugees . . . and then turn us into criminals when we protest or try to protect ourselves. How can we let the government carve up our most valuable land to serve to companies in China? It's our land. Ask the Mbuti,° they can describe every inch of the forest as if it were their own flesh. Am I telling the truth?

Mbuti: A pygmy group.

MAMA: Here's to the truth! (*Kisembe, pleased with his own words, places a cigarette in his mouth. A young rebel soldier quickly lights it for him. Kisembe stares hard at Christian, who averts his gaze, and nervously raises his glass.*)

CHRISTIAN: The truth! (*Mr. Harari uses the awkward silence to interject.*)

MR. HARARI: Has Osembenga shut down production at Yaka-Yaka mine?

KISEMBE: And you are?

MR. HARARI: I'm sorry, Colonel, may I offer you my card? (*Mr. Harari passes Kisembe his card. The rebel leader examines it.*)

KISEMBE: Ha-ra-i?

MR. HARARI: Harari. Yes. Please. Let me buy you a drink. (*Mr. Harari signals Sophie to bring a bottle of whiskey over to Kisembe.*) I handle mostly minerals, some precious stones, but I have contacts for everything. My mobile is always on. (*Sophie pours two glasses.*)

KISEMBE: Thank you. (*Kisembe takes the bottle of whiskey and slips the card into his pocket, by way of dismissing Mr. Harari, who backs away. Mama wraps her arms around Kisembe's shoulders.*)

MAMA: Come, gentlemen. You will be treated like warriors, here. (*Kisembe signals to his men. They follow him toward the door.*)

KISEMBE: I wish we could stay all day, but duty calls.

MAMA: No! So soon? (*Mama signals to Josephine, who refuses to budge, instead sits on Mr. Harari's lap. Mr. Harari tenses.*)

MR. HARARI: (*Whispers.*) Go!

JOSEPHINE: No. (*Kisembe and his men collect their guns and leave. A moment. Relief. Christian slaps his thigh and stands up. He does a spot-on imitation of the haughty swagger of the rebel leader.*)

CHRISTIAN: Girl. Quick. Quick. Bring me a beer, so I can wash it down with Osembenga's blood. (*Sophie and Josephine laugh. Mr. Harari is too nervous to enjoy the show.*)

SOPHIE: Yes, Colonel.

CHRISTIAN: (*Imitating Kisembe.*) Woman, are you addressing me as Colonel?

SOPHIE: Yes. Colonel.

CHRISTIAN: Don't you know who I am? I am from here on in, to be known as the Great Commander of All Things Wise and Wonderful, with the Heart of a Hundred Lions in Battle.

SOPHIE: I'm so sorry, Great Commander of All Things Wise and—

CHRISTIAN: Wonderful with the Heart of a Hundred Lions in Battle. Don't you forget that! (*Christian does a playful mocking warrior dance. Sophie taps out a rhythm on the counter. The drummer joins in. Mama laughs.*)

MAMA: You are a fool! (*Mama carries empty bottles to the back. Unseen, the formidable Commander Osembenga and a sullen soldier, Laurent, enter. They wear black berets and muddy uniforms. A moment. Christian stops his dance abruptly.*)

OSEMBENGA: Don't stop you. Go on.

CHRISTIAN: Commander Osembenga.

OSEMBENGA: Continue. (*Christian finishes his dance, now drained of its verve and humor. Osembenga smiles, and claps his hands. Christian dances until Osembenga stops clapping, releasing him from the dance. Osembenga acknowledges Mr. Harari with a polite nod. The two soldiers ritualistically empty the bullets from their guns.*) Where is Mama?

SOPHIE: She's in the back. (*Yells.*) Mama! Mama!

OSEMBENGA: (*Suspiciously.*) I saw a truck leaving? Whose was it? (*A moment.*)

CHRISTIAN: (*Lying.*) Uh . . . aid worker.

OSEMBENGA: Oh? Good-looking vehicle. Expensive. Eight cylinders.

CHRISTIAN: Yes.

OSEMBENGA: Sturdy. It looked like it could take the road during rainy season.

CHRISTIAN: Probably. (*Osembenga approves.*)

SOPHIE: Mama!

MAMA: (*Annoyed.*) Why are you calling me?! You know I'm busy. (*Mama stops short when she sees Osembenga. She conjures a warm smile.*) Commander Osembenga. Karibu. (*Nervously.*) We . . . how are you? (*Mama glances at the door.*)

OSEMBENGA: Run ragged, if the truth be told. Two Primus, cold, and a pack of cigarettes. (*Mama directs Sophie to get beers for the men. Osembenga strokes Mama's backside. She playfully swats away his hand.*) You look good today.

MAMA: You should have seen me yesterday.

OSEMBENGA: I wish I had, but I was otherwise engaged.

MAMA: Yeah? We heard you had some trouble. Kisembe.

OSEMBENGA: Is that what is being said? Not trouble! Slight irritation. But you'd be pleased to know, we're close to shutting down Kisembe and his militia. We finally have him on the run. He won't be troubling the people here very much longer.

MAMA: Is that so?

OSEMBENGA: My guess, he's heading east. He'll need to come through here. He can't hide from me. It's the only passable road.

MAMA: I saw smoke over the trees.

OSEMBENGA: That bastard and his cronies attacked the hospital.

MR. HARARI: The hospital? Why?

OSEMBENGA: Because they are imbeciles. I don't know. Looking for medicine. Morphine. Who the hell knows? They rounded up and killed mostly Hema patients. (*To Sophie.*) Tsst. Tsst. You, bring me some groundnuts. (*To Mama.*) It was chaos. When we arrived we found the hospital staff tied by their hands and cut up like meat.

LAURENT: One man's heart was missing. (*Sophie covers her mouth with disgust.*)

MAMA: (*Disgusted.*) What?

OSEMBENGA: And he accuses us of being the barbarians? Don't worry, I've given my soldiers the liberty to control the situation. And control it they will. I am afraid this is what must be done. They force our hand. (*Osembenga takes sadistic delight in this notion. Sophie cringes as she places beer and peanuts on the table for Osembenga. He grabs Sophie's wrist and pulls her toward him. Laughing.*) Come here, you pretty pretty thing. (*Osembenga aggressively grabs Sophie around the buttocks and pulls her onto his lap. Laughing.*) What? You don't like what I'm wearing? (*Sophie tries to gently pry herself loose. Christian, sensing tension, moves toward them. Laurent intervenes.*) You don't like men in uniforms? You don't like men, maybe. Is that it? (*A moment. Sophie struggles to free herself. Mama, sensing the tension.*)

MAMA: Sophie, come here. Let—

OSEMBENGA: (*Smiling, Osembenga pulls Sophie onto his lap.*) Hey. We are talking. We are talking, yeah? (*Osembenga gently runs his hand up her leg.*) Jolie fille! Je connais pas votre nom. [Pretty girl! I do not know your name.] (*Sophie tenses. Osembenga moves his hand up her skirt. Sophie gasps and struggles harder.*)

SOPHIE: (*Hisses.*) Let go of me! (*Sophie pushes away, shocked, from Osembenga. Christian rushes in to protect her, as Osembenga lunges for her. Mama blocks him. Laurent rushes to aid Osembenga.*)

MAMA: Sophie, shush! Enough. Commander, ignore her, there are other girls for you. Come. Come.

OSEMBENGA: Bring this girl around back, my men will teach her a lesson. She needs proper schooling. (*Laurent shoves Christian out of the way and grabs Sophie. This is the first time we've seen Mama scared. Sophie spits on Osembenga's feet.*)

MAMA: Sophie. (*Mama, horrified bends down and wipes the spit from Osembenga's shoes. Osembenga glares at Sophie. She shouts as if possessed.*)

SOPHIE: I am dead.

MAMA: No!

SOPHIE: (*Possessed.*) I am dead! *Shetani!* [Satan!] Fuck a corpse! What would that make you? (*Osembenga is thrown. Christian quickly pulls Sophie away.*)

OSEMBENGA: I'm trying to bring order here, and this girl spits on my feet. You see, this is what I have to deal with. This is the problem.

MAMA: Gentlemen, Commander, this is not our way . . . we want you to be comfortable and happy here, let me show you the pleasures of Mama Nadi's. (*A moment. A standoff.*)

OSEMBENGA: Then Mama you show me. (*Osembenga checks his anger. He smiles, and blows a kiss at Sophie. He takes Mama's arm, and pulls her to the back with his man. Sophie desperately scrubs her hands in the basin. Mr. Harari pours himself a healthy drink.*)

MR. HARARI: Okay. Let's not overreact. Everything's going to be fine.

Ruined at the Almeida Theatre in London, 2010: from left to right, Steve Toussaint as Osembenga, Jenny Jules as Mama Nadi, Kehinde Fadipe as Josephine, Pippa Bennett-Warner as Sophie, and Joel Kangudi as a soldier.

CHRISTIAN: (*Whispers.*) Sophie, are you crazy? What are you doing? (*Josephine stops Sophie, who is scrubbing her hands raw.*)

JOSEPHINE: Stop it. Stop it. (*Josephine hugs Sophie tightly.*) Shh. Shhh. (*Mama furiously enters. She slaps Sophie across the face.*)

MAMA: (*Enraged.*) Next time I will put you out for the vultures. I don't care if that was the man who slit your mother's throat. Do you understand me? You could have gotten all of us killed. What do you have to say to me?

SOPHIE: . . . Sorry, Mama.

MAMA: You're lucky the Commander is generous. I had to plead with him to give you another chance. Now you go in there and make sure that his cock is clean. Am I making myself clear?

SOPHIE: Please—

MAMA: Now get outta my sight. (*Mama grabs Sophie and thrusts her into the back. Mr. Harari, Christian and Josephine stare at Mama. A moment. Mama goes behind the bar and pours herself a drink.*) What?

CHRISTIAN: Don't make her do that!

MAMA: What if Osembenga had been more than offended? What then? Who would protect my business, if he turned on me? It is but for the grace of God, that he didn't beat her to the ground. And now I have to give away business to keep him and his filthy soldiers happy.

CHRISTIAN: But if—

MAMA: Not a word from you. You have a problem, then leave.

CHRISTIAN: Business. Just then when you said it, it sounded vulgar, polluted.

MAMA: Are you going to lecture me, Professor? Turn your dirty finger away from me. (*Christian is stung by her words.*)

CHRISTIAN: Mama?

MAMA: What, *Chérie*? (*Mama laughs.*)

CHRISTIAN: (*Wounded.*) Forget it! Bring me another beer. There's my money. (*Christian slams the money down on the counter.*) You understand that, don't you? You like that? There's your fucking money. (*Mama slowly picks up the money and puts it in her apron. She ceremoniously cracks open a beer and places it in front of Christian.*)

MAMA: Drink up, you fucking drunk.

CHRISTIAN: What's wrong with you? (*Christian snatches up his beer and retreats into the corner. He drinks it down quickly.*)

MAMA: You men kill me. You come in here, drink your beer, take your pleasure, and then wanna judge the way I run my "business." The front door swings both ways. I don't force anyone's hand. My girls, ask them, Emilene, Mazima, Josephine, ask them, they'd rather be here, any day, than back out there in their villages where they are taken without regard. They're safer with me, than in their own homes, because this country is picked clean, while men, poets like you, drink beer, eat nuts, and look for someplace to disappear. And I am without mercy, is that what you're saying? Because I give them something other than a beggar's cup. (*With ferocity.*) I didn't come to this place as Mama Nadi, I found her the same way miners find their wealth in the muck. I stumbled off of that road without two twigs to start a fire. I turned a basket of sweets and soggy biscuits into a business. I don't give a damn what any of you think. This is my place, Mama Nadi's. (*Christian begins to exit.*) Of course. (*Mama's words stop him. He walks up to Mama.*)

CHRISTIAN:
    The black rope of water
    towing
    a rusted ferry
    fighting the current of time
    an insatiable flow,
    Drifting, without enough kerosene to get
    through the dark nights.
    The destination
    always a port away

MAMA: (*She spits.*) It's wind. If you can't place it on a scale, it's nothing. (*Christian heads for the door.*) You'll be back when you need another beer.

CHRISTIAN: I don't think so. (*Christian absorbs the blow, then storms outside in a huff. Josephine leads Mr. Harari to the back. Mama is left alone onstage to weigh the enormity of what she has done. Lights fade.*)

Scene 5

Outside of the bar.
    Osembenga and Laurent stumble out of Mama Nadi's place, laughing.

OSEMBENGA: I always like the taste of something new.

FORTUNE: Commander! Commander!

OSEMBENGA: Yes?

FORTUNE: I'm sorry to disturb you, but I . . .

OSEMBENGA: Yes?

FORTUNE: I saw Jerome Kisembe.

OSEMBENGA: Who are you?

FORTUNE: I am Fortune Mukengeshayi, I'm with your brigade.

OSEMBENGA: Jerome Kisembe?

FORTUNE: Yes . . . He was inside Mama Nadi's.

OSEMBENGA: Inside here?

FORTUNE: Yes, I saw him. She was hiding him. I heard him say the rebels are heading south along this road. He will join them tomorrow.

OSEMBENGA: Mama Nadi's?! Here?!

FORTUNE: He just drove south in a white truck! Please, she is holding my wife. I just want to get her back.

OSEMBENGA: (*To Laurent.*) Quick, quick. We'll go after him. Call ahead, prepare the brigade to move out. I'll deal with Mama later! (*They exit with haste.*)

Scene 6

The bar. Dawn.
    Morning light pours into the bar. Mr. Harari paces. His traveling bag is perched near the door. Mama enters, catching him off guard.

MAMA: Would you like a drink while you wait? (*Artillery fire, closer than expected.*)

MR. HARARI: Yes. Thank you. A little palm wine. (*Mama settles her nerves, and pours them both a palm wine.*)

MAMA: It's raining hard, you might wanna wait until—

MR. HARARI: I can't. Thank goodness, I found a lift with one of the aid workers. My driver, fucking idiot, took off last night. (*Jokes.*) Apparently he doesn't care for the sound of gunfire.

MAMA: I told you, you didn't pay him enough.

MR. HARARI: This fucking war, *ya Allah ya azim.*° It's everybody's and nobody's.

MAMA: Tst!

MR. HARARI: It keeps fracturing and redefining itself, militias form overnight and suddenly a drunken footsoldier with a tribal vendetta is a rebel leader and in possession of half of the enriched land, but you can't reason with him, because he's only thinking as far as his next drink.

MAMA: Yes, and what is new?

MR. HARARI: The man I shake hands with in the morning is my enemy by sundown, and why? His whims. Because?! His witch doctor says I'm the enemy. I don't know whose hand to grease other than the one directly in front of me. At least I understood Mobutu's° brand of chaos. Now, I'm a relative beginner, I must relearn the terms every few months, and make new friends, but who? It's difficult to say, so I must befriend everybody and nobody. And it's utterly exhausting.

MAMA: Let all the mother-hating soldiers fight it out. 'Cuz in the end do you think that will change anything here?

MR. HARARI: God only knows. The main road is crowded with folks heading east. There is no shame in leaving, Mama. Part of being in business is knowing when to cut your losses and get out.

MAMA: I have the only pool table in fifty kilometers. Where will people drink if anything happens to me?

MR. HARARI: Eventually you must fly your colors. Take a side.

---

ya Allah ya azim: Literally, by Allah the Supreme Glory.
Mobutu: Mobutu Sese Seko (1930–1997), president of the Democratic Republic of the Congo when it was known as Zaire.

MAMA: He pays me in gold, he pays me in Coltan. What is worth more? You tell me. What is their argument? I don't know. Who will win? Who cares? There's an old proverb: "Two hungry birds fight over a kernel, just then a third one swoops down and carries it off. Whoops!"

MR. HARARI: You are the most devilish of optimists. You, I don't worry so much about you. But what about a lovely girl like Sophie? (*His words weigh heavily on Mama. Mr. Harari knocks back his drink, and heads for the door looking out for his ride.*) Until next time! (*Distant gunfire. Mr. Harari anxiously goes to the doorway. Mama goes to the bar; she appears conflicted. An internal battle.*)

MAMA: Ah . . . One thing, Mr. Harari, before you leave can I ask you a favor.

MR. HARARI: Of course. (*Mama opens the lockbox, and carefully lays out the diamond.*)

MAMA: This. (*Mr. Harari's eyes light up.*)

MR. HARARI: Ah. Your insurance policy.

MAMA: (*With irony.*) Yes. My house, my garden to dig in, and a chief's fortune of cows.

MR. HARARI: You are ready to sell?

MAMA: Yes. Take this. (*Hands him the pamphlet.*) It has the name of a man in Bunia, a doctor. He won't trouble you with questions. Use my name.

MR. HARARI: Slow, slow, what do you want me—

MAMA: Just listen. I want you to take her to—

MR HARARI: (*Confused.*) Josephine? (*Genuinely surprised.*) Be realistic, how would a girl like Josephine survive in the city?

MAMA: No, listen.

MR. HARARI: I can't. She is a country thing, not refined at all.

MAMA: No, listen . . . I'm talking about Sophie. This will raise enough money for an operation, and whatever she needs to get settled.

MR. HARARI: Sophie?

MAMA: Yes.

MR. HARARI: Why? Operation? What?

MAMA: It's a long conversation, and there isn't time.

MR. HARARI: This is more than—

MAMA: Enough for a life. I know.

MR. HARARI: Are you sure? This diamond will fetch a fairly decent price, you can settle over the border in Uganda. Start fresh.

MAMA: I have ten girls here. What will I do with them? Is there enough room for all of us in the car? No. I can't go. Since I was young, people have found reasons to push me out of my home, men have laid claim to my possessions, but I am not running now. This is my place. Mama Nadi's.

MR. HARARI: But I'm not—

MAMA: You do this for me. I don't want the other women to know. So let's do this quickly.

MR. HARARI: And the doctor's name is on the paper. I'm to call when I get there.

MAMA: Yes. And you give Sophie the money. The money for the stone. Understand. Promise me. It's important. All of it.

MR. HARARI: . . . Yes. Are you sure?

MAMA: . . . Yes. (*Mama reluctantly passes the diamond to Mr. Harari.*) Thank you. I'll get her. (*Mama exits. Mr. Harari examines the diamond with absolute delight. An aid worker comes rushing in.*)

AID WORKER: I'm loaded. We have to go now! Now! Three vehicles are coming in fast. We can't be here.

MR. HARARI: But . . . What about—

AID WORKER: (*Panicked.*) Now! I can't wait. C'mon. C'mon. (*Distant gunfire.*)

MR. HARARI: I have to—

AID WORKER: They'll be okay. Us, men, they'll come after us—

MR. HARARI: (*Calls to.*) One minute. Mama! Mama! Come! Mama! I—

AID WORKER: I hafta go! I can't wait. (*The aid worker doesn't have time to listen, he races out. The engine revs.*)

MR. HARARI: Mama! Mama! (*Mr. Harari seems torn, a moment, then he decides. He places the diamond in his pocket and leaves. Silence. Distant gunfire. Mama enters, frantically pulling Sophie.*)

MAMA: When you get there, he has the money to take care of everything. Settle. Make a good life, you hear.

SOPHIE: Why are you doing this for me?

MAMA: Stop, don't ask me stupid questions, just go. Go! (*She tucks a piece of paper into Sophie's hand.*) This is my cousin's wife, all I have is her address. But a motorbike will take you. You say that I am your friend.

SOPHIE: Thank you, Mama, I—

MAMA: No time. You send word through Mr. Harari. Let me know that everything goes well. Okay. (*Sophie hugs Mama. She exits. Mama, elated, goes to pour herself a celebratory drink. She doesn't see Sophie reenter.*)

SOPHIE: He's gone. (*The stage is flooded with intense light. The sound of chaos, shouting, gunfire grows with intensity. Government soldiers pour in. A siege. A white-hot flash. The generator blows. Streams of natural light pour in to the bar. Fortune, Osembenga, Simon, and government soldiers stand over Sophie and Mama.*)

FORTUNE: He was here! I saw him here! (*Osembenga stands over Mama.*)

OSEMBENGA: This soldier said he saw Jerome Kisembe here.

MAMA: This soldier is liar.

FORTUNE: I swear to you! He was here with two men. The same night you were here, Commander!

MAMA: We are friends. Why would I lie to you? This soldier has been menacing us for days. He's crazy. A liar!

FORTUNE: This woman is the devil! She's a witch! She enchanted my wife!

OSEMBENGA: Again. Where is Kisembe?

MAMA: I don't know. Why would I play these games? Don't you think I know better. He is a simple digger. And me, I wouldn't give him what he wants, so he tells tales. Commander, we are friends. You know me. I am with you. Of course. Come, let me get you some whiskey.

OSEMBENGA: *Funga kinua yaké.* [Shut her mouth.] (*Osembenga signals to his soldiers. They ransack the bar. The parrot squawks. Osembenga calmly sits and watches from a chair. He pours himself a whiskey, lights a cigarette as the men turn the place upside down.*)

MAMA: No! (*Fortune takes pleasure in restraining Mama. A soldier drags Josephine from the back. It is chaos. Frightening. Menacing.*)

OSEMBENGA: This can stop. Tell me where, I can find Kisembe.

MAMA: . . . I don't know where he is.

OSEMBENGA: (*Points to Josephine.*) Take that one. (*A soldier grabs Josephine and bends her over the table poised to violate her. The women scream.*)

JOSEPHINE: No! No! Tell him, Mama. He was here.

MAMA: Please! (*Salima enters. A pool of blood forms in the middle of her dress.*)

SALIMA: (*Screams.*) STOP! Stop it!

FORTUNE: Salima!

SALIMA: (*Screams.*) For the love of God, stop this! Haven't you done enough to us? Enough! Enough! (*The soldiers stop abruptly, shocked by Salima's defiant voice.*)

MAMA: What did you do?! (*Fortune violently pushes the soldiers out of the way, and races to Salima.*)

FORTUNE: Salima! Salima!

SALIMA: Fortune. (*Fortune scoops Salima into his arms. Mama breaks away from the soldiers.*)

MAMA: Quick go get some hot water and cloth. Salima look at me. You have to look at me, keep your eyes on me. Don't think of anything else. C'mon look at me. (*Salima smiles triumphantly, she takes Fortune's hand. She turns to Osembenga.*)

SALIMA: (*To soldiers and Osembenga.*) You will not fight your battles on my body anymore. (*Salima collapses to the floor. Fortune cradles Salima in his arms. She dies. Blackout.*)

Scene 7

The sounds of the tropical Ituri rain forest. Bar. The birds quietly chatter.
   Sophie methodically sweeps the dirt floor with a thatched broom. Josephine washes the countertop. Mama stands in the doorway anxiously watching the road.

SOPHIE: (*Sings.*)
   Have another beer, my friend,
   Douse the fire of your fears, my friend.
   Get drunk and foolish on the moment,
   Brush aside the day's heavy judgment.

(*Excited, Mama spots a passing truck.*)

   'Cuz you come here to forget,
   You say drink away all regret,
   And dance like it's the ending.

MAMA: Dust rising.

JOSEPHINE: (*Eagerly.*) Who is it?

MAMA: (*Excited.*) I don't know. Blue helmets heading north. Hello? Hello? (*Mama seductively waves. Nothing. Disappointed, she retreats to the table.*) Damn them. How the hell are we supposed to do business? They're draining our blood.

JOSEPHINE: Hey Sophie, give me a hand. (*Josephine and Sophie pick up the basin of water and exit. Mama buries her face in her hands. Christian enters. He whistles. Mama looks up, doing her best to contain her excitement. Christian brushes the travel dust from his brand-new brown suit.*)

MAMA: Look who it is. The wind could have brought me a paying customer, but instead I get you.

CHRISTIAN: Lovely. I'm glad to see after all these months you haven't lost any of your wonderful charm. You're looking fine as ever.

MAMA: Yeah? I'm making do with nothing. (*Christian smiles.*) Who'd you bribe to get past the road block?

CHRISTIAN: I have my ways, and as it turns out the officer on duty has a fondness for Nigerian soap operas and Belgian chocolates. (*Mama finally smiles.*) I'm surprised to find you're still here.

MAMA: Were you expecting me to disappear into the forest and live off roots with the Mbuti? I'm staying put. The war's on the back of the golddiggers; you follow them, you follow trouble. What are you wearing?

CHRISTIAN: You like?

MAMA: They didn't have your size?

CHRISTIAN: Very funny. *Chérie*, your eyes tell me everything I need to know.

MAMA: Tst!

CHRISTIAN: What you have something in your teeth?

MAMA: Business must be good. Yeah?

CHRISTIAN: No, but a man's got to have at least one smart change of clothing, even in times like these . . . I heard what happened. (*A moment.*)

MAMA: *C'est la vie.*° Salima was a good girl. (*Sophie enters.*)

SOPHIE: Uncle! (*They exchange a long hug.*)

CHRISTIAN: Sophie, *mon amour.* I have something for you.

SOPHIE: *Un livre?*

CHRISTIAN: . . . Yes.

SOPHIE: *Merci.* (*She rips open the brown paper. She pulls out a handful of magazines and a book. A moment.*)

CHRISTIAN: And this. A letter from your mother. Don't expect too much. (*Sophie, shocked, grabs the letter.*)

SOPHIE: (*Overwhelmed.*) Excuse me.

CHRISTIAN: Go! (*Sophie exits.*)

MAMA: I'm surprised to see you. I thought you were through with me.

CHRISTIAN: I was. I didn't come here to see you.

MAMA: (*Wounded.*) Oh?

CHRISTIAN: And—

MAMA: Yes? (*A moment.*) . . . Hello, yes?

C'est la vie: That's life.

CHRISTIAN: (*Hesitantly, but genuinely.*) I . . . I debated whether even to come, but damn it, I missed you. (*Mama laughs.*) You have nothing to say to me?

MAMA: Do you really want me to respond to your foolishness?

CHRISTIAN: (*Wounded.*) You are a mean-spirited woman. I don't know why I expect the sun to shine where only mold thrives. (*His frankness catches Mama off guard.*)

MAMA: I don't like your tone.

CHRISTIAN: We have unfinished "business"!

MAMA: Look around, there's no business here. There's nothing left. (*Christian looks around. He looks at Mama, shakes his head and smiles.*)

CHRISTIAN: (*Blurts.*) Then Mama, settle down with me.

MAMA: Go home!

CHRISTIAN: What?!

MAMA: You heard me, go the hell home. I don't wanna hear it. I have too much on my mind for this shit.

CHRISTIAN: That's all you have to say. I looked death in the eye on the river road. A boy nearly took out my liver with a bayonet. I'm serious, I drop and kiss the ground that he was a romantic, and spared me when I told him I was man on a mission. (*Mama cracks open a cold beer.*)

MAMA: It's cold, why can't you be happy with that?

CHRISTIAN: Because, it isn't what I want? Bring me a Fanta, please. (*Mama smiles and gets him a Fanta.*)

MAMA: I'll put on some music.

CHRISTIAN: What's the point, you never dance with me. (*Mama laughs.*)

MAMA: Oh shut up, relax, I'll roast some groundnuts. Huh? (*A moment.*)

CHRISTIAN: Why not us?

MAMA: What would we do, Professor? How would it work? The two of us? Imagine. You'd wander. I'd get impatient. I see how men do. We'd argue, fight, and I'd grow resentful. You'd grow jealous. We know this story. It's tiresome.

CHRISTIAN: You know everything, don't you? And if I said, I'd stay, help you run things. Make a legitimate business. A shop. Fix the door. Hang the mirror. Protect you. Make love to you.

MAMA: Do I look like I need protection?

CHRISTIAN: No, but you look like you need someone to make love to you.

MAMA: Do I, now?

CHRISTIAN: Yes. How long has it been, Mama, since you allowed a man to touch you? Huh? A man like me, who isn't looking through you for a way home.

MAMA: Enough. God. You're getting pathetic.

CHRISTIAN: Maybe. But damn it against my better judgement . . . I love you.

MAMA: (*With contempt.*) Love. What's the point in all this shit? Love is too fragile a sentiment for out here. Think about what happens to the things we "love." It isn't worth it. Love. It is a poisonous word. It will cost us more than it returns. Don't you think? It'll be an unnecessary burden for people like us. And it'll eventually strangle us!

CHRISTIAN: Do you hear what you're saying?

MAMA: It's the truth. Deal with it!

CHRISTIAN: Hm . . . Why do I bother. If you can't put it on a scale it is nothing, right?! Pardon me. (*Christian, flustered by her response, walks to the door.*)

MAMA: Where are you going?! (*Mama watches suddenly panicked.*) Hey! You heard me. Don't be a baby. (*Christian stops before exiting.*)

CHRISTIAN: We joke. It's fun. But honestly, I'm worn bare. I've been driving this route a long time and I'm getting to the age where I'd like to sleep in the same bed every night. I need familiar company, food that is predictable, conversation that's too easy. If you don't know what I'm talking about, then I'll go. But, please, I'd like to have the truth . . . why not us? (*A moment. Mama says nothing. Christian starts to leave, but her words catch him—*)

MAMA: (*With surprising vulnerability.*) I'm ruined. (*Louder.*) I'm ruined. (*He absorbs her words.*)

CHRISTIAN: God, I don't know what those men did to you, but I'm sorry for it. I may be an idiot for saying so, but I think we, and I speak as a man, can do better. (*He goes to comfort her, she pulls away until he's forced to hold her in a tight embrace.*)

MAMA: No! Don't touch me! No! (*She struggles to free herself eventually succumbing to his heartfelt embrace. He kisses her. Sophie walks in.*)

SOPHIE: Oh, I'm sorry. (*Sophie smiles to herself. Mama pulls away.*)

MAMA: Why are you standing there looking like a lost elephant?

SOPHIE: Sorry, Mama. (*Sophie slips out.*)

MAMA: Don't think this changes anything.

CHRISTIAN: Wait, there.

MAMA: Where are you going? (*Christian straightens his suit.*)

CHRISTIAN: I swear to you, this is the last time I'll ask. (*Recites.*)

> A branch lists to and fro,
> An answer to the insurgent wind,
> A circle dance, grace nearly broken,
> But it ends peacefully, stillness welcome.

(*He holds his hand out to Mama. A long moment. Finally, she takes his hand and he pulls her into his arms. They begin to dance. At first she's a bit stiff and resistant, but slowly gives in. Guitar music: "Rare Bird." Sophie pulls Josephine into the doorway. They watch the pair dance, incredulously.*)

JOSEPHINE: (*Smiling, whispers.*) Go, Mama.

PARROT: Mama! Primus! Mama! Primus! (*Mama and Christian continue their measured dance. Lights slowly fade.*)

COMMENTARY

RANDY GENER

In Defense of *Ruined:* Five Elements That Shape Lynn Nottage's Masterwork   2010

Randy Gener is a senior editor for *American Theatre* magazine and a winner of the 2010 George Jean Nathan Award for best theatrical criticism in the United States. He has won several other awards for his theater writing and is known as an arts curator and an international cultural advisor. His article on *Ruined* examines five major points of contention that help illuminate the significance of the drama.

1. Salima

Seated in the living room of the brownstone in Brooklyn where she grew up and still lives, surrounded by the African and African-American art her parents collected, Lynn Nottage is talking about *Ruined*. She lays emphasis on a precept that guided her in giving flesh-and-blood character to the women and girls in the Democratic Republic of Congo whose experience of being brutally raped is the play's central subject. In using the true stories of these African women, the playwright drew careful lines between documentary reality and theatrical fiction. "The women told me their stories—they didn't *give* me their stories to tell," she says. "I didn't want to write a verbatim play. It would've been a different relationship if they knew I was going to put their exact words on the stage. They would have censored themselves more, become much more self-conscious. Those are their stories, and they are sacred."

It is early summer of 2005, and Nottage is preparing to embark on a second journey to East Africa in order to collect more narratives of these refugee women, all survivors of war, rape and torture at the hands of armed forces. Supported by a Guggenheim Fellowship, accompanied by her husband, filmmaker Tony Gerber, as well as her father and daughter, she is planning to visit refugee camps in Kenya and Uganda for a little over a month. She'd already been there in the summer of 2004, with director Kate Whoriskey, who would help shape and direct the play, but this time around Nottage wants to stay longer. On the first trip, the two women couldn't enter the Congo, because war was still raging in the Ituri Rainforest area and Congolese refugees kept flowing over the border into Uganda. Having worked as a press officer for Amnesty International, Nottage was aware that virtually none of the media narratives provided by Western reporters had investigated the plight of raped and mutilated women whose numbers have continuously risen since the war's official end in 2003. (That situation has worsened, with recent reports of sexual violation of some men and boys.) "I had no idea what play I would find in that war-torn landscape," Nottage says, "but I traveled to the region because I wanted to paint a three-dimensional portrait of the women caught in the middle of armed conflicts; I wanted to understand who they were, beyond their status as victims."

An air of ease and ebullience naturally surrounds Nottage, and that lightness of spirit feels especially disarming when her anecdotes swerve into dark alleys or when her uneasy or fearful reactions to past experiences surface. She recalls the very first Congolese woman who spoke with her, through tears and in a voice barely above a whisper. Her name was Salima. "She related her story in such graphic detail that I remember wanting to cry out for her to stop, but I knew that she had a need to be heard," Nottage says. "She'd walked miles from her refugee camp to share her story with a willing listener." Salima described being dragged from her home, arrested and wrongfully imprisoned by men seeking to arrest her husband. In prison she was beaten and raped by five soldiers. Eventually she found a way to bribe her way out of jail, only to discover that her husband and two of her four children had been abducted. At the time of the interview, Salima still had not learned her family's whereabouts. Her memories so astonished Nottage that "they entered my body in a totally unexpected way," the writer says.

Back in Brooklyn some three years later, as *Ruined* wended its way to a 2008 premiere at the Goodman Theatre of Chicago and the Manhattan Theatre Club, Nottage would sum up her African sojourns in tender language: "I found my play in the painful narratives of Salima and the other Congolese women, in their gentle cadences and the monumental space between their gasps and sighs. I also found my play in the way they occasionally accessed their smiles, as if glimpsing beyond their wounds into the future."

Ruined, which will be one of the most-produced plays of the 2010–11 season, performed this past summer at the Intiman Theatre of Seattle, where Whoriskey recently became artistic director. The Seattle company, which gathers the leading cast members and design team from her original 2008–09 production, remounts the play through Oct. 17 at the Geffen Playhouse in Los Angeles. The play will eventually be brought to South Africa's Market Theatre, where the story will be shared with Congolese refugees in Johannesburg. Ironically, Nottage has yet to set foot in the Congo.

2. Acknowledging Brecht

Allow me to cut the umbilical cord: An original creation, *Ruined* is not—as a few articles and reviews would have it—an adaptation, a version nor a loose recasting of *Mother Courage and Her Children*, Bertolt Brecht's 1939 classic. "People always enter from the thing that is familiar to them," Nottage conjectures. "I am probably to blame for saying, 'Oh, it was inspired by *Mother Courage*'—which it was. But *Ruined* is a huge departure. I didn't want to use a Western theatrical construct. I felt that was totally the antithesis of what I wanted to do with the play." *Ruined* neither apes the thematic concerns nor mimics the gestural interruptions of action in *Mother Courage*. Although the name of *Ruined*'s embittered Mama Nadi dimly echoes the central character's name in Brecht's intellectual epic, that resemblance is merely a tip of the hat. Mama Nadi's courage or cowardice is not a quagmire *Ruined* asks to confront.

There are many ways to define war, just as there are many ways to violate a woman's body. War is, however, a persistent disease whose symptoms recur and break out, like an opportunistic virus. The Congolese women whom Nottage interviewed did indeed react, in French, with mournful pride upon hearing the words "mother" and "courage" spoken together. But the personal resonances those women felt bear no relation to the great capitulation—the totality and finality of defeat—that is Brecht's great subject. The women of *Ruined* are fictional composites of real survivors of sexual violence. As a tribute to the first woman she interviewed, Nottage named one of these composites Salima. She is a simple and uneducated farmer's wife who spent nearly five months in the bush as the sex slave of rebel soldiers. Her monologue recounting the calamitous but "bright and beautiful" day when the men abducted her from her home, and how she was shunned by her husband, her family and her village, is the heartbreaking crux of Act 2.

Ruined takes place entirely in a combination nightclub and brothel in a small mining town in the Congo. Mama Nadi, the club's haughty owner and madam, need only stay put, since the war in the Congo keeps tossing "girls" at her—women in this context are not only less human than men, they are fundamentally the spoils and the discards of the conflict. Like Mother Courage, Mama Nadi profits by taking no sides in the war but her own, yet her actions do not mirror Brecht's template of a wily woman who loses everything, including her children, in a drawn-out war—unlike Mother Courage, Mama Nadi's maternity is merely figurative. She does use her own idiosyncratic ethics ("I put food in the mouths of eight women," she says) to exploit young women for personal gain and political advantage. And yet, although Mama Nadi states that nothing will ever stand in the way of business, her affection for her girls grows in the play, and her actions toward the most damaged of them, 18-year-old Sophie, the chanteuse who is useless for sex, belie her frequent pronouncements.

"I think my play is written from a woman's point of view, so there's much more compassion, there's much more optimism, than in *Mother Courage*," Nottage contends. "Mama embodies the role of 'mama' in a much more traditional way."

Brecht wrote a socialist epic about business during a time of war, where goodness and virtues are not rewarded. Nottage crafted a hard-hitting humanist exposé about the brutalization of women's bodies during the armed conflicts in the Congo. To expose this brutalization, Nottage strives *not* to distance us from its subject. A seamless synthesis of social-justice politics, edge-of-your-seat suspense and uncommon love story, *Ruined* brings audiences emotionally close to the realities of a region where women have been violated and mutilated with sticks and bayonets by soldiers, where families have driven rape victims from their communities, where sexual torture has resulted in sterility or infection or death.

At the same time, *Ruined* sustains, with as much depth and humor as Nottage could muster, the aspects of dignity, integrity, earthbound simplicity and (most emphatically) the implacability she found during her two trips to East Africa. Except for the tellingly named traveling salesman Christian, nobody is allowed to talk politics in Mama Nadi's place. Soldiers must unload their weapons before being serviced. Mama Nadi constantly insists that her bar be treated as a haven of escape and respite for rough-handed miners and drunken soldiers. There's live music and occasional dancing, signs that life goes on no matter what. "The mess is outside," she contends, but the promise of sex in the brothel can never shut out the nation's civil war, which encroaches closer and closer with the appearance of soldiers from various factions, all thoroughly convinced of their murderous righteousness.

3. Politics

None of *Ruined*'s richly drawn characters is an African-American. Nevertheless, *Ruined* earned the 2009 Pulitzer Prize for Drama, normally reserved for plays by an American author, "preferably original in its source and dealing with American life." Perhaps not coincidentally, *Ruined*'s consecration took place during those same heart-stopping months that Barack Obama, whose immigrant father was Kenyan, became our president. In American culture, when blacks advance beyond historically assigned roles, it is usually a point of intrigue. The victory of an American president with African origins sparked a degree of hope abroad that tribal divisions might someday be recognized (if not crumble) and that improved international diplomacy might combat U.S. aggression.

The surge of Iraq-themed plays and anti-war dramas (both fictional and documentary) during the later George W. Bush years mostly vented feelings of ideological upset and political helplessness. Recent U.S. plays about conflict zones—such as Eve Ensler's *Necessary Targets*, about the Bosnian conflict; J.T. Rogers's *The Overwhelming*, about the Rwandan genocide; and practically every U.S. play about the wars in Iraq and Afghanistan—depend on American characters as narrators and protagonists (often they are journalists) as a means of audience entry. *Ruined* commands our respect, because it takes up the cause of the global voiceless who reside outside U.S. boundaries. Nottage's un-chic dramaturgy of naturalism allows sufficient freedom to stir a far-flung narrative into vibrant life.

Sexual violence against women as a side effect of civil war in Africa is, for most Americans, a remote subject. We might shake our heads in horror or numbly watch at the awful reports. Here is a play about gender inequality that transcends our more common hot-button squabbles about pay differentials and glass ceilings and old-boy networks—the stuff we Westerners get anxious or angry or organize tea-parties about. Here is a drama about a phenomenon (Ensler calls it "femicide") that is so extensive, so common, so entrenched as to seem perpetually old news even while it is happening so hellishly.

This tradition of objectifying women during conflicts, dramatized as far back as the extant Greek plays, has stepped up to new levels: Fighters have systematically used rape and murder in the former Yugoslavia, in Rwanda in the 1990s, and currently in Darfur—with the intent to eliminate ethnic groups and to induce forced displacement. The prevalence of rape and other sexual violations in Eastern Congo has been described as the worst in the world. Women, children and even some men are being attacked by multiple assailants, often in public and in front of their neighbors. Even the United Nations' peacekeeping forces have been accused of rape. Sexual violence wasn't recognized as a war crime until June 2008 when the UN Security Council passed Resolution 1820, a small step toward ending what Jan Egeland, the former humanitarian-affairs chief, described as "one of the biggest conspiracies of silence in history."

Ruined's realist zeal prefers, at first, to woo and coax us, because the acts of sexual violence being committed are ghastly and often indescribable. When Nottage lends the most vulnerable of her characters, Salima, a line that crosses the border from the suggestive to direct protest—"You will not fight your battles on my body anymore"—her outcry is desperate and appropriate and hard-won. It works. In black aesthetics, political struggle *is* cultural struggle. Anything less than a cry of rage would mean the worst sort of betrayal; anything other than those words would render women like Salima once again voiceless and unworthy of tragic ennoblement.

4. Hearts of Coltan

Several days before the 2009 opening of *Ruined*, I interviewed Nottage at a Times Square diner.

RANDY GENER: The second time you went to Africa, you interviewed men. What was that experience like?

LYNN NOTTAGE: It was really fascinating, because we traveled throughout the Great Lakes region. In this case, it wasn't Congolese men I talked to. In the northern part of Uganda, we met quite a few mobilized men from the Lord's Resistance Army in a refugee camp. A lot of them divorced themselves of the responsibility. They said, "We put on this uniform. We were given these orders, but we had to comply. That's not who we really are." I expected them to be contrite, apologetic and ashamed. I was shocked, because they could tell their stories divorced of emotion: "And we cut off their lips, and we. . . ." Also I was shocked that people would be around them listening. I thought, "These are war criminals. Why isn't someone arresting them?" But they were listening and not horrified in the way that I was horrified. We interviewed refugee camp members who had been victims of these LRA soldiers and were coexisting with them. That coexistence really confused me.

RANDY GENER: You told me you were making plans to visit the all-female Kenyan village of Umoja, a sanctuary for women escaping violence, genital mutilation and forced marriages.

LYNN NOTTAGE: When I heard about Umoja, I was fascinated by its founder, Rebecca Lolosoli, this woman who started a village of women who had all been shunned by their families or their husbands or had been forced out of their communities because they had been raped, or they rejected hysterectomy for a host of reasons. She managed to form, in the center of this arid northern region of Kenya, a village that is committed to sustaining and nurturing an all-female community. Mama Nadi is not Rebecca. Rebecca is a far more altruistic and nurturing woman than Mama. But I was interested in the dynamics of that: how this woman chief defied odds in this country defined by men. Rebecca is an extremely articulate and passionate advocate for her community. She's been able to get national attention and raise money. I'm part of this women's group; we managed to raise $1,700 worth of supplies and clothing that was sent to her schoolhouse in Umoja.

RANDY GENER: What does Africa mean to you as a playwright or as a citizen of the world?

LYNN NOTTAGE: I want Americans to understand that they have a very deep investment in what happens in Africa and in the Congo. We're beneficiaries of the abundance of resources that exists there. About 90 percent of coltan, the semi-conductive mineral that's used to fuel cell phones and laptops, comes from the Congo. We're invested in the instability there. As long as they can extract coltan cheaply, we continue to buy our cell phones and laptops for very little. I want Americans to acknowledge that we have a stake in the war that's being fought there.

5. Possibility

Trapped in the fear-ridden illogic and dense moral thickets of a hellish war, Mama Nadi thrives. Hers is an act of defiance waged not just over women's bodies but over the ruined body of the Congo herself. "Love is too fragile a sentiment for out here," says Mama Nadi. But it's love and humanity that moves her to action by the play's end. The persistent criticism of Nottage's achievement is that offering Mama Nadi the possibility for romantic love at the play's climax may be too upbeat or false a conclusion for a play about war, rape and survival. The Pulitzer board noted this emotional appeal, characterizing the play as an "affirmation of life and hope amid hopelessness."

The criticism that *Ruined*, emotionally scorching as it is, lacks the ruthless logic of the Brechtian prototype fails to acknowledge that Nottage is a confident yet individual artist who writes big-hearted political stories about the ways of women in the world. The struggle to move on is *Ruined*'s great subject. Yes (without fully giving away the plot), Christian and Mama Nadi do reach some sort of resolution at the close of *Ruined*, but it is a strange denouement, because real happiness remains the dimmest certainty, given the violent outbreaks and bleak realities of war-torn Congo. Will these two find ultimate peace together? Nowhere does the play hint anything as pat as redemption. Christian's entreaties end on a dance of hesitancy.

Righting gender inequality in the developing world, *Ruined* reminds us, continues to be the moral battle of the 21st century. And yet, like others who have seen and documented Africa's horrors firsthand, Nottage offers up in her implacable play a promise of life: Yes, perhaps, the violence will continue to roll on, but this does not mean there are no Congolese men like Christian who are nurturing and loving and supportive, men who will want to form families and relationships with women like Mama Nadi. Nottage does not demonize all African men. Humanist to the core, she seeks to demonstrate that what's obdurate is, in fact, assailable—that although the consequences of gender inequality in Africa are so vast and the statistics those consequences generate are so huge, theatre is still a place that can enlarge our collective feelings of connection and political agency.

Nottage aspires to do more than document what might seem unbearable, outrageous hardships. For the Congolese women and girls Nottage portrays in *Ruined*, gender inequality is far more elemental. It issues from a belief so fixed as to be unimpeachable: that women are less human than men. If we argue, as some critics have, that the damaged women of the Congo aren't capable of change and healing—if we insist that a playwright cannot, as Nottage hopes, "glimpse beyond the wounds into the future"—might it mean that in some deep place most of us believe that ruined women are less than human, too?

Let us hope not. Yes, it's a vicious world. Attitudes change slowly. Good intentions are not enough. Even so. Small steps taken against tragic problems, actions such as writing a play, are the opposite of a vicious circle. And they can be resounding.

Writing about Drama

The act of writing involves making a commitment to ideas, and that commitment helps clarify your thinking. Writing forces you to examine the details, the elements of a play that might otherwise pass unnoticed, and it helps you develop creative interpretations that enrich your appreciation of the plays you read. Besides deepening your own understanding, your writing can contribute to that of your peers and readers, as the commentaries in this book are meant to do.

Because every reader of plays has a unique experience and background, every reader can contribute something to the experience and awareness of others. You will see things that others do not. You will interpret things in a way that others will not. Naturally, every reader's aim is to respect the text, but it is not reasonable to think that there is only one "correct" way to interpret a text. One of the most interesting aspects of writing about drama is that it is usually preceded by discussion, through which a range of possible interpretations begin to appear. When you start to write, you commit yourself to working with certain ideas, and you deepen your thinking about those ideas as you write.

Writing Criticism about Drama

Ordinarily, when you are asked to write about a play, you are expected to produce a critical and analytical study. A critical essay will go beyond simply describing your subjective experience and include a discussion of what the play achieves and how it does so. If you have a choice, you should choose a play that you admire and enjoy. If you have background material on that play, such as a playbill or a newspaper article, or if you have seen a production, these aids will be especially useful in writing.

For a critical study you will need to go far beyond retelling the events of the play. You may have to describe what you believe happens in a given scene or moment, but simply rewriting the plot of the play in your own words does not constitute an interpretation. A critical reading of a play demands that you isolate evidence and comment on it. For example, you may want to quote passages of dialogue or stage directions to point out an essential idea in the drama, but do so in moderation. A string of quotations linked together with a small amount of your commentary will not suffice. Further, make sure that the quotations you use in fact illustrate your point; explain clearly their importance to your discussion.

Approaches to Criticism

Many critical approaches are available to the reader of drama. One approach is to emphasize the response of audience members or readers, recognizing that the audience brings a great deal to a play even before the action begins. The audience's or reader's previous experience with drama influences expectations about what will happen on stage and about how the central characters will behave. Personal and cultural biases also influence how an audience member reacts to the unfolding drama. Reader response criticism pays close attention to these responses and to what causes them.

Another critical approach is to treat the play as the coherent work of a playwright who intends the audience to perceive certain meanings in the play. This approach assumes that a careful analysis, or close reading, of the play will reveal the author's meanings.

Either approach can lead to engaging essays on drama. In the pages that follow, you will find directions on how to pay attention to your responses as an audience member or reader and advice about how to read a play with close attention to dialogue, images, and patterns of action.

Reader Response Criticism

Response criticism depends on a full experience of the text—a good understanding of its meaning as well as of its conventions of staging and performance.

Your responses to various elements of the drama, whether the characters, the setting, the theme, or the dialogue, may change and grow as you see a play or read it through. You might have a very different reaction to a play during a second reading or viewing of it. Keeping a careful record of your responses as you read is a first step in response criticism.

There is, however, a big difference between recording your responses and examining them. Douglas Atkins of the University of Kansas speaks not only of reader response in criticism but also of reader responsibility, by which he means that readers have the responsibility to respond on more than a superficial level when they read drama. This book helps you reach deeper critical levels because you can read each play in light of the history of drama. This book also gives you important background material and commentary from the playwrights and from professional critics. Reading such criticism helps you understand what the critic's role is and what a critic might say about drama.

Reading drama in a historical perspective is important because it can highlight similarities between plays of different eras. Anyone who has read *Oedipus Rex* and *Antigone* will be better prepared to respond to *Hamlet*. The variety of styles and subject matter of the plays presented in this book gives you the opportunity to read and respond to a broad range of drama. The more plays you read carefully, the better you will become at responding to drama and writing about it.

When you write response criticism, keep these guidelines in mind:

1. As you read, make note of the important effects the text has on you. Annotate in the margins moments that are especially effective. Do you find yourself alarmed? Disturbed? Sympathetic or unsympathetic to a character? Do you sense suspense, or are you confused about what is happening? Do you feel personally involved with the action, or does it seem to have nothing to do with you? Do you find the situation funny? What overall response do you find yourself experiencing?

2. By analyzing the following two elements of your response, establish why the play had the effects you experienced. Do you think it would have those effects on others? Have you observed that it does?

   First, determine what it is about the play that causes you to have the response you do. Is it the structure of the play, the way the characters behave or talk? Is it an unusual use of language, allusions to literature you know (or don't know)? Is the society portrayed especially familiar (or especially unfamiliar) to you? What does the author seem to expect the audience to know before the play begins?

Second, determine what it is about you, the reader, that causes you to respond as you do. Were you prepared for the dramatic conventions of the play, in terms of its genre as tragedy, comedy, or tragicomedy or in terms of its place in the history of drama? How did your preparation affect your response? Did you have difficulty interpreting the language of the play? Are you especially responsive to certain kinds of plays because of familiarity?

3. What do your responses to the play tell you about your own limitations, your own expertise, your own values, and your own attitudes toward social behavior, uses of language, and your sense of what is "normal"? Be sure to be willing to face your limitations as well as your strengths.[1]

Reader response criticism is a flexible and useful way to explore possible interpretations of a text. Everyone is capable of responding to drama, and everyone's response will differ depending on his or her preparation and background.

Close Reading

Analyzing a play by close reading means examining the text in detail, looking for patterns that might not be evident with a less attentive approach to the text. Annotation is the key to close reading, since the critic's job is to keep track of elements in the play that, incidental though they may seem alone, imply a greater significance when seen together.

Close reading implies rereading, because the first time through a text, you do not know just what will be meaningful as the play unfolds, and you will want to read it again to confirm and deepen your impressions. You will usually make only a few discoveries the first time through. However, it is important to annotate the text even the first time you read it.

In annotating a play, try following these guidelines:

1. Underline all the speeches and images you think are important. Look for dialogue that you think reveals the play's themes, the true nature of the characters, and the position of the playwright.

2. Watch for repetition of imagery (such as the garden and weed imagery in *Hamlet*) and keep track of it through annotation. Do the same for repeated ideas in the dialogue and for repeated comments on government or religion or psychology. Such repetitions will reveal the importance of such imagery and ideas to the playwright.

3. Highlight in color (or use some other system) to identify various patterns in the text; then examine each pattern before you begin to plan your essay.

Criticism that uses the techniques of close reading pays very careful attention to the elements of drama—plot, characterization, setting, dialogue (use of

---

[1]Adapted from Kathleen McCormick, "Theory in the Reader: Bleich, Holland, and Beyond," *College English* 47 (1985): 838.

language), movement, and theme—that were discussed in the first part of the book in relation to Lady Gregory's *The Rising of the Moon*. As you read a play, keep track of its chief elements; often, they will give you useful ideas for your paper. You may find it helpful to refer to the earlier discussion of the elements in *The Rising of the Moon* (pp. 23–29), because a short critical essay about that play is presented here (pp. 1852–1853).

Annotating the special use of any of the primary elements will help you decide how important they are and whether a close study of them might contribute to an interesting interpretation of the play. You may not want to discuss all the elements in an essay—or, if you do, only one may be truly dominant—but you should be aware of them in any play you write about.

From Prewriting to Final Draft: A Sample Essay on *The Rising of the Moon*

Most good writing results from good planning. When you write criticism about drama, consider these important stages:

1. When possible, choose a play that you enjoy.
2. Annotate the play very carefully.
3. Spend time prewriting.
4. Write a good first draft, then revise for content, organization, style, and mechanics.

The essay on Lady Gregory's *The Rising of the Moon* later in this section involved several stages of writing. First, the writer read and annotated the play. In the process of doing so, she noticed the unusual stage direction beginning the play, *Moonlight*, and noticed also that when the two policemen leave the Sergeant, they take the lantern, but the Sergeant reminds them that it is very lonely waiting there "with nothing but the moon." Second, the writer used the stage directions regarding moonlight to guide her in several important techniques of prewriting, including brainstorming, clustering, freewriting, drafting a trial thesis, and outlining.

The first technique, brainstorming, involved listing ideas, words, or phrases suggested by reading the play. The idea of moonlight and the moon recurred often. Then the writer practiced clustering: beginning with *moon*, a key term developed from brainstorming, then radiating from it all the associations that naturally suggested themselves. (See the cluster diagram on p. 1851.)

Next the writer chose the term *romance*, which had come to mind during her brainstorming, and performed a freewriting exercise around that term. Freewriting is a technique in which a writer takes four or five minutes to write whatever comes to mind. The technique is intended to be done quickly, so the conscious censor has to be turned off. Anything you write in freewriting may be useful, because you may produce ideas you did not know you had.

The following passage is part of the freewriting the student did using *romance* as a key term. The passage is also an example of "invisible writing": the writing was done on a computer and the student turned off the monitor so that she could not censor or erase what she was writing. She could only go forward, as fast as possible!

The setting of the play is completely romantic. In a lot of ways the play wouldn't work in a different setting. When you think about it the moon in the title is what makes all the action possible. Moon associated with darkness, underworld, world of fairies, so the moon is what makes all the action possible. Moon makes Sergeant look at things differently. The moon is the rebel moon — that's what title means. Rebel moon is rising, always rising. So the world the policeman lives in — sun lights up everything in practical and nonromantic way — is like lantern that second policeman brings to dockside. It shows things in a harsh light. Moon shows things in soft light. Without the moon there would be a different play.

The freewriting gave the writer a new direction — discussing the setting of the play, especially the role of light. Thus, the writer's clustering began with the moon, veered off to the concept of the romantic elements in the play, and then came back to the way the moon and the lantern function in the play. The writer was now ready to work up a trial thesis:

Lady Gregory uses light to create a romantic setting that helps us understand the relationship between the rebel and the Sergeant and the values that they each stand for.

Because a writer drafts a thesis before writing an essay, the thesis is like a trial balloon. It may work or it may not. At this point it gives the writer direction.

Next, the student outlined her essay. Because she did not know the outcome of the essay yet, her outline was necessarily sketchy:

I.   Moonlight is associated with romance and rebellion; harsh light of lantern is associated with repressiveness of police.

    A. Rebel is associated with romance.

    B. Sergeant is associated with practicality and the law.

II.   Without the lantern the Sergeant is under the influence of the romantic moon and the rebel.

    A. Sergeant feels resentment about his job.

    B. Rebel sings forbidden song and Sergeant reveals his former sympathies.

    C. Sergeant admits he was romantic when young.

III. Sergeant must choose between moon and lantern.

    A. Sergeant seems ready to arrest rebel.

    B. When police return with lantern the Sergeant sends them away.

    C. Rebel escapes and Sergeant remains in moonlight.

The prewriting strategies of brainstorming, clustering, freewriting, drafting a thesis, and outlining helped the student generate ideas and material for her first draft. After writing this draft, she revised it carefully for organization, clarity, expression, punctuation, and format. What follows is her final draft.

Andrea James

Professor Jacobus

English 233

19 October

The Use of Light in *The Rising of the Moon*

Lady Gregory uses light imagery in *The Rising of the Moon* to contrast rebellion and repressiveness. Her initial stage direction is basic: *Moonlight*. She suggests some of the values associated with moonlight, such as rebellion and romance, caution and secrecy, daring exploits, and even the underworld. All these are set against the policemen, who are governed not by the moon, which casts shadows and makes the world look magical, but by the lantern, which casts a harsh light that even the Sergeant eventually rejects.

The ballad singer, the rebel, is associated with romance from the start: "Dark hair—dark eyes, smooth face. . . . There isn't another man in Ireland would have broken jail the way he did" (26). He is dark, handsome, and recklessly brave. The Sergeant, by contrast, is a practical man, no romantic. He sees that he might have a chance to arrest the rebel and gain the reward for his capture if he stays right on the quay, a likely place for the rebel to escape from. But he unknowingly spoils his chances by refusing to keep the lantern the policemen offer. He tells the policemen, "You can take the lantern. Don't be too long now. It's very lonesome here with nothing but the moon" (26).

What he does not realize is that with the lantern as his guiding light, he will behave like a proper Sergeant. But with the moon to guide him, he will side with the rebel.

It takes only a few minutes for the rebel to show up on the scene. At first, the Sergeant is very tough and abrupt with the rebel, who is disguised as "Jimmy Walsh, a ballad singer." The rebel tells the Sergeant that he is a traveler, that he is from Ennis, and that he has been to Cork. Unlike the Sergeant, who has stayed in one place and is a family man, the ballad singer appears to be a romantic figure, in the sense that he follows his mind to go where he wants to, sings what he wants to, and does what he wants to.

When the ballad singer begins singing, the Sergeant reacts badly, telling the singer, "Stop that noise" (26). Maybe he is envious of the ballad singer's freedom. When the Sergeant tries to make the rebel leave, the rebel instead begins telling stories about the man the Sergeant is looking for. He reminds the Sergeant of deeds done that would frighten anyone. "It was after the time of the attack on the police barrack at Kilmallock. . . . Moonlight . . . just like this" (27). The moonlight of the tale and the moonlight of the setting combine to add mystery and suspense to the situation.

The effect of the rebel's talk — and of the moonlight — is to make the Sergeant feel sorry for himself in a thankless job. "It's little we get but abuse from the people, and no choice but to obey our orders," he says bitterly while sitting on the barrel sharing a pipe with the singer (27). When the rebel sings an illegal song, the Sergeant corrects a few words, revealing his former sympathies with the people. The rebel realizes this, telling the Sergeant, "It was with the people you were, and not with the law you were, when you were a young man" (28). The Sergeant admits that when he was young he too was a romantic, but now that he is older he is practical and law-abiding: "Well, if I was foolish then, that time's gone. . . . I have my duties and I know them" (28).

Pulled by his past and his present, the Sergeant is suddenly forced to choose when the ballad singer's signal to his friend reveals the singer's identity to the Sergeant. He must decide whether his heart is with the world of moonlight or the world of the lantern. He seizes the rebel's hat and wig and seems about to arrest him when the policemen, with their lantern, come back. The Sergeant orders the policemen back to the station, and they offer to leave the lantern with him. But the Sergeant refuses. We know that he will not turn the rebel in. He has chosen the world of moonlight, of the rebel.

Before they leave the policemen try to make the world of the lantern seem the right choice. Policeman B says:

> Well, I thought it might be a comfort to you. I often think when I have it in my hand and can be flashing it about into every dark corner (*doing so*) that it's the same as being beside the fire at home, and the bits of bogwood blazing up now and again. (*Flashes it about, now on the barrel, now on Sergeant.*) (29)

The Sergeant reacts furiously and tells them to get out — "yourselves and your lantern!"

The play ends with the Sergeant giving the hat and wig back to the rebel, obviously having chosen the side of the people. When the rebel leaves, the Sergeant wonders if he himself was crazy for losing his chance at the reward. But as the curtain goes down, the Sergeant is still in the moonlight.

Writing a Review

A review is more than a critical essay because it covers an actual performance of a play. As a reviewer, you write after digesting an evening's entertainment and observing how actors and a director present a production for your enjoyment. Your responsibility is to respond both to the production and to the text of the play; thus, you will discuss the quality of the acting, the effectiveness of the setting, the interpretation of the text, and the power of the direction.

What Is the Purpose of a Review?

Reviews of plays ordinarily appear in daily newspapers or in weekly or semi-weekly publications timely enough to help a prospective playgoer decide whether to see the play. Considering the cost of tickets in contemporary theater, the best reviewers perform a valuable service by letting readers know what they believe is most worth seeing. Regular reviewers, such as Ben Brantley and Charles Isherwood in the *New York Times,* Daniel Mendelsohn of *The New York Review of Books,* and Michael Billington of *The Guardian,* develop their own followings, because playgoers know from experience whether they can rely on these reviewers' judgments.

Another purpose of theater reviews is to set a standard to which producers can aspire. Criticism can promote excellence because experienced and demanding critics force producers of drama to maintain high standards. The power of theater critics in major cities is legendary: more than a few plays have closed prematurely after savage reviews in London, New York, Chicago, and elsewhere. Knowing that they will undergo scrutiny by knowledgeable reviewers convinces writers, directors, actors, and producers to do their best.

What You Need to Write a Good Review

The best reviewers bring three qualifications to their work: experience in the theater, a knowledge of theatrical history, and a sensitivity to dramatic production. Some reviewers have had experience onstage as actors or as production assistants. They are familiar with the process of preparing a play for the stage and in some cases may actually have written for the stage. Other reviewers who have not had such experience have, instead, spent hours in the theater watching plays; their rich experience of seeing a variety of plays enables them to make useful comparisons.

Knowledge of the basics of theater history is indispensable to being a good reviewer. New plays that borrow from the traditions of the Greek chorus or plays that emulate medieval pageants or nineteenth-century melodrama need reviewers who understand their sources. Playwright Suzan-Lori Parks, for example, admits that her work is influenced by that of Bertolt Brecht and Samuel Beckett. She expects her audience to recognize some of that influence, but she knows that her reviewers will spot most or all of it. This book is structured around the history of drama so that readers will better understand drama's roots and evolution. In that sense this book can help a theater enthusiast become a competent reviewer.

Besides knowing the history of drama, a reviewer must also be extremely well read. Some reviewers, for example, have not had the opportunity to see productions of all of Shakespeare's plays, but a good reviewer will have read most of them and can refer to them as necessary. The same is true of the plays of Bernard Shaw, many of which have not been produced in over a dozen years.

In the case of contemporary playwrights, it is common for a reviewer to refer to the playwright's earlier work to put the current production in a useful context. A knowledgeable reviewer knows not only the history of theater but also the work of other playwrights that may be relevant to the play under review.

Most students of theater have enough sensitivity to dramatic productions to write adequate reviews. The most sensitive reviewers will pay close attention to the suitability of the acting and often consider the acting to be of greatest importance, especially if the play is well known. Most contemporary reviews single out actors and comment on their performance in some detail. Reviewers usually know the work of the busiest actors, and in some cases they will make comparisons with an actor's performance in earlier roles. They will also indicate whether the actor has developed further as an artist or has walked mechanically through the part. The reviewer's sensitivity to individual actors is developed in part from past experience, providing a benchmark against which to measure a performance.

No reviewer is going to review *Oedipus Rex* with an eye toward telling us whether it is a good or a bad play; the history of criticism has already done that. The reviewer of *Oedipus Rex,* like the reviewer of any of Sophocles' great plays, will aim to tell us about the quality of the acting or the effectiveness of the setting. Being sensitive to the effective use of lighting, props, costumes, and stage design is essential for any reviewer, but it is even more crucial for a reviewer of classic theater.

Preparing to Review a Classic Play

If you have the opportunity to review a play that is well established—like most of the plays in this collection—you need special preparation. Before seeing the play, besides having read the text, you need to imagine how the play *should* be staged. Once you understand what the play is about and what its implications may be, you need to consult reviews or descriptions of earlier productions. You may do so by referring to the index of any major newspaper or to *New York Theatre Critics' Reviews,* which includes multiple reviews of important productions over the years. The point is to come to the experience of the drama as a fully informed viewer. Knowing how the play has been staged in the past will help you see the innovations and special interpretation of the current production.

Preparing to Review a New Play

Sometime you may have the opportunity to review a new play—one that playgoers, including reviewers, have not had the chance to read in advance. In that case, you need to pay special attention to the dialogue, taking notes when necessary, to follow the development of the drama's ideas and issues. You are still responsible for commenting on the acting and the production, but in the case of a new play, your main responsibility shifts to preparing the prospective audience to understand and respond to the play. They will need to know what the play is about, how it presents the primary issues in the drama, and what is at stake. You may need to refer to the plot, but always do so with an eye toward not giving too much away, especially if the play involves suspense. Ask yourself how much the reader needs to know to decide whether to see the play.

Reviewers of new plays usually include commentary on a new or relatively unknown playwright. The most important information here would be about any previous work of the playwright. The best reviewers will have seen that work and will be prepared to discuss how it relates to the new play at hand. Reviewers of August Wilson, for example, spent time in the late 1980s establishing his credentials as a playwright. Later, when a new play of his was produced, reviewers would usually attempt to describe how the new play fit into the growing body of his work. Because Wilson was in the process of writing a series of plays on African American life, centering on specific decades of the twentieth century, reviewers did readers a service by explaining how each new play fit into Wilson's overall scheme.

Guidelines for Writing Reviews

Good reviewers approach the job of writing reviews from many different angles. Some of the reviews in this book begin with a generalization on a play's theme. Some begin with a personal observation about the play at hand or a personal experience in the theater. Others begin with a note on the background of the playwright, the actors, or the director. There are many ways to write a review. The following suggestions can help you structure your reaction.

1. If you are reviewing a professionally produced play, request a press kit from the theater. These kits usually include a great deal of information that could interest readers.

2. In your review, provide any necessary background on a playwright who is contemporary or relatively unknown. The press kit should contain some information; if not, the program may do so. Check with the press representative or with the box office manager to see whether the playwright is in the house. If so, before the play begins, you may be able to arrange an interview.

3. Before attending a play, be sure to set up a checklist based on this one so that you record the important information:

Author and title of play	Description of the action
What the play is about	Director of the play
The play's main issues	Theater and dates of
The actors, with comments	performance
Your final recommendation	The setting and its
to your readers	effectiveness

Take the list to the theater with you and keep your notes on it. When you begin writing your review, look at the reviews in this book or in your local newspaper. Your review should aim at providing a valuable service for your readers by telling them whether or not you recommend that they attend the performance.

Sample Review

Mel Gussow, in reviewing the Yale Repertory Theatre's production of Molière's *Tartuffe* in 1991 (page 533), focuses not only on the set design but also on the actor playing the title role. Gussow begins by complimenting the director, Walton Jones, by name and then goes on to call attention to the "large mahoganylike doors" that expedite the quick entrances and exits that keep the action of the play moving. Gussow is interested in them because they function in special ways that make them uniquely effective for this play. The man responsible for the "jack-in-the-box" set, Kevin Rupnick, is given credit as well.

In terms of the rhythm of the play, Gussow reminds readers more than once that there is a "breathlessness" to the production because of the speed with which things happen. Directors of a classic play like *Tartuffe* can have a tendency to be so respectful of the text that they let the play drag — but not the director of this production. Gussow does imply a negative criticism in calling the production a "tricked-up approach to Molière," but he quickly explains that it "is enlivened by several performances" and then credits the star playing Tartuffe, Austin Pendleton.

Several paragraphs of the review are about Pendleton's creditable performance. Pendleton is a short man, and Gussow seems amused when he tells us that Pendleton used his stature to good effect, "playing one scene on his knees behind a portable pulpit that is the height of a go-cart." When Gussow tells us that Pendleton's success lies in playing the part as a fanatic, he also tells us that this must be "regarded as a Pendleton specialty" and then cites Pendleton's performance in another drama. A good reviewer will have seen many plays and, when appropriate, call attention to the other achievements of a major figure like Pendleton, which we can compare to the current performance.

Again, because *Tartuffe* is so well known among theatergoers, Gussow tells us almost nothing about what happens. If this play were being performed for the first time, however, he would need to tell us something of what the play is about, describing the action without giving away the entire plot.

Glossary of Dramatic Terms

Act. A major division in the action of a play. Most plays from the Elizabethan era until the nineteenth century were divided into five acts by the playwrights or by later editors. In the nineteenth century many writers began to write four-act plays. Today one-, two-, and three-act plays are most common.

Action. What happens in a play; the events that make up the **plot**.

Agon. The Greek word for "contest." In Greek tragedy the *agon* was often a formal debate in which the **chorus** divided and took the sides of the disputants.

Alienation effect. In his epic drama, Bertolt Brecht (1898–1956) tried to make the familiar unfamiliar (or to alienate it) to show the audience that familiar, seemingly "natural," and therefore unalterable social conditions could be changed. Different devices achieved the alienation effect by calling attention to the theater as theater—stage lights brought in front of the curtain, musicians put onstage instead of hidden in an orchestra pit, placards indicating scene changes and interrupting the linear flow of the action, actors distancing themselves from their characters to invite the audience to analyze and criticize the characters instead of empathizing with them. These alienating devices prevented the audience from losing itself in the illusion of reality. (See **epic drama**.)

Allegory. A literary work that is coherent on at least two levels simultaneously: a literal level consisting of recognizable characters and events and an allegorical level on which the literal characters and events represent moral, political, religious, or other ideas and meanings.

Anagnorisis. Greek term for a character's discovery or recognition of someone or something previously unknown. *Anagnorisis* often paves the way for a reversal of fortune (see *peripeteia*). An example in *Oedipus Rex* is Oedipus's discovery of his true identity.

Antagonist. A character or force in conflict with the **protagonist**. The antagonist is often another character but may also be an intangible force such as nature or society. The dramatic conflict can even take the form of a protagonist's struggle against his or her own character.

Anticlimax. See **plot**.

Antimasque. A parody of the court **masque** developed by Ben Jonson, featuring broad humor, grotesque characters, and ludicrous actions.

Antistrophe. The second of the three parts of the verse ode sung by the **chorus** in Greek drama. While singing the **strophe**, the chorus moved in a dance rhythm from right to left; during the **antistrophe**, it moved from left to right back to its original position. The third part, the **epode**, was sung standing still.

Apron stage. The apron is the part of the stage extending in front of the **proscenium arch**. A stage is an apron stage if all or most of it is in front of any framing structures. The Elizabethan stage, which the audience surrounded on three sides, is an example of an apron stage.

Arena theater. A theater in which the stage is surrounded on all sides by the audience and actors make exits and entrances through the aisles. Used for **theater in the round**.

Arras. A curtain hung at the back of an Elizabethan playhouse to partition off an alcove or booth. The curtain could be pulled back to reveal a room or a cave.

Aside. A short speech made by a character to the audience which, by **convention**, the other characters onstage cannot hear.

Atellan farce. Broad and sometimes coarse popular humor indigenous to the town of Atella in Italy. By the third century BCE, the Romans had imported the Atellan farce, which they continued to modify and develop.

Blank verse. An unrhymed verse form often used in writing drama. Blank verse is composed of ten-syllable lines accented on the second, fourth, sixth, eighth, and tenth syllables (**iambic pentameter**).

Bombast. A loud, pompous speech whose inflated diction is disproportionate to the subject matter it expresses.

Bourgeois drama. Drama that treats middle-class subject matter or characters rather than the lives of the rich and powerful.

Braggart soldier. A **stock character** in comedy who is usually cowardly, parasitical, pompous, and easily victimized by practical jokers. Sir John Falstaff in Shakespeare's *Henry IV* (parts 1, 2) is an example.

Burla (plural, *burle*). Jests or practical jokes that were part of the comic **stage business** in the **commedia dell'arte**.

Buskin. A thick-soled boot possibly worn by Greek tragedians to increase their stature. Later called a *cothurnus* or *kothornos*.

Catastrophe. See **plot**.

Catharsis. The feeling of emotional purgation or release that, according to Aristotle, an audience should feel after watching a tragedy.

Ceremonial drama. Egyptian passion play about the god Osiris.

Character. Any person appearing in a drama or narrative. (Also see **stock character**.)

Chiton. Greek tunic worn by Roman actors.

Choregos. An influential citizen chosen to pay for the training and costuming of the **chorus** in Greek drama competitions. He probably also paid for the musicians and met other financial demands of production not paid for by the state.

Chorus. A masked group that sang and danced in Greek tragedy. The chorus usually chanted in unison, offering advice and commentary on the action but rarely participating. (See **strophe**, **antistrophe**, and **epode**.)

City Dionysia. The most important of the four Athenian festivals in honor of **Dionysus**. This spring festival was the occasion for the first tragedy competitions; comedy was associated with the winter festival, the Lenaea. Also called Great or Greater Dionysia.

Claptrap. A dramatic device designed to get the audience clapping; it is not usually connected to the core of the drama.

Climax. See **plot**.

Closet drama. A drama, usually in verse, meant for reading rather than for performance. Hrosvitha's *Dulcitius*, Percy Bysshe Shelley's *Prometheus Unbound*, and John Milton's *Samson Agonistes* are examples.

Comedy. A type of drama intended to interest and amuse rather than to concern the audience deeply. Although characters experience various discomfitures, the audience feels confident that they will overcome their ill fortune and find happiness at the end.

Comedy of humors. Form of comedy developed by Ben Jonson in the seventeenth century in which characters' actions are determined by the preponderance in their systems of one of the four bodily fluids, or humors—blood, phlegm, choler (yellow bile), and melancholy (black bile). Characters' dispositions are exaggerated and stereotyped; common types are the melancholic and the belligerent bully.

Comedy of manners. Realistic, often satiric comedy concerned with the manners and conventions of high society. Usually refers to the Restoration comedies of late-seventeenth-century England, which feature witty dialogue, or **repartee**. An example is William Congreve's *The Way of the World*.

Drawing room comedy. A type of comedy of manners concerned with life in polite society. The action generally takes place in a drawing room.

Farce. A short dramatic work that depends for its comic effect on exaggerated improbable situations, incongruities, coarse wit, and horseplay.

High comedy. Comedy that appeals to the intellect, often focusing on the pretensions, foolishness, and incongruity of human behavior. Comedy of manners, with its witty dialogue, is a type of high comedy.

Low comedy. Comedy that lacks the intellectual appeal of high comedy, depending instead on boisterous buffoonery, "gags," and jokes for its comic effect.

Middle Comedy. A transitional style of Greek comedy that extended from 400 to about 320 BCE. It marks a change, especially in language, which grew less formal and closer to the way people spoke. Little evidence of Middle Comedy exists, but from surviving statuettes we can surmise that costumes on stage resembled what Athenians actually wore on the street.

New Comedy. Emerging between the fourth and third centuries BCE in ancient Greece, the style that replaced the farcical Old Comedy. New Comedy, usually associated with Menander, is witty and intellectually engaging; it is often thought of as the first high comedy.

Old Comedy. Greek comedy of the fifth century BCE that uses bawdy farce to attack social, religious, and political institutions satirically. Old Comedy is usually associated with Aristophanes.

Sentimental comedy. Comedy populated by stereotypical virtuous **protagonists** and villainous **antagonists** that resolves the domestic trials of middle-class people in a pat, happy ending.

Slapstick. Low comedy that involves little plot or character development but rather consists of physical horseplay or practical jokes.

Comic relief. The use of humorous characters, speeches, or scenes in an otherwise serious or tragic drama.

Commedia dell'arte. Italian low comedy dating from around the mid-sixteenth century in which professional actors playing **stock characters** improvised dialogue to fit a given scenario.

Complication. See **plot**.

Conflict. See **plot.**

Convention. Any feature of a literary work that has become standardized over time, such as the **aside** or the **stock character.** Often refers to an unrealistic device (such as Danish characters speaking English in *Hamlet*) that the audience tacitly agrees to accept.

Coryphaeus. See *koryphaios.*

Cosmic irony. See **irony.**

Cothurnus. See **buskin.**

Craft play. Medieval sacred drama based on Old and New Testament stories. Craft plays were performed outside the church by members of a particular trade guild, and their subject matter often reflected the guild's trade. The fishermen's guild, for example, might present the story of Noah and the flood.

Crisis. Another term for *climax.* See **plot.**

Cycle. A group of medieval **mystery plays** written in the vernacular (the language in common use rather than Latin) for performance outside the church. Cycles, each of which treated biblical stories from creation through the last judgment, are named after the town in which they were produced. Most extant mystery plays are from the York, Chester, Wakefield (Towneley), and N-Town cycles.

Cyclorama. A large painted backdrop, usually curved and covering all of the stage with a complex scene against which the action takes place.

Dadaism. A post–World War I art movement that was in part anti-art; a revolt against pretension in the arts.

Decorum. A quality that exists when the style of a work is appropriate to the speaker, the occasion, and the subject matter. Kings should speak in a "high style" and clowns in a "low style," according to many Renaissance authors. Decorum was a guiding critical principle in neoclassicism.

Defamiliarization effect (or *Verfremdungseffekt*). See **alienation effect.**

Denouement. See **plot.**

Deus ex machina. Latin for "a god out of a machine." In Greek drama, a mechanical device called a *mekane* could lower "gods" onto the stage to solve the seemingly unsolvable problems of mortal characters. Also used to describe a playwright's use of a forced or improbable solution to plot complications—for example, the discovery of a lost will or an inheritance that will pay off the evil landlord.

Dialogue. Spoken interchange or conversation between two or more characters. Also see **soliloquy.**

Diction. A playwright's choice of words or the match between language and subject matter. Also refers collectively to an actor's phrasing, enunciation, and manner of speaking.

Dionysus. Greek nature god of wine, mystic revelry, and irrational impulse. Greek tragedy probably evolved from dramatized ritual choral celebrations in honor of Dionysus. (Also see **City Dionysia.**)

Director. The person responsible for a play's interpretation and staging and for the guidance of the actors.

Disguising. Medieval entertainment featuring a procession of masked actors performing short plays in pantomime; probably the origin of the court **masque.**

Dithyramb. Ancient Greek choral hymn sung and danced to honor **Dionysus.** Originally divided into an improvised story sung by a choral leader and a traditional refrain sung by the **chorus,** it is believed by some to be the origin of Greek tragedy.

Domestic tragedy. A serious play usually focusing on a family and depicting the fall of a middle-class **protagonist** rather than of a powerful or noble hero. An example is Arthur Miller's *Death of a Salesman*, which traces the emotional collapse and eventual suicide of Willy Loman, a traveling salesman. Also called *bourgeois tragedy.*

Double plot. See **plot.**

Drama. A play written in prose or verse that tells a story through **dialogue** and actions performed by actors impersonating the characters of the story.

Dramatic illusion. The illusion of reality created by drama and accepted by the audience for the duration of the play.

Dramatic irony. See **irony.**

Dramatist. The author of a play; playwright.

Dramaturge. One who represents the playwright and guides the production. In some cases, the dramaturge researches different aspects of a production or earlier productions of a play.

Dramaturgy. The art of writing plays.

Drawing room comedy. See **comedy.**

Empathy. The sense of feeling *with* a character. (Distinct from sympathy, which is feeling *for* a character.)

Ensemble acting. Performance by a group of actors, usually members of a **repertory** company, in which the integrated acting of all members is emphasized over individual star performances. The famous nineteenth-century director Constantin Stanislavski promoted this type of acting in the Moscow Art Theatre.

Environmental theater. A term used by Richard Schechner, director of the Performance Group in the late 1960s and early 1970s, to describe his work and the work of other theater companies, including the Bread and Puppet Theatre, Open Theatre, and Living Theatre. He also used the term to describe the indigenous theater of Africa and Asia. Environmental theater occupies the whole of a performance space; it is not confined to a stage separated from the audience. Action can take place in and around the audience, and audience members are often encouraged to participate in the theater event.

Epic theater. A type of theater first associated with German director Erwin Piscator (1893–1966). Bertolt Brecht (1898–1956) used the term to distinguish his own theater from the "dramatic" theater that created the illusion of reality and invited the audience to identify and empathize with the characters. Brecht criticized the dramatic theater for encouraging the audience to believe that social conditions were "natural" and therefore unalterable. According to Brecht, the theater should show human beings as dependent on certain political and economic factors and at the same time as capable of altering them. "The spectator is given the chance to criticize human behavior from a social point of view, and the scene is played as a piece of history," he wrote. Epic drama calls attention to itself as theater, bringing the stage lights in front of the curtain and interrupting the linear flow of the action to help the audience analyze the action and characters onstage. (Also see **alienation effect**.)

Epilogue. A final speech added to the end of a play. An example is Puck's "If we shadows have offended..." speech that ends Shakespeare's *A Midsummer Night's Dream*.

Epitasis. Ancient term for the rising action of a plot. (See **plot**.)

Epode. The third of the three parts of the verse ode sung by the **chorus** in a Greek drama. The epode follows the **strophe** and **antistrophe**.

Existentialism. A post–World War II philosophy that insisted humans had to give their lives value and significance because nothing outside themselves could do so.

Exodos. The concluding scene of a Greek drama, which includes the exit of all characters and the **chorus**.

Exposition. See **plot**.

Expressionism. Early-twentieth-century literary movement in Germany that posited that art should represent powerful emotional states and moods. Expressionists abandon **realism** and **verisimilitude**, producing distorted, nightmarish images of the individual unconscious.

Falling action. See **plot**.

Farce. See **comedy**.

First Folio. The first collected edition of thirty-six of Shakespeare's plays, collected by two of his fellow actors and published posthumously in 1623.

Flies. Space over a stage used to store scenery, lights, curtains, and the like, so that they can be raised and lowered as necessary.

Foil. A character who, through difference or similarity, brings out a particular aspect of another character. Laertes, reacting to the death of his father, acts as a foil for Hamlet.

Foreshadowing. Ominous hints of events to come that help to create an air of suspense in a drama.

Frons scaena. The elaborately decorated facade of the *scaena*, or stage house, used in presenting Roman drama. Also called *scaena frons*.

Hamartia. An error or wrong act through which the fortunes of the **protagonist** are reversed in a tragedy.

High comedy. See **comedy**.

History play. A drama set in a time other than that in which it was written. The term usually refers to Elizabethan

drama, such as Shakespeare's Henry plays, that draws its plots from English historical materials, such as Holinshed's *Chronicles*.

Hubris (or *hybris*). Excessive pride or ambition. In ancient Greek tragedy, hubris often causes the **protagonist**'s fall.

Humor character. A stereotyped character in the comedy of humors (see **comedy**). Clever plots often play on the character's personality distortions (caused by an imbalance of humors), revealing his or her absurdity.

Iambic pentameter. A poetic meter that divides a line into five parts (or feet), each part containing an unaccented syllable followed by an accented syllable. The line "When I consider everything that grows" is an example of iambic pentameter verse.

Imitation. See *mimesis*.

Impressionism. A highly personal style of writing in which an author presents characters, scenes, or moods as they appear to him or her at a particular moment rather than striving for an objectively realistic description.

Interlude. A short play, usually either farcical or moralistic, performed between the courses of a feast or between the acts of a longer play. The interlude thrived during the late fifteenth and early sixteenth centuries in England.

Irony. The use of words to suggest a meaning that is the opposite of the literal meaning, as in "I can't wait to take the exam." Irony is present in a literary work that gives expression to contradictory attitudes or impulses to entertain ambiguity or to maintain detachment.

Cosmic irony. Irony present when destiny or the gods seem to be in favor of the **protagonist** but are actually engineering his or her downfall. Also known as *irony of fate*.

Dramatic irony. Irony present when the outcome of an event or situation is the opposite of what a character expects.

Tragic irony. Irony that exists when a character's lack of complete knowledge or understanding (which the audience possesses) results in his or her fall or has tragic consequences for loved ones. An example from *Oedipus Rex* is Oedipus's declaration that he will stop at nothing to banish King Laios's murderer, whom the audience knows to be Oedipus himself.

Jongleur. Early medieval French musical entertainer who recited lyrics, ballads, and stories. Forerunner of the minstrel.

Koryphaios (or *coryphaeus*). The leader of the **chorus** in Greek drama. Also called the *choragos*.

Kothornos. See **buskin**.

Lazzo (plural, *lazzi*). Comic routines or **stage business** associated with the stock situations and characters of the Italian **commedia dell'arte**. A scenario might, for example, call for the *lazzo* of fear.

Liturgical drama. Short dramatized sections of the medieval church service. Some scholars believe that these playlets evolved into the vernacular **mystery plays,** which were performed outside the church by lay people.

Low comedy. See **comedy.**

Mansion. Scenic structure used in medieval drama to indicate the locale or scene of the action. Mansions were elaborate structures built on pageant wagons to present **mystery plays** outside the church.

Mask. A covering used to disguise or ornament the face; used by actors in Greek drama and revived in the later **commedia dell'arte** and court **masque** to heighten dramatic effect.

Masque (also *mask*). A short but elaborately staged court drama, often mythological and allegorical, principally acted and danced by masked courtiers. (Professional actors often performed the major speaking and singing roles.) Popular in England during the late sixteenth and early seventeenth centuries, masques were often commissioned to honor a particular person or occasion. Ben Jonson was the most important masque writer; the genre's most elaborate sets and costumes were designed by Jonson's occasional partner Inigo Jones. (See **antimasque.**)

Mekane. See *deus ex machina.*

Melodrama. A suspenseful play filled with situations that appeal to the audience's emotions. Justice triumphs in a happy ending; the good characters (completely virtuous) are rewarded, and the bad characters (thoroughly villainous) are punished.

Method acting. A naturalistic technique of acting developed by the Russian director Constantin Stanislavski and adapted for American actors by Lee Strasberg, among others. The Method actor identifies with the character he or she portrays and experiences the emotions called for by the play in an effort to render the character with emotional **verisimilitude.**

Middle Comedy. See **comedy.**

Mimesis. The Greek word for "imitation." Aristotle used the term to define the role of art as an imitation of an action.

Miracle play. A type of medieval sacred drama that depicts the lives of saints, focusing especially on the miracles performed by saints.

Mise-en-scène. The stage setting of a play, including the use of scenery, props, and stage movement.

Moira. Greek word for "fate."

Morality play. Didactic late medieval drama (flourishing in England c. 1400–1550) that uses **allegory** to dramatize some aspects of the Christian moral life. Abstract qualities or entities such as Virtue, Vice, Good Deeds, Knowledge, and Death are cast as characters who discuss with the **protagonist** issues related to salvation and the afterlife. *Everyman* is an example.

Motivation. The reasons for a character's actions in a drama. For drama to be effective, the audience must believe that a character's actions are justified and plausible given what they know about him or her.

Mouth of hell. A stage prop in medieval drama suggesting the entrance to hell. Often in the shape of an open-mouthed monster's head, the mouth of hell was positioned over a pit in the stage that belched smoke and fire and appeared to swallow up sinners.

Mystery play. A sacred medieval play dramatizing biblical events such as the creation, the fall of Adam and Eve, and Christ's birth and resurrection. The genre probably evolved from **liturgical drama;** mystery plays were often incorporated into larger **cycles** of plays.

Naturalism. Literary philosophy popularized during the nineteenth century that casts art's role as the scientifically accurate reflection of a "slice of life." Naturalism is aligned with the belief that each person is a product of heredity and environment, driven by internal and external forces beyond his or her control. August Strindberg's *Miss Julie,* with its focus on reality's sordidness and humankind's powerlessness, draws on naturalism.

Neoclassicism. A movement in sixteenth-century Italy and seventeenth-century France to revive and emulate classical attitudes toward art based on principles of order, harmony, unity, restrained wit, and **decorum.** The neoclassical movement in France gave rise to a corresponding movement in England during the late seventeenth and eighteenth centuries.

New Comedy. See **comedy.**

Ode. A dignified three-part song sung by the **chorus** in Greek drama. The parts are the **strophe,** the **antistrophe,** and the **epode.**

Old Comedy. See **comedy.**

Orchestra. Literally, the "dancing place"; the circular stage where the Greek chorus performed.

Pageant cart. A movable stage or wagon (often called a *pageant wagon*) on which a set was built for the performance of medieval drama. The term *pageant* can also refer to the spectacle itself.

Pallium. Long white cloak or mantle worn by Greek actors or Romans in Greek-based plays.

Pantomime. Silent acting using facial expression, body movement, and gesture to convey the plot and the characters' feelings.

Parodos. The often stately entrance song of the **chorus** in Greek drama. The term also refers to the aisles (plural, *paradoi*) on either side of the orchestra by which the chorus entered the Greek theater.

Pastoral drama. A dramatic form glorifying shepherds and rural life in an idealized natural setting, usually implying a more negative view of urban life.

Pathos. The quality of a drama that evokes pity.

Performance art. An art form that arose in the mid-twentieth century and often mixes media: music, video, film, opera, dance, and spoken text. It was originally defined in terms of artists using a live production for dramatic effect; Anna Deavere Smith's work is a good example. However, the definition has widened to include performances that cross dramatic "boundaries." Dancers Martha Clarke and Pina Bausch, musicians such as Laurie Anderson, and experimental directors such as Richard Foreman have been identified as performance artists.

Peripeteia. A reversal of fortune, for better or worse, for the **protagonist**. Used especially to describe the main character's fall in Greek tragedy.

Phallus. An appendage meant to suggest the penis, added to the front of blatantly comic male characters' costumes in some Greek comedy. Associated chiefly with the Greek **satyr play.**

Play. A literary genre whose plot is usually presented dramatically by actors portraying characters before an audience.

Play-within-the-play. A brief secondary drama presented to or by the characters of a play that reflects or comments on the larger work. An example is the Pyramus and Thisbe episode in Shakespeare's *A Midsummer Night's Dream.*

Plot. The events of a play or narrative; the sequence and relative importance a **dramatist** assigns to these events.

Anticlimax. An unexpectedly trivial or insignificant conclusion to a series of significant events; an unsatisfying resolution that often occurs in place of a conventional climax.

Catastrophe. The outcome or conclusion of a play, usually applied specifically to tragedy. (*Denouement* is a parallel term applied to both comedy and tragedy.)

Climax. The turning point in a drama's action, preceded by the rising action and followed by the falling action. Also known as *crisis.*

Complication. The part of the plot preceding the climax that establishes the entanglements to be untangled in the denouement; part of the rising action.

Conflict. The struggle between the **protagonist** and the **antagonist** that propels the rising action of the plot and is resolved in the denouement.

Denouement. The "unknotting" of the plot's complication; the resolution of a drama's action.

Double plot. A dramatic structure in which two related plots function simultaneously.

Exposition. The presentation of essential information, especially about events that have occurred prior to the first scene of a play. The exposition appears early in the play and initiates the rising action.

Falling action. The events of the plot following the climax and ending in the catastrophe or resolution.

Rising action. The events of the plot leading up to the climax.

Subplot. A secondary plot intertwined with the main plot, often reflecting or commenting on the main plot.

Underplot. Same as *subplot.*

Problem play. A drama that argues a point or presents a problem (usually a social problem). Ibsen was a notable writer of problem plays.

Prologos. In Greek drama, an introductory scene for actor or actors that precedes the entrance of the **chorus**. This **convention** has evolved into the modern dramatic introductory monologue or **prologue.**

Prologue. A preface or introduction preceding the play proper.

Proscaena. The space in front of the *scaena* in a Roman theater.

Proscenium arch. An arched structure over the front of the stage from which a curtain often hangs. The arch frames the action onstage and separates the audience from the action.

Proskenion. The playing space in front of the *skene,* or scene house, in Greek drama.

Protagonist. The main character in a drama. This character is usually the most interesting and sympathetic and is the person involved in the conflict driving the plot.

Protasis. Classical term for the introductory act or exposition of a drama.

Psychomachia. Psychological struggle; a war of souls.

Quem Quaeritis trope. A brief dramatized section of the medieval church's Easter liturgy. The oldest extant **trope** and the probable origin of **liturgical drama,** it enacts the visit of the three Marys to Christ's empty tomb (*quem quaeritis* means "Whom do you seek?" in Latin).

Realism. The literary philosophy holding that art should accurately reproduce an image of life. Avoiding the use of dramatic **conventions** such as **asides** and **soliloquies,** realism depicts ordinary people in ordinary situations. Ibsen's *A Doll House* is an example of realism in drama.

Recognition. See *anagnorisis.*

Repartee. Witty and pointed verbal exchanges usually found in the comedy of manners.

Repertory. A theater company or group of actors that presents a set of plays throughout a season. The term also refers to the set of plays itself.

Restoration comedy. A type of comedy of manners that developed in England in the late seventeenth century, often featuring **repartee** in the service of complex romantic plots. Oliver Goldsmith's *She Stoops to Conquer* is an example.

Revenge tragedy. Sensational tragedy popularized during the Elizabethan age that is notable for bloody plots involving such elements as murder, ghosts, insanity, and crimes of lust.

Reversal. See *peripeteia.*

Riposte. A quick or sharp reply, similar to **repartee.**

Rising action. See **plot.**

Ritual. Repeated formalized or ceremonial practices, many of which have their roots in primitive cultures. Certain theorists hold that primitive ritual evolved into drama.

Satire. A work that makes fun of a social institution or human foible, often in an intellectually sophisticated way, to persuade the audience to share the author's views. Molière's *Tartuffe* contains social satire.

Satyr play. A comic play performed after the tragic trilogy in Greek tragedy competitions. The satyr play provided **comic relief** and was usually a farcical, boisterous treatment of mythological material.

Scaena. The stage house in Roman drama; the facade of the *scaena* (called the *frons scaena*) was often elaborately ornamented.

Scenario. The plot outline around which professional actors of the **commedia dell'arte** improvised their plays. Most scenarios specified the action's sequence and the entrances of the main characters.

Scene. Division of an **act** in a drama. By traditional definition, a scene has no major shift in place or time frame, and it is performed by a fixed group of actors onstage (in French drama, if an actor enters or exits, the group is altered, and the scene, technically, should change). The term also refers to the physical surroundings or locale in which a play's **action** is set.

Scenery. The backdrop and set (furniture and so on) onstage that suggest to the audience the surroundings in which a play's action takes place.

Scenography. Painting of backdrops and hangings.

Senecan tragedy. Tragic drama modeled on plays written by Seneca. The genre usually has five acts and features a **chorus**; it is notable for its thematic concern with bloodshed, revenge, and unnatural crimes. (See **revenge tragedy**.)

Sentimental. Arousing tender emotions in excess of what the situation calls for.

Sentimental comedy. See **comedy**.

Setting. All details of time, location, and environment relating to a play.

Skene. The building or scene house in the Greek theater that probably began as a dressing room and eventually was incorporated into the action as part of the scenery.

Slapstick. See **comedy**.

Slice of life. See **naturalism**.

Social problem play. Another term for **problem play**.

Social realism. Drama that reflects the difficulties of modern life; drama with political content and aimed at reforming society.

Sock. A term derived from the Latin *soccus*, referring to a light slipper or sock worn by Roman comic actors.

Soliloquy. A speech in which an actor, usually alone onstage, utters his or her thoughts aloud, revealing personal feelings. Hamlet's "To be, or not to be" speech is an example.

Spectacle. In Aristotle's terms, the costumes and scenery in a drama—the elements that appeal to the eye.

Stage business. Minor physical action, including an actor's posture and facial expression, and the use of props, all of which make up a particular interpretation of a character.

Stasimon (plural, *stasima*). In a Greek tragedy, a song sung by the **chorus** after it has taken its position. The chorus stands still and is not interrupted by dialogue during the stasimon.

Stichomythia. Dialogue in which two speakers engage in a verbal duel in alternating lines.

Stock character. A stereotypical character type whose behavior, qualities, or beliefs conform to familiar dramatic conventions, such as the clever servant or the **braggart soldier**. Also called *type character*.

Strophe. The first of the three parts of the verse **ode** sung by a Greek **chorus**. While singing the **strophe**, the chorus moves in a dancelike pattern from right to left. See also **antistrophe** and **epode**.

Subplot. See **plot**.

Subtext. A level of meaning implicit in or underlying the surface meaning of a text.

Surrealism. A literary movement flourishing in France during the early twentieth century that valued the unwilled expression of the unconscious (usually as revealed in dreams) over a rendering of "reality" structured by the conscious mind.

Suspense. The sense of tension aroused by an audience's uncertainty about the resolution of dramatic conflicts.

Suspension of disbelief. An audience's willingness to accept the world of the drama as reality during the course of a play.

Symbolism. A literary device in which an object, event, or action is used to suggest a meaning beyond its literal meaning. The lantern in *The Rising of the Moon* has a symbolic function.

Theater. The building in which a play is performed. Also used to refer to drama as an art form.

Theater in the round. The presentation of a play in an arena theater, where the stage is surrounded by the audience.

Theater of the absurd. A type of twentieth-century drama presenting the human condition as meaningless, absurd, and illogical. An example of the genre is Samuel Beckett's *Endgame*.

Theater of cruelty. A type of drama created by Antonin Artaud in the 1930s that uses shock techniques to expose the audience's primitive obsessions with cruelty and sexuality. The purpose was to overwhelm spectators' rational minds, leading them to understand and even participate in the cycle of cruelty and ritual purgation dramatized in the performance.

Theme. Main idea or general topic of a play, which is not always easy to determine. Some plays have several topics that develop simultaneously.

Three unities. Unity of time, action, and locale. Aristotle noted that a play's action usually occurs in one day or a little more and that the plot should reveal clearly ordered actions and incidents moving toward the plot's resolution. Later scholars and critics, especially those in the neoclassical tradition, interpreted Aristotle's ideas as rules and added a third: a play's action should occur in a single locale.

Thrust stage. A stage extending beyond the **proscenium arch,** usually surrounded on three sides by the audience.

Tiring house. From "attiring house," the backstage space in Elizabethan public theaters used for storage and as a dressing room. The term also refers to the changing space beneath the medieval pageant wagon.

Total theater. A concept of the theater as an experience synthesizing all the expressive arts, including music, dance, and lighting.

Tragedy. Serious drama in which a **protagonist,** traditionally of noble position, suffers a series of unhappy events culminating in a catastrophe such as death or spiritual breakdown. Shakespeare's *Hamlet*, which ends with the prince's death, is an example of Elizabethan tragedy.

Tragicomedy. A play that combines elements of tragedy and comedy. Chekhov's *The Cherry Orchard* is an example. Tragicomedies often include a serious plot in which the expected tragic catastrophe is replaced by a happy ending.

Trope. Interpolation into or expansion of an existing medieval liturgical text. These expansions, such as the *Quem Quaeritis* trope, gave rise to **liturgical drama.**

Type character. See **stock character.**

Underplot. See **plot.**

Unity. The sense that the events of a play and the actions of the characters follow one another naturally to form one complete action. Unity is present when characters' behavior seems **motivated** and the work is perceived to be a connected artistic whole. See also **three unities.**

Verfremdungseffekt. German term coined by Bertolt Brecht to mean "alienation." See **alienation effect.**

Verisimilitude. The degree to which a dramatic representation approximates an appearance of reality.

Well-made play. Drama that relies for effect on the suspense generated by its logical, cleverly constructed plot rather than on characterization. Plots often involve a withheld secret, a battle of wits between hero and villain, and a resolution in which the secret is revealed and the **protagonist** saved. The plays of Eugène Scribe (1791–1861) have defined the type.

Contemporary Drama

IMAGE CREDITS

Greek Drama

Roman Drama

Medieval Drama

Renaissance Drama

Late-Seventeenth- and Eighteenth-Century Drama

Nineteenth-Century Drama through the Turn of the Twentieth Century

Drama in the Early and Mid-Twentieth Century

Contemporary Drama